7436

D1415907

7436

NEBRASKANA

BIOGRAPHICAL SKETCHES OF NEBRASKA MEN AND
WOMEN OF ACHIEVEMENT WHO HAVE BEEN
AWARDED LIFE MEMBERSHIP IN

THE NEBRASKANA SOCIETY

Edited by
SARA MULLIN BALDWIN
and
ROBERT MORTON BALDWIN

HEBRON, NEBRASKA
THE BALDWIN COMPANY
1932

212842

WILLIAM JENNINGS BRYAN

To the memory of William Jennings Bryan—brilliant
statesman, silver-tongued orator, prophet of idealism,
champion of the common people, and Nebraska's most
illustrious citizen—this volume is respectfully dedicated
by the editors.

INTRODUCTION

Nebraskana has been completed after two years of intensive effort on the part of a large number of persons. It contains historical data concerning leading Nebraskans who have been elected to life membership in The Nebraskana Society because of outstanding achievement in the business, professional, civic and social life of the state. All selections were made on merit alone and without the knowledge of the subject; no charge of any kind was made for listing any biography, nor was any person required to purchase a copy of the book in order to receive proper recognition.

Every effort has been made to secure the biographies of all prominent Nebraskans, and the material printed has been carefully edited. If the life sketch of any person of achievement has been omitted from these pages it is because, after zealous effort, the editors were unable to obtain it. It will be found that the facts contained herein have an immediate usefulness; their greatest value, however, will come in future years, through the preservation of reliable biographical material.

Copies of *Nebraskana* are being presented to leading university and public libraries throughout the world, and will be preserved in the archives of the Congressional Library in Washington.

The editors believe that a word of appreciation is due the public-spirited citizens and progressive civic organizations without whose co-operation the work could not have been carried out. Especially are they grateful to J. N. Norton and C. L. Clark, whose services as members of the board of governors for The Nebraskana Society were given without remuneration; to Charles E. Day, Arthur DeBoben Werner, Sands F. Woodbridge, Jr., and Vic B. Scherzinger for the art work in the book; to Postmaster H. L. Boyes, for his efficient and courteous co-operation; to the photographers of Nebraska, who supplied the photographs; and to the editors of more than 500 newspapers throughout the state, who so willingly assisted in carrying out the Nebraskana program.

Others whose energetic efforts have brought about the successful publication of *Nebraskana* are:

Helen Baldwin Sherman	Ruth W. Hyers	Mildred Fulton
Gertrude Barbara Wilson	Clinton L. Franklin	L. D. Bennett
David B. Bishoff	Theodore H. Robertson	Evelyn Lyon
M. P. Montgomery	Kathryn M. O'Donnell	O. H. Gooch
Margaret McCarty	Marcella McDonald	Maybel Davis
Myrna Paugh	William S. Sherman	R. G. Bennett
Heber Page	C. W. Montgomery	Charlotte M. Meinen
Leona Young	Claude A. Miller	Virginia Lauer
Eugene Nagey	Eleanor Davenport	Jack Hirrlinger
Narvene Barr	George W. Kline	R. A. Brittain

In the belief that our work will be of lasting benefit to the state, and that this volume has genuine historical value, we present *Nebraskana* to the members of the Society and the general public.

ROBERT MORTON BALDWIN

HONOR ROLL

❦

Following is a roster of those members of The Nebraskana Society to whom particular recognition should be given for the co-operation and financial assistance, without which this volume could not have been published.

Charles Edwin Abbott, Fremont
William James Abbott, Whitman
Ellen Murphy Ackerman, Ainsworth
James George Ackerman, Ainsworth
Thomas Edward Adams, Beatrice
James Edmund Addie, Hastings
John Aden, Carleton
Stuart Elijah Adkins, Arthur
George Simon Agnes, O'Neill
Ainsworth Public School, Ainsworth
Bohumil William Aksamit, Deweese
John H. Albrecht, Deshler
Bess Streeter Aldrich, Elmwood
Arthur Eurasho Allen, Danbury
Charles Edgar Allen, Cozad
Charles Luther Allen, Trenton
Thomas Stinson Allen, Lincoln
William I. Allen, Schuyler
Henry Altschuler, Madison
Carl G. Amick, Loup City
Frederick William Andersen, Cozad
Alfred T. Anderson, Kearney
Andreas Theodore Anderson, Gordon
Charles Barney Anderson, Lincoln
Edna Cochran Anderson, York
Emil Anderson, Minden
Ira C. Anderson, Kearney
Victor Anderson, Stromsburg
Henry S. Andrews, Minden
Orville Alexander Andrews, Lincoln
Leslie C. Anstine, Wood River
Joseph F. Arens, Hartington
Robert McDowell Armstrong, Auburn
Leland Dill Arndt, Blair
Dr. Charles Harrison Arnold, Lincoln
Leonard E. Arnold, Sutherland
Jeanette Mayer Arnstein, Omaha
Carrie Arthur, Scribner
Edwin J. Askwig, Oakland
Wilber Stremmel Aten, Holdrege
Wilber William Aten, Holdrege
Ernest Webster Augustine, Grand Island
Irving Milton Augustine, Grand Island
Otto G. Austin, Newman Grove
Mary Virgie Avery, Humboldt
James Andrew Axtell, Fairbury
Leon Emmons Aylsworth, Lincoln

Fred Bader, Fremont
E. Preston Bailey, Carleton
Allen Crowell Baker, Tecumseh
W. H. Baker, Aurora
Mr. and Mrs. Joseph Pearson Baldwin, Hebron
Grace Ballard, Blair
Harvey Edgar Barbee, Hebron
Grove Ettinger Barber, Lincoln
George Earl Barks, Belden
John D. Barnett, Stanton
Arthur Barney, Kearney
Cass G. Barns, Madison
Charles Cecil Barr, Tilden
Everett Morrison Barr, Burchard
Frank W. Bartos, Wilber
Stanley Bartos, Wilber
John E. Baruth, Alexandria
Conrad Leslie Baskins, North Platte
Harvey Theodore Bates, Carleton
Casper Baumgartner, Scottsbluff
Edward David Beach, Omaha
Roscoe C. Beachler, Reynolds
Charles Edwin Beals, Crete
James O. Beaman, Ceresco
George William Beamer, Gordon
Frank James Bean, Elwood
Beatrice Free Public Library
Adolf Beck, Wilber
James Edmund Bednar, Omaha
Peter Franklin Beghtol, Bennet
Jesse Francis Bejot, Ainsworth
Carroll R. Belden, Omaha
John Ernest Bell, Superior
Harley L. Bellamy, Cambridge
Grace M. B. Benson, Oakland
Harry William Benson, Oakland
Nellie Gray Benson, Lincoln
John Bentley, Sidney
Ida Wilkens Berger, Nehawka
Nelson L. Berger, Nehawka
William H. Berger, Dakota City

Alice Virginia Berryman, Omaha
Cecil Wells Berryman, Omaha
Charles Fred Beushausen, Loup City
James C. Bierbower, Giltner
Arthur Herbert Bivans, North Platte
Joseph Bixby, Geneva
Earl Howell Blackburn, Omaha
Samuel Clarence Blackman, Tilden
Ella Blunk, Grand Island
Clyde L. Bodwell, Lebanon
George Martin Boehler, Omaha
Albert Orr Boggs, Gilead
Homer Bowen, Grand Island
Charles Arthur Bowers, Holdrege
Harry Eugene Bowman, Hastings
Robert James Boyd, Trenton
Clarence C. Boyes, Hebron
Herman Lee Boyes, Hebron
William Edwin Boyes, Hebron
Archie L. Bradstreet, Grand Island
Carmen Brady, Denton
Frank John Brady, Atkinson
John Bell Brain, Omaha
Hjalmer Bernard Branting, Stromsburg
George H. Brewer, Omaha
John T. Brinegar, Belvidere
Otto Herman Brinkman, Lincoln
Charles John Broman, Minden
Alice Brooke, Hastings
William Edgar Brooks, Elgin
Harry H. Brown, Blair
James A. Brown, Lincoln
Lulu Clyde Brown, Stockville
Mentor A. Brown, Kearney
Edward Charles Brt, Abie
Charles Wayland Bryan, Lincoln
James Arthur Bryan, Scottsbluff
Wilbur Franklin Bryant, Hartington
Charles Wallace Buck, Dewitt
A. F. Buechler, Grand Island
Carl Henry Buethe, Elk Creek
Fred John Buntemeyer, Deshler
Earl Haskell Burket, Omaha
Elmer J. Burkett, Lincoln
Joseph Burns, Lincoln
John Wesley Burrows, Gering
George Turner Burt, Elwood
Ben H. Busboom, Crete
Fritz J. Busch, Howells
Otto Buschow, Blue Hill
Benjamin F. Butler, Cambridge
James Arthur Butler, Ewing
Effie Marie Byers, Hastings

Flora B. Cady, Lebanon
Dr. P. L. Cady, Arlington
Samuel S. Caldwell, Omaha
Congrave Clinton Callaway, Fairbury
Eliza Jane Callaway, Fairbury
E. Glenn Callen, Lincoln
Burtis Oakley Callender, North Platte
Jennie Mather Callfas, Omaha
Joseph Robert Cameron, Bennet
H. H. Campbell, Osceola
Joseph New Campbell, Stamford
P. B. Campbell, Osceola
Rev. R. S. Campbell, Lincoln
Joseph Alfred Capwell, Plattsmouth
John Joseph Carey, Petersburg
Swan Carlson, Funk
John Booth Carns, Lincoln
Janet Louise Carpenter, Hastings
Thomas W. Carroll, Lincoln
Stewart Edgar Carskadon, Wilcox
Fred Louis Carsten, Avoca
Clifford Dorwin Carter, Dorchester
Edward Francis Carter, Gering
Harry Glen Carter, Lincoln
Horace Jackson Cary, Kearney
Ernest Edwin Case, Sutton
Elmer Fay Casebolt, Hebron
Roy Lucas Caskey, Big Spring
Yale H. Cavett, Bayard
Albert Bushnell Chain, Seward
Guy C. Chambers, Lincoln
James Chambers, Fairbury
Samuel W. Chambers, Blair
Anna Chatburn, Lincoln
George R. Chatburn, Lincoln
Orville Chatt, Tekamah

Robert Ellsworth Chittick, Stuart
Burton Whitford Christie, Omaha
Anna Gray Clark, Ogallala
Byron Clark, Omaha
Esther Ann Clark, Peru
Lucy Marie Clark, Chadron
Morse Powl Clary, Lewellen
Clara Clyde Clayton, Lincoln
John Leo Cleary, Grand Island
Alice Eliza Cleaver, Falls City
Ralph G. Coad, Omaha
George Edwin Codington, Auburn
Harry Joseph Coffin, Burwell
Leon Minor Cole, Arthur
Raymond Voorhis Cole, Omaha
Roscoe James Cole, Cambridge
Chamber of Commerce, Omaha
Dr. Elbert E. Cone, Oxford
Ulysses Sylvester Conn, Wayne
James D. Conway, Hastings
Harold James Cook, Agate
James Henry Cook, Agate
William Coolidge, Rosalie
Gerald Massey Gilbert Cooper, Rushville
Guy L. Cooper, Humboldt
John William Cooper, Omaha
Charles Finney Copeland, Holdrege
George Corner, Blue Hill
Walter A. Cornish, Shelby
Mabel L. Correll, Cambridge
Jay Timothy Cottingham, Hastings
Major Allen P. Cowgill, Lincoln
Frank B. Cox, Waterloo
John Thomas Cox, Howe
Laurence Madison Coy, Valley
Mabel Cramer, Hastings
Ray A. Crancer, Lincoln
Daniel Craven, Norfolk
Robert Platt Crawford, Lincoln
Howard M. Crilly, Wilber
Edward Porter Cromer, Gering
Charles Robert Cropp, Oxford
Joseph Marshall Crosby, Hayes Center
Leo Jay Crosby, Omaha
James Phillip Crouse, Seward
John L. Currier, Hebron
Carl T. Curtis, Minden
Edward LeRoy Curtis, Rushville

William C. Dahnke, Stratton
Stanley Owen Daily, Minden
Walter Dale, Gothenburg
John Henry Damme, Talmage
Frank Tenney Darrow, Lincoln
Harry Burnham Dart, Brady
Allen Manville Darwin, Virginia
David City Public Schools
Edith Stokes Davidson, Omaha
Edward Llewellyn Davies, Ewing
Clarence Alba Davis, Holdrege
Edward Samuel Davis, North Platte
Grover C. Davis, Homer
Joseph Franklin Davis, Falls City
William H. Davis, Beatrice
Joseph Horn Davison, Ainsworth
Irwell Montgomery Dawson, Madison
Reuben Alwin Dawson, Randolph
Ida Yungblut Day, Lincoln
James Renwick Dean, Lincoln
Quentin Warren Dean, Gering
William Thomas Dearing, Phillips
Bert Decker, Elwood
Rudolph F. Decker, M. D., Byron
C. O. Dedmore, North Platte
Paul Albert DeOgny, Milford
Charles Frederick Diederich, Campbell
Lucia W. Dillenbach, Hastings
Forest Ray Dilts, Wakefield
Charles Docekal, Abie
John J. Dohrn, Grand Island
John Edwin Donaldson, Albion
Dayton Henry Dorn, Big Spring
John Charles Dort, Pawnee City
Lloyd Dort, Lincoln
Harry E. Dorwart, Overton
John Edward Dougherty, York
William James Douglas, Atkinson
Marquis Lafayette Dowell, Salem
Charles Myron Druse, Jr., Cambridge
George Martin Dudley, Norfolk

Gleason A. Dudley, Walthill
Peter William Duffy, O'Neill
John William Dunaway, Overton
William Alpheus Dunlavy, Bloomington
Ballard Dunn, Omaha
Edward E. Duryee, Oxford
Brogan, Ellick & Van Dusen, Omaha
Kittie M. J. Loughridge Dutton, Hastings
William M. Dutton, Sr., Hastings
Albert William Dyer, Exeter

Gilbert Eacker, Schuyler
Glen B. Eastburn, Omaha
A. N. Eaton, Omaha
Guy Wallace Eaton, Maxwell
Roy Wesley Eaton, Omaha
George Agler Eberly, Lincoln
William Ebers, Holdrege
Gottlieb Fredrich Eberspacher, Seward
Charles D. Eby, Leigh
Millard Elmer Eby, Hartington
Edward Herman Eckert, Crete
Frank E. Edgerton, Aurora
Mary Coe Edgerton, Aurora
Andrew J. Edstrom, M. D., Grand Island
Peter Eginton, Sr., Paxton
Frank Ludwig Ehlers, Deshler
Oscar J. Ekstrand, Oakland
Robert Irving Elliott, Chadron
Wilbert Lester Elswick, Gurley
Sarah Saunders Elwell, Springfield
William McLouth Ely, Ainsworth
J. W. Embree, Lodge Pole
Max Emmert, Omaha
Loren William Enyeart, Hayes Center
Ditlev Frederick Enevoldsen, Potter
Andrew Erickson, Campbell
George H. Erickson, Holdrege
Gustavus A. Erickson, Virginia
Henry Erickson, Campbell
Oliver Leo Erickson, Kearney
Clifford F. Eshelman, Red Cloud
Madge Evans, Beatrice
George Evens, Omaha
William F. Evers, Plattsmouth
Samuel Mitchell Ewing, Benkelman
Exeter Public Schools, Exeter

George Otis Fairchild, Kearney
Anna Kemper Fall, Beatrice
Clifford Pervines Fall, Beatrice
Virgil Falloon, Falls City
George Lord Farley, Plattsmouth
Frederick James Farrington, Omaha
Leon C. Farwell, Dubois
William Francis Feehan, Clarks
Elbert Wesley Fellers, Beatrice
Mr. and Mrs. George B. Fergus, Hastings
Joseph Fickel, Gordon
Ruben O. Finch, Cambridge
Ralph Stevenson Finley, Norfolk
Harry Fischer, Omaha
Harry B. Fitch, Omaha
J. S. Fitzsimmons, Elwood
Maude Hammond Fling, Lincoln
H. D. Flory, Pawnee City
Albert Claus Floto, Seward
Dr. Michael J. Ford, Omaha
Ira George Forell, Chester
Harry Alden Forman, Columbus
Eric Forslund, Stromsburg
Fred Charles Foster, Lincoln
Mattie E. Franks Foster, Hebron
John Wesley Fowler, Hershey
C. J. Frankforter, Lincoln
T. Eleanor Frazier, Wauneta
Virgil Sprankle Freas, Beaver City
William Freidell, Dorchester
W. Russell Freidell, Dorchester
Calvin Hervey French, Hastings
John Alexis French, Edison
Ernest L. Fried, Beemer
Matt Friend, Lawrence
Frank Samuel Frisbie, Red Cloud
Andrew Keyser Frolich, Louisville
William Thomas Fry, Holmesville
Otto Fuerst, Scottsbluff
Byron Sylvester Fulk, Atlanta
Clark A. Fulmer, Lincoln
Archie Charles Furman, Danbury
Charles Edward Furman, Danbury
Harry C. Furse, Alma

George E. Garber, Helvey
Charles Walter Garrison, Union
Emma Frances Garrison, Union
Orlie Robert Garwood, Ogallala
Cecil Leon Gatten, Ainsworth
Meta Paula Gemeinhardt, Potter
Benjamin Franklin Gentry, Gering
James Robert Gettys, Omaha
Samuel E. Gilinsky, Omaha
James Ward Gill, Chambers
James Willis Gillette, Norfolk

John Randolph Glassey, Hastings
Elmer Eugene Gockley, Edison
Richard Goehring, Jr., Grand Island
Nathan J. Gold, Lincoln
Ellis Ellsworth Good, Peru
William Larkin Goodell, Minden
George Edwin Gorton, Crawford
Charles Graff, Bancroft
Alice Winifred Graham, Lincoln
Francis Andrew Graham, Lincoln
James R. Graham, Allen
Robert Arnold Graham, York
John Gran, Mead
George Herbert Gray, Columbus
George A. Gregory, Crete
Emmett Henry Gribble, South Sioux City
Kirk Griggs, Omaha
Henry Grosenbach, Mascot
Genevieve Baldwin Guiou, Omaha
John Gumb, Fremont
William Albert Gunderson, Dix
Pleasant Hugh Gupton, Oxford

Blanche Albright Haas, Omaha
Charles William Hadan, Bennington
H. P. Haessler, Leshare
Gustave Hahn, Fremont
Oscar Herman Hahn, Hastings
James M. Hall, Ithaca
William Otto Hall, Reynolds
Eugene Frederick Ham, Benkelman
J. O. Ham, Benkelman
Edward Joseph Hamilton, Wilsonville
Frank James Hamilton, McCook
Lee Thomas Hamilton, Benkelman
Maurine Hamilton, Omaha.
James Waverly Hammond, Geneva
James William Hammond, Holdrege
James Waldo Hancock, Herman
George J. Hand, Alliance
John W. Hann, Wauneta
Anton Hansen, Upland
Peter Hansen, Potter
Roy Blaine Harberg, Springfield
Charles Herbert Harmon, Beatrice
James Joseph Harrington, O'Neill
Arthur Trevenning Harris, Hastings
Riley Clement Harriss, Omaha
John Hartigan, Fairbury
Charles Hartner, Madison
Earle Alonzo Harvey, Fairfield
Jan D. Hasik, David City
George A. Haslam, Fremont
Emil B. Hassel, Holdrege
Hastings Public Library, Hastings
Robert Richardson Hastings, Crete
Thomas Elial Hattel, Surprise
Leo Morgan Hauptman, Burr
Charles W. Havlicek, Crete
William Hawley, North Platte
Frank Martin Hayes, Arthur
William Henry Haywood, Bushnell
Francis Wenger Heagey, Omaha
Marshall Eddmon Hebrew, Lexington
Carl Hehnke, Grand Island
Hettie Josephine Hehnke, St. Edward
Bertin Ellsworth Hendricks, Wahoo
A. E. Henry, Pawnee City
Claude F. Hensel, Lincoln
Kenis P. Herald, Byron
Harry Edward Hester, Beaver City
Clarence Wright Hiatt, Diller
Charles W. Hickey, Bennington
John E. Higgins, Rogers
Ole E. Higgins, Stella
George Grover Hilder, Wymore
Ralph Wright Hill, Hebron
Minnie Grinstead Himes, Humbolt
Leon L. Hines, Benkelman
Alice Hamlin Hinman, Lincoln
William Wyman Hoagland, Omaha
John Hoaglund, Newman Grove
Ernest Howard Hoel, Omaha
Denis Patrick Hogan, Omaha
Henry Hoheisel, Papillion
Pearl Holloway, Fremont
Earl Eugene Hopping, Beaver City
Lulu Horne, Lincoln
Ensley Clinton Houston, Tekamah
Albert Tompkins Howard, Scottsbluff
Edgar Howard, Columbus
Herbert Howarth, Friend
Susan Upson Hoyt, Omaha
Ernest Alfred Hubka, Beatrice
Joseph S. Hubka, Virginia
Lottie Hudson, Crete
Otto Leonhart Huenefeld, Aurora
Grace McCoy Hummel, Gordon
Henry Albert Humrich, Beaver City
Joseph A. Husak, Schuyler
Mason Egbert Hyde, Gothenburg

Charles Reade Imler, Nelson
Royal Clark Inger, Hastings

Arthur James Irvine, Hamlet
Joshua Alvin Isaman, Aurora
May Elizabeth Isaman, Aurora
William Israelson, Hartington

Richard C. James, Falls City
Walter Dudley James, Cambridge
Joseph Jankowski, Ashton
Anthony Louis Jensen, Big Spring
Frank Jensen, Newman Grove
M. P. Jensen, Chappell
Hattie Irene Johns, Aurora
Alvin E. Johnson, Omaha
Carl Oscar Johnson, Lincoln
Czar Clinton Johnson, Lincoln
Dean R. Johnson, Curtis
Frank W. Johnson, Fullerton
George Robert Johnson, Bertrand
Gus Johnson, Ceresco
James Richard Johnson, McCook
John H. Johnson, Herman
R. C. Johnson, Mead
Raymond Samuel Johnson, Beatrice
Reuben A. Johnson, Newman Grove
George F. Jonaitis, Blair
Orel Jones, Oconto
William Lloyd Jones, Wymore
Arthur Lawrence Joseph, Grand Island

Anton C. G. Kaempfer, Bridgeport
Rudolph Ludwig Kaliff, York
James W. Kaura, Dewitt
H. L. Keefe, Walthill
Emma Kees, Beatrice
Riley Lytton Keester, Harlan
Estial C. Keister, Auburn
William Henry Kelligar, Auburn
William Kelly, Wymore
Edwin C. Kelso, North Platte
Edward Louis Kemper, Aurora
George Edward Kennedy, Newman Grove
George Lincoln Kennedy, Brownville
Howard Kennedy, Omaha
John L. Kennedy, Omaha
Bernard V. Kenney, Dodge
Dallas E. Kepler, Bridgeport
William R. Kepner, Osceola
R. H. Kerkow, West Point
Theodore Kerr, M. D., North Platte
Charles Vernon Kettering, Crete
E. R. Keyes, Cambridge
Grace Geneva Kidder, Sargeant
Ita Elizabeth Kiechel, Johnson
Walter Kiechel, Johnson
Hubert Leo Kildare, Paxton
Peter Henry Kilzer, Lebanon
Walter Kimball, Big Spring
Milo D. King, Minden
Ralph Edward King, Danbury
William David King, Whitman
Alva Raymond Kinney, Omaha
Camp KinniKinniK Association, Lincoln
Howard Kirkpatrick, Lincoln
Albert A. Kjar, Lexington
Alois J. Klein, Brainard
Wilhelm Carl Klein, Milford
John Blaine Kline, Hastings
Arthur Klingenberg, Chapman
Harry M. Knabe, Nehawka
John Knickrehm, Jr., Grand Island
Louis Jarrett Knoll, Liberty
S. Jacob Koch, Hershey
George William Koehn, South Sioux City
Gerhard F. Koester, Allen
Carl A. Kollmeyer, Fremont
Andrew Kopperud, Omaha
Walter William Korff, Hebron
Frank Koudele, Weston
Vratislav Joseph Kovarik, Hallam
Alex R. Krause, West Point
Clyde Lauren Krause, Newman Grove
Conrad Krekeler, Gothenburg
Edward Stanley Krikac, Comstock
Mary Eleanor Krisl, Milligan
William Krotter, Stuart
Adolph Jacob Kubitschek, Atkinson
Anna Reed Kuhle, Leigh
Charles R. Kuhle, Leigh
David Henry Kunkel, Osceola
Donald Alden Kunkel, North Platte

Albert LaBounty, Farnam
Thomas Johnson Lahners, Belvidere
Earl Edward Laidig, Danbury
Fred C. Laird, Fremont
Clarence Louis Landen, Omaha
George Winders Lang, Litchfield
Ella M. Langdon, Gretna
John H. Langdon, Gretna
Carl M. Lange, Hartington
Harry H. Lapidus, Omaha
Mary E. LaRocca, Omaha
Henry Larson, Loomis
Lauritz Augustin Larson, McCook

George Wesley Lautenschlager, Swanton
Clyde Conner Leach, Beaver City
George Edwin Leavitt, Crete
John James Ledwith, Lincoln
Daniel Robert Lee, Arcadia
James P. Lee, Omaha
Mabel Lee, Lincoln
Clara Elsa LeHew, Mitchell
Anthony Adam Lembach, Hastings
Frederick William Lentz, Beatrice
Elmer Ellsworth Lesh, Lincoln
August J. Leuthauser, Beemer
Victor Emanuel Levine, Omaha
Mark Levy, Hastings
Nelson Hiram Lewis, Benkelman
Rollie W. Ley, Wayne
O. H. Liebers, Lincoln
George Wallace Lincoln, Lexington
Lincoln Star, Lincoln
Frederic Reinhold Lindberg, Bridgeport
Rev. Anton Link, Sidney
Mr. and Mrs. Earle L. Lionberger,
   Superior
Daniel Webster Livingston, Nebraska City
Francis A. Long, Madison
John Usher Loomis, Omaha
Benjamin Franklin Lorance, Auburn
Gus Lorentz, Loup City
John Arthur Lothrop, Crete
Loup City Public Library, Loup City
Edwin J. Loutzenheiser, Gothenburg
Theodore Lowe, Jr., North Platte
B. Frank Lowery, Davenport
Robert A. Luehrs, Fremont
William Albert Luke, Lincoln
James William Lundy, Sargent
Laura Etta Lundy, Sargent
S. A. Lutgen, Wayne
Don William Lyne, Superior
Ray Orin Lyon, Trenton

James Edmund Mabie, Beaver City
Martin Madison, Goehner
Nellie Throop Magee, Lincoln
George A. Magney, Omaha
John A. Maguire, Lincoln
Thomas Jefferson Majors, Peru
Ada C. Malcolm, Lincoln
Orlando B. Manville, Norfolk
Clarence Sidney Marcy, Hay Springs
William Charles Margrave, Preston
Harry Miller Marquis, Bridgeport
Fred Alexander Marsh, Archer
George W. Marsh, Lincoln
Chester Chancy Marshall, Fremont
Chester G. Marshall, Arlington
George Allison Marshall, Arlington
Frank Thomas Becket Martin, Omaha
Jerry Lewis Martin, Edison
Josephine Sutton Marty, Lincoln
Engalena Josephine Marvel, Giltner
Charles Jacob Mary, Oconto
Edward John Mashek, Abie
Fred G. Mason, Upland
Albert N. Mathers, Gering
August Ferdinand Matzke, Western
Mr. and Mrs. Grover C. May, York
Emma McClelland, Beaver City
Mr. and Mrs. C. A. McCloud, York
Hugh Montgomery McClure, Kearney
Alfred Thomas McCoy, Trenton
Richard McCracken, Springview
Anna Snyder McCullough, Brady
James McCullough, Brady
Oscar Wiley McDaniel, Valentine
Clyde McElmoil, Farnam
Claud Gwinn McGaffin, Bellwood
Edmund G. McGilton, Omaha
Ray B. McIllece, Lawrence
Lillie Muir McKay, Haigler
Henry Clark McKee, Palmyra
Neal Patrick McKee, Atkinson
Robert Lee McKissick, Dunbar
Frederick Walter McNally, O'Neill
A. L. McPherson, Craig
R. V. McPherson, Craig
Hugh Gamble McVicker, Lincoln
Peter Anthony Meehan, York
William Robert Mellor, Lincoln
Bert C. Mendell, Superior
George N. Mendenhall, Fremont
I. J. Merrick, Osceola
Emil Merscheid, North Platte
Ernest M. Merwin, Beaver City
Fletcher N. Merwin, Beaver City
M. Myrtle Merwin, Beaver City
Merta I. Merwin, Beaver City
Anna V. Cornish Metcalf, Omaha
Frank C. Middlebrook, York
Florence Hazen Miller, Crete
Harry D. Miller, Stanton
Harvey J. Miller, Carleton
John H. Miller, Lincoln
Oscar George Miller, Crete

Henry Rufus Miner, Falls City
R. L. Minnick, Stromsburg
Charles Mitchell, Wayne
Orin Wesley Moore, Gering
Edwin Francis Moran, Nebraska City
Joseph W. Morgan, Lexington
R. D. Moritz, Lincoln
Richard Grant Morrison, Loomis
Cyrus Allen Morse, Oxford
Marion Richard Mortensen, Long Pine
Ralph S. Moseley, Lincoln
Fred Carl Mowinkel, Gretna
Carl Clarence Moyer, Ainsworth
William Max August Mueller, Springfield
Sarah T. Muir, Lincoln
Arthur Francis Mullen, Omaha
Wendell E. Mumby, Harrison
Claude C. Munday, Edison
Arbor Day Munger, Lincoln
Cora Ellen Stone Murphy, Page
Myrtle Edna Musser, Rushville
H. Dey Myers, M. D., Howells
Preston B. Myers, Omaha.

Clement Nacke, Hooper
E. Herman Naumann, Columbus
Perry Thomas Naylor, Hastings
Nebraska State Historical Society, Lincoln
Nebraska State Library Commission, Lincoln
Erland N. P. Nelson, Blair
Lemist George Nelson, Bassett
John Wallace Neslund, Cozad
Arthur Lorenzo Neumann, Oakland
Harry George Neumayer, Paxton
John William Neville, Utica
Keith Neville, North Platte
Anne C. Newbigging, Wisner
James Compton Newcomb, Friend
Mr. and Mrs. Everett J. Newkirk, Hastings
Frederick Nielsen, Lexington
Johannes W. Nielsen, Sidney
E. C. Nordlund, Stromsburg
James C. Norgaard, Superior
Charles August Norlin, Surprise
Day C. Norman, Chester
Dan Clifford Norris, Brewster
George W. Norris, McCook
Viola Hinds Norris, Weeping Water
Bernard Norsworthy, Gothenburg
Mrs. Charles Oliver Norton, Kearney
William Fred Novak, Howells
Charles Novotny, Clarkson
Berton Frank Noyes, Hastings
Claire J. Noyes, Hastings
Andrew F. Nuquist, Osceola
Joseph C. Nuss, Wayne
Fred A. Nye, Kearney

Edward James O'Brien, Exeter
Rinehardt Otto Ochsner, Deshler
Viola Emily Rosseter Odendahl, Loup City
Joseph P. O'Gara, Lincoln
Hans C. Olsen, Kearney
George C. Olson, Stromsburg
Omaha Public Library, Omaha
Omaha World-Herald, Omaha
Clyde Oman, Wayne
John Edward Opp, Burwell
Edward Joseph O'Shea, Holdrege
Eugene Daniel O'Sullivan, Omaha
Daniel Lewis Ough, Benkelman
Albert Bernard Outhouse, Loup City
George Edwin Overturf, Hastings
Claire Estelle Owens, Exeter
Griffith John Owens, Benkelman

Bayard H. Paine, Grand Island
Ladimore F. Papik, Dorchester
Edmund M. Parker, Crete
Edward Henry Pauley, York
William George Pauley, Hastings
Jesse Leland Pearl, Burwell
Robert Pease, Beatrice
Charles W. Peasinger, Randolph
Rich Stetson Peckham, Brady
H. Christian Pedersen, Fremont
Ernest Bert Perry, Lincoln
Alexander Peters, Bancroft
Claus F. Peters, Bancroft
Andrew R. Peterson, Wisner
Frank L. Peterson, Valparaiso
Mrs. J. Fred Peterson, Falls City
John Petrow, Fremont
Willard Alonzo Petteys, Wilcox
Harrison McCurdy Pettygrove, Oxford
Robert Frederick Pfeiffer, Kearney
Frank Emery Pfoutz, North Platte
H. E. Phelps, Howells
L. A. Phelps, Fremont
Chandler Noyes Philbrick, Fullerton
Bryce Anton Philips, Bertrand
Albert Phillipson, Holbrook

Peter Phillipson, Holbrook
William Thomas Pickett, Wahoo
Chester Arthur Pierce, Hastings
W. E. Pierson, Osceola
Jane Pinder, Grand Island
Albert Francis Pinkley, Ansley
George LeRoy Pinney, Hastings
Alden Charles Plantz, Rushville
Raymond J. Pool, Lincoln
L. Thomas Poole, Sidney
Erwin Edward Popcke, Blair
John Edward Poquette, Sidney
Myron Jay Posson, Ogallala
Marcus L. Poteet, Lincoln
Bird S. Potter, Gothenburg
Dr. John B. Potts, Omaha
Louise Pound, Lincoln
James Frederick Premer, Benkelman
Gustave Prestegaard, Lincoln
Walter G. Preston, Omaha
Frederick Homer Price, Newman Grove
Rudolf V. Prokop, Hubbard
Robert Morton Proudfit, Friend
Vincent Joseph Prucha, Crete
Francis John Pryor, 3rd, North Platte
Edward Thomas Purinton, Cambridge
Walter George Purtzer, Madison

Gerard V. Rademacher, Crete
Boyd Clyde Radford, Newark
Sanford Eugene Ralsten, Geneva
Orville Alfred Ralston, Ainsworth
Ray E. Ramsay, Lincoln
John Murray Rankin, Cambridge
Robert Hillhouse Rankin, Cambridge
Anton Nelson Rask, Boelus
Kenneth A. Rawson, Dix
August Louis Rebbe, Hooper
William D. Redmond, Mason City
Paul A. Reed, Deshler
William Elbridge Reed, Omaha
William Frederick Reichenberg, Arthur
L. F. Reinecke, Schuyler
Carolyn Renfrew, Hastings
Ferdinand August Reuter, Syracuse
John Walter Reutzel, Trenton
Elmer Mortimer Reynolds, Culbertson
Ralph K. Reynolds, Fairbury
Clarence Edward Rice, Odell
Ernest Joseph Axtell Rice, Ainsworth
Judson LeRoy Rice, Blue Springs
Lloyd Clifford Richardson, Cambridge
Jacob Rickard, Max
Ted Eugene Riddell, Scottsbluff
Charles E. Rider, Imperial
Franz Joseph Riesland, Wood River
John A. Rine, Omaha
Alexander Charles Ring, Hebron
Averilla Ring, Hebron
William Alexander Ring, Hebron
William Ritchie, Jr., Omaha
James Rivett, Lincoln
Antonio R. Rizzuto, Omaha
Joseph Roberts, Fremont
Harold Wiley Robinson, Upland
Lawrence Roswell Robinson, Waterloo
Julius William Ferdinand Roggenkamp,
   Upland
Henry Rohwer, Fort Calhoun
John C. Romer, Minden
James Victor Romigh, North Platte
Charles H. Roper, Lincoln
Lottie W. Rosencrans, Plattsmouth
James Abner Ross, Long Pine
Dave D. Rowe, Fremont
Mark J. Ryan, Pender
George Albert Rydlund, Funk

Harry Evans Sackett, Beatrice
Hermina Reynolds Sackett, Beatrice
Frank J. Sadilek, Wilber
Ira Ernest Sage, Arthur
Frank Eli Sala, Lincoln
Arvid Stanley Samuelson, Axtell
Isaac Theodore Samuelson, Polk
Charles Fredrick Sandahl, Kearney
Daniel Phillip Sanders, Grand Island
Andrew J. Sandstrom, Bertrand
George Emory Newton Sanders, Peru
Arminta Louise Saylor, Bruning
Harvey Wesley Saylor, Bruning
George L. Schaefer, Tekamah
Benjamin Kurtz Schaeffer, Curtis
Elizabeth Elma Schelkopf, Geneva
Henry E. Schemmel, Hooper
Edward August Schenbeck, Gering
Albert L. Schneider, M. D., Brady
Fred David Schneider, Loup City
Louis Scholz, Osceola
Fred Schreiner, Unadilla
Herman Schroeder, Sidney
Herman Gordon Schroeder, Hastings
H. von W. Schulte, Omaha
William Will Schulz, Sidney

Albert Bernard Schuster, Virginia
George Schwake, Lincoln
Mary Dell Schwake, Lincoln
Elmore Charles Schweser, Surprise
T. M. Scott, Hamilton
William Alson Selleck, Lincoln
Victor Seymour, Lincoln
Anna Dorothea Shadbolt, Gordon
Michael Shaheen, Arthur
John Dee Shank, Superior
Lawrence M. Shaw, Osceola
Relvia Ulysses Shaw, Cambridge
Eva Lydia Shearer, Lincoln
Addison Erwin Sheldon, Lincoln
Burton Wallace Sheldon, Ogallala
Lucius A. Sherman, Lincoln
Maurice Fisher Shickley, Ainsworth
Marion E. Shipley, Hooper
Charles Albert Shoff, Grafton
William Edward Shook, Shubert
Abel Vail Shotwell, Omaha
Berton T. Shoup, Sutherland
William Ambrose Shreck, Bertrand
J. Frank Shubert, Shubert
Arthur Harold Shultz, Scribner
Seymour Stephen Sidner, Fremont
Mr. and Mrs. J. M. Silver, Superior
Edward Franklin Sime, Burwell
G. Eli Simon, Cambridge
Osborne Perkins Simon, Culbertson
Henry Sinn, Alexandria
John Edward Sinning, Danbury
Fred Walter Skinner, Ainsworth
Charles Henry Sloan, Geneva.
Clyde C. Smalley, Minden
J. E. Smatlan, Schuyler
Erle Boyd Smiley, Seward
Archie Manley Smith, Pender
Anbrey Adam Smith, St. Edward
Beaman Quincy Smith, Stockville
Clara Lotspeich Smith, Lincoln
Wilber S. Smith, Byron
William John Smith, Omaha
Marietta Snow, Lincoln
Charles Cook Snowden, Davenport
Soren Nielsen Soelberg, Elba
J. M. Sorensen, Fremont
Allan D. Speir, Omaha
C. R. Spicer, Hastings
E. J. Spirk, Wilber
Marion Wilson Spohn, Chester
Edward Herbert Springer, Brady
William George Springer, McCook
Frank Joseph Srb, Dodge
Hugo Frank Srb, Dodge
Joseph John Srb, Dwight
Ben Lynn Stahl, Nelson
Alvah H. Staley, Hastings
Olga Stastny, Omaha
Carl Frederic Steckelberg, Lincoln
Francis J. Stejskal, Crete
Dan Vorhees Stephens, Fremont
Harland U. Stevens, Lincoln
Willis Edie Stewart, Stratton
James Leonard Stivers, Auburn
William Tolbert Stockdale, Chadron
Glenn Earl Stoddard, Alma
Wayne O. Stoehr, Omaha
Arthur Charles Stokes, Omaha
Carl G. Stoll, Lincoln
Robert Irving Stout, Tekamah
St. Paul Public Library, St. Paul
Oscar Strand, Polk
Leonard Stromberg, Oakland
Carl Kennedy Struble, Fremont

Hird Stryker, Omaha
Brantley Elijah Sturdevant, Atkinson
Chester Dwight Sturtevant, Omaha
Louis Suess, McCook
Gustav Sumnick, Waterloo
James A. Sunderland, Omaha
Douglas C. Sutherland, Oakland
Harold W. Swan, Kearney
Carl H. Swanson, Culbertson
W. Otto Swanson, Omaha
Artie O. Swartwood, Fremont
Francis Marion Swartwood, Adams
Charles Arthur Sweet, Palmyra
A. C. R. Swenson, Omaha
Erman Nathan Swett, South Sioux City

W. B. Tagg, Omaha
Earl A. Talhelm, Crete
Dora Alexander Talley, Omaha
Charles William Taylor, Lincoln
Clyde Henry Taylor, Overton
Frank James Taylor, St. Paul
Mary L. Taylor, Raymond
Guy Allen Temple, Lexington
Hardin S. Tennant, Stanton
Dale L. Thomas, Kilgore
Elmer Alonzo Thomas, Hastings
Minnie Florella Thomas, Omana
Charles Y. Thompson, West Point
Arthur C. Thomsen, Omaha
Ingebert Johansen Thomsen, Minden
Bertha Evelyn Mangon Thomson, Lincoln
John Thomssen, Alda
Robert Tichy, Sr., Wilber
August Mathew Tillman, Hooper
Levi Goodsil Todd, Union
Irl D. Tolen, Ord
Earle A. Tolles, Laurel
Edwin Frederick Tonsing, Syracuse
Frank Gordon Tracy, Kearney
George Washington Trine, Red Cloud
Henry Truhlsen, Herman
Nels A. Tuveson, Weston
John S. Twinem, M. D., North Platte
Dr. Albert Franklin Tyler, Omaha
Ace Vern Tyrell, Osceola

Ernest Clarence Uhlig, Sutherland
William Miller Umberger, Elwood
University of Nebraska Library, Lincoln
G. R. Unthank, Lincoln

Clarence A. Valder, Tekamah
Frank Ellsworth Van Cleave, Beaver City
Sarah Van Pelt, Stockville
Guy Van Steenberg, Beaver City
Ralph W. Venrick, Dewitt
Adolph J. Vierling, Omaha
Edwin Vieselmeyer, Deshler
Alice Marie von Bergen, Lincoln
Emil M. von Seggern, West Point

Olin Bennett Waddill, Gordon
Mary Ann Wagoner, Broadwater
Harold P. Waite, McCook
Willis Roseberry Waite, Arcadia
Peter Waldorf, Western
Allan Walker, Dunbar
Irving Seth Walker, Kimball
Charles Glenn Wallace, Hastings
Stanley P. Wallin, Snyder
William Frederick Waltemath, North Platte
William Ballou Wanner, Falls City

Wiley Ray Ward, Overton
Fred C. Warnemunde, Lexington
Charles Joseph Warner, Waverly
Frank Austin Warner, Norfolk
William P. Warner, Dakota City
John Clarence Warren, Beatrice
Willard Bentley Warren, Atkinson
John Wesley Warrick, Meadow Grove
M. C. Warrington, Mason City
Charles William Warwick, Valentine
S. A. Wassum, Tekamah
Guttorm Ellingson Wasthun, Bostwick
Helen Blackman Webendorfer, Beaver City
Pearl Louise Weber, Omaha
H. L. Webster, Tekamah
John Fabian Webster, St. Paul
William Byron Weekes, Ord
Herman Frederick Weigel, Stuart
Andy J. Welch, Milford
Hermann G. Wellensiek, Grand Island
Elizabeth Wentz, Lincoln
Frank Werner, Alma
Harry Jacob Wertman, Milford
George W. Wertz, Schuyler
Clara Street Wescott, Plattsmouth
Elizabeth H. West, Gothenburg
Chattie Coleman Westenius, Stromsburg
Victor Westermark, Benkelman
Frank Elmer Weyer, Hastings
Jennings M. Wheat, Papillion
Grace Mason Wheeler, Lincoln
Kenneth S. Wherry, Pawnee City
Thomas Uridge Whiffen, Dewitt
Harry S. White, Lyons
Herbert T. White, Omaha
Edward Thomas Whiting, Gordon
Fredrick Harvey Whitmore, Valley
George Q. Whitney, Ainsworth
Bernard Whitwer, Tilden
Fred Conrad Wiegman, North Platte
John Henry Wiese, Springfield
T. L. Wiggins, Gothenburg
Elmer Dee Wiley, Bennet
Charles Martel Wilhelmj, M. D., Omaha
Rees Wilkinson, Lincoln
Cora Alice Williams, Elmwood
George Arthur Williams, Fairmont
Robert Henry Willis, Bridgeport
Clarence Oren Wilson, Hastings
Fredric Louis Wilson, Stuart
Howard Stebbins Wilson, Lincoln
Oscar Lee Wilson, Rushville
Waldo Wintersteen, Fremont
Henry Elmer Wolf, Hyannis
Asa Butler Wood, Gering
Wilbur Fisk Wood, Haigler
Sands Forman Woodbridge, Jr., Hastings
Sarah Ladd Woods, Lincoln
James Eugene Woodward, Chester
Clarence C. Worden, Ogallala
Nellie Frances Wullschleger, Leigh

Florence E. Yoder, Lexington
H. S. Yost, Havelock
James Tilton Young, Fremont
Shaw Ruskin Young, Gering

Charles Fred Zabel, Western
William T. Zahradnicek, Johnstown
Nicholas Edward Zehr, Chappell
William Emanuel Zehr, Chappell
Elmo Murray Zike, Edison
Andrew Zoz, Murdock

Charles Edwin Abbott

Charles Edwin Abbott, who has been engaged in the practice of law at Fremont for thirty-three years, was born at Taylorville, Illinois, December 1, 1871. He is the son of Miles J. and Jennie (Scribner) Abbott, the former born at Pana, Illinois, November 17, 1847, a lawyer, newspaper publisher and county judge of Hayes County. He died at Fremont, May 2, 1908. His wife, Jennie, was a native of Kentucky, born July 14, 1847, who died at Omaha, June 24, 1898.

Mr. Abbott attended public and high school, and received his LL. B. degree from Nebraska in 1897. He is a member of Phi Delta Phi. In his 34 years at Fremont he has practiced law continuously, his present partnership being with the firm of Abbott, Dunlap and Corbett.

The partnership enjoys a large and important practice; they have had recent cases, of state-wide importance, in the Nebraska supreme court, involving the constitutionality of school district and electric district laws, in which their contentions that particular laws were each unconstitutional, were upheld.

Mr. Abbott was special counsel for the State of Nebraska, associated with Attorney General Sorensen, in the case brought by 550 State Banks against the state attacking generally the constitutionality of the Depositors Guarantee Fund Law and to enjoin the collection by the state of three million dollars of assessments and also future assessments; decisions in favor of the state were made by the state supreme court and United States supreme court.

He is a Republican and served as city attorney for 12 years, and was delegate to the Republican national convention of 1928. He has extensive banking, real estate and farming interests, and is vice president and director of the Fremont National Bank. Mr. Abbott has declined an important Federal judicial appointment and other positions which would require his removal from Fremont and the abandonment of his active law practice.

On November 28, 1900, he was married to Gertrude Sexton of Fontanelle, Nebraska, at Fremont. They have three children, Katherine Abbott Folsom, born April 12, 1902; Theodore, born March 20, 1903, who died November 13, 1903, and Charles Wade, born May 24, 1906, who was graduated from the academic and law departments of the University of Nebraska, and who is associated with the firm in practice in Fremont. Mr. Abbott is a member of St. James Episcopal Church, the Young Men's Christian Association, the various branches of Masonry, the Elks and Modern Woodmen of America.

He is a member of the American and Nebraska State Bar Associations, and is active in welfare work. Actively interested in Midland College of Fremont, he was for many years a member of the executive committee of its board. Residence: Fremont. (Photograph on Page 10).

Ned Culbertson Abbott

Ned C. Abbott, educator of the blind, writer, and noted lecturer, was born at Fremont, Nebraska, March 9, 1874. Luther Jewett Abbott, his father, was a physician and surgeon, a lecturer, a member of the last territorial legislature, and superintendent of the Nebraska Hospital for the Insane, at Lincoln, Nebraska, 1895-99. He was born at Blue Hill, Hancock County, Maine, September 15, 1831, and was descended from the old Puritan families, Bancrofts, Adams, and Whites. George Abbott, who came to Andover, Massachusetts, in 1640, was an ancestor.

Clara Frances (Culbertson) Abbott, his mother, was a music teacher. Her ancestry was Puritan, and included the Culbertson, Coleman, and Hollister families. She was born at Troy, Miami County, Ohio, February 20, 1835, and died at Fremont, July 19, 1911.

Mr. Abbott was graduated from the Fremont High School in 1892, after which he attended the University of Nebraska, where he was a member of the Union Society, the University debating club. He was given the leading role in *Plautus Captivi* in 1894. He was awarded the A. B. degree in 1896, and the LL. B. degree in 1900. In 1919 he received his M. A. degree. He was admitted to the practice of law at Lincoln in 1900.

He has been engaged in educational work since 1896, and has held various positions as teacher and executive in Nebraska schools. He was a teacher in the Nebraska School for the Blind, at Nebraska City, 1896-98; was principal of the Humboldt High School, 1900-01; superintendent of the Tekamah schools, 1905-1909; was superintendent of the Plattsmouth schools, 1911-13; and since 1915 has been superintendent of the Nebraska School for the Blind.

A resident of Nebraska for 54 years Mr. Abbott has won an enviable position in the regard of his associates in his community and state. He is the author of educational articles, stories, and pamphlets, and has been the editor of various school publications. His most recent work is *Lincoln—Name and Place*, published in 1930. In 1916 he was alumni orator at the University of Nebraska and made the address *Dynamics of Inspiration*. In 1925 he received a medal from Post Number 8 of the American Legion, and in 1927 he was given the Community Service Award by the Nebraska City Rotary Club.

He was married to Lillian Newbranch at Lincoln, June 19, 1901. Mrs. Abbott, who was born at Swedesburg, Henry County, Iowa, is descended from the Swedish families, Newbranch and Rapp. There are four children, Clara Louise, born January 13, 1905, is married to Frederick Ware, sports editor, *World-Herald* at Omaha; Lea, born May 13, 1907, an aviation pilot, is now an instructor at Dallas, Texas; Grace, born November 5, 1908, is a stenographer at Chicago, and Annabel, born April 9, 1916, is a junior in high school.

Mr. Abbott is an independent Democrat, and in 1908 was unsuccessful candidate for state superintendent of schools. In 1891 he was a private in Company E of the First Nebraska National Guards in the Sioux uprising. During the World War he served on the registration advisory board and was a four minute man. He is past president of the Nebraska Sons of the American Revolution.

Mr. Abbott is active in the Rotary Club at Nebraska City; is an honorary member of the Lions Club at Omaha; and an honorary member of the Optimist Club at Lincoln. He is president of the Nebraska State Historical Society; is a director in the American Association of Educators of the Blind, and a director of the University of Nebraska Alumni Association. His social club is the Nebraska City Country Club. Residence: Nebraska City.

William James Abbott

William James Abbott, retired rancher, was born at Wabasha, Minnesota, October 15, 1856, son of George and Ellen (Woods) Abbott. His father was born in Cork, Ireland, and came to America in 1850. He served in the Civil War and died at Nashville, Tennessee, in

CHARLES EDWIN ABBOTT

Skoglund—Fremont

1864. His wife, Ellen, was born in England and died at Minniska, Minnesota, in 1920.

Mr. Abbott has engaged in cattle raising for a number of years, recently retiring. In August, 1891, he was married to Mary Bergerson at Hyannis. Mrs. Abbott was born in Christiania, Norway, May 31, 1866. There are four children, Maud, born August 3, 1892, who married Floyd R. Taylor; Harry, born December 6, 1893, who married Jeanette V. Abbott; Willard, born June 28, 1898, who married Frances G. Gadient; and Lola, born January 21, 1900, who married Edward L. Rasmussen. Harry served in the World War. He is in the garage business at the present time. Willard is the owner of a general store.

Mr. Abbott is a Republican. During 1925 and 1926 he served as county commissioner of Grant County. He is a member of the Odd Fellows, and a former member of the Whitman School Board. Residence: Whitman.

Frank Abegg

Frank Abegg, prominent Alliance broker, was born in Blakesburg, Iowa, April 7, 1895, son of Walter and Kate (Smith) Abegg. His father, who was a banker, died August 28, 1928.

Mr. Abegg has been a resident of Nebraska since May 25, 1912. On November 16, 1915, he was married to Mary Anna Abegg, at Alliance. Mrs. Abegg was born at Alliance, on July 27, 1895. They have ten children.

Mr. Abegg is a Republican. He is president of the Alliance Loan & Investment Company, president of the First National Bank of Minatare, Nebraska, and a director of the Alliance Building & Loan Association. Residence: Alliance.

George P. Abel

George P. Abel, president of the Abel Construction Company of Lincoln, was born at Etna Mills, California, July 6, 1882, son of James and Leasie (Baker) Abel.

His father, born at Peoria, Illinois, was a construction and coal mining engineer in his younger days, but later applied himself to contracting. He is now deceased. His wife was born at Clinton, Iowa, and resides at Lincoln.

The Abel family moved to Nebraska from California while George P. Abel was still a boy, settling at Fremont. Upon leaving high school, Mr. Abel entered the University of Nebraska where he received his degree of Bachelor of Science in civil engineering in 1906. He then entered the employ of the Burlington railroad in the engineering department, where he continued until 1908. At that time he and Charles W. Roberts entered into a business partnership and founded the Abel-Roberts Construction Company. In 1915 the partnership was dissolved, and at that time Mr. Abel became president of the Abel Construction Company, which engages in work all over Nebraska. Mr. Abel has been prominent in civic and business activities for many years, and has served as a director of the First National Bank, as president of the Buffalo Paving Brick Company of Buffalo, Kansas. He is a 32nd degree Scottish Rite Mason and a member of the Shrine, and a member of the Elks. He is a Republican, and a member of the Plymouth Congregational Church.

He is married to Hazel Hempel of Omaha, daughter of Charles Hempel, railroad official of the Union Pacific lines. Mrs. Abel attended Omaha High School and received the Bachelor of Arts degree from the University of Nebraska in 1908. She taught school for a short time prior to her marriage, and since that time has been active in social and club work. She is a member of the Eastern Star and the American Association of University Women. There are five children, Helen, George, Hazel, Alice and Annette Lee. Residence: Lincoln.

Dell Abraham

Born at Sioux Falls, South Dakota, September 12, 1894, Dell Abraham is the son of Charles and Elizabeth (Abdellah) Abraham. Charles Abraham, who is a merchant, was born at Beruth, Syria, January 10, 1866, came to this country 40 years ago, was a farmer for over 10 years, and has been engaged in business since then. Elizabeth (Abdellah) Abraham was born at Beruth, Syria, June 10, 1876.

Mr. Abraham has been a merchant at Ainsworth, for the past 20 years, and is a member of the Ainsworth Commercial Club of which he was secretary for one term and director for two terms. He is affiliated with the Sacred Heart Catholic Church and holds membership in the Modern Woodmen of America. His recreations are fishing, hunting, and reading.

He was united in marriage with Genevieve Saba, at Mankato, Minnesota, April 5, 1919. Mrs. Abraham was born at Mankato, June 5, 1897. They have two children: Dolores, born February 19, 1921; and Ramona, born October 27, 1929. Residence: Ainsworth.

Carl Alfred Abrahamson

C. Alfred Abrahamson was born at Omaha, Nebraska, November 1, 1892, and has lived there all his life. His father, John Alfred Abrahamson, was born at Karlskrona, Sweden, June 21, 1861. His mother, Hanna Mathilda (Nelson) Abrahamson was born at Gothenburg, Sweden, November 22, 1860; her ancestry was Swedish and French.

Mr. Abrahamson was graduated from Central High School in 1911. In 1910 he was mailboy for the United States National Bank; from 1911 to 1917 he held various positions in the Corn Exchange National Bank at Omaha; was manager of the Sioux City office for the Universal Finance Corporation, 1917-20; assistant cashier of the Corn Exchange National Bank, 1921-24; new-business solicitor for the Omaha National Bank, 1924-25; manager of the insurance department of the Omaha National Company, 1925-30; and is now its vice president.

He married Helen Sturgess at Omaha, April 12, 1923. Mrs. Abrahamson was born at Omaha, May 29, 1896. They have one son, John, born July 29, 1925. Mr. Abrahamson served as first lieutenant of the 813th Pioneer Infantry during the World War, and saw active service in the Meuse-Argonne offensive. He is a member of the American Legion, and former vice commander of Omaha Post Number 1, of this organization; a member of the Forty and Eight in which he has held various local offices, and of which he was sergeant-at-arms in 1925.

A member of the Omaha Chamber of Commerce and the Happy Hollow Country Club, he is a Mason and Knight Templar, a Republican, and a member of the Methodist Episcopal Church of Omaha. Residence: Omaha.

Ellen Ackerman

Ellen Ackerman, home maker and club woman, was born at Stillwater, Minnesota, May 13, 1868, daughter of Patrick and Elizabeth (Burden) Murphy.

Her father was born at Bradford, Pennsylvania, September 24, 1842, and died at Ainsworth July 9, 1927. He was a ranchman, a farmer, and politician, whose family came to America from Ireland about 1840. His wife, Elizabeth, was born at Chatham, New Brunswick, February 4, 1844, and died at Ainsworth, January 28, 1919. She was of English descent, and a leader in all civic and cultural movements.

On May 8, 1887, Mrs. Ackerman was married to James George Ackerman at Ainsworth. Mr. Ackerman was born at Ramseys, New Jersey, August 26, 1855, and is a prominent banker and merchant at Ainsworth. (See Nebraskana). Mrs. Ackerman is a Democrat and has served as a member of the board of education. She is author of numerous articles for publication, and for two years was a teacher in the public schools. At the present time she is state director of the General Federation of Women's Clubs for Nebraska.

During the late war she worked on all Red Cross activities and made speeches on Liberty Loan drives. She is a member of the Women's Relief Corps, and from 1912 to 1913 was department president. She is also a member of the American Legion Auxiliary, Ainsworth Woman's Club, and a member of the board of the Alder Free Library of Ainsworth, having held this position since its organization in 1911. She is a member of the Christian Science Church. Her hobby is reading. Residence: Ainsworth. (Photograph in Album).

James George Ackerman

James George Ackerman, retired merchant, broker and banker, of Ainsworth, Nebraska, was born at Ramseys, Bergen County, New Jersey, August 26, 1855, the son of Jacob J. and Elizabeth (Young) Ackerman. His father, a contractor and builder, was born at Crystal Lake, Bergen County, New Jersey, December 23, 1827, and died at Ramseys, September 30, 1868. His ancestors, who moved to Holland from England many centuries ago, came to this country in 1662 and settled in what is now Bergen County, New Jersey; members of the family served in the Revolution and the Civil War.

Elizabeth (Young) Ackerman, wife of Jacob, was born at Ramseys, April 4, 1830, and died at Paterson, New Jersey, October 22, 1896. Her Scotch ancestors settled in America in 1700, and members of the Young family were active in the Revolutionary and Civil Wars.

Mr. Ackerman has been a resident of Brown County for nearly 50 years, and was for many years prominent as a merchant, broker, and banker at Ainsworth. A Democrat, he was a frequent delegate to state conventions, and served as delegate to the Free Silver national convention at Kansas City, Missiouri.

During the World War Mr. Ackerman worked for the Red Cross and took an active part in all Liberty loan drives. He is a member of the Sons of the American Revolution, is affiliated with the Episcopal Church, and holds membership in the Nebraskana Society. His hobby is gardening.

His marriage to Ellen Murphy occurred at Ainsworth, May 8, 1887. Mrs. Ackerman, who was formerly a teacher, is now prominent in club work. At the present time she is General Federation director of Nebraska. She was born of English and Irish parents at Stillwater, Minnesota, May 13, 1868. They have two children: George M., born July 3, 1891, who married Edith May Merten; and Dorothy E., born Aplir 19, 1899, who is married to Kent C. Hartung. George was graduated from the University of Nebraska, and is now state bank examiner at Burlingame, California, while Dorothy was a student at the University of Nebraska for two years before her marriage. Mr. Ackerman has been a Mason fifty-five years, and has held all offices. He holds a fifty year emblem from the grand lodge of Nebraska. He is a Knight Templar, also. Residence Ainsworth. (Photograph in Album).

Franklin George Adams

Franklin George Adams, farmer in Merrick County, Nebraska, has lived in the state all his life. He was born at Clarks, Nebraska, August 18, 1873, the son of William and Amanda May (Cosner) Adams. His father, who was born in West Virginia, was a pioneer homesteader in Merrick County, and served during the Civil War with General Sherman on his famous march to the sea; he died at Clarks in 1897. His mother was born of Pennsylvania Dutch parents at Bureau, Illinois, and died at Clarks in 1903.

Mr. Adams received his education in rural schools. He is a member of the Nebraskana Society, is a Mason,

and for the past 20 years has served on the school board at Clarks. His hobbies are reading and coin collecting and his favorite sport is baseball. He is a Democrat.

His marriage to Lulu Estella Fox occurred at Washougal, Washington, January 2, 1901. Mrs. Adams, who is of Pennsylvania Dutch and Scotch descent, was born at Silver Creek, Nebraska, January 11, 1879. To this marriage the following children were born: Roderick E., October 2, 1901, who died September 13, 1906; Clifford William, March 21, 1906; Audrey Sybil, March 21, 1909, who married George Towman; and Idona Dee, March 2, 1922. Residence: Clarks.

James Henry Adams

James Henry Adams, lawyer, was born in Brighton, Illinois, April 3, 1868, the only son of Reverend William R. Adams. The father was born in New Hampshire, was a graduate of Dartmouth College, and received the degrees of Master of Arts and Bachelor of Theology from Blackburn University. He was ordained a minister of the Presbyterian Church in 1861 and from 1888 to 1900 preached at various points in Nebraska.

James Henry Adams moved with the family to Blairstown, Iowa, at about the age of eleven. In 1888 he was graduated from Coe College with the degree of Bachelor of Arts, and was elected to Phi Kappa Phi, national honorary scholarship society. Thereafter he taught at Hardy, Nebraska, as principal of schools for two years. In 1892 he received the degree of LL. B. from the University of Michigan and has been engaged in the practice of law ever since in the city of Omaha. He has been general counsel of the Bankers Reserve Life Company since 1906.

Mr. Adams is a member of the American, the Nebraska State, and the Omaha Bar Associations. He is a Republican, a member of the Presbyterian Church, being a member of the Permanent Judicial Commission of the General Assembly of that church. He is a 33rd degree Scottish Rite Mason and a member of the Shrine. He was married in 1898 to Clara L. Wigton, who died in 1900. Mr. Adams was married again to Jessie L. Witwer of Cedar Rapids, Iowa, in 1909.

He has three children: Reverend Clarence W. Adams, born in 1900, who was graduated from the University of Nebraska in 1922, and is now a missionary of the Presbyterian Church in northern India; Robert K. Adams, born in 1911, now a junior at Grinnell College; Elizabeth W. Adams, born in 1913, now a sophomore at Grinnell College. Residence: Omaha.

Roy Bennett Adams

Roy B. Adams, one of Nebraska's leading physicians and educators at Lincoln, was born at Martinsville, Morgan County, Indiana, January 10, 1880. George Andrew Adams, his father, was a distinguished lawyer; was a member of the Indiana Legislature, 1883-85-89; and was a member of the board of education at Lincoln, Lancaster County, Nebraska, 1900-03. He served as mayor of Lincoln, 1903-05. His Irish and German ancestors came to America just after the Revolution.

Martha (Bennett) Adams, his mother, who was born at Cory, Clay County, Indiana, February 9, 1853, is descended from Scotch-Irish ancestors who came to America before the French and Indian War.

Dr. Adams attended the public schools of Martinsville, Indiana, and Lincoln, and in 1896 was graduated from Worthington Military Academy. He received his A. B. degree at the University of Nebraska and his M. D. from Rush Medical College. In 1928 he was a student at Columbia University. He is a member of Phi Gamma Delta and Alpha Omega Alpha.

Admitted to the practice of medicine at Lincoln, August, 1908, from that date until 1925 he was engaged in general practice there. Since 1925 he has been school physician at Lincoln. He has been secretary-treasurer of the Nebraska State Medical Association since 1919, and has lived in Nebraska for over 40 years.

During the World War, Dr. Adams served as a member of the draft board. He is a member of the American Medical Association, Nebraska State Medical Association, Lancaster County Medical Society, and the American Public Health Association. He holds membership in the National Educational Association, American Association of School Physicians, and the Lincoln Red Cross. He is a Scottish Rite Mason, and belongs to the Lincoln University Club. He likes to fish and hike, and his hobbies are reading, gardening, and studying mechanics. He is a Republican. Residence: Lincoln.

Thomas Edward Adams

For the past twenty years Thomas Edward Adams has successfully managed and operated the Beatrice Steel Tank Manufacturing Company at Beatrice. He was born at Webster City, Hamilton County, Iowa, August 25, 1871, and for the past 40 years has lived in Nebraska. His father, Thomas Adams, who was a farmer, was born in Kentucky and died in Iowa; his ancestry was Scotch-English and German, and he is a descendant of the distinguished early American Adams family. Martha Ann (Bell) Adams, mother of Thomas Edward Adams, was born in the south, and was descended from Scotch and English farmers.

Mr. Adams was apprenticed to a trade at the age of twelve years and had several years experience in various parts of the country. For twenty years he was connected with a manufacturing company at Beatrice, in several capacities, and in 1911 he organized the Beatrice Steel Tank Manufacturing Company of which he is now president and general manager. Aside from his activities in the latter organization Mr. Adams has a financial interest in industry and real estate.

A Democrat, he has never held public office, but has always taken an interest in public affairs in his community and state. During the World War, Mr. Adams was chairman of war activities in connection with finance in Gage County. He holds membership in the Nebraskana Society.

On June 25, 1899, he was united in marriage with Okolona Miller at Beatrice. Mrs. Adams, who was an educator before her marriage, was born in Illinois, November 9, 1878; her ancestry is Scotch. To this marriage three children were born: Ruth Ann, born April 19, 1901, who married M. E. Dole, superintendent of the Beatrice Steel Tank Manufacturing Company; Thomas Earl, born July 20, 1905, secretary of the Beatrice Steel Tank Manufacturing Company; and James Clifford, born November 3, 1911, who is a student at the University of Nebraska. Mr. Adams is vitally interested in his children's progress and has always maintained a close association with them. Residence: Beatrice.

James Edmund Addie

James E. Addie, prominent lawyer of Hastings, Nebraska, has lived in this state for the past 26 years and has taken an active part in the civic and political affairs of his community. He was born at Cresco, Howard County, Iowa, January 15, 1875, the son of John and Christina (Beveridge) Addie. His father, a farmer, was born in Scotland, February 12, 1843, and died at Cumberland, Wisconsin, May 17, 1920. His mother, whose family came to this country in 1854, was born in Scotland, May 17, 1843, and died at Cumberland, March 2, 1921.

Mr. Addie attended rural school in South Dakota, was a student at Redfield College, at Redfield, South Dakota, and attended Milton College in Wisconsin for two years. In 1902 he was graduated from Valparaiso University with the Bachelor of Arts degree and was awarded highest honors in debating. He received his legal education at what is now the Benjamin Harrison Law School at Indianapolis, Indiana, graduating in 1904.

From 1913 to 1924 Mr. Addie was a law partner of John M. Ragan, and since that date has been engaged in practice alone. He is attorney for the Chicago and Northwestern Railroad Company, the Nebraska National Bank of Hastings, and the State Bank of Juniata, Nebraska. A Republican, he served as county attorney of Adams County from 1919 to 1923, and for four years previous to 1919 he was United States Commissioner at Hastings. He served as president of the School Board at Friend for three years, and has always been interested in the educational welfare of the community. He is a member of the Adams County Bar Association, the Nebraska State Bar Association, and the American Bar Association, is affiliated with the Presbyterian Church, holds membership in the Nebraska State Historical Society, and is a member of the Red Cross. His fraternal organizations include the Elks, Knights of Pythias, and the Odd Fellows. During the World War Mr. Addie was a four minute speaker, and was a member of the questionnaire board at Hastings. He is a member of the Inter-Church Reserve.

Mr. Addie was united in marriage with Ethel Jessie Riggle at Callaway, Nebraska, October 17, 1907. Mrs. Addie, who was a teacher before her marriage, was born in Lucas County, Iowa, August 14, 1880. They had one son, Dwight, born July 5, 1909, who died November 18, 1925. Mr. Addie's recreations are hiking and reading. Residence: Hastings.

Huber Dudley Addison

H. D. Addison, son of John D. and Anna (Wyant) Addison, was born at New Castle, Nebraska, January 17, 1901. His father is a farmer and insurance man and, before her marriage, his mother was a school teacher.

Upon the completion of his elementary education in the New Castle grade school in 1915, Huber D. Addison entered the New Castle High School from which he was graduated in 1919. In June, 1923, he received his LL. B. from the University of Nebraska, where he is a member of Phi Delta Phi.

Since his admission to the bar he has been engaged in active practice, and was recently elected on the Republican ticket as county attorney of Wayne County, now serving. He is a member of the Nebraska State Bar Association, the Independent Order of Odd Fellows, and the First Presbyterian Church.

In February, 1928, he was united in marriage to Alma Lammli, at Lincoln. Mrs. Addison was born at Stanton, Nebraska, in 1901, and before her marriage was a teacher in the public schools. They have a son, John, born November 16, 1929.

Mr. and Mrs. Addison are members of the Wayne Country Club. Residence: Wayne.

John Aden

John Aden, retired farmer and banker, was born at Blumberg, Germany, February 4, 1864, the son of Heye J. and Sente (Habben) Aden. Coming to America at the age of four he was raised in Woodford County, Illinois, and moved to Nebraska in 1890. He lived in Butler County until 1907, and then came to Thayer County. Here he has been active in all civic and educational projects.

He was united in marriage with Katie Doorn, March 12, 1888, at Benson, Illinois. She was born at Wittmund, Germany, May 1, 1867. There are seven children: Etta, born January 5, 1889, who is married to Oscar K. Bauer; Anna, born January 18, 1890, who is married to I. J. Voss; Margaret, born March 5, 1891, who is married to J. H. Swanson; Sente, born October 23, 1892, who is married to Joe Schroeder; John, born September 27, 1894, who is married to Ella Damrow; Sena, born September 27, 1894, and Rose, born September 29, 1904. Sente, Sena, and Rose are all graduates of Nebraska State Teachers

College at Kearney, Nebraska. Sena is teaching at Upland, Nebraska, and Rose is a teacher in Brownell, Kansas.

Mr. Aden was vice president of the Carleton State Bank in 1920 and director in 1921. The Carleton State Bank is now consolidated with the Citizens State Bank. During the World War he was a participant in all civilian war work. His son, John, served in the Army but did not go across. Mr. Aden is affiliated with the Zion Lutheran Church of Carleton. He is director of the Carleton Cemetery Association, a member of The Nebraskana Society, and was a member of the school board from 1897 to 1907, and from 1916 to 1923. Mr. Aden is a Republican. Residence: Carleton. (Photograph in Album).

Stuart Elijah Adkins

Stuart Elijah Adkins, farmer and stockbreeder who has been county treasurer of Arthur County for the past nine years, was born at Salt Rock, West Virginia, September 28, 1875. He has resided in Nebraska for the past 18 years.

His father, Elijah Mortimer Adkins, was a native of Wayne County, West Virginia, born March 29, 1828, who died at Salt Rock, March 30, 1908. He was a farmer, descended from early settlers in West Virginia. His wife, Margaret Price, was born in North Carolina in 1844 and died in Salt Rock, in April, 1903.

On January 6, 1898, Mr. Adkins was married to Eva Leona Rowsey at Salt Rock. She was born on March 12, 1875.

They have nine children, Arlie, born November 30, 1898, who married Mollie Boggs; Emma, born May 28, 1901, who married Charles H. Thompson; Olive, born April 8, 1903, who married Lake M. Crouse; Della, born August 2, 1905, who married Orval W. Meth; Seward, born July 11, 1907, who married Pauline Hurlburt; Zola, born February 22, 1909, who married Arthur Wilson; Oda, born February 6, 1911, who married Marguerite Meth; Eva, born May 28, 1914; and Keith, born November 8, 1916.

Mr. Adkins is a Democrat, a Mason, and a member of the Nebraskana Society. Residence: Arthur.

Joseph Adolphus

Joseph Adolphus, physician and surgeon, was born at Atlanta, Georgia, August 24, 1878, son of Joseph and Emma (Gifford) Adolphus.

His father was a native of Virginia, and a graduate of the University of Pennsylvania where he received his degree of Doctor of Medicine. He served in the Mexican War and was later engaged in the practice of medicine at Des Moines, Iowa, and Lansing, Michigan, and Atlanta. He was a founder of the Georgia College of Medicine and Surgery, and was its president for 25 years. He died on December 2, 1902.

Dr. Adolphus received his education in the public and high schools of Atlanta, and afterward entered the Georgia College of Medicine and Surgery from which he was graduated in 1899. He continued his studies in Creighton University, and was graduated in 1908 with a degree of Doctor of Medicine. He served as interne with the St. Joseph Hospital, and during 1909 took post graduate work from the University of New York.

Dr. Adolphus is a member of the Masons, the Oddfellows, the Elks, the Owls, Moose, Woodmen of the World, Woodmen Circle, The Puritan Union of America, and the Brotherhood of American Yeoman.

He has written for numerous medical journals, and is also the author of articles on medical subjects and some poetry. Among his contributions to literature are the following, *Fickle Love; No Time for Prejudice; An Unsuccessful Politician; Father-Time; Flowers To the Living;* and *Air Castles.* Residence: Lincoln.

George Simon Agnes

George Simon Agnes, prominent lumberman, was born at Akron, Iowa, November 11, 1882, and in August, 1918, took up his residence in Nebraska. His father, Henry Michael Agnes, was born in Milwaukee, Wisconsin, July 25, 1850, and for many years was engaged as a farmer and real estate dealer. He died at Plankinton, South Dakota, July 15, 1916.

Bridget Agnes McInerny, wife of Henry Agnes, was born in County Kilrush, Ireland, and died at Plankinton, on December 9, 1924.

George S. Agnes attended the public schools at Plankinton, and was graduated from high school there in June, 1908. The following year he attended Highland Park College at Des Moines.

On June 30, 1909, he was married to Cora Isabelle Hasbrouck, at Plankinton. She was born at Burlington, Iowa, and died at Mitchell, South Dakota, August 15, 1917. Three children were born to them, George Harlan, on January 21, 1911; Mildred Genevieve, on November 11, 1913; and Mary Virginia, on May 10, 1917.

George is in his second year of pre-medical work at Dubuque, Iowa, while Mildred is attending a school of dress design in Chicago. Mary Virginia is in her first year in high school. On January 16, 1926, Mr. Agnes was married to Margaret Donohoe, at Omaha. She was born at O'Neill, on October 8, 1887, and before her marriage was a teacher of English in the Omaha public schools. They have one daughter, Margaret Lorraine, born November 9, 1926, who has just started to school.

At the present time Mr. Agnes is manager and co-partner in the Seth Noble Lumber Company. He is a member of the Nebraska Lumberman's Association, the Lions Club, the Knights of Columbus, the Red Cross and Salvation Army, the Parent-Teachers' Association, and the O'Neill Country Club. He is a life member of the Nebraskana Society. His favorite sport is baseball and his hobby is gardening. He is a Democrat. Residence: O'Neill. (Photograph in Album).

Hayden William Ahmanson

Hayden W. Ahmanson is a life resident of Omaha, and for the past 11 years has been engaged in the insurance business. Born March 16, 1898, he is the son of William H. and Florence May (Hayden) Ahmanson. His father was born at Omaha, December 16, 1872, and died there May 22, 1925. He was president of the National American Fire Insurance Company at the time of his death.

Mr. Ahmanson attended Omaha High School and Kemper Military Academy, and received his A. B. from the University of Nebraska in 1919. He was awarded an LL. B. from Creighton University College of Law in 1922. From 1912 to 1917 he was employed with the Columbia Fire Underwriters, and during 1919-20, with the Western Adjustment and Inspection Company. Since 1921 he has been associated with the National America Fire Insurance Company, of which he is secretary.

On September 4, 1924, he was married to Aimee Elizabeth Talbod, at Omaha. There are two children, William Hayden, born October 12, 1925, and Robert Howard, born February 14, 1927.

Mr. Ahmanson is a Republican, and a member of Dundee Presbyterian Church. During 1926, he was president of the Junior Chamber of Commerce, and at the present time he is president of the Omaha Kiwanis Club, and a member of his majesty's council, Ak-Sar-Ben. He is a Mason and member of the Blue Goose. His social clubs are the Omaha Athletic and the Happy Hollow Country Club. Residence: Omaha.

Malcolm M. Akin

For the past 29 years Malcolm M. Akin has been engaged in the practice of dentistry at Fairmont, Nebraska, and has been especially prominent in civic affairs there. He was born at Meridian, Nebraska, June 9, 1874, the son of Almon M. and Mary (Mavar) Akin. His father, born at Allens Ferry, New York, August 25, 1833, died at Fairbury, Nebraska, October 15, 1906. He was a pioneer homesteader in Jefferson County, Nebraska, in 1871; he served as county commissioner for several terms, and was a member of the school board for many years; his English ancestors came to America before the Revolution.

His mother, who was born at Aberdeen, Scotland, December 25, 1840, and died at Fairbury, December 25, 1928, was a pioneer home builder; she was a charter member of the Presbyterian Church at Fairbury, and held membership in the Woman's Christian Temperance Union.

Dr. Akin attended the public schools of Jefferson County, was a student at Lincoln Normal University, 1897-98 and at Cotner University, 1895, and in 1902 received the D. D. S. degree at the University of Omaha. He took an active part in debating at Lincoln, was vice president of his graduating class at Omaha Dental College, and was historian of the senior class in the latter institution.

He is interested in farming projects in Jefferson and Fillmore counties. A Republican, he has held the following positions: chairman of the Republican County Committee, 1907-08; member of the Republican State Committee, 1912-13; and presidential elector, 1928.

Dr. Akin is a member of the State Dental Society, is secretary of the Central Nebraska District Dental Society, and is past secretary of the Red Cross. He holds membership in the Young Men's Christian Association, the Fairmont Commercial Club of which he was once secretary, the Nebraskana Society, Masons, and Odd Fellows. He served as secretary of the board of education at Fairmont, 1912-30, was a teacher in the public schools of Jefferson County, 1895-97, and is affiliated with the Federated Congregational Church of Fairmont.

During the World War Dr. Akin served as treasurer of the Red Cross, and was active in the council of defense and in Liberty loan drives. He was a private in Company I, 1st Nebraska Volunteer Infantry during the Spanish American War; he is now a member of the United Spanish War Veterans and Veterans of Foreign Wars.

On December 22, 1903, he married Harriet Althea Chapen at Fairmont. Mrs. Akin, who was at one time secretary and cashier of the Fairmont Creamery, was born at Fairmont, August 23, 1878. Her English ancestors were prominent in the Massachusetts Colony. Their three children are: Frederick M., born December 8, 1904, who is a dentist at Lincoln; Maurice C., born November 6, 1908, who was graduated in journalism at the University of Nebraska; and Jean, born November 12, 1913. Residence: Fairmont.

Bohumil William Aksamit

Bohumil W. Aksamit, pioneer farmer of Nebraska, has lived in Nuckolls County most of his life. He was born at Crete, Saline County, Nebraska, January 1, 1874, the son of Vincent and Mary (Wolesensky) Aksamit. His father, who was born at Pavlov, Czechoslovakia, March 22, 1848, and died at Crete, June 12, 1923, was a farmer; a Republican, he served several terms as county commissioner. His mother was born at Albertstal, Czechoslovakia, in 1854, and died at Crete, January 3, 1903.

Mr. Aksamit has been a director of rural school boards for the past 16 years, and is now a member of the Nebraskana Society and the Modern Woodmen of America, and is banker of the local camp. For four years he acted as precinct assessor, and is secretary of the Community Club at Deweese. His sports are hunting and fishing while his hobby is mechanics. His politics is Republican.

He was united in marriage with Bessie A. Koci at Wilber, Saline County, Nebraska, February 14, 1899. Mrs. Aksamit was born in Bohemia, February 25, 1877. Four children were born to this marriage, three of whom are living: Mary, born March 18, 1900, who died January 26, 1917; Longin, born September 23, 1901; Lillie, born February 23, 1905, who married Perry Kothe, May 15, 1928; and William, born November 2, 1906. Lillie and William are graduates of Edgar High School. Residence: Deweese. (Photograph in Album).

Francis Asbury Alabaster

One of Nebraska's most distinguished educators, Francis A. Alabaster has been a resident of the state since 1893. He was born at Rochester, New York, June 10, 1866, the son of John and Harriet Ann (Bemish) Alabaster. His father, who was of English descent, was born at Geneva, New York, January 2, 1836, and died at Canandaigua, New York, September 7, 1887.

He was a noted clergyman in the Methodist Episcopal Church; was awarded the A. B. and D. D. degrees at Syracuse University; was a lecturer and traveler; and at the time of his death, was pastor of the Trinity Methodist Church in Chicago. His wife, who was of English, Irish, and French descent, was born at Rochester, August 17, 1838, and died at Ann Arbor, Michigan, October 17, 1881.

Dr. Alabaster attended the public schools of New York, and Michigan; and in 1886 was graduated from the Northwestern University Academy. He received the A. B. degree from Northwestern University in 1890, and the A. M. degree, 1898, from the University of Nebraska; and in 1918 was awarded the degree of Doctor of Literature, at Dickinson College, Carlisle, Pennsylvania. During the summers of 1901 and 1902, he was a student at the University of Chicago, and in 1898 to 1900, took post graduate work at the University of Nebraska. He is a member of Phi Beta Kappa and Phi Kappa Phi, at Northwestern, and Pi Gamma Mu, at Nebraska Wesleyan. He was the first president of the Young Men's Christian Association at Northwestern; and served as president of the Alpha Chapter of Phi Kappa Psi there.

Since 1893, he has been professor of classical languages at Nebraska Wesleyan University, and for over 20 years has been dean of the college of liberal arts there. He has been the editor of *University Bulletins* since 1909. He holds membership in the American Philological Association; the American Classical League; the Archaeological Institute of America; Lion's International; The Symposium; and the Nebraskana Society. He is a life member of the Nebraska State Teachers' Association; is affiliated with the First Methodist Episcopal Church of Lincoln; and is a member of the Young Men's Christian Association.

His marriage to Mary Blanche Robinson was solemnized at Omaha, Douglas County, Nebraska, June 27, 1895. Mrs. Alabaster, who is of French and English descent, was born at West Mansfield, Logan County, Ohio, May 2, 1875. Their children are: Wendell, born April 3, 1900, who married Virginia Hardin; Francis T., born November 11, 1903, who married Ellen Rubottom; and Ruth, born November 27, 1907, who married Clair F. Weatherhogg. All of them hold A. B. degrees, granted by the Nebraska Wesleyan University, and Wendell holds an LL. B. degree from the University of Nebraska.

Dr. Alabaster is a Republican. His sports include golfing, hunting and fishing. During the World War he served as a member of the local civic committee. His hobbies are bird study, philately, the cornet, and collecting epitaphs. He is a Mason. Residence: Lincoln.

I. L. Albert

I. L. Albert, lawyer, was born in Clearfield County, Pennsylvania, December 28, 1866, son of Daniel and Barbara (Kethart) Albert, who were born in Clearfield County. They are both deceased.

Mr. Albert attended public school in Pennsylvania,

and in 1876 came to the West, settling in Iowa, where he taught school for a time. Afterward he attended Leander Clark College at Toledo, Iowa, and was graduated with the Bachelor of Arts degree in 1884. During his college days he taught for various periods, and studied law under the professorship of Frank C. Hamie. In 1881 he was admitted to the bar.

After several years practice at Cedar Rapids, he came to Nebraska in 1887, and engaged in practice at Albion. In 1889 he removed to Columbus, where he has since resided.

In 1891 Judge Albert served as county attorney of Platte County, continuing until 1893. In 1898 he was appointed to the bench of the 6th judicial district. From March, 1901, until March, 1907, he was a member of the Nebraska Supreme Court Commission. In 1909 he was retained by the Nebraska State Legislature to write the Bank Guarantee Law. In 1911 he was elected state representative, serving in the sessions of 1911 and 1917, and the special session of 1918.

He was married to Miss Mary Melgum in Iowa. She was born in Canada, daughter of Robert and Eliza Melgum. She died in 1899. Four children were born to them, Daniel, who is deceased; Robert, who is married to Jean Shell and who has two children, Robert M., and Daniel; Frederick C., who was graduated from the University of Nebraska, is a civil engineer; and Mary, who was graduated from the training school for nurses at the Presbyterian Hospital in Chicago. She is deceased. She was married to a physician, who is still living and has a child, Gordon Albert.

In 1902 Judge Albert was married to Jean B. Pauley of Toronto, Canada. She is the daughter of John Pauley, a native of that country. They have three children, Ruth J., who is married to Phillip R. Haffenburger of Columbus; Warren G., and Cliffield B. Residence: Columbus.

Walter Leonard Albin

Walter Leonard Albin, specialist in diseases of the eye, ear, nose and throat, was born at Albany, Missouri, November 9, 1876. He is the son of John Nelson and Mary Jane (Rund) Albin, the former born at Greencastle, Indiana, in 1838. He was a farmer of Scotch-Irish descent, whose death occurred at Albany, August 6, 1906. His wife, Mary Jane, was born at Shelby, Ohio, July 15, 1838, and is still living. She is of German and early American ancestry.

Dr. Albin attended Central Christian College at Albany, and was graduated in 1898 with an A. B. degree. In 1902 he received his M. D. from St. Louis University, and was an honor graduate. From 1904 to 1907, he was surgeon for the Union Pacific Railroad at Lincoln, and from 1916 to 1919, was city physician of University Place. In general practice sixteen years, he took a year's post graduate work in New York, a year in Vienna, and three months in Berlin, in the study of his specialty. He has contributed various articles to the Nebraska State and Lancaster County Medical Societies of which he is a member. He is also a member of the American Medical Association and the Sioux Valley Eye and Ear Academy and the American Interprofessional Institute. He is a Mason and a Republican.

On June 26, 1913, he was married to Anna Fay Hanson at Crete. Mrs. Albin was born at Berea, Kentucky, September 30, 1880. She is a lineal descendant of Gregorias, Alpine king of the Scotts, is interested in art and hand weaving, and is a member of the Garden Club, the American University Club and other civic organizations. There were two children born to their union, Mary Cathern, born April 9, 1914; and Ann Hollis, born January 22, 1917, who died April 1, 1919. Residence: Lincoln.

John H. Albrecht

Born at Collinsville, Madison County, Illinois, on July 31, 1861, John H. Albrecht is the son of Henry and Maria (Kluge) Albrecht. Henry Albrecht was born February 6, 1830, in Saxony, Germany, and was a tailor by profession. Maria, his wife, was born at Glaskow, Schlesien, Germany, August 17, 1838. Both of them died at St. Paul, Illinois; Mr. Albrecht in March 1897, and his wife in April, 1905.

Coming to Nebraska in 1886, John H. Albrecht settled in the town of Friedensau and started farming. On February 28, 1889, he married Emma Ulrike Liermann at Friedensau. Mrs. Albrecht was born at Caledonia, Wisconsin, on June 11, 1869, her parents coming to Nebraska in 1874 and enduring the hardships of the pioneers of those days.

A resident of Nebraska for forty-five years, Mr. Albrecht has been active in political and civic enterprises. A Democrat, he has been chairman of his precinct, a member of the county central committee, and served as county commissioner for one term. For ten years he was a member of the County Fair Board. During the World War he was a solicitor for the Red Cross, and was active in the Salvation Army and War Savings Stamp work.

Mr. Albrecht has been a member of the mission board of the Southern Nebraska district of the Lutheran Church, Missouri Synod, for ten years, was deacon and treasurer of the Lutheran Trinity Congregation of Friedensau twenty years, and is still affiliated with this church.

John H. Albrecht is a member of the Lutheran Laymens' League, the Lutheran Educational Association, the Good Roads Committee, and the Nebraskana Society. He has a family of eight children: Clara, born December 4, 1889, and married to Paul Thiemann; Emilie, born July 22, 1892, and married to H. C. Schardt; Josephine, born May 27, 1894, and married to Julius Kraft; Emma, born March 10, 1896, and married to Edward Schmidt; Erna, born April 30, 1899, and married to Walter Schardt; Rosina, born July 23, 1901, and married to Fred Behle; Florence, born April 14, 1906, and married to Walter Thieme; and Arthur, born November 26, 1908, who is farming the home place; John, who was born August 18, 1901, died on May 16, 1902. Residence: Deshler. (Photograph in Album).

Joseph Garfield Alden

For fourteen years Joseph G. Alden has been editor and publisher of the York Republican, at York, Nebraska. A resident of Nebraska for 52 years, he has always been prominent in civic affairs at York. He was born at Minneapolis, Minnesota, September 7, 1876, the son of William Halbert and Mary (Lightfoot) Alden.

His father, who was a general merchant, was born at Lincklein, New York, June 1, 1831, and died at Aurora, Nebraska, February 12, 1915; he was directly descended from John Alden of Puritan fame. Mary (Lightfoot) Alden, who was born at Canandaigua, New York, November 2, 1848, and died at Aurora, July 16, 1927, was a teacher before her marriage. Her ancestry was English.

Mr. Alden acted as postmaster at Aurora for 12 years, was editor of the Aurora Republican from 1899 to 1909, and is now editor and publisher of the York Republican. A Republican, he was director of the Nebraska State Department of Publicity, 1929-31, was supervisor of the 1930 federal census for the 10th Nebraska district; and is now a committee of one on Christian Science publication for Nebraska.

He is affiliated with the First Church of Christ, Scientist at York, and holds membership in the following professional and community organizations: York County Commercial Club; York Rotary Club; National Editorial Association; Nebraska Press Association; and the Nebraskana Society.

On August 29, 1899, he was married to Eloise Shean at Aurora, Nebraska. Mrs. Alden, who was born in Barry County, Michigan, October 9, 1877, is a Christian

Science parctitioner. She is of Irish and Welsh-Canadian descent. They are the parents of two children: Joseph Maurice, born October 20, 1903, who married Ruth Codington; and Marjorie, born September 4, 1907, who married Dr. Gerald M. Hamilton. Residence: York.

Joseph Maurice Alden

Joseph M. Alden was born at Aurora, Nebraska, October 20, 1903, the son of Joseph Garfield and Alice Eloise (Shean) Alden. His father, a newspaper editor and publisher, was born at Minneapolis, Minnesota, September 7, 1876, and was descended directly from John Alden of Plymouth. His mother, a Christian Science practitioner, was born in Barry County, Michigan, October 9, 1877, of Irish and Welsh-Canadian ancestry.

Mr. Alden was graduated from York High School in 1921, was a student at York College, 1921-23, and attended the University of Nebraska in 1924. He was active in athletics, and was awarded both high school and college letters. He is now advertising manager of the *York Republican*, at York, Nebraska, is a director of the Chamber of Commerce at York, and holds membership in the York Rotary Club. He attends the Church of Christ, Scientist, and is affiliated with the Young Men's Christian Association. His favorite sports are golf and football.

His marriage to Ruth Codington was solemnized at Auburn, Nemaha, County, Nebraska, July 31, 1928. Mrs Alden, who is a high school instructor, was born at Auburn, April 9, 1903. They have one son, John, born April 1, 1930. Residence: York.

Bess Streeter Aldrich

Bess Streeter Aldrich, distinguished writer of Nebraska pioneer and modern life, was born at Cedar Falls, Blackhawk County, Iowa, February 17, 1881. Her father, James Wareham Streeter, an early pioneer in Iowa, was born at Champlain, Clinton County, New York, October 26, 1826, and died at Cedar Falls, Iowa, March 7, 1907. In 1852, he came to Iowa with his father, Zimri Streeter, who became a member of the first Republican Iowa legislature. He is descended from Revolutionary ancestors, among them Dr. John Streeter and Captain Remember Baker.

Mary Wilson (Anderson) Streeter, mother of Mrs. Aldrich, was born in Quebec, Canada, November 15, 1835, and died at Elmwood, Nebraska, August 16, 1916. She was the daughter of Basil and Margaret Anderson; the former a Scotch aristocrat and landed gentleman, the latter a peasant girl whose romantic marriage has been recorded in *A Lantern in Her Hand*.

Mrs. Aldrich received here elementary education in the Iowa public schools and later was graduated from the Iowa State Teachers' College.

On September 24, 1907, she was united in marriage with Charles Sweetzer Aldrich at Cedar Falls, Iowa. Mr. Aldrich, a descendant of colonial ancestors, was a lawyer and banker. He was born at Tipton, Iowa, September 7, 1872, and died at Elmwood, May 3, 1925. There are four children: Mary Eleanor, born February 10, 1909, a graduate of the University of Nebraska and a member of Kappa Alpha Theta, Chi Delta Phi and Pi Lambda Theta; James Whitson, born January 19, 1912, a student at the Chicago Art Institute; Charles Stewart, born September 18, 1913; and Robert Streeter, born June 24, 1920. The two younger children are in public schools.

Mrs. Aldrich is the author of one hundred short stories published in *Century Magazine, American Magazine, The Bookman, Ladies Home Journal, Woman's Home Companion, Delineator, McCalls, Harper's Weekly*, etc. Many of these have resold in England to *Cassels, Pearsons, Woman's Pictorial,* and *Pan*. Her story, *The Man Who Caught the Weather,* published in the *Century Magazine,* was chosen for the 1928 volume of the O. Henry Memorial Award. Her four books, all published by D. Appleton and Company, are: *Mother Mason,* published in 1924; *The Rim of the Prairie,* 1925; *The Cutters,* 1926; and *A Lantern in Her Hand.* The last has gone into its thirtieth edition, has been translated into the Dutch, German and Hungarian languages and is considered one of the outstanding novels of this decade.

She is a member in the following professional organizations: Society of Midland Authors (Chicago); Nebraska State Press Association; Omaha Woman's Press Club; Chi Delta Phi, national literary fraternity; Theta Sigma Chi, national journalistic fraternity; Altrusa Club; Nebraska State Writers' Guild, of which she is past president; and the Quill Club of Lincoln.

She is a member of the Van Fleet Memorial Methodist Church, the P. E. O., the Red Cross and The Woman's Home and Foreign Missionary Society. She is active in civic and religious affairs. The Kiwanis medal was awarded to her for distinguished service to the state for the year 1929. Her home The Elms, is at Elmwood, Nebraska. (Photograph on Page 18).

Carl Milton Aldrich

Carl M. Aldrich was born at Nebraska City, Nebraska, August 26, 1860. His father, John Aldrich, who was born at Norwich, New York, February 23, 1828, and died at Sidney, Delaware County, New York, December 30, 1909, was a teacher and a farmer. He was descended from the Aldrich family of Massachusetts and Rhode Island, George Aldrich, an ancestor, having come from England in 1635.

Mary Jane (Johnston) Aldrich, his mother, who was born at Sidney Plains, New York, March 19, 1833, and died there April 27, 1909, was active in church and club affairs. She was at one time president of the Iowa Women's Christian Temperance Union, and acted as a national officer in that organization. Her parents were Milton and Delia Johnston.

Mr. Aldrich received his education in the grade and high school at Cedar Rapids, Iowa. During his school days he was interested in rowing and was a member of the Cedar Rapids Boat Club. He has lived in Nebraska for thirty years. Since 1876, when he became an office boy, he has been engaged in the packing house business, and today he is vice president and manager of the Morton Gregson Company at Nebraska City.

His marriage to Corinnie May Tackett was solemnized at Shelbyville, Illinois, December 22, 1885. Mrs. Aldrich, who was born at Shelbyville, May 23, 1866, is the daughter of Dr. and Mrs. William J. Tackett. She is of early New England and Virginian ancestry, and is past regent of Otoe Chapter of the Daughters of the American Revolution. Their four children are Glen Tackett, born December 2, 1886, who married Esther Carlson; Carl Milton, Junior, born April 30, 1889, who married Floy Graves; Ralf Johnston, born February 1, 1891, who married Amy Lumby; and Frances Enfield, born March 23, 1900, who married Clyde L. Pursley.

In the World War Mr. Aldrich was a member of the Nebraska City Home Guards, and was active in Red Cross work. His three sons were in army service. He is a member of the following civic and welfare societies: Red Cross, Nebraska City Chamber of Commerce, Omaha Chamber of Commerce, the Rotary Club, Nebraska Territorial Pioneers Association, the Nebraska State Historical Society, and the Nebraskana Society. He is associated with the Boy Scouts of America, and is a member of the Nebraska State Manufacturers' Association, the Nebraska Mayflower Descendants' Society, and the Tuberculosis Eradication Committee.

He is affiliated with St. Mary's Episcopal Church at Nebraska City, serving as senior warden of this body. His social club is the Nebraska City Country Club. Flower gardening and the study of poetry are his hobbies. He is a Republican. Residence: Nebraska City.

Rinehart-Marsden—Omaha

BESS STREETER ALDRICH

Sylvia Stroman Aldrich

Born at Wolcottville, Indiana, April 20, 1870, Sylvia Stroman Aldrich was the daughter of pioneer settlers in Nebraska. Her parents homesteaded in Seward County, near Ulysses, in 1871, on the farm which Mrs. Aldrich still owns.

Mrs. Aldrich attended school in Ulysses. She has taken an active part in the social and civic affairs of her community for many years, and has been especially prominent in religious and welfare work. She is a member of the Methodist Church, the Social Union of which she is president, the Eastern Star, P. E. O., Women's Relief Corps and the Women's Christian Temperance Union.

She is vice president of the library board, is president of the Cemetery Association, and member of Nebraskana Society. She is a regular visitor of the sick and a devoted homemaker. On June 4, 1889, she was united in marriage to C. H. Aldrich at Ulysses. Five sons were born to them, George Stroman; Chester Hardy, Jr.; John Bower, Frederick Schuyler; and Charles Lee, who died in infancy.

Mr. Aldrich, supreme judge of Nebraska and one time its governor, was an outstanding figure in middle-west politics and public affairs. He was born on a farm near Pierpont, Ohio, November 10, 1862, the son of landowners in Ohio. He was a teacher in the public schools for several years prior to his admission to the bar in 1890. Beginning at David City, there he was identified with much important litigation, including prominent criminal cases.

A Republican, Judge Aldrich served as mayor of David City, was a member of the town board for eight years, and was connected with the school board almost continuously. He was elected state senator in 1906, and in 1907 was instrumental in enacting much beneficial legislation. He was the author of the bill reducing rates, known as the Aldrich commodity freight law, and was the author of the railway commission law in 1907.

In 1910 Judge Aldrich was elected governor of Nebraska on the Republican ticket, and in 1918 was elected associate judge of the state supreme court to fill the unexpired term of Francis G. Hamer. Judge Aldrich was a close personal friend of Theodore Roosevelt, whom he entertained in his home at Lincoln on various occasions. He died at the home of his son at Superior, February 27, 1931.

Since Judge Aldrich's death, Mrs. Aldrich has resided at Ulysses with her mother, who is also a widow. Residence: Ulysses.

Hartley Burr Alexander

Hartley Burr Alexander, professor of philosophy of Scripps College, was born at Lincoln, Nebraska, April 9, 1873, son of George Sherman and Abigail Gifford (Smith) Alexander.

The father was born in Cumberland County, Rhode Island, July 10, 1833, and died at Syracuse, Nebraska, May 2, 1894. He was a Methodist Episcopal clergyman and editor of the Syracuse, Nebraska, Journal. In the early 70's he was prominent in Nebraska affairs. His wife, Abigail, was born at Orleans, Massachusetts, July 6, 1835, and died near Bennet, Nebraska, November 13, 1876. Her ancestors came to America with the Plymouth Colony.

Dr. Alexander attended public school at Syracuse, and was graduated from Syracuse High School in 1892. He received his Bachelor of Arts degree at the University of Nebraska in 1897, and his Doctor of Philosophy degree from Columbia University in 1901. A member of Phi Beta Kappa, he received the Butler medal from Columbia University, is past president of the American Philosophical Association, is an honorary member of the American Institute of Architects, and past president of the Southwest Archaeological Federation.

On July 15, 1908, he was married to Nelly King Griggs at Tacoma, Washington. Mrs. Alexander was born at Beatrice, Nebraska, October 11, 1875, and is descended from New England and Pennsylvania colonists and soldiers. To them were born two children, one of whom is living, Hubert, born December 8, 1909; and Beatrice, born March 15, 1912, who died July 4, 1913. (*See Who's Who in America*). Residence: Claremont, California.

John Merriam Alexander

John M. Alexander was born at Sigourney, Iowa, April 28, 1888, the son of Harry Edgar and Katherine (Cogley) Alexander. His father, who was a builder, was born at Sigourney, and was the son of a Mississippi River freighter. His ancestors were early pioneers in New England where they settled near Concord, Massachusetts. Later they came west with General Putnam, beginning the town of Marietta, Ohio. John M. Alexander's mother was born at Sigourney.

Mr. Alexander was educated in the high schools at Richland and Sigourney, and in 1910 was graduated from the University of Nebraska, with an A. B. degree. He was a member of Phi Delta Phi., and during his college days he worked as a freight trucker, and at his graduation he had saved $65.00. He entered the real estate commission business in 1910, and a little later became a builder. He has continued in this profession since that date, and for over 20 years has been a business man of prominence at Lincoln.

He married Helen Abbott Boggs at Lincoln, her birthplace, June 13, 1913. They have four children, John Charles, born January 25, 1915; Robert E., born June 15, 1917; Mary Katharine, born August 29, 1920, and Philip Abbott, born March 20, 1924. Mr. Alexander is a member of the Lincoln Chamber of Commerce and the Eastridge Club. He is fond of golfing, and mechanics. He is a Republican. Residence: Lincoln.

Rose Amanda Alexander

Rose Amanda Alexander, a teacher at Brocksburg, Nebraska, has lived in this state all her life. She was born in Boyd County, Nebraska, May 13, 1892, the daughter of Helge and Rognilda (Johnson) Aarhas, the former a pioneer farmer who was born in Norway in 1848 and died in Boyd County, August 12, 1899. Her mother was born in Norway, October 22, 1850, and died at Whittenburg, Wisconsin, May 11, 1930.

Mrs. Alexander completed the high school course and attended normal school for three summer sessions, teaching in public schools for three years prior to her marriage. On January 21, 1912, she was united in marriage with Charles Arthur Alexander at Butte, Nebraska. Mr. Alexander, who was a farmer, was born of English and Irish descent at Washington, Nebraska, July 10, 1890, and died at Brocksburg, February 10, 1922. Since his death Mrs. Alexander has taught for nine years in the Brocksburg Public School.

To their union the following children were born: Wardell, September 21, 1913; Amber, September 8, 1915; Anita, September 16, 1917; Lois, September 12, 1919; and Charles, September 15, 1921. Amber is a junior in high school at Springview, Nebraska, and Anita is a sophomore in that institution. Residence: Brocksburg.

Joseph E. A. Alexis

Joseph Alexis, one of Nebraska's leading educators, was born near York, Nebraska, July 22, 1885. John Nelson Alexis, his father, was born at Slattakra, Hallands Lan, Sweden, April 4, 1852, and with his parents came to America in 1868, settling at Mediapolis, Iowa. He was a clergyman.

Professor Alexis attended the public schools at Du Bois and Hastings, Pennsylvania; was a student at the Academy of John B. Stetson University, 1898-1900, and was graduated from Whitehall High School at Dover, New Jersey, 1898. He holds the following degrees: A. B. Augustana College, Rock Island, Illinois, 1905; A. M. University of Michigan, 1906; Ph. D., University of Chicago, 1918; Docteur d'universite, University of Paris, 1930. He was a student at the University of Lund, 1911; University of Dijon, 1921; and University of Madrid, 1921. He was a member of the debating team, and was president of his senior class at Augustana College.

From 1907 to 1908, he taught at Coeur d'Alene College in Idaho. Since 1910 he has taught at the University of Nebraska, where he is now professor of romance languages. He is the author of: *German Relatives in 18th Century Prose* (with A. D. Schrag 1919); *First Course in German,* (1919) *First Course in Spanish,* (1925); *In Deutschland,* (with W. K. Pfeiler, 1930); *La Litterature suedoise d' Amerique,* (1930); *Geijerstam's Mina pojkar,* (1911); *Strindberg's Pask; Strindberg's Master Olof* (1921); *Strindberg's Stories and Poems* (1924); *Lazarillo de Tormes* (1927); *Valdes' Riverita* (1928); and *En Espana* (1932). He is a contributor of Encyclopedia Americana.

On August 28, 1917, Professor Alexis was united in marriage with Marjorie Edith Odman, at Valparaiso, Saunders County, Nebraska. Mrs. Alexis, who was born at Mead, Nebraska, May 7, 1894, is the daughter of Swedish parents who came to this country in the 1880's. Their children are: Carl, born August 8, 1918; Josephine, born January 1, 1921; and Marjorie, born July 24, 1927.

He is a member of the Modern Language Association of America; the Linguistic Society of America; and the Swedish Historical Society; he is secretary-treasurer of the Society for the Advancement of Scandinavian Study; and is a member of the Lincoln Chamber of Commerce and the Rotary Club. He is a member of the Grace Lutheran Church of Lincoln, a Republican, and holds membership in the Nebraskana Society. Residence: Lincoln.

James Porter Allan

J. Porter Allan, advertising executive, has lived in this state all his life. He was born at Omaha, September 12, 1897, the son of Donald Buddington and Corlynn Ann (Visscher) Allan. His father, who is an official of the Union Pacific Railroad, was born at Omaha, August 27, 1866; of Scotch ancestry. His mother, whose Holland Dutch ancestors settled in New York, prior to 1700, was born at Watertown, New York, December 24, 1869, and is now regent of the Daughters of the American Revolution, and is regent of C. A. R.

Mr. Allan was graduated from grade school at Omaha, in 1911, and in 1915, was graduated from Central High School there. Since 1917 he has been in business as J. Porter Allan, manufacturers' agents.

In 1924 he served as president of the Omaha Junior Chamber of Commerce. He is a member of the Omaha Club and is affiliated with the Episcopal Church at Omaha. His favorite sport is hunting. Residence: Omaha.

Arthur Eurasho Allen

Arthur Eurasho Allen, county commissioner of Red Willow County, is a native of Brooks, Iowa, born November 13, 1876. His father, Moses Allen, born in Ireland, April 1, 1844, and came to America with his parents in 1845. He served in the Civil War with the 70th Ohio Infantry coming in 1880 to Fillmore County, Nebraska, where he enaged in farming. He died at Laurel, Montana, February 5, 1912. His wife, Barbara Ellen Morris, was born in West Union, Ohio, August 22, 1845, and died at Benkleman, Nebraska, November 2, 1913. She was of German and French descent.

Mr. Allen attended district school in Fillmore County, and was graduated from Danbury High School in 1896. For more than twenty years he was a teacher in rural schools, and since that time has been a farmer. He has been elected county commissioner three times on the Republican ticket, first taking office on January 1, 1923.

He was married to Bessie Maybel Springer at Oberlin, Kansas, May 10, 1899. She was born at Ashland, Nebraska, November 10, 1880, her uncle, William Springer was first sheriff of Red Willow County. They have nine children: Glen, born March 23, 1902; Opal, born March 5, 1905; Ruth, born February 20, 1909; Harold, born November 14, 1907; Earl, born March 12, 1912; Marjorie, born December 6, 1913; Armond, born October 24, 1915; Evelyn, born September 6, 1917; Kathryn, born December 10, 1919; and Zey, born February 6, 1922.

Mr. Allen is interested in boxing, football, baseball and basketball, and devotes much time to reading. He is a member of the Nebraskana Society, and is affiliated with the Congregational Church. Residence: Danbury. (Photograph in Album).

Charles Edgar Allen

Charles Edgar Allen, prominent in the business and political world for many years, was born at Russell, Iowa, January 8, 1865 and came to Nebraska in 1886, primarily in search of a homestead. His first experience was a homestead in Cheyenne County. He located in Cozad, in 1890, and has since resided there. His father, Tandy Allen, a farmer and stockman, was born at Mount Sterling, Kentucky, June 3, 1832, and died at Russell, Iowa, June 2, 1922. His great grandfather, William Allen, was born in County Antrim, Ireland, and came to America, in 1729.

Joanna Smith Van Nice, wife of Tandy Allen, was born in New Winchester, Indiana, February 28, 1835, and died at Russell, December 18, 1923. Primarily a wife and mother, she reared a family of six sons and six daughters to maturity. She and her husband lived together sixty-six years without a death in their home. Her first ancestor in America, Janse Van Nuys, came from Holland in 1651, and in 1673, was appointed magistrate by Governor Clove of New York.

Charles Edgar Allen attended public school and for thirty-seven years was engaged in the retail business and as a banker in Cozad. He is now retired. A Republican, he was for twenty-seven years a member of the local board of education; served as mayor of Cozad, several terms, as councilman, and was state senator from the 30th district two terms.

His marriage to Susan Morrow was solemnized at Gibbon, Nebraska, August 29, 1889. She was born at Hillsboro, Ohio, February 11, 1868, and died at Colorado Springs, July 15, 1919. She was the daughter of Wilson H. and Narcissis Isabel (Patterson) Morrow.

To this union seven children were born: Edith I., born June 7, 1891; Dorothy, born February 9, 1895, who married Dale B. Murphy; Ralph M., born March 7, 1897, who married Marjorie Currant; Edgar Van Nuys, born June 22, 1900, who married Margaret Wise; Hortense L., born July 30, 1902; and Frank P., September 6, 1904, who married Helen Reynolds. Ralph volunteered on May 27, 1917, for service in the United States Army, and was promoted to second lieutenant. Edgar is a member of the staff of internal medicine at Mayo Clinic of Rochester, Minnesota.

On June 14, 1925, Mr. Allen was married to Katherine F. Worley, at Omaha. Mrs. Allen was born in Cass County, Nebraska, in 1876.

Mr. Allen is a member of the First Presbyterian Church of Cozad, is a 32nd degree Mason and Shriner, and an Odd Fellow. He is a member of the Red Cross, the Chamber of Commerce and the Rotary Club, and was recently made a life member of The Nebraskana Society. His favorite sport is golf. Residence: Cozad. (Photograph in Album).

Charles Luther Allen

Charles Luther Allen, now retired, has enjoyed an active and successful career. Born at Chateaugay, New York, May 22, 1859, he is the son of Martin Luther and Isabella (Taylor) Allen, the former of whom came from the same family as Ethan Allen. Martin Luther Allen was born at South Hero, Grand Isle, Vermont, and died at Oregon, Illinois, March 21, 1880. His wife died at Stratton, Nebraska, September 15, 1894.

Educated in public school, Charles Luther Allen was graduated from Oregon, Illinois, High School June 21, 1881. Immediately following his graduation he taught school first in the country near Oregon, Illinois. Then for five years he taught at Woosung, Illinois.

December 25, 1889, he was married to Mary Lucretia Prescott, at Polo, Illinois. She was born at Woosung, Illinois, and died at Trenton, September 13, 1916. They moved to Stratton, Nebraska, settling on a farm north of town, remaining there until the fall of 1894, when he was appointed principal of Stratton Schools.

To them were born three children, John P., November 28, 1890, married Vera Leopold. He is a banker at Trenton. Nina G., born in 1893, married C. R. Arnold; while Helen I., born in 1896, married W. S. Deffenbaugh.

From September, 1894, until December 25, 1895, Mr. Allen taught school at Stratton. On January 1, 1896, he became county clerk of Hitchcock County, elected on the Republican ticket. From 1900, until 1924, he was in the mercantile business at Trenton. Mr. Allen has been a member of the Trenton School Board a total of twenty-one years (1897-1928).

He is a member of the Trenton Commercial Club, the Odd Fellows, Modern Woodmen of America, Ancient Order of United Workmen and the Elks. Recently he was elected to life membership in the Nebraskana Society. On April 24, 1931, he was married to Marie Lawritson, at Trenton. Residence: Trenton.

Clyde Mills Allen

Clyde M. Allen, prominent farmer of Washington County, Nebraska, was born there, May 25, 1878, the son of William Henry and Ruth Emily (Bottorff) Allen. His father, who was a farmer, was born at Paris, Illinois, February 19, 1845, and died in Washington County, August 17, 1922. Five Allen brothers came to America from Scotland, in 1600. His mother, who was born in Clark County, Indiana, May 20, 1844, died at Omaha, Nebraska, April 2, 1916. She was a country school teacher and held membership in the Daughters of the American Revolution; an ancestor, Martin Bottorff, came to America from Switzerland, in 1710.

Mr. Allen attended the country schools of Washington County, and later was a student at the Fremont Normal College. He has lived in Nebraska all his life and has always been a farmer. In the past few years he has written several noteworthy poems, which were published in 1930-31. He is a member of the Washington County Pioneer Association and the Nebraskana Society, and holds membership in Solomon Lodge Number 10, of the the Ancient Free and Accepted Masons, at Fort Calhoun, Nebraska. Politically, Mr. Allen is a Republican.

He was united in marriage with Helen Margaret Pierce at Blair, October 22, 1902. Mrs. Allen, who is descended from eight proven lines of Revolutionary ancestors, was born at Blair, November 22, 1882. Seven children were born to them: Stanley Pierce, born August 2, 1903, who married Margaret Walford; Helen Marr, born May 23, 1905, who died October 13, 1905; Winifred Cora, born February 4, 1908; Ruth May, born May 14, 1911; Margaret, born October 7, 1914; Emily Ann, born October 24, 1917; and Alice Elizabeth, born July 16, 1922. Residence: Blair.

Dougal H. Allen

Dougal H. Allen was born in Hull, Canada, the son of Lemuel and Margaret (McMillan) Allen. His father, a farmer, was born in Canada, and died in Iowa, June 12, 1904; his ancestry was English on the paternal side and Scotch on the maternal side of the family. His mother, whose ancestry was Scotch, was born in Canada and died April 9, 1920.

Mr. Allen's parents were true pioneers of Iowa where they settled in 1871, and endured the same privations and difficult situations that pioneer Nebraskans met. He moved to Nebraska in 1907 with his wife and children and since then has been a rancher and farmer in Holt County where he has assisted in civic and religious affairs for a number of years. He is affiliated with the Methodist Episcopal Church of Emmett, Nebraska, is a member of The Nebraskana Society, and for the past 10 years has served as district president of the Northwestern Church District. During the World War he was active locally in loan drives.

His marriage to Mary Emeline McMillan occurred at Colorado Springs, Colorado, May 4, 1898. Mrs. Allen, who was born in Washington County, Nebraska, December 16, 1870, is the daughter of Daniel and Achsah (Stamford) McMillan. Her father moved from Pittsburg, Pennsylvania, to Nebraska in the fall of 1867 and with three other men homesteaded on the site of what is now the town of Herman, Nebraska.

Daniel McMillan, one of the builders of the middle-west, engaged in ranching and farming throughout the period of years he resided in Nebraska. He was married at Blair, then a hamlet of half a dozen buildings, October 29, 1869.

Mr. Allen and his wife have always been associated with progressive and constructive movements in their community. They have two children: Mollie Bernice, born August 18, 1899, who married George P. Hollopeter; and Robert Russell, born September 21, 1905, who married Bessie Beebe. Robert is a rancher in Holt County. Residence: Emmett.

Katherine Fay Allen

One of Nebraska's foremost women is Katherine Fay Allen, who resides at Cozad. She was born near Rock Bluffs, Nebraska, October 12, 1876, daughter of George Washington and Rachel Matilda (Chalfant) Worley. Her father, born near Springfield, Illinois, November 23, 1835, served in the Civil War with Company K, 16th Kansas Volunteer Cavalry. He also was a member of the 6th Missouri State Militia, government escort to wagon trains across Nebraska following the war. His maternal ancestors were German, and came to America from Edenkoben, on the *Snow Ketty* in 1752. On the paternal side his ancestry was English. Both families were deeply religious, and there were several clergymen on the paternal side.

Rachel Matilda Worley was born at Waynesburg, Pennsylvania, September 13, 1843. Her main interests were in the education and rearing of her family. On the paternal side she was descended from James Madison Chalfant, member of the territorial legislature of 1861, representing Cass and Lancaster Counties. He was a native of Morgantown, Virginia.

Katherine Allen received her education in the public and high school of Elmwood, Nebraska. Her vocation has been newspaper work, and as early as the 1890's she was associate editor of *Weeks Review* published at Elmwood at that time. She has done special work on several newspapers, and was in charge of the Omaha Bureau of Press Clippings in connection with the Thompson Advertising Agency from 1901 to 1908. In May of that year she established the Universal Press Clipping Bureau, which is continuing under her ownership and management.

A Republican in politics, she served three years as

member of the State Board of Control, (1920-23), two years of which she served as chairman, the first woman to serve as chairman of such a board in the United States.

She is the compiler of several memorial books of newspaper clippings of deceased persons of prominence for families. A leader in civic, welfare and club work, she has done much for the Woman's Club. She was first chairman of Americanization work in the Nebraska Federation of Women's Clubs, and of the Omaha Woman's Club. She was one of the promoters and organizers of the first Americanization and foreign night schools in Omaha. During the World War she acted as state chairman of publicity for Liberty Loan drives, and assisted in organizing the first Red Cross work in the state during the war. She was first chairman of the Red Cross committee of the Omaha Woman's Club, and has the first sample bandages brought to Nebraska for war work.

She is a member of the Woman's Relief Corps, and the Daughters of Union Veterans of the Civil War. She is a member of the First Methodist Episcopal Church of Omaha, and of the Omaha Altrusa Club. She is known for her volunteer social service work in Omaha and the state. Residence: Omaha. (Photograph in Album).

Ralph Morrow Allen

Ralph Morrow Allen, who is a leader in business affairs at Cozad, Nebraska, was born in that community March 7, 1897. His father, Charles Edgar Allen, who was born at Russell, Iowa, has served as state senator in Nebraska several terms. (*See Nebraskana*). Sue (Morrow) Allen, his mother, was born in Ohio, and died at Colorado Springs, in July, 1920. She was president of the Cozad Woman's Club and was a talented painter.

Mr. Allen was graduated from the Cozad High School in 1916, and later attended the University of Nebraska. For five years he was manager of the Charles E. Allen Company, and since then has been a partner in the firm Allen & Company. He was president of the Cozad Chamber of Commerce three times, was vice president of the Rotary Club for a time, and is now affiliated with the Presbyterian Church and the Nebraskana Society. He was formerly master of the local Masonic lodge.

He entered the United States Army during the World War and was discharged two years later as a second lieutenant; he is a member of the American Legion. Mr. Allen's favorite sports are football and riding.

On June 25, 1928, he was married at Omaha, to Marjorie C. Currant, who was born at Elmwood, Nebraska, March 2, 1901. They have a daughter, Nancy, born March 15, 1931. Residence: Cozad.

Samuel Allen

Samuel Allen was born in Gallia County, Ohio, March 6, 1844, the son of Richard Allen and Mary E. (Nye) Allen. His father, a farmer, was born in Duchess County, New York, March 10, 1814, and died September 13, 1895. His mother was born at Athens, Ohio, October 1, 1815, and died in Champaign County, Illinois, June 25, 1883.

Mr. Allen attended public schools and the Pine Grove Academy at Pine Grove, Ohio. He married Julia Netta Goodrich on January 27, 1880. Mrs. Allen was born in Champaign County, Illinois, July 4, 1858.

Samuel Allen is affiliated with the First Presbyterian Church at Fairbury, where he has resided since he retired from his farm. He is a Republican and has lived in Nebraska forty-six years. His favorite recreation at the present time is reading. Residence: Fairbury.

Silas Gilbert Allen

Silas Gilbert Allen, physician and surgeon of Stanton, Stanton County, Nebraska, has lived in this state since 1897, and for many years has been active in community affairs. He was born at Harlan, Shelby County, Iowa, April 6, 1875, the son of Daniel Washington and Mary Elizabeth (Bothwell) Allen. His father, who was a farmer, stock raiser, and locomotive engineer, was born in New York County, New York, in 1837, and died at Harlan, April 21, 1901; his ancestry was German and English. His mother, who was born near Anamesa, has been prominent in the Eastern Star for many years; she is of Scotch descent.

Dr. Allen attended public schools and a normal training school, and in 1901 was graduated from the University of Nebraska where he took an active part in football. He served as house physician at the Methodist Hospital in Omaha, 1901, was engaged in the practice of medicine and surgery at Clarkson for 17 years, and practiced at Scottsbluff for five years. He is now engaged in medical practice at Stanton, and is a landowner in Stanton County.

He is a member of the State Medical Society, the American Railway and Elkhorn Valley Surgeons Associations, the Commercial Club of Stanton, and the Nebraskana Society. He is affiliated with the Congregational Church of Stanton, holds membership in the Lions Club, and is a member of the Masons. During the World War Dr. Allen was an active participant in loan drives and relief work for the Red Cross.

His marriage to Louise May Beran was solemnized at Ord, Valley County, Nebraska, October 13, 1904. Mrs. Allen, who was born at Ord, May 9, 1883, was graduated from the Fremont Normal School and later was a teacher in the public schools. They have two children: Daisy Viola, born May 23, 1906; and Sila Gilbert, Jr., born April 3, 1921. Daisy graduated at the University of Nebraska, 1928, and took a secretarial course at the College of Commerce, Long Beach, California; she now has a secretarial position in Syracuse, New York.

Dr. Allen is a member of the Country Club and holds membership in the Republican Party. His favorite sport is football, while his hobby is agriculture. Residence: Stanton.

Thomas Stinson Allen

Thomas S. Allen was born at Paynes Point, Ogle County, Illinois, April 30, 1865, son of Benjamin Franklin and Harriet Maria (Ely) Allen. Benjamin Franklin Allen was born at Campton, New Hampshire, December 10, 1832, and died at Lincoln, Nebraska, December 20, 1915. A farmer, he was a direct descendant of Captain John Allen of the New Hampshire militia in the Revolutionary War.

Mr. Allen's mother was born at Hartford, New York, January 7, 1835, and died in Lincoln, January 24, 1912. Nathaniel Ely, who came to America from England in 1634, is an ancestor.

Upon completion of his public school work, Mr. Allen attended the University of Nebraska where he received his A. B. degree, 1889, and his LL. B., 1891. He was valedictorian of the class of 1889, delivered the class oration and was active in athletics, particularly baseball, the entire four years.

He was admitted to the bar in 1891 at Lincoln, and has practiced law in this state since that time. He was chairman of the Democratic state committee 1904-09, and 1922-1932, and United States district attorney for Nebraska 1915-21. He has been a member of the following law firms: Talbot, Bryan & Allen, 1892-96; Talbot & Allen, 1896-1914; and at the present time the firm of Allen & Requartte.

He is vice president and general attorney for the Service Life Insurance Company; treasurer and general attorney for the Woodman Accident Company; general attorney for Farmers' Mutual Insurance Company of Nebraska; secretary of the Commercial Mutual Surety Company; and general attorney for the Central Health Company.

On June 28, 1898, he was married to Mary Elizabeth Bryan, at Salem, Illinois. Mrs. Allen, who is a daughter

THOMAS STINSON ALLEN

of Judge Silas Lillard Bryan, was an instructor at Ewing College, Illinois.

Mr. Allen is a member of the American Bar Association; Nebraska State Bar Association; the Chamber of Commerce; Knife and Fork Club; Professional Men's Club; Layman's Club; Y. M. C. A.; and the First Baptist Church of Lincoln, Nebraska. He is a Mason, Royal Highlander and Modern Woodman of America. His social clubs are the University Club and the Country Club. His home and office are both in Lincoln. (Photograph on Page 23).

William Irving Allen

William I. Allen, who has resided in Nebraska for the past 45 years, was born at Richmond, Henrico County, Virginia, August 19, 1869, the son of David Jonathan and Mary Ann (Wall) Allen. His father, who was born at Camden, New Jersey, in 1833, and died at Washington, District of Columbia, in 1895, fought in the Mexican War, the Indian Wars, and the Civil War; he was imprisoned in Libby prison during the Civil War; at the time of his death he was superintendent of the Soldiers Cemetery at Washington, D. C.; his Scotch and English ancestors came to America in Colonial days and fought in the Colonial Wars in the Revolution and the War of 1812. His mother was born at Liverpool, England, March 12, 1845, and died at Washington, D. C., September 28, 1883. She was of Scotch-Irish and English descent; her grandfather served with Wellington at Waterloo.

Mr. Allen attended the public schools in Virginia and was graduated from the Richmond Academy in 1895. Later he was a student at Fremont College, Fremont, Nebraska, the University of Omaha, Omaha, Nebraska, and the University of Virginia. He taught in rural schools for three years; was principal of the schools at Gretna, Nebraska, Elkhorn, Nebraska, and Dundee, Nebraska; served as professor of English and mathematics at Dexter Normal College, Dexter, Iowa, 1892-93; was engaged in the practice of law in Omaha, 1894, as a member of the firm Pratt, Allen & Walkup; and in 1895 came to Schuyler, Colfax County, Nebraska, where he has since practiced law.

A Democrat, Mr. Allen has held various public offices in his community and county, among them: city attorney of Schuyler, 1898 to 1903; county attorney of Colfax County, 1904-06, and 1910-14; and county judge, 1906-08. During the campaigns of 1912 and 1916 he was an ardent supporter of Wilson for president.

In the World War he was government appeal agent for Colfax County; was defense council attorney; was a four minute man; and was distinguished by his patriotic addresses which he made all over the state of Nebraska. He is a member of the State Historical Society; the Nebraskana Society; the American Judicature Society; the Izaak Walton League; the Nebraska State Bar Association, and the American Bar Association. He is a member of the Knights of Pythias, serving as Grand Chancellor in 1911, and Supreme Representative, 1915-24; is an Odd Fellow; and is a 32nd degree Mason, and member of the Shrine, having been president of the William McKinley Scottish Rite in 1922. Mr. Allen was president of the County Attorneys' Association, 1913-14; and is at present serving his second year as chairman of the advisory committee of the State Bar Association.

He was united in marriage with Eva Marston Perrine at Omaha, July 7, 1890; she was born of English, French, and Scotch ancestry in Kentucky, October 20, 1870, and died at Omaha, March 2, 1928. To this marriage three children were born, of whom only one is living: Irene, born July 5, 1891, who died December 10, 1893; Ruth born July 7, 1897, who died June 20, 1912; and Esther, born April 20, 1899, who married William G. Hubbard. Esther received her B. S. degree in 1922 at the University of Nebraska where she was awarded Pan Hellenic honors and Phi Beta Kappa membership. She was graduated from the Institute of Musical Art in New York City; received her Bachelor of Music degree at Columbia, and the

A. M. degree at the latter. During 1925-26 she was head of the piano department at East Stroudsburg. She now resides in San Capristano, California.

William Irving Allen married Nellie Arvilla Tagg, nee Imbody, on May 1, 1930. Her father, a soldier in the Civil War, was Lewis Imbody. Mrs. Allen had a brother in the Spanish-American War and two sons in the World War. Dr. Harold E. Tagg, now of Schuyler, served in France as did Lowell Tagg, who died of illness as the troops were being mustered out. Mrs. Allen is a member of the O. E. S., the Rebekahs, the Pythian Sisters. She is past president of the Ladies' Auxiliary and belongs to the Episcopal Church. Residence: Schuyler. (Photograph on Page 25).

Amy Bruner Almy

Amy B. Almy, a resident of Nebraska for the past 56 years and a writer of some distinction, was born at West Point, Nebraska, February 13, 1875. Her father, Uriah Bruner, who was born in Bucks County, Pennsylvania, September 25, 1830, was a teacher, farmer, and lawyer who settled near Omaha, in 1856. He was one of the first regents of the University of Nebraska. His German ancestors, some of whom served in the Revolution, came to America the first part of the 18th century. He died at West Point, July 5, 1905.

Her mother, Amelia Brobst, was born in Leigh County, Pennsylvania, September 20, 1832, and died at West Point, July 22, 1909. She was a pioneer homemaker and the mother of nine children. Her German ancestors came to America in the 18th century.

Mrs. Almy was graduated from the high school at West Point, June, 1891, and in 1896 was awarded the A. B. degree at the University of Nebraska, where she was a member of Delian Literary Society and the English Club. She received her A. M. at Cornell University in 1902. Active in literary circles and civic affairs for many years in Lincoln, she is the author of various short stories, occasional articles, and some verse, published in religious and general magazines.

She was united in marriage to John Edwin Almy at West Point, July 22, 1903. Mr. Almy, who was born at Centralia, Illinois, October 13, 1875, is professor of physics. He is of English ancestry. They have a daughter, Constance Ida, born February 5, 1907, who married Harold Lyman Kipp.

Mrs. Almy is a member of the Nebraska Writers Guild at Lincoln, the Quill Club, and the American Association of University Women. She holds membership in the Red Cross, Native Sons and daughters, the Women's Christian Temperance Union, and the Young Women's Christian Association and Faculty Women's Club, and is affiliated with First Plymouth Congregational Church of Lincoln. Her favorite sports are hiking and taking auto trips. Her hobby is the study of story writing. She is a Republican. Residence: Lincoln.

John Edwin Almy

For over 30 years John E. Almy has been connected with the University of Nebraska, and has taken a prominent place in the educational field. He was born at Centralia, Illinois, October 13, 1875, the son of Horace Manchester and Abbie Colburn (Grinnell) Almy. His father, who was a farmer and stockman, was born at Little Compton, Rhode Island, September 17, 1838, and died at Lincoln, Lancaster County, Nebraska, February, 1891; William Almy came to Massachusetts in 1629, from Leicestershire, England, and was a member of the Aquidneck Colony at Rhode Island, in 1638. Abbie Grinnell was born at Little Compton, March 16, 1837, and died near Ashland, Nebraska, February 6, 1918; she was descended from Matthew Grinnell, a French Huguenot, who emigrated from Burgundy to Newport, Rhode Island, in 1630.

Dr. Almy attended public schools in Lancaster County, and was graduated from the preparatory department

Rinehart-Marsden—Omaha

WILLIAM IRVING ALLEN

of the University of Nebraska, in 1892. He holds the degrees of: B. S., June, 1896, University of Nebraska; A. M., June, 1897, University of Nebraska; Ph. D., Friedrichs Wilhelm University, Berlin, 1900. He was also a student at Cambridge University, England, in 1900. During his college days he was a member of the Union Literary Society, Phi Beta Kappa, Sigma Xi, and was president of his senior class at the University of Nebraska; he was halfback on his class football team, 1894-95-96.

He served as instructor, assistant professor, and professor of physics at the University of Nebraska, all since 1900, and is now professor of experimental physics. He is a member of the Lincoln Chamber of Commerce, the Knife and Fork Club, the Nebraskana Society, and the University Club. He holds membership in the American Association of University Professors, having served as president of the Nebraska section in 1912-13, is a fellow of the American Association for the Advancement of Science, and the American Physical Society. He is affiliated with the First Plymouth Congregational Church, is a member of Red Cross, and the Republican party.

His marriage to Amy Celesta Bruner was solemnized at West Point, Cuming County, Nebraska, July 22, 1903. Mrs. Almy, who is an author and poet of some distinction, was born at West Point, February 13, 1875. Her father, Uriah Bruner, was regent of the University of Nebraska. They have one daughter, Constance Ida, born February 5, 1907, who married Harold L. Kipp of Lincoln.

Dr. Almy is the author of numerous articles on research problems in physics, published in the *Philosophical Magazine, London,* and *Physical Review.* Residence: Lincoln.

Clara Christine Altman

Clara Christine Altman, dean of women at Hastings College, was born at Webber, Kansas, December 25, 1889, daughter of Samuel and Olive Oatman (Cribbs) Altman. Her father was born in Lancaster County, Pennsylvania, July 1, 1852, and is of Dutch descent. Her mother, also a native of Lancaster County, was born August 5, 1860, and is descended from Lord Say, who formed the Saybrook Colony from England.

Miss Altman was graduated from high school at Emporia, Kansas, in 1908, and received her Bachelor of Arts degree from Emporia College, in 1912. She thereafter took post graduate work at Columbia University, Paris University and the University of Madrid, and in 1924, was awarded her Master's degree from the University of Chicago. During her college career she held various class offices, and was made a member of Kappa Delta Pi.

A resident of Nebraska for the past ten years, Miss Altman first came to Hastings as a teacher of modern languages which position she has held since. She was appointed dean of women at Hastings College at the end of her first year. Her professional associations include the National Association of Deans of Women, and the Nebraska State Association of Deans of Women, of which she was president in 1929. She is a member of the First Presbyterian Church of Hastings, and was recently elected to life membership in the Nebraskana Society.

Miss Altman enjoys golf, tennis and hiking, and her hobby is the cello. Residence: Hastings.

Henry Altschuler

Born at Madison, Nebraska, January 21, 1883, Henry Altschuler is the son of Solomon and Mary (Wertheim) Altschuler. His father, who was a farmer, was born near Posen, Germany, and died at Omaha, Nebraska, July 21, 1899; he came to this country in 1855. His mother, who was of Jewish descent, was born at Darmstadt, Germany, and died at Omaha, December 17, 1928.

Mr. Altschuler is a merchant at Madison, Nebraska. He has been a director of the Nebraska Federation of Retailers, is a director of the Nebraska Mutual Burglar Insurance Company, and vice president and director of the Associated Stores Wholesale Company, Inc. He holds membership in the Madison County Historical Society, the National Geographic Society, the Madison Country Club, the Traveling Men's Protective Association, and the Nebraskana Society.

He is district chairman for the Boy Scouts, is a 32nd degree Mason and Shriner, has served as president of the Community Club, and has been treasurer of the Madison County Fair Association. Prior to the World War period he was a first lieutenant in Company H, 4th Nebraska Infantry, and later was county chairman and state director of Near East Relief. His hobby is reading, and his sports include hunting and fishing.

His marriage to Ada Nathan occurred at Des Moines, Iowa, December 27, 1906. She was born at Oskaloosa, Iowa, January 25, 1880, daughter of Moses A. and Hattie Nathan. Residence: Madison. (Photograph in Album).

Otis Theodore Alvison

Otis Theodore Alvison, banker, was born at Bloomfield, Iowa, October 13, 1881. His father, James L. Alvison was born in New York City, July 10, 1846. He was an educator of English descent, who married Charlotte H. Hancock. He died at Long Beach, California, September 12, 1928. Charlotte Hancock Alvison was born on the Ohio River near Corn Island, Indiana, March 21, 1851, and is living in Long Beach. She is also of English descent.

Otis T. Alvison was educated in the public schools of Omaha, and was graduated from Omaha High School in 1899. In August of that year he entered the employ of the Omaha National Bank as a clerk. He has been promoted through various positions to that of vice president which position he has held for the past two years.

He was married to Eleanor Southard at Council Bluffs, Iowa, on December 26, 1906. Mrs. Alvison was born at Morrison, Illinois, and is of Scotch and early American ancestry. They have one daughter, Charlotte Jane, born September 20, 1910.

Mr. Alvison is a Republican. He is a member of the Scottish Rite and Shrine bodies and is also affiliated with the Elks and is a member of the Lions Club. He is active in the civic life of the city and is a member of the Chamber of Commerce, and is treasurer of the Nebraska Humane Society. His clubs are the Omaha Athletic, the Omaha and the Happy Hollow Country. Residence: Omaha.

Ernest Capron Ames

Ernest C. Ames was born at Lincoln, Nebraska, June 14, 1875, and has lived in the state since that time. He has been engaged in the active practice of law at Lincoln, since 1898. His father, John Henry Ames, who was a lawyer and supreme court counsellor, was born in Vermont, of English descent, February 12, 1847, and died at Lincoln, January 18, 1911. His mother was born in Ohio, July 26, 1840, and died at Lincoln. Her ancestry was Dutch and English.

Mr. Ames was graduated from the Lincoln High School in 1892. He was granted his A. B. degree, 1896, and A. M., 1898, at the University of Nebraska where he was a member of Beta Theta Pi, Phi Delta Phi, and Theta Nu Epsilon. He has been a practicing lawyer since his graduation from college and was United States Referee in Bankruptcy. He is now vice president and actuary of the Bankers Life Insurance Company of Nebraska. Politically, he is an independent.

He was married to Grace Alsyne Andrews at Fairbury, Nebraska, October 3, 1907. Mrs. Ames was born at Ann Arbor, Michigan, November 29, 1880, of English descent. There are two children, John Henry, born January 12, 1911; and Margaret Capron, born January 21, 1909.

Mr. Ames is a member of the Lincoln Chamber of Commerce. He holds a fellowship in the American Institute of Actuaries. He is a member of the Masons, Blue Lodge Chapter at Lincoln, Nebraska. He is a member of the Lincoln University Club; Lincoln Country Club; and the Crucible Club. His sports are hiking and fishing, and his hobbies reading and photography. Residence: Lincoln.

Carl Gideon Amick

Carl Gideon Amick, physician and surgeon, was born at Grand Island, Nebraska, July 11, 1896, son of John William and Lillie Mae (Hall) Amick. The father, who is a retired railroad conductor of German origin, was born at Moberly, Missouri, September 16, 1862. His wife, born at Napoleon, Ohio, May 20, 1868, is of Scotch-Irish descent.

Educated in the grade schools of Grand Island, Kearney and St. Paul, Carl Gideon Amick was graduated from high school at Loup City, in 1915. He received his Bachelor of Science degree from the University of Nebraska in 1919, and his Doctor of Medicine degree in 1921. He is a member of the Silver Lynx and of Phi Rho Sigma.

Admitted to practice October 1, 1922, Dr. Amick is now owner and physician and surgeon in charge of the Loup City Hospital and district surgeon for the Union Pacific Railroad. He is medical examiner for the National Red Cross, a member of the Custer County, Nebraska State and American Medical Associations, and holds the rank of first lieutenant in the Medical Reserve Corps. He is a Mason, is fond of hunting and fishing, and enjoys reading.

On November 10, 1923, he was married to Emily Clara Wanek, at Loup City. Mrs. Amick, who is of Bohemian descent, was born at Milligan, Nebraska, February 21, 1901. There are three children, Janet Louise, born November 20, 1924; Ellen Marie, born May 28, 1927; and Arthur Franklin, born March 21, 1930. Residence: Loup City. (Photograph in Album).

B. W. Ammerman

B. W. Ammerman was born at Plymouth, Nebraska, February 19, 1888, the son of Winfield and Ida (Shindoll) Ammerman. His father, who was a farmer, died at Plymouth, in 1922; his ancestry was German and Irish.

Mr. Ammerman has been manager of the Scotia Independent Telephone Company for the past 21 years. He holds membership in the Commercial Club and the Red Cross, is a member of the Village Board of Scotia, Nebraska, is affiliated with the Scotia Methodist Church, and holds membership in the Shrine body of the Masons. His hobbies are reading and mechanics and his favorite sport is baseball. He is also director of the Scotia Municipal Band.

On November 22, 1910, he was married at Plymouth, Nebraska, to Alvina Williamina Sperling, who was born at DeWitt, Nebraska, August 22, 1892. One daughter was born to them: La Verna, May 13, 1914, who died July 13, 1921. Residence: Scotia.

Mildred M. Ammerman

Mildred M. Ammerman, a resident of Nebraska for the past 50 years, was born at Luthersburg, Clarfield County, Pennsylvania, December 8, 1870, the daughter of Walter C. and Elizabeth S. (Pentz) Parker. Her father, a merchant, was born at Crawford, Pennsylvania, April 8, 1814; his Scotch and Irish ancestors came to this country before the Revolution; he died at Eickingville, Pennsylvania, April 8, 1914. Her mother was born at Luthersburg, September 21, 1844, of German parentage, and died at Reynolds, Jefferson County, Nebraska, July 8, 1900.

Mrs. Ammerman attended public school and later was a student at the Lincoln Normal College, Lincoln,

Nebraska. She is affiliated with the Methodist Episcopal Church in which she has been a member of the board of stewards for the past 12 years. She holds membership in the Degree of Honor, Daughters of the American Revolution, Welfare Club, and the Nebraskana Society. She is a Republican.

Of her marriage to U. S. Ammerman one child was born: Helen, born May 19, 1900, who married Paul A. Ude. Residence: Reynolds.

Charles DeWitt Ammon

Charles DeWitt Ammon was born at Raleigh, Saline County, Illinois, June 6, 1887, the son of John Franklin and Adele (Douglas) Ammon. His father, who was for many years a railroad agent, and a merchant, is of German ancestry. His mother, who was born March 3, 1863, and is still living, is of Scotch descent.

Mr. Ammon was graduated from the high school at Benton, Illinois, May, 1903, where he was active in debating and oratorical events. He was in a railroad office for a time; managed a grocery store at Sidell, Illinois, 1904-05; was engaged in the hardware business, 1907-12; and since 1913 has been a manufacturer. He is the owner of the Easy Manufacturing Company at Lincoln, at this time.

He was united in marriage to Emah B. Bruns at Elcampo, Texas, June 23, 1910. Mrs. Ammon, whose ancestry is German, was born at Elcampo, July 18, 1889. They have two children: Robert, born June 8, 1918; and William, born November 3, 1923.

Mr. Ammon is a member of the Lincoln Chamber of Commerce and the Kiwanis Club. He served as county chairman of the Butler County Red Cross in 1918. He is a member of the Modern Woodmen of America and the Young Men's Christian Association. He is a Mason. He is affiliated with the Shrine Country Club, and his sports are golf and hand ball. Residence: Lincoln.

John R. Ammon

John R. Ammon was born at Leavenworth, Indiana, November 25, 1860, the son of George W. and Nancy C. (Peckinpaugh) Ammon. His father, who was a farmer, was born at Madison, Indiana, February 22, 1819, and died at Emmetsburg, Iowa, June 12, 1887; he was vice president and a stockholder in the Ammon, Scott & Company manufacturing concern. His mother, who was president of the local Women's Christian Temperance Union at Emmetsburg, was born at Cape Sandy, Indiana, May 18, 1825, and died at Hammond, Nebraska November 14, 1910.

Mr. Ammon received his education in Iowa where he attended public grade school and a private academy. He was a teacher for a time and engaged in the creamery business at Emmetsburg from 1880 to 1884. He holds membership in the Ancient Order of United Workmen at Hammond, Nebraska, is a member of the Independent Order of Odd Fellows, and is affiliated with Sybrant Evangelical Church. He has been a farmer near Hammond for many years

A Republican, Mr. Ammon served as Republican county chairman, was precinct committeeman for a time, and has attended various state conventions of his party as delegate. He has lived in this state continuously since 1884, and has taken an active part in the progress of his community.

His marriage to Ida Estella Sybrant was solemnized at Sybrant, Nebraska, November 14, 1889. Mrs. Ammon, who is the daughter of David O. and Rozilla Gilbert Sybrant, was born at Guy's Mills, Pennsylvania, July 25, 1864. Their children are: Ben E., born August 29, 1890, who married Estella R. Barker; Harold G., born February 15, 1892, who married Addie A. Welton; and Nancy L., born October 23, 1902. Both sons are farmers in Rock County, Nebraska. Residence: Hammond.

Emma Tracy Amos

Emma Tracy Amos, daughter of Asa and Mary Ann (Shields) Tracy, was born at Cheyenne, Wyoming, March 31, 1881, and came with her family to Kimball County, Nebraska, about 1882. Her father was born at Buffalo, New York, and died at Cheyenne, Wyoming, January 26, 1888. He was a stockman. His father was Irish and his mother English of the Peacock family of Buffalo, a relative of Sir Walter Peacock of London, England.

Mary Ann Shields was born in Illinois, August 2, 1853, and died at Pine Bluff, Wyoming, February 19, 1906. Her father was German and her mother English. The family were early pioneers in Nebraska.

Emma Tracy attended public school at Ogden, Utah, Grand Island, Nebraska, and Cheyenne, Wyoming. On November 5, 1902, she was married to Horace Churchill Amos, a stockman. He was born at Racine, Wisconsin, May 7, 1877. There are two children, Marjorie, born April 3, 1907; and Marian, born May 7, 1912. Marjorie is stenographer for the American State Bank. Marian is graduated from high school.

Mr. Amos is a member of the Episcopal Church and a life member of the Nebraskana Society. Residence: Kimball.

Ross Amspoker

Ross Amspoker, a prominent lawyer of Springview, Nebraska, was born at Nodaway, Iowa, November 18, 1874, the son of Samuel Amspoker and Mary Jane (Caldwell) Amspoker. His father, who was born in Hancock, Ohio, in 1837, and died at Springview, May 28, 1915, was a farmer and stockman who took an active part in political and civic affairs in his community; he served as county treasurer of Keya Paha County for four years. His mother, whose Scotch and Irish ancestors settled in Kentucky, in the early history of the state, was born in Harrison County, Ohio, May 16, 1842, and died at Springview, November 10, 1930.

Mr. Amspoker received his legal education in the college of law of the University of Nebraska. He has been active in the practice of law in northern Nebraska at Springview since his admission to the bar in 1903, and owns several farms in Keya Paha County. A Republican, he served as county treasurer of Keya Paha County for four years, was county attorney for six years, acted as state representative from 1923 to 1925, and was state senator from 1927 to 1931.

He is a member of the local Red Cross, is affiliated with the Congregational Church, and holds membership in the Nebraska State Historical Society. Mr. Amspoker has been interested in banking and farm loan activities for a number of years

On November 14, 1906, he married Getha McKee at Bonesteel, South Dakota. Mrs. Amspoker was born in Armstrong County, Pennsylvania, December 17, 1881. Their two children are: Bernice, born October 23, 1907, who was graduated from the University of Nebraska in 1929; and Ruth Frances, born October 31, 1910, who was graduated from the University of Nebraska in 1931. Residence: Springview.

Harry John Amundson

Harry John Amundson, leading merchant in Hartington, Nebraska, was born at Hartington, on June 8, 1890, son of Andrew and Margaret Ellen (Morrison) Amundson.

Andrew Amundson was born at Occonomowoc, Wisconsin, of American descent for several generations, and engaged in the mercantile business in Cedar County for many years prior to his death on March 28, 1928. His wife, Margaret, was a native of Illinois, whose family was of early American stock.

Educated in the public and high schools of Hartington, after finishing school he entered the business established by his father, which he has since owned and operated. The business was established in 1885, the first general merchandise store in Hartington.

He is a Republican. During the World War he served eighteen months in the United States Army and is a member of the American Legion. A Catholic, he is a member of the local church, as well as the Chamber of Commerce, Lions Club and the Country Club. He is fond of golf and enjoys reading.

Mr. Amundson was married to Alice Loretta Griffin at Des Moines, Iowa, June 8, 1931. Residence: Hartington.

A. E. Andersen

A. E. Andersen was born in Fremont, Nebraska, February 14, 1882, son of Christian S. and Maren J. (Petersen) Andersen. Christian Andersen was born in Denmark, March 28, 1840, and came to the United States in 1861. He was a farmer who served with the First Nebraska Cavalry during the Civil War. He died March 6, 1922. His wife, Maren, was born in Denmark, January 8, 1846, and died January 21, 1902.

Mr. Andersen attended the Fremont public schools, and was graduated from Fremont High School in 1900, when he became a grocery clerk. In 1904 he became bookkeeper for Eddy Brothers Department Store, and later became manager and buyer for them, severing his connection in 1917. He is now partner in the Brunswick Restaurant, and a director of the Equitable Building and Loan Association.

A Republican, Mr. Andersen was defeated for mayor in the Spring of 1917; in January, 1930, he became a member of the City Park Board, serving since that time. He is a director of the Young Men's Christian Association was vice president one year, and member of the board of managers 15 years. He is a member of the Chamber of Commerce, the Fremont Ad Club (president 1915-16) and the Rotary Club (president 1930). His fraternal organization is Elks Lodge No. 514. He is a member of the First Baptist Church, and contributor to the Red Cross and Salvation Army. His sports are football and baseball.

On August 15, 1904, he was married to Orpha Gertrude Palmer, a daughter of Mr. and Mrs. W. J. Palmer, at Wahoo. Mrs. Andersen was born at Stratton, Nebraska, July 6, 1886, of English and Irish descent. She was a milliner prior to her marriage. There is one son, William Dale, born January 21, 1913, who is a sophomore at Midland College. Residence: Fremont.

Charles J. Andersen

Charles J. Andersen, president of the Andersen Company, Incorporated, was born at Herslev, Denmark, March 13, 1864. He is the son of Soren and Christiane Andersen, the former of Kolding, Denmark, born July 6, 1838. He was a saddlemaker and carriage manufacturer, and an officer in the Danish Army. He served in the Danish-German War of 1864. He came to the United States 36 years ago, and died at Omaha on December 7, 1925. His wife, Christiane, was born at Kolding, March 11, 1839, and died at Omaha, January 20, 1913.

Mr. Andersen was educated in the public schools of Denmark until he reached the age of 18 years. He was married on June 1, 1924, to Leda Flick. Mrs. Andersen was born at York, Nebraska, and attended the York public and high schools.

Since coming to America in 1884 he has been engaged in business in Omaha, from 1884-87 in the carriage business. In 1901 he incorporated under the name of Andersen-Millard Company, and from 1904-29 under the name of Andersen Company. He is now president of Andersen Company, Incorporated. A Republican, Mr. Andersen served in the Nebraska legislature from 1905-07. He

FREDERICK WILLIAM ANDERSEN

wrote and introduced the Omaha city charter and helped pass the Omaha water bill, and introduced and helped pass the label law. Hs is a member of the Chamber of Commerce, and the Masons. Residence: Omaha.

Frederick William Andersen

Born at Fremont, Nebraska, March 18, 1882, Frederick William Andersen is the son of Hans and Elese Jacobenne (Jorgensen) Andersen. His father, born in Sillin, Denmark, January 29, 1843, and who died at Cozad, Nebraska, April 16, 1928, was the first farmer to introduce and grow alfalfa in Dawson County; he came to America in 1873. His mother was born in Lollin, Denmark, July 31, 1851.

Mr. Andersen worked as a clerk in Helmers & Jensens general store at Cozad, for a year, 1906-07, and a few years later bought out both partners. He is now president of Andersen's Department Store, is a stockholder in the Farmers Elevator Company and the Co-operative Oil Company, is vice president of the Cozad Mutual Telephone Company, and is active in civic and political affairs.

A Democrat, he served as city councilman 1916-24, was a member of the State Board of Education from 1928 to 1930, and is now secretary of the latter board. He is the author of *The Miracle Merchant*, published in 1925. In 1918 he became a life member of the Red Cross, and since 1928 has been chairman of the City Park Commission. He is president of the Cozad Volunteer Fire Department, is a director of the Chamber of Commerce and the Federation of Retailers, and holds membership in the Nebraskana Society. He has been selected as one of Nebraska's citizens to be represented in the 1932 edition of *Who's Who in Government*. In 1932 he was chosen a Master Merchant of Nebraska, receiving a medal at Lincoln on May 12, 1932.

Mr. Andersen is affiliated with the First Methodist Episcopal Church of Cozad, is a Mason, Shriner and Odd Fellow, and since 1921 has been civic chairman of the Cozad Cemetery Association.

He was united in marriage with Cora May Wallace, at Cozad, June 19, 1907. Mrs. Andersen, who is the daughter of Lieutenant Theobald Scheibel, was born at Philadelphia, Pennsylvania, October 30, 1881. Two children were born to the marriage: Mary Ann, born July 10, 1910, who died July 11, 1910; and Berniece May, born May 29, 1915. Residence: Cozad. (Photograph on Page 29).

Leonard Clarence Andersen

Leonard Clarence Andersen, farm implement dealer and funeral director, was born at Norman, Nebraska, October 24, 1894, son of Anton Marius and Thilda (Olsen) Andersen.

The father, born in Denmark, February 15, 1859, was a farmer and merchant in Nebraska for many years prior to his death at Norman, October 29, 1929. His wife, Thilda, was born in Sweden, September 29, 1854. She resides at Norman.

Mr. Andersen attended country school, and has been in business at Norman almost ever since. He was married to Ruth Hildur Bergsten at Minden, on September 10, 1919, and to them two children were born, Eugene Euclid, born August 11, 1920, and Ivan Dale, born September 3, 1923.

On August 3, 1931, Mr. Andersen was granted a funeral director's license. He served as a private in Company C, 309th Ammunition Train, 84th Division, in the World War. Residence: Norman.

Albert Wilfred Anderson

Albert Wilfred Anderson, physician and surgeon, was born at Callaway, Nebraska, May 6, 1893, and has been a life resident of Nebraska. He is the son of Nels N. and Clara Louise (Bjork) Anderson, both natives of Sweden. Nels Anderson, who is now a retired farmer, was born

October 31, 1858, and his wife, Clara, was born April 14, 1856.

Upon his graduation from Benson High School in 1913, Dr. Anderson entered Creighton University, from which he received his degree of Doctor of Medicine in 1918. Since that time he has been engaged in general practice.

He was united in marriage to Lillie May Hultman at Oakland, Nebraska, August 8, 1918. Mrs. Anderson, who is of Swedish descent, was born in Essex County, Iowa, February 21, 1888.

Dr. Anderson is a member of the American and Nebraska State Medical Associations, and is a life member of the Interstate Postgraduate Association. His religious affiliation is with Grace Lutheran Church, and he is a member also of the Chamber of Commerce and the local Red Cross. Dr. Anderson enjoys hunting and fishing, but his hobby is trap shooting. Residence: West Point.

Alfred Theodore Anderson

Alfred Theodore Anderson, son of August and Ingar (Timmansdotter) Anderson, was born in Skane, Sweden, July 17, 1865, and came to Kearney, at the age of ten.

His father, born in Sweden, August 24, 1841, was a dairyman there, and after coming to America engaged in wagon making and farming. He died at Liberal, Kansas, in October, 1919. His mother, born in Sweden, February 17, 1840, died at Kearney, August 23, 1879.

Mr. Anderson attended the public schools of Kearney, denominational school in Minneapolis, and took special courses in photography. He came to America at the age of two, lived in Knoxville, Galesburg, and Woodhull, Illinois, until 1875, and has since been a resident of Kearney.

Since 1886, Mr. Anderson has operated The Anderson Studio. Prior thereto he was associated with Mr. J. A. Stridborg in the photographic business. During 1924-25, he spent a year traveling and taking photographs in Northwestern Spain. Mr. Anderson is a member of the Photographers' International Association of America. His hobby is cabinet making and the invention and construction of photographic apparatus.

His marriage to Alma Matilda Wickstrom was solemnized in Phelps County, September 11, 1892, and to them three children were born: Ruth, born September 8, 1893; Miriam, born August 17, 1895; and Elizabeth, born November 30, 1913. Miriam is married to Montague H. Worlock; both Miriam and Ruth are photographers, while Elizabeth is a student at Barnard College in New York City.

Mr. Anderson is a Republican. He is a member of the First Baptist Church, the Chamber of Commerce, and the Nebraskana Society. He is a trustee of his church, and during 1907-08, was secretary of the Nebraska State Photographers' Association. From 1906-11, he served on the Kearney School Board. Beginning his career as a photographer at the age of 16, Mr. Anderson recently celebrated his fiftieth anniversary in the business. Residence: Kearney.

Andreas Theodore Anderson

Andreas Theodore Anderson was born at Gelballe, Skanderup, Denmark, July 19, 1885, and came to Nebraska, January 22, 1904, settling in Gordon where he went into the blacksmithing business. He is the son of Andreas and Margrethe Andersen, the former born in Egholt, Denmark, April 9, 1845, and died at Gelballe, Denmark, September 23, 1917. His mother was born in Gesten, Denmark, April 23, 1850, and died at Gelballe, Skanderup, Denmark, December 19, 1931.

From the age of five until the age of 14, Mr. Andersen attended school and on October 1, 1899, was confirmed in the Lutheran Church at Skanderup. Mr. Anderson's grandfather and father were both blacksmiths in Denmark as were his two brothers. In 1914 and 1924 he returned to Denmark for visits. He started in the blacksmithing business for himself at Gordon, Nebraska,

ALFRED T. ANDERSON

Anderson—Kearney

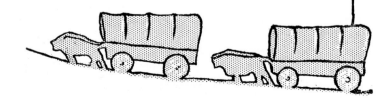

on March 25, 1908, and at the present time is president of the Nebraska Blacksmiths' Association. He is a Republican.

On December 25, 1911, he was married to Elsie Violet Zechman at Gordon. She was born at Easton, Pennsylvania, December 5, 1890. They have three children, Esther, born March 22, 1913; Carl, born July 17, 1914; and Ruth, born March 6, 1916.

Mr. Anderson is a member of the Gordon Methodist Episcopal Church, is president of the local welfare board, and is a steward and Sunday school superintendent in his local church. Residence: Gordon. (Photograph on Page 36).

Anton L. Anderson

Born in Sweden, October 26, 1867, Anton L. Anderson has lived in Nebraska for forty-six years. He is the son of Johannas and Cecilia (Larson) Anderson. His father, who was a custom shoemaker, was born in Sweden, June 23, 1836, and died there on December 18, 1930. His mother, who lived in Sweden all her life, was born August, 1833, and died in February, 1914.

Anton Anderson attended grade school in Sweden, and night school at Lincoln, Nebraska. He was married to Hildegard Nelson at Lincoln, July 3, 1889. Mrs. Anderson was born in Sweden on August 23, 1863. They have two children, Margaret Ellen, born December 17, 1890, now the wife of Bernard E. Warner; and Ferd Emanual, born October 1, 1892, and now married to Helga Torell.

Coming to America in 1885, Mr. Anderson worked on a farm two years and then was associated with the following firms, Harpham Brothers, H. R. Nessley and Company, and Mayer Brothers, all at Lincoln. In 1901 he started in business at Wahoo, Nebraska, where he is now treasurer and general manager of Smith-Hultin-Anderson Company.

During the World War he was active in Red Cross, sold Liberty Bonds and War Saving Stamps, was on the advisory board of the Salvation Army, and was merchant representative of the Saunders County Food Administration. Mr. Anderson was president of the Federation of Nebraska Retailers, 1919-20, president of the Chamber of Commerce in 1921, serving on the executive board of the latter organization, and was a board member in the insurance department fifteen or twenty years.

He holds membership in the Lions Club, of which he was president 1928-29, the Ancient Order of United Workmen, the Modern Woodmen of America, and the Lutheran Brotherhood, of which he was president 1926-27. He is affiliated with the Bethlehem Lutheran Church at Wahoo. Residence: Wahoo.

Arthur Myron Anderson

Born at Oakland, Nebraska, September 21, 1868, Arthur Myron Anderson is the son of John P. and Mathilda A. (Shinstrom) Anderson, the former a native of Ahus, Sweden, born in May, 1835. John P. Anderson came to America in 1857, and settled in Nebraska, where he was a pioneer farmer until his death at Oakland, December 18, 1903. Mathilda A. Shinstrom was born in Sweden, in 1844, and died at Oakland July 4, 1926. She came to America with her parents at the age of two years.

Arthur Myron Anderson was graduated from Oakland High School in 1888, and attended the University of Nebraska, 1889, 1890 and 1891, during which time he was active in football and baseball. He has been a banker most of his life, and at the present time is cashier of the Farmers State Bank of Tekamah, and member of the firm of A. M. Anderson Abstract Company. He is a Republican.

On August 18, 1897, he was united in marriage to Nelle Mae Workman at Tekamah. Mrs. Anderson, who was born in Jefferson County, Iowa, February 2, 1870, is of German ancestry. There are two children, Ralph

M., born April 15, 1899, and Dorothy J., born November 10, 1901.

Mr. Anderson who is a former captain in the Nebraska National Guard, is a member of the Tekamah Chamber of Commerce, the Ancient Free and Accepted Masons and the Independent Order of Odd Fellows. He is fond of fishing. Residence: Tekamah.

Arthur Wesley Anderson

Born at Gothenburg, Nebraska, September 23, 1890, Arthur Wesley Anderson has been a practicing physician at Lexington, since 1922. He is the son of Andrew E. and Posey G. (Ristine) Anderson, the former a retired farmer, who was born in Fairfield, Iowa, May 21, 1854. His parents came to the United States from Sweden, about 1845. Posey G. Ristine was born at Fairfield, October 2, 1864.

Dr. Anderson attended country school, was graduated from Gothenburg High School, received his A. B. from Nebraska Wesleyan University, and his M. D. from Northwestern University. On December 28, 1922, he was married to Marguerite L. Hansen, at Grand Rapids, Michigan. Mrs. Anderson was born at Grand Rapids, August 17, 1902. They have two sons, Arthur W., born June 26, 1924; and Robert D., born March 6, 1929.

With the exception of three and a half years in Iowa, Dr. Anderson has always resided in Nebraska. He served in the Medical Enlisted Reserve during the World War, is a member of the American Legion, the Lexington Chamber of Commerce, the Kiwanis Club, and Hastings Consistory of the Masons. His professional organizations include the American, Nebraska State and Dawson County Medical Societies. Residence: Lexington.

August Nils Anderson

In the general practice of medicine since 1892, August Nils Anderson was born in Sweden, November 16, 1867. He is the son of Nils and Nellie (Nelson) Anderson, both natives of Sweden. Nils Anderson came to America in 1869, and engaged in farming and stock-raising. He served two terms as a member of the Nebraska house of representatives, elected from Filmore County. He died at Shickley, Nebraska, March 1, 1902. Nellie Nelson was born in 1843, and died near Davenport, Nebraska, September 13, 1888.

Dr. Anderson attended district school near Shickley, and was graduated from Edgar High School in June, 1889. In 1892 he was awarded his Doctor of Medicine degree from Rush Medical College, and during 1909 and 1910 was a student at the University of Nebraska. Thereafter he had post graduate work at London, Stockholm and Berlin.

Always in general practice, Dr. Anderson was appointed assistant superintendent of the Norfolk, Nebraska, State Hospital, in 1900, and since that time has practiced at Belvidere. He is a member of the American, Nebraska State and Thayer County Medical Associations.

Dr. Anderson is a Democrat. He is affiliated with the Swedish Lutheran Church of Lincoln, and is a member of the Masons, and The Nebraskana Society. Residence: Belvidere.

August P. Anderson

Born in Sweden, May 22, 1873, August P. Anderson is the son of Andrew and Sophie (Janson) Samuelson. His father, a farmer, was born in Sweden, in 1828, and died there in 1882. Sophie Samuelson was born in Sweden in 1832, and died in 1886.

Coming to Nebraska in 1889, he married Anna Johnson, April 22, 1900. To this union four children were born: Elmer, who is married to Mary LaFollette; Herman, who is married to Evelyn Johnson; Selma; and Anna. Elmer is a college graduate of agricultural engineering; Herman has had three years of college and is now a farmer; Selma is a graduate nurse; and Anna has graduated from high school.

Mr. Anderson is a successful farmer where he has resided for forty-three years. He is treasurer of the Polk County Fair Board, is president of the Farmers Elevator and a number of the other Nebraska state elevator associations, is a member of the board of county commissioners and is a bank director. He is a member of the Modern Woodmen of America, the Odd Fellows, and since 1912 of the school board. Residence: Osceola.

Carl Arcadius Anderson

Carl A. Anderson was born at Horby, Sweden, January 12, 1873, son of Olof and Maria (Thorson) Anderson. His father, born on a farm at Malmohus, Sweden, April, 1832, was a farmer. His mother was born in Horby, Sweden, June 9, 1844, and died there. Carl A. Anderson came to America a few days later, and to Nebraska, December 4, 1888. Here he attended public school and completed a mechanical and electrical engineering course in the International Correspondence Schools.

As a young man he learned the machinist's trade and worked as a journeyman machinist in many shops. He enlisted in the United States Navy on July 7, 1898, as a first class machinist and served aboard the *U. S. S. Iowa, Iris, Isla de Luzon, Marrietta*. He was honorably discharged October 2, 1901.

Entering the automobile service business, he became associated with the J. J. DeRight Oldsmobile Company, and on the death of Mr. DeRight he ventured into business for himself. From January 23, 1913 to April 1, 1920, he operated individually, and on the last mentioned date incorporated for $50,000, with about $36,000 paid up capital. The corporation is a closed one with only three stockholders. Since its inception business has increased each year, until it is now three or four times greater in volume than at the time of the incorporation. The corporation, Carl A. Anderson, Incorporated, holds factory contracts with more than seventeen of the larger accessory and supply houses of the country. Mr. Anderson is president and general manager of the corporation.

He is a member of the United Spanish War Veterans, and he has served as commander of Lee Forby Camp No. 1, Junior Vice Commander in Chief, and now holds the office of Department Commander of Nebraska.

Active in fraternal circles, he is past grand of the Odd Fellows, a Mason and member of the Scottish Rite and Knights Templar and Shrine. He is also an Elk. He is a member of the Chamber of Commerce, The Shrine Luncheon Club and The Nebraskana Society. His chief recreations are reading and traveling, and during his travels he has circumnavigated the globe. Residence. Omaha.

Carl August Anderson

Carl August Anderson, son of August and Christine (Johnson) Anderson, was born at Mead, Nebraska, August 25, 1879.

August Anderson and his wife were natives of Kylingared Parish, in Elfborgs, Sweden. August was born on November 9, 1834, and Christine on April 6, 1838. They were married on February 22, 1866, and soon thereafter set sail for America. Crossing the North Sea from Stockholm to Hull, they traveled by rail to Liverpool, where they went on board the sailship. After a tiresome voyage of more than twenty-one days they reached the coast of Nova Scotia. Here the ship was not allowed to harbor, but was kept at anchor, because of the fact that cholera had broken out on board.

Christine Anderson contracted the disease and for a time her life was endangered, but she eventually recovered. On arriving at Jamestown they discovered that someone had reported them dead, had obtained possession of their trunks and belongings and decamped, leaving them with nothing but the clothes they had on.

For about three months the father worked on a farm, after which he and his wife removed to Bishop Hill, Illinois, and later to Geneseo, Illinois. There they remained until 1867, at which time they came to Nebraska and homesteaded in Saunders County about fourteen miles from Fremont. Trouble pursued them. The mother came through on a passenger train while the father rode with the furniture. The train carrying it was wrecked and the father saved his life by jumping through a window of the car.

After settling in Nebraska hardships and misfortunes continued to descend upon them—grasshoppers devoured their crops for three years in the seventies, leaving hard times and want in their wake, prairie fires frequently raced down upon them, and at one time the sills of their house caught. The eighty acre homestead was sold after a few years and a tract of 160 acres purchased.

The mother's illness during the eighties so impoverished the family that a popular subscription was taken up by neighbors to defray part of the doctor bills. Her partial recovery, however, made the family happy again. During these three years Carl was cared for by neighbors and was nearly adopted by one of the families. Through hardship and the brighter days which followed the family continued to live in the same place until January, 1893, when two of the sons came to Wausa, followed in March of the same year by their parents. August Anderson died at Wausa on November 13, 1896, and his wife on October 6, 1909.

Their five children are: J. Albert, farmer and stockraiser, who lives north of Wausa; Frank Edwin, Swedish Lutheran pastor, who resides at Woodhull, Illinois; Theodore, superintendent of the Swedish National Sanitarium at Denver; Cecilia Gertrude, wife of Charles S. Erickson, who resides in Wausa, and Carl August, the subject of this sketch.

Carl's birthplace was a sod house, partly dug into a sidehill. He resided there until May 30, 1893, when they joined the family in Knox County. He attended the common schools of Saunders County and later was a student at the Wausa public schools. During the years 1893 and 1894 he assisted his brothers in the general merchandise business, and in 1895 began to learn the printer's trade. He kept a case for eight months, then returned to the farm where he worked for a year and a half. Next he spent two years learning the harness maker's trade, and then went back to clerking for sixteen months in a store at Wakefield.

On December 1, 1901, Mr. Anderson purchased a half interest in the *Wausa Gazette* from J. E. Baggstrom who established the journal in partnership with Frank Edwin, now a clergyman at Wodhull, Illinois. The brothers were associated in the publication of the *Gazette* until January 1, 1904, when Carl purchased the remaining half interest and his brother removed to Omaha to take up the wider field of journalism as editor of the *Omaha Posten*, a Swedish weekly.

Mr. Anderson edits a live country paper, full of news, and always boosting for Wausa. The job work ranks well to the front as compared with work turned out by the country shops, and Mr. Anderson enjoys a liberal patronage as his work merits.

In January, 1908, he was appointed postmaster at Wausa, serving a little more than two terms. For three years the work of the *Gazette* was carried on in connection with the postoffice work, but finding this too strenuous Mr. Anderson leased the *Gazette* office. The brothers were again affiliated in the newspaper work until the spring of 1922 when Frank Edwin again severed his connection with the paper.

Since that time Mr. Anderson has been editor in chief of the *Gazette* with the exception of a two year period prior to September 1, 1931, when the position was filled by his second son, Gordon Vladimir. He was undoubtedly at that time the youngest editor in Nebraska, being but nineteen years of age.

Politically, Mr. Anderson has always been a staunch Republican, and has filled various minor political offices. At one time he was candidate for the legislature from his district. He has served as treasurer of the local Red Cross organization since the World War; has been secretary of the Wausa Improvement Club continuously since 1924, and previous to that was president and secretary of the organization at various times. He has taken much interest in good roads and coined the expression "Main Street of North America," which was given to the Meridian Highway, U. S. No. 81.

A member of the Lutheran Church, Mr. Anderson has done much work in behalf of the local church. For more than fourteen years he was choir director, and for a number of years was a member of the board of trustees. For some time he served as treasurer of the congregation. He has always taken an active interest in band work and has been director of the Wausa band for many years, and has directed orchestras at various times.

On August 31, 1904, he was married to Olga E. Monteen at Mead. Mrs. Anderson was a Nebraska girl, the oldest daughter of Mr. and Mrs. Gust Monteen, natives of Sweden. Her mother was Ingrid Berg. Mrs. Anderson's father served as treasurer of the Nebraska Conference of the Swedish Lutheran Church for fourteen years. Her grand uncle, the Reverend S. G. Larson, was one of the pioneer Lutheran ministers of Nebraska.

Mrs. Anderson was graduated from Mead High School and took a teacher's course at Peru Normal School. She taught two successful seasons before her marriage. To them were born three children, Rupert Cedric; Gordon Vladimir and Carmelita Nordica Lucile. The oldest son is a graduate of Augustana College, as is Gordon. In the summer of 1928 both boys were members of the Augustana College band which made a concert tour through Sweden, and upon its completion took a sightseeing trip through Denmark, France, Belgium, Holland and England.

The following two school years Cedric taught in the Battle Creek, Iowa, high schools, having charge of the band and orchestral work. He is now a teacher in the North Platte High School, filling a similar position there. Carmelita has completed two and a half years of college at Augustana, and intends to secure her Bachelor of Arts degree. At present she assists her father in editing and publishing the *Wausa Gazette*. Residence: Wausa.

Carl Emmett Anderson

A druggist, and proprietor of the Anderson Drug Store for the past thirteen years, Carl Emmett Anderson was born at Wall Lake, Iowa, December 14, 1886. He is the son of Jens and Lalie (Calkins) Anderson, the former born in Copenhagen, Denmark, in July, 1859. He came to Nebraska as a young man, where he engaged in farming until his death at Allen, on April 25, 1904. Lalie, wife of Jens Anderson, was born at Shell Rock, New York, in May, 1867, of Irish and Welch descent.

Carl Emmett Anderson attended the public schools of Allen, and Wall Lake, and was graduated from the Fremont College of Pharmacy. From 1904-10, he traveled in various states with a dance orchestra, and for ten years thereafter worked in a drug store. For the past thirteen years he has owned his own store. He is a Republican, a Lutheran, and a member of the Nebraska Pharmaceutical Association. He is a Blue Lodge Mason, and is fond of music and enjoys football.

Mr. Anderson was married to Edna Alice Rakow at Allen, Nebraska, on February 8, 1911. Mrs. Anderson, who was born at Allen, November 5, 1890, of German and French extraction, is extremely active in church and club work. To them were born two children, Wilmer, on November 25, 1912, who attends the University of Nebraska; and Helen L., born October 13, 1914, who is a senior in high school. Residence: Allen.

Charles Anderson

Charles Anderson was born at Lincoln, Lancaster County, Nebraska, August 11, 1876, the son of John and Johana Anderson. His father was born in Sweden, April 25, 1834, came to Lancaster County on July 4, 1875, and died at Ceresco, Saunders County, Nebraska, where he had farmed. His mother, who was born in Sweden, June 14, 1843, reared ten children and was a successful housewife; she died at Ceresco, September 27, 1906.

Mr. Anderson attended the public schools. He was postmaster at Ceresco, 1911-1923, part of which time he was manager of the Ceresco Drug Co. Since 1924 he has been the county assessor of Saunders County.

During the World War he was chairman of the local board of registration, and the War Savings Stamps committee. He is affiliated with the Emanuel Lutheran Church at Ceresco.

Mr. Anderson holds membership in the Nebraskana Society, and is a Republican.

Charles Anderson was united in marriage with Martha Saathoff, who was born at Ceresco, December 6, 1893. They have two children: Pauline, born June 4, 1926, and Charles, born August 30, 1929. Residence: Wahoo.

Charles Barney Anderson

Active as a banker and farm loan investor for the past thirty-five years, Charles Barney Anderson was born at Gaines, Orleans County, New York, June 30, 1865. He is the son of Alva Bingham and Harriett Eliza (Bidelman) Anderson, the former of whom was born at Gaines, May 9, 1836. A farmer his entire life, he died at Albion, New York, August 15, 1886. His father was Matthew Anderson, his grandfather Matthew Anderson and his great grandfather, John Anderson, all of Scotch-Irish descent. Harriett Eliza Bidelman was born at Gaines, May 17, 1840, a daughter of Samuel and granddaughter of Henry Bidelman. She is a leading musician and active in musical circles.

Charles B. Anderson was educated in the district school, and was graduated from Albion High School June 20, 1883. He later attended business college, and engaged in the hardware business at Albion, New York, as bookkeeper and as owner from 1883-87. A resident of Nebraska forty-three years, he was president and cashier of the DeWitt Bank 1887-97; cashier Crete State Bank and vice president 1897-1916. From 1899 to 1918 he was president of the Conservative Investment Company at Crete, and was vice president of the First Trust Company of Lincoln, 1919-24. For more than 10 years he was president of the Conservative Investment Company of Blackwell, and El Reno, Oklahoma, and for the same period was vice president of the Ord State Bank. In addition he has served as a director of other banks, insurance companies, etc. At the present time he is not active except in the handling of investments for a few friends.

A Republican, he was delegate to the national convention of 1896, from the 4th Nebraska Congressional District; served as state senator 1903, from Saline County; served as a member of the state senate from Lancaster County, 1921 and 1923, and from 1908-15, was a member of the board of regents of the University of Nebraska.

Mr. Anderson's first marriage was to May Clarissa Loveland, at Albion. She was born at Albion, New York, September 11, 1865, and died at Crete, January 6, 1900. Of this marriage there are two children: Olsie M., born June 14, 1888, and Delos L., born February 13, 1895, who married Eleanor Lillian Steenburg. On January 15, 1901, Mr. Anderson married Mathilda Anna Miller of Crete. They have four sons and daughters: Marion H., born May 4, 1902, who married Lloyd Hartley Hobson; Margaret B., born April 6, 1904; Helen H., born July 27, 1906, and Charles B., Jr., born October 24, 1910.

Since its organization in Lincoln, Mr. Anderson has been a member of the Kiwanis Club, and has served as a director; he was a member of the school board at Crete, and served thirty years as a trustee of Doane College. A life member of the Chamber of Commerce, he is a former president and a present director of the Social Welfare Society, and is a member of the Nebraska State Historical Society, the Nebraskana Society and the Young Men's Christian Association. He is a York Rite and Scottish Rite Mason and member of the Shrine, and a member of First Plymouth Congregational Church. His clubs are the Eastridge Country Club of Lincoln, and the Golf Club of Alexandria, Minnesota. His sports are golf and fishing.

The sudden death of Mr. Anderson occurred while on his vacation on June 27, 1931, at his summer home at Alexandria, Minnesota.

Charles Olof Anderson

Charles Olof Anderson, lawyer, was born in New York City, March 17, 1874, and for the past 45 years has been a resident of Nebraska. His father, Olof Anderson, who was a shoemaker and farmer, was born at Vase Parish, Sweden, November 21, 1836, and came to America in 1871. His death occurred at Malmo, Nebraska, May 9, 1909. Lena Peterson, wife of Olof Anderson, was born at Jonkoping, Sweden, January 17, 1843, and is still living.

Mr. Anderson attended Luther College at Wahoo, Nebraska, during 1892-93 and in 1916 received the Bachelor of Laws degree at Northwestern University in Chicago. He is a member of Delta Theta Phi.

For a time he engaged in the general merchandise business under the firm name of Holmes & Anderson, and later engaged in the real estate business. While in the latter work he platted the Anderson Addition to Oklahoma City, Oklahoma, and thereafter homesteaded in Tripp County, South Dakota. Since his admission to the bar in 1916 Mr. Anderson has practiced law, first as a member of the firm Battelle, Morgan, Strehlow & Anderson and more recently in the firm of Morgan & Anderson. He is secretary of the Evangelical Covenant Hospital and is affiliated with the First Covenant Church of Omaha.

His marriage to Minnie Marie Isaacson occurred at Aurora, Nebraska, December 28, 1915. Mrs. Anderson whose ancestry is Swedish, was born at Minneapolis, Minnesota, August 28, 1886. They have four children, Hazel Virginia, born September 14, 1916; Lucile Marie, born August 8, 1918; Charles Donald, born July 27, 1920; and Edith Geraldine, born October 29, 1923.

Mr. Anderson is a Democrat. He is a Mason, a member of the Modern Woodmen of America, and a member of the Omaha Bar Association. During the World War he served as a four minute man and was honorably discharged from the United States National Guard. Residence: Omaha.

Chauncey Leroy Anderson

Chauncey Leroy Anderson, physician at Stromsburg, Nebraska, was born there June 14, 1904, the son of Charles Alfred and Lucinda Rebecca (Holmquist) Anderson. His father, who was also a physician, was born in Sweden, January 1, 1870, and died at Stromsburg, March 5, 1921. His mother was born at Stromsburg, February 24, 1876; her ancestry is Swedish.

Dr. Anderson was graduated from the Stromsburg High School in 1922, received the B. Sc. degree at the University of Nebraska, in 1926, and was awarded the M. D. degree there in 1928. For a year he was an interne at Baylor University Hospital at Dallas, Texas. He held membership in Theta Nu, and Alpha Kappa Kappa, at the University of Nebraska.

He is now engaged in medical practice at Stromsburg where he is a member of the Commercial Club, the county, state, and American medical societies, and the First Bap-

tist Church. He is a Mason. Dr. Anderson is independend, politically.

Dr. Anderson was married to Marvelle J. Pielstick, of York, on October 1, 1931. She is a graduate nurse, having completed her course at University Hospital in Omaha. Residence: Stromsburg.

Delmer Scott Anderson

Delmar Scott Anderson, leading Dawson County farmer, was born in Dawson County, Nebraska, October 3, 1882, of pioneer parentage. His father, James Anderson, was born in Denmark, March 21, 1848, and came to the United States in 1868, settling in Illinois. In 1869 he removed to Laramie, Wyoming, where he was connected with the railroad for a short time. He later took a claim near Laramie. He left this claim and moved to Dawson County where he took a homestead in 1877. He made his home in Dawson County until the time of his death at Lexington, September 18, 1927.

Mary Ellon Grafton, wife of James Anderson, was born in Pulaski, Iowa, January 16, 1852, and died at Lexington, June 1, 1930. A devoted wife and mother, she, in later years, devoted much time and effort to community service.

Mr. Anderson attended common school, and has since engaged in farming. He was married to Clara Marion Gregory at Lexington, on November 9, 1904, and to them three children were born: Francis, September 8, 1905, married Lowell Sarnes; Zelda, born August 12, 1908, is a teacher; and Glenrose, born July 4, 1912, is in school. Mrs. Anderson, who has been honored as a Master Homemaker, was born at Seneca, Kansas, June 31, 1883.

Mr. Anderson has served on his local school board, is a member of the Chamber of Commerce, the Kiwanis Club, the Masonic Order, and the Odd Fellows. He has contributed to welfare organizations, including the Red Cross, and during the World War was active in various projects. He is a life member of The Nebraskana Society. Residence: Lexington.

Edna Cochran Anderson

Edna Cochran Anderson, the youngest of nine children, was born on a farm near Waco, York County, Nebraska, February 7, 1878, the daughter of John M. and Harriett Elizabeth (Fox) Cochran. Her father, who was a farmer, died in February, 1879. Her mother died at York, Nebraska, June 30, 1895.

Mrs. Anderson was graduated from York High School in 1895; attended the A. N. Palmer School at Cedar Rapids, Iowa, and the University of Nebraska. During Mrs. Anderson's career as teacher, she was busily engaged in extension work. She was a rural teacher, 1895-98, and again 1903-04; a teacher in village schools, 1904-06, 1907-09; in the city schools of York, 1909 to 1918. During the World War she was engaged in clerical work at Washington, D. C., after which she was travelling instructor for the A. N. Palmer Co. Returning to York, Nebraska, in 1919, she served as principal of Willard School and conducted classes in teacher training at York College until 1923, when she became superintendent of York County Schools. This office she has held for three successive terms. Her services in behalf of rural and village children has been with the same diligence as that which marked her service in city schools.

In 1898, she married Charles E. Anderson, a farmer in York County. One daughter was born, Marjorie, April 29, 1900. The daughter is a graduate of the University of Nebraska, was a Nebraska teacher for six years, then becoming home demonstration agent for Fremont County, Colorado. In April, 1931, she married Laurie Arvid Monson, Smith Hughes instructor in agriculture, Canon City High School, Colorado.

Mrs. Anderson is a member of the First Methodist

ANDREAS THEODORE ANDERSON

Purdy—Gordon

Church at York. She was formerly state chairman of the Rural Department of the Parent-Teacher Association, is chairman of the Junior Red Cross at York, and a member of the Rebekah Lodge. She is a member of the Business and Professional Women's Club, the Nebraska Woman's Educational Club, the national social science honor society of Pi Gamma Mu, and a member of the Nebraskana Society. Residence: York.

Elmo Russell Anderson

Elmo Russell Anderson, manager and part owner of a leading grocery store at York, has lived in this state for 11 years and is prominent in civic organizations there. He was born at Ottumwa, Iowa, February 3, 1900, the son of Loran Clare and Alma Idella (Johns) Anderson. His father, whose ancestry was Scotch-Irish and Dutch, was born at Bloomington, Illinois, June 2, 1871, and died at York, October 29, 1928. His mother was born of Scotch-Irish and Welsh parentage at Moulton, Iowa, February 16, 1874.

Mr. Anderson attended rural schools in Iowa, and in 1921, was graduated from the high school at Cambridge, Nebraska, where he was active in basketball. He was graduated from the York Business College in 1922. He entered the business world in the employ of the Allied Union Store Company, and almost immediately was made manager of the local organization. He remained in that capacity until 1924, when he bought a half interest in the business.

He is a member of the board of the York County Commercial Club, holds membership in the Rotary Club at York, and is affiliated with the York Church of Christ. He is a member of the Masons, Independent Order of Odd Fellows, the Young Men's Christian Association, and the Nebraskana Society. His favorite sport is fishing.

On May 7, 1925, he was united in marriage with Hazel Irene Larkin, at Sidney, Iowa. Mrs. Anderson, who was a bookkeeper before her marriage, was born at Tacoma, Washington, July 5, 1906, of Irish and English parentage. They have a son, James, born May 27, 1926. Residence: York.

Emil Anderson

Emil Anderson, retired farmer of Minden, Nebraska, has lived in that community for the past 55 years and has been outstanding in business and civic affairs. He was born in Sweden, September 14, 1868, the son of Gustaf Victor and Mary (Johnson) Anderson, the former a farmer who was born in Sweden, October 31, 1835, and died at Minden, May 23, 1906. He came from Sweden to Swedesburg, Iowa, about 1868, and returned there about 1871. In 1873, he returned to Nebraska, homesteading where Emil Anderson now resides. His mother was born in Sweden, August 30, 1835, and died at Minden, February 7, 1908.

Mr. Anderson is president of the Kearney County Mutual Insurance Company, is president of the Kearney County Co-operative Creamery, is a director and vice president of the Motala Elevator Company, is a director in the Farmers Elevator Company of Minden, and a stockholder and director in the First National Bank of Minden. A Democrat, he served as a member of the Nebraska Legislature, as a member of the house of representatives 1925, 1931, in both regular and special sessions. He is a trustee of the Bethany Lutheran Church of Axtell, Nebraska, is a member of the Modern Woodmen of America, and holds membership in the Nebraskana Society.

His marriage to Selma Anderson occurred at Minden, April 19, 1913. Mrs. Anderson was born in Sweden, September 19, 1874. Their son, Carl, was born September 1, 1917, and died September 9, 1917. Residence: Minden.

Ira C. Anderson

Born at Gothenburg, Nebraska, August 24, 1883, Ira

C. Anderson is the son of Harriet Elizabeth (Munns) and William Glover Anderson, the latter a distinguished leader in political and civic affairs in his community. The father, born at Fairfield, Indiana, December 28, 1852, died at Wood River, Nebraska, May 28, 1916. He was a pioneer farmer in Nebraska and later engaged in business as a furniture dealer; he received his education at Hartville College, was in the police service for a time, and during his residence in Nebraska served as state representative, a member of the United States Rifle Guard, and the school board; his parents came to this country from County Cork, Ireland. His wife, Harriett, whose parentage was Pennsylvania German, was born in Decatur County, Illinois, September 26, 1853, and died at Kearney, June 4, 1926.

Mr. Anderson attended rural school, was a student at Fremont College, Fremont, Nebraska, and studied embalming at the University of Minnesota. He entered the furniture business at Cozad, Nebraska, where he was employed by the Davis Furniture & Undertaking Company, and a little later conducted a similar business of his own at Wood River, Nebraska. For a time he was employed as salesman for the Orchard Wilhelm Company at Omaha, and for the past 12 years has been the owner and active manager of his own business at Kearney, Nebraska.

He is a trustee and active manager of the William F. Crossley Estate. He has been a director of the Chamber of Commerce at Kearney, for the past 11 years, and holds membership in the Nebraska Funeral Directors Society, the National Funeral Directors Association, the Red Cross, and the Kearney Kiwanis Club. His fraternal organizations include the Elks, Masons, and Odd Fellows Lodges, while his social club is the Kearney Country Club. His religious affiliation is with the Methodist Episcopal Church of Kearney; for several years he has held membership in the Young Men's Christian Association and the Boy Scouts of America, acting as director of the latter.

He married Ada Roseline Mercer, who died at Kearney, December 3, 1921. They have one daughter Margaret Elizabeth Anderson, born December 20, 1915, who is at the present time a student in the Corvallis High School. On June 19, 1924, his marriage to Wilma Ruth Crossley occurred at Kearney. Mrs. Anderson, who was born at Kearney, June 7, 1889, the daughter of W. F. Crossley and Mary A. (Calhoun) Crossley, was graduated from the University of Nebraska, and before her marriage was a school teacher and business woman. Residence: Kearney. (Photograph in Album).

Oscar Bennett Anderson

Oscar B. Anderson was born at Davis, Illinois, October 1, 1889, the son of Olus and Bertha (Matsen) Anderson. His father, who is a farmer, was born at Christiania, Norway, in 1855. His mother was born at Christiania, October 1, 1854.

Mr. Anderson was graduated from the high school at Webb, Iowa, attended the University of Nebraska, and was a student at the Chicago and Lake Geneva Young Men's Christian Association during the summer months.

He entered Young Men's Christian Association work at Evansville, Wisconsin, in 1909, and was physical director for this organization at Columbus, 1909-14. Since 1914, he has been connected with the Lincoln Young Men's Christian Association as director of physical education. He is a member of the National Physical Directors' Society and the Optimists' Club at Lincoln. He is a 32nd degree Mason and Shriner.

During the World War he served overseas for eleven months at Base Hospital Unit Number 49, Verdun Sector. He is a member of the American Legion and the Veterans of Foreign Wars, and is affiliated with Grace Lutheran Church at Lincoln. His social club is the Shrine Country Club. He is independent politically. Residence: Lincoln.

Permelia Anderson

Permelia Anderson was born at Balingslof, Sweden, August 6, 1848, the daughter of Peter and Permelia (Matson) Johnson, and for the past 57 years has been a resident of Nebraska. Her father, who was born in Sweden, December 25, 1823, and died at Stromsburg, Nebraska, July 1, 1898, was a farmer. Her mother was born in Sweden, February 15, 1821, and died at Stromsburg, August 22, 1889.

Mrs. Anderson received her education in the public schools of Lafayette, Illinois. She is a member of the Nebraskana Society, the Red Cross, and St. Edward's Methodist Episcopal Church. Her chief recreations are reading and needlework. Politically, she is a Republican.

She was married to John M. Anderson at Columbus, Nebraska, December 31, 1875. Mr. Anderson, who was a farmer, was born in Sweden and died in Platte County, Nebraska, January 1, 1909; he served in the Union Army during the Civil War for nearly five years and was honorably discharged as lieutenant at the close of the war. Mrs. Anderson donated liberally to war activities during the World War.

To their marriage the following children were born: George, October 11, 1876, who married Maude Simpson; Gertie, May 26, 1878; Mamie, March 18, 1880; Josie E., January 15, 1882, who died September 5, 1882; and Dana, June 17, 1883, who married Madeline Gorius. George is a farmer, Gertie is librarian, and Dana a salesman. Residence: St. Edward.

Ralph Milton Anderson

Ralph Milton, son of Arthur Marion and Nellie (Workman) Anderson, was born at Tekamah, Nebraska, April 14, 1899. His father, who was born at Oakland, September 21, 1868, a former county clerk of Burt County; was a member of the draft board during the World War, and was in the abstract business for some thirty years. At the present time he is cashier of the Farmers State Bank of Tekamah. He is the son of John P. and Mathilda A. (Shinstrom) Anderson who came to the United States in 1857. They were married and settled at Oakland, as pioneer farmers. Both of them died at Oakland.

Nellie Workman was born at Fairfield, Iowa, February 2, 1870. Her father, W. A. Workman, was born at Fairfield, and her mother, Dora S. Herring, who was born at Saarbuck, Germany, came to America at the age of seven years.

Educated in the Tekamah public schools, Ralph Milton Anderson was graduated from Tekamah High School in 1918, and received his LL. B. from the University of Nebraska in 1923. He is a member of Phi Delta Phi and Phi Gamma Delta, and has served as secretary of the latter. He was married to Dorothea Belinda Thomas at Tekamah, on June 4, 1926. Mrs. Anderson, who was born at Tekamah, May 4, 1898, was the daughter of W. B. and Linnie (Nelson) Thomas, and a granddaughter of George P. Thomas, one of the early settlers of Tekamah.

Mr. Anderson is a Republican, and is serving his second term as county attorney of Burt County. He is engaged in the practice of law and affiliated with the A. M. Anderson Abstract Company at Tekamah. He has taken an active part in the civic development of the city, and has served as secretary of the Chamber of Commerce May 1, 1924, to May 1, 1926, and since May 1, 1927. He was president of the organization from May 1, 1926-May 2, 1927, and has been secretary of the Lions Club since May 1, 1927.

A private of Infantry from October 15, 1918, to December 15, 1918, he is a member of the American Legion. He is a member of the First Presbyterian Church, the Masonic Order, the Nebraskana Society and the Nebraska State Bar Association. Residence: Tekamah.

Reuben Leonard Anderson

Reuben L. Anderson, a resident of Stromsburg since 1910, has taken an active part in civic and community affairs for many years. He was born at Kiron, Iowa, July 15, 1889, the son of Andrew J. and Betty (Pearson) Anderson. His father, a farmer, was born in Sweden, December 17, 1837, and died at Stromsburg, February 1, 1918. His mother was born in Sweden, February 27, 1852, and died at Stromsburg, April 16, 1931.

Mr. Anderson attended rural school in Iowa, and in 1904 was a student at the Luther Academy at Wahoo, Nebraska. He clerked in the shoe department of a retail store from 1906 to 1910, when he became owner of a shoe store. From 1919 to 1923 he was manager of the insurance and collection department in a law office, and from 1923 to 1929 he was bookkeeper and assistant cashier in a bank. He is now conducting a general insurance agency.

During the World War Mr. Anderson served in a provisional battalion of Guard and Fire Companies at Camp Mills, Long Island, New York, as a private, and later as corporal and sergeant. He is a member of the American Legion and he has served as adjutant of the local post. He has been a member of the city council of Stromsburg, and served as city clerk, 1915-20 and 1923-28. He is a member of the Nebraskana Society is affiliated with the Lutheran Church, and holds membership in the Republican party.

He was united in marriage with Audrey A. Peterson at Stromsburg, April 15, 1919; she was born there May 9, 1891. They have two children: Robert L., born January 26, 1921; and Betty Jean, born September 3, 1922. Residence: Stromsburg.

Roland Max Anderson

Roland M. Anderson was born at Beloit, Mitchell County, Kansas, June 8, 1879, the son of George Wycliffe and Mary (Townsend) Anderson. His father, who was a sergeant in the Union Army in the Civil War, was the owner and publisher of the Beloit *Gazette* at Beloit, Kansas, and was a member of the legislature in Kansas. His ancestry was Scotch and English; his father invented and built marine steam engines. He was born in Ohio in 1842 and died at Black Rock, Lawrence County, Arkansas, January 14, 1910.

His mother, who was born in Ohio in 1844, was a teacher at Boscabel, Wisconsin, and was a graduate and postgraduate of the New York Chautauqua Academy. Her ancestry was Pennsylvania German. She died at Beloit, September 22, 1924.

Mr. Anderson was graduated from the Beloit High School in 1897. He was awarded his LL. B. at the University of Kansas in 1900, where he was a member of the Green Chapter of Phi Delta Phi, and Sigma Nu. He was admitted to the bar in 1900; was a member of the firm Kagey & Anderson, 1903-17; a member of the firm Foster & Anderson, 1927-29; and since 1929 has been a member of the law firm Sanden, Anderson, Laughlin, & Gradwohl. He is a director and general counsel for the Cornbelt Life Insurance Company of Lincoln.

A Republican, Mr. Anderson served as mayor of Beloit; was judge pro tem of the district court of the 12th Judicial Court; was director of the Speakers Bureau of the Nebraska Republican Committee, 1928-30. He was united in marriage with Mary Bangs Findley at Beloit, May 24, 1903. Mrs. Anderson, who was a member of the Daughters of the American Revolution and the Colonial Dames, was born at Beloit, September 11, 1882, and died there February 22, 1917. Three children were born to them: Park Findley, August 10, 1905, who married Elma Kokko; Roland Max, born June 6, 1911; and Rosemary, born August 23, 1914. Park was a member of Delta Tau Delta at the University of Kansas and the University of Nebraska; he was a member of Phi Delta Phi at George Washington University. Roland was made a member of Sigma Nu at the University of Nebraska.

Mr. Anderson was married to Ruth E. Olson at Lincoln, Nebraska, December 5, 1918; she was graduated from Bethany Linsborg, 1912, studied music for two years at Berlin, and was in lyceum circuit work for two years. She is a member of the Matinee Musicale of Lincoln and Sigma Alpha Iota. She was born at Lincoln, August 10, 1892.

He was a major in the Fourth Kansas Battalion, 1917-18; was made a major at the request of Governor Arthur Capper of Kansas. He was a speaker for the 10th Federal Reserves during the World War. He is a member of the American Bar Association; the Kansas State Bar Association; and the Nebraska State Bar Association. He served as chairman of the Mitchell County Red Cross, 1917, in Kansas. He was a charter member of the Beloit Rotary Club; is a life member of the Kansas Historical Society; and holds membership in The Nebraskana Society. He is a member of the Lincoln Chamber of Commerce. He is a member of the Elks and Odd Fellows, all degrees, and Modern Woodman of America. He is vice president of the Lancaster County Bar Association.

He is a member of the University Club; the Lincoln Country Club; and a life member of the Country Club of Beloit, Kansas. He is president of the Fifty Fifty Club at Lincoln. He is affiliated with the First Presbyterian Church of Beloit. He is fond of golfing, swimming, and big game hunting. His hobbies are reading and Americana. Residence: Lincoln.

Theodore Anderson

A merchant and landowner at Bristow, Nebraska, Theodore Anderson has lived in this state all his life and has always taken an active interest in community and civic affairs. His father, Anders Peter Anderson, who was a pioneer in Burt County, Nebraska, was born at Westphalia, Sweden, May 21, 1833, and died at Oakland, Nebraska, May 23, 1889; he was prominent in church and school affairs at Oakland for many years. His mother, Sarah Gertrude (Adolphdotte) Anderson, who was a leader in the Baptist Church, was born at Mortala, Sweden, in 1833, and died at Oakland, August 19, 1917.

Mr. Anderson completed the eighth grade school and later was a student at Fremont Normal School where he studied commercial subjects. He has cared for the home farm and for the past 20 years has been a merchant at Bristow, and recently served as postmaster there. He is a member of the Yeoman Lodge at Bristow, has served as a member of the school board for 20 years, and is a member of the Commercial Club. During his residence at Oakland he was a member of the school board and the Young Men's Christian Association, and during the World War he was local chairman of the Red Cross, assisting in various loan drives. He is affiliated with the Methodist Episcopal Church and is acting superintendent of the Sunday School.

His marriage to Ollie Sofia Blomquist occurred at Oakland, October 28, 1897. Mrs. Anderson was born in Sweden. They have two children: Francis, born July 16, 1898, who is manager of the Farmers Co-operative Oil Company of Boyd County; and Florence, an adopted daughter, who married Lyle Webster. Residence: Bristow.

Victor Anderson

Victor Anderson, merchant and farmer, was born at Satra, Sandviken, Sweden, March 22, 1865. He was graduated from high school in Sweden, and after coming to America attended the Barnes School of Embalming at Chicago, graduating in 1904.

Anders Anderson, father of Victor, was born in Satra,

Sweden, in 1819, and died there on August 18, 1877. He was a farmer. Karin (Person) Anderson, mother of Victor, was born at Satra in 1821, where she died February 23, 1877.

In 1888 Mr. Anderson married Emma Wilson, who died in 1903. Four children were born to them, Clara; Edwin, who married Olga Elving and who is associated with his father in business; Albert, who married Amy Peterson and who is now in the Stromsburg store; and Erma who lives at home.

On June 22, 1904, he was united in marriage to Charlotte Margareta Samuelson at Stromsburg. She was born there on May 1, 1874, and before her marriage was a nurse. They have four children, Alvina, born April 27, 1905; Carleton, born December 22, 1906; Vernon, born December 22, 1907; and Jeanette, born December 18, 1910. Carleton and Vernon attended the University of Nebraska; while Jeanette is a student at Bethel Academy in St. Paul, Minnesota.

A Democrat, Mr. Anderson was a candidate for state senator in 1930 from the 19th senatorial district, but was defeated by a slight majority. A resident of Nebraska since August 28, 1884, he was a farmer from 1886 to 1903 and since that time has been in the furniture and undertaking business. He was mayor of Stromsburg in 1911.

Mr. Anderson's religious affiliation is with the First Baptist Church of which he is vice president. He is treasurer of the Nebraska state conference of the Baptist Church, and has held the office of president in the Commercial Club, the Stromsburg Hotel Company, the Cemetery Association and the Board of Education. He is a member of the Nebraskana Society, and a leader in every movement for the advancement of his city. Residence: Stromsburg. (Photograph in Album).

Walter Lincoln Anderson

Walter Lincoln Anderson, lawyer, was born at Sidney, Iowa, February 19, 1868. He is the son of Major Albert R. Anderson, Civil War veteran, member of congress and lawyer, and a native of Ohio, and Sarah Jane (Woods) Anderson, a native of Pennsylvania.

Walter Lincoln Anderson is a graduate of the State University of Iowa Collegiate Department (1889) and Law Department (1891). He practiced law at Sidney for one year; at Hot Springs, South Dakota, for seven years, including four years as county attorney; removed to Lincoln, Nebraska, in 1899, where he has since resided and practiced law.

He served in the United States Army in the Spanish American War as a second lieutenant in the Rough Riders; and in the World War as a captain detailed as draft executive for Nebraska and also as paymaster for Nebraska. Prior to his army service in the World War he served as a member of the Draft Board at Lincoln.

He was a member of Lincoln Home Rule Charter Commission (1917); Nebraska Constitutional Convention (1919-1920); and was Speaker of Nebraska house of representatives in sessions of 1921 and 1922. He is a 33rd degree Mason, a Knight Templar, a Shriner and a member of Eastern Star.

Mr. Anderson is a member of United Spanish War Veterans, American Legion, Forty and Eight, Sons of American Revolution, Sons of Civil War Veterans, Kiwanis Club, Lincoln Country Club, Hiram Club and of the American, Nebraska State, and Lancaster County Bar Associations. He has served as director in Lincoln National Bank and in Lincoln and Fremont Joint Stock Land Banks.

In 1902 he married Helen Marie Nance, born in Osceola, Nebraska, a daughter of Governor Albinus Nance. She attended the University of Nebraska and is a member of Eastern Star, the P. E. O., American Legion Auxiliary and Daughters of American Revolution. Residence: Lincoln.

William Ashley Anderson

More than 50 years ago William Ashley Anderson came to Nebraska from Iowa as a pioneer farmer, and since then has contributed towards the civic progress of both his community and state. He was born in Dubuque County, Iowa, April 14, 1853, the son of William I. and Hester (Hillman) Anderson.

His father, a surveyor and civil engineer, was born in Barren County, Kentucky, December 12, 1814, and died at Epworth, Iowa, December 25, 1882. His ancestors came to America in 1745, and settled in Virginia. His mother, Hester (Hillman) Anderson, was born at Bristol, England, May 2, 1817, and died at Epworth, March 4, 1861.

Mr. Anderson attended Epworth Seminary, 1872-74, and since then has been a farmer near Ord. He is a member of the library board at Ord, the Modern Woodmen of America, the Nebraskana Society, the Nebraska State Historical Society, and the Red Cross. His chief aim in life is to be a worthy and progressive citizen of Nebraska. His hobby is science.

On September 5, 1876, he was married to Elizabeth A. Hather at Farley, Iowa. Mrs. Anderson, whose ancestry was English, was born at Farley, September 21, 1857, and died at Kingsbury, California, April 7, 1888; their only son, Roy, died January 17, 1932. On July 26, 1893, Mr. Anderson was united in marriage with Sarah O. Snodgrass. Residence: Ord.

John Joseph Andre

For the past 48 years John Joseph Andre has been an important factor in the building up of Nebraska and his community. He was born at Luxemburg, Iowa, December 1, 1859, the son of John Nick and Catherine (Weis) Andre, the former a farmer who was born at Elvingen, Principality of Luxembourg, February 18, 1821. His father came to America in 1854, and died at Luxemburg, Iowa, December 1, 1880. His mother was born at Niederpalen, Luxembourg, June 26, 1826, and died at Luxemburg, Iowa, March 28, 1906.

Mr. Andre taught in the rural schools of Dubuque County, Iowa, and in the fall of 1883, moved to Raeville, Nebraska, where he established a small store. In 1887, as the town of Petersburg was being organized, he moved to that community and has conducted a mercantile establishment there since. He owns a third interest in the Petersburg Telephone Company, having been connected with that organization since its organization in 1903.

His marriage to Jennie Krier was solemnized at St. Donatus, Iowa, February 5, 1884. Mrs. Andre, who assisted in her husband's business prior to 1903, was born at St. Donatus, December 20, 1863. Their four children are: Nick, born November, 1884, who married Margaret Heinz; Catherine, born in January, 1886, who died in 1928; Frank, born in July, 1887, who married Ann Gertrude Reisdorf; and Claire, born in February, 1889. All are engaged in the mercantile business at Petersburg.

Mr. Andre holds membership in the Red Cross, is affiliated with the St. John The Baptist Catholic Church of Petersburg, and has been connected with every commercial organization in his community. He was a charter member of the Volunteer Fire Department, was treasurer of the village board from 1906 to 1910, and served as a member of the village board at various times prior to 1913. During the World War, Mr. Andre was a member of the Food Control Board.

He acted as a member of the Board of Education from 1901 to 1911, serving as chairman from 1901 to 1905. His hobby is reading. Residence: Petersburg.

Botilla Magdelane Andresen

Botilla M. Andresen was born at Omaha, Nebraska, April 24, 1894, daughter of Peter Fritz and Anna Christine (Rohlff) Andresen. Her father, whose ancestry was Danish and German, was born at Flensburg, Germany, April 19, 1856, and died at Omaha, December 27, 1918.

Her mother, whose ancestry was also German and Danish, was born at Davenport, Iowa, October 15, 1864, and died at Omaha, August 6, 1923.

Miss Andresen received her education in the Castillar and Leavenworth schools at Omaha, and later was a student at Central High School. She is a member of the Altrusa Club of Omaha. She holds membership in the Fontenelle Chapter of the Order of Eastern Star. She is a member of the Nebraskana Society. She is affiliated with Kountze Memorial Lutheran Church of Omaha. Residence: Omaha.

Clayton Farrington Andrews

One of Nebraska's leading surgeons, Clayton Farrington Andrews is a native of the state. He was born at St. Paul, January 4, 1891, son of Ernest Irving and Pearl Josephine (Waite) Andrews. Ernest Andrews was born at Woodstock, Maine, December 5, 1864. He is a banker, and served as chairman of the Howard County Liberty Bond committee in 1918. Of English ancestry, his father's father, J. F. Andrews came from England and settled in Maine in early days. Pearl Waite Andrews was born at Nashua, Iowa, October 4, 1868, descended from the Welsh family of Waites. She is a member and has been state officer in the Order of Eastern Star.

Dr. Andrews was graduated from the St. Paul High School in 1907, and received a Ph. G. from Creighton University in 1909. In 1916 he received his M. D. from the University of Pennsylvania, and in 1923 was awarded the degree of Master of Science in Surgery from the University of Minnesota. During 1910-12 he attended the University of Nebraska. He was president in 1916 of the Deaver Surgical Society at the University of Pennsylvania, and his fraternities are Delta Upsilon and Phi Rho Sigma.

He served with the rank of first lieutenant Medical Corps, with the 134th Infantry, 34th Division, 1917-19, in France 10 months at Base Hospital No. 93, and with the 7th Division. He is a member of the American Legion, the Veterans of Foreign Wars and lieutenant commander of the U. S. Naval Reserve.

On August 28, 1919, he was married to Mildred Rae Wells at New York City. Mrs. Andrews was born at Stanton, Nebraska, April 27, 1895. They have one son, David I., born February 8, 1923. The family attends Holy Trinity Episcopal Church.

Dr. Andrew's professional career is as follows: member of the Army Medical Corps 1917-19; surgical fellowship at the Mayo Clinic, 1919-1923; since 1923 practice in Lincoln. He is chairman of the surgical section at Lincoln General Hospital, attending surgeon at Bryan Memorial Hospital, surgeon Iowa-Nebraska Light and Power Company and the Northern Natural Gas Company. A fellow in the American College of Surgeons, he is also a member of the State and American Medical Associations. He is treasurer of the Lancaster County Medical Society, ex-resident physician at Mayo Clinic, etc. Dr. Andrews has contributed numerous articles on surgery to various state and national magazines.

He is a Scottish Rite Mason, Knight Templar and Shriner, a member of the Chamber of Commerce, the Lions Club, the University and Lincoln Country Clubs. His sport is golf and his hobby philately. Residence: Lincoln.

Henry Seeley Andrews

Henry Seeley Andrews was born at Nemaha, Nebraska, March 28, 1885, the son of Bezaleel Bell and Ida Olive (Seeley) Andrews. His father, who was a surgeon, was born in Putnam County, Ohio, July 3, 1845, of Scotch and Irish parents, and died at Nemaha, November 10, 1915. He was a Civil War veteran; descended from Alexander Hamilton and Sir Charles Bell, and from a long line of doctors and surgeons. His mother, whose ancestry was French, was born at Dayton, Ohio, October 23, 1850, and

HENRY SEELEY ANDREWS

died at Minden, Nebraska, October 10, 1920. She was educated as a physician and nurse.

Dr. Andrews attended the public schools of Stella, Nebraska, received the A. B. degree at the Presbyterian College of Oklahoma, in 1904, and in 1909 was awarded the M. D. degree at the University Medical College in Kansas City, where he was vice president of his graduating class and received scholastic honors. He is surgeon to the Seeley Hospital at Minden, and the Bethphage Mission Hospital at Axtell, Nebraska, and has written various medical articles on case reports.

He holds membership in the Community Commerce Club of Kearney County, is president of the Minden Rotary Club, and a member of the American Medical Association, the Nebraska State Medical Association, and the Adams County Medical Association. He is serving as a member of the school board at Minden, and is affiliated with the First Presbyterian Church there. His chief outside interests are boys vocational guidance and reading. His favorite sport is golfing.

Of his marriage to Louise Hubbard, two children were born: Harry Hubbard, born June 25, 1911; and Thomas, born November 16, 1915. Both sons are studying medicine. He was married to Ella M. Rasmus at Hastings, Nebraska, in 1918.

Dr. Andrews served as captain in the Medical Corps in field hospital work during the World War, and is now a member of the American Legion. Residence: Minden. (Photograph on Page 41).

Kenneth Rae Andrews

Born at Mount Ayr, Iowa, June 1, 1872, Kenneth Rae Andrews is the son of Henry Charles and Mary Frances (Campbell) Andrews. His father, born at North Sydney, Nova Scotia, October 19, 1845, died at Kearney, October 3, 1928. He was a veteran of the Civil War, a lawyer and a member of the Nebraska legislature. His ancestry was English and Scotch. His wife, Mary Frances, was born at Quincy, Florida, June 1, 1848, and died at Kearney, October 10, 1922. An especially active clubwoman, she was of Scotch descent.

Kenneth Rae Andrews attended public school and was graduated from high school on May 28, 1890. For a number of years he has been engaged in the real estate business at Kearney, and from 1916-20, served as mayor, elected on the Republican ticket.

From 1898 to 1902, Mr. Andrews held the rank of captain in the Nebraska National Guard. He is a member of the Red Cross, the Elks, the Nebraskana Society, and the Kearney Country Club. His favorite sport is golfing, and his hobby is reading. Residence: Kearney.

Luther Gilbert Andrews

Luther Gilbert Andrews, insurance executive and musician, was born at Omaha, February 13, 1899, son of Orville Alexander and Jessie (Gilbert) Andrews. Orville A. Andrews was born at Troy Grove, Illinois, November 17, 1870, and is founder and first president of the American States Life Insurance Company. An active worker in many Masonic bodies, he is past master of Lincoln Lodge No. 19, A. F. & A. M. 1916-17; grand master of Masons in Nebraska, A. F. & A. M. 1930-31, and associate patron Electa Chapter No. 8, O. E. S., 1931. His ancestry is Scotch-Irish, the family coming to America in 1638.

Jessie Gilbert Andrews was born at Emington, Illinois, September 19, 1872, and is a member of the Daughters of the American Revolution, past president of the Daughters of Union Veterans of the Civil War and past matron of Electa Chapter No. 8, Order of Eastern Star. She is descended from the Quaker families of Whitaker and Reeder and the Pennsylvania Dutch Hateman family.

Mr. Andrews was graduated from Lincoln High School in 1917, and received his A.B. from the University

of Nebraska in 1924. He was a member of the University Band, the Vikings, Acacia Fraternity, Gamma Lambda, and is past president of Acacia Alumni Association. At the present time he is president of the American Indemnity Company and secretary of the Andrews Insurance Agency. A member of the Lincoln Musicians Association, local No. 462, of the American Federation of Musicians, he served as its president in 1924 and 1925 and member of its board of directors 1923, 1930 and 1931. He has played many musical engagements, including first horn in the following: Omaha Symphony Orchestra, Lincoln Symphony, Nebraska State Band, Lincoln Municipal Band, Stuart Symphony; Strand, Rialto and Brandeis Theatres, Omaha, Rialto and Lincoln Theatres, Lincoln. He was one of the organizers of the Lincoln Symphony, and has served as member of the board of directors, member of the board of personnel and member of the orchestra.

During the World War he was a member of the I. C.O.T.S. at Camp Grant, Illinois; in 1923 he was manager of the American Legion Band at Lincoln and attended the Paris Convention in 1927 with Monohan Post, Sioux City, Iowa. He is a member of Westminster Presbyterian Church and the Nebraskana Society.

Mr. Andrews was married to Helen Leona Clark at Omaha, on November 19, 1921. She was born at Omaha, April 15th, 1899, descended from the English family of Clark, the Pennsylvania Dutch family of Fink and the Scotch-Irish family of McConnell. Their daughter, Jacqueline, was born July 13, 1926. Residence: Lincoln.

Orville Alexander Andrews

A resident of Lincoln for more than thirty-eight years, Orville Alexander Andrews was born at Troy Grove, Illinois, November 17, 1870, son of Luther Ticknor and Anna Elizabeth (Smith) Andrews. Luther Andrews was born at Troy Grove, August 6, 1847, and is still living. He was a pioneer farmer in Kansas, of Scotch-English descent. His wife, Anna Elizabeth, was born at Hagerstown, Maryland, March 3, 1849, and died at Hicksville, Long Island, New York, April 27, 1898. She was of Pennsylvania-Dutch descent, and was particularly active in the work of the Women's Christian Temperance Union.

Orville Andrews attended the public schools of Clay County, and was graduated from Clay Center High School (Kansas) in 1888. In 1891, he attended Kansas State Normal School at Emporia, and held the highest first grade teacher's certificate in the county. Thereafter he taught school three years.

On September 25, 1895, he was married to Jessie Gilbert at Emington, Illinois. Mrs. Andrews was born at Emington, on September 19, 1872, and is of Scotch descent. She was matron of Electra chapter of the Order of Eastern Star at Lincoln, in 1923. There are two sons, Luther G., born February 13, 1899, who married Helen L. Clark; and Orville A. Jr., born January 29, 1904, who married Vera Albers.

Mr. Andrews is a Republican. For twenty-five years he was associated with the Chicago, Burlington and Quincy Railroad, in the traffic department; and for the past thirteen years he has been in the managerial and executive field of the insurance business. He is secretary and treasurer of the American Indemnity Association at the present time. During the World War he was active in Liberty and Victory loan drives, in the Red Cross and as a member of the Y. M. C. A. board. Affiliated with Westminster Presbyterian Church, he has been ruling elder since 1918. He is a former member of the Kansas State Teachers Association, and president of Clay County, Kansas Teachers' Association.

A Mason, he is past master of Lincoln Lodge No. 19, Ancient Free and Accepted Masons, and past grand master of Grand Lodge of Nebraska, (1930-31). He is a member of all the Masonic bodies and the Eastern Star.

His civic memberships include the Hiram International and the Chamber of Commerce. He is a member of The Nebraskana Society. Residence: Lincoln. (Photograph in Album).

Frederick Moore Andrus

Dr. Frederick M. Andrus, distinguished physician and surgeon, was born at Plattsmouth, Cass County, Nebraska, July 29, 1872. His father, Daniel Dart Andrus, was a farmer and stockman in Cass County, and was for many years active in political and educational affairs in his community. He was county chairman of the Republican Committee and as a school director was largely responsible for the development of scientific farm-training in the schools. He was born at Herkimer, Orleans County, New York, November 13, 1832, and died at Weeping Water, Cass County, Nebraska, October 3, 1895. He was of English descent on the maternal side, and was descended from the Irish nobility on the paternal side through a long line of noted New York ancestors.

Louise (Ewing) Andrus, his mother, was of Pennsylvania Dutch descent. She was born at Ossomottamie, Pottowattimie County, Pennsylvania, June 20, 1838, and died at Manley, Cass County, Nebraska, June, 1903.

Dr. Andrus attended the country school at Grand Prairie, until the age of 18, when he entered Manley High School; at the age of 21 he was graduated from the Weeping Water High School. He was a student at the University of Nebraska for two years where he received instruction in the basic science studies. The last two years of his medical course were received at Cotner Medical School. He has since taken post graduate courses in all the principal clinics of Europe and the United States. He was valedictorian of his graduating class in 1900.

A life time resident of Nebraska, Dr. Andrus has won an enviable position in his profession in the last 30 years. He was admitted to the practice of medicine at Lincoln Lancaster County, Nebraska, April 1, 1900, and for the next 10 years was a country doctor and physician in a private hospital. He was engaged in railroad building for 8 years, and from 1903 to 1915 was professor of gynecological surgery at Cotner Medical College. Since 1914 he has been surgeon to St. Elizabeth Hospital and Bryan Memorial Hospital at Lincoln. He is medical director of the Service Life Insurance Company; is director of the American Savings and Loan Company; and is president of the Craftsman Building Association.

He is the author of an article on surgical treatment, published in 1913, and *Correct Shoe*, 1908. He was married to Pearl Shaw at Lincoln, May 3, 1917. Mrs. Andrus, who was born at Decatur, Cass County, Michigan, September 16, 1880, is descended from an old Rhode Island family; her grandfather was judge of the district court.

Dr. Andrus served in the Medical Reserve of the United States Army in 1916-17, and was a member of the National Guard, 1920 to 1921. He is a member of the county, state, and national medical associations; the Community Chest; the Lincoln Chamber of Commerce; the Current Topics Club; and the Hiram Club. He is a Mason, Shriner, and an Elk. He holds membership in the local Young Men's Christian Association, and is affiliated with the following social clubs; University Club; Shrine Country Club; Eastridge Country Club; and the Lincoln Gun Club. He is a member of Westminster Presbyterian Church at Lincoln. His sports are golf, billiards, and hunting. His hobby is keeping a scrapbook of poems, prose, and medical clippings. He is a Republican. Residence: Lincoln.

Edward John Angle

Edward J. Angle was born at Cedarville, Illinois, April 1, 1864, the son of John Bouslough and Jane (Bell) Angle. His father, who was a farmer, was born in Washington County, Maryland, January 17, 1820, and died at

Dakota, Illinois, September 25, 1892. His Swiss ancestors came to America in 1720, and were identified with an early date with the Dunkard and Mennonite churches.

His mother was born in Dauphin County, Pennsylvania, December 19, 1817, and died at Dakota, December 17, 1908. Her Scotch-Irish ancestors came to America early in the 18th century and were active in the Revolution. Among them were the Bells, Swans, Youngs, Wilsons, and Rutherfords. She was vitally interested in educational and religious work.

Dr. Angle, a distinguished physician and dermatologist at Lincoln, Lancaster County, Nebraska, attended the public schools of Cedarville, Illinois; he was graduated from the Madison High School in 1882. In 1886 he was awarded the B. S. degree at the University of Wisconsin; the M. D. degree at the University of Cincinnati, 1887; M. D., University of Pennsylvania, 1895; A. M. University of Nebraska, 1898. He is a member of Sigma Xi and Alpha Tau Omega, University of Nebraska.

He began the practice of medicine at LaSalle, Illinois, in 1888, and remained there in active practice until 1894. After a year in postgraduate work in Philadelphia and New York City, he settled at Lincoln, in 1895, where he has remained. He is the author of numerous medical articles, among them: *Embroyology of the Early Kidney of the Pig; Transactions of the American Microscopical Society*, 1918; and *Parents and Their Problems, National Congress of the Mother*. He was editor of the department of Skin and Genito Urinary Diseases, of the *Western Medical Review*, 1902-1907.

He was united in marriage with Agnes Lillian Wolf at Freeport, Illinois, June 6, 1889. Mrs. Angle, who was born at Freeport, August 8, 1863, is the daughter of Judge George Wolf. Her ancestors settled in Pennsylvania and Virginia early in the history of the country. Five children were born to this union: Sarah Jane, born March 15, 1890, who died August 1, 1903; Florence Bell, born November 28, 1893, who married Guy E. Reed, vice president of the Harris Trust Company of Chicago, and who was queen of the May in her graduating class at the University of Nebraska, where she received Phi Beta Kappa honors; Edward Everett, born January 13, 1896, who married Catharine Dodge, and who is a physician at Lincoln; Barbara Josephine, born March 30, 1898, who died March 23, 1905; and Agnes Evelyn, born September 16, 1904, who married Harrry E. Stevens of Fremont, Nebraska.

Dr. Angle was a member of the Lincoln board of medical examiners during the World War. He is a member of the Sons of the American Revolution and the Society of Colonial Wars. He is a member of the Lancaster County Medical Society; the Nebraska State Medical Society; and the American Medical Association. He holds a fellowship in the American Urological Association, and is a member of the American College of Physical Therapy. He holds membership in the Lincoln Chamber of Commerce; Lincoln Library Board; and is a former member of the Rotary Club.

He is a fellow of the American Association for the Advancement of Science and the American Academy of Social Sciences. He is a member of the Nebraska Academy of Sciences, the Nebraskana Society and the Nebraska State Historical Society. He is affiliated with the various Masonic bodies, including Shrine, and is a member of the University Club and the Shrine Country Club. His sports include fishing and hunting, while his hobby is botany. He is a Republican. Residence: Lincoln.

Everett Edward Angle

Everett E. Angle was born at Lincoln, Nebraska, January 13, 1896, the son of Edward John and Agnes (Wolf) Angle. His father, who was born at Cedarville, Illinois, April 1, 1864, is a physician who specializes in diseases of the skin; he is a charter member of the American Urological Society. He is descended from the following members of the Angle family: Henry, (1740-1810); John, (1776-1826); Daniel, (1790-1835); and John, (1820-1892). Henry Angle came from Switzerland, and settled in Pennsylvania, where he became a soldier in the Revolution.

His mother was born at Freeport, Illinois, August 8, 1863. She is descended from Peter Wolf, (1700-1785) who settled in Pennsylvania when he came to this country from Germany, through the following ancestors: Abraham, (1755-1801); Peter, (1795-1875); George, (1832-1897). The latter was a distinguished judge.

Dr. Angle was graduated from the Lincoln High School in 1914. In 1918 he was graduated from the University of Nebraska with the A. B. degree. He was awarded his M. D. degree at Harvard Medical School in 1921. He was made a member of Sigma Xi, Phi Rho Sigma, and Alpha Tau Omega. He has been a practicing physician in Nebraska for the past 8 years.

His marriage to Catharine Elizabeth Dodge was solemnized at Fremont, Nebraska, September 2, 1920. Mrs. Angle was born at Fremont, August 30, 1896. She is descended from William Dodge who came from England to Salem, Massachusetts, in 1629, and Nicholas Dodge, a Revolutionary War ancestor. They have three children: John C., born August 22, 1923; William Dodge, born January 28, 1926; and Edward Everett, born September 16, 1930.

Dr. Angle served in the Medical Reserve Corps during the World War. A lieutenant in the Reserve Officers' Association, he is a member of the Lancaster County Medical Society; the Nebraska State Medical Society; and the American Medical Association. He holds membership in the American Urological Association, University Club, and the Lincoln Country Club. He is affiliated with the Holy Trinity Episcopal Church at Lincoln, and is a Republican. Residence: Lincoln.

Harry Ray Ankeny

Harry Ray Ankeny, son of Christian and Lavinna (Hicks) Ankeny, was born at Tobias, Nebraska, March 14, 1888. Christian Ankeny, a native of Illinois, was a farmer of Pennsylvania Dutch descent, who died at Tobias, Nebraska. Lavinna Hicks Ankeny was a native of Iowa. She is of Scotch-Irish descent and is still living.

Mr. Ankeny was educated first in the public and high schools of Tobias, and then entered the University of Nebraska where he received his LL. B. During the term 1910-11 he was a member of the track team and received his letter. He was made a member of the Innocents and of Delta Chi fraternity.

Since his admission to the bar he has engaged in general practice in Lincoln. From 1914-16 he was a member of the law firm of Kelley and Ankeny, and from 1921-22 the firm of Cosgrave, Campbell and Ankeny. Since that time he has been practicing alone. He is a member of the American, Nebraska State and Lancaster County Bar Associations, Trinity Methodist Church, the Young Men's Christian Association. He is a Mason, and member of Jewell Lodge No. 149 at Tobias; Lincoln Consistory of Scottish Rite and Sesostris Temple of the Shrine. A Republican, he was appointed deputy county attorney for Lancaster County, serving 1918-20.

His marriage to Beulah Luella Jennings was solemnized at Davenport, Nebraska, November 7, 1914. Mrs. Ankeny was born at Davenport, August 22, 1890, and prior to her marriage was assistant principal of the Geneva High School. There are four children, Clayton Jennings, born November 26, 1916; Harry Ray, born May 8, 1919; June Edith, born November 1, 1923, and Robert Howard, born July 9, 1930.

Grace May Anness

Grace M. Anness was born at Tippecanoe City, Miami County, Ohio, November 9, 1877, the daughter of Charles Davis and Emma Caroline (Boyer) Heikes. Her father, who was a nurseryman in Ohio and Nebraska, was born at Tippecanoe City, November 17, 1852, and died at Salt Lake City, Salt Lake County, Utah, April 7, 1911. His ancestry was Pennsylvania Dutch.

Her mother was born of Scotch Irish parents at Tippecanoe, April 3, 1853, and died at Salt Lake City, April 12, 1923.

Mrs. Anness received her elementary education at Tippecanoe City, Salt Lake City, and the public schools of Beatrice, Nebraska. She studied for a time at the Methodist Seminary at Salt Lake City, and in June, 1897, was awarded the A. B. degree at the University of Utah, being the first Gentile girl to receive a degree at this school. She taught in Nebraska schools for two years and was an instructor in grade and high schools at Salt Lake City for eight years. A resident of Nebraska for 26 years, she has been prominent in social and civic affairs in her community and state.

Her marriage to Wilber Winfred Anness was solemnized at Salt Lake City, June 15, 1904. Mr. Anness, who was a druggist, was born of Scotch parentage at Versailles, Ripley County, Indiana, May 6, 1873, and died at Dunbar, Otoe County, Nebraska, November 2, 1925.

During the World War Mrs. Anness was chairman of the Red Cross in Dunbar, and was distinguished by the award of a medal presented by President Wilson for services rendered her country. She is a member of the Nebraskana Society, is Past Grand Matron of the Eastern Star of Nebraska, and is affiliated with the First Presbyterian Church at Dunbar. Her hobbies are reading and travel, and most of her time during the summer months is spent on trips to various spots of interest in the country. She is a Republican, and a member of the Republican Woman's Club. Residence: Dunbar.

Leslie Clem Anstine

Born at Utica, Nebraska, January 25, 1896, Leslie C. Anstine has been a merchant at Wood River, since 1925. He is the son of George M. and Mary Alice (Kinkade) Anstine, both natives of Industry, Illinois, the former born November 2, 1859, and the latter on September 27, 1862. George M. Anstine is a farmer of English descent, while his wife, a prominent club and church worker, was of Scotch-Irish descent. She died at Seattle, Washington, October 5, 1925.

Leslie C. Anstine was graduated from Utica High School in 1914, attended the Lincoln School of Business, 1922, and the University of Nebraska, 1922-25. He was assistant cashier of the Farmers & Traders Bank at Waco, from 1914-19, with the exception of war service. In 1919-20, he took a homestead on the North Platte irrigation project at Torrington, Wyoming. Since 1925, has been the owner of the Square Deal Grocery at Wood River. He is treasurer, also, of the Wood River Building & Loan Association.

On February 5, 1918, he was married to Alta Hester Remy, at Utica. Mrs. Anstine, who is active in Woman's Club and lodge work, was born at Utica, July 4, 1895, of French and English extraction. They have three children, Janice, born September 2, 1920; Jack, born October 15, 1922; and Leslie Paul, born May 21, 1925.

From 1917-19, Mr. Anstine served in the United States Army with rank of corporal, Company L, 355th Infantry, and was wounded in the St. Mihiel drive, September 12, 1918. He is a member of the American Legion, a member and director of the Chamber of Commerce, a member of the Red Cross, the Odd Fellows and the Methodist Episcopal Church, as well as The Nebraskana Society. Mr. Anstine enjoys golf, hunting and fishing, and is fond of reading. Residence: Wood River. (Photograph in Album).

Fred Irwin Archibald

Fred Irwin Archibald, advertising executive, was born at McCook, Nebraska, October 18, 1893, son of William Wallace and May (Irwin) Archibald.

He attended the University of Nebraska, College of Engineering, where he is a member of Sigma Alpha Epsilon, and on August 11, 1921, was married to Edna Olson at Stromsburg.

For 14 years Mr. Archibald was advertising manager, secretary and treasurer of the Lincoln Star. He was associated with the *Omaha World Herald*, 4 years. He is now vice president and advertising director of the *Omaha Bee-News*.

He is a member of Holy Trinity Episcopal Church, the American Legion, the Chamber of Commerce, the Masons, and the Elks. During the World War he was lieutenant of artillery. Residence: Omaha.

Herman Arends

One of Otoe County's earliest settlers, Herman Arends was born in Illinois, August 26, 1855. He has been a resident of Otoe County since 1859, his family having moved here from his native state. His father, Richard Arends, was born in 1810, and died on his homestead near Syracuse, in 1874. His wife, Mary Teten, died on January 19, 1898.

Mr. Arends was educated in country schools, and has been a farmer all his life. He was married to Lizza Kastner in Otoe County on November 4, 1880. Mrs. Arends died on February 19, 1898. There are seven children, Mary, Leta, Alma, Dora, Richard, Libby and Irena.

During his entire life Mr. Arends has been active in the affairs of his community. He is a member of the Lutheran Church, and takes an interested part in the development of his locality. In addition to the homestead upon which he lives he is an extensive property owner and is looked up to and respected throughout the county. Residence: Talmage.

Joseph Frank Arens

Joseph F. Arens, a lifetime resident of Nebraska, has been engaged in farming in Cedar County for many years. He was born at Bow Valley, Nebraska, May 4, 1881, the son of Theresa (Klienker) Arens, and Frank John Arens. His father was born at Westphalia, Germany, December 21, 1856, and his mother was born there May 21, 1858.

Mr. Arens is interested in civic affairs and is now serving as treasurer of the local school board, is president of the Cedar County Fair Association, and secretary of the Farmers Union at Hartington. He is affiliated with Holy Trinity Catholic Church, is a member of The Nebraskana Society, and is a Democrat.

On November 26, 1907, he was united in marriage with Clara Sarah Schulte at Bow Valley. Mrs. Arens, whose parents were farmers, was born at Fordyce, Nebraska, July 21, 1888, of German descent. Their children are: Caroline, born December 20, 1908; Arthur, born June 29, 1911; Elizabeth, born January 24, 1916; Evelyn, born May 4, 1918; and Jerome Schulte, born December 8, 1916, who is adopted. Residence: Hartington.

George Oscar Armand

George O. Armand was born at Madison, Indiana, May 16, 1895, the son of Christopher J. and Lela Vesta (Bucknell) Armand. His father, who was born at Madison, January 27, 1871, is a farmer whose ancestry is French. His mother was born at Jefferson, Missouri, May 11, 1873.

Mr. Armand, who is an automobile dealer, was the owner and operator of the first bus line in Nebraska, running busses from Beatrice to Lincoln and Lincoln to Grand Island. He is active in community affairs at York, Nebraska, and holds membership in the Parent Teachers Association, the Young Men's Christian Association, the York Rotary Club, and the Nebraskana Society. He served as president of the York Commercial Club in 1920, and for six years has been a member of the board of this organization. He is a member of the First Presbyterian Church, holds membership in the Knights of Pythias, and in 1929 was chairman of the local Red Cross.

He married Alice Viola Headley at Beatrice, Nebraska, September 24, 1919; she was born at Beatrice, December 10, 1896, and was a teacher before her marriage. Two children were born to them: Jane, born October 9, 1924; and Wayne, born April 15, 1928. Mr. Armand is a Republican. His favorite sport is baseball and his hobby is mechanics.

Mr. Armand has been very active in the good roads movement, being chairman of the York County Good Roads Association, and a member of the Nebraska Good Roads Association. He was instrumental in organizing the Nebraska Bus Operators' Association which was responsible for bus legislation in the state. Residence: York.

Arthur Armstrong

Arthur Armstrong, hotel proprietor at Hay Springs, was born in Perth, Ontario, Canada, March 1, 1870, son of Christopher and Jane (McClellen) Armstrong. Christopher Armstrong was born in County Fermanagh, Ireland, April 4, 1823, and died at Hancock, Iowa, April 14, 1913. He was a farmer, who came to the United States in 1846. His wife, Jane, was born in County Antrim, Ireland, April 11, 1836, and died at Hancock, January 11, 1912. She was the mother of 14 children, six boys and eight girls, and reared 13 of them to manhood and womanhood. Her mother died aboard the vessel on which she was coming to America, and was buried at sea.

Mr. Armstrong attended the public school and studied one year at Simpson College, Indiana, Iowa. A farmer in his earlier years, he is now the proprietor of a hotel. He is affiliated with the Methodist Episcopal Church, is a Mason, an Odd Fellow, and a member of the Lions Club.

On September 3, 1902, he was married to Octavia Andrea Nelson at Hancock, Iowa. Mrs. Armstrong was born at Avoca, Iowa, September 3, 1881, of Danish descent. She is a member of the Eastern Star and is affiliated with the Methodist Episcopal Church. She is the daughter of Nels and Annie (Christensen) Nelson, and attended school at Avoca, Iowa. Mr. and Mrs. Armstrong are active in all civic and community work, especially those activities which are good for the morals of their community. There are two children, Marjorie Lorena, born July 26, 1903, who died October 11, 1916; and Claire Mae, born August 17, 1905. Claire is a graduate of the Hay Springs High School and has a Bachelor's degree from the State Normal School at Chadron. Residence: Hay Springs.

Bryan Manford Armstrong

Bryan Manford Armstrong, merchant, was born at Logan, Iowa, April 24, 1896, the son of Joseph Andrew and Rose (Peckinpaugh) Armstrong. His father was a farmer.

Mr. Armstrong attended the public schools of Plainview, Nebraska, and in 1913 was graduated from the high school there. He is a member of the Chamber of Commerce at Valentine, Nebraska, the Rotary Club, the Parent Teachers Association, and the Presbyterian Church. He served in the United States Army during the World War and is now a member of the American Legion. His favorite sport is baseball.

Of his marriage to Florence Erma Wright, which occurred at Knoxville, Iowa, October 10, 1896, two children were born, Jack, on May 1, 1922; and Virginia, born October 23, 1923. Residence: Valentine.

Robert McDowell Armstrong

Robert McDowell Armstrong was born at Auburn, Nebraska, April 29, 1892, son of James McDowell and Eunice Eulalia (Skeen) Armstrong. James Armstrong was born at Galesburg, Illinois, September 18, 1862, and was a farmer and business man of Scotch-Irish descent. He died at San Diego, California, December 28, 1919. Eunice Armstrong was born at Nemaha, April 7, 1864, and resides at Auburn. She is the daughter of Thomas B. Skeen, one of the pioneer settlers of Nebraska in 1854, and is of Scotch descent. An active worker in the Methodist Epsicopal Church, she is a charter member of the Order of Eastern Star at Auburn.

Robert M. Armstrong attended country schools near Auburn, and the Auburn public and high school, having been graduated from the latter in 1909. He entered the University of Nebraska in the fall of 1909 and received his LL. B. June 12, 1913. He played varsity baseball one year, and is a member of Delta Chi fraternity.

His marriage to Alma Grace Plasters of Stella, Nebraska, occurred May 6, 1914. Mrs. Armstrong who is the daughter of Mr. and Mrs. I. L. Plasters of Richardson County, attended the University of Nebraska. There are two children, Robert Eugene, born July 31, 1915, and James Lee, March 27, 1919.

Entering the practice of law at Auburn in 1913, Mr. Armstrong was associated in practice with the late Honorable H. A. Lambert under the firm name of Lambert & Armstrong until 1921. At that time he was elected county judge of Nemaha County, holding office until 1925. He had served as city attorney from 1914 to 1921.

In 1925 he resumed private practice. He is now chairman of the Republican county central committee. He has been secretary-treasurer of the Bagley Oil and Gas Company since its organization in 1918.

In 1918 he enlisted in the Motor Transportation Corps of the United States Army as a private, and served at Camp Johnstone, Florida, and at Camp Dodge, Iowa, until discharged in 1919 with the rank of sergeant. He assisted in the registration with the first draft and was active as a four minute speaker and in Red Cross and other drives.

A charter member of the Auburn Post No. 23, American Legion, he was post commander in 1929. He was chairman of the Red Cross disaster relief committee for Nemaha County. He is a member of the Kiwanis Club, and was president of the Auburn organization in 1925, lieutenant governor of the Nebraska- Iowa district during 1929 and 1930; he was elected governor of the Nebraska-Iowa district 1931. In 1916 he was secretary of the Auburn Chamber of Commerce. He is a member of The Nebraskana Society and the National Geographic Society. A Mason, he belongs to the Royal Arch Chapter, and the Knights Templar. His social club is the Auburn Country, of which he was director several years, and president 1927-28. Golf is his chief sport, and his hobby is landscaping. Residence: Auburn.

Frederick William Arndt

Frederick William Arndt, merchant and executive, was born at Cincinnati, Ohio, May 4, 1862, son of Bernard and Dorretta (Albrecht) Arndt. Bernard Arndt, born in Hamburg, Germany, April 13, 1826, was a cigar manufacturer, who served as a sergeant in the Ohio National Guard. He died at West Point, Nebraska, December 5, 1919. His wife, Dorretta, was born in Bremen, Germany, March 15, 1829, and died at Blair, in 1911

Graduated from elementary schools in Cincinnati, Mr. Arndt attended Blair High School, and was advanced in May, 1877. He has been a resident of Nebraska sixty years, during which time he has engaged as a hardware merchant, automobile dealer and oil distributor. He is president of the Arndt-Snyder Motor Company, vice president of the Blair Building and Loan Association, and treasurer of the N-I Oil Company. He is vice president of the Nebraska Hardware Mutual Insurance Company, treasurer of the Chamber of Commerce and past president of the Nebraska Hardware Association and the Chamber of Commerce.

On April 8, 1886, he was married to Sophia Estelle Riddler at Blair. She was born at Fort Calhoun, Nebraska, of Scotch and English descent, and died at Blair, January 9, 1922. There were three children born to this marriage, Wilfred B., born April 12, 1887, who is an automobile salesman; Mary Josephine, born January 9, 1888, and who is an artist; and Dorrette May, born January 10, 1891, who is a singer and pianist.

Mr. Arndt is a Republican a member of the Methodist Episcopal Church and The Nebraskana Society. He is a member of the Blair Golf Club.

On February 6, 1924, Mr. Arndt was married to Annie Vio Gates at Grand Island, Nebraska. She is a newspaper woman, member of the state senatorial committee, vice chairman of the Washington County central committee 1931, member of the Eastern Star for the past twenty years.

Mr. Arndt is a member of the Masons, Royal Arch Masons, and Knights Templar. Residence: Blair.

Charles Harrison Arnold

Charles Harrison Arnold, physician and surgeon, was born near Dorchester, Nebraska, October 18, 1888, son of Henry and Ann Elizabeth (Gifford) Arnold. His father, a native of Collamer, Indiana, born January 26, 1845, was a farmer in that state, and settled near Dorchester, Nebraska, in 1885. He was a member of the Christian Church, and a Republican. His death occurred at Dorchester, March 17, 1921. His wife, Ann Elizabeth, was born in Michigan, May 21, 1850, and died at Lincoln, June 5, 1925. She was a teacher in the Indiana public schools, and a member of the Christian Church. Her ancestry was English, French and Scotch.

Educated first in the country schools near Dorchester Dr. Arnold was graduated from Dorchester High School in 1908. During the year 1908 he attended Lincoln Business College, and in 1909 attended Cotner University. In 1913 he received his M.D. from the Chicago College of Medicine and Surgery.

His first marriage was to Irma Carlotta Sears at Chicago, January 20, 1912. Mrs. Arnold was born at Aurora, Nebraska, September 12, 1887, and died at Lincoln, March 19, 1926. She was a graduate and registered nurse of Scotch descent. There are two children, Hubert Andrew, born November 15, 1912, who is a junior at the University of Nebraska; and Faith Elizabeth, born September 4, 1914, who is a junior in Lincoln High School.

Dr. Arnold married Mrs. Winifred Owen McCoy of Lincoln, at Colorado Springs, June 11, 1928. A life resident of Nebraska, Dr. Arnold has lived in Lincoln since 1913, when he began the practice of medicine there. For the past seven years he has confined his work to surgery. He is chief surgeon to the Dr. Benjamin F. Bailey Sanitorium, attending surgeon to St. Elizabeth's Hospital, and associate surgeon to Bryan Memorial Hospital. He is a lecturer on surgery to the Bailey Training School for Nurses, also.

In April, 1917, he entered the army and was commissioned first lieutenant in the Medical Corps. He was in service July, 1917, and attached to the Royal Army Medical Corps of England with which he saw service in Flanders and on the Somme; he was at the front for eight months, and was wounded in action June 1, 1918. Promoted to the rank of captain, he engaged in surgery at Base Hospital No. 3 LeTreport, France, until February, 1919. He received his honorable discharge at Camp Dix, New Jersey, in February, 1919, and now holds the rank of major in the Medical Reserves. He is a member of the Reserve Officers Association, the American

Legion, and member and past commander of the Veterans of Foreign Wars.

A director of the Red Cross, he is past president and present director of the Lincoln Automobile Club and director of the American Automobile Association. During 1926-28 he was president of the Cosmopolitan Club. A member of the Hiram Club, he is president of the Interprofessional Club of Lincoln, a member of the Young Men's Christian Association, the Nebraska State Historical Society, the Nebraskana Society, and is listed in *Who's Who in America*. His professional memberships include the American, Nebraska State and Lancaster County Medical Associations, and the Military Surgeons Association. He is a Mason, and past commander of the Knights Templar, past high priest and member of the Shrine, 32nd degree member of Scottish Rite, and a member of the Modern Woodmen of America and the Knights of Pythias. His religious affiliation is with the First Christian Church of Lincoln. He belongs to the Lincoln University Club, Shrine Country and Shrine Golf Clubs. Residence: Lincoln. (Photograph in Album).

Ernst Arnold, Jr.

A leader in business and political affairs at Upland, Nebraska, is Ernst Arnold, Jr., who has lived in this state all his life. He was born at Franklin, Nebraska, April 15, 1881, the son of Caroline (Helfferich) and Ernst Arnold, the latter a farmer who served as the first sheriff of Franklin County, was county treasurer, 1908-12, and acted as county judge in the early history of the state. Ernst Arnold was born in Germany, March 2, 1848, came to America in 1870, and the following year homesteaded in Nebraska. Caroline (Helfferich) Arnold was born in France, November 11, 1850, arrived in this country in 1872, and in 1873 moved to Nebraska.

Mr. Arnold was graduated from the Franklin High School in 1898, attended the Lincoln Business College, was graduated in 1900, and took a short course in an agricultural college at the State University. He served as deputy county treasurer, 1908-12, was secretary of the County Democratic Committee for a number of years, and is now treasurer of the latter organization. He is cashier of the People's Bank at Upland, holds membership in the Commercial Club there, and is treasurer of the Upland Red Cross, president of the 3rd Nebraska Regional Clearing House Association.

During the late war Mr. Arnold acted in the capacity of legal advisor, and was prominent in all activities pertaining to home war work. He is a 32nd degree Mason, a member of Tehama Temple of the Shrine, the Independent Order of Odd Fellows, and holds membership in the Nebraskana Society.

His marriage to Bessie Gertrude Barber was solemnized at Bloomington, Nebraska, October 19, 1910; she was born at Bloomington, May 9, 1882. They have two children: Ernst, III, born January 13, 1913, and Barbara Jean, February 11, 1914, a member of the Upland High School. Residence: Upland.

Leonard E. Arnold

Leonard E. Arnold, proprietor of the Arnold Drug Company at Sutherland, was born at Stockville, Nebraska, December 3, 1900, son of Henry D. and Rachel M. (Smith) Arnold.

His father, who was a carpenter, was born in Kalamazoo, Michigan, July 27, 1870. His family came to America from Germany in 1796. His wife, Rachel M., was born at Fort Wayne, Indiana, June 25, 1877, of English ancestry.

Mr. Arnold attended the public schools of Stockville, and in May, 1917, was graduated from high school there. During the year 1919, Mr. Arnold attended the University of Wyoming, and on May 23, 1923, received the degree of Ph. G. from Valparaiso University. He is a life member of the National Association of Drug Clerks, having received the highest standing in chemistry, in the pharmacy department.

Mr. Arnold assumed various clerkships, including Lynch Pharmacy at Roseland, Nebraska, the Preston Drug Company at Oxford, Nebraska, the Hoopers Pharmacy at Holdrege, Nebraska, the Ogallala Drug Company, Ogallala, Nebraska. He was manager for a time of the Sievers Drug Store at Morrill, and is now the owner of his own store at Sutherland. Mr. Arnold is a Republican, has served as a member of the city council for the past three years. He is the author of *Who Is To Blame* (January, 1932), published in the *National Drug Clerk*.

On March 13, 1925, he was married to Nora C. Miller at Smith Center, Kansas. Mrs. Arnold was born at Holstein, Nebraska, August 30, 1905, the daughter of Fred Sand and Christina (Temm) Miller. She is of German descent. They have one son, Vancen, born August 17, 1927.

Among Mr. Arnold's professional organizations are, the National Association of Drug Clerks, the Nebraska Pharmaceutical Association, and the Platte Valley Pharmaceutical Association. He is a member of the Chamber of Commerce, and has served as its president for two years. He is also a member of the Odd Fellows, and is district deputy grand master. At the present time, he is president of the Platte Valley Pharmaceutical Association. His favorite sports include football, fishing, and hunting, while his hobby is reading. Residence: Sutherland. (Photograph in Album).

Charles Arnot

Charles Arnot, son of Elisha Truesdel and Ruth Ann (Miller) Arnot, was born at Greenville, November 3, 1864. The father, a farmer and stockman, was a Democrat and a veteran of the Civil War, having served with the Confederate Army. Of Scotch descent, his grandfather, Henry Arnot, served in the Revolution. He came from Scotland and settled in Virginia, and was of the House of Balfour, and descended from Mary Queen of Scots. Ruth Ann Miller was born in Wolf Creek, West Virginia, May 7, 1831, and died at Red Sulphur Springs, West Virginia, October 29, 1903. Her husband died there on April 12, 1910. She was a teacher prior to her marriage, and was a vocalist of considerable ability. Her mother came from the north of Ireland and her father from Scotland.

Educated first in public and private schools of Virginia and West Virginia, Mr. Arnot also attended Drake University at Des Moines, Danville College at Danville, Indiana, Valparaiso College, and was graduated from Fremont Normal College in 1891. He taught school in the rural districts of Virginia one year, and in West Virginia one year. He came to Nebraska and taught in rural schools three years, village schools 11 years; served as county superintendent of Dodge County four years, city superintendent for Schuyler eight years, and on July 1, 1915, came to Scribner as cashier and manager of the First National Bank. He is still holding that position, and in 1906 organized the Logan Valley Bank at Uehling, and was its president until 1911, when he sold his interests. Mr. Arnot held the first corn growing contest in the state and while county superintendent devoted much time to organization.

A Democrat he has been active in every Democratic campaign but has held no political offices, except as county superintendent of Schools of Dodge County, as above. He was defeated for the same office in Colfax County by 15 votes in 1894.

On July 17, 1910, he was married to Mabel E. Johnson at Colorado Springs, Colorado. Mrs. Arnot was born at Fremont, November 6, 1887, and is a former

teacher in city grade schools. They have three children:
Ruth Elizabeth, born December 14, 1911, who is a student at Doane College; Charles Pemberton, born March 4, 1917, who has completed his first year in high school; and James William, born July 25, 1927.

Mr. Arnot is the author of several articles of an educational nature, and for fourteen years prior to 1915 was a member of the National Educational Association. He is especially active in community affairs, and is president of the board of directors of the Dodge County Red Cross chapter. He was a member of the commission appointed by Governor Morehead to revise the school laws of Nebraska, and represented the Third Congressional District in the Nebraska State Teachers Association six years. He is a member of the Scribner Chamber of Commerce, the Nebraskana Society and the Nebraska School Masters Club. His fraternal organizations include the Masons, Knights of Pythias, Eastern Star, Modern Woodmen of America and Woodmen of the World. He enjoys especially reading history and fiction. Residence: Scribner.

Leland Dill Arnot

Leland Dill Arnot, dental surgeon, was born at Johnson, Nebraska, July 8, 1900, son of Lycurgus Bernard and Mary Elizabeth (Carmine) Arnot. His father, born near Union, Monroe County, West Virginia, was a farmer. He is a great great grandson of Henry Arnot of the Revolution, who enlisted in New Jersey in 1778 and was a pensioned soldier. His mother came from Ireland and his father from Scotland. Mary Elizabeth Carmine was born on a farm near Galesburg, Illinois, February 9, 1860.

Educated in rural school to the eighth grade until May 26, 1914, Dr. Arnot was graduated from high school at Pawnee City on May 29, 1918, and received the degree of Doctor of Dental Surgery in June, 1924, from the University of Nebraska. There he was made a member of the Green Goblins, the Iron Sphinx, Xi Psi Phi and Beta Theta Pi, of which he was steward in 1923-24.

On May 20, 1925, Dr. Arnot was united in marriage to Esther Philleo at Denver, Colorado. Mrs. Arnot was born at Wayne, Nebraska, September 14, 1905. They have one son, Leland Dill, Jr., born July 7, 1926.

Since his admission in 1924, Dr. Arnot has been actively engaged in practice. He is a member of the American, Nebraska State and Central District Dental Associations, and is serving as president of the last mentioned for the term of 1930-31. During 1925-26 he was president of the Exeter Chamber of Commerce, is a member of the city council (1928-32) and of the school board 1931-34.

Dr. Arnot's religious affiliation is with the Methodist Episcopal Church. He was a four minute speaker and a private in the Student's Army Training Corps at the University during the World War, and is a member of the American Legion. He is also a member of the Odd Fellows, the Nebraskana Society, the Cornhusker Dental Study Club and the University Club at Lincoln. Dr. Arnot's sport is golf and his hobby is landscaping. Residence: Exeter.

Herbert Arnstein

Herbert Arnstein, executive, was born in Omaha, Nebraska, July 6, 1890, son of Sigmund and Theresa Arnstein. He was graduated from Central High School in 1908, and was married to Jeanette Mayer, who was born in Lincoln, May 28, 1898 (*See Nebraskana*).

At the present time Mr. Arnstein is engaged in the mercantile business. He is also real estate owner and an extensive property holder and builder. He is a member of Temple Israel and the Young Men's Christian Association. Residence: Omaha.

Jeanette Mayer Arnstein

Jeanette Mayer Arnstein, who was born at Lincoln, Nebraska, May 28, 1893, is the daughter of Charles and Estelle Mayer, the former a merchant and civic leader of Lincoln, born in New York City, September 13, 1859. He was of German descent, and died in New York, December 7, 1927. Estelle Mayer was also a native of New York, born September 13, 1863. She is of German and American ancestry, and was formerly active in the social, civic and educational life of Lincoln. She now resides in New York City.

Mrs. Arnstein was graduated from Lincoln High School in 1910, and received her A. B. from Wellesley College in Massachusetts in 1914. She is a member of Omaha College Club, Wellesley Club and of Mu Sigma, and the National Council of Jewish Women.

She was married to Herbert Arnstein in 1915. They have three children, Margery, born August 13, 1917; Charles, born October 1, 1922, and Barbara, born December 30, 1924. She is Jewish and a member of Temple Israel. During the World War she was a civilian relief worker, and is now active in the Jewish Women's Welfare Federation, the Community Chest and the Red Cross. She is independent in politics, and is a member of the Nebraska League of Women Voters. She is president of the Omaha section of the National Council of Jewish Women (1930-32), a member of the Omaha Symphony women's committee, the Parent Teachers Association, the American Association of University Women, and the Nebraskana Society. During 1927-29 she was president of the Wellesley Club. Her sports are golf and hiking and her chief recreation is reading. Her clubs are the Omaha Athletic Club and Highland Country Club. Residence: Omaha.

Charles W. Aron

Charles W. Aron was born at Crete, Nebraska, June 28, 1869, the son of Thomas and Elizabeth (Nedela) Aron. His father, who was born in Czechoslovakia, in 1839, was a farmer who came to America in 1867, and settled at Baltimore, Maryland. Later he was married in Chicago, and homesteaded near Crete, where he died October 30, 1908. His mother was born at Msemo, Czechoslovakia, in 1845, and died at Crete, in 1900.

Mr. Aron received his education in the public schools of Saline County. He has been an active farmer for many years. He is a member of the Nebraskana Society, and has served on the district school board for several terms. He has been a member of the Sokol Society for over 40 years. He is a Catholic.

His marriage to Anna Marcelino was solemnized at Crete, October 21, 1896. Mrs. Aron, who was born at Crete, November 19, 1876, is of Bohemian descent on the maternal side and Portuguese through the paternal line. Four children were born to this union, Emma, born November 6, 1897, who married William Tobiska; Otto, born December 7, 1898, who married Hazel Williams; Gertrude, born June 28, 1900, who married William Boles; and Carl, born June 17, 1902, who married Marie Conrad. Residence: Crete.

Edward Fred Aron

Edward F. Aron, owner and manager of the Aron Clothes Shop at Crete, Saline County, Nebraska, has lived in this state all his life. He was born at Crete, October 21, 1881, the son of Charles and Barbara (Dolansky) Aron. His father, who was born in Czechoslovakia, June 9, 1850, and died at Crete, August 18, 1924, was a tailor and merchant for over 50 years. His mother was born in Czechoslovakia, July 8, 1851, and died at Crete, June 4, 1925.

Mr. Aron received his education in the grade and high school at Crete. He is a member of the Community Club, the Nebraska Federation of Retailers, the Allied Clothers, and the Crete Golf Club. He is affiliated with the Methodist Church, is a Scottish Rite Mason, and holds membership in the Nebraskana Society. During the World War he was active in Liberty loan drives. He is a Republican.

His marriage to Frances Amelia Gilbert was solemnized at Johnson, Nemaha County, Nebraska, August 18, 1914. Mrs. Aron was born at Johnson, the daughter of French and Pennsylvania Dutch parents. Two children were born to this marriage: Charles Gilbert, born November 13, 1916; and Ruth Genevieve, born April 1, 1917, who died February 6, 1925. Residence: Crete.

Carlos Epperson Arterburn

Carlos Epperson Arterburn, banker of St. Paul Nebraska, is a lifelong resident of this state. He was born at Imperial, Nebraska, June 12, 1890, the son of Ellsworth E., and Della N. (Epperson) Arterburn. His father, a real estate dealer and abstractor, was born at Kansas, Illinois, February 3, 1862. His French, English and Scotch ancestors came to America prior to the Revolution and later served in that war. Della N. Epperson was born at Oneida, Illinois, February 23, 1865.

Mr. Arterburn attended Nebraska Military Academy until June, 1910, and from 1910 until 1912 was a student at the University of Nebraska where he was a member of Sigma Alpha Epsilon. He played football and basketball at Nebraska Military Academy. For a number of years he has engaged in farming and stockraising at St. Paul, Nebraska, in addition to his banking activities.

From 1913 until 1930 Mr. Arterburn was connected with the St. Paul State Bank and since May, 1930, has served as vice president and chairman of the board of the St. Paul National Bank. He is a Republican.

On September 23, 1914, he was married to Pauline Virginia Paul at St. Paul, Nebraska. Mrs. Arterburn was born at St. Paul, February 3, 1894, of Scotch and English ancestry. They have one son, Carlos Paul, born February 18, 1927.

Mr. Arterburn served as adjutant in the 134th Infantry during the World War. He is a member of the American Legion, the St. Paul Community Club, the Red Cross, and the Masons (Jordan Chapter No. 27, Knights Templar No. 23 of St. Paul, Lincoln Consistory of Lincoln, Nebraska, and Shrine of Hastings). His social club is the Lincoln University Club while his favorite sports are hunting and fishing. Residence: St. Paul.

Carrie Arthur

Carrie Arthur, a lifetime resident of Dodge County, Nebraska, has taken an active part in the business and social world for many years. She was born near Scribner, Dodge County, Nebraska, July 30, 1866, the daughter of James Bard and Caroline (Stoughton) Robinson. Her father, who was born in Union County, Pennsylvania, January 18, 1821, and died at North Bend, Dodge County, Nebraska, February 20, 1907, was a pioneer Nebraskan, and was for many years a miller, merchant, farmer, tavern keeper, and freighter. Her mother, who was born in Northumberland County, Pennsylvania, November 16, 1824, and died at Pebble, Dodge County, Nebraska, October 12, 1884, was a pioneer home maker who knew the perils of Indian warfare and the hardships of the early settlers; she assisted her husband in managing his hotel and was active in church and community work.

Mrs. Arthur attended school at Pebble. She is the sole owner of the Arthur Furniture Company, a furniture and undertaking establishment which she manages with the assistance of her son-in-law, E. J. Spear. She holds membership in the Chamber of Commerce, the Red Cross, the Nebraskana Society, and the Methodist Church of Scribner. Her hobby is reading. Her political affiliation is with the Democratic Party.

She was united in marriage with Thomas L. Arthur at Pebble, March 5, 1884. Mr. Arthur, who was born at Deer Park, LaSalle County, Illinois, June 5, 1853, and died at Scribner, July 8, 1899, was a farm owner in Dodge County for many years. Two children were born to their union: Ray, born May 30, 1885, who died June 2, 1885; and Lou Belle, born April 14, 1887, who married Edward J. Spear. Mr. Spear is a member of the Chamber of Commerce, a Royal Highlander, and a Mason. He has taken an active part in civic affairs and is a Democrat. Mr. and Mrs. Spear have one son, Gifford Arthur, who was born in Scribner, September 27, 1911. A graduate of Scribner High School, he later attended college in Chicago. He is fond of athletics and intends to follow the undertaking and furniture business. Lou Belle was a teacher in the public schools for a time and is now prominent in civic work at Scribner. She does the clerical work in her mother's store; her husband, who is a licensed embalmer and funeral director, is manager of the Arthur Furniture Company. Residence: Scribner. (Photograph in Album).

Elmer Ward Artist

Elmer Ward Artist, county treasurer of Dundy County, was born in Dewitt, Nebraska, May 7, 1883, son of Jacob William and Laura Isabelle (Mathews) Artist.

His father was born in Iowa, March 8, 1856, and died at Benkelman, August 30, 1924. He was a farmer, and also served as county assessor of Dundy County. His ancestry was English. Laura Isabelle Mathews was born at Huntington, Indiana, February 27, 1861, of German descent.

Mr. Artist attended Benkelman Public, and Doane Preparatory School at Crete.

For 22 years, he was engaged in farming, and for the past five years, has been county treasurer of Dundy County. He is also the owner of a service station at Benkelman. He is a Republican.

On December 25, 1907, he was married to Alta May Frasier at Benkelman. She was born there, on February 28, 1887, of French and Scotch Candian descent. Four children were born to them, three of whom are living, Leta Laura, born May 16, 1911; Lila Pearl, born April 12, 1914; Elmer Jacob, born November 11, 1917; and Lucille, born April 24, 1921, who died August 24, 1924.

Mr. Artist attends the Methodist Episcopal Church and is a member of the Chamber of Commerce, the Odd Fellows, and the Ancient Order of United Workmen, joining the Odd Fellows in 1915, and the Workmen, 1907. Residence: Benkelman.

Albert Atchie Ashby

Albert Atchie Ashby, prominent physician and surgeon of Fairmont, Nebraska, was born at Mount Carroll, Illinois, November 3, 1891, the son of Charles L. and Effie (Thompson) Ashby. His father, who is a farmer, was born at Mount Carroll; his ancestors came to this country from England, prior to the Revolution. His mother was born at Mount Carroll, and died at Mount Carroll, Illinois in 1928.

Dr. Ashby was active in basketball, baseball, and track during his school days. He was admitted to the practice of medicine at Chicago Homeopathic Medical College Hospital, Chicago, Illinois, where he was elected to membership in Pi Upsilon Rho Fraternity. He was a member of the medical firm, Drs. Ashby & Ashby at Fairmont, until 1924, since which time he has practiced medicine alone. At present, he is examining physician for the Chicago, Burlington & Quincy Railroad there.

A Republican, he has served as county chairman of various political committees in Fillmore County. He is a member of the school board, Commercial Club, and the following professional organizations: American Medical Association; Nebraska State Medical Society; American Association of Railroad Surgeons. He is a 32nd degree Mason, member of the Shrine and Sesostris Temple, Lincoln, Nebraska, also a member of the Independent Order of Odd Fellows.

During the World War he served as first lieutenant of the Medical Corps, Fort Riley, Kansas, and captain of the Reserves, Camp Devens, Massachusetts. He was commanding hospital officer at Scituate Proving Grounds, Scituate, Massachusetts, for three months. He is now a member of the American Legion. His favorite sport is baseball, and his hobby is overseeing his farms.

Dr. Ashby was married at Independence, Missouri, to Gertrude Ferg, October 29, 1918. Mrs. Ashby, who was a laboratory technician for the City of Topeka, Kansas, before her marriage, was born at Hepler, Kansas, September 20, 1894. Mrs. Ashby was graduated from the Kansas University in 1917. She was instructor at Kansas State Teachers College, Pittsburg, Kansas. To them were born two children: Charles Ferg, February 9, 1920; and Sherman Francis, April 12, 1923. Residence: Fairmont.

George W. Ashford

George W. Ashford, banker and farmer at Homer, Nebraska, was born there July 13, 1875, the son of Thomas and Margaret (Duggan) Ashford. His father, who was a farmer, was born in County Wicklow, Ireland, and died at Homer, April, 1907. His mother was born in County Cork, Ireland, and died at Homer, Nebraska, in April 1916.

Mr. Ashford was graduated from the University of Iowa in 1899 with the degree Ph. G. He is president of the Security State Bank of Homer at the present time, and is active in civic affairs at Homer. He holds membership in the Woodmen of the World, Modern Woodmen of America, Knights of Columbus, the Nebraskana Society, and the Red Cross. He is affiliated with St. Cornelius Catholic Church and is a member of the Democratic Party. His hobby is horses.

On December 15, 1908, he was married to Catherine McLaughlin at Lincoln, Lancaster County, Nebraska; she was born at Lincoln February 22, 1878. They have four children: William, born July 21, 1909; Catherine, born August, 1910; Helen, born September 2, 1913; and Louise, born July 20, 1918. Residence: Homer.

Edwin Johnson Askwig

Edwin J. Askwig, who has been an auctioneer in Nebraska for the past 32 years, has lived in this state all his life, and has been prominent in all civic affairs. He was born at Tekamah, Nebraska, July 10, 1867, the son of James and Dorthea Anne (Tue) Askwig. His father, who was a farmer, was born at LaSalle, Illinois, June 3, 1840, and died at Oakland, Nebraska, September 4, 1917. He was of Norwegian ancestry. His mother was born at Racine, Wisconsin, May 10, 1847, and died at Oakland, September 11, 1916.

Mr. Askwig attended the public schools of Oakland. For over 32 years he has been engaged in the livestock auctioneering business, and is now connected with the Surety National Company at Oakland. During the World War he sold Liberty bonds; was active in all war drives; and was a director for the Red Cross, raising $250,-000 for the latter.

He is a member of all branches of the Masons, and holds membership in the Nebraskana Society and the Burt County Historical Society. He has always been a member of the local Chamber of Commerce, and is a Democrat.

His marriage to Jennie Amelia Krogh was solemnized at Oakland, September 26, 1888. Mrs. Askwig, who was born at Chicago, Cook County, Illinois, December 3, 1866, was a teacher before her marriage. Residence: Oakland.

John Albert Aspegren

Since the spring of 1878, John Albert Aspegren has been a resident of Lincoln. He was born at Osco, Illinois, September 10, 1874, the son of Gust and Anna Lovisa (Erickson) Aspegren. His parents were natives of Sweden, the former born January 31, 1844, and the latter October 16, 1853. The father, who was a farmer, died at Saronville, Nebraska, May 12, 1930.

John A. Aspegren attended country school and was graduated from Lincoln Normal University with the degree of B.D. in 1895. On February 4, 1903, he was married to Lettie C. Benson at Hastings. Mrs. Aspegren is a native of Friend. Three children were born to this union, two of whom are living: Lillian, born November 18, 1903, married Otto E. Skald; Hugo, born August 1, 1915; and Sandford, born January 1, 1904, died April 11, 1915.

Since early manhood Mr. Aspegren has been engaged in the lumber and coal business. He now has extensive interests and is president of the Independent Lumber and Coal Company of Lincoln, and secretary and treasurer of the Aspegren and Strand Lumber Company of Saronville, and the Doniphan Lumber Company of Doniphan, Nebraska. He is a director of all three corporations. An Elk and a Mason, he is a member of St. Paul's Methodist Episcopal Church, and the Lincoln Chamber of Commerce. His hobbies are reading and travel. Residence: Lincoln.

Wilber Stremmel Aten

Wilber Stremmel Aten, lawyer at Holdrege, Nebraska, was born at Ragan, Nebraska, May 19, 1903, the son of Wilber William and Eliza Elizabeth (Stremmel) Aten. His father, a retired farmer and stockman, was born at Rushville, Illinois, December 19, 1872, of Scotch ancestry. His mother, also born at Rushville, is a member of the Woman's Club. She is of German descent.

Mr. Aten attended the public schools of Nodaway County, Missouri, and in 1920 was graduated from the Holdrege High School. He received the LL. B. degree at the University of Nebraska, 1924, where he was a member of Phi Alpha Delta. He has been associated with Clarence A. Davis, former attorney-general of Nebraska, in the practice of law at Holdrege, since July 1, 1924.

He holds membership in the Chamber of Commerce, the Nebraska State Bar Association, the American Bar Association, the Kiwanis Club, and the Lincoln University Club. He is a member of DeMolay, and is Past Master of the Masons. His sports include golfing and tennis.

On June 29, 1927, he was married to Irma Yolanda Hulquist, at Holdrege. Mrs. Aten, who was formerly a teacher, was born in Chicago, October 2, 1903. Mr. Aten was nominated for county attorney of Phelps County, Nebraska, in 1926. Residence: Holdrege. (Photograph in Album).

Wilber William Aten

Wilber William Aten, who has been engaged in the real estate and farm loan business at Holdrege, Nebraska, for many years was born at Rushville, Illinois, December 19, 1871. His father, John Calvin Aten, a farmer, was born in Pennsylvania, of Scotch parentage, September 1, 1842, and died at Ragan, Nebraska, March 19, 1925. Isabelle Trimble, his mother, was born in Scotland, in January, 1846, and was an active church and Sunday School worker for many years; she died at Ragan, September 29, 1926.

Mr. Aten came to Ragan, where he was a farmer and stock shipper, also owned a butcher shop, and was interested in elevators until 1911. He moved to Cozad, in 1912, into Missouri, in 1913, came back to Nebraska, April 5, 1916, locating at Holdrege, and since that time has been one of the most important civic leaders in this section of the state.

He deals in insurance, farm loans and real estate at Holdrege, is a member of the Chamber of Commerce and holds membership in the Red Cross, Salvation Army, and the Methodist Episcopal Church. His social club is the Holdrege Country Club. A Republican, he is serving as county chairman and state committeeman of that party.

He was united in marriage with Eliza Elizabeth Stremmel, at Rushville, Illinois, November 17, 1892. Mrs. Aten, who was a teacher and seamstress before her marriage, was born at Rushville, July 15, 1871. Their children are: Florence, born April 4, 1896, who married John Langford Gilmore; Wilber, born May 19, 1903, who married Irma Yolanda Hulquist; and Paul, born October 6, 1911. Wilber is a prominent attorney at Holdrege, (*see Nebraskana*). Paul is a sophomore in the University of Nebraska. Residence: Holdrege. (Photograph in Album).

Fred Marshall Attebury

Fred Marshall Attebury, cattle rancher, was born at Crete, Nebraska, October 13, 1882, son of Willis and Mary Bell (Mausey) Attebury. His ancestry is English and Scotch.

Upon his graduation from Crete High School in 1902, Mr. Attebury attended Doane College for about a year.

He is a registered druggist in Nebraska and Wyoming, and at the present time is a rancher and cattle feeder. He is a Republican, and a 32nd degree Mason.

His marriage to Myrrh Beatrice Hanson was solemnized at Cheyene, Wyoming, September 6, 1907. Mrs. Attebury was born at Sundance, Wyoming, January 1, 1866. They have two children, Mildred, born July 24, 1915; and Ruth, born October 22, 1922. Residence: Mitchell.

Norman Harry Attwood

Norman Harry Attwood, physiologist and anatomist, was born at Omaha, December 23, 1885. He is the son of James and Anna (Hussie) Attwood, the former a native of Toddington, Bedfordshire, England, born November 30, 1851. He was a liverymen and engaged in the retail hardware business with the John Hussie Hardware Company. He came to America in 1867 and located on the Brewster farm at Irvington, Nebraska, later moving to Omaha. He died at Hawthorne, California, January 14, 1931. His wife, Anna Hussie, was born at Chicago, on May 15, 1863. She taught in district school at French Town, Nebraska, and at Neligh, Nebraska. She was also a teacher of art and music in Omaha. Her father was a moulder in the Union Pacific Shops and later engaged in the hardware business in Omaha for 45 years.

Dr. Attwood attended Holy Family School in Omaha, and St. James in Chicago. Later he entered Creighton Preparatory and received his M. D. from Creighton University in 1920. He is a member of Phi Rho Sigma. From 1904-12 he was a salesman for the John Hussie Hardware Company. Since 1920 he has been a practicing physician, and since 1921 professor of physiology at Creighton Dental College. He is also professor of physiology and anatomy at the St. Joseph Hospital School of Nursing, at Omaha.

He was married to May Hyacinth Jacobson at Omaha, on August 7, 1920. Mrs. Attwood was born at Omaha, May 1, 1887. She is of Danish descent. Dr. Attwood served as a private in the medical corps of the Creighton Student Army Training Corps during the World War. He is a member of the American Legion, and a captain in the Reserve Officers of the Medical Corps, and captain medical department detachment 134th Infantry.

He is a Catholic, and a member of the Holy Name Church. He is a member of the Creighton Alumni Association, a member of the staff of St. Joseph's and Lord Lister Hospitals. He belongs to the American Chemical Association, the Woodmen of the World, and The Nebraskana Society. His favorite sport is riding. His hobby is mechanics. Residence: Omaha.

Raymond Harold Atwood

A leading insurance executive, Raymond Harold Atwood was born and reared at Chester, Nebraska. He was born on August 26, 1880, the son of Sydney DeLoss and Alice Julia (Guile) Atwood. His father, born at Lake Mills, Wisconsin, was an early settler in Nebraska, and was a director of school district No. 54 from 1879-80. A merchant, farmer and educator, he was Chester's first schoolmaster. His death occurred at Corvallis, Oregon, May 14, 1924. His wife, who was also born at Lake Mills, on December 10, 1856, is living.

Mr. Atwood attended Chester High School, graduating in 1898, and was graduated from Doane Academy in 1900. In 1906 he was awarded his Bachelor of Arts degree from Nebraska Wesleyan University, where he was a member of Phi Kappa Tau. He was a letterman at Doane in 1900 and at Nebraska Wesleyan in 1906.

During the year 1907 Mr. Atwood was a merchant in Lincoln, and from 1908-09 was a salesman for the Pacific Mutual Life Insurance Company. From 1909 to 1914 he was a merchant at Chambers, Nebraska, and from 1914-28 engaged in the lumber business at Chester. He is secretary at the present time of the Missouri Valley Life Insurance Company of Lincoln, a director of the Citizens Lumber and Supply Company of Chester, and director of the Missouri Valley Life Insurance Company.

Mr. Atwood is a Master Mason, and belongs to Chester Lodge No. 298, and Council No. 79. He is a member of the United Commercial Travelers, a member of the committee of the local Red Cross, and president of the Chester Community Club. His religious affiliation is with the Chester Methodist Church, and at present he is corresponding secretary of the Chester Young Men's Christian Association. He belongs to the Chester Parent Teacher Association and School District No. 54, and was president of the latter, 1927-28.

During the 1916-18 Mr. Atwood was a second lieutenant in the Chester Home Guard, and from 1914-18 was chairman of Minute Men. He is a Republican.

On June 12, 1906, he was united in marriage to Edith Belle Fellers of DeWitt, their marriage being solemnized at Chester. Mrs. Atwood was born March 5, 1884. There are three children, Pauline, born August 16, 1907, who is principal in the public school at Alexandria; Juliet, born March 15, 1910, who is principal in Thayer, Nebraska; and Raedith, born November 30, 1916. Residence: Chester.

Arthur Jay Auble

Arthur Jay Auble, son of William Lewis and Mattie (Peterson) Auble, was born at Ord, Nebraska, March 30, 1889. His father, born at Newton, New Jersey, November 25, 1857. His grandfather served in the Civil War with the Union Army, and was in the band through the entire war. His father, a farmer, was one of the early settlers in Valley County, where he reared a family of five children, giving all of them a common school education.

His wife, Mattie, was born in Barry, Illinois, in July, 1854. A teacher and an old time singing instructor, she is now active in religious work. Her family settled early in Illinois, her father driving an ox team to the coast in 1849, came back across the Isthmus of Panama to New York, where he had his gold coined. A brother served in the Union Army in the Civil War.

Educated in public school, Arthur Jay Auble excelled in pole vaulting and made a broad jump of 19 feet three inches. A farmer until 1907, he was the owner of an orange grove in California, until July, 1908. He studied watch repairing until the spring of 1909, when he opened a jewelry store at Wolbach. This was sold in the spring of 1910, and the next year was spent with a brother on his farm in Winner, South Dakota. In March, 1911, Mr.

Auble purchased back his store at Wolbach. Thereafter he traded that business for a store at Ord, which he operates in association with his brother who is an optician. He and his brother are interested in an all metal marquise, on which they have the patent, which is being made in Hastings.

On February 23, 1914, Mr. Auble was married to Pauline Andrea Hansen, at Grand Island. She was born at Wolbach, December 3, 1894, of Danish parentage. They have three children living, and one deceased: Leota, born May 4, 1916, who is the official piano player in the high school orchestra; Joycelyn, born October 18, 1918, who is first chair flutist; Don, born June 3, 1926; and Jay, Jr., born June 14, 1924, who died in July, 1924.

Mr. Auble is a Republican. He is a Methodist, a Mason, a member of the Chamber of Commerce, the Parent-Teachers' Association, and the Nebraskana Society. He enjoys golf, and is a member of the Ord Golf Club, while his hobby is mechanics. Residence: Ord.

William Auge

William Auge, son of William and Catherine (Kreuchling) Auge, was born at Ponca, Nebraska, May 4, 1875. His father, a native of Germany, was born in September 1843, and came to Nebraska in 1860. He was a hardware merchant and for ten years was president of the Security Bank of Ponca. His death occurred at Ponca, February 18, 1925. Catherine, wife of William Auge, Sr., was born in Germany, and died at Ponca, in March, 1907.

Educated in the public schools, William Auge, the subject of this sketch, was graduated from Ponca High School in 1892. He was the editor of the school paper and active in school affairs.

On September 22, 1897, he was united in marriage to Emma Drazer at Ponca. Mrs. Auge was born at Martinsburg, June 14, 1875. There is one son, Maxwell, born May 1, 1905, who is a college graduate, and attended the University of Chicago two years. He is engaged in the brokerage business, also.

Mr. Auge is a member of the Salem Lutheran Church, the church choir, and the Masons. His sports are golf, tennis and baseball. Residence: Ponca.

Ernest Webster Augustine

Ernest Webster Augustine, son of Irving Milton and Alice Tabitha (Fitzsimons) Augustine, was born at Bruning, Nebraska, September 13, 1886. His father, born at Grantsville, Maryland, December 28, 1862, is one of Grand Island's most outstanding citizens. For a number of years a newspaper publisher, he is now general manager of The Augustine Company (*see Nebraskana*). His mother, who is of Irish descent, was born at Mineral Point, Wisconsin, July 3, 1860.

Educated in the public schools of Grand Island, Ernest Webster Augustine afterward attended Grand Island College. He was co-editor of the *Free Press* from 1908-12, and in 1908, in conjunction with his father, I. M. Augustine, established The Augustine Company, of which he has since been general manager. This organization manufacturers advertising, calendars, specialties, and various lines of specialty printing.

In addition Mr. Augustine is a director of the Commercial Bank of Grand Island. He is a trustee of Grand Island College, was for a number of years a director of the Chamber of Commerce, and is now a director of the Rotary Club. A former vice president of the local Young Men's Christian Association, he was chairman of the building committee at the time the new building was erected. He is a member of the state committee of the Young Men's Christian Association, has been trustee and treasurer of St. Paul's English Lutheran Church for more than twenty years, and is a Mason (Blue Lodge, Chapter, Knight Templar and Shrine).

A member of the Hall County Historical Society, he is a life member of the Nebraskana Society, this recognition having been given him for his participation in civic and community projects over a long period of years. Mr. Augustine is a heavy real estate holder, and in 1925 erected one of the finest homes in the city. He is a member of the Riverside Country Club, and a Democrat.

On June 15, 1910, he was married to Pernelia Mercedes Spethman, at Grand Island. Mrs. Augustine, who is of German descent, was born at North Loup, Nebraska, July 17, 1886. There are three children: Mercedes, born April 12, 1912, who will graduate this year from Ward Belmont, at Nashville, Tennessee; Webster, born September 24, 1918; and Ernest, Jr., born May 29, 1925. Residence: Grand Island.

Irving Milton Augustine

Irving Milton Augustine, for many years one of the most prominent newspaper men in Nebraska, was born at Grantsville, Maryland, December 28, 1861.

He is the son of Isaac Newton and Amanda Jane (Shultz) Augustine, the former a Lutheran minister who at one time published the *Western Independent Lutheran*. Isaac Newton Augustine was born at Petersburg, Pennsylvania, February 9, 1833, and died at Grand Island, on July 2, 1921. His wife, Amanda Jane, was born at Salisbury, Pennsylvania, October 16, 1835, and died at Grand Island, March 18, 1915. A true minister's wife, she was helpful to him in his work. She was of Pennsylvania Dutch descent.

Irving Milton Augustine was graduated from high school at Hebron, Nebraska, in the 1880's, and attended the University of Nebraska one semester. On November 12, 1885, he was married to Alice Tabitha Fitzsimons, at Carleton, Nebraska. Mrs. Augustine, who is of Irish descent, was born at Mineral Point, Wisconsin, July 3, 1861.

To this union five children were born: Ernest Webster, born on September 13, 1886, who married Pernelia Spethman; Olive Dell, born December 7, 1887, unmarried; Raymond Lloyd, born January 17, 1890, who died September 5, 1898; Howard Milton, born January 14, 1892, who married Dorothy Lynn; and Irving DelMar, born November 29, 1897, who married Ruth M. Mayer.

A staunch Democrat, Mr. Augustine was for a number of years the publisher of the *Grand Island Free Press* and the *Daily Republican*, both Democratic, and strong in their support of Democratic principles.

Now retired, Mr. Augustine formerly published the *Bruning Enterprise*, the *Doniphan Eagle*, the *Free Press* and the *Daily Republican*. Upon retiring from the newspaper field Mr. Augustine, with his son, Ernest, founded the Augustine Company, a co-partnership between father and sons, and long recognized as among the strongest and most successful institutions of its kind in the state. He is, in addition to his holdings in the Augustine Company, a stockholder in the Commercial Bank and Building and Loan Association of Grand Island.

Affiliated with St. Paul's Evangelical Lutheran Church, for his fidelity and long efficient service, the congregation elected him as a life member of its council. He is a member of the Chamber of Commerce, the Hall County Historical Association, the Ancient Order of United Workmen and The Nebraskana Society. His social club is the Riverside Golf Club, and his favorite sports are golf and fishing.

The author of several unpublished manuscripts, he devotes much of his leisure time to writing and expects to publish his works. Residence: Grand Island. (Photograph on Page 53).

James W. Auld

James W. Auld, banker, was born in Marion County, Iowa, April 27, 1876, son of Benjamin G. and Mary M. (Schmidt) Auld.

He was educated in the public schools of Iowa, and in 1893 came to Nebraska. Five years later he established his residence at Red Cloud, and became associated

Locke—Grand Island

IRVING MILTON AUGUSTINE

with the State Bank of Red Cloud, which was founded by his uncle, W. T. Auld, in 1892.

On October 4, 1904, he was married to Jessica Cather, a native of Winchester, Virginia, born August 26, 1881. She was a daughter of early pioneers in Webster County. There are three children, Mary Virginia, William Thomas and Charles Cather. Residence: Red Cloud.

James C. Auman

James Auman, a resident of Nebraska all his life, was born in Kent, Stephenson County, Illinois, and at the age of three, moved to Firth, Nebraska. He has been a resident of the same community since that time, and is the son of William and Mary Elizabeth (Ulsh) Auman. His father, who is a retired farmer, was born at Mifflin, Pennsylvania, January 4, 1847. His mother was born at Mifflin, October 20, 1850, and died at Firth, September 16, 1880.

Mr. Auman attended the rural school of Firth, and later was a student at Hohenschut-Carpenter School of Embalming at Des Moines. He has been an undertaker and furniture dealer for many years, and has engaged in the insurance business for some time. He holds membership in the Parent-Teachers' Association, is affiliated with the Firth Presbyterian Church, and is a member of the Nebraskana Society. He is a Republican.

His marriage to Alydia Abbink was solemnized at Lincoln, Nebraska, June 3, 1896. Mrs. Auman, whose ancestry is Holland Dutch, was born at Holland, Nebraska, August 8, 1874. They have a son, Ralph, born August 28, 1904. He is married and has two children, and resides at Firth.

Francis Gideon Auringer

A leader in the business world at Neligh, Nebraska, Francis Gideon Auringer was born at Albion, Iowa, June 24, 1867, the son of Gideon Francis and Sarah (Sawyer) Auringer. His father, who was born in Onandaga County, New York, October 2, 1832, and died at Marshalltown, Iowa, September 19, 1900, was a painter, glazier, and sign painter. He held membership in the Ancient Free and Accepted Masons at Albion. He was one of the first manufacturers of steel barbed wire and was one of a partnership of small-factory men who managed the wire-production. His grandparents came to this country from Holland and settled in New York.

His mother, who was a tailoress and nurse, was born near Lee Center, Illinois, November 24, 1832, and died at Shell Rock, Iowa, January 6, 1909. She devoted most of her time outside of home activities to caring for the sick in her neighborhood and was known throughout her community for her kindness to the poor. She was the daughter of Joseph Sawyer a drum major in the War of 1812. Her three brothers died in the Civil War.

Mr. Auringer was graduated from the high school at Marshalltown, and at the age of 17 entered the monument business as an apprentice engraver and carver. In 1902 he established the Neligh Marble & Granite Works, and in 1912 incorporated as the Elkhorn Monument Company of which he is now president and manager.

He is a member of the Chamber of Commerce, the Memorial Craftsmen of Nebraska, serving as president three terms, Memorial Craftsmen of America, and the Neligh Rotary Club of which he is president. He was a member of the board of governors of the Memorial Craftsmen of America, serving with Supreme Judge Bayard H. Paine of Grand Island, and is a member of the Red Cross and St. Peters Episcopal Church of Neligh.

He is a member of Trowel Lodge of the Ancient Free and Accepted Masons of Neligh, the Modern Woodmen of America, Knights of the Maccabees, Marshalltown, Iowa, and the Cosmopolitan Lodge of the Knights of Pythias of Marshalltown. He organized the first golf

club in his part of the state, and now holds membership in the Antelope Country Club at Neligh.

Mr. Auringer is a director of the Neligh Cemetery Association, is superintendent of Laurel Hill Cemetery, and has given much time and effort toward making the local cemetery beautiful. He devoted a great deal of effort toward the dedication of a large elm tree in Neligh Riverside Park as a living Legion Memorial, and is interested in birds, trees, and flowers.

During the World War he solicited for the Young Men's Christian Association and personally borrowed money in order to buy government bonds. He was the organizer and first president of the Neligh Rotary Club.

His marriage to Mabel Osman occurred at Marshalltown, May 18, 1892. Mrs. Auringer, who was born at Cedar Rapids, Iowa, April 6, 1866, is the daughter of William Clark Osman and Adah Elizabeth (Bardshaw) Osman. She was a charter member of the P. E. O. Chapter at Neligh, is a communicant of St. Peter's Episcopal Church at Neligh, is a member of the Entre Nous Club, and was a charter member of the Order of Eastern Star, at Marshalltown. They have three children: Osman Francis, born January 19, 1895; Marvin William, born August 28, 1896; and Marion Mae, born February 24, 1904.

Osman Francis was graduated from Neligh High School and was graduated from the Auto School at Detroit. He enlisted in the Motor Ambulance Assembly during the World War and served for 17 months in France, stationed at St. Nazaire. He is a member of the Ancient Free and Accepted Masons, is a member of the Episcopal Church, and resides at Marysville, Michigan.

Marvin William was graduated from Neligh High School and the Academy of Fine Arts in Chicago where he studied under Frederick Grant, the noted illustrator. He is now a successful artist in New York City. He is a member of the Ancient Free and Accepted Masons and the Episcopal Church.

Marion Mae, who married C. D. Wood, of Newport, Rhode Island, was graduated from the Neligh High School and the University of Nebraska where she was a member of Chi Omega. She was a charter member of the P. E. O. at Neligh, and is a communicant in the Episcopal Church.

Mr. Auringer is a member of the Republican Party and the Nebraskana Society. He is interested in golf, football, and baseball. Residence: Neligh.

Fuller Luzerne Austin

Born at Hendley, Nebraska, December 8, 1900, Fuller Luzerne Austin is the son of Fuller Arnold and Bertha (Hanning) Austin. His father, who was born at Dwight, Illinois, August 13, 1878, is the owner of the Austin Advertising Company which operates in thirteen states. His ancestry is traced to the New England States prior to 1800. Bertha Hanning Austin was born at Hendley, also, and was a teacher prior to her marriage. Her forebears were among the first settlers in Ohio.

Mr. Austin attended Hendley High School until 1915; was graduated from Lincoln High School in 1917; received his A.B. from Nebraska in 1922 and his M.A. in 1926. During the World War he was a midshipman at the United States Naval Academy 2 years. At the university he was a member of Phi Delta Kappa, Delta Chi, and a member of the advertising staff of the school paper. He was also on the advertising staff of the paper at Annapolis, and secretary of his class.

Since leaving College Mr. Austin has taught in the Waverly High School, been superintendent of schools at Walton, superintendent of city schools at Gordon, assistant state superintendent of schools; and deputy state superintendent of public instruction; which position he now holds. He is the author of *Waste in Educational Expenditure in Nebraska* (1927); co-author of *Nebraska*

State Course of Study on the Harmful Effects of Alcohol (1929) and *State Aid to the Weak Districts* (1930).

On March 23, 1924, he was united in marriage to Wilmanette Love Drummond at Council Bluffs. Mrs. Austin was born in Lincoln, November 23, 1924. They have two children, Jean Marie, born March 2, 1925, and Fuller Arnold, born November 19, 1927. The family attends Vine Congregational Church at Lincoln.

Mr. Austin is a member of the Nebraska State Teachers Association, the Nebraska Schoolmasters Club, the Masons, Eastern Star, and the Elks. Residence: Lincoln.

Otto George Austin

Born at Colton, South Dakota, December 29, 1888, Otto George Austin is the son of Austin Thomas Austin and Anne Christine (Clauson) Austin. His father, who is a farmer, was born at Telemarken, Norway, May 21, 1848. His mother was born at Telemarken, July 26, 1855, and died at Colton, October 26, 1927.

Mr. Austin attended rural school near Colton and was a student at Luther College Preparatory School, Decorah, Iowa. He received the A. B. degree at Luther College in 1912, and was graduated from the Theological Seminary at St. Paul, Minnesota, in 1916. He has been prominent in religious activities for the past 17 years and has held various pastorates, among them: Trinity Lutheran Church at Sisseton, including Peever, Buffalo Lake, Bethel and Norway, South Dakota, 1916-22; Lake Park, and Nunda Lutheran churches at Nunda, South Dakota, 1922-27; and Trinity Lutheran Church, at Newman Grove, Nebraska, 1927, to the present time.

During 1912 and 1913, Mr. Austin taught in the parochial school at Bode, Iowa. He is a member of the National Geographic Society, was executive secretary of the Roberts County Chapter of the Red Cross, and is affiliated with the Norwegian Lutheran Church of America. During the World War he served as a member of the exemption board of Roberts County and was secretary of the local chapter of the Red Cross. His sports are volley ball and tennis

He was married to Esther Lillian Johnson at Vermillion, South Dakota, December 30, 1919. Mrs. Austin, who was born at Vermillion, South Dakota, March 7, 1895, was formerly prominent in educational affairs as a teacher, and is now an active leader in church affairs. She served as president of the Omaha Circuit Women's Missionary Federation of the Norwegian Lutheran Church of America, for a time. Her father, J. E. Johnson, whose ancestry was Swedish, served in the House of Representatives of South Dakota from 1905 to 1907. They have the following children: Arthur Thomas, born June 23, 1921; Margaret Esther, born January 12, 1923; Paul Richard, born March 23, 1925; Dorothy Lucile, born April 6, 1927; and Donald LeRoy, born April 6, 1927. Residence: Newman Grove. (Photograph in Album).

Mary Virgie Avery

Mary V. Avery was born at Ocean View, Sussex County, Delaware, May 9, 1875. Her father, William McClentic Hudson, who was born at Ocean View, July 27, 1845, of English ancestry, has been a bookkeeper, teacher, and farmer. He is an interested church worker and an enthusiastic temperance advocate.

Her mother, Mary Holloway (Hudson) Hudson, who was born at Roxana, Delaware, February 27, 1847, and died at Lincoln, Nebraska, October 4, 1919, was a devoted homemaker. Although her education was elementary she was vitally interested in the education of her children.

Mrs. Avery attended a country school until 1890 when she entered the Humboldt High School, graduating in 1894 and teaching in a country school one year after her graduation. In 1895 she studied at Banks Shorthand University, in Philadelphia. She has attended the Nebraska Wesleyan University, 1920, when her older daughter,

Gladys entered the university, and the University of Arizona, 1926, when her younger daughter, Zola, entered the university and Mrs. Avery needed to change climate for her health.

A farmer's wife, Mrs. Avery has engaged in many civic and social activities. She is president of the county and local W. C. T. U., attending the national convention at Indianapolis in September 1929 as delegate from four counties; district corresponding secretary of the Woman's Home Missionary Society; state secretary of Bequest and Devise; and temperance secretary of the Richardson County Council of Christian Education.

Aside from her home and social duties she has held various business positions, among them; teacher; assistant bookkeeper and stenographer for the Crane Ice Cream Company, Philadelphia; and stenographer and typist for the Humboldt Steam Mills, Humboldt, Nebraska.

On March 25, 1903, she was married to Charles Orlando Avery at Humboldt, Richardson County, Nebraska. Mr. Avery, who was born at Humboldt, August 17, 1868, is descended from English ancestors on the paternal side and from French and Pennsylvania-Dutch settlers through the maternal line. To this union were born three children, two of whom are living: Gladys, born July 9, 1904, a high school teacher, who married Ralph H. Fletcher, high school superintendent; Zola, a graduate of the University of Nebraska, and a teacher of home economics, born September 17, 1909; and Roger, born June 14, 1914, who died June 19, 1914.

Mrs. Avery is a member of the Humboldt Methodist Episcopal Church. Her hobby is reading. She is a Republican but the principles and character of the candidate determine her vote. She has been a resident of Nebraska for forty-seven years. Residence: Humboldt.

Samuel Avery

Samuel Avery, chancellor emeritus and professor of research in chemistry at the University of Nebraska, was born at Lamoille, Illinois, April 19, 1865. He is the son of Stephen B. and Mary T. Avery.

He received his Bachelor of Arts degree at Doane College in 1887, and has since been awarded the following degrees: Bachelor of Science, University of Nebraska, 1892; Master of Arts, 1894; Doctor of Philosophy, Heidelberg, 1896; Doctor of Laws, Doane College and University of Idaho, 1909. He was married to Mary B. Bennett on August 4, 1897.

Dr. Avery was adjunct professor of chemistry, University of Nebraska, 1896-99; professor of chemistry and chemist at the Agricultural Experiment Station, University of Idaho, 1899-1901; professor of analytical and organic chemistry, University of Nebraska, 1901; professor of agricultural chemistry and chemist, University of Nebraska Experiment Station, 1902-05; head professor of chemistry, 1905-08; acting chancellor, 1908-09; chancellor, 1909-27; since 1927 he has been chancellor emeritus.

He was granted a leave of absence during the World War and served as a member and vice chairman of the chemistry committee of the National Research Council and as a major in the chemistry warfare service of the United States Army. He was head of the university relations unit.

Dr. Avery is an honorary member of the Lincoln Chamber of Commerce and Rotary Club. He is a member of Phi Beta Kappa and Sigma Xi and is a Mason. Residence: Lincoln. (Photograph on Page 56).

Willard Sales Avery

Willard S. Avery, farmer and bank executive at Edgar, Nebraska, has lived in Clay County all his life. He was born at Edgar, February 19, 1881, the son of Orin Austin Avery and Rosalie Audelphin (Hoffman) Avery. His father, who was born in Vermont, February 10, 1837, and died at Edgar, October 1, 1911, was a merchant; he served as captain of the Rhode Island

SAMUEL AVERY

Cavalry during the Civil War. His mother was born in Georgia, October 30, 1846, and died at Edgar, May 13, 1929; her ancestry was German and French.

Mr. Avery attended high school at Edgar, graduating in 1900. He is now a farmer and is serving as vice president of the Edgar State Bank. He is vice president of the school board in his community, is affiliated with the Presbyterian Church, and holds membership in the Nebraskana Society. He is a Mason, a member of the Edgar Lodge No. 67, the Scottish Rite and the Shrine at Hastings. His hobby is mechanics. His political affiliation is with the Republican party.

His marriage to Bertha Fay Miller occurred at Hastings, Adams County, Nebraska, January 23, 1909. Mrs. Avery was born at Edgar, March 20, 1889, the daughter of John G. and Jennie L. (Sanborn) Miller. She is a member of the Eastern Star and has held various positions including that of organist, and is also active in the affairs of the Presbyterian Church. Mr. and Mrs. Avery have four children, Lucile Rosalie, born February 9, 1910; Doris Margaret, born August 11, 1912; Jeanette Louise, born September 4, 1915; and Bobbie Jean, born August 21, 1924. Residence: Edgar.

James Andrew Axtell

For the past 40 years James Andrew Axtell has been prominent in the business world at Fairbury, Nebraska. He was born in Athens County, Ohio, January 13, 1870, the son of Daniel Axtell and Hester Delilah (Clark) Axtell. His father, who was a farmer, was born in Mercer County, Pennsylvania, May 30, 1846, and died at Fairbury, July 11, 1914; his French and English ancestors came to America in the early history of the country and served in the Revolution; he was a soldier in the Civil War.

His mother was born in Athens County, Ohio, March 1, 1848, and died at Fairbury, August 29, 1915; her English ancestors settled in Virginia, and later moved to Tennessee and Ohio.

Mr. Axtell attended rural school, was a student in the Fairbury High School, and was graduated from the Beatrice Business College. A Republican, he has taken a prominent part in political affairs in Nebraska for many years. In 1917, 1919, and 1921, he served as a member of the Nebraska legislature, and at this time he is senator from the 17th district. He has taught in the public schools of Nebraska, has been engaged in farming for the past 30 years, and is also a real estate and insurance man. He is affiliated with the Methodist Church and holds membership in The Nebraskana Society.

His marriage to Olive Shepherd was solemnized at Fairbury, June 2, 1897. Mrs. Axtell, who was a teacher before her marriage, was born in Iowa, January 6, 1876. They have one son, Edwin, born January 19, 1912, who was a student at Wesleyan College and later attended the University of Nebraska.

Mr. Axtell is a member of the Modern Woodmen of America, the Independent Order of Odd Fellows, and is a Knight Templar, Scottish Rite Mason, and Shriner. He was a member of the school board at one time and now holds membership in the Chamber of Commerce and the Farmers Union. His favorite sport is golfing. Residence: Fairbury. (Photograph in Album).

Bertha Owings Aydelotte

Bertha O. Aydelotte, one of Nebraska's outstanding musicians and musical educators, was born at Bradshaw, York County, Nebraska, March 22, 1888. Her father, Christopher Owings, who was born in Randolph County, Missouri, November 15, 1847, was a lumber dealer and stockman; he was a soldier in the Civil War. His ancestry was German, Irish and Scotch. He died at Hot Springs, South Dakota, February 1, 1912. Her mother, Barbara Ann (Roller) Owings, whose ancestry was German, was born at Lafayette, Tippecanoe County, In-

diana, January 28, 1852, and died at Lincoln, Lancaster County, Nebraska, October 29, 1929.

Mrs. Aydelotte was graduated from the high school at Bethany, Nebraska. She received her B. M. degree in voice and piano at the University School of Music, and in 1921, was a post graduate student at this institution. She studied with William Shakespeare in Chicago, 1922-23; and in 1926 took a special course in directorship at Chautauqua Lake. Her B.F.A. degree was granted by the University School of Music, 1922. She was elected to membership in Mu Phi Epsilon, honorary musical sorority.

She has organized several musical companies, among them: *Aydelotte Eight; Aydelotte Peppers; Big Four Quartette; Merry Makers Chorus.* She has composed several songs and musical reviews and literary articles. She has been instructor in the University of Nebraska Conservatory of Music since 1921. She was married at Lincoln, June 3, 1904, to George C. Aydelotte. They have one son, Donald, born December 30, 1906.

Since 1917 Mrs. Aydelotte has been Republican committeewoman in her district. She was captain and treasurer of the Red Cross drive during the late war, and was awarded a medal for service to the nation. She is a member of the Women's Relief Corps and A. N. S. W. V. She is a member of the Lincoln Woman's Club and the Nebraska Music Teachers' Association. She was made past matron, 1918-19, and in 1920 grand organist of Grand Chapter of the Order of Eastern Star.

From 1918 to 1920 Mrs. Aydelotte served as president of the Bethany Woman's Club. She is active in Young Women's Christian Association work and has traveled extensively over the United States and Canada in Chautauqua work. She is a member of Bethany Christian Church. She is fond of tennis and golf. Mrs. Aydelotte made one trip to the Panama Canal during the time it was being constructed, with a musical company. Residence: Lincoln.

Herman Aye

For the past 57 years Herman Aye has lived in Nebraska, and since 1895, he has been active in legal practice in this state. He was born at Blair, Washington County, Nebraska, March 29, 1873, the son of Hans and Caroline (Peck) Aye. His father, who was a carpenter and farmer, was born at Schleswig-Holstein, Germany, August 22, 1840, and died at Blair, January 31, 1901. His mother was born at Schleswig-Holstein, July 21, 1948, and died at Blair, February 2, 1924.

Mr. Aye was graduated from the Blair High School. He was admitted to the practice of law at Blair, May, 1895, and has been engaged in general practice since then. He was county attorney of Washington County from 1898-1902.

On January 9, 1902, he was united in marriage with Nellie Elizabeth Haller, Mrs. Aye, whose ancestry is Swiss, was born in Wisconsin, December 24, 1878. They have three children: Catherine E., born March 10, 1904; Frederick, born June 11, 1907; and Miriam V., born July 3, 1911.

From 1895 to 1911, Mr. Aye practiced law in Blair, and since that time has been engaged in practice at Omaha. Residence: Omaha.

Leon Emmons Aylsworth

Leon Emmons Aylsworth, professor of political science at the University of Nebraska, was born at New Berlin, Chenango County, New York, October 26, 1869, the son of Nelson Olin and Mary (Deming) Aylsworth. Nelson Olin Aylsworth, who was a photographer, pharmacist and farmer, was born at Burlington, New York, August 6, 1846, and died at Euclid, New York, on January 21, 1922. He was descended from Arthur Aylsworth, who came to Rhode Island, from the western part of England, near the Welch border, about 1675.

Mary Deming Aylsworth, who was primarily a home

maker, and the mother of fourteen children, was born at New Berlin, July 8, 1850, and died at Syracuse, New York, on October 16, 1926. Her ancestors, who came from England, settled first in Connecticut, and later in New York, and several members of her family were prominent in military and business affairs.

Professor Aylsworth attended school first in New Berlin and later in Roseville, Illinois, and in Clark County, South Dakota. In 1900, he was awarded his Bachelor of Arts degree at the University of Nebraska, and in 1908, received his Master's degree from the University of Wisconsin. Prior thereto, from 1890 to 1893, he was a student at the State College of South Dakota. He is a member of Phi Beta Kappa, elected in 1900.

During the period Professor Aylsworth was engaged in graduate work he held a scholarship and a fellowship in American history. He was first appointed instructor on the faculty of the University of Nebraska in 1904. He was made adjunct professor in 1908, assistant professor in 1909, associate professor in 1910, and professor in 1918. The author of a number of articles, these were published in the *American Political Science Review* from 1908 to 1930 inclusive.

Professor Aylsworth is a member of the American Political Science Association, and has served a term on its executive council. He is also a member of the National Municipal League, the Social Welfare Society of Lincoln (board member several years, chairman of legal aid committee), the Lincoln Chamber of Commerce, and the Open Forum.

On September 25, 1895, he was united in marriage at Watertown, South Dakota, to Bertha May Fraser, who had been a music teacher for several years. Mrs. Aylsworth was born at New Glasgow, Pictou County, Nova Scotia, April 7, 1874. She is of Scotch, English and Pennsylvania Dutch descent. To them were born three children: Carol, born December 26, 1900, who married Franklyn Faye Yearsley; Donald Fraser, born March 2, 1906; and Lloyd Deming, born August 9, 1913.

Carol was graduated from the University of Nebraska in 1923, and while a student there became a member of Delta Delta Delta. For a time she taught at McCook and Lincoln, and served as instructor in the teachers' college at the state university. Donald was graduated from the university in June, 1931, and immediately entered the service of the S. S. Kresge Company at Cincinnati, Ohio.

Professor Aylsworth is a Progressive Republican. He took an active part in the adoption of the initiative and referendum in Nebraska, and the home rule charter in Lincoln; also in the movement for a convention to revise the state constitution. For many years he has taken a keen interest in seeking to promote more efficient and economical administrative organization and financial methods in the municipal affairs of Lincoln. Recently he was elected to life membership in The Nebraskana Society in recognition of his efforts toward the advancement of his community and state. Professor Aylsworth is a member of All Soul's Unitarian Church at Lincoln. Residence: Lincoln. (Photograph in Album).

Frank Jerome Ayres

Frank Jerome Ayres was born at Galva, Illinois, October 1, 1857, son of John Alonzo and Mary B. Ayres. In 1881, the family came to Nebraska.

He attended the Galva public school and high school, and completed a course at the Davenport Business College in 1881. Upon coming to Nebraska, he engaged in farming in Butler County for a time, retiring to engage in the agricultural implement business at Oakdale. Later he returned to David City, where he established a greenhouse and nursery business. Residence: Omaha.

George T. H. Babcock

George T. H. Babcock, attorney at law, was born at London, Ontario, Canada, January 24, 1868, son of Harvey W. and Olive Jane (Laynge) Babcock.

The father was born at Canajoharie, New York, April 23, 1838, and died January 15, 1896. He was an attorney admitted to practice before the supreme court of New York on January 5, 1859. The first Babcock came to America in 1620; four great uncles of Mr. Babcock served in the Revolutionary War. Olive Jane Laynge was of Irish ancestry.

Mr. Babcock obtained his education in public school and under private tutelage. He was admitted to the bar of Nebraska at Rushville, on December 6, 1890, and has since been in active practice. At the present time he is serving as city attorney of Chadron. He has also held the offices of justice of the peace and United States commissioner. He is a Republican.

On September 27, 1899, he was married to Mary Elizabeth Wright at Chadron, Nebraska. She was born at Escanoba, Wisconsin, October 7, 1875, and at the present time is serving as a member of the Chadron Board of Education. Her mother's family came from Pennsylvania, and her father's from Vermont. There are two children, Catherine Jane, born January 2, 1901, who married Robert H. Nelson and has two children; and George Wright, who was born August 4, 1904, is married and has one child.

A Mason for 40 years, Mr. Babcock is a past master of his local lodge. He was the first exalted ruler of Chadron Lodge No. 1399 of the Elks, and is past district deputy grand exalted ruler. He is a member of the Country Club, the Sons of the American Revolution, the Kiwanis Club (charter member) and Grace Episcopal Church (junior warden 25 years). During the late war he was active in all drives, and was vice-chairman of the liberty loan drive and a member of the home guard company. His favorite sport is golf. Residence: Chadron.

John Backer

John Backer, son of Folker and Geraldine (Schuddie) Backer, was born at Jefferson, Nebraska, December 15, 1882. His father, who was born in Germany, March 30, 1852, was engaged in farming and stockraising in Jefferson County until his death at Fairbury, October 1, 1928. His mother is living.

Mr. Backer attended the rural schools of Jefferson County, and has homesteaded most of his life with the exception of a few years in California. He has a stock of cattle, hogs and colts, but feeds most of his grain and all roughage. He enjoys riding, and ranched in Custer County about eight years.

Mr. Backer's religious affiliation is with the Presbyterian Church, and he is an elder of the church at Alexandria. For twelve years he served as a member of the school board, and he is at the present time director of district No. 52. He is an Odd Fellow, and a member of Temple Lodge No. 78.

On September 25, 1912, he was united in marriage to Iona Mertal Cane at Alexandria. Mrs. Backer was born at Alexandria, January 18, 1888. There are seven children, Marcella Iona, born July 18, 1913; Paula Mavis, born January 21, 1915; Doris Gretchen, born December 19, 1917; John Jr., born June 4, 1919; Charles Truman, born April 14, 1924; Lorane, born September 28, 1924; and Ruthalain, born June 7, 1926. Residence: Alexandria.

Fred Bader

Fred Bader, a resident of Nebraska for the past 44 years, was born at Hugsweier, Lahr, Baden, Germany, November 13, 1870, the son of Karl and Karoline (Lieb)

FRED BADER

Skoglund—Fremont

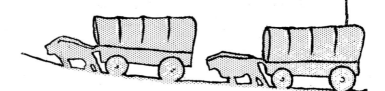

Bader. His father, who was born at Hugsweier, June 4, 1829, and died there November 15, 1912, was tax collector for 47 years and city clerk for 8 years; all his family except him came to America and settled in Nebraska in 1864. His mother was born at Flehingen, Bretten, Baden, Germany, in 1835, and died at Freiburg, Baden, Germany, November 7, 1896. Her mother died when she was still an infant, and she was reared by an uncle.

Mr. Bader attended school in Germany. Starting in the furniture and undertaking business in 1890 with the firm Elsner & Bader, since then he has been a member of the following firms: Bader & Anderson; Bader Brothers Company; Fred Bader Company, and the Fred Bader Funeral Home, Incorporated, of which he is president. He is a director in the Equitable Building & Loan Association, the Union National Bank, the Fremont Hotel Company, and the Chamber of Commerce.

He is a member of the Odd Fellows Temple, the Nebraskana Society, the Red Cross, and the Rotary Club, all of Fremont, Dodge County, Nebraska. He holds membership in the Masons, Odd Fellows (deputy grand master), Knights of Pythias, Rebeccas, and the Eastern Star. He is affiliated with the First Methodist Episcopal Church of Fremont, and is a member of the Young Men's Christian Association. He is a Republican.

On November 20, 1895, he was united in marriage with Laura Cochran at Fremont. Mrs. Bader was born at Ottumwa, Iowa, August 31, 1873. They have two children: Ruth, born November 15, 1896, who attended Northwestern University and was graduated from Van Sant Business College, and who married Mernitz Dewey Jastram; and Marian, born February 17, 1902, who was graduated from Midland College with the A. B. degree, and now teaches in junior high school. Ruth has two children, Rupert Mitchell, six years of age, and Edith Marian who is three.

Mr. Bader attended the Rotary Internationale at Vienna as a delegate in 1931. While in Europe he visited in Germany and traced the Bader family history back to 1660. The church records were destroyed in the ravages of the Thirty Years' War. Residence: Fremont. (Photograph on Page 59).

Lewis Henry Badger

Lewis Henry Badger has resided continuously on the same farm in Fillmore County for the past 63 years, and has taken an important part in the building up of the state and his community. He was born at Piqua, Ohio, October 5, 1856, the son of Henry Lewis and Mary Azubah (Phelps) Badger, both of whom were pioneer settlers in Nebraska. His father, who was born at East Granby, Connecticut, May 26, 1829, and died at Fairmont, Nebraska, July 21, 1905, was a farmer and civil engineer; he was the eighth settler in Fillmore County, helped to organize the county, and was the first county clerk and surveyor. His English ancestors came to America prior to 1640 and were noted as statemen and Revolutionary War soldiers.

His mother was born at Blendon, Ohio, February 1, 1828, and died at Fairmont, January 11, 1894. She completed a college course at Westerville, Ohio, and later taught school in Ohio and Indiana. The Phelps family, which was of English and Scotch descent, settled Dorchester, Massachusetts in 1630, and in 1635 founded the town of Windsor, Connecticut. They helped to make the Blue Laws, and members of the family fought in Colonial and Revolutionary wars.

Mr. Badger attended school in Illinois and in Nebraska in pioneer days. His higher education was gleaned from experience and private study. He has been a farmer and stockraiser for many years and has in recent years modernized and improved the farm he settled in 1868. He is still active in farm work. During the World War he contributed to loan funds and was active in Red Cross affairs; he is a member of the Sons of the American Revolution, and holds membership in

the Masons, Scottish Rite at Lincoln, Mt. Moriah Chapter Number 38 of the Eastern Star, and Hesperian Lodge Number 42 of the Independent Order of Odd Fellows. Mr. Badger is a Republican. His hobbies are relics and guns.

His marriage to Minnie Estell Wies occurred at York, Nebraska, February 27, 1885. Mrs. Badger, who was born at Chillicothe, Ohio, May 26, 1862, was a teacher in the elementary schools in Nebraska and Illinois before her marriage. Of English, Scotch, and German ancestry, she is descended from the Scott family of Virginia; members of the family were active in the Revolution. They have one daughter, Mary Belle, born June 19, 1889, who received the A. B. degree and a teacher's certificate from the University of Nebraska in 1911. Residence: Fairmont.

Byron Howard Baer

Byron Howard Baer, physician at Ashland, Saunders County, Nebraska, has lived in this state all his life. He was born at Omaha, Douglas County, Nebraska, January 18, 1895, the son of Edward Byron and Augusta Louise (Antles) Baer. His father, who was born at Oskaloosa, Mahaska County, Iowa, August 10, 1863, is a retired man; he is Past Master of the Ancient Free and Accepted Masons. His mother, whose ancestry is Scotch and Irish, was born at Mount Union, Henry County, Iowa, September 1, 1872; she is Past Matron of the Order of Eastern Star, and is a member of the P.E.O.

Dr. Baer was graduated from the high school at Stanton, Nebraska, 1914, and in 1919 received his B.S. degree at the University of Nebraska. He was awarded the M.D. degree at the university in 1921; he was active in football in high school, serving as captain of the team for three years and held membership in Phi Delta Theta and Nu Sigma Nu. At this time he is engaged in research work on hay fever and is engaged in general medical practice at Ashland.

He is a member of the American Medical Association, the Nebraska State Medical Association, the Saunders County Medical Society, and the Nebraskana Society. He is chairman of the road committee of the Chamber of Commerce at Ashland, and is affiliated with the Congregational Church there. He is a member of the Masons (Scottish Rite and Shrine), the Boy Scouts, Court of Honor, and the American Legion. He served as a private in the Medical Reserves during the late war.

Dr. Baer is a Republican. He is interested in reading and art, while his sports are angling and hunting. On January 8, 1923, he was married to Mary Augusta Ziegenbein at Omaha, Douglas County, Nebraska. Mrs. Baer was born of German ancestry, at Memphis, Saunders County, Nebraska, June 29, 1896. Their two children are: Mary Jean, born December 15, 1924; and Charles, born August 20, 1928. Residence: Ashland.

Elisha Tarlton Baer

One of Nebraska's distinguished writers and social welfare workers is Elisha Tarlton Baer, who was born at Greensburg, Pennsylvania, May 29, 1872. His father, Philip Snyder Baer, was born at Greensburg, September 13, 1829, and died there November 8, 1906; he was a farmer and served throughout the duration of the Civil War. The first member of the Baer family in this country settled in Lancaster County, Pennsylvania, in 1700, and one ancestor, Philip Steinmetz, served in the Revolution.

His mother, Leah (Steiner) Baer, was born at Greensburg, May 18, 1832, and died there December 12, 1905. She received her education in private German schools, and was descended from ancestors who came to this country in the 18th century.

Mr. Baer attended seminary preparatory school, and was a student at the Iron City Commercial College at Pittsburgh. He entered business with Keystone Coal and Coke Company in 1900, and four years later resigned his position to enter the work of Young Men's Christian Association. He has continued in field work for that organization as general secretary and later secretary of the National Council of New York, until his retirement in recent years. He is the author of a series of verses on various subjects which are being published in serial form at this time.

He is a member of the Rotary Club of Dubuque, Iowa, and a Mason. His affiliation with the Young Men's Christian Association has taken him to Canada, the Philippines, Japan, and the Hawaiian Islands, as well as all over the United States. Mr. Baer's hobby is wood art work, and his outstanding talent is amateur sculpture.

During the World War he was in charge of welfare work among recruits at Camp Funston and helped to organize several finance campaigns. He served with the Tenth Pennsylvania Volunteer Infantry during the Spanish American War. He likes golfing and bowling.

His marriage to Daisy Dale Flesher was solemnized at Greensburg, November 8, 1900. Mrs. Baer, who was born at Weston, Virginia, August 22, 1876, is a member of an old southern family which is descended from Christopher Martin who came to America on the *Mayflower*. They have four children: Arthur MacArthur, born September 12, 1902, who married Henrietta Bartenbach; Elizabeth Leah, born September 14, 1904, who married Loren M. Green; Ida Belle, born June 11, 1907, who married Olie C. Everett; and Kathryn Ann, born August 4, 1916. Arthur owns a cleaning establishment at Grand Island. The three older children received college training. Residence: Grand Island.

Walter Charles Baer

Born at Monroe, Wisconsin, February 11, 1879, Walter Charles Baer is the son of Charles and Anna (Hottinger) Baer. His father was born in Switzerland, coming to America at the age of 19, engaging in the furniture business at York. His death occurred there on July 24, 1923. Anna Hottinger was also born in Switzerland, came to America at the age of three and is still living at York.

Walter C. Baer was a student at York High School; he attended Doane College, where he was a member of the football team; and Western Dental College. On June 25, 1908, he was united in marriage to Bertha Hope Lee at Bellevue, Nebraska.

Mrs. Baer, who was born at Silver Creek, Nebraska, October 4, 1888, is a graduate of Doane College and taught five years at Hastings. She is a direct descendant of Captan Thomas Lee, of Lynn, Connecticut. Her father, Hon. C. H. Lee was a member of the state legislature about 1886. She has resided in Nebraska her entire life, with the exception of five years in Colorado. Mr. and Mrs. Baer have one son, Charles Homer, born September 16, 1914. He is a senior in high school at the present time, is president of the Booster Club, a member of De Molay, the Hi Y and the Congregational Church.

Mr. Baer has lived in Nebraska since he was an infant. During his school days he sold papers, worked in stores, and since he was old enough has been in the furniture business. He is the owner of Baer's Furniture Company at York at the present time. He is a Republican, and for the past eight years has been a member of the York city council.

During the World War he assisted in all relief work, wartime drives, etc. He is a charter member of the Rotary Club, a member of the Chamber of Commerce, (president 1928-29), and the Young Men's Christian Association.

Mr. Baer's religious affiliation is with the First Congregational Church. A Mason, he is a member of the Shrine and Knights Templar bodies. He is also a member of the Odd Fellows and the Knights of Pythias. Mrs. Baer is a member of the Daughters of American Revolution and the Native Sons and Daughters of Nebraska, and is state secretary of the Daughters of American Colonists. Mr. Baer is fond of golf, hunting and fishing, and is a member of the York Country Club. His hobby is reading. Residence: York.

John E. Baggstrom

A resident of Nebraska since September, 1885, John E. Baggstrom, architect, map maker and accountant, was born at Stratford, Iowa, January 10, 1870. His father, Eric Baggstrom, was born at Ljusdahl, Helsingland, Sweden, May 24, 1844. Coming to America in 1866 or 1867, he was the owner of his own homestead and much timberland. He was also a building contractor. His death occurred at Wausa on February 23, 1921.

Ella Olson, wife of Eric Baggstrom, was born in Ofvanaker, Sweden, January 15, 1842, and died at Wausa, on July 14, 1924. She came from a family of Swedish farmers.

John E. Baggstrom attended pioneer country school in Knox County until 1886, and was graduated from Luther College, then Luther Academy in 1898. From 1892 to 1899 he was a school teacher intermittently. From 1898 to 1901 he was in the newspaper business, and was a building contractor from 1901-06. He has practiced architecture as an avocation from 1903 to the present time. From 1906-11 he was bookkeeper for a lumber company, and from 1911-30 was general manager, secretary and treasurer of the Union Telephone Company. He is auditor for the Independent Telephone Company, local treasurer of the Nebraska Central Building and Loan Association and since 1929 has been justice of the peace.

An independent Republican, he has served as township clerk, treasurer and assessor alternately from 1892-1920, was a member of the redistricting committee of the county school 1919-20, and was unsuccessful candidate for county superintendent of schools in 1901.

He was associate editor and founder of the *Wausa Gazette* 1898-1901, and is the author of *The Estimator*, a contractors and carpenters handbook (1902), besides various newspaper and trade paper articles.

On May 6, 1903, he was married to Nelly Anderson at Wausa. She was born in Horja, Skane, Sweden, December 23, 1881. Her family were farmers until the death of her father, when her mother operated a coffee shop.

There are five children, Carl O., born February 13, 1904, who operates an electrical shop; Lilly Althea, born July 19, 1905, who married Carl J. Swanson; Mildred Geneva, born May 12, 1907, who married Rudolph Peterson; Vivian Lucile, born July 31, 1909, who married Emil Shalander; and Dorice Evangeline, born April 7, 1916. She is a junior in high school and the first girl in Wausa to receive a state award in athletics.

Mr. Baggstrom is a member of Tabor Evangelical Lutheran Church, the Wausa Improvement Club (president 1929-30), treasurer of the board of education, 1927-; and a member of the board of directors of Luther College, 1929-31. Since 1925 he has been secretary of his church, since 1931 a trustee, and from 1924-28 was Sunday School superintendent. He was a member of the board of directors of the Nebraska Telephone Association 1926-29. He is a life member of The Nebraskana Society.

His favorite sports are hiking, hunting and fishing, while his hobbies are drawing maps, plats, and plots, reading, landscaping, and planting. Residence: Wausa.

E. PRESTON BAILEY

Day—Hebron

E. Preston Bailey

E. Preston Bailey, retired merchant, farmer and legislator, was born at Carleton, Nebraska, November 11, 1884, son of George Washington, and Saphrona Naomi (Lindsley) Bailey.

George Washington Bailey was born at Circleville, Ohio, February 24, 1847, and served as a drummer boy in the Illinois Infantry during the Civil War for 18 months. He was later a prominent farmer and stockman in Nebraska, and died at Carleton, April 14, 1925. His family moved from northern England to Ireland, and came to America about 1624.

Saphrona Naomi Lindsley was born at Versailles, Kentucky, December 9, 1857, and died at Carleton, June 24, 1916. She was a member of the Order of Eastern Star. Her family came from France with the first settlement in Louisiana. They were Hugenots.

Upon his graduation from Carleton High School, Mr. Bailey entered the University of Nebraska, where he was a student 1908, 1909, and 1910. He was graduated from the following courses at Northwestern University; telegraphy, commercial law, business, and civil engineering. While at Northwestern, he was a member of the football and baseball teams. An Independent Republican, Mr. Bailey opposed Byron Young, in 1912, for county clerk on the Bull Moose ticket, but withdrew in Young's favor after the primaries. He was legislator in Dakota one term, and in Nebraska, four terms. While a member of the legislature in 1923, Mr. Bailey was the author of the Reciprocal School Law, and also the Bovine Tuberculosis Eradication on the Area Plan. During this term he was secretary of both Roads and Bridges and the Railroad Committees. In 1925 he was the author of the Revised Motor Vehicle Laws; introduced and sponsored the first gasoline tax bill in Nebraska; was chairman of the Roads and Bridge Committee; member of the Claims and Deficiencies Committee and Rules and Regulations Committee. In the 1927 session he held the chairmanship of Committee on Committees, which is the highest chairmanship of the legislature. He was also chairman of the house Republican organization, chairman of the Committee on Miscellaneous Subjects, member of Finance Ways and Means Committee, Rules and Regulations Committee and named as chairman of the Committee to ascertain the amount of the State's deficit, and to draft legislation which would prevent a re-occurence of same.

In the 1929 session he was floor leader of the legislature, and served on various important committees. He introduced legislation which abolished the Guaranty Fund Commission. While serving in the legislature he was successful in designating highways known as Wheat Growers Highway and the Golden Rod Highway as state highways, and also was successful in seeing Thayer County's graveling projects fully completed. Through his efforts Thayer County was the first tubercular free area in the State of Nebraska. He placed the first state fish hatchery in Thayer County in 1929.

He was chiefly instrumental in getting through the legislature the legislation which authorized the first state park in Nebraska, at Nebraska City.

He was a road overseer four years, a deputy county clerk of Dakota one year, and was precinct assessor in Nebraska six years. From 1924 to 1928 he was superintendent of advertising of the Republican State Committee. He is a farmer and is associated with the Farmers Elevator Company at Carleton.

On July 18, 1917, he was married to Winifred A. Roberts at Springfield, Nebraska. Mrs. Bailey was born at Springfield, April 13, 1886, the daughter of William and Martha Ann (Jones) Roberts, and was formerly a school teacher. She received her A. B. from Peru Normal College, and held a life certificate. They have three children, Arlene Winifred, born June 14, 1920; E. Preston, born November 20, 1922; and Eileen Rose, born April 14, 1927.

From 1908 until 1912 Mr. Bailey was a member of the United States Reserves. He held the rank of first lieutenant in the home guard at Carleton, 1918-19, and still holds his commission issued by Governor Neville. He was a member of Liberty loan drives and active in Red Cross work in Thayer County during the war. He is a member of the United Brethren Church, the Red Cross, the Young Men's Christian Association, the Chamber of Commerce, and the Community Club of which he is president. He is past master of Gavel Lodge No. 199 of the Masons and a Modern Woodman of America. For 16 years, continuously, he served on the school board at Carleton. He is a member of the state library commission, a member of the University Club, and the Yellow Dogs. His favorite sports are football and baseball, while his hobbies are reading and mechanics. Residence: Carleton. (Photograph on Page 62).

Orestus Andrew Bailey

Orestus A. Bailey was born at Fort Ann, Washington County, New York, October 31, 1861. His father, Lyman Randolph Bailey, who was born at Fort Ann, June 17, 1839, and died at Wenatchee, Washington, was a carpenter and farmer. His ancestry was English.

Mary (Hicks) Bailey, mother of Orestus Bailey, was born at Whitehall, New York, of Irish parents, and died at Akron, Summit County, Ohio, January 8, 1872.

Mr. Bailey, who is a lumber dealer at Crab Orchard, Nebraska, has lived in this state for 53 years. During the World War he was a member of the Johnson County Draft Board. He is a member of the Methodist Episcopal Church of Crab Orchard; the Red Cross; and the Modern Woodmen of America. He is a Republican.

He was married to Harriet Elizabeth Myers at Tecumseh, Nebraska, November 27, 1884. Mrs. Bailey, was born August 8, 1866, and is of Pennsylvania Dutch descent. They have two children: Harriet, born July 21, 1887, who is married to Robert R. Smith; and Carl C., born November 8, 1889, who married Mamie Platt. Residence: Crab Orchard.

Sam Meyer Bailin

Born in Russia, May 10, 1891, Sam Meyer Bailin has lived in Nebraska for the past twenty-one years. He is the son of Meyer and Sonia (Baron) Bailin, the former born in Russia in 1851 and the latter in 1854. Sam M. Bailin attended public school, and on October 19, 1920, was married to Julia Krueger at Sioux City. She was born in Russia, August 15, 1895. They have two children, Larraine, born September 4, 1922; and Willard, born March 22, 1924.

Mr. Bailin is engaged in the general mercantile business at Atkinson. He is a Republican. During the World War he held the rank of first sergeant of Infantry, and for a number of years he has been a member of the American Legion. His favorite recreation is reading. Residence: Atkinson.

Wilfred Wesley Bainbridge

Born at Waverly, Nebraska, March 3, 1875, Wilfred W. Bainbridge has been a prominent farmer in Lancaster County for a number of years. He is the son of Matthew Bainbridge, who was born in Thirlby, Yorkshire, England, June 12, 1847, and who was an early Nebraska farmer. He died at Waverly, September 22, 1929. Anne Lowdon, wife of Matthew Bainbridge, was born in Huntstanworth, Durham, England, October 28, 1846, and died at Waverly on March 16, 1921.

Wilfred W. Bainbridge attended the Camp Creek school in District No. 23, and later attended Lincoln Business College, from which he was graduated on March 7, 1895. He has since been engaged in farming.

On December 28, 1899, he was united in marriage to Olive Mary Mocroft at Waverly. Mrs. Bainbridge, who is of English descent, was born at Neponset, Illinois, September 16, 1877. There is one daughter, Lena Charlotte, born August 3, 1902. Lena was graduated from the University of Nebraska in 1925 and is married to Carroll Lynn Carter. Mr. Carter is manager of the Carter Oil Company at Waverly.

Mr. Bainbridge is a Republican. A Mason, he is affiliated with Unity Lodge No. 163, at Greenwood, Nebraska. He is a member of the Waverly Methodist Church and of the Waverly Farmers Club. Residence: Waverly.

Claire James Baird

Claire James Baird was born at Carthage, Hancock County, Illinois, December 17, 1878, the son of William and Sarah Maria (Allison) Baird. His father, who was a lawyer, was born in Hancock County, in July, 1848, and died at Omaha, Douglas County, Nebraska, July 22, 1923. His ancestry was Scotch. His mother was born in Warren County, Illinois, December 27, 1848, of Scotch and Irish descent.

Mr. Baird received his early education in the public schools at Carthage, and in Omaha, where he was graduated from high school. From 1896 to 1898 he was a student at Monmouth College, Monmouth, Illinois; and from 1900 to 1902 he attended the University of Nebraska Law School. He was made a member of Phi Kappa Psi and Phi Delta Phi.

A resident of Nebraska for 43 years, Mr. Baird has been a member of the firm William Baird and Sons, for many years. He was united in marriage with Adele Louise McHugh at Omaha, September 9, 1908. Mrs. Baird was born at Galena, Jo Daviess County, Illinois, February 10, 1888. They have four children: Barbara Caroline, born October 22, 1909, who married Richard Wagner; William James, born November 22, 1912; Janet, born April 25, 1916; and Adele Louise, born April 7, 1920.

Mr. Baird is a member of the Nebraska State Bar Association and the Douglas County Bar Association. He is a member of the Omaha Chamber of Commerce, and is affiliated with the First Presbyterian Church at Omaha. He is a member of the Omaha Club, the Omaha Country Club, and the Omaha Athletic Club. He is a Republican. Residence: Omaha.

Allen Crowell Baker

Allen Crowell Baker was born at Hawley, Franklin County, Massachusetts, February 8, 1840. Harvey Baker, his father, who was born at Hawley, April 30, 1803, and died there February 14, 1874, was a mechanic and contractor. Edward Baker, an English ancestor arrived in Boston, in 1630, with the large fleet under Governor Winthrop.

Ann Eliza (Carter) Baker, mother of Allen, was born at Hawley, and died at Charlemont, Franklin County, Massachusetts, in February, 1886. She was the daughter of Thomas Carter.

Mr. Baker was educated in the Massachusetts public schools, studying the work now included in the high school course. For fifty-one years he has lived in Nebraska, where he has been an investor of eastern money in mortgages on Nebraska farms, and has engaged in farming and stock raising.

His marriage to Margaret Deborah Taylor was solemnized at East Charlemont, Massachusetts, April 7, 1867. Mrs. Baker, who was born at Rives, Michigan, December 12, 1845, and died at Tecumseh, Johnson County, Nebraska, July 21, 1926, was a teacher and a graduate of the State Normal School at Westhill, Massachusetts. Her ancestors received a grant of 1000 acres of land from the king, early in American history. Residence: Tecumseh.

Alva Avery Baker

A leading farmer of Knox County, Nebraska, Alva Avery Baker has been a resident of that vicinity for the past 47 years. He was born at Greenville, Pennsylvania, June 22, 1860, the son of John Henry and Melissa Melinda (Gelvin) Baker. The former a farmer was born at Greenville, April 6, 1836, and died there, June 16, 1919. His mother, who was always active in church affairs, was born at Kennard, Pennsylvania, March 9, 1837, and died at Greenville, September 4, 1912.

Mr. Baker attended Linn School, and in 1878 was graduated from the Greenville High School. In 1883 he was graduated from Edinboro State Normal College where he was a member of the Potter Society. A Republican, he served as county assessor of Knox County from 1903 to 1907, was state representative from 1919 to 1921, and served as school director from 1893 to 1929. He was a teacher in the public schools of Knox County for 25 years, served as township assessor at Verdigre for seven years, and is now a successful farmer near that community.

He is affiliated with the Methodist Church, holds membership in the Modern Woodmen of America, and the Nebraskana Society. His chief recreation is reading.

Of his marriage to Nellie Abigail Ayers, which occurred at Manning, Nebraska, July 12, 1891, five children were born: Niles, August 23, 1892; Almie, June 18, 1896, who died March 22, 1898; Walker, April 7, 1900, who died January 12, 1902; Nelliebee, September 13, 1903, who married Richard Dean McMillan; and Helen, July 27, 1909.

Mrs. Baker, who was a teacher for a number of years before her marriage, was born at Necedah, Wisconsin, February 26, 1871. Residence: Winetoon.

Benjamin S. Baker

Benjamin S. Baker, lawyer and judge, was born at Sabula, Jackson County, Iowa, February 8, 1850, son of Samuel and Elizabeth (Lewis) Baker.

He received his education in the public schools of Iowa, and received the Bachelor of Didactics and the Bachelor of Laws degrees from Iowa State College.

He was married to Myrtle I. Carroll at Omaha on April 7, 1897.

Admitted to the practice of law in 1874, Judge Baker has been active in practice in Omaha for more than forty years. He has served as a member of the Nebraska Legislature and judge of the District Court, and for some time was judge of the Supreme Court of New Mexico.

Judge Baker enjoys the reputation of being a strong advocate at the bar, popular among his legal brothers and members of the bench. He is a member of the Nebraska State and Omaha Bar Associations, the Chamber of Commerce, the Elks and the Masons. Residence: Omaha.

Chris Baker

Born in the Netherlands, April 7, 1877, Chris Baker has lived in Nebraska for the past thirty-one years. He is the son of Henry Baker, born April 13, 1828, and Sophia Christina (Koster) Baker, born August 5, 1834. Both were natives of the Netherlands.

Henry Baker came to America in 1900. He died in Panama, Lancaster County, Nebraska, on December 28, 1908, and his wife died in Lancaster County.

Chris Baker received his education in his native country. On November 4, 1903, at Firth, Nebraska, he married Johanna Cornelia Kommers whose ancestors were Hollanders. She was born in Firth, Nebraska, August 23, 1883. They have three children: Henry, born July 8, 1905, Abram, born August 17, 1907, and Clarence, born October 26, 1911. Henry is editor of the Summerfield, Kansas, *Sun*.

For three years, during the World War period Mr. Baker was engaged as a slum worker in Chicago, Illinois. He was engaged in general business for twenty years and at present is editor of *The Liberty Journal*. Mr. Baker and his three sons are all fine musicians. He has been leader of bands and orchestras at Panama, Firth and Pella, Nebraska, and organist or pianist in numerous churches of Nebraska. He and his three sons form a male quartette and have often sung at churches and civic occasions.

He is a Republican, belongs to the Nebraskana Society and is affiliated with the Dutch Reformed Church. Residence: Liberty.

Clement Guy Baker

Born at Tilden, Nebraska, April 18, 1886, Clement Guy Baker is the son of Byron Henry and Lanta (Hyatt) Baker. His father, who was a farmer and auctioneer, was born at Burlington, Iowa, December 7, 1852, and died at Tilden, February 21, 1915. His mother, who was a teacher and clubwoman, was born at Peru, Iowa, January 28, 1853, and died at Norfolk, Nebraska, December 26, 1919; she was an active worker in the Methodist Church and the Rebekah Lodge.

Mr. Baker attended a rural school in Madison County, Nebraska, until 1902, and in 1905 was graduated from the Tilden High School. He was a student at Lincoln Business College in 1907 and 1908, and attended the Nebraska State Agricultural College, 1909-1910, where he was awarded honors in dramatics. He took part in dramatic events in high school and served as president of his class for three years.

Since 1910 Mr. Baker has been a stockman, farmer, and auctioneer near Tilden. He is a member of the Farm Bureau, the Farmers Union, the Meadow Grove Community Club, and the Red Cross at Tilden. He served as director of the school board at Tilden from 1916 to 1928, has been superintendent of the Sunday School in the Methodist Church since 1923, and during 1907 and 1908 was a member of the Young Men's Christian Association.

His fraternal organizations include the Odd Fellows Lodge; Masons; and the Royal Highlanders. Mr. Baker's hobby is reading, and his sports include hunting and fishing.

On August 14, 1913, he married Eva May Nelson at Elgin, Nebraska, Mrs. Baker, who was born at Tilden, July 24, 1885, is active in various civic organizations at Tilden, including the Woman's Club, Rebekah Lodge, and the Methodist Sunday School. Her parents, who were natives of Sweden, came to the United States in the middle of the 19th century. They have three children: Lucile Evelyn, born August 6, 1914; Marjorie Helen, born July 29, 1916; and Claudia, born June 21, 1918. Residence: Tilden.

John Samuel Baker

Born of early pioneers in the middlewest, John Samuel Baker has been successfully engaged in farming in Brown County, Nebraska, for many years. He was born near Clarks, Nebraska, February 28, 1876, the son of Samuel and Isabell (Headley) Baker, the former a farmer who settled in Brown County in 1884. His father's ancestry was English and Scotch; he served during the Civil War in the 149th Infantry of the Union Army. His mother, an active Sunday School worker in her younger days, was born in Ohio, October 1, 1848, the daughter of early settlers in Ohio, whose ancestry was English.

Mr. Baker has served on various election boards and school boards at Ainsworth, and has taken a prominent part in the civic affairs of his community. He is a Republican, holds membership in the Nebraskana Society, and is a member of the Modern Woodmen of America. His chief recreations are hunting and reading. During the Spanish-American War, Mr. Baker enlisted in the United States Army, but was not called into active service.

His marriage to Mary Elizabeth Scattergood was solemnized at Johnstown, Nebraska, February 8, 1899. Mrs. Baker, a teacher and musician, was born at Hednesford, England, September 15, 1875, and is descended from the Scattergood and Blake families of Burton-on-Trent, England. To their marriage these children were born: Geneva C., November 27, 1899, who married Charles Leslie Cleal; Marjorie I., February 11, 1901, who married Emil F. Kurpjuweit; and Ruth Mabel, August 29, 1902, who died August 5, 1909. Geneva is a dressmaker and milliner and Marjorie is a nurse. Residence: Ainsworth.

Kenneth Charles Baker

Kenneth Charles Baker, physician and surgeon, was born at Austin, Pennsylvania, April 11, 1901, son of Fred M. and Nellie Mae (Hyde) Baker. The father, an architect and mechanical engineer, was born at Malone, New York, August 26, 1866, and died at Omaha, December 15, 1916. His ancestry was English.

Nellie Mae Hyde was born at Sandusky, New York, December 29, 1878. She is active in church work and holds various offices in the Order of Eastern Star. Her English ancestry is traced to the Puritans of Massachussetts in 1620.

Dr. Baker attended the Omaha Grade School and in 1920 was graduated from the Omaha Central High School. He received the Bachelor of Arts degree from the University of Omaha, 1924, the Bachelor of Science degree from the University of Nebraska, 1926, and the medical degree at the University of Nebraska in 1928. He served as president of his class for two years in the University of Omaha, acting also as athletic manager there, and as athletic manager at the University of Nebraska in 1928. He served as president of Nu Sigma Nu in 1927.

He served his internship at the University Hospital at Omaha from October, 1928, until February, 1930, and since the latter date has been associated in practice with Dr. F. A. Brewster of Holdrege, Nebraska. Dr. Baker is a Republican.

His marriage to Anne Catherine Titus was solemnized at Holdrege, April 4, 1931. Mrs. Baker, whose English and Swedish ancestors helped to settle Holdrege in 1885, was born there April 15, 1910.

Dr. Baker is a member of the First Presbyterian Church of Holdrege, St. John's Lodge of the Masons at Omaha, the Holdrege Chamber of Commerce and the Holdrege Country Club. He is president of the Phelps County Medical Society, 1932, and holds membership in the American Medical Association. His sports include swimming, canoeing, and golfing, while his hobby is etching. Residence: Holdrege.

Ralph A. Baker

Ralph A. Baker, chairman of the board of county commissioners in Cherry County, has been a resident of Valentine for a number of years. He is married to Mary G. Cole, manager of a ladies apparel shop in Valentine, and has the following children, Cole Dale, born February 3, 1922; and Geneva Joyce, born October 16, 1926.

Mr. Baker served in the American Expeditionary Forces during the World War. Residence: Valentine.

Robert Arthur Baker

Robert Arthur Baker, a lawyer at Ainsworth, Nebraska, was born in Hammond County, Iowa, April 16, 1884, and for the past 45 years has been a resident of this state. His father, Edward R. Baker, who is a merchant, was born in Iowa, as was Mary E. (Ballard) Baker, his wife.

Mr. Baker attended a public school at Inman, Nebraska, was a railroad telegrapher and agent from 1902 to 1914, served as deputy treasurer of Holt County, Nebraska, from 1915 to 1917, and was bank cashier from 1918 to 1923. He acted as county judge of Brown County from 1923 to 1929, and since 1929, has been engaged in his own law practice at Ainsworth.

He has been a member of the Red Cross for a number of years, was secretary of the board of education at Ainsworth from 1924 to 1928, and holds membership in the Chamber of Commerce and the Nebraska State Bar Association. His sports are fishing, hunting, and nature study. During the World War Mr. Baker was active in loan drives, and served as legal advisor during the draft period, receiving a medal for service.

His marriage to Laurel Helen Wolfe occurred at O'Neill, Nebraska, March 8, 1905. Mrs. Baker was born in Holt County, Nebraska, August 11, 1883. They have three children: Walter, born April 20, 1907, who married Bettie McCracken; Evelyn, born January 3, 1909; and Raymond, born May 9, 1919. Residence: Ainsworth.

Russell McKelvy Baker

Russell McKelvy Baker, editor and author, was born at Omaha, Nebraska, June 6, 1890, the daughter of Russell Errett McKelvy and Blanche Katherine (Louis) McKelvy. Her father, who was born at Pittsburg, Pennsylvania, September 8, 1854, and died at Omaha, October 19, 1915, was an insurance man. During his college days he was active in athletics and was the first president of the Alpha Chapter of Delta Tau Delta, at Meadville, Pennsylvania. He was descended from Lieutenant John Swisshelm, who served with General Washington at Valley Forge in the Revolution, and John Wonderlich and Melchoir Miller, other Revolutionary War soldiers.

Her mother, who was born at Pittsburg, April 28, 1856, is a distinguished newspaper woman and clubwoman. She is descended from Major Isaac Sadler, 1760-1816, through a long line of soldiers, ministers, and newspaper men.

Mrs. Baker received her elementary education in the public schools of Omaha, and was graduated from the Central High School in 1907. In 1909 she was graduated from the Teachers Training School of Omaha, and for a time was kindergarten teacher in the Webster and Edward Rosewater schools in Omaha.

A life time resident of Omaha, she has taken an active part in the professional world for many years. From 1909 to 1911 she was club and society editor of the Omaha *World Herald*, and at the same time was editor of the *Woman's Page* on this paper. She has written many poems published in school publications and in the *World Herald*.

Perhaps her greatest achievement was the originating of the famous Flag film trailers of which she is the author. These films are produced under the direction of the Daughters of the American Revolution in Nebraska, and depict the historic facts concerning the origin of Flag Day. They are shown in movie houses throughout the country. Mrs. Baker broadcasts this and other information from the Woodmen of the World Radio Station each Flag Day.

Her marriage to Frank W. Baker was solemnized in 1910. Mr. Baker was born in London, September 2, 1887. There are three children: Frank Russell, born May 30, 1911; Frederick McKelvy, born February 23, 1918; and Marjorie Phyllis, born February 9, 1922. Frank Russell is a student at the Municipal University of Omaha, where he is majoring in English and Spanish. He has done a great deal of dramatic work with the Community Playhouse and has contributed several poems to the school papers.

During the recent war Mrs. Baker sold Liberty bonds in the third loan drive and took part in various other war activities. She is Past Regent of the Major Isaac Sadler Chapter of the Daughters of the American Revolution and has served as secretary of the state society in this organization. She is now national vice chairman of the better films committee. She is a member of the Red Cross, the Nebraskana Society, and the Dundee Parent-Teachers' Association. She is affiliated with All Saint's Episcopal Church at Omaha. Her hobby is patriotic education. She is a Republican. Residence: Omaha.

William Hillary Baker

Born at Owensboro, Kentucky, August 19, 1894, William Hillary Baker is the son of George Henry and Rebecka (Bell) Baker. His father, who was born at Indianapolis, Indiana, June 16, 1856, and died at Owensboro, October 31, 1929, was a farmer and tobacco grower; he was a leader in all community activities. Of Scotch-English ancestry, he was descended from a family which settled in Virginia, prior to 1700. Rebecka (Bell) Baker, whose Irish and English ancestors settled in Virginia, in 1700, was born at Owensboro, August 22, 1859. She is still living.

Dr. Baker received his early education in a rural school in Daviess County, Kentucky, was graduated from Kentucky Wesleyan Academy in 1914, and in 1918 awarded the degree of Doctor of Osteopathy at Kirksville College of Osteopathy and Surgery at Kirksville, Missouri. He took a post graduate course at the latter institution in 1920.

His marriage to Alma Zoe Stookey was solemnized at Owensboro, December 5, 1919. Mrs. Baker, who was born at Colchester, Illinois, August 16, 1899, is descended from early settlers who moved from Pennsylvania, to Illinois, in the early history of this country.

Dr. Baker served his internship at Bush Sanitarium, at Louisville, Kentucky, and since 1922, has been actively engaged in his practice at Aurora, Nebraska. He is prominent in civic affairs in Hamilton County, and holds membership in the following professional and community organizations: American Osteopathic Association; Nebraska Osteopathic Association, of which he is president, board of the local Red Cross, Aurora Business Men's Club, of which he was formerly president, Aurora chapter of the Masons, and the Nebraskana Society.

He served as vice president of the Nebraska Osteopathic Association, 1930-31, has been a member of the Aurora Rotary Club since 1924, serving as treasurer in 1926 and 1928, and chairman of the boys' committee, 1924-25. At this time he is president of the Rotary Club. His hobby is service to his community.

During the World War, Dr. Baker was engaged in first aid work in France, Belgium, and Germany, stationed at Field Hospital Section, 114th Sanitary Train, 39th Division. He was commander of the American Legion in 1924, and has been chairman of a committee each year since then. Dr. Baker is a Republican. His favorite sport is football. Residence: Aurora. (Photograph in Album).

Waid E. Balcom

Waid E. Balcom, lawyer, was born in Trego County, Kansas, March 24, 1892, son of Ira G. and Cora (Greene) Balcom. The father was born and reared in Ohio, and as a young man took up a homestead in Trego County. He came to Kearney in 1921.

Mr. Balcom received his early education in the public schools of Arkansas and afterwards attended the Nebraska State Normal School and Teachers College at Kearney. In 1922 he was graduated from the law department of the University of Chicago. During the late war Mr. Balcom was a radio electrician in the United States Navy, serving on the ship *Ireland*.

Mr. Balcom is a Democrat, a member of the American Legion and the Odd Fellows. In 1925 Mr. Balcom was elected City Attorney of Kearney.

He was married to Helen Macauley at Denver. Mrs. Balcom is the daughter of Mr. and Mrs. William R. Macauley, prominent pioneers of Kearney. Mrs. Balcom attended Nebraska State Teachers College at Kearney, where she received the Bachelor of Arts degree, and prior to her marriage was a teacher. Residence: Kearney.

Chloe Christina Baldridge

Chloe Christina Baldridge, educator, and school executive of Lincoln, has lived all her life in the state and has taken a prominent part in the advancement of education. She was born at Fullerton, Nebraska, the daughter of Salem D. and Rachel Ann (Summerville) Baldridge. Her father, a farmer, was born at Irvington, Illinois, March 31, 1863, and died at Fullerton, December 8, 1915; he was the son of John P. and Jane (Janes) Baldridge of Rutherford County, North Carolina; the family was originally English.

Her mother, who was born at Sparta, Illinois, April 22, 1866, was a teacher before her marriage; she is the daughter of Mr. and Mrs. Samuel Summerville who migrated from Ireland to Scotland, and later moved to Randolph County.

Miss Baldridge was graduated from the Fullerton High School; received her A.B. degree from Nebraska Wesleyan University; and her M.A. from the University of Nebraska in August, 1931. She was valedictorian of her high school graduating class and in college was elected to membership in Pi Lambda Theta and Pi Gamma Mu. She has always been intensely interested in education and has devoted her life to various phases of school work. She has held the following positions: rural school teacher; city school teacher; county superintendent of Nance County, 1915-24; director of rural education at the Peru State Teachers' College, Peru, Nebraska, 1924-27; and since 1927 director of rural education, state department of public instruction.

Miss Baldridge is the author of the following: *Rural School Standards Bulletin; Rural and Village High School Bulletin; and Program Discussion Material Bulletin for Nebraska Rural Parent Teachers Associations.* She acted as general chairman for the revision of the Nebraska Elementary Course of Study.

Her membership in professional organizations includes: life membership in the National Educational Association, of which she was a member of the executive committee of the rural department, 1923-26; Nebraska State Teachers Association; and life member of the National Congress of Parents and Teachers. She served as county chairman of the Junior Red Cross of Nance County, 1917-24; and was district chairman of this organization, 1917-24. From 1922-28 she was first vice president, and second vice president of the Nebraska Parent-Teachers Association, and organized the first County Council of the Parent Teachers Association in Nebraska. From 1913-18 she was president of the 7th District of Christian Endeavor, and is now a member of the Fullerton Presbyterian Church. Miss Baldridge holds membership in the Altrusa Club at Lincoln. Residence: Lincoln.

Howard Malcolm Baldrige

Son of one of Omaha's foremost lawyers, Howard Malcolm Baldrige was born in Omaha, June 23, 1894. His father, Howard Hammond Baldrige, was born in Pennsylvania, in June, 1864, and at the time of his death at Miami Beach, Florida, in May, 1928, was one of the leading members of the Omaha bar. He was married to Letitia Blanche Coffey, who is still living.

Howard Malcolm Baldrige was graduated from the Omaha High School, and received his A. B. from Yale University. He entered the University of Nebraska and was awarded his LL. B. at that university. He is a member of Psi Upsilon and was a letterman in football at Yale. Since his admission to the bar in 1921 he has engaged in active practice. He was elected to the state legislature on the Republican ticket and served as a delegate to the Republican national conventions of 1924 and 1928. He was elected to the United States congress for the term 1931-33, at the last election.

On November 30, 1921, he was married to Regina Katherine Connell at Omaha. Mrs. Baldrige was born at Omaha, September 23, 1896. They have three children, Howard Malcolm, Jr., born October 4, 1922; Robert, born November 9, 1924, and Letitia Katherine, born February 9, 1926.

During the World War Mr. Baldrige was a captain of Field Artillery and served overseas. He is a member of the American Legion and the Veterans of Foreign Wars. He is an Elk and a Mason, a member of the Kiwanis Club, the Chamber of Commerce, and the Young Men's Christian Association. He attends the First Baptist Church of Omaha. Residence: Omaha.

Ferman A. Baldwin

Ferman A. Baldwin was born at South Bend, Indiana, May 19, 1872, the son of William Henry and Emma Jane (Gulick) Baldwin. His father, who was a merchant, was born of English and German parents at Granger, Indiana. His mother was born of English and German parents at Harrisburg, Pennsylvania.

Mr. Baldwin was graduated from the Ainsworth High School, and for over 40 years has engaged in banking and the mercantile business at Ainsworth where he is a member of the Game Forestration Parks Commission. He is a member of the Chamber of Commerce, the Ainsworth Country Club, and the Masons. His sports include hunting, fishing and golfing.

On January 3, 1894, he married Alice Reeves Boyd at Ainsworth. Mrs. Baldwin was born at Des Moines, Iowa, October 14, 1873. Their children are: Vivien B., born March 19, 1895, who married Archie F. Johnson; Glenn Addison, born August 6, 1900, who married Janette Arneson; and Lloyd Eugene, born February 12, 1906. Residence: Ainsworth.

Joseph Pearson Baldwin

Joseph Pearson Baldwin is one of the veteran and honored members of the bar of Thayer County, at whose county seat, the city of Hebron, he has engaged in the practice of law for thirty years. As a lawyer Mr. Baldwin early took a place among the foremost practitioners at the bar. Always an eloquent and forceful speaker, he proved himself a vigorous and resourceful trial lawyer and a counsellor of rare and mature judgment. He has been notably successful both as a prosecutor and defender in the trial of criminal cases.

Mr. Baldwin was born at Cookeville, Putnam County, Tennessee, May 25, 1869, a son of William Wiley Baldwin and Nancy Matilda Ann (Pearson) Baldwin. The former was born at Abingdon, Virginia, July 21, 1836, and the latter at Cookeville, Tennessee, in February, 1846. William Wiley Baldwin was a son of Robert Baldwin, who was a son of Kendrick Baldwin, the latter having been a son of John Baldwin, and the family having been founded in Virginia in the Colonial period of American history. John Baldwin was the founder of the family in America. Coming from England, he established his residence in Virginia, whence he went forth as a patriot soldier in the war of the Revolution. In this great conflict his service was continued seven years, and he was six times wounded, notwithstanding which fact he lived to be somewhat more than eighty years of age.

William Wiley Baldwin died at Grandview, Tennes-

Townsend—Lincoln

JOSEPH PEARSON BALDWIN

see, on October 21, 1921. He was by occupation a mechanic, but spent the later years of his life on a farm. He was a soldier in the Union Army in the Civil War, in which he had the rank of lieutenant. He was a staunch Democrat, and in his home community he served in various offices of public trust. Both he and his wife were earnest members of the Methodist Episcopal Church, South, and in this connection it may be noted that the sons of Kendrick Baldwin, three in number, became pioneer clergymen of the Methodist Church. At the time of his death, William Wiley Baldwin was one of the venerable and honored citizens of Grandview, Tennessee. His wife died there on November 14, 1909.

Nancy Matilda Ann Pearson was a daughter of Joseph and Tempie (Clark) Pearson who were pioneer settlers in middle Tennessee, the family lineage tracing back through Mississippi to Irish origin.

The public schools of Tennessee were the medium through which Joseph Pearson Baldwin acquired his early education. He afterwards attended the Grandview Normal Institute in Grandview, Tennessee. Later he carried forward the study of law under the effective preceptorship of John C. Locke of Spring City, Tennessee, and was admitted to the bar in Tennessee, on July 3, 1894. He thereafter engaged in the practice of law at Dayton, Tennessee, until December, 1901, when he engaged in practice in Claude, Texas, for a short time.

In 1902, he came to Nebraska, was here admitted to the bar, and here he has continued his professional activities during the intervening years. His marked success stands in evidence of his ability, his integrity and his personal popularity. He served four terms (1907 to 1915) as prosecuting attorney for Thayer County, Nebraska. He is a Democrat, and in 1928, represented the Democrats of the 4th Congressional District of Nebraska as delegate to the Democratic national convention at Houston, Texas. He and his wife hold membership in the Presbyterian Church.

In the World War period Mr. Baldwin was active in patriotic service in his county where he was a member of all local committees in charge of various war activities. He is a veteran of the Spanish-American War in which he served with the rank of sergeant in the 4th Tennessee Volunteer Infantry with which he saw active duty in Cuba, and was honorably discharged in the spring of 1899.

On the 30th day of January, 1902, at Chattanooga, Tennessee, he was married to Lydia Jane Franklin. She was born and reared in that state, where she was graduated with the degree of Bachelor of Arts from Maryville College as a member of the class of 1895. Mrs. Baldwin gave eleven years of successful service as a teacher in the public schools and in mission work in the Presbyterian and Congregational churches of Tennessee and North Carolina. She is a daughter of John and Nancy Isabel (McAdoo) Franklin. Her father was long engaged in business as a carpenter and builder, and was a Confederate soldier in the Civil War. Of the same ancestral line a distinguished representative was Benjamin Franklin.

Mr. and Mrs. Baldwin have three children, all of whom were born in Hebron, Thayer County, Nebraska. Robert Morton, eldest of the number, was born May 26, 1903, and he is now prosecuting attorney of Thayer County, and is engaged in the publishing business. He married Sara A. Mullin, who is a lawyer. They are the parents of a daughter, Ritchie, born May 4, 1932. Robert was elected delegate to the Democratic national convention at Chicago, from the Fourth Congressional District in 1932. William Orville, the younger son, was born February 1, 1905, and is now engaged in the practice of law with his father in Hebron. He married Iris Miller of Omaha. They have a son, William Orville, Jr., born September 12, 1931. The only daughter, Helen Franklin, was born January 5, 1908, and married William S. Sherman. She has a daughter, Robert Jo, born January 25, 1929. Residence: Hebron. (Photograph on Page 68).

Lydia Franklin Baldwin

Early in the 19th century Bennett C. Franklin left his native North Carolina and crossed the great Smoky Mountains into Tennessee. He settled in the fertile valley of the Tennessee River in what is now Rhea County, and there married Lydia Tunnell, whose family came from Kentucky. To these pioneer parents was born, in 1838, John K. Franklin.

Lydia Jane Franklin is the daughter of John K. Franklin and Nancy Isabelle McAdoo, who was descended from the same branch of the McAdoo family as William Gibbs McAdoo, secretary of the treasury under Woodrow Wilson. Her mother died in 1877. Altho his sympathies were with the Union cause, John K. Franklin was conscripted into the Confederate Army and forced to take the field. He died in 1892. The Franklin family is of Scotch-Irish descent, the first settlers coming to America about the end of the 17th century, several members serving in the Revolution. The McAdoos have been prominent in Southern history for more than two centuries.

After completing her preliminary work in Grand View and Spring City, Tennessee, Lydia Jane Franklin entered the preparatory department of Maryville College in 1887. During the next seven years she completed the regular preparatory course, taught school part of each year, and in 1895 was awarded the Bachelor of Arts degree. Having completed her college course she taught mission schools of the Presbyterian and Congregational churches in the mountains of Tennessee and North Carolina.

On January 30, 1902 she was united in marriage to Joseph Pearson Baldwin whose family had lived in the same county with hers for many years. The ceremony was performed at Chattanooga, Tennessee, by Dr. E. A. Elmore, who was one of the south's leading Presbyterian clergymen, and a trustee of Maryville College. Mr. Baldwin preceded his wife to Nebraska, entering the practice of law at Hebron in the summer of 1902; Mrs. Baldwin joined him a few weeks later.

To their union the following children have been born: Robert Morton, May 26, 1903; William Orville, February 1, 1905; Helen Franklin, January 5, 1908. Robert Morton is county attorney of Thayer County and William Orville is associated with his father in the law practice at Hebron. Robert married Sara A. Mullin of New York, and they have a daughter, Ritchie, born May 4, 1932. Orville married Iris Miller of Omaha. They have one son, William Orville, Jr. Helen married William Seward Sherman, and is the mother of a daughter, Robert Jo "Bobbie Jo."

Since coming to Nebraska Mrs. Baldwin has taken active part in the civic, religious and educational life of her community. A member of the Presbyterian Church, she has worked regularly in the Sunday School and other church organizations, and has served as delegate to various religious conventions. She is a charter member of the Hebron Woman's Club, and has held the offices of president, vice president, and parliamentarian. She has also represented her club at various state, district and county conventions. Residence: Hebron. (Photograph on Page 70).

William Emit Bales

William Emit Bales, postmaster, was born at Venus, Texas, December 27, 1897, and has resided in Nebraska for the past 12 years. He is the son of William S. and Elnora (Futhey) Bales, the former a native of Illinois. The father is of Welch descent and the mother of French descent. They reside at Ardmore, Oklahoma.

Mr. Bales attended the public and high school at Lindsay, Oklahoma, graduating from the latter in 1913. He is at the present time owner and operator of the Hershey Telephone Company and for the past eight years has served as postmaster. He is a Republican. From

Strauss-Peyton—Kansas City

LYDIA FRANKLIN BALDWIN

1917 until 1919 he served in the United States Navy with the rank of Chief Petty Officer.

He is a member of the American Legion, the First Presbyterian Church, and the Odd Fellows, and at the present time is serving as president of the Hershey Community Club. He enjoys golf and football while his hobby is fishing.

On October 29, 1919, he was married to Laura E. Jenkins at Hershey. Mrs. Bales was born at Shenandoah, Iowa, November 25, 1897, and is of English descent. They have one daughter, Wilma, born March 2, 1928. Residence: Hershey.

William Balfour

A native of Danzig, Germany, William Balfour was born April 5, 1845. His father, James Balfour, was a Scotchman, who married Matilda Von Gralath, and who migrated to America with his son in the early 1800's. Matilda Balfour was a native of Germany, who died in Edinburgh, in November, 1850, while enroute to America.

Mr. Balfour has as interesting war record. He and his father enlisted for service with the Union Army in the Civil War in the fall of 1861. His father's regiment was the 45th Illinois Volunteer Infantry, and he held the rank of first lieutenant in Company I of that regiment. His father was wounded at the battle of Fort Donnelson, Tennessee, on February 13, 1862, and again on April 7, 1862, at which time he suffered the loss of his right arm at the shoulder. At the same time William was given a sick furlough and reached their home in Illinois, on May 20, 1862, where his father died. William Balfour was then discharged because of ill health, and later entered the Illinois Soldiers' College.

In 1867, Mr. Balfour migrated west, and purchased a plot of land about thirteen miles northwest from the present site of Nebraska City. He has been a farmer all his life, and well and favorably known throughout the entire community. In 1876, he married Ella Elbina Hughes, whose family were settlers in Pennsylvania. She was born in Otoe County, February 16, 1858, and died on the homestead August 15, 1901. There are nine children, the youngest and the oldest of whom are girls. They are as follows: Myrtle E., born September 13, 1877, who married F. L. Cross, living at Brush, Colorado; Levi C., born June 20, 1879, who died January 17, 1924; Marvin W., born July 10, 1881, who married Libbie Clark and are residing at Caldwell, Idaho; George S., born August 1, 1883, who is living at Oakland, California; Carl, born July 23, 1886, who married Amelia Nutzman living at Nehawka; Max E., born February 8, 1888, married Ruth Hinton, now living at Venice, California; Ernest, born March 18, 1889, died June 3, 1891; Ivan J., born April 19, 1891, who married Eunice Ferguson now living at Union, Nebraska; Ella, born January 26, 1895, who married John A. Kearney, and is now dead.

While he has never taken an active part in politics, Mr. Balfour is affiliated with the Republican party. He has always been a member of the Nebraska City Post No. 24 of the Grand Army of the Republic, and has held the office of post commander and junior vice-president.

During late years he has played the violin over the radio, and has played in many fiddler's contests, but because of two paralytic strokes he is not as active as he would like to be, in spite of his advanced years. Residence: Nebraska City.

Ira R. Ball

Born at Connersville, Indiana, October 12, 1859, Ira R. Ball has resided in Nebraska for the past thirty-seven years. He is the son of Elkanah and Elizabeth A. (Ream) Ball, the former a farmer and a veteran of the Civil War. Elkanah Ball was a native of Tennessee, born May 8, 1825, who served with the 26th Indiana Infantry, and died at Milton, Indiana, May 25, 1906. He

was of Irish descent. His wife, born in Pennsylvania, March 14, 1818, died at Milton, March 28, 1877.

Ira R. Ball attended public school, and on December 22, 1891, was married to Florence Fountain at Anderson, Indiana. Mrs. Ball was born there on August 12, 1870, of English ancestry. To them were born three children, Ora W., born June 11, 1893, who married Floy Edna Dake; Lottie Ann, born October 17, 1895, who married Charles W. Shreve; and Farrie Iris, born November 4, 1899, who married Ernest Zalman.

Mr. Ball is engaged in the dairy business at the present time. In the World War period he was a participant in all civilian drives, and wartime projects. He is a member of the sons of Veterans of the Civil War, is affiliated wth the First Christian Church of Hastings, and was recently elected to the Nebraskana Society. Residence: Hastings.

Alberta Ballard

Alberta Ballard, known to her many friends as Bert, was born in Marion County, Iowa, January 10, 1870. She is the daughter of Alexander and Rebecca Burress (Sumner) Ballard, the former of whom was a native of Virginia. Alexander Ballard, a blacksmith, was born in Grayson County, Virginia, October 10, 1828. He came to Iowa, and later to Nebraska, and died at Fairbury, September 25, 1916. Rebecca, his wife, was born in Hamilton County, Indiana, April 20, 1836, and died at Fairbury, September 25, 1913. During her lifetime she was a member of and an ardent worker in the Women's Christian Temperance Union.

Miss Ballard, who received her education in the public schools of Knoxville, Iowa, and Diller, Nebraska, has been a resident of the state nearly forty-eight years. Formerly a teacher, she has been associated with the Fairbury Post Office since March 11, 1899, and for some time has been assistant postmaster.

She is a Republican, a member of the Methodist Episcopal Church, the Order of Eastern Star, and The Nebraskana Society. Residence: Fairbury.

Carl H. Ballard

Carl H. Ballard, physician and surgeon, was born at Esterville, Iowa, February 5, 1877, son of Ezra Hardin and Amanda F. (Kirkpatrick) Ballard, both of whom are deceased.

Dr. Ballard received his education in the public schools of Esterville, and was graduated from high school in 1895. He attended the University of Michigan from which he received his Doctor of Medicine degree, and thereafter served an internship of two years in a hospital in Grand Rapids, Michigan. Thereafter for a period of one year he was in practice at Three Rivers, Michigan, and in 1903 came to Nebraska where he has since been engaged in practice.

Since 1912, Dr. Ballard has confined his practice exclusively to x-ray. He has served as a member of the staff of the University Hospital, the Swedish Mission Hospital, and Wise Memorial Hospital, and has been associate professor of roentgenology at the University of Nebraska.

Dr. Ballard was married to Ora May Babcock of Three Rivers, Michigan, on April 29, 1903. She is a member of the Society of Mayflower Descendents, and is a direct descendant of John and Priscilla Alden. There are four children: Janet Barbara, Clay Hardin, Bruce Babette, Bonnie Nadine. Residence: Omaha.

Grace Ballard

A distinguished woman lawyer of Nebraska, Grace Ballard was born in Washington County, August 12, 1877, and has lived in this state most of her life. Her father, Martin Ballard, who was born in Grayson County, Kentucky, November 6, 1824, and died at Chadron, Nebraska, February 7, 1889, was a leading lawyer cf Blair, Nebraska. He served as county attorney of Dawes

County, and was engaged in practice at Blair from 1877 to 1885. Her mother, Sarah Darinda (Strong) Ballard, was born at Batemantown, Ohio, November 17, 1840. She was descended from Elias Rano and David Keyes who assisted in establishing American independence; they were natives of New Hampshire and Vermont.

Miss Ballard was graduated from Blair High School, received her degree at Dana College in 1904, and from 1911 to 1914 was a student at the University of Nebraska College of Law where she was president of the senior class, 1913-14. She was engaged in secretarial work for the Bell Telephone Company at Omaha, 1907-10, and for the Lincoln Safe Deposit Company, 1911-14. In 1915 she took a prominent part in the Woman's Suffrage campaign in Pennsylvania and New York, in 1916 carried on the same work in Iowa and Nebraska, beginning the practice of law in 1918.

As a Republican and one of the few women lawyers of Nebraska Miss Ballard has taken an active part in the political life of her state. She served as county attorney of Washington County in 1918-22, and since 1922 has been secretary of the Republican county central committee.

Miss Ballard is a member of the Order of Eastern Star, former chairman of the local Red Cross at Blair, and holds membership in the Methodist Church. She is affiliated with the Daughters of the American Revolution, the Daughters of Founders and Patriots, and the Nebraskana Society. Residence: Blair. (Photograph in Album).

Warren Robert Baller

Born at Trenton, Nebraska, June 19, 1900, Warren Robert Baller is the son of Albert Ernest and Mary Louise (Taylor) Baller. His father, who is employed at the University of Nebraska Agronomy Farm, was born at Bloomington, Illinois, April 22, 1868. His mother, who is employed at the Nebraska State Home For Dependent Children, was born at Bedford, Iowa, March 16, 1872.

Mr. Baller attended the rural schools of Saline County and in May, 1919, was graduated from the high school at DeWitt, Nebraska. He received the A. B. degree at York College, 1923, and the A. M. degree at the University of Nebraska, 1927. He was valedictorian of his senior class in high school, was president of the college Young Men's Christian Association, was active in debating, and received letters in football and track. During the terms of 1927 and 1930, he specialized in psychology, studying at the University of Colorado and Columbia University.

He was an instructor in York Business College, 1921-23, served as principal of the high school at Callaway, Nebraska, and was superintendent of schools at Cheney, Nebraska, 1925-27. At this time he is head of the department of psychology at York College. He is an occasional director of Boy's Work at Young Men's Christian Association conferences, is a member of the board of directors of that organization at York, and holds membership in the York Business Men's Club.

Mr. Baller is a member of the Nebraska Conference of the United Brethren Board of Education, and in president of the York College Alumni Association. His fraternity is Pi Gamma Mu.

He is a class A official in the Nebraska High School Athletic Association; his favorite sports are fishing and golfing. On December 25, 1924, Mr. Baller was united in marriage with Grace Marie Evans at Aurora, Nebraska. Mrs. Baller, who was born at Aurora, January 26, 1903, was graduated from York College and took graduate work at the University of Colorado. At this time she is a part-time English teacher in the high school and college at York. Residence: York.

Oliver Daniel Baltzly

One of Omaha's best known and most loved clergymen is Reverend Oliver D. Baltzly, recently retired as pastor of Kountze Memorial Evangelical Lutheran Church. Dr. Baltzly, who is reputed to be the best known Lutheran pastor in America, has during the past nineteen and a half years increased the Kountze Memorial Church to the largest Lutheran church in America. Under his pastorate the church has received 6736 members and had an enrollment of 806 in the 1931 confirmation class, surpassing any enrollment of Lutheran churches in this country.

Dr. Baltzly was born on a farm near Ponca, Nebraska, October 14, 1871. His father, Simon Peter Baltzly, was born near New Philadelphia, Ohio, November 16, 1829. He was a farmer, active in Republican politics, of Swiss descent. His great grandfather, Peter Baltzly, was brought to America as a baby with three brothers, in 1756, and all served in the American Revolution. Simon Baltzly married Elizabeth Stough, born in Westmoreland County, Pennsylvania, March 20, 1834. She was of German descent, her family having settled in America in pre-Revolutionary days.

Educated in the country schools of Dixon County, Dr. Baltzly was graduated from Ponca High School in 1888 with the grade of 98 plus. From June, 1888, to April, 1889, he attended Fremont Normal School. Entering Wittenberg College at Springfield, Ohio, in September, 1889, he received his A. B. from that institution in June, 1893. In September of that year he entered the Mt. Airy Lutheran Theological Seminary at Philadelphia. In 1901 he was awarded a Ph. D. from Wittenberg College, and in 1912, a D. D. He received an A. B. and an A. M. from Hanna Divinity School in June, 1896, and an LL. D. from Midland College at Fremont, in 1921.

Among the various pastorates he has held in his earlier life are the following: assistant pastor to Dr. Weber at Sunbury, Pennsylvania, summer of 1894; assistant pastor Fifth Lutheran Church July 1, 1895-July 1, 1896; pastor Fifth Lutheran Church, Springfield, Ohio, July 1, 1896-December 1, 1899; pastor St. Luke's Lutheran Church, Mansfield, Ohio, December 1, 1899-June 1, 1911.

On June 1, 1911, he was made pastor of Kountze Memorial Evangelical Lutheran Church at Omaha, and in 1931 was forced to resign his active pastorate because of impaired health. His resignation took effect August 31, 1931. In recognition of his outstanding service to Kountze Memorial Church, the congregation at a congregational meeting on December 9, 1930, unanimously elected Dr. Baltzly pastor emeritus of the church for life.

On June 11, 1896, Dr. Baltzly was united in marriage to Iva A. Taylor, at Galion, Ohio. Mrs. Baltzly was born at Galion, November 19, 1873. They have one daughter, Olive, born September 29, 1897, who was graduated from Wittenberg College in 1919.

Dr. Baltzly has always been active in welfare and social work in the community. He was a member of the board of directors of Wittenberg College from 1902 to 1910, and of the Omaha Library Board from 1924-30. An author of religious works, perhaps his best known are *Death Pot in Christian Science* (now in its third edition); *Catechetical Evangelization* (266 pages, now in its second edition); and *The Morning Order of Worship Made Plain for the Pew.*

Dr. Baltzly is a missionary in spirit, and his church has established four missions in the city, one of which has become a vigorous self-supporting congregation—the Lutheran Church of Our Redeemer, at 24th and Larimore Streets. The other three missions are at 19th and Castellar, 42nd and Bancroft, and 60th and Walnut Streets. All are housed in excellent buildings, which are paid for.

Dr. Baltzly is a member of the Chamber of Commerce and of the Omaha Athletic Club. Residence: Omaha.

John Raymond Bancroft

Born at Barney, Madison County, Iowa, June 27, 1890, John Raymond Bancroft is the son of George Bradley and Hattie Almyra (Sheldon) Bancroft. His father, a clergyman, was born in Lincolnshire, England,

June 19, 1863, and in 1884 came to the United States. His mother, born at Laurel, Maryland, March 8, 1867, died at Lincoln, Nebraska, July 8, 1930. She was of early American stock, her father a veteran of the Civil War.

Dr. Bancroft attended the public schools of Beaver Crossing and Nelson, Nebraska, and Nelson High School. In 1919 he was graduated from the Kirksville (Missouri) College of Osteopathy and Surgery, and in 1918 was president of his class. Since 1919 he has been actively engaged in the practice of osteopathy at Hebron. He holds membership in the American, and Nebraska State Osteopathic Associations, and the American Osteopathic Society of Proctology.

On September 8, 1916, Dr. Bancroft was united in marriage to Lillian Minnie Kaiser at Lincoln. Mrs. Bancroft, who is of German descent, was born at Preston, Nebraska, July 15, 1893. There are three children, Eunice Lorine, born March 27, 1918; Frances Elizabeth, September 16, 1920; and George Raymond, born January 31, 1923. The Bancrofts are justly proud of their fine family.

Dr. Bancroft is a Republican. He is affiliated with the First Methodist Episcopal Church of Hebron, and is a member of The Nebraskana Society, the Red Cross, the Chamber of Commerce and the Kiwanis Club. Residence: Hebron.

William Bryan Bang

William Bryan Bang, son of Michael Christian and Maren (Anderson) Bang, was born in Minden, April 19, 1892. His father was born in Thisted, Denmark, October 5, 1849, and farmed until his retirement in 1916. He came to America in 1872, and helped materially in the development of Kearney County. His wife, Maren, was born in Thisted County, Denmark, December 18, 1856.

Upon leaving rural school in May, 1906, Mr. Bang engaged in farming. He was married on May 31, 1916, to Frieda Louise Berndt at Minden. Mrs. Bang was born in Holstein, May 11, 1892. They have three children, Robert, born July 21, 1918; Elaine, born January 17, 1920; and Willa Jean, born April 4, 1930.

Mr. Bang is a Democrat. He was active in liberty loan and Red Cross drives during the World War, is a member of the United Presbyterian Church, the Nebraskana Society, the Parent Teachers Association (1931-1932), and of the school board (chairman 1930). His hobby is reading. Residence: Minden.

Joseph Frank Bange

Joseph Frank Bange, son of August and Thresa (Schungle) Bange, was born in Medebach, Kreis Brilon, Westphalia, Germany, April 3, 1862. His father was born in Medebach in 1832, a miller and soldier, and died there in 1882. His mother was born in Dreislar, Germany, in 1820, and died at Medebach in 1886.

Educated in the public schools of Medebach, Germany, Mr. Bange specialized in the study of art. After coming to America he studied embalming in Des Moines, and for many years has been engaged as a mortician and furniture dealer in Hartington.

He was married to Mary Josephine Heimes at Hartington on November 21, 1893. Mrs. Bange, who was born at Hartington, assists her husband in his work. There were nine children born to this marriage, seven of whom are living: Alphons, born January 11, 1895, died March 14, 1926; Pauline, born July 16, 1896, married Robert E. Brown; Thresa, born July 14, 1898, married Joseph Obert; August, born November 11, 1900, died February 22, 1904; Leone, born February 17, 1903, married Alfred E. Lee; Brigetta, born October 11, 1908; Cecelia, born August 6, 1910; Marie, born October 19, 1912; and Bernadette, born December 31, 1913.

A Democrat, he has served as county coroner a number of years, and is a member of the Knights of Columbus of which he is trustee and former director. He is affiliated with Holy Trinity Catholic Church, and is a member of the Commercial Club and the Nebraska Funeral Directors Association. He enjoys hunting, reading and target shooting. Residence: Hartington.

Arville Grant Banks

Born at Salem, Indiana, February 5, 1868, Arville Grant Banks is the son of George W. and Wealthy (Gilstrap) Banks. The father was born at Salem, March 10, 1828, and died there on June 10, 1869. His wife, born at Salem, January 12, 1839, died at Alma, Nebraska, February 14, 1916. George W. Banks was a farmer whose ancestors came from Vermont, while his wife's family settled early in Ohio.

Arville Grant Banks attended rural school in Indiana and in Seward County, Nebraska, was graduated from high school at Milford in 1889 and taught rural school for a short period.

For five years he operated a general merchandise store at Trumbull, and after his marriage farmed there and in Harlan County twenty-five years. On March 14, 1899, he was united in marriage to Sara Elsie Schlacter at Pleasant Dale. Mrs. Banks was born at Peoria, Illinois, December 27, 1879, of German and French descent.

There are five children, Vera Irene, born July 31, 1900, who married John F. Clouse; Miles Standish, born January 30, 1902, who married Myrl E. Hardin; Dorothy, born June 10, 1908, who is unmarried; Robert A., born September 14, 1913; and Betty, born May 8, 1920. The four oldest were graduated from Alma High School, Vera and Dorothy have taught in Douglas County, Vera seven years and Dorothy four. Miles was graduated from the State University and is now a practicing dentist in Fairbury. Robert attends Nebraska Wesleyan University.

Mr. Banks is a Republican. He is manager and director of the Equity Elevator, and secretary-treasurer and director of the Co-operative Oil Company. At different periods he has been a member of city and rural school boards. He is a member of the Lions Club, the Masons and the Red Cross, and is affiliated with the First Methodist Episcopal Church of Alma. Residence: Ewing.

Marie Louisa Banks

Maria Louisa Banks was born April 28, 1859, the daughter of John Nelson and Clara Gustava (Anderson) Nelson. Her father, who was born in Sweden and died there in 1867, was a salesman. Her mother was born in Sweden, August 16, 1824, and died at Erhard, Minnesota, in November, 1904.

Mrs. Banks received her education in the public schools of Sweden, and for the past 37 years has lived at Wausa, Nebraska, where she is a successful farmer and president of the Commercial State Bank. She is a member of the Red Cross, the Nebraskana Society, and the Methodist Episcopal Aid Society. Her hobby is reading.

On January 2, 1882, she was married to A. H. Banks at Rockport, Missouri. Mr. Banks, who was a farmer, stockraiser, and banker, was born at Halmstead, Sweden, February 9, 1854, and died at Wausa, May 18, 1931. Nine children were born to them, six sons who are farmers and three daughters who are homemakers and teachers. One daughter is librarian at Wausa at this time. Residence: Wausa.

William Benton Banning

William B. Banning was born September 18, 1869, at Wyoming, Otoe County, Nebraska, the son of William Henry and Eliza Ann (Wilson) Banning. His father was born of English and Swedish parentage at New London, Henry County, Iowa, January 4, 1846, and died at Union, Nebraska, September 19, 1918. He was a farmer.

His mother, of Irish descent, was born at Afton, Union County, Iowa, December 1, 1854, and died at Union, Nebraska, February 26, 1926.

Mr. Banning was graduated from the Lincoln Business College, and the University of Nebraska. At the present time he is cashier of the Bank of Union, at Union, Nebraska. He is a member of the Agricultural Achievement Hall of the University of Nebraska, and is chairman of the board of education at Union.

On September 6, 1899, he married Jennie Elizabeth Roush, at Keosauqua, Van Buren County, Iowa. Mrs. Banning, who was a stenographer before her marriage, was born at Keosauqua, November 17, 1870. She is of German descent. One child, Hollis, was born October 2, 1902, and is now bookkeeper at the Bank of Union.

In the World War Mr. Banning was food administrator for Cass County. He is a member of the Chamber of Commerce, the Modern Woodmen of America, and the Masons. He was State Senator for 2nd District from 1909-11, also from 1923 to 1931. Mr. Banning is a Democrat. He has also been a member on Nebraska State Board of Agriculture for 19 years and at present one of Board of Managers. Residence: Union.

Ira Ellsworth Banta

Ira E. Banta, leading banker, was born at Adams, Indiana, March 4, 1869, the son of Daniel H. and Priscilla (Wheeler) Banta. His father was born at Cynthiana, Kentucky, in 1807, and died at Plainville, Indiana, in August, 1886. During his life he was a clergyman, miller and a farmer. His parents were born in Virginia. Priscilla Banta was born in Kentucky, in 1832, and died at Plainville, in 1890. Her parents were also born in Virginia.

Mr. Banta spent his boyhood days in Indiana, where he attended an elementary school. He later attended Franklin Baptist College at Franklin, Indiana, and National Normal University at Lebanon, Ohio.

A resident of Nebraska since April 4, 1887, he was a country school teacher, deputy county clerk of Polk County for two years, and for thirty-nine years has been associated with the Stromsburg Bank, first as assistant cashier, then as cashier, and for the last seventeen years as president.

On November 28, 1900, he was united in marriage to Mary Alice Roberts at Pilot Grove, Missouri, where she was born October 22, 1872. Mrs. Banta died at Lincoln, Nebraska, February 5, 1919. Three children were born to them: Harold E., born February 9, 1902, who is married to Edith Kiem; Ruth E., born November 18, 1903, and Wallace E., born June 29, 1907, a graduate of the University of Nebraska in 1929, who is married to Peggy Happ. Harold E., is employed by the General Electric Company at Chicago, Wallace E., by the B. F. Goodrich Rubber Company at Boston, Massachusetts, and Ruth E., resides at home.

During the World War Mr. Banta was chairman of all liberty loan drives in Polk County. He is a member of the Red Cross. the Community Club, and the Nebraskana Society. Golfing, football and baseball are his favorite sports and fishing and hunting are his hobbies.

Mr. Banta was married to Emma Olson Danielson on February 12, 1927. Residence: Stromsburg.

Merle Albert Banta

Merle Albert Banta, manager of the Bridgeport Bottling and Storage Company, was born at Chicago, Illinois, November 11, 1891, son of Albert A. and Florence Emma (McMillian) Banta.

In 1913 Mr. Banta was graduated from the high school of Salem, Iowa, and attended Whittier Academy from which he was graduated in 1918. He afterward attended Iowa Wesleyan College two years.

On August 31, 1920, he was married to Dorothy Lamme at Mount Pleasant, Iowa. She was born at Mount Pleasant, March 4, 1898. There are two children, Richard, born July 7, 1925; and Barbara Anne, born April 4, 1928.

At the present time Mr. Banta is serving as president and general manager of the Bridgeport Bottling and Storage Company, Incorporated. He is a member of the Lions Club, the Masons and the American Legion. For two years he held the rank of second lieutenant in the Motor Transport Corps; this was during the World War. He is fond of golf. Residence: Morrill.

Harvey Edgar Barbee

Harvey Edgar Barbee, who has been prominent in educational affairs in Nebraska for the past fifteen years, has lived in this state all his life and has taken an active part in civic projects in his community. He was born at Fairbury, Jefferson County, Nebraska, May 18, 1889, the son of Charles M. and Rosella (Waymire) Barbee. His father, who was born at Portsmouth, Ohio, in 1854, and died at Hebron, Thayer County, Nebraska, July 21, 1931, was a grain dealer; his French ancestors settled in Virginia in the early history of the country and later moved to Ohio.

Mr. Barbee, who is county superintendent of schools in Thayer County, attended the public schools of Jefferson County, and later was a student at York College and Peru State Teacher's College. He was awarded a professional state life certificate by the state department in 1917, and in 1921 received the city life certificate. He has always been connected with educational activities and has held the following professional positions: teacher in Cherry County schools, 1910-11; teacher in Thayer County, 1912-13; superintendent of public schools Byron, Nebraska, 1916-18; and county superintendent of schools in Thayer County, 1918 to date.

For four years Mr. Barbee served as president of the interstate spelling contest, comprising the states of Minnesota, Iowa, Missouri, and South Dakota, and was chairman of the state fair spelling committee for five years. He has devoted a great deal of time to writing and is the author of various songs, short stories, and short novels, among them: We Are Coming Back to You, Montana, a song published in 1918; My Carnation, 1928, a song, Star of Liberty, 1928; The Lure of the Sandhills, published in serial form in a professional publication, 1928.

His marriage to Mary W. Ahlschwede was solemnized at Hebron, June 9, 1917. Mrs. Barbee was a teacher in Thayer County Schools before her marriage and took an active interest in music. She is affiliated with the Presbyterian Church at Hebron, has taught in the Sunday School since girlhood, and is active in various women's affairs in the church. She holds membership in the Nebraska Writers Guild, the Eastern Star, of which she was secretary at one time, and the Hebron Woman's Club, of which she is an active member. Mrs. Barbee is interested in writing, and is the author of two stories, both of which have been published: When Johnny Comes Marching Home Again; and Stony Justice.

To their marriage two children were born: Jack Mahlon, born July 31, 1918; and Gwyn Stanley, born October 23, 1919. Both of the boys are students in the Hebron Public School.

Mr. Barbee holds membership in Pi Gamma Mu, the Presbyterian Church, where he has been superintendent of the Sunday School, is a member of the Masons and Odd Fellows, is affiliated with the Eastern Star. He has been a member of the Nebraska Writers Guild for several years and is a member of the Nebraskana Society. Residence: Hebron. (Photograph on Page 75).

Day—Hebron

HARVEY EDGAR BARBEE

Grove Ettinger Barber

Grove Ettinger Barber, retired professor of the University of Nebraska, was born at Freedom, Ohio, November 1, 1843. He is the son of Myron Alphonso and Marinda Lucetta (Streeter) Barber, the former a farmer of English descent who died at Freedom in 1844. Marinda Streeter was born at Shalersville, Ohio, January 13, 1819, and died at East Des Moines, Iowa, April 19, 1903. Her family came overland from Connecticut in a covered wagon, driven by oxen with horses in the lead, and settled in Shalersville.

Professor Barber attended country school and later Freedom Academy. In 1871 he received a B. A. from Hiram College, in 1874 an A. M., and thereafter took post graduate work at the University of Chicago. He was a student at Hiram College at the time Garfield was president, but was too young to join the company organized by him. He enlisted in the Ohio Volunteers the following year. He was a member of the Alpha Delta Debating Society at Hiram.

On June 24, 1868, he was married to Esther Bates Gardner at Freedom, Ohio. She was born there in 1844, and died in Lincoln on November 28, 1895. Of this marriage there are four children: Lena Aldula, born July 25, 1869, who married L. A. Hussong; Harry Gardner, born April 20, 1871, who married Blanche Davis; Alphonso Grove, born June 24, 1873, who married Ida Herpolsheimer; and Virgil Cassius, born June 24, 1875, who married Lola Tillitson. Mr. Barber was married to Ida E. Mack, who is of Revoluntionary ancestry, on September 3, 1901.

A resident of Nebraska since 1881, he was for nine years professor of Greek and Latin at Hiram College, one year superintendent of public schools at Grand Island, and forty years professor of Roman History and literature at the University of Nebraska. He is the author of *Captivi of Plautus* (1899), a *Synopsis of Latin Grammar* (1894) and *Latin Charts* (1893).

On August 11, 1862, he enlisted in Company I, 104th Ohio Volunteer Infantry, and served as a musician until June 30, 1865, when he was mustered out, lacking about forty days of being three years in service. He is a member and former commander of Appamattox Post of the Grand Army of the Republic at Lincoln. One of the organizers in Chicago of the Classical Association of the Middlewest and South, he served as vice president of the organization, and later was elected president. He is a member of the Philological Association, the Archeological Institute of America, and the Nebraska Art Association of which last he has been president. He is a member also of the National Geographic Society, and has always been a contributor to the Red Cross, Salvation Army, Child Welfare Society, etc. Mr. Barber is a member of the First Christian Church of Lincoln.

Identified with the early educational movements of the state, Mr. Barber was one of the organizers of the Central Nebraska Teachers Association. He was a member of the committee (chairman) that organized the Associated School System of the State; in 1887-88 was dean of the academic faculty of the University and was chairman of the jury of awards of the department of education on Social Economy at the Panama Pacific Exposition in San Francisco in 1915.

After the above sketch was written Professor Barber died at his home in Lincoln, on April 25, 1931. (Photograph in Album).

Jacob A. Barber

Jacob A. Barber, a retired farmer near North Loup, Nebraska, was born at Worchester, Indiana, January 27, 1861, the son of William and Amelia (Graves) Barber. His father, who was born at Harrisburg, Pennsylvania, December 16, 1816, and died at Fullerton, Nebraska, October 5, 1913, was a farmer; he carried mail for the United States government before the days of the railroad; his parents built one of the first houses at Harrisburg and were among the pioneer settlers of that community. His mother was born of English parentage in Ohio in 1819, and died at Hamburg, Iowa, April 10, 1868.

Mr. Barber attended the public school and later taught in Valley County, Nebraska. He began farming on a rented farm in Valley County and in a few years purchased his own land there where he was successful until his retirement a few years ago. He has served as county supervisor, road supervisor, and a member of the local school board, and since 1927 has beeen mayor of North Loup.

He is a member of the Welfare Board at North Loup, has been treasurer of the Independent Order of Odd Fellows for the past six years, and was formerly a member of the Modern Woodmen of America. He is chairman of the North Loup Federal Seed Loan Committee, and is interested in civic improvement and beautifying his community. Mr. Barber's favorite sports are fishing and hunting.

He was married to Harriet Ann Moore at Sidney, Iowa, August 8, 1881. Mrs. Barber was born in Marion County, Ohio, June 3, 1860, and died at North Loup, December 19, 1920. Three children were born to this marriage: Daisy, January 7, 1882, who married Charles Black; Harry, July 14, 1884, who married Berta Goodrich; and Christa, December 24, 1885. Harry is a farmer and is prominent in community affairs. Mr. Barber married Myra W. Thorngate of North Loup, on October 22, 1928. She is the daughter of Reverend C. W. and Ethel (Babcock) Thorngate, pioneer residents of Nebraska. Residence: North Loup.

Peter Thaddeus Barber

For the past 44 years Peter T. Barber has lived in Nebraska. Upon his graduation in 1895, he entered the practice of dentistry in Chadron, Nebraska, where he continued until 1901, then moved to Omaha, where he has since practiced. He was born in Clayton County, Iowa, January 23, 1872, the son of William Clayton and Izora Cornelia (Hutchins) Barber. His father, who was a farmer and ranchman, was born at Clayton County, September 30, 1844, and died at Long Beach, California, December 12, 1916. He was a Civil War veteran who served in the 21st Iowa Infantry. His English ancestors came to this country in 1750. Izora Barber, mother of Peter T. Barber, was born at Malone, New York, May 1, 1851.

Dr. Barber received his elementary education in the country schools and in the Chadron High School. In 1891 he was graduated from Chadron Academy. He was graduated in 1895 from the Chicago College of Dental Surgery. He was elected to membership in Delta Sigma Delta in 1908. From 1904 to 1908 he was professor of operative dentistry at Creighton Dental College. He is now president of the P. T. Barber & Son Dental Supply Company, and is now engaged in the practice of dentistry at Omaha.

He was united in marriage with Mary Ellen Mason at Chadron, June 11, 1893. Mrs. Barber was born at Cheyenne, Wyoming, November 24, 1872. Her ancestry is English. They have the following children: Peter T., born September 13, 1900; Mildred P., born February 19, 1896; Dorothy M., born December 14, 1904; and Harry DeLoss, born April 27, 1911.

Dr. Barber is a member of the Nebraska State Dental Society; the Eastern District Dental Society; the National Dental Society; Odontological Dental Society; and the Professional Men's Club. He is past president of the Nebraska State Dental Society; the Odontological Society; the Tri-City Dental Society; and the Eastern District Dental Society. He is a member of the Omaha Chamber of Commerce, and the Lions Club. He served on the dental examining board during the World War.

He is a member of the following Masonic divisions; Omaha Lodge Number 288; Knights Templar; Commandery; Tangier Temple; and Scottish Rite. He is affiliated with Lowe Avenue Presbyterian Church of Omaha. His hobby is raising dahlias. He is a Republican. Residence: Omaha.

Edward Logan Barker

Edward Logan Barker, editor and postmaster, was born at Tekamah, Nebraska, June 10, 1867, son of Charles E. and Sarah Jane (Ginn) Barker. His father was born at Columbus, Ohio, December 19, 1836, and moved with his parents to Henry County, Iowa, in 1847. Two years later his father, going to the gold fields of California, caused the family to return to Ohio.

In 1853 they again started for Iowa, but cold weather compelled them to stop in Illinois, where they remained three or four years before continuing their journey. When the Civil War broke out Charles Barker was painting a house near Mount Pleasant, and his material becoming exhausted he went into town for a fresh supply. There he found the government calling for three months volunteers, and enlisted on August 10, in Company H, 25th Iowa Infantry and participated in seventeen battles and the Siege of Vicksburg. At Resacca, Georgia, he was wounded in the right leg. During Sherman's march to the sea he had charge of a forage detail and had many adventures. Entering as a drummer boy, he was mustered out of the army as a first lieutenant.

At the close of the war he returned to Oskaloosa, Iowa, where he was joined by his wife. After purchasing a team and wagon, he loaded his personal effects and started overland for Nebraska. Landing on the bank of the Missouri Valley, eight miles east of Tekamah, on September 5, 1865, he lived there ten years until his farm of 253 acres was washed away by the Missouri River. He then moved to Summit township, one and a half miles west of Tekamah, where with the exception of two years spent in Keya Paha County, he resided until his retirement from the farm in the spring of 1910. His death occurred at Tekamah, June 22, 1910. Sarah Jane Ginn, his wife, was born in Newcastle, Indiana, October 30, 1844, and died at Tekamah, July 14, 1906.

Edward Logan Barker attended public and high school at Tekamah, Nebraska. In 1915 he moved to Pender, where he has been active in public life. He is editor of the Pender Republic, and at the present time is also postmaster. He is a Republican, a Presbyterian and a member of the Chamber of Commerce.

On October 8, 1895, he was united in marriage to Nettie Mae Hilsinger at Valentine. Mrs. Barker was born at Little Sioux, Iowa, July 30, 1877, and is assistant editor of the Pender Republic. They have two children, Ethlyn M., born November 17, 1900, who married Waldron F. Wright; and Elaine, born August 15, 1910, who married Norris Kelso. Residence: Pender.

Joseph Barker

Joseph Barker, vice president of the Foster-Barker Company, general insurance agents, was born in Omaha where his parents were early pioneers. His grandfather came from England and settled in Omaha in 1856. His son, Joseph, married Eliza E. Patrick in 1875.

Joseph Barker, the subject of this sketch, was educated in the public schools of Omaha, and in St. Paul's Preparatory School at Concord, New Hampshire. Since 1907 he has been in the insurance business, and has been connected with the Omaha Building and Loan Association, and the Omaha Electric Light and Power Company. He is a member of the firm of the Foster-Barker Company.

On October 31, 1899, he was married to Elizabeth A. Peck. There are four children: Elizabeth E., who married I. J. Bussing; Virginia; Joseph, Jr.; and James. Residence: Omaha.

William E. Barkley

William E. Barkley, son of William E. Barkley, Sr., was born in Indiana, and at the age of 18 came to Nebraska with his parents who settled in Lincoln.

The father was born in Rockport, Indiana, January 24, 1837, and died at Lincoln, July 13, 1905. In August, 1881, he and his family came to Lincoln, where he was subsequently a merchant, a rancher, and a real estate man. In 1894, he became associated with his son in the Lincoln Safe Deposit Company of which he was president at the time of his death. His wife, Nancy E. Hart, was the daughter of Aaron and Isabel (Pye) Hart.

William E. Barkley entered the Lincoln Savings Bank in 1892, and subsequently organized the Lincoln Safe Deposit and Trust Company, and later the Lincoln Trust Company, of which he was president for a time. In 1920, he retired from both to devote his entire attention to the Lincoln Joint Stock Land Bank. Residence: Lincoln.

George Earl Barks

Born at Manson, Iowa, March 23, 1896, George Earl Barks is the son of George W. and Hattie M. (Briggs) Barks. His father, born in Cornell, Iowa, in 1858, was a contractor of German descent, who died at Sioux City, March 31, 1930. His mother was born in Michigan, in 1861, and died at Sioux City, in July, 1918. Her ancestry was Welch and Scotch.

George Earl Barks attended country school and the public schools of Chelsea, South Dakota, and Manson, Iowa. He attended Morningside Academy and Sioux City High School until 1914, and received his A. B. from Morningside College in 1918. He is a member of Pi Kappa Delta and Alpha Tau Delta, was editor of the Collegian Reporter and of the Sioux '18 (annual), and engaged in intercollegiate debate two years.

A resident of Nebraska for the past ten years, Mr. Barks is cashier and director of the First National Bank of Belden, at the present time. He is a Republican, a member of the First Presbyterian Church, the Red Cross and the Parent-Teachers' Association. An Ordinance Sergeant in the World War, he is a member of the American Legion. He also belongs to the Odd Fellows and the Ancient Free and Accepted Masons.

On September 10, 1926, he was united in marriage to Mildred B. V. Bruce at Malmo, Nebraska. Mrs. Barks, who is of Swedish descent, was born at Malmo, July 8, 1901. They have one daughter, Beverly Jean, born December 5, 1927. Residence: Belden. (Photograph in Album).

Erskine M. Barnes

Erskine M. Barnes, physician and surgeon, was born at Plattsmouth, Nebraska, September 21, 1876, son of John W. and Martha B. (Gage) Barnes. His father was born in Bowling Green, Kentucky, and his mother in Illinois. Her father was one of the earliest pioneer clergymen of the Methodist Episcopal Church in the state.

John W. Barnes came to Nebraska in its pioneer days and was connected for many years with the Chicago, Burlington and Quincy railroad. He died at Tecumseh, Nebraska. His wife is also deceased.

At the age of nine years Erskine M. Barnes removed from Plattsmouth, to York, and attended public school there. He entered Lincoln Medical College and was graduated in 1903 with the degree of Doctor of Medicine. From 1903, until 1912, he practiced at Plainview, Nebraska. Since then he has been in practice in Omaha. He is a member of the Nebraska State, the American and the Douglas County Medical Societies.

In 1898, Dr. Barnes served with the Company A, Second Nebraska Volunteer Infantry in the Spanish-American War. During the World War he held the rank of captain in the medical corps, and served as director of field hospitals of the 321st Sanitary Train, 96th division of the American Expeditionary Forces. He served overseas 16 months. At the present time he holds the rank of lieutenant-colonel in the medical division of the Sixth Reserve Corps.

A Republican, he is interested in party politics. He is a member of the American Legion, the Odd Fellows, the Elks, and the Knights of Pythias (past chancellor). On June 10, 1912, he was married to Lillian J. Weber. Residence: Omaha.

Fred Barnes

Born at Reedsburg, Wisconsin, December 28, 1868, Fred Barnes is the son of James Brewster and Alice Jane (Randall) Barnes. His father, was born in Ohio, December 29, 1840, was a farmer who served as county commissioner for a number of years, and was a veteran of the Civil War. He died at Loretto, Nebraska, March 15, 1905. His mother died at Albion, Nebraska, August 29, 1879.

Mr. Barnes has been a farmer in Nebraska for over 40 years and has resided in Boone County for nearly 60 years. He holds membership in the Boone County Pioneers Association, the Territorial Pioneers Association, the Nebraskana Society, and the First Methodist Episcopal Church of Loretto. He is president of the local school board, and is a member of the Modern Woodmen of America. His political connection is with the Democratic party.

His marriage to Minnie Maude Havens was solemnized at Loretto, March 15, 1899. Mrs. Barnes was born at Hopkinton, Iowa, January 21, 1873, and died at Loretto, April 1, 1926. Their three children are Dorsey, born August 18, 1900, who married Betty Bosserman, now residing at Rapid City, South Dakota; Mina, born March 27, 1905, who is living at home and teaching; and Bernard, born, July 24, 1907, who married Valma Myers of Loretto, on Christmas day, 1931. He is still living in the town of his birth, employed by the State of Nebraska in the extension department. A step-daughter, Neva Havens, was born September 17, 1891, at Omaha, and was married to Albert C. Hutchinson in June, 1917. All the children are graduates of the University of Nebraska, except Neva, who obtained her advanced education at Kearney Normal School, and Midland College.

Mr. Barnes is a brother of M. G. Barnes, one of the engineers on the Panama Canal. Residence: Loretto.

Frederick Hall Barnes

Frederick Hall Barnes has lived in Nebraska for the past 63 years and has been prominent in the banking world for many years. He was born at St. Devoin, Nebraska, July 2, 1868, the son of Francis Marion and Mary Jane Barnes. His father, who was born at Baltimore, Maryland, May 1, 1833, and died at Barneston, Nebraska, August 18, 1916, was a retired merchant and stockman for several years before his death. In the early 1860's he freighted from the Missouri River to the mountains. His ancestry was Scotch and German.

His mother, Mary Jane Barnes, whose ancestry was Irish and Indian, was born at Bellvue, Indian Territory, November 17, 1827, and died at Barneston, November 11, 1920.

Mr. Barnes was a student at St. Benedict's College at Atchison, Kansas, for a time. He is a member of the Nebraskana Society, the Masons, and the Elks. His hobby is fishing. His political affiliation is with the Republican Party. Residence: Barneston.

James Dudley Barnes

Born in White County, Indiana, January 17, 1874, James Dudley Barnes is the son of Alexander and Elizabeth (Nutt) Barnes. His father, who was a farmer and merchant, was born in White County, February 24, 1835, and died at Hoopeston, Illinois, March 17, 1919. His

mother was born at Idaville, Indiana, May 25, 1841, and died at Hoopeston, June 22, 1877.

Mr. Barnes was graduated from the Fullerton High School, and in 1898, passed the State Board of Pharmacy entering actively in the management of a drug business in Genoa, Nebraska, being associated with R. A. McMillan of that place. After a partnership lasting six years, Mr. Barnes sold his interests in the store at Genoa, and entered into the drug business at Fullerton, where he still resides. He has been actively engaged in the drug business since 1894, has been stockholder in two banks, acting as vice president and later as president.

He is secretary of the Fullerton Chapter of the American Red Cross, having been active in that capacity for over 13 years, is a member of the Lions Club, and holds membership in the Nebraska Pharmaceutical Association. His hobby is reading.

His marriage to Olive Josephine Shute occurred at Coon Rapids, Iowa, June 26, 1907. Mrs. Barnes was born at Warren, Illinois, September 13, 1877. She is an accomplished musician, having studied in Chicago and other metropolises. They have one daughter, Henrietta Josephine, born August 28, 1910. She is a senior at the University of Nebraska, and following her mother's foot-steps is also a musician. She is a member of Gamma Phi Beta. Residence: Fullerton.

Leonard Colby Barnes

Leonard C. Barnes was born at Blue Springs, Gage County, Nebraska, November 19, 1890. After graduating from the Blue Springs High School in 1908, he attended Peru State Normal School from 1909 to 1910.

He is the son of Charles Reuben and Lydia Ann (Melvin) Barnes, the former born in Michigan, October 27, 1857. Lydia Ann Melvin was born in Ohio, April 26, 1857.

On June 24, 1913, Mr. Barnes was married to Emma Tustin Rise, who was born at Tustin, California, October 7, 1891, and died at Beatrice, Nebraska, June 23, 1925. To them were born two children, Thelma Marie, born October 18, 1914; and Annetta Elizabeth, born April 12, 1917.

Mr. Barnes' marriage to Irene M. Scroggs, was solemnized on August 1, 1926, at Beatrice. She was born August 1, 1889, at Odell, Nebraska. They have one daughter, Dorothy Irene, born September 5, 1927.

He has been a resident of Nebraska his entire life with the exception of one year, 1912 to 1913, while he was employed at Des Moines, Iowa. On January 1, 1914, he began as stenographer for E. G. Drake at Beatrice. He is now assistant office manager of E. G. Drake and Company, farm loans, of Beatrice.

During the World War he was chairman of the Ward Committee at the time of draft registration. He is a member of the board of deacons of the First Presbyterian Church of Beatrice. He is president of the local Kiwanis Club, and was Worshipful Master of Beatrice Lodge No. 26, Ancient Free and Accepted Masons, from June 15, 1931 to June 15, 1932. He is a member of The Nebraskana Society and the Young Men's Christian Association. Residence: Beatrice.

Newell Horace Barnes

Born at Oak Park, Illinois, November 18, 1885, Newell Horace Barnes, cost and mechanical engineer, is the son of Frank Horace and Louisa J. (Newell) Barnes. His father was a native of Wheaton, Illinois, born September 17, 1855. For many years city passenger agent for the Rock Island Railroad, he later served as deputy assessor of Los Angeles County, California. His death occurred at Long Beach, California, on August 18, 1927. His family came to New England from England, previous to 1750; Horace Barnes, father of Frank Horace, settled in Illinois, prior to the Civil War.

Louisa J. Newell was born at Farm Ridge, Illinois, July 18, 1858, and died at Oak Park, October 6, 1892. She was formerly organist at the Oak Park Congregational Church. Her family came to America previous to 1750, and remained in New England until just prior to the Civil War when they moved to Illinois.

Newell Horace Barnes attended the public schools of Oak Park, Illinois, and Lincoln, Nebraska, and was graduated from Lincoln High School in 1904. From 1904 to 1908 he attended the University of Nebraska. In the years 1904 and 1905 he won first place in individual drill in the University of Nebraska Artillery, and was received into membership in Sigma Alpha Epsilon. At Lincoln High School he was a member of the track team and of the Phlogiston Debating Society.

For the past thirty years or thereabout he has been a resident of Nebraska. For two years he was with the Washington Power Company of Spokane, Washington, and with the Cushman Motor Works of Lincoln, sixteen years. He is now engaged in research work in economics.

On August 27, 1908, he was married to Jennie Grace Whitmore at Valley, Nebraska, where she was born on July 11, 1886. Her ancestry is traced to 1723, in New England; her father was a member of the legislatures of both Massachusetts and Nebraska, and a member of the board of regents of the University of Nebraska for many years.

Mr. and Mrs. Barnes had two sons, Burton Horace, born May 6, 1909, who died July 21, 1915, and Frank Whitmore, born March 28, 1910. He is an Eagle Scout, a graduate of Lincoln High School and a member of the class of 1932 at the University.

Mr. Barnes is eligible although not now a member of the Sons of the American Revolution. He is a member of the Society of Automotive Engineers, the National Geographical Society, the Red Cross and Lincoln Lodge No. 210, Ancient Free and Accepted Masons, Lincoln Consistory of the Scottish Rite, and Sesostris Temple of the Mystic Shrine. His hobbies are philately, antiques and Oriental art, and his sports are hiking, and trout fishing. He belongs to the Lincoln Collectors Club and the Bruner Bird Club. Residence: Lincoln.

William John Barnes

Born at Monmouth, Illinois, March 8, 1870, William John Barnes is the son of Reuben Decatur and Elizabeth Augusta (Harret) Barnes. His father, who was a farmer and architect, was born at Ithaca, New York, February 22, 1826, and died at Cotesfield, Nebraska. He was a member of the Home Guard at Leon, Iowa, during the Civil War. His mother, whose father was a physician, was born of English and German parentage at Ithaca, June 29, 1832, and died at Cotesfield, June 29, 1907.

Mr. Barnes was manager of the Farmers Elevator Company at Cotesfield for eight years, served as vice president and secretary-treasurer of the Farmers Mutual Telephone Company at Cotesfield for a number of years, and was instrumental in the organization of both of these companies. He has served as director of the local school board for nine years. He is a Mason.

On December 24, 1902, he married Grace Adelaide Whitney at Cotesfield. Mrs. Barnes, who was prominent in the Women's Christian Temperance Union as president in Howard County for a number of years, is also active in church and civic affairs. She was born at West Ridge, New Hampshire, March 2, 1876. Their children are: William Whitney, born July 12, 1907; and Percy Orville, born June 10, 1909. Residence: Elba.

John David Barnett

A resident of Stanton County since January 5, 1882, John David Barnett was born in Clinton County, Indiana, September 11, 1851, son of John Mathias and Elizabeth (Whitcomb) Barnett.

John Mathias Barnett was a farmer, born in Hardy County, Virginia, March 4, 1823, who died at Michingtown, Indiana, December 18, 1880. His wife, Elizabeth Whitcomb, was born in Clinton County, Indiana, February 8, 1829. The genealogy of her family is traced to 1630, when John Whitcomb and his wife came to America on the *Arabella*. He has a direct line to the time of Henry IV, and is entitled to the arms of Berwick Whitcomb. Elizabeth Whitcomb was eligible to the Colonial Dames, and a direct descendant of General James Cudworth, whom history states was a noted man. She was also eligible to the Daughters of American Revolution under Asa Whitcomb, John Whitcomb and William Parmenter.

John David Barnett attended country school, and upon moving to Nebraska took up farming. Starting with little, he reared a fine family, and is an extensive landowner. He was married to Margaret William Denney, daughter of James Maxwell and Susan (Marty) Denney, at Monticello, Illinois, December 31, 1881. Mrs. Barnett was born at Sunfish, Ohio, December 18, 1855. There are seven children: Blanche Dora, married Charles Lyle Ditman; Jessie Elizabeth, married Louis F. Zander; Campsia Pearl married Maurice G. Barr; Georgia Fern, married Dr. Leonard Collins; Hazel Grace is unmarried; Flonnie Irene, married Edward J. Kerbel; and Leilah Alberta, married Lorence F. Raabe.

Mr. Barnett is a Democrat, and a member of the New England Congregational Church at Stanton. He has always been a great hunter and fisherman. Residence: Stanton.

Mable Barnett

Mable Barnett was born at Garden Grove, Iowa, September 2, 1864, the daughter of Samuel and Eliza Ann (Dilsaver) Gribble. Samuel Gribble was born at Hookway, Devonshire County, England, April 12, 1830, and died at Dakota City, Nebraska, November 9, 1922. He came to America in 1840, and later was a farmer. Eliza Ann Diisaver was born at Delaware, Ohio, November 22, 1842, and died at Dakota City, January 14, 1917.

She is married to George Barnett. They have six children, George, born September 10, 1892; Beulah, born February 5, 1894, who is married to Pat Kelher; Wilfred, born September 17, 1896, who is married to Ethel Johns; Helen, born January 5, 1899, who is married to Willard Chessher; and twins, Dorothy and Doris, born November 24, 1901. Dorothy is married to Anthony Hoffman.

Mrs. Barnett came to Nebraska at the age of twenty-seven. She is a member of the Red Cross, the Auxiliary of American Legion, the Hotel Association, Eastern Star, the Rebeccas, the Royal Neighbors, the Lutheran Guild, and the Trainman Auxiliary. Residence: Dakota City.

Arthur Barney

Born at Kearney, Nebraska, July 7, 1886, Arthur Barney is a successful business man there today. His father, Walter Warren Barney, who was born at Roanoke, Illinois, October 21, 1864, and died at Kearney, February 22, 1915, was a pioneer leader in all activities pertaining to the material and spiritual development of his community. His mother, Anna (Thornton) Barney, who is active in church work, was born at Butler, Missouri, January 29, 1866.

Mr. Barney was graduated from the Kearney High School, was midshipman in the United States Naval Academy, and completed a post-graduate course at Boston Technical and Naval School of Engineering. He was a member of the United States Naval Rifle Team and was awarded a medal for marksmanship. Since 1916, he has been a member of the firm W. W. Barney & Son, is president of the Federal Oil and Warehouse Company, and operates two large tourist parks. A Republican, he served as a member of the city council in 1917.

He has held the following positions in state and local

organizations: president of the Nebraska Association of Building & Loan Associations, 1926; president of the Nebraska Association of Local Insurance Agents, 1917-18; vice president of the Nebraska Association of Real Estate Boards, 1931; member of the advisory board of the Red Cross and the Salvation Army at Kearney; secretary of the Kearney Rotary Club, 1919-26; president of the Kearney School Board, 1925-26; and a member of the Board of Visitors of the United States Naval Academy, appointed by President Coolidge, 1926.

Mr. Barney is a member of the Nebraskana Society, the Fort Kearney Memorial Association, the Naval Athletic Association, Greater Nebraska Association, the Kearney Chamber of Commerce, and the Nebraska Realtors Association. He is an Elk and Mason, and a member of the Methodist Church. He is interested in football, golfing, fishing, and hunting, and holds membership in the Kearney Country Club and the Army and Navy Club of Washington. His hobby is preparing young men for admission to the United States Naval Academy. During the World War he was chief of the canteen service, acted as president of the Kearney Red Cross, and just before the close of the war was commissioned captain in the United States Army.

On June 4, 1909, he married Leta J. Haskell, at Annapolis, Maryland. Mrs. Barney, who is a homemaker and teacher of music, was born at Augusta, Maine, July 16, 1886. She is the niece of Judge Gaslin, a pioneer judge of early Nebraska and is a Daughter of the American Revolution through both sides of the family. They have four children: Walter, born March 29, 1910; Juliette, born April 2, 1912; Haskell, born July 16, 1913; and Amelita, born July 16, 1918. Haskell Barney was recently appointed to service in the Naval Academy by Senator Howell. Walter is an employee of the Standard Oil Co., in Omaha; Juliette is a student at the University of Nebraska, and is a member of Kappa Kappa Gamma. Residence: Kearney. (Photograph in Album).

Ralph Morrison Barney

Ralph Morrison Barney, who was born at Kearney, Nebraska, March 29, 1888, is a leading business man of that community. His father, Walter Warren Barney, who was born in Illinois and died at Kearney, February 22, 1915, was an abstractor and real estate dealer; he was active in state title matters and at the time of his death was serving as president of the State Title Association. Anna (Thornton) Barney, his wife, was of English ancestry.

Mr. Barney was graduated from the Kearney High School in 1906. He has been active in abstract work since 1906 when he was in business with his father, and owns one of the most accurate set of abstract records and books in the state. He is now owner of the abstract firm at Kearney, W. W. Barney & Son, and holds stock in various local companies. He has written several articles published in title papers on matters relative to real estate titles.

A Republican, Mr. Barney served as councilman of Kearney during 1915-16, and is active in all local political affairs. He has been a member of the Rotary Club for the past 10 years, has been an active member of the Chamber of Commerce for over 20 years and is affiliated with St. Lukes Episcopal Church of Kearney. He is a member of the Nebraska State Title Association, the American Title Association, and the Kearney Country Club. His fraternal organizations include the Knights Templar and Scottish Rite bodies of the Masons, and the Shrine. For a number of years he served as secretary-treasurer of the Nebraska State Title Association of which he was president for two terms.

His sports include golfing, fishing, and hunting in his summer home in the Rocky Mountains. On April 19, 1914, he was married to Bethine West at Indianapolis,

Indiana. Mrs. Barney, who is descended from Caesar Rodney, a signer of the Declaration of Independence, was born at St. Paul, Nebraska, February 17, 1889. They have four children: Ralph Warren, born February 12, 1915; Emma Jane, born March 5, 1918; Betty, born March 6, 1919; and William George, born October 31, 1923. Residence: Kearney.

Henry F. Barnhart

Henry F. Barnhart, lawyer, was born in Franklin County, Pennsylvania, September 12, 1857, son of D. S. and Mary A. (Rearich) Barnhart. The father was born in Dawson County, Pennsylvania, and died in 1922. His mother was a native of Baden, Germany, who died in 1872.

Mr. Barnhart obtained his early education in the public schools of Pennsylvania, and the University of Pennsylvania. He attended the University of Iowa from which he was graduated in 1884 with the degree of Bachelor of Laws, and for several months was engaged in practice at Kingsley, Iowa.

He came to Nebraska in 1895, and practiced law at Creighton, then removing to Pierce County, Nebraska, where he served four terms as county attorney. In 1906 he came to Norfolk, where he has since resided. He was appointed referee in bankruptcy in 1916 by Judge Woodrow, and held this office ten years. In 1924 he was Democratic candidate for district judge, but was defeated. In addition to his legal practice Mr. Barnhart is the owner of a truck farm of 12 acres where he maintains his home. He is a member of the Madison County Bar Association, the Nebraska State Bar Association, the Elks, and the Modern Woodmen of America.

He is married to Mattie Stewart, daughter of pioneer settlers in Nebraska, and they have two children, Walter H., who married Woodie V. Lamb; and Mary, who married Charles Abbott of Stanton, Nebraska. Mr. and Mrs. Abbott have one son, Harry. Residence: Norfolk.

John Westhafer Barnhart

For the past 54 years John W. Barnhart has been engaged in the publishing business in Nebraska, and has held various editorial positions on newspapers, some of which he founded. He was born at Mount Joy, Lancaster County, Pennsylvania, November 8, 1856, the son of Israel and Lydia (Bear) Barnhart. His father, who was a contractor and builder, was born at West Manchester, York County, Pennsylvania, September 13, 1827, and died at Mount Joy, June 22, 1904. His German ancestors came to this country before the Revolution.

His mother, who was active in church affairs throughout her life, was born at Mountville, Lancaster County, Pennsylvania, February 11, 1826. Her ancestors were English and German, and were in America before the Revolution. She died at Mount Joy, August 20, 1895.

Mr. Barnhart received his early education in the public schools of Mount Joy, and was graduated from the high school there in 1874. He was a student at Cedar Hill Seminary, 1874-75.

He was editor of the *Sterling News* 1877-78, and during 1879-81, together with C. W. Pool, former Secretary of State, established the *Tecumseh Journal;* in 1881 purchased a half interest of General Victor Vifquain in the *Daily State Democrat* at Lincoln; in 1883 Albert Watkins purchased the Vifquain interest and for a year thereafter the publication continued under the firm name of Watkins & Barnhart. In 1894 he established the *Elk Creek Echo* and continued until 1887, when he removed the plant to Auburn, and founded Nemaha County Herald of which he was editor until 1905, in that year he moved to Omaha, and has since been engaged in the job printing business. He is now president of the *Barnhart Press,* formerly the Waters-Barnhart Printing Company.

Mr. Barnhart is a Democrat. He was assistant chief clerk of the Nebraska legislature, 1898-99; was a member of the Congressional Committee from Nemaha County, 1890-92, both times Bryan was elected to congress. He served on the state election commission at Camp Grant, Illinois, during the World War.

On November 20, 1882, he was married at Tecumseh, Nebraska, to Claribel Chittendon Foster. Mrs. Barnhart, who was born at Greencastle, Indiana, February 2, 1858, is the great great granddaughter of Governor Chittendon of Vermont. The following children were born to them: Dr. Edgar G., born March 11, 1884, who married Gussie Durkes; Katherine E., born November 15, 1886, who married Rev. S. J. Hedelund; Charles B., born January 1, 1889, who is secretary-treasurer of the *Barnhart Press;* Chandler F., born November 20, 1893, who married Lorene Hulse, and who is salesman for the *Barnhart Press;* and Marguerite, born January 2, 1896, who died March 28, 1916. Edgar G., is a physician and surgeon on the staff at Lord Lister Hospital.

Mr. Barnhart is chairman of the fellowship division of the Chamber of Commerce; is a member of the Ad Club, and the Ben Franklin Club. He is a member of the Knights of Pythias and the Pythias Veterans. He is affiliated with All Saints Episcopal Church, and is a member of the Men's Club of that church. He is a member of the Omaha Field Club. His favorite sports are golfing and bowling. Residence: Omaha.

Cass Grove Barns

Born on an eighty acre farm in northern Indiana, October 1, 1848, much the youngest of seven children, Cass Grove Barns is the son of Cyrus and Eliza (Elliott) Barns. His father, born in Onondaga County, New York, April 11, 18.8, died in La Porte County, Indiana, May 23, 1883. His mother, born in Onondaga County, May 23, 1809, died in La Porte County, on February 8, 1887.

Tradition assigns his nationality to England, with a mixture of Scotch-Irish ancestry, which was continued in America by intermarriage. An ancestor, Thomas Barns, of Hartford, Connecticut, came to America about 1630, where he joined a party going west to the Connecticut Valley. He participated in the first great Indiana wars, and was given a six acre tract of land in the city of Hartford, and a farm in the country. After peace was proclaimed he was married and his benign neighbors executed his wife for alleged witchcraft. He married again and from that union the entire line descends directly to Cass Grove Barns, he being the seventh generation. Members of the family participated in the Revolution, and the War of 1812. On the maternal side Mr. Barns' lineage is traced to participants in the two wars also, an uncle having lost his life in filibustering expeditions in attempting to take Canada from England.

Reared on a farm, Cass Grove Barns attended district school when possible and taught in country schools several terms. He later became a medical student with an active physician, a custom which antedates the interneship of the present day. After graduation he practiced in the thickly populated neighborhood where he grew up, later removing to the county seat where there were fifteen or twenty old doctors. He served as township physician 1879-80, and was appointed county physician, having charge of the county hospital, the poor house, jail and out door poor, which gave him a job in addition to his regular practice.

Having bought wild land in Boone County, Nebraska, he succumbed to the western fever and moved to Albion, in April, 1881. For five years the family lived on their farm, where Dr. Barns supervised the farming and cattle feeding and practiced medicine in Albion. In 1886, he moved into town where he engaged in the drug business with another doctor. After a few years business interests interfered with his medical practice and he ceased answering sick calls. However, he has never been clear of practice, and is still a registered physician.

Dr. Barns has served on the United States Pension Board, has been medical examiner for the Modern Woodmen of America, chief surgeon for the Nebraska National Guard, and in 1922 freshened up a bit at Tulane University. To his credit are several years as a member of the school boards of Albion, and rural districts, as well as several terms as president of the Albion Board of Education.

He was drafted to take charge of the Boone county fair, donating his services, and for a period of six years, during the depression and loss of crops of the nineties, was secretary of that organization. The fair was dying under a heavy debt, and as its secretary he was given complete control. In 1898 he left the organization entirely out of debt.

Dr. Barns is a Democrat, and from 1894-98, was postmaster of Albion. In 1897 he had a newspaper to edit, a farm to operate, a fair to manage, postoffice work to do, and in addition was obliged to assume management of the Albion Flouring Mill doing commercial work with a branch store in Omaha, another in Chattanooga, smaller ones here and there. He directed also a traveling salesman. After a year he sold the *Albion Argus,* left the fair, and being an offensive partisan, was let out of the postoffice by McKinley. Thereafter for a period of twenty-two years he operated the milling business, which earned him a lot of money at first. At one time he owned and operated a small mill at Petersburg, Nebraska, but traded it for land in Kimball County.

In 1908, he purchased a large department store in Albion, operating it two years. In 1911, he again bought the *Argus,* selling it in 1917, because of the dearth of labor due to the war. From 1890 to 1904, Dr. Barnes did much Sunday School work and otherwise supported and assisted the Methodist Church.

When his daughters were students at the University he bought the historic D Street home of William Jennings Bryan, where his family lived two or three years, while he remained in Albion. His wife desiring to return to Albion he built a new home there where the family remained until 1923. At that time he purchased the *Madison Star-Mail,* moving to Madison, where he built another home. He sold the paper in April, 1931. Being idle during the past summer he has devoted much of his time to assembling a 75,000 word fiction story of pre-Civil War times.

The World War period injured the milling business greatly. Dr. Barns was assigned to about all the local war projects that did not pay—he was appointed to organize the County Council of Defensane, securing an admirable organization with county officers and precinct chairmen. To this was added a staff of many auxiliary workers. Among them he organized 13 home guard companies, got their officers commissioned and many companies drilled. No Nebraska Red Cross was functioning, and he was chosen to organize it in the county. He became temporary county chairman and secured an excellent permanent one. He circulated food pledge cards, and to grow wheat one year, distributed two carloads of seed, and the next year sent away for 65 single orders of seed. Dr. Barns carried on war construction alone, denying some and forwarding requests for others. He was called upon to support the sale of bonds, and held meetings for food saving.

Dr. Barns was appointed chairman for Taft's League to Enforce Peace, and then to find jobs for returning ex-service men. He announced that he desired to get overseas where things would be peaceful and quiet, and his application for work in the Red Cross, Salvation Army and Young Men's Christian Association went as far as preparing his passport. He was given many recommendations, which apparently were cancelled by other statements that he was worth more at home.

In addition to the foregoing he was government appeal agent between county and district draft boards. He helped recruit a company of infantry which was camped at the fair grounds and inducted into service. He was responsible for the support, which amounted to considerable, but was later paid by the Albion Commercial Club. The camp was given his name.

Prominent in political life over a long period of time, Dr. Barns was twice elected county commissioner of Boone County. In that capacity he opened most of the hilly roads surrounding Albion, and made many dry run bridges. His brother commissioners backed his leadership, and when a cash basis was attained Dr. Barns quit the job. He was nominated for lieutenant governor in 1920, and was defeated; was unsuccessful candidate for state senator from Boone, Antelope and Greeley once by six votes, which on the recount was reduced to three. On the no license ticket he was candidate for mayor of Albion three times, was defeated twice and elected once. Prior to that he had served as chairman of the village board.

On June 24, 1871, Dr. Barns was united in marriage to Isabelle Smith, in Berrien County, Michigan. Mrs. Barns, who was born in London, England, February 21, 1852, came to New York State with her parents as an infant. They lived there until she was about thirteen, when they removed to La Porte County, Indiana. Of this marriage there are four children: Frank Milan, born July 5, 1877, who married Ruth Burch; Viola Florence, born August 28, 1885; Ruby Eliza, born February 12, 1889, who married Samuel C. Waugh; and Donald Grover, born May 21, 1892, who married Margaret McGregor.

Dr. Barns desired his children to become farmers, but it was not to be. Frank graduated in both medicine and dentistry and became professor of head surgery in the Omaha Dental College. He practiced in Omaha, some years, and entered war service as a lieutenant. Promoted to captain and later to major, he was transferred from the base hospital at Houston, Texas, overseas as general surgeon. There he had command of surgical unit No. 7 which followed the battle front and operated on those sent back from the lines. He was in advance sector from Memorial Day to Armistice Day, and thereafter had charge of hospitals in different parts of France. Returning, he was married and settled in Albion, where he enjoys an extensive clinical practice. They have a son and a daughter.

Viola is professor of history at Mount Holyoke College in Massachusetts. She has four degrees, three from Nebraska, and her Doctor of Philosophy from Yale. After majoring in composition in music, and receiving her Bachelor's degree in English, she became an instructor in history at the University of Nebraska. She was a Phi Beta Kappa there, and winner of scholarships, is the author of a history book *The Dominion of New England*, and has several others now in preparation. For several years she was abroad engaged in research work, mostly in London. She has had several fellowships, from June, 1930, to September, 1931, being employed in research work in London, on furlough from college. She has also had a Guggenheim Foundation fellowship.

Ruby received her Bachelor of Arts degree from Nebraska, taught one year in Nebraska schools, and married Samuel C. Waugh, a college classmate. He is now trust officer for the First Trust Company of Lincoln. They have a thirteen year old daughter.

Donald was a Phi Beta Kappa student at Nebraska, receiving his Bachelor of Arts degree and a scholarship to Harvard. There he received his Master's and Doctor's degrees. He taught for a time in the Milton Academy in Boston, and has spent several years in research work in London. In 1922, he was given a traveling fellowship, spent many months at the University of London, the University of Paris, and Cambridge University, finishing at King's College. In 1929 he was given a Guggenheim Foundation fellowship, and has a book in preparation. He was professor of history several years at the University of Oregon, and this year is filling the same position at the University of Washington. His wife, Margaret McGregor of Northhampton, Massachusetts, was also a college worker at the University of Oregon.

Dr. Barns has written several books, the best known being *The Sod House*, published in 1930. His first newspaper work began in 1885, when he became owner of the *Albion Argus*. He was a charter member of the first national bank established in Boone County, and served as director in the First National Bank of Albion 37 years, and about 10 years as vice president. He is a Mason, a Modern Woodman of America, a member of the Nebraska State Historical Society and a life member of The Nebraskana Society. Residence: Madison.

Charles Cecil Barr

Charles Cecil Barr, physician and surgeon of distinction in Madison County, Nebraska, has been a resident of this state for the past 24 years. He was born at Akron, Iowa, July 12, 1884, the son of David and Sarah Barr. His father, who was born at sea in 1845, and died at Sioux City, Iowa, in 1928, was a merchant; whose ancestry was Scotch. His mother died at Waterloo, Iowa, in 1912.

Dr. Barr was graduated from the Sioux City High School in 1903, received the Doctor of Medicine Degree at Sioux City College, 1907, and was awarded membership in the American College of Surgeons in 1930; he held a fellowship in the American College of Surgeons and is a member of Theta Kappa Psi.

At this time Dr. Barr is chief of the surgical staff at Tilden Hospital, Tilden, Nebraska. He is the author of various articles published in medical journals: *Report of a Case of Diabetes Insipidus With a Peculiar Complication*, Nebraska State Medical Journal (1924); and *Carcinoma of Stomach in Young Adults*, Nebraska State Medical Journal (1928).

He holds membership in the Tilden Country Club, the Public Library Board, the Lions Club, Red Cross, and the Nebraskana Society. He is a Master Mason, holding membership in the Shrine and Scottish Rite bodies, and is a member of the Odd Fellows and Elks. His professional organizations include: Five County Medical Society; Nebraska State Medical Society; Elkhorn Medical Society; American Medical Association; and the American College of Surgeons. His favorite sport is golfing, and his hobby is wood work and cabinet making.

For many years Dr. Barr has been very active in civic affairs of his community, having served on the town board and as mayor for four years. During his term as mayor, the village of Tilden was made a city of the second class, mainly through his efforts.

On May 15, 1908, he married Rosa Belle Long, of Sioux City, Iowa, at Dakota City, Nebraska. Mrs. Barr, who was born at Lyons, Nebraska, February 26, 1882, is the daughter of native Missourians. They have four children: Dorothy C., born January 3, 1910; Gwendolyn G., born June 13, 1912; Carl Cecil, born June 21, 1915; and Robert Earl, born February 24, 1920. Ruth, who is an adopted child, was the daughter of Mrs. Lucy Collins, a sister of Mrs. Barr; she was graduated from the University of Nebraska, in 1930. Dorothy received the R. N. degree at the University of Nebraska in 1930. Mrs. Barr holds membership in the Eastern Star and Royal Neighbors, besides other local clubs. Residence: Tilden.

Everett Morrison Barr

Everett M. Barr was born at Liberty, Pawnee County, Nebraska, November 7, 1895. His father, John David Barr, was a farmer, banker, and political leader of Nebraska. Of Scotch ancestry, he was born at Hanover, Jo Daviess County, Illinois, April 16, 1858, and died at Beatrice, Nebraska, October 20, 1928. He served as state senator from 1918 to 1920, and from 1922 to 1924.

Mary Elizabeth (Morrison) Barr, mother of Everett Barr, was born of Scotch-Irish parents at LaPrairie, Illinois, December 5, 1867, and died at Excelsior Springs, Missouri, July 3, 1925.

Mr. Barr received his elementary education in the

country schools of Pawnee County after which he was graduated from the Liberty High School, 1914. In June, 1918, he received the B. S. degree from Tarkio College, Tarkio, Missouri, where he was graduated with the honor *Summa Cum Laude.* He was awarded the M. S. degree at Washington and Jefferson College, Washington, Pennsylvania, in June, 1920. He spent a short time at the University of Colorado, at Boulder. During his stay at Tarkio College he won his letter in football, serving as captain of the team in 1917. He was president of the senior class, 1917-18.

Upon completing his college course Mr. Barr was instructor of chemistry at Washington and Jefferson College for two years. Since that time he has farmed in Nebraska. He is a member of the board of directors of Tarkio College, and has been a member of the district school board, of which he is treasurer, since 1927, and is County Commissioner of Pawnee County.

He was married on October 12, 1921, at Washington, Pennsylvania, to Margaret Eleanor Hawkins. She was born June 20, 1898, at Washington, and died at Pawnee City, Nebraska, August 15, 1923. In 1927 he married Vera Colette Duncan, at Albia, Iowa. She was former music instructor of the public school of Perry, Iowa. There are two children: John David, Jr., born August 10, 1923; and Joseph Lee, born June 9, 1929.

Mr. Barr served as a private in the 23rd training battalion, field artillery, in the late war. He is a member of the Red Cross, the American Legion, and the Mission Creek United Presbyterian Church. His favorite sport is football. He is a Republican. Residence: Liberty.

Joseph Barr

Joseph Barr was born at Hanover, Jo Daviess County, Illinois, March 16, 1860, the son of Robert and Elizabeth (Williamson) Barr. His father, who was a carpenter, was born in Ireland, and died at Hanover, in September, 1859. His mother was born in Ireland, and died at Liberty, Pawnee County, Nebraska, October, 1884.

Mr. Barr has lived in Nebraska 51 years. He was married at Clarinda, Iowa, May 9, 1894, to Christina Hancock, who was born at Alford, Aberdeenshire, Scotland. To this union five children were born. They are: Marie, born February 27, 1895; Ross M., born May 2, 1897, who married Ethel Jorgenson; Edna, born February 17, 1899, who married Newell M. Beatty; Lowell C., born March 3, 1901; and Joseph Harold, born April 9, 1911.

He is affiliated with the United Presbyterian Church at Pawnee City, and is a Republican. Residence: Pawnee City.

Ross Morrison Barr

Ross Morrison Barr, farmer and stockman, was born at Liberty, Nebraska, May 2, 1897. His father, Joseph Barr, was born at Hanover, Jo Daviess County, Illinois, March 16, 1860; and his mother, Christina Hancock, at Alford, Aberdeenshire, Scotland, October 1, 1871. Joseph Barr is a retired farmer and stockman, is president of the Citizens State Bank of Pawnee City, and has been vice president of the State Bank of Liberty.

Ross M. Barr received his early education in rural school until 1913, and attended Tarkio College where he received his Bachelor of Science degree in 1922. He took an active part in all campus activities at Tarkio College; was president of the class of 1921; vice president, treasurer and critic of Tarkio Literary Society, editor of *Tarkiana*, the Tarkio College annual; and president of the Young Men's Christian Association. His interest in athletics has been extensive; he played football at Liberty High School, and both football and baseball at Tarkio College.

On August 12, 1925, his marriage to Ethel Irene Jorgensen was solemnized at Minden, Nebraska. Mrs. Barr, prior to her marriage was a mathematics teacher. She is the daughter of Charles J. and Mary H. Jorgensen, the

former a master farmer of Nebraska, in 1929.

Their daughter, Josephine, born November 18, 1927, has a promising future due to the interest and ability of her parents in educational work.

He is a Republican. He is an elder of the Mission Creek United Presbyterian Church of which he was superintendent for three years, and is also a member of The Nebraskana Society. Residence: Liberty.

William Milton Barr

William M. Barr, chemical engineer of Omaha, Nebraska, was born at West Union, Iowa, August 26, 1878, the son of Robinson Alexander Barr and Nancy Fenner (Slocum) Barr. His father, who was an Iowa business man, was born in Pennsylvania, July 6, 1838, and died at Grinnell, Iowa March 4, 1920; he served in the Civil War for four years. His Scotch ancestors were in America in 1776; his great grandfather served in the Revolution for 7 years; and his grandfather was a soldier in the War of 1812.

His mother was born at Lake Zurich, Illinois, March 23, 1845. Her English ancestors came to America in 1740. She died November 26, 1931.

Mr. Barr was graduated from the high school at Britt, Iowa, in 1894. He holds the following degrees: B. S., University of Iowa, 1902; M. A., Grinnell College, 1904; Ph. D., University of Pennsylvania, 1908. He is a member of Sigma Xi and Phi Gamma Delta. He served as instructor of chemistry at Grinnell College, 1902-05; was assistant instructor of chemistry at the University of Pennsylvania, 1905-06; was chemist for the United States Geology Survey, 1906; was Harrison fellow at the University of Pennsylvania 1907-08; was research chemist for the Mallinckrodt Chemical Works, 1908-09; was professor of engineering chemistry at Iowa State College, 1909-11; was superintendent of the Andrews Chemical Works, at Davenport, Iowa, 1911-12; and was manager of the eastern plant of the Mallinckrodt Chemical Works, 1913-16. Since 1916 he has been consulting chemist of the Union Pacific System, and is now assistant to the vice president in charge of operation.

He is the author of articles on water supply, boiler feed water, locomotive materials, alloy steels, and so on. He is a member of the Omaha Engineers Club; the American Chemical Society; the American Institute of Chemical Engineers; the American Water Works Association; the American Society for Testing Metals; and the American Railway Engineering Association. He is a member of the Omaha Chamber of Commerce and is a Universalist. His sports are golfing and fishing. He is a Mason. Politically, Mr. Barr is a Republican.

His marriage to Anna M. Lyndall was solemnized at St. Louis, Missouri, March 23, 1909. Mrs. Barr, who was born at New Albany, Indiana, was supervisor of music and teacher of voice and piano. Her ancestors came to America from England before the Revolution. They have one son, William, born July 9, 1918. Residence: Omaha.

Emil John Barry

Emil John Barry, farmer and bank director, residing near Weston, Nebraska, has lived in this community all his life. He was born at Weston, November 10, 1881, the son of Anton and Johanna (Johanson) Barry. His father, who is a farmer, was born at Varberg, Sweden, February 22, 1848. His mother was born at Stockholm, Sweden, and died at Weston, November 1, 1910.

Mr. Barry attended the public schools, and later attended Luther College for a time. He is a director in the Farmers & Merchants Bank at Malmo, Nebraska, and has been a farmer in Saunders County for many years. He is affiliated with the Evangelical Lutheran Church in which he is a trustee, is a member of the Farmer's Union and holds membership in the Nebraskana Society. He is a Democrat.

On February 23, 1914, he was united in marriage with Charlotta Fredricka Peterson, at Omaha, Douglas County, Nebraska. Mrs. Barry was born at Wahoo, Saunders County, Nebraska, March 17, 1887. They have two children: Willard, born September 20, 1915, and Donald, born November 13, 1922. Residence: Weston.

Richard August Barry

Richard August Barry was born at Malmo, Nebraska, March 27, 1891, the son of Barney Elof and Anna (Johnson) Barry. His father, a farmer, was born in Sweden, April 24, 1853, and died at Malmo, October 26, 1914. His mother was born at Stockholm, Sweden, September 8, 1852, and died at Wahoo, on January 8, 1921.

Mr. Barry is a farmer near Malmo, and is now serving as director of the Farmers and Merchants Bank of Malmo. He is a director of the school board, is affiliated with the Red Cross, and holds membership in the Nebraskana Society. He is a member of the Masons.

On November 28, 1917, his marriage to Pearl Verna Roslund was solemnized at Omaha; she was born at Weston, Saunders County, Nebraska, December 23, 1898. To this marriage two children were born: Wayne, born June 23, 1921; and Eileen, born January 10, 1923. Residence: Malmo.

Frank A. Barta

Born at Pishelville, Nebraska, December 3, 1876, Frank A. Barta is the son of John and Anna (Schiner) Barta, the former a blacksmith and farmer and a homesteader in Nebraska in 1874. His father was born in Czechoslovakia, January 15, 1847, and died at Pishelville, September 29, 1915. His mother was born in Czechoslovakia, November 28, 1851, and died at Pishelville, August 16, 1926.

Mr. Barta attended rural school and in 1903 was graduated from Wayne Normal School with the B. S. degree. He received the LL. B. degree at the University of Nebraska Law School in 1906, where he received letters in football and baseball, and was a member of the athletic board. He taught school in Knox County, Nebraska, for five years, was engaged in the hardware and implement business for a time, and since then has been a lawyer at Center, Nebraska, in the firm Peterson & Barta.

He was vice president of the Knox County Bank at Verdigre, Nebraska, is attorney for the village of Center, and is a member of the village council. He is city treasurer, was secretary of the Knox County Republican Club for eight years, and during the World War was a member of the committee on Liberty loan drives, was a member of the Home Guards, and served on the registration board.

He holds membership in the Northeastern Bar Association, the Nebraska State Bar Association, and the Masons. His chief recreations are tennis and bridge. He was married to Rose A. Shimanek at Wilber, Nebraska, November 21, 1906. Mrs. Barta who is secretary in the law office of Peterson & Barta, was born at Crete, Nebraska, February 14, 1881. To them two children were born: June Ona, June 1, 1913, who is a teacher; and Janice Ann, April 1, 1916. June is Women's Tennis champion of northeast Nebraska. Residence: Center.

Fred Bartels

Fred Bartels, a farmer and livestock feeder in Dakota County, Nebraska, for the past 50 years, was born at Wenden-Wienburg, Germany, June 1, 1867, the son of Henry and Wilheminia (Herman) Bartels. His father, who was born at Wenden-Wienburg, in April, 1830, and died at Dakota City, Nebraska, July 26, 1910, was a livestock farmer of prominence at the time of his death. His mother, who was an ardent church worker, was born in Germany, May 10, 1843, and died at Dakota City, August 28, 1920.

Mr. Bartels began farming in a drainage district in Nebraska his aim being to drain swamps and divert flooding creeks to the nearest point into the Missouri River. This problem was kept in the courts for twenty years, and in 1916 he succeeded in winning the case in the United States Supreme Court. He has served as a member of the Drainage Board for many years, and through this plan has succeeded in producing the best products of the west. He delivered the first sheep and hogs to the Sioux City Stock Yards, fattened the first sheep in northeastern Nebraska, and has always been successful in stockraising.

He traveled all over the United States in his youth buying sheep and cattle. In 1928, together with his wife, he made a tour of Europe where he investigated farming conditions in England, Belgium, France, and Switzerland; his conclusion, based on observation in those countries, was that northeastern Nebraska farm products are vastly superior to those of other lands.

Mr. Bartels is a member of the German Lutheran Church, has been a member of the local school board at Hubbard, Nebraska, for 22 years, and has had charge of the Taylor Cemetery since 1904. On March 6, 1890, he married Rica Ostemeyer at Dakota City. Mrs. Bartels, whose ancestors have lived in Germany many generations, was born at Bilefield, Germany, January 7, 1871.

These children were born to them: George, born August 10, 1893, who married Frieda Wendte; Minnie, December 20, 1890, who married Charles Heikes; Lena, March 1, 1892, who married Thomas Renz; Mabel, born January 30, 1895; Gertrude, June 12, 1897, who married James Hefferman; Elmer, born July 16, 1899, who married Nell Maloney; Roy, born November 30, 1901, who married Marie Oehlerking; Freddie, February 6, 1906, who married Camilla Hartnett; Ollie, November 11, 1903, who married Catherine Larson; Melvin, August 24, 1908; and Dorothy, October 28, 1909. Residence: Hubbard.

William Sylvester Bartholomew

Born in Bellevue, Nebraska, January 4, 1877, William Sylvester Bartholomew is the son of Arthur Corwin and Charlotte (Florkee) Bartholomew. His father was born in Harpersfield, Ohio, May 24, 1841, and was a carpenter and farmer. He died at Lebanon, Nebraska, August 23, 1925. His ancestry can be traced to English and Welsh settlers in America prior to the Revolution.

Charlotte Florkee was born in Indiana, on January 20, 1848, and died at Lebanon, May 29, 1915. She was the daughter of a Methodist Episcopal minister who came to eastern Nebraska in 1856. A devoted wife and mother, she was an early western mid-wife, eligible to register as a physician at the time the law was passed in Nebraska making registration necessary.

Educated in the country schools of Red Willow County, William Sylvester Bartholomew attended the Wilsonville High School and obtained his remaining credits by examination at the Lincoln Academy in 1903. He attended Cotner University, and received his medical degree from the Lincoln Medical College on April 23, 1907, there he was a member of Tau Alpha Epsilon.

Dr. Bartholomew has been in practice since 1907, and from 1907 until 1918 practiced at Marion, Nebraska. Since 1920 he has been in practice at Lebanon. He is now specializing in obstetrics and gynecology. He is the author of an article on physical examination for marriage licenses published in 1912, and one on sex published in 1931.

From 1918-20, he held the rank of first lieutenant in the Medical Corps, attached to the 37th Infantry United States Army. Prior to entering the service he was a captain in the home guard, and assisted in loan drives. Dr. Bartholomew is a member of the American, Nebraska State and Red Willow County Medical Associations, the

American Legion and the First Presbyterian Church. He is a Mason, an Odd Fellow, a Modern Woodman of American, a member of the Eastern Star and the Independent Order of Foresters. His hobby is construction.

On December 12, 1907, he was married to Beatrice Alma Whited at Cozad, Nebraska. Mrs. Bartholomew was born in Harrisonville, Missouri, September 29, 1886, and is a practical nurse. She is a member of the Eastern Star, the Woman's Christian Temperance Union, the Independent Order of Foresters, and active in co-operative extension work in agriculture and home economics, sponsored by the University of Nebraska. There are four children, Lois Irene, born October 19, 1908, at Marion, Nebraska, who is a registered nurse; Arthur Thomas, born June 16, 1911, at Marion, who was a letterman in basketball four years in high school at Lebanon, and in football and basketball his first year in McCook Junior College; Kent Albert, born March 17, 1914, at Marion, who lettered in basketball his second year in Lebanon High School; and Roland Burrdette, born April 8, 1921, at Lebanon. Residence: Lebanon.

Arthur Monroe Bartlett

Arthur Monroe Bartlett, prominent farmer and ranchman, was born at Prescott, Massachusetts, December 26, 1860, and has been a continuous resident of Nebraska, since May 19, 1884. He is the son of Alfred Esery and Rebecca Leah (Putnam) Bartlett. The father was born at Amherst, Massachusetts, February 27, 1837, and died in Audubon County, Iowa, April 10, 1897. He was a farmer descended from Josiah Bartlett who came to America in the Mayflower. Rebecca, his wife, was born at Amherst, October 7, 1840, and died at Los Angeles, April 27, 1915. She was a graduate of the Ladies' Seminary at Wilbraham, Vermont. The Putnam family was English.

Mr. Bartlett attended common school and has since been a farmer and rancher. A Republican, he served three years as commissioner of Dawes County, four years as sheriff of Dawes County, and twenty years as president of the Dawes County Farm Bureau. Mr. Bartlett was a delegate to the Republican national convention in Kansas City, in 1928.

On December 15, 1880, he was married to Ada Linetta Shrauger at Exira, Iowa. She is the daughter of John and Anna (Olmstead) Shrauger. Mrs. Bartlett was born at Rock Island, Illinois, March 6, 1863, of German descent. They have one son, Alfred, born August 21, 1882. Residence: Chadron.

William Allen Bartlett

William Allen Bartlett, retired farmer and business man, prominent in Valley County for many years, was born at Montour, Iowa, November 4, 1872. He is the son of Daniel Simpson and Hannah Miranda (Ford) Bartlett, the former a soldier in Company H, 12th Vermont Volunteers in the Civil War.

Daniel Simpson, born at Litchfield, New Hampshire, November 8, 1835, died at Grinnell, Iowa, June 28, 1912. A carpenter and cabinet maker, he came to Tama County, Iowa, in 1866, and to Valley County, Nebraska, in 1880. He traced his ancestry to the early settlement of New Hampshire, and is said to have been descended from Josiah Bartlett, a signer of the Declaration of Independence.

Hannah M. Ford, his wife, was born at Newberry, Vermont, May 3, 1835, and died at Ord, January 11, 1887. She was active in the work of her church. Her father, Ross C. Ford, was born at Fairfax, New Hampshire, June 7, 1793, and served in the War of 1812. Her mother, Reuben Leighton's daughter, was born March 7, 1796, and died in Lowell, Massachusetts, in February, 1879.

William Allen Bartlett attended country school, Ord High School and the Western Normal College at Lincoln

1892-93. He taught in the rural schools of Valley County for about 9 years, and until he was elected county assessor in 1914, farmed in Valley County. He was county assessor 1914 and 1915, was elected county clerk and recorder of deeds two terms 1916-17, 1918-19, was postmaster at Ord 1920, 21, 22, and 23, and served as mayor two terms. He is a Democrat.

His marriage to Susan Una Hull was solemnized at Ord, Nebraska, November 10, 1897. She was born at Atkinson, Illinois, September 1, 1879. She is the daughter of William C. and Susan (Benedict) Hull. There are four children, Ida Blanche Gilmore, born October 24, 1901, who lives in Lincoln; Helen Una Nelson, born August 20, 1903, who resides at Omaha; Murl May, born April 21, 1906, who lives at Ord; and Daniel Clarke, born June 17, 1908, editor of the *Arcadia Weekly*.

Mr. Bartlett was clerk of the Selective Service Board during the World War, and is a life member of the Civil Legion. For the past fifteen or twenty years he has been a member of the Knights of Pythias, and for many years he has been a member of various school and township boards. He is affiliated with the First Presbyterian Church of Ord, and is a life member of The Nebraskana Society. Baseball as a spectator is his favorite sport. Residence: Ord.

William Clarence Bartlett

Born at Centerville, Iowa, January 7, 1879, William Clarence Bartlett has resided in Nebraska for twenty-eight years, and during all of that time has been a physician and surgeon in private practice.

He is the son of Abner Mathew and Julia Ann (Wright) Bartlett, the former, a farmer, born in Cardington, Ohio, March 13, 1850. He is of Scotch and English descent, his ancestors having come to America prior to the Revolution. The mother, born in Centerville, Iowa, August 11, 1849, died at Larned, Kansas, August 7, 1914. She was of Irish descent.

Dr. Bartlett attended common school until 1895, and thereafter was a student at Central Normal College and Kansas Wesleyan University. He received his medical degree from Central Medical College in 1904, and came directly to Alma where he has since practiced, with the exception of the time spent in army service. He was a member of the Medical Corps, U. S. Army, with the rank of first lieutenant July 10, 1917, promoted to captain May 14, 1918, and was discharged April 18, 1919. Dr. Bartlett was in command of Section "F", U. S. Army Base Hospital, Fort Riley, Kansas. He is local surgeon for the C. B. & Q. Railroad at present.

He is a member of the American Legion, the American, Nebraska State and Harlan County (secretary) Medical Associations and the Railway Surgeons Association. A director of the Lions Club, he is also a member of the city council, and was delegate to the Democratic National Convention in Houston in 1928. For three years he was a member of the Alma School Board.

On December 26, 1906, Dr. Bartlett was married to Grace C. Sturdevant at Tecumseh, Nebraska. A school teacher before marriage, Mrs. Bartlett was born at Atkinson, Nebraska, October 12, 1885, of pre-Revolutionary ancestry. They have two daughters, Helen, born February 9, 1909, a graduate of the University of Nebraska School of Journalism; and Marian, born September 5, 1911, who is specializing in dietetics at the University. Residence: Alma.

James Earl Bartley

Born at Powhatan, Kansas, January 27, 1890, James Earl Bartley is the son of William Randall and Sarah Ann (Ranshaw) Bartley. His father, a farmer, was born in Virginia on May 8, 1863, and his mother in Kansas on April 7, 1868.

James Earl Bartley attended public school in Kansas until 1906, and for a time was a student at the Jennings, Kansas, High School. He completed his course at Nebraska Wesleyan Academy, and in 1925 received his Bachelor of Arts degree from Nebraska Wesleyan University. His Master of Arts degree was awarded by the University of Nebraska in 1930. Mr. Bartley was a member of the Wesleyan male quartet four years, was a member of Pi Gamma Mu and the Botany Club. He was graduated in music in 1916.

His marriage to Neva Leona McNiel was solemnized at Otoe, Iowa, August 16, 1916. Mrs. Bartley, a native of North Loup, was born December 8, 1893, of Scotch and Irish parentage. They have two sons, Ernest Randall, born May 11, 1919, and Richard Lee, born January 11, 1923.

Mr. Bartley's entire career has been devoted to teaching, with the following exceptions: He was city treasurer, elected on the Republican ticket, of University Place 3 years; bookkeeper of the First National Bank a year and a half; assistant cashier five and a half years, and cashier 3 years, of the Citizens State Bank of Lincoln. Junior High school principal during 1924-25, Mr. Bartley was principal of the Burke, South Dakota, High School the year 1925-26, and superintendent of schools at Bennet, Nebraska, from 1926-28. During 1929-30 he was the holder of a scholarship in business research at the University of Nebraska. At the present time Mr. Bartley is head of the department of business at Dana College.

During the World War Mr. Bartley had charge of the sale of Liberty Bonds, and held the rank of first sergeant in the Nebraska Home Guard. He is a member of the Nebraska State Teachers Association, the Symposium of University Place, and from 1920-23 he was school treasurer. His religious affiliation is with the First Methodist Episcopal Church of Lincoln.

Mr. Bartley's hobbies are music and the industrial arts, while his favorite sports are baseball and tennis. Residence: Blair.

Neva Leona Bartley

Neva Leona Bartley, daughter of Levi and Minnie (Foutts) McNiel, was born at North Loup, Nebraska, December 8, 1894. Her father, who was of Scotch-Irish descent was born at Withville, Virginia, November 2, 1860, and died at Lincoln, October 22, 1927. A Methodist minister for more than forty years, he was a graduate of Athen's School of Theology. His wife, who was born in Iowa, February 5, 1870, is of English and French extraction.

Educated in the public schools of Nebraska, Missouri, South Dakota, Minnesota and Oregon, Mrs. Bartley was graduated from the eighth grade at Wakonda, South Dakota, and from the Stromsburg, Nebraska, High School. In 1916 she was awarded her Bachelor of Arts degree from Nebraska Wesleyan University, where she was secretary of her class. A member of Alpha Epsilon, now Beta Phi Alpha, she was its president in 1916.

On August 16, 1916, she was united in marriage to James Earl Bartley at Otoe, Iowa. Mr. Bartley, who is a teacher, was born at Powhatan, Kansas, January 27, 1890. There are two sons, Ernest Randall, born May 11, 1919; and Richard Lee, born January 11, 1923.

Mrs. Bartley has taught for several years, serving as head of the English departments in the junior and senior high schools at Burke, South Dakota, and principal of the Bennet, Nebraska, high school. She has been a teacher in the Daily Vacation Bible School in Lincoln, and is now part time teacher at Dana College.

She is a member of the First Methodist Episcopal Church of Lincoln, the Red Cross, Eastern Star and The Nebraskana Society. Her social clubs include the Monday Afternoon Club of Blair, and the Dana College Faculty Women's Club of Blair. Residence: Blair.

Frank W. Bartos

Frank W. Bartos, one of the state's most prominent lawyers, has lived in Nebraska for the past 47 years and since 1900 has been engaged in the active practice of law. He was born in Bohemia, August 1, 1878, the son of Frank and Katerina (Bauer) Bartos. His father, who was a tailor, was born in Bohemia, and died at Wilber, Saline County, Nebraska.

His mother was born in Bohemia and died at Wilber. Mr. Bartos was graduated from the Wilber High School June, 1896, and later was a student at the University of Nebraska College of Law where he received his LL. B. degree and was admitted to the bar at Lincoln, Lancaster County, Nebraska, June 7, 1900. He began the practice of law alone and a little later organized the firm Bartos, Bartos & Placek, of which he is senior member.

He is a director of the Home Guardian Life Insurance Company of Lincoln, and is a director of the Bank of Wilber. A Democrat, Mr. Bartos served as state senator in 1909 and 1911. During the past decade he has become known as one of Nebraska's most eloquent orators and has at this time a legal practice extending over the entire middle west.

His marriage to Anna Svacina was solemnized at Omaha, October 21, 1903. Mrs. Bartos was born at Omaha, January 21, 1879. They have two children: Camile, born January 12, 1905, who married Otto Placek; and Helen, born July 30, 1909, who married Victor Dvorak. Residence: Wilber. (Photograph on Page 87).

Stanley Bartos

For the past 45 years Stanley Bartos has lived in Nebraska, and since 1907 he has been engaged in the practice of law. He was born in Czechoslovakia, June 29, 1883, the son of Frank and Katerina (Bauer) Bartos. His father, who was a tailor, was born in Czechoslovakia, August 10, 1834, came to America in 1885, and died at Wilber, Saline County, Nebraska, September 6, 1915. His mother was born in Czechoslovakia, November 19, 1843, and died at Wilber, June 15, 1923.

Mr. Bartos was graduated from the Wilber High School in 1902, and from 1904 to 1907 was a student at the University of Nebraska where he received his LL. B. degree. He was elected to membership in Theta Kappa Nu. He was a country school teacher for two and a half years, and practiced law as the junior member of the firm Bartos & Bartos until 1927, when the firm changed to Bartos, Bartos & Placek.

His marriage to Theresa Othelia Beck was solemnized in Gage County, Nebraska, October 29, 1907. Mrs. Bartos, who was born in Saline County, September 25, 1887, is prominent in social affairs at Wilber, and has taken an active part in various local theatricals. They have five children: Theresa, born October 24, 1908, who was awarded the A. B. degree at Lindenwood College, St. Charles, Missouri, and who is teaching in the Wilber High School; Blanche, born August 8, 1910, who is a student at the University of Nebraska; Stanley F., born February 1, 1913, who is a student at Wentworth Military Academy at Lexington, Missouri; Dorothy, born December 2, 1916; and Mary, born April 14, 1921.

Mr. Bartos is a member of the Knights of Pythias and the Nebraskana Society. He served as a member of the Wilber school board, 1921-22. His hobby is raising flowers. He is a Republican. Residence: Wilber. (Photograph on Page 88).

John E. Baruth

John E. Baruth was born at Alexandria, Nebraska, December 3, 1885. He received a common school education in District No. 10 in Jefferson County, and was graduated in 1905.

Fredrick Baruth, father of John E. Baruth, was born in Germany, and came to Manitowoc, Wisconsin, when he

FRANK W. BARTOS

Townsend—Lincoln

STANLEY BARTOS

was about three years old. He is an outstanding resident and one of Thayer County's most successful farmers. Louise (Hamann) Baruth, mother of John, was born in Germany, and died at Alexandria, Nebraska, August 26, 1924.

John Baruth's marriage to Emma Proett took place at Alexandria, November 22, 1911. She was born at Herman, Missouri, June 15, 1888, and to this union was born two children: Raymond Edward, born November 13, 1912, and Vernon Dwight, born January 29, 1917. Both boys are students and are helpers in their home on the farm.

During the late war Mr. Baruth participated in civilian relief work and in loan drives. He is a member of the Red Cross, and an elder in the First Presbyterian Church of Alexandria. His hobby is mechanics. Mr. Baruth has always been active in the civic organizations of his community and through such splendid efforts was elected to and made a life member of the Nebraskana Society. Mr. Baruth is an independent Republican, however, he has never aspired to any office although he has always been interested in politics. Residence: Alexandria. (Photograph in Album).

Conrad Leslie Baskins

Conrad Leslie Baskins, lawyer, was born at North Platte, Nebraska, January 30, 1889, and is the son of Charles Wesley and Florence Rose (Ranck) Baskins.

His father, who was a locomotive engineer for the Union Pacific Railroad, of Scotch ancestry, was born at Benue, Pennsylvania, March 6, 1860. His wife, Florence Rose, was born at New Columbia, Pennsylvania, December 24, 1853, of French ancestry. The parents are residing at North Platte. Mr. Baskins retired on a pension August 1, 1925.

In June, 1902, Mr. Baskins was graduated from North Platte Schools, and on May 24, 1906, was graduated from North Platte High School. He received the Bachelor of Arts and the Master of Arts degrees from Bucknell University, at Lewisburg, Pennsylvania, in 1910 and 1912, respectively, and on June 12, 1913, was awarded the Bachelor of Laws degree from the University of Nebraska. While at Bucknell he was a member of the football team in 1909.

Admitted to the bar of Nebraska on June 12, 1913, Mr. Baskins has practiced law since that time, and is now a member of the firm Beeler, Crosby and Baskins of North Platte. He is a Democrat.

His marriage to Leah Elizabeth Jenkins was solemnized at Sunbury, Pennsylvania, December 31, 1913. Mrs. Baskins was born at Milton, Pennsylvania, July 28, 1888, and is of Welsh descent. They have two children, Charles William, born July 24, 1920; and Robert Leslie, born July 6, 1924.

During the World War, Mr. Baskins served with the 13th training battery of the Field Artillery Reserve Training School at Louisville, Kentucky. He is a member of the American Legion and the Forty and Eight. His fraternal organizations include the Elks, the Odd Fellows, and the Knights of Pythias. His club is the North Platte Country Club. Residence: North Platte. (Photograph in Album).

Arthur Harold Bass

Born at Carleton, Nebraska, December 14, 1905, Arthur Harold Bass is the son of Mayo and Mary Estella (Weinbar) Bass. His father, who is a farmer, was born at Iola, Kansas, January 26, 1872, the son of Zeno Bass, a farmer and banker. His mother was born at Hastings, Iowa, April 30, 1872.

Mr. Bass attended the public schools of Geneva, Nebraska, and in 1924 was graduated from Central City High School. Later he was a student at Nebraska Central College and the University of Nebraska. He was employed as stenographer in the law office of Waring & Waring at Geneva, and in the office of John C. Martin of Central City, Nebraska. During his college days he was employed by the Supreme Court Commission and at this time he is official reporter for the Eleventh Judicial District of Nebraska.

A Republican, he received appointment as secretary to Supreme Judge George A. Eberly serving from 1929 to 1930. He holds membership in the Nebraska Shorthand Reporters Association, the National Shorthand Reporters Association, and the First Christian Church of Grand Island. His fraternal societies are: Masons; and Elks. He is interested in golf and football.

His marriage to Ruby Elnora Nicholas was solemnized at Central City, Nebraska, November 24, 1927. Mrs. Bass, who was born at Palmer, Nebraska, June 23, 1906, is the daughter of A. C. Nicholas who is cashier of the Central City National Bank, and Francina (Campbell) Nicholas. They have two children: Orval, born April 20, 1929; and Merlyn Elaine, born September 29, 1931. Residence: Grand Island.

Charles Kelly Bassett

Charles Kelley Bassett, editor of the *Grant County Tribune* was born at Abingdon, Illinois, February 24, 1859, and has resided in Nebraska for 27 years. His father, George Bassett, was born in New York State, January 9, 1809, and died at Abingdon, June 17, 1889. He was a general merchant of French and Irish descent. His wife, Nancy, was born in Brown County, Ohio, February 28, 1818, and died at Abingdon, May 1, 1906. Her ancestry was Irish.

Mr. Bassett attended district school and on July 1, 1905, was married to Birdie Belle White at La Moure, North Dakota. Mrs. Bassett was born at Onalaska, Minnesota, July 22, 1878.

Mr. Bassett has been in the newspaper business almost ever since coming to Nebraska, and is also the owner of a moving picture theatre. He started to work in a printing office in 1873, and established his first newspaper at Abingdon, Illinois, in 1877. He is a member of Lions International Club, is a 32nd degree Mason and member of the Shrine. He is a member of the Knights of Pythias, the Eagles, and the Odd Fellows (all degrees, including the degree of chivalry). Residence: Hyannis.

Harvey Theodore Bates

Born at Carleton, Nebraska, October 2, 1881, Harvey Theodore Bates is the son of Walter C. and Mary (Keim) Bates. His father, who was born at Troy, New York, January 17, 1842, died at Carleton, February 24, 1930. He was a well borer, farmer and nurseryman, and a veteran of the Civil War. For eight years prior to his death he had been retired. His wife was born at Meyersdale, Pennsylvania, May 10, 1850, and died at Carleton, January 28, 1930. Her ancestry was German.

Harvey Theodore Bates attended public school, took some work at the University of Nebraska, and completed a course at Lincoln Business College. He also had a course in pharmacy. On October 3, 1906, he was united in marriage to Eva May Miller at Carleton. Mrs. Bates, who is of Pennsylvania German descent, was born at Waterloo, Iowa, June 6, 1882.

Mr. Bates has been a resident of Nebraska for more than forty-nine years, and at the present time is secretary-treasurer of the Farmers Mutual Insurance Company of Thayer County. He is chairman of the Board of Education for District No. 26, and a member of the Progressive Brethren Church of Carleton. Recently he was awarded life membership in the Nebraskana Society. Although Mr. and Mrs. Bates have no children of their own, they have made a home for LaVerne Fitton and her brother Donald Fitton. They also have one adopted daughter, Mary Katherine, born January 30, 1925. Residence: Carleton. (Photograph in Album).

Luke Manning Bates

Luke Manning Bates, newspaper publisher since 1900, was born at Hartford, Connecticut, October 18, 1877. He is the son of John Mallory and Sarah Maria (Glazier) Bates, the former of whom was born at Wallingford, Connecticut, January 3, 1846. John Mallory Bates was a clergyman of the Episcopal Church and held two degrees, the Bachelor of Arts degree and the Master of Arts degree, from Trinity College in Hartford, Connecticut. He was a fellow of the American Association for the Advancement of Science a botanist and ornithologist, and a member of Phi Beta Kappa (*See Who's Who in America*). His English ancestors fought in the Revolutionary war. He died in May, 1930.

Sarah Maria Glazier, his wife, was born in Hartford, Connecticut, in March 1846, and died at Lincoln, in October, 1919. She was graduated from Vassar College in 1867, and was the first professor of mathematics and astronomy at Wellesly. She was also a member of Phi Beta Kappa, and her English ancestors fought in the Revolution.

Mr. Bates attended private schools, and in 1899, received the degree of Bachelor of Laws from the University of Nebraska. He is a member of Phi Delta Phi.

From 1900 until 1906 he was publisher of the *Long Pine Journal*. Since 1916 he has been publisher and editor of the *Valentine Republican*. Admitted to the practice of law in June, 1899, he has held the office of county attorney and county commissioner of Brown County, 1900-1904. He was register of the United States Land Office at Valentine from 1906 until 1916, and for many years has been chairman of the Republican county central committee.

He has been twice married, the second time in August, 1919, to Minnie Adamson at Valentine. They have four children, Helen K., John M., George E., and Sarah M. Helen is a graduate in home economics and is now with the Edison Illuminating Company of Boston.

During the late war Mr. Bates was secretary of the Cherry County Council of Defense. He has been secretary of the Masons for many years. Recently he was made a life member of The Nebraskana Society. His hobby is books. Residence: Valentine.

John Henry Bath

John H. Bath was born at Washington, Daviess County, Indiana, November 4, 1878, the son of Peter and Anna Magdalena (Houser) Bath. His father, a butcher, was born at Washington, April, 1849, and died there, May, 1881; his parents were born in Germany. His mother was born at Schaffhausen, Switzerland, October 3, 1845.

Mr. Bath attended the public schools of Omaha until the age of 13 when he entered the wholesale dry goods business. In 1907, he was a florist assistant. Since then he has been in business for himself, and is now proprietor and owner of the Bath Florist Company. He is director in the Omaha Wimsett System Company.

On May 26, 1906, he was united in marriage with Maude Adelaide Quarnstrom at Omaha; she was born of Swedish parentage at Omaha, in 1884, and died there December, 1924. One son was born to this marriage: John H., Junior, born October 19, 1911, who died May 8, 1930. Mr. Bath's marriage to Mary MacIntosh was solemnized at Omaha, October 15, 1925. Mrs. Bath was awarded the A. B. degree at the University of Nebraska in 1907, and was a teacher at Central High School for 12 years. She served as president of the Women's Overseas Service League, 1926; and was treasurer of the Omaha College Club, 1911, and 1929-31. They have a son, Hubert MacIntosh, born November 22, 1929.

Mr. Bath was a member of the Nebraska National Guards in 1900-1905; he resigned as first lieutenant. During the World War he was active in various loan drives and war relief work. He is a member of the Chamber of Commerce; the Ad-Sell League; and the Omaha Automobile Association. He is a life member of the Society of American Florists, and is a member of the Omaha Florists Club, serving as secretary of the latter in 1906, and president, 1918-19.

Since 1923 he has been a member of the Omaha Rotary Club. He holds membership in the following fraternal organizations: Elks; Woodmen of the World; Royal Arcanum; and Ak-Sar-Ben. He is a member of the Omaha Walking Club, and since 1923 has been a member of the Omaha Field Club. He is interested in the following sports: golf, hiking, chess, checkers, bridge. His hobby is gardening. He is a member of the Young Men's Christian Association, and is a Republican. (Deceased September 18, 1931).

Roy Batie

Roy Batie, successful stockman and farmer of Overton, Nebraska, was born at Orient, Iowa, January 15, 1884, and for the past 47 years has been a resident of Nebraska. His father, William John Batie, was the son of Jerry and Jane Heslep (Telfer) Batie. He was a farmer, born at London, Canada, June 29, 1855; his Scotch and English ancestors moved to Canada from Northumberland County, England, in 1820. He was married to Caroline Bonus at Orient, Iowa, December 4, 1882. The mother, who was a practical nurse, was born at North Andover, Wisconsin, November 15, 1858, and died at Overton, January 3, 1902. Her father, Edward Bonus, came to this country from England in 1844, and died at Bloomington, October 28, 1879. His wife, Sarah Jane Edwards, came from England at the age of twelve and died at Bloomington in 1883.

Mr. Batie is a breeder of thorough-bred stock, Shorthorn cattle, Poland China hogs, and fine varieties of chickens. He holds membership in the Farmers Elevator Company of Overton, serving as director since its organization. He has been a member of the Dawson County Farm Bureau since its origin, and for the past three years has served on the local school board.

He is affiliated with the Overton Methodist Episcopal Church, is a member of the Red Cross, and holds membership in the Odd Fellows and Modern Woodmen of America. His hobbies are reading and flowers. Politically, Mr. Batie is a Republican.

On June 15, 1920, he married Beulah Edith Ward at Overton. Mrs. Batie, who was a teacher and has served as general secretary of the Young Women's Christian Association, was born at Overton, August 25, 1889. She is a graduate of Kearney State Teachers College, 1909, and Nebraska Wesleyan University, 1913. They have a son: Leroy Ward, born January 17, 1922. Residence: Overton.

John Wilson Battin

John W. Battin, distinguished lawyer and judge of Omaha, Douglas County, Nebraska, was born at Albany, New York, February 6, 1868. His father, Isaac Battin, who was an engineering executive, was born at Millville, Columbia County, Pennsylvania, July 13, 1831, and died at Swarthmore, Delaware County, Pennsylvania, February 12, 1915. His ancestry was English. Nancy (Wilson) Battin, mother of John, was an ardent temperance advocate. She was born at Danville, Montour County, Pennsylvania, October 11, 1840, and died at Millville, April 1, 1918. Her ancestry was German and English.

Judge Battin attended the public schools of Albany, New York, and was graduated from the high school there in 1884. He was a student at the Omaha Law School for a time and in 1890, was awarded his Ph. B. at Cornell University. He was class orator at Cornell University; was a member of the Banjo and Mandolin Club; was elected to Delta Upsilon, and was one of the editors of the Cornell Magazine.

He was engaged in the practice of law in Omaha, from

1893 to 1929. Since 1929 he has been judge of the municipal court at Omaha appointed by Governor Weaver. He was re-elected in November, 1930. He has served as a member of the house of representatives from Douglas County. He has been in Nebraska for the past forty years.

He is a member of the Nebraska State Bar Association; the Omaha Bar Association; Omaha Chamber of Commerce. He is an Elk, an Eeagle, and a Mason. He is affiliated with Trinity Cathedral at Omaha. His favorite sport is golf and his hobby is gardening.

Judge Battin married Lila Josephine Lathrop Brown, who was born December 20, 1877, at Grand Rapids, Michigan. Mrs. Battin is eligible to the Daughters of the American Revolution, Daughters of 1812 and Colonial Dames. Their marriage took place on March 28, 1907. Residence: Omaha.

Ralph G. Batty

Ralph G. Batty was born at Alma, Nebraska, August 31, 1891, the son of E. H. Batty. His father, a real estate man, died at San Leandro, California, in 1930; his ancestry was English. His mother, who was also of English descent, died at Lincoln, November, 1920.

Mr. Batty received his early education in the public schools of Alma; was graduated from the Hastings High School; and received his B. S. degree in 1915 from Hastings College. Later he was a student at the University of Nebraska. He served as principal of the Harvard High School, 1916-17; was appointed state chemist in 1917, and remained in that position until his death, August 6, 1929.

He was affiliated with the Trinity Methodist Episcopal Church for many years, and was a member of the American Chemical Society. Recently, he was honored with membership in the Nebraskana Society. His marriage to Gouldene F. Batty was solemnized at Lincoln, August 21, 1916. Mrs. Batty was born at Lincoln, August 21, 1916. Their children are: Elmer E., born June 6, 1918; and Ralph G., born November 11, 1921.

Charles W. Bauer

Charles W. Bauer, educator and professor of chemistry at Creighton University, was born at Hastings, Nebraska, June 6, 1899. His father, Conrad Arthur Bauer, was born at Krastowec, Russia, January 30, 1873, of German descent. He arrived in New York, in April, 1899, and was naturalized September 5, 1905. He is a farmer. He married Kathryn Margaret Stroh, born at Krastowec, July 10, 1873.

Mr. Bauer was graduated from St. Anthony, Idaho, High School in May, 1919. In 1921 he received his Ph. G. and Ph. C. from Valparaiso University. He entered Creighton University and received his B. S. in August, 1927, and his M. A. in August, 1929. He attended Idaho University the summer of 1923, and Chicago University the summer of 1930. In high school he was active in football, basketball and track, and won a gold medal as best all around athlete in high school. He is a member of Phi Delta Chi and Phi Delta Psi.

In 1921 he was chemist for the Utah Idaho Sugar Company at Sugar City, Idaho, and was analytical chemist for the U. S. Steel Company at Gary, Indiana, during 1922. From 1922-24 he was professor of science at St. Anthony High School. Since 1924 he has been professor of chemistry at Creighton College of Pharmacy. He is also a consulting chemist. He is the author of *Teaching the Meaning of Chemical Structure* (1927); *The Chemistry of a Common Incompatability—Borax on Glycerine* (1929); and the *Relationship of Chemical Structure to Pharmacological Action* (1927).

Professor Bauer is a Republican. He is affiliated with the First Presbyterian Church of Omaha, and a member of the Young People's Society of which he was president in 1928. He is a member of the Nebraska Pharmaceutical Association, the American Pharmaceutical Association, and the American Association for the Advancement of Science. He is a Mason. His sport is golf and his hobby is chemotherapy. On August 27, 1931, he was married to Ruth L. Litton. Residence: Omaha.

Edwin Ayres Baugh

Edwin A. Baugh was born at Andover, Henry County, Illinois, March 11, 1861, the son of Lincoln Sevier and Anne Eliza (Jellison) Baugh. His father, who was a merchant and miller, was born at Greenville, Tennessee, March 17, 1832, and died at Arkansas City, Cowley County, Kansas, August, 1916; he was sergeant in Company C, 112th Regiment of the Illinois Volunteers in the Civil War; his ancestry was Holland Dutch; he is descended from early settlers in the Carolinas. His mother, who was of Irish descent, was born at Venango, Pennsylvania, and died at Arkansas City, July, 1899.

Mr. Baugh has lived in Nebraska for 51 years. From 1885 to 1888 he was postmaster at Oakland, Burt County, Nebraska, and since 1926 has held this position there. He is a Democrat. He is a member of the Sons of Veterans; the Nebraska State Historical Society; and the Nebraskana Society. He holds membership in the Oakland Chamber of Commerce, the Masons, and the Red Cross.

He was united in marriage with Ada Beatrice Cornell at Fremont, Dodge County, Nebraska, April 6, 1887. Mrs. Baugh, whose ancestry was English, was born at Ontario, Canada, April 16, 1864, and died at Omaha, Douglas County, Nebraska, July 2, 1928. Their children are: Leland Arthur, born February 25, 1891; Kenneth Cornell, born January 15, 1899; and Alton Edwin, born May 18, 1900. Residence: Oakland.

Christian Ferdinand Baum

For more than 55 years Christian F. Baum has been a farmer at Dodge, Dodge County, Nebraska. He was born at Sangerhausen, Germany, January 10, 1839. At this time he is 92 years of age and is living with his daughter in Dodge. He served four years in the German army before he came to America.

He was united in marriage with Emilie Richard who was born at Pomeru, Germany, May 15, 1848, and died December 26, 1926. Five children were born to them. Those living are Arthur Carl, a farmer living near Dodge; William Charles, who is in the commission business at Omaha; and Hilda, who married William Ralston, of Dodge. Residence: Dodge.

Herman Ewald Julius Frederick Bauman

Herman "Heinie" Ewald Bauman, wholesale grain merchant, was born at Eau Claire, Wisconsin, March 28, 1887, son of August and Maria (Maas) Bauman.

The father was born in Germany, January 18, 1854, and came to the United States by way of Glasglow and New York in 1883. He was a merchant tailor, whose death occurred at Eau Claire, February 8, 1908. His wife, Maria, was born in Germany, February 22, 1859, and died at Minneapolis, Minnesota, in April 1926. She was married in Germany and came to the United States with her husband in 1883.

Heinie Bauman attended Eau Claire public and high school, and the Eau Claire Business College one year. He was graduated from high school in June, 1905, and afterward took a correspondence course from LaSalle Extension University. He also had two years of extension work from the University of Minnesota.

A grain man all of his mature life, Mr. Bauman has managed grain offices at Lincoln, Hastings, Wichita, Denver, and Sidney. For three years he was cashier for grain firms at Duluth and Minneapolis. At the present time, he is manager of the Sidney office of the Nebraska-Iowa Grain Company.

A former member of the Naval Militia at Duluth, Minnesota, Mr. Bauman served in the United States Navy during the World War. He was commander of Sidney Post No. 17 of the American Legion in 1931 and 1932, and broke all previous records for membership in this post, making it the largest post in western Nebraska. He was vice-district commander of the 4th district of Nebraska in 1932. He is affiliated with the German Lutheran Church, is a member of the Red Cross, the Chamber of Commerce, and the Elks. He is also a member of the Omaha Grain Exchange.

Among the sports in which Mr. Bauman is interested are American Legion Junior baseball, ice hockey, golf, bowling, and rifle shooting. He also enjoys tennis, swimming, wrestling, and boxing and held the Sidney Club championship in 1928. He is a director of the Sidney Country Club, president of the Sidney Rifle Club and manager of the Sidney Ice Hockey Club. While in Hastings Mr. Bauman was president of the Commercial Bowlers League. Residence: Sidney.

Edward Martin Baumann

Edward M. Baumann, who was born at West Point, Nebraska, October 27, 1881, has lived in this state all his life. His father, Otto Andrew Baumann was born in Bavaria, Germany, November 3, 1836, and died at West Point, January 21, 1904. He was a merchant, hotelman, and banker; was active in all enterprises to build up various city factories and establishments; and was chairman of the village board, councilman, and mayor.

Helena (Zepf) Baumann, mother of Edward Baumann, was born at Aldingen, Wittenberg, Germany, April 18, 1847, and died at West Point, February 13, 1929.

Mr. Baumann attended the West Point public schools, the Lutheran Parochial School, and in 1898, was graduated from the West Point High School. He studied business law, shorthand, and bookkeeping at the Gem City Business College, Quincy, Illinois, where he was graduated in 1901; was a student at the University of Nebraska for two years, and was elected to membership in Delta Tau Delta.

He worked in a store from 1901 to 1903; was assistant to Warden Beemer at the Nebraska State Prison, 1903-06; and in 1906 entered the mercantile business. He is now a member of the firm The Baumann Company—Northeast Nebraska's Popular Department Store; secretary of the Refinite Company; and a director of the Cornbelt Life Insurance Company. He is editor of the store paper *The Daylight Messenger*, and was one of the first ten master merchants selected for membership by the *Nebraska Merchant*. A Republican, he has served on various committees, and has been chairman of the Republican County Central Committee.

During the World War Mr. Baumann was active on loan drive committees and served as chairman of the Red Cross drives. He is a member of the West Point Community Club; was a member of the committee to draft the constitution and by-laws; has been a director since its organization in 1922; and has served as vice president and president of the organization. From 1913 to 1922 he was a member of the local school board, serving as secretary two years and president two years.

Mr. Baumann was chairman of the committee that erected the West Point Hotel; is secretary of the Cuming County Agricultural Society; is a charter member of the West Point Lions Club; and holds membership in the Nebraskana Society. He was a member of the West Point Rifles, a national guard company organized after the Spanish American War, holding the ranks of first sergeant and second lieutenant. His social club is the Cuming County University of Nebraska Alumni Club. His hobby is boosting his community; and his religious affiliation is with St. Paul's Evangelical Lutheran Church of West Point.

On June 12, 1907, he was united in marriage with Emma Mary Kloke at West Point. Mrs. Baumann, whose ancestry is Swiss and German, was born at West Point, January 29, 1883. Before her marriage she worked in a bank and a real estate office at West Point. Eight children were born to their marriage, seven of whom are living: Ada, born April 3, 1908, who married Howard D. McEachen; Otto, born August 29, 1909; Alice, born March 28, 1911; Marie, born April 10, 1912, who died August, 1912; Ruth, born June 17, 1913; Paul, born December 25, 1914; Robert, born March 31, 1923; and Marjorie, born November 21, 1924.

Ada was graduated from the University of Nebraska, 1928, where she was elected to Pi Lambda Theta and Phi Beta Kappa. She taught in the Norfolk High School for one year, and is now part time teacher in the Meadow Grove School where her husband is superintendent; she organized the first commercial course in that school. Otto was graduated from the University of Nebraska, 1930, where he was junior student manager of football and senior student manager of baseball. He was formerly treasurer and buyer for the Fraternal Co-operative Association; and is now associated with his father in business. Ruth was graduated from the West Point High School in 1929, and was valedictorian of her graduating class. Alice is married to Lawrence R. Lashley, and resides in Tulsa. Ruth has completed one year at Lindenwood, and planned to enter the university in the fall of 1931. Residence: West Point.

Casper Baumgartner

Casper Baumgartner, merchant, was born at Columbus, Nebraska, November 28, 1895, son of Martin and Ursula (Marty) Baumgartner. The father, who was born in Switzerland, died at Columbus, Nebraska, in 1901. His wife died there in 1909.

Mr. Baumgartner attended public schools, and was graduated from Columbus High School in 1915. Since leaving school he has been a merchant, and at the present time is the proprietor of the Scottsbluff Variety Store. He is independent in politics.

He is married to Myrtice Amber Edwards, daughter of Howard and Weltha Carolina Edwards. She was born at Oakdale, Nebraska, August 1, 1897. They have three children, Richard, born October 12, 1924; Patricia, born March 15, 1927; and Jerold, born February 27, 1929.

During the late war, Mr. Baumgartner served with the American Expeditionary Forces with the rank of corporal in the 338th Field Artillery, 88th division. He is a member of the American Legion, the Red Cross, the Chamber of Commerce, the Elks, and the Parent-Teachers' Association. His religious affiliation is with the Lutheran Church. He enjoys golf, while his hobby is current-events. Residence: Scottsbluff.

Martin Baumgartner

Martin Baumgartner, merchant, was born at Columbus, Nebraska, July 24, 1893, son of Martin and Ursula (Marty) Baumgartner. His parents were Swiss.

Mr. Baumgartner received his education from the public schools of Columbus, and afterward attended night school. For a number of years he has been a prominent merchant.

On September 20, 1916, he was married to Evelyn Frakes at Kearney. Mrs. Baumgartner was born in Meade County, Kentucky, February 13, 1896. They have three children, Imogene Ursula, Albert Martin, and Evelyn Adeline.

Mr. Baumgartner is a member of the Rotary Club, the Chamber of Commerce, and of the German Lutheran Church. Residence: Kearney.

Edward David Beach

Born in Columbia County, Wisconsin, December 8, 1865, Edward David Beach has been a prominent resident of Nebraska for a number of years. His father, Lyman Beach, was born in Luzerne, New York, June 20, 1825, and died at Exeter, Nebraska, October 3, 1906. A farmer, he was intensely patriotic, and during the Civil War was rejected for service on account of physical disability. His ancestry in America is traced to 1635, when John Beach came from Derbyshire, England, and settled in New Haven, Connecticut. He died in 1667, at Wallingford, Connecticut. Benjamin Beach, grandfather of Lyman Beach, served seven years in the Revolutionary Army.

Clarissa Diana Green, wife of Lyman Beach, was born in Catteraugus County, New York, October 9, 1831, and died at Omaha, January 9, 1923. She was a member of the Methodist Episcopal Church for 75 years. Her ancestry was traced to Timothy Green, born in Connecticut, August 9, 1723, and who married Eunice Ellsworth of Windsor, Connecticut, a cousin of Oliver Ellsworth, chief justice of the United States Supreme Court. Timothy Green died November 1, 1796.

On September 1, 1886, Edward David Beach was married to Minnie Estelle Fisher at Exeter. Mrs. Beach was born at Morrison, Illinois, February 22, 1865, and died at Omaha, August 2, 1922. She was a school teacher before her marriage. Her father was German and her mother, Irish. To Mr. and Mrs. Beach were born seven children, all of whom are living: Bessie C., born August 14, 1888, married Joseph Henry Clouse; Verna L., born July 11, 1890; Rena R., born April 1, 1895, married Lee Roy Chesney; Ruey B., born March 26, 1898, married John Thomas Freeland; Hazel D., born September 21, 1900; Glenn E., born March 16, 1903, married Thelma O. Lewis; and Ivy G., born February 9, 1906.

As a boy Mr. Beach moved from his native Wisconsin to Sterling, Illinois, and in 1879 settled in Exeter, Nebraska. As a young man, he was engaged in farming and stock raising. In 1907 he removed to Lincoln, where he was actively engaged in the fire, tornado, and hail insurance business as president of the Nebraska National Insurance Company for 25 years. From 1912 until 1915 he was special agent of the Home Fire Insurance Company of New York. In 1921 he removed to Omaha, and from 1925 until 1927, he was manager of the Nebraska Hail Adjustment Bureau. At the present time he is connected with the Lincoln Joint Stock Land Bank and the Lincoln Trust Company.

A Republican, he is an active and enthusiastic party worker. At 23 years of age, in 1888, he was elected to the county board of supervisors of Fillmore County, holding the office two terms, part of that time as chairman. In 1903, he was again elected to the same office and during this term was elected secretary of the State Association of County Commissioners and Supervisors, serving two years. In 1908 he was treasurer of the Traveling Men's Taft Club of Lincoln.

For many years he was a member of the Republican State Committee, and chairman of the committee from 1916 until 1919. He managed the campaign of Charles Evans Hughes in Nebraska for president of the United States in 1916, and again handled the party campaign in 1918 which resulted in a complete victory. *The Omaha Bee* of November 8, 1918, said editorially: "His labors as chairman were arduous, but his courage was superb, and his leadership generous and effective. The Republicans of Nebraska owe much to this man, who stuck to his work and won."

In July, 1917, Mr. Beach was appointed by Governor Neville (Democrat) as Republican member of the State Soldiers Voting Commission, whose duty it was to collect the vote of Nebraska soldiers wherever the state troops might be located and return the votes to Nebraska. During the years 1919 and 1920, he was state fire marshal.

From 1883 until 1886, Mr. Beach was a member of Company G of the Nebraska National Guard. During the late war he contributed time and effort to all loan drives, the Red Cross, and other wartime activities. He is a Methodist, and for 42 years has been a member of the Independent Order of Odd Fellows. Recently he was made a life member of The Nebraskana Society. His hobby is high protective tariff for the benefit of the American farmer. Residence: Omaha. (Photograph on Page 94).

Roscoe C. Beachler

Roscoe C. Beachler, a farmer and stockman, was born at Reynolds, Nebraska, May 12, 1883, son of Jerome Edward and Sarah Alice (Moss) Beachler. Jerome E. Beachler, a native of Anderson, Indiana, was born on December 30, 1854, and when a young man taught school in Indiana. Later he came to Nebraska where he engaged as a farmer and hardware and implement dealer until his death at Reynolds, on April 19, 1922. Sarah Alice, his wife, was born in Anderson, Indiana, April 14, 1860, and died at Reynolds, March 27, 1885.

Educated in rural schools, Mr. Beachler engaged in farming from early youth, and is also a stockraiser at the present time. In addition he has some insurance connections. He is a Democrat, and active in local politics, and from 1912-30 was a member of the local school board.

On November 14, 1906, he was united in marriage to Leona Payne, at Reynolds, her birthplace. She was born November 10, 1887, and prior to her marriage was a teacher. There are eight children: Ira, born September 21, 1907; Bernice, born June 6, 1909; Bessie, born March 6, 1911; Roscoe, born October 3, 1913; Floy, born January 1, 1915; Leora, born November 10, 1916; Marie, born May 18, 1919, and Betty, born August 21, 1926.

Mr. Beachler is a member and active in the work of the Methodist Church, and is a life member of the Nebraskana Society. Residence: Reynolds. (Photograph in Album).

Gaylord Vincent Beadle

Gaylord Vincent Beadle, one of Fort Calhoun's outstanding citizens, was born in Forest City, Iowa, October 7, 1893, son of James Ernest and Anna Christine (Drugg) Beadle. His father, who is a railway engineer, was born in Cedar Falls, Iowa, March 15, 1866, descended from settlers in Vermont, several generations ago. Anna Christine, his wife, was born in Forest City, June 26, 1875, and is a member of the Federated Women's Club and the Women's Christian Temperance Union. She is of Swedish descent, her family active in the steel industry in Sweden.

Upon his graduation from the public school of Council Bluffs in 1909, Mr. Beadle attended the Council Bluffs High School from which he was graduated in 1913. He was active in athletics, especially football. From 1913-14, he was stock clerk for Charles E. Walters Company, and held positions from transit clerk to receiving teller in the Corn Exchange National Bank 1914-16. Mr. Beadle served in the World War in the Medical Service, and is a member of the American Legion.

In 1919 he opened a garage and farm implement store at Fort Calhoun, which he has since operated. A Republican, he is active in local politics, and has served as alderman, committeeman, etc. He is a Scottish Rite Mason and member of the Shrine, and of the National Masonic Research Society. He also belongs to the Parent-Teachers' Association, the Young Men's Christian Association and The Nebraskana Society. His favorite sports are football and fishing, and his hobby is mechanics.

On February 28, 1922, he was united in marriage to Hazel Belle Knott at Council Bluffs. Mrs. Beadle was born there on February 15, 1892. They have one daughter, Patricia Anna, born April 14, 1924. Residence: Fort Calhoun.

EDWARD DAVID BEACH

Heyn—Omaha

Henry J. Beal

Henry J. Beal, county attorney of Douglas County, was born in Omaha, April 13, 1886, son of Henry H. and Mary (Paulson) Beal. The father, who was of German ancestry, died at Omaha, in 1918. The mother was born in Bredsted, Germany.

Mr. Beal attended the public school of Omaha, and received the degrees of Master of Oratory and Bachelor of Laws from Creighton University. He also attended Inland Technical School of Chicago.

On February 14, 1908, he was married to Lillian Winkler at Papillion. Mrs. Beal was born at Soukuelle, Wisconsin, of German ancestry.

Mr. Beal has been in the practice of law and prominent in Republican politics for a number of years. He served four years as deputy county attorney of Douglas County and for a number of years has been county attorney. He is the author of *Beals Criminal Forms*.

He is a member of Kountz Memorial Lutheran Church, the American Bar Association, Ak-Sar-Ben, Woodmen of the World, the Knights and Ladies of Security, Young Men's Christian Association, the Elks, and the Masons. Residence: Omaha.

Charles Edwin Beals

For the past 14 years Charles E. Beals has been prominent in the political and business affairs of Crete, Saline County, Nebraska. He was born at Carrollton, Carroll County, Missouri, September 14, 1883, the son of Chauncey A. and Eliza C. (Stroup) Beals. His father was born in Indiana, July 22, 1861, and was in the postal service until his retirement several years ago. His mother was born at Carrollton, June 27, 1863.

Mr. Beals attended rural schools and for two years was a student at Baker University at Baldwin, Kansas, where he took part in athletics, as a member of the football, basketball, and baseball teams. For 14 years he was express agent for the Adams Express Company, the American Railway Express Company, and the Railway Express Company, and was in the transportation department of the Santa Fe at Kansas City, and the Burlington at Lincoln. In 1930 he was appointed postmaster at Crete. He is also president of the Farmers and Merchants Gas and Oil Company.

A Republican, Mr. Beals has served his community through various offices, among them: city clerk, six years; mayor, two years; president of the League of Nebraska Municipalities, 1929-30; chairman of the legislative committee of this league; and secretary-treasurer of the league, 1928-. He is the editor of the *Nebraska Municipal Reviews*.

Mr. Beals holds membership in the Nebraskana Society and the Independent Order of the Odd Fellows. He is a member of the Belmont Heights Methodist Episcopal Church of Lincoln, Nebraska. His sports include tennis and hunting.

On May 13, 1903, he was married to Clara Edith Griffis at Baldwin, Douglas County, Kansas. Mrs. Beals was born at Baldwin, September 6, 1884; she is descended from a pioneer Michigan family. Two children were born to them, one of whom is living: Lucille Edna, born June 27, 1904; and Charles Elton, born August 20, 1913, who died August 10, 1914. Lucille is a graduate of Crete High School; received her A. B. degree at Doane College; was awarded the A. M. degree at Northwestern University; and is now professor and head of the speech department of Tarkio College, Tarkio, Missouri. Residence: Crete. (Photograph in Album).

James Orville Beaman

James Orville Beaman was born at Savannah, Iowa, September 19, 1854, the son of Alonzo and Elizabeth (Kelly) Beaman. Alonzo Beaman, a farmer and a soldier in the Mexican and Civil Wars, was born in Cincinnati, Ohio, December 13, 1825, and died at Bartley, Nebraska, October 19, 1896. His wife, Elizabeth, was born in Boone County, Missouri, August 17, 1829, and died at Savannah, Iowa, August 14, 1859.

Mr. Beaman attended public schools, and in 1882 purchased land in Rock Creek precinct of Saunders County, which he still owns. He is now retired after an active life as a farmer. During the period 1895-1930 he served as moderator, director, treasurer and president of various school districts in Nebraska. A Democrat, he was an unsuccessful candidate for the state legislature. He is affiliated with the Ceresco Methodist Episcopal Church, is active in the Red Cross, and is a member of the Nebraskana Society.

On March 23, 1879 Mr. Beaman was united in marriage to Mary Ann Ethell, at Ceresco. She was born in Davis County, Iowa, August 18, 1853, and died at Ceresco, on May 1, 1904. Two children were born to them: Grace Ethell, on March 23, 1880; and James Otis, on December 8, 1888. Grace attended Nebraska Wesleyan University, and Otis, who married Edna Harriett Walter, has three sons: Loren O., 23, a graduate of Ceresco High School; Francis Jennings, 20, a sophomore at the University of Nebraska; and Ivan Fred, 16, a senior in Ceresco High School. Residence: Ceresco. (Photograph in Album).

George William Beamer

George William Beamer, farmer and real estate agent, was born at Netawaka, Kansas, July 10, 1875, son of George William and Alta Luella (Graham) Beamer.

His father, born in Erie, Pennsylvania, January 24, 1850, was a farmer his entire life time. He died at Gordon, Nebraska, August 21, 1921. His grandfather emigrated from Baaron on Rhine, Germany, in the year 1840, and settled near Erie, Pennsylvania. He was married to Jane Smith in 1846. Alta Luella Graham was born in Keokuk, Iowa, March 2, 1856, and died at Jacksonville, Florida, April 1, 1930. Her ancestors were Scotch-Irish.

Mr. Beamer attended common schools to the 10th grade in a pioneer Nebraska school house, and during the years 1894 and 1895, attended high school at Valentine. He has resided in Nebraska 45 years, and is now manager of the Beamer Realty Company. He also has extensive land holdings. A Democrat, he was candidate for county clerk in 1900, defeated by two votes, and a candidate for state representative in 1924, defeated by 26 votes.

His marriage to Minnie Marie Hills was solemnized at Rushville, Nebraska, November 7, 1900. Mrs. Beamer was born at Neligh, January 31, 1880. Mr. and Mrs. Beamer have brought up three foster children, and are bringing up their three grandchildren. Mrs. Beamer is the daughter of Steven and Phoebe (Trowbridge) Hills. They were early pioneers of Sheridan County.

For 22 consecutive years Mr. Beamer was director of a country school board. He is chairman of the Civic League of Sheridan County, a member of the Anti-Saloon League, and is affiliated with the Methodist Episcopal Church. Residence: Gordon. (Photograph on Page 96).

Frank James Bean

A pioneer farmer in Nebraska, Frank James Bean has been a resident of this state for the past 61 years, and still resides on the farm he homesteaded in Gosper County, in 1883. He was born at Avoca, Wisconsin, November 26, 1860, the son of William Sevier Bean and Sophronia (Gear) Bean. His father, who was a miner and farmer, was born in Pike County, Missouri, November 30, 1812, and died at Elwood, Nebraska, August 4, 1896. His mother was born at Alton, Illinois, November 3, 1819, and died at Elwood, July 11, 1912.

Mr. Bean organized the Elwood Coal & Lumber Company in 1907, and served as manager of that company for 16 years. During this time he became manager of the

Purdy—Gordon

GEORGE WILLIAM BEAMER

Elwood Shipping Association and has served in that capacity for 20 years. He has always been actively engaged in farming and stock raising until his retirement in recent years. He is connected with the First National Bank.

He was married at Orleans, Nebraska, December 24, 1889, to Mary Elizabeth Hull. Mrs. Bean was born of Scotch parentage at Boone, Iowa, August 11, 1865. Five children were born to them: Elva, born October 20, 1890, who married Lester Withers; Floyd, born November 26, 1892, who married Grace Muller; Marcia, born March 31, 1894, who married Delmer Long; Marie, born March 18, 1905, who died August 20, 1907; and John, born March 18, 1905, who is at Overton, operating a drug store. Residence: Elwood.

Robert H. Beatty

Robert H. Beatty, lawyer, was born at Brady, Nebraska, July 29, 1887, son of William and Mary E. (Burke) Beatty. The father was born in Ireland, and the mother in the United States.

In 1909, Mr. Beatty was graduated from Brady High School, and in 1912, received the Bachelor of Laws degree from the University of Nebraska. There he was a member of the Order of the Coif.

On July 8, 1917, he was married to Ethel A. Brown at Lexington, Nebraska. She was born at Brady, Nebraska. They have two children, Margaret Jane, born September 14, 1919; and Mildred Louise, born June 28, 1921.

From 1912 until 1916, Mr. Beatty practiced law, and then became employed with Wilcox and Halligan, serving until July, 1919. They then formed the firm of Halligan and Beatty, of which firm he is still a member. His professional memberships include, the Nebraska State Bar Association, the Western Nebraska Bar Association, and the American Association. Since 1919, Mr. Beatty, as a member of one of the leading law firms of western Nebraska, has taken part in most of the important litigations in that part of the state. He is now senior member of the firm, J. J. Halligan having died in July, 1930.

Mr. Beatty is a member of the Elks, the Odd Fellows, the Knights of Pythias, the Modern Woodmen of America, and the Masons (Shrine). He was in Officer's Heavy Artillery Training Camp at Camp Taylor, Kentucky, during the World War. He enjoys hunting and fishing, while his favorite sport is golf. Residence: North Platte.

Eugene Mark Beaty

Eugene Mark Beaty was born at Blair, Nebraska, May 30, 1886, son of Eugene S. and Lucretia (Maun) Beaty. His father, who was a contractor, was born at Bedford, Massachusetts, December 10, 1855, of English descent. His death occurred at Blair, January 2, 1921. Lucretia Maun was born of Irish parentage at Brownville, Nebraska, October 20, 1862.

Upon his graduation from Blair High School, in 1903, Eugene Mark Beaty entered the Armour Institute of Technology from which he received his B. S. in 1908. He is a member of Tau Beta Pi. After graduation, Mr. Beaty entered the contracting business, following in the footsteps of his father, and at the present time in secretary-treasurer of the Beaty Contracting Company at Blair.

He was married to Bess Lee Roberts at Blair, February 20, 1912. Mrs. Beaty was born at Blair, August 8, 1886. They have one daughter, Betty, born December 13, 1918. The Beatys are Catholics, and attend St. Francis Borgia Church. Mr. Beaty is a Republican, a member of the Blair Chamber of Commerce and the Ad-Sell League at Omaha. He is active in civic and educational work, and is a member of the Blair Library Board. His club is the Blair Golf Club, and his favorite sport is fishing. Residence: Blair.

Sam Beber

Sam Beber was born at Minsk, Russia, September 27, 1901, the son of Israel and Rosa (Greenglass) Beber. His father, who was born in Russia, was a grocer who came to America in 1905.

Mr. Beber attended the Kellom, Long, and Webster schools of Omaha. In 1919, he was graduated from Central High School, and in 1923 he received his LL. B. degree at Creighton University where he was graduated with the highest honors awarded, Magna Cum Laude. He was admitted to the bar at Omaha, June 2, 1923, and since that time has been engaged in legal practice. He was first associated with Isidor Ziegler, and in 1924 he formed the firm of Stalmaster & Beber. In 1930, he organized the firm, Fradenburg, Stalmaster & Beber. He has lived in Nebraska for 22 years.

He was united in marriage with Helen Riekes at Omaha, August 2, 1925. Mrs. Beber was born at Kapula, Russia, December 18, 1903. In 1930 he was made president of the Jewish Philanthropies, and in 1931, he became second vice president of the Jewish Community Center and Welfare Federation. He served as secretary of the latter organization from 1928 to 1930. He is a member of the Conservative Synagogue.

Mr. Beber has been a member of B'nai Brith since 1924; in 1930 he was elected second vice president of District Grand Lodge Number 6. He is founder and president of the Supreme Advisory Council of Aleph Zadik Aleph. He is a member of the Nebraskana Society. He is a member of the Youth Commission of the Citizens Committee of One Thousand for Law Enforcement. He is a member of the Omaha Bar Association, the Nebraska State Bar Association, and is a Republican. His favorite sport is golf. His hobby is social work. Residence: Omaha.

Adolf Beck

For the past 61 years Adolf Beck has lived in Nebraska and for 25 years has been president of the Bank of Wilber. He was born in Jones County, Iowa, August 11, 1863, the son of Vaclav and Theresa (Pavlista) Beck. His father, who was a farmer and stockman, was born in Czechoslovakia, February 12, 1826, and died in Gage County, Nebraska, August 11, 1908; he was a soldier in the Austria-Italian War; his German parents came to America in 1855, settled in Iowa, and in 1870 moved to Saline County, Nebraska. His mother was born in Czechoslovakia, May 2, 1830, and died in Saline County, February 1, 1917.

Mr. Beck attended the rural schools of Saline County. He has been a farmer and banker in Saline County for many years. He is now retired from active business, but is still president of the Bank of Wilber. He is interested in horticulture. He is a Democrat. He is a Freethinker.

His marriage to Mary Nemec was solemnized at Wilber, December 24, 1881. Mrs. Beck, who was a prominent clubwoman in her community for many years, was born in Czechoslovakia, March 9, 1867, and died at Wilber, April 5, 1925. Four children were born to them: Theresa Othelia, born September 25, 1887, who married Stanley Bartos; Blanche, born January 1, 1889, who married Frank P. Cerveny; Edward A., born November 6, 1891, who married Alice Bartos; and Alice A., born March 17, 1895, who married Leonard Chaloupka. Edward is assistant cashier and vice president of the Bank of Wilber. Residence: Wilber. (Photograph on Page 98).

Clarence S. Beck

Clarence S. Beck, lawyer, was born at Kellerton, Iowa, February 4, 1898, son of Sherman T. and Emma E. (Foltz) Beck.

Upon his graduation from high school at Hot Springs, South Dakota, in 1917, Mr. Beck entered the United States Army. He served from July 16, 1917 until June 24, 1919, and was with the American Expeditionary Forces from September 17, 1918, until June 16, 1919. He at-

ADOLF BECK

tended the University of Nebraska, and received his Bachelor of Laws degree in 1923.

His marriage to Helen R. Martin was solemnized at Portland, Oregon, June 2, 1927. Mrs. Beck was born at Craig, Nebraska, April 14, 1901.

Since September 12, 1923, Mr. Beck has been in active practice at North Platte. A Republican, he has served as county attorney of Lincoln County since February 11, 1929.

He is a member of Phi Alpha Delta, the Elks (past exalted ruler), the Masons, the Country Club, the American Legion (past commander) and the Forty and Eight. His sports include golf, hunting and fishing. Residence: North Platte.

Theophilus Christian Beck

Theophilus Christian Beck, banker, was born in Gasconade County, Missouri, November 15, 1859, son of Christian and Rosine (Menzenmeier) Beck. His father, a minister, was born at Eichelberg, Germany, July 16, 1829, and died at Seward, in May, 1922. Rosine Menzenmeier was born in Germany and died at Pinkney, Missouri, in May, 1872. She was a teacher.

Mr. Beck attended Elmhurst College and for 26 years was engaged in farming. He served as county superintendent of schools for six years, was county assessor of Seward County, Nebraska, for four years, city clerk one year, and county clerk for one year. For the past 12 years he has served as assistant cashier of the Cattle National Bank of Seward.

His marriage to Kate Crouch occurred at Ulysses, Nebraska, March 7, 1887. Mrs. Beck was born at Philadelphia, December 17, 1864. They have five children, Carl Leslie; Walter Everett; Emma Kate; Ella Mary; and Norma Rosina. The sons are farmers while the girls are teachers. Mr. Beck is a member of the Red Cross, Chamber of Commerce, the Masons, and the First Presbyterian Church of Seward. Residence: Seward.

John Henry Becker

John Henry Becker was born December 2, 1892, at Gibson, Jefferson County, Nebraska, the son of John Becker and Katherina (Theiss) Becker. His father was born in Niederaufleiden, Hessen-Darmstadt, Germany, November 6, 1856. He received military training in Germany and was honorably discharged from service. He came to America in June, 1882, and has been successful as a farmer. Mrs. Becker was born in Normandy County, Ontario, Canada, July 7, 1863, and died at Plymouth, Jefferson County, Nebraska, March 5, 1922.

Mr. Becker attended the grade schools. On January 27, 1916, at Plymouth, he was married to Mathilda Carolina Groenemeyer. Mrs. Becker was born in Plymouth, March 4, 1894, the daughter of Fred and Louise (Brandt) Groenemeyer. To this union seven children were born; Ruth, October 23, 1916; Irene, January 31, 1918; Alice, June 23, 1920; Leila, March 29, 1922; John April 12, 1925; Leon, May 22, 1928; and Marlyn, August 27, 1930.

John H. Becker is affiliated with the Lutheran Church. He was chairman of the Democratic committee for the Gibson precinct and was chairman of the war society in 1919. He has been a director on the school board since 1919 and has held the offices of chairman and secretary in the Farmer's Union local No. 1482, which he represented in 1924 and 1930 at the Omaha State Convention. Mr. Becker is a member of the Nebraskana Society. His favorite recreations are baseball and reading. Residence: Plymouth.

Loraine Alfred Becker

Loraine A. Becker, known in the newspaper world as Larry Becker, has lived in Nebraska all his life, and has been in the newspaper business since 1911. He was born at DeWitt, Saline County, Nebraska, July 19, 1897, the son of Charles John and Louise M. (Inderlied) Becker. His father, who was engaged in the meat business, was born in Canada, August 6, 1866, and died at Lincoln, November 4, 1910. His mother was born in Germany, March 11, 1875.

Mr. Becker attended the public and high schools of Lincoln. He entered the office of the *Lincoln Star* as an office boy; later was a reporter; and in 1921 was made city editor of that paper. He holds this position now.

His marriage to Marian Wallace Henninger was solemnized at Lincoln, May 25, 1921. Mrs. Becker, who was born at Pawnee City, Nebraska, July 2, 1897, was formerly a newspaper feature writer and woman's club editor. She is of Scotch-Irish descent. They have one son, Larry Wallace, born June 9, 1927.

Mr. Becker is a member of the Nebraska Writers Guild and the Nebraskana Society. He is a member of Lincoln Lodge Number 19, of the Masons, and holds membership in the Saturday Nite Dancing Club, and the Cornhusker Dancing Club, of Lincoln. He is affiliated with the First Presbyterian Church of Lincoln, and is a Democrat.

Wesley Charles Becker

Wesley C. Becker was born at Kansas City, Missouri, December 27, 1891, the son of Gustav Adolph and Louise Elizabeth (Fricke) Becker. His father, who was a pioneer in Nebraska and a clergyman in the Methodist Church, was born at Karlschue, Germany, August 8, 1864, and died at Lincoln, Nebraska, October 10, 1910. His German and French ancestors came to America in 1881. His mother, who is of German descent was born at Papillion, Nebraska, February 4, 1866.

Dr. Becker was graduated from the high school at St. Joseph, Missouri, in 1908. He was awarded the following degrees: A. B., University of Nebraska, 1912; A. M., University of Nebraska, 1914; M. D., Rush Medical College, 1915. He was elected a member of Sigma Xi, Delta Tau Delta, and Nu Sigma Nu, and in 1926 he studied at the University of Vienna. He won his N in track at the University of Nebraska.

He was admitted to the practice of medicine at Chicago, June 10, 1916, and has been a practicing surgeon in Nebraska since that date. He is the author of numerous medical articles. He is president of the People's Savings & Loan Association at Lincoln, and is a director in the Fremont Joint Stock Land Bank there.

He married Marie Mason at Greenwood, Cass County, Nebraska, August 11, 1913. Mrs. Becker, whose ancestry is Scotch-Irish, was born at Lincoln, April 30, 1892. They have four children: Arnetta, born July 11, 1914; Alice Louise, born June 24, 1921; Patricia Ann, born May 21, 1925; and Jacqueline, born October 15, 1930.

Since 1917, Dr. Becker has been a captain in the medical corps, and during the World War saw active service. He is a member of the American Legion. He is a member of Lancaster Medical Society; Nebraska State Medical Society; American Medical Association; the Lincoln Chamber of Commerce; and the Lions Club. He is an Elk and a Mason. He is a member of the University Club and the Lincoln Country Club. He is a golf and tennis enthusiast. He is affiliated with Trinity Methodist Episcopal Church at Lincoln, and is a Republican. Residence: Lincoln.

Edith Beckman

Edith Beckman, lawyer and musician, was born at Omaha, daughter of Joseph Anton and Ida Mary (Kleffner) Beckman. Joseph Beckman was born at Steinfield, Oldenburgh, Germany, March 12, 1850. In 1830 his father, a shipbuilder, came to America and settled in Philadelphia, where he worked in the shipyards until 1842, returning to Germany in that year. Joseph Beckman owned and operated the second cigar factory and store in Omaha in 1871, in the old Merchants National Bank Building, in which he employed twenty-eight men. He died at Omaha, July 4, 1922. Ida Mary Kleffner, his wife, was born at Dubuque, Iowa, November 11, 1856, and died at Omaha, May 9, 1910. Her father, George Kleffner, settled in Nebraska in 1856. She was of German and Spanish descent, a lover of music and art, and intensely interested in her home.

Miss Beckman received her early education under her mother's tutelage, and later entered St. Peter's parochial school. She attended St. Berchman's Academy and received her LL. B. from the University of Omaha Night Law School. She also studied and taught music under Jean P. Duffield from 1910 to 1918. At that time she became private secretary to John C. Wharton, noted jurist, and studied law in his office until his death on May 7, 1924. In November, 1925, she opened her present office where she is engaged in the general practice of law, specializing in real property, wills and probate work.

She is the author of *Alumnae Notes* contributed to *The Golden Record* in addition to short articles for newspapers and magazines.

Perhaps her most particular interest outside her profession is the Nebraska Pioneers' Memorial Association of which she is secretary-treasurer. The purpose of the society is the erection of a monument to the memory of the spirit of the pioneers of Nebraska, and the preservation of early Nebraska history.

She is also active in various professional associations. A member of the American, the Nebraska State and Omaha-Douglas County Bar Associations, she is vice president for Nebraska of the National Association of Women Lawyers, which office she has held since 1926. She was president of the Omaha Women Lawyers from 1926-30. She is a member of the Douglas County Law Library, and the Nebraska and Omaha League of Women Voters. In that connection she is chairman of the committee on the legal status of women in Nebraska.

Miss Beckman is a Catholic, and a member of St. Peter's Church. She is affiliated with the International Federation of Catholic Alumna, and the Catholic Daughters of America. She is legislative chairman for Nebraska, of the former organization. Particularly active in civic and welfare work, she is a member of the child survey group of the Council of Social Agencies. She has been a member of the Women's Division of the Chamber of Commerce since 1925, and served as its president from 1928-29. Her hobbies are music, art, dramatics, reading and journalism. Residence: Omaha.

Edwin Walton Bedford

Edwin Walton Bedford, real estate executive, was born in Omaha, August 27, 1886, son of Jefferson William and Mary Octavia (LeSueur) Bedford. His father was born in Lexington, Missouri, June 3, 1845, and died at Omaha, September 17, 1917. He was very prominent in the public affairs of Omaha (member of the City Council several terms) was state representative and state senator, and at the time of his death was Douglas County commissioner. He was a member of the Sons of the American Revolution, and directly descended from one of the signers of the constitution. Mary Octavia LeSueur was born in St. Louis, Missouri, April 24, 1849, and died at Omaha, August 22, 1922. She was directly descended from the old French families of LeSueur and Dumain.

Mr. Bedford received his early education in the public schools and later attended Missouri State Normal School. He was married on October 27, 1909, to Alice Eliza Bolton at Omaha. Mrs. Bedford was born at Logan, Iowa, April 26, 1877.

Mr. Bedford has been engaged in the real estate business since 1907. At the present time he is a member of the firm of Stuht-Bedford Company. During the late war he served with the 62nd Balloon Company. He is a member of Calvary Baptist Church, the American Legion, the Chamber of Commerce, the Masons and the Omaha Real Estate Board. Residence: Omaha.

Britannia Bednar

Britannia Bednar, clubwoman and educator, was born at Mooreshill, Indiana, December 27, 1879, the daughter of William Turpen and Sarah Elmira (Heaton) Daughters. Her father, an engineer, was born at Mooreshill, August 8, 1834, and died at Coeur d'Alene, Idaho, July 28, 1916. His English ancestors settled in Delaware and Maryland as early as 1714. His wife, Sarah, was born at Mooreshill, December 6, 1841, and died at Coeur d'Alene on February 11, 1907. She traced her ancestry back nine American generations to Governor Theophilus Heaton (Eaton) who served as colonial governor of New Haven Colony for 19 years.

Britannia Bednar attended the public schools of Kansas, the preparatory school of the University of Idaho, and in 1905 received the Bachelor of Arts degree at the University of Nebraska. Later she took graduate work in sociology and education at the latter instiution. She received the Kaufman scholarship at the University of Idaho, was a member of the Ladies Chorus and Varsity Viff of the University of Idaho, and was a charter member and one of the founders of Phi Omega Phi at the University of Nebraska.

She taught in the public schools of Washington and Idaho from 1906 until 1909, and during the year 1909-10 served as assistant in the education department at the University of Nebraska. A Republican, she was one of the five women to speak for woman's suffrage on July 4, 1913, in Nebraska. She is a member of the executive board of the First Congregational Church of Omaha, serving as head of the Women's Missionary Society of that body, was a member of the Central High Parent Teachers Association, 1924-28, and at this time holds membership in the Dundee Parent Teachers Association. From 1926 until 1930 she acted as vice president of the Camp Fire and in 1929 was an active member of the Social Settlement Association.

Mrs. Bednar was president of the Omaha branch of the American Association of University Women, 1924-26, during which time the publication of college news was organized and sections in international relations and education were started. She was leader of the Dundee Round Table in Adolescence, 1926-28, was chairman of the Omaha Mother-Daughter Week, 1928, 29, 30, and was chairman of industrial work of the Young Women's Christian Association and counsellor of Omaha branch of the American Association of University Women 1926-27. A member of the Eastern Star, she served as Worthy Matron of Chapter No. 52 and was Grand Representative of the state of Tennessee. Her club is the Happy Hollow Country Club of Omaha, while her chief recreations are reading, golfing and hiking.

Her marriage to James Edmund Bednar occurred at Lincoln, Nebraska, June 16, 1910. Mr. Bednar, a lawyer, was born at Wymore, Nebraska, September 28, 1882. They have two children, James Edmund Bednar, II, born October 13, 1911; and Bryce Renwick Bednar, born August 3, 1916. James is a member of the National Honor Society, is a talented pianist, and is a member of the debating team at Leland Stanford University where he is a student. Residence: Omaha.

James Edmund Bednar

James Edmund Bednar, lawyer, was born in Gage County, Nebraska, September 28, 1882, son of Albert and Johanna (Peroutka) Bednar. The father was born in Czechoslovakia, April 23, 1837, and died at Odell, September 21, 1914. He was a cabinet maker and farmer who came to America in 1876, and pioneered on the Otoe and Missouri Indian Reservation. His wife, Johanna, was born in Czechoslovakia, in 1840 and died at Odell on December 15, 1925.

Mr. Bednar attended rural school in Gage County and in 1903 was graduated from Wymore High School. He received the B. A. degree from the University of Nebraska in 1907; and the LL. B. degree in 1910. In 1906 he attended Nebraska Wesleyan. He is a member of Delta Sigma Rho, Phi Alpha Tau and Delta Chi, and was a member of the debate team which defeated the University of Illinois in 1907.

On June 16, 1910, he was married to Brittania Daughters, at Lincoln. Mrs. Bednar was born at Moores Hill, Indiana, and formerly taught in the public schools of Washington and Idaho. During 1909-10 she was assistant in the department of education of the University of Nebraska.

Mr. and Mrs. Bednar have two children, James Edmund, II, born October 13, 1911, and Bryce Renwick, born August 3, 1916. James is a graduate of Omaha Central High School with membership in the national honor society, captain of Company F (Flag Company), the Susan Paxton Latin prize, etc. He is a pianist, and is now a student at Leland Stanford University and a member of its debating team. He is a member of Phi Gamma Delta and assistant manager of Chaparal. Bryce Renwick is a prominent violinist.

Since June 16, 1910, Mr. Bednar has been active in the practice of law at Omaha. He is a Mason (32nd degree, Scottish Rite, K. C. C. H., Shrine; past grand patron, Order of Eastern Star). He is a member of the First Central Congregational Church, the Nebraska State and Douglas County Bar Associations, the Chamber of Commerce, the Ad-Sell League and the Nebraskana Society. His club is the Happy Hollow Club. His favorite sport is golf and he is a member of the Hole-In-One Club. Residence: Omaha.

Leroy Beebout

One of the leaders in the political and business affairs of Johnstown, Nebraska, is LeRoy Beebout, who was born at Salem, Ohio, October 5, 1881, the son of William Larmer and Lettie Margaret (Price) Beebout. His father, who was a farmer, was born in Ohio, July 19, 1849, and died at Eden, Idaho. His mother, who was born at Richmond, Ohio, August 27, 1851, and died at Eden, January 14, 1926, was active in religious affairs and work of the Women's Christian Temperance Union. Her father was a Presbyterian minister in Ohio and Nebraska.

Mr. Beebout has been editor of the *Johnstown Enterprise* since 1906 having formerly been a farmer and carpenter. He has engaged in the insurance business since 1913 in addition to publishing the newspaper. After receiving a common school education in a sod school house in Blaine County, Nebraska, he entered upon his editorial career without any previous experience in publishing or editing. He is active in his community in all civic matters, and holds membership in the Johnstown Methodist Episcopal Church, of which he is chairman of the board of trustees; School Board, of which he is secretary; Nebraskana Society; and the Modern Woodmen of America.

During the World War he served as second lieutenant in the home guard company, was a member of the registration board, acted as chairman of the Council of Defense, and was prominent in Liberty loan and Red Cross drives. A Republican, he has served as county commissioner of Brown County, 1914-1924, was candidate for legislature in 1927, and served as chairman of the City Council of Johnstown for several terms.

His marriage to Rosa Akert was solemnized at Oak-

dale, Nebraska, May 20, 1913. Mrs. Beebout, whose parents were natives of Switzerland, was born at Coleridge, Nebraska, April 11, 1894. To them the following children were born: Lois P., January 12, 1914; Leona Fae, August 7, 1919; Allan Dee, January 11, 1921; Merlin Frederick, June 25, 1923; Ardis Ione, January 4, 1916; Willard Leroy, April 1, 1917; William Larmer, July 20, 1929; and Shirley Ann, born December 26, 1927. Residence: Johnstown.

Edwin Dewey Beech

Edwin Dewey Beech was born at Meadow Grove, Nebraska, August 24, 1898, and is now engaged in the practice of law at Pierce, Nebraska. His father, Joseph Isaac Beech, who was born in Iowa, October 15, 1860, is a retired hardware merchant. His mother was born in New York, and died at Meadow Grove, July 20, 1919.

Mr. Beech was graduated from the Meadow Grove High School in 1916, and in 1923, received the LL. B. degree at the University of Nebraska where he was a member of the Order of the Coif, Sigma Phi Epsilon and Phi Alpha Delta. He is now serving as county attorney of Pierce County, and holds membership in the Lions Club at Pierce. He is a member of the Nebraska State Bar Association, is a Mason, and holds membership in the Pierce University Club and the American Legion.

On August 11, 1928, he married Clara Olive Roberts at Lincoln, Nebraska. Mrs. Beech, who was a teacher in the high school at Neligh, Nebraska, prior to her marriage, was born at Dorchester, Nebraska, September 1, 1901, of Scotch parentage. Residence: Pierce.

George Allen Beecher

Right Reverend George A. Beecher, bishop of the Episcopal Church in western Nebraska, was born at Monmouth, Illinois, February 3, 1868, son of Benjamin Jonah and Mercy Ann (Boland) Beecher. His father, a native of Minerva, New York, was born in 1832, and died at Kearney, Nebraska, March 28, 1888. He was of Scotch, Irish and English descent; a school teacher, farmer and merchant. Bishop Beecher's mother was born at Parishville, St. Lawrence County, New York, in 1837. She also died at Kearney in 1903.

After the completion of his elementary education in the public schools at Kearney, he attended the University of Nebraska from 1886 to 1889. After the death of his father, Mr. Beecher became a student under the tutorship of the late Rev. Robert W. Oliver, D. D., rector of St. Luke's Church, Kearney, Nebraska. For one year he taught in the Stone School House one mile east of Kearney. He then became a candidate for Holy Orders under the Rt. Rev. George Worthington, D. D., then Bishop of Nebraska. In 1892 he graduated from the Philadelphia Divinity School and was ordained to the Deaconate and Priesthood in the little old Episcopal frame church in Kearney.

He was sent by Bishop Graves, then Bishop of The Platte, to Old Fort Sidney in the west end of the state, where he was given charge of the missions extending from Fort Sidney to North Platte on the East, and to the Wyoming line on the West, including the North Platte Valley which was then very sparsely settled. This territory required a trip of 250 miles overland each month with pony team and buggy.

His marriage to Florence Idella George, who was born at Kenosha, Wisconsin, April 22, 1867, was solemnized in St. Luke's Church, Racine, Wisconsin, on June 22, 1893. At the time of their residence in Fort Sidney, Nebraska, the United States Government was trying the experiment of making soldiers out of the younger generation of Indians from the Agencies of the Dakotas. The young parson grasped this opportunity for real missionary work and began, with the consent of the Commanding Officer, to conduct day and night schools for the men and non-commissioned officers of this company of Indians stationed at Fort Sidney. As the result of this enterprise, recognition was given to Company I of the 21st United States Infantry for its proficiency in drill formation, improvement of conduct, loyalty, and obedience.

In the fall of 1895, a year after Fort Sidney was abandoned, Rev. and Mrs. Beecher moved to North Platte, where Mr. Beecher became, for eight years, the rector of the Church of Our Saviour.

Six children were born to Rev. and Mrs. Beecher. The first, Pauline Helen, born at Fort Sidney, died in infancy. Ruth Allen, born in North Platte, March 26, 1896, became a graduate of Brownell Hall, a Church Boarding School for girls in Omaha, attended the State University of Nebraska, and later married Captain Adrian R. Brian of the United States Army. George Sanford, born in North Platte in 1896, died in infancy. Elizabeth Knox, born in North Platte, January 18, 1900, attended Brownell Hall, is a graduate of the National Cathedral School in Washington, D. C., also of St. Faith's Training School, New York City, and took post-graduate work in Columbia University. For a few years she was Field Secretary in the Department of Religious Education under the National Branch of the Woman's Auxiliary. She was married to Rev. Frederic A. McNeil in St. Mark's Pro-Cathedral, Hastings, April 21, 1931, and now resides in Phoenix, Arizona. Mary, twin sister of Elizabeth Knox died, in infancy. Sanford Dent, the only son living, was born in North Platte, February 22, 1902. He attended the Kearney Military Academy in Kearney, Nebraska, the Episcopal High School, Alexandria, Virginia, is a graduate of Hobart College, and also a graduate of the Law School of the University of Pennsylvania, Philadelphia. He was married to Miss Sarah Horter of Germantown, Philadelphia, in June, 1930, and is associated with the Attorney General of Pennsylvania, in charge of the Department of Revenue in the State Capitol at Harrisburg.

Mr. Beecher was very active during the Spanish-American War. He was unofficially associated with the reorganization of Company E, of North Platte, before going to the front. After leaving North Platte he became the rector of St. Luke's Church, Kearney, and chaplain of the Kearney Military Academy. In 1904 he accepted the unanimous call of the vestry to become the dean and rector of Trinity Cathedral Parish, Omaha. He was installed as dean by Bishop Worthington in the fall of 1904. During his deanship he became actively engaged in the social welfare work of the community and was intimately associated with the work of the Juvenile Court, from which docket, many young boys and girls were paroled to him for his personal help and direction through the crucial years of their young lives. He was instrumental in the organization of the Juvenile Court, and the inauguration of the system of court trials of first offenders which abolished some of the old-time court proceedings. Tables were arranged for the young boys and girls who became victims of evil surroundings and temptations, where the judge himself sat at the end of the table with the children and those interested in their welfare and where the group was more like that of a family. Mr. Beecher was a member of the Newsboys' Club, and for nearly twenty years fostered a club of young lads through all of his parish experience.

After his installation as dean of Trinity Cathedral, Omaha, he became the chaplain of the Fifth Regiment of the Nebraska National Guard, which position he occupied from 1906 to 1916, including active service with the troops on the Mexican Border just previous to the World War.

He was a charter member of the American Institute of Criminal Law and Criminology; a member of the American Prison Association and also of the International Prison Association; president of the Nebraska

Humane Society, vice-president of the Child Labor Commission; member of the Nebraska Branch of the National Commission for Treatment of Cancer; Grand Chaplain of the Grand Lodge A. F. & A. M. of Nebraska.

'n 1898 he was official delegate representing the Missionary District of Western Nebraska at the General Convention of the Protestant Episcopal Church held in Washington, D. C. At the General Convention held in Cincinnati, Ohio, in October, 1910, he was unanimously elected to succeed the Rt. Rev. Anson R. Graves, D. D., as bishop of the Missionary District of Kearney (later Western Nebraska). He was consecrated bishop in Trinity Cathedral, Omaha, on St. Andrew's Day, November 30, 1910. Those taking part in this consecration were: 1. Rt. Rev. Daniel S. Tuttle, D. D., LL. D., D. C. L., presiding bishop; 2. Rt. Rev. Alexander Charles Garret, D. D., S. T. D., bishop of Dallas. 3. Rt. Rev. Anson R. Graves, D. D., S. T. D., bishop of Kearney (Western Nebraska); 4. Rt. Rev. Frank R. Millspaugh, D. D., LL. D., bishop of Kansas; 5. Rt. Rev. Arthur Llewelyn Williams, D. D., S. T. D., Bishop of Nebraska; 6. Rt. Rev. Theodore Nevin Morrison, D. D., LL. D., bishop of Iowa; 7. Rt. Rev. Nathaniel Seymore Thomas, D. D., LL. D., bishop of Wyoming.

As bishop he became the president of the Kearney Military Academy, retaining his official position above referred to.

Bishop Beecher is the author of numerous pastoral letters, public addresses, biographical books, journals, etc., and is editor of the *Western Nebraska Churchman*. Previous to and during the World War, Bishop Beecher was actively engaged in various groups of public speakers in the campaign for voluntary enlistments. He was the first organizer of the Adams County branch of the American Red Cross, and became a charter member of that organization.

He was initiated into the Masonic fraternity at Fort Sidney, Nebraska, afterwards serving as Master of the Lodge in North Platte. He is at present a member of the George Lininger Lodge No. 268 at Omaha; a Knight Templar, and a 32nd Degree Mason with the honorary degree of K. C. C. H. He is also a member of the Knights of Pythias in Hastings, Nebraska, and a member of the Elks Lodge No. 39 in Omaha. Although he is a member of the Hastings Country Club, Bishop Beecher finds his favorite sport in horse-back riding, and in June, 1930, together with three young lads, a covered wagon, team of mules, wrangler, and cook, he rode the Oregon Trail from the crossing of the Blue south of Hastings to Fort Laramie, Wyoming, a distance of 500 miles. A history of this trip over the Oregon Trail will appear in his book of reminiscences which the bishop is preparing for publication.

For the past twenty years he has resided at 919 North St. Joseph Avenue, Hastings, Nebraska. (Photograph on Page 103).

William Charles Beer

William C. Beer was born at Princeville, Peoria County, Illinois, September 24, 1858, where he attended elementary school into the eighth grade, in a pioneer country schoolhouse.

His father, William Beer, Sr., was born at Allegany, Pennsylvania, June 26, 1819, and died at Wymore, Nebraska, December 21, 1899. He was a farmer. Adaline (Belshee) Beer, his wife, was born in Ohio, March 23, 1827, and died at Wymore, Nebraska, January 6, 1906. She was of German and Scotch descent.

On March 23, 1881, he was united in marriage to Alice Moseley at Alexandria, Nebraska. Mrs. Beer, who was of Pennsylvania-German ancestry, was born at Dixon, Illinois, January 14, 1860. Her death occurred at Alexandria, Nebraska, September 14, 1899. They had six children: J. L., born March 5, 1882, who was married to Alma M. Goodman, and died September 19, 1910, F. H., born December 23, 1884, who is married to

GEORGE ALLEN BEECHER

Mabel Simmons; Edna M., born July 24, 1886, who is married to Myron H. Decker; Charles, born December 25, 1888, who is married to Maude Cory; Ida A., born December 21, 1890, who died January 2, 1898; and Albert L., born October 27, 1896, who died December 24, 1918.

Mr. Beer has been a resident of Nebraska for fifty years, and has been an undertaker and embalmer for twenty-five years. At the present time he is also in the insurance business.

He is local Red Cross president, is a Mason, and holds membership in the Eastern Star, as well as The Nebraskana Society. Residence: Alexandria.

Orrin Leroy Beeson

Orrin Leroy Beeson, who has been a dentist at Beatrice, Gage County, Nebraska, for the past 30 years, was born at Marshalltown, Iowa, February 18, 1869. His father, Wilson Bruce Beeson, a farmer, was born at Columbiana, Ohio, August 12, 1841, and died at Marshalltown, August 30, 1923; he was a direct descendant of Edward Beeson who came from England to America in 1682; his father was a member of Company C, 8th Iowa Cavalry, during the Civil War, and was imprisoned for 16 weeks in the Andersonville prison. His mother, whose ancestors were Quakers, was born in Ohio, August 6, 1839, and died at Marshalltown.

Dr. Beeson attended the public school at Marshalltown, and later attended a commercial and music school at Vaiparaiso, Indiana. He was graduated from Lake Forest University, dental department, where he was a member of Delta Sigma Delta. He has held the following positions: violin instructor at Advent College, Mendota, Illinois, 1892-93; expert machinist for the McCormick Company, 1893-99; and is now a member of the dental department of the Hepperlen Clinic, at Beatrice. With his brother-in-law, he owns and manages a 12,000 acre ranch in Nebraska.

He is a member of the child welfare committee of the Kiwanis Club, is affiliated with the Centenary Methodist Episcopal Church at Beatrice, and holds membership in the Young Men's Christian Association. He is a member of the district, state, and national dental societies, is a member of the medical staff at Lutheran Hospital, and holds membership in the Chamber of Commerce and the Nebraskana Society. He has been a member of the local school board for seven years, and has taken an active part in musical affairs in the Methodist Church and Kiwanis Club. His social club is the Beatrice Country Club, while his sports include golfing, fishing, and motoring.

Dr. Beeson is a Mason, is affiliated with the Red Cross, and is a member of the Republican Party. He has lived in Nebraska for the past 38 years and has always been interested in the progress of his community and state.

His marriage to Hannah Floretta Quein was solemnized at Beatrice, September 19, 1899. Mrs. Beeson, who is descended from Queen Victoria, through the maternal side, was born at Zanesville, Ohio, July 8, 1869, the daughter of Amos and Elizabeth Quein. Two children were born to this marriage: Martha, born March 26, 1902; and Ruth, born August 12, 1903. Dr. and Mrs. Beeson have provided a home for three other children. Residence: Beatrice.

Peter Franklin Beghtol

Peter F. Beghtol, who has been engaged in the drug business at Bennet, Lancaster County, Nebraska, since 1883, was born at Industry, McDonough County, Illinois, December 27, 1857. His father, Uram Beghtol, who was a merchant, was born at Louisville, Kentucky, October 20, 1820, and died at Holdrege, Phelps County, Nebraska, December 19, 1906; his ancestry was German. His mother, Martha (Vance) Beghtol, was born at Memphis, Tennessee, February 2, 1823, and died at Holdrege, Phelps County, Nebraska, April 9, 1906.

Mr. Beghtol attended the public schools of Illinois, and in 1874 was graduated from the Industry High School. He was a clerk in a drug store for a time, and then moved to Bennet, where he now owns his own drug store. A Republican, he was elected state senator from Lancaster County in 1902 and 1904, and has always been interested in civic and political affairs.

His marriage to Ella Lawton Kenyon, was solemnized at Industry, October 2, 1879. Mrs. Beghtol was born at Bloomington, Illinois, January 15, 1857, and died at Bennet, April 9, 1928. Two children were born to their marriage: Scott K., born May 12, 1881, who is now engaged in the grocery business at Portland, Oregon; and Maxwell, Va., born May 25, 1886, who is a lawyer at Lincoln.

Mr. Beghtol is a Mason, and holds life membership in the Nebraskana Society. Residence: Bennet.

Arnold Behrens

For the past 27 years Arnold Behrens has been actively engaged in farming near Holdrege, Nebraska. He was born at Wichita, Kansas, February 10, 1878, the son of Henry and Eva (Gise) Behrens. His father, who was a world-wide traveler and explorer, was for many years a diamond and gold miner, and later was a farmer and stockraiser; he was born at Hanover, Germany, December 18, 1831, and died at Clearwater, Kansas, April 29, 1921. His mother was born at Baden, Germany, March 14, 1845, and died at Clearwater, February 1, 1926.

Mr. Behrens served in Company K, 30th Infantry as a corporal in the Spanish American War, and at this time is a member of the Veterans of Foreign Wars. He holds membership in William Lewis Camp of the Spanish American Veterans, at Lincoln, Nebraska, and is director of the Phelps County Soldiers Relief Organization. He is affiliated with the Methodist Episcopal Church, the Modern Woodmen of America, and the Nebraskana Society.

His marriage to Amanda Olivia Davidson was solemnized at Holdrege, March 31, 1907. Mrs. Behrens, the daughter of Gustaf and Caroline (Carlson) Davidson, was born at Holdrege, February 28, 1878. To this marriage two children were born: Roy Arnold, January 15, 1908; and Everett, May 22, 1912. Residence: Holdrege.

Jesse Francis Bejot

Born at Ainsworth, Nebraska, November 14, 1885, Jesse Francis Bejot is the son of Joseph Cincinnatus and Mary Emma (Sinele) Bejot. His father, who is a land owner and financier, was born of French parents at Chicago, Illinois, January 6, 1859. His mother, a typical pioneer homemaker in Nebraska, was born at Elvaston, Illinois, June 16, 1860, and died at Long Pine, Nebraska, February 9, 1931; she was descended from a former mayor of Paris, France.

Mr. Bejot attended school in Brown County until 1904, when he was graduated from a rural high school there. In 1923, he completed a course in business and banking at Massey Business College, Jaksonville, Florida. He has been a successful farmer for many years and recently has been engaged in the loan and brokerage business at Ainsworth, where he is vice president of the Citizens State Bank. He is a director in the Western Union Life Insurance Company of Lincoln, Nebraska. He is an extensive landowner.

During the World War Mr. Bejot bought war bonds and contributed liberally to Red Cross activities. He is a member of the Order of Odd Fellows, serving as chairman of the trustees of the local lodge, and holds membership in the Rebekah Lodge, and the Nebraskana Society. He is fond of reading and playing checkers.

Mr. Bejot was appointed chairman of the Taxpayers

League Investigating Committee of Brown County, in 1932. Politically, independent, he takes an active interest in all farm movements. Residence: Ainsworth. (Photograph in Album).

Paul Henry Bek

Paul Henry Bek, county judge of Seward County, was born at Seward, August 26, 1894, son of Paul William and Ida Sophia (Wulf) Bek. He attended public school at Seward, was later graduated from Concordia Teachers College, and was a student at the University of Nebraska, 1926-27-28.

Mr. Bek is a Republican. He served 20 months with the rank of corporal in the American Expeditionary Forces, and served in Siberia for 18 months, participating in engagements with hostile Bolsheviki near Vladivostok in Siberia.

He is a member of the American Legion, the Infantry Officers Reserve Corps (2nd lieutenant), St. Johns Evangelcial Lutheran Church, the Red Cross (chairman Seward County chapter), the Chamber of Commerce (secretary 1922-), the Rotary Club (charter member), the Nebraskana Society and the Nebraska Alumni Association. His hobby is photography. Residence: Seward.

Carroll Reed Belden

One of Omaha's leading merchants is Carroll R. Belden, who for the past 20 years has been engaged in business in the city. Born in Omaha, August 14, 1888, he is the son of Charles Carroll and Della Viola (Reed) Belden. His father was born at Mesopotamia, Ohio, August 5, 1849, and was a merchant whose Scotch ancestors settled in Connecticut prior to the Revolution. He died at Omaha, November 17, 1925.

Della Viola Belden was born at Farmington, Ohio, October 16, 1860. She is of Scotch-Irish descent, her ancesters having been pre-Revolutionary settlers in Vermont.

Upon his graduation from Omaha High School in 1906, Carroll R. Belden entered Amherst College, from which he received his B. S. in 1911. He is a member of Beta Theta Pi. On December 27, 1913 he was married to Fannie Arnetta Brown, at Madison, Wisconsin. Mrs. Belden was born at Mason City, Iowa, March 3, 1890, and is of Scotch-Irish descent.

Following in his father's footsteps, Carroll Belden has been active as a merchant since he reached maturity. He is president of Thompson Belden and Company and vice president of Seymour Belden Company. He is a Republican and a member of First Central Congregational Church. His clubs are the Omaha Club and the Omaha Country Club. Residence: Omaha.

David William Bell

David William Bell, physician and surgeon, was born at Arlington, Nebraska, January 12, 1879, son of William A. and Lydia E. (Reid) Bell. His father who was born at Quincy, Illinois, September 23, 1847, was a retired farmer and real estate dealer at the time of his death in Omaha, September 3, 1915. He was of Scotch-Irish descent. His wife, Lydia, was born at Omaha, October 28, 1850, and is also of Scotch-Irish descent on one side, and Pennsylvania Dutch on the other.

Dr. Bell attended Papillion schools and received his Ph. G. from the Omaha College of Pharmacy in 1902. He attended the University of Nebraska 1899-1900, and received his M. D. from Creighton Medical College. In 1898 he attended Shenandoah Normal School. He is a member of Phi Rho Sigma, and a member of the faculty of Creighton College of Medicine, College of Pharmacy and College of Dentistry.

On December 25, 1902, he was married to Anna Mathilda Zwiebel at Papillion. Mrs. Bell was born at Papillion, March 14, 1880, of French and German descent. There are two children: Beatrice M., born December 5, 1903, and Traber David, born September 13, 1907.

Dr. Bell is a Democrat and during his years of residence has engaged in the practice of pharmacy, medicine and surgery. He was a private in the Students Army Training Corps at Creighton University, and is a member of the Omaha-Douglas County, Nebraska State and American Medical Associations. He is a Methodist, a member of the Knights of Pythias and the Nebraskana Society. His hobbies are medical research and reading. Residence: Papillion.

Fred Bell

Fred Bell, a resident of Thayer County, Nebraska, since 1882, was born at Eden, Iowa, August 19, 1869, the son of David and Bessie (Gooden) Bell. His father, who was a farmer and fruit raiser, was born at Bilsby, England, September 16, 1841, and died at Palmwood, Australia; his family had lived at Lincolnshire, England, for many generations. His mother was born at Lincolnshire, May, 1842, and died during Fred Bell's early boyhood.

Mr. Bell received his education in the public schools of Iowa. He has been a farmer near Hebron, Nebraska, for many years and for the past five years has served as county commissioner of Thayer County. He is a Democrat. Mr. Bell holds membership in the Masons and Odd Fellows, is affiliated with the Methodist Church and is a member of The Nebraskana Society. For 11 years he has been a member of the school board of District 51. His sports are baseball and horse racing, and his hobby is good horses.

On October 26, 1904, he was married to Sophia Knapp at Hebron. Mrs. Bell was born of German parentage at Papillion, Nebraska, May 20, 1872. Residence: Hebron.

Jesse Durnell Bell

Jesse Durnell Bell, son of Jesse Durnell Bell, Sr., and Hattie M. (Derby) Bell, was born September 1, 1878, at what is now Bellwood, Nebraska. His father was born at New Albany, Floyd County, Indiana, October 22, 1836. He was a merchant in Woodhull, Illinois, and came to Butler County, Nebraska, where he settled and later founded the town of Bellwood. He was also one of the founders of the Methodist Church in Bellwood, of which he was Sunday School superintendent for many years. He died at Bellwood, January 4, 1889.

His mother was born at Lockport, New York, June 26, 1849, the daughter of Lydia (Pinkney) Derby and Benjamin Derby, who was a Civil War veteran. Hattie Bell Lloyd died at Long Beach, California, November 5, 1919. Mrs. Derby was educated musically and in 1878 brought the first piano into the Platte Valley country.

Jesse Bell attended the Bellwood elementary schools and received his high school work at Nebraska Wesleyan University. He then studied a general course, and agriculture, for three years at the University of Nebraska, and in 1902, graduated from the Iowa State College at Ames, where he received a degree, Bachelor of Agricultural Science.

Ada Belle McFall became his wife, January 21, 1903, at Lincoln, Nebraska. She was born in Listwell, Ontario, Canada, April 21, 1878, the daughter of William G. McFall, a pioneer merchant of Lincoln, and Mary McFall. The latter died in 1918. Mrs. Bell taught in the kindergarten before her marriage. To this union five children were born: Dorothy C., November 23, 1903, who is married to Aubrey Becker, Jesse Donald, June 14, 1905; Robert McFall, January 7, 1907; Richard Wilton, April 5, 1909, and Patricia, September 5, 1916, who died March 10, 1918, at Long Beach, California. The children have attended Bellwood schools, Long Beach High School and the University of Nebraska.

Mr. Bell has lived on his farm in Nebraska for fifty-two years, is a member of the Republican party, has served on the Bellwood school board twenty years, was on township board twelve years, and has been a steward and trustee on the Methodist Church board for twenty-five years. In 1902 he was elected cashier of the Bellwood Bank and served until 1917, when he was elected presidnt of the bank. In 1920, he retired from business and now supervises the work on his farms.

During the war, Mr. Bell was local registrar for men entering the service. He is a member of the Odd Fellows, the Nebraskana Society, and is a member of the State Historical Society. He holds membership in the Masonic Lodge at David City, Nebraska. Reading and touring are Mr. Bell's favorite recreations. Residence: Bellwood.

John Ernest Bell

John Ernest Bell, stockman and farmer near Superior, Nebraska, was born at New Matamoras, Ohio, October 3, 1893, and since 1906 has been a resident of this state. His father, John D. Bell, who was a farmer, was born at New Matamoras, March 23, 1844, and died at Superior, April 7, 1921. His mother, Hulda (Riggs) Bell, was born at New Matamoras, August 22, 1866.

Mr. Bell attended school at New Matamoras, and in 1913 was graduated from the high school at Hardy, Nebraska. He was awarded the B. S. degree at Nebraska University in 1917 where he was active in athletics, being a member of the basketball team.

He served as instructor of agriculture and athletics at Harris, Iowa, 1917-18, was instructor in a camp school of the United States Army from 1918 to 1919, and acted as athletic coach at Hardy High School in 1919. He had an undefeated basketball team for one year and was unusually successful in managing the various athletic teams with which he was connected. Mr. Bell is now manager of the Superior Stock Farm where he maintains one of the largest herds of pure bred Hampshire hogs in Nebraska. He owns a farm of 500 acres of which 100 acres are under irrigation, and all of which is highly productive.

Mr. Bell is a member of the Nebraskana Society, is affiliated with the Methodist Church, and holds membership in the American Legion. He is a member of the Young Men's Christian Association of the University of Nebraska. He served as a corporal during the World War and was stationed at Camp Dodge where he acted as instructor. His hobby is basketball.

His marriage to Lucy Stout Keifer was solemnized at Bostwick, Nebraska, June 12, 1923. Mrs. Bell, who was a high school teacher before her marriage, was born at Bostwick, August 8, 1889. Among her distinguished ancestors were: General J. Warren Keifer of Ohio; Major General Keifer, who served in the Civil and Spanish American wars, and who was speaker of the house of representatives at Washington; and J. Warren Keifer, Jr., her father, who served in the Nebraska Legislature in 1907. Their three children are: John Ernest, Jr., born December 21, 1925; Warren James, born September 6, 1928; Julia Evaline, born September 17, 1931. Residence: Superior. (Photograph in Album).

Ortha Constantine Bell

Ortha C. Bell, a resident of Nebraska for the past 59 years, has been a leader in the political and civic life of Lincoln for many years. He was born on a farm in Cass County, Indiana, April 30, 1847, the son of George William and Marrietta (Thomas) Bell. His father, who was born at Georgetown, Cass County, Indiana, April 30, 1824, first enlisted as a musician in the Regimental Band of Indiana in the Civil War; later he re-enlisted in the

cavalry and was discharged at the close of the war as a captain. He was the son of Major Daniel Bell of Maryland. He died at Hagerman, Idaho, March 10, 1899. Marrietta Bell, mother of Ortha, was born in Susquehannah, Pennsylvania, and died at Farm Ridge, LaSalle County, Illinois, November 29, 1869.

Mr. Bell has had an interesting and varied career as a soldier, public official, and a business man. He enlisted for service in the Union army early in the Civil War as a bugle boy, and served in the battles of Nashville, Franklin, Pulaski, and Sulphur Trestle. He had previously studied in the log school house in the early 50's, and had attended an academy at Princeton, Indiana. Upon the completion of his war service he entered a printing office as an apprentice; a little later he studied to be a telegraph operator and became the first operator at Havana, Illinois. In 1870 he moved to Texas, where he became a cowboy; he found work on a ranch where he became later a private secretary and bookkeeper for the owner.

In 1872 he moved to Lincoln, and became connected with the Conover & Druse Shoe Shop. Two years later he became a salesman for a time, and in 1880, he was appointed deputy county clerk of Lancaster County. Since that time he has been in state and county service continuously. He has held the following positions: deputy county clerk, 1880-1886; county clerk, 1886-1890; deputy secretary of state, 1890-1891; deputy county register of deeds, 1910-1915; county assessor, 1916-1921; deputy county assessor, 1921-25; and county assessor, 1925-1931. He is a Republican.

From 1897 to 1900 Mr. Bell was receiver for the First National Bank at Red Cloud, Nebraska. From 1900 to 1905 he was manager of the Capitol Hotel at Lincoln. He was editor of the Galveston *News* in 1876. He is now assistant assessor of Lancaster County. An article published in the *Lincoln Star,* January 4, 1931, tells the story of his life and is a sincere tribute to him from the people of Lincoln.

His marriage to Minnie DeEtte Polley was solemnized at Lincoln, December 10, 1874. Mrs. Bell was born in Herkimer County, New York, October 25, 1854. She is the granddaughter of William D. Polley. Two children were born to this union: Jane B., born March 9, 1877, who married Frank S. Ringer; Hazel B., born in 1888, who married E. Boyd Smith.

Mr. Bell is a member of the Grand Army of the Republic; was appointed chief bugler for the department of Nebraska in 1885; and was made department commander in 1924. He is a life member of the Lincoln Chamber of Commerce; has been president of the Nebraska County Assessors Association for the past 14 years, and is active in all welfare societies. He is a member of the Odd Fellows. He holds membership in the Nebraska Pioneer's Association and the Nebraskana Society. For the past 45 years he has been a member of the First Christian Church of Lincoln.

He is a member of the Young Men's Christian Association. He has been a deacon in his church for the last forty years and has been a member of the choir there for several years. He is a musician and singer of some note and has been a member of the G. A. R. Quartette for a long time. Mr. Bell was not a candidate for re-election to public office in 1931 because he feels that younger men should carry on the state and county affairs. Residence: Lincoln.

Truman Thaddeus Bell

One of Howard County's outstanding lawyers, Truman Thaddeus Bell was born in Crawford County, Indiana, September 2, 1859, and came to Nebraska in 1874, at the age of fifteen. His father, James Madison Bell, who was a farmer of early American ancestry, died in 1897. His mother, Mary Esther Conrad, died in 1921.

Truman T. Bell attended public school and was graduated from Grand Island High School. He received his Bachelor of Laws degree from the University of Michigan Law School in June, 1885, and has since been in active practice. A Republican, he served as city attorney of St. Paul for twenty years, and as county attorney two terms.

He was married to Mary Ella Orcutt at Rochester, New York, in September, 1888, and to them three children were born, Percival H., born June 21, 1889, who died June 23, 1916; Beulah, born July 16, 1890, married Thomas C. Minnich; and Bernice, born October 22, 1897, married George R. Field. Mrs. Bell, was born at Vienna, Virginia, September 29, 1860.

Mr. Bell was a four minute speaker during the World War period, and for seven years served as president of the local Red Cross organization. He is a member of the Communitiy Club, The Nebraskana Society and the Ancient Free and Accepted Masons and the Shrine. His social club is the St. Paul Golf Club. Residence: St. Paul.

W. Glen Bell

W. Glen Bell, who is an educator at Newman Grove, Nebraska, was born at Tabor, Iowa, June 28, 1897, the son of Willis B. and Judith Anne (Wyant) Bell. His father, who was a farmer and business man, was born in Ohio, May 27, 1862, of English descent, and died at Tabor, November 19, 1926. His mother, whose ancestry ·; Pennsylvania Dutch, was born at Silver City, Iowa, June 9, 1869, and is living today.

Mr. Bell was graduated from Tabor College Academy in 1915, received the A. B. degree at Tabor College in 1919, and was awarded the A. M. degree at the University of Iowa in 1932. He took a prominent part in the Young Men's Christian Association at Tabor College, was active in music affairs, and played football. He attended summer school at Lake Geneva, Wisconsin, in 1916.

He has held the following professional positions: superintendent of schools at Kiron, Iowa, 1919-21; superintendent of schools at Lehigh, Iowa, 1921-23; head of the department of social science, Norfolk Senior High School, 1923-26; superintendent of schools at Allen, Nebraska, 1926-29; and superintendent of cshools at Newman Grove since 1929. He is a member of the National Educational Association, the Nebraska State Teachers Association, the Red Cross, and the Masons.

Mr. Bell served as president of the Young Men's Christian Association at Tabor College, 1917-18, was a member of the Lions Club of Norfolk, 1924-26, and is now a member of The Nebraskana Society. His hobbies are reading and music, and his favorite sports are hunting and golfing.

Of his marriage to Clara Alice Watkins, three children were born: Glen, May 3, 1923; Wendell, January 16, 1925; and William, June 19, 1926. Mrs. Bell, who was formerly a teacher, was born of English and Welsh ancestry at Iowa City, Iowa, July 27, 1899. Residence: Newman Grove.

Harley LeRoy Bellamy

Harley LeRoy Bellamy, who is a pharmacist at Cambridge, Nebraska, was born at Decatur, Illinois, November 29, 1889, the son of John and Sarah Jane (Denton) Bellamy. His father, a carpenter, was born in Illinois, in October, 1857, and died at Blackfoot, Illinois, in August, 1929. His mother was born in Illinois, September 1, 1862, and died at Blackfoot, in August, 1929.

Mr. Bellamy was graduated from the Cambridge High School in 1905, and received the Ph. G. degree at Northwestern University in 1910. He has been in the drug business as partner and manager of the Bellamy & Dold Company at Cambridge, since 1910. He holds member-

ship in the Rotary Club, the Community Club, the Congregational Church, and the Masonic order, at Cambridge. His recreations are reading, tennis, baseball, and golf.

On November 12, 1913, he married Gertrude May Picthall at McCook, Nebraska. Mrs. Bellamy was born at Aurora, Nebraska, December 8, 1889. Their two children are: Robert, born March 2, 1915; and Donald, born February 1, 1917. Residence: Cambridge.

Oren Allin Beltzer

One of the leading executives of Grand Island, Nebraska, is Oren Allin Beltzer, president of the Grand Island Trust Company. He was born at Stratton, Nebraska, March 20, 1888, the son of Jacob Edwin and Margaret (Thompson) Beltzer. His father, who was a nurseryman, was born of Pennsylvania Dutch and Welsh ancestry, in Ohio, 1848. He came to Nebraska after the Civil War, settling near Stratton. He died at Arapahoe, Nebraska. His mother, whose ancestry was English and Scotch, was born in Missouri, in 1855, and died at Atwood, Kansas.

Mr. Beltzer was graduated from the Arapahoe High School, was a student at the University of Nebraska where he held all offices in Kappa Sigma, and received letter in football and baseball, captain both teams 1909-10. Later he attended the University of Pennsylvania.

At this time he is president of the Grand Island Trust Company, is president of the Grand Island Finance Company, and is active in civic affairs at Grand Island. At one time Mr. Beltzer was engaged in professional baseball, and prior to holding his present position was in the real estate business.

He is a member of the Grand Island Chamber of Commerce, the Red Cross, the Elks, and The Nebraskana Society. His social clubs include: Riverside Golf Club; Eastridge Golf Club; and his favorite sport is golfing. He is independent, politically.

Of his marriage to Nell Marie Schreff three children were born: Betty Jane, December 27, 1911, who died September 29, 1913; Jimmie, born November 21, 1918; and Joanne, born July 9, 1919. Residence: Grand Island.

Eugene Henry Bemis

Born at Sutton, Nebraska, July 4, 1882, Eugene Henry Bemis is the son of George Whitfield Bemis and Ada (Gray) Bemis. His father was a distinguished lawyer at York, Nebraska, where he was once mayor, and at Sutton where he served as district attorney for the Fifth District. His mother is a talented musician and writer.

Mr. Bemis has been engaged in the newspaper business many years and is associate editor of the *New Teller* at York. He has written a few stories for magazines and lyrics for J. A. Parks compositions. He is actively interested in music and music composition and has arranged hundreds of programs for various community events. He acted as song leader at a recent district convention of the Rotary Club, originated the county school parade at York, which is now an annual feature, and was largely responsible for the festoon lighting system which has been used in York since the first fall festival several years ago.

His wife, who was Kittie Houston, of York, is associated with him in the publication of the *New Teller*.

He is a member of the York Chamber of Commerce, the Young Men's Christian Association, York Rotary Club, Elks, and Knights of Pythias. An expert advertising man, Mr. Bemis was the author of *Song of the Willys-Knight,* an advertisement in rhyme, of which ten million copies were distributed. His favorite sport is golfing. Residence: York.

Florence Olive Bemis

For the past several years Florence Olive Bemis has been prominent in club activities at York, York County, Nebraska. She was born at Brookings, South Dakota, July 16, 1895, the daughter of Harvey Asa and Olive (Johnson) Stevens. Her father, owner and manager of a large ranch, was born January 7, 1866, the son of John Nelson Stevens and Elizabeth Ann (Swartz) Stevens. Her mother, who is an educated and intellectual woman, was born in Wisconsin, July 30, 1870.

Mrs. Bemis was graduated from the high school at Brookings. She is a member of the Young Men's Christian Association Auxiliary, the Parent Teachers Association, The Nebraskana Society, and the Methodist Episcopal Guild. She holds membership in the Neighbors Club at York. During the World War she was prominent in hospital visitation work at Fort Logan, Colorado, where her husband was in the army service, and took part in all Red Cross activities. She is eligible to the membership in the Daughters of the American Revolution, is local president of the American Legion Auxiliary, and has held every office in that unit. She is a member of the Eight and Forty Club of Nebraska.

Her marriage to Wendell P. Bemis was solemnized at Rochester, Minnesota, September 2, 1913. She has one son, Wendell Whitfield, born November 22, 1916, who is the youngest member of the junior class in the York High School. Mrs. Bemis is a Republican. Residence: York.

Nathaniel Gustave Bender

Nathaniel Gustave Bender, a leading executive at Sutton, Nebraska, has been prominent in business and civic affairs in the state for many years. He was born at Sutton, July 9, 1884, the son of Eugenia (Reuss) Bender and Jacob Bender. Jacob Bender, who was born at Galoi, Russia, August 21, 1854, and died at Sutton, November 14, 1928, was a homesteader in Nebraska in 1875; he was engaged in the implement business at Sutton from 1884 until his death in 1928, and served as president of the Mid-west Implement Dealers Association of Nebraska and Iowa at one time. He was mayor of Sutton for several terms, served as a member of the legislature in 1925 and house of representatives in Nebraska, and was a leader in state affairs.

Eugenia (Reuss) Bender, his mother, was born at Galoi, December 19, 1853, and died at Sutton, May 2, 1898. Of German descent, she came to America in 1875. She was an active church worker and was interested in music.

Mr. Bender attended the public schools of Sutton where he was graduated from high school in 1904, and later was a student at the University of Nebraska. He was awarded letters in high school for football, baseball, and track. He entered the business world with the firm of Jacob Bender & Son, and except for a brief period when he was European representative for an implement company, has been connected with that organization.

He is stockholder in the City State Bank of Sutton and spends part of his time in looking after various farm interests. Mr. Bender is a Republican, and has held the following positions in his community and state; member of the board of education of Sutton, four years; city engineer of Sutton; chairman of the Republican Central Committee for Clay County for four terms; and member of the Republican State Central Committee.

He served as a member of the library board for a time, and is a member of the Sutton Cemetery Association and was chairman of the local Red Cross from 1917 to 1918. He holds membership in the following fraternal organizations; Independent Order of Odd Fellows; Masons, Blue Lodge, Chapter, Royal Arch, Scottish Rite, Shrine. He served as representative from Tehama Shrine Temple to the Imperial International Council at Toronto, Canada, in 1930.

Mr. Bender was president of the Mid-west Implement Dealers Association in 1929 and 1930, was vice president of the National Federation of Implement Dealers Associations, 1930, and was elected president of the latter in 1931. He is a former member of the executive board of the Sutton Community Club, is a supporter of the Young Men's Christian Association, and holds membership in the University Club of Nebraska. He is affiliated with the First Congregational Church of Sutton. His sports include golfing, fishing, and hunting, and his hobbies are reading, mechanics, and flowers. In 1910 he acted as American representative for American Manufacturered Agricultural Implements, in Europe, with headquarters at Budapest, Hungary, and Odessa, Russia.

During the World War Mr. Bender was a member of the Home Guards and was chairman of the Liberty loan drives in his district. He married Clara Henrietta Landmann at Scotland, South Dakota, January 11, 1912. Mrs. Bender, who was a teacher in South Dakota prior to her marriage graduated from Milwaukee Downer Seminary at Milwaukee, Wisconsin, in 1908. She was born of German parents at Scotland, September 15, 1887. Mrs. Bender is a member of the Sutton Chapter No. 54 of the Order of the Eastern Star, and was matron in 1931. She was president of the P. E. O. Sisters in 1920-21-22. They have four children, all of whom are in school; Gretchen, born January 23, 1914; Paul J., born October 15, 1916; Frederick G., born October 13, 1922; and Wallace, born January 18, 1926. Residence: Sutton.

Nels August Bengtson

Nels A. Bengtson, geographer and educator at the University of Nebraska, was born at Navlinge, Skane Province, Sweden, May 22, 1879. His father, August Bengtson, who is a retired farmer, was born in Sweden in 1854. Hannah (Johnsson) Bengtson, his mother, was born in Sweden, in 1853, and died at Shickley, Fillmore County, Nebraska, May 14, 1926.

Professor Bengtson attended the rural schools of Fillmore County, and in 1897 was graduated from the Shickley High School. He holds the following degrees: A. B., 1907, University of Nebraska; A. M., 1908, University of Nebraska; Ph. D., 1927, Clark University. During the summer of 1904 he was a student at Cornell University. He is a member of Sigma Xi, and in 1929-30 he served as president of the Nebraska chapter of this society. He is a member of Sigma Phi Epsilon.

He was a rural school teacher for two years; high school principal at St. Paul, Nebraska, for one year; professor of geography at Peru State Teachers College, three years; instructor in the summer session at Cornell University, 1912, the University of Virginia, 1913, University of Wisconsin, 1925, Columbia University, 1929-30-31-32; and since 1908 has been professor of geography at the University of Nebraska. In 1929 he was made chairman of the department of geography at the latter institution. He was consulting geologist in charge of field investigations in Honduras, 1920, in Ecuador, 1922, and in Venezuela, 1927.

In 1918, Professor Bengtson was breadstuffs expert for the United States War Trade Board, and in 1919 he was appointed Trade Commissioner to Norway. He is the author of: *Physical Geography Manual*, 1913; *The Wheat Industry*, 1915; *Commercial Handbook of Norway*, 1920; and *Pupils' Workbook in Geography of Nebraska*, 1925. He has acted as Councillor of Economic Geography at Worcestor, Massachusetts, and has written numerous articles on educational and geographical subjects.

He has lived in Nebraska since September, 1880. On June 14, 1902, he was united in marriage with Iva M. Maxcy at Peru, Nemaha County, Nebraska. Mrs. Bengtson was born at Bramwell, West Virginia, June 14, 1882. There are five children: Juanita, born April 22, 1903, who married Robert H. Downing; Paulus, born October 26,

1904; Rowena, born December 2, 1910; Ruth, born January 9, 1919; and Martha, born July 9, 1921.

He is a member of the Association of American Geographers, having served as vice president of this society in 1923; was president of National Council of Geography Teachers in 1929; and holds a fellowship in the American Association for the Advancement of Science. He is a Mason. His favorite sport is walking. Politically, Professor Bengtson is an independent Democrat. He is affiliated with the First Unitarian Church of Worcester, Massachusetts, and he is a member of the Nebraskana Society. Residence: Sutton.

Abram Elting Bennett

One of Nebraska's leading neuropsychiatrists, Dr. Abram E. Bennett is a native of the state. He was born at Alliance, January 12, 1898, son of Charles Elting and Bertha (Kinsey) Bennett. His father, born at Marshall, Michigan, March 6, 1872, is a conductor on the C. B. & Q. R. R., and is descended from Holland Dutch and English settlers in America prior to the American Revolution. His mother, born at Genoa, Nebraska, October 30, 1876, was a music teacher, of Holland Dutch ancestry.

Upon his graduation from Alliance High School in 1915, Dr. Bennett entered the University of Nebraska, from which he received a B. Sc. in 1919, and an M. D. in 1921. He took post-graduate work at Philadelphia General Hospital 1921-23, Philadelphia Orthopedic and Nervous Infirmary 1923, and Johns Hopkins University in 1924. He is a member of Alpha Omega Alpha, Sigma Phi Epsilon and Phi Rho Sigma.

On September 18, 1923, he was united in marriage to Evelyn Rose Langfang of Dover, New Jersey, at Philadelphia. Mrs. Bennett was born June 20, 1902, and is of German and French descent. Their three children are: Foster, born December 30, 1924; Ann, born May 27, 1926, and Jean, born January 1, 1930.

Since 1924 Dr. Bennett has been engaged in private practice in association with Dr. G. Alexander Young, of Omaha. He is the author of about twenty medical publications in the fields of neurology and psychiatry since 1921. He is a member of the American Medical Editors and Authors Association, and instructor in neuropsychiatry at the University of Nebraska. He is secretary of the Red Arrow Burner Company of Omaha.

During the World War he was a private in the S. A. T. C. He is a Mason, and is diplomat of the National Board of Medical Examiners. His professional organizations include the American Medical Association, the Nebraska State Medical Association and the Omaha-Douglas County Medical Society, of which he was council member 1928-30. Residence: Omaha.

Mary Bennett

One of Nebraska's oldest pioneer women is Mary Humphrey Bennett, who has lived in the state since 1873. She was born at Groton, Tompkins County, New York, October 19, 1846, the daughter of Margaret (Lamberson) and John Humphrey. Her father, a farmer, was born at Trenton, New Jersey, April 8, 1776, and died at Plainfield, New Jersey, March 5, 1870; his ancestry was English. Her mother was born at West Dryden, New York, August 29, 1805, of English parentage, and died at McLean, April 14, 1882.

Mrs. Bennett is a member of the Rebekah Lodge, is affiliated with the Methodish Church, and holds membership in the Daughters of the American Revolution. During the World War she bought Liberty bonds and assisted in all relief work.

Her marriage to Ashley Bennett was solemnized at Hudson, Wisconsin, June 13, 1868. Mr. Bennett was born at Argile, Wisconsin, October 12, 1846, and died at Sutton, October 16, 1927; he was a farmer. Their son, Floyd, was born May 12, 1878. Residence: Sutton.

Grace Margaret Bohne Benson

Born at Grand Island, Nebraska, February 14, 1882, Grace Margaret Benson has lived in this state practically all her life and at this time is an outstanding figure in women's affairs. Her father, Alfred Herman Bohne, who was a furniture dealer, was born at Beardstown, Illinois, August 27, 1842, and died at Grand Island, July 21, 1891; he served in the 33rd Illinois Infantry during the Civil War. He was of German descent, and was related to the founder of Beardstown who was an officer in Washington's army during the Revolution.

Eliza Margaret (Craig) Bohne, mother of Grace Benson, was born at Springfield, Illinois, November 22, 1842, and died at Rochester, New York, May 15, 1913. She was an educator, served as matron at Doane College, Crete, Nebraska, and was always active in civic and social welfare work. Her ancestry was Scotch.

Mrs. Benson attended the public schools of Grand Island, and in 1901 was graduated from Crete High School. She was a student at Doane College, 1901-04, New York University, 1911-12, Vineland Institute, and the New York School of Philanthropy. She taught at East Northfield, Massachusetts from 1905 to 1906, was active in the schools of Springfield, 1907, and from 1907 to 1913 served as director of the Child Study Laboratory; she is the author of *Report of Child Study Laboratory* (1913).

Her marriage to Harry William Benson was solemnized at Rochester, October 14, 1913. Dr. Benson, who is a physician and surgeon at Oakland, Nebraska, was born at Argo, Nebraska, February 23, 1876, of Swedish parentage. Their two children are: Louise Margaret, born December 10, 1918; and Barbara, born August 31, 1921.

Mrs. Benson holds membership in the Nebraska State Historical Society, the Native Sons and Daughters, and the Red Cross, is serving as secretary-treasurer of the Oakland Library Board, and is chairman of the Burt County Tuberculosis Campaign and Clinic. She is past member of the Academy of Political and Social Science, is member-at-large of the Conference of Social Workers, and at this time is acting as director of the Nebraska Tuberculosis Association. From 1927 to 1929, she was president of the Oakland Woman's Club in which she is still prominent.

She is affiliated with the Presbyterian Church and is a member of the local Parent Teachers' Association. Her favorite sport is motoring, and her hobbies are gardening and child welfare. Politically, Mrs. Benson is independent. For the past six years she has been a member of the League of Women Voters in Nebraska. Her published report of the Child Study Laboratory entered into the second edition and is considered a thorough and comprehensive study. Residence: Oakland. (Photograph in Album).

Harry D. Benson

Harry Benson, grain dealer, was born at Tiskilwa, Illinois, August 17, 1859, son of Darius L. and Esther M. (Golding) Benson. He received an elementary education.

His father was born at Worcester, Massachusetts, March 9, 1883. During his life he was a farmer. His ancestors came from England in 1636, landing six miles below Plymouth Rock. His death occurred at Shenandoah, Iowa, August 16, 1916. Esther M. Golding, mother of Harry, was born in Cambridge County, England, October 6, 1833, and died at Shenandoah, March 5, 1916.

His marriage to Lenore Smith was solemnized at Marysville, Missouri, June 29, 1887. She was born at Canton, Illinois, April 29, 1861.

Mr. Benson has been a resident of Nebraska for thirty-three years. A Republican, he served in Kansas Legislature during the years of 1889 to 1891. He is a member of the Nebraskana Society and his secret organization is the Independent Order of the Odd Fellows. Residence: Fairbury.

Rinehart-Marsden—Omaha

HARRY WILLIAM BENSON

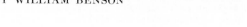

Harry William Benson

Harry William Benson, physician and surgeon, was born at Argo, Nebraska, February 23, 1876, son of Torsten and Elna (Johansson) Bengtson. Torsten Bengtson, who was born at Vaby, Malmo, Sweden, April 18, 1836, came to America, September 15, 1868, and engaged in farming in Burt County until his death at Oakland, March 15, 1916. His wife, Elna, was born at Lanekar, Forstorp, Sweden, February 12, 1841, and died at Omaha, April 21, 1891. She was a typical pioneer mother.

Dr. Benson attended the public and high schools of Omaha, and received his M. D. from the University of Nebraska in 1903. He is a member of Phi Rho Sigma. A resident of Nebraska all his life, he has been engaged in active practice since 1903, and is a member of the American, Nebraska State and Burt County Medical Associations. His life as a country doctor has been an inspiration and example. He has made a splendid contribution to the life of his community, and has taken an active part in civic and welfare projects. He is a member and former president (1929-30) of the Nebraska Academy of Opthalmology and Otolaryngology, and is a fellow of the American College of Physicians. A life long member of the First Lutheran Church, he served as president of the Lutheran Brotherhood 1928-29, chairman of the Red Cross 1929-31, and president of the Chamber of Commerce in 1926. Dr. Benson is the author of the following: *Preclinical Medicine* (Burt County, December 16, 1926); *Social Problems with Illustrating Cases* (Woman's Club, 1930); *The Crucifixion and The Phophecies* (Lutheran Brotherhood, 1929); *Some Complications of Para-nasal Sinus Disease* (State Academy, May, 1926; Burt County, December 4, 1928); *Intestinal Infection* (Burt County, June 24, 1924); *Hay Fever; Treatment by Pollen Extract* (December 2, 1922); *Etiology of Nephritis* (Burt County, June 5, 1923); *Gastric Ulcer* (Burt County, February 2, 1931; *Acute Conjunctivitis; A Report on a Case of Cerebral Abscess; Epidemic Dysentery* (Printed Bulletin of the State Institution of Iowa, 1905); *Synopsis of 164 Cases of Measles.*

He was married to Grace Margaret Bohne at Rochester, New York, October 14, 1913. Mrs. Benson, who was born at Grand Island, Nebraska, February 14, 1882, is of German and Scotch descent. Before her marriage she was director of the child study laboratory of the Rochester public schools. There are two daughters, Louise Margaret, born December 10, 1918, and Barbara Elna, born August 31, 1921.

Dr. Benson is a Democrat, a Mason, and a member of the Nebraska State Historical Society, the Nebraskana Society, the Native Sons and Daughters of Nebraska, and the Parent-Teachers' Association. In his few spare moments he enjoys golf and reading. Residence: Oakland. (Photograph on Page 110).

John Linus Benson

John Linus Benson, a resident of Nebraska for the past 60 years, was born at Kinnekulle, Sweden, November 6, 1867, the son of Nels Johan Benson and Lena (Kajsa) Benson. His father, who came to this country in 1868, was born at Lidskopinz, Sweden, October 29, 1848, and died at Saronville, Nebraska, December 17, 1930. His mother was born at Lidskopinz, October 18, 1844, and died at Saronville, June 21, 1930.

Mr. Benson has been a prominent stock buyer for over thirty years as well as an extensive feeder of hogs and cattle. He is a Democrat, has been a county commissioner, a member of the Nebraskana Society and a member of the Saron Evangelical Lutheran Church.

On November 1, 1893, he was married to Mathilde Batzeba Malm at Saronville. She was born in Sweden, January 16, 1866. To their marriage five children were born: Linnea, on July 12, 1894, who married Elmer Nuss at Saronville, November 29, 1916; Judith, on February 4, 1896, who married George Carlson, at Saronville,

August 25, 1920, and who died February 17, 1926; Sigrid, on March 18, 1898, who married Alvin Hultman at Saronville, November 1, 1921; Hildur, on October 14, 1900, who married Roger Anderson at Saronville, November 17, 1920; and Bernice, on April 8, 1905, who married Leonard Johnson at Saronville, August 14, 1928. Residence: Saronville.

Nellie Gray Benson

On January 24, 1879, Nellie Gray Benson was born at Johnstown, Licking County, Ohio, daughter of Tilton and Angenora Meeker (Dean) Hill. Her father, also a native of Johnstown, was born on September 30, 1836. A farmer and lawyer, he held the rank of captain and served as a recruiting officer in the Civil War. His ancestry was English, Irish and Scotch. He died at Lincoln, on January 23, 1906. His wife, Angenora, was born at Newark, New Jersey, September 19, 1843, and died at Silver Creek, Nebraska, January 3, 1911.

Mrs. Benson was educated in the school of Schuyler and Silver Creek, receiving a third grade teacher's certificate at the age of fourteen years. She later attended Fremont Normal College. Her marriage to DeAlton Benson was solemnized at Silver Creek on June 3, 1903. Mr. Benson was born at Silver Creek, on December 22, 1875, and is engaged in farming and the insurance business.

There are three children of this marriage, Hazel Lorene, born June 16, 1907, who is a senior at the University of Nebraska; Emmett Hill, born July 20, 1911, who is a graduate of the Lincoln School of Commerce; and Gilbert Eugene, born October 22, 1913, who graduated from high school in 1931.

In addition to her duties as a homemaker and mother, Mrs. Benson has been active in public life for a number of years. She taught school for ten years, and was a member of the board of the County Farm Bureau for seven years. After serving two years as a member of the State Farm Bureau she was elected vice president of the State Farm Bureau Federation, serving in that capacity a year and a half, and as president for three years and a half. She is the only woman ever to serve as state president of that organization. She was home and committee chairman of the Nebraska Farm Bureau Federation 1924-28. Also active in Democratic politics she was Democratic committeewoman from Polk County, and was elected alternate delegate to the last Democratic National Convention from the Fourth District.

She is a member of the Osceola Methodist Episcopal Church, the Pythian Sisters, (state secretary, 1909) the Royal Highlanders and The Nebraskana Society. At the present time she is a member of the Nebraska State Board of Control, with offices in the State Capitol. Residence: Lincoln. (Photograph on Page 112).

Peter L. Benthack

Peter L. Benthack, homeopathic physician and surgeon, was born at Scharmbeck, Winsen, Germany, June 26, 1867, and for the past 54 years has resided in Nebraska.

His father, Hans Peter Benthack, was born at Stelle, Germany, July 3, 1828, and was a minister. He died at Columbus, Nebraska, April 28, 1893. His wife, Kathrine Dorethea Tidge, was also born in Stelle, on April 7, 1841, and died at Columbus, Nebraska, in March, 1912.

Admitted to the practice of medicine on April 9, 1900, at Platte Center, Dr. Benthack has practiced for 32 years in Nebraska, 14 of which were at Platte Center, and 18 in Chadron. He also has some interests in farm land and livestock.

He is married to Wilhelminne Wetgen, who was born at Grosrosenweide, Winsen, Germany, June 5, 1868. Her family came to Platte County in 1881. Their children are as follows, Emil, born February 10, 1892; Amanda, born February 7, 1893; Selma, born June 18, 1894, who

Townsend—Lincoln

NELLIE GRAY BENSON

died May 28, 1905; Walter, born May 8, 1896; Minnie, born December 21, 1897; Alvine, born December 17, 1899; Gus, born November 2, 1901; Adolph, born July 16, 1903; Ella, born September 9, 1904; Selma, born February 14, 1907; Louis, born October 8, 1908; and Elsie, born August 9, 1910.

Dr. Benthack is a Republican. He is a member of the American Iinstitute of Homeopathy, the International Hanemamnan Association, and the Colorado Homeopathy Association. He was baptized in the Baptist Church in Hamburg, Germany, April 19, 1874. He is a member of the Chadron Chamber of Commerce, and the Modern Woodmen of America. Residence: Chadron.

John A. Bentley

John Alexander Bentley, real estate operator, was born at Tama, Iowa, May 17, 1876, and has resided in Nebraska for the past 25 years. He is the son of C. Byron and Sarah A. (Carroll) Bentley, the former of whom was born at Dayton, Ohio, in November, 1840. He was a brick manufacturer and contractor, a leading Republican, and a member of the township board, the school board and the board of alderman. He filled all chairs in the Odd Fellows Lodge. His ancestry was English and Scotch, and he was the son of J. A. and Maria (Ogan) Bentley, the former of Green County, Ohio, and the latter of Kentucky.

Sarah A. Carroll was born in Georgetown, Ohio, in 1843, and died at Tama, Iowa, December 15, 1908. She was an active clubwoman and church worker and the daughter of J. H. Carroll of Georgetown, Ohio, who was a descendant of Charles Carrol of Carrolton a signer of the Declaration of Independence.

John Alexander Bentley attended grammar and high school at Tama, Iowa, and was graduated from Western College at Toledo, Iowa, from which he received his business degree.

On June 3, 1896, he was married to Bertha Mae Phillips at Toledo, Iowa. Mrs. Bentley was born at Toledo, April 3, 1876, daughter of Alford and Ella (Clark) Phillips and granddaughter of Gaius and Mary (Kountz) Allison of Easton, Pennsylvania. To Mr. and Mrs. Bentley were born four children, Alford Phillips, March 23, 1897, who died May 30, 1919; Charlton Blair, born November 29, 1898, whose first wife was Sybil Rood and his second wife was Beata Busenbark; Genevieve Allison, March 7, 1901, who married Carter H. Dunaway; and Leslie Eugene, born April 1, 1906.

Mr. Bentley is a Republican. He is an extensive real estate operator and active in the development of land in western Nebraska, eastern Colorado, and western Kansas. He is president of the Bentley Land Company and has indirect connections with the Equitable Life Insurance Company of Iowa, and the Struble and Stiger Loan Company of Toledo.

He is a member of the Methodist Church, the Chamber of Commerce, the Rotary Club (retired), the Masons, the Modern Woodmen of America, the Nebraskana Society, and for a number of years was a member of the school board. He is a member of the Sidney Country Club and member of its board of directors and one of its former presidents. He enjoys sports and horses, and is a member of the Gun Club. Residence: Sidney. (Photograph in Album).

John Schuyler Bentley

John S. Bentley, newspaper man and sports editor of the *Nebraska State Journal*, was born at Hutchinson, Reno County, Kansas, October 19, 1898, the son of George Smith and Cora (Button) Bentley. His father was born at Aledo, Illinois, and died at Hutchinson.

Mr. Bentley attended the grade school at Hutchinson, and in 1916 was graduated from the Hutchinson High School. Later he was a student at the University of Nebraska, where he was a member of Beta Theta Pi. He has

been connected with the *Nebraska State Journal* for the past ten years as sports editor. He was advertising manager of the First Trust Company of Lincoln for one year.

On March 15, 1924, he was married to Ethel Elmira Weidner at Kansas City, Missouri. Mrs. Bentley was born at Omaha, Douglas County, Nebraska. During the World War Mr. Bentley served as coxswain in the United States Naval Reserve Forces. He is a Mason. Politically, he is a Republican. His favorite sport in golfing, and his hobby reading. Residence: Lincoln.

Seward Ralph Benton

One of the prominent bankers of Hall County, Nebraska, is Seward Ralph Benton who was born in that county, October 17, 1885, the son of Charles Seward and Ida Maria (Squire) Benton. His father, a farmer, was born at Lowville, New York, July 27, 1844, homesteaded in Hall County in 1872, and died at Cairo, Nebraska, July 11, 1913. His English ancestors came to this country in 1633. Ida (Squire) Benton, who was born at Portage County, Wisconsin, October 5, 1859, and is still living, is a devoted home-maker.

Mr. Benton was a stenographer for the Chicago, Burlington & Quincy Railroad at Alliance, Nebraska, from 1902 to 1904, engaged in farming, 1904-05, and from 1905 to 1912, was an implement and automobile dealer at Cairo. He managed his ranch in Keith County, Nebraska, from 1912 to 1915, and at this time is vice president and director of the State Bank of Cairo, Nebraska.

He holds membership in the Independent Order of Odd Fellows, and is affiliated with the Nebraskana Society. His favorite sport is golfing. Politically, Mr. Benton is a Republican.

His marriage to Grace Mae Sponsler was solemnized at Cairo, September 25, 1907. Mrs. Benton was born at Riverton, Illinois, May 7, 1890. They have two children: Charles William, born April 3, 1910, who married Evelyn Mary Smith, and who is a farmer near Cairo, and Jane Helen, born April 23, 1922. Residence: Cairo.

Joseph Venceslaus Beran

Joseph Venceslaus Beran, farmer and railway agent, was born on a farm near Ord, November 19, 1895, son of Joseph V. and Vernie (Petska) Beran. The father was born in Bohemia, May 11, 1873, and in 1891 came to the United States. He is now a retired farmer. His wife, Vernie, was born in Iowa, September 19, 1875. Her ancestry is Bohemian.

On June 3, 1910, Mr. Beran was graduated from high school at Ord, and on June 12, 1912, was graduated from Spalding College. Since that time he has been a farmer and railway agent for the Chicago, Burlington and Quincy Railroad.

His marriage to Eva Dominica Kalkowski was solemnized at Ashton, June 3, 1919. Mrs. Beran was born at Ashton, April 7, 1897, of Polish descent. They have six children all living, Emanuel, born April 12, 1920; Raymond, born May 27, 1922; Joseph, born October 4, 1924; Ivan, born October 15, 1926; Catherine, born February 14, 1930; and Phyllis, born February 14, 1930.

Mr. Beran is a member of St. Francis Catholic Church and the Knights of Columbus. His favorite sport is football, while his hobby is mechanics. During the late war he was a member of the Home Guards. Residence: Ashton.

Theophil Herman Berg

Born at Augusta, Missouri, October 18, 1879, Theophil H. Berg has been a resident of Nebraska, since 1883, and city clerk of Lincoln, since 1913. He is the son of John and Emily Katharine (Beimdick) Berg, the former a native of Germany, born November 24, 1834. He came to America as a child, and served in the Missouri Home

Guards during the Civil War. Himself a farmer, he was descended from a line of German tillers of the soil. He died at Lincoln, January 17, 1917.

Emily Katharine Beimdick was born in St. Charles County, Missouri, March 27, 1846, and died at Pleasant Dale, Nebraska, November 10, 1901. She was of German descent.

Theophil H. Berg attended the public schools, and was graduated from Lincoln Business College in 1901. In that year he entered the employ of Leach and Plym, architects, and from 1902 to 1904, was associated with H. O. Barber and Sons, grain dealers. During 1905 and 1906, he was a clerk in the office of the city clerk of Lincoln, and during 1907, was assistant secretary of the Lincoln Commercial Club. Appointed deputy clerk of the district court in 1908, he served until 1913, since which time he has been city clerk. He is a Republican. At the present time he is president of the Midwest Savings and Loan Association. From April, 1921, to January, 1926, he was editor of the *Nebraska Municipal Review*. He is the author of *The City of Lincoln, Its Foundation, Development and Government* (1916).

Mr. Berg is a member of St. Paul's Evangelical Church, the Red Cross, Lincoln Chamber of Commerce, the Optimist Club, of which he is now president, the National Geographic Society, the Nebraskana Society and the Y. M. C. A. His fraternal organizations include the Masons, Maccabees, and the Ancient Order of United Workmen. His favorite sport is bowling, and his hobby is magic.

On September 26, 1906, he was united in marriage to Clara Augusta Kapke, at Lincoln. Mrs. Berg was born at Emerald, Nebraska, April 22, 1884, the daughter of a Civil War soldier. They have two children: Helen, born September 28, 1907, and Harold, born March 22, 1912. Residence: Lincoln.

Ida Wilkens Berger

Ida Wilkens Berger has had an interesting and varied career. She is the daughter of Louis W. and Katherine (Krieg) Wilkens, and was born at DeWitt, Nebraska, June 23, 1884. Her father was born at Frankfort-on-Main, Germany, October 5, 1858, and came to America in 1876. He received his elementary, high school and college training in Germany. In Saline County, Nebraska, he was an extensive landowner, stockman and farmer. He died at DeWitt, February 18, 1909.

Louis W. Wilkens married Katherine Krieg, who was born at Chicago, March 2, 1859. She is still living. She received her elementary education in the public schools of Chicago, came to Nebraska with her parents in 1873 and attended Doane College 2 years. An active member of the Twentieth Century Club at DeWitt, 10 years, she has been a member of the Lincoln Women's Club 10 years, and a member of the Order of Eastern Star since 1911.

Ida Wilkens Berger received her B. S. in home economics from the University of Nebraska in 1921, and a teacher's life certificate at the same time; she attended Peru Normal School the summer of 1901, and the two Fremont Normal School terms 1903-04, besides attending Wesleyan University one semester in 1908. She was a member of the Home Economics Club at the University of Nebraska. Her marriage to Nelson L. Berger was solemnized at Lincoln, April 9, 1924. Mr. Berger was born at Hemingford, Nebraska, September 23, 1888 (See *Nebraskana*).

A life resident of Nebraska, she was a teacher in the rural schools of DeWitt from 1901-04, and in the primary department of the DeWitt public schools from 1905-08. She taught in the Lincoln public schools 1908-10. From 1910-12 she gave private instruction in water color and china painting. In 1921 she was made assistant county agent of Cass County, continuing until 1924, when she married.

During the World War she served as chairman of the DeWitt Red Cross for one year. Since 1911 she has been a member of the Order of Eastern Star. She has held many offices in that order. For the past nine years she has been a member of the Rebekah Lodge and has filled all offices in the Nehawka chapter. She is also a member of the Nebraskana Society, the Nehawka Library Board and was state president of the Home Economics department of Organized Agriculture 1927 and 1928. In 1928 she was delegated to the National Convention of Farm Women held at Edgewater Beach Hotel, Chicago, and represented Nebraska and Kansas. She was selected as one of the judging committee by *The Farmers Wife Magazine* to assist in the selection of master farm homemakers of 1929-30-31. Among her social and cultural clubs are the Nebraska Federation of Women's Clubs, Nehawka Woman's Club. She was a member of the Twentieth Century Club at DeWitt. She was district chairman of the Nebraska Federation of Women's Clubs for rural clubs and rural life two years, and appeared on the state program in 1928 with the subject *Rural Women and the State Federation*, which paper was placed in the state reciprocity bureau. She was president of the Cass County Federation 2 years, and secretary-treasurer 4 years. During the 7 years she has been a member of the Triangle Club she has held many offices.

She is a lover of nature, and is particularly interested in gardening and flowers. Her hobby is attending conventions. Residence: Nehawka. (Photograph on Page 115).

Nelson L. Berger

A farmer, stockman and landowner, Nelson L. Berger is descended from Jacob and Catherine Berger, natives of Germany, who emigrated to the United States about 1770. John Berger, born about 1775, and who died about 1855, was the son of Jacob and Catherine. He married Margaret Hedrick. Nelson Berger's grandfather was Enos Berger, son of John, born in 1815. He married Elizabeth Wallace, in Indiana, May 18, 1839.

On the maternal side Mr. Berger is the grandson of Nelson McReynolds and Martha Henderson. Nelson McReynolds was born in Abingdon, Virginia, June 6, 1808, and at one time owned three hundred acres of land in Tennesee. This he sold and purchased 500 acres in Carroll County, Mo. In 1865 he came to Nebraska, and at the time of his death owned 400 acres near Nehawka. Mollie L. McReynolds, a daughter of Nelson McReynolds, married John P. Berger, who was born in 1855 and died in 1930. To this union four children were born. Nelson L. Berger, one of the younger of the children, lives on the home place which has been in the family three generations, it being originally owned by his grandfather, Nelson McReynolds, who purchased the land in 1865. In 1929 the home was destroyed by fire and in 1930 Nelson L. Berger built a new nine room house, strictly modern in every respect, with beautiful trees and a well kept lawn, surrounded by an attractive fence bordered with flowers and shrubs, making it one of the most pleasant homes in the county.

Nelson L. Berger has been engaged as a farmer and stockman all of his life. He was born at Hemingford, Nebraska, September 23, 1888. He is a member of the Nebraska Crop Growers Association, of the Agricultural College of the University of Nebraska, and for two years was vice-president of the first district. In 1926 he was winner of a silver medal in the Cass County corn yield contest. In 1928 he was the winner of the state prize for the second highest yield of 102 bushels. In 1929 he was made a member of the State 100 Bushels Club, to which only 12 men were eligible. His marriage to Ida Wilkens took place at Lincoln, April 9, 1924 (see *Nebraskana*).

Mr. Berger is a member of the following secret and fraternal organizations: The Odd Fellows and the Rebekah Lodge of Nehawka, the Knights of Pythias, having held all offices, and of the following Masonic orders: Nehawka Lodge, Ancient Free and Accepted Masons, Scottish Rite, Sesostris Temple, Lincoln, and of the Ancient

IDA WILKENS BERGER

Hauck-Skoglund—Lincoln

NELSON L. BERGER

Hauck-Skoglund—Lincoln

Arabic Order, Nobles of the Mystic Shrine at Lincoln. As a member of the last mentioned body he attended the national conclave held at Des Moines, Iowa, in 1920. At present he is serving as director and vice president of the Farmers' Grain Elevator of Nehawka, having been recently re-elected to the office. Residence: Nehawka. (Photograph on Page 116).

William Henry Berger

William Henry Berger, son of August Frederick and Lucy Ann (Murdock) Berger, was born at Dakota City, Nebraska, March 9, 1866. His father, born in Behren, Germany, August 24, 1832, came to America in 1859, and served with Company I, 2nd Nebraska Cavalry during the Civil War. A pioneer farmer, he died at Phillipsburg, Kansas, October 24, 1910. His wife, Lucy Ann Murdock, was born in Toronto, Canada, April 22, 1840, daughter of John Murdock, who was of Scottish birth and Hannah Hutchinson, daughter of Lord Hutchinson of England. She died at Dakota City, November 9, 1921.

Educated in the public schools, Mr. Berger has been a farmer since early manhood. He is active in agricultural organizations, and is president of the Omadi Cooperative Grain Company and a member of the board of directors of the Midwest Research Laboratory of Sioux City.

On January 18, 1893, he was married to Anna Maria Ochander at Homer, Nebraska. Mrs. Berger was born at Homer, January 15, 1874, and to them were born the following children: Laura E., born August 3, 1894, married Orville L. Legg; William M., born February 13, 1897, who married Jennie Esther Thomas; Francis F., born June 8, 1900, died February 7, 1901; Edna M., born December 9, 1901, who married George E. Billgren; Anna M., born March 30, 1904, married Ross Gourley; George E., born July 27, 1906; and Maurice E., born December 16, 1910. All of the children are farming except William, who is an engineer and Maurice who is serving in the United States Navy.

During the World War Mr. Berger was active in Red Cross, Loan and other drives. He is a member of the First Methodist Episcopal Church at Dakota City, a member of the South Sioux City Chamber of Commerce, and is past noble grand of the Odd Fellows and a member of the Rebekahs. His hobby is mechanics. Residence: Dakota City. (Photograph in Album).

Charles Emil Berggren

A resident of Kearney County, Nebraska, for the past 45 years, Charles Emil Berggren, born May 25, 1877, is the son of Gustaf and Lena Berggren. His father, who was a blacksmith, was born in Sweden, October 1, 1849, and died at Ragan, Nebraska, August 14, 1925. He moved to Holdrege, Nebraska, in the fall of 1885. His mother was born in Sweden and died there in 1880.

Mr. Berggren located in Wilcox in 1903, where he became a blacksmith and a machinist. He is a member of the Modern Woodmen of America.

On August 17, 1904, he was married to Ella C. Carlson of Wilcox. To them were born four children: Ralph Kenneth, born July 28, 1906, who married Merna Evelyn Kailey, of Holdrege, Nebraska, on June 16, 1925; Clarence Harvey, born March 5, 1909, who married Dorothy E. Termin, of Wilcox, August 14, 1931; Dorothy Marie, born February 6, 1917; and Margaret Alvena, born December 19, 1919. Residence: Wilcox.

Joseph Fredrick Berggren

Joseph Fredrick Berggren, lawyer in Nebraska for nearly 30 years, was born at Wahoo, Saunders County, Nebraska, August 20, 1877, the son of Nils B. and Hanna (Johnston) Berggren. His father, who was born in Sweden, September 19, 1842, and died at Wahoo, December 6, 1899, was a landscape gardener, farmer, and stock-raiser; he was a pioneer in Saunders County and was prominent in the advancement of his community. His mother was born in Sweden, July 28, 1847, and now resides in Wahoo.

Mr. Berggren was graduated from the Wahoo High School, and was awarded the A. B. degree 1903, and LL. B., 1903 at the University of Nebraska where he held membership in Phi Delta Phi. He is now attorney for several corporations in addition to his regular law practice at Wahoo. A Democrat, he served as county attorney of Saunders County from 1910 to 1914. He is a member of the Wahoo Lions Club, the State Bar Society, Odd Fellows, and Knights of Pythias.

During the World War, Mr. Berggren served as a member of the Civilian Relief Committee in Saunders County, and was active in Red Cross work. He is affiliated with the Congregational Church at Wahoo. He is interested in agriculture, and his favorite sport is football.

His marriage to Elva Gillilan, was solemnized at Wahoo, June 30, 1909. Mrs. Berggren was born at Linn, Iowa, January 6, 1886. They have one daughter, Josephine, born June 25, 1910. She is now teaching in the public school at Nebraska City. Residence: Wahoo.

Albert Bergland

For the past 44 years Albert Bergland has been engaged in farming near Loomis, Nebraska. He was born at Galesburg, Illinois, February 27, 1864, the son of Louis and Hannah (Erickson) Bergland, the former a contractor and builder. His father, who was descended from the Russian nobility, was born at Sundsvall, Sweden, December 5, 1826, and died at Galesburg, Illinois, in June, 1897. His mother was born at Silverborg, Sweden, January 20, 1836, and died at Galesburg, February 20, 1923.

Mr. Bergland attended high school at Galesburg. He is a member of the Nebraskana Society, is affiliated with the Republican party, and holds membership in the Independent Order of Odd Fellows. His hobby is reading.

On May 23, 1889, he was married at Denver, Colorado, to Augusta A. Edmunds who was born at Huskvarna, Sweden, February 16, 1867. They have five children: Ruth, born June 9, 1890, who married Edwin Davis; Eugene, born October 26, 1894; Alice, born January 5, 1897, who married Howard A. Sherman; May, born September 8, 1898, who married Earl F. Sherman; and Bert, born December 18, 1908. Residence: Loomis.

Edwin A. Bergman

Edwin A. Bergman, prominent farmer, was born in Kimball County, Nebraska, November 26, 1886, son of Andrew and Johanna (Sjobloom) Bergman.

The father was born in Sweden, June 3, 1852, and pioneered in western Nebraska among the first settlers in 1885. He is a retired rancher. His wife, also born in Sweden, in August, 1850, was a pioneer also in the north divide of Kimball County.

Mr. Bergman attended country school through the 8th grade and was graduated from Kimball High School in 1904. While there he was active as a member of the baseball team.

Mr. Bergman was born on the farm on which he now resides, was the first extensive wheat grower in western Nebraska and an exponent of summer tilling. He is the director of school district No. 13 of Kimball County, an ex-member of the board of regents of the Kimball City High School, and a member of the farm bureau and county fair board. He is a former member of the Lions Club at Kimball and is now a member of the Kimball Country Club. During the late war, he was chairman of local loan drives.

On August 5, 1913, he was married to Etta Mae

Lathrop at Kimball. Mrs. Bergman was born at Prescott, Iowa, November 9, 1893. They have eight children, all living, Raymond, born May 22, 1914; Harold, June 15, 1916; Jessie, February 28, 1918; Joan, March 1, 1920; Edwin, February 24, 1921; Ralph, July 12, 1923; Betty, November 22, 1924; and William, July 26, 1926. Residence: Kimball.

Bernie D. Berkheimer

Bernie D. Berkheimer, banker, was born at Ashland, Nebraska, December 23, 1895, son of Adam and Alice J. (Donner) Berkheimer. Both parents were born in the United States, the paternal grandparents being Dutch and the maternal being German.

Upon his graduation from Ashland High School, Mr. Berkheimer attended Bellevue College and the University of Nebraska. He has engaged in the lumber business in Gordon and Casper, Wyoming, and since 1919 has been in the banking business at Gordon. He enlisted in the Coast Artillery Corps, December 14, 1917, and was commissioned a second lieutenant of Coast Artillery, on July 26, 1918.

On June 16, 1919, he was married to Regina Grace Fritz at Gordon, Nebraska. She was born there on April 2, 1894. They have one son, Richard Lee, born May 17, 1927.

Mr. Berkheimer is a Republican. He is a member of the First Presbyterian Church of Gordon, the Masonic Lodge, the Order of Eastern Star, and the Kiwanis Club. His favorite sport is golf. Residence: Gordon.

Henriette Bernstein

Henriette Bernstein, county superintendent of schools of Hall County, was born at Grand Island, Nebraska, July 28, 1894. She is the daughter of Henry and Anna (Dumke) Bodmer, the former a chemist of Swiss ancestry, and the latter of German ancestry.

Mrs. Bernstein attended the public schools of Grand Island and received her Bachelor of Arts degree from Grand Island College in 1926. She was also a student at Boulier University. From 1912-18 she taught in the public schools of Hall County, and from 1919-20 was engaged in secretarial work. Returning to the teaching profession in 1922, she continued therein until 1926, when she was elected to her present position as county superintendent.

She is affiliated with the English Lutheran Church and was recently made a life member of The Nebraskana Society. Her favorite sports are hunting, fishing and golf and her hobby is gardening. Residence: Grand Island.

Alice Virginia Berryman

Alice Virginia (Davis) Berryman was born at North Platte, Nebraska, December 5, 1889. She is the daughter of George Warren and Alice (Clark) Davis. Her father, a farmer, was manager of the Barton farm in Sarpy County until his death at Omaha, on October 28, 1923. She is of *Mayflower* ancestry, and an aunt Mary Smith Lockwood, was one of the three founders of the Daughters of the American Revolution. Her ancestors were among the founders of Smith College. Mrs. Berryman is a niece of Mrs. Guy Barton of Omaha.

Educated in the Omaha public schools, Mrs. Berryman was graduated from the South Omaha High School with honors; she studied in Paris with Swayne, a pupil of Leschetizky, in Switzerland, and with Rudolph Ganz. She made her New York debut in 1915 at the Princess Theatre, and has appeared in individual recitals both in this country and abroad, and in joint recitals with Mr. Berryman in the east and the middlewestern states. She has also given two concerts in Paris. She was formerly head of the piano normal training department of the University Conservatory of Omaha, and now has a private piano class.

Her marriage to Cecil Wells Berryman was solemnized at Omaha, December 19, 1916, (see *Nebraskana*). Mrs. Berryman is the author of numerous articles for the *Musical Observer, Music News* and others. She is a member of the P. E. O., of the Omaha Clef Club, the Nebraska State Teachers Association and The Omaha Music Teachers Association. She is a Presbyterian and is eligible to the Daughters of the American Revolution. Her hobby is gardening. Residence: Omaha.

Cecil Wells Berryman

For the past 15 years Cecil W. Berryman has been a leading Nebraska pianist and recitalist. Born at Central City, Nebraska, April 21, 1888, he is the son of Edward Price and Daisy (Wells) Berryman. His father, born at Owensboro, Kentucky, April 22, 1862, died at Omaha, December 10, 1924. He was descended from early English settlers in Virginia. During his lifetime he served as colonel on the staff of Governor Shallenberger, and was a member of the Omaha park board. Daisy (Wells) Berryman, who is living, was born at Janesville, Wisconsin, November 4, 1865. She is of English and French descent, a musician and teacher of piano.

Cecil W. Berryman was graduated from Central High School at Omaha. In 1910 he studied piano, composition and theory in Paris with Wager Swayne and Emile Schwartz of the Paris Conservatoire Nationale. In 1916, he was married to Alice Virginia Davis, likewise a musician. Mrs. Berryman was born at North Platte, December 5, 1889, and before her marriage was a teacher of piano, and is at present teacher of normal classes at the University of Omaha. There are three children, Edward, born February 8, 1920; Warren, born February 24, 1922, and Rudolph, born February 25, 1929. The children are musically inclined, and the two older ones have given five public recitals.

Before his marriage Mr. Berryman gave many recitals in Paris, and in the east and midwest. Since then he has appeared with Mrs. Berryman in many joint recitals. He is the author of a song recorded by Victor, and of many articles in *Etude* and *Musical Observer*. He has written many piano compositions, concerto, violin sonata, songs, etc. From 1916-18 he was music critic for the *Omaha Nebraskan*. He was formerly head of the department of piano and theory, University Conservatory of Music at Omaha, and is now private instructor of piano and composition.

Mrs. Berryman made her New York debut in 1915, and like her husband is the author of many musical articles. Her great aunt was one of the founders of the Daughters of the American Revolution. She is descended also from the founder of Smith College.

Mr. Berryman's sister, Elizabeth Gagnebin, born August 23, 1895, is a graduate of Omaha University. She took post graduate work at Chicago University, and has been a teacher in the department of dietetics at Technical High School for ten years.

During the year 1907 Mr. Berryman was first lieutenant in the Central High School Band. He is affiliated with the Omaha Clef Club, and has served as president and treasurer. He is a member of the Nebraska Writers Guild. He was formerly a member and vice president of the Nebraska State Music Teachers' Association and member of the board of directors of the Omaha Music Teachers' Association. He is a member of Wheeler Memorial Presbyterian Church. His hobby is hiking with his family. Residence: Omaha.

Hans P. Bertelsen

Hans P. Bertelson, retired clergyman, was born in Denmark, February 15, 1846, son of Bertel Paulsen and Anna Marguerite (Hansen) Bertelsen.

Mr. Bertelsen was graduated from Augsburg Seminary at Minneapolis, Minnesota, and for the past 47

CHARLES FRED BEUSHAUSEN

years has been a resident of Nebraska. A clergyman for many years, he filled various pastorates in the Danish Lutheran Church until his retirement several years ago.

He was married to Anna Marguerite Hansen, at Hampton, Nebraska, and there are four children of this marriage, as follows: Anna, born August 12, 1881; Martin, born November 1, 1883; Ella, born October 5, 1892, and Sena, born August 3, 1895.

Mr. Bertelsen is a Republican. Residence: Blair.

Gustav Frank Beschorner

Gutav Frank Beschorner, insurance man and fraternal worker, is a native of Herautz, Moravia, Austria, born May 28, 1880. He is the son of Anton and Rosalia (Kaupe) Beschorner. Anton Beschorner was born at Herautz, on April 14, 1837, and engaged in farming and in the transfer business. He died at his birthplace on February 1, 1904. His wife, Rosalia, was born at Landskron, Bohemia, Austria, June 5, 1849. Of the German race, her family lives in present day Czechoslovakia. She came to America in 1904, and is still living.

During the time he has been in America Mr. Beschorner has served in various capacities—as a student, bookkeeper, traveling salesman, editor, auditor, and insurance salesman, in which last he is now engaged. During the sessions of 1915, 1917, and 1918 he was bookkeeper of the Nebraska state senate, and during 1916 to 1917 he was editor of *Die Welt-Post*, German weekly at Lincoln.

On October 23, 1913, he was married to Clara Amanda Bartzat at Lincoln. Mrs. Beschorner, who was born at Lincoln on June 27, 1890, died there on October 6, 1918. There are two daughters, Elsie Mathilda, born September 8, 1914, and Frieda, born November 7, 1917, died November 28, 1917.

A member of the United Lutheran Church in America, he served as representative of the National Lutheran Council on the staff of the American Relief Administration (Hoover organization) in Russia from January to December, 1922, and supervisor of 95 kitchens operating to feed 22,000 children in the famine district of the German Volga, Republic in the Soviet Union.

He is a member of the United Commercial Travelers, the Sons of Herman, the Eagles, and the Blue Lodge, Royal Arch Chapter (of which he is a past high priest), Royal and Select Council (of which he is a Past Master), Knight Templar and Shrine bodies of Masonry in Lincoln. Residence: Lincoln.

John George Beste

John G. Beste was born in Cedar County, Nebraska, June 28, 1881, the son of Theodore and Catherine (Brocke) Beste. His father, who was a farmer, served as county commissioner of Cedar County for nine years; he was born in Westphalia, Germany, March 14, 1850, and died at Hartington, Cedar County, Nebraska, January 20, 1930; he came to this country in 1869. His mother was born of German parentage, at Wheeling, West Virginia, January 4, 1853, and died in Cedar County, January 13, 1887.

Mr. Beste received his education in the grade and high schools at Hartington. He has been engaged in banking since 1902, and today is vice president of the First National Bank of Hartington. A Democrat, he served as a member of the board of education for six years, was mayor of Hartington one term, and city councilman several terms.

During the World War he was county chairman of the United War Work in Cedar County. He is director in the Chamber of Commerce, is a member of the Red Cross, and is affiliated with Holy Trinity Catholic Church. He holds membership in the Nebraskana Society, and has held the various positions in the Knights of Columbus. His hobby is mechanics.

On June 27, 1906, he was married to Lucy Maud Morrison, at Vermilion, South Dakota. Mrs. Beste was born at Vermilion, April 27, 1883. They have two children: Myrtle C., born January 17, 1912; and Dorothy, born July 15, 1913. Residence: Hartington.

Charles Fred Beushausen

Born in New York, New York, August 23, 1876, Charles Fred Beushausen came to Nebraska with his parents, August and Mathilda (Beck) Beushausen, fifty-two years ago. His father, born in Hamburg, Germany, in 1840, came to America where he became a farmer, settling near Ashton, in Sherman County in the fall of 1878. He was a soldier in the German army before his immigration. His death occurred at Loup City, June 24, 1914. His wife, Mathilda, born in Baden Baden, Germany, died at Loup City, December 14, 1914.

Charles Fred Beushausen attended country school, was graduated from high school at Ashton, and was a student at Lincoln Normal University one year. He taught in a sod school house the first of a three year term, and later was manager for the E. G. Taylor Grain Company. In 1906 he was elected county clerk on the Democratic ticket, being re-elected in 1908. For nine years dating from September, 1912, he served as postmaster of Loup City.

Mr. Beushausen was elected to the Nebraska house of representatives in the fall of 1922, and filed for lieutenant governor of Nebraska in November, 1931. He is at the present time the owner and publisher of the *Sherman County Times*, is secretary of the Loup City Community Club, secretary of the Board of Education, secretary of the Sherman County Fair Association and treasurer of the Loup City Township library.

During the World War Mr. Beushausen was chairman for war Saving Stamp drives, county chairman of Y. M. C. A. drives and county chairman of the 5th Liberty Loan. He is a member of the Methodist Church, is past president of the Rotary Club, a Mason, Modern Woodman of America, an Odd Fellow and a Knight of Pythias. He is a life member of the Nebraskana Society, and his favorite sport is golf. Residence: Loup City. (Photograph on Page 119).

John Harrie Beveridge

John Harrie Beveridge, superintendent of schools at Omaha, was born in Highland County, Ohio, January 21, 1869, son of John Thomas and Eliza E. (Steen) Beveridge.

Mr. Beveridge attended the public school and in 1892 received the Bachelor of Science degree from the National Normal University at Lebanon, Ohio. He received the Masters degree from Ohio University, which university, in 1917, made him a Doctor of Pedagogy. In 1915 Mr. Beveridge received the Master of Arts degree from Columbia University.

On July 7, 1897, he was married to Florence M. Haselton. Their children are Lenore and Wendell.

From 1897 until 1902, Mr. Beveridge was principal of schools at Glidden, Iowa, and from 1902 until 1908, was superintendent at Missouri Valley, Iowa. Coming to Council Bluffs, in 1908, he served as superintendent there until 1917. Since July 1, 1917, he has held his present position of superintendent of the schools of Omaha.

Mr. Beveridge is a member of the Department of Superintendents, the Nebraska State Teachers' Association, the Nebraska Schoolmasters' Club, the National Editorial Association, and the Masons. Residence: Omaha.

John Henry Bexten

John Henry Bexten, accountant and banker, was born at Quincy, Illinois, February 6, 1860, and for the past fifty-two years has been a resident of Nebraska. He is the son of Henry Hermann and Fredericka W. (Kipp) Bexten. Henry Bexten was born in Germany, August 30, 1833. He was a merchant and farmer, and came to America in 1852. He died at Omaha, February 1, 1906. Fredericka (Kipp) Bexten was born in Germany, December 25, 1838, and died at Omaha, May 26, 1930.

Educated in the public schools of Quincy, until 1872, Mr. Bexten came to Nebraska in March, 1878. He started his business career as bookkeeper for Henry Ruff & Company of Quincy. From January 1, 1880, to December 1, 1884, he was confidential bookkeeper for Haines Brothers Company. On December 21, 1886, he entered the First National Bank of Omaha, and on the date of his retirement, January 10, 1929, held the position of cashier. He is director and treasurer of Carter Lake Club and director and treasurer of Stuntz Hall Association.

His marriage to Martha Abbie Noyes was solemnized at Hastings, Nebraska, December 25, 1882. Mrs. Bexten was born in Illinois, February 25, 1863. There are three children, J. H. Edward, born at Omaha, December 25, 1883, who died March 4, 1885; Louis Noyes, born at Hastings, July 17, 1885, teacher at Omaha Central High School, and graduate of Armour School of Technology at Chicago; and L. Merta, born at Omaha, May 15, 1887.

Mr. Bexten is a Republican. He is affiliated with Trinity Methodist Episcopal Church. His fraternal organizations include the Knights of Pythias and the Fraternal Aid Union. His favorite sport is bowling and his hobby is reading. Residence: Omaha.

John Beynon

Since 1912, John Beynon has been active in the business affairs of Burwell, Nebraska. He was born at Willow Springs, Nebraska, January 3, 1887, the son of David Saunders and Christina Jennie (Corneli) Beynon, the former a druggist at Burwell, for over 38 years, and later postmaster there. His father, whose ancestry was Welsh, was born at Albia, Iowa, December 5, 1856, and died at Douglas, Wyoming, July 10, 1926. His mother was born of German and Irish parents at Albia, April 21, 1868.

Mr. Beynon was graduated from the Burwell High School in 1903, was a clothing merchant for a time, engaged in the drug business for several years, and since 1917 has been the owner and manager of a grocery establishment. He is a member of the Red Cross, Masonic Lodge, and the Nebraskana Society, and for a number of years was president of the local School Board.

On June 26, 1910, he was married to Alvena C. Grunkemeyer at Burwell. Mrs. Beynon, whose ancestry was German, was born at Phillips, Nebraska, March 7, 1889. They have one daughter, Gwendolyn, born September 28, 1914, who was graduated from the Burwell High School in 1932.

Mr. Beynon is a Republican. His favorite sports are baseball and football. Residence: Burwell.

Dana Xenophon Bible

Dana X. Bible, football coach at the University of Nebraska, was born at Jefferson City, Jefferson County, Tennessee, October 8, 1891. His father, Jonathan David Bible, who was born at Mosheim, Cooke County, Tennessee, October 9, 1863, is a teacher and farmer; his ancestry is Scotch-Irish. His mother was born of German parentage at Washburn, Grainger County, Tennessee, October 19, 1870.

Mr. Bible was graduated from the high school at Jefferson City, and later was a student at Carson-Newman College, the University of North Carolina, Ohio State University, and Center College. He was graduated with the A. B. degree from Carson-Newman, in 1912, where he won his college letters in football, basketball, and baseball. He is a member of Delta Kappa Epsilon Fraternity. He coached at Mississippi College, L. S. U., Texas A. and M., and is now head coach of football at the University of Nebraska. He has written various athletic articles for magazines and newspapers.

He was united in marriage with Rowena Rhodes at Fort Worth, Tarrant County, Texas, December 19, 1923. Mrs. Bible was born at Bryan, Brazos County, Texas, January 17, 1892. They have one daughter, Barbara Nancy, born March 25, 1929.

Mr. Bible was a lieutenant in the air service, serving overseas with the 22nd Aero Squadron during the World War. He is a member of the Lincoln Red Cross, the Chamber of Commerce, and the Lincoln Rotary Club. He is trustee of the Football Coaches Association of America. His social clubs are the University Club and the Lincoln Country Club. He is a member of the Masons, and a Shriner. His religious affiliation is with the First Baptist Church at Lincoln. He is interested in golf and all college sports. He is a Republican. Residence: Lincoln.

Clarence Hanks Bickel

On March 6, 1886, Clarence H. Bickel was born in Independence, Kansas. His father, Charley C. Bickel, was born at Graham, Missouri, on April 13, 1884; he is a contractor. Mary S. Hanks, his mother, was born at Nebraska City on February 7, 1870, and died in Lincoln, on August 10, 1919.

Mr. Bickel was graduated from Nebraska Wesleyan University with a Bachelor of Arts degree. On May 5, 1909, he was married to Mabel A. Overton, who was born at Nebraska City, November 9, 1887; she is of English descent. The Bickels have two children, Grace, born April 19, 1910, and Myron, born February 7, 1913.

For many years Mr. Bickel has been active as a Mason; he is a member of the First Methodist Episcopal Church of Lincoln. In politics he affiliates with the Democratic party. He was formerly a member of the state democratic committee. He engaged in banking from 1909 to 1923. He is now manager of the thrift department for the Lincoln Liberty Life Insurance Company. Residence: Lincoln.

Harold Bickford

On December 13, 1899, Harold Bickford was born at Curtis, Frontier County, Nebraska, the son of John William and Frances (Baxter) Bickford. His father, who was born at Plymouth, Hancock County, Illinois, April 20, 1860, was a railroad agent in the early days in Nebraska; and was a member of the town board of Curtis, and Smithfield, Nebraska. His paternal grandfather was of pure English stock; his paternal grandmother, who was born at Baltimore, Maryland, was of Holland Dutch descent. He died at Lincoln, Lancaster County, Nebraska, June 22, 1922.

His mother was born in Schuyler County, Illinois, January 29, 1865. Her maternal ancestors were prominent in the history of Virginia. She is of English, Scotch, Welsh, and Irish ancestry.

Mr. Bickford attended the public schools of Smithfield, Kenesaw, and Lincoln, and in 1919 was graduated from the Lincoln High School. He was awarded his LL. B. degree at the University of Nebraska in 1923, where he was elected to membership in Phi Alpha Delta, Acacia, and Delta Phi Gamma. He has been engaged in the practice of law at Lincoln since his admission to the bar on June 1, 1923, and his lived in Nebraska all his life.

His marriage to Marjorie Frances Cooper was solemnized at Seward, Nebraska, January 23, 1926. Mrs. Bickford, who was born at Geneva, Nebraska, September 7, 1902, is in the society department of the *Nebraska State Journal.* Her maternal grandparents were members of the Fulton and Burleigh families of Ohio and Pennsylvania.

Mr. Bickford is a member of the Nebraska State Bar Association and the Lancaster County Bar Association. He holds membership in the Cosmopolitan Luncheon Club, at Lincoln. He is a Mason, Scottish Rite and Shrine; and an Elk. He is a Republican. Residence: Lincoln.

Marjorie Frances Cooper Bickford

Marjorie Bickford, a resident of this state all her life, was born at Geneva, September 7, 1902, the daughter of George B. and Tessa Ruth (Fulton) Cooper. Her father, who is a salesman, was born at Canton, Illinois, December 13, 1874; he is descended from English ancestors who went to Holland as religious dissenters and came to America with the Dutch in colonial times; two Cooper brothers settled in this country, one in New York, and one in Pennsylvania, and George Cooper is descended from the latter branch.

Her mother was born at New Boston, Illinois, December 4, 1875. She is descended through the maternal side from the Burleighs, of Ohio, who originally came from Scotland, and Ireland; the Fultons were Irish, and settled in Indiana and Westmoreland County, Pennsylvania.

Mrs. Bickford was graduated from the Lincoln High School in 1919, and in 1923, received the A. B. degree from the University of Nebraska where she was a member of Phi Omega Pi. For several years she has been connected with the society department of the *Nebraska State Journal* at Lincoln. She is a member of the Nebraskana Society.

On January 26, 1926, she was united in marriage with Harold Bickford at Seward, Nebraska. Mr. Bickford, who is a lawyer, was born at Curtis, Nebraska, December 13, 1899. His parents, Mr. and Mrs. J. W. Bickford, were pioneers in western Nebraska, the former serving as station agent for the Burlington Railroad for many years. Residence: Lincoln.

James C. Bierbower

James C. Bierbower, newspaper man, was born at Arrowsmith, Illinois, October 21, 1886, son of Jonathan and Margaret J. (Cavett) Bierbower.

The father was born in Brown County, Ohio, September 10, 1845, and died at Giltner, June 23, 1923. He served with Company B, 39th Illinois Volunteer Infantry in the Civil War, and at the time of his death was a retired farmer. His wife, Margaret, was born in Posey County, Indiana, October 24, 1851, and died at Giltner, August 2, 1914. Her ancestry was English.

Mr. Bierbower was graduated from Giltner High School in 1906, and afterward attended Fremont College, York College, and Kearney normal school. For six years thereafter he was a public school teacher, and since June 12, 1912, has been editor and publisher of the *Giltner Gazette*. He is an independent Republican.

On August 6, 1919, he was married to Margaret B. Luby, at Harvard. Mrs. Bierbower was born at Giltner, January 8, 1897, of Irish and American ancestry. Seven children were born to their union, six of whom are still living: June M., born July 29, 1920; Margaret E., born December 9, 1921; James J., born March 17, 1923; Dorothy Joan, born July 21, 1924; Mary Lou. born March 31, 1926; Robert L., born October 28, 1927; Barbara Jean, born April 6, 1929, who died December 27, 1929.

Mr. Bierbower served in the World War. He is a member of the Ancient Free and Accepted Masons, of the Modern Woodmen of America, and The Nebraskana Society. He is fond of all forms of athletics. Residence: Giltner.

Elmer Henry Biermann

Elmer H. Biermann, a banker in Nebraska, for the past 17 years, was born at Dakota City, January 3, 1895, the son of William and Sophie (Runge) Biermann. His father, a retired farmer, was born at Steimbke, Germany, December 18, 1866. His mother was born at Steimbke, August 10, 1869.

Mr. Biermann was graduated from the Sioux City High School, Iowa, in 1913, and later was a student at Capitol City Commercial College at Des Moines, Iowa. He has been cashier and director of the bank of Dakota City, Nebraska, and has been engaged in the insurance business at South Sioux City for a number of years.

He is a member of the South Sioux City Commercial Club, the Nebraskana Society, and the American Legion. He is affiliated with the Salem German Lutheran Church at Dakota City. During the World War he served as sergeant major of the 8th ammunition train, and was active in loan drives.

On September 8, 1926, he was married to Maurine Agatha Pomeroy, at South Sioux City. Mrs. Biermann, who is of Scotch-Irish descent, was born at Ponca, Dixon County, Nebraska, December 16, 1898. Residence: South Sioux City.

Anson Hardin Bigelow

Anson Hardin Bigelow, prominent lawyer, was born at Buckley, Illinois, August 23, 1867, son of Anson Hardin and Mary (Brazeil) Bigelow.

The father was born in Rochester, New York, August 12, 1832, and died at Omaha, November 24, 1914. The Bigelow family coming to America in 1652, from England, settled first in Connecticut and Massachusetts. Mary Brazeil was born in Londonderry, Ireland, April 18, 1839, and died at Beaver Falls, Minnesota, in May, 1886. Her ancestry was Irish and French. Her father was one of the earliest pioneers of Renville County.

Mr. Bigelow was graduated from Omaha High School in 1884, and received the Bachelor of Science degree from the University of Nebraska in 1887, and the Bachelor of Laws degree from Creighton in 1912.

On January 1, 1891, he was married to Margaret Hynes at Omaha. Mrs. Bigelow was born in Pittston, Pennsylvania, July 21, 1867, and was killed in the tornado at Omaha, on March 23, 1913. There is one daughter of this marriage, Ellen Lucile, who married Leo A. Paige. His marriage to Harriet LeMaster Agnew was solemnized on February 22, 1914. She has the following children, Portia Lee, who married Benjamin A. Arkin; Ilma, who married West B. Bonnifield; and Thomas Joseph.

In 1891, Mr. Bigelow served as clerk of the house of representatives. In 1919 he was elected a member of the Constitutional Convention of 1919-20. He was elected a member of the South Dakota house of representatives, in 1911, was candidate for congress on the Republican primary of 1914, and a delegate to the Progressive National Convention of 1916, and a member of its platform committee, from Nebraska.

In 1922, Mr. Bigelow was a candidate for United States Senator on the Progressive ticket. He is the author of the following, *Elements of Arithmetic* (1911 Bigelow and Arnold); *Trust Relationship Between Corporation Directors and Stockholders* (Central Law Journal, June, 1912); *Model Parliamentary House in Law Schools* (Central Law Journal, 1914).

Mr. Bigelow is a member of the First Presbyterian Church, the Elks, Modern Woodmen of America, and Royal Highlanders. Residence: Omaha.

Edward Marvin Bigelow

Edward Marvin Bigelow, insurance and real estate operator, was born at Newport, Minnesota, October 25, 1869, son of Gilbert Marvin and Matilda (Cooley) Bigelow. Gilbert M. Bigelow was born in Bellow Falls, Vermont, April 1, 1834, and served in the Civil War with the Union army. He died at Aspen, Colorado, January 18, 1899. His wife, Matilda, was born in Champlain, New York, in 1835, and died at Newport, in 1880.

Mr. Bigelow attended public school and supplemented his education by night school study. From 1889 until 1905, he was the owner of a steam laundry. From that time until 1917, he was the owner of the Bigelow Gas Light Company. Since 1917 he has been engaged in the real estate and insurance business. From 1920 until

1925, he was secretary of the Bridgeport Electric Light and Power Company. Independent in politics, he served as county assessor of Morrill County, 1921-1922, elected on Republican ticket.

On February 21, 1892, he was married to Emma Aurora Benson at Hudson, Wisconsin. Mrs. Bigelow was born at St. Peter, Minnesota, March 16, 1869. She is an artist, and a member of the Eastern Star.

From November, 1917, until February, 1919, Mr. Bigelow was a member of the Morrill County fuel committee. He was local chairman of the American Red Cross from 1918 until 1925, and has served from 1929 until the present time. He is the past president of the Lions Club at Bridgeport, and has been a mmber of the Masons since 1894, he is also a member of the Eastern Star. Residence: Bridgeport.

Eugene A. Bigelow

Eugene A. Bigelow, retired farmer and ranchman, was born in LeClaire, Iowa, June 23, 1884, son of Benjamin F. and Rachel (Fairly) Bigelow. His ancestry is American Yankee.

After leaving country school, he took up a pre-emption homestead in Nebraska, and afterward took up a Kinkaid homestead. He has always been active as a farmer and ranchman, and taken much interest in Republican politics. He is an Odd Fellow, and a member of the Nebraskana Society.

On December 25, 1883, he was married to Elizabeth C. Cope at Newton, Iowa. Mrs. Bigelow was born at Clinton, Illinois, June 28, 1860. To them five children were born, Mabel, October 26, 1885; Lee, December 1, 1887; Del, March 27, 1890; Cleo, September 11, 1893; and Ray, March 4, 1895. Residence: Harrison.

Mabel Emily Bigelow

Mabel Emily Bigelow, postmistress at Ulysses, was born at Ulysses, on May 1, 1884, daughter of Robert Chappell and Florilla Lovina (Mattoon) Bigelow. Robert Bigelow was born in Brookfield, Vermont, March 23, 1841, and died at Ulysses on July 4, 1904. A veteran of the Civil War, he was confined in Libby Prison for several weeks. He participated in the Battle of Gettysburg and others. Of English descent, he traced his ancestry to Mayflower passengers.

Florilla Mattoon was born in Norwich, Vermont, March 11, 1843, of Irish and English descent. Until her death at Ulysses, on March 31, 1929, she was active in the work of her church, and was a member of the Women's Relief Corps.

Mabel Emily Bigelow was educated in the public and high schools, and graduated from Ulysses High School on May 17, 1901. In 1908 she became assistant postmistress, and in 1924 was appointed postmistress, which position she now holds.

A Republican in politics, she is a member of the Christian Church, and the Rebekahs and Royal Neighbors of America. She is a member also of the Nebraskana Society. Miss Bigelow devotes her leisure time to reading. Residence: Ulysses.

Edward Ernest Bilon

Born at Wahoo, Nebraska, July 2, 1899, Edward Ernest Bilon is the son of Louis Bernard and Anna (Koudele) Bilon. His father, who was a optometrist, was born of French and Czechoslovakian parentage July 9, 1871, and died at Columbus, Nebraska, January 10, 1930. His mother was born at Wahoo, December 29, 1875.

Mr. Bilon was graduated from the high school at Kearney, Nebraska, in 1916, and received the degree Doctor of Optometry at Needles Institute in 1921. He served as office assistant in Kearney, 1915, was book-keeper for the A. C. Killian Company of Kearney, 1916, was assistant purchasing agent for the Morris Packing Company of Omaha, 1917, and in 1918 owned the Employers Reference Company of Omaha. He is now the owner and operator of the Bilon Optical Company at Grand Island.

He is a member of the Grand Island Chamber of Commerce, the Red Cross, Salvation Army American Optical Association, the local lodge of the Elks and The Nebraskana Society. He holds membership in the Woodland Country Club and the American Legion. Mr. Bilon's favorite sports are golf and football.

His marriage to Christine Henriette Jensen was solemnized at Omaha, September 21, 1922. Mrs. Bilon, whose ancestry is Danish, was born at Omaha, April 11, 1906. They have two children: Thomas, born July 19, 1926; and Donna Lee, born July 16, 1929. Residence: Grand Island.

Veggo Walter Binderup

Veggo Walter Binderup was born at Adams County, Nebraska, May 12, 1875, the son of George Werner and Lorenze (Bjering) Binderup. His father, who was instructor in a Danish university, was born at Copenhagen, Denmark, in 1826, and came to Adams County in 1874. He died at Minden, Nebraska, April 15, 1915; he served as an officer in the Danish Army in the war with Germany, and later was in the King's service as an insurance adjuster. His mother was born at Viley, Denmark, in 1816, and died at Minden, in December, 1927.

Mr. Binderup attended Hastings College for a time. He is the author of an article *Among the Bees*, published in 65 newspapers. He is a teacher of nature study in the Kearney County rural and city schools, and is also instructor in the same subject at Dana Seminary, Blair, Nebraska. His favorite sport is hunting, while his hobby is the study of bees. He was elected president of the Nebraska Honey Producers' Association 5 years, and is now an honorary member and vice president.

Of his marriage to Dora Mohel Eriksen two children were born: Catherine, who is a student nurse at the University Hospital in Omaha, Nebraska; and George W., who is in business at Minden. Residence: Minden.

Frank Albert Birchell

Frank Albert Birchell, merchant, was born at Sylvania, Wisconsin, May 14, 1875, son of James and Christine (Meinzer) Birchell.

His father, a native of Yorkshire, England, came to America in 1845, and died at Racine, Wisconsin, March 3, 1917. He was a farmer. His wife, Christine, was born in Germany, in 1845, and died at Racine, in June, 1902.

In 1890, Mr. Birchell was graduated from public school at Sylvania, and in 1903, began business in partnership with W. R. Woolfenden, now deceased, in the firm of the Gering Mercantile Company. This company is still owned and operated by Mr. Birchell as partner and manager. He is also an extensive land owner and farmer. For nearly 30 years he has been a prominent merchant at Gering.

On December 25, 1898, he was married to Lulu Belle Woolfenden at Stratton, Nebraska. She was born at Racine, Wisconsin, March 1, 1873. She is the daughter of James H. and Lucy (Vincent) Woolfenden, who were prominent pioneer settlers of Stratton, Nebraska. Her father was a merchant. She attended school at Stratton, and is a member of the Eastern Star and the Gering Woman's Literary Club. They have one daughter, Helen, born October 9, 1908, who was graduated from the University of Colorado with the class of 1930.

Mr. Birchell's religious affiliation is with St. Timothy's Episcopal Church. He is a member of the Ancient Free and Accepted Masons, the Royal Arch Masons, the

Eastern Star, the Modern Woodmen of America and the Elks. His civic and professional organizations include the Federation of Nebraska Merchants and the Chamber of Commerce. He has served for more than 20 years on the local board of education, and is a member of the Gering Golf Club. His hobby is hard work. Residence: Gering.

Peder Rudolph Birk

One of the leading bankers of Grand Island, Nebraska, is Peder Rudolph Birk who has lived in this state all his life. He was born at Omaha, Nebraska, December 17, 1887, the son of Christian Pederson and Hansine (Petersen) Birk. His father, who was born at Horsens, Denmark, May 15, 1865, is a carpenter and has served as a member of Grand Island City Council for ten years. His mother was born in Denmark, January 16, 1873.

Mr. Birk was graduated from the Grand Island High School in 1904, and studied banking and accounting at the Grand Island Baptist College. He entered the First National Bank of Grand Island, in 1911, as a messenger boy and has progressed steadily in this organization until today when he is first assistant cashier and assistant trust officer, serving as a junior executive officer.

He holds membership in the Chamber of Commerce, was formerly a member of the Kiwanis Club, and is affiliated with the First Presbyterian Church of Grand Island. His social club is the Woodlawn Golf Club. He is a Mason, is now treasurer of the Knights Templar, is a Royal Arch Mason, and is a member of the Shrine. At one time he served as president of the Masonic Building Board at Grand Island.

Mr. Birk was married at Grand Island, June 12, 1912, to Agnes Adair Livingston. Mrs. Birk, who is a vocal teacher and musical director, was born of Scotch parents at Trenton, New Jersey, December 4, 1887. They have two children: Mary Jean, born September 7, 1917; and Barbara Agnes, born August 17, 1915. Residence: Grand Island.

John Martin Birkner

John Martin Birkner, physician and surgeon, was born in Germany May 29, 1856, and has resided in Nebraska since April 28, 1886. He is the son of Frederick Heinrich and Maria Claudia (Wilkins) Birkner.

Dr. Birkner attended school in Germany, and received his medical degree from the Missouri Medical College at St. Louis in 1886. He attended the Pharmacy College there 1880-82.

From 1880 until 1886 he was in the drug business in St. Louis, and from 1886 until 1899 practiced medicine and surgery at Sutton, Nebraska. Since 1899 he has been in practice in Lincoln. He is a member of the Nebraska State and Lancaster County Medical Associations, the Chamber of Commerce, and Lincoln Lodge No. 19 of the Ancient Free and Accepted Masons; Mt. Moriah Commandery and the Order of Eastern Star.

The possessor of a fine military record, Dr. Birkner is a member of the American Legion, the Veterans of Foreign Wars, the Military Order of the World War and the Association of Military Surgeons, etc. His religious affiliation is with the Holy Trinity Episcopal Church of Lincoln.

On November 1, 1883, he was married to Elvira Caroline Emily Middleton at St. Louis. She was born there on June 14, 1860. Four children are living and one deceased: Carrie, born December 19, 1884, died July 14, 1885; Hugh Ernest, born May 1, 1886; Alma Catherine, born May 11, 1887; Arwin Middleton, born September 30, 1888, and Gisela Julia, born January 12, 1891. Residence: Lincoln.

Robert Birrell

A leading farmer and stockraiser in Thayer County for many years, Robert Birrell was born in Kennoway, Scotland, February 18, 1856. The son of Robert and Agnes (Thompson) Birrell, he left home at the age of 17, settling in Fairbury, Illinois, where he remained three years. Desiring to visit Scotland again, he first took out citizenship papers and spent a year in Scotland. At the end of that time he returned to America, spending six months in Fairbury, Illinois, then removing to Chester, where he has continuously resided.

Mr. Birrell's father was born in Kennoway, and died at Methal, Scotland, in February, 1868. He was a contractor. His wife, who was born at Kennoway, December 25, 1823, came with her six children to America after her husband's death, providing for and rearing them all to maturity. Her death occurred at Chester, June 28, 1881.

At the time Mr. Birrell settled at Chester he lived on a farm about a quarter of a mile from his present home. He has owned the farm on which he now lives for more than forty years. On December 28, 1887, he was united in marriage to Margaret Shearer at Hebron. Mrs. Birrell was born at New Lisbon, Wisconsin, October 23, 1864, and died at Chester, November, 1889. There is one child of this marriage, Grace, born October 21, 1888, who is married to John G. Kuhlman.

Mr. Birrell was later married to Elizabeth Kirkwood Ingersoll, born at Fairbury, Illinois, November 25, 1866. She is of Scotch ancestry. They have two daughters, Rachael, born April 19, 1896, who married Joe S. Hunt, and Ruth, born April 19, 1896, who married David Spafford.

Mr. Birrell is a Democrat. During the World War he had charge of loan drives and subscribed liberally to them. He is a member of the Presbyterian Church, the Modern Woodmen of America, and for more than thirty years has served on the school board of District 95 of Thayer County.

Mr. Birrell's hobby is fine horses, and he has for years bred and owned purebred Clysdales, one of which was imported from Scotland. He has always been interested in and worked for every project for the advancement of his community. Recently, in recognition of his efforts he was awarded life membership in The Nebraskana Society. Residence: Chester.

Ira Birt

Ira Birt, farmer and dairyman, was born at Hickman, Nebraska, May 27, 1886. He is the son of Charles H. and Mary Margaret (Heupel) Birt, the former of whom was born at Lafayette, Indiana, February 24, 1854. A farmer for many years, he died at Hickman, July 2, 1897. His wife, who was born at Lancaster, Wisconsin, June 2, 1854, died at Hickman, January 24, 1930.

Mr. Birt was educated in the public schools of Hickman until 1900, when he began to farm. On February 19, 1908, he was married to Clara Wissel at Hickman, her birthplace. Mrs. Birt was born September 2, 1885.

There are four children, Irene, born April 11, 1912; Ross, born February 24, 1914; Earl, born July 10, 1916; and Myrtle, born August 8, 1918. Irene has graduated from high school, Ross is a senior, Earl is a sophomore and Myrtle is in the eighth grade.

Mr. Birt has always resided at Hickman. He is a member of the Presbyterian Church there, served as a deacon ten years, and at the present time is an elder of the church. For ten years he has served on the school board of Hickman High School. He is a member of the Nebraskana Society, and during the World War was a participant in all civilian war and relief drives. Residence: Hickman.

William Bischof, Junior

William Bischof was born at Nebraska City, Otoe County, Nebraska, October 24, 1866, the son of William and Kunnigunda (Zimmerer) Bischof. His father, who was a hardware merchant, was born at Nuremburg, Germany, in 1835, and died at Nebraska City, March 17, 1917.

His mother was born at Fritlingen, Wurtemberg, Germany, in 1837, and died at Nebraska City, July 7, 1884.

Mr. Bischof was graduated from the Nebraska City Episcopal College. From 1884 to 1888, he attended the United States Naval Academy. He has lived in Nebraska all his life and for three years was colonel in the Second Infantry of the Nebraska National Guards; having been captain for three years and lieutenant colonel for six years. At the present time he is salesman for the Great Western Stove Company, and is president of the King Drill Manufacturing Company.

He is a member of the United Commercial Travelers Association and the Travelers Protective Association, an Odd Fellow and an Elk. Residence: Nebraska City.

Alfred S. Bishop

Alfred S. Bishop was born at St. Paul, Decatur County, Indiana, October 8, 1877. He is the son of Robert and Mary Alphenas (Jessup) Bishop. Robert Bishop was born in Virginia on September 27, 1847, and died at Los Angeles, California, September 26, 1928. He was a railroad agent. Mary A. Jessup was born in the State of New York, June 24, 1885, and is now living at the age of seventy-six years.

Mr. Bishop received his education in elementary schools. Before coming to Nebraska in 1904, he was a railroad telegrapher, and a station agent, and since 1904, he has been train dispatcher, and night chief dispatcher. He is now chief train dispatcher on the Rock Island Lines.

He was married to Bessie Bailey Johnsen September 3, 1899, at El Paso, Texas. They have one daughter, Jessie, born July 26, 1900, who is married to Marion George Bloom.

He is a Republican, is a member of The Nebraskana Society, and holds membership in the Elks. Touring by auto and reading are his hobbies. Residence: Fairbury.

Arch Lee Bishop

Arch Lee Bishop, distinguished lawyer, banker, and landowner of Wheeler County, has been a resident of this state for the past 52 years. He was born in Nova Scotia, July 29, 1866, the son of George Nelson and Elizabeth (Wood) Bishop. His father, who was a sea captain, came to Nebraska in 1879, and took up a homestead in Wheeler County.

Mr. Bishop has been president of the State Bank of Bartlett, Nebraska, since it was chartered in 1906, and is now an active stockholder and director in that organization. He has spent the past 35 years building and improving on un-cultivated land and now owns nearly 50 farms ranging in size from 40 acres to 2200 acres. He has owned stock in the Bankers Loan Company of Omaha, the South Ford Bank, and the City National Bank of Omaha.

He is a Democrat and served for 17 years as county attorney of Wheeler County. He is a member of the Nebraska State Bar Association and The Nebraskana Society. His favorite sports are hunting and fishing.

Of his marriage to Ida J. Anderson, the following children were born: Vida, who married George A. Brown; Bertha, who married Francis Tobin; Pearl Larson, who is married; Clifford, who is employed by the Standard Oil Company at Alliance, Nebraska; George, who resides at Grand Island; Harold; Hubert, who is cashier of the Bartlett State Bank; Genevieve; Josephine, who married Gerald Krueger; Oliver, who married Jessie Bignell, and who is a merchant; and Adelia, who married Walter Plugge Ranch. The following are the children of his marriage to Martha H. Detwiler: William; Elinor; Dean; Robert; and Mary Anne. Residence: Bartlett.

John Skilton Bishop

John S. Bishop, prominent lawyer and legislator of Nebraska, was born at Lyons, Wayne County, New York, September 3, 1861; John Calvin Bishop, his father, who was born at Rose, Wayne County, New York, February 7, 1829, was a teacher, farmer, United States government surveyor, and reporter, for thirty years. He was descended from John Bishop who came from England in the first Guilford Connecticut company in 1639, and who was the second man to sign the Plantation Covenant. He died at Lyons, August 20, 1897.

Mary Skilton (Avery) Bishop, his mother, who was a teacher before her marriage, was born at Lyons, May 13, 1824, and died there November 9, 1910. She was descended from Henry Skilton and the Croton Averys, both distinguished families whose genealogy has been carefully preserved.

Mr. Bishop attended the country school, took a commercial course at Lyons Union School, and took a preparatory course for college, graduating in 1881. He received his A. B. and C. E. degrees at Union College, Schenectady, New York, 1884. He was awarded his LL. B. at Albany Law School in 1887. He completed the full classical and engineering courses at Union College in three years, and was an honor student.

He has been engaged in the practice of law since 1887, and has held various civic and political positions in Lincoln. He was secretary of different organizations of retail merchants in Lincoln; organized the Nebraska Credit Company; and edited and published the *Blue Book* for 10 years. A Republican, he served on the city council from 1903 to 1908; was unsuccessful candidate for county judge and city attorney; and was elected state representative in 1928 and 1930.

He married Cora Lucy Knapp at Rose, Wayne County, New York, June 20, 1894. A teacher for ten years, she was born at Rose, January 20, 1866, and died at Lincoln, September 23, 1929. She was of German, and English descent. To their union three children were born, Anna Mary, born August 20, 1896, who married Lawrence Eugene Wentz; Grace Margaret, born February 14, 1901, who died December 16, 1901; Charlotte Sherman, born May 25, 1903, who was adopted and married Frederick J. Miller, a dentist; and Sarah Jeanette, born December 16, 1908, who died June 22, 1909. Mr. Bishop was united in marriage to Mrs. Alice J. Cornell, February 14, 1931, at Omaha, Nebraska.

Mr. Bishop is a member of the Sons of the American Revolution; a member of the Legal Aid Committee of the Social Welfare Society for over 30 years; a member of the Lincoln Chamber of Commerce since 1902; and was formerly a member of the Knife and Fork Club. He is a member of the First Baptist Church of Lincoln, and has served as church clerk since 1910. He is a member of all Masonic bodies from Blue Lodge to Shrine. Residence: Lincoln.

Nelson Edward Bishop

Nelson Edward Bishop was born April 23, 1879, in Seward County, Nebraska, the son of Thomas Henry and Anna (Smith) Bishop. His father was born at Troy, New York, August 28, 1843, and died at Pleasant Dale, Nebraska, March 16, 1926. He served in the twenty-third Wisconsin Infantry during the Civil War. His ancestors were Scotch and Irish. His mother was born at Salem, Salem County, Wisconsin, March 3, 1854, of English parentage, and died at Pleasant Dale, February 4, 1913. She taught school and was a member of the Eastern Star.

Mr. Bishop received his education in the elementary schools and the Milford High School, from which he was graduated in 1899. On October 15, 1916, he was united in marriage to Emma Mauner, at Crawford, Nebraska. She was born in Davis County, Iowa, February 13, 1885, of German and French parentage, and is a registered nurse. They have two children: Wilmer Julius, born August 14, 1918, and Bernadine Bethel, born December 17, 1920.

Nelson Bishop was a rural mail carrier for twelve years, was in the merchandising business for a year. He has been a farmer for some time.

From September 1899-1901 he served in the Philippine Insurrection as a private in Company D of the Thirty-ninth Infantry. He is a member of Camp Lewis of the Spanish War Veterans, at Lincoln.

He is affiliated with the First Methodist Episcopal Church at Pleasant Dale, is a member of the Commercial Club and the Parent Teachers' Association; holds membership in the Ancient Free and Accepted Masons and is a member of the Nebraskana Society. Residence: Pleasant Dale.

Arthur Herbert Bivans

Arthur Herbert Bivans, son of George G. and Elizabeth (Campbell) Bivans was born at Trinidad, Colorado, July 16, 1891. His father was born in Ohio, May 26, 1858, and died at Guthrie, Oklahoma, in September, 1905. He was a teacher in the public schools of Georgetown, Ohio, and later a paperhanger, painter and farmer. His Scotch-Irish and English ancestors have been in America several generations.

Elizabeth Campbell was born in West Virginia, May 29, 1861, and died at Miami, Florida, February 27, 1930. Before her marriage she was a teacher in schools in eastern Nebraska. She was a direct descendant of John and Priscilla Alden, who came over on the Mayflower in 1620.

On October 21, 1914, Mr. Bivans was married to Venola Julia Lewis at Ojus, Florida, and came to North Platte in October, 1918. Mrs. Bivans was born at Santa Ana, California, September 18, 1887. She was a graduate of the high school at Downs, Kansas, attended Washburn College at Topeka, Kansas, and before her marriage was a public school teacher. She traces her genealogy to early colonial settlers from England, and her ancestry on her father's side is Welsh and French. She is a member of the Methodist Episcopal Church, the Women's Home Missionary Society, the Nebraska Federation of Women's Clubs, and the Parent Teachers' Association. At the present time she is engaged in welfare work for the benefit of the unemployed under the supervision of the Parent Teachers' Association and the North Platte Woman's Club. They have three children, Margaret, born July 18, 1915, who is valedictorian of her class of 1932 of which there are 111 members; Roberta, born May 14, 1918; and Caryl, born May 5, 1924.

Mr. Bivans is a Republican. He has been city letter carrier at North Platte for the past eleven years, and is a member of the First Methodist Episcopal Church. Since 1920 he has been a member of the official board of the Methodist Episcopal Church. Since 1925 he has been chairman of the world's service committee and since that time has been treasurer of the Sunday School. During 1930 and 1931 he was secretary and treasurer of the Inter-church Reserve, and at the present time is serving as vice-president.

During 1929, 1930 and 1931, Mr. Bivans was vice-president of the Nebraska State Association of the National Association of Letter Carriers. He is serving as its president at the present time. He is also a member of the Parent Teachers Association. His favorite sports are tennis and croquet. Residence: North Platte. (Photograph in Album).

Ammi Leander Bixby

Ammi Leander Bixby, one of Nebraska's leading columnists and editors, was born at Potsdam, New York, April 21, 1856, son of Alfred and Catharine (Willson) Bixby. His father, born at Jerico, Vermont, February 17, 1815, was a farmer and stock raiser, and a descendant of Joseph Bixby who came to America in 1640. He died at Pawnee Reservation, August 21, 1878. His wife, Catharine, was born at Sharon, Vermont, April 26, 1818. She was a teacher and singer. The family came from Leeds, England, and settled in America, in 1638. She died at Garrison, Nebraska, January 10, 1899.

Ammi L. Bixby received his education in the common schools and attended medical college one year. In 1881 he started in the newspaper game at Fullerton, Nebraska, and was in business for himself at various places in Nebraska and Colorado, over a period of years. Since 1892 he has been associated with the *Nebraska State Journal,* of which he is now associate editor. He is the author of *Driftwood, Memories, Bix Abroad, Bix in America,* etc., and is an extensive reader and lecturer.

He was married to Mary Adel Bates at Fairmont, Minnesota, May 14, 1878. Mrs. Bixby, who was born at Dodgville, Wisconsin, June 21, 1856, died at Lincoln, on March 8, 1928. There were five children born to their marriage, four of whom are living: Alfred Leroy, born August 29, 1879; Anna Katherine, born December 30, 1880; Florence Lillian, born April 10, 1883, who died August 27, 1894; Bessie May, born September 17, 1884, and Alice Lorena, born October 7, 1891.

Mr. Bixby is a Republican, but has never aspired to public office. He is a member of the Sons of the American Revolution, and served as state president one year. He holds honorary memberships in the Hiram and Kiwanis Clubs, and is a Mason and Modern Woodman of America. For several years he was a member of the Lincoln Board of Education, and he is now a member of the State Historical and the Nebraskana Societies. The family attends Trinity Methodist Episcopal Church. Mr. Bixby is a member of the Laymen's Club. His hobby is decent behavior. Residence: Lincoln.

Joseph Bixby

Joseph Bixby, distinguished physician and surgeon of Nebraska, was born at Minonk, Illinois, June 27, 1875, the son of Joseph and Sarah (Todd) Bixby. His father, who was born at Kenne, New Hampshire, November 9, 1833, and died at Diller, Nebraska, August 28, 1897, was a seaman on a whaling ship, serving later as assistant engineer for the Tiffin and Ohio Railroad; he was consecutively a farmer, grain dealer, and hardware merchant, and served as past chancellor of the Knights of Pythias and past master of the Ancient Free and Accepted Masons. He was descended from Joseph Bixby who was born at Little Waldinford, England, in 1620; the first Bixby came to America in 1647.

Sarah (Todd) Bixby, mother of Dr. Bixby, was born in McComb County, Ohio, July 15, 1836, and died at Strang, Nebraska, March 21, 1900. She was active in the Order of Eastern Star, Woman's Relief Corp, the Women's Christian Temperance Union, and the Methodist Church. She was a member of the distinguished Todd family of Ohio, and was a cousin of the second wife of Abraham Lincoln.

Dr. Bixby attended public school, was graduated from Lincoln Business College, and was a student at the University of Nebraska. In 1900 he was graduated from the University Medical College at Kansas City. He has been engaged in the practice of medicine and surgery continuously since 1900, has numerous farming interests in Fillmore County, and is vice president and director of the Western Union Life Insurance Company of Lincoln, Nebraska.

He holds membership in the Nebraska State Medical Association of which he is past vice president, the American Medical Association, the Fillmore County Medical Society, Red Cross, and the Young Men's Christian Association. Dr. Bixby is president of the Geneva Chamber of Commerce, is a member of the Nebraskana Society,

JOSEPH BIXBY

and was formerly a member of the first Library Commission of Geneva. During the World War he served as a member of the advisory board and a member of the examining board. He is a charter and life member of the Civil Legion, is affiliated with the Congregational Church of Geneva, is past patron of the Chapter 180 of the Eastern Star.

A Mason, Dr. Bixby is Past Master of Geneva Lodge Number 79, and is a member of the Lincoln Consistory and Sesostris Temple. His hobby is reading. His political preference is the Republican Party.

His marriage to Josephine Pangle was solemnized at York, Nebraska, September 14, 1917. Mrs. Bixby, who was born at Geneva, September 22, 1891, and died there July 3, 1925, was the daughter of Vance Bush Pangle, who was a pioneer settler in Fillmore County and a Civil War veteran. Members of the Pangle family were prominent in America as early as 1774 and were pioneer settlers of Virginia and Ohio. They have two children: Joseph, Jr., born August 25, 1918, who is a student in Pembroke School, Kansas City; and John Richard, who was born June 10, 1924, a student in the Geneva Public School. Residence: Geneva. (Photograph on Page 127).

Horace Owen Bixler

Horace Owen Bixler was born at Hayes Center, Nebraska, October 20, 1887, the son of Lewis Albert and Ulrika (Peterson) Bixler. His father, whose ancestry was Pennsylvania Dutch, was born at Markelville, Pennsylvania, February 12, 1854, and died at Palisade, Nebraska, February 8, 1921. His mother was born in Sweden, February 9, 1864.

Mr. Bixler received the A. B. degree at Nebraska Wesleyan University in 1922, and was awarded the A. M. degree at the University of Nebraska in 1927. He was a student at the University of Colorado summer school, 1924, and Claremont College summer school, 1930. He taught in rural schools for two years, was a grade school teacher for three years, served as county superintendent of Hayes County for four years. For the past 13 years he has been superintendent of Nebraska schools, and is at present superintendent of the Perkins County High School at Grant, Nebraska.

He holds membership in the Nebraska State Teachers' Association, the National Education Association, the Nebraska Schoolmasters Club, Phi Delta Kappa Fraternity, and the Grant Commercial Club. He is a Mason and a member of the Nebraskana Society. His hobby is music, while his favorite sport is golfing.

On November 18, 1914, he was united in marriage with Lucy Inez Brown at Grafton, Nebraska. Mrs. Bixler, whose ancestry is English, was born at Stuart, Nebraska. They have one child: Dean Allison, born October 24, 1919. Residence: Grant.

Charles M. Black

Charles M. Black, retired farmer and banker, and one of the most outstanding citizens of North Bend, was born at Lexington, Rock Bridge County, Virginia, November 11, 1856. He is the son of James and Cassie (Moore) Black, who were both natives of Virginia. James Black was born in Franklin County, June 8, 1810, and died at North Bend, on February 19, 1896. He was a farmer of German ancestry. His wife, Cassie Moore, was born in Buchanan, Virginia, October 10, 1815, and died at North Bend, August 9, 1895. Her ancestry was English.

Upon finishing country school, Mr. Black started farming, and continued over a period of years, gradually increasing his holdings until now he is an extensive landowner. He has also been active as a banker, and at the present time is vice-president and a director of the First National Bank of North Bend. In politics he is a member of the Democratic party, and has served as supervisor of Dodge County. Mr. Black is a member of the Metho-

dist Church, the Red Cross, and The Nebraskana Society.

He was married to Mary Ann Scott at North Bend, on April 29, 1880. Mrs. Black was born in Philadelphia, August 14, 1860, of Irish ancestry. There are three children, Myrtle Mae, born February 16, 1882, who married Oscar David Funk; Theola Isabella, born February 21, 1887, who married Robert A. McWhorter, and David Wilson, born May 28, 1900, who married Sadie Mae Scott. Residence: North Bend.

Leonard Harry Black

Leonard Harry Black, owner and manager of a general store at Verdel, Nebraska, has lived in this state his entire life. He was born at Verdel, September 20, 1896, the son of William and Susanna Black, the former an early settler in Knox County, Nebraska. His father was born near Council Bluffs, Iowa, July 4, 1854, and died at Verdel, Nebraska, May 21, 1929. His mother was born at Griswold, Nebraska, September 17, 1867.

Mr. Black attended the Verdel High School and studied business at York College for a year. He was employed by the Farmers Co-operative Association for four years, and since 1919 has owned his own mercantile establishment. He is a member of the Verdel Presbyterian Church, the Red Cross, and the Nebraskana Society.

During the World War he served for six months with the American Expeditionary Forces in France, has been post commander of the American Legion for two years, and is now finance officer of that organization. His chief recreations are hunting and fishing. He is an Odd Fellow.

On September 11, 1919, he was married at Bloomfield, Nebraska, to Laura Dever, who was born in that community, June 15, 1897. They have one child: Melba, born September 1, 1920. Residence: Verdel.

Oswald Ragan Black

Oswald R. Black, known throughout Nebraska as "Oz" Black, popular newspaper cartoonist and art director, has lived in this state for the past 25 years. He was born at Neoga, Illinois, October 29, 1898, the son of Eben Ringo and Julia Cynthia (Ragan) Black. His father, whose ancestry is English and Dutch, was born near Dallas, Texas, May 22, 1860. His mother, a music teacher and an active church worker, was born of Scotch-Irish parents at New Winchester, Indiana, April 29, 1867.

Mr. Black attended the public schools of Cheyenne, Wyoming, and was graduated from the high school at Lincoln, Lancaster County, Nebraska, in 1917. He was a student at the University of Nebraska from 1918 to 1923, where he was sports editor of the *Daily Nebraskan,* and was art editor of *Awgwan.* He was a member of Sigma Delta Chi, journalistic fraternity.

He served as newspaper reporter and cartoonist of the *Lincoln Star* where he conducted the widely known feature, *Here in Lincoln,* 1919-1927; and was commercial artist in Lincoln from 1928 to 1930. Since 1930 he has been cartoonist and art director on the *Nebraska State Journal,* drawing a full page Sunday cartoon feature under the title, *Here In Lincoln.*

His marriage to Alona Carpenter was solemnized at Chicago, March 17, 1923. Mrs. Black, who was born at Knoxville, Iowa, November 14, 1899, is a primary teacher and a writer for children's magazines. They have two children: Virginia Hains, born June 24, 1924; and Judith Louise, born April 11, 1930.

During the World War Mr. Black was a private in the Student's Army Training Corps at the University of Nebraska. He is a member of the American Legion; the Lincoln Chamber of Commerce; and the Lions Club. He is a director of the People's City Mission at Lincoln; was a director of the Lincoln Advertising Club, 1927; and is a member of the Nebraskana Society and an elder of

Westminster Church. Since 1929, he has been sponsor of the Lincoln Hi Y Club, and is a member of the Boy's Work Committee of the Young Men's Christian Association. Politically, Mr. Black is an independent. Residence: Lincoln.

William Conant Black

William Conant Black, milling executive at Beatrice, Gage County, Nebraska, has been a resident of the state for over 30 years and is prominent in civic organizations in his community. He was born at Sycamore, Dekalb County, Illinois, June 3, 1878, the son of William and Mary (Conant) Black. His father, who was a miller, was born in Ireland and died at Beatrice, February 4, 1919. His mother was born in New York and died at Beatrice, January 19, 1920.

Mr. Black received his education in the public school of Youngston, Ohio. He is president of the Black Brothers Flour Mills at Beatrice, is vice president of the First National Bank of Beatrice, and is active in the Beatrice Chamber of Commerce and the Rotary Club. He holds membership in The Nebraskana Society, the Elks, Young Men's Christian Association, and the Presbyterian Church at Beatrice.

He was united in marriage at Beatrice, August 12, 1901, with Ivy Bell Howey, who was born at Kenanee, Illinois. Their children are: Frances, born March 25, 1903; William, born April 28, 1906; and Beatrice, born February 4, 1909. Residence: Beatrice.

Earl Howell Blackburn

Earl H. Blackburn was born at Fairbury, Nebraska, January 28, 1888. He is the son of Nathan Carson and Hannah (Furry) Blackburn. His father was born at Pleasantville, Bedford County, Pennsylvania, February 13, 1861, and is engaged in the flour milling business with his son under the name of the Blackburn Milling Co. He is of English and German descent. Hannah Blackburn, his wife, who is of Holland Dutch descent was born at New Enterprise, Bedford County, Pennsylvania, December 10, 1865.

At two years, in 1863, N. C. Blackburn was orphaned through the death of his father in Andersonville prison, the story of which makes one of the saddest pages in the history of the Civil War. He was the youngest of six children in the family. At the close of the Civil War, in appreciation of the services of the men who had given their lives to the cause of the country, the Pennsylvania state legislature created the Soldiers' Orphan School at Harrisburg to educate and to care for the orphans between 10 and 16 years of age who survived the conflict. Here the head of the Blackburn firm of today was nurtured, with one visit a year to the home of his mother. At 16 he was sent back to his home. After about a year he succeeded in obtaining employment at the Pleasantville Mills at wages fixed at $4 a month and with no specified number of hours of labor.

Nebraska has counted Mr. Blackburn among her millers since 1883. In that year he and Mr. Furry decided to move to Nebraska in the hope of finding larger opportunities. As a new mill was then under construction in Endicott, Mr. Blackburn went there for employment. The job he obtained paid $40 a month. When he came to the state, Nebraska produced only spring wheat, but experiments had just started with turkey red winter wheat. Mr. Blackburn was therefore a witness to the transition of Nebraska into the ranks of hard winter wheat growers.

Earl H. Blackburn attended the Fairbury High School two years, and removed with his parents to St. Edward, Nebraska where he was graduated in 1904. During 1906-07 he attended the University of Nebraska. His fraternity is Beta Theta Pi.

Since leaving the University he has been engaged in the milling business, first as a partner in the Blackburn and Furry Mills at St. Edward, Nebraska, and later as vice president of the Nebraska Consolidated Mills Com-

pany of Grand Island. He is now in business with his father and his brother, Glenn, as partner and manager of the Blackburn Milling Company of Omaha.

On May 15, 1910, he was united in marriage with Bertha Jean Brown at Alva, Oklahoma. Mrs. Blackburn was born at Robinson, Illinois, October 19, 1886. There are two children, Nadine, born February 24, 1912, married Walter Cassel and John, born February 24, 1915.

Mr. Blackburn is a Republican. He has always been active in civic and fraternal work and is a member of the Chamber of Commerce of Omaha and of the Omaha High School Parent Teachers Association. While at Grand Island he was a member of the Rotary Club during 1921-22. He is a Protestant and a member of the Masonic Order. Residence: Omaha.

Hobert Lee Blackledge

Hobert Lee Blackledge, lawyer at Kearney, Nebraska, for the past few years, was born at Red Cloud, Nebraska, August 18, 1900, the son of Lewis H. and Margaret Edith (Lawrence) Blackledge. His father, who was born in Monroe County, Ohio, January 10, 1868, is a distinguished lawyer, and since 1920, has been judge of the 10th Judicial District of Nebraska. The family genealogy which dates to 1682, when the first member came to America from England, is traced through the following members of the Blackledge family: David, Samuel, William, Robert, Thomas, and William.

His mother was born in La Salle County, Illinois, March 26, 1872, and died at Red Cloud, September 17, 1920. Hobert Lee Blackledge was graduated from the Red Cloud High School in 1918, and in 1925 received the Bachelor of Laws degree at the University of Nebraska where he was a member of Phi Delta Phi, Gamma Lambda, and Kappa Sigma of which he served as president. He practiced law at Grand Island, Nebraska, 1925-29, and was city attorney part of that time; he is now junior member of the law firm Miller & Blackledge.

Mr. Blackledge is a member of the American Bar Association, the Nebraska State Bar Association, Kearney Chamber of Commerce, the New England Historic Genealogical Society, Bucks County Historical Society (of Pennsylvania), and the Nebraskana Society. He is a member of the Kearney Country Club, the American Legion, the Elks, and Scottish Rite Body of the Masons. Politically, he is a Democrat.

On October 1, 1930, his marriage to Helen Negley occurred at Council Bluffs, Iowa. Mrs. Blackledge, who was born at Coyle, Oklahoma, December 2, 1903, is a direct descendant of Roger Williams through Obadiah Edmunds, a Revolutionary soldier, and of Daniel Perrine, The Huguenot. Residence: Kearney.

Samuel Clarence Blackman

One of Nebraska's leading newspaper editors, Samuel Clarence Blackman was born at Naperville, Illinois, September 26, 1867, the son of Francis Wilson and Clarissa (Warne) Blackman. His father, a farmer and lumberman, was born of German and English parents at Rochester, New York, February 22, 1823, and died at West Side, Iowa, February 6, 1902; his ancestors settled in America in colonial times. Clarissa (Warne) Blackman, his mother, was born near Aurora, Illinois, August 28, 1830, and died at West Side, April 2, 1891. Her great-grandfather was one of the 20 proprietors of West Jersey.

Mr. Blackman attended school at West Side, was graduated from the high school at Geneva, Illinois, in 1888, and later was a student at Wheaton College. He taught in a rural school for three years, was employed in a newspaper office at West Side for a time, and served as postmaster there until 1905. He was editor and publisher of the *Madison Chronicle*, Madison, Nebraska, 1905-1909, and in 1917 bought the *Citizen* at Tilden, of which he is still editor. He has served as president and secretary of school boards in all the above communities.

He served for several years as secretary of the Madison County Agricultural Society, was one of the promoters of the public library at Madison, and today holds membership in the following civic and fraternal organizations: Tilden Chamber of Commerce; Red Cross; Lions Club; Modern Woodmen of America; and Royal Highlanders. He is a member of the Tilden Country Club, is affiliated with the First Methodist Church of Tilden, and holds membership in the Nebraskana Society.

A Republican, Mr. Blackman has served as a member of the county and state central committees; was register of deeds of Madison County, 1909-12, and was elected state representative from District 50, in 1930.

He was married to Grace Lockwood, daughter of A. C. Lockwood, a Civil War veteran, at Newton, Iowa, November 10, 1892. Mrs. Blackman, whose ancestry was English, was born at Monroe, Iowa, August 22, 1873, and died at Madison, November 30, 1912. She was active in church affairs and held membership in the Woman's Club. To this marriage four children were born: Lloyd C., February 9, 1894, who married Alice Hoagland; Lucille C., January 8, 1898, who married Louis A. Olson; Leslie F., October 27, 1900, who married Cleonice Smith; and Francis E., August 22, 1907, who married Vivene Cunningham.

Lloyd C. is at the head of the dental department of Pelton Clinic at Elgin, Illinois. Leslie F. is connected with the registry department of the Omaha Postoffice. Francis E. is a publisher, and is associated with his father in business, and Lucille is engaged in secretarial work at Lincoln, Nebraska. On June 19, 1919, Mr. Blackman was united in marriage to Edith Cunningham at Council Bluffs, Iowa. She is the daughter of William S. and Mary (Mossbarger) Cunningham, pioneers who homesteaded north of Tilden, in 1879. Mr. Cunningham served in the Civil War. Residence: Tilden. (Photograph in Album).

Samuel Holmes Stout Blackwell

Samuel Blackwell, prominent banker and executive of Omaha, Douglas County, Nebraska, has lived in this state since 1886. He was born at Hopewell, Mercer County, New Jersey, April 12, 1867, the son of Nelson Daniel and Anna (Stout) Blackwell. His father, who was born at Hopewell, March 11, 1834, and died at Lawrenceville, New Jersey, December, 1921, was a merchant; he occupied the same store building used by his father and grandfather. He was a director and officer of several banks and for many years was active in the business and civic life of his community. He was descended from Robert and Mary (Manning) Blackwell; the latter was a daughter of Captain John Manning who settled in New York, in 1676. He was also descended from Captain Ralph Hunt of Long Island, and through the maternal line was descended from: Captain Content Titus, born in 1643, who was the son of John and Mary (Reed) Moore; Rev. John Prudden, born 1645, died 1725; and Judge William Green. He was a direct descendant of Captain Stephen Blackwell and Colonel John VanCleve, who were officers in the Revolution.

Anna (Stout) Blackwell, mother of Samuel Blackwell, was born at Stoutsburg, Somerset County, New Jersey, June 30, 1840, and died at Hopewell, December 4, 1906. She was a graduate of Pennington Seminary and was active in literary club work. She was a direct descendant of Richard and Penelope Van Princes Stout who are credited with being the first settlers of New Jersey. Among her noted ancestors are: Rev. Obadiah Holmes, born 1606, died 1682; Colonel Joseph Stout; and Jonathan Stout. She is a direct descendant of the Revolutionary War soldiers: Samuel Stout; Abraham Cruser; Rudolph Hagaman; and Benjamin Van Kirk.

Mr. Blackwell first attended school at the Hopewell Seminary and later the New Jersey State Model School, where he ranked second in a class of fifty scholars. He was graduated from Stewart's College and later took a special course of law. He started his business career in the Union State Bank of Harvard, Nebraska, about 1887, and resigned his position there in 1893 to become cashier of the First National Bank at Princeton, New Jersey, which was near his boyhood home. About ten years later, he purchased the controlling interest of a bank at Friend, Nebraska, and moved there to take over the management thereof. After about five years he sold his interest in this bank and moved to Afton, Iowa, to become president of the Savings Bank of Afton, which he had recently purchased, and where he remained as president and manager until the organization of the Federal Land Bank of Omaha, in 1917, when he sold his interests at Afton, to take the position of assistant registrar of the Federal Land Bank of Omaha, and shortly thereafter was appointed registrar, which position he holds at the present time. Mr. Blackwell is also registrar of several other banks of the Eighth Federal Land Bank District. He has always taken an active interest in civic affairs and community clubwork wherever he resided and is a member of the Omaha Red Cross, Community Chest, Chamber of Commerce, Advertising-Selling League and the Omaha Athletic Club.

He is a member of the Sons of the American Revolution. During the war, he was active in loan drives and Red Cross affairs. He is a member of the Military Affairs Committee of the Omaha Chamber of Commerce, a member of the Presbyterian Church and the Young Men's Christian Association; he is an Odd Fellow, a thirty-second degree Mason, and a member of the Shrine. In politics, he is a Republican; his favorite sports are football and golf, and his hobby, flowers.

His marriage to Bessie Walker Bartine was solemnized at Princeton, New Jersey, June 29, 1899. Mrs. Blackwell was born at Princeton, September 2, 1868. Her French Huguenot ancestors came to America in 1685; she is a direct descendant of Sir Francis Drake and of Edward Hunt, who settled on Long Island many years prior to the Revolution. Three children were born to them: Sarah, who died at the age of three years; Mary was graduated from Central High School at Omaha, and from Choate's School in Boston, had two years at Wheaton College, was graduated from the University of Wisconsin in 1930, and is now doing personnel work for the Northwestern Bell Telephone Company in Omaha; Elizabeth, who also was graduated from Central High School and Choate School at Boston, afterward entered the University of Wisconsin. Both are members of Kappa Alpha Theta. Residence: Omaha.

Edward Samuel Blair

Edward S. Blair, who has been engaged in the practice of medicine in Nebraska for the past 37 years, was born at Forreston, Illinois, June 17, 1857. His father Matthew Blair, who was born at Parish of Raloo, County Antrim, Ireland, May 14, 1823, and died at Forreston, May 21, 1891, was a carriage maker; he served as captain in the Civil War; his ancestry was traced to Brice Blair, born in Scotland, in 1600, who moved to Ireland, in 1625. His mother, Sarah Ann Blair, was born in Crawford County, Pennsylvania, December 23, 1827, and died at Naperville, Illinois, September 5, 1913; she is also descended from Brice Blair.

Dr. Blair attended the high school at Belvedere, Illinois, and the preparatory department of Allegheny College, at Meadville, Pennsylvania, 1878 to 1880, 1880 to 1884; received the A. B. degree at Allegheny College in 1884, and in 1887 was awarded the M. D. degree at the University of Michigan, at Ann Arbor. He was elected to membership in Phi Delta Theta, and is now a member of the Golden Legion chapter of this society, by reason of his 50 years membership.

A lecturer on hygiene in the Sioux City College of Medicine, 1894, he was state medical examiner for the insurance department of the Modern Woodmen of America for four years with the office of headquarters physician, and for 30 years was secretary of the United States Pension Board and examining surgeon. He is now engaged in general practice. He is the author of an article on influenza, published in the proceedings of the Nebraska State Medical Society, in 1902.

During the World War he was a member of the Medical Advisory Board for Wayne County. He is a member of the Nebraska State Medical Society, and the district medical society composed of Cedar, Dixon, Dakota, Thurston, and Wayne counties. In 1905 he was a member of the school board and library board at Wayne, and from 1909 to 1929, was secretary of the official board of the Methodist Episcopal Church at Wayne. He is a member of the Nebraskana Society, is affiliated with Chapter 120 of the Ancient Free and Accepted Masons, and is a Republican.

On August 14, 1889, he was united in marriage with Ida Rosetta Williams, at Amboy, Lee County, Illinois. Mrs. Blair, who is city librarian at Wayne, was born June 8, 1867. Four children were born to their marriage: Helen, born June 24, 1890, who married Dr. George F. Hodgson; Harold M., born November 29, 1891, who married Anna Harms; Robert P., born December 16, 1895, who died July 7, 1902; and Alice D., born August 20, 1901, who married Dr. William M. Hawkins, a veterinarian, who was graduated from the Iowa State College, 1921, where his wife was a student. Residence: Wayne.

William Joseph Blake

Born at Philadelphia, Pennsylvania, April 10, 1859, William Joseph Blake has resided in Nebraska for the past forty-four years, where he has engaged extensively in farming.

His father, Joseph Andrew Blake, was born in Miltenberg, Bavaria, Germany, in 1813, came to America in 1845, where he served as an interpreter. His death occurred at Wheaton, Illinois, in 1870.

His mother, born at Miltonberg, in 1821, died at Naperville, Illinois, in 1908.

William Joseph Blake attended public school. On October 18, 1884, he was married to Mary Lena Bortsch at Somanck, Illinois. She was born at Elbing, West Prussia, Germany, November 7, 1860. To them were born seven children, four of whom are living.

Mary, born August 27, 1888, married Oscar Knutson; Fred, born December 22, 1890; Eleanor, born November 15, 1893, who married Arthur John Iverson; Walter, born April 23, 1899, who married Lucy Ellen Peterson; Henry, born December 19, 1885, died in 1890; William, born September 30, 1887, died in 1890; and George, born May 19, 1897, died in 1898.

Mr. Blake served five years with the Illinois State Militia before coming to Nebraska. He is a Catholic and a member of the Nebraskana Society. Residence: Brewster.

Anton Charles Blatny

Anton C. Blatny was born at Linwood, Nebraska, July 11, 1900, son of Anton Peter and Marie Otilla (Homolka) Blatny. His education was received in elementary schools, and a semester in high school at Linwood.

Anton, father of Anton Jr., was born at Linwood, May 19, 1877, and died at Linwood, November 16, 1927. His life occupation was farming. He is of Bohemian descent. Marie, his wife, was born in Linwood, May 21, 1879, and died there, February 10, 1914.

Mr. Blatny has lived in Nebraska his entire life, his occupation is farming. Being secretary of Butler and Saunders Counties drainage, district No. 3, is one of his business connections.

Although not active in politics, he is a Republican. He is a baptized Catholic. Reading is his hobby. Residence: Linwood. (Photograph in Album).

Daniel Victor Blatter

Daniel Victor Blatter, banker, was born in Tuscarawas County, Ohio, September 7, 1866, and on March 14, 1884, settled in Nebraska.

His father, John Blatter, was born in Tuscarawas County, Ohio, November 4, 1839, and died at Baltimore, Maryland, April 14, 1901. He was a merchant who served with the 98th Ohio Volunteer Infantry in the Civil War. His father and mother came to the United States from Switzerland in 1830. John Blatter married Mary Jane Demuth. She was of a Pennsylvania Dutch family who came originally from Moravia in Bohemia.

Mr. Blatter attended the public schools of Baltimore and the Baltimore City College. On coming to Nebraska he worked in the post office one year, and entered the service of Thompson and Baker, bankers, on April 1, 1885. He has been in the same bank since that time. The name of the bank is now the Albion National Bank. It was organized under the name of Thompson and Baker in December, 1881.

Mr. Blatter was married to Gertrude Mae Letson at Albion on June 5, 1889. She was born at Sparta, Wisconsin, September 5, 1869, and died at Albion, July 25, 1904. Six children were born to them, John and Edward, who died in infancy; Donald, born August 14, 1891, who married Laura Knight; Roger, born August 22, 1894, who married Eva Fleming; Oscar, born December 31, 1899, who married Helen Hardin; and Dorothy, born July 15, 1901. On April 14, 1910, Mr. Blatter was married to Carrie Edna Ross, nee Boots. She died at Albion, March 30, 1928.

During the late war Mr. Blatter was county chairman of War Saving Stamp drives. He is a member of Albion Congregational Church, is a Mason and a member of the Modern Woodmen of America. He is a life member of the Nebraskana Society, and a member of the Nebraska State Historical Society. During the World War he was chairman of Boone County Red Cross, and at the present time is a trustee of Doane College. Residence: Albion.

Frank Robert Blincow

Frank Robert Blincow was born at Fairmont, Nebraska, November 3, 1872, the son of William and Betsey Wykes (Howe) Blincow. His father, who was born at Long Buckby, England, December 7, 1831, and died at Colby, Kansas, July 10, 1903, was a farmer in Thomas County, Kansas, where he served as county judge and clerk of the court; his English ancestors came to this country in 1872. His mother was born at Long Buckby, January 26, 1838, and died at Norton, Kansas, December 17, 1915.

Mr. Blincow attended the rural schools of York County, Nebraska. He has been a farmer near Oxford, Nebraska, for many years, and at this time is a stockholder in the Oxford Co-operative Oil Company, the Oxford Equity Creamery, and the Farmers Equity Elevator in which he is a director. From 1912 to 1920, he served as a member of School District Number 17, and since 1925, has been a member of the Oxford Public School Board. He is one of the local people who made it possible to erect the Oxford General Hospital, and is a member of its board of directors. He is affiliated with the Methodist Episcopal Church.

Of his marriage to Millie Priscilla Brown three children were born: Harlan Robert, March 17, 1899, who served in the military training school in the late war and who married Mary Catherine Bailey; Ethel Irene, November 21, 1902, who married Kenneth Aikins; and Homer Brown, December 10, 1909. All the children were graduated from the Oxford High School. Residence: Oxford.

Morris Joslin Blish

Morris J. Blish was born at Lincoln, Lancaster County, Nebraska, April 21, 1889, the son of Frank May and Louise Ann (Joslin) Blish. His father, who was born at Wilmington, Illinois, June 30, 1867, is manager of R. G. Dun & Company at Kansas City, Missouri. His Welsh ancestors came to America early in the 17th century. His mother was born in Tioga County, New York, February 11, 1866.

Mr. Blish attended the public schools of Lincoln and Omaha, and in 1907 was graduated from the Omaha High School. In 1912 he was graduated from the University of Nebraska with the B. S. degree; M. A., 1913. He was awarded the Ph. D. degree at the University of Minnesota, in 1915. He was elected to the following fraternities in college: Sigma Xi, Gamma Sigma Delta, Phi Kappa Phi, Phi Lambda Upsilon, Phi Gamma Delta, and Alpha Chi Sigma.

He served as assistant chemist at the Montana Agricultural Experiment Station, 1916-22, at Bozeman, Montana. Since 1922 he has been chemist of the Agricultural Experiment Station at Lincoln. He is the author of scientific papers in various technical journals on agricultural biochemical subjects.

He was married to Vera Buell at San Francisco, California, April 21, 1921. Mrs. Blish was born at Livermore, Iowa, January 29, 1889. They have one daughter: Mary Louise, born October 15, 1922.

Mr. Blish was a second lieutenant in the American Expeditionary Forces during the World War, and in 1929 was made a major in the Chemical War Service Reserves. He is a member of the American Chemical Society; holds a fellowship in the American Association for the Advancement of Science; and was president of the American Association of Cereal Chemists, 1923-25. He is a member of the Eastridge Club at Lincoln, and his favorite sport is golfing. Residence: Lincoln.

Rodney Bliss

Rodney Bliss, physician and surgeon, was born at York, Nebraska, August 9, 1878, son of David Cleveland and Sophia Christiana (Hart) Bliss.

Dr. Bliss received his Bachelor of Arts degree from the University of Nebraska in 1901, and attended the University of Chicago, and Rush Medical College, 1901-04. He was an interne in Cook County and St. Luke's Hospitals from 1904 to 1906.

On April 25, 1907, he was married to Clara Jane Dimmick, at Chicago.

Mr. Bliss is a member of the First Presbyterian Church, the Omaha-Douglas County Medical Society, the American Medical Association, and is a fellow of the American College of Surgeons. He is a member of the Missouri Valley Medical Association, the Elkhorn Valley Medical Association and the Young Men's Christian Association. His clubs are the University and Happy Hollow. Residence: Omaha.

Herman C. Blobaum

Born in Stift Quernheim, Westfalen, Germany, February 4, 1879, Herman C. Blobaum is the son of Herman Blobaum and Marie Louise (Nunnencampf) Blobaum. His father was born in Stift Quernheim, Germany, in 1841, and died in Cowles, Webster County, Nebraska, in September, 1909. He came to America in 1881 and was a farmer and Mason. His mother was born in Stift Quernheim, Westfalen, Germany, March 29, 1843, and died in Rosemont, Webster County, Nebraska, May 23, 1913.

Herman Blobaum was educated in the grade schools in Gage County. His marriage to Anna Marie Louise Spilker, born in Clatonia, Gage County, Nebraska, February 25, 1884, took place in DeWitt, Nebraska, April 26, 1906. To this union nine children were born: Alfred,

April 14, 1907; Marie, May 1, 1909; Ester, January 19, 1911; Alma, April 6, 1913; Werner, May 10, 1916; Louise, February 28, 1918; Martha, December 20, 1920; Victor, September 29, 1923; and Robert, July 31, 1928.

Mr. Blobaum is affiliated with the Evangelical Lutheran Friedens Church near Jansen, Nebraska. He was treasurer of the DeWitt school board for ten years and treasurer of the Fairbury school board six years. He is a director of the Farmers Elevator in Jansen, at the present time. Residence: Fairbury.

Herman Otto Bloch

Herman Otto Bloch was born at Milton, Nebraska, January 31, 1892, the son of Johann Gustave and Emelie Louisa Caroline (Schievelbein) Bloch. His father, who was a blacksmith, was born at Kamionke, Germany, December 25, 1852, and died at Milton, September 8, 1907; he settled in Gosper County, Nebraska, in 1881. His mother, whose parents were farmers at Greuenberg, Germany, was born in that community August 28, 1852.

Mr. Bloch attended the Christian Day School at Milton until 1906, received the Bachelor of Pedagogy degree at Fremont Normal College in 1919, and was a student at the Lutheran Normal School at Seward. He has been principal of Trinity Evangelical Lutheran School at Blue Hill, Nebraska, since 1922. The pupils of Trinity School are housed in a new modern school, having four class rooms, a fine auditorium, a library, toilet rooms, has a steam heating plant and is equipped with electric lights. The school has at present three teachers. Mr. Bloch was instrumental in having this building erected. He is affiliated with the Trinity Evangelical Lutheran Church of the Missouri Synod serving as secretary since 1922, in his local congregation, and holds membership in the Aid Association for Lutherans and the National Lutheran Education Association.

His sports are baseball, tennis, and fishing, and his hobby is playing the violin. He is a Republican. On July 16, 1914, he was united in marriage with Wilhelmine Martha Zimmerman at Seward. Mrs. Bloch, whose German parents were farmers, was born at Seward April 1, 1885. She received her education in the Christian Day School at Middle Creek, and attended the Seward Normal College for about one year. She was a milliner before her marriage.

There are six children, all living: Verona Emelie, born November 1, 1917; Waldemar Dietrich, born December 3, 1919; Victor Kurt, born December 6, 1921; Norman Herman, born October 3, 1923; Lorenz Lewis, born August 23, 1925; and Charlotte Catherine, born August 21, 1927. Verona is interested in music, taking her early instructions from her father. Residence: Blue Hill.

Andrew Bernard Blomstrom

Born at Ceresco, Nebraska, September 29, 1891, Andrew Bernard Blomstrom is the son of Nels and Johanna (Nelson) Blomstrom. His father, who was a farmer and rural mail carrier, was born at Varmland, Sweden, February 25, 1851, and died at Ceresco, Nebraska, July 12, 1920; he came to America in July, 1870. His mother was born at Varmland, June 7, 1851, came to America in 1872, and died at Ceresco, February 18, 1920.

Mr. Blomstrom attended public school in Saunders County, Nebraska, and was a student at Lincoln Business College for a year. Since 1921 he has been business manager of the Farmers Union Co-operative at Ceresco, and at this time is director of that organization and the Saunders County Farmers Union Oil Association.

He holds membership in the Nebraskana Society, the Masons, Ancient Order of United Workmen of Nebraska, Order of Eastern Star, and the Ceresco Commercial Club of which he was chairman in 1929. He is a Republican and has served as city clerk, for six years, treasurer of the Volunteer Fire Department, eight years, treasurer of the Masonic Lodge, and member of the board of stewards of the Methodist Episcopal Church. His favorite sports are baseball and football.

Mr. Blomstrom was chairman of the War Savings Stamps Committee, 1918, during the World War. He was united in marriage with Jeanne Lois Cutts at Maryville, Missouri, October 20, 1926. Mrs. Blomstrom, who was born at Omaha, Nebraska, May 19, 1891, was the daughter of Thomas M. and Samantha (Frater) Cutts. They have a son, Dale Clifton, born December 13, 1927. Residence: Ceresco.

Alvin Frederick Bloom

Born at Red Oak, Iowa, February 9, 1885, Alvin Bloom is the son of the late John Frederick Bloom, who came to America from Sweden in 1871. John Frederick Bloom was born November 2, 1854, and died at Omaha, October 30, 1918. He was president of J. F. Bloom and Company, monument and mausoleum manufacturers, at the time of his death. His wife, Emma F. Bloom, born in Sweden, on June 3, 1860, came to America in 1873.

Alvin F. Bloom attended Red Oak and Council Bluffs public schools and attended Omaha High School. He was in the employ of the Chicago, Burlington and Quincy Railroad from 1902 until he became associated with the *Omaha Bee* in 1904. In 1907 he entered the firm established by his father, J. F. Bloom and Company, of which he is secretary-treasurer.

He was married to Irene Mae Tetard at Omaha, on June 12, 1912. Mrs. Bloom was born at Omaha, November 1, 1887, and is of Pennsylvania Dutch, Irish and French descent. There are three children: Marjorie Aileen, born July 3, 1918; Louise Irene, born May 18, 1922, and Marie Fredericka, born February 10, 1926.

Mr. Bloom is active in various civic and fraternal organizations. During the World War he assisted in various loan drives and other activities. He is a member of the Chamber of Commerce and the Rotary Club; past president of Rotary Club and past secretary; Capitol Lodge of the Ancient Free and Accepted Masons, and Elks Lodge No. 39. He is past president of Omaha Manufacturers Association and past president of the Nebraska Manufacturers Association.

He is a Republican in politics, and a member of Kountze Memorial Lutheran Church. His clubs are the Carter Lake Club and the Omaha Athletic Club. His favorite sports are fishing and hunting. Residence. Omaha.

Marion G. Bloom

Born at Guide Rock, Nebraska, February 23, 1896, Marion G. Bloom is the son of Levi and Minnie (Karnatz) Bloom. His father, a native of Marion, Iowa, was born July 14, 1862. He is a farmer. His mother was born at Chicago, Illinois, September 2, 1873.

Marion G. Bloom attended rural school to the eighth grade, completing his course in 1910; in 1914 he completed the twelfth grade in the Red Cloud School.

From 1914-17 he was a teacher in the public schools, and from 1917-19 was in the railway mail service. Since 1920 he has been assistant postmaster at Red Cloud. He was secretary-treasurer of the Commercial Club 1927-28; secretary of the Lions Club 1929-31; and from 1920-21 and 1922, was scoutmaster.

Mr. Bloom is a member of the Red Cross, the Modern Woodmen of America and the Ancient Free and Accepted Masons of which he is past master. He is a life member of the Nebraskana Society. His sports are hunting and fishing, and his hobby is gardening.

On January 1, 1920, Mr. Bloom was married to Jessie Bishop at Fairbury. Mrs. Bloom was born at El Paso, Texas, July 26, 1900. To them were born three children: Marjorie Lee, born February 17, 1921, died March 2, 1923; Richard Alfred, born January 23, 1924; and Marion Louise, born April 6, 1929. Residence: Red Cloud.

Will Clark Bloom

Will Clark Bloom, county superintendent of schools of Dawson County, was born at Spring Ranch, Nebraska, June 30, 1878, son of Peter Bartholomew and Anna Frances (Felk) Bloom.

The father was born at Sunbury, Pennsylvania, July 8, 1844, and is a farmer. His ancestry is Pennsylvania Dutch. His wife, Anna, was born in Harrisburg, Pennsylvania, July 28, 1860, and died at Brady, Nebraska, February 11, 1921. Her ancestry was also Pennsylvania Dutch.

Mr. Bloom was graduated from rural schools of Lincoln County, in 1894, and during the year 1897 and 1898, attended Grand Island Business College. He was a student at Fremont Normal College from 1900 until 1901, and during the years 1906, 1907, and 1908, was a student at Nebraska State Teachers College. In his school days, he was active in baseball and basketball.

After three years teaching in rural schools in Lincoln County, Mr. Bloom became superintendent of the city schools of Moorefield, Nebraska, holding that position four years and was superintendent of city schools at Farnum, four years. He has been county superintendent of Dawson County school for 18 years. A Democrat, he was deputy county treasurer 1912, 1913, 1914.

He was married on July 3, 1901 to Eatha L. Folden at Stockville, Nebraska. She was born at Dayton, Ohio, November 24, 1877, descended from early settlers in Virginia. They have four children, Velma, born September 11, 1905; Mildred, born May 4, 1909; Kenneth, born May 20, 1911; and Marguerite, born February 18, 1914.

Velma received her Bachelor of Science degree from the University of Nebraska, where she was a member of Kappa Delta sorority. At the present time, she is kindergarten supervisor of Lexington city schools. Mildred attended the University of Nebraska one year, and is a stenographer in Lexington. Kenneth is attending the University of Nebraska his second year, taking the electrical engineering course, while Marguerite is in her first year at the University of Nebraska, where she is taking a course in physical education.

During the late war, Mr. Bloom was county chairman of the American Red Cross, director of loan drives, and chairman of the war savings stamp committee. He is a member of the Nebraska State Teachers' Association, the County Superintendents' Association, the Chamber of Commerce, and the Kiwanis Club. During 1930 and 1931, he was grand master of Nebraska Odd Fellows.

He enjoys hunting, both small and big game, his last big game hunt being in Canada, in November and December, 1930. His hobbies are reading, civic and fraternal work. Residence: Lexington.

Frederick Ferdinand Blum

Frederick Ferdinand Blum, retired farmer, was born at Kyrets, Bradenburg, Germany, July 26, 1851, son of August and Dorothea (Buckholz) Blum. His father who was born at Neichstaat, Bradenburg, Germany, on the desert, died at Kyrets, in November, 1886. He was a blacksmith and farmer, and a private in the German army. Dorothea, his wife, died at Kyrets, in September, 1876.

Mr. Blum attended the public schools of Germany, and came to Nebraska in 1870. On February 14, 1874, he was married to Fredericka Lamprecht at Omaha. Mrs. Blum was born at Kyrets, Germany, February 22, 1851. There are three children, Otto, who married Mary Becker; Emma, who married Henry B. Rohwer; and Marie, who married Ben Schomer. They are all farmers.

A farmer and fruit grower all his life, Mr. Blum is now retired. He was elected mayor of Millard, Nebraska, on the Republican ticket, and served from 1904-10 For twenty-three years he was president of the school board of District 18, and has served 34 years as a director of the Douglas County German Mutual Fire Insurance Company of Elkhorn. Fourteen years of this time he was also treasurer.

He is a member of St. Paul's German Lutheran Church of Millard, of which he has been a trustee 20 years. He is also a member of the Red Cross and the Nebraskana Society, and a contributor to the Salvation Army. His hobby is growing fruits and flowers. Residence: Millard.

Ella Blunk

Born near Grand Island, October 24, 1888, Ella Blunk is the daughter of Adolf and Juliane Margarete (Schmidt) Blunk. Her father, born in Schicren, Schleswig-Holstein, Germany, April 12, 1854, came to America in 1871. He was a farmer and manager of brick yards, and a Republican. His death occurred at Grand Island, March 4, 1910. His wife, born in Ostenfeld, Schleswig-Holstein, Germany, January 28, 1862, died at Grand Island, March 1, 1928. She came to the United States in 1886.

Ella Blunk attended elementary school at Doniphan and Grand Island, and the Grand Island and Aurora High Schools until 1907. The following two years she attended the University of Nebraska, and during 1912, 13 and 14 attended summer sessions at Kearney Normal School. She received her Bachelor of Arts degree in 1917, and her Master of Arts degree in 1927, from the University of Nebraska. She was valedictorian of her high school class at Aurora, in 1907, and was elected to Pi Lambda Theta at the university.

Miss Blunk taught two years, 1909-10, 1910-11 in District No. 71, Hall County, and since then has been a teacher in the Grand Island public schools. Her first year was as second and third grade teacher in the Lincoln School, after which she taught German in the seventh and eighth grades five years.

Since that time she has taught in the senior high school, first German, then science, later normal training and now German again. In addition she serves as registrar and in other ways assists the principal. During 1927-28 she was secretary of District No. 4, of the Nebraska State Teachers Association, and 1929-30 was vice president of the Nebraska Women's Educational Association.

She is a member of the American Association of University Women, the National Educational Association, the Order of Eastern Star, the Business and Professional Women, the Red Cross and the Salvation Army.

Miss Blunk is affiliated with St. Paul's English Lutheran Church, and is a life member of the Nebraskana Society. Residence: Grand Island.

Manuel William Boals

Born at Dakota City, Nebraska, June 5, 1902, Manuel William Boals is the son of Bernard Manuel and Etta (Beermann) Boals. His father, a farmer, was born in Dakota City, September 19, 1876. His mother was born in Dakota City, September 21, 1877, and died there June 5, 1902.

Manuel William Boals was educated in the grade schools of Dakota City, and was graduated from Fayette, Idaho, High School in 1921. He attended the National Business Training School at Sioux City, Iowa, and the University of Nebraska, where he was a member of the Pershing Rifles.

Mr. Boals has two children, Bernard, born May 27, 1926, and Dorothy Carol, born August 27, 1930.

Since leaving school he has been engaged in the bond business. He is a Republican, and a member of the Boals Methodist Episcopal Church, the Red Cross and the Nebraskana Society. His favorite diversion is reading. Residence: South Sioux City.

George Robert Boardmann

George Robert Boardman, executive, was born at Imperial, Nebraska, August 2, 1902, son of William Henry and Nellie Louisa (Kortright) Boardman. The father was born in New York City, October 31, 1855, and the mother on July 15, 1865.

Mr. Boardman received his education in public school, and in 1919 was graduated from the Chase County High School. In 1926 he received the Bachelor of Science degree from the University of Nebraska. He was a letterman in basketball, a member of the high school swimming team, and is a master swimmer, at Nebraska.

Since leaving college Mr. Boardman has been forest clerk in the United States Department of Agriculture, a teacher in Boyles Business College, and assistant scout executive of the Omaha Council of the Boy Scouts of America. He has served also as camp director of the Omaha Area Council.

He is a member of the Methodist Episcopal Church, the Red Cross, the Chamber of Commerce and the Masons. Residence: Omaha.

Thomas W. Bockes

Thomas W. Bockes, lawyer, was born at Central City, Nebraska, March 20, 1885, son of George David and Ada (Howe) Bockes. His father was born in Cattaraugus County, New York. His mother, also born in Cattaraugus County in 1859, died at Central City, December 20, 1918.

Educated in public school, Mr. Bockes was graduated from high school and in 1908 received the Bachelor of Laws degree from the University of Nebraska where he was a member of Theta Kappa Nu and Phi Delta Phi.

On June 27, 1925, he was married to Doris Lorna Corn at Fremont. She was born in Richardson County, Nebraska, February 7, 1904.

Since his admission to the bar, Mr. Bockes has been in active practice. For three years he was a member of the firm of Hall, Woods and Pound at Lincoln, and for eight years was a member of the firm of Martin and Bockes. He withdrew from the latter to become assistant general attorney for the Union Pacific Railway System.

Mr. Bockes is a member of the Presbyterian Church, the American, Nebraska State and Omaha Bar Associations, the Chamber of Commerce and the Masons. Residence: Omaha.

Henry Louis Bode

Born at Myerdale, Sommerset County, Pennsylvania, December 22, 1876, Henry Louis Bode has been a resident of Nebraska 47 years. He is the son of Henry and Caroline (Ebbecka) Bode, the former of whom was born in Germany, October 11, 1845. He was a German miner and farmer who came to America in 1872, after having served in the Franko-Prussian War, and settled in Nebraska. He died at Exeter, Nebraska, April 30, 1906. His wife, who still survives him, was born in Germany, June 22, 1850.

Mr. Bode was educated in country schools, and as a youth became engaged in farming. He is now an extensive landowner and prosperous in his chosen work. Active in civic and community affairs he participated in Liberty Loan and Red Cross drives and other patriotic work during the World War. He is a Lutheran and member of the Odd Fellows, and the Nebraskana Society. His favorite sport is baseball and he enjoys baseball games immensely.

He was married to Ida May Burton at Friend, October 8, 1902. Mrs. Bode was born at Friend, June 30, 1881. They have four children, Mae, born July 10, 1904, who married W. T. Shiffs; Lena, born January 19, 1906, who married Francis Drake; Henrietta, born April 21, 1911, who married Olin Porter; and Bud, born September 27, 1917. Residence: Friend.

Clyde L. Bodwell

A resident of Red Willow County since 1878, Clyde L. Bodwell was born at Des Moines, Iowa, June 18, 1868, son of Alvin P. and Jennie M. (Garrett) Bodwell.

The father was born at Alfred, Ohio, December 7, 1839, and died at Lebanon, February 15, 1925. He was a farmer of Scotch descent. His wife, Jennie, was born in Hyland County, Ohio, March 3, 1842, and died at Lebanon, August 15, 1930.

Mr. Bodwell attended public school and for many years has been the proprietor of a general mercantile store at Lebanon.

On October 31, 1892, he was married to Fannie M. Murphy, at Indianola, Nebraska. Mrs. Bodwell was born in Harrison County, Missouri, September 23, 1868, and died at Lebanon, March 30, 1926. She was a life member of the Red Cross, and was the daughter of William Murphy, who was born in Kentucky, and whose family came from Ireland. There is one son of this marriage, Rea E., born December 3, 1898, who was an aviator in the World War. On May 8, 1918, he was stationed at Caruthers Field, Fort Worth, Texas, where he was an instructor. On November 30, 1929, he was married to Muriel Steed of Omaha Nebraska.

On May 29, 1927, Mr. Bodwell was married to Pearl Garrett of Lebanon Nebraska. Mr. Bodwell is a Mason, a member of the Southwest Nebraska Historical Society, a member of the Red Cross and of the Presbyterian Church. He was elected to life membership in the Nebraskana Society in 1931. Residence: Lebanon.

Francis Boehler

Francis Boehler, farmer, was born at Beatrice, Nebraska, November 10, 1883, son of Conrad and Amelia (Spittley) Boehler. The father was born in Baden, Germany, October 16, 1849, and came to the United States in 1872. He located first at Lincoln, and in 1878, moved to Beatrice. From 1893 until his death, on May 20, 1930, he lived at Alma. His wife, Amelia, was born in Lincoln, Illinois, February 7, 1857, and died at Alma, November 14, 1926.

Mr. Boehler attended country school, and since reaching maturity, has engaged in farming. He is a Democrat, a member of St. Joseph's Catholic Church, the Modern Woodmen of America, the Knights of Columbus, the Nebraskana Society, and for 15 years has been president of his local school board. His hobby is mechanics.

He was married to Matilda Teresa Colgan at Orleans, Nebraska, January 29, 1908. Mrs. Boehler was born at Wyoming, Illinois, January 1, 1884, of Irish ancestry. They have one son, Clement Conrad, born November 5, 1910. He is a student at Creighton Medical College, at this time, and was graduated from Alma High School in 1928. Residence: Alma.

George Martin Boehler

George M. Boehler was born at Beatrice, Gage County, Nebraska, April 6, 1888, and has lived in this state all his life. His father, Conrad Boehler, was born in Germany, and died at Alma, Harlan County, Nebraska, May 16, 1930; he was a business man. Amelia (Spittley) Boehler, his mother, was born at Lincoln, Illinois, and died at Alma, November 14, 1927.

Dr. Boehler, who is a dental surgeon at Omaha, Douglas County, Nebraska, was graduated from the Alma High School, and later received his D. D. S. degree from the Creighton University Dental College at Omaha. He was a student at Northwestern University, Cambridge, in England, and Queen's College of Arts. He is a member of Delta Sigma Delta, honorary fraternity.

He was for 10 years a member of the State Dental Examining Board, and is past president of the Nebraska Dental Board, Creighton Dental Alumni, and the South West District Dental Association. He is the author of various articles on dentistry published in dental magazines and papers.

During the World War, Dr. Boehler was stationed in France, with Base Hospital Number 49; was commissioned lieutenant and later was promoted to major of the dental reserves. He is a member of the Reserve Officers Association and the American Legion. His social clubs are: University Club, Omaha Club, and Omaha Country Club. Residence: Omaha.

Adolph Don Boehm

Born at Grand Island, January 25, 1883, Adolph Don Boehm is the son of George Adolph and Catherine Amelia (Lange) Boehm. The father, a native of Wurtemberg, Germany, was born March 25, 1847, and at the age of twenty came to the United States. He was a brewer at Grand Island, where he died February 18, 1883. His wife, Catherine, was born at Main, Germany, September 28, 1850, and is still living at Grand Island.

Adolph Don Boehm attended the Grand Island public schools, from which he was graduated in 1901, as president of his high school class. He played football four years there, and afterward attended college one year. For a period of about thirty years Mr. Boehm was a member of the firm of the Independent Publishing Company, as manager of the circulation and advertising departments. He is a stockholder in that corporation, was formerly a director of the Commercial State Bank, and for the past two years has been in the real estate and insurance business at Grand Island.

On June 24, 1908, he was married to Helen Adela Noehrn at Grand Island. Mrs. Boehm, who was born at Chapman, Nebraska, October 29, 1888, is of German descent. Three children were born to them, one of whom is deceased: George H., born August 11, 1911, died January 21, 1921; Adolph, Jr., born May 31, 1916; and Robert Frederick, born March 30, 1926.

Mr. Boehm is a Republican. He is an English Lutheran, a member of the Nebraskana Society, the Hall County Historical Society, the Chamber of Commerce, the Elks, the Liederkranz Society, and the Plattdeutsch Verein. Residence: Grand Island.

Albert Orr Boggs

A general merchant for the past twenty-four years, Albert Orr Boggs has resided in Nebraska fifty-seven years. He was born at Granby, Missouri, October 12, 1867, son of James and Mary (Hostetter) Boggs. His father was born in Pennsylvania, January 10, 1835, and served three years in the Civil War with the rank of corporal. Later he engaged in farming, and died at Blue Springs, Nebraska, in January, 1918. Mary Hostetter was born at Clinton, Indiana, September 26, 1839, and died at Endicott, Nebraska, in July, 1885. She was a teacher whose mother traced her ancestry to early settlers in Virginia, and whose father was German.

Mr. Boggs attended the Endicott public schools and completed a business course at Burlington, Iowa. For about eleven years he was a country school teacher, and later a poultry buyer and general merchant. He is the author of an article on the *Care and Production of Eggs* (Mesco Book, August, 1915); and an article on advertising in the Federated Merchants Bulletin (1917).

On May 16, 1897, he was united in marriage to Alice Welsh at Endicott. Mrs. Boggs, who was born at Fairbury, March 21, 1877, is of Irish extraction. Her mother's name was Harrison, and she came from Harrisonville, Virginia. She is a flower gardener. There is one daughter, Marguerite M., born May 6, 1898, who is married to George F. Dutton.

Mr. Boggs is a Republican. For a time he was a member of the Modern Woodmen of America, and he is now affiliated with the Royal Neighbors of America and is a member of the Nebraskana Society. Residence: Gilead.

Charles Summer Boggs

Charles S. Boggs, who has been a physician in Nebraska for the past 46 years, was born at North Manchester, Indiana, June 19, 1857, the son of Lewis Boen and Virginia Rebecca (Frazer) Boggs. His father, who was also a physician, was born at North Manchester, September 3, 1828, and died at Oklahoma City, Oklahoma, July 28, 1923. His mother was born at LaPorte, Indiana, March 28, 1836, and died at Oklahoma City, March 28, 1923.

Dr. Boggs was graduated from the medical department of the University of Nebraska at Lincoln in 1884 and since that time has been engaged in medical practice at Filley, Nebraska. He is a progressive Republican and a Mason.

His marriage to Mary C. Faulder was solemnized in Gage County, September 28, 1882. Mrs. Boggs was born in Maryland, December 28, 1860. One child was born to them, Mabel M., born November 15, 1884, who died December 17, 1904. Residence: Filley.

John James Boggs

John James Boggs, distinguished educator and clergyman of Nebraska, was born at Independence, Iowa, February 23, 1865, the son of John Marshall and Adeline (Marshall) Boggs. His father, who was also a clergyman, was born in Washington County, Pennsylvania, in 1818, and died at Independence, September 1, 1872; his ancestry was Scotch-Irish. His mother was born of Scotch-Irish parentage in Richland County, Ohio, in 1828, and died at San Bernardino, California, in 1907.

Dr. Boggs attended high school at Independence, was awarded the A. B. degree at Lake Forest College in Illinois, 1888, and received the D. D. degree at Hastings College in 1929. He was a student at Chicago University for a time, and was graduated from McCormick Theological Seminary. He taught in a government school at Okayama, Japan, 1888-91, was engaged in missionary educational work at Canton, China, 1894-1915, and 1917-18, and served as professor of Latin and Greek at Rollins College, Florida, 1918-20. Since 1920 he has been professor of Latin and Greek at Hastings College, Hastings, Nebraska. Dr. Boggs has travelled extensively in Europe, the Far East and the Near East.

His marriage to Ruth Chapman Bliss was solemnized at Canton, April 22, 1896. Mrs. Boggs, who was a missionary physician to women and children in a China clinic, was born at Longmeadow, Hampden County, Massachussetts, November 3, 1866, and died at Hastings, Adams County, Nebraska, October 18, 1930. Her English ancestors came to America in 1636. One child was born to this union, Agnes Louise.

Dr. Boggs holds membership in the Classical Association of the Middlewest and South, the Classical League, and the Archaelogical Institute of America. He is a Republican, and is affiliated with the Presbytery of Chicago. Residence: Hastings.

William F. Bogle

A leading educator in Lincoln County, Nebraska, is William F. Bogle who was born at Bramwell, West Virginia, June 22, 1904. His father, William H. Bogle, who was a farmer, was born in Virginia, March 21, 1872. Alice S. Wallace, his mother, was born in Virginia, November 26. 1871.

Mr. Bogle was graduated from Peru Demonstration School in 1918, was graduated from the Peru Preparatory School in 1922, and in 1927 received the A. B. degree at Peru State Teachers College where he was a member of Tri Beta. He was awarded the B. S. degree in Pharmacy at the University of Nebraska in 1930. He served as instructor and coach of athletics at Adams and Alma, Nebraska, was superintendent of schools at Wellfleet,

Nebraska, and is now superintendent of schools at Wallace, Nebraska.

He is a member of the State Teachers Association, the Nebraska Pharmaceutical Association, the Red Cross, and the Nebraskana Society, and is a Mason.

On July 23, 1927, he was married to Opal M. Slick at Denver, Colorado. Mrs. Bogle, who is a teacher, was born at Pawnee Rock, Kansas, February 18, 1903. Residence: Wallace.

Floyd Loomis Bollen

Floyd L. Bollen, lawyer at Friend, Saline County, Nebraska, was born at Wells, Minnesota, January 18, 1875, the son of George and Ella (Loomis) Bollen. His father, who was a farmer and business man, was born at Geneseo, Henry County, Illinois, November, 1849, and died at Norfolk, Madison County, Nebraska, March, 1921. His mother was born at Canisteo, New York, December 10, 1852; her English ancestors came to America before the Revolution.

Mr. Bollen attended the grade schools of Illinois and Nebraska, and was a student in high school at Coleridge, Nebraska. He was a student at Fremont College where he was graduated in 1897. He was awarded his LL. B. degree at the University of Nebraska, in 1906.

From 1897 to 1899, he was an instructor in the public schools of Tilden, Nebraska; and from 1907 to 1911 taught at Bonesteel, South Dakota. Since 1911 he has been engaged in the practice of law. He is now city attorney of Friend, Nebraska. An Independent Democrat, Mr. Bollen served as a member of the Nebraska legislature in 1913.

During the World War he was active in loan drives; assisted in questionnaire work; and was a Four Minute speaker. He is a member of the Nebraska Bar Association and the Saline County Bar Society. He holds membership in the Friend Chamber of Commerce and the Nebraskana Society. He is a member of the following fraternal organizations: Modern Woodmen of America; Royal Highlanders; Knights of Pythias; and Independent Order of the Odd Fellows. He is affiliated with the Friend Congregational Church.

On January 7, 1902, he was married to Ray Katie Jennings at Fremont, Dodge County, Nebraska. Mrs. Bollen, who was born in Iowa, September 1, 1879, was formerly a high school teacher; her ancestry is English. Four children were born to their marriage: Lowell, born February 10, 1903; Emerson, born June 4, 1904, who married Jessie Nichols; Ruth, born May 30, 1906, who married Don. W. Thompson; and Ralph L., born August 31, 1909, who died January 18, 1928. Lowell was graduated from the University of Nebraska, and is an engineer. Emerson, also a university graduate is an engineer. Mr. Bollen has lived in Nebraska for the past 42 years. Residence: Friend.

Henry Bolton

A merchant and farmer in Colfax County many years, Henry Bolton was born near Nauvoo, Illinois, September 7, 1854. He is the son of Charles and Elizabeth (Wilsey) Holton, the former born in Hull, England, August 29, 1829. He came to America in 1847, settling in Hancock County, Illinois, where he engaged in farming. He was a studious man, who took much interest in reading, and who died near Nauvoo, on January 10, 1908. His wife, Elizabeth Wilsey, was born in Hamilton County, New York, August 1, 1835, and died near Nauvoo on January 11, 1923.

Henry Bolton attended rural schools, and had two years academic work at Fort Madison, Iowa. Later he was graduated from Bailey's Business College at Keokuk. For the past fifty-two years he has resided in Nebraska. Entering the mercantile business at Malvern, Iowa, in 1874, he removed to Red Oak, in 1875, and to Nebraska, in 1878. He located at Schuyler, where he is still engaged in business under the name of Henry Bolton & Son.

On October 8, 1881, Mr. Bolton was united in marriage to Nancy Ella Sheldon. Mrs. Bolton, who was born near Monmouth, Illinois, died at Schuyler, in April, 1887. Two children were born to them: Daisy, on August 1, 1882, and Addison L. on December 26, 1885. Daisy married Allen Sharp and resides at Stanton. Addison married Hazel Prince of Grand Island, and is now in business with his father. Residence: Schuyler.

Ella Wheeler Bond

Born at Farina, Illinois, April 26, 1874, Ella Wheeler Bond is the daughter of Elnathan J. and Sarah Ann (Wheeler) Bond. Her father, born at Lost Creek, West Virginia, February 5, 1828, was a physician and diagnostician, a graduate of Rush Medical College.

He was a talented singer, a choir director and a deep reader. His family, mostly English, though partly Welch on the maternal side, has been in America many generations, and produced musical directors, lawyers and authors. His parents were married in 1809. His death occurred at Ord, July 17, 1901.

Sarah Ann Wheeler was born at Thedford, Vermont, April 22, 1842, of Mayflower English and Irish descent. An educator, teacher of music, vocalist and choir director, she was fond of art, specialized in English, and was a tireless reader. She was a sister of Ella Wheeler Wilcox and of M. P. Wheeler, the poets. Her father was a violin master and carriage maker, while her mother was devoted to the letters. The ancestry of the family is traced to Ethan Allen. The parents of Ella Wheeler Bond were married on December 6, 1866. Her mother's grandmother was the first white child born in Thedford, Vermont, (1767).

Miss Bond received her diploma from the New York College of Music in 1892, and in the same year sang under William R. Chapman at the Patti Festival in a chorus of 1000 voices. During 1891-92, she sang under Walter Damrosch in the Oratorio Society (500 voices). She sang under John Finley Williamson with 1500 voices at Lincoln, and has been a choir director and organist as well as teacher for more than thirty years.

During the late war she prepared many programs, and at various times has appeared in Chautauqua and concert work over the state.

In 1920 she was made a member of the extension department of the National Academy of Music at Carnegie Hall, New York, and in 1928, was certified as a teacher of the Towsley University System of Musical Kindergarten. During the season of 1922-23, she was pianist for the People's National Opera Society (Rollin Bond, director) at Washington, D. C. Miss Bond was a student of vocal art under Colen Clarke White in 1922-23 at Washington.

A soloist, composer and writer, as well as a teacher, during the World War she was a member of programs for various benefits. She is a member of the Eastern Star, the Nebraska State Teachers Association, and was recently made a life member of The Nebraskana Society. Residence: Ord.

James R. Bond

James R. Bond, son of John Bond and Rachel (Metcalf) Bond, was born at Maryville, Nodaway County, Missouri, March 6, 1859. His father was born at Kington, St. Michael County, Welto, England, April 18, 1824, and was a Democrat. He was among the first settlers of Washington County, Kansas, and was a pioneer blacksmith. He died at Washington, Kansas, January 2, 1902.

His mother was born in Ashland, Ohio, April 21, 1828, and died at Washington, Kansas, in August, 1900. Her parents were descended from early Maryland families.

Mr. Bond attended the public schools. On September 19, 1888, he was married to Katie Parrish at Wash-

ington, Kansas, where she died, on April 22, 1912. On September 19, 1916, he was married to Katherina Rider.

Mr. Bond has lived in Nebraska eleven years and is successful as a farmer. He is a Democrat and holds membership in the Nebraskana Society. Residence: Fairbury.

Luther Bonham

Luther Bonham, banker, was born in Mound City, Missouri, April 10, 1886, son of Isaiah Bonham. His mother's name was Blevins. The father was born in Indiana, in July, 1846, and died at Fairbury, January 31, 1920. He was a prominent livestockman and banker. The mother was born in Mound City, in July, 1859, and was formerly a public school teacher.

Mr. Bonham attended public school and was graduated from Campbell University. In January, 1911, he was married to Myrtle Fisher at Red Cloud. She was born at Hubbell, March 31, 1887.

A Democrat, Mr. Bonham served in the Nebraska legislature in 1913. He is president of the First National Bank of Fairbury at the present time. Residence: Fairbury.

Lewis L. Booth

Born in Lee County, Illinois, April 3, 1866, L. L. Booth was a pioneer farmer in Nebraska in the early history of this state. Reuben Booth, his father, who was born in Canada, May 6, 1833, and died at Sutton, Nebraska, March 19, 1925, was a farmer; his ancestry was Irish and English. His mother, Maria (Throop) Booth, was born in eastern Canada, January 25, 1838, of Scotch and English parents, and died at Sutton, March 11, 1927.

Mr. Booth attended a rural school after coming to Nebraska, and since then has been a farmer in Clay County. He is a member of the Independent Order of Odd Fellows, and has been Noble Grand, holds membership in The Nebraskana Society, and is affiliated with the Methodist Church.

He married Caroline E. Swallow at Sutton, September 3, 1890. Mrs. Booth, whose ancestry is Pennsylvania Dutch, was born at McLean, Illinois, September 24, 1870. Mrs. Booth is a member of the Royal Neighbors, and has been Oracle of the local lodge. Their children are: Onie, born March 11, 1894; Rhoda A., born April 16, 1897; Ora, born September 26, 1900, who married Harold E. Brown; and Byron, born March 18, 1904, who married Zadie A. Cory. Rhoda married Allen B. Connell. Residence: Sutton.

Helen Amanda Borsheim

Helen Amanda Borsheim, born at Dundas, Canada, June 9, 1855, is the daughter of John Henry Fenton, born at Dublin, Ireland, February 16, 1818. An inventor, he came to America four months prior to the Civil War. He formed his company, serving the duration of the war. He was the youngest son of Honorable John P. Fenton, of Dublin. His wife, Helena Clifton, was born at Clifton, England, August 3, 1828. She was the daughter of the Honorable Claud E. Clifton, for whom the town was named. The town was named after the Clifton family in recognition for services rendered the crown. She died at Indianapolis, September 5, 1876; her husband survived her until November, 1905.

Mrs. Helen A. Borsheim was educated in the public and high schools of Indianapolis. On December 10, 1871, she was married to Louis Andrew Borsheim at Indianapolis. There are two children, John Louis, since the death of his father, known as Louis A., born September 22, 1872, and Alfred Fenton, born March 16, 1874.

Upon the death of her husband, March 27, 1922, Mrs. Helen Borsheim became his successor in business, and later, with her son, Louis, formed the Louis A. Borsheim

Corporation which is one of the oldest firms in the city. She is active in civic and cultural work, especially in the Woman's Christian Temperance Union. In 1909 she was largely instrumental with others in securing the national convention of that body for Omaha, at which time she was made a world delegate to the World Convention at Glasgow, Scotland. She served as president of the local organization for two years.

Her religious affiliation is now with the Dundee Presbyterian Church. In 1899 she was a delegate to the National Epworth League. She is a member of the Young Women's Christian Association, in which she was chairman of the devotional committee three years. Residence: Omaha.

Paul E. Boslaugh

Born at Mapleton, Iowa, June 13, 1881, Paul E. Boslaugh, leading trial lawyer of Hastings, has been a resident of Nebraska for more than twenty-nine years. He is the son of Jasper and Anna Martha (McCleery) Boslaugh, the former a farmer and a veteran of the Civil War. Jasper Boslaugh was born in Pennsylvania, of Dutch ancestry, and after the Civil War removed to Iowa, his death occurring at Castana, Iowa, in 1912. Anna Martha McCleery, his wife, who was born in Indiana in 1851, is of English descent.

Paul E. Boslaugh attended public school, and was graduated from high school. He received his LL. B. from the University of Nebraska in 1903, and in that year was admitted to the practice of law. For the past eighteen years he has been a member of the law firm of Stiner and Boslaugh at Hastings. He is a director of the First National Bank of Hastings and of the First Trust Company of Hastings. His professional associations include the Adams County, Nebraska State and American Bar Associations.

On June 1, 1910, he was united in marriage to Ann Viola Herzog of Harvard. Mrs. Boslaugh, who is of German and English extraction, was born at Harvard, July 8, 1884. They have two children, Genevieve E., born March 7, 1911; and Leslie, born September 4, 1917. Genevieve is now in her third year at the University of Nebraska and a member of Gamma Phi Beta sorority.

Mr. Boslaugh is a Republican. He is a member of the Chamber of Commerce, the Rotary Club, the Hastings School Board (director 6 years), the Masons, Knights of Pythias, Elks, and the D. O. K. K. His favorite outdoor recreation is golf, although he enjoys watching college football games. His clubs are the Lincoln University Club and the Hastings Country Club. Mr. Boslaugh participated in all civilian projects during the World War, and is a member of the Sons of Veterans of the Civil War. Residence: Hastings.

Charles M. Bosley

Born at Burlington Junction, Missouri, March 17, 1899, Charles M. Bosley has resided in Nebraska twenty-six years. His father, Augustus M. Bosley, was born in Clinton, Illinois, December 1, 1866, of Irish and German parentage. He is a farmer. His mother, Effie N. (Sinclair) Bosley, was born at Rockport, Missouri, August 20, 1877. Of Irish descent, she was a teacher and a homemaker.

Charles M. Bosley attended Pawnee City High School, from which he was graduated in 1915. Thereafter he was a student at Peru State Normal College, 1916-17. Upon the completion of his legal studies he was admitted to the bar June 15, 1927. Mr. Bosley was registered in the law office H. P. Armitage of Trenton, Nebraska, June 15, 1922, and was admitted to practice in all state courts and the United States District Courts of Nebraska. Prior to that he was a school teacher, teaching in the rural schools of Pawnee County, Nebraska, an automobile salesman and a banker. Mr.

Bosley was unsuccessful candidate for state representative on the Republican ticket in 1928.

On January 1, 1920, he was married to Verna M. Gruver at Palisade, Nebraska. Mrs. Bosley, born at Hayes Center, Nebraska, December 15, 1901, is of Dutch descent. They have two children, Warren G., born January 1, 1922; and Robert C., born March 14, 1925.

Mr. Bosley served in the United States Navy during the World War, enlisting in the early part of 1918, spending about thirteen months at the Great Lakes Naval Training Station, and was honorably discharged on February 1, 1919. He is a member of the John L. Sullivan Post No. 318 the American Legion, at Palisade, Nebraska. He is past local commander, county commander, state executive committeeman, and department commander of Nebraska. He is a Mason, a member of Palisade Lodge No. 216 of Palisade, Nebraska, a member of the Nebraska State Bar Association, the Red Cross, the Commercial Club and the Methodist Episcopal Church. He is a life member of the Nebraskana Society. Residence: Palisade.

Ernest Bossemeyer, Jr.

A resident of Nebraska for the past 50 years is Ernest Bossemeyer, Jr., who was born at Union, Iowa, October 22, 1871, the son of Ernest and Anna (Ackerman) Bossemeyer. His father, who was a farmer and merchant, was born in Lengerich, Germany, June 18, 1838, and died at Superior, Nebraska, in 1929. His mother was born at Hesse-Cassel, Germany, August 12, 1846, and died at Superior, March 9, 1924.

Mr. Bossemeyer attended the rural schools of Iowa and Nebraska. He started in business with a small feed store in 1891, and today owns a half interest in the firm of Bossemeyer Brothers, a grain and feed manufacturing establishment. He is a member of the National Grain Dealers Association, the Nebraska Grain Dealers Association, the Superior Chamber of Commerce, the Christian Science Church of Superior, is a Mason and Odd Fellow, and holds membership in the Young Men's Christian Association.

On June 13, 1897, he was married to Lulu May Aldrich in Jewell County, Kansas. Mrs. Bossemeyer who was born at Cedar Falls, Iowa, August 17, 1876, and is the daughter of Ziba S. and Flora V. (Egbert) Aldrich. Mr. Bossemeyer's chief recreations are golfing, tennis, and reading. Residence: Superior.

Ray Alonzo Bothwell

Ray Alonzo Bothwell was born at Reynolds, Nebraska, July 14, 1884, son of Alonzo Hector and Ida Belle (Williams) Bothwell. His father, who was born in Victoria, Illinois, December 10, 1855, came to Reynolds in 1881, as one of its first settlers. For many years a merchant and banker, he is now a druggist and mortician. Ida, his wife, was born in Marion, Iowa, September 24, 1859, and died at Reynolds, November 17, 1914. Of Irish descent, she was a teacher, a splendid business woman, and was for some time postmistress at Old Ida, Kansas, where she lived many years.

Mr. Bothwell attended the public and high schools of Reynolds, and was graduated in 1899. While in school he was active in baseball. Since leaving school he has engaged as an automobile and an insurance agent, and is now in business with his father as a druggist and mortician.

On June 12, 1917, he was united in marriage to Fannie Melbina Dunn of Kansas City, Missouri. They have two children, Gail, born February 4, 1916, who is a student in high school and an outstanding basketball player; and Idonna, born April 29, 1912, who is a student at Nebraska Wesleyan University. Mr.

Bothwell's first marriage was to Bessie Rebecca May. She was born at Reynolds, and died there some years ago.

Mr. Bothwell is a Democrat, and active in local politics. He has always been a member of the Reynolds Methodist Episcopal Church, and for fifteen years served as superintendent of its Sunday School. A Mason, he is also a member of the Eastern Star. In recognition of his work for the advancement of his community, he was recently awarded life membership in the Nebraskana Society. He is also a member of the Parent Teachers Association of Reynolds. Mr. Bothwell's hobby is carpentry. Residence: Reynolds.

Michael Bouc

Born in Czechoslovakia, June 15, 1870, Michael Bouc is the son of Jacob and Margaret (Toupal) Bouc, the latter born in Czechoslovakia, in 1844. Jacob Bouc was born in Czechoslovakia, in 1841, and died at Weston, Nebraska, in 1913, where his parents had settled in 1880 after coming to America.

Mr. Bouc attended public school, and was united in marriage with Frances Wotipka, February 11, 1894, at Weston, Nebraska. Mrs. Bouc was born in Texas, in 1875. To this union ten children were born: Louis, December 1, 1897; Joe, February 14, 1898; Agnes, September 2, 1901; Ludvik, April 10, 1902; Emil, December 22, 1903; Adolph, December 24, 1905; Margaret, September 5, 1907; John, May 7, 1909; Cycil, July 29, 1912; and Helen, September 13, 1914.

A successful farmer for many years Mr. Bouc has resided in Nebraska fifty-one years. He is affiliated with the St. Vitus Catholic Church, and he holds membership in the Catholic Workmen Lodge, and the Nebraskana Society. Reading is his favorite pastime. Residence: Valparaiso.

James Francis Bourret

James Francis Bourret, rancher, was born at Washburn, Wisconsin, November 6, 1867, son of Peter and Mary (Cross) Bourret. His father was born in Dubuque, Iowa, November 20, 1842, and was a rancher until his death at Hot Springs, South Dakota, on June 16, 1905. He was of French descent.

Mary Cross was born at Kilkearny, Ireland, January 1, 1838, and died at Torrington, Wyoming, January 6, 1922. She came to the United States from Ireland with her parents as a child.

Mr. Bourret attended the grade schools at Highland, Wisconsin, and for 45 years has been a rancher in Nebraska. He is a member of St. Mary's Catholic Church, Woodmen of the World, and a director of the school district board of district 81 of Sioux County. He enjoys baseball and basketball as a spectator. He is a Democrat.

On November 3, 1896, he was married to Jennie Lacy at Ardmore, South Dakota. She was born at Nevada, Iowa, December 20, 1878. Their four children are as follows: Grace Margaret, born February 15, 1901, who is a school teacher and is married to William D. Powell; Francis John, born December 20, 1904, who is a rancher, and married to Fern Eberspetcher; James Lacy, born July 23, 1914, who is a junior in high school; and Ina Marie, born April 19, 1922.

James was awarded the degree of Nebraska State Farmer, F. F. A., 1931, and American Farmer, F. F. A., 1931. Residence: Harrison.

William Henry Bousfield

William Henry Bousfield, banker, was born at Brownville, Nebraska, January 24, 1868, son of John C. and Esther (Haywood) Bousfield. John C. Bousfield was born at Hull, England, in 1842, and came to America in his early youth. He settled in Nebraska, in the 1860's, where he entered the grain business. He was a Republican and served as treasurer of Nemaha County one term. He died at Denver, Colorado, in October, 1927.

Esther Haywood Bousfield was born in Indiana, in 1846, and prior to her marriage was a teacher. She was active in the Methodist Episcopal Church until her death at Brownville, in May, 1876.

William H. Bousfield attended the public and high school of Auburn, and was graduated from the latter in 1885. In 1894 he entered the employ of the First National Bank, as bookkeeper. Thereafter he was made assistant cashier, and is now a director and cashier of that bank. A Republican, he served as city clerk for ten years.

On August 3, 1905, he was married to Dorothy Franklin, at Des Moines, Iowa. Mrs. Bousfield was born at Hiawatha, Kansas, and is of Pennsylvania Dutch descent. She is a member of the Order of Eastern Star, the Round Dozen Club and is affiliated with the Episcopal Church.

During the World War, Mr. Bousfield was chairman of a war saving stamp loan, and was a participant in all loan drives and active in the sale of Liberty Bonds. He is a member of the Y. M. C. A. He attends the Methodist Episcopal Church. He is a former vice president of the Nebraska Bankers Association, and for two years served as director of the Chamber of Commerce. He belongs to all branches of the Masonic order, and is a former member of the Elks, Modern Woodmen of America, Woodmen of the World, Odd Fellows, and Knights of Pythias. Both he and Mrs. Bousfield are members of the Auburn Country Club. He has an active interest in all sports, but especially ball games. Residence: Auburn.

Guy A. Bouton

Guy A. Bouton, farmer, son of Albert A. and Alice A. (Strong) Bouton, was born in Bellwood, Nebraska, September 16, 1878.

Albert A. Bouton was born October 28, 1837, at Milburg, New York. He was a farmer and a soldier in the Civil War, whose death occurred at Wood River, Nebraska, February 9, 1920. Alice, his wife, was born at Friendship, New York, on July 6, 1845, and died at Bellwood, August 19, 1918.

Guy A. Bouton was united in marriage with Stella I. Flake on March 2, 1904, at Bellwood. She was born at Lone Tree, Iowa, December 22, 1880. They have one daughter, Elma, born October 11, 1906.

Mr. Bouton's political preference is that of the Republican Party, and at various times he has served as election judge.

He is a member of the Farmers Co-operative Association, The Nebraskana Society, the Masons, was director of the school board during 1906 to 1921, and secretary of the Parent-Teachers Association. His home is at Bellwood.

Homer Bowen

Homer Bowen, a resident of Nebraska for the past 32 years, was born at Vales Mills, Ohio, January 22, 1876, of English, Irish and French descent. He is the son of William Jasper and Harriett (Chapman) Bowen. His father, a farmer and an ardent member of the Democratic party, who was born at Vales Mills, December 4, 1849, and died at Columbus, Ohio, June 17, 1929. His mother, a teacher before her marriage, was born at Wilkesville, Ohio, October 26, 1849, and died at Vales Mills, September 13, 1911; she was descended from Miles Standish and leaders in the Massachusetts Colony who came to this country from England.

Mr. Bowen attended the Academy at Wilkesville, and was a student at Creighton College of Pharmacy, at Omaha, Nebraska, 1908. He taught school in Ohio, 1894-1900, was a teacher at Wood River and Phillips, 1900-06, and has since been in the drug business. Since 1914, he has been a pharmacist at Grand Island, Nebraska, where he holds an interest in two drug stores.

He was the first president of the Grand Island Cosmopolitan Club, served on the local school board, president 1919 to 1921, and holds membership in the Chamber of Commerce, the Grand Island Credit Association and the Nebraska Pharmaceutical Association. Mr. Bowen is a Mason and is affiliated with the First Presbyterian Church of Grand Island. His hobby is flower gardening and his social club is the Woodland Golf Club. He is a Republican.

His marriage to Bertha Brown occurred at Cody, Wyoming, March 4, 1912. Mrs. Bowen, whose father was a captain in the Civil War, was born of English ancestry at Champaign, Illinois, August 26, 1876. They have one daughter, Harriet, born September 28, 1913, who attended Lindenwood College for Women, and is now a student at the University of Nebraska. Residence: Grand Island. (Photograph in Album).

Charles Arthur Bowers

A leader in Nebraska's educational field, Charles Arthur Bowers, was born at Beatrice, Nebraska, December 4, 1890, son of Edward Franklin and Della (Lupher) Bowers. His father, who was a pioneer minister in the United Brethren Church in Nebraska, was born at Saugerties, New York, January 17, 1854, and died at York, Nebraska, April 6, 1906; he was presiding elder of the eastern Nebraska district at various times. His father, who was of German descent, was also a clergyman.

His mother was born near Monmouth, Illinois, December 17, 1864, of Pennsylvania Dutch parentage, and died at York, June 24, 1924. She was a rural school teacher in Saline County, Nebraska, before her marriage and served as state president of the Woman's Foreign Missionary Society of the United Brethren Church in later years. Her ancestors were farmers in Pennsylvania.

Mr. Bowers attended the public school of York, and in 1909, was graduated from York Academy. He was awarded the Bachelor of Arts degree at York College in 1913. At this time he has completed the requirement for a Master of Arts degree which will be granted him from the University of Nebraska during the next year. He holds membership in Omicron Chapter of Phi Delta Kappa of the University of Nebraska.

His professional career is as follows: teacher of science and athletic coach at St. Edward, Nebraska, 1914; superintendent of schools at Cowles, Nebraska, 1915-17; instructor in science and history at the Nebraska School of Agriculture, Curtis, 1919-21; superintendent of public schools at Exeter, Nebraska, 1921-26; and superintendent of schools at Ord, Nebraska, 1926-30. He is now superintendent of schools at Holdrege, Nebraska, where he is also active in civic affairs.

Mr. Bowers is a member of the Holdrege Chamber of Commerce, is past president of the Ord Chamber of Commerce, is past president of the Ord Rotary Club, and holds membership in the Holdrege Rotary Club. He is a life member of the National Educational Association, is vice president of District Five of the Nebraska State Teachers Association, and is a contributing member of the Young Men's Christian Association. He is affiliated with the First Methodist Episcopal Church and holds membership in the Nebraskana Society and the Nebraska State Historical Society. On February 1, 1932, Mr. Bowers became executive secretary of the Nebraska State Teachers Association at Lincoln, where he now resides.

During the World War he was commissioned first lieutenant of Infantry and was assigned to active duty at Camp Dodge, Iowa, December 15, 1917. He served in France for ten months and participated in the battles of Haute-Alsace and Meuse-Argonne. He is a member of the executive committee of Martin Horn Post Number 66 of the American Legion, and is past commander of Fidelity Post Number 38 of Ord.

On June 18, 1918, he was married to Elma Grace Squires, at Hastings. Mrs. Bowers, who was a teacher prior to her marriage, was born near Fairfield, Nebraska, May 9, 1890, of English parentage. They have four children: John Edward, born October 12, 1920; Elma Jean, born December 30, 1923; Robert Squires, born September 7, 1925; and Gretchen Mae, born July 16, 1930. Residence: Holdrege. (Photograph in Album).

Frank Earl Bowers

Frank E. Bowers, educator and school executive, has lived in Nebraska for the past 45 years. He was born at Frankton, Indiana, March 26, 1883, the son of William Anderson and Harriet Virginia (Helsley) Bowers. His father, who was a farmer and voice instructor, was born at Sulphur Springs, Indiana, March 6, 1852, and died at Pickrell, Nebraska, July 28, 1930; his ancestry was German. His mother was born at Timberville, Virginia, February 14, 1853, and died at Franklin, March 26, 1931. Her German ancestors emigrated to the Virginia Colony prior to the Revolution.

Mr. Bowers attended the rural schools of Gage and Franklin counties; was graduated from the high school at Odell, Nebraska, 1902; and received a diploma at the Nebraska State Teachers College at Peru, 1913. He was a student at the University of Nebraska, 1928-30, where he held membership in Phi Delta Kappa.

He has held the following positions: teacher in rural schools, 1902-06; superintendent of the Rockford Schools, 1907-09; superintendent of public schools at Barneston, Nebraska, 1909-12; superintendent of schools at Papillion, Nebraska, 1913-18; superintendent of schools at Arapahoe, Nebraska, 1921-27. He was engaged in the implement retail business from 1919-21. Since 1927 he has been state supervisor in secondary education in the office of the state superintendent of public instruction.

On August 29, 1906, he was married to Bessie Belle Sharp at Liberty, Gage County, Nebraska. Mrs. Bowers was born at Liberty, July 11, 1884. Their two children are: Doren W., born June 4, 1909; and Loree E., born May 10, 1915.

During 1918 and 1919 Mr. Bowers served overseas with the American Young Men's Christian Association. He was county director of the Boys' Working Reserve in Sarpy County, during the war, and served as a member of the Advisory Registration Board, 1917-18. He is a member of the Nebraskana Society, the State Historical Society, the Odd Fellows, and the Masons. He has been a member of the Nebraska State Teachers Association since 1921, and in 1925 was district president of this organization in district five. He served as president of the Nebraska State Declamatory Association, 1923-24, was scoutmaster of the Boy Scouts of America, 1923-25, and held membership in the Red Cross, 1922-27. He is a Republican. He is interested in all out of door sports and is fond of reading. Residence: Lincoln.

Harry Eugene Bowman

On September 10, 1870, Harry Eugene Bowman was born at Lathrop, Missouri. His parents, Vincent and Elizabeth (Calder) Bowman, were natives of Ohio. Vincent Bowman was born in Brown County, January 19, 1831, where his family engaged in farming. He served for a short time as judge of the probate court, and died at San Antonio, Texas, December 7, 1913. His father was born in Amherst County, Virginia, in 1792, and his father's father in England. His father's grandfather was born in Switzerland.

Elizabeth Calder was born in Ohio, December 28, 1830,

and died at Cameron, Missouri, April 28, 1907. Her father was a native of Scotland, born in 1785.

Educated first in country school, Harry Eugene Bowman graduated from Missouri Wesleyan College (now Baker University, Baldwin, Kansas), in 1892, and attended business college at Cameron, Missouri. In 1892 Mr. Bowman became a bookkeeper in a lumber yard at Lawrence, Nebraska, from 1894 until 1910 he was manager of the business, and from 1910 to 1914 engaged in the milling business. For the last seventeen years he has been in real estate loans and insurance, and at present is the owner of H. E. Bowman and Company at Hastings. He is also a stockholder in the Hastings National Bank, and the owner of several farms.

On June 19, 1895, he was united in marriage to Effie Mae Fitch at Lawrence, Nebraska. She was born in Mason County, West Virginia, August 2, 1869, and died at Hastings, February 17, 1926. Her father, a Kentuckian, served in the Civil War. Mr. Bowman was married on July 3, 1928, to Bess Phillips, at Mankato, Minnesota. Mrs. Bowman was born at Patoka, Illinois, January 23, 1887.

A Republican, Mr. Bowman was a member of the Nebraska legislature the session of 1905-06, and from 1918-28, was a member of the Hastings city council. During the late war he was active in all civilian projects, and from 1926-32 has been a director of the local chapter of the Red Cross.

Mr. Bowman is one of Hastings' outstanding citizens, and is a leader in all efforts toward the betterment of his city and state. In 1930 he was president of the Chamber of Commerce, and since 1920 he has been a member of its board of directors. From 1906-14 he served as a member of the Lawrence School Board. He is affiliated with the First Methodist Episcopal Church, is a 32nd degree Mason and member of the Shrine, and is a member of the Young Men's Christian Association. Mr. Bowman was supervisor of the 1930 census for District 10 of Nebraska, composed of seven counties near Hastings. Residence: Hastings. (Photograph in Album).

Charles Johnston Boyd

Charles Johnston Boyd, a resident of Nebraska for the past 30 years, was born at Des Moines, Iowa, April 30, 1866, the son of Cyrus and Maggie (Johnston) Boyd. His father, who was born in Ohio, May 27, 1837, and died at Omaha, Nebraska, July 22, 1914, was a veteran of the Civil War and served as county clerk of Brown County, Nebraska; his ancestry was Scotch and Irish. His mother, whose ancestry was English and Scotch, was born at Keokuk, Iowa, May 13, 1840, and died at Ainsworth, Nebraska, August 12, 1898.

Mr. Boyd attended the public school until 1879, and for a number of years was a railroad agent and dispatcher. He has been engaged in the nursery and orchard business for the past 30 years at Ainsworth, and holds membership in the Nebraska State Horticultural Society. His hobby is reading.

He was united in marriage with Mary Addie Fowler at Dennison, Ohio, December 28, 1911. Mrs. Boyd was born of English parents in Iowa, April 21, 1872, and died at Ainsworth, May 28, 1929. They have a daughter, Margaret, born August 30, 1912. Residence: Ainsworth.

James William Boyd

James William Boyd, a lifetime resident of Nebraska, is the son of James Archibald and May (Robertson) Boyd. He was born at Kearney, Nebraska, July 15, 1896, and for many years has been active in business and civic affairs in his community. His father, who was born at Morrison, Illinois, was cashier of the Farmers State Bank at Kearney for 40 years, and is now retired from the banking business. His mother, an active club worker and church leader, was born at Morrison, of Scotch parentage.

Mr. Boyd was graduated from the Kearney High School in 1914, and from Culver Military Academy in 1915. He was a student at the University of Nebraska, where he was a member of Phi Gamma Delta and the Iron Sphinx, was chairman of the Freshman Hop, and was awarded the freshman scholarship cup of Phi Gamma Delta in 1917. From 1919 to 1925, Mr. Boyd was teller in the Farmers State Bank at Kearney, and since that date has been part owner and manager of the Golden Eagle Clothing Store there.

He is a member of the Kearney Chamber of Commerce, the Kearney Country Club, and the First Presbyterian Church. He is a Mason, holds membership in the Pinochle Club, and is interested in golfing, swimming, hunting, and fishing. His hobby is reading. On June 21, 1917, he enlisted in the United States Army, sailed for France the following month and was line sergeant for the remainder of the World War. He is a member of the American Legion as executive committeeman, and is a member of the Veterans of the Foreign Wars.

He was united in marriage with Nan Henrietta Mattson, at Wahoo, Nebraska, February 18, 1930. Mrs. Boyd, who was a private secretary prior to her marriage, was born in Sweden in 1903. Mr. Boyd has one daughter by a former marriage, Bobette, born March 25, 1919, who is a student at Brownell Hall in Omaha. Residence: Kearney.

Joseph Wesley Boyd

Joseph W. Boyd, lawyer, was born at Eckley, Colorado, November 3, 1894, and for twenty-eight years has resided in Nebraska. The son of Robert James and Barbara Elizabeth (Schwerer) Boyd, his father was a farmer and stockraiser. Robert J. Boyd was born in Newark, New Jersey, January 22, 1853, of a Scotch father and Irish mother. He died at Trenton, January 26, 1922. His wife, Barbara, was born at Blandinsville, Illinois, January 7, 1858, and is still living. Her parents were immigrants from Germany.

Educated in the public and high schools of Trenton, Nebraska, Joseph W. Boyd was graduated in May, 1913, and was a letterman there three years in basketball, baseball and football. He attended Peru State Teachers College, where he won first prize on the junior debating team, was editor in chief of the *Peruvian* (1916), and earned letters in football, basketball and baseball (1915-16). In January, 1923, Mr. Boyd was awarded his Bachelor of Laws degree from the University of Nebraska, with Order of the Coif. He is a member of Delta Theta Phi.

During 1916-17, Mr. Boyd was athletic coach and teacher of mathematics in the David City High School, and from 1917-20 was a farmer. From March, 1923, until January, 1924, he was engaged in the practice of law at Norfolk, and since the last date has practiced at Superior. For a time prior to 1926, he was a member of the law firm of Agee, Kiechel and Boyd, but since then has been in private practice. A Republican, he was defeated in the primary election of 1930 for nomination as county attorney, and at the present time is precinct chairman of the Nuckolls County central committee.

His marriage to Gladys Chaney was solemnized at Riverton, Iowa, July 10, 1917. Mrs. Boyd was born at Riverton, January 3, 1896. There is one child living and one deceased: Don Allison, born April 7, 1926; and Eleanor Joan, born August 12, 1924, who died July 5, 1925.

Mr. Boyd's religious affiliation is with the Methodist Episcopal Church. Since April, 1924, he has been a member of the Kiwanis Club, and for five years he served as secretary of the local club. At the present time he is lieutenant governor of Division V, Nebraska-Iowa District of Kiwanis International. A Mason, he is a member and officer of Superior Lodge No. 121, Ancient Free and Accepted Masons, a member of Tadmore Chapter No. 17, Royal Arch Masons, Damascus Council No. 14, Royal and

Select Masons, and Palmyra Commandery, No. 27, of the Knights Templar.

A lover of all sports, Mr. Boyd is particularly fond of golf. He maintains a membership in the University of Nebraska Club at Superior, and is a life member of The Nebraskana Society. He also belongs to the Nebraska State Bar Association and the Chamber of Commerce. Residence: Superior.

Robert Catron Boyd

Since November 22, 1884, Robert C. Boyd has been a resident of Nemaha County. Born at Upton, Franklin County, Pennsylvania, October 25, 1866, he is the son of Robert James and Susan C. (White) Boyd. Robert Boyd was born in southern Pennsylvania, January 4, 1834, and until about 25 years before his death was a merchant. During the Civil War he was captain of a regiment of Pennsylvania Volunteer Cavalry. He was of Scotch-Irish descent, the family being early settlers in Pennsylvania. Susan C. White was a native of Fulton County, Pennsylvania. Her father was English, and her mother of German birth. Her father was a physician. She died at Upton, Pennsylvania, August 20, 1897, while Robert J. Boyd died at Upton, December 30, 1922.

On April 24, 1890, Robert C. Boyd was married to Lillie B. Angle, at Welsh Run, Pennsylvania. Mrs. Boyd was a native of Welsh Run, born July 21, 1868. She is an active worker in the Presbyterian Church, and in welfare and community affairs. She is a member of the Order of Eastern Star and of the Daughters of the American Revolution. They have four children: Avis Angle, born February 6, 1891. Avis attended Stout Institute, was graduated from Bellevue College, and studied at Johns Hopkins University. She married William C. Atwater, and is active in the League of Women Voters, the Y. W. C. A., and the Woman's Club. She lives at Springfield, Massachusetts.

The second child, Mary Jane, was born June 28, 1895. She was graduated from South Institute, attended Nebraska University for one year, and has taught school in Nebraska and Minnesota, and is now home demonstration agent at Blue Earth, Minnesota. William N., born July 8, 1899, attended Mercersburg Academy (Pennsylvania) one year, and is special agent for the American Fire Insurance Company at Fremont. He is married to Carrie Hanks, and is the father of two sons.

John C., born December 26, 1905, attended Mercersburg Academy three years, Roxbury School at Cheshire, Massachusetts, one year, and is employed in the Carson National Bank.

Mr. Boyd is a Republican, and has served as secretary of the Republican county central committee and was a member of the state Republican central committee one term.

Entering the banking business upon his arrival in Nebraska forty-six years ago, Mr. Boyd has remained in it ever since. He started as bookkeeper, and is now cashier of the Carson National Bank. He is also president of the First National Bank at Johnson, Nebraska.

During the World War he was active in the sale of bonds, in which his bank went over the top in each drive, and was active in Red Cross work and other drives. He has been affiliated with the Presbyterian Church for many years and is an elder. He is a member of the Y. M. C. A., and president of the Nemaha area of the Boy Scouts of America, which embraces five counties. For the past eight years he has been treasurer of the local Red Cross organization, and is now president of the Kiwanis Club. He is a 32nd degree Mason, and a member of the Shrine, and a life member of the Lincoln Lodge of the Elks. He is also an Odd Fellow and member of the Ancient Order of United Workmen. His social club is the Auburn Country, and his hobby is golf. Residence: Auburn.

Robert James Boyd

Robert James Boyd, postmaster at Trenton, Nebraska, was born at Yuma, Colorado, February 24, 1893, and has resided in Nebraska for the past 28 years.

His father, Robert James Boyd, Sr., was born at Patterson, New Jersey, January 22, 1853, and died at Trenton, Nebraska, January 26, 1923. He was a lumberman and business man of Scotch-Irish descent. His wife, Barbara Elizabeth Schwerer, was born at Blandinsville, Illinois, January 6, 1859, and is still living at Trenton, Nebraska. Her ancestry is German.

Mr. Boyd attended the public schools, was graduated from high school and from the state normal school at Peru, Nebraska, in 1915. For two years thereafter he taught in Elmwood, Nebraska, High School. He then farmed for seven years near Trenton, Nebraska. For the past eight years he has been postmaster of Trenton.

During the late war Mr. Boyd served overseas one year as a private in the 137th Regiment, 35th Division. He participated in the St. Mihiel Offensive; Meuse-Argonne Offensive; Sondernach Offensive; and served on two sectors. He is a member of the American Legion, past commander of Stellges-Baker Post No. 337, past adjutant, and finance officer of his local post. He is a member of the League of Postmasters, the Commercial Club, and the Masons, a member of King Cyrus Chapter No. 35, Royal Arch Masons in McCook, Nebraska, and St. John Commandery No. 16, Knights Templar.

On June 25, 1919, he was married to Maude Harrison at Gering, Nebraska. Mrs. Boyd, who is of English and German ancestry, was born at Trenton, Nebraska, February 25, 1898. They have two children, Geraldine, born June 9, 1920; and Leonard, born June 6, 1924. Residence: Trenton.

Peter Friedrich Boyens

A pioneer furniture dealer at Plainview, Nebraska, Peter Friedrich Boyens was born in Germany, June 11, 1861, and has lived in Nebraska for the past 44 years. His father, Henry Boyens, who was a farmer, was born in Germany, and died at Denison, Iowa. His mother was born in Germany, and died at Denison.

Mr. Boyens is a mortician and furniture dealer, and holds membership in various civic organizations at Plainview, including Lions Club; the Commercial Club; the Red Cross; and the local undertakers society. He is affiliated with Zion Lutheran Church and holds membership in the Plainview Country Club. His favorite sport is golfing.

On October 7, 1894, he was united in marriage at Creighton, Nebraska, with Bertha Looft. Mrs. Boyens was born in Germany. Politically, Mr. Boyens is a Republican. Residence: Plainview.

William R. Boyer

William R. Boyer physician and surgeon, was born at Lena, Stephenson County, Illinois, April 2, 1871, and in 1882 came to Nebraska.

Dr. Boyer attended the public school, and was graduated from Falls City High School in 1886. He was graduated from the Hahnemann Medical College in 1894.

In 1916 he established the Pawnee Hospital, and in 1921 the Pawnee Medical Unit, by amalgamating all Pawnee City physicians into one firm. This association has continued for a period of eleven years.

Dr. Boyer is a member of the Pawnee County, Nebraska State, and American Medical Associations. He is also a member of the Nebraska State Historical Society. Residence: Pawnee City.

Clarence Clinton "Chick" Boyes

Clarence Clinton "Chick" Boyes, was born at Belleville, Kansas, February 9, 1890, son of Herman Lee and Marila Catherine (Wagner) Boyes.

His father was born in Geneva, New York, August 20, 1866, and has been postmaster of Hebron, for a number of years. His wife, Marila, was born in Oregon, Illinois, December 11, 1866, and since its organization in 1919, has been a member of the board of the Hebron Public Library. (See Nebraskana).

In 1909, Mr. Boyes was graduated from Hebron High School, and the following year attended the University of Nebraska. He was a school teacher for a short period, and musician and dramatic manager for the Hebron opera house and the picture theatre in 1914, 1915, and 1916. For one year, following, he was in Canada, and for five years in the United States with dramatic stock companies. Since that time, he has been the owner and manager of the Chick Boyes Players of Hebron.

He was married on July 8, 1914 to Florence Edna Gallant, at Hebron. She was born at Hebron, August 4, 1893, and is active in dramatic work with her husband.

Mr. Boyes is a Republican. He is a member of the Royal Highlanders, the Masons, and the Shrine, and a member of the Hebron Golf Club. His favorite sports are golf and hunting. Residence: Hebron. (Photograph in Album).

Herman Lee Boyes

Born at Geneva, New York, August 20, 1866, Herman Lee Boyes is the son of William Henry and Eliza Sarah (Wolverton) Boyes. His father, who was born at Monterey, New York, April 17, 1838, was a farmer and market gardener, who specialized in growing potatoes, at Geneva. He went west with Horace Greeley, came back in a stage coach and settled on a homestead in Republic County, Kansas, in 1870. His ancestry was English on the paternal side, his father having come to America in 1805. His mother, who was Irish came to the United States at the age of 19. William Henry Boyes died at Hebron, Nebraska, in October, 1923.

Eliza Sarah Wolverton was born at Tyrone, New York, October 8, 1842. After her graduation from Starkey Seminary, at Geneva, she taught school, first in New York State and later in Kansas, and was a member of the Teachers County Examination board. Her father was born in Germany and her mother in France. They were married in the United States. Eliza Wolverton Boyes died at Hebron, December 19, 1904.

Educated in a sod school house in Republic County, Kansas, Herman L. Boyes attended County Teachers Institute in Republic County, at Belleville, Kansas. Born on a farm, he engaged in farming and market gardening at Belleville and at Hebron until 1900. Thereafter he spent five years as a traveling salesman, and in January 1906 was elected clerk of the district court of Thayer County, on the Republican ticket.

Continuing in that office until October 1, 1923, he resigned upon his appointment as postmaster. He served two terms as mayor of Hebron (1921-23), and is still serving as postmaster. Mr. Boyes has never been defeated in any election.

On November 15, 1887, he was united in marriage to Marila Catherine Wagner at Belleville. Mrs. Boyes, who was born at Oregon, Illinois, December 11, 1866, attended the Marysville, Missouri, High School and Academy. She was a school teacher and bookkeeper for a time prior to her marriage. A member of the library board since the library was organized, she has been its secretary since 1923. Her parents were born in Maryland, and her grandparents in Germany.

To them were born three children, two of whom are living: Clarence C. "Chick," was born at Belleville, February 9, 1890. He is married to Florence Gallant, and is an actor and the owner of the Chick Boyes Players.

Bessie Belle, born October 1, 1888, is married to Walter Clarence Hess. They operate the Hebron Dairy Store. Floyd Lee, born June 11, 1891, died January 23, 1892. Prior to her marriage Bessie was a school teacher and postal clerk.

A Mason, Mr. Boyes is a member of the Royal Arch and Knight Templar bodies at Hebron, and Sesostris Temple of the Shrine at Lincoln. He is also a member of the Modern Woodmen of America, the Royal Highlanders and the Odd Fellows. From 1899 to 1918 he was chief of the Hebron Fire Department, and in 1912 was president of the Nebraska State Volunteer Firemen's Association.

From 1914-16 Mr. Boyes was a member of the Hebron School board, and during the World War was a member of the Home Guard, active in loan and Red Cross drives, and was a member of the finance committee of the Red Cross at Hebron. He is a Methodist. A member of the Hebron Golf Club, he enjoys golf, baseball and hiking, while his hobbies are reading and mechanics. Residence: Hebron. (Photograph in Album).

William Edwin Boyes

Born at Belleville, Kansas, October 25, 1889, William Edwin Boyes is the son of Elmer Ellsworth and Rosalind (Thompson) Boyes. His father, a grocer and market gardener, was born at Geneva, New York, November 27, 1861, and died at Hebron, October 22, 1924. His grandfather came to America in 1805 from England. His wife, Rosalind was born at Prairie du Chien, Wisconsin, October 30, 1865, and traces her lineage to pre-Revolutionary settlers.

William E. Boyes was graduated from Hebron High School in June, 1908, attended the University of Nebraska two years, and was graduated from the voice department of the Hebron College School of Music in June 1926. For eighteen years he engaged in the grocery business with his father, and for the past three years he has been the owner of Boyes Bootery. He is also administrator of the E. E. Boyes Estate. For some time he has been a member of the park board.

On June 28, 1911, he was united in marriage to Bessie Bell Kleppinger at Fairmont. Mrs. Boyes was born at Carleton, Nebraska, April 13, 1890. There are three children: Phyllis, born July 27, 1912, was graduated from Hebron High School. She has graduated from Hebron College (teacher's and piano school) and is teaching at Morrill, Nebraska. William, Jr., born December 11, 1915, is a junior in high school, and assists his father in his business. Earl Melvin, who is an excellent pianist, is a freshman in high school.

Mr. Boyes is a member of the First Methodist Episcopal Church, the Chamber of Commerce, Kiwanis Club, Masons, Order of Eastern Star and the Nebraskana Society. He has an exceptional voice, is fond of singing and amateur theatricals, and enjoys a game of golf occasionally. Residence: Hebron. (Photograph in Album).

Earl Mills Boyington

Earl Mills Boyington, banker, was born at Osawatomie, Kansas, September 29, 1893, the son of John and Alda (Syphrit) Boyington. His father died at Bird City, Kansas, in 1918. His mother died at Osawatomie, October 1, 1893.

Mr. Boyington was graduated from the Kemper Military School at Boonville, Missouri in 1911, attended Baker University at Baldwin, Kansas, and was a student in mechanical engineering at the University of Kansas.

He is treasurer of the local Young Men's Christian Association, is affiliated with the Presbyterian Church, and holds membership in the Independent Order of Odd Fellows, the Modern Woodmen of America, and the Ancient Order of United Workmen. He is Past High Priest of the Royal Arch Masonry, is a member of the Salina

Consistory and Shrine and holds the 32nd degree. Mr. Boyington is Worthy Patron of the Order of Eastern Star. His sports include baseball, tennis, volley ball, and handball.

On November 29, 1916, he married Essie Mae McDonald at Hutchinson, Kansas. Mrs. Boyington was born at Holton, Kansas, November 16, 1893. Residence: McCook.

John Morris Boyle

John Morris Boyle, teacher, was born at Ralston, Oklahoma, May 13, 1902. He is the son of John and Cora Nettie (Bradley) Boyle, the former of Canadian birth and of Scotch-Irish descent. The mother was born in Illinois, daughter of J. D. Bradley, a veteran of the Civil War.

He attended grade school in Otoe and Pawnee Counties, Oklahoma, and Gordon, Nebraska, entering high school at Gordon, and graduating from Casper, Wyoming in 1923. He received his Bachelor of Science degree in education from the University of Nebraska in 1929.

On July 16, 1927, he was married to Zona Tessel Beutler at Humboldt, Nebraska. Mrs. Boyle was born at Humboldt, Nebraska, July 16, 1901. She attended the rural schools of Richardson County, Nebraska, graduating from the high school at Humboldt in 1919, later attending the state university with credits for three years work. Her parents were both born and raised near Humboldt, Nebraska, of Swiss descent. Mr. and Mrs. Boyle were the parents of one child, Sammy Gene, born June 8, 1929, who died in infancy.

During the school years of 1926-27-28, Mr. Boyle taught in the high school of Stella, Nebraska, and for the past two years has been superintendent of schools at Haigler, Nebraska. Previous to that time he was principal of the Haigler High School.

A regret expressed by Mr. Boyle is that during his school days he was unable to take an active part in the athletics of his school, because of his inability to spare the time from his other duties that enabled him to attend school and college.

Both Mr. and Mrs. Boyle are actively identified with the Methodist Episcopal Church in which they hold memebership. Residence: Haigler.

William Lincoln Bozarth

For the past 48 years William L. Bozarth has lived in Nebraska where he has been successful in the business world. He was born at Chapin, Illinois, September 1, 1865, the son of John Carlack and Harriet (Tichnor) Bozarth. His father, who was a farmer and grain and livestock dealer, was born at Chapin, December 26, 1826, and died at San Jose, California, January, 1911; his ancestry was French. His mother was born in Chapin, Illinois, in 1832, and died at Beatrice, Nebraska, in 1901.

Mr. Bozarth received his education in the public schools. He has been retired from active business for several years and maintains his home at Hebron where he is chiefly interested in gardening and improving his lawn and grounds. Politically, he is a Democrat. Recently he was elected to membership in the Nebraskana Society.

He married Delana Poole at Beatrice, December 31, 1885; she was born at Chapin, May 2, 1866, of English parentage, and died at Long Beach, California, May 2, 1924. Four children were born to this marriage: Walter N., born January 29, 1888, who married Edith Tichnor; Genevieve G., born May 23, 1890, who married Christian W. Alschwede; Olive B., born January 26, 1892, who married H. B. Wright; and Elton P., born October 2, 1901, who is a physician. Walter N. and all his family were killed in an automobile accident August 23, 1931.

On October 16, 1925, Mr. Bozarth was married to Minnie R. Hyland at Stockton, Kansas. Mr. and Mrs.

Bozarth attend the First Presbyterian Church at Hebron. Residence: Hebron.

Waldorf Hartman Brach

Born at Hastings, Nebraska, March 11, 1895, Waldorf Hartman Brach is the son of William and Charlotte (Hartman) Brach. His father, a native of Germany, born April 3, 1854, came to Racine, Wisconsin, in 1865, and to Nebraska in 1876. Here he was for many years in the mercantile business, for forty years as president of Wolbach & Brach. He died at Hastings, on March 21, 1921. His wife was born at Grand Rapids, Michigan, April 21, 1861.

Waldorf H. Brach attended the public schools of Hastings, and was graduated from high school there. At the present time he is president of Wolbach and Brach, and is a director of the Nebraska National Bank. During the World War he was sergeant of Company F, 355th Infantry, 89th Division, and is now a member of the American Legion.

On September 10, 1924, Mr. Brach was united in marriage to Helen Marie Youngson, at Minden. Mrs. Brach, who is of German and Danish extraction, was born at Minden, April 20, 1899. The family attends the Presbyterian Church at Hastings.

A Mason, Mr. Brach is a member of the Shrine, and belongs to the Elks and the Hastings Chamber of Commerce. Recently he was elected to life membership in the Nebraskana Society. He is a Democrat. Residence: Hastings.

Benjamin H. Bracken

Benjamin H. Bracken was born at Wallace, Kansas, August 16, 1888, the son of Reed P. and Floretta Jane (Erskine) Bracken. Reed P. Bracken, his father, was born in Pennsylvania, October 17, 1842; he served as a Civil War soldier; his Scotch ancestors came to this country prior to the Revolution. His mother, whose ancestry is English, was born in Ohio, December 16, 1854, and died at Hastings, Nebraska, November 30, 1926.

Mr. Bracken was graduated from the preparatory department of Emporia College in Kansas, was graduated from Hastings College with the B. S. degree in 1913, and in 1917, attended the college of law at the University of Nebraska. He served as superintendent of schools at Potter, Nebraska, 1914-16, was superintendent of schools at Minden, Nebraska, 1919-22, and since 1922, has been engaged in the practice of law at Minden, in the firm King & Bracken.

He was united in marriage with Helen Octavia Jones at Hastings, August 27, 1919. Mrs. Bracken, who was born at Hastings, December 16, 1893, is a member of the Daughters of the American Revolution; her ancestors were natives of New England and New York. Their children are: Octavia Jane, born October 30, 1920; and Benjamin Howard, born June 27, 1928.

He was president of the Community Commerce Club for two years and was director for a number of years, was president of the board of education, 1929-31, and was a charter member of the Minden Rotary club. He is a member of the Nebraska State Bar Association, the American Bar Association, the Masons, and the Knights of Pythias.

He is affiliated with the First Presbyterian Church of Minden, and holds membership in the American Legion. During the World War he held the rank of second lieutenant, served in France, from 1917 to 1919, and was honorably discharged February 22, 1919. He is a Republican. Residence: Minden.

Daniel Chester Bradbury

Daniel Chester Bradbury was born at Oskaloosa, Iowa, September 6, 1888, the son of Daniel and Mary (Conner) Bradbury. His father, who was a merchant, was born in

County Kent, England, in 1847, and died at Oskaloosa, February 12, 1921. His mother, who was of Scotch-Irish and Welsh ancestry, was born in Iowa, February 10, 1849, and died at Oskaloosa, March 16, 1927; she was the granddaughter of John Stanley.

Mr. Bradbury was graduated from the Oskaloosa High School in 1907, and studied a year at the University of Iowa. He served as manager of a clothing store at Albion, Iowa, for two years, and traveling salesman for a clothing firm for three years, and is now owner and manager of a cleaning plant at Alliance, Nebraska.

He is a member of the Chamber of Commerce of which he is vice president, is past president of the Rotary Club, and holds membership in the Masons and Elks. His social club is the Alliance Country Club of which he is director. He is affiliated with the American Legion, acting as post commander at Alliance.

His marriage to Jessie Garfield Andrew was solemnized at Chariton, Iowa, December 30, 1917. Mrs. Bradbury, whose father served in the Civil War, was born at Chariton, September 10, 1886. Residence: Alliance.

Leah Bellman Bradbury

Leah B. Bradbury was born at Omaha, Nebraska, the daughter of Mark and Eva (Kahn) Bellman. Her father, a merchant, was born March 7, 1858, and died at Omaha, March 11, 1902. Her mother was born April 14, 1861, and died at Omara, February 23, 1923.

Mrs. Bradbury received her education in the grade and high schools of Omaha. She has been active in public life in Omaha for the past 25 years and has served every administration of the Chamber of Commerce since 1904. She is now secretary of the Membership Service Bureau of the Omaha Chamber of Commerce.

Her marriage to William Jay Bradbury was solemnized at David City, Nebraska, May 19, 1928. Dr. Bradbury, who was born at Platteville, Wisconsin, is an Omaha dentist.

She is a member of the National Geographic Society; the Nebraskana Society; the Women's Division of the Chamber of Commerce; and the Red Cross. She holds membership in the Order of Eastern Star; the Altrusa Club; and the Delphian Society. She is a Republican. Residence: Omaha.

Juliana Braddock

Juliana Braddock, ranchwoman, was born at Nevada, Iowa, March 10, 1879, daughter of John H. and Theodora T. (Tow) Jacobson. The father was born in Norway, July 4, 1854, and died at Chadron, Nebraska, October 9, 1930. He was a farmer and ranchman who came to America from Norway with his parents at the age of one year. Theodora T. Tow was born in Norway, July 28, 1854 and died at Mullen, Nebraska, January 1, 1928. She came to the United States at the age of 13 with her parents.

Juliana Jacobson attended district school in Sheridan County and high school in Rushville.

On March 28, 1899, she was married to William Braddock at Chadron, Nebraska. Mr. Braddock was born at Marshalltown, Iowa, December 26, 1856, and died at Chadron, January 7, 1917. He was a prominent ranchman, of English ancestry. There are two children, Gladys, born April 24, 1900, who married Alford Lee Isham, and Wilma Doris, born February 10, 1906, who is single.

Mrs. Braddock has been a resident of Nebraska since 1885. In her early life she taught school, and after her marriage made a home for her husband. Since his death she has managed the ranch raising registered Hereford cattle, draft and saddle horses, Duroc-Jersey hogs, and White Leghorn chickens in addition to raising alfalfa hay.

Mrs. Braddock is active in the Chadron Women's Club which was organized in her home in 1909. She is a member of the board of education of the Chadron Public Schools also. She enjoys horseback riding, while her hobbies are reading and the study of present day economics. Residence: Chadron.

Harry Elwyn Bradford

Harry Elwyn Bradford, educator at the University of Nebraska since 1912, has lived in this state for the past 47 years, and has taken a prominent part in educational activities. He was born at Sheboygan, Wisconsin, February 12, 1878, the son of Dewitt A. and Almeda Velma (Crocker) Bradford. His father, who was born at Plymouth, Wisconsin, in 1848, and died at Minden, Nebraska, October 12, 1902, was a merchant. He was descended from the Bradford family who came from England in the early history of the country and settled in Massachusetts. His mother was born at Sheboygan, in 1853, and died at Lincoln, Nebraska, October 4, 1912; she was directly descended from Priscilla Alden.

Professor Bradford attended the public schools of Nebraska, and in 1897 was graduated from the Orleans Academy. He received the A. B. degree, 1904, and the A. M. degree, 1917, from the University of Nebraska. He is a member of Gamma Sigma Delta, Alpha Gamma Rho and Alpha Zeta. He was a student at Columbia University in New York City in 1922. In 1932 he received the Ph. D. degree from Cornell University, Ithaca, New York.

He taught in high school, was principal of city schools, and superintendent, at Chadron, Aurora, and Kearney, Nebraska. He has been professor of vocational education at the University of Nebraska since 1912, serving as chairman of the department. He is the author of *Geography and Agriculture of Nebraska.* He is a member of the Nebraska State Teachers' Association, American Vocational Association, the Lincoln Chamber of Commerce, and the Nebraskana Society. He is a member of the Rotary Club and of the Masonic Order. He is affiliated with First Plymouth Congregational Church at Lincoln. His sport is golf, and his hobby is music.

He was married to Ethel King at Geneva, Nebraska, December 27, 1904. Mrs. Bradford was born at Bedford, Iowa, June 25, 1880. They have one daughter, Eloise, born December 11, 1911. Politically, Professor Bradford is an independent. Residence: Lincoln.

Edward Leonidas Bradley

Edward L. Bradley, distinguished lawyer of Nebraska, has lived in this state for over 40 years and has engaged in the practice of law at Omaha, since 1896. He was born at Springfield, Sangamon County, Illinois, November 1, 1870, the son of Leonidas Hamline and Abagail Lucretia (Manly) Bradley. His father, who was born at Patriot, Ohio, July 23, 1842, and died at Omaha, May 6, 1913, was a lawyer; he was assistant acting adjutant general at Fort Pickering, Tennessee, during the Civil War; he received his A. B. and A. M. degrees at Ohio Wesleyan University.

His mother was born in Marshall County, Illinois, May 3, 1847, and died at Omaha, August 19, 1927. She was graduated from the Bettie Stuart Institute at Springfield; she was the oldest daughter of Uri Manly, lawyer, state senator, probate judge, and a member of the Illinois constitutional convention. He was quartermaster in the United States Army.

Mr. Bradley was graduated from the Omaha Central High School in 1891, and in 1896 was awarded the LL. B. degree at the University of Omaha. He was a student at the University of Pennsylvania, 1891-92. He was editor of the Omaha High School *Register*, 1890-91.

He was united in marriage with Luna May Powell at Omaha, June 17, 1903. Mrs. Bradley was born at Sand Lake, Michigan, October 4, 1881, the only daughter of George S. and Lucy J. Powell. They have two children, Edward Leonidas, and George H.

Mr. Bradley is a member of the Nebraskana Society. During the World War he was a four minute man and a member of the Douglas County Advisory Board. He was the founder of the Omaha law class which afterward became merged in, and known as, the law department of the University of Omaha. He was the founder of the Omaha Avocation Club later known as the Concord Club. He was connected with the founding of the Omaha Athletic Club. He is justice of the supreme forum, of the Loyal Order of Moose, and a Mason, Nebraska Lodge Number 1, Tangier Temple, Shrine, Mount Calvary Commandery, and Knight Templar. He is past regent of the Royal Arcanum. He is a Republican. Residence: Omaha.

Edwin Bruce Bradley

One of the leading professional men at Spencer, Nebraska, is Edwin Bruce Bradley, who was born at Charles City, Iowa, June 12, 1879, the son of John Stratton and Susan Martin (Newell) Bradley. He was graduated from the high school at Charles City, Iowa, in 1896, and received the M. D. degree at Rush Medical College in 1903, where he was a member of Delta Tau Delta and Nu Sigma Nu.

Dr. Bradley was admitted to the practice of medicine at Chicago, Illinois, in 1903, and since 1912 has been a practicing physician at Spencer. He is a director in the Spencer State Bank, holds membership in the Nebraska Society, and is a Mason. His political affiliation is with the Republican party.

On March 6, 1911, he was married at Des Moines, Iowa, to Josephine Momsen, who was born at Grand View, South Dakota. Residence: Spencer.

Elmer Leo Bradley

Elmer Leo Bradley was born at Exeter, Nebraska, June 25, 1897, the son of Frank M. and Lizetta M. (Schneider) Bradley. His father, who is a retired business man, was born in Pennsylvania, February 8, 1861; his ancestry is Irish. His mother was born of German parentage, in Iowa, February 20, 1868.

Mr. Bradley attended the country schools of Fillmore County, Nebraska, and in 1913, was graduated from the high school at Geneva. He was assistant cashier of the Hebron State Bank for a time, was secretary-treasurer of the Shickley Grain Company, and is now cashier of the Shickley State Bank, Shickley, Nebraska.

A Republican, he served as township treasurer for four years, village trustee two years, and mayor of Shickley, two years. He is affiliated with St. Mary's Catholic Church at Shickley, holds membership in the Knights of Columbus, and is a member of the Nebraskana Society. Mr. Bradley served as a first class private in the World War and is a member of the American Legion.

On June 30, 1920, he was married to Addie P. Spangler, in Fillmore County. Mrs. Bradley was born in Chase County, Nebraska, May 14, 1896, and for six years prior to her marriage was county superintendent of schools in that county. They have four children: Elmer Leo, Jr., born November 14, 1921; Betty Joan, born January 13, 1925; Gene Marie, born August 13, 1928; and Paul Francis, born August 2, 1931. Residence: Shickley.

DeEmmett Bradshaw

DeEmmett Bradshaw, a prominent lawyer of Omaha, Douglas County, Nebraska, was born at Izard, Arkansas, the son of David Corroll and Emily Frances (Meredith) Bradshaw. His father, who was born in Tennessee, and died in Arkansas, in 1907, was a farmer. His mother was born in Mississippi, April 3, 1837, and is still living in Arkansas.

Mr. Bradshaw attended the country schools of Arkansas, and later was a student at the national normal university at Lebanon, Ohio, where he was graduated with a B. S. Degree. He also graduated from the Arkansas Law School. He has practiced law at Omaha since 1916, and is now general attorney for the Woodmen of the World Life Insurance Company. A Democrat, Mr. Bradshaw held the offices of chairman of the city Democrat Committee at Little Rock, Arkansas, and some other offices.

He was president of the Arkansas Humane Society, and the Arkansas Sunday School Association. He was affiliated with the Methodist Episcopal Church of Little Rock, and was superintendent of the Sunday School for 12 years, and is now a member of the First Methodist Church of Omaha. His Omaha clubs include: Happy Hollow, Omaha Athletic, and Omaha Club. He is a Mason and a member of the Woodmen of the World.

He married Nellie Shorthill at Little Rock. Mrs. Bradshaw is a musician and composer; she was born in McDonald County, Missouri. Three children were born to them: Melba, born May 21, 1899, who married John B. Dawson, who was graduated from the law school at the University of Nebraska; Ellen Frances, born January 10, 1905, who married Mason S. Zerbe, a graduate of Ames College; and DeEmmett, born April 5, 1903, who died June 30, 1916. Residence: Omaha.

Archie Lee Bradstreet

Archie Lee Bradstreet was born at Sanborn, Iowa, January 19, 1888, the son of E. Thomas and Mary Luella Bradstreet, and for the past 31 years has been a resident of Grand Island, Nebraska.

His father who was formerly a state senator of Nebraska, was born at Quasqueton, Iowa, February 14, 1866, and is a descendant of a colonial governor of Massachusetts. He was united in marriage to Mary Luella Bidinger on November 25, 1886, at Quasqueton, Iowa. He went to Sanborn, Iowa, and in the fall of 1888 removed to Sioux City, Iowa, and in 1900 located at Grand Island, Nebraska. Mrs. Bradstreet, whose ancestry is Scotch and German, was born at Quasqueton, June 24, 1867, and died at Lincoln, Nebraska, in February, 1919.

Mr. Bradstreet was graduated from the Sioux City High School and later attended business college there. At this time he is secretary-treasurer of the Bradstreet & Clemens Company of Grand Island, Nebraska, and is a member of the Grand Island bodies of the Elks and Masons. He is a member of the Woodland Golf Club and his chief recreations are golfing, reading, and hunting. He is the holder of 48 medals and cups which he has won at different times, both in Wyoming and Nebraska.

His marriage to Helen Anna Lykke was solemnized at Grand Island, August 9, 1912. Mrs. Bradstreet, whose ancestry is Danish, was born at Grand Island, March 16, 1889. To them were born, Hazel, December 28, 1916; Thomas, January 24, 1918, who died May 6, 1922; and Marian, September 20, 1919. Residence: Grand Island. (Photograph in Album).

Archie Lee Bradt

Born at Ord, Nebraska, June 11, 1882, Archie Lee Bradt is the son of Aaron V. and Clara Jane (Blodgett) Bradt. His father, who was a farmer and served as second lieutenant in the Union Army during the Civil War, was born of Dutch and Irish parents at Amsterdam, New York, October 17, 1836, and died at Ord, July 20, 1906. His mother, whose ancestry was Dutch, was born at Clinton, Wisconsin, February 11, 1858.

Mr. Bradt clerked in a mercantile establishment for seven years, was a drayman and expressman for eight years, engaged in farming and the dairy business for seven years, and for over 10 years was the proprietor of a cafe. For the past three years he has operated an oil station at Ord, where he is active in civic affairs.

He served as director in the local Chamber of Commerce during 1923 and 1924, was president of the Fire Department, 1910-12, was a member of the local Library Board in 1924, and served on the Ord School Board from 1920 to 1924. Since 1906 he has been a member of the Masons.

His marriage to Myrtle Josephine Peterson was solemnized at Ord, June 19, 1907. Mrs. Bradt, whose ancestry is Norwegian, was born at Creston, Iowa, December 16, 1884. They have three children: Evelyn, born January 21, 1908, who married Lores McMindes; Frances, born August 25, 1909; and Ruth, born August 26, 1911. Ruth and Frances are stenographers. Mr. Bradt is active in politics and is a progressive Democrat. Residence: Ord.

Carmen Brady

Carmen Brady, daughter of Dwight Albert and Florence Cornelia (Shafer) Jones, was born at Milford, Nebraska, March 1, 1889. Her father, who was born at Fowler, Ohio, March 1, 1852, is a stockman. Her mother was born at Cortland, Ohio, April 12, 1856.

Mrs. Brady attended the rural school of District No. 76 in Seward County until 1903, Pleasant Dale High School, 1904, and Nebraska Wesleyan Academy 1905-08, graduating in 1908. In 1913 she took special work at the University of Colorado. After teaching in the rural schools of Seward County two years she taught the primary room of the Denton grade school two years, 1910-11; and was married to Clarence Carlos Brady at Pleasant Dale, Nebraska, May 21, 1914. She was divorced from him in 1926. There is one daughter, Dorothy, born July 29, 1918, who is a student at the Malcolm Studio of Expression at Lincoln.

At the present time Mrs. Brady is looking after the business interests of her father who is a retired farmer and stockman. A Republican, she has served on election boards, as a committeewoman and as census enumerator. She is the author of several poems and songs used in school and community activities. A leader in educational work, she is at the present time a member and president of both the Parent-Teachers' Association and the Board of Education. She is a member of the Methodist Episcopal Church, and of the church board and the Ladies' Aid Society. She is affiliated with the Southeast Seward County Home Circle Club, of which she was secretary two years, 1922-23. She is fond of writing poetry, and growing flowers, and is a member of The Nebraskana Society. Residence: Denton. (Photograph in Album).

Frank John Brady

A leading business executive of Atkinson, Nebraska, is Frank John Brady, who is manager of a coal, grain, and hay business in that community. He was born at Atkinson, September 15, 1894, the son of John Franklin and Ella (Shaw) Brady, the former a rancher and business man, who was born at Kankakee, Illinois, October 20, 1857, of French and Irish parents. His father, who was in the coal and grain business for a number of years, died at Atkinson, September 1, 1931. His mother, whose ancestry was Irish, was born at Joliet, Illinois, April 14, 1864.

Mr. Brady was graduated from the Atkinson High School in 1914, and from 1914 to 1917 and in 1920 he was a student at the University of Nebraska where he was a member of Alpha Sigma Phi. He worked in a bank for a time, was purchasing agent for the Game, Forestation & Parks Commission, and is now manager of the J. F. Brady Company at Atkinson.

He served as vice president of the Nebraska Division of the Izaak Walton League, 1924, was state president, 1925-29, served as a member of the National Executive Committee in 1926, and was national director of that organization, 1925 to 1931. He is a member of the Atkinson Commercial Club, the Booster Club, Lions Club, and the Atkinson Country Club. Mr. Brady is a Scottish Rite Mason, is affiliated with the Presbyterian Church, and holds membership in the American Legion of which he was adjutant in 1920 and in 1931. He is interested in football, golfing, fishing, and hunting.

During the World War he served as ordnance sergeant, and participated in the engagements at Champagne-Marne, Meuse-Argonne, Aisne-Marne, and St. Mi-

hiel, with the American Expeditionary Forces. A Republican, he was once a candidate for the state senate.

On July 12, 1930, he was married at Red Oak, Iowa, to Louella Theolyn Olson. who was born of Norwegian parents at Rudd, Iowa, January 24, 1903. Residence: Atkinson. (Photograph on Page 148).

Thomas Edmund Brady

Thomas Edmund Brady, lawyer, was born in Cayuga County, New York, January 29, 1871, and since 1906 has been a resident of Nebraska. His father, John Brady, was born in Prescott, Canada, January 29, 1827, and came to New York, in 1847. He was a farmer, a soldier and sailor. He died at Dunlap, Iowa, November 1, 1905. He married Mary Welch, a native of Waterford, Ireland. Mrs. Brady died at Dunlap, March 4, 1897.

Upon his graduation from Dunlap High School in 1891, Thomas E. Brady entered the State University of Iowa, where he received his LL. B. in June, 1897. Since that time he has been actively engaged in the practice of law.

His marriage to Pearl Evangeline Randall was solemnized at Dunlap, June 23, 1897. Mrs. Brady was born at Pomeroy, Iowa, February 24, 1872, and is of American descent for several generations. She is state inspector of labor for Nebraska. There is one son, Richard Randall, born July 15, 1900. He is married to Patti Atkisson, and is engaged in the practice of medicine at Livingston, Montana.

Mr. Brady is a Republican. During the World War he was secretary of draft board number four of Douglas County. He is affiliated with the First Central Congregational Church. He is a member of the Sons of Union Veterans, the Nebraska State Bar Association, the Omaha-Douglas County Bar Association, The Nebraskana Society, and of the Odd Fellows, the Modern Woodmen of America and the Royal Neighbors of America. Residence: Omaha.

Robert Lee Bragg

Born at Hinton, West Virginia, November 16, 1867, Robert Lee Bragg has been a resident of Nebraska for forty-nine years. He is the son of John Hudson and Caroline (Hopkins) Bragg, the former a farmer of French descent, who is deceased. Caroline Hopkins was born in Pipertown, West Virginia, and died at Elwood, on September 10, 1909.

Educated in country schools, Robert Lee Bragg has been prominent in the affairs of his community almost ever since. As a young man he learned the barber's trade, which he is still following. He is now serving his twentieth year as chairman of the county board, and is in his fourteenth year as sheriff of Gosper County.

During the World War period he served as chairman of the war board, and was appointed clerk of the board at the close of the war. He was also active in loan drives and Red Cross work. He is a member of the Modern Woodmen of America, and for forty-one years has been an Odd Fellow. He is affiliated with the Methodist Episcopal Church, and the Epworth League, the Commercial Club and The Nebraskana Society. He enjoys football and hiking, and his hobby is music.

On September 20, 1895, Mr. Bragg was married to Nettie Margaret Moore at Montrose, Colorado. She was born at Dorchester, Nebraska, on September 15, 1876, the daughter of J. J. and Margaret Moore. To them eight children were born, one of whom died in infancy. The others are: William Lee, born October 4, 1896; Ivan, born September 10, 1899, died December 15, 1919; Beulah, born February 11, 1901; Helen, born March 15, 1903; Louis, born September 4, 1905; Earl, born May 3, 1907; and Francis, born October 5, 1912. William Lee works on the railroad, while Lewis and Earl are teaching in high school. Beulah is married to William McKenzie, and Helen to Ben Houlden. Residence: Elwood.

Barnett—Lincoln

FRANK JOHN BRADY

JOHN BELL BRAIN

Heyn—Omaha

John Bell Brain

John Bell Brain, son of Edwin Bell and Melvina Free-love (Leech) Brain, was born at Defiance, Iowa, February 18, 1888. Edwin Bell Brain was born in London, England, March 27, 1852. He settled first in Iowa and then in Nebraska, where he served as county treasurer of Rock County. He was founder and president of the Omaha School Supply Company at the time of his death in Omaha, March 26, 1923. His wife, Melvina Brain, was born in Lucas, Iowa, August 8, 1872.

Educated in the Omaha public schools, Mr. Brain was graduated from Central High School in June, 1907, and attended the University of Nebraska from 1908-11, when he received his LL.B. He is a member of Phi Delta Phi and Phi Gamma Delta.

Upon his graduation from college he entered upon his business career in association with his father. After his father's death in 1923 he became president of the National School Supply Dealers Association. He is president of the Omaha School Supply Company, president of the Omaha Central Radio Company, the Omaha Central Paper Company, the Chicago School Supply Company and the Kansas City School Supply Company.

He was elected to the Nebraska state house of representatives from Douglas County in 1913 on the Republican ticket, and is active in party politics.

He held the rank of sergeant in the Nebraska State Militia from 1915-17, and participated in all Liberty loan drives during the World War. He attends Dundee Presbyterian Church and is a member of the Young Men's Christian Association.

He is a Mason and a member of the Shrine, and also an Elk and Modern Woodman of America. He is a Rotarian and member of the A. B. C. Club and the Chamber of Commerce. His favorite sport is golf and his hobby is philately. He is a member of the Omaha Athletic Club and Happy Hollow Country Club·

On June 4, 1912 he was married to Jessie Spence at Omaha. Mrs. Brain, who is of Scotch descent, was born at Kearney, Nebraska, April 15, 1890. There are three children born to them, two of whom are deceased. Dorothy L., born September 18, 1914, died November 13, 1914; and Robert W., born December 28, 1917, died January 1, 1918. John B., Jr., born December 11, 1915, is living. Residence: Omaha. (Photograph on Page 149).

Alanson Pullman Brainard

Alanson Pullman Brainard was born August 21, 1870, in Saunders County, Nebraska, the son of Henry Harrison Brainard and Cornelia (Pullman) Brainard. His father was born at Norway, Herkimer County, New York, August 14, 1847, and was a farmer and member of the New York Volunteers in the Civil War. He is the eighth descendant of Daniel Brainard, the first of the family of Brainards having come to this country in 1649 and settled near Haddam, Connecticut. Henry H. Brainard came to Nebraska in 1868, and homesteaded near Cedar Bluffs, Nebraska. His brother, Brigadier General D. L. Brainard, was a member of the Greeley Polar Expedition and now resides in Washington, D. C. Henry Brainard was a director in the Farmer's and Merchant's Bank at Cedar Bluffs, was a Mason, a member of the Eastern Star and the Woodman of the World.

Alanson Brainard's mother was born at Norway, New York, July 11, 1844, and died in Cedar Bluffs, January 17, 1922. She was educated in a private seminary, and was the daughter of Isaac and Carolina (Bly) Pullman. She was affiliated with the Episcopal Church of Fremont and was a member of the Woman's Club.

Mr. Brainard attended rural school and the Fremont High School. He was united in marriage to Amelia Frahm Brunner, June 28, 1905, at Fremont, where she was born January 4, 1877. To this union three children were born: Charles, April 11, 1906, who died April 14, 1906; Alanson David, September 15, 1907, is a graduate of

Midland College, class of 1928, and is married to Clara Stafford; and Hollis Harrison, February 2, 1910.

Alanson is superintendent of the schools at Carleton, Nebraska, and Hollis is a second lieutenant in the Officer's Reserve Corps of the United States Army, and was chosen as Saunders County's best young citizen in 1928.

Mr. Brainard is a Democrat. He has lived in Nebraska since 1870, during which time he has engaged in farming. Residence: Cedar Bluffs.

Henry Allen Brainerd

Henry Allen Brainerd, newspaper man and historian, was born at Boston, Massachusetts, November 4, 1857, son of Henry Hall and Maria Lucy (Stetson) Brainerd.

The father was born at South Hadley, Massachusetts, June 13, 1832, and died at Providence, Rhode Island, October 28, 1901. He was a commercial traveler, practically all his life, crossed the Atlantic several times. Lyman Brainerd was a tanner in St. Albans, Vermont, who was killed about 1856, from a fall through an elevator. He was a descendent from the 6th child of Daniel Brainerd, the first member of the family in the United States.

Maria Lucy Stetson was born in Greene, Maine, September 16, 1832, and died at Charlestown, Massachusetts, September 14, 1862. She died when Henry Allen Brainerd was four years of age. She was what would be called today a deaconess in the Methodist Episcopal Church, and did much good among the poor of the city. Turner Stetson and Thankful Lombard are her ancestors. Her father was born in 1788, and died in 1847, while her mother was born in 1795, and died in 1848. They were married in 1811.

Mr. Brainerd attended public school in Boston, and Providence, Rhode Island. He attended the Kent's Hill Seminary, in Maine, 1878-79, and Middletown University for a short time. Afterwards he attended the night sessions of Brown University at Providence. He started in the printing business in 1865 at Boston. He was graduated from Bryant and Stratton's Business College at Providence in 1875, the youngest graduate at the university, at that time. For a short time he worked on the newspapers in Boston, Providence, New York, Chicago, and other large cities.

Mr. Brainerd came to Nebraska in 1883, and was a newspaper man in Lincoln, Milford, Sutton, Bennett, Chester and Hebron. At the present time, he is engaged in writing features and short stories for various papers. He is the author of *Nebraska Press History, History of the Young Men's Christian Association, 1844-1890,* and several short articles, in addition to newspaper stories. A Republican, he was one of the three organizers of the first Blaine and Logan Club at Milford, organized the first Ladies Marching Club at Milford in 1890, and the first Broom Brigade, McKinley Marching Club in 1896 at Chester.

On August 17, 1892, he was married to Clara Castle at Seward. Mrs. Brainerd was born at Buffalo Prairie, Illinois, November 11, 1868, daughter of Lemuel Melvin and Helen (Moffett) Castle, who were married in Rock Island, Illinois, on November 8, 1866. Mr. and Mrs. Brainerd have five children, Helen, born May 4, 1893, married Raymond J. Ditzler, and they live at Douglas, Wyoming. Gladys LaVerne, born October 16, 1894, married J. M. Kornder, and they live at Armour, South Dakota. Ona Marguerite, born November 16, 1900, is married to William H. Amstutz, and resides at Newark, New Jersey. Marion Lelibeth, born December 23, 1902, married C. J. Rhodes, of Peoria, Illinois. Henry Hall, the youngest child, was born December 13, 1903.

At various times, Mr. Brainerd has held membership in the National Guards of Maine, Rhode Island, and at Nebraska. He was a member of the Lincoln Home

HENRY ALLEN BRAINERD

Dole—Lincoln

Guard during the late war. Born a Methodist, he is now a member of St. Paul's Methodist Episcopal Church at Lincoln. In past years he has been a member of various fraternal organizations, but at the present time holds membership only in the Odd Fellows. He is a member of the Sons of the Revolution, the Territorial Pioneers Association, the Nebraskana Society, and the Lincoln Young Men's Christian Association, in which he has a life membership. Residence: Lincoln. (Photograph on Page 151).

Carl Burton Brande

Carl Burton Brande, editor and publisher of Pierce, Nebraska, was born at Money Creek, Minnesota, January 9, 1873, the son of Alfred Gerry Brande and Mary Caroline (Smith) Brande. His father, who was a clergyman, was born at West Gardner, Maine, August 22, 1840, and died at Pierce, January 10, 1928; he served in the 11th Maine Infantry and the 2nd Maine Cavalry during the Civil War; he was a direct descendant of Rev. John Robinson of the Pilgrims of Holland, and of Revolutionary ancestors. His mother, who was active in the Woman's Club and the Order of Eastern Star, was born at Gilmington, New Hampshire, June 3, 1841, and died at Pierce, November 3, 1929.

Mr. Brande is a member of the Pierce Community Club, the Lions Club, and the Congregational Church. His fraternal organizations are: Masons; Independent Order of Odd Fellows; and the Woodmen of the World. Residence: Pierce.

Frank Henry Brandes

Frank Henry Brandes, automobile executive, was born at Exeter, Nebraska, May 19, 1882. He is the son of Deadrich August and Katherine (Brandes) Brandes, both natives of Germany. Deadrich Brandes was born at Liferdale, October 20, 1843, and came to Nebraska in 1870, where he engaged in farming until his death at Hastings, on October 12, 1909. As a young man he served in the war with Prussia. Katherine, his wife, was born at Hanover, July 21, 1848, and died at Wilber on February 25, 1885.

Educated in rural schools, Frank Henry Brandes entered the implement business in 1910 under the firm name of Jones and Brandes Company. In 1912 he engaged in the automobile business, and in 1918 went into business for himself. At the present time he is the owner of F. H. Brandes Company; president and general manager of the Brandes Motors, Incorporated, of Mankato, Minnesota.

Mr. Brandes was married to Millie Estelle Hilton at Hastings, Nebraska, November 30, 1905. They have two children, Ethel, born October 21, 1906, who attended college and studied the pipe organ; and Edwin, born August 9, 1908, who received his degree from the University of Nebraska, and is now assistant manager of Brandes Motors at Mankato.

A leader in every civic project, Mr. Brandes is a member of the good roads committee of the Chamber of Commerce at the present time. He has always been a staunch supporter of law and order, and took a leading part in the apprehension of the murderer of Carl Moore, a salesman in his employ in 1924.

Mr. Brandes' religious affiliation is with the Zion Lutheran Church. He is an Elk and a member of the Masons and Shrine, the Red Cross and The Nebraskana Society. His hobby is mechanics. Residence: Hastings.

Mary Brandfas

Mary Brandfas, who is an educator and civic leader at Burwell, Nebraska, was born at Erina, Nebraska, June 11, 1895, the daughter of John and Hannah (McDonald) Quinn. Her father, who was a pioneer farmer in Nebraska, was born of Irish parents at Prince Edwards, Massachussetts, December 9, 1853, and died at

Burwell, February 11, 1928. Her mother, a teacher, was born of Scotch-Irish parentage, at Springfield, Illinois, December 9, 1866.

She was graduated from the Burwell High School in 1915, and attended the Kearney State Teachers College where she was president of the Aespasian Dramatic Club. She was a rural teacher for two years, 1915-17, served as grade teacher, 1917-18, and was high school mathematics instructor, 1918-22. She was principal of the high school and normal training instructor at Burwell from 1922 to 1929, was again a rural school teacher for a year, and for the past two years has served as principal of the Kent School.

She served as vice president of the Parent Teachers Association in 1924, is a member of the Nebraska Teachers Association, and holds membership in the Rebecca Lodge and the Royal Neighbors of America. Mrs. Brandfas was president of the Woman's Country Club, from 1928 to 1929, and served as secretary-treasurer, 1929-30. She has engaged in teaching for over 16 years and is vitally interested in her profession.

Her marriage occurred at Smith Center, Kansas, October 11, 1923. Residence: Burwell.

Emelia Hanigsen Brandt

Emelia Hanigsen Brandt, physician and surgeon, was born at Fergus Falls, Minnesota, March 20, 1881, daughter of Henry and Christine (Traeger) Hanigsen.

She received her A. B. and Ph. G. degrees from Fremont College, and her medical degree from the University of Nebraska.

On August 6, 1903, she was married to Henry Frederick Brandt at Fergus Falls.

At the present time Dr. Brandt is specializing in internal medicine. She was admitted to practice in Omaha on June 4, 1918. She is a member of The First Methodist Church, the National Medical Women's Association, the Nebraska Association of Medical Women, the American Medical Association, the Nebraska State Medical Association, the Omaha-Douglas County Medical Society, and the Omaha Women's Medical Society. Residence: Omaha.

Joseph Michael Brannan

Joseph M. Brannan, a lifetime resident of Nebraska, was born at St. John, Dakota County, Nebraska, June 8, 1858, the son of Joseph and Margaret (O'Brien) Brannan. His father, who was a merchant, was born at Dublin, Ireland, January 2, 1827, and died at Jackson, Nebraska, August 10, 1901; he came to this country in 1829. His mother was born at New Palace, County Limerick, Ireland, November 3, 1832, and died at Jackson, April 10, 1920.

Mr. Brannan has been a farmer at Jackson, most of his life, and is now retired. He is a member of the board of education at Jackson, is affiliated with St. Patrick's Catholic Church, holds membership in the Nebraskana Society, and is a Democrat.

His marriage to Mittie Maher was solemnized at Jackson, September 5, 1889; she was born at Galena, Jo Daviess County, Illinois, June 4, 1870, of Irish and English parentage, and died at Jackson, January 8, 1895. Two children were born to this marriage: Margaret, born February 2, 1891; Sylvester, born September 6, 1892. Of Mr. Brannan's marriage to Nellie Frummell, one child was born: Mary Josephine, born October 8, 1908. Residence: Jackson.

Hjalmer Benard Branting

Hjalmer Benard Branting was born at Osceola, Nebraska, May 23, 1898, the son of Otto Frederick and Hilma Amelia (Jones) Branting. His father, a farmer, business man and county commissioner, was born in Sweden, June 19, 1869. His mother, who came with her parents to Polk County in 1878, was born at Winona, Marshall County, Illinois, May 9, 1870.

Mr. Branting attended rural school and in 1916 was graduated from Luther College at Wahoo, Nebraska. For eight years he was connected with the general mercantile business, for six years was engaged in the implement business at Osceola, and for six years was engaged in that business at Stromsburg. During the World War he assisted in loan drives. He is a member of the Red Cross, the Midwest Implement Dealers Association, the Nebraskana Society, and Salem Lutheran Church of Stromsburg. He likes to fish and hike.

His marriage to May Sarah Louise Gustafson took place at Axtell, Kearney County, Nebraska, June 9, 1920. Mrs. Branting was a nurse before her marriage. They have one child, Kermit, born July 14, 1921. Residence: Stromsburg.

Mary Bratt

Dr. Mary Bratt, physician and surgeon of Beaver City, was born at Arapahoe, Nebraska, November 2, 1894, the daughter of Reuben W. and Daisey (Clark) Bratt. Reuben W. Bratt was born near San Jose, Illinois, March 25, 1865, of English descent. He came to Nebraska in 1890 and settled on a farm four miles south of Arapahoe, where he now resides. His wife, Daisey Clark, was born in Charleston, Illinois, November 13, 1876, of German and Dutch descent. She came to Nebraska with her parents in 1879 and settled on a farm near Arapahoe. Six children were born to their union, Mary, born November 2, 1894; Lawrence W., born June 28, 1896, who is now in the theological school at Boston and has a charge at Hillsboro, New Hampshire; Wesley R., born April 3, 1899, who is now instructor at Hastings College; Elmer C., born November 12, 1901, who is now instructor in Lehigh University at Bethlehem, Pennsylvania; Orin J., born January 24, 1904, who is auditor for the Continental Oil Company of Nebraska; Clara May, born August 26, 1908, who is a teacher in the high school at Franklin; and Dr. Mary Bratt.

Dr. Mary Bratt attended public school and was graduated from high school at Arapahoe in 1912. She taught rural schools in Furnas County for three years and attended Kearney State Normal College two years. The following three years she was principal of the high school at Cordova, Nebraska. She later attended the University of Nebraska, where she was elected to membership in Nu Sigma Phi. There she received her Bachelor of Arts and her degree of Doctor of Medicine.

Following her graduation from medical college Dr. Bratt spent one year internship at the Methodist Hospital at Omaha, and one year as resident physician and surgeon at the Methodist Hospital at St. Joseph, Missouri. From 1925 until 1930 she practiced in Arapahoe. In the fall of 1930 she was sent to Sleeper Davis Hospital in Peiping, China, as a medical missionary under the Women's Foreign Missionary Society of the Methodist Church, but was forced to return because of ill health. She then located in Beaver City, where she is now practicing.

She is an outstanding citizen, and greatly devoted to her medical practice. She is a member of the Methodist Church and a life member of the Nebraskana Society. Residence: Beaver City.

Fritz Brauer

Fritz Brauer, prominent retired farmer, was born in Essen, Germany. January 22, 1860, and came to the United States in September, 1878.

His father, John Fred Brauer, was born in Essen, Germany, in 1822, and died at Malcolm, Nebraska, in October, 1878. He was a farmer.

Elizabeth Tuhnhorst was born in Bohnte, Germany, in 1834, and died at Lincoln, in 1925.

Mr. Brauer attended public school at Essen, Germany,

and soon thereafter became engaged in farming. He came to this country when 18 years old and worked for his mother until he was married. He then farmed for himself near Malcolm, Lancaster County, until 1892, when he removed to Sidney, Cheyenne County, where he took a homestead of 160 acres, 14 miles southeast of Sidney. He bought more land from time to time and his ranch now consists of 1600 acres. He is now retired from active work, but has managed for the last eight years the Farmers Elevator. He is a Republican.

On October 23, 1883, he was married to Albertina Oldenburg, at Malcolm, Nebraska. She was born in Germany, February 13, 1863, and died at Sidney, Nebraska, April 26, 1915. To them were born the following children: Emma; Bertha; Carl; Walter; Mathilda; Richard; Arthur; Clara; George; and Helen. All the children were born in Nebraska. On May 22, 1922, Mr. Brauer was married to Mrs. Emma Teufert. The second wife had three children by a former marriage.

Mr. Brauer is a member of St. Paul's Lutheran Church. He is fond of driving, while his hobby is reading. Residence: Sidney.

Charles Bray

In the fall of 1861, Charles Bray moved with his parents to Otoe County, in what was then known only as Nebraska territory. A resident of the state since that time, he has seen much of the early pioneer days and the great progress of the west as civilization came in. He recalls the freighters being drawn across the prairie by plodding oxen teams, on their way to the far west in the days before the railroad. His father, Nathaniel Bray, who was a farmer, was born in New York, June 8, 1827, and died at Syracuse, Otoe County, Nebraska, July 6, 1883.

His mother, Emily G. (Daymen) Bray, was born in New York, January 16, 1831, and died at Syracuse, September 14, 1904. She was the mother of seven children, one of whom, Daniel Bray, was a charter member of the Nebraska Sportsman Association, a pioneer buffalo hunter, and held state championship in shooting.

Mr. Bray received his education in a small school in Nursery Hill, the nearest stage coach stop, and lived in this vicinity until his marriage, when he moved to Oakdale, Antelope County, Nebraska, where he and his wife made their home in a dugout. Late in 1893 they returned to Syracuse and purchased a farm which Mr. Bray at the age of 70 still owns and operates. One of the interesting stories told by pioneer settlers, taken from the files of the *News Press*, published in 1868, is: "Nathaniel Bray, of Nursery Hill lost two horses. He suspected roving Pawnees of the crime, followed them to their village and made them give up the animals."

His marriage to Cynthia Edna Waterman was solemnized at Syracuse, March 10, 1883. Mrs. Bray was born at China, Wyoming County, New York, October 11, 1863. Her parents, Eli Webster Waterman and Louisa (Spencer) Waterman, moved to Otoe County in 1875, and were energetic and prosperous farm people.

There are two children: Edith, born March 26, 1884, who married George Kramer, a farmer at Syracuse; and Walter, born September 27, 1885, who married Emma Scheel, is farming on a large scale at Bird City, Kansas.

Mr. Bray is a member of the Nebraskana Society, and was a member of the Good Templars, a lodge which does not exist now. He is a member of the Congregational Church of Syracuse. He was a Republican until recent years. Residence: Syracuse.

Daniel Harvey Braymer

Daniel Harvey Braymer, mechanical and electrical engineer, was born at Hebron, New York, November 29, 1883, son of George Winfield and Jennie Cordelia (Smith) Braymer. His father was born at Hebron, March 13, 1861, and is a farmer of Swiss-German descent. His mother was born at North Hebron, February 29, 1864, and was a teacher prior to her marriage. She is past grand matron of the Order of Eastern Star, and is of Scotch and English descent.

Mr. Braymer was graduated from the Granville (New York) High School in 1902, and received his higher education from Cornell University. He received his A. B., in Engineering Chemistry in 1906, and his M. E. in Electric and Mechanical Engineering in 1908. From 1910 to 1925 he was engaged in editorial work with the W. R. C. Smith Publishing Company of Atlanta, Georgia, the Gage Publishing Company of New York, and the McGraw Publishing Company and the McGraw-Hill Company of New York and Chicago. Since 1925 he has been in private practice as a consulting mechanical and electrical engineer in Omaha.

He is the author of *American Hydroelectric Practice* (1917); *Armature Winding and Motor Repair* (1919); *Rewinding Small Motors* (1925); *Repair Shop Diagrams and Connecting Tables* (1927); *Rewinding and Connecting A. C. Motors* (1932). He has served as editor of *Electrical Engineering* (Atlanta); *Electrical Record* (New York); and as managing editor and later editor-in-chief of the *Electrical World*. He was editorial director of *Industrial Engineering* (Chicago).

He is a member of the American Institute of Electrical Engineers and of the American Society of Mechanical Engineers.

He was married to Ruth Marie McGuire at Chicago, August 29, 1925. Mrs. Braymer was born at Omaha, October 8, 1892, and is of Irish descent. Mr. Braymer is a member of the University Club, and is a Democrat. Residence: Omaha.

Charles Brazda

For the past 32 years Charles Brazda has been engaged as a photographer at Dodge, Nebraska. He was born at Racine, Wisconsin, November 2, 1869, the son of Frank and Catherine (Pavel) Brazda. His father, who was a farmer, was born at Vlasim, Bohemia, October, 1839, and died in Dodge County, February 20, 1919. His mother was born in Bohemia, in 1845, and died at Racine, August 6, 1881.

Mr. Brazda was graduated from the Racine public school in 1883, and until 1899 lived on a farm. In 1899 he moved to Dodge, and has since been a photographer there. He has resided in Nebraska for 47 years. For a number of years he was a member of the village board at Dodge, and for more than twenty years has been a member of the school board there. He holds membership in the Dodge Commercial Club; the Nebraskana Society; the Modern Woodmen of America, and Z C B J, Bohemian fraternal society. His political affiliation is with the Democratic Party.

His marriage to Christina Mathilda (Bartosh) was solemnized at West Point, Cuming County, Nebraska, November 27, 1894. Mrs. Brazda was born in Dodge County, April 14, 1871, the daughter of Frank and Christina (Legro) Bartosh; her father was a farmer. They have two children: Daniel Steven, born December 7, 1895, who married Gladys Munro; and Adolph William, born January 11, 1899, who married Ellie Carter. Both were graduated from college with M. D. degrees. Daniel S. is now a doctor at Blossburg, Pennsylvania, while Adolph W. is practicing at Stockton, California. Residence: Dodge.

Henry Bredthauer

Henry Bredthauer, automobile dealer, was born at Ord, Nebraska, May 4, 1888, son of William and Dorothy (Vogeler) Bredthauer. William Bredthauer was born in Steinhude, Schaumburg, Lippe, Germany, April 1, 1845, and came to America in June, 1883. He was a farmer and stock dealer until his death at Scotia, February 28, 1914.

Dorothy Vogeler was born in Mardorf, Hanover, Germany, February 11, 1852, and died at Scotia, January 9, 1927. She was an active church worker, of a family of private bankers.

Educated in grade school until 1905, Henry Bredthauer attended Kearney Normal School in 1906, and Boyles College at Omaha, in 1907. On June 16, 1913, he was married to Cecile M. Daily, daughter of Mr. and Mrs. W. E. Daily, pioneer Nebraskans, at Scotia. Mrs. Bredthauer was born at Greeley, January 20, 1891.

To Mr. and Mrs. Bredthauer three children were born, Dale, on July 31, 1915; Dean, on December 12, 1919, and William, on June 19, 1927. The family attends the Lutheran Church at Scotia.

Mr. Bredthauer is an automobile dealer at Scotia, with a branch at Wyoming, Colorado. He is treasurer of the Dominion Oil Corporation, has served twelve years on the town council (chairman 3 terms); president of the Scotia Business Men's Club 1922-28; and is a member of the Lions International. He is a member of the Red Cross, the Parent-Teachers' Association, and the Nebraskana Society, and is fond of golf, football and baseball. He is a Republican. Residence: Scotia.

Carl Theodore Bremer

Carl T. Bremer, farmer of Hamilton County, Nebraska, has lived in this state all his life and has taken an active part in the political and civic affairs of his community and state for many years. He was born at York, April 28, 1886, the son of John Henry Christian and Mary (Schrader) Bremer. His father, a farmer, who was born at Hanover Germany, September 23, 1847, and died at York, April 18, 1911, was a Democratic candidate for state representative from York County in 1902; he came to America in 1867 and a few years later homesteaded in Fillmore County, Nebraska.

Mary (Schrader) Bremer, mother of Carl Bremer, was born in Stephenson County, Illinois, August 23, 1858, and died at York, September 30, 1901. Her ancestry was German.

Mr. Bremer attended the public schools of York and was a student at York College for a time. A Democrat, he was a member of the 1931 Nebraska Legislature. He has been moderator of the local school board since 1929, is a member of the Nebraskana Society, and is member of the Presbyterian Church.

His marriage to Emma Elizabeth Jeske occurred at York, September 12, 1916. Mrs. Bremer was born at Adrain, Minnesota, December 24, 1891, of German parentage. They have two children: Mary Jean, born September 3, 1917; and Betty, born August 25, 1920. Residence: Aurora.

John George Bremer

Born at Davenport, Iowa, November 16, 1872, John George Bremer has resided in Nebraska since March 20, 1889. The son of John George Bremer, Sr., his father was born at Gluckstadt, Schleswig, Holstein, Germany, December 27, 1838, and died at Ord, Nebraska, November 21, 1919.

The father, a cooper and farmer, served in Company H, 86th Illinois Volunteer Infantry during the Civil War. He was the son of a farmer, and the grandson of a sailor on a Danish war vessel. He was a charter member of St. John's Lutheran Church of Mira Valley, Nebraska.

His wife, Bertha Wilhelmina Prien, was born in Pomerania, Germany, February 8, 1846. She was a nurse whose death occurred at Ord on April 1, 1929.

John George Bremer attended parochial and public schools, being graduated in June, 1887. For about two years he farmed in Iowa, coming then to Nebraska where he has since continued in his chosen occupation. At the present time he is director and secretary of the Farmers Grain and Supply Company of Ord.

A progressive Republican, he was county supervisor four years, 1905-08, chairman of the county board three years, clerk of the township of Enterprise and assessor of Enterprise Township. He was unsuccessful candidate for state representative in 1916.

On May 22, 1907, he was married to Elsie Wilhelmina Vogeler at Ord, her birthplace. Mrs. Bremer was born March 1, 1888.

To them were born eight children, seven of whom are living: James, August 17, 1908; George, January 4, 1910; William, February 24, 1912; Lois, November 27, 1914; Ava, March 19, 1916; Franklin and Frances, twins, July 20, 1919; and John, Jr., born June 10, 1923, who died August 14, 1923.

Mr. Bremer's favorite recreations are baseball and reading. He is a member of St. John's Evangelical Lutheran Church of Mira Valley, has served as treasurer of School District No. 15 of Valley County since 1914, and is a life member of The Nebraskana Society. During the World War he participated in all civilian activities, including Red Cross and Liberty bond drives. Residence: Ord.

William Charles Brenke

William Charles Brenke, distinguished educator of Nebraska, was born at Berlin, Germany, April 12, 1874, the son of Fred William and Wilhelmina (Klopper) Brenke. His father, who was born at Lippstadt, Germany, in 1846, and died at Chicago, Illinois, in 1917, was a merchant. His mother was born at Lippstadt, 1848, and died at Chicago, 1923.

Professor Brenke attended the Chicago public schools and in 1892, was graduated from the Northwest Division High School there. He holds the following degrees: A. B., 1896; B. S., 1897; M. S., 1898; all at the University of Illinois. He was awarded the Ph. D. degree at Harvard University in 1907.

He was instructor at the University of Illinois, 1896-1904, was fellow and instructor at Harvard University, 1904-07, and since 1907 has been assistant professor and professor of mathematics at the University of Nebraska. He is the author of *Algebra and Trigonometry*, (1910); *Geometry*, (1916); *Trigonometry*, (1917); *Advanced Algebra*, (1919); and *Calculus*, (1912), besides various research papers.

He married Kate Read at Grand Ridge, Illinois, August 16, 1898; Mrs. Brenke was born at Grand Ridge, October 2, 1872. Their children are: Katherine, born August 9, 1900, who married R. T. Dunstan; and Bernice, born August 16, 1902.

Professor Brenke is a member of the American Mathematics Society, the American Association for the Advancement of Science, the Mathematical Association of America, the Nebraska Academy of Science, of Sigma Xi, and Deutche Mathematikes Verein. He holds membership in the Nebraskana Society and is a member of the Lincoln University Club. He is affiliated with the First Presbyterian Church of Lincoln. Residence: Lincoln.

Lee Brenner

Lee Brenner, son of Martin and Catherine (Lang) Brenner, was born at Muscatine, Iowa, November 13, 1869. His parents were natives of Germany, the former a farmer. His father died at Fremont, in 1901, and his mother at Wilton Junction, Iowa, about 1876.

Mr. Brenner attended the public schools and Fremont Normal School and engaged first in farming. Later he learned the tinsmith's and plumbing trade, and later engaged in the automobile business. For the past thirty years he has engaged as a funeral director.

On June 30, 1895, he was married to Leva Rea at Coleridge, Nebraska. Mrs. Brenner, who was born in Boone, Iowa, October 4, 1880, was of Scotch and German parentage. They have four children: Vera Agnes, born February 3, 1896, who married Russell L. Larson; Gladys Elizabeth, born March 30, 1899, who married John A.

Abts; Ed. Douglas, born November 5, 1906, who married Anna McDonald; and Phyllis Leva Lee, born August 9, 1917.

Until recently Mr. Brenner has been a Republican. He is a Protestant, and a member of the Modern Woodmen of America and the Funeral Directors' Association of Nebraska. He is a life member of The Nebraskana Society, and enjoys hunting and fishing. Residence: Randolph.

Arthur P. Bressler

Arthur P. Bressler, contractor and farmer, was born in Genoa, Nebraska, July 31, 1891, son of Isaac and Lura Lavina (Phillips) Bressler. His father is of Pennsylvania Dutch and his mother of early American ancestry.

For a number of years after completing his public school education, Mr. Bressler was a contractor and builder at Gering. He is now engaged solely in farming. A Republican, he was mayor of Gering two terms, 1926-1930. He is a Royal Arch Mason, member of the Modern Woodmen of America, member of the Scotts Bluff County Red Cross (chairman), and a member of the Christian Church.

On June 10, 1916, he was married to Anna Margaret Roberts at Gering. She was born at Atlantic, Iowa, April 18, 1897. There are three children, Alice, born July 20, 1919; Ruth, born August 22, 1921; and Donald, born April 5, 1923. Residence: Gering.

John Tannehill Bressler

One of Nebraska's pioneer bankers and leading citizens, John T. Bressler has lived in this state since April, 1870, and has taken a prominent part in civic affairs at Wayne, for many years. He was born at Warriors Mark, Huntington County, Pennsylvania, January 14, 1849, the son of Daniel and Mary Ann (Tannehill) Bressler. His father, who was a cooper, was born in Center County, Pennsylvania, November 8, 1808, and died at Fostoria, Pennsylvania; his ancestry was German. His mother was born in Blair County, and died at Fostoria, September, 1880.

Mr. Bressler organized and managed the first bank in Wayne County, which was known as the Logan Valley Bank, 1880. In September, 1885, the bank was re-organized as the First National Bank of Wayne, with Mr. Bressler serving as president. He is chairman of the board of the First National Bank at Wayne, at this time, and spends much of his time in managing his large number of farms in northeast Nebraska.

A Republican, he has held an important place in Nebraska politics for the past 35 years, and has held the following public offices: state senator, 1895; delegate to the Republican Convention, 1896; county treasurer, 1877, and 1879; member of notificiation committee to inform William McKinley of his nomination as president; delegate to all the Republican National Conventions until 1928, with the exception of 1924; government director of the Union Pacific Railroad, appointed by President McKinley, 1897.

During the World War Mr. Bressler served as chairman of the Wayne County Council of Defense and as Wayne County Fuel Administrator, and was county appeal agent in that county. He is a life member of the Red Cross, and holds membership in the Nebraska State Historical Society, the Nebraskana Society, and the Wayne Kiwanis Club. He is affiliated with the First Presbyterian Church at Wayne, and is a trustee of the Omaha Theological Seminary at Omaha, Nebraska. He is a 33rd degree Mason; charter member of the chapter and commandery at Norfolk; charter member Wayne Lodge No. 120; member of Consistory Number One at Omaha; life member of Tangier Temple, Omaha. His social clubs include, Wayne Country Club, Wayne; West Okoboji Country Club, of Okoboji, Iowa; and the Omaha Athletic Club, Omaha. His hobby is reading history.

He was united in marriage with Julia Fair at Dakota City, Nebraska, July 21, 1880. Mrs. Bressler was born in Indiana County, Pennsylvania, January 14, 1859. Six children were born to this union, of whom five are living: Maud, born November 9, 1881, who married O. A. Harker, Jr.; Ruth, born August 13, 1886, who married Amos T. Claycomb; Kate, born May 15, 1888, who married W. E. Von Seggern; John T. Jr., born May 15, 1894, who married Helen Main; Dorothy, born May 17, 1897; and George, born February, 1884, who died September 15, 1885. John T. Jr., is president of the First National Bank at Wayne. Residence: Wayne.

Miles John Breuer

Miles J. Breuer, noted Nebraska physician, was born in Chicago, January 3, 1889. His father, Charles Hugh Breuer, was a physician and surgeon, who wrote a great deal of popular medical material in the Czech language for the Czechoslovak press in America. He was born at Pardubice, Czechoslovakia, and is descended from a family of mechanics, founders, and glass blowers. He is now retired. Barbara (Hulla) Breuer, mother of Miles J. Breuer, was born at Pilsen, Czechoslovakia. Her ancestors were carpenters and cabinet makers.

Dr. Breuer was graduated from the high school at Crete, Nebraska, in 1906. He was granted his A. B. and A. M. degrees at the University of Texas, in 1911, and was awarded his M. D. at Rush Medical College, University of Chicago, in 1915. He was a student at the University of Chicago during the summer terms of 1909 and 1910. He was valedictorian and class prophet at Crete High School, and class poet at the University of Texas. He was elected to Phi Beta Kappa, Sigma Xi, and Phi Gamma Mu.

Admitted to the practice of medicine at Lincoln, June 1915, he engaged in general practice until 1927. Since 1927 he has been a specialist in diagnosis and internal medicine. He is attendant in Internal Medicine on the staff of the Bryan Memorial Hospital and the Lincoln General Hospital at Lincoln. He holds the position of chairman of the Pathology Department at Bryan Memorial Hospital, and at the Lincoln General Hospital. He is the author of various technical medical articles; numerous short stories; a novel published serially in a magazine; and a volume *Index of Physiotherapy Technic*. He is associate editor of *Social Science*.

He was united in marriage with Julia Etta Strejc at Omaha, Douglas County, Nebraska, January 3, 1916. Mrs. Breuer, whose ancestry is Czechoslovakian, was born at Table Rock, Pawnee County, Nebraska, April 13, 1891. They have three children: Rosalie Eva, born September 12, 1917; Stanley Marcel, born September 6, 1921; and Mildred Renee, born November 18, 1926. Rosalie shows tendencies toward creative art; Stanley will probably enter business, and Mildred is musically inclined.

Dr. Breuer served as first lieutenant in the medical corps with Nebraska Base Hospital Number 49 in France, during the World War. He is a member of the executive committee of the Nebraska State Tuberculosis Association, and was formerly a member of the board of directors of the Social Welfare Society of Lincoln. He holds a fellowship in the following: American Medical Association; American Public Health Association; and the American College of Physicians.

He is a member of the International Optimist Club, serving as secretary, 1921-27, and president since 1929. He is a 30th degree Mason. From 1915 to 1927 he was Scoutmaster in Lincoln, and in 1927, was the organizer of *Wolf-Cub*, a junior scout movement in Lincoln. He is now a member of the executive committee of this organization. His favorite sport is hiking. His hobbies include: amateur photography; short-story writing; and mechanical shop work. He is affiliated with the Elm Park Methodist Church of Lincoln. Residence: Lincoln.

George Herkimer Brewer

Born at Norwich, New York, March 20, 1856, George H. Brewer has been a resident of Nebraska forty-three years. He is the son of Herkimer Willis and Emily (Day) Brewer, both natives of New York State. Herkimer W. Brewer was born at Plymouth, New York, July 20, 1831, and died at Norwich, in April, 1896. He was a farmer. His wife, Emily, was born at Norwich, November 27, 1835, and died there in May, 1911.

George H. Brewer was educated in the public schools and at Norwich Academy. He began his business career as a member of the firm of Brewer and Sullivan, furniture dealers and undertakers in 1888. In 1892, he became head of the firm of Brewer, Sloane and Company which continued until 1898. This firm conducted both a furniture and undertaking business. Upon dissolution of the partnership, Mr. Brewer continued in the funeral directing business until July, 1928, when a consolidation of the Brewer Funeral Home with Korisko Brothers was effected under the firm name of Brewer-Korisko Funeral Home. Mr. Brewer assumed the presidency of the organization.

Mr. Brewer has been active in funeral work for forty-three years a record established by few men. For fourteen years he was a member of the state board of examiners for embalming. He was married to Julia Etta Young at Minden, Nebraska, on February 20, 1890. Mrs. Brewer was born at Manhattan, Illinois, April 1, 1871. They have one daughter, Edith.

A Republican, Mr. Brewer has always been active in the affairs of South Omaha, and is regarded as a leading citizen. During the World War he was a participant in loan and other drives, and is a member of the Red Cross, the Chamber of Commerce, Kiwanis Club, Elks, Modern Woodmen of America, the Odd Fellows, and all Masonic bodies. Residence: Omaha. (Photograph in Album).

Wilbur Millard Brewer

Wilbur Millard Brewer was born in Verdon, Richardson County, Nebraska, April 20, 1902. He is the son of Willard and Cora Ellen (Hart) Brewer, the former a minister. He attended elementary school at York, Cario, Hastings, Alma, and Thayer, Nebraska, High School at Thayer, Deshler and Edgar, Nebraska, graduating in 1921, and from Hastings Business College in 1923. He took part in athletics when in high school at Deshler and Edgar.

Wilbur Brewer was united in marriage to Mildred Erma Nisely on January 7, 1924, at Mankato, Kansas. She was born at Edgar, Nebraska, August 3, 1904. They are the parents of two sons, Robert, born October 10, 1924; and Buddy Monroe, born December 13, 1926.

Mr. Brewer started as a clerk with the Twidale Shoe Company at Hastings and was promoted to manager of the Twidale Shoe Company at Fairbury, in January, 1925.

He is a Republican and a member of the Presbyterian Church of Fairbury, Nebraska. He is also a member of The Nebraskana Society, Red Cross, the Fairbury Junior and Senior Chamber of Commerce, being secretary of the junior organization in 1929 and 1930, the Modern Woodmen of America, the Parent Teachers Association of which he has been elected vice president of Central Ward for the present year, Young Men's Christian Association, and the Fairbury Country Club. Golf is his favorite sport and reading is his hobby. Residence: Fairbury.

Jesse Sylvester Brice

Jesse Sylvester Brice, ranchman and secretary of the Antioch Telephone Company, was born at Grant City, Missouri, July 18, 1883, son of William Hugh and Mary (Van Metre) Brice.

The father, who was descended from early English settlers in Virginia, died at Antioch, September 3, 1910. His wife, Mary, was born in Sweedona, Illinois, May 2, 1857, of Scotch and German ancestry.

Mr. Brice attended the public schools at Kearney, and has since been a rancher and active in community and civic affairs. He is a Republican, and has served as precinct assessor and director of the school board. He has resided in Nebraska since 1888.

On April 26, 1905, he was married to Mary Alpha Clack, at Edgar. She was born at Verdun, Illinois, September 15, 1884. To them were born four children, Bernard, December 25, 1907; Clifford, April 29, 1910; Edna Elizabeth, October 18, 1920; and Byron, on March 14, 1923. Clifford is married to Gretel Dentler of Alliance, their marriage having been solemnized September 3, 1931.

Mr. Brice is a member of the Methodist Episcopal Church, the Nebraskana Society, and the Masons, of which he is a 32nd degree member. At the present time, he is master of Alliance Lodge No. 183. Residence: Antioch.

Samuel Aughey Bridenbaugh

Samuel A. Bridenbaugh, retired farmer, was born at Homer, Pennsylvania, December 26, 1860, and has been a resident of Nebraska sixty-six years. His father, John Bridenbaugh, was born at Huntington, Pennsylvania, a millwright and farmer. He served in the Civil War, and was an early settler in Nebraska; his death occurred at Dakota City, December 25, 1897. Margaret Ellen Wertz, wife of John Bridenbaugh, was also born in Huntington, and died at Dakota City, December 29, 1892.

Educated in the common schools of Nebraska, Samuel A. Bridenbaugh farmed for many years, and has always been an outstanding citizen of his community. He was treasurer of the school board from 1903-12, and is a member of the Chamber of Commerce and the Masons. His hobby is stockraising. He is a Republican and a member of the First Lutheran Church.

He was married to Tina Irene Owens at Dakota City, on February 11, 1891, and to their union four children were born. Samuel Hal, born November 26, 1891, married Ruth Vivian Kline; Elda Lorraine, born October 9, 1892, married George W. Zentmire; Jessie Margaret, born February 21, 1896, married Kenneth C. Fouts; and Lloyd Donald, born April 1, 1898, married Harriet Anderson. Mrs. Bridenbaugh, who was born at Sioux City, Iowa, February 14, 1871, is the daughter of William N. and Elizabeth C. Owens. Residence: South Sioux City.

Willson Orton Bridges

Willson Orton Bridges, physician and surgeon, was born at Coteau Landing, Canada, April 30, 1856, son of Banjamin Willson and Mary Elizabeth (Pease) Bridges.

He received his medical degree from the University of New York in 1879, and the Doctor of Laws degree from the University of Nebraska in 1917. He is a member of Alpha Omega and Phi Rho Sigma. Dr. Bridges has served as professor of medicine at the University of Nebraska, and is now a professor emeritus. He is a member of the Omaha, Missouri Valley and Nebraska State Medical Associations, the Chamber of Commerce, Ak-Sar-Ben of which he was king in 1928, and is a member of the Omaha Country Club and the Century Club. Residence: Omaha.

Clark Briggs

The son of Nebraska's earliest settlers, Clark Briggs was born at Hooper, Nebraska, January 3, 1871, and for many years has been engaged in the newspaper business. His father, Asa Briggs, a stockman and farmer, came to Nebraska in 1858 and settled in Dodge County; he was born at Kalamazoo, Michigan, January 25, 1845, of

English ancestry, and died at Springview, Nebraska, in August, 1921. Ottie (Clark) Briggs, his mother, whose parents came to Nebraska in 1859 and were prominent in the early history of the state, was born in Illinois, January 26, 1851, of English parentage. She died at Springview, February 11, 1924.

Mr. Briggs attended the public schools of Fullerton and Alliance, Nebraska, and at the age of 15 entered the newspaper field as an apprentice on a pioneer newspaper at Box Butte, Nebraska. He is editor of the *Springview Herald* and the *Primrose Record*, and resides at Springview where he is a member of the Red Cross. His hobbies are reading and traveling.

On February 24, 1897, he was married at Scribner, Nebraska, to Eva Jane Rich, who was born there of English parents August 14, 1876. Their two children are: Hulda Mae, born May 30, 1904, who married George A. Hallock; and James Buren, born June 16, 1908. Residence: Springview.

Fred Henry Brigham

For nearly 60 years Fred Henry Brigham has lived in Nebraska where he has engaged in farming. He was born in Jones County, Iowa, March 4, 1870, the son of Milan Henry and Phoebe (White) Brigham. His father, who was a farmer, was born in New York, April 9, 1819, of English ancestry, and died at Osceola, Nebraska, April 11, 1894. His mother, who was a tailoress, was born in Wisconsin, May 3, 1830, and died at Osceola, April 24, 1879.

Mr. Brigham, who is a retired farmer, attended a country school near Shelby, Nebraska. He was in partnership with the Brigham Brothers Hardware Company 1913-1914. He then returned to the farm and now resides in Shelby. His father came to Nebraska in 1872, and homesteaded on the farm which Mr. Brigham owns and which his son manages.

He was united in marriage with Mattie Eva Vanderbilt, February 16, 1898, at Shelby. Mrs. Brigham, who was born at Hastings, Nebraska, September 24, 1876, is of Irish and Dutch descent. To this union two children were born: Jean, born May 11, 1899, who is director of a nursery school in Pittsburgh; and Rex, born June 4, 1901, who married Blanch Ingalls, and who is a farmer and stockman.

Mr. Brigham holds membership in the Nebraskana Society, and the Royal Highlanders, and has been a member of the board of education of Shelby, for the past four years. Residence: Shelby.

John T. Brinegar

John T. Brinegar was born at Murry, Sangamon County, Illinois, May 20, 1878, the son of John and Nancy Ann (Johnson) Brinegar. His father was born in Bath County, Kentucky, October 5, 1841, and died at Belvidere, Thayer County, Nebraska, December 28, 1908. His ancestors came to America before the Revolutionary War. He was a farmer, carpenter, and an unusually clever machinist.

His mother was born at Bath County, Kentucky, March 31, 1841, and died at Belvidere, Nebraska, May 20, 1915. Her ancestors also came to the United States before the Revolutionary War.

Mr. Brinegar attended high school at Hebron, Nebraska. On September 20, 1908, he married Sarah Jane Bowen, who was born at St. Joseph, DeColb County, Missouri, June 3, 1880. They have two children: Joyce, born June 15, 1913, and Marjorie, born October 7, 1915. Joyce attends Hebron College at Hebron, and Marjorie is a junior at the Belvidere High School.

John Brinegar lived in Nebraska fifty-one years, and during most of that time has been a farmer. He is a Democrat and holds membership in the following organizations: the Red Cross, Independent Order of Odd

Fellows and the Nebraskana Society, and is past president and secretary of the school board at Belvidere.

During the World War Mr. Brinegar served in the Nebraska Home Guards and assisted in giving instructions to men who were going to the training camps. Reading is his favorite recreation. Residence: Belvidere. (Photograph in Album).

Fred A. Brink

Fred A. Brink, druggist, was born at Fremont, Nebraska, April 28, 1888, son of Earl C. and Millie A. (Herfurth) Brink. The father, who was born in Illinois, October 10, 1858, is a musician and a registered and graduate pharmacist, of Holland-Dutch ancestry. His wife, Millie, was born in Wisconsin, in September, 1862, of German descent.

In 1909, Mr. Brink was graduated in pharmacy from Creighton University, and from that time until 1918, was an employee in drug stores. Since 1918 he has had a store of his own at Hershey. He is a member of the Masons and the Presbyterian Church.

His marriage to Alice M. Stuart was solemnized at Omaha, December 20, 1914. She was born at North Platte, Nebraska, September 13, 1892. Her mother, Clara (Owens) Stuart was born on June 13, 1868, at Chatfield, Minnesota. There are two children, Frederick, born August 11, 1918; and Charles, born December 1, 1920. Both children were born at Hershey. Residence: Hershey.

James Washington Brink

Born at Mankato, Minnesota, December 3, 1878, James Brink is the son of William Augustus and Isabelle (Moore) Brink. His father, who was a farmer, was born at LaCrosse, Wisconsin, September 19, 1839. He served four years and eleven months in the Civil War, and died at Lyons, Nebraska, June 2, 1914. He was of New York Dutch descent. Isabelle, wife of William A. Brink, was born in County Cork, Ireland, February 12, 1843, and died at Lyons, November 15, 1913. She came to America with her parents at the age of seven.

Mr. Brink attended Lyons public and high schools, but did not graduate from the latter. His career has been chiefly in the editorial and publishing field, and he has served as editor of the following: *The Bentley Argus*, one year, *Dixon County World* and *Dixon Herald* two years, and the *Rosalie Rip-Saw* for the past twenty-three years.

On April 1, 1901, he was united in marriage to Besse Mae Taylor at Lyons. Mrs. Brink, who is a printer, was born at Blair, January 20, 1883. They have six children: Don T., born May 4, 1902, who married Irma Jennewein; Enid M., born May 16, 1904, who married L. V. Morgan; Winona, born May 3, 1906, who married O. B. Oxford; Natalie, born October 3, 1908, who married P. R. Salisbury; Ciona, born October 3, 1911, and Roberta, born August 1, 1914.

Mr. Brink was a member of Company E, Third Nebraska Volunteers in the Spanish-American War, and is a member of the United Spanish War Veterans. During the World War he was a member of the local draft board. He is affiliated with the Methodist Episcopal Church, and is a member of the Red Cross and the Nebraska State Historical Society. His sport is hunting, and his hobby is the propagation of wild water fowl. Residence: Rosalie.

Otto Herman Brinkman

Otto H. Brinkman, a lifetime resident of Lincoln, Lancaster County, Nebraska, was born there October 6, 1892, the son of Fredrick and Johanna (Radatz) Brinkman. His father, who was born in Germany and died at Lincoln, in 1926, was a railroad man for 36 years. His mother was born in Germany.

From 1906-17, he was connected with the Woodruff Printing Co.; from 1917-19, was manager of the Terminal

Printing Co.; 1919-1920, was with the Beacon Press, and in 1920 organized the Wekesser-Brinkman Co. Mr. Brinkman is still a member of the Wekesser-Brinkman Company. He is also secretary-treasurer of the Wekesser-Brinkman-Robinson Insurance Savings Plan, organized in 1931. He is a member of the Young Men's Christian Association; is a Mason, a member of the Scottish Rite and Shrine; and holds membership in the Nebraskana Society, and the Lincoln Auto Club. For the past 11 years he has been engaged in Boy Scout work at Lincoln, holding the positions of scoutmaster, district commissioner, and at present, commissioner. He is affiliated with St. Paul's Evangelical Church at Lincoln; and is a member of the Republican Party.

His marriage to Mary Elizabeth Helrich was solemnized at Mason City, Iowa, August 26, 1920. Mrs. Brinkman was born at Valparaiso, Nebraska, November 26, 1891. Their three children are: Allen, born February 5, 1919; Betty, born May 25, 1925; and Donnald, born October 12, 1929. Residence: Lincoln. (Photograph in Album).

Clarence Leslie Brittain

A lifetime resident of this state Clarence Leslie Brittain was born at Tilden, Nebraska, December 24, 1894, the son of William Benjamin Brittain and Mabel Laura Heckman. His father, who was born in Champaign County, Illinois, December 28, 1870, of German and English parentage, is a farmer. His mother, whose ancestry is Scotch and Irish, was born at Tama, Iowa, April 29, 1872.

Mr. Brittain was a carpenter employed by the firm Lytle & Thornton at Neligh, Nebraska, from 1912 to 1914, was employed by the Miller Brothers Contracting Company at Norfolk, 1914-15, and worked for L. C. Peterson at Tilden, Nebraska, 1915-16. Since 1926 he has been the owner of a cabinet and millwork business at Norfolk, Nebraska.

He is a member of the Chamber of Commerce, The Nebraskana Society, and the First Methodist Church at Norfolk; he is a Mason. From March, 1918, to January, 1919, he served as a sergeant in the United States Army overseas, stationed in France from March 4, 1918—January 19, 1919, with active service in the St. Mihiel and Argonne sectors. He is now a member of the American Legion and the Veterans of the Foreign Wars. His favorite sport is golfing, and his hobby is reading.

His marriage to Emma Evelyn Allison occurred at Chadron, Nebraska, June 25, 1919. Mrs. Brittan was born of Swedish parents at Crawford, Nebraska, February 8, 1898. Their children are: Dwan, born April 10, 1920; and Robert, born March 29, 1928. Residence: Norfolk.

James E. Brittain

James E. Brittain was born at Wayne, Wayne County, Nebraska, December 11, 1893, the son of James I. and Mary L. (Roberts) Brittain. His father, a pioneer in Nebraska in 1876, was a distinguished lawyer, judge, and statesman in Wayne County, born in Lee County, Illinois, January 9, 1853, and died at Wayne, January 25, 1918; he served as a member of the legislature, 1881, was district attorney, 1884-86, was mayor of Wayne for several terms, and served as county judge of Wayne County, 1909-18. Members of the Brittain family were in America as early as 1660; Zeboeth Brittain served in the Revolution.

His mother was born at Red Bank, New Jersey, February 21, 1851. She is the granddaughter of Joseph Roberts of Monmouth County, New Jersey, 1782-1804, who was of Scotch descent.

Mr. Brittain was graduated from the Wayne High School in 1910. He was a student at the State Normal School for a time, and holds the following degrees from the University of Nebraska: A. B., 1914; LL. B., 1916;

A. M., 1922. He was elected to membership in Sigma Chi and Phi Delta Phi, honorary legal fraternity, and served as president of the Freshman class. He has held the following public offices in Wayne County: county judge, 1918; deputy county attorney, 1922-26. He has been engaged in the practice of law at Wayne, since 1922, and city attorney since 1926.

He is a member of the Nebraskana Society, and the First Presbyterian Church of Wayne. He is the author of *Administration of Justice in Nebraska, and A History of Wayne County*. His favorite sport is golfing.

His marriage to Marie Gettman was solemnized in 1929. Mrs. Brittain was born in Norfolk, Nebraska, in 1895. Residence: Wayne.

Jefferson Hoover Broady

Jefferson H. Broady, distinguished lawyer and judge, was born at Brownville, Nemaha County, Nebraska, the son of Jefferson H. and Nancy Jane (McDonald) Broady. His father, who was born in Adams County, Illinois, April, 1844, was a lawyer, a member of the constitutional convention in 1875, and district attorney, 1876-78. He served as district judge from 1880 to 1891. His Scotch ancestors came to America where they settled in Virginia and Tennessee early in the history of the country. He died at Lincoln, October, 1908.

His mother was born at Baileyville, Centre County, Pennsylvania, 1845, and died at Lincoln, October, 1919. Her maternal and paternal ancestors came from Scotland at an early date and settled in Pennsylvania.

Judge Broady was graduated from the high school at Lincoln, and in 1904 was granted his LL. B. degree at the University of Nebraska, where he was a member of Beta Theta Pi and Phi Delta Phi. He was admitted to the bar at Lincoln, June, 1904, and from that date until 1907, he was engaged in legal editorial work on the staff of law publishing companies in Minnesota, New York, Ohio, and Nebraska. He was the editor of *Nebraska Synopted Digest*, a four volume law publication, 1910.

In 1911, he was appointed a member of the commission to revise the Nebraska statutes, by the Supreme Court and the governor. The revised statutes for 1913 were published by this commission. In May, 1923, he was appointed judge of the district court, third district; he was re-elected in 1924, and again in 1928.

On November 25, 1909, Judge Broady was married to Margaretta Jenkins at Mifflin, Pennsylvania. Mrs. Broady, whose ancestry is Scotch-Irish, was born at Mifflin. They have four children: John H., born September, 1910; Margaret, born September, 1912; Elizabeth, born September, 1915; and Jefferson, born April, 1917.

He is a member of various civic and welfare organizations, and is a member of the State Historical Society and the Nebraskana Society. A member of the Masons, Scottish Rite, Shrine, he is also affiliated with the First Presbyterian Church of Lincoln. Residence: Lincoln.

Andrew Brock

Andrew Brock, president of the Citizens State Bank of Blair, Nebraska, was born at Naderup, Jylland, Denmark, November 18, 1868. He is the son of Andrew and Julia (Christensen) Brock, both born at Naderup. Andrew Brock immigated to this country in 1872, the year after the death of his wife at Naderup, and was a farmer until his death, July 14, 1931, at Minden, Nebraska. Andrew Brock received his education in the elementary schools of Denmark.

On September 25, 1896, he was married to Carrie Christensen, at St. Paul, Nebraska. She is assistant cashier of the Citizens State Bank of Blair, Nebraska. Their children are Ernest, born June 18, 1897, and Myron, born May 6, 1906. Ernest is a graduate of the University of Nebraska, and is in the automobile business at Auburn. He married Margaret Roberts of Columbus. Myron is assistant cashier of the Citizens State Bank.

Mr. Brock has been in Nebraska for forty-three years. He is a member of the local Chamber of Commerce, the Modern Woodmen of America, the Masons, Danish Brotherhood, and the Nebraskana Society. Residence: Blair.

Paul Brockmann

Paul Brockmann, a lifetime resident of Nebraska, was born at West Point, on February 16, 1894. His father, Fred Brockmann, a farmer, was born at Manitowoc, Wisconsin, August 18, 1855, and died at West Point, September 9, 1912. His mother, Pauline Louise Schleusner, was born at Bernbaum, Germany, April 13, 1860, and died at West Point, January 24, 1924.

Mr. Brockmann was graduated from the grade school at West Point. He is now engaged in farming and stockraising in Cuming County. He is a member of the Farmers Union; is affiliated with St. Paul's Lutheran Church, at West Point; and holds membership in the Nebraskana Society. His hobby is reading.

During the late war Mr. Brockmann served as a private in the medical corps, engaged in hospital work; he is a member of the American Legion. His political preference is the Republican Party.

On August 30, 1921, his marriage to Ida Fischer was solemnized at West Point. They have one daughter, Eileen, born July 27, 1927. Residence: West Point.

David Owen Brodhead

David Owen Brodhead, stockman and farmer, was born at Gabe Rock, seven miles west of Harrisburg, Nebraska, January 16, 1894, son of John V. and Margaret I. (Cronn) Brodhead. The father was born at Dingman, Pennsylvania, December 29, 1854, and died at Kimball, Nebraska, September 4, 1928. He was a farmer and ranchman who homesteaded in Banner County in 1886. His wife, Margaret, was born at Lehman, Pennsylvania, October 14, 1857. She was a devoted housewife and homemaker, and died March 23, 1932, at Norwood, Colorado. The homestead is still retained by David Owen Brodhead.

Mr. Brodhead was graduated from public school at Harrisburg, and has since engaged in farming and stockraising. He is a member of the Knights of Pythias, the Harrisburg Methodist Community Church, and the Harrisburg School Board. He was elected treasurer in June, 1928, and is still serving. Politically, he is a Republican.

His marriage to Alice V. Wyatt was solemnized at Scottsbluff, Nebraska. Mrs. Brodhead was born at Bighorn, 17 miles east of Harrisburg, Nebraska, June 19, 1891, the daughter of William E. and Susan C. (Duncan) Wyatt. Her father homesteaded in Banner County on Pumpkin Creek in 1885. He was born in Iowa, November 1, 1859, and died at Harrisburg, January 16, 1906. Her mother was born in Iowa, November 21, 1857, and died April 3, 1928. The Wyatt homestead is now owned by the son, Clyde O. Wyatt. Mrs. Brodhead is a member of the Methodist Community Church, and the Church Improvement Club, and has served as secretary and treasurer since 1928. She served as secretary of the Red Cross for four years. Mr. and Mrs. Brodhead have one son, Dwight, born December 9, 1916, who is a member of the Methodist Community Church. Residence: Harrisburg.

Francis Albert Brogan

A native of DeWitt, Iowa, born December 6, 1860, Francis A. Brogan has been a leading member of the Nebraska bar for many years. He is the son of Francis and Ann (Cummins) Brogan. The former, a farmer, was born at Lifford, County Donegal, Ireland, March 17, 1822, and came to America in 1838. He died at Hartford, Kansas, August 16, 1905.

Ann Cummins Brogan was born at Athy, County Kildare, Ireland, in May of 1837. She came to America in 1850, and died at Los Angeles, May 1, 1921.

Francis A. Brogan attended the elementary schools of Kansas, and St. Benedict's College at Atchison. In 1883 he received his A. B. from Georgetown College, and during 1884-85 attended Harvard University Law School. He was the winner of the Merrick Debating Medal at Georgetown in 1882, and valedictorian in 1883.

He was first admitted to the bar at Emporia, Kansas, in June, 1885, and began the practice of law in the office of C. N. Sterry of that city. From 1886 to 1888 he was local attorney for the Atchison, Topeka and Sante Fe Railroad Company. In 1888 he came to Omaha, where he was admitted to the bar of Nebraska, and where he has since been engaged in practice. In 1918 he organized the law firm of Brogan and Ellick, and from 1919-29 was senior member of the firm of Brogan, Ellick and Raymond. He is now senior member of the firm of Brogan, Ellick and Van Dusen.

He was married to Maude Haskell Perley at Emporia, October 17, 1888. Mrs. Brogan was born at Emporia, September 1, 1869, and is descended from Allan Perley, who settled in Massachusetts Bay Colony in 1630. They have two children, Albert Perley, born July 22, 1889, married Mary Cleo Rice. He is professor of philosophy at the University of Texas. They have two children, Mary Rice and Francis Albert. The younger son, Maurice Perley, was born November 20, 1896, and married Marjorie Rutter. He is commercial engineer with the Northwestern Bell Telephone Company at Omaha, and they have three children, Thomas Edward, Francis Allen and Maude Elizabeth.

Mr. Brogan is a Republican. He was candidate for county attorney of Lyon County, Kansas in 1886; chairman of the Business men's Sound Money League of Omaha, in 1896, and candidate for chief justice of Nebraska in 1914. During 1916-18 he was president of the Nebraska branch of the National Security League.

He is a member of the Omaha Bar Association and was president of that body in 1905. During 1909 he was president of the Nebraska State Bar Association. A member of the American Bar Association, he was member of general counsel in 1911, and vice president for Nebraska, 1922. He was director of the Chamber of Commerce from 1916-29, and its president in 1920. From 1916-20 he was a member of the Omaha school board. He is an Elk, a member of the Woodmen of the World, the Nebraska State Historical Society and The Nebraskana Society. He is a member of the Omaha Club, and a charter member of the Omaha University Club and of the Omaha Country Club. Residence: Omaha.

Samuel Brolliar

A resident of Nebraska since June 2, 1863, Samuel Brolliar is a pioneer clergyman and editor. He was born February 25, 1852, son of William and Sara (Miller) Brolliar, both of whom were early settlers, who died many years ago.

He was married to Florence I. Garton, at Wilber, January 5, 1879. She was born in Benton County, Iowa, June 6, 1859, and died December 23, 1929, at Wilber. To them seven children were born, five of whom are living: Gertie M., born June 16, 1880, married Henry White; Walter R., born June 11, 1881, married Rose Terry; Francis M., born August 11, 1882, married Pearl Irvin; Earl M., born August 9, 1884; Gladys M., born August 23, 1897, married Robert Hawes; Samuel F., died in infancy; Ernest, born March 17, 1890, served in the World War, and died April 5, 1920, in Portland, Oregon.

Mr. Brolliar has been a minister and editor many years, and is editor of the *Saline County Democrat*. He is a member of the Reorganized Church of Jesus Christ of the Latter Day Saints, and of The Nebraskana Society. Residence: Wilber.

Charles John Broman

Charles John Broman, who has been a merchant at Minden, Nebraska, for more than 44 years, was born in Sweden, August 20, 1871. His father, Alfred Broman, a farmer, was born in Sweden in 1843, came to America, in 1872, and died at Denver, Colorado, November 21, 1927. Caroline (Johnson) Broman, his mother, was born in Sweden, in 1846, and died at Axtell, Nebraska, January 26, 1892.

Mr. Broman is serving as county clerk at Minden, at this time. He holds membership in the Modern Woodmen of America, the Royal Highlanders, the Minden Commercial Club, and Nazareth Lutheran Church of Minden.

He was united in marriage with Ida Sophia Carson, June 17, 1893. She was born in Sweden, September 5, 1868. Their daughter, Mabel, was born May 7, 1899. In 1925 Miss Broman married Walter Scarbrouh. They have two children, Walter Jr., and Donald. Residence: Minden.

Alice Brooke

Alice Brooke, pioneer of Nebraska, was born at Somerset, Pulaski County, Kentucky, September 22, 1866, the daughter of Eli and Anna Bell Dutton Strumk. Her father, who was a farmer and a Civil War veteran, was born at Somerset, August 30, 1846, and died at Juniata, Adams County, Nebraska, February 18, 1895: he was of German, Scotch, and Irish ancestry. Her mother, whose ancestors were English and German, and was born at Somerset, December 15, 1847, and is still living.

Mrs. Brooke was graduated from Cotner University and for eight years was a school teacher. For many years she has been an optometrist in addition to household duties. She served for eight years on the school board, and is a member of the board of directors of the Hastings Museum. Perhaps her greatest achievement was the organizing and building of Sunnyside Home for the Aged at Hastings, of which she is now a member of the board of directors.

In the late war Mrs. Brooke was active in loan drives and Red Cross affairs. She is a Democrat. She is married to Albert Henry Brooke; they have two children, Donavon Albert and William Henry both of whom are college graduates and registered pharmacists.

Mrs. Brooke has been active in the Nebraska Federation of Woman's Clubs since 1906, holding various positions, and now is chairman of law observance and delinquency. She is on the executive board of the League of Women Voters of Nebraska. Her church is the First Congregational Church of Hastings. Residence: Hastings.

Albert Munsell Brooking

Albert Munsell Brooking, known throughout the middle west as the owner of the largest collection of its kind in this country, has lived in Nebraska, since 1885, and has been prominent in the business world in the vicinity of Hastings, for many years. He was born at Macomb. Illinois, January 12, 1880, the son of Lucian Threshley and Jennie (Munsell) Brooking. His father, who was a grain dealer and newspaper writer, was born at Cyene, Texas, January 5, 1860, and is still living; his ancestors came to this country from England, before the Revolution. His mother, whose French ancestors came to America, with LaFayette, was born at Hamilton, Iowa, in 1861. The Brooking family has been represented in every war fought by the United States.

Mr. Brooking was in the grain business until 1926, when he became director of the Hastings Museum, a collection valued at $70,000. He is vitally interested in building up the museum for the city of Hastings, and hopes to hand down to posterity a noteworthy collection. He is the author of many scientific articles, and holds membership in the Nebraska Ornithological Society and other scientific organizations. He is a member of the Nebraska State Historical Society, the Kansas State Historical Society, the Nebraskana Society, and the Hastings Chamber of Commerce.

On August 19, 1931, Mr. Brooking discovered the remains of a mammoth near Angus, Nebraska, where it had been buried probably more than 100,000 years. Under the left shoulder was found a stone arrow head of the Folsom type. This is the first direct evidence discovered in this state to substantiate the claim of various scientists that man roamed the Nebraska plains at the same time that these immense beasts were alive. He has the further distinction of bringing to science a previously undiscovered type of giant prehistoric buffalo, the skull and horn cores of which have a spread of more than six feet; this head was discovered at Dorchester.

Mr. Brooking has done much research and exploratory work in archaeological and ornithological lines, and in his early life was a big game hunter and traveler of note. He was married to Bertha Foreman, who died in 1911; one child, Eleanor, was born to them March 18, 1907; she is the wife of Kenneth Oliver, who is an air mail pilot. On June 14, 1913, he was united in marriage with Katherine Schneider at Toledo, Ohio. Mrs. Brooking was born in Lenaway County, Michigan, in 1880.

Mr. Brooking is the owner of a collection of more than 3000 mounted birds, most of which were mounted under his supervision. This was the largest private collection in the United States in 1926, when it was added to the Hastings Museum. This collection, together with his Indian relics, mammals and fossil remains probably constitutes the largest museum display ever assembled by one man. Mr. Brooking has willed all these exhibits to the city of Hastings. Residence: Hastings.

Lucian Threshley Brooking

Lucian Threshley Brooking, a retired business man at Funk, Nebraska, was born in Texas, January 4, 1858, the son of William Thomas and Louisana (Walker) Brooking. His father, who was a farmer and grocer, was born at Morgantown, Kentucky, May 6, 1824, and died at Macomb, Illinois, February 7, 1910; he was a soldier in the Morman War. His mother was born in Kentucky, July 2, 1833, and died at Macomb, January 5, 1902.

Mr. Brooking attended private school. He was a farmer until 1883, engaged in the grocery business for two years, and was engaged in the grain business from 1887 to 1905. He has a keen interest in politics, and has written various articles on politics, economy, crime and history for Nebraska newspapers.

He served as chief registrar and legal advisor at Funk, was president of the Red Cross, served as chairman of the Council of Defense, was a member of the secret service, and had charge of soliciting for the Red Cross and Young Men's Christian Association during the World War. He is interested in amateur magic, bridge, and the violin.

On March 11, 1879, he married Jennie Munsell at Hamilton, Iowa. Mrs. Brooking was born at Hamilton, February 25, 1859. Four children were born to them: Albert M., January 12, 1880, who married Katherine Schneider; Mabel, July 1, 1882, who died April 3, 1883; William T., March 27, 1885, who married Belva Smith; and Edward E., July 11, 1887, who married Pauline White. Residence: Funk.

William Edgar Brooks

Born at Mount Vernon, Iowa, March 29, 1858, William Edgar Brooks is the son of James Stuart and Melissa Ann (Jones) Brooks. His father, who was a carpenter, was born in Oneida County, New York, September 27, 1830, and died at Elgin, Nebraska, February 28, 1903. James Brooks served in Company A, 13th Iowa Infantry, during the Civil War, until 1862, when he was wounded.

Three Brooks brothers, Charles, Abner, and Reuben, arrived in America in 1648, settling at Boston, Massachusetts.

His mother was born in Ohio, of Welsh and English descent. Prior to her marriage, she taught school near Blue Grass, Iowa. She died at Osborne, Kansas, in February, 1898.

Mr. Brooks attended elementary schools at Mount Vernon, Iowa, and Osborne, Kansas. He began farming near Elgin, and in 1892 became engaged in the retail hardware and furniture business in Elgin, where he is now the owner of a hardware store. He is a member of the Commercial Club, the Nebraska Hardware Dealers Association, the Nebraska Funeral Directors' Association, the Lions Club, and the local Red Cross. From 1893, to 1920, he served as director of the Elgin Public Schools; his fraternal organizations include the Masons, Blue Lodge, Chapter, and Commandery bodies.

He was married to Anna May Fee at Stanwood, Iowa, March 25, 1885. Mrs. Brooks was born in Bradford County, Pennsylvania, November 21, 1866, daughter of Richard and Nancy (Forsythe) Fee, both born in Ireland. They have a daughter, Genevieve, born July 30, 1892, who married Rollie Cleveland Huffman. Mr. Brooks is interested in reading and landscape gardening. He holds membership in the Nebraskana Society. Residence: Elgin. (Photograph on Page 162).

Elroy A. Broughton

Elroy A. Broughton, postmaster at Venango, was born in Swan County, Indiana, February 3, 1861, son of Orvil and Mary Jane (Wright) Broughton. The father was born in Ohio, April 6, 1837, and died at Redfield, South Dakota, in October, 1913. A veteran of the Civil War he was later a merchant. His ancestry was English and Holland Dutch. His wife, Mary Jane, was born in New York State, March 21, 1839, and died in Swan County, Indiana, in 1893. She was of Scotch-Irish descent.

Mr. Broughton attended public schools and from 1897 until 1916, was a railroad agent. From 1917 until 1920, he was manager of the Farmers Equity Union. In his earlier days from 1886 until 1889, he was band master of the Kearney Industrial School. He is a Republican, and for the past 10 years has been postmaster.

On December 25, 1888, he was married to Augusta Sophia Peter at Dorchester. Mrs. Broughton was born on the Isle of Rugen, Germany, May 16, 1862. To them were born seven children, six of whom are living, Janie M., born June 3, 1890, married Emery A. Watkins; Frederick O., born December 29, 1891, married Irma Conover; Elroy A., Jr., born October 1, 1893, died in February, 1909; Delores V., born August 23, 1895; Roland R., born July 3, 1898, married Leota Miner; Lois Irene, born January 6, 1901, married M. L. Sachs; Donald, born June 5, 1904, married Sonia Christensen. Janie married a farmer, Frederick is a railroad engineer, Delores is a nurse, Roland is a farmer, Lois Irene is a teacher and nurse, and Donald is an aviator.

Mr. Broughton is a Republican. He came to Nebraska in 1885, settling in Kearney, and later homesteading in eastern Colorado. He went there in 1889, and came to Nebraska in 1897. Since 1888, he has been superintendent of Sunday School of the Congregational Church. He is a member of the Modern Woodmen of America. Residence: Venango.

Edgar Merl Brouse

Edgar Merl Brouse, experiment substation superintendent, was born at Stratton, Nebraska, September 26, 1892, son of John Louis and Sarah Marguerite (Hepler) Brouse.

The father, a contractor and carpenter of German ancestry, was born in Highland County, Ohio, May 3, 1865, and died at Stratton, August 5, 1921. His wife, Sarah, was born at Kitanning, Pennsylvania, June 7, 1864, and

Westland—Neligh

WILLIAM EDGAR BROOKS

died at Stratton, April 25, 1920. Her ancestry was German and English.

Upon his graduation from public school in 1911 at Stratton, Mr. Brouse attended the Nebraska School of Agriculture until 1913. In 1918 he received his Bachelor of Science degree in agriculture from the University of Nebraska, where he was a member of Alpha Zeta and the Union Literary Society.

Since leaving school Mr. Brouse has been continuously employed by the University of Nebraska as extension agronomist, one year, and since that time as experiment substation superintendent.

On June 10, 1919, he was married to Hazel May French at Page, Nebraska. She was born at Page, December 25, 1893, of German and English ancestry. She was a school teacher before her marriage. There are two children: Betty Jean, born November 7, 1921; and Harold Arthur, born February 10, 1925.

Mr. Brouse is a member of the First Methodist Episcopal Church at Valentine, the Rotary Club, the Masons, and the Odd Fellows. He enjoys hunting and fishing, while his hobby is reading. Residence: Valentine.

Alfred Jerome Brown

One of Nebraska's foremost surgeons is Dr. Alfred Jerome Brown, who has been in practice for nearly thirty years, eleven of which have been in this state. Dr. Brown was born in New York City, August 27, 1878, son of Edward Flint and Eleanor (Bonney) Brown. His father was born at Sebago, Maine, in October, 1839. A lawyer, he was president of the New York county committee, president of the Reform Club, president of the board of trustees of Bridgton Academy (Maine). Of English descent, his family came to America in 1630; an ancestor David Brown, was captain of the Concord Minute Men. Edward F. Brown died in New York City in October, 1909. His wife, Eleanor, was born in New York City, March 4, 1849. She is still living, and is a daughter of Benjamin West Bonney, judge of the Supreme Court of the State of New York, and member of the Board of Trustees of Dartmouth College. She is of English and Holland Dutch descent.

Dr. Brown attended Yale School in New York, until 1895, when he entered Yale University, receiving his A. B. in 1899. In 1903 he was awarded an M. D., from the College of Physicians and Surgeons of Columbia University. A member of Sigma Xi and Phi Rho Sigma, he was awarded first Harsen prize and first Harsen clinical prize, from Columbia in 1903.

He was married to Grace Elting Overton of Brooklyn, at Plainfield, New Jersey, July 11, 1906. Their two children are Eleanor Bonney, born July 30, 1907, and Katherine Frances, born August 25, 1913. Eleanor was graduated from Smith College in 1928, and Katherine is now attending that school.

From 1903 to 1905, Dr. Brown was interne at Presbyterian Hospital, New York; he was assistant in anatomy and surgery at Columbia until 1913, and associate in surgery there until 1918. He was visiting surgeon at New York Orthopedic Hospital, New Jersey Orthopedic Hospital, Vanderbilt Clinic, New York, and first surgical division of Bellevue Hospital, New York, to 1918.

A major in the Medical Corps in the World War, he was chief surgeon, Debarkation Hospital No. 2, Staten Island, and in charge of coal region at Scranton, Pennsylvania. During the summer of 1918, he was surgical director of Evacuation Hospital No. 37, Joinville, France, and surgeon consultant, 40th division, Castres, France. He is now a lieutenant-colonel U. S. M. R. C.

A resident of Omaha for the past 11 years, he is associate professor of surgery at the College of Medicine of the University of Nebraska. He is also a director of the Physicians Health Association of Omaha. He is the author of *Old Masterpieces in Surgery* (1928), *History of Surgery in Nelson's Looseleaf Surgery* (1928); besides many scientific articles.

Dr. Brown is a member of the First Presbyterian Church of Omaha. He is also a member of the American Medical Association, and the American College of Surgeons. He is former first vice president of the Western Surgical Association and a fellow of the American Surgical Society. He is a member of the Red Cross and past district trustee of the Omaha Kiwanis Club. His sport is golf, and his hobby books. Residence: Omaha.

Charles Samuel Brown

Charles S. Brown, banker and business executive, was born at Agency City, Iowa, February 3, 1879. He is the son of Samuel M. and Marilla (Derby) Brown. Samuel M. Brown was born at Greencastle, Indiana, January 24, 1840. He died in Aurora, March 30, 1916. He was identified with the lumber industry and took an active part in the development of Seward County. Mrs. Samuel M. Brown was born in Licking County, Ohio, October 6, 1846. She has been active in civic improvement.

Charles S. Brown attended the Seward High School and from 1898 to 1901 attended Wesleyan University. While in college he was a member of the Everett literary society.

In order to assist in making his college expenses he worked in the money order department of the Lincoln post office. In 1901 he was placed in charge of Station A, a sub-station of the Lincoln post office at the State University. In the organization of this branch he was highly successful and won statewide recognition for efficiency. He entered the banking business at Aurora January 1, 1907, and is now vice president of the Fidelity State Bank of Aurora.

He married Nettie A. Steinmeyer at Clatonia June 7, 1905, (*see biography*). There are three children: Kenneth Henry, born June 20, 1908; who is a junior in the University of Nebraska; Eleanor G., born January 21, 1911, a junior in the Wesleyan University; and Bessie Belle, born April 6, 1914; a senior in the Aurora High School.

Mr. Brown took a prominent part in the Liberty Loan drives and World War organization. He is a member of the Rotary Club, the Country Club, the Masons and the Nebraskana Society. Residence: Aurora.

Frank Prentice Brown

Frank P. Brown was born at Yutan, Saunders County, Nebraska, August 15, 1879, the son of Joshua Prentice and Lena (Cerney) Brown. His father, who was born at Brookfield, New York, October 31, 1841, and died at Omaha, Douglas County, Nebraska, September, 1923, was a pioneer in Nebraska in 1863; he was engaged in freighting across the plains for several years; helped build the Union Pacific Railroad; and later established milling concerns in Butler and Saunders Counties. Of English and Scotch ancestry, he was directly descended from Thomas and Mary Brown who came from Worcestershire, England, to Lynn, Massachusetts, in 1628.

His mother was born at Vienna, Austria, December 23, 1859. She is active in the affairs of the Presbyterian Church.

Mr. Brown attended the public schools of Douglas County and later was graduated from high school there. He has been a horticulturist, mail carrier, owner of a feed and milling business, and a hay and grain wholesaler. He is now vice president and secretary of Edward A. Knapp Company of Omaha. He is a director in the Omaha Hay Exchange. He is president of the Masonic Temple Craft, Masonic Lodge 281, Omaha.

He was united in marriage with Maude Jeanette Johnson at Omaha, June 14, 1905. Mrs. Brown, who was a teacher before her marriage, was born at York, Nebraska, December 10, 1880; her parents moved from Illinois to

Nebraska in the early days of the state. They have one daughter: Dorothy M., born March 22, 1906; she was awarded the A. B. degree at Grinnell College where she was elected to membership in Phi Beta Kappa.

During the World War Mr. Brown was active in Liberty loan, Red Cross, and Saving Stamps drives, and served as a member of the Council of Defense. For years he has been a leader in Omaha's civic and business life. He is a member of the Florence Improvement Club; was formerly a member of the Omaha Chamber of Commerce; and for enght years was a director of the Douglas County Agricultural Society.

He holds membership in the State Horticulture Society; Ak-Sar-Ben; the Red Cross; and the Nebraskana Society. He was at one time a member of the Florence school board. He is Past Master of the Florence Lodge 281 of the Ancient Free and Accepted Masons; Scottish Rite; Royal Arch; and Shrine. He is a member of the Order of the Eastern Star and the Independent Order of the Odd Fellows, of which he is past noble grand. His social club is Dundee Golf Club. His sports are: golfing, bowling and fishing. He is a Republican. Residence: Omaha.

Harry Herbert Brown

Harry Herbert Brown, son of Hugh Clark and Mary Almyra (Goff) Brown, was born at Fremont, Nebraska, July 15, 1882. His father, who was born in Fairfield, Iowa, September 9, 1850, settled in Fremont, in 1870. He engaged in farming and stock raising for many years, and later engaged in the machinery business in Fremont. He is descended from early settlers in America. Mary Almyra Goff was born in Augusta, Oneida County, New York, October 19, 1849, and came to Nebraska in 1869, where she was one of the state's first school teachers. Her death occurred at Lincoln, June 6, 1928.

Educated in the public and high schools of Fremont, Harry H. Brown was graduated from the latter in 1900, and attended the University of Nebraska 1905 and 1906, during which time he was a member of the Glee Club. On October 22, 1914, he was married to Edna Mae Woods, daughter of James Edward and Artie (Trailer) Woods at Walnut, Iowa. Mrs. Brown was born at Marne, Iowa, February 5, 1889, of American descent for several generations. There are four children, Herbert E., born March 30, 1916; Dorothy L., born April 1, 1917; Evelyn M., born December 30, 1919, and Ralph W., born July 28, 1923.

A well driller since leaving school, Mr. Brown operated at Fremont several years, moving to Knox County in 1913, where wells were from 600 to 1000 feet deep. In 1916 he removed to Lincoln, where he purchased an interest in the Plattner Yale Manufacturing Company, manufacturers of windmills and water supplies. In 1919 he came to Blair, where he has since engaged in business. He now operates several machines in Northeastern Nebraska.

Mr. Brown is a Republican and a member of the Congregational Church. During the years 1928, '29, and '30, he was president of the Nebraska Well Drillers Association, and assisted in organization of the association. He belongs to Washington Lodge No. 21, Ancient Free and Accepted Masons, is associate patron of the Eastern Star, and is a member of the Blair Chamber of Commerce, the Nebraskan Society and the Blair School Board, of which he is now president. Residence: Blair. (Photograph in Album).

Howard F. Brown

Howard F. Brown was born at Council Bluffs, Iowa, June 16, 1907, son of Samuel W. and Pearl Ray (McCloud) Brown.

He was graduated from Chadron Public School in 1921, and from the preparatory high school in 1925. He completed a two year commercial course at the Chadron Teachers College, and in July, 1931, received a diploma from the International Accountants Society.

His marriage to N. Bonne Potter was solemnized at Deadwood, South Dakota, July 2, 1928. Mrs. Brown was born in Shelby, Iowa, April 11, 1908.

For three years after leaving school Mr. Brown was manager of the Chadron Furniture Company. At the present time he is the owner of a grocery store. He was secretary of the Harrison Lions Club, 1931-32. His hobby is collecting coins, while he enjoys horseshoes, tennis, and bridge. Residence: Harrison.

Hugh Richmond Brown

One of the younger members of the newspaper profession in Nebraska, Hugh Richmond Brown is the manager of the *Kearney Daily Hub* and during the past few years has attained recognition in the professional world. He was born at Kearney April 17, 1899, the son of Mentor A. and Sophie G. (Schmidt) Brown, the former a distinguished editor and publisher at Kearney.

Mr. Brown was graduated from the Kearney High School in 1917, is a director in the Kearney Savings & Loan Association, is president of the Kearney Chamber of Commerce, and is past lieutenant governor of the Nebraska-Iowa District of the Kiwanis Club, and has also been president of the local club. He was chairman of the County Red Cross, is secretary of the Kearney Library Board, is affiliated with St. Luke's Episcopal Church and holds membership in the Kearney Country Club.

Of his marriage to Dora Stenehjem, which occurred at Spring Grove, Minnesota, on September 9, 1923, two children were born: Dorothy Jean; and Patsy Mae. Mr. Brown is a Republican, a member of The Nebraskana Society and an Elk. Residence: Kearney.

James Arthur Brown

James Arthur Brown, who was born in Cedar County, Iowa, July 14, 1869, has been a lawyer at Lincoln, Lancaster County, Nebraska, for the past 34 years. His father, Francis Marion Brown, a farmer, teacher, and civic leader, was born in Jay County, Indiana, May 15, 1837, and died at Shannon, Union County, Iowa, May, 1919; he served as a private in Company I, 46th Iowa Volnteer Infantry, during the Civil War and was a prisoner of war for nine months at Cahaba, Alabama; his ancestry was Scotch-Irish; his father was born on the Atlantic Ocean coming from Ireland to America, while his mother's family settled in America before the Revolution.

Elizabeth Priscilla (Kester) Brown, his mother, was born in Crawford County, Ohio, August 27, 1842, and died at Shannon, August, 1916. She was prominent in religious and welfare work for many years, and held membership in: Women's Christian Temperance Union; Woman's Foreign Missionary Society; the Home Missionary Society; and the Women's Relief Corps. Her Dutch ancestors settled in Pennsylvania before the Revolution, and some of them served in that war.

Mr. Brown attended the rural schools from 1875 to 1889; taught in rural school during the winter months of 1890-01-02-03-04-05; received the B. S. degree, 1889, and the M. S. Degree, 1896, at the South Dakota State College; and in 1898 was awarded his Bachelor of Laws degree from Nebraska University. He was president of the senior class; was a member of the debating team; and was winner of the oratorical contest in 1893.

From 1898 to 1912 Mr. Brown was associated with Hon. Charles O. Whedon; from 1912-15, was a member of the law firm Stewart, Williams & Brown; from 1917-22, was a member of the firm Burr & Brown; was a member of the firm Burr, Brown, & Dibble, 1922-25; and was a member of the firm Letton, Brown, & Dibble, 1925-28. He is now president of the Dwelling House Insurance Company at Lincoln; is vice president of the Douglas Manufacturing Company; and is director of and attorney for the Home Savings & Loan Association at Lincoln.

A Republican, he served as a member of the Nebraska legislature 1927-28. He is a member of the Hiram Club; the Red Cross; the Nebraskana Society; the National Geographic Society; and the Young Men's Christian Association. He served as president of the school board from 1905 to 1915. He is affiliated with the First Methodist Episcopal Church of Lincoln; is a member of the University Club; and holds membership in North Star Lodge Number 227 of the Ancient Free and Accepted Masons.

He was married to Ida Dibble at Moody, South Dakota, March 4, 1896. Mrs. Brown, who was born in Howard County, Iowa, November 20, 1872, died at Lincoln, June 21, 1927. Five children were born to this marriage: Elizabeth, born October 9, 1899; Frances Marion, born May 15, 1901, who married Rev. George E. Mitchell; James Lowell, born August 14, 1907; Ida Lois, born August 14, 1907, who married Henry Huff; and William Oscar, born March 14, 1909, who married Mildred Farnsworth, August 15, 1931. Mr. Brown was married to Edith I. Foster at Grand Island, Nebraska, August 18, 1930. She is recorder for the Nebraska University. She is the mother of three children, Myrtha, who married Dr. Wilber E. Deacon; Hugh and Walter who are at home. Residence: Lincoln.

John Brown

John Brown, successful farmer in Clay County, Nebraska, has lived in this state since 1878, when he came to Sutton from Illinois. He was born in Lee County, Illinois, August 3, 1863, the son of Hiram C. and Lucy Ann (Bidwell) Brown. His father, a stockraiser and farmer, was born in Steuben County, Indiana, April 28, 1837, and died at Sutton, Nebraska, September 15, 1909. His mother was born in Wayne County, Pennsylvania, August 12, 1840, and died at Sutton, April 28, 1910; her ancestry was Scotch.

Mr. Brown received his education in pioneer rural schools in Illinois. On March 17, 1886, he was united in marriage with Fidelia L. Gormon in Clay County. Mrs. Brown was born of Scotch-Irish parents in Wayne County, Pennsylvania, November 15, 1851, and died at Sutton, November 17, 1927. Two children were born to this marriage: Erma, January 30, 1887; and a son, born October 29, 1889, who died in infancy.

He holds membership in the Nebraskana Society, is affiliated with the Congregational Church of Sutton, and is a member of the Democratic party. Residence: Sutton.

Julius Philip Brown

Julius Philip Brown, physician and surgeon since 1924, was born at Omaha, December 20, 1900, son of Joseph Philip and Antonia (Kysela) Brown.

He attended the public and high schools of Omaha, received his B. Sc., from the University of Omaha in 1922, and the degree of Doctor of Medicine from the University of Nebraska in 1924. He is a member of Phi Sigma Phi and Phi Chi.

On November 27, 1928, he was married to Sophia Maye Wefso at Stanton. She was born at Dustin, Nebraska, April 7, 1902, and is a graduate nurse. Dr. Brown is a member of the American, Nebraska State and Holt County Medical Associations, the Masons and Knights Templar. He enjoys golf. Residence: O'Neill.

Lulu Clyde Brown

Born at Franklin, Illinois, September 20, 1874, Lulu Clyde Brown has been a resident of Nebraska for the past 47 years and has taken a prominent part in civic and educational affairs there. She is the daughter of James Henry and Sarah Jane (Southard) Nall, the

former a teacher and contractor, who was born at Carlinville, Illinois, March 20, 1835, and died at Grand Island, Nebraska, February 26, 1920. Her father, who served in the Civil War, owned and operated the first brickyard in Frontier County, Nebraska; his ancestors were southerners. All the brick used in Frontier County at that time was manufactured by him at Stockwell.

Her mother, who was born at Pikeville, Tennessee, August 3, 1844, and died at Stockville, Nebraska, December 9, 1904, was a teacher prior to her marriage. Her family had lived in the south for many generations.

Mrs. Brown attended the public schools of Stockville. She was appointed postmistress in that village August 1, 1924, and has held the position continuously since then. She is vice president of the Frontier County Southwest Nebraska Historical Society, served four years as treasurer of the local school board, and was a charter member of the Kensington Social Club. She is affiliated with the First Congregational Church of Stockville, is a member of the Royal Neighbors of America, and holds membership in the Nebraskana Society.

On April 14, 1892, she was united in marriage with Ellsworth Dayton Brown at Stockville. Mr. Brown, who was clerk of the district court for 11 years, was born at Bethesda, Ohio, July 23, 1865, and died at Stockville, October 3, 1918. His ancestors were pioneers of the Shenandoah Valley of Virginia. They have four children: Martha Dimon, born March 3, 1893, she is living in Denver, Colorado; Ethel Elizabeth, born January 15, 1900, who married Lewis Verne Hogoboom, they are living in Pauline, Nebraska; Richard Dayton, born August 9, 1904, who married Marie Agnes Lloyd, living in Denver, Colorado; and Rex Raeburn, born February 15, 1908, who is at home with his mother. Residence: Stockville. (Photograph in Album).

Mentor Alsworth Brown

Born at Janesville, Wisconsin, February 19, 1853, Mentor Alsworth Brown, newspaper publisher and editor, is the son of Jeremiah and Ann Hancelia (Pound) Brown. The father, born in Ohio, served in the Civil War with the 25th Wisconsin Volunteers, and died while with Sherman on his march to the sea, April 14, 1864. He was a teacher and a physician of Anglo-Saxon ancestry. His wife, born in December, 1826, was a student and teacher, whose parents were Quakers. Both were graduates of Milton (Wisconsin) College. She died at Jamestown, on April 22, 1854, when Mentor A. Brown was little more than a year old.

Mr. Brown became a printer's apprentice at the age of thirteen in Jefferson, Iowa, and at the age of seventeen came to Nebraska, working for a short time in the summer of 1870, at Nebraska City. Thereafter he worked for a few weeks in the Redfield Job Printing office at Omaha, and was recommended for a place with W. R. Vaughan, a job printer at Council Bluffs. During the spring and summer of 1871 he was a compositor for the *Daily Nonpareil*, and was then recommended for foremanship of the *Express* office at Beatrice.

Continuing there until January 1, 1874, Mr. Brown purchased a half interest in the *Express*, the senior member of the firm being Theodore Coleman, a newspaper pioneer in Nebraska, and a brilliant editor. When A. S. Paddock was elected to the senate, Mr. Coleman accompanied him to Washington, as his private secretary, and soon thereafter sold his half interest in the paper to L. W. Colby. Mr. Colby soon purchased Mr. Brown's share of the paper also, and in the early months of 1877, Mr. Brown, then aged twenty-three, purchased a half interest in the *Fairbury Gazette*. Shortly afterward he resold the business to his former partner, George Cross, and being footloose again, started for Beatrice with the intention of establishing a paper there. On the way he met I.

MENTOR A. BROWN

W. Colby, and after a short talk by the roadside became sole owner of the *Express*.

From that time on the growth of the town and of the paper was rapid. The paper was published in the form of a daily in January, 1884. In 1888, Mr. Brown received a tempting offer to sell his interests in the *Express*, and a few months later he was located in Kearney, in the vortex of the boom. Negotiating for the purchase of the *Central Nebraska Press*, then owned by Rice Eaton and J. P. Johnson, he was successful, a corporation being formed with Mr. Eaton and J. T. Cassel as minor stockholders. The name of the paper was changed to the *Hub*, and the first copy of the paper printed on October 22, 1888.

Very soon afterward the boomers subsidized a new morning daily with the associated press franchise, a corps of brilliant young newspaper men from Boston, and a unionized detail of printers from Denver, and the *Daily Enterprise* became the journalistic sensation of the west. When the boom collapsed and the *Enterprise* blew up, Mr. Brown was found still plugging along as editor and manager of his paper, giving Kearney a good newspaper service. Other competition, just as dangerous, was encountered and outlived. The *Hub* has built up one of model printing and newspaper plants of the state, housed in its own building, with a well paid corps of managers, solicitors, reporters and skilled workmen and a leased wire telegraphic service.

Mr. Brown, now dean of Nebraska editors, writes a column of editorial daily, renders first aid when necessary, and watches closely the various branches of the newspaper, printing and bookbinding departments. In 1906 he was appointed postmaster of Kearney, holding that office until 1914. He is a Republican, takes an active interest in party politics, but has never run for elective office, except for presidential elector in 1904. He was electoral messenger in 1905.

Twice married, Mr. Brown has three sons and two daughters living, two sons deceased. There are twelve grand children, and five great grand children. The daughters are Mrs. C. E. Eustice, of Omaha, and Mrs. G. H. Connell, of Oakland, California. Ulysses, the oldest son, is publisher of the *Arnold Sentinel*; Oliver F. is in the printing business at Lincoln; while Hugh R. is manager of the *Kearney Daily Hub*.

Since 1914, Mr. Brown's entire attention has been given to his paper and the general interests of his business. He has kept himself fit by frequent attendance on the golf links. More conservative in late years in some respects, he is more radical as a booster for development and in his support of the highest political and social standards, asserting that hard work and the simple virtues will make this a great country. His hobbies are history and economics and the advancement of Nebraska.

Mr. Brown is affiliated with St. Luke's Episcopal Church, is a member of the Chamber of Commerce, the Rotary Club and the Elks, and a contributor to all welfare work, giving service as well as money. He is past president of the Nebraska State Press Association, a life member of The Nebraskana Society, and a member of the Kearney Country Club. He is a baseball and football fan. Residence: Kearney. (Photograph on Page 166).

Nettie Steinmeyer Brown

Nettie Steinmeyer Brown was born at Clatonia, Nebraska, April 23, 1880, the daughter of John H. and Sarah (Unland) Steinmeyer. Her father is a prominent stockman and banker of Gage County. He was born in Germany May 17, 1853, and has always been active in political and agricultural organization matters. Mrs. Steinmeyer was born at Beardstown, Illinois, April 19, 1857.

Nettie Steinmeyer Brown attended Nebraska Wesleyan University in 1903. She is a member of the Wil-

lard Society. Her marriage to Charles S. Brown took place at Clatonia, June 7, 1905. (*See Nebraskana*).

Norris Brown, lawyer and former United States senWoman's club and is active in the work of the Methodist church. Residence: Aurora.

Norris Brown

Norris Brown, lawyer and former United States senator, was born at Maquoketa, Iowa, May 2, 1863, the son of William Henry Harrison and Eliza Ann Phelps Brown. He received the A. B. degree at the University of Iowa, 1883, and the A. M. degree, 1885. He was admitted to the bar in 1884. A Republican, Mr. Brown has been prominent in city, state, and national politics for many years, and has held the following offices: deputy county attorney; county attorney of Buffalo County, 1892-96; deputy attorney general, 1900-04; attorney general of Nebraska, 1904-06; and United States senator, 1907-13.

Since 1912, he has been a member of the law firm Brown, Baxter, VanDusen, & Ryan at Omaha. He is a member of the Omaha Club; Omaha Commercial Club; Country Club; Palimpsest; and the University Club, and the Nebraskana Society. He is a Mason, and he is affiliated with the Congregational Church.

He married Lula K. Beeler who was born at Perry, Iowa, November 28, 1865. Residence: Omaha.

Raymond Lindsey Brown

Raymond Lindsey Brown, owner of the Brown Stationery Company, was born at Louisville, Nebraska, July 1, 1896, son of Horace E. and May (Lindsey) Brown. Mr. Brown was born at Mt. Pleasant, Iowa, May 19, 1867. Mrs. Brown was born at Boise, Idaho, September 4, 1870, both now reside at Scottsbluff, Nebraska.

He attended Scottsbluff High School and the University of Nebraska, and was formerly owner of the Brown Drug Company.

On December 25, 1917, he was married to Zona Irene Cline at Scottsbluff, Nebraska. Mrs. Brown was born at Creston, Iowa, November 28, 1898. They have one daughter, Helen Irene, born September 4, 1922.

A Republican, Mr. Brown is now serving as city councilman of Scottsbluff. He is a member of the Masons, the Scottsbluff Country Club, and the Presbyterian Church. His favorite sports are golf and hunting. Residence: Scottsbluff.

Richard Carney Brown

Richard Carney Brown, executive, was born at Holdrege, Nebraska, July 8, 1906, the son of Eben E. and Edna Elvira (Carney) Brown. His father, born at New London, Iowa, July 22, 1879, is a merchant, and one of the founders and now president of the Brown Ekberg Company, Inc. His parents were Swedish immigrants, most of whose lives in America were spent on a farm in Phelps County. Edna E. Carney was born at Germantown, Ohio, June 21, 1881, of Pennsylvania Dutch and Irish extraction.

Educated in the public schools of Holdrege, Richard C. Brown was graduated from high school there in June, 1923. In June, 1927, he received the degree of Bachelor of Science in Business Administration from the University of Nebraska, where he was valedictorian, treasurer and president of the Nebraska chapter of Sigma Chi, a member of the Kosmet Club, Beta Gamma Sigma and Phi Beta Kappa.

In February, 1928, he entered the employ of Brown-Ekberg Company, and is now manager of the store established at Hastings, on August 30, 1930. On July 8, of that year he was married to Frances Hooper at Holdrege. Mrs. Brown was born at Oxford, Nebraska, May 20, 1905.

Mr. Brown is a Democrat. A 32nd degree Scottish

Rite Mason, he is also a member of the Knights of Pythias. He is affiliated with the First Presbyterian Church of Hastings, is a member of the Red Cross, Chamber of Commerce, Lions Club, Young Men's Christian Association and The Nebraskana Society. Residence: Hastings.

Robert Given Brown

Robert Given Brown, pioneer lawyer at Sutton, Nebraska, has been a resident of the state since 1871 when he moved to Clay County from Illinois. He was born in Clark County, Illinois, October 4, 1847, the son of Samuel Robinson and Mary Rare (Howell) Brown. His father, who was a farmer, was born in Virginia, in 1810, and died in Clark County, in 1855. His mother was born in Kentucky in 1815 and died at Sioux Falls, South Dakota, in 1897. Both parents were of English descent.

Mr. Brown attended country school and the high school at Marshall, Illinois. He was admitted to the bar at Springfield in 1870, and for many years has been one of the foremost lawyers of Nebraska; he is now retired. He has been a member of the Nebraska State Bar Association, holds membership in the Red Cross, and is a member of the school board of which he served as the first director in 1872. He was awarded a medal by the U. S. Government during the World War for legal service.

A Democrat, Mr. Brown has played an important part in the political affairs of his state and community in the following positions; first treasurer of Clay County, 1871; legal advisor of the county; delegate at large to the Republican National Convention at Cincinnati, 1876; mayor of Sutton; and state senator, 1887. He moved to Clay County in the spring of 1871 and assisted in the organization of the county.

He married Ella Belinda Constable at Marshall, May 4, 1881; her ancestry is Scotch and French. Four children were born to this marriage: Alice Mary, born March 11, 1882, who died in 1929; Jess Belinda, born November 29, 1883, who married Ralph Waldo Giffen; Mabel Roberta, born in December, 1889, who married Anthony William Burg; and Robert Grant, who died in infancy. Mr. Brown is a Mason. Residence: Sutton.

William Arthur Brown

William Arthur Brown, publisher of the *Friend Sentinel*, was born at Loup City, Nebraska, July 8, 1889, son of Edward Arthur and Lavinia (Goldsworthy) Brown. The father was born in Batavia, Illinois, September 20, 1864, and died at Friend, December 21, 1922. He was publisher of the *Friend Sentinel*, postmaster at Friend, and served in the Nebraska legislature 1907, 1909. His wife, Lavinia, was born in Wales, June 5, 1868, of English ancestry.

Mr. Brown attended public school at Loup City and began his newspaper career on the *Sherman County Times*. He has been associated with the Claflin Printing Company and the *Lincoln Daily Star*, and since October, 1911, has resided at Friend.

On September 3, 1913, he was married to Weir Eugenia Lenox at Friend. She was born at Sterling, Colorado, June 9, 1889. There are two children, Grace Elizabeth, born March 7, 1915; and Sarah Lavina, born March 24, 1920.

A Democrat, Mr. Brown has been a member of the board of education, and the city council. He was delegate to the general conference of the Methodist Episcopal Church, 1928-32, and during 1926-27, was president of the Nebraska Press Association. He is a member of the Friend Chamber of Commerce. Residence: Friend.

Thorne Browne

Thorne Browne, former newspaper man and a leading business executive of Lincoln, Lancaster County, Nebraska, was born in Macoupin County, Illinois. His father, Elliott LeRoy Browne, who was a farmer and a mechanic, was born at Rome, New York, August 7, 1845, and died at Edgar, Clay County, Nebraska, June 21, 1921. His ancestry is Scotch-Irish. Elizabeth (Pierson) Browne, mother of Thorne, was born of English parentage at St. Louis, Missouri, August 7, 1851.

Mr. Browne was graduated from the Edgar High School in 1898, and in 1907, was granted his A. B. degree at the University of Nebraska, where he was a member of Phi Beta Kappa. He was president of the senior class in 1907, was editor of the year book, and was a member of Alpha Theta Chi Fraternity.

He was a teacher in the public schools from 1898 to 1903; was a member of the editorial staff of the Nebraska State Journal, 1907-15; acted as assistant director of the Legislative Reference Bureau, 1915; was industrial commissioner of the Omaha Chamber of Commerce for eight months in 1926 and 1927; and since 1927 has been managing director of the middlewest division of the National Electric Light Association, and of the Nebraska section of this organization.

A Republican, Mr. Browne was secretary of the state railway commission, 1916-19; was a member of this commission by appointment, 1919-20, and by election, 1921-26; and was defeated for renomination in 1926.

His marriage to Zoe Lou Chenoweth was solemnized at Ohiowa, Fillmore County, Nebraska, June 12, 1910. Mrs. Browne was born at Hubbell, Thayer County, Nebraska, December 8, 1883. Her Welsh-Irish ancestors came to America in 1635. Two children were born to this marriage: Donald, born February 20, 1911, who died November 20, 1917; and Betty May, born October 25, 1919.

Mr. Browne was a cadet at the University of Nebraska, and is a member of the Chamber of Commerce and the Kiwanis Club of Lincoln. He holds membership in the Lincoln University Club of Lincoln, and the Congregational Church of Lincoln. Residence: Lincoln.

Edith Wright Brownell

Edith Wright Brownell, clubwoman, was born at Schuyler, Nebraska, August 30, 1886, daughter of Henry Chester and Carrie Elizabeth (Sumner) Wright. Her father, who was born at Hyde Park, Vermont, January 21, 1847, was a lumberman. He died at Schuyler, on March 14, 1922. His wife, Carrie Elizabeth, was born at Appleton (McLain's Mills), Maine, June 28, 1853, and died at Schuyler, September 13, 1922. She served a three year term as first president of the Schuyler Civic Club. She was grand matron and grand treasurer of the Order of Eastern Star of Nebraska, and had ten ancestors who served in the Revolutionary War. John Howland, Mayflower passenger and Elizabeth Tilley, were among her forebears.

Upon the completion of her elementary education in the Schuyler grade school, Edith Wright attended Schuyler High School from which she was graduated in 1904. From September, 1904, until June, 1906, she attended the University of Nebraska, where she was a member of Delta Gamma.

On October 2, 1912, she was united in marriage to Rainsford Ormond Brownell, at Schuyler. Mr. Brownell was born at Liverpool, England, February 8, 1882, and is engaged in the banking business. They have one daughter, Winifred Edith, born July 10, 1913.

Mrs. Brownell is a Republican, and a member of the Daughters of the American Revolution, and the Society of Mayflower Descendants. She organized, and was first secretary of the local chapter of the Red Cross, and is a past president of the Civic Club of Schuyler. She is also a member of the Eastern Star, and of Holy Trinity Episcopal Church and the Woman's Auxiliary. Residence: Schuyler.

Rainsford Charles Brownell

Born at Dorchester, New Brunswick, Canada, January 12, 1860, Rainsford C. Brownell, bank executive, philanthropist, and outstanding civic and political leader, is the son of John Harvey and Mary Black (Taylor) Brownell.

John Harvey Brownell was born at Dorchester, New Brunswick, was an operator of mills at that place, and a political office holder throughout his life. He was a descendant of a family of English aristocrats who emigrated to Canada, in 1750. His wife was born at Dorchester, and she, too, was a descendant of English aristocracy, her family settling in Canada in 1800. Both Mr. and Mrs. Brownell died at their country home in Saunders County, Nebraska; Mr. Brownell in 1866, and his wife on January 18, 1904.

Rainsford C. Brownell attended public school, and on June 15, 1904, at North Bend, Nebraska, was married to Cedelia May Easom, a teacher and executive secretary. Mrs. Brownell was born at Morse Bluff, Nebraska, December 3, 1871. Her mother was of English parentage, and her father's ancestors were Kentuckians. She is a member of the Woman's Club, the P. E. O., the Eastern Star, and the Parent-Teachers' Association.

A resident of this state for fifty-nine years, Mr. Brownell was a pioneer settler in Nebraska, coming with his parents from Canada to Saunders County, April 22, 1872. He is president of the Bank of Morse Bluff, and has extensive farming interests and connections. Much of his time has been spent in active politics; he was postmaster at Cedar Hill, during the years 1885 to 1895, and a member of the state legislature in 1895, elected on the Republican ticket.

Always outstanding in civic work, he possesses letters of recognition from ex-President Woodrow Wilson, and former Governor Neville, for his service in the registration of men for the war on September 12, 1918; was sergeant in the Home Guards, acted on every loan drive during the World War, and was chairman of many Red Cross drives, an organization the local chapter of which he is now vice-president. For thirty years he has been a member of the Cedar Hill School Board, and for two years has served in that capacity in North Bend.

Mr. Brownell holds membership in the Community Club, the Red Cross, the Masons, and the Shrine, and is affiliated with the North Bend Methodist Episcopal Church where he is trustee and steward of the board.

Horse breeding and raising is another interest of Mr. Brownell's. He owns a stock farm on Cedar Hill, and has raised and owned some of the fastest standard-bred horses in Nebraska. One of these horses, the famous gelding *Spill*, won numerous cash prizes and established a record on the turf of this state.

Mr. and Mrs. Brownell live in an attractive old colonial home in the beautiful residential section of North Bend, and their hospitality is known to a large acquaintance of friends throughout the county and state. They have two children, Agnes Mary Collins, a child of a former marriage of Mrs. Brownell's, and born January 2, 1896; and Donald Rainsford, born November 9, 1905.

Agnes Mary Collins is married to Richard E. Janssen. She is a graduate of Francis Shiner Academy, Mount Carol, Illinois, and holds an M. A. degree from Northwestern University. She is an accomplished musician, and the mother of two children, Richard, Jr., and Martha May. Donald Rainsford Brownell is a graduate of the Hill Preparatory School at Pottstown, Pennsylvania, and the Babson Institute of Boston, Massachusetts. He holds a position of chief statistician for the Tidewater Oil Corporation of Boston, Massachusetts. Residence: North Bend.

Rainsford Ormond Brownell

Born at Liverpool, England, February 8, 1882, Rainsford Ormond Brownell has been a resident of Nebraska for the past forty years. He is the son of William Taylor and Ida (Fowler) Brownell, the former a native of St. John, New Brunswick, Canada. William Taylor Brownell was a sea captain of Scotch-Irish descent, who died at Burwell, Nebraska, in 1903. His wife, Ida, was born in Nova Scotia of French and English extraction.

Mr. Brownell attended Fremont High School, the Fremont Normal College, and was graduated in 1901. He was also a student at the University of Nebraska. At the university he was made a member of Acacia Fraternity.

His marriage to Edith Wright was solemnized at Schuyler, where Mrs. Brownell was born, August 30, 1886. She is of English descent. There is one child, Winifred, born July 10, 1913.

For some years Mr. Brownell was active in educational work, three years as a teacher in country school, three years as superintendent of school at Alexandria, four years as principal of the Schuyler High School, and four months as superintendent of the Hooper Schools. He is at the present time cashier and director of the Schuyler State Bank, and the Schuyler Savings Bank, and from 1926-29 was a member of the Guarantee Fund Commission.

Mr. Brownell is a Republican. While at the university he was a member of the cadets, with ranks from private, Company A, to sergeant; and during the World War was a member of the Home Guard. He is an Episcopalian, a member of the Knights of Pythias, the Masons and the Odd Fellows, and is also a member of the Chamber of Commerce. His hobby is gardening. Residence: Schuyler.

Edward Charles Brt

Banker and merchant, Edward Charles Brt, was born at Crete, Saline County, Nebraska, March 13, 1882. He is the son of Frank Brt and Theresa (Janecek) Brt. His father was born at Lhota Rybova, Sobeslav County, Tabor, State, Czechoslovakia, in 1845. His parents were peasants and land tillers, and came to the United States in 1871. He received military training in Austria Hungary, and served as a musician in the military band. He died at Crete, Saline County, Nebraska, December 30, 1928.

His mother was born in Dolany, Pilsen County, Czechoslovakia, May 28, 1855. Her parents were successful farmers and she was interested in reading and beneficial community work. She died at Crete, April 4, 1925.

Mr. Brt attended Crete High School, Omaha Commercial College, in 1900, and the summer school session of the Teacher's College at Emporia, Kansas, in 1926, where he studied music and received honors. Martha Marie Henke became his wife at Crete, April 26, 1917. She was born at Western, Saline County, Nebraska, of German parentage. Her parents farmed and she had experience as a clerk and house keeper. To this union four children were born; Genevieve, May 12, 1918, who died April 15, 1925, Edward Blaine, May 9, 1924, Donnalee, September 13, 1927, and Carolyn, March 18, 1931.

Edward Brt was in the mercantile business from 1907-17, at Madison and Crete, Nebraska, then entered the City National Bank and a year later the Tobias State Bank, as bookkeeper. Later he worked for the Saline County Bank at Western, Nebraska, as the assistant cashier, which position he held for ten years. At present he is cashier in the Abie State Bank and is a trustee for the depositors committee. He is a director of the Abie State Bank and also has the position of city treasurer.

Mr. Brt is affiliated with the Evangelical Church, is secretary and a director of the Abie school board and has held membership in the Royal Highlanders for twenty-five years. He is a member of the Nebraskana Society. Music is his hobby. He plays a cornet and for the past thirty-five years has participated in many musical occasions. Residence: Abie. (Photograph in Album).

Carl Wilhelm Bruce

Carl W. Bruce, pioneer Nebraska farmer and banker, was born at Dalarna, Sweden, November 18, 1861, the son of Lars P. and Greta E. (Soderburg) Bruce. His father, a farmer, was born in Dalarna, April 18, 1831, and died at Malmo, Nebraska, July 13, 1907. He came to America in 1868, and settled at Omaha. Greta E. Soderburg was a typical pioneer woman, born at Dalarna, January 24, 1833, and who died at Malmo, on September 23, 1902.

Mr. Bruce received his education in the public schools and soon became a farmer and cattle feeder. After some years he entered the real estate and banking business, and is now president of the Farmers and Merchants Bank at Malmo. A Republican, he has been actively interested in political affairs in his community and state for many years, and has served as chairman of the Saunders County Republican central committee several times.

He is a member of the Nebraskana Society, is affiliated with the Swedish Mission Church at Malmo, and holds membership in the Woodmen of the World. During the World War he took part in war saving stamp sales. His recreations include hunting, fishing and reading.

On March 2, 1898, Mr. Bruce was married to Emma C. Nordquist at Malmo. She was born at Dalarno, on January 30, 1869. They have the following children: Clifford, born January 13, 1899, who attended a mechanical school, and who is in the oil business; Mildred, born July 18, 1901, who received a business education, and who married Earl Barks; Leila, born October 14, 1905, who attended the State University two years, and Genevieve, born December 8, 1908, who attended the State University. Leila and Genevieve are teachers. Residence: Malmo.

Clark Bruce

Clark Bruce, educator of the blind, was born in Dearborn County, Indiana, November 15, 1861, the son of Amos and Sarah Ann (Clements) Bruce. His father, whose family came from Scotland, was born in Indiana, in 1826, and died in Burt County, Nebraska. He was a farmer.

His mother was of English descent, was born in Indiana, and died in Burt County.

Mr. Bruce received his education at the School for the Blind at Nebraska City, where he was graduated in 1886. Later he studied for eight months at the Ohio School for the Blind at Columbus, Ohio. He has lived in Nebraska City since 1874, and for forty years has been a teacher of industrial art at the School for the Blind. Aside from his school activities he is an expert piano tuner and teaches this subject to his students.

On June 16, 1897, he was married to Mamie Leonora Gray at Bellevue, Sarpy County, Nebraska. Mrs. Bruce, whose ancestry is Scotch, was born at Marton, Michigan, May 16, 1878. She is a nurse. Three children were born to this union: Robert C., born June 24, 1898, who married Hannah Hibbard; Alta, born May 20, 1901, who married James Freeman; and Clark, born October 4, 1902, who married Viola Fitzeham.

Mr. Bruce is president of the Nebraska Association of Workers for the Blind, and president of the Greggsport Parent-Teachers' Association. He is a member of the Highland Nobles, and is affiliated with the First Methodist Church at Nebraska City. His hobby is gardening. He is a Republican. Residence: Nebraska City.

Charles Henry Brugh

A leader in the professional and civic world at York, Nebraska, Charles Henry Brugh, has been a resident of this state for over 37 years. He was born in Livingston County, Illinois, December 7, 1888, the son of Charles Lewis and Mollie Belle (Snider) Brugh. His father, who was a farmer, was born in Botetourt County, Virginia, May 17, 1851. He came to Nebraska in 1893 and settled near Alma in 1894, where he resided until his death, March 18, 1923. His mother, whose German ancestry dates to the Fishburn family of Virginia (1740), was born at Troutville, Virginia, January 29, 1863.

Dr. Brugh attended rural school in Harlan County, Nebraska, and in 1910 was graduated from the Alma High School. He received the D. D. S. degree at Creighton University in 1913. He has been engaged in the practice of dentistry since 1913 and at this time is president of the Southwestern District Dental Society, is director and treasurer of the Missouri Valley Life Insurance Company of Lincoln.

He is a member of the York County Commercial Club, has been a member of the board of directors of the Young Men's Christian Association since 1926, and is a member of the Red Cross and Salvation Army. He holds membership in the following: Odd Fellows; Masons; Elks; Knights of Pythias; Nebraskana Society; and the First Methodist Episcopal Church of York. His favorite sport is football, and his hobbies include mechanics and touring by automobile. Politically, Dr. Brugh is independent.

He was married to Muriel Ruth Adams at Lincoln, Nebraska, May 20, 1916. Mrs. Brugh was born at Phillips, Nebraska, May 1, 1894; her father's ancestors came to America from England prior to 1880 and her mother's family came from Switzerland in 1775. They have four children: Janice Marie, born August 5, 1918; Charles Henry, born April 6, 1921; Elroy Alfred, born April 19, 1922; and Donalea, born October 4, 1925. Residence: York.

Charles Henry Brugh

A life resident of Nebraska, Charles Henry Brugh was born at Fremont, July 5, 1867. He is the son of Elijah G. and Mary E. (Bowman) Brugh, pioneers in Nebraska in its early days. Elijah Brugh was born in Hartford City, Indiana, August 17, 1846, and at the time of his death at Fremont, on March 9, 1919, was a retired farmer.

Mary E. Bowman was born in Virginia, April 5, 1839, and came with her husband to Nebraska. She died at Fremont, on May 14, 1926. Charles Henry Brugh was educated in the public schools, and later married Anna Lydick. To them were born three children: Earl E., born March 26, 1889, who married Earley Flesher; C. Stewart, born January 2, 1891, who married Helen Randall; and Ethel B., born February 18, 1892.

Mr. Brugh has always been a leader in his community, and has been a Republican all his life. He is a member of the Presbyterian Church, the Masonic order and The Nebraskana Society. Residence: Fremont.

Emmet Stewart Brumbaugh

Emmet S. Brumbaugh, prominent lawyer at Omaha, Douglas County, Nebraska, was born at Logansport, Cass County, Indiana, November 13, 1888. His father, Theodore Everett Brumbaugh, who was born in Elkhart County, Indiana, November 22, 1863, and died at Omaha, July 15, 1915, was a traveling salesman for the National Cash Register Company; his ancestry was Pennsylvania Dutch and Scotch. His mother, who is of English and Scotch descent, was born at Logansport, November 2, 1865.

Mr. Brumbaugh was graduated from the high school at Logansport, in 1907. He was awarded the A. B., 1912, and LL. B. degree, 1913, at the University of Indiana. He was a student at De Pauw University at Greencastle, Indiana, 1909-10. While attending University of Indiana, he was a member of the honorary law fraternity Phi Delta Phi and was president of the board of managers of *Arbutus*, the year book, 1913. He is now a member of the law firm Gray & Brumbaugh of Omaha. He has lived in this state for 18 years.

He was married to Lucille Maud Gray at Brooklyn,

New York, March 23, 1918. Mrs. Brumbaugh was born at Winimac, Indiana, January 5, 1887; she is of Scotch-Irish descent. They have one daughter, Lucille, born June 9, 1923.

Mr. Brumbaugh was auditor of masters accounts for the United States Shipping Board, the Emergency Fleet Corporation at New York City, 1918-19. He is a member of the Omaha Bar Association; the Nebraska State Bar Association; and the American Bar Association. He holds membership in the Elks; of which he is esteemed Leading Knight; Knights of Pythias; Ancient Order of United Workmen of Iowa, and is member of 2nd division; and the Security Benefit Association. He is a member and elder of the First Presbyterian Church of Omaha. His sport is golf. He is a Republican. Residence: Omaha.

Dee Andrew Brumley

Dee Andrew Brumley, manager of the J. C. Penney Company at Superior, was born at Greenville, Tennessee, May 20, 1899, and is the son of David Andrew and Martha Adlyn (Fraker) Brumley.

He was educated in public school, and has been connected with the mercantile business practically all his mature life. For four years he was a salesman with the W. J. Johnston Mercantile Company at Lamar, Colorado, and for the past seven years has been associated with the J. C. Penney Company as store manager, the last three years at Superior.

On August 31, 1920, he was united in marriage to Bertha Rowena Knisley, at Checotah, Oklahoma, her birthplace. Mrs. Brumley was born September 8, 1904. There are two children, Martha Lee, born June 5, 1927; and Mary Dee, born January 28, 1929.

Mr. Brumley is independent in politics. During the late war he had eighteen months' service in the Philippine Islands, and for a number of years has been a member of the American Legion. He is a member of the Chamber of Commerce, the Kiwanis Club, the Masons, and the Methodist Church. Mr. Brumley's club is the Superior Country Club. Residence: Superior.

Percy A. Brundage

Percy A. Brundage was born at Orange, New Jersey, October 9, 1864, the son of Abner and Sarah Jane (Harrison) Brundage. His father was born at Orange, August 2, 1830, and died at Tecumseh, Nebraska, February, 1906.

Sarah Brundage, his mother, was born at Orange, December, 1838, and died at Tecumseh, June, 1908.

Mr. Brundage received his education at Ashland School, East Orange, New Jersey. A Republican, he has been postmaster at Tecumseh for 24 years, and for 26 years has been president of the Tecumseh Building and Loan Association. He is one of the publishers of the Tecumseh Chieftain, and is a director in the Farmers' State Bank. He has been a resident of Nebraska for the last 51 years.

On May 4, 1892, he was united in marriage with Lelia Dew, at Tecumseh. Mrs. Brundage, who was born in Tecumseh, December 9, 1867, died August 29, 1923. Four children were born to this marriage, two of whom are living: Alan, born November 3, 1894, who died April, 1919; Anna, born January 31, 1897, who married Merl E. Townsend; Mary, born May 3, 1903, who married Bryce Crawford, junior; and Jean, born August 11, 1911, who died July, 1916.

Mr. Brundage is a Mason and Knight of Pythias. He is a member of the First Presbyterian Church at Tecumseh. Residence: Tecumseh.

Thomas J. W. Bruning

Thomas J. W. Bruning was born at Minonk, Woodford County, Illinois, March 21, 1878, the son of Frank D.

and Lena Engle (Lehners) Bruning. His father, who was a successful banker, was born in Germany, April 10, 1850, and died at Bruning, February 27, 1931. His mother was born in Germany, March 27, 1854, and died at Bruning, April 10, 1890.

Mr. Bruning who is a Republican, has lived in Nebraska for the past 50 years during which time he has been a farmer, and for 15 years has served as constable and street, light, and water commissioner of Bruning. He is a member of Trinity Lutheran Church, and holds membership in the local Red Cross chapter, the Bruning Community Club, and The Nebraskana Society.

His marriage to Tena M. Block was solemnized at Bruning, June 26, 1902. Mrs. Bruning was born in Livingston County, Illinois, September 1, 1878. Residence: Bruning.

Benjamin John Brunke

Benjamin John Brunke, a lifelong resident of this state, was born at Campbell, Nebraska, November 1, 1886, the son of John Conrad and Mary Agnes (Dusek) Brunke, and is now living on the same place where he was born 46 years ago. His father, a farmer, was born at Rockville, Wisconsin, May 1, 1856, and died at Campbell, November 27, 1920. His mother was born in Bohemia, May 7, 1867.

He has been a member of the Modern Woodmen of America, has been treasurer of the local school board since 1921, was formerly a deacon in the Presbyterian Church, and holds membership in the Red Cross and the Farmers Union at Campbell.

On March 22, 1910, he married Carolina Louise Koch at Campbell. Mrs. Brunke, whose ancestry is German, was born at Campbell, November 28, 1889. They have two children: Allen Vincent, born July 23, 1912; and Jerome Clayton, born September 29, 1924. Allen is studying veterinary surgery at Kansas State Agricultural College at Manhattan, Kansas. Residence: Campbell.

Charles H. Brunner

Charles H. Brunner, one of Fremont's leading citizens, was born at Muscatine, Iowa, December 31, 1853. He is the son of Dr. Henry and Ernestine (Denkman) Brunner, the former a native of Germany, and a physician. He died at Fremont, in June, 1881. His wife, Ernestine was also a native of Germany, and died at Long Beach, California, in 1923.

Mr. Brunner attended public and high school, and was graduated from the University of Michigan in 1880, as a pharmaceutical chemist. A resident of Nebraska for 60 years, he has been engaged in business in Fremont during a large part of that time. At present he is senior member of the firm, Brunner Drug Company, and a director of the Fremont National Bank.

On September 19, 1888, he was married to Lizzie Knoell at Fremont. Mrs. Brunner was born at Fremont, on March 15, 1865. There are no children. Mr. and Mrs. Brunner are Democrats, but inclined to vote for the man rather than adhere closely to party politics.

Mr. Bruner is an Agnostic. He is a member of the Masons, the Odd Fellows and the Woodmen of the World, and for a number of years was a member of the School Board of Fremont. His hobby is reading. Residence: Fremont.

Harvey J. Bruns

Harvey J. Bruns, farmer, was born at Talmage, Nebraska, November 15, 1890. He is the son of John O. and Fannie (Weber) Bruns, the former a native of Germany, who was born January 10, 1858. His wife, Fannie, was born in Sterling, Nebraska, in December, 1859, and died at Excelsior Springs, Arkansas, in June, 1898. She was of pioneer Nebraska parentage.

Mr. Bruns attended the public school and has since

CHARLES WAYLAND BRYAN

engaged in farming. He is a Democrat, active and interested in party politics. At the present time he is farming an 860-acre farm in Deuel County. He moved there 15 years ago from Otoe County. He is a member of Zion Lutheran Church, the Nebraskana Society, and for 15 years has been a director of the local school board. His hobby is driving a good team of mules.

He was married to Pearl Viola Bischoff, at Talmage, on April 23, 1912. Mrs. Bruns was born at Nebraska City, June 5, 1892. They have four children: Carl, born August 10, 1915; Glenn, born February 28, 1920; Irene, born April 12, 1922; and Dale, born July 21, 1924. The children love to help their father around the farm. Residence: Chappell.

Charles Wayland Bryan

Charles Wayland Bryan, eminent Statesman and political leader of Nebraska, was born at Salem, Illinois, February 10, 1867. His father, Silas Lillard Bryan, was circuit judge of Illinois for twelve years; served two terms in the Illinois state senate and was a member of the constitutional convention of 1872. He was born in Culpepper County, Virginia, in 1822. Mary Elizabeth (Jennings) Bryan, mother of Charles W. Bryan, was born near Walnut Hill, Illinois, in 1834.

Mr. Bryan received his elementary education in the public schools of Salem, Illinois, and later attended the University of Chicago and Illinois College. On November 29, 1892, he was married to Bessie Louise Brokaw, at Salem. To their union three children were born: Silas Millard, a captain in the World War, who is a practicing attorney in Minneapolis; Virginia, who is deceased; and Marylouise, who married W. E. Harnsberger, a banker at Ashland, Nebraska.

Since 1891 Mr. Bryan has been a resident of Lincoln. From 1897-1902 he was a colonel on the governor's staff, and from 1901-23 was publisher and associate editor of *The Commoner*, William Jennings Bryan being editor. For several years he was editor and proprietor of the *American Homestead*. During the life-time of his brother, the late William Jennings Bryan, he was closely associated with him as political secretary, publisher and business agent from 1897 until his death in 1925. Also active in farming and stock raising, he is well konwn as a lecturer on economics and government.

The following is quoted in part from *Who's Who in Lincoln*, published in 1928: mayor of Lincoln, 1915-17; city commissioner 1921-22; governor of Nebraska January, 1923, to January, 1925; Democratic candidate for governor, 1926; also 1928. Mr. Bryan was elected governor over Arthur J. Weaver in 1930. As candidate for vice president he was on the national ticket with John W. Davis, presidential candidate.

As mayor of Lincoln Mr. Bryan established a municipal employment bureau and legal aid department for wage-earners; extended and developed city parks and playgrounds, and as chairman of the Lincoln Park board helped to establish the Lincoln Park System and zoo. He took the first formal action in establishing the Lincoln General Hospital and contributed the first money for it. Governor Bryan advocates the initiative, referendum and recall in municipal and state governmental affairs, and advocates also municipal ownership of public utilities to protect the public against profiteering.

As mayor of Lincoln Governor Bryan secured the payment of widow's pensions in cash, which formerly were paid in orders on stores for goods. A city official and as chairman of the municipal ownership forces of Lincoln he secured a reduction in the price of ice, cooking gas, electric light and power rates. He established a municipal coal yard and reduced the retail price of coal about $4.00 a ton, making an annual saving to Lincoln coal consumers of $150,000. The legality and constitutionality of this municipal coal yard was upheld by the district and supreme courts of Nebraska.

Governor Bryan advocated and secured an amendment to the Lincoln city charter in 1924 permitting the establishment of a gasoline filling station which has operated for several years, and has resulted in a saving of several cents a gallon in the retail price of gasoline. The constitutionality of this municipal enterprise or utility has been upheld by the district and supreme courts of Nebraska, and by the supreme court of the United States. Governor Bryan suggested this plan of municipal competition to regulate monopolies after regulation through the courts had proven ineffective. He advocated government ownership and development of natural waterpower of the state and nation, such as Muscle Shoales and the Boulder project to regulate light and power rates.

As governor of Nebraska his first term Mr. Bryan reorganized the state government, reducing the number of employees more than one-half, and reducing taxes for state purposes 33 per cent as compared with preceding administrations. He established a state gasoline filling station at Lincoln and threatened to establish one in each town throughout the state, thereby securing a reduction in the price of gasoline of about 6 cents per gallon, resulting in an annual saving to consumers of the state of about eleven million dollars, which continued until the day he retired from office. He also established competition throughout the state in the sale of coal by buying coal and supplying it to towns and cities to be sold through public officials or public agents at reasonable prices, thereby saving coal consumers about $4.00 per ton, and amounting to an annual saving of about ten million dollars to the people of Nebraska.

In 1930 Mr. Bryan was again elected governor of Nebraska, the only candidate on the Democratic state ticket elected, his majority being 6500 while for the remaining state offices Republicans were elected by average majorities of about 75,000. Mr. Bryan ran on a platform pledging reduced cost of state government. After a battle for tax reduction, fought through the longest session of the legislature ever held in Nebraska, and a special session, Governor Bryan succeeded in reducing the cost of the state government twenty-five per cent or upwards of three and one-half million dollars. He also effected a reduction in the cost of road-building of thirty-two per cent by re-establishing competitive bidding, saving three million of dollars out of the yearly road funds, and building fifteen hundred miles of additional road or a total of 2700 miles of road as compared with about 850 miles for the preceding year.

When the depression, supplemented by draught in parts of Nebraska, made relief measures necessary, Governor Bryan directed that state road funds be spent for road development in the affected communities, and that the work be done by hand labor and teams instead of machinery. In this way distressed citizens could maintain their self-respect by earning money to sustain them and their families during the winter and not be compelled to accept charity or dole.

Governor Bryan helped secure and upheld the bank guarantee of deposits law in Nebraska which resulted in the payment in full to depositors of all bank deposits in failed banks during the 15 years the law was in force in Nebraska. Governor Bryan favors a guarantee of bank deposits for both state and national banks. He is a firm believer in the Jeffersonian democratic principle of "Equal rights to all and special privileges to none."

Governor Bryan affiliates with the Baptist Church, is a member of the Lincoln Chamber of Commerce and the Kiwanis Club. His fraternal organizations include the Odd Fellows, the Modern Woodmen of America and the Elks. He is a member of the Lincoln Country Club. Residence: Lincoln. (Photograph on Page 172).

JAMES ARTHUR BRYAN

Steiner—Scottsbluff

James Arthur Bryan

James Arthur Bryan was born at Lebanon, Illinois, June 18, 1862, son of William Jefferson and Margaret Jane Bryan.

The father was born in Wayne County, Indiana, December 24, 1827, and died at Newkirk, Oklahoma, in November, 1907. He was a prominent Republican a farmer and banker, whose grandfather came from Ireland. His wife, Margaret Jane, was born in Lebanon, Illinois, and died there in July, 1875. Her grandfather also came from Ireland. Mr. Bryan attended common country school.

In 1889 he started a grocery store in Ashland, Nebraska, but gave too much credit and had too small capital so was not successful. Later in Lincoln he had the same experience. In 1907 he moved to Scottsbluff, where he located on a homestead. After proving up on his homestead he traded for the H. P. Lewis Company. He moved to Henry, Nebraska, where he started a strictly cash grocery store, which was successful for a few months. Later he sold out and moved to Lingle, Wyoming, where he started a grocery store on a very small scale. In a few months he bought a lot, built a store building, and continued in business strictly for cash for a year and a half. He then sold out and come to Scottsbluff in 1915, where he now operates a cash store.

On May 29, 1889, he was married to Ella May Hays at Lebanon, Illinois. Mrs. Bryan was born at Lebanon, Illinois, June 11, 1862, and was a teacher in the public schools of Belleville, Illinois, six years and at Ashland, Nebraska, one year. Her parents came from Scotland and Ireland, and were pioneer settlers in Illinois. Her father was James Hays and her mother was America Jane Higgins. Mrs. Bryan attended country schools at Lebanon, Illinois. She is past county and local president of the Women's Christian Temperance Union and is a member of the Christian Church.

Mr. and Mrs. Bryan have had eight children, three of whom are living, Roland Arthur, born February 18, 1890, died September 7, 1890; Floyd Kenneth, born March 7, 1891, died June 29, 1891; Almon Victor, born July 12, 1895, married Thelda Jones; Almira, born January 20, 1895, died February 25, 1900; Lloyd McKinley, born October 12, 1896, married Jessie McCann; Margaret America, born July 16, 1898, married Earl S. Manthe; Anna Elizabeth, born November 24, 1899, died October 5, 1900; and LeRoy, born July 8, 1901, died October 3, 1901, Almon Victor is a banker and farmer. Lloyd McKinley is in partnership with his father in the grocery business at Scottsbluff. Lloyd served in the World War and is a member of the Commercial Club of Scottsbluff and the Masons. Almon is a Mason. There are four great grandchildren, Jean Anne Bryan, Welma Jane Bryan, Richard Earl Bryan, and Margaret Ann Manthe.

Mr. Bryan is a member of the Christian Church of Scottsbluff, the Commercial Club, is a Republican and a life member of the Nebraskana Society. Residence: Scottsbluff. (Photograph on Page 174).

Robert Raymond Bryan

Robert R. Bryan, clergyman, was born at Hookstown, Pennsylvania, March 21, 1889. He is the son of Robert Miller and Isabelle (Swaney) Bryan.

He received the following degrees: A. B., Westminster College, 1910; A. M., Princeton University, 1915. He attended Princeton Seminary, University of Nebraska and Columbia University.

Since 1923 he has been active in civic affairs at Omaha, where he is pastor of the Central United Presbyterian Church. Residence: Omaha.

William Jennings Bryan

William Jennings Bryan, the great commoner, was born in Salem, Illinois, March 19, 1860. Some of the Bryan ancestry is traced to Ireland and some to Wales, while other branches have followed through the Irish into English history. However, Judge Silas Lillard Bryan states that the family is of Irish extraction.

Judge Silas Lillard, father of William Jennings Bryan, was born near Sperryville in what was then Culpepper, but is now a part of Rappahannock County, Virginia, November 4, 1822.

He was elected to the state senate of Illinois in 1852 or 1853, serving eight years. In 1860 he was elected to the bench of the circuit court, where he served for twelve years. In 1872, as a member of a convention which framed the constitution of Illinois, he introduced a resolution declaring it to be the sense of the convention that all offices, legislative, executive, and judicial provided for by the constitution should be filled by the people. Before his election to the bench and after retirement therefrom he practiced law in Marion and adjoining counties.

Mariah Elizabeth Jennings, wife of Silas, was born near Walnut Hill, Illinois, May 24, 1834. She attended the public schools of the neighborhood and when nearly grown was the pupil of Silas L. Bryan, who was nearly twelve years her senior. She was a woman of excellent sense and superior management. Her husband's frequent absence from home threw upon her a large portion of the responsibility for the care and discipline of the family.

After her husband's death she removed from the farm to Salem. She always took a deep interest in the political fortunes of her son, William, and he always felt indebted to her, equally with his father, for counsel and instruction. After a lingering illness she died June 27, 1896.

The Bryan, Lillard, and Jennings families all belonged to the middle class. They were very industrious, law abiding, God fearing people. No member ever became very rich and none was very poor. Farming has been the occupation of the majority, while others have followed the legal and medical professions and mercantile pursuits.

William Jennings Bryan was always sturdy and happy and fond of play. One of his early ambitions was to be a minister. However, this soon gave place to determination to become a lawyer "like father." When he was six years old his father purchased a large farm near Salem, Illinois; here he studied, worked, and played until ten years of age, his mother being his only teacher. He learned to read quite early; after committing his lessons to memory he stood on a little table and spoke them to his mother. This is, perhaps, his first recorded effort at speech making. His work was feeding the deer, which his father kept in the small park, and helping to care for the pigs and chickens. His favorite sport was rabbit hunting with dogs.

At the age of ten, William Jennings Bryan entered the public schools at Salem. Not what one would call an especially brilliant student, he never failed during his school attendance. It was during his early school years that he developed an interest in the work of literary and debating societies. His father's congressional campaign in 1872 was his first political awakening, and from that time on he always cherished the thought of entering public life. His idea was first to win a reputation and secure a competency at the bar, but he seized the unexpected opportunity which came to him in 1890. At the age of fifteen he entered Whipple Academy, the preparatory department of Illinois College at Jacksonville. With this step he began a changed life. Vacation always found him at home, but for eight years he led the life of a student and then took up his profession. His parents wished him to take a classical course, and while sometimes grumbling over his Latin and Greek, he many times recognized the wisdom of their choice. Of these two languages Latin was his preference. He had a strong leaning for mathematics and especially toward geometry and believed that the mental discipline acquired through this study was later useful in argument. We believe it will be extremely interesting to every boy who reads this sketch to know of his record on this point. During his first year at the academy he declaimed Patrick Henry's masterpiece, and not only failed to win a prize but ranked well down the list. Nothing daunted, the second year found him again entered with *The Palmetto and the Pine* as his subject. This time he ranked third. The next as his subject. This time he ranked third. The next year when a freshman, he tried for a prize in Latin prose and won half of the second prize. In his sophomore year he entered another contest with an essay on *Labor* and this time the first prize rewarded his work. Again in his junior year an oration upon *Individual Powers* gave him the first prize. This winning of the Junior prize entitled him to represent Illinois College in the intercollegiate oratorical contest which was held at Galesburg, Illinois, in the fall of 1880.

At the time of his graduation he was elected class orator by his class, and having the highest rank in scholarship during the four years course, delivered the valedictory address. The graduating exercises of Illinois College occurred in June 1881. When fall came he entered the Union College of Law at Chicago. On July 4, 1883, began the practice of his profession in Jacksonville, Illinois. During the next six months, the struggle encountered by all young professional men began. During the few years that followed politics lost none of its charms and each campaign found Mr. Bryan speaking.

Three years after graduation, it might be well to mention, he attended the commencement at Illinois College, delivered the Masters oration, and received his degree. The subject being *American Citizenship*.

In 1887, legal business called him to Kansas and Iowa and he spent a day in Lincoln with a former law classmate, A. R. Talbot. Mr. Bryan was greatly impressed by the beauty and business enterprise of Lincoln, and with the unlimited advantages which a growing capital furnished a young lawyer. Returning to Illinois full of enthusiasm for the west, he made plans to remove to Lincoln. We might again mention that no political ambitions were responsible for the change as the city, county, and state were strongly Republican. Arriving in Lincoln, October 1, 1887, a partnership was formed with Mr. Talbot.

Mr. Bryan did not distinguish himself particularly as a lawyer. He entered the practice at 23 and left it at 30. He became actively connected with the Democratic organization in Nebraska almost immediately after coming to the state, for early in the spring of 1888 he made a political speech at Seward.

In 1890, without opposition for the nomination in his own party, Mr. Bryan was elected to congress. He was re-elected to congress in 1892. In the spring of 1894 he announced that he would not be a candidate for re-election, but had decided to stand as a candidate for the United States senate. He was nominated for that office by the unanimous vote of the democratic state convention, but was unsuccessful in the election. The defeat, a disappointment, did not discourage Mr. Bryan. On September 1, 1894, he became chief of the editorial staff of the *Omaha World Herald,* continuing until nominated for president in 1896.

From that date until the last national convention he gave a portion of his time to newspaper work. It might be mentioned that two of Mr. Bryan's most important speeches were delivered, one at Tammany Hall, July 4, 1892, and the other at the National Cemetery at Arlington, May 30, 1894. President Cleveland and four of his cabinet were in attendance on the latter occasion.

As a delegate in the Democratic National Convention of 1896, he delivered the oration in favor of the free coinage of silver, known as the "Cross of Gold" speech, which won him the nomination for the presidency. He traveled more than 18,000 miles during this campaign, speaking at almost every stopping place. He was, however, defeated by William McKinley, receiving 176 electoral votes against McKinley's 271.

Then the Spanish War came, and on the day war was declared Mr. Bryan telegraphed his services to President McKinley. Without any experience Mr. Bryan could not be assigned to the staff. However, Governor Holcomb of Nebraska authorized him to raise a regiment which was known as the Third Nebraska Regiment of Volunteer Infantry for the Spanish American War. He became its colonel.

In 1900 Mr. Bryan was again nominated for the presidency. He made a most brilliant and active campaign but again was defeated, receiving 155 electoral votes against 292 for William McKinley. About this time Mr. Bryan established a political magazine at Lincoln, which was known as the *Commoner*. In 1906 he toured the world, contributing articles to newspapers and magazines thereafter. In 1908 he was nominated for president a third time at Denver, but was defeated by William Howard Taft.

On March 4, 1913, he took the office of secretary of state in the cabinet of President Woodrow Wilson, resigning on June 9, 1915. During this time he negotiated thirty treaties with governments which represented three-fourths of the world's population. Mr. Bryan was the author of *The First Battle* (1897); *Under Other Flags* (1904); *The Old World and Its Ways* (1907); besides numerous articles in magazines and newspapers throughout the world. In 1916 the question of state prohibition became the dominant issue in Nebraska, and Mr. Bryan made a tour of the state in support of the movement. In 1920 he made his last campaign in the state, when he was a candidate for delegate from Nebraska to the convention at San Francisco.

For thirty years Mr. Bryan was in the public eye as a champion of the common people, and probably has had no equal in American history in ability to put his sentiment into eloquent and stirring words. No man in history has spoken to so many people. Perhaps there will be equals but never a superior in the power of his eloquence.

To Mr. and Mrs. Bryan were born three children; Ruth Baird, now Mrs. Reginald Owen, was born October 2, 1885. William Jennings Bryan, Jr., was born June 24, 1889, and Grace Dexter, now Mrs. Richard L. Hargreaves, was born February 17, 1891.

William Jennings Bryan died at Dayton, Tennessee, July 26, 1925. (Photograph on Page 3).

Gordon Folsom Bryant

Born at Tekamah, May 6, 1887, Gordon Folsom Bryant has been a lifelong resident of Burt County. He is the son of Edward Washburn and Rose (Folsom) Bryant, the former a native of Barre, Massachusetts, who came to Nebraska in its early days. He was born December 13, 1847, and died at Tekamah, November 15, 1919. He engaged in the lumber, coal and building material business in one location for more than fifty years. His wife, Rose Folsom, was born at Attica, New York, November 23, 1858, and is the daughter of B. R. Folsom, who homesteaded the townsite of Tekamah; she is also a second cousin of Mrs. Frances Folsom, wife of President Cleveland.

Gordon Folsom Bryant attended Tekamah public schools until 1905, and attended Worcester (Massachusetts) Academy one year. After leaving school he entered the business of his father, with whom he was associated twenty-five years, and upon his death became the owner and manager. In addition to this he is the owner of four farms adjoining Tekamah, and engages in stock-feeding and raising.

He was married to Anne Radcliffe at Sidney, Nebraska, January 27, 1921. Mrs. Bryant, who is a reader and student of literature, was born at Sidney, October 7, 1893. There are two sons, Gordon, born February 14, 1921, and Jack, born October 5, 1926. The family belongs to the Presbyterian Church.

Mr. Bryant is independent in politics, and is a member

of the Chamber of Commerce, the Lions Club and the Red Cross. He enjoys golf, and is a member of the Tekamah Country Club. Residence: Tekamah.

James Howard Bryant

James H. Bryant was born at Mooresville, Indiana, September 15, 1866, the son of Bowater and Lucetta Ann (Warthen) Bryant. His father was born at Mooresville, September 9, 1840, and died at Norcatur, Kansas, April 4, 1916. His mother was born at Mooresville, and died at Norcatur, Kansas, July 12, 1924, the mother of eleven children. Her ancestry on her mother's side, dates back to the celebrated temperance worker, Josiah Dow.

On September 6, 1906, Mr. Bryant was united in marriage with Laura A. Emerick, at Lincoln, Nebraska. She was born at Butler, Pennsylvania, December 6, 1871, her ancestry dating to Hessie Castle Armstedt, in Germany. To this union three children were born: Lyle, born March 16, 1908, who is now married to Lulu Lewien; Eulalia, born September 30, 1910; and Roma, born April 12, 1913. Lyle has been connected with the department of public works for four years, and Eulalia and Roma are both successful school teachers.

A resident of Nebraska sixty years, Mr. Bryant has served three times as census enumerator, and four years as precinct assessor. He was the first mail carrier at Carleton, was owner and editor of the *Carleton Leader* for five and one-half years, and was in the real estate business for four years.

During the World War he bought bonds and donated liberally to the Red Cross. He holds membership with the Modern Woodmen of America, is an Ancient Free and Accepted Mason, a veteran free Mason, and a member of the Low Twelve Club. Reading baseball news is his hobby. Residence: Carleton.

Wilbur Franklin Bryant

Wilbur Franklin Bryant, distinguished lawyer and judge of Nebraska, has lived in this state for the past 55 years, and has taken a prominent place in the legal world during that time. He was born at Dalton, Coos County, New Hampshire, March 21, 1851, the son of George Washington and Nancy Marinda (Parker) Bryant. His father, who was a doctor of divinity, and held the A. M. degree, was a soldier in the War of the Rebellion; he was born at Enfield, Grafton County, New Hampshire, March 30, 1825, and died at New York City, June 16, 1901; his English and Irish ancestors came to England with William the Conqueror. His mother, who was a musician, was born at Concord, Essex County, Vermont, September 1, 1830, and died at New York City, December 24, 1900; her ancestors served in the Revolution.

Mr. Bryant attended Kimball Union Academy and Dartmouth College. He was president of his class at Kimball, and held membership in Kappa Kappa Kappa at Dartmouth College. After the age of fifty he studied under Professor Ross at the University of Nebraska. He is the author of: *Life of Louis Riel; Historical Men of Nazareth; Did Virgil Write the Aeneid; Letter to a Young Law Student;* a speech against the parochial schools in which he advocated compulsory attendance in public school. He is the editor of *Campaign Post.* He been engaged in law practice for many years, has tried twenty-two homicide cases and received a conviction in each of them.

He is a Democrat, and has held the following positions: district attorney for six districts in Nebraska; county judge for two years in Cuming County; county judge for 17 years in Cedar County; state insurance commissioner until the supreme court declared it unconstitutional for him to hold the office; postmaster for three years in Cedar County; deputy provost marshal during the World War, and colonel in the state militia; and reporter of the supreme court of Nebraska for six years.

Judge Bryant voted against state prohibition in 1917,

but believing in law enforcement, he fed convicted bootleggers on bread and water. The associated press blazed this over three continents. It was published over America, and even in China and Turkey. *The New York Times* and the *Springfield (Mass.) Republican* censured Bryant severely.

He is a member of the American Bar Association. While he was in Lincoln, he was one of the directors of the State Organization of Charities and Collections. He has been a delegate to numerous conventions, among them the Catholic World Congress in 1893. He is affiliated with Holy Trinity Catholic Church at Hartington.

He was interested in war activities in Cedar County in 1918. All of his sons served, one of them being totally disabled. He is a member of the Nebraskana Society.

Mr. Bryant's marriage to Kate Saunders was solemnized at Springfield, Bon Homme County, South Dakota, October 1, 1881. Mrs. Bryant, who is librarian at Hartington, was born at Waucapona, Cedar County, Nebraska, July 25, 1861. She is of Holland Dutch ancestry. Their children are: Ita, an instructor in the Teachers College at Valley City, North Dakota; Ethel, who is now a high school teacher in the Lincoln High School; Eugene, who married Eloise Engle, and who is totally disabled as a result of the World War; Donovan, who is a journalist; and George, born June 20, 1900, who was an educator, and who died September 25, 1923. Ita is also an educator, while Donovan is on the staff of the Bee News at Omaha. Residence: Hartington. (Photograph on Page 178).

John Anton Brym

Born in Provice, Czechoslovakia, January 1, 1883, John Anton Brym is the son of Anton and Frantiska (Macek) Brym, both of whom came to America in 1884, and both of whom are living.

John Anton Brym attended public school, and from 1899 to 1900, was in the mercantile business. During the year 1901, he was manager of the Republican Publishing Company, 1902-07 was a grain buyer and postmaster at Loma, Nebraska. From 1907-12, he owned and operated a general merchandise business at Dwight, Nebraska, and from that time until 1922 was a realtor and auctioneer at Dwight. He became vice president of the First National Bank of David City in 1922, and since 1930 has been its president.

On February 3, 1902, he was united in marriage to Fanny Maresh, at Dwight. There were two children: Mary, born August 21, 1902, who died May 9, 1903; and Emma, born November 2, 1905, is married to Alexander L. Pohl, who is connected with the First National Bank.

Mr. Brym is a Democrat. He has resided in Nebraska forty-seven years, is an outstanding figure in his community, and is a member of the Nebraskana Society. During the World War he was a four minute speaker, and a member of the Butler County Council of Defense.

He is a member of St. Mary's Church, and was chairman of its building committee in 1915, when the new church and school were erected, is secretary of Butler County 4-H Clubs, and is a member of the school board. He is a member of the Modern Woodmen of America, and the Chamber of Commerce, and was a member of the committee on civic improvements of the latter in 1925. During 1912-20 Mr. Brym was mayor of Dwight. Residence: David City.

Carl Holland Bryner

Carl Holland Bryner was born at Callaway, Custer County, Nebraska, January 6, 1889. He is the son of Isaac and Matilda Arsino (Sayre) Bryner, the former a merchant and photographer, whose Welsh and German ancestors came to America in 1757. Isaac Bryner was born at Uniontown, Pennsylvania, April 1, 1858, and died at Callaway, March 2, 1929. His wife, Matilda, was born at Sandyville, West Virginia, April 26, 1860. She is an expert embroiderer and formerly was a teacher of the art.

Richards—Hartington

WILBUR FRANKLIN BRYANT

She is of English and French descent and still living.

Dr. Bryner was graduated from Callaway High School 1908, and was class historian. He attended Omaha University during 1914 and 1915, and Creighton University of Arts College during 1915 and 1916. He received his D. D. S. from Creighton Dental College in 1919, and is a member of Delta Sigma Delta.

He was married to Cozie Ellen Bryner at Grand Island, September 18, 1910. Mrs. Bryner was born at Shell Creek, Nebraska, December 1, 1889, and is of English descent. They have three children, Jean Ellen, born January 26, 1919; Patricia Carlene, born August 24, 1924, and Charles Robert, born June 14, 1929.

Upon his graduation from high school Dr. Bryner spent two years as a photographer, and three years as head clerk in a grocery store. He was later head clerk and manager of a shoe store for seven years. In 1919, he entered the active practice of dentistry and has the honor of having received the first appointment as dental surgeon for the Missouri Pacific Railway, in which capacity he has served five years. His appointment was the first ever given for any railroad.

On September 18, 1917, he enlisted as a private in the United States Army, and took the examination and was given the rank of first lieutenant, but never served; he was discharged on December 8, 1918. He is a member of the First Methodist Church, and of all bodies of York and Scottish Rite Masonry, including the Shrine and Shrine Patrol. He is a member of the Omaha, Nebraska State, and National Dental Societies. His club is the Lakewood County Club. He enjoys golf and fishing, and his hobby is mechanics. Residence: Omaha.

James Monroe Bryson

James Monroe Bryson, a farmer in Nebraska for several years, has been a resident of this state all his life. He was born at Grand Island, Nebraska, July 5, 1900, the son of Silas Young and Julia (Zuver) Bryson, the former a farmer who was born at Adams, Nebraska, October 26, 1867, and died at Grand Island, September 13, 1921. His mother was born in Gage County, Nebraska, March 7, 1872, and died at Grand Island, December 31, 1929.

Mr. Bryson attended Grand Island College in 1915, and since 1917 has been engaged in farming near Grand Island. He is a Democrat, holds membership in the Methodist Church, and is a member of the Nebraskana Society.

His marriage to Mary Ellen Caveny occurred at Wood River, Nebraska, December 26, 1923. Mrs. Bryson, who was formerly a teacher, was born at Wood River, October 6, 1896. To them three children were born: Robert James, October 29, 1925; Helen Jean, May 14, 1927; and Gerald Lee, December 13, 1930. Residence: Grand Island.

Albert Edward Buchanan

Albert Edward Buchanan, one of the leading physicians in Dodge County, was born at Chatham Hill, Smyth County, Virginia, August 21, 1872. His father, Hickman Spiller Buchanan, was born in Smyth County, September 12, 1847, and died there March 31, 1899. He was a farmer and cattle raiser, descended from Scotch-Irish settlers 1720-30, who were soldiers in the Revolution and the Confederate Army, and prominent in the development of southwestern Virginia. Among them were state legislators, congressmen and presidents. Laura Marie (Sexton) Buchanan, wife of Hickman, was born in 1850, and died in Smyth County, August 10, 1925. She was of English and Scotch-Irish descent.

Dr. Buchanan attended Marion High School and Holston High School until 1890, and received his A. B. from Emery and Henry College in 1896. In 1900 he was graduated from the Medical College of Virginia, and was admitted to practice by competitive examination. A member of the Callipean Literary Society, he twice represented it in public debate (1892-93), and in 1895 was the winner of the debater's medal. He is a member of Sigma Alpha Epsilon (chapter Pi), and of Pi Mu which is now merged with Phi Chi. He was a member of the football team of Emery & Henry College 1892-94.

On June 12, 1901, he was united in marriage to Ada Grace Pratt at Pleasant Grove, Virginia. Mrs. Buchanan was born at Chatham Hill, Virginia, October 29, 1876, and is a member of the Presbyterian Church and the American Legion Auxiliary. She is descended from early English and Scotch settlers in Virginia. There are three children: George Warren, born June 8, 1902; Edna Virginia, born December 7, 1903, and Laura Marie, born January 29, 1907. George is a graduate of Fremont High School, received his A. B. and LL. B. from the University of Nebraska and is a practicing attorney at Seattle, Washington. Edna graduated from Fremont High School and the National Kindergarten at Chicago, and is teaching in Kansas City, Missouri. Laura, who was also graduated from Fremont High School, received her A. B. from the University of Nebraska, and is a teacher of English at Saint Paul, Nebraska.

Dr. Buchanan taught in the public schools of Smyth County, 1893-94, and was assistant principal of the Marion, Virginia, High School 1896-97. From 1900-03 he was engaged in the practice of medicine in Smyth County; from 1903-10, at Cedar Bluffs, Nebraska, and since 1910 at Fremont.

He served in the Medical Corps with the rank of captain, and was assigned to Camp Meade, Maryland. Following his discharge he was a captain in the Medical Reserve five years, and promoted to the rank of major, which he holds at the present time. Since its organization he has been a member of the American Legion, and a medical member of the State Fund Relief Committee, Department of Nebraska, 1924-; a member of the General Welfare Committee, and Child Welfare Committee. He was present at the organization of Henry Teigeler, Jr. Post No. 20, at Fremont, and also at the organization of the State Department. He was third commander of Post No. 20, and served as delegate from that post to the Annual State Department Conventions every year but one. He has also been delegate to the National American Legion Conventions at Kansas City, San Francisco, Saint Paul, San Antonio, Louisville and Boston.

He is a member of the Reserve Officers' Association, the Military Surgeons of the United States, and the Forty and Eight. His professional memberships include the Dodge County, Nebraska State, Sioux Valley, Elkhorn Valley, Missouri Valley and American Medical Associations. He is a former member of the Red Cross and Salvation Army, serving as chairman of the emergency medical committee.

Dr. Buchanan is a Master Mason, and member of the Knights Templar, 32nd degree, Scottish Rite and Shrine. He is a former member of the Board of Education, and is a member of the First Presbyterian Church, the Nebraskana Society, and the Retail Merchants' Association. His hobby is working in the American Legion Department of Nebraska. Residence: Fremont.

Louis Buchholz

Louis Buchholz was born at Barada, Richardson County, Nebraska, June 16, 1879, the son of August and Johannah (Rife) Buchholz. His father, who was born at Baden, Germany, April 28, 1834, and died at Falls City, Richardson County, Nebraska, October 7, 1911, was a farmer who came to America in 1851.

His mother was born at Wurtemberg, Germany, August 15, 1838, and died at Falls City, May 11, 1915.

Mr. Buchholz was educated in the country schools after which he studied business. A Democrat, he is county commissioner of Richardson County at the present time.

He is a farmer and purebred stock breeder, dealing in shorthorn cattle and Percheron horses.

He was married to Edith Koso, at Falls City, May 20, 1902. Mrs. Buchholz was born at Falls City, August 28, 1883. To their union four children were born, three of whom are living. They are: Arthur J., born July 2, 1903, who married Anna Halbert; Nelson M., born June 20, 1905, who died August 26, 1911; Henry Clay, born August 19, 1908, who married Lois Wileman; and Bernice, born January 20, 1913.

Mr. Buchholz has no church affiliation, but is a firm believer in the practice of the golden rule. His hobby is reading. Residence: Falls City.

John Buchta

John Buchta was born at Edwardsville, Illinois, December 26, 1860, the son of John and Sophia Henrietta (Kaiser) Buchta. John Buchta was born at Jesen, Bavaria, Germany, May 6, 1821, and died at Osceola, Nebraska, November 16, 1909. He was a farmer. He was a member of Captain Seed's Company, crossing the plains to California in 1849, and returning in 1852 to Illinois by way of Panama and New York. Sophia H. Buchta was born at Mark Selbitz, Bavaria, Germany, January 8, 1829, and died at Osceola, Nebraska, May 31, 1910.

Mr. Buchta received his elementary education from a country school near Edwardsville, Illinois.

His marriage to Sevilla Heitzman was solemnized at Osceola, March 21, 1893. She is a native of Urban, Pennsylvania, and was born October 31, 1861. They have three children: J. William, born September 18, 1895, who is married to Viola L. Koerner; Verna Ruth, born December 7, 1896, who is married to LeRoy Rhodes; and Alverto Henrietta, born October 9, 1899, who is married to Walter W. Herrmann. All three children are graduates of the University of Nebraska.

Mr. Buchta has been a resident of Nebraska for forty-eight years, and is now a retired farmer. He holds membership in the Independent Order of Odd Fellows, and the Nebraskana Society. Residence: Osceola.

Charles Henry Buck

Charles Henry Buck, automobile dealer, was born at Crete, Saline County, Nebraska, October 11, 1883. He is the son of Jess M. and Mina Buck. Jess M. Buck was a farmer, for many years prior to his death which occurred at Buffalo, Montana.

Mr. Buch attended public school and was a high school student. At the present time he is engaged in automobile business at Davenport.

He was married to Mary A. Keim on December 18, 1914, at Davenport, Nebraska. Mrs. Buck was born at Rockwood, Pennsylvania, December 16, 1888. Residence: Davenport.

Charles Wallace Buck

For over 62 years Charles W. Buck has lived in Saline County, Nebraska, where he has been prominent in business and civic affairs. He was born at DeWitt, February 18, 1869, the son of Charles Harvey and Ophelia Henrietta (Knox) Buck. His father, who was a farmer, was born at Barrington, Cook County, Illinois, October 26, 1843, and died at DeWitt, August 29, 1928. He served for many years as a member of the board of education; was a Democrat; and held membership in the Grand Army of the Republic, the Modern Woodmen of America, and the Ancient Order of United Workmen. He was of English descent.

His mother, whose ancestry was Scotch, was born of Quaker parentage at Elgin, Illinois, August 16, 1845, and died at DeWitt, April 9, 1914. She was a teacher and was active in the work of the Woman's Christian Temperance Union.

Mr. Buck attended grade school in Saline County, but received most of his education through his own experience and personal application. He has been a farmer for many years and has held various positions in farmers' organizations, among them secretary of the Farmers Elevator Company, 16 years; president of the Saline County Livestock Breeders Association; secretary of the DeWitt Duroc Breeders Association; secretary of the DeWitt Poultry Show; and director of the County Farm Bureau.

He is proprietor of the Cloverdale Stock Farm near DeWitt; is a stockholder in the Farmers and Merchants Bank; director and manager of the DeWitt Sales Pavilion Association, of which he has been president; and for 29 years has been an agent for the Farmers Mutual Insurance Company. Mr. Buck is the editor of a weekly column in the *DeWitt Times News,* and is the author of *Early History of the Community.*

His marriage to Emma Beckner was solemnized at DeWitt, February 26, 1896. Mrs. Buck was born at Conn, Grey County, Province of Ontario, Canada, April 26, 1871; she is of German descent. Their three children are: Emma Luella, born April 18, 1898, who married Arthur W. Farrall; Charles Wallace, born January 6, 1903, who married Katherine Lanore Heckart, a home economics teacher; and Glenn Augustus, born May 21, 1905, who married Sylvia Hernie Lewis, a French teacher. Luella is a home economics teacher; Charles Wallace is interested in vocational agriculture; Glenn specialized in agricultural journalism; and Arthur W. Farrall was an instructor in the University of California for six years and is now research engineer in Chicago.

Mr. Buck took an active part in Red Cross and Liberty Loan drives, and Council of Defense work during the World War. He is a member of the Red Cross; Near East Relief; Civic Service Club; Parent Teachers' Association; and the Nebraskana Society. He is an officer and member of the Municipal Band; has been a member of the board of education for 26 years, serving consecutively as president, treasurer, and secretary; and is a member of the Saline County Re-districting Board.

Mr. Buck is a member of the official board of the Methodist Episcopal Church of DeWitt, and takes a prominent part in religious activities. His hobbies are reading, writing, and educational work of all kinds. He is a football enthusiast. Politically, he is an Independent. Residence: DeWitt.

Ralph Joseph Buck

Ralph Joseph Buck, retired lumberman of Sutton, Nebraska, has lived in the state for 28 years. He was born at Monica, Illinois, October 7, 1878, the son of John Mortimer and Susie Zadee (Clute) Buck. His father, who was born in Cayuga County, New York, January 25, 1847, and died at Sutton, September 19, 1925, was a farmer and a veteran of the Civil War; he was a member of the Congregational Church and the Independent Order of Odd Fellows Encampment. His mother, who was born at Monica, August 25, 1857, is a member of the Congregational Church, the Rebekah Lodge, Degree of Honor, and the Daughters of the American Revolution.

Mr. Buck attended school in Illinois and Nebraska and in 1898 was graduated from the Sutton High School. He received the B. S. Degree at the University of Nebraska in 1903; he served as president of the senior class both in high school and at the university. For several years Mr. Buck was engaged in educational work, and later was connected with a retail lumber firm in Idaho. He is now retired.

A Republican, he has served as a member of the Nebraska legislature, was a member of the school board for nine years, acting as president for three years, and was town treasurer for three years, in Idaho. He holds membership in the Sutton Community Club, the Independent Order of Odd Fellows, the Masons, and The Nebraskana Society. He is affiliated with the Congregational Church of Sutton. His hobbies are checkers and chess.

He was married to Mabel Louise Hoerger at Sutton, November 29, 1905. Mrs. Buck, whose grandfather served in the Civil War, was born at Sutton, September 18, 1879. They have one daughter, Kathryn Louise, born June 12, 1913.

During the World War Mr. Buck served as a member of local committees in relief and loan activities. Residence: Sutton.

Roscoe Buck

Roscoe Buck was born in Buckfield, Maine, September 18, 1880, the son of King Romanzo and Isabella (Farrar) Buck. His father, who was a farmer and served in the Civil War, was born at Buckfield, in 1847, and died at Boston, Massachusetts, in October, 1914; he was a descendant of Abija Buck who settled at Salem in 1635 having come to this country from England on the *Increase*. His mother, who was also descended from early settlers in America, was born at Hartford, Maine, November 25, 1849.

Mr. Buck attended the high school at Wellesley Hills, Massachussetts, until 1896, and on May 14, 1898 joined the United States Marine Corps, serving five years in Cuba, the Philippines and China. He was connected with the Zeno Manufacturing Company in Chicago from 1905 to 1909, and in 1909 homesteaded in Tripp County, South Dakota. The following year he moved to Nebraska, where he engaged in farming until 1912 when he became connected with the Stockman Bank at Springview as assistant cashier. Since 1915 he has served as postmaster at Springview where he is active in civic and welfare affairs.

He has been secretary-treasurer of the American Red Cross in Keya Paha County for the past 13 years. Mr. Buck served as a private in the United States Marine Corps for five years, participating in the Boxer Rebellion, *U. S. S. Machais*, Cuba and the Philippines, and was wounded in the battle of Tient-Sin, China, in 1900. He served as county chairman of the Citizens Military Training Camp in Keya Paha County, for the past four years, and is Past Commander of the Post No. 926 of Veterans of Foreign Wars, at Springview.

His chief past-time are reading and the radio. On February 27, 1906, he was married to Estelle Marie Burns at Chicago. Mrs. Buck, who is assistant postmaster at Springview, was born of French parents at Windsor, Canada, March 12, 1883.

William Ernest Buckendorf

For the past 25 years William Ernest Buckendorf has been editor and publisher of the *Rock County Leader*. He was born at South Bend, Indiana, May 4, 1882, son of Louis August and Joanna (Stemwell) Buckendorf.

His father, born in Hanover, Germany, March 31, 1847, died at Norfolk, December 25, 1919. He was a florist and landscape gardener. He planned and landscaped the Studebaker estate at South Bend, Indiana, the Norfolk Insane Hospital and the Harvey Estate in Otoe County. He came to the United States at the age of 19, following the completion of his education in which he specialized in flori-horticulture and landscaping. His wife, Joanna, was born in LaPorte, Indiana, April 29, 1859. She is a floriculturist.

Mr. Buckendorf attended the Norfolk public schools, private school, and business college. He is a Republican and served as state representative 1929-30, 1931-32, from the 78th district. He has served as city clerk at various times and is a member of the city council. For two terms he was a member of the local school board and he has been chairman of the Republican central committee.

On May 31, 1907, he was married to Mallie Opal Stockwell at Bassett. Mrs. Buckendorf was born at Bassett and traces her ancestry to Nathan Hale on her father's side.

He took active part in all war time drives, Red Cross, bond sales and food conservation. He is a member of the Methodist Episcopal Church. Mr. Buckendorf has always been active in civic affairs, is a member of the executive committee of the Rock County Red Cross, a member of the board of directors and of the executive committee of the Lions Club, past noble grand and past district deputy grand master of Bassett Lodge No. 242 of the Odd Fellows. He enjoys hunting and fishing while his hobbies are reading, mechanics, gardening and growing flowers. Residence: Bassett.

Frederick Watson Buckley

Frederick Watson Buckley, physician and surgeon since 1907, was born in Fulton County, Pennsylvania, January 16, 1881. The son of Jacob Lawrence and Emma Grace (Benedict) Buckley, his father was born in Fulton County, October 5, 1844. A farmer, he was a corporal with the 22nd Pennsylvania Cavalry from 1864-65, and settled in Iowa in its early days. He was of Irish and Dutch extraction, his paternal grandfather having come from Ireland about 1770. His death occurred at Beatrice, November 5, 1925. Emma Grace Benedict was born in Fulton County March 23, 1854, and now resides at Shelby, Iowa. She is descended from Welch and German settlers in Colonial times.

Dr. Buckley was graduated from the Shelby, Iowa, high school in 1899, and attended the University of Iowa 1900-03, completing two years pre-medical and two years medical work. He received his M. D. from Northwestern University in 1907, later attending the New York Post Graduate Medical School, and taking work at Vienna, Austria. While at the University of Iowa he was a member of the sophomore debate team in 1902, was elected to Phi Rho Sigma and was a letterman in football 1901, 1902, 1903.

Since his graduation Dr. Buckley has been actively engaged in practice. He has been a resident of the state for the past twenty years, and is one of the leading professional men in his locality. During the World War he held the rank of first lieutenant in the Medical Corps, and was stationed at Base Hospital No. 49, American Expeditionary Forces. Dr. Buckley's professional memberships include the American, Nebraska State and Gage County Medical Societies, and he is also a member of the American Legion, the Red Cross, Chamber of Commerce (director), Kiwanis Club (president 1927) the Elks, Masons and Young Men's Christian Association (director).

His religious affiliation is with the Methodist Episcopal Church, and his political preference is that of the Republican party. He is a member of the Beatrice Country Club, and is fond of golf and hiking.

On May 23, 1917, he was united in marriage to Louise Emaline Sabin, at Beatrice. Mrs. Buckley, who is of English descent, was born at Beatrice, August 23, 1885. There are three children: Frederick, born April 13, 1918; Lawrence, born August 17, 1920; and Barbara, born September 21, 1924.

Orville Edson Buckley

A leading business man and public spirited citizen, Orville Edson Buckley is a life resident of Nebraska. Born at Lyons, on August 1, 1877, he is the son of Edward Forknal and Ann Jane (Clements) Buckley. His father, born in England, March 17, 1843, came to Nebraska as a young man, and engaged in farming until his death at Lyons on March 10, 1887. His mother was born in Lodi, Wisconsin, August 21, 1864, and is still living.

Mr. Buckley attended the Lyons public school and for a time attended Fremont Normal School. During

1898-99 he attended the Nebraska Agricultural School and during 1900-03 the University of Nebraska.

Since 1910 he has been the owner of a hardware and implement business at Winnebago, and operates a farm nearby. A Republican, he was a member of the county central committee in 1920, and has been delegate to state conventions and census enumerator for Logan township.

His marriage to Frances Marie Reed was solemnized at Bancroft, Nebraska, June 24, 1908. Mrs. Buckley was born at Wyoming, Iowa, September 21, 1880, and was a school teacher prior to her marriage. They have three children, Dorothy, born December 6, 1910, a graduate of Wayne State Teachers College, who teaches in the schools of South Sioux City; Lois, born July 29, 1913, and Frances, born July 31, 1915, attending high school.

Mr. Buckley is active in fraternal circles, and is a 32nd degree member of Sioux City Consistory, of Scottish Rite Masons; a charter member of Winnebago Lodge No. 309, Ancient Free and Accepted Masons, in which he has held the offices of treasurer, secretary, junior warden and worshipful master. Besides nine years service on the School Board of District No. 17, he has been chairman of the village board four years, and member six years. He is a director of the local Boy Scout work, and leader and teacher of the Ready Helpers Sunday School Class, of the Winnebago Presbyterian Church, vice president of the Red Cross, and a member of the Chamber of Commerce. He enjoys reading and the theatre, but his hobby is really boys' activities.

During the World War he was a member of the Home Guard and committeeman on loan drives. Residence: Winnebago.

Arthur Eugene Bucklin

Arthur Eugene Bucklin, merchant at Atkinson for a number of years, was born at Aurora, Nebraska, May 22, 1877, the son of David Emanuel and Hattie Jane (Hawkins) Bucklin. His father was born at Kankakee, Illinois, and died in North Dakota, in May, 1925. He was a real estate dealer. His wife, Hattie, was born at Kankakee, November 19, 1852.

Upon the completion of his public school education, Mr. Bucklin entered the mercantile business. On November 16, 1898, he was married to Anna Lorretta Eaton at Marquette, Nebraska. Mrs. Bucklin was born at Pitsford, Michigan, July 6, 1878. Their only child, Harold, born January 10, 1901, died December 23, 1902.

Mr. Bucklin is a Republican. He is a member of the Methodist Episcopal Church, the Red Cross, the Lions Club and the Odd Fellows. He is also a member of the Atkinson Country Club. His favorite sport is golf. Residence: Atkinson.

Charles Rhine Bucy

Born at Staplehurst, Nebraska, June 27, 1886, Charles Rhine Bucy has for many years been a prominent farmer. He is the son of Hezekiah and Lydia Anna (Renner) Bucy, pioneer Nebraskans. Hezekiah Bucy was born in Coschocton County, Ohio, June 6, 1858, and came to Nebraska in 1880. He died at Wolbach, on February 27, 1927. His wife was born at Vermont, Illinois, April 6, 1852, the daughter of William Renner. She died at Cushing, Nebraska, August 8, 1930.

Charles Rhine Bucy attended rural schools in district 91 of Seward County and district 34 of Howard County, until 1904. In 1907 he entered the York College Academy, being graduated in 1911. In 1909 he was graduated from York College with the degree of Bachelor of Accounts.

On August 5, 1914, Mr. Bucy was married to Blanche Iona Gilmore, at Blue Valley. Mrs. Bucy was born at Blue Valley, December 26, 1890, her father having been a pioneer settler in Nebraska in 1866. Their infant son died at birth. Sebastian Gilmore is a homesteader, living on the place originally settled. His father built the first frame house in York County which is still standing.

Mr. Bucy held a teaching position in rural school one year, and since that time has engaged in farming. A Democrat, he is township chairman of the county central committee at the present time. During the World War he was active in all civilian relief drives, was assistant chairman of war saving stamp drives, and was chairman of the Armenian relief drive. His religious affiliation is with the First Church of Christ, Scientist, at York.

From 1907 to 1911, Mr. Bucy was a member of the Young Men's Christian Association, and during the years 1930-31 has served as moderator of School District No. 7. He was a member of the Red Cross 1915, 16, and 17, and is a former member of the Modern Woodmen of America. His hobby is reading. Residence: York.

A. F. Buechler

A. F. Buechler, editor of *The Daily Independent* at Grand Island was born at Stanton, Illinois, January 20, 1869, son of Christian and Hanna Louise (Niehaus) Buechler.

The father, a clergyman, was born near Mannheim, Germany, and came to the United States in 1865. He died in 1920. His wife, Hanna Louise, was born in Germany and came to the United States with her parents as a child. Her death occurred in 1908.

A. F. Buechler attended public school, and received the Bachelor of Arts degree from Capital University at Columbus, Ohio. Starting in the newspaper game as office boy, he became reporter, partner, and later editor. He has been a director of the Grand Island Chamber of Commerce for the past twenty-six years, and is now serving as its president.

He is editor and vice president of the Independent Publishing Company, and is the editor-in-chief of the *History of Hall County* (1917). An independent Republican, he was postmaster from 1911-15, and has served as secretary of the county committee and as a member of the state executive committee.

On November 26, 1891, Mr. Buechler was married to Lydia Leonore Boehm at Grand Island. Mrs. Buechler is a native of Omaha. They have four children: Theodore Earl, a graduate of West Point in 1917, is a captain in the United States Army and is married to Mary Elizabeth Taylor. Ethel Hanna married A. A. Roeser, an insurance man. Walter Edward, who is city editor of *The Daily Independent*, held the rank of corporal in the army, serving overseas. He volunteered for service and did not reach the age of 21 until after the war. Catherine Louise, married Harold Buenz, who is in the mercantile business.

During the World War Mr. Buechler was secretary of the Hall County war activities committee, a director of the Hall County Red Cross, and a member of the county food committee. He is secretary of the Hall County Historical Society, a director of the Nebraska State Historical Society and a life member of the Nebraskana Society. He has been director of the Red Cross and the Salvation Army, and is a member of the St. Paul's English Lutheran Church, and of the Young Men's Christian Association Building Association. His club is the University.

An organizer of the present Chamber of Commerce in 1906, he was secretary the first five years, served as president in 1931, and vice president 1932. He has always been a director of the organization. Residence: Grand Island. (Photograph in Album).

Dexter Clark Buell

Dexter C. Buell, educator and railroad man at Omaha, Douglas County, Nebraska, was born at Chicago, September 13, 1881. George Cook Buell, his father, who was a lawyer, was born at Burlington, Des Moines County,

Iowa, July 22, 1853, and died at Pittsburgh, Pennsylvania, December 28, 1911. His Holland Dutch ancestors came to America more than 300 years ago.

Katherine Dexter (Clark) Buell, his mother, was born at Rockford, Winnebago County, Illinois, December 28, 1861. She was formerly active in club affairs and musical work. She is a descendent of Stephen Hopkins who came to America in the *Mayflower*; she holds membership in the Daughters of the American Revolution.

Mr. Buell was graduated from the Chicago Manual Training School in 1897. He was awarded the following degrees at Purdue University: B. S. in mechanical engineering, 1899; and M. E., 1902. He was secretary of his class and was a member of Phi Gamma Delta Fraternity.

He has been engaged in many branches of railroad work, and is now owner and director of the Railway Educational Bureau, at Omaha. He is the author of numerous texts, and railroad papers written for engineering societies. He has lived in Nebraska for the past 26 years.

On January 17, 1911, he was united in marriage with Elsie Cleaver at Chicago. Mrs. Buell, who was born at Chicago, May 23, 1886, and died at Omaha, August 15, 1913, was a direct descendant of John and Priscilla Alden of *Mayflower* fame. Two children were born to this marriage: Elaine Clark, born December 18, 1911; and Richard Cleaver, born July 31, 1913.

His marriage to Elma Jane Milliken was solemnized at Fremont, Nebraska, October 2, 1915; she was born at Pleasant Valley, Dodge County, Nebraska, July 25, 1887. They have three children: Robert Landis, born August 30, 1916; Dexter Clark, Jr., born April 6, 1918; and John Barrett, born January 4, 1925.

During the World War, Mr. Buell was a commander in the United States Naval Reserve, and was in charge of building and erection of naval railway guns in France. He is now commander of the Naval Reserve Force of Nebraska. He is an honorary member of the Pittsburgh Railway Club; is past president of the International Railway Fuel Association; and is a member of the American Society of Mechanical Engineers.

He is a director of the Family Welfare Association; is a member of the Omaha Chamber of Commerce and the Rotary Club. He is a Mason. His social clubs include: University Club; Happy Hollow Club; and Phi Gamma Delta Club of New York. His hobbies are books and philately. He is a member of the First Presbyterian Church of Omaha. He is a Republican. Residence: Omaha.

Carl Henry Buethe

Carl Buethe was born at Hessen, Germany, May 15, 1850, son of Carl and Wilhelmine (Bueltemeier) Buethe. His father, who was born in Germany and died at Elk Creek, Johnson County, Nebraska, February 9, 1899, was an early settler in Nebraska. He came to America from Germany in 1858. Wilhelmine Buethe, a native of Hessen, Germany, came to America with her family, in the middle 1800's· She died at Elk Creek, September 29, 1874.

On July 30, 1876, Mr. Buethe was married to Louisa S. Sodman, at Elk Creek. Mrs. Buethe was born of German parents at Dubuque, Iowa, September 4, 1859, and died August 27, 1923. There were eleven children, ten of whom are still living. They are as follows: Sophie, born November 3, 1877, who married Diedrich Schrader; Minnie, born July 20, 1879, who married John H. Johnson; Chris, born September 17, 1881, who married Lydia Buethe; Carl, born September 15, 1883, who married Beatrice Morris; Christine, born September 27, 1885, who married Emil Stutheit; Dick, born October 26, 1887; Gotlieb, born January 22, 1890, died October 31, 1891; Walter, born February 11, 1892, who married Lottie Shafer; Herbert, born March 14, 1896; Stella, born September 25, 1898, who married Walter Tiede; and Henry, born April 3, 1903, who married Ada Sodman.

Educated in the country schools of Johnson County,

Mr. Buethe early entered the political field. From January 1, 1884, to January 1, 1887, and from January 1, 1890, to January 1, 1893, he served as county commissioner of Johnson County. Elected in 1901 by the Republican party as member of the Nebraska State Legislature, he served one term.

After more than fifty years of active life as a farmer, he is now retired. He still maintains, however, directorship in the State Bank of Elk Creek. He is affiliated with the Lutheran Church, and holds membership in St. Peter's Church at Elk Creek. He is a member of the Lutheran Layman's League. During the World War he was active in the various drives and was a member of the Nebraska Council of Defense. He has been guardian for children more than 30 years. Residence: Elk Creek.

James C. Buffington

James C. Buffington, executive, was born in Louisa County, Iowa, July 14, 1866, son of David Sleeth and Nancy Ann (Getts) Buffington.

David Sleeth Buffington was born in Ohio, in 1844, and died in Louisa County, Iowa, in May, 1914. He was of Scotch-Irish ancestry. His wife, Ann Getts, was born in Pennsylvania, in 1845, and died at Chariton, Iowa, on January 27, 1902. She was a mother of twelve children.

Mr. Buffington was educated in public schools, and on October 31, 1899, was married to May Griffis at Des Moines, Iowa. They have two children, Ruth, who was graduated from LaSell Seminary; and James, seventeen, who was graduated from the Missouri Military Academy.

Mr. Buffington has been engaged in insurance work for many years, and for about 30 years has been president of the Guarantee Fund Life Association.

He is a member of the First Methodist Episcopal Church, the Red Cross, the Chamber of Commerce, the Young Men's Christian Association, the Modern Woodmen of America, and the Elks. His clubs are the Happy Hollow Country Club and the Omaha Athletic Club. Residence: Omaha.

Edna Dean Bullock

Edna Dean Bullock, director of the Nebraska Legislative Reference Bureau, was born at North Lewisburg, Ohio, April 26, 1869, daughter of Charles Goodrich and Miriam Daniels (Sweet) Bullock. Her father, a native of Chautauqua County, New York, was born on October 4, 1839. He was at the time of his death at Lincoln, February 14, 1925, a retired contractor and builder, whose ancestors came to Plymouth from England, in 1643, settling at Rehoboth, Massachusetts and Swansea, Rhode Island, migrating to Dutchess County, New York, prior to the Revolution.

Miriam (Sweet) Bullock was born at West Liberty, Logan County, Ohio, August 10, 1844, and died at Lincoln, September 7, 1928. She was descended from the Sweet family which migrated from western Pennsylvania to Ohio, just after the Revolution, and from the Guyton family, Huguenot settlers in Baltimore County, Maryland.

After completing her elementary work in the Lincoln public schools, Miss Bullock attended the preparatory department of the University of Nebraska, and entering the University received her B. L. in 1889. She is a member of the Palladian Society. In 1895, she received her B. L. S. from the New York State Library School. She has engaged in library and bibliographical work in twelve states. From 1901 to 1906, she was first secretary of the Nebraska Public Library Commission. From 1909-10, she was on the editorial staff of the H. W. Wilson Publishing Company. During 1894 and 1897-98, she was cataloger at the University of Nebraska Library; and since 1911 she has held positions with the Nebraska Legislative Reference Bureau, until 1921, as librarian, and since that time as director.

During the World War she had two months service

in the foreign information department of the American Red Cross Headquarters at Washington, and now assists in Red Cross work through the Community Chest. She is a member of All Soul's Unitarian Church, the Nebraska League of Women Voters, the American and the Nebraska Library Associations. Her club is the University. Her hobby is gardening. Residence: Lincoln.

Motier Carlos Bullock

The Reverend Motier Carlos Bullock was born at Elba, Michigan, March 26, 1877, son of Carlos Alonzo and Nellie Elizabeth (Litle) Bullock.

His father, born at Elba, September 3, 1855, was a farmer of early American descent. He died at Goodrich, Michigan, March 4, 1931. Mary Elizabeth Litle was born at Chili, New York, March 31, 1856, she is also descended from early settlers in America.

Mr. Bullock attended district school in Elba Township, Michigan, and was graduated from high school at Hadley, Michigan, in 1893. In 1902 he received his Bachelor of Divinity degree from the Oberlin Graduate School of Theology at Oberlin, Ohio. He was ordained to the ministry June 22, 1906, and has held various pastorates in Michigan, Ohio, New York, Kansas, Texas, Oklahoma and Nebraska for the Congregational Church. At the present time he is pastor of the First Congregational Church of McCook, Nebraska.

On June 25, 1902, he was married to Myrtle DeWitt at Blanchard, Michigan. Mrs. Bullock was born at New Hope, New York, August 12, 1877. There are three children, Doris, born August 3, 1903, who married C. Wesley Israel; Carlos, born September 21, 1907; and Mark, born August 20, 1911. Carlos is a graduate architect, while Mark is a student at the University of Nebraska.

Mr. Bullock is an independent Democrat. During the World War he served for one year as secretary of the Young Men's Christian Association while in England and France with the American Expeditionary Forces. At the present time he is a member of the Southwestern Association of Congregational Churches and Ministers, an honorary member of the McCook Chamber of Commerce, vice president of the McCook Rotary Club, and is active in the Young Men's Christian Association work. He holds membership in the Masons, the Knights Templar, the Eastern Star, and is eminent commander of St. John Commandery No. 16. His favorite sports are tennis and volley-ball, and his hobby is bird study. Residence: McCook.

Wardie Elmo Bullock

Born at Franklin, Nebraska, May 17, 1897, Wardie Elmo Bullock is the son of Guy Bernard and Mary Elizabeth (Chelf) Bullock. His father, who is engaged in the hardware business, and was county commissioner for eight years at Madrid, Nebraska, was born at Keithsburg, Illinois, August 19, 1874; he served as chairman of the town board for four years. His mother, whose ancestry is traced to Daniel Boone in Kentucky, was born at Bradfordsville, Kentucky, February 1, 1874.

Mr. Bullock was a student in the public schools of Madrid until 1916 when he studied principles of business at Kearney State Normal College. He is manager of the firm of Bullock & Bullock at Madrid, and formerly engaged in the automobile and insurance business there. He has served as precinct assessor and a member of the town board. Mr. Bullock is a member of the Methodist Episcopal Church and the Independent Order of Odd Fellows.

His marriage to Ruby Florence Mann occurred at Louisville, Kentucky, April 11, 1921. Mrs. Bullock, who is descended from an old southern family, was born at Bradfordsville, September 18, 1901. She is president of the Ladies Aid Society of the Methodist Episcopal Church, is bookkeeper for her husband's firm, and is

treasurer of the Madrid Consolidated School. Their three children are: Audrey Marilyn, July 4, 1922; Joyce Gay, born December 16, 1924; and Mary Jean, born October 20, 1929. Residence: Madrid.

Fred John Buntemeyer

Fred J. Buntemeyer, grain and lumber dealer, was born at Oshholt, Oldenburg, Germany, May 5, 1882. His parents, Gerhard Buntemeyer and Elizabeth Louisa (Bollman) Buntemeyer, were born at Oldenburg, Germany; his father on May 20, 1829, and his mother on November 15, 1837. Gerhard Buntemeyer died at Zwischenahn, Oldenburg, August, 1911, and his wife in February, 1911, at the same town.

Mr. Buntemeyer was graduated from public school in May, 1896. He married Alvina Louisa Mundt at Crete, on April 21, 1910. She was born at Crete, Nebraska, on February 21, 1888. Their three children are: Carl, born March 18, 1911; Dorothy, born March 3, 1913; and Irma, born April 18, 1916.

Mr. Buntemeyer has resided in Nebraska for twenty-seven years, was associated with the Crete Telephone Company during the years 1906 and 1907, and is now manager and part owner of the elevator and lumberyard at Deshler, Nebraska.

He is affiliated with the American Lutheran Church, is a member of the Red Cross, the Commercial Club, and the Nebraskana Society. His favorite sport is golf. Residence: Deshler.

Byron George Burbank

Byron George Burbank was born near Northfield, Minnesota, August 26, 1860, and for the past forty-six years has been a resident of Omaha. He is the son of Edy Mulcahie and Sarah Richardson, the former a school teacher and farmer, and a soldier in the Union Army during the Civil War. He served four years, and took part in Sherman's march to the sea. He was born in the North of Ireland, about 1835, and died near Platte City, Missouri, in June, 1884. His mother died when he was 8 months of age, and he was raised by her sister, Mary Burbank, and took that family name.

Sarah Richardson was born in Michigan, about 1837, and died near Northfield, Minnesota, in 1861. She was a direct descendant of Amos Richardson who settled in Boston in 1634. He was prominent in colonial life and one of the first lawyers in America.

Byron G. Burbank received his early education in a country school, and was graduated from Elgin Academy in June, 1880, and later attended Heidelberg University. From 1880 to 1883 he was principal of the Bryon, Illinois, High School, and from 1883-84 was principal of the Mount Morris High School. He holds a life teacher's certificate in that state. In 1885, he was admitted to the bar at Chicago, and for forty-three years was engaged in practice in all the state and federal courts of Omaha and nearby states. He retired from active practice on June 1, 1928.

He was married November 26, 1881. There are two children of this marriage, Byron M., born September 15, 1886, and Wayne, born July 20, 1897. On June 6, 1906, Mr. Burbank was married to Jane Breckenridge Brown of the Breckenridge family of Omaha. They have one son, Forrest B., born June 7, 1909, who is a senior at Harvard.

Mr. Burbank is a Republican. He has been a candidate for congress, chairman of the fourth judicial central committee, chairman of the Douglas County Republican central committee, and member of the executive committee of the Republican state central committee. He is a member of the American, Nebraska State, and Omaha-Douglas County Bar Associations. A Mason, he belongs to the Blue Lodge, Royal Arch, Knights Templar, Scottish Rite and Shrine Bodies. For about thirty years he has been a member of the Omaha Club. During the past few years he has travelled extensively, and has visited all the provinces of Canada, and every state in the Union except four. His hobby is the study of German language. Residence: Omaha.

Harry H. Burden

Harry H. Burden, elevator manager, was born at Campbell, Nebraska, December 22, 1883, son of William Arthur and Nettie L. (Crosby) Burden.

The father was born at Peoria, Illinois, September 26, 1856, and came to Nebraska in 1871 located in Webster County and resided there until his death at Campbell, Nebraska, March 13, 1931. His wife, Nettie, was born at Janesville, Wisconsin, July 31, 1861, her ancestry is Scotch-Irish. She is residing with her daughter, Mrs. Lee Walker, at Red Cloud at the present time.

Mr. Burden was graduated from Campbell High School and attended the Hastings Business College one term. He was owner of the Mirage moving picture theatre from 1912 until March 23, 1929, and at the present time he is the owner of Burden's Confectionery, and is manager of the local elevator. A Democrat, he has been a member of the city council for more than 15 years, and for more than eight years, has served on the board of education. He served one four year term as a member of the county board of supervisors of Kearney County, and was chairman of the board one year.

On November 15, 1911, he was married to Hazel Millicent Leafgren at Axtell. She was born at Axtell, November 5, 1893, and is manager of Burden's Confectionery. Her father was Swedish, and her mother Irish. They have four children, Norma Irene, born September 13, 1912; Vera Mae, born August 17, 1918; Dorothy Marie, born November 6, 1919; and Doris Mildred, her twin, born November 6, 1919. Norma was graduated from Axtell High School, and is now attending Kearney State Teachers College.

Mr. Burden is a member of the Masons, and the Nebraskana Society. He enjoys a game of golf at the Axtell Golf Club, of which he is a member. Residence: Axtell.

George Henry Burdette

George H. Burdette was born at Palestine, West Virginia, January 15, 1877, son of John and Caroline (Moses) Burdette. His father and mother were born in Roanoke County, West Virginia, and died at Frankton, Madison County, Indiana.

Mr. Burdette, who is a farmer, and hog and cattle breeder, was left an orphan at the age of twelve. For twenty-nine years he has lived in Nebraska where he has specialized in the breeding and sale of Duroc Jersey hogs. He was at one time chairman of the board of trustees in the county fair, and superintendent of the live stock department of that organization. For the past ten years he has held Duroc Jersey sales.

On June 14, 1905, at Auburn, Nebraska, he was married to Gertrude Conner, who was born in Auburn, August 29, 1880. They have one daughter, Nina, who is a school teacher, and a son, John, who is attending high school.

During the World War Mr. Burdette was a member of the home guards, and took an active part in liberty loan and Red Cross drives. He is a director of the school board of district number six, having held this position since 1904. He is president of the board of deacons in the Church of Christ, and treasurer of the Living Link Committee. He is a member of the Independent Order of Odd Fellows. Residence: Auburn.

Clarence William Burdick

One of the leading business executives of Grand Island, Nebraska, is Clarence William Burdick who has been a resident of this state all his life. He was born at Westerville, Nebraska, January 26, 1891, the son of George Joel and Nellie Mae (Grierson) Burdick. His father, who was a real estate dealer, was born of Scotch-Irish and French parents at DeRytter, New York, November 15, 1865, and died at Los Angeles, California, December 28, 1927. His mother, who is a member of the Women's Relief Corps and the Order of Eastern Star, was born at Morrison, Illinois, June 26, 1868, and resides in Los Angeles. Her parents, who were natives of Scotland, established the first grist mill in Custer County, Nebraska.

Mr. Burdick was graduated from the Hastings High School in 1910, was a student at Grand Island Baptist College, and studied at the Armour Institute. He was employed by the Hastings Machine Works during 1908 and 1909, was electrician for the Grand Island Electric Company, 1912-13, and since 1913 has served as city electrician and electrical engineer of the city of Grand Island where he is water, light, and ice commissioner.

His marriage to Genevieve Susan Druliner was solemnized at Grand Island, October 22, 1913. Mrs. Burdick was born at Giltner, Nebraska, June 24, 1894. Their son, Roger Nevin, was born September 24, 1919.

Mr. Burdick is a member of the Parent-Teachers Association, the Woodland Country Club, and the Trinity Methodist Episcopal Church of Grand Island. His civic and professional organizations include: Chamber of Commerce; Nebraska League of Municipalities; the Engineers Club of Grand Island; the Red Cross; and The Nebraskana Society; Mr. Burdick is a member of the Order of Eastern Star and holds membership in these bodies of the Masons; Shrine; Knights Templar; and Commandery. He is interested in mechanics and reading, and likes to golf. Residence: Grand Island.

George W. Burgess

George W. Burgess was born in Green County, New York, December 14, 1852, the son of Harvey Smith Burgess and Caroline (Brewer) Burgess. His father, who is a farmer, was born in Green County, New York, of English parentage. His mother was also born in Green County, of German ancestry.

George Burgess attended public school. He united in marriage with Maria A. Boane, at Ulysses, Nebraska, in 1875. She was born at Geneseo, Illinois, July 10, 1856, of English parentage. To this union four children were born: Georgie, who died at the age of four years; Amy, who married Dr. W. D. Jones, who is now deceased; Howard, who died at the age of seven months; and Neal, who died when he was seven years of age.

Harvey Smith Burgess homesteaded two miles from Rising City in 1871. George W. Burgess took up a homestead in Antelope County, in 1882. He lived there three years, traveled for a time, and returned to Rising City, in 1894, where he has since resided.

During his 60 years residence in Nebraska, Mr. Burgess has engaged in various lines of endeavor, but for some time has been in the insurance business. He is affiliated with the Republican party, and is a member of the Nebraskana Society. Residence: Rising City.

Allen Gilmore Burke

Allen Gilmore Burke, son of David William and Isabella (Gilmore) Burke, was born on a farm in Cuming County, Nebraska, on September 8, 1877. His father was born in Perth, Ontario, September 15, 1838, and died at the age of seventy-three. His mother was born in Scotland, in 1840, and died in 1882. David William Burke took a homestead eight miles west of Bancroft, in 1868.

Allen Burke attended rural school and the Bancroft,

Nebraska, High School from March, 1894, until 1896. He then attended the University of Nebraska, receiving the degree of Bachelor of Science in 1902, and a Bachelor of Laws degree in 1903.

On May 8, 1906, at Omaha, Nebraska, he married Emily Margaret McManus, who was born in Galena, Illinois, on June 7, 1880. To this union three children were born; Hyle Gilmore, August 29, 1907; Margaret, Isabella, October 14, 1916, and Dorothy Elaine, July 27, 1921. Hyle received a Bachelor of Arts degree at the State University in 1929, is a student in law college, and has assisted in editing the law bulletin.

Mr. Burke served as a member of the house of representatives from 1923-31, on the Republican ticket. He was speaker of the house in 1925, and Republican floor leader 1929, 30, 31, and chairman of the finance committee in 1931. During the administration of Governor Weaver, Mr. Burke gave much attention to the five million dollar deficit that had been incurred. He aided in devising the plan that resulted in wiping out the deficit and leaving a balance in the state treasury.

He has been a member of the board of directors of the Citizens Bank in Bancroft, for the last seventeen years, was secretary-treasurer of the Bancroft Telephone Company for a number of years, and was a member of the village board for ten years.

He has resided in Nebraska for fifty-three years and is a member of the Nebraskana Society. He is affiliated with the Presbyterian Church in Bancroft. Mr. Burke holds membership in Bancroft Lodge No. 145 of the Ancient Free and Accepted Masons, is a member of Jordan Commandery No. 15, Knights Templar in Blair, and is a member of Tangier Temple of Shrine.

Mr. Burke has always been interested in agriculture, and is an extensive land owner. Residence: Bancroft.

Charles Ernest Burke

Charles Ernest Burke, leading professional man at Bassett, Nebraska, has been engaged in the practice of dentistry at Bassett since 1924. He was born at Bodarc, Nebraska, November 14, 1896, the son of Julius Brace and Chloe Catherine (Pfost) Burke. His father, a clergyman, was born at Charleston, West Virginia, April 13, 1860, and died at Albion, Nebraska, May 21, 1929. His mother was born at Charleston, February 22, 1864, and died at Adams, Nebraska, February 16, 1928.

Dr. Burke was graduated from the high school at Stuart, Nebraska, in 1914, and in 1924, received the degree Doctor of Dental Surgery at the University of Nebraska where he was president of the Dental Students Association. He served as vice president of his fraternity, Xi Psi Phi.

He is a member of the Lions International, the Red Cross, and the Masons, and for a number of years has served as a member of the School Board and the Bassett Town Board. He served as sergeant in the Medical Corps of the United States Army during the World War, and at this time is a member of the American Legion. His favorite sport is football.

His marriage to Alice Wilhelmina Wefso occurred at St. Edward, Nebraska, May 25, 1920. Mrs. Burke, who was a teacher in the Stuart Public Schools for four years prior to her marriage, was born at Dustin, Nebraska, November 5, 1900. They have two children: Mary Jeanette, born February 19, 1925; and Charles James, born March 7, 1929. Dr. Burke is a Republican and holds membership in The Nebraskana Society. Residence: Bassett.

Donald J. Burke

Donald J. Burke, lawyer, educator, and business executive, has lived in Nebraska for the past 26 years. He was born at Council Bluffs, Iowa, February 25, 1891, the son of Finley and Parthenia (Jefferis) Burke. His father, who was born in West Virginia, and died at Council Bluffs in 1903, practiced law at Council Bluffs for many years and was probably Iowa's most distinguished lawyer; his Irish and Scotch ancestors settled in America in the early history of the country.

His mother was born at Council Bluffs, and died there in 1928. Her paternal ancestors were early Americans; her mother was born in Ireland.

Mr. Burke attended the public schools of Council Bluffs, and received his LL. B. at Creighton University School of Law where he was graduated with cum laude honors. He was elected to the law fraternity, Delta Theta Phi. He practiced law from 1912-17, and for the next two and a half years was First Lieutenant of Infantry in the United States Army; he served one year in France and Germany with the 88th and 2nd divisions, 1917-19. After the war he was professor of law at Creighton University for 9 years, 1919-1928. Since then he has been vice president of the George H. Lee Company at Omaha.

He is a member of the American Legion. He holds membership in: Omaha Chamber of Commerce; the Rotary Club; Douglas County Bar Association; and the Interprofessional Men's Club. He is a member of St. Cecilia's Cathedral at Omaha, and is affiliated with the Knights of Columbus. He was formerly a member of the American Bar Association. He is a Democrat.

His marriage to Ivy Lee was solemnized at Omaha, August 18, 1917. Mrs. Burke was born at Exeter, Nebraska; her maternal and paternal grandparents were born in England. They have three children: Joseph, born August 2, 1918; Mary Catherine, born June 30, 1920; and Margaret, born December 16, 1921. Residence: Omaha.

Mabelle Baker Burke

One of Nebraska's leading business women Mabelle Baker Burke was born at Damariscotta, Maine, the daughter of Nathaniel Palmer Baker and Annie Mary (Benner) Baker. Her father, who was a merchant, was born at Bristol, Maine and died at Damariscotta, December 31, 1900, having served in Company I, 21st Regiment of the Maine Infantry during the Civil War. Her mother, a descendant of Seward Poland who served in the Revolution, was born at Bristol of English descent; she is a member of the Kearney P. E. O. and Daughters of the American Revolution.

Mrs. Burke was graduated from Lincoln Academy at New Castle, Maine, and was a student at Kearney State Teachers College, Kearney, Nebraska. For a number of years she was associated with the Forgan-Haskell Investment Company of Omaha, assisted in the offices of the county clerk and register of deeds, and for over 12 years published a daily report of instruments filed in Buffalo County. She is now serving her fifth consecutive term as city clerk of Kearney and is active in various civic organizations there.

She holds membership in the Business and Professional Women's Club, the Red Cross, P. E. O., The Nebraskana Society, and the First Methodist Church of Kearney. Mrs. Burke is a Republican and is a member of the Fort Kearney Chapter of the Daughters of the American Revolution.

Her marriage to Milton Edward Burke was solemnized at Omaha, Nebraska, September 25, 1907. Mr. Burke, who was a banker and business executive, was born at Kearney and died there June 23, 1911; his paternal grandfather, Gustave Fredrick Burke, served in the Civil War. They have one son, Nathaniel Baker Burke, who married Mabel Matzke. He is district agent for the John Hancock Mutual Life Insurance Company at Grand Island, Nebraska. They have one daughter, Louisa Ann. Residence: Kearney.

Thomas Nicholas Burke

Thomas Nicholas Burke, a physician and surgeon in Nebraska since 1904, was born at Calhoun, Iowa, August 31, 1875. His father, Peter Burke, was born in Kil-

EARL HASKELL BURKET

Heyn—Omaha

cullen, County Kildare, Ireland, February 14, 1828. After serving with the United States Marine Corps in the Civil War, he became a pioneer farmer in Iowa. His death occurred at Elkhorn, on October 9, 1912. His parents were Irish immigrants to America in 1854. Mary Kennedy, wife of Peter Burke, was born in County Tipperary, Ireland, February 14, 1828, and died at Elkhorn, February 15, 1923. Of Norman-Irish stock, her parents came to America in 1862.

Dr. Burke attended public and parochial schools and was graduated from academy in 1894. He was a student at Creighton University 1894-97, and Creighton Medical College 1900-04, receiving his degree of Doctor of Medicine from the last mentioned institution. Since 1904 he has been in active practice at Elkhorn.

On July 26, 1905, Dr. Burke was united in marriage to Catherine Cecelia Beirne at Omaha. Mrs. Burke, who was born at Atlantic, in May, 1884, died at Norfolk, February 25, 1918, leaving three children: Peter F., born January 3, 1907; William M., born April 5, 1908; and John J., born March 6, 1911. All of them are in school. Residence: Elkhorn.

Earl Haskell Burket

Earl Haskell Burket was born at Omaha, Nebraska, October 14, 1888, son of Henry Kennedy and Ella M. (Haskell) Burket. His father, who was a funeral director, was born at Grand Detour, Illinois, October 24, 1850, and died at Omaha, December 27, 1922. His mother was born at Tiskilwa, Illinois, February 26, 1854, and died at Omaha, July 22, 1929.

Mr. Burket was graduated from the Omaha High School and later attended Colgate University, where he was a member of Delta Kappa Epsilon. He has lived in Nebraska 42 years. The H. K. Burket Funeral Chapel was established in 1876 at Creston, Iowa. In 1883 the family came to Omaha, where Henry K. Burket entered the undertaking business. The business is the oldest established firm in Omaha. Mr. Burket has been connected with the business since June 1914, and is owner of the H. K. Burket and Son Funeral Chapel.

He was married to Harriet Copley at Omaha, March 21, 1917. Mrs. Burket was born in Omaha. They have one son, Copley, born September 30, 1923.

Mr. Burket is a member of the Chamber of Commerce, the Rotary Club, and the Pro Tem Club. He is a Scottish Rite Mason, Knight Templar and member of the Shrine. His clubs are the Omaha Club, the University Club and the Happy Hollow Country Club. He is a member of the First Baptist Church. His hobby is trees. Residence: Omaha. (Photograph on Page 187).

Homer Kauffman Burket

One of Lincoln's foremost business men, and a leader in civic and fraternal circles, Homer Burket was born on a farm in Lee County, Illinois, May 19, 1858. His father, Peter Burket, was born in Blair County, Pennsylvania, December 5, 1820, and died in Cedar County, Iowa, on September 14, 1874. He was a farmer, whose family came to America from Germany about 1750.

Peter Burket married Elizabeth Eberle, who was born at Huntingdon, Pennsylvania, March 22, 1823. She was of German and Swiss ancestry, and died in Cedar County, Iowa, June 9, 1881.

Homer K. Burket received his elementary education in the schools of Lee County, Illinois, and Tipton, Iowa. He was graduated from the Tipton High School in 1877. On May 19, 1885, he was united in marriage to Ella Gibson at Creston, Iowa. Mrs. Burket is a native of Dixon, Iowa, and of Scotch and German descent. There are two children of this marriage, John G., born February 16, 1886, who is married to Margaret Sargent and residing in Lincoln; and Ethel, born March 4, 1888. She was graduated from the University of Nebraska, and attended school in Washington, D. C., and in Vienna, where she

studied music. She is married to Dr. M. F. Russell of Great Bend, Kansas.

Since 1893, Mr. Burket has been a resident of Nebraska, and for many years has been engaged in the building and loan business. He is a former president of the Nebraska State Bank, and at the present time is president of the Nebraska State Building Company, the Nebraska Central Building and Loan Association, and formerly of the First National Bank of Bridgeport. A Republican in politics he has filled various public offices, both in Illinois and Nebraska. Among them he was city treasurer of Creston, Iowa, coroner of Union County, Iowa; city alderman in Lincoln, 1912-13, and member of the house of representatives in 1913 of Nebraska.

During 1914 and '15, he served as president of the Lincoln Chamber of Commerce, and in 1927 was president of the Rotary Club. His clubs include the Candle Light Club and the Lincoln Country Club. For six years he was a member of the board of education. He is a thirty-second degree Mason, and a member of the Young Men's Christian Association. At present he is a member of Advisory Water Board of Lincoln. Residence: Lincoln.

Elmer Jacob Burkett

Elmer J. Burkett was born on a farm in Mills County, Iowa, December 1, 1867, the son of Henry W. and Catherine (Kearney) Burkett. His father, whose ancestry was Pennsylvania Dutch, was born in Blair County, Pennsylvania, August 26, 1842, and died at Glenwood, Mills County, Iowa, September 11, 1923.

His mother was born in Holt County, Missouri, March 7, 1848, and died at Glenwood, July 28, 1908.

Mr. Burkett attended the public schools at Silver City, Iowa, and in 1890, was graduated from Tabor College with the degrees B. A. and B. L. He was awarded his LL. B. and LL. M. degrees at the University of Nebraska, in 1893 and 1895, respectively. He was president of the senior class at Tabor College, 1890; was president of the law class at the University of Nebraska, 1893; and was elected to membership in the Innocents and Phi Delta Phi.

He has been engaged in the practice of law since 1893, at Lincoln, Lancaster County, Nebraska. For the past 20 years he has been director of the First National Bank and the First Trust Company of Lincoln. A Republican, he served as a member of the Nebraska legislature in 1897; was member of United States congress, 1899-1905; and was United States Senator from 1905 to 1911. He has always taken an active part in state and national political affairs. He is the author of *Outline of History*, a textbook for use in the public school (1890). He was editor of *Phideltian* at Tabor College.

On September 1, 1891, he was united in marriage with Fannie Fern Wright at Glenwood. Mrs. Burkett, who was born in Mills County, September 16, 1869, is descended on the maternal side from Governor John Webster of Massachusetts. They have three children: Lenore C., born July 22, 1893, who married Rolla C. Van Kirk; Josephine S., born June 22, 1895, who married Raymond R. Farquhar; and Helen F., born May 6, 1901, who married Marvin M. Meyers. Lenore is a professional musician, and is at the head of the Fine Arts department of Cotner University.

During the World War Mr. Burkett was active in loan drives and was a member of the home guard. He has been president of the board of trustees of Nebraska Annual Conference of the Methodist Episcopal Church for the last 15 years. He is a member of the county, state, and national bar associations, and holds membership in the Lincoln Chamber of Commerce.

He is affiliated with the Nebraskana Society and the Nebraska State Historical Society. He is a member of the Ancient and Accepted Scottish Rite Masonry, Sesostris Temple, Ancient Arabic Order of the Nobles of the Mystic Shrine. He is a member of the following frater-

ELMER J. BURKETT

Townsend—Lincoln

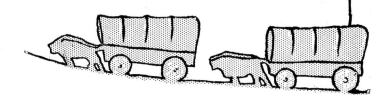

nal organizations: Woodmen of the World; Modern Woodmen of America; Ancient Order of United Workmen; and Royal Highlanders.

He is a member of the University Club, the Lincoln Country Club, the Lincoln Auto Club, and the Shrine Club. His hobby is reading. Mr. Burkett has been a resident of Nebraska for the past 40 years. Residence: Lincoln. (Photograph on Page 189).

Elmer Burkholder

Elmer Burkholder, farmer, was born at Lancaster, Pennsylvania, August 23, 1883, son of Peter and Martha (Keller) Burkholder. Peter Burkholder was a farmer, born at Lancaster, Pennsylvania, August 26, 1845, and who died at Octavia, Nebraska, May 23, 1919. His ancestors were Swiss, coming to America early in the sixteenth century. Martha Burkholder was born at Ephrata, Pennsylvania, March 28, 1853. Her ancestors, also Swiss, came to this country early in the seventeenth century.

On May 30, 1918, he was married to Susie Mable Rothrock, at Davenport, Nebraska. She was born December 4, 1884, at Davenport. To this union were born five children: Robert Elmer, born January 11, 1921; Helen Aileen, born December 5, 1922; John Henry, born July 11, 1925; Donald Lyman, born January 19, 1927; and Wendell Eugene, born June 24, 1928.

Mr. Burkholder is a Republican, and has been a resident of Nebraska his entire life. He has served on local boards and as secretary of his local telephone company, and during the World War was a supporter of the various loan drives and relief activities. A Protestant, he is a member of the Octavia Church of the Brethren.

He is now a member of The Nebraskana Society, Parent-Teachers' Association, has been secretary of the board of education since 1927, and is a member of the Red Cross. His pastime is reading. Residence: Octavia.

William Mawer Burkitt

William Mawer Burkitt, merchant, was born at Alford, England, January 12, 1841, and came to America with his parents in 1851. His father, William Burkitt, was born in South Lincolnshire, England, and died at Lyndon, Illinois, in 1875 or 1876. He was a baker. His wife, Eleanor Mawer, also born in South Lincolnshire, died at Lyndon in 1875 or 1876.

Mr. Burkitt attended public school in Alford, England, and Plover, Wisconsin. He was a farmer in Lyndon for about 10 years, from 1860, and afterward a clerk in a grocery store in Amboy, Illinois, for about a year. He then entered the mercantile business in Lyndon, continuing until 1879. For about two years he was a farmer near Mapleton, Iowa. He was a hardware merchant in the same town for about the same length of time, and a furniture dealer in Pierce, Nebraska, from 1884 until 1886. Since 1887 he has been in the general merchandise business in Whitney.

He is a member of Warring Memorial Methodist Episcopal Church, (charter member), a charter member of the Masonic Lodge at Lyndon, Illinois, and from 1917 until 1921, was a member of the Red Cross.

On January 2, 1866, Mr. Burkitt was married to Delia Semanthe Deming at Lyndon, Illinois. She was born in New York, July 6, 1833, and died at Mapleton, Iowa, September 6, 1881. Her English and French ancestors came to America in 1630.

There are five children of this marriage, Eleanor A., born December 22, 1868, who married William Sherman Gillan; Delia M., December 22, 1868; William Deming, born August 31, 1871, who married Susan O. Thomas; John Mawer, born July 18, 1874, who died September 21, 1882; and Joseph Alfred, born September 12, 1876, who died March 26, 1879. On December 16, 1882, Mr. Burkitt was married to Hannah M. Deming, who died February 17, 1912. Residence: Whitney.

Francis Joseph Burkley

Francis Joseph Burkley was born at Omaha, October 24, 1857. He is the son of Vincent and Theresa (Stelzer) Burkley, the former of whom was born in Germany, on April 5, 1818. Vincent Burkley came to America in 1837, and for many years was connected with the *Omaha Herald*, the *Omaha World* and the *Omaha World-Herald*. He also served as collector of customs at Omaha, under President Cleveland. Until his death in 1898 he was an outstanding citizen of Omaha. His wife, Theresa Burkley, was born in Germany, June 6, 1824, and died at Omaha, April 27, 1909.

Mr. Burkley received his education in the Omaha public schools and later entered the newspaper business. He afterward became one of the incorporators and publishers of the *Omaha World* and *Omaha World-Herald*. He was married at Chillicothe, Ohio, in 1888. Mrs. Burkley died at Omaha, in 1903, leaving two children, Agnes, who married J. M. Harding and Mary, who married Lawrence Brinker.

A Democrat, Mr. Burkley began his political career as member of the Omaha city council from 1894-1903. From 1885 to 1892 he was business manager of the *World* and of the *World Herald*. He is president of the Burkley Envelope and Printing Company, and past chairman of the board of directors of the Metropolitan Utilities District of Omaha. He is a member of the board of regents of Creighton University, and a member of the board of directors of the U. S. National Bank. He has been active in the civic, political and business life of Omaha for more than 50 years.

He is a member of St. Cecilia's Cathedral. During the World War he was active on Red Cross, Liberty loan and other drives. He is a member of the Chamber of Commerce and of the Omaha Country Clubs. Residence: Omaha.

Harry Vincent Burkley

Harry Vincent Burkley, who was born in Omaha, on May 8, 1865, is the son of Vincent Burkley who was born in Germany, April 5, 1818, and who came to America in 1837, settling first in Columbus, Ohio.

Vincent Burkley came to Omaha in 1855, and brought his family in 1856. He was the first clothing merchant, later engaging in the newspaper business, and in 1856 was one of the incorporators of Columbus, Nebraska. He died at Omaha, July 4, 1898.

Mr. Burkley was educated in the public schools of Omaha, and attended Creighton University. On September 30, 1896, he was married to Angela Wickham, at Council Bluffs, Iowa. Mrs. Burkley was born at Council Bluffs, December 9, 1871, and died in Omaha, February 8, 1920. There are four children: Harry, born February 24, 1899; Robert, born January 20, 1901, who married Martha R. Bradford; Eleanor, born April 26, 1902, married Daniel F. McCarthy; and Francis, born February 16, 1910.

Mr. Burkley is a life resident of Omaha, and has been engaged as a manufacturer and printer most of his life. He is now vice president of the Burkley Envelope and Printing Co. A Catholic, he is a member of St. Cecilia's Cathedral. He is a Democrat, a member of the Chamber of Commerce, and the Knights of Columbus. His clubs are the Omaha Club and the Omaha Country Club. Residence: Omaha.

Paul Christopher Burmeister

Paul C. Burmeister was born at Yutan, Nebraska, August 24, 1893, the son of Charles and Mary (Karloff) Burmeister. His father, who was a farmer, was born in Germany, September 29, 1862. His mother, whose ancestry is German, was born at Wakena, Illinois, December 16, 1873.

Mr. Burmeister attended the public schools at Yutan, and later was a student at Fremont Normal College for

EDGAR ALBERT BURNETT

two terms. He served as rural mail carrier, was clerk in a store for a year, and was a hardware, furniture, and undertaking man for several years. He is now president of the Saunders County Finance Company, and is a member of the Burmeister Brothers Real Estate Loans and Insurance Company, in association with Karl J. Burmeister.

A Republican, he served in the county treasurer's office of Saunders County, 1917-26, and as county clerk, deputy, and treasurer. He holds membership in the Wahoo Chamber of Commerce, of which he is a director, and the Wahoo City Council. He is a member of the Nebraskana Society, the Wahoo Golf Club, and the Red Cross. His favorite sport is golfing.

Mr. Burmeister is affiliated with the Lutheran Church at Yutan, and is a member of the Knights of Pythias. He was married to Genevieve Theodora Swanson, daughter of John and Hannah (Johnson) Swanson, at Wahoo, October 21, 1921. Mrs. Burmeister, who was a graduate nurse at the Presbyterian Hospital at Omaha, Nebraska, before her marriage, was born at Weston, Saunders County, Nebraska, January 29, 1898. They have one son, Charles John, May 19, 1930. Residence: Wahoo.

Edgar Albert Burnett

Chancellor of the University of Nebraska since 1928, Edgar A. Burnett was born at Hartland, Michigan, October 17, 1865. He is the son of Ellsworth Solon and Eliza Mary (Crane) Burnett. On the paternal side the family is descended from Robert Belknap, who came from England in 1637. Jonathan, father of Ellsworth, was born in 1838. Ellsworth Burnett died in Shiawassee County, Michigan, February 2, 1895.

Eliza Crane was born at Skinnerville, New York in 1839, and died at Chicago, February 29, 1916. She is descended from the Crane family of colonial times, one of whom came from England about 1655.

Dr. Burnett attended district and high school in Michigan; in 1887 he received his B. Sc. from the Michigan State Agricultural College which also awarded him an honorary D. Sc. in 1917. He is a member of Sigma Xi, Alpha Zeta and Gamma Sigma Delta, and recently was made an honorary member of Phi Beta Kappa.

On June 22, 1899, he was married to Nellie E. Folsom at Brookings, South Dakota. Mrs. Burnett is a native of Herman, New York. Their one child, Knox, was born on August 19, 1903. He is married to Lela Mae Randall, and is engaged in the practice of architecture.

Dr. Burnett has been a resident of Nebraska since 1899, when he became professor of animal husbandry at the state university. In 1909, he was made dean of the agricultural college, and in 1928 he was made chancellor. From 1901 to 1928 he was director of the Nebraska Agricultural Experimental Station. He is the author of various books and pamphlets on animal husbandry, etc. He is a director of the Federal Land Bank. During 1925-1926, he was president of the Association of Land-Grant Colleges.

During the World War he was a member of the American Educational Corps, in charge of agricultural lectures in First Army, A. E. F., University of Beaune, France. He is affiliated with the First Plymouth Congregational Church of Lincoln.

He holds membership in the following organizations: Sons of the American Revolution, National Educational Association, Lincoln Chamber of Commerce, Kiwanis Club, American Association for the Advancement of Science, and the Y. M. C. A. His social club is the University Club of Lincoln, and his favorite recreation is golf. Residence: Lincoln. (Photograph on Page 191).

Charles Edwin Burnham

On July 21, 1860, at West Troy, Walworth County, Wisconsin, Charles E. Burnham was born, son of Charles Lansing and Amanda Malvina (Hicks) Burnham. His father, who was a merchant, was born at Oswego, New York, March 6, 1836, and died at Tilden, Madison County, Nebraska, November 3, 1902.

His mother was born in Oswego County, New York, March 13, 1841, and died at Tilden, Nebraska, July 4, 1929.

At the age of 15 Mr. Burnham entered the employ of the S. C. & P. Railway, at Sioux City, as clerk. When the office of the company was moved to Missouri Valley, Iowa, he went with them remaining until 1881. At that time he became associated with the C. St. P. M. & O. Railway at St. Paul. He resigned in 1882 and removed to Burnett (now Tilden), Nebraska, and engaged in the mercantile business until 1887. Entering the banking business at Burnett, in 1904, he purchased an interest in the Norfolk State Bank. He is now president of the Norfolk National Bank and the Norfolk Savings Bank; a director of the Haskins State Bank, and of the Federal Reserve Bank of Kansas City.

An active member of various banking associations, he has served as president and member of the taxation committee of the Nebraska Bankers Association, and as member of the executive committee of the American Bankers Association.

He was married at Council Bluffs, Iowa, May 24, 1881 to Lona Adelaide Loper. Mrs. Burnham was born near Adel, Iowa, January 2, 1862. They have one daughter, Faie B., born October 2, 1882, who is married to Eugene G. White.

During the World War Mr. Burnham was chairman of the committee in charge of northeastern Nebraska loan drives. He is secretary of the committee for the relief and care of orphans. He is a member of the Episcopal church, the Y. M. C. A. and the Kiwanis Club.

Mr. Burnham is a Mason and served as grand master in 1904. He is a Republican. His hobby is reading. His home is at Norfolk.

Silas Henry Burnham

For the past fifty years Silas H. Burnham has been a resident of Nebraska, and during this time has been in the banking business. He was born at Harrison, Cumberland County, Maine, April 12, 1848, the son of Sumner and Christiana (Washburn) Burnham. His father, who was born at Harrison, was a farmer, and for many years was president of the Norway National Bank at Norway, Maine. He was of English descent. He died at Norway, in 1878. Silas Burnham's mother was born at Harrison, and died at Portland, Cumberland County, Maine, at the age of 99.

Mr. Burnham attended the public schools of Norway, and the Hebron Academy. He was graduated with the A. B. degree at Dartmouth College in 1874, where he was especially active in music and dramatics; he took part in various athletic affairs particularly football and baseball. He was elected to membership in Psi Upsilon.

He was admitted to the bar at Norway, in 1875, and for the next four years was engaged in the practice of law there. Since then he has been in the banking business. He is chairman of the board of the First National Bank and the First Trust Company of Lincoln. He is vice-president of the Lincoln Telephone & Telegraph Company; and is vice president of the Lincoln Telephone Securities Company.

He was united in marriage with Elizabeth Lewis at Glasgow, Barren County, Kentucky, in 1876. Mrs. Burnham was born at Glasgow, in 1854. Her father was a general in the Orphan Brigade of the Confederate Army in the Civil War. They have four children: Sayde, who married George W. Holmes of Lincoln; Joseph, who married Clara Watts of Carbondale, Pennsylvania; Louise, who married Willard S. Yates of Lincoln; and Silas Henry, who married Helen Chapin and later Alice Hallasey, of Los Angeles.

Mr. Burnham is a member of the American Bankers Association; the Nebraska Bankers Association; Lincoln Chamber of Commerce; and the Elks. He holds membership in the Nebraska State Historical Society and the Nebraskana Society. He is a member of Lincoln Country Club and Lincoln University Club. He is interested in golf, football, and baseball. His hobby is bridge. He is a member of the First Plymouth Congregational Church of Lincoln. He is a Republican. Residence: Lincoln.

Sumner Burnham

Sumner Burnham, farmer and stock raiser, was born in Cass County, Nebraska, June 23, 1882, son of Horace and Elizabeth (Frost) Burnham. His father was a farmer born in Maine who died at Westerville, Nebraska, in March, 1903. His mother was also born in Maine, and died at Westerville in 1888.

In 1895 Mr. Burnham was graduated from rural school in Lancaster County, and the following two years attended the Lincoln Business College.

From 1898 until 1906 he was bookkeeper at the First National Bank of Lincoln, and the following two years was assistant cashier of the First National Bank at Scottsbluff. From 1909 until 1913 he was assistant cashier of the Scottsbluff National Bank, and from 1913 until 1918 was secretary-treasurer and manager of the York Brick and Tile Company. Since that time he has engaged exclusively in farming and stock raising.

His marriage to Jessie Pearl Dixon was solemnized at Lincoln, on July 15, 1905. Mrs. Burnham was born at Roachdale, Indiana, March 19, 1883. They have two daughters, Frances, born March 13, 1910, who is a teacher of Latin and English at Hay Springs High School and who has the Bachelor of Arts degree; and Margaret, born September 21, 1912, who is secretary to the superintendent of the Bayard City Schools.

Mr. Burnham is a Republican. He is affiliated with the Congregational Church, is a member of the Masons, and from 1918 until 1924 was a member of the local school board. Residence: Bayard.

Joseph Burns

Joseph Burns, contractor and hydraulic engineer, was born in County Roscommon, Ireland, the son of William and Mary Burns. William Burns, a farmer, brought his family to America in 1861, and died at Hartford, Connecticut in 1900. His wife, Mary, who was a native of Scotland, died in Ireland in 1851.

Self educated, Mr. Burns was engaged as a contractor and engineer from early manhood. He was married to Anna Carl at Meriden, Connecticut, on December 15, 1869. Mrs. Burns was born in Scotland on February 22, 1849, and died at Lincoln on January 4, 1922. To their marriage eight children were born: Howard, born June 1, 1873, who married Blanche McGinnis, and who died in 1924; Daisy, born February 22, 1876, who married William E. Taylor, and who died October 9, 1930; Deana, born April 13, 1878, who married William P. Heath and who died February 11, 1930; Charles, born August 1, 1880, who married Bessie Bixby; Nelle, born February 22, 1883, who married Alfred C. Goodwin; Mollie, born December 20, 1885, who married Fred R. Slade; George, born January 11, 1887, who married Lillian Wicks; Joseph, Jr., born December 11, 1892, who married Winnie Burns.

About forty-eight years ago Mr. Burns brought his family to Nebraska where he always resided. A Republican, he has been active in politics, and has held the following offices: city councilman 1890-91; state representative 1893-95; 1899-1905; state senator 1907.

Mr. Burns invented and patented the section well augur at Monticello, Iowa, in 1870, the tool which made it possible for the early Nebraska settlers to secure water at a small cost and which did more to settle the state of Nebraska than any other implement. With this augur it was possible for three men to bore and curb a well 125 feet deep in two days.

As the water in many sections of the state was more than 125 feet from the surface, the digging of these wells without this augur was a slow and very expensive process. Mr. Burns also introduced the battery of drove wells system in Nebraska, and drove and connected up to one pump eighty wells which furnished Lincoln with three and a half million gallons of water per day. This was in 1886, and was considered by the *Scientific American* and the *Engineering News* as a feat of engineering.

The same year Mr. Burns planned for the city of Hastings water plant six individual eight inch pipe wells from which he guaranteed one million gallons of water a day. With much ridicule from representatives of pump companies who declared it could not be done, he furnished a bond and completed the job which proved to be a great success.

Shortly after this, and with the use of the battery well system, the cities of Nebraska and railroad companies in the state abandoned the dug well plan. Mr. Burns introduced also what was known as tubular wells, and assisted Walker and Lockwood, wellmen, in introducing their rotary well method, now so generally in use over the United States. He was the first man west of the Alleghenys to introduce the Foley air lift now in extensive use.

He was the first man to introduce pumping for irrigation in 1893, and at the time of his recent death was actively engaged in the well contracting business.

His hobby was the public ownership of utilities. He was a member of the City Civic League, and had an enviable reputation for service to his city and state. (Photograph in Album).

Lyle Willis Burns

Lyle Willis Burns, life insurance executive, was born at Scribner, Nebraska, February 9, 1898, son of John Edward and Nellie (Burrows) Burns. John Edward Burns was born in New York State June 22, 1868, and now lives at Loveland, Colorado. His mother was born at Platte Center, Nebraska, January 29, 1872, and died at Longmont, Colorado, September 17, 1929. His father's ancestry was Scotch, tracing back to Robert Burns, and the mother's ancestry is English.

Mr. Burns attended public school, and in 1915 was graduated from Manual Training High School at Denver, Colorado.

He was married on March 31, 1919, to Clora Nica McCane at Denver. She was born in Kentucky, June 24, 1896, the daughter of Francis Marion and Margaret Helen (Kyle) McCane. The father was born in Bracken County, Kentucky, March 14th, 1860. Mother was born also in Bracken County, August 15th, 1860, and died at Denver, March 11, 1912. They have two children, John W., born April 1, 1920; and Frances McCane, born February 9, 1922.

From 1920 until 1928 Mr. Burns engaged in the mercantile business, at Lafayette, Colorado, one year, Mitchell, Nebraska, 5 years, and Gering, two years, and from 1928 until 1930 was city clerk at Gering. He became postal clerk in 1928, and since October of that year has been supervisor of the Penn Mutual Life Insurance Company for western Nebraska.

During the late war Mr. Burns served with the 338th Tank Corps in Company C. He is now a member of the American Legion. His hobbies are hunting and baseball. He is a Republican. Residence: Gering.

Melissa Elisabeth Burns

Melissa Elisabeth (Getter) Burns was born in Medina County, Ohio, July 24, 1838, of English, Irish, Dutch and German descent. A teacher in the rural schools of Indiana, she was married to Edward Clark Burns at Ovid, Michigan, October 15, 1865. Mr. Burns was born in Phelpstown, New York, November 13, 1838, son of John Flowers and Eunice (Noyes) Burns. His father was an axmaker, born in Philadelphia, of Scotch and English descent, and a descendant of Robert Burns, the Scottish poet. His mother was born in New Hampshire, September 27, 1810, and died at Scribner, March 10, 1894. She was of Scotch and English descent also.

To Edward and Melissa Burns were born ten children, seven boys and three girls, five of whom were teachers in Dodge County Schools. Frank O., who died in May, 1908, was born in Indiana, as were John E., Robert L., Mark G., Willis P., Birge E., Jesse C., Mary E. Elnora, and Dolly were born in Scribner. Robert L. and Birge E., were both railroad men, and reside in California. Mark G., who was a newspaper man in South Dakota, for many years, now owns a fruit farm in central California. Willis P., who was a volunteer with Company E, 3rd Nebraska Infantry, died of typhoid in Jacksonville, Florida. All her children are Republicans.

Mr. and Mrs. Burns came to Dodge County in June, 1869. He held many public offices, including justice of the peace four years, county commissioner six years, postmaster of Scribner, four years, member of the legislature one term, and deputy state oil inspector four years. He died in office. He was the author of the act giving a bounty to beet growers, and also of the act reducing county commissioners in rural counties to three.

Edward C. Burns was the first man to enlist for the Civil War in 1861, from Steuben County, Indiana. He held the rank of corporal in Company B, 4th Michigan Infantry, 3rd Brigade, 1st Division, 5th Army Corps. He participated in the Battle of Bull Run (first battle), and at Gettysburg. His division was the one which repulsed Pickett at Little Round Top. He was captured and was a prisoner of war for one year, four months in Libbey Prison in Richmond, Virginia, and eight months in Andersonville Prison, Georgia. He was paroled and exchanged on February 8, 1865, having served four years and six months, but never regained his health fully after his suffering in southern prisons.

Mr. Burns was a member of the Masonic Order, and adjutant of the D. A. Woodbury Post of the Grand Army of the Republic. He was a trustee of the Methodist Episcopal Church, and chairman of the town board of Scribner, for fourteen years. He died at his home in Scribner, Nebraska, after a long illness, on May 30, 1908.

William Wesley Burr

William W. Burr, prominent Nebraska educator, was born at Goodland, Jasper County, Indiana, March 26, 1880. His father, Elliott Remus Burr, who was a farmer and a Civil War veteran, was born at Cuba, Allegheny County, New York, August 2, 1842, and died at St. Cloud, Florida, March 27, 1918. He was of Scotch, Irish, and English descent. Sarah Jane (Vorheis) Burr, his mother, was born at Friendship, Allegheny County, New York, May 7, 1842, and died at Goodland, Indiana, September 17, 1887.

Professor Burr received his elementary education in the public schools of Indiana and Virginia. He was graduated from the University of Nebraska College of Agriculture in 1906, with the B. S. degree. He was a student at Virginia Polytechnic Institute, 1899-1900. He was made a member of Alpha Zeta, Sigma Xi, Gamma Sigma Delta fraternities at the University of Nebraska.

From 1906 to 1912, he was assistant in dry land agriculture at North Platte Experiment Station; was assistant agronomist of the United States Department of Ag-

riculture, 1913-16; was agronomist at the University of Nebraska, 1916; was assistant director of the University of Nebraska Experiment Station, 1919-28; was acting dean of the College of Agriculture, 1927. Since 1928 he has been dean of the College of Agriculture and director of the Agricultural Experiment Station at the University of Nebraska.

He is the author of numerous experiment station bulletins, chiefly concerning dry-land agriculture. He is contributing editor of *Book of Rural Life.* He has lived in Nebraska for the past 27 years.

Professor Burr was married to Aurelia Marion Scott at Lincoln, Lancaster County, Nebraska, January 1, 1919. Mrs. Burr, whose ancestry is Scotch, was born at Taylor, Loup County, Nebraska, June 7, 1890. They have two children: Della Jean, born December 27, 1920; and William Wesley, Junior, born March 12, 1923.

Mr. Burr served as chairman of the federal and state seed committee during the World War. He is a member of the Nebraska State Teachers Association; the American Society of Agronomy; vice president, 1926-30, president, 1931; Nebraska Academy of Science; American Association for the Advancement of Science; and International Congress of Soil Science. He holds membership in the Red Cross; Community Chest; Chamber of Commerce, serving as director in 1931; and the Parent-Teachers' Association. He was a member of the board of directors and vice president of the Lincoln Kiwanis Club for two years; and holds membership in the Nebraskana Society and the Nebraska State Historical Society. He is a member of the Masonic Blue Lodge, Scottish Rite (Knight Commander of Court of Honor), and Shrine.

His social clubs are the University Club, Polemic Club. and Shrine Country Club. He is a member of First Plymouth Congregational Church of Lincoln, and is a Republican. Residence: Lincoln.

John Wesley Burrows

John Wesley Burrows, executive, was born in Dows, Iowa, August 22, 1874, son of Chester William and Jane (Gurney) Burrows. The father and mother were born in England, and came to the United States in 1852, settling in Wisconsin. They later removed to Iowa and were prominent pioneer settlers.

Upon his graduation from high school Mr. Burrows engaged in railroad work. Starting as a telegraph operator, he was time-keeper, accountant, ticket agent, cashier, chief clerk to the superintendent and conductor in 20 years of service. He was engaged in clerical work for the Central Colorado Power Company six months, and was in the United States Reclamation service for a year at Mitchell, Nebraska. He was in the hotel business at Greeley, Colorado, four years. The balance of his time has been spent in county work. A Republican, he has been county clerk of Scotts Bluff County since 1920. Mr. Burrows was deputy county clerk two years prior to his appointment as county clerk.

On March 20, 1917, he was married to Edith Mary (Comer) Funk, at Greeley, Colorado. Mrs. Burrows is a graduate of Greeley High School, and is the daughter of Robert W. and Hanna (Stevens) Comer. She has two children by a former marriage, Charles and Annabel. She was born at Detroit, Michigan, August 12, 1884. Mr. and Mrs. Burrows have one daughter, Carol Rosalie, born February 28, 1922.

Mr. Burrows is a member of the Methodist Church, the Masons and Scottish Rite. Residence: Gering.

Oliver P. Burrows

Oliver P. Burrows, real estate, loan and insurance broker, was born at Dows, Iowa, August 26, 1871, son of Chester William and Jane (Gurney) Burrows. His parents came to the United States from England in 1852.

In May, 1890, Mr. Burrows was graduated from the

Dows, Iowa, High School, and in 1899 from the Cedar Rapids Business College at Cedar Rapids, Iowa. He taught school from 1893 to 1898.

On August 14, 1907, he was married to Gertrude MacDonald at Sauk Center, Minnesota. Mrs. Burrows was born at Minneapolis, December 28, 1880. She is a member of the Eastern Star, Rebekahs, Woman's Club and the Methodist Episcopal Church, and is president of the Parent Teacher's Association at Mitchell. They have three children, Donald O., born August 12, 1909; Gurney E., born January 31, 1912; and Gertrude C., born January 8, 1914. Donald O. and Gurney E. are both students of the Chadron State Normal.

For ten years Mr. Burrows was engaged in the United States Reclamation Service. He was associated with the Burlington Cedar Rapids and Northern Railway for one year, and was engaged in banking for one year.

Active in Republican politics Mr. Burrows has been justice of the peace for about 12 years and a member of the school board 16 years. He is a member of the Methodist Episcopal Church, the Masons, and the Odd Fellows. Residence: Mitchell.

Russell Melvin Burruss

Born at Alexandria, Nebraska, February 10, 1888, Russell M. Burruss is the son of Joseph Gordon and Hattie (Phelps) Burruss. His father, a lumberman, of English descent, was born at Lynchburg, Virginia, and died at Lincoln, in 1912. His mother, a native of Illinois, died at Lincoln, in 1907.

Mr. Burruss was graduated from Lincoln High School in 1904, and attended the University of Nebraska during 1906-07-08. He was a member of Sigma Alpha Epsilon, and was active in basketball and track.

On January 12, 1910, he was married to Sarah Margaret Martin. Mrs. Burruss, who is of Scotch descent, was born at South Omaha, in 1890. There are two children, Robert, born November 16, 1917, and John, born April 9, 1916.

A resident of Nebraska for forty years, Mr. Burruss has been engaged in the live stock commission business for more than fifteen years. Among his business associations are the Phelps-Burruss Lumber Company; Martin Brothers Live Stock Commission Co. of Omaha and Chicago. He is a member of the Omaha Live Stock Exchange, also.

Mr. Burruss is a member of the Elks and of the Omaha Athletic Club and Field Club. His favorite sports are football and golf. Residence: Omaha.

Albert Henry Burt

Born at Elwood, Nebraska, January 4, 1886, Albert Henry Burt is the son of Gordon Turner and Catherine (Lawson) Burt. His father, who was a minister in the Christian Church, was born in Illinois, and died at Stamford, Nebraska, February 2, 1911. His mother was born in Illinois and died at Stamford, December 28, 1924.

Mr. Burt was graduated from the Elwood High School in 1905, and the following year was employed by Rudge & Guenzel Company of Lincoln. He moved to Stamford in 1906 where he was associated in business with his father until 1908 when he entered the civil service. He is a rural mail carrier at this time, is secretary and a stockholder in the Stamford Oil & Supply Company, and is connected with the Cowles Oil Company and the Farmers & Merchants Oil Company as a stockholder and officer.

A member of the Stamford Christian Church, Mr. Burt is active in that organization as superintendent of the Sunday School, teacher, and chairman of the official board. His hobby is traveling and he has visited most places of interest in the United States. His favorite sports are golf and tennis.

His marriage to Maude Tracey took place at Lincoln, Nebraska, December 30, 1906. Mrs. Burt, whose ancestry is Scotch and Irish, was born at Elwood, November 24, 1888. Residence: Stamford.

George Turner Burt

Born at Wilber, Nebraska, September 24, 1877, George Turner Burt is the son of Gordon Turner and Catherine Your (Lawson) Burt. His father, a native of Illinois, born March 15, 1856, was a clergyman, whose death occurred at Stamford, Nebraska, February 14, 1911. His mother, who was born in Illinois, June 12, 1856, died at Stamford, on January 18, 1920.

Educated in public school, Mr. Burt was for some time a grain buyer. He was elected county treasurer of Gosper County on the Democratic ticket two terms, and is now manager of a lumber yard, director of the Home Bank, the Elwood Co-operative Oil Company, the Equity Elevator, the Community Improvement Company, and secretary of the Elwood Community Club.

On October 15, 1899, Mr. Burt was married to Sadie Estella Hicks at Elwood. Mrs. Burt was born at Boone, Iowa, March 26, 1883. There are three children, Klyte, born December 29, 1902, who married Doris Kelly, and who is a student at the University of Nebraska; Homer, born September 22, 1904, who married Letha Gembler, and who is employed by Rudge & Guenzel at Lincoln; and La Vera, born June 2, 1906, who married James Murphy, and is connected with the department of public works at Lincoln.

Mr. Burt has lived in Nebraska, since birth. He was treasurer of the local Red Cross organization during the World War and participated in other civilian wartime projects. He is a member of various commercial, welfare and educational organizations, and was recently made a member of the Nebraskana Society. Residence: Elwood.

Ben H. Busboom

Ben H. Busboom, merchant and farmer of Crete, Saline County, Nebraska, was born at Crete, February 9, 1890, the son of pioneer Nebraskans Ben H. and Johanna (Sleep) Busboom. His father, who was a farmer, was born in Germany, March 21, 1862, and died at Crete, March 29, 1926; he came to America in 1870 when he settled in Illinois, and in 1888 settled in Saline County. His mother was born in Germany, September 12, 1866; came to this country with her parents in 1870 and settled in Illinois; and in 1875 moved to Crete.

Mr. Busboom was graduated from the Crete High School where he participated in track and basketball activities. In 1922 he began work with the Farmer's Union in the implement department. In 1927 he organized an implement business for himself. He is the owner and manager of the Busboom & Stone Implement Company, and has retained 255 acres of farm land for cultivation.

On December 11, 1912, his marriage to Elizabeth Katherine Schultz was solemnized at Crete. Mrs. Busboom was born in Lancaster County, Nebraska, October 22, 1893; her ancestry is German. They have four children: Evelyn, born December 21, 1913; Dorothy, born November 24, 1915; Edward, born December 1, 1918; and Clarence, born January 3, 1920.

Mr. Busboom's children have all attended the district school at Crete, where his parents and he received their education. He is a member of the Crete Community Club and the Nebraskana Society. For the past 15 years he has been an active member of the district school board. He is affiliated with the German Congregational Church of Crete. He is interested in all out of door sports. He is a Democrat. Residence: Crete.

Fritz John Busch

Fritz J. Busch was born at Strokirchen, Mecklenburg, Germany, July 31, 1855, the son of Christian John and Dorothea (Mueller) Busch. His father was a farmer in

Germany. His mother died at Strokirchen, September 13, 1865. Mr. Busch received his education in Germany. He arrived in Schuyler, Nebraska, July 15, 1870, and started to work on a farm at $70.00 per year.

In 1872, he was connected with the firm Wells & Nieman, Millers and Grain Buyers, which position he held for eight years; he was compelled to give up this work because of ill health. Later he returned to farm work, and in 1896 moved to Howells, and went into business. He organized a stock company to build a flour mill; he was successful in building a 75 barrel capacity flour mill of which he is now president and general manager. The mill has twice been enlarged and today it has a 500 barrel capacity and is a thriving concern. He is also interested in a general merchandise store.

Mr. Busch is a member of the Red Cross and the Nebraskana Society. He is a Mason, a Democrat, and holds membership in the Trinity Lutheran Church of Howells.

He was married to Minnie Mary Brumm, at Schuyler, July 22, 1881. Mrs. Busch was born at Middleton, Dane County, Wisconsin, October 17, 1858, and died at Howells, September 28, 1915. The following children were born to them: Mary S., born May 3, 1882, who married Dr. H. Dey Myers; Herman, born September 15, 1892, who died October 5, 1892; Rudolph F., born October 18, 1883, who married Bertha Phelps; Minnie D., born November 10, 1890, who died February 10, 1895; John, born December 20, 1886, who died December 21, 1886; John W., born February 13, 1888, who died May 13, 1888; and Caroline S., born February 10, 1889, who married P. J. Kulhanck. Mr. Busch was united in marriage with Minnie H. Nieman, at Schuyler, May 20, 1919. Residence: Howells. (Photograph in Album).

Alfred Otto Buschow

Alfred Otto Buschow was born in Blue Hill, Nebraska, August 8, 1894, and in 1929 was elected the youngest Master Farmer in Nebraska. He is the son of Frank Charles and Marie (Kublanch) Buschow, the former born in Brauburch, Germany, November 25, 1847. Frank Charles Buschow was a cabinet maker by trade in Germany, and an early pioneer in Webster County. He had much to do with the development of his community. After his retirement from the farm he was a justice of the peace until his death at Blue Hill on December 16, 1922. His wife, Marie, was born in Brauburch, Germany, July 2, 1868, and is still living.

Mr. Buschow attended public school and afterward started farming. He then traveled for a year over the United States and Canada, working in lumber camps on the west coast, and then in one of the largest dairies there. He has exhibited at the Nebraska State Fair for 15 consecutive years and possesses many first premium ribbons. He also exhibited at the National Dairy Show in St. Louis, in 1931. Returning in the spring 1912, he engaged in the purebred stock business and is now a breeder of purebred livestock. At the present time he is president of the Nebraska Guernsey Breeders Association, and active and interested in 4-H Club work. He is a member of Guilds Gopatis (National Honor Roll), of which he has been vice president, the Nebraska Dairymens Association, the Nebraska Dairy Development Society, the Greater Nebraska Club, (charter member), the Lincoln Chamber of Commerce, and the Nebraska Dairy Herd Improvement Association. He is a Mason, a member of Hastings Consistory, and a member of the Nebraskana Society. He is a member of St. Paul's Lutheran Church and is a liberal giver to all worthy causes.

During the late war he was a corporal in the United States Army and participated in three battles, Fliry, St. Mihiel, and Meuse-Argonne. He is a member of Shirley Post No. 176 of the American Legion and has been an officer of that organization.

On November 18, 1920, he was married to Helen Elca Suchland at Hastings. Mrs. Buschow was born at Hastings, August 10, 1896. Her father was born in Baden, Germany, and her mother in Switzerland, her mother comes of the Swiss nobility. The Buschows have three children, Dale Everett, born September 7, 1921; Bernard Vaughn, born December 7, 1922; and Rosemary, born January 16, 1926. Residence: Blue Hill. (Photograph on Page 197).

Nelson Burt Bush

Nelson Burt Bush, railroad passenger and freight agent at Red Cloud for a number of years, was born at Ellington, New York, June 25, 1877, son of Collins L. and Ella Ernestine (Round) Bush.

The father, a farmer died at Ellington in the winter of 1884. The mother is still living and is residing at Oberlin, Kansas. Mr. Bush attended public school, was graduated from high school in 1894, at Oberlin, Kansas, and taught school two terms in Decatur County, Kansas.

He was married on April 17, 1900, to Elsie Louise Burgess at McCook. Mrs. Bush was born near Arapahoe, Nebraska, March 25, 1880, daughter of Frank D. and Florence E. Burgess. There are two children, Lynn H., born March 25, 1901, who married Mildred C. Borin who is in the incurance business at Red Cloud; and Eugene C., born September 30, 1903, who married Ilah L. Barrett who is a railway telegrapher and relief agent on the McCook division of the Chicago, Burlington and Quincy Railroad.

Mr. Bush has been prominent in civic organizations for some years, has been president of the Red Cloud Ad Club, 1928-30, and president of the Lions Club, 1930-1932. He is a member of the Red Cloud Methodist Church and its brotherhood, the Red Cross, the Masons, and the Isaak Walton League. His favorite sport is golf. Residence: Red Cloud.

Louis Bernard Bushman

Louis Bernard Bushman, oculist and aurist, was born at Omaha, March 29, 1877, the son of William and Wilhelmina (Litzen) Bushman.

He received his medical degree from Creighton University in 1903, and took post graduate work in London and Vienna.

He was married on October 20, 1915, to Evangeline Homan at Omaha.

His professional organizations include the American Medical Association, the Nebraska State Medical Association, the Douglas County Medical Association and the American College of Surgeons. Residence: Omaha.

Herbert Martin Bushnell

Herbert Martin Bushnell, banker, was born at Lincoln, Nebraska, July 1, 1893, son of Herbert Martin and Elsie Nevada (Campbell) Bushnell.

His father was born July 20, 1855, at Moria, New York, and died at Lincoln, January 1, 1920. He was a publisher and a former postmaster, and at one time was president of the Nebraska State Association of Commercial Clubs, and president of the Nebraska Sons of the American Revolution. His wife, Elsie, was born November 12, 1858, and was former president of the Lincoln Woman's Club and the Nebraska Federation of Women's Clubs.

Mr. Bushnell was educated in the Lincoln Public and High Schools, and received his Bachelor of Laws degree from the University of Nebraska in 1915, there he was a member of Phi Gamma Delta. He is a Republican, a member and former secretary of the Chamber of Commerce at Alliance. He is former executive secretary of the Federal Food Administration of Nebraska, and at the present time is the director of the United States Trust Company and director of the United Staes National Bank. He was admitted to the practice of law in Nebraska in 1915. He is a former director of the

Blackford—Blue Hill

ALFRED OTTO BUSCHOW

Nebraska Sons of the American Revolution, and a member of the Chamber of Commerce. His clubs are the University Club, the Omaha Country Club, and the Athletic Club. Residence: Omaha.

Howard Lewis Bushnell

Howard Lewis Bushnell, retired merchant, was born at Johnsonville, Ohio, January 18, 1850, son of Lewis and Elizabeth Ann (Treat) Bushnell.

Lewis Bushnell was born in Johnsonville, Ohio, March 23, 1818, and died there on December 6, 1903. He was a farmer and dairyman.

The Bushnell genealogy, gives the Tribe of Daniel, the great, great grandfather of Howard Lewis Bushnell, as Daniel Bushnell, who was born December 18, 1763, and died August 12, 1842. He was a captain in the Revolution, serving seven years, and it is thought that some of his sons were also in that war. Captain Alexander Bushnell, with his son Daniel and others of the family, came from Connecticut about 1804, and settled in Hartford, Ohio.

The great grandfather, Daniel Bushnell, was twice married, his first wife being Rebecca Banning, by whom he had ten children, Lewis B., Lydia (twice married but had no children), Ziba B. married Amasa Webb, Amoret B. married Sylvester Borden, Daniel M. B. married Minerva Coe (first son was Ralph S. B.), Clarrissa married Josiah Fenney, George W. B. (physician).

Neither Hiram nor Rhoda were ever married. Elijah's second wife was Eunice Brockway, and the names of the children were, Newton, Rebecca, Alexander, Joseph 1st., Joseph 2nd., Philena, and Benjamin.

Elizabeth Ann Treat, wife of Lewis Bushnell, was born in Vienna, Ohio, July 4, 1821, and died at Johnsonville, Ohio, February 22, 1894. She was a teacher before her marriage.

On September 18, 1876, Howard Lewis Bushnell married Kit Clark at Vienna, Ohio. She was born at Vienna, December 12, 1853. To them six children were born, four of whom are living, Ira, born July 17, 1880, married Rachel Brown; Bert, born December 12, 1882, married Lottie People; Mary, born July 25, 1884, married Claude Walter Brown; Hugh, born April 12, 1886, died August 21, 1892; Charles, born July 28, 1887, married Esther Neeland; and Carrie, born June 3, 1890, married Clarence Canfield and died February 11, 1918.

Mr. Bushnell has been a resident of Nebraska for 44 years and during much of that time was a merchant at Hemingford. He is a member of the Congregational Church, the Odd Fellows, and the Nebraskana Society. Residence: Hemingford.

Benjamin Franklin Butler

Benjamin Franklin Butler was born at Calhoun, Iowa, June 20, 1881, the son of Harvey Gibson and Ida (Wills) Butler. His father, who was a miller, was born at Springfield, Illinois, September 20, 1847, and died at Los Angeles, California, November 20, 1928; his ancestry was English. His mother was born in Iowa, October 1, 1862, and died at Cambridge, Nebraska, November 11, 1891.

Mr. Butler was graduated from the Cambridge High School in 1898, and received the Bachelor of Laws degree from the University of Nebraska in 1907. He was a student at Doane College, from 1899 to 1901, and while a student at the University of Nebraska, was a member of Phi Delta Phi, Acacia, and president of Junior Laws.

A Republican, he served as county attorney of Furnas County, 1914-16, and as a member of the Nebraska Constitutional Convention, 1919-20. He is a member of the law firm Butler & James at Cambridge. Mr. Butler holds membership in the American Bar Association, the Nebraska Bar Association, Southwestern Nebraska Bar Association, the Cambridge Community Club, the Cambridge Rotary Club, and the Nebraska State Historical Society. He is affiliated with the First Congregational Church of

Cambridge, holds membership in the Young Men's Christian Association, and is a member of the Cambridge Golf Club.

His fraternal organizations include the Elks, Odd Fellows, Modern Woodmen of America, and the Masons, (Scottish Rite and Shrine). His favorite sports are golfing and riding. During the World War Mr. Butler was active in Liberty loan drives and Four Minute work. He was married at Beaver City, Nebraska, January 29, 1913, the Maudlee Lewelling who was born at Western, Nebraska, April 8, 1889. Residence: Cambridge. (Photograph in Album).

Guy Butler

Guy Butler, who has been in the drug business at Lincoln since 1920, was born at Missouri Valley, Iowa, August 16, 1879, and has resided in Nebraska forty years. He is the son of H. G. and Ida (Wills) Butler. H. G. Butler died at Los Angeles, on November 11, 1928, and his wife at Cambridge, Nebraska, November 12, 1890.

Mr. Butler is a graduate in pharmacy of the Northwestern School of Pharmacy. He is the senior member of the firm of Butler-Wagey Drug Company at Lincoln, at the present time has been a member of the Nebraska Pharmacentical Association for 15 years and has served on the pharmacy examining board.

His marriage to Nellie Rosenfelt took place at Cambridge, Nebraska, April 22, 1903. Mrs. Butler was born at Cambridge, July 30, 1880. There are two children, Helen, born May 4, 1904, who is a graduate nurse, and Kenneth, born April 12, 1905, who is a graduate embalmer. They are members of the Second Baptist Church of Lincoln. Mr. Butler is a member of the Chamber of Commerce. He enjoys football more than any other sport. Residence: Lincoln.

Hugh Alfred Butler

Born at Missouri Valley, Iowa, February 28, 1878, Hugh A. Butler is the son of Harvey Gibson and Ida (Wills) Butler. Harvey G. Butler was born in Sangamon County, Illinois, September 20, 1846, and was descended of early settlers in Kentucky, near Louisville. He died at Los Angeles, November 11, 1927. His wife, Ida Wills, was born in Harrison County, Iowa, January 7. She died at Cambridge, November 12, 1891.

Upon his completion of grade school in the country schools of Iowa and Nebraska, Mr. Butler entered the Cambridge High School and was graduated in June, 1895.

He was active in athletics and debate while in college. He received an S. B. degree from Doane College in June, 1859, and died at Cambridge, Nebraska, November 12, 1891.

On February 5, 1903, he was married to Fay Johnson of Crete, at Aurora, Nebraska. Mrs. Butler traces her ancestry on both sides to the *Mayflower*, through Governor Bradford. Their children were Lawrence, born June 14, 1909, died July 15, 1909, and Robert, born December 28, 1912, died March 21, 1925.

After eight years with the Chicago, Burlington and Quincy Railroad, as construction engineer, Mr. Butler was engaged with the Crete Mills ten years as manager at Curtis and Crete. Since 1918 he has been in business for himself, and is now president of the Butler-Welsh Grain Company. He is a member of the Salvation Army Advisory Board of Omaha, president of the National Grain Dealers Association, the Omaha Grain Exchange and member of the Chicago Board of Trade. He is one of the trustees of Doane College, and a member of the board of education of Omaha. He is affiliated with the First Central Congregational Church of Omaha, and is a member of the Rotary Club, the Modern Woodmen of America, the Chamber of Commerce, the Odd Fellows and the Masons. His clubs are the University Club, the Omaha Athletic Club, the Happy Hollow Country Club and the Omaha Field Club. He is fond of hunting, and enjoys taking movies of his hunting trips. Residence: Omaha.

James Arthur Butler

James Arthur Butler, a former newspaper editor and farmer, was born at Stoney Fork, Pennsylvania, December 15, 1861, and in 1868 came to Benton County, Iowa, and came to Nebraska in October, 1879. In 1880-1881 he taught at the Riverside School in a dugout. His father, Welman Sumner Butler, a farmer, was born at Keene, New Hampshire, April 4, 1824, and died at Ewing, Nebraska, April 3, 1913; his ancestry was Irish and English. Eliza Ann (Catlin) Butler, his mother, was born at Otsego, New York, October 26, 1827, and for many years was a teacher; she died at Ewing, November 26, 1908.

Mr. Butler acted as editor of the *Public Opinion* at Orchard, Nebraska, from 1890 to 1891, and for a number of years was a farmer in Antelope County, Nebraska. He entered the United States service as a mail carrier in 1903 and continued in that capacity until 1931 when he was retired. He is president of the Ewing Commercial Club, is chairman of the relief committee of the Red Cross, and since 1925 has served as president of the local school board, having been a member of that board since 1914. Mr. Butler is treasurer of the village board of Ewing. His hobby is good government, and his political preference is the Democratic party.

On September 14, 1887, he married Ora Comstock at Ewing. Mrs. Butler, who was born at Cascade, Iowa, May 13, 1868, was a teacher until after her marriage. The following children were born to this marriage: Pearl, November 21, 1888, who died December 31, 1896; Ruby, January 6, 1891; Winifred, April 24, 1893, who married Ora Switzer; Mildred, April 6, 1895, who married Wilbur Bennett, and who died January 30, 1919; Jay, February 17, 1898; Kay, November 11, 1900, who died July 25, 1901; Gretchen, July 11, 1902; Alberta, April 3, 1905; Donald, April 8, 1908; and Cleo, December 31, 1910. Residence: Ewing. (Photograph in Album).

Willis Myron Butler

Willis Myron Butler was born at Phillipsville, Pennsylvania, February 16, 1870, the son of Richard Emory and Charlotte Annette (Rockwood) Butler. His father, a blacksmith, was born at Phillipsville, August 12, 1843; his ancestors coming from Schuyler, New York. His mother was born at Erie City, Pennsylvania, August 5, 1847, of French and English parentage; her father, who was born in Massachusetts, served in the Revolution. Both parents now reside at Ashland.

Mr. Butler, who has lived in Nebraska for 50 years, is now president of the Butler Dry Goods Company at Ashland. He is a member of the Ashland Chamber of Commerce, is affiliated with the Congregational Church, holds membership in the Nebraskana Society, and for several years has been a member of the Ashland School Board. He is a member of the Scottish Rite and Shrine bodies, and is past master of Pomegranite Lodge No. 110 of the Ancient Free and Accepted Masons.

His marriage to Ella Edna Vandeman was solemnized at Ashland, October 19, 1894. Mrs. Butler was born at Youngstown, Ohio, April 19, 1871. They have two children: Hazel, born September 12, 1895, who married Eugene F. Adams; and Dwight W., born September 22, 1897, who married Freda Voght, and who is now associated with his father in business. Mr. Butler is a Republican. Residence: Ashland.

Gordon Bryan Butterfield

Gordon Bryan Butterfield, has been a resident of Norfolk for about 12 years, and is district manager of the Mutual Life Insurance Company of New York, at Norfolk. He was born at Fort Crook, Nebraska, September 25, 1896, the son of Charles Adolph and Sophia Ann (Julyan) Butterfield, the former a lifetime resident of this state. His mother was born in England, October 30, 1860, and came to America at the age of 13. His father was born February 9, 1857, at Belleville, Nebraska.

Mr. Butterfield attended the Wood Lake High School and later completed a stenography course at Boyles College in Omaha, Nebraska. He was connected with the Wood Lake Bank for a year, served in the United States Army during the War, was connected with the Chicago & Northwestern Railway Company for nearly three years, and served as stenographer and bookkeeper for The Butterfield Company for six years. He has been district manager of the Mutual Life Insurance Company of New York for the past six years.

He is a member of the National Association of Life Underwriters, the Norfolk Chamber of Commerce, and the First Presbyterian Church of Norfolk. He is a Mason, a member of the Eastern Star, and of the Meridian Heights Golf Club. He is interested in prehistoric relics, while his favorite sports are golfing, hunting, and fishing.

During the World War he served as sergeant of Company F, 109th Supply Train, 34th Division, of the United States Army, and was overseas for eight months. He is a member of the American Legion and the Veterans of Foreign Wars.

On December 25, 1921, he married Mary Jane Nightingale at Chadron, Nebraska. She is the daughter of Isaac N. and Mary Lilly (Bush) Nightingale. Her mother was born March 27, 1867, and her father on June 2, 1859, both in Fon du lac County, Wisconsin. Mrs. Butterfield, who was formerly a stenographer and bookkeeper, was born at Norfolk, February 28, 1898. They have one son, Gale Eugene, born June 29, 1931. Residence: Norfolk.

William Spencer Butterfield

William Spencer Butterfield, farmer and real estate operator, was born at Columbus, Wisconsin, October 21, 1889. His father, William Henry Butterfield, was born at Albany, New York, April 16, 1843. He was a very successful real estate, livestock and lumber dealer at the time of his death at Norfolk on April 18, 1916.

Josephine Dayton, wife of William Henry Butterfield, was born at Albany, September 26, 1848, and died at Norfolk on February 27, 1930. She was a member of the Daughters of the American Revolution.

Educated in the preparatory department at Lake Forest, Illinois, until 1907, Mr. Butterfield later attended Norfolk High School. During the years 1908-11 he was a student at Iowa State College where he was a member of Sigma Sigma and Phi Gamma Delta.

An extensive farmer, Mr. Butterfield, is also in the real estate business as vice president and secretary of The Butterfield Company. He is a Republican. During the World War he was called for service, passed and placed in the commissary department as a first lieutenant, but due to his extensive farm and feeding operations was never called into active service.

Mr. Butterfield is an Episcopalian and a Republican. He is a member of the Chamber of Commerce, the Rotary Club, the Masons (Scottish Rite), the Elks and the Nebraskana Society. At the present time he is serving as secretary-treasurer of U. S. Highway No. 20 Association. His clubs are the Athletic and the Norfolk Country Club and his favorite sports are golf and football. Residence: Osmond.

Frank Porter Button

Frank Porter Button, automobile dealer, was born at Doniphan, Nebraska, August 24, 1897, son of Jesse

Porter and Annie May (Clendinin) Button. The father, who was born at Doniphan, February 12, 1872, is a rural mail carrier. His wife, Annie, was born in Illinois, February 16, 1871.

Upon his graduation from Doniphan High School in 1912, Mr. Button entered Grand Island College from which he received the Bachelor of Arts degree. He was the editor of *Volante,* a college publication and editor of the *Islander,* college annual. He was also active in football and track.

For a short time Mr. Button was principal of high school at Sterling, Nebraska, and since that time has been in the automobile business. He was in the aviation service in the World War, and now holds rank of second lieutenant in the reserve corps. He is a Democrat.

On January 8, 1922, he was married to Lola Luella Brehm at Ogallala. Mrs. Button was born at Talmage, July 21, 1903. They have two children, Joseph Frank, born March 18, 1927; and Nancy Jane, born May 3, 1930.

Mr. Button is a member of the Congregational Church, the Commercial Club, the Rotary Club, and the Masons. He enjoys all outdoor sports, while his hobby is shooting. Residence: Ogallala.

Paul Buzek

Paul Buzek, one of the earliest settlers in Nebraska, was born in Czechoslovakia in December, 1859, the son of Paul and Marie Buzek, and for 63 years has lived in this state. His father, who was a farmer, was born in Czechoslovakia, and died at Milligan. His mother was born in Czechoslovakia, and died in Saline County, Nebraska, in the winter of 1887.

Mr. Buzek attended school in Czechoslovakia and in Saline County. He has been a member of the school board near Milligan for many years and holds membership at this time in the Nebraskana Society. His sports include wrestling, boxing, and hunting, and his hobby is reading.

His marriage to Anna Marie Braum occurred at Geneva, Nebraska, in November, 1887. Mrs. Buzek was born in Czechoslovakia, November 15, 1867, and died at Milligan, August 13, 1925. To their marriage the following children were born: William, December 4, 1888, who married Libbye Horlivy; Emma, May 5, 1890, who married Albert Soukup; Rudolph, May 31, 1891, who married Anna Nadherny; Alice, September 7, 1895, who married Albert Kassik; Bohumil, August 5, 1894, who married Anna Chadim; Lou, December 28, 1896; Harry, May 25, 1898, who married Helen Suda; Alba, November 25, 1892; Edward, January 25, 1900, who married Mollye Placek; Anne, January 6, 1902, who married Edward Placek; Marie, February 14, 1903; Velma, February 26, 1904; Mildred, September 16, 1907; Milo, March 24, 1905, who married Mildred Hines; Emil, September 6, 1909; and Lad, March 24, 1905, who died May, 1905. Residence: Milligan.

Charles E. Byars

Charles E. Byars, for thirty-five years editor and publisher of the *Valley Enterprise,* was born at Valley, Nebraska, May 28, 1866. He is the son of Harrel Byars, born at Nashville, Tennessee, February 12, 1840, and Kathryn C. Saunders, born at Shelbyville, Missouri, December 29, 1838.

Harrel Byars, who was descended from early Scotch-Irish settlers in Tennessee, moved to Missouri, settling in Shelby County, when a boy. There he married, and together with his family was a pioneer settler in Valley in 1862. Until his death at Napa, California, March 5, 1923, he was a farmer and breeder of pure-bred stock. Kathryn, his wife, was the mother of nine children. She traced her ancestry back to early settlers in America, also. Her death occurred at Valley, on March 10, 1915.

Educated in country school a few months of the year, in a log house, Charles E. Byars had no opportunity to attend high school, for there were none at that time, but he did attend short terms at Fremont Normal School, and at the time Dr. Bessey was acting chancellor was a student at the University of Nebraska one year.

For thirty-five years Mr. Byars was editor of the *Valley Enterprise,* retiring to conduct a real estate and fire insurance office. At the present time he also operates the Valley Theatre. A Republican, he served in the Nebraska legislature its 1925 session, where he made an enviable record. Understanding thoroughly the needs of the agricultural districts, he ably represented his constituency, and his record was fearless, clean and above criticism.

His marriage to Hattie E. Hallenbeck was solemnized at Valley, Nebraska, October 11, 1891. She was born at Millard on January 12, 1868, and died at Valley, August 5, 1898. There is one child of this marriage, Bulah, born September 3, 1892. On October 26, 1899, he was married to Jennie M. Standen, who was born at Elkhorn, March 18, 1874. They have one son and two daughters, Marie, born July 6, 1902, who married Lieutenant William J. Chapman of the United States Aviation Corps; Alfred E., born September 23, 1908; and Charlotte, born January 11, 1914.

A leader in civic and religious work, Mr. Byars is a member of the Presbyterian Church, active in Sabbath school work, and a member of the State Board of the Nebraska Council of Christian Education. He is a participant in Red Cross work and in commercial organizations, and is a member of the Modern Woodmen of America and the Masonic Order. His historical memberships include the Native Sons of Nebraska, The Nebraska Territorial Association and The Nebraskana Society. Residence: Valley.

Effie Marie Byers

Effie Marie Byers, educator and clubwoman, was born at Oskaloosa, Iowa, November 16, 1881, and is the daughter of George Playford and Mary Frances (Pike) Craft. Her father, born at Fayette County, Pennsylvania, August 2, 1850, was a farmer and stockfeeder. His death occurred at Aurora, Nebraska, February 23, 1914. Her mother was born at Cincinnati, August 30, 1860, and died at Aurora, August 14, 1922. A teacher, she was educated at Ames College, and was of New England Yankee descent.

Educated in country school and Aurora High School, Effie Marie Craft began teaching at the age of sixteen years, and continued seven years. On January 5, 1904, she was united in marriage to C. E. Byers, lumber executive and bank director, at Aurora. There are three children, John Harold, born May 22, 1905, who married Daisy Anderson of Hastings, Nebraska; Virgil Craft, born August 23, 1907; and Helen Charlene, born December 25, 1910. Mrs. Byers is a Democrat, and served as delegate at large, as well as delegate from the 5th district to the national convention at Houston, Texas, in 1928. She is a member of the Red Cross, and was exceptionally active in the American Defense Society as well as active in loan drives during the World War period; is a Rotary Ann, a member of the Young Women's Christian Association and attends the First Presbyterian Church at Hastings.

Her fraternal and cultural organizations include the P. E. O., the Order of Eastern Star, the Pythian Sisters, the Hastings Woman's Club, the Little Theatre and Alpha Delphian. She was recently elected to life membership in The Nebraskana Society in recognition of her effort toward the advancement of her community and state. Residence: Hastings. (Photograph on Page 201).

Cornelius Bykerk

Cornelius Bykerk, real estate and insurance executive of Havelock, Nebraska, was born at Firth, Lancaster County, Nebraska, February 14, 1892. His father, An-

EFFIE MARIE BYERS

drew Bykerk, was born at Dunkirk, New York, March 3, 1859, and died at Firth, May 3, 1927; he was a merchant and farmer, who served on the school board and the village board for many years; he was a Republican. His mother, Angeline (Zwerink) Bykerk, was born at Sheboygan, Wisconsin, July 23, 1859, and died at Havelock, June 20, 1927. Her ancestors were Holland Dutch.

Mr. Bykerk was graduated from the Firth High School in 1907. He was bookkeeper for the Marshall Oil Company, 1912-18; was secretary of the Lincoln Stove Repair Company, 1918-25; and since 1925 has been the owner and manager of a real estate and insurance business at Havelock. He is the Havelock representative of the Lincoln Community Chest; is secretary of the Lions Club; and is a member of the Nebraskana Society. His hobby is mechanics. He likes to golf. He is a member of the First Methodist Church of Havelock. During the World War he was active in loan drives and Red Cross affairs. He is a Democrat.

His marriage to Henrietta Elizabeth Herberts was solemnized at Firth, July 14, 1914. Mrs. Bykerk was born of Holland Dutch parents, at Holland, Lancaster County, Nebraska, January 9, 1894. Their children are: Norman H., born August 27, 1915; Donald N., born February 13, 1926; and Jean Elaine, born May 30, 1927. Residence: Havelock.

Clara Schneider Byrne

Clara Schneider Byrne, daughter of R. B. and Isabella Diana (Spangler) Schneider, was born at Fremont, Nebraska, March 30, 1890. Her father, who was born at Beardstown, Illinois, February 25, 1853, was engaged in the grain business, and came early to Nebraska. He was a Republican national committeeman in 1900, and a member of its executive committee in 1908. Of German descent, his parents came to America via New Orleans and the Mississippi River to St. Louis, in 1835.

Isabella Spangler Schneider was a native of Freeburg, Pennsylvania, born October 3, 1849, and resides at Fremont. Clara Schneider was graduated from Fremont High School in 1907, and entered the University of Nebraska where she studied one year. In 1911 she was graduated from Wellesley College with the degree of B. A. She is a member of Delta Gamma and Zeta Alpha.

On November 17, 1920, she was married to Harry Stephenson Byrne at Fremont. Mr. Byrne, who was born at Baltimore, June 28, 1878, is an attorney and insurance executive (see Nebraskana). There are three children: Isabella, born June 10, 1922; Barbara, born January 13, 1925, and Henry Schneider, born June 22, 1929.

Mrs. Byrne has been active in the welfare and civic life of Omaha for some time. She was a member of the White House Conference on Child Welfare and Protection held at Washington, by President Hoover, in 1930, and was a member of the executive committee of the Council of Social Agencies from 1927-30. During 1926 she was head of the Omaha Junior League Day Nursery, and was second vice president of the Omaha Junior League in 1926, and first vice president in 1927 and 1928. During 1918 she served overseas with the Red Cross Canteen Service. She is a member of the American Legion Auxiliary and the Women's Overseas Service League.

She attends the First Presbyterian Church of Omaha, and is a member of the Dundee School Parent Teachers Association. She is active in all sports, especially tennis and golf. She is a member of the University Club, the Omaha Club, and Happy Hollow Country Club. Residence: Omaha.

Harry Stephenson Byrne

Harry Stephenson Byrne was born at Baltimore, Maryland, June 28, 1878. He is the son of William Mathew and Ella Still (Stephenson) Byrne, the former a newspaper man, born in New York City, in 1850. He married Ella Still Stephenson, of Baltimore, who died at Omaha, in October, 1916. William Mathew Byrne died at Baltimore, in May, 1905. Ella Still Stephenson was the daughter of Joseph B. Stephenson, born in Newcastle, England, and who married Ellen Still, who was born in Baltimore.

Harry S. Byrne attended the public schools of Baltimore, and was graduated from Baltimore City College in 1898. He was manager of the football and other teams at Baltimore City College, and entered Johns Hopkins University at Baltimore, from which he received his A. B. in 1901. He attended the University of Maryland, from 1901 to 1903, and from 1903 to 1905 inclusive attended the University of Omaha, from which he was awarded his LL. B. in 1905. He was class president of Johns Hopkins in 1899, delegate to the international convention at University of Glasgow, Scotland, in 1901, member of the declaiming team in 1898, and of the debating team in 1899. He was president of the university senate in 1901. At the University of Maryland he was head of the local chapter of Kappa Sigma, for which he was district grand master and national catalogue editor. He was manager of the university Lacrosse team of Johns Hopkins and secretary-treasurer of the Intercollegiate Lacrosse Association.

He was married to Clara Schneider at Fremont, Nebraska, on November 17, 1920. (See Nebraskana).

A Republican, Mr. Byrne has been active in his party for the past twenty-five years. He was presidential elector-at-large for Nebraska in 1917; alternate delegate-at-large, Republican national convention in 1928; and has served as a member of the Douglas County and Nebraska State Republican committees for many years.

He is the author of various articles on athletics, politics, good roads, insurance and other subjects. Since 1901, he has engaged in the insurance business, and has been a lawyer, although not in active practice, since 1905. He is the owner of Harry S. Byrne and Company, general insurance and surety bonds, and a former director of the Nye and Jenks Grain Company. He is treasurer and director of the Omaha Auto Association, and a director of the Nebraska Good Roads Association.

During the World War Mr. Byrne was a candidate for commission in the Quartermaster Officers Reserve Corps at Camp Joseph E. Johnston, Jacksonville, Florida. He assisted in the various Liberty Loan drives, was on the U. S. Food Administration committee, and participated in various Red Cross activities. He is a member of the American Legion and has served on the executive committee of the Omaha Post as a delegate to the state convention and other capacities.

For many years Mr. Byrne has been active in educational and civic work in Omaha. He is a member of the Dundee School Parent Teachers Association, a director of the Omaha Public Library, a member of the First Presbyterian Church and the Y. M. C. A.

Among the professional and scientific organizations in which he holds membership are the Omaha and Nebraska State Bar Associations, the National Council of the National Economic League (Boston), the Nebraska and Omaha Associations of Insurance Agents, the National Association of Casualty and Surety Underwriters, a member of the Academy of Political Science (New York), American Economic Association, of which he is a director, the American Library Association, etc.

His clubs are the Omaha Club, the University Club, and Happy Hollow Country Club. His hobby is reading. Residence: Omaha.

Mary O. Byrne

Mary O. Byrne, wife of Thomas F. B. Byrne, was born September 15, 1879, a daughter of John and Joanna (Foley) Bolin. Her father, who was city police judge of Greeley, was of Irish Canadian descent. He was born at Keene, Canada, June 25, 1850, and died at Greeley, March 26, 1922. His wife, Joanna, was born in Ireland, March 10, 1857.

Mary O. Byrne attended public and high schools at

Greeley and on January 14, 1901, was married to Thomas Francis Byrne at Greeley. (*See Nebraskana*).

Mrs. Byrne has been active in Democratic politics for some time, and has served as delegate to state conventions at various times, and is at present a committee-woman. Before her marriage she was a bookkeeper for J. J. Collins store, and is now associated with her husband in the same capacity.

During the late war she was chairman of the Red Cross activities, a member of the council of defense, the Service League, and was Red Cross and Liberty Loan chairman. She is a member of the Sacred Heart Catholic Church, president of its Altar Society, chairman of the local Parent Teachers Association, and is a member of the Commercial Club and the Royal Highlanders. During the war she won a service medal, and was first chairman and organizer of the local Red Cross unit. Her favorite diversions are golf, tennis, and bridge. Recently she was made a life member of the Nebraskana Society. Her hobby is reading. Residence: Greeley.

Thomas Francis Byrne

Thomas Francis Byrne, prominent automobile dealer at Greeley, was born at Westport, Ireland, December 18, 1872, son of John Cementine and Mary (Broderick) Byrne. His father was born at Westport, Ireland, and died at Greeley, March 28, 1924. He was prominent in political circles, and served as county judge of Greeley County. His wife, Mary, was born at Westport, Ireland, and is still living.

Mr. Byrne attended public and high school at Greeley, and soon thereafter engaged in farming. For some time he has been an automobile dealer and is now the owner of the Chevrolet Garage. He is a director of the Agricultural board, and the Telephone Company at Greeley. He is a Democrat.

On January 14, 1901, he was married to Mary Oreanna Bolin at Greeley. Mrs. Byrne was born at Keene, Canada, September 15, 1879, and is of Canadian ancestry. Three children were born to them, Thomas Francis, born September 28, 1913, who died in infancy; Maryjo, born December 8, 1914; and Rita, born March 29, 1920. Maryjo is a stenographer.

Mr. Byrne is a Catholic and a member of Sacred Heart Church and the Knights of Columbus. He is a member of the school board, trustee of the church, member of the city council and the city board, and a member also of the Red Cross. Recently he was made a life member of the Nebraskana Society. He is fond of golf and enjoys reading. Residence: Greeley.

Albert H. Byrum

Albert H. Byrum, attorney at law, was born in Jo Daviess County, Illinois, December 31, 1858, son of Almond B. and Almyra C. (Hoyt) Byrum.

His father was born in Ohio, and died at Stockton, Illinois. He was a farmer. His wife, Almyra, was born in New York State and died at Stockton.

Mr. Byrum attended public school in Illinois and took a special course at Mt. Morris College and at Valparaiso University, at Valparaiso, Indiana.

He came to Nebraska in March, 1884, and has since been engaged in the practice of law. He is a Republican, served as county judge of Franklin County two terms, 1888-92, and was afterwards county attorney two terms. He served as state representative three terms, 1918-19, 1920-21, and 1924-25. He was a member of the constitutional convention of 1919.

In the past Mr. Byrum has been editor of two or three country newspapers. At the present time he is president of the Naponee Miling Company and president of the Bloomington State Bank, newly organized.

In June, 1889, he was married to Jennie E. Chapman at Blue Hill. She was born in Iowa and died at Bloomington. Before her marriage she was a teacher in city schools. There are two children, Albert Hoyt, born July 23, 1891, who married Bessie Sheets, of Franklin; and Ruth, born August 26, 1892, who married Claud Wilmot, living at Naponee.

Mr. Byrum has always been prominent in political and civic work. He was coal administrator and a member of the Council of Defense during the World War. He is a Protestant, a life member of the Nebraskana Society, and Bloomington Lodge No. 76 Ancient Free and Accepted Masons. Residence: Bloomington.

Addison Edgerton Cady

Addison Edgerton Cady, prominent banker at Grand Island, Nebraska, was born at Schuyler, Nebraska, April 22, 1884, and has always lived in this state. His father, Addison Edgerton Cady, was born at Watertown, Wisconsin, December 7, 1853, and died at St. Paul, October 14, 1918; he was a banker and wholesale grocer and served as a member of the senate and legislature in Nebraska; he was a candidate for the United States Congress, 1896, and for governor at the time Aldrich was elected. His mother was born of Irish and German parentage at Fondulac, Wisconsin, January 8, 1856, and died at St. Paul March 16, 1909.

Mr. Cady was graduated from St. Paul High School and Shattuck Military Academy where he played football and was active in track. He is president of the Nebraska Trust Company at Grand Island and is vice president of the Nebraska National Bank. He is a member of the Grand Island Chamber of Commerce, the Rotary Club, St. Stephens Episcopal Church, and The Nebraskana Society.

He holds membership in the Lincoln University Club, the Riverside Country Club, the Masonic Lodge, and the Elks. His recreations include golfing, bowling, hunting and fishing. For over 13 years he served as captain of the Nebraska National Guards.

His marriage to Lucile Kotik occurred at St. Paul, October 7, 1909. Mrs. Cady was born at St. Paul, June 16, 1885. They have one son, Addison, born October 12, 1912, who was graduated from Shattuck Military School and is a freshman at the University of Nebraska where he is a member of Delta Upsilon. Residence: Grand Island.

Flora B. Cady

Flora B. Cady, educator, was born at York, Nebraska, January 17, 1882, daughter of Madison Greeley and Sarah S. (Paugh) Demaree. Her father was born in Rexville, Indiana, November 10, 1854, and was among the early settlers in western Nebraska. He died at Long Beach, California, February 17, 1920. His wife, Sarah, was born in Ripley County, Indiana, November 8, 1860, and died at Long Beach, February 20, 1925. She was active in church and club work.

Upon her graduation from Wilsonville elementary schools in 1896, Mrs. Cady attended Wilsonville High School from which she was graduated in 1900. She has a state life teacher's certificate, all her work having been taken at the State Teachers' College, Kearney, Nebraska, from 1923 to 1932, in summer sessions. She was valedictorian of her high school class in 1900, at Wilsonville, and made the honor roll in college in 1930 and 1931.

For three years she was a teacher in the Wilsonville schools and is now teaching her fourteenth year in the primary department at Lebanon, Nebraska. At the present time Mrs. Cady is compiling a history of Red Willow County. She is a member of the Community Presbyterian Church, the Nebraska State Teachers' Association, the Red Cross, the Women's Christian Temperance Union, and the Mission Circle of her church. Her hobby is art.

Her marriage to Harmon E. Cady was solemnized at Wilsonville, Nebraska, June 14, 1905. Mr. Cady was born at Wilsonville, July 30, 1880, and is descended from New England Yankee settlers. They have one daughter,

Aletha May, born July 23, 1911, who was graduated from State Teachers' College, Kearney, Nebraska, in 1931. She is a teacher at Cedar Bluffs, Nebraska. Residence: Lebanon.

Pearl LeRoy Cady

Pearl LeRoy Cady, son of Frederick Clinton and Alvina (Dale) Cady, was born and raised on a farm west of Bellwood, Nebraska, of pioneer parentage. His grandfather, who was a graduate of Cornell University, came west as a contractor and built bridges over the Loup River at Columbus, for the Union Pacific. He brought with him his son, Frederick, who was born at Battle Creek, Michigan, August 29, 1859. Frederick Clinton Cady has been a pioneer farmer in Nebraska since 1883. His wife, Alvina Dale, was born at Albia, Iowa, October 24, 1862, and is of Revolutionary descent.

Pearl LeRoy Cady grew to manhood on a farm, and attended country school. He was graduated from high school at Columbus, and received his B. Sc. and Ph. D. from Fremont Normal College in 1905, and 1906, after which he taught school three years. Always a lover of animals, he attended Kansas City Veterinary College from which he received his D. V. S. in 1910.

On September 10th, of that year, he was married to Margaret L. Larson at Fremont, her birthplace. There are three sons, Duane LeRoy, born September 13, 1911; Richard Ellsworth, born April 4, 1915, and John Dale, born June 26, 1918.

Dr. Cady is engaged in the practice of veterinary medicine, and is president of the Missouri Valley Veterinary Association. A Democrat, he has served as mayor of Arlington, and is president of Collins and Cady Company, Inc., of West Point. Dr. Cady has served his community, state and nation in matters pertaining to veterinary medicine and disease control, and has held many offices of honor and trust. During the World War he raised over $10,000 for the Red Cross.

He is a member of the First Congregational Church of Arlington, the Arlington Commercial Club, the Young Men's Christian Association and the Parent-Teachers' Association of which last he was president in 1930.

Perhaps his greatest interest outside his profession is work among boys' organizations. He enjoys golf and baseball and likes to fish, hunt and travel. He is a Mason, Knight Templar and member of the Shrine, and his professional organizations include the Nebraska Veterinary Medical Association of which he was president in 1916, the Missouri Valley Veterinary Association, and the American Veterinary Medical Association of which he was regional secretary in 1925. Dr. Cady's social club is the Fremont Country Club. Residence: Arlington.

James Robert Cain, Jr.

James Robert Cain, Jr., banker, was born at Falls City, Nebraska, August 4, 1876, son of James Robert and Martha (Kirk) Cain.

He attended public school at Falls City, and was graduated from high school there. He is an honorary member of Acacia fraternity at the University of Nebraska.

His marriage to Minnie Haggard was solemnized at Seneca, Kansas, August 24, 1898.

A Republican, Mr. Cain has served as mayor and treasurer, and president of the board of education at Stella, Nebraska, as state representative and state senator. He has served also as president of the Omaha Bankers Club, and is a member of the Chamber of Commerce, the Ad-Sell League, Ak-Sar-Ben, the Omaha Council of Churches, and the Masons. Residence: Omaha.

Jean Benson Cain

Jean B. Cain, distinguished lawyer and judge, was born at Falls City, Nebraska, November 25, 1890. His father, James Robert Cain, a merchant and banker, was born on a farm in Platte County, Missouri, December 29, 1820. Of American born parents he was descended from Scotch and English ancestors. A Mason, he was Most Worshipful Master of the Grand Lodge of Nebraska. For many years he was county treasurer of Richardson County, Nebraska.

His mother, Nettie Jane (Ingram) Cain, who was born at Fairview, Iowa, January 22, 1863, and died at Rock Island, Illinois, June 16, 1826, was the daughter of English parents, James and Julia Ann (Hakes) Ingram. She was an active church worker and a profound student of the Bible.

Mr. Cain attended the Falls City grade and high schools graduating in the spring of 1910. He received the degree LL. B. June 12, 1913, at the University of Nebraska. During his college career he was president of the first year law class, in 1911, and was president of Phi Delta Theta Fraternity in 1913.

Judge Cain was admitted to the bar at Falls City, June 12, 1913, and has practiced law in Nebraska since that time. He has held many public offices during his career, among them: county judge of Richardson County, 1917; city attorney, 1916; and member of the city council, 1927-28. In 1917 he was the Republican candidate for county attorney, but was defeated at the general election.

He entered the World War as first lieutenant of the Nebraska national guard, and was promoted to the position of captain of the infantry, serving 18 months. He has been a member of the American Legion since its organization; was vice president of the temporary state American Legion, 1919; was chairman of the committee to administer relief to soldiers; and served on the state fund relief committee of Nebraska for seven years, and is former state commander.

Mr. Cain is a member of the Nebraska State Bar Association, and was president of the Richardson County Bar Association from 1926 to 1928. He is a member of the Falls City Chamber of Commerce. He is an Elk, exalted ruler in 1928; a Mason, Blue Lodge, Chapter, and Commandery. Residence: Falls City.

Edwin Gallt Caine

Edwin Gallt Caine, former lumberman and now a general merchant, was born at Whitewater, Wisconsin, December 1, 1864, and has resided in Nebraska since December 29, 1900.

His father, Edwin Ruthven Caine, was born in Ludlowville, New York, October 15, 1820, and died at Yankton, South Dakota, October 12, 1868. He was a gunner on the African cruiser *Saratoga* 1843-44, and later a merchant at Whitewater. His father was Irish, and his mother was English.

Helen M. Gallt, wife of Edwin R. Caine, was born at Weedsport, New York, June 12, 1833, and died at Indianola, Nebraska, February 25, 1907. Her father was Scotch, and her mother of German ancestry.

Mr. Caine attended public school and the state normal school at Whitewater. For 30 years he was engaged in the lumber business, of the 30, in Indianola for about 22 years. Since that time, he has been a general merchant, with the exception of the years 1928, 1929, and 1930. He is the owner of E. G. Caine's store. A Republican, he has always taken an active interest in state and national political issues.

He is a member of the Indianola Commercial Club, and the Brotherhood of American Yeomen. For three years 1921, 1922 and 1923, he was mayor of Indianola.

Mr. Caine was first married at Milwaukee, Wisconsin, on February 21, 1883. On May 25, 1897, he was married to Effie Hart at Humeston, Iowa. Mrs. Caine was born in Wayne County, Iowa, May 22, 1875. Of the first marriage there are two children, Edna Frances, born at Keokuk, Iowa, April 27, 1884, is married to J. L. Loewenstein, a lumberman at Bayard. Warren Edwin, born September 30, 1885, married Lydia Charlotte Ohlendorf. He is a farmer, north of Indianola. Of the second marriage there are four children, Howard Hart, born May 29, 1899, at North English, Iowa, who married Gertrude Mary Plourd, is in business with his father. Helen Mar, born November 17, 1900, at North English, Iowa, is married to John J. Foley. He owns a 640 acre farm and is a farmer and cattleman north of Indianola. Walter Ruthven, born June 12, 1903, is a chiropractor. Lewis Gallt, born September 20, 1905, is also a chiropractor. Walter resides at McCook.

Mr. Caine has six grandchildren, and four great grandchildren. All of his children, grandchildren, and great grandchildren are living. Residence: Indianola.

Albert William Caldwell

Born at West Liberty, West Virginia, December 26, 1854, Albert William Caldwell has been a farmer and horticulturist in Nebraska since 1874.

His father, John Caldwell, was born in West Liberty, February 5, 1826, and died at Elgin, June 6, 1900. He was a pioneer Nebraska farmer of English, Irish and Welch descent.

Rachel Priscilla Darling, wife of John Caldwell, was born in West Liberty, July 6, 1829, and died at Lisbon, Iowa, November 13, 1867. She was of English and Welch descent.

Albert William Caldwell attended public school in West Virginia. He is a Socialist, a Protestant, a member of the Elgin Commercial Club, the Modern Woodmen of America, the Nebraska Territorial Pioneers Association and the Nebraskana Society. His hobby is reading. Residence: Elgin.

Samuel Smith Caldwell

Samuel S. Caldwell was born at Omaha, November 25, 1875, son of Smith Samuel Caldwell and Henrietta McGraff Bush. His father, who was born at Marion, New York, September 4, 1834, died at Omaha in 1885. He was a banker, and president of the United States National Bank. He served as mayor of Omaha, and was president of the Republican Valley Railroad. Henrietta Bush Caldwell was born in Tioga, Tioga County, Pennsylvania, September 23, 1840. She died at Tioga, in 1915.

Mr. Caldwell was educated in the public schools of Omaha; attended Creighton, and later Phillip Andover Academy. He has been a member of the Coal Hill Coal Company for many years, and is vice president of the Douglas Truck Manufacturing Company. He is a director of the United States National Bank and the City Fuel and Supply Company of Des Moines.

On June 24, 1904, he was married to Fredericka Manderson Wessells at Hannibal, Missouri. Mrs. Caldwell is a granddaughter of General H. W. Wessells of the United States Army, and a descendant of Charles Adams of Connecticut. They have two children, Julia, born November 11, 1905, who was graduated from Emma Willard School in 1925 and from Smith College in 1928; and Samuel, born June 20, 1910, who was graduated from Andover Academy in 1922, and who attends Yale University.

During the World War Mr. Caldwell was vice chairman of the Omaha Red Cross Campaign committee and chairman of the Omaha War Camp Community Service. He is active in educational and civic work, and is treasurer of the Young Men's Christian Association and a trustee of the Young Women's Christian Association. He is a member of All Saint's Episcopal Church, the Chamber of Commerce and the Nebraska Motor Transport Corporation. His clubs are the University Club and the Omaha Country Club. He is fond of tennis, and his special interests are in unemployment and social insurance. Residence: Omaha.

Charles Adelbert Calkins

Born in Polk County, Nebraska, December 25, 1880, Charles Adelbert Calkins is the son of Kirkland and Loralla Virginia (Williams) Calkins. His father, who

was a pioneer farmer in Polk County, in 1872, was born at Watertown, New York, of English, French and Irish descent, October 27, 1840, and died at York, Nebraska, February 14, 1920. His mother was born of English parentage at Great Valley, New York, December 12, 1845, and died at York, March 18, 1930.

Dr. Calkins was graduated from the York High School, was a student at York College, and in 1903 received the D. D. S. degree at the University of Omaha. He took a post graduate course at Mayo Brothers School in Chicago, and at Bosworth College. He was active in football at the University of Omaha. Since 1903, he has been engaged in the practice of dentistry at York, Nebraska, and has taken an active interest in farming.

He is a member of the Central Nebraska Study Club, the Young Men's Christian Association, the state, national, and district dental associations, and the Red Cross. He is a member of the Odd Fellows, the Knights Templar body of the Masons, is affiliated with the United Brethren Church of York, and holds membership in the Nebraskana Society. He served as captain of Company A, First Nebraska National Guard for five years prior to the Philippine trouble, and during the World War gave his services for an hour each day to war activities. He is a member of the Sons of Veterans and the Sons of the American Revolution.

Dr. Calkins is independent, politically, and has served as a member of the York City Council. His favorite sports are hunting and fishing. On September 22, 1904, he was married to Olga Wiig, at Omaha, Nebraska. Mrs. Calkins was born at Omaha, June 17, 1881, and died at York, October 30, 1929. Their two children are: Ardyth M., born June 17, 1905, who married D. W. Fiester; and Kirkland Jack, born August 21, 1912. Ardyth is a medical student at the University of Nebraska. Kirkland attended York College and is now a teacher.

Dr. Calkins can trace his family history to the period prior to the formation of the Anglo-Saxon race. He is also a descendant of the French Huguenot, Solomon Jaques; among his ancestors are the Van Rensselaer and Knickerbocker families of Holland. Residence: York.

James Turner Calkins

For over 50 years James T. Calkins has lived at Friend, and has been a leader in political and civic undertakings in the state. He was born at Merton, Wisconsin, March 28, 1867, the son of Abram Daton and Margaret (Rankin) Calkins. His father, who was a farmer, was born at Austerliz, New York, August 14, 1819, and died at Friend, December 14, 1897; he was a direct descendant of Hugh Calkins who was born in England in 1600, emigrated to America in 1640, and landed at Plymouth, Massachusetts. His mother, who was of Irish ancestry, was born in Massachusetts, April 13, 1835, and died at Friend, July 3, 1907.

Mr. Calkins attended the Friend High School for three years. He is now assistant cashier of the First National Bank of Friend. A Democrat, he served as chairman of the County Central Committee in 1898; and was a member of the 27th session of the Nebraska legislature representing Saline County in 1901 and 1902. During the World War he was a member of the Liberty loan drive county committee.

He is a member of the Red Cross; Chamber of Commerce; Young Men's Christian Association; and the Nebraskana Society. He was vice president of the board of education, 1928-29, and is now a member of the Friend Parent Teachers Association. He holds membership in the National Geographic Society. He is a Mason, Odd Fellow, and Modern Woodman of America. His hobby is reading. He is affiliated with the First Methodist Church of Friend.

Mr. Calkins was united in marriage with Mary Elizabeth Hoschouer at Kearney, Nebraska, December 28, 1892. Mrs. Calkins, who is of Dutch descent, was born at Rossburg, Dark County, Ohio, February 5, 1875. The following children were born to this union: Julian, born February 23, 1895, who married Donna Coykendall; Mildred, born November 23, 1904, who died September 1, 1930, and who was married to Reinhardt Redman; Leslie, born January 15, 1909; and Edyth, born March 14, 1911. Julian is a World War veteran; he served in the 3rd division of the 4th infantry, and was wounded at the second battle of the Marne, July 26, 1918. Residence: Friend.

Congrave Clinton Callaway

Congrave C. Callaway of Fairbury, Nebraska, was born in Howard County, Missouri, August 27, 1835, son of Ambrose and Susan (Jackson) Callaway. Ambrose Callaway, a Revolutionary War veteran, who was born in Bedford County, Virginia, in the year 1795. Ambrose was a justice of peace, constable, and later a farmer until his death on October 18, 1861. Susan Callaway was born in Tennessee, July 28, 1799, and died in Carroll County, Missouri, June 15, 1867.

Congrave Callaway received a common school education and since 1869 he has been a resident of Nebraska, living continuously on the farm which he homesteaded at that time.

On June 12, 1870, he married Eliza Jane Browning, daughter of Josiah Browning, who was a grandson of Captain Francio Browning, a Revolutionary War captain. Before her marriage she was a milliner and dressmaker. Her death occurred June 10, 1841, near Fairbury. They had eight children: Etta, born March 7, 1871, who is married to Ralph Gray; Joe, born December 11, 1872, married to Mattie Diller; Susie, born September 18, 1874; Mattie, born August 9, 1876, married to Edgar Shoebotham; Agnes, born April 1, 1878; Clinton, born February 26, 1880, was married to Elizabeth Henderson, died August 13, 1912; William, born December 9, 1882, married Elizabeth Henderson.

Before the Civil War, Mr. Callaway joined the Presbyterian Church. He was a captain in the Confederate Army in the Civil War, served on his local school board from 1878 to 1900, and is a member of the Nebraskana Society. He died February 9, 1932. (Photograph in Album).

Eliza Jane Callaway

Born in Russel County, Virginia, September 19, 1841, Eliza Jane Callaway died at Fairbury, Nebraska, June 10, 1919. She was the daughter of Josiah D. and Martha Birdine (Honaker) Browning, both of prominent Virginia families. Josiah Browning was born in Russel County, May 14, 1819, and died at Fairbury, October 5, 1893. A cabinet maker by trade, he was active in public life, and served as county commissioner of Jefferson County for some years. His grandfather, Francis Browning, was a Revolutionary War soldier. Martha, his wife, was born in Russel County, January 17, 1821, and died at Fairbury, March 11, 1880. Her grandfather was also a soldier in the Revolutionary War.

On June 12, 1870, Eliza Jane Browning was united in marriage to Congrave Clinton Callaway, at Fairbury. Mr. Callaway was born in Howard County, Missouri, August 27, 1835, and for many years was a farmer and stock raiser in Jefferson County. To them were born eight children, seven of whom are living: Etta, born March 7, 1871, married Ralph L. Gray; Joseph, born December 11, 1872, married Mattie Diller; Susie, born September 18, 1874; Agnes, born April 1, 1878; Mattie, born August 9, 1876, who married Edgar Shoebotham; Clinton, born February 26, 1880, who married Elizabeth Henderson, and who died August 13, 1912; William, born December 9, 1882, who married Odella Diller; and Charles, born April 1, 1885, who married Elizabeth Henderson.

A resident of Nebraska fifty-five years, at the time of her death, Mrs. Callaway was one of Fairbury's most interesting personages.

She was always active in church and welfare work, and was a member of the Presbyterian Church and the Red Cross. She was an early Nebraska pioneer, and a member of the Nebraska Territorial Association. Her political affiliation was with the Democratic party. (Photograph in Album).

Ernest Glenn Callen

E. Glenn Callen was born at McCook, Nebraska, September 11, 1894, son of Samuel Edward Callen and Dora (Beyrer) Callen. His father, who was born in Illinois, March 3, 1861, is a railway passenger conductor, whose ancestry is Scotch-Irish. His mother, who is of German descent, was born in Indiana, April 12, 1864.

Professor Callen received his early education in the public schools of McCook, where he was graduated from high school in 1914. He was awarded the A. B. degree at Nebraska Wesleyan University, 1919; the A. M. degree at the University of Nebraska, 1921; and was a student at the University of Wisconsin for a time. On January 29, 1932, he received his Ph. D. from the University of Nebraska. He is a member of Phi Kappa Phi, Pi Gamma Mu, and Pi Kappa Delta.

He served as critic teacher at Wesleyan Teachers' College, 1919-22; was assistant professor of economics and sociology, Nebraska Wesleyan University, 1922-27; and since 1927, has been professor of political science and sociology at Nebraska Wesleyan University. He is the author of *Administration of Nebraska Workman's Compensation Law*, published at Lincoln, 1921; and various articles on taxation and labor questions. He has been prominent in civic affairs as applied to sociological problems for several years; served as secretary of the Nebraska Compensation Survey Commission, 1928-29; and since 1929, has been a member of the Lincoln commission of stabilization of employment. He is a member of the board of directors of the Lincoln Social Welfare Society and the Lincoln Council of Social Agencies.

His marriage to Frances M. Day was solemnized at Lennox, South Dakota, July 28, 1924. Mrs. Callen, who is of English descent, was born in Iowa, June 3, 1899.

Professor Callen holds membership in the following organizations: American Political Science Association (1925); American Sociological Society (1928); American Labor Legislation Association (1928); and the American Association of University Professors (1929). He is a Mason. His political affiliation is with the Republican party. Residence: Lincoln.

Burtis Oakley Callender

Burtis O. Callender, oil dealer, was born in Indiana, April 7, 1875, son of David N. and Mary Anna (Rickley) Callender. His parents came to Nebraska in 1878 and have resided here ever since. The father is Scotch-Irish and the mother is of Swiss descent.

The father was born in Ohio, June 1, 1854, and died at Stapleton, January 23, 1932. The mother was born in Switzerland in September, 1874, and died at Stapleton, January 23, 1924.

Mr. Callender attended public school of Gandy, Nebraska, and business college at Lincoln. He now is in the gas and oil business at North Platte. For a number of years he was engaged in the lumber business at Keystone, Nebraska. He is a member of the Odd Fellows, and is affiliated with the Presbyterian Church. His favorite sport is baseball.

On October 27, 1903, he was married to Minnie Evelyn Crawford at Grand Island. She was born in Iowa, April 5, 1873, the daughter of James H. and Elizabeth J. (Niles) Crawford. They have four children, Alburta, born February 25, 1905; Walter, born October 19, 1909;

JENNIE MATHER CALLFAS

and Richard and Bernard, twins, born January 12, 1913. James H. Crawford was born in Putman County, Indiana, September 26, 1847, and died at Stapleton, Nebraska, in September, 1911. His wife was born in Illinois, May 3, 1845, and died at North Platte, in October, 1923. Residence: North Platte. (Photograph in Album).

Jennie Mather Callfas

Jennie Mather Callfas, physician and prominent clubwoman, was born in Toronto, Canada, March 20, 1876, daughter of Eli and Emily Matilda (Dease) Mather. The father, born in Scotland in 1854, died at Walsingham, Canada, in 1881. He was a farmer and stock raiser.

Emily Matilda Dease was born in Canada, September 19, 1851, and died at Omaha, November 9, 1909. She was a teacher in her younger days.

Dr. Callfas attended public and high school and the University of Toronto, from which she was graduated in 1894. She came to the United States, entering Barns University Medical School at St. Louis, from which she was graduated with honors on May 3, 1904. Previously she had been graduated with high honors from the College of Music of Toronto.

Her marriage to William F. Callfas was solemnized at St. Louis, and until 1907 they engaged in the practice of medicine there, removing to Omaha at that time. During the World's Fair in 1904 Dr. Callfas was the only woman physician in the hospital on the fairgrounds.

Since taking up her residence in Omaha Dr. Callfas has enjoyed an extensive practice. She is a member of the First Methodist Church, and active in all its auxiliaries. During the World War she was a member of the board of the Council of Defense and active in the Red Cross. She has served three four-year terms as Democratic national committeewoman; has been a member of the Public Welfare Board five years, and for four years was a member of the Board of Education. She was the first woman ever elected to this position in Omaha, and for two years served with eleven men. Residence: Omaha. (Photograph on Page 207).

William Frederick Callfas

William F. Callfas, prominent Omaha physician and surgeon, has been in active practice there since 1907. At that time he came to the state from St. Louis, where he was married to Jennie Mather. She is a prominent physician, and former Democratic national committeewoman. (See Nebraskana).

Dr. Callfas is a member of various professional and civic organizations, and has been outstanding in the medical profession for many years. Residence: Omaha. (Photograph on Page 209).

Cora Hardy Calvert

Cora Hardy Calvert, pioneer civic leader of Nebraska, was born at Gainesville, Wyoming County, New York, July 29, 1861, the daughter of Harvey Wesley and Charlotte Clement (Abbott) Hardy. Her father, who was born at Gainesville, October 29, 1825, and died at Lincoln, January 10, 1913, was a merchant. He moved to Lincoln, in 1871, and was a furniture dealer there until his death; a prohibitionist, he served as mayor of Lincoln, and was candidate for governor of Nebraska on the prohibition ticket; Thomas Hardy, an English ancestor, came to America in 1630, with Governor Winthrop.

Her mother was born at Ogden, New York, April 6, 1831, and died at Lincoln, March 19, 1891. She was an active club worker and prominent in the Woman's Christian Temperance Union; in 1852, she was graduated from the Ingham Female Seminary at LeRoy, New York. She was descended from George Abbott who came to America from England, in 1640, and from Robert Clement who settled in Massachusetts, in 1642.

Mrs. Calvert was graduated from the elementary school at Lincoln, in 1876, and in 1880 was graduated from Lincoln High School. She was a student at the University of Nebraska for a time. She has always been interested in the social and civic affairs of her community, is affiliated with First Plymouth Congregational Church, and holds membership in the Nebraskana Society, Colonial Dames, the Lincoln Country Club, Fortnightly Club and Lotus Club.

Her marriage to Thomas Elwood Calvert was solemnized at Lincoln, November 1, 1911. Mr. Calvert, who was born at Newton Square, Delaware County, Pennsylvania, September 10, 1849, and died at Lincoln, December 19, 1916, was descended from the Quaker ancestor, John Calvert, who came to Pennsylvania with William Penn, in 1685. He was graduated from the scientific course at Yale, in 1870; was first assistant engineer for the Chicago, Burlington & Quincy Railroad; was chief engineer of this railroad west of the Missouri River; served as general superintendent of lines west of the Missouri River; and later was chief engineer with an office in Chicago. He came to Nebraska in 1871.

Mr. Calvert was a member of the National Engineering Society; the Young Men's Christian Association; Yale University Club; and the Lincoln Chamber of Commerce. His hobbies were mechanics and music. Both Mr. and Mrs. Calvert have been affiliated with the Republican party for many years. Residence: Lincoln.

John Hargreaves Calvert

Born at Cook, Nebraska, November 23, 1901, John Hargreaves Calvert is the son of John and Agnes Annie (Davis) Calvert. His father, who was a chaplain in France connected with the Young Men's Christian Association during the World War and is a minister in the Methodist Church, was born at Newmillerdam, England, April 3, 1870; he came to America in 1896. His mother, who is a leader in women's affairs and a talented public speaker, was born at Wakefield, England, January 21, 1865. Her father was a soldier in the British Army at one time.

Dr. Calvert was graduated from Benson High School in Omaha, Nebraska, in 1921, was graduated from Nebraska Wesleyan University in 1925, and received the M. D. degree at the University of Nebraska Medical School in 1929. He was a member of Phi Kappa Phi and Phi Chi at the University of Nebraska, and was active in basketball, track, tennis, and football, at Nebraska Wesleyan University.

He served his internship at Henry Ford's Hospital at Detroit, Michigan, and since then has been engaged in general medical practice at Pierce, Nebraska. He is a member of the Five County Medical Society, Nebraska Medical Society, and the American Medical Society. He is county and city physician, is county chairman of the first aid supervision of the Red Cross, is a member of the Pierce Commercial Club, and holds membership in the Lions Club and the Masons. He is affiliated with the Methodist Episcopal Church and is a member of the Nebraskana Society. His favorite sport is tennis.

He was united in marriage with Alma Christine Goebel at York, Nebraska, June 12, 1929. Mrs. Calvert, whose ancestry is German, was born at Overton, Nebraska, October 12, 1903. They have one son, John, Jr., born February 29, 1931. Residence: Pierce.

Joseph Robert Cameron

Joseph Robert Cameron, physician and surgeon, was born at Mission Creek, Nebraska, July 29, 1878, son of James and Charlotte (McKee) Cameron. His father, who was born at Glasgow, Scotland, April 26, 1844, came of the Cameron clan, and migrated to America alone at the age of fourteen. A farmer, he died at Beaver City, Nebraska, July 14, 1915. His wife, Charlotte, was born at Spade, Indiana, December 7, 1856, and died at Beaver City, January 26, 1887. Her great grandfather was a

WILLIAM FREDERICK CALLFAS

soldier in the Revolution and her mother came from England.

Upon his graduation from Beaver City High School in 1898, Dr. Cameron attended Creighton University and the University of Illinois, from which he received his M. D. in 1905. He was admitted to the practice of medicine in Nebraska in February, 1906.

During the Spanish American War and the Philippine Insurrection Dr. Cameron was a private in Company H., First Nebraska Volunteer Infantry. Thereafter, and at the age of 21 he was elected sheriff of Furnas County, being the youngest man in the state to have been elected to that office. There he served two years, then entering medical college.

Dr. Cameron held the rank of captain in the Medical corps in Mexican Border Service in 1916, and had charge of military registration for Bennett and locality in the World War. He is a member of the United Spanish War Veterans.

He is a Christian, a member of the American, Nebraska State and Lancaster County Medical Associations, the Chamber of Commerce, Modern Woodmen of America, the Masons and Mystic Shrine, and during 1926-27, served as mayor of Bennet.

On September 5, 1905, he was united in marriage to Veda Corbin of Beaver City, Nebraska. Their marriage took place at Ashland, Oregon. There were two children born to this union, Evelyn, born December 15, 1909, died July 16, 1916; and Dale Corbin, born July 10, 1912. He is a pre-medic student at the University of Nebraska. Residence: Bennet. (Photograph in Album).

Melville D. Cameron

Melville D. Cameron, investment banker, was born at Arlington, Ohio, July 10, 1858, son of Wallen and Sarah Jane (Woods) Cameron. The father, born in Ohio, October 31, 1833, died at Schuyler, Nebraska, in April, 1915. The mother was born in Columbiana County, Ohio, February 2, 1839, and died at Schuyler January 15, 1927.

Mr. Cameron attended public school at Schuyler and the Nebraska Conference Seminary at York. He has been president of the Peters National Bank and vice president of the Peters Trust Company.

He was married at South Bend, Indiana, to Viola Jennings, who was born there on July 29, 1875. She is the daughter of the Rev. Jesse W. Jennings.

Mr. Cameron is a Republican. He is a member of the First Methodist Episcopal Church of Omaha, the Red Cross, the Young Men's Christian Association, the Chamber of Commerce, the Odd Fellows, the Masons, the Nebraska State Historical Society and the board of trustees of Nebraska Wesleyan University. His club is the Omaha Club. Residence: Omaha.

William Cara Cameron

William Cara (W. C.) Cameron, farmer and stock raiser, was born at Genesco, Illinois, April 17, 1863, son of Lorenzo Dow and Sarah (Demming) Cameron. His father, born at Brockville, Canada, August 9, 1817, was a farmer of Scotch descent, who die din Washington County, Nebraska, October 30, 1894. His mother, also born in Brockville, November 3, 1823, died in Washington County, March 29, 1885.

Mr. Cameron received his education in a country school, and soon thereafter engaged in farming and stockraising. He has been a resident of Nebraska since September, 1865, and is a member of the Pioneer and Old Settlers Association, and The Nebraskana Society. He is a Methodist.

On December 23, 1886, he was united in marriage to Harriet Ruth Wilson, at Spika, Nebraska. Mrs. Cameron, who was born at De Soto, Nebraska, January 7, 1867, is of Irish descent. There are five children, Sadie, born February 12, 1888, who married James C. Broderson; Whit, born September 9, 1891, who married Emily Van Valin; Malcolm, born July 22, 1893, who married Emma Holstein; Mary, born April 21, 1895, who married Frank D. Broderson; and Ruth, born December 25, 1896, who married Henry Jackson. They are all engaged in farming.

Mr. Cameron is an outstanding farmer in his locality and his hobby is raising pure bred hogs. He was recently made a life member of the Nebraskana Society in recognition of his work for the advancement of his community and state. Residence: Herman.

Alexander James Campbell

Born at Miles, Iowa, March 26, 1867, Alexander James Campbell has been for many years a prominent farmer in Valley County. He is the son of Daniel and Agnes (Watson) Campbell, the former a native of Edinburgh, Scotland.

Daniel Campbell, who was left fatherless at an early age, walked six miles to his work as a stone cutter for two years to live with his widowed mother. He came to America in 1848, on a sailing vessel, came by boat up the Hudson River and Erie Canal to Buffalo, and over Lake Erie to Toledo. From there he came overland to Lyons, in Clinton County, Iowa. He died in Clinton County on October 8, 1875.

Agnes Watson Campbell was born in Perthshire, Scotland, in March 1843, and died at Reinbeck, Iowa, September 23, 1913. A Scottish Protestant of sturdy religious character, she was much interested in community activities and church work.

Alexander James Campbell attended district school and during 1886-87 attended Northern Illinois College to prepare for teaching. Receiving a first grade teacher's certificate, he taught three years in Grundy County, Iowa, in the same school. Thereafter he completed a course in bookkeeping through the Young Men's Christian Association Night School, and during 1890-91 attended Ames Agricultural College. He held the freshman class record in the 100 yard dash in 1890, and was a member of the Crescent Society at Ames.

On May 18, 1898, he was married to Minnie Ruth Anderson at Spencer, Iowa. Mrs. Campbell, who was born at Peosta, Iowa, October 27, 1867, was a teacher and stenographer before marriage. Of Revolutionary ancestry, she is eligible to the Daughters of the American Revolution. There are three children living, and one deceased. Ervin Ray, born April 25, 1899; Mary Elizabeth, born March 25, 1903, died April 10, 1903; Allen James, born February 5, 1906, who married Gladys Minard; and John Watson, born November 19, 1910.

All were graduated from the Ord High School, John winning a scholarship to the Agricultural College of the State University for a short course in agriculture. He has completed one year. While in high school James was called the "one man team." He set a new record in the hurdle race at the Hastings Invitation Meet; won two firsts and one second event in the State High School Track Meet at Lincoln in 1925. He attended the Citizen's Military Training Camp 1924-25, and scored second in rifle practice. He was sent with the Des Moines rifle team to Camp Perry, Ohio, placing third in army rifle target practice, competing with boys from all the states. In 1927 he was graduated from the Coin Electric School at Chicago.

Mr. Campbell was employed by A. Treadway & Sons Hardware Company at Dubuque, Iowa, from 1892 until 1901, when he came to Ord, and engaged in farming. He has served on the local school board for many years, and for ten years has been township assessor. He is a Republican. During the World War period he was township peace officer and assisted in Red Cross drives. He is a member of the executive board of the Methodist

Episcopal Church at Ord, and a life member of The Nebraskana Society. He devotes much time to reading. Residence: Valley.

Daniel Roy Campbell

Daniel Roy Campbell, implement dealer, was born in Hamilton, Canada, August 31, 1868, son of Joseph Randall and Hannah (Featherstone) Campbell. His parents were Scotch, and English, who came to the United States in 1873.

Mr. Campbell attended public school only, and has been in the implement business since reaching the age of 22. He spent three and a half years in Australia for the McCormick Harvestering Machine Company at one time. He has been active in Republican politics for a number of years and has held city offices including city alderman and treasurer. He is a member of the Chamber of Commerce, and the Episcopal Church. He is a 32nd degree Mason, and a former member of Company G of the Iowa National Guard. He enjoys baseball, plays golf, and is a member of the Sidney Country Club.

On April 10, 1901, he was married to Dorothea Agnes Wright at Melbourne, Australia. Mrs. Campbell was born at Melbourne, April 8, 1878. They have two children, Rupert Daniel, born August 31, 1904; and Elvira Margarite, born February 14, 1910. Residence: Sidney.

George Moral Campbell

George Moral Campbell, one of Nebraska's pioneer farmers, was born at Nortenhill, New York, March 17, 1871, the son of Nelson Gerard and Ann Elizabeth (Nelson) Campbell. His father, who was one of the oldest settlers in Knox County, Nebraska, was born at Freehold, New York, July 16, 1848, and died at Crofton, Nebraska, October 8, 1925; he served as justice of the peace in Knox County for 12 years, and for 16 years was township assessor of Herrick Township.

His mother, whose ancestors were Dutch and Swedish Quakers, was born at Nortenhill, December 17, 1849, and died at Crofton, November 24, 1919.

Mr. Campbell received his education in one of the typical log school houses of early Nebraska days, attending school for three months each year. He has always taken an active interest in history, politics, and civic affairs in his state and community, and has held the following business positions at Crofton: farm implement dealer, two years; manager of a threshing crew, 15 years; carpenter; blacksmith; and stockman and farmer. He owns land in both Iowa and Nebraska.

He is a member of the Northwestern Telephone Company, is a member of the Modern Woodmen of America, and holds membership in the Nebraskana Society. His chief recreations are hiking, reading, and mechanics. Residence: Crofton.

Henry Hiram Campbell

Henry Hiram Campbell, editor, county judge, and lawyer, was born at Fontenelle, Iowa, December 2, 1865, the son of Benjamin Crawford and Elizabeth Ann (Scott) Campbell. His father, who was a farmer, was born in Ohio, and died at Osceola, Nebraska, January 14, 1908; he was a soldier for three years with Company H of the 21st Missouri Regiment during the Civil War; his ancestors came to this country nearly three hundred years ago from Scotland. His mother, whose ancestry was Scotch and Dutch, was born in Indiana, and died at Lincoln, Nebraska, March 28, 1921.

Judge Campbell was graduated from Osceola High School in 1888 where he was valedictorian of his class. He has been active in various capacities in Polk County, serving as postmaster, 1898-1906; editor of the *Osceola Record*, 1890-1903; county judge of Polk County, 1906-

15; teacher in rural schools; and bank clerk for a year and a half. He is now a lawyer at Osceola. During the World War he was government legal representative under the draft board and chairman of the council of defense of Polk County.

He holds membership in the local and state bar associations; Red Cross; Osceola Community Club; Osceola Lodge No. 65 of the Ancient Free and Accepted Masons (Master May 1914-1915); Osceola Country Club; Young Men's Christian Association; and the Nebraskana Society. He was a member of the board of education at Osceola for eight years. Golfing and baseball are his favorite sports.

He was married to Anna Teele July 2, 1890. Mrs. Campbell was born at Riceville, Iowa, February 21, 1865, and is a prominent clubwoman. They have four children: Harold Ray, a graduate of the University of Nebraska in 1916, who married Matilda C. Long; Phil B., a graduate of the university in 1920, who married Dorothy Garber; Esther, who graduated from the university in 1921, and who is married to Chester R. Beck; and Robert B., who married Blanche Gramlich. The three sons and son-in-law volunteered for service in the World War. Residence: Osceola. (Photograph in Album).

Jacob Newton Campbell

Jacob N. Campbell was born at Watson, Missouri, March 31, 1865, the son of Archibald Severe and Nancy (Jones) Campbell. His father, who was born at Greenville, Tennessee, May 26, 1836, and died at Fullerton, Nebraska, June 13, 1918, was a farmer. His mother was born at Greenville, December 25, 1833, and died at Fullerton, 1910.

Mr. Campbell attended school in Missouri, at Watson and Rockport, and later was a student at Peru State Normal School for a year. He is president and treasurer of the Nebraska Iowa Packing Company; is secretary of the Nebraska Millers Association; and is secretary of the Nebraska Grain Dealers Association. He served as state senator, 1893-95; was representative from Nance, Merrick and Polk counties; and was superintendent of the Nebraska State Industrial School at Kearney, 1900. He is a Democrat.

He was married to Carrie Lamberth Horn at Watson, Missouri, March 22, 1887; she was born at Watson, June 1, 1869, and died at Fullerton, October 4, 1916. Six children were born to their marriage: Valore P., born January 26, 1888, who married Mildred Knight; Harry L., born November 7, 1889, who married Marguerite Haley; Archie W., born December 21, 1891, who married Mabel Kisner; Joel W., born April 13, 1893, who married Bernice Mitchell; Bryan, born February 21, 1898, who married Evelyn Burke; and Marjorie B., born December 22, 1900, who married Richard Hartigan of Fairbury.

Mr. Campbell was a four minute speaker during the World War. He is a member of the Omaha Chamber of Commerce. He is a Mason. He is affiliated with the First Presbyterian Church of Omaha. Residence: Omaha.

Joseph New Campbell

Joseph New Campbell, a physician at Stamford, Nebraska, for the past 30 years, has lived in this state all his life. He was born at York, Nebraska, August 10, 1880, the son of William Thomas and Mary (New) Campbell. His father, who was a farmer, was born at Johnstown, Pennsylvania, June 10, 1844, and died at College View, Nebraska, April 5, 1928; his father came to this country from Glasgow, Scotland. His mother was born at Jacksonville, Illinois, October 6, 1844, and died at College View, January 1, 1927.

Dr. Campbell attended the rural schools of Gospel County, Nebraska, and in 1896, was graduated from the Smithfield High School. He received the M. D. degree from Lincoln Medical College affiliated with Cotner

University, and since 1902 has been engaged in the practice of medicine continuously at Stamford. He is a
member of the Nebraska State Medical Association, the
Republican Valley Medical Association, and the Harlan
County Medical Society, having served as coroner of
the latter county for a period of years. He is a member
of the Nebraskana Society, has served on the local school
board for the past 20 years, and holds membership in
these bodies of the Masons: Blue Lodge, Chapter, Knight
Templar, and Shrine.

He was united in marriage with Anna Nielsen at
Stamford, June 21, 1905. Mrs. Campbell was born at
Stamford, August 7, 1883. Two children were born to
them: Donald, born February 23, 1907, who died August
22, 1930; and Darrell, born December 4, 1911, who is a
student at the University of Nebraska Medical College.
Donald was graduated from the University of Nebraska
with the A. B. degree in 1928 and received the LL. B.
degree in 1930.

Dr. Campbell's hobby is chess and his favorite sport
is golfing. Residence: Stamford. (Photograph in Album).

Phillips Brooks Campbell

Born at Osceola, Nebraska, September 7, 1893, Phillips Brooks Campbell is the son of Henry H. and Anna
Richard (Teele) Campbell. His father, who is a lawyer
(see *Nebraskana*) was born at Fontanelle, Iowa, December 2, 1865. He is the son of Benjamin C. and Elizabeth
(Scott) Campbell, early pioneers in Polk County. Henry
H. Campbell is a former county judge and during the
World War was chairman of the Polk County Council of
Defense.

Anna Richard Teele was born in Iowa, February 21,
1872, the daughter of an early Iowa minister. For many
years she has been a member and an active worker in the
Osceola Woman's Club.

Phillips Brooks Campbell was graduated from Osceola
High School in 1911. Thereafter he entered the University of Nebraska, from which he received his Bachelor of
Science degree. On July 5, 1917, he enlisted in the Field
Artillery of the Regular Army, and was thereafter promoted to the ranks of corporal and sergeant. On July
12, 1918, he was commissioned a second lieutenant, and
while with the American Expeditionary Forces attended
the University of Nancy, in France.

Mr. Campbell was a member of the football and baseball teams while in high school, and during the years
1909 and 1910, was a member of the debate team. In 1911
he was valedictorian of his class. Upon leaving the university, Mr. Campbell became a traveling salesman for
the Liebers Equipment Company of Lincoln, continuing
until January 1, 1921. At that time he became associated
with the law offices of King, Bittner and Campbell at
Osceola, until 1924, when he was admitted to the bar and
became a member of the law firm of Campbell and Campbell.

A Republican, for four years Mr. Campbell served as
chairman of the Polk County Republican central committee. He has also served as member of the Osceola
city council for two years, from the first ward. He was
defeated for the office of county attorney in 1930.

On June 2, 1923, he was united in marriage to Dorothy
Ann Garber at Geneva. Mrs. Campbell, who was born at
Hubbell, June 18, 1900, is the daughter of Martin W. Garber. Mr. Garber hauled the first load of lumber into Red
Cloud, Nebraska, where his father was a pioneer settler.
Mrs. Campbell is a member of the Daughters of the American Revolution, and is serving as secretary of the local
chapter. She is former president of the American Legion
Auxiliary, and past matron of the local chapter of the
Order of Eastern Star. There is one son, Henry Crawford, born November 13, 1926.

Mr. Campbell is a member of the American Legion at
Osceola. A member of the executive committee for many

years, he is past commander of the Osceola post, and has
been service officer since 1921. He is a member of the
First Methodist Episcopal Church, the Red Cross, Salvation Army, the Young Men's Christian Association,
and is past master of Masons. He also belongs to the
Nebraska State and Polk County Bar Associations, the
Osceola Community Club, the Nebraskana Society and the
Osceola Country Club. His favorite sport is golf, and his
hobby is reading. Residence: Osceola. (Photograph in
Album).

Robert Sheeler Campbell

Robert Sheeler Campbell, clergyman and educator,
was born at Bristol, Tennessee, February 27, 1877, son of
James Charles and Eliza Anne (Campbell) Campbell. A
native of Lebanon, Tennessee, James C. Campbell was
born August 19, 1834. On the paternal side he is descended from Thomas and Alexander Campbell, who were famous religious leaders. He was also a direct descendant
of General John Sevier, brigadier general under George
Washington and governor of Tennessee for six terms.
James C. Campbell died at Ironton, Ohio, January 23,
1916, after sixty years as an outstanding minister.

Eliza Anne Campbell was born at Lebanon, February
12, 1835. The wife of a minister and the mother of four,
she was a character builder and assistant to her husband.
She died at Winnsboro, Texas, September 12, 1911. Her
ancestry included politically and religiously prominent
figures of Virginia.

While Mr. Campbell was still young his family removed to Indiana, where he received his education in the
public and high schools of Winamac. Thereafter he completed his high school education in the Monroe High
School, at Monroe, Wisconsin, in June, 1893. He then attended Normal College and the International Bible College, and received a full course of college training under
his father and private teachers of the South.

On April 19, 1903, he was united in marriage to Mary
Emma Roberts at Hedricks, Iowa. Mrs. Campbell was
born in Taylor County, Iowa, March 29, 1883. She is a
musician and assistant to Mr. Campbell. Her ancestry
is early American on the paternal side and French on the
maternal. There is one child, Mary Evangeline, born
February 19, 1919.

An independent Republican, Mr. Campbell's great
grandfather was six terms governor of Tennessee, the organizer of the state and the holder of many other offices.

At the present time Mr. Campbell is promotional secretary of fourteen Bible colleges and a national evangelist.
He was ordained in September, 1893. He is affiliated
with the East Lincoln Christian Church, and is a member
of the Interdenominational Evangelistic Association, the
National Evangelistic Association, besides national and
local literary societies. He is a member of The Nebraskana Society, the Odd Fellows, Modern Woodmen of
America, and the Knights of Pythias. He enjoys baseball. His hobby is reading, and particularly history.
Residence: Lincoln. (Photograph in Album).

Ralph Oliver Canaday

Ralph Oliver Canaday, lawyer, was born at Minden, Nebraska, April 4, 1891, son of Joseph Sylvester
and Mary Jane (Winters) Canaday. The father, born
in Indiana, came as a comparatively young man to Nebraska. A farmer, he has served as superintendent of
Kearney County, and in 1897 and 1899 was state senator
from Kearney County. Mary Jane Winters was born in
Crawford County, Illinois, November 8, 1866, of
American and English descent.

Educated in public schools, Ralph Oliver Canaday
was graduated from Minden High School in 1909, received his A. B. degree from the University of Nebraska
in 1915, and his LL. B. in 1918. He is a member of Phi

Alpha Delta, and was treasurer of his senior class in 1915.

His marriage to Violet Pansy Neuman was solemnized at Bridgeport, November 27, 1919. Mrs. Canaday was born in Cheyenne County, Nebraska, May 16, 1898. There are three children, Eunice Mary, born November 28, 1920; Shirley Rae, born March 23, 1923; and Raymond Sylvester, born June 29, 1925.

Locating in Bridgeport on the 19th of March, 1919, Mr. Canaday was associated with William Ritchie, Jr. He was for a time a member of the firm of Ritchie, Chase, Canaday & Swenson with offices in Omaha and Bridgeport, and is now in practice in Hastings.

Mr. Canaday enlisted as a private in the 4th Officers Training Camp at Camp Dodge, Iowa, in May, 1918, was commissioned second lieutenant in August, 1918, assigned to Company D, 88th Infantry, 19th Division. Prior to entering the service he was secretary of the Kearney County Red Cross.

Mr. Canaday is a member of the American, Nebraska State and Western Nebraska Bar Associations, the Red Cross, the American Legion, and has served as president of the Bridgeport School Board. He is a life member of the Nebraskana Society, and an Ancient Free and Accepted Mason. His club is the Bridgeport Country Club. Residence: Hastings.

Albert Luther Candy

Albert L. Candy was born at Jonesboro, Grant County, Indiana, March 12, 1857, the son of Jacob and Hannah (Schaeffer) Candy. His father, a carpenter and farmer, was born of German parents at Nittany Hall, Centre County, Pennsylvania, January 16, 1820, and died at Jonesboro, September 1, 1907. His mother, whose ancestry was German, was born at Nittany Hall, August 20, 1824, and died at Jonesboro, December 22, 1902.

Professor Candy attended the rural schools of Indiana, and later was a student at Jonesboro High School. In 1892, he was granted the A. B. degree at the University of Kansas; A. M., 1893. He was awarded the Ph. D. degree at the University of Nebraska, in 1898. He was a student at Northern Indiana Normal School, 1884-86. He was elected to membership in Sigma Xi.

He has been a leading educator in Nebraska since 1892, and is now professor of mathematics at the University of Nebraska; he has been chairman of this department since 1918. He is the author of the following: *Analytic Geometry*, 1900-04-09; *Theorem on Transversals* (his doctor's thesis), 1896; *Solution of Equation of N degree*, 1920; *Elimination of Skidding in Motor Cars*, 1920; and *Cyclic Operations on Determinants*, 1923.

A Republican, Professor Candy served as alderman of the city of Lincoln, 1909-13. He was married to Eda L. McCain at Goodland, Newton County, Indiana, August 26, 1886. Mrs. Candy, who was born at Washington, Davies County, Indiana, May 7, 1865, of Scotch and English parents, was an artist. She died at Goodland, April 23, 1893. One child was born to this union: Albert McCain, born February 4, 1888; he was graduated from the University of Nebraska with the B. S. degree in engineering, 1909, received his E. E. degree in 1928, and is now an engineer with the Westinghouse Company.

On June 27, 1895, he was united in marriage at Long Island, New York, with Ella Van Brunt, who was born January 26, 1855, at Smithtown, Long Island. One child was born to them, May 8, 1897, who died in infancy.

He is a member of the following welfare and civic organizations: Red Cross; Community Chest; Social Welfare Society, of which he was a member of the board of directors, 1902-27, and president, 1903-13. He served as vice-president of the latter from 1913 to 1927. He is a member of American Association for the Advancement of Science; American Mathematics Society; Mathematical Association of America; and American Association of University Professors. He is a member of Pi Mu Epsilon. He is affiliated with the First Presbyterian Church of Lincoln. Residence: Lincoln.

Joseph Alfred Capwell

On October 5, 1888, Alfred J. Capwell was born at Factoryville, Wyoming County, Pennsylvania, son of Joseph Allison and Hattie Elizabeth (Dickson) Capwell. His father, who was born of French ancestry at Factoryville, April 3, 1854, and died there April 1, 1896, was a farmer and teacher.

His mother was born of Scotch Irish parents at Sycamore, DeKalb County, Illinois, July 6, 1856, and died at Lincoln, Nebraska, May 9, 1930. She was a teacher.

Mr. Capwell was graduated from the Elmwood, Nebraska, High School in 1908, and received his LL. B. degree at the University of Nebraska in 1914. He was admitted to the practice of law, June, 1914, and has devoted his entire time to it since that date. He has lived in Nebraska for 27 years and has engaged in general law practice during that time, serving also as special attorney for the Continental Construction Corporation.

A Democrat, he served as secretary of the Cass County Democratic Central Committee in 1916; was chairman of this organization 1928-30; and was a member of the State Democratic central committee, acting on the executive committee of the latter. In 1924 he was county attorney of Cass County, and since 1926 has been city attorney of Plattsmouth, Nebraska.

He married Nita B. Samek, August 12, 1925, at Harvard, Nebraska.

Mrs. Capwell is a graduate of the University School of Music where she majored in piano. She is a reader, and a member of the faculty of the Omaha Conservatory of Music. She was born of Bohemian and English parents at Weston, Saunders County, Nebraska, May 5, 1896. The Capwells have adopted two children, Bonnie Jean, born August 19, 1927, and Joseph R., born June 10, 1918.

Mr. Capwell served in the United States Regular Army, 1917-19, in the Coast Artillery Corps; was private, corporal, sergeant, and sergeant-major; is now first lieutenant of the 17th Infantry in the Regular Army Reserves. He is a member of the American Legion and the Reserve Officers' Association.

He is a member of the Chamber of Commerce, and is affiliated with the First Methodist Church, at Plattsmouth, Nebraska. He is a Mason, Blue Lodge, Scottish Rite, 32nd degree, Royal Arch, and Shrine. He is a member of the Nebraskana Society and the Nebraska State Bar Association. His hobby is sports. He is fond of hiking, shooting and football. Residence: Plattsmouth.

John Joseph Carey

A distinguished lawyer and editor of Petersburg, Nebraska, John Joseph Carey was born at Montreal, Canada, September 17, 1870, the son of John and Ellen (Trainor) Carey. His father, a farmer, was born at Utica, New York, of Irish parentage. His mother, whose ancestry was also Irish, was born at Montreal, Canada.

Mr. Carey came to Nebraska in 1871, when his father homesteaded in Saunders County. He taught in country schools at the age of 17, and has in his possession and is using a watch purchased with his first earnings. He farmed in the summer and taught in the winter for several years.

From 1890, until 1900 Mr. Carey taught in the Fremont Normal College, having the English, Latin, and mathematics departments. During that time he published two editions of a teachers hand-book of English grammar under the title of *Plain Facts on English Grammar*. He has engaged in the real estate business, practiced law, and been the editor of the *Petersburg Index* at Petersburg, Nebraska, during the 61 years of his residence in this state. He has held office as chairman of the village board and as village treasurer.

Mr. Carey is affiliated with the St. John The Baptist Catholic Church of Petersburg, and is a member of the Nebraskana Society. He was married to Martha Ann Carraher at Columbus, Nebraska, September 12, 1900. They have four children, Patrick J., Miriam, Flavian, and Madonna.

During the World War Mr. Carey was active as a member of the examining board for Boone County, as well as in Red Cross work and the sale of Liberty bonds. Residence: Petersburg.

Leon Rex Carey

Leon Rex Carey, executive, was born at Bancroft, Nebraska, February 6, 1888, son of James Edward Lynch and Delia (Gage) Carey.

The father, who was born in New York State, entered the farm implement business at Bancroft in 1878, in which he continued until 1918 when he retired. His was the oldest retail implement firm in Nebraska. Delia Gage, his wife, was born in Mason County, Iowa, December 31, 1861, and died at Denver, November 18, 1923. She was for years a member of the board of education at Bancroft, and active in the Nebraska Federation of Women's Clubs in which she held state office. Her ancestry was Dutch.

Leon Rex Carey was graduated from Bancroft High School in June, 1904, and received the degree of Bachelor of Science from Bellevue College in June, 1909. He was a member of the debating team, 1906-07; and the football team at Bellevue 1906, 1907, 1908; the track team 1908; and his football team held the championship for Nebraska secondary colleges all three years.

He is married to Letha Faye Scherer, their marriage having been solemnized at Denver, Colorado. Mrs. Carey was born in Cheyenne County, Nebraska, and is a graduate nurse.

From 1909 until 1912 Mr. Carey was instructor in mathematics and athletics in the Watertown, South Dakota High School. He homesteaded in Duchesne County, Utah, from 1913 until 1916, was with the United States Bureau of Reclamation, Salt River Project, Arizona, in 1917. From October, 1917, until May, 1919, Mr. Carey served in the United States Army as a private, Headquarters Company, 158th Infantry, and for nine months served with the American Expeditionary Forces in France. For two years thereafter, Mr. Carey was levelman to assistant engineer for the Wyoming State Highway Department, and held the position of transitman to chief of party in the United States Bureau of Public Roads.

In January, 1927, Mr. Carey started in business at Dalton, Nebraska, as a member of the firm of the Carey Brothers Oil Company. He has served as a member of the town council of Dalton 1930-32, and while a resident of Utah, was a member of the Duchesne County Board of Education, 1914-1915. Mr. Carey is a member of the American Legion, the Nebraska Independent Oil Men's Association, the Masons, the Odd Fellows, and from 1921 until 1926 was a member of the American Association of Engineers. He enjoys football, hunting and fishing, while his hobby is reading. Residence: Dalton.

Nellie M. Carey

Born at Hebron, Nebraska, January 5, 1891, Nellie M. Carey, is the daughter of John and Zaidee Ella (Gifford) Carey. Her father, a native of Martinsville, Ohio, was born October 31, 1858. He is a retired farmer and real estate agent. Her mother, who was a teacher prior to her marriage, was born in New Jersey, August 16, 1863.

Nellie M. Carey attended the public schools of Hebron and the Hebron and Villisca (Iowa) High Schools, and received her Bachelor of Arts degree from Nebraska Wesleyan University in 1915. Afterward she had post graduate work at the University of Nebraska, the University of California and the Library School of the New York Public Library, from which she received her certificate in 1926.

Following her graduation from college Miss Carey taught in the public schools for a number of years. She became the librarian of the Hastings Carnegie Library in 1926 and on October 1, 1931 became secretary of the Nebraska Library Commission. She is president (1931) of the Nebraska Library Association, and is a member of the American Library Association.

During 1928-29 Miss Carey was president of the Hasting Business and Professional Women's Club. She has also served as the state emblem chairman and as district membership chairman. She is a Methodist, a member of the Young Women's Christian Association, the Eastern Star and The Nebraskana Society. Residence: Lincoln.

Charles Eugene Carhart

Charles E. Carhart, prominent lumberman at Wayne, Nebraska, was born at Platteville, Wisconsin, February 23, 1875, the son of John Samuel and Elizabeth (Ivey) Carhart. His father, who was born near Platteville, April 5, 1849, is a retired farmer; his French ancestors migrated from France to England with William the Conqueror, and his grandfather came to America in 1845. His mother, whose ancestors came from County Cornwall, England, was born near Platteville, May 29, 1851.

Mr. Carhart was graduated from the Mapleton High School in 1894, and in 1895 was graduated from the Capitol City Commercial College. He entered business as a bookkeeper at Des Moines, Iowa, in 1895. In 1900 he entered business for himself; and now owns lumber yards at Wayne, Pierce, Hartington, and Randolph, Nebraska, as well as real estate holdings and other interests. He is proprietor of the Carhart Lumber Company.

He is past president of the Kiwanis Club, is chairman of the board of education, and holds membership in the Young Men's Christian Association, the Nebraskana Society, and the Red Cross. He is past master of the Masons. His social club is the Wayne Country Club. During the World War Mr. Carhart took an active part in Red Cross work in Wayne County. He is a Republican. His favorite sport is fishing, while his hobby is agriculture.

His marriage to Mary Ethel Miller was solemnized at Mapleton, Iowa, June 7, 1899. Mrs. Carhart, who was a teacher before her marriage, was born near Mapleton, April 5, 1875; she is descended from colonial ancestors. Four children were born to this marriage: Ralph, born May 14, 1900, who married Fauniel Senter; John, born January 27, 1902, who married Winifred Main; Elsie, born April 21, 1909; and Charles, born February 27, 1911, who died July 21, 1928. Ralph and John are in the lumber business, and Elsie is a student at the University of Nebraska. Residence: Wayne.

Thomas Carlon

Judge Thomas Carlon, who was a leader in the professional and civic affairs of Nebraska for many years, was born at Albany, New York, December 18, 1853. He received his early education in New York and Illinois, and for a number of years taught in the public schools of the latter.

He moved to O'Neill in the early history of that community, was admitted to the bar shortly afterwards, and became one of the leading lawyers of Holt County, where he served as county judge and city attorney in addition to his private practice. He was identified with every progressive activity of his county in both political and civic enterprise, and held membership in the Knights of

THOMAS CARLON

Columbus and the Workmen division of that organization.

In 1899, Judge Carlon moved to Denver, Colorado, where he served as county judge for a number of years and was connected with much important litigation. Until his death in 1927, he continued to take an active interest in religious, economic, and professional affairs.

He was married to May Sparks at O'Neill, Nebraska, June 25, 1885. Mrs. Carlon, the daughter of Mr. and Mrs. Darwin Sparks, received her eduction in the public schools of Wisconsin and came to Nebraska with her parents in pioneer days. She was a devoted wife and mother and took a prominent part in social and welfare work in her community. She died at Denver, Colorado, several years prior to her husband's death.

To this marriage eight children were born, of whom only five are living today: Mrs. Bert Shoemaker of O'Neill; Mrs. W. J. Hammond, of O'Neill; Mrs. L. E. Soukup, of Fort Lauderdale, Florida; Mrs. L. B. Duffy, of Jackson, Minnesota; and Grace Carlon, of Denver, Colorado. There are thirteen grandchildren of Judge Carlon, Harold, Donald, Lester, and Richard Shoemaker; Will, Mary, and Harriett Hammond; Patrick, Robert, and Mary Duffy; and Robert and John Soukup.

Mr. Carlon was buried from St. Patrick's Catholic Church and interment was made in Calvary Cemetery in O'Neill. (Photograph on Page 215).

Estella Geil Carlsen

Estella Geil Carlsen was born at Norwalk, Iowa, December 7, 1886, and has resided in Nebraska for nearly forty-three years. She is the daughter of Jacob and Leah (Beery) Geil, the former of whom was born May 16, 1854, and died January 16, 1927. He was a clergyman. Leah Beery Geil was born August 21, 1853, and died January 12, 1907.

On May 8, 1910, Estella Geil was married to Carl Christian Carlsen at Omaha. Mr. Carlsen was born in Howard County, Nebraska, March 28, 1884, and is one of Lincoln's leading bankers. They have three children: Carl Richard, born August 7, 1911; Leah Jane, born January 18, 1915; and Joseph Blair, born March 3, 1920.

Mrs. Carlsen is active in club work, and is a member of the Parent-Teachers' Association. She is a Protestant. Residence: Lincoln.

Arthur Magnus Carlson

One of the leading merchants of Axtell, Nebraska, is Arthur Magnus Carlson, a lifetime resident of Kearney County. He was born at Axtell, July 7, 1886, the son of John Magnus and Matildah Christine Carlson. His father, who was born in Sweden, July 14, 1852, came to this country in 1881, and died at Axtell, September 1, 1919. His mother was born in Sweden, April 23, 1859, and died at Axtell, May 20, 1929; she was active in church work most of her life.

Mr. Carlson attended the Axtell High School where he was graduated in 1901, and from 1907 to 1908 was a student at Nebraska State Normal School where he was a member of the college band. He took an active part in baseball, football, and track, in high school. He served as a clerk for five years and in 1915 entered business for himself as a merchant.

He is a member of the Volunteer Fire Department, is a former secretary of the Commercial Club, and holds membership in the village board at Axtell. He is affiliated with Trinity Lutheran Church, is a Master Workman of the Ancient Order of United Workmen, and is a member of the church choir and male chorus. His hobbies include oil painting, drawing, and reading.

On December 27, 1914, he was married at Axtell to Ida Wilhelmina Johnson. Mrs. Carlson, whose ancestry is Swedish, was born in Kearney County, Nebraska, July 28, 1889. They have three children: Phillip, born November 16, 1915; Leslie, born February 18, 1919; and Marilyn, September 25, 1931. Residence: Axtell.

Luther Martin Carlson

Luther Martin Carlson, was born at Galva, Illinois, April 13, 1871, son of Charles August and Johannah (Anderson) Carlson.

The father, born in Sweden, August 4, 1844, came to America in 1869, settling first in Illinois. He came to Nebraska in February, 1873, moved to Thomas County, Kansas, in 1886, and died in Nebraska, October 31, 1898. His wife, Johannah, was born in Sweden, March 4, 1839, and died in Nebraska, October 31, 1898.

Mr. Carlson attended country schools. He was married to Lorraine Gurney at Lincoln, June 21, 1910, and to them one daughter was born, Mary Louise on January 12, 1916. Mrs. Carlson was born at Brooks, Iowa, April 29, 1892, and is of English descent.

For some time Mr. Carlson has been the owner and manager of the Carlson Mattress and Auto Top Works at Grand Island. This company specializes in the manufacture of auto tops, curtains, cushions and other accessories, and in the making of mattresses, pillows, cushions and upholstery, as well as awnings and tents.

Mr. Carlson is a member of the Church of the Nazarene, the Red Cross, Chamber of Commerce, the Young Men's Christian Association and The Nebraskana Society. His leisure time is largely devoted to reading. Residence: Grand Island.

Swan Carlson

As a farmer in Phelps County, Nebraska, for the past 40 years, Swan Carlson has taken an active part in civic and business affairs. He was born at Urshult, Sweden, March 23, 1877, the son of Carl M. and Helena Swenson. His father, who was a farmer at Urshult all his life, was born November 11, 1845, and died May 29, 1930, in Sweden. His mother was born at Urshult, Sweden, in 1843, and died there in 1889.

Mr. Carlson received all of his education in Sweden. He is a successful farmer near Funk, Nebraska, and is president and a director in the Funk Grain and Elevator Company. A Democrat, he served as justice of the peace of Anderson Township from 1919 to 1930. He is an honorary member of the Chamber of Commerce of Lincoln, is affiliated with the Fridhem Lutheran Church, and has served as moderator, director and treasurer of the local school over a period of years.

Perhaps his greatest achievement is shown by his election to membership in the Master Farmers Club of Nebraska. During the World War Mr. Carlson was a member of the Council of Defense and was prominent in loan drives and local Red Cross work. He was united in marriage with Anna M. Olson at Holdrege, March 13, 1901. Mrs. Carlson was born at Trollhattan, Sweden, July 28, 1884, and is the daughter of Mr. and Mrs. A. M. Schild. Mrs. Carlson's parents are still living in Sweden.

There are eight children in the Carlson family: Adolph, born February 19, 1903; Harry, born December 28, 1904, who married Louise Bell; Walter, born January 7, 1907; Phillip, born August 1, 1909; Paul, born January 22, 1911; Edwin, born May 23, 1917; Melaine, born February 20, 1919; Ann, born November 10, 1925. Two of the children are farmers, one is business manager of the Bachrach Studio, Cleveland, Ohio, and the others are students. Paul is attending the University of Nebraska, while Phillip is a student at the Kearney State Teachers College. Residence: Funk. (Photograph in Album).

Richard Ernest Carlyon

Richard Ernest Carlyon, clergyman, was born at Ishpeming, Michigan, June 2, 1895, son of Thomas Henry and Elizabeth Jane (Bennett) Carlyon. His father was born in Camborne, England, February 19, 1858, and died at Ishpeming, Michigan, April 13, 1924. He was a miner who came to America in 1885. Elizabeth Bennett was born in Camborne, England, June 12, 1861, and died at Iron Mountain, Michigan, August 26, 1926.

Upon his graduation from the Ishpeming public school, Mr. Carlyon entered the Ishpeming High School from which he was graduated in June, 1913. He attended Morningside College, 1925-28, and was a member of Sigma Theta Rho, the Glee Club and Chapel Choir. He has filled various pastorates in Nebraska during his ten years of residence, including the Methodist Church at Chambers 1922-25; Dakota City 1925-27; Dakota City-Homer 1927-29 and South Sioux City, 1929.

On October 4, 1923, he was married to Ruth Lillian Wolters at Emerson, Nebraska. Mrs. Carlyon was born at Independence, Iowa, August 6, 1902. There are three children; Donald, born August 14, 1924; Margaret, born August 3, 1926, and Hilda, born September 13, 1928. Mr. Carlyon is a Republican. From September 4, 1917, to September 6, 1919, he served in the United States Navy, starting as a landsman for radio, and rated as a radio electrician first class at the close of his service. He is a member and pastor of Boals Methodist Church and a member of the Sioux City Ministerial Association (Sioux City, Ia.).

He is a Mason, a member of the Order of Eastern Star and the Odd Fellows, as well as The Nebraskana Society and the Sioux City Young Men's Christian Association. His hobby is recreational leadership. Residence: South Sioux City.

William Wilford Carmichael

William Wilford Carmichael, executive, was born in Mercer County, Pennsylvania, November 15, 1872, son of Hiram and Elizabeth (Fowler) Carmichael.

The father was born in Mercer County, September 12, 1825, and died at Table Rock, Nebraska, January 24, 1901. His mother, Charlotte Wibble, was born July 4, 1783, and his father served in the War of 1812, and the Indian Wars.

Elizabeth Fowler was born in Staffordshire, England, September 7, 1828, and died at Table Rock, April 26, 1903. Her mother, Margaret Mears, was born May 5, 1791.

Mr. Carmichael attended Peru State Normal School and the Omaha Business College.

He was married to Della Adeline Stratton at Omaha, on June 9, 1900. She was born at Verdon, Nebraska. September 29, 1876. They have three children, Orlo, Margaret and Neil.

Mr. Carmichael is a Democrat. He is a former member of the Omaha Board of Education, and a candidate for state senate in 1924. He taught school from 1890 until 1897, and was later associated with the C. N. Dietz Lumber Company for many years. He is now president of the Carmichael Lumber Company, which recently bought the interests of that company. Residence: Omaha.

Noble Lyle Carmody

Noble Lyle Carmody, automobile dealer, was born at Portland, Oregon, December 17, 1895, and for the past 30 years has resided in Nebraska. He is the son of Henry and Stella (Phillips) Carmody, the former of whom died at Norfolk, Nebraska, on September 8, 1927, and the latter on January 2, 1927.

Mr. Carmody attended public schools at Meadow Grove, Nebraska. At the present time he is Ford salesman at Chadron. He is a Republican, a member of the First Methodist Episcopal Church, the Chamber of Commerce, and the Modern Woodmen of America. He is also a member of the Chadron Country Club, enjoys golf. hunting, and fishing, and is fond of reading.

On April 8, 1915, he was married to Nettie Lucille Ives at Alliance, Nebraska. Mrs. Carmody was born at Tilden, Nebraska, March 4, 1896. They have three

daughters, Lilyan LaJeanne, born April 2, 1916; Margaret Grace, born October 11, 1917; and Annette Lucille born July 19, 1927. Residence: Chadron.

John Booth Carns

For the past 46 years Rev. John B. Carns has been a clergyman of the Methodist Episcopal Church. He was born at Leesburg, Carroll County, Ohio, July 17, 1844, the son of William and Lydia (Booth) Carns. His father, who was a physician, was born in 1805, and died at New Cumberland, Ohio, in 1888. His ancestry was English, Scotch and Irish.

His mother was born in Ohio, in 1810, and died at New Cumberland, in 1892, after a life of service in her community as the wife of a physician. Her ancestry was English and Welsh.

Rev. Carns attended the public school of Shepherdtown, Ohio, and in 1871, was graduated from Mount Union College. He was awarded the following degrees: A. M., Illinois Wesleyan University at Bloomington; Ph. D., at Illinois Wesleyan; and D. D. in South Carolina, in 1880. He was editor of the first Nebraska temperance paper. A Republican, he served as a member of two Republican State Conventions.

He married Isabel Smith at New Cumberland, October 11, 1868. Mrs. Carns who was born at New Cumberland, February 15, 1844, of German parentage, was a school teacher and was an active church worker throughout her life. She died at Lincoln, Lancaster County, Nebraska, December 24, 1928. Six children were born to their marriage, four of whom are living. They are: Dessie, who married W. M. Cox; Mary I., who married J. A. Quick; Florence, who married Leo Brown, December 28, 1917; Laura B.; Ruth Estelle, who married Leonard L. Chambers, and Foss De Pauw, who married Grace Zink, and who died January 28, 1928.

On December 7, 1930, Rev. Carns was married at Bluffton, Wells County, Indiana, to Luella J. Stansbury-Kenagy. He is a member of the Ecumenical Conference, acting as delegate to the conference in London, in 1901. He is a clergyman of the Nebraska Annual Conference of the Methodist Episcopal Church. He is chaplain of the Lincoln Masonic Lodge. Perhaps his most notable claim to distinction was his organization of the Nebraska Anti-Saloon League in 1898 of which he was state superintendent 11 years. Politically, he is a Republican. Residence: Lincoln.

Eddie Eugene Carpenter

Born at Champaign. Illinois, March 22, 1861, Eddie Eugene Carpenter has been a resident of Kearney County, Nebraska, for the past 58 years, and has played an important part in the progress of his community and state. His father, Thomas Carpenter, who was a contractor and builder, was born at Sandy Hook, New York, in 1812, and died at Tolono, Illinois, in June, 1875. Thomas Carpenter, who was of English descent, helped to build the New York and Erie Canal, and constructed many of the stations of the Central Railroad south of Chicago in early days.

His mother, Catherine (Belinger) Carpenter, was born at Rochester, New York, and died at Lowell, Nebraska, July 7, 1901. She was a descendant of the Belinger family of New York, and her mother was born and reared in Mohawk Valley, New York.

Mr. Carpenter is director of the Platte Valley Development Company at Lowell, is director of the Gibbon Exchange Bank at Gibbon, Nebraska, serving as vice president of the latter institution. He is serving his 14th year as postmaster at Lowell, and has formerly served as treasurer of the local school board, justice of the peace, town treasurer and notary public.

In the early days of the middlewest Mr. Carpenter

made the long and arduous journey to Nebraska by way of covered wagon, and later traveled to California and back in the same manner. His step-father served as post surgeon at Fort Kearney, Nebraska, when the state was still a partly settled country.

Mr. Carpenter is a member of the Modern Woodmen of America, the National Geographic Society, and the Nebraskana Society. His hobby is music, and he is interested in architecture.

On September 17, 1888, he married Hattie Amelia Cotten at Lowell. Mrs. Carpenter, who is assistant postmaster at Lowell, was born of Scotch, English and Irish extraction, in Fayette County, Iowa, October 8, 1871. They have the following children: Edwin F., born October 4, 1889; Roy I., born January 25, 1891; Viola A., born June 22, 1892; Berniece C., born March 24, 1901, and Arthur E., born December 3, 1893. Residence: Lowell.

Janet Louise Carpenter

Janet Louise Carpenter, educator, was born at Sturbridge, Massachusetts, June 28, 1871, of pre-Revolutionary English stock. Her father, Henry Merritt Carpenter, who is still living, was born at Southbridge, Massachusetts, December 8, 1839. In early life he learned the carriage trimming trade, and was later a harness maker. During the Civil War he served with Company B, 15th Massachusetts Infantry. His wife, Sophronia Allen (Fuller) Carpenter, was born at Sturbridge, September 4, 1842, and died at Hastings, January 9, 1906. Her family, as well as her husband's was represented by soldiers in the Revolutionary War.

Educated in the public schools of Marengo, Iowa, from 1880-84, Miss Carpenter was a student at Hastings, from 1884-88; received her A. B. in 1892, and her A. M. in 1895, from Hastings College; and attended summer school at the University of Chicago, 1899, 1902, 1913, 1924; the University of Washington, 1917, and the University of Colorado, the summer of 1928. Miss Carpenter is a member of Pi Gamma Mu, honorary sociological fraternity.

During the years 1895 to 1899, Miss Carpenter taught Latin and Greek at Highland College in Kansas, and from 1899 to 1906 was teacher of Greek at Kansas City University. Becoming a member of the faculty of Hastings College in 1906, Miss Carpenter is now head of its English department.

She is especially devoted to reading in physics and economics, is affiliated with the First Presbyterian Church at Hastings, and is a member of The Nebraskana Society, and the Hastings Library Board. Residence, Hastings.

Milton Henry Carrig

One of Nebraska's professional leaders is Milton Henry Carrig who has been engaged in the practice of medicine and surgery at Stuart, for the past eight years. He was born in Platte County, Nebraska, April 21, 1900, the son of Charles Joseph and Elizabeth (Hancy) Carrig. His father, who was born in Platte County, January 21, 1868, is a livestock dealer and landower. His mother, whose ancestry is Irish, was born in Platte County, March 19, 1868.

Dr. Carrig attended St. Bonaventure Parochial School at Columbus, Nebraska, was graduated from the high school at Columbus, in 1918, and received the B. S. degree at Creighton University at Omaha, in 1922. He was awarded the M. D. degree at Creighton University in 1924 where he was president of the Eta Chapter of Phi Rho Sigma in 1924.

He is a member of the Holt County Medical Society, the Nebraska State Medical Society, and the American Medical Society. He is a fourth degree member of the Knights of Columbus, is affiliated with St. Boniface Catholic Church, and holds membership in the Lions International. During the World War he was a member of the Students Army Training Corps at Creighton University, and at this time holds membership in the American Legion.

His marriage to Louise Patricia Kerz was solemnized at Chicago, May 24, 1928. Mrs. Carrig, whose ancestry is German, was born at Galena, Illinois, October 28, 1903. They have one son, James Arnold, born September 9, 1928. Residence: Stuart.

John Anthony Carrigan

John A. Carrigan, who has practiced law at Blair Nebraska, for the past seven years, has always resided in Nebraska. He was born at Blair, July 2, 1901, the son of Edmund Burke and Frances Margaret Carrigan. His father, who was district judge, was born at Blair, November 2, 1869, and was a pioneer lawyer in Nebraska; he died at Blair, December 8, 1927. His mother was born in Pennsylvania, April 26, 1871. His grandfather, John A. Carrigan, practiced law at Blair for twenty years.

Mr. Carrigan was graduated from the Blair High School in 1918, and received the LL. B. degree at the University of Michigan, where he was a member of Beta Theta Pi and Phi Alpha Delta. He was a student at the University of Nebraska for a time. Since June 24, 1924, he has been engaged in the practice of law at Blair. A Republican, he served as county chairman of the Hoover-Curtis Campaign Club, and is vitally interested in the political affairs of his state and community. He holds membership in St. Mary's Episcopal Church at Blair; and is a Mason, Royal Arch, Knight Templar. Residence: Blair.

Frank Leslie Carroll

Frank L. Carroll was born at Tecumseh, Johnson County, Nebraska, the son of Charles Calvin and Maria (Sherman) Carroll. His father, who was a farmer, was born at Lowell, Massachusetts, October 26, 1844, and died at Canton, Illinois, January 5, 1915; he served in the 8th Missouri Infantry and the 11th Illinois Cavalry during the Civil War. Maria Sherman Carroll was born at Mansfield, Ohio, November, 1850, and died at Canton, May 10, 1908. Her family was related to the families of General Sherman and Senator Sherman.

Mr. Carroll attended the rural schools of Illinois, and the Canton High School. He owned and operated the *Ashland Gazette* and the *St. Paul Republican* for some time, and is now president of the Sun Publishing Company, and is editor of the *Schuyler Sun* at Schuyler, Nebraska. From 1899 to May 1908 he served as postmaster at Manito, Illinois. A Republican, he served a short term in the Nebraska legislature in 1923, when Governor McKelvie appointed him to succeed Donald McLeod in special session to reduce appropriations. He has lived in Nebraska for 22 years. He is a member of the Schuyler Chamber of Commerce, the Nebraskana Society, and Holy Trinity Episcopal Church at Schuyler. He is a Mason and Modern Woodman of America. His favorite sport is golf.

His marriage to Besse Lee Carman was solemnized at Princeville, Peoria County, Illinois, November 23, 1898. Mrs. Carroll was born at Princeville, April 1, 1884. Her maternal ancestors who were of the Hyde family, came from England. Residence: Schuyler.

Thomas William Carroll

Thomas William Carroll was born at Manitowoc, Wisconsin, November 10, 1872. Richard Carroll, his father, a farmer, was born in Ireland, and died at Holdrege, Phelps County, Nebraska, April 3, 1891. Mary (Clark) Carroll was born in Ireland and died at Holdrege, April 1, 1891.

Mr. Carroll received his early education in the public and high schools at Holdrege. Later he was a student at the Orleans Business College. He has lived in Nebraska for the past 42 years and has been prominent politically for many years. He is a special agent and insurance adjuster. He served as sheriff of Harlan County, Nebraska, three terms; was deputy United States marshal for the district of Nebraska, eight years; federal prohibition agent 1921-23, and was state sheriff of Nebraska, 1923-25. He is a Democrat.

On November 15, 1893, his marriage to May Travis was solemnized at Orleans, Harlan County, Nebraska. Mrs. Carroll was born at Peterboro, Ontario, Canada, September 27, 1873. Eight children were born to this union: Frances, who married Francis J. Kane. She died January 27, 1924. Raymond L., who married Alta J. Nelson; Helena, who married William J. Griffin; Mary, who married R. F. Moran; Irene, who married M. H. Layton; Genevieve; Joseph; and Thomas.

He is a member of the Knights of Columbus, 4th degree, and is a Modern Woodman of America. For six years he was a member of the board of education at Alma, and was its president for two years. He is interested in all athletics. He is a member of St. Mary's Cathedral at Lincoln. Residence: Lincoln.

Stewart Edgar Carskadon

Stewart Edgar Carskadon was born at Dunkinsville, Adams County, Ohio, July 4, 1877, the son of William and Charlotte (Jones) Carskadon. His father, who was a farmer, was born at Manchester, Ohio, October 21, 1836, and died at Wilcox, Nebraska, December 3, 1931. His mother was born at Manchester, October 20, 1840, and died at Wilcox, April 15, 1920.

Mr. Carskadon has delivered mail on the same route for the past 29 years at Wilcox. He is a member of the Parent-Teachers' Association, was formerly president of the school board, and holds membership in the following fraternal organizations: Ancient Order of United Workmen; Order of Eastern Star; Rebekahs; Masons; Modern Woodmen of America; and the Independent Order of Odd Fellows.

On February 25, 1902, Mr. Carskadon was married to Sadie Coridella Whitlatch at Holdrege, Nebraska. Mrs. Carskadon was born at Parkersburg, Virginia, February 16, 1884. She is a member of the Eastern Star, Rebekahs, R N. A., and the Community Church. They have five children: Jennie Lucille, born September 19, 1911, who married Kenneth W. Beahm, and is living on a farm near Ragan, Nebraska; Helen Elizabeth, born October 29, 1913; Phillip Edgar, born March 30, 1918; Paul Herman, born February 17, 1920, who died January 7, 1921; and Margaret Eleanor, born August 5, 1924. Residence: Wilcox. (Photograph in Album).

James Charles Carson

James Charles Carson, president of the Carson Ranch, Incorporated, was born in County Monaghan, Ireland, July 4, 1864, and for the past 50 years has resided in Nebraska.

His father, Charles Leslie Carson, was born in County Monaghan, and died there in 1900. He was a farmer and linen manufacturer, of Scotch-Irish ancestry. His mother, Matilda Kidd, was born in County Armagh, Ireland, and died in County Monaghan, in 1903. Her ancestry was also Scotch-Irish.

James Charles Carson attended public school at Castle Shane, Ireland, and Model School in County Monaghan.

For 20 years after coming to America Mr. Carson was a hardware salesman, and was a director of the corporation which he represented. He is at the present time extensively engaged in ranching as above. During the late war Mr. Carson was active in Liberty loan drives,

in registering citizens for the military draft, and as a member of the Food Conservation Committee. He is a member of the Presbyterian Church, the Masons, and his clubs include the Omaha Club and the Omaha Athletic Club. His hobbies are reading and hunting.

His marriage to Maud Hunter was solemnized at Brooklyn in July, 1920. Mrs. Carson is a native of Warren, Ohio. Residence: Irwin.

Rosanna Carson

Rosanna Carson, prominent woman executive of Nebraska, was born at Brownville, Nebraska, June 4, 1872, the daughter of John Lind and Mary (Masters) Carson. Her father, who was born at Mercersburg, Pennsylvania, August 30, 1832, and died at Lincoln, December 30, 1897, was a pioneer Nebraska banker, who served as captain of the commissary department during the Civil War. His father and mother were James Oliver Carson and Rosanna Marshall (White) Carson; and his grandfather and mother, David Carson and Jean Oliver Carson, who came from Ulster, Ireland; the Whites, who were English, were natives of Maryland and New Jersey.

Miss Carson's mother was born in Wayne County, Ohio, July 20, 1835, and died at Lincoln, December 31, 1901; she was the daughter of John and Mary Caven Masters, who moved from Wayne County, Ohio, to Oregon, Missouri.

Miss Carson was graduated from Miss Aiken's School for Young Ladies in June, 1891, and later attended the University of Nebraska where she was a member of Kappa Alpha Theta. She is now vice president of the Carson National Bank of Auburn, Nebraska. During the World War she was state chairman of the Young Women's Christian Association. She holds membership in the Red Cross; Native Sons and Daughters of Nebraska; University Club of Lincoln; Country Club; Athenea Club; Lotus Club; Copper Kettle Club, and the Nebraskana Society. She is a member of the First Presbyterian Church of Lincoln; and holds membership in the Colonial Dames and the Daughters of the American Revolution. She is a Republican. Residence: Lincoln.

Fred Louis Carsten

Fred L. Carsten was born on a farm near Avoca, Otoe County, Nebraska, November 25, 1886, the son of Louis and Sarah Selma (Haeffner) Carsten. His father, who was born at Dunbar, Otoe County, Nebraska, July 19, 1863, is a retired farmer, now living in Avoca. His ancestry is French on the maternal side; his father was German.

His mother was born at Alsace Lorraine, France, September 22, 1864, and died at Omaha, Nebraska, February 22, 1928.

He attended Iowa Wesleyan at Mount Pleasant, Iowa, and the Lincoln Business College at Lincoln, Nebraska. He has lived in Nebraska for 44 years and has been a farmer all his life. He was united in marriage with Nancy Ethel Fleshman at Omaha, Nebraska, May 3, 1911. Mrs. Carsten, who was born at Avoca, December 17, 1887, is the daughter of pioneers who came to Nebraska from Indiana in 1885. Her father was a Civil War veteran. They have one son, Calvin, born November 11, 1915.

During the war Mr. Carsten was chairman of the Liberty Loan sales committee. He is a member of the Red Cross; the Parents Teachers' Association; the library board at Avoca, and is president of the Cass County Fair Association, serving his third term. He is a member of the Nebraskana Society, a Mason, and an Odd Fellow. He is a member of the Congregational Church and superintendent of Sunday School. His favorite sport is golf, and his hobby is horses. He is a Democrat. Residence. Avoca.

CLIFFORD DORWIN CARTER

Clifford Dorwin Carter

C. Dorwin Carter was born at Alexandria, Thayer County, Nebraska, August 4, 1903, the son of William G., and Silvia Mary (Dinnis) Carter. His father, who is a real estate man, was born in Illinois; his ancestry is English. His mother was born in Missouri; she is of English and Irish descent.

Mr. Carter attended the grade school of Table Rock, Nebraska, and later was graduated from the high school at Hebron, Nebraska. He was a student at Peru State Teachers' College, and was awarded his B. S. degree at the University of Nebraska, where he later took graduate work for his master's degree in education. He attended the University of Notre Dame for a time. He is a member of Phi Epsilon Kappa. He was granted college letters in football at Peru; served as all-state college guard in 1923; and was a member of the football squad at the University of Nebraska in 1930.

He was superintendent of the Orafino Consolidated School, 1924-27; was superintendent of the Honey Creek Consolidated School at Salem, Nebraska, 1927-28; and is now superintendent of schools at Dorchester, Nebraska. He is a member of the School Men's Association, and the Nebraska State Teachers' Association. He is a Mason. He is affiliated with the Presbyterian Church of Hebron.

He was united in marriage with Opal May Jackson, at Sidney, Fremont County, Iowa, July 19, 1924. Mrs. Carter, who was born at Woodston, Kansas, April 24, 1905, is a music teacher; her ancestry is English and Irish. Residence: Dorchester. (Photograph on Page 220).

Edward Francis Carter

Edward Francis Carter, judge of the District Court of the 17th Judicial District of Nebraska, was born at Middlebranch, Nebraska, March 11, 1897, son of Edward Charles and Allie Margaret (Waring) Carter. The father was born in New Jersey, April 9, 1870, and is a miller of English descent. The mother, who is of Scotch descent, was born in Iowa, August 12, 1878.

Mr. Carter attended the public and high schools of Beaver City, and in June, 1919, received the Bachelor of Law degree from the University of Nebraska. There he was a member of the Order of the Coif and Phi Alpha Delta. From 1919 until April, 1927, he engaged in the practice of law at Bayard.

A Republican, he was county chairman of the Republican county central committee in 1924-26, was a candidate for county attorney of Morrill County 1922, 1926, and on April 26, 1927, was appointed district judge by Governor Adam McMullen. In 1928, he was re-elected, and in 1932 is a candidate for that office.

On June 2, 1920, he was married to Vera Marie Hofrichter at Bruning. Mrs. Carter was born at Bellwood, February 12, 1899, of German descent. She is the daughter of Benjamin and Martha (Mennenga) Hofrichter. Mrs. Carter is a member of the Eastern Star and the Woman's Club. They have four children, Dolores Jean, born July 23, 1921; Lyle A., born December 22, 1922; Edward F., born March 23, 1928; and Robert L., born March 24, 1932.

Among Judge Carter's professional organizations are, the American and Nebraska State and Scottsbluff Bar Associations, and the Western Nebraska Bar Association. He is a member of the Masons, the Knights of Pythias, the Scottsbluff Lions Club, and the Gering Chamber of Commerce, as well as the American Legion. During the World War, he served as a private in the United States Army. His clubs are the Scottsbluff and Gering Country Clubs, and his favorite sport is golf. Residence: Gering. (Photograph on Page 222).

George Alexander Carter

Born at Chicago, Illinois, December 4, 1868, George Alexander Carter is the son of James and Agnes (Low)

Carter. His father, who was born near Dublin, Ireland, March 15, 1821, and died at Superior, Nebraska, July 19, 1897, was employed by the English Army in his youth as a horse trainer, and later moved to Chicago, where he was a member of the police force; he settled in Nuckolls County, Nebraska, in 1884.

His mother was born at Kerry Muir, Scotland, September 18, 1831, and died at Superior, August 17, 1906. She came to America in 1843, and settled at Peoria, Illinois, and later moved to Chicago. She organized the Valley Home Society at Superior.

Mr. Carter received his education in suburban schools of Chicago, and since 1884 has been a farmer and stockman near Superior. He is a member of the school board and Parent-Teachers' Association, is affiliated with the First Presbyterian Church of Superior, and holds membership in the Independent Order of Odd Fellows. He is especially interested in raising Angus cattle.

He married Jessie Margaret McConnell who was born at Washington, Iowa, April 14, 1869, and died at Superior, August 26, 1925. His marriage to Edna Worden occurred at Bovina Center, New York, September 10, 1927. They have two daughters, Marguerite Hattie and Enid Ann. Residence: Superior.

Harry Glenn Carter

Harry G. Carter, meteorologist of the United States Weather Bureau, was born in Dixon County, Nebraska, February 8, 1883, and has been a resident of this state practically all his life. His father, Emory E. Carter, was a school teacher and justice of the peace for many years. Anna Marie (Johnson) Carter, his mother, was a school teacher before her marriage.

Mr. Carter attended grade and high school at Ponca, Nebraska, and later took special work at the University of Nebraska. He entered the newspaper business at Ponca and later was a newspaper man at Ponca and Newcastle, Nebraska. In 1904 he entered the United States Weather Bureau; was appointed assistant director of the Nebraska section, 1913; and was authorized weather forecaster, February, 1918. Since 1918 he has been meteorologist and assistant director of the Nebraska section of the United States Weather Bureau. During 1929 he was instructor of meteorology and air navigation in the Mutual Flyers Club.

He is the author of various articles dealing with weather and climate, effect of weather on crops, rain insurance, and other meteorological studies. He was admitted to his profession at Lincoln, Lancaster County, Nebraska, November, 1918.

He was united in marriage with Grace Beatrice Fritts at Lincoln, September 5, 1905. Mrs. Carter, who was born at Peoria, Illinois, October 15, 1883, was a music teacher prior to marriage. Their children are: Richard E., born October 29, 1910, who is an observer in the United States Weather Bureau; and Dorothy G., born June 29, 1915, who is a student at Lincoln High School.

Mr. Carter volunteered for service in the World War but was exempted as a necessary government employee. He is a member of the Federal Business Association, of which he is secretary; the American Meteorological Society; and the Nebraska Academy of Science. He holds membership in the Nebraskana Society, and is affiliated with the Presbyterian Church. He is a Mason. He is a Republican. Residence: Lincoln. (Photograph in Album).

Lew Arthur Carter

Lew Arthur Carter, physician and surgeon, was born at Henderson, Iowa, November 20, 1875, son of Elijah Benjamin and Josie (Boswell) Carter. He received his medical degree from the Kansas City Hahnemann University and has been in active practice since 1903. He is a Republican and has held various minor offices.

On November 25, 1896, he was married to Lola V.

EDWARD FRANCIS CARTER

Wells at Washington, Kansas. There are three children, Vera, born October 24, 1897, who married Arthur Blum; Eunice, born December 18, 1904, who married Joel I. Smith; and Marjorie, born July 24, 1910, who married Vance Beghtol.

Dr. Carter is United States pension examiner. He is a member of the Nebraska State Medical Association, the Red Cross, the Lions Club, the Odd Fellows, and the O'Neill Country Club. He was president of the board of education from 1928-31. Residence: O'Neill.

Thomas Hough Carter

A resident of Nebraska for the past fifty-seven years, Thomas H. Carter was born at Richmond, New York, June 16, 1872. He is the son of Oliver France and Harriet (Mallet) Carter, the former a native of Burwell, England. Oliver France Carter was born on December 24, 1833, and came to America in 1849, and to Nebraska in 1873. He was a miller and milling executive until his death at Ashland, in February, 1883. His wife, Harriet, was born in Richmond, New York, in 1841, and died at Ashland, in January, 1891. She was of English descent.

Thomas H. Carter attended the public schools of Ashland, until 1885, and during that year was water boy on railroad construction. From 1886 to 1889, he was a farm hand, and from 1889 to 1892, was helper in the Ashland Mill and Electric Light Company. In 1892, he became associated with the Wetherald Brothers as second miller, and from 1903, until 1908, was superintendent for them.

In the year 1908, Mr. Carter purchased the mill, operating as Bozarth and Carter, and in 1918 became sole owner. He built the hydro-electric plant in 1921, disposing of it in 1924, and was one of the organizers of the Northern Nebraska Power Company in 1926. In addition he has newspaper interests and is the owner of considerable farm acreage.

Mr. Carter has always been active in Republican politics in Thayer County, serving as city councilman 1902-05, member of the board of education 1912-15, and as mayor of Hebron, 1915-18. During the World War he was county chairman of the Red Cross, chairman of the county council of defense and government appeal agent. He was the organizer of the Bull Moose party in Thayer County in 1912.

On July 15, 1893, Mr. Carter was married to Maude Rebecka Clarke, at Hebron. Mrs. Carter, who was born at Salem, Nebraska, December 10, 1873, died at Hebron, April 18, 1931. There were five children born to their union, three of whom are living: Edna, born February 20, 1895, married Will Long; Edith, born March 13, 1897, married William H. Bauman; Thomas, born September 9, 1901, died September 3, 1905; Adelene, born March 7, 1910; and Newton, born October 11, 1918, who died February 18, 1919. Residence: Hebron.

W. Lyndal Carter

One of the leading merchants at Columbus, Nebraska, is W. Lyndal Carter who was born at Chariton, Iowa, January 10, 1901, the son of Edward Grant and Ida (McMains) Carter. His father, who was born at Chariton, February 9, 1872, of French descent, has served as a furniture salesman for 32 years and is now engaged in the furniture business independently; he is descended, through the maternal line, from Robert Edwards of Scotland. His mother, whose ancestry is Scotch and Irish, was born at Chariton, February 11, 1877.

Mr. Carter was graduated from the Columbus High School in 1919, and is the owner and manager of the Baer Shoe Company of that city. He holds membership in the Community Orchestra, the City Band, and the Chamber of Commerce of Columbus. He is affiliated with St. Bonaventures Catholic Church, holds membership in The Nebraskana Society, and is interested in music and reading. His favorite sport is hunting.

His marriage to Kathryn Louise Greisen occurred at Columbus, April 24, 1923. Mrs. Carter, who is of German descent, was born at Columbus, April 16, 1902. They have three children: Roberta Jean, born April 16, 1924; Virginia Lee, born May 14, 1928; and Kathryn Joyce, born December 30, 1926, who died January 20, 1927. Residence: Columbus.

Carl C. Cartney

Carl C. Cartney, banker and lawyer of Lincoln, was born in Clay County, Nebraska, December 24, 1881, the son of George and Bridget (Carrabine) Cartney. His father, who was born in Ireland, died at Tilden, Antelope County, Nebraska, in 1910. His mother, whose ancestry is Irish, was born in Canada.

Mr. Cartney was graduated from the Lincoln High School; attended the state normal school; and in 1922 was graduated from the University of Nebraska with the degree LL. B. He was elected to membership in Phi Alpha Delta. He has lived in Nebraska all his life and from 1905 to 1919, was engaged in the banking business, holding the following positions: assistant cashier; cashier; vice president; and president.

He was united in marriage with Grace L. Walker at Grand Island, Hall County, Nebraska, June 16, 1915. Mrs. Cartney, whose ancestry is German, was born in Somerset County, Pennsylvania. She is a banker. They have a daughter, Kathryn, born January 1, 1917.

Mr. Cartney was active in loan drives and Red Cross activities during the late war. He is a member of the Lancaster County Bar Society; the Nebraska State Bar Society; and the American Bar Association. He is a member of the York Rite and Shrine bodies of the Masons. He is a member of Holy Trinity Episcopal Church of Lincoln, and is independent politically. Residence: Lincoln.

Gilbert L. Carver

Gilbert L. Carver, who is engaged in the insurance business at Kearney, Nebraska, has lived in this state all his life. He was born at Cambridge, Nebraska, July 4, 1893, the son of Stephen L. and Nora Ann (Montgomery) Carver. His father, who is a retired farmer, was born at Nashville, Tennessee, April 8, 1861. His mother was born at Woodruff, Kansas, November 20, 1869.

Mr. Carver attended the East Valley Rural School in Red Willow County, Nebraska, was graduated from the Cambridge High School in 1914, and later attended York United Brethren College and the Lincoln Business College. He is engaged in the insurance business at Kearney, independently, and takes a prominent part in civic affairs there. He is a member of the Kearney Chamber of Commerce, is affiliated with the Methodist Episcopal Church of Kearney, and holds membership in the Parent Teachers Association and the local Masonic Lodge. He is serving as a member of the Kearney City Library Board at this time.

During the World War Mr. Carver served in the United States Army, and at this time is a member of the American Legion. His favorite sport is golfing. He is a member of the Democratic party and holds membership in The Nebraskana Society.

His marriage to Marguerite Grace Didriksen occurred at Kearney, June 9, 1920; she was born in the community, November 25, 1894. To them were born: Boyd William, April 11, 1923; and Doris Louise, January 9, 1925. Residence: Kearney.

Horace Jackson Cary

Horace Jackson Cary was born in Buffalo County, Nebraska, December 27, 1888, the son of Lyman and Lavina (Rines) Cary.

His father, who was a stockman and farmer, served as county treasurer of Buffalo County for three terms and was treasurer of Tama County, Iowa, for two terms; he was born at Turner, Maine, July 18, 1847, and died at Kearney, Nebraska, December 10, 1924; he was a direct descendant of Governor William Bradford, John Alden and Elder William Brewster, all of *Mayflower* fame, and was descended from Daniel French, Cornelius Waldo, and Ephriam Cary. His mother was descended from Daniel Jackson of Revolutionary times.

Mr. Cary was graduated from the Kearney High School in 1906, and in 1910 received the B. S. degree at the University of Nebraska, where he majored in civil engineering. He is a stockman and farmer near Kearney, is past president of the Kearney Rotary Club, is president of the School Board, and is past secretary of the Farm Bureau. At this time he is president of the Ravenna Bank, and is a director in the Fort Kearney State Bank.

He holds membership in the local Parent-Teachers' Association, is a director in the Chamber of Commerce, and holds membership in the Country Club and the Masonic Lodge. Politically, he is independent.

On April 15, 1914, he married Lucile Elizabeth Nye at Kearney. Mrs. Cary, who was born at Kearney, March 27, 1894, is the daughter of Fred Allen Nye, a lawyer, and Helen Barlow Nye. She is past regent of the Fort Kearney chapter of the Daughters of the American Revolution, is vice state regent of that organization, and has served as state recording secretary and state auditor.

Among her Revolutionary ancestors were Iram Nye and Samuel Scott. They have three children: Helen Rines, born May 25, 1916; Margaret Zoe, born May 30, 1918; and Horace Jackson, born December 26, 1920. Residence: Kearney.

Jacob Casal

Jacob Casal, a farmer in Cedar County, Nebraska, for the past 44 years, was born at Schiers, Switzerland, April 22, 1870, the son of Jacob and Luisa (Senteler) Casal. His father, who was a clerk, was born at Schiers, in 1843, and died at Angeslem, France, 1870. His mother was born at Schiers, in 1844, and died at Davos, Switzerland, 1914.

Mr. Casal was graduated from school in 1886. He is a member of the Nebraskana Society, the Hope Reformed Church at Belden, and the Republican party.

He was married to Maria Rieder at Schiers, October 25, 1876; she was born in Switzerland, August 30, 1877. They have five children: Luisa, born October 11, 1897, who married Herman Benck; George, born March 7, 1899, who married Martha Cunningham; Barbara, born January 25, 1901, who married Carl Bring; Hilda, born January 23, 1903; and Emma, born June 22, 1907. Mr. Casal, who has extensive land interests, has always taken an extremely active interest in community affairs, particularly along agricultural lines. Resdence: Belden.

Ernest Edwin Case

Ernest E. Case was born near Brighton, Iowa, September 9, 1869, the son of Samuel John and Mary Parthena (Horton) Case, and since 1871 has been a successful farmer in Nebraska. Coming to Nebraska with his parents and one brother, Charles, in a covered wagon where they homesteaded, he now lives with his sister, Maude. She is a member of Butler Johnson Chapter of the Daughters of the American Revolution and has acted as regent.

His father, who was also a farmer, was born in Connecticut, November 17, 1842, and died near Sutton, Nebraska, May 13, 1912; he was descended from John Case who came to America from England in 1635 and was one of the founders of Simsbury, Connecticut. His mother

was born near Fredonia, Ohio, June 2, 1841, and died near Sutton, April 13, 1922. She was descended from Barnabas Horton who came to America from England in 1640; John Howland and John Tilley, who came to this country on the *Mayflower,* were also ancestors.

Mr. Case received his education in the Sutton High School. He is a member of the local school board, the board of directors of the Sutton Farmers Elevator Company, and the Sutton Co-operative Oil Company and is its vice president. He is affiliated with the First Congregational Church of Sutton, and his political affiliation is with the Democratic Party. He was township assessor, 1895-96, and was elected a life member in the Nebraskana Society in 1931. Residence: Sutton.

James Dodds Case

James Dodd Case, physician and surgeon, was born in Adams County, Nebraska, August 2, 1875, son of Robert Gable and Louisa (Glidewell) Case. He attended public school at Bridgecreek, Missouri, and Liberty, Kansas, and in 1893, was graduated from the academy at Bennet, Nebraska. He attended Cotner University and in 1901 received his medical degree from that institution.

His marriage to Agnes Frances Morgan was solemnized at Bennet on March 25, 1897. Mrs. Case was born at Pittsburg, Pennsylvania. There are two children, Richard J., and Ruth.

Dr. Case has been in active practice since 1901. He is a member of the Eclectic Medical Society, the Young Men's Christian Association and the First Christian Church. He was secretary of the State Health Department, 1915-17; superintendent o fthe State Hospital for the Insane, 1917-18, and secretary of the Department of Public Welfare, 1923-24. Residence: Lincoln.

Elmer Fay Casebolt

Elmer Fay Casebolt, manager of the Thayer County Motor Company at Hebron, Nebraska, has always lived in this state. He was born on a farm in Thayer County, September 2, 1897, the son of William J. and Jennie (McMurphy) Casebolt. His father, who was a farmer, was born at Ashville, Kentucky, January 31, 1856, and died at Hebron, February 28, 1929; he was of English descent.

His mother, who was born at Lincoln, Illinois, May 19, 1869, of Scotch Irish parentage, is active in the P. E. O.'s and holds membership in the Order of Eastern Star. She now resides at Hebron where she was a business woman for many years.

Mr. Casebolt attended the Hebron High School and has always been in the automobile business in that community. For a number of years he was employed by the Thayer County Motor Company of which he is now manager.

His marriage to Hazel Richey was solemnized at Marysville, Kansas, May 22, 1918. Mrs. Casebolt, who was born at Waterville, Kansas, September 13, 1897, was a teacher in Thayer County schools prior to her marriage, and since then has been actively interested in women's affairs at Hebron. She holds membership in the Woman's Club, has assisted in various programs in church and social activities, and through her dramatic ability has contributed to many local entertainments. Of Irish and English descent, she is the daughter of Oscar A. and Emogene (Lawrence) Richey.

Their two children are: William Oscar, born December 26, 1920; and Robert Dean, born March 21, 1931. Mr. Casebolt is a Democrat, a Mason, and a member of the Nebraskana Society. With his wife he is a member of the First Presbyterian Church at Hebron and the Merrimix Club. He is interested in all outdoor sports, especially hunting and fishing. Residence: Hebron.

Roy L. Caskey

Roy Lucas Caskey, son of William and Barbara Ellen (Imes) Caskey, was born at North Bend, Iowa, February 15, 1891, and for thirty-six years has resided in Nebraska. Hs fater was born in Indiana, March 4, 1858, son of Robert and Susan (Freland) Caskey. William Caskey was a farmer and harness maker in earlier life, and later associated with the Denver and Rio Grande Railroad.

Barbara Ellen Imes was born in Iowa, January 18, 1859, and died at Big Spring on March 10, 1930. She was the daughter of John and Barbara (Miller) Imes.

Roy Lucas Caskey was graduated from public school at Big Spring in the class of 1908, and first engaged in farming. Later he moved into the town of Big Spring and entered the electrical business. He hung the first light meter and pumped the first water in the town, and in 1920 was appointed city electrician. He held that position until 1927 when the light plant was sold to the Public Service Company of Colorado, and was elected to the same position with that company.

Mr. Lucas is also serving as village clerk and water superintendent. He is a progressive Republican. He is a member of the Red Cross, the Odd Fellows and the Big Spring Golf Club and until 1930, when electricians were barred, was a member of the Modern Woodmen of America. His favorite sport is golf, while his hobby is photography. Residence: Big Spring. (Photograph on Page 226).

Jacob H. Casper

Jacob H. Casper, farmer and real estate dealer, was born at Benson, Illinois, January 6, 1861, the son of Garret and Teda (Conrad) Casper. Garrett Casper was born at Ostelburg, Aurich, Germany, September 27, 1821, and died at Milford, Illinois, June 24, 1901. He was a carpenter and a farmer. Teda Casper was born at Moorhousen, Eastfresland, Germany, January 26, 1841, and died at Bruning, March 26, 1929. She was the daughter of Dick and Emma (Poppenge) Conrad, who died in the early nineties.

On February 15, 1883, Jacob Casper was united in marriage with Augusta Taddiken, who was born at Wardewarden, Oldenburg, Germany, August 12, 1861. She is the daughter of H. R. and Magerta Taddiken. Mr. and Mrs. Casper have six children, C. J., who is married to Florence Patrow; Robert H., who is married to Agnes Russell; Tracy, who is married to Frank Kreizinger; John, who is married to Maude Niblack; Henry R., who is married to Louise Martin; and Fred W., who is married to Nona Bushnell.

A resident of Nebraska for forty-eight years, Mr. Casper was the justice of the peace in Butler County, for ten years, and has been a farmer and a real estate man, for many years.

He is a Democrat. His religious affiliation is with the American Trinity Lutheran Church at Bruning, Nebraska. He is a life member of the Nebraskana Society. Residence: Bruning.

Albert Thomas Cassel

Albert T. Cassel was born at Nebraska City, Nebraska, February 5, 1870, the son of Job and Mary (Harmon) Cassel. His father, who was a farmer and served as state representative from Otoe County, was born at Attica, Indiana, December 7, 1834, and died at Lincoln, May 8, 1922. His mother was born at New Marlboro, Massachusetts, August 20, 1845, and died at Lincoln, December 29, 1912.

Mr. Cassel attended a country school near Nebraska City until 1886; he was graduated from high school at Nebraska City in 1890; and in 1894 was awarded the S. B. degree at Doane College, Crete, Nebraska. He was a member of the local fraternity, Delta Kappa Pi,

at Doane College. He worked on a farm until 1894 when he became night clerk for the Missouri Pacific Railway Company at Weeping Water, Nebraska. A year later he entered the Bank of Palmyra, at Palmyra, Nebraska, as assistant cashier. He served as assistant cashier of the Farmers Bank at Nebraska City for several years; was assistant cashier of the Anaconda Mines at Butte, Montana for five years; was traveling salesman for the Omaha Packing Company for one year; and was cashier of the Bank of Palmyra for nearly 20 years. He is now treasurer and business manager of Doane College at Crete.

He was united in marriage with Mary Alvira Richards at Lincoln, October 2, 1912. Mrs. Cassel was born at Wabash, Cass County, Nebraska, May 15, 1884. They have two children: Jean R., born October 15, 1913; and Donald Edwin, born August 23, 1915.

During the war Mr. Cassel was chairman of all loan drives at Palmyra. He served as president of the Crete Rotary Club, 1927-28. He is a member of Union Lodge Number 287 of the Masons at Palmyra; 32nd degree Scottish Rite of Lincoln; and Sesostris Temple of the Ancient and Arabic Order of the Nobles of the Mystic Shrine, of Lincoln. His favorite sport is golf. His hobbies are: birds; trees; and landscaping. He is a Republican. He is a member of the First Congregational Church of Crete. Residence: Crete.

David Cassell

For the past 46 years David Cassell has been highly successful as a farmer in Clay County, Nebraska. He was born at Morrison, Illinois, September 17, 1864, the son of James and Isabella (Maxwell) Cassell. His father, a farmer, was born at Dunkirk, Scotland, January 28, 1822, and died at Morrison, March 19, 1882. His mother was born at Dunkirk, September 28, 1828, and died at Ong, November 26, 1908.

Mr. Cassell is a member of the Independent Order of Odd Fellows, and holds membership in the Nebraskana Society. He took an active part in Red Cross drives in Clay County during the World War. His political preference is the Republican party.

He married Maggie Alice Rowlison at Hoxie, Kansas, April 7, 1890. Mrs. Cassell, who was born at Kirksville, Missouri, January 29, 1868, is a descendant of the early American Putnam family. Her great-great-grandfather served in the Revolution, while her father was a Civil War soldier.

To this union the following children were born: Jessie, born February 19, 1891, who married William John Karnatz; James, born April 11, 1892, who married Myrtle Florence Lindburg; Harry, born August 1, 1894, who married Emma Pauline Manning; Leonard, born March 18, 1897, who married Pearl Ruth Swanson; Gladys, born February 7, 1902; Leland, born December 28, 1904; Arthur, born April 14, 1907; Wayne, born December 17, 1909; Mildred, born May 22, 1912. James served in the World War with Company G, 355th Infantry, 89th Division. Leonard served at the Great Lakes Naval Training Station. Residence: Ong.

Waldron Alvin Cassidy

Waldron A. Cassidy, leading physician of Omaha, was born at Shelby, Iowa, April 12, 1895. George Alvin Cassidy, his father, who was born at Rawdon Township, Montcalm, Quebec, September 4, 1859, is a physician. His ancestry is Scotch-Irish. He came to the United States in 1891. Bertha Amelia (Dixon) Cassidy, mother of Waldron A. Cassidy, was born at Pickering, Ontario, May 29, 1867. She was graduated from Alma College in Canada. Her ancestry is Scotch-Irish.

Dr. Cassidy was graduated from the Shelby High School in 1912, and in 1916, was awarded the A. B. degee at the University of Denver, at Denver, Colorado. He re-

ROY LUCAS CASKEY

ceived his M. D. degree at the University of Nebraska, in 1918. He was made a member of Sigma Phi Epsilon, and Nu Sigma Nu.

He was admitted to the practice of medicine at Omaha, June, 1918, and has been engaged in the fields of medicine and education since that date. He was made assistant surgeon in the United States Navy, 1918. He is a member of the firm: Callfas, Potts, Cassidy, Judd and Stokes. He is instructor in oto-laryngology at the University of Nebraska College of Medicine, and has been certified by the American Board of Oto-laryngology.

Dr. Cassidy is the author of the following: *Apparent Pituary Tumor With Restoration of Vision*, March, 1922; *Unusual Circular Lesion of the Retina*, June, 1922; *Acute Retrobulbar Optic Neuritis of Paranasal Sinus Origin*, November, 1925; *Vertigo, Secondary to Paranasal Sinus Infection*, November, 1927; *and Cerebellar Pontile Angle Tumor, With Report of a Case*, March, 1931.

His marriage to Grace Dowling Ketcham was solemnized at Brooklyn, New York, November 18, 1920. Mrs. Cassidy, who is of Scotch-Irish descent, was born at Brooklyn, New York, August 24, 1894. They have a daughter, Gloria Lynn, born June 18, 1925.

Dr. Cassidy took a post graduate course in the United States Naval Medical School the summer of 1918; he was an enterne in the United States Navy Hospital, 1918-20. He is a member of the following professional organizations: Douglas County Medical Society; Nebraska State Medical Society; American Medical Association; Omaha and Council Bluffs Eye and Ear Society; Sioux Valley Eye, and Ear Society; and the Omaha Clinical Club. He is a member of the Omaha Country Club, and is a Republican. Residence: Omaha.

John Laurence Casteel

John Laurence Casteel was born at Randolph, Nebraska, December 17, 1903, the son of William Edgar and Geneva Ann (Bell) Casteel. His father, who was born near Burlington, Iowa, April 5, 1874, is a rural mail carrier. His ancestors followed Daniel Boone into Tennessee and Kentucky, moved from there to Indiana, Illinois, and Iowa, and later came to Nebraska. His mother was born near Taylorsville, Illinois, April 25, 1875; she is descended from early settlers in Indiana, Illinois, and Nebraska.

Professor Casteel was graduated from high school at Randolph, Nebraska, in 1921; in 1927, was awarded the A. B. degree with highest honors at Nebraska Wesleyan University; and in 1929 received his A. M. degree at Northwestern University. During the summer of 1928 he was a student at the University of Nebraska. He was awarded second place in scholarship honors in his college graduating class; was prominent in debating and oratory; and was elected to membership in Phi Kappa Phi; Pi Gamma Mu, Pi Kappa Delta, Delta Sigma Rho, and Delta Omega Phi.

His professional activities are as follows: fellowship in the school of speech of Northwestern University, 1927-28; instructor at Northwestern University, 1928-30; instructor, during the summer sessions, at the Asheville Normal, Asheville, North Carolina, 1929-30. He is now acting head of the department of public speaking at Nebraska Wesleyan University.

Professor Casteel is an Independent, politically. His hobby is writing. He was united in marriage at Lincoln, Lancaster County, Nebraska, June 8, 1929, with Audeline Jean Boughn. Mrs. Casteel was born at Pittsburg, Kansas, May 14, 1907. Residence: Lincoln.

Roy L. Caswell

Roy L. Caswell, who has been a merchant at Wilcox, Nebraska, for the past 13 years, was born in Phillips County, Kansas, August 11, 1889, the son of Arthur G. and Julia Belle (Kesslar) Caswell. His father was born at Mount Sterling, Wisconsin, November 16, 1862, and

his mother was born at Auburn, Illinois, October 18, 1864.

Mr. Caswell is a member of the Independent Order of Odd Fellows, the Nebraskana Society, and the American Legion of Wilcox. He is vitally interested in the economic, political, and religious aspects of our present civilization, and enjoys the radio.

His marriage to Cecille Lucetta Richmond occurred at McDonald, Kansas, June 14, 1914. Mrs. Caswell was born at McDonald, May 10, 1895. They have one son, Robert, born March 4, 1920. Residence: Wilcox.

Willa (Sibert) Cather

Willa Sibert Cather, author, was born in Winchester, Virginia, December 7, 1876, daughter of Charles F. and Mary Virginia (Boak) Cather.

Miss Cather attended the University of Nebraska from which she received the Bachelor of Arts degree in 1895, and the degree of Bachelor of Letters in 1917. In 1924 she was awarded a Bachelor of Letters degree from the University of Michigan, and in 1928 from Columbia University.

From 1897, until 1901, Miss Cather was engaged in newspaper work. She was associate editor of *McClures Magazines* from 1906 until 1912.

Among Miss Cather's contributions to literature are: *April Starlight* (1903); the *Troll Garden* (1905); *Alexander Bridge* (1912); *O Pioneers* (1913); *The Bohemian Girl* (1912); *The Song of the Lark* (1915); *My Antonia* (1918); *Youth and the Bright Medusa* (1920); *One of Ours* (Pulitzer Prize Novel, 1922); *A Lost Lady* (1922); *The Professor's House* (1925); *My Model Enemy* (1926); and *Death Comes for the Archbishop* (1927). Residence: New York.

James Henry Catron

James H. Catron, pioneer farmer and banker of Nebraska City, Otoe County, Nebraska, was born at Nebraska City, March 2, 1872, the son of James Henry and Dora (Ewing) Catron. His father was a farmer, banker, rancher, and freighter in the early days in Nebraska. He was born in Lafayette County, Missouri, December 12, 1832, the son of Dutch parents who came from Holland and homesteaded in Lafayette County, clearing the wild timber and building their own log house. He died at San Antonio, Texas, March 2, 1914.

His mother's parents were among the first settlers in Lafayette County, and she was born there November 15, 1844. She died at Nebraska City, June, 1918.

Mr. Catron received his education in the public schools of Nebraska City, and later attended Drury College, at Springfield, Missouri. As a boy he started to work in the Farmers' Bank of Nebraska City, and in 1890, he opened the Bank of Palmyra, Palmyra, Nebraska, acting as its cashier. He later became president of this institution, and in 1914 was made president of the Farmers' Bank at Nebraska City. He has engaged in commercial apple and cherry growing, farming, ranching, and the wholesale grocery business, aside from his banking activities. At this time he is president of the Farmers Bank, and the Bank of Palmyra.

He was united in marriage with Ruth MacCuaig at Nebraska City. Mrs. Catron was born at Nebraska City, October 31, 1884. Her ancestry is Scotch and English.

Mr. Catron is a Rotarian and a Mason. His chief interest outside of business hours is apple raising and growing fruit trees. Residence: Nebraska City.

Grace Adele Cavanaugh

Grace Adele Cavanaugh, children's librarian at the public library, Wayne, Wayne County, Nebraska, was born at Galesburg, Knox County, Illinois, January 11, 1868, the daughter of Samuel House and Mary Lucinda (Cossite) McMakin. Her father, who was born in Ohio,

June 11, 1835, and died at Wayne, was a decorator; he served in the Illinois Cavalry during the Civil War; his ancestry was Scotch. Her mother was born at Marion, Kentucky, November 29, 1849. Her ancestry is French, and the line has been traced back to Henry II, Duke of Orleans, born in 1519.

Mrs. Cavanaugh was graduated from the Galva High School, and later attended school in Wayne. She was a school teacher for a number of years, but for the past 15 years she has been in library work. She is now children's librarian at the Wayne Public Library.

During the World War she was active in the Red Cross in Wayne County. She is a member of the Douglas King Chapter of the Daughters of the American Revolution, the Order of Eastern Star, and the Nebraskana Society. She served as president of the Wayne Woman's Club in 1923, and now holds membership in the Country Club at Wayne and the Wayne Presbyterian Church. She has been a member of the Eastern Star for the past 32 years. Politically, she is a Republican.

On September 26, 1891, she was married to Daniel Joseph Cavanaugh at Madison, Nebraska. Mr. Cavanaugh, who was employed by the State Highway Commission for many years, was born at Dubuque, Iowa, May 29, 1864, and died at Wayne, June 22, 1930; he was of Irish and French descent. They have one son: Arthur, born July 28, 1892, who married Neva Jane Orr. He conducts a general loan and insurance agency at Wayne. Residence: Wayne.

Yale H. Cavett

For the past 15 years Yale H. Cavett has been prominent as a lawyer and a civic leader at Bayard, Nebraska. He was born at Phillips, Nebraska, August 22, 1891, the son of Thomas Wilson and Martha Lois (Hatch) Cavett. His father, who was born in Indiana, April 23, 1847, is a retired farmer and stock raiser. His mother, whose ancestry is Welsh, was born at Towanda, Illinois, March 26, 1855.

Mr. Cavett was graduated from the Hastings High School in 1912, and in 1916 received the LL. B. degree at the University of Nebraska. He is attorney for the First National Bank of Bayard, was mayor of that city from 1922 to 1924, and is city attorney at the present time. He holds membership in the Nebraska State Bar Association, the Morrill County Bar Association, the Red Cross, and the Nebraskana Society. Mr. Cavett is a 32nd degree, Scottish Rite Mason.

During the late war he served as sergeant in Company A, 355th Infantry, 89th Division, and is now County Commander of the American Legion of which he was formerly post Commander. His hobby is gardening, and his favorite sport is golfing.

On September 21, 1927, he was united in marriage with Clara Juergens at Minatare, Nebraska; she was born at Minatare. Mrs. Cavett is the daughter of Otto and Anna (Kah) Juergens, pioneer residents of Scotts Bluff County, Nebraska. Residence: Bayard.

Glenn Clinton Chadderdon

Glenn Clinton Chadderdon was born at Freedom, Nebraska, May 28, 1892, the son of George Darrow and Sarah (Saulvester) Chadderdon. His father, who was born in Sagamore County, Michigan, January 17, 1859, and died at Curtis, Nebraska, October 4, 1917, was a teacher, serving as county superintendent of schools in Frontier County, Nebraska, 1890-91, and superintendent of public schools at Bartley, Nebraska; he homesteaded in Frontier County in 1885.

His mother, who is active in church work and is a member of the Order of Eastern Star and the Woman's Club, was born at Dewitt, Illinois, October 9, 1869. She is the daughter of Irish and English parents, Mary Ann Gambrel and Nicholas Saulvester.

Mr. Chadderdon was graduated from the Stockville

High School in 1907, was graduated from the Kearney State Teachers College in 1914, and was a student at the University of Nebraska College of Law in 1930. He was valedictorian of the graduating class in high school, was prominent in debating at Kearney State Teachers College, and served as president of the junior and senior classes at the latter institution.

He taught in rural schools in Frontier County during 1908-11, was principal of the schools at Amherst and Wood River, Nebraska, and served as county superintendent of Frontier County schools from 1915-18. In 1911 Mr. Chadderdon had the distinction of teaching in the last sod schoolhouse in Frontier County, in the last year of its existence. He is now general manager and secretary of the Cambridge Motor Company at Cambridge, Nebraska. From 1918 to 1920, he was postmaster at Cambridge.

Mr. Chadderdon was secretary of the Cambridge Rotary Club, 1927-30, was secretary of the Cambridge Board of Education, 1923-30, and at this time is a member of the Southwest Nebraska Historical Society, the Red Cross, Masonic Lodge, and the Cambridge Community Club. He served as president of the Southwest Nebraska District Epworth League of the Methodist Church, 1924-28, acting as treasurer of the summer institute of that organization, and a member of the finance commission of the Nebraska Conference of the Methodist Church, 1924-30. He was a delegate to the Methodist International General Conference at Kansas City, in 1928.

His marriage to Edith May Jesse was solemnized at Carleton, Nebraska, August 29, 1915. Mrs. Chadderdon was born at Ohiowa, Nebraska, October 25, 1893. Their two children are, Darrell Glenn, born August 28, 1917; and Norris Max, born November 28, 1919. Residence: Cambridge.

Albert Bushnell Chain

Albert Bushnell Chain was born at Seward, Nebraska, April 25, 1885, the son of Jacob Mathew Chain and Amelia Frances (Simms) Chain. His father, a pharmacist, was born at Norristown, Pennsylvania, July 2, 1837, of German-Irish parentage, and died at Utica, Seward County, Nebraska, July 17, 1907. His mother was born at Lewistown, Illinois, February 26, 1843, and died at Seward, April 15, 1927. Her ancestors were Scotch and English and several of them were of prominence in the Civil War.

Mr. Chain attended the Seward and Utica, Nebraska, public schools, and was graduated from York High School in 1906. He was a student at the University of Nebraska for three and one half years, and there was a member of Phi Kappa Psi.

From 1913-29, he was owner of a furniture and undertaking business and at present he is part owner of the firm of Chain and Wood. He is connected with the First Trust Company, the Seward Lumber and Fuel Company, is a director of Kay's Petroleum Company and owner of the Chain and Smith Natural Gas Production Company.

He is a past member of Company A of the first Nebraska Infantry. For six years Mr. Chain was a member of the Seward School Board (president 1923 and 1924) and was president of the Library Board for two years. He is affiliated with the Grace Methodist Episcopal Church and is a member of the Young Men's Christian Association. He is a Royal Arch, Scottish Rite, thirty second degree Mason and is a member and president of the Rotary Club (1931-32). He holds membership in the Nebraska Funeral Directors Association and the Seward Chamber of Commerce.

On December 31, 1912, at York, Nebraska, he was united in marriage with Abby Elvira Hall, who was born at Marquette, July 19, 1887. They have three children, Virginia, born January 8, 1918, Priscilla Frances, born February 2, 1920, and John Hardie, born March 1, 1923.

Mechanics and golf are Mr. Chain's chief diversions. Residence: Seward.

Nettie Chain

Nettie Chain was born at Swan Creek, Illinois, August 25, 1871, and has been a resident of Nebraska since 1885. Her father, Archibald T. O'Neall, a farmer and teacher, was born March 1, 1846, and died at Swan Creek, August 11, 1875. Her mother, Elizabeth J. (Hughen) O'Neall, who was a teacher before her marriage, was born March 24, 1848, and died January 5, 1927.

Mrs. Chain, who is active in social and community affairs at York, received her education in the public schools of Illinois, and Seward County, Nebraska. She was a Red Cross worker during the World War, was worthy matron of Grace chapter of the Eastern Star, 1919-20, was past most excellent chief of the Pythian Sisters, 1921, and was noble grand of the Evening Star chapter of the Rebekah Lodge. She is a member of David Bryant chapter of the Daughters of the American Revolution at York, and is affiliated with the First Presbyterian Church.

Her marriage to James H. Chain was solemnized at Lincoln, November 29, 1893. Mr. Chain, who was a merchant, was born at Lewistown, Illinois, September 21, 1868, and died at York, May 31, 1922. They have one daughter, Mabel, born October 19, 1895, who married Clyde A. Little of York; she has two daughters, Jere Louise and Helen Jane Little.

Mrs. Chain is a member of the Benevolent and Protective Order of Does, and the Nebraskana Society. She is a Democrat. Residence: York.

Edward Chaloupka

Edward Chaloupka was born at Wilber, Nebraska, April 5, 1878. He received his elementary education in the Wilber public schools, and was graduated from Wilber High School. He attended Highland Park College at Des Moines, Iowa, and received his M. D. from Creighton University. In 1905, he was admitted to the practice of medicine, and has since been so engaged. He is professor of gynecology and obstetrics at Creighton Medical College.

He is married to Anna Krcma, of Omaha, and has four children. He is a Republican and a member of the Presbyterian Church. He served in the Spanish American War, and during the World War participated in the usual civilian activities. His favorite sports are hunting, fishing and golf. Residence: Omaha.

Guy Cleveland Chambers

Guy C. Chambers, a resident of Nebraska all his life, has been engaged in the practice of law at Lincoln, since 1916. He was born at Sidney, Cheyenne County, Nebraska, July 26, 1891, the son of Charles P. and Susan (Sanderson) Chambers. His father, who was born in Indiana, November 12, 1859, of Scotch and English parentage, is a ranchman in Cheyenne County; he served as county superintendent of schools, 1891-1901; and was county judge, 1915-25. His mother, who was born in Indiana, August 17, 1869, is of Irish and Pennsylvania Dutch ancestry.

Mr. Chambers was graduated from the Sidney High School in 1909; was a student at the Peru State Teachers College, Peru, Nebraska; and in 1916 was granted the LL. B. degree at the University of Nebraska. He was honored by election to Order of the Coif; was varsity debater; Ivy Day orator, 1916; and was made a member of Delta Sigma Rho, Delta Upsilon, and Phi Delta Phi. He has been a member of the faculty of the College of Law at the University of Nebraska since 1923.

On September 24, 1921, his marriage to Grace V. Rood was solemnized at Minneapolis, Minnesota. Mrs. Chambers was born at Omaha, Nebraska, April 5, 1892. Their two children are: Robert, born May 23, 1923; and Susan, born April 25, 1926.

Mr. Chambers taught school at Sunol, Nebraska, 1909; at Danbury, and Indianola, Nebraska, 1910; and at Chap-

pell, Nebraska, where he was principal of schools, 1911-13. In 1916 he served as assistant attorney for the Rock Island Railway Company. He was a member of following law firms at Lincoln: Holmes, Chambers & Mann, 1925; Holmes & Chambers, 1928; and Holmes, Chambers & Holland, and is attorney for Nebraska for the Rock Island Railway Company.

During the World War Mr. Chambers served in the United States Army in France, and has since been commissioned captain of the J. A. G. D. Reserve Corps. He holds membership in the American Bar Association; the Nebraska State Bar Association; the Lancaster County Bar Association; the Lions Club; and the Nebraskana Society. He is affiliated with Holy Trinity Episcopal Church of Lincoln. Residence: Lincoln. (Photograph in Album).

James Chambers

James Chambers was born at Washington, Indiana, April 16, 1855, the son of Robert Chapman and Martha Jane (Harris) Chambers. Robert, the father, was born in North Carolina January 17, 1825, and died at Tarkio, Missouri, April 10, 1883. He was a farmer and stockman of Irish ancestry, and kept the Rockport Landing on the Missouri River, 1867-69. His wife, Martha Jane, was born in Washington, Indiana, January 29, 1834, of German parentage, and died at Tarkio on December 31, 1925.

Mr. Chambers attended rural school near Tarkio, and on December 24, 1876, was united in marriage to Susannah Shackelford at Tarkio. She was born at Marion, Indiana, July 6, 1859, of Scotch-Irish and Dutch parentage, and died at Fairbury on July 30, 1919. To this union five children were born, Lena, on November 23, 1877, who died July 15, 1880; Lela, July 15, 1882, who died July 12, 1884; Pearl, February 7, 1883, who is married to Albert E. Renner; Bessie, October 15, 1885, who is the wife of Delbert L. Boone, and Margaret, born September 13, 1887. Mr. Chambers has six grandchildren.

On April 9, 1881, Mr. Chambers crossed the Missouri River at Brownville, Missouri, on an old steam ferry, with a lumber wagon and a span of horses. He recalls the blizzard of 1888 in which many persons were frozen, and on September 13, 1890, settled on a farm near Fairbury. He experienced the drowth of 1893 when it was necessary to kill the young stock as soon as it was born because there was no feed. In 1894 the year of 10c corn nearly two hundred of his pigs died of the cholera.

Mr. Chambers was the first man to raise army mules for the world market, from 1900 to 1908, and at one time sold ninety mules to I. Bonham for $11,700. Always a cattle feeder, he has sold at least 40,000 head.

It is interesting to note that in 1931 Mr. Chambers crossed the Missouri at the point he crossed in 1881, and found very few changes and improvements had been made during the fifty years which had elapsed.

A Republican, Mr. Chambers was county commissioner for part of one term. Now retired after forty years of active farming and stock raising, he was one of the first three farmers to plant alfalfa in Nebraska, and erected the first hay barn equipped with a track and carrier in Jefferson County. He is a member of the Nebraskana Society. Residence: Fairbury. (Photograph in Album).

Robert Otis Chambers

Robert Otis Chambers, real estate and insurance man, was born at Sidney, Nebraska, May 8, 1889, son of Charles P. and Susan (Sanderson) Chambers. His ancestry is Scotch-Irish, English, Irish and Pennsylvania Dutch.

Upon the completion of his high school education at Sidney, Mr. Chambers attended Alliance Junior Normal School and Chadron State Teachers College.

Mr. Chambers taught school for thirteen years, including seven years as superintendent at Minatare. He was city clerk of Minatare ten years and secretary of the Minatare Volunteer Fire Department. For five years he has served as mayor of Minatare. He is a member of the board of directors of the Pathfinder Irrigation District, and has served as president for a number of years. He is a former president of the State Irrigation Association and Associated Chambers of Commerce of North Platte Valley.

He is a Democrat, and was county chairman of the Democratic County Committee, 1930-1932, and a candidate for secretary of state in 1932. He is a member of the Lions Club, the Odd Fellows, and the Episcopal Church.

On May 29, 1912, he was married to Helen W. Schroeder at Greeley. Mrs. Chambers was born at Alexandria, Minnesota, March 27, 1885. They have four children, Robert E., born February 27, 1913; Frederick C., born March 3, 1914; Dorothy Helen, born January 19, 1917; and Glen D., born September 11, 1919. Residence: Minatare.

Samuel William Chambers

Samuel W. Chambers, one of Nebraska's leading executives, was born at Peru, Nebraska, February 18, 1859, the son of James and Ann (Davidson) Chambers. His father, who was a retired farmer for several years before his death, was born at Cincinnati, Ohio, October 4, 1828, and died at Peru, April 4, 1891; his ancestry was English. His mother, who was of Scotch descent, was born at Cincinnati, August 11, 1826, and died at Rochester, Fulton County, Indiana, February 18, 1871.

Mr. Chambers has lived in Nebraska practically all his life. For over 20 years he served as a railroad agent and operator; and for the past 30 years has been in the real estate loans, banking and building and loan association businesses. He is now secretary-treasurer and director of the Blair Building & Loan Association, at Blair, Nebraska, and is a member of the Blair Chamber of Commerce, the Nebraskana Society, the Masons, and the Modern Woodmen of America. He is affiliated with the Episcopal Church at Blair; is a member of the Red Cross; and holds membership in the Democratic Party.

His marriage to Gertrude Emma Beals was solemnized at Geneva, Nebraska, September 10, 1887. Mrs. Chambers was born at Geneva, September 10, 1870, and died at Blair, January 2, 1930. Her parents were born in Massachusetts. Two children were born to them: Lloyd, born September 2, 1888, who married Bertha Moore, and Mona M., born August 26, 1899, who married Ross E. Deets.

His grandchildren are Dorothy Deets, born January 26, 1920; Dolores Deets, born July 20, 1922; and Billy Chambers nine years of age. Residence: Blair. (Photograph in Album).

George E. Chapman

For the past 30 years Dr. George E. Chapman has been a clergyman in the Presbyterian Church and has been an educator in both religious and academic subjects. He was born in Defiance County, Ohio, October 4, 1870, the son of George W. Chapman and Fannie (Hull) Chapman. His father, who was born in Canada, February 27, 1834, and died in Wisconsin, February 24, 1910, originally lived in Connecticutt and moved to Ohio in the early history of that state; he was a builder.

Fannie (Hull) Chapman, who was descended from the Hulls of Revolutionary fame, was born in St. Lawrence County, New York, in 1841, and died at Spooner, Wisconsin, May 24, 1925. Her family came to America from England early in the history of this country.

Dr. Chapman attended high school in Farmer and Hickville, Ohio, and in 1890 received the B. C. S. degree at Tri-State Normal College in Angola, Indiana. He was

awarded the A. B. degree at Leander Clark (now Coe) College in 1909 and in 1922 received the honorary degree of Doctor of Divinity. He was a member of the Philomathian Society. During the past 25 years Dr. Chapman has been active in religious and educational affairs, chiefly in Iowa and Nebraska, holding the following positions: pastor at Blanchardville, Wisconsin, three years; pastor at Ontario, Wisconsin, two years; instructor at Leander Clark, Toledo, Iowa, six years; pastor at Toledo, 1910-18; pastor First Presbyterian Church at Knoxville, Iowa, 1918-23; secretary of the Chamber of Commerce at Knoxville, 1923-24; pastor of Presbyterian Church at Colfax, Iowa, 1924; and since 1928, pastor of the First Presbyterian Church at Hebron.

At Toledo he served as a member of the school board for several terms. He now holds membership in the Hebron Kiwanis Club, the Red Cross, the Nebraskana Society, and the Nebraska City Presbytery. He is a member of the Hebron Golf Club, while his favorite sport is golfing. His hobby is mechanics.

His marriage to Aimee Cornell was solemnized at Knoxville, Iowa, October 5, 1921. Mrs. Chapman is of German and English descent. To their marriage one child was born; Margaret Carolena, born August 28, 1922, who is in school. Politically, Dr. Chapman is a Republican. Residence: Hebron.

Elwood Blake Chappell

Elwood Blake Chappell, judge of the district court, was born at Osmond, Nebraska, May 4, 1889, son of William Henry and Pleasant May (Turner) Chappell. The father, born in Petersburg, Indiana, July 24, 1867, is a lawyer, has served in the Oklahoma legislature and is now judge of the criminal court of appeals of Oklahoma. The mother was born at De Peyster, New York, August 27, 1869, and died at Lincoln, August 16, 1919.

Judge Chappell received his Bachelor of Laws degree in 1916 and his Bachelor of Arts degree in 1923 from the University of Nebraska, at which he has been a lecturer since 1925. He was associated with T. F. A. Williams in the practice of law 1916-25; was first municipal judge of Lincoln 1925-28, and was made judge of the 3rd judicial district of Nebraska in 1929. He is a Republican.

On April 10, 1918, he was married to Myra May Stenner at Plattsmouth. She was born at Bartley, Nebraska, February 9, 1899. There are three children, True, born June 13, 1919; James, born February 15, 1924; and Mary, born May 11, 1926.

Judge Chappell is a member of the Judge Advocate General's Reserves (captain), the American Legion, the Disabled Veterans of America, the Officers Reserve Corps and the Forty and Eight. He is a member of the First Christian Church, the Chamber of Commerce, the Lions Club, the Masons, the Parent Teachers Association, and the Young Men's Christian Association. His club is the Shrine Club. Residence: Lincoln.

George Washington Chappell

Born at Algiers, Indiana, April 7, 1869, George Washington Chappell is the son of Moses Lane and Nancy Delilah (Freeland) Chappell. His father, who was a farmer, was born at Algiers, in 1822, and died there in August, 1886; he served with Company I, 58th Regiment during the Civil War, and was with Sherman on his march to the sea. His mother was born at Washington, Indiana, and died at Lincoln, April 1, 1911.

Mr. Chappell engaged in farming until 1900, was a rancher from 1900 to 1919, and for the past 13 years has been engaged in the real estate and insurance business in Ainsworth, Nebraska. He was elected to the Nebraska Legislature in 1912 on the Republican ticket, and served as county clerk of Logan County during 1897 and 1898. He is affiliated with the Methodist Episcopal Church, holds membership in the Ainsworth Commercial

Club, and is a member of the Modern Woodmen of America.

His marriage to Hila Virginia Perkins was solemnized at Louisville, Kentucky, November 17, 1904. Mrs. Chappell, who was a teacher in a southern girls' school prior to her marriage, was born in Missouri, December 12, 1874, and died at Omaha, Nebraska, April 19, 1924. They have two children: Kenneth G., born August 2, 1907, who married Frances Williams; and Gladys, born June 9, 1911, who married Urban Hawkins. Residence: Ainsworth.

James Robinson Chappell

One of the leading members of the dental profession in Nebraska, James Robinson Chappell was born at Minden, September 20, 1892. His parents, both natives of Indiana, were pioneer settlers of the state. McLeod Washington Chappell, his father, was born in Petersburg, Pike County, Indiana, in 1853, of pre-Revolutionary ancestry. His father was a captain in the Civil War, and he was a lumberman, his death occurring at Minden, Nebraska, in 1925. Nancy Ann Arthur, wife of McLeod Washington Chappell, was born in Washington, Daviess County, Indiana, August 12, 1860, of early Colonial ancestry.

Dr. Chappell was graduated from Minden High School in 1911, and received his degree of Doctor of Dental Surgery from Lincoln Dental College, which is now a part of the University of Nebraska, in 1917. He is a member of Delta Sigma Delta and the Palladian Literary Society.

Since July, 1917, Dr. Chappell has been in active practice, and was a member of the dental firm of Drs. Hopfer and Chappell at Minden for five years; since 1922 he has practiced at Hastings. His professional memberships include the American Dental Association, the Northwestern District Dental Society, of which he has served as president, vice president and secretary, and the Nebraska State Dental Society of which he has been delegate to the council.

On August 22, 1922, Dr. Chappell was married to Blanche Eathel Weeks at Hastings. They have two sons: James Carroll, born May 30, 1924; and William Robinson, born April 23, 1928. The family attends the First Methodist Episcopal Church at Hastings, while Dr. Chappell is also a member of the Chamber of Commerce, the Lions International, the Masons, the Young Men's Christian Association, and The Nebraskana Society. Residence: Hastings.

James Vaclav Charvat

James V. Charvat was born at Psany, Bohemia, September 21, 1887, the son of Vaclav and Ana (Fronkova) Charvat. His father, who was the manager of a large estate in Bohemia, was born at Divice, in 1844, and died at Smolnice, Bohemia, April 5, 1931; he was active in the struggle for religious tolerance under the Austrian rule, serving in the war of 1866. His mother, whose parents were farmers, was born at Divice, in 1848, and died at Smolnice, February 9, 1910.

Mr. Charvat attended rural and high school in Bohemia, where he was graduated in 1904, and was a student at Lincoln Business College, Lincoln, Nebraska, 1913-14. He has been a type-setter, farm hand, bank clerk, bank executive, real estate and insurance man, and notary. A Democrat, he served as village justice of the peace at Milligan.

He is chairman of the Sokol Athletic Organization, is a member of the Nebraskana Society, and holds membership in the Milligan Chamber of Commerce of which he was chairman in 1929. He was reared in the Catholic Church, later joined the Methodist Episcopal Church, and finally decided that one church should prevail among all civilized nations. During the war he served as first class private, First Gunner Battery D, 72nd Artillery, and was in overseas service during 1918-19. Prior to his enlistment he was a member of the Home Guard and was active in Liberty Loan drives and Red Cross affairs.

He is a member of the American Legion Post 240 at Milligan, of which he was Commander in 1927.

Mr. Charvat's hobby is reading historical, political, and economic works. He married Christine Bernasek at Oklahoma City, Oklahoma, November 24, 1924. Mrs. Charvat was born at Milligan, April 2, 1885. They have a daughter, Venus Christine, born August 23, 1925. Residence: Milligan.

Clinton Chase

Clinton Chase, distinguished judge of the district court of Stanton County, Nebraska, has lived in this state all his life and for many years has been prominent in political and civic affairs in his community. He was born at Papillion, Nebraska, July 29, 1878, the son of John Nelson and Mary (Miller) Chase. His father, who was born at Plattsburg, New York, April 1, 1827, and died at Papillion, March 6, 1918, was a farmer in Sarpy County for many years and served as county commissioner and representative to the state legislature of Nebraska. His ancestry was English.

His mother, who was a teacher in public schools before her marriage, was born at Long Point, Illinois, October 4, 1841, and died at Papillion, September 13, 1921. She was of English and German descent.

Judge Chase was a student at the University of Nebraska where he received both a general education and law work, and in 1906, received the LL. B. degree there. A Democrat, he served Stanton County as county attorney, 1909-13, and since 1924, has been judge of the 9th Judicial District. He holds membership in the State Bar Association, the 9th Judicial District Bar Association, the Stanton Commercial Men's Club, and the Red Cross. He is a member of the Nebraskana Society, Masons, Elks, and Knights of Pythias.

His marriage to Minnie Van Housen was solemnized at Omaha, May 11, 1910. Mrs. Chase whose ancestry is Scotch and Holland Dutch, was born at Schuyler, Nebraska, September 19, 1886. Their children are: Jeanette Mae, born March 21, 1914; and Gale Jane, born January 19, 1921.

Judge Chase is interested in reading philosophy and biography. His favorite sport is golfing. Residence: Stanton.

F. Pearl Chase

F. Pearl Chase, educator and clubwoman at Johnstown, Nebraska, has been a resident of this state all her life. She was born at Johnstown, November 24, 1888, the daughter of Byron M. and Annie M. (Golden) Chase. Her father, who was a farmer, was born at Virogua, Wisconsin, May 15, 1856, and died at Johnstown, March 6, 1919; his ancestry was English. Her mother, a teacher for many years, was born at Russel, Kentucky, January 28, 1857, of English and German extraction.

Miss Chase attended a rural school until 1900, was graduated from the academy at Grand Island, Nebraska, in 1908, and received her A. B. degree in 1912 at Grand Island College. She was awarded the A. M. degree at Grand Island College in 1914, and later attended summer school at the University of Colorado.

She is a member of the Royal Neighbors of America and the Baptist Church of Polk, Nebraska. She was formerly an active member of the Young Women's Christian Association, and is now a member of the Ainsworth Woman's Club. Her chief recreations are reading and hiking. She is independent politically. Residence: Johnstown.

Leon Wilson Chase

Leon Wilson Chase, one of Nebraska's leading business executives, has lived in Nebraska for the past 46 years. He was born at Jacksonville, Vermont, August 27, 1877, the son of Fred Wilson and Anna (Murdock) Chase. His father, a farmer, was born at Jacksonville,

June 16, 1853, and died at Pawnee City, Nebraska, November 28, 1926; in 1922, he was awarded the certificate of honor from the University of Nebraska, for distinguished service to agriculture in Nebraska; he was a direct descendant of Aquilla Chase, who was born in England, in 1618; he has traced his ancestry to Revolutionary soldiers through three distinct lines.

Anna (Murdock) Chase, mother of Leon, was born at Whitingham, Vermont, June 9, 1856, and is still living. She is descended from pre-Revolutionary stock in America.

Mr. Chase was graduated from the Pawnee City High School, and in 1904 received the B. S. degree in mechanical engineering at the University of Nebraska. He holds an honorary M. E. degree granted by the University of Nebraska, and the degree of Agricultural Engineering from Ames University. He is a member of Sigma Xi and Sigma Tau, Alpha Zeta, and is an honorary member of the Farm House.

He served as professor of agricultural engineering at the University of Nebraska, 1905-20. In 1919 he organized the Chase Plow Company at Lincoln, Nebraska, and has been president and manager of this organization since that time. He is the author of numerous newspaper and magazine articles, and is joint author of *Farm Machinery and Farm Motors.* He served as major in the ordnance department of the United States Army during the World War, and is now lieutenant-colonel of the Ordnance Reserves. He holds membership in the Sons of the American Revolution, the American Legion, and the Reserve Officers Association.

Mr. Chase is a member of the Lincoln Chamber of Commerce; the Nebraskana Society; the University Club; the Lincoln Country Club; and the Polemic Club. His professional organizations include: Lincoln Engineers Club; and the American Society of Agricultural Engineers. He is affiliated with the Second Presbyterian Church of Lincoln.

Mr. Chase is a charter member of the American Society of Agricultural Engineers, (past president and past secretary); treasurer of the Nebraska Manufacturers Association, vice president of the National Association of Farm Equipment Manufacturers; and a former member of the American Society of Mechanical Engineers; the Society for the Promotion of Engineering Education; and the Society of Automotive Engineers.

He was united in marriage at Logan, Harrison County, Iowa, August 16, 1905, with Susan Mills Barnhart. Mrs. Chase, who is of Revolutionary descent, was born at Logan, April 15, 1877. Four children were born to this marriage: Fred M., born August 6, 1906; Frances, born August 5, 1908, who died February 13, 1913; Eleanor, born August 5, 1917; and Suzannah Leona, born March 15, 1914.

Mr. Chase is a Republican, politically. He is interested in all of out door sports, especially golfing. Residence: Lincoln.

Susan Barnhart Chase

Susan Barnhart Chase was born at Logan, Iowa, the daughter of John Willis and Susan Mills (Hicks) Barnhart. Her father, who was born in Herkimer County, Pennsylvania, November 30, 1837, and died at St. Paul, Minnesota, March 18, 1899, was a lawyer; he was graduated from the University of Michigan law department; his ancestry was German on the paternal side and English through the maternal line. Her mother was born at Saratoga, New York, September 10, 1840; she received her education at a young ladies' seminary at Ann Arbor, and was one of the charter members of the Women's Foreign Missionary Society of the Presbyterian Church. Her father's ancestors were English Quakers while her mother was descended from the Wheeler family which came from England, in 1658.

Mrs. Chase was graduated from the High School at Minneapolis, in 1899, after attending the public schools

of Logan, Iowa. In 1905, she received an A. B. degree at the University of Nebraska, where she was a member of the Palladian Literary Society. She has been a homemaker and school instructor for many years, and has held the following professional positions: teacher in rural schools in Iowa; fifth grade teacher at Logan; high school teacher at Ida Grove; German teacher at the University of Nebraska during her senior year there.

Her marriage to Leon Wilson Chase was solemnized at Logan, August 16, 1905. Mr. Chase was born at Jacksonville, Windham County, Vermont, August 27, 1877; his English ancestors fought in the Revolution. He is manager of the Chase Plow Company at Lincoln. Of the four children born to this union, three are living. They are: Fred, born August 6, 1906; Leona, born March 15, 1914; and Eleanor, born August 5, 1917. Frances, born August 5, 1908, died February 13, 1913.

Mrs. Chase is a member of the Daughters of the American Revolution and the American Legion Auxiliary. She is a member of the board of directors of the Young Women's Christian Association; has been a member of the Lincoln Board of Education since 1925; and holds membership in the Parent-Teachers' Association. She is affiliated with the Second Presbyterian Church of Lincoln; is a member of the P. E. O. and of the Nebraskana Society. Politically, she is an independent Republican. Residence: Lincoln.

Anna M. Chatburn

Anna M. Chatburn, homemaker and clubwoman, was born at Plattsmouth, Nebraska, August 27, 1865, daughter of Michael Bennett and America Anne (Baker) Murphy. Her father, who was a native of Ireland, born September 18, 1834, died at Long Beach, California, September 16, 1913. A harness maker by trade, he later engaged in the mercantile business and as a railway postal clerk, in the last mentioned capacity making the first through run on the Union Pacific from Omaha to Ogden, Utah. Michael Bennett was the son of Robert and Catherine (Barry) Bennett. Robert was the son of John and Catherine Barry the daughter of John and Nellie (Emmens) Barry, all of Ireland.

America Anne Murphy was born at Ottumwa, Iowa, February 24, 1840, and died at Plattsmouth, Nebraska, September 23, 1865. She was the daughter of William L. Baker, born March 19, 1817, who died March 16, 1878, and his wife, Sallie L. Higdon, born March 26, 1813, and who died December 30, 1861. They were married September 13, 1838. Sallie was the daughter of Gabriel and Rebecka Davis, who was born in 1793. Their marriage took place about 1810. Gabriel Higdon was born in 1789 and died about 1860. He was the son of Joseph Higdon, born June 18, 1759, and who died on February 6, 1836.

Tradition places Gabriel Higdon as a soldier in the War of 1812. Joseph Higdon was a soldier in the Revolution as a private and corporal of cavalry in the Virginia militia. He removed to Kentucky soon after the Revolution and received a pension January 13, 1834, of $110.00 per month at which time he was seventy-five years old.

William L. Baker was a son of Josias Baker, born April 8, 1793, who died January 6, 1853, and Polly Gillock, who was born May 19, 1795, and died June 6, 1845. Josias Baker (1) was the son of Josias Baker and his wife, Elizabeth Herndon. The last named Josias was the son of a Josias Baker, who was a soldier in the French and Indian War under Colonel George Washington. Polly Gillock was the daughter of Lawrence Gillock (probably a soldier in the Revolution) and his wife, Elizabeth.

Rebecka Davis, above mentioned, was the daughter of Isham Davis and Winneford Woodward. A pension was granted to Isham Davis on application made out October 10, 1832; and later one was granted to his widow on application executed April 22, 1843. The pension

ANNA M. CHATBURN

Townsend--Lincoln

record shows they had children, but their names were not given.

Anna Chatburn attended the Plattsmouth Schools, afterward teaching five years in these schools, and had about ten years work in Chautauqua reading courses. She is an honorary member of Phi Omega Pi, University of Nebraska. She was married to George Richard Chatburn at Plattsmouth, July 21, 1889, (See *Nebraskana*). There were three children born to their union, Mary Frances, born April 6, 1891, who is director of music for the City of Springfield, Illinois, and in charge of school music for the Parent-Teacher Association for the State of Illinois; Alice, born August 2, 1897, died ugust 3, 1897; George Richard, born September 9, 1900, is head geologist in the organization of Mr. Tom Johnson of Wichita, Kansas.

Mrs. Chatburn is a Republican, and for the past fifteen years has served as precinct committeewoman; several times she has been a delegate to county and state conventions. During the World War she was active in Red Cross, and is now a member of that organization and the Community Chest. During the years 1921-22 and 1922-23 she was president of the Lincoln Woman's Club, and served as first president of the Lincoln Parent-Teachers Association, which was the first of its kind in the city. A member of the Order of Eastern Star, she served as Worthy Matron of Electa Chapter No. 8 in 1912; Grand Lecturess in 1926, and district supervisor for several years. She is a member of the Nebraskana Society, the Nebraska Pioneers, Native Sons and Daughters, and the Daughters of the American Revolution. Her religious affiliation is with the Second Presbyterian Church. Residence: Lincoln. (Photograph on Page 233).

George Richard Chatburn

George Richard Chatburn, since 1894, a member of the faculty of the University of Nebraska, was born near Magnolia, Harrison County, Iowa, December 24, 1863. He is the son of Jonas Wellington and Mary (Burton) Chatburn, the former of whom was born at Clitherow, Lancashire, England, March 11, 1821. Jonas Wellington Chatburn attended a private school in England and at the age of 14 was apprenticed to a calico printer, serving seven years. He did not like the trade, as printing at that time was done by the use of blocks. However, he used his inventive faculties and made a model of a rotary printer, which he left in the shop when he came to America in 1844. When he visited England 29 years later he found nearly all the calico and wall paper being printed by just such a cylindrical press.

At about the age of 21 Mr. Chatburn became interested in the Chartist movement, and he with others decided to emigrate to America. With his wife and two children he embarked for the United States in a sailing vessel, and after a three months' trip landed practically penniless in America. After about six years in Philadelphia they decided to come west, traveling to Pittsburgh by rail, then by boat down the Ohio and up the Mississippi and Missouri to Council Bluffs, then known as Kanesville. After a momentous trip they arrived at their destination and Mr. Chatburn went into the hills and squatted upon a small parcel of land. After farming this for three years he removed to Harrison County, Iowa. While living near Council Bluffs between his farming activities he did some carpenter work and erected several grist mills, which were among the first in Iowa. From 1853, when he moved to Harrison County, until his death at Harlan, Iowa, on March 31, 1902, Mr. Chatburn was the owner and operator of various mills, the last of which, erected shortly after 1867 was known as the Harlans Flouring Mills, a landmark throughout the whole of western Iowa.

The family of Jonas Chatburn was English; one of his grandfathers was a soldier in India, Spain and at the Battle of Waterloo under the Duke of Wellington.

Mary Burton, wife of Jonas, was born in Wiswell, Lancashire, England, July 26, 1821. In addition to her duties as a wife and mother she was noted for her skill as a nurse and her willingness to assist in all kinds of sickness. The Burton family according to tradition, lost their land through confiscation during one of the English wars.

George R. Chatburn, son of this notable couple, attended elementary schools at and near Harlan, Iowa, from 1868 to 1876, and in 1880 was graduated from the Harlan High School. He attended Iowa State College 1880-84, receiving a B.C.E. on the last mentioned date, and in 1907, was awarded an M. A. from the University of Nebraska. In 1910 he was given the degree of C. E. from Iowa State College. His honors include Sigma Xi, Phi Kappa Phi, Sigma Tau, Acacia (charter membership at Nebraska) and selection as a junior orator during his junior year in college. In 1928 he was made a doctor of engineering by Iowa State College.

Of his marriage to Anna Murphy three children were born, two of whom are living (See *Nebraskana*).

A member of the Republican party, Mr. Chatburn was precinct chairman from 1916-1930. As a young man he worked in his father's mill and on his father's farm. From 1884 to 1885 he taught in the district schools of Shelby County, Iowa, and from 1891-94 was principal at Plattsmouth. From 1889-91, he was superintendent of Humboldt public schools, and from 1891-94 served as superintendent of the Wymore city schools.

From 1894 to 1905, he was instructor and adjunct professor of mathematics and civil engineering at the University of Nebraska; from 1905, to the present time he has been associate professor and professor of applied mechanics, and head of the department of applied mechanics and engineering drawing. During 1926-27, he served as dean of men. Especially active in committee work, he was chairman of the University Scholarship committee from its inception until 1930, and chairman of the Student Loan committee from 1920 to 1931. For several years he was chairman of the Student Organization committee, and from 1901 to 1931, was chairman of the Scholarship committee of the Engineering College.

During the World War, Mr. Chatburn was regularly enlisted in the Nebraska Home Guards and was discharged at the close of the war. He was also active in the organization of the Student Army Training Corps, and when this was taken over by the government, and the name changed to Reserve Officers Training Corps, all of the students became soldiers in the United States Army. Military drill was in charge of U. S. Army officers, while the work of instruction was left with the college. Scholastic instruction under Dean Ferguson was given to Mr. Chatburn.

Although a Christian in the broad sense of a belief in Christ, he is not a member of any church, but has attended Second Presbyterian Church at Lincoln with Mrs. Chatburn, who is a member.

He is a charter member of the American Interprofessional Institute, the Nebraskana Society, the Nebraska State Historical Society, Red Cross, Community Chest, American Association for the Advancement of Science, Nebraska Academy of Sciences, American Association of University Professors, Nebraska School Masters Club, etc. Since 1909, he has been a member of the Society for the Promotion of Engineering Education, and has held the following offices: president, 1916-17; vice president, 1915-16; member of council, 1912.

His secret and fraternal organizations include membership in Lincoln Lodge No. 19, Ancient Free and Accepted Masons (worshipful master, 1911-12); Royal and Select Masters, Lincoln Council No. 4; Lincoln Chapter No. 6, Royal Arch Masons; Mt. Moriah Commandery No. 4, Knights Templar (eminent commander 1912-13); Ancient and Accepted Scottish Rite Masons, 33rd degree (commander council 1922-23); Ancient Arabic Order

Townsend––Lincoln

GEORGE RICHARD CHATBURN

Nobles of the Mystic Shrine (potentate of Sesostris Temple, 1918-19; imperial representative, 1918); Order of Eastern Star, Electa Chapter No. 8 (worthy patron, 1908-09; grand patron of Nebraska, 1914-15); Veteran Masons Organization of Nebraska.

Dr. Chatburn is interested in good roads, and is fond of reading. His club is the University. Residence: Lincoln. (Photograph on Page 235).

Orville Chatt

Orville Chatt, son of John William and Mary Ellen (Harris) Chatt, was born in Tekamah, Nebraska, December 3, 1893, and for the past fifteen years has been active in the legal and political life of Tekamah. His father was born at Highland, Wisconsin, December 9, 1849, and died at Enid, Oklahoma, February 12, 1916. A farmer and stockman, his ancestry was entirely English. Mary Ellen, his wife, was born at Avoca, Wisconsin, July 30, 1858, of Scotch-Irish descent, and is living.

Mr. Chatt was graduated from Tekamah High School in 1910, and received his A. B. from Phillips University in 1913. Active in dramatics and debate he is a member of Phi Delta Phi and Phi Gamma Delta. He attended the University of Nebraska, receiving his LL. B. in 1916, and his J. D. in 1917. During 1910, '11 and '12 he played baseball, tennis and football at Phillips, and 1914, '15 and '16 played tennis at the University of Nebraska.

Since his admission to the bar Mr. Chatt has been in active practice and served as county attorney 1917-19, and county judge 1921-28. He is secretary-treasurer of the Tekamah Investment Company at the present time. A sergeant first class, in Air Service Headquarters in the World War, he is a member of the American Legion and a first lieutenant in the United States Reserves. He is a 32nd degree Mason, a member of the Lions Club and the Community Club, and is affiliated with the Methodist Episcopal Church of Tekamah. His professional memberships include the Nebraska State and Burt County Bar Associations.

On June 3, 1919, he was united in marriage to Willa Harbert at Ada, Oklahoma. Mrs. Chatt, who is of English descent, was born at Sherman, Texas, March 30, 1893. They have one son, John Orville, born November 17, 1925. Residence: Tekamah.

William Beverly Cheek

William Beverly Cheek was born at Indianapolis, Indiana, November 22, 1862. His father, Omer Tousey Cheek, was a railroad builder, born at Cincinnati, Ohio, in 1840. He was a soldier in the Civil War, and a descendant of Sir John Cheek, the American branch of whose family came to Virginia, in 1698. Omer Cheek married Mary Robeson, who was a native of England, of the family of Lord Beverly. She was born June 3, 1840, and died at Omaha, August 10, 1912. Omer Tousey Cheek died at Kansas City, Missouri, January 9, 1912.

William Beverly Cheek was graduated from public school in 1877, and attended Wabash College, Crawfordsville, Indiana, from 1877 to 1879. From 1883 to 1914, he was with the Chicago, Burlington and Quincy Railroad as train dispatcher, agent and general agent, resigning to become manager of the western department of the Hartford Fire Insurance Company. He is a stockholder in several Nebraska corporations.

On March 25, 1884, he was united in marriage with Mamie Murray of Hamilton, Ohio. Mrs. Cheek was born May 23, 1862, and her parents came from Scotland, in 1850. They have two children: Mabel, born May 30, 1885, married Eugene Arnold Rose; William Harrison, born May 8, 1888, married Merle Cooper. Both Mr. Cheek's son and his son-in-law are engaged in the live stock business at Omaha.

Mr. Cheek was chairman of the stock yard district of Omaha, for the sale of Liberty bonds during the World War. A member of Wheeler Memorial Presbyterian Church, he has been an elder since 1918. He was a member and president of the Omaha School Board from 1899-1901, and member of the Omaha Library Board from 1902-08. He is one of the foremost members of the Chamber of Commerce, and is chairman of the public highways committee. He is a director of the Omaha Auto Club and of the American Automobile Association, and vice president of the Nebraska Good Roads Association.

He is a member of the Elks and of the Kiwanis Club, and is the builder and organizer of Lakewood Country Club. He enjoys golf, but his hobbies are reading and the good road movement. He is a Democrat. Residence: Omaha.

Luke Henry Cheney

Luke Henry Cheney, lawyer, was born at Randolph, New York, June 27, 1864, son of Matthew Benjamin and Lucy (Stanley) Cheney.

The father born in Kiantone, New York, May 20, 1839, was a farmer and a miner in California from August, 1855, until August, 1860. He served as captain of Company G, 154th New York Volunteer Infantry, and was state senator from Lancaster County, Nebraska, from 1879 until 1881. His death occurred at Lincoln, July 5, 1915. The Cheney family came from England to Massachusetts in 1634. Ebenezer Cheney, great grandfather of Luke Henry Cheney, was a Revolutionary soldier.

Lucy Stanley was born in Randolph, New York, May 29, 1835, and died at Lincoln, January 5, 1911. She was of English descent, and her grandfather, Joseph Stanley, was a soldier in the Revolution.

Educated first in country school, Mr. Cheney next attended Latin school then called preparatory at the University of Nebraska, there he received his Bachelor of Arts degree in 1887. He received his Bachelor of Laws degree in 1889 from the University of Michigan, and in the same year was admitted to the bar of both Michigan and Nebraska. A Republican, he was county attorney of Frontier County, 1899-1909, 1918-1923, city attorney of McCook, 1926-27, 1931-32; and secretary of the Frontier County Fair 1897-1917.

Mr. Cheney has resided in Nebraska since September 1, 1870. He came first to Lincoln, and in 1891 removed to Frontier County. Since 1923 he has been a resident of Red Willow County.

On November 14, 1894, he was married to Clara Maud Vance at Laurens, Iowa. Mrs. Cheney was born at State Center, Iowa, March 23, 1875. Her father, William Vance, was a Canadian, a lieutenant in the 75th Illinois Volunteer Infantry during the Civil War. Her mother, Jennie Bradbury, was a native of Maine, of English descent. Mr. and Mrs. Cheney have three children living and one deceased: Dorothy, born September 8, 1895, is married to Ray F. Powers; Matthew Vance, born ugust 16, 1897, died October 18, 1909; Newel S., born February 13, 1902; and Wendell P., born August 15, 1909. All were born at Stockville.

In 1885 Mr. Cheney joined the Nebraska National Guard and received the commission of first lieutenant, Company D, First Regiment. He was captain of the same company during 1887 and 1888 at Lincoln. During the World War he was secretary of Frontier County Council of Defense, director of War Saving Division of Frontier County, chairman of the coal committee and a member of the draft committee. He is the director at the present time of the Associated Charities, a member of the Chamber of Commerce, the 14th Judicial District Bar Association, the Nebraska State Bar Association, and the American Bar Association. His religious affiliation is with the Congregational Church of McCook. He is a member of McCook Board of Education (1925 to date), and in 1924 was president of the University of Nebraska Club at McCook.

Mr. Cheney is a member of the Modern Woodmen of America; the Elks; the Ancient Free and Accepted Masons (past master); Royal Arch Masons (high priest); a member of Sesostris Temple of the Shrine at Lincoln; the Order of Eastern Star (past patron); St. John's Commandery No. 16 of the Knights Templar (past eminent commander); Royal and Select Masters (past thrice illustrious master). He is a member of the Southwest Nebraska Historical Society, the Nebraska State Historical Society, and the Nebraskana Society. Residence: McCook.

Abner Kenneth Chestem

A farmer and stockman since 1919, Abner Kenneth Chestem was born at Decatur, Nebraska, May 13, 1892, son of O. A. and Valborg Chestem. His father, who was born in Norway, in 1866, is a retired farmer. His mother, also a native of Norway, died at Decatur, November 17, 1907.

Mr. Chestem was graduated in 1915 from the University of Nebraska School of Agriculture, and from 1915-17, was a steward at the State Hospital at Kearney. From then until the World War he was employed by a potash company at Hoffland, Nebraska, when he entered the service. He held the rank of sergeant in the 355th Infantry, and participated in the St. Mihiel and Argonne engagements.

In 1919, he returned to Nebraska where he has been engaged as a farmer and stockman. He is a director and president of the Burt County Co-operative Oil Company, a director of the Farm Bureau and president of the Farmers Union, Local No. 500. Since 1925 he has been a school director, and also serves as a member of the executive committee of the American Legion. He is a Master Mason and member of the Royal Arch body. His sport is hunting and his hobby marksmanship.

On August 10, 1916, he was married to Frances I. Foltz at Kearney. Mrs. Chestem, who was a trained nurse prior to her marriage, was born in Lancaster County, Pennsylvania. There are four daughters, Olena, born May 29, 1918; Mary, born December 29, 1919; Martha, born April 9, 1923, and Ruth, born September 3, 1926. Residence: Tekamah.

Emil Gottfrid Chinlund

One of the outstanding clergymen of Nebraska is Emil Gottfrid Chinlund who has been in the ministry for the past 32 years. He was born at Chicago, Illinois, January 18, 1872, the son of Charles Gustaf and Charlotta Wilhelmina (Nelson) Chinlund. His father, who was connected with the Engberg-Holmberg Publishing Company of Chicago for a number of years, was born at Hossna, Sweden, September 4, 1849, and died at Chicago, June 8, 1918. His mother was born at Bjurback, Sweden, April 24, 1851.

Dr. Chinlund received his elementary education in the public schools of Chicago, was graduated from Augustana College with the A. B. degree in 1896, and was a student at the University of Nebraska from 1902 to 1905. He was awarded the degree Doctor of Sacred Theology in 1922. At this time he is director of the Immanuel Deaconess Institute at Omaha, Nebraska, and is editor of the *Deaconess Banner.*

He holds membership in the Omaha Chamber of Commerce, the Fellowship Club, the Ministerial Union, the Augustana Historical Society, the Young Men's Christian Association, and the Nebraskana Society. He is especially interested in music.

His marriage to Alma Josephine Swenson occurred at Chicago, October 30, 1901. Mrs. Chinlund, whose ancestry is Swedish, was born at Chicago, September 24, 1871. Dr. Chinlund is a member of the Red Cross and the Republican party. Residence: Omaha.

Robert Ellsworth Chittick

Robert Ellsworth Chittick, druggist and postmaster at Stuart, was born in Muscatine County, Iowa, July 12, 1867, son of James and Jennie (Rosemann) Chittick. The father, born in Ohio, in 1835, died at Stuart, Iowa, January 12, 1925. He was a farmer of Irish descent. His mother, born in Ohio, in 1835, died at Stuart, Iowa, July 7, 1903. She was of German descent.

Mr. Chittick attended public school in Stuart, Iowa, being graduated from high school in May, 1884. He later attended Simpson College where he was a member of Alpha Tau Omega. For the past forty-one years he has been engaged in the drug business at Stuart. He is president of the Stuart Farmers Co-operative Creamery. He is a Republican, and has served as treasurer of Holt County, in addition to being postmaster.

On July 7, 1891, he was married to Sarah Lorena Sturdevant at Atkinson. She was born at Mead, November 8, 1872, and was a teacher prior to marriage. There are six children, Martin B., born April 18, 1892; Robert E., Jr., born November 26, 1893; Florence L., born December 6, 1898; Rupert A., born October 5, 1900; Ethel C., born February 5, 1909; and Ralph J., born May 28, 1912. Four are registered pharmacists, while one is a physician.

A member of the school board for the past twenty-five years, Mr. Chittick is serving his fourth year as its president. He is a Methodist, a Mason and a life member of the Nebraskana Society. Residence: Stuart.

Waldo Christensen

A life time resident of Lyons, Nebraska, Waldo Christensen was born there July 29, 1883, and for the past 20 years has been engaged in farming. His father, Chris Christensen, was born in Denmark, December 27, 1841. On the 4th of July, 1867, he walked with Ole Larson from Omaha and each of them took up a homestead on the same section in Bell Creek Township, six miles east of Lyons. He still owns the farm. His mother was born in Denmark, October 24, 1851, and died at Boise, Idaho, August 8, 1918.

Mr. Christensen attended the district school in Burt County where he was graduated in 1896. He attended Lyons High School for two years, and was a student at the school of Agriculture of the University of Nebraska for three years. In 1910 he received the A. B. degree at Midland College. He received college letters in football, basketball, and baseball, at Midland College. He served as justice of the peace in Logan Township, 1922-24, and 1930-32.

He was united in marriage with Dora Clementine Young at Craig, Nebraska, January 18, 1911. Mrs. Christensen was born at Craig, September 2, 1885. Her paternal grandparents moved from Columbus, Ohio, in a covered wagon in 1856, and were among the first settlers in Burt County. They had the first white child born in that part of the country. Her father, Andrew Young, was a year old baby when he came to Burt County; he lived there 71 years, and was vitally interested in stories of the pioneer days and the old settlers. He died in 1927.

They have five children: Ruth Ione, born February 2, 1912, who is a sophomore at Midland College; Gladys Irene, born April 10, 1915; Paul Eldred, born April 5, 1918; Eleanor Marie, born August 3, 1920; and Franklin, born August 24, 1924.

Mr. Christensen is a member of The Nebraskana Society. Since 1928 he has been superintendent of the Sunday School of the Divide Center Presbyterian Church; he was Sunday School teacher from 1911 to 1928; and has been an elder in the church since 1928. His sports include basketball, baseball, and football. His hobby is cattle feeding. Residence: Lyons.

BURTON WHITFORD CHRISTIE

Burton Whitford Christie

Burton W. Christie, physician and educator is a native of Creston, Iowa. He was born August 22, 1877, son of William Henry and Sarah Maria (Whitford) Christie. His father, also a physician, was a veteran of the Civil War. He came to Omaha in 1887, and was professor of internal medicine at the University of Nebraska Medical College. He also served as president of the Omaha School Board. His ancestors came to America prior to the Revolution and were represented both in that war and the Mexican War. William Henry Christie died at Omaha, June 10, 1909.

Sarah Whitford Christie was born in Johnsons Grove, Illinois, March 7, 1848, and taught school in Illinois before her marriage. She was president of the Omaha Women's Relief Corps for many years prior to her death on January 5, 1905. She was of English and Scotch descent, her ancestors having come to the United States prior to the Revolution. She was descended from the well known Carpenter and Conklin families.

Upon his graduation from Omaha High School in 1895, Dr. Christie entered the University of Nebraska, receiving his B. Sc. degree in 1899 and his M. D. in 1902. He ranked first in scholarship in his medical graduating class in 1902. While at the university he was active as a tennis player. He is a member of Phi Kappa Psi and Phi Rho Sigma.

On June 24, 1902 he was married to Florence Lois Gridley at Omaha. Mrs. Christie was born at Friend, Nebraska, May 17, 1879, and is descended from the noted family of Admiral Gridley. There are four children, Page, born October 25, 1903, who married Marguerite Tamisea; Barbara, born December 27, 1905, who married Eldon Kiffin; Florance, born October 29, 1907, who married Dale Thornton Segrist; and Billy Burton, born July 19, 1915.

Dr. Christie has been in practice since 1902. He is the author of a monograph *Anterior-polio-myelo-encephalitis* (1917). From 1902 to 1922 he was assistant professor of pediatrics at the University of Nebraska, and in 1913 was president of the Omaha-Douglas County Medical Society. He is a director of the Lininger Implement Company. He is a Republican.

He served as a corporal in Company M, 2nd Nebraska Volunteer Infantry in 1898, and is a member of the United Spanish War Veterans. From 1920 to 1928 he was a fellow in the American College of Physicians. He has been a member of the American Medical Association since 1922. A member of the Omaha Chamber of Commerce, he was a member of the executive committee 1917, 18 and 19. He has belonged to the Rotary Club since 1902, and to the Masonic lodge since 1902. He is a member of the Omaha Humane Society. His sport is golf. He is a member of the Omaha Field Club. Residence: Omaha. (Photograph on Page 238).

George Christopher

George Christopher, farmer and rancher, was born at Lincoln, Nebraska, July 2, 1876, son of James and Marie (Hanson) Christopher. The father, a native of Jutland, Denmark, was born April 13, 1832, and came to the United States in March, 1864. He was a Republican, active in politics and engaged in farming until his death at Lincoln on October 11, 1918.

Marie Hanson Christopher was born in Jutland, Denmark, November 16, 1843, and died at Lincoln, Nebraska, February 14, 1900. She was a professional mid-wife of Danish ancestry.

Mr. Christopher attended public schools, and is now a partly retired rancher and farmer. He is a partner with his son in business, and for three years was president and general manager of the Douglas Motor Manufacturing Company of Lincoln, Nebraska. A Republican in national politics, he is independent in local and state politics.

On December 23, 1896, he was married to Almina A.

Ellis at Panama, Nebraska. Mrs. Christopher was born at Panama, Nebraska, October 31, 1872, and died at Lincoln, Nebraska, December 26, 1911. Mr. and Mrs. Christopher had the following children, Paul M., born July 3, 1897, who married Chloe Morey; Raymond J., born December 31, 1899, who married Almira Bachelor; George E., born June 4, 1904; Roy M., born May 8, 1909, who married Elmira Tate.

On June 30, 1915, Mr. Christopher was married to Mabel E. Slawson, graduate nurse at Omaha, Nebraska. They have two children, Merritt J., born June 25, 1918; and Robert D., born July 27, 1927. Paul is a salesman, Raymond is a storekeeper, while George, Jr., and Roy M. are ranchers.

During the late war Mr. Christopher was active in all civilian projects. He is a member of the Methodist Church at the present time although he was born and raised a Lutheran. He is a member of the Omaha Chamber of Commerce, the Omaha Kiwanis Club, the Modern Woodmen of America, the Odd Fellows and the Masons. He enjoys hunting and fishing while his hobbies are his home and his business. Residence: Valentine.

James Baird Christopher

James Baird Christopher, county commissioner of Thayer County since 1924, was born in Jersey County, Illinois, September 16, 1858, the son of John and Mary Elizabeth (Baird) Christopher. His father was a native of Ohio, born August 9, 1832. He was a farmer, whose ancestors came from Germany. Mary Elizabeth Baird was born in New Jersey, September 13, 1836, of English and Scotch extraction. She died at Albia, Iowa, October 8, 1908, her husband having died at Carleton, August 28, 1902.

Educated in the public schools, Mr. Christopher has farmed continuously since youth. For the past forty-five years he has been a resident of Thayer County, where he has extensive agricultural interests. He is a member of Carleton Methodist Episcopal Church, and Gavel Lodge No. 199 of the Ancient Free and Accepted Masons. He is a Republican.

On November 2, 1881, Mr. Christopher was married to Nora Mignon Palmer at Kemper, Illinois. Mrs. Christopher was born at Kemper, August 10, 1862. There is one son, Rei, born January 9, 1884, who is married to Martha Chaffee, of Warren, Ohio.

Rei Christopher is superintendent of a band and orchestra at Pueblo, Colorado, which position he has held for the past eight years. He is a graduate of Dana Institute at Warren, Ohio. He also taught at Dana Institute for about six years. At the time he graduated from this school it was the only one of its kind in the country. Mr. Christopher was also a member of Sousa's band prior to the World War. They have two daughters. Residence: Carleton.

John J. R. Claassen

John Claassen, master farmer near Beatrice, Gage County, Nebraska, has lived in this state all his life. He was born at Beatrice, October 23, 1885, the son of Aaron E. and Anna (Jansen) Claassen. His father, who was also a farmer, was born in Germany, May 28, 1850, and died at Beatrice, September 8, 1929; he was the son of Johann and Katherine (Enns) Claassen. His mother, the daughter of Cornelius and Helena (von Riesen) Jansen, was born in Germany, March 23, 1856, and died at Beatrice, October 16, 1924.

Mr. Claassen received his education in Kansas, and in 1910 was graduated from the School of Agriculture at Lincoln, Nebraska. He holds membership in the Farmer's Union, is a director in the local school, and is a member of the Nebraskana Society. He is affiliated with the Second Mennonite Church at Beatrice.

His marriage to Christine Catharine Penner was solemnized at Newton, Harvey County, Kansas, March

14, 1914. Mrs. Claassen was born at Lehigh, Marion County, Kansas, September 12, 1889, the daughter of Heinrich D. and Katharine (Dalke) Penner. Their children are: Anna Dorothy, born January 24, 1915; Paul Gerhard, born May 10, 1917; John Carl, born July 7, 1919; Donald Aaron, born January 27, 1923; and Waldo Frederic, born July 11, 1926.

During the World War Mr. Claassen was a member of the Liberty loan drive committee in Gage County. Residence: Beatrice.

Jason Lewis Claflin

Jason L. Claflin was born at Coudersport, Potter County, Pennsylvania, June 26, 1858, the son of Rufus Tingley and Lavina Margaret (Lewis) Claflin. His father, who was a pioneer clergyman in Pennsylvania, served as superintendent of schools in Potter County in 1865. He was born in Rhode Island, May 22, 1820, and died at Fremont, Dodge County, Nebraska, March 4, 1893. His Scotch ancestors came to America about 1620. Lavina Claflin, mother of Jason, was born near Buffalo, New York, October 22, 1835, and died at Lincoln, June 28, 1918.

Mr. Claflin received his education in the public schools of Coudersport. He was editor of the St. Paul *Phonograph,* 1885-93; was editor of the Ord *Journal,* 1894-1904; and has been engaged in the active printing business in Lincoln and its vicinity since 1904. He published a newspaper in Lincoln for 10 years; in 1909 he organized the Claflin Printing Company, of which he is now president.

He is a member of the Lions Club of Lincoln, and the Young Men's Christian Association. He is an honorary member of the Woman's Christian Temperance Union. He is interested in all public questions, and is especially interested in having an unbiased and fair outlook on all moral and religious questions, and is affiliated with the First Methodist Epscopal Church of Lincoln.

His marriage to Mamie Mildred Perkins was solemnized at Cairo, Hall County, Nebraska, February 10, 1886. Residence: Lincoln.

Henry Luther Clapp

Henry L. Clapp was born at Elmwood, Cass County, Nebraska, August 29, 1888, the son of Henry L. and Sarah Jane (Conn) Clapp. His father, who was born at Watertown, New York, November 2, 1840, and died at Elmwood, March 13, 1921, was a farmer who owned large tracts of land.

His mother was born at New Castle, Indiana, September 7, 1848, and died at Elmwood, February 8, 1922.

Mr. Clapp was graduated from the Elmwood High School in 1906, and from 1906 to 1908, was a student at the University of Nebraska, where he was a member of Sigma Alpha Epsilon. A lifetime resident of Nebraska, he is a farmer and stock raiser, and is a director in the Elmwood State Bank.

At Lincoln, Nebraska, February 28, 1920, he was united in marriage with Grace Ellen Bailey, who was born at Alvo, Cass County, Nebraska, November 3, 1892. Mrs. Clapp was a teacher in the Cass County schools and an assistant in Lincoln postoffice before her marriage. There is one son, Robert, born November 13, 1925.

Mr. Clapp served in the World War in Company F, 350 Infantry, 88th Division, and today is a member of the American Legion. He is affiliated with the Methodist Episcopal Church at Elmwood, and is a member of the Knights of Pythias and the Odd Fellows. His social club is the Revelers Dancing Club, of Lincoln. Residence: Elmwood.

Hiram Cornell Clapp

Hiram Cornell Clapp, merchant and executive, was born in Allegan, Michigan, May 11, 1878, and for the past thirty years has resided in Nebraska. He is the son of Irving Fletcher and Delora Alvira (Sherwood) Clapp, the former born in New York State, June 10, 1838. He was a merchant at Allegan, Michigan, and died at McCook on February 27, 1910. Delora Alvira Sherwood was born in Otsego, Michigan, October 28, 1843, and is still living.

Mr. Clapp was graduated from high school at Allegan in 1895 and started as a bookkeeper and merchandise salesman in a drygoods store. Later he accepted a managing position in Stuart, Iowa, and from there came to McCook as manager of a drygoods store. In November, 1905, he started in business for himself, retiring in 1926. In 1929 he opened a store for women, which he still owns. He is vice president of the McCook Trust Company.

Active in every civic and community project, Mr. Clapp is a former president (1925-26-27) of the Chamber of Commerce, and is a member of its board of directors; is vice president of the Kiwanis Club; a member of the board of directors of the Young Men's Christian Association; a Mason (Tehama Shrine of Hastings), and a member of the local and national Red Cross organizations.

During the World War period he was a participant in all civilian activities. He is a member of the McCook Country Club, is affiliated with the First Congregational Church, and is a member of The Nebraskana Society, the Nebraska State and McCook Historical Societies. As a sport he prefers golf, while his hobbies are business, bridge and reading.

On August 22, 1900, he was married to Cora Earl Born at Allegan, Michigan. She was born at Coopersville, Michigan, and died at McCook, June 30, 1924.

On November 10, 1927, Mr. Clapp was united in marriage to Bertha Asten Lussen in Brooklyn, New York. There are two children, Elsie Asten, born September 29, 1928, and Patricia Ruth, born November 11, 1930, of whom their parents are justly proud. Residence: McCook.

Raymond Gustavus Clapp

Raymond Gustavus Clapp, educator and physician, was born at Northampton, Massachusetts, May 31, 1875. He is the son of Willis Warner and Luanna Allen (Blood) Clapp, the former born at Easthampton, Massachusetts, in July 1844. A traveling salesman for many years, he died at Northampton in November 1910. On the maternal side he was descended from General Seth Pomeroy. Luanna, his wife, was born at Westfield, Massachusetts, December 10, 1845, and is of early New England ancestry.

Dr. Clapp was graduated from the elementry schools of Northampton in 1891, and attended Northampton High School one year. Thereafter he was a student at Williston Seminary three years, but did not graduate. He received his Ph. B. from Yale University in 1899 and his M. D. from the College of Physicians and Surgeons at Keokuk, Iowa. At Yale he held a varsity letter in track and gymnastics, and was captain of the gymnastic team in 1899. From 1898-1904 he held the world's record for pole vault, and was individual inter-collegiate gymnastic champion in 1899. His fraternities are Theta Delta Chi and Phi Epsilon Kappa.

On August 19, 1903, he was married to Anne Louise Barr at Jamestown, New York. Mrs. Clapp was born at Lancaster, Pennsylvania, March 4, 1871. There are two daughters, Catherine, born November 20, 1909, who received her A. B. from the University of Nebraska in 1930, and is an instructor at Brownell Hall; and Margaret, born June 27, 1912. The family attends the First Presbyterian Church of Lincoln.

From 1899-1903 Professor Clapp was physical director of the Young Men's Christian Association at Keokuk, and from 1900-1902 was coach of track at Iowa State College. In October, 1902, he came to Nebraska as professor of physical education at the University, and has since continued. For a number of years he was also coach of basketball, track, gymnastics, fencing and wrestling. From 1899-1914 he was instructor in physical education at the Chautauqua, New York, Summer School of Physical Education, and dean of same 1909-14. During the summers of 1919 and 1920 he was instructor of hygiene and medical advisor at the University of Chicago. From 1927-29, inclusive, he was instructor of physical education at Cornell University.

During the World War he was director of first aid, Lincoln chapter of the American Red Cross, and still retains his membership in the organization. His professional memberships include the Society of Directors of Physical Education in Colleges, the American Association of University Professors, the American Medical Association and the National Collegiate Athletic Association. He is a member of the Nebraskana Society and the University Club of Lincoln. Residence: Lincoln.

Anna Gray Clark

Anna Gray Clark was born at Oxford, in Butler County, Ohio, daughter of Richard and Mary Milligan (Webb) Gray. Her father was born in Cincinnati, Ohio. November 15, 1815, and died at Ogallala, Nebraska. September 24, 1896.

Richard Gray was Scotch, the son of William Gray, who was the son of Robert Gray, who served seven years in the Revolutionary War under Putnam, Washington and others. He made three enlistments, went up the hill at Stony Point and often made up regimental accounts by the dim light of Tories' windows. As commissioned officers were not paid at the close of the war, he received no remuneration until years afterward, when he was allowed to purchase land between Cincinnati and Hamilton at the rate of $1.25 per acre. The transfer was signed by the president of the United States. This land is still retained in the family and the buildings have been preserved. He married a woman of the same name, but no relation, making the subject of this sketch related to two families of Revolutionary fame. Ex-congressman Gray and Judge George L. Gray, both of Indiana, and W. C. Gray, a prolific writer, now deceased, of Chicago, were paternal relatives of Richard Gray. He was also connected to Whitelaw Reid and Congressman Woods of the early history of Indiana and Ohio. Richard Gray's father was a lawyer and his great grandfather one of the earliest teachers in Cincinnati, after he purchased land there in 1804.

Mary Milligan Webb was born near Hagerstown, Maryland, October 23, 1824, and died at Pleasant Plain, Iowa, on August 18, 1860. She was the daughter of Peter Webb, a Baptist minister of much respect in the South. Her family has become almost extinct since the Civil War. Two of her uncles served in the War of 1812. Mary M. Webb was an educator, especially strong in English and technical grammar. She was educated under the governess regime of the South, and spent much time aiding students in Ohio University. She died in 1865.

Anna Gray Clark began her education with her mother after the southern system and knew but little of public school life until she began to teach which was at a very early age. Thereafter she took post graduate work in Mt. Pleasant, Iowa, languages in Howes Academy and science in Wesleyan University. College societies were little known when she made her greatest efforts. Through life she has held positions usually filled by men. She has studied hard to attain them and keep abreast of the age. She has had charge of Madrid, Grant, Big Springs and other schools. While supervising the Stromsburg schools she observed the rapid advance in Nebraska land and through a syndicate formed by C. H. Morrill of that city she aided in selling large tracts of Union Pacific lands. In the mean time she taught in Summer Schools and Normal Institutes. Before leaving Polk County she served two terms as County Superintendent of Schools after which she joined the western procession

and located in Keith County where she followed the advice she had given others and filed on a Homestead. Since that time she has served two terms as County Superintendent of Schools of Keith County after which she purchased and operated the Keith County News for nearly five years. She is a Jefferson Democrat and has been honored on State Committees. She served as Chairwoman on the Tax Revision of Woman's League Voters. In faith she is a United Presbyterian, but has worked with the Congregational Church in later years. She has enjoyed aiding and fostering a Woman's Library Association of which she became a charter member twenty-seven years ago when women drove over ungraded roads for twenty miles to attend a meeting. The activities of this little band of women were far reaching in their results. At first they organized as a Woman's Club for mutual improvement and a closer relationship between neighbors and friends. They were cultured women and soon planned a course of study. Mrs. W. A. Paxton, a woman whose generosity was only equaled by her ability to organize, gathered the young girls of these families into a King's Daughters Circle, and the foundation of a prosperous village was established. A postoffice, church, and library building which is now supplied with nearly 2600 books with a paid librarian, and many other accessories which pertain to the public good have put the village of Keystone on the map. Aside from other duties of a business life, Mrs. Clark has written for Short Story Magazine, also Poetry Daily Drift and old time history of life on the plains. Though practically retired she continues to write of the West as she saw it first before it was despoiled by civilization. Residence: Ogallala. (Photograph in Album).

Benjamin Franklin Clark

Born in Washington County, Kentucky, September 11, 1891, Benjamin Franklin Clark is the son of Ben and Martha Frances (Blackerby) Clark. His father, who was interested in music and was a vocal instructor for many years, was born at Danville, Kentucky, August 17, 1859, and died at Ainsworth, Nebraska, December 15, 1923. His ancestors originally settled in Virginia, and later established homes in Kentucky where they were forced to live in forts as protection from the Indians. The grandfather of Benjamin Clark was a slave holder at the time of the Civil War but was a union sympathiser.

His mother was born at Stanford, Kentucky, June 6, 1865, and died at Ainsworth, Nebraska, August 5, 1911. Her ancestors came to this country from England where the family estate still is held intact by the heirs. Her father was an inventor and held many patents recorded in Washington, D. C.

Mr. Clark attended the elementary schools of Illinois. He has been a rancher and farmer near Ainsworth for a number of years, and is director of the Ainsworth Creamery Company. He is appraiser for the South Pine Local and the National Farm Loan Association.

He is a director in the local school board, is affiliated with Highland Grove Church, and holds membership in The Nebraskana Society. His hobby is mechanics.

On November 25, 1917, he was married to Ethel May Morrow at Johnstown. Mrs. Clark, who taught school before her marriage, was born at Modale, Iowa, December 25, 1895. To them were born two children: Evelyn, February 5, 1919; and Wayne, February 1, 1923. Both the children studied music. Residence: Ainsworth.

Byron Clark

On April 24, 1856, Timothy Byron Clark was born at Spring Lake, Illinois. His parents were Timothy and Anna (Benninnger) Clark, the former born near Amity, Pennsylvania, September 6, 1820. Orphaned at an early age he became apprenticed to a tailor, and later became a pioneer farmer in Nebraska. Tradition in the family is to the effect that his ancestry goes to Abra Clark, one of

BYRON CLARK

the signers of the Declaration of Independence. He was of Scotch-Irish descent, and died at Weeping Water, Nebraska, November 11, 1901.

Timothy Clark married Anna Benninnger, daughter of the first founder of an iron forge, at Johnstown, Pennsylvania, which developed into an historic plant. It was located on government land, and because he failed to get a patent, he was ousted by Yankee patentees. Anna Benninnger was born in Westmoreland County, May 27, 1817, and came to Nebraska as a pioneer with her husband. She died at Plattsmouth, June 25, 1895.

Timothy Byron Clark was educated in public and high schools, and took one years preparatory work at the University of Nebraska. A farm lad until 22, he studied law in the office of George S. Smith, former U. S. Surveyor General, of the District of Nebraska, and Jesse B. Strode, district attorney, congressman and district judge. He was admitted to the Nebraska bar in November, 1880. On January 1, 1881, he entered private practice, continuing until January 1, 1912, when he entered the exclusive service of the Chicago, Burlington and Quincy Railroad Company. He is solicitor, law department, of that company for Nebraska, Kansas and South Dakota.

He married Minnie Crocker Murphy at Plattsmouth, May 5, 1881. She was born at Ottumwa, Iowa, June 12, 1860, and died at Plattsmouth, October 30, 1905. She was the daughter of Michael Murphy, an Irish emigrant, and her mother, who was of the Baker family, was eligible to the Daughters of the American Revolution.

He was later married to Margaret Tower Farley, born July 5, 1875, who died June 18, 1930. She was the daughter of Henry W. Farley of Weeping Water, once a noted educator at Boston, who came to Nebraska for the benefit of his health. There are two children, Earle, born February 28, 1882, who married Ida Belle Crum, and who died March 22, 1917; and Helen, born September 29, 1891.

Mr. Clark is a Republican and a member of the Presbyterian Church. He holds membership in the Chamber of Commerce at Omaha, and at Lincoln, and is a Mason and an Elk. During the World War he was a four minute speaker. His clubs include the Omaha University Club, the Happy Hollow Country Club, the Omaha Athletic Club and the Omaha Club. Residence: Omaha. (Photograph on Page 242).

Chester Melville Clark

Chester M. Clark was born at Lewiston, Nebraska, July 13, 1884, the son of Isaac Melville and Sarah (Skillman) Clark. His father, a prosperous farmer of Scotch, Irish, and Pennsylvania Dutch descent, was born at Coshocton, Ohio, October 18, 1848, and died at Whittier, California, October, 1922. He was interested in church work and gave large sums to church schools, foreign missions and other religious organizations.

His mother, who was born at Lorraine, Ohio, April 12, 1858, and died at Lincoln, Nebraska, July 28, 1914, was educated at Oberlin College, and was an active church worker. Her ancestry is traced to the house of Stuart of England, on the maternal side.

Mr. Clark was graduated from Wesleyan Academy at Lincoln, Nebraska, in 1904, and received his B. S. in June, 1908, from Wesleyan University. He was a member of the Orophilian Society, which later became a fraternity.

He was state representative from Pawnee County, in 1930, and from 1918 to 1927 was the secretary of the Lewiston school board.

On September 22, 1909, he was married to Dora Moulton at Swanton. Mrs. Clark, who was born at Swanton, November 30, 1886, is a descendant of Sir Robert Moulton and Millard Fillmore. Before her marriage she was a teacher in the public schools of Swanton and Wilber. They have two children, Ronald Moulton, born March 19, 1914; and Chester Dean, born November 29, 1919. Ronald has shown at several of the leading county fairs, and has won

40 ribbons and first place in the Guernsey class at the 1930 state fair.

Mr. Clark is a member of the Lewiston Methodist Episcopal Church, of which he has been superintendent of Sunday school for fifteen years. He is a member of the Red Cross. His hobbies are reading and beautifying his home grounds. He raises registered Guernsey cattle and has the record of selling the highest priced cattle ever sold on an open market. Residence: Burchard.

Clarence Leon Clark

Clarence L. Clark, a lifetime resident of Nebraska, has been prominent in the legal world since 1914. He was born at Lincoln, Lancaster County, Nebraska, March 27, 1890, the son of John Homer and Julia Addie (Hawkes) Clark. His early education was received in the public schools of Lincoln, and in 1908 he was graduated from the Lincoln High School.

He was awarded the A. B. degree at the University of Nebraska in 1912; and in 1914 was graduated from the law department with an LL. B. degree. During his college days he was a member of the Nebraska Inter-collegiate Debate Team; the University Dramatic Club; and the University Glee Club. He was national counsellor for Sigma Tau Delta, and served as national president of Phi Alpha Tau. He has been engaged in general law practice since his admission to the bar in 1914.

A Democrat, Mr. Clark has taken an active part in the political life of his community and state for the last decade. He was secretary of the Democratic County Central Committee, 1922-30; and since 1930 has been chairman of this organization. He has served as a member of the Board of Insanity since 1920.

His marriage to Lenor S. Fitzgerald was solemnized at Omaha, Douglas County, Nebraska, December 14, 1921. He was lieutenant of the University Cadets and during the World War was in the World War Air Service, unassigned.

He is a member of the American Legion and the Forty and Eight. He holds membership in the following professional and civic organizations: Lancaster County Bar Association; Nebraska State Bar Association; American Bar Association; the Lincoln Chamber of Commerce; the Nebraskana Society; and the State Historical Society. He is president of the Knife and Fork Club. He is an Elk, a Mason and member of Lancaster Lodge No. 54, Scottish Rite, Shrine. His social clubs are the University Club; and Eastridge Country Club. He is affiliated with St. Paul's Methodist Church at Lincoln. Residence: Lincoln. (Photograph on Page 244).

Esther Ann Clark

Since September, 1896, Esther Ann Clark has been a resident of Nebraska, and since September, 1898, she has been a teacher at Peru State Teachers College. A native of Ohio, she was born at Wheat Ridge, Adams County, daughter of Samuel Ellison and Sarah Ann (Kirker) Clark.

Her father was a teacher and farmer, born near Philadelphia. A soldier in the Civil War, he was captain of Company E, 91st Ohio Volunteer Infantry, and was killed in the Battle of Cloyd Mountain, West Virginia, May 9, 1864. He was of Scotch-Irish ancestry, the family having settled in America early in the 19th century.

Sarah Ann Kirker was born near West Union, Adams County, Ohio, and died at Great Bend, Kansas, September 25, 1900. She was descended from Scotch-Irish pioneers; her two grandfathers, Thomas Kirker and William Williamson, served in the Revolution, and Thomas Kirker was second governor of Ohio. While Ohio was still a territory, in 1800, these two great men, together with a group of neighboring planters, left their homes near Fair Forest, South Carolina, and settled in southern Ohio, in order that they might free their slaves. This self-exile was one of the earliest movements for the cause of abolition. Mrs. Clark, herself, although primarily inter-

CLARENCE LEON CLARK

ested in her home and family, was an earnest worker in the women's crusade against the saloon which later became the W. C. T. U.

Esther Ann Clark was educated first in the village schools of West Union and later graduated from West Union High School, although at that time there was no formal graduation. In 1885 she received her A. B. from National Normal University at Lebanon, Ohio, and in 1890 was awarded her M. A., and taught English and Latin in that college from 1885-96. In 1897 she received her A. B. from the University of Nebraska, and during 1897 and 1898 she took graduate work at Yale University. She is a member of Sigma Tau Delta.

A Republican, Miss Clark is interested in prohibition and a proponent of world Peace. Reared a Presbyterian, she is truly a Christian. She is a member of the Methodist Episcopal Church at Peru.

Since she first entered Peru as a teacher of Latin in 1898, her entire life has been devoted to education. She has been head of the Latin department since her arrival and since 1919 has also been teacher of Spanish. She loves her work, and her chief pride is in the achievements of the men and women who have studied under her. She is the author of *Student's Aid to Caesar* (1915), together with various educational articles. Her avocation, however, is writing poetry, especially for children. Her poems have appeared in various magazines.

Among her social and cultural clubs are the Peru Women's Club, the P. E. O. and the Nebraska Writers Guild. She is also a member of the Nebraska State Teachers Association, Classical Association of the Middle West and South, and the Nebraska Women's Educational Club. She is a member of the Red Cross, and also of the W. C. T. U. and the Anti-Saloon League of America. She has always been an active worker in the College Y. W. C. A. Residence: Peru.

George Edward Clark

George Edward Clark, a farmer in Antelope County, Nebraska, since 1881, was born at Union, Iowa, November 20, 1868. His father, George Edward Clark, who was a farmer, was born in New York, October 8, 1836, and died at Elgin, Nebraska, in 1917. His mother was born at Lavonia, New York, October 4, 1839, and died at Claremont, California, February 5, 1912.

Mr. Clark is a member of the Park Church at Elgin, has served as a member of the local school board, and holds membership in the Nebraskana Society. His marriage to Florence Matilda Howe occurred at Neligh, Nebraska, January 22, 1895. Mrs. Clark, who was a teacher before her marriage, was born in Indiana, December 9, 1871, and died at Elgin, Nebraska, August 26, 1913. Six children were born to their marriage: Marjorie, January 27, 1898, who died April 6, 1908; Myrtle E., April 28, 1899; Leland, October 15, 1901; Alice L., March 22, 1907; Bernice F., July 14, 1913; and Bernard, July 14, 1913. Residence: Elgin.

Lucy Marie Clark

Lucy Marie Clark, head of the department of English at Chadron State Normal College, was born at St. Martin's, Ohio, December 1, 1869, daughter of Adam Dominic and Maria (Derivan) Clark.

Miss Clark's father was also born in St. Martin's, Ohio, on October 15, 1839, descended from Irish settlers in Pennsylvania, and in Perry County, Ohio, in 1790. He died at Tecumseh, Nebraska, October 4, 1891. The mother, born at Portumna, near Galway, parish of Kalimer, Ireland, February 14, 1847, now resides at Lincoln, Nebraska, near the capitol. She is 85 years of age. Her father, Hugh Derivan, was an Irish scholar.

Miss Clark attended Ursuline Academy at St. Martin's and was graduated from the Tecumseh High School in 1888. She received her Bachelor of Arts degree in 1903 from the University of Nebraska, and in 1926 received her Masters degree. She was Phi Beta Kappa at graduation, is a life member of the Nebraska Alumni Association, and of the National Educational Association.

Miss Clark began teaching in the grade schools of Tecumseh, was later principal of the Tecumseh High School, and then head of the Department of English at the Lincoln, Nebraska, High School, and in 1911 became head of the department of English at Chadron State Normal College. She is teacher of journalism also, and director of publicity for the college.

Early in the World War Miss Clark represented Chadron at a conference of women workers held at Lincoln. She later was one of several prominent speakers in this section. She was also a member of the Red Cross board at Chadron. At the present time she is a member of St. Patrick's Catholic Church. Her favorite sport is golf. Residence: Chadron. (Photograph in Album).

Reuben Valentine Clark

One of Nebraska's most prominent educators and school executives is Reuben Valentine Clark of Kearney, who is superintendent of the Nebraska State Industrial School there. He was born at Ribott, Illinois, November 25, 1876, the son of Reuben and Louisa M. (Doty) Clark. His father, who was a farmer and salesman, was born in England April 11, 1825, and died at Kearney, Nebraska, November 10, 1920. His mother was born in Vermont, May 26, 1833, of Dutch descent, and died at Denver, Colorado, in 1914.

Mr. Clark was graduated from York High School in 1896 and was a student at the United Brethren College at York, Nebraska, for a time. He served as superintendent of schools at Clay Center, Nebraska, from 1898 to 1905, was superintendent at Harvard, Nebraska, 1905-13, and since 1913 has served in his present position at Kearney. He is affiliated with the Presbyterian Church of Kearney, is a Mason and an Elk, and holds membership in The Nebraskana Society.

On July 20, 1899, he was married to Elizabeth H. Heal at Wilcox, Nebraska. Mrs. Clark, whose ancestry is Scotch and Irish, was born in Wisconsin, May 6, 1877. Five children were born to this marriage: Marion, August 9, 1902; Elizabeth, January 29, 1907; Helen, January 22, 1909; Ruth, January 2, 1914; and Reuben, February 8, 1917. Residence: Kearney.

Rose B. Clark

Rose B. Clark, educator and school executive of Nebraska, was born at Wheat Ridge, Adams County, Ohio. Her father, Andrew Reed Clark, who was born at Wheat Ridge, Ohio, served as a volunteer in the Civil War; his father fought in the War of 1812. Her mother, Celia (Arbuthnot) Clark was born in Ohio, and died at Pawnee City, Nebraska. She was descended from a long line of Scotch ancestors who were educators, ministers, and writers.

Miss Clark attended the grade and high schools at Pawnee City, Nebraska, and after her graduation from high school was a student at the University of Nebraska where she was awarded the A. B. degree, 1904, and A. M., 1918. At various times during 1912-15-20-22-28, she was a student at the University of Chicago. She was awarded Phi Beta Kappa and Phi Kappa Phi membership.

She has been a high school principal, and an instructor at Peru State Teachers' College. She is now professor of education at Nebraska Wesleyan University. She is the author of: *Geography for the Grades*, 1920; *A Geography of Nebraska*, 1922; and *Unit Studies in Geography*, 1924.

She is a member of the Nebraska State Teachers' Association; National Council of Geography Teachers; the department of supervisors and directors of instruction of the National Educational Association; and the Altrusa

Club of Lincoln. Her hobbies are reading and motoring. She is a member of the First Methodist Episcopal Church of University Place, Lincoln. Politically, Miss Clark is an Independent. Residence: Lincoln.

Wilber Dale Clark

Wilber Dale Clark, banker, was born at Fillmore, Missouri, April 26, 1892, son of Samuel Milton and Catherine (Sayres) Clark.

He attended public and high school, and on August 31, 1915, was married to Ethyl Johnston at St. Joseph, Missouri.

Mr. Clark is a member of the Methodist Church, the Kiwanis Club, the Chamber of Commerce, the Elks and the Athletic Club. Residence: Omaha.

William Clark

William Clark, a general merchant at Page, was born at Oakland, Iowa, March 4, 1879, son of William and Martha Ann (Humbert) Clark. The father was born in Youngstown, Ohio, March 1, 1837, and died at Oakland, January 7, 1926. He was a farmer and a Republican. His ancestry was Scotch-Irish. His wife, Martha Ann, was born in Covington County, Indiana, November 14, 1842, and died at Oakland, Iowa, November 11, 1910. She was of Canadian French descent.

Mr. Clark attended country school, and for some years thereafter was a farmer. For three years he was in the livestock commission business at South Omaha, and for the past seven years has been in the produce and general merchandise business in his present location. He is senior partner and manager of William Clark & Sons.

On October 17, 1900, he was married to Susie Ethel Bay at Oakland. Mrs. Clark was born at Avoca, Iowa, April 5, 1878, of English ancestry. They have four children, Velna, born August 16, 1903; Fred L., born December 5, 1905, who married Lena Holbrook; W. Foy, born February 19, 1908, who married Louise Nissen; and Delbert V., born February 14, 1910. The boys are all associated with their father in his business.

Mr. Clark is an independent Republican. He is a member of the Methodist Church, the Red Cross, the Ancient Free and Accepted Masons, and the Odd Fellows. Residence: Page.

Harvey L. Clarke

A leading professional man in Fairbury, Nebraska, forty-four years, Harvey L. Clarke was born at Aylmer, Canada, June 10, 1858, the son of Lewis J. Clarke and Deborah Ann (Teeple) Clarke. His father was born in Suffolk County, England in 1809, and was a farmer. Mrs. Clarke was born in Elgin County, Ontario, Canada, in 1819, of Canadian parentage.

Dr. Clarke attended high school at Aylmer, Ontario, and the Normal School at Toronto, in 1879. He received the degree of Doctor of Medicine, at the New York Homeopathic Medical College in New York City, in 1882, and also a degree from the homeopathic department of the University of Michigan, at Ann Arbor. He is a member of the Hahnemanian Society of the University of Michigan and for twenty years has been a member of the American Institute of Homeopathy.

He was united in marriage to Alice E. Corwin, April 30, 1884, in Niagara County, New York. Mrs. Clarke was born January 10, 1860. She is a member of the Daughters of the American Revolution, and a home-maker. Her father, C. R. Corwin, was born in New Jersey of English parentage. Her mother, Sara M. Wilson, was born in New York State of Holland Dutch descent.

To this union two children were born, Corwin S., born February 11, 1880, is married to Marcia Brainard; and Harvey L., born October 9, 1900, is married to Beverly Wurtele. Corwin was graduated from the homeopathic medical department of the University of Michigan where

he also received the B. S. degree, and is practicing in Jackson, Michigan. Harvey is also a graduate of the medical department of the University of Michigan. He took his interneship in Kings County Hospital at Brooklyn, New York. He is practicing in North Platte, Nebraska.

Dr. Clarke was admitted to the practice of medicine in 1886, at Fairbury, where he has since been engaged. He was county physician three years and chairman of the board of health for one year. Dr. Clarke is affiliated with the First Baptist Church at Fairbury and is an independent in politics. Among his fraternal organizations are the Woodmen of the World, Modern Woodmen of America, and the Knights and Ladies of Security. He is also a member of the National Geographic Society and the Nebraskana Society, while his hobby is building. Residence: Fairbury.

Morse Powl Clary

Morse Powl Clary, a farmer and rancher, was born in Quincy, Iowa, October 20, 1858, son of Denis Batty and Rachel Ann (Hooper) Clary. The father was born in Fredricksburg, Maryland, September 1, 1822, and died at Lewellen, October 21, 1909. He was a clergyman of English and German descent. Rachel Ann Hooper was born at Fort Wayne, Indiana, June 15, 1831, and died at Indianola, Iowa, July 7, 1876. Her ancestry was Scotch.

On January 21, 1881, Mr. Clary was married to Louisa Custard McNaught at Indianola. She was born at Centerville, Illinois, August 3, 1860, of Scotch-Irish ancestry. They have eight children, all living. March D., born July 20, 1882, who is a business college graduate; May Roxanna, born January 19, 1884; Frank Tracy, born August 22, 1885, who is a graduate of business college; Genoa Rachel, born October 23, 1887, who is graduated from high school; Josie June, born May 4, 1891, who was graduated from college and is a teacher in Lewellen; Ray Spencer, born January 5, 1887, who was a band master in the World War; Oren Vernon, born March 26, 1899; and Cora Maud, born December 20, 1901.

Mr. Clary came to Nebraska 46 years ago, and was one of the organizers of the Farmers State bank of Lewellen, and its president for three years. He homesteaded in Garden County in 1886, and now owns 3200 acres of land in Ash Hollow and vicinity. A Republican, he was county commissioner of Deuel County, 1892-98, and of Garden County 1910-16. For 42 years he has been school treasurer and for 11 years treasurer of the Garden County Agricultural Society. He has also served as precinct committeeman.

He is affiliated with the Methodist Church, is a member of the Red Cross, the Masons, the Nebraska State Historical Society, and is a life member of the Nebraskana Society. His hobby is reading. Residence: Lewellen. (Photograph in Album).

Fred D. Classen

A resident of Nebraska all his life, Fred D. Classen was born at Glenvil, Nebraska, September 7, 1895, the son of George and Emma A. (Schlipman) Classen. His father, born in Germany, July 22, 1863, came to America as a young man and has since farmed in the state. His mother was born at Quincy, Illinois, November 14, 1871, and is of German descent.

Fred D. Classen received his education in the public schools of district No. 75, and since leaving school has engaged in farming. On May 26, 1925, he was united in marriage to Bernice Marguerite Kober at Hastings. Mrs. Classen, who is the daughter of Bertram and Carrie (Hyland) Kober, was born at Hastings on December 16, 1907. There are two children, Elizabeth Jean, born July 16, 1926; and Gerald Fred, born September 23, 1930.

Mr. Classen is a Republican and active in local poli-

CLARA CLYDE CLAYTON

Hauck-Skoglund—Lincoln

tics. Since 1929 he has been a member of the Parent Teachers Association and the Red Cross. He attends St. Paul Lutheran Church at Hastings, and is a life member of The Nebraskana Society. Residence: Glenvil.

Clara Clyde Clayton

Clara Clyde Clayton, educator and clubwoman, was born at Wisner, Nebraska, January 10, 1877, daughter of Charles Taylor and Lillie R. (Sharp) Richardson. Her father was born at Brier Hill, New York, December 7, 1850. A farmer and lumber dealer, he also served as postmaster. His death occurred at Cambridge, Nebraska, February 23, 1925. Of English and Dutch ancestry, his grandfather went from Vermont to New York about 1840; his father married a descendant of Mohawk Dutch families. Lillie Sharp Richardson was born at Richland Center, Wisconsin, May 27, 1854, and died at Cambridge, Nebraska, July 7, 1914. A teacher, clubwoman and active church worker, she was descended from Scotch-English settlers in Virginia, prior to the French and Indian War.

Upon the completion of her high school work at Wisner High School in 1890, Mrs. Clayton attended Gates Congregational College as well as Normal School at Fremont and Lincoln. She has served as a teacher in the high schools of Wisner, Nebraska, Canton, South Dakota, and Cambridge, Nebraska. Her marriage to Curtis Stanton Clayton was solemnized at Minneapolis, July 17, 1901. Mr. Clayton was born at Siam, Iowa, August 19, 1876, of Scotch-Irish and Pennsylvania Dutch descent, and is an accountant and salesman. Their children, one of whom is deceased, are as follows: Charles Curtis, born June 3, 1902, who married Elizabeth Elliott. He is assistant city editor of the *St. Louis Globe Democrat*. Ruth Beatrice, born December 25, 1905, is a normal training teacher. Genevieve Maud, born May 14, 1908, is a Camp Fire executive. Lloyd Vinton, born July 9, 1910, died December 23, 1914.

Mrs. Clayton is a Democrat, and has been extremely active in party politics, serving as a member of the state central committee in 1922. She was head of the Child Welfare Bureau under Governor Charles W. Bryan, 1923-24, and has been re-appointed under the present Bryan administration. A leader in civic work she is state president of the Woman's Christian Temperance Union, and has contributed many articles to the *Union Worker*, its state paper. In addition she has written much for the Nebraska Parent-Teacher. Since the organization of the Parent-Teachers' Association she has been a member of the state board, and has also served as chairman of the bulletin committee and parliamentarian. In addition to her present position in the W. C. T. U. she served as local president, county president and state vice president 1920-25, and since that date has served as president as above. She is a member of Westminster Presbyterian Church. Her hobby is reading. Residence: Lincoln. (Photograph on Page 247).

John Leo Cleary

Born at Grand Island, October 17, 1878, John Leo Cleary has been a practicing lawyer there since June, 1902. He is the son of James and Joanna (Danahy) Cleary, both natives of Ireland. James Cleary, who was a merchant, died at Grand Island on May 21, 1927.

John L. Cleary attended the public schools of Grand Island, and received his Bachelor of Laws degree from the University of Nebraska where he was a member of Phi Delta Phi. In addition he was a student at St. Benedict's College and Notre Dame University.

Admitted to the practice of law in 1902, Mr. Cleary practiced alone in Grand Island until 1923, after which he was a member of the firm of Horth, Ryan, Cleary and Suhr; next of the firm of Horth, Cleary and Suhr; and is now a member of the firm of Cleary, Suhr and Davis, as senior member. A Democrat, he served as county at-torney of Hall County 1909-1913; and mayor of Grand Island 1917-21.

On June 10, 1910, Mr. Cleary was united in marriage to Frances Jane Cunningham at Grand Island. Mrs. Cleary died there on December 12, 1921. To them was born one daughter, Frances Jane, on January 24, 1914. She is a student at St. Mary-of-the-Woods College, in Indiana. On April 21, 1928, Mr. Cleary married Celia R. Swanson.

Mr. Cleary is a director of the First National Bank of Grand Island, a member and past president of the Nebraska State Bar Association and a member of the American Bar Association. He is an Elk, a member of the Grand Island Chamber of Commerce, department commander and national patriotic instructor of the United Spanish War Veterans. He was a member of the 2nd Nebraska Volunteer Infantry in the Spanish American War, serving with Company M.

Mr. Cleary is a life member of The Nebraskana Society, a member of the University Club and Riverside Golf Club. His religious affiliation is with St. Mary's Catholic Church of Grand Island. Residence: Grand Island. (Photograph in Album).

Alice Eliza Cleaver

Alice E. Cleaver, one of Nebraska's most noted artists, was born at Racine, Wisconsin, the daughter of John Lawson and Rosa Emily Eliza (Barker) Cleaver. Her father, who was born at Salem, New Jersey, June 26, 1842, and died at Falls City, Richardson County, Nebraska, March 17, 1918, was an insurance man and expert bookkeeper, acting in the Nebraska senate as such for many years. Peter Kleaver, his direct ancestor came to America from Germany in 1683 and became a member of the Society of Friends.

Her mother, who was born at Clinton, Hickman County, Kentucky, May 16, 1847, was a teacher and botanist. Her maternal grandfather, James Markham, was a commodore in the Virginia Navy.

Soon after her graduation from the Falls City High School, Miss Cleaver began to win recognition in the world of art. Her real academic training was begun at the University of Nebraska, after which she enrolled in the Chicago Art Institute, where for four years she studied, paying practically all of her tuition with scholarship funds which she won with her paintings. In 1904 she was graduated with the highest honors of her class, and was awarded a traveling scholarship. It was her good fortune while in Chicago to study under the famous Vanderpoel (winning first prize for an original composition), and later at Philadelphia she was a student of William Chase and Cecilia Beaux. Her next educational step was a year's work in Paris where she was under the direction of Lucien Simon and Louis Biloul. During her stay in France two of her pictures were accepted for an exclusive art exhibition of women's paintings. In 1914 she returned to America just as the World War began.

Miss Cleaver, who is a member of the Nebraska Hall of Fame, and Who's Who of American Artists published by the American Federation of Arts in Washington, D. C., has won prizes and scholarships through her paintings, and has shown them in exhibits in the large cities abroad and in the United States. Her representative productions have been shown in Paris, Chicago, Milwaukee, Kansas City, Omaha, Minneapolis, and Lincoln; some of her paintings have been permanently hung in the Vanderpoel collection in Chicago. Some years ago the Santa Fe railroad commissioned her to go to New Mexico and Arizona to produce paintings of the Pueblo Indians. She completed seven canvases, one of which hangs in the Chicago office of the railroad, another in their Denver office, and two in Kansas City. The largest and most striking of the group hangs at the El Tovar Hotel at the Grand Canyon of Arizona.

Visitors at the public library of Falls City are attracted by the *Cast Room* which hangs permanently there.

It was this picture, exhibited as part of the Women's Club Exhibit in the St. Louis exposition, that, in the opinion of Professor H. E. Barbour of the University of Nebraska, helped win the medal for Nebraska. The model used in the foreground of the picture was Vachel Lindsay, America's vagabond poet. Lindsay was a student with Miss Cleaver and in his story, *The Lady Poverty,* published in 1911, he portrayed her as the heroine.

Perhaps her most satisfying recognition from her home state came in 1922 when she won the John L. Webster prize for the best group painting at the exhibition of Nebraska artists at Omaha, and was awarded second place in the entire collection.

Miss Cleaver is an accomplished violinist and violin teacher, having studied music at the University of Nebraska School of Music, and at Chicago Music College. Her pupils have won various musical honors in high school contests. She is a member of the Music Club of Falls City, the Woman's Club, and the Nebraskana Society. She is a Republican and is affiliated with the First Presbyterian Church of Falls City. Residence: Falls City.

Bryon Isaac Clements

On February 17, 1865, Byron I. Clements was born at Marcellus, Onanadaga County, New York, the son of John and Sarah (Barnett) Clements. His father, who was born at Somersetshire, England, October 26, 1838, and died at Elmwood, Cass County, Nebraska, August 2, 1899, was a farmer, merchant, and public office holder. He came with his parents from England, in 1841. He served as county commissioner of Cass County for several years, and from 1871 to 1875 he was in business in Lincoln.

His mother, who was a housewife and interested church worker, was born at Somersetshire, April 23, 1840, and died at Elmwood, May 30, 1908.

Mr. Clements attended the Peru State Teachers' College for two years, and was a student at the University of Nebraska for one semester. He received a second grade teacher's certificate from Peru. He has lived in Nebraska for sixty three years, during which time he has been a teacher, farmer, furniture dealer, undertaker, and banker. He served as county coroner in Cass County for nine years. At the present time he is vice president of the American Exchange Bank, and is an undertaker at Elmwood.

On September 23, 1885, he was united in marriage with Ida Minnie Bailey, at Elmwood. Mrs. Clements, who was born in Tioga County, Pennsylvania, April 27, 1867, is of early American and Pennsylvania German descent. There are six children: Guy Leland, born January 13, 1888, who married Marie Lorenz, and who is a banker and lawyer; Alma Hattie, born February 27, 1889, who is a doctor's assistant; Sanford L., born March 18, 1892, who married Hattie Renswold; Orley D., born September 2, 1894, who married Emma Kunz, and who is postmaster; Leroy Dick, born October 23, 1896, who married Gladys Maine, and is state supervisor of vocational agriculture, and Vernon, born February 27, 1898, who married Opal Turner, and is an undertaker and electrician. Four of the sons served in the World War.

Mr. Clements is a member of the State Historical Society; the Nebraskana Society, the Odd Fellows, the Elmwood Chamber of Commerce, and the Nebraska Undertakers' Association. He is a member of the Red Cross, and the Peter Van Fleet Memorial Methodist Episcopal Church. He is fond of hunting and fishing, and plays golf and chess. He is a Republican. Residence: Elmwood.

Leroy D. Clements

Leroy D. Clements was born at Elmwood, Nebraska, October 23, 1896, the son of Byron Isaac and Minnie Ida (Bailey) Clements. His father, who was born in New York State, February 17, 1865, has been county coroner, a farmer, undertaker, and banker. His ancestry is English. His mother was born at Tioga County, Pennsylvania, April 27, 1868, and is a musician and is active in the Rebecca Lodge. Her ancestry is Pennsylvania Dutch.

Mr. Clements was graduated from the Elmwood High School in 1915, and in 1923 was awarded the B. S. degree at the University of Nebraska. He was a student at Peru State Teachers College, 1913; was a graduate student at Colorado Agricultural College, 1929; and was granted a fellowship in agricultural education at the latter institution in 1931. He was a member of the Peru Men's Glee Club and Orchestra Club, 1917-18; held membership in the Dramatic Club at Peru, 1918; and was a member of the University of Nebraska Band, 1921-22. He was a charter member of Phi Tau Theta.

He has held the following positions: teacher at Sargeant Bluffs, Iowa, 1919-20; principal of schools at Alvo, Nebraska, 1921; vocational instructor in agriculture at Stromsburg, Nebraska, 1923-24-25; vocational agricultural instructor at Beatrice, Nebraska; 1925-26-27-28-29; and since 1929 has been state supervisor of Vocational Agriculture Education for Nebraska. He is the author of various articles on vocational education, 1930-31.

Mr. Clemnets served as second class musician in the 211th Engineers Regimental Band, and is a member of the American Legion. He holds membership in the American Vocational Association; the Nebraska State Teacher's Association; the Nebraska Vocational Agricultural Association; the Nebraska School Masters Club. He is a member of the Alpha Tau Alpha, and The Nebraskana Society.

He served as a member of the Agriculture Committee at Beatrice, in the Kiwanis club, 1926-29; and is a member of the Committee on Vocational Guidance and Placement, Kiwanis Club of Lincoln. During 1924 and 1925 he was a member of the Parent Teacher's Association at Stromsburg, and in 1921-22 was a member of the Young Men's Christian Association. He is affiliated with the Grace Methodist Episcopal Church of Lincoln. Mr. Clements is a Republican. His hobbies are music, photography, wood-work, and reading, while his favorite sport is fishing.

His marriage to Gladys Norene Mayne was solemnized at Lincoln June 18, 1924. Mrs. Clements, who is interested in music and art, was born at Shelby, Iowa, March 21, 1902; her ancestry is Irish and Pennsylvania Dutch. Residence: Lincoln.

Etta Jeanette Cleveland

Etta J. Cleveland was born at Coaticook, Standstead, Province of Quebec, Canada, July 15, 1867. Her father, Oliver Hanks, who was a farmer, was born in New York in 1824, and died at Coaticook, March 10, 1876. Her mother, Persis (Cooly) Hanks, was born at Whitefield, New Hampshire, June 10, 1827, and died at Falls City, Richardson County, Nebraska, December 25, 1901.

Mrs. Cleveland received her education at the Coaticook Academy and the Catholic Convent at Coaticook. She has been a resident of Nebraska for 47 years and has taken an interested part in the civic, social, and business affairs of her community for many years. She entered the business world at Ord, Nebraska, in 1884, and has been engaged in business with her husband, the late F. W. Cleveland of Nebraska City, as follows: Coaticook, 1888; Alliance, Nebraska, 1889; Denver, for four years; Falls City, Nebraska, 10 years; and Nebraska City for the last 25 years. Since the death of her husband the business has been carried on by their son, F. S. Cleveland.

Her marriage to F. W. Cleveland was solemnized at Coaticook, January 3, 1884. There are two children: Frederick S., born February 12, 1886; and Etta Jeanette, born January 25, 1889, who married Francis Baldwin Hall.

She is a member of St. Mary's Episcopal Church at Nebraska City.

Henry LaRue Click

Henry LaRue Click, prominent farmer and vice-president of the State Farmers Union was born in Gage County, Nebraska, February 19, 1882.

His father, Phylander Washington Click, was born in Ohio, October 31, 1844, and died at Denver, July 21, 1927. He was in the Civil War two years, serving with the Indiana volunteers. His wife, Sarah Ellen Parish, was born at Fort Wayne, Indiana, March 20, 1848, and died at Filley, Nebraska, August 22, 1920.

Mr. Click attended the public schools of Gage County and has since engaged in farming.

On April 8, 1903, he was married at Cortland. Mrs. Click was born at Adams, Nebraska, March 8, 1884, of English descent. They have three children, Marian, born January 16, 1908, who married Paul Sampson Chambers; Margaret, born July 9, 1910, who is a teacher; and Ruth Ellen, born July 12, 1916, who is a student.

Mr. Click is a Democrat. He is past director of the State Farmers Union, of which he is now vice-president. He is a member of the local board of the Nebraska Children's Home Society, is affiliated with Grand View Baptist Church, and is an Odd Fellow. His favorite sports are baseball and horseshoes. Residence: Chadron.

Henry Emerson Clifford

Henry Emerson Clifford, lawyer and city clerk of Grand Island, was born at South Paris, Maine, September 19, 1853, son of Jonathan Kendall and Harriett Newell (Hall) Clifford. The father, born in South Paris, January 1, 1820, was a farmer and a carpenter. His wife, also born at South Paris, December 5, 1825, was of English descent. Henry Emerson Clifford was united in marriage to Hattie E. Whitney, July 6, 1882, at Shirley, Massachusetts, and they have two children born to this union, Leon Emerson and Nona Beth. Hattie E. (Whitney) Clifford died December 4, 1931.

Leon Emerson Clifford, born at Grand Island, Nebraska, April 2, 1883, now lives in Randolph, Massachusetts. He married Maude Kenney and they have two children: Hugh Emerson, born January 6, 1912; and Hazle Beth, born February 6, 1917. Nona Beth Clifford, born at Grand Island, February 23, 1890, is a graduate of Grand Island High School and is now teaching in Columbus, Nebraska.

Henry Emerson Clifford attended country school and studied law in the offices of William Austin Williams at Worcester, Massachusetts, and the law offices of Othman Ali Abbott at Grand Island. He was admitted to the bar in Hall County, January 9, 1883.

Mr. Clifford came to Nebraska, March 1, 1882, and has made his home in Grand Island since that date. He was first elected to the office of justice of the peace about 1883, served for one term; was elected city clerk for one term in 1885; was assessor of the city of Grand Island 1887-88; was elected county judge of Hall County and served for three terms from January 1890 to 1896.

In 1901 he was elected member of the city council and was re-elected in 1903 and 1905. In March 1906 he was appointed city clerk and has been re-elected every two year term since that date. Mr. Clifford was never defeated but once and that was by Judge J. H. Mullen, about 1905, and in 1889 Mr. Clifford had defeated him. He is a Republican.

Mr. Clifford's religious affiliation is with the First Congregational Church of Grand Island. He is a member of The Nebraskana Society. Residence: Grand Island.

Edgar Cline

On January 31, 1890, Edgar Cline was born at Greenleaf, Washington County, Kansas, the son of Laurence and Mary (Flear) Cline. His father, who was a brick contractor, was born in Ontario, Canada, March 16, 1853.

He is descended from German ancestors who came to this country about 1850.

His mother was born at Lincolnshire, England, November 25, 1853. She was a member of the Church of England, and during her younger years was an active church worker.

Dr. Cline, who has practiced law in Nebraska for over 17 years, was a student at Creighton College for one year; and attended Creighton Medical College four years, where he was graduated in 1913. He served one year's internship in the St. Joseph Hospital, at Omaha. His M. D. was received at Creighton, where he was a member of Phi Beta Pi.

His marriage to Abbie Ann Thompson was solemnized at Manhattan, Kansas, January 19, 1918. Mrs. Cline, who was born at Humboldt, Richardson County, Nebraska, November 21, 1894, is of English and German ancestry. She is a member of the American Legion Auxiliary, the Order of Eastern Star, and the Auburn Country Club.

From 1914 to 1916, Dr. Cline was associated with Dr. Dillon, under the name Dillon & Cline. Since that time he has engaged in general medical practice.

During the late war he was a captain in the Medical Corps, from 1917 to May, 1919. He is a member of the American Legion; is secretary of the Red Cross; and is service officer for the American Legion.

A member of the county and state medical associations, he is also an active member of the Chamber of Commerce at Auburn. He is a Mason, Auburn Lodge Number 124, York Rite. His social club is the Auburn Country Club. He is affiliated with the Episcopal Church of Auburn. Dr. Cline's favorite sport is golf, and he is an ardent baseball enthusiast. He is a Republican. Residence: Auburn.

Frank Cline

Frank Cline, son of Lawrence and Mary (Flear) Cline, was born in Lansing, Michigan, May 3, 1875. His father was a native of Canada, born March 16, 1853, who later settled in Michigan. He married Mary Flear, who was born in England, November 25, 1854.

Mr. Cline attended Auburn High School, where he was graduated in May, 1894. In 1897 he was graduated from Kansas City College of Pharmacy. He was valedictorian of his class. On September 2, 1901, he was united in marriage with Lucile Ely, at Auburn, Nebraska. They have one son, Frank, Jr., born March 13, 1917, who attends Auburn High School. He is a member of the Glee Club, the Junior Band and the high school orchestra.

A Republican, Mr. Cline is chairman of the Republican county central committee, and active in the work of his party. He has been engaged in the drug business for the past thirty-two years, and has owned his own store for twenty-seven years. It contains a wallpaper, paint and glass department, gift shop and soda fountain. He has just finished the erection of the post office building at Auburn, with all new equipment.

During the war he was active in all loan drives, etc. He is president of the Auburn Chamber of Commerce, and active in the upbuilding of the city. He is a member of the Nebraska Pharmaceutical Association. A Mason, he is a Knight Templar. His social club is the Auburn Country Club. Residence: Auburn.

Lucile Cline

Lucile Cline, wife of Frank Cline, was born at Auburn, July 13, 1876, daughter of James Fitz and Mary Ann De-Lay Ely. Her father, a farmer and stockman, was born at Springfield, New York, May 18, 1843, and is still living. He is descended from English settlers in America about 1625. He is a direct descendant of Warren Ely, whose father, Simeon Ely served in the Revolution, and who witnessed the execution of General Andre and the surrender of General Burgoyne. He married Mary Ann DeLay, who was born in Appanoose County, Iowa, July

10, 1852, and died at Auburn, October 5, 1904. She was French, a daughter of Joseph DeLay.

Mrs. Cline graduated from Auburn High School in 1895, and attended business college and conservatory at Quincy, Illinois, in 1899. She was president of her class at Auburn High School. She is a member of P. E. O., and held offices of guard, recording secretary and now vice president.

Since her marriage on September 2, 1901, she has been active in club and community work in Auburn and vicinity. A member of the Daughters of the American Revolution, she was regent of Ann Froissart chapter 1928-29; she is also state historian, state chairman of historical research, member of the national committee on historical research and member of the Arbor Lodge committee. Affiliated with the First Methodist Church, she was president of the Ladies' Aid four years, and is member of the official board. She was matron of O. E. S. two years, and was an officer in Ada chapter Number 2 for sixteen years. She has filled most of the offices in Ada chapter.

For the past 16 years she has been closely associated in business with her husband, and does the buying for the gift and wall paper departments. She is state president of the Ladies' Auxiliary Pharmaceutical Association, elected in June, 1930, at Omaha. She was formerly active in the Parents-Teachers' Association, and is a member of the Red Cross, and vice president of the local Welfare Society. Her social clubs include the Auburn Country, where she was first chairman of the ladies' committee, and the Bridge Luncheon Club, of which she has served as president.

Mrs. Cline has one son, Frank, Jr., born March 13, 1917, who attends Auburn High School and is active in music. Residence: Auburn.

Jennie Closs

Jennie Closs, daughter of Morris and Annie Jones, was born near Wymore, Nebraska, on the farm of her parents, March 16, 1881. Morris Closs was born in Wales, Great Britain, in the year 1846 and came to this country, where he later became engaged in farming. He died on December 25, 1928, at Wymore. Annie Jones, the mother of Jennie Closs, was born at Belmont, Wisconsin, December 9, 1858. She is now living at the age of seventy-three years.

Jennie Closs received her early education, which consisted of the elementary grades, in a country school.

She was united in marriage to E. H. Closs at her farm home near Wymore, March 9, 1904. To this union were born three children, Ellsworth, born January 3, 1909; Maldwyn, born December 25, 1911, and Elvira, born October 23, 1913. They are all graduates of the Wymore High School.

Mr. Closs died August 18, 1930, leaving his wife and children to manage the two hundred and forty acre farm on which they reside.

Mrs. Closs is a member of the Bethel Presbyterian Church. She gave her assistance in garment making for the Red Cross during the World War. She is a member of The Nebraskana Society, the Ladies Aid Society, of which she was president in 1927. Residence: Wymore.

Frank Clough

Frank Clough, prominent in banking circles for many years, but now retired, was born at Bishop Wilten, Yorkshire, England, May 6, 1864. He is the son of George and Mary (Jordan) Clough the former born at New-Port, Yorkshire, October 3, 1821, and the latter at New-Port, March 8, 1823. George Clough was a farmer, who came to America in 1878, with his family, locating near Allen, Nebraska, where he died on September 10, 1893. His wife survived him until April, 1900.

Educated in Mechanics Institute in England, Mr. Clough was a banker for many years until his recent retirement. He was married to Bessie Sarah Frantz at

Allen, on October 3, 1889. She was born in Verona, Dana County, Wisconsin. Of this marriage there are seven children: Edna May, born July 5, 1890, who married D. C. Travers; William W., born August 16, 1891, who married Florence Herrick; Fay J., born September 1, 1893, who married Beva Harris; Martin H., born February 18, 1895, who married Lucile Goodner; Floyd F., born June 27, 1898, who married Marie Gaughran; Benjamin F., born September 29, 1901, who married Ruby Wheeler; and Bessie B., born October 8, 1906, who attended Wayne Normal College.

Mr. Clough was local registrar, and active in the sale of Liberty bonds during the World War, receiving a medal from the government for patriotic service. He is a member of the First Methodist Church of Allen, and the Ancient Free and Accepted Masons and the Odd Fellows. He is a life member of The Nebraskana Society. Residence: Allen.

Augustus Davis Cloyd

For the past 46 years Augustus D. Cloyd has been a practicing physician in Nebraska, and has taken an active part in the civic and welfare affairs of Omaha. He was born at Fayette, Howard County, Missouri, February 17, 1860, the son of John Wesley and Eliza Jane (Basye) Cloyd. His father, who was born at Boonsboro, Howard County, Missouri, September 4, 1826, and died at Fayette, May 30, 1891, was a farmer, and served in the Confederate Army during the Civil War; his ancestry was Scotch-Irish. His mother, who was of English descent, was born in Culpepper County, Virginia, June 2, 1826, and died at Fayette, December 6, 1910.

Dr. Cloyd attended Central College at Fayette, and later was graduated from Missouri Medical College at St. Louis, Missouri. He was admitted to the practice of medicine at Falls City, Nebraska, March, 1886, and since that date has been active in the medical world in Nebraska. He has been medical director of the Woodmen of the World since 1898. He is the author of *Genealogy of the Cloyd, Basye, and Tapp Families in America,* published in 1912. He has contributed many articles to various medical and fraternal journals.

His marriage to Nina E. Smith was solemnized at St. Louis, April 14, 1896. Mrs. Cloyd, who was born December 3, 1871, has traced her English ancestry back to the year 1400. They have one son: Augustus David, born June 15, 1898, who married Jean Hampton; he was awarded his A. B. degree at Amherst College in 1920, and his M. D. degree at the University of Nebraska, 1925, and is in successful practice in Omaha.

Dr. Cloyd is a member of the Douglas County Medical Society; the Nebraska State Medical Society, and the American Medical Association. He was the organizer and is the president of the Omaha Spanish Club. Perhaps his greatest achievement was his work for the Nebraska Tuberculosis Association of which he was co-founder and is a director. He holds membership in the Omaha Chamber of Commerce, the Young Men's Christian Association, and the Woodmen of the World. He is a Mason. His social club is the Happy Hollow Country Club of Omaha. He is affiliated with the First Baptist Church of Omaha. Politically, Dr. Cloyd is an independent Democrat. Residence: Omaha.

Ralph George Coad

Ralph George Coad, a life time resident of Nebraska, has been active in the political and legal affairs of Omaha, for the past twenty years. He was born at Omaha, Douglas County, Nebraska, June 17, 1889, the son of John F. and Ellen M. (Leahy) Coad. His father, who was born in Ireland, December 5, 1842, led an interesting life and was a prominent figure in the west in pioneer days. He was a rancher, banker, real estate man, who came to

America in 1849. He was director of the Metropolitan Utilities District from the time of its creation in 1903 to 1910; president of the Packers National Bank of South Omaha, and director of the Merchants National Bank of Omaha; was a freighter between Omaha and Denver before the days of the railroad; and was a contractor who supplied all the United States army posts in western Nebraska and Wyoming with hay and wood. He died at Omaha, October 15, 1910.

His mother, who was born in Ireland, was the first pupil at the old Catholic Convent at Nebraska City, and settled with her parents in Nemaha County in 1855 when that county was practically unsettled. She died at Omaha, December 18, 1923.

Mr. Coad was graduated from the grade schools at Omaha in 1903, and in 1907 was graduated from the high school department of Creighton University. He was awarded his A. B. degree at the University of Nebraska, 1911; and received the LL. B. at Columbia Law School at Columbia University, New York City, 1913. He was a member of Phi Delta Theta fraternity. During his high school days he was captain of the football team.

He is secretary of the Coad Real Estate Company; is secretary of the Clark Land & Development Company; is director of the Maple Grove Land & Livestock Company; Argonant Real Estate Company, a subsidiary of General Motors; and is attorney for the Packers National Bank of Omaha, and for the Nebraska division of General Motors.

Mr. Coad was elected to a six year term as director of the Metropolitan Utilities District of Omaha, January 1, 1931, succeeding his brother, William J. Coad, who had served as a director since 1913. In 1922 he served as vice chairman of the Democratic Central Committee.

He was united in marriage February 17, 1920, at New York City, to Laura Lyttleton Callahan. Mrs. Coad is a daughter of a prominent physician and surgeon at Staten Island, New York. They have two children: Laura L., born October 2, 1923; and Adeline V., born October 28, 1925.

During the World War Mr. Coad was first lieutenant of the air service from May 12, 1917, to December 12, 1918. He is first vice-commander of the American Legion in Douglas County; was one of the organizers of this body in Omaha and in Nebraska; and attended the caucus which organized the American Legion in St. Louis in 1919.

He is a member of the Omaha Bar Association and the Nebraska State Bar Association. In 1925 he served as president of the United Improvement Club of Omaha. He is a member of St. Margaret Mary's Church at Omaha. He is a member of the Parent Teachers' Association and the Nebraskana Society. Residence: Omaha.

Frank Jefferson Coates

One of Nebraska's pioneer bankers and executives is Frank Jefferson Coates who has been a resident of this state for over 60 years. He was born at Boscobel, Wisconsin, January 16, 1868, the son of Francis Jefferson Coates and Rachel Susanna (Drew) Coates. His father, a farmer and a Civil War veteran, 7th Wisconsin Infantry, died at Dorchester, Nebraska, January 20, 1880.

Mr. Coates attended school at Boscobel, Wisconsin, and at Dorchester. He is president of the Grand Island National Bank, the Dolan Fruit Company, and is director in the Ulry Talbert Company. He holds membership in The Nebraskana Society, is affiliated with the First Presbyterian Church of Grand Island, and is a 32nd degree Mason. He is a member of the Sons of Veterans of which he has been state commander.

Mr. Coates was united in marriage to Mary Mattes on October 12, 1887. There are four children, George Francis, Mercer Mattes, Lucile Marie, and Evelyn Ruth. Of his marriage to Harriet Evelyn Ferris the following children were born: Stanley Ferris; and Donald Robert. Mr. Coates likes to golf. Residence: Grand Island.

Frank Emerson Coatsworth

Frank E. Coatsworth was born at Toronto, Ontario, Canada, May 18, 1878, the son of John Taylor and Rebecca (Reid) Coatsworth. His father, who was born at Toronto, September 12, 1851, of English descent, is a contractor. His mother was born near Barrie, Ontario, Canada, September 19, 1851; she is of Scotch-Irish descent.

Mr. Coatsworth received his education in the public schools of Omaha, Douglas County, Nebraska; was president of his freshman class in high school; and was a member of the Demosthenian Debating Society at Omaha High School. He has lived in Nebraska since 1883 and is now president of the Queen Incubator Company of Lincoln, Nebraska. He has written several magazine articles on business management.

His marriage to Maude Carolyn Brooks was solemnized at Mitchellville, Polk County, Iowa, August 7, 1902. Mrs. Coatsworth was born at Clarion, Wright County, Iowa, November 30, 1880. Their two children are: Reed Hamilton, born November 5, 1906, who married Geraldine Jones; and Franklyn Bard, born April 3, 1915. Reed Hamilton is executive and manager of the Queen Incubator Company of Lincoln.

Mr. Coatsworth is president of The Incubators Manufacturers Association of America; was president of the Rotary Club 1924-25; is past president of the Hiram Club; Lincoln chapter of the Isaak Walton League, and of the Rotary Club. He is a member of the Elks Lodge Number 39 of Lincoln, and holds membership in the Scottish Rite and York Rite Masonic Lodge. His social clubs are the University Club and the Lincoln Country Club. Residence: Lincoln.

Robert LeRoy Cochran

Robert LeRoy Cochran, state engineer and secretary of the Department of Public Works, was born at Avoca, Nebraska, January 28, 1886. He is the son of Charles A. and Jane (Wilkinson) Cochran, the former born at Galena, Illinois, September 18, 1848. A farmer of Scotch-Irish descent, he died at Brady, Nebraska, December 7, 1914. Jane, his wife, was a native of Illinois of English descent.

Mr. Cochran attended Brady High School from which he was graduated in 1906. In 1910 he received his B. Sc. in C. E. from the University of Nebraska. From 1911-15 he was county engineer of Lincoln County, and from 1915 to 1917 was state bridge inspector and deputy state engineer. Enlisting in 1917 he was stationed at Fort Snelling and Fort Monroe three months, and served overseas with the rank of first lieutenant and captain of artillery. At the present time he is a member of the Officers Reserve Corps wih the rank of lieutenant-colonel. Upon his discharge he became state engineer in 1923, which position he still holds. His memberships include the American Society of Civil Engineers, the Engineer's Club of Lincoln, the Chamber of Commerce, American Legion, and Veterans of Foreign Wars. He is a former member of the Rotary and Lions Clubs, and is a Mason, Knight Templar, member of the Scottish Rite and Shrine, and the Elks. He likes hiking and enjoys reading and working on his lawn and garden.

On March 18, 1919, he was married to Aileen Gantt at North Platte. Mrs. Cochran was born there on November 4, 1888. They have two children, Mary Aileen, born December 25, 1922, and Robert LeRoy, born August 16, 1924. Residence: Lincoln.

George Edwin Codington

Born in Tulala, Illinois, December 1, 1868, George E. Codington has been a resident of Nebraska more than forty years. His father, Joseph W. Codington was born in Illinois in 1840. A farmer, he was of English descent, and was active in his church and community. Together with his wife, Charlotte (Jones) Codington, he came to

Nebraska in 1888, bringing his family with him. Charlotte Codington was a native of Ohio, and of Irish parentage. She died at Auburn in 1913. Joseph W. Codington died at Auburn in 1903.

George Codington attended the country and village schools in and near Tulala, and after coming to Nebraska completed a business course at Cotner University. By training and heridity a farmer, he has always been interested in the upbuilding of the community. He is a Democrat and served as Nemaha county treasurer from 1900-04. His marriage to Mamie Idella Dixon was solemnized at Falls City, June 5, 1901. Mrs. Codington is descended on the maternal side from early Dutch settlers in Pennsylvania. She is active in the community and is a member of the Woman's Club, and holds office in the Order of Eastern Star. Both she and Mr. Codington are members of the First Church of Christ, in which he has been a deacon for many years. Their only daughter, Ruth, was born March 8, 1902. She attended William Woods Girls' School at Fulton, Missouri, and is a graduate of the University of Nebraska. She is a member of Phi Mu, the P. E. O. Sisterhood and the Daughters of the American Revolution. Prior to her marriage to Joseph M. Alden of York she taught French and English five years. There is one son, John Codington Alden.

During his business career Mr. Codington has been active in the promotion and advancement of the interests of the city. He was for twenty years manager of the Auburn Telephone Company, which was later merged with the Lincoln Telephone Company, and is still a director of that organization. For six years he was president of the Nemaha County Bank, and for the past seven or eight years he has been a member of the Auburn Building and Loan Association. In addition he has extensive farming interests.

A member of the Nebraska Council of Defense during the World War, Mr. Codington was active in the various loan drives and in Red Cross work. For twelve years he served as member of the school board, and has always been active in the Boy Scout organization. He is a member of the Chamber of Commerce and was its president two years. He is also a Kiwanian and Woodman of the World. Residence: Auburn.

Harry B. Coffee

Harry B. Coffee, real estate and insurance man, was born in Sioux County, Nebraska, March 16, 1890, son of Samuel Buffington and Elizabeth (Tisdale) Coffee. His ancestry is Scotch-Irish, a grandfather having been a colonel in the Confederate army during the Civil War.

Mr. Coffee attended public and high schools and was graduated from the University of Nebraska in 1913 with a Bachelor of Arts degree. He is at the present time managing extensive real estate holdings, is the president of the Coffee Cattle Company, a $100,000.00 corporation. He is a member of the Rotary Club, the Elks and the Masons. During the late war he held the rank of second lieutenant in the air service. His favorite sport is traveling. Residence: Chadron.

Rex Tisdale Coffee

Rex Tisdale Coffee, a stockman, was born at Georgetown, Texas, February 27, 1892, son of Samuel Buffington and Mary Elizabeth (Tisdale) Coffee.

The father, a stockman of Irish descent, was descended from General Coffee, defender of New Orleans and Atlanta. He died at Harrison, Nebraska, October 1, 1900. His wife, Mary Elizabeth Tisdale, is living.

Mr. Coffee was graduated from Chadron High School in 1911, and received the Bachelor of Science degree from Chadron State College. During 1911 and 1912, he attended the University of Nebraska. One of the best athletes in northwestern Nebraska, Mr. Coffee was active in athletics, both in college and in high school. He received a football letter three years at Chadron, a letter in track one year, and three letters in basketball.

In 1915, he acquired 1800 acres of unimproved land, and today has 2800 acres of land, all well improved. He has 300 acres in alfalfa, 200 acres in farm ground, and has a herd of 300 head of cattle, all registered.

On June 15, 1918, he was married to Ermine Carmean at Chadron. She was born at Fairfax, Missouri, November 17, 1895. They have two children, Jeane, born March 1, 1921; and Rex T. Jr., born March 28, 1923.

Mr. Coffee is a Democrat. He is a member of the Methodist Episcopal Church, the Chamber of Commerce, the Masons, and the school board, of which he is a director. He is a member of the Harrison Country Club. His favorite sport is baseball. Residence: Harrison.

Harry Joseph Coffin

Born at Boston, Massachusetts, January 11, 1860, Harry Joseph Coffin, who is now retired, was for many years active in the lumber business in Nebraska.

He is the son of Henry Joseph and Harriet Frances (Merriam) Coffin, the former born at Columbia Falls, Maine, July 7, 1830. Henry J. Coffin was a wood carver and furniture manufacturer of the old school, who designed piano legs and lyres for pedals, and was the winner of several prizes when wood carving was in vogue. In his Boston shop in 1870 he employed about thirty persons. Of English ancestry, he was a descendant of Tristram Coffin.

Harriet Frances Merriam was born at Boston, February 21, 1835, and was descended from English settlers who were continental soldiers, living at Merriam Corners, between Lexington and Concord, Massachusetts, in 1770. She died at Burwell, Nebraska, October 2, 1928, while her husband died on September 2, 1894.

Harry Joseph Coffin attended primary and grammar school, and West Roxbury High School at Jamaica Plains. Later he was a student at Chauncey Hall in Boston.

Coming to Nebraska nearly fifty-four years ago, he first was a piano tuner. From 1877, until 1892, he engaged in farming and thereafter was a lumber dealer thirty years. During part of that time he also engaged in the mercantile business under the names of Bunnell and Coffin and the Burwell Mercantile Company.

An independent Republican, Mr. Coffin served as justice of the peace in 1889, school director in 1890, county commissioner in 1892, and from 1919 to 1925, was a member of the school board. He also served three terms as a member of the town board.

At the present time Mr. Coffin is a director of the First State Bank of Burwell. While in school in 1875, he was a member of the Boston High School regiment, and during the World War was chairman of the Garfield County Council of Defense and chairman of the Victory loan. He is affiliated with the Congregational Church, the Wranglers Club, the Odd Fellows and the Masons. In the archives of the family at Nantucket, Massachusetts, is a letter written by Benjamin Franklin, addressed to his kinfolks, the Coffins.

On May 1, 1893, Mr. Coffin was married to Mary Halloran at Inman, Nebraska. Mrs. Coffin, who was born at Rockford, Iowa, October 29, 1866, is half Irish and half English. She was a teacher in the public schools for eight years prior to her marriage.

Mrs. Coffin is eligible to the Women's Relief Corps, her father having served as a Union soldier in the Civil War. She is a member of the Order of Eastern Star, the Rebekas, the Congregational Church, and is a former member of the Carnegie Library board. She is past president of the Burwell Women's Club.

There are three children living, Frances, born August 13, 1895, who married Frank Earnest DeLashmutt; Olive, born November 2, 1898, who married Ralph Leo Walker; and Margaret, born November 25, 1900. Henry, born

November 25, 1900, died April 14, 1901. Frances and Olive were teachers prior to marriage. Margaret, who taught for a time is now in business college. Residence: Burwell. (Photograph in Album).

Berta Coffman

Berta Coffman was born in Winnisheik County, Iowa, April 14, 1872, the daughter of Lewis and Ruthey (Farnham) Grandy. Her father, who was a farmer, was born in Canada, June 6, 1836, and died at Hebron, Thayer County, Nebraska, January 5, 1903; his parents came to this country in 1872. Her mother, a descendant of John Quincy Adams, was born at East Liberty, Ohio, April 29, 1846, and died at Fairbury, Jefferson County, Nebraska, October 27, 1930.

Mrs. Coffman was graduated from the Fairbury High School in 1889, and for many years has been prominent in civic and social affairs in Jefferson County. She is the author of various songs, poems, and plays used in local community work, and is a member of the Fairbury Methodist Episcopal Church. She is a member of the Woman's Club, is ex-president of the local Red Cross, and is a member of the Nebraskana Society. At various times she has superintended the woman's division in county fair work. She is independent, politically.

Her marriage to Milton Abraham Coffman was solemnized at Fairbury, November 9, 1892. Mr. Coffman, who is a farmer and stockman, was born at Palmyra, Warren County, Iowa, September 15, 1868. To their marriage three children were born: Helen, born September 8, 1893, who is a candy jobber; Milton, born March 11, 1903, who married Charlotte Gantz; and Lucille, born May 27, 1908. Milton is a sheep rancher; he is baritone soloist for several musical organizations at Casper, Wyoming. Lucille is a school teacher and soloist of note. Residence: Fairbury.

Frank Cohee

Born at Beemer, Nebraska, December 1, 1887, Frank Cohee is the son of Cornelius Alexander and Minerva Frances (Cannon) Cohee. His father, who was a farmer, was born in Indiana, in October, 1838, and died at Beemer, January 20, 1921; he served with the 10th Illinois Cavalry for over four years during the Civil War as sergeant, scout, and dispatch carrier. His mother, whose ancestry was Welch, was born in Menard County, Illinois, in 1849, and died at Beemer, Nebraska, July 22, 1909; she was a cousin of the founder of the Grand Army of the Republic, and her father was a cousin of the noted Uncle Joe Cannon.

Mr. Cohee was graduated from the Beemer High School and for a number of years has been a farmer near Elgin. He is a director in the Elgin Creamery Association, is affiliated with the Methodist Church of Elgin, and holds membership in the Masons and Order of Eastern Star. He is a member of the Home Guards, is active in Red Cross and relief affairs, and holds membership in the Nebraskana Society.

His marriage to Sadie Elizabeth Ayr took place at Lyons, Nebraska, December 17, 1913. Mrs. Cohee, who was a teacher, was born of Irish and Dutch parentage at Lyons, October 20, 1887, and died at Beemer, December 15, 1915. One daughter was born to them: Evelyn, December 15, 1915, who is a student in the Elgin High School. Mr. Cohee was married to Luella Henrietta Herrmann at West Point, Nebraska, September 12, 1923. She was a commercial teacher and stenographer prior to her marriage. Residence: Elgin.

Walter Coker

Walter Coker, general merchant at Sutherland, was born at Montfort, Wisconsin, October 17, 1871, son of John and Adelaide (Calame) Coker.

His father, born in Cornwall, England, October 29, 1829, died at Sutherland, September 17, 1914. He was a farmer and stockman. His wife, Adelaide, was born at Aniton, Wisconsin, February 14, 1840, and died at Sutherland, April 29, 1920. Her father, Peter Calame, was born in France, and her mother, Sarah Lamb (Calame) in County Down, Ireland.

Mr. Coker attended North Platte High School, and worked as a cow hand from 1890 until 1896 for the John Bratt ranch. From that time until 1900, he was employed by a government contractor delivering beef cattle to the Sioux Indians at Pine Ridge, and Rosebud reservations of South Dakota. In 1900 he went into the hay business, buying and selling until 1913 when he opened the general merchandise store under the name of E. & W. Coker at Sutherland, and continued in this business until April, 1931, at which time Mr. Coker purchased the interest of Ed Coker, and since then he has operated the store under the name of Cokers Store.

On December 27, 1899, he was married to Eva Leuella Peyton at Gordon, Nebraska. Mrs. Coker was born at Walker, Iowa, May 13, 1879, and before her marriage was a school teacher in Cherry County. She came from Walker, Iowa, with her parents who homesteaded south of Chadron, in 1885. There are two children, Mainard, born November 13, 1901, who works in the store with his father; and Lucille, born May 13, 1908, who was a graduate of the University of Nebraska in the class of 1930, is a members of Alpha Phi Sorority, and is completing her second term teaching the high school at Dalton.

Mr. Coker has resided in Nebraska since 1885. He is a member of the Sutherland Presbyterian Church, and the Sutherland Lodge of the Ancient Free and Accepted Masons. Residence: Sutherland.

William Orlin Colburn

William Orlin Colburn has been a distinguished physician at Lincoln, Nebraska, since 1904. He was born at Warren, Jo Daviess County, Illinois, August 5, 1880, the son of William Robinson and Ruth (Bradley) Colburn. His father, who was a hardware merchant, was born at Champion, New York, May 6, 1833, and died at Waterloo, Blackhawk County, Iowa, May 1, 1914. He was a first lieutenant in the Civil War. His ancestry was Scotch.

His mother was born at White Pigeon, Michigan, July 15, 1837, and died at Waterloo, September 17, 1917. She was of English descent.

Dr. Colburn was graduated from the Dexter High School at Dexter, Iowa, in 1893, and in 1897 was graduated from Dexter Normal School. He was a student at the University of Iowa, 1900-02, and was awarded his M. D. degree at Northwestern University Medical College where he was graduated in 1904.

He was admitted to the practice of medicine at Lincoln, September, 1904. From 1904 to 1915 he was engaged in general medical practice and since 1915 he has been a specialist in pediatrics. He is the founder and chief physician of the Lincoln Children's Clinic. He is the author of numerous articles appearing annually in the Nebraska State Medical Journal.

He was married to Ethel Reighter at Kansas City, Missouri, October 18, 1905. Mrs. Colburn was born at Bedford, Taylor County, Iowa, January 27, 1879. They have one daughter: Carolyn, born October 15, 1924.

Dr. Colburn is a member of the following professional organizations: American Academy of Pediatrics; American Medical Association; Central States Pediatric Society; Nebraska State Medical Society; and Lancaster Medical Society. He is a member of the Rotary Club and the Chamber of Commerce at Lincoln. He is a 32nd degree Mason, and a member of Lincoln Lodge Number 19, Lincoln Consistory, Valley of Lincoln, Orient of Nebraska, and Scottish Rite. He holds membership in the Young Men's Christian Association and the First Presbyterian Church of Lincoln. He is a Republican, and his hobby is travel. Residence: Lincoln.

Demmitt C. Cole

Demmitt C. Cole, prominent banker of Polk County, Nebraska, has lived in this state for over 54 years and has been active in the educational and business affairs of his county. He was born at Rising City, Butler County, Nebraska, June 9, 1874, the son of Lorenzo Dow and Julia Matilda (Lemon) Cole. His father, who was a farmer in Butler County for many years, was born near Cincinnati, Ohio, February 22, 1847, and died at Surprise, Nebraska, November 1, 1920. His mother was born in Indiana, June 24, 1853, and died at Rising City, May 9, 1915.

Mr. Cole was a student at the David City High School and later attended Bryant Normal at Stromsburg, Nebraska. From 1892 to 1901 he taught in country and city schools, and from 1901 to 1904 he served as county superintendent of schools in Polk County. For the next three years he was engaged in farming; in 1909 he organized the Shelby State Bank, serving as cashier for thirteen years. He is now president of the bank and is serving as president of the State Bank of Surprise.

He was united in marriage with Maude Edna Lott, July 21, 1896, at Rising City. To this marriage four children were born: Otis D., born April 24, 1906; Richard M., born December 29, 1909, who married Leah Watkins; Lester D., born May 7, 1911; and Leonard L., born January 26, 1917. Otis, Richard, and Lester are all university graduates.

Mr. Cole is affiliated with the Methodist Church of Shelby, and holds membership in the Red Cross, the Independent Order of Odd Fellows, and the Nebraskana Society. Residence: Shelby.

Harold Sterigere Cole

Harold Sterigere Cole was born at Oakdale, Nebraska, April 2, 1891. Willis Woodington Cole, his father, who was born at Towanda, Pennsylvania, September 10, 1858, was a registered pharmacist and served as postmaster, state drug inspector, and state representative: he died at Lincoln, Nebraska, January 10, 1926. Charlotte Rena Shenefelt, his mother, who is prominent in club affairs, music and dramatics, was born in Huntington County, Pennsylvania, December 21, 1869. Her parents were farmers.

Mr. Cole was graduated from the Neligh High School in 1908 and from 1908 to 1911 was a student at Nebraska Wesleyan University where he received college letters in baseball and football. He was employed as sub-railway mail clerk for a short time, was assistant postmaster at Neligh for three years, engaged in professional baseball for a time, and since the World War has been a rural mail carrier. He served as private and as corporal in Company D, 341st Machine Gun Battalion in the St. Mihiel and Meuse Argonne engagements during the war, and since 1930 has been commander of the Neligh post of the American Legion.

He is interested in football, baseball, and other sports but is no longer active as a player; he has helped coach various football teams and was manager and coach of the state champion baseball team of the American Legion Juniors for 1931. He is a member of the Neligh Volunteer Fire Department. Politically he is a Republican.

On November 23, 1922, Mr. Cole was married to Mirtie Iona Elliot Bolton, at Fullerton, Nebraska. Mrs. Cole, whose ancestry is Scotch-Dutch, was born at Gresham, Nebraska, February 16, 1888. An infant daughter born to them August 2, 1925, died at birth. They have an adopted son, Eugene Willis, born April 21, 1927. The following children are Mrs. Cole's by a former marriage; Eva Nancy Bolton; Jeanette Gertrude Bolton; and James Bolton. Residence: Neligh.

Leon Minor Cole

Leon Minor Cole, county clerk of Arthur County, was born at Strang, Fillmore County, Nebraska, September 5, 1903, son of Delbert Dean and Anna Mary (Eck) Cole. The father was born in Nuckolls County, Nebraska, June 11, 1880, and is a banker at Keystone, Nebraska. His mother was born in Pennsylvania, November 14, 1881.

Mr. Cole attended public and high school in Arthur County, and from 1922 until November, 1929, was editor of the *Arthur Enterprise*. At the present time he is county clerk of Arthur County.

He is married to Ruth Elizabeth Wilson who was born at Red Cloud, March 6, 1908. They have one daughter, Shirley Ann, born July 16, 1929.

Mr. Cole is a member of the Odd Fellows and the Nebraskana Society. He enjoys baseball, while his hobby is reading. Residence: Arthur.

Maynard Copeland Cole

Maynard C. Cole was born at East Norton, Bristol County, Massachusetts, October 5, 1877. His father, Ansel Orlester Cole, who was born at Rehoboth, Massachusetts, April 12, 1853, was secretary of the M. A. Disbrow and Company for many years, and was factory superintendent of this company at Lyons, Iowa, at one time; he is descended from Captain Simeon Cole; the Cole family came from the Isle of Wight, Wales, to America early in the 16th century.

His mother, Martha Louise (Copeland) Cole, who was born at Norton, Bristol County, Massachusetts, June 15, 1857, was a direct descendant of John Alden and Captain Miles Standish. She attended Wheaton College at Norton, and was a talented musician; she died early in her married life, April 16, 1884, at Attleboro, Massachusetts.

Mr. Cole was graduated from the high school at Clinton, Iowa, June, 1896, and in 1900, received the B. S. degree from Northwestern University at Evanston, Illinois. He was a member of the glee club and the University Quartette, and was awarded Phi Beta Kappa honors. He served as secretary of Beta Theta Pi, 1898-1899.

In 1900 he entered the employ of M. A. Disbrow and Company. He is now secretary and assistant treasurer of this organization, which is a woodworking industry.

His marriage to Florence Edith Moody was solemnized at Omaha April 15, 1903. Mrs. Cole, who was born at Bellows Falls, Vermont, December 23, 1878, is descended from a long line of illustrious ancestors, among them: Richard Trent, first governor of Connecticut; and Sir Robert Whitney, who in turn was descended from William the Conqueror. Three children were born to them: Helen Copeland, born December 29, 1905; Gertrude Sager, born May 28, 1907, who died March 16, 1924;and Florence Moody, born December 3, 1912, who died of injuries received in the tornado of 1913, April 16, 1913. Helen was graduated from Northwestern University in 1928, and is now on the staff of that institution as assistant to the personnel director.

Mr. Cole served as captain in Liberty loan drives during the late war. He is a member of the Sons of the American Revolution and is secretary of the Nebraska Society of Mayflower Descendants. He is a member of the Omaha Chamber of Commerce; the Parent Teachers Association; the Red Cross; The Nebraskana Society; and the local Young Men's Christian Association. He is a member of the University Club. He is a member of the Episcopal Church and is secretary of the Vestry of Trinity Cathedral. He likes golf, baseball, football, and hiking. He has lived in Omaha for the past 30 years. He is a Republican. Residence: Omaha.

Raymond Voorhis Cole

Raymond Voorhis Cole, funeral director, was born at Troy, New York, March 12, 1869, and came to Nebraska in 1895. He is the son of Thomas and Polly (Raymond) Cole, the former of whom is a descendant of John Jacob

Cole (Kroll in Holland), who settled in Duchess County, New York about 1622. Thomas Cole was born at Troy, December 13, 1824, and was a horticulturist and agriculturist all his life. He died at Troy, November 5, 1904. His wife, Polly Raymond, was born in Westchester County, New York, in April, 1830, and died at Troy in 1921. She was of French descent, and several of her ancestors served in the Revolutionary War.

Mr. Cole attended Union Classical Institute at Schenectady, New York, and was graduated in 1889. He also attended Union College at Schenectady, and Rutgers College, at New Brunswick, New Jersey, from 1889-1892. He is a member of Delta Kappa Epsilon. He has been engaged in the undertaking business most of his life, and has been president of the Cole-McKay Mortuary since its organization.

He was married to Lena B. Vanderzee at Troy, New York, September 10, 1890. Mrs. Cole was born at Troy, December 21, 1871, daughter of Edgar F. Vanderzee who served with the 169th New York Volunteers in the Civil War. They have two children, Sara Raymond, born May 8, 1894, who married William T. Usinger. She was graduated from the University of Nebraska and was a Phi Beta Kappa. Evelyn Lucy, born September 8, 1903, married Roderick D. Clark.

Mr. Cole is a Republican. He attends the First Presbyterian Church of Omaha, and is an elder in the church. He is a member of the Chamber of Commerce, and Omaha Lodge No. 2, of the Odd Fellows. He is past master of Right Angle Lodge No. 303, Ancient Free and Accepted Masons, past high priest of Delta Chapter No. 60, Royal Arch Masons, and member of Mt. Calvary Commandery and the Scottish Rite body. He is also a member of Omaha Lodge No. 39 of the Elks. Residence: Lincoln.

Roscoe James Cole

Born at Farnam, Nebraska, June 1, 1889, Roscoe James Cole is the son of Charles Gilbert and Sylvia Ann (Phillips) Cole. His father, a farmer, was born of German parents in Iowa, and died at Cambridge, Nebraska, on September 3, 1924. His mother, whose ancestry is Swedish, was born in Missouri, September 16, 1860, and died at Cambridge, August 2, 1928.

Mr. Cole attended District School Number 55 in Frontier County, Nebraska, and was a student at Cambridge High School. He is manager of the branch office at Cambridge of the Jerpe Commission Company of Omaha, Nebraska, is a member of the Cambridge Community Club, and holds membership in the First Congregational Church of Cambridge. He is a Mason. He served as Master of Lodge Number 150, in 1927 and 1928.

He married Bessie Newcomb at Cambridge, February 21, 1909. Mrs. Cole, who was a rural school teacher for some time before her marriage, died at Cambridge, June 1, 1927. One child was born to this marriage, Virginia June 4, 1917. On December 26, 1928, Mr. Cole was united in marriage with Etta M. Kinder. Residence: Cambridge.

Roy Olin Cole

Roy O. Cole was born at Plattsmouth, Cass County. Nebraska, October 7, 1887. He is the son of Shadrach Olin and Caroline (Cook) Cole. His father, who was a farmer and real estate investments dealer, was born at Fort Madison, Lee County, Iowa, October 23, 1854. He is descended from English, Scotch, and Dutch ancestors, who settled in Nebraska in 1857. He lives on a farm that his grandfather purchased more than seventy years ago.

Caroline Cole was born at Plattsmouth, March 19, 1863. Her parents came to America from Germany, and migrated to Nebraska in 1856; they were among the first pioneers in the western states.

Mr. Cole received his education in district schools and studied at home for several years. A resident of Nebras-

ka for 43 years, he has been engaged in the various phases of agriculture since his boyhood. At the present time he owns and manages extensive farming operations.

He married Virgia Pearl Keefer, at Alvo, Cass County, Nebraska, May 9, 1918. Mrs. Cole was born at Alvo, January 4, 1890, of Dutch Irish parents. Before her marriage she was a music instructor. There are three children: Robert Roy, born July 21, 1925; Eloise Pearl, born December 20, 1927; and Margaret, born January 8, 1931.

Mr. Cole is a Republican. He is a member of the Red Cross; the Plattsmouth Chamber of Commerce, serving on the board of directors of this organization; the agricultural committee; the Mynard Community Club, having served on various committees in this society. He is a member of the Masons, Royal Arch No. 3, commandery of Knights Templar Number 5, and Home Chapter Number 189 Eastern Star. He is a member of the National Rifle Association. His hobby is firearms. He is especially fond of hunting and mountain climbing. Residence: Mynard.

W. H. Cole

Now retired after a successful career, W. H. Cole was born at Boston, Massachusetts, September 5, 1861, and for fifty-eight years has resided in Nebraska. His father, David Cole, a merchant, of Irish descent, died in Arkansas. His mother, born in Ireland, died at Lexington, Nebraska.

Mr. Cole was first married to Emma Belle Caldwell at Lexington. She was born at Louden, Iowa, June 26, 1864, and died at Lexington, September 11, 1921. His second marriage was to Lucinda Martin at Boulder, Colorado, on May 28, 1924.

A Republican, Mr. Cole has always taken an active interest in party politics. He is affiliated with the First Presbyterian Church of Lexington, is a Mason, Knight Templar and Shriner, a member of the Red Cross and the Lexington Country Club. Hs is a life member of The Nebraskana Society. Residence: Lexington.

Walter Ernest Cole

One of the leading ranchmen of Custer County, Nebraska, is Walter Ernest Cole, who was born at Kewanee, Illinois, August 22, 1886, the son of Joseph Talbert and Sarah E. (Frazier) Cole. His father, who is a farmer, was born of English ancestry at Kewanee, July 9, 1862. His mother was born at Hopedale, Ohio, January 8, 1861.

Mr. Cole is a farmer and stockman near Broken Bow, Nebraska, and is president of the Central Nebraska Breeders Association. He is serving as a director of the Custer County Fair Association at this time, and holds membership in the Republican party and the Nebraskana Society.

He is married to Myrtle Love Watts who was a teacher prior to her marriage. Mrs. Cole, whose ancestry is chiefly English, was born at Monroe, Nebraska, October 13, 1895. They have two children: Wanda May, born May 1, 1921; and Claude Joseph, born November 22, 1923. Residence: Broken Bow.

William Alphonzo Cole

An outstanding business executive of Franklin County, William Alphonzo Cole has been an abstracter at Bloomington, since 1882. He was born at Coldwater, Michigan, October 5, 1856, the son of John W. and Mary A. (Card) Cole, and has resided continuously in Nebraska for the past 55 years. His father, a hotel proprietor and farmer, was born at Bennington, Vermont, and died at Coldwater, in 1920. His mother was born at Rochester, New York, in 1830, and died at Chicago, in 1910.

Mr. Cole served as county clerk of Franklin County for six years, 1892-98, and was receiver for the First National Bank of Superior, Nebraska, from 1914 to 1917. He is manager of the Franklin County Abstract Company of Bloomington, at this time, and holds membership in the American Title Association and the Nebraska Abstracters Association.

He was a member of the Knights of Pythias, is chiefly interested in political economy, and is a member of the Nebraskana Society. His favorite sporting interest is trotting and pacing horses. During the late war he served as food administrator for Franklin County, and was correspondent of the War Department and the Department of Justice.

Mr. Cole was married to Fannie Burns at Belleville, Kansas, in 1900. Mrs. Cole was born at Sheridan, Missouri, in 1877, and died at Lincoln, Nebraska, in 1923. Their three children are: Fonzo Katherine, who married C. W. Nobiling; Ilow, who married George Soker, and Elizabeth, who married Reuben Volz. Residence: Bloomington.

Adelbert Pitman Coleman

Adelbert P. Coleman, who has resided in Nebraska all his life, was born near Waverly, February 22, 1879, the son of Richard Edwin and Eliza (Birdsall) Coleman. His father, who was born in Illinois, July 19, 1849, is now a retired farmer who served in the Civil War. His mother was born in Canada in 1856, and died near Memphis, Nebraska, February, 1889.

Mr. Coleman was graduated from high school at Greenwood, Nebraska, in 1895, and attended Creighton University Law School, 1912-13. He was telegraph operator and station agent from 1897 to 1910, was employed by the First National Bank at Walthill during the World War, and was an employee in a law office at Walthill for five years. Since 1919 he has been engaged in the practice of law there, serving as village clerk and village attorney. A Democrat, he has been United States Commissioner since 1924.

He has always been interested in local politics and has been prominent for some time in community affairs. He is a member of the board of directors of the Thurston County Fair and Speed Association. He was unsuccessful candidate for county attorney for Thurston County in 1930. He is a member of the Nebraska State Bar Association, the Lions Club, the Nebraskana Society, and the board of education at Walthill. He served as president of the Commercial Club in 1927.

Mr. Coleman is Present Master of the Masonic Lodge, having held membership in that society since 1910. During the World War he assisted with questionnaires and did other clerical work. He is a member of the First Presbyterian Church of Walthill. His hobby is reading. He likes to golf.

On May 1, 1901, he was united in marriage with Maud Estelle King at Greenwood, Cass County, Nebraska. Mrs. Coleman was born at Louisville, Cass County, Nebraska, December 31, 1879. They have two children: Edwin, born October 1, 1904, who was graduated from the University of Nebraska and is now a teacher in the high school at Spearfish, South Dakota. Edith Grace, who married John Gerald Crandall, resides at Seattle, Washington. Residence: Walthill.

Beach Coleman

Beach Coleman, lawyer, was born at Asbury, Pennsylvania, May 15, 1871, son of John Clinton and Elizabeth (Ammerman) Coleman. His ancestry is English and Dutch.

Mr. Coleman came to Nebraska in the year 1878, and in 1895 received the Bachelor of Letters degree from Nebraska Wesleyan University. In 1897 he was awarded the Bachelor of Laws degree from the University of Nebraska. He has since been in active practice.

On January 5, 1898, Mr. Coleman was married to Mae McFadden at Holbrook, Nebraska. Mrs. Coleman was born in Arcola, Illinois, August 17, 1875. Two chil-

dren were born to them, Ada Lee, on November 30, 1920; and Margaret, on April 4, 1908, who died July 27, 1915.

Mr. Coleman is a Methodist. He is a member of the Masons, the Lions Club, and Phi Delta Phi, legal fraternity. His hobby is fishing. Residence: Scottsbluff.

Thomas Bernard Coleman

Thomas Bernard Coleman is the son of Thomas Coleman, a pioneer Nebraskan, who located at Falls City shortly after the Civil War. Thomas Coleman was a harness maker by trade, who enlisted in the Civil War and served during the whole war. He married Anna Ryan, and to this union Thomas Bernard Coleman was born on January 11, 1876. Thomas Coleman died at Falls City, on January 8, 1877. His wife survived him until October 20, 1923, when her death occurred at Lincoln.

Upon his graduation from the Falls City High School in 1892, Mr. Coleman became a drug clerk and later a traveling salesman. For more than thirty years he has been associated with the Pittsburgh Plate Glass Company at Omaha. Since 1928 he has been manager of that company, and in addition is a director of the following corporations: The Nebraska Power Company, the Omaha Manufacturer's Association and the Nebraska Manufacturer's Association. He is also a director of the Chamber of Commerce.

He was married to Margaret Theresa Cassidy at Omaha, October 21, 1912. Mrs. Coleman was born at Omaha, August 18, 1879, and is of early American ancestry. There are two children: Thomas B., Jr., born January 1, 1903, at Omaha, who married Dorothy Davidson. He is a graduate of the arts college of Creighton University. Marian M., who was born March 16, 1907, at Omaha, married Dr. Gilbert C. Struble. She was graduated from St. Mary's Seminary and Duchesne.

During the War Mr. Coleman participated in the various war drives, and was a member of the Nebraska Council of Defense. He attends St. Cecilia's Cathedral, and is a member of the Knights of Columbus. He is a member of the Nebraska Paint Club, the Omaha Athletic Club and the Omaha Club. His favorite sports are hunting, baseball and football. Residence: Omaha.

Dell Blaine Colgrove

Dell Blaine Colgrove, farmer and stockraiser of Gage County, Nebraska, has lived in this state all his life. He was born at Odell, Gage County, Nebraska, March 3, 1890, the son of James Franklin and Mary Ann (With) Colgrove. His father, who was a settler in Gage County on the Otoe Indian Reservation, was born in Steuben County, New York, July 31, 1853; his ancestors were successful farmers and stockmen in New York. His mother, the daughter of John W. and Elizabeth (Clark) With, was born at Smyrna, Delaware, June 8, 1855. She was an unusual home-maker and for many years cared for her invalid husband. Her ancestors were farmers in Delaware for several generations.

Mr. Colgrove is president of the elevator board of the Farmers' Union Elevator at Krider and the Farmers Union Co-operative Association. He is the owner and overseer of 760 acres of land in Gage County and 1097 acres in Jefferson County; in addition to this he feeds 200 head of cattle and pastures 300. He is past grand head of the Odd Fellows at Odell, and at present is noble grand, is a member of the Republican party, and holds membership in the Nebraskana Society. For the past 20 years he served as a member of the school board. He is a director of the Odell Telephone Company.

At one time Mr. Colgrove acted as justice of the peace in Paddock township. He was married to Celia Etta Whitton at Beatrice, Gage County, Nebraska, December 28, 1910. Mrs. Colgrove, who was a teacher before her marriage, was born at Wymore, Nebraska, March 27, 1887, the daughter of Richard and Lucinda Whitton, early settlers in Gage County. They have five children: Eugene, born April 20, 1914; Thelma, born January 23, 1917; Wanda, born August 9, 1920; Merle, born January 21, 1926; and Wayne, born May 1, 1928. Beulah and Verne are now deceased; Eugene and Thelma are students in high school.

James F. Colgrove, father of Dell Blaine Colgrove, was one of the earliest settlers on what was formerly the Otoe Indian reservations, coming into Gage County in about 1878. This land was wholly unimproved as it had been but recently opened for settlement and it had been a part of the Otoe Indian reservation. Mr. Colgrove became one of the most extensive land-owners and stockmen of the county and at the time of his retirement had accumulated about 3000 acres, which he divided among his family of seven children. Mr. Colgrove died July 27, 1931, at Odell, Nebraska. Residence: Odell.

Clinton Ellsworth Collett

Clinton Ellsworth Collett, superintendent of schools at Lexington, was born a twin at Portland, Indiana, January 24, 1884, and since the age of three has resided almost continuously in Nebraska. His twin sister, Mrs. Clara E. Johnson, lives with her family at Clinton, Iowa.

His father, David Wells Collett, was a native of Warren County, Ohio, born January 24, 1850, and died at Omaha, March 26, 1924. A farmer, he was a pioneer settler in Nebraska, having lived in Cherry County from 1887 until 1910.

Mary Angeline Finch, wife of David Collett, was born in Portland, Indiana, July 25, 1852, and died at Rosalie, Nebraska, December 26, 1928.

Mr. Collett attended Cherry County rural schools until 1899, was graduated from Valentine High School in 1902, received his Bachelor of Arts degree from Nebraska Wesleyan University in 1908 and his Master's degree from the University of Nebraska in 1917. He is a member of Phi Delta Kappa. During 1929-30 he took post graduate work at Columbia University.

On August 14, 1912, he was married to Grace Wolvin at Utica. Mrs. Collett was born at Utica, September 4, 1885. They are members of the Lexington Methodist Episcopal Church.

Mr. Collett is a Republican, a member of the Masons, the Chamber of Commerce, the Kiwanis Club, the Nebraska State Teachers Association and the National Education Association. He is a life member of the Nebraskana Society. From 1915 until 1917 he served as a member of the Nebraska National Guard. Residence: Lexington.

Charles Herman Collier

A merchant at Grant since 1890, Charles Herman Collier was born at Champaign, Illinois, January 24, 1861. He is the son of Joseph J. and Mary (Adler) Collier, the former of whom was born in England, June 21, 1832. He was a carpenter by trade, who died at York, Nebraska, in December, 1909. His wife, Mary, was born in Germany and died at York, January 7, 1908.

Mr. Collier attended public school and has been a merchant for many years. From 1880 until 1890 he was a clerk in a general store at York. He is a Republican, a Mason, and an Odd Fellow.

His marriage to Amelia Doerffel was solemnized at York, May 26, 1892. Mrs. Collier was born at Buffalo, New York, March 12, 1866. They have one son, Gerald W., born May 14, 1893, who married Dora Richmond, of Grant, Nebraska, and is associated in business with his father. Residence: Grant.

Andrew Gordon Collins

Andrew Gordon Collins, retired banker, was born in Shrewsbury, Pennsylvania, April 3, 1847, son of Cornelius Collins. He attended public school and college at Millersville, Pennsylvania, and since 1880 has resided in Nebraska.

Mr. Collins has two children living, a daughter Mrs Gertrude M. Marsh, and a son, Cornelius. He is a Republican. Engaged in the banking business at Hebron for many years, he was until his retirement president of the Hebron State Bank. He is a member and has long been active in the First Presbyterian Church. Residence: Hebron.

Cornelius Collins

Cornelius Collins, president of the Hebron State Bank, was born at Hebron, July 29, 1884, son of Andrew Gordon and Rosa (Beck) Collins. The father was born in Shewsbury, Pennsylvania, April 3, 1847, (see Nebraskana). The mother was born in York County, Pennsylvania, and died at Hebron.

On June 13, 1911, Mr. Collins was married to Grace Cooley at Kenesaw, Nebraska. She was born at Kenesaw, Nebraska. There are two children, John, born in 1918 and Cornelius B., born in 1912.

Mr. Collins is a Republican. He is a Mason and a member of the First Presbyterian Church of Hebron. His favorite sport is golf. Residence: Hebron.

Lillie Lenora Coltman

One of Nebraska's pioneer homemakers and civic leaders is Lillie Lenora Coltman, who has been a resident of the state for nearly 48 years. She was born at Syracuse, New York, December 20, 1855, the daughter of Charles and Fannie (Walshe) Worker. Her father, who was a farmer, was born at Ailso, England, November 5, 1829, and died at Pierce, Nebraska, May 28, 1925; he served as quartermaster sergeant in the Civil War.

Her mother who was a nurse and seamstress, was a well-educated and widely traveled woman; some of her brothers were teachers in Ireland and the family was composed of highly intellectual men and women. She was born at Glynn, Ireland, June 20, 1835, and died at Pierce, May 1, 1888.

Mrs. Coltman attended school but a short time but has always been a student and reader. She is still active, at the age of 75, in civic and social affairs at Meadow Grove, Nebraska, and has always taken a prominent part in women's affairs in her community. She is a member of the Methodist Church of Meadow Grove where she is a member of the Aid Society and the Missionary Society.

She holds membership in the Madison County Historical Society, the Nebraskana Society, and the Women's Relief Corps of Norfolk. Her social clubs include the Rebekah Lodge of Tilden, Nebraska, and the Royal Neighbors Lodge of Meadow Grove.

Mrs. Coltman's father, Colonel Worker, who left a family of small children to enlist in the army during the Civil War, was the last survivor of the first Republican National Convention of 1856.

She was married to William Coltman, a brick moulder and farmer. He was born at Galena, Illinois, of English and German parents, August 21, 1844, and died at Meadow Grove, November 8, 1921. He served with the 45th Illinois Infantry during the Civil War. Four children were born to them, all of whom died in infancy. Residence: Meadow Grove.

John Hay Comstock

John H. Comstock was born at Lincoln, Lancaster County, Nebraska, March 28, 1904, the son of Wilmer Beecher and Jessie (Spurck) Comstock. His father, who was a prominent Lincoln lawyer and judge, served as a member of the Lincoln City Council at one time. He was born of English and French descent, at White Pigeon, St. Joseph County, Michigan, October 20, 1867.

His mother, who was born at Ulysses, Butler County,

Nebraska, February 8, 1874, has been active in civic and educational affairs in Lincoln for many years. She holds offices in the Lincoln League of Women Voters, and the Parent-Teachers' Association, and is a member of the American Association of University Women. Her father was of German extraction; her mother came to America from Ireland, in 1852.

Mr. Comstock was a student at the McKinley, Everett and McKinley Preparatory School, where he was graduated in 1918. In 1920 he was graduated from the Lincoln High School. He was awarded the following degrees at the University of Nebraska: B. S., 1924; and LL. B., with cum laude honors, 1927. He won his college letter in track at the University of Nebraska in 1926; was awarded The Order of the Coif; and was president of his class in 1927. He was elected to membership in Phi Alpha Delta and Alpha Kappa Psi. He was student editor of *Nebraska Law Bulletin,* 1920-27.

He was admitted to the bar at Lincoln, June 4, 1927, and since then has been associated with the law firm Comstock & Comstock, engaged in the active practice of law. He was elected representative from District 35 to the Nebraska Legislature, in 1931. He is a Republican.

He is a member of the Unitarian Church at Lincoln.

Mr. Comstock is a member of the Lancaster Bar Association, the Nebraska State Bar Association, and the Junior Chamber of Commerce at Lincoln. He likes hunting, golfing, hiking, camping, and fishing, and his hobby is horse racing and riding. Residence: Lincoln.

John Parker Comstock, Jr.

John Parker Comstock, Jr., was born at Hastings, Nebraska, son of John Parker and Louise (Davis) Comstock. John Parker Comstock, Sr., was born at Nelsonville, Ohio, February 9, 1869, descended from English settlers in America prior to the Revolution. He died at Omaha, in August, 1930. Louise Davis Comstock is a native of Iowa, of English descent.

Upon his graduation from Central High School in 1920, Mr. Comstock entered the University of Michigan, and spent four and one half years there, then entering Creighton University. He received his LL. B. and Ph. B. in 1927. He is a member of Phi Gamma Delta and Gamma Eta Gamma. Upon his admission to the bar he entered the practice of law at Omaha. He is a Republican and a Mason. He attends Miller Park Presbyterian Church. His professional organizations include the Nebraska State and Omaha-Douglas County Bar Associations, and the Barristers Club of which he was president in 1929. His club is the University Club.

He was married to Bess M. Anderson of Council Bluffs, Iowa, August 18, 1929. Residence: Omaha.

Carl Austin Conant

Carl Austin Conant, retired business man of South Sioux City, Nebraska, has lived in this state for the past 26 years. He was born at Burton, Ohio, August 2, 1866, the son of Austin Gardner and Eleanor (Joslin) Conant. His father, a farmer, who was born at Maple Grove, Ohio, and died at Burton, June, 1901, was descended from English ancestors who came to America in 1623 and settled at Salem, Massachusetts. His mother, who was also of English descent, was born at Mesopotamia, Ohio, in 1844, and died at Burton, March, 1880.

Mr. Conant, who is now retired from active business, was formerly a contractor. He served as a member of the board of education in Dakota County, 1905,-1917, and is now a member of the Commercial Club and the Nebraskana Society. He is independent in politics.

He married Margaret Teresa Breslin at Sioux City, Iowa, March 30. 1891. Mrs. Conant, who is of Irish descent, was born at Green Bay, Wisconsin, March 4, 1866. Five children were born to this marriage: Eleanor, born May 6, 1893, who died June 3, 1895; Lee Austin, born

November 15, 1894; Elmer Gardner, born July 9, 1896; Frank Arthur, born May 14, 1900; and Lillie Margaret, born October 12, 1902.

Harley Conant

Harley Conant, hotel operator, was born in Cherokee, Iowa, July 11, 1875, and obtained his education in the public schools of Iowa and Nebraska.

In 1893 he became employed by a manufacturing concern in Omaha, and in 1898 volunteered for service in the Spanish-American War with the Second Nebraska Volunteer Infantry. For several years after the war he was engaged in the grain business in Omaha, and since 1905 has been in the hotel business. He organized the Conant Hotel Company and has been its president since 1918.

Mr. Conant is a member of the Omaha Club, the Omaha Athletic Club, the Omaha Field Club, and the Happy Hollow Country Club. He is a Rotarian, and a member of the First Congregational Church. He is a member and past president of the Omaha Hotel Men's Association, and is past vice president of the Northwestern Hotel Men's Association. Residence: Omaha.

Elbert Ernest Cone

Elbert Ernest Cone, a physician at Oxford, Nebraska, for many years, has been continuously engaged in the practice of medicine for the past 40 years. He was born at Nebraska City, June 25, 1866, the son of Edgar Whitefield Cone and Emma (Bates) Cone. The former, a carpenter, was born at Geneseo, Illinois, March 30, 1838, and died at Holdrege, Nebraska, August 14, 1908. His father, who served in the Civil War, was descended from Daniel Cone who settled in Connecticut in 1662. His mother, whose parents were natives of Connecticut, was born in that state December 8, 1838, and died at Holdrege, August 2, 1915.

Dr. Cone has been prominent in the medical world for many years and is now house physician of the Oxford General Hospital. He is a stockholder in this hospital, is a member of the Nebraska Medical Society and the Furnas County Medical Society, and holds membership in The Nebraskana Society and the Masons. His favorite sport is baseball. He is a Republican.

On August 19, 1889, he was married at Akron, Colorado, to Lina Boller, who was born at Elcador, Iowa, and died at Oxford, March 5, 1928. They have a daughter, Inez, born June 1, 1890. She married Homer T. Heaton and now resides at Seattle, Washington. Dr. Cone is a member of the American Legion, having served in the Medical Corps for nearly two years during the World War. Residence: Oxford. (Photograph in Album).

Trenmor Cone

Nearly sixty-two years ago, among the coal hills of southeastern Iowa, a son was born to William J. and Helen Heiness Cone. The former, a six foot, red headed Irishman, was a lawyer. His wife was a beautiful Holland Dutch girl. This son, Trenmor Cone, came with his parents who were homesteaders in Nebraska fifty-one or more years ago.

He was educated in public schools and received a first grade teachers' certificate, and taught in Nebraska schools. He is a farmer, an extensive miner and sand shipper. Rejected for military service, because of his age, he helped to feed, clothe and sustain those who were permitted to bare their breasts to the enemy, and is still helping to pension the worthy and the unworthy.

A farmer, teacher, lawyer and preacher of equal rights to all, a professional kicker on the subject of the poor paying taxes for the rich, he assists in all things to save a few real people for posterity. Primarily proud of being a Nebraskan, in his younger days, Mr. Cone was what is called a joiner, but for the past twenty years has not belonged to any fraternal organizations.

He is a father and a grandfather, and is still a student, whose hobby is to fill his mind with all the facts it will retain, and to be an all around good sport. He has served seven sessions in the House since 1907, trying to reduce taxes and taxes keep going higher. Residence: Valley.

J E Conklin

J E Conklin, banker, was born in Hubbell, Nebraska, November 23, 1889, son of William Hamilton and Lou (Arbuthnot) Conklin. The father was born in Moravia, New York, January 23, 1840, the son of Elisha and Martha (Richardson) Conklin. He located in Hubbell, in 1880, founding the Hubbell Bank in 1881, and was a prominent Thayer County banker until his death on December 3, 1924. His wife, Lou, was born in Oil City, Pennsylvania, January 24, 1850, the daughter of James G. and Mary C. (Fogle) Arbuthnot, and is past worthy grand matron of the Order of Eastern Star in Nebraska.

Mr. Conklin attended public and high schools in Hubbell, graduating from the latter in 1904. In 1908 he was graduated from Phillips Exeter Academy, Exeter, New Hampshire. He is a member of Kappa Delta Pi. At the present time he is president of the Hubbell Bank. He is a Democrat.

On March 29, 1911, he was married to Wilhelmina Barrett at Hubbell, the daughter of William and Lorena (Montgomery) Barrett. She was born at Frankfort, Kansas. Mrs. Conklin is a descendant of Arthur Barrett, who served in the Revolutionary War. She is regent of the Oregon Trail Chapter of the Daughters of the American Revolution at Hebron, and is chaplain of the state Daughters of the American Revolution organization. Mr. and Mrs. Conklin have two children, Wilhelmina Ruth, born May 19, 1920; and William J., born May 2, 1923.

During the late war Mr. Conklin was a member of the I. C. O. T. S. at Camp Pike, Arkansas. He is a member of the American Legion, the Methodist Episcopal Church, and Ancient Free and Accepted Masons, Scottish Rite and Shrine as well as the Odd Fellows and the Parent-Teachers' Association. Residence: Hubbell.

Francis Marion Conn

Francis Marion Conn was born in Pulaski County, Indiana, July 25, 1862, and since 1879 has resided in Nebraska. His father, Andrew Jackson Conn, was born in Pennsylvania, of Dutch ancestry and came to Nebraska as a pioneer farmer in 1879. His wife, Nancy Ann Blue, was born in Ohio, of French descent.

Mr. Conn attended public schools and since then has been a farmer and rancher. He has also been a merchant, and has served as assistant postmaster and postmaster at Pine City, South Dakota. At the present time, he is in the real estate business and manages his own properties. He is the owner of a large ranch in Sheridan County.

On April 1, 1885, he was married to Minnie Maud Roby in Keya Paha County, Nebraska. To them were born five children, four of whom are living, Clem K., born in 1896, died January 16, 1918, he was married to Marie Talbott; Edna B., Ila F., May E., and Irene M. are still living.

Mr. Conn is a Democrat, a member of the Congregational Church and of the Masons. Residence: Chadron.

Ulysses Sylvester Conn

Ulysses Sylvester Conn, noted educator, was born at Middletown, Indiana, March 16, 1865, son of Charles and Mary C. (Jones) Conn. Charles, the father, was born in Middletown, October 31, 1838, and died there in April, 1910. He was an extensive farmer and a Republican. Mary C. Jones was born in Henry County, Indiana, April 9, 1827, and died in Middletown in April, 1900.

Educated first in country schools in Henry County,

Ulysses S. Conn was a student at the Spiceland, Indiana, Academy. He attended National Normal University at Lebanon, Ohio, and Valparaiso University, receiving his A. B. in 1891, and his M. A. in 1901. He studied at the University of Chicago and received an LL. D. from the Nebraska Wesleyan University.

Dr. Conn resided in Nebraska from 1892 to 1901, and during this time was consecutively a member of the faculty at the Fremont College, Wayne Normal College and Superintendent of schools at Wayne. During these years he did a great deal of lecturing before educational organizations and during the summer devoted practically all of his time to instruction in teachers institutes in Nebraska. In 1901 he was president of the Nebraska State Teachers' Association.

From 1901 to 1906 he was engaged in business as a life insurance executive in Minneapolis, Minnesota, and later as a retail merchant in Fargo, North Dakota. In 1906 he returned to Nebraska and again entered school work as head of the department of mathematics at Fremont College, Fremont, Nebraska. Later he was superintendent of schools at Columbus, Nebraska.

In 1910, by act of the legislature, the Nebraska Normal College at Wayne, a private institution, was bought and made a state normal school. This school opened September 19, 1910, with Dr. Conn as its president, and he has served in that capacity since.

He is a Republican, a Presbyterian, and member of the Kiwanis Club, the Masons, the North Central Association of Colleges and Secondary Schools, the American Association of Teachers Colleges, and the National Education Association. He enjoys golf and is a member of the Wayne Country Club.

On August 23, 1893, he was united in marriage to Cammie C. Conn at Valparaiso, Indiana. Mrs. Conn is a native of Iowa, born April 29, 1870. There is one child, Ardath, born February 7, 1898. Residence: Wayne. (Photograph in Album).

William Thomas Connell

William Thomas Connell, leading merchant of Allen, Nebraska, was born in Cork, Ireland, April 8, 1882, and has been a resident of Nebraska forty-six years. He is the son of Richard and Elizabeth Anne (Kingston) Connel, the former of whom was born in County Cork, Ireland, January 18, 1846. He came to America in the Spring of 1884 and settled in Nebraska, where he engaged in farming until his death on December 17, 1916. Elizabeth Anne Kingston was born in Ireland, in January 1851, and died in Nebraska in January 1917.

Educated in Springbank public school and Allen High School, Mr. Connell also attended Nebraska Wesleyan University. For many years he has engaged in the mercantile business in Allen, where he has been active in Republican politics. He is a member of the Chamber of Commerce and the Allen School Board, and is a Mason, a member of the National Geographic Society and the Nebraskana Society. He is fond of hiking and of horses.

Of his marriage to Anna Laura Kellogg, who was born at Allen, June 3, 1882, there is one daughter, Wilma Lillian, born March 1, 1919. Residence: Allen.

Cornelius Francis Connolly

Cornelius F. Connolly was born at Omaha, Douglas County, Nebraska, January 19, 1892. James Joseph Connolly, his father, who was a retail shoe merchant, was born in Ireland, February 22, 1862, and died at Omaha, September 19, 1891. Rose Ann (Smith) Connolly, his mother, who was a pioneer Omahan, was born at Des Moines, Polk County, Iowa. Her ancestry was Irish.

Mr. Connolly attended the Holy Family School at Omaha, and in 1915, was awarded the degree LL. B. at Creighton University. He was admitted to the bar in Nebraska, May 3, 1915, and has practiced law in Omaha since then. He is now a member of the law firm Crofoot, Fraser, Connolly & Stryker, at Omaha.

On August 30, 1916, he was married to Nelle Jane Coulton at Omaha. Mrs. Connolly, who is Canadian and Irish, was born at Marshalltown, Marshall County, Iowa, January 22, 1892. Five children were born to this union: Rosemary, born September 1, 1917; Margaret Helen, born May 3, 1919; Cornelius, Jr., born December 24, 1920; Jeanne Francis, born May 26, 1924; and David William, born January 23, 1929.

Mr. Connolly is a member of the Omaha Bar Association, the Parent-Teachers' Association, and the Young Men's Christian Association. He is an Elk. He is affiliated with the Blessed Sacrament Church; he is a member of the Knights of Columbus. He is a Democrat. Residence: Omaha.

James Patrick Connolly

James Patrick Connolly, dentist, was born at Phoenixville, Pennsylvania, June 3, 1865, son of Patrick Meaney and Cecelia (O'Hara) Connolly.

Dr. Connolly attended high school at Omaha, and received his degree of Doctor of Dental Surgery from Creighton University. On September 10, 1890, he was married to Pauline Sander at Omaha.

Dr. Connolly is a Democrat, and has served as county commissioner, a member of the Nebraska legislature, and in 1924 was candidate for lieutenant governor. Residence: Omaha.

Alexander Arthur Conrad

Alexander A. Conrad, prominent physician of Saline County, was born at Crete, April 6, 1890, the son of Arthur Charles and Dora (Broz) Conrad. His father, who was a physician, was born at Breslau, Germany, May 8, 1850, came to America in 1875, and in 1880, moved to Crete, where he died August 18, 1907. His mother was born at Praha, Bohemia, September 1, 1870.

Dr. Conrad was graduated from the Crete High School in 1909, and for a time was a student at Doane College. He was awarded his M. D. degree at the College of Medicine of Creighton University, Omaha, and later studied in the post graduate department of Harvard Medical School. He won letters in track and basketball in high school, and was elected to membership in Phi Rho Sigma at Creighton University.

He was interne for one year at St. Vincent's Hospital, at Portland, Oregon, and since July, 1916, has been engaged in the practice of medicine at Crete. He is the author of *Treatment of Pneumonia*, published in the *Nebraska Medical Journal*, February, 1931.

His marriage to Eugenia Haight was solemnized at Shawnee, Pottowatamie County, Oklahoma, June 12, 1918. Mrs. Conrad was born at Crete, June 26, 1891. Their two daughters are: Mary Jean, born November 29, 1920; and Patricia Margaret, born April 19, 1924.

Dr. Conrad served as first lieutenant in the Medical Reserves. He is a member of the Saline County Medical Society of which he is past president; is past president 7th Councilor District Medical Society, and is a member of the Nebraska State Medical Society; and is present chairman of the program committee of the latter organization. He is chairman of the disaster-preparedness committee of the Red Cross; is instructor in first aid for the Camp Fire Girls; and is past president of the Crete Community Club.

He served as a member of the board of directors of the Crete Rotary Club for one year; and is a member of the state Young Men's Christian Association and the Nebraskana Society. He is affiliated with the Congregational Church at Crete. His social club is the Crete Golf Club. He is a Mason. His sports include golf and tennis, and his hobby is reading. Residence: Crete.

Clifton L. Contryman

Clifton L. Contryman, who is president of the Citizens State Bank of Ogallala, was born at Nehawka, Nebraska, January 31, 1871, son of R. Emett and Mary (McConnahay) Contryman.

His father was born in Canada and died at Weeping Water, Nebraska. He was a farmer of German descent. His wife, Mary, was born at Jamestown, Pennsylvania, and died at Weeping Water. She was a teacher in her early life and was a graduate of Westminster College, Pennsylvania. Her ancestry was Scotch-Irish.

Upon the completion of his early education at Weeping Water Academy in 1890, Mr. Contryman entered the University of Nebraska, from which he received the degree of Bachelor of Science in 1897. He was a farmer until he reached the age of 38 years, and for the past 23 years has been a banker. He is a Republican, a member and former treasurer of the County Red Cross, a member of the Commercial Club, the Rotary Club, and the Masons. For ten years he was a member of the Ogallala school board.

On February 20, 1918, he was married to Nelle Morrell at Palmyra, Nebraska. She is the daughter of Elijah and Elizabeth Morrell. Mrs. Contryman was born at Palmyra of English descent. They have two sons, Dale M., born February 14, 1911, who is a junior at the University of Nebraska; and Allan M., born October 17, 1913, who is a sophomore at the University of Nebraska. Residence: Ogallala.

James D. Conway

Born at Creston, Iowa, October 2, 1903, James D. Conway is the son of Matthew and Mary (Clarke) Conway. His father was born in Adams County, Iowa, March 23, 1878, and his mother in County Mayo, Ireland, March 27, 1878. She died at Creston, on June 3, 1921,

Mr. Conway attended the public schools and St. Malachy's parochial school in Creston, until 1916, and St. Berchman's High School at Marion, Iowa, and the Des Moines Catholic Academy until 1921. He received his Bachelor of Arts degree from Columbia College, at Dubuque, Iowa, in 1924, and his degree of Bachelor of Laws from Creighton University, 1926, and received the following athletic honors: three letters in high school football and three letters in high school basketball at Des Moines, two letters each in football and basketball at Columbia College, and three basketball letters at Creighton University. Mr. Conway is a member of the Athens Club, and was president of his senior law class, and president of Delta Theta Phi in 1926.

Since his admission to the bar in 1926, he has been in active practice, and is director and secretary of the Hastings Loan and Finance Company. He was candidate for county judge of Adams County in 1928, and is a member of the Nebraska State and Adams County Bar Associations. During 1929 he was president of the Junior Chamber of Commerce, and from 1929-30, was advocate of the Knights of Columbus. He attends St. Cecilia's Catholic Church, and is a member of the Elks and The Nebraskana Society. His social club is the Hastings Country Club.

On September 2, 1929, he was married at Omaha, to Grace Dwyer. Mrs. Conway was born at Auburn, Nebraska, September 23, 1909. Residence: Hastings. (Photograph on Page 262).

Arthur Ellsworth Cook

For over 30 years Arthur E. Cook has been a practicing physician at Randolph, Cedar County, Nebraska. He was born at Ionia, Dixon County, Nebraska, December 22, 1870, the son of Sylvester and Katherine Elizabeth (Stewart) Cook. His father, who was a farmer, was born at Worcester, Worcester County, Massachusetts, December 21, 1839, and died at New Castle, Dixon Coun-

Nelson—Hastings

JAMES D. CONWAY

ty, Nebraska, November 19, 1907; his English ancestors probably came to America in the *Mayflower*. His mother was born at Hamilton, Ontario, Canada, November 16, 1850, and died at New Castle May 19, 1922. Her father, William W. Stewart, was Canadian-English, and her mother, Mary Small, was born in Dublin, Ireland, of English and Irish parentage.

Dr. Cook attended public school in Dixon County, high school at Columbus, Nebraska, and received his M. D. degree at the Sioux City College of Medicine in 1898. He served his internship at the Samaritan Hospital, Sioux City, and entered the practice of medicine at Alpena, South Dakota. For the past 32 years he has been a physician at Randolph where he is a director in the Security National Bank, and is a landowner. He is the author of numerous medical articles published in medical journals during the past 25 years.

During the World War he was captain of the local company of the National Home Guard, and was commissioned first lieutenant in the Medical Corps, U. S. Army. He holds membership in the following: Cedar County Medical Society; Nebraska State Medical Association; the American Medical Association; V. M. S.; E. M. S.; and American Railway Surgeons. He served as councilor of the District Nebraska State Medical Association for 14 years, and is at the present time president elect of this state organization. He was president of he Elk Horn Valley Medical Society, 1928, was a member of the Board of Education of the Randolph Schools for 18 years, and during the war was president of the Red Cross at Randolph. He has been treasurer and president of the local school board at various times. He now holds membership in the Nebraska State Historical Society, and the Nebraskana Society. His social club is the Randolph Golf Club.

He was married at Sioux City, Woodbury County, Iowa, July 30, 1889, to Mary Belle Hosmer. Mrs. Cook, who was a trained nurse in a woman's hospital in Chicago, was born at Havre de Grace, Hartford County, Maryland, October 29, 1867, and died at Randolph, Cedar County, Nebraska, February 7, 1920. She was the daughter of Elbridge Warren Hosmer, and India Woodhouse; Harriet Hosmer, the noted sculptress, was Elbridge Hosmer's cousin.

Their children are Stuart Hosmer, born November 10, 1900, who married Myrtle Amanda Jensen; Alice Elizabeth, born January 27, 1902, who married Harley Fillmore Edlund; and Kenneth Warren, born March 14, 1904, who married Marjorie Pease. Stuart H. is a physician at Randolph. Kenneth W. is serving on the staff of the Pasadena *Star News* in California. Alice Elizabeth now resides in Chicago.

On November 17, 1926, Dr. Cook was married to Helen Rebecca Peverett-Buol at Lincoln, Nebraska. He is local surgeon for the C. B. & Q. Railway and the C. St. P. M. & O. Railway Company. His hobbies are reading, mechanics, collecting curios and old firearms, while his sports include golfing, fishing, and hunting. Residence: Randolph.

Dean Charles Cook

Born at Blair, Nebraska, January 2, 1896, Dean Charles Cook is the son of Charles and Elizabeth (Renard) Cook. His father, a banker, was born at Sandy Hook, Kentucky, May 26, 1855. His father, Edwin Cook, served as captain in Company K of the Kentucky Volunteer Army during the Civil War. His mother, who was born in Washington County, Nebraska, December 25, 1860, and died at Wausa, Nebraska, December 25, 1902, was graduated from the Blair High School and was prominent in the Methodist Episcopal Church for a number of years.

Mr. Cook attended St. John's Military Academy. He served as a bank executive from 1915 to 1927, was connected with the Spencer State Bank, 1927 to 1929, and since 1929 has been secretary-treasurer of the O'Neill

Agricultural Credit Corporation. He is a member of the Red Cross, the Commercial Club of Spencer, Nebraska, and the Spencer School Board. His chief recreations are golfing and reading.

During the World War he served as second lieutenant in the United States Army Air Service, and since 1924 has been commander of the Spencer American Legion Post. He is independent, politically.

His marriage to Marie Anna Ziegler occurred at Beaver Dam, Wisconsin, September 8, 1921. Mrs. Cook, whose parents were natives of Wisconsin, was born at Marysville, October 9, 1896. They have four children: Louis Lucian, August 12, 1922; Dean Charles, March 14, 1924; Mary Elizabeth, March 27, 1927; and Martha Ann, July 15, 1928. Residence: O'Neill.

Fred M. Cook

Fred M. Cook, credit executive, was born at Kingsville, Kansas, April 1, 1886, son of William F. and Angie (Meredith) Cook. William F. Cook, who was born at Lecompton, Kansas, in 1856, is a retired furniture dealer and mortician. His wife, Angie, was born at Mammoth Cave, Kentucky, in 1856.

Educated in the public schools, Mr. Cook attended Baptist College at Grand Island, and from 1908-20 was publisher of the *Kansas Optimist* at Jamestown, Kansas. During 1921 he was an editorial writer for the *Sioux City Daily Tribune*, and from 1923-27 was publisher of the *Marengo Pioneer* at Marengo, Iowa. In 1925 he was the organizer of the Pioneer Service Company, Incorporated, at Marengo, which has developed into a state-wide credit corporation, and finally into an interstate association. Its national headquarters are located in Hastings, and state offices are located in some twenty states. Mr. Cook is president of the corporation.

On September 18, 1907, Mr. Cook was united in marriage to Clara B. Lambing at Waterman, Illinois. Mrs. Cook was born at Weeping Water, Nebraska, June 3, 1885. They have four children, Ruth Delight, born June 24, 1908; Edwin, born June 12, 1910; George, born August 29, 1912; and Ted Pershing, born June 7, 1917.

Mr. Cook is an independent Democrat, and served as postmaster at Jamestown under the Wilson administration 1913-20. During the late war he was a promoter of and participant in Red Cross, Young Men's Christian Association and Liberty Loan Drives, and other civilian projects. He is a Presbyterian, a member of the Knights of Pythias, the Elks and the Odd Fellows. At the present time he is chairman of the publicity committee of the Hastings Rotary Club, a member of the Hastings Chamber of Commerce and the Nebraskana Society. His social clubs are the Hillside Golf and the Knights of Pythias Golf Clubs at Hastings. Resident: Hastings.

Hal V. Cook

Hal V. Cook, lumberman, was born at Tecumseh, Nebraska, December 29, 1878, son of Charles C. and Emma (Cady) Cook.

Charles C. Cook was born at Ives Grove, Wisconsin, January 28, 1847, and was a farmer until his death at Tecumseh, August 18, 1915. His parents came to the United States about 1840. Emma Cady, his wife, was born at Centerville, Michigan, August 20, 1856, and died at Tecumseh, August 9, 1910.

Mr. Cook attended the public and high schools at Tecumseh, and was graduated from Lincoln Business College in 1897. From that time until 1910, he resided in Kansas, since that time he has been a resident of Nebraska. He is now manager for the J. H. Melville Lumber Company at Ogallala.

On May 29, 1901, he was married to Grace D. Feldner at Topeka, Kansas. She was born at Marietta, Ohio, May 21, 1881. They have two children, Berniece, born

HAROLD JAMES COOK

July 8, 1902, at Washington, Kansas; and Erdene, born January 6, 1910, at Kansas City, Missouri.

Mr. Cook is a Protestant. He is a member of the Rotary Club, the Odd Fellows, and the Modern Woodmen of America. Residence: Ogallala.

Harold James Cook

Harold J. Cook, consulting geologist, ranchman and naturalist, was born at Cheyenne, Wyoming, July 31, 1887, son of James Henry Cook, noted naturalist (see *Nebraskana*). James H. Cook was born at Kalamazoo, Michigan, August 26, 1858; and is directly descended from Captain James Cook, the famous British explorer and navigator, who discovered the Hawaiian Islands, Cook's Inlet, etc. He married Kate Graham who was born at Three Rivers, Michigan, June 28, 1867. She is a woman of remarkable ability and many accomplishments. Her ancestory is English, Irish and Scotch.

Harold J. Cook received his early education in country schools in Kansas and in home training and private tutelage. He attended Lincoln High School and Lincoln Academy. During 1906-07 and 1908, he studied at the University of Nebraska, and during 1909-10 at Columbia University Post Graduate School. He has been awarded honorary membership in Phi Sigma, and is a member of Delta Epsilon and Sigma Gamma Epsilon.

His marriage to Eleanor Barbour of Lincoln, Nebraska, took place October 13, 1910. There are four children of this marriage: Margaret, born October 17, 1911; Dorothy, born June 1, 1913; Winifred, born July 15, 1915 and Eleanor, born October 9, 1917. The children have all shown marked musical ability, have been honor students in the various schools attended, are athletic, and unusually versatile. Mr. Cook's second marriage was to Margaret F. Crozier, an educator, musician and naturalist of French and English descent.

A rancher in Nebraska since early boyhood, he has been a consulting geologist since 1916, making examinations of oil and mining properties for many concerns and individuals. He was honorary curator of the Colorado Museum of Natural History at Denver from 1926-28 and curator of palaeontology 1928-30. He is vice-president of the United States Land and Cattle Company of Cimarron, New Mexico, and co-founder with his father, James H. Cook, of the Cook Museum of Natural History at Agate. He is joint owner of the Agate Springs Ranch, and is a member of the advisory board of the Petroleum Research Corporation.

He is a charter member of the Nebraska State Park Board, and served six years. He has charge of educational work for the Colorado Museum in nature study, co-operating with the Denver city school administration officials. An author and lecturer of note he has written over fifty publication on geology, palaeontology, archaeology, together with numerous popular and semi-popular articles in various magazines. His illustrated lectures include the subjects of fossils and fossil collecting, evolution, numerous phases of historic and commercial geology, the antiquity of man in America, and other related subjects. He is the discoverer, in Nebraska, of Hesperopithecus haroldcookii, oldest known near relative of the human race.

He carries membership in the following scientific and educational organizations: American Association of Petroleum Geologists, American Institute of Mining and Metallurgical Engineers, Society of Economic Geologists and Palaeontologists, F. A. A., Palaeontological Society of America, Geological Society of America, American Association of Mammalogists, Colorado-

Wyoming Academy of Science, Nebraska Academy of Science, etc. He holds honorary life memberships in the American Museum of Natural History, New York, the Archaeological Society of America, the American Naturalists Association, American Forestry Association, etc., etc. His social clubs are the Teknik and The Research Group, both of Denver. He resides at Agate. (Photograph on Page 264).

James Henry Cook

James Henry Cook, naturalist and ranch owner, was born at Kalamazoo, Michigan, August 26, 1858, the son of Elizabeth (Shaw) and Henry Cook. His mother, who died in 1860, was of Scotch-Irish descent. His father was English, directly descended from Captain James Cook, the famous Bristish navigator who discovered the Hawaiian Islands. A ship owner and captain, he was born at Portsmouth, England, came to America in 1836, and died at Menden, Michigan, December 10, 1910.

Mr. Cook, whose life work has been natural history research, has had interesting and varied experiences. As a boy, after the Civil War, he helped lay out routes and drive cattle over all important cattle trails north from Texas. He was guide and scout with the Texas Rangers in the early '70s; organizer and manager of a large ranch, transporting over 50,000 cattle into south western New Mexico, 1881-86; purchaser and builder of his present holdings at Agate Springs Ranch, Agate, Nebraska. This ranch was purchased and improved in 1887, and today is the site of the world-famous Agate Springs Fossil Quarries which were discovered by Mr. Cook in 1878. Together with his son, Harold J. Cook, he is co-owner and founder of the Cook Museum of Natural History at Agate.

He served as civilian scout for the United States troops in the Geronimo campaign in New Mexico, 1885-86, and was wounded in an Indian ambush in southwest Texas, in the early '70s.

On September 28, 1886 he was married to Kate Graham at Cheyenne, Wyoming. Mrs. Cook, who is of Scotch, Welsh and Irish descent, was born at Three Rivers, St. Joseph County, Michigan, June 28, 1867. Two children were born to this marriage; Harold James, born July 31, 1887, who married Eleanor Barbour, and John Graham, born May 28, 1898, who died December 11, 1919.

Mr. Cook is the author of several books on natural history, among them: *Fifty Years on the Old Frontier*, published by Yale University Press; and *Wild Horses of the Plains*.

He was chairman of the Sioux County Council of Defense in Nebraska; and is associate companion of the Order of Indian Wars (medal); Winners of the West, camp number 11, at St. Joseph, Missouri; honorary member of the Grand Army of the Republic and of the Boy Scouts of America. He is a member of the Nebraska State Historical Society; Old Fort Laramie Historical Society; and the American Institute of Local Science.

Hunting and fishing are his favorite out of door sports, while his hobbies are: archaeology; vertebrate palaeontology; geology; collecting semi-precious stones. He has been a lecturer on *Western American History; Indian Sign Language; Evolution as Illustrated in Fossil Vertebrates*. Mr. Cook has lived in Agate for 43 years. (Photograph on Page 266).

LeRoy Edwin Cook

LeRoy Edwin Cook, manager of the Johnson Fruit Company, was born at Leigh, Nebraska, December 25, 1896, son of Elmer Beaver and Harriet Endly (Hiscox) Cook.

The father, born in Illinois, July 31, 1868, is the son

JAMES HENRY COOK

of John C. Cook, who was born in Hamilton, Ohio, and who was a veteran of the Civil War. Elmer Beaver Cook is a traveling salesman, land appraiser and collector. His wife, Harriet Endly, was born at Lisbon, Ohio, May 28, 1867, and died at Hastings, June 30, 1919. She was a school teacher and dressmaker. Her father, James Hiscox, was born at Stratford-on-Avon, England and came to the United States at the age of nineteen. He was a trade-tailor and miller. Her mother was of Welch descent.

Mr. Cook attended public school at Craig, Leigh, Wayne, Norfolk, and Hastings, Nebraska, until 1910, and high school at Sioux Falls, South Dakota, Shenandoah, Iowa, and Hastings, Nebraska, graduating in June, 1914. From September, 1914, until March 13, 1917, he was a student at Hastings College, where he was a member of Eta Phi Lambda and active in basketball, football and track. He was captain of the basketball team in 1916. Entering the mercantile business in 1920, he became manager of the Hastings Basket System No. 1 at the that time and since 1921 has been manager of the Johnson Fruit Company. He held the rank of first lieutenant in he 22nd United States Infantry during the World War and is a member of the American Legion. His religious affiliation is with the Congregational Church.

He is a member of the Chamber of Commerce, the Rotary Club, the Ancient Free and Accepted Masons, being past master of the McCook Lodge No. 135, the Scottish Rite Masons, and the Shrine, as well as the Y. M. C. A. and the Patime Tennis Club. His favorite sport is tennis.

On June 21, 1920, he was married to Audra Irene Wilkinson at Lincoln. Mrs. Cook was born at Avoca, Nebraska, February 18, 1897, and before her marriage was a school teacher in Lincoln. She is a member of the Eastern Star, being past matron, and an active member of the Congregational Church. Residence: McCook.

Virgil Harold Cook

Virgil Harold Cook was born at Unionville, Missouri, November 17, 1894, son of Stark John David and Ruth Ann (Comstock) Cook.

The father was born at Taylorville, Kentucky, May 8, 1852, and died at Unionville, Missouri, October 2, 1902. He was a carpenter and a member of the police force. His wife, Ruth, was born at Unionville, Missouri, September 20, 1850, and died at Fairbury, Nebraska, June 25, 1923.

Mr. Cook attended the public school, and from 1919 until the present time has been in the express business. From 1913 to 1917 he was a carpenter, and before that for three years engaged in farming. He is a Republican.

On November 24, 1921, he was married to Minnie Uhlken at Crawford. Mrs. Cook was born at Crawford, February 14, 1900, of German ancestry. They have one son, Franklin Allen, born August 30, 1923.

During the late war Mr. Cook served in the United States Army as private first class in the 89th division. He participated in the following engagements, Lucey Sector, S. Mihiel, Eavezin Sector, and the Meuse Argonne. From 1924 until 1929 he was vice-commander of the American Legion and in 1930 was again elected to the same office, in which he still continues. He was adjutant during 1929 and 1930, and from 1922 until the present time has been a member of the executive committee.

He is a member of the Chamber of Commerce, the Moose, the Nebraskana Society, and the Volunteer Firemen, of which he is secretary at the present time. His favorite sports are football and hiking, while his hobby is reading. Residence: Crawford.

Willis Ellsworth Cook

Willis E. Cook, pioneer railroad man in Nebraska, has been a resident of this state for over 43 years. He was born at Marseilles, Ohio, February 3, 1867, the son of Simon Brown and Julia Cordileras (Hildreth) Cook. His father, a farmer, was born in Pennsylvania, October 10, 1840, and died at Marseilles, June 6, 1909. His mother was born in New York, August 1, 1842, and died at Marseilles, March 24, 1909.

Mr. Cook attended country schools and the public school at Marseilles where he was graduated from high school in 1886. Later he took a short business course at Lincoln, Nebraska. In the spring of 1891 he entered the service of the Chicago & Northwestern Railway Company as telegrapher at Exeter, Nebraska. He was transferred to Linwood, Nebraska, in 1892, and four months later was appointed agent at Nora, Nebraska, where he remained until 1905. For the next 20 years he was agent at Stanton, Nebraska, and in 1926, he was transferred to Hastings, Nebraska, where he is agent for the same railroad company.

He is a member of the Lion's Club, the Modern Woodmen of America, Young Men's Christian Association, the Hastings Chamber of Commerce, and the Red Cross. Mr. Cook served as president of the Red Cross during the World War, and is a member of the Sons of Veterans. He is affiliated with the Methodist Episcopal Church, and holds membership in the Republican Party. While living at Stanton he was city clerk for 8 years resigning when transferred to Hastings.

His marriage to Nettie Belle Manning occurred at Exeter, Nebraska, August 24, 1892; she was born at Polo, Illinois, on December 7, 1868. To this union the following children were born: Loren, born June 21 1899, who married Janette Rasmussen; Enid, born May 8, 1901, who married Delbert Charles Irwin; and Paul, born September 6, 1908, who died March 16, 1911. Loren is a traveling salesman for the Carpenter Paper Corporation of Omaha, having been connected with this organization for the past 13 years. Enid is a graduate of Nebraska Wesleyan University, and prior to her marriage was a music teacher, her husband is a chiropodist. Residence: Hastings.

Edward Lewis Cooley

Edward Lewis Cooley, son of Roswell Day and Mary Jane (Kile) Cooley, was born at Waverly, Nebraska, June 11, 1880. His father, born at Warren, Ohio, February 21, 1838, was a pioneer Nebraska farmer. His death occurred at Waverly, October 30, 1913. His wife, was born at Quebec, Canada, February 15, 1843, and died at Lincoln, May 30, 1915. A teacher before coming to Nebraska, her father was a blacksmith and inventor, and an operator for the underground railroad, assisting slaves to escape to Canada.

Educated in the public and high schools of Waverly, Edward L. Cooley was graduated in 1900, and thereafter attended the Nebraska School of Agriculture for a year. On February 27, 1906, he was united in marriage to Sally Edith Landis at Waverly. Mrs. Cooley was born at Strawn, Illinois, August 21, 1883.

There are six children, Marian, born June 21, 1907, who married Clarence A. Althouse; Margaret, born February 16, 1910; Lucile, born September 30, 1912, who married John C. Martin; Kathryn, born March 1, 1917; Betty Jean, born October 11, 1920, and Lewis, born February 26, 1926.

Mr. Cooley is a Republican and active in local politics. He was a member of the Congregational Church at Waverly until it was disbanded, and holds membership in the Red Cross, the Parent Teachers Association, the Modern Woodmen of America and the Masons. His club is the Waverly Farmers Club and his hobby is reading. Residence: Waverly.

John Emerson Cooley

John Emerson Cooley, a farmer and ranchman near Clearwater, Nebraska, has resided in that community since 1882. He was born at Mineral, Ohio, December 7,

1870, the son of George Washington and Emretta Ada-
lene (McGill) Cooley. His father, who was born at Albany, Ohio, February 29, 1848, is a farmer and rancher,
and has spent a great deal of time and effort to promote
public interest in welfare work.

His mother, who was vitally interested in all civic and
welfare activities, was born at Athens, Ohio, on December 9, 1846, and died at Neligh, Nebraska, April 21, 1920.
Her parents, who were of Scotch descent, were prosperous
plantation owners in Virginia.

Mr. Cooley attended rural school in Antelope County,
and was a student at Gates Academy at Neligh for a number of years. Later he studied at the University of Nebraska, and the agricultural school of the University of
Iowa. He has taught in the public schools of Nebraska,
but has spent most of his life in agricultural activities,
always striving to build up the practical side of farming.

He is interested in promoting modern methods of
farming and farm improvement, and has taken an active
interest in educational, civic, political, and community affairs. Mr. Cooley is a member of the Farmers Union, the
state and county fair associations, the Independent Order
of Odd Fellows, and the Ancient Order of United Workmen. He is a contributor to the Red Cross, Salvation
Army, and the Methodist Church. His hobby is helping
young people, and his favorite pastimes are reading and
mechanics.

On September 24, 1902, his marriage to Irena Melissa
DePeel occurred at Clearwater, Nebraska. Mrs. Cooley,
who was born at Sparta, Canada, March 5, 1880, is prominent in church work and affairs of the 4-H Club. She is
descended from English and German ancestors on the
maternal side, and traces her father's family to 1750
in France. They have a son, George Michael, who is married to Francis Elizabeth Hickman; he is a farmer. Residence: Clearwater.

Margaret Elizabeth Cooley

Margaret Elizabeth Cooley, nee McMurry, was born
at Vincennes, Indiana, August 11, 1850, daughter of
Albert and Sarah (McClure) McMurry. Her father,
who was born in Green County, Kentucky, April 29,
1818, was a farmer of Scotch-Irish descent. He died
at Waverly, August 7, 1879. His wife, Sarah, was born
in Vincennes, Indiana, February 24, 1823, and died at
Greeley, Kansas, about November, 1888. Of Scotch descent her family records show her ancestors as soldiers
in the Revolution.

Educated in the public schools, Mrs. Cooley has been
an outstanding citizen of Nebraska since October, 1869.
On May 28, 1871, she was united in marriage to Richard
S. Cooley, at Greenwood. Mr. Cooley was born in Johnson, Trumbull County, Ohio, July 29, 1842, and died at
Waverly, August 3, 1928, after an active and successful life as a farmer. His ancestry is traced to the Pilgrims of Massachusetts and Connecticut.

There were born to this union five children, three of
whom are deceased: Clarence Jay, born February 22,
1872, died October 5, 1895; Thomas Allen, born February
11, 1876, died January 7, 1897; Mae, born April 27, 1878,
married Alvin J. Todd; Ella, born October 10, 1882,
married George O. Tutton; and Nora, born July 31,
1891, died December 16, 1895.

Mr. Cooley was a veteran of the Civil War, having
served with the 6th Ohio Cavalry, and Mrs. Cooley is a
member of the Women's Relief Corps. She is affiliated
with the Waverly Methodist Church, and is a member
of the Red Cross, Ladies Aid Society and the Missionary
Society. Her hobby is reading. Residence: Waverly.

William Coolidge

For the past 54 years William Coolidge has lived in
this state where he has taken an active part in the economic and civic affairs of his community. He was born
at Columbus, Nebraska, October 15, 1871, the son of Henry

Promroy and Theda Wheeler Coolidge. His father, who
was born in Taswell County, Illinois, October 6, 1835, and
died at Hot Springs, South Dakota, September 24, 1918,
was a tinner and hardware merchant. He served in the
8th Iowa Cavalry during the Civil War; his Scotch ancestors came to America in 1530, and settled in Massachusetts. His mother, who was interested in all civic affairs, was born at Flowerfield, Michigan, August 5, 1841,
died at Columbus, Nebraska, 1924. Her ancestors came
to this country prior to the Revolution.

Mr. Coolidge was graduated in 1888 from the Columbus
High School where he was class valedictorian. He spent
seven years in the Burlington coach shops at Plattsmouth,
and for 30 years has been engaged in the general merchandise business in Thurston County. A Republican,
he has served as deputy county clerk of Cass County, 1894
to 1900; town board member at Rosalie, 15 years; school
board member for 15 years. He is a member of the Nebraskana Society. His hobby is reading. During the
World War Mr. Coolidge was an active participant in all
patriotic work, especially in loan drives.

He was married to Martha Lois Smith at Plattsmouth,
February 14, 1893. She was born, of English parentage,
at Plattsmouth, December 13, 1873, and died at Rosalie,
December 23, 1927. Four children were born to this marriage: Theda, born July 6, 1895, who married John M.
Rose; Ruth, born June 17, 1897, who married A. P. Witt-
huhn; William, born June 20, 1899, who married Florence
La Velle; and Helen, born May 31, 1914, who died December 25, 1915.

On February 17, 1930, Mr. Coolidge was united in marriage with Ina Southwick. Residence: Rosalie. (Photograph in Album).

Charles L. Cooper

Charles L. Cooper, president of the Farmers State
Bank of Wallace, was born at St. Charles, Missouri,
August 15, 1871.

His father, Charles Cooper, was a native of West
Virginia, born April 18, 1845. He was a minister of the
Methodist Episcopal Church. He died at Agency, Iowa,
November 19, 1921.

Mr. Cooper was married on May 4, 1897, to Marie
Schaupp at Arcadia. They have one daughter, Marie,
born December 4, 1906.

Mr. Cooper is a Republican. He has resided in Nebraska since March 1, 1883, and for many years has been
prominent in the development of his community. Residence: Wallace.

Gerald Massey Gilbert Cooper

Gerald Massey Gilbert Cooper, editor and publisher,
was born at London, England, January 19, 1862, son of
George Armytage and Dinah Julia (Jones) Cooper.

The father, born in Yorkshire, England, died in London, about 1890. He was a lawyer, lecturer, and public
entertainer, whose ancestry is traceable to Charles I. His
wife, Dinah, was born in London, and died at Binley,
Yorkshire, England, April 1, 1903. She was an operatic
singer, a public entertainer, and a leader of music. Her
ancestry was Welsh and Jewish.

As a boy before settling in Nebraska, Mr. Cooper
traveled throughout England, Scotland and Wales with
his parents, who were entertainers. He received his early education in public and private schools in England,
and in April, 1892, came to Sheridan, where he has since
resided.

A singer and dancer as a boy until he reached the age
of twelve and a half, after retiring from the show business
his father apprenticed him to the printers trade at Barrows in Furnas. He was for two years thereafter in a
sportsmen's outfitting shop in London, with his brother.
For the past 54 years, he has been in the printing and publishing business, nine years on the *Barrow Herald*, in
Lancashire, England, five years in London, and 40 years

in Nebraska. He served three years in Company E 10th Lancashire (England) Rifles. Although reared an Episcopalian, he is now a member of the Methodist Episcopal Church (life member and trustee).

A Republican, Mr. Cooper has held various minor offices, including that of Justice of the Peace for five years and member of the Rushville School Board for five years During the late war he was a member of the County Council of Defense. He is a member of the Red Cross, and has been director and treasurer of that organization He is also a Mason, a member of the State Historical Society, and a member of the Chamber of Commerce. His hobbies are painting and drawing.

On June 4, 1897, he was married to Emma Lydia Hetzel at Gordon. Mrs. Cooper was born at Boone, Iowa, November 4, 1873, and for ten years was associated in business with her husband. They have two children, Vera Grace, born October 4, 1900, who married Ross D. Rash; and Gerald F., born May 9, 1903, who married Clara Benner. Residence: Rushville. (Photograph in Album).

Guy Lester Cooper

On July 3, 1880, Guy L. Cooper was born at Humboldt, Richardson County, Nebraska. Orrin Alonzo Cooper, his father, a pioneer Nebraska miller and grain dealer, was born on a farm in Cayuga County, New York, November 18, 1849, and died at Humboldt, March 23, 1923. For many years he was mayor of Humboldt. His ancestry was German and English.

Calista Ellen (Merrifield) Cooper, mother of Guy, was born of English parentage on a farm in Benton County, Iowa, September 25, 1858, and died at Humboldt, October 20, 1905. She was an active club worker.

Mr. Cooper attended the Humboldt High School where he was graduated in 1898, after which he was a student at the University of Nebraska for two years. He was a member of Alpha Theta Chi at the University. From 1900 to 1922 he was associated with his father in the milling and grain business. Since 1922 he has been in charge of the O. A. Cooper Company, Incorporated, with milling, grain, livestock, farming, ice-manufacturing and other interests. He is president of the O. A. Cooper Company. He has lived in Nebraska his entire life.

He was married to Josephine Lovina Bruun, at Humboldt, May 24, 1905. Mrs. Cooper, who was born at Muscatine, Iowa, August 12, 1885, is of Danish and English ancestry. There are four children, Guy Lester, born February 9, 1907, who married Evelyn Mae Kerr; Charles Albert, born October 21, 1908; John Robert, born January 1, 1911, who married Virginia Agnes Lee; and Calista, born April 27, 1914. Guy Lester and John Robert are associated with their father in business, Guy a graduate of the University of Nebraska where he was a member of Alpha Theta Chi. Charles Albert is a graduate of the University of Nebraska and a member of Alpha Theta Chi and Phi Beta Kappa; he is now attending diplomatic school at Washington, D. C.

Mr. Cooper was a first lieutenant in the home guards during the World War, later was in service at Fort Snelling, Minnesota. He was active in Red Cross Drives at Humboldt, and was chairman of the local Y. M. C. A. war drives. For 18 years he has been a member of the Humboldt school board, and at the present time is president of the organization. He is a Mason, Shriner, a member of the Independent Order of the Odd Fellows, and an active member of the Humboldt Chamber of Commerce, the Nebraskana Society, and the American Legion. He is a Republican. Residence: Humboldt.

Harold Cooper

Born at Bolton, England, September 29, 1881, the Reverend Harold Cooper is the son of George and Ellen (Harwood) Cooper. His father who was also born at Bolton, is a business man there. His mother died at Bolton, in 1929.

Mr. Cooper attended public school, Lancashire College and the University of Manchester. He won special honors in oriental languages, and is a lecturer of considerable note on World Travel. He has crossed the Atlantic sixteen times, and has traveled around the world once, spending nearly five years in India.

A lecturer before Rotary, Kiwanis, Shriners, Lions, Exchange, Civitan, Trojan, Altruian and various other clubs, he has also appeared before colleges and student gatherings throughout the middle west. Among his lectures are Around the *World in Topsy Turvy Time; Migrating with the Immigrant; India—Strange Customs of a Strange Land: Japan—The Key to the Orient; Seeing Europe Through a Parson's Eyes; Don't be a Punkah Wallah;* and *The Lure of the Arctic.*

On February 25, 1906, Mr. Cooper was married to Harriet Shugart at Marion, Indiana, her birthplace. Mrs. Cooper, who was born September 24, 1885, is descended from early Quaker settlers in Indiana.

In 1915, Mr. Cooper was chaplain of Red Cross in Manchester, England. He is a member of the First Congregational Church of Crete, and the South India United Church. He is president of the Nebraska Council of Christian Education, and a member of the Commission on International Relations. He is a member of the Rotary Club and the Masons. Residence: Crete.

Horatio Franklin Cooper

Horatio Franklin Cooper, who is a farmer in Webster County, Nebraska, was born at Waukon, Iowa, March 26, 1852, and for he past 54 years has been a resident of Nebraska. His father, Harmon Squire Cooper, also a farmer, was born in Vermont, September 8, 1824, and died at Waukon, October 28, 1920. His mother, Jane Eliza Gilbert Cooper, was born in New York, January 5, 1835, and died at Forest City, Iowa, July 4, 1915.

Mr. Cooper was graduated from the Waukon High School, was a teacher for a time, and is now retired at Guide Rock, Nebraska. He was united in marriage with Matilda Jane Dunbar at Guide Rock, April 24, 1880. Mrs. Cooper, whose parents were farmers, was born in Illinois, February 28, 1861. Their children are: Chester, born October 5, 1882; Elsie, born May 4, 1881; and Winnie, born September 24, 1889. Mr. Cooper is a Democrat. Residence: Guide Rock.

John William Cooper

Active in the legal and political life of Omaha for many years, John W. Cooper is one of the most outstanding members of the Nebraska bar. Born at Hartford, Ohio County, Indiana, October 17, 1867, he is the son of Thomas Nelson and Mary Pugsley (Epsey) Cooper. His father, born at Hartford, April 25, 1830, was a farmer whose English ancestors came to America and fought in the Revolution. He died at Rising Sun, Indiana, March 1, 1889.

Mary Espey Cooper was a native of Rising Sun, born June 30, 1842. Her ancestry was also English, and members of the family served in the Revolutionary War. She died at Omaha, March 19, 1901.

John W. Cooper received his education in the public and high schools of Indiana, and was admitted to the practice of law at Kingman, Kansas, June 3, 1889, at the age of twenty-one. He is admitted to all state and federal courts, including the United States Supreme Court. A Republican, he was elected to the Nebraska state senate and served from 1918-30, and is now serving as senator from Omaha. He is president pro tempore of the state senate, and is a member of the Nebraska-Iowa Joint Boundary Commission, and serves as secretary of that body. For the past thirty-eight years he has been active in the public life of the state. He is a Methodist, a member of the Odd Fellows and the Knights of Pythias. He is a member also of the Omaha Philosophical Society. He is fond of reading and hiking. Residence: Omaha. (Photograph in Album).

Louisa J. Cooper

For the past 47 years Louisa J. Cooper has lived in Nebraska where she has been prominent in educational, civic, and welfare activities. She was born at Newcastle, Laurence County, Pennsylvania, the daughter of James and Cynthia (Dunlap) Tidball. Her father, who was a building contractor, was born at Mahoning, Ohio, June 5, 1805, and died at Moberly, Missouri, September 5, 1883; his ancestry was English and Scotch. Her mother was born at Warren, Ohio, August 1, 1812, of English and Welsh parentage, and died at Crete, Saline County, Nebraska, May 25, 1886.

Mrs. Cooper attended high school at Newcastle and received her higher education through private study. She has been a leader in the Woman's Christian Temperance Union for many years, and has always been identified with religious affairs in her community. She served as a member of the Crete Library Board for over 40 years, acting as president of that organization for 17 years, and in 1929 was appointed president emeritus by the mayor and city council. For 43 years she has been a member of the Round Table Club, the oldest organization of women in Nebraska. She was also one of the organizers of the Women's Association of the First Congregational Church where she is a regular attendant.

At one time, as a member of the State Society of the home for the Friendless, she served as state corresponding secretary; she was secretary of the local organization in this society and acted as delegate to various conventions. During the World War she was an active Red Cross worker.

Her marriage to Daniel Cargill Cooper was solemnized at Newcastle, September 13, 1866. Mr. Cooper, who was a Presbyterian clergyman, was born at Xenia, Ohio. His death occurred at McComb, Hancock County, Ohio, February 9, 1882. His English and Scotch-Irish ancestors were distinguished educators. To this union four children were born: James Walton, who married Lucy Mathews; Carrie Louisa, who married Dr. W. H. Pallett; Edward Cargill; and Alice Mary, who died in infancy. James was awarded the A. B. degree at Doane College, A. M. at Chicago University; Ph. D., at Columbia University. He was professor of romance languages in Whitman College for twenty-one years, and died June 24, 1919. Carrie received the A. B. degree at Doane, and Edward was dental surgeon until his death on October 20, 1930.

Mrs. Cooper was recently elected to membership in the Nebraskana Society. She is a Republican. Her chief recreation is reading. Residence: Crete.

Charles Finney Copeland

Charles Finney Copeland, a prominent author and poet who lives at Holdrege, Nebraska, was born at Clinton, Kansas, March 9, 1863, the son of Jonathan and Serepta (Curtis) Copeland. His father, who was a home missionary and minister, was born at Charlton, Massachussetts, July 19, 1817, and died at Loma, Colorado, March 17, 1912.

Rev. Jonathan Copeland moved from New York to Kansas in 1857 to help make it free soil territory, and was active in caring for the wounded and dying people after Quantrell's raid on Lawrence, Kansas. He was an abolitionist and an ardent prohibitionist, and believed that politics and religion should be distinctly correlated. He was descended from Lawrence Copeland who came to America on a later trip of the *Mayflower;* Lawrence Copeland's son married the granddaughter of John and Priscilla Alden. Lawrence Copeland died at the age of 100 years, December 31, 1699.

Serepta (Curtis) Copeland, who was a teacher in public and private schools in New York, was born February 9, 1820, and died at Durango, Colorado, April 8, 1900. Mrs. Copeland was the daughter of Nathaniel Curtis and the granddaughter of Sylvester Finney, a soldier in the Revolution.

Mr. Copeland received his education at home under the tutelage of his parents and attended the public schools of Kansas and Iowa. As a boy he was employed in a printing shop and has been engaged in that business intermittently throughout his entire business career. He is at the present time starting the publication of a small quarterly publication called the *Hope and Help Headlight* which will contain his own literary productions. He is the author of *Poems of Inspiration,* which has gone into its second edition, and the *Copeland Genealogy,* which is placed in all state historical libraries, and many booklets published in non-commercial form. Because of the wide spread popularity of his poems, Mr. Copeland plans to establish a gift-volume enterprise which will send his literary works into all parts of the country.

He is a member of the Republican party, and has always been an advocate of prohibition. He was employed in the postal service of the United States Government for many years, and because of the regulations of the government does not enter into political activities. He is a member of the Red Cross, the Anti-saloon League of America, and the Lincoln Branch of the Railway Mail Association. He was a charter member of the American Eugenics Society, is affiliated with the First Methodist Church of Holdrege having been active in that body for the past 33 years, and holds membership in the Nebraskana Society.

Mr. Copeland's hobby is literature, and he devotes a great deal of his spare time in seeking expressive phrases and original thoughts. In his younger days he was interested in educational activities and received scholastic honors in every teacher's examination and county test. He strives in all his poems to bring to his public, inspiration and enjoyment.

His marriage to Harriett Gennette Knowlton was solemnized at Springfield, Colorado, May 29, 1890. Mrs. Copeland, who is the daughter of Ellis Augustus Knowlton and Julia Maria (Simmons) Knowlton, was born at Owatonna, Minnesota, July 19, 1870. Their three children are: LeRoy Newton, born November 23, 1895, who is a printer and linotype expert; Bernice, born October 13, 1900, who married James William Young; and Paul LaVerne, born April 13, 1905, who married Gertrude Phelps. Paul Laverne is an instructor in the physics department of the Massachussetts Institute of Technology, Cambridge. Residence: Holdrege. (Photograph in Album).

Plenna Reuben Copple

Since 1906 Plenna Reuben Copple has been engaged in the practice of dentistry at Fullerton, Nebraska. He was born near Centralia, Illinois, July 29, 1876, the son of Charles and Lucy Melvina (Jackson) Copple, the former a farmer who was born near Centralia, June 16, 1852, and died at Fullerton, January 16, 1927. His father's ancestors came to this country from Holland in the early days of America and settled at New Amsterdam. His mother was born near Irvington, Illinois, April 17, 1851, and died at Fullerton, March 10, 1893.

Dr. Copple attended school in a sod building in pioneer days, and received his dental education at Northwestern University, Chicago, where he was graduated with the D. D. S. degree in 1902. He had formerly attended Anderson Normal University in Indiana and taught school in Nance County, Nebraska. He was treasurer of the junior class of Northwestern University and was a member of Delta Sigma Delta.

At this time he is a member of the Northwestern

District Dental Society, the Nebraska State Dental Society, and the American Dental Association. He is a Mason and Modern Woodman, is a corresponding member of the Young Men's Christian Association, and is affiliated with the First Methodist Episcopal Church. His sports are golfing and hunting.

On September 10, 1902, he married Grace Tranbarger at Anderson. Mrs. Copple, ancestry is German, was born at Perkinsville, Indiana, September 15, 1880. Residence: Fullerton.

C. E. Corey

For the past 30 years C. E. Corey has lived at Omaha, Douglas County, Nebraska, and acted as manager and treasurer of the Corey & McKenzie Printing Company. He was born at York, York County, Nebraska, May 26, 1872, the son of A. G. and Mary C. (Gilmore) Corey. His father, who was born in Wisconsin, and died at Lincoln, Nebraska, in 1928, was a farmer and merchant, and for many years was postmaster at Fairfield, Nebraska; he was a soldier in the Civil War. His mother was born in Pennsylvania; she is still living.

Mr. Corey attended the public schools and later was a student at Fairfield College. His early years in business were spent in the newspaper field; he was the editor of the Swanton *Echo*, and the Fairfield *Messenger*. For the past 30 years he has been manager and treasurer of the Corey & McKenzie Printing Company. He has lived in Nebraska his entire life. He is a Democrat.

On November 31, 1903, he was united in marriage with Virginia H. Peterson at Omaha; she was born at Omaha, August 26, 1880. They have two children: Marjorie, born November 19, 1907, who married K. C. Russell; and Audrey, born February 17, 1909, who married William S. Rush.

He holds membership in the Red Cross; Sales Managers Society; Omaha Concord Club, of which he was president in 1919; and the Omaha Chamber of Commerce, of which he was a director for one year. He was president of the Ben Franklin Club for 8 years. He was Omaha chairman of war saving societies during the war. Residence: Omaha.

Fred Dudley Cornell

Fred D. Cornell was born at Kansas City, Wyandotte County, Kansas, July 20, 1869, the son of Dudley Emerson and Annie M. (Speck) Cornell. His father, who was born at Saratoga, New York, January 15, 1837, and died at Kansas City, February 11, 1911, was a general passenger agent for the Kansas Pacific Railroad for many years; he was a major in the Civil War, and served as brigadier general in the Kansas State Militia; and served as mayor of Kansas City, 1885, and 1909; Thomas Cornell, an ancestor, settled in Rhode Island, in 1634. His mother was born at Philadelphia, May 16, 1849, and died at Charleston, South Carolina, April 2, 1928. She was state regent for the Daughters of the American Revolution.

Mr. Cornell was assistant city ticket agent for the Union Pacific Railroad at Kansas City, 1889-94; was passenger and ticket agent for the Missouri Pacific Railway at Lincoln, Nebraska, 1894-1911; was engaged in the real estate and insurance business, 1911-1920; and since 1920 has been secretary of the Scottish Rite Bodies and recorder for Sesostris Temple of the Ancient and Accepted Order of Nobles of the Mystic Shrine. He is also secretary of the Scottish Rite Educational Welfare Association.

In 1915 he was secretary of the Lincoln City Charter Convention. During the World War he was a four minute speaker, and was active in Liberty loan drives and Red Cross work. Mr. Cornell is a member of the Lincoln Country Club; is a life member of the Lincoln Chamber of Commerce; and since 1911 has held membership in the Rotary Club. He is a 33rd degree Mason and Shriner, and is a member of the Modern Woodmen of America, the

Order of the Eastern Star, and the Nebraskana Society. His sports include golf, football, and baseball. He is a Republican.

On June 26, 1894, he was united in marriage with Eliza Martha Mott, at Independence, Missouri. Mrs. Cornell was born at Independence, September 18, 1871, and died at Lincoln, August 12, 1928. Their daughter, Carol, was born October 29, 1904. Residence: Lincoln.

John Cass Cornell

John Cass Cornell, president of the Cornell Supply Company of Lincoln, was born in Richmond, McHenry County, Illinois, August 6, 1869. His father, Albert Willard Cornell, came from Lancashire, England when a boy, and lived in Illinois, where he followed the dental profession. He also served in the Civil War and died in Illinois, January 23, 1872. He was married to Augusta H. Burrows, daughter of John Smith and Maria (Spory) Burrows.

When Mr. Cornell was 14 years of age, the family established a residence at Ord, and there he completed his education in the public schools. He served an apprenticeship in the coppersmith and sheet metal workers trade, and from 1891 until 1892 and part of 1893 he followed his trade at Grand Island and Fremont. In April, 1893, he went to work in a hardware store at Alliance, and while there he and his brother, Charles D., also engaged in cattle business.

In October, 1899, Mr. Cornell returned to Ord and purchased a hardware store. In 1911 he sold his business and moved to Lincoln. There he founded the Cornell Supply Company, a wholesale plumbing and heating business.

Mr. Cornell is a member of the Presbyterian Church, and is a Democrat. He is a Mason, Knight Templar and a member of the Shrine, and in 1925, was elected chief rabban of Sesostris Temple at Lincoln. He is a member of the Kiwanis Club, the Chamber of Commerce, and the National Chamber of Commerce.

On October 11, 1898, he was married to Blanche Tupper. They have two daughters, Mary Ann and Charlotte. Residence: Lincoln.

George Corner

George Corner, automobile dealer, was born at Blue Hill, Nebraska, December 2, 1888, son of Martin Beebe and Louisa Mary (Huff) Corner.

His father who was a farmer of Democratic affiliations, was born in Volinia, Michigan, September 5, 1863. His family came to America from England in 1825. His wife, Louisa, was born in Volinia, October 27, 1866. Her father was born in Pennsylvania in 1845 and fought in the Civil War. She is a musical instructor.

Mr. Corner was graduated from the public schools of Cassopolis in 1903, and attended Red Cloud High School. He learned the jewelry business and followed that until the age of twenty-one, when he farmed and raised stock for five years. In the fall of 1916 he took over the Ford Sales and Service organization at Blue Hill. At the present time he is the manager and owner of the Ford garage and the Home Oil Company, distributors of gas and lubricating oils in his immediate vicinity and surrounding territory.

His marriage to Della DeEtte Morrison was solemnized at Red Cloud, on December 29, 1909. Mrs. Corner was born at Ravenna, Nebraska, May 5, 1890, daughter of David Morrison, an Englishman. They have two children, Ellen Geraldine, born January 11, 1913; and James Martin, born August 27, 1920. Ellen is a teacher in Nebraska rural schools.

Mr. Corner is a member of the Blue Hill Chamber of Commerce, the Red Cross, the Woodmen of the World, the Masons and the Eastern Star, and at the present time is serving as president of his local school board. Residence: Blue Hill.

Kenneth Aaron Cornish

Kenneth Aaron Cornish was born at Osceola, Nebraska, May 29, 1896, the son of Walter Adnarm and Georgia A. (Lohr) Cornish. His father, who is a newspaper editor, was born at Ross Station, Indiana, March 31, 1853. His mother was born in Bedford County, Pennsylvania, June 15, 1858.

Mr. Cornish was graduated from the high school at Shelby, Nebraska, in 1915, and later was a student at the University of Nebraska where he was elected to membership in Phi Sigma Kappa. He served as assistant cashier of the Farmers State Bank at Osceola, from 1921 to 1925, taught one term in a rural school in Polk County in 1915, and is at this time county treasurer of Polk County.

A Democrat, he has twice been elected city clerk of Osceola. He holds membership in the Nebraskana Society, the Osceola Community Club, and the Osceola Methodist Church. He is president and chairman of the legislative committee of the State Associations of County Treasurers of which he was formerly treasurer, served as local treasurer of the Red Cross, 1927-28, and is past commander, past adjutant, and past treasurer of the American Legion Post at Osceola.

His marriage to Ruth Pauline Smith occurred at Osceola, September 15, 1920. Mrs. Cornish was born at Osceola, November 13, 1899. During the World War Mr. Cornish served for 15 months overseas with the United States Naval Forces on the following United States ships: *George Washington; Carola; Flag Ship.* His chief recreations are golfing, hunting, and reading. Residence. Osceola.

Walter A. Cornish

A resident of Nebraska since 1873, Walter A. Cornish has been engaged in the publishing business for over 25 years, and is today editor and publisher of the *Shelby Sun* at Shelby, Nebraska. He was born in Lake County, Indiana, March 31, 1853, the son of Aaron and Rebekah Jane (Loomis) Cornish. His father, who was a farmer, was born in Michigan, in 1826, of English ancestry, and died at Blaine, Washington, April 2, 1894. His mother was born in Pennsylvania, in 1832, and died at Everett, Washington, 1918.

Mr. Cornish has served as county surveyor of Polk County since 1922, and was chairman of the village board at Shelby for a number of years. He is a Democrat, is affiliated with the United Brethren Church of Shelby, and holds membership in the Nebraskana Society. He is past grand of the Independent Order of Odd Fellows.

He was united in marriage with Georgia Ann Lohr, February 5, 1882, at Osceola, Nebraska. Mrs. Cornish was born in Somerset County, Pennsylvania, June 15, 1857. Two children were born to this marriage: Roy A., born August 10, 1884, who died February 26, 1930, and who was married to Viola M. Otter. There are two children of this marriage: Allan and Robert Rex. Kenneth A., the second son, was born May 29, 1896, and on September 15, 1920, was married to Ruth Pauline Smith at Osceola. He is now serving his second term as treasurer of Polk County. Residence: Shelby.

Ulysses S. Cornwell

Ulysses S. Cornwell, who has been engaged in farming in Nebraska for the past 45 years, was born at Medora, Indiana, January 18, 1864. He has lived in this state for 62 years and has been active in the educational and civic life of his community for over half a century, and is county commissioner at the present time. His father, Floyd Cornwell, who was born at Louisville, Kentucky, April 4, 1834, and died at Paola, Kansas, January 18, 1909, was a horse shoer and blacksmith during the Civil War; he had the distinction of shoeing General

Grant's horse. His mother, whose ancestry was Scotch, was born at Pea Ridge, Indiana, February 29, 1840, and died at Paola, November 6, 1928.

Mr. Cornwell attended the grade and public school at Blair, Nebraska. He has been chairman of the Red Cross at Walthill, Nebraska, has served on the school board for 18 years, and is a member of the Nebraskana Society. During the World War, he was a member of the Council of Defense, and took part in the sale of Liberty Bonds. He is a member of the Lions Club, is affiliated with the Penticostal Church and is a Democrat. His hobby is reading.

He was married to Susan Thompson at Blair, on December 31, 1890. Mrs. Cornwell, whose ancestry is English, was born at Omaha, March 7, 1873. They have twelve children, all of whom are living: William, born November 29, 1891, who married Alta Chambers; Thornton, born December 5, 1893, who married Elsie Martin; Ethel, born November 4, 1895, who married Ira Snyder; Deforest, born March 20, 1898, who married Vesta Riggs; Elsie, born February 20, 1900, who married George Snyder; Ruth, born October 25, 1902, who married Lester Jacobson; Elmer, born January 7, 1905; Bryant F., born April 28, 1907, who married Violet Morrow; Kenneth, born June 9, 1909, who married Bessie Bahr; Alfred W., born October 25, 1911; Harold, born June 8, 1915; Helen, born September 2, 1917. Resiednce: Walthill.

Earnest Erasmus Correll

One of the outstanding figures in the civic and professional life of Hebron, Nebraska, is Earnest Erasmus Correll, a lifelong resident of that community. He was born at Hebron, October 7, 1871, the son of Erasmus Michael and Lucy Lozier (Wilder) Correll, and for many years has been prominent in political and educational activities there.

Erasmus Michael Correll, a pioneer leader of Thayer County, Nebraska, was born August 14, 1846, and received his early education in the public schools of Rockford, Illinois. He studied at the University of the Pacific, at Santa Clara, California, in 1860, and in 1865 attended Eureka College in Illinois. As a civil engineer he surveyed the site for Hebron in 1869, and in 1871 established the *Hebron Journal,* which has continued through many years as a newspaper representative of its community. He served as second lieutenant of Company A, First Regiment of the Nebraska State Militia, an organization formed primarily as protection against the Indian attacks.

A man of unusual intellect and versatility, Mr. Correll was a successful lawyer in conjunction with his editorial work, and was instrumental in promoting many constructive movements in Thayer County. He was a staunch Republican, and in 1881 served as representative in the Nebraska State Legislature where he was the author of a woman's suffrage amendment, a bill later defeated at the polls. In 1881 he was elected national president of the American Suffrage Association, in 1892 was elected state senator (elected president of that body). He served as a member of the military staffs of Governors Dawes, Thayer, and Crounse, and later acted as quartermaster general of the Nebraska State Militia.

Lucy Lozier (Wilder) Correll, mother of Earnest E. Correll and the daughter of George and Elmira (Bunker) Wilder, was descended through the maternal line from the Bunker and Breed families, owners of battleground famed in the Revolution. Among her American colonial ancestors were these distinguished statesmen and early settlers; Thomas Rogers and his son, Lieutenant Joseph Rogers, both of whom came from England on the *Mayflower* in 1620; Assistant-governor Stephen Hopkins who came to this country with his daughter. Constance, on the *Mayflower;* Thomas Prence, fourth governor of the Plymouth Colony; Assistant-governor William Collier; Captain Benjamin Bunker, of Revolu-

EARNEST ERASMUS CORRELL

tionary fame; and Captain John Fowle of Massachussetts

She was a gracious and talented gentlewoman who left an indelible impress on her community and state. She was organizing regent of the Oregon Trail Chapter of the Daughters of the American Revolution, served as state president of the Nebraska Women's Suffrage Association, and was state historian of the Nebraska Daughters of the American Revolution. An able newspaper woman, she gave effective service as assistant editor of the *Hebron Journal,* and upon the death of her husband became its editor. Through his Holland Dutch ancestors, the Van Der Cooks, Mr. Correll traced the line back to William, Prince of Orange; one of the collateral family lines was that of Reuben, the artist.

Earnest E. Correll received his education in the Hebron schools and the state university, and through association with his father learned the rudiments of the printing and publishing business. The *Hebron Journal* which is still in the possession of the Correll family since its founding, maintains its high standards and principles under his able management.

Mr. Correll has been influential in both county and state affairs throughout his career, has taken an active interest in local political campaigns, and in 1910 was state president of the Roosevelt Progressive Association. He was appointed by the United States Government to membership on the war campaign committee in Thayer County, 1918, and later was made a member of the Committee on Prisons and Prison Labor. During the World War he served as secretary of the Thayer County Council of Defense, and was an enthusiastic worker in advancing patriotic measures.

He is affiliated with Bethlehem Commandery, Knights Templar, of the Masonic Order, and holds membership in the Sons of the American Revolution, the Modern Woodmen of America, The Mayflower Society, and the Ancient Order of United Workmen.

His marriage to Olive Robbins Hazard was solemnized at Hebron, June 22, 1910. Mrs. Correll, who is widely known in Nebraska through her social and civic attainments, is the daughter of Omar Elisha Hazard, pioneer merchant at Hebron, and Harriet Adeline Robbins Hazard. She has served as treasurer of the state organization of the Daughters of the American Revolution, has held various local offices in the Hebron's Woman's Club, and served as corresponding secretary of the Nebraska Federation of Women's Clubs. She acted as chairman of the Women's Council of Defense during the late war, and in 1927 was alternate delegate to the Republican National Convention held at Kansas City. She was again elected to attend the National Convention in Chicago, 1932.

Mrs. Correll is a descendant of colonial American families on both the maternal and paternal side. Her ancestry includes such notables as: Joshua Robbins, who served in the Revolution; Governor Welles of Connecticut; and Commodore Oliver Hazard Perry, hero of the naval battle of Lake Erie in the War of 1812. Mr. and Mrs. Correll have two children, Donald Hazard and Earnest E., Jr. Residence Hebron. (Photograph on Page 273).

Mable Leona Correll

A distinguished educator and business woman at Cambridge, Nebraska, Mable Leona Correll is a lifetime resident of this state. She was born at Cambridge, January 30, 1891, the daughter of Joseph Orange Correll and Jennie Estella (Denney) Correll. Her father, who was born at Silver Lake, Indiana, May 6, 1867, came to Cambridge in 1886, and is engaged in the livestock, insurance and real estate business in Furnas County, Nebraska. He served as a member of the Fuel Administration Committee during the World War. His ancestry is Pennsylvania German, French and English. His wife, Jennie, whose ancestry is German and French, came to Cambridge in 1884. She was born at Warsaw, Indiana, July 27, 1869.

Miss Correll attended the country schools of Frontier County, Nebraska, and in 1910 was graduated from the Cambridge High School. She received the Bachelor of Arts degree at the University of Nebraska in 1914, and in 1927 received the Master of Arts degree at Columbia University in New York City. She was valedictorian of her graduating class at Cambridge High School.

She served as a grade school teacher at Cambridge until 1916 when she became instructor of history and English in the high school there. In 1919 she was made principal of the Cambridge schools where she served until 1924 when she entered the high school of Superior, Nebraska, as history and English teacher, and dean of girls. Since 1929 she has been the owner and manager of the Ladies Ready-to-Wear Store at Cambridge.

Miss Correll is a member of the Commercial Club, the Red Cross, the Nebraska Women's Educational Club, the American Historical Association, and the Nebraskana Society. She is a life member of the University of Nebraska Alumni Association, is a member of the Research Club of Cambridge, and holds membership in the Order of Eastern Star and the National Geographic Society. She is affiliated with the First Presbyterian Church of Superior, Nebraska. Her chief recreations are hiking, reading, and gardening. Residence: Cambridge. (Photograph in Album).

Festus Corrothers

Festus Corrothers, leading rancher and outstanding Democrat of Grant County, was born in Taylor County, Virginia, April 9, 1856, son of Samuel and Harriet (Poe) Corrothers.

The father, who was of Scotch descent, was an early farmer and stockman in West Virginia. He died in West Virginia. The mother was born in Taylor County, Virginia, and died there in 1912.

Mr. Corrothers was educated in common schools and has been a stockman almost ever since. At the present time he is the owner and general manager of the Z-0 Ranch. He is a Democrat, and served 18 years as county commissioner of Grant County. He has been a leader in Democratic politics in his community, and was a member of the Constitutional Convention in 1919-20. Mr. Corrothers has been a resident of Nebraska for more than 40 years. He is a Universalist.

Mr. Corrothers married Anzina Isner in September, 1889. She was born April 18, 1864, and died January 8, 1914. They had one son Ney, who died in 1895. Residence: Whitman.

Earl LeRoy Coryell

Born at Brock, Nebraska, August 9, 1899, Earl L. Coryell is the son of George and Myrtle (Brown) Coryell. His father, who was born at Janesville, Wisconsin, April 16, 1864, was president of the Coryell Oil Company at Lincoln. His death came suddenly at Albany, Georgia, December 30, 1928. For many years he was prominent in civic, political and fraternal activities. He was a Republican and a Mason, a member of the Shrine, and served as master of the Ancient Free and Accepted Masons. He was president of the Nebraska Independent Oil Men, a member of the Salvation Army Board, and an active church worker. He was the son of Richard Coryell who homesteaded in Nemaha County in 1867; of French Huguenot ancestry, his forebearers settled in New Jersey and served with George Washington in the Revolutionary War. Myrtle Brown Coryell was born at Brock, Nebraska, May 23, 1875, of English and Scotch descent. Well educated, she is an active clubwoman and church worker, and is a past matron of the Eastern Star.

Earl Coryell attended the Brock public and high schools, being graduated from the latter in June, 1917. In June, 1922, he received his A. B., from the University of Nebraska. Active in student affairs he was manager of the *Daily Nebraskan,* business manager of University

Week, a member of the *Awgwan* staff and the Vikings and a member of Phi Kappa Psi.

At the age of 22, during his senior year at the university Mr. Coryell became associated with his father in the operation of retail gasoline service stations under the name of the Coryell Oil Company; in 1927, the properties were sold, and Earl Coryell organized the Earl Coryell Company of which he is sole owner, taking a 99-year lease on one-fourth of the city block at 14th and N streets, in the heart of Lincoln. On this site he has erected the largest gasoline, oil and greasing service station in Nebraska.

On August 12, 1926, Mr. Coryell was married to Margaret Nell Stidworthy at Lincoln. She was born at Homer, Nebraska, September 22, 1902, and until her marriage was a kindergarten instructor at the University.

During the World War he was stationed at Fort Sheridan, Illinois. He is a Mason, and member of Lodge No. 19, Ancient Free and Accepted Masons at Lincoln, 32nd degree Scottish Rite, Knight Templar, member of Sesostris Temple of the Mystic Shrine and Sesostris Shrine Patrol. A member of the Junior Chamber of Commerce he served as director during 1927-28. He was the first business manager of the Lincoln Symphony Orchestra, a Junior Chamber of Commerce activity. He is now a member of the Chamber of Commerce, the Lions Club, the Hiram Club; member and former president of the Lincoln Automobile Club; president of the Nebraska Motor Club, president of the Lincoln Baseball Association and member of the American Legion and University Club.

His religious affiliation is with the Episcopal Church of the Holy Trinity, of which he has been vestryman since 1930. Residence: Lincoln.

Jay Timothy Cottingham

Born at Etna, LaFayette County, Wisconsin, April 6, 1886, Jay Timothy Cottingham is the son of Anthony Hunt and Elizabeth Ann (Keating) Cottingham. Anthony Cottingham was born in Bainbridge, Swalesdale, Yorkshire County, England, November 17, 1850, and was brought to America by his parents at the age of four years. He engaged in farming all his life, and died at Mount Vernon, South Dakota, February 7, 1920. His wife, Elizabeth, was born in Etna, June 5, 1858, and is still living. She is of Scotch-Irish descent.

Mr. Cottingham was graduated from the Shullsburg, Wisconsin High School and received his Bachelor of Science degree from South Dakota State College in 1911. During 1910-11, he was editor of the *Collegian* (weekly), and in 1911, won first place on the debate team, of which he had been a member since 1909.

On August 17, 1918, Mr. Cottingham was united in marriage to Gladys Emma Murray, at Sioux City, Iowa. She was born at Chicago, February 20, 1894. There are three children: Donald, born September 20, 1924; Mary, born November 1, 1926, and Bruce, born September 26, 1928.

Mr. Cottingham entered the employ of the Fullerton Lumber Company at Mount Vernon, South Dakota, as assistant manager in 1912, and was removed to Murdo, as manager for the years 1913-14. He was transferred to Sioux City, Iowa, in 1915, as cashier, holding this position two years. From 1917 to July, 1918, he was cashier of the Newton Lumber Company at Colorado Springs, Colorado. With the exception of two months spent as a private in the United States Army, he served as auditor of the Bonneville Lumber Company at Salt Lake City, during the years 1918 and 1919. During 1920-22, he was manager of the Byers Lumber Company at Hastings, and since 1923, has been joint owner and general manager of the Oliver Lumber Company and its branch yards, with headquarters at Hastings.

Mr. Cottingham is a member of Post No. 11 of the American Legion, is a Scottish Rite Mason, and member of the Shrine, and is a member of the Red Cross. At

the present time he is a director of the Hastings Young Men's Christian Association, is a director and past president of the Chamber of Commerce, a director of the Nebraska Lumber Merchants Association, a director of the Kiwanis Club, and director of the Northwestern Retail Coal Dealers Association of Minneapolis. His social club is the Hastings Country Club. Residence: Hastings.

Lewis Emory Cottle

Lewis Emory Cottle, lawyer, was born in Macon County, Illinois, November 11, 1873, and with the exception of four years in Idaho, one in Mexico, and one in France, has resided in Nebraska since 1881.

His father, James Weeks Cottle, was born in Somersetshire, England, November 7, 1841, and came to the United States about 1850. He was a farmer, who served in Company G, 149th New York Infantry during the Civil War. His death occurred at Edgar, Nebraska, May 13, 1912.

Lucinda Jane DeMotte, wife of James Weeks Cottle, was born in Taylorville, Illinois, December 25, 1848, and died at Edgar, December 1, 1923. Her ancestry was French and Dutch.

Upon the completion of his high school education in 1895, Mr. Cottle attended the University of Nebraska in which he received his Bachelor of Arts degree in 1901, and his Bachelor of Laws degree in 1902.

Mr. Cottle was admitted to the bar of Nebraska in 1902, and that of Idaho in 1904, and since leaving school has practiced law almost continuously. From 1907 until 1910 he was a member of the law firm of Christy and Cottle at Edgar, and from 1919 until 1928 was a member of the law firm of Olsen and Cottle at Gering. Since 1928 he has practiced independently. He is a Republican.

On October 16, 1910, he was married to Daisy Williams at Geneva, her birthplace. Mr. and Mrs. Cottle are members of the First Methodist Church at Gering.

During the Spanish-American War Mr. Cottle was a private in Company M, Second Nebraska Volunteer Infantry. From May 12, 1917, until July 2, 1919, he served in the United States Army. He held the rank of captain in Company D, 317th Service Battalion and served one year in France. For several years he was a major in Judge Advocate General's Reserve. He is a member of the American Legion, and the United Spanish War Veterans.

A Mason, Mr. Cottle is a member of Edgar Lodge No. 67, Ancient Free and Accepted Masons, and Oregon Trail Chapter No. 65 Royal Arch Masons. He is a member of the Red Cross, the Gering Chamber of Commerce, the Nebraska State Historical Society, the Scotts Bluff County and Nebraska bar associations. He is a member of the alumni association of the University of Nebraska and the Gering Golf Club. His sports are fishing and hunting. Residence: Gering.

Bern Raymond Coulter

Born in Cheyenne County, Nebraska, November 13, 1895, Bern Raymond Coulter is the son of Warren B. and Vie I. (Hendricks) Coulter. His father, who is a farmer and rancher, was born in Illinois, April 19, 1863. His mother was born in Illinois, November 24, 1863.

Mr. Coulter attended the rural schools of Cheyenne and Morrill counties, Nebraska, and in 1914 was graduated from the Bridgeport High School. He received the LL. B. degree in 1921 at the University of Nebraska where he was a member of the Order of Coif, and Phi Alpha Delta. Since 1922 he has beeen engaged in the practice of law as a member of the firm Neighbors & Coulter at Bridgeport. A Republican, he served as a member of the Nebraska House of Representatives, 1925, 1927, 1929, was speaker of the house 1920, 30, and in 1930 was candidate for lieutenant governor of Nebraska.

He is a member of the Morrill County Bar Society,

the Western Nebraska Bar Society, the Nebraska State Bar Association, and the American Legislators Association. His marriage to Esther Mae Scott occurred at Gering, Nebraska, September 9, 1927. Mrs. Coulter, who was a nurse, was born at Bridgeport, April 15, 1900. They have one son: Calvin L., born January 4, 1930, and a daughter, Madelyn Ann, born January 18, 1932. Residence: Bridgeport.

Harry Ginter Counsman

Harry G. Counsman was born at Omaha, Nebraska, August 24, 1861, and has lived there all his life. His father, Jacob Miles Counsman, who was born at Hollidaysburg, Pennsylvania, December 2, 1837, and died at Omaha, December 12, 1926, was a general building contractor, and a member of the Omaha city council 1888-1889. His ancestry was German. His mother, Arabelle (Redman) Counsman, whose ancestors were German, was born at Hollidaysburg, August 10, 1838, and died at Omaha May 26, 1927.

Mr. Counsman received his education in the Omaha public schools. A Republican, he served as county assessor, 1912-16-20-24, and is now Douglas County Commissioner. He is a member of the Red Cross, Chamber of Commerce, Young Men's Christian Association, and The Nebraskana Society. His social clubs are the Omaha Field Club, and the Prettiest Mile Club. He is an Elk, a Mason, Knight Templar and Shriner, and a member of the Woodmen of the World. His sport is golf.

On July 10, 1884, he was married to Yuba Kate Bailey at Council Bluffs, Iowa; she was born at Warren, Ohio, March 10, 1863. Her ancestry is English. They have two children: Harry, who married Dorothy Rice, and who resides at Lexington; and Maude, who married John L. Baumann, and resides at Hastings. Residence: Omaha.

Cecil Calvert Coursey

Cecil Calvert Coursey, prominent architect, was born at Topeka, Kansas, July 12, 1898, son of Fred Washington and Nellie Jane (Onion) Coursey. His ancestry is English and Pennsylvania Dutch.

Mr. Coursey attended public and high schools at Topeka, the Commercial Art School of Chicago, and the American Correspondence School of Chicago.

He was married on November 22, 1921, to Lena Christina Keiser at Alliance, Nebraska. She was born at Alliance, April 22, 1902. They have two daughters, Betty Jane, born February 1, 1923; and Marjorie Ann, born April 21, 1929.

For the past three years Mr. Coursey has practiced at North Platte, Nebraska. He is the designer of the Medical Building at Alliance; the Irrigation Building at Bridgeport, Nebraska; the high schools at Paxton and Ogallala, Nebraska; and the Catholic Church at Paxton.

During the late war Mr. Coursey served in the United States Navy. He is fond of fishing and hunting, baseball, football, and reading. He is a member of the American Legion, the Forty and Eight, Blue Lodge of the Masons, the Elks, the Rotary Club, and the Chamber of Commerce. Residence: North Platte.

William J. Courtright

William J. Courtright was born in Clinton County, Iowa, July 29, 1862, son of Ira F. and Mary (Shirley) Courtright, the former a farmer who died in Clinton County, in 1865.

He was married to Mary Reeves, at Sibley, Iowa, November 27, 1881. Mrs. Courtright was born March 26, 1862. They have two children, Carrol C., born June 8, 1886, who is a hardware merchant, and Marie, born May 14, 1895, who is a nutritionist.

Mr. Courtright is a Republican, and held the rank of major in the 2nd Nebraska National Guards until his resignation about 1891. He has been engaged in the practice of law since his admission to the bar in February, 1888, and is an outstanding member of the legal profession in his part of the state.

He is a member of the Methodist Church of Fremont, and former president of the Young Men's Christian Association. His hobby is garden flowers. Residence: Fremont.

William Poppleton Cowan

William Poppleton Cowan, lawyer, was born at Omaha, Nebraska, February 28, 1876, son of John and Celia Maria (Fay) Cowan. He was educated in the public schools of Omaha, and was admitted to the bar of Nebraska on June 16, 1898. He has always resided in Nebraska, and since his admission has been actively engaged in the practice of his profession.

From January, 1906, until July, 1914, he was county judge of Stanton County, elected on the Democratic ticket, and from 1916, until 1922, served as county attorney of Stanton County. He is active in the civic and professional life of his community, and a member of St. Peter's Catholic Church. He is also a member of the Nebraskana Society, and during the World War was government appeal agent for Stanton County. Residence: Stanton.

Allen Parker Cowgill

Allen P. Cowgill, retired army officer of Lincoln, Lancaster County, Nebraska, was born at Paducah, McCracken County, Kentucky, July 17, 1890, the son of Warwick Miller and Alice Blake (Parker) Cowgill. His father, who was an eye, ear, and nose specialist, was born at Hickman, Kentucky, in 1856, and died at Lincoln, in 1919; his ancestors settled near Philadelphia in William Penn's time. His mother was born at St. Louis, Missouri, in 1864; she is descended from early New England settlers.

Major Cowgill was graduated from the Lincoln High School in 1907; was a student at the University of Nebraska, 1907-09; and was graduated from the United States Military Academy, 1914. In 1916 he was graduated from the Engineer School of the United States Army, and in 1930 was awarded the A. M. degree at the University of Nebraska.

His career is as follows: entered West Point, 1910; was graduated and commissioned 2nd lieutenant, 1914; served in the Corps of the Engineers in the grades of 2nd lieutenant to major, 1914 to 1921; and was retired for disability incident to the service, 1921. He is now a retired major; is a graduate student studying for the degree of Doctor of Philosophy in mathematics at the University of Nebraska; and is the owner of the Cowgill Coal Company at Lincoln.

An Independent, Major Cowgill served as councilman and superintendent of streets and public improvements for the city of Lincoln. He is a member of the Engineer's Club of Lincoln, the Society of American Military Engineers, and the Nebraskana Society. A member of the Modern Woodmen of America, he is affiliated with the Episcopal Church of the Holy Trinity at Lincoln.

His marriage to Helen Mary Schwind was solemnized at Francitas, Texas, September 1, 1915. Mrs. Cowgill was born at Lincoln. They have three children: Mary Allen, born August 9, 1916; Helen Louise, born May 1, 1919; and William Parker, born January 30, 1921. Residence: Lincoln. (Photograph in Album).

George Cowton

Born at Scalby, Yorkshire, England, May 7, 1889, George Cowton came with his parents, James Harold and Emma (Thompson) Cowton, to America on July 1, 1904. His father, born in Yorkshire, England, February 5, 1862, is a cabinet maker. His mother was born in England, January 14, 1864.

George Cowton attended elementary school in Scarborough, England, until he reached the age of fourteen when he left school. After coming to America he attended high school one semester at Hastings, in the junior class.

On June 18, 1913, Mr. Cowton was married to Emma Hass at Grand Island. She is of German parentage, and was born in Grand Island, August 23, 1891. They have one daughter, Jean Ann, born December 27, 1916. She is in her junior year at high school, and makes a hobby of swimming.

Upon leaving school Mr. Cowton was office boy for eleven months for an attorney, a Mr. Costello, in Scarborough. The winter of 1904 he was office boy for the American Beet Sugar Factory at Grand Island, and during 1905-06 and part of 1907 was clerk in the store of S. N. Wolbach Sons. The balance of that year he was an insurance salesman for the Wamberg-Underwood Company.

In 1908 Mr. Cowton was a salesman for the Grand Island Real estate and Investment Company, and during 1909, 1910, and until October, 1911, was associated with Henry Allan in the insurance business. In October, 1911, he purchased the agency from Henry Allan. At the same time he was appointed deputy clerk, United States District Court, Grand Island Division, which position he, still holds. He is secretary-treasurer of the American Securities Company also.

Mr. Cowton is a Republican. He was a member of the Home Guards and on loan drive committees during the World War, is a member of the board of directors of the local Boy Scouts, president of the Nebraska Life Underwriters Association, 1931-32, immediate past president of the Grand Island Life Underwriters Association 1930-31, past president the Chamber of Commerce 1923-24, and at the present time a member of its board of directors.

He has served as president of the Rotary Club, was chairman of the program committee 1931-32, ,and is president of the Grand Island High School Athletic Board. He is an Elk, Mason and Knight Templar. A member of the Riverside Country Club, he is a member of The Nebraskana Society, and an admiral in Lieutenant Governor Metcalfe's State Navy. Mr. Cowton enjoys golf and bowling. His hobby is writing insurance, and on September 29, 1925, he broke the world's record by writing 122 life insurance applications in one day. He holds the record in the Equitable Life Assurance Company for writing at least one application for life insurance each week for six hundred and twenty nine consecutive weeks, which still holds. He is a member of the Quarter Million Club, Equitable Life, New York, for 1931. Residence: Grand Island.

Frank B. Cox

Frank B. Cox, editor and publisher, was born at Forney, Texas, August 28, 1883, son of M. J. and Lydia A. (Brazeale) Cox. His father, a native of Illinois, was born May 4, 1854, of English parentage. He was one of the best known editors in the South, and died at San Marcos, Texas, in 1920. His wife, Lydia, was born in Arkansas, January 20, 1861, and is living.

Mr. Cox attended puble school and afterward spent fifteen years on various papers throughout the United States. He was employed on the *Omaha Bee* and the Omaha Daily News for eight years. He is now the owner and publisher of the *Waterloo Gazette*, the *Elkhorn Exchange*, the *Bennington Herald* and the *Millard Courier*.

On March 5, 1910, he was married to Blanche Mabel Jesse at Oklahoma City, Oklahoma. Mrs. Cox was born at Des Moines, Iowa, October 24, 1883. There are two children, Frances B., born April 24, 1912, and Frederic, born September 17, 1915.

Mr. Cox is a Republican, and from 1920-28, was secretary of the Douglas County Agricultural Society. He is a member of the Ancient Free and Accepted Masons, and the Nebraskana Society, a charter member of the Nebras-

kana Society, and is fond of reading and fishing. Residence: Waterloo. (Photograph in Album).

Gilbert Morris Cox

Gilbert Morris Cox, who was born at Cedar Rapids, Nebraska, August 17, 1887, is the son of Jacob William and Elizabeth Louise (King) Cox. His father, a farmer, was born of German parents at Clear Lake, Iowa, May 29, 1861. His mother, who was a teacher for a number of years before her marriage, was born at Dubuque, Iowa, January 11, 1867; her ancestry was Irish.

Mr. Cox has been a farmer near Cedar Rapids for 30 years and is a progressive leader in civic affairs in Boone County. On January 29, 1913, he married Emma Caroline Peterson at Cedar Rapids. Mrs. Cox, who was born at Lindsay, Nebraska, July 17, 1886, is of Danish descent. To these were born: William C., January 31, 1914; Maurice L., May 5, 1916; Margaret A., June 20, 1919; Betty Louise, August 8, 1926; and Edwin F., November 30, 1929. Residence: Cedar Rapids.

Harold Herbert Cox

Born at York, Nebraska, February 1, 1898, Harold Herbert Cox has been engaged in the practice of dentistry and dental surgery for the past ten years. He is the son of Lincoln and Lillie Estelle (Moores) Cox, both of whom are residents of Nebraska. Lincoln Cox who was born at Indian Springs, Indiana, in 1862, is a cement contractor, and is descended from early Scotch-Irish settlers in Indiana. He traces his ancestry to Daniel Boone. His wife was born in Dixon, Illinois, in 1867, daughter of George D. Moores, whose family settled early in that state.

Harold H. Cox attended York public schools, and graduated from high school there in 1916. In 1922, he received the degree of Doctor of Dental Surgery from the University of Nebraska, where he had previously been made a member of Delta Sigma Delta. Before entering the university he studied pharmacy and served as a drug store apprentice.

On September 7, 1921, he was united in marriage to Florence Marie Ankeny at York. Mrs. Cox, who traces her ancestry to Stephen Hopkins, was born at Prescott, Iowa, September 6, 1898. She is a member of the D. A. R. and the Mayflower Society. There are three children: Harold Richard, born October 8, 1922; Barbara Jean, born September 15, 1924, and Marilyn Louise, born June 28, 1927.

During the World War, Dr. Cox was a private in the dental department of the Students Army Training Corps. He is now a member of the American Legion, the Junior Chamber of Commerce, the Red Cross and Midwest Lodge No. 317 of the Masons. He is affiliated with the Methodist Episcopal Church, and holds life membership in the Nebraskana Society.

Dr. Cox's hobbies are philately, reading and the scientific study of dentistry. Residence: Hastings.

John Thomas Cox

On August 13, 1869, John T. Cox was born at Edinburg, Johnson County, Indiana. Joseph Denise Cox, his father, was born at Germantown, Montgomery County, Ohio, October 19, 1840, and died on December 18, 1930. His ancestry was French and English.

His mother, Sarah Rachael (Adams) Cox was descended from English Quakers. She was born in Bucks County, Pennsylvania, June 20, 1845, and died at Howe, Nemaha County, Nebraska, in 1925.

Mr. Cox received his education in the public schools of Indianapolis, Indiana. He has lived in Nebraska for 33 years, and at the present time is vice president of the Bank of Howe, at Howe, Nebraska.

On January 18, 1892 he was married at Indianapolis to

Jessie Lane Scott, who was born of English parents at Crawfordsville, Montgomery County, Indiana, January 9, 1867. Four children were born to them, two of whom are living. They are Jessie M., born November 29, 1894, who married Chester L. Ames (deceased), and who was graduated from the Lincoln School of Music; Denise A., born July 25, 1900, who died March 15, 1907; John T., Junior, born January 26, 1904, who was awarded the A. B. degree at the University of Nebraska, 1930, and is now geologist for the Ohio Oil Company at Bakerfield, California; and Joseph D., born March 3, 1907, who died in October, 1907.

During the late war Mr. Cox was food and coal commissioner and was active in all loan drives at that time. He is a member of the Red Cross and the Nebraskana Society; has been treasurer of the school board for over 20 years; is a member of the Masons, Odd Fellows, Knights of Pythias, and the Woodmen of the World. He is affiliated with the Presbyterian Church and is a Republican. His favorite sport is golf. Mr. Cox's hobby is the care and producton of flowers. Residence: Howe.

Laurence Madison Coy

Born at Omaha, Nebraska, December 25, 1887, Laurence Madison Coy is the son of Charles Herbert and Amelia Sophia (Madison) Coy. Charles H. Coy was born in West Hebron, Washington County, New York, August 14, 1857, a descendant of Sir Robert Carey of the British nobility. He is a seedsman and the inventor of smokeless powder, and is a graduate of Claverick Military Academy. Amelia, his wife, was born in West Hebron, March 25, 1858, and was graduated from Elmira (New York) College. A former president of the Valley Woman's Club, she is descended in the direct line from President Madison. Her father and her brother practiced medicine together for 110 years at West Hebron.

Laurence Madison Coy was graduated from the 8th grade of the Mary A. Livermore School at Melrose, Massachusetts, in 1901, and from the 9th grade, Washington School at Melrose in 1902. In 1907 he was graduated from Melrose High School, after graduating from the Valley High School the year of 1906. Mr. Coy attended Dartmouth College during 1907-08, and the University of Nebraska 1908-10. At Melrose High School he was a letterman in football, and was a member of the freshman team at Dartmouth, where he was also a Phi Sigma Kappa. At the university he was a member of the Dramatic Club.

On September 8, 1915, he was united in marriage to Margaret Carolyn McCoid of Logan, Iowa. Mrs. Coy was born December 7, 1892, and is descended from Daniel Boone on the paternal side, and on her mother's side of the family is descended from the Purdums, an old English family of ecclesiastics and the nobility. They have one son, Laurence Madison, born August 31, 1916. A first class Boy Scout, he lettered in basketball, football, track and tennis at Valley High School.

Mr. Coy has been a resident of Nebraska thirty years. Formerly secretary of the C. Herbert Coy Seed Company of Valley, he is at the present time manager of the succeeding firm of O. and M. Seed Company at Valley. He is a Republican.

He held the rank of private (sharpshooter) with the 15th regiment of United States Marines during the World War, and is a member of the Marine Corps Reserve, past commander of Claude H. Montgomery Post No. 58 of the American Legion, and past department vice-commander of the American Legion of the State of Nebraska.

Among his civic and professional memberships are the Chamber of Commerce, the American Seed Trade Association, the Western Seedsman Association, and the Southern Seedman Association. He served as president of the Commercial Club in 1917, was a member of the village council seven terms and has been mayor three terms.

He is a past master of the Masons, and a member of the Methodist Episcopal Church.

Mr. Coy enjoys reading, and is fond of golf, tennis, football and baseball. Residence: Valley.

Francis Coyle

Francis Coyle, an early settler and farmer of Merrick County, Nebraska, has lived in this state since 1868. He was born at Athol, New York, March 7, 1848, the son of Patrick and Catherine (Sleven) Coyle. His father, who was born in Scotland, was a farmer. His mother was born in County Tyrone, Ireland, and died at Athol.

Mr. Coyle attended district school and studied in an academy for a year. He was engaged in the livery business at Clarks for two years, and has since been a successful farmer near there. He has lived near Clarks, since 1868, and has played an important part in the progress of his community.

During the Civil War, Mr. Coyle served in the quartermasters department; at the age of 14 he acted as messenger boy in the Union Army. He is affiliated with St. Peter's Catholic Church of Clarks, and holds membership in the Nebraskana Society. His hobby is reading. Mr. Coyle is now retired. He is a Democrat.

He was married to Isabelle Traynor at Louiseville, Kentucky, November 18, 1868. Mrs. Coyle was born at Louisville, and died at Clarks, April 22, 1869. Of his marriage to Julia Gates, which occurred at Columbus, Nebraska, October 23, 1873, three children were born: Charles, who is engaged in the commission business at Omaha; Francis, who died at the age of 12 years; and Isabelle, who married a farmer near Clarks. Residence: Clarks.

Fred Elias Craig

Born at Strahn, Iowa, September 11, 1878, Fred Elias Craig is the son of John and Emma I. (Parks) Crag. His father, who was a farmer and stockman, was born at Janesville, Wisconsin, March 18, 1851, and was prominent as a member of various educational and religious organizations at Creston, Nebraska; he died at Creston, November 14, 1926; his ancestry was Scotch. His mother, who took an active part in church work, was born at Janesville, May 21, 1856, and died at Creston, September 6, 1927.

Mr. Craig attended the grade and high schools at Creston, and then engaged in farming in Platte County for seven years. He was cashier in the First National Bank at Lubbock, Texas, for seven years, and since 1916, has been a farmer near Creston. He is a member of the Republican party, is affiliated with the Presbyterian Church of Creston, and is Past Grand of the Independent Order of Odd Fellows. He has been secretary of the local school board since 1915.

He married Alpha Marie Nash at Creston, January 28, 1899. Mrs. Craig, whose ancestry is Scotch and English, was born at Pickering, Missouri, November 8, 1879. Three children were born to them, of whom only one is living: Lola, born January 28, 1900, who married Alex McDonald, and who taught school for four years after which she was a student at the University of Nebraska where she held membership in Kappa Delta. Irma, who was born March 27, 1906, died June 10, 1906, and Earl Fred, who was born July 31, 1910, died June 21, 1913. Mr. Craig's hobby is reading. Residence: Creston.

Jesse Vincent Craig

Jesse Vincent Craig was born at Lehigh Gap, Pennsylvania, October 13, 1876, son of William and Martha Elizabeth (Gish) Craig, both natives of Pennsylvania. The former was born at Lehigh Gap, April 22, 1841, son of Thomas Craig, who was born in 1797.

Mr. Craig attended public school at Blue Springs, and was graduated from high school at Wymore. He attended the Creighton College of Law and the University of Nebraska.

On June 12, 1896, he enlisted in Company C, First Nebraska Infantry and enlisted for service in the Spanish-American War in 1898. He served in the quartermaster department in the Philippine Islands from July 20, 1898, until the following December. He was commissioned captain of Company K, First Infantry, Nebraska National Guard on December 8, 1909, and was honorably discharged, February 28, 1914. On March 11, 1914, he was commissioned captain and assistant quartermaster in the Nebraska National Guard, and on April 16 of that year was commissioned a major and assistant quartermaster of the Quartermaster Corps. On September 16, 1914, he was commissioned Chief of Ordnance of the Nebraska department of the National Guard, and at the expiration of his commission received his honorable discharge on January 8, 1915.

Mr. Craig has been active in the Republican party and has attended several national conventions. He is an honorary member of the Veterans of Foreign Wars, a Scottish Rite Mason and a member of the Shrine.

On November 7, 1901, he was married to Beatrice Crowley Fenton, daughter of Erie W. and Addie Fenton. Arthur C., the only son, was born August 13, 1903, and is a graduate of the University of Nebraska, from which he received the Bachelor of Arts degree and the Bachelor of Laws degree. Rsidence: Lincoln.

Albert Irvin Cram

Born in Clinton County, Iowa, November 16, 1871, Albert Irvin Cram has resided in Nebraska since the fall of 1883. His father, Wilber Irvin Cram was born at Crown Point, New York, August 18, 1846. Until his death at Burwell, March 20, 1918, he was a prominent farmer and stockman.

The family was originally von Cram, the family having come from Germany to England in 1620, and from England to Exeter or Boston in 1637. Honour Elizabeth Filby, wife of Wilber Irvin Cram, was born near Norfolk, Downham, England, December 7, 1845, and died at Burwell, May 17, 1928.

Albert Irvin Cram attended public school until 1891, and thereafter was a student at the David City High School. Entering the banking business in 1893 he continued until 1897, and from 1908 to 1910. He was a bank director 1910-19, and since that time has been president of the Farmers Bank of Burwell.

In the year 1897 he organized the A. I. Cram Company, lumber and coal, which he still operates. Since 1916 he has also been engaged in the building contracting business under the same name, and for the past two years has been taking state highway contracts. He is a Republican, and for the past ten years has been chairman of the Republican county central committee.

Mr. Cram's marriage to Effie Violet Wilson was solemnized at Ballagh, Nebraska, September 1, 1897. Mrs. Cram was born at Knoxville, Iowa, December 14, 1876, and in her earlier years was a teacher. Her father was a native of Ohio, while her mother was born in Indiana.

There are three children living, Besse Iola, born September 22, 1898, married Frank William Bieser, a banker at Steamboat Springs, Colorado; Jay Irvin, born July 23, 1900, died December 20, 1905; Roy Spencer, born February 3, 1903, married Edith Frease; he is a practicing physician at Burwell; Honor Elva, born February 3, 1906, married Charles A. Frease, a physician of Los Angeles. All are graduates of the University of Nebraska, with various degrees.

From 1916-23 Mr. Cram was chairman of Liberty loan drives for Burwell, and from 1917-21 he was chairman and from 1921-32 treasurer of the Garfield County Red Cross. He was a member also of the county War Board from 1917-19.

He is affiliated with the First Congregational

Church, is a member of the Wranglers Club, the Chamber of Commerce, (1923-32), the Nebraska Lumber Merchants Association (1898-1932), the Masons, Eastern Star, the Nebraskana Society and the National Geographic Society.

From 1907-21 he was a member of the Burwell school board, with the exception of two years 1912, 1913. Since 1916 he has been a member of the Burwell Golf Club. His hobby is building houses. Residence: Burwell.

William Frederick Cramb

William Frederick Cramb, editor, was born at Mendota, Illinois, October 23, 1871, and for the past fifty one years has been a resident of Nebraska. He is the son of James Oliver and Lydia Alphonsine (Kelsey) Cramb, the former a clergyman of the Methodist Episcopal Church, a farmer and member of the Nebraska legislature. James O. Cramb was born at Parsonsfield, Maine, September 9, 1833, and died at Kirksville, Missouri, in June, 1904. Of New England Yankee descent, his grandfather was a captain in the Revolutionary Army and his father was a farmer.

Lydia A. Kelsey, wife of James, was born in Troy Grove, Illinois, October 23, 1841, and died at Boston, April 17, 1917. The mother of twelve children, ten of whom lived to maturity, she was a college graduate and an ardent student. She was also of New England ancestry, her father a banker and her great grandfather a Puritan minister and head of a church.

Educated entirely through his own effort, Mr. Cramb was graduated from Fairbury High School in 1891, attended the University of Nebraska and its law school and was admitted to the bar in Jefferson County in 1894. Since January 1, 1897, he has been editor of the *Fairbury Journal*, and from 1894 until 1898 was engaged in the practice of law. At the present time, in addition to his editorial capacity, he engages in farm management, makes loans and acts as consultant in minor matters of law.

His marriage to Cora Helen Garnsey was solemnized at Fairbury on December 26, 1894, and to them was born a daughter, Pauline, on December 10, 1900. She is married to Harold L. Nuckolls. Mrs. Cramb, who was born at Hastings, on November 19, 1874, is descended from New York Yankees, who were probably French and English.

Independent in politics, Mr. Cramb was candidate for the congress and has been a candidate for the legislature and the office of county judge. He is a life member of the Red Cross, former secretary and director of the Chamber of Commerce, and a member of the Modern Woodmen and the Nebraskana Society. An ardent hiker, he is the owner of a forty-acre improved camping ground, one of the finest in the state. Hs hobby is architecture, and he designed and built three of the show places in Fairbury and vicinity. Residence: Fairbury.

Glenn William Cramer

Glenn William Cramer, newspaper editor and publisher of Nebraska, has lived in this state all his life and has been engaged in newspaper work since 1907. He was born at Albion, Nebraska, July 1, 1884, the son of Morris Wesley and Sarah Etta (Leavitt) Cramer, the former a farmer, who died at Boone, Nebraska, in 1896.

Mr. Cramer was graduated from the University of Nebraska School of Agriculture in 1907, having completed the high school course at Albion in 1903. He was connected with the firm publishing the *Albion Weekly News* from 1907 to 1918, and in 1918 purchased that paper from A. W. Ladd. He is an active worker in the Methodist Episcopal Church, holds membership in the Albion Commercial Club, and is a member of the Nebraska Young Men's Christian Association. He is a member of the Red Cross and the Modern Woodmen of America. A Republican, he was defeated for the legislature in 1926.

He was married at Albion, July 6, 1909, to Ruth May Moore. Mrs. Cramer, who is a reporter on the *Albion Weekly News*, was born at Schuyler, Nebraska, May 25, 1891. Residence: Albion.

Mabel Cramer

Mabel Cramer, a lifetime resident of Hastings, Nebraska, was born there on July 27, 1884, the daughter of Alexander Harrison and Ella Elizabeth (Cox) Cramer. Her father, who was a real estate and insurance man, and a pioneer in Adams County, always interested in the growth of Hastings, was born in Herkimer County, New York, January 31, 1852, and died at Hastings, on February 17, 1926. His mother was a New Englander, and his father was of German descent. Ella Elizabeth Cox is of English and Scotch ancestry; her parents, who were Quakers, moved from Indiana to Nebraska, settling in Glenvil.

Edna Cramer Jacobson, only sister of Mabel Cramer, and the wife of Henry F. Jacobson, was born January 24, 1881, and died February 16, 1931. Mr. Jacobson died in 1928, at the age of 51. Their three children now live with Miss Cramer. They are Mary Elizabeth, born March 31, 1909; Helen Leone, born May 27, 1917; and Dorothy Edna, born June 27 1921. Mrs. Jacobson was an accomplished musician, and before her marriage was one of the foremost teachers of piano in Hastings. In recent years she resumed her work and was associated with the Hastings College Conservatory. She was always in demand for programs and recitals.

Miss Cramer was graduated from Hastings High School in 1902, and in 1907 received her Bachelor of Arts degree from the University of Nebraska. Until the death of her father she was associated with him in the real estate and insurance business. She has since that time carried on the business in her own name and now has a general insurance, real estate and loan business.

Miss Cramer has always been active in civic and community affairs and has taken an interest in local and national politics. She is a member of the League of Women Voters, the Business and Professional Women's Club, the Young Women's Christian Association, and the First Presbyterian Church of Hastings. She is a member of the Nebraskana Society, and during the late war was secretary of the Adams County Red Cross. She is interested in flowers and gardening, and enjoys outdoor life and traveling. Her political affiliation is with the Republican party. Miss Cramer is active in Federated Woman's Club work, and has held various offices in past years. Residence: Hastings.

George Aloysius Crancer

A resident of Nebraska since about 1886, George A. Crancer was born at Saint Louis, Missouri, October 25, 1861. He is the son of Valentine and Catherine (Douglas) Crancer, the former born in Germany. Until his death in 1926 he was engaged in the mercantile business in Saint Louis, having come to America with his parents at the age of nine. His wife, Catherine, was born at New Orleans, Louisiana, and died at Saint Louis in 1919. She was the daughter of Hardin Douglas, who emigrated from Scotland, and upon the early death of her parents made her home with her grandfather, Jeremiah Buckley.

George A. Crancer attended the public schools of Saint Louis, afterward removing to Nebraska. On August 12, 1891, he was married to Lillian May Yott at Lincoln. Mrs. Crancer was born at Cleveland, Ohio, February 25, 1873, of *Mayflower descent*. There is one son, Ray Ayotte, born July 13, 1892, whose three children make their home with their grandparents.

At the present time Mr. Crancer is president of the G. A. Crancer Mercantile Company, and is noted as an international chess problem composer, being the author of *Chess Problems and Chess Compositions*. He is a member of the Chamber of Commerce and the Lincoln Country Club. His favorite sport is golf, and his hobby is chess. Residence: Lincoln.

Ray Ayotte Crancer

Ray A. Crancer was born at Lincoln, Lancaster County, Nebraska, July 13, 1892, and for some years has been a prominent business executive there. His father, George Aloysius Crancer, who is president of the G. A. Crancer Company at Lincoln, was born at St. Louis, Missouri, in 1862; his ancestry is German and Scotch. Mame Yott (Burkett) Crancer, whose French and English ancestors settled in America in colonial days, was born at Cleveland, Ohio, February 15, 1872; some of her ancestors came to this country in the *Mayflower*.

Mr. Crancer was graduated from the Lincoln High School in 1909, and was awarded the A. B. and LL. B. degrees at the University of Nebraska in 1913; he was a member of Phi Gamma Delta at the University of Nebraska. He is now vice president and manager of the G. A. Crancer Company and the Central Radio Company; and is connected with the Glenn Crancer Company of Omaha, and Crancers Incorporated. He was admitted to the practice of law at Lincoln, in 1913.

He holds membership in the Chamber of Commerce, National Association of Music Merchants, the Parent-Teachers' Association and the Nebraskana Society. His social clubs are the University Club and the Lincoln Country Club. Included in his sports are golf, tennis and bowling. His hobby is chess.

Mr. Crancer was married to Mamie Anderson at Boise, Idaho, January 29, 1914. Mrs. Crancer was born at Shelby, Nebraska, June 14, 1895, and died at Lincoln, April 25, 1925. Three children were born to them: Catherine, born November 18, 1915; Ray, born December 18, 1920; and George, born July 20, 1922. On December 25, 1928, Mr. Crancer was united in marriage with Jeanne Howard. Residence: Lincoln.

Howard Wallace Crandall

One of Nebraska's leading business men is Howard Wallace Crandall who was born at Bremen, Illinois, June 21, 1875, and since 1884 has been a resident of this state. His father, Albert W. Crandall, who is a retired farmer, was born at Bremen, December 14, 1849, and is descended from ancestors who settled at Westerly, Rhode Island, in 1634. Mary Ann (Stokes) Crandall, his mother, was born in England, July 8, 1854.

Mr. Crandall was graduated from the high school at Creighton, Nebraska, and for a number of years was in the grain and lumber business. He served as county treasurer of Knox County from 1910 to 1914, was in the insurance business for a time, and at this time is assistant receiver in the Nebraska Trade and Commerce Department. A Democrat, he served as county assessor from 1902 to 1910.

He is affiliated with the Ancient Free and Accepted Masons at Creighton, holds membership in the Red Cross, and is a member of the Nebraskana Society.

On September 1, 1897, he was married to Clara Matilda at Niobrara, Nebraska. Mrs. Crandall, whose ancestry is German, was born at Bloomington, Illinois, January 21, 1876. Their two children are: Lorena Marie, born August 9, 1898; and Leonard Milford, born March 5, 1900. Residence: Winetoon.

Charles Milton Craven

Charles M. Craven, who lived in Nebraska since 1886, was born at Monroe, Green County, Wisconsin, April 30, 1867, the son of Regin and Anna (Miller) Craven. His father, whose ancestry was English, Irish, and German, was born in Green County, Pennsylvania, December 28, 1828, and died at Wayne, Wayne County, Nebraska, July 21, 1913; he was a brickmaker. His mother was born in Northampton County, Pennsylvania, January 3, 1842, of Pennsylvania Dutch descent.

He was graduated from the Monroe High School June 22, 1884, for two years was a country school teacher, and later was a farmer for a time. Since 1888 he has been engaged in the photography business at Wayne. He is now director in the First National Bank at Wayne, is a member of the Young Men's Christian Association, and the Nebraskana Society. In 1928 he served as president of the Kiwanis Club. He is a life member of the Red Cross, is affiliated with the First Presbyterian Church at Wayne, and holds membership in the Photographic Association of Amercia. His social club is the Wayne Country Club, and his favorite sport is golfing.

During the World War he was prominent in Red Cross work and Young Men's Christian Association activities. He is a Republican. On October 30, 1890, he was married to Nettie Childs at Parker, South Dakota. Mrs. Craven, who was a school teacher at one time, was born at Middletown, New York, January 10, 1870, and died at Wayne, January 17, 1895; her ancestry was German. Mr. Craven was married to Hattie Olga Boethin in Minnesota, May 31, 1911. To his first marriage one child was born, Alma, born October 30, 1894, who married Ralph Waldo Hahn. Residence: Wayne.

Daniel Craven

Daniel Craven, who has been engaged in business at Norfolk, Nebraska, for the past 33 years, was born in England, October 31, 1865, the son of George and Esther (Large) Craven. His father, who was a Methodist minister, was born in England and died at Hamilton, Canada. His mother, whose ancestry was also English, died at Exeter, Nebraska.

Mr. Craven was married at Exeter, Nebraska, January 9, 1895, to Carrie Barbur. Mrs. Craven, who was a teacher before her marriage, was born in Fillmore County, Nebraska, May 26, 1871, in a dug out. In this early Nebraska home was organized the first Protestant Church in that part of the country. The nearest source of supplies was Lincoln, a distance of 46 miles, a trip of three days under the best of conditions with horses. They have seven children: Helen, born April 5, 1896; Abbie, born December 25, 1898, who married Thorvald Haines; Charlotte, born October 23, 1900; Marion L., born November 5, 1902, who married Dorothy Drebert; Robert L., born October 17, 1904, who married Lucille Dean; Ira L., born September 15, 1906; and Victor M., born January 29, 1910, who married Stella Carrico. Residence: Norfolk.

Albert O. Crawford

Albert O. Crawford, rancher and farmer, was born near Winterset, Iowa, June 17, 1868, son of James M. and Mary M. (Harmon) Crawford. The father was born in Indiana, January 9, 1835, and was an early settler in Nebraska. He died at Seneca, December 2, 1906. Mary M. Harmon was born near Burlington, Iowa, March 17, 1848, and died at Seneca, Nebraska, August 9, 1918. Her ancestry was Irish and German.

Mr. Crawford attended Buffalo school house in Madison County, Iowa, and in 1883, settled in Boone County. Since 1888, he has resided in Thomas County, where he has been prominent as a rancher and farmer and in local politics. A Democrat, he served one term as county commissioner and for a number of years has been county surveyor. He is a member of the Modern Woodmen of America and the Nebraskana Society.

On November 8, 1899, he was married to Hilma C. Anderson at Seneca. She was born at Princeton, Illinois, May 16, 1872, of Swedish parentage. Four children were

born to them, three of whom are living, Anna M., born September 20, 1900, who married N. M. Anderson; Bud E., born April 21, 1904; Ora, born December 16, 1906, who died February 13, 1909; and Alvo O., born May 19, 1909. Residence: Seneca.

Bryce Crawford, Junior

Bryce Crawford, Jr., son of Bryce Crawford, county judge of Douglas County, was born at Omaha, May 14, 1899. His father was born at Sparta, Illinois, of Scotch parentage, June 12, 1867. His mother, Agnes Love Crawford, was born in Lawrence, Kansas, October 15, 1870. She is of Scotch and Irish descent.

Both of Bryce Crawford's grandfathers served in the Civil War.

Mr. Crawford was graduated from Lake School, in 1913, and from Omaha Central High School in 1917. He received his LL. B. from the University of Nebraska in 1922. He is a member of Phi Kappa Psi, and Phi Delta Phi, and while at the university played tennis.

He was married to Mary Lelia Brundage at Tecumseh, May 2, 1925. Mrs. Crawford, who is of English and German descent, was born at Tecumseh, May 5, 1903. They have two children, Bryce III, born June 2, 1927, and Anne, born February 15, 1930.

Since his admission to the bar in July, 1922, Mr. Crawford has been engaged in the practice of law. He was elected on the Republican ticket as assistant county attorney of Douglas County for the term 1926-30. During the world war he was a student aviator, in the Naval Aviation Service. He is a member of the American Legion. His religious affiliation is with the First Presbyterian Church. He belongs to the Junior Chamber of Commerce, the Community Club, and the Nebraska State and Douglas County Bar Associations. His sports are golf and squash, and his clubs are the Omaha Club and Happy Hollow Country Club. Residence: Omaha.

Frank Elmer Crawford

Frank Elmer Crawford, lawyer and postmaster, was born in Wymore, Nebraska, August 22, 1877, son of James and Carrie Jane (Lott) Crawford. James Crawford was born in New York City, New York, October 25, 1847. His father, and family of eights boys and two girls, migrated from Ireland only a short time prior to the birth of James. James Crawford was a Civil War veteran, belonged to Company G, 64th Illinois Infantry, and was active in Grand Army of the Republic organization. He engaged in farming, and served several terms as county commissioner.

Carrie Jane Crawford, mother of Frank, was the daughter of Mr. and Mrs. Monroe Lott. Monroe Lott, a German minister, came to this country at a very early date and was one of the first homesteaders in Nebraska. Carrie Lott was born at Blue Springs, Nebraska, May 4, 1863. She was prominent in the Women's Relief Corps.

After graduating from high school at Wymore on June 3, 1898, Frank Crawford became a student at the University of Nebraska, and graduated in 1903 receiving his Bachelor of Laws degree.

His wife, Jennie May Smith, who was born at Wymore, September 16, 1884. Her parents, A. K. and Kate M. (Newton) Smith, were early settlers in Nebraska. To Mr. and Mrs. Crawford was born a daughter, Kathleen, on January 14, 1912. She was a student of the University of Nebraska and was later married to Harlan Amos. Mrs. Crawford died January 28, 1912, at Wymore, Nebraska.

On April 30, 1914, Mr. Crawford's marriage to Maude L. Clark was solemnized. Her father, W. H. Clark, has been associated with the legal department of the Burlington for the past thirty years. A daughter, Virginia, was born to them on May 22, 1920.

Mr. Crawford is a Republican. He has resided in this state for fifty-four years, and during this time he spent ten years as a police judge, thirteen years practicing law prior to the World War, and at the present time is postmaster in Wymore.

During the War he was captain of Company F, 134th infantry and Company E, 11th Infantry. While overseas he participated in the Meuse-Argonne engagement. He also served through the Mexican Border campaign.

Mr. Crawford is a member of the Wymore Bapitst Church, serving as superintendent of the Sunday school for nine years, and is a member of the Young Men's Christian Association. He is active in the Gage County Bar Association and State Bar Association, Wymore Community Club, is chairman of the Boy Scout committee, and is a member of the Kiwanis, American Legion, Independent Order of the Odd Fellows, Maccabees, Woodmen of the World, Royal Highlanders, Ben Hur, Security Benefit Association, Nebraska State Historical Society, The Nebraskana Society, National Council of Northern Baptist Men, and serves on the Wymore school board. Mr. Crawford's hobby is military technic. Residence: Wymore.

Robert Platt Crawford

Robert Platt Crawford, author and educator of Nebraska, has lived in this state for the past 20 years. He was born at Council Bluffs, Iowa, December 7, 1893, the son of Nelson Antrim and Fanny Vandercook Crawford. His father, who was a lawyer, was born at East Fairfield, Columbiana County, Ohio, May 18, 1853, and died at Lincoln, Lancaster County, Nebraska, October 20, 1927. His mother was born at Milwaukee, Wisconsin.

Professor Crawford was graduated from the Council Bluffs High School in 1912. He was awarded the A. B degree at the University of Nebraska in 1917, and in 1926 received the A. M. degree from Columbia University in New York. He was reporter for the *Nebraska State Journal*, Lincoln, 1914-16, was agricultural editor for the University of Nebraska, 1917-18, was assistant editor of the United States Department of Agriculture at Washington, 1918, and was associate editor of the *Nebraska Farmer*, 1919-21. He was engaged in historical research work for the College of Agriculture of the University of Nebraska, 1922, and established a course in agricultural journalism at this institution, 1922. In 1923 he was assistant professor, in 1924 associate professor, and since 1926 has been professor of agricultural journalism. Since 1928 he has also been assistant to the chancellor of the University of Nebraska.

He is the author of *These Fifty Years*, 1925, (a book) and *The Magazine Article*, 1931, (a book). He has contributed many articles to leading magazines, and has traveled to every part of the United States in studying economic situations. He holds membership in the following professional organizations: Nebraska Writers' Guild, serving as secretary, 1925-26, and president, 1928-29; American Country Life Association; the American Farm Economic Association; the National Economic League; American Association of Teachers of Journalism; National Association of Teachers of Marketing and Advertising; American College Publicity Association; American Association of Agricultural College Editors; American Association of University Professors, serving as secretary of the University of Nebraska chapter 1928 and 1929; and the Nebraskana Society.

He is a member of the Chamber of Commerce, the Kiwanis Club, and the University Club of Lincoln, and is affiliated with the Presbyterian Church. During the World War, Professor Crawford served in the United States Army, and is now a member of the American Legion. His favorite sport is horseback riding. He is a Republican. Residence: Lincoln. (Photograph in Album).

John Martin Creamer

John Martin Creamer, cashier of the Farmers State Bank of Ogallala, was born in Mills County, Iowa, September 9, 1881, and the following years was brought to Nebraska by his parents. His father, Cyrus LaFayette Creamer, was born in Missouri, January 15, 1851. He was a farmer whose death occurred at Elmwood, Nebraska, May 14, 1925. His mother, Clara Jane, was born in Illinois, November 24, 1861.

Mr. Creamer received his education in public school and business college. He has been in the banking business since 1903. He is a Republican. During the World War he was food commissioner of Banner County, and active in other loan and war activities. He is a member of Ogallala Methodist Episcopal Church, the Ancient Free and Accepted Masons, the Odd Fellows, and the Modern Woodmen of America.

His marriage to Mabel Ruth VanEvery was solemnized at Wabash, Nebraska, December 29, 1909. Mrs. Creamer was born in Cass County, Nebraska, February 2, 1881. They have one daughter, Ruth born March 11, 1921. Residence: Ogallala.

Sanford Preston Cresap

Sanford P. Cresap was born at St. Charles, St. Charles County, Missouri, April 26, 1869, the son of William Sanford and Ann Maria (White) Cresap. His father, who was a physician, was born in Maryland, and died at St. Charles, in 1882. He was directly descended from Thomas Cresap who migrated from Yorkshire, England, in 1751, and settled in Maryland. His ancestors served in the Indian wars and the Revolution.

His mother was born at Richmond, Henrico County, Virginia, and died at St. Louis, Missouri, in 1912. Her ancestors came from England to Virginia where they were prominent for many years in civic affairs.

Mr. Cresap has lived in Nebraska for the past 19 years. He attended the public schools at St. Charles, Missouri, and later was a student at the following colleges: Central College at Fayette, Missouri; American School of Classic Studies at Rome. He was awarded a medal for honors in declamation and oratory at Central College. Before coming to Nebraska he held the following pastorates, in the Methodist Missouri Conference; Maryville; Moberly; Columbia; and St. Joseph. He is now retired.

His marriage to Sarah Martha Payne was solemnized at Payne, Fremont County, Iowa, December 27, 1894. Mrs. Cresap was born in Howard County, Missouri, the daughter of Rev. Moses U. Payne, a pioneer farmer of southwestern Iowa.

Mr. Cresap was prominent during the World War in all the various loan drives and relief work. He is president of the Otoe Chapter of the Red Cross, and is president of Associated Charities at Nebraska City. He was president of the Nebraska City Chamber of Commerce for ten years, and was president of the Nebraska Chamber of Commerce for one year. He is national director of the Izaak Walton League of America and from 1929 to 1930 was president of the Nebraska division of this organization.

He is a member of the Sons of the Revolution; and is a director and vice chairman of the state committee of the Young Men's Christian Association. His favorite sport is fishing. He is a Democrat. Residence: Nebraska City.

Howard McKee Crilly

Howard M. Crilly, newspaper publisher and editor of Wilber, Saline County, Nebraska, was born at Riverton, Franklin County, Nebraska, September 6, 1894. His father, Hugh Crilly, who was born at Belfast, Ireland, in 1855, is a real estate and insurance man at Campbell, Nebraska. His mother, Mary Caroline (Merriott) Crilly, was born at Chicago, Illinois, 1860, and died at Campbell, January 16, 1930.

Mr. Crilly was graduated from the Campbell High School in 1912; was a student at the University of Nebraska for one year; and in 1917 was graduated from Peru State Teachers' College. He was a member of the Bushnell Guild Fraternity at the University of Nebraska in 1916. He was the editor of newspapers consecutively at Campbell, Bird City, Kansas, and McCook, Nebraska. Since 1925 he has been editor of the Wilber *Republican*.

He was united in marriage with Lenore Nadene Hagel at Beatrice, Nebraska, October 26, 1921. They have two children: Donn, born May 7, 1927; and Janis, born July 20, 1928.

During the World War Mr. Crilly was a corporal in the 24th Machine Gun Battalion, 1918-19. He is a member of the American Legion. He served as president of the Wilber Commercial Club in 1930; is a member of the board of directors of the Wilber Rotary Club; and is a member of the Nebraskana Society. He is a Mason and a Knight of Pythias. He is a member of the Congregational Church. He is an Independent in politics. Residence: Wilber.

Neil Louis Criss

Neil Louis Criss, physician and later insurance executive, was born at Sac City, Iowa, August 13, 1886. His parents were James Louis and Villa M. (Wodell) Criss, the former a merchant and insurance man, born in Pennsylvania. He died at Omaha in February, 1918. Villa Wodell Criss died at Omaha, in October, 1924.

Neil L. Criss was educated in the public schools of Omaha, and received his M. D. from Creighton University in 1912. He was secretary and treasurer of his senior class, and is a member of Phi Rho Sigma. He is unmarried. After being engaged in the practice of medicine three years, he entered the insurance field as assistant manager of the Mutual Benefit and Health and Accident Association. He is now assistant treasurer and medical director of the last mentioned company and medical director and treasurer of the United Benefit Life Insurance Company.

During the World War he was first lieutenant, Medical Section of Air Service. He belongs to the American Legion, and the Red Cross. His religious affiliation is with the First Presbyterian Church. He is a member of the Elks Lodge No. 39, and the Chamber of Commerce. He is interested in all sports, but golf particularly. His clubs are the Omaha Athletic and the Omaha Field Clubs. Residence: Omaha.

Edwin Darling Crites

Edwin Darling Crites, lawyer, was born at Plattsmouth, Nebraska, January 29, 1884, son of Albert Wallace and Mary (Minnie) Caroline (Hayt) Crites. The families, which are of Pennsylvania Dutch and English extraction, came to America about 1650.

Mr. Crites attended public school at Chadron and Lincoln high school. He received his Bachelor of Arts degree from the University of Nebraska in 1906. At the present time Mr. Crites is senior member of the firm of E. D. and F. A. Crites, president of the Chadron Building and Loan Association, and a member of the board of directors of the First National Bank of Chadron.

He is serving as a member of the state normal board, is past grand master of Masons of Nebraska, a member of the Sons of the American Revolution, and of the Mayflower Descendants. He is a Democrat. Residence: Chadron.

Frederick Augustus Crites

Frederick Augustus Crites, attorney and counselor at law, was born at Plattsmouth, Nebraska, July 1, 1885, son of Albert Wallace and Minnie Caroline (Hayt) Crites.

Albert W. Crites was born in the town of Waterford,

Wisconsin, May 12, 1848, and died at Chadron, August 23, 1915. His family originated in Pennsylvania. Its forbears having come to America about 1650. Albert W. Crites was a lawyer and past grand master of the Masons, and served as district judge of the 16th Judicial District of Nebraska. His wife, Minnie Caroline, was born at Bellevue, Michigan, January 11, 1846, and died at Chadron, March 2, 1926. She was a Daughter of the American Revolution, and past grand matron of the Order of Eastern Star. Her family originated in England, her mother being a lineal descendant of the Southworth family, a branch of which came over in the *Mayflower*.

Mr. Crites was graduated from Lincoln High School, and from the University of Nebraska in 1909, with the degree of Bachelor of Arts. He is a member of Sigma Nu fraternity.

Since June 11, 1913, Mr. Crites has been active in the practice of law. From 1918 until 1930, he served as county attorney of Dawes County, and from 1914 until 1927, was referee in bankruptcy for the Chadron division.

On August 18, 1914, he was married to Marion Smith Hart at Kansas City, Missouri. Mrs. Crites was born at Colwick, Kansas, July 4, 1888. They have three children, Wallace, born February 1, 1915; Sherman, born January 12, 1918, and Marion, born January 11, 1925.

Mr. Crites is a Democrat. He is affiliated with the Congregational Church, is a member of the Chadron Chamber of Commerce, the Nebraska State Bar Association, the Kiwanis Club, the Masons, and the Elks. For more than 20 years he has served as a member of the Chadron board of education, serving as president five years of his time. His club is the Chadron Country Club. He enjoys hunting and fishing. Residence: Chadron.

Marion Smith Crites

Marion Smith Crites, daughter of Sherman Elisha and Caroline (Smith) Hart, was born at Colwick, Kansas, July 4, 1888. She has resided in Nebraska for the past 27 years.

Her father, Sherman Elisha Hart, was born at Guilford, Connecticut, July 17, 1862. He is a salesman, a lineal descendant of John Hart, the first graduate of Yale. His wife, Caroline, was born in Marietta, Ohio, November 4, 1868, and was graduated from the Lincoln Conservatory of Music. She is a member of the Ames Amateurs, and is a lineal descendant of the Courtney family of England.

Upon her graduation from Lincoln High School in 1905, Marion Smith Hart entered the University of Nebraska, from which she was graduated with a Bachelor of Arts degree. She is a member of Alpha Omicron Pi.

Her marriage to Frederick August Crites was solemnized at Kansas City, Missouri, April 18, 1914. They have three children, Wallace, born February 1, 1915; Sherman, born January 12, 1918; and Marion, born January 11, 1925.

Mrs. Crites is a Republican. She is a member of the Congregational Church, the Order of the Eastern Star, and the P. E. O. Sisterhood. Her club is the Chadron Country Club. She enjoys reading. Residence: Chadron.

Charles Gifford Crittendon

Charles G. Crittendon, business executive of Lincoln, was born at Buffalo, New York, November 14, 1863. His father, Myron Lyman Crittendon, a grain merchant, was born at Buckland, Massachusetts, March 31, 1822, and died at Buffalo, April 28, 1913; his English ancestors came to America in 1584. Parthenia (Morse) Crittendon, his mother, was born at Charlemont, Massachusetts, August 28, 1826, and died at Buffalo, April 2 1920; she was of English descent.

Mr. Crittendon attended public schools and was a

student in business college for two years. He has lived in this state for the past 36 years and has held the following positions: treasurer of Harris & Company; vice president and president of the Central Granaries Company; and president of the Crittendon Grain Company. He now holds the latter position. He is a member of the Lincoln Chamber of Commerce and for many years was a member of the Lincoln Rotary Club. He is affiliated with St. Matthews Episcopal Church at Lincoln; is a member of The Nebraskana Society; and is a member of the Republican Party.

His marriage to Marian Elizabeth Brown was solemnized at Buffalo, August 10, 1892. Mrs. Crittendon was born at Buffalo, May 66, 1865. They have one child: Cornelia, born May 14, 1895, who is assistant professor of languages at Kansas State Agricultural College, Manhattan, Kansas. Residence: Lincoln.

Lodowick Fitch Crofoot

Lodowick Fitch Crofoot, lawyer, was born at Pontiac, Michigan, October 9, 1865, son of Michael E. and Annie E. (Fitch) Crofoot.

He attended the public and high schools of Pontiac, and in 1888 received the Bachelor of Laws degree from the University of Michigan.

On June 25, 1896, he was married to Mary Nash at Omaha. The children are Edward B., Lodowick F., Jr., David N., Michael J., and Virginia.

Mr. Crofoot is active in the practice of law, and is a member of the American, Nebraska State and Omaha Bar Associations. His clubs are the Omaha Country Club the Omaha Club and the New York and Eastern Yacht Clubs. Residence: Omaha.

Mary Nash Crofoot

Mary Nash was born at Omaha, April 26, 1875, and is the daughter of Edward Watrous and Catherine (Barbeau) Nash. Her father, who was born at Akron, Ohio, April 8, 1846, was a business man and was president of the American Smelter Company. He died at Omaha, July 22, 1905. Catherine Barbeau Nash was a native of Quebec, Canada, born April 18, 1848. She was of French Canadian and Irish descent. She died at Omaha, November 3, 1928.

Mary Nash was educated in the convent of the Sacred Heart in Omaha and New York. On June 25, 1896, she was married to Lodowick Fitch Crofoot at Omaha. Mr. Crofoot is a lawyer, born at Pontiac, Michigan, October 9, 1865. They have five children, Edward, born December 26, 1898, who married Josephine Ellick; Virginia, born March 29, 1900; Lodowick, born January 6, 1902; David, born November 16, 1908, and Michael, born September 6, 1911. Edward is a lawyer.

Mrs. Crofoot, whose main interest out side her home is music, has done much for the cultural development of Omaha along musical lines. She has been instrumental in bringing many musicians to Omaha, and in the development of musical appreciation. She is a member of the Catholic Church of St. Margaret Mary. Residence: Omaha.

Edward Porter Cromer

Edward Porter Cromer, son of John Basor and Mary Catherine (Hedrick) Cromer, was born at Muncie, Indiana, January 18, 1860. His father was born at Hagerstown, Pennsylvania, and died at Irving, Illinois, in 1898. He was a blacksmith, a preacher and a farmer, and a strong advocate of prohibition. His ancestors came from Holland. His wife, Mary Catherine, was born in Maryland, and died at Louisville, Kentucky, in 1910.

Educated first in the country schools of Montgomery County, Illinois, Mr. Cromer received his academic education at Hillsboro, Illinois, and after 23 years in Nebraska, Mr. Cromer was made a Master Farmer of Nebraska on January 8, 1927. A Republican, he was elected state

representative November 5, 1930, and is a candidate for re-election.

He was married to Ida Jane Kerr at Hillsboro, Illinois, August 16, 1883. She was a teacher of Scotch descent, born at Greenfield, Ohio, November 12, 1861. Mrs. Cromer is the daughter of Sampel P. and Catherine (Howard) Kerr. She attended country schools near Hillsboro. Illinois, and was a student at Hillsboro Academy one year, and Indianapolis, Indiana, two years. To them were born four children, Rowena Clare on March 31, 1888, who married Earl M. Kendall, and is a graduate of Wesleyan University and took a post graduate course in music at Boston, Massachusetts; George Chalmers, born on March 3, 1890, was a student at the University of Nebraska, and married Freda Henach of Scribner, Nebraska and married George A. Coughran, residing at Gering; Ida Gladine, born January 29, 1892, was graduated from the University of Nebraska, and married George A. Coughran, and who resides at Gering; and Miriam Edna, born on July 3, 1897, who was also graduated from the University of Nebraska, and married Charles M. Jefferay. Gladine and Miriam are teachers, and George is a farmer.

On August 16, 1929, Mr. Cromer was elected first honorary president of the Oregon Trail Association at Gering. He has been active in the introduction and extension of irrigation in western Nebraska, since 1900. His hobby is the breeding of registered Percheron horses.

For the past 44 years he has been a member of the Methodist Episcopal Church at Gering, he is a member of the Red Cross, the Chamber of Commerce, and is director of the Scottsbluff Agricultural Society. He is a member of the Nebraska State Historical Society and a life member of the Nebraskana Society. Residence: Gering.

Julius Dennis Cronin

Julius Dennis Cronin was born near O'Neill, May 29, 1895, the son of Dennis H. and Katherine (Lorge) Cronin. His father, who was born at Heola, Michigan, January 10, 1869, was an outstanding newspaper publisher, served as a member of the Nebraska Legislature and the Nebraska Senate for several terms, and has been United States Marshall for the past ten years; he is editor and publisher of the Frontier at O'Neill. His mother, whose ancestry is German, was born at Festina, Iowa, August 24, 1871, and died at O'Neill, April 6, 1911.

Mr. Cronin was graduated from the O'Neill High School, and in 1916 received the LL. B. degree at Creighton University where he was a member of Delta Theta Phi. He has been engaged in the practice of law at O'Neill since 1919, and is now serving his third term as county attorney of Holt County. He holds membership in the County Attorneys' Association of which he was president in 1930, is a member of the Nebraska Bar Association, and holds membership in the Elks and the Knights of Columbus. He is affiliated with St. Patrick's Catholic Church of O'Neill. During the World War Mr. Cronin served as first class sergeant in the 137th Aero Squadron, and was overseas for 13 months in France and England. He is now a member of the American Legion. Residence: O'Neill.

William Sherman Crook

One of Nebraska's pioneer farmers is William Sherman Crook, who was born at Dodgeville, Wisconsin, November 7, 1866, the son of John and Jennie (Maitland) Crook. His father, who was a farmer, and who served for four years in the Union Army during the Civil War, was born at Bolton, England, March 24, 1840, and died at Meadow Grove, Nebraska, August 13, 1929. His mother was born in Scotland, in 1845, came to this country with her parents in 1848, and died at Meadow Grove, in 1915.

Mr. Crook served as county commissioner from 1915 to 1918, in Madison County, Nebraska, and since 1923, has held that office. He is affiliated with the Meadow Grove Methodist Episcopal Church and holds membership in the Nebraskana Society and the Republican party. He

EDWARD PORTER CROMER

has been a farmer near Norfolk, Nebraska for over 40 years.

His marriage to Grace Muffly was solemnized at Meadow Grove, December 20, 1891. Mrs. Crook, whose ancestry is English and Pennsylvania Dutch, was born at Red Oak, Iowa, February 25, 1872, and died at Meadow Grove, April 1, 1916. Three children were born to them. Ralph E., born December 9, 1892, who married Eunice Edwards; Ruth M., born March 11, 1900; and Jack M., born September 2, 1906, who married Frances Connaughton. Residence: Meadow Grove.

Charles Robert Cropp

For the past fourteen years Charles Robert Cropp has been manager of the Farmer's Co-operative Equity Union at Oxford. He was born in Orleans, Nebraska, January 28, 1893, son of George William and Georgia (Matheny) Cropp, the former a railroad man. The father was born in Romney, West Virginia, December 12, 1853, of a family of early English settlers, and died at Lincoln, Nebraska, December 19, 1911. Georgia Matheny was a native of Keyser, West Virginia, born January 19, 1856, who died at Oxford, Nebraska, July 18, 1900.

Charles Robert Cropp attended public school at Oxford and at Almena, Kansas, and was graduated from high school at Almena. Thereafter he attended Kansas State Agricultural College 1910-16. He has been a farmer and dairyman since maturity, and has held his present position, as stated above, for fourteen years. He has been a member of the school board since 1925 and its secretary since 1926, with the exception of one year.

On February 17, 1913, he was married to Lydia M. Kellner at Oxford. Mrs. Cropp, who was born in Alta Vista, Kansas, January 28, 1893, is of German parentage. There are five children, Lorena Mae, born November 23, 1913; James Hobart, February 19, 1918; Ruth Maxine, December 1, 1919; Benjamin Robert, August 20, 1921; and Barbara Beth, September 11, 1923.

Mr. Cropp is a Republican. He is a member of the Red Cross, the Lions Club, the Odd Fellows, Modern Woodmen of America and the Nebraskana Society, and is affiliated with the Methodist Episcopal Church. He enjoys baseball and basketball, while his hobbies are breeding tropical aquarium fish and collecting old coins. Residence: Oxford.

Joseph Marshall Crosby

Joseph Marshall Crosby, abstractor of title, was born in Lincoln, Nebraska, July 20, 1875, son of Richard Madison and Nancy Husenstein (Stone) Crosby.

His father was born at Danville, Indiana, January 29, 1849, and was a mining and civil engineer, until his death at Imperial, October 19, 1918. His father was James Richard Crosby, born in Mason County, Kentucky, March 10, 1820. James Richard Crosby married Henrietta Boggs Daniel, and they had 15 children, 13 boys and two girls. He died November 30, 1899.

Nancy Husenstein Stone was born in Switzerland, and died at Kearney, in June, 1879. She was the daughter of Joseph and Franciska Husenstein (called Stone in America), and had only one sister, Sophia, who married Thomas Patz and lives in Crete, Nebraska.

Mr. Crosby attended Buffalo County public school, and finished at Fremont Normal in 1904. He lived on his father's farm from 1888 until 1892, and from 1897 until 1905, taught in the public schools. Since that time, he has been an abstractor of title, and is the sole owner at the present time of the Hayes County Abstract Company. A Republican, he served as county treasurer of Hayes County 1917-1922, and as county judge 1925-1928.

His marriage to Eva Leora West was solemnized at Hayes Center, December 25, 1906. Mrs. Crosby was born at Hayes Center, March 28, 1887, the daughter of William W. and Nora (Ratcliff) West. They have two children, Claire Izola, born February 5, 1908, who married Charles Alva Counce August 1, 1926; they have three children: Shirley May, Eugene Dwayne, and Richard Crosby; and Walter Floyd, born April 28, 1914.

During the World War, Mr. Crosby was chairman of the Hayes County Chapter of the American Red Cross, continuing until 1926. He was reared a Methodist, but as there was no church of that organization at Hayes Center, he is affiliated with the Congregational Church. He was a member of the Odd Fellows ten years, and from 1917 until 1922, was regent of Hayes County High School. His hobby is fishing. Residence: Hayes Center.

Leo Jay Crosby

Leo Jay Crosby, the subject of this sketch, is the son of Joseph and Emily Maude (Johnson) Crosby, pioneers in the Arizona Territory. Joseph Crosby was born in Salt Lake City, Utah, December 15, 1857, descended from English immigrants to America in 1632. His wife, Emily, was born at Spring Lake Villa, Utah, November 26, 1863. Together they went to Arizona Territory, where Leo Jay Crosby was born, March 3, 1884. His birth place was St. Johns, in Apache County. Emily Crosby was of Scotch-English descent; her grandfather, Joseph Ellis Johnson, published the first newspaper in Nebraska, the *Arrow*, in Omaha in 1854. Joseph Crosby returned to Salt Lake City, where he died on September 7, 1896.

Leo Jay Crosby was graduated from Panguitch High School in 1899, and attended Brigham Young University from 1900-02. He was active in track and basketball at the university. Prior to June, 1916, he was engaged in general sales work and studied in the law office of a practicing attorney. In May, 1919, he engaged in the title business, as secretary of the Kerr Title Guarantee and Abstract Company, and in September, 1922, he entered business for himself. He consolidated with the Midland Title Company in April, 1928, and is secretary and treasurer of that organization.

On May 26, 1913, he was married to Hazel M. Lucas of Creighton, Nebraska. Their marriage took place at Council Bluffs, Iowa. Mr. Crosby has been prominent in political, fraternal and civic organizations for many years. A Republican, he was unsuccessful candidate for the position of clerk of the district court in 1924. He was president of the Nebraska Title Association in 1928, and a member of the legislative committee of the American Title Association in 1929. He is a member of the Red Cross, and was on the executive committee of the Boy Scouts organization 1929, 1930, and 1931. He is also a member of the council. He is at the present time president of the Ad-Sell League, and a member of the Concord Club.

His military record is extensive. He was enlisted in the Nebraska National Guard on March 23, 1914, and was promoted to sergeant on January 4, 1915. On August 14, 1915, he was honorably discharged to accept a commission as second lieutenant. He was promoted to first lieutenant on June 2, 1916, and to captain, Company D., 4th Infantry, April 9, 1917. He saw Mexican Border service under the call of the President, June 18, 1916, to January 15, 1917. On March 23, 1917, he was mustered into service of the United States under call of the president. On March 25, 1917, he reported for federal service, and served until his discharge on April 1, 1918, with rank of captain, Field Artillery. He accepted appointment as captain of Field Artillery in the Officer's Reserve Corps on May 30, 1919, and is now a colonel of Field Artillery.

From 1919 to 1929 he was a member of the executive committee of the Omaha Post No. 1, American Legion, and in 1930 was commander of the post. A member of the Reserve Officers Association, he was president in 1924. For the term 1930-32 he is a member of the state council, Nebraska department of the Reserve Officers Association. He is also a member of the Military Order of the World War. In 1927 he was president of the Sojourners, and in 1930 was appointed commander of the Heroes of '76.

His fraternal organizations include Omaha Lodge No. 39 of the Elks, Mizpah Lodge of the Ancient Free and Accepted Masons, Delta Chapter No. 60, Royal Arch Masons, and the Scottish Rite body, of which he is a 32nd degree member. He is a member of the National Geographic Society and the Nebraskana Society. His social club is the Omaha Club. He is fond of golf and polo, and enjoys reading. Residence: Omaha.

Mainard Elery Crosby

Mainard Elery Crosby, lawyer, was born at Hastings, Nebraska, September 26, 1884, son of Elery Adelbert and Lucy Amelia (Powers) Crosby.

The father was born at Cherry Valley, Illinois, December 11, 1858, and is a farmer. He is the son of Sidney Asof and Julia Crosby. Lucy Amelia Powers was born in Adams County, Nebraska, September 24, 1862. She is the daughter of John H. Powers of the Populist Party and a candidate for governor at one time.

Mr. Crosby attended Sutherland High School until 1902, received his Bachelor of Laws degree from the University of Nebraska in 1908. He is a member of Phi Delta Phi.

From 1902 until 1904, Mr. Crosby was superintendent of city schools at Bayard, Nebraska. From 1908 until 1913, he practiced law independently, and from 1913 until 1919, was a member of the firm of Beeler and Crosby. Since 1919 he has been a member of the firm Beeler, Crosby and Baskins.

A Republican, he has served as a member of the city council 1915-1919; city attorney 1919-1921; and mayor of North Platte 1923-1927.

On October 2, 1909, he was married to Cora May Berkey at Davenport. Mrs. Crosby was born at Davenport, Nebraska, June 16, 1883, daughter of James M. and Anna Berkey. She is a graduate of the University of Nebraska receiving her Bachelor of Arts degree in 1908. She is a member of the Altrusa Club; the Federation of Women's Clubs (past president both local and county); the Travel and Study Club; the Chapter AK of the P. E. O. Sisterhood; a sponsor of the Campfire Girls and Girl Reserves; and a member of the First Presbyterian Church. They have three children, Robert B., born March 26, 1911, who is a student at Harvard Law School; Horace E., born March 25, 1916; and Lucy Ann, born November 1, 1923.

During the World War, Mr. Crosby was a four minute speaker and a liberty loan speaker. He is a member of the First Presbyterian Church of North Platte, the American and Nebraska State Bar Associations, the Kiwanis Club, the Elks, Masons, and the Odd Fellows. He is a member of the University Club and the North Platte Country Club. He enjoys golf and hiking, while his hobby is reading. Residence: North Platte.

Raymond M. Crossman

On January 5, 1887, Raymond M. Crossman was born at Atkinson, Holt County, Nebraska, and has lived in this state all his life. His father, Arthur C. Crossman, who was a merchant and real estate dealer, was born at Burlington, Vermont, July 30, 1851, and died at Omaha, Douglas County, Nebraska, October 18, 1918. Clara (Hart) Crossman, his mother, was born at Saltsburg, Indiana County, Pennsylvania. She is the great granddaughter of John Hart a signer of the Declaration of Independence.

Mr. Crossman was graduated from the Atkinson High School in 1903, where he was valedictorian of his class. He was graduated from Bellevue Academy in 1904; was awarded the B. S. degree at Bellevue College in 1908; and was granted his J. D. degree at the University of Michigan, 1911. He was a member of the baseball team at Bellevue College for four years, serving as captain one year; and was a member of the class baseball team at the University of Michigan for three years.

He became associated in law practice with the firm Brome, Ellick, & Brome, in 1911; was a member of the firm Morsman, Maxwell & Crossman, 1913-19; and in 1919 became a member of the firm Crossman & Munger. He is now senior member of the firm Crossman, Munger, & Barton.

His marriage to Leila Margaret Ostenberg was solemnized at Mead, Saunders County, Nebraska, April 15, 1914. Mrs. Crossman was born at Mead. They have two children: Raymond, Jr., born August 3, 1918; and Margaret Joan, born October 27, 1925.

He is a member of the Omaha Bar Association; Nebraska State Bar Association, having served for many years as treasurer of this organization; Commercial Law League of America; and the American Bar Association. He holds membership in the Omaha Chamber of Commerce and the Nebraskana Society.

He has been a member of the Kiwanis Club since 1920; was lieutenant governor of the Nebraska-Iowa district, 1922; and was governor, 1923; he served as chairman of the International Committee on Laws and Regulations, 1923; was an international trustee, 1924-27; was chairman of the finance committee for six years; was international treasurer 1927-1920; and is now immediate international past president of this organization.

He holds membership in the Omaha Club; is a Mason. and is affiliated with Dundee Presbyterian Church of Omaha. He is a Republican. Residence: Omaha.

James Phillip Crouse

Born at Seward, Nebraska, April 3, 1872, James Phillip Crouse is the son of Daniel Webster and Sarah Matilda (Randall) Crouse. His grandfather was born in Germany, and came to America at the age of 18. His father, who was born in Maquan, Illinois, July 12, 1845, was a farmer. He enlisted for service in the Civil War with the 11th Illinois Cavalry, and later settled in Nebraska. He died at Seward, Nebraska, May 30, 1915. His mother was Scotch-Irish.

Sarah Matilda Randall was born at Lewiston, Illinois, January 16, 1850, and died at Seward, on December 10. 1927, survived by ten children. She was the daughter of James H. Randall, a native of Kentucky, who married a member of the Hull family. She was a cousin of Ed. Hull of Peoria, Illinois, and of the late Caroline Hull Doty.

James Phillip Crouse attended public school, in later years working in the summer on the farm and attending school in the winter. As a child he endured the hardships incident to pioneer life in the 1870's, and as a young farmer survived the terrible drowth of 1894 and 1895.

From 1894 until 1897 Mr. Crouse operated a farm and for three years thereafter worked for Paul Herpolsheimer in the farm implement business. Then he entered the employ of the McCormick Harvester Company as a salesman and expert, being sent to Utah and Idaho in 1903 in connection with this work. During the year 1904 he was associated with F. N. Wullenwaker in the implement business at Seward, and in 1905 returned to the Herpolsheimer firm.

From 1906-11, inclusive, Mr. Crouse was blockman for the International Harvester Company at McCook, and during 1912-13 at Seward. He returned to McCook, in 1914, remaining there until he entered the implement business at Seward in connection with the Babson-Deckman Implement Company in 1916.

Continuing in this connection until June, 1919, he then became manager of a like business for the International Harvester Company at Seward. At the end of that year he purchased the company's interest and since that time has operated his own business.

On December 26, 1906, he was united in marriage to Stella May Cole at Seward. Mrs. Crouse, who is the

Gumbel—Seward

JAMES PHILLIP CROUSE

mother of three children, was born at Moline, Illinois, May 23, 1869. The children are: Elizabeth, born August 7, 1908, who was graduated from Seward High School, taught school two years, attended Hastings College two years, and then taught in the Seward schools two years. She is married to Kenneth J. Freese, and resides at Franklin, where Mr. Freese is connected with the Exchange Bank.

Martha, the second daughter, was born February 22, 1911, and is employed by the Iowa-Nebraska Power Company at Seward. She attended Hastings College one year, and is a member of the Seward Municipal Band. Dorothy, born December 28, 1912, attended Hastings College one year and is now a student at the University of Nebraska.

A Republican, with independent tendencies, Mr. Crouse has served as a member of the Seward city council three years, and as a member of the Seward board of education. During the World War period he was a member of the Red Cross and the Welfare Board. At the present time he is a member of the board of directors of the Chamber of Commerce, in which he has also served as vice president. As a 32nd degree, Scottish Rite Mason and member of the Shrine, he has held all of the appointive and elective offices of the local lodge, and is a member also of the Royal Highlanders and the Modern Woodmen of America. He is fond of baseball and football. During the years 1900-1901 he was a member of the Seward Fire Department, and for some time was a member of their running team in state tournaments. Residence: Seward. (Photograph on Page 288).

John Sebastian Crouse

John Sebastian Crouse, farmer and stockraiser, was born at Hartsburg, Illinois, January 9, 1882, son of John and Kathrine Caroline (Rohrer) Crouse. John Crouse, Sr., was a native of Lucasville, Ohio, born December 19, 1848, whose parents migrated from Germany. Until his death at Chester on February 22, 1911, he was a prominent farmer there. His wife, who was born at Jacksonville, Illinois, August 24, 1858, was of German parentage. Her parents came to the United States in their youth and were married here.

Educated in the rural schools of Thayer County until June, 1899, Mr. Crouse was a student at Chester High School the winter months of 1899, 1900 and 1901. At the present time he is an outstanding farmer and stockraiser, and holds extensive agricultural interests.

Of his marriage to Alta Harriett Thomas there are four children living and one deceased: Paul D., born on August 14, 1920, died August 26, 1927; Wilbert Earl, born August 21, 1922; Ruth Fern, born December 27, 1924; John Eldon, born July 10, 1927; and Elmer Lewis, born April 20, 1929. Mrs. Crouse, who is the daughter of George H. and Rosa (Heckel) Thomas, was born at Dwight, Illinois, October 23, 1886.

Mr. Crouse is an independent Democrat. For a number of years he has been a member of the local Red Cross and a member of its committee. From 1917 to date he has been a member of the school board, and has served as its secretary since 1921. He is affiliated with the Church of Christ at Chester. Residence: Chester.

Samuel Thomas Crouse

Samuel Thomas Crouse, who has lived in Nebraska all his life, has been engaged in the drug business at Osceola, since 1915. He was born at Osceola, September 28, 1898, the son of Charles and Elizabeth (Bennett) Crouse. His father was born at Wheeling, West Virginia, August 7, 1861, of German parentage, and died at Osceola, Nebraska, August 4, 1901. His mother was born at Wheeling, West Virginia, September 30, 1861.

Mr. Crouse attended Kearney State Normal School, and the University of Nebraska, and in 1915 received the degree Ph. G. He took part in football and baseball

activities in high school and college. At this time he is a member of the firm Crouse-Tex Drug Company, is a member of the Osceola Community Club, and holds membership in the school board. He is a Mason and Odd Fellow, and is affailiated with the Methodist Church. His favorite sport is golf.

His marriage to Pearl Dora Humiston was solemnized at Shelby, Nebraska, September 5, 1918. Mrs. Crouse, who is a druggist, was born at Shelby, November 17, 1899. They have a son, Murray, born August 7, 1920. Mr. Crouse is a Democrat. Residence: Osceola.

Charles Felix Crowley

Charles Felix Crowley, educator and chemist, was born at Detroit, Michigan, May 17, 1869. His father, John Jerome Crowley, was born and died at Detroit. He was a pharmacist, and served as a hospital steward in the Civil War; his parents came from Ireland. He married Delphine Van Damme, a native of Ghent, Belgium, who was an organist and school teacher, and who died at Detroit.

Professor Crowley was educated first in the schools of Detroit; he received his A. B. from Detroit University in 1887; his A. M., from the same university; he received a Ph. C. from the University of Michigan, in 1889, an M. D. from Creighton University in 1901, and an LL. D. in 1925.

He was married to Marie Euphemia Blay, at Detroit, September 22, 1897. Mrs. Crowley was born at Detroit, October 15, 1870. There are three children: Creighton F., born December 30, 1901; Edward D., born September 19, 1903, and Charles B., born November 28, 1906. Edward is a graduate of Annapolis, and a lieutenant in the United States Navy.

Professor Crowley has been a resident of Omaha, since 1894, and has been city chemist since 1902. He is a Democrat. Since 1894, he has been associated with Creighton University as research professor of chemistry. He was Nebraska member of the Naval Consulting Board from the American Chemical Society during the World War, and holds membership in the American Chemical Society, the American Association for the Advancement of Science and the American Institute of Chemical Engineers. He is a member of St. Cecilia's Cathedral, and the Knights of Columbus. His social clubs are the Omaha Athletic Club and the Happy Hollow Club. Residence: Omaha.

James Francis Crowley

Born at Ottumwa, Iowa, April 9, 1879, James Francis Crowley is the son of Jerome Joseph and Agnes (Carney) Crowley. His father, a wholesale grocer, was born at Ottumwa, May 1, 1853, and died in Berlin, Germany, January 18, 1905. He traced his ancestry to early settlers in Louisiana, a town in that state having been named for the family. Agnes Carney was born in Liverpool, England, April 21, 1856, and died at Hastings on December 18, 1928.

James Francis Crowley attended Hastings Public Schools and St. Marys, at St. Marys, Kansas. He has been in active practice in Nebraska since his admission to the bar on June 13, 1901; has served as justice of the peace at Hastings for about twenty years; and served as Adams County Judge in 1920. He is a Republican.

On June 10, 1915, he was united in marriage to Margaret Blanch Cantwell at Hastings, her birthplace. There are three children, John J., born August 9, 1916; James Francis, born October 18, 1917; and Mary Helen, born December 27, 1924.

During the late war Mr. Crowley was a four minute speaker, chairman of the registration board, and chairman of district loan drives. His professional organizations include the Adams County Bar Association, of which he is a former president, and the Nebraska State Bar Association. A Catholic, he is a member of St. Cecilia's Catholic Church, a fourth degree Knight of Columbus, and during 1914-15 was district deputy of the latter organization.

For the past thirty years Mr. Crowley has been a member of the Elks, and he is at the present time president of the Adams County Humane Society. Mrs. Crowley is very active in civic work, especially in the Parent Teachers Association. Residence: Hastings.

Forrest Newton Croxson

Forrest N. Croxson was born at Koleen, Green County, Indiana, December 10, 1876, the son of William Henry and Evalyn (Mitchell) Croxson. His father was born at Tarrytown, New York, December 9, 1843, and died at Texarkana, Arkansas, October 10, 1909. His mother was born near Bloomington, Indiana, March 28, 1857.

Mr. Croxson attended the public schools of Arkansas, where he was graduated in 1888. In 1899 he was employed by the M. M. Cohn Company at Little Rock, Arkansas. Later he was advanced to bookkeeper for this firm. In 1908, he became connected with the Equitable Life Assurance Society. At this time he is agency manager of the Omaha agency Equitable Life Assurance Society. A Republican, Mr. Croxson was elected commissioner for two years in Pulaski County, Arkansas, 1909-10.

His marriage to Kathryn Carpenter was solemnized at Arkadelphia, Clark County, Arkansas, September 19, 1906. They have one daughter, Jane Croxson, who was born January 10, 1908.

During the late war Mr. Croxson was Y. M. C. A. secretary in France, attached to the 103rd infantry of the 26th division, was with them at Chateau Thierry, September 12, 1988; at San Mihiel, July 18, 1918, and the Argonne. He was active in Liberty loan drives and Red Cross affairs.

He is past president of the Life Underwriters Association and the Life Managers' Association of Omaha. He is a member of the Omaha Chamber of Commerce, the Red Cross, and Community Chest, National Geographical Society. He is a member of Ak-Sar-Ben. He is an Elk and a Mason. His clubs are: University Club; Happy Hollow Club; Omaha Club; and Athletic Club. He is affiliated with the First Central Congregational Church. His favorite sports are golf and football. Residence: Omaha.

Edwin Elijah Crue

Edwin Elijah Crue, who is now retired, was born in Cook County, Illinois, July 7, 1859. He is the son of Valentine and Cornelia (Smith) Crue, the former born in Worms, Hesse, Germany, in 1828. Valentine Crue came to America in 1837. His death occurred in Madison, Nebraska, July 5, 1906. His wife, Cornelia, was born at Morristown, New Jersey, April 16, 1826, and died at Madison, December 6, 1896. Her grandfather, Lieutenant Elijah Smith, served in the New Jersey militia in the Revolutionary War.

Mr. Crue attended country school near Elgin, Illinois, and was later a student at Elgin Academy. He has been a resident of Nebraska 51 years and from 1889 until 1911, was the owner of a grain and livestock company at Tilden.

On March 9, 1892, he was married to Ida Fanny Warren at Tilden. Mrs. Crue was born at Rutland, Dane County, Wisconsin, September 20, 1855, and died at Tilden, October 25, 1928. She was descended from Governor John Webster, fifth governor of the colony of Connecticut, and also David Landon and Captain Abner Baldwin, who served in the Connecticut militia in the Revolutionary War.

There are two children: Charlotte, and Margaret, who married M. L. Biggs. Both are members of the Daughters of the American Revolution they graduated from the Nebraska State University, where they were members of Phi Beta Kappa.

From 1892 until 1898, Mr. Crue served on the town board of Tilden. He is a former member of the Modern Woodmen of America and Royal Highlanders, is a life member of the Red Cross and the Nebraskana Society, and from 1892 until 1901, was a member of the Tilden school board. His club is the Tilden Country Club, and his favorite sports are golf and fishing. Residence: Tilden.

Hugh Marcus Crumbliss

Born near Kingston, Tennessee, March 6, 1863, Hugh Marcus Crumbliss was the son of George Washington and Cordelia Matilda (Luttrell) Crumbliss. George Crumbliss was born March 10, 1832, near Kingston, of English parentage and died in David City, Nebraska, September 1, 1908. His wife was born in Knoxville, Tennessee, September 1, 1828, and died March 27, 1903, in Tamora, Nebraska. She was of Scotch and English parentage and taught school before her marriage.

Hugh Marcus Crumbliss was educated in public school in Kingston and has studied much at home. On March 9, 1898, at Hillsdale, Iowa, he married Stella Ann Hodges. She was born November 18, 1868, in Hillsdale. To this union three children were born an infant child, October 7, 1901, who died October 10, 1901; Bernice, June 10, 1905; and Walter Marcus, August 3, 1906. Bernice is married to Howard Orin Matson and has a Bachelor of Arts degree from the Manhattan Bible College. Walter has a Bachelor of Arts degree from Nebraska Wesleyan University. He is engaged in farming.

Mr. Crumbliss is manager of the Blue Mound stock farm and is a member of the Farmer's Grain and Supply Company. He is affiliated with the Ulysses Methodist Episcopal Church and the Republican party. He is a 32nd degree Scottish Rite Mason, and is president of the Ulysses township library, a member of the Red Cross and of The Nebraskana Society. Residence: Ulysses.

John J. Cubbon

A farmer until about thirteen years ago, John J. Cubbon was born in Elizabeth, Illinois, March 25, 1862. He is the son of Thomas and Margaret (Quey) Cubbon, the former born at Raby, near Peel on the Isle of Man. Captain of the ships Vixen and Elinor, sailing vessels, he later came to America and became a farmer in Illinois. His ancestry was Scotch-Irish. He died at Elizabeth, Illinois, August 15, 1906. Margaret Quey was born near Peel, Isle of Man, and died at Galena, August 10, 1893. Her ancestry was Scotch-Irish also.

Educated in public school, John J. Cubbon attended Mount Morris Seminary at Mount Morris, Illinois, one term. In March, 1890, he came to Nebraska, farming at Nora until the spring of 1918. Since that time he has been in the implement business at Nelson. He is a William Jennings Bryan Democrat, a member of the Nelson Methodist Episcopal Church, and of the Chamber of Commerce.

On March 28, 1888, he was united in marriage to Ida May Kevern at Elizabeth. Mrs. Cubbon, who was born at Elizabeth, January 28, 1872, is of English parentage. There is one daughter, Cora Alberta, born November 20, 1889, who is married to George D. Thayer. Residence: Nelson.

George Joseph Cullen

For the past 40 years George J. Cullen has lived in Nebraska and for the past several years has been president of the Grand Grocery Company. He was born at San Francisco, California, November 30, 1880, the son of Gerald James and Fannie (Gould) Cullen. His father, who was the son of Gerald Cullen, a shipbuilder of Sligo, Ireland, was a collector of customs at the Port of San Francisco.

Mr. Cullen was a student in the San Francisco public schools and was graduated from the high school at Lincoln, Nebraska. He is now president of the Grand Grocery Company there. He is a member of the Red

Cross, the Young Men's Christian Association, and the Modern Woodmen of America. He is a Mason. His sport is golf. He is a Republican.

On August 1, 1906, he was united in marriage with Carrie Mae Corbin at Lincoln. Mrs. Cullen was born at Lincoln, November 12, 1888, and is descended from an old Virginia family closely related to Robert E. Lee. Their two sons are: Richard, born November 9, 1914; and George, Junior, born March 16, 1917. Residence: Lincoln.

Joseph Aloysius Cullen

Since his admission to practice in 1916, Joseph Aloysius Cullen has been a dentist at Kearney. He was born on a farm in Fulda, Minnesota, May 17, 1893, son of Michael and Anna (Wynne) Cullen. The father, born in County Sligo, Ireland, September 22, 1852, is living; while the mother born in County Roscommon, Ireland, died at Fulda, January 13, 1914.

Dr. Cullen was graduated from Fulda High School in 1912, and worked for a year as bookkeeper for the Farmers Elevator and Creamery Company before he entered Creighton University. He was active in athletics in high school, and at Creighton, from which he received the degree of Doctor of Dental Surgery in April, 1916, was a member of Xi Psi Phi.

On June 16, 1920, he was married to Mae Ethel Smith at Bloomington. Mrs. Cullen, a teacher before marriage, was born at Franklin, Nebraska, October 22, 1895. Three children were born to them, Charles, on May 5, 1921, who died August 18, 1924; Joseph, born January 23, 1925; and Richard, born March 4, 1927.

Dr. Cullen is a Democrat. Entering the United States Army as a first lieutenant in the Dental Corps, he was discharged with the rank of captain. He participated in the Somme Sector, June 21-August 18, 1918, Meuse, September 18-October 21, 1918, and Troyon engagement October 23-November 11, 1918. He is a member of the American Legion and the Veterans of Foreign Wars.

He is a member of St. James Catholic Church, the Knights of Columbus, of which he was grand knight 1928-29, the Chamber of Commerce, the District, State and National Dental Associations and The Nebraskana Society. His hobby is Boy Scout work. Residence: Kearney.

Judson Alexander Cummings

Judson A. Cummings, druggist, was born in Delhi, Delaware County, Iowa, February 15, 1853. Ephraime Cummings, father of Judson, was born in Milford, New York, February 1, 1824. He was a farmer until his death which occurred October 29, 1895, at his home at Delhi, Iowa. Lucinda (Stone) Cummings, mother of Judson, was born in Milford, New York, February 15, 1829, and died at Delhi, Iowa, September 11, 1896.

Mr. Cummings was united in marriage to Florence Breach June 13, 1877, at Delhi. She is of Pennsylvania Dutch ancestry, and was born in North Umberland County, Pennsylvania. To them were born eight children, Lewis, born July 18, 1878; Ira, born February 7, 1880; Cora, born June 1, 1882; Arlington, born December 31, 1883; Alonzo, born June 15, 1885; Lester, born August 2, 1887; Jaso, born June 1, 1889; and Richard, born May 19, 1891.

During his forty-four years in Nebraska, Mr. Cummings has been in the drug business first with A. Stone in Delhi, and later alone in Beatrice, Tobias, and now in Daykin, Nebraska. He was admitted to the practice of his profession in 1878 at Delhi.

Affiliated with the First Baptist Church of Tobias, Nebraska, he is also a member of the Nebraskana Society, and was a member of the school board at Tobias most of his residence there. He is a baseball fan, and his hobby is reading. Residence: Daykin.

Morris Burt Cummins

Born at Ord, Nebraska, August 1, 1888, Morris Burt Cummins is the son of Frank Clinton and Alsa Brace (Cummings) Cummins. His father, who served as county judge of Valley County, Nebraska, from 1892 to 1896, was born at Akron, New York, February 19, 1855, and served as a soldier in the Indian War; he died at Arcadia, Nebraska, September 13, 1918; his ancestry was Irish and Scotch.

His mother, whose ancestry was Irish, was born at Akron, New York, August 28, 1860, and died at North Loup, Nebraska, December 10, 1925. She attended Cornell Academy.

Mr. Cummins was connected with the Cummins Brothers Hardware Company at North Loup for three years, and for the past 12 years has been an auctioneer there. He served as director of the Ord County Cooperative Creamery acting as president of that organization for a time. He was a member of the federal grand jury of Omaha, Nebraska, is president of the Valley County Sunday School Association, has been treasurer of his local school district for nine years, and is a Mason and an Odd Fellow.

His marriage to Myrtle Alma Knapp occurred near Loup City, January 1, 1908. Mrs. Cummins was born at Loup City, December 16, 1887. They have four children: Alma, born December 10, 1908, who married Clyde Lester Baker; Corwin, born November 12, 1912; Vivian, born December 1, 1916; and Wauneta, born April 9, 1918. Residence: North Loup.

Donald Horton Cunningham

Donald H. Cunningham, son of E. Cunningham and Jenny Belle (Horton) Cunningham, was born July 27, 1886, in Gilman, Marshall County, Iowa. His father, born in Juniata, Pennsylvania, March 6, 1852 of Scotch parentage, was an editor and auctioneer. His mother was born on August 31, 1860, of English and Scotch parentage. She died in Wayne, May 1, 1914.

Donald Cunningham was graduated from the Wayne High School in 1903 and then attended the Iowa State College in Ames, where he received the degree of Bachelor of Scientific Agriculture. He belonged to the Alpha Zeta and was a Phi Gamma Delta.

He married Freda J. Ellis at Wayne, Nebraska, September 22, 1914. She was born in Wayne on September 11, 1891, of German-Irish parentage. They have a son, Robert, born August 17, 1917.

Mr. Cunningham is a republican and has resided in Nebraska thirty-nine years. He managed a ranch in Idaho six years, was mayor of Wayne two years and is connected with the Sioux City Stock Yards Company in for whom he has worked for one year. At present he is an auctioneer. He is affiliated with the Presbyterian Church and is a member of the Masons, the Elks, and the Kiwanis Club. He is president of the Wayne Library Board and holds a position in the Juvenile Court Office of Wayne County. He is a member of the Nebraskana Society. Riding and reading are his favorite recreations. Residence: Wayne.

M. O. Cunningham

For the last 30 years M. O. Cunningham has been engaged in the practice of law in Nebraska, and has taken part in the civic affairs of Omaha. He was born at Red Key, Jay County, Indiana, September 18, 1869, the son of Burlington and Elizabeth Starr (Matts) Cunningham. His father, who was a farmer, was born at Front Royal, Warren County, Virginia, August 4, 1841, and died at Bloomfield, Knox County, Nebraska, November 30, 1930. His ancestry was Scotch-Irish. His mother was born at Fairview, Randolph County, Indiana, and died at Dallas, Iowa, January 6, 1879. Her ancestry was Scotch-Irish.

Mr. Cunningham attended the rural schools, and in

1895, was graduated from the Wayne Normal School with the degree B. S. He was awarded the LL. B. degree at the University of Nebraska in 1898. He is engaged in general practice in Omaha; is attorney for the U. S. Brush Company; and is a director and secretary of the latter organization. He is director and attorney for the Metropolitan Building & Loan Association.

He was united in marriage with Jennie D. Brown at Vermillion, South Dakota, February 15, 1899. Mrs. Cunningham was born at Emerson, Mills County, Iowa, July 27, 1873. They have one daughter, Ruth Miller, born December 11, 1903; she is a music instructor.

During the World War, Mr. Cunningham was in the treasury department of the United States and British governments. He is a member of the Nebraska State Bar Association, and the Douglas County Bar Association, and a conservative Republican. Residence: Omaha.

John L. Currier

John L. Currier, son of Alfred and Elizabeth (Martin) Currier, was born at Greenville, Pennsylvania, December 6, 1856. His father, who was born at Erie, Pennsylvania, came to Nebraska in 1878. His family had resided in Pennsylvania for several generations, originally coming from England. Members of his family served in the Revolution. Alfred Currier was an early Nebraska pioneer farmer, and died here in 1901. His wife, a native of Butler County, Pennsylvania, was descended from English pioneer settlers in that state. She died in Thayer County, in February, 1904.

Educated in country schools in Illinois, John L. Currier came to Nebraska fifty-four years ago. He is the only farmer in Thayer County who has resided on the same place more than fifty years, and was a settler here before railroads were built. For twenty-five years he auctioneered in addition to his farming activities, and has been more than successful in his undertakings.

On March 21, 1888, Mr. Currier was united in marriage to Amy Corliss at Hebron. Mrs. Currier, who was born at St. Albans, Vermont, January 13, 1857, taught school prior to her marriage. She is descended from early English settlers in America. To them were born two children, Sarah A., born January 5, 1889, who is married to Charles Wills; and Joseph, born August 21, 1899, who is a farmer.

Mr. Currier is a Republican. He and his family attended the Christian Church, while he is also a member of The Nebraskana Society. Residence: Hebron. (Photograph in Album).

Carl T. Curtis

Carl T. Curtis, county attorney of Kearney County, was born at Minden, Nebraska, March 15, 1905, son of Frank O. and Alberta May (Smith) Curtis. His father, a retired farmer of Swedish descent, was born at Galesburg, Illinois, February 22, 1865. For a number of years he has been active in Democratic and Populist politics, and has served as a member of the board of county commissioners. His mother, whose ancestry is English, was born in Warren County, Illinois, December 5, 1868.

Upon his graduation from Minden High School Carl T. Curtis was a student at Nebraska Wesleyan University where he was a member of Beta Kappa. Afterward he attended the University of Nebraska. Prior to his admission to the bar in 1930, he served as principal of the Minden public school. He was elected county attorney in 1930 by the largest majority ever given a candidate for any Kearney County office.

He is county general chairman of the 1931-32 Northern Nebraska drouth relief committee. He is a member of the Nebraska State Bar Association, the Kearney County Historical Society and The Nebraskana Society. His religious affiliation is with the First Presbyterian Church of Minden. He is an Odd Fellow, and a Democrat.

His marriage to Lois Irene Wylie Atwater was solemnized at Minden, June 6, 1931. Mrs. Curtis, who was born at Omaha, August 16, 1903, is the daughter of Robert M. and Clara (Smith) Wylie and the foster daughter of Orland D. and Laura Wylie Atwater. She was a teacher in the Minden public school before her marriage. Residence: Minden. (Photograph in Album).

Wesley Lyman Curtis

A native Nebraskan, Dr. Wesley Lyman Curtis has been engaged in the practice of medicine since 1896. He was born in Johnson County, January 7, 1870, son of Harrison J. and Mary Elizabeth (Cannon) Curtis. His father, who was born in St. Lawrence County, New York, on August 16, 1839, was of English stock, his ancestors having settled first in Connecticut, and later in New York. A farmer by occupation, he enlisted and served in the Civil War, and came to Nebraska shortly after its close. He died at Dannebrog, June 11, 1894. His wife, Mary Elizabeth, was born at Elsberry, Missouri, September 14, 1840, and died at Cook, Nebraska, January 3, 1908. Her ancestry was Scotch-Irish.

Upon completion of his public school work Dr. Curtis attended Grand Island Baptist College. Later he entered Rush Medical College from which he was graduated with an M. D. on May 27, 1896. Thereupon he entered active practice, continuing until 1906. The following year he was surgeon in the Coast and Geodetic Survey on the Philippine Islands, and during 1906-07 served as resident surgeon at St. Paul's Hospital at Manila. Since 1909 he has specialized in eye, ear, nose and throat, part of this time in association with Dr. Hompes. His professional memberships include the Lancaster County, Nebraska State and American Medical Associations, the American College of Surgeons and the Academy of Ophthalmalogy and Otolaryngology.

Dr. Curtis' first marriage was to R. Minta Campbell of Thornton, Indiana. She was born February 23, 1871, and died at Lincoln May 4, 1924. There were four children, three of whom are living: Martha E., born August 29, 1901; John C., born August 3, 1900, who died August 11, 1900; Donald W., born January 20, 1904, who married Gladys Emert; and Mary C., born July 15, 1908, who married Dr. John C. Peterson.

He was married to Alice E. Long on September 15, 1925. Mrs. Curtis who is a daughter of A. J. and Bessie A. Evens, was born at David City, November 9, 1878.

Dr. Curtis is a Mason, and member of the Blue Lodge and Scottish Rite bodies. He is also a member of the Kiwanis Club. Residence: Lincoln.

Edward LeRoy Curtiss

Edward LeRoy Curtiss, lumber merchant, was born at Bassett, Nebraska, May 19, 1898, son of George Emerson and Ada (Richards) Curtiss.

The father was born in Warren, Ohio, October 4, 1868, and is a merchant of English descent. His wife, Ada, was born at Bassett, Nebraska, September 16, 1878; her ancestry is English also.

Mr. Curtiss was graduated from Rock County High School in 1916 and attended the University of Nebraska two years. Since leaving college, he has been associated with the H. W. Galleher Lumber Company at Bassett, starting as bookkeeper and was promoted to the managership of the Cornbelt Lumber Company at Rushville, in 1925.

A Republican, Mr. Curtiss is interested and active in local politics. He served as a private in the World Was and is now a member of the American Legion. Since 1929, he has served as secretary-treasurer of the Rushville Chamber of Commerce. He is a Methodist, a Mason, and a member of the Red Cross. His favorite sports are hunting and fishing, while his hobby is reading.

His marriage to Eda Caroline Peterson occurred at Valentine, Nebraska, August 30, 1925. Mrs. Curtiss was born at Long Pine, March 1, 1903. She is of Swedish ancestry. She attended school at Long Pine and is a member of the Woman's Club, and the Eastern Star. She is the daughter of Isaac and Clara E. (Bethge) Peterson. They have one son, Jack, born June 15, 1928. Residence: Rushville.

Herbert Dewey Curtiss

Herbert Dewey Curtiss, lawyer, was born at Bassett, Nebraska, August 28, 1885, son of Charles Henry and Martha (Abby) Curtiss. His father, who was a farmer, of English descent, died at Bassett. His mother was born in Ohio, and died at Bassett. She was of French and English descent.

Mr. Curtiss attended the Bassett public and high school and Bellevue Academy. He received the Bachelor of Laws degree from the University of Nebraska in 1915. His A. B. degree was awarded in 1912 at Bellevue College. While at Bellevue he was a member of the debating club. Mr. Curtiss received football letters, 1909, 1910, 1911, and 1912, and letters in track, 1909, 1910, 1911, and 1912. He coached football at Cotner University in 1913 and 1914.

On November 17, 1915, he was married to Zilpha Edna Thurber, at Craig, Nebraska. She was born at Yuma, Colorado, January 12, 1892. There are four children: David William, born September 9, 1916; Eugene Herbert, June 7, 1918; Elizabeth Clare, May 23, 1920; and Harold Thurber, August 2, 1921.

Mr. Curtiss is a member of the Methodist Episcopal Church, the Modern Woodmen of America, the Odd Fellows, the Masons, and the Nebraskana Societ. He was secretary of the School Board from 1916 to 1926. He enjoys football, golf, hunting, fishing and reading. Residence: Bassett.

Herbert Louis Cushing

Since 1908 Herbert L. Cushing has been active in the educational field in Nebraska. He was born at Ord, Valley County, Nebraska, October 30, 1890, and has lived all his life in this state. His father, Francis Marion Cushing, who was born in Potter County, Pennsylvania, December 7, 1847, is a bridge builder and surveyor in central and northwestern Nebraska, and a hunter and trapper in the North Long Valley, and miner in the Black Hills. He settled in Valley County in 1872, and spent four years in the Black Hills, 1876-1880. He has been a deacon and trustee in the First Baptist Church at Ord, for many years. He is descended, through a long line of illustrious ancestors, from William the Conqueror, and lists among his relatives and ancestors such notables as Caleb Cushing, Frank Hamilton Cushing, and Governor Cushing of Massachusetts. The first members of his family to come to America arrived on the *Griffin* and settled at Bingham, Massachusetts.

Kate Adelaide (Bassett) Cushing, who was born at Potter, Pennsylvania, June 19, 1860, is an enthusiastic church worker. She was active in the Women's Christian Temperance Union.

Mr. Cushing was graduated from the Ord High School in 1908. He holds the following degrees: A. B., Grand Island College, 1914; A. M., University of Nebraska, 1930. In 1922 he was a student at the University of Chicago. He was a member of the debating team at Grand Island College for two years; was captain of the basketball team, 1912; and was made a member of Phi Delta Kappa. He was editor of *Volante*, a college publication, 1912.

He is the author of: *Early Days of the Nebraska State Teachers Association*, volume 9, 1929; *Whats and Whys of the Federal Constitution*, 1928; and various stories of Valley County pioneers published in the Ord *Quiz*, 1921.

His marriage to Annie Laurie Van Broekloven was solemnized at Ord, September 17, 1915. Mrs. Cushing, who was born at Elwood, Gosper County, Nebraska, June 25, 1897, is the granddaughter of S. C. Thomas, a Civil War veteran. She was a teacher before her marriage. There are three children: Thomas Caleb, born July 10, 1916; Mae Margaret, born February 2, 1918; and Herbert Louis, Jr., born March 5, 1920.

Mr. Cushing was awarded a medal in recognition of his war work in connection with Liberty loan drives. He is eligible to membership in the Sons of the American Revolution. He is a member of the Nebraska State Teachers' Association; the National Educational Association; and the Nebraskana Society. He was a member of the board of the Valley County Red Cross, 1922-24; and was president of the college Young Men's Christian Association for a semester during his stay at Grand Island College. He is a member of Ord Lodge Number 103 of the Masonic Lodge. He holds membership in the Nebraska Schoolmasters Club. He is affiliated with the First Baptist Church at Lincoln. Politically, Mr. Cushing, is an Independent Democrat. Residence: Lincoln.

Marion Jay Cushing

One of Valley County's prominent farmers is Marion Jay Cushing, who was born at Ord, Nebraska, September 11, 1887, and has been a resident of the state all his life. His father, Francis Marion Cushing, who was born at Ulysses, Pennsylvania, December 7, 1847, was a pioneer settler in Valley County, Nebraska, was hunter for the first surveying party, and was a gold prospector and miner in the Black Hills in 1876; his English ancestors came to America during the 16th century, and members of the family served in all the early American wars; Chief Justice William Cushing administered the oath of office to George Washington in 1789.

His mother, Kate Adelaide (Bassett) Cushing, whose ancestors were French Acadians, was born at Ulysses, June 17, 1860. Mr. Cushing attended the public school at Ord and school training in 1903. At Grand Island Baptist College he was noted as an amateur baseball pitcher from 1906-12. He was a farmer from 1904 to 1921, acted as vice president of the Ord State Bank from 1918 to 1921, was president and manager of the Ord State Bank from 1921 to 1925, and since 1925 has engaged in farming near Ord.

A Republican, he was state representative from the 77th district from 1928 to 1932. He is a member of the Knights of Pythias, is a member of the Baptist Church, and holds membership in The Nebraskana Society. His favorite sports are fishing and hunting, and his hobby is politics.

On December 30, 1912, he married Ruth Odell Work at Ord, Nebraska. Mrs. Cushing, who is a musician, was born at Ord, April 16, 1893. Two children were born to them: Robert Leavitt, April 12, 1914; and Marion Grace, February 21, 1916. Residence: Ord.

Anna Gray Cutler

Anna Gray Cutler, educator, businesswoman and author, has lived in Nebraska all her life and for many years has been active in the social and civic life of her community. She was born at Sutton, Nebraska, December 28, 1876, the daughter of George Whitfield and Ada Augusta (Gray) Bemis, and is the wife of Robert Erwin Cutler.

Her father, who was born at Mayfield, New York, September 1, 1846, and died at York, Nebraska, March 4, 1915, was a distinguished lawyer in New York and Nebraska. He served as district attorney in Nebraska where he was later mayor of York, city attorney, and police magistrate. He was the son of Phineas and Eleanor (Day) Bemis, and was the grandson of Isaac Bemis (John, John, John, John, Joseph of Watertown, Massachusetts) and Mary (Stevens) Bemis who came to Massachusetts from England in colonial days. Isaac Bemis served in the Revolution.

Her mother was born at Marion, Linn County, Iowa, December 16, 1848, and was descended from the Gray family who came to America in the 1600's; Lord John Gray, Captain Matthew Fuller, The Reverend John Lathrop, John Cass, and Henry Rowley were among her ancestors. She received her education at the Female Seminary at Cedar Rapids, Iowa. At this time she holds membership in two music clubs, Daughters of the American Revolution, Mayflower Society, American Legion Auxiliary, and the Women's Christian Temperance Union.

Mrs. Cutler was graduated from York High School and York College. She was a school teacher for nine years and for five years was the manager of a wholesale music firm, J. A. Parks Company. She is the author of verse, articles, and short stories published in the following magazines: *Point of View; Field and Stream; The Harp; Poet's Scroll; The Oracle; The Legionnaire; The Household Magazine; The Nebraska Farmer; The National; The American;* and the *Youth's Companion.*

She is past president, past state chaplain, state chairman of legislation, of the American Legion Auxiliary, is a member of the Eight and Forty Club, holds membership in the Daughters of the American Revolution, the United States Daughters of 1812, and the Nebraska Society of Mayflower Descendants. In 1925 she was state chairman of legislation of the Women's Christian Temperance Union, and for 12 years has been president of the Amateur Musicale Club. She was head of the literature department of the York Woman's Club in 1930, has been Most Excellent Chief of the Pythian Sisters since 1930, and is a member of the Native Sons and Daughters.

Mrs. Cutler is affiliated with the First Methodist Episcopal Church of York. Her hobby is genealogy. Residence: York.

John Leo Cutright

John Leo Cutright, lawyer and statesman, was born at Lincoln, Nebraska, October 31, 1891. He is the son of John William and Hannah (Hultgren) Cutright, the former a noted journalist and editor. John William Cutright was born at Chillicothe, Illinois, December 8, 1855, and died at Lincoln, September 28, 1921. His family appears to have had its headquarters in Peoria, Illinois. John W. Cutright's mother died when he was a small child, and his father re-married. There were a number of half-brothers and sisters as well as full. One of his full brothers, Nathaniel Cutright, was until his recent death a wealthy and influential citizen of Peoria, and a number of the family reside there.

The original Cutright family seems to have come from West Virginia. It would appear that a certain Peter Cutright came originally from Virginia and settled in Illinois, where he presumably was the progenitor of the family in that vicinity. Members of the family who still reside in West Virginia, are members of the Daughters of the Revolution, and it is apparent that the Cutrights originally settled there in pre-Revolutionary times.

John W. Cutright first read law in Illinois, and later drifted into the newspaper field. He, together with Hon. Edgar Howard, came west as tramp printers, and he seems to have worked on various newspapers until some time in the late 80's when he took up his work in Plattsmouth. There he met Hannah Hultgren, who was born in Sweden, July 5, 1858. Later he established *The Plattsmouth Journal* in conjunction with the father of Charles Sherman, now sports editor of the *Lincoln Daily Star.*

Later John W. Cutright became closely associated in a journalistic and political way with the late William Jennings Bryan. It is said that when Mr. Bryan first ran for Congress he consulted Mr. Cutright. Mr. Cutright approved, and later wrote what he considered the first article concerning Mr. Bryan's candidacy for national political office. Thereafter, when Mr. Bryan was

in Congress, Mr. Cutright was his private secretary, and traveled with him in that capacity in his first presidential campaign. Up until the time of the Democratic Convention in St. Louis, at which time Mr. Cutright, like many others, turned against him, Mr. Bryan and he were to a considerable extent associated in the work of the Democratic party in Nebraska.

Mr. Cutright worked in various reportorial and editorial capacities on newspapers in Plattsmouth, Lincoln and Omaha, and in 1906 left Lincoln to become editor of the *Peoria Journal.* After a few months, however, he returned to Nebraska, and in 1910, became editor of the *Lincoln Daily Star,* continuing in that capacity until about 1918. Early in that year he and his wife arranged to go on a homestead south of Buffalo, Wyoming, and were given a testimonial dinner on February 26, of that year, at the Hotel Lincoln. The roster of complimentarians includes sixty-eight of the political, legal and civic leaders of the state. At this time he was presented with a draft for the purchase of a new Ford car. After spending three years on the homestead he returned to Nebraska, and at the time of his death was Omaha correspondent for the Lincoln Journal.

John Leo Cutright attended the public schools of Omaha and Lincoln, and Wesleyan Preparatory and Omaha High Schools. He received his LL. B. from the University of Nebraska in 1914, and while there took an active part in basketball and track. He was a member of interclass teams and running distance and cross country intercollegiate meets. He was his sophomore class president, associate editor of *The Nebraskan,* and was a member of Sigma Delta Chi, Alpha Tau Omega, the Innocents, the Kosmet Club, the Iron Sphinx, and the Spikes.

With reference to his own political history, John L. Cutright states that any positions he has held are attributable almost entirely to his father's influence. While in the sixth grade in the Normal public school near Lincoln, he won a $5.00 prize given for scholarship by Mr. Bryan. With the money his mother purchased a picture for the school. Two years later, upon his graduation he won a scholarship which entitled him to enter Nebraska Wesleyan, where he spent two years. Later, when he was about to graduate from the University, Mr. Bryan told his father that he would see that he got an appointment in the consular service. In June, 1914, he received an appointment to Coburg, a small city in southern Germany, and he arrived there on July 1, 1914. Finding, however, that his lack of German was a handicap, he wrote the Department of State for a post where he could be of more service.

The war, however, interrupted communication to such an extent that it was several months before he was transferred as vice-consul at Nottingham, England. At this time he was requested by his father to return home, but when he reached his post was advised by his chief that a letter he had written from Coburg, had been published in the *World Herald,* and that if he endeavored to accept his position he would be protested by the English. Upon returning to London, he cabled the Department of State, and received a cable from Mr. Bryan to the effect that his letter would necessitate his withdrawal.

Returning to America, through his father's influence, he secured a position in the law department of the Union Pacific, where he remained a year and a half. Several months later he was appointed assistant attorney general under Willis E. Reed, serving about a year and a half. Shortly afterward he enlisted in the Air Service and in July, of 1918, was called into the service. He took a three month's ground school course, was in concentration for a month at Camp Dick, Texas, and was then transferred to the Heavy Artillery School of Fire at Fort Monroe, Virginia, remaining there until the Armistice.

After the war, Mr. Cutright became associated, in the legal profession with T. W. Blackburn. Here he remained about a year and a half. Removing to Fremont, where he was associated with a leading law firm for a short time, he has since engaged in general practice. Mr. Cutright is a member of the Commercial Law League of America, the American, Nebraska State and Dodge County Bar Associations. He is a Christian Scientist. Among his civic, fraternal and patroitic organizations are the American Legion, the Red Cross, the Fremont Chamber of Commerce, the Retail Merchants Association, the Elks and the Young Men's Christian Association. Mr. Cutright's sports are swimming, skating, hiking and basketball. Residence: Fremont.

James Charles Dahlman

James Charles Dahlman was born at Yorktown, Texas, December 15, 1856, son of Charles and Mary Dahlman.

The father, a ranchman, was descended from German settlers in America, in 1845.

Mr. Dahlman attended public schools, and on December 18, 1885, was married to Harriet Abbott at Union, Iowa. There are two daughters, Ruth, who married C. C. Baughman, of Washington, D. C.; and Dorothy.

Mr. Dahlman served as sheriff of Dawes County, Nebraska, six years, and as mayor of Chadron, two years. For four years he was a member and chairman of the Democratic state committee and for eight years served as national committeeman.

Mr. Dahlman, one of Omaha's most beloved citizens, served as mayor nearly 25 years, and in 1928 was elected delegate at large to the Democratic national convention. He was a member of the Community Chest, the Chamber of Commerce, the Young Men's Christian Association, the Library Commission, the Fraternal Aid Union, the Royal Arcanum, the Woodmen of the World, the Ancient Order of United Workmen, the Moose and the Elks. He was president of the Americanization League. (Deceased).

Gust Dahlstedt

For nearly half a century Gust Dahlstedt has been engaged in farming in Phelps County, Nebraska. He was born in Sweden, December 12, 1862, the son of Gustaf Person and Anna Christina Dahlstedt. His father, who was a farmer in Phelps County, was born at Kisa, Sweden, April 26, 1823, and died at Holdrege, November 1, 1909. His mother was born at Eneby Parish, Sweden, in 1823, and died at Holdrege, December 1, 1896.

Mr. Dahlstedt is affiliated with the Loomis Evangelical Mission Church and holds membership in the Nebraska Society. Politically, he is a member of the Democratic party.

He married Mathilda Kristina Johnson at Holdrege, August 26, 1903. Of the four children born to this marriage, two are living: Ruth, born June 16, 1904, who died February 6, 1920; Alice, born September 15, 1905; Carl, born February 11, 1907; and David, born July 18, 1909, who died in infancy. Residence: Holdrege.

Peter Dahlsten

Peter Dahlsten, prominent Wheeler County farmer, was born at McGregor, Iowa, December 4, 1862, son of Carl and Karin (Hansen) Dahlsten. The father, born in Sweden, December 12, 1822, came to the United States in 1857, and was a farmer until his death in Madison County on November 2, 1906. His wife, Karin, also born in Sweden, July 31, 1827, died in Madison County, February 17, 1884.

Mr. Dahlsten attended common school and has since been a farmer and rancher. Independent in politics, he was postmaster of Ericson six years; a member of the Nebraska legislature in the session of 1901; county treasurer of Wheeler County, 1902-09; county clerk, 1909 13; county commissioner of Wheeler County four years, 1917-18 and 1919-20.

His marriage to Hannah E. McCort was solemnized at Palmyra, December 25, 1893. Mrs. Dahlsten was born in Otoe County, January 13, 1874. To them were born four children, Sarah Belle, December 7, 1894, who married Howard Williams; Anna M., January 1, 1899, who married Carl Asimus; Carl H., born June 6, 1896, who married Alice Nelson; and Peter G., born November 2, 1910, who is a farmer. Sarah Belle was a teacher before her marriage. Carl H. is a a farmer, and Anna is a musician and elocutionist.

Mr. Dahlsten is a member of the First Lutheran Church of Ericson, the Ancient Order of United Workmen and the Modern Woodmen of America. Recently, he was made a life member of the Nebraskana Society. Residence: Ericson.

Christ Dahmke

Christ Dahmke, son of F. W. and Louis (Wallhenrich) Dahmke, was born in Kiel, Germany, January 9, 1865. His father and mother were both natives of Germany, and his mother died there in 1900 and his father in 1910.

For the past forty-six years Mr. Dahmke has been a resident of Nebraska, and a successful farmer for many years. On August 14, 1892, he was married to Emma Suhl in Sarpy County, Nebraska, her birthplace. There are six children, Marie, born July 15, 1893; Fred, born November 4, 1894, who married Marie Dahmke; Louise, born May 31, 1897, who married A. Loschousky; Emil, born August 14, 1899; Claus, born July 4, 1901; and Freda, born June 17, 1903, who married G. Fundaburg.

Mr. Dahmke is a Republican, and has held various local offices, among them membership on the town board and the school board, and that of assessor. He is a member and treasurer of the school board at the present time, and attends St. Paul's Lutheran Church. Residence: Millard.

William C. Dahnke

William C. Dahnke, realtor and insurance writer, was born at Stratton, Nebraska, November 10, 1886, son of William J. and Ida M. (Molkenthin) Dahnke. The father, born in Mecklenberg, Schwerein, Germany, July 6, 1861, is a retired farmer, who came to America as a young man in 1873. His wife, Ida M., was born in Eirenberg, West Prussia, Germany, March 14, 1863.

Mr. Dahnke attended country grade schools and Stratton High School and in 1912 was graduated from Franklin Academy, Franklin, Nebraska. He attended the University of Nebraska two years, 1912-1913 and 1913-1914. While at the Franklin Academy he took first place in dramatics, 1911; was a member of the debating club and for a time was a member of the football team, although working his way through school.

He taught in country schools two terms, 1908 and 1909, and from 1915 until 1918 was general manager of the Farmers Co-operative Company at Stratton, Nebraska. He was private first class in training camp and on medical duty at Camp Grant, Illinois, during the World War, from September, 1918, until June, 1919. Returning from the war he was again associated with the Farmers Co-operative Company until 1924. He was a bank cashier from 1924 until 1929. Since then he has operated a real estate and insurance agency. Mr. Dahnke is secretary-treasurer of the Doane National Farm Loan Association; from 1926 until 1929 was president of the State Bank of Stratton, and during 1930, 1931 and 1932 was cashier of the Farmers Company, Inc. He is the owner and proprietor of Dahnke Realty and Insurance Company and the owner of a 320 acre farm eleven miles southeast of Stratton, a combination stock and grain farm.

On April 19, 1918, he was married to Minnie Myrtle Richards at Stratton, and has made his home on a five acre tract purchased prior to his marriage. Mrs. Dahnke was born at Stratton, the daughter of A. Richards, a farmer, formerly of Fairbury, Nebraska, and is a member of the American Legion Auxiliary, Woman's Club and takes an active interest in the affairs of the Methodist Church of which she is a member. Her mother is Tillie

(Wiser) Richards. There are two children: Dorothy A., born June 12, 1920, at Stratton; and Leonard L., born July 26, 1921, at Stratton. The children are both music-ally inclined and are exceptional students in their school work.

Mr. Dahnke is a Republican. He is a charter member of William Egle Post No. 281 of the American Legion, treasurer of the Methodist Episcopal Church, and a member of the Red Cross. He is the present secretary of the Chamber of Commerce, a member of the school board, police magistrate and for several years has been a member of the town board. His hobby is hard and conscientious work. Residence: Stratton. (Photograph in Album).

William Frederich Dahnke

A resident of this state for the past 44 years, William Frederich Dahnke was born at Quaslin, Germany, December 3, 1868, the son of Fred and Anna Maria (Ganzlien) Dahnke. His father, who was a brickmolder was born in Germany, and died there in 1868. His mother was born at Quaslin, Germany, February 18, 1845, and died at Tilden, February 4, 1921.

Mr. Dahnke has been successfully engaged in farm-ing in Madison County, Nebraska, for many years, was di-rector of the Farmers Elevator Company at Tilden, and was president of the latter organization from 1915 until 1927. He is agent for the Battle Creek Mutual Insurance Company with which he has been connected for 25 years, and is now serving as a member of the board of directors. From 1900 to 1907, he was treasurer of the school board, District Number 4, and from 1902 to 1917, was sec-retary-treasurer of the Evangelical Lutheran Immanuel Church at Tilden. He is a member of the Nebraskana So-ciety, and the Tilden Community Club of which he was vice president from 1914 to 1928. In 1890, he enlisted in the United States Army in the campaign against the Sioux Indians, was promoted to the rank of corporal in 1893, and was honorably discharged in that year. He served as first lieutenant in the Nebraska Home Guard during the World War and solicited funds for training camp expenses.

His marriage to Wilhelmine Caroline Hoepfinger was solemnized at Tilden, March 11, 1894. Mrs. Dahnke was born at Pierce, Nebraska, March 15, 1874. They have five children: Henry, born May 16, 1895; Bertha, born October 20, 1897; Mathilda, born December 28, 1900, who grad-uated from Tilden High School, is a public school teacher and who married Albert Bruveleit; Helena, born Feb-ruary 20, 1906, who married Charles C. Hansen; Irvin, born September 23, 1909, who married Clara Roder. Helena was graduated from Tilden High School in 1923, was a bookkeeper in an elevator for two years, and is now in nurse's training at York, Nebraska.

A Democrat, Mr. Dahnke was a member of the Madi-son County Democratic Central Committee, and for four years acted as precinct assessor. Residence: Tilden.

William Peter Dailey

One of the leading bankers of Holt County, Nebraska, is William Peter Dailey who is a lifelong resident of this state. He was born at Emmet, Nebraska, December 19, 1883, the son of John and Ellen (Curry) Dailey, the form-er a farmer who died at O'Neill, Nebraska, October 3, 1899. His mother died at O'Neill, in October, 1916.

Mr. Dailey attended a rural school until 1904, and for over a year studied at Fremont Normal College. He served as clerk in the First National Bank, O'Neill, Ne-braska, from 1905 to 1907, and since 1907, has been cash-ier of the Emmet State Bank. His religious affiliation is with the Epiphany Catholic Church of Emmet.

He was united in marriage with Frances C. Menish, at O'Neill, September 6, 1910. Mrs. Dailey was born at O'Neill, in November, 1882; they have two children, John,

born February 8, 1913, and Arthur, born March 4, 1917. Mr. Dailey is a member of the Democratic party. Resi-dence: Emmet.

Stanley Owen Daily

Stanley Owen Daily, farmer, was born at Stansbury, Missouri, March 22, 1888, son of William Levi and Fran-ces Isabel (Smith) Daily. His father was born in Kansas, May 11, 1860, and died at Bethany, Missouri, October 1, 1900. He was a farmer, who also taught school and prac-ticed law. His wife, Frances, was born at Bethany, Miss-ouri, January 8, 1863, and is now living at New Hampton, Missouri. Her father was born in Scotland.

Mr. Daily attended public schools at Bethany, Miss-ouri, and has been a farmer since reaching maturity. He has a fine herd of pure bred Holstein cattle, and in 1930 was awarded the championship medal of the state for but-ter fat production, averaging 533.1 pounds per cow. In 1914, he became light weight wrestling champion of the world. Vivid in Mr. Daily's memory is his first match with Billiter, of Toledo, Ohio, in February, 1914. With the championship at stake the contestants wrestled for four hours and fifteen minutes to a draw. Then in June of the same year they met again at Lincoln, for the champ-ionship which Mr. Daily won. The first fall was made in four minutes and forty-five seconds, and the second in forty-nine minutes. During Mr. Daily's wrestling career he participated in over fourteen hundred matches.

On March 12, 1913, he married Martha Lyden at Keene, Nebraska. Mrs. Daily was born at Keene, October 15, 1889, of Danish and German ancestry. They have seven children, Gladys, born January 15, 1914; Joseph, born October 29, 1915; Juniata and June, born December 15, 1917; Stanley, born February 5, 1920; and Ruth and Rob-ert, born September 1, 1923. Gladys is graduated from high school and is a nurse, Joseph and June are in high school, and the rest of the children are in grade school.

Mr. Daily is a member of the Lutheran Church. He is a Democrat. His favorite sports are wrestling and box-ing, while his hobby is reading. In 1931 he was elected to life membership in the Nebraskana Society. Residence: Minden. (Photograph in Album).

Walter Dale

Walter Dale, who has been engaged in the business affairs of Gothenburg, Nebraska, for many years, is a lifelong resident of this state. He was born at Stroms-burg, Nebraska, April 23, 1876, the son of John and Josephine Caroline (Carlson) Dale. His father, who was a merchant, was born in Sweden, November 14, 1848, came to America in 1869, and died at Stromsburg, September 26, 1882. His mother was born at Four Corners, Iowa, December 17, 1848, of Swedish parents, and died at Goth-enburg, May 9, 1927.

Mr. Dale was graduated from the Stromsburg High School in 1893, and was a student at the university of Ne-braska, during 1895-96. He is president of the Corn-husker Hardware Company of Gothenburg, and owns an interest in the Cornhusker Hardware Company of Cozad, Nebraska. He is a member of the Red Cross, the Goth-enburg Commercial Club, the Modern Woodmen of Amer-ica, and Masonic bodies. His social club is the local Coun-try Club, and his favorite sports are golfing, hunting and football. He is interested in mechanics and gardening.

His marriage to Alma Chasta Johnson was solemnized at Stromsburg, August 16, 1920. Mrs. Dale was born at Stromsburg, October 3, 1883, of Swedish ancestry. Resi-dence: Gothenburg.

Merrill John Allen Dalrymple

The Reverend Merrill John Allen Dalrymple was born at Birmingham, Iowa, September 22, 1903, son of Henry Allen and Elsie (Lewis) Dalrymple.

The father was born in Hapkinton, Iowa, June 23,

1870, and is a clergyman. His wife, Elsie, was born in New York State, September 25, 1874. Her uncle, Bishop Wilson Sealy Lewis, was president of Morning Side College of Sioux City, Iowa, and later Bishop to China, in the Methodist Episcopal Church.

Mr. Dalrymple received the Bachelor of Arts degree from Iowa Wesleyan College at Mt. Pleasant, Iowa, on June 1, 1928. Prior thereto he attended Yankton College for three years. In 1930 he was a student at the Chicago Theological Seminary.

Ordained to the Congregational Church in April, 1930, he is serving at the present time as pastor of the First Congregational Church of Burwell. He is a member of the Loup Valley Association of Congregational Churches and Ministers, and at the present time is serving as moderator. He is a member of the Wrangler Club and the Nebraskana Society. His hobby is reading.

On June 1, 1927, he was married to Helen Marie Dexheimer at Yankton, South Dakota. Mrs. Dalrymple was born at Nelson, Nebraska, January 25, 1904. She received her Bachelor of Arts degree from Yankton College in 1926, and was a teacher before her marriage. They have one son, Dean, born July 19, 1928. Residence: Burwell.

Frederick Trenck Daly

Born in Chillicothe, Iowa, June 17, 1884, Frederick T. Daly, dentist, has resided in Nebraska twenty-seven years. His father, Eugene Sylvester Daly, was born at Pittsfield, Vermont, and died at Hot Springs, South Dakota, May 6, 1928. He was a clergyman of Irish descent, who received his Doctor of Laws degree from Cornell University. His wife, Martha Alyce (Correll) Daly died at Cambridge, Nebraska, June 21, 1921.

Dr. Daly attended public school in Iowa, was graduated from Milton High School in 1902 and received the degree of Doctor of Dental Surgery in 1906 from the University of Iowa. He is a member of Psi Omega.

On September 19, 1906, he was married to Bessie Logan Reed at Pulaski, Iowa, and to them were born four children: Frederic, born December 4, 1907; Margaret, born December 4, 1907, who married Arthur E. Easter; Ellen, born May 15, 1916; and Mary Lou, born September 10, 1919. Frederic and Margaret were graduated from the University of Nebraska in 1929 with the degree of Bachelor of Arts.

Since his admission in 1906, Dr. Daly has been in continuous practice. He is a member of the American Dental Association, the Nebraska State Dental and Furnas County Dental Societies. He is a member of the Methodist Church, the Red Cross (was chairman during the World War), the Rotary Club, the Masons, the Cambridge School Board (past president), and the American Full Denture Association. He enjoys golf, horseback riding and tennis. Residence: Cambridge.

Leo Guenther Dambach

Leo Guenther Dambach, druggist was born at Hayes Center, Nebraska, September 3, 1896, son of Jacob and Carrie (Erdman) Dambach. The father was born at Frankfort on Oder, Germany, in 1862, and came to America in 1881. He was a druggist from April, 1885, at Hayes Center, until his death at Hayes Center, March 7, 1913. His wife, Carrie, was born at Frankfort on Main, Germany, in 1867.

Mr. Dambach attended Hayes Center schools until May, 1909, and in June, 1916, was graduated from Polytechnic High School of Los Angeles, California. In 1917 he was a student at the University of Southern California.

A resident of Nebraska 28 years, Mr. Dambach has been proprietor of Dambach Pharmacy at Palisade, Nebraska, and Hayes Center for a number of years. He served 6 years as a member of the board of trustees of Palisade, and chairman of the board of trustees for four years.

He was married to Clara Constance Kehler, October 26, 1926, who was born at Bladen, Nebraska, January 25, 1901. They have two children, John, born December 6, 1928; and James, born January 2, 1931.

Mr. Dambach is a Protestant, and in politics is independent. His favorite sports are golf and tennis, while his hobby is reading. Residence: Palisade.

Arthur Kent Dame

Arthur Kent Dame, lawyer and legal author, was born at Orford, New Hampshire, October 8, 1860. He is the son of Henry Augustus and Harriett Frances (Moulton) Dame, the former born at Orford, July 15, 1826. A farmer and town officer, he was descended from John Dame of Chester, England, who emigrated to America in 1630; four other lines of the family trace back in America to the 17th century; Theodore Dame (1750-1799) was a lieutenant in a New Hampshire regiment in the Quebec Expedition. Henry Dame died at Newbury, Vermont, June 24, 1879.

His wife, Harriett, was born at Lyman, New Hampshire, November 24, 1839, and died at Fremont, April 5, 1926. Of English descent her ancestry is traced to Sir Guy de Molton, who came to England with William the Conqueror; five other lines trace to the 17th century in America.

Upon the completion of his elementary education in the public schools of Newbury, Mr. Dame attended St. Johnsbury Academy at St. Johnsbury, Vermont, graduating in 1878. He received his A. B. from Dartmouth College in 1882, and is a member of Kappa Kappa Kappa. Admitted to the bar of Michigan at Muskegon, in 1885, he came to Nebraska in November 1887, and was admitted to practice here at the November term of 1888. In addition to his legal practice he has written various law text books, including *Probate and Administration* (1st ed. 1902; 2nd ed. 1915; 3rd ed. 1928); *Nebraska Inferior Court Practice* (1st ed. 1918; 2nd ed. in preparation). He is co-author with Ralph S. Moseley of Lincoln *Dame and Moseley's Nebraska Digest* (1929; 6 volumes).

A Democrat, Mr. Dame served as justice of the peace of Dodge County 27 years, and police judge of Fremont five years, the last term being 1925-27. He has had various banking connections.

From 1881-91 he was a private in the Nebraska National Guard, and company clerk for Company E, 1st Regiment. He served in the Sioux Indian Campaign of January, 1891, and was stationed on the White River, northeast of Chadron. During the World War he was a member of the Food Conservation Commission. Since 1895 he has been a member of the Sons of the American Revolution. He is a member of the First Congregational Church of Fremont, the Dodge County Bar Association, and the Nebraska State Bar Association of which he is now president. He is an Odd Fellow, Red Man and member of the Ancient Order of United Workmen, The Nebraskana Society and the Young Men's Christian Association. His social club is the Dartmouth Alumni Association of the Plains, of Omaha. He has always been interested in American history, more especially the political and economic aspects, rather than the military. He enjoys reading and chess, mountain climbing and long walks. Residence: Fremont.

John Henry Damme

John H. Damme was born at Berger, Franklin County, Missouri, September 21, 1853. His father, William Damme, who was a farmer, was born at Borgholshausen, Germany, August 5, 1829, and in 1836 came to America where he served in the Union Army during the Civil War. He died at Berger, in January, 1896.

His mother was born at Borgohlshausen, January 22, 1834. She is still living.

Mr. Damme has lived in Nebraska since 1875, and has been a merchant since 1882. He is vice president of the

Bank of Talmage, at Talmage, Otoe County, Nebraska; is chairman of the Talmage Lumber Company; and is a director of the Bank of Sterling, Sterling, Nebraska. A Republican, he has been mayor of Talmage and a member of the school board on several occasions. Since 1912 he has been chairman of the Drainage Board.

He was united in marriage with Caroline Charlotte Holtgrave at Beauford, Franklin County, Missouri, October 16, 1884. Mrs. Damme was born of German parentage at Beauford, August 17, 1864. There were six children born to this union, four of whom are living. They are: John, born October 12, 1885, who died March 8, 1919; Henry H., born May 16, 1898, who is a merchant at McAllen, Texas; William H., born March 14, 1903, who is a graduate of the University of Nebraska; Emma C., born October 29, who is a student at the University of Nebraska; Theodore F., born July 22, 1907, who is a graduate of the University of Nebraska; and Sophia, born in 1889, who died January, 1901.

Mr. Damme sold bonds in the first loan drive during the recent war. He is a member of the Talmage Chamber of Commerce, the National Geographic Society, and the Nebraskana Society. He is affiliated with Zion's Evangelical Church. His hobby is reading. Residence: Talmage.

Marion Lee Daniel

Born at Bellwood, Nebraska, September 27, 1889, Marion Lee Daniel is the owner of the Daniel Studio at Columbus. He is the son of Thomas William and Emma Ella (Corbett) Daniel, the former a carpenter, born in Ohio in 1859. His mother was born in Canada in 1868.

Mr. Daniel was graduated from high school at Schuyler, Nebraska, in 1911. On March 4, 1923, he was married to Freda Emma Gass at Columbus. Mrs. Daniel was born at Columbus on November 9, 1895. Her parents are Samuel and Anna (Hoeffer) Gass.

During the World War Mr. Daniel was in Remount Service at Camp Funston, Kansas. He is a member of the American Legion, the Photographers of America, the Chamber of Commerce, the Lions Club, the Young Men's Christian Association and The Nebraskana Society. Residence: Columbus.

August Danielson

Born at Ogden, Iowa, May 29, 1871, August Danielson is the son of Peter Magnus and Sarah Lena (Andersdotter) Danielson. His father, born at Alvastad, Kronolergs Lan, Sweden, February 1, 1835, came to America in 1868. Here he established a home on the prairie in what was known as Swede Valley, where the nearest neighbor was four miles away. He died at Ogden, Iowa, March 9, 1910. His wife, born at Moheda, Sweden, August 10, 1833, was an accomplished woman who did much to assist new settlers in the middle west. She died at Ogden, on February 26, 1886.

August Danielson received a country school education and later completed a business course. For a number of years he has maintained a real estate, insurance, loans and rentals business in his own name.

On June 26, 1907, he was united in marriage to Ida Louise Younger at Alexandria, Minnesota. Mrs. Danielson, who was born at Alexandria, August 16, 1876, died at Wausa, on April 11, 1919. There are four children, Sarah, born August 10, 1908; Luella, born October 22, 1909; Lester, born July 9, 1912, and George, born February 20, 1915. Mrs. Danielson was a music teacher, and a great granddaughter of Professor Junger, director of music at Uppsala Laroverk. Sarah and Luella are school teachers and Lester is in his second year in college.

During the late war Mr. Danielson was a member of the Council of Defense, chairman of four loan drives and a member of the exemption board. He is a member of the Mission Church, the Red Cross and the Nebraskana Society. His hobby is reading. A Republican, he has been a member of the school board nine years (president four years) and a member of the village board six years (chairman three years). Residence: Wausa.

Fred J. Dankers

Fred J. Dankers, cashier of the First National Bank of Madison, was born at Corning, Missouri, August 31, 1874, son of Henry A. and Elizabeth (Gunkel) Dankers. Henry Dankers was born in Germany on May 20, 1830, came to America at the age of six, and died at Corning on July 20, 1913. His wife, also born in Germany, in 1846, and died at Corning, March 28, 1887.

Educated in Corning public schools, Fred J. Dankers was graduated from Northwestern Normal College at Stansberry, Missouri, in 1896, and took up his residence in Madison County in 1907.

He was married to Tude Hochstutter at Corning on April 16, 1902, and to them was born one daughter, Emma E., on July 23, 1904. She taught in rural schools two years, then attended Nebraska Wesleyan University three years, was graduated from Northwestern University and from the National Kindergarten School in Chicago. For the past four years she has been a teacher in the public schools of Evanston, Illinois. Mrs. Dankers who is descended from Ulrich Hochstutter of Revolutionary War fame, was born at Craig, Missouri, June 11, 1884.

Mr. Dankers was treasurer of the local Red Cross organization during the World War period and for twelve years thereafter. He assisted in all war time activities, and for a period of nineteen years served as city clerk of Madison. He is a life member of the Madison County Agricultural Society, and of The Nebraskana Society, and a member of the Chamber of Commerce, the Masons and the Modern Woodmen of America. He attends the Presbyterian Church. His favorite sports are baseball and golf. Residence: Madison.

Roy Howard Danly

Born at Axtell, Nebraska, November 30, 1888, Roy Howard Danly is the son of George Everett and Sarrah Elizabeth (Secrist) Danly. His father, who was born of New England parentage at Sycamore, Illinois, December 29, 1855, and died at Axtell, July 7, 1926, was a farmer. His mother, whose parents were natives of Pennsylvania, was born at Princeton, Illinois, September 19, 1857, and died at Hutchinson, Kansas, January 20, 1932; she was a teacher in Sunday School.

Mr. Danly attended Axtell High School and in 1914 received the B. S. degree in agriculture at the University of Nebraska where he was a member of the oratorio chorus. He had previously attended the Nebraska State Teachers College at Kearney, where he was active in athletics and a member of the college band, orchestra and glee club.

He has served as private secretary to Congressman W. E. Andrews, of the Fifth Nebraska District, was employed in a bank for a time, engaged in the real estate business, and is now a farmer near Axtell. He is affiliated with the Methodist Episcopal Church of Kearney, Nebraska, and holds membership in the Nebraskana Society. Mr. Danly is fond of baseball, football, and hiking, while his hobby is travel. During the late war he took an active part in all Liberty loan drives except the first. Residence: Axtell.

Frank Tenney Darrow

Frank Tenney Darrow, civil engineer and railroad man, was born at Corning, Iowa, September 2, 1875, son of Lew Ellsworth and Sara Eucebe (Carpenter) Darrow. His father was born at Clarendon, New York, September 25, 1843. He was a banker who served with the 151st New

York Volunteers in the Civil War. His ancestors, who were Scotch-Irish came to America, about 1760, and served in the Revolution. He died at Willmette, Illinois, May 13, 1922. His wife, Sara, born at Barre, New York, September 3, 1846, died at Corry, Pennsylvania, March 7, 1894. Her family was descended from early settlers in Vermont.

Mr. Darrow attended the Corning public schools, Corning Academy, and the preparatory department of Portland University, Oregon, before being graduated from Corry High School in 1894. He received the degree of civil engineer from Allegheny College in 1897, and was president of his class. He is an honorary member of Sigma Tau.

On January 2, 1906 he was married to Eunice Davis at Lincoln. Mrs. Darrow was born at Mount Pleasant, Nebraska, June 10, 1881. Her father, Stephen Davis, came to Nebraska from North Carolina in 1856. Her mother, Kate (Winslow) Davis, came by boat to Nebraska City in 1863. They have one child, Josephine, born May 3, 1914.

Mr. Darrow is a Republican, and a member of Trinity Methodist Episcopal Church. Since July, 1897, he has been associated with the civil engineering department of the Chicago, Burlington and Quincy Railroad, serving in all grades up to assistant chief engineer. From May to September, 1905, he was manager of the International Contract Company at Seattle, Washington. From 1921-23, he was a director of the American Society of Civil Engineers, and now is a member of the American Railway Engineering Association, the Chamber of Commerce, Interprofessional Institute, and the State Historical Society. Residence: Lincoln. (Photograph in Album).

Harry Burnham Dart

Harry Burnham Dart was born at Wyanet, Illinois, June 17, 1875, and has been a resident of Nebraska for 25 years. He came to Nebraska, in May, 1907, working as extra operator under the Nebraska division of the Union Pacific and in 1908, settled permanently in Brady. He is the son of Alonzo and Elizabeth Ellen (Shurtleff) Dart, both of whom are of English descent.

His father was born in Lincoln, Vermont, July 31, 1835, and was in the grain and elevator business at Wyanet, Illinois, for a number of years and died at Chicago, Illinois. His mother was born in Centerville, Knox County, Illinois, September 30, 1841, and died at Wyanet, Illinois, February 12, 1893.

Mr. Dart attended the public and high schools at Wyanet, Illinois, and for a number of years has been connected with the Union Pacific Railroads, of which he is now station agent at Brady. Formerly he was associated with the Chicago, Rock Island and Pacific Railroad.

He was married to Amelia Heitz, of Depue, Illinois. Mrs. Amelia (Heitz) Dart was born in Depue, Illinois, January 3, 1881, daughter of Samule and Barbara Heitz of German descent and died at Brady. Three children were born to them, Harold Carl, September 12, 1901, married Ruth Fowles. He is in the maintenance department of the Southern Pacific, and is residing at San Leandro, California. Frederick Sheldon, born May 20, 1905, is district park ranger in the Yellowstone National Park; and Lucile Isabel, born April 18, 1910, is a student in the University of Nebraska, completing her second term in music and fine arts.

Mr. Dart is a member of the Masons, the Odd Fellows, the Modern Woodmen of America, and the Nebraskana Society, and is president of the school board of District No. 6, of Lincoln County. Residence: Brady.

Allen Manvile Darwin

Allen Manvile Darwin, grain buyer and bank executive at Virginia, Nebraska, has lived in this state for the past 46 years. He was born at Atlantic, Iowa, April 29, 1883, the son of George Edward and Emma (Taylor) Darwin. His father, who was born in England, and died at Virginia, October 8, 1909, was a butcher and farmer. His mother was born in France, and died at Virginia, December 11, 1911.

Mr. Darwin is manager of the Farmers Co-operative Company, is director of the Citizens State Bank, is serving as treasurer of Sherman Township, and is secretary of the Virginia Telephone Company. He holds membership in the Nebraskana Society, the Modern Woodmen of America, the Republican party, and the Masons.

His marriage to Leola Belle White occurred at Beatrice, Gage County, Nebraska, October 5, 1916; she was born at Beatrice, October 8, 1892. Their two sons are: Willis, born July 12, 1918; and Edwin, born November 12, 1923. Residence: Virginia. (Photograph in Album).

William G. J. Dau

William G. J. Dau, farmer and executive, was born in Holstein, Germany, December 24, 1868, son of Peter John and Margatha (Shoemaker) Dau. His father was born in Holstein, Germany, January 7, 1839, and his mother on February 18, 1841. The family came to America in 1872, settled in Fremont and lived there until 1879, when the father engaged in farming. Peter J. Dau died at Hooper, August 1, 1896, and Margatha Shoemaker Dau on June 17, 1916.

Mr. Dau attended school at Fremont Normal College, and has been a farmer all his life. He is active in the development of his community, and is mayor and chairman of the village trustees and president of the Hooper Telephone Company. During 1915, 1917 he served as representative in the state legislature, elected on the Democratic ticket.

On March 23, 1893, Mr. Dau was united in marriage to Anna Kathrine Studt, daughter of John and Lena (Reimeis) Studt at Hooper. They have two children: Peter J., born December 22, 1894, who married Charlotte Hoefner; and Lillian A., born April 8, 1898, who married Ray A. Edelmaier. Both attended Fremont Normal College. Peter Dau lives in Hooper and Mrs. Edelmaier resides on the family homestead near Hooper. Residence: Hooper.

James Henry Davey

James Henry Davey, Thayer County farmer, was born in Ontanagan County, Michigan, December 23, 1862, son of James and Isobelle (Wales) Davey.

The father was born in Cornwall, England, and was a miner for many years. He came to Nebraska, in 1877, settling in Thayer County. He was much interested in church work, and sang in the choir. He died in Thayer County. His wife, Isobelle Wales, was born in Guernsey, England, and died in Thayer County.

Mr. Davey attended rural school, and from 1874 until 1876, worked in the copper mines in Michigan. He farmed in Nebraska, in 1879, and in 1880, went to the gold mines of Colorado. He farmed in Nebraska again until 1896, when he returned to the gold mines, remaining two years. He then returned to Nebraska, where he has since farmed. For more than 20 years, he has been treasurer of local school board. A Democrat, he has held the position of central committeeman for Stoddard precinct for the past 15 years.

During the homesteading period in Oklahoma, Mr. Davey spent over two years in that state where he drew a plot of ground in the homestead free land distribution. He returned to Nebraska and purchased land near Beaver City, and a little later bought extensive land interests at Yuma, Colorado. For over 15 years he and his brother managed the Stoddard Elevator, and directly after that he entered the implement business. He is now once more active in farming near Hebron. Residence: Hebron.

Albert Carl Davidson

Since 1899, Albert Carl Davidson has been engaged in the practice of dentistry, living most of this time at Holdrege, Nebraska. He was born at Lake Station, Indiana, November 26, 1866, the son of Gustaf and Carolina (Carlson) Davidson. His father, who was a farmer, was born in Sweden, May 31, 1821, and died at Holdrege, January 8, 1899. His mother was born in Sweden, September 4, 1843, and died at Holdrege, April 20, 1920.

Dr. Davidson received the D. D. S. degree at Northwestern University Dental School in Chicago, where he was offered a position as instructor after graduation. For eight years he practiced dentistry at Chariton, Iowa, and since then has been continuously engaged in his profession at Holdrege. He is a member of the First Methodist Church where he is a teacher in the Sunday School, and was formerly a member of various community organizations at Holdrege. Dr. Davidson was a member of the official board of the First Methodist Episcopal Church.

His marriage to Amanda Augusta Wedean occurred at Wilcox, Nebraska, March 27, 1895. Mrs. Davidson was born of Swedish parents in Jefferson County, Iowa, September 24, 1876. They have two children: Vernon Arthur Carl, who is a florist at Denver, Colorado; and Alberta Pauline, born April 26, 1906, who was graduated from the State Teachers College, and is a commercial teacher. She was awarded the championship in shorthand in the state of Nebraska, in 1924. Residence: Holdrege.

Edith Stokes Davidson

Edith Stokes Davidson was born at Philadelphia, Pennsylvania, August 8, 1881, the daughter of Lisle and Mary Etta (Burnham) Stokes. Her father, who was born at Moorsetown, New Jersey, January 17, 1845, and died at Philadelphia, February 13, 1896, was engaged in the real estate business. He was of English ancestry and was a member of the Society of Friends.

Her mother was born at Springfield, Massachusetts, April 6, 1847, and died at Los Angeles, California, September 12, 1926.

Mrs. Davidson received her education in the public school and in the Friend's School in Philadelphia. Later she was a student at Dana Hall, Wellesley, Massachusetts. She has lived in Nebraska for 14 years.

Her marriage to James E. Davidson was solemnized at Philadelphia, April 15, 1903. Mr. Davidson is president of the Nebraska Power Company. There are three children: Dorothy, born May 6, 1904, who married Thomas B. Coleman, Junior; James E., born January 10, 1906; and John Stokes, born September 8, 1907.

During the World War Mrs. Davidson engaged in canteen work and Belgian relief. She is a member of the Red Cross, is president of the Omaha Drama League, and is director of the Visiting Nurse Association. She is active in the Friends of Music Society. She is a member of the board of directors of the Y. W. C. A. residence and member of the membership committee of the Tuesday Musicale Club. She is affiliated with the Trinity Cathedral, and is a Republican. Residence: Omaha.

James Davidson

A leading business man at O'Neill, Nebraska, is James Davidson, who has been a resident of that community for the past 55 years. He was born in Stockton County, Indiana, December 6, 1871, the son of Owen Evans and Rebecca (Hilligas) Davidson. His father, who was born in Coshocton County, Ohio, September 10, 1838, and died at O'Neill, October 15, 1905, was a carpenter and served in the 121st Indiana Volunteer Infantry during the Civil War. His mother, who reared a family of 10 children, was born in Harrison County, Ohio, January 4, 1841, and died at O'Neill, October 25, 1928.

Mr. Davidson is manager and owner of a plumbing and heating establishment at O'Neill. He is a member of the National Geographic Society and the Nebraskana Society, and many years ago served as a member of the Nebraska National Guards. His hobby is fishing.

He married Anna Hansen at O'Neill, November 7, 1893. Mrs. Davidson, whose parents came to this country from Denmark, was born in New York, March 27, 1872. They have eleven children: John, born May 19, 1894, who married Edith J. Sexsmith; Clyde, born April 7, 1896, who married Stella Hoover; Edward, born July 1, 1898, who married Catherine Morrison; Ralph, born November 3, 1900, who married Margaret Degnan; Dorothy, born May 5, 1903, who married J. Fred Degnan; James Edgar, born June 8, 1905; Frances Fay, born August 30, 1907, who married Floyd Hardesty; Lloyd Evans, born January 31, 1910; Frank, born March 2, 1912; Eileen, born April 10, 1916; and Owen, born November 11, 1918. Residence: O'Neill.

William Edward Davidson

William Edward Davidson, formerly a dentist, and at this time a florist at Hastings, has lived in this state since 1876. He was born at East Gary, Indiana, November 13, 1870, and for over 30 years has been active in civic projects in his community. His father, Gustaf Davidson, who was a farmer, was born in Sweden, April 20, 1821, came to America in 1846, and died at Holdrege, December 6, 1898. His mother was born in Sweden, March 6, 1843, and died at Holdrege, April 19, 1920.

Dr. Davidson received his education in the Holdrege High School where he was graduated, 1895, and in 1900 was awarded the D. D. S. degree at Northwestern University. From 1900 to 1910, he practiced dentistry, when because of failing health he entered the florist business. He is now proprietor and manager of the Davidson Floral Company at Hastings, Adams County, Nebraska. He is independent, politically; from 1915 to 1919 he served as mayor of Holdrege, Nebraska.

He is a member of the Red Cross, Chamber of Commerce, Rotary Club, and the Young Men's Christian Association; is president of the Nebraska State Florist Society; and is a member of the board of directors of the Salvation Army. His fraternal organizations include: Elks, Modern Woodmen of America, Knights of Pythias, and Masons (Shrine). He holds membership in the Hillside Golf Club, is affiliated with the First Methodist Episcopal Church of Hastings, and is a member of the Nebraskana Society. His hobby is plant study.

On May 20, 1900, he was united in marriage with Clara A. Wedean at Spaulding, Adair County, Iowa; she was born at Agency City, Iowa, January 5, 1875. To this union the following children were born: Oliver W., born November 2, 1901; Russell W., born October 2, 1903; Louise, born January 20, 1905, who died August 30, 1923; William Edward, born August 5, 1914, who died June 12, 1915; Paul Benjamin, April 17, 1919. Russell was graduated from the University of Illinois, in 1927, and is now a landscape architect with the Rockefeller Development at Cleveland, Ohio. Residence: Hastings.

Edward Llewellyn Davies

A hardware merchant at Ewing for the past twenty-eight years, Edward Llewellyn Davies is the son of Evan Mathias and Mary Ann (Bowen) Davies. He was born at Glenburn, Pennsylvania, April 13, 1877, and came to Nebraska forty-seven years ago.

Evan Mathias Davies was a native of Wales, born April 23, 1837, and who died at Ewing, June 4, 1892. He was a contractor and builder. His wife, Mary Ann, born in Dowlas, Wales, August 2, 1842, was a teacher in her younger days, and later raised a family of eight children on the farm. Her father was a merchant in the same location 50 years, and was also a teacher of voice. Her brother, David Bowen, was an accomplished pianist.

Educated first in public school, Edward L. Davies

attended high school two years and was graduated from Fremont Normal Business College on August 2, 1902. He farmed for a while, and has since engaged in the hardware business. For eight years he also owned and operated a moving picture theatre.

He was married to Pearle Louella Peeler at Lynch, Nebraska, November 25, 1908. She was born at Clinton, Missouri, July 24, 1883. There are three children, Everal, born June 4, 1910, who married Stanley Reamer, and who resides in David City; Eloise, born September 27, 1912; and Claude Edward, born July 6, 1916. He has one granddaughter, Marlene Eloise, born February 25, 1931.

Eloise won the state essay contest sponsored by Omicrom Nu, the national honorary home economics society at the University of Nebraska in 1927, and the state contest sponsored by the American Chemical Society in 1928-29. She was valedictorian of her class at Ewing High School at the age of 16. Mrs. Davies studied at the convent in O'Neill and later taught at Bristow and Dusten. She has conducted private art classes since her marriage.

Mr. Davies is a Republican, served as a member of the village board fourteen years, and held the office of mayor eight years. He is a member of the Masons, the Modern Woodmen of America and the Red Cross and The Nebraskana Society, and has been a member of the Ewing band for twenty years. His hobbies are mechanics, radio, hunting, and fishing. Residence: Ewing. (Photograph in Album).

Rupert Arthur Davies

For the past 31 years, Rupert A. Davies has practiced medicine at Arlington, Nebraska, and has been prominent in civic and educational activities there. He was born at Fremont, February 9, 1875, the son of James and Mary Elizabeth (Williams) Davies. His father, a druggist, was born in Wales, came to America in 1869, and died at Fremont, in 1878. His mother was born in Wales, and died at Fremont, in 1911.

Dr. Davies attended the Fremont public school, and in 1900, received the M. D. degree at Rush Medical College; he was a student at the University of Chicago, for a time. He is now practicing physician and surgeon at Arlington, is a member of the board of directors of the Arlington State Bank, and is connected with the Farmers Grain & Lumber Company.

For a number of years he served on the school board, and for the past ten years he has been a member of the board of trustees of Arlington. He is past president of the Elkhorn Valley Medicinal Society. Dr. Davies was married to Mary Elizabeth Blackburn, at Arlington, December 3, 1902. Mrs. Davies was born at Arlington, January 15, 1876. Residence: Arlington.

Archie C. Davis

Archie C. Davis, abstracter of titles, was born at Ord, Nebraska, November 15, 1886, son of John I. and Alice A. (Hutchins) Davis. His ancestry is Welsh and English.

Upon the completion of his high school education, Mr. Davis attended Grand Island Business College. He has been elected clerk of the district court three terms beginning November 1, 1921, and is still serving. He is also county clerk. He is a Republican. He is a member of the Odd Fellows, the Ancient Free and Accepted Masons, and the Modern Woodmen of America. His hobbies are baseball and golf.

On October 25, 1911, he was married to Nella Mae McClarey at Harrison, Nebraska. She was born near Clear Field, Iowa, November 13, 1890. There are two children, Thea Fay, born December 18, 1912; and Bonne Jeane, born September 1, 1918. Residence: Harrison.

Camille Hall Davis

Camille Hall Davis, who has lived in Nebraska all her life and has taken a prominent part in civic affairs, was born at Lincoln, Nebraska, July 19, 1886. Her father, Charles Leland Hall, a distinguished lawyer, and judge of the district court, was born in Ohio, December 15, 1855, and died at Lincoln August 24, 1898; his ancestry was English. Her mother, Clara Lillian (Stanhope) Hall, was born of English parentage, in Ohio, September 12, 1858.

Mrs. Davis was graduated from Lincoln High School in 1903, and in 1907 was a student at the University of Nebraska where she held membership in Kappa Alpha Theta. She is now president of the Nebraska League of Women Voters, is a member of the Lincoln Park Board, holds membership in the Lincoln Symphony Orchestra board, and is a board member of the Community Chest at Lincoln.

She is a member of the board of the Nebraska Art Association, holds membership in the Nebraskana Society, and is affiliated with All Souls Unitarian Church at Lincoln.

Her marriage to Ellery Davis was solemnized at Lincoln. Mr. Davis who is an architect, was born at Lake City, Columbia County, Florida, February 21, 1887. His ancestry is English. They have two children: Ellery Hall, born December 23, 1912; and Mary Helen, born June 3, 1915. Residence: Lincoln.

Charles Edward Davis

Charles Edward Davis, who has been a dentist at Oxford, Nebraska, for the past 15 years, was born in that community February 17, 1893, the son of Fred Harrison and Elizabeth Ann (Smallbrood) Davis. His father, who has served as head chef in the same hotel for the past 30 years, was born in London, England, in 1863. His mother, an active member of the Eastern Star and the P. E. O., was born of French parents at St. Joseph, Missouri, in 1865, and died at Oxford, January 29, 1931.

Dr. Davis was graduated from the Oxford High School in 1911, received the D. D. S. degree at Creighton University in 1916, where he was a member of Delta Sigma Delta, and since then has been one of the leading professional men at Oxford. He holds membership in the American Dental Association, the Nebraska Dental Association, the Lions Club, and the Masonic Lodge. He is a member of the Oxford School Board, the Oxford Country Club, and the First Presbyterian Church. His chief recreations are golfing, fishing, and reading.

He served as first lieutenant in the Dental Reserve Corps during the World War, connected with a hospital in France, and from 1920 to 1925 was captain of the Reserve Corps. Dr. Davis is affiliated with the Democratic party and The Nebraskana Society.

On December 31, 1917, he married Gladys Ethel Neuerberg at Houston, Texas. Mrs. Davis, who was a teacher prior to her marriage, was born at Oxford, August 14, 1896; her ancestry is Swedish and German. Their children are: Dean H., born August 15, 1920; and Donna Elizabeth, November 5, 1922. Residence: Oxford.

Clarence Alba Davis

Clarence Alba Davis, prominent in political and professional affairs at Holdrege, Nebraska, has been engaged in the practice of law there for the past 16 years. He was born at Beaver City, November 21, 1892, son of Thomas Milburn and Nannie (Gelvin) Davis. His father, who was born at Hillsboro, Ohio, May 14, 1854, and died at Rochester, Minnesota, August 12, 1919, was a distinguished banker and served as president of the Bankers Association; he was past grand master of the Nebraska Masons. His mother, whose ancestry was

Ebers—Holdrege

CLARENCE ALBA DAVIS

Scotch, was born in Washington County, Iowa, September 12, 1856.

Mr. Davis was graduated from Beaver City High School in 1910, received the A. B. degree from Nebraska Wesleyan University in 1913, and in 1916 was awarded the LL. B. degree at Harvard Law School. He was valedictorian of his graduating class at Wesleyan, was active in debating, served as junior class president, and held membership in Pi Kappa Delta and Everett. He received a letter in track and tennis at Wesleyan and was state champion in tennis 1913-14-15.

Since his admission to the bar in 1916, Mr. Davis has been a leader in civic affairs at Holdrege. A Republican, he served as attorney general of Nebraska, 1919-23, was a member of the Uniform Laws Commission, 1922-24, and served as delegate to the Republican National Convention in 1928. He is a member of the Nebraska State Bar Association, the American Bar Association, the Holdrege Chamber of Commerce, and the Lincoln Chamber of Commerce.

Mr. Davis is a former member of the board of governors of the Nebraska State Historical Society, The Nebraskana Society, and the First Methodist Church of Holdrege. He was formerly a member of the Lincoln Kiwanis Club, and is now a member of the University Club of Omaha, the Lincoln Country Club, and Happy Hollow Club of Omaha. His favorite sports are golfing and tennis. He is a captain in the Judge Advocate General Reserve.

He was united in marriage with Florence Wells at Schuyler, Nebraska, August 2, 1916. They have one son, Thomas Milburn, born March 25, 1918. Residence: Holdrege. (Photograph on Page 302).

Clarence M. Davis

Born at Harrison, Nebraska, July 12, 1894, Clarence M. Davis is the son of Asa Carleton and Sarah Amanda (Gifford) Davis. His father, who was manager of a lumber yard for a time, and later was in the real estate business at Lead, South Dakota, was born at Ewing, Illinois, and died at Texarkana, Texas, in September, 1915.

Mr. Davis attended the public schools of Lead, and in 1916, received the LL. B. degree at the University of South Dakota. He was unusually prominent in college activities in the following capacities: a member of the university debating team three times; debated Ames, Drake, and Kansas State College, was president of the Mask and Wig Club, 1915-16; was assistant editor of the University Paper; and held membership in Lambda Chi Alpha; Phi Delta Phi; and Tau Kappa Alpha. He was consul for the Ames Inn of Phi Delta Phi and organized the local chapter of Sigma Delta Upsilon, which later became a chapter of Lambda Chi Alpha.

He was a member of the firm Davis & Shield, at Salem, South Dakota, 1916-19, Davis & Davis, of Ord, 1920-27, Davis & Vogeltanz, since 1928. He is director in the Ord Creamery Company of Ord, Nebraska, is a member of the Chamber of Commerce, and was formerly president of the Ord Community Club. Mr. Davis was president of the Rotary Club for two years, has served on the library board since 1927, and in 1918, was vice chairman of the Red Cross. He holds membership in the American Bar Association, the Commercial Law League of America, the Nebraska Bar Association, the Valley County Bar Association, all bodies of the Masons, the Odd Fellows. He was Grand Master of the Grand Council of Royal and Select Master Masons in Nebraska, in 1926, and the Nebraskana Society.

During the late war he acted as chairman of the Four Minute Men of McCook County, South Dakota, was connected with the legal advisory board, and was fuel administrator, locally. He is a member of the Civil Legion at this time. As a member of the Republican party, Mr. Davis has taken an active part in county and state political affairs for the past 15 years. He was county chair-

man of McCook County, 1917-20, was a member of the state committee, served as vice chairman of the Republican Committee of Valley County for several years, was alternate delegate to the Republican Convention at Cleveland, 1924, served as city attorney of Ord, from 1928 to 1930, and since 1927, has been a member of the township library board. In April, 1932, he was elected delegate to the Republican National Convention at Chicago from the 5th Congressional District of Nebraska.

He married Ida A. Bakker at Salem, December 1, 1918. Mrs. Davis, who was a teacher prior to her marriage, was born in the Netherlands, July 3, 1894. Two children were born to them: Virginia, born June 9, 1921; and Beverly, September 23, 1923. Mr. Davis is the author of several articles on the history of the Black Hills of South Dakota. Residence: Ord.

Claude A. Davis

One of the leading lawyers at Grand Island, Nebraska, Claude A. Davis has resided in this state for more than 30 years. He was born at Mount Vernon, Illinois, May 21, 1882, the son of Amanda (Gifford) Davis and Asa C. Davis, the latter a lumberman who was born in Franklin County, Illinois, September 27, 1856, and died at Texarkana, Texas, September 27, 1915. His mother was also born in Franklin County, November 14, 1863.

Mr. Davis attended the grade school at Custer, South Dakota, was graduated from the Lead High School, and in 1906, received the LL. B. degree at the University of Nebraska, where he was a member of Order of Coif and Delta Upsilon. He was elected to membership in Phi Delta Phi.

Since his admission to the bar in 1906, he has been a member of the law firm Davis & Davis at Ord, and Cleary, Suhr, & Davis at Grand Island. He served as county attorney of Valley County, Nebraska, 1909-13, and was judge of the Supreme Court Commission, 1928-31. Mr. Davis is a member of the Grand Island Chamber of Commerce, the American Bar Association, the Nebraska State Bar Association, and the Hall County Bar Association. He is a Mason and Elk, and his social club is the University Club of Lincoln, Nebraska.

He was united in marriage with Mary Carlota Smith, at Ord, Nebraska, July 25, 1909. Mrs. Davis, whose ancestors came to this country in the *Mayflower*, was born at Ord, August 17, 1885. Their children are: Carlota, born September 12, 1910; Eldon, born July 11, 1912; and Dean, born January 3, 1916. Residence: Grand Island.

Edward Samuel Davis

Edward Samuel Davis, executive, was born at Stacyville, Iowa, December 18, 1869, son of Thomas A. and Mary (Lawrence) Davis. The father, born in Carmarthenshire, Wales, July 12, 1818, came to America in 1832. His wife was born in Carmarthenshire, Wales, November 12, 1830, and came to America in 1840.

In May, 1887, Mr. Davis was graduated from high school at Indianola, Iowa. He was in the hardware business from 1885 until 1900; Sidney, Iowa, until 1891, Broken Bow, Nebraska, from 1891 until 1894, and from 1894, until 1900, at North Platte, Nebraska. He served as deputy county treasurer from 1900 until 1904, in Lincoln County, Nebraska. He was county treasurer from 1904-08, also of Lincoln County, Nebraska; postmaster from 1911, until 1916, of North Platte, Nebraska; and grand secretary of the Grand Lodge I. O. O. F. of Nebraska from 1923, until the present time. He is also a member of the Kiwanis Club. He is a great lover of nature and enjoys fishing, and is also devoted to history and pioneer life.

On October 12, 1892, he was married to Clara Leona Eskew, at Sidney, Iowa. She was born at Sidney, Iowa, January 25, 1872. They have two children, William Edward, born February 3, 1900, who married Alberta Callender, who served in Students Army Training Corps at Ames, Iowa, during the war and is also a graduate of the University of Nebraska; and Robert Lee, born August 17, 1909, who is single. Both children were born at North Platte.

During the late war, Mr. Davis was an active participant in all bond and loan drives as a five minute man. He is a Republican, and has served as state representative during the sessions of 1919 to 1921 in the Nebraska state legislature. Residence: North Platte.

Edwin Davis

Edwin Davis, surgeon, was born in Lake City, Florida, December 13, 1888, son of Ellery W. and Annie Turner (Wright) Davis.

Dr. Davis received the Bachelor of Arts degree from the University of Nebraska, and his medical degree from Johns Hopkins Medical School in 1912. He is a member of Phi Beta Kappa, Sigma Xi and Phi Rho Sigma.

On September 20, 1921, he was married to Dorothy Baiback at Omaha.

A Republican, Dr. Davis is interested in politics. He is the author of about 40 medical articles, dealing with various phases of his profession.

Dr. Davis' professional organizations include the Omaha-Douglas County, and Nebraska State Medical Society, the American Medical Association, the American Association of Genito-Urinary Surgeons, the American Urological Association and the American College of Surgeons. Residence: Omaha.

Ellery Lothrop Davis

Ellery Davis, noted architect, was born at Lake City, Florida, February 21, 1887, son of Ellery Williams and Annie (Wright) Davis. His father was born at Oconomowoc, Wisconsin, March 29, 1857, and was professor of mathematics and dean of the College of Arts and Sciences at the University of Nebraska until his death at Lincoln on February 2, 1918. His wife, Annie, was born at Lake City, September 10, 1855, and is still living.

In 1894 the family removed to Lincoln, where Lothrop attended the public and high schools, graduating in 1903, with the honor of being valedictorian. In 1907 he received his A. B. from the University of Nebraska, and in 1909 his B. Arch. from Columbia University. He is a member of Sigma Xi.

On March 30, 1912, he was married to Mary Camille Hall at Lincoln. There are two children, Ellery Hall, born December 23, 1912; Mary Helen, born June 3, 1915.

A resident of Nebraska since 1894, Mr. Davis has practiced architecture both in partnership and individually, since 1909, and has designed many school and business buildings in Lincoln and throughout Nebraska, including many of the University of Nebraska buildings. At the present time he is a member of the firm of Davis and Wilson in partnership with W. F. Wilson. A Mason, he is a member of the Scottish Rite and Shrine. He is a member of the American Institute of Architects and the Lincoln Chamber of Commerce. His clubs are the University and the Lincoln Country, and his hobby is chess. Residence: Lincoln.

Ellsworth Elmer Davis

Born of pioneer Nebraska parentage, Ellsworth E. Davis has lived in this state practically all his life. He was born in Williams County, Ohio, November 24, 1862, the son of Walter and Elizabeth (Welton) Davis. His father, who was a farmer, was born in Pennsylvania, in 1829, and died at Columbus, Ohio, in 1865. His mother, whose ancestry was English, was born in Ohio, September 23, 1837, and died at Central City, Nebraska, January 3, 1921.

Mr. Davis is a Republican, and has served on the vil-

lage board for a total of 11 years, acting as chairman for six years. For over 29 years he has been a member of the Clarks Fire Company. He has been a barber at Clarks, since 1888.

On November 23, 1884, he was united in marriage with Eva Luella Headley. Mrs. Davis, whose ancestry is English and German, was born in Williams County, Ohio, March 24, 1864. Four children were born to them, two of whom are living; Lena, born March 13, 1886, who married Homer Chandler, and who died October 9, 1919; Walter, born March 25, 1895, who married Florence Hansen; Viva, born October 7, 1897, who married Sylvester Whetstine; and Helen, born June 12, 1899, who died in September, 1901. Walter has been in the employ of the Union Pacific Railway Company for 19 years. Residence: Clarks.

Freda Martha Davis

Freda Martha Davis, editor and clubwoman, was born at Lincoln, Nebraska. She received her education in the public and high schools of Lincoln and attended the University of Nebraska during 1920, 21 and 22. She married W. Leroy Davis, who is a traveling salesman. They have no children.

Mrs. Davis was associated with the *Lincoln Daily Star* during 1916 and 1917. She has held various offices in the state and local Federation of Women's Clubs, and the League of Women's Voters, and the American Association of University Women. At the time suffrage was granted to women she was an officer in the Lancaster County Suffrage Association.

A Republican, she was elected alternate delegate at large to the Republican National Convention in 1928. At the present time she is an officer in the League of Women Voters, and a member of the American Association of University Women. Residence: Lincoln.

Frederick Hamilton Davis

One of the outstanding business executives of Madison, Nebraska, is Frederick Hamilton Davis, who was born in Madison County, July 14, 1873, the son of Angeline (Bunce) and George Davis. George Davis, who was born in Jefferson County, Iowa, January 29, 1852, and died at Alma, Nebraska, January 30, 1907, was a homesteader in Madison County, where he later served as commissioner and sheriff; he was a leader in all political and civic affairs in his community, and was admired and liked by his many friends.

Otho Davis, grandfather of Frederick Davis, was born in Kentucky, the family having come there from Wales, in the early history of the state. Angeline (Bunce) Davis was born in Missouri, October 6, 1854.

Mr. Davis attended the grade school at Madison, and later was a student at the normal college at Fremont, Nebraska. For the past 17 years he has served as postmaster at Madison, and prior to that was secretary of the Madison County Building & Loan Association for 10 years; he continues to act as director and auditor of the latter organization at this time. He is also a salesman for the Woods Brothers Securities Company of Lincoln, is secretary of the Madison Cemetery Association, and holds membership in the Madison Community Club.

He holds membership in the Royal Highlanders, and the following Masonic bodies: Nebraska Globe Lodge, Number 113, Consistory, Number 2, Sesostris Temple; Shrine. He was president of the Tri County Old Settlers Association in 1926, which comprises three counties, and is now vice president of that organization. Mr. Davis' social club is the Madison Golf Club, and his favorite sports are golfing, fishing, and motor-boating. He is affiliated with the First Presbyterian Church of Madison, is a member of the Red Cross, and holds membership in the Nebraskana Society.

His marriage to Hattie Belle Tratch occurred at Madison, October 1, 1903. Mrs. Davis, whose family organized the county of Madison, was born there, October 29, 1873, and died at Norfolk, March 15, 1925. Three children were born to them: Doris F., July 14, 1904; Mary A., January 14, 1907, who married Ray Garvin; and Irmabelle, October 25, 1913. Both the Thatch and Davis families were among the leaders in Madison County in pioneer days, and held important offices in the community government.

Mr. Davis married Clara Louisa Kaul, August 5, 1928. She was graduated from Madison High School, and for 23 years was employed in various county offices, acting as clerk in the office of the county judge, clerk of the district court, and county treasurer.

Doris F. Davis was graduated from the University of Nebraska, and is now a teacher at Madison. Mary A. Davis was graduated from the Madison High School, served in the post office as a clerk, and was deputy register of deeds in Madison County. Residence: Madison.

Gladys Irene Davis

At Elk Creek, Johnson County, Nebraska, Gladys I. Davis was born October 17, 1894, the daughter of Edgar Thomas and Etta Alice (Young) Parker. Her father was born at Mount Sterling, Brown County, Illinois, February 16, 1863, and died at Pawnee City, Pawnee County, Nebraska, September 15, 1900. Her mother, who was a clubwoman was born at Elizabeth, Jo Davis County, Illinois, March 23, 1863.

Mrs. Davis attended the Pawnee City grade school, and in 1913 was graduated from the Pawnee City High School. In 1913 and 1914 she was a student at the Lincoln Business College. From 1914 to 1916 she served Pawnee County as clerk of the county court; from 1916 to 1926 she was bookkeeper and stenographer for Wherry Brothers, at Pawnee City. A Republican, she is a member of the Republican Central Committee.

On June 16, 1926, she was married at Pawnee City, to Cecil Albert Davis who is a car salesman for Wherry Brothers at Pawnee City. Mr. Davis was born at Seneca, Nemaha County, Kansas, February 16, 1897.

During the World War she was a member of the Florence Nightingale Red Cross, and at the present time she is a member of the Pawnee County chapter of Red Cross, where she served as a member of the executive committee. She is a member of the Nebraskana Society, the Twentieth Century Club, and the Methodist Episcopal Church of DuBois, Nebraska. She is a member of the Rebeccas and the Pythian Sisters. Residence: DuBois.

Grover Cleveland Davis

Grover Cleveland Davis has lived in Nebraska all his life and has taken an active part in civic and political affairs in his community. He was born at Homer, Dakota County, Nebraska, October 17, 1884, the son of Josiah Willard and Mary Josephine (Ockander) Davis. His father, who was born at Guilford, Maine, June 2, 1826, and died at Homer, February 21, 1915, was a miller, merchant, hotelman, and postmaster; he moved to Dakota County in 1860, and was prominent in Nebraska as a county commissioner, 1873-76; was a member of the legislature in 1882, was also a candidate for the senate in 1882, on the Democratic ticket, but was defeated by a narrow margin. He was of New England Puritan ancestry, and a veteran of the Mexican War.

His mother was born at Gothland, Sweden, March 1, 1845, and died at Homer, December 8, 1928.

Judge Davis attended business college for two years, was connected with the Western Union Telegraph Company for a year, was a barber for 20 years, and engaged in the insurance business for six years. He served as sport writer for the *Homer Star* for a year, and is now a member of the firm O'Dell & Davis, Real Estate. He is mayor of Homer, is president of the board of health, and is a member of the Progress Club. A Democrat, Judge Davis served as village councilman for sixteen years, and served

as judge of the justice court for six years. He is now a candidate for the legislature on the Democratic ticket.

He holds membership in the Masons, Yeoman, Red Cross, Homer Fire Department, and the Nebraskana Society. He was registration clerk in draft department during the World War, and was a member of the National Home Guards. His hobby is the study of current events.

His marriage to Mattie Luella Miles was solemnized at Omaha, Douglas County, Nebraska, December 22, 1910. Mrs. Davis, whose ancestry is Irish and German, was born at Prosper, Fillmore County, Minnesota, December 22, 1891. To this marriage three children were born, two of whom are living: Woodrow, born January 18, 1913; Mildred, born January 14, 1918, who died February 15, 1921; and Lois, born August 9, 1924. Residence: Homer. (Photograph in Album).

Horace Mansell Davis

Horace Mansell Davis, editor and author, was born on the homestead of his father near Scotia, Greeley County, Nebraska, September 14, 1873, the second white child to be born in the county. His parents, Mansell and Mary Matilda (Rood) Davis, were pioneer settlers in Nebraska. His father, who was born at Fredonia, New York, December 5, 1848, was a teacher, surveyor and farmer of Welch stock who represented the 3rd generation of his family in America. He died near Scotia, November 6, 1917.

Mary Matilda Rood was born at Richford, Wisconsin, August 27, 1853, and resides at North Loup, Nebraska. A teacher, and president of the Woman's Club at North Loup, she was the first woman to settle on a homestead in Greeley County, in 1872, having come by ox team from Wisconsin. Of English descent, her grandfather, George Thorngate, came to America as a British soldier in the War of 1812.

Until 1891 Mr. Davis attended country and high school at North Loup, and during 1893-94 and 1895-96 was a student at Milton College (Wisconsin). During the summers of 1896 and 1897 he attended the University of Nebraska, and received his B. A. from Lincoln Normal University in 1898. At Milton he was a member of the baseball team.

Mr. Davis was married to Besse June Fackler at Ord, Nebraska, July 18, 1901. Mrs. Davis was born at Astoria, Illinois, June 17, 1881, of early Virginia stock. They have three sons, Mansell F., born April 30, 1902, who married Frances Carrothers; he is associated with the National Board of Fire Insurance Underwriters, and resides at Columbus, Ohio. Keith T., born May 25, 1907, was a graduate in engineering from the University of Nebraska in 1929, and married Jennie McClung, June 5, 1931. H. Richmond, born November 12, 1911, is a student at the University.

Mr. Davis' career has been varied. For several years he taught school, and later was editor of many papers and magazines, including the *Omaha New-Nebraskan,* the *Ord Journal, Broken Bow Herald, Greeley Leader-Independent,* and the *Nebraska Highways.* A Democrat, he was from 1901-03 clerk of the district court of Valley County, and in 1909 was clerk of the Nebraska senate. Postmaster at Ord from 1915-18, he was clerk of the house of representatives 1911, 1913, 1915 and 1917. For eight years he was publicity director for public utilities and part owner in several publications. An extensive landowner, he does some farming and is a director of the Capitol Fire Insurance Company, the S. E. Nebraska Development Company, and the Nebraska Publishing Company (secretary).

During the World War he was active in the Council of Defense, a four minute speaker and chairman of the Red Cross. His professional associations include the Nebraska Press Association, and the Professional Men's Club.

He is a member of the Masons, Elks, and Knights of

Pythias, the Knife and Fork Club, the Nebraskana Society and the Nebraska Pioneers and Nebraska State Historical Society. His clubs are Eastridge Country and Antelope Golf Clubs. Residence: Lincoln.

Ida Woolsey Davis

Ida Woolsey Davis was born of pioneer Nebraska parents December 30, 1875, at Nebraska City, Otoe County, Nebraska. Edmund Elting Woolsey, her father, who was born at New Paltz, Ulster County, New York, March 16, 1834 and died at Nebraska City, June 20, 1919, was a farmer and landowner who came to Nebraska, in 1857. He was of English descent.

Her mother, Helen M. (Tuxbury) Woolsey, of English ancestry, was born at Windsor, Vermont, April 15, 1838, and died at Nebraska City, December 24, 1917.

A lifetime resident of Nebraska, Mrs. Davis has taken an active part in civic and religious affairs for many years. Her education was received at St. Kathrine's Hall, Davenport, Iowa, where she was graduated in 1892.

On October 20, 1906, she was married to William Curtis Davis, at Nebraska City. Mr. Davis, who is a farmer, was born at Nebraska City, October 27, 1879. There are three children: Helen, born May 3, 1908; William Woolsey, born September 9, 1911; and Florence Josephine, born January 30, 1917.

Mrs. Davis is a member of the Does. She is affiliated with the St. Mary's Episcopal Church, and is a member of various church organizations. Among them are: Girl's Friendly Society; Episcopal Auxiliary; and the Episcopal Guild. Her social clubs are the Nebraska City Country Club and the Bridge Club. Her favorite sport is golf.

Joseph Franklin Davis

On April 25, 1878, at Brinkley, Monroe County, Arkansas, Joseph F. Davis was born, son of John Wesley and Saphronia Angeline (Dodson) Davis. His father, who was born at Paducah, Kentucky, December 20, 1836, and died at Brinkley, February 12, 1880, was of Welsh descent. He was a cabinet maker.

His mother, who was of Irish ancestry, was born at Summerville, Fayette County, Tennessee, March 13, 1853, and died at Texarkana, Texas, March 24, 1915. She was active in church work.

Mr. Davis was graduated from high school in 1896, after which he attended Ouachita College where he was a member of the Philomathean Society, and was active in athletics. Mr. Davis' career has been an interesting one, and his progress in the business world has been steady. He has been a clerk in the St. Louis Southwestern Railway Company; a section laborer; section foreman; construction foreman; and brakeman. In the Missouri Pacific Railway Company he was gang foreman; roadmaster; general roadmaster; division engineer; and assistant superintendent. Today he is superintendent of the Omaha-Northern Kansas division of the Missouri Pacific lines, at Falls City, Nebraska.

He was united in marriage with Kathryn Keevil, at Beemis, Woodruff County, Arkansas, on May 3, 1903. Mrs. Davis, who was born at Clarendon, Monroe County, Arkansas, June 11, 1882, is of Irish and English ancestry. There are two sons, Joseph, born December 13, 1908, who is a machinist's apprentice; and John, born February 24, 1915, who is a student in the Falls City High School.

In the late war Mr. Davis was an active participant in the Victory Loan, and Liberty Loan drives. He is a member of the Chamber of Commerce of Falls City, the Rotary Club, and the Traffic Club of St. Joseph, Missouri. He is a Mason, Shriner, member of Blue Lodge, 32nd degree Scottish Rite, Grotto. He is a Republican and a member of the Baptist Church. (Photograph on Page 307).

Russell Arnell Davis

Russell Arnell Davis, abstracter, was born at Fairbury, Jefferson County, Nebraska, December 7, 1893. He is the son of J. Monroe Davis and Jane Elizabeth (Arnell) Davis, the latter born in LaSalle County, Illinois, November 5, 1854, and who taught school before her marriage. She is a direct descendant of the English Wolcotts of Revolutionary fame; and is president of the Nebraska section of the Wolcott Society of America. J. Monroe Davis was born in Indiana, July 1, 1852, of Welsh parentage. He is a bonded abstracter.

Mr. Davis was graduated from the Fairbury High School in 1911. He received the degree of Bachelor of Arts at Wesleyan University, in 1915, and was president of the local fraternity, Everett. He married Maria Dawson, at Bennet, Lancaster County, Nebraska, October 14, 1915. Mrs. Davis was born in Bennet, on October 14, 1895. Their son, J. Monroe Jr., was born September 13, 1920, at Fairfield, Idaho.

Russell Davis was elected alternate delegate to the presidential convention of the Republican party in 1924, was city clerk in 1917, and has been a councilman since 1926.

He is editor of the *Davis' Daily Abstract*. He learned the abstract business under his father, with whom he was in partnership from 1915-17. He has been manager of the business since 1920. He was, from 1919-20, manager of the Camas Abstract Company, at Fairfield, Idaho, and was secretary of the Fairbury National Farm Loan Association, 1929-30. He is connected with the New York Title and Mortgage Company, and has authority to issue title insurance.

Mr. Davis is affiliated with the Methodist Church, the Masons, (Consistory, and Shrine) and the Eastern Star. During the World War he was quartermaster in the United States Army, from October 4, 1917, to December 20, 1918, stationed at Ft. Logan, Colorado, Madison Barracks, New York, and Ft. Myer, Virginia. He is a member of the American Legion, and has been a service officer of Jefferson County, Post No. 24 since November 16, 1927.

Secretary of the Nebraska Title Association in 1921-22, he has been president since 1929, and is a member of the executive committee in the Abstracters Section of the American Title Association. He is a member of the following organizations; the Young Men's Christian Association, the Chamber of Commerce (president 1923), the Rotary Club, and the Nebraskana Society. He is a member of the Fairbury Country Club. Golf, tennis and swimming are his favorite sports. Residence: Fairbury.

Searl S. Davis

Searl S. Davis was born at Murray, Cass County, Nebraska, June 10, 1887, the son of Stephen Meek and Mary Lucina (Minford) Davis. His father, who was born in Andrew County, Missouri, July 24, 1847, and died at Plattsmouth, Cass County, Nebraska, February 10, 1904, was a farmer and landowner in Nebraska; he was a Civil War Veteran; his Welsh ancestors came to Surrey County, North Carolina in pre-Revolutionary days.

His mother was born at Webster, Scioto County, Ohio, April 17, 1861. She has always been interested in church activities. She is of Scotch-Irish descent on the paternal side and Swedish and English through the maternal line; William White, who came to America on the Mayflower, was an ancestor.

Mr. Davis attended the rural schools in Cass County, and in 1905 was graduated from the Lincoln High School. He was awarded the A. B. degree in 1909 from the University of Nebraska, and was a graduate student at University of Chicago, and the University of Wisconsin. He was a member of the German Club, cadet bank, class debating team, dramatic club, and the conservatory orchestra.

He served as instructor and professor in rhetoric at the University of Nebraska, 1910-17; was engaged in farming and raising livestock, 1917-22; and since 1922 has been in the investment business. A Republican, he was

JOSEPH FRANKLIN DAVIS

secretary of the County Central Committee. He was the editor of the Cass County *Farm Bureau News.*

Mr. Davis is a member of the Red Cross, and has held the following offices in civic organizations; president of the Chamber of Commerce, 1923-26; president of the Plattsmouth Rotary Club, 1927; president of the Plattsmouth School Board, 1924-27. He is a member of the above and the following: Parent-Teachers' Association; City Council of Plattsmouth; Nebraskana Society; State Young Men's Christian Association; University Club of Lincoln; and the Shrine Country Club of Lincoln.

During the World War he was a four minute speaker and was chairman of the Liberty loan committee for his precinct. He is a Mason, Scottish Rite, 33rd Degree. He is affiliated with the Christian Science Society of Plattsmouth. His sport is hiking. His hobbies are: reading, and livestock.

Mr. Davis was married at Dayton, Montgomery County, Ohio, September 29, 1917, to Leila Frances Corbin. Mrs. Davis was born at Vandalia, Ohio, February 2, 1888. Her ancestors of Scotch-Irish descent, were early settlers in Pennsylvania. They have three children: Stephen Meek, September 17, 1918; Corbin James, April 14, 1923; and Elizabeth, June 22, 1928.

Troy L. Davis

Troy L. Davis, mayor of Weeping Water, Nebraska, was born near Murray, Nebraska, August 5, 1873. His father, Stephen Meek Davis, who was a Civil War veteran, was born at Savannah, Missouri, July 24, 1847, and died at Plattsmouth, Cass County, Nebraska, February 10, 1904. He was a farmer, and took an active interest in politics, educational and church work.

Jane Davis, mother of Troy Davis, was of Irish and German extraction. She was known and loved throughout her community for her kindness and helpfulness to everyone. She was born in Ohio, July 19, 1851, and died near Murray, November 27, 1876.

Mr. Davis attended a country school, and was a student at the University of Nebraska in 1892, and the Fremont Normal School in 1893. From 1894 to 1897 he was a farmer, after which he entered the clothing and shoe business in Weeping Water. In 1899, he sold his store and returned to the farm for three years. In 1902, he started in the hardware and furniture business, selling this in 1905 when he engaged in milling. In the same year he moved to Lincoln, and there was active in real estate, building houses to sell. He returned to Weeping Water, in 1909, and has remained there since that date.

He served as state representative from Cass County, from the sixth district, in 1923, 1927, and 1929, and 1931. He has been mayor of Weeping Water for the last eight years.

He married Ella Estella Stevens at Bethany, Harrison County, Missouri, August 22, 1894. Mrs. Davis, who was a school teacher before her marriage, was born near Bethany, October 17, 1873. She is of English descent.

Mr. Davis is a member of the Chamber of Commerce, having been its president for several years; and a member of the Nebraskana Society. He is affiliated with the First Church of Christ, Scientist. His hobby is reading.

William H. Davis

William H. Davis, abstracter, was born at Wilber, Nebraska, September 5, 1869, where he attended elementary school and completed his high school course.

He is the son of Samuel D. and Mary A. (Young) Davis. Samuel Davis, a lawyer, was born in Licking County, Ohio, and his father was born in Wales, Great Britain. Samuel Davis died at Wilber, Nebraska, January 13, 1907. Mary A. Davis who is of German descent, was born in Licking County, Ohio, and died October 7, 1924, at Wilber, Nebraska.

On October 14, 1889, Mr. Davis was united in marriage

to Edith M. VanDuyn, who was born in Wilber, December 21, 1871. Before her marriage she was a school teacher. Their children are Lillian F., Eva., Rena D., Letha M., and William V.

During the sixty-one years that Mr. Davis has lived in this state he has been active in the business world. He first held the position of bookkeeper until he became interested in abstract work. Later he enlarged his business and added insurance and loans. He is now the president and owner of the Gage County Abstract Company at Beatrice, Nebraska.

Mr. Davis has done much toward the betterment of his community. During the World War he participated in loan drives and took an active part in Young Men's Christian Association work. He was secretary of the school board at Wilber, from 1907 to 1909, and is a member of the First Christian Church of Beatrice. His membership in numerous organizations is also a mark of the interest that he shows in his community. They include the Chamber of Commerce, Rotary Club, Masons, Modern Woodmen of America and the Highlanders. He is also a member of The Nebraskana Society.

Joseph Horn Davison

Joseph Horn Davison, farmer and rancher, and also president of the Citizens State Bank, was born at Oxford, New Jersey, June 30, 1860, son of Lewis and Mary (Horn) Davison. His father was born in Oxford, in 1828, and was a farmer of Scotch descent. His wife, Mary, was born at Riverton, Pennsylvania, and died at Butzville, New Jersey, September 10, 1874.

Mr. Davison attended common school, and in November, 1883, settled in Nebraska. Beginning as a day laborer, he was later a butcher, and then a coal dealer and operator of a grain elevator. For a number of years he was a livestock buyer, rancher and stock breeder, and implement dealer. He still maintains his interest in farming and ranching, and is president of the Citizens State Bank of Ainsworth, Nebraska.

On November 16, 1889, he married Idora Rathburn at Ainsworth. Mrs. Davison was born at Cairo, Ohio, August 10, 1870. To them were born seven children, all of whom are living, Lewis Augustus, born October 8, 1891, married Faith Ravenscroft; Vivian Katrina, born March 7, 1893, married Frank Dodds; William J. Bryan, born November 27, 1896, married Fern Cheny; John Dewey, born October 5, 1898; Mary Susan, born September 22, 1906, married Leonard Swett; Joseph Horn, born October 3, 1908; and Sara Helen, born December 24, 1909.

Mr. Davison has always been an influence in his community. Recently he was elected to life membership in the Nebraskana Society in recognition of his interest toward the advancement of his community and state. Residence: Ainsworth. (Photograph in Album).

Irwell Montgomery Dawson

A resident of Nebraska for the past 61 years, Irwell Montgomery Dawson was born near Milwaukee, Wisconson, the son of George Wolstenholme and Alice Ann (Wolfenden) Dawson. His father, born at Nuttal Lane, England, January 12, 1827, died at Duluth, Minnesota, September 19, 1908. He was a farmer and was especially interested in horticulture and landscape gardening. His mother was born at Oldham, England, June 13, 1824, and died at Blair, Nebraska, February 21, 1871.

Mr. Dawson attended the public school of Blair, and was a student at Elliot's Business College at Burlington, Iowa. He served as post office clerk at Blair, was associated with the Crowell Lumber & Grain Company for several years, and for the past 35 years has been land manager and local representative of the Stuart Investment Company of Lincoln. He is a director of the Madison County Building & Loan Association at Madison, and secured the site of the Carnegie Library.

He is a member of he Madison Community Club, the Madison County Historical Society, and the Nebraskana Society. He was formerly a member of the Kiwanis Club, and for over 16 years was a trustee and treasurer of the First Presbyterian Church. He is a Mason and a member of the Modern Woodmen of America. During the World War he served in loan drives and Liberty bond sales. In the face of adverse opinion as to the value of sweet clover as a ground builder Mr. Dawson was a firm believer in its value and staunchly advocated its use. The universal opinion now prevails that there is no better soil builder.

His marriage to Florence Nightingale Crawford occurred at West Point, Nebraska, July 12, 1899. Mrs. Dawson, who was born at Bangor, Pennsylvania, was formerly a teacher in public schools, and is now a piano instructor. She is a member of the Daughters of the American Revolution and the P. E. O. Her ancestral line is that of George Wolf who was seventh governor of the State of Pennsylvania, and the founder of the public school system of Pennsylvania. They have a daughter, Alice, born June 11, 1912, who was graduated from Stephens College, Columbia, Missouri, where she was a member of Phi Theta Kappa, an honorary society, and while a student there she was honored with a scholarship. She is now a student at the University of Nebraska, where she has affiliated with the Gamma Phi Beta Sorority. Residence: Madison. (Photograph in Album).

Reuben Alwin Dawson

Reuben Alwin Dawson, one of Cedar County's leading educators, was born in Big Stone City, Roberts County, South Dakota, on July 18, 1893. He is the son of Joseph Frederick and Elizabeth (McDonald) Dawson. His father was born in Wisconsin, August 15, 1857, followed the occupation of a millwright, and died in Lynch, Nebraska, May 15, 1916. His father migrated to the United States from England. Elizabeth M. Dawson, was born in Canada, on January 3, 1862, of Scotch and English parentage and died in Lynch on August 4, 1930.

Reuben Dawson was graduated from the Corona, South Dakota, public school in 1907, then attended Windom Institute in Montevideo, Minnesota, until his graduation in 1911, at which time he entered Yankton College where he continued for one term. After his first year of college at Yankton it was necessary for Mr. Dawson to remain at home until 1915, assisting his father. The finances for his additional college work were obtained through his own efforts. He recalls that he washed dishes, waited table and did many other odd jobs to earn his board and room.

He received his Bachelor of Arts degree at the Nebraska Teachers College in 1921, and in 1930, he became a Master of Arts at Columbia University in New York City. During the time he attended Yankton and Wayne he received letters for football, basketball, and track in both schools.

Elsa Johanna Mildner became Mr. Dawson's wife on July 22, 1919, in Wayne, Nebraska, where she was born, March 2, 1895. She was a teacher of German descent. They have two sons: Richard, born January 12, 1925, and Robert C., born May 26, 1930.

Mr. Dawson was superintendent of schools in Brunswick, Nebraska, 1916-17, 1919-20; was superintendent in Battlecreek, Nebraska, 1918-19; was an instructor in the Osmond, Nebraska, High School 1920-21 and served as instructor at Wayne College during the summer of 1921. Since 1921 he has been in the employ of the Randolph school and has been superintendent since 1923.

Mr. Dawson was first sergeant in the United States Army in 1917, and second lieutenant in the Officers Reserve Corps from 1918-23. He is a member of the American Legion.

He is affiliated with the Presbyterian Church, is a Republican, a member of the Nebraska State Teacher's Association and treasurer at the present time of the third district. His fraternal organizations are the Lions and the Masons. He is a member of the Nebraskana Society and the Red Cross. Golf is his favorite sport and mechanics is his hobby. (Photograph in Album).

William Albert Dawson

One of the foremost of Wymore citizens is William Albert Dawson, who was born in Stark, Illinois, November 28, 1872, son of Lusian Dawson, born in Ohio, September 9, 1842, and Elizabeth (Taylor) Dawson, born in Lancashire, England, February 5, 1850. John L. Dawson was in the Civil War three years and was a successful farmer. His wife came to this country from England at the age of five.

William Dawson was educated in the Wymore elementary and high schools. In 1895, he went to Lincoln Business College. He farmed until he was thirty-one years of age and engaged in the mercantile business until recently. At present he is retired from business.

Mr. Dawson married Francis Mae Chapman, who was born in Illinois, July 19, 1876, and died in Wymore, Nebraska, November 4, 1915. They were married February 28, 1900, in Wymore. Their two children, Loren and Irene, born November 6, 1901, and April 3, 1909, have both been graduated from the Nebraska University. Loren has completed a civil engineering course.

William A. Dawson is director of the Farmers and Merchants Bank and the Wymore Building and Loan Association. He belongs to the Ancient Free and Accepted Masons and the Nebraskana Society, and has lived in the state for forty three years. Residence: Wymore.

Carl Eugene Day

Carl E. Day was born at Weeping Water, Cass County, Nebraska, October 9, 1876. His father, Eugene Ithamer Day, who was a farmer, was born at Sheffield, Loranin County, Ohio, April 12, 1847, and died at Weeping Water, July 5, 1894. He is descended from early American settlers who came from Rivee Dee, near Chester, England; Robert Day, a Puritan of Hartford, Connecticut, was one of his ancestors.

His mother, Mary Louis (Carter) Day, was a teacher before her marriage. Of English descent, she was born at Sheffield, June 9, 1848, and died at Weeping Water, October 4, 1929.

Mr. Day studied during his childhood under a private tutor, after which he was a student in the Weeping Water High School, and the Weeping Water Academy. In 1897-98-99, he attended Tabor College, Tabor, Iowa, and in 1900 received his A. B. degree from Oberlin College. He was engaged in athletics, baseball and football, while at Tabor.

A resident of Nebraska for 54 years, he has always engaged in farming and stockraising, and often makes speeches before farm bodies. He holds land in Florida. Mr. Day is vice-president of the Grain Growers' Association; was vice president of the County Fair Association; has been a member of the local school board since 1915, and is now president of that organization. He is a trustee in the First Congregational Church.

He married Ida Laura Cowles, October 6, 1903, at Cambridge, Nebraska. Mrs. Day, who was born at Marshalltown, Iowa, September 24, 1874, is a musician. There are two children: Eugene, born December 19, 1904, who married Lenora Kruse; and John R., born April 29, 1912. Mr. Day is fond of football and golf. He is a Republican.

Day—Hebron

C. E. DAY

Charles Eugene Day

Charles Eugene Day, photographer, was born at Abingdon, Illinois, October 1, 1881, and came to Nebraska at the age of five with his parents. His father, Jefferson Eugene Day, was born at Prairie City, Illinois, and died at Strang, Nebraska, in 1929. He was of English Yankee descent, his grandfather was born in New York. His wife, Mary Ann Catt, was born in Indiana in 1853 and died at Bruning in 1908. She was of Pennsylvania Dutch ancestry.

In 1899 Mr. Day was graduated from Bruning High School. He has been a photographer at Hebron for more than 30 years, having served his apprenticeship with Griffin Studio. He is the owner of the Day Studio. A Democrat, he is serving his sixth year as a member of the town council, and for twelve years was a member of the school board.

On December 16, 1902, he was married to Laura Effie Hendrick at Bruning. Mrs. Day was born at Lushton, Nebraska, May 4, 1883, and was a teacher before her marriage. She is of English descent, tracing her ancestry to Robert Morris, one of the signers of the Declaration of Independence. She is a charter member of the Pollyanna Club, and a member of the Eastern Star and the Woman's Club.

There are five children, Eugene Drew, born March 7, 1905, married Marie Willy; Lee Allen, born October 4, 1908, married Dorothy Vandervoort; Charlene, born June 13, 1910, married Elmer Beisner; Dorothy, born March 2, 1918; Charles Jr., born September 12, 1920; and Robert Dwain, born April 2, 1925. Eugene is in business with his father while Lee is a shoe salesman.

Mr. Day is a trustee of the First Christian Church, is a member of the Red Cross, the Chamber of Commerce, the Masons (Blue Lodge and Chapter), the Nebraskana Society, and the Nebraska Photographers Association. He enjoys football and basketball and is a member of the Hebron Golf Club. His hobby is reading. Residence: Hebron. (Photograph on Page 310).

Frederick Ira Day

Born at Superior, Nebraska, February 10, 1888, Frederick Ira Day is the son of George Leverett and Isabelle (Barber) Day. His father, who is a lumber dealer, is the son of Ira Church and Orcelia (Greenleaf) Day and was born at Whitewater, Wisconsin, January 25, 1857. He has been prominent in Republican politics for many years, serving as state senator in 1903, and delegate to the Republican National Convention in 1900. His Welsh ancestors came to America in the 17th century and members of the family were related to the poet, John Greenleaf Whittier.

Isabelle (Barber) Day was born at Horicon, Wisconsin, April 8, 1857; her grandfather, Hiram Barber, was a pioneer in Wisconsin; she is also descended from Roger Sherman, signer of the Declaration of Independence. She is a member of the P. E. O., Red Cross, and for many years was a member of the Superior library board. She was an instructor in Milwaukee College.

Mr. Day was graduated from the Superior High School in 1905, and was a student at the University of Nebraska, for a year, holding membership in Alpha Theta Chi. He has been the active manager of the firm Day & Frees at Superior, Nebraska, for several years, acting as co-partner with his father since 1906. He has been vice president of the Superior Board of Education for the past three years, is a member of the Chamber of Commerce and the Kiwanis Club, and has been identified with various committees of the Salvation Army and the Near East Relief.

He holds membership in the Knights Templar and Shrine bodies of the Masons, is a member of the Nebraskana Society, and is affiliated with the First Presbyterian Church where he has been elder, Sunday School superintendent, and choir member for many years.

Mr. Day's social club is the Superior Country Club,

and his favorite sports are golf and tennis. On December 3, 1914, he married Katherine Hole at Fairbury, Nebraska. Mrs. Day, who was a teacher in high school prior to her marriage, was born of English parents at Fairbury, January 15, 1889. She is the daughter of Henry F. and Susan D. (Cadwalader) Hole and is descended from the Sharpless and Cadwalader families. Of their three children, two are living: Elizabeth, born September 27, 1917; and George Frederick, born July 1, 1925. Isabelle, who was born August 30, 1919, died September 18, 1930. Residence: Superior.

Ida Yungblut Day

Ida Yungblut Day was born at Carson, Iowa, January 29, 1879, the daughter of John Rainey and Melissa A. (Cooper) McComb. Her father who was a native of Pennsylvania, born February 16, 1839, was a farmer who served in the Civil War with Company G, 76th Pennsylvania Volunteer Infantry. His grandfather, James McComb, who served in the Revolution, held the rank of general in the War of 1812. John McComb died at Minden, Nebraska, April 7, 1903. His wife, Melissa, was born near Ottumwa, Iowa, February 26, 1854, and died at Omaha, February 24, 1921. Her mother was of the Barker family.

Mrs. Day attended the public schools of Indianola, Iowa, and Minden, Nebraska, High School. Thereafter she was a student at Nebraska Wesleyan University summer session and attended many other summer school terms. When a young girl she was the winner of three declamatory contests. Her first marriage was to Dr. Charles Yungblut at Sutton, Nebraska. Dr. Yungblut was born at Marietta, Ohio, March 18, 1871, and was a dentist by profession. His death occurred at Lincoln, on January 25, 1919. Of this marriage there are three children: Donald Charles, born January 29, 1909, is a student at the University of Nebraska Dental College, and is a member of Xi Psi Phi fraternity. Dorothy Louise, born July 17, 1911, was a fine arts student and member of Kappa Phi at the University, and is married to Mark Simons, who is a senior at the University of Nebraska College of Law. Janet Lucile, born January 1, 1916, is a student in high school.

On April 24, 1927, Mrs. Day was married to Wilbur W. Day of Lincoln. He was born at Topeka, Illinois, November 13, 1863, and is superintendent of agencies, of the Bankers Life Insurance Company of Nebraska.

Mrs. Day taught three years in the rural schools of Kearney County, and seven years in the fifth grade of the Minden city schools. After the death of Dr. Yungblut she managed her home and business affairs. For several years she has been active in educational, civic and cultural projects and has filled various offices.

During the years 1926-30, she was state president of the Nebraska Congress of Parents and Teachers, and 1925-26, was president of the Lincoln City Council of the Parent-Teachers' Association. Prior to the organization of the P. T. A. she was president of the Mothers Club at Normal School. She is a member of the National Education Association, and a national life member of the National Congress of Parents and Teachers. She is a member of Deborah Avery chapter of the Daughters of the American Revolution and Sara D. Gillespie Tent of the Daughters of Union Veterans. Past matron of Electa chapter of the Order of Eastern Star, she is a member of Hall in the Grove, and has had four years study in Hellenic Circle of Chautauqua.

She belongs to the Young Woman's Christian Association, the Nebraska Art Association, the Matinee Musical and the Nebraskana Society. Her religious affiliation is with the St. Paul Methodist Episcopal Church of Lincoln, but before her marriage to Mr. Day was a member of the First Plymouth Congregational Church. Mrs. Day has visited most of the national parks in the United States, likes traveling, reading and art, and spent last summer in Europe. Residence: Lincoln. (Photograph on Page 312).

Townsend—Lincoln

IDA YUNGBLUT DAY

L. B. Day

L. B. Day, distinguished associate justice of the supreme court of Nebraska, was born at Wetboro, Atchinson County, Missouri, February 3, 1889, the son of Frank and Sarah Jane Day. His father was born in Illinois.

Judge Day attended the public schools of Boone County, and in 1907 was graduated from the Albion High School. He was awarded his A. B. degree at Creighton University, 1911; A. M., 1913; and LL. B., 1914.

He was admitted to the bar at Omaha, Douglas County, Nebraska, May 5, 1914. He served as judge of the district court at Omaha, from November 10, 1920, to January 3, 1929; and since 1929 has been associate justice of the supreme court of Nebraska. He is a Democrat.

His marriage to Neva Emma Grimwood was solemnized at Oxford Junction, Iowa, April 10, 1916. Mrs. Day was born in Boone County, Iowa, September 4, 1889. They have two children: Frank Edmund, born May 21, 1918; and Robert G., born April 6, 1921.

Judge Day is a member of the Nebraska State Bar Association; the Omaha Bar Association; and the American Bar Association. He holds membership in: Ak-Sar-Ben; Concord Club; and the Parent Teachers' Association. He is a director of the National Probation Association. He is a member of the Modern Woodmen of America; the Elks; Masons; Order of the Eastern Star; and Knights of Pythias. He likes golf. He is affiliated with Westminster Presbyterian Church of Omaha.

Roy Walter Deal

Roy W. Deal was born at Davenport, Nebraska, July 25, 1889, the son of Elmer Ellsworth and Kate (Walter) Deal. His father, whose English ancestors came to America in the early part of the 18th century, was born in Somerset County, Pennsylvania, October 5, 1864, and died at Davenport, April 15, 1927. His mother was born in Somerset County, April 12, 1867. She is of Swiss and Scotch descent. Her grandfather was a titled landholder in Switzerland.

Mr. Deal was graduated from the Davenport High School in 1910. He was awarded the A. B. degree at Nebraska Wesleyan University in 1917, received the A. M. degree at the University of Nebraska in 1924, and the Ph. D. degree at the same institution in 1931. He was also a student at the University of Chicago. He was elected to membership in Phi Kappa Phi, Pi Gamma Mu, Psi Chi, Phi Delta Kappa, Sigma Xi, and Delta Omega Phi, serving as president of the latter. He was awarded the junior class scholarship at Wesleyan University, and was active in track, baseball, and basketball in high school.

He was engaged in the general merchandise business at Davenport, 1910-11, taught in the public schools at Davenport, 1912-13, 1913-14, and was superintendent of the schools at North Loup, 1916-17. He served as professor of manual training at Nebraska Wesleyan University, 1919, was director of the secondary schools, 1925, and is today professor of education and personnel director at Wesleyan.

His marriage to Edith Alice Fiddock was solemnized at Elsie, Perkins County, Nebraska, December 25, 1922. Mrs. Deal, who was formerly a teacher, was born at Louisville, Nebraska, May 2, 1901; her ancestry is French, German, and English. They have three children, Duane, born May 17, 1924; Bruce, born September 20, 1927; and Erwin, born November 20, 1929.

Professor Deal is a member of the following: Nebraska State Teachers' Association; National Educational Association; the Parent Teachers' Association; Nebraskana Society; Young Men's Christian Association; Red Cross; and the Lions Club of which he is past president. He is a member of the executive committee of the Lincoln Community Chest, holds membership in the Symposium at University Place, and is a member of the University Place Club. His sports include golf, tennis, hunt-

ing, and gymnasium activities, while his hobbies are mechanics and photography.

He served as seaman, gunner, carpenter's mate, and chief petty officer on the United States ship *Swallow*, during the World War, and was active in Red Cross and Liberty loan drives. He is affiliated with the First Methodist Episcopal Church at Lincoln, and is a member of the Republican party. Residence: Lincoln.

Earl Julius Dean

Earl Julius Dean, leading merchant and business executive of York, Nebraska, has been a resident of that community all his life and takes an active part in civic affairs there. He was born at York, July 29, 1889, the son of Nathaniel A. and Belinda (Heller) Dean. His father, who was born in Allegheny County, Maryland, January 29, 1850, and died at York, March 28, 1928, was treasurer of York College from its organization until his death; he was the first man to sign the petition to Governor Butler for the permanent organization of York County. His mother was born in Apinous County, Iowa, May 20, 1854, and died at York, January 29, 1926.

Mr. Dean was graduated from York High School in 1909, and the following year was a student at the University of Nebraska. He was active in track and basketball during his high school days. At this time he is manager and partner in the Dean & Company Home Furnishing Store, is secretary and treasurer of the York Theatres Corporation, and is secretary-treasurer of the York Building Corporation and the York Burial Vault Company.

He is a member of the Knights of Pythias, the York Commercial Club, the York Country Club, and the Nebraskana Society. He is interested in mechanics, and his favorite sport is golfing. He was united in marriage with Mary Ophelia Barnes at Auburn, Nebraska, August 21, 1918; she was born in Nemaha County, November 28, 1891. They have a son, Billie, born July 18, 1919. Mr. Dean is a Republican. Residence: York.

Edwin Blanchard Dean

Edwin B. Dean, educator, is a son of Samuel Chase Dean and Augusta Elizabeth (Abbott) Dean. He was born at Satara, Bombay Presidency, India, July 21, 1866. Dr. Dean's father was a clergyman, a zealous missionary in India, and in Nebraska in pioneer days. He was a graduate of Williston Seminary, 1849; Amherst College, 1853; and Andover Seminary, 1856. He was a descendant on the maternal side, of William Chase of Massachusetts and of John Dean of Taunton, Massachusetts. He died at South Bend, Cass County, Nebraska, September 9, 1890.

Edwin Dean's mother was born at Ahmednager, Bombay Presidency, India, April 8, 1835, of American parentage. She was educated at Mount Holyoke College. As a widow, at the age of sixty-five she returned to India as a missionary, remaining five years. She died at Minneapolis, Minnesota, February 12, 1916. She is descended from George Abbott, of Andover, Massachusetts, 1645, and William Wilson, of Massachusetts, 1635.

Dr. Dean attended Bella Vista School, Steele City, Nebraska until 1881. In 1884 he was graduated from Doane Academy. He has received the following degrees; A. B., Doane College, 1888; A. B., Amherst College, 1889; M. A., 1904; B. D., Chicago Theological Seminary, 1893; D. D., Doane College, 1917.

During his career he has held various educational and religious positions. He was pastor of First Church, Wilmette, Illinois, 1893-99; minister of First Church, Northfield, Minnesota, 1905-20; assistant to president and chairman of the board of deans, Carleton College, Northfield, Minnesota, 1920-25. Since January, 1925,

EDWIN BLANCHARD DEAN

he has been president of Doane College at Crete. He is the author of many newspaper and magazine articles.

He was united in marriage with Georgia DeCou at Omaha, Nebraska, July 8, 1896. Mrs. Dean was born at West Union, Fayette County, Iowa, November 11, 1867. On the maternal side she is descended from Richard Everett, of Dedham, Massachusetts, (1636); Isaac DeCou, Newcastle, Maryland, is also an ancestor. Their two children are: Berta DeCou, born November 1, 1900, a graduate of Carleton College and teacher in the Clinton School at Lincoln; Carol Chase, married to Glenn Ralph Oertli, and a graduate of Carleton College.

During the war Dr. Dean was a member of the war personnel board; National War Work Council of Y. M. C. A., New York, of which he was headquarters chaplain in Paris; chairman of the committee in charge of the *S. S. Haverford*, arriving in Philadelphia August 1, 1919.

In Northfield, Minnesota, he was scoutmaster and scout commissioner from 1910 to 1920. At various times he has been a member of the Nebraska Association of Church Colleges, (president); Association of Colleges of the Congregational Affiliation, (president 1928-29); Nebraska Schoolmasters Club. In 1930 he was appointed commissioner on Institutions of Higher Education of the North Central Association. He is a director of the Nebraska Congregational Conference and a member of the commission on Interchurch Relations of the National Council of Congregational Churches. His social club is the Amherst Club, New York City. His residence is Doane College, Crete, Nebraska. (Photograph on Page 314).

James Renwick Dean

James Renwick Dean, judge of the Supreme Court of Nebraska, was born at Saint Louis, Missouri, September 15, 1862. He is a son of Henry and Ellen Margaret (Armour) Dean, both of Scotch-Irish ancestry. His father was a leather merchant with interests in St. Louis and Pittsburgh.

After receiving his preparatory education in the public schools, Judge Dean entered the law school of the University of Michigan where he was graduated with the degree of LL. B., in 1885. While at Ann Arbor he supplemented his regular work with lectures in the literary department of the university. He is a member of Phi Alpha Delta (honorary).

Upon his graduation he practiced law in Chicago and in 1890 he removed to Broken Bow, Nebraska. From 1895 to 1899 he was county attorney of Custer County and thereafter he served three terms as city attorney of Broken Bow, and was there, for ten years, a member of the board of education. He was presidential elector-at-large during the year 1912.

Appointed judge of the Supreme Court of Nebraska by Governor Sheldon for the term 1909-1910, the judge was after elected for the six year term, namely, from 1917 to 1923, on a non-political ballot, and was re-elected for the 1923-1929 term, and is now serving his third elective term. He is a member of the American Bar Association.

In 1906, Judge Dean was commissioner to the Presbyterian General Assembly of that year. He is a member of the First Presbyterian Church of Broken Bow, and is a member of the Presbyterian Synodical Council, and is president of the *Westminster Foundation*, which relates to the welfare of Presbyterian and other students at the state university. His social and fraternal memberships include the Hiram Club, Knife and Fork Club, the Masons (32 degree, Knight Templar) and the Odd Fellows.

On January 14, 1892, he was united in marriage to Jennie E. Sutton at Broken Bow. Mrs. Dean is a member of the Daughters of the American Revolution; her mother's family is of Pilgrim stock and her father was of Scotch ancestry. They have two children, Dorothy, who

married Ross L. Sine and now resides in San Francisco, California. They have one daughter, Jane, aged 5 years. Paul H. Dean married Hazel Burns and they reside in Broken Bow. They have two sons, Paul, aged 11 years, and Henry, aged 9 years. Residence: Lincoln. (Photograph on Page 316).

Quentin Warren Dean

Quentin Warren Dean, tire dealer, was born at Swink, Colorado, August 11, 1906, son of Donald Stowe and Mary Barnard (Partridge) Dean. His family is English and Scotch, having come to America about 1700.

His great grandfather, Col. Robert W. Barnard, was born in Georgetown, D. C., on the site of the United States Observatory, then called Normanstown. He entered service at the beginning of the Civil War under General George H. Thomas, and commanded Nashville, Tennessee, until its close. Thereafter he was in command of various posts until his death at Baton Rouge.

His grandfather, John Warren Partridge, was graduated from Yale and Yale Seminary. He was pastor of the Fort Collins Presbyterian Church when he died in 1898.

Mr. Dean was graduated from Gering High School in 1925, and at the present time is engaged in the automobile tire business. He is a Royal Arch Mason, a member of the Odd Fellows, the Commercial Club, the Volunteer Firemen, and is a former member of the Nebraska National Guard. He is independent, politically.

On December 30, 1925, he was married to Leona Ethel Onstatt, at Gering, her birthplace. She was born April 10, 1909. Mr. and Mrs. Dean have two children, Dorothy, born September 22, 1926; and Vivienne, born December 8, 1927.

Mr. Dean's hobbies are his home and his family. Residence: Gering. (Photograph in Album).

George Claude Dearing

George Claude Dearing, prominent in civic affairs at Brule for many years, was born at Palmyra, Iowa, November 13, 1874, son of John Franklin and Sarah (Hickey) Dearing.

His father was born in Frankfort, Kentucky, April 11, 1834, descended from early settlers in that state. His death occurred at Hastings, Iowa, April 27, 1902. His wife, Sarah, was born in Springfield, Illinois, May 8, 1838, and died in Knox County, Nebraska, January 18, 1911.

Mr. Dearing attended the public schools of Hastings, Iowa, until 1892, and in 1900 came to Nebraska. He was a traveling salesman five years, operated a farm and ranch for the next 13 years, and for the past 12 years has been postmaster. He was elected mayor of Hastings, Iowa, at the age of 21 on the Republican ticket, the youngest mayor ever to have been elected in the state.

His marriage to Cora Elizabeth Cox was solemnized at Hastings, Iowa, February 20, 1895. Mrs. Dearing was born at Hastings, March 25, 1872. There are three children, John W., born February 13, 1896, who is a rural mail carrier; Waldo H., born December 14, 1898, who is a restaurant owner; Stanley R., born May 10, 1910, who is the owner of a garage. Mr. Dearing was active in all loan drives in the World War. He is a member of the Brule Congregational Church. Residence: Brule.

William Thomas Dearing

A resident of Nebraska for the past 58 years, William Thomas Dearing was born at Jacksonville, Illinois, November 21, 1858, the son of Edward and Lydia (Wilson) Dearing. His father was born at Oakhampton, England, May 10, 1844, and homesteaded in Hamilton County one and one-fourth miles southeast of Bunker Hill Post Office in April 1873. He died at Grand Island, July 7, 1919. His mother was born at Pecek, England, February 20, 1849; her parents came to America in 1853 and settled

Hauck-Skoglund—Lincoln

JAMES RENWICK DEAN

at New Orleans. Mr. and Mrs. Edward Dearing were united in marriage at Jacksonville, Illinois, February 22, 1868. Mrs. Dearing is at the present time living with her daughter, Mrs. L. B. Underwood at Burley, Idaho.

Mr. Dearing was a farmer near Phillips, Nebraska, for many years. He and his wife were also engaged in the mercantile business for 18 years at Phillips. He is now president of the Farmers Lumber Company and president of the Bank of Phillips. He is a member of the Red Cross, the Masons, and the local school board. His political affiliation is with the Democratic party.

His marriage to Emma Mary Kirkpatrick occurred at Omaha, June 2, 1898. Mrs. Dearing was born at Colona, Illinois, October 9, 1877, the daughter of James and Elizabeth (Sharp) Kirkpatrick of Grand Island. She is a member of the Red Cross at Phillips. Residence: Phillips. (Photograph in Album).

William Henry DeCamp

William Henry DeCamp was born at Clearwater, Nebraska, February 11, 1876, the son of Marshall Alburn DeCamp and Susan (Anderson) DeCamp. His father, who was a farmer and stockraiser in Antelope County for 40 years, was county judge, county commissioner, and a member of the county board at Clearwater. He was born at Dubuque, Iowa, June 20, 1848, and died at San Diego, California, July 10, 1925; his French Huguenots ancestors were banished from France in 1597, took refuge in Holland, and migrated to America in 1607 settling at Jamestown, Virginia.

His mother, who was born at Dubuque, Iowa, September 18, 1846, and died at Littleton, Colorado, February 22, 1920, was a teacher; her English and Welsh ancestors were prominent in America in colonial and Revolutionary times.

Mr. DeCamp was graduated from the Clearwater High School in 1896, and except for a short time spent in Montana, has been a resident of Nebraska all his life. He entered the blacksmith business at the age of 13 years and was active at Clearwater for 25 years, but throughout his entire life has been interested in agriculture. During the past two years he has been engaged in the well and windmill business in partnership with his sons.

A Republican, he has served as justice of the peace and police magistrate at Clearwater, and during the last 30 years has been county central committeeman of the Republican party. He is a member of the Nebraska State Historical Society, has served as a member of the local school board. He is interested in outdoor sports and his hobby is mechanics.

His marriage to Fannie Minerva Hewitt was solemnized at Neligh, Nebraska, January 19, 1905. Mrs. DeCamp, whose Scotch and English ancentors were prominent in America in the colonial period, was born at Elgin, Illinois, July 29, 1875. She was instructor in the mathematics department of the University of Nebraska, 1897-98. Seven children were born to them: Frances C., November 3, 1905; William Hewitt, August 5, 1907, who married Blanche Marion Healey; Marcus Alfred, March 17, 1909; Susan Alice, July 31, 1910; Merritt Henry, November 15, 1913; Charles Marshall, April 1, 1915; and Josephine Adelaide, September 14, 1917.

William was graduated from the Clearwater High School, was a student at the University of Nebraska for two years, and is now in business at Omaha, Nebraska. Marcus is in business with his father. Residence: Clearwater.

Bert Decker

Born at Hopeville, Iowa, October 2, 1880, Bert Decker is the son of Adam Haeshbearger and Susan Jane (Shields) Decker. His father, who was a farmer, was born in Illinois, February 26, 1851, and died at Lexington, Nebraska, December 13, 1928; his ancestors, who were of German, Irish, and Pennsylvania Dutch descent, were

natives of New Jersey. His mother was born at Mount Air, Iowa, December 20, 1860, the daughter of John and Elizabeth (Camel) Shields.

Mr. Decker received his elementary training in a rural school and in 1903 was graduated from the Grand Island Business College, Grand Island, Nebraska. He has been a farmer near Elwood, Nebraska, most of his life and is director and general superintendent of the Gosper County Agricultural Society. He has served as director of the local school board over a period of 18 years, holds membership in the Elwood Community Club, and is affiliated with the Methodist Episcopal Church of Elwood. He is a member of all branches of the Odd Fellows Lodge, and is president of the Gosper County Sunday School Convention. His favorite recreations are baseball and hunting.

He was united in marriage with Gertrude Eunice Brown at North Platte, Nebraska, December 29, 1909. Mrs. Decker, who was formerly a school teacher, was born at Stuart, Nebraska, August 13, 1884, the daughter of Thomas Johnson Brown and Anna M. White. Their two children are: Lucille, born December 6, 1912; and Berdena E., born March 7, 1915. Lucille is a violin instructor and is a member of the National Honorary Society of High Schools, and is teaching in the rural schools of Dawson County, while Berdena is a pianist, and is teaching school in Gosper County. Residence: Elwood. (Photograph in Album).

Rudolph Frederick Decker

Rudolph F. Decker, physician, was born at Fowler, Adams County, Illinois, July 20, 1881. His father, Henry A. Decker, was a native of Hadersleben, Germany, who was born June 12, 1851. Coming to America in May, 1872, he was for forty-five years active in the Lutheran ministry, and is now retired. His wife, Sophie Muenstermann, was born at Hoenebach, Hesse-Cassel, Germany, January 6, 1852, and came to America with him.

Educated first in the public and parochial schools of Bureau County, Illinois, Dr. Decker was a student in the academic department of Wartburg College, at Clinton, Iowa, and received his Bachelor of Arts from that college on June 13, 1901. From 1902-04 he attended the medical department of the State University of Iowa, and from 1904-05 attended Rush Medical College at Chicago. On June 4, 1906, he was awarded his medical degree from Jefferson Medical College at Philadelphia.

During 1901 and 1902, Dr. Decker taught school in Bureau County, After leaving medical school he served an internship at the Milwaukee Hospital (Wisconsin) from July 1, 1906 to July 1, 1907. A resident of Byron since January 20, 1908, Dr. Decker has been in the active practice of medicine the entire period.

A Republican, he has held various public offices, serving as a member of the board of trustees of Byron, 1910-17, 1920-31, and as chairman of the board 1911-17. He has been a member of the Byron board of health 1912-31, and the Thayer County Board 1928-31. Since 1920 he has served as village clerk, and since 1912 as Republican precinct committeeman.

On September 20, 1916, Dr. Decker was united in marriage to Theodora Proehl, at Mendota, Illinois. Mrs. Decker, who was born at Castleton, Illinois, August 4, 1888, is the daughter of the Reverend Carl and Engel (Schwartz) Proehl. Four children were born to this union: Rudolph F., July 27, 1917; Edgar C., November 19, 1925; Martin T., November 10, 1927; and Dorothy I., June 1, 1929.

During the World War period Dr. Decker held the rank of first lieutenant in the Medical Corps, and from October 16, 1918, to January 29, 1919, was in service at Fort Riley, Kansas, Camp Humphreys, Virginia, Franklin Cantonment, Maryland and Camp Dodge, Iowa. Prior to his active service he was a member of the Medical Advisory Board of Thayer County, and chairman for Byron precinct of Red Cross drives. At the present time he holds the rank of first lieutenant in the Medical Reserves, is a member of the Association of Military Surgeons, and was first adjutant of Saxton Post No. 180 of the American Legion at Hebron.

Dr. Decker's professional memberships include the Thayer County Medical Society of which he was president 1913-14 and secretary 1920-31; the Nebraska State Medical Association, the American Medical Association, and the District Medical Society of which he has been secretary since 1926.

A member and secretary of the Byron chapter of the Red Cross, Dr. Decker is also secretary of the Byron Community Club, a member of St. Paul's Evangelical Lutheran Church and a life member of the Nebraskana Society. His hobbies are philately and politics. Residence: Byron. (Photograph in Album).

Clinton Orla Dedmore

Clinton Orla Dedmore, photographer, was born at Fairmont, Nebraska, where he has spent most of his life. His parents were born in Iowa where they lived until their children were grown, then moving to Nebraska where they spent the remainder of their lives. The father served in the Civil War and died at North Platte, at the age of 89.

Clinton O. Dedmore, better known as "Lucky" Dedmore, after living in Illinois for a short time located in North Platte, where he entered the photograph business in April, 1919. He is now located at 210 E. 6th Street of that city. Residence: North Platte. (Photograph in Album).

Russell Franklin Dedrick

Russell Franklin Dedrick, banker, was born at Lodgepole, Nebraska, October 17, 1892, son of Swan and Lillian May (Camden) Dedrick. The father was born in Sweden, May 16, 1857, and is a rancher and business man. He came to America in 1863. His mother was Swedish and his father was German. Lillian May Camden was born in Otoe County, Nebraska, November 16, 1863, her mother of French descent and her father a Scotchman.

Mr. Dedrick attended public school in Sidney and was graduated from Sidney High School in 1911. From 1919 until 1926 he was cashier of the Farmers State Bank of Dalton, and since 1927 has been cashier of the American State Bank of Sidney. He is also a director. His marriage to Edna Clare Rowan was solemnized at Sacramento, California, December 13, 1918. Mrs. Dedrick was born at Sidney, April 24, 1898. They have two children, Franklin, born October 11, 1919; and Jack, born July 2, 1926.

Mr. Dedrick is a Democrat. He held the rank of second lieutenant in the Reserve Military Aviation, and Air Service during the World War. He is a member of the American Legion and the Masons. Residence: Sidney.

Francis George Deglman

The Reverend Francis G. Deglman, educator, was born at Mankato, Minnesota, September 17, 1881. He is the son of Anthony and Louise (Reuther) Deglman, the former an early settler in Minnesota, who was a cabinet maker by trade. His father was born at Rosshaupt, Bohemia, November 18, 1845, and came to America in his youth. He married Louise Reuther, born at Cross Plaines, Wisconsin, April 23, 1851, who died at Mankato, November 17, 1924.

Upon his graduation from St. Peter and Paul's Parochial School at Mankato, in June, 1893, Father Deglman entered Loyola Latin School and was graduated in June, 1897. He received his A. B. from Campion College, Praire du Chien, Wisconsin, in 1904, and his A. M. from St. Louis University, in 1911.

From 1904-09 he was a teacher at St. John's College at Toledo, and from 1914-17 at Gonzaga Hall, St. Louis University. He was successively teacher, principal, superintendent of Campion College 1917-18, 1918-25, and 1925-27. He has been teacher and dean of boys at Creighton University High School since 1927. Father Deglman is the author of numerous articles in the *Classical Bulletin*, St. Louis. He is a Democrat. He was school representative of Reserve Officers Training Corps, 1919-25, and professor in Campion Students Army Training Corps, 1918. He has been a member of the Society of Jesus, since 1897, and of the Jesuit Historical Association since 1923. Since 1922 he has been a member of the Jesuit Educational Association, and has been president of the Classical Association since 1928. He is a Knight of Columbus. His hobbies are reading and boys. Residence: Omaha.

Clayton William DeLamatre

Clayton W. DeLamatre was born in Kimball, Ohio, July 15, 1860. He is the son of Delding DeLamatre, Sr., and Elizabeth (O'Leary) DeLamatre. His father was born in Hyde Park, Duchess County, New York, in February, 1819, died at Kimball, Ohio, January 23, 1881. He was a farmer whose first paternal ancestors came to America in 1652. His mother, Elizabeth O. Delamatre, was born in Ireland, April 25, 1826, and died at Kimball, on May 15, 1890.

Clayton W. DeLamatre attended district school in Erie County, Ohio, and was graduated from the Monroeville, Ohio, High School in 1876. He earned his A. B. at Ohio State University in June, 1884, and his LL. B. at Cincinnati Law School in May, 1886. He is a member of Beta Theta Pi.

He married Martha Ann Sargeant at Kimball, Ohio, October 5, 1887. Mrs. DeLamatre was born in Kimball, October 5, 1861. Her father was born in England, and her mother on the Isle of Man. Their two children are: Harry C., born August 8, 1888, who is in practice with his father; and Howard W., born March 15, 1892, who is a farmer.

Since 1890, he has been engaged in the practice of law in Omaha. For six years he was a member of the law firm of Bradley and DeLamatre, and then he practiced alone until 1915, when he took his son, Harry C. into the firm with him, under the name of DeLamatre and DeLamatre. He is a Republican, and a member of Trinity Methodist Episcopal Church.

He is a member of the American Bar Association, the Nebraska State Bar Association, and the Omaha-Douglas County Bar Association. He is attorney and trustee of the Nebraska Conference of the Methodist Episcopal Hospital and Deaconess Home, of which he has been president, and of which he is now vice president. Residence: Omaha.

Harry Clayton DeLamatre

Claude LeMaitre, first ancestor of the DeLamatre family in America, came with the Dutch in 1652. He was a French Huguenot, and settled in New York, where the name was changed to DeLamatre. Harry Clayton DeLamatre is the son of Clayton William DeLamatre, who was born in Kimball, Erie County, Ohio, July 15, 1860. He is one of Omaha's well known lawyers. His paternal grandmother was born in Ireland. Clayton William DeLamatre married Martha Ann Sargeant, who was born at Sandusky, Ohio, October 5, 1861. She is the daughter of William G. Sargeant, born in Staffordshire, England, and Margaret Gill, born on the Isle of Man.

Upon his graduation from Omaha High School in 1907, Harry C. DeLamatre entered the University of Nebraska, where in 1915 he received his B. A. and LL. B. He received a football letter at Cornell College, Mount Vernon, Iowa, which he attended from 1907-11. He also received a letter in football from the University of Nebraska in 1914. He is a member of Phi Delta Theta and Phi Delta Phi.

He was admitted to practice in June, 1915, and became a member of the law firm of DeLamatre and DeLamatre, in association with his father, and with whom he is still practicing. He was a second lieutenant in the balloon branch of the U. S. Air Service during the World War.

He was married to Gladys Erwin Tallmage at Omaha, December 17, 1921. Mrs. DeLamatre is a native of Omaha, born February 10, 1895. Prior to her marriage she was a teacher in the Omaha grade schools. Both sides of her family is traced to pre-Revolutionary days in America. They have one daughter, Joan, born March 31, 1929.

Mr. DeLamatre is a Republican, a member of the American Legion, and the Chamber of Commerce. He attends Trinity Methodist Church. His professional organizations are the Nebraska State and Omaha-Douglas County Bar Associations and the Inter-professional Institute. He is a Mason. His sport is golf. He is also a member of the Board of Trustees for Stuntz Hall for Girls of Omaha. Residence: Omaha.

Charles Gerald DeLancey, Sr.

Charles Gerald DeLancey, Sr., commercial artist, was born at Laurel, Nebraska, September 6, 1899, son of Lawson Walter and Sarah Jane (Philbric) DeLancey.

Lawson Walter DeLancey was born in Ohio, about 1848, and homesteaded in Cedar County, Nebraska, about 1880. He was an honest, successful Christian farmer until his death at Albany, Oregon, in November, 1914. He was of French and Pennsylvania Dutch descent, some of his cousins fought in the Civil War. His wife, Sarah Jane, was born in Illinois, about 1853, and died at Albany, in June, 1921. She was a school teacher and an ardent church worker, of Scotch-Irish descent.

Charles Gerald DeLancey attended country schools in Sheridan, Benton and Linn Counties, Oregon, and was graduated at Scio, Oregon, in 1913. He was graduated from Albany, Oregon, High School in 1917, and was cartoonist for the high school annual, *Whirlwind*, 1916-1917. He received a class letter in baseball also.

From 1917 until 1918, Mr. DeLancey was a farm hand in northeastern Nebraska, and the following year was employed in the Northwest Steel Shipyards. Coming to Nebraska in 1920, he was ranch manager in Cherry County until 1924, and the following four years was salesman for the J. R. Watkins Company in the north half of Antelope County.

The following year Mr. DeLancey engaged in farming, and since 1929, has been postoffice clerk at Gordon. He is also a sign painter and showcard writer under the name of DeLancey Signs.

On May 16, 1920, he was married to Orpha Claire Wingett, at Orchard, Nebraska. She was born at Laurel, June 6, 1900, of Pennsylvania Dutch and Irish descent. Three children were born to them, two of whom are living; Robert, born October 19, 1921; Duane Lawson, born August 14, 1926, who died April 11, 1929; and Charles Gerald, Jr., born July 5, 1929.

During the late war, Mr. DeLancey served as a private in Company E., Student Army Training Corps, United States Army, October 1, 1918, to November 18, 1918. He is a member of Sturdevant Post of the American Legion at Gordon, affiliated with the First Methodist Episcopal Church, he is financial secretary of the church board, and a member of the Men's Brotherhood. He is also a member of the United National Association of post office clerks. He is a football fan, and is fond of drawing, painting, animal draftsmanship and writing poetry. Residence: Gordon.

Leo Achille Narcis DeLanney

Leo DeLanney, surgeon and educator at Omaha, Douglas County, Nebraska, has lived in this state for 38 years, and for the past 24 years has practiced medicine at Omaha.

He was born at Topeka, Kansas, June 6, 1884. His father, Achille DeLanney, who was born at Mons, Belgium, in 1850, was a lawyer and notare in Belgium, and at the time of his death was counsel for Belgium. He migrated to the United States with his family in 1871. He died at Omaha, in 1913. His mother, Emelie (Nolance) DeLanney, was born at Liege, Belgium, in 1850, of Belgian and Dutch descent. She is still living.

Mr. DeLanney was graduated from the South Omaha High School in 1902, and in 1908 was awarded his M. D. degree at Creighton University. He is now assistant professor in surgery at Creighton University.

He married Bertha Fredericka Hettfeldt at Omaha, August 29, 1912. Mrs. DeLanney was born of German parentage at Omaha, January 11, 1890. They have one son, Leo Henry, born September 1, 1926. During the World War Dr. DeLanney served as first lieutenant in the medical corps of the United States Army, from July, 1918, to August, 1919. He was a Four Minute Man before he entered active service.

He was the organizer and is past commander of Henry Fiers Post American Legion at Belgrade, Nebraska. He is a member of the Omaha, Douglas County, Medical Society; the Nebraska State Medical Society; and the American Medical Association. He holds membership in the Concord Club and the Nebraskana Society. He is a Mason. He is a Democrat. Residence: Omaha.

Frank Ernest DeLashmutt

Frank Ernest DeLashmutt, lumberman, was born at Pacific Junction, Iowa, August 30, 1890, son of Dudley Wilson and Susie (Adams) DeLashmutt.

His father was born in Eddyville, Iowa, January 18, 1857, and is a rancher. His mother was born at St. Louis, Missouri, August 25, 1867.

Mr. DeLashmutt attended public school at Pacific Junction, and Boulevard North Side High School at Denver, Colorado.

On June 18, 1919, he was married to Frances Coffin at Burwell. Mrs. DeLashmutt was born at Burwell, August 13, 1895. They have three children, Harry, born May 31, 1920; Leslie, born August 5, 1922; and Keith, born January 7, 1924.

At the present time, Mr. DeLashmutt is the owner of the Burwell Lumber and Coal Company. He is a member of the American Legion (treasurer four years), and the Soldiers Relief Association (treasurer four years). During the late war, he served as a private in the United States Army. He affiliated with the Congregational Church, and is a member of the Nebraska Lumber Merchant's Association, the Wranglers Club, the Masons and Eastern Star, and the school board (director four years). His favorite sport is football, while his hobby is reading. Residence: Burwell.

William Newton Delzell

William N. Delzell, noted educator and executive, was born near Delphi, Correll County, Indiana, October 24, 1868. His father, Solomon Delzell, who was born near Knoxville, Tennessee, June 29, 1829, and died at Holliday's corner, Hancock County, West Virginia, January 30, 1901, was a farmer who served with the 142d Indiana Volunteers in the Civil War; he was totally blind upon his return from the war. His Scotch and Irish ancestors came to Pennsylvania about 1780.

Jane (Davis) Delzell, his mother, was born of Welsh parentage in Columbia County, Ohio, February 22, 1835, and died at Holliday's Corner, December 20, 1921. Her mother was a descendant of the early William Penn Colony settlers; her father was born in Virginia.

Mr. Delzell received his elementary education in the public schools of Indiana and Nebraska, after which he attended the Nebraska State Teacher's College, the University of Ann Harbor, Michigan, and the University of Colorado.

Always especially interested in all educational affairs

he has held various positions in schools, both as teacher and in executive positions. For one year he was principal of the Unadilla public schools; superintendent at Dunbar, for three years; was superintendent of the Syracuse public schools five years; was connected with the University Publishing Company of Lincoln for three years; and in 1905 became assistant instructor in the mathematics department of the Peru State Teachers' College. In 1906 he was elected head of the commerce department at Peru; was promoted to position of vice president and was placed in charge of field work in 1918. He was elected executive dean and extension director of the Peru State Teachers' College in 1921, and is in this position at the present time. He has lived in Nebraska, since 1883.

He was united in marriage with Dora Ann Wilson, at Nebraska City, Nebraska, June 19, 1900. Mrs. Delzell, who was born at Nebraska City, July 21, 1874, and died at Peru, May 14, 1920, was a member of an old Virginia family, and a descendant of Light Horse Harry Lee. There are four children: Esther, born May 20, 1902, who received her A. B. degree from Peru State Teachers' College, and who married Samuel Brownell; Mark, born October 21, 1904, a graduate of Peru College, who is now superintendent of schools at Clay Center, Nebraska, having received his master's degree from Columbia University; James Wilson, born September 7, 1907, who is coach and science instructor in the school at Sidney, Iowa; and Donna Jane, born March 30, 1911, who is a junior at Peru State Teachers' College. On August 28, 1928, Mr. Delzell was married to Mary Ogg, who has served for five years as a missionary in China.

For 58 years he has been a member of the Presbyterian Church, but at present time he engages in work in the Baptist Church. He is a member of the Peru Chamber of Commerce; the State Teachers' Association; and the School Masters' Club. He is chairman of the program committee of the Kiwanis Club, and is a life member of the National Educational Association. He is affiliated with the Y. M. C. A., the Masons, and Knights of Pythias. He is a Republican. Residence: Peru.

Elmer N. Demaray

Elmer N. Demaray was born at Canton, Minnesota, February 11, 1887, the son of Melvin J. and Mary E. (Gray) Demaray. His father, who is a rancher, was born at London, Canada, May 8, 1861, of French parentage. His mother, whose ancestry is English and German, was born at Newburg, Minnesota, July 23, 1865.

Mr. Demaray attended public school at Canton, and in 1907, was graduated from the high school at Cedar Rapids, Iowa, where he received seven letters in athletics. A Republican, he served as county treasurer of Blaine County from 1923 to 1927, and since 1927 has been county clerk there. He is a member of the Ancient Order of United Workmen, is affiliated with the Congregational Church, and holds membership in the Nebraskana Society.

During the World War, Mr. Demaray served as wagoner in the 83rd Division, and is now a member of the American Legion. He likes baseball and fishing. He was married at Brewster, December 16, 1911, to Ethel Norris; she was born of Scotch and German parents at Abbie, Nebraska, March 12, 1892, and died at Cincinnati, Ohio, December 9, 1915. On June 20, 1917, Mr. Demaray married Renna M. Smithson at Cincinnati. Two children were born to the latter marriage: Maxine, May 18, 1918, who died December 20, 1928; and Dorothy Ann, September 21, 1926. Residence: Brewster.

Horace Grove Deming

Horace Grove Deming, who has been professor of chemistry at the University of Nebraska since 1918, was born at San Bernardino, California, February 25, 1885. His father, Joseph Jefferson Deming, was born in Franklin County, Indiana, in 1854. Nettie (Morey)

Deming, his mother, was born at Rutland, Vermont.

Dr. Deming received his B. S. degree in chemical engineering at the University of Washington in 1907, and in 1911 was awarded the Ph. D. degree at the University of Wisconsin.

He is the author of the following: *General Chemistry*, 1923, 1925, 1930; *Exercises in General Chemistry*. 1924. 1925, 1930; *In the Realm of Carbon*, 1930; *College Chemistry* (a service course in chemistry), 1932; and various articles in chemical, mathematical and educational journals since 1911. He holds membership in the American Chemical Society, the American Society for the Advancement of Science, and The Nebraskana Society.

On September 12, 1908, he was united in marriage with Elsie Madeline Ball at Port Angeles, Washington, and they have the following children: Joseph Horace; Florence Eleanor; Margaret Linette; Kelvin Ball; Frank Andrew; and Philip Harvey. Joseph graduated from the University of Nebraska in the summer of 1930. Eleanor is a member of the class of 1932, and Margaret of the class of 1933. Residence: Lincoln.

William Joseph Dendinger

William Dendinger, farmer, stock feeder and dealer, was born at Hartington, Nebraska, May 25, 1884. He is the son of John Anthony and Elizabeth (Donahue) Dendinger, the former a farmer and builder of German descent. John A. Dendinger was born at Buffalo, New York, October 4, 1856, and resides at Hartington. His wife, Elizabeth, was born at Erie, Pennsylvania, August 23, 1854, and died at Hartington, May 22, 1930. She was of Irish descent, and prior to her marriage was a teacher.

Educated in country schools to the eighth grade, William Joseph Dendinger later attended Fremont Normal for a short period. For the past forty-seven years he has been engaged in farming, stockraising and feeding, and has taken an active part in the affairs of his community.

On September 2, 1913, he was united in marriage to Martha Katherine Burgel at Hartington. To them were born the following children: Nell, born June 8, 1916; Marion, born November 28, 1917; Harriett, born July 23, 1919; Katherine, born November 18, 1921; and Roger, born May 16, 1924. Mrs. Dendinger was born at Hartington on December 3, 1886.

The family are members of Holy Trinity Catholic Church at Hartington, and Mr. Dendinger is a member of the Knights of Columbus. For a number of years he was director of district schools. He is fond of reading and his sport is baseball. Residence: Hartington.

Albert John Denman

Albert John Denman, one of the prominent executives of Grand Island, was born there, January 11, 1881, the son of John William and Ida May (Huhn) Denman. His father, a stockraiser and farmer, was born at Bloomington, Illinois, November 15, 1854, came to Nebraska and located at Peru in 1855, moving to Hall County in 1871, he resided in and near Grand Island until the time of his death, November 26, 1926. He was united in marriage to Ida Mary Huhn January, 1880. His mother was born at McArthur, Ohio, September 30, 1860, and came to Nebraska and settled in the southeastern part of Hall County, January 1, 1884.

Mr. Denman was graduated from the Grand Island High School and later attended business college in that community. He entered the employ of the American Beet Sugar Company at Norfolk, Nebraska, in 1901, and has been continuously employed by that firm in various capacities since then. At this time he is manager of the Grand Island factory of the same organization, and is a director in the Nebraska National Bank of Grand Island.

For the past 15 years he has served as a member of

the board of directors of the Grand Island Chamber of Commerce, is a member of the School Board at the present time, and is serving as president of the Grand Island Rotary Club. He is vice president of the Nebraska Manufacturers Association. In 1927 and 1928, he was president of the Grand Island Chamber of Commerce. Mr. Denman holds membership in the following: Masonic Lodge; Travelers Protective Association; Elks; United Commercial Travelers; Grand Island Leiderkranz Society; Hall County Historical Society, and The Nebraskana Society. He has been president of the Young Men's Christian Association for two years and is affiliated with the First Methodist Church.

Mr. Denman is a member of the Red Cross, is a regular contributor to the Salvation Army, and is affiliated with the Republican party. His favorite sports are golfing, baseball, and bowling.

His marriage to Augusta Matilda Giese occurred at Grand Island, April 4, 1905. Mrs. Denman was born at Grand Island, June 7, 1884. They have two children: Florence, born March 28, 1911; and Gertrude, born November 3, 1907. Florence attended Wesleyan University and Gertrude was a student at Grand Island Baptist College. Residence: Grand Island.

Arthur James Denney

Arthur James Denney, distinguished lawyer of Fairbury, Jefferson County, Nebraska, has lived in this state most of his life and has been in public service in Jefferson County for many years. He was born at Daykin, Jefferson County, Nebraska, August 24, 1889, the son of Charles Henry and Dora A. (Reesman) Denney. His father, who was also a lawyer, was born in 1860.

Mr. Denney was graduated from the Fairbury High School in 1907, and in 1919, was awarded the LL. B. degree at Creighton Law School. He was active in football, basketball, and track, during his high school days. A Republican, Mr. Denney served as postal clerk for the government from 1908 to 1920, and since 1923 has been county attorney of Jefferson County. He is a member of the Fairbury Chamber of Commerce, the Nebraska State Bar Association, and the Nebraskana Society.

He is past president of the Elks, is affiliated with the Quaker Church, and is a member of the school board at Fairbury. He holds membership in the Young Men's Christian Association, the Independent Order of the Odd Fellows, and the Fairbury Country Club. He is a Mason, Knight Templar and Royal Arch.

Mr. Denney was united in marriage with Helen Lucile Weaver at Fairbury, Nebraska, June 3, 1913. Mrs. Denney, who was born at McFarlane, Kansas, April 19, 1896, is First Reader of the Christian Science Church at Fairbury. Their children are Max, born September 19, 1914; Maxine, born September 19, 1914; Robert, born April 11, 1916; and Richard J., born October 5, 1924. Residence: Fairbury.

Charles Henry Denney

A leading professional man in Jefferson County, for fifty-one years, Charles Henry Denney, born at Lee, Iowa, September 18, 1860, is the son of James Cook Denney and Sarah Elizabeth (Wickersham) Denney. His father was born at Preble, Ohio, June 29, 1820. He was a farmer and preacher and died at Fairbury, Nebraska, January 1, 1896.

His mother was born at Kokomo, Indiana, and taught school before her marriage. She died in Lee County, Iowa, in 1862.

Charles Denney attended the public schools. He was united in marriage to Dora Alice Reesman on July 9, 1888, at Fairbury, Nebraska. She was born in Stevens County, Illinois, September 29, 1869. To this union five children were born; Arthur J., August 24, 1889, who is married to Helen (Weaver) Denney; Edna S., September, 1890, the wife of Herbert Knight; Bernice, in Sep-

tember, 1894, married to Raymond Reynolds; Vernon C., in September, 1896, who died January 16, 1918; and Harold Edward, December 28, 1910, who married Sophia Denney. Arthur is county attorney of Jefferson County for his third term. Edna lives in Baltimore, Maryland, and Bernice's husband is a railroad conductor. Vernon was killed accidently during training for the World War. Harold is a projectionist at a theatre.

Mr. Denney was unsuccessful as a candidate for congress in 1918, on the Republican ticket. He has been city clerk, city attorney, mayor at two different periods, and was county attorney from 1898-1902. He was admitted to the bar on March 17, 1891, at Fairbury, and has practiced law there since that time. At present he is associated with his son in the firm Denney and Denney.

Mr. Denney is the director of the Daykin Lumber Company, and was a member of the Fuel Board during the War. He is a member of the Nebraska Bar Association and has been a member of the Fairbury Board of Education for fifteen years, holding the presidency of the latter fourteen years.

He is affiliated with the Quaker Church, and is a member of the Young Men's Christian Association. He is a Chapter Mason, Knight Templar, and Shriner, a member of the Nebraskana Society, the Modern Woodmen of America, the Degree of Honor and the Court of Honor. He holds membership in the Chamber of Commerce at Fairbury, and is a member of the Royal Highlanders. Residence: Fairbury.

Paul Albert DeOgny

A physician and surgeon since 1901, Paul Albert DeOgny was born at Nebraska City, Nebraska, September 8, 1877, and has been engaged in practice in Nebraska since 1908.

The son of Charles Louis and Susan (Rapp) DeOgny, he is descended on the paternal side from a family which originated in the French Pyrenees Mountains. Later they moved to what is now Pas-de-Calais, where the first artesian well was dug, and the name of Artois was given to the region. The family was Huguenot, and escaped from France in 1572, during the Massacre of St. Bartholomew, locating in Geneva, Switzerland. There Charles Louis DeOgny was born on August 2, 1834. He came to America in 1861, and received his citizenship papers on June 8, 1874. Here he entered the drug business, in which he engaged for many years prior to his death at Wichita, Kansas, August 19, 1914.

Susan Rapp was also born in Geneva, Switzerland, on October 1, 1839, of German and French extraction. She died at Salina, Kansas, May 6, 1923.

Educated in the public schools of Lincoln, Dr. DeOgny was graduated from Lincoln High School and received his M. D. from the Eclectic Medical College at Cincinnati, in 1909. He was admitted to practice in Kansas, on August 22, 1901, and in Nebraska on June 10, 1909. He was president of State Eclectic Medical Association for three years, 1929, 1930, and 1931. His professional organizations include the Nebraska State Eclectic Medical Association, the National Eclectic Medical Association, the Nebraska State and Seward County Medical Associations and the American Association of Railway Surgeons.

Dr. DeOgny served as a private in the 3rd Nebraska Volunteer Infantry in the Spanish American War, and is a member of the United Spanish War Veterans.

On November 1, 1902, he was married to Lyda Pearl Mathers at Wichita. Mrs. DeOgny was born at Benton, Kansas, February 9, 1880, of Scotch-Irish descent. They have one daughter, Lucile Aileen born August 23, 1903. She married Harold Carl Pauley, and they have three sons, Harold Clay, Richard Wayne, and Paul A.

Dr. DeOgny is a member of the First Baptist Church of Lincoln, the Milford Chamber of Commerce, and Library Board, the Red Cross, and the Young Men's Christian Association. He is a Mason, and member of Blue Lodge, Consistory and Shrine, and the Modern Woodmen

Townsend—Lincoln

PAUL ALBERT DeOGNY

of America. He is a life member of the Nebraskana Society, and is affiliated with the Republican party. Dr. DeOgny enjoys golf and tennis, and is a member of the Seward Golf Club. He is interested in boys and boys' work, and his hobby is the Pioneer Club. Dr. DeOgny is one of five members selected to serve on National Council of Medical Education.

He is a member of the National Eclectic Council on Medical Education and of the Nebraska Medical Examining Board. He is also a member of the executive committee of the Young Men's Christian Associations of Nebraska. Residence: Milford. (Photograph on Page 322).

Edna Holland dePutron

Edna Holland dePutron was born at Falls City, Nebraska, the daughter of George Wesley and Ida (Shock) Holland. Her father, who was a banker and graduate lawyer, was born on a farm in Iowa, and died at Falls City, Nebraska, May 30, 1919. Her mother was born in Ohio and died at Lincoln, January 10, 1923.

Mrs. dePutron was graduated from the Falls City High School in 1900, and 1905, she was awarded her A. B. degree at the University of Nebraska. She was chapter treasurer and president of Pi Beta Phi.

On November 8, 1905, she was married to Roy Lee dePutron at Fall City. Mr. dePutron, who was born at Lincoln, November 16, 1878, and died there October 24, 1917, was associated with the Eastman Kodak Company for many years. Two children were born to this union: Georgia, born October 1, 1906, who died November 25, 1915; and Mary Mabel, born October 3, 1914.

Mrs. dePutron is a member of St. Paul's Methodist Episcopal Church at Lincoln. She is a member of the Lincoln University Club and the Lincoln Country Club. His favorite sport is golf. Residence: Lincoln.

Frederick M. Deutsch

One of Norfolk's most promising younger lawyers, Frederick M. Deutsch is a life resident of Nebraska. Born at Talmage, September 4, 1898, he is the son of Fred and Mary Ellen (Moran) Deutsch. His father, a retired farmer, was born in Lee County, Iowa, to which place his parents emigrated from Bavaria. Fred Deutsch died at Hastings, on December 2, 1912.

Mary Ellen (Moran) Deutsch was a native of Wheeling, West Virginia. Her parents emigrated from County Cork, Ireland. Until her death at Hastings, March 22, 1916, she was prominent in club work, and a member of the Hastings Woman's Club. She attended the University of Nebraska.

Frederick M. Deutsch attended the Hastings public schools, received his academic work at Spalding College, and the University of Nebraska and was awarded his Bachelor of Laws degree by the latter. He is a member of Sigma Chi and Theta Nu Epsilon.

Admitted to the bar of Nebraska in June, 1921, he is admitted also in the United States district and circuit courts. He is engaged in active practice and is a member of the following professional organizations: The American Bar Association, the Nebraska State Bar Association, the Ninth Judicial District Bar Association and the International Association of Insurance Counsel.

At the present time Mr. Deutsch is president of the Norfolk Chamber of Commerce. He is a member of the Church of the Sacred Heart, the Knights of Columbus, the Elks and Eagles, and the Norfolk Country Club. He enlisted in the United States Naval Reserve Forces in the late war, and is a member of the American Legion, the Red Cross and the Salvation Army, and was recently made a life member of the Nebraskana Society. He is much interested in sports generally. Residence: Norfolk.

Robert W. Devoe

Robert W. Devoe, a resident of Nebraska for the past 48 years, has been engaged in the practice of law at Lincoln, since 1914. He was born at Lebanon, Nebraska, February 7, 1882, the son of Elmore E. and Sarah (Casement) Devoe. His father, who is a banker, was born at Kankakee, Illinois, December 20, 1856; his ancestry is French. His mother was born in Canada, June 30, 1856, and died at Lebanon, March 4, 1911; she was of Scotch descent.

Mr. Devoe was graduated from the Franklin Academy in 1901, and in 1909 was awarded the LL. B. degree at the University of Nebraska where he held membership in Theta Kappa Nu and Delta Chi. He was a member of the law firm Devoe & Swanson, from 1911 to 1914, and since 1914, he has been a member of the firm of Peterson & Devoe at Lincoln.

A Republican, Mr. Devoe has been prominent in state politics for many years and has held various public offices at Lincoln, among them, chairman of the state central committee; clerk of the district court in Red Willow County, 1904-08; county attorney of Cheyenne County, 1911 to 1915. In 1916 he was a candidate for attorney general of the state of Nebraska. He is the editor of the bar section of the *Nebraska Law Bulletin*.

During the World War he served as federal food administrator in Lancaster County. He holds membership in the American Bar Association; the Nebraska State Bar Association, of which he was president in 1928; the Uniform Law Congress; Lincoln Chamber of Commerce; and the Nebraskana Society.

Mr. Devoe is a member of the University Club and the Lincoln Country Club; and holds membership in Lincoln Lodge No. 19, of the Ancient Free and Accepted Masons, Scottish Rite and Shrine. His favorite sport is golfing.

He was married to Maud Sovern at Wilsonville, Nebraska, May 18, 1904. Mrs. Devoe was born at Wilsonville, March 17, 1881. They have two children, Melba, born March 13, 1916, and Robert, born May 17, 1918. Residence: Lincoln.

Lillie Estella DeVore

Lillie Estella DeVore, prominent educator at Fairbury, Jefferson County, Nebraska, has lived in this state since 1878, and has been active in club affairs for many years. She was born in Huntington County, Indiana, April 21, 1875, the daughter of George DeVore and Harriett Eliza (Hardy) DeVore. Her father, who is a farmer, was born near Salem, Columbiana County, Ohio, December 11, 1848, of Irish and German parentage. Her mother, who was a teacher, was born at Medina, Ohio, May 31, 1846; her ancestors were English and were *Mayflower* descendants; she is descended from General Goff, Governor Bradford, and ten Revolutionary soldiers.

Miss DeVore attended rural school, the Fairbury High School, Lincoln Normal School, and Wesleyan State Normal. She is affiliated with the Church of Christ, is a member of the Nebraskana Society, and holds membership in the Rebekah Lodge. She is independent, politically. Residence: Fairbury.

Joshua Shipley Devries

Joshua Shipley Devries, physician and surgeon, was born in Carroll County, Maryland, September 23, 1864, son of Elias Perry and Elizabeth (Shipley) Devries. His father, who was born in Carroll County, December 26, 1829, came to Nebraska in 1878, and died at Fontanelle, Nebraska. His wife, Elizabeth, was born in Carroll County, Maryland, in 1834, and died there June 22, 1870.

Dr. Devries attended common school, and received part of his education under private tutelage. He received his M. D. from the University of Nebraska College of Medicine, and was admitted to practice on March 22, 1888. He has resided in Nebraska fifty-three years, and has been an outstanding resident of his community at all times.

He was married to Miriam Woodman at Omaha, on August 27, 1889. Mrs. Devries was born at Chicago, August 30, 1867, and to them six sons and daughters were born, all but one of whom are living: James Arthur Woodman, born June 28, 1890; Perry Oscar, born June 20, 1892, married Allana McArthur; Miriam Gertrude, born April 20, 1895, married Carl Gilbert Byorth; Herbert Joshua Shipley, born September 5, 1898, married Inez Bond; Donald Eugene, born April 9, 1903, a graduate of the University Law College in 1928, who married Alice Miller; and Elizabeth Ruth, born February 9, 1902, died in January, 1903.

Dr. Devries is an Episcopalian, and a member of the American, Nebraska State and Dodge County Medical Associations. For six years he was a member of the school board, and his fraternal organizations include the Modern Woodmen of America, the Woodmen of the World, the Eagles, Elks, and Odd Fellows. He is a 32nd degree Mason, and a member of the Knights Templar and Shrine. Residence: Fremont.

Fred Girard Dewey

Fred Girard Dewey, one of Coleridge's leading physicians, was born December 3, 1880, in Fairbank, Iowa. He is the son of Joseph Frank Dewey and Esther Mary (Thompson) Dewey, the latter born at Sturgeon Bay, Wisconsin in 1856. His father was born in Ohio, in 1851, and was a jeweler, by trade. His ancestry is traceable to Tom Dewey, who came to America in 1600; he died in Sioux City, Iowa, May 3, 1928.

Upon completion of his high school work in Moville, Iowa, in 1898, Fred Dewey attended the University of Illinois. There he received his degree, Doctor of Medicine in 1906. He is a member of Alpha Kappa Kappa, and Alpha Omega Alpha.

He was united in marriage with Faye Leone Hampton on August 6, 1908, in Cassopolis, Michigan. Mrs. Dewey was born in Creighton, Nebraska, July 3, 1887, and traced her ancestry to Joseph Reed who was in the Revolutionary War. Their children are: Reed Hampton, born November 26, 1911. and Barbara Louise, born November 20, 1916.

Mr. Dewey practiced medicine at Moville, Iowa, for three years, was a doctor at Hartington, Nebraska, nine months and then moved to Coleridge, where he is now a physician. He is affiliated with the Congregational Church and the Republican party.

He holds membership in the county, state and American medical associations, is a member of the Missouri Valley Medical Society, and is a member of the Masonic order. He is a member of the Red Cross, the Booster Club and the school board in Coleridge. Reading is Mr. Dewey's favorite recreation. Residence: Coleridge.

Wilbur E. Dewey

A native of Burt County, Nebraska, born May 29, 1886, Wilbur E. Dewey is the son of James Edward and Cora A. (Davis) Dewey. His father, a building contractor, was born at Muscatine, Iowa, May 12, 1858, and is still living. He is the son of an English father, born in Indiana, and an Irish mother who came to America at the age of 16. Cora (Davis) Dewey was born in Burt County, November 18, 1863. Her father was of German descent, born in Ohio, and her mother was French, brought to America when a baby.

Mr. Dewey was educated in the public schools, and attended business college. He was a bookkeeper on the Burlington Railroad in 1904, and bookkeeper and collector for L. Flescher 1905-06. In 1907 he entered the employ of the H. E. Frederickson Auto Company as a mechanic. In March, 1908, he entered the motorcycle and bicycle business for himself, and continued until August 1, 1918, when he entered the general garage business. In April, 1921, he entered the automobile sales business as direct dealer for the Chevrolet automobile. He is president of the Dewey Chevrolet Company, and president of the Omaha Auto Dealers Parts Company.

On March 10, 1921, he was married to Virginia Katherine Kalteier at Omaha. Mrs. Dewey was born at Omaha, April 9, 1897. Mr. Dewey has one child by a former marriage, Jack Edward, born January 11, 1918.

Mr. Dewey is a Democrat. He was mechanical instructor of motorcycles at Ft. Omaha, in 1918. He is a member of the Omaha Auto Trade Association and of the National Auto Dealers Association. He belongs to the Ad-Sell League, and is a Mason. His sports are hunting and fishing, and his hobby is mechanics. Residence: Omaha.

Kate Dibble

Kate Dibble, postmaster at Surprise, Nebraska, was born at Dodgeville, Wisconsin, May 17, 1870. She is the daughter of Thomas and Rachel Thomas, the former of whom was a Civil War soldier, miner and farmer. Thomas Thomas was born in Llawyno, Glanmorganshire, South Wales. Rachel Thomas was born in Glanmorganshire, August 30, 1823, and died at Surprise, January 17, 1905. She was the mother of fifteen children.

Mrs. Dibble was educated in the public schools and received a teachers certificate. She was married to H. B. Dibble at Surprise, March 1, 1900. There is one daughter, Rachel Anise, now Mrs. Harold Reichwein. A Republican, Mrs. Dibble has served as postmaster at Surprise, since June 1, 1903, and prior to that time was assistant postmaster five years.

Always active in civic and fraternal affairs she was first president of the Red Cross in the World War; is president of the Daughters of Union Veterans of the Civil War; secretary of Arcadia chapter of the Eastern Star, of which she was first matron when the chapter was first organized in 1895. She is a member of the Parent-Teachers' Association, Baptist Church, and the Nebraskana Society. Residence: Surprise.

Ota A. Dick

Ota A. Dick, who is a leading druggist at Arapahoe, Nebraska, was born at Claypool, Indiana, June 19, 1880, the son of James Henry and Mary Alice (Hollingsworth) Dick. His father, who was born at Claypool, September 2, 1853, and died at Cambridge, Nebraska, September 8, 1919, was a farmer whose ancestors were natives of Pennsylvania. His mother was born at Indianapolis, February 6, 1861.

Mr. Dick attended the public schools of Frontier County, Nebraska, farmed for several years, and for a time was a member of the firm Crawford-Dick Pharmacy Company in Otis, Colorado. He was a member of the firm Dick Brothers Oil Company of Cambridge, Nebraska, and at this time owns his drug store at Arapahoe.

He is a member of the Nebraska Pharmaceutical Association, the Rotary Club, the Red Cross, and the Masons. He was a member of the Parent Teachers Association at Otis, Colorado, from 1916 to 1919, was a director in the Consolidated Rural School at Orafina in 1925, and holds membership in The Nebraskana Society. He is interested in music and likes golf. Mr. Dick served as a four minute speaker during the World War and subscribed to all loan drives.

On October 8, 1902, he married Maud Corder at Cambridge. Mrs. Dick, who was born at Cincinnati, Ohio, June 13, 1881, the daughter of David F. and Elizabeth (Horn) Corder. Five children were born to them: James Corder, October 26, 1904, who died July 7, 1906; Paul Lee, born July 7, 1907, who married Anita Beryl Cawthra and is a teacher; Frank Graydon, born June 9, 1912, who died August 24, 1917; Victor Lawrence, September 22, 1915; and Justin Hugh, February 7, 1919. Paul received the A. B. degree at McPherson College in 1927.

Mr. Dick is a member of the Republican Party. He has lived in Nebraska for over 35 years and has always been identified with progressive civic activities. Residence: Arapahoe.

Ivan Roy Dickerson

Born at Atkinson, Nebraska, December 3, 1886, Ivan Roy Dickerson is the son of William A. and Eva K. (Davis) Dickerson. William A. Dickerson was born in Springfield, Ohio, July 6, 1850, and died at Atkinson, January 27, 1932. His wife, who was born in Minnesota, December 27, 1864, is living.

Mr. Dickerson attended the Atkinson public and high school until his graduation in 1904. In April, 1907, he became employed by the First National Bank, and during the more than twenty years of his service with that bank has held all positions up to and including his present position of cashier.

On June 7, 1917, he was married to Fannie Pearl Linville at Atkinson. She was born at Glenwood, Iowa, June 25, 1891. There are three children living, one deceased. Roy Linville, born December 3, 1918; Lewis William, September 24, 1923; Robert Ray, July 3, 1925, died July 20, 1930; and Harold Eugene, January 10, 1927.

Mr. Dickerson is a Republican and a Protestant, a member of the Royal Highlanders, the Nebraskana Society and the Atkinson Country Club. Residence: Atkinson.

Harry Earle Dickinson

Harry E. Dickinson was born at St. Charles, Minnesota, October 29, 1868, and since early youth has been in the railroad business. He is the son of Jeremiah and Mary Elmira (Pike) Dickinson. His father who was a grain man, died at Balaton, Minnesota, February 20, 1898. His mother died at Balaton, November 4, 1889.

Upon his graduation from high school, Mr. Dickinson commenced railroading as an operator, and following through various capacities to his present position as general superintendent of the Chicago and Northwestern Railway Company. He has been a resident of Nebraska for eleven years. He was married to Hattie Brown Cleveland, of Rochester, Minnesota, who was born August 5, 1869.

Mr. Dickinson is a Republican. He belongs to the first Congregational Church of Omaha. His civic and fraternal organizations include the Chamber of Commerce, Rotary Club, Elks, and Modern Woodmen of America. He also belongs to the Y. M. C. A., the Travelers Aid, the Salvation Army and the Community Chest. His club is the Omaha Athletic Club. Residence: Omaha.

Robert R. Dickson

A distinguished lawyer and judge of the district court at O'Neill, Nebraska, is Robert R. Dickson who was born in Rock County, Wisconsin, November 21, 1863, the son of John and Margaret MacElroy Dickson. His father, who was a farmer, was born in County Derry, Ireland, and died at Osage, Mitchell County, Iowa, December 22, 1896; his parents came to this country from Ireland in 1862, and settled in Iowa in 1870. His mother was born in County Derry, and died at Osage, Mitchell County, Iowa, February 14, 1911.

Judge Dickson attended public school in Iowa, and since 1887 has been active in the practice of law at O'Neill, Nebraska. A Republican, he served as mayor in his community, 1893-94, and since 1911 has been judge of the district court of the 15th judicial district. He is a member of the Red Cross, is a regular attendant at the Presbyterian Church of O'Neill, and holds membership in the O'Neill Country Club and the Omaha Athletic Club. He was grand master of Masons of Nebraska, 1924-25.

During the World War he served as chairman of the Council of Defense of Holt County. On June 14, 1900, he was united in marriage with Marion Skirving at O'Neill. Mrs. Dickson, whose ancestry is Scotch, was born at Jefferson, Iowa, March 6, 1878. They have three children: Marjorie, who attended Rockford College, was a student at the University of Nebraska where she held membership in Kappa Alpha Theta, and is now engaged in secretarial work; Marion, who was graduated from St. Mary's Academy and now lives at home; and Nancy, who was graduated from St. Mary's Academy, is now a teacher. Residence: O'Neill.

Charles Frederick Diederich

Charles Frederick Diederich, farmer, was born in Madison, Indiana, October 12, 1861, and has resided in Nebraska for 48 years.

His father Conrad John Diederich, was born in Cascel, Hessian, Germany, May 3, 1821, and died at Madison, Indiana, June 9, 1898. He was a farmer and stone mason. He came to America in 1848. His wife, Susannah Maria Gieling, was born in Hasfurt, Bavaria, Germany, September 5, 1827, and died at Indianapolis, Indiana, May 20, 1918. She had 11 children, seven of whom she reared to manhood and womanhood.

Mr. Diederich attended country school, and started in farming in Nebraska with $500.00. A farmer and stockman ever since, Mr. Diederich raises spotted Poland China hogs and is also a breeder of Angus cattle. He is the owner, at the present time, of 3700 acres of land, all unencumbered. At the present time, he is a stockholder and a member of the depositors committee of the Bank of Campbell, which recently failed.

An Independent Republican, he has served as county supervisor four years, a member of the school board 40 years, county assessor four years, township clerk six years, township treasurer six years, and justice of the peace six years. For 35 years continuously, he has been government crop reporter.

On April 23, 1902, he was married to Emma Rosch at Minden. Mrs. Diederich was born at Cadillac, Michigan, November 4, 1875, of German ancestry. Mr. and Mrs. Diederich have four children, three of whom are living. Susannah, born December 28, 1904, married Alexander Grams; Elizabeth, born January 28, 1907; Mary Louisa, born September 22, 1908; and Lillian Florence, twin of Mary, born September 22, 1908, who died May 8, 1909. Elizabeth and Mary are at home.

In addition to their own family, Mr. and Mrs. Diederich have helped to rear three sons of a widowed sister. Their names are, Nicholas, Charles and George Appel, who is a missionary in China. They also reared another boy, Guy Stevens, and have two orphan children of a niece six and eight years old, whose names are Roy and Dale Glebe.

Mr. Diederich is a member of the Presbyterian Church of Campbell, the Odd Fellows, and the Nebraskana Society. Residence: Campbell. (Photograph on Page 226).

Edward Henry Dierks

Edward H. Dierks has lived in Nebraska for the past 39 years, and for the last decade has been prominent in the Lincoln business world. He was born at Clinton, Iowa, January 4, 1890, the son of Henry and Caroline Edith Dierks. His father, who was a lumberman, was born at Clinton, and died at Broken Bow, Nebraska. His ancestry was German. His mother was born at Clinton, of German parentage. She is still living.

Mr. Dierks attended the Elliott School at Lincoln, Nebraska, and the Kentucky Military Academy at Louisville, Kentucky. Later he was a student at the University of Nebraska. He is now president of the Dierks-Drumm Lumber Company.

On May 28, 1914, he was united in marriage with Sarah Ruth Jones, at Columbus, Nebraska. Mrs. Dierks was

CHARLES FREDERICK DIEDERICH

born at Llanally, Wales, February 26, 1890. They have a daughter, Ruth Louise, born October 16, 1917.

Mr. Dierks is a life member of the Lincoln Chamber of Commerce. He is a member of the Nebraska Art Association, and the Nebraskana Society. He is a Mason, Blue Lodge Number 19, Scottish Rite, York Rite, and Shrine, all of Lincoln, Nebraska. He is a member of the Lincoln University Club, the Lincoln Country Club, and the Shrine Country Club. He is affiliated with St. Matthew's Episcopal Church. His hobby is fishing. He is a Republican. Residence: Lincoln.

John Merton Dierks

John M. Dierks, lawyer of Nebraska City, Otoe County, Nebraska, was born on a ranch in Holt County, Nebraska, November 6, 1902. His father, Merton Henry Dierks, who was born at Joliet, Will County, Illinois, July 10, 1872, is a livestock ranchman at Ewing, Nebraska. His father came to America from Germany, in 1859.

Letha Lula Glassburn, his mother, who was a teacher for several years in rural schools, was born at Valparaiso, Saunders County, Nebraska, November 1, 1876. Her father, who was of German descent, was a teamster in the Civil War, and was a county judge and county clerk of Wheeler County, Nebraska. Her mother was French.

Mr. Dierks received his elementary education in the public schools of Holt County, and was graduated from the Ewing High School in 1919. He was awarded his A. B. degree in 1923, at the University of Nebraska; he received the degree LL. B. at the Harvard Law School in in 1926. He was admitted to the bar at Lincoln, Nebraska, July 2, 1926, and to the Missouri bar at Jefferson City, Missouri, November 23, 1926. In the fall of 1926, he was associated with the firm Bowersock, Fizzell & Rhodes of Kansas City, Missouri. From February 19, 1927, to December 20, 1927, he was in law practice with D. W. Livinston at Nebraska City.

Mr. Dierks has lived all his life in Nebraska. He was elected county judge of Otoe County on the non-political ticket, November 6, 1928, having previously filled the unexpired term of his predecessor by appointment of the county board. On February 1, 1931, he resigned this office on which date he formed a law partnership with Paul Jessen under the firm name of Jessen and Dierks. He is a Republican.

He was united in marriage with Mary Antoinette Mullen, at Lincoln, Nebraska, August 21, 1926. Mrs. Dierks was born at O'Neill, Holt County, Nebraska, July 3, 1902. Her mother was of Irish descent and her father is English. They have a son, John Merton, II, born April 16, 1927.

He was in R. O. T. C. work at the University of Nebraska while attending there. He is a member of the Nebraska State Bar Association, the Otoe County Bar Association, and the Nebraska City Chamber of Commerce. He is associated with the Red Cross, and from June, 1929, to June, 1930, was president of the Nebraska City Lions Club. He is a member of the Nebraskana Society, and is affiliated with the Methodist Church. His social club is the Nebraska City Country Club. His favorite sport is hunting. Riding is his hobby. Residence: Nebraska City.

Carl Everitt Diers

Carl Everitt Diers, born February 6, 1893, in Ulysses, Nebraska, is the son of Henry Diers, born in Clayton County, Iowa, October 1, 1859, and Winifred (Towner) Diers who was born February 7, 1869, in Ulysses, Nebraska.

Mr. Diers attended grade school until 1906, when he entered Ulysses High School, graduating in 1910. In 1911, he attended the State University and 1912-13, was a student at Northwestern Dental College. He received the degree of Doctor of Dental Surgery at Northwestern University in 1913, and belongs to Xi Psi Phi, also Theta Nu Epsilon.

On September 18, 1919, at Ulysses, Nebraska, Mr. Diers married Luetta Emma Gubser. She was born December 4, 1891, in Rising City, Nebraska. They have three children: Donald Dean, born April 23, 1922, and Catherine M., born June 11, 1927, and Robert R., born September 26, 1928.

Dr. Diers practiced dentistry in Hastings, Nebraska, in 1915, managed a general merchandise store in Scottsbluff, Nebraska, 1919-20, and at present is owner of a general store in Ulysses, Nebraska.

He held the rank of sergeant, first class in Service Park Unit No. 350 of the Motor Transport Corps and participated in one major military operation, Vittoria Venita. He is a member of the American Legion and is chairman of the Ulysses Chapter of American Red Cross. He is affiliated with the Church of Christ in Ulysses, the Elks Lodge, the Odd Fellows Lodge and is an Ancient Free and Accepted Mason. He is a member of Ulysses town board and the Board of Education and the Democratic party. Raising rabbits is Dr. Dier's avocation. Residence: Ulysses.

Louis Henry Diers

Louis Henry Diers, county treasurer of Seward County, was born at Seward, September 16, 1875, son of Herman and Anna Diers. He was graduated from Lincoln Medical College in 1897, and from the College of Physicians and Surgeons of Chicago, in 1899. A Democrat, he has served as mayor, councilman, township clerk and township assessor, as well as county supervisor.

On June 18, 1905, he was married to Blanch Foster Gordon at Logansport. She was born at Spencer, Indiana, November 18, 1879. There are two children, Gordon, born May 18, 1915; and Muriel, born March 21, 1920.

Dr. Diers is a member of the Seward Chamber of Commerce, the Young Men's Christian Association and holds the rank of first lieutenant in the Nebraska National Guard (Medical Corps). Residence: Seward.

Theodore Carl Diers

Theodore C. Diers, prominent educator and business man of Nebraska, was born at Seward, December 4, 1880, the son of Herman and Annie Catherine (Schulte) Diers. His father, who was a merchant, was born at the province of Oldenburg, Germany, March 23, 1845, and came to America with his parents Johan Heinrich and Margarette (Sehfken) Diers, in 1854; he died at Seward, December 25, 1924. His mother, the daughter of Henry and Marie (Waterman) Schulte, was born at New Bremen, Ohio, December 8, 1849.

Mr. Diers attended the Seward city schools; was a student at Concordia Seminary at Seward; and in 1899 was graduated from the Lincoln Business College at Lincoln, Nebraska. He was a student at Chicago Musical College, 1903-05; was awarded the B. O. degree there in 1925; and in 1931 received the B. F. A. degree at the University of Nebraska. He is a member of Phi Mu Alpha, professional music fraternity.

He has held the following positions: assistant cashier, First National Bank at Seward; cashier and president, Clearmont State Bank, Clearmont, Wyoming; and cashier of the Citizen State Bank, Sheridan, Wyoming. He is now director of radio and instructor in radio broadcasting at the University of Nebraska.

Mr. Diers is the author of the song, *My Nebraska*, published in 1929, and various poems and articles. He is the editor of the *Rotary Propelor*, at Lincoln. A Democrat, he has taken an active part in state and national politics for many years and has served in the following capacities: member of the Wyoming house of representatives, 1911; member of the state senate, 1913-15; chairman of the Democratic State Convention in Wyoming, 1920; delegate to the National Democratic Convention, 1920; alternate, Democratic National Convention, 1924. During the war he served as a member of the Wyoming State Council for the National Defense, and was federal food administrator for the state of Wyoming.

Mr. Diers was a professional actor for four years, supporting such notables as Joe Weber, Aubrey Boucicault, E. M. Holland, and James K. Hackett; he acted as stage manager for the latter. He is secretary of the Nebraska Writers Guild; is a life member of the Red Cross; and from 1918 to 1924 was a member of the board of directors in both the Red Cross and Salvation Army, at Sheridan, Wyoming. He is past exalted ruler of the Elks; is past potentate of Kalif Temple of the Shrine, and holds membership in all Masonic bodies. He holds membership in the Native Sons and Daughters, the Nebraskana Society, and is a member and director of the Rotary Club. From 1920 to 1924 he was a member of the board of directors of the Young Men's Christian Association at Sheridan. His hobby is reading.

His marriage to Sylvia Jeanette Cole was solemnized at Lincoln, September 25, 1929. Mrs. Diers, who is a voice teacher, was born at Lincoln, August 15, 1903, the daughter of John D. and Marie Cole. Residence: Lincoln.

Charles N. Dietz

For the past fifty years Charles N. Dietz has been a figure of prominence in Omaha. He was born at Oneonta, Otsego County, New York, July 18, 1853, of the ancient house of Dietz in Nassau, Germany.

At one time the family name was pronounced von Diez, as is attested by a painting which now hangs in the Dietz home in Omaha. It portrays an incident in Thirty Years' War, done by one von Diez, an ancestor of Mr. Dietz. The family settled in the Mohawk Valley where his father, Gould Price Dietz was born February 17, 1828, and passed away in December, 1902, at Omaha. His mother, Leonora Cook, was born of English parents at Oneonta, New York, May 5, 1834, and passed away in October, 1920, at Omaha.

It was in the late fifties that the Dietz family moved to Anamosa, Iowa, and afterward when Charles N. Dietz located in Omaha, the family also came to Omaha. In 1868, Mr. Dietz became a student at Iowa State College at Ames, Iowa, and was the first student to enroll in this institution. He was graduated with a B. S. degree. He has been active in civic and business affairs in Omaha since 1880, and has won an enviable measure of success.

Fifty years ago Mr. Dietz organized the C. N. Dietz Lumber Company, which continued in business until January 1, 1931, at which time the outstate yards were sold to the Rivett Lumber and Coal Company of Omaha, the retail Omaha yard was sold to the Carmichael Lumber Company of Omaha, and the wholesale business is now being liquidated.

In 1889, Mr. Dietz organized the Sheridan Coal Co., with mines at Dietz, Wyoming, which company he directed until 1903, when he sold his interest.

He served as president of the Omaha Public Library Board for a period of fifteen years and upon his retirement in 1930, the city council created the position of president emeritus of the library board and conferred the title upon Mr. Dietz for life.

Mr. Dietz is a life member of the American Forestry Association and the National Geographic Society. He is a member of the Academy of Political Science and the National Aeronautic Association. He belongs to the Omaha Club, the Omaha Country Club, the Omaha Athletic Club, the University Club, and is also a member of the Omaha Chamber of Commerce, and Ak-Sar-Ben. His lodge memberships include a life membership in the Elks, and Masonic Order; and he is a charter member of the Mystic Shrine of Lincoln and Omaha. In politics Mr. Dietz is a Republican.

His marriage was solemnized at Nashville, Tennessee, July 21, 1880 to Nettie Fowler Woodford. Mrs. Dietz, whose ancestors were New Englanders, was born at Burlington, Wisconsin.

Reading and traveling are Mr. Dietz' hobbies. His home contains a very large and well selected library, and also many interesting souvenirs and paintings which were collected during his extensive travels. Residence: Omaha.

John A. Dietz

John A. Dietz, farmer and insurance dealer of Broken Bow, Nebraska, was born at Jordan, Wisconsin, July 25, 1864, and for the past 45 years has lived in Nebraska. His father, Jacob Dietz, was born at Danville, Pennsylvania, June 4, 1831, and died at Monroe, Wisconsin, November 21, 1927; he was a farmer and merchant who served in the Civil War, and during his younger days was a school teacher. His mother, Frances Elizabeth (Meacham) Dietz, was born at Ellicottville, New York, August 25, 1841, and for a number of years was a rural school teacher; she died at Monroe, January 18, 1917. Her ancestry was Scotch and English.

Mr. Dietz has been both a farmer and insurance man at Broken Bow and is now retired. He served as a member of the Nebraska state legislature from 1925 to 1927, and was a member of the rural school board in his community for over 30 years. He holds membership in the Grange, and was master of the State Grange in 1927. He belongs to the Farmers Union Association, the Public Service Club of Broken Bow, the Odd Fellows and Masons. His hobby is the study of nature.

His marriage to Jessie May Taylor was solemnized at Kearney, Nebraska, January 7, 1888. Mrs. Dietz, whose parents were English, was born at Jordan, December 11, 1869, and died at Broken Bow, January 19, 1921. Their children are: Eva L., born May 13, 1889; C. L., born December 31, 1891, who married Marguerite Holden; Stacy T., born February 27, 1894, who married Mamie Warring; Elsie F., twin of Stacy T., born February 27, 1894; Howard, born March 31, 1896, who married Jessie May Wilson; Donald F., born June 11, 1904; and Delma L., born September 15, 1909, who married Charles Watts of Broken Bow; C. L. was graduated from the University of Nebraska, was a soil analyist for the government at the University of Missouri for three years, and is now farming with his father. He has been master of the State Grange, 1930-33. Residence: Broken Bow.

Miner Calvin Dill

Miner Calvin Dill, insurance man, farmer and educator, was born in Tippecanoe County, Indiana, July 29, 1852, son of William Harrison and Mary Ellen (Kellogg) Dill. The father was born in Ross County, Ohio, February 13, 1815, and died at Belvidere, June 19, 1893. He was descended from David Dill (born in Scotland, 1605), Francis Dill (born in Scotland, 1648), John Dill (born in Ireland, 1671), and Matthew Dill (born in Ireland, 1698). Matthew came from Ireland in 1710, to southeastern Pennsylvania. He was a captain in the French and Indian Wars, while his son, Matthew was a colonel in the Revolution.

Mary Ellen Kellogg was born in Dayton, Ohio, January 12, 1822, and died at Belvidere, on February 20, 1898. Her family came from the Netherlands.

Miner Dill attended country school, and was a student for a short time at the Universalist University at Logansport, Indiana. He has resided in Nebraska fifty-two years, and for thirty-seven years has been president of the Farmers Mutual Insurance Company of Thayer County. A Bryan Democrat, he was unsuccessful candidate for state representative.

On December 28, 1880, he was married to Lydia Ann Busard at Logansport. She was born in Pulaski County, Indiana, February 23, 1861. They celebrated their golden wedding on December 28, 1930, with 150 guests. Their children are: Bertha M., born November 1, 1881, who married Charles A. Phelps; Earl P., born November 19, 1883, who married Nell Trumble; Clara E., born January 5, 1886, who married J. C. Bartel; Richard E., born February 5, 1889, who married Rebanis Sisler; Ethel B., born April 21, 1891, and Besse M., born November 27, 1896, who married Joe E. Bowen.

Mr. Dill is a member of the Church of Christ, the Red Cross, and the Nebraskana Society. For a number of years he was a member of the Modern Woodmen of America, and from 1884, until about 1914, was a member and treasurer of School District No. 48. Residence: Belvidere.

Lucia Wolcott Dillenbach

Lucia Dillenbach, clerk of the district court of Adams County, was born on the banks of the Kalamazoo River, in Michigan, the daughter of Daniel and Emily (Hawes) Dillenbach. Her father, whose paternal ancestors came with the Palatinites to the Mohawk Valley, was born at Sprakers Basin, New York, August 9, 1813. His mother was a granddaughter of Sir Thomas Ansley of England. Prior to his death in Hastings, April 12, 1905, Daniel Dillenbach had won for himself a reputation as a farmer and stockman. A strong and fearless man, he was the first to introduce alfalfa in his section of Nebraska, and one of the first to plant ornamental and fruit trees about his farm.

Emily Hawes, wife of Daniel Dillenbach, was born at Carlisle, New York, August 7, 1833. She was a direct descendant of Roger Wolcott, Jr., judge of the superior court of Connecticut, a major general and one of the censors of the laws of the colony; he was born in 1704, married Mary Newberry and his death occurred in 1758. She was also related to John Burroughs, the naturalist, and to Mary J. Holmes, the novelist, and the Lord family of New York. Her death occurred at Hastings, April 3, 1905, seven days before the death of her husband.

Lucia Wolcott Dillenbach received a business education, and at the age of fifteen began her work in the commercial world. She was bookkeeper and stenographer for the Clarke-Buchanan Company for many years. She completed a home course in short story writing with Columbia University, and is now taking a lyric course there. She had completed a course in dramatic art under private tutelage. All of this study has been carried on after office hours. In 1921 Miss Dillenbach was elected on the Republican ticket to the office of clerk of the district court, which position she still fills. She is a member of the board of commissioners of insanity of Adams County. She is the author of various unpublished works, including one novel and numerous short stories, and enjoys writing poetry also.

Miss Dillenbach is a member of the Daughters of the American Revolution and is eligible to the Colonial Dames. Her civic and cultural organizations include the Business and Professional Women's Club, the Chamber of Commerce, the Order of Eastern Star of which she is a former chaplain, the National Geographic Society, the Nebraskana Society and the National Travel Club of New York City. She is a member also of the First Presbyterian Church of Hastings, the Red Cross, the Young Women's Christian Association and the Woman's Club. Her favorite sport is hiking, and her hobby is flowers.

The books and records of Miss Dillenbach's office are kept in perfect condition and the accountants have stated that her work is not excelled by any similar office in the state. Miss Dillenbach believes that every person should assert his own personality and develop his own abilities, cultivating the art of self expression, rather than basing his beliefs and actions on the thoughts of others. It is part of her philosophy that an unexpressed thought is nevertheless real, that it carries with it a reflection of the mood and is communicated by facial expression and actions; in this way bright colored thoughts lend their enthusiasm to others. Residence: Hastings. (Photograph on Page 330).

Forest Earl Dillman

Forest Earl Dillman, investment banker, was born at Curtis, Nebraska, September 8, 1887. He is the son of Clarence Benton and Maren (Whitham) Dillman, the former of whom was born at Wenona, Illinois, January 30, 1855, and died at Curtis, Nebraska, January 7, 1931. He was a farmer, whose ancestors came to America from Germany during the Revolutionary times. Maren Whitham was born at Elk Grove, Wisconsin, December 3, 1862, and is still living. Her ancestry is Scotch and English.

Mr. Dillman attended public and high schools at Curtis, and was graduated from the latter in 1903.

On May 28, 1913, he was married to Blanche M. Taylor at Curtis, Nebraska. Mrs. Dillman was born at Raymer, Colorado, January 18, 1891, and is of English and Irish descent. Their children are, Dorthy E., born June 1, 1914, at Curtis, Nebraska; Blanche Elinor, born July 25, 1915, at Curtis, Nebraska; and Forest Earl, Jr., born May 20, 1921, at Oshkosh, Nebraska.

A banker most of his life, Mr. Dillman began as assistant cashier of the Security State Bank of Curtis, which position he held ten years. Later he was cashier of the First State Bank of Traer, Kansas, for five years, and for eight years was assistant cashier of the Farmers and Merchants State Bank of McCook. Two years thereafter he was manager, secretary and treasurer of the McCook Finance Company. He is at the present time holding that position and is also manager of the McCook Credit Association, and is associated with Dillman and Burke Agency, Insurance, Loans, and Investments.

During 1917 and 1918 Mr. Dillman was active as a member of Kansas Council of National Defense. He is a member of the Associated Credit Bureaus of Nebraska, the National Retail Credit Association of St. Louis, Missouri, the McCook Chamber of Commerce, the Southwestern Nebraska Historical Society, and the Nebraskana Society. He is affiliated with the First Congregational Church at McCook, a member of the Red Cross, and the Ancient Free and Accepted Masons, (senior warden of McCook Lodge No. 135).

Mrs. Dillman is a member of the Order of Eastern Star and the Parent Teachers Association.

He is fond of hiking, hunting, and fishing, while his hobby is work. Residence: McCook.

Forest Ray Dilts

Forest Ray Dilts, who has lived in Nebraska for the past 48 years and has been a successful farmer there, was born at Tipton, Iowa, July 6, 1881. His father, Levi Dilts, also a farmer, was born at Mansfield, Ohio, January 10, 1842, and died at Wakefield, Nebraska, December 24, 1915; his ancestry was German. His mother, whose ancestry is also German, was born at Tipton, February 19, 1859.

Mr. Dilts received his education in the rural and public schools of Dixon County, and in 1898 was graduated from the Wakefield High School. He is a member of the Nebraskana Society, is a Mason, and holds membership in the Republican party. His hobby is reading. Residence: Wakefield. (Photograph in Album).

Charles Edwin Dinsmoor

Charles Edwin Dinsmoor, flour milling executive, was born at Coolville, Ohio, December 26, 1865, and has resided in Nebraska for the past forty-one years. He is the son of Charles and Fannie (Wells) Dinsmoor, the former a native of New Hampshire. Charles Dinsmoor was a farmer, whose death occurred at Coolville, in 1879. Fannie Wells was born at Oxford, Ohio, June 29, 1834, and died at Hastings, in August, 1926.

On July 12, 1921, Mr. Dinsmoor was united in mar-

Nelson—Hastings

LUCIA WOLCOTT DILLENBACH

riage to Marjorie Arzelia Rowell at Goffstown, New Hampshire. Mrs. Dinsmoor was born at Goffstown, on January 6, 1886.

Mr. Dinsmoor is at the present time manager of the Hastings unit of the Nebraska Consolidated Mills Company, and a director in the corporation. He is a Republican, and a member and director of the Hastings Chamber of Commerce and a member of the Rotary Club.

His religious affiliation is with the First Methodist Church of Hastings, and he holds membership in the Young Men's Christian Association (president, 1890), the Scottish Rite Masons and Shrine. His club is the Hillside Golf Club. Residence: Hastings.

Roy William Dirks

At Johnson, Nemaha County, Nebraska, Roy W. Dirks was born on June 14, 1886. His father, Henry Dirks, was a pioneer of Nebraska, who came to Nemaha County in 1865. A thrifty and prosperous farmer, he owned 320 acres of the finest Nebraska land. Born at Springfield, Illinois, February 11, 1852, he is descended from German ancestors who came to America in 1846. He died at Hobart, Kiowa County, Oklahoma, April 13, 1923.

Mary E. (Rademacher) Dirks, his mother, was descended from German ancestors who came to America in 1852, and who settled near Springfield, Illinois, later moving to Nemaha County where they homesteaded. She was a typical pioneer homemaker, sharing in all the hardships which confronted the early Nebraska settlers. She was born in Springfield, Illinois, November 4, 1858, and is still living.

Mr. Dirks was graduated from the Johnson High School in 1902, where he was president of his class and valedictorian. From 1904 to 1906, he was a student at the Peru Normal at Peru, Nebraska, and was active in baseball and track. In 1906 he was elected assistant cashier of the bank at Johnson, which position he filled until 1912, when he was elected cashier of the Auburn State Bank where he has remained since that date.

He was married to Rose Pohlman, at Kansas City, Missouri, January 25, 1911. Mrs. Dirks, who was born at Johnson, January 4, 1888, is the daughter of a Civil War veteran who was a political power in Nebraska for many years. He was twice elected to the Nebraska legislature on the Republican ticket, and was county commissioner for several terms. Two children were born to this marriage: Helen Belle, born October 3, 1912, who is a freshman at the University of Nebraska; and Margie, born December 25, 1917, who attends the grade school at Auburn.

A resident of Nebraska all his life, Mr. Dirks assisted in organizing liberty loan drives during the World War, and handled all subscriptions made through his bank, always going over the quota assigned to his territory. He was also a member of the home guards. For the last six years he has been treasurer of the Business Men's Association; was treasurer of the Auburn Country Club; was a charter member of the Kiwanis Club, organized in 1924; has been a member of the Auburn Improvement Club since 1920; and is a member of the Parent-Teachers' Association. He is an Odd Fellow, a member of the Nebraskana Society, and is affiliated with the Presbyterian Church of Auburn. He is champion golfer of the Southern Nebraska Golf Association, and won the loving cup in 1924. His hobby is beautifying the home. Residence: Auburn.

Charles Aaron Ditloff

Charles A. Ditloff, who has been engaged in diversified farming near Bradshaw, York County, Nebraska, for the past 21 years, has lived in this state since 1884. He was born at Halmstad, Drangserd, Sweden, March 12, 1863, the son of Carl John and Johanna Eva (Arvidson) Ditloff. His father was born at Drangserd, Sweden,

January 15, 1825, and for four years was in military training; he died at Holmstad, June 10, 1893. His mother, a graduate of a Swedish School, was born at Kinnared, Hallan, Sweden, December 16, 1833, and died at Folkenborg, October 6, 1907.

Mr. Ditloff attended school in Sweden until 1878, and in 1881 was graduated from a Lutheran College there. He has lived on the same 240-acre farm in York County for 21 years. In 1880 he came to America, settling originally in Philadelphia, moved to Salina, Kansas, and three years later came to Nebraska. He is a member of the Independent Order of Odd Fellows, Modern Woodmen of America, the Nebraskana Society, and the Lutheran Church. During the World War he was active in the sale of Liberty bonds.

He was united in marriage with Clemma Eaton at Lincoln, Nebraska, October 10, 1904. Mrs. Ditloff, who was born at Unionville, Iowa, August 11, 1867, is interested in all educational affairs; her hobby is flower gardening. Her father was of English descent, while her mother's ancestry was Dutch. They have two children: Hazel, born August 14, 1907; and George, born September 8, 1910. Both are graduates of the Bradshaw High School, where George was awarded a letter in basketball. He manages a small apiary, is practicing diversified farming, and is raising registered Hampshire hogs. Hazel is an instructor in York County Schools, and was formerly a student at Peru State Teachers College and York College. Residence: Bradshaw.

Gilbert Harry Doane

Gilbert H. Doane, librarian at the University of Nebraska, author and editor, was born at Fairfield, Franklin County, Vermont, January 28, 1897. His father, Harry Harvey Doane, who was proprietor of a farm, teacher, and superintendent of schools, was born at Bakersfield, Franklin County, Vermont; he is descended from John Doane, Plymouth, 1629, Thomas Rogers, of the *Mayflower*, Rev. John Sherman and Mary (Launce) Sherman, George Hubbard, and John Maynard.

Charlotte Maude (Gilbert) Doane, his mother, who was born at Fairfield, June 28, 1872, has been a teacher and superintendent of schools. She is descended from the following ancestors: Thomas Gilbert, whose wife, Lydia Gilbert was hung as a witch in Connecticut; George Soule of the *Mayflower;* Thomas Hungerford; Thomas Ufford; and Governor Symonds.

Professor Doane attended the public schools of Fairfield, and in 1914 was graduated from the Springfield High School. He was awarded the A. B. degree at Colgate College, 1918. He was a graduate student at the University of Arizona, the University of Michigan, and the University of Nebraska.

He has held the following positions: assistant at the Colgate University Library, 1914-18; librarian, United States Naval Training Station, Newport, Rhode Island, 1918-20; assistant in the New York State Library, 1921; assistant librarian at the University of Arizona, 1921-22; assistant librarian at the University of Michigan, 1921-25; and since 1925 librarian at the University of Nebraska. He is the author of: *Legend of the Book,* 1924, and is a contributor to the Dictionary of American Biography and other professional and literary magazines. He is the editor of: *Nebraska and Midwest Genealogical Record;* and is review editor of the *New Haven Genealogical Magazine.*

His marriage to Susan Howland Sherman was solemnized at Elliot, in the parish of Pomfret, Connecticut, June 23, 1923. Mrs. Doane was born at Newport, Newport County, Rhode Island, September 13, 1895. She is descended from John Howland; Francis Cook; John Chilton, all of the *Mayflower.* Among her illustrious ancestors are: Governor Arnold; Governor Coggeshall; and

GILBERT H. DOANE

Dole—Lincoln

Governor Clark. Their daughter, Cynthia Gilbert, was born August 2, 1924.

Professor Doane served in the United States Navy, 1918-19. He is a member of the American Library Association; the Nebraska Literary Association, of which he was president in 1930; and the Bibliographical Society of America. He holds membership in: Vermont Historical Society; Nebraska Historical Society; and the Nebraskana Society. He is a member of the Nebraska Public Library Commission. He is a member of the University Club at Lincoln; the First Edition Club, London; the Society of Mayflower Descendants; and the Baronial Order of Runnemede. He is a member of the Episcopal Church and is a Mason. His hobbies are: reading; genealogy; and book collecting. He is a Republican. Residence: Lincoln. (Photograph on Page 332).

Jennings B. Dobbin

Jennings B. Dobbin, educator, was born at Haskins, Nebraska, May 17, 1897, son of Joseph and Hattie Anna (Kelley) Dobbin.

He attended public schools, was a student at Nebraska Wesleyan, 1916-1918, and was graduated from LaSalle Extension University in banking and finance.

On August 10, 1920, he was married to Della Myrll Liston. Mrs. Dobbin was born at Roseland, Nebraska, September 26, 1898. They have three children, Dorothy Dell, born October 18, 1922; Marilyn Rae, born May 8, 1927; and Nadyanne Jo, born November 6, 1929.

At one time Mr. Dobbin was assistant cashier of the bank at Manville, Wyoming. He is now a teacher in the Gering city schools. He is a member of Theta Phi Sigma at Nebraska Wesleyan University, is affiliated with the Methodist Episcopal Church, and is a past noble grand of Western Lodge No. 229 of the Odd Fellows. He is a member of the Nebraska State Teachers' Association, and the Gering post of the American Legion. His hobbies are football, reading and wood working. He is a Democrat. Residence, Gering.

Harry Thompson Dobbins

Harry T. Dobbins, prominent newspaper man of Lincoln, has lived in this state for the past 47 years. He was born at Williamsburg, Pennsylvania, January 4, 1865, the son of C. Thomas and Clarissa Sidney (Aek) Dobbins. His father, who was a merchant, was born at Newry, Blair County, Pennsylvania, and died at Lincoln, April 11, 1886; his ancestors came from Ireland to America, in 1820. His mother was born at Williamsburg, and died there April 2, 1867.

Mr. Dobbins attended the public schools of Williamsburg, and in 1880 was graduated from the high school at Huntingdon, Pennsylvania. He was connected with the *Evening News*, at Lincoln, of which he was part owner, 1892-98. This newspaper was later purchased by the *State Journal;* he is now associate editor of the latter and conducts a column of comment in the *Evening Journal* which uses the editorial page of the *Morning Journal*. From 1886 to 1888, Mr. Dobbins was editor and part owner of the *Capitol City Courier,* now defunct.

He is the author of innumerable articles published in magazines, trade papers, financial, insurance, and banking periodicals. A Republican, he has been a frequent delegate to state, congressional, county, and city conventions. In 1906-08 he served as a member of the state committee of the Republican Party, and in 1904 was chairman of the Republican Lancaster County Central Committee.

Mr. Dobbins is a member of the State Society for the Friendless; the Red Cross; the Chamber of Commerce; the Nebraskana Society; and the Lincoln Automobile Club. He is an honorary member of the Lincoln Life Underwriters Association, and the Lincoln Typographical Union. Since 1887, he has been a member of the Lincoln Library Board of which he is now vice president. He

is affiliated with the First Plymouth Congregational Church, of which he is deacon, and the Young Men's Christian Association. He is a member of the Nebraska Writers' Guild.

He was married to Mary Lorena Highlands at Yates City, Illinois, January 11, 1887. Mrs. Dobbins was born at Ipavam, Knox County, Illinois, June 26, 1866. One child was born to their marriage: Harry Sidney, born September 11, 1893, who died August 15, 1911. Residence: Lincoln.

Frank G. Dobrovolny

Frank G. Dobrovolny was born in Bohemia, March 24, 1873, the son of Jacob and Marie (Hosek) Dobrovolny. His father, who was born in Bohemia, March 19, 1843, and died at Du Bois, Pawnee County, Nebraska, October 13, 1916, was a farmer.

His mother was born in Bohemia, December 28, 1847, and died at Du Bois, September 15, 1922.

Mr. Doborovolny is a farmer who has lived in Nebraska for 38 years. He has conducted Bohemian funerals for his people in Pawnee and adjoining counties for the past 27 years. On July 4, 1896 he was married at DuBois to Anna Karas, who was born at Bohemia, May 4, 1879. Three children were born to them: Bessie, born September, 1898, who married Lud E. Shinn, and who died February 14, 1928; Anna, born May 4, 1900, who married John Rakosnik; and Ludwik E., born October 19, 1902, an electrical engineer who married Evelyn Layman.

He took part in loan drives and Red Cross affairs in the late war. He is a member of the Western Bohemian Fraternal Association and has been secretary of Jan Kollar Lodge No. 101 for 29 years. A free thinker, he is a member of the Jan Hus Memorial Church, at Chicago. Residence: Pawnee City.

Charles Docekal

Born in Czechoslovakia, November 2, 1873, Charles Docekal is the son of John and Marie (Svoboda) Docekal. His father was born in Czechoslovakia, came to the United States in 1877, where he engaged in farming until his death at Abie. Charles Docekal's mother was also born in Czechoslovakia and died at Abie.

On May 10, 1896, he was united in marriage with Marie Veprak, who was born in Czechoslovakia. They have two children: Emil, born June 16, 1897, and Ben, born October 4, 1900. Emil is a station agent and Ben is in the employee of the telephone company.

A resident of Nebraska fifty-four years, Mr. Docekal is a leading business man and banker. He farmed for about eight years and at the present time he is secretary of the Abie Milling Company and president of the Abie State Bank.

Mr. Docekal was captain of Home Guard during the late war. He is a member of Z. C. B. J. and the American Sokol Union and the Nebraskana Society. He is affiliated with the Democratic party, has served on the county central committee, and as a member of the school board and for twenty-two years was chairman of the village board. Residence: Abie. (Photograph in Album).

Charles Francis Dodge

Charles F. Dodge, pioneer banker of Fremont, Nebraska, was born in Bureau County, Illinois, August 27, 1862, and for nearly 60 years has been prominent in public affairs in Dodge County. His father, George Addison Dodge, was born in Maine, July 17, 1819, where he served as a member of the legislature for several terms in the 1850's. He died at Dodge, Nebraska, September 22, 1895. In his honor the town of Dodge was named. He was descended from a long line of illustrious ancestors, among them, Elisha, Nicholas, Nicholas II., Robert,

William, and William Dodge, II. The latter landed at Salem, Massachusetts, June 29, 1629.

His mother was born in Maine, March 31, 1819, and died at Louisiana, Missouri, August 6, 1892. She was a teacher in the public schools of Maine for several years and was the daughter of Daniel and Elizabeth Catharine (Dennett) Marshall, and the granddaughter of John Marshall who fought in the Revolution and the War of 1812.

Mr. Dodge was graduated from the Fremont high school in 1879; from 1882 to 1893 he was cashier of the Farmers & Merchants National Bank at Fremont, serving as director and vice president of that institution. Since 1913 he has served as president of the Fremont National Bank. He was formerly a member of the Fremont school board, is affiliated with the Episcopal Church, and holds membership in the Nebraskana Society. During the World War he was awarded a medal by the United States Government in recognition of his service in loan drives and war activities. He is a Republican.

He was united in marriage with Eva Clarendon at Marysville, Missouri, May 10, 1893. Mrs. Dodge, the daughter of Alvin and Marcia Ann (Hopkins) Clarendon, was born at Council Bluffs, Iowa, May 9, 1869, and died at Fremont, February 15, 1929. Three children were born to them: Catherine, born August 31, 1896, who married Dr. Everett E. Angle of Lincoln, September 2, 1920, and was graduated from the State University in 1918; Margaret, born November 15, 1898, who died May 9, 1919; and Caroline, born January 13, 1908, who married William Harland Kearns, October 24, 1931. She is a graduate of the State University, class of 1929.

On January 14, 1931, Mr. Dodge was united in marriage with Nona Turner of Fremont. Mr. Dodge's hobby is gardening. Residence: Fremont.

John J. Dohrn

John J. Dohrn was born at Marne, Germany, March 7, 1860, the son of Peter and Ange (Hargens) Dohrn. His father, who was a farmer in Germany was born at Marne, in 1810, and died there in 1866. His mother, a dressmaker, was born at Marne, February 29, 1819, and died on the trip to America, September 24, 1888, and was buried at sea.

Mr. Dohrn learned the carpenter's trade in Germany and in 1882 came to America where he was employed for four years by Charles Gunther, carpenter contractor at Grand Island. He began working for the Chicago Lumber Company at Grand Island, Nebraska, in 1886, as yard manager, was made manager of the company in 1907, and held the latter position until he was retired on a pension in 1927.

He served as a member of the Grand Island School Board from 1906 to 1915, acting as president for one year, and is now affiliated with the German Lutheran Church, the Sons of Herman and the Low German Society. His chief recreations are reading and walking.

On September 16, 1888, he married Mary Heldt at Grand Island. Mrs. Dohrn, whose parents were natives of Germany, was born at Dehme, October 23, 1870. To them were born: Martha, October 12, 1889, who married Harry Oldson, December 24, 1908; Anna, October 5, 1891, who married W. T. Detweiler, June 24, 1915; and Alma, January 21, 1893, who married Frank L. Scoville, June 12, 1918. Residence: Grand Island. (Photograph in Album).

Francis Farrell Dolan

Francis Farrell Dolan was born at Maxwell, Nebraska, October 22, 1884. He is the son of Peter Farrell and Anna G. (Kelleher) Dolan, the former a native of County Cavin, Ireland, born March 19, 1840. Peter Farrell Dolan was a pioneer railroader and rancher who came to the United States in 1860, settling in Nebraska about 1868. He was naturalized in 1864 by the Surrogate Court in New York. He died at Maxwell, March 29, 1897. His wife, Anna, was born in New York City, June 26, 1852, the daughter of William and Mary (Geenty) Kelleher, and died at Milwaukee, Wisconsin, July 2, 1921. She was a country school teacher in Iowa in her youth.

Her father was born in County Longford, Ireland, in 1818 and came to this country in 1845, settling in New York City and later homesteading near Lansing, Iowa, in 1856. Although a farmer, he was educated for the engineering profession and was a capable mathematician. He married Mary Geenty in New York City. She is of the same family as Charles Carroll of Carrollton, a signer of the Declaration of Independence.

Dr. Dolan attended country school at Maxwell and was graduated from the high school at Lansing, Iowa, in 1902. In 1910 he received the degree of Doctor of Comparative Medicine from the Chicago Veterinary College, and during the following year was interne in the Chicago Veterinary College. In May, 1911, he located in Willow City, North Dakota, practising there until 1918 when he entered military service. In 1920 he located in Maxwell and has practised there since that time. He is now admitted to practice in five states. He is a member of Alpha Psi and in 1909 was a member of the football team at Chicago Veterinary College.

He was married to Rose Cathleen Conmy at Pembina, North Dakota, September 7, 1916. Mrs. Dolan was born at Neche, North Dakota, November 1, 1891, the daughter of Edward Walsh and Celina (Parenteau) Conmy. She was graduated from the University of North Dakota in 1910 and is a member of Kappa Alpha Theta. Her father was born in Ireland, and her mother in Minnesota, of French parentage. They have five children, Anna Mary, born August 4, 1917; Edward F., born March 27, 1921; William Joseph, born August 25, 1925; Cathleen Mae, born May 24, 1928; and Peter F., born July 2, 1931.

With the exception of his school days and nine years spent in North Dakota, Dr. Dolan has been a resident of Nebraska his entire life. He is the author of numerous articles published in veterinary magazines and has been in veterinary practice since 1910. He served under the president of the Chicago Veterinary College one year, was assistant state veterinarian in North Daktota for five years, and in practice in North Dakota for nine years. He has served two summers with the United States Bureau of Animal Industry. From 1918 until 1919 he held the rank of second lieutenant in the Veterinary Corps. He is a member of the American Legion, was adjutant of Fort McPherson Post for six years, commander in 1932, and county commander of Lincoln County in 1932.

Dr. Dolan is a Catholic and a charter member of the Knights of Columbus (St. Mary's Council, Grand Island, and St. Patrick's Council, North Platte). He is affiliated with St. Patrick's Church of North Platte also. He is a member of he Nebraska Veterinary Association, the Central Nebraska Veterinary Association, and served as secretary of the latter in 1928 and as president in 1929. His hobbies are writing and wild life. Residence: Maxwell.

Joseph Lewis Dollins

Born at Scottsville, Kentucky, December 25, 1864, Joseph Lewis Dollins was a prominent Dawson County farmer for many years. He is now retired. His father, Joseph Alexander Dollins, was born in Tennessee, September 22, 1823. Originally a brick mason he was later a farmer. His death occurred at Scottsville in February, 1902. He came from early settlers in America. Agnes C. Waller, wife of Joseph Alexander Dollins, was born in Scottsville, where her death occurred in March, 1897.

Joseph Lewis Dollins attended public school near

Scottsville, and forty-five years ago came to Nebraska where he homesteaded in Perkins County in 1887. He sold his farm in 1892 and moved to Cozad, Nebraska, where he has since made his home. On February 22, 1911, he was married to Cora S. Whitney at Scottsville, her birthplace. She was born October 17, 1877. There were two children born to them, Mabel, on January 29, 1912; and Russell, born May 22, 1913, who died May 12, 1918. Mabel is a senior at the University of Nebraska at the present time. She attends the state normal school at Kearney from 1928 until 1930.

Mr. Dollins is a Republican and a Protestant. He served on the rural school board, 1923-24, is a member of the Nebraskana Society, and devotes much of his leisure time to reading. Residence: Cozad.

Guy Bayley Dolson

Guy Bayley Dolson, distinguished English professor at Nebraska Wesleyan University, was born at New Paltz, New York, September 6, 1893. His father, George Dolson, who was born at Highland, Ulster County, New York October 9, 1856, and died there April 24, 1916, was a blacksmith and wheelwright; he was the great-great-great-great-grandson of Captain Jan Gerritsen Van Dalsen who came to New Amsterdam (New York) from Holland before 1648. Adeline (Wiley) Dolson, mother of Guy Dolson, was born at Highland, October 30, 1859, and died at New Paltz, August 22, 1908; she was the daughter of James Wiley, born September 22, 1815, died November 29, 1903, and Sarah (Atkins) Wiley, born June 2, 1812, died November 27, 1897.

Dr. Dolson attended school at Libertyville, New York, and in 1911 was graduated from the New Paltz High School. He was graduated from the New Paltz State Normal School, 1913, was awarded the A. B. degree at Cornell University, 1918, the A. M., 1920, and Ph. D., 1926. He was awarded Phi Beta Kappa honors and was vice president of the Delphic Fraternity, and was also made an honorary member of Phi Kappa Phi.

He served as instructor in English at the University of Buffalo, 1922-24, was professor of English at the College of the Pacific, 1926-28, was principal of the East Moriches Public Schools, New York, 1913-15, and was head of the department of English at the Boys Preparatory School at Indianapolis, Indiana, 1920-22. Since 1928 he has been head of the department of English at Nebraska Wesleyan University.

He is the author of: *I. T., Translator of Boethius*, 1921; *Imprisoned English Authors and the Consolation of Philosophy of Boethius*, 1922; *Boethius' Consolation of Philosophy in English Literature during the 18th Century*, 1922; *Southey and Landor and the Consolation of Philosophy*, 1922; and *Did Caxton Translate "De Consolatione Philosophiae" of Boethius*, 1926.

Dr. Dolson served as instructor in the United States School of Aerial Photography at Rochester, New York, 1918. He is a member of the Medieval Academy of America, the Modern Language Association of America, the American Association of University Professors, the Nebraskana Society, and the Lincoln Civic Music Association. He is affiliated with the First Methodist Church of Lincoln, is a member of the Red Cross, and holds membership in the Odd Fellows. He is a member of the American Legion.

His sports include hiking and fishing, while his hobby is collecting valuable old books of scholarly interest. He was married to Marguerite Kathryn Allhusen at Poughkeepsie, Dutches County, New York, September 12, 1925. Mrs. Dolson, who was the daughter of Henry and Henrietta Allhusen, was born at Melville, Suffolk County, New York, September 1, 1893. They have two children: Marguerite May, born November 11, 1927; and Ruth Elaine, born January 19, 1931. Politically, Mr. Dolson is an Independent.

Mr. Dolson's nephew, Teunis Dolson, who lives in New York, is named for the first Teunis Van Dalsen who died in 1766 at the age of 102 years. The Dolson family is one of the oldest in Manhattan, and members of the family, including John Dolson, served in the American Revolution. Residence: Lincoln.

Lawrence Anthony Donahoe

Lawrence Anthony Donahoe, dentist, was born at Omaha, Nebraska, May 16, 1887, son of Anthony Joseph and Mary Ann (Pickett) Donahoe.

His father was born in Alleghany County, Pennsylvania, June 3, 1864, and is passenger pilot for the Missouri Pacific Railway at the Union Station in Omaha. He is the former president of the Central Labor Union of Omaha, labor and political leader, and was elected to the Constitutional Convention of 1920. His wife, Mary Ann, was born at Omaha, March 3, 1867, and died there on March 1, 1895. She was a student of literature, and a reader in her leisure time. Her father, who was Irish, was grading contractor and a dealer in draft horses.

Dr. Donahoe attended Holy Family Parochial School until June 1900, and was graduated from the academic department of Creighton University in 1904. He received his degree of Bachelor of Dental Surgery from Creighton University in April 1916, where he was a member of Delta Sigma Delta.

From 1904 until 1908, Dr. Donahoe was general yard master's clerk for the Missouri Pacific Railway, and from 1908 until 1910, was in the Civil Engineering Department. He was in the Oil Inspecting Department at the State House in Lincoln, during 1911 and 1912, and then entered dental college. He has been in active practice since 1916.

He is a Republican, and held a commission in the Pure Food and Oil Inspection Department under Governor Chester Aldrich, 1911-12. He is a member of St. Patrick's Catholic Church, and the Knights of Columbus (past grand knight, local council, district deputy four years, present state treasurer, state council).

Dr. and Mrs. Donahoe have had four children, three ganized the dental clinic of Cheyenne County in 1923 and 1924 under the local Red Cross direction. At the present time he is vice-president of the Lions Club, and a member of the Nebraska State Board of Dental Examiners (1929-1934). His favorite sports are golf and hand ball. He is a member of the American and Nebraska State Dental Associations.

On April 30, 1916, he was married to Ann Margaret Schifferle at Omaha. Mrs. Donahoe was born at Creston, Iowa, of Swiss and Irish descent. Her father is a graduate of Rush Medical College.

Dr. and Mrs. Donahue have had four children, three of whom are living, Edward, born April 12, 1917; Patricia, born December 17, 1920, who died February 11, 1925; Harry, born February 24, 1927; and Margaret-Mary, born September 28, 1928. Residence: Sidney.

John Edwin Donaldson

One of Nebraska's foremost farmers, and a leader in the organization and management of farm project clubs, John Edwin Donaldson resides at Albion. He was born at College Springs, Iowa, March 8, 1881, the son of William and Agnes Gertrude (Graham) Donaldson. His father, who served as county commissioner of Wheeler County, and who was a farmer and breeder of improved livestock, was born near Glasgow, Scotland, February 26, 1848, and died in Sacramento County, California, September 12, 1919. He came to America in 1857 and settled in Columbiana County, Ohio, moving to College Springs, Iowa, in 1874, and to Cumminsville in Wheeler County, Nebraska, in 1882.

Agnes (Graham) Donaldson, mother of John E., was born in Salineville, Ohio, April 30, 1843, and died at

Campbell, California, July 29, 1916. She was a teacher for many years and was much interested in church activities. Her ancestry was Scotch-Irish.

Mr. Donaldson attended the public schools of Cumminsville, a rural school in Boone County, and the Albion High School. He was a student at the University of Nebraska School of Agriculture for a term. For the past 30 years he has been prominent in the production of Shorthorn cattle and Percheron horses, and has been the outstanding leader of Boone County in farm organizations.

He served as director of the Albion Livestock Shipping Association from 1909 until 1928, and was president of that organization for eight years. He has been director and trustee of the Albion Elevator Company since 1910, and was director of the Boone County Farmers Mutual Insurance Company for several years prior to 1925. He was one of the organizers of the Boone County Farm Bureau of which he is now president, and is the leader of the Boone County All Breeds Baby Beef Club, formerly known as the Boone County Shorthorn Calf Club.

An article in the *Nebraska Farmer*, which gives a brief resume of Mr. Donaldson's life and achievements, states that perhaps his most constructive work has been with the management and organization of 4-H Clubs in Boone County. He is a member of the First Methodist Church of Albion, and was a director of his local school board for 15 years. Recently he was elected to membership in the Nebraskana Society.

Mr. Donaldson is one of the 1928 Master Farmers of Nebraska and is an active member in the Master Farmer Club. During the World War he was awarded a medal for service in Liberty loan drives. His hobby is boys' and girls' club work. He is a Democrat.

On March 8, 1905, he was united in marriage with Frances Sophronia Porter at Albion. Mrs. Donaldson, who is a leader in girls clubs and is president of the Mount Pleasant Homemakers Club, was born at Grove Creek, Iowa, May 10, 1883. She is the daughter of John F. and Mary Ellen (Houston) Porter.

They have four children, Ellen, born May 28, 1906, who was graduated from the home economics department of the University of Nebraska in 1930, and who is assistant county agent of Burt County, Nebraska. In 1928 she was awarded a $250 cash prize with the distinction of being the champion 4-H Club leader in her community. Charles F., born December 5, 1908, is a farmer near Albion. Dorothy, born January 18, 1912, was a member of the *R* Busy Needle Workers and won first prize at the Nebraska State Fair in 1928, having made the best complete costume. The costume was then exhibited at he National Club Congress in Chicago, and won third prize. In 1928 she showed the first prize 4-H Club Shorthorn heifer at the Nebraska State Fair and was a member of the Baby Beef Club of 1929. Roy W. was born May 9, 1914. Residence: Albion.

Margaret Hitchcock Doorly

Margaret Hitchcock Doorly was born at Omaha, Douglas County, Nebraska, May 31, 1884, the daughter of Gilbert Monell Hitchcock and Jessie (Crounse) Hitchcock. Her father, long a Nebraska leader, was born at Omaha, September 18, 1859. In 1885 he established the *Omaha Evening World*, and in 1889 purchased the *Morning Herald* which he consolidated with the former as the *World Herald*, of which he has since been publisher. He served as a member of the United States congress and later was United States senator.

Her mother was born at Fort Plain, New York, July 12, 1862, and died at Washington, District of Columbia, May 8, 1925. She was the daughter of Lorenzo Crounse, former governor of Nebraska, judge of the Nebraska

Supreme Court, and assistant treasurer of the United States. She was a talented pianist.

Mrs. Doorly has been prominent in social circles and welfare activities at Omaha for many years. On September 6, 1904, her marriage to Henry Doorly was solemnized at Omaha. Mr. Doorly, who was born at Barbados, British West Indies, November 9, 1879, is the business manager for the *World Herald*. They have three children: Katherine, born June 27, 1905, who married Dr. Richard H. Young; Gilbert, born July 8, 1907; and Margaret, born November 5, 1913. Mrs. Doorly is affiliated with the St. Barnabas Episcopal Church of Omaha. She resides at Fairacres. Residence: Omaha.

H. B. Dopf

H. B. Dopf, banker, was born in Rockport, Missouri, October 4, 1886, son of John D. and Mary (Burnett) Dopf.

The father was born in Germany, and was the editor of the first Republican newspaper in northwestern Missouri, the founder of the first bank in Atchison County, Missouri, and the founder of the Northwestern Missouri Press Association.

Mr. Dopf attended the high school at Rockport, Missouri, and was later a student at Columbia University. In 1904 he was associated with Swift and Company at St. Joseph, and in 1905 the Blanchard Livestock Commission Company of St. Joseph. In 1907 he was assistant postmaster at Rockport and in 1908 assistant postmaster at Fullerton, Nebraska. In 1910 he was associated with a furniture and undertaking establishment at Fullerton, and from 1912-14 was a traveling salesman. From 1918 until 1921 he was editor of the *Wolbach Messenger* and the *Blaine County Booster*. Since 1921 he has been president of the Farmers State Bank of Brule and engaged in the insurance and farm loan business.

He was first married to Florence Kern, who died at Wolbach, Nebraska, November 19, 1918. There are two children of this marriage, Robert Wade, born March 19, 1916; and Mary Louise, born July 30, 1918. His second marriage was to Flossie Stafford, of Brule.

During the World War Mr. Dopf was active in all civilian projects. He is a member of the Nebraska State Bankers Association, the Red Cross, the Elks, the Nebraskana Society, and the Parent Teachers Association. He enjoys hunting, fishing, golf, baseball, football, skating and swimming. His hobbies are reading, mechanics, building, and lawns. Residence: Brule.

John Harrison Doran

John Harrison Doran was born at Beaver, Iowa, August 6, 1888, the son of Thomas Henry and Ettie Eliza (Satterlee) Doran. His father, who for over 30 years was a banker and lumberman, was a livestock and land owner, and served as state representative in Nebraska; he was prominent in all civic affairs and in state politics until his death at Burwell, Nebraska, August 25, 1925. His mother died at Burwell in 1906.

Mr. Doran was graduated from the Burwell High School in 1905, attended the Kearney Military Academy, and was a student at the Lincoln Business College. He served as partner in the Burwell Hardware Company, 1905-07, was connected with the Cram Lumber Company, 1907-10, was a partner in the lumber firm of Doran, Johnson & Troxell, 1911-26, and was active in the Farmers Bank at Burwell, 1916-19, being vice president from 1917 to 1919. He owns a garage at Burwell and holds extensive land and stock interests there. Mr. Doran is president of the Western Finance Company.

He is a member and former director of the Commercial Club, is affiliated with the Ancient Free and Accepted Masons, and holds membership in the Nebraskana Society. Mr. Doran was one of the organizers of the Nebraska Big Rodeo, of which he is vice president and arena director, and is serving as director of the Rodeo Association of America, an organization with headquarters in California. During the World War he served in loan drives and was a member of the local advisory board at Burwell.

On May 10, 1916, he married Jessamine Agnes Flynn at North Platte, Nebraska. Their children are: Jack, born December 29, 1917; Tom, born December 5, 1918; Dorothy, born August 6, 1921; Elinor, born October 12, 1922; Bob, born March 22, 1924; and Billy, born June 19, 1925. Residence: Burwell.

Dayton Henry Dorn

Dayton Henry Dorn, merchant, was born at Big Spring, Nebraska, April 22, 1905, son of Frank and Kate Rodella (Henry) Dorn.

The father was born at Weisbaden, Germany, in May, 1862, and came to America about 1880 as a day laborer. At the present time he is an extensive landowner, the operator of a general store, and a lumber and grain elevator business. His wife, Kate, was born in Mucatine, Iowa, March 17, 1878, and is active in church organizations and the Eastern Star. Her grandparents came to the United States from County Tyrone, Ireland.

Upon his graduation from rural high school in 1922 Mr. Dorn entered the University of Nebraska where he was awarded the Bachelor of Arts degree in 1926. While there he was secretary of Pi Kappa Phi. At the present time he is in business with his father.

On June 11, 1930, he was married to Virginia Ellis McCoy at North Platte. She was born at Thomson, Illinois, November 5, 1909, of Scotch-Irish descent.

Mr. Dorn is a Republican. He is affiliated with the Big Spring Methodist Episcopal Church, and is an 18th degree Mason and member of the Scottish Rite, and the Independent Order of Odd Fellows. He is an executive officer of the Big Spring Rifle Club at the present time and a member of the Big Spring Golf Club. His hobbies are shooting and golf. During the late war he was a member of the Reserve Officers Training Corps at the University of Nebraska. Residence: Big Spring. (Photograph in Album).

William Henry Dorrance

William Henry Dorrance, one of Omaha's leading citizens, was born on a farm near Tobias, Fillmore County, Nebraska, March 5, 1880. His father, Frank Bird Dorrance was born at Scotts, Michigan, October 1, 1854, and is now a retired farmer. He is descended from French Huguenots who came to Jamestown, Virginia, the first, a clergyman, coming in 1607. Frank B. Dorrance married Harriet Catherine McLeod, a native of New York, born April 26, 1863. Her parents came from Edinburgh, Scotland, and settled in New York. She died at Fort Crook, Nebraska, May 26, 1904.

Until he was twelve years of age William Henry Dorrance was educated in rural country schools, and then entered the elementary school at Tobias. He was graduated from Tobias High School in 1898, when he came to Omaha. In order to secure his commercial education it was necessary for him to work his way, carrying papers and washing dishes in a restaurant for his meals and sleeping in a funeral establishment at night. Through this connection he studied embalming, and later entered the business which he has made his life work.

In 1900 he entered the office of the superintendent of the Union Pacific Railroad as stenographer, and in the fall of that year was promoted to time keeper of train and engine men. On December 30, 1901, he resigned to engage in business. On July 1, 1901, together with E. F. Brailey, he organized the firm of Brailey and Dorrance, Funeral Directors. The business was conducted as a

partnership until April 1, 1922, when Mr. Dorrance became sole owner. He is also secretary and member of the board of directors of the Platinum Metals Corporation.

He was married to Mae Mary Robinson at Council Bluffs, Iowa, November 27, 1902. Mrs. Dorrance was born at Ashland, Nebraska, February 8, 1879. There were two children of the marriage, both of whom died in childhood: William H., Jr., born March 8, 1905; who died January 31, 1911; and Gretchen, born March 1, 1907, who died February 8, 1911.

Mr. Dorrance has always been active in professional organizations. He was president of the Nebraska Funeral Directors Association in 1909; president of the State Embalmers Examining Board 1928, 29, 30 and 31; and president of The Conference of Embalmers Examining Board of the United States, Inc., 1930-31. A member of the Chamber of Commerce, he is on the advisory committee of the Funeral Service Bureau of America.

During the World War he served on loan drives committees of the Chamber of Commerce. He attends Kountze Memorial Lutheran Church. His fraternal organizations include the Elks, Moose, Modern Woodmen of America, and the Masons, in which he is a member of the Knights Templar and Shrine bodies. His hobby is mechanics. Residence: Omaha.

Francis Patrick Dorsey

Francis P. Dorsey was born at Grantsville, Garrett County, Maryland, September 15, 1867, the son of Patrick and Sarah Jane (McCuster) Dorsey. His father, who was born at Columbus, Ohio, in 1820, and died at Grantsville, January 10, 1902, was a lumberman. His mother was born at Mount Savidge, Maryland, in 1829, and died at Grantsville, May 15, 1884.

Dr. Dorsey, who has been a practicing physician in Cedar County for the past 35 years, was graduated from the Grantsville High School, and received his M. D. degree at the University of Louisville, Kentucky, 1895. He was a student at Notre Dame and the University of Maryland. He is a member of the Chamber of Commerce, the American Legion, the Cedar County Medical Society, the Nebraska State Medical Society, and the American Medical Association. He is a member of the Country Club. His hobbies are reading and the study of chemistry.

During the World War he served as captain in the United States Medical Corps. He is a Democrat, and is a member of the Nebraskana Society.

His marriage was solemnized at Sioux City, Iowa, February 2, 1902, when he married Sarah Louise Larch. Mrs. Dorsey, who is a musician, was born at Yankton, South Dakota, in 1880; her ancestry is German. They have four children: Francis P., born February, 1903; Louise, born 1906, who married H. McCochrane; James, born 1911; and Donald, born 1912. Francis is a physican who was graduated from the medical department of Northwestern University in 1927. Residence: Hartington.

Charles Lloyd Dort

Charles Lloyd Dort was born at Burchard, Nebraska, January 18, 1884. His father, John Charles Dort, who is a lawyer, was born near Delavan, Wisconsin, December 28, 1857, and is a member of the Dort family who settled in New York in 1600, several of whom were active in the Revolution.

Catherine J. Lloyd, mother of Lloyd, was born at Toulon, Illinois, the daughter of Stephen and Phoebe Jane Lloyd. Ancestors on the maternal side came from Wales to Pennsylvania, and paternal ancestors were early residents of Ebensburg, Pennsylvania. Her brother, James

Darsie Lloyd, is the father of Harold Lloyd, the famous moving picture star.

Graduated from Pawnee City Academy in 1902, Charles Lloyd Dort taught in a country school and then entered the University of Nebraska. In 1908 he received his Bachelor of Laws degree and completed five years of a six year course. He received a letter in baseball and is a member of Beta Theta Pi.

Admitted to the bar in June, 1908, Lloyd Dort practiced in Kansas City from 1909-1917, where he was assistant counsel for two interurban railways and several investment companies. At the close of the World War he formed a law partnership with Jean B. Cain at Falls City, which was most harmonious, and which was not dissolved until November 1, 1929. In March of that year he debated Clarence A. Darrow of Chicago, at the Liberty Theatre in Lincoln.

Except for his residence in Kansas City, Mr. Dort has lived in Nebraska all his life. In politics he is a Republican, and from 1920 to 1929 was assistant attorney general of Nebraska. He was Commissioner of Insurance and Securities of Nebraska for more than a year, and in his first year was made a member of the executive committee of the National Convention of Insurance Commissioners, an unusual honor.

On January 1, 1907, he was married to Elizabeth Mabel McCready at Pawnee City. Mrs. Dort, who was born at Pawnee City, died at Lincoln on September 23, 1921. She was of Scotch, French and German ancestry, her father, the Reverend Robert J. McCready, D. D., having been a pioneer minister in Nebraska. She is a descendant of the noted actor, McCready.

Of this marriage there are two children: Mignon, born August 18, 1908, and Douglas, born October 27, 1915.

Mr. Dort volunteered for war service, and entered as a private in the 3rd Battalian, Company 2, Infantry Officers Training School. He was active in wartime speeches and drives until Officers Training School opened for him. He is a member of the American Legion and the Forty and Eight, the Sons of the American Revolution, the Nebraska State and Lancaster County Bar Associations, the Elks and the First Christian Church of Lincoln. His favorite sports are fishing and golf, while his hobby is reading. At the present time Mr. Dort is engaged in the practice of law in Lincoln, giving much attention to insurance law and insurance cases. Residence: Lincoln. (Photograph in Album).

John Charles Dort

On December 28, 1857, John Charles Dort was born near Delavan, Wisconsin. He is the son of Charles and Ada Cordelia (Pattyson) Dort, the former of whom, a farmer and business man, was born at Belfast, New York, August 13, 1833. Charles Dort's ancestors came to America in 1660. He was a cripple, and was twice rejected for military service in the Civil War. He was a Republican, a member of the Methodist Episcopal Church and a singer of note. His death occurred at Cawker City, Kansas, on February 1, 1908. His father, John Dort the first, was born in New Hampshire, January 1, 1805.

Ada Pattyson, mother of John Charles Dort, was educated in public schools and academies in New York State. Of distinguished ancestry, she was an educator and church worker of much prominence. Her father, who was English, was a veteran of the Mexican War. In his family were many outstanding characters, most of whom were public officials, school executives and teachers. Mrs. Dort was born in Cattaraugus County, New York, December 17, 1836, and died at her home near Pawnee City on November 2, 1882.

As a farmer boy, John Charles Dort taught a country school, after which he entered the mercantile business, remaining seventeen years He was admitted to the practice of law in Nebraska by the first board of examiners

for admission in 1895, and has been active in practice in the courts of Nebraska, Colorado, and other state and federal courts.

Mr. Dort, who has lived in Nebraska 68 years, is vitally interested in farming and agriculture conditions in Nebraska. During the World War he took an active part in patriotic work, the sale of bonds, three minute speeches and presenting questionnaires.

He was married to Catherine Jane Lloyd at Burchard, Nebraska, March 20, 1883. Mrs. Dort was of Welsh descent on both sides of her family, the only aunt of Harold Lloyd, famous screen star. Born at Cherry Tree, Pennsylvania, May 6, 1858, she was the only daughter of Stephen and Phoebe J. Lloyd. She was active in church and club work, and above all was a homemaker. One son, Charles Lloyd, a lawyer, veteran of the World War, member of the American Legion, the Christian Church, and other organizations, was born January 18, 1884. He was for nine years assistant attorney general of Nebraska, and later served as state insurance commissioner. He married Elizabeth Mabel McCready.

John Charles Dort was a country town postmaster under President Harrison, and for nearly 10 years was county attorney of Pawnee County. He is a member of the Commercial Law League of America, the American, Nebraska State, Lancaster and Pawnee County Bar Associations. His various other memberships include the Modern Woodmen of America, the Ancient Order of United Workmen and the Nebraska State Historical Society. He is a member of the Sons of the American Revolution, the Royal Arch, Knights Templar and Shrine bodies of Masonry, and the Eastern Star, and is an elder and member of the official board of the Christian Church. Residence: Pawnee City. (Photograph in Album).

Harry Edward Dorwart

One of the younger members of the medical profession of Dawson County, is Harry Edward Dorwart, who is engaged in the practice of medicine and surgery at Overton. He was born at Friend, Nebraska, March 13, 1903, the son of Daniel C. and Anna I. (Reilly) Dorwart. His father, who was a dentist, was born at Friend, October 5, 1873, and died there, May 4, 1930. His mother, who was born at Peoria, Illinois, October 15, 1873, is the daughter of Thomas and Margaret (Breen) Reilly, natives of County Cork, Ireland.

Dr. Dorwart was graduated from the Friend High School in 1921, was a student at the University of Nebraska, 1921-23, and in 1927 received the M. D. degree at Creighton University where he was president of Phi Chi. He has practiced his profession at Overton since 1927, with the exception of the two and one half years, 1927 to 1930, he spent in Cleveland, Ohio, in post graduate work, majoring in surgery, and is active in community affairs there. He holds membership in the Lions Club, the Dawson County Medical Society, the Nebraska State Medical Society, and the Country Club of Lexington, Nebraska.

He is a member of the Nebraskana Society and is affiliated with Immaculate Conception Catholic Church at Elm Creek, Nebraska. Among his favorite recreations are: football; hunting; fishing; reading; and flower gardening.

Dr. Dorwart married Emily May Waters at Omaha, Nebraska, October 7, 1931. Mrs. Dorwart was born at Westerville, Nebraska, August 27, 1907, the daughter of W. W. and Stella (Brown) Waters, of Lexington. Residence: Overton.

Edward Adolph Dosek

Edward Adolph Dosek was born December 1, 1898, in Wahoo, Nebraska, the son of Wencil Frank Dosek and Frances (Ceck) Dosek. His father was born in Bohemia, and was postmaster in Dwight, Nebraska, at which time he was vice president of the Postmaster's Association. Mrs. Dosek was born in Bohemia.

Mr. Dosek attended the Dwight High School, the Fremont Normal College and the University of Nebraska, professional State Teacher's Certificate.

His marriage to Philomena Catherine Kabourek took place in Dwight, November 25, 1919. She was born April 29, 1898, in Brainard, Nebraska . Their children are Edwin Francis, born October 9, 1921, Rita Marie born November 26 1923, Jerome, born March 14, 1925, and Marie Alice, August 30, 1929.

Edward Dosek taught in rural school four years and in the Dwight schools two years. He is affiliated with the Immaculate Conception Catholic Church and the Knights of Columbus. Mr. Dosek is secretary of the Ulysses Commercial Club and is a member of the Nebraskana Society. Residence: Ulysses.

Charles William Doty

Charles W. Doty was born at Darlington, Wisconsin, June 6, 1861, the son of George Doty. His father died at Camp Randall, Madison County, Wisconsin, in 1861, and his mother died at Baraboo, Wisconsin.

Dr. Doty, who has been a physician and surgeon at Beaver Crossing since 1888, received his high school education at Darlington, and later attended Rush Medical College in Chicago, where he was graduated in 1888. In connection with his medical practice, he has been connected with the drug business at Beaver Crossing for many years.

He served as coroner of Seward County for some time, was state senator from both Seward and Butler counties for 12 years, and for the past 40 years has been United States Pension Examiner. During the World War he was active in Liberty loan drives, acted as chairman of the Four Minute Men, and took part in Red Cross work.

Dr. Doty is a member of the Nebraska State Medical Society, the Seward County Medical Society, and the Beaver Crossing Chamber of Commerce. He is a Mason and an Odd Fellow, and is affiliated with the Democratic party.

He was married to Jane Caroline Schreiter at Darlington, June 4, 1891. Mrs. Doty, who was born at Darlington, October 26, 1864, is of German and English descent. They have two children: Helen S., born July 8, 1895, who married Roscoe E. Shutt; and David A., born December 24, 1900, who married Alice O'Brien. Helen is a graduate of the University of Nebraska, where she held membership in Delta Gamma and the Mortar Board. David is a physician and surgeon at Denver, Colorado, and is also a graduate of the University of Nebraska. Residence: Beaver Crossing.

Howard McGregor Doty

Howard McGregor Doty, assistant cashier of the First National Bank of Hastings, was born at Trumbull, Nebraska, March 8, 1897, and has resided in Adams County all his life. He is the son of Charles and Mary Lytel (McGregor) Doty, both of whom are living. Charles Doty was born in Plano, Illinois, July 31, 1862, of Holland Dutch and English descent, and is a farmer. His wife, who was born at Iowa City, Iowa, April 6, 1868, is of Scotch and English descent.

Educated in School District No. 59 of Adams County, Nebraska, Mr. Doty was graduated from Hastings High School in 1915, and immediately entered the employ of the First National Bank. He has advanced through various positions to that of assistant cashier of that organization.

He was united in marriage to Dorothy Jane Matticks at Hastings on October 18, 1928. Mrs. Doty, who was born at Ridge Farm, Illinois, May 3, 1900, is of Welsh extraction. They have no children. Mr. Doty is a Republican. He was a private in the Air Service of the Regular United States Army during the war period, and is a member of the American Legion.

Active in the civic and fraternal life of his city, Mr. Doty is a member of the Chamber of Commerce, the Kiwanis Club, the Red Cross, the Elks and the Masons. In the last mentioned he is a member of all branches except 32nd degree Masonry. Mr. Doty's religious affiliation is with the Methodist Episcopal Church. His hobby is reading. Residence: Hastings.

James Mouton Doty

James Mouton Doty retired farmer and banker, and one of Stanton County's foremost citizens, was born on the farm of his father in Iowa, December 6, 1857. He is the son of Luther and Mary (Hillborn) Doty, the former a teacher and successful farmer. Luther Doty was born in Richland County, Ohio, August 15, 1826, of Scotch-Irish and Dutch ancestry, and died at Pilger, October 2, 1895. Mary, his wife, died in 1880.

After attending public school, Mr. Doty engaged in farming. He is serving as vice president of the Farmer's National Bank and a member of its board of directors. A Democrat, he was unsuccessful candidate for the state legislature, and has been chairman of the local school board twenty successive terms. His religious affiliation is with the Methodist Episcopal Church.

Mr. Doty's ancestry is traced to the *Mayflower*, and he is eligible to the Sons of the American Revolution. He is a member of the Modern Woodmen of America, and in recognition of his activities toward the advancement of his community he has been awarded life membership in The Nebraskana Society.

On January 26, 1881, Mr. Doty was married to Nettie M. Simpson at Shelby, Iowa. Mrs. Doty was born in Clinton County, Iowa, December 6, 1861, and died at Pilger, July 6, 1931. She was of French, Irish and English descent. To them were born five children four of whom are living: Ivan, born March 31, 1882, married Cythia Rhudy, and died June 2, 1927; Glen, born January 13, 1891, married Fern Nellor; Lloyd, born April 23, 1892, married Lovina Snyder; Elta, born September 5, 1894 married Kile R. Martin; and Elna, born February 6, 1900, married Grant A. Lothrop. Residence: Pilger.

Frank Ellis Doud

Born at Plattsmouth, Nebraska, July 25, 1864, Frank Ellis Doud is the son of John Fletcher and Lovisa Bickwell (Ellis) Doud. His father, who was a student, scholar, and teacher, was born at North Hero, Vermont, April 2, 1824, and for a number of years engaged in farming; he died at Plattsmouth. His mother, who was a teacher and musician, was born at Potsdam, New York, September 12, 1826, and died at Plattsmouth, September 1, 1890. She was graduated from the Miss Willard Seminary at Poughkeepsie, New York, and later was a governess in South Carolina.

Mr. Doud attended the Plattsmouth High School, and for two years was a contributor on the *Franklin County Tribune* at Bloomington, Nebraska, where he resided. For the past 16 years he has served as president of the Bloomington Equity Exchange. Politically, he is a Democrat.

He was married to Minnie Carroll at Shenandoah, Iowa, in September, 1890. Mrs. Doud, whose ancestry is Scotch and Irish, was born at Decatur, Illinois, in 1868. To them were born four children: Ralph, who married Kate Miller of Plattsmouth; Keitha, who married Charles Swanda, of Chicago; Wayne, who married Vera Helfrich, of Bloomington; and Ruth, who married Carl Osterbehr, of Franklin. Residence: Bloomington.

John Edward Dougherty

John Edward Dougherty, lawyer at York, Nebraska, has been a resident of this state all his life. He was born at York, February 11, 1899, the son of John and Julia Hanna (Hayes) Dougherty. His mother was born at Peoria, Illinois, August 23, 1859, and died at York, June 12, 1927.

Mr. Dougherty was graduated from St. Mary's High School in 1918, was a student at St. Mary's College in the art department for a time, and received the LL. B. degree at Creighton University in 1927. He was editor-in-chief of Creighton literary publications, was class president in 1926, and held membership in Alpha Sigma Tau and Gamma Eta Gamma, legal fraternity. He was awarded an honor key.

Since his admission to the bar in 1927, Mr. Dougherty has been engaged in legal practice at York where he is a member of the York Rotary Club, the Commercial Club, and St. Joseph's Catholic Church. He is a member of the Nebraska State Bar Association, the American Bar Association, The Nebraskana Society, and the Elks. In 1918 he was a member of the Student Army Training Corps at St. Mary's College.

He was united in marriage with Lola Esther Brooks at Omaha, on November 20, 1930. Mrs. Dougherty, who was a private secretary before her marriage, was born at Grand Island, January 16, 1904, and died at York, September 19, 1930. Mr. Dougherty's recreations include hunting, camping, fishing and golfing. He is a Democrat. Residence: York.

Mattie Marguerite Douglas

Mattie M. Douglas, clubwoman and community worker of Cass County, Nebraska, was born at New Virginia, Iowa, June 12, 1866. She is the daughter of George W. and Letticia (Irwin) Hylton. Her father, a merchant and farmer, was born in Hendrix County, Indiana, September 22, 1837, and died at Elmwood, Nebraska, September 12, 1923. He is descended from English and French ancestors.

Her mother, a teacher and housewife, was born of Presbyterian Scotch-Irish parents at Ballybay, Ireland, April 9, 1841, and died at Elmwood, February 19, 1923.

Mrs. Douglas has spent her adult years in social service, political activity, and community club work. In 1901, she was graduated from Weeping Water Academy, and later attended Doane College, at Crete, and the normal college in Lincoln, earning her way. For several years she taught in the public schools, and has held many offices in the local clubs and churches. She served as county and precinct chairman of the Republican party, and as committee-woman for this organization. She has taken part in several home talent plays in her church; is a painter of some ability, having won several prizes at state fairs; and was recently elected president of the Cass County Federation of Woman's Club. A member of the Elmwood library board, her aim is service to her community.

On June 20, 1894, she was united in marriage with George H. Douglas, at Elmwood. Dr. Douglas, who is a physician and surgeon, is a graduate of Washington University, St. Louis.

Born at Clayton, Illinois, June 30, 1863, he is a descendant of the Revolutionary War soldier, Joseph Douglas, who came to Rockingham County, Virginia, from Scotland. Three children were born to this marriage, two of whom are deceased. Leland Dwight, was born July 31, 1897, and died October 3, 1909. Jamie Irwin was born May 13, 1910, and died November 28, 1911. Ellen Marie, who was born June 6, 1906, is a graduate of Wesleyan University, at Lincoln, and was married to Dr. T. A. Pitts, of Columbia, South Carolina, September 7, 1928. A niece of Dr. Douglas, Alma L. Murray, has lived in their home since her early childhood. She is a graduate of the University of Nebraska, and is principal of the high school at Campbell, Nebraska.

Mrs. Douglas has lived in Nebraska for 39 years. She is a member of the Order of Eastern Star, the Rebekahs, and the Royal Neighbors. She is affiliated with the Methodist Episcopal Church of Elmwood. She has served as a reporter for one Lincoln and one Omaha paper for a number of years. Her hobbies are painting and dramatics. She is a Republican. Residence: Elmwood.

William James Douglas

William James Douglas, prominent physician and surgeon, was born at Pekin, Maryland, August 6, 1878, and has resided in Nebraska for the past forty-two years.

His father, William J. Douglas, was born in Glasgow, Scotland, and died at Leadville, Colorado, in 1876. He came to the United States, settling in Maryland in 1856. He was prominent in public affairs. His wife, Catherine Reid, was born in London, England, and died at Omaha, February, 1927. Her ancestry was Irish and English.

Dr. Douglas attended the public schools of Omaha and was graduated from high school there in 1896. In 1900 he received the degree of Bachelor of Medicine from the Nebraska State University, and since that time has been in active practice. A Republican, he has served as mayor of Atkinson several terms, and as councilman eight terms. He is chairman of the Holt County Red Cross, and surgeon at the Atkinson General Hospital.

His marriage to Anna May Campbell was solemnized at Atkinson, Nebraska. Mrs. Douglas was born at O'Neill, Nebraska, January 16, 1887, of Irish descent. They have one daughter, Cathryn D., born October 29, 1905, who is married to David Adler of Evanstown, Illinois. She is a graduate of Duchesne College at Omaha and attended the University of Nebraska and the Washington University, St. Louis.

During the World War Dr. Douglas held the rank of captain in the medical section of the United States Army, attached to the 86th Infantry, 18th Division. He was also a Four Minute speaker and a member of the Advisory Council. At the present time he is a member of the Reserve Officers Association, and is a major and executive officer of the 123rd General Hospital of Lincoln, Nebraska.

Among his professional organizations are the American, the Nebraska State, and Elkhorn Valley Medical Societies. He is counsellor of the Nebraska State Medical Society. He is a member of the Lions Club at Atkinson, the Elks, Knights of Columbus, Woodmen of the World, and Modern Woodmen of America. His hobby is the promotion of civic welfare. His favorite sport is golf. Residence: Atkinson. (Photograph on Page 341).

William Arthur Dowding

Born at Seward, Nebraska, January 19, 1888, William Arthur Dowding is the son of James Alfred and Emma Sarah (Roberts) Dowding. His father, who was a jeweler and watch maker, was born at Red Hill, England, May 19, 1848, and is still living; he came to this country in the late 1860's from England. His mother, who was a devout church worker and a member of the Order of Eastern Star, was born at Westhope, England, on May 30, 1858, and died at Seward, January 31, 1930.

Mr. Dowding attended the public schools at Seward and in 1907 was graduated from the high school there. He was prominent in dramatics in high school, was president of the senior class, and is a member of various municipal and fraternal bands at Seward. He is active in swimming and was examiner for the American Red Cross in life saving.

After graduation from high school Mr. Dowding became connected with the office work of his county

WILLIAM JAMES DOUGLAS, M. D.

government and after four years in this work moved to Omaha, Nebraska, where he was employed by the Chicago, Burlington & Quincy Railroad Company. Later he served as a salesman and for the past few years has been connected with the Postal Service at Seward. He was a member of the board of education for two terms, in the capacity of secretary, and for several years has been assistant scout master and swimming instructor for the American Red Cross. He is a Royal Arch Mason, Knight Templar and Shrine member, and holds membership in the Welfare Society and the Red Cross. He is an elder in the First Presbyterian Church of Seward, is a member of the Nebraskana Society, and has always been an ardent promoter of civic affairs.

He married Edna M. Thompson at Albion, Nebraska, June 18, 1913. Mrs. Dowding, whose ancestry is Scotch and Pennsylvania Dutch, was born in Seward County, January 12, 1889. Three children were born to their marriage: James, May 22, 1914; Billy, September 16, 1918; and John, April 28, 1925. Residence: Seward.

Marquis LaFayette Dowell

Marquis L. Dowell, farmer, banker and merchant of Salem, Richardson County, Nebraska, was born May 3, 1865, at Edmonton, Metcalfe County, Kentucky. John Sandy Dowell, his father, who was born at Albemarle, Virginia, May 9, 1819, and died at Beechville, Metcalfe County, Kentucky, May 22, 1889, was a tobacco merchant who was a prominent citizen in the south. A Democrat, he cast his first vote for Henry Clay. He was a Mason, and was affiliated with the Baptist church.

Marquis L. Dowell was educated in the public schools of Kentucky. A resident of Nebraska for forty-seven years he has been, consecutively, a steam shovel engineer for eleven years; a merchant for thirty-two years; and at the present time is president of the Bank of Salem, and has farming interests near that town. In 1889 he helped engineer the cut and approach for the C. B. & Q. railroad bridge at Rulo, Nebraska.

On December 24, 1890, he was married to Harriet Lucy Davis at Salem. Mrs. Dowell, who was born at Fayette, Wisconsin, on June 28, 1869, is of English descent and is a member of the Daughters of the American Revolution.

Mr. Dowell is a life member of the Red Cross and during the World War was local chairman of the food conservation committee and a member of the various loan drives committees. He is a member of The Nebraskana Society, the Parent-Teachers Association, and the First Congregational Church of Salem. He is a Mason and a member of the Democratic party. His hobby is reading. Residence: Salem.

William Leo Dowling

Born at Randolph, Iowa, May 8, 1880, William Leo Dowling has lived in Nebraska most of his life. His father, Solomon Miller Dowling, a farmer, was born at New London, Canada, January 5, 1851, and died at Madison, Nebraska, November 23, 1930; his ancestry was Irish. Martha (Dilts) Dowling, his mother, whose ancestry was Scotch, was born at Wabash, Indiana, July 5, 1849, and died at Madison, October 30, 1911.

Mr. Dowling attended the high school at Madison, was a student at Fremont College. He was a student at the University of Nebraska from 1901 to 1903 where he was a member of the N Club and Alpha Theta Chi. He received a university letter in track and football.

Since 1908, when he was admitted to the bar, Mr. Dowling has been engaged in the practice of law at Madison in the following law firms: Allen & Dowling; Dowling, Warner & Moyer; Dowling, Theilen & Dougherty. He was county attorney of Madison County, 1915-17, 1917-19, and in 1924 was a candidate for judge of

the Supreme Court of Nebraska. He is a member of the American Bar Association, the Nebraska Bar Association, the Kiwanis Club, Nebraska State Historical Society, and the Nebraskana Society His fraternal organizations are Masons, Odd Fellows, Knights of Pythias, and the Elks. His favorite sport is golf.

On August 21, 1906, he was married to Willa Cartha Allen at Madison. Mrs. Dowling, who was born at Ackley, Iowa, March 16, 1882, is the daughter of William V. Allen, United States senator, and is descended from Captain A. Allen, an officer in the American Revolution. Blanche (Mott) Allen, mother of Mrs. Dowling traces her ancestry to the American Revolution. She was born August 17, 1847. William V. Allen, father of Mrs. Dowling, was born January 28, 1847, in Madison County, Ohio, and died January 12, 1924. At the time of his death he was judge of the 9th Judicial District Court.

To Mr. and Mrs. Dowling were born four children, Imogene, July 4, 1907; Lyle Robert, January 4, 1909; John William, June 24, 1911; and Allen Vincent, February 4, 1913. Lyle is associate editor of the Omaha World Herald. John W. is a graduate student and instructor at the University of Wisconsin. Residence: Madison.

Lorin George Downing

Lorin George Downing, a resident of Nebraska for the past 45 years, was born at Juneau, Wisconsin, July 28, 1883, the son of George and Lavinia (Skinner) Downing. His father, who is vice president of the Peerless Laundry Company of Los Angeles, California, was born at Bristol, Vermont, January 27, 1854. His mother was born in Nova Scotia, November 7, 1853.

Mr. Downing received his education in the Kearney High School, Kearney, Nebraska, and the Chicago Business College. After his return from business college, Mr. Downing clerked for his father who was operating the George H. Downing Lumber and Coal Yards, which is now the Tollefsen and Elliott Lumber and Coal Company. He has been president and general manager of the Kearney Laundry and Dry Cleaning Company at Kearney for the past 27 years. He is a member of the Kearney Chamber of Commerce and Rotary Club, and holds membership in the Red Cross and St. Luke Episcopal Church. He is a member of the Elks, Masons, and the Kearney Country Club.

He was married at Kearney, June 18, 1905, to Armada Maddux who was born at Buda, Nebraska, in October, 1887. They have two children, Rollin, born August 3, 1906, who married Bernice Bailey; and Willis, born September 22, 1907. They are both connected in business with their father. Residence: Kearney.

Dora Goodson Doyle

Dora G. Doyle was born at Birmingham, Van Buren County, Iowa, the daughter of Solomon and Elizabeth (Harris) Goodson. Her father was a real estate dealer. Her mother was extremely active in religious affairs.

Mrs. Doyle attended the public school at Mount Pleasant, Iowa, and later was a student at the Birmingham College. Since 1921 she has been policewoman at Lincoln, Lancaster County, Nebraska. She has lived in this state for the past 47 years. She is a member of the International Association of Policewomen; the Red Cross; Social Welfare Society; and the Fraternal Aid Union.

She is a member of the Young Women's Christian Association, and the Women's Christian Temperance Union. She is affiliated with St. Paul's Methodist Episcopal Church of Lincoln. She is a Republican.

She was united in marriage with Shelton Edward Doyle at Ottumwa, Iowa, May 29, 1870. Mr. Doyle, who was a contractor, was born at Clayton, Illinois, and died at Lincoln, May 29, 1899. Five children were born to them: Harry, who married Elizabeth Ryan, and who died September 12, 1928; Mabel, who married George Vanderpool; Irene, who died in 1884; James Shelton, who married Virginia Nicholas; and Edwin Eugene who married Margaret Barnes. Residence: Lincoln.

James Bartholomew Doyle

J. B. Doyle, merchant, was born at Ponca, Nebraska, April 23, 1891, son of Bartholomew and Margaret Eletha (Burke) Doyle. His father was born in Chatham, Canada, March 20, 1853, and died in Ponca, December 6, 1912. His mother, who was born at Galena, Illinois, April 9, 1853, is of Irish descent.

Upon the completion of his elementary education in the Ponca public school, J. B. Doyle attended Ponca High School, graduating in 1909. He was married to Ethel Lione Rice at Ponca, January 14, 1914. Mrs. Doyle was born in Dixon County, Nebraska, August 20, 1893. There are four children, Margaret Elvira, born May 18, 1916; Mary Phyllis, born September 2, 1917; James Elmer, born May 23, 1921, and Elizabeth Ann, born October 17, 1925.

Mr. Doyle has always resided in Dixon County, and after leaving school worked for ten years for William Lester. For the past twelve years he has been the owner and operator of his own meat market at Ponca. He is a Democrat. He was a member of the Home Guard during the World War, and is a member of the Red Cross. A Catholic, he attends St. Joseph's Church and is a member of the Knights of Columbus and the Woodmen of the World. Residence: Ponca.

Louis Frederick Doyle

Louis Frederick Doyle, clergyman, and educator, was born at St. Louis, Missouri, February 27, 1891. He is the son of John L. and Adelia B. (Lyons) Doyle, the former a miner, born in Ireland, who came to America about 1865. He was born in 1844, and died at St. Louis, in April, 1905. His wife, Adelia, was born in County Mayo, Ireland, in December, 1850, and came to America when a young girl.

Father Doyle was graduated from Yeatman High School at St. Louis, in June, 1910, and entered St. Louis University, where he received his A. B. in 1921, and his A. M. in 1927. He was ordained to the Roman Catholic priesthood on June 16, 1926. He is an author of considerable note, and the following are some of his more outstanding works: *Dark Roses* (drama); *France* (drama); *The Master-Builder* (poem); *Renunciation* (poem), and *Courage* (poem), all of which were written between 1925-28. He is associate professor of English literature at Creighton University.

Father Doyle is interested in amateur dramatics. He is an honorary member of the Knight of Columbus, a member of the Jesuit Educational Association, and of the Nebraskana Society. Residence: Omaha.

Hugh Drake

Hugh Drake, lawyer and member of the Nebraska State Railway Commission, was born at Humphrey, Nebraska, August 3, 1891. His parents, Royal and Florence (Henderson) Drake, were of Colonial ancestry. The former was born at Muscatine, Iowa, October 25, 1859, and the latter in Illinois, October 12, 1866.

Mr. Drake was graduated from Humphrey High School in 1907, and entered the law school of the University of Nebraska. While still in school he took the state bar examination, and was admitted to practice by the Supreme Court of Nebraska in 1914.

In 1923 he was elected county attorney of Buffalo County on the Republican ticket, serving until 1927. Over a period of years he has been active in Republican county central committee work. In December 1928 he

resigned from the practice of law to become secretary of the Nebraska State Railway Commission. He was elected a member of the commission in 1931, for a term of six years. He is a member of the Nebraska State Bar Association, also.

He was married to Bonnie Hess at Wayne, Nebraska, on December 29, 1925. Mrs. Drake was born at Chambers, Nebraska, May 12, 1900. There is one son, Hugh Hess, born April 30, 1928. They are members of St. Mathews Episcopal Church at Lincoln.

During the World War Mr. Drake served three years with rank from private to first lieutenant. Since leaving the service in 1919 he has been a member of the American Legion and the Reserve Officers Association. A Mason for the past twenty years, he has been an Elk for 10 years, and a member of the Kiwanis Club since 1922. His sport is golf and his hobby is mechanics. Residence: Lincoln.

Oscar Andrew Drake

A leading professional man at Kearney, Nebraska, Oscar Andrew Drake is successfully engaged in the practice of law there. He was born at Humphrey, Nebraska, November 22, 1897, the son of Royal Prentice and Florence (Henderson) Drake, the former a lawyer at Muscatine, Iowa.

Mr. Drake was graduated from the high school at Humphrey, Nebraska, in 1914, and in 1921, was awarded the LL. B. degree at the University of Nebraska, where he was a member of the debating team and held membership in Phi Alpha Delta, Delta Sigma Rho, and Sigma Nu. He was admitted to the bar on November 20, 1918, and has been practicing at Kearney, Nebraska, ever since. He was the youngest man to ever pass the bar examination in the state of Nebraska.

He is a member of the Nebraska State Bar Association, is affiliated with the First Presbyterian Church of Kearney, and holds membership in the Kearney Chamber of Commerce and the Kearney Country Club. He is a member of the Royal Highlanders and of Kearney Chapter Number 23, Mount Hebron Commandery Number 12, Knights Templar, all bodies of the Ancient Free and Accepted Masons. His sports include golfing, basketball, and trout fishing.

He was united in marriage with Miriam Eckhardt at Virogqua, Wisconsin, August 20, 1927. Mrs. Drake, whose ancestry is Scotch and German, was born at Sylvan, Wisconsin, August 12, 1903. Mr. Drake has been chairman of the Republican Central Committee in Buffalo County, Nebraska, for several years. Residence: Kearney.

Robert Zale Drake

Robert Zale Drake, bridge builder, inventor and scientist, was born at Holton, Kansas, September 11, 1869, son of George W. and Martha M. (Parrott) Drake. George W. Drake was born at Zanesville, Ohio, September 8, 1832, and died at Holton, Kansas, August 19, 1899. He was a ranchman, contractor and banker, and was admitted to the bar, although he never practiced. He served in the Civil War from 1861-65. His ancestry was English. His wife, Martha M. Parrott, was born at Coshocton, Ohio, November 10, 1841, and died at Holton, March 22, 1909. Prior to her marriage she was a school teacher. She was of Irish descent.

Robert Z. Drake attended elementary schools from 1874-80 and was graduated from Holton High School in 1885. He attended a short term at Campbell University at Holton, Kansas, and has since been in the bridge building business. He was married to Minnie De Bra Miles at Kansas City, Missouri, June 6, 1893. She was born at Winchester, Indiana, July 6, 1865, and died at Redlands, California, May 30, 1900. She was of English descent. There are two children of this marriage, Grace, born January 16, 1897, who married Gottardo Tenchini, and Mary, born September 16, 1901, who married Peter Kiewit. Mr. Drake was married to Margaret Jean Truland at Omaha, on September 5, 1900. Mrs. Drake was born at Aberdeen, Mississippi, September 20, 1862. Before her marriage she was an accountant. Her ancestry is Irish.

Mr. Drake has been building bridges for the past forty years, approximately, and has not been connected with any association or combination during that time, but acts and bids entirely independent of other concerns. He was the originator of the standardized bridge, and the inventor of the transverse joist standardized bridge, as well as the multiple punch used in its manufacture. During his career he has erected more than thirty thousand bridges between the Mississippi River and the Pacific coast. He is also the inventor of the steel substructure pile, which, while being driven, picks up and attaches to itself two earthen cores, thereby making it possible to secure a perfect substructure for bridges, buildings, etc. There are now standing more than twenty-five thousand bridges on these steel pile substructures. Probably ninety-five per cent of the steel bridges in Nebraska are on this type of piling.

He was an early, if not the first observer of what may be called the negative or expulsive actions of wood cells when they are the cells of a piece of lumber, and first made commercially practicable the use and benefit to be had from this negative or expulsive cell action. The process, Called *Cold Sesoning of Lumber* was discovered by Mr. Drake. He invented the machinery, appliances and designed the standardized structures necessary in the art of cold seasoning. By this method lumber can be made 100% stronger, very much tougher, brighter in color and lighter in weight than by any other known process. It does not readily decay.

Mr. Drake is the owner of the Standard Bridge Company and the Standard Sesoning Society. He is not generally an officer in corporations in which he is interested. He is admitted to practice bridge and structural engineering in states requiring it. He has written newspaper articles and letters on steel pile substructures and on standardized bridge construction, and also on cold sesoning of lumber.

In politics, he is a Progressive. He is a member of the First Methodist Church of Omaha, and of the Masons and Elks. In communities where he has much business he belongs to the Chamber of Commerce. He is also a member of the United Commercial Travelers, and the Nebraskana Society.

His hobby is work for others. He believes that exhausting toil for human beings makes them in each act stronger and better men. He has had more happiness in life than any person known to him. He believes that most of the sorrow of the world comes from people who are living in some materially fine state trying to arouse in others admiration and consequent envy of this state of living. Residence: Omaha.

Francis S. Drath

Francis S. Drath was born at Herndon, Kansas, August 30, 1904, the son of F. H. and Mercedes (Miller) Drath. He was graduated from the Herndon Public School in 1917, and in 1921 was graduated from high school in Decatur County, Kansas. He was awarded his A. B. degree at the University of Nebraska in 1925.

He became a newspaper reporter in 1925, and two years later entered the editorial field. At the present time he is associate editor of the *Nebraska State Journal* at Lincoln. He has lived in Nebraska for the past 10 years.

On June 20, 1927, he was united in marriage with Pauline E. Campbell at Lincoln. Mrs. Drath, who is a designer, was born at Lincoln. Mr. Drath is a member of the Nebraskana Society. He is independent in politics. Residence: Lincoln.

Thomas Joseph Dredla

Thomas Joseph Dredla, distinguished lawyer of Saline County, has taken a prominent part in community affairs at Crete for some years. He was born at Crete, November 21, 1892, the son of Anton and Bessie (Drasky) Dredla. His father, who was engaged in the banking and insurance business for many years, was born at Zdar, Czechoslovakia, December 1, 1868, and died at Crete, May 26, 1931; he came to America on May 15, 1877. His mother was born in Czechoslovakia, August 16, 1870.

Mr. Dredla was graduated from Crete High School in 1911, and in 1915 received the LL. B. degree from the University of Nebraska. He is attorney for the Crete State Bank, the Farmers State Bank at Kramer, Nebraska, the Crete Conservative Mortgage Company at Crete, and the Crete Mills. He is a director in the Crete Loan and Savings Association, is a member of the Community Club and The Nebraskana Society.

During the World War Mr. Dredla was a four minute man and assisted in Red Cross and loan drives. He is a member of the American Bar Association, the Nebraska State Bar Association, and the Saline County Bar Association. He is a Mason, and a member of the Independent Order of Odd Fellows, Order of Eastern Star, and Z C B J. His hobby is travel.

A Republican, he has held the following public offices: county attorney of Saline County, 1918-23; 1927-31; chairman of the Republican county central committee, 1920-25; 1927-31; city attorney of Crete five years.

His marriage to Elsie Amelia Shebl was solemnized at Lincoln, Nebraska, September 15, 1915; she was born at Ravenna, Nebraska, March 1, 1893. Two children were born to them, Marion Elizabeth, July 20, 1919; and Thomas Joseph, Jr., November 20, 1921. Residence: Crete. (Photograph on Page 345).

Albert Vernon Dresher

Albert Vernon Dresher was born at Lock Haven, Pennsylvania, August 17, 1874, of a family of pioneer settlers in that state. His father, Samuel Dresher, was born at Centre Hall, Centre County, Pennsylvania, April 1, 1844, the third generation of the family in America. He served in the Civil War three years and eight months, and was wounded in the Battle of the Wilderness, later coming to Nebraska where he established a building contracting business. He died in Omaha, March 25, 1907.

Samuel Dresher married Helen Maurey, who was born at Williamsgrove, Pennsylvania, November 14, 1851. Her father was born at Frenchville, Pennsylvania, of French and German parentage, and her mother in Berkes County, of German and Holland-Dutch ancestry. Helen Maurey Dresher died at Clarinda, Iowa, August 1, 1915.

For more than thirty years Albert V. Dresher has been in business in Omaha. He is president of Dresher Brothers, Inc., and president of Dresher The Tailor, and is a member of the American Chemical Company, the Chamber of Commerce, the Omaha Executives Club, the Rotary Club and the National Association of Dyers and Cleaners of Washington, D. C., of which he is vice president.

He is also a member of the Mundatechnical Society of America and his fraternal organizations include the Modern Woodmen of America, the Woodmen of the World, the Knights of Pythias, the Elks and Eagles. He is a member of the Masons, and of the Scottish Rite and Shrine. His clubs are the Omaha Athletic and the Happy Hollow. He is a Lutheran and a Democrat.

On November 30, 1898, he was united in marriage to Nellie E. Garver, at Grant City, Missouri. Mrs. Dresher was born at Grant City, December 26, 1881, and is of German descent. Residence: Omaha.

THOMAS JOSEPH DREDLA

Herbert R. Dressler

Herbert R. Dressler, prominent banker of Nemaha County, Nebraska, was born in Nemaha County, November 12, 1892. His father, John I. Dressler, who is a farmer, was born in 1852 of German parentage. His mother, Bena (Hartman) Dressler, died in Nemaha County in 1899.

Mr. Dressler attended the public schools of Nemaha County and in 1908 was graduated from the Nemaha High School. Later he was graduated from the Nebraska State Teachers College at Peru. He attended the law school at the University of Nebraska where he was a member of Phi Alpha Delta.

He entered the banking business as bookkeeper at the Bank of Nemaha; was later made assistant cashier, cashier, and director. He served as cashier and director of the Bank of Ashby at Ashby, Nebraska, for a time. He was superintendent of schools at Johnson, Nebraska, for several terms. He is now cashier of the Bank of Nemaha; has been in the invoice department of Swift & Company at Omaha and connected with the War Finance Corporation at Omaha.

He married Helen May Hutcheson at Brush, Morgan County, Colorado, November 6, 1919. Mrs. Dressler was born at Blanchard, Page County, Iowa, October 31, 1895. They have two children: Barbara, born September 24, 1922; and Margaret, born June 20, 1925.

Mr. Dressler was an instructor in the Radio Theory School at Great Lakes, Illinois, in the navy department during the World War. He is a member of the American Legion at Auburn. He is a member of the Parent Teachers' Association; and is now serving as secretary of the school board at Nemaha. He is an Odd Fellow. He is affiliated with the Methodist Church. Politically, he is an independent. Residence: Nemaha.

Gerald Montgomery Drew

Gerald Montgomery Drew, lawyer, was born at Plattsmouth, Nebraska, June 9, 1875, son of Alva and Emily (Colvin) Drew.

He attended public and high schools at Plattsmouth, and was afterward a student at the University of Omaha Law School. He received his Bachelor of Laws degree from the University of Nebraska in 1902, since which time he has been active in the practice of law.

He is a member of the Nebraska State and Omaha Bar Association, the Red Cross, and the Masons. Residence: Omaha.

Glen Robert Driscoll

Glen R. Driscoll, leather executive of Omaha, was born at Altoona, Iowa, January 8, 1895, the son of Arthur and Alice May (Hughes) Driscoll. He attended the grade schools of Iowa, and at the age of 14, began his business career in the employ of the wholesale leather company of Thomas A. Mansfield at Des Moines. In 1912 he became a traveling salesman for Henry Kleine & Company of Chicago, and later entered the leather business for himself, when he organized the Driscoll-Stanley Company at Omaha, July 1, 1923.

In 1928, he purchased his partner's interest in the concern and changed the firm name to the Driscoll Leather Company. He is now president, treasurer, and general manager of this organization. He is interested in all civic affairs and is a member of the Omaha Chamber of Commerce and the Omaha Rotary Club. He is a Mason, and is affiliated with the First Presbyterian Church of Omaha. His favorite sport is golf.

His marriage to Sarah May Patterson was solemnized at Des Moines, Iowa, December 25, 1916. Mrs. Driscoll was born at Des Moines, October 17, 1894. Four children were born to them; John, born June 16, 1919, who died

February 28, 1930; Barbara Jean, born July 28, 1925; Carolyn Ann, born September 21, 1927; and Sallie May, born January 17, 1931. Residence: Omaha.

Charles Myron Druse, Jr.

Since 1919 Charles Myron Druse, Jr., has been engaged in the insurance, loans and real estate business at Cambridge, Nebraska. He was born at Friend, March 27, 1897, son of Charles Myron and Mary Elizabeth (Stephen) Druse. His father, born at Earlville, Illinois, April 19, 1863, came to Nebraska in 1880 and was consecutively a store keeper, postmaster, and insurance man. He is descended from John Druse who came to America from Scotland in 1784 and settled in Otsego County, New York, later moving to Portland, New York, where he owned extensive land interests. John Druse was an ardent Whig and took a prominent part in the political affairs of his state.

Mary Elizabeth (Stephens) Druse, a leader in club work and educational activities for a number of years, was born at Taylorville, Illinois, September 11, 1870, and died at Cambridge, Nebraska, October 14, 1924. Her Dutch ancestors were pioneers in Ohio and Illinois in the early days, and her parents, James W. and Clara Stephens settled on a farm near Friend, Nebraska, in 1878.

Mr. Druse attended the public schools of Friend, Cambridge, and York, Nebraska, graduating from high school at Cambridge in 1915. He was a student at the University of Nebraska, 1915-17, where he was active in athletics and held membership in Sigma Nu. He is owner of the C. M. Druse Insurance & Real Estate Agency, at Cambridge, and holds membership in the Cambridge Community Club, the Cambridge Rotary Club, the Red Cross, and the Nebraskana Society. He is a member also of the American Legion and St. Paul's Episcopal Church.

On August 24, 1922, he married Hazel Jeannette Banwell at Norton, Kansas. Mrs. Druse, who was born at Orleans, Nebraska, August 24, 1904, was a bank clerk prior to her marriage. She is descended from the Sprague family who emigrated from England on the ship *Ann* and landed at Plymouth in 1623. Her grandfather, Dr. W. H. Banwell, was captain in the Civil War.

Mr. Druse's recreations include football, baseball, and reading. Residence: Cambridge.

Lawrence Dry

Lawrence Dry, clergyman of the Christian Church, was born at Chester, Nebraska, October 5, 1892, the son of Harley and Mary (Krause) Dry. His father, a farmer, was born at Allendale, Missouri, October 28, 1869, and was descended from early Americans. His mother was born at Bloomington, Illinois, August 16, 1874.

Mr. Dry served as pastor of the Peru Christian Church from 1914 to 1915. He was graduated from the Chester High School in 1911, received the A. B. degree at Cotner College in 1915, and was awarded the B. D. degree at Yale University in 1922. He was associate pastor of the First Christian Church of Lincoln, Nebraska, 1916-19, was pastor of the Mill Plain Union Church at Waterbury, Connecticut, 1927-32, and is now pastor of the Federated Church at Mitchell, Nebraska.

He is president of the Red Cross, is a member of the Mitchell Commercial Club, and holds membership in the Parent-Teachers' Association and the Masons. His social club is the Mitchell Country Club, and his favorite sport is golfing. Politically, he is a Republican.

On June 9, 1915, he married Bessie Adams at Lincoln, Nebraska. Mrs. Dry was born at Chester, August 16, 1892. They have two children: Elizabeth, born March 30, 1917; and Barbara, born June 12, 1922. Residence: Mitchell.

William Dry

William Dry, civic leader and farmer at Chester, Nebraska, has lived in this state since 1884. He was born at Allendale, Missouri, August 15, 1882, the son of Daniel and Rebecca Dry. His father, also a farmer, was born at Ducon, Illinois, April 4, 1845, and died at Chester, May 23, 1911; he was a Civil War veteran. His mother was born of English parentage at Salem, Indiana, February 18, 1842, and died at Chester, November 13, 1922.

Mr. Dry was active as a member of the high school debating team and in 1902 was graduated from the Chester High School. Later he attended business college at Lincoln for a year. From 1915 to 1918 he operated a general mercantile store, and has been a farmer in Thayer County since 1902. He is especially interested in church and school progress and has served as president of the board of the Church of Christ of Chester, Nebraska, for nearly 20 years. Since 1929 he has served as president of the board of education of the Chester High School.

During the World War Mr. Dry acted as a member of the county food board. He is an Ancient Free and Accepted Mason, and holds membership in the Odd Fellows and Nebraskana Society. He was married to Mae Isadora Harris at Chester, March 6, 1907. She was born at Shelbyville, Indiana, November 24, 1884, and died at Chester, April 13 1923. Five children were born to them: Doris, October 14, 1908; who married Clifford Palmer; Paul, August 21, 1910; Dean, April 1, 1912, who died February 26, 1913; Ruth, March 29, 1914; and Daniel, March 4, 1916. Doris lives near Chester, Paul is in the Orient, while Ruth and Daniel are living at home. Mr. Dry was married to Ella M. Crouse, November 24, 1926, at Chester. Residence: Chester.

Adolf Dudek

Adolf Dudek was born in Colfax County, Nebraska, October 13, 1889, the son of Frank and Josephine Dudek. His father, who was a farmer, was born in Czechoslovakia, came to the United States in 1877, and settled at Clarkson, Nebraska, where he died May 26, 1918. His mother was born in Czechoslovakia and came to this country in 1877. She died in Colfax County, May, 1891.

Mr. Dudek attended rural school and later took a commercial and teacher's course at Fremont Normal School, where he was graduated. He was a country school teacher for two years and in 1910 became cashier of the Citizens State Bank at Orchard, Nebraska. Since 1912 he has been cashier of the Farmers State Bank at Clarkson. He is a Democrat and served for about eight years on the Clarkson City Board.

He was married at Omaha, on December 2, 1913, to Mary Alva Telply. Mrs. Dudek was born at Colfax, October 3, 1890. Their daughter, Ardyth Elaine, was born August 2, 1914.

During the World War Mr. Dudek took part in all loan drives in his community. He is a member of the Red Cross; has been president of the Commercial Club for the past three years; and holds membership in The Nebraskana Society. He is a Mason. His religious affiliation is with the New Zion Presbyterian Church at Clarkson. His hobby is reading. Residence: Clarkson.

Emil E. Dudek

Emil E. Dudek, leading banker at Clarkson, was born April 14, 1884, son of Frank and Josephine (Fajman) Dudek. Frank Dudek was born in Nove Mesto, Moravia, January 14, 1846, and died at Clarkson, May 14, 1918. His wife, a native of Czechoslovakia, died at Clarkson in May, 1892.

Mr. Dudek attended public school and thereafter was a student at Fremont Normal College 1909-10. In Oc-

tober, 1911, he accepted a position as bookkeeper with the Farmers State Bank of Clarkson. In January, 1912, he was made assistant cashier, and in April, 1921, was made vice president, which position he now holds.

His marriage to Jennie Indra was solemnized at Clarkson, February 23, 1914, and to their union four children were born: Edmund E., born November 20, 1914, a student at the University of Nebraska; Frank J., and Helen J., twins, born February 28, 1919; and Richard A., September 3, 1926.

Always a leader in his community, Mr. Dudek is a member of the Board of Education since 1920. During five years of that time he has served as treasurer, and during 1928-30 was secretary. Mr. Dudek was elected chairman 1930-31 and again elected for another year in July, 1931.

A member of the Commercial Club for many years, he was elected treasurer of that organization in May, 1925, holding the position until May, 1929. During the World War Mr. Dudek was a member and drilled with the Clarkson Home Guard organization. He is a member of the New Zion Presbyterian Church and the Red Cross, and is a Democrat. Residence: Clarkson.

George Martin Dudley

George Martin Dudley, president of the Dudley Laundry Company, was born near La Porte, Indiana, February 17, 1873, son of George and Mary Anna (Reynolds) Dudley. The father, who was a liveryman, was born November 24, 1843, and died at Norfolk, April 24, 1916. Mary Anna Reynolds, daughter of Louis and Matilda (Wooster) Reynolds, was born August 9, 1842, and died at Norfolk, October 14, 1893. George Dudley served during the Civil War as a member of the Seventh Indiana Cavalry.

Mr. Dudley attended public school at Norfolk, and thereafter from 1901 until September 1, 1916, operated a transfer business there. On January 2, 1925, he incorporated under the name of the Dudley Laundry Company, with himself as president, the laundry business which he started on a small scale in 1916. At the present time forty persons are employed by this company, which also operates a linen and towel supply service, and a dry cleaning service.

Of his marriage to Hattie Louisa Boeck, there are two children, Darrel Darus, born at Norfolk, November 27, 1901; and Bonita Charlotte, born October 5, 1907. Darrel who is secretary-treasurer of the Dudley Laundry Company, married Joanna Roberts, at Norfolk, September 24, 1924, they have two sons: George Robert, born August 7, 1927, and Darrel Douglas, born July 15, 1928. Bonita Charlotte married Frank Roy Denton, at Lincoln, October 28, 1927; they have one daughter, Louise Ann, born September 1, 1928. Mrs. Dudley was born in Germany, February 17, 1877, daughter of John and Louisa (Schultz) Boeck.

Mr. Dudley is a Republican. He has resided in Nebraska since 1887, and has been prominent in civic affairs at Norfolk for some time. He is affiliated with the Trinity Episcopal Church, is a member of the Chamber of Commerce (director 3 years), the Rotary Club, and is a life member of The Nebraskana Society. He served as president of the Nebraska Laundry Owners Assocation in 1925. Residence: Norfolk. (Photograph in Album).

Gleason A. Dudley

Gleason A. Dudley, editor of the *Walthill Times* at Walthill, Thurston County, Nebraska, since 1911, was born near Ashmore, Coles County, Illinois, August 23, 1868. His father, Eli Dudley, who was a farmer, was born near Ashmore, January 17, 1840, and died at Ashmore, August 29, 1920; an ancestor, Governor Thomas

Dudley, came to this country in 1629, and settled in Massachusetts, serving as the second governor of the Massachusetts Bay Colony.

His mother, Margaret Nash (Brown) Dudley, was born at Madison, Indiana, July 5, 1841, and died at Charleston, Coles County, Illinois, April 14, 1922. She was of Scotch descent through the paternal line and of Irish ancestry on the maternal side.

Mr. Dudley attended rural school and a private academy at Ashmore, and in 1898 was graduated from the University of Chicago with the A. B. Degree. Previous to that he attended Illinois State Normal College, for a time. He was teacher of physics at the Sioux City High School from 1898 to 1904, was the manager of a lumber yard for four years, and has served as editor of the *Walthill Times* since that date. He is the owner of Illinois real estate which he inherited.

During the World War, Mr. Dudley took an active part in various activities through his newspaper. He is a member of the Lions Club of Walthill, the Nebraskana Society, the Red Cross, and the Walthill Presbyterian Church, and served 6 years on the local Board of Education. He is a Mason, and is a member of the Odd Fellows and the Knights of Pythias. He is a Republican.

His marriage to Carrie Ida Selby was solemnized at Council Bluffs, Iowa. Mrs. Dudley, who was supervisor of music in the Walthill High School for 14 years, was born near Maxwell, Story County, Iowa, December 12, 1873. They have one daughter, Margaret Selby, born March 7, 1906, who was graduated from the Walthill High School in 1924, and also was graduated from the Western College for Women, at Oxford, Ohio, June, 1928, and is now a teacher in the Cincinnati public schools. Residence: Walthill. (Photograph in Album).

Frederick Charles Duerfeldt

Frederick Charles Duerfeldt, Ford dealer, was born at Williamsville, Nebraska, June 30, 1867, son of Frederick Charles and Catherine (Schnapp) Duerfeldt.

His father was born in Preisen, Germany, March 6, 1830, and died at Williamsville, Nebraska, May 2, 1877. He was a cigarmaker. His wife, Catherine, was born in Preisen, Germany, September 26, 1831, and died at Williamsville, November 29, 1876.

Upon leaving country school, Mr. Duerfeldt became a rancher. For a number of years thereafter, he was a lumber dealer and then became engaged in the automobile business. For some time he handled Buick cars and at the present time handles the Ford dealership at Gordon. He is a Republican and has served several years on town and county boards.

He was married on May 1, 1894, to Mary Elizabeth Margrave at Gordon. Mrs. Duerfedt was born at Albany, Nebraska, January 6, 1873. To them were born five children, four of whom are living: George, born January 3, 1896, married Florence Ulton, and is in business in California; Fred Thomas, born March 24, 1898, died May 6, 1898; Kathyrn, born November 13, 1900; Clifford, born November 10, 1902, married Jane Seaman; and Leonard, born January 6, 1906. Clifford is lieutenant in the United States Navy, while Kathryn is a lawyer's secretary at Gordon.

Mr. Duerfeldt is a member of the Presbyterian Church and the Kiwanis Club. Residence: Gordon.

William Parker Duey

William Parker Duey, farmer, was born in Carlisle Springs, Pennsylvania, September 4, 1879, son of Joseph and Amanda (Wolf) Duey. The father was born at Carlisle Springs, October 6, 1855, and died at Chester, November 27, 1920. The mother was born at Carlisle Springs, May 31, 1855, and died at Chester, October 6, 1906.

Since his graduation from the Chester public schools in 1899, William P. Duey has been engaged in farming. On April 30, 1902, he was married to Hannah George at Superior. She was born in Republic County, Kansas, November 18, 1881. Their children are as follows: Ruth, born April 26, 1903; died December 17, 1905; Grace, born January 2, 1906, married Harlan Ray; Edith, born September 24, 1909, married Eugene Nesmith; and Beth, born born April 1, 1914.

Mr. Duey is a member of the Methodist Episcopal Church. Residence: Chester.

Francis Michael Duffy

Francis Michael Duffy, physician, was born at Williamsburg, Iowa, March 4, 1896, son of John James and Bridget H. (Murphy) Duffy.

In 1914 Dr. Duffy was graduated from public school at Williamsburg, and in 1916 was graduated from high school there. He received his Masters degree and his medical degree from Creighton University.

His marriage to Ruth Ann Kelly was solemnized at Omaha, October 24, 1923. Dr. Duffy is a member of the American and Douglas County Medical Association and the Nebraska Academy of Science. Residence: Omaha.

James Albert Duffy

The Right Reverend James Albert Duffy, former bishop of Grand Island, and now titular bishop of Silando, was born at St. Paul, Minnesota, September 13, 1873, son of James J. and Johanna (Shiely) Duffy.

His father, born in Ennis, County Clare, Ireland, in 1843, came to America about 1858. He was a stonemason, builder and contractor, whose death occurred at St. Paul, Minnesota, in July 1879. His wife, Johanna, was born in New York City, in 1847, and died at St. Paul, in September, 1879.

Bishop Duffy was first educated in parochial schools, and from 1887-93 was a student in the academic department of St. Thomas Seminary. His ecclesiastical studies were pursued at St. Paul Seminary at St. Paul, Minnesota, which is affiliated with the Catholic University of America, at Washington, D. C.

He was ordained a priest at St. Paul, on May 27, 1899, and from that time until 1902 served as assistant pastor at Minneapolis. From 1902-04 he was pastor of St. Anne's Church, Le Soeur, Minnesota, and from 1904 until 1913 was rector of the Cathedral of Cheyenne, Wyoming.

Appointed bishop of Kearney in 1913, he moved to Grand Island when that city was made the See of the Diocese in 1917. There he served until 1931, when he resigned on account of ill health. As stated by the press "Bishop Duffy has been responsible for an enormous development of the Catholic Church in the 40,000 square miles which constitutes the Diocese of Grand Island. The most conspicuous of his works was the building and consecration of the beautiful Cathedral at Grand Island. Likewise it was a historic achievement when he founded the Nebraska edition of *The Register* in February of last year, and put it into every home of the diocese."

The growth of the diocese under his administration is a testimonial of real leadership. Upon his resignation Bishop Duffy was named titular bishop of Silando.

During the World War period he was an active participant in wartime activities. A member of the Red Cross in 1917, he has been a contributing member annually since that time. He is a member of the Chamber of Commerce and a life member of The Nebraskana Society, also of the Riverside Golf Club of Grand Island. Residence: Grand Island.

Peter William Duffy

Peter William Duffy, who has been a resident of Nebraska since 1887, is the son of Francis and Sarah (Mitchell) Duffy. His father, who was a farmer, was born at Belfast, Ireland, June 16, 1828, and died at Saratoga, Nebraska, February 19, 1898. His mother, the daughter of William Micthell and Esther (Gleason) Mitchell, was born in County Tipperary, Ireland, in 1843, and died at Genesee, Wisconsin, March 3, 1871.

Mr. Duffy was elected sheriff of Holt County for the first time in 1916, and has served five terms in this office. He has been a farmer and rancher near O'Neill, Nebraska, for nearly 40 years, and is active in community organizations there. He is affiliated with St. Patrick's Catholic Church, is a member of the Elks and the Knights of Columbus, and holds membership in The Nebraskana Society. His political preference is the Democratic party. Residence: O'Neill. (Photograph in Album).

Marie Dugan

Marie Dugan, newspaper woman, was born at Allen, Nebraska, the daughter of Horace and Joanna (Cavanagh) Dugan. Her father, who is a farmer, was born at Collins Station, Lancaster County, Pennsylvania, of Irish and German ancestry. His father was born in York County, Pennsylvania, and his grandfather in Ireland, coming to this country when a boy. His mother was a member of the von Kline family. Marie Dugan's mother was born on the family homestead near Allen, Nebraska, February 5, 1861. She was a teacher before her marriage. Her ancestry is French and Irish; the Cavanaghs having come to this country in 1842, and her great grandfather and grandmother having homesteaded in Nebraska in 1855.

Miss Dugan attended the rural schools of Nebraska and Missouri, and was graduated from St. Catherine's Academy at Jackson, Nebraska. She was also a student at Wayne Normal School and the University of Nebraska. She is now editor of the telegraph news department of the *Evening State Journal*, and has charge of the *Your Problems* department of the paper.

A member of the Quill, and Theta Sigma Phi. She is a member of the Catholic Daughters of America, and affiliated with St. Mary's Cathedral. Her hobbies are writing and reading and she has written several poems published in the *Household Magazine*. Politically, she is independent. Residence: Lincoln.

Raymond Hugh Duke

A merchant since 1903, Raymond Hugh Duke has been the owner and manager of a drug business at Mason City since 1905. He was born at Oxford, Indiana, April 27, 1880, son of Charles Newton and Elizabeth Naomi (McConnell) Duke. His father, a farmer, stockraiser and merchant, now retired, was born at Hamilton, Ohio, December 11, 1848, of Irish and English descent.

Elizabeth Naomi, his wife, was born in Oxford, Indiana, March 6, 1853, of Scotch ancestry. She is a member of the Daughters of the American Revolution.

Raymond H. Duke attended public school at Summerset, Iowa, and high school at Goodland, Indiana and Mason City, Nebraska. He afterward was a student at the Captial City Commercial College of Des Moines, and attended the Creighton College of Pharmacy.

A farmer until 1903, he was in the implement business one year and from 1903-05 was in the general merchandise business. He has since been a druggist. A Republican, he was justice of the peace 1922-26 and 1930-; has served as a member of the Custer County Republican central committee and of the village board, and at the present time is a member of the township board. He is secretary and treasurer of the Rat Lake Club, a member of the Mason City Golf Club, and is fond of golf, hunting and fishing.

During the World War he was registrar on the local draft board, secretary of the local Council of Defense, and a participant in other wartime activities. He is a

Mason, and past patron of the Order of Eastern Star, is affiliated with the Mason City Baptist Church, and is a member of the National Association of Retail Druggists.

On August 18, 1903, he was married to Zada Amsberry at Mason City. (*See Nebraskana*). They have one son, Ferris Ray, born July 8, 1904. Residence: Mason City.

Zada Duke

Born near the same home in which she now resides at Mason City, June 11, 1880, Zada Duke is the daughter of John Allan and Mary Catherin (Buckley) Amsberry. Her father, a farmer and stock raiser, was born at South Side, West Virginia, September 11, 1850, and came as an early pioneer settler to Nebraska, in 1878-79. He was a member of the state legislature 1929-30. Her mother, born at South Side, January 17, 1861, died at Mason City, Nebraska, May 2, 1918.

Zada Amsberry attended public school and was graduated from high school at Mason City, in May, 1896. During the year 1901-02, she was a student at Grand Island College. On August 18, 1903, she was married to Raymond Hugh Duke at Mason City. Mr. Duke, who is a pharmacist, was born at Oxford, Indiana, April 27, 1880. They have one son, Ferris Ray, born July 8, 1904.

Mrs. Duke has always taken an active part in Republican politics, is a member of the League of Women Voters, and has served as clerk and judge at general elections. Since 1905 she has assisted her husband in his drug business. During the late war she was local chairman of Liberty Loan and home demonstration food drives, etc.

She is a member of General George A. Custer chapter of the Daughters of the American Revolution, and its chaplain. She is affiliated with the Mason City Baptist Church, is past worthy matron of the Order of Eastern Star, and a life member of the Nebraskana Society. Her favorite sports are fishing, hunting and golf, while her hobbies are reading and club work. Residence: Mason City.

John William Dunaway

Born at McConnelsville, Ohio, October 29, 1853, John William Dunaway is the son of John Bartlett and Margaret (Cassidy) Dunaway. His father, born at Uniontown, Pennsylvania, January 27, 1825, was a salt manufacturer, whose father came from County Down, Ireland, in the 1760's. John Bartlett Dunaway was orphaned at the age of twelve and left to face the world alone. He was an Abraham Lincoln Democrat, an underground railway conductor and a private in the State Home Guard. He died at Overton, Nebraska, August 10, 1886.

Margaret Cassidy, wife of John Bartlett Dunaway, was born in McConnelsville, Ohio, and died at Overton, Nebraska. An active church and Sunday School worker, she was Irish on the paternal side and Pennsylvania Dutch on the maternal side.

John William Dunaway completed his high school course in May, 1869, receiving highest grade. On October 14, 1875, he was married to Evangeline Porter at Sherwoodsburg, Ohio, where she was born April 13, 1853. To them were born four children: Ernest Malcolm, born August 17, 1876, married Anna Brownell; Lida M., born October 30, 1879, married William A. Boucher; Everett B., born June 4, 1884, married Harriet McGinnis; and Emmett H., born March 27, 18889, married Dorothy Denney.

Mr. Dunaway sold harvesting goods for thirteen years and then went on the road for the Deering Harvester Company. For the past thirty-two years he has been city clerk, and in addition now holds the office of police judge and handles real estate and insurance. A progressive Democrat, he voted for President Hoover. Mr. Dunaway was formerly editor of the Overton Herald 19 years, and its owner 21 years.

He is the proud possessor of a medal direct from Washington which was made from a stolen German cannon and given for Red Cross collections and for the chairman of the precinct Council of Defense. His son, Emmett H. Dunaway, who held the rank of captain in the World War, now holds the rank in the Infantry Reserve Corps.

Mr. Dunaway is affiliated with the Methodist Episcopal Church. He is a Mason (Chapter to Commandery), a member of the Brotherhood, and for twenty years was a member of the board of education. Recently he was made a life member of The Nebraskana Society. Residence: Overton.

William Fredrick Dunbar

An outstanding farmer of Custer County, Nebraska, is William Frederick Dunbar whose parents were among the early builders of the state. He was born at Dunbar, Nebraska, November 11, 1864, the son of John and Anna Elizabeth (Watson) Dunbar, both of whom were pioneer settlers in Nebraska. His father, a farmer, was born in County Ulster, Ireland, in 1820, and died at Dunbar, in August, 1903, having served as a member of the justice court from 1858 to 1882; his appointment to the latter position was signed by Queen Victoria. His mother, whose father operated a plantation in the West Indies in the early 1830's, was born in County Ulster, in 1830, and died at Dunbar, in May, 1903.

Mr. Dunbar's parents came to Nebraska in the fall of 1856 through Chicago and St. Louis, making the trip from St. Louis by steamboat and landing at Nebraska City. They took a prominent part in early day Nebraska history and were among the first settlers of Otoe County.

Mr. Dunbar, who is a progressive farmer near Comstock, Nebraska, is vice president of the Conover Telephone Company of Sargent, and is president of the Comstock Independent Telephone Company. He holds membership in the Red Cross and the Nebraskana Society, and formerly served as a member of the justice court and as city assessor at Comstock.

He was married to Charlotte Elizabeth Latter at Dunbar, March 12, 1888. Mrs. Dunbar, whose ancestry is German, was born at Freien Dietz, Germany, July 20, 1870. They have the following children: Charlotte, born May 1, 1889, who married Robert H. Stone; Mamie Elizabeth, born November 17, 1890, who married Robert W. Hille; Wilda Beulah, born January 25, 1893, who married Edward S. Skolil, a banker; William Vernon, born September 8, 1897, who married Eunice Davis; Vesta Leona, born May 29, 1900, who married Professor Alva T. Friend; and John Frederick, born March 27, 1907, who is employed by the Bank of America, Los Angeles, California. William Vernon is a physician and surgeon at San Pedro, California. Residence: Comstock.

Robert Ross Duncan

Robert Ross Duncan, retired banker, was born at Buffalo, New York, February 17, 1857, son of James and Christeen (Ross) Duncan. His father, born in Aberdeen, Scotland, February 25, 1821, was a farmer whose death occurred at Ashkum, Illinois, March 9, 1908. The mother, also born in Aberdeen, on May 1, 1820, died at Ashkum on August 22, 1881.

Mr. Duncan attended public school, and for fifteen and a half years engaged in the hardware and implement business. Thereafter, for twenty-five years he was a banker, eleven years as cashier and fourteen years as president. In 1930 the bank paid its depositors in full and closed out the bank. At the present time Mr. Duncan is engaged in the insurance business.

He was married on May 5, 1890, to Agnes Temple-

ton McDonald at Ashkum. Mrs. Duncan, who was born at Chicago, November 6, 1861, is of Scotch descent.

Mr. Duncan is a Republican. He was chairman of a committee selling war saving stamps and bonds during the World War, is a 32nd degree Mason (Scottish Rite, Consistory No. 1, Omaha). For a number of years he served on the local school board, where he held the offices of president and treasurer. His favorite sport is baseball. Residence: Merna.

Alexander James Dunlap

Alexander James Dunlap was born at Washington Court House, Ohio, February 7, 1882, son of Samuel Crothers and Molly (James) Dunlap. His father was a farmer, born in Greenfield, Ohio, April 21, 1861, whose Scotch-Irish ancestors settled in America in 1690. He married Mollie James at Greenfield, Ohio, where she was born May 28, 1862, of Scotch-Irish and German decent.

In 1883 the Dunlap family came to Nebraska where Alexander J. Dunlap entered the Hastings public schools. He was graduated from Hastings High School in 1901, and received his B. Sc. from Hastings College in 1905. At that college he established five intercollegiate records in track, winning five letters. He later entered the law school of the University of Nebraska where he received his LL. B. in 1916. He was a member of the "N" Club and a letterman at the university two years.

From 1910 to 1917 he was superintendent of schools at Cambridge, Stromsburg and Central City, Nebraska. From 1919 to 1922, he was manager of the Western Good Road Service Company, and from 1925-30, was dean of the college of commerce of the University of Omaha. Since 1931 he has been executive dean.

He is the author of several syndicated publications, including *Unbeaten Paths, The Old Home Town* and *The Old Farm,* together with two books of verse *Shelled Corn* and *Goldenrod,* the last mentioned appearing in 1921.

Mr. Dunlap has always been active in politics, and was secretary of the Republican state central committee during 1918-19. He served as county attorney of Merrick County, elected on the Republican ticket, 1918-19, and as executive secretary of the Republican state central committee 1920-21. He was executive secretary of the Coolidge League of Nebraska, 1923-24.

During the War he was active in the usual drives, and was a member of the Four Minute Men, working principally in theatres; and is one of the three men accredited with the political movement and legislative enactments which resulted in the organization of the University of Omaha.

He is much in demand as an entertainer and lecturer, and fills approximately one hundred engagements a year as entertainer and lecturer on business subjects. His religious affiliation is with the Miller Park Presbyterian Church. He is a member of the National Educational Association and the Nebraska State Teachers' Association, and is a Mason.

On August 10, 1910, he was married to Caroline McCue at Hastings, Nebraska. Mrs. Dunlap was born at Afton, Virginia, October 6, 1883, and is of English and Scotch-Irish decent. Prior to her marriage she was a teacher. There are three children: Richard Leonidas, born April 18, 1912; Robert Alexander, born October 1, 1914, and John McCue, born December 20, 1918. Mr. Dunlap's hobbies are writing and aeronautics. Residence: Omaha.

Maynard W. Dunlap

Maynard W. Dunlap was born at Edgemont, Fall River, South Dakota, July 9, 1899, the son of George Allen and Flory Dunlap. His father, who was a general contractor, was born at McQuon, Illinois, July 29, 1856, and died at Tecumseh, Nebraska, August 6, 1930, the son of Dr. A. J. Dunlap. His mother, who was born at Ro-

WILLIAM ALPHEUS DUNLAVY

chester, New York, January 21, 1862, was the daughter of David and Maria Mook, early settlers in Johnson County.

Mr. Dunlap was graduated from the Tecumseh High School in 1917, and later was a student at the University of Nebraska, where he was a member of Alpha Tau Omega. He has lived in Nebraska for 26 years, and is now cashier of the Farmers State Bank, at Douglas, Nebraska.

His marriage to Helen A. Jobes was solemnized at Tecumseh, June 15, 1921. Mrs. Dunlap, the daughter of J. L. and Ella Jobes, was born at Johnson County, Nebraska, March 11, 1900. They have four children: George Allan, born June 7, 1925; Don Lee, born December 21, 1928; Jay Loren, born November 15, 1930; and Paul David, born November 15, 1930.

During the World War, Mr. Dunlap was a private in the S. A. T. C. at the University of Nebraska. He is a Mason, and is affiliated with the Methodist Episcopal Church at Douglas. Residence: Douglas.

William Alpheus Dunlavy

Born in Deersville, Ohio, June 26, 1856, William Alpheus Dunlavy is the son of James and Lucretia Taylor (Glandon) Dunlavy. The father, born in Deersville, February 22, 1825, was a school teacher, farmer and stockman, a breeder of Durham cattle and Chester White hogs. An ardent member of the Methodist Episcopal Church, he was a strong Whig and later a Republican. His father, born in Dublin, Ireland, came to America as a child in 1800, and married Elisabeth McBeth. She was of Irish descent, born in Pennsylvania.

Lucretia Taylor Glandon was born near Deersville, Ohio, March 10, 1829, and died at Holdrege, Nebraska, May 28, 1903. Her husband preceded her in death at Rushville, Illinois, January 18, 1869. Left a widow while very young, she was extremely devoted to her children, her chief outside interest being the Methodist Episcopal Church. Her parents were Pennsylvanians, her father, William Glandon, of Scotch extraction. Her mother's maiden name was Mary Magdalene Peacock.

William A. Dunlavy received his early education in country school, and later took Bishop J. H. Vincent's correspondence Chautauqua course, which he has supplemented by nights of study and reading. In early manhood he taught school five years, and has since engaged in farming and stock raising, at the present time in association with Newton R. Betts.

He was a member of the commission which appeared before Food Commissioner Herbert Hoover in the interests of stockmen of Nebraska on March 12, 1918, appointed by Governor Keith Neville. On November 1, 1918, he was appointed state and federal government representative in all farm bureau activities in Franklin County, by Governor Neville.

On August 29, 1880, he was married to Effie Gabriel at Rushville, Illinois, and they celebrated their golden wedding anniversary in 1930. Mrs. Dunlavy, who was born at Payson, Illinois, June 11, 1861, is fond of reading, music and travel. She and Mr. Dunlavy have visited Porto Rico and the Hawaiian Islands for study, recreation and pleasure, but have always taken much comfort in returning to their beautiful home in Franklin County.

Mrs. Dunlavy is the daughter of William Rowell and Sarah Elizabeth (Collins) Gabriel, the former of whom was a direct descendant of Abraham Gabriel, a private soldier in the Revolutionary War. There are four children, Alva James, born November 7, 1881, who married Doris Cole; Jessie, born April 5, 1883, who married Harvey Godfrey McComb; Vernon Atwell, born October 21, 1887, who married Elizabeth Warrick; and Lucretia, born January 4, 1890, who married Newton Riley Betts.

Alva is a dentist in Honolulu, Jessie is head of the extension service department of Oregon; Vernon is principal of high school and a fruit farmer at Sonora, California; while Lucretia and her family are on her father's farm in Franklin County. All are independent politically.

Mr. Dunlavy has been a member of the Methodist Episcopal Church for fifty-five years and has been active in Sunday School work. He has been a member of the Epworth League for many years, and for a number of years has been on the school board. He is a member of the Red Cross, and the local temperance organizations, and is a life member of The Nebraskana Society. Perhaps his greatest interests are traveling and collecting relics and souveniers from land and sea in American and foreign lands, but he also enjoys hiking in Yellowstone Park, the Grand Canyon and the Petrified Forests of Arizona. Residence: Bloomington. (Photograph on Page 351).

Arthur Leroy Dunn

A leading educator in Grand Island, Arthur Leroy Dunn has resided in Nebraska for the past twenty-seven years. He was born at Greenleaf, Kansas, April 18, 1886, son of Benjamin Joseph and Mary Elizabeth (Rines) Dunn. His father, who held the rank of first sergeant in the 9th Pennsylvania Volunteer Cavalry 1861-65, was born at Towanda, New Jersey, April 2, 1840. He died at Greenleaf, Kansas, September 18, 1891. He was of Scotch-Irish and Pennsylvania Dutch descent.

Mary Elizabeth Rines, his wife, was a native of Asberry, New Jersey, born March 9, 1845. She is the granddaughter of Obadiah Evans, who enlisted in the Revolutionary War with the First Establishment from the New Jersey Continental Line, on February 28, 1776, and who served until the end of the war.

Mr. Dunn attended country school, high school and business college, and afterward taught for a time in public schools. He then worked for a lumber company for a short period. His life work has been teaching in business colleges, in later years supplemented by managerial work along the same lines. At the present time he is president of the Grand Island Business College, and a director of the Nebraska College of Commerce at Hastings.

His marriage to Astella Clara Gingherick was solemnized at Grand Island, June 14, 1911, and to them was born one daughter, Nina Leanore, on August 2, 1915. Mrs. Dunn was born at Chadron, Nebraska, September 21, 1889.

Mr. Dunn is affiliated with the First Methodist Episcopal Church, is a member of the Chambers of Commerce at Grand Island and Hastings and is a life member of the Nebraskana Society. He is a Master Mason (Ashlar Lodge No. 33; 32nd degree, Hastings Consistory) and a member of Tehama Temple of the Shrine. He is also a member of Elks Lodge No. 604. Residence: Grand Island.

Ballard Dunn

Ballard Dunn, perhaps the best known newspaper man in Nebraska, is a native of Indianapolis, born September 16, 1877. He is the son of William McCullough and Amy (Talbot) Dunn. William McCullough Dunn, born at Lawrenceville, Indiana, January 8, 1844, was a physician who matriculated at Rush Medical College, receiving his M. D. from Louisville Medical College. He was engaged in the practice of medicine forty-five years. He died at Los Angeles in 1924. His wife, Amy Talbot Dunn, was a native of Kentucky. In early life she was associated with the original temperance and equal rights workers, Frances Willard and Elizabeth Cady Stanton. She died in Los Angeles in 1916.

Ballard Dunn's maternal grandfather was a grandson of Sarah Ballard, sister of Bland Ballard, who with his family went into Kentucky over the wilderness trial from Virginia with the first settlers who followed Daniel Boone, and who with all his family except a brother, James, and sister, Sarah, were massacred by Indians. Both the Dunn

BALLARD DUNN

and Talbot families have been in America for many generations.

Upon the completion of his elementary education in the country schools of Crawford County, Missouri, Mr. Dunn attended St. Louis High School two years. He received his LL.B. from the law department of Washington University in 1898 and in 1899 entered the newspaper field, in association with the *St. Louis Chronicle* and then the *Colorado Springs Gazette.* He continued with that paper one year, and then became connected with the *Chicago Inter-Ocean.* He has been associated successively with the *Chicago Daily News,* the *Chicago Evening Journal* (editor), and the *Omaha Bee-News* (editor in chief 1924-29). He is now editor and publisher of *The Omaha Journal.*

He served in the Spanish American War as a private First Missouri Volunteers. He holds the rank of major in the Special Reserves, and during the world war was chief of the bureau for suggestions and complaints of the United States Railroad Administration. In 1919 he was assistant chief of the Bureau of War Risk Insurance. He is a member of the United Spanish War Veterans.

On July 27, 1907, he was married to Eleanor Reese at Chicago. Mrs. Dunn was born at Chicago, December 24, 1876, and is of Danish descent.

Mr. Dunn is a Republican and during his career in Chicago was a member and president of the Cook County civil service commission. He is not affiliated with any church, but attends Christian Science meetings. He is an Elk and a Mason and a member of the Chamber of Commerce and Omaha Athletic Club. His hobby is the study of history, economics, philosophy and psychology. Residence: Omaha. (Photograph on Page 353).

I. J. Dunn

For the past 30 years I. J. Dunn has been a leading lawyer at Omaha, and has taken an active part in the political affairs of his community and state. He was born in Sarpy County, Nebraska, the son of pioneer Nebraskans, February 1, 1868, and has lived in Nebraska all his life. His father, Michael Dunn, was born in Tipperary, Ireland, in 1826, and in 1866 moved to Sarpy County, Nebraska, where he settled on a quarter-section of government land under the preemption law. He still owned the land at the time of his death at Papillion, on November 14, 1900. His mother was born of Scotch and Irish parents in County Antrim, Ireland, in 1836, and died at Papillion, October, 1926.

Mr. Dunn attended the rural schools of Sarpy county and later was a student at Creighton College for a time. He was admitted to the bar in 1900, and at the present time is a member of the firm Ziegler and Dunn at Omaha.

A Democrat, he was deputy county attorney of Douglas County, 1898-1902; assistant city attorney of Omaha, 1906-11; delegate at large to the Democratic national convention at Denver, 1908, and at Baltimore, 1912; was nominated, but declined the nomination, for congress, in 1896.

He is a member of the Nebraska Pioneer Organization, and the Douglas County Pioneer Society, an Elk, and a member of the Omaha Field Club. He is fond of out of doors recreations, including golfing, fishing, hunting, and hiking, and is a Catholic.

He was united in marriage to Maude M. Wingrove at St. Louis, Missouri, April, 1900. Mrs. Dunn was a teacher before her marriage. She is of an old English family at Buckhannon, Upshur County, West Virginia. Residence: Omaha.

Lester Lloyd Dunn

Lester L. Dunn, a lawyer at Lincoln, for the past 11 years, was born at Atlantic, Iowa, November 29, 1890, the son of Albert Lawrence and Carolyn Hester (Stier)

Dunn. His father, who was a merchant and broker, was born at Vinton, Iowa, July 4, 1866, and died at Atlantic, May 30, 1908; his ancestry was Irish. His mother was born at Davenport, Iowa, May 30, 1872 of German descent.

Mr. Dunn was graduated from the Lincoln Academy in 1914, after receiving his grade school education in Iowa. He was awarded the LL. B. degree at the University of Nebraska, where he won honors in public speaking and was president of his junior class. There he was also elected to membership in Delta Chi and Phi Alpha Tau. Since his admission to the bar at Lincoln, March 24, 1919, he has been engaged in the general practice of law there, except from 1920 to 1924, when he was counsel to the compensation commission and chief of the division of workmen's compensation, State of Nebraska. He has lived in Nebraska for 20 years.

He married Aetna Patricia Eakin at Lincoln, June 4, 1919. Mrs. Dunn was born at Little Rock, Arkansas, July 17, 1894 and is of Irish and English descent. Mr. Dunn served in the World War, and is a member of the American Legion. He is also a member of the Nebraska State Bar Association, the Lancaster County Bar Association, the Lincoln Chamber of Commerce, Red Cross, Salvation Army, and the Young Men's Christian Association. He is a 32nd degree Mason, and is affiliated with Westminster Presbyterian Church at Lincoln. His favorite sport is hiking. Residence: Lincoln.

Albert Chester Dunning

A resident of Nebraska for the past 50 years, Albert Chester Dunning is now a retired grain dealer of Shelby, Polk County, Nebraska. He was born at Shelby, April 6, 1881, the son of Frank and Katherine (Clark) Dunning. His father, who was born at Watson, Michigan, September 18, 1851, of German parentage, was a farmer; he died at Shelby, January 18, 1923. His mother, whose French and Canadian parents came to this country in 1867, was born at Dodgeville, Wisconsin.

Mr. Dunning was formerly president of the Shelby Grain Company and had been in the grain business continuously until he retired in 1929. He is a director in the Shelby State Bank, and is a member of the Red Cross, the Shelby Commercial Club, the Odd Fellows, the Ancient Order of United Workmen, and the Nebraskana Society. He is a Democrat.

On December 14, 1904, he was united in marriage with Josephine Thelen at Shelby. Mrs. Dunning was born at Shelby, July 17, 1883. She is a member of the Eastern Star, and is past president of the Woman's Club and the Methodist Episcopal Church Society. Her German ancestors settled in Hackberry Precinct in 1869. Their son, John Ray, who was born September 24, 1907, is married to Esther Laura Blevins. He is a graduate of Nebraska Wesleyan University where he held membership in Phi Kappa Tau and Phi Kappa Phi, and is now instructor in the physics department at Columbia University. Residence: Shelby.

George Bela Durkee

George Bela Durkee, for many years prominent in agricultural life in Adams County, was born at Big Rock, Illinois, December 28, 1859. He is the son of Nathan Dimick and Angeline Jewitt (Wood) Durkee, both descended from early New England settlers. Nathan Durkee was born in New Hampshire, March 6, 1830, and died at Hansen, Nebraska, January 1, 1895. His wife was born at Berkshire, Vermont, November 30, 1832, and died at Big Rock, February 15, 1886.

Mr. Durkee attended country school and came to Nebraska about forty-eight years ago. He has engaged in farming for many years, and has served as a member of the county board of Adams County, the Adams County fair board, and for five years was president of the Farm Central Insurance Company. He is now retired.

He was married to Belle Wallis at Sandwich, Illinois, March 14, 1883, and to them were born two children: Minnie, born August 27, 1884, who married W. E. Christopher; and Grace Edith, born December 11, 1888, who married Arnold Bauman. Both are farmers.

Mr. Durkee is a Republican. He is a member of the Presbyterian Church, has served on the school board seventeen years, and is a member and director of the Chamber of Commerce. A 32nd degree Mason, also a member of the Young Men's Christian Association and the Red Cross. Fishing is his favorite sport.

Mrs. Durkee, who was born at Somonauk, Illinois, November 1, 1859, died at Hastings, November 28, 1925. Residence: Hastings.

Edward Eugene Duryee

Born at Lexington, Nebraska, September 12, 1884, Edward Eugene Duryee is the son of Edward Joseph and Julia Catherine (Conlin) Duryee. His father, whose ancestry was French, was born at New York, July 15, 1857, and died at Lexington, January 4, 1922. His mother, whose parents were Irish, was born in Canada, November 29, 1860, and died at Lexington, August 12, 1915.

Mr. Duryee was graduated from the Lexington High School, and in 1906 received the Ph. G. degree at Highland Park College of Pharmacy, Des Moines, Iowa. He clerked in drug stores at Lexington; Overton, Smithfield, Broken Bow, Nebraska; and Des Moines, Iowa. He is the owner and manager of the Duryee Drug Company at Oxford, Nebraska, and is the manufacturer of Duryee's Stomach Powder, Duryee's Throat Gargle, and Eedo's Laxative Tablets.

He is a member of the Nebraska State Pharmaceutical Association, the National Association Board of Pharmacy, the American Pharmaceutical Association, and the National Association of Retail Druggists. He has been president of the Oxford Board of Education for eight years, is president of the State Board of Pharmacy Examiners, and holds membership in the Society of American Magicians and I. B. M. He is a member of the Knights Templar and Shrine bodies of the Masons, is past master of Rawalt Lodge Number 138, and holds membership in the Independent Order of Odd Fellows. His hobby is sleight of hand tricks.

Mr. Duryee is a registered pharmacist in Nebraska and has a certificate to practice in any one of twenty-five other states. He is affiliated with the Republican party and holds membership in the Nebraskana Society.

Of his marriage to Josephine Knapple, two children were born: Merle, September 6, 1905, who was graduated from a four-year course in pharmacy at the University of Nebraska; and Ruth, April 10, 1907, who is a senior in the college of arts and sciences at the University of Nebraska. Residence: Oxford. (Photograph in Album).

Anton Dusatko

For the past fifty-five years Anton Dusatko has been a farmer and business man at Clarkson, Nebraska. He was born at Caslav, Czechoslovakia, June 11, 1861, the son of James and Barbara (Turek) Dusatko. His father, who was a farmer, was born at Caslav, 1826, and died at Abie, Nebraska, June 8, 1880; he came to this country in 1876. His mother was born at Caslav, in 1832, and died at Abie, December 18, 1912.

Mr. Dustako who has been prominent in Colfax County public affairs for many years, received most of his education by hard work and private study, much of his studying being done at night schools. He was engaged in farming for five years; and for over 35 years

has been in the lumber, grain, and coal business. He is now president of the Anoka Lumber and Grain Company of Anoka, Nebraska; and is a director of the State Farmers Insurance Company of Omaha.

A Democrat, he was unsuccessful candidate for representative from Colfax County in 1926. He served for several years as a member of the town board at Clarkson; was director of the Clarkson schools for five years; and was treasurer of the local Red Cross, 1917-29. He is a member of the Clarkson Commercial Club; the Czech Historical Club of Nebraska; the Nebraskana Society; and Z. C. B. J.

During the late war he helped to sell war bonds and savings stamps and was a generous contributor to war loan funds. He is affiliated with the New Zion Presbyterian Church at Clarkson. His hobbies and sports are reading; studying; fishing and hunting.

Mr. Dusatko was married to Anna Margaret Marsh at Linwood, Butler County, Nebraska, March 1, 1888. Mrs. Dusatko was born at Pittsburg, Pennsylvania, February 15, 1868. Their children are as follows: Anna Louise, born September 22, 1888, who married Joseph T. Votava; Ida Mathilda, born February 8, 1893, who married Boies H. Turk; Bertha Mary, born June 9, 1895, who married Joseph Pekar; Olga Ozina, born September 4, 1900, who married Cline C. Finlay; and Alan Albert, born October 30, 1903, who married Christina Foyt. All the children were given high school and university training. Residence: Clarkson.

Frank Benham DuTeil

Frank B. DuTeil, a merchant at Lincoln, since 1889, was born at LaFayette, Indiana, October 19, 1869. His father, Claude Charles DuTeil, who was born in Tippecanoe County, March 14, 1830, and died at LaFayette, in 1880, was a mechanic. He served as first lieutenant of the 16th Indiana Artillery during the Civil War and was of French and English descent.

His mother was born at Warren, Ohio, December 20, 1832, and died at Lincoln, September 2, 1916. She was of Dutch descent on the maternal side and Welch through the paternal line.

Mr. DuTeil was graduated from the Lincoln High School in 1889. Engaged in the wholesale and retail tobacco business in Lincoln for over 40 years, and is now the owner and manager of F. A. Brown Company.

During the World War he engaged in clerical work and was active in loan drives at various times; in 1898 he was a private in Company F of the Nebraska National Guard. He holds membership in the Chamber of Commerce, the University Club, the Shrine Club, and the Nebraskana Society, and his fraternal organizations include the Masons, Modern Woodmen of America, and Elks.

He was united in marriage with Clare Sophia Wolf at Lincoln, June 3, 1903. Mrs. DuTeil, who was a bookkeeper before her marriage, was born at Lincoln, May 19, 1875. Residence: Lincoln.

Albert Frank Dutton

Albert Frank Dutton, hardware and implement dealer, was born in Deweese, Nebraska, June 27, 1896, son of William Albert and Katie (Wagner) Dutton.

The father was born in Illinois, December 4, 1862, and is a farmer. His ancestry is mostly English. The mother was born in Germany, October 14, 1866.

Mr. Dutton attended the public school, Minatare High School, and had one year in business college. During his high school days, he played basketball two years.

Since leaving school, Mr. Dutton has been engaged in the hardware and implement business, and is the owner of the Dutton Implement Company at Bridgeport and

Nelson—Hastings

KITTIE M. J. LOUGHRIDGE DUTTON

Gering, at the present time. In addition, he has extended farming interests. He is a Republican.

His marriage to Helen Faye Townsend was solemnized at Minatare, September 6, 1916. She is president of the Eastern Star Kensington at Bridgeport and is a member of the Parent Teachers Association. Mrs. Dutton was born at Randolph, Iowa, March 11, 1897. They have two children, Alberta, born April 11, 1918; and Howard, born October 14, 1921.

At the present time, Mr. Dutton is a member of the Bridgeport Lions Club, the Parent-Teachers Association, the Masonic Lodge, and the Business Men's Club. His favorite sport is volleyball while his hobby is mechanics. He is a Methodist. Residence: Bridgeport.

Kittie M. J. Loughridge Dutton

Born at Oskaloosa, Iowa, May 20, 1860, Kittie Maria Jane Loughridge is the daughter of Reverend John Mitchel and Emily (Bean) Loughridge. Her father, who was a minister of the United Presbyterian Church, had seven children, six of whom were boys.

Educated in the public schools, Kittie Loughridge was graduated from Oskaloosa High School in 1883, and thereafter taught in the public schools of Iowa. At the time of her marriage to William M. Dutton, on November 24, 1887, she was school principal at Centerville, Iowa.

A resident of Hastings for many years, Mrs. Dutton has been intensely interested always in the advancement of her community. One of the six organizers of the Hastings Woman's Club in 1906, she is now serving as its president, her term of office expiring in 1933. She is affiliated with St. Mark's Pro-Cathedral and during 1927-29 was president of the Daughters of St. Mark's.

At the Trans-Mississippi Exposition in 1898, Mrs. Dutton was elected to represent the women of the 5th district on the ladies' board. She also was the organizer of the first P. E. O. Sisterhood in Hastings in 1889.

One of the founders and organizers of the Sunnyside Home for the Aged, she has been a member of its board since its inception, and for a number of years she has been a member of the board of the Young Women's Christian Association.

Mrs. Dutton has devoted much of her life to public affairs, and enjoys activity. Particularly does she like golf and motoring, in which she indulges frequently. Residence: Hastings. (Photograph on Page 356).

William M. Dutton, Sr.

One of the leading merchants of Hastings for many years, William M. Dutton, Sr., was born at Oskaloosa, Iowa, March 1, 1859. He is the son of Basil T. and Mary (Wendle) Dutton, the former a native of Ohio, who came as a carpenter and builder to Iowa in its early days. He was of Holland Dutch descent, his family having come to America in the 17th century. Basil T. Dutton died at Hastings on May 17, 1907. His wife, May, a native of New Jersey, was born on August 12, and died April 12, 1879. She was of French Huguenot extraction.

William M. Dutton, Sr., attended public school and was graduated from high school, thereafter entering the mercantile business. He is a member of the Knights of Pythias, and has always taken an active part in every effort toward the advancement of his state.

Of his marriage to Kittie M. J. Loughridge, there are four children: Florence May, born March 19, 1889, who is a graduate of the University of Nebraska and is married to Barton Green of Lincoln; George Reynolds, born January 22, 1891, who is married to Helen Koehler; Armilda, born January 24, 1898, who was graduated from Mills College in California, and is married to Gerould Scott of Kearney; and William Manderville, Jr., born August 16, 1900. Mrs. Dutton, who was born at Oskaloosa, Iowa, May 20, 1860, of English and Scotch Irish

ancestry was a teacher prior to marriage, and has always been active in civic and club work.

In 1886, Mr. Dutton founded J. H. Haney & Company, a wholesale harness and saddlery concern. This business prospered and expanded throughout the years of its existence, and the firm was one of the pioneers in the automobile business. At the time of the death of one of the original partners the partnership was dissolved, and the firm was incorporated to continue to operate the business under the name W. M. Dutton & Sons Company. This firm was one of the first to enter the radio and electrical appliances field. As new lines developed, the enterprising nature of Mr. Dutton was such that his firm was usually one of the first in the field. Mr. Dutton retired from the business in 1928, and since that time the business has continued its record of development and expansion.

During his entire life Mr. Dutton has been interested in all civic activities along business lines, including the Chamber of Commerce, the Adams County Fair, the Old Soldiers' Tri-State Reunion in 1898, which included Nebraska, Kansas and Colorado, and Nebraska's first street fair in 1889. On January 15, 1899, he was commissioned colonel on the staff of Governor William A. Poynter. From 1925 to 1927, he was active as a member of the Tri-County Project committee, organized for the purpose of storing the water of the Platte River for irrigation and power. Residence: Hastings. (Photograph on Page 358).

Eugene Duval

Eugene Duval has been a prominent railroad man in Nebraska for the past 45 years, and has always been active in Omaha's civic and business affairs. He was born at King, Ontario, Canada, July 26, 1862, the son of Hilair and Mary Ann (Gannon) Duval. His father, who was a railroad agent, was born at Garden Island, Canada, in 1835, and died at Richmond, Michigan, September 18, 1913. His parents, Solomon and Clarisse Duval, who were born in Canada, were of French extraction.

His mother was born at King, Ontario, Canada, in 1838, and died at Richmond, Michigan, August 15, 1919. She was the daughter of Mathew and Mary Gannon who moved from Ireland to Canada, in 1825.

In 1865, Mr. Duval moved with his parents to New Haven, Michigan, where he learned telegraphy in his father's office. He attended public school at New Haven, and parochial school at Mt. Clemens, Michigan, and in 1877 began working for the Grand Trunk Railway as telegrapher; he learned shorthand and was employed by the Griffin Car Wheel Company at Detroit, 1882; was stenographer for the superintendent of the Wabash Railway at Peon, Indiana, until 1885; stenographer general superintendent's office; and the Union Pacific Railroad at Omaha, 1886. He served as stenographer in the quartermaster department of the United States Army, 1887, and was stenographer and telegraph operator of general western agent, Milwaukee Railroad, Omaha, from 1892 to 1897.

Mr. Duval was made contracting agent of the Milwaukee Railroad in 1897; was promoted to assistant general western agent, 1902; and was made general agent, 1915. He is now general agent of the Chicago, Milwaukee, St. Paul, & Pacific Railroad, at Omaha, and is a member of the board of directors of the Provident Loan Society of Omaha.

On June 29, 1886, he was married to Estelle Caroline Carter, at Omaha. Mrs. Duval was born at Astoria, Illinois, September 28, 1865, the daughter of Dilworth and Emily Carter. Their children are: Hilair Dilworth, born January 4, 1888, at Omaha, who married Grace Hartman of New Albany, Indiana; and Mary Alice, born at Omaha, October 8, 1893, who married Rollin H. Sturtevant. Hilair is manager of the American Radiator Company at

WILLIAM M. DUTTON, SR.

Nelson—Hastings

Norfolk, Virginia. Mary Alice, who is a talented singer, is interested in welfare work in Kansas City, Missouri.

Mr. Duval was a private in the home guards during the late war, and took an active part in Liberty loan drives. He is a member of the Red Cross, the Kiwanis Club, Chamber of Commerce, and Ak-Sar-Ben, and holds membership in the Old Time Telegraphers Society, the Elks, Woodmen of the World, and Royal Arcanum. He is a member of the Omaha Club and the Athletic Club. Residence: Omaha.

Aubrey Hobart Duxbury

Aubrey H. Duxbury, lawyer and county judge of Cass County, Nebraska, was born at Stanberry, Missouri, November 4, 1896. His father, Franklin Pierce Duxbury, who was a blacksmith, was born at Fond du Lac, Fond du Lac County, Wisconsin, and died at St. Joseph, Missouri. James Duxbury, grandfather of Aubrey, came to America from Lancastershire County, England, in its early days. His mother, Mollie (Blue) Duxbury, was born on a farm near Island City, Gentry County, Missouri, February 2, 1877. She is the daughter of Thomas Blue, who was born in Roseville, Illinois, and Mary Ellen (Gillett) Blue, a native of Ohio.

Judge Duxbury was graduated from Plattsmouth High School in 1916, and attended the United States Naval Radio School at Harvard University, Cambridge, Massachusetts, for eight months. During his boyhood he was a delivery boy on the *News-Herald* at Plattsmouth, Nebraska. For eleven years he was employed as a clerk in the retail store of H. M. Soennichsen, working after school hours and on holidays. Later he studied law in the law office of A. L. Tidd, and A. G. Cole, and was admitted to the Nebraska State Bar on June 20, 1920.

From April, 1921, to April, 1924, he was city clerk of Plattsmouth. County judge of Cass County since January 8, 1925, at the present time he is co-partner in the firm of A. H. & R. M. Duxbury Insurance Agency, at Plattsmouth.

He enlisted in the United States Navy, March 15, 1918, serving as radio operator and electrician throughout the rest of the World War. From 1920 to 1921, he was commander of Hugh J. Kerns Post 56, of the American Legion, and for the past nine years he has been post-service officer of this organization. He is a home service secretary of the Cass County chapter of the American Red Cross, and is vice president of the Plattsmouth chapter of this society.

Judge Duxbury is chairman of the civic improvement committee of the Plattsmouth Chamber of Commerce; chairman of the community service committees; has been superintendent of the Methodist Episcopal Sunday School for the past nine years; is president of the Young Men's Bible Class, of his church; is a member of the Rotary International. He is a Mason, and past master of Lodge Number 6, of Plattsmouth, past high priest of the Nebraska chapter number 3, present Generalissimo of Mount Zion Commandery No. 5, Knights Templar; a member of the Elks, the Eastern Star. He is a member of the Y. M. C. A., of Omaha, Nebraska, and is now enrolled in this society's night school where he is studying public speaking.

An ardent enthusiast of sports, Judge Duxbury is a member of the Plattsmouth Business Men's Gymnasium Class, where he plays volley ball. His hobby is reading good books. Residence: Plattsmouth.

Emil Andy Dwehus

Emil Andy Dwehus was born at Nysted, Nebraska, November 14, 1897, the son of Emil and Olina (Anderson) Dwehus. His father, who is president of the Rockville State Bank, was born in Germany, and came to this country at the age of 17. His mother was born in Denmark, and came to this country at the age of 14.

Mr. Dwehus served as bookkeeper for the Rockville State Bank at the age of 16, and three years later became assistant cashier of that institution. He was cashier of the Rockville State Bank for a time, was cashier of the Farmers Bank of Alda, Nebraska, and cashier of the State Bank of Dannebrog from 1928-32. Since January 1, 1932, he has been president of the State Bank of Dannebrog, of which he was organizer. He is a director in the Rockville State Bank at this time.

He is a member of the Dannebrog Commercial Club, the Masons, the Odd Fellows, and the Nebraskana Society, and is serving as treasurer of School District Number 4 at Dannebrog. His sports include baseball and golf, while his hobby is electricity. Mr. Dwehus is a Democrat, and is affiliated with the Lutheran Church.

He married Marie Florentine Ohlsen at Loup City, Nebraska, July 20, 1922. Mrs. Dwehus, who is of German descent, was born at Loup City, May 10, 1896. They have three children: Dorothy, born August 16, 1925; Joan, born December 19, 1929; and Emil, born December 23, 1931. Residence: Dannebrog.

Albert William Dyer

Born in Wallingford, England, March 3, 1871, Albert William Dyer is the son of William and Jane (Sevelle) Dyer. His father, who was a farmer and a rural school teacher, was born in Wallingford, September 8, 1842, and died at Exeter, Nebraska, September 23, 1901. His mother was born in Wallingford, and died at Exeter, September 20, 1880.

Mr. Dyer has been engaged in the implement business for the past 29 years.

He is president of the Mid-West Implement Dealers' Association at this time at Exeter, and has been a resident of this state for the past 60 years. He holds membership in the Modern Woodmen of America, is affiliated with the Methodist Church, and is a member of the Nebraskana Society.

He was married to Sophia Amerita Hussmann at Exeter, November 20, 1900. She was of German descent, and died at Exeter, August 31, 1916. On January 4, 1921, he married Pearl Clover, who had two sons by a former marriage. Mr. Dyer has given his step-sons liberal education. Delphin studied for two years at the University of Nebraska, and Clarence was graduated from the University of Nebraska in 1931. Residence: Exeter. (Photograph in Album).

Thomas Boyd Dysart

Thomas Boyd Dysart, lawyer, was born at Newcastle, Ohio, July 30, 1871, son of William and Margaret L. (Twinem) Dysart. Mr. Dysart attended public school at Superior, and in 1899 he received the Bachelor of Laws degree from the University of Michigan. He received his Master of Laws degree from the University of Omaha.

A Republican, Mr. Dysart was state representative in 1921-22, and state senator in 1925. He is the author of *Mortgage Foreclosure in Nebraska* (1923); *Tax Lien Foreclosure in Nebraska* (1925), and *Federal Court Liens in Nebraska* (1927).

Among his professional organizations are the American, Nebraska State and Omaha Bar Association. He is an Elk, a member of the Knights of Pythias, of the Ad-Sell League, and the Kiwanis Club. His club is the Athletic. Residence: Omaha.

Gilbert Eacker

Gilbert Eacker, son of J. I. and Hattie (Smith) Eacker, was born at Mount Carroll, Illinois, December 21, 1879. His father, who was born at Chat, New York, in March, 1853, is a farmer, most of whose ancestors came from Holland. His mother, who was born in Wisconsin, in September, 1855, is descended from early settlers in Pennsylvania.

Educated in the public schools, Gilbert Eacker has been engaged in business in Schuyler for a number of years, and at the present time is president of the Eacker Motor Company of Schuyler. He was married to Lina Oleson, at Columbus, on June 8, 1904. Mrs. Eacker was born at Albion, Nebraska, December 22, 1879, of Danish descent. There are three children, Valma, born January 4, 1907, who is a teacher; Gerald, born July 18, 1912; and Howard, born September 22, 1915. All of them attended the University of Nebraska.

Mr. Eacker is a Presbyterian, a Mason, Woodman, Knight of Pythias, and an Odd Fellow. He is a Scout master in the Boy Scouts of America, a member of the Chamber of Commerce, the Lions Club and the Nebraskana Society. Residence: Schuyler.

Fred Eason

Fred Eason was born in Ohio, December 15, 1866, the son of Richard and Lucy (Howlett) Eason. They were both born in England, later coming to this country, where he became engaged in farming. Mr. Eason died at North Bend, Dodge County, Nebraska, August 31, 1896, and his wife died at North Bend, July 2, 1878.

On December 28, 1892, Fred Mason was united in marriage with Bert Acom, who was born at Jacksonville, Illinois, July 27, 1871. Their children are: Myrtle, born October 15, 1893, who is married to Vernon E. Rand, and who was graduated from the University of Nebraska in 1915; Alice, born April 24, 1895, who is married to Wilmer W. Boyd, and who attended the university for three years; Richard, born June 24, 1901; died September 1, 1909; Thomas, born September 1, 1911, a senior at the university; and Edith, born December 16, 1915.

Mr. Eason came to the state of Nebraska at the age of six, and has lived 46 years on his home place. His political preference is that of the Democratic party. He is president of the Farmers' Insurance Company, and president of the board of directors of the Farmer's Co-operative Association.

He is a member of the Red Cross, the North Bend Community Club, the Modern Woodmen of America, the Dodge County Historical Society, and the Nebraskana Society. He is also a member of the Parent-Teacher Association and has been chairman of the school board since 1904. Residence: North Bend.

Glen B. Eastburn

Glen B. Eastburn was born at Webster, Iowa, May 10, 1894, son of William W. and Mary E. (Stephenson) East-burn. His father, who was born in Lake County, Indiana, June 16, 1852, was a graduate of the State University of Iowa, and a physician. He traced his ancestry to Eastbourne, England, in the 12th century. Several of his forebears came to America before the Revolution and served in that war.

Mary E. Stephenson was born in Webster, Iowa, February 14, 1870. She received a B. A. degree from Grinnell. A number of her relatives reside at Bradford, England; her father came to America in 1868.

Mr. Eastburn received his elementary education in the Los Angeles public schools, and was graduated from the Sigourney (Iowa) High School. He is a graduate in business accounting from Valparaiso University, and attended the State University of Iowa three years, leaving to serve in the World War as second lieutenant of Field Artillery.

For the past ten years he has been engaged in commercial organization. He was assistant secretary of the Iowa State Association two years, secretary of the Marshailtown (Iowa) Chamber of Commerce three years, industrial commissioner of the Sioux City Chamber of Commerce one year, manager of the industrial department of the Omaha Chamber of Commerce one year, and is now commissioner of the Omaha Chamber of Commerce. In addition he is secretary of the Industrial Development Corporation, member of the board of managers of the National Institute for Commercial Executives at Northwestern University, and secretary-treasurer of the American Industrial Development Council.

He was married to Mary Fern Culbertson at Des Moines, Iowa, June 18, 1919. Mrs. Eastburn was born at Greenfield, Iowa, July 16, 1894. She is of English descent and a member of the Daughters of the American Revolution. She was graduated from Drake University and the University of Colorado. Mr. and Mrs. Eastburn have three children: Ruth Emily, born January 10, 1922; James W., born February 10, 1928, and Joan, born July 15, 1930.

Mr. Eastburn is a member of Dundee Presbyterian Church. He is a member of the American Legion, the Chamber of Commerce, the National Association of Commercial Secretaries, and the Nebraskana Society. His sport is golf and his hobby is his children. Residence: Omaha.

Fred Ralph Easterday

Fred R. Easterday, prominent executive of Nebraska, has lived in this state for the past 48 years. He was born at Carthage, Illinois, August 24, 1875, the son of Levi F. M. and Abbie (Hunsaker) Easterday. His father, who was born near Steubenville, Ohio, October 21, 1839, and died at Lincoln, Lancaster County, Nebraska, February 17, 1913, was a university professor for many years, serving as professor of mathematics and astronomy at Carthage College, Illinois, from 1870 to 1883. Thereafter he held this position at the University of Nebraska, 1883-85. He was a banker and business man from 1885 to 1913, and his ancestry was German and Scotch-Irish. His mother, whose ancestry was Pennsylvania Dutch, was born at Fairhaven, Ohio, September 20, 1853.

Mr. Easterday attended the grade and high schools at Lincoln. He was employed at the Nebraska State Industrial School at Kearney from February 1, 1897, to December 1, 1897; was clerk and teller at the First National Bank, Lincoln, from December 1, 1897, to January 15, 1913; and was assistant secretary of the First Trust Company of Lincoln, from January 13, 1913, to January 15, 1927. Since 1927, he has been secretary of the First Trust Company, and is also secretary of the First National Corporation and the First Securities Corporation.

He holds membership in the following: Red Cross, Community Chest, Chamber of Commerce, National Geographic Society, and the Nebraskana Society. He is a charter member of the Lions Club at Lincoln, and is at present serving on its board of governors. During the World War Mr. Easterday participated in all Liberty loan drives. He is affiliated with the First Presbyterian Church of Lincoln, is an elder of this church. A member of the Order of the Eastern Star he holds membership in the Masons, Shrine and Scottish Rite bodies. He is a member of the Lincoln Country Club, and is interested in golf and football. His hobby is gardening.

On April 17, 1902, his marriage to Grace May Bowen was solemnized at Avoca, Iowa. Mrs. Easterday, who was born at New Sharon, Iowa, June 4, 1880, is editor of the Nebraska Parent-Teacher, is secretary of the Lincoln Recreation Board, and is a member of the Lincoln Park Board. She is of Welch and German descent. They have two children: Fred Ralph, born November 14, 1910; and Daniel Charles, born December 7, 1912. Both children are students at the University of Nebraska, where they hold membership in Delta Sigma Lambda. Fred Ralph is first lieutenant in the Reserve Officer's Training Corps.

Mr. Easterday is a Democrat, and is vitally interested in the economic and political affairs of his community and state. Residence: Lincoln.

Grace Bowen Easterday

Grace Bowen Easterday, one of Lincoln's leading civic and educational workers, was born at New Sharon, Iowa, June 4, 1880. Her parents are Charles Thomas and Jennie C. (Wood) Bowen, the former a native of Sharon, Pennsylvania, born April 15, 1856. He came to Iowa as a young man, where he engaged in the drug business, and later in the insurance business. His death occurred at Avoca, Iowa, July 3, 1914. Jennie Wood Bowen, who is still living, was born at Iowa City, Iowa, November 19, 1862.

Upon the completion of her public school work at Avoca, Grace Bowen was a student at Avoca High School, being graduated in 1900. Thereafter she attended the University of Nebraska. On April 17, 1902, she was united in marriage to Fred Ralph Easterday. Mr. Easterday was born at Carthage, Illinois, August 24, 1875, of German and Scotch Irish parentage. He is secretary of the First Trust Company of Lincoln. There are two children of this marriage, Fred Ralph, born November 14, 1910, and Daniel Charles, born December 7, 1912. Both are students at the University of Nebraska and members of Delta Sigma Lambda. Fred is a first lieutenant in the R. O. T. C.

During her residence in Lincoln Mrs. Easterday has taken an active part in educational work particularly. From April 1926 to May 1927 she was editor of the *Nebraska Parent-Teacher*, and since February 1930 she has held the same office. Since 1922 she has been state chairman of recreation of the Parent-Teachers Association.

A writer of some merit, she is the author of numerous articles, and is a member of the Quill Club and the Nebraska Writers Guild. During the World War she was active in Red Cross work, and for some time she has been a member of the Young Women's Christian Association. She is secretary of the Lincoln Recreation Board and a member of the Lincoln Park Board.

Mrs. Easterday attends the First Presbyterian Church of Lincoln and is a member of the Eastern Star, The Nebraskana Society and the Nebraska State Historical Society. Her hobby is reading. Residence: Lincoln.

Lyman H. Eastman

One of the outstanding farmers in Franklin County, Lyman H. Eastman has been a resident of Nebraska for the past 54 years. Coming to Nebraska with his parents in the fall of 1878 in a Prairie Schooner leading two milk cows, they located 12 miles southeast of Lincoln, near Roca. Mr. Eastman's first employment was in a stone quarry where he earned and saved enough money to buy a team of horses and some farm implements. Then in 1885, he came farther west and purchased 320 acres of land from the B. & M. Railroad of Nebraska, at $10.00 per acre. He experienced all the hardships of the early pioneers. He was born at Belmont, Wisconsin, February 16, 1859, the son of James S. and Nancy Ann (Hazel) Eastman, the former a farmer who was born at Hazell Green, Wisconsin, May 28, 1828, of English and German parentage; and died at Campbell, March 8, 1919. His mother, whose parents were Kentuckians, was born at Galena, Illinois, January 15, 1834, and died at Campbell, February 4, 1891.

Mr. Eastman attended a rural school in Wisconsin. He is now a retired farmer, living in Campbell where he is active in community affairs. A Democrat, he served as a member of the state legislature in 1909 and 1911, was supervisor of Franklin County from 1907 to 1909, and from 1914 to 1923 was postmaster of Campbell. He was secretary of the Campbell Board of Education from 1926 to 1929, and is a member of the local lodge of the Odd Fellows, and is past noble grand, and a member of the Nebraskana Society. Mr. Eastman's hobby is reading.

His marriage to Alma Armenia Palmer occurred at Lincoln, Nebraska, June 6, 1884. Mrs. Eastman, who is a devoted homemaker, was born at Belmont, Wisconsin, April 18, 1864. They have an adopted daughter, Ruth, born February 24, 1907, who married Dr. Roy E. Hanson at Clay Center, Nebraska, November 11, 1927. Residence: Campbell.

Osgood Tilton Eastman

Osgood T. Eastman was born at South Braintree, Massachusetts, January 18, 1865, the son of Lucius Root and Octavia Yale (Smith) Eastman. His father, who was a clergyman, was born at Sharon, Massachusetts, January 25, 1839, and died at Framingham, Massachusetts, October 26, 1916. His ancestors were in America in 1636. His mother was descended from the Smith and Yale families prominent in New England for the past 200 years. She was born at Worcester, Massachusetts, May 15, 1843, and died at Holyoke, Massachusetts, June 20, 1866.

Mr. Eastman, who has been a banker and prominent business man of Omaha, for many years, was graduated from the Framingham High School in 1881, and received his A. B. from Amherst College in 1886. He was active in football, 1884-85, and was elected to membership in Theta Delta Chi.

A manufacturing chemist at Chicago, 1390-1908, he was assistant cashier of the First National Bank of Omaha, 1910-17; vice president of the Merchants National Bank, 1920-26; and since 1927 has been business manager of the Omaha schools. He served as manager of the Omaha branch of the Federal Reserve Bank from 1917 to 1920. He is a Republican.

His marriage to Nellie Burns was solemnized at Omaha, September 30, 1891. Mrs. Eastman, who was born at Omaha, April 25, 1866, is descended from Samuel Burns of Dungannon, Ireland. Three children were born to them: Helen, born December 7, 1895, who died January 26, 1921; Octavia Yale, born March 26, 1899, who died August 31, 1902; and Margaret Burns, born April 17, 1902.

During the World War Mr. Eastman was district manager of Liberty loans, during the time he was manager of the Omaha branch of the Federal Reserve Bank. He is past master and treasurer of his local lodge of the Masons and is affiliated with the First Central Congregational Church of Omaha. Residence: Omaha.

Henry Monroe Easton

Born at Mason City, Illinois, July 23, 1864, Henry Monroe Easton has been a prominent farmer in Nebraska for many years. He is the son of Alcinous and Mary Jane (Doan) Easton, both natives of Ohio. Alcinous Easton was born at Warren, Ohio, July 25, 1837, of early New England ancestry. He engaged in farming near Cambridge, Nebraska, for many years prior to his death there on January 7, 1907. His wife, born at Lake County, Ohio, October 25, 1841, was descended from early settlers in Virginia. She died at Cambridge, March 23, 1906.

Henry Monroe Easton attended country school, and has engaged in farming most of his life. He was married on February 28, 1888, to Louisa Carrie Wagner at Hebron. Mrs. Easton, a native of LaSalle County, Illinois, was born June 6, 1866. There are two children, Clinton, born February 9, 1889, who married Florence Rainy; and Leola, born April 20, 1891, who married Hershel Howard. Clinton is a farmer.

Mr. Easton is independent in politics. He is a freethinker. Residence: Hebron.

Thomas J. Easton

Thomas J. Easton, lawyer and publisher, was born at Glenwood, Missouri, December 2, 1873, son of George

McCulloch and Lydia Stuyvesant (Haney) Easton. His ancestry is Welsh, English, German, and Scotch.

After his graduation from high school, Mr. Easton attended Kahoka College, from which he received his Bachelor of Science degree. For a number of years he has been engaged in the practice of law, the operation of farms, and in the publishing business. He is a member of the Odd Fellows and the Brotherhood of American Yeomen. He is a baseball fan.

On June 26, 1905, he was married to Minnie Belle Garrett at Green City, Missouri. She was born at Knox City, Missouri, October 10, 1882. There are three children, James R., born May 13, 1906; Helen R., born September 1, 1918; and Edgar, born June 9, 1920.

Mr. Easton is a Republican. Residence: Bushnell.

Albert Nathaniel Eaton

Albert N. Eaton was born at Quincy, Massachusetts, August 25, 1859, the son of Nathaniel Hubbard Eaton and Mary Ann (Jones) Eaton. His father was born at Portsmouth, New Hampshire, August 20, 1828, and died at Wellsville, Kansas, August 12, 1898.

His mother was born at Lincoln, Massachusetts, June 10, 1828, and died at Tonganoxie, Kansas. She was of New England descent.

Mr. Eaton was graduated from the public schools and soon after this entered the business world. He was owner of a general merchandise store at Peabody, Kansas, before coming to Omaha. He is now the owner and president of the A. N. Eaton Metal Products at Omaha, president of the Eaton Metal Products Company at Denver, Colorado, and president of the A. N. Eaton Metal Products Company of Billings, Montana. He has lived in Nebraska for 29 years.

He is a member of the Steel Tank Association, the Omaha Chamber of Commerce, and the Rotary Club. For the past four years he has served on the school board and has been affiliated with the Y. M. C. A. for many years. He is a member of the Shrine Club and Woodmen of the World. He is a member of the North Presbyterian Church. He is a Republican. Residence: Omaha.

Guy Wallace Eaton

One of Nebraska's leading educators is Guy Wallace Eaton who was born at Lafayette, Indiana, April 6, 1876, the son of Charles Wesley and Frances Adeline (Moore) Eaton. His father, who was a distinguished lawyer in Indiana, was born at Eaton Hill, New York, March 20, 1834, and died at Davenport, Nebraska, June 4, 1901; he served in the Civil War as a sergeant and was present when Lincoln was shot.

His mother, a homemaker and clubwoman, was born at McDonough, New York, October 29, 1836, and died at Chapman, Nebraska, December 16, 1919. She served in public schools as a teacher prior to her marriage, was prominent in the Women's Relief Corps, and served as president of the Women's Christian Temperance Union.

Mr. Eaton attended Fremont College, Kearney Teachers College, and the University of Nebraska. He received the A. B. degree from Fremont College in 1902. He was active in athletics during his high school and college days and served as secretary-treasurer and president of the Nebraska Declamatory Association. His professional career is as follows: teacher and superintendent of city schools in various Nebraska communities, principal of the state normal at Valentine, Nebraska; employee of the Department of Public Instruction at Lincoln, Nebraska; and institute instructor and lecturer. He is now superintendent of schools at Maxwell, Nebraska.

His marriage to Kittie May Joyce occurred at Shickley, Nebraska, December 24, 1896. Mrs. Eaton, a teacher, was born at Milo, Iowa, October 12, 1875. She is a member of the Methodist Episcopal Church and takes an active part in its different organizations. She is also

a member of the organization known as the War Mothers, the Rebekahs, and the Eastern Star.

Their three children are, Harry F., born December 1, 1900, who married Cora A. Waldo; Edgar O., born November 13, 1902, who married Velma Deering; and Fern E., born September 23, 1910, who married Malcolm J. Thomas. Harry, who is a rural mail carrier at Cozad, Nebraska, served in the World War, and is a member of the American Legion. Edgar is manager of the J. C. Penney Company at Biloxi, Mississippi. Fern's husband is assistant manager of the J. C. Penney Company at Baton Rouge, Louisiana.

Mr. Eaton is a member of the local Red Cross (chairman, 1931), and was a member of the Commercial Club at DeWitt and at Cozad, Nebraska, is affiliated with the Methodist Episcopal Church of Cozad, and holds membership in the Nebraska State Teachers' Association and the National Geographic Society of Washington, D. C. He holds membership in the Independent Order of Odd Fellows, having affiliated with all branches, and the Masons.

During the World War he served as a four minute speaker at DeWitt where he was sergeant in the Home Guard. He has been captain of the Sons of Veterans at Davenport, Nebraska, and is a member of the state body of that organization. His hobby is farming and gardening, while his sports include golfing, hunting, and fishing. Residence: Maxwell. (Photograph in Album).

Paul H. Eaton

Born at Phillips, Nebraska, September 23, 1889, Paul H. Eaton is the son of Eugene Edward and Etta Charity (Fligg) Eaton. His father, who was an early settler in Nebraska, was born at Denmark, Iowa, January 3, 1851, and died at Stratton, Nebraska, April 6, 1906; he was descended from the following line of English ancestors on the paternal side: John, who settled in Massachusetts in 1635; John II, 1636; William, 1677; Josiah, 1711; Ebenezer, 1744; Jonas, 1776; Ebenezer Ansel, 1810.

His mother was born at Hillsboro, Iowa, September 15, 1853, and now resides at Whittier, California. Her paternal ancestor, William Fligg, came to this country in 1795, and settled in Illinois.

Mr. Eaton attended school at Stratton, Nebraska, where he was graduated from high school in 1907. He studied at Doane College, Crete, Nebraska, 1907-08, was a student at the University of Nebraska, 1908-10, and studied law at the University of Nebraska, where he was active in the Literary Society. From 1919 to 1923 he was assistant cashier and director of the Broadwater Bank, and since 1917 has been engaged in the practice of law.

A Republican, he served as assistant clerk in the Department of Banking in charge of the Guarantee Fund assessments, 1911-12, was assistant bookkeeper in the office of the State Auditor of Public Accounts, in 1913-14. He was appointed by the Judges of the Supreme Court of Nebraska as bailiff of the court and assistant state librarian, 1914.

Mr. Eaton is a member of the Morrill County Bar Association, the Nebraska State Bar Association, the Red Cross, the Nebraskana Society. He is an elder in the Presbyterian Church and holds membership in the Ancient Free and Accepted Masons, Lodge Number 19, at Lincoln, Nebraska.

He was united in marriage with Anna Marie Ketler at Benkelman, Nebraska, April 17, 1911. Mrs. Eaton, whose ancestry is German, was born at Mercer, Pennsylvania. She is a member of the Eastern Star and the Presbyterian Church. Mrs. Eaton is the daughter of John and Clara (Cummings) Ketler. She is a graduate of Fremont Normal College and Zanarian College at Columbus, Ohio. She also attended the University of Ohio. They have two children: Pauline Marie, born

Skoglund—Omaha

ROY WESLEY EATON

March 12, 1914, who was graduated from the Broadwater High School and is now a freshman at Doane College; and Gene Clair, born May 26, 1925. Residence: Broadwater.

residents of South Sioux City. Mr. Ebel, in recognition of his work for the advancement of his state, has been awarded a life membership in The Nebraskana Society. Residence: South Sioux City.

Roy Wesley Eaton

Born at Lafayette, Indiana, June 11, 1878, Roy Wesley Eaton has been a continuous resident of Nebraska since 1879. He is the son of Charles Wesley and Frances Adaline (Moore) Eaton, the former an educator, farmer and soldier of German and English Descent. Charles Wesley Eaton was born at Willet, New York, March 30, 1834, and died at Davenport, Nebraska, June 4, 1901. His wife, Frances Moore, was born at McDonough, New York, August 29, 1836, and died at Chapman, Nebraska, December 16, 1919. She was of English descent, and during the Civil War served as a nurse. Thereafter she was a teacher in the public schools.

Roy W. Eaton attended Happy Hollow School in Thayer County until 1894, and was graduated from Davenport High School in 1896. In 1903, Mr. Eaton received the degree of Bachelor of Arts from Fremont College, and in 1904 received the degree of Bachelor of Pedagogy, and in 1905 the degree of Bachelor of Science from the same institution. He received another Bachelor of Arts degree from the University of Nebraska in 1913, and in 1920, was awarded his Master's degrees from that university. His fraternity is Pi Gamma Mu. During 1924, Mr. Eaton attended Harvard University.

On June 3, 1903, he was united in marriage to Daisie Serena Hansen at Wymore. Mrs. Eaton, who was born at Creston, Iowa, October, 2 1878, is of Danish and Swedish descent. They have one son, Waldo, born September 8, 1906. He is a graduate of Iowa State College at Ames, and is married to Helen B. Docekal.

Mr. Eaton is known throughout the middlewest as an educator and author of educational pamphlets and textbooks, and has attended scores of grade school contests and teachers' institutes as a lecturer and conductor. He is included in *Who's Who in North American Authors.* He is a member of the firm Omaha School Supply Company and editor of the *Middlewest School Review.*

Among his textbooks are: *Eaton's Graded Speller,* (1914); *True Blue Contest Speller,* (1914); *Eaton's Contest Arithmetic,* (1914); *Eaton's True Blue Bible Contest,* (1918); *True Blue Picture Study,* (1918); *True Blue Geography Note Book,* (1920); *Silent Reading Text,* (1924); *Nature Study,* (1929); *True Blue Grammar Review,* (1929); *True Blue Book Review,* (1929). He is the editor of the *Middlewest School Review.*

Mr. Eaton is a Republican, a Methodist, a 32nd degree Mason, and holds the rank of lieutenant in the Nebraska National Guard. Residence: Omaha. (Photograph on Page 363).

William Ebel

William Ebel, retired farmer, was born in Lengen, Brandenburg, Germany, July 4, 1864, son of George W. and Minnie Ebel. His father, a native of Lengen, was a carpenter. His mother was also born in Lengen.

Mr. Ebel attended common schools, and shortly thereafter engaged in farming. He has resided in Nebraska forty-five years, and is now retired. He is a Democrat, a member of St. John's Lutheran Church, and the Modern Woodmen of America.

In 1887, shortly after coming to Nebraska, he was united in marriage to Lizzie Harder, a native of Wisconsin. They have eight children, Annie, Minnie, Albert, Eddie, Louis, Robert, Lily and Mabel.

Mr. and Mrs. Ebel are active in the life of their community and especially in the church, and are outstanding

George Agler Eberly

George Agler Eberly, son of John and Mary (Agler) Eberly, was born at Fort Wayne, Indiana, February 9, 1871. His father was born in Stark County, Ohio, January 25, 1839, and died at Stanton, Nebraska, April 2, 1914. A farmer from 1873 to 1879, he served as county clerk of Stanton County from 1880 to 1884. From that time on he was a banker, and at the time of his death was president of the Stanton National Bank. He saw service in the Civil War from September 9, 1861 to November, 1865 with the 19th Ohio Volunteer Infantry. Of Pennsylvania Dutch ancestry, his family came from Switzerland to America in 1727, settling in Pennsylvania, and later migrating to Ohio. It was at Wilmot, Ohio, that Mary Agler was born, on January 22, 1843. She was a school teacher in early life, and was descended from settlers near Keedysville, Maryland, prior to the Revolution. Her grandfather served in General Wayne's Indian campaign. Her death occurred at Stanton, on September 18, 1925.

Upon his graduation from the Stanton High School in 1888, Judge Eberly read law in the office of W. W. Young. He attended the University of Michigan receiving his LL. B. in 1892 and his LL. M. in 1893. He was valedictorian of his high school class and president of the Post Graduate Law Class at Michigan in 1893. He followed the general practice of law at Stanton, and on May 15, 1898, enlisted for service in the Spanish-American War with rank of sergeant, serving until September 11, 1898. From 1902-17 he held successively the rank of captain, major and colonel in the Nebraska National Guard, and was appointed colonel of infantry in the United States Reserve Corps in February, 1917. He was commander of the Fourth Nebraska Infantry on Mexican Border Service 1916-17, and was ordered to active duty in Officers Training Camp on May 5, 1917, serving as colonel of infantry, Officers Reserve Corps, and major, National Army until December 3, 1918. While in military service at Camp Dodge, Iowa, in 1917, he was in charge of a Liberty loan drive. He is a member of the Reserve Officers Association, the American Legion, the Forty and Eight, the Military Order of the World War, the United Spanish War Veterans and the Sons of Union Veterans, of which he is past state commander.

His political career has been a long one. From 1899-1903 and 1905-09 he was county attorney of Stanton County, and in 1908 was chairman of the Republican Congressional committee. In July, 1925, he was appointed associate justice of the Supreme Court of Nebraska, and was unopposed for the term commencing January 8, 1931.

Judge Eberly is a director of the Stanton National Bank. He has long been a member of the New England Congregational Church at Stanton, and is a 32nd degree Mason, Shriner, a member of Ben Hur, the Modern Woodmen of America and the Sons of Herman. He is a Kiwanian, a member of the Hiram International, the Red Cross, The Nebraskana Society and the Nebraska State Historical Society. His club is the Lincoln University, and his hobby is military science.

His family consists of his wife, the former Rose Psota, and two children. Mrs. Eberly was born at West Point, Nebraska, November 30, 1877. Her grandparents imigrated from Bohemia to America in 1869. She is a teacher of music. Their children are Lloyd A., born November 21, 1900, who died April 18, 1910; Lola A., born September 8, 1904, George Donald, born March 21, 1912. Lola graduated from the University of Nebraska with an A. B. degree in 1927, and George Donald who was graduated from Lincoln High School in 1929, is a student in engineering at the University of Nebraska. Residence: Lincoln. (Photograph on Page 365).

Townsend—Lincoln

GEORGE AGLER EBERLY

William Ebers

William Ebers was born in Pleidelsheim, Marbach, Wurttemburg, Germany, September 2, 1875, the son of Christian Frederick and Catherine Louise (Kloepfer) Eberspacher. His father, who was a farmer, was born in Germany, May 2, 1837, and died in Seward County, Nebraska, September 10, 1926. His mother was born in Germany, August 28, 1835, and died in Seward County, February 2, 1916.

Mr. Ebers attended the public schools of Seward County, and in 1898 was graduated from the Wesleyan University at Mount Pleasant, Iowa. Following his graduation, he was employed as a bookkeeper for a building contractor in Omaha. Two years later, Mr. Ebers accepted a position as bill clerk and city salesman for a wholesale building material company where he remained for four years. The next two years Mr. Ebers was identified with a commercial rating company in Omaha. He has been engaged in the photograph business at Holdrege, Nebraska for over twenty years, and has been a resident of this state for over half a century. He served as city treasurer of Phelps County from 1917 to 1922, and is now completing his sixth year as city assessor at Holdrege.

He holds membership in the Missouri Valley and the Nebraska Photographers Associations, is a charter member of the Rotary Club of Holdrege, and holds membership in the Holdrege Chamber of Commerce. He is past master, past high priest and past commander of the Masonic fraternities of Holdrege, and a member of Sesostris Temple, Lincoln.

On September 2, 1902, he was married to Charlotte Matilda Maier, at Papillion, Nebraska. She was born at Wathena, Kansas, February 20, 1879.

Mr. Ebers has affiliated primarily with the Republican party. Residence: Holdrege. (Photograph in Album).

Gottlieb Frederich Eberspacher

A resident of Nebraska since 1880, when he came to America with his parents, Gottlieb Frederich Eberspacher is the son of Christian F. and Katharine Marie Eberspacher. Christian Eberspacher was born at Pleidelsheim, Wurttemberg, Germany, May 2, 1837, of a German family which produced several sculptors. He was a farmer, but excelled in free hand drawing and in printing, was a talented musician and singer. He died at Seward, Nebraska, in September, 1926.

Katharine Marie Klopfer was born in Pleidelsheim, August 28, 1835, of a family which contained several physicians. Her mother's brothers served in the war with Napoleon. She was well educated, and was a fine singer. Her death occurred at Seward, on February 2, 1916.

Gottlieb Eberspacher was one of a family of six boys and three girls, and as there was plenty of help on his father's farm, he was permitted to hire out at the age of eleven to a farmer in York County, at a wage of $45.00 a year. He plied farming assiduously, and was quick to observe the most efficient methods of farming and stock-raising, and then, beginning for himself, he pursued this policy of making even the best better if possible. He is a breeder of pure-bred stock; his small grain is inspected and certified by the Nebraska Crop Growers Association, and much of it is sold for seed.

Mr. Eberspacher was chosen Master Farmer in 1930; has been president of the Farmers Elevator at Goehner; and has served as precinct assessor over a period of ten years. He is a Republican. During the World War Mr. Eberspacher served on the local Council of Defense and was official representative of the state and federal governments in all farm bureau activities in Seward County, under appointment of Governor Keith Neville.

Gottlieb Eberspacher is a member of the Salem Methodist Church. He is a lover of music, and his children are all active in musical circles. His hobby is to improve his farm and methods of farming to obtain the best and largest yielding crops, and raising good pure-bred stock of various kinds.

On August 3, 1899, he was united in marriage to Anna M. Luecke of Cortland, Nebraska. Mrs. Eberspacher was born at New Hall, Iowa, August 21, 1878. There are eleven children, as follows: Floyd R., born June 21, 1900; Elmer E., born March 23, 1902; Myrtle S., born June 2, 1904; Florence May, born May 4, 1906; John G., born August 13, 1908; Homer H., born March 1, 1911; Harold G., born August 9, 1912; Luella A., born May 25, 1915; Phoebe K., born July 14, 1918; Lois F., born December 19, 1920; and James W., born February 22, 1923.

One daughter, Myrtle, taught in the public schools for a period of five years, and another daughter, Florence, is a graduate nurse of the State University Hospital at Omaha. Three sons are farming for themselves, two are taking care of the home farm, and the others are attending school.

Mr. Eberspacher was one of the first leaders in 4-H Club work, and continued over a period of many years. His children have been unusually prominent in the affairs of this organization—Homer, with two of his cousins, Milton and Raymond, comprised the State Livestock Judging Team representing Nebraska at the International Stock Show at Chicago, in 1930, and were placed third among the 23 teams representing various states. Homer also had the Grand Champion Poland China fat barrow at the Ak-Sar-Ben stock show at Omaha, in 1930.

Harold was champion showman at the Ak-Sar-Ben in 1930, and is a member of the Livestock Judging team representing Nebraska at the International Stock Show at Chicago for 1931-32. This team took third place among the 17 teams representing their several states. Among the high men in the individual classes, Harold Eberspacher was third, took first on swine judging and won the $200 agricultural college scholarship offered by the Chicago Association of Commerce.

Mr. Eberspacher has always believed that the Biblical dictum, "What soever a man soweth that shall he also reap" expresses an inexorable law that affects the spiritual and financial status, and finally the destiny of man and nations. This affected his attitude toward God very early in life and resulted in a fixed habit of putting God first in everything. In other words, his objective or purpose in every relationship of life has been to act in harmony with his Creator and Redeemer as fully as possible, to know His will and honor His great name. He has found that such a concern about His will brings His blessing on every phase of life and gives a satisfaction to the human heart that earthly accessions and possessions cannot otherwise do. Residence: Seward. (Photograph in Album).

Friedrick William Ebinger

Friedrick William Ebinger, a leading merchant at Plainview, Nebraska, was born at Nurtmgen, Wurttemburg, Germany May 1, 1866, the son of Karl and Christine (Miller) Ebinger. Karl Ebinger who was street commissioner in his community, was born at Nurtmgen, February 26, 1814, and died there February 21, 1899. His mother was born at Nurtmgen, January 9, 1822, and died there November 21, 1892.

Mr. Ebinger attended seminary school until his confirmation in 1880 and the following year moved to Plattsmouth, Nebraska. He has been a hardware merchant since 1885 and at this time is senior member of the firm Ebinger Hardware Company. A Democrat, he has held the following public offices: member of city council at Plattsmouth, Nebraska, 1904-06; member city council at Plainview, 1907 to 1909; mayor of Plainview, 1921-24. He holds membership in the Masons and Order of Eastern Star.

His marriage occurred at Plattsmouth, May 21, 1899; his wife was born at Plattsmouth, January 1, 1870. T꜠

them were born these children: Karl G., April 6, 1890; Anna Louise, March 14, 1895; and Friedrich William, March 8, 1906. Residence: Plainview.

William John Ebsen

William John Ebsen has been a farmer in Nebraska for the past 57 years and is today active in educational and civic affairs at Bostwick. He was born in Illinois, September 15, 1869, the son of Peter F. and Mary Elizabeth (Krebs) Ebsen. His father, who was born in Germany, April 22, 1835, and died at Cedar Bluffs, Nebraska, September 29, 1910, was a farmer and stockman and served as vice president of the Farmers & Merchants Bank of Cedar Bluffs for several years; he came to America in 1850. His mother was born in Germany February 13, 1843, and died at Cedar Bluffs, May 13, 1891.

Mr. Ebsen attended public school at Cedar Bluffs. He is a member of the Nebraskana Society, and for the past 15 years has served as president of the Bostwick School Board. His political affiliation is with the Democratic party.

His marriage to Rosa Lichtenberg occurred at Wahoo, Nebraska. Mrs. Ebsen was born at Cedar Bluffs, August 12, 1877. Her father was born in Germany, came to America in 1861 where he engaged in farming, and in 1862 enlisted in the Civil War. They have three children: Leonard William, born December 30, 1901, who married Ruby Mae Good; Mabel Rosa, born December 20, 1905; and Alice Clarabel, born February 10, 1910. Leonard is a farmer. Residence: Bostwick.

Charles Daniel Eby

Since 1904 Charles D. Eby has been engaged in the practice of medicine in Nebraska, where he has lived his entire life. His father, John W. Eby, was born at Canton, Ohio, April 4, 1848, and died at Aurora, Oregon, December 12, 1924; his ancestry was German. His mother was born at Liberty Mills, Wabash County, Indiana, June 9, 1850, and died at Seattle, Washington, July 9, 1927. She was of Scotch descent.

Dr. Eby attended academy and later was a student at Grand Island College. He received the M. D. degree at the University of Nebraska in 1904, and is now engaged in medical practice at Leigh, Nebraska. He is a member of the Nebraska State Medical Society; the American Medical Association; and the Colfax County Medical Society. He is a member of the Leigh Chamber of Commerce and the Nebraskana Society, and a Republican, a 32nd degree Mason.

He was united in marriage with Mamie Lydia Dorothy Bowers at Wahoo, Nebraska, February 11, 1909. Mrs. Eby, who is descendant of Betsy Ross on the maternal side, was born at Leigh, August 17, 1889. Three children were born to them: Charles, born September 6, 1910, who died June 6, 1926; Olive Dell, born February 18, 1915; and Charlotte Maxine, born January 22, 1927. Residence: Leigh. (Photograph in Album).

Millard Elmer Eby

Millard E. Eby, a lifetime resident of Nebraska, has been engaged in the practice of dentistry at Hartington, Cedar County, Nebraska, since May 15, 1901. He was born at St. James, Cedar County, Nebraska, January 16, 1878, the son of Jacob H. and Sarah Ann (White) Eby. His father, who was a farmer and high school janitor for over 40 years, was born at Freeport, Illinois, October 23, 1848, and died at Hartington, September 29, 1930; his father, John Eby, who was a farmer, was born in Pennsylvania of German and English parentage. His mother, whose parents were Virginians, was born at Danville, Virginia, December 19, 1852, and is still living.

Dr. Eby was graduated from the Hartington High School in 1896, attended the University of Nebraska for

a year, and was then graduated from the Louisville College of Dentistry with the D. D. S. degree. He received his tuition each year as a scholarship for honors, and upon graduation was awarded a gold medal for all-around efficiency during his three years' work. He was active in college athletic events.

Active in dental practice in the same office building for the past 31 years, he is also president of the Hartington Building & Loan Association, and has been an extensive land owner in Nebraska for many years. A Republican, he has always taken an interest in community and state political affairs. He is a member of the local Commercial Club, the Nebraskana Society, and the Hartington Country Club; holds membership in the state and national dental societies and is affiliated with the First Congregational Church at Hartington. During the World War he was secretary of the Medical Advisory Board, since he was unable to pass the requirements for aviation service.

Dr. Eby was married to Edna Taylor at Sioux City, Iowa, June 21, 1905. Mrs. Eby, who is a niece of Professor Fossler of Lincoln, was born at Huron, South Dakota, October 25, 1882. She is active in the Congregational Church. They have four children: Helen, born June 15, 1907; Ruth, born January 27, 1909; Howard, born May 1, 1912; and Grace, born July 2, 1916. Ruth and Helen will graduate from the University of Nebraska in 1932, while Howard is a sophomore in the dental department at the University of Nebraska. Residence: Hartington. (Photograph in Album).

Edward Herman Eckert

Edward H. Eckert, justice of the peace for Saline County, Nebraska, was born at Heinrichsfelde, Pommern, Germany, May 11, 1858. His father, Wilhelm Eckert, who was a farmer, was born at Dramburg, Pommern, Germany, and died there in 1869. His mother, Emilie (Glanz) Eckert, died at Heinrichsfelde in 1880.

Judge Eckert was graduated from high school in Germany, in 1875, and attended the State Teachers Seminary at Pyritz, Germany, 1875-8. He was a teacher in the public school from that date until 1882, when he moved to America, and settled at Fontanelle, Nebraska. He worked on a farm until 1884; was teacher of German at the Theological Seminary at Crete, Saline County, Nebraska, 1884-6; acted as clerk in a real estate office, 1886-8; was bookkeeper in the First National Bank of Crete, 1888-1900; was cashier of the Irrigators Bank of Scottsbluff, Nebraska, until 1901; and engaged in the real estate business at Crete.

A Republican, Judge Eckert was a member of the Crete City Council for six years and since 1925 has been police judge of Crete, and justice of the peace for Saline County. He has lived in Nebraska for 49 years, and has taken an active part in the advancement of Saline County. He holds membership in the Crete Community Club; the Sons of Herman; the Nebraskana Society; and the Knights of Pythias. During 1907 and 1908, he was a member of the local school board. He is affiliated with the German Congregational Church of Crete, Nebraska.

On August 27, 1903, he was united in marriage with Henriette Sophia Blume, at Crete. Mrs. Eckert was born at Lebenstedt, Braunschweig, Germany, November 28, 1854. Residence: Crete. (Photograph in Album).

Allen Barnett Edee

Allen B. Edee, merchant and banker of Pawnee City, was born at Jonesville, Indiana, December 7, 1861, son of Charles Thomas and Virginia Frances Edee. His father, who was born at Utica, New York, and died April 12, 1895, was a banker and merchant.

His mother was born at Louisville, Kentucky, November 7, 1835, and died March 23, 1916.

A resident of Nebraska for 49 years, Mr. Edee has taken an active part in the civic and economic life of the state. He is a member of the Presbyterian Church and the Commercial Club.

He was united in marriage with Minnie Maude Comford at Omaha, Nebraska. Mrs. Edee, who was born at Spring Lake, Michigan, is of Scotch ancestry. To their marriage were born four children: Allen, born October 23, 1896, who married Helen Readey; Gretchen, born March 19, 1899, who married Pierce A. Jensen; Alfred, born October 27, 1900; and Gwendolyn, born January, 1903, who married Dr. Ray Vinsant. Residence: Pawnee City.

Frank Eugene Edgerton

Frank Eugene Edgerton, journalist, author, orator, and a leading member of the Nebraska bar, was born at Woodbine, Iowa, September 29, 1875. He is the son of Leroy A. and Mary (Luke) Edgerton. His father, Leroy A. Edgerton, was born at Ripon, Wisconsin, March 1, 1848, and died at Woodbine, Iowa, February 7, 1904. He was a farmer and a direct descendant of Richard Edgerton, one of the founders of Norwich, Connecticut. Mary Luke Edgerton was born in Baldwinsville, New York, July 14, 1848, and died in Woodbine, Iowa, August 18, 1918.

Frank E. Edgerton entered the University of Nebraska, in 1896, after taking preparatory work at the Woodbine, Iowa, Normal School. He was president of the senior class, was prominent in oratory and debating and was graduated in 1900, receiving his A. B. degree. He taught in the Fremont schools and joined the staff of the Lincoln Star where he remained until he became private secretary to Senator Norris Brown. He held this position from 1907 to 1910. During this time he attended George Washington University, receiving the degrees of LL. B. and LL. M. He was assistant attorney general of Nebraska from 1911 to 1915, and then joined the law firm of Hainer & Craft, which later became Hainer, Craft & Edgerton, and is now Craft, Edgerton & Fraizer. He was county attorney of Hamilton County, 1919-1920.

In politics he has taken a prominent part since his college days. As a journalist he assisted in the crusade which led to the establishment of the railway commission and the nomination of Norris Brown for the United States Senate and George L. Sheldon for governor. In 1908 he reported the Republican National Convention at Chicago, and the Democratic National Convention at Denver. In 1926, he was a candidate for the Republican congressional nomination.

Mr. Edgerton is a member of the Nebraska Writers' Guild. Besides numerous speeches, editorials and feature stories, he is the author of The Story of the Federal Constitution, The State Constitution and Motoring Through Europe. He has been a constant contributor to newspapers and magazines since 1900.

He is a member of the Sons of the American Revolution, the Mayflower Descendants, the Nebraska State Bar Association and the American Bar Association. He is a member of the Church of Christ in Aurora, and is affiliated with the Red Cross. He is a member of the Modern Woodmen of America, the Scottish Rite and the Shrine. He was the organizer and the first president of the Aurora Rotary club.

For more than ten years he has been interested in practical farming. His hobby is golf.

He was married to Mary Nettie Coe (see biography) at Woodbine, Iowa, April 2, 1902. There are three children. Harold Eugene was born April 6, 1903. He is a graduate of the University of Nebraska, 1925, a member of Acacia, and is now instructor in electrical engineering at Massachusetts Institute of Technology, Cambridge, Massachusetts, where he has received the degree of Doctor of Philosophy in electrical engineering. He married Esther Garrett, who was graduated from the state university in 1927. They have a daughter, Mary Louise, born April 3, 1931. Mary Ellen Edgerton was born October 27, 1904. She is a journalist and musician and was graduated from the University of Nebraska, in 1926. She is a member of Alpha Phi. She married Welch Pogue, University of Nebraska, 1925, and a graduate of the Harvard Law School. For one year Mr. and Mrs. Pogue resided in Paris, where Mr. Pogue practiced law in the Paris office of Ropes, Gray, Boyden & Perkins. He is now practicing law in Boston. Mr. and Mrs. Pogue have one child, Richard Welch, born April 26, 1929.

Margaret Coe Edgerton was born May 2, 1912. She spent a year at Radcliffe and is a sophomore at the University of Nebraska. She is a talented writer, and is specializing in journalism. She is a member of Alpha Phi.

In the summer of 1930, Mr. and Mrs. Edgerton and Margaret took an extended tour of Europe, traveling by auto and visiting unfrequented spots. Residence: Aurora. (Photograph on Page 369).

Mary Coe Edgerton

Mary Coe Edgerton, musician, club woman and home builder, was born at Woodbine, Iowa, March 2, 1875, daughter of Josiah and Jessie (Kinnis) Coe. Her father was a banker, farmer and stock raiser. He was born in Nelsonville, Ohio, June 16, 1843, and died in Woodbine, Iowa, May 20, 1915. The Coe family, coming from England, took a prominent part in the early settlement of Connecticut, came as pioneers to Ohio, and afterwards to Iowa.

Jessie Kinnis was born in Perth, Scotland, June 16, 1843. She was of the Maclaren clan and died in Woodbine, Iowa, November 9, 1919.

Mary Coe Edgerton attended the Woodbine Normal College, and was a student in the musical department of Oberlin College. She married Frank Eugene Edgerton, at Woodbine, Iowa, April 2, 1902. (See biography). She was one of the organizers of the Fremont Chapter of P E O and has served as president of the Aurora chapter. She is a member of the Daughters of the American Revolution, and has been an active worker in the First Christian Church of Aurora. She was president of the Aurora Woman's Club in 1923, and was president of the League of Women Voters in 1930. She is a member of the Country Club, and is keenly interested in music and civic improvement. Residence: Aurora.

Albert Edholm

Albert Edholm was born at Milton, Morgan County, Utah, June 9, 1864. Lars Peter Edholm, his father, who was born at Krongede, Sweden, July 25, 1825, was a farmer who came to America with his father, Bengt Larson, and crossed the western plains twice before the railroads came into the new country. He was a graduate of Upsala University in Sweden, and served as probate judge after settling in Utah. Johanna Justina Edholm, his mother, was born in Sweden and died at Omaha, Nebraska, January, 1895.

Mr. Edholm attended the Omaha public schools until 1879, and always ranked high in scholastic honors. In 1887 he homesteaded in Wyoming, where he remained until 1888. From 1890-1921 he operated Albert Edholm Retail Jewel Shop in a street level store. Since then he has had an upstairs location.

His marriage to Susie Lee Erskine was solemnized at St. Louis, Missouri, March 20, 1890. Mrs. Edholm was born at Huntsville, Alabama, September 6, 1869. To this union were born two children: Bessie, born December 5, 1891, who married Clyde J. Drouillard; and Janet, born November 23, 1893, who married Ralph E. Conrad.

On November 17, 1900, Mr. Edholm was married to Mrs. K. J. Donnelly, at Omaha. They have one daughter, Camilla, born November 19, 1901. She is a school teacher.

Mr. Edholm was a member of Company C of the Home Guards in which he served as corporal, during the war. He was a diligent worker for funds for the cyclone sufferers in Omaha. He is a member of the Omaha & Council Bluffs Jewelers Guild, and is serving on the member-

FRANK E. EDGERTON

ship committee of the Omaha Chamber of Commerce; and is a member of the Noonday Club and the Nebraskana Society. A Scottish Rite Mason, and Shriner, he is affiliated with First Church of Christ Scientist, Omaha, and is a member of the comforts committee of this church. His social clubs are the Carter Lake Club, in Omaha, and the Dewey Lake Club, in Cherry County, Nebraska. His favorite sports are angling, fly and bait casting, and his hobby is philately. Residence: Omaha.

H. H. Ediger

H. H. Ediger, a pioneer farmer in York County, Nebraska, has lived near Henderson for the past 56 years. He was born at Alexandertol, Russia, October 23, 1865, the son of Cornelius and Agnes (Dohl) Ediger. His father, who was born in Russia, May 11, 1827, and died at Hampton, Hamilton County, Nebraska, April 30, 1898, was a farmer and came to this country in 1875. His mother was born in Russia, August 23, 1827, and died at Hampton, April 28, 1910.

Mr. Ediger was married at Petersburg, Boone County, Nebraska, January 22, 1889, to Anna Baerg. Mrs. Ediger, who is an energetic farm woman, was born at Lichenau, Russia, October 28, 1867. Their children are: Henry, born May 3, 1892; John, born March 9, 1894; Anna, born July 10, 1896; Peter, born October 21, 1899; Chris, born July 9, 1902; Jacob, born September 3, 1905; and Tena, born September 28, 1907. All their children are farmers.

Mr. Ediger is affiliated with the Mennonite Brethren Church. Residence: Henderson.

William Edmonds

William Edmonds, physician and surgeon since 1900, was born at Fredonia, New York, February 1, 1871. He is the son of Richard and Rebecca (Cattelle) Edmonds, the former a contractor and builder of English descent, who died at Fredonia, in 1916. Rebecca Cattelle is a native of England.

Dr. Edmonds received his elementary education in the Fredonia public schools, and attended the Fredonia Normal School. He studied medicine at the Jefferson School in Philadelphia, and received his M. D. in 1900.

On April 10, 1904, he was married to Mary Martha MacVean at Chicago. She is a physician, specializing in diseases of the eye, ear, nose and throat in Nebraska City. They have two daughters, Mary, born December 31, 1905, who married George Mayer; and Edith Elizabeth, born September 5, 1908, who married Merle Hasselbalch.

Dr. Edmonds has been engaged in the practice of medicine and surgery in Nebraska City, for twenty-six years. For the past seven years he has been physician for the Morton-Gregson Packing Company. He has been prominent in professional organizations for many years, and is a member of the Nebraska State Medical Society, and vice president of the Otoe County Medical Society. At the present time he is giving a course in life saving, first aid, etc., to men in Nebraska City. A captain in the Reserve Officers' Association he was commissioned first lieutenant in the Medical Corps in the World War.

He is a member of the American Legion, the Masons and Odd Fellows, and is a member of the Episcopal Church, and has served as a vestryman and on various music committees in the church. He devotes much time to Boy Scout work, giving first aid instruction, and hiking. His hobby is collecting Indian souvenirs and relics. Residence: Nebraska City.

Andrew J. Edstrom

One of the outstanding physicians and surgeons of Nebraska, Andrew J. Edstrom has been engaged in practice for many years. He was born at Skorped, Sweden, August 14, 1878, the son of John A. and Christina (Olnilson) Edstrom. His father, who is a blacksmith and stone cutter, was born at Skorped, May 12, 1854. His mother was born in Sweden, January 10, 1857, and died at Duluth, Minnesota, May 2, 1928.

Dr. Edstrom completed his high school education at Bethel Academy in 1911, and in 1915, received the M. D. degree from Creighton Medical College at Omaha. He was president of his senior class at Bethel Academy in 1911. At this time he is the manager of the Medical, Physical and Electro-Therapeutic Clinic with hospitals at Grand Island, Columbus, York, and Stromsburg, Nebraska, with several physicians in his employ. At one time he owned a private hospital at Clyde, Kansas. He resides at Stromsburg, where he is affiliated with the First Baptist Church.

He is a member of the Hall County Medical Society, the Nebraska State Medical Society, and the American Medical Association. He is a Scottish Rite Mason and Shriner.

On April 6, 1900, he was married at Quamba, Minnesota, to Freeda M. Lundeen, who was born at Borsho, Sweden, December 6, 1884, and died several years ago. Four children were born to this marriage: Minne, born November 20, who died January 22, 1901; Alice Victoria, October 22, 1901, who died August 30, 1904; Edith Christine, born September 22, 1903; and Alice Dorothy, born February 13, 1906. He married Amy A. Johnson at Kiron, Iowa, in 1913; she died May 20, 1927. Alice received the B. S. degree at Manhattan, Kansas, in 1924, and the M. D. degree at the University of Nebraska. Edith received the R. N. degree from the Nebraska University Hospital in Omaha, Nebraska, and the B. S. degree from the University of Nebraska. Edith is a teacher in a nurses training school at Flint, Michigan, and for three years prior to this time was a teacher in nurses training schools in Pennsylvania and New Jersey. Residence: Grand Island. (Photograph in Album).

Charles Busby Edwards

Born at Lexington, Nebraska, September 30, 1889, Charles Busby Edwards, physician and surgeon, is the son of John Henry and Amanda Belle (Busby) Edwards. His father, born at Findley, Ohio, October 21, 1865, was a merchant, stockman and landowner, who died at Beaver City, January 28, 1924. He was the son of Ephriam Edwards, born in Tunbridge Wells, Kent County, England, on November 2, 1843, and Lucinda Huff, his wife, born in Hancock County, Ohio, October 7, 1846. Amanda Belle Busby was born at Jewett, Ohio, September 3, 1865, daughter of Shadrach and Sarah (Galbraith) Busby.

Charles Edwards attended Beaver City public school, Peru State Normal College and received his medical degree from Creighton University. He was made a member of Phi Beta Pi and was active in baseball while in college.

On December 31, 1921, Dr. Edwards was united in marriage to Lillian Margaret Arendt at Lincoln. Mrs. Edwards was born at Elm Creek, Nebraska, October 14, 1898. There are two sons, Charles C., born September 16, 1923; and Marlin Keith, born May 23, 1927; both were born at Overton.

Dr. Edwards is a Republican. He served two years in the World War with the ranks of lieutenant and captain, one year of which was overseas service with Base Hospital No. 10. He is a member of the American Legion, the Veterans of Foreign Wars, the Chamber of Commerce, Rotary Club, the Elks and the Masons. His professional organizations include the American Medical Association and the Buffalo County Medical Society. He is fond of sport, and is a member of the Kearney Country Club. Residence: Kearney.

Clarence Arthur Edwards

In 1884 Clarence Arthur Edwards came to Nebraska from his native state, Illinois, and for many years has been a leader in the business life of Dawson and Buffalo

Counties. He was born at Moline, Illinois, November 17, 1859, son of Herbert Root and Harriet M. (Gordon) Edwards.

Herbert Root Edwards, a mason and later a farmer, was born at Guilford, Vermont, December 3, 1826, and died at Orion, Illinois, in November, 1874. William Edwards, the earliest known forebear of the family, was born in Coventry, Connecticut, July 25, 1741, and his son, Benajah, was born there on May 3, 1772.

Harriet M. Gordon, who was a school teacher, and of pioneer parentage, was born in Wayne County, Michigan, July 10, 1833. She died at Geneseo, Illinois, December 25, 1929. Her ancestry was traced to the Gordon family, members of which settled in the Salem Colony in Massachusetts, and one of whom was Abner Gordon.

Clarence Arthur Edwards attended rural and village schools and was later a student at Northern Indiana Normal School. From 1881-84, he was resident engineer for the Burlington, Cedar Rapids and Northern Railway. During the years 1886 to 1891, he was county surveyor of Dawson County, and from 1894 to 1901, was engineer and manager of the Gothenburg Power and Irrigation Canal. From 1902-13, he was county surveyor of Buffalo County and city engineer of Kearney.

In 1913, Mr. Edwards became superintendent of the Gothenburg Light and Power Company, serving until 1920, when he became highway commissioner for a term of four years. At the present time he is city engineer of Gothenburg.

His marriage to Vina Luhm was solemnized at Manchester, Iowa, April 14, 1885. Mrs. Edwards, who is of German parentage, was born at Watertown, Wisconsin, March 21, 1862. There are five children living and one deceased:

Florence, born June 20, 1888; Dan Gordon, June 2, 1892, who married Ethel Arbuckle; Herbert Christian, Jr., born January 10, 1894, who married Dorothy Rhodes; Gladys H., born February 8, 1898, who married Glenn H. Mahen; Frank C., born August 28, 1901, who married Dorothy Sack; and Edward, born August 28, 1901, who died in May, 1902. Gordon is superintendent of the Gothenburg Light and Power Company; Herbert is an engineer for the Packard Motor Company, and Frank is superintendent of an excavation company.

Mr. Edwards is a member of the American Association of Engineers, the Modern Woodmen of America, the Washington Memorial Association and The Nebraskana Society. Residence: Gothenburg.

Clifford E. O. Edwards

A lifetime resident of Nebraska is Clifford E. O. Edwards, who is a cement contractor at Kearney. He was born at Gibbon, Nebraska, August 20, 1892, the son of E. R. Edwards and Lulu (Blair) Edwards. His father, who was a farmer and cement contractor, was born in Wisconsin, and died at Kearney, June 24, 1923. His mother was born at Denver, Colorado, February 20, 1868.

Mr. Edwards attended the Kearney Military Academy until 1913, and since then has been in business at Kearney. He is a member of the Chamber of Commerce and Kiwanis Club, is affiliated with St. Luke's Church, and holds membership in the Country Club and the Elks. His favorite sport is hunting. During the World War, Mr. Edwards served as a first class private in the Marine Corps of the United States and is now a member of the American Legion.

He was married at Kearney, July 8, 1922, to Amelia Marguerite Romano, who was born at Omaha, Nebraska, August 4, 1894. To this marriage were born: Jean Lou, July 11, 1923; Clifford, Jr., September 3, 1924; and Donald B., April 13, 1928. Residence: Kearney.

Lewis Clifford Edwards

In a frontier cabin of stone and hewn logs, near what is now Glen Rock, Nebraska, Lewis Clifford Edwards was born on September 28, 1878. The son of true pioneers, Andrew Jay and Elvira Isabelle (Mullins) Edwards, his parents were natives of Ohio and Indiana, respectively. Andrew J. Edwards, left an orphan, was reared by an uncle, James Ammons, who took him to South Bend, Indiana, where he grew to manhood. During the first year of the Civil War he enlisted with Company B, 48th Indiana Volunteer Infantry. The 48th Indiana Infantry, which was organized at Goshen, Indiana, in 1861, fought at Fort Donelson in February, 1862, and was at the seige of Corinth, Mississippi, in May, 1862. It then joined in the pursuit of General Price and fought at the Battle of Iuka, in September, 1862, where 116 of its men were killed out of the 420 engaged. In October of that year, it took part in the second battle of Corinth, under General Rosecrans, and later joined Grant's army, with which it pushed to the rear of Vicksburg and took part in the skirmish of Forty Hills, on May 3, 1863. Later in that month it participated in the battle of Raymond, Mississippi, on the 13th, and at Champion Hills on the 14th, where it lost 33 killed and wounded. On May 22, 1863, it took part in the assault on Tunnell Hill, and the Vicksburg forts. The regiment re-enlisted as a veteran organization in January, 1864, and later they joined Sherman's army on its march from Atlanta to the sea. Following the capture of Savannah they took part in the campaign through the Carolinas to Raleigh, thence to Petersburg, Va., and on to Washington, from which they were transferred to Louisville, Kentucky, where they were mustered out on July 15, 1865. Andrew J. Edwards was transferred to the Veteran's Reserve Corps on September 22, 1863, and re-enlisted on June 23, 1863, for three years additional service.

During the last year of the war he came to Nebraska, and located at Omaha, where he was employed on various stage lines as a driver. He then entered the employ of the Union Pacific in construction work, and was stationed at Fort Laramie, Wyoming for some period of time. Upon his return to Nebraska he was again employed on mail and stage lines out of Omaha. He made his home in Otoe County for several years, and after farming in Nemaha County some years located at Humboldt, in 1885. He died there on November 15, 1906.

His wife, Elvira Isabelle Mullins, was born in Crawford, Indiana, April 26, 1849. She is the daughter of Lewis Clasby and Elizabeth (Hume) Mullins. Her father was the son of Lindsey and Millie (Sutherd) Mullins, of Virginia. Elizabeth Hume was a daughter of John Gray Hume. To this marriage the following children were born: Gila J. of Lincoln; Lewis Clifford of Falls City; Warren C. of Lincoln; Calvert T., of Lincoln; Marcia, who married H. M. Bradley of Lincoln, and Jesse Lee, who died in Nemaha County.

Lewis C. Edwards attended the public schools of Glen Rock and Humboldt, later serving an apprenticeship in a photograph gallery at Humboldt, after which he entered the office of the *Humboldt Standard*, in 1890. Learning the trade of printer, he then entered the employ of the *Humboldt Enterprise*. In 1901, he realized his ambition of becoming a paper owner, and purchased the *Humboldt Standard*. He operated and edited this paper for about five years, later entering a partnership with Oliver Hall, under the firm name of Edwards & Hall. A Democrat, he was in November, 1905, elected register of deeds for Richardson County. At the expiration of his term of four years he was re-elected, holding office a total of nine years. In November, 1916, he was candidate on the Democratic ticket for state senator, and carried his home county by a large majority, although he took no active part in the campaign. From 1915-20, he was deputy clerk of the district court of Richardson County.

On September 28, 1909, his marriage to Jessie Elvira Paxton was solemnized at Nebraska City. Mrs. Edwards was born near Chambers, Nebraska, in January, 1890. She is a daughter of Dr. Galen C. and Laura B. (Cain) Paxton of Falls City, the latter being a daughter of William R. Cain, who with his wife, settled in Richardson County in pioneer days. Dr. Paxton is the son of William L. Paxton, also a pioneer in Richardson County. The Edwards have one child, Bettye Isabelle, born March 31, 1911. She graduated from Falls City High School and attended Stephens College for Women, and Peru State Teachers College.

Mr. Edwards is one of the recognized Democratic leaders of Richardson County. Since 1924 he has been managers of the firm of Edwards-Goldsmith Abstract Company. During his varied business career he has devoted much time to writing. He is the author of *Edwards History of Richardson County*. He is a true lover of history, a student of archaeology, and has contributed to some valuable research work along the banks of the Missouri River, where he, with others, has unearthed various skeletal remains, ornaments, etc., which have been pronounced remains of a prehistoric race by persons of authority on the subject. He is a member of the Nebraska Historical Society, The Nebraskana Society, etc. He and his wife are affiliated with St. Thomas Episcopal Church. He is a Mason and an Odd Fellow. Residence: Falls City.

Thomas Aloysius Egan

Born at Chicago, Illinois, November 13, 1884, Thomas Aloysius Egan is the son of John and Ellen Bunyan Egan. His father, a native of Ireland, came to America in 1880, and died at Chicago, in 1910. His mother, also born in Ireland, is still living.

Thomas Egan was educated in Holy Family and St. Ingnatius Schools in Chicago, attended Loyola University, and received his A. B. and M. A. degrees from St. Louis University in 1908 and 1910 respectively. He was ordained to the Jesuit order in 1918.

Since 1920 he has been professor of sociology at Creighton University. He is a member of the Catholic Church, the American Sociological Society and the American Philosophical Society. Residence: Omaha.

Max Jacob Egge

Max Jacob Egge, a resident of Nebraska all his life, has been engaged in the jewelry and optical business at Grand Island for the past 36 years. He was born at Grand Island, May 4, 1871, the son of Adolph Peter and Ottielie Marie (Rosenkranz) Egge. His father, who was born at Holstein, Germany, December 5, 1845, and died at Grand Island, June 30, 1900, was a coal merchant. His mother was born at Holstein, October 26, 1850, and died at Grand Island, April 25, 1908.

Mr. Egge attended school at Grand Island, and then entered the jewelry business there, later becoming an optometrist. A Republican, he has been chairman of the County Central Committee for six years, was city treasurer for two terms, and served as city councilman for two terms. He is past president of the Chamber of Commerce and Rotary Club, and is affiliated with the First Christian Church of Grand Island.

He is an Elk, holds membership in the Shrine Body of the Masons, and is a member of the Grand Island Golf Club. His marriage to Ada Florence Casad was solemnized at Cortland, Nebraska, December 7, 1899. Mrs. Egge, who was a school teacher before her marriage, was born at Oskaloosa, Iowa, March 29, 1873. Residence: Grand Island.

Harold Everett Eggers

Harold Everett Eggers, physician and surgeon, was born at Royalton, Wisconsin, March 1, 1882, son of Frederic and Louise (Matchiniski) Eggers.

He obtained his medical degree from Rush Medical

College in 1909, his Bachelor of Science degree in 1903, and his Masters degree in 1905 from the University of Wisconsin. There he was a member of Phi Beta Kappa.

His marriage to Eunice Cartwright was solemnized at Chicago, on November 15, 1911.

Dr. Eggers is the author of many pathological articles. He was a fellow of pathology at the University of Chicago, in 1905-06, and a graduate fellow in pathology at Rush Medical College, 1910-1911. From 1911 until 1916, he was professor of pathology at Harvard Medical School.

During the World War he held ranks from lieutenant to major, and is now a lieutenant colonel in the Medical Reserve Corps. Residence: Omaha.

Peter Eginton, Sr.

Peter Eginton, Sr., livestock buyer and feeder, was born in Kluken, County West Mead, Ireland, May 28, 1883, son of George and Elizabeth (Ray) Eginton. He came to the United States, November 4, 1884, with his parents. His father homesteaded in Keith County in 1884, and resided there until his death on August 3, 1928. The homestead is still retained in the possession of the Eginton family.

His mother, a devoted homemaker, died on the homestead, June 29, 1923. There were six children in the family, five of whom are still living, Dan, born March 12, 1881; Katherine, born October 1, 1882; Peter, born May 28, 1883; Sadie, born September 8, 1884; and Elizabeth, born November 4, 1891; and Prudence, August 29, 1893. Dan, Katherine, Peter and Sadie were all born in Ireland; Dan died in July, 1906.

Mr. Eginton was married on March 16, 1919, to Freda Harriet Fritsche at Ogallala, Nebraska. She was born in Osborne, Kansas, January 24, 1896, the daughter of August John and Bertha Anne Fritsche. She is a member of the Lutheran Church and the Order of the Eastern Star. They have one daughter, Elizabeth Ann, born February 29, 1920; and one son, Peter, Jr., born December 7, 1921.

Mr. Eginton is a Republican, is affiliated with the Episcopal Church, a member of the Ancient Free and Accepted Masons, the Ancient Arabic Order of the Nobles of the Mystic Shrine, and is fond of all sports. Residence: Paxton. (Photograph on Page 373).

Frank Ludwig Ehlers

Frank L. Ehlers was born at Fort Atkinson, Wisconsin, August 20, 1871, the son of John and Wilhelmine Ehlers. John Ehlers, a farmer, was born in Germany, and died at Atkinson, Wisconsin. Wilhelmine, wife of John, was born in Germany, in March, 1848, and lives in Hebron. He attended public school to the seventh grade and then entered parochial school for a term of three years.

Amelia (Schoenfeld) Ehlers, wife of Frank L. Ehlers, was born at Friedensau, Nebraska, April 21, 1876. Their marriage took place at Deshler, Nebraska, February 19, 1895. To this union were born six children: Ella, born January 11, 1896, who is married to Herbert Harms; Wilbur Carl, born March 12, 1900, who is married to Anna Schoene; Delma, born July 7, 1904, who is married to Dwoyd Schroel; Edgar, born May 1, 1906; Roy, born March 16, 1908; and Orville, born August 13, 1912. These children are all living on farms.

Mr. Ehlers is a successful farmer and a breeder of pure bred Shorthorn cattle. He is a stockholder in the Deshler Grain Company, and is associated with the Deshler Co-operative Creamery Company. During the World War he was active in home defense work, and purchased a large amount of bonds and participated in Red Cross work. He is still a member of the Red Cross. His religious affiliation is with the Lutheran Church of Friendensau, Nebraska. Mr. Ehlers is one of Thayer County's most highly respected citizens and in recogni-

PETER EGINTON, SR.

Dedmore—North Platte

tion of his work for the advancement of his community he has been awarded life membership in the Nebraskana Society. Mr. Ehlers is a Democrat. Residence: Deshler. (Photograph in Album).

Walter Richard Ehlers

Walter Richard Ehlers, grain and livestock dealer was born at Scribner, Nebraska, August 20, 1895, son of William P. and Emma K. (Hendricks) Ehlers. His father and mother were both born in Germany, and at the present time are residing at Dix. Prior to coming to Dix, Mr. Ehlers was a farmer and livestock dealer at Scribner, Nebraska.

Upon his graduation from Scribner High School in 1913, Mr. Ehlers entered the bank at Malcolm, Nebraska, where he was employed until 1916. He became assistant cashier of the Logan Valley Bank at Uehling, Nebraska, in 1916, holding that position until 1918. He served in the United States Army in 1918 with the rank of sergeant first class, and in 1931 was county commander of the Kimball County organization of the American Legion.

From 1919 until 1922 Mr. Ehlers was cashier and president of the Citizens State Bank at Dix. Since that time he has been in the grain and livestock business, selling his bank in 1922 to the Farmers State Bank of Dix. He is chairman of the village board at Dix, and is a Republican.

On November 11, 1919, he was married to Clara Sievers at Omaha. Mrs. Ehlers was born at Scribner, Nebraska, November 11, 1896. They have two children, Carrol Walter, born in August, 1920; and Kenneth Warren, born in August, 1922.

Mr. Ehlers is a Protestant. He is a member of the Red Cross, the Masons, the Odd Fellows, of which he is past Noble Grand, and from 1922-1925 was treasurer of school district number two. He is fond of baseball, and was coach on the Fort Sheridan army baseball team in the summer of 1919. He also enjoys golf. Residence: Dix.

Frank A. Eichberg

Frank A. Eichberg was born at Hoengroph, Germany, January 1, 1858, the son of John and Minnie Eichberg. His father, a farmer, was born in Germany and died at Columbus, Wisconsin. His mother was also a native of Germany.

Mr. Eichberg has been a farmer in Madison County for the past 52 years, and is a stockholder in the Van Sicle Paint Company of Tilden, Nebraska. He is a member of the Nebraska State Historical Society, is affiliated with the Methodist Episcopal Church, and holds membership in the Nebraskana Society.

He was united in marriage with Ernestine Minnie Groening at Waterloo, Wisconsin, February 15, 1885. Mrs. Eichberg was born in Germany, March 16, 1861, and died at Tilden, February 21, 1922. Four children were born to them: Lilly Mae, November 8, 1887, who married Dwight O. Whitehorn; Lydia Louise, August 3, 1891, who died November 9, 1928; Frank H., born July 3, 1893, who married Dorothy Eichberg; and Arvid Charles, April 28, 1895, who married Lillie Wettier. Residence: Tilden.

George Charles Eicher

On March 17, 1890, George C. Eicher was born at Toledo, Ohio, the son of Charles F. and Grace Margaret (Harkey) Eicher. He attended the public and high schools of Toledo, and was married to Alice Marie Schroeder there. Mrs. Eicher was born at Toledo, November 21, 1896.

His father was born at Mount Pleasant, Pennsylvania, November 19, 1852, and is in the newspaper business, his ancestors coming to America from Germany, in 1720. His mother was the daughter of the Reverend Sid-

ney Levi Harkey, D. D., prominent Lutheran clergyman and educator. She was born at Quincy, Illinois, October 23, 1861, and died at Toledo, July 2, 1928.

Mr. Eicher is the father of two children, Grove, born February 16, 1918; and Irene, born May 30, 1926. He is a Republican and has been in the feed manufacturing business for twenty-six years. He started as office boy and is now general manager of one of the largest mills in the state of Nebraska, The G. E. Conkey Company. He is a director also of the Dresch Laboratories Company of Toledo, Ohio, manufacturers of dental materials.

Among the organizations to which Mr. Eicher belongs are the First Lutheran Church, of Nebraska City, the Chamber of Commerce, Rotary Club, and the Elks. He is also a Mason. His clubs are Heather Downs Golf Club (Toledo), Nebraska City Country Club, and Omaha Athletic Club. His hobby is reading. Residence: Nebraska City.

Arwin Calvin Eiker

Arwin Calvin Eiker, farmer and stock feeder, was born in Webster City, Iowa, October 19, 1888, and came to Nebraska 32 years ago. His father was born in Galesburg, Illinois, in January, 1858, and is now a retired farmer. His mother, Sallie McCook Stafford, was born at Columbus, Ohio, in November, 1863. His parents are now residing at Ogallala, Nebraska.

Mr. Eiker attended public school, and has since engaged in farming.

On September 27, 1911, he was married to Edith Harrison at Big Spring. Mrs. Eiker was born at Grant, Nebraska, December 12, 1891. She is a member of the Big Spring Methodist Church, the Royal Neighbors and is president of the South Side Progressive Club of Big Spring.

To Mr. and Mrs. Eiker were born three children, two of whom are living, Harrison, September 18, 1913, died June 22, 1917; Louise, on April 19, 1918; and Calvin, on December 30, 1924. The children are members of the 4-H club. Louise was a member of the Beef Dairy and Sheep Clubs, 1931, and is taking an active part in them this year. She is also a member of the Girl Scouts and the Knighthood of Youth Club.

Mr. Eiker is a member of the Big Spring Methodist Church, Modern Woodmen of America of which he served as officer 1910-29, the Odd Fellows, the Parent-Teachers' Association, and from 1913 until 1917 was director of school district No. 3. He has taken an active part in all 4-H club work and has been a club leader the past three years. His favorite sport is golf, while his hobbies are reading and mechanics. Residence: Big Spring.

Roy David Eiker

Roy David Eiker, electrical dealer, was born at Blairsburg, Iowa, January 30, 1886, son of Calvin Armstrong and Sallie McCook (Stafford) Eiker.

The father was born in Knoxville, Illinois, December 23, 1858, and until 1918 was a farmer. He is now a honey producer. He is active in civic work and was first president and co-organizer of the Keith County Agricultural Society, his ancestry is Pennsylvania Dutch. The mother, Sallie McCook, was born in Columbus, Ohio, November 2, 1861. Her father, J. A. Stafford, organized Company K of Columbus, Ohio, and was elected captain, serving through the entire war.

Mr. Eiker attended country school. He came from Iowa to Polk County in 1898 and moved to Keith County in 1905. He farmed until 1918 when he moved to Ogallala. He built the artificial ice plant there in 1920 and sold it in 1922. At that time he went into the electrical contracting business. In addition he handles the Delcolight and Frigidaire dealership for three counties.

He was married in 1910 to Dora Pearl Caskey of Big Springs, Nebraska. She died at Ogallala, November 23, 1918. There are two children of this marriage, Eva Naomi, born May 29, 1911; and Harlow Earl, born February 8, 1913.

Mr. Eiker's second marriage was to Edna Mae Mc-Leod, daughter of Charles McLeod, a farmer and banker and state representative from Stanton County several terms and also a member of the constitutional convention. They were married at Stanton, January 17, 1923. There are two children of this marriage, Lois Ann, born July 1, 1925; and Zola Mae, born March 7, 1928. Eva will graduate from Children Hospital as a nurse this year; Harlow was just graduated from Ogallala High School.

Mr. Eiker is a Republican. In 1908 he joined the Presbyterian Church and in 1918 his membership was transferred to the Congregational Church. He is district deputy grand master of the Odd Fellows at the present time, and is a member of the Commercial Club and the Rotary Club. Formerly he enjoyed playing tennis and at the present time his favorite sport is golf. His hobby is mechanics. Residence: Ogallala.

Julius Joseph Eimers

Julius Joseph Eimers, newspaper man and abstractor, has lived at South Sioux City, Dakota County, Nebraska, since 1887. He was born at Peterson, Clay County, Iowa, January 29, 1871, the son of Joseph and Mary (Schwartz) Eimers. His father, who was a mechanic, was born in Germany, and died at Storm Lake, Buena Vista County, Iowa, 1884. His mother was born in Germany and died at Denver, Colorado, in 1895.

Mr. Eimers received his education in the public and high schools of Storm Lake, Iowa, and then moved to South Sioux City where he was the publisher of the *Dakota County Record*, 1895-1909. He is now the owner and manager of the Dakota County Abstract Company, is vice president of the Nebraska State Bank, and is vice president and director of the Nebraska State Bank at South Sioux City. From 1900 to 1908 he served as county judge in Dakota County.

During the World War Mr. Eimers served as chairman of the Red Cross of South Sioux City, was chairman of the Dakota County Chapter of the Red Cross, and acted as county food administrator. He holds membership in the American Title Association, is a Mason, and is a member of the Odd Fellows and Modern Woodmen of America. He was president of the board of education 1910-18, was president of the South Sioux City Commercial Club, 1929, and is affiliated with the Presbyterian Church. His favorite recreations are fishing and reading.

He married Mary Luella Stamm at Sioux City, Iowa, November 25, 1903; she was born at Lena, Illinois, January 4, 1877. Their daughter, Marion, who was born March 23, 1907, was graduated from the University of Nebraska and is married to George F. Branigan. Mr. Branigan is an educator. Residence: South Sioux City.

John Jacob Eisele

Born at Cedar Creek, Nebraska, May 10, 1880, the son of John Jacob Eisele and Sarah A. (Berge) Eisele, John Jacob Eisele, Jr., has been a resident of this state all his life. His father, who was born at Wurtemberg, Germany, August 29, 1839, and died at Lincoln, Nebraska, was a farmer. He was living at Atlanta, Georgia, at the beginning of the Civil War, and unable to escape draft into the southern army in any other way he fled to Mexico, returning at the end of the war. The parents of Sarah A. (Berge) Eisele were natives of Pennsylvania where the family had lived for several generations.

Mr. Eisele received his education in a rural school near Douglas, Nebraska, and since completion of his education has been a farmer near Juniata, Nebraska. He is president of the Parent Teachers Association, and is superintendent of the Baptist Sunday School. His hobby is reading.

He was united in marriage with Amelia Pauline Basch

at Hastings, Nebraska, April 11, 1906; she was born at Juniata, April 30, 1879, of German parentage. Their children are: Harold, born January 23, 1908; and Ray, born January 31, 1909. Harold was graduated from Grand Island College in 1929 and in 1931 received the Masters degree. Ray is a student at Hastings College. Residence: Juniata.

Gustaf Enoch Ekstrand

Gustaf Enoch Ekstrand was born at Chicago, Illinois, October 15, 1889, the son of Gustaf Nelson and Charlotta (Swanson) Ekstrand. His father was born in Sweden, November 17, 1854, came to America in 1887, where he was a farmer, and died at Stromsburg, Nebraska, December 2, 1930. His mother was born at Smalan, Sweden, November 23, 1854, and came to this country with her husband.

Mr. Ekstrand, who is a salesman for the Rystrom Company at Stromsburg, has lived in Nebraska for over 30 years. He is a member of the Nebraskana Society, was chairman of the Red Cross roll call for Polk County for three years, was chairman of the Citizens' Military Training Camp for Polk County for three years, and is now chairman of the local Boy Scouts. A Republican, he was the defeated candidate for county clerk in 1930.

During the World War he was corporal of the 75th Company, 6th Regiment of the United States Marines, and the 2nd division of the American Expeditionary Forces. While overseas, he participated in the Meuse-Argonne engagement, marched to the Rhine, and was in the Army of Occupation in Germany.

He was united in marriage with Hilda Henrietta Peterson at Omaha, Nebraska, May 21, 1921. Mrs. Ekstrand, who is of Swedish parentage, was born at Omaha, September 5, 1889. Four children were born to them: Arnold E., born April 15, 1923; James G., born March 19, 1924; Elizabeth Ann, born October 20, 1926, died July 6 1930; and Margaret L., born February 27, 1929.

Mr. Ekstrand has served 3 years as post commander and 2 years as post adjutant of the local post of the American Legion. Residence: Stromsburg.

Oscar John Ekstrand

Born at Ulrickshamn, Elfsborgs, Lan, Sweden, March 17, 1883, Oscar John Ekstrand has been a resident of Nebraska 47 years. He is the son of Swan August and Marie Christine (Gustafson) Ekstrand, the former born at Ulrickshamn, June 10, 1841. He arrived in America May 16, 1884, a laborer and penniless, settling in Nebraska, where he became a successful farmer. He died at Oakland, December 16, 1910. Marie Christine Gustafson was born in Ulrickshamn, May 22, 1859, and makes her home with her son, Oscar.

Oscar Ekstrand attended country schools, and followed in the footsteps of his father, as a farmer. He manages his own farm and dairy and is president of the Burt County Fair Association, the Logan Valley Federal Farm Loan Association, and is connected with the First National Bank, is secretary of the Farmers Co-operative Union and director of the Farmers Mutual Insurance Company. He was awarded the master farmer's gold medal, class of 1930. A Republican, he is active in local politics and is district committeeman.

On May 26, 1909, he was married to Clara Christine Nelson at Omaha. Mrs. Ekstrand was born at Oakland, April 13, 1886, of Swedish parents. There are six children, Leila Marie, born March 20, 1910; Clarice Mae, born May 24, 1911; Enid Elaine, born October 26, 1912; Arlene June, born June 22, 1914; Elwin Francis, born January 5, 1916, and Inez Dorene, born May 17, 1917. Four of the children are graduates of Oakland High School, and the two youngest still attend it. Lula Marie was graduated from the University in 1930; Clarice May finishes in 1932; and Enid is a graduate of the Lincoln School of Commerce.

During the late War, Mr. Ekstrand was a member of

several committees on Liberty Loan drives and other activities. He was president of the Oakland P. T. A. in 1929, and a director of the school district No. 48 from 1914-1923. He is a director of the Burt County Farm Bureau, attends the First Swedish Baptist Church, and is a member of the Masons, Eastern Star, Modern Woodmen of America and the Vikings. He is the owner of the Oakland Golf Links, but is not a member, his favorite sport being baseball. Residence: Oakland. (Photograph in Album).

Charles Elmer Eldred

Charles Elmer Eldred, judge of the district court, was born at Argyle, Wisconsin, June 30, 1870, son of Charles Carroll and Euphema Jane (Hunnell) Eldred.

The father was born in New York state, November 12, 1832, and died at Kansas City, Missouri, July 23, 1914. He was a carpenter and contractor. His wife, Euphema, was born in Indiana, in 1832, and died at Argyle, Wisconsin, in October, 1875.

Judge Eldred attended common schools in Owego Mills, Wisconsin, and was graduated from high school at Argyle.

He was admitted to the bar in Phillipsburg, Kansas, on January 16, 1890, and in 1901 was elected mayor of McCook. He held this office three successive terms. He was county judge of Red Willow County, Nebraska, part of 1901 and 1902, and county attorney for two terms beginning January, 1903.

Since 1920 he has been judge of the 14th Judicial District of Nebraska, and is a candidate without opposition for re-election at this time. He is a Republican.

On August 18, 1892, he was married to Jessie Anne Pratt at Phillipsburg, Kansas. Mrs. Eldred was born at Brooklyn, New York, February 19, 1869. There are three children, William Carroll, born August 15, 1893, who married Mary Russell; Charles Pratt, born April 28, 1897, who married Opal Nelson; and John Elliot, born September 11, 1905, who married Agra Genho.

Judge Eldred is a member of the American, Nebraska State, and the 14th Judicial District Bar Associations. He is a Modern Woodman of America, a Mason, Blue Lodge No. 135 at McCook, Chapter No. 35, and the Royal Arch Masons. He is a member of the Ancient Order of United Workmen, and the Young Men's Christian Association. His favorite sport is golf. Residence: McCook.

Robert Bruce Eldredge

Robert Bruce Eldredge, physician and surgeon, was born at York, Nebraska, November 14, 1898, son of Delmer Cornelius and Cora (Gilbert) Eldredge.

He was graduated from Central High School at Omaha, in 1916, and received his medical degree from the University of Nebraska in 1922.

His marriage to Katherine Gohery was solemnized at Omaha, on May 11, 1920.

Dr. Eldrege is a member of the American, Douglas County and Omaha Medical Associations, the Nebraska-Iowa Pediatric Society, and the University of Nebraska College of Medicine. Residence: Omaha.

Israel Curtis Eller

Born at Brookville, Iowa, December 17, 1853, Israel Curtis Eller has been in public life in Washington County nearly fifty years, and has a distinguished record. He is the son of Harvey and Mary Caroline (Vannoy) Eller, the former of whom was born at Wilksboro, North Carolina, March 24, 1819. A farmer all his life, he died at Farson, Wapello County, Iowa, November 3, 1906. He was descended from Christian Eller who came from Rotterdam to Philadelphia October 9, 1747, and whose descendants removed to North Carolina.

Mary Caroline Vannoy was also a native of Wilks County, North Carolina, born February 18, 1823. Her ancestry is said to include a soldier under Cromwell, who after the Reformation removed to Staten Island and from there to New Jersey and thence to North Carolina. Her grandfather, Nathaniel Vannoy, fought under Colonel Benjamin Cleveland at Kings Mountain.

Israel Curtis Eller attended country school and Central University at Pella, Iowa, 1876-80. He was admitted to the bar at Tekamah, in November, 1882, and has since been engaged in practice with the exception of time spent in public office. A Republican, he was clerk of the district court of Washington County January 1, 1884-January 1, 1892; appointed county judge October 1, 1893-January 1, 1894; clerk of the district court July 1, 1908-11; county judge 1911-19; 1925-34; and city clerk of Blair and member of the state legislature from Burt and Washington Counties in 1907.

He was married to Ellen Elizabeth Kamp at Blair, on November 3, 1886. Mrs. Eller was born at East Troy, Wisconsin, February 9, 1861, and died at Blair, June 14, 1914. She was Swiss on the maternal side and English on the paternal. Before her marriage she was a teacher. There were three children William Curtis, born March 6, 1888, died December 27, 1900. Mary Louise, born August 26, 1893, married Harry L. Morris; and Frances Pauline, born January 24, 1897, married Ralph J. Roush.

Judge Eller is a member of the Baptist Church, the Masons and Odd Fellows. During 1904-11 he was a member of the city school board of Blair. He is a member of the Nebraskana Society at the present time. Residence: Blair.

Louis F. Ellermeier

For the past 62 years Louis F. Ellermeier has lived in Nebraska, and for 42 years has been engaged in the grain business at Swanton. He was born at Qunicy, Illinois, October 20, 1864, the son of E. L. and Mary (Stork) Ellermeier. His father, born in Germany, August 31, 1837, in 1853 moved to America with his parents. He homesteaded in 1869 settling in Jefferson County, Nebraska; he served in the Civil War, 1861-64; he died at Swanton, December 13, 1922. His mother was born in Germany in 1833 and died in Jefferson County, July 26, 1876.

Mr. Ellermeier attended grade school and business college. He has been a grain merchant at Swanton for 42 years. He engaged in loan drives, food administration work, and Red Cross activities at Swanton, during the World War. He is a Mason. His political affiliation has always been with the Republican Party.

He was united in marriage with Evelyn McBride at Swanton, July 24, 1895. Mrs. Ellermeier, whose ancestry is Scotch, was born at Winterset, Iowa, July 26, 1866. They have two children: Dwight R. born June 19, 1896, who married Sadie Ann Krejnek; and Frank D., born July 24, 1902, who married Stella M. Hopkins.

Mr. Ellermeier holds membership in the Nebraskana Society, and is vitally interested in civic improvement and community affairs. Residence: Swanton.

Alfred George Ellick

For the past thirty years Alfred G. Ellick has been engaged in the practice of law at Omaha. He was born at Fremont, Dodge County, Nebraska, August 29, 1878, the son of Francis Ignatius and Josephine (Lauth) Ellick, and has lived in Nebraska all his life.

Graduated from the Fremont High School in 1897, in 1900 he was awarded the LL. B. degree at the University of Michigan. He was admitted to the bar in Michigan and Nebraska in 1900, and served as assistant city attorney of Omaha, 1904-05; deputy county attorney of Douglas County, 1906-12; assistant general attorney for the Union Pacific Railway Company, 1912-18. He has been associated with the following law firms in general practice: Brome, Ellick & Brome, 1910-12; Brogan, Ellick & Raymond, 1918-28; and Brogan, Ellick & Van Dusen since 1928.

He was united in marriage with Frances Purvis at Omaha, December 16, 1903. Mrs. Ellick was born at Omaha. They have three children: Josephine, who married Edward B. Crofoot; Robert P.; and Alfred G.

Mr. Ellick served as captain of Company A of the Nebraska Home Guards, in Omaha, and was, during the participation of the United States in the World War, chairman of Four Minute Men. He holds membership in the Omaha Bar Association, Nebraska State Bar Association, and the American Bar Association, and is a member of the Nebraska State Historical Society, the Nebraskana Society, the University Club, and the Omaha Country Club.

His absorbing interest outside of the business world is football and golf; he served as coach of the Haskell Indians football team, 1900-01, and coach of the Creighton football team, 1902. He is a Mason. Residence: Omaha.

Lillian Artman Elliott

Born in Cuming County, Nebraska, February 12, 1880, Lillian Artman Elliott is the daughter of John C. and Kathryn (Artman) High. She was educated in the public schools of West Point, and was graduated from high school in the class of 1896.

She was married to James C. Elliott, at West Point, and to them were born the following children: David Donald, born January 27, 1899, who received his A. B. and LL. B. from the University of Nebraska, and is now associated with the Veterans Bureau; Thomas Myron, born February 16, 1906, who received his A. B. degree at Nebraska and is athletic director at Kearney High School; James Drake, born November 20, 1908; Dorothy Rose, born October 26, 1911, married Chester William Paul; Grace Carolyn, born February 12, 1914; and Robert Burton, born April 7, 1918. James attended the University of Nebraska three years, and the two youngest children are attending school at the present time.

Mrs. Elliott was associate editor with her husband of the *West Point Republican*, 1901 to 1916, and since 1924 has been postmaster at West Point. She is a Republican, a member of the American Legion Auxiliary, the Woman's Federated Clubs and the Business and Professional Women's Club. Her religious affiliation is with the Grace Lutheran Church. During the World War she was a member of the Red Cross Nurses's Class and devoted much time to community knitting. Her hobby is art.

James C. Elliott was prominent in state politics for many years. He was county attorney, clerk of the district court, held several city offices and was Republican candidate for congress in the 3rd district in 1911. Residence: West Point.

Robert Irving Elliott

Since 1916, Dr. Robert Elliott has been president of the Nebraska State Normal College at Chadron. He is the son of John and Marion Elizabeth (Tobey) Elliott, and was born at Worth, Cook County, Illinois, April 18, 1883. His father, who died at Lincoln in March, 1925, was a banker and stock grower of Irish and English descent. His mother was a native of Worth, and died at Lincoln in 1927. She was of French ancestry, and during the latter part of her life was active in the local Woman's Club, once serving as its president.

Upon his graduation from the Winside, Nebraska, High School in 1899, Dr. Elliott entered Nebraska Normal College at Wayne, receiving a B. S. in 1901; in 1914 he was awarded an A. B. at the University of Nebraska. He secured his M. A. at Columbia University in 1928. Active in debate, he was a member of Delta Sigma Rho. He is also a member of Phi Alpha Tau, Phi Gamma Delta and the Acacia.

On November 27, 1912 he was united in marriage with Annie L. Babcock of Arkansas. They have one child, Robert Irving, born November 17, 1917.

Dr. Elliott entered the teaching profession in the rural schools of Stanton County in 1901; in 1903 he was made superintendent of the Pilger (Nebraska) schools, continuing until 1905. During that year he was summer school instructor at Nebraska Normal College. From August, 1905 to January 1, 1906, he was Wayne County superintendent of schools; superintendent, Chadron city schools 1908-09; superintendent, Broken Bow city schools, September, 1909 to January 1, 1912; deputy state superintendent of public instruction of Nebraska, 1912-15. From January, 1915 to August, 1916, he was head of the department of mathematics at Nebraska Teacher's College at Kearney.

He has been a resident of Chadron for the past fifteen years, and is a member of the Chamber of Commerce and Rotary Club. He is a Congregationalist, affiliated with the Chadron Community Church. He is active in the Y. M. C. A., and is a member of the American Association of Teachers of Colleges, North Central Association of Colleges and Secondary Schools, and the Nebraska State Teachers Association. Dr. Elliott's chief recreations are golf and hiking. Residence: Chadron. (Photograph on Page 378).

Ruth Elliott

An outstanding figure in the educational affairs of Nebraska is Ruth Elliott who is serving as dean of women at Kearney State Teachers' College. She was born at Superior, Nebraska, September 1, 1879, the daughter of James Firman and Emeline (Cameron) Harris. Her father, who was born at Zanesville, Ohio, May 10, 1839, and died at Hildreth, Nebraska, February 21, 1920, was a pioneer farmer and cattleman in Nebraska and Kansas, in 1867; he was the leader of the freight wagons which crossed the plains of the middlewest during homestead days.

Her mother, who was born in Ontario, Canada, November 29, 1847, and died at Kearney, Nebraska, February 6, 1923, was a teacher and a leader in her community; she served as president of the Woman's Club for a number of years, and prior to coming to America, had attended a girl's seminary in Canada.

Mrs. Elliott was graduated from the high school at Bostwick, Nebraska, in 1893, attended York College for a year, and received a two-year diploma from the State Teachers' College at Peru, Nebraska. She received the A. B. degree at Kearney State Teachers' College, and in recent years has studied at the San Diego Teachers' College in California, and the University of Nebraska. She was president of the debating club at Peru, and served as president of her class.

She began her teaching career in rural schools, and has served as high school teacher, school principal, high school superintendent and county superintendent in various Nebraska schools. Mrs. Elliott is now dean of women at Kearney State Teachers' College, and is prominent in social and professional affairs at Kearney. She is a member of the Kearney Woman's Club, the Order of Eastern Star, the National Educational Association, the National Association of Deans of Women, and the Young Women's Christian Association.

Mrs. Elliott is the owner of the Elliott Motor Lodge Camp at Kearney. She is affiliated with the Kearney Methodist Episcopal Church, is a member of the Nebraskana Society, and was formerly president of the Franklin County Council of Defense. Her hobby is landscap-

ROBERT IRVING ELLIOTT

ing, and she is particularly interested in beautifying the college campus.

On July 21, 1904, she married George Herman Erfman, at Hildreth, Nebraska. Mr. Erfman, who was born at Blue Hill, Nebraska, May 20, 1879, and died at Hildreth, October 5, 1918, was a merchant. She was united in marriage with J. S. Elliott, at Kearney, April 19, 1921. Mr. Elliott was college registrar at Kearney, and was formerly a member of the Nebraska legislature. Residence: Kearney.

Harry Hiram Ellis

One of the leading professional men at Holdrege, Nebraska, Harry Hiram Ellis has been engaged in the practice of law there since his admission to the bar in 1917. He was born at Linden, Iowa, April 15, 1894, and is the son of William Franklin Ellis and Minnie Grace (Moore) Ellis. His father, who was born at Panora, Iowa, August 22, 1867, has been a farmer, grocer, telephone executive, and banker; his ancestry is Scotch and Irish. His mother, who was prominent in the Order of Eastern Star at Beaver City, was born at Linden, Iowa, January 21, 1873.

Mr. Ellis was graduated from the high school at Beaver City, Nebraska, in 1911. He was a student at Peru State School, Peru, Nebraska, and in 1917 received the Bachelor of Laws degree at the University of Nebraska where he was a member of Acacia and Phi Delta Phi. He was awarded letters in athletics at Peru State Normal College, was Missouri Valley Intercollegiate Doubles champion in tennis in 1916, and was Nebraska state doubles champion in tennis, 1913-14-15.

He has practiced law continuously at Holdrege since the World War, serving as county attorney of Phelps County from 1922 to 1926. He is a member of the Nebraska State Bar Association, the Holdrege Chamber of Commerce, and the Masonic Lodge. During the war he served as a private and sergeant in the 58th Infantry, 4th Division of the United States Army, and was wounded in action in Argonne Forest, France. He is affiliated with the Methodist Church of Holdrege, and holds membership in the Nebraskana Society.

His marriage to Verle Alta Farlow occurred at Des Moines, Iowa, June 26, 1919. Mrs. Ellis was born at Farnhamville, Iowa, August 4, 1895. Their two children are: Vera Maxine, born October 27, 1920; and William Farlow, born August 17, 1923. Mr. Ellis is especially interested in tennis and bridge. Residence: Holdrege.

Harvey Joy Ellis

Harvey Joy Ellis, retired newspaper man, was born at Plymouth, Ohio, April 4, 1867, son of Lindley Faris and Rebecca Jane (Hobson) Ellis.

Lindley Ellis was born at Plymouth, Ohio, March 3, 1840, and died at Genoa, Nebraska, December 30, 1884. He was a builder and contractor, who served four years and eight months with the 2nd West Virginia Cavalry during the Civil War. At the time of his death, he was in the hardware and grain elevator business. He was a Republican, whose father was Irish, the son of Michael Ellis and Elizabeth Murphy. Michael Ellis was born January 28, 1760, Elizabeth Murphy was born April 13, 1761, and they were married October 16, 1779.

Rebecca Jane Hobson was born at Plymouth, Ohio, June 16, 1845, and died at Alliance, July 31, 1906. She was the daughter of Samuel N. and Belinda (Naylor) Hobson, who were English Quakers.

Educated in common schools, Harvey J. Ellis was compelled to leave beacuse of the death of his father. He was the eldest of a family of five, and when his father died, went to work at the printing trade, which he had learned during vacations. From July, 1892, until October, 1914, he was the editor and owner of the *Alliance Semi-Weekly Times.* He was delegate to the Republican National Convention at Chicago in June, 1904, and from April, 1906, until October 15, 1915, was receiver of public

moneys at the United States Land Office at Alliance. During this period of time he also had a half partnership in a garage business.

At the time that Mr. Ellis entered the newspaper business there were five newspapers in Alliance. With the exception of one, he absorbed the others, including the *Guide,* which was moved to Alliance from Hemingford, Nebraska. Starting with practically nothing, Mr. Ellis erected a $30,000 building in 1900, and was always considered one of the live newspaper men of the state.

Two years following the death of the father in the spring of 1886, Mrs. Ellis and her family moved to Box Butte County, where the mother had filed on a homestead six miles from the place where Alliance now stands. They endured many of the hardships of pioneering during their first few years residence in this county. The country had just been opened and was then practically unsettled. There was no railroad there at that time. Hay Springs and Sidney were the nearest railroad points, and lumber and fuel had to be hauled 50 miles with no bridges or roads.

Of Mr. Ellis's marriage to Minne Ursula Sturgeon there is one child, Olive N. His second marriage occurred January 28, 1903, when he was married to Beatrice M. Holt, daughter of Isaac Holt of Omaha.

There are three children of this marriage, Irma, born March 2, 1904, who was married on February 9, 1926, to Eugene C. Leggett, editor of the *Quiz* at Ord, Nebraska. Ethelyn, the second daughter was born December 19, 1905, and is a graduate in journalism. She attended Columbia University and is employed as a writer for the *Omaha Bee News.* Wade H., the only son, was born December 21, 1907, and is now a student in law college at Creighton University.

Mr. Ellis was a member of the first brass band in Alliance and continued more than 40 years. At the time of his retirement two years ago, he was president of the municipal band. He was a charter member of Elks Lodge No. 961, and has been chairman of the house committee fourteen years. He is also a charter member of Lodge No. 733 of the Modern Woodmen of America and held many high offices during the years of his membership. He was a charter member also of Lodge No. 183 of the Ancient Free and Accepted Masons. Mr. Ellis was compelled to retire from the newspaper business because of impaired health. Residence: Alliance.

Corinth Elsmith

Corinth Elsmith, for a number of years county judge of Keith County, was born in Morristown, New Jersey, June 9, 1870, son of David M. Elsmith, a native of that state.

He attended public school in New Jersey and New York, and practiced pharmacy there before coming to Nebraska, in 1898. He was a cowboy for six years in Keith County, and then became manager of the Ogallala Trust Company until 1909. During 1909 he established an undertaking business. In 1915 he was appointed county judge to fill a vacancy and was elected to that office in 1918.

Mr. Elsmith is a 32nd degree Mason, and a member of the Shrine. His religious affiliation is with the Episcopal Church. He has taken an active part in the work of the Commercial Club for a number of years.

He was married to Amy G. Clough of Denver, Colorado, on January 7, 1909. She was educated in the public schools of Kansas, Chicago and Denver. She is a member of the Eastern Star and an Episcopalian. They have one daughter, Frances Elizabeth. Residence: Ogallala.

Wilbert Lester Elswick

Wilbert Lester Elswick, publisher and printer, was born at Moravia, Iowa, May 4, 1873, son of Andrew R. and Jane R. (Dinwiddie) Elswick. The father, who was an attorney, died at Crawford, Nebraska, in September, 1894. The mother died at Guernsey, Wyoming, in 1906.

Mr. Elswick attended high school in Nebraska, and since boyhood has been in the printing business. He came to Nebraska in 1876. He has owned and operated papers at Crawford; Hemingford; Spearfish, South Dakota; Milford, Utah; Sheridan, Wyoming; and at Gurley. At the present time Mr. Elswick is the editor and publisher of the *Gurley Gazette*. He serve as city clerk of Crawford for 10 years and is now justice of the peace at Gurley.

He was married in June, 1895, to Ellen Marie Smith at Chadron. They have one daughter, Jennie, born March 20, 1896, who is married to Robert Earl Ware. She resides in Cheyenne, Wyoming.

Mr. Elswick is a member of the Nebraska State Press Association, the Gurley Business Men's Association, of which he is now president, the Knights of Pythias, of which he is past grand chancellor of Nebraska, the Odd Fellows, and the Woodmen Circle. Residence: Gurley. (Photograph in Album).

Sarah Saunders Elwell

Sarah S. Elwell, daughter of William Henry and Minnie Dora (Bruns) Saunders, was born at Bazile Mills, Knox County, Nebraska, November 23, 1899. Her father, who was of English ancestry, came to Knox County with his parents at the age of two years. He was born in Stillwater, New York, October 8, 1867, and died at Lincoln, Nebraska, April 19, 1919. He lived in Nebraska practically all his life and was engaged in the hardware business.

Minnie Saunders, who was German, was born in Niobrara, Nebraska, October 9, 1870. Part of her childhood, however, was spent in Germany, where she received her early education.

Mrs. Elwell attended the Bazile Mills and Winneton grade schools, and was graduated from Creighton High School in 1916. She attended Wayne Normal School from 1916 to 1918, and was awarded the degree of Bachelor of Fine Arts, from the University of Nebraska. She was a member of Alpha Rho Tau, Delta Omicron (a musical sorority), and for four years was district president of Phi Mu.

She married Joseph Money Elwell, Junior, at Lincoln, June 18, 1925. Mr. Elwell was born at Springfield, Nebraska, May 31, 1894. They have one son, Joseph Money, third, born July 24, 1929.

Mrs. Elwell, who is a well-known and talented musician, was assistant professor of theory and harmony at the School of Fine Arts of the University of Nebraska, 1923-25. For two years she was musical supervisor in the public schools of Lyons, Nebraska. At the present time she is voice and piano instructor, and chorus director at Springfield.

Among her activities in club work is membership in various welfare and civic organizations. She is vice president of the county federation of Woman's Clubs; chairman of the Springfield library board; chairman of the annual roll call of the local Red Cross; a member of the Parent-Teachers Association and chairman of the board of stewards of the Methodist Church. She is a member of the Order of Eastern Star, and in 1928 was vice president of the Nebraska University Alumnae Association. She is a Republican. Residence: Springfield.

Edward Hudson Ely

On October 13, 1882, Edward H. Ely was born at Auburn, Nebraska. His father, James Fitz Ely, who was of English ancestry, was born at Springfield, New York, May 18, 1843. He is a farmer and stockman. Mary Ann (DeLay) Ely, his wife, was born in Appanoose County, Iowa, July 10, 1852, and died at Auburn, October 5, 1904.

She was the daughter of Joseph DeLay, whose ancestry was French.

Mr. Ely, who is a farmer, stockman and grain dealer, was graduated from the Auburn High School, after which he attended the Lincoln Business College, 1899-1900. He has lived in Nebraska all his life and since 1921, has engaged in farming and stockraising. In 1924 he also became a seed and grain dealer. For 14 years he was director and secretary of the county fair board, and for two years was president of the Farmers' Union. He is a director in the J. W. Kerns Lumber Company and is vice president of the Auburn Hotel Company.

On January 20, 1909, he married Laura Sophia Kerns at Auburn. Mrs. Ely, of Irish descent, was born at Auburn, March 8, 1885. To this union seven children were born, one of whom is deceased. They are: Laura, born November 19, 1909, who died November 19, 1919; Edward, born September 19, 1911; Mary Alice, born January 22, 1913; Eugene, born January 8, 1915; Charles, born June 20, 1916; William, born November 11, 1919, and Richard, born December 11, 1924.

Mr. Ely was active in loan drives during the World War. He is a member of the Parent-Teachers' Association, is a fourth degree Knight of Columbus, and is a member of St. Joseph's Catholic Church, serving as trustee and church committeeman. His favorite sport is golf, and he is a member of the Country Club. Residence: Auburn.

Samuel Ervin Ely

One of the pioneer merchants of Nebraska is Samuel Ervin Ely who has always lived in this state. He was born at Guide Rock, Nebraska, September 29, 1879, in a dug-out. His home was later made into a sod house, which is the type of houses in which the early settlers of Nebraska lived. He is the son of Charles Taylor and Harriet Adaline (Watt) Ely, the former a carpenter and farmer who was born in West Virginia, September 11, 1838, and died at Guide Rock, November 12, 1915. His mother, who was born at Perrysville, Indiana, January 13, 1849, and died at Guide Rock, April 22, 1920, was an active worker, was a member of the Women's Christian Temperance Union, and was a charter member of the Rebekah Lodge, at Guide Rock.

Mr. Ely was graduated from the Guide Rock High Schools in 1897, which was the first class to graduate there. He was connected with the R. S. Proudfit Company of Lincoln for 27 years, and served as a member of the board of directors of that organization for ten years. At this time he is the owner and manager of a hardware store at Naponee and a lumber yard there. He is secretary of the local school board, is a Mason, and holds membership in the Nebraskana Society. His favorite sport is baseball.

On October 25, 1905, he married Elsie May Vaughan at Guide Rock. Mrs. Ely was born at Unadilla, Nebraska, October 26, 1888, born of Pennsylvania German parents. Their children are: Maurine Gertrude, born September 16, 1906, at Guide Rock, who married John Craig Haines, residing at Franklin; Paul, born December 14, 1908, at Reynolds, who married Bernice Bernadine Kingsbury, residing at Naponee; Clarice Adaline, born January 9, 1913, at Reynolds, who is a teacher; and Leona May, born September 13, 1918, in Naponee. Maurine taught school for five years, and Paul was graduated from the University of Nebraska with the BB. S. degree, in 1931. Residence: Naponee.

William McLouth Ely

A distinguished lawyer in Nebraska, is William McLouth Ely, who was born at Marion, New York, September 21, 1875, the son of William Brown and Mary Frances (Potter) Ely. William Brown Ely, who was a leading physician, and at one time the president of Nebraska State Medical Society, was born in Connecticut, March 5, 1842, and died at Ainsworth, Nebraska, June 23, 1921. Mary Frances (Potter) Ely was born at Marion, New York, July 6, 1844, and died at Ainsworth, November 7, 1926.

Mr. Ely attended the public schools at Penfield, New York, and Marion Collegiate Institute, was graduated from the Ainsworth High School in 1892, and in 1900 received the Bachelor of Laws degree at the University of Nebraska, where he was a member of Alpha Tau Omega. He has engaged in the practice of law at Ainsworth, since 1900, and has taken a prominent part in the political and civic affairs of his community.

A Republican, Mr. Ely served as county attorney of Brown County, Nebraska, 1903-07, was county judge of Brown County in 1899, and in 1928 was defeated candidate for district judge. He is a director in the National Bank of Ainsworth, is a member of the Ainsworth Commercial Club, and holds membership in the Country Club there. He holds membership in the American Bar Association, the Nebraska State Bar Association, the Red Cross, Nebraskana Society, and the Young Men's Christian Association.

During the late war he was chairman of the Four Minute Men, served as a member of the legal advisory board and the Home Guard, and was active as a member of the War Savings Committee. His fraternal organizations include the Royal Arch and Commandery bodies of the Masons, the Independent Order of Odd Fellows, and the Woodmen of the World.

On June 7, 1905, Judge Ely was married at Ainsworth to Grace Maude Chesnut, who was born at Denver, Colorado, May 8, 1881. They have two children: Samuel C., born January 9, 1910, who is a law student at the University of Nebraska where he holds membership in Alpha Sigma Phi; and Rebecca Frances, born January 30, 1923. Residence: Ainsworth.

Jehu Whitfield Embree

The Reverend Jehu Whitfield Embree, pastor of the Methodist Episcopal Church at Lodgepole since September, 1931, was born at Richland, Iowa, March 21, 1867, son of Noah and Margaret (Lyon) Embree.

The father was born in Indiana, February 22, 1833, and died at Merna, Nebraska, in March, 1909. He was a farmer. His father was Jesse Embree and his grandfather, John Embree. Margaret Lyon was born at Richland, Iowa, June 29, 1841, and died at Callaway, Nebraska, in July, 1898. She was the daughter of Fredrick F. and Rachel (Harris) Lyon.

Dr. Embree attended country school, Gibbon Collegiate Institute, and Nebraska Wesleyan University. From the latter he received the Bachelor of Philosophy and Doctor of Divinity degrees. He was the editor of *The Nebraska Wesleyan*, and president of the Everett Literary Society one term while in school.

On September 20, 1887, he was married to Bessie Frances Anderson at Syracuse. Mrs. Embree was born at Darlington, Wisconsin, May 25, 1869. They have four children. Eva Edith, born March 18, 1892, married Glenn R. Haworth; Arthur Lee, born November 8, 1893, married Edith Forbes; Robert Lester, born December 31, 1896, married Olive Grace Lare; Frances, born March 17, 1917, was adopted March 8, 1924. She is a freshman in high school. Arthur and Robert are both Methodist ministers.

Dr. Embree has resided in Nebraska nearly 62 years. His professional history has been as follows:

From September, 1888, until May 31, 1891, he taught in public schools. From September, 1891, until September, 1892, he was pastor in Lincoln at Asbury and Lucy Peters Memorial Methodist Churches. From September, 1892, until December 31, 1892, he was pastor at Cheyneys

and Hickman. He joined the Nebraska Annual Conference of the Methodist Episcopal Church on trial September 17, 1893, and was ordained a deacon at Beatrice, by Bishop John M. Walden on that day. From January 1, 1893, until September, 1894, he was pastor at Roca, Hickman, Denton, Bowers' School House and Jamaica. From September, 1894, until 1895 he was pastor at Davey and Valley View.

On September 25, 1895, he was made a full member of the conference, and on September 25, 1898, was ordained an elder at Fairbury by Bishop James N. Fitzgerald. From September, 1895, until September, 1897, he was pastor at Alvo, Nebraska, and from that time until September, 1898, he was pastor at Waverly. From September, 1898, until September, 1901, he was pastor at Emmanuel Church in Lincoln, and from September, 1901, until September, 1902, was pastor at Hebron. Following his pastorate at Hebron, he was pastor at Osceola, two years, next becoming pastor at Tecumseh, remaining until September, 1906. From September 1906 until September, 1909, he was pastor at Superior, and from September, 1909, until September, 1910, was pastor at Geneva.

At that time he became district superintendent of the Nebraska City District, continuing until September, 1916. From that time until September, 1923, he was district superintendent of the Hastings District. From September, 1923, until September, 1924, he was field secretary of the Conference Claimants Society. Given a year's leave of absence in September, 1923, Dr. Embree secured subscriptions for the Hamline University in St. Paul, Minnesota, until December 24, 1924, when he was appointed to the pastorate at Crawford on January 1, 1925. There he remained until September, 1927, when he became pastor at Alliance. In September, 1928, he became pastor at Gordon, remaining until September, 1931.

Dr. Embree is the author of the *District Superintendent's Record Book*. Recently he was made a life member of the Nebraskana Society. Residence: Lodgepole. (Photograph in Album).

Robert Lester Embree

The Reverend Robert Lester Embree, clergyman, was born at University Place, Nebraska, December 31, 1896, son of Jehu Whitfield and Bessie Frances (Anderson) Embree. The father was born in Keokuk, Iowa, March 21, 1867, son of Jesse and Mary (Hollingsworth) Embree. He is a clergyman of the Methodist Episcopal Church. Bessie Frances Anderson was born at Darlington, Wisconsin, May 25, 1869, daughter of Jesse W. and Anna C. (McConnell) Anderson.

Educated in the public schools of Osceola, Tecumseh, Superior, and Geneva, from 1902 until 1910, Mr. Embree entered University Place High School in 1910 and was graduated in 1914. In 1918 he received the Bachelor of Arts degree at the Wesleyan University.

From 1918 until 1920 Mr. Embree engaged as a high school principal at Lyons, Nebraska. He was superintendent at Hemingford, 1920-22, and was engaged in mercantile work, 1922-24. He entered the ministry in 1924, serving at Minatare until 1927, and from 1927 until 1931 was pastor at Rushville. Since 1931 he has been pastor of the Methodist Episcopal Church at Broken Bow.

He is married to Olive Grace Lare, their marriage having been solemnized at Brock, Nebraska, August 12, 1918. Mrs. Embree was born at Brock, July 14, 1895. Five children were born to them, four of whom are living. Francis, born February 14, 1921, died February 16, 1921; Lester, born February 9, 1922; Dorothy, born August 25, 1925; Donald, born August 25, 1925; and Roberta, born March 30, 1930.

During the late war Mr. Embree was a four minute

speaker. He is a member of the Nebraska Conference
of the Methodist Episcopal Church, the Pilot Lodge No.
240 of the Ancient Free and Accepted Masons at Lyons,
and of the Nebraskana Society. He enjoys all out door
sports, while his hobbies are manual training and reading.
Residence: Broken Bow.

J. D. Emerick

Since 1913, J. D. Emerick has operated an abstract
and insurance business at Alliance. He was born in
Mills County, Iowa, September 26, 1881, son of Frank
Andrew and Della (Paterson) Emerick. The father was
born in Malvern, Iowa, January 14, 1859, and is a farmer of Irish and German descent. Della, his wife, was
born at Mills County, Iowa, and died in Crawford, Nebraska, February 15, 1902.

In 1904 Mr. Emerick was graduated from public
school at Alliance, and in 1906 became city ticket agent
for the Chicago, Burlington, and Quincy Railroad. He
continued in that capacity until 1912 when he took up
his present occupation. He is a Republican.

He was married to Anna Rebecca Chambers at Sidney, Nebraska, on August 25, 1918. Mrs. Emerick was
born in Cheyenne County, Nebraska, and before her
marriage was a public school teacher. Mrs. Emerick is
a graduate of Peru State Normal. She taught in the
grade and high schools of Alliance, before her marriage
and is now president of the council of the Girl Reserves
and is past matron of the Order of Eastern Star, chapter
Allyol. She is vice-president of the Ladies Guild of the
Episcopal Church where she is a Sunday school teacher
also. She is the daughter of C. P. Chambers of Sidney,
Nebraska.

Mr. Emerick is a member of the Chamber of Commerce, the Masons, the Red Cross, the American and
Nebraska Title Association, and is affiliated with St.
Matthews Episcopal Church. His favorite sports are
football, fishing and hunting. Residence: Alliance.

Raymond Emerson

Raymond Emerson, who is one of the leading merchants at Lexington, Nebraska, was born at Brandon,
Minnesota, September 26, 1881. His father, Theodore
Almiran Emerson, who was a farmer for many years,
was born at Wolcotville, Indiana, November 29, 1843,
and died at Ulysses, Nebraska, June 30, 1925. His mother, Mary (Bower) Emerson, whose ancestry was German, was born in Wolcotville and died there in 1905.

Mr. Emerson received his early education in rural
schools and studied for a year at the Minnesota School
of Agriculture. Since 1905 he has been engaged in the
furniture and undertaking business at Lexington.

A Republican, he was a member of the special and
regular sessions of the Nebraska legislature in 1930 and
1931. He is a Mason, an Odd Fellow, and is affiliated
with The Nebraskana Society.

Of his marriage to Murthey Goodwin, which occurred
at Wolcotville, September 28, 1902, one son was born:
Wilbur, August 16, 1909. Residence: Lexington.

William W. Emick

William W. Emick, a general merchant, was born at
Orrville, Ohio, April 22, 1872, and has resided in Nebraska 27 years.

His father, Adam Emick, was born at Berne, Germany, August 6, 1828, and came to America with his
parents at two. He was a farmer and carpenter and
general mechanic. His wife, Catherine, was born in
Pennsylvania, February 2, 1833, and died at Orrville,
May 20, 1884. She was of Pennsylvania German descent.
Adam Emick died at Orrville, Ohio, December 26, 1914.

William W. Emick attended public school, and for
a number of years has been in the mercantile business.
He also has real estate interests in various parts of the
country. He is a Democrat, and a member of the Elks.
He is much interested in sports, generally.

On January 12, 1910, he was married to Myrtle Frye
at Hot Springs, South Dakota. She was born at Buffalo Gap, South Dakota, and died at Scottsbluff, December 27, 1914. There is one child of this marriage,
Myrtle, born October 3, 1914.

Mr. Emick was next married to Julia Cooney at
Scottsbluff, Nebraska, on September 15, 1917. Mrs.
Emick was born October 14, 1888, at Sargent, Nebraska,
the daughter of John and Mary (Conners) Cooney. She
attended country schools at Sargent and finished at
Broken Bow. She taught school for several years after-
which she took up the nursing profession, receiving her
training at Roper Hospital, Charleston, South Carolina.
Entering the hospital in 1912, she served two years in
training and three years in professional nursing and
at that time received her diploma. She later passed the
state examination in Nebraska and at present retains
her certificate as a registered nurse. She is a member
of the Woman's Club and is affiliated with the Minatare
Federated Church.

Mr. Emick have three children, Wilma, born November 8, 1918; William, born July 18, 1920; and Helen,
born April 23, 1923. Since locating in Minatare, Nebraska, eleven years ago, Mr. Emick has been engaged
in the mercantile business. Previous to this time he
lived in Scottsbluff, Nebraska, for nine years, during
which time he held the position as secretary of the Elks
Lodge there. He was one of the promoters of the lodge
at Scottsbluff, having transferred his membership there
from Alliance, Nebraska, at which place he had held
membership for a number of years. He held the position
as secretary and treasurer of the Farmers Mutual Insurance Company, a local company with its main office
in Scottsbluff. After holding ths position for four and
a half years he refused the re-election for another term,
and took up other lines of insurance with which he continued until moving to Minatare.

He is a charter member of the Lions Club at Minatare,
Nebraska. Residence: Minatare.

Max Emmert

Son of one of Iowa's foremost physicians and statesmen, Max Emmert is one of Nebraska's outstanding
physicians. He was born at Atlantic, Iowa, August 18,
1883, and has been a resident of Nebraska for the past
fifteen years. His father, Joseph Martin Emmert, was
born in Franklin County, Maryland, June 9, 1846, and is
of German descent. He came to Iowa in 1873, bringing
with him his wife, Ida Elizabeth Washabaugh, who was
born at Chambersburg, Pennsylvania, May 10, 1852. She
was of German descent, her family coming from Germany
in 1752.

Joseph Martin Emmert was a physician, and served
as president of the Iowa State Medical Association and
the Cass County, Iowa Medical Society. He was an active figure in Democratic politics, served as a member of
the Iowa state senate and of the state board of parole. He
died at Atlantic, July 15, 1909.

Max Emmert was graduated from Corning (Iowa)
Academy in 1901, and received his A. B. from the State
University of Iowa in 1905. He entered Johns Hopkins
University and received his M. D. in 1909. He is a mem-
ber of Sigma Nu and Nu Sigma Nu.

On October 23, 1912 he was married to Virginia Davis
Cuykendall at Atlantic. Mrs. Emmert was born at Ham-
ilton, Canada, September 15, 1888, and is of Holland
Dutch descent. They have three children, Max, Jr., born
July 28, 1913; Harriet, born November 15, 1917; and Jean-
nette, born September 15, 1921.

In politics Dr. Emmert is a Democrat. During the
World War he was a member of the Advisory Medical
Board and local examining board. He is a Presbyterian.

Dr. Emmert is the author of the following articles:
Colon Bacillus Infection (Iowa State Medical Journal,

May 14, 1915) ; *Tumors of the Female Breast* (Iowa State Medical Journal, June 15, 1910) ; *Diatetics and Therapeutics of Auto-Intoxication* (Iowa State Medical Journal, August 1910) ; *Pathological Aspect of the Tonsils* (Cass County Society, July 1908) ; *Abdominal Adhesions* (Cass County Society, September 12, 1910) ; *Symptomatology and Treatment early Tubal Pregnancy* (Iowa State Medical Association, May 17, 1911) ; *A Typical Case of Exfoliativa Dermititis* (Iowa State Medical Journal, November 1909) ; *Adhesive Complications of the Right Abdomen; Chronic Systic Mastitis* (Nebraska State Medical Association, April 27, 1922) ; *Malignant Sarcomas* (Douglas County Medical Society, November 26, 1919) ; *Pelvic Conditions Producing Bladder Complications* (Nebraska State Medical Association, May 1918) ; *Diverticulitis and Peridiverticulitis* (Nebraska State Medical Association 1919) ; *Rat-Bite Fever* (Nebraska State Medical Journal, September 1922) ; *Loose Bodies in the Abdominal Cavity* (Surgery, Gynecology and Obstetrics, November 1918) ; *Gangrene of the Appendix* (Iowa State Medical Society, February 1916) ; *Arterio-schlerosis* (Iowa State Medical Journal, February, 1913) ; *Clinical Diagnosis of Tumors of the Breast* (Botna Valley Medical Society, September 15, 1920) ; *Carcinoma of the Vulva* (Elkhorn Valley Medical Society, March 17, 1925) ; Report of case of *Acute Lymphatic Leukaemia, Secondary Infection of the Tongue* (November 1923) ; Case Report *Large Ovarian Cyst* (Nebraska State Medical Journal, June 1924) ; Case Report *Schlattors Disease* (Journal of Radiology, 1925) ; *The Appendico-Biliary Snydrome* (Nebraska State Medical Journal, December 1924) ; *Oration on Surgery* (Iowa State Medical Journal, July 1926) ; *Tuberculosis Peritonitis* (Nebraska State Medical Journal, April 1927) ; *Sarcoma and Elephantiasis* (Nebraska State Medical Journal, November 1928) ; *Chairman's Address,* Nebraska Section of the American College of Surgeons, (Nebraska State Medical Journal, April, 1930). He is a member of the surgical staff of Evangelical Covenant Hospital, and has served as president. He is past president of the Nebraska Section of the American College of Surgeons of which he is a member. Dr. Emmert is a member of the American Medical Association and the Nebraska State and Douglas County Medical Societies, and is president of the Nebraska Children's Home Society.

Dr. Emmert is past international director of the Lions International, and past vice president of the local organization. He is a Mason and member of the Scottish Rite and Srine. He seeks his relaxation in golf. Residence: Omaha.

Roland Finch Emmett

Born at Arapahoe, Nerbaska, Roland Finch Emmett is serving as cashier of the Citizens State Bank in that community, and is unusually prominent in the civic organizations there. He was born November 2, 1891, the son of Edward E. and Kathleen (Finch) Emmett, the former a distinguished banker of Lincoln, Nebraska. He was born at Havana, Illinois, June 17, 1865, and died at Lincoln, February 15, 1930. His mother was born at Omaha, Nebraska, February 5, 1870. She was the daughter of Rolando J. and Louise (Boener) Finch.

Mr. Emmett was graduated from the Lincoln High School in 1909 and was a student at the University of Nebraska for the following three years. He is cashier, and a director in the Citizens State Bank of Arapahoe, is vice president of the Furnas County Red Cross, is president of the Community Club, and is acting as president of the local Rotary Club.

His fraternal societies are the following Masonic bodies; Lodge Number 293 at Arapahoe; Scottish Rite, Hastings, Nebraska; and Shrine, Hastings, Nebraska. Mr. Emmett is treasurer of the local school board, is affiliated with the Episcopal Church, and holds membership in the Nebraskana Society. During the World War he served as second lieutenant in the Field Artillery of the United States Army and at this time is vice commander of the American Legion.

On October 20, 1920, he was married at Arapahoe to Twyla Tull, who was born at Mediapolis, Iowa, April 20, 1897. She is the daughter of James L. and Ellen (Shields) Tull. They have a son, Roland Edward, born October 20, 1926. Mr. Emmett is a Republican. Residence: Arapahoe.

John Edwards Enders

For the past 48 years John Edward Enders has been a rancher near Ainsworth, Nebraska. He was born at Cedar Rapids, Iowa, January 12, 1858, the son of Fredrick and Rachel Minnie (Carns) Enders, the former a farmer who was born at Albany, New York, January 16, 1826, and died at Cedar Rapids, Iowa, December 1, 1902. His mother, who was a teacher for a number of years prior to her marriage, was born in Mercer County, Pennsylvania, March 18, 1827, and died at Cedar Rapids, in March, 1878; her parents were pioneers in Cedar County.

Mr. Enders was graduated from the Cedar Rapids High School in 1879, and was a student at Coe College in 1880. He has always been a rancher in Brown County, Nebraska, and for the past 30 years has served on the school board in his community. He is a member of the Blue Lodge and Silver Cord bodies of the Masons, and holds membership in the Nebraskana Society. He was defeated candidate for county commissioner of Brown County in 1894, in a close political battle, and since then has never aspired to public office.

On June 25, 1890, he married Emma Marie Day at Lakeland, Nebraska. Mrs. Enders was born at Round Prairie, Wisconsin, January 7, 1872. The following children were born to them: Harry L., July 2, 1892, who married Hazel Lewis; Fred L., January 8, 1902; Frank Graham, August 1, 1905, who married Ethel Wrasch; Helen Ruth, December 3, 1907, who married Harry Wilson; and Rachel Maria, born November 3, 1913, who died in October, 1917. Residence: Ainsworth.

Ditlev Frederick Enevoldsen

Ditlev Frederick Enevoldsen, banker, was born at Boelus, Nebraska, October 26, 1896, son of Hans Christian and Elsie (Anderson) Enevoldsen. His father homesteaded in Howard County May 24, 1882. After retiring in 1924, he moved to Dannebrog where he resided until his death, March 21, 1932. His mother died at Dannebrog, August 9, 1929. His parents were of Danish descent.

Mr. Enevoldsen attended country school to the eighth grade, and completed a business course at St. Paul Business College at St. Paul, Nebraska.

On September 28, 1921, he was married to Ella Izola Wiekhorst at Potter. She was born at North Bend, Nebraska, September 27, 1899, the daughter of Ferdinand Bertha (Horstman) Wiekhorst. She is a member of the Methodist Church, the Eastern Star, and the Legion Auxiliary. They have two children, Charlotte, born December 2, 1923; and Donald, born September 16, 1925.

From September, 1918, until October, 1919, Mr. Enevoldsen served in the United States Army. A Republican, he is a member of the American Legion Post No. 291, the Community Club, and the Masons. His favorite sports are golf and hunting. Residence: Potter.

George England

For the past 53 years George England has lived in Nebraska where he has been a farmer, stock buyer, and stock feeder for many years. He was born at Lafayette,

Indiana, July 26, 1875, the son of Gust and Carolina (Palmer) England. His father, who was a farmer, was born at Grenna, Sweden, March 15, 1838, and died at Saronville, Nebraska, April 25, 1930, came to this country in 1858. His mother was born at Junkoping, Sweden, September 11, 1848.

Mr. England received his education in the public schools of Eldorado, Nebraska, and has been engaged in farm work most of his life. A Democrat, he served as supervisor of Clay County, 1914-27, and committeeman since 1912. During the World War he made loan drives in his county, acting also as registrar, and from 1911 to 1926 was an active member of the school board at Eldorado. He is a Mason and holds membership in the Nebraskana Society.

His marriage to Edith Victoria Anderson was solemnized at Lincoln, Nebraska, March 11, 1903. Mrs. England was born at Saronville, September 14, 1881. They have three children: Earl, born December 13, 1903, who married Elsie Youngsen; Evelyn, born April 1, 1906, who is a stenographer; and Clayton, born July 29, 1909. Earl and Clayton are farmers. Residence: Eldorado.

Thomas William Engles

Born on the farm of his father in LaSalle County, Illinois, October 31, 1858, Thomas W. Engles has been a resident of Nemaha County since 1860. At that time his father, Peter Engles, brought his wife and family to Nebraska, where he pre-empted a section of land in Nemaha County. Peter Engles was born in Metz, Germany, in 1825, and died on his homestead April 25, 1881. This homestead is still in the possession of the family. Peter Engles was the son of William and Katherine (Reck) Engles. After serving three years in the German Army, he came to America in 1848 and participated in the gold rush to California, in 1849.

Mary Ann Meath Engles, wife of Peter, was born in County Mayo, Ireland, in 1835, daughter of Thomas and Eleanor (Conway) Meath. She came to America while still a girl and prior to her marriage was a teacher. She died at Auburn, February 16, 1897.

On May 4, 1886, at LaSalle, Illinois, William Engles was united in marriage to Belinda Mary Halligan. Mrs. Engles was born at LaSalle, October 3, 1858. Her father was a plantation owner at Savannah, Georgia, and her brother, Thomas P. Halligan, was first judge of LaSalle County. She died at Kansas City, Missouri, July 12, 1925, leaving four children living. They are: Albert, born August 30, 1888, married Beatrice Ryan; Mary; Emily; Thomas A., born March 12, 1898, married Florence Zimmer. Two children died in infancy, a son, born May 4, 1887, died May 4, 1887, and another, born January 2, 1890, died the same day.

For more than 68 years William Engles has been active in the life of his community. He has always been extensively interested in farming and stock-raising, and during later years established a lumber and coal company, which he thereafter gave into the charge of his son, Thomas. He still devotes most of his time to his agricultural and breeding interests. A Catholic, he attends St. Joseph's Church. His hobby is reading. Residence: Auburn.

James Thomas English

James Thomas English, lawyer, was born at Omaha, October 26, 1893, son of James Patrick and Margaret Agnes (Dalton) English. He received his Bachelor of Arts degree from Creighton University in 1916 and his Bachelor of Laws degree in 1920.

On June 18, 1918, he was married to Genevieve Eileen Dross at Omaha. She was born there on August 2, 1895. There is one son, James, born May 19, 1926.

Mr. English is a member of the American Legion, having served in the United States Navy as a second class seaman in the World War. He is a member of St. Margaret Mary's Catholic Church, the Nebraska State and Omaha Bar Associations, and the Knights of Columbus (advocate). Residence: Omaha.

Oscar L. Engstrom

Oscar L. Engstrom was born at Axtell, Nebraska, July 20, 1884, the son of John E. and Johanna F. (Belfrage) Engstrom. His father, a farmer, was born at Smalan, Sweden, April 3, 1839, and died at Axtell, July 16, 1921. His mother was born at Wesende, Sweden, December 28, 1849, and died at Axtell, April 29, 1930.

Mr. Engstrom, who is a progressive farmer at Axtell, attended public school there and later studied at business college. He has been a member of the local school board since 1920, is a member of Bethany Lutheran Church, and holds membership in the Nebraskana Society. His hobby is reading.

On August 29, 1916, he married Anna Maria Anderberg at Wakefield, Nebraska; she was born in Sweden. To them one son was born: Emmett, November 13, 1917. Residence: Axtell.

Loren William Enyeart

Loren William Enyeart was born at Liberty Mills, Indiana, March 12, 1879, the son of John Wesley and Erma Jane (Park) Enyeart. His father, who was a farmer and a Civil War veteran, was born in Indiana, April 12, 1845, and died at Lincoln, Nebraska, May 15, 1906. His mother, whose ancestry was Scotch-Irish, was born in Sullivan County, Ohio, December 22, 1853, and died at Milford, Nebraska, January 27, 1922.

Mr. Enyeart was graduated from the Culbertson High School in 1897. He was editor and publisher of the *Hayes Center Times* at Hayes Center, Nebraska, for over 20 years, served as county treasurer of Hayes County for four years (1908-1912), and for the past 16 years has been postmaster there. He is a member of the Hayes County Chamber of Commerce and the Red Cross of which he has been secretary for the past 10 years. During the World War he was county chairman of Hayes County of the Food and Fuel Administration. He is also a member of the Southwestern Nebraska Historical Society and the Nebraskana Society. He is a member of Palisade Lodge No. 216, Ancient Free and Accepted Masons.

On November 18, 1903, he was married at Hayes Center, to Frances G. Potts, who was born in Pennsylvania, November 5, 1881. They have four children: Florence R., born November 25, 1904, who married H. M. Counce at Chester, Nebraska, in November, 1926; Charles R., born May 20, 1907, who married Vivian Sloan at McCook, Nebraska, July 2, 1930; John R., born October 10, 1911; and Kenneth R., born June 2, 1914, who is still in school and working in a bank. Florence, who received an A. B. degree at the University of Nebraska in 1925, is a teacher. Charles is assistant postmaster, and John is a licensed air craft pilot. Residence: Hayes Center. (Photograph in Album).

Jacob M. Epp

Jacob M. Epp was born in York County, Nebraska, April 23, 1881, and for the past 35 years has been a farmer there. His father, Heinrich P. Epp, who was a farmer, was born in South Russia, January 25, 1857, came to America in 1874, and died at Henderson, Nebraska, August 11 1929. Margaretha (Wall) Epp, mother of Jacob Epp, was born in South Russia, October 26, 1859, and died at Henderson, April 22, 1927.

Mr. Epp has been a member of the board of education in District Number 31 for nine years, and is actively interested in all community affairs. He is affiliated with Bethesda Church of Henderson, (trustee 12 years), is a member of the Republican Party, and holds membership in the Nebraskana Society.

On June 18, 1903 he was united in marriage with Maria Peters at Henderson. Mrs. Epp was born in York County, February 26, 1882. Seven children were born to this marriage, Willard, born May 18, 1908; Emma, born March 30, 1906, who married Dietrich E. Peters; Minnie, born May 21, 1910, who married Henry R. Regier; Louise, born September 8, 1912, who married Albert A. Buller; Robert, born March 2, 1914; Herman, born February 4, 1916; and Geannetta, born March 28, 1919. Residence: Henderson.

Richard John Epp

Richard J. Epp, publisher, was born at Fairbury, Nebraska, November 3, 1901, the son of John Jacob and Mary (Geisbrecht) Epp. John Jacob Epp, born in Germany, March 27, 1872, is a milk distributor. Mary Epp was born in Germany, November 28, 1878.

Richard J. Epp, was graduated from Fairbury High School in 1920. There he was active in football. Thereafter he attended the University of Nebraska at Lincoln for three semesters.

He was united in marriage with Lela Ware, June 14, 1926, at Fairbury, Nebraska. She was born at Powell, Nebraska, August 9, 1906. They have two children: Margaret Louise, born September 22, 1927, and Joan Marie, born May 19, 1929.

Mr. Epp has been editor of the *Bruning Banner* for some years. His religious affiliation is with the Methodist Church of Bruning. He is a member of the Bruning Community Club and the Nebraskana Society. Residence: Bruning.

Eugene C. Eppley

Eugene C. Eppley was born at Akron, Ohio, April 8, 1884. He is the son of Owen and Jessie C. (Phillips) Eppley. He was graduated from Culver Military Academy at Culver, Indiana, in 1901, and attended Standford University in 1902-03.

Mr. Eppley entered the hotel business in 1903 with the McKinley Hotel at Canton, Ohio. He has built up a large hotel organization and operates many of the leading hotels of the country from Pittsburgh to the Pacific Coast. The position of president of the Eppley Hotels Company, with executive offices in Omaha, is held by Mr. Eppley.

Among the hotels under the direction of the Eppley organization are the following: Hotel Norfolk, Norfolk, Nebraska; Hotel Lincoln, Hotel Capital and Hotel Lindell of Lincoln, Nebraska; Hotel Fontenelle, Hotel Rome and the Logan Apartment Hotel of Omaha, Nebraska; Hotel Cataract and Hotel Carpenter of Sioux Falls, South Dakota; Hotel Warrior, Sioux City, Hotel Martin and Hotel West, Sioux City, Iowa; Hotel Tallcorn, Marshalltown, Iowa; Hotel Chieftain, Council Bluffs, Iowa; Hotel Montrose and Hotel Magnus, Cedar Rapids, Iowa; Hotel Seelbach, Louisville, Kentucky; Hotel Fort Pitt and Hotel William Penn, Pittsburgh, Pennsylvania; Hotel Alexandria of Los Angeles, California, and the Elms Hotel of Excelsior Springs, Missouri.

During the World War, Mr. Eppley served as national fuel administrator for hotels. He is a director of the Greater Omaha Association and the Omaha Chamber of Commerce. For three terms he served as president of the Hotel Men's Mutual Benefit Association of the United States and Canada. He is a member of Chi Psi, of which he has served as member of the executive council.

In 1926, Mr. Eppley was awarded a special distinction when he was decorated with the Gold Cross of Social Welfare by the French government. He is a Mason and a member of the Shrine. His clubs include the Elks, Omaha Club, Omaha Field Club, the Omaha Country and the Omaha Athletic Club. Residence: Omaha.

Edward Charles Epsten

Edward C. Epsten, president of the Epsten Lithographing Company of Omaha, was born at Rochester, New York, December 24, 1874. He is the son of Edward Arthur and Belle (Perry) Epsten. Edward Arthur Epsten was born at Rochester, New York, in 1851; the family originated in Belgium, emigrated to Germany and thence to America. Belle Perry Epsten was born in Rochester, January 7, 1854, and died at Rochester, November 12, 1927. She was a teacher of dramatic art, music and elocution, of English and Welsh descent. Her mother was of the Perry family.

Edward C. Epsten was educated in the public and high schools of Rochester, graduating in 1892. For some years he conducted an art studio and was assistant instructor at the Milwaukee School of Fine Arts. In 1910 he came to Omaha, where he founded the Epsten Lithographing Company, the first strictly lithographing firm in Nebraska.

He was married to Katherine Louise Krein at Rochester, July 3, 1895. Mrs. Epsten was born at Wayland, New York, June 6, 1876, and is of German descent. To their union three children were born, Edward J., born January 7, 1897, married Helen Bechtold. He is secretary-treasurer and general manager of the Epsten Lithographing Company. Robert F., born June 21, 1911, is a senior at Creighton University, and Thomas P., born April 30, 1913, is a senior at St. Mary's High School, St. Mary's, Kansas.

Mr. Epsten is a Republican. He is a member of St. Cecilia's Cathedral and the Knights of Columbus. His civic and fraternal organizations include the Chamber of Commerce, the Ad-Sell League, the Kiwanis Club and the Elks. He is fond of golf, hiking, fishing and hunting, and his avocation is oil and water color painting. His indoor recreation is reading. Residence: Omaha.

Andrew Erickson

One of the outstanding leaders in business and civic affairs at Campbell, Nebraska, is Andrew Erickson, who has resided in this community since 1873. He was born at Kongsvinger, Norway, October 12, 1855, the son of Erick and Karen (Amundson) Erickson. His father, a farmer, was born at Konsvinger and died at Campbell. His mother was also a native of Norway and died at Campbell.

Mr. Erickson was a pioneer farmer in Franklin County, Nebraska, and in 1910 became active in business at Campbell. He has been president of the Citizens Lumber Company since 1905, has acted as vice president of the Farmers State Bank since 1915, and has been a director in the latter organization since 1904. At this time he is a member of the Zion Lutheran Church at Campbell and the Nebraskana Society.

He was married at Campbell, January 8, 1882, to Helena Tollefson, who was born at Bergen, Norway, July 6, 1859. She was a daughter of Hans and Martha O. (Olson) Tollefson. The six children born to this marriage were: Edwin, September 22, 1883, who married Marie Bowers; Henry, born October 23, 1885, who married Hazel Vivian South; Bertha Carolina, July 26, 1887, who married Carl Lindgren; Matilda Olena, born April 7, 1889, who married Alphonse W. Gagnon; Emma Louise, October 27, 1891, who married Frank Gary Abel; and Anna Maria, August 15, 1893.

Mr. Erickson was active in the Republican Party as a member of the Nebraska Legislature in 1913; he served as state senator in 1919. He homesteaded in 1876 about 5 miles south of Campbell, living in a dug-out after which a sod house was added to the home and in this dug-out both of his sons were born. During the early days on his claim Mr. Erickson recalls many visits by the Pawnee Indians who were on their way to the buffalo feeding ground which was an annual hunt every fall. Residence: Campbell. (Photograph on Page 386).

ANDREW ERICKSON

George Henry Erickson

George Henry Erickson, merchant, was born at Holdrege, Nebraska, March 12, 1890, son of Henry and Laura (Larson) Erickson. His father, born in Drumand, Norway, March 22, 1862, is now retired. His mother, who was born at Drumand, June 2, 1864, died at Holdrege, in February, 1925.

Mr. Erickson attended the Holdrege public schools. On September 8, 1919, he was married to Clara Victoria Swanson, at Lincoln, and to them four children were born: George Roland, born March 22, 1924; James Frederick, born September 22, 1925; Raymond Alden, born January 12, 1929; and Gloria Aldine, on January 12, 1929.

Mrs. Erickson, who was born at Omaha, July 12, 1894, is of Swedish descent. She is a member of the American Legion Auxiliary, the Woman's Club, and the Mother's Club.

For a number of years Mr. Erickson has been engaged in business at Holdrege, and at the present time is the owner and manager of the Erickson Paint Store. A Republican, he has served as a member of the city council four years, as its chairman one year. During this period eleven miles of paving were put in Holdrege, as well as a sewage disposal plant.

During the World War, Mr. Erickson served with Company C, 355th Infantry; was in overseas service in France, June 4, 1918, to January 9, 1919; and was wounded at Toul. He served as first commander of Martin Horn Post No. 66 of the American Legion at Holdrege. Mr. Erickson is a member of the First Methodist Church, the Odd Fellows, the executive board of the Community Welfare Association, and the board of directors of the Chamber of Commerce.

He enjoys hunting and golf and holds membership in the Holdrege Country Club. Recently he was made a life member of The Nebraskana Society. Residence: Holdrege.

Gustavus A. Erickson

Gustavus A. Erickson, retired farmer of Gage County, Nebraska, has lived in this state since 1884 and has taken an active part in economic and civic affairs in his county for many years. His father, Peter Erickson, who was born in Sweden, December, 1834, and died at Virginia, Gage County, Nebraska, November 22, 1901, was also a farmer. Susan Erickson, his mother, was born in Sweden and died at Virginia, August 16, 1923.

Mr. Erickson, who is now a stock buyer and is president of the Virginia State Bank, received his education in the rural schools of Gage County. He is a member of the Christian Church at Virginia, and for the past 30 years has been a member of the school board there. During the World War he served as chairman of the Red Cross in his community.

His marriage to Mary E. Mangus was solemnized at Virginia, January 15, 1893. Mrs. Erickson was born in Illinois, January 29, 1873. Five children were born to this union: Oliver L., born April 26, 1895, who married Amelia Barnard; Walter E., born December 20, 1896, who married Nina Raynor; Nellie M., born August 4, 1898, who died September 13, 1890; Edith V., born September 4, 1890, who married George Weiss; and Elva G., born October 29, 1894, who married William Lawson, and lives in Omaha. Oliver is in the nursery and seed business at Kearney and Walter is a banker at Filley. William Lawson is a traveling salesman. Residence: Virginia. (Photograph in Album).

Henry Erickson

Henry Erickson, successful lumber dealer at Campbell, Nebraska, was born there October 23, 1885, the son of Andrew and Helena (Tollefson) Erickson. His father, who is a retired farmer and lumberman, was born at Kongsvinger, Norway, October 12, 1855; he served as

a member of the Nebraska Legislature in 1913 and in 1919 was state senator. His mother was born at Bergen, Norway, July 8, 1859.

Mr. Erickson was graduated from Hastings Business College, Hastings, Nebraska, in 1907. He entered business with the Citizens Lumber Company in 1908 as a yard man, and since 1911 has been manager of that organization of which he is also secretary. He traveled for the Handy-Minor Lumber Company of Denver, Colorado, as salesman for a brief period. He has been a member of the village board at Campbell for several terms, is a member of the Volunteer Fire Department, and for several years was chairman of the Campbell Community Club.

He served as secretary of the village school board, 1923-24, was chairman of the Four Minute Men at Campbell during the World War, and served as a member of the Campbell Home Guard, 1917-18. Mr. Erickson is affiliated with the Campbell Presbyterian Church, is a member of the Nebraskana Society, and holds membership in the following fraternal organizations: Eastern Star; Odd Fellows; Rebekah Lodge; the Bladen Lodge No. 319 Ancient Free and Accepted Masons; and the Scottish Rite and Shrine at Hastings. His social club is the Campbell Country Club and his favorite sport is golfing.

His marriage to Hazel Vivian South was solemnized at Strang, Nebraska, on September 12, 1916. Mrs. Erickson, whose ancestry is Scotch and Irish, was born at Stewart, Iowa, September 12, 1895. They had two children: Patricia Dawn, born September 13, 1926; and Hope Diane, born February 20, 1928. Both children died in infancy. Mrs. Erickson is worthy matron of Hildreth Chapter No. 170 Order of Eastern Star. A Royal Neighbor, she is a member of the Christian Church at Cumberland, Iowa, active in church work and takes an active interest in the affairs of her community and home, especially her flower garden. Residence: Campbell.

Oliver Leo Erickson

Oliver Leo Erickson was born at Virginia, Nebraska, April 26, 1895, the son of Gustavus Adolphus and Mary (Mangus) Erickson. His father, who was a farmer, stockman and banker, was born near Galesburg, Illinois, August 2, 1871; he served on school boards for several years. His mother, whose ancestry is Pennsylvania Dutch, was born in Illinois, January 29, 1874.

Mr. Erickson was graduated from the high school at Beatrice, Nebraska, in 1914, received the D. D. S. degree at Creighton University at Omaha, in 1919, where he was a member of Xi Psi Phi. For a time he engaged in farming in Gage County, Nebraska, was engaged in the practice of dentistry at Kearney, for five years, and since 1924, has been proprietor of the Kearney Floral & Nursery Company. He is a director of the Buffalo County Fair Association.

He holds membership in the Chamber of Commerce, the Kiwanis Club of which he was secretary in 1922, the Fort Kearney Memorial Association, the Nebraska State Florists Society of which he is a director, the Red Cross, and the Nebraskana Society. He is affiliated with the Methodist Church and from 1927-31, was a member of the city council at Kearney. He served as a private in the United States Army during the World War, and is now a member of the American Legion. His hobby is attending football games.

On October 23, 1919, Mr. Erickson was married to Corrinne Amelia Barnard at Beatrice. She was born at Filley, Nebraska, October 23, 1895. They have four children: Mary Erdine, born November 1, 1920; Virginia Jeanne, born April 8, 1922; Evelyn Ann, born August 8, 1925; and Oliver Leo, Jr., born September 17, 1927. Mr. Erickson is a member of the Masons, (chapter), the Elks and the Odd Fellows. Residence: Kearney.

Leonard Everett Eriksen

Leonard Everett Eriksen, banker, was born at Council Bluffs, Iowa, September 14, 1903, son of Erik Peter and Laura Louise (Leonard) Eriksen.

Erik Peter Eriksen was born in Chicago, Illinois, November 4, 1870, of Danish parentage. He is a retired farmer and mail carrier. His wife, Laura, was born in Decatur, Iowa, February 3, 1871. Her parents were born in Ireland.

Upon the completion of his elementary education in the rural schools of Cherry County, Mr. Eriksen attended Hooker County High School, from which he was graduated on May 18, 1921. Thereafter for four years he taught in the public schools of Cherry and Hooker counties. At the present time he is assistant cashier of the Citizens State Bank of Mullen. He is a Democrat.

In 1924 he attended Citizens Military Training Camp at Des Moines, Iowa. He is a member of St. Joseph's Episcopal Church, Mullen Lodge No. 282 of the Ancient Free and Accepted Masons, and Winifred Chapter No. 292 of the Order of Eastern Star. Residence: Mullen.

H. L. Ernst

Colonel H. L. Ernst, farmer and stock dealer, was born at Graf, Nebraska, August 8, 1880. His father, William Henry Ernst, was born in Hanover, Germany, March 28, 1845. He was a member of the state legislature and a breeder of Percheron horses and Hereford and Shorthorn cattle. He died at Tecumseh, March 3, 1917. Louise Catherine (Hahn) Ernst was born in Germany, January 17, 1849. She resides at Tecumseh.

Colonel Ernst was educated in the country schools of Nebraska, and attended the State Agricultural College two years. On February 18, 1904, he was married to Marie Hannah Schomerus, at Johnson, Nebraska. Mrs. Ernst was born at Syracuse, on March 20, 1883. Their only son, Mark W., was born May 5, 1906, and is a registered pharmacist.

Mr. Ernst is a Republican. During his entire life he has been a farmer and auctioneer, and in the World War he donated his services and held twenty-four Red Cross sales in various towns in southeastern Nebraska. He is a member and deacon of the Presbyterian Church, a member of the Chamber of Commerce, Kiwanis Club and Modern Woodmen of America, and is secretary of Nemaha County fair board. His social club is the Country Club. He is interested in golf, duck hunting, fishing and football. Residence: Auburn.

Edward Floyd Ervin

Edward Floyd Ervin, banker, was born at Danbury, Nebraska, September 2, 1890, son of Edward and Eliza (Wingerter) Ervin.

The father was born at Charleston, Ohio, January 18, 1850. He came to Red Willow County in 1879, where he is now a retired farmer. His ancestry is German. His wife, Eliza, was born in Monroe County, Ohio, September 13, 1856. Her father came to the United States from Germany in 1840, and her mother in 1856.

Mr. Ervin attended public school and business college, otherwise he is self-educated. During 1918, he was sergeant instructor at military training school at the University of Nebraska. There he also taught engineering classes in the agricultural college. There are perhaps few graduates from the eighth grade, who can state that they have taught in the state university. While there Mr. Ervin had the first office in the new agricultural engineering building.

In January 1910, he went into the farm implement and automobile business for himself continuing until 1920, when he became cashier of the bank of Danbury. In 1931 he was elected president of that bank, and is still holding that office. He is also a director of the Beaver Valley Telephone Company. A Republican, he has served as mayor of Danbury for eight years.

On May 22, 1918, he was married to Elna Madeleine McDonald at Danbury. Mrs. Ervin was born at Danbury, May 13, 1892, of English and Scotch descent. They have two children, Floyd McDonald, born December 24, 1919; and Roger Edward, born October 9, 1921.

Mr. Ervin is a member of the American Legion, active in the Red Cross, and is a Mason and Shriner. His religious affiliation is with the Congregational Church. He enjoys golf, and is a member of the Parkhurst Golf Club. He spends his summer vacation fishing. His hobbies are reading and automobiles. Residence: Danbury.

Blanch Mendell Erwin

Blanch Mendell Erwin, daughter of George Henry and Margaret (Miller) Mendell, was born in Laughlinstown, West Moreland County, Pennsylvania, March 11, 1860, and has been a resident of Nuckolls County for the past 50 years.

Her father was born in Ligonier, West Moreland County Pennsylvania, May 12, 1838, and died at Superior, Nebraska. He was a tanner and a farmer and a veteran of the Civil War. His family came from Massachusetts, where they were engaged in the mercantile business and settled in New York City. Mr. Mendell served with Company H, 32nd Ohio Volunteers in the Civil War for three years, and afterward received a pension.

Margaret Miller Mendell was born at Scranton, Pennsylvania, January 16, 1838, and died at Superior, March 11, 1906. Her maternal progenitors were Samuel and Mary (Garver) Neely, who both died in West Moreland County.

Samuel Neely was a soldier in the Revolutionary War, who fought under Generals Wayne and Harrison, and was wounded in the knee and in later years received a pension from the government. He served as a private in the Dulchess County Militia of New York. (See *Roberts' New York in the Revolution*).

Sarah J. Neely, daughter of Samuel and Mary (Garver) Neely, was born near West Newton, West Moreland County, Pennsylvania, September 27, 1814. She married Phillip Miller at West Newton, Pennsylvania, in 1837. She was one of nine children, and was a survivor of the Johnstown Flood in 1889. Sarah and Phillip Miller had twelve children. She died in Johnstown, Pennsylvania, in 1903.

Margaret Miller, daughter of Sarah and Phillip Miller, was born at Scranton, Pennsylvania, January 16, 1838, and died at Superior, Nebraska, March 11, 1906. She married George Henry Mendell on May 26, 1859, at Johnstown, Pennsylvania.

Blanche Mendell, the eldest of ten children, was educated first in the common schools of Shamburg, Pennsylvania, and later attended a girl's boarding school at Ligonier.

On December 22, 1875, she was married to Alem Britten Erwin at Tecumseh. He was born at Milton, Pennsylvania, October 24, 1845, and died at Superior, Nebraska, August 13, 1907. A farmer, he served as a private in Company G, 156 Illinois Volunteer Infantry from 1864 until 1865, being discharged September 20, of the last year. To Mr. and Mrs. Erwin were born twelve children as follows: Margaret Miller, born September 24, 1876, married William Gabby Weir. William P., born November 22, 1877, married Grace Louise Dysart. Maud Blanch, born April 13, 1882, married William Albert Lunt. Atley Charles, born September 26, 1886, married Sadie Donahue, while Alfred Daniel, born the same day, married Pearl Merganthler. Mary G., born March 7, 1889, married Lawrence J. Arnold. Florence A., born December 12, 1890, married George A. Garrison. Mendell L., born February 17, 1893, married Mary Janette Wood. Lloyd

Britten, born March 4, 1895, married Hallie Macy. Maurice W., born July 24, 1898, married Ruth Marten.

Lloyd Britten was a soldier in the World War, who volunteered with Company A, 53rd Artillery (Ammunition Train) and served in the Coast Artillery Corps of the American Expeditionary Forces. He drove a truck in the ammunition train which carried supplies to the army in the Argonne Forest.

Maurice W. Erwin enlisted in the United States Marines as a member of the 317th Company, Battalion M. He was stationed at Marine Barracks, Paris Island, South Carolina and later in the Brooklyn Navy Yard at New York. In 1918 when about to sail for France, he was taken from the ship with influenza and was put in the Naval Hospital in Brooklyn, beside a friend, one of five boys from his home town who enlisted together. They remained together in camp, and would have all sailed together.

For a number of years after the death of her husband, Mrs. Erwin managed the home farm. She is now retired. She is affiliated with the Republican party, is a member of the Woman's Relief Corps, the American Legion Auxiliary, and is eligible for the Daughters of the American Revolution.

Her religious affiliation is with the Methodist Episcopal Church of Superior, she is a member of the Degree of Honor, the Auxiliary of the Woodmen of the World, and was recently made a life member of the Nebraskana Society. Residence: Superior.

Frank Henry Carl Erxleben

Frank H. C. Erxleben, one of Wayne County's most outstanding citizens, was born at La Porte, Nebraska, December 31, 1871. He is the son of Carl Fredrick William Franz and Caroline Christina (Weisser) Erxleben, both natives of Germany. Carl Erxleben was born in Erfurt, Saxony, March 12, 1842, and came to America at the age of 14. A pioneer homesteader in Wayne County, he was a carpenter and farmer, and beginning in 1872 served as county commissioner of Wayne County six years. His death occurred at Wayne, on September 14, 1905. Caroline, wife of Carl, was born in Studtgard, Wurttemburg, Germany, May 30, 1848, and died at Wayne September 13, 1891.

Educated in the public schools, Frank H. C. Erxleben has engaged as a farmer and banker successively all his life. He is chairman of the County Board of Wayne County, and has been a member of the board, elected on the Republican ticket, three successive terms. He is also former president of the Farmers State Bank of Altona.

On February 14, 1901, he was united in marriage to Emma Augusta Schach at Altona. Mrs. Erxleben, who was born at Wisner, on December 24, 1881, is of German descent. There are five children, Clara, born January 15, 1902, who married W. H. Hall; Esther, born December 4, 1903; Irven born May 23, 1905; Frances, born July 23, 1907; and Lloyd, born April 14, 1915. Esther and Frances are teachers, Irven a transport pilot, and Lloyd attends high school.

Mr. Erxleben is a member of Grace Evangelical Lutheran Church, and during the World War participated in all civilian projects. His hobby is mechanics. Residence: Wayne.

Clifford Franklin Eshelman

Clifford Franklin Eshelman was born at Canton, Illinois, August 6, 1889, the son of Benjamin Elliot and Ella Irene (Negly) Eshelman. His father, who was born at Canton, Illinois, November 1, 1860, and died at Red Cloud, Nebraska, August 3, 1926, was a farmer; his parents were natives of Pennsylvania. His mother, who was born at Canton, November 28, 1861, died at Anthony, Kansas, July 26, 1928.

Mr. Eshelman was a student in rural schools in Webster County, Nebraska, until 1904, was a student at Mount

Morris College, 1912-13, and attended the School of Agriculture and the Red Cloud Business College. A progressive farmer near Red Cloud, he is president of the Webster County Farm Bureau Board, is vice president of the Republican Valley Turkey Growers Association, and was first secretary of the Farmers Union Association Local 1222 at Red Cloud, when they organized in 1917.

Originally he was a member of the Church of Brethren, and due to the fact a great many of the members moved elsewhere and some had passed away, the membership became unable to support a pastor so he transferred his membership to the Congregational Church. He is a teacher of the Men's Bible Class of the Congregational Church of Red Cloud, and serves as a member of the board of that church. He is a regular attendant at the Organized Agriculture Meeting at the Lincoln College of Agriculture, is a member of the Red Cross, and holds membership in the Nebraska Society. Mr. Eshelman was awarded second place in the Nebraska Pig Crop Contest for two consecutive years, 1926 and 1927. His hobby is mechanics, and his favorite outdoor recreation is hunting. Politically he is Independent.

On August 30, 1916, he was united in marriage with Ruth Eleanor Johnston, daughter of Alfred and Clara (Kitchell) Johnston, of Red Cloud. Mrs. Eshelman, who served as principal of the Red Cloud High School for several years prior to her marriage, was born at Downs, Illinois, October 23, 1890. Both her maternal and paternal grandfathers served in the Civil War in the Union Army. They have two sons and two adopted daughters: Philip, born January 16, 1918, is a member of the Webster County Baby Beef 4-H Club; Richard, born July 1, 1925; Doris, born June 18, 1916, is a high school student and has been a member of the Let-Us-Win 4-H Club, taking sewing and cooking; and Elizabeth, born November 28, 1918, has also been a member in the Let-Us-Win 4-H Club, taking sewing and cooking. Residence: Red Cloud. (Photograph in Album).

Glenn Aulden Etter

Born at Niobrara, Nebraska, October 21, 1892, Glenn Aulden Etter has served as cashier of the First National Bank of Minatare, since May 14, 1929.

His father, Franklin Pierce Etter, was born in Cass County, Indiana, January 9, 1859, of Pennsylvania Dutch ancestry. The mother, Minnie Peosta Breniman, was born in Dubuque, Iowa, March 13, 1860, and died at Niobrara, Nebraska, November 24, 1927. Before her marriage she was a musical instructor. She was Pennsylvania Dutch descent on the father's side and Yankee on the mother's side. Her mother's ancestry having been traced to the *Mayflower*.

In May, 1909, Mr. Etter was graduated from the Niobrara High School, and for three years thereafter was employed by the Whipple Hardware in Niobrara. The four years following he was employed by the McClintock Hardware Company of Verdel, and afterward was associated with the Farmers Union there. He began his banking career as assistant cashier of the First State Bank, of Bazile Mills, Nebraska, and served two years. Thereafter for nine and one-half years, he was cashier of the First National Bank of Wellington, Colorado. He is a Democrat.

His marriage to Hanna Jorgensen was solemnized on January 2, 1917, at Verdel. She was born on the Isle of Fyn, Denmark, July 17, 1888, the daughter of Anders C. and Karen (Sorensen) Jorgensen. She and her parents are natives of Denmark, and are pioneer settlers of Nebraska. She attended school in Knox County, and is a member of the Minatare Woman's Club and the Rebekah Lodge.

Mr. Etter attends the Christian Science Church at Scottsbluff, Nebraska. For five years he served as secretary of the Wellington, Colorado, Commercial Club. At the present time he is a member of the Minatare Lions

Club, the Nebraskana Society, the Woodmen of the World, the Odd Fellows, and the Masons. He was active in all drives during the World War. He is fond of tennis, while his hobby is the promotion of community welfare, religious education and prohibition. Residence: Minatare.

Carroll D. Evans, Jr.

Born at Columbus, Nebraska, March 19, 1892, Carroll D. Evans, Jr., physician and surgeon, is the son of Carroll D. and Lorena Rose (North) Evans. The father, born at Tarentum, Pennsylvania, Mary 26, 1856, of English and Welsh Revolutionary ancestry, has been prominent in Nebraska for many years. A physician and surgeon, he has been surgeon general of Nebraska, and has served as grand commander of the Knights Templar of Nebraska.

Lorena Rose North was born at Columbus, Nebraska, February 18, 1865. She is a lineal descendant of Revolutionary War soldiers, and the daughter of J. E. North, collector of internal revenue at Omaha, 1893-97.

Carroll D. Evans, Jr., attended Columbus public schools and was graduated from high school in 1909. He was a student at the University of Nebraska, 1909-10, the University of Pennsylvania, 1910-11, and received his medical degree from Jefferson Medical College in Philadelphia, in 1916. His fraternities include Phi Delta Theta, Phi Alpha Sigma and Theta Nu Epsilon.

On April 6, 1918, he was married to Margaret Miller McHenry, at Denison, Iowa. Mrs. Evans, who traces her descent to participants in the Revolutionary War, was born at Denison, April 8, 1892. They have one daughter, Carolyn-Jean, born September 28, 1923.

In active practice at Columbus, since 1917, Dr. Evans is a member of the firm of Drs. Evans, Evans and Evans.

Dr. Evans held the rank of first lieutenant in the Medical Corps in the World War, and served as squadron surgeon, Lafayette Escadrille, 1918. Since 1924, he has held the rank of captain, Medical Corps, N. N. G., and in 1920, served as commander of Hartman Post No. 84, of the American Legion.

He was exalted ruler of the Elks, 1924, commander of Gethsemene Commandery, 1922, and grand generalissimo, Knights Templar of Nebraska, 1931. He is a member of the Knights of the Red Cross of Constantine, the Nebraskana Society and the Chamber of Commerce, and is affiliated with Grace Episcopal Church. His professional memberships include the American, Nebraska State and Platte County Medical Associations, and from 1925-29, he was secretary of the last mentioned organization. Residence: Columbus.

Dallas Gates Evans

Dallas G. Evans, banker in Dakota County for the past 29 years, was born at Hastings, Mills County, Iowa, March 30, 1876, the son of James and Annie (Barr) Evans. His father who was a farmer, was born at Springfield, Illinois, February 11, 1843, and died at South Sioux City, Nebraska, October 11, 1911; his Scotch and Welsh ancestors came to this country about 1700. His mother, whose ancestry is German, was born in Indiana, September 30, 1840.

Mr. Evans has been a merchant, county treasurer of Dakota County, and banker, for many years. He is now serving as cashier of the Home State Bank at Homer. He is a member of the Odd Fellows, the Red Cross, the Nebraskana Society, and the Masons. He has served on the local school board and during the war he was active in loan drives and Red Cross work. He is an Independent, politically.

He was united in marriage with Helen H. Shearer at Ida Grove, Ida County, Iowa, May 14, 1903. Mrs. Evans was born, of Dutch parentage, at Denison, Iowa,

July 25, 1877. They have three children: Harold, born September 14, 1907, who married Lorna Barnard; Anna B., born September 18, 1904, who married Henry E. Ley; and Dallas, born December 22, 1912. Residence: Homer.

George Alexander Evans

George Alexander Evans, sheriff of Loup County, was born in Madison County, Iowa, November 26, 1863, and for more than forty-five years has resided in Nebraska. His father, Hugh Evans was born in Washington County, Indiana, October 22, 1836, and his mother, Susan Katherine Davis, in Lawrence County, Indiana, December 28, 1839.

Hugh Evans, a farmer and merchant for many years, died in Fontanelle, Iowa, February 9, 1913. His paternal grandfather came from Wales to America. Susan Katherine Davis died at Fontanelle on August 19, 1916.

Educated in rural schools in Nebraska, George Alexander Evans has been a farmer for a number of years. He is now sheriff of Loup County, also, elected on an independent ticket. He was married to Nettie Jane Hooper in Loup County, on June 30, 1890. Mrs. Evans was born in Piatt County, Illinois, November 16, 1869. There are four children, as follows: Christena, born January 2, 1891, taught school for fourteen years, served as postmistress at Taylor, for nearly six years, and is now a linotype operator. Mahala, born February 22, 1894, married John Ward; Ina, born March 12, 1896, married Ervin Holley who is now deceased; while Blanche, born November 19, 1898, married Dana Newberry.

Mr. Evans is prominent in community affairs at Taylor, and was recently made a life member of The Nebraskana Society. Residence: Taylor.

Virden Elvon Evans

A leading merchant and banker of Grand Island, Nebraska, is Virden Elvon Evans who has resided in Howard and Hall Counties for the past 48 years. He was born at Henderson, Iowa, April 2, 1883, the son of John W. and Maggie (McMullen) Evans, the former a farmer who was born in Ohio, June 18, 1860. His mother was born of Irish parents at Galesburg, Illinois, January 14, 1863.

Mr. Evans was a student at the St. Paul Business College from 1901 to 1905, and since 1905 has been a leader in the banking mercantile business of Grand Island. He has held the following positions in the professional world: cashier of the Cushing State Bank, 1906-11; president of the Glass-Evans-Auto Company, 1908-28; president of the State Bank of Grand Island for five years. At this time he is president of the American Securities Company, and is a director in the First National Bank of Grand Island.

During the World War he was instrumental in raising a $13,000 fund for the Red Cross, and was active in various loan projects. Mr. Evans is a member of the Grand Island Chamber of Commerce, is affiliated with the First Presbyterian Church, and has held membership in the Riverside Country Club and the Woodland Country Club of Grand Island. His sports include trap shooting; golfing; hunting; and fishing.

On September 2, 1905, he was united in marriage with Lida C. Paulsen at St. Paul, Nebraska. Mrs. Evans, who was a clerk before her marriage, was born at Dannebrog, Nebraska, July 1, 1887. They have two children: Gordon, born December 3, 1909, a student at the University of Nebraska; and Clayton, born February 14, 1913, who is a student at the Grand Island Junior College. Mrs. Evans is of Danish descent.

Mr. Evans is a member of the Nebraskana Society, and is affiliated with the Democratic party. Residence: Grand Island.

George Evens

George Evens was born at Westboro, Atchison County, Missouri, November 14, 1879, the son of Joseph Louis and Annie Eliza (Herron) Evens. His father, who is a farmer, was born at Dubuque, Dubuque County, Iowa, April 26, 1849. His ancestry is English and Welsh.

His mother, whose ancestry was Scotch, was born at Shelbyville, Shelby County, Indiana, October 4, 1855, and died at Portland, Oregon, November 10, 1930.

Mr. Evens was graduated from the high school at Creston, Nebraska, and later was a student at the Nebraska State Normal School, Peru, Nebraska; Fremont Normal School, Fremont, Nebraska; and the University of Omaha. He was awarded an LL.B. degree at the University of Omaha. He was valedictorian of his class in high school.

He was admitted to the bar at Omaha, June 21, 1921. For the past seven years he has practiced law in Omaha; for a time he was associated with Judge Thomsen of the firm Thomsen, Mossman & Standeven. For the last two years he has been associated with Judge W. W. Slabaugh. He is a member of the Nebraska State Bar Association. He has lived in Nebraska for 38 years.

On June 16, 1909 he was united in marriage with Florence Sullivan at Wellington, Sumner County, Kansas. Mrs. Evens who is of Scotch Irish descent, was born at Dover, Mason County, Kentucky, July 24, 1881. There are two children: Marjorie M., born March 1, 1910; and Marion C., born June 16, 1918.

Mr. Evens is a member of the North Side Christian Church, at Omaha. He is a Democrat. His hobby is reading. Residence: Omaha.

Mrs. J. S. Everett

A leader in social and civic affairs at Scotia, Nebraska, Mrs. J. S. Everett was born at Geneva, Wisconsin, February 20, 1874, the daughter of Andrew Burritt Acker and Eleanor Catherine (Eick) Acker. Her father, who was a farmer and stockraiser, was born in New York, May 23, 1850, and died at Clarks, South Dakota, October 8, 1921; his ancestry was German. Her mother, a descendant of the Dow family of New England, was born at Hagertown, New Jersey, April 28, 1844.

Mrs. Everett attended an elementary school at Council Bluffs, Iowa, and received her high school education at Harlan, Iowa, where she was a leader in dramatics and music. She taught the first school at Lindsay, Nebraska, and has always been a progressive and civic-minded community leader. She is a member of the Parent Teachers Association at Scotia, is a member of the official board of the Methodist Church, is serving as vice president of the Woman's Foreign Missionary Society, and is treasurer of the Ladies Aid Society.

She has served as treasurer of the church board for a period of 12 years, has been corresponding secretary of the Woman's Club of Scotia for eight years, and is chairman of the health study department of the Royal Neighbors Society. Mrs. Everett is especially interested in home-building and rearing her children and grandchildren.

Of her marriage to Jacob A. Sheridan, which occurred near Beemer, Nebraska, January 1, 1891, two children were born: Jessie, November 19, 1891, who married Robert W. Vogt, and who died July 10, 1924; and Jay Clinton, April 6, 1900, who married Mary Josephine Coy. Mrs. Everett is a Progressive. Residence: Scotia.

Jacob Sheridan Everett

Jacob Sheridan Everett, farmer and stockman, was born January 9, 1868, son of John and Margaret Regina (St. Clair) Everett. His father, born at Danville, Pennsylvania, December 21, 1823, died at Chariton, Iowa, Jan-

uary 26, 1908. He was a soldier throughout the Civil War. His wife, Margaret, was born at Danville, October 11, 1843, and died at Chariton, December 10, 1915. She was of Pennsylvania Dutch and French ancestry.

Mr. Everett attained his education in the public schools. He has always been a farmer and stock raiser, and for a number of years lived on a ranch of 800 acres, 14 miles north of Scotia. At the present time he resides on 80 acres on the edge of Scotia, and is the owner of about 1600 acres of wheat land near Tribune, Kansas.

On January 1, 1891, he was married to Bertie Arletta Acker, at Beemer. Mrs. Everett was born at Geneva Lake, Wisconsin, February 20, 1874. They have one child living and one deceased. Jessie LaVern, born November 19, 1891, married Robert W. Vogt, and died July 10, 1924. Jay Clinton, born April 6, 1900, married Mary Josephine Coy.

Mr. Everett is a Socialist. He is a stockholder in the Co-operative Elevator Company, the Co-operative Creamery Company, and the Co-operative Oil Station, all of Scotia, and a member of the Co-operative Wheat Growers Association of Kansas City, Missouri. His hobby is setting out trees of all kinds and improving farm land. His favorite sport is hiking. Residence: Scotia.

Chauncey E. Everhart

A resident of Nebraska for the past 43 years Chauncey E. Everhart was born at Poneto, Indiana, June 11, 1885, the son of John and Sarah Mary (Durbin) Everhart. His father, who was a farmer, was born in Ohio, in 1829, and died at Neligh, December 20, 1901; his ancestry was Pennsylvania Dutch. His mother, whose ancestry was Irish and Scotch, was born in Wells County, Indiana, August 15, 1846, and died at Neligh, January 13, 1913.

Mr. Everhart was graduated from the Gates Academy at Neligh in 1906, and immediately entered the employ of the *Neligh Register* as job man and press man. He is now editor of the *Orchard News*, is a member of the Orchard Chamber of Commerce, and holds membership in the Nebraskana Society. He is affiliated with the United Brethren Church, and is a member of the Independent Order of Odd Fellows.

His marriage to Olive May Meuret was solemnized at Orchard, November 6, 1909. Mrs. Everhart, who is a newspaper publisher, was born at Shirland, Illinois, March 1, 1889. Her maternal grandparents came to this country from France, and her paternal grandparents were English. Three children were born to them: Lucile E., born February 26, 1911, who died September 15, 1911; Harold V., born October 19, 1912; and Leona E., born August 15, 1915. Residence: Orchard.

William Frederick Evers

At Plattsmouth, Nebraska, William F. Evers was born May 6, 1894, the son of Peter and Mary Margaret (Ohlenhausen) Evers. His father, born at Schleswig, Germany, August 14, 1870, was a farmer, who came to Nebraska, in 1887. His mother was born in Peoria, Illinois, June 29, 1875. Her ancestors came from Hessen Damstadt, Germany, her father, a von Ohlenhausen.

Mr. Evers received his education in the Plattsmouth city schools, and attended the German school during the summer months. He has lived in Nebraska for 35 years during which time has been a railway employee for four years, a contract carpenter, and superintendent of the Masonic Home. He has held the latter position since 1920.

He married Pearl Frank Schwenneker at Plattsmouth, June 5, 1913. Mrs. Evers, who was born at Plattsmouth, is the daughter of a German father and a French and English mother. They have three children: Billy Earl, born March 9, 1920; Raymond Frederick, born May 6, 1925; and Mary Vesta, born January 22, 1927.

During the late war Mr. Evers was a four minute man,

and was a member of the home guards of Plattsmouth, in 1917. He is a member of the Chamber of Commerce, serving as a director of this organization; was a charter member of the Rotary Club at Plattsmouth; and is a member of the Red Cross. He is a Mason, and a member of the First Methodist Episcopal Church. Residence: Plattsmouth. (Photograph in Album).

Samuel Mitchell Ewing

Born in Bedford County, Virginia, November 6, 1851, Samuel Mitchell Ewing has been a farmer and banker in Dundy County, Nebraska, since 1885. His father, William Ewing, a farmer, was born in Bedford County, Virginia, December 26, 1813, and died in Dundy County, May 9, 1896; he was descended from Robert Ewing, who was born in 1715, in County Londonderry, Ireland, and a grandson of Mitchell Ewing and Nancy (Beard) Ewing, who moved to Bedford County.

His mother, Lydia (Patterson) Ewing, whose ancestry was Scotch and Irish, was born in Washington County, Pennsylvania, May 22, 1825, and died in Bedford County, Virginia, December 29, 1860. She is a descendant of James Patterson who was born in Ireland, in 1708, and settled in Lancaster County, Pennsylvania, in 1728.

Mr. Ewing was graduated from the Bryan & Stratton Commercial and Banking School at Ewalt College, Pittsburg, Pennsylvania, in 1873. He homesteaded in Dundy County in 1885, and is still farming on the original farm near Benkelman, Nebraska. A Democrat, he was an ardent Al Smith supporter, has served in the Nebraska Legislature, 1917, where he fought ardently for the rights of the West, has acted as county commissioner for six years, 1892-1898, and was formerly a councilman and school officer over a period of 19 years.

For the past 50 years he has been a Master Mason, being a member of Justice Lodge No. 180 at Benkelman. He has been active in the affairs of this lodge of which he is now treasurer, having held this position for the past 14 years. He is also treasurer of the Cemetery Association. He is a member of the Nebraskana Society, and is affiliated with the Presbyterian Church. His hobby is fish propagation.

He was united in marriage with Addie Belle Hamilton, in Dundy County, March 8, 1888. Mrs. Ewing, who was a teacher, was born in Clay County, Illinois, April 28, 1870, and died at Benkelman, Nebraska, March 4, 1925. Her parents died in Canada. Of the eleven children born to them, nine are living: May, born May 22, 1889, who married Charles O. Nelson; Lenna, born January 11, 1892, who married Jess E. Purdy; Henry, born July 6, 1894, who married Alice Hester; Ida, born May 23, 1897, who married Clifford J. Toler; Harriet, born August 3, 1899, who died June 10, 1924; Ann, born July 30, 1902, who married John McEvoy; Samuel, born November 22, 1904, who married Gladys Piper, and who died May 1, 1931; Merle, born July 6, 1907, who married Dorothy Smith; Florence, March 22, 1909; Gladys, born March 17, 1911; and Robert, born September 12, 1913. Residence: Benklelman. (Photograph in Album).

William J. Ewing

William J. Ewing, banker, was born at Falmouth, Indiana, July 27, 1875. He is the son of John Thomas and Emeline Ewing, the former a farmer who was born, October 25, 1847, at Miami, Indiana, and died at Exeter, Nebraska, in October, 1921. He was of Scotch Irish descent. His mother, whose ancestry was Irish, was born at Miami in September, 1851, and died at Dalton, Nebraska, December 19, 1928. Her mother came to America from Ireland with her parents at the age of three.

Mr. Ewing attended high school at Reynolds, Nebraska. He engaged in the mercantile business for a time at Exeter, was a lumberman for 14 years, and for the past 15 years has served as president of the Dalton State Bank. He was chairman of the council of defense during the World War and has been a prominent citizen of Dalton since 1906. He is a member of the Modern Woodmen of America, the Independent Order of Odd Fellows, the school board, and The Nebraskana Society. His hobby is reading, and his favorite sport golfing. He is a Republican.

His marriage to Elsie (Poole) Ewing occurred at Dalton, November 14, 1908. She is the daughter of Sidney and Dora (Castle) Poole. Mrs. Ewing was born at Hennepin, Illinois, December 18, 1883. They have two children: Bessie, born September 14, 1909, who married J. F. Creswell; and Clara, born September 19, 1911. Residence: Dalton.

Fred Harman Eyler

Fred H. Eyler, investment banker, was born at Omaha, Nebraska, February 13, 1898, son of John Albert and Minnie Dell (Harman) Eyler. His father, who was born at Xenia, Ohio, June 5, 1856, and died at Omaha, January 30, 1930, was of Dutch descent. His mother, whose ancestry was Dutch, Swedish and Irish, was born at Springfield, Ohio, September 5, 1858.

Mr. Eyler attended Lothrop School at Omaha, until 1911, and in 1915 was graduated from the Omaha Central High School. Thereafter he was a student at the University of Nebraska, and the United States Military Academy. A clerk for the Nebraska Power Company for three years. He was in the loan department of the Omaha National Bank for seven years; was vice president of the Drovers and Merchants Bank at St. Joseph, Missouri, for four years; and was manager of the Chicago office of the Omaha National Company for one year. He is now treasurer of the Omaha National Company at Omaha, Nebraska.

His marriage to Nellie Ewall was solemnized at Omaha, June 26, 1926. Mrs. Eyler was born at Council Bluffs, Iowa, March 15, 1899. They have one son: John Frederick, born January 9, 1930. Mr. Eyler was a cadet in the United States Military Academy for a time. He is a member of the American Legion.

He holds membership in: Omaha Chamber of Commerce; American Institute of Banking, (president of Omaha Chapter, 1925, and St. Joseph Chapter, 1926); and the Nebraskana Society.

He is a Mason and an Odd Fellow, is affiliated with the First Presbyterian Church of Omaha, and belongs to the Athletic Club. His sports are golf, tennis, and skating. Residence: Omaha.

Frank Fafeita

Frank Fafeita, veteran merchant of Ord, Nebraska, has lived in this state over 48 years. He was born at Hyskov, Czechoslovakia, July 30, 1869, the son of Kate and John Fafeita. His father, who was a tailor, died at St. Paul, Nebraska, September 8, 1904. His mother died at St. Paul, November 21, 1894.

Mr. Fafeita is retired from active business now. He was in business for 15 years at Elba, and 15 years at Ord. He is a member of Z. C. B. J., the Modern Woodmen of America, and St. Mary's Catholic Church. His chief recreations are golfing and reading.

Of his marriage to Emma L. Novak are the following children: Emil R., born February 29, 1892; and Frank J., born September 13, 1893, who is a merchant. Emil is cashier in the Nebraska State Bank at Ord. Mr. Fafeita is affiliated with the Republican party and holds membership in the Nebraskana Society. Residence: Ord.

Charles Lander Fahnestock

For the past 30 years Charles L. Fahnestock has been engaged in the practice of medicine at Lincoln, Nebraska.

He was born at Wanda, Illinois, July 5, 1874, the son of Jacob K., and Nancy E. (Lander) Fahnestock. His father, who was a country storekeeper, was born at Muncy, Pennsylvania, and died at Wanda, Illinois, November 1, 1899. His German ancestors came to this country in 1726. His mother was born at Hopkinsville, Kentucky, June 21, 1847, and died at St. Louis, Missouri, in November, 1909.

Dr. Fahnestock was graduated from high school in 1892; and in 1896 received the M. D. degree at Washington University at St. Louis, Missouri. From 1896-1907 he was with the St. Louis City Hospital; during 1897-98 he practiced in St. Louis, and during 1898-99 practiced in Aurora, Illinois. Coming to McCook in 1899, he practiced there until September, 1921, when he was transferred to Lincoln as district surgeon and examiner for the Burlington Railroad Company. During 1907-1908 he was mayor of McCook.

During the World War, Dr. Fahnestock served as captain in the Medical Corps and is now a member of the American Legion, of which he was post commander in 1920. He holds membership in the American Medical Association, the Nebraska State and Lancaster County Medical Societies. In 1920 and 1921 he served as president of the Young Men's Christian Association at McCook, and is now a member of the Hiram Club and The Nebraskana Society. He is an Elk, and a Mason, holding membership in the York Rite, Sesostris Temple of the Shrine, and the Shrine Country Club of Lincoln. His favorite sport is fishing.

His marriage to Anne E. Anderson was solemnized at Lincoln, August 19, 1902. Mrs. Fahnestock was born at Granville, Pennsylvania, May 10, 1875. Their children are Margaret J., born January 17, 1906, who is a science teacher; and Dale R., born December 4, 1907, who is a senior at the University of Nebraska.

Dr. Fahnestock is a Republican. He is affiliated with the First Plymouth Congregational Church at Lincoln. Residence: Lincoln.

George Otis Fairchild

Born at Blanchard, Missouri, March 10, 1875, George Otis Fairchild has been a resident of Nebraska for the past 40 years. His father, Levi Fairchild, who was a farmer and a veteran of the Civil War, was born at St. Thomas, Ontario, January 25, 1844. His mother was born at Corridon, Indiana, January 5, 1848, and was a teacher for several years before her marriage.

Mr. Fairchild was graduated from the high school at Leavenworth, Kansas, in 1895, and later attended the Lincoln Normal University. He taught school for two years, was in the drug business at Loomis, for four years, was a hardware merchant for a period of eight years, and for over 20 years engaged in the automobile business. He now owns and operates the Fairchild Motor Company at Kearney, Nebraska, and manages his thousand-acre farm in Kimball County, Nebraska.

He served as president of the Chamber of Commerce at Kearney, 1925-27, was president of the Kearney Rotary Club, 1928-29, and acted as president of the Kearney School Board, 1928-29. Mr. Fairchild is a member of the Red Cross, the Kearney Country Club, the First Presbyterian Church, the Elks and Masons. His chief recreations are golfing and reading.

His marriage to Lelia Charlotte Pedley, was solemnized at Bertrand, Nebraska, September 20, 1899. Mrs. Fairchild, who was a teacher before her marriage, was born at Murray, Iowa, June 23, 1877. They have two children: Nellie, born June 9, 1901, who married Dr. Harold L. Averill; and Dorothy, born January 10, 1926, who married Joseph E. Wellman. Nellie was graduated from Leland Stanford University with the A. B. degree, and

Dorothy received the B. S. degree from the University of Nebraska. Residence: Kearney.

Mary Ann Fairchild

Mary Ann Fairchild was born in London, England, the daughter of George and Mary (Hitchcock) Spurway. Her father, who was also born in London, on May 5, 1845, came to America where he engaged in the contracting business until his death at Detroit in 1926. His wife, Mary, was born in London about September 20, 1845, and is living in Springfield, Illinois.

Upon the completion of her grade school education she attended high school and business college at Springfield, and came to Nebraska in 1904. Of her marriage to James Donville Fairchild there are two children, Mary Eleanor, born December 4, 1892, who married Robert Waters Turner. She is a musician. Donville Seymour, born December 8, 1900, married Kathryn Smith, of Lincoln, Nebraska; he is employed in the actuarial department of the Woodmen of the World at Omaha.

For the past 18 years Mrs. Fairchild has been connected with the State Insurance Department, as clerk, chief clerk, assistant chief and deputy commissioner; at the present time she is assistant to the Commissioner of Insurance and Securities. She is a member of the Red Cross, the Lincoln Chamber of Commerce, The Nebraskana Society and Holy Trinity Episcopal Church. Residence: Lincoln.

Nora May Fairchild

Nora May Fairchild, physician, was born at Lebanon, Ohio, February 28, 1884, daughter of George William and Etta Marlowe (Wright) Fairchild.

She received her medical degree from the University of Nebraska in 1906 and for a number of years has been associated with Drs. Gifford, Patton, Callfas and Potts.

She is a member of Central Congregational Church, the American, Nebraska State and Douglas County Medical Associations, and the American Academy of Ophthalmology and Oto-Laryngology, as well as the Nebraska Association of Medical Women. Residence: Omaha.

Wiliam H. Faling

William H. Faling was born in Jefferson County, New York, March 3, 1848, the son of David and Betsy (Wheeler) Faling. His father, who was a farmer and justice of the peace in his community, was born in New York and died at Fiatt, Illinois, in February, 1878; his ancestry was German. His mother was born in Jefferson County and died at Fiatt, in April, 1898. She was of early American ancestry.

Mr. Faling attended Free Will Baptist Academy at Prairie City, Illinois. He has been engaged in the real estate and loan business for many years at Cambridge, Nebraska, and has been a resident of the state for 57 years, and a resident of Cambridge for 52 years. A Republican, he served as the first chairman of the board of trustees of Cambridge in 1885, when Cambridge was incorporated as a city. He is a member of the Cambridge Community Club, the Red Cross, and the Foreign Missionary Society of the Congregational Church. He is a Mason.

During the World War Mr. Faling served as secretary of the Home Guards, bought bonds, and assisted in various war-time drives. He married Anna E. Stewart at Cuba, Illinois, May 23, 1877. Mrs. Faling was born at Alexandria, Ohio, August 6, 1851, the daughter of Richard and Philena (Twining) Stewart. She died at Cambridge, Nebraska, January 3, 1926. They had one daughter, Lena Ethel, born May 18, 1883, who died in 1885. Residence: Cambridge.

Roszell—Beatrice

ANNA KEMPER FALL

Anna Kemper Fall

Born at Lancaster, Wisconsin, February 22, 1865, Anna Kemper Fall is the daughter of George John and Anna Elizabeth (Wohmelsdorf) Kemper. Her father, a native of Schiller by Berleburg, Prussia, Germany, came to America and settled in Wisconsin in 1844. He was descended from a family of educators and clergymen, who were prominent in the development of their home community in Germany. George John Kemper was born on June 14, 1822, and died at Aurora, Nebraska, February 7, 1898, after a long and highly successful life as a landowner and farmer.

Anna Elizabeth Wohmelsdorf was born at Schiller by Berleburg, on February 29, 1824, of a family of soldiers and cabinetmakers. She was essentially a wife and mother, and devoted her entire life to her family. Her death occurred at Aurora, May 26, 1920.

Educated in the elementary schools of Lancaster, Wisconsin, until 1882, Mrs. Fall later attended the State Normal School at Platteville, Wisconsin. Two years later she removed to Nebraska, and on June 17, 1885, was united in marriage to Clifford Pervines Fall at Aurora. Dr. Fall, who is a physician and surgeon, was born at Thorntown, Indiana, February 9, 1863 (see Nebraskana). There were four children born to their marriage, two of whom are deceased; Crystal, born May 23, 1886, who died September 30, 1894; Hazel, born August 14, 1890, who married C. F. Shaffer; William, born August 21, 1900, who died August 22, 1902; and Frederic, born January 27, 1903, who married Ruth Nichols of Beatrice.

While most of her life has been devoted to the rearing of her family, Mrs. Fall has found opportunity to do much for the advancement of her community. She is a member of the Presbyterian Church, and has taken an active part in its affairs. During 1917 and 1918 she was a member and president of the local chapter of the Red Cross, and during 1930 and 1931 served as president of the Beatrice School Board, in which she has held membership for the past six years.

During the past fourteen years she has been a member of the Young Women's Christian Association, and has held the offices of local and district president. She is also a member of the Eastern Star, the P. E. O. and The Nebraskana Society. Both she and Dr. Fall are members of the Beatrice County Club. Residence: Beatrice. (Photograph on Page 394).

Clifford Pervines Fall

Clifford Pervines Fall, physician and surgeon, was born in Boone County, Indiana, February 9, 1863, son of David and Anna (Kernodle) Fall. His father, a farmer, was born in North Carolina in 1814, and died in Boone County, Indiana, in 1869. An early settler in Indiana, he hauled freight from Cincinnati to Chicago with ox teams before the day of railroads. He was a cousin of Daniel Boone.

Dr. Fall's mother was born in Virginia, February 22, 1816, and died at Thorntown, Indiana, November 28, 1880. Her father, a southern planter, sold his slaves before the Civil War retaining only one whom he educated for the ministry after giving him his freedom.

Dr. Fall received his elementary education at a Quaker school in Indiana. He was graduated from the Physician's and Surgeon's College, Chicago, in 1888. Study at Chicago Polyclinic and two European post-graduate tours completed his education. While going to school he worked on a farm and later taught school in Aurora, Nebraska. In 1888 he settled in Beatrice where he established the Beatrice Sanitarium.

On June 17, 1885, his marriage to Anna Kemper was solemnized at Aurora, Nebraska. Mrs. Fall who is active in civic and social affairs, was born at Lan-

caster, Wisconsin, February 22, 1865. She is past president of the local and district Y. W. C. A., and president of the school board in Beatrice. Of the four children born to this marriage, two are deceased; Crystal, born May 23, 1886, who died September 30, 1894; William, born August 21, 1900, died August 22nd, 1902. Hazel, born August 14, 1890, is the wife of Carl S. Shaffer, manager of the Gage County Electric Company at Beatrice. Frederick, born January 27, 1903, is a graduate of the Chicago University of Law and lives in San Antonio, Texas.

A Democrat, Dr. Fall was an unsuccessful candidate for nomination to congress in 1922. He has been president and director of the Beatrice Building and Loan Association since its organization twenty-seven years ago.

As first lieutenant he served in the Spanish American War, where he was special contract surgeon, and during the World War was a member of the local advisory board. He is a member of the American Medical Association, the Nebraska State Medical Association, the Gage County Medical Society, and the American Railway Medical Association. Dr. Fall is a member of the Kiwanis Club and the Beatrice Country Club. He is a 32nd degree Mason and an Elk.

Dr. Fall was first president of Beatrice Kiwanis Club and is responsible for the wonderful organization of this club in Beatrice. Residence: Beatrice. (Photograph on Page 396).

Henry H. Falldorf

Born at Nienburg, Germany, September 7, 1864, Henry H. Falldorf has resided in Nebraska 58 years, and has taken an active part in the development of his community and state. He is the son of Henry H. and Maria (Holmann) Falldorf, the former born at Bohkope, Germany, August 6, 1834, and the latter at Siedenburg, Germany.

Henry H. Falldorf, Sr., came to America in the early 1880's, where he engaged in farming until his death at Grand Island, on May 30, 1922. His wife died at Sutholz, Germany, in April, 1872.

Educated in public schools in Germany, and in Grand Island, Henry Falldorf, the subject of this sketch, was for a number of years in the general contracting business. He is now retired. He is a Mason, and a Lutheran. Mr. Falldorf has taken an active interest in Republican politics, and at the present time is serving as city councilman. Recently he was elected to life membership in The Nebraskana Society.

On May 17, 1887, he was united in marriage to Maria I. Timpke, at Grand Island. Mrs. Falldorf was born there on August 21, 1866, of German parentage. There is one daughter, Emilie, born January 4, 1888, who married Albert T. Hein. Residence: Grand Island.

Oscar Otto Fallert

Born at Holbrook, Nebraska, November 4, 1892, Oscar Otto Fallert is the son of Fidel and Louisa Mary (Kammerer) Fallert. His father, who was a farmer and stockraiser, was born in Germany, February 28, 1844, and came to Holbrook, and took a homestead in 1879. He died at Holbrook, April 20, 1929. His mother was born at Alsace Lorraine, Germany, January 6, 1853, and came to this country in 1858, settling at Hamilton, Ohio.

Mr. Fallert was employed by the H. G. Miller Company, 1909-11, the Teeter & Homan Company, 1911-15, and the S. F. Davis Company, 1915-18. After the World War he once more entered the employ of the S. F. Davis Company for a year when he became manager of the Farmers Store at Holbrook.

He is a member of the St. Germanus Catholic Church, has been a member of the Parent-Teachers' Association since 1925, and has served on the city council since 1925.

CLIFFORD PERVINES FALL

He is a member of the Western Merchants Association, the Woodmen of the World of which he is Sovereign Commander, and the Knights of Columbus. His hobby is mechanics and his favorite sport is golfing.

During the World War he served as a private in Campany B, 24th Machine Gun Battalion. He is adjutant of the American Legion at Holbrook. On June 15, 1921, Mr. Fallert married Carrie Margaret Meyerle at Arapahoe, Nebraska. Mrs. Fallert, who is of German descent, was born at Holbrook, September 14, 1894. She was a teacher before her marriage, teaching two terms at Edison, two terms at Holbrook, and ten terms in city schools. Residence: Holbrook.

Virgil Falloon

Virgil Falloon, lawyer and county judge of Richardson County, was born at Falls City, Richardson County, Nebraska, May 30, 1891. Edwin Falloon, his father, was born at Montreal, Canada, July 26, 1853, and died at Falls City, March 28, 1917. Emma Viola (Stump) Falloon, his mother, was born at Williamsville, (formerly Stump's Station) Richardson County, Nebraska.

Mr. Falloon was graduated from the Falls City High School in 1909, and in 1913 received the A. B. degree from the University of Ohio where he was president of the sophomore class, and was president of Gamma chapter of Phi Delta Theta.

Judge Falloon was admitted to the bar at Lincoln, in December, 1916, and since that time has practiced law in this state. From 1923 to 1929 he was editor of the *Falls City Journal;* he has been county judge of Richardson County since 1917. He is president of the Journal Publishing Company and is a director in the Falls City State Bank.

On December 31, 1921 he was married at Denver, Colorado, to Mabel Traxler who was born at Edgar, Clay County, Nebraska, January 20, 1894. There are three children Virgil, born April 25, 1924; Virginia, born November 11, 1925; and Marian, born September 19, 1926.

Judge Falloon is a member of the bar association, the Red Cross, and the board of education. During 1926 he was vice president of the Chamber of Commerce, and has been a director of this organization since 1926. In 1924 he acted as president of the Rotary Club; was secretary of this club in 1923, 1928, 1929, and 1930. He is a member of the Elks; the Odd Fellows, all bodies; and all branches of the Masons. He is a member of The Nebraskana Society and the Elks Country Club. His hobby is football. Residence: Falls City. (Photograph on Page 398).

George Lord Farley

On June 3, 1866 George L. Farley was born at Weeping Water, Cass County, Nebraska. His father, Henry Woods Farley, a farmer and teacher, was prominent in Nebraska politics for many years, serving as a member of the Nebraska House of Representatives in 1875. Descended from early New England Welsh and English ancestors, he was born at Hollis, Nashua County, New Hampshire, April 12, 1820, and died at Weeping Water, January 14, 1885.

Sarah Elizabeth (Chamberlain) Farley, his mother, who was born at Quincy, Norfolk County, Massachusetts, May 19, 1830, and died at Weeping Water, June 5, 1881, was an active church worker. Her ancestors were early settlers in New England.

His early education was received in the public schools of Weeping Water, and in 1891 he was graduated from the Weeping Water Academy. Mr. Farley has lived in Nebraska all his life and has taken an interested part in the economic and political life of the state. From 1900 to 1908 he was editor of the *Plattsmouth Evening News,* and the *Semi-Weekly News-Herald,* after which he engaged in the real estate and insurance business for several years.

A Republican, he has held various public offices, among them that of county superintendent of schools

three terms; county assessor one term; deputy county treasurer two years; and today is serving his second term as county commissioner of Cass County.

His marriage to Mary Hoadley Baird was solemnized at Plattsmouth, January 19, 1904. Mrs. Farley, who was born at Plattsmouth, August 2, 1878, was a teacher in the Plattsmouth school for eight years before her marriage. She is the daughter of Dr. John T. Baird, of Scotch descent, a Presbyterian pioneer minister, who for over 30 years was stated clerk of the Presbyterian synod of Nebraska. Her mother was of English descent. To this union were born twin daughters, Edith M. and Helen L., born May 13, 1905. Both became public school teachers; Edith is married to Charles E. Tunnell, and lives at Plattsmouth.

Mr. Farley was a member of the home guard in the late war, was a four minute speaker and a solicitor in loan drives. He is a member of the Red Cross, the Chamber of Commerce, the Modern Woodmen of America, and the Security Benefit Association. He is affiliated with the First Presbyterian Church of Plattsmouth, and is a member of the Nebraskana Society. His hobby is reading. Residence: Plattsmouth.

George Alfred Farman, Jr.

A leading professional man at Ainsworth, Nebraska, is George Alfred Farman, Jr., who has been engaged in the practice of law there since 1922. He was born at Ainsworth, November 19, 1898, the son of George Alfred and Lou Irene Richmond, the former a druggist who was born at Lockridge, Iowa, August 8, 1859. His mother was born at Berlin, Illinois, December 9, 1867, and died at Ainsworth, September 8, 1918.

Mr. Farman was graduated from the Ainsworth High School, 1916, where he was valedictorian of the senior class, and in 1920 received the LL. B. degree at the University of Nebraska where he held membership in Alpha Sigma Phi and Phi Alpha Delta. He has practiced law continuously since 1922, and since 1925, has been a member of the law firm Scattergood & Farman. A Republican, he served as mayor of Ainsworth, from 1924 to 1926, was state representative from District 78, 1927-29, and is at this time city attorney at Ainsworth.

On June 6, 1928, he married Hertha Lochmiller, of Ainsworth, Nebraska. He holds membership in the Nebraska Bar Association, the Nebraskana Society, and the Ainsworth Commercial Club of which he was president in 1927. Mr. Farman is a Mason, and a member of the American Legion. Residence: Ainsworth.

Earle Edwin Farnsworth

An outstanding figure in the professional life of Grand Island, Nebraska, is Dr. Earle Edwin Farnsworth, who has been engaged in the practice of medicine there for the past 20 years. He was born at Middlebury, Vermont, May 24, 1881, the son of Luther and Delia (Pearson) Farnsworth, the former a retired druggist. His father, who was born at Ogdensburg, New York, March 27, 1852, is the son of Edwin Farnsworth, a native of Lawrence County, New York.

His mother, whose ancestry is Scotch, was born in New York, September 27, 1885, and died at Grand Island, July 8, 1929.

Dr. Farnsworth was graduated from the Grand Island public school in 1899, was a student at the University of Nebraska, 1899-1902, and was a member of Phi Delta Theta. He received the A. B. degree at Cornell University in 1903. He was a student at the Creighton Pharmacy College, 1906, was awarded the M. D. degree at Harvard Medical College, Boston, where he was a member of Phi Rho Sigma.

He engaged in a partnership medical practice at Grand Island from 1912 to 1922, and since 1922 has served as secretary-treasurer of the Grand Island Clinic.

Martin—Falls City

VIRGIL FALLOON

He is the author of: *Etiological Factors of Pneumonia* and *Treatise on Poliomyelitis Epidemics*. He is a member of the Hall County Medical Society, the Nebraska Medical Society, the American Medical Association, and the American College of Physicians in which he holds a fellowship.

Dr. Farnsworth was a charter member of the Rotary Club, is a life member of the Hall County Historical Society, is president of the staff of the St. Francis Hospital, and holds membership in the Grand Island Commercial Club. He is a Mason, Elk, and a member of the University Club and the Grand Island Riverside Club. He is especially interested in boys' work, and his sports include tennis, football, baseball, and golf.

On June 27, 1912, he was married to Jessie Kistle at LeMars, Iowa. Mrs. Farnsworth, the daughter of William T. Kistle, and Elizabeth (Wallace) Kistle, was born at LeMars, November 29, 1890. They have two children: William Kistle, born July 6, 1916; and Richard Pearson, born December 31, 1925. Residence: Grand Island.

Frederick James Farrington

A pioneer in the agricultural implement business, Frederick James Farrington, has been a resident of Omaha since 1903. He is the son of Levi and Marie (Young) Farrington, and was born at Romeo, Michigan, August 20, 1876. Levi Farrington was a native of Canada, born December 13, 1846. He came to the United States as a boy and homesteaded in South Dakota. He died at Palouse City, Washington in 1910. His wife, Marie Farrington, was also a Canadian. She was born in 1856, and died at Omaha in 1914.

Frederick J. Farrington first attended the country schools near Aberdeen, South Dakota, and later attended St. Thomas High School in North Dakota. He later entered Hamlin University at St. Paul, remained there a short time and still later attended the Minneapolis School of Business.

At the age of 18 he entered the agricultural implement business, and has spent his entire business life in its various phases. He has handled labor, sales, service, collections, credits, accounting, advertising and managing in the wholesale and retail branches. He is managing director of the John Deere Plow Company at Omaha, and president of the Overlook Investment Company.

On December 21, 1899 he was united in marriage with Katie Gertrude Van Camp at St. Thomas, North Dakota. Mrs. Farrington was born in Canada, June 7, 1879.

Mr. Farrington is active in the civic life of the city, and is a member of the Chamber of Commerce, the Omaha Traffic Bureau and the Nebraska Dairy Development Society. He is affiliated with the First Methodist Church of Omaha, and is a member of the Young Men's Christian Association. He is a member of Elks Lodge No. 39 of Omaha. His social club is the Omaha Athletic. His chief interests in life are his family, home, business and friends. Residence: Omaha.

James Robert Farris

James Robert Farris, lawyer and state purchasing agent, was born at Cedar Rapids, Iowa, July 11, 1875. His father, Matthew Robert Farris, was born at Clayton County, Iowa. A pioneer to western Nebraska in 1880 he was a railroad and government contractor. His parents came from Scotland in 1836 and settled in Iowa, where his father became a large land owner. His mother was a direct descendant of Robert Bruce. Her maiden name was Grace Roan, and her mother's maiden name was Elizabeth Hart. Matthew R. Farris married Mary Ann Wilson, who was a native of Pennsylvania, and who came to Nebraska with him. Her parents were born and married in Scotland.

Educated first in the country schools of Valentine, Nebraska, James R. Farris was graduated from Valen-

tine High School, and later from Lincoln Business College. He took special courses at the University of Nebraska, and received his B. L. from LaSalle University of Chicago.

From 1892-96 he was the editor of a weekly newspaper, the *Cherry County Independent,* and during 1897-98 was instructor in printing at the State Industrial School for Boys at Kearney. He was chief clerk in the office of the Adjutant General of Nebraska preparing the official report of activities of Nebraska troops in the Spanish American War, 1899-1900. During 1901-02 he was assistant to the clerk of the Supreme Court of Nebraska, and during 1902 was office manager of the Dwelling House Mutual Insurance Company. Going to Ames in 1903 he was secretary to the general manager of the Standard Cattle Company and in 1904 engaged in real estate as a member of the firm of Weber and Farris.

He was general superintendent of the publication office of *The Commoner,* 1905-22; purchasing agent for the State of Nebraska, 1923-24; office manager of the State Coal Company 1925-28; manager of the Lincoln Municipal Coal Yard and Gasoline Station 1929-30, and was appointed Nebraska State Purchasing Agent again in January, 1931. A Democrat, he was secretary of the Populist state committee at one time; member of the Democratic state committee and its secretary, and was defeated for city commissioner of Lincoln in 1925.

On January 14, 1903, Mr. Farris was united in marriage to Marie Alice Battreall of Muncie, Indiana, at Omaha, Nebraska. Mrs. Farris is of French and Irish descent. They have two daughters, Vera Elizabeth, 25, who married Lynn Cunningham; and Helen Melvina, 20, who married Ernest M. Yardley.

Rejected for service in the Spanish American War because of physical disability, Mr. Farris served 3 years in the Nebraska National Guard at Valentine, and was a wagon boss in the Sioux Indian War. He is a Christian, and was a Sunday School teacher for 14 years. He is a member of the Chamber of Commerce, the East Lincoln Civic League, the Knights of Pythias, Modern Woodmen of America, the Fraternal Aid Union and the Young Men's Christian Association. His hobby is municipal ownership. Residence: Lincoln.

Leon C. Farwell

On a farm near Preemption, Mercer County, Illinois, Leon C. Farwell was born, on October 24, 1883, the son of Horace and Margaret (Park) Farwell. His father, who was born at Preemption, October 24, 1857, is a farmer. His mother, of Irish ancestry, was born at Aledo, Mercer County, Illinois, October 29, 1857, and died at DuBois, Pawnee County, Nebraska, January 7, 1903. She was prominent in all church and religious affairs.

As a boy, Mr. Farwell attended country school in Illinois, and the public schools of DuBois, later working on his father's farm until he was twenty-one years old. He studied for one term at the Lincoln Business College. As he was the eldest of four children he left home to work, entering the State Bank of DuBois, December 15, 1905, as a bookkeeper. He held, consecutively, the positions of assistant cashier, cashier, and member of the board of directors, starting with a salary of ninety cents a day. During his twenty-five years with the DuBois bank he has, through panics, inflation and deflation, been faithfully on the job, never failing to be at work. The bank has always paid a dividend, even through the various business depressions. Today, in perfect health, Mr. Farwell operates and lives on a small farm adjoining DuBois, where he performs some farm tasks each day in addition to his business affairs.

A leader in his community, he has held a large number of offices and civic positions. Among them are cashier and director of the State Bank of DuBois; president of the Pawnee County Bankers Association; director in the Fourth Regional Clearing House Association; director of the Pawnee County Fair Association; school treasurer; treasurer of the Red Cross; village treasurer; treasurer of the telephone company, of which he is a stockholder; notary public; and administrator and guardian.

Mr. Farwell was vitally interested in, and took an active part in the establishment and location of highway number 98, in Nebraska, and highway number 63, in Kansas. In the World War he put the Pawnee County quota over the top, on loan drives, and raised large sums for the Red Cross. He is a member of the Parent-Teachers' Association, the Community Service Club, and the Nebraska Good Roads Association.

On October 23, 1912, he was married to Evelyn Florence Dorrance, at Lincoln, Nebraska. Mrs. Farwell was born at Pawnee City, Nebraska, December 25, 1887. Their three children are: Florence Louise, born February 12, 1915, who holds an attendance record at school; Laura Phannetta, born October 24, 1916; and Mary Ellen, born October 29, 1919. The girls are active in the Methodist Church and belong to the orchestra and school band.

Mr. Farwell is a Knight of Pythias, a Mason, and a Shriner. His favorite sports are hunting and fishing. Residence: DuBois.

David Samuel Fase

David Samuel Fase, county treasurer of Sarpy County, was born at Papillion, January 19, 1870. He is the son of Andrew Fase, who was born in Germany, June 27, 1837, and died at Papillion, November 11, 1912. He was a farmer, and married Sophia Timme, born in Germany, October 15, 1844. She is still living.

David S. Fase was educated in the public schools of Sarpy County, and later attended Fremont Normal and Business College. He married Margaret Lees at Council Bluffs, Iowa, December 26, 1899. Mrs. Fase was born at Council Bluffs, April 23, 1877, of English and Irish descent. There are two children: Raymond S. was born September 4, 1903, and married Leona Harder, of Millard, Nebraska; Dorothy May, born August 26, 1908, graduated from the University of Nebraska in June, 1930.

Mr. Fase is a Republican. He has been a banker all of his life, until elected county treasurer. He had served two terms in that office, when he was re-elected in 1930 for a third term. During the World War he was active in Liberty Loan drives and the war savings stamp campaign. About twelve years ago he was secretary of the Papillion school board, and was active in the Parent-Teachers' Association.

He is a member of the Masons, and Modern Woodmen and of the Nebraskana Society. His hobbies are his home, garden and flowers. He is a member of St. Paul's Methodist Episcopal Church and of the brotherhood of that church. Residence: Papillion.

Hiram Albert Fecht

Hiram Albert Fecht, retired farmer and banker, has resided in Nebraska for the past 45 years. He was born at Wiessens, Hanover, Germany, March 5, 1862, son of Albert Jacob and Tatje (Huls) Fecht. The father was born in Wiessens, Germany, where he died. He was a farmer and landowner.

Mr. Fecht attended public schools in Germany, and on September 26, 1889, was married to Martha Sophia Germann at Weyerts, Nebraska. Mrs. Fecht was born at Tuscola, Illinois, December 13, 1871, her father and mother both born in Mecklenburg. Seven children were born to them, two of whom are desceased. Matilda and Henrietta were born April 6, 1890. Matilda died August 9, 1890, while Henrietta married Arthur Borcher. Anna, born March 15, 1892, married Clyde B. Toof; Albert, born July 23, 1894, married Anna Hessel; Sophia, born January 13, 1898, died March 20, 1898; Viola, born Oc-

tober 10, 1905, married Herman M. Staley; and Arthur, born March 21, 1908, married Doris Krebs.

Mr. Fecht is a Republican. He served as a member of the local school board for 26 years, and is affiliated with Emmanuel Lutheran Church. Residence: Dalton.

Margaret Sophie Fedde

Margaret S. Fedde was born at Irvington, Douglas County, Nebraska, and has lived in this state all her life. Her father, Christian Fedde, who is an agriculturist, was born at Delve, Germany, October 14, 1850, and came to America in 1868. Her mother, Magaretha Helena (Glandt) Fedde, was born at Busum, Germany, January 22, 1851, and died at Omaha, Douglas County, Nebraska, November 13, 1923.

Miss Fedde attended the rural schools and later was graduated from the Omaha High School. In 1914 she received her A. B. degree at the University of Nebraska, and in 1922 she was awarded the A. M. degree at Columbia University. During the summer of 1927 she was a student at Chicago University. She was elected to Omicron Nu, Phi Upsilon Omicron, and Delta Delta Delta. From February, 1931, until June, 1931, she attended Columbia University. During the summers of 1925 and 1931, she traveled abroad.

She has held various educational positions in Nebraska; and taught in the rural schools one year; was principal of the public high school at Benson, Nebraska; and was instructor in the home economics department at the University of Nebraska from 1914 to 1919. She has been chairman of the home economics department of the University of Nebraska since 1919.

Miss Fedde is a member of the state and national home economics associations, and of the American Association of University Women. She is a member of the League of Women Voters and the Red Cross. She is now serving as chairman of the advisory board of the University Young Women's Christian Association. She is affiliated with the First Plymouth Congregational Church of Lincoln. Her club is the University Club. Her sports are golf and hiking. Reading is her hobby. She has been grand president of Omicron Nu, a national honor society in home economics, for three years. She has been grand vice president of this society for two years. Residence: Lincoln.

William Francis Feehan

One of the leading farmers in Merrick County, Nebraska, William Francis Feehan has resided in this state all his life. He was born at Clarks, Nebraska, January 14, 1884, the son of Daniel and Elizabeth (McCarthy) Feehan. His father, who was a farmer and stockman, was born in County Cork, Ireland, and died at Clarks, August 9, 1906; he came to this country from Ireland, in 1875, settled in Rock Island, Illinois, and pioneered in Nebraska in 1876. His mother was born in County Cork and died at Clarks, February 9, 1925.

Mr. Feehan is a farmer, stockman, and landowner near Clarks, and is serving as vice president of the Farmers State Bank there. He is affiliated with St. Peters Catholic Church, and from 1924 to 1929 was a member of the Knights of Columbus. He took an active part in loan drives during the World War. Residence: Clarks. (Photograph in Album).

Henry Luther Feistner

Born on a farm in Nemaha County, Nebraska, December 3, 1875, Henry L. Feistner is the son of John Michel and Barbara (Muller) Feistner. His father was born in Bavaria, Germany, October 3, 1841, and died at Johnson, Nebraska, June 24, 1912. He was a farmer. His mother was born in Bavaria, August 21, 1843, and died at Johnson, September 21, 1916.

Mr. Feistner was educated in rural schools and later attended the University Veterinary College, Kansas City, where he received the degree of D. V. S. Since March 3, 1903 he has been a veterinarian at Auburn, Nebraska. A Democrat, and life time resident of Nebraska, he served as a member of the state examining board from 1922 to 1924, and acted as chairman of the Nemaha County Democratic Central Committee from 1920 to 1930.

He married Alice Young Ely at Auburn, October 5, 1908. She is of Scotch, Irish and French descent; was born in Nemaha County, March 26, 1878, and died at Auburn, January 31 1917. To this union were born two children; Ely, born August 16, 1909, a graduate of Auburn High School and a student at Peru State Teachers' College; and Henry Luther, born May 28, 1913, a graduate of Auburn High School and a student at Peru State Teachers' College. His marriage to Flora Anderson took place at Lincoln, Nebraska, February 17, 1923; she was born in Nemaha County, February 23, 1888 and was graduated from the Peru State Teachers' College. She taught for 6 years in Auburn and one year at Beatrice.

Mr. Feistner has taken an active part in the educational and civic affairs of his community. He has served on school boards, was president of the board of education in the Auburn public schools for many years, and has held various other executive positions. He is a member of the Nebraska Veterinary Medical Association and the Red Cross. He is also a very active Boy Scout worker and has been sponsor of the local De Molay Lodge. He is affiliated with the Lutheran Church. Residence: Auburn.

Elbert Wesley Fellers

A leading Nebraska dentist, Dr. Elbert Wesley Fellers was born at DeWitt, Nebraska, February 12, 1882, the son of Wesley Fellers, born in Findlay, Ohio, October 31, 1849, and Susan Isabelle (Cherry) Fellers, born at Springfield, Illinois, April 21, 1856. Dr. Elbert Fellers' paternal ancestors were Dutch and came to this country in 1809. His mother was of Scotch ancestry. Wesley Fellers died in Chester, Nebraska, October 9, 1929.

Dr. Fellers attended the Chester, Nebraska, public school until his graduation from high school in 1900. In 1906 he received his degree of Doctor of Dental Surgery at the Nebraska University. He belongs to the Xi Psi Phi fraternity and took part in base ball activities in college.

Floy Zella Kissick became Dr. Fellers' wife, June 11, 1907, at Cody, Wyoming. She was of the 6th generation in descent from Sir Francis Bacon. Their daughter, Verona, was born August 6, 1910, and is teaching in the kindergarten department in the schools at Providence, Rhode Island, and is touring Europe at present. Their son, Harold Lloyd Fellers, was born March 7, 1917, and died the same day.

Dr. Fellers' only political experience was as a member of the Board of Education in the Beatrice public schools from 1919-29. He was admitted to the practice of dentistry in June, 1906, and has practiced in this state all of his life. He taught prosthetic dentistry three years at the University of Nebraska, and demonstrated in the infirmary, was a member of the Nebraska State Board of Dental examiners for seven years, is now president of the Nebraska State Dental Society and is a member of the Southeastern Dental Society and the National Dental Association.

During the World War he was a member of the medical examining board for Gage County. He is a captain in the Dental Reserve of the United States Army, and is a member of the Gage County Reserve Officers Association.

He is affiliated with the Presbyterian Church and holds membership in the Order of the Ancient Free and Accepted Masons. Dr. Fellers is director of the Citizens Lumber and Supply Company with headquarters at Chester, director of the Missouri Valley Life Insurance Company, was director of the Young Men's Christian Association in 1919-21, is a director of the Beatrice Chamber of Commerce, and is a member of the Nebraskana Society.

He belongs to the Rotary Club, and the Beatrice Country Club, and his favorite sports are golf and shooting. Residence: Beatrice. (Photograph in Album).

William Alpheus Fellers

Born at DeWitt, Saline County, Nebraska, January 6, 1877, William A. Fellers is the son of Wesley Fellers and Susan Isabelle (Cherry) Fellers. Wesley Fellers was born at Findlay, Hancock County, Ohio, October 31, 1847, and died at Chester, Nebraska, October 31, 1927. During his life he was an active farmer, and served one term as county commissioner of Gage County. Susan Isabelle Fellers was born at Springfield, Illinois, April 21, 1856, and is now president of both county and local Women's Christian Temperance Union. Mrs. Feller's father was a farmer, and was active in politics, having served two terms in the Nebraska legislature.

William A. Fellers attended high school and was graduated from business college at Lincoln, Nebraska, in 1897. On May 24, 1904, at York, Nebraska, he married Edith Donnell. They have two children: Mildred, born July 16, 1905, and now the wife of Donald A. Cramer; and Donneline, born November 1, 1910. Mildred received a Bachelor of Fine Arts degree at Nebraska Wesleyan, at Lincoln, where she served as president of Sigma Alpha Iota. Donneline is a graduate of Chester High School.

A Republican, Mr. Fellers has twice received the nomination for state representative, but was defeated at the general elections. He was yard man and bookkeeper for the Brown Lumber Company of Chester, 1897, to 1900, manager of the lumber yard of the Foster Lumber Company, at Burlington, Colorado, 1900 to 1903, and for two years was traveling salesman for Von Steen Company of Beatrice. In 1913 he purchased the lumber yard at Chester, and one year later organized the Citizens Lumber and Supply Company, of which he is now president and general manager. He is also vice-president and director of the Missouri Valley Life Insurance Company.

Mr. Fellers is a member of the Methodist Episcopal Church of Chester, and served in the General Conference of the Methodist Church for eight years, being a delegate to two national conventions. He holds a membership in the Masons, The Nebraskana Society, and the Parent-Teacher Association. Residence: Chester.

George Alonzo Felton

George Alonzo Felton, pioneer Nebraska farmer, was born at Franklin, Vermont, July 21, 1850. He is the son of Alonzo and Mary (Tenney) Felton, both natives of Vermont, who were among the early settlers of the middle west. Alonzo Felton was born in Franklin, on March 20, 1820, and was descended from the Felton family which came from England in 1636; he represented the 8th generation in America.

Mary Tenney, whose family came to America in 1637, was born at Orwell, Vermont, March 8, 1822. Her genealogy is traced eight generations in America. She died at Edgar, Nebraska, in December, 1910, while her husband died at Oberlin, Ohio, October 20, 1867.

George Alonzo Felton attended common school, and came west to Nebraska in 1871. A pioneer settler, he has farmed all his life, and has in addition, taken an active part in the affairs of his community. Long a resident of Nuckolls County, he can recall among other things, when there were only fifty voters in the county. A Democrat, active in party politics, he served in the Nebraska legislature, as a member of the house of representatives in 1891 and 1893.

His marriage to Anna Mary Littrell was solemnized at Nelson on April 22, 1874, and to them were born eight children: Emory E., born April 25, 1875, who married Bertha Halloway, who is deceased; Alice, born April 16, 1876, who married Stanley Adamson; Zella, born September 13, 1879, who married Ira Overton; Sarah, born March 7, 1882, who married Edgar Moore; Charles, born October 8, 1883, who died October 25, 1902; Jennie, born April 4, 1890, who married C. Humerickhouse; Bertha, born April 4, 1891, who married Charles Runga, and who died March 25, 1829; and Stella, born February 28, 1898, who married Duil Kay.

During the World War Mr. Felton participated in loan drives and other civilian activities. He is a member of the Church of Christ at Angus, Nebraska, and is a life member of The Nebraskana Society. Residence: Nelson.

Harold A. Fenner

Harold A. Fenner, osteopathic physician and surgeon, was born at Almond, New York, January 5, 1894, son of Andrew Jackson and Alveretta Margarette (Barrett) Fenner. His ancestry is English, the Fenner family having settled in Rhode Island in the early days of that colony.

Dr. Fenner was graduated from Hornell High School in 1911, and received the Bachelor of Osteopathy degree from the College of Osteopathic Physicians and Surgeons in 1915. In 1916 he received the degree of Doctor of Medicine from the Pacific Medical College.

On January 15, 1920, he was married to Ruth E. Dixon at Des Moines, Iowa. She was born at Fort Dodge, Iowa, March 29, 1896. They have one son, Harold Allen, born April 12, 1924.

At the present time Dr. Fenner is the owner of the North Platte Osteopathic Hospital and Sanitarium. He is a member of the Nebraska Osteopathic Association, the American Osteopathic Association and is a fellow of the American College of Osteopathic Surgeons. His favorite sport is hunting. He is affiliated with the Republican party. Residence: North Platte.

C. H. Fenstermacher

C. H. Fenstermacher, physician and surgeon, was born at Marcellus, Michigan, March 2, 1873, son of Christian Alford and Margaret L. (Hill) Fenstermacher.

The father, a native of Catawasia, Pennsylvania, was born February 4, 1839, and died at Marcellus, May 8, 1917. He was a farmer of German descent. His wife, born in Park, Michigan, July 13, 1847, died in Cass County, Michigan, December 15, 1928. She was of Irish and New England Yankee descent.

Dr. Fenstermacher attended public school and was graduated from the University of Louisville, Kentucky, in 1900. He was married to Rhoda Olive Griffith at Sargent, Nebraska, November 10, 1913, and to them two children were born, Inez, on November 1, 1914; and Robert, on March 28, 1919. Mrs. Fenstermacher was born at Callaway, February 20, 1888, daughter of George A. and Cyndonia Griffith.

Dr. Fenstermacher is a Methodist, a Mason and an Odd Fellow. Residence: Sargent.

George B. Fergus

George B. Fergus, a resident of Nebraska for the past 47 years, was born at Logansport, Indiana, January 31, 1883, the son of James C. and Lucy (Zeiler) Fergus. His father was a rural mail carrier for many years at Hastings, Adams County, Nebraska.

Mr. Fergus, who is the owner and manager of the Fergus Transfer & Storage at Hastings, has been a successful executive there and is active in all community projects. He is a member of the American Insurance Union, the Independent Order of Odd Fellows, and the Nebraskana Society. He has been a member of the Hastings Volunteer Fire Department for 15 years, is a member of the Sons of Veterans, is affiliated with the First Baptist Church, and is a charter member of the Inter-Church Reserve. He is a Republican.

On March 20, 1906, he was united in marriage with Frederica E. Conrad at Hastings. Mrs. Fergus, who was born at Crete, Saline County, Nebraska, March 19, 1887, is cashier of the American Insurance Union. They have one daughter: Thelma Belle, born March 29, 1909, who is her father's clerk and secretary. Residence: Hastings.

Elmer Ross Ferguson

Elmer Ross Ferguson, prominent Brown County farmer, was born in Rawley, Iowa, April 25, 1879, and has resided in Nebraska for the past forty-seven years.

His father, a farmer, was born in Fort Wayne, Indiana, September 24, 1843, and served as a corporal in the 88th Volunteer Indiana Infantry in the Civil War. He participated in Sherman's march to the sea. His death occurred at Ainsworth in September, 1901. His parents came to the United States from Scotland.

Melissa Winn, wife of John Y. Ferguson, was born at Benton, Wisconsin, March 30, 1856, and died at Ainsworth, May 29, 1913. She led a typical pioneer life, coming to Brown County in the spring of 1884. She was a member of the Women's Relief Corps. Her parents came to the United States from England.

In the spring of 1884, two families, those of John Y. Ferguson and John Fernau came to Brown County, Nebraska, from Buchanan County, Iowa. Coming early to prepare for spring and summer work, they found that winter was not over in Nebraska. Their families and their stock lived under one roof until other shelter could be provided.

The Fergusons settled on a homestead seven and one-half miles northeast of Ainsworth on Bone Creek, and the Fernaus just west of them. Among the early reminiscences of Ross, the second son of the Fergusons, is the following tale. One bright winter day he, together with a younger brother and an older sister, was trying to keep warm in a little sod school house and at the same time gain a fair degree of knowledge. Suddenly as if from nowhere a storm descended upon them, so terrific and so deadly that stories of it have been handed down through the years as the storm of '88.

Before noon Sam Miles, a farmer living northwest of the school house came and took the children going north and west. About two o'clock, Nellie Brunner, a brave pioneer teacher, took the two remaining families, the Fernaus and Fergusons, and tied them together with a long old fashioned scarf, placing the youngest of the lot, Joe Ferguson, next to herself. She led the march to the Fernau home, a matter of three-fourths of a mile. This was in a direct line with the storm and thus made her successful where other brave women failed because of having to face the storm. Old timers remember how darkness came early in the day. Between four and five o'clock Mrs. Ferguson became so agitated about her three children that it became a matter of which parent should go after them. Not be outdone, Mr. Ferguson donned his wraps and showed his true Scotch blood in braving the cold and storm to walk the mile to the neighbors. It was a drastic undertaking as many lost their lives in attempting much shorter distances. However, guided by the One who always leads us aright if we but choose to listen, he found his way safely across canyons, some places where only a few feet to right or left would have meant a drop into a snow filled gulch. Mr. Ferguson found his children safe and once more guided in his path, he reached home and his beloved wife and baby. They stayed in their new home despite the hardships. Then came the drouth and panic of 1894 and 1895 making matters worse. They did not weaken and were rewarded by a fine crop in 1896.

In 1901 when the father was taken from the Ferguson home, Ross took up the load where his father had left off. The family finances were still suffering pitifully from the hard years in the 90's. It meant hard work for everyone, with planning and sacrificing. In 1908 he passed his charges on to his brother and struck out for himself, taking as the lady of his choice Blanche Murray, who also moved to Brown County with her parents in 1884. The next year they were blessed with a baby girl, Grace, who has followed in her mother's footsteps in choosing teaching as a vocation.

Mr. Ferguson is the sort who showed his pioneer breeding by being ready to answer the call of a friend or neighbor who needed help. He has lived a life of loving devotion and today is highly honored and respected in his own community. "Not widely but deeply known."

Blanche Keturah Murray, wife of Ross Ferguson, was born at Decorah, Illinois, June 7, 1881. She was the daughter of pioneers in Brown County, her father born in Dublin, Ireland, and her mother in America, eligible to the Daughters of the American Revolution. Mr. Ferguson is a Republican. He was active in Red Cross and in all other civilian activities during the late war, is a member of the Woodmen of the World, the Odd Fellows, and the Rebekahs, and from 1900 until 1925 was director of the school board of District No. 1 of Brown County. He enjoys hunting and fishing, while his hobby is reading. Residence: Ainsworth.

Olin Jerome Ferguson

Olin Jerome Ferguson has been dean of the College of Engineering at the University of Nebraska for the past 11 years and has been engaged in engineering and educational work in Nebraska for many years. He was born at Annawan, Henry County, Illinois, November 21, 1875, the son of Henry Jerome and Mary Catherine (Troyer) Ferguson. His father, who was born at Smyrna, Chenango County, New York, July 19, 1848, was a farmer, school teacher, and bank cashier. John Tower, from whom he is descended, arrived in America in 1637, and Samuel Ferguson, another ancestor, came to this country from Ireland, and settled in Boston, in 1718. Other notables from whom he is descended were: Clement Bates, who came to America in 1635; William Knox; and Captain Anthony Collamore. Henry J. Ferguson died at Dorchester, Nebraska, May, 1887.

His mother, who was born at Walsingham, Canada, June 11, 1851, is descended from a long line of well-known ancestors, among them Michael Troyer, who came to this country from Switzerland and became a celebrated hunter in western Pennsylvania.

Professor Ferguson attended the country schools of Saline County, and in 1890 was graduated from the Dorchester High School. Later he was a student at the University of Nebraska, where he was granted his B. S. degree in electrical engineering in 1903. In 1909 he received the M. E. E. degree from Union University at Schenectady, New York. He is a member of Sigma Xi and Sigma Tau.

A bookkeeper in the Dorchester State Bank, 1892; he was country school teacher, 1895-98; tester and design engineer for the General Electric Company, 1903-05, holding this position during several subsequent summer months; was instructor and associate professor of electrical engineering at Union College, 1905-12; and since 1912 has been professor of electrical engineering and chairman of this department at the University of Nebraska. He was acting dean of the College of Engineering at the University of Nebraska, 1918-19; and was made dean in 1920. He is also director of the engineering experiment station.

The author of textbooks *Elements of Electrical Trans-*

mission (1911), *Electric Lighting* (1920), and he has also written various scientific articles. A resident of the state from 1879 to 1903, he has lived here continuously since 1912. He was united in marriage with Hannah Miller Ferriss at Schenectady, New York, June 6, 1907. Mrs. Ferguson was born at Albany, New York, June 26, 1883, and is descended from Samuel Ferriss who came to Connecticut, from England, in 1658; from John Akin who came to Massachusetts from Scotland, in 1860; and from John Alden of colonial fame. Four children were born to this marriage, Elizabeth Alden, born July 10, 1908; Richard Ferriss, March 21, 1911; Robert Olin, born August 2, 1920; and Ruth Hannah, born April 11, 1922.

Professor Ferguson has been major in the Officers Reserve Corps since 1923. He was a director of war training courses in the students Army Training Corps at the University of Nebraska, 1918-19. He is a member of the Society for the Promotion of Electrical Engineering (vice president 1923-24); in a member of the National Electric Light Association; the American Interprofessional Institute; the American Association of University Professors; and is a fellow in the American Institute of Electrical Engineers, (vice president 1927-29). He is a member of the Lincoln Engineers Club, the Rotary Club, and the Lincoln Chamber of Commerce. His social club is the Lincoln University Club.

Professor Ferguson is affiliated with the First Baptist Church at Lincoln. His hobby is the study of genealogical records. Residence: Lincoln.

Floyd Lisle Ferrell

Floyd Lisle Ferrell, banker, was born at Wallace, Nebraska, December 27, 1896, son of Edward Reed and Josephine (Barnbrugg) Ferrell.

Graduated from the Nebraska School of Agriculture at Curtis, he was married to Margaret May Filbert on February 4, 1918, at North Platte, Nebraska. Mrs. Ferrell was born at North Platte, April 30, 1897. They have one daughter, Marjorie Jean, born January 26, 1925.

At the present time Mr. Ferrell is serving as cashier of the Nebraska State Bank at Oshkosh, Nebraska. He is affiliated with the Presbyterian Church, is a member of the Masons, and the Oshkosh Country Club. He is a Democrat. Residence: Oshkosh.

Earl William Fetter

Earl William Fetter, physician and surgeon, was born at Oakland, Iowa, December 10, 1886, son of William Lawrence and Millie (German) Fetter. The father was a newspaper man.

Dr. Fetter attended public and high school at Oakland, Iowa, and received the degree of Doctor of Medicine from Creighton University. He also attended the University of Missouri and took post-graduate work at the University of Vienna and at Cornell University, in New York.

He has been admitted to practice since 1909, and is a member of the American, Nebraska State, and Lincoln County Medical Associations. During the late war, he was a captain in the Medical Corps. He is a member of the American Legion.

On May 29, 1914, he was married to Hazel Pauline Ellsworth at North Platte. She was born in Douglas County, Nebraska, April 11, 1894. They have one daughter, Jeanne, born November 2, 1916.

A Republican, Dr. Fetter has always taken an active interest in party politics. He is a member of the Chamber of Commerce, the Kiwanis Club, the Red Cross, the Elks, the Modern Woodmen of America, and the Nebraskana Society. His club is the North Platte Country Club, his favorite sport is football. Residence: North Platte.

Elmina Jenny Fichter

A resident of Nebraska for the past 41 years, Elmina Jenny Fichter was born near Dover, New Jersey, January 9, 1864, the daughter of David Meeker DeCamp and Margaret (Tebo) DeCamp. Her father, who pioneered in Iowa in 1870, was born in Morris County, New Jersey, September 8, 1831, and died at Randolph, Iowa, October 8, 1910. His parents were American born.

Her mother, who has been active in community and civic affairs for many years, was born near Dover, New Jersey, January 7, 1842.

Mrs. Fichter is a member of the Royal Highlanders, the Happy Hour Club, and the I. T. Club at Meadow Grove, Nebraska, and is affiliated with the Highland Christian Church there. She is president of the M. F. H. Guild. During the World War she took an active part in Red Cross relief work and devoted much of her time to knitting for the soldiers.

On February 1, 1888, her marriage to Judson B. Fitcher was solemnized at Randolph. Mr. Fichter, who was a farmer, was born at Dover, September 19, 1863, and died at Meadow Grove, December 27, 1912. To their marriage the following children were born: Raymond, January 25, 1889, who married Phyllis Collins; Margaret L., December 8, 1890, who died July 23, 1919; Edith F., December 27, 1892, who married Dave Hale; Iantha, January 5, 1895, who married Curtis Oimsted; M. Ruth, March 14, 1897, who married John Horrocks; Alvin L., July 31, 1901, and Judson B., August 22, 1903, who married Evadine Quart. Residence: Meadow Grove.

Joseph Fickel

Joseph Fickel, for many years one of the most prominent ranchers in Sheridan County, was born in Putnam County, Ohio, December 17, 1859, son of Eli and Martha (Madden) Fickel.

The father, born in Perry County, Ohio, November 13, 1830, died at Malvern, Iowa, July 9, 1919. He was a farmer, a kind and generous neighbor, a staunch friend and a great lover of righteousness. He was one of the best known and most highly respected citizen of Malvern. His wife, Martha Madden, died March 19, 1879. Mr. Fickel came to Nebraska March 26, 1885. He homesteaded in Sheridan County and still maintains his homestead. Mr. Fickel was the only one to settle permanently in his locality. He at present is owner of 1,760 acres of land, all of which is located in Sheridan County.

Mr. Fickel attended public school, and on November 29, 1899, was married to Esther Nelson at Gordon. She was born in Denmark, April 2, 1877. Mrs. Fickel came to Cherry County with her parents in 1885. They have three children, Martha, born August 29, 1900, who is now Mrs. Martha Poulsen; Dorothy, born March 14, 1902; and Arthur, born March 26, 1910.

In politics Mr. Fickel is an independent Democrat. He is a member of the Gordon Methodist Episcopal Church, the Yeoman Lodge, and the Nebraskana Society. Residence: Gordon.

Bohdan Anton Filipi

Bohdan A. Filipi was born at Malcin, Czechoslovakia, July 4, 1880, and for the past 25 years has been a missionary and clergyman in Nebraska. His father, Anton Filipi, who was a teacher and superintendent of schools, was born at Teleci, Czechoslovakia, February 20, 1850, and died at Prosec, Czechoslovakia, February 6, 1930; he studied in Hungary, and was an accomplished musician, expert linguist, and spent much time in reading and studying. His mother, who was born at Korakovany, Czechoslovakia, and died at Caslav, July 8, 1922, was a homemaker and the mother of six children.

Mr. Filipi attended school in Czechoslovakia, and was graduated as an honor student in 1899. He was a student at Union Theological Seminary, at New York, 1899-

1900, and the Western Theological Seminary, Pittsburgh, 1900-02. He was a missionary in Pittsburgh, Pennsylvania, 1904-06; pastor of the Bohemian Presbyterian Church at Omaha, 1906-13; and since 1914, has been pastor of the Presbyterian Church of Clarkson, Nebraska. He is the author of articles published in the *Homiletic Review*, and is a contributor to the *Christian Journal*, a Bohemian paper.

He was united in marriage with Mary Sedlak, at Pittsburgh, March 24, 1903. Mrs. Filipi was born at Pittsburgh, March 19, 1883. They have four children: Theodore A., born March 1, 1904, who married Olga Novotny; Alice M., born June 21, 1909; Lillian K., born August 8, 1913; and Paul T., born July 27, 1918. Theodore A. is a research engineer at Newark, New Jersey. Alice M. is a high school teacher at Ohiowa, Nebraska.

Mr. Filipi was county chairman of the Red Cross during the World War and took an active part in all loan drives. He is a member of the Clarkson Chamber of Commerce, and for the past seven years has been a member of the Clarkson School Board. His hobbies are mechanics, and gardening. He is a Mason, and is a member of the Nebraskana Society. Residence: Clarkson.

Ruben Osben Finch

Ruben Osben Finch was born at Cambridge, Nebraska, January 10, 1884, the son of William Osben and Anna Josephine (Stenner) Finch. His father, who was a pioneer farmer in Furnas County, Nebraska, in 1872, was born near Potsdam, New York, November 5, 1858, and died at Trenton, Nebraska, March 10, 1930. His mother, whose German ancestors were tailors for many generations, was born at Bromen Haven, Germany, May 26, 1864, and is living today on her farm near Trenton. Her father Anton Stenner, who was an early pioneer of western Kansas, moved to Rawlins County, Kansas, in 1876 and was killed in an Indian raid near what is now known as Lewdell, Kansas, on October 1, 1878.

Mr. Finch was graduated from the Indianola High School in 1903, worked for a year for the Union Pacific Railroad, and a little later entered the electrical business. He has been water and light commissioner and general superintendent of the Municipal Light, Water, & Ice Works at Cambridge for the past 10 years. For the past two years he has served as general chairman of the Cambridge Red Cross, is president of the Cambridge Rotary Club at this time, and is serving as scout master at Cambridge.

He is a member of the Ancient Free and Accepted Masons, holds membership in the Nebraska State Historical Society, the Nebraskana Society, and the First Congregational Church of Cambridge. He is interested in mechanics, likes to golf, and is particularly fond of all kinds of boys' activities.

Mr. Finch was married at Fairmont, Nebraska, October 11, 1916, to Grace Alice Daniels who was born at Campbell, Nebraska, March 30, 1886. Mrs. Finch is president of the Congregational Ladies Aid Society, an officer of the Eastern Star, and a member of the Twentieth Century Club. Residence: Cambridge. (Photograph in Album).

Charles Finegan

Charles Finegan, banker, was born at Sparland, Illinois, April 26, 1880, son of Patrick and Elizabeth (Cahill) Finegan. His father was born in Ireland, and died at Harvard, Nebraska, March 20, 1908. His mother was also born in Ireland and died at Harvard, October 15, 1913.

Upon the completion of his education in the Stockham public school, Mr. Finegan entered the banking business. At the present time he is cashier of the Bank of Hyannis, and president of the Bank of Bingham, Nebraska.

On July 7, 1914, he was married to Ada Mae Hayward at Alliance. She was born at Hyannis on January 21, 1891. They have one son, Robert, born August 7, 1916.

During the World War Mr. Finegan was chairman of Grant County Liberty Loans. He is a member of the Catholic Church and the Lions Club. His favorite sport is golf. Residence: Hyannis.

Jacob M. Finkelstein

Jacob M. Finkelstein, lawyer, was born in Russia, May 7, 1906, the son of Isaac Reuben and Sarah Finkelstein. His father, who came to America from Russia, in 1904, is a retired bakery proprietor, whose ancestors were learned rabbis. His mother, who is also Russia born, is the mother of eight children, five of whom are university graduates.

Mr. Finkelstein was graduated from the Lincoln High School in 1923; received his A. B. degree, 1928, and his LL. B. degree in 1929, at the University of Nebraska, where he was also a member of Delta Sigma Rho and Sigma Alpha Mu. He was prominent in debating at the university and was awarded law scholarships for two semesters.

From 1928-29 he was a member of the law firm Jeary & Johnson; from 1929 to 1931 was a member of the firm Mockett & Finkelstein; and since 1931, has been engaged in private law practice at Lincoln. A resident of Nebraska for 25 years, he is active in civic affairs and holds membership in the Young Men's Republican Club.

He is a member of the Lancaster County Bar Association, the Nebraska State Bar Association, the Young Men's Christian Association, the Nebraskana Society and the Independent Order of the Odd Fellows. Senior deputy and past grand president of the Aleph Zadik Aleph of the B'nai Brith; he is affiliated with Tifereth Israel Snynagogue, and is a member of B'nai Brith. His sports include tennis, handball, golf, and hiking. Residence: Lincoln.

Beverly Arthur Finkle

Beverly Arthur Finkle, physician and surgeon, has been a resident of Nebraska fourteen years. He was born in McPherson County, Kansas, January 10, 1884, son of Arthur D. and Frances Fay (Meek) Finkle. Arthur Finkle, born in New York State March 6, 1852, was a liveryman and horse buyer of Holland-Dutch descent. He died at Cherokee, Oklahoma, May 11, 1929. Fay, his wife, was born in Ohio, November 16, 1861, of Scotch-Irish descent. She was an educator and music teacher before her marriage.

Educated in the grade and high school of Galva, Kansas, Dr. Finkle attended Kansas Normal School, and from 1903 to 1909, was a teacher. From 1909 to 1912, he attended Ensworth Medical College, and in May, 1913, received his M. D. from the Chicago College of Medicine and Surgery. He was admitted to practice in Nebraska, June 4, 1918.

During the years 1913-17, he was assistant physician, School for the Feebleminded, at Faribault, Minnesota. From 1917-18, he was assistant superintendent at the Insane Hospital at Norfolk, Nebraska, and from 1918-21, was superintendent of the Orthopedic Hospital at Lincoln.

At the present time he is medical officer at the State Penitentiary, and State Reformatory, head of the obstetrical department of St. Elizabeth's Hospital, and member of the board of St. Elizabeth's Training School. He was married to Edna C. Whalen, at St. Joseph, Missouri, August 13, 1913. Mrs. Finkle was born at St. Joseph, November 27, 1890, of Irish descent. There are four children: Beverly, Jr., born October 11, 1915; Jerry, born

September 22, 1917; Joan, born December 3, 1923, and Nancy, born December 9, 1927.

Dr. Finkle is a captain in the Medical Reserve Corps, and a member of the Nebraska State and Lancaster County Medical Societies. He is the author of "Typhoid Epidemic following Immunization" (May, 1914). A Catholic, he is a member of the Blessed Sacrament Church, and of the Knights of Columbus. His club is Eastridge Country. He is a member of the Elks and of the Lincoln Chamber of Commerce. Residence: Lincoln.

Ethan Clyde Finlay

Ethan C. Finlay, educator and lawyer of Omaha, was born at Trinway, Ohio, October 4, 1878, the son of William Austin and Caroline L. (Taylor) Finlay. His father, who was a drover, was born in Ohio, and died at Greenwood, Nebraska; his ancestry was Scotch Irish. His mother was born in Ohio, in 1853.

Mr. Finlay was graduated from the high school at Greenwood, in 1896. He was awarded his A. B. degree at the University of Nebraska where he completed a teachers course in addition to his regular studies, and received the LL. B. degree at the University of Omaha Night School. Later he completed a course in the American Institute of Banking. He attended the University of Chicago in the summer of 1918, and in 1916-17 was a student at the University of Omaha where he completed his master's thesis; which was withdrawn later. He won the gold medal for oratory at the University of Omaha Law School, and represented the American Institute of Bankers in intersectional debates and oratorical contests for three years.

After serving as assistant principal of the Greenwood High School, 1901-02, he was head of the department of mathematics and assistant principal at the South Omaha High School, 1902-09; and during this time, had a half interest in a coal and feed business, a decorative company, and a construction company. From 1909 to 1915 he was in civil service in the Philippines, and was connected with the Live Stock National Bank of Omaha, from 1918 to 1927 as cashier. Since 1927 he has been engaged in general practice of law at Omaha. He has never aspired to a public office but has frequently campaigned on the behalf of other candidates. He is a Republican.

Mr. Finlay is a member of the Omaha Bar Association and the Nebraska State Bar Association. Until 1927 he was an active member of the Omaha Chamber of Commerce. He was a member of the Elks from 1912 to 1927. Since 1928 he has been instructor in Negotiable Instruments at the University of Omaha Night Law School, and during 1931, was instructor in the American Institute of Banking. Residence: Omaha.

Kenneth Stewart Finlayson

Kenneth Stewart Finlayson, lawyer, was born at Portree, Inverness, Scotland, February 15, 1888, son of John McRae and Anne Stewart (Kelly) Finlayson.

Mr. Finlayson received his Bachelor of Laws degree from Skerry College, in Glasgow, and later attended the University of Omaha.

He was married on October 18, 1913, to Laura Inez Waterman.

For the past eighteen years Mr. Finlayson has resided in Omaha. He is a member of the Presbyterian Church, the American, Nebraska State and Omaha Bar Associations, the Chamber of Commerce, and the Masons. Residence: Omaha.

James Douglas Finley

James Douglas Finley, postmaster at Sargent, was born there on April 22, 1897, son of George Milton and Irene (Farritor) Finley.

The father, born in Bloomington, Indiana, May 18.

1874, is a livestock buyer of Irish descent, while the mother, born at Streator, Illinois, November 4, 1873, is of Irish descent also. She was a teacher prior to her marriage.

Mr. Finley was graduated from Sargent High School in 1916, and from Chillicothe Business College in 1920. For four years he taught in the rural schools of Custer County, and since that time has been postmaster. He is a Republican.

He was married on April 6, 1920 to Marie Nell Stokes at Chillicothe. She was born at Sargent, July 29, 1900, of English ancestry. There are two children, Anita Marie, born February 9, 1921, and Jimmy Douglas, born May 29, 1922.

During the World War Mr. Finley served as a first class private with the 15th Company, Coast Artillery Corps, and was later acting clerk. Thereafter he was transferred to Battery E, 39th R. R. Artillery, unassigned. He is a member of the American Legion, the Methodist Episcopal Church, the Masons and the Nebraskana Society. His favorite sport is football and his hobby is reading. Residence: Sargent.

Ralph Stevenson Finley

Born at Kingsville, Missouri, February 17, 1884, the son of Theodore Thomas and Sarah Ellen (Stevenson) Finley, Ralph S. Finley has been prominent in public affairs at Norfolk, Nebraska, since 1913. His father, who was a retired farmer and merchant for several years before his death, was born at Sparta, Illinois, September 8, 1851, and died there August 7, 1925; his grandfather, who was of Irish descent, was a native of South Carolina, and moved to Sparta, in 1820. His mother was born of English parentage at Elkhorn, Illinois, April 5, 1855, and died at Norfolk, December 16, 1929; her father, John Stevenson, settled at Sparta, in 1829.

Mr. Finley attended high school at Sparta, where he was active in football and baseball. He was salesman for T. M. James & Sons of Kansas City, Missouri, 1905-10; for Niles & Moser Company of Kansas City, 1910-18, and has been engaged in the grain and coal business in Norfolk, since 1920. He is the owner and manager of the Finley Coal, Grain & Ice Company at Norfolk, is a stockholder in the State Bank of Norfolk, and is chairman of the board of the Nebraska State Bank Liquidation Corporation.

A Republican, he served as a member of the Republican State Central Committee in 1928, and has been a member of the city and county committees several times. For the past eight years he has acted as a member of the Norfolk Public Library Board, is past director, secretary, and president of the Rotary Club, was a member of the National Waterways Committee, and served on the Board of Appraisal of the University of Nebraska. He has been a director of the Chamber of Commerce for five years; has been a member of the board of trustees of the Salvation Army for five years, and at this time is local treasurer of the Red Cross. Mr. Finley is a Mason, (Royal Arch, Consistory, Knights Templar, and Shrine) and an Elk. He is affiliated with the Norfolk Country Club and holds membership in the Norfolk Congregational Church. His sports include golfing and football.

During the World War he served as warehouse and supply manager for the Young Men's Christian Association at Winchester, England. His marriage to Florence Buford Rees, occurred at Norfolk, October 2, 1917. Mrs. Finley, whose parentage was Welsh and Irish, was born at Norfolk, December 6, 1892, and died there August 31, 1923. One child was born to them: Ted, born February 18, 1923.

On July 6, 1925, Mr. Finley was married at Norfolk, to Irene Eide, daughter of Ole E. and Hannah (Finstad) Eide. She is of Norweigian descent, and was born at Chaseburg, Wisconsin, August 25, 1899. Residence: Norfolk.

Alphonse Thomas Fiore

Alphonse T. Fiore, well known educator of Omaha, was born at Nelson, British Columbia, July 13, 1905. Gildo Thomas Fiore, his father, was born at Naples, Italy, and died at Nelson, in 1909. He was a mining engineer. His mother, Rose Mary (Delanti) Fiore, was born at Palermo, Italy.

Mr. Fiore attended private school at Mount Angel, Oregon, and was graduated from high school there. From 1921 to 1925 he was a student at Columbia University at Portland, Oregon; from 1925 to 1929 attended Creighton University, where he was awarded the degrees Ph. B., 1927, and M. A., 1929. While at Creighton he was a member of Alpha Chi Kappa and at Columbia University he was a member of the History and Language Club, and the debating society. He was vice president of his senior class, chairman of the student body activities, and was valedictorian of his graduating class.

At this time Mr. Fiore is instructor of social sciences at Creighton High School. He is the author of *Benedict XV, Pope of Peace; Christian Education;* an essay, *Ballad of White Horse,* printed 1922-23; 1924 by the *Columbia Press* at Portland.

A member of the Creighton Parent-Teachers' Association and the Nebraskana Society, he is affiliated with St. Mary's Catholic Church at Omaha, and is a member of the Knights of Columbus. He is a member of the Columbia University Club at Portland, Oregon. His sports are golf, hiking, and football, and his hobby is reading folk lore of other countries. He is actively engaged in social welfare work among the Italian group in South Omaha. Residence: Omaha.

Harry Fischer

Harry Fischer, senior member of the law firm of Fischer, Fischer and Fischer, was born in Flonheim, Germany, January 28, 1869, and came to Omaha in 1888. He is the son of Michael and Elizabeth (Brueck) Fischer, the former of whom was born in Flonheim, Germany, March 2, 1835, and died there October 15, 1907. He was a cooper and farmer, and a corporal in the German Army. His grandfather was a soldier in Napoleon's Army twenty-one years. The first written record of the family appeared in 1287. Elizabeth Brueck was born at Uffhofen, Germany, September 2, 1835, and died at Flonheim, December 9, 1896. She was descended from Baron von Schweitzer, who was extremely prominent in the Middle Ages in Germany.

Mr. Fischer was educated in the elementary schools of Germany, and when he came to Nebraska entered the Omaha School of Law where he was awarded his LL. B. On June 18, 1902, he was united in marriage to Clara Rostin, who was born at Wahoo, August 2, 1883. They have four children, Herbert W., 27, who is engaged in the practice of law with him; Mary E., 25, who is head of the English department at Chadron High School; Margaret R., who is in law practice with her father; and Howard H., who is 20.

Since 1898, Mr. Fischer has been engaged in the practice of law, and was formerly head of the firm of Fischer and Fischer, in partnership with his son, Herbert. The present firm includes also his daughter, Margaret. He has been secretary of the Omaha Wholesale Produce Market since 1902. He is the author of *Land of Freedom* (1896). He is a member of Kountze Memorial Evangelical Lutheran Church of Omaha. His civic organizations include the Chamber of Commerce, the Ad Sell League and Ak-Sar-Ben. He is a member of the Omaha-Douglas County, Nebraska State and American Bar Associations. A Mason, he is a member of St. John's Lodge, Tangier Temple and Shrine. He is one of the trustees of Midland College at Fremont, and a member of its executive committee. Residence: Omaha.

Herbert William Fischer

One of Omaha's rising young lawyers is Herbert W. Fischer, son of Harry Fischer, prominent attorney. Harry Fischer was born at Flonheim, Germany, January 28, 1869, and came to America while a young man. He married Clara Rostin, who was born at Wahoo, Nebraska, August 2, 1883.

On the paternal side the Fischer family is descended from a soldier in the army of Napoleon; the record of the family has been traced to 1287. On the maternal side, through the Brueck family, the line is traced through Baron von Schweitzer, an outstanding figure in Germany during the Middle Ages.

Herbert W. Fischer's mother was of Swedish descent, her parents having come to America in their youth. Her father was one of the pioneer settlers of Saunders County.

Upon his graduation from Central High School in 1921, Herbert Fischer entered the University of Omaha, from which he received his A. B. and LL. B. in 1925. He was editor of the *Weekly Gateway* and of the *Annual Gateway,* chairman of the Gala Day committee, president of the Pan Hellenic Council and of the German Club, member of the Spanish Club and French Club and treasurer of the junior class 1923-24. A member of Lambda Phi, local fraternity, he is at the present time president of the alumni chapter. He was president of Alpha Sigma Lambda 1923-25, secretary 1921-23, president of the alumni association 1927-28, and is now secretary.

Born May 27, 1903, he was admitted to the bar June 17, 1924, and has since been associated with his father, and since 1929 with his father and sister, Margaret, in the law firm of Fischer, Fischer & Fischer. Since January, 1929, he has been secretary of the University of Omaha Night Law School. He is treasurer of the Hospice of the Luther League of Nebraska, an eleemosynary institution. He is affiliated with Kountze Memorial Evangelical Lutheran Church and is president of the Luther League of Nebraska, vice president of the Luther League of America, president of Kountze Memorial Luther League, secretary of the Mid-West Regional Luther League and superintendent of Kountze Memorial Sunday School.

In politics Mr. Fischer is a Republican. He is a member of the Ad-Sell League, the Chamber of Commerce and of Ak-Sar-Ben and holds membership in the Nebraska State Bar and Omaha-Douglas County Bar Associations. He is fond of hiking. His hobbies are philately and magic, and he is a member of Society of American Magicians, and International Brotherhood of Magicians. Residence: Omaha.

Margaret Ruth Fischer

Margaret Ruth Fischer, one of Omaha's youngest lawyers, was born at Omaha, December 17, 1906. She is the daughter of Harry Fischer, well known attorney, and Clara (Rostin) Fischer. (See *Nebraskana.*) Miss Fischer was graduated from Central High School in 1924, and received her A. B. from the University of Omaha, in 1928. In June, 1929, she received her LL. B., and entered the practice of law with her father and her brother, Herbert W. Fischer. While at the University of Omaha she was selected for Gamma Sigma Phi, was class secretary during her third year, vice president her fourth year, and was president of the College Y. W. C. A.

A member of Kountze Memorial Evangelical Lutheran Church, the women's division of the Chamber of Commerce, and the Nebraska State Bar Association, she is interested in reading and dramatics. Residence: Omaha.

Edward Cole Fisher

One of Nebraska's younger lawyers, Edward Cole Fisher was born at Lincoln, April 16, 1900, the son of Edward Spencer and Ida May (Keester) Fisher. His father, who was born at Dundas, Minnesota, December 17, 1874, is night supervisor of the Lincoln Telephone Company. His mother was born at Athens, Missouri, June 29, 1875.

Mr. Fisher attended Whittier grade school, Lincoln High School and received his LL. B. degree from the University of Nebraska, June 5, 1922. He is a member of Delta Theta Phi. He was married to Hazel Faye Poorbaugh at Lincoln, April 16, 1930. Mrs. Fisher was born in Somerset County, Pennsylvania, July 18, 1899, and was a librarian prior to her marriage.

He is a member of Vine Congregational Church, a member of the Nebraska State Bar Association, and of the Lincoln Chamber of Commerce. He is a Royal Arch Mason, and a member of the American Legion. From October 12, 1918, to December 13, 1918, he was a member of the Student Army Training Corps of the University of Nebraska.

Mr. Fisher enjoys golf, hand ball and hunting, spends much time reading, and is fond of carpenter work and gardening. Residence: Lincoln.

George Lee Fisher

George Lee Fisher, one of Omaha's most prominent architects, was born in Pontiac, Michigan, August 21, 1856, son of Charles Ernest and Mary E. (Lee) Fisher.

Mr. Fisher was graduated from Pontiac High School in 1874, and received the degree of civil engineer from the University of Michigan in 1880.

He was married to Addie Grace Bower at Clarkston, Michigan, on November 23, 1882. Their children are Robert Clarence, and Edith Jeanette.

For nearly 50 years Mr. Fisher has resided in Omaha, where he has been engaged in the practice of architecture, part of the time as a member of Fisher and Lawrie. He is a member of the Plymouth Congregational Church, the Chamber of Commerce and the Professional Men's and Engineer's Clubs. Residence: Omaha.

Jacob Fisher

Jacob Fisher, successful business man and prominent civic leader, has lived at Hastings, Adams County, Nebraska, for the past 54 years. He was born at Aschbach, Germany, March 3, 1839, the son of Matthew and Frances (Rhinehardt) Fisher, and came to America by himself at the age of sixteen years.

He learned the bakery and confectionary trade in Baltimore, Maryland, and at the outbreak of the Civil War joined the Union Army. He has served as councilman, mayor, and postmaster at Hastings, and as a pioneer citizen of Adams County was a leader in all progressive activities. He was a director in the Nebraska National Bank for the past 28 years, and now at the age of 93 years takes an active interest in political and business events.

Mr. Fisher has been a Mason for over 50 years, is a member of the Shrine, Knights Templar, and is past commander. His hobby is gardening. He was united in marriage with Lucretia Long at Brookfield, Missouri, September 29, 1867. Mrs. Fisher, who was born at Springfield, Fayette County, Pennsylvania, and died at Hastings, January 5, 1891, was the daughter of Nathan Long, a cabinet maker. The latter served as postmaster under Abraham Lincoln. Five daughters and three sons were born to this marriage, all of whom are living: Fred W.; Flora G.; Emma G.; Elizabeth E.; George J.; Katherine L.; Alice; and Jacob, Jr.

Mr. Fisher is a member of the Grand Army of the Republic, and the Nebraskana Society. Residence: Hastings.

Joseph McConnell Fisher

In 1877 Joseph McConnell Fisher came to Polk County, Nebraska. He homesteaded in Colorado in 1886 and came to Valley County, Nebraska, in 1892, and has been a progressive farmer in that vicinity since that time. He was born in Polk County, Iowa, January 7, 1863, the son of John Anderson and Mary Ann (Harvey) Fisher. His father, who was a farmer, was born in Kentucky, May 23, 1825, of Scotch and English parentage, and died in Valley County, May 13, 1899. His mother, whose ancestry was Pennsylvania Dutch and Irish, was born in Indiana in 1832, and died in Polk County, Iowa, June 1, 1868.

Mr. Fisher attended a rural school. He has served as a member of the county board of supervisors in Valley County, is a member of the board of directors of the Loup Valley Independent Telephone Company, having served in that organization since its establishment in 1906, and has held various township offices, including: precinct assessor; village board member; chairman of the village board.

He married Nellie Olive Clark in Valley County, September 16, 1894. Mrs. Fisher, whose father was a native of Illinois, was born in Clinton County, Illinois, January 18, 1873. Her mother was born in New York. The three children born to this marriage are: Rollan E., June 26, 1895, who married Ille Stewart; Harold C., September 19, 1899, who married Neva Anderson; and J. Donald, November 30, 1908. Rollan operates a filling station at York, Nebraska, and H. C. is a farmer. J. Donald is engaged in teaching in public schools. Mr. Fisher is a progressive Democrat. Residence: North Loup.

Fred B. Fitch

Fred B. Fitch, district agent for the Banker's Life Company of DesMoines, Iowa, was born at Roseburg, Oregon, December 17, 1890, but has resided in Nebraska nearly all his life. He is the son of Peter and Minerva Fitch. The former, a native of Missouri, was born August 20, 1865. Peter Fitch was a stockman, the son of a veteran of the Civil War. He died at Norfolk, Nebraska, July 31, 1927. His wife, Minerva, was born in Ohio, July 27, 1867. Her father was a captain in the Union Army during the Civil War, and died in 1928, at the age of 92.

Mr. Fitch completed high school at Merriman, Nebraska, in 1905, and during the following year attended Boyles Business College. He received a scholastic scholarship at the time of his graduation from high school. While in school he was active in baseball. For several years after leaving school, Mr. Fitch was a breeder of Hereford cattle. He served as president of the Northwestern Nebraska Hereford Association for eight years. In 1931 he was club leader for the 4-H Baby Beef Club. At the present time, Mr. Fitch is district agent for the Banker's Life Company of Des Moines, Iowa. He has served on the school board for several years, and during the late war supported all civilian activities. He is a member of the Methodist Church at Gordon, the Modern Woodmen of America, and the Parent-Teachers Association. His favorite sports include baseball and basketball, while his hobbies are mechanics, better livestock, and 4-H Club work.

He was married on July 9, 1910, to Frances M. Logsdon at Geneva, Nebraska. Mrs. Fitch was born at Shickley, Nebraska, July 19, 1887, daughter of a prominent Fillmore County citizen and a state representative. Mr. and Mrs. Fitch have three children, Lyle C., born May 22, 1913, who is attending State Normal School at Chadron; Helen F., born February 18, 1917; and Val L., born March 10, 1923. Residence: Gordon.

Harry Bige Fitch

Harry B. Fitch, advertising man of Omaha, was born at Tekamah, Burt County, Nebraska, April 29, 1887. His father, William Ray Fitch, was a mechanic. He was born in Indiana, July, 1852, and died at Denver, Colorado, August, 1926. His ancestry was Scotch-Irish. Josephine (West) Fitch, mother of Harry, was born in Indiana, April, 1853, and died at Omaha, in 1904.

Mr. Fitch received his early education in the public schools and later was a student at business college. He is a water color artist and salesman, and is in charge of the Omaha office of Barron G. Collier, Incorporated, a national street car advertising firm. He has lived in Nebraska practically all his life.

His marriage to Maybelle Anna Boon, at Blair, Nebraska, was solemnized July 3, 1911. Mrs. Fitch was born at Omaha, May 4, 1889, of Scotch-Irish parents. They have two children: Virginia, born July 27, 1915, who is in high school; and Don Lee, born May 17, 1930.

He is a member of the Omaha Chamber of Commerce; is a former director of the Omaha Ad-sell League; and is a past director in charge of publicity for the Izaak Walton League. He is now chairman of the *Tribe of Yessir* fun organization of the Chamber of Commerce.

Mr. Fitch has served as vice president of the Hiram International Club. He is a member of the Masonic Lodge, Scottish Rite Masons; Tangier Temple Shrine. He was publicity man for the Omaha Western League Baseball Club for one year. He is intensely interested in forest and wild life conservation. His favorite sports are angling and hunting. Politically, he is an independent. He is a student of Christian Science. Residence: Omaha.

James Joseph Fitzgerald, Jr.

James J. Fitzgerald, prominent lawyer of Omaha, Douglas County, Nebraska, was born at Omaha, August 26, 1903, the son of James Joseph and Katie Ann (O'Rourke) Fitzgerald. His father, who was born at Caher, Tipperary, Ireland, August 29, 1869, is secretary of the Commercial Savings & Loan Association, and is a director of the Livestock National Bank at Omaha. His mother was born at Sebula, Iowa, July 24, 1875.

Mr. Fitzgerald was graduated from St. Bridget's Parochial School in 1917, and in 1921 was graduated from the Creighton University High School. He was awarded the A. B. degree at Creighton University in 1925, and the LL. B. degree in 1927. He served as speaker of the house at Creighton Law College in 1926, and was singles tennis champion at Creighton that year.

Admitted to the bar in Nebraska, in 1927, he is now associated in the practice of law with the firm Brogan, Ellick & Van Dusen, at Omaha.

During the World War Mr. Fitzgerald was a member of the Reserve Officers' Training Corps. He is a member of the Omaha Bar Association; the Nebraska State Bar Association; and the Barrister's Club, of which he was secretary-treasurer in 1929. He holds membership in the Omaha Chamber of Commerce; the University Club; and the Omaha Tennis Club. He is affiliated with St. Bridget's Catholic Church and is a member of the Knights of Columbus. His sports are tennis, golf and squash. He is a Democrat. Residence: Omaha.

James M. Fitzgerald

James M. Fitzgerald, lawyer and judge, was born at Chicago, Illinois, August 7, 1874, son of John J. and Mary Fitzgerald. In 1903 he received his Bachelor of Arts degree from the University of Nebraska, and in 1906 received the Bachelor of Laws degree from the University of Michigan.

His marriage to Mabel Garvey was solemnized at Omaha on January 15, 1908. There are two children,

James and Eugene. Mr. Fitzgerald is a Democrat. He has served as deputy county attorney seven years, and as district judge. He is a member of the Catholic Church, the Knights of Columbus, the Red Cross and the Elks. Residence: Omaha.

Edward Joseph Fitzpatrick

Edward Joseph Fitzpatrick, son of Joseph and Catherine (Davey) Fitzpatrick, has been a resident of Nebraska for the past fifty-one years. His father, born in Ireland, came to America as a young man, farming in Lancaster County, near Davey, until his death in January, 1911. His mother, born in County Sligo, Ireland, died on the farm, near Davey, June 21, 1901.

Mr. Fitzpatrick attended country school in Stark County, Illinois, and after coming to Nebraska, was married in January, 1894, to Julia Elizabeth Healy. There are three children, John Vincent, Helen, who married William Barret, and Catherine, who married Edward J. O'Donnell.

With the exception of three months in Wisconsin, in the winter of 1881, and a few months as a mule driver on railroad grade work, Mr. Fitzpatrick has engaged in farming all his mature life. At the present time in addition to his farm holdings he is connected with the Farmers Co-operative Grain Company at Davey, and a member of the finance board of the Lancaster County Farm Bureau Federation.

During the World War he was precinct chairman of the Council of Defense and precinct captain of all loan drives. A Catholic, he is a member of St. Mary's Church at Davey. Recently he was elected to life membership in the Nebraskana Society in recognition of his work for the advancement of his community. Residence: Davey.

Thomas J. Fitzpatrick

Thomas J. Fitzpatrick, curator of the department of botany of the University of Nebraska, was born at Centerville, Iowa, April 2, 1868, son of Francis Marion and Rebecca (Seals) Fitzpatrick.

He received the Bachelor of Science degree from the University of Iowa, in 1893, and the Master of Science degree in 1895. He taught in various schools and colleges from 1887 until 1913, since when he has been successively assistant professor of botany, and curator of the herbarium. He has written many literary and technical articles and is the author of *Refinesque*, a sketch of his life with bibliography, 1911, etc.

On August 26, 1896, Mr. Fitzpatrick was married to Mary Frances Linder, who descends from the counts of von Linderhof, prominent in the early history of Tyrol, at Iowa City, Iowa. There are two children: Frederick L., born May 6, 1900 who married Margaret Smith; and Lilian L., born February 2, 1902.

Mr. Fitzpatrick is interested in the history of science, literature, Americana and fine printing. He is a life member of the State Historical Society of Iowa, a member of the Mississippi Valley Historical Association, a life fellow of the Iowa Academy of Science, etc., etc. Residence: Lincoln.

Walter Joseph Fitzpatrick

Walter Joseph Fitzpatrick, dentist, was born at Greeley, Nebraska, November 21, 1907, son of James Louis and Ella (Killeen) Fitzpatrick.

His father was born in Ireland, 1875, and died at Greeley, Nebraska, in October, 1929. He was prominent as a business man, and served for eight years as treasurer of Greeley County. His mother resides at Greeley.

Dr. Fitzpatrick attended the public schools of Greeley, and was graduated from Greeley High School. In 1929, he received the degree of Doctor of Dental

Surgery from Creighton Dental College, where he was a member of Xi Psi Phi. Since 1929, he has been in active practice in North Platte.

He is a member of St. Patrick's Catholic Church, the Nebraska State Dental Society, the Chamber of Commerce, and the Elks. Residence: North Platte.

Albert P. Fitzsimmons

Albert P. Fitzsimmons, physician and surgeon, was born in Louisa County, Iowa, February 7, 1869. John Fitzsimmons, his father, who was born in County Longford, Ireland, August 14, 1825, and died in 1900, was a farmer and stockman. Catharine (Moss) Fitzsimmons, his mother, who was born in Indiana, April 7, 1838, was an energetic farmer's wife and the mother of a large family. She died at Prescott, Arizona, May 29, 1910.

Dr. Fitzsimmons, who holds the degrees A. B., and M. D., has lived in Nebraska all his life, where he is medical director in a building and loan company, is a director in the bank at Tecumseh, and owns and farms about 1500 acres of land. For two years he was on the Manila Municipal Board of the Philippine Islands, was treasurer of the Islands for four years, and was a director of the Mint of the Philippine Islands for two years.

First married to Clara Dean at Pawnee City, Nebraska, his wife, who was born in Illinois, died at Tecumseh, May 25, 1904. One daughter was born to them, Lenore, born November 16, 1903. On July 12, 1913, he was married to Nellie Reed, at Schuyler, Nebraska. Their daughter, Katherine, was born October 30, 1914, at Manila, Philippine Islands.

Dr. Fitzsimmons served as first lieutenant (assistant surgeon) in the 3rd Nebraska Volunteer Infantry for one year; was assistant surgeon in the United State Army for two years; was in active service in Cuba and the Philippine Islands for a time; and for two years was surgeon general of the Nebraska National Guard, with the rank of colonel. He served five years in the United States Medical Reserve Corps; and during the World War had charge of the United States government bond issues in the Philippine Islands. He is a member of the Association of Military Surgeons, the Veterans of Foreign Wars, and the United Spanish War Veterans.

He is a member of the various state, district, and national medical associations; the Red Cross, the Commercial Club, the Kiwanis Club, the Nebraska State Historical Society, and the Nebraskana Society. President of the Tecumseh school board, he is a member of the Elks, and all branches of the Masons, and is affiliated with the Presbyterian Church. His favorite sports are shooting, golf, and football. Residence: Tecumseh.

John S. Fitzsimmons

A pioneer resident of Gosper County, Nebraska, John S. Fitzsimmons came to the state 46 years ago and has been engaged in the real estate and insurance business at Elwood for the past 12 years. Prior to that time he was engaged in farming and stock raising.

He was born at Centralia, Illinois, November 10, 1868, the son of Michael E. and Mary Fitzsimmons. His father, a contractor and farmer, was born at Dover, Ireland, in 1816, and died at Dallas, Texas, in October, 1887. His mother, whose ancestry was German, was born at New York, in 1824, and died there in 1870.

Mr. Fitzsimmons is a member of the Commercial Club, the Elwood Parent Teachers Association, the library board, and the Christian Church at Elwood. He holds membership in Ancient Free and Accepted Masons, the Independent Order of Odd Fellows, and the Nebraskana Society. He is interested in instrumental and vocal music and enjoys reading. His sports include basketball, baseball, and golf.

On April 10, 1893, he was united in marriage with

Nellie May Chambers at Elwood. Mrs. Fitzsimmons, who was formerly a rural school teacher, was born at Newton, Indiana, December 24, 1872. Four children were born to them: Homer E., January 22, 1894, who died August 24, 1894; Harold J., October 4, 1895; and Perry R., born September 6, 1906, who is in the furniture business at Oxford and is a musician. Harold is cashier in the Securities State Bank of Oxford. He served in the 339th Field Artillery band during the World War.

Mr. Fitzsimmons is a member of the Bible class at Elwood, which he helped organize several years ago. Residence: Elwood. (Photograph in Album).

Edward Joseph Flanagan

Edward Joseph Flanagan, clergyman, was born in County Roscommon, Ireland, son of John Joseph and Nora Marie (Larkin) Flanagan.

His father was born in Ballymoe, County Roscommon, June 24, 1831, and died at Omaha, April 13, 1923. His mother was also born in Roscommon County.

Father Flanagan is the director of Father Flanagan's Boy's Home, and has served as president of the Omaha Welfare Board. He is a member of the Knights of Columbus. Residence: Omaha.

Claude Copley Flansburg

Claude C. Flansburg, pioneer lawyer in Nebraska, was born on a farm in Knox County, Illinois, June 1, 1857, the son of Nelson and Catherine (Walker) Flansburg. His father, who was born in Delaware County, New York, August 8, 1832, and died at Chicago, December, 1906, was a manufacturer. He served as captain in the Civil War for three years; his ancestry was Danish. His mother was born at New York City, October 11, 1836, and died October 20, 1880; her ancestry was English and French.

Mr. Flansburg was graduated from the University of Illinois and was admitted to the bar September 24, 1879. He served as county attorney of Harlan County, Nebraska, 1886; was city attorney of Lincoln, 1910-12; and was a member of the Constitutional Convention, 1919-20. In 1907, he was president of the Nebraska State Bar Association. He is now a member of the Nebraskana Society and is a lifetime deacon of the First Baptist Church of Lincoln.

He was united in marriage with Clarissa Wilkinson at Galva, Henry County, Illinois, February 2, 1881. Mrs. Flansburg, who is of English and Scotch-Irish descent, was born at Peoria, Illinois. Five children were born to them, three of whom are living: Leonard, born May 3, 1882, who married Francis Westervelt; Harry, born February 12, 1884, who married Mary Allensworth; Allan, born August 20, 1886, who died October 22, 1928; he was married to Lucie Cotton; Claude, born November 17, 1889, who married Alice Brooks; and Robert, born February 3, 1893, who was killed in action in the battle of Xivray in France, June 16, 1918. Residence: Lincoln.

Wellington Flansburg

Wellington Flansburg, successful farmer in Butler County, Nebraska, has lived near Surprise, for the past 51 years. He was born in Albany County, New York, July 15, 1849, the son of Peter and Jane Ann (VanWormer) Flansburg. His father, whose Dutch ancestors came to America over 200 years ago, was born in Albany County, June 5, 1823, and died in Cedar County, Iowa, November 28, 1922; he was a farmer. Jane (VanWormer) Flansburg, mother of Wellington Flansburg, was born at Albany, May 2, 1827, and died in Cedar County, May 18, 1910. Her Dutch ancestors came to America in 1620.

Mr. Flansburg is affiliated with the Lutheran Church, holds membership in the Republican Party, and is a member of the Nebraskana Society. He married Ellen Sisty in Butler County, March 6, 1882. Mrs. Flansburg, whose ancestors were natives of Maine and Pennsylvania, was born in Henry County, Ohio, December 19, 1859, and died in Butler County, September 1, 1929. Three children were born to this marriage: Warren, December 28, 1882; Frank, May 27, 1884; and Ralph, July 8, 1890. Residence: Surprise.

William Ota Fleenor

William Ota Fleenor, superintendent of the Gering and Fort Larmie Irrigation District, was born in Jonesville, Virginia, November 30, 1886, son of Sydney J. and Martha S. (Leedy) Fleenor. Now residing at Morrill, Nebraska. The father was born in 1852 and the mother in 1862 both at Jonesville, Virginia. His family have been Americans for several generations.

Upon the completion of his education in the Jonesville, Institute, Mr. Fleenor was employed with the United States Reclamation Service (1909-1927). Since that time he has been associated with the Gering Fort Larmie Irrigation District. He is a member of the Odd Fellows and the Nebraskana Society. His political affiliation is with the Republican party.

On December 9, 1914, he was married to Mae Naomia Townsend at Gering. She was born in Texas, May 13, 1896. The daughter of William Lewis and Addie (Hopkins) Townsend. William being born in Quincy, Adams County, Illinois, January 18, 1856, and died at Morrill, Nebraska, October 9, 1919. Addie Townsend was born in Ohio, July 15th, 1860, and now resides at Burbank, California. They have four children, Kenneth, born May 18, 1916; Merle, born March 11, 1918; Margherita, born July 1, 1920; and Wilma, born April 18, 1922. Hobby, hunting. Residence: Gering.

Edward John Fleetwood

For the last 47 years Edward J. Fleetwood has lived in Nebraska, and since 1902, has been a practicing physician in this state. He was born in Sweden, February 25, 1872, the son of August and Anna Mary (Johnson) Fleetwood. His father, who was born in Sweden, died at Colorado Springs, Colorado, in 1924. His mother was born in Sweden and died at Wakefield, Dixon County, Nebraska, in 1920.

Dr. Fleetwood attended Hastings College from 1894 to 1897, and in 1902 was graduated from the University of Nebraska with the degree M. D. He was united in marriage with Inez Elizabeth Hultquist at Osceola, Polk County, Nebraska, September 16, 1903. Mrs. Fleetwood, whose ancestry is Swedish, was born at Osceola, March 2, 1879. They have four children; Evangeline Adell, born July 2, 1905; Vivian Ann Mays, born February 15, 1908; Marian Elizabeth, born November 4, 1912; and Virginia Ellen, born June 9, 1917.

During the World War Dr. Fleetwood was chairman of the Medical Advisory Board for Dixon County, and was a four minute speaker. He is a member of the Nebraska State Medical Association and the American Medical Association, and is a Republican. Residence: Lincoln.

Harry Burke Fleharty

Harry Burke Fleharty, son of Henry Clay and Marjory Ellen (Cullison) Fleharty, was born in Mercer County, Illinois, July 1, 1872. He has been a resident of Nebraska during practically his entire lifetime. His father was born in Maryland, in October, 1831, and died at Omaha, in June, 1918. He was a farmer of Irish descent, whose ancestors were pre-Revolutionary settlers in America. Marjory Cullison Fleharty died at Lexington, Nebraska, in June, 1906.

Harry B. Fleharty was educated in the public schools

of Nebraska, after which he took up the study of law and was admitted to practice in Frontier County in March of 1894. Since that time he has been in active practice, and in addition has held public offices. From 1897 to 1898, he was secretary to Governor Leedy of Kansas; in 1904 he became city attorney of South Omaha, continuing in office until 1908; from 1914-17 he was city solicitor of Omaha, and was re-elected in 1930. He was candidate on the Democratic ticket for attorney general of Nebraska, in 1924, and Democratic nominee for congress from the second district of Nebraska, in 1928.

On October 22, 1912, at Kansas City, Mo., he was united in marriage to Maud Doersam. Mrs. Fleharty was born at Waddams Grove, Illinois, February 13, 1882.

Mr. Fleharty was active in the national loan drives during the World War. He is a member of the Nebraska State and Omaha-Douglas County Bar Associations, and of the Methodist Episcopal Church. He is fond of horseback riding and his hobby is nature study. Residence: Omaha.

Irene Louretta Fleming

Irene L. Fleming, one of Nebraska's most distinguished women executives, was born at York, York County, Nebraska, January 24, 1894, the daughter of Oscar and Mathilda Johanna (Sandall) Froid. Her father, who owned and operated a shoe store for many years, was born at Tisrum, Sweden, October 7, 1853, and died at York, December 2, 1899; he came to America in 1867, at the age of 14. Her mother, whose ancestry is Swedish, was born at Fairfield, Iowa, July 25, 1859. She was church organist and choir leader at Fairfield, Iowa, and York, Nebraska.

Mrs. Fleming attended the public schools of York, and in 1911, was graduated from the McCool High School, where she was secretary of her class for two years, and was a member of the high school mixed quartette. She studied at the York Commercial College in 1920. She has held the following positions in the business world: secretary and bookkeeper, Laurel National Bank; secretary to the president of the York Milling & Grain Company; secretary to the general manager of the Milling & Grain Company of Denver, Colorado; and bookkeeper for the Nebraska Gas and Electric Company at York.

She is now serving her sixth year as state secretary-treasurer of the American Legion Auxiliary, department of Nebraska, and is editor of the *Legion Auxiliary Star*, the official publication of the Nebraska American Legion Auxiliary. Mrs. Fleming is a member of the First Congregational Church of York; is a member of the Temple Chapter of the Eastern Star at Lincoln; and holds membership in the Nebraskana Society. During the World War she served as secretary of a Red Cross Unit and was active in various war time drives. Her sports include hiking, camping and fishing. Mrs. Fleming is an Independent, politically. Her hobbies are landscaping and china painting.

On November 14, 1927, she was united in marriage with Ivan Ellsworth Fleming at Lincoln. Mr. Fleming, who was born at Lincoln, September 23, 1894, is a commercial artist. His ancestry is English and Scotch-Irish. Residence: Lincoln.

Paul Dow Fleming

Paul Dow Fleming, a dentist at Beaver City, Nebraska, was born in that community, June 11, 1895, the son of Pierce and Nellie May (Rogers) Fleming. His father, who has been rural mail carrier continuously since 1905, was born at Osage Mission, Kansas, April 16, 1874; he is of Scotch-Irish descent. His mother, a music teacher, was born at Bogard, Missouri, November 24, 1872, and died at Wilsonville, Nebraska, August 21, 1921.

Dr. Fleming received the degree Doctor of Dental

Surgery at the University of Nebraska, in 1919. Since that time he has been engaged in the practice of dentistry at Beaver City where he is active in all civic affairs. He holds membership in the Rotary Club, the Beaver City Community Club, the Southwest Nebraska Dental Association, Nebraska State Dental Association, National Dental Association, and the Beaver City Board of Education. He is a Mason and is affiliated with the Beaver City Methodist Church.

During the World War Dr. Fleming served as a first class private in the 178th Brigade of the United States Army, and since 1919 has been a member of the American Legion. He was a private in the Medical Enlisted Reserve Corps from November 6, 1917, to November 5, 1923. His hobby is music and his sports include fishing and tennis.

He was united in marriage with Rosa Dana Fulis at Hugo, Colorado, June 16, 1919. Mrs. Fleming, who was a public school teacher for a time before her marriage, was born at Beaver City, November 17, 1894. They have three children: Paul E., born May 20, 1920; Max W., born November 28, 1922; and Betty J., born November 30, 1923. Residence: Beaver City.

William Cleo Fleming

William Cleo Fleming, executive, was born at Beaver City, November 15, 1889, son of William Sebastin and Laura Ann (Payton) Fleming.

The father was born in Mulberry Grove, Illinois, August 26, 1866. He is a farmer and leader in community life. His parents were Scotch-Irish, native born, his father, William Fleming, a veteran of the Civil War. Laura Ann, wife of William Sebastian Fleming, was born in Wakenda, Missouri, February 10, 1869. She is a homemaker, active in club and church work. Her parents were Scotch-Irish, native born, her father, Daniel Payton, a Civil War veteran. He served with the United States Cavalry and was an Indian scout and fighter. Many members of her family attained success in the atrical profession.

Mr. Fleming was graduated from public school in district 92 of Beaver City, in 1908, and completed a four year course at Beaver City High School in three years, graduating in 1911. He attended the University of Nebraska, during the years 1912-13, 1913-14, and 1914-15. From 1912 until 1915, he was a member of the Pershing Rifles, and during 1914, held the rank of first lieutenant in the Pershing Rifles. In high school he was a member of the football and basketball teams, during 1910 and 1911.

From 1915 until 1917, inclusive, Mr. Fleming was a salesman for the Lord Auto Company of Lincoln. He was a private in the Nebraska National Guard from 1910 until 1911, and sergeant of the Lincoln Light Infantry 1914-1916. In 1916, he was in service on the Mexican border. He was a cadet in the air service at the University of California, and at Mather Field, California, in 1918. And in 1919, went to Alberta to operate his feed and stock farm. He remained there until 1928. From November until April of each year, he lived in Kansas City. At the present time, Mr. Fleming is manager of the Perry Sheets Lumber Company of Beaver City, and a director and part owner of the Valley Lumber Company, which maintains three yards. The Perry Sheets Lumber Company operates ten yards.

His first marriage was to Jeannette Estelle Sublette, from whom he was divorced in March, 1927. In June, 1928, he was married to Irma Luella Sheets, who was graduated from the University of Nebraska in 1923.

Mr. Fleming is a Republican. He is a member of the American Legion (commander of post No. 313 in 1928; adjutant post 313 in 1929; adjutant post 28 in 1932). In 1929, he was chairman of the Red Cross at

Lebanon, Nebraska, and in 1931, served as vice-president of the Community Club of Beaver City. He is a member of the Rotary Club and the Methodist Church. He enjoys motoring and reading. Residence: Beaver City.

C. C. Fletcher

C. C. Fletcher, a resident of Thayer County, Nebraska, for the past 52 years, was born in Illinois, November 4, 1858. His father, Robert Green Fletcher, who died in 1911, was a native Kentuckian and was descended from English ancestors who came to America on the *Mayflower* and settled in Virginia; they moved to Kentucky during Daniel Boone's lifetime. His mother was born in Pennsylvania.

Mr. Fletcher has lived at Hebron since its founding and has been prominent in the advancement of all civic affairs in Thayer County for many years. For 15 years he was the owner of a barber shop and for the following 15 years owned and managed a circus. For over 20 years he served as an active member of the Hebron Park Board, and was one of the organizers of the Hebron Park System, acquiring title for the city and assisting in the planning of the park. He has built and promoted several of Hebron's business buildings which he still owns and rents to various concerns.

For three years Mr. Fletcher served in the Nebraska National Guard. He is a member of the Nebraskana Society and was formerly affiliated with the Knights of Pythias. His favorite sport is baseball, while his hobby is horse races. Residence: Hebron.

Larkin Jefferson Fletcher

A farmer and homesteader in Nebraska since March 4, 1872, Larkin Jefferson Fletcher was born at Winchester, Illinois, February 24, 1852. His father, Christopher Columbus Fletcher was born in Adair County, Kentucky, May 7, 1831, of early Scotch-Irish settlers. During the Civil War he held the rank of second lieutenant in the 34th Iowa Infantry, and thereafter was a farmer. His death occurred at Superior, August 3, 1890. Christopher Fletcher married Martha Biggers Young. She was born at Winchester, October 28, 1834, and died at Superior, August 2, 1890. She was the daughter of J. B. and Linda Myra (Edmondson) Young, the former born in 1801 and the latter in 1811. Christopher Fletcher died on the way to his wife's funeral.

Larkin Jefferson Fletcher attended common school at the time his father was serving in the Civil War, and assisted his mother in earning a living for the family. Coming to Nebraska in 1872, he homesteaded in what is now Nuckolls County, and still owns his homestead. He is retired at the present time.

His first marriage was to Fannie E. Carlon. She was the daughter of Joseph and Margaret (Orr) Carlon, and died at Oak, May 22, 1890. There were four children born to this marriage, Ira, born December 28, 1877; Harry, born September 30, 1881, who married Rose Shepperd and who died May 4, 1908; Joseph C., born April 8, 1883; Raymond, born February 27, 1888, who married Winnie Corman.

On August 16, 1893, he was united in marriage to Hester LaFollette Fleming at Saint Joseph, Missouri, and to them were born two children: Dora, born August 22, 1894, who married Harry Temple; and Frank, November 4, 1899, who is unmarried.

Mr. Fletcher is a Democrat. He is affiliated with the Christian Church at Oak, and was recently elected to life membership in the Nebraskana Society. Residence: Oak.

Maude Hammond Fling

Maude Hammond Fling was born at Tipton, Cedar County, Iowa, March 19, 1873, the daughter of Charles and Anna Rosaltha (Kirby) Hammond. Her father, who was a banker and real estate man, was born at Guilford, Penobscot County, Maine, April 29, 1829, and died at Lincoln, Lancaster County, Nebraska, June 17, 1916. He traced his ancestry through his parents, Willard and Susan (Gower) Hammond, to the *Mayflower* and the Revolution.

Her mother, who was born at Towanda, Bradford County, Pennsylvania, December 6, 1845, is the daughter of Job P. Kirby who was born at Nichols, New York, in 1815, and Jemima (Coolbaugh) Kirby of Revolution descent.

Mrs. Fling attended the elementary schools of Tipton, and in 1890 was graduated from the high school at Lincoln, Nebraska. She has attended the following schools: University of Nebraska, A. B., 1894; M. A., 1896; The American Institute of Applied Music, New York City, 1922; Yale University Graduate School, 1894-5, 1897-8; Barrett Business College, Chicago, 1903; and Columbia University, summer of 1911. She is a member of Phi Beta Kappa; was awarded a scholarship at Yale in the classics; is a charter member of the Musical Art Club at Lincoln; and a member of the Palladian Society at the University of Nebraska. She was president of the Irving Society at the Lincoln High School.

Mrs. Fling has been a resident of Nebraska for the past 46 years, and has been prominent in educational circles for 25 years. She has held various executive and educational positions, among them: teacher of Latin in the Lincoln High School, 1896-98; teacher of Latin and commercial branches at Bloom Township High School at Chicago Heights, 1904-07; instructor in Latin, Greek, and Pedagogy at the University of Wyoming, 1907-12; primary teacher at the University School for Girls at Chicago, 1903-04; teacher of music in the Hartley Settlement, New York, 1918-20. In 1903 she was stenographer for the Benjamin H. Sanborn & Company at Chicago; and the same year she became complaint adjustor for Revell's Furniture Store. In 1923 she was made vice-president of the Hammond Investment Company of Lincoln, and to-day still holds that position

She is the author of the following articles: *Glimpses of Women on a World Cruise; Sobs and Smiles of Farming; Midwest Farms.* In 1908 she was editor of the Latin magazine, *Caduceator.*

She was married to Allan Clements Fling at Lincoln, Nebraska. Mr. Fling, who was superintendent of schools at Nebraska City, Nebraska, was born at Portland, Maine, in 1870, and died at Oshkosh, Wisconsin, 1904.

During the World War, Mrs. Fling served as district leader in Red Cross drives for Liberty loans in Chicago. She is a member of the Daughters of the American Revolution and the Mayflower Society. She is a member of the Business and Professional Women's Club at Lincoln; the Nebraska Writers Guild; and the Nebraskana Society. She is a member of the Lincoln Country Club and the American Association of University Women. In 1922 she served as secretary of the Women's Automobile Club in New York City.

Mrs. Fling has given much of her attention in the last eight years to farm lands in Arkansas and the middlewest where she has spent some time planning their cultivation and the erection of new buildings. She is a member of the Episcopal Holy Trinity Church at Lincoln. She is a Republican. Residence: Lincoln.

Merton Estlic Flock

Merton Estlic Flock was born near York, Nebraska, May 10, 1871, son of Morris Fankbonel and Elizabeth (Ellis) Flock.

His father was born in Ohio, June 9, 1845, and died at Maywood, Nebraska, May 20, 1914. He was a farmer, a soldier in the Civil War, and was of German descent. His wife, Elizabeth, was born in Illinois, October 1, 1849, and died at Omaha, Nebraska, April 24, 1911.

For 27 years after leaving school, Mr. Flock engaged

in farming, in Frontier County, Nebraska. For the past six years he has been in the wholesale and retail oil business. He is a Republican, a member of the Modern Woodmen of America, and the Odd Fellows. His favorite pastime is playing cards.

On September 22, 1892, he was married to Clara Jane Fouse at Blue Valley, Nebraska. Mrs. Flock was born at Beaver Crossing, Nebraska, March 28, 1875. To them were born three children, two of whom are living, Chester, born September 30, 1893, at McCool Junction, Nebraska; Minnie, born July 10, 1898, at Maywood, Nebraska, who married Gilbert Johnson. She died April 1, 1919; and Erma, born June 27, 1910, at Maywood, Nebraska; Chester married Hattie Easton of Maywood, and has two children, a boy, Leon, and a girl, Maxine. Erma married Johnnie Bauer. They have one son, Doran. Residence: Maywood.

Francis Arthur Flood

Francis A. Flood, Nebraska lecturer and writer, has been a resident of this state since 1900. He was born at Oakland, Pottawatamie County, Iowa, November 13, 1896, the son of James Francis and Jennie L. (Meeks) Flood. His father, a farmer, was born in Mills County, Iowa, August 15, 1865; his father, James Flood, was born in County Clare, Ireland, while his mother was a native of England; both of them came to the United States at the age of twenty. Jennie (Meeks) Flood, mother of Francis, was born in Michigan, August 11, 1867, the daughter of English parents.

Mr. Flood attended the rural school in precinct A in Seward County, and in 1914 was graduated from the University Place High School. He received his A. B. degree at the University of Nebraska in 1920; was a member of Alpha Gamma Rho; and was awarded his university letter in track, high hurdles, and high jump, 1918 and 1919.

From 1914 to 1916, he served as a clerk for the Southern Pacific Railway in California; was an instructor in the high school at Steele City, Nebraska, 1922; homesteaded in Wyoming, 1920-22; was instructor at the School of Agriculture of the University of Nebraska, 1922-23; was instructor at the Iowa State College, Ames, Iowa, 1923-24; and was associate editor of *The Nebraska Farmer*, 1924-29. He is now a travel editor and lecturer for a syndicate of agricultural magazines, at Lincoln, Nebraska.

During the World War Mr. Flood served in the United States Navy as a seaman. He is a member of the American Legion; is affiliated with the Westminster Presbyterian Church at Lincoln; and holds membership in the Nebraskana Society. From 1928 to 1930, he was a member of the Lincoln Rotary Club. His favorite sport is tennis.

On June 27, 1925, he was united in marriage with Helen Janet Maitland, at Lincoln. Mrs. Flood was born at Detroit, Michigan, October 30, 1900; her maternal grandparents were born in Ireland, and her father, who was an inventor, was born in Scotland. They have a daughter, Barbara Joan, born June 15, 1929, and a boy, Francis, Jr., born October 2, 1931. Residence: Lincoln.

Harry Davis Flory

Harry D. Flory was born at Pawnee City, Nebraska, December 26, 1884, the son of George Saylor and Ann (Davis) Flory. His father, whose French Huguenot ancestors settled at New Rochelle, New York, about the middle of the 17th century, was born at Staunton, Virginia, June 7, 1854. He is a retired druggist.

His mother, whose parents came from Aberdare, Wales, to Wisconsin, in 1856, was born at Spring Green, Sauk County, Wisconsin, September 21, 1860, and died at Pawnee City, March 19, 1928. She was an active worker in the Woman's Club and Sunday School.

Mr. Flory is a graduate of the Pawnee City High School, where he played baseball and football. On May 30, 1896, he began printing with the Pawnee Press, having carried papers on the Daily Press for six months prior to that date. Editor and publisher of the Pawnee Republican, he has been with that paper continuously for 24 years.

He married Florence Elizabeth Nye, at Lincoln, Nebraska, October 8, 1914. Mrs. Flory, who was born at Tate, Pawnee County, Nebraska, June 26, 1885, was graduated from the University of Nebraska in 1911. Her father was a member of the well known Nye and Fairbanks families. Her mother was of Scotch-Irish descent. They have two sons; Harry Davis, Junior, born March 27, 1917; and William Nelson, born June 28, 1927.

Mr. Flory took part in liberty loan and Red Cross drives in the late war. He is a member of the Nebraska Press Association, of which he has been director for the past ten years; the National Editorial Association; the Pawnee Public Service Club, acting as secretary for five years; and the State Historical Society. He is a member of the First Presbyterian Church of Pawnee City. He is a Mason. His hobby is reading, and golf and tennis are his favorite sports. His club is the Fairview Golf Club. Residence: Pawnee City.

Orville Henry Flory

Dr. Orville Henry Flory has been a resident of Nebraska since 1883, residing at Albion, Nebraska. He was born at South Bend, Indiana, August 27, 1869, the son of William and Mary (Sturgis) Flory. His father, who was also a physician, was born in Cass County, Indiana, April 11, 1843, and died at St. Edward, Nebraska, December 1, 1898; his French Huguenot ancestors came to this country before the Revolution. His mother, whose ancestry was English, Irish, and Scotch, was born in Bond County, Illinois, January 16, 1850, and died at St. Edward, January 12, 1905.

Dr. Flory attended school in Indiana until 1883 when he moved to Nebraska with his parents. He received the M. D. degree at Kansas City Medical College in 1891, and for the next twelve years was engaged in the practice of medicine at St. Edward. From 1903 to 1916 he served as president of the First National Bank at St. Edward, and then returned to his farm. He is now retired. A Democrat, he served as a member of the board of education for 18 years, and during the World War was a member of the Food Commission Board. He is a Mason.

He was married to Anna Johnson Davison at St. Edward, June 2, 1892. Mrs. Flory, whose ancestry is Scotch-Irish and English, was born at Leyden, Illinois, June 2, 1869. They have two children: Robert D., born June 26, 1893, who is a lawyer and state commander of the American Legion; and Donald W., born July 15, 1898, who is a farmer and poultryman. Residence: St. Edward.

Max William Flothow

Max William Flothow, physician, and surgeon, was born at Omaha, Nebraska, April 6, 1890, son of Max and Marie (Harms) Flothow.

The father was born in Hamburg, Germany, on September 22, 1864, and died at Omaha, February 29, 1928. He came to the United States in 1886. His wife, Marie, was born in Ludwisburg, Germany, September 14, 1868.

Dr. Flothow received his medical degree from Creighton University in 1913, where he was a member of Phi Rho Sigma.

He was married on March 25, 1914, to Rena Redman at Salt Lake City.

Dr. Flothow is a Republican, and since 1921 has been engaged in the practice of surgery and gynecology. He held the rank of lieutenant junior grade in the United States Navy during the World War. He is a member of the Nebraska State and Douglas County Medical Association and the American Legion. Residence: Omaha.

Albert Claus Floto

Albert C. Floto, was born in Griswold, Iowa, October 19, 1899. His education consisted of the elementary eight grades from which he was graduated in 1914; he then entered Griswold high school, completing the work in 1918. Later he attended Iowa State College and then the University of Iowa where he received his degree of Bachelor of Science in Mechanical and Electrical Engineering in 1923. Mr. Floto ranked with the upper one-fourth of his class. He was a member of the Triangle and was eligible to Tau Beta Pi.

Charles Floto, father of Albert, was born near Mt. Morris, Illinois. His principle occupation in life was that of a cattle speculator. He died near Griswold, Iowa, which was the birthplace of his wife Margaret. Both of Mr. Floto's parents were of German descent.

On June 30, 1922, Albert C. Floto was united in marriage to Leona Marie Baughman, at Griswold. She was born at Griswold, on May 20, 1900. They have one daughter, Barbara Joanna, born May 29, 1923.

Mr. Floto was a private in the United States Army, Quarter Master's Corps during the World War. He was made a major in the Reserve Officers Training Corps at the University of Iowa. He is a member of the American Legion, the American Institute of Mechanical Engineers, the Red Cross, the Seward Welfare Society, the Chamber of Commerce, Rotary Club, Elks, the Young Men's Christian Association and the Nebraskana Society. His social club is the Oak Ridge Golf Club.

Mr. Floto is intensely interested in golf and baseball, while his hobbies are fishing and reading.

His present position is that of district manager for the Seward district of the Iowa-Nebraska Light and Power Company. He started as a lineman with the same company in 1918, and has always been in their employ with the exception of four years while in school. Residence: Seward. (Photograph in Album).

Walter Flynn

Walter Flynn, dentist, was born at David City, Nebraska, August 22, 1872, and is the son of Frank and Sarah (Martin) Flynn. Educated in the public school of David City, he attended Northwestern University, at Chicago, Illinois, and received his Doctor of Dental Surgery degree in 1899. He has practiced dentistry in Ulysses, for thirty-three years.

His marriage to Mary Alice Walter, daughter of Jacob Leonard Walter of Rising City, took place November 5, 1900. To them were born two children, Walter Francis, August 7, 1901, who graduated from the University of Nebraska in 1924. He is married to Evelyn Keith, of Hebron; and Marial, born November 9, 1903, a graduate of the university in 1926. Evelyn has two sons, Francis Keith, born July 22, 1929, and Walter M., born July 7, 1931.

Mr. Flynn's political affiliation is with the Democratic party. He is a member of the Congregational Church, the Masons, and the Nebraskana Society, and has served on the board of education for several years. His home is at Ulysses.

Edward Francis Fogarty

Edward F. Fogarty, lawyer, was born at Omaha, January 5, 1898, son of Frank and Elizabeth (Costello) Fogarty. His father was born at Joliet, Illinois, February 14, 1861, and his mother was born at Ballaghaderien, County Mayo, Ireland, May 12, 1869. They are both living.

Edward Fogarty was educated in the parochial and high schools of Omaha, and attended Creighton Univers-

ity, where he received his A. B. in 1919, and his LL. B. in 1924. Since his admission to the bar in that year he has been active in the practice of law in Omaha. He is a Republican. During the World War he served as a private in the U. S. Army. A Catholic, he attends Sacred Heart Church and is a member of the Knights of Columbus. He is a member of the Omaha-Douglas County Bar Association. Residence: Omaha.

Emil Folda

Emil Folda, one of Nebraska's most prominent bankers, was born at Manitowac, Wisconsin, May 16, 1866, the son of John and Josephine (Sinkula) Folda. His father, who was born in the village of Holofousy, Bohemia, August 26, 1836, and died on a farm in Colfax County, Nebraska, December 30, 1895, was a farmer for many years 12 miles north of Schuyler, where he settled in 1869; he was an intimate friend of Jay Sterling Morton, and was active in Democratic politics; served with the army in Europe, and moved to America with his parents in 1860, settling in Wisconsin. His mother was born at Prodeslady, Bohemia, January 6, 1845, came to this country with her parents, and died on a farm in Colfax County, February 4, 1879.

Mr. Folda attended rural schools in Colfax County where he lived on a farm with his parents. His father's farm was located on the land where a Catholic Church now stands, near which a school building has been erected. In 1887, he became a clerk at Schuyler, Nebraska, in a general merchandise store owned by his uncle, Frank Folda; the latter was a candidate for state treasurer in 1879, on the Democratic ticket, and in 1888, was candidate for lieutenant governor with John A. McShane.

Mr. Folda entered the banking business in 1889, at Linwood; moved to David City; was assistant cashier of the First National Bank there, and in 1893 returned to Linwood, and took charge of the Linwood bank as cashier. In 1911 he moved to Clarkson, where he is now president of the bank. At one time he was president of four banks; he is now president of the Linwood Farmers' and Merchants Bank; is vice president of the Pilger State Bank; is stockholder in more than a dozen banks; and is a director in the Clarkson State Bank, the Farmers & Merchants Bank, and the Pilger State Bank.

Mr. Folda is a Democrat, and has always been active in politics in Nebraska; has held some minor offices; and has attended various state conventions. He has not been able to devote a great deal of time to campaigns, and has not accepted nominations for important offices.

His son served as corporal of Company M, 355th Infantry, 89th Division, was in the battle of St. Mihiel on September 12, 1918, and was killed near Romagne, 1918. Mr. Folda was chairman of the Red Cross; was chairman of the Council of Defense; was chairman of the four minute men; and was a member of nearly all war time committees. The local post office building was donated to the government at Clarkson for war activities.

Several years ago, Mr. Folda was president of the Commercial Club of Clarkson; was a member of the Nebraska Bank Guarantee Fund Commission, 1923-26; was a member of the village board for several years; and served as chairman of the school board at Linwood, for some time. He holds membership in these historical organizations: Nebraska State Historical Society; Nebraska Territorial Pioneer Association; Czech Nebraska Historical Association; and the Nebraskana Society.

His fraternal affiliation includes membership in: Modern Woodmen of America; Woodmen of the World; Royal Neighbors of America; Z. C. B. J., of which he was supreme treasurer for 13 years; Knights of Pythias; and C. S. D. P. J.

Mr. Folda was married to Emily Peschek at David City, Nebraska; she was born at Schuyler, October 13, 1875, and died April 20, 1904. Two children were born to this marriage: Albin, born December 17, 1894, who was killed in France, October 21, 1918; and Laura, born February 15, 1898, who married Joseph A. Kucera, and now has two children: Emil Joseph, aged 6, and John Folda Kuvera, aged 4.

On September 13, 1905, he was united in marriage with Tony Sadilek at Wilber, Saline County, Nebraska. Mrs. Folda was an assistant in the District Court of Wilber, at the age of 16; later worked for Attorney Foss, of Crete, Roscoe Pound, and Supreme Judge Letton who was prominent in Republican political circles. One daughter was born to them: Olga, born November 5, 1906, who married Professor Orin Stepanek of the University of Nebraska.

Albin Folda was assistant cashier of the Clarkson State Bank until he entered the army in the World War. Residence: Clarkson.

Eugene Arthur Follmer

A farmer and stockraiser at Oak, Nebraska, Eugene Arthur Follmer was born at Nelson, November 24, 1880. The son of George Dallas and Eva Minnie (Smith) Follmer, his father was a native of Montour County, Pennsylvania, born July 17, 1844. An early settler in Nuckolls County, he was in the real estate business, was appointed first county treasurer, holding office seven years, and was elected land commissioner of Nebraska, serving two terms 1900-02. His death occurred at Oak, May 29, 1914. George D. Follmer traced his ancestry to his great grandfather, who settled in Pennsylvania, coming from Germany in 1723. Eva Minnie Smith was born in Jackson County, Michigan, August 5, 1855; her family were early pioneers in Iowa.

Eugene Arthur Follmer was educated first in Oak public schools, was graduated from Lincoln (Nebraska) High School and attended the University of Nebraska. A letterman in football at the university, he was also a member of Alpha Tau Omega. Since leaving school he has been engaged in stockraising at Oak. He is unmarried. His political affiliation is with the Republican party, and he is a Mason and Shriner. Residence: Oak.

Eva Minnie Smith Follmer

Eva Minnie Smith Follmer, daughter of Samuel Masterson and Mariah (Mills) Smith, was born in Jackson County, Michigan, August 5, 1855. Her father, born at Canandaigua, New York, July 21, 1825, was a pioneer farmer, merchant and manufacturer at Grant, Iowa, and a soldier in the Mexican War. His death occurred at San Diego, California, October 10, 1914. Mariah Mills, his wife, was born at Ridgway, New York, October 14, 1831, and died at San Diego, November 21, 1915. She was Scotch, descended from the Bruce family.

Educated in public and select schools, Mrs. Follmer completed a college course in English through Chautauqua, and after her children became college students continued her studies with them at the University of Nebraska.

She was married to George Dallas Follmer at Grant, Iowa, January 29, 1874, and at the present time has fifty descendants. Mr. Follmer, who died at Oak, Nebraska, May 29, 1914, was a prominent farmer, stockraiser, real estate dealer and politician in Nebraska for many years. He was born in Montour County, Pennsylvania, July 17, 1844. After his death Mrs. Follmer took over the operation of the farms and other business interests in which he had been active.

Their children are as follows: Clarence S., born January 9, 1875, married Grace Ewing; Harry R., born May 7, 1878, married Mary S. Crawford; Eugene A., born November 24, 1880; Ralph W., born July 11, 1884, married Marie Yunker; Katherine, born June 22, 1887; Pansy M., born June 18, 1890, married J. B. Blue; Florence Fern, born April 4, 1897, married Ray J. Lowrey.

During her fifty-seven years' residence in Nebraska Mrs. Follmer has been active in the development of her community. She is a member of the University Extension Club, the Better Homes and Gardens, the Eastern Star, the P. E. O. Sisterhood, and was the organizer of the first Parent-Teachers' Association in her county. During her long membership in the Christian Church she has taken an interested part in Sunday School and church work, and has for some time been a member of the Kings Daughters. The first court ever held in Nelson was in the house that afterwards became the Follmer home, which was also the first house in Nelson.

Mrs. Follmer is a Republican and during the World War was active in Red Cross Work and a purchaser of bonds. Her hobby is her Sunday School work. Recently she was elected to life membership in the Nebraskana Society in recognition of her achievements in the advancement of her community. Residence: Oak.

Anna Miller Folsom

Anna Miller Folsom, a resident of Nebraska for over 40 years, was born at Brooklyn, Kings County, New York, November 21, 1865. Her father, Ezekiel Hoag Miller, who was a dentist, was born at New York City, September 11, 1837, and died at Nyack, Rockland County, New York, April 24, 1910; his ancestors came from England. Her mother, Phebe Caroline (Underhill) Folsom was born, of English ancestry, at New York, November 24, 1841, and died at Nyack, April 20, 1891.

Mrs. Folsom received her education under a private tutor until she was ready for high school, when she attended Friends Seminary, at Rutherford Place, New York. She has always been active in welfare work at Lincoln, Nebraska, and holds membership there in the Young Women's Christian Association; and the Presbyterian Church. She is a member of the Country Club of Lincoln, and the Nebraskana Society. Her hobby is reading.

Her marriage was solemnized at Nyack, October 21, 1891. She has two children: Willard Miller, born February 27, 1894; and Phebe, born May 19, 1895. Her political affiliation is with the Republican party. Residence: Lincoln.

Ruth Whitmore Folsom

Ruth Whitmore Folsom was born at Valley, Nebraska, December 8, 1895, the daughter of William Gunn and Ida Jane (Knowlton) Whitmore. Her father, who was born at Sunderland, Massachusetts, June 23, 1849, served one term in the Massachusetts legislature before coming to Nebraska in 1878. He was prominent in political and civic affairs in Nebraska for many years, serving as a member of the Nebraska legislature, 1885-87, 1887-89. He was regent of the Nebraska University for 13 years, acting as president of the board of regents part of that time. He is a direct descendent of Joseph Whitmore who came to America in 1620, from England, where the family line is traced back to English nobility. Several of his ancestors were officers in the Revolution.

Her mother was born at Dew Plain, Michigan, June 14, 1858. She has held various state offices in the Federated Woman's Club and the Home Economics Association. Her ancestry is traced directly back to 1066, when the first Knowlton was knighted by William the Conqueror. Several of her ancestors were active in the Revolution.

Mrs. Folsom attended the Valley public school and was graduated from the Valley High School in 1913. In 1917, she was awarded the A. B. degree at the University of Nebraska, where she was a member of the Mystic Fish, freshman honorary society, and Valkyrie, senior honorary society. She was secretary of the sophomore class at the University of Nebraska, and was treasurer and president of Alpha Chi Omega.

She has lived in Nebraska her entire life, and is prominent in social and civic affairs there. She has been secretary of the Lincoln Junior League; is a member of the Parent-Teachers' Association; and holds membership in the Nebraskana Society. During the World War Mrs. Folsom took part in Red Cross Work, and is a member of the American Legion Auxiliary. Her social clubs include: Lincoln University Club and Lincoln Country Club.

On June 15, 1918, her marriage to Willard Miller Folsom was solemnized at Valley. Mr. Folsom, who is secretary of the Nebraska Central Building & Loan Association, was born at Lincoln, Lancaster County, Nebraska, February 27, 1894. His ancestors settled in America in colonial times and members of the Folsom family served in the Revolution. Their children are: Willard Whitmore, born August 19, 1920; Lowe Ricketts, born March 20, 1922; and Burton Whitmore, born March 21, 1925. Residence: Lincoln.

Willard Miller Folsom

Willard Miller Folsom, son of Morris Willard and Anna (Miller) Folsom, was born at Lincoln, Nebraska, February 27, 1894. His father, who was a banker and the organizer of the Nebraska Central Building and Loan Association, was born at the American Legation in Canton, China, June 30, 1866. His ancestors were English settlers in America prior to the Revolution. His death occurred at Lincoln, March 21, 1923. Anna Miller, his wife, was born at Brooklyn, New York, November 21, 1865. She is of English descent.

Willard Folsom was graduated from Prescott grade school in 1908, and from Lincoln High School in 1912. Entering the University of Nebraska, he was awarded his A. B., in 1916, and his LL. B., in 1919. His fraternities are Phi Delta Phi and Beta Theta Pi. He earned a letter in golf and was a member of the Kosmet Club.

On June 15, 1918, he was married to Ruth Irene Whitmore at her birthplace, Valley, Nebraska. Mrs. Folsom, who was born December 8, 1895, is of English descent; several ancestors served in the Revolution. They have three children, Willard Whitmore, born August 19, 1920; Lowe Ricketts, born March 20, 1922, and Burton Whitmore, born March 21, 1925.

For several years Mr. Folsom was a director of the Nebraska State Bank of Lincoln, and later assistant secretary and then secretary of the Nebraska Central Building and Loan Association. From May 12, 1917, to January 19, 1919, he served with the rank of 2nd lieutenant in the 338th Field Artillery. He is a member of the Red Cross, the American Legion, the Chamber of Commerce, the Parent-Teachers' Association, and the Young Men's Christian Association of which last he is a director. A Mason, he belongs to the Scottish Rite and Shrine Bodies. He is a member of the Nebraskana Society. The following are his social clubs: Lincoln Country Club, Lincoln University Club, and the Shrine Country Club. His sport is golf. Residence: Lincoln.

Alfred Fonda

Alfred Fonda, a prominent farmer in Custer County, Nebraska, was born at Cohoes, New York, October 20, 1851, the son of Henry and Alida M. (Link) Fonda. His father, a farmer and a soldier in the Civil War, was born in New York in 1827 and died in Albany County, New York, in 1889; his ancestors, who came to this country from Holland, were among the first settlers on the Mohawk River. His mother, whose ancestry is Dutch, was born in New York, in 1833, and died at Albany County, New York, in 1916.

Mr. Fonda served as county supervisor at Oconto, Nebraska, from 1902 to 1906. He is a member of the Independent Order of Odd Fellows, is affiliated with the Republican party, and holds membership in the Nebraskana Society. He has been a resident of this state for the past 44 years.

On September 7, 1884, he was married to Helena Jean Turnbull at Gloster, New Jersey. Mrs. Fonda, whose ancestry is Scotch, was born in Cataraugus County, New York, March 29, 1858. They have four children: Elvira Alida, born August 28, 1885; Indah Pearl, December 7, 1889; and twin sons, Roy and Troy, born August 19, 1892. Troy has been employed by the Chicago Burlington & Quincy Railroad for the past 10 years, and Roy owns a garage in Las Vegas, Nevada. Both sons served in the late war. Residence: Oconto.

Michael Joseph Ford

By profession a physician, Dr. Michael Joseph Ford, has taken for his avocation work among boys. Dr. Ford was born at Newcastle-on-Tyne, England, May 10, 1872, and came to America as an infant. His father, Michael Joseph Ford was a native of County Sligo, Ireland, a shoemaker by trade, who came to Omaha in 1882 from Maryland. He died at Omaha, November 5, 1905. His wife, Bridget (Rowan) Ford was born in County Mayo, Ireland. She died at Omaha in 1912.

Upon his graduation from Omaha High School, Dr. Ford entered Creighton University, where he received his M. D. and was valedictorian of his class, in 1901. He took post-graduate work at Johns Hopkins University; at Bellevue Hospital (New York and at Harvard), and had private work in surgery with Dr. Ferguson of Chicago. He is a member of Phi Rho Sigma.

He married Ida Bertha Biurvall at Omaha, August 11, 1897. Mrs. Ford was born in Chicago, January 1, 1873, and is of Norwegian and Swedish descent. There are two children. Barton H., born November 5, 1901, who is married to Teresa Christman. He is district manager for the John Hancock Life Insurance Company at Sioux City, Iowa. Edwin J., born February 14, 1903, is representative for Charles Ward Company, electrical supplies, of Kansas City.

A Republican, Dr. Ford is a national speaker for his party. He is the author of many articles on medicine and surgery. He was formerly the editor and owner of the *Switchmen's Journal of North America* and *Creighton Medical Bulletin*. He is a director of the Physicians Casualty Association. In 1916 he erected the Ford Hospital, which he has since operated. A Catholic, he is a member of St. Cecilia's Cathedral. He is a member of the Douglas County Medical Association, the Nebraska State Medical Association, the American Medical Association, the Missouri Valley Medical Association and the Elkhorn Medical Association. He is a life member of the Switchmen's Union and of the Old Settlers of Nebraska. He is a member of the Triangle Club, Boys Work Club, Elks Club, Woodmen of the World and physician to the Independent Order of Foresters. His club is the Omaha Athletic, and his sports are swimming and boxing. Residence: Omaha. (Photograph on Page 417).

Ralph Waldo Ford

Ralph W. Ford was born near Bertrand, in Gosper County, Nebraska, April 24, 1899, the son of Roy and Virginia Gilpen (Bowen) Ford. His father, who was a stockman and farmer, was born in Illinois, January 19, 1873. His mother was born in New Jersey, August 10, 1875.

Mr. Ford attended the rural schools of Gosper County, and in 1917 was graduated from the Bertrand High School. He received the LL. B. degree at the University of Nebraska, June 5, 1922, and was elected to Pi Kaption and the Lansaster County Bar Association, is a Mason, and a member of the Young Men's Christian Association. Residence: Lincoln.

On August 21, 1923, he married Oakle Morey Cochran at Holdrege, Nebraska. Mrs. Ford was born at Benedict, Nebraska, November 9, 1899. Their children are: Jack, born August 10, 1925; and Richard, born February 24, 1929.

Mr. Ford served in the United States army during the

DR. MICHAEL J. FORD

Heyn—Omaha

World War, and is a member of the American Legion. He holds membership in the Nebraska State Bar Association and the Lancaster County Bar Association, is a Mason, and a member of the Young Men's Christian Association. Residence: Lincoln.

Roy Bowen Ford

Roy B. Ford was born near Bertrand, in Gosper County, Nebraska, April 30, 1897, and has lived in this state all his life. His father, Roy Ford, who is a farmer and stockman, was born in Illinois, January 19, 1873. His ancestry is English. His mother, who was born at Camden, New Jersey, August 10, 1875, is descended from Scotch English ancestors who came to this country in 1740.

Mr. Ford attended the rural schools of Gosper County, Nebraska, and was graduated from the high school at Bertrand, Nebraska, in 1915. He was awarded the A. B. degree at the University of Nebraska where he was president of Pi Kappa Phi, 1919. Since his admission to the bar, June 21, 1921, he has engaged in general law practice at Lincoln, Lancaster County, Nebraska, specializing as insurance and trade association counsel. He is associated in practice with his brother, Ralph W. Ford.

He was united in marriage with Ethel Beatrice Tousley at Crookston, Minnesota, May 9, 1920. Mrs. Ford was born at Fargo, North Dakota, April 3, 1899; she is descended from early English settlers in America. They have the following children: Robert Bowen, born October 28, 1921; Virginia Mae, born November 10, 1922; and Bruce, born September 25, 1926.

Mr. Ford was a member of the Pershing Rifles at the University of Nebraska, the Cadet Rifle Team, Quartermaster Cadet Regiment, and in 1918 he enlisted in the Officers Training Camp of Fort Sheridan, Illinois. He was commissioned second lieutenant of infantry, special assignment, personnel adjutant's school, and was personnel adjutant in charge of the Student Army Training Corp at Fargo, North Dakota.

He is a member of the American Legion, the Nebraska and Lancaster County Bar Associations. He also holds membership in the Lincoln Chamber of Commerce, the Lions Club, and the Nebraskana Society. He is a Mason, a member of the Sheridan Parent-Teachers' Association and the Lincoln Young Men's Christian Association, and is affiliated with Westminster Presbyterian Church of Lincoln. His hobbies are fishing and hunting. Residence: Lincoln.

Charles Fordyce

Charles Fordyce, leading Nebraska educator, was born at Bloomington, Illinois, February 7, 1857, the son of Lebbeus, and Martha Ellen (Stephens) Fordyce. His father, who was born at Zanesville, Ohio, July, 1833, and died at Houston, Texas, April, 1915, was a cabinet maker; he was of Scotch descent. His mother who was born at Columbus, Ohio, June 1833, died in 1913. She was of English and German descent.

Dr. Fordyce received his early education at Prairie College, Gridley, Illinois, and was graduated from high school in 1879. He holds the following degrees: diploma, State Normal University of Illinois, 1882; A. M., Nebraska Wesleyan University, 1893; B. S., University of Nebraska, 1896; A. M., University of Nebraska, 1898; Ph. D., University of Nebraska, 1900. He was a student at De Pauw University, 1892; University of Chicago, 1904; Columbia University, 1912-13; and Harvard University, 1929. He is a member of Sigma Xi and Phi Delta Kappa.

He served as professor at Nebraska Wesleyan University, 1893-1908; was dean of the college of liberal arts at the latter, 1896-1908; was dean of the college of education, University of Nebraska, 1908-21; and since 1921 has been in the department of measurements and research. He is the author of *Monographs of Cladocera of Nebraska*, and *Scale for Measuring the Achievements in Reading*. He is associate editor of *The New Reference Library* and the *Journal of Educational Research*. Dr. Fordyce has lived in Nebraska for the past 45 years.

He holds membership in the following: Nebraska State Teachers Association; the National Education Association; the Rotary Club; the Optimist Club; and the Nebraskana Society. He has been chairman of the Nebraska State Young Men's Christian Association since 1928; is chairman of the research committee in the personnel division of the National Council of the Young Men's Christian Association; and is a member of the St. Paul's Methodist Church at Lincoln. During the late war he served as lecturer under the Fosdick Commission, 1918. Politically, Dr. Fordyce is a Republican.

He was married to Marie Priscilla Gray at El Paso, Woodford County, Illinois, June 8, 1882. Mrs. Fordyce was born at Hudson, Illinois, May 19, 1860; her ancestry is English and Irish. Three children were born to this marriage: Claude Powell, born March 6, 1893, who is a physician, and is now medical advisor for Merck Company, New York; Glen Gray, born October 30, 1887, who is executive for the Boy Scouts of America at Iowa City, Iowa, and Mildred Marie, born June 15, 1893, who died August 15, 1894. Residence: Lincoln.

Claude Powell Fordyce

Claude P. Fordyce, physician, author and editor, was born at McLean, Iowa, March 6, 1883, son of Charles and Marie (Gray) Fordyce. His mother, who was of Scotch ancestry, is active in P. E. O. and Woman's Club. His father, a noted educator, received the degrees of A. M. and Ph. D. at the University of Nebraska, and has been responsible for many advanced education measures in that institution. Since 1921 he has been at the head of the department of educational measurements and research.

Dr. Fordyce was at one time a student at the Illinois State Normal University. He has received the following degrees: A. B., Nebraska Wesleyan University, 1905; B. S., 1907; M. D., Washington University, 1910. He was a student at the University of Nebraska, 1907-08, where a scholarship in zoology was awarded him. While there he was appointed special representative for the governor of Nebraska to the National Conference on State Parks; at one time he was on the board of directors of the latter. He is a member of Sigma Chi, and Nu Sigma Nu.

The author of over 200 special feature magazine articles on nature, among them are: *Trail Craft* and *Touring-Afoot*. For eight years he was editor of the recreation department of the *Outdoor Life Magazine* in Denver. He is at the present time assistant editor of the *Journal of the American Medical Association* and *Hygeia*, Chicago. In 1930 he was appointed assistant editor of the American Medical Association.

He was married at Falls City, Nebraska, June 22, 1910, to Dora Maude Maddox. Mrs. Fordyce, who is of German descent, was born at Falls City. They have one child, Marileen Ann, born September 29, 1916.

Dr. Fordyce was admitted to the practice of his profession at Broken Bow, Nebraska, June, 1910. He is a member of The American Medical Association; Nebraska State Medical Association; Nebraska Writers' Guild, of which he is president; the advisory board of the National Safety Council of Chicago; and Academy of Science, in Nebraska. During the war he was on the bureau of examinations for the draft. A Methodist, he is a member of the Heminway Church, at Evanston, Illinois.

Motor boating, hiking and camping are his favorite sports. He is vice-commodore of the Missouri Valley Boat Racing Association, and editor of the motor boating department of *Outdoor Life*, Denver.

Dr. Fordyce is a member of the Odd Fellows Lodge.

DR. CLAUDE POWELL FORDYCE

He is a Democrat. His home and office are in Falls City. (Photograph on Page 419).

Harry Franklin Fore

Harry F. Fore was born at Albany, Gentry County, Missouri, March 25, 1879, the son of John Warren and Rose (Owen) Fore. His father, who was a farmer, was born in Iowa, February 8, 1849, and died at Albany, June 18, 1912. His ancestors were Frenchmen who came through Netherlands to America in 1750. His mother was born of Welsh and English parentage in Texas, February 22, 1854, and died at Albany, March 12, 1884.

Dean Fore attended the country schools of Missouri, and the town school at Gentryville, Missouri, and in 1900 was graduated from Stanberry Normal School. He was awarded the A. B. degree at the University of Missouri, in 1905, and a B. S. in Education in 1906. He attended the University of Chicago during the summer sessions of 1907, 1908, 1909, 1910, 1911, 1920, 1921, and 1923, and was awarded a fellowship in English at the University of Chicago, in 1924. Active in debating, he was a member of the Union Literary Society; was elected to membership in Sigma Delta Chi; and was a member of Tau Kappa Alpha and Delta Tau Delta.

Principal of the high school at Van Buren, Arkansas, 1905 to 1907, he was instructor in English at the A. and M. College in Mississippi, 1907-08; and was associate professor of English at Purdue University from 1908 to 1928. He is now head of the English department and acting dean of the graduate school at Creighton University. He is the author of *Life of Josiah Gilbert Holland*; *Courtley Love in Shakespeare*; both of which will be published soon. He has contributed various articles to *The Nation*.

On July 8, 1913, he was united in marriage with Valpey Cottle Trimble. Mrs. Fore, who is of English descent, was born at Memphis, Tennessee, July 2, 1888. They have three children: Elizabeth, born June 14, 1914; Frances, born February 22, 1916; and Louise, born January 12, 1918.

During the World War, Dean Fore was on the publicity committee and was a speaker in various loan campaigns. He is a member of the Business and Professional Men's Club. His sports are fishing and golf, and his hobby collecting Americana. Resilence: Omaha.

Ira George Forell

Ira George Forell, insurance executive and member of the Nebraska legislature, was born at Dwight, Illinois, February 11, 1881. He is the son of August George and Nancy Melissa (Thomas) Forell, the former a member of the von Forell family of Germany. August George Forell was born at Buffalo, New York, October 1, 1850, and died at Chester, Nebraska, March 24, 1925. An outstanding resident of his community, a farmer by occupation, his progenitor, Adolph von Forell belonged to the military or "King's family," which entitled him to the honorary sub-title of "von."

August George Forell was married to Nancy M. Thomas of Round Grove, Illinois. She was born January 20, 1856, of Pennsylvania Dutch ancestry, and died at Chester, Nebraska, May 19, 1919.

Educated in the rural schools of Thayer County, Ira G. Forell was graduated from Chester High School in May, 1898, and received his Bachelor of Arts degree from the University of Nebraska on June 8, 1912. He is a member of Acacia and Phi Rho Sigma, and in 1909 served as treasurer and representative to grand conclave of Acacia.

On December 19, 1927, Mr. Forell was united in marriage at Cecelia Sophie Wehrs at Omaha. Mrs. Forell, who was born at Milford, Nebraska, is of German and French descent, and traces her ancestry to Count von Moltke. They have one daughter, Mary Cecelia, born February 28, 1931.

A Democrat, Mr. Forell was defeated for election to the Nebraska house of representatives in 1924 and 1926, and was successful in November 1930. He is the author of *Hogs on the Farm*, published in the *Ozark Countryman* (1915). A farmer and rural school teacher for a number of years, he has been associated with the Farmers Mutual Insurance Company of Thayer County for some time, and is vice president of the organization. He has been a director also.

During the World War Mr. Forell was chairman of the local school district thrift stamp drive, and the 5th Liberty loan drive. He has been a member of the Red Cross, and since 1913 has been a director of School Board District No. 58. During the years 1915-17 he was a member of the Chester Community Club. His fraternal organizations include the Masons and Eastern Star, he is a 32nd degree Mason and a member of the Shrine and past master of Chester Lodge of the Ancient Free and Accepted Masons.

Mr. Forell holds life membership in the Nebraska Alumni Association, and was elected to the board of directors in June, 1931. He is past president of the Thayer County group of the University of Nebraska Alumni, and during 1903, 06, 07, and 08 was a member of the Young Men's Christian Association at the University. He also served as treasurer of that organization in 1907.

A member of Ak-Sar-Ben, and the Order of the Yellow Dog, he is also a member of the University Club by courtesy. Mr. Forell's hobbies are reading, philosophy and politics. Residence: Chester.

Harry Alden Foreman

Born at Sterling, Nebraska, October 2, 1888, Harry Alden Foreman is the son of Charles Elmer and Ida Ann (Atkins) Foreman. His father, who was a farmer and stockman, was born at Altoona, Pennsylvania, of German parentage, August 12, 1865, and died at Lincoln, Nebraska, December 19, 1919. His mother, who was a teacher before her marriage, was born at Minonk, Illinois, February 14, 1865; she is descended directly from John Alden and Priscilla Mullins, of *Mayflower* fame.

Mr. Foreman attended grade school at Adams, Nebraska, and was graduated from the high school at Central City, Nebraska; later he studied normal training for two years at the Nebraska School of Business at Lincoln. He taught in the business department of Nebraska Central College, at Central City, for five years, was commercial instructor in Brown's Business College at Colorado Springs, Colorado, and is now manager of the Columbus Fuel & Storage Company at Columbus, Nebraska. He is endowment trustee of the Nebraska Central College at this time.

On June 3, 1913, Mr. Foreman was united in marriage with Inez Esther Taber, daughter of James C. and Clara (Roberts) Taber, at Central City. Mrs. Foreman, who was a missionary in Japan, for five years and taught in American public schools prior to her marriage, was born at Marshalltown, Iowa, June 1, 1879. They have two children: Esther, born January 31, 1914; and Charles, born August 13, 1918.

Mr. Foreman is a member of the board of directors of the Columbus Chamber of Commerce, is affiliated with the Young Men's Christian Association and the Nebraskana Society. He is interested in baseball, football, and mechanics. During the World War he acted as postmaster at Rokeby, Nebraska, and was awarded medals for his activities in the sale of War Saving Stamps and Liberty bonds. He is a Republican. Residence: Columbus.

George Forgan

George Forgan, prominent Omaha banker, was born in Linlichdowshire, Scotland, July 1, 1871, son of Peter Liddle and Grace (MacMillan) Forgan. The father was born in St. Andrew, Scotland, April 2, 1833, and died there on May 6, 1915. He was a banker. His wife, Grace, was born in Glasgow, Scotland, July 22, 1833, and died at Omaha, July 25, 1926.

Mr. Forgan received his education in Scotland. On June 12, 1894, he was married to Mabel Cole at Omaha. She was born at Baraboo, Wisconsin, April 10, 1875. At the present time Mr. Forgan is the owner of the Forgan Investment Company. He is a member of Westminster Presbyterian Church, the Masons, and the Woodmen of the World. Residence: Omaha.

Eric Forslund

An outstanding merchant of Stromsburg, Nebraska, Eric Forslund was born in Darana, Sweden, May 17, 1866, the son of Johan and Johanna Forslund. Johan Forslund was born in Sweden, October, 1830, and died at Stromsburg, in 1900. His wife was born in Sweden on July 15, 1834, and died there during the summer of 1880.

Mr. Forslund attended public school and junior high school, and later the Agricultural College at Lincoln, Nebraska. On February 28, 1890, he married Emma Carlson. Mrs. Forslund was born at Falun, Dalarna, in Sweden, April 8, 1864. Two children were born to them, Lillie, in November, 1890, and now the wife of Hartwig Flodman; and Sigrid, born in July, 1892, now the wife of Delbert Query. Sigrid, who was a school teacher before her marriage, has two daughters, Ruth, aged 10, and Lillie Marie, aged 6. Mr. and Mrs. Flodman have a son, Earl, aged 13.

A farmer for twenty-five years, Mr. Forslund was in the grain business in Polk, Nebraska, for five years, and for the past fifteen years has been the proprietor of a grocery store. Politically he is a Democrat and has served as mayor of Polk, Nebraska, for two terms, as justice of the peace in Stromsburg two terms, and for six years as assessor in the Stromsburg precinct.

Mr. Forslund is a member of the Swedish Free Church of Stromsburg, holds a membership in the Red Cross, the Stromsburg Commercial Club, and The Nebraskana Society. He has served on the Stromsburg board of education, and for two years has been president of the Young Men's Christian Association. Fishing is his hobby. Residence: Stromsburg. (Photograph in Album).

R. T. Fosnot

R. T. Fosnot, distinguished educator and school executive of Nebraska, has lived in Nebraska all his life and has taken an active part in the progress of education. He was born at Davenport, Nebraska, September 16, 1886, the son of C. C. and Ida (Hefflinger) Fosnot. His father, a farmer, was born at Newville, Pennsylvania, March 17, 1860; he is of Scotch and German descent. His mother, whose ancestry is German, was born at Newville, October 25, 1859.

Mr. Fosnot attended the rural schools of Thayer County, and in 1905 was graduated from the Davenport High School. He holds the following degrees: B. E., Peru State Teachers College, Peru, Nebraska; A. B., Nebraska Wesleyan University, 1912; and A. M., University of Nebraska, 1915. He is now superintendent of the public schools at Schuyler, Colfax County, Nebraska.

His marriage to Lestia Irene Simmons was solemnized at Omaha, Douglas County, Nebraska, November 3, 1915. Mrs. Fosnot, who was born in Kansas, March 12, 1892, was formerly a school superintendent. They have two children: Jeannette, born February 23, 1917; and Glenn, born July 2, 1919.

Mr. Fosnot is a member of the Chamber of Commerce; the Nebraskana Society; and the Red Cross. He is a life member of the National Educational Association and the Nebraska State Teachers Association; is affiliated with the Presbyterian Church; and is a member of the Masons. His sports are: golfing, scouting, and fishing. Residence: Schuyler.

Charles Eber Foster

Charles Eber Foster, judge of the district court, was born at LaFayette, Illinois, December 6, 1877. His father, Ira George Foster, was born at Meadville, Pennsylvania, October 22, 1842. He was a tinsmith, hardware merchant and lumber merchant, and served three years in the Civil War. He came to Nebraska when a young man, and died at Nelson, Nebraska, October 17, 1916. His wife, Emmogene Wentworth, was born in Bennington, Vermont, November 2, 1848. Essentially a homemaker, she was active in the church and in club and lodge work, and was eligible to the Daughters of the American Revolution through both her father and her mother. She died at Nelson, August 29, 1926.

Upon his graduation from Nelson High School, Judge Foster attended the University of Nebraska and received his LL. B. in 1900. A member of the Maxwell Debating Society and the Union Society; he was also active in athletics, particularly baseball, football and track.

His political career has extended over a period of twenty-five years, and he has served as member of various Republican committees and conventions, and as police magistrate and deputy county attorney, municipal judge and now district judge, all at Omaha.

He is the author of various short stories, newspaper articles, etc. During his thirty years of active practice in the law he has handled and been connected with many known cases, both civil and criminal.

During his university days he was a member of the University Cadets, and later a member of the National Guard. During the World War he was a member of the draft board, and active in loan drives, recruiting and Red Cross work. He is a member of the Officers Reserve Corps, the Sons of Veterans, the Sons of the American Revolution, and the Heroes of '76.

A member of the First Presbyterian Church of Omaha, and the Young Men's Christian Association, he is active in all civic enterprises, and is an enthusiastic worker with children, especially those that are under-privileged.

His professional organizations include the American Bar Association, the Nebraska State Bar Association and the Omaha-Douglas County Bar. He is a member of the Ad-Sell League, the Chamber of Commerce, and the Kiwanis Club. He is a member also of the Ancient Free and Accepted Masons, Scottish Rite, Shrine, Royal Arch, Eastern Star and other bodies. He is fond of golf, hiking and swimming, and his hobby is the collecting of old law books. His clubs are the University Club, the Omaha Field Club and the Omaha Walking Club. Residence: Omaha.

Fred Charles Foster

Fred Charles Foster was born at Lincoln, Nebraska, December 13, 1880, son of John Lewis and Mary Ceneska (Damrow) Foster. John Lewis Foster, who was born at Remington, Indiana, February 5, 1856, was a physician many years. He was descended from English settlers in America prior to the Revolution, and died at Tyler, Texas, August 1, 1899. His wife, Mary, was born at Williamsport, Indiana, January 21, 1858, of German and English descent. For thirty-eight years she has been a teacher in the Lincoln public schools.

Mr. Foster was graduated from Lincoln schools in 1894, and received his LL. B. at the University of Nebraska, in 1903. He is a member of Alpha Tau Omega and Phi Delta Phi. He has been engaged in the practice of law since his admission to the bar in 1903, and was deputy county attorney of Lancaster County in 1901; city attorney of Lincoln, 1911-15, elected on the Republican ticket and member of the home rule charter convention, city of Lincoln.

On September 23, 1904, he was married to Beulah Livesay of Hebron, Nebraska, at Council Bluffs, Iowa. Mrs. Foster was born December 14, 1879.

Mr. Foster is a member of the American, Nebraska State and Lancaster County Bar Associations, and the Rotary Club. A Mason, he belongs to the Blue Lodge, Scottish Rite and Shrine bodies. His club is the Lincoln Country Club, and his favorite sport is fishing. Residence: Lincoln.

Henry Hubbard Foster

Henry H. Foster was born at Buffalo, New York, December 3, 1876. For the past ten years he has been one of Nebraska's leading legal educators and since 1926 he has been dean of the college of law at the University of Nebraska. His father, Hubbard A. Foster, who was a graduate of the Harvard Medical School, was born at Adrian, Ohio, November 22, 1847, and died at Buffalo, June 6, 1902. His ancestors were New Englanders, and he was a Civil War veteran. Florence A. (Jenkins) Foster, mother of Henry H. Foster, was born at East Bridgewater, Massachusetts, March 29, 1848, of New England ancestry, and died at Lincoln, September 3, 1923.

Dean Foster was graduated from Central High School at Buffalo, in 1894. He was awarded the degree A. B., at Cornell University, 1899, and LL. B., at Harvard, 1908. He was made a member of the Alpha Chapter of Sigma Xi at Cornell, 1899, and of Phi Delta Phi. Principal of Franklin School at Peoria, Illinois, 1899-1902; he was associate professor of education at the New Jersey State Normal School, 1902-04; began the practice of law at Peoria, 1908; and was professor of law at the University of Oklahoma, 1910-20.

Since 1920, he has been professor of law at the University of Nebraska. He is dean of the law school there and is legal alvisor to the Board of Regents. During his college days he was the author of a thesis published in Volume XII of *American Junior Psychology*. He is the author of various articles on real estate law appearing in the *Nebraska Law Bulletin*, the University of Pennsylvania *Law Review* and other legal periodicals. With W. A. Seavey, he was founder of the *Nebraska Law Bulletin*.

His marriage to Emma Beatrice Adams was solemnized at Peoria, Illinois, December 29, 1910. Mrs. Foster, whose ancestry is Scotch, was born at Haverstraw, New York, January 21, 1873. There are three children: Henry H., Jr., born December 3, 1911; Margaret Adams, born December 20, 1913; and Virginia Beatrice, born February 18, 1917.

Dean Foster is a member of: American Bar Association; Nebraska State Bar Association; Lancaster County Bar Association; the Lincoln Chamber of Commerce; and the Lincoln Rotary Club. He is a Mason, a member of the University Club, and has served as president of Cornell Alumni Club of Lincoln. He is affiliated with the First Plymouth Congregational Church. Residence: Lincoln.

James Espey Foster

For the past 40 years James E. Foster has lived at Omaha, and has taken an active part in the civic and business affairs of his community and state. He was born at Steubeuville, Ohio, March 23, 1878, the son of George Marshall and Sally Jane (Wallace) Foster. His father, who was born at Carnegie, Pennsylvania, April 17, 1852, died at Park Ridge, Illinois, September 25, 1923. His mother was born at Steubenville.

Mr. Foster received his education in the public and high schools of Omaha. He entered business in the employ of the Aetna Insurance Company in the northwest department at Omaha, and remained in this company for 14 years. For two years he was manager of a local insurance agency at Omaha, and for five years was chief examiner of the Columbia Fire Underwriters Agency of the Nationai Fire Insurance Company.

Resigning from the latter position in 1919, to become secretary-treasurer of the National American Fire Insurance Company, he was made president and treasurer of this organization in 1925.

Mr. Foster is married to Mary Virginia Robinson, who was born at Council Bluffs. He is a member of the Chamber of Commerce, the Young Men's Christian Association, and the Omaha Athletic Club. He is affiliated with the Episcopal Church at Omaha, and is a member of Happy Hollow Club. Residence: Omaha.

Margaret Vera Foster

Margaret Vera Foster, educator and club woman at York, Nebraska, has lived in this state all her life, is prominent in every civic and educational undertaking in her community. She was born at Hartington, Cedar County, Nebraska, October 16, 1887, the daughter of Jacob Napoleon Lemon and Margaret Missouri (Jones). Her father, who was a real estate dealer, was born at Harrisburg, Pennsylvania, July 12, 1851; his parents came to this country from England. He is deceased.

Her mother was born at St. Louis, Missouri, July 16, 1857. Her parents came to America from Wales, and her father, Lewis E. Jones, Sr., who was the author of many historical articles, was at one time the owner and editor of the *Christian Advocate*. She died in March, 1932.

Mrs. Foster was graduated from the Hartington High School in 1906. She received the A. B. degree in 1910 from the Nebraska Wesleyan University where she was president of the junior class, 1909, treasurer of the Young Women's Christian Association, 1908, and president of Alpha Epsilon, 1909-10. She was valedictorian of her graduating class in high school at Hartington, 1906.

She served as superintendent of the public schools at North Loup, Nebraska, 1910-13, and was principal of the Edison school in York, 1914-17. In recent years Mrs. Foster has acted as substitute teacher in both the grade and high school at York. She is a member of the Parent-Teacher's Association at York, and the Red Cross. She is guardian of Jobs' Daughters, which she organized at York in 1930, served as president of the Eastern Star Kensington in 1928, and as Worthy Matron of the Eastern Star in 1930, was president of the Young Men's Christian Association Auxiliary, 1926-28, and acted as secretary of the Woman's Club in 1921. She holds membership in the Nebraska Teachers' Association, is affiliated with the Methodist Episcopal Church at York, and is a member of the Nebraskana Society. Her social club is the York Country Club.

Her marriage to Leslie Everett Foster occurred at University Place, Lancaster County, Nebraska, June 7, 1913. Mr. Foster, who was born at Giltner, Hamilton County, Nebraska, January 17, 1888, is in the dry cleaning business, and is the author of books and articles on dry cleaning. His grandfather, Jonathan Foster was a lieutenant in the Civil War. They have three children, all of whom are honor roll students in school. They are: Arthur Hubert, born November 9, 1917; Robert Gayle, born December 5, 1919; and Dorothy Maxine, born May 18, 1922. Mrs. Foster is a Republican. Residence: York.

Mattie E. Franks Foster

Mattie E. Franks, daughter of George Milton and Mary Jane (Holsey) Franks, was born at Maryville, Missouri, June 23, 1866. Her father was born at Quincy, Illinois, March 7, 1842, and died at Maryville, September 10, 1869. Her mother was a native of St. Joseph, Missouri, born March 6, 1844, and died at Rockford,

Nebraska, November 16, 1898. Both parents were of German descent.

Educated in a pioneer school near Jewell Center, now Mankato, Kansas, she attended school from 1876 to 1881, three months of each year. She received her education in the early pioneer days, living on a Kansas homestead. School days were only three months a year. The school house was made of sod with the ground for a floor. The teacher's salary was $15.00 a month. Conditions were not as acceptable as now for an education, but it was much more appreciated. A Sunday school was organized and a lyceum course also, but no church services were held for a year or more. Mrs. Foster has used every opportunity to improve her education through church and church organizations, the Federation of Woman's Club, the Woman's Christian Temperance Union, and in missionary and welfare work. Conditions were not so favorable for an education at that time as they now are, but Mrs. Foster has used every opportunity for advancing her intellectual development.

In her pioneer school days children were compelled to combine recreation with activities to increase efficiency. Horseback riding was one of her hobbies at that time. In the winter the children made prairie chicken traps, and placed them on the ground at the edge of cornfields. Each day it was her duty to look after the traps and bring in the game. She would get on to her saddle horse, take her gray hound and a gunny sack, and on the way would scare the rabbits and the hound would run them down. Her leisure time spent in this matter was always profitable for prairie chickens were very plentiful and they all enjoyed the game that helped supply their daily food during the winter months.

On February 2, 1882, she was united in marriage to Charles N. Foster. To this union three children were born, Charles Oscar, July 15, 1884, who died December 4, 1896; Mary Estella, born December 2, 1882, who died May 3, 1909; and James Albert, born January 23, 1886, who died March 10, 1911.

At the time of her marriage the ox team was used to break up the sod and prepare it for farming and also to break the sod for building houses. Sometimes Mrs. Foster would yoke the oxen to the wagon and drive them to the field while Mr. Foster was sharpening the breaking plow. Then when they wanted to go to the post-office to take and get the mail, they would ride a mule on the errand, and many of the neighbors would go with them on horseback and sometimes races were run. That was the real pioneer life in western Kansas in the eighties. The prairie schooners were great in number going west and seeking for gold. Altho she has no children of her own, at the present time, Mrs. Foster took into her home two orphan children, one two weeks old and the other three and a half, rearing them to maturity. John Wesley Neyhart, the boy, is married to Evelyn Farver, and Mary Catherine is married to Willard Campbell. Both are graduates of Hebron High School.

In 1910 Mrs. Foster was elected a member of the Woman's Christian Temperance Union, and during the entire period of her membership she has been an active worker for the cause of temperance. For some time she was county president of the organization, and for three years she was state director of non-alcoholic flavorings. At the present time she is state director of non-alcohol fruit products.

Over this period of time she has attended eighteen state, five national and two world conventions. Her greatest desire is to help raise humanity to a higher life of Christian citizenship and civic righteousness.

A member of the Presbyteran Church for the past twenty years, Mrs. Foster was elected secretary-treasurer of the Missionary Society four years, and president one year. She has been a member of the welfare board of the Hebron Woman's Club six years, and has taken a prominent part in the collection of food, clothing and other necessaries and has spent much time in personal service for the poor and sick.

She has always taken an active part in Red Cross Work, and during the World War especially assisted in packing clothes, knitting and sending boxes overseas. The author of various papers and articles for the Woman's Club, the Women's Christian Temperance Union and the Missionary Society, she has covered subjects of an educational, religious, welfare and civic nature. She has brought home reports from the scores of conventions attended and read them at local meetings.

Among the conventions to which she has been a delegate for the Women's Christian Temperance Union are the following: Fairbury, 1910, Central City, 1912; Fremont, 1913, Hastings, 1914, Omaha, 1916, Lincoln, 1917, Fremont, 1918, York, 1919, David City, 1920, Columbus, 1921, Lincoln, 1922, Hastings, 1923, North Platte, 1924, Fremont, 1925, Kearney, 1926, Grand Island, 1928, and Fairbury 1929. She was also delegate to the national conventions at Columbus, Ohio, 1923, Chicago, 1924, and Detroit, 1925. In 1925 she attended the Anti-Saloon League National Convention at Chicago, and in 1927 the World's League against Alcoholism at Winona Lake, Indiana, where fifty-one countries were represented. In addition she was delegate to the national Women's Christian Temperance Union convention at Minneapolis in 1927, at Niagara Falls, New York, in 1931, and the World's convention at Toronto, Canada, in 1931.

From 1912-20 Mrs. Foster was traveling representative for the Spirella Corset Company of Meadville, Pennsylvania, and from 1910-14 represented the Franco American Hygienic Company of Chicago.

Independent in politics, she attended the Woman's Suffrage convention at Omaha, 1912, 1914. She also attended the Parent Teachers State Convention in 1926, and the Nebraska Conference of Social Workers at Lincoln, in 1921. As a representative of the Presbyterian Missionary Society she attended the convention at Omaha in 1925, Aurora in 1924, Nebraska City in 1928 and Beatrice in 1931. She attended the Nebraska Federation of Women's Clubs district convention at Aurora in 1924, Gilead in 1926, Stromsburg in 1928, and Carleton in 1927, and the state conventions at Lincoln in 1927 and Fairbury in 1922. Residence: Hebron. (Photograph in Album).

John Wesley Fowler

For the past 26 years John Wesley Fowler has been engaged in the livestock business at Hershey, Nebraska. He was born at Stewartsville, Missouri, March 25, 1877, the son of John Wesley and Cornelia Jane (Weddle) Fowler. His father, whose ancestry is Scotch and English, was born in Illinois, in 1840, and died at Stewartsville, Missouri, February 12, 1877; he was a farmer and served in the Union Army during the Civil War.

Mr. Fowler's mother was born at Stewartsville, June 8, 1850, was a homesteader in Kansas in 1877, and died at Beatrice, Nebraska, August 26, 1924. Her father was of Pennsylvania Dutch extraction and her mother's ancestry was French.

Mr. Fowler received his education in the public schools of Lebanon, Kansas. He engaged in farming for many years, but recently has been a livestock buyer and seller. He is a member of the school board at Hershey, is affiliated with the Methodist Episcopal Church, and holds membership in the Independent Order of Odd Fellows. He is a former member of the Elks and Yeomen.

His marriage to Bertha Leota Anderson occurred at Smith Center, Kansas, May 10, 1899. Mrs. Fowler, whose grandfather came to this country from Ireland, was born at Birmingham, Iowa, November 23, 1876. Mrs. Fowler's mother was born near Birmingham, Iowa, and died in 1882. Her father was also born in Iowa and died at Jetmore, Kansas. They have reared and educated three adopted children: John, born February 18,

1899, who married Annie Miller; Vern, born December 20, 1908; and Gladys, born September 29, 1908, who married Cecil Miller. Residence: Hershey.

Thomas Herbertson Fowler

One of Fremont's outstanding citizens, Thomas Herbertson Fowler has been a resident of Nebraska forty-five years. He was born at Tenafly, New Jersey, May 28, 1867, son of William Kirk and Mary Ann (Stirling) Fowler. His father was born at Auchtermuchty, Fifeshire, Scotland, July 6, 1822, and died at North Bend, Nebraska, January 28, 1895. He was a banker and livestock breeder, who came to America in 1851. His wife, Mary Ann, was born in Stirling, Scotland, in 1838, and died at Otisco Center, New York, in 1871; she also came to America in 1851.

Thomas H. Fowler attended the public and high schools of the city of New York, and the College of New York during 1881-82. In 1890 he became cashier of the National Bank of North Bend, continuing until 1912, when he became cashier of the First National Bank of North Bend. During 1920-25, he was vice president of the Union National Bank of Fremont. A Republican, he was elected county treasurer of Dodge County for the term 1927-31, and was re-elected in the fall of 1930 for the term 1931-35.

On April 24, 1894, Mr. Fowler was married to Minnie Harris Johnson at Los Gatos, California. Mrs. Fowler was born in Allegheny, Pennsylvania, February 7, 1871, and died at Fremont, May 1, 1930. She was a teacher prior to her marriage and was of Scotch-Irish descent. There are three children: Mary Stirling, born June 6, 1897, who married George W. Warrenburg; Richard Herbertson, born November 20, 1900, who married Rosamond Seacrest; and Margery Allison, born October 12, 1902, who married Clifford Dahl.

Mr. Fowler is a member of the First Presbyterian Church of Fremont, the Chamber of Commerce, Kiwanis Club (vice president) and the Young Men's Christian Association. Residence: Fremont.

George A. Fox

George A. Fox, manager of the grain elevator at Bertrand, Nebraska, was born in that community, April 9, 1881, the son of George and Rosa (Simmon) Fox. His father, was born in Bohemia, January 15, 1853, and died at Bertrand, February 6, 1907. He was united in marriage to Rosa Simmon in Wisconsin, 1879, just prior to starting for Nebraska. His mother was born in Bohemia, June 2, 1860, and died at Bertrand, May 28, 1923.

Mr. Fox served as manager in the Bertrand Lumber Yard under the ownership of Roy Ford, 1908-12, 1917-28, and the Perry Lumber Yard, as manager, 1928-30, and at the present time is manager of the Bertrand Equity Exchange Elevator. He is a Democrat. He is a member of the Community Club, is treasurer of the School Board, and is affiliated with the First Congregational Church. He is serving as church trustee, church clerk, also secretary-treasurer of the Men's Brotherhood Class. His favorite sport is walking while his hobby is mechanics.

His marriage to Dora Dell Ferry, daughter of Silas A. and Amy (Coe) Ferry, occurred at Lexington, Nebraska, September 24, 1908. Mrs. Fox was born at Gove, Kansas, August 26, 1888, and died at Bertrand, December 9, 1921. Their two children are: Doris D., born September 11, 1910, who married Chester E. Anderson; and George F., born January 24, 1921. Doris is a stenographer in the Livestock Exchange at Omaha. Residence: Bertrand.

John Monroe Fox

John Monroe Fox, for the past fifteen years general manager and auditor of the Yates Lumber and Coal Company, was born at Conrad, Iowa, December 14, 1881. He is the son of Henry Stroh and Hattie Alvira (Thorpe) Fox.

Henry Fox was born at Kingston, Pennsylvania November 14, 1849, his mother of Holland Dutch birth, and his father a native born American. A lumberman in early life, he was a farmer at the time of his marriage, and spent the last twenty years of his life in the general mercantile business. He died at Balgrade, Nebraska, January 9, 1912.

Hattie Alvira Thorpe was born at Lorraine, Ohio, September 17, 1861, and died at Lincoln, October 28, 1927. The Thorpe family is of Irish and Welsh descent, her uncle, Uriah Blake Thorpe, having been one of the hardy pioneers of Sandusky County, Ohio, when Indians were more numerous than whites.

Educated in the public schools of Brainard and Mead, Nebraska, John Monroe Fox was graduated from Mead High School in 1899, took some work at the University of Nebraska, and completed a six month's course at Lincoln Business College. Upon leaving school he entered the freight department of the Burlington, and after eight months there accepted a stenographic and bookkeeping position with the Yates Lumber and Coal Company of Lincoln, on February 3, 1907. He has been associated with this firm continuously since that time.

On March 6, 1905, he was married to Martha Elizabeth Primley at Lincoln. Mrs. Fox was born at Mead, April 10, 1881, her parents having emigrated to Nebraska from Illinois. The Fox family came to Nebraska in 1888, first locating at Brainard, Butler County. Mrs. Fox's father, William F. Primley was born April 29, 1844, in Mercer County, Illinois, and died April 7, 1919, at Aledo, Illinois. He enlisted when a young boy and his first engagement was in the Battle of Look Out Mountain, he made the march with Sherman to the Sea. He was editor of the *Mead Advocate* at Mead, Nebraska, a well known publisher and a writer of current events in verse. They have one daughter, Naomi, born April 19, 1906, who is married to Dr. Corliss Myers Totman, a dentist, at Elmwood, Nebraska.

Mr. Fox is independent in politics. He attends the Methodist Church, is a member of the Red Cross, the Business Men's Club, and the Parent Teachers Association. He was recently made a life member of the Nebraskana Society. Among his favorite recreations are golfing and hunting, and he is an ardent football fan. Residence: Scotia.

Roy Emerson Fox

Roy Emerson Fox was born at York, Nebraska, January 18, 1890, the son of Leroy Carson and Eva Jane (Gelvin) Fox. His father, who was for many years a farmer, teacher, and telegraph operator, was born at Bushnell, Illinois, September 11, 1862; his ancestry is Scotch, Welsh, and Irish. His mother, who was born in Iowa, March 12, 1867, is descended from Pennsylvania Dutch ancestors.

Mr. Fox attended a rural school, and in 1911 was graduated from the York High School. From 1912 to 1913, he was a student at the United Brethren College at York. He was a farmer until 1918, served as assistant manager of the Farmers Grain Association at Benedict, Nebraska, from 1919 to 1924, and since 1924 has been manager of the Farmers Grain Association at Thayer, Nebraska.

A Republican, Mr. Fox served as village trustee for four years and acted as mayor of Thayer, for two years. He has lived in York County all his life and is a member of the Methodist Church and the Independent Order of Odd Fellows there. He holds membership in the Nebraskana Society and the American Legion. His favorite sports are baseball and hunting.

His marriage to Juanita Mae Bell was solemnized at Benedict, February 22, 1916. Mrs. Fox was born at Benedict, March 8, 1901, and died at Mason City, Custer County, Nebraska, January 26, 1918. One child was born to this union, Hazel, February 21, 1917. On November 21, 1920, Mr. Fox was married at York, to Catherine Berger. Two children were born to them: Warren, born December 24, 1921, who died September 10, 1923; and Wayne, born September 10, 1924. Residence: Thayer.

Joseph Barnett Fradenburg

Joseph B. Fradenburg was born at Saint Joseph, Missouri, August 16, 1880. His father, Joseph Barnett Fradenburg, was a native of New Jerusalem, New York, decented from Dutch settlers in that vicinity. He died at Omaha. His wife, Lucy Lee Ledgerwood of Centralia, Illinois, was descended from early settlers in New England. She died at Omaha, and had been a resident of Nebraska since 1885.

Mr. Fradenburg was graduated from Omaha High School, and entered the University of Nebraska, where he received his LL. B. in 1901. He is a member of Alpha Theta Chi and Phi Delta Phi. Upon his admission to the bar he took up the active practice of law, and was formerly a member of the law firm of Fradenburg & Matthews. He is now senior member of the firm of Fradenburg, Stalmaster & Beber, and is also active in the business world, being connected with the O. K. Hardware Company and with the Sand-Gravel Company of which he has served as president.

On July 7, 1904, he was united in marriage with Cora Lee Hyer, at Omaha. Mrs. Fradenburg was born at Marietta, Ohio, March 5, 1880, and is of New England ancestry. They have two children, William, born July 9, 1915, and Elizabeth, born June 16, 1908, who is married to Stanley Kalish.

Mr. Fradenburg has always been active in the Masonic Lodge, and in 1921 was grand master of Ancient Free and Accepted Masons of Nebraska. An Episcopalian, he attends Trinity Cathedral. He is fond of golf, is a member of the Omaha Field Club and the Omaha Athletic Club. He is a member of the American Bar Association, the Nebraska State Bar Association and the Omaha-Douglas County Bar. Residence: Omaha.

Cecil Cooper Fraizer

Cecil Cooper Fraizer was born at Montpelier, Indiana, June 15, 1892, the son of Alvin J. and Amelia Haworth (Cooper) Fraizer. His father, who is a druggist, was born in Henry County, Indiana, of Scotch ancestry. His mother was born, of English parentage, in Henry County.

Mr. Fraizer, who is a prominent lawyer and civic leader at Aurora, Nebraska, received his education in the public and high schools of Muncie, Indiana, where he was graduated in 1910. He was a student at the University of Pennsylvania, at Philadelphia, 1910-11, where he was active in debating and public speaking and was elected to membership in the Philmathean Society. He received the LL. B. degree at George Washington University in 1914, and was president of the local chapter of Sigma Alpha Epsilon in 1914.

During his high school days Mr. Fraizer worked in a drug store, and was employed in the law office of Charles H. Bates at Washington, while he studied at the university. From 1914 to 1917, he continued in the employe of the latter law firm, and in 1917 became a member of the firm Hainer, Craft, Edgerton, & Fraizer, at Aurora, of which he is still a member.

A Republican, he served as city attorney of Aurora, 1919, was deputy county attorney of Hamilton County, Nebraska, 1919-21, and was chairman of the Fourth District of the Hoover-for-president Club in 1928; he has been a delegate to various Republican State Conventions. He is a member of the Rotary Club, of which he was president in 1926 and 1927, the Aurora Business Men's Club, serving as a member of its board of directors, and the Aurora Country Club of which he is president. He holds membership in the American Bar Association, was formerly vice president of the Nebraska State Bar Association, and in 1927 was chairman of the Hamilton County Chapter of the Red Cross. He was a member of the Young Men's Christian Association for a number of years, and is still a contributor to that organization. During 1926 and 1927, he served as a member of the Aurora School Board.

During the World War he was chief petty officer in the United States Navy, and served in the Intelligence Service of the 9th, 10th and 11th Naval Districts at Chicago, in connection with the Great Lakes Naval Training Station. He was a charter member and one of the organizers of the Lester S. Harter Post Number 42 of the American Legion at Aurora, and has held various executive offices in that organization: member executive committee, 1923-24; department commander, 1927; member National Americanism Commission of the American Legion, 1925-31; member of the State Fund Relief Committee, 1927; and delegate to national convention at New Orleans, Omaha, and Boston.

Since the war, Mr. Fraizer has spent a tremendous amount of time assisting ex-service men in obtaining compensation from the United States Government, and has been of invaluable service to soldiers and their dependents. The Nebraska Soldier Relief Committee of which he is chairman has charge of the expenditure of a hundred thousand dollars a year for the relief of needy ex-service men and their families, this being the annual income from the two million dollar fund appropriated by the state legislature. Only one other state in the Union has such a fund.

Mr. Fraizer was married to Nelle Elizabeth McCarthy at Denver, Colorado, October 22, 1916. Mrs. Fraizer, who was formerly a teacher, was born at Anderson, Indiana, September 26, 1892. Their son, Theodore J., was born January 21, 1919. Residence: Aurora.

Clarence Lefever France

For the past fifty years Clarence L. France has been a resident of Nebraska. During that time he has been engaged in farming, and for thirty years he has been a member of the Syracuse board of education.

He is the son of Oliver DeVine and Mary Agnes (Crist) France. His father was born in Ulster County, New York, and was of Dutch descent; he was a scythe maker. His mother was of Scotch descent, born at Orange, New York, and was a teacher in the public schools.

Clarence L. France was born at Orange, New York, October 25, 1858. He attended the common schools of New York State, and came to Nebraska at the age of 24. On December 19, 1883 he was married to Evagene Andrews, at Syracuse, Nebraska. Mrs. France was a school teacher before her marriage and was of German descent. She was born in New York State, May 6, 1863, and died December 3, 1930.

There are fourteen children living, all of whom are married and have homes of their own, except one son who served in the Navy during the World War, and has been promoted to the rank of commissioned officer.

Mr. France served one term in the Nebraska legislature. He is a member of the Syracuse Congregational Church, and is a 32nd degree Mason. Residence: Syracuse.

Harry Whiting Francis

Harry W. Francis, who has been a practicing physician at Bancroft, Nebraska, for the past 35 years, was

C. J. FRANKFORTER

Dole—Lincoln

born at Oquawka, Illinois, October 12, 1866. His father, James F. Francis, who was a lumberman and farmer, was born in West Virginia, and died at Seward, June 27, 1883. Lizzie H. Francis, his wife, died at Seward, January 1, 1890.

Dr. Francis was graduated from the Seward High School and in 1896 was awarded the M. D. degree at Omaha Medical College. He holds membership in the Nebraska State Medical Association; the Cuming County Medical Society; and the American Medical Association. He is president of the Elkhorn Medical Association; is a member of the village board at Bancroft; and is a life member of the Red Cross. He holds membership in the Modern Woodmen of America, the Masons, and the Nebraskana Society.

During the World War Dr. Francis served as captain of the medical corps at Camp Pike, Arkansas; he is a member of the American Legion. His political affiliation is with the Democratic Party.

On June 4, 1890, he was united in marriage with Cora R. Nelson, at Knoxville, Illinois. Mrs. Francis, daughter of William Jackson and Lora Smith, was born at Galesburg, Illinois, August 6, 1868. They have five children: Floyd Vincent, born November 26, 1898, who attended the University of Nebraska; Myrton, born May 12, 1903; Marvyn Bliss, born August 7, 1904, a graduate of the University of Nebraska in 1930; Minnie, born September 11, 1906; Norton L., born March 21, 1910, University of Nebraska, class of 1931. Residence: Bancroft.

Clarence Jackson Frankforter

C. J. Frankforter, one of Nebraska's leading educators, was born in Lincoln, October 30, 1885. He is the son of Jacob W. and Rebecca Jane (Jackson) Frankforter, the former of whom was born in Wood County, Ohio, August 17, 1844. Active in business, he served as a Union soldier in the Civil War, with the 86th and 144th Ohio Volunteer Infantry. His father, who was of German birth, came to America very early in the 19th century and engaged as a lumberman and farmer in the early days of Ohio.

Rebecca Jane Jackson, wife of Jacob, was born in Henry County, Ohio, August 25, 1849, and died in Lincoln, February 4, 1920. Active in church work and the Women's Relief Corps, she was of German and Scotch-Irish descent, and a first cousin of General Stonewall Jackson.

Clarence J. Frankforter attended the Lincoln public and High School, and was graduated from the latter in 1903. He received his B. Sc., from the University of Nebraska in 1908, his A. M., 1909, and took special work at the University of Minnesota for his Ph. D. His thesis was turned in and accepted, but when the time for his examinations arrived he was in service for the World War. He served as a captain of Infantry 86th Division, and Captain, Chemical Warfare at Edgewood Arsenal and was then commandant at the University to reorganize the Reserve Officers Training Corps in 1919. He is a colonel of Infantry Reserve, commanding the 356th Infantry at the present time, and a member of the American Legion, the Reserve Officers Association (former commander), Forty and Eight (former chef de gare).

Mr. Frankforter is a member of Sigma Xi, Phi Lambda Upsilon and Sigma Gamma Epsilon, Scabbard and Blade Alpha Chi Sigma (National Officer 1910-12), Alpha Tau Omega. He was major of the Cadet Battalion at the University in 1908, and a member of the class football team. Since that same year he has been a member of the faculty of the University, beginning as assistant instructor. For twenty years he has been consulting and analytical chemist in addition to his teaching. He is now assistant professor of chemistry, and technical director, vice president and a member of the board of directors of the Frankforter Oil Process, Inc., recently organized in

Nebraska for the development of a method of removing sulphur from oil. Mr. Frankforter holds a United States and several foreign patents on this process. He is the author of several articles on scientific subjects in the *Journal of the American Chemical Society, the Journal of the American Ceramic Society* and the *Oil News.*

Professor Frankforter was married to Grace M. Hull at Lincoln, on June 25, 1908. Mrs. Frankforter was born at Unadilla, Nebraska, July 24, 1885, descended from early settlers from England, in Virginia and Kentucky. She is active in church and club work. There are three children, Dorothy, born January 9, 1914, who is a national honor student from Lincoln High School, and a freshman at the University; Jackson, born March 20, 1920; and Betty, born January 29, 1925.

Formerly active in football and baseball, Professor Frankforter is still interested in them as a spectator; he does some hiking and shooting, and during the World War was an expert rifle and pistol shot. A graduate of the Conservatory in 1903, he enjoys music, and is an accomplished pianist. As he says, he is a crank on auto-mechanics. Perhaps his greatest interest aside from his profession, is in young men. He does some special executive and advisory work with them in the University, and is a faculty member of the Interfraternity Council. During the summer of 1929, he commanded a Citizens Military Training Camp at Fort Crook, and also commanded one during the summer of 1931, at Fort Snelling.

He is a member of the American Chemical Society, the American Ceramic Society, and is a former president, and for several years acted as secretary-treasurer of the local section of the former. He is a member of the Nebraskana Society, and Mrs. Frankforter is a member of the Parent-Teachers' Association. Residence: Lincoln. (Photograph on Page 426).

William Charles Fraser

William C. Fraser was born at Walnut, Iowa, June 20, 1887, the son of William E. and Dora (Burton) Fraser. His father, who was born June 2, 1859, at Tiskilwa, Illinois, was a hotel proprietor; his ancestry is Scotch and Irish. He died October 11, 1929. His mother was born at Bussey, Iowa, July 8, 1860, and died at Omaha, Douglas County, Nebraska, May 8, 1927; her ancestry was English.

Mr. Fraser was graduated from the high school at Walnut, and in 1908 received his LL. B. degree at Creighton University. He has been engaged in the practice of law at Omaha, since 1908. He is now a member of the firm Crofoot, Fraser, Connolly, & Stryker. He has lived in this state for the past 26 years.

He was united in marriage with Mabel Gray, September 22, 1909, at Omaha. Mrs. Fraser, who was born at Hull, Iowa, August 8, 1887, is of German and English descent. They have four children: Dorothy, 20; Mary 17; Robert, 16; and Barbara Ann, 3.

Mr. Fraser is a member of the Nebraska State Bar Association; the Omaha Bar Association; American Bar Association; and the Ad-Sell League. He was president of the Omaha Bar Association in 1926; was chairman of the legal education committee of the Nebraska Bar Association, 1928; and is president of the Community Chest of Omaha. He is active in the Boy Scouts of America, and former president of the Omaha Council. He is affiliated with the St. Margaret Mary's Catholic Church of Omaha, and the Knights of Columbus and was Grand Knight of Omaha Council during war time. His social clubs are: the Omaha Athletic Club, Omaha Club, and Happy Hollow Club. His sports include golfing and hunting, and his hobby is reading. He holds membership in the Nebraskana Society. He is a member of the board of directors and the Executive Committee of the Chamber of Commerce and was a member of the Omaha Public Library Board for three years. Residence: Omaha.

T. Eleanor Frasier

T. Eleanor Frasier, editor of the *Wauneta Breeze,* an independent newspaper, was born at Vassar, Michigan, October 1, 1888, and for the past 15 years has resided in Nebraska. She is the daughter of David and Mary Ann in (McInnes) Stevens. Her father, born at Tuscola, Michigan, November 5, 1865, died at Vassar, Michigan, in February, 1890. Her mother was born at Westminster, Ontario, Canada, June 22, 1866, and at the present time makes her home in Wauneta.

Mrs. Frasier attended high school at Marlette and Saginaw, Michigan. On April 26, 1910, she was married to William Marshall Frasier at Saginaw, Michigan. Mr. Frasier, who was an editor for many years, owned and operated the *Wauneta Breeze* from April, 1920, until September, 1929, and was also postmaster from January, 1929, until September of the same year. He was Republican committeeman, past master of lodge No. 217 of the Ancient Free and Accepted Masons, patron of the Eastern Star, an Odd Fellow, and noble grand during one term. He was born at Flynn, Michigan, September 5, 1888, and died at Omaha, September 16, 1929. Three children were born to them, two of whom are living, Harold T., April 22, 1911, who is attending the Colorado Teachers College at Greeley, Colorado; Burnell, July 12, 1913, who is in high school; and William, born November 6, 1915, who died February 12, 1923.

In May, 1931, Mrs. Frasier edited a special edition called History and Development of Wauneta that is of special interest and was profusely illustrated. She is a member of the Methodist Episcopal Church, where she is a member of the official board, the Nebraska Press Association, the National Editors Association, the Order of Eastern Star, past matron of Wauneta Lodge No. 295, the Parent Teachers Association, and the Federated Woman's Club. She is affiliated with the Republican party. Residence: Wauneta.

Mason Amadon Frazell

Mason Amadoon Frazell, a lifelong resident of this state, was born at Hiawatha, Nebraska, May 27, 1894, the son of Jacob Hiram and Ida Irene (Blakeman) Frazell. His father, who was born in Ohio, March 29, 1845, is a farmer who served in Company E of the 10th Illinois Infantry during the Civil War; his ancestry is French Huguenot and Holland Dutch. His mother was born January 7, 1850, and died at Lake Worth, Florida, August 22, 1928.

Rev. Frazell attended the rural school of Dundy County, Nebraska, was graduated from the academy at Franklin, Nebraska, in 1914, and later attended Wesleyan University. He served as a rural school teacher for two years, was a mail carrier for the United States Government for three years, and for the past seven years has served as priest in charge of the Ewing Mission Field of the protestant Episcopal Church at Ewing, Nebraska.

He has served as a member of the Ewing Board of Education since 1926, acting as secretary, is a member of the local board of the Red Cross, and holds membership in the local Lions Club. His hobby is mechanics. During the World War Rev. Frazell was a private in Ambulance Company 354, 89th Division of the United States Army, serving in engagements at St. Mihiel and Argonne.

His marriage to Marietta Maxwell Purcell was solemnized at Broken Bow, Nebraska, June 1, 1920. Mrs. Frazell, who was formerly a practising registered nurse, was born of Irish parentage at Broken Bow, May 4, 1896. They have four children: Frances Lucilla, born January 4, 1922; Theodore Mason, born October 2, 1923; Jennie Margaret, born August 13, 1925; and Carolyn Mary, born March 16, 1928. Residence: Ewing.

Louis Wood Frazier

A resident of Nebraska for the past 61 years, Louis Wood Frazier was born at Martins Ferry, Ohio, December 2, 1869, the son of Joseph and Talitha (Spence) Frazier. His father, who was a newspaper editor, was born at Mt. Pleasant, Ohio, June 11, 1826, and died at Fairmont, Nebraska, August 13, 1891. He served as lieutenant in Company G, 15th Ohio Volunteer Infantry during the Civil War; his ancestry was Scotch.

Talitha (Spence) Frazier, mother of Louis Frazier, was a homemaker and a talented artist. She was born in Harrison County, Ohio, December 1, 1837, of Irish parentage, and died at Fairmont, Nebraska, January 28, 1903.

Mr. Frazier has been editor and publisher of the *Fillmore Chronicle* since July 1, 1885, and has been active in civic affairs at Fairmont during that period. He is a member of the Nebraska State Historical Society, the Nebraskana Society, and the district, state, and national press associations. A charter member of the Fairmont Commercial Club, he has always been interested in the progress of his community. He is a Scottish Rite Mason, and Shriner.

An independent Republican, Mr. Frazier served as state printer of Nebraska from 1903 to 1909, and was postmaster at Fairmont, from 1909 to 1913. He married Anna Shoff at Grafton, Nebraska, April 7, 1902. Mrs. Frazier, who is a newspaper reporter, was born of German and English parentage at Mt. Pleasant, Iowa, November 30, 1867. Their son, Donald, who was born July 20, 1903, married Ethel Brown. He is an electrician and builder of federal airways and landing fields, and is a construction engineer. Residence: Fairmont.

Carleton Earl Freas

For the past 45 years Carleton Earl Freas has been engaged in the general merchandise business at Beaver City, Nebraska. He was born at Ringgold, Pennsylvania, March 22, 1869, the son of Jacob Hubert and Maggie Angeline (Sprankle) Freas. His father, who was a farmer and homesteader in Furnas County, Nebraska, in 1875, was born at Ringgold in 1839 and died at Beaver City, November 6, 1878. His mother, a teacher in Pennsylvania and a pioneer homemaker in Nebraska, was born at Grange, Pennsylvania, May 6, 1840, and died at Beaver City, October 12, 1926.

Mr. Freas is a member of the Beaver City Community Club, the Red Cross, The Nebraskana Society, the Masons, and the Rotary Club of which he was president in 1927. He is affiliated with the Methodist Episcopal Church at Beaver City. During the World War he was food control committeeman in Furnas County. He is a Republican.

On February 4, 1901, he was married at Beaver City to Rosetta Alexander. Mrs. Freas was born at Bennett, Nebraska, August 30, 1874. They have three children: Harold, born December 6, 1901, who married Bernice Louise Simmons; Mildred, born August 20, 1904, who married Claude E. Berreckman; and Carleton Earl, Jr., born May 16, 1906. Harold and Carleton are merchants. Mildred's husband is a retail merchandise manager located at Gothenburg. Residence: Beaver City.

Virgil Sprankle Freas

A resident of Nebraska for the past 57 years, Virgil Sprankle Freas in the son of Jacob H. and Angeline Maggie (Sprankle) Freas. He was born at Ringgold, Pennsylvania, September 9, 1867, and for many years has been a successful merchant at Beaver City, Nebraska. His father, who was a farmer and served as captain of the 105th Pennsylvania Infantry during the Civil War, was born at Ringgold, April 21, 1839, and died at Beaver City, November 6, 1878. His mother was born at Hamilton,

Pennsylvania, May 6, 1839, and died at Beaver City, October 11, 1926.

Mr. Freas received his education in the public schools of Beaver City, and for the past 45 years has been engaged in the merchandise business at Beaver City. He holds membership in the Odd Fellows Lodge and was noble grand of the order in 1920, in the Rotary Club was sergeant of arms since 1928, and the Red Cross, being a life member. His political affiliation is with the Republican party.

He was united in marriage with Jeanette Wainwright, at Beaver City, January 22, 1896. Mrs. Freas was born at Adrian, Michigan, March 1, 1867. They have one daughter, Dorothy Lucile, born October 26, 1900, who married Arthur Hubbard at Beaver City, on June 26, 1919. To them were born three children, Jeanette, April 13, 1920; Phyllis, August 21, 1921; and Marion, October 12, 1925. Residence: Beaver City. (Photograph in Album).

John William Frederick

A distinguished banker of Callaway, Nebraska, is John William Frederick who is a lifelong resident of this state. He was born at Gothenburg, Nebraska, September 25, 1885, the son of John George and Amanda Elizabeth (Sellars) Frederick. His father, who is a banker, was born at Falls City, Nebraska, of French and German parents, and is still living at Callaway. His mother, who was a teacher prior to her marriage, was born at Falls City, August 1, 1864.

Mr. Frederick was graduated from the Callaway High School in 1902, and the following year studied at Boyles Business College. He was bookkeeper for various business firms, was a clerk in a grocery store, bought livestock for a time, and in 1906 entered the banking business. He has been cashier of the Farmers State Bank of Callaway for 25 years.

He is treasurer of the Chamber of Commerce, is treasurer of the Rotary Club and the Callaway School Board, and holds membership in the Elks, Modern Woodmen of America, and the Royal Highlanders. He is a member of the Consistory and Shrine bodies of the Masons and the Independent Order of Odd Fellows. His social club is the local golf club, and his favorite sports are fishing, hunting and baseball.

His marriage to Olive Ellen Pershall was solemnized at Broken Bow, Nebraska, May 10, 1909. Mrs. Frederick, whose ancestry is Welsh, was born at Hillsdale, Iowa, March 19, 1881. Residence: Callaway.

John Earl Freeland

One of the leading business men at Axtell, Nebraska, is John Earl Freeland, who was born there, February 15, 1900, and is now a successful furniture dealer and undertaker there. His father, John Swan Freeland, was engaged in the furniture and undertaking business at Axtell for over 40 years; he was born in Sweden, March 5, 1855, and died at Axtell, May 8, 1930, after a resident of nearly 50 years in that community. His mother, Esther Opetele (Pearson) Freeland, was born at Galesburg, Illinois, December 21, 1869.

Mr. Freeland was graduated from the high school at Minden, Nebraska, in 1918. He was engaged in business with his father until 1930, and is now operating the establishment independently at Axtell, where he is a director in the community band. He is affiliated with the First Presbyterian Church of Axtell, is a member of the Nebraska Funeral Directors Association, and holds membership in the Modern Woodmen of America. He is a member of the Shrine and Scottish Rite bodies of the Masons, and holds membership in the Republican party.

He was united in marriage with Elsie Signild Braum Peterson at Axtell, April 17, 1924. Mrs. Freeland was born at New York City, June 10, 1901. Residence: Axtell.

Truman Freeland

Born at Rock Island, Illinois, February 22, 1852, Truman Freeland, pioneer Nebraskan, has resided in Garfield County for the past sixty years.

His father, William Calvin Freeland, was a native of Kentucky, born January 19, 1825, a farmer and mechanic. He died in Texas County, Missouri, in 1914. His mother, born in Indiana, April 9, 1825, died in Garfield County, Nebraska, in October, 1909. Her maiden name was Mary A. Cox.

Truman Freeland came to Nebraska, in 1870, settling two years later in Garfield County, where he built the first frame house. He was the second settler, the first, Charlie Jones, having preceded him by ten days. His nearest neighbor, Marion Littlefield, was killed by Indians near the Freeland home.

Mr. Freeland assisted in the original survey of Custer and Loup Counties in the early 1870's, and helped build the first bridge across the Platte River in Nebraska. On February 3, 1874, he was married to Almira Jane Russel at Rock Island, Illinois. She was born in Vermont, June 19, 1832 and died in Garfield County in October, 1905. There are two children of his second marriage, which occurred December 31, 1908; Elmer Calvin, born November 2, 1909, who was graduated from Burwell High School; and Jesse A., born April 29, 1912, who passed the eighth grade in district school.

The author of many articles for newspapers and magazines in Nebraska and elsewhere, Mr. Freeland's book of poems *My Thoughts*, published in 1912, is very beautiful. He has also written a history of Garfield County, which he has not yet published. He is a believer in the Golden Rule. He is a member of The Nebraskana Society and the Old Settlers' Association of Garfield County. Residence: Burwell.

Robert Miller Freeman

Born at Rural Retreat, Virginia, February 24, 1886, Robert M. Freeman is the owner of a truckline business in Nickerson, Nebraska. His father, Albert David Freeman, a retired farmer, was born at Rural Retreat, Virginia, May 31, 1859, as was his wife, Zobedia (Miller) Freeman, on January 21, 1860.

Mr. Freeman attended grade school and on January 20, 1909, at Groseclose, Virginia, married Beulah Elizabeth Dutton, a school teacher. Mrs. Freeman was also born at Rural Retreat, April 11, 1885.

Mr. and Mrs. Freeman have two children: Garland Lozerne, born July 31, 1911, and Lloyd David, born August 27, 1914.

Always active in civic progress, Robert M. Freeman has been serving on the school board at Nickerson, Nebraska, since 1926, and on the town board since 1924. He was a member of the Red Cross during the years 1916 to 1918, and is now a member of the Ancient Order of United Workmen and the Odd Fellows. Mr. Freeman is affiliated with the Nickerson Methodist Church. He has been a resident of this state for twenty-two years and is a Democrat. Residence: Nickerson.

William Freidell

William Freidell, a Nebraska pioneer merchant of half a century, is the son of Frederick and Anna M. (Kramer) Freidell. The father, born in Heimbrum, Hesse-Darmstadt, Germany, July 6, 1812, settled in Dansville, New York, where William Freidell was born June 7, 1858.

In 1879, lured by the exciting stories of the opportunities of the golden west, he came to Nebraska, and secured his first job with the firm of Stein & Kramer, of Kearney. Kearney at that time was the junction of the Burlington Railroad. The country was made up mostly of Swedes, and ranchers would drive from 25 to 200 miles to do their shopping. Because of the distance, many of them driving teams of oxen, trips would be made about twice a year, and would often take from three to five days.

The change from New York State to Nebraska was very great, and Mr. Freidell received his first thrill when he joined Dr. C. D. Dildine, who drove a horse and buggy from Kearney to three miles southeast of Minden, to see a sick child. A heavy snow fell in the afternoon and the trails and roads became so covered that they were obliged to spend the night in a sod house.

In 1880, the boom was on in the Republican Valley, and William Freidell opened a branch store for his firm in Bloomington. The following year he was transferred to Republican City, and remained there until the crops were destroyed by hot winds. The stock was moved to Sutton, Nebraska, and there he managed the store until the firm sold out, when he accepted a position with the firm of C. Armstrong of Sutton.

Mr. Freidell, having confidence in Nebraska, opened a business for himself at Dorchester, in 1883, and has resided there ever since. From that year until 1892, the firm was William Freidell & Company, Wolf & Baltzley, of Crete, being the other members of the firm. In 1892 Mr. Freidell took over the business, and a year later took in W. P. Hanley as a partner. Thus the business was operated until 1896, when the big fire destroyed most of the business section of Dorchester. This caused a heavy loss to Mr. Freidell, and in the fall of 1896 he started at the bottom of the ladder again with borrowed money. He has steadily progressed during all these years, and after fifty-nine years of continuous retail experience, is cited as one of the oldest pioneer merchants operating in Nebraska.

He is able to recall the period in the nineties when farmers sold eggs at three cents a dozen and merchants didn't want them at that price; and remembers when corn on the ear sold at eight cents a bushel, and farmers used it for fuel rather than buy coal.

During the forty-nine years of his residence in Dorchester, he has always been classed as a Democrat, yet he has stepped from the ranks when he saw better men on the other ticket. He has served fifteen years on the city council and twenty-five on the board of education, sixteen of which were as its secretary. In 1890, he was a vital figure in the building of the new brick high school at a cost of $10,000.

Mr. Freidell is a member of the Methodist Church, and a Mason. He served as master of Doric Lodge No. 118, Ancient Free and Accepted Masons, for many years, was secretary five years and delegate to grand lodge many times. He is a member of the Order of Eastern Star and was recently made a life member of The Nebraskana Society.

On December 7, 1884, Mr. Freidell was married to Ida Egolf, daughter of Jeremiah Egolf, a pioneer settler of Saline County. Mrs. Freidell lived in a sod house near the present town of Dorchester, when she came from Indiana in a covered wagon. She died on January 7, 1928.

To this union five children were born, two of whom died in childhood. The three remaining are: W. Russell Freidell, who has active charge of his father's business at Dorchester; Dr. Hugh F. Freidell, a prominent physician of Santa Barbara, California; and Mrs. Rhea (Freidell) Schultz of Omaha. Residence: Dorchester. (Photograph in Album).

W. Russell Freidell

W. Russell Freidell, World War veteran, Sunday School worker and Nebraska merchant, is the son of William and Ida Freidell of Dorchester, Nebraska.

His father, born in Dansville, New York, June 7, 1858, came to Nebraska in 1879, and is one of the oldest pioneer merchants still operating in Nebraska (see Nebraskana). His mother, born in Columbia City, Indiana, September 7, 1863, died at Dorchester, on January 7, 1928. She was the daughter of pioneer settlers who came from Indiana, in a covered wagon.

W. Russell Freidell was born in Dorchester, February 3, 1890, and most of his business experience has been in association with his father in the mercantile business. He received his education in the Dorchester public schools, graduating in 1907, and later attended the University of Nebraska. When but a young man he became very active in Sunday School work, and in 1910 was elected secretary and treasurer of the Saline County Sunday School Association. He served in that office three years and was then elected president.

During that period, for the first time in thirty-seven years he brought Saline County to the very top of the list of star counties in the state and took first awards given each year for the statistical report drives. He also published the History of Saline County Sunday School Work, which dated to May 26, 1874, and placed it in the hands of every Sunday School worker in Saline County.

In October, 1915, he opened a general merchandise store of his own at Arapahoe, Nebraska, operating it until the outbreak of the World War, when he sold his business and returned to Dorchester.

On December 4, 1917, he enlisted as a first class private in the Quartermaster Corps of the Regular Army, at Fort Omaha. He was ordered to Camp Joseph E. Johnson at Jacksonville, Florida, on December 24, 1917, where, together with fourteen other Quartermaster men he was sent to Camp Park Field at Millington, Tennessee, to take charge of the Quartermaster warehouse on that flying field. This detachment remained there during the rest of the war. During that time Mr. Freidell was advanced to the rank of sergeant, and had charge of all class A property on the field. In August, 1918, he escaped possible death when an airplane in which he was riding fell 2000 feet, landing in a tree. On April 3, 1919, special orders came to discharge Mr. Freidell, and after being sent to Camp Funston, Kansas, he was given his final discharge from the 1st Company 164th D. B. Brigade.

Since his return from the army he has managed his father's general merchandise store at Dorchester. He is unmarried. He is a member of August Post No. 264 of the American Legion at Dorchester; is a Master Mason, and past master of Doric Lodge No. 118, Ancient Free and Accepted Masons at Dorchester; he belongs to the Lincoln Consistory of 32nd degree Masons, and to Sesostris Temple of the Shrine. He is a member of the Eastern Star, and the Methodist Church. He is a member of the Shrine Country Club at Lincoln, and was recently made a life member of The Nebraskana Society. Residence, Dorchester. (Photograph in Album).

Calvin Hervey French

Clergyman and educator, Calvin Hervey French, was born at Williamsburg, Clermont County, Ohio, June 13, 1862. He is the son of Charles Porter and Mary Jane (Brown) French. His father, who was born at Lindley's Mills, in Washington County, Pennsylvania, 1828, and died at Grand Ridge, in La Salle County, Illinois, 1870, also was a clergyman. He was descended from a Scotch great grandfather who came to America from Glasgow prior to the Revolutionary War and settled in Germantown, Philadelphia; with one son he participated in that war.

Mary Jane French, his mother, was born at Triadelphia, Ohio County, West Virginia, in 1830, and died at Huron, South Dakota, in 1910. She was the great-grand-daughter of William Brown who held a record as soldier in the Revolutionary War.

Dr. French has been awarded the following degrees: A. B., Lake Forest College, Illinois, 1888; A. M., 1891; D. D., Wooster College, Ohio, 1904; LL. D., Huron College, South Dakota, 1913; D. D., Lake Forest College, Illinois, 1928. Dr. French received the degree of Doctor of Divinity from Lake Forest College on the 40th anniversary of his graduation from that institution.

He was married to Anna Elizabeth Long at College Springs, Iowa, in July, 1897. Mrs. French, who was

CALVIN HERVEY FRENCH

born at College Springs, November 27, 1869, is of Scotch-Irish descent. There are three children: Robert Calvin, born January 13, 1899, an oil chemist; Ralph Voorhees, June 22, 1903, a banker in the far east; and Charles Louis, September 18, 1907, who is in business.

Dr. French has held various positions in educational and religious fields. He was pastor of the Presbyterian Church, Scotland, South Dakota, from 1891-1898; president of Huron College, 1898-1913; associate secretary of the Presbyterian College board, New York, 1913-17; president of Rollins College, Florida, 1917-19. Since 1920 he has been president of Hastings College.

Dr. French is a member of the Presbyterian Church, the Hastings Presbytery, and the Y. M. C. A. Aside from his religious affiliations he is active in the Red Cross, Rotary Club and the Hastings Chamber of Commerce, the Union League Club, Chicago, and the Town Hall Club of New York. His chief outdoor activity is golf. He resides at Hastings. (Photograph on Page 431).

John Alexis French

John Alexis French, a resident of this state practically all his life, was born at Edison, Nebraska, July 8, 1876, the son of Ira and Martha Melvina (Wells) French. His father, who was a farmer and carpenter, was born at Zionville, Indiana, October 16, 1848, and died at Edison, Nebraska, April 12, 1922; he was county commissioner in Furnas County from 1900 to 1906, where he homesteaded in 1873, one mile south and three miles west of Edison. His mother was born in Indiana, September 3, 1853, and died at Edison, February 14, 1893.

Mr. French engaged in the grain business at Edison, was with the Minden Grain Company for a year, was connected with the Updike Grain Company for six years at Edison, and for the past 20 years has been manager of the Farmers' Co-operative Grain Association there. He is a member of the Christian Church and of its official board, the Modern Woodmen of America and posses a certifi- Modern Woodmen of America and possesses a certificate of efficiency issued by the association in 1905, and signed by the head clerk, C. W. Hawes, testifying as to his efficient handling of all matters as local clerk of Camp No. 9180 at Edison, which office he has held for 27 years. He has been a member of the Edison village board, and at various times has served on the school board in his community, and was chairman of the board and its treasurer for one year. His hobby is reading.

On April 7, 1894, he married Kate Ostrom at Elwood, Nebraska. Mrs. French, whose ancestry is Pennsylvania Dutch and English, was born at Christy, Wisconsin, June 11, 1878, and is particularly active in church work and a member of the Farm Bureau Club. They are residing in the home built by Mr. French in 1906, a period of 26 years. Five children were born to this marriage, Freda Malvina, March 21, 1896, who married Hal H. Harlan, at Kearney, Nebraska, in 1917; Dale Alexis, born August 27, 1900, who married Jane Learned on August 27, 1921, at Holdrege, Nebraska; Mae Belle, born December 21, 1904, who married James T. Pierce on December 24, 1930, at Norton, Kansas; Bonnie Avery, born February 6, 1908, and at present is superintendent of schools at Loomis, Nebraska; and Lois, born August 16, 1910, who died September 20, 1916. Mr. French is affiliated with the Republican party. Residence: Edison. (Photograph in Album).

Latta Snider Frew

Latta S. Frew was born at Hastings, Nebraska, October 25, 1888, the daughter of John and Adda (Latta) Snider. Her father, who was born at Alden, Iowa, 1860, has been a lawyer at Hastings for many years and has served as county attorney and county judge of Adams County. His ancestry is German. Her mother, who was born in Iowa, in 1861, taught in the public schools at Hastings, for 10 years after her marriage and later served as deputy in her husband's office; she is of Scotch-Irish descent.

Mrs. Frew was graduated from the Hastings High School in 1906; received her A. B. from Nebraska Wesleyan University; and in 1912 was graduated from the music department of that institution. During her college days she was active in the Young Women's Christian Association, and was elected to membership in the Orophilian Society. She was granted her A. M. degree in English at Columbia University, 1919 German and music instructor in the high school at Humboldt, Nebraska, 1912-13, she held this position in the Hastings High School from 1913 to 1918.

In 1930 she taught in the Illinois Women's College at Jacksonville, Illinois; received the B. S. degree in library science at the University of Seattle, Washington, 1921; and was assistant in the Seattle Public Library in the circulation department for a year. She has lived in Nebraska practically all her life.

On June 8, 1922, she was married to Thomas A. Frew, near Seattle. She is a member of the Dorchester Methodist Episcopal Church, and the Women's Foreign Missionary Society. She holds membership in the Nebraskana Society and the Literary Guild Club. Her hobbies are reading and music. She is a Democrat. Residence: Dorchester.

Thomas A. Frew

On February 21, 1883, Thomas A. Frew was born at Crete, Nebraska, the son of John and Sarah (Booth) Frew. His father was born at Kilsyth, County Storlingshire, Scotland, September 12, 1841, came to America in the early 1870's and was a farmer at Dorchester, for many years. He died at Dorchester, November 26, 1921. His wife was born at Yorkshire, England, in 1855, and died in Saline County, June 6, 1908.

Mr. Frew, who has farmed in Nebraska for over 30 years, attended the district school near Crete. He is a member of the local school board, and holds membership in the Nebraskana Society and the Dorchester Methodist Church.

He married Willa B. Melvin at Fremont, Nebraska, December 27, 1916. She was principal of the Dorchester public schools before her marriage, and was born at Princeton, Missouri, July 25, 1880, and died at Crete, July 6, 1921. One child was born to this union, Elsie Elisabeth, born March 3, 1919. Mr. Frew was united in marriage with Latta Snider, June 8, 1922. They have four children: Helen Louise, born March 12, 1923; John Snider, born September 26, 1925; Latta Katherine, born June 15, 1927; and Dorothy Dunn, born May 3, 1929. Residence: Dorchester.

Clarence Elmer Frey

Clarence E. Frey was born at Lincoln, Nebraska, November 14, 1889, the son of Clarence Hayes Frey and Clara Ann (Sidles) Frey. His father, who was born at Carlisle, Pennsylvania, July 27, 1865, was a pioneer florist in Lincoln, where he founded the firm of Frey and Frey. This florist establishment was Lincoln's largest retail and wholesale business. He is now retired. H. H. Frey, father of Clarence H. Frey was a florist of Dutch descent; his mother, who was English, was a teacher.

Dr. Frey's mother was born in Stevenson County, Illinois, November 20, 1864. She was the daughter of Charles Sidles, a Civil War veteran, and Sarah Lowery Sidles. Now an invalid she has been very active in Methodist church work.

Dr. Frey attended the Lincoln grade schools, the normal high school and Nebraska Wesleyan Academy. He was a student at Nebraska Wesleyan University, and the College of Pharmacy of the University of Nebraska, and in 1919 was granted his M. D. at the Eclectic Medical College at Cincinnati, Ohio. He was president of Franklin Literary Society at Wesleyan University.

After serving as interne at the Christ Hospital at Cincinnati for two years, Dr. Frey was resident physician at St. Elizabeth's hospital at Lincoln for one year. He is now engaged in private medical practice and is a member of the staff at St. Elizabeth's Hospital. He is the author of numerous medical articles and a book, *Shep,* a child's story of a dog, published in 1899.

He was married to Julia Elizabeth Van Pamele at Omaha, Douglas County, Nebraska, January 23, 1913. Mrs. Frey, who was born at Patterson, New Jersey, May 12, 1892, is a descendent of the house of Noe of the Belgian nobility. They have one son: Clarence Van Pamele, born March 2, 1914, who is a student at Lincoln High School; he has written some promising poetry which has been published.

Dr. Frey is a member of the Lancaster County Medical Society, the Nebraska State Medical Society, American Medical Association, Elkhorn Valley Medical Society, International Post-graduate Medical Society, and the Missouri Valley Medical Association. He is a member of the National Geographic Society and the American Association for the Advancement of Science, the Lincoln Chamber of Commerce, the Red Cross, and the Anti-Saloon League of Nebraska. He is a Mason, member of Ben Hur, and the Yeoman. His hobbies are the study of philosophy, psychology, and bee-keeping. Residence: Lincoln.

John Joseph Freymann

John J. Freymann, educator and physician at Omaha, was born at LeMars, Plymouth County, Iowa, December 13, 1889. His father, Nicholas Freymann, who was a grain merchant, was born in Jackson County, Iowa, February 22, 1854, and died at LeMars, August 28, 1920. His parents came from the Grand Duchy of Luxemburg, to America. Elizabeth (Wentink) Freymann, his mother, was born at Port Washington, Wisconsin, and died at LeMars, November 19, 1891. Her anceestors came from Holland.

Dr. Freymann attended school at St. Catherine's School, Oyens, Iowa, 1905; Campion High School; and Prairie du Chien High School, from which he was graduated in 1908. He was graduated from Marquette University with the degree A. B., 1911; A. M., 1913. He received his M. D. at Creighton University in 1917. He was a member of Phi Rho Sigma, medical fraternity. He was admitted to the practice of medicine in Douglas County, November 19, 1919, and has been prominent in educational and medical work since that date.

During 1917-18-19, he was medical officer in the United States Navy. Now lieutenant commander in the Medical Corps of the United States Naval Reserve he is medical officer of the 43rd Fleet Reserve Division stationed at Omaha. He is a member of the Douglas County Medical Society; the Nebraska State Medical Society; the Interstate Post Graduate Medical Society; and the American Medical Association. He is a member of the faculty at Creighton University Medical School, and holds membership in the Nebraskana Society, the National Geographic Society, and the Omaha Executives Association. His social club is the Omaha Athletic Club. He is a Democrat.

On May 31, 1919, he was united in marriage with Marion Wicks at Philadelphia. Mrs. Freymann was born at Los Angeles, California. Four children were born to this union: Moxley Sorrel, born January 13, 1921, who died June 4, 1921; John Gordon, born April 9, 1922; Moye Nicholas, born September 2, 1925; and Jarvis, born February 28, 1927. Residence: Omaha.

Charles B. Fricke

Born at Madison, Nebraska, January 6, 1884, Charles B. Fricke is the son of Herman and Johanna (Ruegge) Fricke. His father, a farmer and implement dealer, was born in Hanover, Germany, April 17, 1843, and died at Omaha, May 20, 1931. His wife, Johanna, was born in Hanover, May 20, 1850, and died at Omaha August 30, 1932.

Charles B. Fricke was graduated from Madison High School in 1904, and received the degree of Doctor of Pharmacy from the Philadelphia College of Pharmacy in 1906. From that time until 1911 he was instructor at the Creighton College of Pharmacy, and since then has been in business at Council Bluffs, Iowa, and Columbus, Nebraska.

Mr. Fricke is vice president of the First Investment Company, and vice president of the Equitable Building and Loan Association at Columbus. Active in civic and community affairs, he has been president of the Columbus Credit Bureau (1927), president of the Lions Club (1927), president of the Young Men's Christian Association (1930) and master of the Columbus Lodge of the Ancient Free and Accepted Masons (1929). He is affiliated with the Federated Church, is a member of The Nebraskana Society and the Wayside Country Club. He enjoys fishing and golf.

On June 1913 Mr. Fricke was married to Laura May Smith at Council Bluffs. She was born at Stratford, Ontario, February 14, 1892, the daughter of Robert H. and Ellen M. Smith. There are three children, Jean, born August 30, 1920; Doris, born June 13, 1927; and Mary, born August 30, 1931. Residence: Columbus.

Henry Friday

Henry Friday, one of the earliest settlers of Pierce County, Nebraska, was born at Bielefeld, Germany, April 20, 1858, and for the past 50 years has engaged in contracting and building near Osmond, Nebraska. He is the son of Christian Friday and Florentine Friday, the former a paper manufacturer who was born at Bielefeld. His mother was a native of Bielefeld, and died there in 1880.

Mr. Friday was graduated from the public school at at Bielefeld, Germany, and since then has engaged in contracting and building near there. He is connected with the Farmers Lumber Yard, the Farmers Elevator Company, and is a member of the First Presbyterian Church of Osmond. He has been a Mason for the past 30 years.

Upon his arrival in this country Mr. Friday settled first in Illinois, coming to Nebraska two years later where he homesteaded in Holt County. He was married at Davenport, Iowa, January 24, 1910, to Anna Wichmann, who was born at Round Grove, Iowa, November 25, 1872. They have a daughter, Dorothy E., born April 6, 1914. Residence: Osmond.

Ernest Leslie Fried

Ernest L. Fried, who has lived in this state all his life, was born at Fremont, Nebraska, September 10, 1873, the son of Carl August and Mary Anna (Gustofson) Fried. His father, who was born in Sweden, and died at Omaha, August 16, 1887, was for many years manager and buyer for Lee, Fried & Company, a firm which he organized in 1880. His mother was born in Sweden and died at Omaha, December 1, 1916.

Mr. Fried attended the Izard and Lake schools at Omaha, and for two years was a student at the Omaha High School. From 1891 to 1895 he was a clerk for the company, Lobeck & Linn, at Omaha; was stock keeper and salesman for W. J. Broatch, 1895-99; acted as salesman and buyer for the James Morton & Son Company at Omaha, 1900 to 1913; and since 1913 has owned and operated a hardware store at Beemer, Cuming County, Nebraska.

A Republican, he has held the following public offices:

village treasurer, 1914-15; member of the cemetery board, 1921-2-3; member of the park board, 1922-3-4; member of the town board, 1917-18, 1925-31; and chairman of the town board, 1918, 1928-31. He served as secretary of the Beemer School Board from November 2, 1920, to June 9, 1924; was chairman of the Beemer Community Club, 1930-31; and is a member of the Nebraska Retail Hardware Dealers Association.

Mr. Fried is a member of the Lions Club; the Beemer Red Cross; and the Nebraskana Society. He holds membership in and is past master of Beemer Lodge Number 253 of the Ancient Free and Accepted Masons; a member of Nebraska Lodge Number 1, at Omaha; a Shriner, and member of Tangier Temple, at Omaha. He likes to fish, while his hobby is philately. During the World War he served as a member of the home guards and served on the committee for Red Cross collections.

His marriage to Elizabeth Craddock was solemnized at Omaha, September 4, 1901. Mrs. Fried was born at Nebraska City, Otoe County, Nebraska, August 3, 1872, and died at Beemer, March 20 1919. They have a son, Rolland, born March 7, 1907, who is in charge of electrical and radio work in his father's store. He married Herta Iden on November 23, 1930. Rolland was graduated from Beemer High School and attended Wayne College one year. Residence: Beemer. (Photograph in Album).

Matt Friend

Born at Johnsburgh, Illinois, June 30, 1870, the son of Joseph and Anna (Wagner) Friend, Matt Friend has lived in Nebraska for the past 52 years. His father, who was a building contractor and furniture dealer, was born in Germany, March 7, 1829, and died at Lawrence, Nebraska, August 25, 1893. His mother was born in Germany, April 1, 1828, and died at Lawrence, March 24, 1899.

Mr. Friend was employed on a cattle ranch for five years, was clerk in a bank for four years, and for over 20 years was a contractor and builder. He has been engaged in the hardware and furniture business at Lawrence for the past 20 years.

He married Kathrene Wiebeler at Lawrence, February 6, 1894; she was born at Fort Madison, Iowa, of German parentage. Nine children were born to them, all of whom are living: G. S., born June 7, 1895; I. J., March 7, 1900; May, March 7, 1902; Eileen, May 6, 1904; Frank J., December 17, 1905; Pat J., March 17, 1909; Anna E., November 26, 1907; Virginia, January 4, 1911; and Matt C., July 7, 1917.

Mr. Friend is a member of the Booster Club, is affiliated with Sacred Heart Catholic Church, and holds membership in the Knights of Columbus. He served as secretary of the local school board in 1921 and at this time he is acting as treasurer of that organization. He has been a member of the Modern Woodmen of America since 1896; from 1917 to 1918, he was chairman of the Red Cross at Lawrence. His favorite sport is golfing. Residence: Lawrence.

Charles Augustus Fries

Charles A. Fries, a resident of Nebraska for the past 53 years, was born at Omaha, Nebraska, July 26, 1877, the son of Johanna (Thoelecke) and Gustave A. Fries.

Mr. Fries, who is a merchant, deals in draperies and interior decorations, and established his business at Omaha, May 1, 1916. He is a member of Company L., First membership in the Omaha Chamber of Commerce and the Nebraska Regiment of the Thurston Rifles. He holds Community Chest; is past president of the Triangle Club; and is a director of the Executive Association.

He is a 32nd degree Scottish Rite Mason, Shriner, and member of the Royal Order of Jesters and Shrine Patrol. He is affiliated with the Kountze Memorial Lutheran Church.

His marriage to Minnie Sorenson was solemnized at Cheyenne, Wyoming, January 27, 1904. Mrs. Fries was born at North Platte, Nebraska. Their two children are: Alan Willis, born March 10, 1905; and Charles Jr., born August 21, 1910. Residence: Omaha.

Albert Henry Friesen

Born at Jansen, Jefferson County, Nebraska, March 22, 1896, Albert Henry Friesen is the son of Henry A. and Maggie (Thiessen) Friesen. His father, who is a native of Germany, came to America about fifty-six years ago, and is a prominent merchant in Nebraska. His mother, who was born at Jansen, April 6, 1884, is the daughter of John P. Thiessen who served as state representative two years.

Mr. Friesen attended public school and shortly thereafter engaged as a clerk and hardware salesman. In 1917 he entered the automobile business for himself, and is now proprietor of the Jansen Auto Company. During the World War he served with the American Expeditionary Forces with the 116th Field Signal Battalion, 42nd Division.

On August 9, 1920, Mr. Friesen was married to Helen Brown at Lincoln. She was born at Henderson, Nebraska, September 4, 1899. Both Mr. and Mrs. Friesen are active in civic and cultural circles. He is a Mason and a member of the Business Men's Club, the Red Cross and The Nebraskana Society; while his hobbies are mechanics and reading. Residence: Jansen.

Frank Lee Frink

Born at Clarence, Iowa, September 25, 1865, Frank Lee Frink is the son of E. P. and Eliza (Root) Frink. His father, who was a carpenter, was born at Buffalo, New York, in 1837, and died at Wisner, Nebraska, in June, 1884; his ancestry was English. His mother, whose ancestry is English, was born at Erie, New York, and died at Clarence, in 1881.

Dr. Frink was graduated from the Clarence High School and received his medical education at the University of Louisville in Kentucky where he was awarded a gold medal for scholastic attainment. He has been prominent as a physician and surgeon at Newman Grove, Nebraska, for the past 50 years and at this time is serving as mayor there.

He is chairman of the Old Settlers Association of Madison County, is chairman of the Red Cross, and holds membership in the state and county medical societies. He is a member of the Modern Woodmen of America and the Masons. During the World War Dr. Frink served as captain of the Medical Department, and at the same time is a member of the Medical Reserves and the American Legion. His favorite sport is big game hunting.

On October 6, 1887, his marriage to Ida Vestilla Person was solemnized at Fremont. Mrs. Frink, whose ancestry is Pennsylvania German; was born at Allentown, Pennsylvania, April 2, 1871. Three children were born to them: Amy B., born April 19, 1891; Bessie, April 23, 1893, who died in April, 1905; and Hazel A., July 29, 1895. Dr. Frink is a Republican and holds membership in The Nebraskana Society. Residence: Newman Grove.

Frank Samuel Frisbie

Frank Samuel Frisbie, who has been a resident of Nebraska for the past 56 years, was born at Grandview, Iowa, September 30, 1871, the son of Ichobod and Hannah Tompkins (Patmor) Frisbie. His father, who was a pioneer miller in Nebraska, and built the first mill west of Blue Springs, in 1874, (this being the first mill on the Republican River in Nebraska), was born at Southington, Connecticut, December 8, 1835, and died at Red Cloud, Nebraska, August 24, 1918; he was a veteran of the Civil War, having served as hospital steward in the 35th Iowa Regiment.

Ichobod Culpepper Frisbie, grandfather of Ichobod Frisbie, served in the 6th Brigade of the Farmington Regiment during the Revolution, and the father of Ichobod Frisbie died as a prisoner of war at Marlinico, West Indies, in 1766. Hannah Tompkins (Patmor) Frisbie, was born in Ohio, March 27, 1837, and died at Red Cloud, Nebraska, May 12, 1884.

Mr. Frisbie attended rural school and attended the high school at Red Cloud, Nebraska. He is secretary-treasurer of the Amboy Milling & Elevator Company at Red Cloud, where he has been a farmer and livestock raiser for many years, and is director of the local school board there. He is affiliated with the Methodist Church, in which he is a steward, and holds membership in the Nebraska Historical Society and the Nebraskana Society. He is a director of the Farm Bureau, and secretary-treasurer of the Amboy Telephone Company. He has always been a Republican, and has served as county committeeman.

On June 16, 1895, he was married at Red Cloud, to Lora E. McBride, who was born at Winterset, Iowa, April 27, 1868; Mrs. Frisbie, who was a teacher prior to her marriage, is the daughter of pioneer homesteaders in Nebraska.

They have one daughter, Josephine, born June 26, 1903, who was graduated from the University of Nebraska, in 1927. She was president of the Mortar Board, served as president of Vestals of the Lamp, was chosen as May Queen in 1927, and held membership in the Classical Club and the Young Women's Christian Association, serving as a member of the staff of the latter organization. She received her Masters degree at the university in 1928, and at this time is instructor in English and Latin at Norfolk Junior College. In 1931, she made a European tour. Residence: Red Cloud.

Sylvester William Frisbie

Born at Grand View, Iowa, November 2, 1873, Sylvester William Frisbie is the son of Ichobod and Hannah (Patmor) Frisbie. His father, who was a miller and grain dealer, was born at Southington, Connecticut, December 8, 1835, and died at Red Cloud, Nebraska, August 18, 1918; he was a soldier in the 35th Iowa Regiment during the Civil War.

Mr. Frisbie was a teacher in his younger days, and for many years has been a mill owner and grain dealer at Red Cloud, in the same milling establishment his father organized in 1874. He is president of the Farmers Independent Telephone Company, is affiliated with the Methodist Episcopal Church at Red Cloud, and holds membership in the Blue Lodge, Royal Arch, and Knights Templar bodies of the Masons.

On February 12, 1903, his marriage to Mary Florence Beal occurred at Red Cloud. Mrs. Frisbie, who was a teacher prior to her marriage, was born at Monroe, Iowa, January 19, 1871. Her father, Isaiah Beal was a captain in the Union Army during the Civil War. They have two children: Howard L., born March 18, 1905; and Patricia Gertrude, born June 27, 1913. Howard will graduate in June from the University of Nebraska Medical School, and will interne in White Grady Hospital, Atlanta, Georgia. Patricia is a student at Doane College, Crete, Nebraska. Residence: Red Cloud.

George E. Fritzer

George E. Fritzer, who is a farmer and banker at Edison, Nebraska, is a lifelong resident of this state and for many years has been prominent in business affairs in his community. He was born in Furnas County, Nebraska, July 7, 1885, the son of Peter and Augusta Agnes (Hanks) Fritzer, the former a native of Luxemburg, Germany. His father, who was born June 21, 1844, served as a private in the 104th Ohio Infantry. His mother was born of German parents at Massilon, Ohio, March 19, 1845, and died in Furnas County, September 10, 1911.

Mr. Fritzer is president of the Farmers & Merchants Bank of Edison, and has been a farmer there all his life. He holds membership in the Republican party, and is affiliated with the Nebraskana Society. His favorite sport is baseball.

On June 23, 1925, he was married at Kansas City, Missouri, to Edna Lee Crist, who was born at Marion, Kansas, June 13, 1890. Mrs. Fritzer is of English and Dutch extraction. Residence: Edison.

Andrew Keyser Frolich

Andrew Keyser Frolich was born at Kristianssand, Norway, March 5, 1887. John Keyser Frolich, his father, was born at Oslo, Norway, February 8, 1858, and died at Kristianssand, November 13, 1927. He was an architect. His mother, Beate (Corneliussen) Frolich was born at Kristianssand, February 23, 1861. She is still living.

Mr. Frolich, who received his elementary education in Norway, was awarded a degree in the mechanical and electrical engineering department at Ilmenau, Germany. He served in the Norwegian regular army. In the early days of his career he was mechanical engineer in the company Rjukan Salper Fabrick, of Rjukan, Norway, 1910-13; he was superintendent of the firm Marriott & Seligman, of Libau, Russia, 1913-18 and was assistant superintendent of the Dalen Portland Cement Company of Brevik, Norway, 1918-24.

In 1924 Mr. Frolich arrived in America and became connected with the Ash Grove Lime and Portland Cement Company as draftsman, and later was their chief draftsman at Chanute, Kansas. In 1927 he was transferred to Louisville, Nebraska, where he was in charge of the designing and building of this company's new cement plant. He has been in this firm as superintendent since operation commenced in 1929.

Mr. Frolich was married at Kristianssand, Norway, March 1, 1919, to Louise Lysholm Selleg. Mrs. Frolich was born at Oslo, Norway, October 26, 1891. They have one child, Louise, Born March 12, 1920. He is a Republican and is a member of the Lutheran Church. Residence: Louisville. (Photograph on Page 436).

David From

David From was born in Mercer County, Pennsylvania, August 14, 1851, the son of Daniel and Mary (Flasher) From. Daniel From was born in Pennsylvania and died in Iowa, in May, 1880. He was a farmer and a soldier in the Civil War. His brother James From died in 1912, came to Butler County in 1871, and he came two years later. Mary From was born in Pennsylvania, and died in Butler County, Nebraska, June 23, 1884.

David From was united in marriage with Rosanna McKellips at Columbus, Nebraska, October 4, 1879. She was born in Hancock County, Illinois, January 2, 1861, and is a direct descendant of Charles Carrol. To them were born six children, Arthur, born August 31, 1880, who is married to Abbie Stafford; Moro, born September 20, 1881; Marie, born June 10, 1885, who is married to B. L. Story; Guy D., born December 20, 1891, who is married to Ferne Dollison; Wreatha, born September 15, 1893, who is married to Martin Stoddard; and Harold David, born April 7, 1900, who is married to Hazel Kilgore. He was a soldier in the World War.

A farmer in Nebraska for fifty-six years Mr. From is now retired. He is a Protestant and a member of the Nebraskana Society.

Guy D. From

Guy D. From, son of David and Rosanna (McKellips) From, was born in David City, Butler County, Nebraska, December 20, 1891. David From, a pioneer farmer, now retired, was born in Nuisser County, Pennsylvania,

Skoglund—Omaha

ANDREW KEYSER FROLICH

August 14, 1851. He is of German descent. His wife, Rosanna, was born in Hancock County, Illinois, January 2, 1861, a direct descendant of Charles Carroll, a signer of the Declaration of Independence.

Upon the completion of his elementary education, Guy D. From attended David City High School, from which he was graduated in 1912, and where he tied for second valedictory honors. In 1914, he completed his work at the School of Agriculture of the University of Nebraska.

His marriage to Ferne Adella Dolison was solemnized at Seward on August 6, 1916. Mrs. From was born in David City, September 13, 1895. They have three children, Floy Ferne, born September 29, 1917; Eleanor Rose, born November 20, 1920, and Marilyn Maxine, born December 10, 1924.

A resident of Nebraska since birth, Mr. From has always engaged in farming. He is a Republican, a member of the David City Methodist Church and the Nebraskana Society. He is particularly interested in music. Residence: David City.

Elbert James Frost

A farmer and stockman at Coleridge, Elbert James Frost was born at Merrill, Iowa, April 12, 1883. He is the son of William and Elizabeth (Stinton) Frost, the former a farmer and grain and livestock dealer, born at Wallington, Suffolk, England, February 15, 1845. He died at Merrill, October 13, 1908. His wife, Elizabeth, was born in England, March 22, 1847, daughter of William and Hannah Stinton.

Elbert James Frost attended public school, and came to Nebraska in 1911. Here he has engaged successfully in the operation of farms and as a stockraiser. He was married to Mable Sloan near Sioux City, Iowa, February 20, 1907. Mrs. Frost, who is the daughter of Thomas Oliver and Mary (Benton) Sloan, was born near Sioux City, June 3, 1886.

Mr. Frost is a Republican and takes an active interest in the work of his party. He is a Protestant and a member of the Red Cross. Recently he was awarded life membership in the Nebraskana Society, in appreciation of his efforts toward the advancement of his community and state. Residence: Coleridge.

Hubert Melvin A. Frost

Hubert Melvin A. Frost, lawyer and certified public accountant, was born at Uehling, Nebraska, August 2, 1891. His father, Andrew Frost, was born in Sweden, January 25, 1863, and was brought to America by his parents in 1865. A farmer and rancher, he is a former member of the Nebraska state legislature. He married Mary Victoria Anderson, who was born at Hooper, Nebraska, July 16, 1869, and who died at Uehling, April 21, 1928. She was of Swedish descent.

Mr. Frost was graduated from Fremont High School in 1909, and received his A. B. from the University of Nebraska in 1913. He was awarded an LL. B. from Creighton University in 1923 and an LL. M. from Columbia University in 1924. He was licensed to practice as a certified public accountant at Omaha, on May 1, 1922. His fraternities are Kappa Sigma, Delta Theta Phi and Alpha Chi Sigma.

On May 17, 1930, he was united in marriage with Ruby Vera Bruce at Uehling, Nebraska. Mrs. Frost was born at Mead, Nebraska, February 19, 1904, and is of Swedish descent.

Until 1924, Mr. Frost taught school and worked for accounting firms, and at that time opened an office in Omaha. He is a member of the firm of Frost and Frost, law and accounting offices, and is a director of the Nelson Ranching Company, Ltd. During the World War he was in the Chemical Warfare Service. He is a member of the American Legion, the American Institute of Accountants, the Nebraska State Bar Association and the Omaha-Douglas County Bar Association, and the Co-operative Club. A Scottish Rite Mason, he is a member of the Shrine and an Odd Fellow. His clubs are the Omaha Athletic Club and the University Club. He is fond of golf and reading. Residence: Omaha.

Lincoln Frost

Judge of the district court for the third judicial district of Nebraska intermittently since 1898, for a total period of seventeen years, Lincoln Frost is an outstanding figure in Nebraska. Born at Colesburg, Iowa, January 14, 1861, he has been a resident of Nebraska since 1868. His father, Lyman Frost, was born in New Hampshire, January 10, 1821, and when a young man came to Iowa, and later to Nebraska, operating saw mills in both states in the manufacture of lumber. He married Laura Augusta Gray, a native of New York, who died at Palo Alto, California, in 1899.

Lincoln Frost attended the Frost School which was in the second school district organized in Lancaster County, and later attended Lincoln High School for a period of seven months. In 1886 he received his A. B. at the University of Nebraska, and then spent a year in post graduate work at Johns Hopkins University. At the state university he was made a member of Phi Beta Kappa.

Prior to 1898 he was a member of the law firm of Sawyer, Snell and Frost; in December of that year he was made judge of the third judicial district and by subsequent elections served continuously until January 1912. He was appointed to fill the vacancy caused by the assination of Judge Morning for the term March 1924-January 1925, and was later elected for the term beginning January 1929 and is still serving as district judge under this election. From January 1925 until January 1929 he was secretary of the state department of Public Welfare.

Judge Frost was married to Jennie C. Bonnell at Lincoln on November 19, 1890. Mrs. Frost was born at Fort Madison, Iowa, February 14, 1869. She is a member of the Daughters of the American Revolution. She was graduated from the University of Nebraska in 1889 where she was made member of Phi Beta Kappa. Three children were born to this union, two of whom are living: Florence, born January 16, 1892, who married John E. Baird, died April 23, 1916; Harold B., born October 5, 1893, married Jeannette Butcher; and Lincoln, Jr., born January 14, 1907.

For many years Judge Frost has been vice president and a member of the board of directors of the Midwest Life Insurance Company. He has served as president of the Lincoln Social Service Club for ten years—its first president; and is president of the Lancaster County Humane Society, and president and director of the Society for the Friendless. During seven years of the time he has served as district judge he handled the work of the Juvenile Court.

He is a member of the American, Nebraska State and Lancaster County Bar Associations, the Red Cross, the National Probation Association, the National Conference of Social work, the National Child Labor Committee, the American Prison Association and the National Committee on Prisons and Prison Labor.

For the past thirty-five years he has been a member of the Lincoln Chamber of Commerce. He is a 32nd degree Mason and a Modern Woodmen and a member of the Y. M. C. A. Judge Frost enjoys golf, and his hobby is social service work. Residence: Lincoln.

Charles W. Fruit

Charles W. Fruit, county judge of Arthur County, was born in Sangamon County, Illinois, August 20, 1880, and has resided in Nebraska for the past 19 years. He is the son of James Thomas and Margurite (McDomial) Fruit. The father was born in Sangamon County in 1855, and died in Smith County, Kansas, November 21,

1919. He was a farmer. His wife, Margurite, was born in Sangamon County, October 24, 1845. She is still living.

Judge Fruit was graduated from public school in Smith County, and has been county judge for the past three years. He served in the United States Army three years, is a veteran of the Spanish American War, and a member of the United Spanish War Veterans, Roosevelt Camp No. 14 Scotts Bluff. He is an Odd Fellow. His hobby is reading.

On May 10, 1905, he was married to Agnes Irene Ryan at Red Cloud. Mrs. Fruit was born in Smith County, Kansas, April 3, 1888. Mr. and Mrs. Fruit have four children, Velma, born May 1, 1910, married H. Jack Honn; Fernola, born September 9, 1919; Marguerite, born November 21, 1920; and Marcelene, born July 11, 1923. Residence: Keystone.

Sidney Thomas Frum

For over twenty years Sidney Thomas Frum has been engaged in the practice of law at South Sioux City, Nebraska, where he is active in community affairs. He was born at Danbury, Woodbury County, Iowa, November 16, 1886, the son of Christopher C. and Alice (Hodgson) Frum. His father, who was born near Morgantown, West Virginia, August 16, 1853, and died at Sioux City, Iowa, May 20, 1919, was a farmer and for several years was supervisor in Woodbury and Thurston counties. His mother was born in Illinois, July 8, 1857, and died at Minneapolis, Minnesota, November 20, 1920.

Mr. Frum was graduated from the Danbury High School in 1903, and in 1909 was awarded the LL. B. degree at the University of Nebraska, where he held membership in Acacia. He was active in football at the university during 1907 and 1908. A Republican, he served as county attorney of Dakota County, 1912-16, and 1922-26. He holds membership in the South Sioux City Commercial Club, the Masons, Nebraskana Society, and the Red Cross. He is affiliated with the First Presbyterian Church.

He was married to Alice Reynolds Pomeroy at Shelby, Iowa. Mrs. Frum, who was born at Shelby, Shelby County, Iowa, July 8, 1890, is a prominent clubwoman and is now serving as president of the Woman's Club for the third district. To this marriage two children were born: Virginia, born October 2, 1917; and Catherine, born August 28, 1915, who died February 11, 1919.

Mr. Frum served in all Liberty loan drives during the World War, was active in Red Cross drives, and took part in registration work. His sports are golfing and fishing. Residence: South Sioux City.

William Thomas Fry

William T. Fry, farmer and stockman, was born at South English, Keokuk County, Iowa, July 29, 1864. He received his earlier education at Locust Grove and Prairie, Nebraska, and later attended Campbell Normal Business and Banking College and received his diploma on June 4, 1885.

John, father of William, was born at Waynesboro, Virginia, May 7, 1822. He was a teamster, driving seven or eight horses to covered wagons, hauling flour from the Shenandoah Valley, Virginia, to Richmond, returning with loads of freight. Later he was a farmer. His death occurred in Pawnee County, Nebraska, August 19, 1900.

Sarah (Coffman) Fry, mother of William, was born near Staunton, Virginia, June 3, 1831, and died near Homesville, Nebraska, September 20, 1914. Her parents came from Pennsylvania and settled in the Shenandoah Valley in 1804. Her father's barn was used as a hospital during the Civil War.

Mr. Fry was united in marriage to Mary Ella Dorrance on October 15, 1896. Her ancestors came from Scotland and Ireland. She was born near Pawnee City, Nebraska, October 27, 1872. She was a school teacher for six years

before her marriage. They have six children, John Gilmore, who is married to Eoe Fletcher; Cyrus W., who is married to Lois Elwood; Vera, who is married to Dean Taylor; William C.; Lawrence A., and Katheryn E.

He has been a resident of Nebraska for fifty-one years. In 1926, he was selected as one of the first master farmers in Nebraska. He is now serving his twenty-ninth year on the board of education 14 years in Riverview Consolidated School. During the World War he participated in loan drives.

A member of the South Beatrice Brethren Church, he is also a member of the Kiwanis Club, the Masons, Red Cross and The Nebraska Hall of Agricultural Achievement. He is president of the Gage County Fair and Agricultural Society, and is chairman of the agricultural committee of the Nebraska-Iowa district of Kiwanis. His hobby is reading. Residence: Holmsville. (Photograph in Album).

Otto Fuerst

Otto Fuerst, general manager of the Platte Valley Telephone Corporation, was born at Kewanee, Illinois, March 27, 1882, son of Fred Fuerst who came from Germany when a boy and died at Battle Creek, Nebraska, May 27, 1931, at the age of 87 years.

On August 12, 1906, he was married to Martha Wolfe at Batttle Creek, Nebraska. She was born at Norfolk, Nebraska, October 20, 1885. There are two sons, Martin Otto, born December 3, 1907 at Norfolk, Nebraska, who married Dorthy Evans, daughter of Winifred Evans. They have one daughter, now living at Sturgis, South Dakota. Harry William, born March 18, 1911, at Columbus, Nebraska, is in attendance at the Boeig Air School at Oakland, California.

Mr. Fuerst has been engaged in telephone work since 1898, starting his work at Norfolk, Nebraska, and leaving there in 1908, to go to Madison, Nebraska. Leaving there he served as general manager of Platte County Independent Telephone at Columbus, Nebraska, leaving there in 1914 for Chadron, Nebraska, where he served as plant superintendent until 1919, moving to Scotts Bluff and he served as plant superintendent until 1928, then taking over the management of the Platte Valley Telephone Corporation, which position he still holds.

He is a member of the Masons, the Rotary Club, the Nebraskana Society, and the Telephone Pioneers of America. Residence: Gering.

William Charles Fuerst

William Charles Fuerst, telephone executive, was born at Battle Creek, Nebraska, June 26, 1898, son of William Bernard and Anna E. (Wolfe) Fuerst. His ancestry is German.

Mr. Fuerst attended public and high school, and was a student two and a half years in the Seward Lutheran Teachers Seminary.

He was married on July 12, 1922, to Beulah Pauline Koenig at Torrington, Wyoming. Mrs. Fuerst was born at Scottsbluff, Nebraska, August 27, 1902. Mr. and Mrs. Fuerst have two children, Bernard, born September 1, 1923; and Dorothy, born September 1, 1925.

At the present time Mr. Fuerst is serving as district manager of the Northwestern Bell Telephone Company. He is a member of the Volunteer Fire department, and the Lions Club. His hobbies are golf and fishing. Residence: Bayard.

Phillip John Fuesler

Phillip John Fuesler was born at Friedrichstal, Germany, September 18, 1871, and since 1890 has been in business in Nebraska. His father, Phillip John Fuesler, who was a carpenter and contractor, was born at Friedrichstal, October 29, 1804, and died there January 13, 1872, after serving several terms as mayor of the city; his ancestors were driven from Holland early in the 17th century because of religious dissension. His mother, who was born at Friedrichstal, November 11, 1824, and died there December 26, 1880, was descended from French Huguenot ancestors who left France in the 17th century because of religious persecution.

Mr. Fuesler worked as a journeyman tailor for ten years and from 1900 to 1930, when he retired, he was a tailor at Norfolk, Nebraska. He had served his apprenticeship in Germany. As a Republican he was city councilman from 1908 to 1912 and in 1914 was unsuccessful candidate for city mayor of Norfolk. He has been a member of the Norfolk Chamber of Commerce for over 30 years and is now a member of the Kiwanis Club and Grace Lutheran Church.

During the World War he served as a member of the registration board at Norfolk, sold Liberty bonds, and was active in the Red Cross. He likes to hunt.

On September 18, 1892, he was married to Rosa Broecker at Norfolk. Mrs. Fuesler, whose parents were natives of Germany, was born at La Porte, Indiana, March 3, 1874. She is the daughter of John and Friedericke Broecker. They have six children: Nora, born April 2, 1893, who married W. H. Strong; Arthur, born July 19, 1895, who married Ruth Zwicky; Eric, born December 9, 1896, who married Myrthel House; Mabel, born February 20, 1899, who married Dr. H. A. Askey; Clarence, born June 21, 1901, who married Malray Warrick; and Ruth, born February 16, 1911. Residence: Norfolk.

Hayes M. Fuhr

Hayes M. Fuhr, director of conservatory for Hastings College, was born at Lewistown, Illinois, January 25, 1891. He is the son of William Stanley and Mary Rachel (Maguire) Fuhr, the former a dentist, born at Allegheny, Pennsylvania, September 2, 1847. Mary Rachel Maguire was born in Kentucky, August 20, 1857, of Irish ancestry.

Upon his graduation from Macomb (Illinois) High School in 1909, Mr. Fuhr entered Western Illinois State Teachers' College from which he was graduated. Here he received honors in dramatics, music and oratory. Later he attended Bush Conservatory at Chicago, from which he received his Bachelor of Music degree. He received his B. A. degree from Hastings College in 1928.

From 1910 to 1912, inclusive, Mr. Fuhr was director of voice at Culver Military Academy at Culver, Indiana, and since 1912 has been director of Hastings College Conservatory. During his residence in Hastings, Mr. Fuhr has taken an active part in civic and cultural work. He is a member of the First Presbyterian Church, (of which he is a member of the session and director of music), the Red Cross and Young Men's Christian Association, the Rotary Club of which he has twice been a director, and the Masonic Lodge (Scottish Rite, Shrine). He is also a member of the Nebraskana Society. His hobbies are reading and writing, and his favorite sport is golf at the Hastings Country Club.

On June 30, 1915, Mr. Fuhr was united in mrariage to Ruth Ann Johnson at Fairfield, Iowa. Mrs. Fuhr, who is an accomplished pianist, was born at Holyoke, Colorado, December 25, 1890. There is one son, Edgar Stanley, born February 1, 1918. Residence: Hastings.

Byron Sylvester Fulk

Born at Strawn, Illinois, September 26, 1877, Byron Sylvester Fulk is the son of Martin Alexander and Ida May (Hopkins) Fulk. The father, born in Green County, Indiana, May 18, 1854, is a retired farmer, merchant, and banker of German descent, and is the son of Joseph Fulk. He is now living in Atlanta. Ida May Hopkins, his wife, was born April 2, 1858, of Scotch descent. She

was the daughter of Joseph and Louise Sempson (Henline) Hopkins. Louise Henline was the first white child born in McClean County, Illinois.

Byron Sylvester Fulk attended public school in Strawn, Illinois, and Harlan, Phelps County, Nebraska. His father moved to Nebraska when Byron was nine years old. Mr. Fulk has engaged in farming all of his life since reaching maturity. His specialty is hog raising, and he is much interested in master farming, having kept a farm record for about five years. From 1921-29, he was a director on the school board, and he has always taken an active interest in community affairs. With the exception of nine months, Mr. Fulk has lived 34 years on the same farm, his parent's home. During his lifetime he has officiated at 150 or more funerals, and has in several instances acted as undertaker.

On December 28, 1897, he was married to Bertha Evelyn Pritchard at Beaver City. Mrs. Fulk, who was born at Exeter, December 14, 1875, died at Atlanta, November 19, 1931. She was the daughter of John and Ellen (Lonsdale) Pritchard. Her parents were both born in Hampshire, England, and came to this country in 1849, when they were children. There are five children, Dothan Pritchard, born November 20, 1898, who married Dollie Read; Ora Ellen, born December 2, 1900, who married Lawrence Ossie David; Florence Fern, born January 14, 1904, who married Lars P. Christensen; Velda Mae, born September 22, 1907; and Delwin Martin, born February 26, 1912. Dothan is a farmer, while Fern and Velda are registered nurses. Delwin is a farmer with his father.

Mr. Fulk is a member of the Atlanta Seventh Day Adventist Church, is a supporter of the Red Cross, a Republican, and a member of the Nebraskana Society. He has been active in the affairs of the Atlanta Farmers Institute during its 24 years of existence, and for several years acted as president. He enjoys reading. Residence: Atlanta. (Photograph in Album).

Charles J. Fulk

Charles J. Fulk, merchant and executive, was born at Lyons, Indiana, November 16, 1896, son of James W. and Delitha (Workman) Fulk.

James W. Fulk was born in Greene County, Indiana, in 1862, of Holland, Dutch and Irish descent. He is a farmer. His wife, Delitha, was born in Greene County, Indiana, in 1864, of Dutch descent.

Mr. Fulk attended the schools of Bloomfield, Indiana, until his graduation in 1914. He was thereafter a student at the College of Business Administration at the University of Nebraska. From 1919 until 1925 he was secretary-treasurer of Burke and Harpole Company at Bayard. He has been in the mercantile business for himself at Dickens and Wallace since that time and is a partner and general manager of the Charles J. Fulk Company.

On April 21, 1921, he was married to Marion Barbara Berwick at Bridgeport. Mrs. Fulk was born in Illinois, February 12, 1897, of French and Irish descent. There are two children, Barbara Lee, born June 8, 1927; and Patricia Lou, born May 4, 1930.

During the World War, Mr. Fulk served in the United States Navy with the rank of seaman. He is a member of the American Legion, the First Baptist Church of Bloomfield, Indiana, the Red Cross, the Masons, and the Harper Golf Club. His favorite sport is golf, while his hobby is reading. Residence: Wallace.

Clark Adelbert Fulmer

Clark A. Fulmer, who has lived in Nebraska for the past 50 years, was born at Marcellus, Onondaga County, New York, April 22, 1867. His father, David Morgan Fulmer, who was a farmer, was born in New York, February 4, 1831, and died at Gibbon, Buffalo County, Nebraska, September 18, 1900. His ancestry was Dutch and English. Ellen Elizabeth (Longstreet) Fulmer, mother of Clark, was born in Onondaga Valley, Onondaga County, New York, September 10, 1838, and died at Gibbon, March 20, 1930. Her English ancestors, Oliver Breed and Comfort Tyler, were Revolutionary War soldiers. Her family history is included in *The Breed Family*, by J. Howard Breed, published in 1892.

Mr. Fulmer attended the grade school at Marcellus, and the high school at Gibbon; later he completed the high school course at Nebraska Baptist Seminary. He was awarded the Ph. B. degree at Nebraska Wesleyan University in 1898; received the A. M. degree at the University of Nebraska, 1910; and was granted the LL. D. at Grand Island College in 1914. He was elected to membership in Phi Delta Kappa, Phi Kappa Phi, and Pi Gamma Mu.

He has served as superintendent of schools in the following Nebraska towns: Gibbon; Edgar; Pawnee City; and Beatrice. From 1908 to 1911 he was dean of the college of Liberal Arts at Wesleyan University; was acting chancellor, 1910-11; and chancellor, 1911-17. Since January 1, 1918, he has been state director of Vocational Education.

He is the author of: *Civil Government of Nebraska;* numerous contributions to professional magazines on *Vocational Education, Vocational Guidance, School Administration,* and *Education.* He is the editor of *Vocational Education,* published in Nebraska.

His marriage to Evalena Anna Ingham, was solemnized at Gibbon, June 23, 1887. Mrs. Fulmer, who was born at Upper Alton, Madison County, Illinois, August 2, 1867, was a teacher before her marriage. She is a descendant of Governor Bradford, and is a member of the Society of Mayflower Descendants. Four children were born to their union; Ellis Ingham, born April 12, 1891, who married Ruth Files; Elbert, born April 12, 1891, who died October 16, 1891; Miriam, born May 17, 1894, who married Irvin Henry Vogel; and Pauline, born November 4, 1895, who married Joseph H. Ruliffson, Jr.

Mr. Fulmer served as special federal agent for war training in Nebraska during the World War; he was chairman of the school and college activities committee of the Federal Food Administration for Nebraska. He is a member of the National Educational Association; the Nebraska Schoolmasters Club; the National Association of State Directors of Vocational Agriculture; and American Vocational Association. He holds membership in the Red Cross; Nebraska Conference of Social Work; Lincoln Chamber of Commerce; and the Rotary Club, of which he was a director, 1929-30. He is affiliated with the Candlelight Club and the Young Men's Christian Association.

He is a Mason, a Knight Templar, and Modern Woodman of America. He is a member of St. Paul's Methodist Episcopal Church of Lincoln. He is a Republican. Residence: Lincoln.

William D. Funk

Since the spring of 1892 William D. Funk has been engaged in the practice of law at Bloomfield, Nebraska, where he has led in community activities. He was born at Iowa City, Iowa, September 18, 1856, the son of Joseph and Leah (Steely) Funk. His father, who was a shoemaker and a farmer, was born at Frostburg, Maryland, March 21, 1816, and died at Nashua, Iowa, March 9, 1895; his Swiss and German ancestors settled at Germantown, Pennsylvania, in 1709.

Leah (Steely) Funk, whose ancestry was English and Scotch, was born at Levistown, Pennsylvania, April 2, 1830, and died at Nashua, April 12, 1912.

Mr. Funk was graduated from the law school of the University of Iowa in 1886. He has practiced law continuously since 1888 and has resided at Bloomfield most of that time. He is at the present time one of the directors of the Farmers and Merchants Bank, and was formerly a stockholder and director in the Nebraska State Bank of Bloomfield.

A Republican, Mr. Funk served as county attorney of Knox County for two terms, was city attorney for many years, and was a candidate for the Nebraska senate. He is a member of the District Bar Association, the Nebraska State Bar Association, the Bloomfield Commercial Club, and the Red Cross. He was Grand High Priest of the Royal Arch Masons of Nebraska in 1918 and 1919, and formerly served on the Bloomfield School Board. His chief recreation is farming.

On October 22, 1883, he married Cora Abigail King at Blairstown. Mrs. Funk, whose English ancestors were merchants, farmers and lawyers, was born at Lyndon, Illinois, October 12, 1860. Of this marriage four children were born: Hazel K., March 19, 1886, who married R. B. Miller; Angeline, April 2, 1889, who is a stenographer; Samuel W., January 25, 1891, who married Minnie B. Funk; Owen K., September 13, 1893, who married Ruby F. Funk, and who is a farmer. Samuel is also a farmer. Residence: Bloomfield.

Archie Charles Furman

Archie Charles Furman was born at Mehoopany, Pennsylvania, October 3, 1869, is editor and owner with his son, Charles Edward Furman, of the *South Side Sentinel,* operating the paper in conjunction with the neighboring towns of Lebanon and Marion, Nebraska. He is the son of Granville S. and Wanda Jane (Campbell) Furman.

Mr. Furman received his early education at Lacyville and Towanda, Pennsylvania, and upon removing with his parents to a homestead near Oberlin, Kansas, in 1879, attended school in sod school houses. He continued to live near Oberlin, until his marriage in April, 1891, to Mattie Ann Van Pelt.

In 1892, Mr. Furman removed to Danbury, Nebraska, where he engaged in barbering and photography and where in 1897 he took up newspaper work, publishing the *Danbury News.* In 1904 he removed to Fort Collins, Colorado, where he operated a barber shop and job printing establishment, remaining there until 1909. In the summer of 1909, Mr. Furman returned to Nebraska, locating at Marion, where he merged the *Danbury News* with the *Marion Enterprise* under the name of the *South Side Sentinel.* There he also served as postmaster. In 1924 he moved his printing and publishing establishment to Danbury, where he erected a one story building and continued in the publishing business.

Mr. and Mrs. Furman have five children, Hazel Winslow, born July 25, 1893, who is teaching in the English department at Hastings College; Bessie Irene, born December 2, 1894, who is now connected with the Associated Press, Washington, D. C.; Nellie Lucille, born April 30, 1896, resides with her father and brother Charles, and who is associate editor of the *Sentinel,* a linotypist, and has had experience in all branches of newspaper work; Donald Archie, born February 1, 1900, who married Fayette Haase of Amherst, Nebraska; and Charles Edward, born August 4, 1902, who manages the *South Side Sentinel* with his father.

Mr. Furman is affiliated with the Methodist Church, and is a life member of the Nebraskana Society. His politics are non-partisan. Residence: Danbury. (Photograph on Page 228).

Charles Edward Furman

Born at Danbury, Nebraska, August 4, 1902, Charles Edward Furman is the son of Archie Charles and Mattie Ann (Van Pelt) Furman. Archie Charles Furman was born at Mehoopany, Pennsylvania, October 3, 1869, and is editor of the *South Side Sentinel.* His wife, born at State Center, Iowa, April 4, 1869, is a doctor of osteopathy.

Charles Furman was graduated from the Kearney High School in 1919, and since that time has been associated with his father in business. He is business man-

ARCHIE CHARLES FURMAN

Nelson—McCook

ager of the *South Side Sentinel,* published at Danbury, Nebraska.

A member of the Danbury Methodist Episcopal Church and the Masons, Mr. Furman is also a member of the Nebraskana Society. His hobby is mechanics. Residence: Danbury.

Thomas Ross Furry

A leader in business and civic affairs at Superior, Nebraska, is Thomas Ross Furry who has resided in this state for nearly 50 years. He was born at New Enterprise, Pennsylvania, March 6, 1876, the son of Leonard E. and Cornelia (Border) Furry. His father, who was born at New Enterprise, May 29, 1851, and died at Franklin, Nebraska, November 14, 1927, was engaged in the livestock, grain, and milling business for many years, and was an unusually good judge of cattle; he was of German descent.

His mother, Cornelia (Border) Furry, was born at New Enterprise, January 11, 1851, and died at Omaha, Nebraska, June 3, 1907; her ancestry was English and Irish.

Mr. Furry was graduated from high school in 1892, and from that time until 1900 was telegraph operator for the Burlington Railroad Company, and from 1900 until 1904 was brakeman for the Burlington and Sante Fe Railroad, western division in Los Angeles. From 1904, until 1916, he was engaged in the livestock and grain business with his father and brother at Franklin. Since 1916 he has been president and manager of the Blue Cross Serum Company at Superior. He is a member of the Chamber of Commerce, the Masonic Lodge and the Modern Woodmen of America.

On March 30, 1906, he was married to Maude Frances Peery at Franklin. Mrs. Furry, who was born at Franklin, September 26, 1871, and died at Superior, July 22, 1929, was prominent in club affairs and held membership in the P. E. O., Daughters of the American Revolution, and the Woman's Club. Of Scotch-Irish parentage, she was the first white child born in Franklin County. Four children were born to this marriage, Thomas E., January 26, 1907, who married Lucille Lourey; Margaret L., January 30, 1909, who attended the University of Nebraska, where she was a member of Alpha Phi; Cornelia, February 22, 1911, who is studying piano at Bethany College, Lindsborg, Kansas; and Mary E., November 8, 1914, who is a high school student at Superior.

Mr. Furry is a member of the Nebraskana Society, and is affiliated with the Republican party. Residence: Superior.

Harry C. Furse

Harry C. Furse, who has been a newspaper editor and publisher at Alma, Nebraska, since 1882, was born at Milwood, Ohio, June 8, 1875, the son of Thomas and Mary Jane (Sandercock) Furse. His father, who was a custom shoemaker and dealer, was born at Plymouth, England, May 12, 1845, and died at Alma in July, 1894. His mother was born at Plymouth, October 17, 1846, and died at Alma, March 15, 1899.

Mr. Furse attended the Alma High School, and since 1882 has been editor and publisher of the *Harlan County Journal.* A Democrat, he served as postmaster at Alma under the Wilson administration, has been city treasurer for two years, was city clerk for six years, served as city councilman for six years, and was township clerk for eight consecutive years. He has served as a member of the Alma School Board for the past two years, is a member of the Odd Fellows, Modern Woodmen of America, and the Lions Club.

His marriage to Bertha Evelyn Dow occurred at Alma, June 8, 1898; Mrs. Furse, who was a teacher at one time, was born at Richland, Wisconsin, June 15, 1876. They have seven children: Merle D., August 30, 1899, who married Thelma Wood at Alma, in July, 1923; Harry Garold, born September 11, 1901, who married

Elsie Foltz at Phillipsburg, Kansas, in December, 1923; Ronald Roy, born August 16, 1904, who married Georgia Glandon in November, 1924; Dean, February 10, 1912; Gersham, September 29, 1906, who married Dorothy Banks on March 14, 1932; Hope, September 25, 1915; and Hubert, January 23, 1918. Residence: Alma.

Arthur Emile Gadbois

Arthur Emile Gadbois, who is a leader in the professional affairs of Norfolk, Nebraska, was born at Sioux City, Iowa, November 30, 1875, and for the past 30 years has been a practising physician at Norfolk. His father, Alphonse Gadbois, who was a farmer and lumber dealer, was born in Canada, and died at Sioux City, December 1, 1917; his ancestry was French. His mother, Sarah (Allard) Gadbois, whose ancestors were natives of Canada, was born at Jefferson, South Dakota, May 1, 1855.

Dr. Gadbois attended public school and seminary at Nicolet, Canada, and received the M. D. degree at Creighton University at Omaha. He is an eye, ear, nose, and throat specialist in the Norfolk Clinic at this time, and holds membership in the Nebraska State Medical Society, the American Medical Association, the American Academy of Physicians, and the Elkhorn Valley Eye, Ear, Nose and Throat Academy.

He is a director in the DeLay National Bank, is a director in the Allied Security Investment Company, and is connected with the Allied Building & Loan Association of Norfolk. Dr. Gadbois is a member of the Chamber of Commerce, was formerly president of the Lions Club, is affiliated with the Sacred Heart Church, and is an Elk and Modern Woodman. He served as captain of the Medical Reserve Corps during the World War and at this time is an active member of the American Legion at Norfolk. His social club is the Norfolk Country Club.

His marriage to Marie Josephine Desparois occurred at Sioux City, January 27, 1904. Mrs. Gadbois, whose ancestry was French Canadian, was born at Sioux City, May 30, 1882, the daughter of pioneer Iowans. Four children were born to their marriage: Guy, November 3, 1904, who married Marcella Folda; Robert, born September 5, 1909; Richard, September 5, 1909, who married Margaret Donahue; and Betty, April 17, 1916. His sons are graduates of Creighton University. Residence: Norfolk.

Clarence James Galbraith

Clarence J. Galbraith was born in Fairbury, Nebraska, April 16, 1891. He is the son of George B. and Annie (Rosenberger) Galbraith. George B. Calbraith was born in Glasgow, Scotland, June 4, 1860, coming to America while a youth and later entering the nursery business. His death occurred March 25, 1910, at Needles, California. Annie Rosenberger, mother of Clarence, was born in Pennsylvania, March 18, 1865, of Pennsylvania Dutch ancestry.

After receiving his elementary education he was graduated from high school in 1910. Soon thereafter he entered the mercantile business. He has been a resident of Nebraska his entire life. Although he is not active in politics, he is affiliated with the Democratic party.

He was married to Edna Ellen Shoebotham, who is of English Canadian descent, September 18, 1912, at Fairbury, Nebraska. She was born at Fairbury, January 26, 1892. They are the parents of four children, Ruthanna, born September 29, 1913; George, born March 17, 1915; Maxine, born January 10, 1917; and Catherine, born February 9, 1919.

He is a member of the Christian Church of Fairbury, The Nebraskana Society, the Chamber of Commerce and Kiwanis Club. During 1925-26 he was a member of the Fairbury School Board. Residence: Fairbury.

Claude Eugene Galbraith

Born at Beemer, Nebraska, September 25, 1893, Claude E. Galbraith is the son of William H. and Alta L. (Cohee) Galbraith. William H. Calbraith was born in Peoria, Illinois, November 30, 1866, and is a farmer of Irish descent. His wife, Alta, was born at Atlantic, Iowa, January 19, 1868, and before her marriage was a teacher.

Claude E. Galbraith was graduated from grade school in 1908 and from Beemer High School in 1911. During the years 1915, 1916 and 1917 he attended the University of Nebraska, where he was made a member of Sigma Nu. During 1911, 1912 and the year of 1913-14 he taught in the schools of district No. 28 in Cuming County, and since that time has been engaged as a farmer and stockman.

On June 29, 1918, he was married to Edna Marie Blomgren, at Des Moines, Iowa. Mrs. Galbraith was born at Gowrie, Iowa, January 31, 1898. There are three children, Margaret Lou, born July 24, 1920; William Gene, born January 22, 1926; and Frances Ailene, born November 22, 1927.

Mr. Galbraith is an independent Democrat. During the world war he held the rank of first lieutenant of Infantry as a machine gunner. He is a member of the American Legion, a director of school district No. 19, and a member of the First Methodist Episcopal Church. A Mason, he is a member of the Scottish Rite, and Master of Beemer Lodge No. 253. He also belongs to the Eastern Star and the Nebraskana Society. He enjoys reading. Residence: Beemer.

Clarence Willard Gale

On July 12, 1886, Clarence Willard Gale was born in Adams County, Nebraska, son of Charles Fremont Gale and Aldula Gertrude (Garrison) Gale. Charles F. Gale was born in Michigan, of Scotch parentage. He was in the newspaper business and was an author. He died in Beatrice, Nebraska, 1916. His wife was born in Illinois and is still living.

Clarence Willard Gale was graduated from Beatrice High School in 1904. On August 4, 1909, he married Gladys Lottie Majors at Peru, Nebraska. She was born in Peru, February 3, 1890, the daughter of Honorable Thomas J. Majors. They have two daughters; Clair Frances, born May 16, 1911, and Doris, born September 6, 1913, both students at Stevens College.

Mr. Gale worked as an apprentice in Beatrice for J. C. Barkhurst 1904-07 and then started in the photographer's business for himself. At the present he is owner of an art store.

He is affiliated with the Republican party and is a member of the Centenary Methodist Episcopal Church. Mr. Gale has lived in Nebraska forty-four years most of which time he lived in Beatrice, where he has been president of the Chamber of Commerce two terms, 1930-31.

He is a member of the Young Men's Christian Association, the Beatrice Country Club, the Rotary Club, the Elks lodge, the Nebraskana Society and the Order of the Ancient Free and Accepted Masons. Mr. Gale was secretary of the Missouri Valley Photographers Association, 1924-28, and president in 1929. He has had four years' military training in the Nebraska National Guard.

Mr. Gale plays golf and enjoys photography as a pastime. Residence: Beatrice.

James P. Gallagher

In 1878 James P. Gallagher came to Nebraska with his parents who settled in O'Neill at a time when the town consisted of a few sod homes, a blacksmith shop, and village post office. He was born at Scranton, Pennsylvania, February 15, 1871, the son of Bridget (Erwin) and Michael G. Gallagher, the latter a rancher

and successful farmer who was born in Ireland and died at O'Neill, December 22, 1916. His mother, who is living today, was born in Pennsylvania.

Mr. Gallagher acquired a grade school education but received his business training through practical application in a general store at O'Neill. He assisted his father in the cattle-buying business for about ten years, and then established his own mercantile business which he still manages. Four of his brothers and two nephews are practicing physicians.

He is a member of the Ancient Order of United Workmen, and is affiliated with St. Patricks Catholic Church at O'Neill. Mr. Gallagher was a charter member and one of the organizers of the local Knights of Columbus at O'Neill and has since then taken a prominent part in the affairs of that society. His favorite recreations are reading and fishing. During the World War he contributed liberally to Red Cross activities and bought Liberty bonds.

His marriage to Winifred McInery was solemnized at O'Neill, October 10, 1906. They have three children, all of whom are students in college: Helen and Hilda, twin daughters, born March 28, 1909; and Frank, born April 30, 1911. Residence: O'Neill.

Paul C. Gallagher

Paul C. Gallagher, wholesale grocer, was born at Omaha, Nebraska, son of Ben and Winifred (Keogh) Gallagher. His father was born in Ottumwa, Iowa, and died in 1900. His mother was born in Belleville, Ontario, Canada, and died in 1920.

Mr. Gallagher is married to Rachel M. Kincade, who was born in Kansas City, Missouri. Mr. Gallagher is secretary and treasurer of Paxton and Gallagher Company. Residence: Omaha.

Rachel Kincade Gallagher

Rachel Kincade was born at Fort Scott, Kansas, daughter of George Percy and Emily Elizabeth (Crowe) Kincade. Her father, who was born at Athens, Ohio, January 2, 1867, is a real estate operator, whose ancestors came from England about 1700. Emily Elizabeth Crowe was born at Fort Scott on January 8, 1867, and is of Scotch descent.

Upon the completion of her education in the West Port High School at Kansas City, Rachel Kincade attended Smith College, at Northampton, Massachusetts. She was married to Paul C. Gallagher at Kansas City, on March 24, 1915, and has since made her home in Omaha. Two children were born to this marriage, Jean Dudley, born April 17, 1916, and Anne, born December 11, 1925. Mrs. Gallagher is a Democrat.

For the past sixteen years she has been prominent in the civic and cultural development of Omaha. Among the organizations in which she has been active are the Omaha Art Institute, of which she served as secretary from 1922 to 1924, and from 1928 to the present. She is a member of the Junior League, and served as its president in 1919. During the ten years from 1919 to 1929, she wrote numerous articles which appeared in the *Junior League Magazine*, and she is the author of various articles appearing in the *Christian Science Monitor*. A member of St. Cecilia's Cathedral, she is also a member of the National Council of Catholic Women.

During the World War she was a participant in Red Cross canteen work, a member of the Christmas Bureau, etc. She belongs to the Omaha Club, and her sport is golf. Residence: Omaha.

Nellie Rose Gallant

Born at Defiance, Ohio, September 15, 1868, Nellie Rose Gallant is the daughter of William Henry and Sarah (Black) Bridenbaugh. Her father, a native of Lancaster, Ohio, was born May 22, 1833. Her father, a native of Lancaster, Ohio, was born May 22, 1833. A carpenter, he served three years in the Civil War with the 100th Ohio Volunteers, and was a member of the Grand Army of the Republic. His grandfather, a clockmaker, came to America from Baden, Germany, when his father was 8 years of age. William Henry Bridenbaugh died at Defiance, Ohio, November 7, 1901.

Sarah Black was born in Butler County, Ohio, February 9, 1836. Devoted to her home, she was also active in the work of her church. Her mother was of Pennsylvania Dutch descent, while her father was Irish, and came from the same family as that of William Black, Commissioner of Pensions, and S. S. Cox, Democratic leader of Ohio.

Nellie Rose Bridenbaugh attended the elementary schools of Defiance, and completed private school and junior college in 1886. In 1928 she was graduated from Peru State Normal School, having completed her course through summer school courses and absentia work. She has also attended Defiance College and the University of Nebraska.

On March 19, 1890, she was united in marriage to William Gallant at Hebron. Mr. Gallant, who is a farmer and real estate dealer, was born at Danville, Illinois, September 30, 1849. On the paternal side he is French and on the maternal side is of English descent. To their union six children were born, as follows:

Margaret Ella, born December 27, 1890, is married to W. E. van Natta; Florence Edna, born August 4, 1893, married Clarence C. (Chick) Boyes; Dorothy, born November 29, 1897, married R. H. Wise; Richard Bridenbaugh, born March 23, 1900, married Geraldine Mae Bane; Kathleen, born August 1, 1903, married Willard Henderson; and Nellie, born November 7, 1907. All of the children except Florence and Nellie reside in California. Nellie is a beautician, Dorothy is a trained nurse, and Florence is engaged in dramatic work with her husband in the Chick Boyes Players.

Mrs. Gallant began her teaching career in 1885 in the public schools of Ohio. Thereafter she taught five years in Nebraska, and in 1912 resumed her work, teaching for fourteen years in the grade school of Hebron, and serving as principal for five years. She has written numerous articles, including *Bible in the Public Schools,* they having appeared in the State Teachers Journal, and in other state and county periodicals and papers.

During the World War Mrs. Gallant was especially active, and performed much clerical work during that period. She is affiliated with the Methodist Episcopal Church, is a member of the Nebraskana Society, the Ladies Bible Club of Hebron, and the Hebron Woman's Club. In 1931, she was elected delegate to the state convention of the Federation of Women's Clubs. Mrs. Gallant's hobby is reading. Residence: Hebron.

Jesse McClelland Galloway

Born at Crawfordsville, Indiana, March 24, 1867, Jesse McClelland Galloway has been an outstanding citizen of Saunders County for thirty-five years. He is the son of William and Rachel Ellen (Bailey) Galloway, the former born at Hamilton, Ohio, March 22, 1821. A farmer by trade, he spent nearly half his life as a farmer, and died at Linnsburg, Indiana, December 2, 1888. The Galloway family came from the north and west of Ireland.

Rachel Ellen Bailey was born at Culpepper, Virginia, April 18, 1828, and died at Mace, Indiana, March 26, 1892. Her life was devoted to homemaking. The Baileys were directly descended from Pennsylvania Dutch settlers who came to the United States in early Colonial days, as did the Galloways.

Judge Galloway attended rural and grade schools in Mace, Indiana, from which he was graduated in the spring of 1882. In lieu of high school he attended the

preparatory department of Wabash College, and the Summer Normal School, preparatory to teaching. He was graduated from the Law College of the University of Michigan June 21, 1905, and was admitted to practice in that state and in Nebraska in the summer of 1905. He was elected at the open university election, Secretary of the Debating and Oratorical Society of the University of Michigan, in 1904.

A teacher in country grades, to and through high school, Judge Galloway served twelve years, nine of which were as superintendent. From November, 1898, to 1901, he served as county superintendent of schools, elected on the Democratic ticket, two terms. He was elected city attorney of Wahoo, serving eight years; and in November, 1906, was elected county attorney of Saunders County, and was re-elected to the same office in November, 1908. Appointed county judge on February 1, 1930, he was elected to that office on November 4, 1930, and still serves.

On June 18, 1893, he was married to Bertha Ellen Fletcher, at Ashland, Nebraska. Mrs. Galloway, a native of Parkersburg, Indiana, was born February 28, 1877, of Dutch extraction on her father's side, and French on her mother's. There are two children, Lucille, born October 5, 1894, who is married to a banker in Santa Ana, California. Cecil, born July 8, 1899, is married and resides at Wahoo. He served as county attorney four years, and is now engaged in the practice of law.

Always active in civic affairs, Judge Galloway was called upon as a Four Minute speaker throughout Saunders County, and participated in other civilian war work. He has always been identified with either the Christian, Presbyterian or Baptist Churches, but is not a member of any local church. He enjoys reading historical and philosophic works, and is a member of The Nebraskana Society. Residence: Wahoo.

John William Gamble

John William Gamble, manufacturer, was born at Springfield, Nebraska, September 8, 1879, the son of William Wallace and Annie (Morrison) Gamble.

Mr. Gamble received his B. E. degree from Peru State Normal School in 1908, and his Bachelor of Arts degree from the University of Nebraska in 1912.

He is married to Elizabeth Caroline Keefer, who was born in Delaware, Ohio, July 12, 1870. From 1906 until 1908 he was superintendent of schools in Cass County. From 1919 until 1924 he was vice-president of the First National Bank of Omaha. He has served as president of the Standard Chemical Manufacturing Company, the American Machinery and Supply Company and the Don Lee Furniture Company, and a director of the First National Bank of Omaha. He is a member of the Westminster Presbyterian Church.

During the late war Mr. Gamble was a four minute speaker and active in loan drives.

He is a member of the Chamber of Commerce, the Manufacturers Association, the Community Playhouse, Ak-Sar-Ben, and the Masons. Residence: Omaha.

Everitt Jay Gano

Born at Little Valley, New York, August 30, 1862, Everitt Jay Gano has been a resident of Nebraska intermittently since 1880. He is the son of Jay and Jane (Ellis) Gano, both of whom were natives of New York. The father was born at Middletown, in 1828, and died at Frankfort, Kansas, in November, 1912. He was a farmer, whose ancestors came to the United States in the 16th century. His wife, Jane, was born at Middletown, in 1836, and died at Frankfort, in 1911.

Everitt Jay Gano attended the public schools, and engaged immediately in the retail business, which he has continued forty-four years. He is an outstanding merchant and member of his community. He is a Republican and a member of the Presbyterian Church, the Red Cross and the Masons.

His marriage to Carrie Frances Brown was solemnized at Frankfort, Kansas, November 27, 1887. Mrs. Gano was born at Henderson, Illinois, August 31, 1865, and died at Tekamah, February 10, 1923. On August 10, 1924, Mr. Gano was married to Julia A. Rhodes. Residence: Tekamah.

John Francis Ganson

Since 1910, John Francis Ganson has been a leading merchant at Hershey. He was born at Urbana, Ohio, August 23, 1863, son of Lewis Allen and Louise Rebecca (Harper) Ganson.

The father was born in Urbana, Ohio, and died at Kearney, Nebraska. He was a farmer who served in the 95th Ohio Infantry for three years, and was confined in Libby prison for four months. His father was Francis Ganson, born in Pennsylvania, of Danish parentage. Louise Rebecca, wife of Lewis Allen Ganson, was born in Urbana, Ohio, and during the time her husband was at the front in the Northern army cared for her home and family. Her father was John Harper, an Englishman, and her mother was Sarah Sparks, who was of Scotch parentage.

Mr. Ganson attended country school until the age of 17, when he went to Mechanicsburg, Ohio, to attend high school there for two years. From 1898 until November, 1902, he was in the employ of the Union Pacific Railroad. In 1902, Mr. Ganson came to Hershey as manager of the W. W. Young lumber, hardware, and coal business. He remained in that position until 1910, when he purchased the general store from Martin Mickleson which he has since operated under the name of the Ganson & Ganson Department Store.

His marriage to Adella Ann Cisney was solemnized at Hastings, June 13, 1888. Mrs. Ganson was born at Silver Lake, Indiana, July 24, 1869, daughter of George E. and Mathilda Cisney. Mr. Cisney is a contractor and builder at Hastings. There were three children born to them: Florence, August 14, 1889, who died October 14, 1898; Mable, August 15, 1891, who died September 7, 1892; and Blanche, December 10, 1894, who is married to J. Verne Brewer. Blanche and her husband reside at Omaha, where he is an insurance adjuster.

Mr. and Mrs. Ganson have been residents of the state since 1886 and 1873, respectively. Mr. Ganson is the author of a few articles to farm journals in his earlier days. He is a member of the Hershey Methodist Episcopal Church, the Commercial Club, the Modern Woodmen of America and The Nebraskana Society. His hobbies are mechanics and home gardening. Residence: Hershey.

George E. Garber

George E. Garber, merchant and postmaster, at Helvey, was born in Webster County, Iowa, July 20, 1866. He is the son of William and Jane (Wark) Garber, the former a carpenter and farmer. William Garber, who was born in Rockingham County, Virginia, September 25, 1833, was of Dutch and English descent. His death occurred at Scandia, Kansas. Jane, his wife, was born in Tuscarawas County, Ohio, May 13, 1838, and died at Scandia, Kansas, March 12, 1908. She was of Irish and English descent.

An exceptional student, George E. Garber attended district school, and later entered the general merchandise business, in which he has been engaged for many years. A Republican, he has been postmaster at Helvey since April, 1930.

On January 17, 1892, Mr. Garber was united in marriage to Minnie Florence Warren at Scandia. Mrs. Garber, who was born at Glenwood, Missouri, January 31, 1871, died at Scandia, March 5, 1905. To them were born four children: Lester Warren, born March 16, 1893, who died December 11, 1901; Chester C., born June 18, 1902, who married Ione Chambers, and who resides at Randolph, Iowa; Grace Esther, born April 13, 1895, who married Melza Brown, a clergyman, and who resides at Denver; and Warren, born February 28, 1905, who married Verna Harvey. Chester is associated with the Standard Oil Company, Grace's husband is pastor of the Nazarene Church at Denver, Warren is purchasing agent for the Western Public Service Company at Holdrege.

Mr. Garber was married to Lela M. Durand, daughter of O. H. and E. (Amlin) Durand on December 25, 1907. She was born April 21, 1878, daughter of O. H. Durand who was State Commander of the Grand Army of the Republic in 1914. He was a very prominent Republican and one of the first members of the State Historical Society. They have one son, Herbert D., who was born September 24, 1909, and who married Roberta Gaston. He is a printer.

Mr. Garber has been a resident of Nebraska since January, 1908, and has always taken an active interest in the affairs of his community and state. He is a member of the Presbyterian Church at Fairbury, and is a life member of The Nebraskana Society. Reseidence: Helvey. (Photograph in Album).

Alvin John Gard

Born at Beaver Crossing, Nebraska, May 10, 1887, Alvin John Gard is the son of Joseph and Sophia (Billhorn) Gard. His father was born at Crown Point, Indiana, in 1864, and was one of Seward County's pioneers. A carpenter and farmer, his homestead was purchased from the B. and M. Railroad, and is still intact. His parents came to America in the early 1800's. Joseph Gard died at Beaver Crossing, February 5, 1889. His wife, Sophia Billhorn, was born in Bavaria, Germany, November 10, 1856, and came to the United States at the age of 14 years. She was a pioneer wife and mother in Seward county, and lived on the original farm nearly fifty years prior to her death at York on February 2, 1929.

Alvin John Gard attended the public schools of Seward County, and since leaving school has always engaged in farming. From 1911-14 he was a director of the local school board, and was re-elected and served part of a second term. He is director (1931-32) of the Beaver Crossing Community Club, and an associate member of the Chamber of Commerce. During 1917-18-19 he held membership in the Red Cross, and was a participant in all drives during the war period. He attends the Methodist Episcopal Church. His hobbies are mechanics and carpentry, and his sports are hunting and an occasional game of billiards.

On January 26, 1921, Mr. Gard was united in marriage to Ruth Pratt at Omaha. Mrs. Gard, who was born at Beaver Crossing, October 30, 1900, was a teacher prior to her marriage. With the exception of her grandfather on the maternal side, who was German, she is descended from early English settlers in America. There are three sons, John Alvin, born February 2, 1922, who was Nebraska's grand champion boy at the State Fair of 1928, with a score of 97.7; Gene Arthur, born November 9, 1923; and Don Irvin, born June 18, 1926. Residence: Beaver Crossing.

Albert Johnston Gardner

A leader in the professional activities of Orleans, Nebraska, is Dr. Albert Johnston Gardner who was born at Brookfield, Missouri, April 28, 1873. His father, Johnston C. Gardner, who was born at Rimersburg, Pennsylvania, March 25, 1843, is now retired; he was a soldier in the Civil War and fought in the battle of Gettysburg. He is still living and resides in Kansas City. His mother, Elizabeth Jane (Spivey), whose ancestry was Scotch, was born at Wheeling, West Virginia, April

20, 1850, and died at Quincy, Illinois, July 31, 1922. She was descended from General Winfield Scott.

Dr. Gardner was graduated from an academy at Brookfield, was a student at Washington University where he received the M. D. degree in 1901, and attended the University of Michigan, 1887-88. He is a member of the medical fraternity Nu Sigma Nu. From 1901 to 1905 he served as medical examiner for the Chicago, Burlington & Quincy Railroad at St. Joseph, Missouri, Alliance and Wymore, Nebraska, and since 1905 has been engaged in the private practice of medicine at Orleans, Nebraska.

He was married to Nell Gertrude Fort at Red Cloud, Nebraska, June 24, 1905. Mrs. Gardner, whose parents were Scotch and Irish, was born at Brownsville, Nebraska, April 24, 1882. They have one son, Albert Fort, born January 28, 1911, who is a student at the University of Nebraska.

Dr. Gardner was delegate to the Republican National convention held in 1922 and 1916. He is a member of the county, state, district, and national medical associations, is chairman of the county chapter of the Red Cross, and is past president of the Orleans Rotary Club which he helped organize. He is a 32nd degree Mason and Shrine member, is affiliated with the First Presbyterian Church of Orleans, and holds membership in the Nebraskana Society. His favorite sport is tennis.

During the World War Dr. Gardner served as captain in the Medical Reserve Corps of the United States Army and prior to that had been active in the National Guard of Missouri for five years. He has been a resident of Nebraska for the past 30 years and is licensed to practice medicine in Missouri, Indiana, and Nebraska. Residence: Orleans.

Anna Monroe Gardner

Anna Monroe Gardner was born at Lexington, Dawson County, Nebraska, August 6, 1874, the daughter of E. D. and Annie (Monroe) Johnson. Her father, who was a real estate man and hotel keeper, was born of English parents at Farmington, Maine, February 23, 1839, and died at Lexington, March 6, 1907. Her mother, who is of Scotch descent, was born at Pictou, Nova Scotia, May 10, 1849.

Mrs. Gardner received her early education in public schools and boarding school, and later attended business college. She holds membership in the Red Cross; the Nebraskana Society; and the Eastern Star. She is affiliated with Holy Trinity Episcopal Church at Lincoln, Nebraska. She is a member of the Democratic Party.

Her marriage to Fred Gardner was solemnized at Lincoln, January 1, 1896. Mr. Gardner, who was born at London, England, February 4, 1863, is a jeweler. Four children were born to them: Kenneth, born March 14, 1897, who died July 14, 1897; Walter, born May 16, 1898, who married Florence Graves; Fred, born September 4, 1904, who married Henrietta Claussen; and Louise, born April 21, 1907, who married Russel Doty, Walter is in business with his father; Fred is in business in Omaha.

During the World War Walter Gardner served in the United State Army in France for one year. He is now first lieutenant in the Officers Reserve Corps, and is a member of the American Legion. Fred Gardner, Jr., is second lieutenant in the Officers Reserve Corps. Residence: Lincoln.

Walter Johnson Gardner

Walter J. Gardner was born at Lincoln, Nebraska, May 16, 1898, and has lived there all his life. His father, Fred Gardner, who was born at London, England, February 4, 1864, is a jeweler. Anna Monroe (Johnson) Gardner, his mother, was born at Lexington, Dawson County, Nebraska, August 6, 1878. She was active in Red Cross work during the World War.

Mr. Gardner was graduated from the Lincoln High School in 1917, and later was a student at the University of Nebraska, where he was elected to membership in Alpha Tau Omega. He has been in the retail jewelry business since 1919, and is now a partner in the firm Fred Gardner & Son, Jewelers.

He was united in marriage with Florence Lillian Graves at Lincoln, February 4, 1921. Mrs. Gardner, who was born at Grand Island, Hall County, Nebraska, January 16, 1900. They have two children: Sidney Ann, born November 13, 1921; and Walter J., Jr., born April 22, 1924.

During the World War Mr. Gardner served as sergeant, 108th Ammunition Train, 58th Field Artillery Brigade, 33rd Division. He is now first lieutenant of the 341st Field Artillery, United States Army Reserve Corps; is past president of the local chapter of the Reserve Officers Association; is a member of the Lincoln Junior Chamber of Commerce; and is affiliated with Westminster Presbyterian Church of Lincoln. He also holds membership in the Nebraskana Society and the Masons, (Consistory, Shrine). Residence: Lincoln.

William Henry Gardner

William Henry Gardner, educator and school executive, was born at Lee Center, Illinois, July 19, 1855, the son of Joseph and Hannah Maria (Shaw) Gardner. His father, who was born at Hornby, Steuben County, New York, July 9, 1823, and died at Del Norte, Rio Grande County, Colorado, July 2, 1894, was a public official for many years, serving on the board of education, and as justice of the peace and police judge. He was descended from James Sweet Gardner and Malinda Hammond Gardner, of New England.

His mother, who was born at Lewiston, New York, August 17, 1829, and died at Del Norte, January 17, 1878, was a teacher. She was the daughter of William and Sarah Aldrich Shaw.

Mr. Gardner's elementary education was received in the public schools of Ashton, Illinois. Later he attended Rock River Seminary, at Mount Morris, Illinois, for two years, and received the A. B. degree at Nebraska Wesleyan University, in 1910. His A. M. degree was awarded by the University of Nebraska, in 1911. From 1896 to 1898, he was editor of the *University Place Gazette*. For thirty-seven years he has taken part in the educational activities of Nebraska, holding the following positions: superintendent of city schools at Pawnee City, Tecumseh, Auburn, Wymore, Nebraska City, and Fremont; principal of the junior normal school at North Platte for two terms; head of the consolidated Smith-Hughes Schools at Virginia, for three years; and county superintendent of schools in Lancaster County for three terms.

On July 3, 1878, he was married to Elizabeth Nesbitt at Hanover, Jo Davies County, Illinois. Mrs. Gardner was born at Hanover, June 5, 1858, the daughter of John and Jane (Moffett) Nesbitt. Her ancestry is Scotch-Irish. Five children were born to them, four of whom are living. Gertrude H., born May 14, 1879, who married Albert Nelson Dafoe, is a graduate of Nebraska Wesleyan University and the University of Nebraska, and was a teacher in the Kearney Normal School, at Kearney, Nebraska, fourteen years. Mary E., born April 19, 1882, who married James F. Powell, is a graduate of Nebraska Wesleyan and the University of Nebraska, and was a high school instructor for six years. John M., born May 1, 1886, who married Allie Furlong, is an architect at Denver. Charles H., born November 13, 1888, who married Anna Madden, is a civil engineer; he was a lieutenant in France, in the World War. Erma J., was born May 8, 1892, and died on January 4, 1893.

Mr. Gardner is a member of the National Educational Association, the Nebraska State Educational Association, the Nebraska State Historical Society and the Nebraskana Society. He is a Mason, Knight Templar, and a member of the Y. M. C. A. and a life member of the American Bible Society. He is affiliated with the Methodist Episcopal Church. Residence: Tecumseh.

Merlin Robert Garey

Born at Beaver City, Nebraska, January 17, 1900, Merlin Robert Garey is the son of Harry B. and Lena (Wittenbach) Garey. His father, who is a leading farmer near Beaver City and is prominent in community affairs there, was born in Pennsylvania, July 23, 1876. His mother, who is particularly interested in church work, was born in West Virginia, July 5, 1879; her father, who was born in Germany,served in the Prussian Army, and her mother was a native of Switzerland.

Mr. Garey attended a rural school and in 1918 was graduated from the Beaver City High School. He attended the University of Nebraska where he was graduated with the Bachelor of Science degree in Business Administration in 1922; he was elected to membership in Alpha Kappa Psi. He served as a bank clerk at Beaver City, 1918, was connected with the Wilsonville State Bank, 1922-29, and since 1929 has been cashier and manager of the Farmers & Merchants Bank at Edison, Nebraska.

On June 30, 1925, his marriage to Cora Viola Johnson occurred at Wilsonville; she was born of Irish ancestry at Wilsonville, March 17, 1902. Their two children are: Neal Robert, born June 2, 1926; and Marjory Ann, born June 1, 1930.

Mr. Garey is secretary-treasurer of the Edison Commercial Club, is affiliated with the Church of Christ at Edison, and holds membership in the Nebraskana Society and the Masonic Lodge. He is interested in gardening and football. Residence: Edison.

John Dunmire Garmire

Born at Mount Vernon, Ohio, January 18, 1861, John D. Garmire has long been one of the most influential residents of Thayer County. He is the son of Daniel and Elizabeth (Dunmire) Garmire, both natives of Ohio. Daniel Garmire, whose German ancestors settled in Maryland about four generations ago, was born at Benton, Ohio, June 12, 1823, and was a farmer and stockraiser. He died at Benton, January 29, 1901. His wife Elizabeth, was born at Cadiz Junction, Harrison County, Ohio, December 21, 1828, and died at Benton, March 25, 1895. She was of Pennsylvania Dutch descent.

John D. Garmire attended district school at Benton, Ohio, and Normal School at Millersburg. He taught for four years in Ohio, and coming west engaged in the lumber and hardware business. He is an extensive landowner, and at the present time is an independent adjuster of all types of losses except life insurance.

On May 14, 1883, he was united in marriage to Rosa Barbara Kleppinger at Walnut, Iowa. Mrs. Garmire, who was born at Machunk, Pennsylvania, May 14, 1863, is of Pennsylvania Dutch extraction. There are four daughters: Iva M., born July 23, 1884, who married Roy R. Lockwood; Beatrice E., born December 1, 1888, who married Charles S. Hoyt; Bernice V., born December 1, 1888, who married Dr. Milton J. Powell; and Delma M., born November 6, 1892, who married Charles T. Wilson.

Mr. Garmire is a Democrat. His fraternal organizations include the Elks (No. 1203), Modern Woodmen of America (No. 578), the Independent Order of Odd Fellows and the Knights of Pythias (both lodges have surrendered their charters). He is a member of the Omaha Chamber of Commerce, the Red Cross and the Nebraskana Society. Residence: Hebron.

Charles Walter Garrison

Charles W. Garrison was born near Union, Cass County, Nebraska, on the same farm that he occupies today. His father, George Washington Garrison, who was a farmer, was born at Clayton, Indiana, June 10, 1835, and died at Union, April 29, 1914.

His mother, Amelia Ann (Newton) Garrison, of Pennsylvania Dutch ancestry, was born in Pittsburg, Pennsylvania, in 1836, and died at Union, July 25, 1894.

Mr. Garrison resides on a farm which has been conceded by many to be the most beautiful country home in the state. It is located on the land where his father farmed for many years. On the high land overlooking the Missouri river, it includes an architecturally perfect house with a landscaped garden, and shrubs and flowers of almost every kind.

As a boy he worked on the farm and attended country school, later graduating from the Union High School. On December 30, 1896, he was married to Emma Frances Sans, at Rock Bluffs, Nebraska. Mrs. Garrison, who was born at Rock Bluffs, August 23, 1878, is of German and French descent. Her grandfather was a direct descendant of John Hardin. Seven children were born to Mr. and Mrs. Garrison, five of whom are living. They are: Ruth, Born September 14, 1897, who married Paul Hanley; Beulah, born September 14, 1897, who died February 29, 1910; Virgie Dee, born April 21, 1900, who died February 29, 1925, and was married to Glenn Todd; Flora A., born June 11, 1901, who married Arnold Fahrlander; Clifton K., born November 25, 1903, who married Margaret Swan; George A., born October 16, 1907; and Margaret A., born July 22, 1909, who married John G. Howard. Four of the children are high school graduates; one daughter attended the University of Nebraska; another studied business; and a third took a teacher's course at the Peru State Teachers' College. George is a graduate of the University of Nebraska College of Agriculture. Both sons are Masons.

Mr. Garrison, whose farming is diversified, is a strong believer in county agent work, and has co-operated with the Cass County Agent in several activities. In 1928 he was appointed one of the Master Farmers of Nebraska and was awarded a gold medal in recognition of this honor. A resident of Nebraska for his entire life, he has been prominent in his community in civic and county affairs.

He is a member of the Master Farmers' Club; the Farm Bureau; the Farmers' Union; the Red Cross; and the Nebraska Society. He is affiliated with the Union Baptist Church. He is a Republican. Residence: Union.

Emma Frances Garrison

Emma Frances Garrison, wife of Charles Walter Garrison, was born at Rock Bluffs, Nebraska, August 23, 1878, of German and French extraction. One of her grandfathers was a direct descendant of John Hardin.

She attended public school and on December 30, 1896, was married to Charles Walter Garrison at Rock Bluffs. To them were born the following children: Ruth, September 14, 1897, who married Paul Hanley; Beulah, twin of Ruth, who died February 29, 1900; Virgie Dee, born April 21, 1900, who married Glen Todd, and who died February 29, 1925; Flora A., born June 11, 1901, who married Arnold Fahrlander; Clifton K., born November 25, 1903, who married Margaret Swan; George A., born October 16, 1907; and Margaret, born July 22, 1909.

Mrs. Garrison is extremely proud of her fine family. She is a member of the Union Baptist Church, the Red Cross and the Nebraskana Society. Residence: Union.

Francis Brown Garrison

Francis Brown Garrison was born at Missouri Valley, Iowa, September 11, 1896, the son of Edgar Soloman Garrison and Edith Mariam (Clouser) Garrison. His father, who was born at Clarence, Iowa, January 10, 1873, and died at Horconcitos, Panama, July 15, 1915, was a distinguished lawyer and judge of the district courts in Panama Canal Zone. The latter traveled extensively in Venzuela and South American Countries for several years; his father, the grandfather of Francis Garrison, was a lawyer and capitalist in Dennison, Iowa.

His mother was born in Pennsylvania. She is a direct descendant of the John Brown of Civil War and Abolitionist fame. Mr. Garrison was graduated from the Abraham Lincoln High School at Council Bluffs, Iowa, in 1915, and in 1918, received the degree of Doctor of Dental Surgery at Creighton University Dental College where he was a member of Xi Psi Phi. He has practiced dentistry at Oakdale for the past 14 years.

He is a member of the Northeast Nebraska District Dental Society, the Nebraska State Dental Society, and the American Dental Society. Dr. Garrison is a Master Mason, and holds membership in the Royal Arch and Council bodies of that organization. He is a member of the Nebraskana Society, the Republican Party, and the American Legion. During the World War he served as a private in the Medical Reserve Corps. His sports include bass fishing and hunting.

On May 10, 1930, he was married to Helen A. Hana at Le Mars, Iowa. She was born at Elgin, Nebraska, September 8, 1904. Residence: Oakdale.

Samuel Jefferson Garrison

Samuel Jefferson Garrison, farmer and cattle raiser, was born in Peoria, Illinois, May 25, 1874, son of Lemuel Jefferson and Isabelle (Wayson) Garrison.

The father, born in Ohio, was a soldier in the Civil War, and later a farmer. He died at Burwell, and was closely related to Henry Hudson thru the maternal line. His father was born on the Isle of Man. Isabelle Wayson's father came from England, and married Elizabeth Hunter. She is deceased.

Samuel Jefferson Garrison attended the public schools of Elmwood, Illinois, from which he was graduated on May 15, 1897. He was a member of the track team there, and held the state record of 22.4 for the 220 yard dash.

Since 1890 Mr. Garrison has operated the same farm. He introduced Red Polled cattle in Garfield County, and operated one of the first dairies in his locality. He was married to Luella Isabelle Compton at Burwell on December 29, 1905, and to them were born three children: Rowene, October 27, 1906, who married Ray O. Bissell; Lemuel J., born September 2, 1913; and Linn Compton, born August 2, 1919. Mrs. Garrison was born at Thomastown, Minnesota, August 22, 1885.

The Garrison and Compton families have been farmers as far back as they can be traced. They were all pioneers in Pennsylvania, Ohio, Illinois, Minnesota and Nebraska. There are five generations on the mother's side now living, the oldest of each generation being a woman. Four generations reside on the home farm at this time and three generations have attended the local district school.

Mr. Garrison is a member of the First Congregational Church, and was recently made a life member of The Nebraskana Society. During the World War period he recruited skilled labor for the government. Residence: Burwell.

Orlie Robert Garwood

Orlie Robert Garwood, mayor of Ogallala, was born at Marquette, Nebraska, October 2, 1889, son of Miller and Amelia (Austin) Garwood. The father is a native of Pennsylvania, born March 21, 1852. He is a retired farmer, and lives at Aurora. His wife, Amelia, was born in Illinois, May 31, 1852.

Mr. Garwood attended public schools and Aurora Business College in Hamilton County. He has been in the grocery and meat business for a number of years at Ogallala. He was elected on the People's ticket as mayor of Ogallala in 1930, the first mayor to be elected in Ogallala by the people.

On February 22, 1911, he was married to Abbie Jane Mourer at Aurora. She was born at Benkleman, November 2, 1887. Mr. Garwood is a Methodist, a member of the Commercial Club and the Masons. Residence: Ogallala. (Photograph in Album).

John Edward Gaskill

John Edward Gaskill was born at Waverly, Nebraska, September 13, 1879, the son of George Washington and Johanna (Hurley) Gaskill. George Washington Gaskill was born at Bluffton, Ohio, October 20, 1846, and homesteaded near Waverly, in 1869. He is interested in dairying. His family, which was English and Scotch, came from England and settled in Burlington, New Jersey, in the late 1700's.

Johanna Hurley, who was born at Dover, Ohio, April 10, 1852, died at Lincoln, July 6, 1904. Her parents came from Milton, Ireland, sailing about 1840, shortly after the great famine. Mr. Gaskill recalls his grandfather telling of the voyage which took seven weeks, and of the violent storm in which the vessel was nearly wrecked.

Mr. Gaskill attended the public schools of Waverly, and the Lincoln High School. He traveled out of Lincoln from 1898 to 1903 for a music firm. In 1903, he settled in Nebraska City, and entered the music business for himself. Since that time he has been the owner and manager of the Gaskill Music Company. He has increased his business during these years, and at the present time maintains a stock at Auburn, also.

He was married to Mamie N. Beard at Broken Bow, Nebraska, September 18, 1901. There are three children: Louise, born in June, 1902, who married Edwin Moran; Eunice F., born in August, 1908; and Forrest D., born in August, 1910.

Mr. Gaskill is a Republican. He is affiliated with the First Presbyterian Church of Nebraska City, and is a member of the Young Men's Christian Association. He is a member of the Red Cross, the Chamber of Commerce, the Rotary Club, the Nebraska State Historical Society and the Nebraskana Society. His most prized possession is his collection of historical pictures of eastern Nebraska, several of which have been turned over to the State Historical Society.

His fraternal organizations include the Elks, the Woodmen of the World and the Modern Woodmen of America. He belongs to the Nebraska City Country Club. Residence: Nebraska City.

Mamie N. Gaskill

A native of Kentucky, Mamie N. Gaskill has been a resident of Nebraska about thirty years. She was born at Albany, January 10, 1880, daughter of William D. and Mary (Reneau) Beard. Her father was also a native of Kentucky. His father left Ireland and came to Kentucky, where he homesteaded in the early days of the state.

Mary Reneau was born in Kentucky, daughter of a French clergyman, who was one of the founders of the Christian Church, and a noted religious educator in that state.

Mamie N. Gaskill attended the public and high schools of Kentucky, and was graduated in 1896. She was married to John Edward Gaskill at Broken Bow, Nebraska, September 18, 1901. There are three children: Louise, who graduated from Hardin College, Missouri, and who is a teacher in home economics; Eunice who is majoring in piano at the University of Nebraska, and who is a member of Alpha Omicron Pi; and Forrest, who is a member of Phi Kappa Psi, and is majoring in chemistry at the University of Nebraska.

Before her marriage Mrs. Gaskill was a teacher in Kentucky. She is now associated with her husband in the Gaskill Music Store at Nebraska City. She was especially active in Red Cross work during the World War and is still a member of the organization. She is a member of the First Presbyterian Church. She is a member of the civics department of the Nebraska City Woman's Club, and a member of the Music Club and the Eastern Star. Her social club is the Nebraska City Country Club. Residence: Nebraska City.

Sherlock Bronson Gass

Sherlock B. Gass, Nebraska educator and professor of English at the University of Nebraska, has lived in this state for the past 26 years. He was born at Mansfield, Richland County, Ohio, October 17, 1878, the son of Florien Preston and Harriet Elizabeth (Bronson) Gass. His father, who was a business man, was born at Mansfield, December 18, 1850, and died at St. Petersburg, Florida, February, 1924. He was directly descended from Benjamin Gass who came to Philadelphia from Antrin, Ireland, in 1690. Sherlock B. Gass' mother was born at Sandusky, Ohio, August 25, 1855.

Professor Gass attended the public schools of Mansfield and Chicago, and was graduated from Steele High School at Dayton, Ohio. He was awarded his Ph. B., at Chicago, 1904. In 1905 he was instructor in rhetoric at the University of Nebraska. Since 1916 he has been professor of English in this institution. He is the author of *A Lover of the Chair*, 1919; *Criers of the Shops*, 1925; and *A Tap on the Shoulder*, 1929.

He was married to Alice Virginia Dougan at Lincoln, Lancaster County, Nebraska, June 7, 1926. Mrs. Gass was born at St. Louis, Missouri, September 17, 1905. They have one son: Geoffrey, born July 18, 1928.

Professor Gass is a member of the Lincoln University Club and the Sierra Club, of California. He is an independent. Residence: Lincoln.

Clarence Ray Gates

As an educator and school executive Clarence Ray Gates has been active in professional affairs in Nebraska for over 25 years. He was born at Baker, Kansas, December 23, 1885, the son of James Lyman and Annie Vio (Racey) Gates. His father, who was a railroad station agent and telegrapher, was born in Athens County, Ohio, October 29, 1851, and died at Stella, Nebraska, January 10, 1897; his English and Scotch ancestors came to America in 1638.

Annie Vio (Racey) Gates, his mother, who was born at Beloit, Wisconsin, April 9, 1864, has been editor of several Nebraska weekly newspapers including the *Blair Tribune*. She has written many feature articles for newspapers and is active in political affairs in her community and state. Her ancestry is English.

Mr. Gates attended the public schools of Baker, Kansas, Stella, Falls City, and Auburn, Nebraska, completing his high school education at the latter in 1903. He was graduated from the Nebraska State Teachers College at Peru in 1907, receiving the B. Ed. degree in 1911, was awarded the A. B. degree at the University of Nebraska in 1916, and received the A. M. degree at Columbia University in 1920. He was a member of the inter-state debating team at Peru State Teachers College, was president of various literary and debating societies, and was president of the senior summer class in 1916. He was elected to membership in Phi Delta Kappa and took a prominent part in dramatics.

At the age of 13 Mr. Gates became a messenger boy for the Missouri Pacific Railway Company at Auburn and later held various positions in this organization. He has served as principal in the high schools at Oak-

land, Nebraska City, and Blair, Nebraska, and has been superintendent of schools at Pilger, West Point, Columbus, and Grand Island, Nebraska. During various summer terms he has been instructor in the University of Nebraska, Peru State Teachers College, Kearney State Teachers College, and Grand Island College.

At this time he is superintendent of public schools at Grand Island where he is active in civic and religious affairs. He is the author of *The Management of Smaller Schools*, 1923, and numerous magazine articles. Mr. Gates is president of the Nebraska State Teachers Association, was president of the Nebraska Schoolmasters' Club in 1925, is a member of the National Education Association and the National Society for the Study of Education, and holds membership in the board of directors of the Nebraska Tuberculosis Association.

He is affiliated with Trinity Methodist Episcopal Church, holding membership in the board of trustees, is a member of the Grand Island Chamber of Commerce, and holds membership in the Grand Island Rotary Club of which he was president in 1927. He holds membership in the Woodland Country Club of Grand Island. He has been a member of the Men's Work Commission of the Methodist Episcopal Church since 1928, is a member of the 1932 General Conference Council of that organization, and is a member of the Board of Trustees of Nebraska Wesleyan University.

During the World War he served as a Four Minute Speaker and assisted in loan drives. His favorite sport is golfing. He is a member of Ancient Free and Accepted Masons and Royal Arch Masons and holds membership in the Red Cross. He is listed in *Who's Who in America*.

He was united in marriage with Maude Beatrice Nixon at Omaha, Nebraska, September 1, 1909. Mrs. Gates, whose English ancestors came to America about 1650, was born near Clarinda, Iowa, February 19, 1886. Their two children are: Esther, born July 18, 1913; and Clarence, born October 2, 1927. Esther is a sophomore at Lindenwood College. Residence: Grand Island.

Elmer Charles Gates

Elmer Charles Gates was born at Clarks, Nebraska, April 20, 1900, son of Francis C. and Rua Adeline (Wright) Gates. The father was born in Clarks, March 6, 1873, and is a farmer. His wife, Rua, was born at Weeping Water, September 22, 1883.

In June, 1918, Mr. Gates was graduated from Clarks High School, and afterward completed a special course in journalism at the University of Missouri.

He was married on December 25, 1921, to Evelyn Annette Buscher at Hastings. Mrs. Gates was born at Thomasboro, Illinois, September 23, 1903. They have two children, Marcia Jean, born May 3, 1923; and Dorothy Mae, born February 7, 1926.

Mr. Gates is a Republican. He served as a sergeant in the medical detachment, 1st infantry, regular army during 1918 and 1919, and is a member of the American Legion. He is state secretary of the Nebraska State Association of the National Association of Letter Carriers, and of all branches of the Odd Fellows. He is affiliated with the Christian Church. His hobby is organization work in connection with letter carriers association. Residence: Hastings.

George Minor Gates

George Minor Gates, clergyman, lawyer and author, was born at Oquawka, Henderson County, Illinois, son of David and Edith Frances (Rust) Gates. David Gates was born in Trumbull County, Ohio, January 9, 1833, and died at Table Rock, Nebraska, February 13, 1899. A farmer, he was always a Republican. He was descended from General Gates of Revolutionary fame, and the Reverand Stephen Gates, of Ipswich, England, who with his wife, Ann Schute, settled in New England in 1638, at Hingham, Massachusetts. He died June 9, 1662. A Congregationalist minister, he served in the Indian and Colonial wars. Mathias Gates, father of David Gates fought in the War of 1812 with the Ohio militia, and for services was awarded a military land warrant, No. 7993, which is on record in Washington.

Edith Frances Rust was born at Galesburg, Illinois, in 1842, and died at Oakland, Iowa, in October 1873. She attended the Galesburg Schools, married David Gates on May 6, 1868, and was the mother of five sons and one daughter, Annie, now Mrs. Campbell of Hastings, Nebraska. The Rust family came from Pennsylvania.

George M. Gates attended high school at White Cloud, Kansas, until 1878 and at Salem, Nebraska, 1879. He took college course at Cornell College 1880-82, and was graduated with an LL. B. from the State University of Kansas in 1884. A leader in oratory both in Cornell and Kansas State, he was second in line for state oratorical honors at Kansas and met William A. Quail, later an honored bishop of the Methodist Church.

On August 16, 1882, he was united in marriage to Celia Ann Clark at Morrison, Illinois. She is a daughter of John Calvin Clark who served in the Civil War with the 131st Iowa Infantry, and died in Andersonville Prison in 1862. She was born in Iowa, on May 22, 1862, and is believed to be a descendant of Clark of the Lewis and Clark expedition. She was graduated from Cornell College and is a member of Philomathean Society. There are seven sons and daughters, as follows: W. Edgar, born July 4, 1883, a coal dealer at Lincoln, who married Fannie Noyes. Cecil Clark, born July 14, 1885, a banker in Lincoln, who married Margaret Mulder. Bernice Edith, born August 13, 1888, a music teacher, who married Malcolm Showalter, who is in the life insurance business at Sioux City, Iowa. LeRoy Mallieu, born June 22, 1891, state entomologist, married Mattie Taviner. George Milton, born March 10, 1893, a garageman at Lincoln, married Louise Goddie. Lloyd Emerson, born in 1898, a garageman in Lincoln, married Lenora Biggs. Frances Cella, born March 14, 1902, married Lee H. Willitson.

Mr. Gates has been active as a clergyman, lecturer, lawyer and author for many years. He has written, among others, the following: *First Log Cabin in Lincoln, Nebraska,* 1928, *Through Story Land, Scenic Wonders,* etc. He practiced law at Stella, Omaha and Lincoln, has officiated at 556 weddings and as many funerals and has been called upon to give addresses in leading churches and for high school commencements. He was formerly lecturer at th University of Nebraska and Nebraska Wesleyan, and has given travel talks before high schools and educational bodies.

In 1891 he was ordained a Methodist minister at the Nebraska Conference of 1891, and served at Peru, Table Rock, Fairmont, Schuyler, Lincoln and Syracuse. He is a member of the University Place Business Men's Association, Knights of Pythias, Odd Fellows, Rebekahs, Knights Templar and Shrine bodies of the Masons. He is a member also of the Nebraska Writers and Authors Guild and The Nebraskana Society. Residence: Lincoln.

Jed Mills Gates

On November 29, 1862, Jed M. Gates, banker and retired farmer, was born at Gilmore, Sarpy County, Nebraska. He is the son of Amos and Samantha (Arnett) Gates, both of whom are deceased. His father, a farmer. stock raiser, and banker, was active in the political life of Nebraska, serving for many years as state representative. He was born at West Jefferson, Madison County, Ohio, September 5, 1829, and died at Gilmore, Nebraska, August 5, 1905. His wife, who was a school teacher, was born at West Jefferson, December 24, 1832, and died at Gilmore.

Mr. Gates was educated in the country schools and later attended Creighton College at Omaha. A resident of Nebraska all his life, he has been prominent in business and political circles for many years. He is a stock raiser and feeder; has been connected with the Packer's National Bank of South Omaha; and was at one time secretary of the *Papillion Times.* A Democrat, he has served three terms in the senate, and two terms in the house of representatives.

He was united in marriage January 9, 1884, at Gilmore, with Elizabeth Marion Trumble. Mrs. Gates, the daughter of A. W. Trumble of Hulberton, New York, was born in Bellevue, Nebraska, December 1, 1885. She is interested in banking and farming. Six children were born to this marriage: Delia S., born April 26, 1885, who married LeRoy Miller; Amos W., born November 29, 1886, who married Margaret Gretchen Godfrey; Fred T., born April 1, 1889, who married Marie E. Beals; Ida Maud, born February 21, 1891, who married Clair F. King; Harold Bryan, born October 4, 1894, who married Lora M. Gehringer; and Thomas Kelly, born July 17, 1905, who

Mr. Gates served on executive committees and was active in all drives during the World War. He is a member of the Red Cross and has served on the local school board for 21 years. A 32nd degree Mason, and Modern Woodman of America, he is also a member of the Anderson Grove Presbyterian Church of Fort Crook. Residence: Fort Crook.

Cecil Leon Gatten

Cecil Leon Gatten, son of Thomas and Fannie (Jeanes) Gatten, was born at Brighton, Illinois, December 31, 1888, and for the past eight years has resided at Ainsworth, Nebraska. His father, born at Barnesville, Ohio, May 3, 1854, was a gardener and well known flower grower. He was the son of an Ohio schoolmaster, whose family came to America, from England, probably about 1700. Thomas Gatten died at Davenport, Iowa, July 10, 1926.

Fannie Jeanes, wife of Thomas, was born at Ibberton, Dorsetshire, England, January 2, 1864, and died at Carroll, Iowa, July 31, 1917. She was the daughter of a small landowner in England, an excellent seamstress and a splendid cook.

Dr. Gatten attended public school in Carroll County, Iowa, and was graduated from the four year course in three years. There he was valedictorian of his class, and represented his school in various oratorical contests.

From 1907 to 1910, Dr. Gatten attended the State University of Iowa, (a Whitney Carr Scholarship), working for board and room as well as other expenses. He was a member of the college choral club and assistant in entomology while in college.

His marriage to Olive Stella Hoffmann was solemnized at Iowa City, Iowa, June 11, 1910. Mrs. Gatten, who was born at Riverside, Iowa, February 27, 1890, is descended from early German settlers in Illinois; her father a veteran of the Civil War. She is a breeder of purebred Black Orpingtons, and a winner at the Chicago Show in 1930. There are three children: Emma Lynnette, born June 10, 1911, who is a sophomore at the University of Nebraska, majoring in home economics, and an honor student; George Thomas, born December 2, 1913, is a freshman in dairy husbandry at the University of Nebraska; while Modesta Frances, born March 14, 1916, is in high school.

Dr. Gatten was registered for pre-medic work his senior year in college, when circumstances forced him to leave school. The winter of 1912 he was principal of the Lanesboro, Iowa, High School, then returning to Iowa City. His next connection was with the Singer Sewing Machine Company. Later he held the position of manager for Johnson and Washington Counties, with a store in Iowa City, at that time being the youngest store manager in the company's employ.

The idea of practicing the healing art was still with him, and as the university had now begun to require two years pre-medical work, and Iowa City offered so little in the way of part time employment, he decided to go to Des Moines, in an effort to find a means of attending Still College. There his activity as a collector precluded any chance of college, and after a hard winter he was offered the position of manager at Newton, Iowa. After several months in the country, an argument arose regarding an advanced position with the company, and Dr. Gatten resigned.

Then followed almost a year with the Bollhoefer Mercantile Company in their grocery and collection departments at Colfax, Iowa. The death of his wife's father called them to Hills, Iowa, and there they became the owners of a small cement block plant. The following fall term, not being rushed with work, he taught district school. The so-called "worst school in the county" offered better money, for the spring term, and there he successfully taught what was known as "Pokertown" School.

The following summer was passed in hard work, and brought him the opportunity of becoming princpial of the Ollie, Iowa, High School. But business called until mid summer, and the war made shipping almost impossible. So, having used up most of the cement blocks in building a home, Dr. and Mrs. Gatten decided to go where war work was going on.

It was a question of distance which made him choose Rock Island, instead of Des Moines. Applying for work in the morning, he went to work in the afternoon. Advancement came rapidly, and as the night foreman needed an assistant, his ability with a pencil and paper helped him ahead. Only the hundred of volunteer workmen who went through the hours of hellish rush will appreciate what the men in charge went through. Men were driven night and day to their utmost to get out badly wanted weapons.

After the war, the experimental tanks came to Dr. Gatten's attention, and Mark VIII parts were a nightmare. Unrest, uncertainty and continual reduction of forces were followed by his taking a collection and sales position with the Bernard Manufacturing Company of Iowa City. Finally he entered the Palmer School of Chiropractic at Davenport, and graduation found him with all A grades but one. He passed the National Board of Chiropractic examiners and then the Iowa board with one of the highest grades ever given. After one year's practice he removed to Ainsworth. In March, 1927, Dr. Gatten was graduated from the Dearborn College of Osteopathy with the degree of Doctor of Osteopathy.

Dr. Gatten is an outstanding citizen of Ainsworth. He has served for the past eighteen months as president of the Ainsworth Commercial Club, and was recently elected president for 1932. He is justifiably proud of the various activities of that organization during his term of office. These include the arrangement and publication of the Fish and Game booklet of which 3000 have been distributed; the open house celebration with 11,000 visitors; an increase in membership from 47 to 100; the leasing and licensing of the airport and building of a hangar; the poultry show; large community Christmas trees with treats to more than 1250, in 1931; a loaded car of food for Oklahoma drouth sufferers; and several unusually large banquets.

Dr. Gatten is a member of the Nebraska Chiropractors Association, a member of the executive committee of the Lincoln Chiropractic College of Indianapolis, manager of the Municipal Band. He is past consul of the Modern Woodmen of America, and past grand of the Odd Fellows.

A fine bass singer, Dr. Gatten has nearly always been connected with a church choir. He was the author of the class poem at Palmer, and was the assistant editor of the *History of Johnson County, Iowa,* some years ago. He is vice president of the Ainsworth Parents-Teachers' Association and a life member of The Nebraskana Society. His favorite sport is football, while his hobby is books— except essays. He is a rapid and omnivorous reader, Residence: Ainsworth. (Photograph in Album).

Abdon M. Gdanitz

Born at Detroit, Michigan, July 30, 1870, Abdon M. Gdanitz is the son of Edward and Josephine (Ruchniewiec) Gdanitz. The father, a native of West Prussia, Europe, came to America in 1867. He was a cabinet maker by trade, who later became a farmer. He died at Elba, Nebraska, October 24, 1908. His wife, born in West Prussia, died at Elba, in November, 1921.

Abdon M. Gdanitz attended public school in Detroit, and for the past fifty-five years has resided in Howard County, Nebraska. For fourteen years he served as postmaster of Farwell and for thirty-six years has been engaged in the general merchandise business. He is, at the present time, president of A. M. Gdanitz & Sons. A Republican, for fourteen years he has been and still is, city treasurer of Farwell.

His marriage to Katherine Lorkowski was solemnized at St. Paul on June 26, 1895. Mrs. Gdanitz, who is a milliner, assists her husband in his merchantile business in addition to her home duties. There are four sons, Isadore A., born May 10, 1897, who married Anna Demuth; Roman, born July 4, 1896, who married Regina Ann Jankowski; Edmund A., born May 14, 1903, who died April 20, 1909; and Anselm L., born January 17, 1907, who married Frances Flannagan.

Isadore, who served in the World War, is a merchant at Loup City, Nebraska; Roman A., is and for the past five years has been a merchant and insurance man at Farwell. He was for a time the Old Line and is now a member of the Nebraska Hail Adjustment Bureau. Anselm, who now spells his name Danitz, is a dentist at Omaha. The family is Catholic, and affiliated with St. Anthony's Church at Farwell.

Mr. Gdanitz participated vigorously in all wartime activities during the World War. He is a member of the Red Cross, the Federation of Nebraska Retailers, the Ancient Order of United Workmen, The Nebraskana Society, and has served many terms as a member of school boards. He is fond of baseball and enjoys out of door life. Residence: Farwell.

John F. Geesen

John F. Geesen, who has been engaged as a merchant tailor for the past forty-six years, was born in Romsloh, Germany, October 17, 1863. He is the son of Ahlrich Geesen who was also born in Germany and who was deputy sheriff and tax collector.

Educated in public school until 1880, Mr. Geesen learned the tailoring trade and in 1885 settled in Nebraska where he has since been engaged in business. At the present time he is president of the Geesen Company, Inc., vice president of the Seward Lumber Company, and president of the Seward Building and Loan Association.

Mr. Geesen is married to Gertrude Scheibel and they have six children and seven grandchildren. The children are as follows: Clara, who married Edward Green; Edward, who married Ruth Ashby; Josephine, who is unmarried; Marie, who married A. M. Perley; Margaret, who married Stenne Halverson; and Leonard who married Margaret Parker.

Always active in civic and educational work Mr. Geesen was for twelve years a member of the school board and for twelve years a member of the city council. He is president of the welfare board, and a member of the Chamber of Commerce, the Rotary Club, the Modern Woodmen of America, and the Nebraskana Society.

He is a Catholic, and a member of St. Vincent's Church and the Knights of Columbus. In politics he is an independent Republican. Residence: Seward.

Edgar Sharp Beattie Geesaman

A resident of Nebraska 42 years, Edgar S. B. Geesaman has practiced medicine at Fort Calhoun, since 1914. He was born at Minneapolis, Minnesota, December

23, 1887. His father, George E. Geesaman, was born at Shippenburg, Pennsylvania, 1843, and died at Minneapolis, January, 1889; his ancestors came from Holland, originally; he was a merchant for many years at Minneapolis. Martha E. (Elliott) Geesaman was born of Scotch-Irish parents at Shiprenburg, December 13, 1857, and died at Omaha, Douglas County, Nebraska, September 2, 1923.

Dr. Geesaman received his early education in the public schools at Osceola, Nebraska, and in 1907 was graduated from the high school there. He was awarded the M. D. degree at Creighton Medical College in 1912, where he was elected to membership in Phi Rho Sigma.

On August 29, 1917, he was united in marriage to Clara Catharine Rohwer at Fort Calhoun. Mrs. Geesaman was born at Fort Calhoun, June 9, 1893. Three children were born to them, two of whom are living: George Donald, born October 22, 1919, who died October 29, 1919; Edgar Rohwer, born August 2, 1921; and Richard Elliott, born March 17, 1923.

Dr. Geesaman is a Mason, a member of the Nebraska State Medical Society and the Washington County Medical Society. He has always been interested in civic affairs in his community, and is at the present time a member of the local Red Cross and the Salvation Army. He is treasurer of the school board, and is an active member in the Parent-Teachers' Association at Fort Calhoun. His hobby is reading and his favorite sports are football and baseball. Residence: Fort Calhoun.

Max Geisler

Max Geisler was born at Breslau, Germany, April 5, 1864, the son of Adolf and Sophia (Weiss) Geisler. His father, who was a real estate dealer in Germany, was born at Breslau, August 18, 1816, and died there in 1886. His mother was born at Breslau, December 7, 1836, and died in March, 1918.

Mr. Geisler was graduated from high school in 1881, and has been a bird and animal dealer in Omaha, since that date. He owns and is president of the Max Geisler Bird Company of Omaha; owns a warehouse at Omaha; and an import house in New York City. He also has an import house at Hanover, Germany.

He was married to Marie Elsner at Omaha, December 26, 1893. Mrs. Geisler was born at Breslau, Germany, August 15, 1870. They have the following children: May, born October 4, 1894; Howard, born May 10, 1896; Alvan, born January 16, 1898; Herbert, born October 29, 1900; Max, Jr., born September 26, 1905; Pearl, born September 26, 1908; and Richard, born June 16, 1910. All of their children are connected with the business of importing birds and animals, and the manufacturing of bird and animal food.

Mr. Geisler has lived in Nebraska for over forty years, and is a member of the Chamber of Commerce and the Omaha Athletic Club. He is a Mason, and a member of the Lutheran Church. He is fond of fishing and traveling. Residence: Omaha.

George Washington Gell

Born of pioneer Nebraska parents, George Washington Gell has lived in this state all his life and for the past 35 years has been a farmer in Clay County. He was born at Sutton, Nebraska, May 5, 1874, the son of Robert and Ellen (Silverlock) Gell. His father, a farmer, was born at London, England, April 4, 1843, and died at Lincoln, Nebraska, June 29, 1895; he moved to Canada from England in 1851 and came to America in 1869. His mother was born in London, December 3, 1842, and died at Edgar, Nebraska, February 15, 1915.

Mr. Gell received his education in rural schools in Nebraska. He is now retired and is a member of the depositors committee of the Exchange Bank of Ong, Nebraska. For six years he has been a member of the local school board. His religious affiliation is with the Methodist Episcopal Church of Ong.

On December 27, 1905, he was married to Olive Mae Dodge at Geneva. Mrs. Gell, who was born at Shickley, Nebraska, October 27, 1880, was formerly a teacher and postmistress. To this marriage the following children were born: Harry, January 6, 1907, who married Bertha E. Schmidt; Wilson, February 10, 1909, who married Josephine A. Stickell. Both are farmers, and received high school education. Mr. and Mrs. Gell have one grandchild Donna Mae Gell, born March 11, 1931.

Mr. Gell is a Democrat. His favorite sports are baseball and horseback riding, while his hobby is good draft and saddle horses. Residence: Shickley.

William Gellatly

William Gellatly was born in Dane County, Wisconsin, May 24, 1857, the son of William and Margaret (Cameron) Gellatly. For over 54 years he has lived in Clay County, Nebraska, where he has been successfully engaged in farming. Mr. Gellatly recalls the hardships of early pioneer life, including the periods when corn was cheaper to burn than coal. His father, who was also a farmer, was born at Perth, Scotland, March 10, 1834, and died at Sutton, Nebraska, November 24, 1888; he came to this country in 1856. His mother, who was born at Perthshire, Scotland, June 11, 1836, and died at Sutton, December 17, 1918, came to America in 1856.

Mr. Gellatly is a member of the Independent Order of Odd Fellows, and is affiliated with the Congregational Church at Sutton. He married Louie M. Campbell at Sutton, September 20, 1893; she was born at Peoria County, Illinois, December 27, 1870, of Scotch, Manx, and Welsh, descent. She is a member of the Royal Neighbors and Rebekahs. They have one daughter, Martha Margaret, born August 9, 1894, who is also a member of the Royal Neighbors and Rebekahs. Residence: Sutton.

Meta Paula Gemeinhardt

Meta Paula Gemeinhardt, educator, was born at Frohna, Missouri, daughter of C. G. and Julia Magdalena (Fiehler) Gemeinhardt. Her father was born at Frohna, August 31, 1874, and is a farmer, grain cultivator and a poultry raiser. His wife, Julia, was born at Frohna, January 29, 1878. She has six daughters. She is active in club work. Her great-grandparents came from Saxon, Germany, and her parents were American born. Her father was a lumberman.

Miss Gemeinhardt attended Lutheran parochial school at Gurley, and afterward was a student in the public school of Dalton and Potter, Nebraska. She was graduated from high school in Potter, in 1926, and has a teacher's certificate. She won the eighth grade scholarship of Cheyenne County in 1922, high school scholarship in 1926, and received $100 toward entering some church college. During 1925-26 she was a member of the basketball team of Potter High School.

For the past five years she has taught in rural schools and at the present time is instructor of Clover Dale School in Potter. She is a member of St. Paul's Lutheran Church, and in 1927 served as secretary of the local Parent Teachers Association. She has been secretary and chairman of the entertainment committee of the Walther League, of the home society, also. Miss Gemeinhardt's leisure has been devoted to reading, music, and dramatics. She is talented as a musician, plays the piano and sings mezzo soprano. She has had a year and a half of voice training and has performed solo, duet, trio and quartette work before the public repeatedly. She has also taken a leading part in amateur plays in college, high school, and community entertainments. Her favorite sports are tennis, hiking, swimming, and basketball. Residence: Potter. (Photograph in Album).

John A. Gentleman

John A. Gentleman, funeral director, was born at Omaha, August 6, 1881, son of Thomas F. and Catherine Mary (Furlong) Gentleman.

Mr. Gentleman attended the Holy Family parochial school, and was graduated in 1893. In 1898 he was graduated from Creighton University.

Mr. Gentleman is the owner of the John A. Gentleman Mortuary. He is a Roman Catholic and a member of St. Peter's Church. He is a member of the Chamber of Commerce, the Ad-Sell League, the Elks and the Knights of Columbus. Residence: Omaha.

Benjamin Franklin Gentry

Benjamin Franklin Gentry, real estate, insurance, and loan executive, was born in Gilford, Missouri, March 24, 1861, and for the past 60 years has resided in Nebraska.

He is the son of William Ellis and Rebecca (Wiles) Gentry, the former of whom died at Gilford, Missouri, in January, 1862, and the later in Cass County, Nebraska. The father died of typhoid fever contracted from exposure while serving in the Union Army during the Civil War. The mother was the daughter of Thomas Wiles of Mills County, Iowa, and a sister of Captain Isaac Wiles of Plattsmouth, Nebraska.

Mr. Gentry attended public and high school at Plattsmouth, Nebraska, and was graduated from the Valparaiso Normal School at Valparaiso, Indiana. From 1909 unitl the present time he has been president and owner of the Scotts Bluff County Abstract Company. Since 1918 he has been secretary and treasurer of the Gering National Farm Loan Association. He is a Republican, and was the first county clerk of Scotts Bluff County, serving from 1889 until 1892, and is now serving as police judge at Gering. Since 1923 Mr. Gentry has been agent for the Nebraska State Building and Loan Association of Fremont.

On November 30, 1890, he was married to Cora Elizabeth Johnson at Gering, Nebraska. Mrs. Gentry was born at Elmwood, Nebraska, April 4, 1869, and is vice president of the Scotts Bluff County Abstract Company. She attended school at Weeping Water, Nebraska, and was graduated from the Ohio Northern University at Ada, Ohio. She taught school in early pioneer days and was issued the first 1st grade certificate in Scotts Bluff County. Mrs. Gentry is the daughter of Colonel Daniel D. and Elizabeth A. (Lathrop) Johnson. Her Father was a pioneer citizen of Scotts Bluff County and was prominent in the irrigation projects of the North Platte Valley.

Mrs. Gentry is past deputy county clerk and a member of the Eastern Star. There are four children, Harold Ellis, born July 8, 1893, who married Jessie M. Wells, and is county surveyor of Scotts Bluff County and is past chief chemist for the Great Western Sugar Company at Gering, and was the youngest chief chemist in their service at that time; Willard Max, born October 20, 1896, who married Emily M. Nystrom, is a member of Phi Kappa Phi, Alpha Omega Alpha, Phi Rho Sigma and Delta Omega Phi; Elizabeth, born August 28, 1898; and William Johnson, born December 31, 1903, who married Esther H. Nystrom is a member of Phi Chi, Delta Omega Phi and is a prominent physician and surgeon at Gering.

All four children attended the University of Nebraska. Max and William were graduated from Nebraska Wesleyan University, and later from the medical department of the University of Nebraska. Elizabeth was graduated in home economics from Nebraska University. At the present time Max is a Methodist Episcopal Medical missionary at Chungking, China.

Mr. Gentry is a charter member of Gering Lodge No. 201 of the Ancient Free and Accepted Masons, a member of the Modern Woodmen of America, and the National and Nebraska State Title Associations. From 1892 until 1909 he was a member of the school board of district No. 25 in Scotts Bluff County, and from 1909 until 1926 was a member of the city school board at Gering. Since 1929 he has been a member of the cemetery committee at Gering.

Mr. Gentry has had a very active career. In 1886 he and his brother-in-law, S. W. Ripley, irrigated a small tract of land on Winters Creek which was the first irrigation done in the North Platte Valley. He has been prominent in all irrigation projects, and served on the board of directors on the Nine Mile Canal and the Minatare Canal. He was the first treasurer of the Farmer's Irrigation district.

In November, 1890, Mr. Gentry saved the life of Sheriff Milton Blyle as he was attempting to arrest a man charged with cattle theft. The man pulled a gun on the sheriff and Mr. Gentry grabbed the man's arm, the shot went through Mr. Gentry's trouser leg, narrowly missing his foot. The sheriff was unarmed at the time that Mr. Gentry helped arrest George S. Arnold who murdered George Burton in 1888.

Among Mr. Gentry's favorite sports are football and basketball, while his hobbies are gardening, flowers and shrub growing. Mr. and Mrs. Gentry are both charter members of the Methodist Episcopal Church at Gering. Residence: Gering. (Photograph in Album).

Cora Elizabeth Gentry

Cora Elizabeth Gentry, wife of Benjamin Franklin Gentry, was born at Elmwood, Nebraska, April 4, 1879, daughter of Daniel D. and Elizabeth A. (Lathrop) Johnson. Her father was a pioneer citizen of Scotts Bluff County, and prominent in irrigation projects of the North Platte valley.

She attended school at Weeping Water, and was graduated from Valparaiso Normal School and the Ohio Northern University at Ada, Ohio. She taught school in pioneer days, and was issued the first first grade certificate in Scotts Bluff County.

On November 30, 1890, she was married to Benjamin Franklin Gentry at Gering. Mr. Gentry was born at Gilford, Missouri, March 24, 1861. There are four children, Harold Ellis, born July 8, 1893, who married Jessie M. Wells; Willard Max, born October 20, 1896, who married Emily E. Nystrom; Elizabeth, born August 28, 1898; and William Johnson, born December 31, 1903, who married Esther H. Nystrom. (See Nebraskana).

At the present time Mrs. Gentry is an abstracter and is serving as vice president of the Scotts Bluff County Abstract Company. She has served as deputy county clerk of Scotts Bluff County, and is a member of the Order of Eastern Star. Residence: Gering. (Photograph in Album).

Burton Arthur George

Burton George, manufacturer and merchant was born at Brookfield, Wisconsin, October 15, 1871. He is the son of William A. and Mary M. (Barnes) George, the former of whom was an editor and publisher, who served two enlistments in the Union Army with the 5th Wisconsin Regiment in the Civil War. His paternal grandfather was a farmer and justice of the peace in Pennsylvania, and a homesteader in Nebraska.

Mr. George attended the public schools of Hartford, Wisconsin, and Exeter, Nebraska, and on October 15, 1893, was married to Lillie B. Bridges at Lincoln. Mrs. George is a native of What Cheer, Iowa, and a grand daughter of an Iowa legislator. The George's have with them a nephew, Burton Bridges, a graduate of the University of Nebraska, and a member of Sigma Mu.

For the past forty-six years Mr. George has lived in Lincoln. He was associated with the *Daily State Democrat,* later the *Daily Call,* for seven years, and for about a year and a half with the *State Journal*. In 1894 he went into business for himself under the firm name of George Brothers, Printers, of which he is still a member. He is also a director of the Cushman Motor Works. Since 1915 he has been active in good roads work, and has served in various capacities with organizations engaged in this work. He was chairman of the legislative committee on good roads when Nebraska first accepted federal aid in 1917 and is present chairman of this committee. A Republican, Mr. George was city councilman for seven years, and has been active in party politics. Mr. George is a member of the First Plymouth Congregational Church.

During the World War he was president of the Lincoln Chamber of Commerce, and for several years was a member of the board of directors. As a Rotarian he is a charter member of the Lincoln organization and was its first secretary and first statistician. Active in welfare work, he has contributed much effort to Community Chest, Boy Scouts and Y. M. C. A., and Y. W. C. A. drives. He is past president of the Lincoln Auto Club, and the D. L. D. Highway Association.

Mr. George is a 32nd degree Scottish Rite Mason and past potentate of Sesostris Temple of the Shrine, a member of the Royal Neighbors of America, the Royal Highlanders, the Macabees and the Modern Woodmen of America. He is a former member of the Izaak Walton League, an honorary member of the Lincoln Typographical Union, and a member of the Sons of Veterans and the Lincoln Fine Arts Association. His clubs are the Lincoln Country, the Fifty-Fifty Dancing Club and the Shrine Country Club, and is a member of the executive committee which planned and built the latter named club. Residence: Lincoln.

Charles Carlton George

Charles Carlton George, prominent real estate operator, was born in Galesburg, Illinois, March 21, 1863, son of John Wesley and Mary Elizabeth (Younger) George.

He received his Bachelor of Science degree from Knox College in 1885, and his Master of Science in 1888. On Dcember 14, 1905, he was married to Idella Louise Hamlin. She was born at Boston, Massachusetts, and was a graduate of Radcliffe College.

Mr. George is a Republican. He was a member of the firm of Potter & George for a number of years and is now president of George Brothers. For a number of years he has been active in banking and loan associations. He is a member of the Chamber of Commerce and a former director of that organization, and has been a director of the Community Chest for a number of years. He has been trustee of Knox College, and a member of the International Chamber of Commerce. His clubs are the Omaha Club, the University Club, the Country Club, and Happy Hollow Club. Residence: Omaha.

Idella Hamlin George

Idella H. George was born at Boston, Massachusetts, November 6, 1878, the daughter of Dana Billings and Helena (McCuaig) George. Her father was born at Waterford, Maine, August 22, 1839, and died at Boston, October 2, 1903. Her mother, whose ancestry was Scotch, was born April 4, 1849, and died at Omaha, March 4, 1926.

Mrs. George was a student at the Boston public school and a girls high school in Boston. In 1901 she received her A. B. degree at Radcliffe. She has made her home in Nebraska for the past 28 years.

On December 14, 1905, her marriage to Charles Carlton George was solemnized at Chicago, Illinois. Mr. George, who was born at Galesburg, Illinois, March 23, 1863, is of English descent. He is engaged in the real estate, insurance, and investment business. Their daughter, Mary, was born September 24, 1912. Residence: Omaha.

Jacob C. George

Jacob C. George was born near Hampton, Nebraska, February 8, 1878, the son of Christian and Rosena (Ormon) George. His father, who was born at Odessa, Russia, April 1, 1850, and died at Aurora, Nebraska, September 2, 1931, was a farmer. His mother was born at Odessa, October 22, 1853, and is still living.

Mr. George received his education in country schools. Today he is one of the leading farmers in Hamilton County, Nebraska, and is a member of the Farmers Union Store, serving as a board member for the past nine years. Since 1911, he has been a member of the school board.

He is affiliated with Hampton Methodist Church, and holds membership in the Nebraskana Society. During the World War he served in loan drives. On October 21, 1900, he was married to Elizabeth Nicholas at Stockholm, Nebraska. Mrs. George, whose ancestry is German, was born near Stockholm, September 13, 1877.

Their children are: Esther, born January 12, 1903, who married William Hahle; Elma, born March 7, 1905, who married Crystal Cook; Frances, born September 7, 1908; Mildred, born February 8, 1910; Ruth, born August 17, 1911; Willis, born March 2, 1913; and Edmond, born October 11, 1920. Esther and Elmer are farmers, Frances is a teacher, and the other children live at home. Residence: Hampton.

Lycurgus George

Born at Washington, Iowa, January 10, 1859, Lycurgus George is the son of William and Nancy Jane (Meek) George. William George was born in Carrol County, Ohio, in 1822 and came to Nebraska in 1883, after spending several years in Washington County, Iowa. He was a farmer at Bostwick until his death on March 17, 1904. His wife, Nancy Jane, was a native of Tuscarawas County, Ohio, born March 21, 1825, of Scotch-Irish descent. Her death occurred in Jewell County, Kansas, in October 1905.

Lycurgus George was educated in common schools, and came to Nebraska in 1892. With the exception of the years 1905-08 he has resided in the state in the same precinct and county. On October 6, 1887 he was united in marriage to Ella Emma Cook at Washington, Iowa. Mrs. George, who is of Scotch-Irish descent, was born at Huntsville, Ohio, June 5, 1859.

Four children were born to their union, Mary Agnes, August 19, 1888; William Floyd, June 19, 1892, who married Elma Dishman, and who died November 27, 1928; Acena, March 19, 1895, who married Virgil Dixon; and Frank Lycurgus, April 27, 1898, who married Fern I. Parsons.

Mr. George is a Republican. He is affiliated with the Bostwick Methodist Episcopal Church, and is a life member of The Nebraskana Society. He has served as precinct assessor for several terms. Residence: Bostwick.

William Hamby George

William Hamby George, one of Dakota County's outstanding farmers, was born in Lexington, Ohio, February 18, 1843, and died at his home in South Sioux City, September 12, 1912. He was the son of John B. and Eliza (Hittle) George, both natives of Pennsylvania.

John B. George was born at Frankfort, Pennsylvania, April 12, 1820, and died at Circleville, Ohio, December 27, 1845, when William Hamby George was less than two years of age. His wife, Eliza, was born in Obermilfort Township, Pennsylvania, December 23, 1816, and died at Circleville, Ohio, January 8, 1894. Both were of German descent, and John B. George was an ordained minister of the United Brethren Church.

Educated in common schools, Mr. George engaged in farming in Ohio, and in 1888, came to Nebraska where he continued this occupation. He had an enviable war record, having enlisted in the Union Army for the duration of the Civil War (1861-64). His service of three years and three month's was with the 64th Ohio Volunteer Infantry, under General Sherman. A member of the Grand Army of the Republic, he was a member also of the Odd Fellows and The Nebraskana Society.

Always active in Democratic politics, Mr. George served his party well, and was elected delegate to the National Convention of 1908 at Kansas City. He was a participant in all projects for the betterment of his community and state, and among other things served as a member of the South Sioux City School Board 12 consecutive years.

On February 19, 1890, he was united in marriage to Libby Beck, at Waverly, Iowa. Mrs. George, who still survives him, was born in Cottage Grove, Illinois, January 24, 1856. To them were born five children, four of whom are living: Earl B., born February 9, 1891, married Minnie Larson; Glen G., born August 11, 1892, died April 4, 1924; Ralph H., born March 19, 1894, married Edna Falin; Gladys S., born November 9, 1897; and Marie R., born February 19, 1900. Residence: South Sioux City.

Herbert Franklin Gerald

Herbert F. Gerald, physician and educator of Omaha, Nebraska, was born at Turner Falls, Franklin County, Massachusetts, September 5, 1881. His father, Franklin Gerald, was born at Benton, Fairfield County, Maine, June 25, 1848, and died at Turner Falls, November 25, 1925. He was a business man and was actively engaged in political affairs many years, serving as selectman several terms. He was descended from an English family who settled in Maine, in 1700.

His mother, Loraine (Spearin) Gerald, who was born at Alexander, Maine, August 6, 1847, and died at Turner Falls, May 19, 1924, traced her ancestry to the Chase family who came to America from England, in 1630.

Dr. Gerald was graduated from the Turner Falls High School in 1896, and holds the following degrees: Ph. G., Massachusetts College of Pharmacy, 1902; B. S., Creighton University, 1927; M. D., Tuft Medical School, 1909. He was, for a time, a student at Harvard University where he received special instruction in chemistry. He was president of his graduating class at Tuft Medical School, 1909, and was a member of Phi Delta Chi and Phi Rho Sigma.

He was admitted to practice medicine at Omaha, 1918; Boston, 1909; and Des Moines, Iowa, 1914. A resident of Nebraska since 1912, he has held the following positions: manager of a drug store, 1902-04; instructor at the Massachusetts College of Pharmacy, 1904-09, interne at the Worcester City Hospital, 1910-11; engaged in general practice at Haverhill, Massachusetts, 1911-12; and instructor at Creighton Medical School 1912. Since 1912 he has been associated with Creighton Medical School as professor of pharmocology. He is chairman of the Junior Council there, is a member of the Advisory Board, and is at the head of the departments of Physiology and Pharmocology.

His marriage to Emma Florence Park was solemnized at West Harwich, Barnstable County, Massachusetts, August 15, 1914. Mrs. Gerald was born at Cebu, Philippines, July 15, 1889, and is a descendant of Perigrin White of Mayflower fame. They have two children: Curtis, born May 22, 1915; and Park, born June 30, 1921.

Dr. Gerald is a member of the Omaha-Douglas County Medical Association; the Nebraska State Medical Association; and the American Medical Association. He is a member of the Nebraska State; the American Pharmaceutical Associations and American Association for the Advancement of Science, the Red Cross, the Professional Men's Club, and the Parent-Teachers' Association. He is affiliated with the Miller Park Presbyterian Church at Omaha. His favorite sports are tennis and golf, and his hobby is mechanics. Residence: Omaha.

Edwin H. Gerhart

A leading banker at Newman Grove, Nebraska, is Edwin H. Gerhart, who has been a resident of Madison County for the past 37 years. He was born at Reamstown, Pennsylvania, August 20, 1870, the son of William and Maria (Mishler) Gerhart. His father, who was born in Lancaster County, Pennsylvania, in 1822, and died there in 1898, was a farmer; he was of German descent. Maria (Mishler) Gerhart was born at Reamstown, August 21, 1833, of German parentage, and died at Reinholds, Pennsylvania, in 1900.

Mr. Gerhart attended rural schools in Pennsylvania, received the B. E. degree at Millersville State Normal School at Millersville, Pennsylvania, in 1892, and was awarded the B. S. degree at Wayne Normal College, Wayne, Nebraska, in 1896. He was prominent in educational work for several years, serving as superintendent of the public schools at Newman Grove, 1894-98, and superintendent of public schools at Hooper, Nebraska, 1898-99. From 1899 to 1912 he was connected with the First National Bank of Newman Grove as cashier and since 1912 has been president of that institution. He is president of the Newman Grove Improvement Society.

He is a member of the Tri County Community Club at Newman Grove, the Red Cross, and The Nebraskana Society. He is affiliated with the Methodist Episcopal Church there and is a member of the following fraternal organizations: Modern Woodmen of America; Independent Order of Odd Fellows; and Masons, Scottish Rite and York Rite of the Shrine.

Mr. Gerhart is a Republican, and has held the following political and civic positions: member of the state legislature, 1919; member of the State Normal Board, 1921-23; secretary of the Newman Grove School Board for 19 years; and candidate for regent of the University of Nebraska. He is interested in golfing and gardening. During the World War he served as a Minute Man, Red Cross lecturer, and Liberty loan promoter.

He was united in marriage with Kathryn Daum at Cordelia, Pennsylvania, August 21, 1894. Mrs. Gerhart, whose ancestry is German, was born at Cordelia, May 26, 1871. Two children were born to them: Kathryn E., February 12, 1896; and Harold Lincoln, December 17, 1897, who married Dorothy E. Hallgren. Kathryn was graduated from the University of Nebraska in 1917 and is now teaching German in the high school at Fremont, Nebraska. Harold was graduated from the University of Nebraska in 1920 and is vice president of the First National Bank of Newman Grove. Residence: Newman Grove.

Reuben Firman Getty

Reuben Firman Getty was born at Jones Station, Butler County, Ohio, December 11, 1857, the son of Robert and Sarah (Emerick) Getty. His father, who was a farmer, was born at Norristown, Montgomery County, Pennsylvania, in 1816, and died at Waco, Nebraska, October 14, 1884; his ancestry was Scotch. His mother was born in Pennsylvania in 1830 and died at Logansport, Indiana, January 21, 1872.

Mr. Getty received his education in a rural school near Lafayette, Indiana. He has been a member of the township board of Waco for the past 30 years, and since 1897 has served on the school board there. He is a member of the Odd Fellows, the Modern Woodmen of America, the Rebekahs, and the local Red Cross. He is a teacher in the Sunday School of the Methodist Episcopal Church at Waco; his original church membership was with the Evangelical Association near Lafayette, Indiana.

During the World War Mr. Getty served as a member of the council of defense. His hobbies are reading and radio. He was married to Mae Evelyn Garton at

Skoglund—Omaha

JAMES ROBERT GETTYS

Benedict, Nebraska, March 12, 1890. Mrs. Getty, who was formerly a teacher, was born near Clyde, Ohio, May 7, 1870.

To this union the following children were born: Robert, born May 19, 1891, who married Anna Bell; Amy, born Mary 14, 1893, who died August 31, 1894; Grace, born April 26, 1897, who married Frank S. Walter; Hayward, born October 24, 1898; Millard, born August 9, 1900; and Wayne, born August 25, 1902, who died May 23, 1907; Beth, born August 29, 1904; Ervin, born August 16, 1907; and Norris, born May 13, 1915. Residence: Waco.

James Robert Gettys

James Robert Gettys was born in Jasper County, Iowa, August 3, 1868, the son of Joseph and Rebecca Frances (Wilson) Gettys. His father, who was born in Richland County, Ohio, September 15, 1834, was a farmer and homesteader in Kansas, in 1870. He was a corporal in Company D of the 40th Iowa Volunteer Infantry, and was the great grandson of Samuel Gettys, who came from Donegal, Ireland, and settled in Lancaster County, Pennsylvania, in 1740, where he founded the City of Gettysburg. He died at Prairie View, Kansas, June 25, 1895.

Rebecca Frances Wilson was born in Arkansas, May 11, 1838, and was the granddaughter of Jesse Wilson of Delaware. She was the daughter of Robert White and Johanna (Demars) Wilson, the latter of whom was born in Kentucky of French parentage. She died at Newton, Iowa, October 8, 1920.

Dr. Gettys received his early education in the public schools of Kansas and was a student at McPherson Normal College at Republican City, Nebraska, for a time. In 1897, he was graduated from Nebraska Wesleyan University with the Bachelor of Arts degree, and from 1905-07 took post graduate work at the University of Nebraska. He was awarded the degree of Doctor of Divinity by Nebraska Wesleyan University in 1912 and was elected to membership in Phi Kappa Phi and Theta Phi Sigma.

Ordained to the ministry in 1888, he joined the West Nebraska Conference of the Methodist Episcopal Church in Minden in September of that year. He was business manager of the Topical Bible Publication in 1897; was pastor at DeWitt 1897-99, at Hebron 1899-1901; served as superintendent of the Beatrice district 1901-07; was pastor at David City 1908-12; was pastor of the First Church at Grand Island 1912, First Church of University Place, Lincoln, 1913; was financial director of the Conference Claimants Society 1916-21; and superintendent of the Beatrice district 1921-27. Since 1928 he has been financial secretary of the Board of Pensions.

Dr. Gettys has been delegate to general conference of the Methodist Episcopal Church six times. He is the author of *The Upper Trail* (1913); and *Who's Who in the Universe* (1922). He is a Republican, a 32nd degree, Scottish Rite Mason, and a member of the Nebraskana Society. Since 1888 he has resided in Nebraska.

On October 27, 1890, he was united in marriage to Cora Estella Scofield at Hendley, Nebraska. Mrs. Gettys, who was born in Cherokee County, Iowa, May 17, 1869, is the granddaughter of John Henry and Louisa (Doyle) Scofield of New York City, and a daughter of John Francis and Mary (Gillis) Scofield. There are four children, Lloyd Bryant, born October 19, 1893, who was graduated from Nebraska Wesleyan University with the Bachelor of Arts degree; Flora Frances, born August 27, 1896, who is a world-famous soprano and is especially known for her achievements in Italy, and who took her Bachelor of Arts degree from the University in 1917; Cora Luella, born October 17, 1898, who was awarded the Bachelor of Arts and Master of Arts degrees by the University of Nebraska and the degree of Doctor of Philosophy at the University of Illinois; and Margaret, born November 19, 1901, who was graduated from the University of Nebraska with the degrees of Bachelor of Arts and Bachelor of Laws. Lloyd married Ruth Elaine Crosthwaite; and Margaret married Benjamin A. Hall. Residence: Lincoln. (Photograph on Page 456).

Charles Kimball Gibbons

Charles Kimball Gibbons, son of Henry and Emma Jane (Drew) Gibbons, was born at Kearney, Nebraska, December 13, 1876, and since 1903 has been engaged in the practice of medicine and surgery in Nebraska. His father, born in Ireland, about 1840, came to America about 1866, and was a prominent Mason in Nebraska. At the time of his death at Kearney, August 22, 1923, he was retired. His mother, who was born in Illinois, in 1852, died at Kearney on October 19, 1911. Her father died from starvation in Andersonville prison in the Civil War.

Dr. Gibbons attended Shattuck Military Academy until 1895, and received his degree of Doctor of Medicine from Northwestern University in 1902. His fraternity is Phi Rho Sigma. Dr. Gibbons served his internship at Passavant Memorial Hospital at Chicago, and returning to Nebraska in 1903, established his present practice. At the present time he specializes in surgery. During the World War he served one year with the rank of major at Base Hospital No. 111, in France. For ten years he has been a member of the Medical Corps of the Nebraska National Guard.

On June 25, 1902, Dr. Gibbons was married to Nellie June Downing at Kearney. Mrs. Gibbons, who is the daughter of R. L. Downing, was born at Kearney, December 7, 1879. They have one daughter, Nancy Jane, born February 21, 1907, who is married to John Henry.

Dr. Gibbons is a Republican. He is a member of the Elks and all Masonic orders, and is affiliated with St. Luke's Episcopal Church. His professional organizations include the American Medical Association, the Nebraska State Medical Association and the Buffalo County Medical Society. He is a member of the Red Cross, the Commercial Club, the Nebraskana Society, and the Kearney Country Club. He is fond of golf, while his hobby is art. Residence: Kearney.

Charles Henry Gietzen

Charles Henry Gietzen, dentist, was born at Fremont, Nebraska, August 2, 1876, son of Henry and Louisa (Voight) Gietzen.

He attended public schools at Fremont and Humphrey, Nebraska, and was graduated from high school at Humphrey in 1893. In 1900 he received the degree of Bachelor of Dental Surgery from Northwestern University.

His marriage to Florence O. Sammons was solemnized on August 10, 1923.

He is the author of scientific papers on dentistry, various poems, and is now dental clinician and lecturer. His professional organizations include the American Dental Association, the Minnesota Dental Association, the Omaha District Dental Society (president, 1928), the Nebraska State Dental Association, the Tri-City Dental Association (president, 1916). He is a Scottish Rite Mason and a member of the Shrine. Residence: Omaha.

Frank Thurston Gifford

Born at Rome, Wisconsin, May 24, 1879, Frank Thurston Gifford is the son of Francis Marion and Maria (Thurston) Gifford. The father, born in Erie, Pennsylvania, December 15, 1842, was a farmer, who served in the Civil War and who died at Ord, in October, 1926. His ancestors came from Germany at the time Catholicism forced Protestants out. Maria Thurston was born at Kennebec, Maine, and died at Ord on

January 9, 1905. She was a rural school teacher in younger days, and was later president of the local Women's Christian Temperance Union. Her ancestry was traced to the Norsemen.

Frank Thurston Gifford attended public school, and soon thereafter became a farmer. He was the owner and manager of a stockyards at Burwell for five years, and at the present time has extensive farming interests and serves as solicitor for the Nebraska Producers Commission firm of Omaha.

On January 19, 1905, he was married to Opal Vero Garnick at Ord. Mrs. Gifford, who is of English descent, was born at Ceresco, Nebraska, July 22, 1882. There are two children, Thurston, born October 14, 1906; and Gail, born April 5, 1911.

Mr. Gifford is a Democrat. He was recently made a life member of the Nebraskana Society. His favorite recreation is reading. Residence: Ord.

Sanford Robinson Gifford

Sanford Robinson Gifford, physician and surgeon, was born at Omaha, Nebraska, January 8, 1892, the son of Harold and Mary Louise (Millard) Gifford.

His father, who was born November 14, 1858, is now deceased. He received his education from Cornell University and the University of Michigan, and was one of the most prominent physicians of the state, a specialist in diseases of the eye. His wife, Mary, was born May 1, 1864.

Dr. Gifford received the Bachelor of Arts degree at Cornell University in 1913, and his medical degree from the University of Nebraska in 1918. In 1923 he received the Master of Science degree from the University of Nebraska.

His marriage to Mary Alice Carter was solemnized on July 11, 1917. Dr. Gifford is the author of scientific articles pertaining to opthalmology. He is a member of the firm of Drs. Gifford, Patton, Callfas, and Potts, and during the World War held the rank of first lieutenant in the medical corps. Residence: Omaha.

Clair Vernon Gilbert

Clair Vernon Gilbert was born at Fitchburg, Wisconsin, December 17, 1885, the son of Charles Lafayette and Mary Ella (Shaw) Gilbert. His father, who was a farmer, was born at Steuben, New York, June 15,1842. He was a veteran of the Civil War and served four and a half years in the 8th Wisconsin, Eagle Regiment. He died at Grand Island, Nebraska, February 14, 1929. His wife, Mary Ella, was born at Janesville, Wisconsin, February 22, 1852, and died at Broadwater, Nebraska, March 26, 1912.

Mr. Gilbert, who operates three farms in Morrill County, Nebraska, was a student at the Kansas State Agricultural College for a time. He homesteaded in Morrill County in 1908, was a garage proprietor until 1918, and since then has been assistant postmaster at Broadwater. He is precinct committeeman, is a member of the Chamber of Commerce, and holds membership in the Woodmen of the World and the Masonic Lodge, (32nd degree and Shrine). His hobby is golfing.

His marriage to Eva May Rickman was solemnized at Phillipsburg, Kansas, July 9, 1905. Mrs. Gilbert, who is a teacher and has served as postmaster at Broadwater since 1919, was born at Russell, Iowa, November 15, 1886. She is the daughter of the Reverend Thomas M. Rickman, state temperance lecturer for the Women's Christian Temperance Union in Ohio. He was a Baptist minister at Ames, removing to Manhattan, Kansas, where he was a minister for five years. Joshua D. Rickman, brother of Mrs. Gilbert's father, was superintendent of printing on the faculty at Kansas State Agricultural College for 17 years. Her mother was Mary Ann Stolte, who was of German descent. Residence: Broadwater.

Emma Crooks Gilbert

Emma Crooks Gilbert, dean of Women at Nebraska Wesleyan University, has lived in this state for the past 42 years. She was born near Gunnison, Colorado, July 18, 1879, the daughter of John Thornton and Mary Ann (Ghent) Crooks. Her father, who was a clergyman, was born in Virginia, January 15, 1857, and died at Pilger, Stanton County, Nebraska, September 10, 1896; he was of Scotch descent. Her mother, who is Irish, was born at Greenup, Kentucky, December 27, 1859.,

Mrs. Gilbert attended the public schools of Colorado, was a student in the schools at Scribner, Nebraska, and in 1895 was graduated from the Pilger High School. She attended Nebraska Wesleyan University for a time where she held membership in Alpha Delta Theta. She has been dean of women at Nebraska Wesleyan for several years.

She was united in marriage with Marvin Edwin Gilbert at Lincoln, Lancaster County, Nebraska, January 8, 1902. Dr. Gilbert, who was born at Sidney, New York, October 16, 1873, is a distinguished clergyman and educator at Nebraska Wesleyan University. Two children were born to this marriage. John Dawson, who was born October 5, 1903, was a student at Nebraska Wesleyan University and Syracuse University, and was married to Marjorie B. Miltz; he died March 20, 1930. Lauren Edwin, born April 8, 1911, was graduated from Nebraska Wesleyan University at the age of 19; he was awarded Phi Beta Kappa membership.

Mrs. Gilbert is a member of the National Association of Deans of Women; is affiliated with the First Methodist Church of Lincoln; holds membership in the Nebraskana Society; and is a member of the local Red Cross organization. She is at present state president of the P. E. O.; is Young Women's Christian Association advisor; and is a member of the Eastern Star. She is a Republican. Residence: Lincoln.

Marvin Edwin Gilbert

For the past 50 years Marvin E. Gilbert has lived in Nebraska and for over 30 years has taken an active part in the religious and educational life of the state. He was born at Sidney, Delaware County, New York, October 16, 1873, the son of Henry William and Sarah Ann (Wells) Gilbert. His father, who was born in Delaware County in 1835, and died at Omaha, Douglas County, Nebraska, 1918, was a carpenter; he served with the First New York Engineers; his ancestry was Scotch Irish.

His mother was born in Delaware County, May, 1837, and died at Weeping Water, Cass County, Nebraska, 1899. She held membership in the Daughters of the American Revolution.

Dr. Gilbert was a student in the public schools of Weeping Water and in 1900 was graduated from the Wesleyan University High School. He was awarded the B. S. degree at Nebraska Wesleyan University in 1906, and the D. D. degree, 1916. He attended the University of Nebraska for a time. During his college career he served as class president in his junior year; was a member of the debating team for two years; received college letters from Nebraska Wesleyan University and the University of Nebraska; and was a member of Phi Kappa Tau.

Since 1899 he has been a minister in the Nebraska Conference. He served as district superintendent for 12 years in three different districts, and for the past six years has been secretary of the extension department at Nebraska Wesleyan University. He is a member of the Lincoln Chamber of Commerce; the Young Men's Christian Association; the National Travel Club; and the Nebraskana Society. He is affiliated with the

Methodist Episcopal Church and holds membership in the following fraternal organizations: Masons; Eastern Star; and the Lions Club. He is a Republican.

His marriage to Emma Frances Crooks was solemnized at Lincoln, Nebraska, January 8, 1902. Mrs. Gilbert, who was born at Gunnison, Colorado, July 18, 1879, is dean of women at Nebraska Wesleyan University. Two children were born to their marriage, one of whom is living: John Dawson, born October 5, 1903, was a student at Nebraska Wesleyan University and Syracuse University, and married Marjorie N. Miltz—he died March 20, 1930; and Lauren Edwin, born April 8, 1911, who was graduated from Nebraska Wesleyan University at the age of 19, with Phi Beta Kappa honors. Residence: Lincoln.

William Henry Gildersleeve

For the past 49 years William H. Gildersleeve has lived in Nebraska where he is known as a successful stockman and landowner. He was born at St. Charles, King County, Illinois, March 29, 1860, the son of Moses and Eliza Bell Gildersleeve. His father, who was a farmer, was born at East Northport, New York, March 10, 1829, and died at Wayne, Nebraska, January 26, 1892. He was descended from the Gildersleeve family of England, which in the year of 1165 was called Gyldersleve. Sirvase Paganet de Gyldersleve, an ancestor, was cup bearer to the king from 1165 to 1200. In 1932 members of the family settled in Long Island; members of the Paganet family were descended from Ahlmen, King of Kent, 775-95.

Mr. Gildersleeve was active during the World War in the sale of loan bonds, and was especially prominent in the Young Men's Christian Association drives. He is affiliated with the First Presbyterian Church, is a member of the Nebraskana Society, and holds membership in the Red Cross. His sports include motoring and fishing.

He was united in marriage with Mary Catherine Cunningham at Wayne, June 18, 1884. Mrs. Gildersleeve, who is the daughter of David and Virginia Cunningham was born at Mifflinton, February 8, 1863. Their children are as follows: Alice Mae, born April 9, 1886, who married Lee A. Young; Franklin, born July 3, 1888, who died June 10, 1910; Cella Bell, born November 23, 1891, who married Harry F. Radaker; Lloyd, born July 20, 1893, who died November 25, 1918; Wilma Evelyn, born July 12, 1903, and Elizabeth, born July 2, 1900, who married J. R. Phillips. Wilma is secretary to the president of Doane College at Crete.

Mr. Gildersleeve is a Republican. He is still actively engaged in the cattle business. Residence: Wayne.

Herbert Session Giles

Born at Friend, Nebraska, June 13, 1888, Herbert Session Giles is a life resident of Nebraska. His father, Daniel Samuel Giles was a farmer of Pennsylvania Dutch descent, born at Pulaski, Iowa, January 17, 1863. He died at Juniata on January 7, 1926. His mother, Olive Lena Lancaster, was born at Moweaqua, Illinois, January 1, 1870, and is of English, Irish and Dutch extraction.

Herbert S. Giles received his education in the public schools of Juniata, and entered upon his life as a *farmer*. On August 26, 1908, he was married to Charity W. Benight at Juniata. Mrs. Giles, whose father was a veteran of the Civil War, was born in Brooks, Iowa, August 22, 1890. There are three children:

Wayne, born May 15, 1909, married Ruth Jones; Melvin, born October 6, 1911; and Harley, born October 4, 1913. Wayne attended Hastings College and the Georgia School of Technology, while Melvin and Harley are students at Hastings College at the present time.

Mr. Giles is a member of the Juniata Methodist Episcopal Church, the Modern Woodmen of America, the Nebraskana Society, the Parent Teachers Association and the local school board of which he is president. His hobby is mechanics. Residence: Juniata.

James Skewis Gilham

One of the outstanding leaders in the professional and political world of Nebraska is James Skewis Gilham who has been a resident of this state for the past 57 years. He was born at Shullsburg, Wisconsin, January 14, 1852, the son of William and Anne (Skewis) Gilham. His father, who was a miner, was born at Canterbury, England, October 16, 1817, and came to the United States in 1848; he died at Red Cloud, Nebraska, May 31, 1880. His mother was born at Camborne, England, September 1, 1822, and died at Red Cloud, April 20, 1915; she came to this country in 1849.

Mr. Gilham attended school at Shullsburg, Wisconsin, and in 1872 received the A. B. degree at Beloit College. Since 1874 when he was admitted to the bar, he has been a prominent lawyer at Red Cloud and has been distinguished as an energetic and progressive citizen of Webster County. He is known as one of the leaders in the promotion of the Republican Valley and is recognized throughout the state for his oratorical and literary ability.

He served as a member of the state legislature of Nebraska, in 1877, the youngest man to serve in any Nebraska law body, was county superintendent of Webster County in 1876, and served as county attorney in 1886. He is the author of an essay on Bryan's *Prince of Peace*. Mr. Gilham is nominally president of the local bar association at Red Cloud, is president of the Webster County Old Settlers Club, and holds membership in the Nebraskana Society. He is a Mason. In 1892 he served as a member of the school board in his community.

On June 20, 1877, he was married to Eliza Elinor Tulleys at Red Cloud.

Mrs. Gilham, who was the daughter of Dr. W. I. Tulleys, and is descended from the southern Lee family, was born at Clinton, Illinois, March 17, 1860, and died at Red Cloud, February 18, 1925. Three children were born: Anna Josephine, born August 18, 1880, who died February 21, 1900; Harry Tulleys, born August 25, 1886, who married Edith Ranney; and James Edward, born February 15, 1891, who died August 15, 1893. Residence: Red Cloud.

Samuel Earl Gilinsky

Samuel E. Gilinsky was born at Council Bluffs, Iowa, June 1, 1885, the son of Barney and Lena (Levy) Gilinsky. His mother, was born in the west suburb of Warsaw, Poland, March 4, 1862, and died at Council Bluffs, November 20, 1928. His father in the east suburb of Warsaw, December 10, 1861.

In 1902 Mr. Gilinsky was graduated from the Council Bluffs High School. He has been a resident of Nebraska since 1918, and has been active in Omaha's welfare and commercial affairs since that date. He is now president of the Gilinsky Fruit Company of Omaha.

He was united in marriage with Minnie Zemurray at New Orleans, Louisiana, December 26, 1917. Mrs. Gilinsky was born at Selma, Alabama, April 22, 1893. They have three children: Armand, born September 24, 1918; Sari, born November 8, 1920, and Morton Lewis, born February 9, 1924.

Mr. Gilinsky is a member of the Jewish Welfare Society at Omaha. His social clubs are: Highland Club; and Omaha Athletic Club. He is affiliated with Temple Israel at Omaha. His hobby is reading. He is a Republican, and a member of the Chamber of Commerce. Residence: Omaha.

J. S. Gill

J. S. Gill, successful farmer and livestock feeder of Burt County, Nebraska, has lived in this state for the past 46 years. He was born at Mont Clair, Indiana, December 4, 1880, the son of J. T. Gill and Mary Isabelle (Weddle) Gill. His father, whose ancestry is Scotch and Irish, was born at Floyd, Floyd County, Virginia, April 16, 1855. His mother was born at Floyd, January 11, 1859, and died at Tekamah, Burt County, Nebraska, September 19, 1927; she was of German descent.

Mr. Gill is now serving as county supervisor of Burt County, is president of the Burt County Co-operative Oil Company which was organized five years ago, and is a member of the Tekamah Chamber of Commerce in which he has held various offices. He holds membership in the Red Cross, Nebraska State Historical Society, Nebraskana Society, Odd Fellows, and the Silver Creek Baptist Church. He has been treasurer of the local school board for 17 years and for the past three years has served as director. His hobby is reading.

His marriage to Dora Heth was solemnized at Clarence, Cedar County, Iowa, March 8, 1904. Mrs. Gill, who was formerly a teacher, was born of English and German parents at Clarence, January 6, 1881. Six children were born to this marriage: Ina Imogene, born December 1, 1905, who died March 17, 1906; Clarence H., born August 17, 1908; Glenn T., born March 8, 1910; James T., born July 5, 1913; Virginia B., born September 10, 1911; and Anna Belle, born February 6. Mr. Giill is a Democrat. Residence: Tekamah.

James Ward Gill

Born at Tekamah, Nebraska, December 1, 1880, James Ward Gill has been a practicing physician and surgeon since September 11, 1912. His father, Thomas H. Gill, a native of Pennsylvania, was born December 5, 1842, and resides at Tekamah. He is a retired farmer and a veteran of the Civil War, of Scotch-Irish and Pennsylvania German descent.

Margaret Ann Cornelius, his wife, was born in Pennsylvania, April 16, 1852, and died at Tekamah, April 1, 1925. She was also of Scotch-Irish and Pennsylvania German descent.

James Ward Gill was graduated from high school at Tekamah in 1896, and received his Doctor of Medicine degree from Cotner University in 1912. He was offered valedictory honors in college, but declined in favor of Dr. H. R. Murphy of Singapore, India. He is a member of Tau Alpha Epsilon.

Dr. Gill was married to Bertha Marie Wetz at Omaha, June 14, 1911, and to them four children were born, one of whom is living: Melba, born September 29, 1922; Olline, born March 18, 1914, died at birth; Lorraine, born August 5, 1916, died July 21, 1919; and Nadine, born January 30, 1918, died October 15, 1920.

Dr. Gill has been an outstanding figure in community affairs for a number of years. He has been chairman of the village board for ten years, director of the school board ten years, and for four years has been president of the 8th Councilor District Medical Society.

Vice president of the Holt County chapter of the American Red Cross, he is a member of the Nebraska State and Holt County Medical Associations, and is a member of the Parent Teachers Association, the Nebraskana Society, the Garfield Lodge No. 95 of the Ancient Free and Accepted Masons and the Medical Officers Reserve. Dr. Gill has served two enlistments in the Nebraska National Guard, with Company F, 2nd Regiment, enlisting as a private and being promoted to the rank of sergeant. Residence: Chambers.

Gale Harold Gillan

Gale Harold Gillan, executive, was born near York, Nebraska, May 10, 1904, son of Samuel Wallace and Mary (Hammond) Gillan. His father, born in Balleymena, County Antrim, Ireland, February 8, 1871, came to America with his father, Alex Gillan, settling in Illinois, in 1873, arriving on June 16. Coming to Nebraska in 1883 he engaged in farming until 1920, and since that time has been in the wholesale bakery business.

Mary Hammond Gillan was born in Exeter, Nebraska, January 25, 1875. Her father, Henry Hammond, was kidnapped at the age of seven, escaped at the age of 14, when he enlisted in the Union Army and served four years in the Civil War. Thereafter he came to Nebraska, homesteaded and married here, and reared his family. Mary Hammond is active in club work, and is a member of the Daughters of the American Revolution, the Women's Relief Corps, the Does and others.

Educated in the public schools of District 14 in York County until 1919, Gale H. Gillan attended Exeter High School in 1919-20, and was graduated from York High School in 1923. In 1927 he received his Bachelor of Science degree in Economics from the University of Nebraska, and in 1929, attended the United Brethren College at York, taking post graduate work. Mr. Gillan is a member of Sigma Nu, and at Exter was a member of the football team; at York was a member of the football, basketball and baseball teams.

After his graduation in 1927, Mr. Gillan became manager of and partner in the York Sanitary Bakery (wholesale and retail), continuing to date. On August 3, 1930, he was united in marriage to Katherine Margaret Reynolds at Seward. Mrs. Gillan was born at Seward, October 21, 1909.

Mr. Gillan is a Democrat. His religious affiliation is with the Holy Trinity Episcopal Church at York. A member of the Elks, he has been an officer of his local lodge since 1928. He belongs to the Young Men's Christian Association, the Rotary Club, and the Nebraskana Society, and has held the office of vice-president in the Northwest District of Nebraska Master Bakers Association the years of 1930, 1931.

A member of the board of directors of the York County Commercial Club 1929-31, he is now serving as vice president of the organization. Interested in travel, reading and civic work, Mr. Gillan enjoys golf, handball and volleyball. Residence: York.

Trevelyan Erwin Gillaspie

Trevelyan E. Gillaspie was born at Victor, Iowa, June 9, 1892, the son of Thomas Erwin and Nora Almeda (Atherton) Gillaspie. His father, who is a life insurance man, was born in Iowa County, Iowa, June 5, 1868, of Scotch descent. His mother, who is of Pennsylvania Dutch descent, was born in Poweshiek, Iowa, May 5, 1870.

Mr. Gillaspie was graduated from high school in 1909, and in 1910 was graduated from commercial college. He has lived in Nebraska for the last 16 years, and is now postmaster at Lincoln. A Republican, he served as city commissioner of Lincoln, in 1926, 27, 28.

His marriage to Ivy May Waller was solemnized at Clear Lake, Cerro Gordo County, Iowa, June 25, 1914. Mrs. Gillaspie was born at Clear Lake, July 7th, 1894. Their three children are: Donita Waller, born July 14, 1915; Robert Emmett, born April 29, 1922; and Patricia May, born May 26, 1926.

In the World War Mr. Gillaspie was in the United States Naval Aviation Service. He is a member of the American Legion and the Reserve Officers Association, the National Postmasters Association, the Lincoln Chamber of Commerce, the Red Cross, and the Salvation Army. He served as president of the Lions Club, 1928-29, and is a member of the local Young Men's Christian Association. A Mason, he belongs to Lincoln Lodge Number 54, Lincoln Consistory and Sesostris Temple of the Shrine. He is a member of the Shrine Country Club at Lincoln, and is affiliated with St. Paul's Methodist Church of Lincoln. Residence: Lincoln.

William Marshall Giller

William Marshall Giller, lawyer, was born at Whitehall, Illinois, January 11, 1860, the son of Edward Alfred Giller who was born in Manchester, England, in 1821, and who came to America at the age of 18, settling in Illinois. He became a successful farmer, and was master of the Illinois State Grange for several years. He married Augusta Ladd, who was born at Windsor, Vermont, in 1830. They had eleven children, six of whom are living. Edward A. Giller died at Whitehall in March, 1907, and Augusta Ladd Giller died there in September, 1919.

William M. Giller received his early education in country schools. He attended high school at Ann Arbor, Michigan, being graduated in 1882, and received his A. B. from the University of Michigan, and his LL. B. from the University of Chicago.

Admitted to the bar in 1888, for the past forty years he has been a member of the law firm of Weaver and Giller, and has been engaged in active practice during all that time.

He was married to Elsie Conant, at Omaha, on December 25, 1907. Mrs. Giller was born at Cherokee, Iowa, December 13, 1873, and has one son Richard Conant Giller, aged 31, by a former marriage. They have one daughter, Maxine, born July 1, 1910, who married Pierce Peters of Glenwood, Minnesota.

During the World War he was a four minute speaker and otherwise active. He is a member of the American, Nebraska State and Omaha-Douglas County Bar Associations. He attends the First Central Congregational Church. His fraternal organizations are the Elks, Masons, Woodmen of the World, Modern Woodmen of America and the Royal Arcanum. He is a member of the Happy Hollow Country Club, and enjoys hiking. Residence: Omaha.

John Valentine Gillespie

John V. Gillespie, jeweler at Randolph, has lived in Nebraska all his life. He was born at Gretna, the son of Michael Joseph and Elizabeth (Conner) Gillespie, December 27, 1881. His father, a farmer and insurance agent, was born at Joliet, Illinois, January 19, 1851, and died at Randolph, Nebraska, May 18, 1930; his ancestry was Irish. His mother was born at Gretna, April 17, 1858; her parents were pioneers of Sarpy County, coming to Nebraska when the territory was inhabited by Indians.

Mr. Gillespie attended rural school and in 1900 was a student at the Omaha Commercial College. He was a farmer until the age of 21, was clerk in the Union Pacific headquarters for two years, was employed in the Armour Packing Company office for one year, served as clerk for the Woodmen of the World Insurance Company for three years, and since then has been partner in a jewelry firm at Randolph with his brother, Francis W. Gillespie.

During the World War he served as chairman of the welfare work in Cedar County, was a member of the council of defense, and took part in loan drives. He is a member of the Red Cross, and was chairman of the committee that managed the $16,000 campaign during the war. He acted as chairman of the Commercial Club, 1918-19-20, is a member of the Woodmen of the World, and holds membership in the Nebraskana Society. He is a Modern Woodmen and a Democrat. He is affiliated with St. Francis de Chantal Catholic Church and is a member of the Knights of Columbus. His sport is golf, and his main interest in life is advising and aiding young men and women. Residence: Randolph.

Mabel Gillespie

Mabel Gillespie, newspaper woman and congresswoman, is a native of Ord, Nebraska, daughter of Hjalmar and Catheryn (Jensen) Gudmundsen. Her father, who died at Ord, July 6, 1930, was born at Nysted, Denmark. He had served as a county official in Valley County for more than 30 years, and was county judge for 21 years. His ancestors came from Iceland to Denmark; both his grandfathers were orators and statesmen. Hjalmar Gudmundsen was captain of Company I, Nebraska Volunteer Cavalry in the Spanish-American War, and had a long and honorable military career. When he first came to America he joined the army and saw service on the Mexican Border and elsewhere. Catheryn Gudmundsen, his wife, was a native of Denmark. She died at Ord, Nebraska, when Mrs. Gillespie was a child.

Mrs. Gillespie attended school at Ord and Superior, graduating from high school at Superior. She graduated also from the Kearney State Teachers' College in 1915. She was married to William C. Gillespie at Omaha, in 1919.

From 1917-19, she was a member of the reportorial staff of the *Omaha Bee* and was the first woman to do straight news assignments on a metropolitan newspaper. A Democrat, she was the first woman to take the oath of office as state representative in January, 1925. She served during the terms 1925-27-29, special session 1930, was was re-elected in 1931. Her hobbies are reading and writing. Residence: Gretna.

Peter Leo Gillespie

Peter Leo Gillespie was born in Pottsville, Pennsylvania, September 2, 1875, the son of Hugh Francis Gillespie. Hugh Francis Gillespie was born in Pottsville, Pennsylvania, January 2, 1846, while Ellen Cecilia Salmon, his wife was born in Pottsville, Pennsylvania, June 12, 1847.

His father was a locomotive engineer for the Chicago, Burlington and Quincy Railroad Company; he was of Scotch-Irish ancestry and his father served in the Mexican War and in the Civil War. Ellen Salmon Gillespie was also of Scotch-Irish parentage. Mr. Gillespie died January 10, 1915, and his wife died June 16, 1929. Their home was in Omaha, Nebraska.

Peter L. Gillespie received his education in the Wymore, Nebraska, elementary school, Wymore High School and then attended the Creighton, Nebraska, Academy in 1895. He received a degree of Bachelor of Arts at Creighton in 1897, Master of Arts in 1899 and Doctor of Medicine in 1901. He continued his education in New York City where he took a post graduate course in the School of Medicine, 1914-16. Mr. Gillespie received scholastic honors in medicine and was class valedictorian.

He married Stella Rosalie Mercer, November 4, 1903, at Omaha, Nebraska. They have two children: Howard, born January 13, 1911, and Eleanor, born July 22, 1912. Howard is a student of the University of Nebraska and is a sports writer for the *Nebraska State Journal*. Eleanor is a student at Creighton College in Omaha, Nebraska.

Mrs. Gillespie was born in Salem, Illinois, June 15, 1882. She is of Scotch-Irish Revolutionary ancestry. She is a club woman and the state officer in the Children of the American Revolution.

Peter L. Gillespie came to Nebraska, in October of 1888, and has been in the general practice of medicine since 1902 at which time he had completed a year's service as interne at the St. Joseph's Hospital in Omaha, Nebraska.

During the war he was in charge of the local enlistment company. He belongs to Daughters of the American Revolution by proxy and to the St. Mary's Church at Wymore, Nebraska, the Red Cross, the Knights of Columbus and the Wymore Chamber of Commerce. From 1905 to 1931 Mr. Gillespie was the medical examiner of the Knights of Columbus. He holds membership in the Gage County Medical Society and is a member of the Beatrice and Wymore, Nebraska, Country Clubs. He is an Elk, and is particularly fond of golfing, reading and gardening. Residence: Wymore.

James Willis Gillette

One of the leading business men of Norfolk, Nebraska, James Willis Gillette has lived in the state all of his adult life. He was born at Newman Grove, Nebraska, March 8, 1887, the son of W. Stephen and Blanche (Hoffman) Gillette. His father, a physician and a member of the Grand Army of the Republic, was born at Fairfax, Vermont, July 28, 1844, and died at Worcester, Vermont, May 21, 1902.

His grandfather, C. Willis Gillette, a marble carver, lived in Stowe, Vermont, where he died in 1896. The first American ancestor of the Gillette family was Jonathan, a French Hugenot, who escaped from France to England with William the Conqueror, and came to America about ten years after the Mayflower, settling in Massachusetts.

Mr. Gillette's mother, whose ancestry was German, was born in New York, and died at Newman Grove, June, 1901. She was for years one of Newman Grove's most prominent and beloved residents, and in the early days served as postmistress there.

Mr. Gillette attended Goddard Seminary at Barre, Vermont. For a number of years has been the owner and manager of the Gillette Creamery Company at Norfolk, Nebraska, which he founded January 1, 1917. He holds membership in the Chamber of Commerce, is a Mason, (Scottish Rite and York Rite), and during 1929 and 1930 was treasurer of the Young Men's Christian Association. He is very active in Boy Scout work.

His marriage to Birdie C. Kuhl occurred at Norfolk, September 15, 1915. Mrs. Gillette, whose ancestry is German, was born at Norfolk, October 15, 1891. She is the daughter of Gus and Emma (Kluckhohn) Kuhl. They have three children: Richard Willis, born January 9, 1918; Mary L., born October 11, 1919; and J. Stephen, born August 2, 1927. Residence: Norfolk. (Photograph in Album).

Edward Encil Gilmore

For 57 years Edward Encil Gilmore has lived in Nebraska where he has been a farmer for many years. He was born in LaSalle County, Illinois, May 25, 1869, the son of Jonas and Jane (Stanford) Gilmore. His father, a farmer, was born in Fayette County, Pennsylvania, April 5, 1842, and died at Blue Vale, York County, Nebraska, August 26, 1910; his ancestry was Dutch. Jane (Standford) Gilmore was born at Wheeling, Marshall County, West Virginia, June 1, 1844, and died at McCool Junction, York County, Nebraska, March 9, 1930.

Mr. Gilmore owns and operates a farm near McCool Junction. He is a Democrat. His marriage to Sarah Catherine Eastman was solemnized at Seward, Seward County, Nebraska, March 15, 1889. Mrs. Gilmore, whose ancestry was Dutch, was born at Forest City, Holt County, Missouri, November 12 1869. Mrs. Gilmore is president of the McCool Women's Christian Temperance Union.

They have two children: Richard, born January 17, 1892, who married Margaret May Donovan; and Alberta, born November 22, 1893, who married Frank Klone. Richard is a veterinarian, and Alberta is a beauty operator.

Mr. Gilmore's chief recreation is reading. Residence: McCool Junction.

Raymond McCreary Gilmore

Raymond McCreary Gilmore, dentist, was born at Auburn, Nebraska, January 5, 1896, son of Albert David and Elizabeth Culbertson (Curtis) Gilmore.

His father was born in Greencastle, Indiana, and died at Auburn, November 24, 1918. He was a merchant, whose Scotch-Irish ancestors came to Virginia about 1650. His wife, Elizabeth Culbertson, was born in Troy, Ohio, and is a member of the Daughters of the American Revolution through the Culbertson line.

In 1909 Dr. Gilmore was graduated from the public schools at Lincoln, Nebraska, and in 1913 from high school at Mondamin, Iowa. He attended Bellevue College, the University of Chicago, and Creighton University of Omaha, and was admitted to practice in June, 1923. He was a member of Alpha Sigma Tau at Creighton, Delta Sigma Delta at Creighton, and was president of the local chapter in 1923. While at Bellevue College he was a member of the football team in 1914 and 1915.

His marriage to Emma Jane Ward was solemnized at Rushville, Nebraska, December 28, 1922. Mrs. Gilmore was born at Albany, Nebraska, September 1, 1896. They have three children, Helen, born May 6, 1925; Pauline, born August 16, 1926; and Barbara Jane, born August 18, 1930.

Dr. Gilmore is a Republican. He was ordnance sergeant in the United States Army during the World War, participated in the Toul defensive sector, the St. Mihiel, Meuse Argonne, and served in the army of occupation. He is a member of the American Legion and the Veterans of Foreign Wars.

His professional organizations include, the American Dental Society, the Nebraska State Dental Society, and the Northwestern District Dental Society. He is affiliated with the Kearney Presbyterian Church, is a member of the Chamber of Commerce, the Kiwanis Club, the Masons, the State Historical Society, and the Kearney School Board. He is fond of golf and fishing, and is a member of the Kearney Country Club. Residence: Kearney.

Robert Gilmore

Robert Gilmore, prominent physician and surgeon, was born in Belfast, Ireland, June 4, 1856, son of James and Jean (McRoberts) Gilmore.

Dr. Gilmore received his education in public schools, and from Queen's University at Belfast. He was graduated from the Royal College of Physicians and surgeons at Edinburgh, Scotland, and in 1880 was given his medical degree by the Queen's University of Ireland, at Dublin.

In 1880 Dr. Gilmore came to Nebraska where he has carried on a general practice. He has served as president of the Central States Investment Company and the Central States Land Company, and as vice president of the Skinner Manufacturing Company of Omaha.

He is a Royal Arch Mason, an Elk, and a member of the Omaha and the Country Club. He is a Democrat, and is affiliated with the Presbyterian Church.

On October 21, 1884, he was married to Gretta Campbell Burrows at North Lodge, Ireland. They have one daughter, Amy Kathleen, who is married to R. M. Switzler. (*See Who's Who in Omaha*). Residence: Omaha.

James Gilmour

James Gilmour, was born in Rock Bluffs, Nebraska, May 24, 1869, the son of William and Lucy Ellen (Towner) Gilmour. William Gilmour was born in Orchard Lake, Michigan, September 20, 1838, and came to Nebraska in 1853. He fought in the Civil War, freighted across the plains and knew Peter A. Sarpy and Logan Fontanelle at Bellview, Nebraska, as friends. His father was a native of Scotland and his mother was a direct descendant of General Braddock, who was the first governor of Massachusetts.

James Gilmour's mother was born in Bates County, Missouri, January 4, 1848, the daughter of Reverend A. Towner, pioneer and Methodist minister of Scotch descent. Her mother was Hester Vought, of Pennsylvania Dutch parentage. William Gilmour died in Plattsmouth, Nebraska, January 28, 1928, and his wife in Sioux City, Iowa, December 11, 1924.

Mr. Gilmour married Louella Jane Snyder, May 30, 1894, at Plattsmouth. Her ancestors were from Virginia. She was born in Plattsmouth, on April 19, 1872, and taught school before her marriage. They have no children.

During the World War Mr. Gilmour was a member of the Home Guards and he is a member of the Red Cross. He is affiliated with the Christian Church of Ulysses, Nebraska, and the Odd Fellows Lodge. He is independent in politics, has resided in Nebraska sixty-two years, and is a member of the Nebraskana Society. Residence: Ulysses.

Herbert Dewey Gish

Herbert D. Gish, director of athletics at the University of Nebraska, was born at Abilene, Kansas, June 2, 1898. His father, Nathan Engle Gish, who was born at Maytown, Lancaster County, Pennsylvania, August 14, 1874, was a business man and traveling salesman. He died at Lincoln, February 18, 1925. Mary Josephine (Gibson) Gish, his wife, was born at Abilene, October 3, 1873. She is of English descent.

Mr. Gish received his education in the public schools of Kansas and Nebraska, and in 1918 was graduated from the Lincoln High School. He was awarded his B. S. degree in business administration at the University of Nebraska in 1922, and was a student at the University of Michigan, during the summer of 1926. A member of Sigma Alpha Epsilon, he was also active in track for three years at the University of Nebraska.

General assistant in the athletic department of the University of Nebraska from 1922 to 1925; he was acting director of athletics from March, 1925, to May, 1927; and since 1927 he has been director of intercollegiate and intramural athletics at that institution. He has lived in Nebraska for 12 years.

He was united in marriage with Irene Florence Graham at Manhattan, Riley County, Kansas, June 7, 1923. Mrs. Gish was born at White City, Kansas, March 4, 1898. There are two children: Mary Jo, born October 6, 1924; and Herbert G., born December 20, 1928.

Mr. Gish served as a private in the Student Army Training Corp in 1918, and is a member of the American Legion. A member of the board of directors of the Rotary club, 1930-31, he is a member of the Chamber of Commerce, and is a member of the Nebraskana Society. He is a Scottish Rite Mason and Shriner, and his social clubs are the University Club and Shrine Country Club. He is affiliated with Westminster Presbyterian Church of Lincoln, and is fond of golfing, hunting, and fishing. Residence: Lincoln.

Annie Reavis Gist

Annie Reavis Gist, clubwoman, was born at Falls City, April 7, 1865, the daughter of Isham and Annie Dorrington Reavis. Her father, who was born at Chandersville, Illinois, January 28, 1836, and died in Falls City, 1865, was a distinguished lawyer and judge of the United States Court of the Arizona territory. His ancestors came to North Carolina, in 1620; his great great grandfather, the first Isham Reavis, served in the battle of King's Mountain. His father settled in Illinois in its early days. Her mother, who was born at Whitestown, Oneida County,

New York, October 24, 1845, was a teacher and church worker.

Mrs. Gist attended the Falls City High School, and she was graduated from the Jacksonville Woman's College in 1884, where she was valedictorian of her class and was awarded the degrees A. B., M. A., and B. F. A. She was a member of Pi Beta Phi.

At Falls City, she was married to Thomas Jefferson Gist on September 5, 1888. Mr. Gist, who was born at Tipton, Missouri, May 2, 1863, is a banker, and traces his ancestry from Revolutionary times. Four children were born to this union: Isham Reavis, born July 22, 1890, died at Fort Riley, Kansas, in the service of his country, October 21, 1918; Silas Frank, born October 29, 1893; Anna Margaret, born May 3, 1897, who married Edwin Morehead; and Elizabeth Webster, born August 9, 1899, who married Dr. Millard U. Burton.

Mrs. Gist was in charge of seven counties in liberty loan drives during the World War, and helped raise funds for building hostess houses. For 12 years she has been a member of the Red Cross, of which she has been president of the county chapter for the last five years. She is a member of the Daughters of the American Revolution, the auxiliary of the Disabled Veterans of America, the auxiliary of the American Legion, the State Historical Society and the Nebraskana Society. For twenty-five years she has been on the library board of Falls City. She is a member of the Eastern Star and the Methodist Episcopal Church, where she has played the pipe organ for over twenty years. Her hobbies are reading and music. Residence: Falls City.

Claus Wilhelm Glandt

Claus Wilhelm Glandt, building contractor, real estate and insurance man, was born at Deichhausen, Ditmarschen, Holstein, Germany on April 8, 1871. His father, Peter Glandt, born in Holland, in 1820, was a miller, whose death occurred at Deichhausen on July 4, 1885. Peter Glandt married Katharine Thode, a native of Busum, born in 1838, and whose death occurred at Deichhausen in 1877.

Educated in grade school at Deichhausen, Claus Wilhelm Glandt came to America as a youth, and about thirty-five years ago entered the building contracting business, and later took up insurance and real estate work. He started his business at Elkhorn, a few years later removing to Bennington where he is senior member of the firm of C. W. Glandt and Sons.

Of his marriage to Kathrine Alvina Stoltenberg three children are living and three are deceased. Carl, born October 12, 1876, died in 1903, as did Wilhelm, born September 24, 1898. Rudolph P., born April 1, 1901, married Helen Margaret Roe; Arthur R., born August 13, 1903, married Maude Vaughn; Otto W., born November 1, 1906 is unmarried, and Emma K., born March 20, 1910, died December 20, 1910.

Rudolph, Arthur and Otto are associated with their father in business. Mrs. Glandt was born at Barsbeck, Propsti, Holstein, Germany on June 30, 1873.

Mr. Glandt is a Republican. He is a member of St. John's Evangelical Lutheran Church, the Bennington Plattdutcher Verein, the Commercial Club and the Nebraskana Society. His hobby is mechanics. Residence: Bennington.

Lee A. Glassburn

Lee A. Glassburn, publisher of the *Fillmore County News*, was born in Miami County, Indiana, February 1, 1869, son of Andrew and Mary Frances (Willie) Glassburn. The father was born in Johnson County, Indiana, October 26, 1837, and died at Glenwood, Iowa, September 17, 1927. The mother was born in Kentucky, August 8, 1842, and died at Glenwood, August 5, 1899.

On December 23, 1926, Mr. Glassburn was married

to Mary A. Allison at Silver City, Iowa, her birthplace. Two children were born to them, Vera on May 25, 1898, who married Warren L. Strickland, and Mildred, born April 1, 1900, who died February 15, 1925.

Mr. Glassburn has owned and published the *Melbourne Record* at Melbourne, Iowa, and the *Seymour Leader* at Seymour, Iowa, in addition to his present paper. A Republican, he was candidate for the legislature in 1930. He was secretary of the Commercial Club in 1929, is a member of the Methodist Episcopal Church and the Masons. Residence: Exeter.

John Randolph Glassey

John Randolph Glassey, clergyman and educator, was born at Fort Morgan, Colorado, October 19, 1895, son of John Henry and Nell (Fitz-Randolph) Glassey. His father, a native of Markethill, County Armagh, Ireland, born December 11, 1856, is of Protestant Irish stock. He came to America in 1869, and settled in Colorado before the railroads were built, and became a pioneer rancher. His wife, Nell, was born in La Grange, Indiana, October 28, 1869, and died at Fort Morgan, April 3, 1926. She was of early Colonial extraction, and a member of the Daughters of the American Revolution. She was a music teacher of unusual ability.

Educated in the public and high schools of Fort Morgan, Mr. Glassey was graduated from the latter in 1914. He attended the University of Nebraska his freshman year 1914-15, and Rollins College in Florida 1918-19, graduating from Hastings College with a Bachelor of Arts degree in 1921. Mr. Glassey next attended Columbia University for a summer session. He received his Bachelor of Theology degree from Princeton University in 1924 and his Master's degree from New York University later.

Mr. Glassey has been a member of the glee clubs of each school he has attended, was president of his junior class, president of his club at Princeton, and in addition is a member of Phi Alpha (Rollins), and has a letter in the 400 yard canoe race at Rollins. An ordained minister of the Presbyterian Church, Mr. Glassey is a member of the Synod of Nebraska. A member of the Red Cross, also, he has served as divisional chairman in drives of the organization, is a member of the Lions Club, the Young Men's Christian Association, Pi Gamma Mu, and Tri Gamma Literary Society. A resident of Nebraska since 1924 since that time he has been professor of Bible at Hastings College.

On June 24, 1930, he was united in marriage to Marion Lucile Fabrique at Wichita, Kansas. Mrs. Glassey was born at Chester, Nebraska, October 10, 1907, of French and Scotch ancestry. A graduate of Hastings College with the Bachelor of Arts degree in 1927, she is now working for her master's degree.

Mr. Glassey is a member of the Hillside Golf Club, while his hobby is entertaining. Residence: Hastings.

Alvin Edward Glaze

At the age of thirteen Alvin Edward Glaze left the farm of his father, and went to Allen, Nebraska to learn the printers' trade. He was born at Danbury, Iowa, January 28, 1904, son of Oscar Nathan and Martha (Race) Glaze, the former a pioneer farmer in Wheeler County, now retired. Oscar N. Glaze was born in Kentucky, March 4, 1863, of Yankee ancestry. His wife, Martha, was born in Iowa.

Alvin Edward Glaze attended public school at Allen, Nebraska, and was graduated from high school in May, 1923. After learning the printing trade, Mr. Glaze worked at Allen and Hartington, Nebraska, and Sioux City, Iowa, and in April, 1930, became editor of the *Plainview News*.

He was married on January 24, 1927, to Eunice

Margaret Prouse at Sioux City. Mrs. Glaze was born at Ponca, Nebraska, April 22, 1906. There is one daughter, Marilyn Ann., born at Sioux City, Iowa, November 4, 1927. Mr. Glaze is a Republican. Recently he was elected to life membership in the Nebraskana Society. Residence: Plainview.

Harold Francis Gleason

Harold Francis Gleason, lumber executive, was born at Platte Center, Nebraska, August 24, 1895. His father, Thomas Henry Gleason, was born in Columbus, September 12, 1859. He is of Irish descent, for many years in the general mercantile business, and now retired after twenty-three years as a rural mail carrier. His mother, Margaret Agnes Hennessey, was born at Omaha, March 15, 1870, her parents having come from Ireland.

Mr. Gleason attended St. Joseph's parochial school, from which he was graduated in 1912. For three years thereafter he was engaged in the automobile business, and for the past eighteen years has been in the lumber business, now as manager for G. W. Viergutz.

He is a Republican, a member of St. Joseph's Catholic Church, and a member and post commander of the American Legion. During the World War he served eighteen months in the Naval Aviation Service. Mr. Gleason is a member of the Nebraskana Society and the Chamber of Commerce. His favorite sport is golf, and his social club is the Wayside Country Club. Residence: Platte Center.

Jacob Glur

Born at Columbus, Nebraska, May 11, 1896, Jacob Glur is the son of Jacob and Anna Glur. His father, born in Switzerland, came to America as a young man, and was engaged in business at Columbus until his death on December 22, 1913. His mother was also a native of Switzerland.

Jacob Glur, the subject of this sketch, attended the public school at Columbus, and was graduated from Columbus High School. He attended York College 1916-17, where he participated in basketball, football and track.

On August 17, 1926, he was married to Anna W. Witt at Columbus. Mrs. Glur was born at Scribner on June 30, 1905. There are two daughters, Carolyn, born September 8, 1928; and Margaret, born May 11, 1931.

Upon leaving school Mr. Glur entered business, and is now secretary-treasurer of the Glur Cement Works. He held the rank of sergeant first class in the World War, is a member of the Reserve Corps, and is affiliated with the Evangelical Lutheran Church. He is a Mason and an Elk, a member of the Red Cross, the Columbus School Board and the Young Men's Christian Association, and a life member of the Nebraskana Society. His favorite sport is football. Residence: Columbus.

William Joseph Glynn

William Joseph Glynn, a resident of Merrick County, Nebraska, for the past 42 years, was born at Balitore, Ireland, January 13, 1879. His father, Thomas George Glynn, a farmer, was born at Balitore, January 22, 1847, and came to America in 1888. Mary Ann Glynn, hiis mother, was born at Ridge, County Carlow, Ireland, in 1845, and died at Brule, Nebraska, February 19, 1894.

Mr. Glynn has been successfully engaged in farming for many years. He is affiliated with St. Mark's Episcopal Church and holds membership in the Nebraskana Society. His hobby is carpenter work.

His marriage to Elizabeth Watchorn occurred at Palmer, Nebraska, December 31, 1901. Mrs. Glynn was born at Augharue, Ireland, February 8, 1877. Their three children are: Ernest, born August 3, 1903, who married Hazel Stone; Osvil, born October 17, 1907, who married Grace Weber; and Elizabeth, born September 16, 1912, who is a student in business college. Residence: Palmer.

Elmer Eugene Gockley

Elmer Eugene Gockley, postmaster at Edison, Nebraska, was born at Sycamore, Illinois, March 9, 1878, son of Levi D. and Matilda (Bentz) Gockley. His father, a carpenter and contractor, whose French ancestors came to America in 1732, was born at Kleinfeltersville, Pennsylvania, January 10, 1835. His death occurred at Haigler, Nebraska, October 17, 1923.

Matilda Bentz, his mother, was born June 3, 1840, at Brubaker, Pennsylvania, and died at Haigler, Nebraska, on July 16, 1928. She was a descendent of the early German settlers of Pennsylvania.

Mr. Gockley attended the public schools of Illinois, and in the early 1890's came to Nebraska. He clerked in a general merchandise store at Holbrook, Nebraska, from 1898-1900, and farmed from 1900 until 1915. From that time until 1919 he was a grain buyer at Edison, Nebraska, and since 1919 has served as postmaster. Mr. Gockley is a Republican.

His marriage to Elnora Snyder was solemnized at Cambridge, Nebraska, September 23, 1900, and to them two children were born, Evalyn Fae, and Ralph Eugene. Both children were graduated from the Edison, Nebraska, High School.

Mrs. Gockley was born at Columbia City, Indiana, December 7, 1879. She takes active interest in the Church of Christ, in which the entire family holds membership. She is active in the work of the American Legion Auxiliary, the Women's Christian Temperance Union, but is principally interested in her home.

Mr. Gockley recently was made a life member of the Nebraskana Society in recognition of his efforts toward the development of his community and state. He is at the present time trying to get the information together relative to his ancestors, and has in his possession a chest, originally the property of his French ancestors, brought to America in the 17th century.

Each year the Gockley relatives meet in Hershey Park, Pennsylvania, the reunion lasting several days. At each reunion the attendance increases. Residence: Edison.

Richard Goehring, Jr.

Richard Goehring, Jr., president and general manager of Goehring-Sothman Company, was born at Grand Island, Nebraska, August 18, 1887. His father, Richard Ernest Goehring was born in Saxony in 1850. He was of the German Lutheran faith, coming from Germany in 1869. An early settler in Nebraska, he was a lumber merchant and president of the Equitable Building and Loan Association prior to his death on November 30, 1929. His wife, Pauline Wagoner, was born in Germany in 1863 and died at Grand Island on March 16, 1930.

Educated in the public and high schools of Grand Island, Richard Goehring, Jr., was also a student at Grand Island Baptist College. From 1908-10 he was the director of a popular concert orchestra and from 1910-12 was manager of the George A. Hoagland Lumber Company at Columbus. Removing to Grand Island in 1914 as manager of the same company he continued with the organization until 1919, at which time he founded the Goehring-Sothman Company.

From 1926-29 he was president of the Grand Island Brick Works. He is a member of the traffic committee of the Chamber of Commerce, a charter member of the Kiwanis Club, an Elk and an Eagle, and a member of the Hall County Historical Society and The Nebraskana Society. His religious affiliation is with the Presbyterian Church, his sport is golf and his hobby is mechanics.

Of his marriage to Ina Viola Kayser there is one daughter, Helen, born August 13, 1913. She was graduated from Grand Island High School, studied voice and dancing in New York in the fall of 1930, and in Los Angeles in 1931. Mrs. Goehring, who was born at Hastings, June 4, 1891, was a pianist and teacher of more than average ability. Her death occurred at Grand Island on December 10, 1930. Residence: Grand Island.

Ira Alonzo Goff

Born at Beloit, Iowa, March 20, 1878, Ira Alonzo Goff has resided in Nebraska since 1907.

He is the son of John Frederick and Mary Louisa (Hunt) Goff, the former of whom is now retired. The father was born at Nicholsville, Michigan, July 8, 1854, and is of English descent. The mother was born at Table Rock, Nebraska, September 13, 1858, and died at Aitkin, Minnesota, in September, 1924. Her ancestry was also English.

Mr. Goff received his early education in country and small town schools, and from 1910 until 1916 was a railway station agent and telegraph operator. Since 1916 he has been cashier of the First National Bank of Hay Springs.

On December 24, 1900, he was married to Mary Caroline Albright at Beloit. Mrs. Goff was born at Beloit, November 7, 1880, of German ancestry. They have two children, LaRue E., born September 26, 1907; and Iris A., born June 11, 1911. LaRue is a banker, while Iris is a student in medical school.

Mr. Goff is a Republican. He is affiliated with the Reorganized Church of Later Day Saints at Deloit, is a member of the Red Cross, the Hay Springs and Rural Community Club, the Lions Club, the Masons, and the Camp Sheridan Memorial Association. He is also a member of various educational associations. He enjoys outdoor sports, and is a member of the Izaak Walton League. His favorite sport is golf. Residence: Hay Springs.

LaRue Errol Goff

LaRue Errol Goff, assistant cashier of the First National Bank of Hay Springs, was born at Kiron, Iowa, September 26, 1906, son of Ira Alonzo and Mary Caroline (Albright) Goff.

His father was born at Beloit, Iowa, March 20, 1878, and is a banker of English descent. His mother was born at Beloit, November 6, 1880, and is a member of the Delphian Society.

Mr. Goff was graduated from public school at Hay Springs in 1920 and from the Hay Springs High School in 1924. Thereafter, he attended the University of Nebraska, where he is a member of Kappa Rho Sigma. In 1927, Mr. Goff entered the employ of the Hastings Motor Company. During the same year he became associated with the First National Bank of Hay Springs, of which he has been assistant cashier since 1928. He was a member of the Reserve Officers Training Corps for two years, and held the rank of first sergeant. He is a Protestant, a member of the Red Cross, and a member of the Hay Springs and Rural Improvement Club. From 1924 until 1927, he was a member of the National Engineering Society and the American Society of Mechanical Engineers. His favorite sports are golf, hunting and fishing, while his hobby is mechanics. Residence: Hay Springs.

Laurence Archibald Goines

Laurence Archibald Goines, city manager of Alliance, was born in New York City, July 23, 1886, and received the Bachelor of Science degree in civil engineering at the University of Wyoming in 1912.

On July 29, 1911, he was married to Lulu May Mead at Laramie, Wyoming. She was born in Carbon County, Wyoming, October 4, 1888. There are five children, William H., born in 1912; Marguerite K., born in 1913; Laurence A., born in 1915; Patricia E., born in 1918; and Dorothy Jeanne, born in 1922.

For ten years including the period of his university attendance, Mr. Goines was engaged in subordinate engineering and construction work in United States, Canada, and Mexico, for seven and one-half years with the Costilla Estates Development Company in Colorado and New Mexico. During five years of the time he was responsible for engineering work, and for two and one-half years was executive assistant to the general manager of the parent company and its subsidiaries. For nine and one-half months he was engaged in private engineering practice in Ogallala, Nebraska, and for three and one-fourth years was general manager of the Buckfield Plantations in South Carolina. Since June 1, 1925, he has held the position of city manager of Alliance, that position being appointive, non-political, and non-partisan. He is the author of several articles on municipal administration.

Durng the late war Mr. Goines was instructor for draft troops. He served 18 months in Colorado National Guard (Federalized service) with the rank of first sergeant. He is a member of the American Legion.

Mr. Goines' professional organizations include the American Society of Civil Engineers, the Colorado Society of Engineers, the International Association of City Managers, and the League of Nebraska Municipalities, of which he is vice president.

Mr. Goines is a member of the Ancient Free and Accepted Masons Lodge No. 44 at Alamosa, Colorado, Scottish Rite at Pueblo, Colorado, and the Order of Eastern Star at Alliance, Nebraska. He is a member of the Guardian Council of Job's Daughters at Alliance, and a member of the Alliance Chamber of Commerce. Residence: Alliance.

Joseph Gardner Goings

One of Nebraska's outstanding farmers, Joseph Gardner Goings was born at Bloomington, Illinois, July 19, 1862, the son of Joseph and Mary Ann McCoy Goings. His father, a farmer was born in Virginia in 1812, and died at Minden, Nebraska, in 1891. His mother was born in Woodford County, Illinois, in 1832, and died at Bloomington, Nebraska in 1915.

In 1863, Mr. Goings moved with his parents to Davids County, Missouri, lived in Mills County, Iowa, for a period of three years, and in 1876 moved to Rocks County, Kansas. Since 1882 he has farmed continuously and has taken a prominent part in agricultural projects in Nebraska, Missouri, and Oklahoma. He served as director of the Farmers Co-operative Association at Kansas City, Missouri, acting as president of the board of that organization for two years. In 1919 he moved to Kearney, Nebraska, and two years later purchased the farm he now occupies at Wilcox, Nebraska, land comprising 960 acres.

Mr. Goings is treasurer of the Pleasant View School Board, is a member of the Nebraskana Society, and holds membership in the Democratic party. His hobby is reading.

Of his marriage to Ida D. Babb one daughter was born, Hazel, October 13, 1899. On December 27, 1913, he married Hattie L. Fulkerson at Salt Lake City, Utah. She was born April 19, 1886, at Warrensburg, Missouri, the daughter of William and Anna (Keen) Fulkerson. Previous to her marriage Mrs. Goings was educated at the Warrensburg Normal School, graduating in 1909. She taught in Washington, Montana, Nevada, and Utah.

Mrs. Goings's paternal grandfather was an extensive land and slave owner in Missouri in the early days and was a physician and surgeon of prominence.

Mr. and Mrs. Goings' children are: Leona, born October 13, 1915; Antha L., July 6, 1917; and Dorris J., born September 21, 1918. Residence: Wilcox.

Nathan Jules Gold

Nathan Jules Gold, one of Nebraska's leading executives, was born at Hampton, Iowa, May 28, 1894, son of William and Pauline (Mayer) Gold. His father who was born at Plattsburg, New York, March 27, 1862, has been president of Gold and Company for many years. He is of German descent. His wife, Pauline, was born in New York City, on July 9, 1863. She was a teacher prior to her marriage, and died at Lincoln, December 29, 1918.

Nathan Gold attended the Lincoln public and high schools and the University of Nebraska, the latter as a special student. Since early youth he has been associated with Gold and Company, and for a number of years has been vice president of the organization. He is also a director of the Security Mutual Life Insurance Company.

On May 25, 1922, he married Evelyn Putzel Baum at Philadelphia, Mrs. Gold's birthplace. There are two children, William II, born March 17, 1925, and Louise, born September 29, 1926.

During the World War Mr. Gold enlisted in the first officer's training camp at Ft. Snelling, Minnesota, later served at Camp Dodge, Iowa, and Madison Barracks, N. Y., and spent fourteen months in France. He is a member of the American Legion, the Veterans of Foreign Wars, and the Red Cross and Community Chest, and has served as a member of the board of directors of both last mentioned organizations. He is a Mason, and member of the Scottish Rite and Shrine bodies, the Rotary Club, the Lincoln Chamber of Commerce, the National Retail Dry Goods Association and the Nebraskana Society. His clubs are the Lincoln University and Country Clubs, and his sport is riding horses. Residence: Lincoln.

Louis Goldsmith

Louis Goldsmith, son of Bennett and Helena (Olcovich) Goldsmith, was born at West Point, Nebraska, January 19, 1878, and for many years has been a member of the firm of L. Goldsmith and Company. His father was born at Kempen, Germany, July 29, 1844, and came to Beaufort, South Carolina, in 1866. Later he came to Nebraska where he engaged in the mercantile business served as mayor of West Point and state representative in 1893. He died at West Point on August 9, 1893. Helena, his wife, was born in Kempen, Germany, February 20, 1846 and is still living.

Mr. Goldsmith attended the West Point schools and was graduated in June 1895. In 1896 he attended Elliott's Business College at Burlington, Iowa. He is the owner of L. Goldsmith and Company, a member of the Red Cross, the Community Club and the Masons. His political affiliation is with the Republican party. Mr. Goldsmith is fond of reading.

On June 21, 1915, he was united in marriage to Emily Margaret Fisher at Davenport, Iowa. Mrs. Goldsmith was born at Dietikon, Zurich, Switzerland, April 14, 1878, and before her marriage was a nurse. They have no children. Residence: West Point.

Abe Goldstein

Abe Goldstein, one of Omaha's most prominent merchants, was born at St. Paul, Minnesota, December 25, 1880. His father, Reuben Goldstein, was born in Russia, and died at Omaha, Douglas County, Nebraska; he was a merchant. His mother was born in a small town in Germany, and died at Omaha.

Mr. Goldstein attended the public schools of Nebraska, and from 1888 to 1903 worked in stores in Clay Center, Fairbury, and Nebraska City. In 1903 he began his own business at Centerville, Iowa, and stayed there for 17 years. In 1921, he moved to Omaha, where he is now president of Goldstein-Chapman's department store Carman's Silk Shop, Incorporated and Natelson's.

During the late war Mr. Goldstein served as city chairman of the war stamp drives and was chairman of the speakers bureau for Appanoose County, in Iowa. He is a member of the Red Crss, Chamber af Commerce, the Nebraskana Society, the Highland Club, Woodmen of the World, Modern Woodmen of America, and the Masons.

His marriage to Anna Chapman was solemnized at Centerville, Iowa. Mrs. Goldstein was born at Des Moines, Iowa. Two children were born to them: Rosaline, born February 20, 1906; and Herman, born May 19, 1914. Residence: Omaha.

Frank E. Golson

Frank E. Golson, prominent Loup County farmer and rancher, was born in Wakesha County, Michigan, March 11, 1872, and for the past fifty-six years has resided in Nebraska.

James Christy Golson, his father, was born on Granden Island, Canada, March 7, 1840, came to the United States as a young man and served three years and three months in the Civil War. He was an early settler in Nebraska, where he was a farmer and ranchman until his death at Brewster, April 21, 1910.

Alice Adela Trainor, wife of James C. Golson, was born in Maryland, April 4, 1845, and died at Milburn, Nebraska, December 16, 1922. She was a typical pioneer homemaker, devoted to her husband and family.

Frank G. Golson was educated in country school, and thereafter followed in his father's footsteps. He has been a farmer and rancher for thirty years, has a ranch of 2420 acres, a farm of about 300 acres, and is joint owner with his brother of another farm and cattle ranch of 380 acres, well improved. His home farm and ranch are well improved, and he employs quite a large number of men. He has bred registered Hereford cattle from the beginning, has Percheron horses and breeds Duroc hogs. In addition to his work in this line, he has filled the office of county surveyor of Loup County for the past thirty years, also.

He is one of the most outstanding men in his locality, and was recently elected to life membership in the Nebraskana Society. Residence: Moulton.

Herbert E. Gooch

Herbert E. Gooch was born in Chicago, Illinois, September 10, 1878, son of Herbert E. and Lotta (Amsden) Gooch. The father was born in England, and came to the United States as a young man settling in Chicago.

After the death of his father, while still a young boy, Mr. Gooch moved to St. Paul, Minnesota, with his mother. At the age of ten he left school and received the balance of his education in the school of experience.

He moved to Nebraska in 1904, establishing a grainbrokerage business. At the present time he is the president of the Gooch Milling & Elevator Company and of the Good Food Products Company which were organized by him.

Mr. Gooch is a Democrat, a 32nd degree Mason, and a member of the Nobles of the Mystic Shrine. He is a member of the Sons of the American Revolution, the Nebraska State Historical Society, the Lincoln Chamber of Commerce, the Lincoln Country Club and the Eastridge Country Club.

He is married to Jessie Holloway of St. Paul, Minnesota. She is a member of the Woman's Club, and the Lincoln and Eastridge Country Clubs. There are three children, Amsden, Herbert E., Jr., and Ann. Residence: Lincoln.

Benjamin F. Good

Benjamin Franklin Good, retired lawyer, was born in Bloomfield, Iowa, April 2, 1860, son of John and Margaret Frances (Bothamer) Good. John Good was born in County Cork, Ireland, about 1820, and died at Bloomfield in October 1878. He was a farmer and livestock breeder of English descent, whose ancestors moved to Ireland in 1620; one was a member of Lord Bandon's colony and lived near Bandon, coming to the United States about 1849.

Margaret Frances Bothamer was born near Bandon, Ireland, about 1820, and died at Bloomfield in August, 1900. She and her husband were pioneers in Wisconsin and Iowa, and resided on farms in both states. Originaliy English, the family became part of Lord Bandon's colony about 1620.

Educated first in common schools, Benjamin F. Good attended Southern Iowa Normal School at Bloomfield, 2 years, graduating in 1883. He took some special work in languages and history at the State University of Iowa, 1883,-85; attended the law school, receiving his LL. B. in 1885. He is a member of Phi Delta Phi.

On June 11, 1890, he was married to Jennie Jessen, a native of Nebraska City, born in 1864. She was of Danish-American ancestry, and a teacher before marriage. There are two children of this marriage: Anabel, born May 19, 1891, who has two sons and one daughter, and lives at Clinton, Iowa. She attended Smith College and took her degree at the University of Nebraska. Paul F., born March 16, 1893, took his B. A. at Amherst at the age of 20, was a Rhodes Scholar, and attended Oxford University 3 years where he took his degree in 1917. His master's degree was received four years later. He enlisted in the World war as an ensign in the U. S. Naval Reserve Force. He is married and has four sons, and is engaged in the practice of law at Lincoln. Jennie Jessen Good died at Lincoln in April, 1916.

On July 28, 1917, Mr. Good was married to Louise M. Allen. She is a graduate of the University of Nebraska (1906), M. A., 1907, and a member of Sigma Xi, and Kappa Delta. They have one daughter, Margaret Frances, born November 7, 1918.

Upon his admission to the bar in June, 1885, Judge Good entered the practice of law at Wahoo. He was a member of the law firm of Good and Good at Wahoo for fifteen years, until his election as judge of the district court (1900-1912). From 1912 to 1925 he practiced at Lincoln where he was associated with his son, Paul F., and with Arthur Richardson, under the firm name of Good, Richardson and Good. In 1925 he retired because of ill health and removed to Beverly Hills, California. Judge Good is a Democrat. He is co-author of *Good and Corcoran's Law Digest and Instructions to Juries,* (1903).

During the World War he was a four minute speaker and active in war projects. He is a member of Beverly Hills Community Church and The Nebraskana Society. His clubs are the University of Lincoln and the Men's Club of Beverly Hills. Residence: Lincoln.

Edward Ellsworth Good

Edward E. Good, lawyer and justice of the Supreme Court of Nebraska, was born at Bloomfield, Iowa, May 13, 1862. His father, William Henry Good, was born in Halifax County, Virginia, February 23, 1797. He was a farmer and stockman and married Mary Ann McCullough. He died at Bloomfield, January 12, 1874. Mary Ann McCullough was a native of Indiana, born in June, 1829, and who died in Bloomfield February 11, 1884.

Judge Good attended country and high school in Iowa and Southern Iowa Normal School at Bloomfield. He received his LL. B. from the State University of Iowa, and was admitted to the practice of law at Iowa City

June 24, 1885. That year he came to Nebraska and established a practice at Wahoo. From 1885 to 1900 he was a junior member of the law firm of Good and Good; and from 1900 to 1902 senior member of the firm of Good and Slama. During the periods 1902-08 and 1909-12 he was a member of the firm of Simpson and Good.

He is a Republican, and served as county attorney of Saunders County from 1895 and 1896. Commissioner of the Supreme Court of Nebraska during 1908 and 1909, he was elected judge of the District Court from the 5th Judicial District in November, 1911, and was re-elected in 1916 and 1920. He was elected Justice of the Supreme Court of Nebraska for the term 1923-28, and was re-elected and still serves.

His marriage to Orpha Jane Gillilan was solmnized at Central City, Iowa, July 8, 1885. Mrs. Good was born at Central City, January 10, 1862. They are members of the First Congregational Church at Wahoo. A Mason, he belongs to the Royal Arch and Scottish Rite bodies, and the Eastern Star. His other fraternal memberships include the Modern Woodmen of America, the Knights of Pythias, Elks, and Ancient Order of United Workmen. He is also a Kiwanian. His clubs are the University Club of Lincoln and the Shrine Country Club. Residence: Lincoln.

Ellis Ellsworth Good

Ellis E. Good was born in Nemaha County, May 20, 1863, son of Jacob and Barbara Ellen (Lash) Good. His father was a farmer and in later years was the organizer and president of the Bank of Brock, the Murray State Bank, and the Citizens State Bank of Peru, all Nebraska banks. The son of Salathiel and Eulalia (Templin) Good, he was born in Henry County, Indiana, February 12, 1838, and died at Peru, Nebraska, March 20, 1913.

His mother, the daughter of a pioneer family in Nemaha County, was born at Finley, Ohio, September 26, 1843, and died at Peru, August 7, 1912.

Mr. Good was educated in the country schools and at Peru State Teachers' College where he was graduated in 1887. He has lived all his life in Nebraska and has been prominent in the business and educational activities of the state for many years. From January 1, 1889, to September 1, 1891, he was superintendent of schools at Elmwood after which he was superintendent of the Valentine schools for four years.

One of the organizers of the Lincoln Liberty Insurance Company, he has been a director in that company since its origin. He was one of the organizers and a director of the Bank of Brock, at Brock, Nebraska, and of the Bank of Murray, at Murray. From 1895 to 1913 he was cashier of the Citizens' State Bank of Peru, and has been president of it since that date.

Mr. Good, who is a Republican, served five sessions in the Nebraska legislature; he was representative from Nemaha and Johnson counties, 1903; was senator from the same district, 1905; and was representative from Nemaha County, 1917, 1919, 1921.

He was united in marriage with Ida Eleanor Church at Auburn, Nebraska, September 12, 1889. Mrs. Good, who was born at Mason City, Iowa, is the daughter of Jarvis and Sabra (Van Patter) Church. Her ancestry is traced to the Revolution.

During the war Mr. Good was active through his bank in liberty loan drives. He is a member of the state and national bankers' associations; the Kiwanis club; the Peru Chamber of Commerce, having served as its president; and the Red Cross. He is a Mason, of which he is a past Master, Peru Lodge number 14, Scottish Rite, Shrine.

He is affiliated with the Methodist Episcopal Church. (Deceased).

Jesse S. Good

Jesse S. Good, who has been engaged in the general collection and loan business at Cozad for 40 years, was born at Sandwich, Illinois, August 11, 1867. He is the son of Stephen W. and Rosetta (Hastie) Good. Stephen W. Good was a farmer of English descent, whose death occurred at Fairmont, Nebraska, February 25, 1887. His wife, Rosetta, was a native of New York State, of Scotch ancestry, who died at Cozad in 1922.

Educated in the public schools of Fairmont, Jesse S. Good was graduated from high school there, and on February 21, 1889, was married to Ethel W. Riggs at Cozad. Mrs. Good, who was born at Cincinnati, Ohio, died at Cozad on September 23, 1925. There are two children, Robert R., who married Fern Griffith; and Dorothy C., who married Ivan D. Wood.

Mr. Good is an independent Republican. He has lived in Nebraska for the past fifty-six years, is vice president of the Cozad Chamber of Commerce, a 32nd degree Mason and a Rotarian. He is president of the Cozad Public Library and was recently made a life member of The Nebraskana Society. Residence: Cozad.

Paul Francis Good

Paul F. Good was born at Wahoo, Nebraska, March 16, 1893, and has lived in this state all his life. His father, Benjamin Franklin Good, who was born near Bloomfield, Davis County, Iowa, April 2, 1860, is a distinguished lawyer and judge having served as judge of the district court of the fifth judicial district in Nebraska; his ancestry is Irish. Jennie (Jessen) Good, his mother, was born at Nebraska City, Otoe County, Nebraska, May 12, 1865, and died at Lincoln, Lancaster County, Nebraska, April 6, 1916. Before her marriage she was a teacher in the public schools at Wahoo. Her Scotch ancestors came to America before the Revolution; her parents were territorial pioneers of Nebraska.

Mr. Good was graduated from the Wahoo High School in 1909. He holds the following degrees: M. A., Oxford University, England, 1921; A. B. in jurisprudence, Oxford, 1917; B. A., Amherst College, 1913, where he was a member of Phi Beta Kappa. He was a student at the University of Nebraska Law School, 1913-14, and was there a member of Phi Delta Phi. He was admitted to the bar at Lincoln, June 1919, and since that date has been engaged in the practice of law there.

On September 1, 1917, he was united in marriage with Dorothy Frances Collins at Clyst St. George, Devon, England. Mrs. Good was born at Exeter, Devon, England, October 20, 1898. They have four children: John Paul, born August 3, 1918; Robert James, born August 13, 1920; David Martin, born February 20, 1922; and Anthony Jessen, born June 23, 1928.

Mr. Good is a director of the First National Bank at Wahoo. He holds membership in: American Bar Association; Nebraska State Bar Association; Lancaster County Bar Association; Lincoln Chamber of Commerce; and the Nebraskana Society. Since 1924 he has been a director of the Young Men's Christian Association; is a member of the budget committee of the Lincoln Community chest; since May, 1929, has been a member of the Lincoln Board of Education; and holds membership in the Lincoln Kiwanis Club and the Parent Teachers Association.

His social club is the Lincoln University Club; he is affiliated with the Holy Trinity Episcopal Church of Lincoln. His favorite sport is swimming, while his hobby is reading. During the World War Mr. Good served as an ensign in the United States Naval Reserve Force under Admiral Wilson, commander of the United States Naval Forces at Brest, France.

He is a member of the American Legion. Politically he is a Democrat. Residence: Lincoln.

WILLIAM ERNEST GOODHUE

William Larkin Goodell

Born at Sacramento, California, September 19, 1897, William Larkin Goodell is the son of William Yates and Nora May (Flint) Goodell. At the age of 4 years he left California with his parents locating on a farm near Wahoo, Nebraska. They remained here two years and later moved to a farm six miles northeast of Norfolk, Nebraska.

He received his elementary training in a rural school two miles from his home, and remained on the farm until entering the academy at Cotner College. His father, a farmer, was born at Syracuse, New York, April 11, 1867. His mother was born at Gallatin, Missouri, July 19, 1870.

Mr. Goodell was graduated from Cotner College Academy in 1922, was a student at Cotner College for three years, where he was active in debating and music. While there he worked at various occupations to pay for his schooling, including the business management of the college paper during the school years, 1921-22. He was a member of the championship debating team in 1924, and held membership in Phi Kappa Delta. He served as student pastor at Waco, Salem, and Murray, Nebraska, 1921-22, held a pastorate at Valparaiso, Nebraska, 1922-25, was resident pastor at David City, Nebraska, 1926, and served at Indianola, Nebraska, 1927-29. He has been pastor of the First Church of Christ, of Minden, Nebraska, since 1930. He is president of the local ministerial association, and also president of the sixth district Churches of Christ in Nebraska.

Mr. Goodell is a member of the Nebraskana Society. He has been a resident of Nebraska for the past 30 years and for the past decade has devoted his entire time to religious activities in various communities. He is a Republican.

On July 14, 1920, he was married to Grace Crystal Will at Falls City, Nebraska. Mrs. Goodell, who was a stenographer and bookkeeper prior to her marriage, was born at Falls City, August 14, 1897. She attended Cotner Academy, and was the associate business manager of the *Cotner Collegian* during the school years of 1920-21. To this marriage were born the following children: Will Edward, June 15, 1921; Robert Yates, June 15, 1923; Dorothy Ellen, February 13, 1925; and Virginia May, March 31, 1927. Residence: Minden. (Photograph in Album).

William Ernest Goodhue

William Ernest Goodhue, lawyer, was born in Cheshire County, New Hampshire, February 18, 1860, and has been a resident of Nebraska since March 20, 1884. His father, Nathaniel Gage Goodhue, was born at Newport, Massachusetts, August 17, 1820, and died at Carleton, February 11, 1888. He was a minister of the Congregational Church, descended from William Goodhue who came from England 19 years after the Mayflower sailed.

Nathaniel Goodhue married Lucinda Almira Osborn. She was born at Attica, New York, June 30, 1829, and died at Carleton, February 2, 1888. She was a successful wife and mother, and under her training William E. Goodhue received part of his early education.

On October 11, 1911, he was united in marriage to Ada Jamison, at Lincoln. She was born at Mediapolis, Iowa, in 1860, and died at Mediapolis on June 22, 1926. Mr. Goodhue was married to Delila Colson, on August 15, 1928.

Active in the practice of law for many years, Judge Goodhue has always been active in Republican politics, and served two terms as county judge and one term as county attorney of Thayer County. He is a member of the Nebraska State Bar Association, the Red Cross, the

Nebraskana Society, and for many years has been affiliated with the First Presbyterian Church of Hebron. His hobby is reading. (Deceased 1932). (Photograph on Page 469).

George Leonard Gordon

George Leonard Gordon, merchant, was born at Nashua, New Hampshire, December 6, 1878, son of Arthur C. and Susan C. (Kimball) Gordon. His ancestry is Scotch English on both sides, his family having come to America between 1760 and 1770.

Mr. Gordon attended the public and high schools at Nashua, and at the present time is the operator of the Gering Mercantile Company. He is a Republican, a Methodist and a Mason. His hobbies are golf, fishing and hunting.

On July 7, 1908, he was married to Florence V. Woolfenden at Gering. Mrs. Gordon was born at Racine, Wisconsin, July 3, 1886, and died at Omaha, October 13, 1928. Residence: Gering.

George Edwin Gorton

George Edwin Gorton, pharmacist, has lived in Dawes County, Nebraska, since 1889. He was born at Ypsilanti, Michigan, March 3, 1864, the son of Edwin Delos and Janes Elizabeth (Kriseley) Gorton. His father, a harness maker and a non-commissioned officer in the Civil War, was born at Ypsilanti, November 3, 1833, and died at Crawford, Nebraska, October 8, 1891; he served as postmaster under President Cleveland's administration. His mother, who devoted time and energy to all community affairs, was born at Seneca Falls, New York, March 21, 1838, and died at Crawford, October 6, 1925.

Mr. Gorton received most of his education in study at home and studied pharmacy at the University of Illinois where he received the Ph. G. degree. He has engaged in business at Crawford for the past 40 years and has been one of the builders of his state and community. Mr. Gorton holds membership in the Red Cross and the Nebraskana Society. During the World War he served as chairman of the Four Minute Men and was active in loan drives. He was one of the organizers of the Sons of Veterans at Crawford. He is a member of the Lincoln Farm Association, and is president of the City Taxpayers League. He is past secretary of the Crawford Chamber of Commerce, past chairman of the Republican county committee and past delegate to the Republican state convention.

His marriage to Ora Pearle Cowlick occurred at Cheyenne, Wyoming, July 15, 1899. Mrs. Gorton, who was a teacher before her marriage, was born at Bryan, Ohio, July 16, 1874. They have four children, Alice, born November 8, 1902, who married Carl W. Peters; Edwin, born May 10, 1911; Frances Jane, born July 17, 1915; and Mildred Louise, born November 24, 1918. Alice graduated from the Crawford High School and attended the University at Lincoln two years and graduated from the Emerson College of Oratory at Boston, Massachusetts. Prior to her marriage she was engaged in dramatic work. Edwin is a student at the University of Nebraska. Residence: Crawford. (Photograph on Page 471).

Charles Albert Goss

Chief Justice Charles A. Goss, of the Supreme Court of the State of Nebraska, has made his residence in Omaha since April 14, 1886. He was born in Edinburg, Portage County, Ohio, December 10, 1863. His father, Alfred Ruggles Goss was born in Fall River, Massachussets, August 30, 1834, and died at Omaha, July 25, 1898. He was a country merchant whose father was born in Massachusetts, while his mother came to this country from Scotland in early girlhood.

Lumiere—Crawford

GEORGE EDWIN GORTON

CHARLES ALBERT GOSS

Lumiere—Crawford

GEORGE EDWIN GORTON

CHARLES ALBERT GOSS

The mother of Judge Goss was Martha Carr, who was born in Edinburg, Ohio, November 26, 1837. She died at Cleveland, Ohio, in January, 1919. Her father was a Methodist minister and her mother a cousin of William H. Seward.

On October 4, 1890, Charles A. Goss was united in marriage to Carrie Shimp of Alliance, Ohio. They have one daughter, Catherine Goss Pollock. In 1885 Mr. Goss was awarded an A. B. degree by Mount Union College; in 1888 he received his A. M. He was admitted to the Nebraska bar at Omaha, December 10, 1887.

Soon after beginning the practice of law he interested himself in politics and became a member of the Nebraska house of representatives in 1893. From 1906-10 he served as United States Attorney for the district of Nebraska. He was judge of the fourth Nebraska district in 1920 and held this office until 1927, when he was elevated to the position of chief justice of the Nebraska Supreme Court.

He is a member of the American Bar Association, Douglas County Bar Association and Nebraska State Bar Association. In 1908 he was president of the Douglas County Bar Association. Judge Goss is a member of the American Law Institute, and Society of Colonial Wars. He is a 32nd degree Mason. Among the social clubs in Which he belongs are the University Club of Lincoln, the Elks Club and the Lincoln Country Club. Chief Justice Goss maintains a residence in Lincoln, altho his legal place of residence is at Omaha. Residence: Lincoln. (Photograph on Page 472).

Victor Raymond Gould

Victor Raymond Gould, the subject of this sketch, is the son of a pioneer contractor and builder in Omaha. His father, Franklin Pierce Gould, was born at Belfast, New York, in 1853, and came to Nebraska as a young man. He established a general contracting business, which he operated until his death at Omaha, on January 24, 1916. He was married to Ella Atkins, who was born at Bradford, Pennsylvania, February 14, 1857. She is of English ancestry, and a member of the Daughters of the American Revolution.

Victor Raymond Gould was born on July 12, 1882, and has made his home in Nebraska practically all of his life. Graduated from Lake School at Omaha, he attended Omaha High School, Culver Military Academy, and the University of Nebraska, where he majored in civil engineering. He was made a member of the Vikings in 1902, and was president of Sigma Chi from 1904-05.

From 1916 to 1927 he was secretary-treasurer and general manager of F. P. Gould and Son, the company established by his father. In 1927 he organized the V. Ray Gould Company, of which he is the owner. Among the various outstanding buildings which he has erected are the Burlington Station at Omaha, and Omaha Technical High School.

On October 3, 1906, Mr. Gould was married to Elizabeth Thorne Heacock at Falls City. Mrs. Gould was born at Falls City, July 2, 1882, and is of English and Canadian ancestry. They have three children: Marjorie, born November 25, 1909; Virginia, born June 23, 1916; and Janice, born October 22, 1917.

During the World War Mr. Gould was captain of a Home Guard Company. He is a Mason and member of the Shrine, and was potentate of Tangier Temple in 1930. A member of the Omaha Builders Exchange, the Nebraska Builders Association and the Chamber of Commerce, from 1913-28 he was a member of the Rotary Club. He is a Presbyterian and a member of the Nebraskana Society. His clubs are the Omaha Field Club and the Omaha Athletic Club, and his favorite sports are golf, hunting and fishing. Residence: Omaha.

Blaine Chester Grabill

Blaine Chester Grabill, county treasurer of Cheyenne County, was born at Hudson, South Dakota, February 20, 1896, son of Issac Elmer and Amanda (Frisbie) Grabill.

The father, who was a merchant, farmer and grain buyer, was born at Brownston, Pennsylvania, in May, 1866. His wife, Amanda, was born at Lime Springs, Iowa, in 1871.

Mr. Grabill was graduated from Sidney High School, and received the Bachelor of Science degree from the University of Nebraska. While there he was a member of the university band, president, vice-president and house manager of Delta Upsilon. He was a member of the high school basketball team four years at Sidney.

Mr. Grabill has served as western manager for the Trans-Mississippi Grain Company of Omaha, and the Butler-Welsh Grain Company, and later for the Updike Grain Corporation.

On September 2, 1922, he was married to Margaret Beth Lanham at Sidney. They have one daughter, Kathryn Louise, born January 21, 1931. Mrs. Grabill was born at Stromsburg, Nebraska, October 3, 1901, a direct descendent of Governor Treat of the New England Colony.

During the late war, Mr. Grabill held the rank of second lieutenant in the air corps. He is a charter member of Sidney Post No. 17 of the American Legion, and has served as first and second vice-commander for several years. He is a member of the Presbyterian Church, the Lions Club, the Masons, and the Sidney Country Club. His favorite sport is golf, while his hobby is music. Residence: Sidney.

Charles Graff

Charles Graff, farmer, legislator, banker and leader in economic thought, has been prominent in the state for more than forty years. He came to Bancroft in Cuming County forty-seven years ago and took up a homestead. He has developed his original holdings into three splendid farms.

Mr. Graff was born at Mackinaw, Tazewell County, Illinois, February 16, 1863, the son of Valentin and Elisabeth (Wullenwaber) Graff. His father, a farmer, was born in Germany, in 1832, and died at Minier, January 28, 1903. Elisabeth (Wullenwaber) Graff was born in November, 1841, and died in September, 1922, at Minier. Her ancestry was German and she was the mother of thirteen children.

Valentin Graff served in the German army. He was progressive in thought, a leader of the people of his community. In his pioneer days, he preached on occasion and was an earnest worker for social and economic progress. From his father, Charles Graff inherited his interest in public affairs and his independence of thought and action.

Charles Graff attended the rural schools of Illinois He homesteaded near Bancroft, broke the prairie soil baching in his shack. On February 12, 1885, Mr. Graff was united in marriage with Mary Elisabeth Waldemeyer at Manito, Mason County, Illinois. Mrs. Graff was born at Manito, July 24, 1864. She is of German descent. Five children were born. Robert V., born 1885, who married Margaret Burke. He attended the University of Nebraska Agricultural College, farmed for a time and is now engaged in the oil business in Bancroft.

Arthur N., born 1887, enlisted in the World War from Minnesota, and died in the service, a victim of the flu epidemic in 1918. Charles Floyd was born in 1889, and died in 1899; R. Chester was born in 1891, attended the State University Agricultural College and is now a farmer and pure bred stock breeder. He married Ida Hansen. Leona was born in 1893. She married Floyd L. Cary and resides on a farm near Bancroft.

In his financial success Mr. Graff attributes much

Jacobs—Oakland

CHARLES GRAFF

credit to the resourcefulness, energy and spirit of his wife. She encouraged him in his political and economic independence of thought, directed the education of the children, met the adversities of pioneer conditions and has been an earnest worker in the religious and social advancement of her community.

In the development of Agriculture, Mr. Graff has been prominently identified. He has been connected with all the co-operative movements, for many years was president of the Farmers' Grain Company, and has been a worker with all the telephone and marketing organizations.

For 21 years he has been president of the Red Polled Cattle Club of America. For many years he was president of the Nebraska Improved Live Stock Breeders Association. In these two organizations his work has aroused national interest. For five years he was president of the county fair organization.

On April 14, 1924, Mr. Graff's services to agriculture were recognized by the University of Nebraska, the Board of Regents and the Chancellor of the University signing a testimonial substantially as follows: "In recognition of his eminent services in the development of agriculture and in appreciation of his labors as a Breeder of Pure Bred Live Stock and a promoter of Farmers' Organizations, The Board of Regents of the University of Nebraska, on recommendation of the College of Agriculture has voted this testimonial to Charles Graff."

DeWitt C. Wing says of him:

"Mr. Graff was recently honored by the University of Nebraska in recognition of his long and distinguished service in behalf of Nebraska agriculture. His personality, as well as his work as a farmer and Red Polled cattle breeder, is a perennial inspiration to those who know him. To sit on a porch step or a bale of hay and talk with this big, good-natured, successful stockman and fine citizen is a privilege and a pleasure. He is unique in the manner in which he saunters along, fills his pipe and meets his friends. He is of the kindly, self-reliant earth-man type of commanding individuality, trained by first hand contacts with living things and hard facts outdoors in all weathers."

His work on the State Board of Agriculture has also brought him into national prominence. For twenty years he has been on the board and held various superintendencies, has been a member of the board of managers and was president for two years. As a member of the board, he laid the foundations for making the state fair a clean cut educational institution with its amusements on a high plane. He ousted gambling and fought cheap concessions. In his annual report, after discussing these changes, he declared:

"Once again I wish to call your attention to the past evil, not because I have fears of your not being able to handle it, but just to jog your memory and call your attention to the fact that it remains a big problem unsolved." Other objectional features in state and county fair were eliminated during his administration.

Beginning with his vote for James G. Blaine, in 1884, Mr. Graff has been a political free thinker while nominally a Democrat. He was a member of the legislature in 1907-9, and was twice defeated for state senator. He was chairman of the banking committee in 1909, and a member of the joint banking committee created by the joint committee. He had much to do with outlining the bank guarantee act. In 1926, he was drafted as a Democratic candidate for governor and was defeated for the nomination in the primary.

In 1918, he moved to Bancroft, leaving three modern equipped farms in charge of his children. He has served as mayor of Bancroft during the major period of his residence in the town. For a number of years he has been president of the Citizens Bank. For this responsibility his study of banking problems has peculiarly fitted him.

Mr. Graff is a life member of the Red Cross and holds membership in the State Historical Society and the Nebraskana Society. He is a Mason, and a member of the Order of the Eastern Star. He is affiliated with the Presbyterian Church. He is an excellent speaker with a tendency to entertain his audience with adroit humor. Aroused on some political or economic theme he deals sledge hammer blows at his antagonists but emerges from the combat without any personal feeling against his opponents. Residence: Bancroft. (Photograph on Page 474).

Alice Winnifred Graham

Alice Winnifred Graham, physician and surgeon, was born at Schuyler, Nebraska, May 23, 1875, daughter of Charles M. Mapes was born October 12, 1830, in Cayuga October 12, 1830, who came to Nebraska with his family, where he engaged in farming and stockraising. His wife, Hannah, was born at Newville, Indiana, July 17, 1845. She was a teacher prior to her marriage, and was a direct descendent of Ethan Allen. She died at Schuyler on November 2, 1894, her husband surviving her until February 2, 1906.

Dr. Graham attended rural schools, Fremont Normal, and Creighton University. On May 5, 1905 she was graduated from Barnes Medical College with an M. D. She is a member of Chapter K of the P. E. O. Sisterhood. From 1902 until her marriage in 1908 she was the owner of the Mapes Drug Company at Craig, Nebraska. She married Francis Andrew Graham, a physician and surgeon of Lincoln, at Schuyler. Dr. Francis Graham was born at North Bend, Nebraska, March 24, 1862.

Since her admission to practice of medicine she has been actively engaged, and is now a member of the staff of St. Elizabeth's Hospital at Lincoln. She is licensed to practice in Missouri, Colorado, and Nebraska. Dr. Graham is a member of the Daughters of the American Revolution National No. 178256, and of the Eastern Star and Rebekahs. Her medical associations include the American Medical Association, the Nebraska State Medical Association and the Lancaster County Medical Association. She is a fellow in physio-therapy as well. Her church is the Plymouth Congregational. Residence: Lincoln. (Photograph in Album.)

Francis Andrew Graham

For over forty-two years Francis A. Graham has been a physician at Lincoln, Lancaster County, Nebraska. He was born in Dodge County, Nebraska, March 24, 1862, the son of Delilah Retan (Stewart) Graham and James H. Graham. His father, who was a farmer, was born in Columbiana County, Ohio, August 15, 1834, and died in Dodge County, July 10, 1890; his Irish ancestors came to this country about 1831. His mother was born of Scotch ancestry, in Indiana, March 30, 1831, and died at Lincoln, at the age of 90 years, 2 months and 3 days.

Dr. Graham attended rural school, was a student at Monmouth College, 1881-3, and later was a student at Omaha Medical College. He received post graduate instruction at New York Polyclinic, 1891-92, and was admitted to the practice of medicine at Lincoln, September 10, 1891. He has been engaged in practice there since April 3, 1889. He served as county coroner of Lancaster County for eight years, and since 1916 he has been a member of the Insanity Board. He has been a Nebraska resident all his life.

He was married to Alice Winnifred Mapes-Goldsbury in Colfax County, Nebraska, October 13, 1908. Mrs. Graham, who is a physician, was born in Colfax County, May 23, 1875. Her father was a farmer; one of her brothers is a lawyer.

Dr. Graham is a member of the County Medical Association and the American Medical Association. He is a member of the Lincoln Kiwanis Club, the Masons, Elks, and the Knights of Pythias. His hobbies are hunting and fishing. Residence: Lincoln. (Photograph in Album).

James Robert Graham

James R. Graham, physician and surgeon, was born at Irving, Iowa, October 8, 1878, and has been a resident of Nebraska 27 years. His parents, James Harlow and Ida (Breckenridge) Graham, were residents of Iowa for many years. His father, a native of New York, was born June 29, 1859, of Scotch-Irish ancestry. He was a physician and surgeon, who died at Manilla, Iowa, February 19, 1927. His mother, Ida Breckenridge, was born in Ohio, and died at Manilla.

Dr. Graham attended the public and high schools of Manilla, and attended the Keokuk Medical College two years. In 1903, he received his M. D. from the University of Nebraska. After graduation he practiced one year with his father at Manilla, and since that time has been in practice in Allen. A Republican, he served as county coroner several years. He is a member of the Nebraska State and Tri-County Medical Associations, and of the Board of Education, and is affiliated with the English Lutheran Church.

On April 2, 1905, he was united in marriage to Beryl E. Hathaway, at Manning, Iowa. Mrs. Graham, who was born at Bennington, Kansas, April 4, 1884, is of English descent, and active in church and community affairs. They have two children, Harlow, born April 5, 1906, who married Gladys Carlson; and Wendell, born October 13, 1913. Residence: Allen. (Photograph in Album).

Robert Arnold Graham

Robert Arnold Graham was born at Crete, Nebraska, December 4, 1886, the son of Calhoun and Emma (Deems) Graham. His father was born in Ireland, June 21, 1859, and died at Crete, in 1923. His mother was born in Pennsylvania, October 20, 1862.

Mr. Graham was graduated from the Crete High School, was a student at Doane College at Crete, for two years, and was graduated from the University of Nebraska where he was a member of Sigma Tau, engineering fraternity. He was awarded letters in track at both Doane College and the University of Nebraska.

He was resident engineer for the Nebraska Portland Cement Company at Superior, Nebraska, one year, 1914, was sales manager of the American Electric Company at St. Joseph, Missouri, 1915-1922, was sales manager of the Tungsten Spark Plug Company at St. Joseph, one year, was manager of the Graham Electric Company, 1924-25, and since 1925 has been district manager of the Iowa Nebraska Light & Power Company at York.

Mr. Graham is a member of the York County Commercial Club, the York Rotary Club, Parent Teachers Association, and the Young Men's Christian Association. His sports include hunting, fishing, and football, and his hobbies are geology and paleontology.

Of his marriage to Ethel Ann Shippen four children were born: Robert A., Jr., June 1, 1912, is taking his second year in the York College; John B., October 16, 1913, is taking his first year in the York College; Glenn E., May 31, 1917; and William E., September 17, 1920 Residence: York. (Photograph in Album).

Robert Hamel Graham

A resident of Nebraska for 57 years, Robert Hamel Graham was for many years one of the leading educators and school executives of the state. He was born at Irving, Illinois, June 13, 1870, the son of Perry F. and Mariah Emily (Marks) Graham. His father, who was born at Deer Creek, Ohio, April 2, 1839, and died at Hastings, Nebraska, October 2, 1921 was a farmer; some of his Scotch English ancestors came to America before the Revolution and later members of the family came to this country as English fugitive sailors during the War of 1812.

His mother was born in Mifflin County, Pennsylvania,

June 20, 1846, and died at Clay Center, Nebraska, November 14, 1893. She was of Scotch, Irish, and German descent.

Mr. Graham attended the rural schools of Clay County; was a student at Fairfield College for a time; and in 1898 was graduated from the University of Nebraska with the A. B. degree. He held membership as a charter member in Alpha Tau Omega at the University of Nebraska. In 1921 he took a post graduate course at Columbia University.

He was actively interested in the educational life of Nebraska for over 30 years and held the position of superintendent of city schools at the following places: Arapahoe, Nebraska, four years; West Point, Nebraska, four years; Wymore, Nebraska, seven years; Sutton, Nebraska five years; Auburn, Nebraska, three years; and Canton, South Dakota, two years. In January, 1927, he was made deputy state superintendent of schools in Nebraska and held this position until his death in 1929. Mr. Graham was a contributor to various educational periodicals for several years.

In 1904-05-06 he was secretary of the Nebraska State Teachers' Association; was secretary of the school board at Auburn, 1925-27; and held membership in the Auburn Kiwanis Club. He was a member of the Country Club at Auburn, 1924-27; was affiliated with the Tabernacle Christian Church; and was a member of the Sons of Veterans. He was a Mason.

His marriage to Bernice Rice Gore was solemnized at Lincoln in January, 1918. She died at Denver, Colorado, August, 1921. One child was born to this marriage: Roberta, born April 11, 1919. On August 14, 1923, he was united in marriage with Doretta Brehm at Council Bluffs, Iowa. Mrs. Graham, who was a teacher before her marriage, is the daughter of Mr. and Mrs. Henry Brehm of Sutton, Nebraska. They have one son, Robert Lee, born August 16, 1929.

Mr. Graham came to Nebraska in April, 1872, and was prominent in civic and educational affairs, until his death at Lincoln, Lancaster County, Nebraska, June 10, 1929. His favorite recreation was reading. His out of door sport was golf. Residence: Lincoln.

Robert O. Graham

For the past 20 years Robert O. Graham, motor securities executive, has lived in Nebraska. He was born at Hannibal, Missouri, August 31, 1888, the son of Robert H. and Harriett L. (Robison) Graham. His father, who was an engineer, was born at Greensburg, Pennsylvania, 1848, and died at Hannibal, January, 1915; his ancestry was Scotch. His mother, who is of English descent, was born at LaHarpe, Illinois, 1859.

Mr. Graham attended the public schools of Hannibal. He is now president of the Motor Securities Company at Hastings, is a member of the Chamber of Commerce and the Young Men's Christian Association, and holds membership in the Nebraskana Society. His fraternal and social organization includes the Hastings Country Club and the Elks. He is a Republican.

On June 24, 1911, Mr. Graham was united in marriage with Margaret L. Guffey at Des Moines, Iowa. Mrs. Graham, whose ancestors were English, was born at Unionville, Missouri, November 3, 1888. They have one son, Robert, born April 21, 1912. Residence: Hastings.

Wilson Thompson Graham

Wilson T. Graham was born at Morning Sun, Louisa County, Iowa, October 15, 1863, the son of James Harvey and Mary Jane (Brown) Graham. His father, who was a physician and surgeon, was born in Todd County, Kentucky, and died at Morning Sun. His mother was born at Morning Sun, Ohio, and died in Morning Sun, Iowa.

Mr. Graham was graduated from high school in 1882,

and in 1885 was graduated from Monmouth College where he ranked high in scholastic awards. He has been a successful business man in Omaha where he has engaged in real estate and loans for the past 43 years. He was a charter member of the University of Omaha, and is now a regent of the Municipal University of Omaha.

On November 23, 1887, he was united in marriage with Elizabeth Ann Cunningham. Mrs. Graham, who was born at Morning Sun, Iowa, June 21, 1862, died at Omaha, February 22, 1931. Four children were born to them: George, born June 30, 1889, who died August 25, 1913; Harold, born August 5, 1892; Victor, born July 14, 1896; and Mary born October 6, 1900 All of them are graduates of the Omaha High School and the Nebraska State University.

During the World War Mr. Graham was active in Liberty loan drives. He is an ardent prohibitionist. A former director of the Omaha Young Men's Christian Association; for 20 years he has been secretary of the board of trustees of the University of Omaha; and was formerly president of the Omaha Real Estate Board. He is a member of the Central United Presbyterian Church of Omaha, and a Republican. Residence: Omaha.

Harry Kelsall Grainger

Harry Kelsall Grainger, president of Grainger Brothers Company, was born at Lincoln, October 7, 1893. He is the son of Harry Bates and Emma A. (Norbury) Grainger. Harry Bates Grainger was born at Manchester, Lancashire, England, August 19, 1859, the son of a draper, Joseph Grainger. In 1881, he came to America where he founded and built up the firms of Grainger Brothers Company and J. Grainger and Company, with offices at Lincoln, Fairbury, Holdrege and McCook. He died at Lincoln on September 27, 1927. Emma N. Norbury was born at Lombard, Illinois, August 27, 1862. She is of English and French Huguenot descent.

Upon the completion of his elementary education in Everett School, Harry K. Grainger attended Shattuck School at Faribault, Minnesota, graduating in 1912. He attended the University of Nebraska for two years and received his A. B. from Amherst College in 1917. At Nebraska, he was made a member of Sigma Chi.

On December 3, 1919, he was united in marriage to Louise Hite at Fairmont, West Virginia. Mrs. Grainger, who was born at Kingmont, West Virginia, September 1, 1901, is a direct descendant of Colonel John Hite of the Revolutionary War. There is one son, Rolfe Hite, born March 16, 1926.

In August, 1919, Mr. Grainger entered the employ of Grainger Brothers Company in Lincoln, and on January 14, 1927, was made president. He is vice-president also of J. Grainger Company of Holdrege. He is a member of the First Presbyterian Church of Lincoln, a Mason, Elk and Kiwanian.

In the World War he was connected with the Air Service from May 1, 1917, to July 29, 1919. From August 15, 1917, to July 10, 1919, he served overseas and took part in the Battle of Chateau-Thierry, the Aisne Offensive, St. Mihiel and Meuse-Argonne engagements with the 1st U. S. Aero Squadron and 9th Aero Squadron. He also served with the 142 French Escadrille. At the present time he holds the rank of captain in the United States Reserves, and is a member of the American Legion.

His sport is golf, and his hobby is horses. His social clubs are the University Club, the Lincoln Country Club and the Amherst Club of New York. Residence: Lincoln.

Adam H. Gramlich

Adam H. Gramlich, pioneer Nebraskan, has lived at Papillion Nebraska, for the past 58 years. He was born at Papillion, February 25, 1873, the son of Alois and Matilda (Watkins) Gramlich. His father, who was born at Hessen, Dam Stadt, Germany, August 28, 1829, and died at Papillion, September 10, 1910, was a farmer who

came to America in 1846. His mother was born at Oakford, Illinois, and died February 2, 1882. Her ancestry was Scotch.

Mr. Gramlich was a student in the Western Normal College of Shenandoah, Iowa, and later was a student at Fremont Normal School. He also was a student at the Western Normal College at Lincoln, 1892-93. He has been a farmer in Sarpy County all his adult years. From 1919, to 1923, he served as county commissioner of Sarpy County. He is a Democrat.

His marriage to Matilda Margaret Lutz, was solemnized at Papillion, December 20, 1899. Mrs. Gramlich, who is of German descent, was born in LaSalle County, Illinois, January 13, 1877. Their children are: Blanche, born June 11, 1902, who married Robert B. Campbell, and is a graduate of the University of Nebraska; Hazel, born May 18, 1913, who is a graduate of Papillion High School, and is attending Wesleyan University at Lincoln, Nebraska.

Mr. Gramlich is a Mason, and a Modern Woodmen of America, and a member of the Parent-Teachers' Association at Papillion. Residence: Papillion.

Amos Kirby Gramlich

Amos Gramlich was born at Springfield, Nebraska, June 7, 1902, the son of George Kirby and Eva Christina (Lutz) Gramlich. His father, who was born at Papillion, Nebraska, July 27, 1869, is the son of a German immigrant to this country in 1848, and an English and Irish mother who was born at Illinois. He was one of the first ten master farmers selected in Nebraska. His wife was born in Ottowa, Illinois, May, 1870, and died at Papillion, Nebraska, December 10, 1925.

Mr. Gramlich received his diploma at the Nebraska School of Agriculture in 1926; receiving his B. C. degree from College of Agriculture, University of Nebraska. He was a member of the University of Nebraska stock judging teams, 1925-26, and was editor of the *Cornhusker Countryman*. He was also president of Alpha Gamma Rho in 1926.

On January 21, 1928, he was married to Helen Elizabeth Voorhees, at Lincoln, Nebraska. Mrs. Gramlich was born at Lincoln, May 16, 1905. They have one son George Richard, born December 27, 1930.

He has lived in Nebraska all his life, and is now part owner and manager of Keto's Corner Farm near Fort Crook, Nebraska. Mr. Gramlich is a second lieutenant in the Infantry Reserves. He is a Mason, and a member of Anderson Grove Presbyterian Church. His hobby is flying, and he owns and operates his own plane. Residence: Papillion.

Howard John Gramlich

Howard J. Gramlich, noted educator of the University of Nebraska, has lived in Nebraska all his lfie, and has been interested in the various civic and educational organizations of his community for several years. He was born at South Omaha, Nebraska, January 26, 1889, the son of John W. and Joanna M. Gramlich. His father was born at Papillion, Sarpy County, Nebraska, and died at South Omaha, February 12, 1893; he was a farmer and commission merchant. Alois Gramlich, father of John W. Gramlich, was born in Germany, in 1825, and settled in Sarpy County, Nebraska, in 1855. He was one of the three first settlers there, the oldest child of S. W. Gramlich and was the first white child born in that country. His wife was born at Petersburg, Illinois, November 25, 1855. She is still living.

Professor Gramlich attended rural schools for a time and worked on his uncle's farm. He was graduated from the South Omaha High School in 1905, and in 1911, was graduated from the University of Nebraska where he held membership in Gamma Sigma Delta, Alpha Zeta, and the Acacia. He is now chairman of the department of animal husbandry at the University of Nebraska and is the author of various livestock articles and bulletins on educational subjects.

He was united in marriage at Bancroft, Cuming County, Nebraska, January 16, 1915, to Mabel Daniels. Mrs. Gramlich was born at Bancroft, Nebraska, February 6, 1888; she was a home economics instructor before her marriage. Two children were born to them: Herbert Howard, born January 15, 1923, who died January 24, 1923; and Lois Alice, born November 13, 1924.

Professor Gramlich was Nebraska representative of the War Industries Board during the World War. He holds membership in the American Society of Animal Production, of which he was president in 1929, Lincoln Chamber of Commerce, the Nebraska Academy of Science, the Kiwanis Club, the Young Men's Christian Association, and the Nebraskana Society. He is a Mason, Scottish Rite and Shrine, and Modern Woodman of America.

He is a member of the Nebraska State Historical Society and the Nebraskana Society, and his social club is the Shrine Country Club of Lincoln. His favorite recreation is golfing. Residence: Lincoln.

Samuel Watkins Gramlich

Known throughout his entire community as a farmer and Shorthorn breeder, Samuel W. Gramlich has now retired after an interesting and eventful life. His father, Alois Gramlich, was born in Hessen, Germany, August 28, 1829. After attending school there for about 8 years he sailed for America on the *Cathrina Jackson*, a sail ship, in 1846, the voyage taking three months. He settled in Illinois, where he met and married Matilda Watkins. Samuel was born at Bellevue, Nebraska Territory, January 18, 1856. Matilda Gramlich had in all eleven children, eight of whom are now living. While her schooling was somewhat meager, her chief endeavor was to see that her children were properly educated. Her ancestry is traced to the Watkins family, noted in early American history, on the paternal side, and to General Greene of the Revolution on the matrenal side.

The education of Samuel Gramlich was begun in a school held in the granary of a neighbor on June, 1862. The teacher in charge of the school was Frances Whittington. On September 14, 1880, his marriage to Edith Almira Trumble was solemnized at Bellevue. Mrs. Gramlich was born there, on September 8, 1861, before the state was admitted to the Union. There are nine of the fourteen children of their marriage still living. The children are: Matilda, born July 16, 1881; Abner W., born June 11, 1883, died July 16, 1894; Ruth, born February 23, 1885, died March 16, 1885; Alice Maud, born May 30, 1886, who married Philip A. Frazeur on November 7, 1906; Alois Trumble, born March 19, 1888; Cordelia, born March 16, 1891, who married Herman Borman on January 15, 1919; Frederick, born September 21, 1893, who married Alice Grell on March 27, 1917; Barbara E., born March 13, 1896, who married Norman Bryan Calaway on August 11, 1925; Edith, born July 13, 1898; Mary, born November 14, 1900; Mattie C., born January 13, 1904; Samuel Kirby, born May 15, 1906, died November 26, 1906; baby, born July 28, 1908, died August 7, 1908; and Edna E., born December 29, 1910, died January 13, 1911. The girls of the family have all been teachers, one son is a college graduate and one an electrical engineer with the General Electric Company.

For many years Mr. Gramlich has been associated with the Fairview Methodist Episcopal Church. During the war he contributed to Red Cross and other organizations. Always interested in agricultural life, he believes that success and happiness come only by hard work. He was a member of two pioneer secret societies in Nebraska, the Sons of Temperance and the Farmers Grange, organized in 1873 and 74. He is also affiliated with Lodge No. 473 of the Nebraska Territorial Pioneers. Residence: Fort Crook.

John Gran

John Gran, who was born in Hof Parish near Vadstena, Sweden, February 13, 1844, has been a resident of Nebraska since 1868, and has always lived on Nebraska farms. At the age of twelve years he began to earn his own living, attending school only a part of each year and working on various farms a part of every day. He was employed by the Northwestern Railway Company for a time in 1869 upon his arrival in America, and the same year moved to Nebraska where he finally homesteaded in Saunders County.

He has known all the privations and difficulties of pioneer days in the middlewest and through the years has acquired 540 acres of land with a home which he built largely himself. Mr. Gran is vitally interested and enthusiastic about farm work and as a successful farmer has taken an active interest in the education of his children and the improvement of his community.

His father, Anders Gran, who was born in 1816 and died in 1904, was a carpenter in Sweden. His mother, Johanna Hermanson, was born in 1815, and died in 1879. Mr. Gran served on the school board at Mead for eight years, was a trustee in the Swedish Evangelical Lutheran Church for nine years, and served as deacon for 36 years. He holds membership in the Nebraskana Society.

His marriage to Emma Christina Gren was solemnized in Saunders County, August 2, 1871. Mrs. Gran, who was born in Stra Parish, near Vadstena, Sweden, March 18, 1843, and died at Omaha, Douglas County, Nebraska, September 3, 1903, was descended from soldiers who fought under Gustavious Adolphus in the Thirty Year War. Six children were born to this marriage, three of whom are living: William, who married Georgia Maude Mason; Ida, who died in infancy; John Edwin, who died at the age of fifteen; Selma, who was graduated from the State University in 1901; Ellen Amanda, who attended the University in 1906 and 1907; Oscar Fred, who died at the age of eight; William, who graduated from the University in the class of 1897, is a civil engineer at Lincoln, and was formerly an instructor at the University of Nebraska for two years; he has two children.

Mr. Gran's hobby is trees; he has planted thousands of them on his farm, and has often transplanted them from other land to his own. He is especially fond of reading. Residence: Mead. (Photograph in Album).

Richard W. Grant

On January 5, 1862, at New Berlin, Illinois, Richard Withgot Grant was born, son of John Nelson and Emma (Batty) Grant. His father was born in Kentucky, and followed the occupation of contractor. The ancestors of John Nelson Grant held title to the land on which the town of Lexington, Kentucky, is located; such title remains in the Grant family name. John Nelson Grant died at Beatrice, Nebraska, on August 24, 1894. His wife was born in Manchester, England, and died in Seattle, Washington.

Richard W. Grant received his education in rural and town schools and the University of Illinois. On August 30, 1887, he married Ida May Schell at Beatrice. She was born in Peoria, Illinois; was talented as an artist and reared a family of seven. The children are: Emalyn, born July 15, 1888, who is the wife of Robert E. Kyle; Olive, born July 2, 1890, now Mrs. Henry M. Randall; Esther, born January 29, 1892, now the wife of Ralph O. Sheldon; Richard Schell, born October 18, 1894, and married to Norma West; Rachel, born October 5, 1896, who is the wife of Harvey T. Smith; Joseph N., born October 13, 1898, who married Olga McGirr, and John H., born April 13, 1910.

Mr. Grant has been an architect since 1886, and during his general practice of the profession, has done much work for the various state institutions. He is a member of the Christian Church in Beatrice, belongs to the Republican party, and has lived in the state for sixty-two years.

Richard W. Grant was the first member of the Park Commission at Beatrice, where he landscaped all the city parks. He belongs to the Blue lodge of the Ancient Free and Accepted Masons, is a Royal Highlander, Modern Woodman of America and belongs to the Young Men's Christian Association. He is an extensive reader and a successful floral culturist. Residence: Beatrice.

Charles Luther Graves

Charles L. Graves, lawyer and judge, was born near Glenwood, Mills County, Iowa, November 23, 1861, the son of William Wilber and Mahala Pearl (Graves) Graves. His father, who was born at Knoxville, Tennessee, July 19, 1818, and died at Rock Bluffs, Cass County, Nebraska, April 6, 1895, was a brick maker and mason. He is descended from an old southern family prominent in Tennessee since Boston Graves, grandfather of William Graves, served in the Revolution.

His mother, who was born at Knoxville, September 24, 1820, and died at Peru, Nebraska, August 27, 1919, was the daughter of Henry Graves, a doctor and minister in Tennessee.

Judge Graves attended the district schools where he was a pupil of the late Judge B. S. Ramsey. He received his legal education in the law office of Beeson & Sullivan, at Plattsmouth, Nebraska, and in 1886 was admitted to the bar, beginning the practice of law at Union, Nebraska, where he made his home until three years ago when he moved to Plattsmouth. From 1889 to 1925, he was secretary and promoter of the Old Settlers' Association, at Union; was editor of the *Ledger* at the same time, during which he practiced law continuously. A Republican, Judge Graves has served as police judge at Plattsmouth for the past three years, and is justice of the peace there at this time.

He was united in marriage with Alice Jane Graves, at Plattsmouth, December 18, 1887. Mrs. Graves was born in Carroll County, Missouri, March 18, 1866, and died at Union, January 9, 1912. Her parents were Tennesseans. There are three children: Harry E., born February 19, 1889, whose wife is deceased; Verna L., born December 18, 1890, who married Harry D. Royal, and Leola A., born June 15, 1893, who married Michael A. Derieg. All reside in Lincoln.

Judge Graves was chairman of the four minute men, Liberty precinct, Cass County, during the World War. He is a member of the Cass County Bar Association, the Plattsmouth Chamber of Commerce, and the Nebraskana Society. His sport is baseball, and he is interested in band music, having played in bands for many years. Residence: Plattsmouth.

George Washington Graves

George W. Graves, retired farmer of Gage County, Nebraska, has lived in this state for the past 38 years. He was born in Jo Daviess County, Illinois, December 6, 1860, the son of Homer and Amyra (McComber) Graves. His father, who was a carpenter and farmer, was born in Ohio, March 31, 1811, and died in Jo Daviess County, August 5, 1898; his ancestry was English. His mother, of Scotch descent, was born in New York, February 23, 1822, and died in Illinois, July 23, 1865.

Mr. Graves is a member of the Nebraskana Society, is affiliated with the Methodist Church, and holds membership in the Republican party.

He was married to Flora Matilda Waldo, December 3, 1891. Mrs. Graves was born in Jo Daviess County, March 13, 1865, and is of French descent. Their two children are: Blanche, born March 12, 1893, who married Chase Burrows; and Clara, born August 1, 1894. Residence: Adams.

Guy T. Graves

The honorable Guy T. Graves, judge of the eighth judicial district of Nebraska for a quarter of a century, the first county attorney of Thurston County, and an eminent civic organizer and public leader, was born on a farm in Butler County, Iowa, in 1862. At the age of five he was taken by his parents to another farm near Dunlop, Iowa, where he grew up, attending the country schools and later graduating from the Western Iowa Normal College. He began teaching school, and as a member of that profession went with his parents in 1884 to Dakota County, Nebraska, which then included the present county of Thurston. Acquiring a farm in the Omaha Indian reservation when that land was thrown open for settlement by the government, Mr. Graves alternately farmed and taught school, reading law during intervals in Dakota City.

Admitted to the bar in 1887, he located in Pender, and two years later was elected county attorney for the newly formed county of Thurston. In 1891, he married Gertrude Lockhart of Red Oak, Iowa, and to their marriage was born a son, Guy T. Graves, Jr., now a lawyer in Los Angeles. Their only other child died in infancy.

Elected to the district court in 1899, Judge Graves served in this capacity continuously until his death in October, 1924. He was an ardent Democrat, but was elected on a fusion ticket his first term, his successive elections to this office never being opposed by either party because of the confidence and respect which his character as a jurist commanded. During the World War he was chairman of the council of defense in his district.

Although not identified with any church or religious creed, Judge Graves was tolerant of them all, and without discrimination, was a quiet giver to charity. He was a member of no lodges and his only recreation outside of court was reading. Residence: Pender.

Carl R. Gray

Carl R. Gray, president of the Union Pacific System, was born at Princeton, Arkansas, September 28, 1867, son of Oliver Crosby and Virginia LaFayette (Davis) Gray.

He received his secondary education in the preparatory department of the University of Arkansas, and the degree of Doctor of Laws from Maryland State College of Agriculture. On December 6, 1886, he was married to Harriette Flora. She was born at Liberty, Kansas, September 17, 1869. Their children are Carl Raymond, Jr., Russell Davis, and Howard Kramer.

Mr. Gray began his career with the St. Louis-San Francisco Railroad in 1883, and has been promoted through various positions until he is at the present time president of the Union Pacific System. He is a director of the First National Bank of Chicago, a member of the First Baptist Church, and a member of the Metropolitan Club (New York), the Chicago Club (Chicago), the University, Omaha, Athletic and Country Clubs of Omaha. (*See Who's Who in America; Who's Who in Omaha.*) Residence: Omaha.

Emmet Gray

Born at Macon, Nebraska, January 22, 1880, Emmet Gray is the son of Walter and Mary (Hubbard) Gray. His father, who was a farmer, was born at Southoe, England, November 28, 1850, came to America in 1870, and died at Hastings, Nebraska, April 20, 1928. His mother was born at Southoe, July 3, 1847, and died at Upland, Nebraska, October 3, 1925.

Mr. Gray has been a farmer in Franklin County, Nebraska, for many years, and is active in civic affairs at Upland. He holds membership in the Modern Woodmen of America, the Independent Order of Odd Fellows, and the United Brethren Church of which he is a trustee and member. From 1919 to 1929 he served as a member of the local school board, acting as president of that organization for two years and secretary for two years. His chief recreations are reading and baseball.

On March 2, 1910, he married Ida Martha Steinke at Upland. Mrs. Gray, whose ancestry is German, was born at Upland, September 1, 1889. She is a member of the Rebekahs, and is active in the affairs of her church the United Bretheren. Their two children are: Richard Walter, born May 5, 1911; and Doris Augusta, born October 12, 1912. Both are students of the Hastings College, Richard being a member of the senior class. Residence: Upland.

George Adams Gray

George Adams Gray, prominent banker at Coleridge, Nebraska, was born at Ardee, Ireland, December 9, 1868, the son of James and Marion (Adams) Gray. He attended school in Ireland and came to this country in 1889. Since 1902 he has been president of the Coleridge National Bank which was organized that year.

He is a member of the American Association for the Advancement of Science, the Congregational Church of Coleridge, and the Nebraskana Society. He is a Mason. Mr. Gray has lived in Nebraska for the past 42 years and has always been interested in the advancement of his community and state. He is a Republican.

On July 10, 1912, he was married to Wilhelmina Eliza Wells at Catleblayney, Monaghan County, Ireland. Mrs. Gray, who was born in County Monaghan, is the daughter of Captain John Wells, of the 81st Regiment of the Royal County Down.

They have four children: Emily M., born April 2, 1913; James L., born June 30, 1914; George A., born January 25, 1916; and Amy F., born August 15, 1918. Emily was graduated from St. Mary's Hall, Faribault, Minnesota, while George and James are students at Shattuck Military School at Faribault. Residence: Coleridge.

George Herbert Gray

George H. Gray, banker, was born at Rome City, Indiana, February 27, 1868. Of pioneer parentage, he has been a resident of Nebraska 58 years. His father, George Henry Gray, was born at Bridgeport, Connecticut, February 27, 1838. He was a successful merchant and a soldier in the Civil War. He died at Central City, on February 12, 1875. He married Louisa W. Caswell, born at Vergennes, Vermont, June 5, 1839, who came to Nebraska with him. She was active in the church and for twenty-two years was superintendent of the primary department of Central City public schools.

Mr. Gray graduated from Central City High School, and attended Nebraska Central College. He was president of its literary club several terms.

He was married to Hettie Rogers Tindall on June 1, 1892. She was born at Lafayette, Indiana, March 1, 1872. She is the daughter of Reverend D. K. and Hannah M. Tindall. Naomi, their only child, was born March 13, 1893. She is married to Dr. Otis Martin, of Omaha.

In 1887 Mr. Gray entered the grocery and queensware business at Central City, continuing until 1902, when he became cashier of the Central City National Bank. He was made president of that organization, and in 1919 was made president of the Duncan (Nebraska) State Bank and the Bank of Tarnov, Nebraska. He is now president also of the First Investment and Securities Company of Columbus.

Always active in civic and educational affairs, he is a member of the board of trustees of the Nebraska Methodist Hospital at Omaha, of Nebraska Wesleyan University, and of the Nebraska Conference of the Methodist Episcopal Church (president).

During the war he was organizer and chairman of Liberty Loan and Red Cross drives in Merrick County. He is a life member of the Red Cross and of the Welfare Board. National councilor of the United States Chamber of Commerce, he was for sixteen years president of the Central City organization.

He is affiliated with the First Methodist Church of Central City. He is a thirty-second degree Mason and member of the Shrine; Modern Woodmen and Macabees. He is a member of the state committee of the Y. M. C. A. He is a member of the Nebraskana Society and of the Nebraska State Historical Society. His favorite sport is baseball and his hobbies are reading and boys' activites. His home is 2909 15th St., Columbus. (Photograph on Page 481).

Charles E. Green

For many years a leading banker in Thayer County, Charles E. Green was born at Hebron, December 19, 1877. His parents, William and Mary Green, were natives of Lincoln, England, who came to America in 1859. William Green who was retired at the time of his death on December 19, 1913, was a prominent figure in the early life of the county. His wife, who was born May 6, 1836, at Lincoln, England, died at Hebron, May 18, 1926. She was the daughter of a squire.

Charles E. Green attended public and high school, and almost immediately entered into the banking business. For the past twenty-nine years he has been associated with the Thayer County Bank, of which he has been president for some time.

He was united in marriage to Adella Switzer, at Kearney, Nebraska, in October, 1913. Mrs. Green, who was born at Steinauer, Nebraska, December 26, 1888, is of the Switzer family. Mr. and Mrs. Green are members of the Christian Church.

Mr. Green was chairman of Liberty loan drives and active in all civilian projects in the World War. He is a member of the Nebraska State Historical Society, the Nebraskana Society, the Ancient Free and Accepted Masons and the Elks. Residence: Hebron.

Walter Scott Green

A successful merchant at Burwell, Nebraska, Walter Scott Green was born at Rushford, Minnesota, March 22, 1870, the son of John and Mary Green. John Green, a contractor and stone mason, was born at Ogdensburg, New York, December 14, 1835, and died at Rushford, in December, 1903, his ancestry was English. Mary Green, his mother, was born at Buffalo, New York, September 13, 1845.

Mr. Green served for 17 years with the Burlington Railway Company, and is now engaged in the merchandise business at Burwell. He is a member of the Elks, the Modern Woodmen of America, and the Nebraskana Society. His favorite sport is golfing.

He was united in marriage with Mary Ella Beers at Crete, Nebraska. Mrs. Green, whose parents came from Massachusetts, was born at Crete and died at Burwell, December 27, 1911. To this marriage were born: Lulu, June 6, 1892; Mabel, June 4, 1894; Clarence, January 31, 1896; and Charles, January 11, 1903. Of his marriage to Alma Florence Davis, which occurred at St. Joseph, Missouri, in 1915, one daughter was born: Ellen, December 27, 1918. Residence: Burwell.

Abraham Greenberg

Abraham Greenberg was born in New York City, June 16, 1892, the son of Harry Greenberg, who came to America from Russia in 1886, and who is a merchant and active in Republican politics. Harry Greenberg married Jennie Slobodinsky, who was born in Kief, Russia, in 1870, and who came to America in 1889.

After being graduated from Omaha High School in

GEORGE HERBERT GRAY

1909, Abraham Greenberg entered the University of Nebraska, from which he was awarded his B. Sc. in 1913, and his M. D. in 1915. During 1918 he attended the Neurological Institute at New York City. He is a member of Phi Delta Epsilon. He was married to Blooma Kogan at Minneapolis, on June 14, 1922. Mrs. Greenberg, who was born at Minneapolis, on December 14, 1901, is of Russian Jewish descent. They have three children, Beverly Ramona, born April 6, 1923; Renee Joyce, born December 8, 1924, and Phylliss Doretto, born October 21, 1928.

Upon his admission to practice in 1915, Dr. Greenberg took up the active practice of medicine. From 1919-25 he was a member of the surgical staff at the University of Nebraska, and has been a member of the staff of Wise Memorial Hospital since 1917. He is now associate member of the staff of Clarkson Memorial Hospital. From 1917-19 he was first lieutenant in the Medical Corps, attached to American Red Cross Medical Hospital No. 5, Base Hospital No. 49, and commanding officer Ambulance Company No. 157. He is a member of the American Legion and the Forty and Eight.

Dr. Greenberg is a member of the Conservative Jewish Synagogue of Omaha, and is extremely active in Jewish welfare and social work. He is a member of the executive committee of the Jewish Welfare Federation and in 1929 was first vice president of the Jewish Philanthropies. A director of the Jewish Community Center, serving from 1925-30, he is a member of the Hebrew Club and B'nai Brith.

His professional organizations include the Douglas County Medical Society, the Elkhorn Valley Medical Society, the Association of Military Surgeons and the American Medical Association of which he is a fellow. He is a member of the Red Cross, the Dundee Parent-Teachers' Association, the Modern Woodmen of America, and the Odd Fellows. His clubs include the Omaha Athletic Club, and the Highland Country Club. His sport is golf and his favorite recreation is bridge. Residence: Omaha.

Robert James Greene

Robert James Greene, lawyer, was born at Delphi, Indiana, October 22, 1862, son of James Wilson and Catherine Elizabeth (Organ) Greene. He has the degrees of A. B., LL. B., and A. M., and has been in active practice in Lincoln for many years.

On December 9, 1887, he was married to Maude Miller at Lafayette, Indiana. She was born there on December 7, 1861. Mr. Greene is a Republican. He is a member of the American, Nebraska State and Lancaster County Bar Association, and of the Chamber of Commerce, the University Club, the Red Deer Club and the Lincoln Country Club. Residence: Lincoln.

R. R. Greenland

As a pioneer rancher and farmer of Nebraska, R. R. Greenland came to Nebraska nearly 60 years ago, enduring all the privations and hardships of the early days in the middlewest and taking an active part in the building of the state. He was born at Colfax, Pennsylvania, August 22, 1853, the son of Ezra and Elizabeth (Madden) Greenland. His father, who was a farmer and laborer, was born at Carlisle, Pennsylvania, in October, 1819, and died at Colfax, in December, 1891. His mother was born at Orlisonia, Pennsylvania, in 1823, and died at Colfax, August 1, 1870; her ancestry was Irish.

Mr. Greenland worked in the mines of Pennsylvania during his boyhood, and for eight years was a cowhand in Nebraska; since then he has been engaged in ranching in Blaine County, Nebraska. He is president of the Purdum State Bank, at Purdum, Nebraska, is a member of the Nebraska State Historical Society, and holds membership in the Nebraskana Society.

He was married at Ord, Nebraska, in January, 1883.

Mrs. Greenland was born in Webster County, Iowa, June 14, 1865. The following children were borne to them: Richard J., born November 8, 1883; George W., born August 12, 1885, who died October 8, 1885; Albert E., born September 12, 1886, who married Henrietta Marsburg; Robert N., born September 12, 1889, who died September 16, 1891; Ruth H., born December 3, 1891, who died in June, 1904; Ruby E., born December 2, 1896, who died in June 1904; and Harold W., borne March 5, 1900, who died in August, 1902. Residence: Purdum.

David Westbrook Greenleaf

A banker for more than thirty years, David Westbook Greenleaf was born at Wolowich, Maine, November 4, 1870, son of Silas Holt and Arabella Augusta (Farnham) Greenleaf. Silas, who was born at Westport, Maine, April 5, 1832, was a sea captain twenty-five years, and in later life came to Nebraska where he engaged in farming. He died at Tekamah in 1902. Of English descent, his ancestors came to America in 1632, settling at Newburyport, Massachusetts, and were active in the early life of New England.

Arabella Farnham Greenleaf was born at Woolwich, Maine, November 13, 1843, and died at Los Angeles, May 1, 1920. As a young woman she taught in the public schools of Bath, Maine. She was also descended from early English settlers in New England.

David Westbrook Greenleaf was graduated from Tekamah High School in 1888 and from Western Normal Business College at Shenandoah, Iowa, in 1890. He has been a banker practically all the time since leaving school, and was first associated with the First National Bank of Tekamah. Later he served with the Chelsea, Michigan, Savings Bank four years, and for the past twenty-five years has been connected with the Farmers State Bank of Tekamah, of which he is now president.

On June 12 1901, he was united in marriage to Ida Dorothea Schumacher at Chelsea, Michigan. Mrs. Greenleaf, who was born at Chelsea, February 1, 1875, was a saleswoman and manager of the silk department of a department store before her marriage. Her father was born in Germany and her mother in Ann Arbor, Michigan. There are three children of this marriage, Mariane Enid, born February 2, 1904, who is a teacher; Ruth Schleicher, born May 13, 1905, who is a stenographer and bookkeeper and Dorothy Augusta, born January 30, 1907, who is a teacher.

Mr. Greenleaf is a Republican, and active in party politics. He was local chairman for enlistment in the Citizen's Military Training Camps for a number of years, and local treasurer of the Red Cross and chairman for all bond issues and savings stamps drives in Tekamah during the late war.

For ten years he was a member of the school board, and he is at the present time a member of the First Presbyterian Church, the Chamber of Commerce, the State Young Men's Christian Association, the Odd Fellows, Odd Fellows Encampment and the Rebekahs. During his early life Mr. Greenleaf taught in the country schools in the winter and farmed in the summer. He is fond of reading. Residence: Tekamah.

Walter Lee Greenslit

Born at Surprise, Butler County, Nebraska, March 5, 1885, Walter Lee Greenslit is the son of Walter Henry and Catherine Cecelia (Ammerman) Greenslit. His father was born at Scotland, Connecticut, September 30, 1855, and has been engaged in the lumber business at Surprise for nearly half a century. One of the oldest lumbermen in the state in point of service, he is also engaged in the banking business. The family came from England between 1620 and 1666, one line on the *Mayflower*, settling at Plymouth, Barnstable, Andover and

Lynn, Massachusetts. Walter Henry Greenslit's wife, Catherine, was born at Asbury, Pennsylvania, January 13, 1852, and died at Surprise, December 9, 1928. A teacher for ten years prior to her marriage, she was one of the founders and an active worker in the Methodist Church and a charter member of the Womans Christian Temperance Union. Her ancestors came from Holland and England and were early settlers in New York City, New Jersey and Pennsylvania.

Walter Lee Greenslit attended the public and high schools of Surprise, and was graduated from Nebraska Wesleyan Academy in 1904. In 1908 he received a B. A. degree each from the University of Nebraska and Nebraska Wesleyan University. At Nebraska Wesleyan he was editor in chief of the *Coyote*, treasurer of the Athletic Association, member of the Y. M. C. A. Cabinet, and Everett Fraternity, and was a member of the committee that established the first fraternity house in Nebraska Wesleyan. At the University of Nebraska he was a member of Sigma Alpha Epsilon and a member of the editorial staff of the *Daily Nebraskan*. Active in athletics, he was a member of the baseball team 1906, 1907, and the basketball team, 1907, at Nebraska Wesleyan.

On December 30, 1908, he was married to Mollie Hannah Stewart at Surprise. Mrs. Greenslit was born at Warren, Minnesota, January 27, 1886. She is a former teacher and a great granddaughter of Joseph Stewart who in 1815 was commended by the 14th Congress for distinguished service in the War of 1812. They have one son, Frank Stewart, born September 26, 1912, a freshman at the University of Nebraska, and member of Sigma Alpha Epsilon.

Mr. Greenslit's career began in 1908 when he served as high school principal at Gothenburg, Nebraska. From 1909-13 he was principal and later superintendent of schools at Scottsbluff. In 1913-14 he was an instructor in the Lincoln High School, leaving to become credit man for the University Publishing Company of which he became secretary-treasurer in 1916. He still holds that office in addition to the following: secretary-treasurer Superior School Supply Company, Kansas City, Missouri; secretary Greenslit Lumber Company of Ravenna, Nebraska, Stapleton, Stanton and Ashland; president of the Everett Building Society and treasurer of the Business Education Bureau. He is a former editor of the *Nebraska Teacher*.

On October 14, 1903, he enlisted in the second regiment band of the National Guard and was discharged on October 13, 1906. During the World War he assisted in Loan drives, Red Cross and other activities. He is a member of the California Society of Coloniel Wars; the Lincoln City Mission (board of directors); the Chamber of Commerce of which he has served on various committees; the Nebraska Society of Mayflower Descendants, etc.

A Kiwanian since the organization of the club, he has served on many of its committees, and he is a charter member of the Lincoln Hiram Club and past president of Hiram International. Since 1920 he has been a trustee of Nebraska Wesleyan University, and is a member of the executive committee. A member of the Nebraska State Teachers Association, of which he was district president, the Alumni Association of the University of Nebraska, he is also a member and past president of the Alumni Association of Nebraska Wesleyan. He is a Republican.

His professional memberships include the Lincoln branch of the National Credit Men's Association, of which he is ex-president; the National School Supply Association, etc. He is an honorary member of the Lincoln Musicians Union, and a member of the Young Men's Christian Association. A member of St. Paul's Methodist Episcopal Church, he is also a member of its official board.

Mr. Greenslit enjoys baseball, basketball, football and hiking. His hobby is genealogy. Residence: Lincoln.

Edwin Stanton Gregg

Edwin S. Gregg was born of a pioneer Nebraska family, at Nebraska City, October 25, 1861. James Harrington Gregg, his father, who was born at Wheeling, Ohio County, Virginia, April 20, 1820, and died near Nebraska City, October, 1888, was one of Nebraska City's leading citizens for many years. In 1854 he established the Platt Valley Nursery, and later platted and owned the Greggsport Addition to the city. He served as mayor of Nebraska City in 1858. His ancestry was Scotch.

Elizabeth Jane (Bloss) Gregg, his wife, who was born in Treble County, Ohio, November 18, 1830, and died at San Jose, California, July, 1914, was descended from early Pennsylvania Dutch ancestors.

Mr. Gregg has lived in Nebraska City all his life, and is an electrician there at the present time. His marriage to Jesse Tait was solemnized at Council Bluffs, Iowa, November 29, 1913. Mrs. Gregg was born near Nebraska City, October 21, 1886. Her grandfather, James Nelson Tait, was a member of the firm Ashton & Tait, merchants whose brick store building was south of the new Waugonsie Mridge at Nebraska City. He was wharfmaster and had charge of all boats that landed there. Mr. and Mrs. Gregg have three children: Dorothy, born February 21, 1915; Elizabeth, born October 18, 1916; and Paul Stanton, born January 25, 1919.

He is a member of the Fourteenth Street School Parent-Teachers' Association. His family is affiliated with St. Mary's Episcopal Church. Residence: Nebraska City.

Fred Marion Gregg

Fred Marion Gregg, head of the department of psychology of Nebraska Wesleyan University was born at Nevada, Ohio, March 7, 1867, son of William Smith and Louisa Jane (Welty) Gregg.

He received his A. B. degree from Ohio Northern University in 1894, and his A. M. from the University of Chicago in 1915. He attended the University of Nebraska, 1929-31.

On June 30, 1898, he was married to Carrie Pettis Cockerill at Washington Court House, Ohio. She was born at Lincoln, Missouri, December 18, 1868. Their children are: Genevieve, born August 21, 1899, who married Frank W. Hubbard; Otis, born March 15, 1904; and Helen, born April 19, 1905, who married Arthur Von Thaden.

Professor Gregg is the author of *Manual of Parliamentary Law* (1910); *Hygiene as Nature Study* (1917); *Hygiene by Experiment* (1923); *Courses of Study in Character and Health Education in Nebraska* (1927), revised (1929), etc. He was president of the Nebraska State Teachers Association 1917-19, chairman of child hygiene station, Parent Teachers Association of Nebraska 1930, and is a member of the American Association for the Advancement of Science, the American Psychological Association, the First Methodist Episcopal Church, etc. Residence: Lincoln.

George Albert Gregory

George A. Gregory was born at Hillsdale, Michigan, November 19, 1851, the son of George and Jane (Bross) Gregory. His father, who was a farmer, was born in Jackson County, New York, 1826, and died at Council Bluffs, Iowa, in 1912; his Scotch ancestors were members of the Alpine Clan. His mother was born in Cattaraugus County, New York, and died at Crete, Saline County, Nebraska, October, 1881; her Dutch ancestors, who settled in Pennsylvania in the early history of the country, served in the Revolution.

Mr. Gregory, who is a horticulturist at Crete, was

graduated from the Crete High School in 1878. He was awarded his A. B. degree at Doane College in 1882. He helped to organize Gates College at Neligh, Nebraska, and for a time was at the head of the institution; he was botany instructor in addition to his executive duties. In 1894 he moved to Oregon where he was superintendent of schools for three years at Medford, and was county superintendent for two years.

Returning to Crete, in 1900, he was superintendent of public schools and during the summer months was a student at Amherst University, Chicago University, and Yale, where he specialized in mathematics, botany, and German. He was active in debating during his college days, and was a member of the Hesperian Society. In 1909 he was appointed normal training inspector for Nebraska normal schools and traveled throughout the state visiting all the accredited schools. In 1916 he was recalled to Crete to serve as superintendent of schools; he remained in this capacity until 1919 when he retired to the Bonivu Gardens to engage in growing flowers, plants, shrubbery, and trees.

He was united in marriage with Mary Mattrassa Foss at Crete, December 16, 1884. Mrs. Gregory, who was born at Grafton, New Hampshire, November 22, 1858, was graduated from Doane College in 1881, and taught school before her marriage. She is of Scotch and English descent. They have two children: Annadora, born April 15, 1893, who will receive her Ph. D. degree at the University of Nebraska this year; and Mary Alberta, born March 26, 1898, who married E. J. Stowell of Ann Arbor, Michigan.

Mr. Gregory is a member of the Knights of Pythias, the Knights and Ladies of Security. He is a trustee of Doane College and is a member of the committee for developing the grounds and buildings of the campus. He is a member of the Nebraskana Society. He is affiliated with the First Congregational Church of Crete. His hobby is horticulture. He is a Republican. Mr. Gregory has lived in Nebraska for 58 years, and has made many projects for the development of education.

In 1904 the Crete Plan in Domestic Science was developed by him and was successfully used in many states, was recognized by leading educators and was discussed in articles in newspapers and educational magazines all over the United States. He introduced basketball in the Crete schools in 1901; Omaha and Lincoln schools were the only other schools in Nebraska where the game was played at that time. Mr. Gregory has developed a method of addition which is used successfully in many schools. Residence: Crete.

Emmett H. Gribble

A banker and farmer for many years, Emmett H. Gribble was born in Decatur County, Iowa, May 1, 1865. His parents, both of whom are deceased were Barnabas and Ellen (Walden) Gribble. Barnabas Gribble, who was a farmer of English descent, died at Dakota City, Nebraska, May 28, 1916. His wife, a native of Ohio, died in Dakota City, March 26, 1889. She was of German and Irish extraction.

Emmett H. Gribble was educated in rural schools. Now retired he was a successful farmer for many years, and later engaged in banking. At the present time he is president of the Nebraska State Bank at South Sioux City. He was married to Ida M. Savidge at South Sioux City on May 31, 1893, and to them two children were born, Harold, born May 29, 1894, who married Gertrude Hubbell; and Emmett, born April 2, 1896, who died July 2, 1896. Harold is a graduate of the University of Nebraska.

Mr. Gribble is a Democrat and active in local politics. A resident of the state 65 years, he has taken much interest in its development. Among other things he has served as a member of the Board of Education, is a member of the board of elders of the First Presbyterian Church, and is a member of the Commercial Club. His

fraternal affiliations include the Modern Woodmen of America, the Woodmen of the World and the Modern Brotherhood of America. His hobby is mechanics. Residence: South Sioux City. (Photograph in Album).

David Gurney Griffiths

For the past fourteen years superintendent of the Lincoln State Hospital, David Gurney Griffiths is an outstanding member of the medical profession. He was born at Verdon, Nebraska, November 27, 1875, son of David and Mary Ellen (Young) Griffiths. His father who was born at Sugar Creek, Pennsylvania, October 27, 1845, was a farmer, who came to Nebraska just after the Civil War. His parents came to America from Wales about a year prior to his birth. His wife, Mary Ellen, was born in Ridgeway, Wisconsin, August 20, 1851. The father died at Verdon on November 6, 1918, and the mother on October 19, 1925.

Dr. Griffiths attended the Verdon High School and thereafter the Peru State Normal School for two years. He was graduated from the medical department of the University of Nebraska with an M. D. in 1902. On June 25 of the same year he was married to Nora May Moore at Wymore, Nebraska. She was born at Blue Rapids, Kansas, May 18, 1877, and was a teacher of Dutch, Irish and Scotch descent. They have one son, Heath, born September 20, 1903. He is married to Blanche Martz. He and his wife are both graduates of the University, she having also been graduated from the conservatory. Heath is a member of Delta Tau Delta, and at present is an undertaker in Lincoln. His wife is a member of Alpha Phi sorority. They have one child, Joyce M., born December 6, 1929.

From 1913 to 1916 Dr. Griffiths was a member of the staff of Lincoln State Hospital; and from February 1, 1916, to November 1, 1919, was superintendent of the Institution for the Feebleminded at Beatrice. Returning to Lincoln in 1919 he was made superintendent of Lincoln State Hospital, which position he still holds. He is active in the Red Cross and state and county welfare work, and is a member of the American Medical Association, the Lancaster County Medical Association, the District Psychiatric Association, and in 1917 was president of the Gage County Medical Society.

Since 1917, he has been a member of the Rotary Club. A Blue Lodge, Scottish Rite Mason and member of the Shrine, he is also a member of the Nebraska Art Association, the Lincoln Chamber of Commerce, the Nebraskana Society and the Young Men's Christian Association. His hobby is reading and his club is the Shrine Country. Residence: Lincoln.

Kirk Griggs

Kirk Griggs was born at Beatrice, Gage County, Nebraska, January 8, 1878, the son of Lewis Theodore Griggs and Carrie Edith (Gale) Griggs. His father was a lawyer and rancher in Wyoming, and served as county attorney of Weston County, Wyoming for several years. He was a soldier in the 11th Indiana Cavalry in the Civil War. He was descended from *Mayflower* pilgrims; one of his ancestors was a soldier in the Revolution. He was born at Jefferson City, Indiana, April 17, 1841, and died at Newcastle, Weston County, Wyoming, November 9, 1907.

His mother was born in Pennsylvania, and at an early age was left an orphan. She was the first school teacher in Gage County, Nebraska. She died at Atchison, Kansas, June 11, 1885.

Mr. Griggs attended the public schools of Beatrice and Lincoln, Nebraska, and was later graduated from the high school at Newcastle. Since a university course was not available he finished his higher education through private instruction and correspondence courses.

He entered the business world as auditor for the Kilpatrick Brothers Company at Beatrice. He was cashier of the First National Bank at Hastings; was secretary of

KIRK GRIGGS

Skoglund—Omaha

the department of Trade and Commerce at Lincoln; and is now president of the Occidental Building and Loan Association of Omaha. From 1914 to 1918 he was engaged in farming and stock raising. He is a director of the Omaha and Council Bluffs Street Railway Company. He is the author of various addresses and essays published in Nebraska papers and periodicals.

His marriage to Mabel Clare Pyrtle was solemnized at Kansas City, Missouri, June 12, 1901. Mrs. Griggs, who was born at Riverton, Iowa, December 3, 1878, was a teacher in the public schools at Beatrice before her marriage. They have five children: Theodore K., born August 18, 1902; Roger M., born August 2, 1903; Gale E., born November 6, 1904; Jessie M., born April 17, 1906; and Mary V., born August 8, 1919. Theodore is married to Lois Elma Hankins. Roger married Alice Bradford Waters. Gale is a graduate of Annapolis with the rank of lieutenant; he has seen service abroad, both in European and Asiatic waters.

Mr. Griggs was active during the World War on loan drive committees. He is a member of the Red Cross, the Community Chest, and the Omaha Chamber of Commerce. He is chairman of the Bureau of Publicity of the latter organization; is a member of the Rotary Club; and is now president of the Native Sons and Daughters of Nebraska. He is a Mason, and holds membership in the Young Men's Christian Association and the Nebraskana Society. He is a member of the Omaha Field Club. He is a Republican. His religious affiliation is with the First Christian Church of Omaha. His sport is golf. His hobby is the impounding and use of waste waters in Nebraska for irrigation purposes. Residence: Omaha. (Photograph on Page 485).

James Franklin Grim

James Franklin Grim, a retired farmer at Cozad, Nebraska, was born in Washington County, Pennsylvania, February 20, 1857, the son of Alfred and Elizabeth (Ferrel) Grim. His father, who was born in Greene County, Pennsylvania, March 7, 1821, and died at Creston, Iowa, January 5, 1894, was a teacher and farmer who received his education at Washington & Jefferson College in Pennsylvania; his ancestry was German through the paternal line and Scotch on the maternal side of the family. His mother, of English and German descent, was born in Washington County, October 30, 1829, and died at Lenox, Iowa, May 15, 1916.

Mr. Grim attended college for two years at Eureka, Illinois, and since then has been a progressive and energetic farmer near Cozad. He is affiliated with the Christian Church and holds membership in The Nebraskana Society.

He was united in marriage with Mary Malinda Pickerill at Eureka. Mrs. Grim was born at Cazenovia, Illinois, December 1, 1860. They have two children: Carl, born December 13, 1889, who married Edith Shull, is living in Lexington, and is county clerk of Dawson County; and Zella, born August 8, 1894, who married Arthur Munson, and resides at Cozad. Mr. Grim is a member of the Republican party. Residence: Cozad.

James Jay Grimm

Engaged in the practice of law at Wilber since 1901, James Jay Grimm has been a resident of Nebraska since birth. He was born at Pleasant Hill, in Saline County, June 10, 1878, son of Joseph H. and Esther E. (Hess) Grimm. Joseph H. Grimm, who was also a lawyer died at Wilber, Nebraska, January 15, 1911. His wife, Esther, died at Denver, June 17, 1907.

Upon his graduation from Wilber high school, Mr. Grimm entered the university in the fall of that year, and received his LL. B. in 1901. He has since been engaged in practice and has been a member of the law firm of J. H. Grimm and Son, and Grimm and Grimm. He

served as county judge of Saline County from January 1912 to January 1925. He is a Republican. His military service was with the Nebraska National Guard, of which he was a member from 1897 to 1907. He held the rank of major of infantry until he resigned his commission. During the World War he was chairman of the board for the preparation of questionnaires, a four minute speaker, etc. He is a member of the Nebraska State Bar Association and The Nebraskana Society.

Mr. Grimm was married to Alma J. George at Atlantic, Iowa, February 28, 1918. Mrs. Grimm was born at Annawan, Illinois, May 31, 1892. They have three children, Jeanne Mabelle, born December 25, 1918; Betty June, born July 18, 1920, and Marvin J., born October 10, 1925. Residence: Wilber.

Dwight Palmer Griswold

Dwight Palmer Griswold, editor of the *Gordon Journal*, was born in Harrison, Nebraska, November 27, 1893, son of Dwight Hubbard and Clarissa (Palmer) Griswold.

The father was born in Blakesburg, Iowa, November 18, 1860, and was a pioneer in western Nebraska. At the time of his death at Cheyenne, Wyoming, December 7, 1928, he was president of the First National Bank of Gordon. His wife, Clarissa, was born in Wisconsin, January 17, 1862.

Mr. Griswold attended the Gordon High School two years and the Kearney Military Academy two years, graduating in 1910. In 1914 he received the Bachelor of Arts degree from the University of Nebraska. Prior thereto he was a student at Nebraska Wesleyan University for two years. He was a member of the college debating team at Nebraska Wesleyan, and active in football and baseball through his whole school career. His fraternity is Alpha Tau Omega.

A Republican, Mr. Griswold served as a member of the Nebraska house of representatives in 1921; member of the Nebraska state senate, 1925, 1927, and 1929; and is Republican nominee for governor, 1932. He is editor of the Gordon Journal, and is director of the First National Bank of Gordon.

On September 25, 1919, he was married to Erma Elliott at Yorkville, Illinois. Mrs. Griswold was born at Yorkville, April 2, 1893. They have two children, Dorothy Helen, born August 21, 1922; and Dwight Elliott, born March 20, 1926.

During the late war Mr. Griswold served from July 1917, until December, 1918, holding the rank of captain in the field artillery at the time of his discharge. From June, 1916, until January, 1917, he was sergeant in the fourth Nebraska Infantry on the Mexican border. He is a member of the American Legion (state commander in 1930), the First Presbyterian Church at Gordon, the Nebraska Press Association (president in 1931). He is a Mason. Residence: Gordon.

Henry Grosenbach

Henry Grosenbach, retired farmer of Mascot, Nebraska, was born in Tazewell County, Illinois, July 8, 1851, and has been a resident of Nebraska for the past 45 years. His father, Jacob Grosenbach, also a farmer, was born in Germany, July 29, 1823, and died in Tazewell County, February 9, 1902. His mother, Elizabeth (Rorebach) Grosenbach was born in Germany and died in Tazewell County at the age of 73.

Mr. Grosenbach learned the carpenter trade when a young man, and for a number of years followed his trade. He has erected a number of homes in Mascot. He was the owner of a general store at Mascot for five years, and for the past 20 years has been a lumberman and farmer there. He retired from farming 25 years ago but still owns farm land in Harlan County. He was treasurer of the school board of district No. 34 for about 20 years, and holds membership in the Nebraskana Society. Politically, he is independent.

His marriage to Norah Ella Ficht was solemnized in Tazewell County, November 12, 1874. Mrs. Grosenbach, whose ancestry is German, was born in Tazewell County, December 20, 1853. Of the seven children born to their marriage, six are living, Henry J., who married Ella Poehlman, and who died November 12, 1922; Edward L., who married Eva Maude Meglemre; Lizzy M., who married Amel O. Bloom; Dan C., who married Elsa E. Keene; Katie A., who married Dan W. Troutman; John W., who married Jennie Engel; and Sam, who married Dora Sandage. Mr. and Mrs. Grosenbach, their six children and their families are all members of Mascot Evangelical Church. Residence: Mascot. (Photograph in Album).

Daniel John Gross

Daniel J. Gross was born at Avoca, Iowa, March 18, 1897. His father, George Charles Gross was born at Le Claire, Iowa, May 10, 1866, and was a farmer and stockman of French descent. He died at Walnut, Iowa, March 13, 1926. His wife, Ellen Rosalie (McCarthy) Gross, was born in Missouri, January 19, 1876. She is of Irish descent.

Upon his graduation from Walnut High School in 1913, Mr. Gross entered Creighton University, from which he received an LL. B. in 1916. During 1917 and 1918 he attended Georgetown University at Washington, D. C. He was active in debate and a member of Delta Theta Phi. At both universities he participated in football.

Since his admission to the bar at Omaha, in June, 1920, Mr. Gross has been actively engaged in practice. A Republican he was assistant county attorney of Douglas County 1922, 23, 24, 25, and tax attorney of the city of Omaha and of Douglas County 1926, 27, 28, and 29. Chief petty officer in the United States Navy during the World War, he is a lieutenant in the U. S. Army Reserve Corps, at the present time. He is a member of the Catholic Church of St. Margaret Mary, and grand knight of the Knights of Columbus, is affiliated with the Elks, the American Legion and the Chamber of Commerce, and is a member of the national, state and local bar associations. His club is the Lakewood Country. Residence: Omaha.

Emiel Edward Grosse

Emiel Edward Grosse, son of William and Wilhelmine (Lierman) Grosse, was born at Husterford, Wisconsin, December 16, 1875. His father was born near Berlin, Germany, March 27, 1823, and was a contractor and carpenter when he first came to the United States in 1852. From 1862-65 he served in the Union Army in the Civil War. His wife, who was born in Germany, July 6, 1838, died on the home farm in Cuming County, Nebraska, April 2, 1884.

Mr. Grosse attended public schools and German Lutheran Schools, and from 1883 to 1897 worked on the farm. In 1898 he started in the implement business as a salesman and bookkeeper for Fred Wiggers at Wisner, and on January 16, 1901, he purchased an implement business in Beemer. He disposed of this in 1911 and worked as a traveling salesman until 1916, when he again engaged in the business he now operates. He is also in the motion picture business.

A Republican, he was elected member of the village board in 1902, serving four years, and was re-elected in 1917. In 1924 he was elected Cuming County commissioner for four years, and was chairman of the board.

He was married to Nettie Lizzie Klosner at West Point, Nebraska, October 27, 1898. Mrs. Grosse was born at St. Louis, September 25, 1875. They have three children, Verna, born August 4, 1899 who was graduated

from high school and had a business course. She worked as a stenographer and bookkeeper two years, and was a milliner three years and is married to Walter Schweers. They have three children, Joelene, Kermit and Russell. Grace, born October 30, 1901, died May 11, 1903; Rosada, born December 23, 1905, was graduated from high school and has worked two years in the Beemer Telephone office and two years as clerk and bookkeeper. She is married to Budd Chilcott, a farmer and pure bred livestock breeder, near Wayne.

Mr. Grosse is a member of St. John's Evangelical Lutheran Church, the Red Cross, of which he is a committeeman, the Beemer Improvement Association and the Nebraskana Society. He served as an elder in the church four years. He is a member of the Beemer Community Club, and is a baseball fan. Residence: Beemer.

Ludwig Edmund Grosskopff

Ludwig E. Grosskopff, physician and surgeon, was born at Osnabrueck, Germany, January 19, 1896, the son of Clemens and Elisabeth (Commes) Grosskepff. His father, who is a prominent physician was born in Osnabrueck, July 30, 1860. His mother was born at Bonn, on the River Rhine, Germany.

Dr. Grosskopff attended Real gymnasium at Bromberg, Germany, was a student at Westphalian-Wilhelm University of Muenster, 1919-20, and studied at the University of Bonn, 1920-22, where he received his M. D. degree December 3, 1922. He was president of the Markominnia at Muenster, and was the winner of two rowing races.

He entered the World War as a private in the Field Artillery of the German Army, August 2, 1914, and was advanced to first lieutenant in January 1916. He is a member of the American Medical Association, the Red Cross, the Deshler Commercial Club, and the Nebraskana Society. Rowing, swimming and skating are his favorite sports, while reading and flowers are his hobbies.

His marriage to Johanna Maria Werner was solemnized at Omaha, Nebraska, April 22, 1926. Mrs. Grosskopff was born at Gelsenkirchen, Rhineland, Germany, March 13, 1899. Residence: Deshler.

Phillip Theodore Grove

Phillip Theodore Grove, clerk of the district court of Box Butte County, was born at Alliance, Nebraska, December 1, 1898, son of Arthur Henry and Matilda (Zobel) Grove. Their ancestors came from Germany.

In 1918 Mr. Grove was graduated from the Alliance Public Schools. From 1923 until 1925 was a student at the University of Nebraska College of Dentistry and was obliged to leave school on account of an injury to his hand.

On June 8, 1920, he was married to Beulah Rozella Reddish at Alliance. Mrs. Grove was born at Indianola, Iowa, May 4. 1897. Their three children are: Phyllis Mae, born September 5, 1924; Raymond Lloyd, born December 12, 1927; and Robert Arthur, born December 28, 1929. For some time after returning from the army Mr. Grove was engaged in farming and ranching. Since January 8, 1931, he has been clerk of the district court, elected on the Democratic ticket. He is a member of the American Legion, the Veterans of Foreign Wars, and saw foreign service in the United States Army from April 9, 1917, the date of his enlistment, until his discharge on June 25, 1919. His hobby is athletics. Residence: Alliance:

George Albert Grubb

George A. Grubb was born in Pawnee County, Nebraska, February 18, 1880, the son of William Henry and Mary Jane (Clark) Grubb. His father, who was born near Dayton, Ohio, February 11, 1856, is a retired farmer, whose ancestry is Pennsylvania Dutch and Swiss. His mother, was born in Indiana, June 30, 1854, and died at Lincoln, Lancaster County, Nebraska, February 28, 1928.

Dr. Grubb, who is dean of the college of dentistry at the University of Nebraska, attended the rural schools near DuBois, Nebraska, and was graduated from the Pawnee City High School in 1899. He was awarded his A. B. in 1923, and his D. D. S. in 1912, from the University of Nebraska where he is a member of Omicron Kappa Upsilon. He served as supreme president of Xi Psi Phi, dental fraternity, 1929-31.

During 1901 and 1902 he was a country school teacher in Pawnee County; taught in the grade school at Ashland, 1904-05; was ward principal in the Wahoo schools, 1905-08; was ward principal at Auburn, 1909; and from 1912-23 was engaged in the private practice of dentistry at Lincoln.

He was married to Amy Shively at Lincoln, January 7, 1913. Mrs. Grubb, who was a high school teacher, instructing in mathematics, English, and dramatics, was born in Indiana, October 25, 1879. She is of Pennsylvania Dutch descent.

During the World War Dr. Grubb served as a member of the physical appeal boards for Lancaster County; this board was composed of three physicians and one dentist. He is a member of the Cornhusker Study Club; Lincoln District Dental Club; Nebraska Dental Association; and the American Association of Dental Schools. He holds membership in the Lincoln Chamber of Commerce; the Kiwanis Club; and the Young Men's Christian Association.

He is a member of Lancaster Lodge Number 54 of the Masons, Lincoln University Club, Eastridge Country Club, the Lincoln Auto Club, and the Professional Men's Club. He is a member of the Methodist Episcopal Church of Lincoln, and is a Republican. Residence: Lincoln.

John August Grueber

Born at Schwarlingen, Hanover, Germany, January 25, 1874, John August Grueber is the son of Henry Christopher Wilhelm Grueber and Katherine Margarete (Boesch) Grueber. His father was born at Gilberdingen, Germany, May 10, 1829. A cabinet maker and later a farmer, he served in the German army in the war against Denmark and came to America in March, 1882, settling in Nemaha County, Nebraska, and later moving to Thayer County. He died at Byron, Thayer County, Nebraska, January 23, 1923. His wife, Katherine, was born at Helvesiek, Hanover, Germany, December 3, 1844, and died at Byron, December 26, 1917.

John Grueber attended school two years in Germany, rural school in this country, and at the Seminary in Dubuque, Iowa, he completed a two years preparatory course and a three years seminary course. On August 18, 1904, at Parkston, Hutchinson County, South Dakota, he was united in marriage to Emily Doering. Mrs. Grueber was born at Parkston, on January 15, 1882. Her father had been mayor of a village in Russia. They have three children: Augusta, born at Tripp, South Dakota, August 14, 1905; Frank J., born at Sioux City, Iowa, November 26, 1910, and Marcella, born August 14, 1922, at Deshler, Nebraska.

Mr. Grueber was admitted to the pastorate at Dubuque, Iowa, June 24, 1895, and since then he has been a pastor in Iowa, Illinois, South Dakota, and has lived in Nebraska twelve years. He was editor of the *Herington Lutheraner,* published at Herington, Kansas, 1906-10. At present he is pastor of the Zion Lutheran Church at Deshler, Nebraska, is a member of the American Lutheran Church, and holds membership in the Lutheran Brotherhood and the Lutheran Mutual Aid. He is also a member of the Nebraskana Society. Residence: Deshler.

Paul Henry Grumann

Paul Henry Grumann, educator, was born in Indianapolis, Indiana, October 4, 1872, son of Albert Urban and Augusta Wilhelmina (Storch) Grumann. He received his early education in the Indianapolis public and high schools, and received his Master of Arts degree from the University of Indiana in 1900.

On August 26, 1891, he was married to Katherine Frances Coleston at Indianapolis. Their children are: Herbert Richard; Norma (Mrs. William Rotton), and Katherine Anna.

He was instructor at Butler University 1891-92, teacher of manual training in the Indianapolis High School 1892-1900, and since 1900 has been a member of the faculty of the University of Nebraska, from 1912-1931 as director of the school of Fine Arts. He is now director, Society Liberal Arts, Joslyn Memorial, Omaha.

Professor Grumann is a member of the Modern Language Association, the Chamber of Commerce, the Omaha Club and Omaha Country Club. His religious affiliation is with the First Unitarian Church. Residence: Omaha.

Henry August Grummert

Henry August Grummert was born at Holtzhausen, Westphalien, Germany, August 1, 1876, the son of Earnest Henry and Marie Charlott (Wickermerir) Grummert. His father, who was a butcher, was born at Holtzhausen, August 14, 1831, came to America in 1881 and was a farmer near Jansen, Jefferson County, Nebraska. He died at Jansen, July 14, 1916. His mother was born at Holtzhausen, December 11, 1834, and died April 12, 1917, at Jansen.

Mr. Grummert has lived in Nebraska for fifty years, is affiliated with the Lutheran Friedensau Evangelical Church at Jansen, and is a member of the Nebraskana Society. He was married to Anna Margretha Pholmann at Beatrice, Gage County, Nebraska, August 29, 1901. Mrs. Grummert was born at Clatonia, Nebraska, December 12, 1880. Six children were born to this union: Dora, born July 12, 1902, who died December 3, 1918; Ernest, born August 7, 1904, who married Elizabeth T. Fleckel; Ella, born February 2, 1907, who married William Bocklemann; Meta, born November 23, 1909, who married Harry Weichel; Adolph, born April 15, 1914; and Hulda, born April 25, 1917. Residence: Jansen.

Genevieve Baldwin Guiou

Genevieve Baldwin Guiou was born at Council Bluffs, Iowa, September 20, 1879. She is the daughter of John Nehemiah and Lilla (Holcomb) Baldwin. Her father was a native of Council Bluffs, born July 9, 1857. He was a lawyer, and was general solicitor for the Union Pacific Railway until his death in Omaha, on April 19, 1908. Of early American stock, his grandfather, Caleb Baldwin, was a judge of the Supreme Court of Iowa.

Lilla Holcomb Baldwin was born at Bloomington, Illinois, January 10, 1860. She is still living. Mrs. Guiou was graduated from Miss Hersey's School at Boston, in 1897, and from Vassar College with an A. B. in 1901.

She came to Nebraska in 1906, and on June 1, 1911, was united in marriage with Arthur Pounsford Guiou. Mr. Guiou was a lumber merchant, born at Omaha, July 11, 1870, and died there April 12, 1923. There are four children, Charles Baldwin, born March 29, 1912, who attends Amherst College; Joan Pounsford, born September 11, 1913; Echo Hathaway, born April 6, 1917, and Sarah Pounsford, born April 4, 1920.

At the present time Mrs. Guiou is head of the women's department of the First Trust Company of Omaha. She is extremely active in civic and cultural work, and is president of the Orthopaedic Association and member of the Creche board. She is a member of the women's division of the Chamber of Commerce, of the Omaha Drama League, the Omaha Symphony Orchestra and the Community Playhouse.

She belongs to the Parent-Teachers Association of Central High School. During the World War she was an active civilian worker, and assisted in machine knitting and the making of soldier's socks. She was formerly vice president of the Guiou Lumber Company. Residence: Omaha.

John Gumb

John Gumb, son of Phillip and Barbara (Kobberger) Gumb, was born at Bensheim, Hessen-darmstadt, Germany, June 29, 1860, and came to Nebraska, in 1881. His father was born at Bensheim, and died in Chicago. He was a brick mason. His mother was also born in Bensheim, and died at Chicago.

Mr. Gumb attended the public schools and the Hannstein School of Mechanics at Chicago. At the present time he is manager of the produce business conducted by the Fremont Beverage Company. In 1923, he was elected to the Nebraska state senate on the Democratic ticket, and was unsuccessful candidate in 1925.

He was married to Elizabeth Catherine Nuernberger at Chicago, August 15, 1886. Mrs. Gumb was born at Peru, Illinois, August 19, 1864. There are five children, Phillip G., born May 17, 1888, married Bessie A. Dodendorf, and is assistant foreman of the car department of the Chicago and Northwestern Rairoad; Fritz, born September 7, 1891, married Ada McGee, and is a musician; John, born October 7, 1895, married Hazel Whalen, and is a lawyer; Harold, born December 2, 1903, married Julia Ann Tawney, he is also a lawyer; George A., born November 2, 1908, is an accountant.

Mr. Gumb is a member of St. James Episcopal Church, the United States Chamber of Commerce, the Elks, Eagles, Sons of Herman, Woodmen of the World, the Nebraska Poultry and Egg Association, and the Nebraskana Society. He is also a member of the Izaak Walton League. His hobby is mechanics. Residence: Fremont. (Photograph in Album).

William Albert Gunderson

William Albert Gunderson, postmaster at Dix, Nebraska, was born there on September 13, 1898, son of Nels and Thora (Gunderson) Gunderson. His father was born in Norway, and his mother at Pleasanton, Nebraska. She is of Danish descent. His parents are residing at Dix, where his father is acting as county assessor.

Mr. Gunderson attended public school, and from 1919 until 1924 was a Standard Oil Company agent. He was manager of the Linn Hardware Company at Dix from February 7, 1925 until December 10, 1928, at which time he became postmaster. He is a Republican.

His marriage to Carrie Louise Kronberg was solemnized at Kimball, August 19, 1919. Mrs. Gunderson was born at Blair, Nebraska, May 5, 1899, and is assistant postmaster at the present time. They have one daughter, Opal, born July 5, 1920.

During the late war Mr. Gunderson was chauffeur in the Air Service Flying School at Langely Field, Virginia. He is a member of the American Legion at Dix, is present adjutant and past post commander. He is a member of the Lutheran Church, the Odd Fellows (vice grand), and the Modern Woodmen of America (clerk). His favorite sport is golf. Residence: Dix.

Pleasant Hugh Gupton

Pleasant Hugh Gupton, proprietor of a hotel at Oxford, Nebraska, was born at Longview, Kentucky, April 5, 1850, son of Granville Monroe and Emma Jane (Bondurant) Gupton. The father, a carpenter of Irish descent, was born in Green County, Kentucky, March 24, 1827, and died in Ballard County, Kentucky, July 14, 1899. His wife, born in Longview, died in Ballard County, April 27, 1876. She was of French extraction, her maiden name having been Bondurant.

Mr. Gupton attended country school and commercial college at Evansville, Indiana, and about forty-two years has resided in Nebraska. He was the operator of two grain elevators for twenty-five years at Oxford, a flour miller two years at Oxford, a merchant twenty years, and at the present time operates two hotels at Oxford. He is a Democrat, and for about four years, prior to his coming to Nebraska, served as sheriff and treasurer of Ballard County, Kentucky.

His marriage to Mattie D. Cooper, was solemnized at Pekin, Illinois, November 20, 1883. Mrs. Gupton, who was born at Pekin, November 12, 1854, is active in club work in her community. She is the daughter of Thomas Cooper. There are five children living, and one deceased: Ella, born in 1884; Mabel in 1885; Tom in 1888; Mary, born in 1891, died September 11, 1912; Cleveland, born in 1893; and Leonard, born in 1894.

Mr. Gupton has been active in politics all his life, and for a number of years served as mayor of Oxford. He is a member of the Baptist Church, the Red Cross, the Modern Woodmen of America, the American Hotel Association of the United States and Canada, and the Nebraskana Society. Residence: Oxford. (Photograph in Album).

Frances Arminta Gustafson

Frances Arminta Gustafson, musician and club woman, was born at Minburn, Iowa, September 24, 1887, daughter of Thomas Johnston and Emily Jane (Brenton) West.

Her father was born in Johnson County, Indiana, January 21, 1837, and died at Minburn, Iowa, October 4, 1903. He was a farmer, whose father came from England, and his mother was born in Vermont, of English and Scotch descent. Emily Jane Brenton was born in Johnson County, Indiana, March 26, 1851, and died at Minburn, February 18, 1915. She was a teacher and a lover of music, descended from Colonial stock. Among her Revolutionary ancestors were members of the Brenton, Glenn, Clark, and McClain family.

In 1904, Mrs. Gustafson was graduated from the Minburn High School, and during the summer terms of 1904 and 1906, attended the William Farr Normal School. During the summer of 1908, she attended Drake University. She later taught in the Bridgeport city schools, from January 1, 1907, until May, 1910. She now teaches music and private classes in English. A Democrat, Mrs. Gustafson has served on the school board six years.

At the present time, she is the first 6th district chairman of the Parent-Teachers Association, past matron of the Order of Eastern Star, a member of the Red Cross, and a member of the Daughters of the American Revolution. She is secretary of the Bridgeport Woman's Club, and is a member of the Presbyterian Church.

She is married to Wallace Henry Gustafson, who was born at Dayton, Iowa, October 17, 1886. He is an engineer on the Burlington Railroad and is a member of the Masons. They have two children, John Raymond, born December 17, 1912, who is a student at the State Agricultural School, Ames, Iowa; and Emily Lucile, born January 12, 1916, who is an accomplished violinist. Residence: Bridgeport.

Oscar Gustafson

A resident of Nebraska for the past 42 years, Oscar Gustafson has been successful as a farmer and business man in Newman Grove. He was born at Hastholmon, Sweden, December 1, 1871, the son of Eric Gustaf and Caroline Johnson. His father, a farmer, was born at

Heyn—Omaha

BLANCHE LUCILE ALBRIGHT HAAS

Hastholmon, and died there in 1901. His mother was born in Hastholmon, February 8, 1845, and died there October 12, 1927.

Mr. Gustafson is a member of the Tri County Community Club, the Red Cross, and the Nebraskana Society. He is affiliated with Zion Lutheran Church at Newman Grove and is a member of the Independent Order of Odd Fellows. A Republican, he served as city councilman for 10 years and was city assessor for eight years. He has been a farmer, implement dealer, and well-driller at Newman Grove. At the present time he is assessor for the Shell Creek precinct in Madison County, Nebraska.

On June 20, 1906, he married Betty Lindo, daughter of Carl Henry and Minna (Terngren) Lindo, at Newman Grove. Mrs. Gustafson was born at Newman Grove. Mrs. Gustafson was born at Newman Grove, of Swedish parents, October 30, 1885. Her parents settled in Madison County in 1883. They were pioneer settlers and endured many hardships. They have a daughter, Mernie, born April 11, 1909, who married Emil Fahrlander. Residence: Newman Grove.

Blanche Lucile Albright Haas

One of Nebraska's most charming vocalists and composers, Blanche Albright Haas, is a native Nebraskan. She was born at Pawnee City, August 1, 1888, daughter of John Daniel and Ida Jane (Bowles) Albright. Her father, born at Armington, Illinois, May 10, 1856, was, until his retirement, a leading land and livestock owner, and was from 1914-18 county treasurer of Pawnee County. His grandfather Albright came to America from Germany. Ida Jane (Bowles) Albright was also a native of Armington, Illinois, born January 13, 1860. Before her marriage she was a teacher, and a graduate of the Illinois State Normal School. She was very active in church and civic work, woman's suffrage and the W. C. T. U., until her death at Pawnee on December 5, 1925. Her ancestry was English.

Mrs. Haas began her education in district number thirteen of Pawnee County, and was graduated from Pawnee City High School in 1906. During 1907-08 and 1909-10 she attended the University of Nebraska, where she was a member of Delta Delta Delta sorority. She married Fred Lipp Haas at Pawnee City, April 12, 1911. Mr. Haas, who was born in Pawnee City, December 2, 1887, is president and general manager of Haas Brothers Co. of Omaha. He is a member of the Rotary Club. They have one child, F. Lowell, born June 15, 1914. During 1931 he was elected to membership in the National Honor Society. He was graduated from high school in 1931 and now attends Dartmouth College.

By preference Mrs. Haas is a Republican. Her main interest is in things musical. She is a highly talented singer, and has composed the music for many songs, including: *Cradle Song, A Home; The Harbinger; My Lady Spring; and Twilight Hours.* She is a member of the Friends of Music, and is corresponding secretary of chapter B. N. of the P. E. O. Sisterhood. She is chairman of courtesy of Central High School Parents Teachers Association, and corresponding secretary of the Omaha College Club, a branch of the American Association of University Women. She is affiliated with the First Methodist Church of Omaha, and is a member of the Nebraskana Society. Her clubs are the University Club and Happy Hollow Country Club. Residence: Omaha. (Photograph on Page 490).

Fred Lipp Haas

For the past 16 years Fred L. Haas has been one of the prominent business executives at Omaha, and has taken an active part in civic affairs there. He was born at Pawnee City, Pawnee County, Nebraska,

December 2, 1887, the son of Christian B. and Savilla (Lipp) Haas, and has lived in this state practically all his life. His father, who was a merchant, was born at Petersburg, Mahoning County, Ohio, June 16, 1851, and died at Pawnee City September 5, 1909; his ancestors came from Wittenberg, Germany. His mother was born at Petersburg, May 11, 1851, and died at Pawnee City, September 15, 1926. Her ancestors came to America from Luxemburg, Germany.

Mr. Haas received his education in the grade and high schools at Pawnee City. He has held the following positions in the business world: clerk for the A. B. Edee Dry Goods Company at Pawnee City; travelling salesman for the Farrell-Spence Company of Chicago; manager of the ready-to-wear department of the Rorabaugh-Wiley Dry Goods Company at Hutchinson, Kansas. He is now president and general manager of the Haas Brothers Company, a ladies' specialty store at Omaha.

He holds membership in the Nebraskana Society, the Parent Teachers' Association, and the First Methodist Church of Omaha. In 1926 he served as a member of the board of directors of the Chamber of Commerce at Omaha, and from 1925 to 1927 was president of the Associated Retailers. He is a member of the Rotary Club. His social clubs include: University Club; Harry Hollow Club. He likes to golf and motor.

On April 12, 1911, he was married to Blanche Lucile Albright at Pawnee City. Mrs. Haas, who is a well-known clubwoman in Omaha, is a soloist and the author of several musical compositions; she was born at Pawnee City. They have one son, F. Loweil, born June 15, 1914. He was graduated from Central High School in 1931, where he was elected to the National Honor Society and was captain of the Cadet Board: he is attending Dartmouth College. Residence: Omaha.

William W. Hackney, Jr.

William W. Hackney, Jr., banker, was born at Brownville, Nebraska, May 31, 1875. He attended public school, and entered the preparatory department of the University of Nebraska, from which he was graduated with the Bachelor of Science degree in 1897. He attended Eastman Business College at Poughkeepsie, New York, and started out in his banking career as a messenger for the old Columbia National Bank of Lincoln. He is married to Anna E. Elmgren.

In 1907 he was assistant cashier of that bank, when it merged with the First National Bank. In October, 1907, he was made assistant cashier of the Central National Bank at its organization. He became vice president in 1918, and in May, 1923, became president.

Mr. Hackney is a Scottish Rite Mason, and in 1909 served as illustrious potentate of the Mystic Shrine. He has served as treasurer of the Lincoln Rotary Club also. Residence: Lincoln.

Charles William Hadan

Charles William Hadan, plumbing contractor, was born in Winside, Nebraska, August 15, 1897. He is the son of Carl William and Anna Marie (Glandt) Hadan. His father was born at Brandenburg, Germany, July 15, 1853, and came to America in 1883, where he engaged in farming. He died at Winside on November 21, 1914. Anna Marie Glandt, his wife, was born in Holstein, Germany, July 23, 1862.

Mr. Hadan attended public school, and started in his present line of business in 1917. He is engaged in the plumbing, heating and electrical business, and during the past fourteen years its volume has steadily increased, and he has purchased his own building. He conducts as fine a business of its kind as can be found in the state, and is justly proud of it.

On June 2, 1920, he was united in marriage to Clara Margaret Witte at Omaha. Mrs. Hadan is a native of Elkhorn. There are three children, Arlene Ione, born May 30, 1922; Bernette Wilberta, born June 19, 1924, and Myra Lea, born December 3, 1926.

Mr. Hadan is a Republican. He attends St. John's Lutheran Church, and is a Mason and Modern Woodman of America. He also belongs to the Nebraska Plumbers Association, the Bennington Commercial Club, and The Nebraskana Society. His hobby is mechanics. Residence: Bennington. (Photograph in Album).

Richard Hadley

Richard Hadley was born at Cedar Rapids, Nebraska, February 17, 1900, son of Seth Smith and Addie (Bowen) Hadley. His father was born in Indiana, June 10, 1848, and died at Cedar Rapids, April 21, 1911; he was a banker, lumberman, and miller. His English ancestors were in America in the early colonial days.

His mother was born in Ohio, July 30, 1865. Her Irish ancestors came to America before the Revolution. Mr. Hadley, who is a bank examiner at Lincoln, attended the public school at Cedar Rapids, Everett grade school of Lincoln, and in 1917, was graduated from the Lincoln High School. He received his A. B. degree in 1921, at the University of Nebraska, where he was president of the senior class and held membership in Sigma Delta Chi and Phi Gamma Delta.

He was married at Weeping Water, Nebraska, April 26, 1922. Mrs. Hadley was born at Weeping Water, October 26, 1902; her ancestry is Scotch-Irish. Their children are Robert, born September 15, 1924; and Jean, born August 19, 1926.

Mr. Hadley served during the World War in 19th Observation Battalion, Camp Taylor, Kentucky. He is a member of the American Legion, and is affiliated with the Episcopal Church of Lincoln. Residence: Lincoln.

Hugo Paul Haessler

A banker and farmer, Hugo Paul Haessler was born at Beatrice, Nebraska, April 14, 1896, the son of Traugott William and Henrietta (Hansmeier) Haessler. His father was born in Germany in January, 1846, and came to the United States in 1867. A Lutheran minister, he was a pioneer missionary in Nebraska, coming to the state in 1867. He died at Holstein, March 21, 1907. His wife, Henrietta, was born in Germany, February 3, 1861, and died at Deshler, in February, 1928.

Hugo Haessler attended elementary and high schools and had some military training. After having been assistant cashier in the German American Bank at Deshler, he entered the army service. He was promoted from a private to a lieutenant in the eighteen months that he served, eleven of which were in France. Later, he was cashier in the bank at Ruskin, Nebraska, and from 1921-1925 he was cashier of the Leshara State Bank, of which he has been president since 1925. He is secretary and manager of the Farmers Oil and Truck Company at Leshara, and engages in the insurance business and in farming.

On November 2, 1920, at Lawrence, Kansas, he was united in marriage to Florence Esther Dunigan, who was born at Guthrie, Oklahoma, July 19, 1895. She is a graduate of the University of Kansas in 1917, and taught school before her marriage. Their son, George, was born November 2, 1922.

Mr. Haessler is affiliated with the Trinity Lutheran Church at Fremont, Nebraska. He was active in the Liberty loan drive before entering war service, is a member of the Red Cross and a Republican. Baseball and reading are his favorite recreations. Residence: Leshara. (Photograph in Album).

Ella Margaret Hagedorn

Ella Margaret Hagedorn, clubwoman, was born at Hay Springs, Nebraska, September 6, 1892, daughter of William and Margaret (Eckles) Waterman.

She was educated in Doane College and Oberlin College at Oberlin, Ohio, and on December 15, 1919 was married to William Hagedorn at Chadron, Nebraska. Mr. Hagedorn was born in Peoria, Illinois.

Mrs. Hagedorn is a member of the American Legion Auxiliary, the Order of Eastern Star, the Nebraska Federation of Women's Clubs, and is affiliated with the Congregational Church. Residence: Hay Springs.

George Edward Hager

For the past thirty-two years George Edward Hager has been engaged in the practice of law in Nebraska, and nearly all of that time in Lincoln. He was born in Appanoose County, Iowa, February 28, 1874, son of Jacob and Margaret (Croft) Hager. Jacob Hager, a native of Ross County, Ohio, born March 17, 1836, was a farmer. In politics he was a Republican and was active in the work of his party. During the Civil War he served with the 36th Iowa Infantry. His ancestry was Pennsylvania Dutch, early settlers in America. His wife, Margaret, was born in New Bedford, Pennsylvania, April 21, 1844, and she also was descended from early Pennsylvania Dutch settlers.

George E. Hager attended the public school at Clay Center and received his A. B. from the University of Nebraska in 1898. In 1899 he was graduated from the Law College of the University. In 1896 he participated in the Center-Laimer-Quaintence Oratorical contest, and in 1897 was president of the Union Boys Debating Club.

After his admission to the bar in 1899 he took up the active practice of law, practicing at Plattsmouth for a short time, and then removing to Lincoln. From 1900 to 1906 he was a member of the firm of Kirkpatrick and Hager, and from 1920-22 of the law firm of McCarty and Hager. During the balance of said period Mr. Hager was in practice for himself. He has since been engaged in active practice. In addition to his legal activities Mr. Hager has taken an active part in Republican politics. He served as assistant postmaster of Lincoln from 1906-11, as deputy county attorney of Lancaster County 1911-14 and county attorney 1914-16.

On November 28, 1900, he was married to Jennie Harris at Chicago. Mrs. Hager, who was born at Johnstown, Pennsylvania, January 28, 1876, is descended from early Welsh settlers in that state. There are two children, Margaret Rees, born September 22, 1902, who was graduated from Lincoln High School and from the University of Nebraska with a B. A. degree in 1924. She married Dwight S. McVicker. Gwendolyn, who was born July 21, 1910, is now a junior at the University of Nebraska.

Mr. Hager is interested in many of the larger undertakings in Lincoln. He is a member of the board of directors of the Lincoln Trust Company, the Dwelling House Insurance Company, and is vice president of the Home Savings and Loan Association. In addition he is vice president of the Byran Memorial Hospital, secretary of the Union Lumber and Mercantile Company, and secretary and treasurer of the Auditorium Building Corporation.

The Hagers are members of Trinity Methodist Episcopal Church of Lincoln. Among Mr. Hager's professional memberships are the following: The American Bar Association, the Nebraska State Bar Association, the Lancaster County Bar Association and the American Inter-professional Institute. He is a member of the Modern Woodmen of America, the Masons, the Young Men's Christian Association, the Chamber of Commerce and the Sons of Civil War Veterans. He is interested in farming and stockraising and is fond of golf. His club is the Open Forum. Residence: Lincoln.

Helen Lynch Hager

Helen Lynch Hager, stockgrower and clubwoman, was born at St. Louis, Missouri, November 6, 1882, daughter of Thomas Richard and Anne (Lyons) Lynch.

Her father was born in Woodford, County Galway, Ireland, June 2, 1841, and came to the United States in 1866. He was a railroad builder and stockgrower, who helped to build the Union Pacific to Salt Lake City. He was the hero of the Sappa Creek Indian raid in Kansas, and was appointed the first county commissioner to organize Grant County, Nebraska. He died at Omaha, December 6, 1901. His wife, Anne, was born in Woodford, County Galway, Ireland, February 27, 1849, and died at Los Angeles, May 6, 1926. She was a pioneer homemaker.

Upon the completion of her early education in the Omaha public school, Helen Lynch attended St. Mary's College at South Bend, Indiana.

On November 17, 1923, she was married to Ross Hager at Denver, Colorado. He was born in Cowles, Nebraska, August 14, 1894, of Scotch-Irish ancestry. He is a prominent stockgrower.

Mrs. Hager is a member of the Catholic Church, the American Legion Auxiliary, Women's Benefit Association, and is director of the local school board. Her hobby is traveling. Residence: Hyannis.

Ross Hager

Ross Hager, stock breeder, was born at Cowles, Nebraska, August 14, 1894, son of George Washington and Eliza (Buster) Hager.

The father was born at Freedom, Wisconsin, October 20, 1851, and is a farmer, of Scotch-Irish ancestry. He moved with his family by ox team from Wisconsin to the place where Fremont now stands in 1855. His wife, Eliza, was born at Plattsmouth, Nebraska, April 1, 1860, and is of Scotch-Irish ancestry. She was a pioneer homemaker in the early days in Nebraska.

Mr. Hager attended public school, and has since engaged in stock raising.

He was married on November 17, 1923, to Helen Frances Lynch at Denver, Colorado. She was born at St. Louis, Missouri, November 6, 1882. After the death of her father, she operated the home land. Her ancestry is Irish.

During the late war Mr. Hager served in the United States Army with the rank of sergeant. He is a member of the American Legion, and the Masons. He is a dog fancier, and is fond of hunting. Residence: Hyannis.

Thomas Charles Hagerman

One of Nerbaska's pioneer farmers is Thomas Charles Hagerman who has lived in Nebraska for the past 48 years and is now retired. He was born at Hagerstown, Maryland, January 7, 1851, the son of William Andrew and Hetty (Mickey) Hagerman. His father, a brickmaker and farmer, was born at Gettysburg, Pennsylvania, of German parents, and died at Downsville, Washington County, Maryland, July 3, 1887. His mother, who was of French descent was born at Cashtown, Pennsylvania, and died at Downsville, Maryland.

Mr. Hagerman has been mayor of Filley, Nebraska, for many years, and served as president and secretary of the high school there for a time. He is a member of the board of the Methodist Episcopal Church at Filley, is affiliated with the Red Cross, and holds membership in the Republican Party. He is a member of the Modern Woodmen of America, Royal Neighbors of America, and the Nebraskana Society.

He was united in marriage with Mary Ellen Hutgell at Boonsboro, Washington County, Maryland, October 12, 1873. Mrs. Hagerman was born at Boonsboro. Five children were born to this marriage, four of whom are living: Nannie Elizabeth, born September 11, 1874, who married Dr. J. J. Williams; Alice, born February 15, 1877, who married E. W. Starlin, and who died February 13, 1913; Ada, born November 30, 1878, who married Earl Norcross; William, born October 11, 1881, who married Joyce Clark; and Luther, born July 3, 1887, who married Eva Clark. Residence: Filley.

Fred Raymond Haggart

Fred Raymond Haggart, a leading banker of St. Paul, Nebraska, was born in that community, May 1, 1886, the son of James Arch and Joanna (O'Hollaren) Haggart. His father, who is a lawyer, was born in St. Lawrence County, New York, June 14, 1854, and is descended from Scotch and Welsh ancestors. His mother, a prominent club worker, was born in Adams County, Wisconsin, October 22, 1862, of Irish descent.

Mr. Haggart was graduated from the St. Paul High School in 1903, attended St. Paul Business College, 1903-04, and was a student at the University of Nebraska, 1904-06. He was elected to membership in Delta Tau Delta at the University of Nebraska where he also took an active part in athletic events.

He entered the banking business at St. Paul in 1906, acting first as bookkeeper. He is now vice president and cashier of the St. Paul National Bank, and has served as chairman of the executive counsel of Nebraska Bankers Association. He is a member of the St. Paul Community Club, the Red Cross, the Nebraskana Society, and the First Presbyterian Church of St. Paul. His social club is the St. Paul Golf Club, and his chief recreations are golfing, football, basketball and tennis.

Mr. Haggart was married at Davenport, Iowa, September 18, 1912, to Freda Louise Weidenpesch, who was born at Chicago, Illinois, June 21, 1888. Mrs. Haggart, who was a milliner prior to her marriage, is a descendant of Robert Schuman, noted musician and composer, and of General Keller who commanded Napoleon's forces on the left bank of the Rhine at the battle of Waterloo. They have one daughter, Elaine, borne October 2, 1913, who was graduated from St. Paul High School with honors and is now a student at Hastings College.

Mr. Haggart is a progressive Republican and a member of the Republican county central committee. Mr. Haggart's hobbies are gardening and golf. Residence: St. Paul.

Gustave Hahn

Born in a sod house in Colfax County, Nebraska, May 17, 1871, Gustave Hahn is the son of Peter and Elizabeth (Backhaus) Hahn. His father, who was born in Nordendorf, Hanover, Germany, March 3, 1827, came to America in 1869 and homesteaded 9 miles from Schuyler, Nebraska. He died in Colfax County on December 1, 1903. Elizabeth, his wife, was born in Nordendorf, March 5, 1834, and died in Colfax County on September 22, 1890.

Gustave Hahn attended rural schools and engaged in farming until 1905, when he entered the implement and banking business. He is a director of the First National Bank of Leigh at the present time.

On October 21, 1896, he was married to Anna Herling. Mrs. Hahn was born at Hilchenbach, Westfalen, Germany, November 23, 1879. They have two sons, Arnold, born August 23, 1900, who married Iona Marjory Metzinger; and Harry, born June 21, 1903, who married Gladyce Lucille Botsch. Arnold is deputy state game warden, and Harry is assistant cashier of the First National Bank of Leigh. Both sons are graduates of Leigh High School and Midland College.

Mr. Hahn is a member of the Odd Fellows, the Ne-

OSCAR HERMAN HAHN

Nelson—Hastings

braskana Society and St. Johns Lutheran Church of Leigh, while Mrs. Hahn assisted in organizing the Sunday School at St. Johns, and served as Sunday School superintendent ten years. Residence: Leigh. (Photograph in Album).

Oscar Herman Hahn

A physician and surgeon at Hastings, since 1910, Oscar Herman Hahn was born at Home, Kansas, June 17, 1885, son of Herman Ludwig and Augusta Caroline (Zimmerling) Hahn. His father, born near Danzig, Germany, February 2, 1858, died at St. Joseph, Missouri, December 25, 1926. His parents remained in Germany, where a sister now resides. One brother died in Germany, while four of them settled in America. Augusta Caroline, wife of Herman Hahn, was born near Westphalen, Germany, October 31, 1865, and migrated with her parents to a farm in Marshall County, Kansas, in 1877. She now resides in St. Joseph.

Dr. Hahn attended public school at St. Joseph and later entered Union College at College View, Nebraska. He received the degree of Doctor of Medicine from Ensworth Medical College in May, 1908, and afterward took postpraduate work in New York, and various other American clinics. After two years' practice at Home, Kansas, he removed to Hastings where he was superintendent of the Nebraska Sanitarium five years. In 1910 he was admitted to practice in Nebraska by reciprocity, and in 1925 was licensed to practice in California.

On October 20, 1908, Dr. Hahn was united in marriage to Anna Corinne Didrickson at St. Joseph. Mrs. Hahn, whose parents came from Sweden, and were married in America, was born at St. Joseph, December 24, 1884. They have two daughters, Elinore Caroline, born May 30, 1910, who is a senior in Union College; and Eldine Adelia, born May 23, 1914, who is a senior in Hastings High School.

Dr. Hahn is a Republican. During the World War he was appointed first lieutenant but could not fill his appointment because of illness. He is a member of Hastings Post No. 11 of the American Legion.

Among his professional memberships are the American, Nebraska State and Adams County Medical Associations, and at the present time he is a member of the surgical staff of Mary Lanning Memorial Hospital. Dr. Hahn is a member of Hastings Lodge No. 159 of the Elks, is a life member of The Nebraskana Society, and during 1926 served as president of the Lions Club of Hastings. His hobbies are fish and flowers, mechanics and architecture. Residence: Hastings. (Photograph on Page 494).

Elmer Wallace Haight

Elmer Wallace Haight, born at Honey Creek, Wisconsin, October 22, 1862, is the son of Lewis Bailey and Elizabeth Irene (Estey) Haight. Lewis Haight was born in Adrian, Michigan, September 21, 1835, of Canadian-English parentage, and died at David City, Nebraska, April 22 1902. He homesteaded just west of David City in 1871. Elizabeth Estey Haight was born in Massachusetts, February 10, 1835, and died in David City, April 1, 1924.

In 1882, Elmer W. Haight completed his studies in the district school. Mr. Haight married Flora Burr, March 10, 1898, at David City. She was of English descent, born in Atlantic, Iowa, July 26, 1876. To this union three children were born: Ernest Byron, July 20, 1899; Lewis Cyrus, July 18, 1901, and Elton Vaughn, May 13, 1906, who died August 5, 1923. Ernest and Lewis are operating the original homestead on a share rental basis. Both are graduates of the state university, class of 1923. Ernest Haight was the first graduate of the agricultural engineering college to receive Phi Beta Kappa.

During the World War period Mr. Haight belonged to the Home Guard for three years. He is affiliated with the First Baptist Church in David City, is a member of the Nebraskana Society, and a Republican. Croquet is his favorite sport and pastime. He has resided in Nebraska for sixty years. Residence: David City.

Julius J. Hairhouse

Born at Roensahl by Elberfeld, Westphalen, Germany, in 1885, Julius J. Hairhouse, retired jeweler of Fremont, Nebraska, is the son of Frederick Hairhouse and Henrietta (Plate) Hairhouse. Frederick Hairhouse was a baker.

Mr. Hairhouse attended public school in Germany and studied under private tutelage in America. On February 17, 1884, at Fremont, Nebraska, he married Mary M. Herre, a dressmaker. Mrs. Hairhouse was born at Belvedere, New Jersey, August 28, 1863. They have two children living, Mrs. Henry Haman, of Fremont, Nebraska, born November 16, 1884, and Mrs. Lloyd W. Phillips of Omaha, born April 28, 1891. A third child, Cecil Hairhouse, was born January 8, 1895, and died on January 17, of the same year.

A resident of Nebraska for fifty-five years, Mr. Hairhouse is a member of the Congregational Church of Fremont, and a Republican. Residence: Fremont.

Ezra Frederick Haist

Ezra Frederick Haist, district superintendent of the Evangelical Church, was born at Golden Lake, Ontario, Canada, August 12, 1880, son of George Frederick and Mary Anna (Ruf) Haist.

His father, born in Wurtemburg, Germany, September 15, 1843, has been a minister of the gospel all his life. He came to Canada in 1867, to New York State in 1909, and to Colorado in 1921. His mother died when he was a child and his father at the age of 68. His father was a poor man when he came to Canada, and is now in comfortable circumstances.

Mary Ann Ruf was born in Etten Heim Muenster, Baden, Germany, October 5, 1847, and died at Hanover, Ontario, June 11, 1902. Her family all remained in Germany. She was a French cook before coming to America in 1867. After her marriage she was a devoted wife and mother, an earnest Christian, and active in young peoples' religious work. She was a public speaker and a student of Christian literature.

Ezra F. Haist attended public school, high school and normal college, and was graduated from Seminary at Naperville, Illinois, in 1902.

Ordained to the ministry while at Wakerton, Ontario, June 29, 1902, he served in various pastorates from 1902 until 1928, since which he has been district superintendent for the Kearney district of the Evangelical Church. He is a member of the Nebraska Conference of the Evangelical Church, the Masons (1914-), the Red Cross (chairman at Culbertson 1917-21), and during 1918 was county organizer of Near East relief work. His favorite recreation is kodaking and his hobby is travel.

On May 13, 1903, he was married to Emma Sophia Bertram at Drumbo, Ontario. Mrs. Haist, who was born at Bright, Ontario, October 6, 1877, is a public speaker and an ardent religious wrker. There are six children, Frank F., born October 8, 1904, who married Elizabeth Hovey; Harry F., July 1, 1906; Ruby Marie, July 19, 1908, who died March 11, 1909; Edna Florence, June 19, 1910; Elmo Murrary, September 23, 1915; and Ruth Florence, August 29, 1922. The two oldest sons live in Hollywood and Los Angeles, respectively. There is one grandchild, Frank Fredrick Hovey, born March 12, 1929. Residence: Kearney.

Peter Hakanson

One of Nebraska's pioneer farmers is Peter Hakanson who was born at Cordova, Illinois, August 25,

1858, the son of John and Hannah (Pearson) Hakanson. His father, who was a farmer, was born in Sweden in March, 1818, and died at Wahoo, Nebraska, March 9, 1899. Hannah (Pearson) Hakanson was born in Sweden in 1823, and died at Fairfield, Nebraska, July 9, 1892.

Mr. Hakanson attended the public schools of Geneseo, Illinois, Mount Pleasant, Iowa, and Fairfield. Coming to Nebraska in the fall of 1874 with his parents in covered wagons, the only stock they possessed was 12 head of horses and some farm machinery and household goods. Mr. Hakanson's parents bought a relinquishment and located four miles east of Fairfield on the Sandy where they lived in a sod house for a period of about six weeks while their frame dwelling was under construction. He remembers how the tribe of Omaha Indians would camp within throwing distance of the home, and also remembers of seeing the emigrant trains of between 40 and 50 wagons going farther west. His greatest recollection is a cyclone that visited the Fairfield territory May 24, 1903, and completely demolished their home and all out buildings and of his warning to his family to take to the cellar only in time to escape the storm. He is a progressive farmer near Fairfield at this time and takes an active part in civic and educational affairs there. A Republican, he served as a member of the Nebraska House of Representatives in 1921. He is affiliated with the Fairfield Christian Church and serves as deacon and trustee, is a member of the Men and Millions Club, and from 1885 to 1926 served on the local school board. His hobby is reading.

On January 1, 1879, he was married at Edgar, Nebraska, to Mary Elizabeth Jayne who was born at Aurora, Illinois, January 31, 1859. To them were born: Elinor Hanna, on November 15, 1879; John Edwin, on October 24, 1881, who married Jessie Riddel at Fairfield in 1903; William Leonard, on August 14, 1882, who married Lora Leach at Edgar in 1910; and Ruth Viola, on January 12, 1890, died at Fairfield in December, 1924.

Mr. and Mrs. Hakanson agree that at this time their proudest possession is a great grand-daughter, Betty Louise Schliep, born May 10, 1929. Residence: Fairfield.

H. Halderson

H. Halderson, Republican candidate for congress from the Third District of Nebraska in the election of 1932, attended the University of Nebraska where he received his Bachelor of Laws degree, and was also a student at the University of South Dakota. His parents came from Norway, in 1866.

A practicing lawyer in Nebraska for twenty-five years, Mr. Halderson was born in a log house on a pioneer homestead, and has written the *History of Pioneers* and *The Small Town Will Survive*. He is listed in *Who's Who in the Central States*.

In 1906 Mr. Halderson wrote the Republican progressive platform which provided for a two-cent fare, the anti-pass law, primary law, and railway commission. In 1912 he was alternate delegate to the Republican national convention at Chicago, elected by a large majority from the 3rd district. In 1915 he was the original proponent of the law for summoning jurors by mail. This law has saved the counties of Nebraska more than $100,000 thus far.

Mr. Halderson is the author of *Taxation for Federal Purposes*, published in the *Central Law Journal* and the *Congressional Record*. He was Republican nominee for congress in 1930.

He has been attorney for the Board of Foreign Missions of the Methodist Episcopal Church, and a member of the Volunteer Firemen of Newman Grove for 21 years.

He is a member of the American Bar Association and the Civil Legion, and was recently elected to life membership in the Nebraskana Society.

During 1912-15 Mr. Halderson was one of the leading tennis players in Nebraska, and in former years he managed the local baseball team. He is a Mason and an Odd Fellow, a member of the Madison County Historical Association and the Tri County Community Club.

On September 10, 1910 he was united in marriage to Gertrude Kenagy at Milford, Nebraska. Mrs. Halderson, who died in 1922, was a high school teacher. She was the daughter of Mr. and Mrs. David P. Kenagy of Milford, Nebraska. There are two children, Maxwell Hayes, who is 19 and Lewellyn Dean, 17. Residence: Newman Grove.

Clarence Edward Haley

Born at Valentine, Nebraska, October 11, 1894, Clarence Edward Haley is the son of William Edgar and Emma Genevieve (McNichols) Haley. Clarence Haley, who was born in Woodbury County, Iowa, October 4, 1863, is an abstractor of Irish descent. His wife, Emma was born in Fondulac, Wisconsin, January 29, 1871, and is also of Irish descent.

Clarence Edward Haley was educated in the public and high schools of Valentine and was graduated from the latter in 1914. He thereafter attended the University of Nebraska, from which he received his LL. B. in 1921. He is a member and former president of Delta Tau Delta.

Upon his admission to the bar, Mr. Haley engaged in active practice, and has served as county attorney of Cedar County two terms, elected on the Democratic ticket. He was married to Lucile Johnson at Iowa, August 9, 1928. Mrs. Haley, who is of Irish and English descent, was born at Charter Oak, Iowa, May 26, 1901.

Mr. Haley is a member of Holy Trinity Catholic Church. At the present time he is secretary-treasurer of the Lions Club and president of the Hartington Library Board. He belongs to the Red Cross and the Commercial Club, and is a member of the Hartington Country Club. His favorite sport is golf and his hobby is reading. Residence: Hartington.

Francis Baldwin Hall

Francis B. Hall was born at Barnston, Stanstead, Quebec, September 27, 1887. His father, George Benjamin Hall, who was born at Barnston, December 21, 1852, of English descent, is a farmer and a maple produce dealer. He holds a 25 year service medal in the Canadian militia. His wife, Jennie Eva (Baldwin) Hall, was born at Barnston, June 20, 1863, and died there September 20, 1927. She was a member of the English Baldwin family and traced her ancestry to Cromwell's time.

Mr. Hall was graduated from the Barnston Model School in 1903; was a student at the Methodist Business College at Stanstead, 1904, and the Ontario Business College at Belleville, Ontario, 1905. He entered the business world as bookkeeper for the J. S. Mitchell Company, wholesale hardware firm, in 1907. From 1907 to 1909 he served as secretary and treasurer of the Eastern Townships Dairy Produce Company; was connected with the Penman Limited, Knitgoods Manufacturers as a bookkeeper, 1909-10; was with the Eastern Townships Bank and the Canadian Bank of Commerse, 1910-11; was office manager of Penman Limited from 1912 to 1916; and was London manager of this company from 1916 to 1920.

In 1921 he moved to Nebraska City, where he became department manager for F. W. Cleveland & Son. He has continued in this position for the past ten years. In 1928 he became a naturalized citizen of the United States.

His marriage to Etta Jeanette Cleveland was solemnized at Nebraska City, April 20, 1914. Mrs. Hall was born at Coaticook, Stanstead, Quebec, Canada, January 25, 1889, the daughter of F. W. and Etta (Hanks) Cleveland. They have one daughter: Hazel Margaret, born January 24, 1918.

Mr. Hall is a member of the Nebraska City Chamber of Commerce, and in 1927 was on the board of directors of this organization. He is a Mason, and past master of Ashlar Lodge Number 31, of the Grand Lodge of Quebec He is affiliated with St. Mary's Episcopal Church at Nebraska City, and is a Republican. Residence: Nebraska City.

Fred C. Hall

Fred C. Hall, a resident of Nebraska for the past 51 years, was born at Prairie Home, Nebraska, February 28, 1880. His father, John Hall, a farmer, was born in England, June 9, 1850, and died at Prairie Home, September 28, 1925; he came to America in 1854. His mother, Caroline (Oades) Hall, was born in Canada, February 23, 1854, of English parentage, and died at Prairie Home, March 29, 1913.

Mr. Hall was a farmer and hardware merchant for more than seven years, and is now connected with the Continental Oil Company at Lincoln. He is a Republican, and served as councilman of Havelock, Nebraska, and mayor of the city, May 1, 1926, to May 1, 1930.

His marriage to Daisy Florence Kerrhard, was solemnized at Red Oak, Iowa. Mrs. Hall was born at Red Oak, October 7, 1879; her ancestry is English. They have three children: Ralph, born February 12, 1904; Harold, born June 24, 1907; and Violet, born January 2, 1911.

Mr. Hall is a Mason, a member of the Modern Woodmen of America, and is treasurer of the Havelock Farmers Institute. Residence: Havelock.

Harry Bigelow Hall

Harry Bigelow Hall was born at Vesta, Nebraska, July 12, 1891, the son of Walter Perry and Margaret Ellen (Long) Hall. His father, who was born at Vesta, May 7, 1865, has been a merchant and real estate agent for many years and has served as county assessor. His mother was born at Dubuque, Iowa, December 6, 1871.

Mr. Hall was graduated from the Beaver City High School in 1907, was connected with the bank at Beaver City for 23 years, and is now business manager of the Brewster Hospital at Holdrege, Nebraska. He is a member of the First Christian Church of Beaver City, is a Mason, and holds membership in The Nebraskana Society, and was the first commander of the Beaver City American Legion Post.

He is married to Florence Catherine Rummel, who was born at Plattsmouth, Nebraska, June 2, 1893, of German parentage. She was formerly a school teacher. They have two children: Margaret Louise, December 27, 1925; and Joan Elizabeth, June 28, 1930. Mr. Hall served as a wagoner in evacuation ambulance Company 28 of the United States Army for a year in France during the World War. Residence: Holdrege.

James Michael Hall

James M. Hall, prominent as a banker, farmer, and stock-raiser, has been cashier of The Farmers State Bank of Ithaca, Nebraska, for twenty-nine years. He came to Nebraska, when a boy four years old with his parents in a covered wagon. He was born at Bradford, Indiana, on September 24, 1864. His father was Edward Hall, who was born in County Carlow, Ireland, on August 15, 1817, and came to America in 1832. His mother, Elizabeth (McGrath) Hall, also of Irish ancestry, was born in Lancaster County, Pennsylvania, on October 6, 1823. Both Mr. and Mrs. Edward Hall died on the farm they purchased and settled on when they first came to Nebraska. It was school land situated sixteen miles west of Omaha, near Elkhorn, in Douglas County, on what is now Federal Highway No. 16. Here, Edward Hall passed away on December 28, 1883, and his wife on October 21, 1894. They were persuaded to move from their Indiana home to Nebraska by one of their older sons, the late Dr. P. L. Hall, a well known pioneer physician and banker of Saunders County, Nebraska, and later a banker at Lincoln, Nebraska. P. L. Hall came to Nebraska in 1868, to work for the Union Pacific railroad, and helped in building its line west from Fremont. One of his recollections of this time was that they lived largely on wild game with occasional consignments of food from the east, and in rare instances, shipments of side meat. He returned to Indiana, in 1869, and induced his parents and eight brothers and sisters to join a covered wagon train and come with him to Nebraska. Of these nine brothers and sisters and the tenth brother, Charles, born in Nebraska, six survive, and they all still make their homes in Nebraska: John W. at Valley; Robert, at South Omaha; Edward, at Roseland; Charles, at South Omaha; James M., at Ithaca; and the one sister, Mrs. Eliza King, at Papillion.

James M. Hall assisted his parents on their Nebraska farm and struggled to secure an education. He attended Iron Bluff School in Douglas County, and was graduated from Rohrbaugh's Business College in Omaha. After his father's death, he remained on the home farm until 1900. Then for two years, he was on another farm near Elkhorn. In 1902, he disposed of his farm interests and purchased a home at Ithaca, and stock in the only bank at that place and assumed his present duties.

James M. Hall has served as president of the Saunders County Bankers Association. He also has been a member of the executive committee for Saunders County of the First Nebraska Regional Clearing House Association of Fremont. During the World War, associated with A. J. Alson, he did executive work on the Red Cross drives and the quotas from his community were always oversubscribed. He is a Democrat, but has never been active in politics as a partisan. He is vice president of the Ithaca Community Club, a member of the Modern Woodmen, and recently elected to membership in the Nebraskana Society. He married Anna E. Willhoft, at Omaha on January 1, 1895. Mrs. Hall was born in Chicago, Illinois, on February 12, 1874. She is of German descent and was baptized and confirmed in the Lutheran Church at Davenport, Iowa. She has always been interested in the social development of the community, is a member of the Royal Neighbors of America and during the World War was active in Red Cross work. She was vice-chairman of the local branch of the Red Cross, and was awarded the distinguished service medal for her work in garment making and knitting. In 1926, she was elected president of the Ithaca Homemakers, a University Extension Project Club, and when the next year, this became a federated Woman's Club, she was a charter member.

One son, Glenn J., was born to Mr. and Mrs. Hall, on December 11, 1895. He died on September 20, 1923, at Waterloo, Nebraska. His widow, who was Gladys C. Condron, of Valley, Nebraska, and their two sons, James Ellsworth and Kenneth Glenn, live in Omaha, Nebraska. Residence: Ithaca. (Photograph in Album).

Matthew Alexander Hall

For the past 42 years Matthew A. Hall has lived in Nebraska, and has been prominent in the legal world. He was born near Toronto, Canada, July 31, 1862, the son of Thomas Hewiston and Janet (Burns) Hall. His father, who was born at Scarboro, York County, Canada, March 4, 1834, and died at Souris, Manitoba, Canada, October 20, 1897, was a merchant, farmer, and stockbreeder. His grandfather came from Alston, England, to Canada, in 1832, and became a pioneer farmer in Scarboro Township.

His mother, Janet (Burns) Hall, was born at York

Mills, York, Canada, September 25, 1837, and died at Minneapolis, Minnesota, June 12, 1917. Her family came from Lanarkshire, Scotland, to Canada, about 1775.

Mr. Hall attended the public schools of York County, and in 1880 was awarded a second class non-professional teachers certificate at the Collegiate Institute at Toronto. He obtained his LL. B. degree in 1888 from the University of Wisconsin Law College where he was a member of Phi Delta Theta and served as president of his class in 1888.

Admitted to the bar at Madison, Wisconsin, June 20, 1888, since 1890 he has been a member of the law firm now known as Montgomery, Hall, Young and Johnsen. He served as a member of the state senate, 1903-04, elected on the Republican ticket.

His marriage to Isabella May Wurtele was solemnized at Sorel, Richelieu Province, Canada, September 2, 1890. Mrs. Hall, who was born at St. David, Quebec, Canada, May 20, 1868, is descended from United Empire Loyalists. Four children were born to this union: Percy Wurtele, born September 15, 1892, who married Frances Gaslin; Charles Alexander, born September 9, 1894, who married Mildred Rockwell, and who died November 4, 1927; Donald James, born November 6, 1897; and Robert Andrew, born September 9, 1906.

Mr. Hall is a member of the Omaha Bar Association; and the American Bar Association. He holds membership in the Red Cross; has been a director of the Young Men's Christian Association; Boy Scouts and Humane Society; and is a member of the University Club at Omaha. He is a Mason, and is affiliated with the First Presbyterian Church of Omaha. Residence: Omaha.

Summer Seward Hall

Sumner Seward Hall, farmer and stockraiser, was born at Osceola, Iowa, February 16, 1857, son of James and Elizabeth (Cassell) Hall. His father was born at Alexandria, Indiana, June 23, 1826. A Republican, he served as sheriff of Clark County, Iowa, and served in the Civil War with the 2nd Company of Iowa Volunteer Cavalry. He took a soldier's homestead in Nebraska on March 5, 1869, at the landoffice in Lincoln, and later served as representative in the Nebraska legislature. His death occurred at Elmwood, Nebraska, July 26, 1906. Elizabeth Cassell, his wife, was born at Alexandria, Indiana, September 24, 1824, and died at Eight Mile Grove, Cass County, Nebraska, July 27, 1893. She was the daughter of a German preacher.

Mr. Hall attended the public schools, and the Plattsmouth High School. He has been a continuous resident of Nebraska since about 1865. One of his earliest occupations was as transcribing clerk in the Surveyor General's Office at Plattsmouth in 1882. He also taught school in Cass County, Nebraska, three winters. Aside from his extensive farming operations, he has filled many public offices in his community. He is a Republican, and was legislative candidate from Cuming County during the movement for woman suffrage, but was defeated. He has served as township assessor and school director, and the fiscal agent for the government at the First Reserve Bank of Kansas City expressed sincere appreciation for his loyal co-operation in the sale of the Fourth Liberty Loan. He is a member of the Commercial Club, and the First Presbyterian Church, as well as the Nebraskana Society.

On March 29, 1887, he was united in marriage to Lucy Helen Tillotson at Bancroft. Mrs. Hall was born at Hastings, Michigan, September 30, 1861, and is descended from John Tillotson, English settler in 1634, who traced his ancestry to Archbishop John Tillotson. For a number of years before her marriage Mrs. Hall taught in the public schools.

There were five children born to them, three of whom are living. They are as follows: Grace E., born January 16, 1888, who married Dr. George E. Hartman; John Tillotson, born December 25, 1890, who was a sergeant

in the Ordnance Department in the World War, and who married Catherine Thomas; Frank Sumner, born March 8, 1893, died April 21, 1895; Genevieve May, born September 24, 1896, died October 7, 1928; and Seward Ralph, born April 6, 1904. Both girls were teachers. Ralph is a great lover of music.

Mr. Hall's hobby is good roads and he has been responsible for several good roads projects in his community. Residence: Bancroft.

William Otto Hall

Since 1915, William Otto Hall has been active in Jefferson County as a lumberman and merchant. He was born at Northwood, Iowa, December 30, 1876, the son of George Riddle and Anna Esther (Curtis) Hall. His father, a carpenter and school teacher, was born at Troy, New York, June 9, 1835, and died at York, Nebraska, March 4, 1913. His mother was born at Meadville, Pennsylvania, November 22, 1840, and died at Villard, Minnesota, July 2, 1923.

Coming to Nebraska at the age of nineteen, Mr. Hall attended York College four years. His previous educational advantages were only those offered by the district school. Attracted by circulars sent out by York College, and realizing the advantages to be gained by a higher education, he resolved to secure these for himself. He hired out to neighboring farmers and saved his earnings. However, on the eve of his departure for college he was robbed of the money he had earned and saved, and hoping to find employment to pay his way, on New Year's Eve, 1896, arrived at York. He enrolled as a student. His funds were small, but he found work sufficient to stay in school.

Later he built a home near the college for his parents, and thus other members of the family had the opportunity to receive a college education.

He was manager of a lumber and hardware store for Edwards and Bradford Lumber Company at Brownville, from 1907-15; and was manager of the Proudfit Lumber Company at Reynolds, 1915-20. Since 1920, he has been the owner and manager of a general store at Reynolds. He is affiliated with the Methodist Church, is a member of the Federation of Nebraska Retailers, and a life member of the Nebraskana Society.

On March 25, 1908, he was married to Emma Marie Stache, at York. Mrs. Hall, who was born at York, was graduated from York High School and received a life teacher's certificate from York College. Prior to her marriage she taught school. She is the daughter of Ernest Edward Stache, who was born in Trebnitz, Germany, December 21, 1842, and Follina Stache, who was born at Emden, Germany, July 16, 1851. Mr. and Mrs. Stache came to York County in its early days as one of the first pioneer families. Mr. Stache had learned the saddler's trade in his native land, and for many years owned and operated a harness and shoe store at York. At his death, December 12, 1905, he was one of the oldest business men in the community.

Mr. and Mrs. Hall are the parents of four children: Genevieve, Clarence and Helen who were born at Brownville, and Ernest, who was born at Reynolds. Genevieve, who married Emory G. Priefert, graduated from Peru State Normal College in 1931, with the Bachelor of Arts degree. Clarence and Helen are at present enrolled as students in the college at Peru. The youngest, Ernest, is attending public school at Reynolds.

Mr. Hall has always taken a very active interest in the education and training of his children. His life and experience furnish a fine example of what ambition, integrity and perseverance can accomplish. Residence: Reynolds. (Photograph in Album).

Effegene Hallock

Born at Union, Iowa, February 18, 1878, Effegene Hallock is the daughter of Uriah and Cynthia (Hinshaw) Moorman. Her father was born in Henry County, Indiana, August 9, 1842, and died at Ord, on

April 6, 1921. He was a farmer and carpenter whose great grandfather came from Ireland to South Carolina, the family later migrating to Indiana.

Her mother, Cynthia Hinshaw, was born in Henry County, Indiana, February 2, 1844, and died at Ord May 14, 1925. She was of a family of early settlers in South Carolina.

Effegene Moorman attended the country schools of Iowa and Nebraska, and in June, 1897, was graduated from Ord High School. On December 9, 1900, she was married to Harry Orrin Hallock at Ord. Mr. Hallock was born at Muscatine, Iowa, February 9, 1878, and died at Omaha, November 27, 1921.

Mr. and Mrs. Hallock farmed for a number of years, and about twenty-one years ago went into the hotel business. They have one son, Chester E., born February 25, 1902, who married Lena Nelson. He was graduated from Burwell High School, and has always been in the hotel business, from February, 1925, until August, 1931 as manager of the Hays Hotel at Central City.

Mrs. Hallock has resided in Garfield County since 1895. She is the owner and manager of the Burwell Hotel, a member of the Methodist Church, the Order of Eastern Star and the Nebraskana Society. Residence: Burwell.

David L. Hallquist

David L. Hallquist was born at Stromsburg, Nebraska, October 20, 1875, the son of Lars and Elizabeth (Ostrom) Halquist. His father was born at Ockelbo, Sweden, February 27, 1842, and died at Stromsburg, July 10, 1918. He was a successful farmer at Altona, Illinois from 1869 to 1871 and came to Nebraska and settled in Polk County in 1872, before Stromsburg was founded. Elizabeth Hallquist was born at Gafole, Sweden, October 30, 1847, and died at Stromsburg, April 15, 1930. She was the mother of six children. Her father was a blacksmith, and her mother died when she was but five years old.

Mr. Hallquist attended public and business college. Coming to Nebraska 55 years ago, he has been a successful farmer most of that time. He is a Democrat and holds membership in Stromsburg Lodge No. 126 of the Masons, and the Nebraskana Society.

He was united in marriage with Clara Josephine Anderson, September 9, 1903, at Osceola, Nebraska. She was born at Stromsburg, August 22, 1882, the daughter of Mr. and Mrs. Alfred Anderson. Her father was an early pioneer and harness maker. They have two children, Leonard E., born April 9, 1905; and Clayton D., born May 20, 1919. Residence: Stromsburg.

Lloyd Dickson Halsted

Lloyd D. Halsted was born at Tecumseh, Johnson County, Nebraska, January 1, 1891, the son of Charles Henry and Ann Ellen (Adams) Halsted. His father, who is retired from active business, is a member of the Grand Army of the Republic, having served full time in the Civil War.

Mr. Halsted, who is an educator, received his early education in the Tecumseh schools where he was graduated in 1908. He was graduated in 1912 from the University of Nebraska, receiving his A. B. He is a member of Phi Beta Kappa. For some time he was a student at the University of Southern California where he was a member of Gamma Epsilon fraternity, and in 1927 he was awarded the M. A. degree at Columbia University. A resident of Nebraska all his life, he has held various educational and executive positions in the public schools. He was superintendent of schools at Hendley, Nebraska, 1912-15; superintendent at Shubert, 1915-17; principal at Tecumseh, 1919-23; and since 1923 has been superintendent at Tecumseh.

During the late war Mr. Halsted was a corporal, bat-

tery E. 338 field artillery in the American Expeditionary Forces. He is a member of the American Legion and since 1923 has been a member of the Kiwanis Club, and is a Mason. He is affiliated with the Methodist Church. Residence: Tecumseh.

Eugene Frederick Ham

Eugene Frederick Ham, grain dealer, was born at Benkelman, Nebraska, March 21, 1832, son of Joseph Oscar and Martha Emmeline (Thompson) Ham.

The father was born in Maquoketa, Iowa, April 19, 1854, and was a pioneer homesteader in Dundy County Nebraska, in 1885. He acquired large land holdings there and has been prominent in community affairs for many years. His ancestors have been in America for several generations. His wife, Martha, was born in St. Joseph, Missouri, on June 4, 1860. She was a typical pioneer mother. Her ancestors have taken part in every war in which the United States has been engaged.

Mr. Ham attended the public school in Dundy County, Nebraska, and was graduated in 1908. In 1912, he was graduated from Benkelman High School, and the following year attended the University of Nebraska.

In 1914, he became associated with the Kellogg Grain Company of Benkelman, Nebraska, and has since been a partner in the firm of the Independent Elevators with elevators at Benkelman, Parks and Doane, Nebraska. He also has interests in various other business concerns. His politics are independent.

In April, 1917, he was married to Edna McEvoy of Benkelman, Nebraska, at McCook, Nebraska. Mrs. Ham died at Benkelman, Nebraska, January 15, 1920. They have one son, John Everett, born March 7, 1918.

On December 30, 1926, Mr. Hahn was married to Hazel Frank of Minden, Nebraska, at Kansas City, Missouri. Mrs. Ham attended Hastings College in 1919-21; 3 summer terms at the University of Nebraska, and 2 at the University of Colorado.

Mr. Ham is a member of the Elks, and the Woodmen of the World. He is a member of the Lions Club being a director, which he assisted in organizing in 1931. A member of the Chamber of Commerce (1925-1932), he is an active Red Cross worker and assists in every welfare drive. From 1920 until 1925, he served on the local school board, in the capacity of secretary and at the present time is a member of the Parent Teachers Association. He enjoys golf, and is a part owner of a nine hole golf course. Residence: Benkelman.

Joseph O. Ham

Joseph O. Ham, retired farmer and stock raiser, was borne at Maquoketa, Iowa, April 19, 1854, son of John and Justina (Pool) Ham.

His father was born in Canterbury, New Hampshire, February 14, 1828, and died at Maryville, Missouri, March 1, 1920; his parents came from England. He was a farmer. His wife was born at Cuyahoga Falls, Ohio, August 13, 1835, and died at Maryville, Missouri, October 28, 1925. Her father was born in Connecticut.

Mr. Ham attended the rural schools of Nodaway County, Missouri, and the city schools of Maryville. He is a Republican and has been county assessor of Dundy County from 1908 to 1912. Coming to Dundy County in a covered wagon with Mrs. Ham's brother, J. L. Thompson, in 1886, he located on a homestead about four miles northeast of Benkelman where he made his home until April, 1919. Mr. and Mrs. Ham have spent all of their time in Benkelman and vicinity, with the exception of two months while visiting relatives in Missouri, since locating there. Mr. Ham started with three cows and a calf and in 1902 had increased his herd to more than 400 head. On March 20, 1901, a blizzard struck the country, lasting for three days and nights before abating. The loss in cattle was terrific, in some cases a total loss, and in 30 years to the day another blizzard of two days of the same intensity visited the country with no serious loss of cattle, but with the loss of the life of a school boy, Boyd Edwards, in an effort to reach his home from school a distance of about one half a mile. Mr. Ham recalls when, speaking of drouth, that from August, 1892 until May 1895 there was no rainfall other than a light sprinkle. He requests that the readers understand that that condition did not always exist as many good crops and years have been experienced by him.

He is a member of the First Methodist Episcopal Church, the Red Cross, the Ancient Free and Accepted Masons, and for 28 years was a member of rural school boards and for nine years of city school boards.

His marriage to Martha E. Thompson was solemnized near Gilford, Missouri, December 30, 1877. Mrs. Ham was born near St. Joseph, June 4, 1860. There are six children, Roy A., born near Maryville, Missouri, May 6, 1880, married Jennie M. Roberts, of Benkelman, Nebraska, June 17, 1908; Ray O., born near Gilford, Missouri, March 20, 1882, married Nellie Foster; Grace E., born near Gilford, Missouri, September 23, 1883, married Chesney C. Foster; Earl D., born near Gilford, October 1, 1885, married Mayme Bond; John P., born near Benkelman, Nebraska, February 13, 1889, married Elva Finch; and Eugene F., born near Benkelman, March 21, 1892, was first married to Edna McEvoy of Benkelman, Nebraska. His present wife is Hazel Frank, to whom he was married December 30, 1926. She was born at Norman, Nebraska. Residence: Benkelman. (Photograph in Album).

William Hamann

William Hamann was born near Berlin, Germany, October 10, 1852, the son of John and Dorothy (Clasen) Hamann. His father, who was a carpenter and farmer, was born near Berlin, September, 1820, and died at Crete, Nebraska, November, 1905; he came to America in 1866, and in 1869 homesteaded in Nebraska. His mother was born near Berlin, February, 1821, came with her husband to America, and died at Crete, November, 1906.

Mr. Hamann, a retired farmer, has lived in Nebraska for 62 years, and has always made the welfare of his community his object, having taken part in church activities with the German Congregational Church at Wilber.

On July 3, 1906, he was united in marriage with Minne Scherling at Crete. Mrs. Hamann was born near Berlin, September 14, 1875. Their children are: Arthur, born August 29, 1907; and Gunther, born August 24, 1908. Residence: Wilber.

Robert Black Hamer

Grandson of one of Nebraska's most illustrious judges, Francis G. Hamer, Justice of the Supreme Court, Robert Black Hamer is the third generation to follow the legal profession. He was born at Kearney, Nebraska, April 22, 1906, the son of Thomas Franis Hamer, who was born at Kearney, November 6, 1877. He is of Scotch, Irish and English descent, whose ancestors on both sides came to America about 1720. He is engaged in the practice of law at Kerney. His wife, Ada Chesdey (Black) Hamer, was born at Kearney, January 22, 1878, and died there September 20, 1906. Her ancestors came to the United States about 1800.

Robert B. Hamer was graduated from Kearney High School in 1924, and received his LL. B., *cum laude*, from the University of Nebraska on June 7, 1930. He attended Nebraska State Teachers College from September, 1924-May, 1927. He received the Order of the Coif his senior year at the university, and is a member of Phi Delta Phi.

Upon his admission to the bar he became associated in practice with the law firm of Brogan, Ellick and Van

Dusen, of Omaha. He is a member of the Barristers Club of Omaha, and the Nebraska Bar Association. He is a member also of The Nebraskana Society. During 1929-30 he was associate editor of the *Nebraska Law Bulletin*.

He was married to Edith Lorene Marts at Lincoln, November 1, 1930. Mrs. Hamer was born at Wilsonville, Nebraska, March 15, 1907, and is of Dutch, French and English descent, and is distantly related to Generals Grant and Sheridan.

Mr. Hamer is a member of the Omaha University Club. He likes to go to football games, and enjoys hunting and fishing. Residence: Lincoln.

Agnes Elmore Hamilton

Agnes E. Hamilton was born at Rushville, Nebraska, February 2, 1893, the daughter of John Patrick and Neceity Philomenia (Cook) Elmore. Her father, who was born at Weston, Missouri, March 17, 1863, is a railroad contractor. Her mother, born at Oceana, Wyoming County, West Virginia, March 17, 1866, was the daughter of pioneer settlers and slave owners in West Virginia.

Mrs. Hamilton received her education at St. Agnes Academy at Alliance, Nebraska. She is now president of the American Legion Auxiliary at Omaha, Unit Number 1, is a member of the Red Cross, and holds membership in the Nebraskana Society. She is a member of the Royal Highlanders, the North Omaha Woman's Club, North High Parent-Teachers' Association, and Holy Angels Parents-Teachers' Association, and is affiliated with Holy Angels Catholic Church. Her hobby is music. Residence: Omaha.

Edward Joseph Hamilton

A resident of Nebraska, since 1891, Edward Joseph Hamilton was born near Iowa City, Iowa, October 17, 1875, son of Cornelius Piper and Clarinda Jane (Hamilton) Hamilton. Cornelius Hamilton was born in Washington County, Iowa, March 29, 1855, of Scotch-Irish ancestry; while his wife was born in Johnson County, Iowa, February 15, 1855, of Scotch ancestry.

Edward Joseph Hamilton was graduated from Wilsonville High School in 1897, and in 1905 was graduated from the Creighton College of Pharmacy. He is a registered pharmacist in Nebraska, and followed that work in Omaha, about one year, and at Wilsonville, for seven years. For a number of years he has been in the real estate and investment business at Wilsonville.

On July 5, 1910, he was married to Helen Lucinda Johnson at Wray, Colorado. Mrs. Hamilton, who is Scotch-Irish, was born at Rensselaer, Indiana, April 8, 1872.

Mr. Hamilton is a Republican, a member of the Wilsonville Commercial Club, the Modern Woodmen of America, the Masons, Knights Templar and Shrine. He is a life member of the Nebraskana Society. His hobby is reading. Residence: Wilsonville. (Photograph in Album).

Frank James Hamilton

Frank James Hamilton, telephone executive, was born at St. Edward, Nebraska, September 27, 1886, son of Ira McClain and Clara May (Watson) Hamilton.

The father, born in Carlisle, Pennsylvania, January 1, 1859, is now retired and resides at McCook. He started the first newspapers in St. Edward and in Plainview, Nebraska. He is of Dutch and Scotch-Irish descent. The mother, born in Bellevue, Nebraska, January 10, 1865, of Swedish descent, resides in McCook.

Mr. Hamilton attended public school to the eleventh grade at Plainview quitting to go to work for the Nebraska Telephone Company. He started for them at Norfolk as a collector, has been troubleman, wire chief, and manager at various places and in various states, namely: Belle Fourche, South Dakota; Lexington, Nebraska; Wood River, Nebraska; Sheridan and Buffalo, Wyoming; Denver, Elizabeth and Yampa, Colorado; Lincoln, Nebraska; Wayne, Nebraska; Minot, South Dakota; Rugby, North Dakota; Drake, North Dakota; Kenmare, North Dakota; Kalispel, Montana; Ainsworth, Nebraska, O'Neill, Nebraska, and West Point, Nebraska.

At the present time he is local manager for the Northwestern Bell Telephone Company.

On February 9, 1919, he was married to Mabel Cart at Kenmare, North Dakota. Mrs. Hamilton was born at New Virginia, Iowa, August 14, 1894, descended from early settlers in Virginia who served in the Revolution. There are four children, Kenneth, born December 23, 1919; Lenora, born September 4, 1921; Fredric, born March 29, 1923; and Beryl, born July 19, 1924.

For three years Mr. Hamilton held the rank of corporal in the Nebraska National Guard. Since 1929 he has been chairman of the first aid and life saving committee of the Red Cross. He is a member of the First Baptist Church, the Chamber of Commerce, and the Masons. He was secretary of the Southwest Nebraska Historical Society for one year and helped to organize it in 1928. Since 1929 he has been a member of the board of directors of the Young Men's Christian Association. From May 1925, until July, 1930, he was secretary of the Rotary Club of McCook and from July, 1930 until July, 1931, was its president. Mr. Hamilton instigated the idea of inviting a central gathering of Boy Scouts in McCook in 1924, from Benkelman, Stratton, Trenton in Nebraska and Norton and Hoxie in Kansas. His hobby is gardening. Residence: McCook.

Fred Franklin Hamilton

Fred Franklin Hamilton, lumberman, was born at Benton, Tennessee, January 3, 1895, and for the past 21 years has resided in Nebraska.

His father, William Chancey Hamilton, was born in Indiana, January 28, 1869, and died at Cleveland, Tennessee, March 8, 1908. His father was a farmer, who served as sheriff of Polk County, Tennessee. His wife, Cora Ann Hatcher, was born at Benton, Tennessee, February 24, 1873, and died at Cleveland, December 4, 1906.

Mr. Hamilton attended public school until 1910. For the past 11 years, he has been manager of the Bridgeport Lumber Company. He is a Republican, a Methodist, and is worshipful master of Masonic Lodge No. 285, and is a member of the Parent-Teachers' Association, and the Bridgeport Country Club. His favorite sport is volleyball, while his hobbies are hunting and fishing.

On April 8, 1917, he was married to Zoa Belle McLaughlin at Stockville. Mrs. Hamilton was born at Moorefield, Nebraska, January 16, 1897. Mrs. Hamilton is vice president of the Parent-Teachers' Association and a member of the Eastern Star. She is the daughter of Robert and Annie (Wood) McLaughlin. To them were born five children, four of whom are living, William Mervin, born February 22, 1918; John Colby, born August 11, 1919; Elizabeth Ann, born June 13, 1921; Fred Albert, born January 31, 1923, who died February 12, 1929; and Mary Lee, born October 20, 1925. Residence: Bridgeport.

Lee Thomas Hamilton

Lee Thomas Hamilton, druggist, was born at Burchard, Nebraska, August 20, 1894, son of William Clemence and Evelyn (Logan) Hamilton. The father, who was born in Clay County, Illinois, of Scotch-Irish ancestry, was county judge of Dundy County, Nebraska, prior to his death at Benkelman, March 31, 1924. His wife, Evelyn Logan, was a native of Pennsylvania, born November 30, 1870 at Pittsburg, who died at Benkelman, February 11, 1905.

In 1910 Mr. Hamilton was graduated from Benkelman public school and in 1924 the Benkelman High

School. At the present time he is a member of the firm of the Hamilton Drug Company, and a co-partner in various real estate holdings. A Republican, he served as a member of the city council four years and was mayor four years.

He was married to Maude Lucille Davis at Sterling, Colorado, April 10, 1915, and to them one daughter was born, Doris Evelyn, on October 16, 1916. Mrs. Hamilton was born at Riverton, Iowa, January 10, 1894. She has always been active in the affairs of the Woman's Club, but is most interested in the affairs of her home and family.

Mr. Hamilton's religious affiliation is with the United Presbyterian Church of Benkelman. He is a member of the Chamber of Commerce, the Masons, Justice Lodge No. 180 of Benkelman, the Red Cross, and the Nebraskana Society. He enjoys playing golf and watching football games. His hobby is reading newspapers. Residence: Benkelman.

Maurine Hamilton

Maurine Hamilton is a native of Omaha, born October 6, 1894. Her father, Arthur H. Murdock, was born at Penn Yan, New York, August 13, 1863. He came to Nebraska in 1878 and to Omaha forty-three years ago. He is a prominent lawyer and business man. Her mother, Ana Merrill Murdock, was born at Farmington, Illinois, October 18, 1870. She is of English ancestry and is active in the civic life of Omaha and in club work.

Mrs. Hamilton was graduated from South Omaha High School in 1912, and received her B. A. from the University of Nebraska in 1916. On December 22, 1918 she was united in marriage to Charles William Hamilton, Jr., at Washington, D. C. Mr. Hamilton, who was born at Omaha, August 12, 1890, is a descendant of Governor Cummins, first territorial governor of Nebraska. He was graduated from Creighton University in 1913, and served as captain with the 127th Field Artillery during the World War. He is a member of the firm of Hamilton and Company, insurance and bonds. Mr. and Mrs. Hamilton have one daughter, Mae Louise, born April 22, 1923.

Mrs. Hamilton is a Republican and a member of the executive board of the Omaha League of Women Voters. She is also a member of St. Cecilia's Cathedral. Mr. Hamilton has received the papal decoration of Knight of St. Gregory, of which there are only a few in America. They are members of the Omaha Club and the Omaha Country Club. Residence: Omaha.

Thomas Price Hamilton

Thomas Price Hamilton, stock farmer and banker, was born in Atchinson County, Missouri, March 3, 1862, son of Thomas Jefferson and Sarah Elizabeth (Buster) Hamilton. The father was born in Hamilton County, Kentucky, June 8, 1829, and died at Rockport, Missouri, July 11, 1889. He was a farmer. His wife, Sarah, was born in the Town of Charles, in Johnson County, Missouri, February 20, 1836, and died at Rockport, January 14, 1913.

Mr. Hamilton attended public schools and since has engaged in farming and stock raising. At the present time he is the owner of extensive farming interests and is president of the Citizens State Bank at Thedford. He is an independent Democrat.

On January 25, 1888, he was married to Lucy at Rockport. Mrs. Hamilton was born at Rockport, January 3, 1868. They have two children, Jesse Earl, born December 24, 1888, and Lloyd Lester, born October 12, 1897.

Mr. Hamilton has been a resident of Nebraska for 46 years. He is a member of the Nebraska State Historical Society and the Nebraskana Society. He is an agnostic. Residence: Thedford.

Irwin Allen Hammer

Irwin Allen Hammer is a native of Missouri, born at Mount Vernon, June 5, 1894. His father, William Huston Hammer, was born at Mount Vernon, September 27, 1866, and is the son of Allen and Sarah (Toliver) Hammer. William Hammer married Lula Fay Hillhouse, born at Mount Vernon on October 2, 1874. She is the daughter of Irwin Hillhouse, and a granddaughter of Dob Hillhouse. On the maternal side her grandparents were William and Ellen (Shook) Allen.

In 1912 Irwin A. Hammer was graduated from Mount Vernon High School and entered Park College, Parkville, Missouri, where he received his A. B. in 1920. His studies were interrupted by the World War, when he enlisted on April 20, 1917, with the Fifth Field Artillery. He was transferred to the medical department of the Fifth Field Artillery and was promoted to sergeant of the medical department and transferred to the Sixth Field Artillery in 1918. He served with the American Expeditionary Forces for twenty-six months and was discharged in September, 1919. While abroad he attended the University of Toulouse (France) one quarter.

During 1920 and 1921 he was superintendent of schools at Knob Noster, Missouri, and at Copeland, Kansas, 1921-22, Wilmore, Kansas, 1922-24, Cawker City, Kansas, 1924-27. In that year he received his M. A. from the University of Colorado. He attended the University of Minnesota for one year 1927-28, working toward his Ph. D.

While at the University of Minnesota he was an instructor, and coming to Omaha, in 1928, he was made head of the department of education and sociology of the University of Omaha. In 1929 he was made head of the department of education, and is now dean of the department.

He was married to Annie Catherine Smith at Knob Noster, June 1, 1921. Mrs. Hammer was born at Warrenburg, Missouri, July 16, 1901, and is the daughter of Joseph J. and Ida D. (Allen) Smith. They have two children, Margie Helen, born May 28, 1922, and Donald Irwin, born April 22, 1926.

Mr. Hammer was active in track at high school and college, and a member of the debate team at Park College. He is a member of Kappa Delta Pi, Pi Gamma Mu and Alpha Kappa Delta, and is honorary member and faculty sponsor of Alpha Sigma Lambda at the University of Omaha.

He is a member and elder in the Miller Park Presbyterian Church, a member of the Parent-Teachers' Association, the Young Men's Christian Association and a member of the educational committee of the Nebraska Covered Wagon Troop of the Boy Scouts. Active in civic work he was captain of a Community Chest team in the 1930 drive, and is a member of the Chamber of Commerce.

His educational organizations include the Nebraska State Teachers' Association, the National Education Association and the National Society for the Advancement of Educational Sociology. His favorite sports are golf, basketball, handball and swimming. He is fond of reading, hiking and woodworking. His clubs are the University Faculty Club, and the Birchwood Club. He is a Mason. Residence: Omaha.

James Waverly Hammond

James Waverly Hammond was born at Exeter, Nebraska, May 30, 1903, the son of Henry George and Ada (Bryd) Hammond. His father, who is a barber, was born at Exeter, March 27, 1879, of Scotch and Irish parentage. His mother, whose ancestry is English and French, was born at Lonsdale, Illinois, May 16, 1880. Her great uncle, Colonel Kilibrew, served under General Lee.

Mr. Hammond attended the public school at Exeter, and in 1924 was graduated from the high school at Hugo, Colorado. He was engaged in the barber business at Exeter, 1916-20, and at Downey, California, 1921-22. In

1924 he served as deputy county clerk of Fillmore County, Nebraska, was unsuccessful candidate for county judge in 1927, and in 1930 was elected county attorney on the Republican ticket. He was bookkeeper for the Economy Paint Mills at Geneva, 1928, and was employed in the Hiatt Barber Shop at Geneva, for a time in 1929.

He is a member of the Nebraskana Society and is a Scottish Rite Mason. His sports include: golfing, hunting and fishing. On December 25, 1927, he was united in marriage with Rose Lela Peterson at Geneva. Mrs. Hammond, who was a teacher before her marriage, was born at Geneva, April 8, 1905; her ancestry is Swedish and Irish. Their two children are: James Waverly, born January 30, 1929, and Paul David, born August 4, 1931. Residence: Geneva. (Photograph in Album).

James William Hammond

A distinguished editor and publisher of Nebraska, James William Hammond has lived in this state all his life. He was born in Nemaha County, Nebraska, April 25, 1872, the son of Martha Jane (Hurst) and Robert Hammond. His father, a farmer, was born in Pike County, Illinois, January 19, 1839, and died at Freedom, Nebraska, September 10, 1900. His mother, whose ancestry is English and Irish, was born in Brown County, Illinois, October 19, 1843, and died at Versailles, Illinois, September 10, 1875.

Mr. Hammond was graduated from the Cook High School, Cook, Nebraska, 1893, and later attended the Peru State Normal College. He has been editor and publisher of the *Cook Courier*, the *Cambridge Clarion* and the *Fairbury Times*, all in Nebraska, and at this time is editor and publisher of the *Holdrege Citizen*. He holds membership in the Nebraska Press Association, the Holdrege Chamber of Commerce, Red Cross, the Nebraska State Historical Society, Nebraskana Society, and the Rotary Club, of which he was president in 1925. He is a Mason and an Odd Fellow.

His marriage to Charlotte Luella Willcox occurred at Cook, February 8, 1899. Mrs. Hammond was born at Shenandoah, Iowa, April 19, 1882. They have two children: Opal, born September 30, 1902, who married Warren A. Girch; and Dean, born December 4, 1907. Opal was graduated from Cambridge High School, completed a course at the Peru State Teachers College, and taught school for six years prior to her marriage. Dean was graduated from the University of Nebraska, where he received Phi Beta Kappa honors, was editor in chief of the *Daily Nebraskan* during his senior year; he is connected with the Lincoln office of the United Press Association at this time.

In 1917 and 1919, Mr. Hammond was a member of the Nebraska State Senate, representing the 21st district. He is a progressive Republican. Residence: Holdrege. (Photograph in Album).

Raymond Winfred Hammond

A printer and Publisher for many years, Raymond Winfred Hammond was born at Fremont, July 25, 1880. He is the son of Frank and Nettie (Hammer) Hammond, the former born in Marshall County, Iowa, July 9, 1858. Frank Hammond is president of the Crystal Refrigerator Company, the Hammond Printing Company, the Union National Bank and the Equitable Building and Loan Association. He is of Quaker descent. His wife, Nettie, was born in Henry County, Iowa, January 9, 1858, and died at Fremont, March 5, 1931. She was also of Quaker descent, and was a member of the Woman's Club and active in church work.

Raymond W. Hammond attended Fremont public school, and was graduated from Fremont High School in 1898. During 1900-02, he attended Armour Institute of Technology. After attending college he returned to Fremont, in 1902, to take a position in the office of the Hammond Printing Company, founded by his father. In 1906, when the latter took over the management of the Sure Hatch Incubator Company, now the Crystal Refrigerator Company, he became manager of the publishing house. He is now vice president and manager of the Hammond Printing Company, commercial printers and publishers of the *Fremont Tribune* since 1879. He is also a director of the Crystal Refrigerator Company.

On December 15, 1903, Mr. Hammond was married to Frances Arms Misner, at Chicago. Mrs. Hammond was born at Muskegon, Michigan, June 25, 1883, and is of Scotch-Canadian descent. There are two sons, Egbert, born August 24, 1912, and Raymond, Jr., born April 1, 1917.

Mr. Hammond is a Republican. He is a member of the First Methodist Episcopal Church of Fremont, the Masons, and the Young Men's Christian Association. He is president of the Nebraska Daily Newspaper Association, past president of the Fremont Chamber of Commerce (1921) and past president of the Nebraska Manufacturers Association (1927). He was first president of the local Rotary Club (1919-21). During the World War he was active in Liberty Loan and Red Cross work. His sports are golf and fishing, and his hobby is reading. Residence: Fremont.

William James Hammond

William James Hammond, lawyer, was born at Omaha, February 7, 1890, son of Arthur John and Sarah (Fitzsimmons) Hammond. He attended public and high school at O'Neill and St. Thomas College, St. Paul, Minnesota, and since 1914 has been actively engaged in the practice of law.

On June 18, 1913, he was married to Lillian Elizabeth Carlon at O'Neill. She was born there August 28, 1890. They have three children, William, born April 8, 1914; Mary, born August 26, 1915; and Harriett, born June 17, 1920.

Mr. Hammond is a member of the Nebraska State Bar Association, St. Patricks Catholic Church, and is affiliated with the Democratic party. He enjoys golf and fishing. Residence: O'Neill.

Edward Finley Hancock

Edward Finley Hancock, pioneer farmer of Nebraska was born at Confidence, Iowa, October 24, 1867, the son of Marion A. and Nancy (Neal) Hancock. His father was born at Gosport, Indiana, May 22, 1842, and died at Lincoln, Nebraska, April 8, 1924; he was a farmer. His mother was born at Plainfield, Indiana, May 4, 1844, and died at Benkelman, Nebraska, August 10, 1924.

Mr. Hancock was a student at Christian College, Fairfield, Nebraska, 1888-89. He is a member of the Church of Christ and holds membership in the Nebraskana Society. On December 5, 1894, he was married to Belle Tingley at Fairfield. Mrs. Hancock, who was born at Rushville, Indiana, August 19, 1870, is descended from Palmer Tingley who came to America in 1614.

Their three children are George T., born June 3, 1896, who married Anna Irene Baker; Grace, born October 13, 1897, who married Elmo G. McReynolds; and Marjorie, born December 5, 1899, who married Joseph Wesley Hall. George is a motor mechanic, Elmo McReynolds is the owner and operator of funeral coaches, while Joseph Hall is a traveling salesman. Residence: Fairfield.

James Waldo Hancock

James W. Hancock, stockman and farm implement dealer, has lived in this state all his life. He was born at Tekamah, Burt County, Nebraska, October 16, 1886, the son of James Kinnison and Sarah Etta (Rankin) Han-

Pennsylvania, December 6, 1842, and died at Tekamah, July 5, 1923, was a farmer; J. K. Hancock served in Company E, 149th Pennsylvania Volunteers, Bucktail Brigade, during the Civil War. His mother was born at Curvensville, Anderson County, Pennsylvania, May 12, 1856, of Scotch-Irish parentage. She has always been active in church work.

James W. Hancock attended country school in Burt County, and was a student at Fremont Normal College. He is the owner of a cattle and hog feeding ranch and operates a 320 acre farm. He is the owner of an implement business at Herman, Tekamah, and Blair, Nebraska, and is manager of the Nicholas Oil Corporation Bulk Station at Herman.

A member of the Red Cross, from 1923-27, he served on the local school board. During the war he was in charge of loan drives in his community. He is a Republican. He holds membership in the Nebraskana Society.

He has been a member of the city council 12 successive years, acted as city treasurer 10 years, and was first implement dealer in Nebraska to give free delivery of farm equipment.

His marriage to Blanche Wilmina Smith was solemnized at Omaha, Nebraska, October 26, 1908. Mrs. Hancock was born of Scotch-Irish parents at Omaha, January 13, 1888. Their children are: Paul, born July 26, 1910; Harold, a junior at the University of Nebraska, born July 16, 1912; Lee, born September 16, 1914; and Lucille, born March 20, 1916. Residence: Herman.

Roy Hancock

Roy Hancock, son of James Kinnison and Sarah Etta (Rankin) Hancock, was born at Tekamah, Nebraska, May 24, 1899. James Hancock was a native of Clearfield, Pennsylvania, born December 6, 1842, who died at Tekamah, July 5, 1923. A farmer, he was of Scotch-Irish descent, and served four years in the Civil War. His wife, Sarah Etta, was born at Smithsburgh, Indiana County, Pennsylvania, May 12, 1859. She is of Scotch descent.

Educated first in the Tekamah public schools, Roy Hancock was graduated from the high school in May, 1918, and has since been engaged as a retail merchant. He is now a member of the firm of Hancock Implement Company of Tekamah. On February 12, 1927, he was united in marriage to Edith Van Patter of Neligh. Mrs. Hancock, who was born June 16, 1899, was a Domestic Science teacher prior to her marriage, and is of Danish descent. Their marriage was solemnized at Omaha.

Mr. Hancock is a Republican. He served in the World War, and is a member of the American Legion and the Red Cross. His religious affiliation is with the Methodist Church at Tekamah. He is a member of the Chamber of Commerce, the Masons and the Lions Club. Residence: Tekamah.

R. K. Hancock

R. K. Hancock was born in Tekamah, Burt County, Nebraska, on August 1, 1884, the son of James K. Hancock and Sarah E. (Rankin) Hancock. His father was born in Clearfield, Pennsylvania, in 1842, and died in Tekamah, on July 5, 1923. Sarah E. Rankin was also born in Clearfield, Pennsylvania, on May 27, 1859.

Mr. Hancock attended the public schools and the Fremont Normal College, he then attended the Fremont Business College. On December 5, 1911, at Tekamah, he was married to Belle Smith, daughter of William D. and Mary (Dudgeon) Smith. She was born February 14, 1891. To this union five children were born; Kenneth, March 3, 1912, Leonard, March 7, 1917, Marjorie, September 4, 1919, Raymond, March 7, 1924, and R. K. Junior, August 26, 1927. Kenneth is employed by the Burt County Herald.

On February 1, 1910, Mr. Hancock accepted the position as bookkeeper in the Farmer's State Bank in Tekamah, was later elected assistant cashier in the Burt County State Bank, and in 1914 he was elected cashier, which position he holds at present. He is president of the Burt County Bankers' Association and president of the Lions Club.

Mr. Hancock was active in all of the World War Liberty loan drives, is a member of the Red Cross, and of the Home Guards. He is affiliated with the Methodist Church; is secretary of the board of education and holds membership in the Chamber of Commerce, and in the Nebraskana Society. Residence: Tekamah.

George J. Hand

George J. Hand, one of Nebraska's outstanding physicians and surgeons, was born at Vermillion, South Dakota, August 2, 1875, and came to Hay Springs, Nebraska, with his parents in 1885, in a covered wagon before the railroad was built or the town located. All freight at that time was transported by wagon trains from Valentine and Sidney.

His father, Redmond Hand, was born in County Roscommon, Ireland, January 31, 1840. He was hotel proprietor at Vermillion, until the flood of 1881, and later was a railroad contractor, farmer and rancher. He came to the United States in 1850, and died at Hay Springs, on May 16, 1916. His wife, Mary Ann Keough, was born at Gelena, Illinois, February 2, 1840, and died at Alliance, June 14, 1917. She was a devoted pioneer wife and mother.

Dr. Hand attended various schools in Iowa, Nebraska, Wyoming, and Colorado, and was graduated from high school at Hay Springs in 1897. He attended Chadron Academy in 1898, and received the degree of Doctor of Medicine from the University of Iowa, in 1904, where he served his internship. He was a member of the Hannemannian Society, and secured his internship by competitive examination. While at Chadron Academy, he participated in the annual field contest in 1898, winning 14 first places and two second places out of a 19 event contest. Dr. Hand was at Vermillion, South Dakota, during the historical flood of 1881, in which the whole town was destroyed. He has been a prominent resident of Nebraska for the past 48 years, and has had a very interesting and colorful career.

His first marriage was to Mame Laravae at Alliance, in 1908. She was born at Whitehall, New York, in 1877, and died at Boise, Idaho, in April 1925. She was a school teacher, prior to her marriage. Four children were born to them, Frances G., on October 26, 1909, who died March 19, 1913; Helen, born November 2, 1911; Arch, born August 7, 1913; and Odette, born December 16, 1920.

On December 31, 1917, Dr. Hand was married to Nellie M. Luten of Omaha. They have two children, Darlene, born December 1, 1919; and Shirley Nell, born August 21, 1926. She is the daughter of Russell and Florence Belle (Lewis) Luten.

Dr. Hand has ben in active practice since 1904. He is ex-president of St. Joseph's Hospital of Alliance Nebraska, former president of the Box Butte County Medical Association, former president of the 12th Councillor District Medical Society of Nebraska, and during the World War, was on the advisory board. For some time, he was health officer of the city of Alliance.

For the past six years, Dr. Hand has had a class in boxing. He has 100 boys, and no charges are made for pupils from 7 to 21 years of age. His hobbies are athletics and children. Residence: Alliance.

Jiles William Haney

Jiles Haney, educator and chairman of the department of mechanical engineering at the University of Nebraska, was born at Guin, Alabama, November 17, 1886. His father, Willis Jiles Haney, who is a farmer, was born of Scotch Irish parentage in Alabama, in 1867. Emma Frances (McDonald) Haney, his mother, whose ancestry is Scotch-Irish, was born in Georgia, in 1868.

Professor Haney was graduated from the high school at Bloomfield, Missouri, in 1908. He holds the following degrees; B. S., in mechanical engineering at the University of Missouri, in 1913; M. C., 1914; M. A., 1915. He was a student and teacher at Pennsylvania State College, 1916-18, where his graduate course was completed. He was valedictorian of his senior class in high school; was a member of Sigma Xi, and Sigma Tau, at the University of Nebraska, 1920; and was president of the junior class at the University of Missouri. He is a member of Theta Chi at the University of Nebraska, and is now faculty adviser of this fraternity.

He was instructor in the mechanical engineering department at Pennsylvania State College, 1916-18; was assistant professor at the University of Nebraska, 1919-20; was associate professor there, 1920-26; and since 1926 has been professor of this department. Since 1927 he has been chairman of the mechanical engineering department at the University of Nebraska.

He is the co-author of: *Transmission of Heat Through Boiler Tubes.* He was married to Mary Aileen Martin at Lees Summit, Missouri, June 11, 1916. Mrs. Haney was born at Lees Summit, November 25, 1894. They have a daughter, Mary Maxine, born March 20, 1919.

During the World War Professor Haney was civilian instructor in the Army Auto-Mechanic and Truck Driving School at Pennsylvania State College; has been captain of the Reserve Officers Corps, 1925-30; and is a Major of the latter organization at this time. He is a member of the American Society of Mechanical Engineers; the Society for the Promotion of Engineering Education; and the Inter-professional Men's Institute. He was president of the Engineer's Club of Lincoln, 1928.

In 1930 he served as president of the Optimist Club. He is a member of the Open Forum Club; the Hiram Club; the Nebraska Academy of Science; and in 1931 was made president of the Nebraska-Kansas section of the Society for the Promotion of Engineering Education. His religious affiliation is with the Presbyterian Church of Lincoln. He is a member of the Masons, Scottish Rite and Shrine. His social clubs are the Shrine Country Club and the University Faculty Dancing Club. He enjoys golfing, camping, and fishing. Professor Haney is politically inclined toward Democratic principles. Residence: Lincoln.

William Porter Haney

William Porter Haney, ear, nose, and throat specialist, was born in Omaha, February 5, 1877, son of Edwin and Inez A. (Porter) Haney.

Dr. Haney received his early education in the public schools of Omaha, and was awarded his medical degree from the Rush Medical College. He was married to Josephine Elizabeth Williams at Omaha, December 9, 1916.

Dr. Haney is a Republican. He has been in active practice since his admission in 1903, and is a member of the Douglas County, the American, and the Nebraska State Medical Associations. He is also a member of the American Academy of Oto-laryngology. He is a Mason, Knight Templar, and a member of the Shrine. Residence: Omaha.

William Thomas Haney

William Thomas Haney, leading rancher of Arthur County, was born at Sullivan, Illinois, August 30, 1862, and came with his parents to the sandhills of Nebraska in 1872. His father, Isaac, was born in Illinois, and died at Moore, Nebraska. He was a rancher. His wife, Eliza Duty, was born in Moline, Illinois, and died at Mullen, Nebraska. She was of Irish descent. Her father was killed by the Indians near Hebron in the early 1860's.

Mr. Haney has been a rancher for many years, and has always been prominent in his community in Democratic politics. He was married on November 3, 1896, to Sarah Gibson at Tryon, Nebraska. Mrs. Haney was born in Keokok, Iowa, October 31, 1873. To them were born six children: Violet, born July 24, 1898, who married Edgar B. Deidel; Lulu, born March 19, 1900, who married Clyde D. Wilson; Nancy, born November 25, 1901, who married Edward C. Frost; William, born September 23, 1902, who married Mary E. Morris; Fern, born November 25, 1906; and Roy, born March 31. Residence: Lena.

Herman Charles Hanke

Herman Charley Hanke, who has lived in Nebraska for the past 50 years, was born in Germany, December, 1872, the son of Anton and Mathilda (Beling) Hanke. His father, who was a farmer, was born in Germany and died there in 1878. His mother was born in Germany and died at Ithaca, Nebraska, June 2, 1915.

Mr. Hanke has always been a farmer near Ithaca. He was married to Minnie Zamson at Archer, Nebraska; she was born at Archer, April 27, 1876. They have the following children: Albert, born August 29, 1898; Mabel, born December 7, 1900; Mae, born December 7, 1900; Silas, born September 21, 1904; Mildred, born September 1, 1911; and Clarence, born September 6, 1913.

Mr. Hanke is a member of the Nebraskana Society, and is affiliated with the Evangelical Church. He has been treasurer of the school board of District No. 30 for the past 32 years and has been director of the board for the past three years. His hobby is reading. He is a Republican. Residence: Ithaca.

Firman James Hanks

Firman James Hanks, trucker, was born at Rising City, July 19, 1888, son of John Jeremiah and Emma Jane (Balliet) Hanks. His father, who was born in Iowa, September 15, 1863, is a farmer. His mother was born in Pennsylvania, January 16, 1867.

Mr. Hanks attended the public schools of Butler County, and since then has been a trucker. On June 3, 1924, he was married to Pauline Frances Beckoff at Thedford. Mrs. Hanks was born at Thedford, July 10, 1898. To them were born three children, two of whom are living, Floyd James, December 3, 1925; Carolyn May, February 14, 1928. Louise Mathilda, born December 23, 1926, died January 28, 1927.

Mr. Hanks is a Democrat. He served as a first class private in the 4th United States Infantry, 3rd Division, and was promoted to the rank of corporal. He participated in the Champagne-Marne Defensive, July 15-18, 1918, the Aisne-Marne Offensive, July 18-28, 1918, St. Mihiel Offensive, September 12-16, 1918, the Meuse-Argonne Offensive, September 26, 1918, Hill 204 West of Chateau Thierry, June 14-18, 1918, and from December 16, 1918 until August 9, 1919, served in the Army of Occupation. He is a charter member of Steidley-Kayton Post No. 230, of the American Legion. Residence: Thedford.

Stewart Bruce Hanley

Stewart Bduce Hanley, superintendent of schools at Grant, was born at Kearney, Nebraska, June 30, 1900, son of Benjamin Franklin and Leona Eel (Detamore) Hanley. The father was born at Homer, Illinois, and is a retired merchant of Irish descent.

Stewart Bruce Hanley was graduated from the eighth grade at Mount Lincoln School near Grand Junction, Colorado, and attended the public schools of Callaway, Nebraska, Lodi, Nebraska and completed his high school course at Kearney Normal School of which he is a graduate. The summer of 1925 he attended the University of Nebraska. He is a letter man in cross country events and a member of State Championship Team at Kearney State Teachers College in 1929.

On July 16, 1921, Mr. Hanley was married to Ada Emma Haring at Franklin. She was born at Riverton, Nebraska, March 11, 1899, and was a teacher in the public schools of Nebraska for ten years. They have a son, Theodore, born February 28, 1929.

Mr. Hanley is a Republican. He taught school one year at Hildreth, Nebraska, in charge of the seventh and eighth grades, and in charge of high school athletics and dramatics. He also served three years at Pleasanton, Nebraska, in the same capacity, and two years at Milburn as superintendent of consolidated school. For the past three years he has held the position of superintendent of the Grant grade school.

Mr. Hanley is a member of the Congregational Church at Grant, of the Nebraska State Teachers Association, and for three years was scoutmaster of Troop Number 1 at Grant. He enjoys golf, basketball, and hiking, reading and working with boys. Residence: Grant.

John W. Hann

John W. Hann, a resident of Nebraska since 1886, was born at Dansville, New York, September 9, 1862, son of C. F. and Nettie (Owen) Hann. His father, born at Danville, New York, was a wagon maker until his death in 1894 at Wayland, New York. His mother, born at Danville, New York, died at Wayland, New York, in 1925.

Mr. Hann attended public school at Wayland, New York, and for 42 years was the editor of the *Wauneta Breeze*. Disposing of his interests in the paper in 1920, he is now postmaster of Wauneta. He was one of the early settlers of Wauneta and remembers that when he first arrived there, the now flourishing little city had but one business building and a sod house. He has served many terms on the local town board and was mayor at different times. He has also served on the school board and is a member of the Ancient Order of United Woodmen. He was active on the Methodist Church board in the early days.

He was married to Grace M. Baker on October 8, 1888 at Wauneta, Nebraska. To them were born two children, Dorothy D., September 9, 1892; and Beulah A., September 16, 1900. Dorothy married C. A. Laurence of Fairmont, Nebraska, on August 9, 1910, at Wauneta. To them were born three children, Mildred D.; John Leland; and Rex Dean, Beulas married Fred W. Olmsted of Wauneta, January 18, 1918. They have one son, Fred Wayne. Residence: Wauneta.

Don Emerson Hanna

Don Emerson Hanna, cattle rancher, was born in Blaine County, Nebraska, March 3, 1887, son of John Milton and Della (Hazen) Hanna. His father was born in Fontenelle, Iowa, March 15, 1858, and came to the sand hills of Nebraska in 1881 to work for the Rankin Cattle Company. He has resided there since. He is descended from Scotch-Irish settlers in Pennsylvania. His wife, Della, was born in Painesville, Ohio, December 8, 1869, and died in Custer County, Nebraska, November 28, 1919.

Mr. Hanna attended public schools and since reaching the age of 21 has been in the cattle business. He owns and operates a 12,000 acre ranch stocked with 1500 cattle. He is a member of the executive committee of the Nebraska Stock Growers Association, and in 1930 was elected county commissioner of Cherry County.

He is treasurer of the local school board, a member of the Masons, and of the Union Church of Brownlee (trustee). His hobbies are bridge and good cow horses.

On April 5, 1911, he was married to Wynona Severance at Thedford.

Mrs. Hanna was born at Hugoton, Kansas, December 19, 1891. She is the daughter of Hiram B. and Pearl (Pound) Severance. She attended high school in Kansas City, Missouri, and is a member of the Eastern Star, and the Woman's Club. Mr. and Mrs. Hanna have three children, Don Jr., born December 30, 1912; Francis, born November 20, 1915; and Bobbie, born November 5, 1920. Residence: Brownlee.

Harry Clayton Hanna

Harry Clayton Hanna, real estate dealer and former banker of Superior, Nebraska, has lived in this state for 42 years, and has been active in civic affairs in his community for many years. He was born near Tipton, Iowa, October 27, 1881, the son of Joseph Baird and Sarah Ann (Kessler) Hanna. His father, who was born in Iowa, October 22, 1855, is a retired stockman. His mother was born in Iowa, October 12, 1859.

Mr. Hanna attended business college at Lincoln, Nebraska, was engaged in banking from 1907 until 1918, and for several years has been in the real estate and insurance business. He owns land in Colorado. He is a member of the Chamber of Commerce, Odd Fellows Lodge Number 87, the Superior Country Club, and the Nebraska Society. For 15 years he has served as city treasurer at Superior. He is a Republican.

He married Arabelle Jessie Peart, the daughter of James Peart. Mrs. Hanna, who was a school teacher before her marriage, was born in Pennsylvania, June 6, 1893. Mr. Hanna's favorite recreations are golfing and fishing. He is affiliated with the First Presbyterian Church. Residence: Superior.

Anton Hansen

Since 1884, Anton Hansen has been engaged in the mercantile business at Upland, Nebraska. He was born in Denmark, April 24, 1865, the son of Nels and Karen (Jensen) Hansen, the former a mechanic who was born in Denmark, March 22, 1838, and died at Upland, July 20, 1920. His mother was born in Denmark, February 5, 1842, and died at Upland, November 20, 1925.

Mr. Hansen received his education in the public schools of Denmark, and in 1882, came to America, settling in Michigan. Two years later he moved to Nebraska, and is now president and manager of the Hansen Brothers, Incorporated. He holds membership in the Midwest Implement Dealers Association, the Nebraska Retail Hardware Dealers, and the Retail Hardware Mutual Insurance Company, serving as director in each of these organizations.

He is a member of the Independent Order of Odd Fellows, the Modern Woodmen of America, and the Methodist Episcopal Church of Upland, and the Methodist Brotherhood. From 1909 to 1912, Mr. Hansen served as director of the local school board. His hobbies are reading and mechanics.

He was united in marriage with Katharine Barbara Schechtler, at Hastings, Nebraska, October 20, 1890; she was born at St. Gallen, Switzerland, April 26, 1866. Their children are: Clarence Herbert, born in 1891, who is a farmer near Upland; Edward L., born in 1896, who is a merchant; and Wilfred Jennings, born in 1897, who is in the mercantile business. Mr. Hansen is a member of the Democratic party. Residence: Upland. (Photograph in Album).

Christian Hansen

Christian Hansen, educator, was born on a farm near Oakland, Burt County, Nebraska, son of Nels and Cedsel Marie (Christensen) Hansen. His father, who was a farmer, was born in Copenhagen, Denmark, March 6, 1848, and died at Oakland, on July 16, 1912. His wife, Cedsel Marie, was born in Noestved, Denmark, and died at Lyons, Nebraska, December 25, 1924.

Upon finishing country school Christian Hansen attended the Blair and Lyons High Schools, and received his A. B. from Midland College in 1897. He also attended Fremont Normal School, and Augustana College, and from the latter was awarded his L. H. D. in 1921. He is a member of Phi Beta Kappa and Alpha Sigma Phi.

On December 25, 1898, he was united in marriage to Ida M. Hultberg, at Lyons, Nebraska. Mrs. Hansen was born in Rock Island, Illinois, September 18, 1872, and is of Swedish descent. Of this marriage there are seven children: Harold E., born May 18, 1902, who is an accountant at the Union Pacific Headquarters in Omaha; Lillian, born April 13, 1900, was married September 9, 1921; Paul V., born March 5, 1905, who is supervisor of the Reliance Life Insurance Company; Elliott G., born July 3, 1917; Lois G., born December 10, 1909, who is a teacher; Winston C., born February 21, 1911, who is engaged in the stocks and bonds business; and Ernest W., born January 4, 1913.

Mr. Hansen's life has been devoted principally to teaching or executive educational work. He is the author of various educational pamphlets, and at the present time is head of the teacher training department of Dana College.

During the World War he was a four minute speaker, and active in civilian welfare work. He is a member of the First Lutheran Church, the Chamber of Commerce, the Nebraskana Society and the Nebraska Academy of Sciences. He enjoys football and tennis, and his hobby is the study of psychology. Residence: Blair.

Elmer Marion Hansen

Elmer M. Hansen was born at St. Paul, Nebraska, March 22, 1893, the son of Niels Peter and Marie (Jensen) Hansen. His father, who was born in Denmark, June 3, 1863, and died at Lincoln, October 22, 1927, was a pharmacist; he was chairman of the Republican state central committee; was food commissioner of Nebraska under the administration of Governor Aldrich. He came to the United States in 1881, and settled in Howard County, Nebraska. His mother was born at Copenhagen, Denmark, December 13, 1870.

Dr. Hansen was a student in the public school at Kearney, Nebraska, and in 1911 was graduated from the Lincoln High School where he was president of the senior class. He received his Bachelor of Science degree in 1915, and his medical degree in 1927, from the University of Nebraska. He held membership in Sigma Xi, Phi Gamma Delta, Phi Chi, and Phi Delta Chi.

After his graduation from the university he was city chemist and bacteriologist for the city of Lincoln for two years; was proprietor of a pharmacy at Shickley, Nebraska, until 1923, when he re-entered the university to study medicine. He was interne at the University Hospital for two years and was then resident interne at the Chicago Lying-in Hospital for six months. Since that time he has been engaged in the practice of medicine at Lincoln. He is associated with the Lincoln Clinic, his practice limited to obstetrics.

On March 7, 1918, he was married to Ramona Troup at Lincoln. Mrs. Hansen was born at Warsaw, Indiana, January 26, 1894. They have a daughter, Mary Adelaide, born January 10, 1922. He has lived in Nebraska all his life.

Dr. Hansen was commissioned second lieutenant of the Military Reserve of Nebraska, 1915. He was president of the Red Cross chapter at Shickley, 1917-18; is a member of the Lancaster County Medical Society; the Nebraska State Medical Association; the American Medical Association; and the Central Association of Obstetricians and Gynecologists. He is a member of the medical advisory committee of the Lancaster County Red Cross, and holds membership in the Randolph Parent-Teachers' Association at Lincoln; the Kiwanis Club; and the Nebraskana Society. He is a member of the Lancaster Lodge Number 54 of the Ancient Free and Accepted Masons. His sport is golfing. His hobby is medical reading. He is a member of Westminster Presbyterian Church, and a Republican. Dr. Hansen is attending obstetrician at Bryan Memorial Hospital and also at Lincoln General Hospital. Residence: Lincoln.

Hans C. Hansen

Hans C. Hansen, farmer and stock raiser, was born at Hemingford, Nebraska, August 6, 1888, son of Chris and Marie (Peterson) Hansen.

His father was born at Horsens, Denmark, August 21, 1866, and came to the United States in 1885. He is a retired farmer. His wife, Marie, was born in Horsens, Denmark, March 2, 1863, and died at Hemingford, November 5, 1922.

Mr. Hansen attended public school and the high school at Hemingford, Nebraska. He is a prominent stock raiser and farmer, and at the present time is director of the Farmers Union of District No. 1 of Nebraska.

On May 23, 1916, he was married to Sena Jensen at Blair, Nebraska. She was born at Blair, April 13, 1892, of Danish ancestry. There are three children, Norman, born September 22, 1918; Dale, born October 18, 1931; and Donald, his twin born October 18, 1931.

During the late war Mr. Hansen was active in Red Cross and other drives. He is a member of the Hemingford Congregational Church. Residence: Hemingford.

J. Meyer Hansen

J. Meyer Hansen, retired farmer of Saline County, Nebraska, was born at Brons, Denmark, May 7, 1867, and for the past 34 years has been a resident of Nebraska. His father, Knud Hansen, a merchant, was born at Brons, March 7, 1827, and died there November 8, 1878. His mother, Marie (Larsen) Hansen, was born at Astrup, Denmark, April 6. 1837, and died at Elkhorn, Iowa, March 30, 1896. She was an expert needlewoman and a poet.

Mr. Hansen attended public school and for three years was a student at Elkhorn College, Iowa. He has always been interested in the educational and civic life of his community. Upon his retirement from farm activities he traveled extensively with his family; visited his old home in Denmark, and the battlefields of France, and spent some time in Germany, Norway, Sweden, and Belgium. Before the trip a few days were spent in Washington, D. C.

During the late war Mr. Hansen was active in the sale of Liberty bonds. For the past 28 years he has served as moderator for the Friend school board. He is a member of St. John's Danish Lutheran Church at Cordova, Nebraska, and the Red Cross.

He was united in marriage with Mary Mason at Friend, November 10, 1897. Born at Davenport, Iowa, September 6, 1866, she died at Friend, October 14, 1905. She was a teacher and landscape painter. On December 4, 1907, he married Marie Johansen at Friend. Mrs. Hansen was born September 8, 1888, the daughter of Mr. and Mrs. H. C. Johansen. She is a member and president of the local Ladies' Aid Society. They have two children: Mary Hil-

ma, born October 11, 1908; and Emilie Mathilde Dagmar, born October 16, 1912. Both girls were students at Grand View College, Des Moines, Iowa. Residence: Friend.

Peter Hansen

Peter Hansen was born at Elsborg, Denmark, August 14, 1875, son of Niels and Maren (Nielsen) Hansen. Niels Hansen was born at Elsborg, Denmark, March 2, 1840. He was a blacksmith most of his life, and was a farmer the later part of his life. His ancestors were all blacksmiths back as far as 800 A. D. He came to the United States September 6, 1883, and received his naturalization papers May, 1890. He homesteaded in Howard County, Nebraska, in 1890. The homestead is now in the possession of the oldest boy, Thomas H. Hansen. Mr. Hansen died at Denver, Colorado, June 20, 1909. He was a member of the Lutheran Church. His wife, Maren, was born at Elsborg, December 10, 1846. She was a seamstress, a member of the Lutheran Church and a devoted homemaker. She died in Howard County, March 28, 1900.

Mr. Hansen came to the United States with his father, and for the past 12 years has been a merchant at Potter. Prior to that time he was connected with the Union Pacific Railroad. He is a member of the Masons, has been Past Master for 27 years, the Woodmen of the World, the Veterans Free Mason Society of Nebraska, the Masonic Research Society, and the Methodist Episcopal Church. During the World War he was a sergeant in the home guard.

He was married on January 20, 1903, to Rose Viola Hansen at Dannebrog, Nebraska. Mrs. Hansen was born at Jackson, Nebraska, January 20, 1879. She is a member of the Methodist Episcopal Church, the Order of Eastern Star, secretary of the Ladies' Aid Society, and president of the Missionary Society. They have two children, a boy and a girl, who died in infancy.

Mr. Hansen is fond of golfing, hunting and fishing, and enjoys playing horseshoes. Residence: Potter.

Alfred Leif Hanson

Alfred Leif Hanson, public auditor and accountant, was born at Fremont, Nebraska, July 5, 1892, son of James Ferdinand and Lelia Stanton (Wightman) Hanson. He attended public and high school at Fremont and from 1906 until 1918 was engaged in a clerical capacity with the Alfalfa Products Company, the Standard Live Stock Commission Company of South Omaha and the Nye-Schneider-Fowler Co. Since 1918 he has been vice president of the firm J. F. Hanson and Company, and the Hanson Audit Company. He is secretary of the Farmland Fremont & Railroad Drainage District, succeeding his father in office.

On June 3, 1914, he was married to Neta Fern Clark at York. She was born at Charleston, Nebraska, July 19, 1891. Three children are living and one deceased: Eugene Stanton, born June 4, 1915; Bernita Jane, born August 19, 1919, died August 24, 1919; RobertEverett, born March 26, 1926; and Mary Ellen, born November 10, 1927.

Mr. Hanson is a Republican. He is a member of the First Methodist Episcopal Church, the Rotary Club (secretary 1931), and the Nebraska State Historical Society. His hobby is gardening. Residence: Fremont.

Harold G. Hanson

Born at Little Sioux, Iowa, March 25, 1896, Harold G. Hanson is the son of Charles Laurence and Dora Ella (Gleason) Hanson. His father, who was a farmer, was born at Ejusburg, Denmark, May 1, 1859. After spending two years in Australia, he came to America in 1879 and was a rancher in Colorado for twenty-five years.

His mother, born in Little Sioux, October 24, 1877, is a graduate of Fremont Normal School. She is of English descent.

Harold G. Hanson attended Little Sioux public and high schools and was graduated from the latter in 1914. In 1914 and 1915 he was a student at the University of Iowa, and in 1927 received his degree of Doctor of Dental Surgery from Creighton Dental College. He was a member of the track team at Iowa, and served as treasurer of Delta Sigma Delta in college.

During the World War he served twenty-three months with the rank of private, 13 months of which was overseas. While in the army he played football with the 90th Division. He is a member of the American Legion, the Ancient Free and Accepted Masons and the Royal Arch Masons. His religious affiliation is with the Methodist Episcopal Church at Little Sioux.

Dr. Hanson has been a farmer and teacher, and since his admission to practice as a dentist. He is a member of the Nebraska State Dental Association. He is a Republican, and a member of the Nebraskana Society.

On December 22, 1919, he was united in marriage to Florence M. Liedl at Minneapolis. Mrs. Hanson was born at Furgus Falls, Minnesota, December 17, 1897. Residence: Crofton.

Herman Frederick Hanson

Herman Frederick Hanson, *clerk* of the *district court* of Custer County, was born at Helsingborg, Sweden, September 16, 1878, and on July 2, 1881 came to Nebraska with his mother from Sweden.

His father, Peter Hanson, was born at Ystad, Sweden, January 13, 1854, and came to Nebraska City on October 15, 1880, and was section and extra gang foreman on the Union Pacific and Burlington Railroads. Later he engaged in farming, and is now retired.

Petronella Olson, wife of Peter Hanson, was born in Landscrona, Sweden, September 20, 1848, and died at Broken Bow, May 29, 1918. Herman Frederick Hanson, completed the sixth grade in the public schools of Nebraska, and received the balance of his common school and the equivalent of his high school education at Valparaiso University, in Indiana. On March 25, 187, he was graduated from a business course there.

His first work after leaving college was teaching a country school in Sedgwick County, Colorado. He has engaged in clerical work for the Union Pacific Railroad Company, the Union Pacific Coal Company, and the United States Reclamation Service. From 1909 to 1921, he was engaged in the abstract business at Broken Bow, and since 1921 has been clerk of the district court, elected on the Republican ticket.

On March 7, 1914, Mr. Hanson was married to Sybil Adele Guthery at Lincoln.

During the World War period Mr. Hanson helped in connection with selective service, loan and Red Cross drives, and volunteered for service as cost accountant, but was not accepted. He is a member of the First Presbyterian Church, the Public Service Club, the Masons, Modern Woodmen of America and The Nebraskana Society. Residence: Broken Bow.

James R. Hanson

James R. Hanson, public auditor and accountant. was born at Fremont, Nebraska, February 7, 1888, son of James Ferdinand and Lelia Stanton (Wightman) Hanson. He attended public and high school and Fremont Normal College, and since leaving school has been associated with various firms.

From 1919-20 he was office manager for the Fremont Joint Stock Land Bank, and in 1921 became president of J. F. Hanson & Company, and manager of the Hanson Audit Company. He is vice president of the Louis E. May Company, investment securities, of Fremont. He is a Republican and active in politics.

On September 30, 1924, he was married to Jay Emma Robinson at Council Bluffs. She was born near Ainsworth, Nebraska, May 24, 1892. There are four children, Marjory, born December 23, 1925; James, born February 27, 1927; Barbara, born March 28, 1928; and Richard, born May 23, 1931.

Mr. Hanson is a member of the Red Cross, the Chamber of Commerce, the Rotary Club, the Elks and Odd Fellows, the Nebraska State Historical Society, the Fremont library board, the American Legion (chaplain), and the Methodist Episcopal Church. He has held various offices in many of these organizations, most of them over a period of years. Residence: Fremont.

Vernon Louis Hanson

Vernon Louis Hanson, ranchman, was born at Oakland, Nebraska, April 13, 1882, son of Robert M. and Mary Ellen (Kessler) Hanson. The father was born near Nestved, Denmark, June 11, 1842, and died at Crawford, Nebraska, July 28, 1901. He was a farmer, and came to the United States in 1869. His wife, Mary Ellen Kessler, was born in Chester, Pennsylvania, January 23, 1855, and died at Hay Springs, Nebraska, April 4, 1927. She was German on the maternal side.

Mr. Hanson graduated from high school at Crawford, Nebraska, on May 22, 1902, and completed a correspondence course in pharmacy on February 11, 1904.

For eight years he was a drug clerk, and for eight years was the owner of a drug store. For the past 16 years he has been a ranchman. He is an independent Democrat.

On June 10, 1910, he was married to Mildred Caroline Warneke at Omaha. Mrs. Hanson was born at Odebolt, Iowa, November 5, 1882, of German ancestry. To Mr. and Mrs. Hanson were born three children, Wendell, born May 20, 1911, who died February 20, 1928; Verna L., born September 1, 1912, who married Frank G. Boggs; and Edna Mae, born July 16, 1914. After completing her high school course at Harrison, Verna attended University of Nebraska two years. Edna Mae is teaching at the present time.

Mr. Hanson's hobby is the breeding of registered Hereford cattle. He is a member of the board of regents of the Sioux County High School, a member of the Odd Fellows, and the Brotherhood of American Yeomen. Residence: Harrison.

Walter Allyn Hanthorn

Since 1879 Walter Allyn Hanthorn has lived on the same farm in Nuckolls County, Nebraska, near Superior. He was born at Abingdon, Illinois, September 18, 1873, the son of James and Sarah Elizabeth (Teel) Hanthorn. His father, who was born at Chambersburg, Pennsylvania, January 14, 1836, and died at Cadams, Nebraska, November 12, 1903, was a farmer, stockraiser, and teacher; he served in the Nebraska Legislature, and in Company K, 55th Illinois Volunteer Infantry, and was wounded in the Battle of Shiloh during the Civil War. His mother, who was a teacher, received her education at Lombard University in Illinois. She was born at Girard, Illinois, June 3, 1848, and died at Nelson, Nebraska; she is descended from a member of the Allyn family who brought Lafayette to America on his own ship.

Mr. Hanthorn attended elementary school at Cadams, was graduated from the Superior High School in 1893, and later attended the University of Nebraska. He taught school at Smyrna, Cadams, Nora, and Superior, Nebraska, and was a teacher in rural schools for a time. For the past 20 years he has been a successful farmer and stockraiser near Superior. A Republican, he was a candidate for county treasurer of Nuckolls County in 1905 and 1926.

He is a member of the Nebraskana Society and is affiliated with the Methodist Episcopal Church of Nora. During the World War he served as a member of the Council of Defense in Nuckolls County. His marriage to Anna Orpha Ellison, daughter of George Wilmot and Mary Agnes (Reynolds) Ellison, occurred at Cadams, February 20, 1907. Mrs. Hanthorn, who was a teacher prior to her marriage, was born at Friend, Nebraska, January 18, 1883; her French Huguenot ancestors came to America in colonial times.

To this marriage the following children were born: Gladys Orpha, born December 19, 1907, who died January 5, 1908; Allyn Ellison, born November 29, 1908, who died June 24, 1929; Eunice Elizabeth, born March 21, 1910; James Emerson, born February 13, 1912; George Wilmot, born October 10, 1913; Walter Willis, born December 18, 1915, who died November 27, 1918; Herbert Genung, born April 28, 1917; and Lindell Loren, born September 12, 1920. Residence: Superior.

John Benjamin Happel

John Benjamin Happel, clerk of the district court of Thayer County, was born in Warsaw, Illinois, February 20, 1898, son of Henry and Delphena (Cammack) Happel.

His father was born in Hessen-Darmstadt, Germany, September 4, 1860, and died at Hebron, October 19, 1913. He was a farmer and a director of the First National Bank of Hebron. His wife, Delphena, was born in Indiana, October 25, 1872, and died at Lincoln, May 9, 1925.

Mr. Happel attended public school and for some time was a farmer. He was employed by the Deshler Telephone Company for four years, and was deputy county treasurer three years and a half. Later, he was the owner of the Vienna Bakery at Deshler, for four years.

On March 19, 1929, he was married to Suzanne Elizabeth Huge at Abilene, Kansas. Mrs. Happel was born at Tampa, Kansas, November 18, 1907. They have one daughter, Connie-Sue, born June 30, 1931.

Mr. Happel is a Methodist and a Mason. He is a member of the Hebron Country Club and enjoys golf. Residence: Hebron.

Roy Blaine Harberg

For more than twenty years, Roy Blaine Harberg has been an outstanding figure in the business and community life of Omaha and Springfield, Nebraska. Born at Omaha, March 8, 1887, he is a son of John Henry and Margaret Dorothy (Mohrman) Harberg. His father was born at Garnavillo, Iowa, November 7, 1859, and at the time of his death, October 14, 1925, he was secretary of the wholesale hardware firm of Wright & Wilhelmy Company, at Omaha. His parents were natives of Mecklenberg-Schwerin, Germany. Margaret Dorothy (Mohrman) Harberg was born at Garnavillo, Iowa, June 4, 1856, and died at Omaha, March 6, 1929. Her family was German, originally coming from the vicinity of Hamburg.

Roy Harberg received his education in the public and high schools of Omaha, and was graduated from Omaha High School in 1904. On June 19, 1913, he was married to Irene Anne Bergers of Omaha. She was born at Fremont, on October 4, 1895. There are two children, John, born August 30, 1914, and Doris, born October 11, 1920.

A Republican, Mr. Harberg was appointed chairman of the Sarpy County Republican Central committee in 1920. He has been a resident of the state since birth, and has been a resident of Springfield for some years. He is president of the Harberg Lumber Company and secretary-treasurer of the Metz Construction Company. He is also a member of the board of directors of Wright & Wilhelmy Company of Omaha.

During the World War he was chairman for Sarpy County of the Red Cross Drive, and participated in all loan and other drives. From 1920-22 he was a member of the Springfield school board. He is a Lutheran and a member of St. Mark's Lutheran Church at Omaha. He is a member of the executive committee of the Sarpy County Red Cross organization.

He is affiliated with the following: Associated General Contractors of America, Nebraska Lumber Dealers Association, National Geographic Society, The Nebraskana Society, Knights of Ak-Sar-Ben, etc. A Mason, he belongs to Springfield Lodge No. 112, Ancient Free and Accepted Masons, Nebraska Consistory, Ancient and Accepted Order Scottish Rite Masons at Omaha, and Tangier Temple, Ancient Arabac Order, Nobles of the Mystic Shrine at Omaha. His sports include golf and fishing, and his hobby is reading. Residence: Springfield.

Bert Marshall Hardenbrook

A lawyer for the past 26 years, Bert Marshall Hardenbrook was born near Albia, Iowa, July 20, 1874. His father, John Clifford Hardenbrook, who was an employee of the Standard Oil Company, was born at Mt. Gillead, Ohio, August 20, 1849, and died at Fremont, Nebraska, February 20, 1928; Ludwig Hardenbrook, an ancestor, was a soldier of the Revolution and after the war settled in Ohio. His mother, Margaret Mary (Marshall) Hardenbrook, was born near Keokuk, Iowa, February 20, 1850, and died at Fremont, April 20, 1930.

Mr. Hardenbrook was graduated from high school and in 1896 was graduated from Fremont Normal School. He served as superintendent of schools at Marion, South Dakota, for 11 years, and practiced law in South and North Dakota before coming to Nebraska. He is now senior member of the law firm of Hardenbrook & Misko. A Republican, he served for nearly 10 years as county attorney of Valley County, was candidate for nomination for attorney general of Nebraska in 1930, and served as president of the County Attorneys Association of Nebraska from 1924 to 1928. He has written many articles on crime and criminology.

He is a member of the Chamber of Commerce of which he was secretary at one time, The Nebraskana Society, the American Bar Association, the Nebraska State Bar Association and the Valley County Bar Association of which he is president. He was president of the board of education at Arcadia, 1916-17, was a member of the Ord school board, 1921-23, and is a member of the Odd Fellows and Masons. He is a member of the First Methodist Church of Ord.

On August 20, 1899, he was married to Lorinda Carrie Kinkaid at Marion, South Dakota. Mrs. Hardenbrook was born near Rochester, Minnesota, April 1, 1870, and died at Ord, February 18, 1918. These children were born to them: Luella Joice, May 16, 1902, who married Forest Johnson; Samuel Clifford, July 3, 1904, who died February 2, 1908; Daryl Kenneth, February 3, 1907; and Nona Norene, June 14, 1909.

Mr. Hardenbrook married Minnie Viola Smith; she was deputy county clerk prior to her marriage. His son-in-law, Forest, operates the Ord City Bakery, Nona is a teacher. and Daryl K. is a printer and publisher. During the World War he served as chairman of the Valley County Council of Defense and government appeal agent. He enlisted for service in the Spanish American War in 1898 but was not mustered into federal service. Residence: Ord.

Jesse McMillan Harding

Jesse McMillan Harding, manufacturer, was born in Wisner, Nebraska, August 20, 1887, son of Charles and Onetah (McMillan) Harding. He received his masters degree from Yale University in 1909, where he was a member of Phi Beta Kappa and Phi Gamma Delta.

His marriage to Agnes Miriam Burkley was solemnized at Omaha, on October 16, 1912. Mr. Harding has been a member of the firm of the Harding Cream Company for a number of years. He is a member of Saint Cecelia's Catholic Church, the American Legion, the Chamber of Commerce, the Rotary Club, and is active in the Omaha Symphony Orchestra Society. Residence: Omaha.

Arthur Shereburne Hardy

Arthur Shereburne Hardy, proprietor of the Commercial Hotel at Sidney, was born July 13, 1882, son of Edwin C. and Margaret (Spaithe) Hardy. His father was born at Mount Vernon, District of Columbia, and died at Chicago, in 1916. He was an editorial writer and dramatic critic of English descent. His wife, Margaret, was born at Berea, Ohio, and died at Chicago, in 1915. Her ancestry was Dutch.

Upon his graduation from the Omaha High School, Mr. Hardy entered the University of Nebraska, where he received the degree of Bachelor of Science in electrical engineering. He is a member of Kappa Sigma.

On March 13, 1909 he was married to Mabel Clare Boydston, at Ord. Mrs. Hardy was born at Grant City, Missouri, August 22, 1883, of *Mayflower* ancestry, tracing back to Robert Bruce. Five children were born to them, Arthur, on March 28, 1913; Lois, on March 9, 1916; Lucille, on July 29, 1917; and Betty and Bobby, on March 20, 1924. Bobby died on July 25, 1924.

Mr. Hardy is a Republican. He has resided in Nebraska for the past 48 years, and in 1910 held the rank of second lieutenant in the Millard Rifles at Omaha. He is a member of the Presbyterian Church, active in Community Chest work, a member of the Commercial Club, the Rotary Club, and the Masons. For seven years he was a member of the Sidney School Board, serving as president in 1928. His club is the Sidney Country Club, and his favorite sport is golf. Residence: Sidney.

Gertrude Laws Hardy

Gertrude L. Hardy, a resident of Nebraska for the past 54 years, was born at Richland Center, Wisconsin, February 24, 1871, the daughter of Gilbert LaFayette and Josephine (Lawrence) Laws. Her father was an educator and editor in Wisconsin and Nebraska for many years and was prominent in Nebraska politics and civic affairs. A Civil War veteran, he was principal of the high school at Richland Center, served as registrar in the United States Land Office at McCook, Nebraska, 1883-86, was secretary of state, 1886-89, congressman from the Nebraska Third District, 1889-91, and was a member of the State Board of Transportation. He died at Lincoln, April 25, 1907, and was descended from Scotch-Irish ancestors who came to America in 1733.

Her mother was born at Paterson, New York, April 24, 1844, and died at Lincoln, July 6, 1927. Her ancestry was French and English. She received her education at the University of Wisconsin, and before her marriage was a teacher.

Mrs. Hardy attended district school at Orleans, Nebraska, and in 1886 was graduated from high school at McCook, Nebraska. In 1890 she was graduated with the degree A. B. at the University of Nebraska, where she was elected to Phi Beta Kappa and Mortar Board. She is a member of Kappa Alpha Theta.

Her marriage to William Edwin Hardy at Enid, Oklahoma, January 9, 1895. Mr. Hardy, who was born at Gainesville, Wyoming County, New York, August 5, 1863, is a merchant in Lincoln, and is active in civic affairs there.

Mrs. Hardy is a member of the Association of American University Women; the League of Women Voters; and the Astronomical Society of the Pacific. She holds membership in the Nebraskana Society and the Red Cross; and is affiliated with Sorosis, Fortnightly Club, Copper Kettle Club, and Matinee Musicale. She is a member of All Souls Unitarian Church at Lincoln, and is a Republican. Residence: Lincoln.

William Edwin Hardy

Since 1871 William E. Hardy has lived in Nebraska and for many years has been a leader in community affairs and civic enterprises in Lincoln. He was born at Gainesville, New York, August 5, 1863. His father, Harvey Wesley Hardy, who was born at Gainesville, in 1825, was a merchant, descended directly from Thomas Hardy who came to America from England, and settled in Massachusetts in 1630. He died at Lincoln, Lancaster, Nebraska, January, 1913.

Charlotte Clement (Abbott) Hardy, his mother, was born at Churchville, New York, and died at Lincoln, March 19, 1897. Her ancestry was English.

Mr. Hardy attended the elementary schools of Lancaster County, and in 1880 was graduated from the Lincoln High School. He was later a student at the University of Nebraska, and was awarded an honorary A. M. degree. A member of the national grand council of Sigma Chi, he served as chairman of the national board of grand trustees.

He is affiliated with most of Lincoln's community and welfare clubs, and has served as city alderman. He is president of the Hardy Furniture Company; a director of the Federal Reserve Bank, at Omaha, Nebraska and a director in the Lincoln Trust Company. He was appointed a member of the Nebraska Capitol Commission in 1919, and served until the completion of the building.

On January 9, 1895, he was united in marriage with Gertrude Hardenberg Laws at Enid, Oklahoma. Mrs. Hardy was born at Richland Center, Richland County, Wisconsin, February 24, 1871. She is of Scotch Irish decent.

Mr. Hardy directed all his efforts to war work in 1917 and 1918; was chairman of the Lancaster County chapter of the Red Cross; and was chairman of the Liberty Loan drives. He is a member of the Red Cross and the Social Welfare Society at Lincoln; past president of the Lincoln Chamber of Commerce; a member of the Hiram Club; and is past president of the Nebraska State Historical Society. He holds membership in the National Archaeological Society and the Nebraskana Society, and is a 32nd degree Mason.

His social clubs are: University Club; Country Club of Lincoln; Round Table; Candle Light Club; The Club; and the Canadian Alpine Club. He is fond of golfing, while his hobbies are reading and architecture. He is a member of All Soul's Unitarian Church at Lincoln. Residence: Lincoln.

Charles Herbert Harman

For nearly 30 years Charles Herbert Harman has been active in the business world in Nebraska, and is now prominent in civic affairs at Beatrice. He was born at Tecumseh, Nebraska, February 26, 1886, the son of John Sinclair and Sadie Elizabeth (Gardner) Harman. His father, who was born at Hillsboro, Ohio, April 26, 1848, and died at Tecumseh, December 30, 1922, was a hardware merchant at Tecumseh, for 42 years. He was grand commander of Nebraska in 1919, was grand high priest of Nebraska, 1900-01, and from 1898 to 1922, was grand treasurer of the Grand Council. His paternal grandfather came from Germany in the early 1700's, settled in Philadelphia, and after the Revolution moved to Virginia. His grandmother was born in London.

Sadie (Gardner) Harman, mother of Charles H. Harman, was born near London, England. Her father, who was also English born, was a merchant in London, before he came to America.

Mr. Harman was graduated from the Tecumseh High School, May 28, 1905. He has had the following experience in the business world: clerk for the Burlington Railroad at Omaha, 1905-06; clerk for the Lee Glass Hardware Company, 1906-08; assistant for the E. L. Dodder Funeral Directors, 1909-11; assistant for the W. W. Scott Funeral Firm, Beatrice, 1912-22. In 1921 he organized the Scott-Harman Funeral Directors which since 1926 has been Harman-Johnson.

He acted as vice president of the Kiwanis Club at its organization, served as a member of the board of directors of the Young Men's Christian Association at Beatrice, 1924-7, and is now a member of the Nebraskana Society and the Beatrice Country Club. He is affiliated with the First Presbyterian Church at Beatrice, is a member of the Republican party, and holds membership in the Masons. He is a member of Beatrice Lodge Number 26, of the latter organization, Raboni Livingston Chapter Number 10, Rabonia Council Number 9, and Mt. Hermon Commandery Number 7. He likes to golf; his hobby is philately.

His marriage to Jennie Tombrinck was solemnized at Omaha, Douglas County, Nebraska, June 26, 1912. Mrs. Harman, who is a trained nurse, was born at Omaha, January 16, 1889. Their two children are: John Sinclair, born November 17, 1913; and Sarah Elizabeth, born December 13, 1915. Residence: Beatrice.

August Henry Harms

For more than fifty years August H. Harms has been engaged in the mercantile business in Hooper. He was born in Oldenburgh, Germany, April 5, 1856, the son of Gerhard and Anna Sophie (Schraeder) Harms. Gerhard Harms was born in Streck, Oldenburgh, Germany, April 1, 1817, and died at Hooper, September 18, 1895. He was a pioneer farmer who came to Nebraska, April 4, 1870. His wife, Anna, was born in Hatten, Oldenburgh, Germany, December 31, 1821, and died at Hooper, October 9, 1905.

August Harms was educated in the rural schools of Germany, and came to America with his parents at the age of fourteen. A shoemaker and watchmaker, he has been a merchant since 1880. He is a Lutheran, a member of the Maccabees, and of the Nebraskana Society. He was married to Anna B. Bodewig, at Fremont, March 26, 1883. Mrs. Harms was born in East Prussia, Germany, October 27, 1863.

They have had nine children, seven of whom are living: Gerhard, born March 14, 1884, died February 17, 1890; Anna M. S., born August 29, 1885, married H. P. Dressen; Minnie A., born September 12. 1887, died February 6, 1890; Harry F., born January 7, 1890; Barbara A., born January 24, 1892; Coletta H., born March 7, 1894, married F. L. Hoskinson; August F., born March 22, 1896, married Louise Reviellac; Jerome P., born February 10, 1898, married Eleanore Spheeler; and Gordon J., born November 20, 1903, married Mary Bates. Residence: Hooper.

Charles W. W. Harms

Charles W. W. Harms, physician, was born at Kansas City, Kansas, September 5, 1889, son of Charles Christian and Mary (Seng) Harms. He received his Bachelor of Science degree in 1912, his master's degree in 1914 and his medical degree in 1914 from the University of Nebraska.

On September 4, 1926, he was married to Velma V. Rains at Wahoo. She was born at McPherson, Kansas, March 16, 1903. There is one daughter, Marilyn Jean, born June 8, 1930.

From 1914 until 1917 Dr. Harms practiced in Omaha.

He served with Hospital Train No. 45, in the American Expeditionary Forces with the rank of first lieutenant in the World War, and since 1919 has been in practice in Lincoln. He is a Republican.

He is a member of the American Legion, the American, Nebraska State and Lancaster County Medical Associations, the Military Surgeons of America, the Royal Arch Masons, the American Association for the Advancement of Science and the Nebraska Academy of Sciences. Residence: Lincoln.

William Michael Harnan

William Michael Harnan, rancher, was born in Springfield, Illinois, October 12, 1868, son of William and Mary (Halligan) Harnan. The father was born in County Queen, Ireland, March 17, 1817, and died at Woodriver, Nebraska, April 27, 1898. He was a farmer whose Irish ancestors came to America in 1828. Mary Halligan was born at Port Arlington, Ireland, October 20, 1834, and died at Wood River, Nebraska, on November 23, 1893.

Educated in country schools, Mr. Harnan was a farmer until the age of 21, and since that time has been a rancher. He owned a ranch 40 miles south of Cody, Nebraska, 40 miles from a railroad, and resided there from 1890 to 1923, when he moved into Gordon. He still maintains some ranching interests.

He was married on December 26, 1900, to Mary Matilda Russell at Valentine. Mrs. Harnan was born at Whiting, Iowa, November 24, 1874, and died at Gordon, January 31, 1928.

Mr. Harnan is a Democrat. He is a member of St. Leo's Catholic Church at Gordon, the Knights of Columbus, and the Modern Woodmen of America. His favorite sport is fishing. Residence: Gordon.

Dana Earl Harper

Dana Earl Harper was born at Beaver City, Nebraska, October 3, 1897, the son of Ross J. and Margaret (Jones) Harper. His father, who was a lawyer, was born at Kokomo, Indiana, February 21, 1867.

Mr. Harper was graduated from the Beaver City High School in 1916, and in 1921 received the LL. B. degree at the University of Nebraska where he held membership in Sigma Phi Epsilon and Phi Alpha Delta. He has been engaged in the practice of law at Gothenburg, Nebraska, since 1921. He is a Democrat.

On June 19, 1921, he married Florence Mae Smith at Dorchester, Nebraska. She is the daughter of Thomas E. and Millie (Benedict) Smith. Their three children are: Patricia Lou, born in 1924; Shirley May, born in 1926; and Jerry Dana, born in May, 1931. Residence: Gothenburg.

Harry W. Harper

Harry W. Harper, automobile dealer, was born at Newburg, Iowa, February 1, 1879, son of Thomas and Olive (Brown) Harper. The father, a carpenter and farmer, died at Fort Dodge, Iowa, in February, 1886, while his wife, Olive, who was born at Worcester, Massachusetts, October 13, 1837, is still living.

On July 8, 1900, Mr. Harper was married to Linda L. Mann at Valentine. They have five children, Eva Allen, Harrison, Douglas, and Stephen.

Mr. Harper has been a resident of Nebraska for thirty-six years, and at the present time is the owner of the Harper Automobile Company. He is a member of the Odd Fellows, and was recently elected to membership in the Nebraskana Society. Residence: Valentine.

O'Neill Photo Company—O'Neill

JAMES JOSEPH HARRINGTON

James Joseph Harrington

James Joseph Harrington, lawyer and former judge of the district court, was born at Lindsey, Ontario, Canada, October 29, 1868. He is the son of John and Margaret (Carroll) Harrington, the former a farmer. John Harrington was born in County Tipperary, Ireland, and immigrated to Canada as a young man. He died at Lindsey in 1897.

His mother, born in County Tipperary, Ireland, died at O'Neill, Nebraska. James J. Harrington attended the Lindsey Separate School, was graduated from high school in 1886, and came to the United States on January 23, 1887. A graduate of the Omaha Commercial College in 1889, he received his Bachelor of Laws degree from the University of Michigan in 1894.

In June of that year he was admitted to the bar at O'Neill, Nebraska, and from 1900 until 1912 served as judge of the district court for the 15th judicial district. At that time he retired to resume the active practice of law. Judge Harrington is a Democrat.

He was married on October 26, 1898, to Minnie E. Daly at O'Neill. Mrs. Harrington, who was born at Washburn, Illinois, December 13, 1873, confines her activities to her home and family. They have one daughter, Helen T., born August 1, 1899, who is married to Earl F. Buelow. She was graduated from St. Mary's Academy at O'Neill, and from the University of Nebraska with the degree of Bachelor of Arts. Mr. Buelow, who is a lawyer, is district attorney at Racine, Wisconsin, where they reside.

Judge Harrington has always been prominent in his community. At the time he was elected judge he was only 31 years of age, the youngest district judge ever to have been elected at that time in the state. He has been president of the Holt County Bar Association since 1900, is a member of the Nebraska State Bar Association, the Red Cross, the Commercial Club, the Woodmen of the World, Modern Woodmen of America and the Royal Highlanders.

A Catholic, Judge Harrington is a member of St. Patrick's Church and the Knights of Columbus. He enjoys golf and hiking, and holds membership in the O'Neill Country Club. He is a life member of the Nebraskana Society. Residence: O'Neill. (Photograph on Page 512).

Arthur Trevenning Harris

Arthur Trevenning Harris, one of Nebraska's most distinguished physicians, surgeons and X-ray specialists, was born at Grahamstown, Cape Province, South Africa, August 22, 1894. His father, Robert Osborn Harris, who was a building contractor, was born at Marazion, England, April 6, 1856, and at the age of twenty-four removed to South Africa, where his death occurred on May 5, 1898. His mother, Lydia Dinah Elliott, was born in Trapps Valley, South Africa, October 23, 1860. Her father was of Scotch descent while her mother was Irish.

Dr. Harris attended the Victoria High School at Grahamstown, and in 1912 entered Rhodes University division of the University of South Africa. He was awarded the degrees of Bachelor of Medicine and Bachelor of Surgery in 1919, at the University of Edinburgh, Scotland. He was awarded honors in anatomy and histology in college, and is now a specialist in X-ray. Dr. Harris practiced in South Africa before coming to the United States, and was roentgenologist and pathologist to the Methodist Hospital at Gary, Indiana, prior to his residence in Nebraska. He is the owner and operator of an X-ray and physiotherapy laboratory at Hastings, at the present time.

He is the author of *Prenatal Diagnosis of Anencephaly with Spina Bifida*, published in the *American Journal of Roentgenology and Radium Therapy* (1929), *Duodenal Diverticula* (1932), is an honorary member of the Adams County Medical Society, and a member of the American Medical Association. He also holds membership in the Nebraskana Society, the Kiwanis Club, the National Geographic Society and St. Mark's Cathedral. He is interested in birbs, and is serving as president of the Brooking Bird Club. His favorite sport in hiking, and his hobby, ornithology.

During 1916-17, Dr. Harris served with the rank of second lieutenant with the Argyll and Sutherland Highlanders, with service in Egypt and Salonica. Thereafter from 1921-28, he was surgeon to St. John's Ambulance Association at Cape Town, and from 1922-28, held the rank of captain in the South African Medical Corps.

He has three children: Marjorie Trevenning, born October 3, 1920; Sheila Trevenning, born May 5, 1922, and Derek Trevenning, born September 17, 1923.

On November 4, 1931, he was married to Helen Elizabeth Chick, daughter of the late Ferdinand and Mrs. Mary Chick of Hastings. She received the degree of Bachelor of Science in Education at the University of Nebraska in 1926. Residence: Hastings. (Photograph in Album).

George Arthur Harris

Born at Piasa, Illinois, August 7, 1871, George Arthur Harris has been a Nebraska physician since 1895. He is the son of William Johnson and Louise Ann (Brailey) Harris, the former a Canadian. William Harris born at Frankford, Ontario, December 28, 1848, was a physician of Welch descent, who died at Beatrice on January 25, 1901. His wife was born at Concord, Massachusetts, July 28, 1848, and died at Beatrice on May 26, 1920.

George Arthur Harris attended Beatrice public and high schools, and was a student and member of Phi Rho Sigma at the University of Illinois. During his 39 years residence in Nebraska he has been in active practice most of the time, and during 1915-16 was a major in the Medical Corps. He is a 32nd degree Mason and member of the Shrine, a member of the Valley Commercial Club, The Nebraskana Society and the Methodist Church.

On March 29, 1916, he was united in marriage to Grace Mary Coy at Waterloo, Nebraska. Mrs. Harris was born at Greenwich, New York, June 19, 1878. They have one son, William Donald, born February 23, 1901.

Dr. Harris is a Republican. His favorite sports are fishing and hunting, while his hobby is cabinet work. Residence: Valley.

Maud Enid Harris

Maud Enid Harris, clubwoman, was born at Birmingham, Iowa, March 14, 1871, daughter of Anthony Wayne and Eliza Jane (Camblin) Walmer. Her ancestry is English, Holland Dutch and Welsh, in America for several generations.

Maud Enid Walmer attended public and high schools at Leavenworth, Kansas, and was graduated from high school at Holdrege, Nebraska, in 1890. She has done much institute and Chautauqua work, and has studied at home extensively.

On September 18, 1895, she was married to Royal Lory Harris at Holdrege. Mr. Harris was born near Oskaloosa, Iowa, June 19, 1868. There are six children, Florence Eleanor, born January 6, 1897, who married Burk White; Clarence Edgar, born February 2, 1899, who died March 22, 1899; Ernest Elton, born September 7, 1900, who married Irene Mae Boag; Samuel Sterling, born September 29, 1902, who married Vesta King; Miriam Maud, born October 28, 1905, who married William Lowell Wooding; and Sherman Wayne, born January 28, 1909.

Mrs. Harris is a Republican. She and her husband are the owners of a large farm, but are now retired. She is county president of the Women's Christian Temperance Union, and active in club and cultural work. Residence: Alliance.

Heyn—Omaha

RILEY CLEMENT HARRISS

Riley Clement Harriss

Riley Clement Harriss is a native of Arthur, Illinois, born December 28, 1881. He is the son of Sion and Mary Frances (Richards) Harriss, the former a native of Wayne County, Illinois. Sion Harriss was born January 3, 1847, and has been a farmer all his life. His wife, Mary Frances Richards was born in Moultry County, Illinois, December 2, 1860. She was formerly a teacher, and is of English descent.

Riley C. Harriss was educated in the elementary schools of Jefferson County, Nebraska, and was graduated from Fairbury High School in 1905. He served as county superintendent of Jefferson County schools from 1908 to 1915. He was elected on the Republican ticket to the Nebraska state senate and served four years, the 1919 and 1921 sessions. During the 1919 session Mr. Harriss took an active part as a member of the state senate in the passage of the bill which carried an appropriation of five million dollars for the erection of Nebraska's new capitol building.

In 1912 he began writing insurance for the Bankers Life Insurance Company of Nebraska. In 1922 he was promoted to the Omaha branch as general agent. He is a member of the National Underwriters Association, the Nebraska Life Underwriters Managers Club, and is a charter member of the Fairbury Kiwanis Club. He is a member of the Omaha Chamber of Commerce, the Omaha Parent Teachers Association, the Y. M. C. A., The Nebransakana Society and the Red Cross. He is a 32nd degree Mason. His hobby is golf.

He was married to Alice Mary Hunt at Fairbury, Nebraska, June 15, 1911. Mrs. Harriss was born at Belvidere, Nebraska, October 14, 1887. The genealogy of her family reveals that she is a direct descendant of William the Conqueror. There are three children living and one dead: Clement Lowell, born August 2, 1912, who attends Harvard University; Donald Hunt, born September 24, 1915; Marion Elizabeth, born December 25, 1917, and Robert Mendell, born November 22, 1922, who died November 30, 1928. Residence: Omaha. (Photograph on Page 514).

Howard LeRoy Harse

For nearly 20 years Howard LeRoy Harse has been one of the owners and manager of the Queen City Laundry at Hastings, Nebraska. He was born at Miller, Buffalo County, Nebraska, October 20, 1886, the son of John and Abbie Jane (Cassel) Harse. His father, who was a ranchman and livestock dealer, was born at Christchurch, England, October 17, 1850, and died there October 4, 1924; he came to America in 1864. His mother was born in Iowa, May, 1862, and died at Omaha, Nebraska, March 5, 1911; her father was of Pennsylvania Dutch descent, while her mother's parents were English.

Mr. Harse attended the Hastings High School where he was awarded a letter for activities in football events. He was employed by a railway company at Omaha for two years and at Alamosa and Gunnison, Colorado, for four years. From 1913 to 1916 he operated his father's stock ranch, and since 1916 has been in his own business at Hastings. He is a director in the Great Plains Aircraft Company.

He is a member of the Chamber of Commerce and the Hastings Country Club, and from 1923 to 1929 was a member of the Hastings Kiwanis Club, acting as president of the latter organization in 1926. During the World War he served in the United States Army, stationed at Camp Grant, Rockford, Illinois. He is now a member of the American Legion and is affiliated with St. Marks Episcopal Church at Hastings. Mr. Harse is interested in hunting and fishing and likes the out of doors.

He was married at Hastings, March 23, 1918, to Gertrude Adelade Benedict, who was born at Hastings,

August 4, 1892. Her ancestry is English. Their three children are: Janet, born March 5, 1921; William, born March 3, 1923; and Robert, born April 2, 1926. Residence: Hastings.

John. A. Harshfield

John A. Harshfield, rancher and breeder of Hereford beef cattle, was born at Osage Mission, Kansas, (now St. Paul), May 4, 1875, son of John Thomas and Caroline (Shoptaugh) Harshfield.

John Thomas Harshfield was born in Green County, Indiana, February 11, 1843, and died at Sutherland, October 18, 1906. He was a farmer and later a merchant, and still later a stockfarmer. In his last years he became a hotel manager. He was descended from early German, English and Irish settlers in the United States. His wife, Caroline, died at St. Paul, Kansas, in 1881. She was of pre-Revolutionary ancestry.

Mr. Harshfield attended public school, and for many years has been engaged in ranching. He has written a series of articles on economics and stories of the old west, and is one of the few old-timers in Lincoln County.

On April 11, 1898, he was married to Etta Carrico at North Platte. Mrs. Harshfield was born at Parsons, Kansas, March 29, 1879. She is descended from settlers in America who came with Lord Baltimore. There are five children: Olive, born May 13, 1900; Walter, born July 2, 1902; Alva, born July 18, 1905; Wilbert, born January 24, 1908; and Gladys, born June 9, 1912.

During the World War Mr. Harshfield was active in almost every drive. He is a member of the Odd Fellows, the Nebraskana Society, the Old Settlers Club of Lincoln County, and for 25 years has been director of school districts number 103 and 104. He was the organizer, and is still a member of the Antelopes. His hobby is reading. Residence: Sutherland.

Earl F. Hart

Earl F. Hart was born at Edgar, Nebraska, November 23, 1888. His father, William Alonzo Hart, who is a retired farmer, was born at Waverly, Illinois, January 30, 1859. His mother, Eliza Ella (Nall) Hart, was born at Franklin, Illinois, April 1, 1864.

Mr. Hart attended rural school district number 77 and was graduated from the Edgar High School in 1906. Later he was a student at Nebraska Wesleyan University. He was a farmer for several years, and at this time operates a grain and coal business at Edgar; he is also the manager and owner of grain elevators at Alexandria and Glenvil, Nebraska, and is secretary-treasurer of the Hart-Bohling Grain Company.

He holds membership in the Lions Club, is affiliated with the Methodist Episcopal Church at Edgar, and is a member of the Nebraskana Society. His sports are hunting and fishing. He is a member of the Masonic Lodge Number 167 at Edgar, Chapter Number 22, Royal Arch, Tehama Temple at Hastings. He is a Democrat.

On October 26, 1910, he was married at Edgar to Inez Elizabeth Ferree. Mrs. Hart was born at Edgar, November 29, 1888. Three children were born to this marriage: Robert, born May 1, 1912, who is operating a grain elevator at Alexandria for the Hart-Bohling Grain Company; an infant son born March 9, 1916; and Gordon, born February 24, 1925, who died June 1, 1930. Mrs. Hart is a member and recording secretary of the P. E. O. Residence: Edgar.

Harry Hills Hart

Harry Hills Hart, son of Samuel Ira and Jane (Mills) Hart, was born at Richland, Iowa, April 18, 1867. Samuel Ira Hart was born in Ohio, in 1824, and farmed in Iowa and Nebraska until his death at Allen, Nebraska, in June, 1900. Jane Mills Hart was born in Indiana, in 1834, and died at Moscow, Colorado, in March, 1928.

Upon the completion of his elementary education, Mr. Hart farmed for some time, and later engaged in the automobile business. At the present time he is dealer for Ford cars at Ponca. A Republican he has served as sheriff and county judge during his sixty-four years of residence.

He was married to Nellie R. Isom, at Allen, Nebraska, November 24, 1888. Mrs. Hart was born in Janesville, Wisconsin, December 18, 1867, and is active in her husband's business. There were three children born to this marriage: Alta, born in 1890, died in 1895; Zeta, born in 1897, married George Carter, and died in March, 1931; Lamont, born January 12, 1904, married Esther Wendte.

Mr. Hart is a member of Salem Lutheran Church, the Red Cross, Lions Club and the Nebraskana Society. He is an Odd Fellow, a Mason, and a member of the Shrine. His favorite sport is golf. Residence: Ponca.

John Crandall Hartigan

A leading professional man in Fairbury, Nebraska, John Crandall Hartigan, born May 20, 1870, at Kansas City, Missouri, is the son of Michel Angelo Hartigan and Martha (Crandall) Hartigan. His father was born at Carbondale, Pennsylvania, and died at Fort Dodge, Iowa, March 19, 1920. He was of Irish parentage and was a lawyer. His mother was born at Oswego, New York, of English and Dutch parentage, and died at Fort Dodge, September 10, 1921.

John Hartigan was graduated from the Plattsmouth High School in 1887 and then attended Hastings College. He was admitted to the bar at Hastings, Nebraska, in May 1889. From 1890-91 he was mayor of Fairbury and has been city attorney of Fairbury. He was Adjutant General of Nebraska from 1909-1911.

On January 5, 1895, he was married to Nelle Gertrude Brown at Hastings, Nebraska. Mrs. Hartigan, born at Sibley, Iowa, October 6, 1874, is of English parentage. To this union three children were born; John, Merrell, January 2, 1897; Kathleen, February 13, 1898; and Richard, January 7, 1907.

Mr. Hartigan is a Democrat and is a member of the State Bar Association. He was a second lieutenant in the Second United States Volunteers in the Spanish American War (serving as captain colonel, and brigadier general). He is a former member of the National Guard, was chairman of the Jefferson County Council of Defense, and is a United Spanish War veteran.

He holds membership in the Fairbury Commercial Club, the Rotary Club, the Elks, the Modern Woodmen of America, the Independent Order of Odd Fellows, the Fairbury Country Club, and the Fairbury Park Board. Golf is his favorite recreation. Residence: Fairbury.

Gordon Adelbert Hartman

Gordon Adelbert Hartman, pharmacist and owner of a drug store at Gresham, Nebraska, has lived in this state for the past 30 years. He was born at Moulton, Iowa, June 19, 1891, the son of Morgan Eagle and Myrtle Elizabeth (Dodge) Hartman. His father, a farmer, was born of Pennsylvania Dutch ancestors, at Pottstown, Pennsylvania, October 4, 1857. His mother was born at Le Souer, Minnesota, March 31, 1867, the daughter of Liva Pixley and Elisha Ashcraft Dodge.

Mr. Hartman attended the public schools of Clarinda, Iowa; McCook, Nebraska; Falls City, Nebraska; Kansas City, Missouri; Eureka Springs, Arkansas; and Plattsmouth, Nebraska. In 1909 he was graduated from the McCook High School; he was employed by C. R. Woodworth, druggist, at McCook during his high school days and continued to work in the drug store there until 1913. He was employed by the Richardson

Drug Company of Omaha during 1914 and at the same time studied pharmacy under a Creighton professor. For a time he worked for J. L. Brandeis & Sons, and from 1915 to 1921 was connected with the Jerome Drug Company of York, Nebraska. He now owns and manages his own drug store at Gresham.

He has been active in civic affairs at Gresham for several years, holding the following positions: chairman of the Red Cross, 1929-30; member of the local school board, two years; justice of the peace; and police judge. He is now a member of the York County Red Cross Committee, the Young Men's Christian Association, Nebraska Pharmaceutical Association, and the Nebraskana Society. He is affiliated with the Gresham Methodist Church and holds membership in the Masons and Odd Fellows Lodge. He is interested in football, while his hobby is reading.

His marriage to Tressa Trean Rector was solemnized at McCook, Nebraska, December 25, 1913. Mrs. Hartman was born at Miltonvale, Kansas, February 7, 1888, the daughter of Mary Humphrey Rector and Oscar Newton Rector. They have two children: M. Adelbert, born August 27, 1916; and Stanley R., born October 31, 1922. Residence: Gresham.

Charles Hartner

Since 1915 Charles Hartner has been prominent as a physician and surgeon at Madison, Nebraska. He was born at Leonardville, Kansas, June 21, 1889, son of Paul and Pauline Hartner. His father, who was a farmer, was born in Germany, October 23, 1863, and now resides at Clay Center, Kansas. His mother, Pauline Frederike (Brodt) Hartner, was born in Germany, December 18, 1868.

Dr. Hartner has six brothers and three sisters, Paul, of Riley, Kansas; Fred, of Clay Center, Kansas; Will, of Clay Center, Kansas; the Reverend Henry, who is pastor of Trinity Lutheran Church of Lincoln; Ernest and Herman of Clay Center; Minnie Hartner Kahre of Clay Center; Rose Hartner Tonn of Clay Center; and Pauline Louise, a teacher of music at Hollywood, California.

Dr. Hartner attended night school where he received the equivalent of a high school education, and was later graduated from the American School of Osteopathy with the degree of Doctor of Osteopathy. Receiving his degree in 1915, prior thereto and in 1911 Dr. Hartner entered York Business College where he attained further education and where he discovered his adaptability for penmanship. He is a member of the Stillonian Club.

During 1927, 1928, and 1929, Dr. Hartner was a member of the Trinity Lutheran School board at Madison and was chairman of Trinity Lutheran Church, 1929. He was its treasurer from 1924 until 1926 inclusive. He is a member of the Madison Community Club, the Lions Club, the Nebraskana Society, and the Red Cross. His professional organizations include the following: the American Osteopathic Association, the Nebraska Osteopathic Association, and the Northeast Nebraska Osteopathic Association. He is affiliated with the Trinity Lutheran Church at Madison, and is a member of the Madison Country Club.

He was married to Alma Dorothy Whemhoff at Clay Center, Kansas, April 22, 1915. Mrs. Hartner, whose parents were German, was born at Clay Center, Kansas, March 25, 1892. Their children are: Lawrence, born March 30, 1916; Helen, born June 10, 1917; and Gerald, an adopted child, born May 11, 1929. Lawrence and Helen are students in high school.

For a period of ten years Dr. Hartner has been secretary and treasurer for the local branch of the Aid Associations for Lutherans as well as their local medical examiner. Residence: Madison. (Photograph on Page 517).

Taylor—Madison

CHARLES HARTNER

Nebraska Photo Company—Hastings

EARLE ALONZO HARVEY

Daniel Hartnett

Daniel Hartnett, who has lived in Nebraska for over 70 years, and has had a prominent part in the building up of the state, was born at St. Charles, Missouri, August 31, 1856, the son of John and Margaret (Fitzpatrick) Hartnett. His father, a farmer, was born in County Limerick, Ireland, 1816, and died at Hubbard, Dakota County, Nebraska, October 5, 1893. His mother was born in County Limerick, in 1825, and died at St. John's Dakota County, Nebraska, February 10, 1864.

Mr. Hartnett is treasurer of School District Number 7, at Hubbard, is affiliated with St. Mary's Church, and holds membership in the Nebraskana Society. He was active in the Red Cross during the World War. He is a Democrat.

His marriage to Margaret Case was solemnized at Sioux City, Doodbury County, Iowa, June 16, 1885. Mrs. Hartnett was born at Osburn, Canada, December 25, 1858. The following children were born to this marriage: Joseph, born March 23, 1886, who married Ethel Rice, and who died March 14, 1925; John E., born September 11, 1887, who married Mary E. Calihan; Mary C., born June 15, 1889, who married John C. Hayes; Thomas K., born September 16, 1891, who married Alma Fredrickson; Margruette, born June 14, 1893, who married Owen E. Beacom; Daniel, born April 11, 1896, who married Pearl Harty; James B., born January 6, 1898, who married Claire Kavanaugh; William P., born September 5, 1901, who married Elnor Lynch; and Raymond H., born January 14, 1904, who married Mabel Babbs. Residence: Hubbard.

Andrew Harvey

Andrew Harvey, physician and surgeon, was born at North Bend, Nebraska, October 26, 1884, the son of Andrew and Margaret (Ritchie) Harvey. His father, who was born at Ayr, Ayrshire, Scotland, April 1, 1843, and died at North Bend, August 22, 1922, was a farmer and fruit grower. His mother was born at Dundee Scotland, November 22, 1846, and died at North Bend, April 30, 1926.

Dr. Harvey attended rural school and in 1903 was graduated from the North Bend High School. He received the B. S. degree at Bellevue College, and the M. D. degree at the University of Nebraska, 1913. There he was secretary-treasurer of Phi Rho Sigma. For a time he was a science teacher in the high school at Fergus Falls, Minnesota, and since 1913 has been engaged in the practice of medicine at Fremont.

During the World War Dr. Harvey served as a member of the draft board in Dodge County. He is a member of the Nebraska State Medical Society, and holds a fellowship in the American Medical Association. He is a member of the Rotary Club at Fremont, the Nebraskana Society, the Young Men's Christian Association, and the Fremont Golf Club. He is a Mason, Knight Templar, Shrine. He is affiliated with the First Presbyterian Church of Fremont.

On October 22, 1913, he was married to Mabel Isabelle Thone at North Bend. Mrs. Harvey, whose ancestry is Scotch and Irish, was born at North Bend, October 8, 1888. They have the following children: Dorothy Jean, born September 20, 1915; Alexander, born November 10, 1917; and Donald Andrew, born February 28, 1925. Dr. Harvey is an independent, politically. His hobbies are reading, biography, and history, and his favorite sport is golf. Residence: Fremont.

Earle Alonzo Harvey

Earle Alonzo Harvey, physician and surgeon at Fairfield, Clay County, Nebraska, has lived in this state for the past 45 years. He was born at Newark, Kearney County, Nebraska, May 25, 1886, the son of Alonzo Abraham and Mary Louise (Maurer) Harvey. His father, who is a farmer, was born at Racine, Wisconsin, March 15, 1856; his father, Henry Harvey, was born in Lincolnshire, England, in 1829, and came to this country in 1841; his mother was born in America of English parents.

Dr. Harvey's mother, who was a school teacher, was born at Waukegon, Michigan, May 29, 1857; her ancestry was German. Dr. Harvey was graduated from the Gandy High School in 1907; attended Hastings College in 1908; in 1917 was awarded the M. D. and D. P. H. degrees at Eclectic Medical University, and has had considerable post graduate work in surgery. He has been engaged in the practice of medicine and surgery since 1917, and holds membership in the county, state, and American Medical Societies. Now city physician, he served as president of the Fairfield Commercial Club in 1930, is a member of the board of education, and is a member of the Methodist Church at Fairfield. Dr. Harvey holds a commission as first lieutenant in the Medical Reserves. His hobby is hunting.

He was united in marriage with Jennie L. Frank at Heartwell, Nebraska, January 6, 1909. Mrs. Harvey, who is a nurse, was born at Heartwell, January 3, 1886. Their children are: Keith A., born July 15, 1912, now a pre-medic student at Wesleyan; Paul F., born September 30, 1914, and Lloyd R., born June 19, 1919. Dr. Harvey is a Republican. He is a Mason, a member of the Eastern Star and the Woodmen. Residence: Fairfield. (Photograph on Page 518).

Kitty B. Harvey

Born at Wells, Minnesota, July 23, 1867, Kitty B. Harvey has resided in Nebraska for the past fifty-four years. She is the daughter of Edward Henry and Eliza (Obrian) Taylor, early settlers in Nebraska.

Edward Henry Taylor was born in Fulton County, New York, February 27, 1835, enlisted in the Civil War in 1862, with the 147th Illinois Infantry and served until the end of the War. He was a farmer and stockman until his death at Sargent on August 22, 1907.

Eliza Taylor, wife of Edward, was born in Vales Mills, New York, November 20, 1835, and died at Taylor Nebraska, June 26, 1901. She was a fine Christian homemaker and mother, and a member of the Woman's Relief Corps.

On August 15, 1883, Kitty A. Taylor was married to James H. Harvey at Loup City. Mr. Harvey was born in West Virginia in 1844, and died at Taylor, January 8, 1922. He was a farmer and stock raiser, and a veteran of the Civil War.

There are six children, James Clarence, born October 8, 1884, married Mary Thompson; John L., born February 18, 1886, married Maud Pierce; Nellie May, born October 16, 1885, married Will Bromwich; Harry, born December 16, 1892, married Hattie Lenke; Ruth, born September 8, 1896, married Leslie Galbreath; and William McKinley, born June 4, 1899, who married Lois Alder.

Mrs. Harvey is a member of the Taylor Congregational Church, the Red Cross, the Royal Neighbors of America, The Nebraskana Society and the Kent Corner Club. Residence: Taylor.

Robert George Harvey

Robert George Harvey, banker, was born at Farwell, Nebraska, December 21, 1889, son of James and Anna (Hadden) Harvey. Mr. Harvey's ancestry is Scotch, his family having settled in America about 1843.

Upon the completion of his public school education Mr. Harvey went to the St. Paul Business College.

On September 3, 1919, he was married to Beatrice Hayden Atkins at Gering. She was born at Elgin, Nebraska, July 3, 1892.

Mr. Harvey served with the 164th Depot Brigade

at Camp Funston, Kansas, during the World War. He is a Republican, a Presbyterian and a Mason. Residence: Gering.

Jan D. Hasik

Born at Zverotice, Tabor County, Czechoslovakia, April 9, 1874, Jan D. Hasik, is the son of Matej Hasik and Katerina (Dusek) Hasik. His father was born in Zverotice, Czechoslovakia, October 24, 1847, and came to the United States in the fall of the year, 1879. His ancestors were farmers in which occupation he was also engaged, in connection with blacksmithing. He died July 6, 1915, at Abie, Nebraska. His mother was born at Zverotice, September 13, 1848, and is living with her son.

Jan Hasik was graduated from the Abie High School in 1891. He was united in marriage with Emma Ruby Faytinger, September 21, 1898, at Abie, Nebraska, where she was born July 29, 1881. To this union were born five children: Otto, October 5, 1900, a graduate of Kearney State Normal School, who is married and has been superintendent of schools for seven years; Milo, April 20, 1902, took a two year course at the State University and is a mechanic; Clarence, December 13, 1903, who is a farmer; Dorothy, August 28, 1905, who is a teacher; and Irene, April 12, 1911, who also teaches scnool. Both daughters attended college at Kearney and the University of Nebraska.

Mr. Hasik taught school from 1894-1903, was a rural mail carrier from 1904-10, since which time he has been a farmer and dairyman. He was a member of the Nebraska legislature from 1911-13, elected on the Republican ticket. He has also been city clerk and justice of peace. Mr. Hasik has contributed many articles concerning general farming to *The Hospodar*, a leading Bohemian farm paper.

During the World War he was active in the loan drives, fund drives, Red Cross and Young Men's Christian Association work. Jan Hasik was a member of the State Board of Agriculture for six years; is a charter member of the Nebraska Crop Growers Association, and is a member of the State Dairy Association. He holds membership in the State Historical Society, the National Geographic Society and the Nebraskana Society. From 1929-31 he was a member of the Deer Creek Parent Teacher's Association, and was a moderator of School District No. 26. He is a member of the David City Commercial Club, and Knights of Pythias, and the Western Bohemian Fraternal Association. Reading farm and dairy articles is Mr. Hasik's hobby. Residence: David City.

William Wesley Haskell

William Wesley Haskell, founder of the *Ord Quiz*, was born at Earlville, Illinois, January 23, 1857, and since November 9, 1881, has resided in Nebraska.

His father, Sylvester Smith Haskell, was a farmer, descended from one of the three Haskells who came from England, and was also descended from General Putnam. He died at Ord. His wife, who was a lineal descendant of a brother of Ethan Allen, also died at Ord.

Mr. Haskell attended common school, and was a student for a time at Northwestern University. He earned his way through his junior year, when he was compelled to leave school because of lack of funds. He became part owner of the Ord townsite; founded and edited the *Ord Quiz* for thirty-six years. Mr. Haskell is the former owner of the Ord gas plant, and was, until recent years, an extensive landowner. For a number of years he was a member of the Modern Woodmen of America, and at the present time is a life member of The Nebraskana Society. He is a Methodist.

On November 6, 1881, he was married to Cecelia Victoria Cutler at Chicago. Mrs. Haskell was born in Van Buren County, Michigan, November 22, 1858, and is descended from the Sprague family. Five children were born to them, Zilpha, Winifred (Mrs. Herman N. Mattley); Cosa Dell (wife of Dr. D. N. Lindberg); John Roscoe, who married Ruth Wilson; and Zerna Mae. Zilpha and Zerna are both deceased. Residence: Ord.

George Alfred Haslam

Born at Fremont, February 10, 1899, George Alfred Haslam is the son of George James and Mary Elizabeth (Dern) Haslam. His father was born in Manchester, England, May 10, 1858, and came to America in 1886. A physician and surgeon, he was an outstanding member of his profession and a fellow of the American College of Surgeons. His death occurred at Fremont, April 23, 1923. His wife, Mary, was born at Fremont, December 18, 1870, of German parentage.

Dr. Haslam was graduated from Fremont High School in June, 1917, received his A. B. in 1921, B. S. in 1922, and his M. D. in 1924. The A. B. and B. S. degrees were from the University of Nebraska while his M. D. was awarded by the University of Pennsylvania. He is a member of the La Place Surgical Society and Phi Rho Sigma from Pennsylvania, and Delta Upsilon from the University of Nebraska.

On September 2, 1922, he was united in marriage to Gertrude Valentine Miller, daughter of John A. and Florence Valentine Miller at Kearney, Nebraska. Mrs. Haslam was born at Kearney, January 7, 1901, and traces her ancestry to colonial days in America. There are two sons, George J., born April 27, 1925, and John A., born November 9, 1927.

In the active practice of surgery since 1926, Dr. Haslam is a member of the American, Nebraska State and Dodge County Medical Societies. He served as a second lieutenant of Infantry in the World War, and is a member of the American Legion. He enjoys golf, and is fond of gardening. He occasionally delivers addresses. Residence: Fremont. (Photograph in Album).

Emil Bernhard Hassel

Emil Bernhard Hassel was born at Loomis, Nebraska, October 24, 1884, the son of John Erick and Benga (Bodelson) Hassel. His father, who was born at Vestmanland, Sweden, October 19, 1850, came to this country in 1879, and has engaged in farming in Nebraska since then. His mother was born at Skane, Sweden, January 11, 1850, and died at Portland, Oregon, in May, 1918.

Mr. Hassel attended rural school in Phelps County, Nebraska, and studied in the business department of Luther College at Wahoo, Nebraska, for a time. He was a farmer until 1908, when he entered the employ of the Kranquest Implement Company, and since then has been connected with the Farmers Union Exchange of Holdrege. Nebraska, and the Nichols & Shepherd Threshing Machine Company of Lincoln. At this time he is serving as county treasurer of Phelps County.

He holds membership in the Holdrege Chamber of Commerce, is affiliated with the Bethel Lutheran Church of Holdrege, and holds membership in the Red Cross. He is a Mason, an Odd Fellow, and a Republican. His hobby is mechanics.

On February 17, 1909, he married Emma Amanda Swanson at Holdrege. Mrs. Hassel was born at Atlanta, Nebraska, August 4, 1888. Mrs. Hassel's parents came to America in 1880, settling in Indiana where they remained three years. They then came to Nebraska, where they spent the remainder of their lives. Mr. and Mrs. Hassel have one son, La Monte Bernhard, born June 20, 1920. Residence: Holdrege. (Photograph in Album).

Earl L. Hasselbalch

Earl L. Hasselbalch was born at St. Edward, Nebraska, June 27, 1901, the son of Nels Christian and Anna Christina (Anderson) Hasselbalch. His father, a merchant, was born at Bodense, Denmark, August 2, 1858, and died at St. Edward, July 14, 1926; he came to America in 1880, and was a resident of St. Edward from 1883 until his death, holding various city offices in his community. His mother was born in Denmark, February 15, 1862, and came to this country in 1867, and makes her home at St. Edward.

Mr. Hasselbalch attended Culver Military Academy at Culver, Indiana, was graduated from St. Edward High School in 1919, received the B. S. degree at the University of Nebraska in 1923, and was awarded the J. D. degree at Stanford University in 1926. His fraternities were Phi Sigma Kappa and Delta Theta Phi.

A Republican, he served as state representative from Boone County in 1929 and at this time is city attorney of St. Edward where he is also engaged in general legal practice. He is affiliated with the First Presbyterian Church of St. Edward and is a member of The Nebraskana Society.

His marriage to Nellie Mae Burke was solemnized at St. Edward, August 16, 1928. Mrs. Hasselbalch was born at Harrison, Nebraska, May 18, 1904. Residence: St. Edward.

Joseph Hassler

Joseph Hassler, grain and lumber dealer, was born in Lyons, Iowa, September 17, 1861, and for the past 55 years has resided in Nebraska. He is the son of Joseph and Magdeline Hassler.

The father was born in Baden, Germany, March 14, 1834, and engaged in the building contracting business until his death at Exeter, June 20, 1925. His wife, Magdeline, was born in Chicago, Illinois, June 10, 1840, and died at Exeter, Nebraska, January 23, 1907.

On December 27, 1898, Mr. Hassler was married to Minta Ellen Boyer at Golden, Colorado. Mrs. Hassler was born at Victoria, Illinois, August 26, 1875, and has resided in Nebraska for 45 years. Mr. and Mrs. Hassler have four children, Josephine, born September 3, 1903, who married V. C. Forbes; Lena, born May 11, 1905, who married R. A. Freeman; Gretchen, born August 3, 1909; and Kathleen, born January 6, 1916. Residence: Culbertson.

Charles Edward Hastert

On June 3, 1873, Charles E. Hastert was born, at Chicago, Illinois, the son of Nicholas and Catherine (Shuh) Hastert. His father, who was born at Luxemburg, December 6, 1842, and died at Alton, Iowa, December 8, 1914, came to this country in 1860, and settled in Chicago. His mother was born at Sandweiler, Luxemburg, October 17, 1861, and died at Alton, March 25, 1918.

Mr. Hastert has been a resident of Nebraska for 54 years, and is the owner of a hardware store at Shelby, Nebraska. He was married to Lena Albena Schlentz at David City, Nebraska, February 3, 1898. They have seven children: Bernard, born November 22, 1898, who died July 9, 1916; Louis A., born July 17, 1900, who married Rose Gabriel; Viola C., born November 12, 1903, who married William Lux; Clarence J., born October 12, 1906, who is a civil engineer in Peru; Francis C., born November 7, 1911, who is a student at the University of Nebraska; Marie, born November 25, 1913; and Margaret, born September 27, 1915. Residence: Shelby.

Robert Richardson Hastings

Robert R. Hastings, distinguished lawyer, and a life time resident of Crete, Nebraska, was born there November 27, 1888, the son of George Henry and Helen Mary (Richardson) Hastings. His father, who was born at Coral, McHenry County, Illinois, August 26, 1848; practiced law at Crete, from 1871 until his death; he served as attorney general of Nebraska from 1892 to 1896; he died at Crete, July 24, 1926. His mother was born at Aurora, Kane County, Illinois, October 3, 1850, and died at Crete, January 24, 1925.

Mr. Hastings was graduated from the Crete High School, May 25, 1906. He was awarded his A. B. degree at Doane College in 1910; and received the LL. B. degree at the University of Nebraska in 1913. He was a member of the Doane College debating team for three years; was president of the junior class, 1908-09; and was president of the junior law class at the University of Nebraska, 1911-12. He was a member of Pi Kappa Delta at Doane College and Delta Chi at the University of Nebraska. He was awarded college letters in track, both at Doane College and the University of Nebraska.

He was first associated with the law firm of Hastings & Ireland at Crete, and later was a member of the firm Hastings & Hastings. He is now in practice alone. He is president of the Crete Loan & Savings Association, and is a stockholder in the Crete State Bank. He was an active war worker in 1917-18; was active in the Red Cross; was a patriotic speaker; and assisted the draft board. He is a member of the Sons of the American Revolution, Nebraska State Bar Association, Saline County Bar Association, Crete Chamber of Commerce, and the Nebraskana Society. He served as secretary of the Crete Rotary Club in 1923-24. He is a member of Crete Lodge Number 37 of the Masons, Royal Arch, at Crete, Mount Moriah Commandry Number 4 at Lincoln, Sesostris Temple, Lincoln, and Nobles of the Mystic Shrine, Lincoln. His social club is the Shrine Country Club at Lincoln. His hobby is horticulture. He is a Republican.

Mr. Hastings was married at Lincoln, Lancaster County, Nebraska, July 28, 1915, to Edith Mae Lapp. Mrs. Hastings was born at Cold Water, Branch County, Michigan, June 23, 1887. They have a daughter, Anna Mae, born April 18, 1922. Residence: Crete.

William Charles Hastings

Since 1903 William Charles Hastings has been a dentist at Newman Grove, Nebraska, where he is also active in civic and professional organizations. He was born at Emmetsburg, Iowa, August 15, 1876, the son of Charles William and Sarah Ann (Wright) Hastings, the former a grain buyer and farmer. His father was born at Manitowoc, Wisconsin, October 10, 1850, the son of Charles Hastings and Lucinda Harrison, and died at Retlaw, Canada, April 15, 1915. His mother, who is the daughter of John Wright and Harriett McKay, was born at West Falls, New York, May 1, 1857, and died at Ryegate, Montana, August 10, 1928.

Dr. Hastings was graduated from the Ruthven High School in 1892, and received the D. D. S. degree at Keokuk Medical College in Iowa, in 1903. He was employed in the office of the *Ruthven Free Press* for a time, was connected with the W. E. Wilson Drug Company of Ruthven as a pharmacist, and since 1903 has successfully practiced dentistry at Newman Grove.

He holds membership in the District Medical Society, the Nebraska State Dental Society, the Five County Medical Society, and the Nebraska Gold Foil Club. He served as chairman of the Red Cross in Madison County, Nebraska, during the World War and was lieutenant of the local Home Guards. Dr. Hastings is a member of the committee of the Boy Scouts of America, has been president of the local library board since 1920, and was formerly president of the local school board. He is a Master Mason and an Odd Fellow. His hobby is flower gardening, while his sports include golfing and shooting.

His marriage to Maude Mae Doty occurred at Newman Grove, June 1, 1908. Mrs. Hastings, who was a teacher before her marriage, was born at Casville, Wisconsin, April 10, 1883, the daughter of John and Lucinda (Halstead) Doty, and died at Newman Grove, March 15, 1913. They have one daughter, Gretchen, born January 22, 1913, who is a senior at the University of Nebraska. On November 12, 1919, Dr. Hastings was united in marriage with Margaret Hansen of Tilden, Nebraska. Their son, William, was born January 22, 1921. Mrs. Hastings is very active in Woman's Club work and is president of the Newman Grove Woman's Club and is vice president of the local P. E. O. chapter. Residence: Newman Grove.

William Granger Hastings

One of the most beloved figures in the legal and judicial life of Nebraska, is William Granger Hastings. Judge Hastings was born at Woodstock, Illinois, April 9, 1853. His father, Carlisle Hastings, was born in Suffield Township, Connecticut, April 12, 1815. He was county superintendent of public instruction, county sheriff of McHenry County, Illinois, 1852-53, and laid out the school districts of that county in 1839. He was decended from Thomas Hastings of Ipswich, England, who settled at Watertown, Massachusetts, in 1632. He died at Coral, Illinois, March 21, 1901. Hannah Granger, wife of Carlisle Hastings, was born at Suffield Township May 11, 1817, and died at Coral, March 19, 1903. She was descended from John Granger who settled on Block Island in Long Island Sound in 1628.

Until he reached the age of fourteen William G. Hastings attended district school in McHenry County, Illinois, and then attended high school at Marengo, Illinois, two winters. Thereafter he taught district school two winters, and later entered the University of Chicago, where he received his A. B. in 1876. He wrote the sophomore prize essay at the University of Chicago in 1874, and was elected to Delta Kappa Epsilon at the same university. In 1924 he received his LL. D. from the University of Nebraska. In 1900 he was the winner of a $2,000 prize from the American Philosophical Society. He has been a member of Phi Beta Kappa since 1898.

Fifty-four years ago he came to Nebraska. From 1877 to 1892, he was engaged in active legal practice in Saline County. On January 1, 1892, he was made judge of the seventh judicial district. He is a Democrat and served as state senator from 1885 to 1887, and as county attorney of Saline County from 1890-91. In 1896 he was again elected judge of the seven district, serving until 1900. From 1901 to 1904 he was Supreme Court Commissioner, and from 1904 to 1921 was teacher of law at the University of Nebraska Law School. Since 1923 he has been judge of the fourth judicial district of Nebraska, which district embraces Douglas, Washington and Burt Counties. He is the author of *Police Power*, the American Philosophical Society prize essay above referred to, and of a translation from the Russian of Korkunov's *General Theory of Law*.

On October 20, 1880, he was united in marriage to Elizabeth Hackley, in McHenry County, Illinois. Mrs. Hastings, who was born in Allegany, Michigan, September 12, 1851, died at Omaha, June 18, 1922. She was the granddaughter, on the maternal side, of Dirk Lansing of Lansingburg, New York, and the granddaughter of Professor Hackley of Hartford, Connecticut. Their two children are Helen, born June 20, 1882, who before her marriage to George Buckland was auditor of the State Bank of Lincoln; and Laura, born May 12, 1884, who is unmarried. Residence: Omaha.

William Albert Hatcher

William Albert Hatcher, a lumber and hardware dealer, was born at Benton, Tennessee, May 22, 1875, son of William and Caroline (Cameron) Hatcher.

His father was born at Sevierville, Tennessee, and died at Benton, October 14, 1903. He was a farmer. His wife was born and died at Benton.

Mr. Hatcher attended common county school at Benton and for the past 29 years has lived in Nebraska. At the present time he is president of the W. A. Hatcher Lumber Company, is president of the Commercial Club, a member of the Congregational Church and of the Masons.

On February 10, 1909, he was married to Eva May Burt at Smithfield, Nebraska. She was born at Granville, Illinois, January 1, 1885. Residence: Venango.

Thomas Elial Hattel

On December 4, 1899, Thomas E. Hattel was born in Thayer, Nebraska, son of Charles Hattel, who was of French parentage, and Mary Jane (Owens) Hattel. Charles Hattel took a homestead one mile south of Thayer, and lived in that community all his life. His mother was born July 26, 1857, in Montgomeryshire, North Wales. She is living; her husband died in Thayer, Nebraska, July 11, 1901.

Thomas Hattel attended the Thayer, Nebraska, grade school, and entered high school in Gresham, Nebraska, where he played basketball for two years. He was graduated in 1919.

Mr. Hattel taught school five years in York and Polk counties, worked two years for the Chicago and Northwestern Railroad Company; worked four years as assistant cashier in the Shelby State Bank, and has been a cashier in the State Bank of Surprise, Nebraska, for two years.

Mildred May Curry, born July 7, 1902, in Superior, Nuckolls County, Nebraska, became Mr. Hattel's wife in York, Nebraska, August 22, 1922. Mrs. Hattel is of French-Irish parentage. They have two children: Norma Lucille, born May 24, 1923, and Thomas Jr., born September 12, 1924.

Mr. Hattel is director of the State Bank of Surprise, Nebraska, president of the Community Club, treasurer of Read Township, city clerk, and secretary of the Parent-Teachers' Association in Surprise. He is a Republican and a Protestant, is a member of the Red Cross, and is a member of the order of the Ancient Free and Accepted Masons.

Thomas Hattel is a member of the Nebraskana Society. He has had success in raising and showing pure bred White Wyandotte chickens which is his avocation. Residence: Surprise.

Dean Allan Hatten

Dean Allan Hatten was born at Fullerton, Nebraska, September 25, 1898, the son of William Price and Belle (Fiske) Hatten. His father, who was born at Hamburg, Iowa, was cashier of the Fullerton National Bank for 23 years, was treasurer of Nance County, Nebraska for several years, and is now retired. His mother was born at Cuba, New York.

Mr. Hatten was graduated from Fullerton High School, where he was active in athletics, attended Hastings College for a year, and was a student at the University of Nebraska for a year. He served in the Fullerton National Bank for a year, was cashier of the Lancaster County Bank at Waverly, Nebraska, for two years, acted as vice president of the Farmers State Bank at Belgrade, Nebraska, for nearly three years, and for over a year sold bank supplies. He has been the owner and manager of the Grand Island Credit Association at Grand Island, Nebraska for the past eight years.

He holds membership in the Kiwanis Club, of which he was trustee and secretary for a number of years, is affiliated with the First Presbyterian Church of Grand Island and is serving on the membership committee of the Grand Island Chamber of Commerce. His sports include golfing and swimming and he is a member of the Fairview Golf Association. His hobby is bridge. Mr. Hatten was connected with every Liberty loan and war stamp campaign in his county during the World War.

He married Lillian Mina Blofield of Fullerton, Nebraska. Mrs. Hatten, whose ancestry is English, was born at Palmer, Nebraska. They have one daughter, Annabella, born June 7, 1918. Residence: Grand Island.

Arthur Edsell Hauke

For the past 54 years Arthur Edsell Hauke has lived in Nebraska where he has been a leader in the business and agricultural world. He was born in Clinton County, Iowa, August 22, 1868, the son of Samuel Wesley and Hannah (Livingston) Hauke, the former a clergyman, teacher, and farmer. Samuel Hauke, who was a descendent of Countess Van Hauke of Holland, was born in Lycoming County, Pennsylvania, December 1, 1844, came to Nebraska from Iowa in 1878, and died at Wood River, Nebraska, December 16, 1881.

Hannah (Livingston) Hauke, whose father was a descendant of David Livingston, the African explorer, was born in Lawrence County, Pennsylvania, November 26, 1847.

Mr. Hauke attended rural and city schools in Hall County. He has been a farmer near Wood River for many years, serving as president of the Hall County Farm Bureau, president of the Wood River Chautauqua Association, and a director in the Wood River Building & Loan Association, is president of the local chapter of the Nebraska Children's Home Society in Wood River, and is serving as president of the Wood River Chamber of Commerce.

He served as director of the local school board from 1902 to 1920, is a member of the Red Cross and The Nebraskana Society, and is affiliated with the Methodist Episcopal Church. During the World War he served as member of the Council of Defense, was assistant chairman of the Red Cross Committee, and participated in loan drives of various kinds. He is a Mason and Odd Fellow.

Mr. Hauke is a profound student and reader. He has held various public offices at Wood River, including: justice of the peace; township treasurer; assessor. His favorite sport is football.

He was married at Wood River, February 17, 1891, to Sadie Hannah Barrick who was born at Wood River, November 27, 1872. Six children were born to their marriage, four of whom are living: Myrtle, December 19, 1891, who married Donald L. Garrison; Lena, August 12, 1893; Lavern, January 9, 1896, who married Irene Blanchard, and who died May 17, 1926; Anna, February 7, 1899, who married Lex A. Wescott; Ralph, born May 26, 1901, who died January 3, 1902; and Arthur, December 12, 1902. Lena is district extension agent at the College of Agriculture at Fallon, Nevada, and Arthur is connected with the Rural Economics Department of the Michigan College of Agriculture. Residence: Wood River.

Leo Morgan Hauptman

One of Nebraska's most promising younger men is Leo Morgan Hauptman, superintendent of public schools at Burr. Mr. Hauptman was born on a farm three miles northeast of Julian, in Otoe County, on June 3, 1909. His father, Lee William Hauptman, a farmer, was born one and a half miles north of Julian, on May 16, 1884. Lee William Hauptman's father was born in Prussia, in 1833, and died in America, in 1890. His mother was born in Covington, Kentucky, in 1848, and died in 1919.

Lee W. Hauptman married Albert Lorena Elwell, who was born at Tabor, Iowa, September 24, 1885. Her father was born at Stoneham, Massachusetts in 1851, and is still living; her mother, who was born at Tabor, in 1865, died in 1887. Of Scotch-Irish descent, the family is descended from Elbridge Gerry, signer of the Declaration of Independence and vice-president of the United States, and from George Walton, also a signer, both on the paternal side.

Leo Morgan Hauptman attended the town and country schools of Otoe County, and was graduated from country school with highest honors in Otoe County's first examination in 1923. From 1923-27 he attended the Nebraska City High School, his average grades being 92.96, the third highest among fifty-six students. He entered Peru State Teacher's College in 1927, and has reached the rank of senior in the college. He was granted a first grade state teacher's certificate from Peru, in 1929. During the summers of 1929 and 1930, he attended Peru, and during the summers of 1927 and 1928 he was editorial assistant for the *Nebraska Daily News-Press*. During the fall of 1926 he was Nebraska City manager of the *Omaha Daily News*, and from December, 1926 to May, 1927, was assistant instructor in shorthand and typewriting in the Nebraska City night school.

Mr. Hauptman has received many scholastic honors. He is a member of Kappa Delta Pi, national honorary educational fraternity; Pi Gamma Mu, national honor social science fraternity; Sigma Tau Delta, national honorary professional English fraternity; national honorary society for journalists in high school, and also national honor society for students in high schools; the Philomathean Literary Society of which he was treasurer in 1928; the Peru Dramatic Club, of which he was president in 1928. Mr. Hauptman has taken leading parts in many of the eleven dramatic productions he has appeared in, and has directed five major productions. He was the winner of the Daughters of the American Revolution Award for excellency in history in Nebraska City, and of the highest award in civics from the *Nebraska Daily News-Press;* and first place in sectional academic Civics contest at Peru.

In 1929 he was associate editor of *The Peruvian,* Peru College Annual; he is the author of a series of newspaper articles of an historical nature published in *The Nebraska Daily News-Press* and *Omaha World Herald* in 1927 and 1928. In 1929 he wrote *Martin Stowell, Conductor Underground Railroad,* the original copy of which is in the Peru College Library, and for some time he has been engaged on the biography of Hon. Thomas Jefferson Majors, one of Nebraska's most prominent and best beloved men.

On August 24, 1930, Mr. Hauptman was married to Lucile Marie Lash, at Auburn. Mrs. Hauptman was born north of Auburn, on December 7, 1908, of Pennsylvania Dutch and Scotch-Irish parentage. She is a teacher in the public school of Burr and an artist. Mrs. Hauptman is a graduate of Peru State Teacher's College with an A. B. degree in January, 1932. She is a charter member of Kappa Omicron Phi, National Honorary-Professional Home Economic Fraternity.

For the past two years Mr. Hauptman has been superintendent of the Burr public schools, and was elected for a third term but resigned so he and Mrs. Hauptman could complete their degrees at Peru during 1931-1932. In addition to this work, he carries on his historical research work, and plans soon to enter the field of journalism. He is the author of a one-act play, *The Test of Time,* not yet published. His hobby is the collection and filing of newspaper articles, and local historical research.

Mr. Hauptman is extremely active in religious and civic work, and has devoted much of his time to local affairs. While in high school he managed the collection of $100 for near East Relief, and while in Peru, during the summer of 1928, represented the Young Men's Christian Association at a summer camp in Estes Park and in state meetings. He is a member of the Methodist Episcopal Church at Nebraska City; was treasurer of the Young People's Branch of the Woman's Christian Temperance Union in 1926, president in 1927, and treasurer of the Ep-

Pitstick—Nebraska City

LEO MORGAN HAUPTMAN

worth League in 1924, and first vice president 1925-28.

His professional organizations include the Nebraska State Teacher's Association, and the National Educational Association. He is secretary of the Burr Parent-Teachers Association. On March 11, 1924, he was taken into the Boy Scouts, and acted as scribe and treasurer. Since June 8, 1927, he has been a member of the Nebraska City chapter of De Molay. He is a member of the Nebraskana Society.

During the time he has been superintendent of schools he has added a fourth teacher, the twelfth grade, secured up to date text books, organized a Parent-Teacher's Association, sponsored and directed six plays, built a new set of scenery, made the first systematic count and record of library books, and improved the health and safety of his children.

Mr. and Mrs. Hauptman spent the summer of 1931 in Association Camp, out of Estes Park, in Colorado, where Mr. Hauptman was desk clerk at the camp. Residence: Burr. (Photograph on Page 525).

Henry Hauschild

Henry Hauschild was born at Schleswig, Germany, November 22, 1856, the son of Peter Hauschild and Sophia (Hintz) Hauschild of Hilstein, Germany. His father born at Schleswig, died at Nebraska City, Otoe County, Nebraska, September 12, 1916. His mother was born at Schleswig, and died at Syracuse, Nebraska, October 12, 1916.

A resident of Nebraska for 53 years, his civic spirit endeared him to his many friends and neighbors in his community. He was married at Nebraska City, Otoe County, March 27, 1877, to Cecilia Wehling. Mrs. Hauschild was born at Schleswig, August 30, 1853, and died at Syracuse, October 8, 1930. There were two children born to this union: Helena, born April 16, 1879, who married Chirs. F. Reimer, and now lives on a farm; and John P., born October 11, 1882, who farmed for some time and now lives in Syracuse.

Mr. Hauschild was a member of the Luther Memorial Church. His death, in 1928, was a distinct loss to the state and his community. He is remembered by his many friends and business associates as a man of kindness and integrity.

John P. Hauschild

John P. Hauschild was born at Nebraska City, Nebraska, October 11, 1882. His father, Henry Hauschild, who was a farmer, was born at Schleswig, Holstein, Germany, November 22, 1856, and died at Syracuse, Otoe County, Nebraska, March 6, 1928. Cecilia (Wehling) Hauschild, his wife, was born at Schleswig, August 30, 1853, and died at Syracuse, October 8, 1930.

Mr. Hauschild attended the rural schools of Otoe County. A resident of Nebraska all his life, he lived on a farm near Syracuse, until January 19, 1920, when he retired.

He was united in marriage with Anna Marie Bartels at Syracuse, March 5, 1908. Mrs. Hauschild was born in New York City, February 9, 1888. There are two children: Harry, born March 3, 1914, who is a student in high school; and La Verna, born August 17, 1918. Mr. Hauschild is affiliated with the Luther Memorial Church at Syracuse.

Lloyd Ranaldo Haven

Lloyd Ranaldo Haven, son of James Platte and Laura Elizabeth (Waterberry) Haven, was born at Nickerson, Nebraska, September 4, 1882. James Platte Haven, who is now retired, was born in Anamosa, Iowa, July 7, 1859; his ancestry was English, dating to 1662, in America. His wife, Laura, was born in Quincy, Illinois, April 6, 1862, and died at Fremont, November 21, 1923. Her parents were German and came to America in 1848.

Lloyd R. Haven attended Fremont public schools and was graduated from Fremont High School in 1901. He received a letter in athletics, and later attended the University of Nebraska two years. For the past twenty-seven years he has been the proprietor of the Haven Cleaning Works.

He was married to Pearl Amber Ryan at Wahoo, Nebraska, June 21, 1902. Mrs. Haven was born at Fremont, January 9, 1885. They have one daughter, Amber, born January 24, 1908, who received her A. B. from Midland College in 1929. Mr. and Mrs. Haven are members of the First Congregational Church, and he belongs to the Red Cross, Boy Scouts of America, DeMolay, Masons and Eagles. His hobbies are public speaking and boys' work. Residence: Fremont.

Charles W. Havlicek

Charles W. Havlicek, a resident of the state for the past 65 years, has been a jeweler at Crete, Nebraska, for 35 years. He was born at Manitowoc, Kewanee County, Wisconsin, July 28, 1865, the son of Vaclav and Katherine (Kucera) Havlicek. His father, who was a mason and farmer, was born at Melnik, Czechoslovakia, April 15, 1823, and died at Bluff City, Kansas, May 10, 1907. His mother was born in Czechoslovakia, July, 1836, and died at Bluff City, October 27, 1915.

Mr. Havlicek was a student in Crete schools, and then entered the jewelry business at Crete. After selling his jewelry business he began the operation of a music store. He is a member of the Nebraskana Society, the Woodmen of the World, Z. C. B. J., and T. J. S.

On June 17, 1890, he was married to Anna Shebl, at vakia, December 8, 1868. Mrs. Havlicek was born in Kramous, Czechoslovakia, December 8, 1868. They have four children; Lumir, born August 11, 1895, who is a musician; Charles L., born February 15, 1897; Joseph W., born December 13, 1896; and Libby L., born September 1, 1906, who is employed as stenographer with the Fairmont Creamery Company. Lumir served in the World War, and is director of the 110th Medical Regiment Band. Charles served in the navy during the war as electrician. He is now station operator for the Edison Electric Company at Long Beach, California. Joseph is a civil service electrician on the gulf coast at New Orleans. Residence: Crete.

Fielden Thomas Hawks

Fielden Thomas Hawks, farmer, was born in Easton, Illinois, August 18, 1863, son of James and Abigail (Bales) Hawks. The father was born in Green County, Kentucky, and died at Easton, Illinois. The mother, also born in Green County, died in Mason County, Illinois.

On January 5, 1886, Mr. Hawks was married to Sarah Lizzie Stone at Easton, her birth place. There are four children, Ollie M., born September 24, 1886; Thomas, born January 6, 1887; William, born January 30, 1890; and Loyd, born August 10, 1893, died November 23, 1907; and Earl, born November 2, 1893.

Mr. Hawks has been a farmer all his life. He is a Democrat, a member of the Modern Woodmen of America, and the Ancient Order of United Workmen. He has served on the school board 37 years and as county commissioner four years. Residence: Bruning.

William Hawley

William Hawley, executive, was born at North Platte, Nebraska, September 29, 1883, son of John and Lucie (McDonald) Hawley. The mother is of Irish, and the father of English descent, their parents having come to the United States about 1875. His father operated the first hotel in North Platte which was known as the Hawley House. It was badly damaged by fire in 1893, remodeled and renamed to Commercial Hotel and was located where the Maloney Furniture Store now stands. In his later years he was a farmer near Sutherland, and died there in March, 1894. His mother died in North Platte, 1887.

For a number of years Mr. Hawley was a railroad man for the Union Pacific, starting as brakeman, was promoted to conductor, train dispatcher, and then chief train dispatcher retiring on account of his health. He engaged in the theatrical business, forming a partnership with Keith Neville operating the Keith, Sun and Crystal Theatres. The partnership was dissolved and Mr. Hawley engaged in the ice and coal business, known as the Artificial Ice and Coal Company of which he is secretary-treasurer and general manager. He is a Democrat, a member of the Elks, the Brotherhood of Railway Trainmen, the Chamber of Commerce of which he was director, 1929-30, and the Knights of Columbus and past member of the Kiwanis Club. He enjoys hunting.

On August 10, 1910, he was married to Mary Irene O'Brien at North Platte, Nebraska. She was born at Council Bluffs, Iowa, July 31, 1892. There are two children, John, born March 9, 1914, is completing his second year of high school at North Platte and is captain of the basketball team. The team is the winner of the 1932 regional tournament and is competing in the state tournament at Lincoln. He was picked as all conference end in football, 1931; and their second son, William, was born January 28, 1928. Residence: North Platte. (Photograph in Album).

Cecil Clyde Hawthorne

A pioneer merchant in Valley County, Nebraska, is Cecil Clyde Hawthorne who was born at Meadville, Pennsylvania, April 25, 1872, the son of Boone Marion and Sarah Isabelle (Coulter) Hawthorne. His father, who was a pioneer farmer in Nebraska, was born at Franklin, Pennsylvania, October 8, 1844, and died at Arcadia, Nebraska, February 25, 1928. His mother, who was a teacher, was born at Franklin and died at Kearney, Nebraska, October 16, 1884. She was the organizer of the first Sunday School at Arcadia, Nebraska, and named the town.

Mr. Hawthorne was engaged in the milling business from 1890 to 1898, and from 1898 to 1924 was a hardware merchant at Arcadia. He has been active in the real estate and insurance business there since 1924, is affiliated with the First Congregational Church, and holds membership in the Masonic Lodge.

On March 28, 1899, he was married to Augusta Doris Peters at Burwell, Nebraska. Mrs. Hawthorne, the daughter of Charles and Louisa (Schulz) Peters, was born at Chabanse, August 28, 1876. Three children were born to this marriage: Doris Aimee, June 16, 1908, who died August 17, 1917; Cecil, April 1, 1911, who died September 17, 1921; John Boone, June 18, 1921; and four adopted children, Donald, January 5, 1914; Sam, October 4, 1915; Elaine, December 15, 1916; and Neva, April 20, 1919. Residence: Arcadia.

Frederick George Hawxby

Frederick George Hawxby, lawyer, and former member of the Nebraska legislature, was born on a farm near Nemaha, December 10, 1871. His father was English, born in Ripon, Yorkshire, England, January 29, 1833. A butcher by trade, he came from a middle class family, his brother was a foreman on a large farm in Yorkshire, under whom he was instructed. His father came from England to Illinois in 1857. Settling in southeastern Nebraska in 1860, he broke prairie there and in Iowa. He became a successful farmer and stockman. Always a lover of blooded animals he did much to encourage breeding of pure bred stock. He was a member of the district school board for many years and was an exponent of higher education. Coming to Nemaha County in 1860, he freighted across the plains to Denver with oxen. He was prominent in the Masonic order. His death occurred at Auburn, October 21, 1922.

Hannah Maria Hodkin, wife of William Hawxby, was born in Yorkshire, England, September 7, 1847. She was the daughter of George and Martha Hodkin. She received her early education in New Hampshire; and worked in the cotton mills until she was thirteen years of age. At that time, her father having enlisted for service in the Civil War, she came with her mother to Nebraska. She was an accomplished musician and a talented teacher of music. For many years she was organist of the Episcopal Church at Brownville, and later at Nemaha. A leader in community life, she was loved by everyone. Her father was a distinguished soldier in the Nebraska Volunteer Cavalry.

Frederick G. Hawxby attended country school in the Maple Grove district near his father's farm and the village school at Nemaha. He attended normal school at Shenandoah, Iowa. He received his B. D., from the Western Normal College at Shenandoah, Iowa, in 1891, A. B., from the University of Nebraska in 1899, and was graduated from the college of law with a B. L. in 1901. He also has the degree of B. Ped., from Lincoln Normal School.

Active in debate while in college, he was a member of the Union Literary Society, and the Debating Club. He represented the university three successive years in interstate debate, and held place in oratorical contest. He was class president his junior year, and was also president of the Union Society. He was a member of the Innocents, and was active in basketball and gymnasium work.

His marriage to Pearl Norton was solemnized at Talmage, November 17, 1909. Mrs. Hawxby was the daughter of Hugh and Myra Norton, the former a Missouri-Pacific employee of more than 42 years standing, and agent at Brock, Plattsmouth and Panama. She, herself was a nurse prior to her marriage. She was born at Wyoming, Nebraska, March 23, 1888. There are two children of their marriage: Margaret, born February 20, 1911, is a graduate of Auburn High School, third highest in a class of 53. She took a year's training in nursing at the Methodist Episcopal Hospital in Omaha. While in high school she took active part in dramatics and was a member of the debate team. An accomplished pianist, she is also athletic, an accomplished swimmer. She is active in church and Bible School also. Ruth, born August 7, 1913, was graduated from Auburn High School in June, 1930, and now attends Peru State Teachers College. She was a member of the high school orchestra, and won honors in declamatory work and in school plays. She is active also in church and Sunday School work. She is an accomplished violinist. She is specializing in commercial work and accounting at Peru.

Mr. Hawxby is now a Democrat. He was formerly a Populist. From 1900-01 he was a member of the 27th session of the Nebraska legislature from Nemaha County. He served as county attorney from 1910-14, inclusive, and from 1916-20 was county judge. He was nominated for regent of the state university, and although he ran 2000 ahead of his ticket, was unsuccessful in the election. While a member of the legislature he introduced and secured the passage of the first rural high school bill; also helped draft, introduced and secured the passage of the present inheritance tax law of Nebraska.

After teaching school three years, two of which were as superintendent at Britton, South Dakota, Mr. Hawxby commenced the practice of law in 1901, when he was admitted to practice in the Supreme Court and the United States District Court. Later he was admitted to practice in the United States Federal Court. For a year or so he was in partnership with G. W. Cornell, at South Auburn; then he practiced a year at Humbolt. In 1903 he entered a partnership with Hon. John S. Stull, former district judge, which continued until the latter's death in 1910. After leaving the county judge's office he was in partnership with H. A. Lambert until his death in 1924, when he became junior member of the firm of Neal & Hawxby, which terminated upon the death of Judge Neal in 1926. Since that time he has engaged in private practice.

He has always taken an active interest in school affairs, and in advancing the livestock and farming industry. He is agent for the Stull estate farms in Nemaha County. He is associate counsel for the Nemaha County Bank, and was for seven years local attorney for the Burlington Railroad.

While attending Lincoln Normal School he belonged to the military unit with the 3rd Regiment of Cadets. During the World War he was chairman of four minute men for Nemaha County, secretary of the Nebraska Council of Defense, member of the legal advisory board, and was especially active in the drives for Red Cross and Y. M. C. A. funds when Nemaha County exceeded its quota.

Although reared an Episcopalian, after his marriage he became a member of the Christian Church at Auburn. He is a member of the Auburn Chamber of Commerce, the Nebraska State Historical Society, The Nebraskana Society, and the Y. M. C. A. He is a member of the Auburn City Library Board, and a former member of the school board. He served as member of the Board of Education of Auburn High School, of which he was secretary three years, and president two years. He is a member of the Auburn P. T. A., a Mason, and a member of the Auburn Country Club.

Mr. Hawxby particularly recalls that he rode horseback from his farm home to the village school at Mahaska, two winters. When he entered the University of Nebraska in the fall of 1895, he specialized in history and English. During his entire time at the University he was self-supporting, earning his tuition as paper boy, cashier of a boarding club and as agent for a laundry. Residence: Auburn.

Joseph Oscar Hay

Joseph Oscar Hay, one of the leading bankers of Scotts Bluff County, Nebraska, was born at Berlin, Pennsylvania, January 7, 1889, the son of William Joseph Rupp Hay and Nellie (Mason) Hay. His father, a farmer, was born at Berlin, Pennsylvania, December 26, 1866. His mother was born at Berlin, Pennsylvania, November 1, 1867.

Mr. Hay attended the rural schools of Somerset County, Pennsylvania, and was a student at Valporaiso University for a year. He served as assistant cashier of the Exchange Bank at Ong, Nebraska, 1915-17, was assistant cashier of the First National Bank at Friend, Nebraska, 1919-20, and since 1924, has been cashier of the Farmers State Bank at McGrew, Nebraska.

He is a member of the Odd Fellows, is affiliated with the Presbyterian Church, and holds membership in the Nebraskana Society. During the World War he served as Captain 351st Infantry at Camp Dodge, Iowa. After serving overseas he was promoted to major of infantry and served on the staff of 1st Division in Germany. At this time he is a member of the American Legion. Residence: McGrew.

Frank Martin Hayes

Frank Martin Hayes, farmer and sheriff of Arthur County, was born at Batesville, Ohio, March 26, 1865, son of Martin and Nancy (Miller) Hayes.

The father was born in Quaker City, Ohio, April 10, 1834, and was a farmer until his death at Oakland, April 15, 1892. His grandfather came from Wales. Nancy Miller was born at Batesville, Ohio, in 1830, and died at Batesville, Ohio, June 6, 1906. She was of English descent.

Mr. Hayes attended public school at Millwood Township, Ohio, and has engaged in farming most of his life. He is a Mason and a Republican. His hobbies are hunting, fishing and out door sports. Residence: Arthur.

James Barratt Haynes

James Barratt Haynes has lived in Nebraska for 50 years, and during that time has taken an active part in the business life of the state. He was born at Indianola, Iowa, July 2, 1859, the son of James and Emily (Barratt) Haynes. His father, a Methodist clergyman, was born near Wheeling, West Virginia, and died at Omaha, in 1901. His English ancestors settled in New Jersey, in the early history of this country.

His mother was born in Clarke County, Ohio, in 1834. Her grandfather, John Farnam, who was English, was a New Hampshire minute man who fought in the Revolution. She was active in social welfare and charity affairs in Omaha for many years. She died at Omaha, 1908.

Mr. Haynes received all of his education by reading and studying without the aid of teachers. He has always been a student. Since 1907 he has been president of the Haynes Advertising Company of Omaha. He was at one time managing editor of the *Omaha Bee.* He is the author of History of the *Trans-Mississippi International Exposition,* published at Omaha, 1898; a sketch of the late General Silas A. Strickland; *Recent Survey of Municipal Universities* in 1930. He acted as private secretary to the late Joseph H. Millard, United States senator from Nebraska.

He was united in marriage with Katie Strickland at Omaha, in 1884. Mrs. Haynes, whose ancestors were English, was born at Omaha, in 1865. They have one son, James Wilbur, born June 23, 1891.

During the late war Mr. Haynes was active in Douglas County on various relief committees. He is a member of the Omaha Chamber of Commerce and the Continental Club. His hobby is reading. He is a Republican. Residence: Omaha.

Mulford Mansfield Haynes

Mulford Mansfield Haynes, who has lived in Nebraska since 1877, was born at Kewanee, Illinois, November 16, 1867, the son of Elias Perkins and Johanna (Barrows) Haynes. His father, who was a ship carpenter, and farmer, was born at New London, Connecticut, January 26, 1810, and died at Hastings, Nebraska, March 10, 1893. His mother was born at Mansfield, Connecticut, October 4, 1827, and died at Hastings, November 1, 1896.

Mr. Haynes was graduated from the Hastings High School. He has been a successful merchant at Hastings for many years and is now connected with the Haynes Brothers Decorating Company there. He is affiliated with the Christian Church, holds membership in the Masonic Lodge, and is a member of the Nebraskana Society. His chief recreations are football, basketball, and the study of mechanics.

On March 31, 1897, he was married to Ida Emily Gilbreth at Hastings. Mrs. Haynes, who is the daughter of John Gilbreth and Lydia Jane (Hunter) Gilbreth, was born near Montreal, Canada, April 4, 1876. They have four children: Gilbert, born February 1, 1898, who married Gladys Kunselman; Dorothy, born January 9, 1900, who married Claire R. Bower; Katherine, born August 28, 1908, who married John Fitzgerald; and John Whitney, born March 4, 1913. Residence: Hastings.

William Henry Haywood

William Henry Haywood, hardware merchant, was born at Monongahela, Pennsylvania, December 16, 1870, son of Albert Haywood. His father was born in England and died at Monongahela in 1878. He was a coal operator. His mother was born in Ireland and died in 1879.

Mr. Haywood attended public school and has been a resident of Nebraska since 1892. He is a Republican, a member of the Knights of Pythias, the Ancient Free and Accepted Masons, and the Shrine. His sports include hunting, baseball and tennis. He is a member of the fire department and the American Geographic Society. Residence: Bushnell.

Walter William Head

Walter William Head, nationally known financier, business executive, and civic leader, was an important figure in the economic affairs of Omaha, Nebraska, for nearly fifteen years. He was born on a farm near Adrian, Illinois, December 18, 1877, the son of Alfred Walter and Margaret Jane (Lambert) Head. Alfred W. Head, who was born February 2, 1835, and died October 30, 1921, moved from Hancock County, Illinois, to western Missouri when his son was a small boy, and settled near Stewartsville.

Mr. Head acquired his preliminary education in the public schools of Missouri and later attended the Missouri State Normal School. For five years he was engaged in teaching, first in Buchanan County, Missouri, and later acting as principal of the public schools at DeKalb, Missouri. At the close of the school year of 1901 he accepted a position with the Derge Campbell Banking Company for the duration of the summer, and at the close of the next school year (1902) severed his connection with the school to become a cashier of the bank.

The experience gained in this village bank proved exceptionally valuable as a preparation for his career in the banking world, since the business of the bank was entirely handled by Mr. Head and the president of that institution. He engaged as a clerk and teller in the American National Bank at St. Joseph for a year, and for the next three years was cashier and manager of the newly organized DeKalb State Bank of DeKalb, Missouri; during this period he took over the deposits of the Derge Campbell Banking Company and liquidated the latter institution. Subsequently, he served for two years as a bank examiner.

From 1908 to 1917 he served as cashier of the American National Bank at St. Joseph, and in 1917 was elected vice president of the Omaha National Bank. He was advanced to the presidency of the latter institution in 1920, and served as the bank's chief executive officer until January, 1929, when he was made president of the State Bank of Chicago. In November, 1931, he became president of the Mars Plan Corporation of America.

He was elected president of the National Bank Division of the American Banker's Association at the convention held in St. Louis in 1919. In 1921 he was made second vice president of the American Banker's Association, was elected vice president of that organization in 1922, and was elected president in 1923 at the Atlantic City convention. He served for several years as a member of the International High Commission assigned to the Nicaraguan Group.

Throughout his career Mr. Head has taken an active interest in social, civic, and religious affairs in the various communities in which he has lived. While a resident of DeKalb, he served as village trustee and mayor, was prominent in the Masonic Lodge, and was Sunday School superintendent and Bible School teacher. At St. Joseph he acted as president of the Chamber of Commerce, was chairman of the Interstate Agricultural Congress, was president of the Young Men's Christian Association, and for a period of six years was a member of the Republican State Committee. In 1913 he assisted in the organization of the St. Joseph Life Insurance Company, now the American Union Life Insurance

Company, of which he is still chairman of the board.

At Omaha Mr. Head was president of the Chamber of Commerce and the Young Men's Christian Association in which he has always been active. For eight years he served as a member of the board of regents of the well-known Roman Catholic institution of learning, Creighton University, resigning that position upon his removal to Chicago in 1929. He has acted as trustee of Hastings College for over six years, and since 1925 has been similarly connected with Grinnell College, Grinnell, Iowa. He was a member of the Nebraska State Capitol Commission (1919-31) which is in charge of the erection of that commonwealth's new capitol scheduled for completion in 1931.

During the entire period of his residence in Omaha he taught the Men's Bible Class at the First Presbyterian Church, and during that time was a member of the board of trustees of the House of Hope (Omaha's home for the aged). Since 1929 Mr. Head has been a teacher in St. Andrews Bible Class and is a member of the session of the First Presbyterian Church of Chicago as well as the general council of the Presbyterian Church. He acted as treasurer and a member of the board of governors of the Child Saving Institute, was chairman of the Nebraska American Red Cross, and the Omaha Committee of the United World War Campaign (1918). Throughout the period of the United States participation in the World War he was a major in the Nebraska Home Guards. For several years he was treasurer of the Republican State Central Committee of Nebraska.

Mr. Head has been prominently associated with the Boy Scout Movement in the following capacities: president of the Omaha Council of Boy Scouts of America, four years; chairman of Region Eight, comprising the states of Iowa, Nebraska, Missouri, Kansas, Colorado, and Wyoming, three years; member of the National Executive Council since 1919; vice president of the National Council, 1921; and president of the council since 1926. In 1922 he was elected delegate to the International Scout Conference in Paris, and in 1924 was a delegate to the International Scout Conference at Copenhagen. He served for many years as a member of the International Committee of the Young Men's Christian Association, and for a number of years has been a member of the general board of that association as well as treasurer and chairman of the finance committee of its national council. He was the first and only chairman of the national Father and Son Committee and for many years was a member of the National Thrift Committee.

Mr. Head was president of the Nebraska Power Company during his stay in this state, and is now chairman of that organization. He is a director of the United States Fidelity and Guaranty Company of Baltimore, is a director and member of the finance committee of the Chicago, St. Paul, Minneapolis & Omaha Railway Company, is director of the New York Fire Insurance Company, and holds membership in nearly thirty other corporations.

He holds membership in the following: board of trustees of the International Council of Religious Education; board of trustees of the Young Men's Christian Association College of Chicago; board of managers of the Young Men's Christian Association of Chicago; advisory council of Augustana Hospital, Chicago; board of directors of the Chicago Boys' Clubs; and the Presbyterian Church Extension Board of the Chicago Presbytery. He is chairman of the Finance Committee of the Illinois Chamber of Commerce and the Boys' Week Committee of the Rotary International.

Mr. Head's social clubs include: the Chicago Club; the Union League Club; Mid-day Club; Medinah Athletic Club; Bob O'Link Golf Club; the Old Elm Club; Glen View Golf Club; and Knollwood Golf Club of Chicago. He has always been interested in farming, and owns and operates about 3000 acres of rich farming

Rinehart-Marsden—Omaha

DR. FRANCIS WENGER HEAGEY

land near St. Joseph on which is located his country home, Wilver Dell.

On March 7, 1900, he was united in marriage at DeKalb with Della Thompson, daughter of John J. Thompson, a farmer of that place. Mr. and Mrs. Head have a daughter who is now Mrs. Raymond A. Baur. Residence: New York.

Francis Wenger Heagey

Francis Wenger Heagey was born at Bareville, Lancaster County, Pennsylvania, June 20, 1884. His parents were Henry Frederick Cronice and Sara Elizabeth (Wenger) Heagey. His father, born at Table Rock, Pennsylvania, February 9, 1865, is a physician of Scotch, Irish and French descent. His wife, Sara Elizabeth, was born at Bareville, April 16, 1864, and is of Pennsylvania German descent.

Dr. Heagey was graduated from the Cochranville, Pennsylvania, High School in 1904. He entered Princeton University where he was graduated with an A. B. in 1908. He received his M. D. from Columbia University in 1912. He was valedictorian of his high school class. He played on the champion inter-collegiate association football team at Columbia University, and received the monogram C. A. F.

He was married to Islay VanKleek McDougall, at Ottawa, Canada, December 23, 1916. Mrs. Heagey was born at Stratford, Ontario, Canada, June 20, 1888, and is of Scotch and Dutch descent. There are four children: Mary, born December 21, 1917; Frances, born December 1, 1918; Elinor, born February 10, 1925, and Suzanne, born August 23, 1926.

Dr. Heagey was resident physician Colon Hospital, Panama, 1911, private pavilion, St. Luke's Hospital, New York, 1914-15, assistant professor of anatomy and medicine, Creighton University, 1916-19, associate in the office of Dr. A. D. Dunn 1919-23. Since that time he has been engaged in private practice, and is associate professor of medicine at Creighton University.

Dr. Heagey is the author of the following: *Epidemic Encephalitis* (with Dr. A. D. Dunn, Oct., 1920); *The Cerebellar Manifestations of Epidemic Encephalitis* (September 10, 1922); *Epidemic Encephalitis in Relation to Anterior Poliomyelitis* (September 1922); *Symptoms of Colonic Disturbances* (1924); *Cervical Adenitis* (Nebraska State Medical Journal); *Relation of Internal Medicine to the General Practice of Medicine* (July, 1927); and *Treatment of Epidemic Encephalitis* (1929).

During the World War he was full time medical teacher, and is Captain in the Medical Reserve Corps. He is a Republican and a member of the First Presbyterian Church. His professional organizations include the American Medical Association, The American College of Surgeons, the Nebraska State Medical Association, the National Tuberculosis Association, Nebraska State Tuberculosis Association (president 1930-), the American Public Health Association, and the Omaha-Douglas County Medical Association. He is a member of the Lions Club and of the Chamber of Commerce. He was vice president of the local Lions Club during 1927-28. He is also a member of the American Association for Scientific Research. His clubs are the Professional Men's, the Omaha Club and the Omaha Country Club. His sport is golf and his hobby is books. Residence: Omaha. (Photograph on Page 529).

Edward Joseph Healey

Born at Scranton, Pennsylvania, June 24, 1872, Edward Joseph Healey is the son of Anthony and Mary (Kelly) Healey. His father, born in Bellin, County Mayo, Ireland, December 25, 1829, came to America June 11, 1865, and worked as a coal miner for twelve years.

In 1877 he came to Knox County, Nebraska, locating on a farm seven miles northwest of Creighton, where he died March 1, 1904. His wife, born at Crossmolina, County Mayo, June 30, 1831, died at Creighton on November 25, 1925.

Edward Joseph Healey attended country school to the eighth grade, and was graduated from high school in 1890. A farmer until he reached the age of twenty-five, he then entered the hardware business in which he has spent most of his life. A Democrat, he is at the present time a member of the city council.

On June 21, 1905, Mr. Healey was married to Catherine Edith Doyle at Creighton. Mrs. Healey, who is of Irish descent, was born at Clarence, Iowa, September 28, 1879. They have two children, Helen, born October 22, 1902; and Francis, born October 23, 1906; who was graduated from high school in 1923, and who entered Creighton University in 1927, graduating in pharmacy in 1930.

Mr. Healey is a member of St. Ludgers Catholic Church and the Knights of Columbus. He is a member of the Red Cross, the Elks, the Nebraskana Society and the Nebraska Hardware Dealers Association, as well as the Creighton Golf Club. His hobby is beautifying his home and its surroundings. Residence: Creighton.

George Arthur Heath

George Arthur Heath, physician and surgeon, was born at Athens, Ohio, February 10, 1873, son of James Herbert and Isabelle (Tope) Heath. His father, a farmer, was born at Richmondale, Ohio, December 24, 1845, and died at Geneva, Nebraska, January 14, 1910. His mother was born at Jackson, Ohio, November 15, 1844, and died at Geneva, January 11, 1911.

Dr. Heath attended public and high school at Geneva, and received the degree of Doctor of Medicine from Illinois Medical College at Chicago, in 1897. He has been in practice in Nebraska since 1907.

His marriage to Addie Belle Wagoner was solemnized at Mason City, Illinois, on September 1, 1898. There are two children, Bernice, born July 1, 1899, who married Ray Otten; and James Barton, born December 11, 1901.

Dr. Heath is a Republican. His professional and civic organizations include the American, Nebraska State and Jefferson County Medical Associations, the Chamber of Commerce, the Rotary Club (charter member, former president), the Elks, Masons, Ancient Order of United Workmen, and the Modern Woodmen of America. Residence: Fairbury.

William Parkhill Heath

William Parkhill Heath, salesman and rancher, was born at Detroit, Michigan, March 15, 1876, son of Oscar Theodore and Hanna (Mahana) Heath.

The father was born in Staten Island, New York, October 26, 1835, and died at Lincoln, March 10, 1918. He was a contractor and builder, whose ancestors served in the Revolutionary War. Hanna, his wife, was born at Rochester, New York, December 25, 1847, and died at Lincoln, June 15, 1915. Her father was a shoe manufacturer, of Irish descent.

Shortly after Mr. Heath's graduation from high school in Creston, he came to Nebraska, and for 24 years was a salesman for the United States Supply Company of Omaha. At the present time he operates a 1440 acre ranch and farm and has other town property. He is a Republican, a member of Grace Episcopal Church, of the Masons, Elks, and Y. M. C. A., as well as the Red Cross. His outdoor sports include baseball and golf, while he also enjoys bridge and dancing.

On June 29, 1903, he was married to Josephine Maud Burns at Chicago. Mrs. Heath was born at Fort Madison, Iowa, April 13, 1878, died at Chadron, February 11, 1930. They have one child, Jerry, born August 18, 1921. Residence: Chadron.

Horace Wheelock Hebbard

For the past 52 years Horace W. Hebbard has been connected with the *Nebraska State Journal* at Lincoln. Born at Galesburg, Illinois, December 30, 1858, he is the son of Albert and Martha (Bigelow) Hebbard. His father, who was a carpenter, was born in Connecticut in 1811, and died at Galesburg, August, 1860. His mother was born in Oswego County, New York, September 30, 1825.

Mr. Hebbard received his education in the public schools of Illinois, and the Aledo Academy at Aledo, Illinois. He was employed by the *Aledo Record* for six years, and since then has been with the *Nebraska State Journal* of which he is now department manager. He is a Republican.

He was united in marriage with Lotta Hurd, at Charles City, Iowa, November 24, 1886. Mrs. Hebbard, who was a teacher before her marriage, was born at Racine, Wisconsin, the daughter of Jabez and Elizabeth Hurd. She died at Lincoln, March 22, 1911. One child was born to this marriage: Ralph, born January 15, 1888, who has been connected with the Bank of Italy (now the Bank of America) at San Diego, California, since 1912; he served overseas for 18 months during the World War. Mr. Hebbard was married to Mrs. Clara Felix, October 2, 1916, at Aledo.

A member of the Buswell Students' Association, he is affiliated with the First Church of Christ, Scientist at Lincoln; and holds membership in the Nebraskana Society. Residence: Lincoln.

Frank Andrew Hebenstreit

Frank A. Hebenstreit was born at Shullsburg, Wisconsin, April 12, 1891, the son of Andrew and Catherine (McCarten) Hebenstreit. His father, of German ancestry, was born at Shullsburg, in 1863. He was a banker and farmer, and served as chairman of the county board for many years. His mother, who was of Irish and German parentage, was born at Kendall, Lafayette County, Wisconsin, in 1869.

Mr. Hebenstreit was graduated from the Shullsburg High School in 1905, where he won letters in baseball and football, and was captain of the baseball team. He attended the University of Wisconsin, 1911-12, and in 1915 was awarded the degree LL. B. at the Creighton University, College of Law. There he was dean of Delta Theta Phi. Admitted to the bar in Nebraska, May 3, 1915, he has practiced law since that time. A Democrat, he was city councilman of Falls City from 1917 to 1918; and was city attorney of Falls City from 1922 to 1930. He has been a resident of Nebraska for 18 years.

He was united in marriage with Irene Helen O'Neill at Omaha, Nebraska, February 1, 1917. Mrs. Hebenstreit was born of Irish parentage at Peru, Illinois, March 29, 1893. Four children were born to their marriage: John, born November 10, 1918; Frank, born November 13, 1921; Joseph, born July 8, 1925; and James, born July 8, 1925.

During the World War Mr. Hebenstreit was on the liberty loan committee, and was a four minute speaker. He is a member of the Red Cross; the Chamber of Commerce; the Falls City Booster Club, of which he is secretary; the Richardson County Bar Association; and the Nebraska Bar Association. He is a member of the Knights of Columbus, the Benevolent and Protective Order of Elks; and from 1923 to 1924 was a member of the Rotary Club. He is affiliated with St. Peter's and St. Paul's Church, at Falls City. His hobby is golf, and his social club is the Falls City Country Club. Residence: Falls City.

Marshall Eddmon Hebrew

Marshall Eddmon Hebrew has been a prominent Nebraska photographer for many years. He is the propriet-

or of the Hebrew Studio at Lexington, where he is active in the social and business affairs of the city. Residence: Lexington. (Photograph in Album).

Cornelius Theodore Heckt

Cornelius Theodore Heckt was born at St. Helena, Nebraska, December 13, 1884, the son of Theodore Frederick Heckt and Catharina (Christensen) Heckt. His father, who was a shoe cobbler in Germany for over 50 years, was born at Plonn, Germany, October 19, 1844, and died at Wynot, Nebraska, April 20, 1912. His mother was born in Denmark, May 20, 1845, and died at Sioux City, Iowa, August 19, 1927.

Mr. Heckt was engaged in the banking business from 1906 to 1929 and since 1929 has been proprietor of the Commercial Hotel at Bloomfield, Nebraska. A Republican, he served as a member of the Nebraska Senate in 1925. He was president of the Board of Education for six years, served as treasurer of the local chapter of the Red Cross at Bloomfield from 1919 to 1929, and is now a member of the Bloomfield Community Club.

He is affiliated with the First Methodist Episcopal Church and holds membership in the following Masonic bodies: Royal Arch; Knights Templar; Scottish Rite; and Mystic Shrine. He attended Citizens Military Training Camp at Camp Steever, Wisconsin, in 1918 and took an active part in all loan drives during the World War.

His marriage to Christene Amelia Hovland occurred at Sioux City, August 20, 1907. Mrs. Heckt was born at Utsire, Norway, April 10, 1880. They have two children: Bernice K., born May 16, 1908; and Eunice M. born October 31, 1911. Bernice K. has been in the banking business for the past three years and Eunice is a senior at Clarkson Hospital in Omaha. Residence: Bloomfield.

Verne Hedge

Verne Hedge, executive and banker, and former mayor of Lincoln, was born near Montezuma, Iowa, September 3, 1877. He is the son of Porter and Martha Ellen (Kisor) Hedge. The former born in Coshocton County, Ohio, June 21, 1848, was a lawyer and abstractor. He served with the 51st Ohio Volunteer Infantry in the Civil War, and was one of the founders of Cotner University. Of English stock, the original name was Hedges; they settled in America in pre-Revolutionary days. Martha Ellen Kisor was born near Union Mills, Iowa, May 13, 1853, and in her younger years was active in the Ladies' Aid and the Missionary Society of the First Christian Church of Lincoln. Her father was of German descent, and her mother of the English Braddock family of the Revolutionary period.

Mr. Hedge received his education in the Lincoln grade and high school and the University of Nebraska, from which he received a B. A. and B. Sc. in C. E. in 1903. He is a member of Kappa Sigma, Sigma Tau, the Vikings, Innocents, Theta Nu Epsilon, and the Pershing Rifles. He is a member of the Engineering Society, president of Kappa Sigma chapter, and district grand master of the same, and supreme executive committeeman thereof. During 1926 he was president of the Alumni Association of the University of Nebraska.

On May 24, 1905 he was married to Grace Bennett of Lincoln, Nebraska. There are three children: John Richard, born January 15, 1909, who graduated from Lincoln High School in 1926 and the University of Nebraska in 1930; Willard Charles who graduated from Lincoln High School in 1928, and who was born October 27, 1911; and who is a senior at the university; and Elizabeth Ann, born August 17, 1917, who attends Irving Junior High School.

For a number of years Mr. Hedge has been active in public affairs in Nebraska. A Republican, he was mayor of Lincoln 1927-29, and since 1929 has been chairman of the Municipal Airport Board. He has been a trustee of Wyuka Cemetery since 1913.

From 1898 to 1903 he was a civil engineer for the Chicago, Burlington and Quincy Railroad, and entered into his present business, that of abstracts of title and title insurance, upon the death of his father in 1903. He is a director of the Lincoln Trust Company, and the State Securities Company and American Savings and Loan Association.

During the World War he drilled Class "A" Men, and was generally active in wartime projects. He is a member of the Nebraska Title Association, and was its president in 1915. He has been vice president several times. In 1925 he was vice president of the American Title Association, of which he is a member. In 1926 he served as president of the Lincoln Chamber of Commerce. President of the Rotary Club in 1921, he was district governor in 1923. He is a member of the Lincoln Executives Club, the Hiram Club (president 1931), the Elks, and is a 33rd degree Mason. He is a member of the Shrine, and was potentate of Sesostris Temple in 1929. He is a member of the Sons of Veterans, the First Christian Church of Lincoln, and the Young Men's Christian Association. His clubs are the University, Shrine and Lincoln Country. Residence: Lincoln.

Lizzie Neville Hedges

Lizzie Neville Hedges was born at Williamsport, Ohio, August 19, 1861. Her father, Rochester Hedges, was a native of Virginia, born April 13, 1826. He married Katherine Acenith Lowe, a school teacher in Ohio, and together they came west and homesteaded in Otoe County. Rochester Hedges was an early day farmer. His family was of English descent, and slave owners in Virginia. He served as state representative and was always active in the affairs of his community and state. He died at Syracuse, October 12, 1893.

Katherine Lowe Hedges was of French Huguenot descent. She was well educated and an extensive reader. After her husband's death she managed his farm and reared her three children. She died at Syracuse, October 23, 1923.

Brought to Nebraska as an infant by her parents, Lizzie Hedges has been a resident of Otoe County for nearly seventy years. She and her two brothers make their home on the homestead of their father and mother. They are active in community civic affairs. Residence: Syracuse.

John Albert Hedlund

A lifetime resident of Nebraska, John Albert Hedlund was born at Ceresco, September 22, 1872, the son of Christian and Mathilda (Norman) Hedlund. His father, who was a pioneer farmer and homesteader in Nebraska, was born in Halland, Sweden, May 26, 1836, and died at Swedeburg, Nebraska, February 3, 1930; he came to America in 1869. His mother was born at Vestergotland, Sweden, November 1, 1851.

Mr. Hedlund has been a partner in the hardware and plumbing firm of Swanson & Hedlund since 1912, and at the present time owns a one-third interest in the Ceresco Motor Company.

He is a member of the Nebraskana Society, was the organizer and leader of one of the first community bands in Ceresco, and is affiliated with the Evangelical Christian Church at Swedburg. He is a Republican. His recreations include mechanics and hunting.

His marriage to Alice Swanson was solemnized at Ceresco, May 23, 1912. Mrs. Hedlund, who worked at Ceresco, before her marriage, was born at Skane, Sweden, January 13, 1875. They have two children: Norma, born June 6, 1913, who attends Midland College; and Aaron, born May 6, 1916. Residence: Ceresco.

Carl Hehnke

A lifelong resident of Grand Island, Carl Hehnke is a progressive hardware merchant there, and for a number of years has taken an active part in the civic life of the city. He was born at Grand Island, November 30, 1881, the son of Hermann Henry and Marie (Schroeder) Hehnke, the former a hardware dealer who was born in Germany, and died at Grand Island, June 19, 1916. His mother was born in Germany, in 1847, and died at Grand Island, December 22, 1912. Mr. and Mrs. Hehnke settled at Grand Island, in 1880.

Mr. Hehnke received his education in the Grand Island public and high schools. He was connected with the Leavitt Sugar Factory for a year after completing his education, and since then has been in the firm Hehnke & Lohmann Hardware Company of which he is secretary. He is serving as councilman of the second ward of Grand Island, at this time, is president of the Retail Merchants Association, and is affiliated with the English Lutheran Church there. He is a Mason.

On April 20, 1910, he was married at Lexington, Nebraska, to Dora Veit. She was born at Grand Island, October 28, 1885. They have three children: Oscar, born in 1911; Wilma, born in 1915; and Carl Lewis, born in 1919. Residence: Grand Island. (Photograph in Album).

Hettie Josephine Hehnke

For nearly 30 years Hettie Josephine Hehnke has been engaged in educational activities at St. Edward, Nebraska, where she has lived for 46 years. She was born at Davenport, Iowa, September 27, 1879, the daughter of John Jacob and Mary Amelia (Vieths) Hehnke. Her father, a farmer, was born at Schlesing, Germany, October 20, 1844, and died at St. Edward, Nebraska, July 23, 1931; his father, Jacob Hehnke, died in 1850, in Germany, and his mother, Margaret Hehnke, died at sea in 1873, just before the ship sailed into New York Harbor.

Mary (Vieths) Hehnke was born in Illinois, September 25, 1852, and died at St. Edward, November 4, 1925. She was always active in helping her neighbors, and was vitally interested in giving her children a thorough education. Her father, Ditmer Vieths, was born at Holstein, Germany, and died at Potter, Nebraska, in 1917. Her mother, Sarah (Burger) Vieths, was born in Pennsylvania, and died at St. Edward, in 1892.

Miss Hehnke received most of her early education in the rural schools of Boone County, where she was graduated in 1895. She passed the teachers' examinations in 1895, and then was a student in the St. Edward High School for three years. In the fall of 1899, she began her study at Peru State Normal College, and in 1910, was graduated from that institution, attending school for a period, and then teaching to support herself in her determination to secure an education. In the summer of 1917, she took a course in Palmer Penmanship at Cedar Rapids, Iowa.

She has taught in the following schools: District 54, rural, three years; District 8, rural, two years; St. Edward, 1905-06; Campbell, Nebraska, 1906-08; Hooper, Nebraska, 1908-09; Superior, Nebraska, 1910-12; District 5, rural, 1912-13; and St. Edward, since 1913. She is now supervisor of the grammar department of the St. Edward public school.

Miss Hehnke is a member of the program committee of the Parent-Teachers' Association, the Nebraskana Society, and the Red Cross. She has held all offices in the Rebecca Lodge, is a charter member of Chapter D. V. of the P. E. O. at St. Edward, and holds membership in the Nebraska State Teachers' Association. In 1896, she affiliated with the First Presbyterian Church of St. Edward, where she has been an exceptionally active member of Christian Endeavor for many years. She has taught

HETTIE JOSEPHINE HEHNKE

Wilson—Albion

Sunday School classes, and from 1913-18, was superintendent. Since 1925, she has taught a boys' and young men's class of which she is justly proud. Her hobby is flower gardening. Residence: St. Edward. (Photograph on Page 533).

Samuel Aughay Heikes

For the past 38 years Samuel A. Heikes has farmed on the same land in Dakota County, Nebraska. He was born in Juniata County, Pennsylvania, the son of Jacob Robert and Mary Jane (Aughoy) Heikes, and has been a Nebraska resident for 58 years. His father, who was a farmer, also, was born at Mifflin, Pennsylvania, October 5, 1817, and died at Wakefield, Nebraska, May 24, 1898; he was a Civil War soldier. His mother, whose French Huguenot ancestors came to America in 1704, was born at Mifflin, Pennsylvania, July 15, 1840, and died at Wakefield, July 8, 1924.

Mr. Heikes is a member of the Nebraskana Society, is affiliated with the Salem Lutheran Church, and is a 32nd degree Mason, holding membership in the Scottish Rite. During the World War he took an active part in Red Cross drives and other patriotic work.

He married Lena Evelyn Waldvogel, at Dakota City, August 29, 1888. Mrs. Heikes, who was a teacher before her marriage, was born at Union Center, Wisconsin, November 7, 1866; her ancestors were French, Swiss, and German. Their children are: Blanche, born February 11, 1890, who married Charles R. Kate; Vernon, born October 30, 1893, who married Dorothy Ford; Marion, born November 6, 1896, who married Herman Lueder; Samuel, born November 11, 1898; Warren, born August 8, 1904, who married Mildred Ream; Lola, born August 12, 1900, who married M. L. Flack; and Geraldine, born August 10, 1907, who married Clair Sloan. All but one are college graduates. Residence: Dakota City.

John C. Hein

John C. Hein was born at Des Moines, Iowa, March 5, 1874, son of Detlef and Anna (Jess) Hein, and practically all his life has been a resident of Nebraska. His father was born in Germany, May 10, 1852, and was a merchant until his death at Fremont, on April 6, 1912. His wife, Anna, was born in Germany, July 15, 1852, and died at Fremont, October 6, 1930.

Mr. Hein attended public school and Fremont Normal College, and was active in baseball. For some years he was engaged in the mercantile business, and later as a real estate dealer. A Democrat, he has served as a member of the Board of Public Works, and is a director of the Equitable Building and Loan Association. He is a member and director of the Fremont Chamber of Commerce, and a member of the Dodge County chapter of the Red Cross. During the World War he was treasurer of the later, and chairman of Liberty Loan drives. He is a Rotarian, Elk and Eagle and a member of the Christian Science Church. His favorite sport is golf and his hobby is reading.

On June 21, 1899, he was married to Lydia Marie Larson at Fremont. Mrs. Hein, who is of Swedish descent, was born at Omaha, March 6, 1874. Residence: Fremont.

Ernst Heinrichs

A farmer in Kiowa precinct all his life, Ernst Heinrichs was born there on April 13, 1880. His parents, William and Minnie (Smith) Heinrichs were natives of Germany. The former was a prominent farmer in Thayer County until his death in 1916. Minnie Smith, who was a successful wife and mother, also died in Thayer County.

Ernst Heinrichs attended Kiowa precinct public and parochial schools, and in early youth began his life occupation of farming. He has met with much success and is the owner of extensive interests at the present time.

On April 25, 1901, Mr. Heinrichs was united in marriage to Lydia Harms at Kiowa. Mrs. Heinrichs, whose parents emigrated to America from Germany, was born in Thayer County, March 6, 1881. Seven of their eight children are living: Edna, born July 29, 1902, married Alvin Ehlers, who is now deceased; Hattie, born January 10, 1904, married Doyle Grone; Walter, born October 22, 1909; Harry, born January, 1914, died in infancy; Edwin, born August 1, 1915; Doyle, born December 26, 1920; and Arnold and Donald, twins, born August 1, 1923.

Mr. Heinrichs is a Republican and active in local politics. He is a member of the Lutheran Church and The Nebraskana Society, and his favorite sport is fishing. Residence: Kiowa.

Norman John Heinzelman

Norman J. Heinzelman was born January 1, 1892, at Verdon, Nebraska. The son of John August and Sena (Jorn) Heinzelman, his father, a flour miller, was born of German parents at Verdon, February 20, 1870, and died at Falls City, January 24, 1924. His mother was born at Corning, Missouri, December 23, 1871. Her ancestry is German.

Mr. Heinzelman received his education in the public schools of Verdon. A resident of Nebraska for 38 years, he is a member of the city council at Falls City, and owns and operates the Falls City Auto Supply Company.

He was married to Lucy May Schuetz at Humbolt, Richardson County, Nebraska. Mrs. Heinzelman, who is of Swiss descent, was born at Humbolt, November 8, 1897. Their two children are: Donald Bruce, born March 16, 1921; and Robert Jean, born February 11, 1923. Both sons attend the grade school.

He served during the World War as a corporal, and was in charge of motor supply train No. 429. In 1928 he was commander of the Falls City Post No. 102 of the American Legion, and in 1930 was county commander of this organization. He is a member of the Board of directors of the Red Cross; is president of the Chamber of Commerce; and chairman of the board of directors of the Falls City Community Chest. He is an Elk and a member of the Rotary Club, and the Methodist Church at Falls City. His social club is the Falls City Country Club. Residence: Falls City.

Albert Anthony Held

Albert A. Held, son of Frank and Mary Christina Held, was born at Geneva, Nebraska, November 6, 1891. His parents were natives of Germany, the former a tailor, who came to America at the outbreak of the French and Indian War. Frank Held died at Geneva, December 15, 1917; his wife is still living.

Mr. Held attended the Geneva public schools and was graduated from high school there in 1912. After leaving school he entered the banking business and for four years was teller and assistant cashier of the Geneva State Bank. Thereafter for two years he served as cashier of the Trumbull State Bank at Trumbull. During the World War he held the rank of sergeant in the 18th Company, 164th Depot Brigade at Camp Funston.

Upon his return to civilian life he became cashier of the Farmers State Bank of Ayr, Nebraska, where he served six years, leaving to enter the state banking department where he remained four years. For the last two years he has been assistant vice president of the National Bank of Commerce at Lincoln.

Mr. Held was married to Minnie Grace Pratt, at Omaha, June 19, 1918. Mrs. Held was born at Albion, Nebraska, May 8, 1890. There are two children, Sidney N., born May 13, 1920, and Carolyn M., born November 7, 1922.

Among Mr. Held's memberships in civic, religious and fraternal organizations are the following: The American

Legion, the Modern Woodmen of America, the Young Men's Christian Association, Trinity M. E. Church and the Cosmopolitan Club. His favorite sport is hiking. Residence: Lincoln.

Walter Henry Hellman

Walter Henry Hellman, a leader in the religious and educational affairs of Nebraska, was born at Kansas City, Kansas, January 23, 1897, the son of Frederick William and Anna Elizabeth (Paul) Hellman. His father, who is a wholesale drug dealer, was born in Germany, October 12, 1859, and came to America in 1870. His mother was born in Germany, May 20, 1868, and died at Kansas City, Missouri, August 1, 1928.

Mr. Hellman attended Longfellow School in Kansas City until 1911, and in 1915, was graduated from Hebron Academy at Hebron, Nebraska. He was awarded the Bachelor of Arts degree in theology at Capital University in 1918, was a student of the Capital University Graduate School of Theology, 1921, and received the Master of Arts degree at Washington State College in 1927. His fraternities were Phi Kappa Phi and Pi Gamma Mu.

As an educator, school executive, and clergyman, Mr. Hellman has held the following positions: clergyman, Port Angeles, Washington, 1921-25; student pastor at Pullman, Washington, 1925-27; member of the teaching staff at Washington State College, 1926-27; vice president of Spokane College, 1927-29; dean of men and head of the English department at Pacific Lutheran College, Parkland, Washington, 1929-30; and president of Hebron College and Academy since 1930.

Mr. Hellman holds membership in the local Kiwanis Club and Red Cross, is affiliated with Grace Lutheran Church, and is a member of the Nebraskana Society. His hobbies are writing and music and his favorite sport is golfing.

On June 1, 1921, his marriage to Agnes Adelle Klingler was solemnized at Lenexa, Kansas. Mrs. Hellman was born at Somerset, Ohio. Four children were born to this marriage: Thilda Anne, July 4, 1923; Robert Walter, November 17, 1924; Daphne Louise, September 30, 1926; and Donna Delle, July 2, 1929. Residence. Hebron.

Carl William Helmstadter

Carl William Helmstadter, educator and vocational counsellor, was born at Crete, Nebraska, August 20, 1901. He is the son of Wilhelm and Fredericka (Inderlied) Helmstadter, the former of whom was formerly a business man and merchant at Crete, but now is in business at Beatrice. He was born at Baden Baden, Germany, September 9, 1858, and came to America as a young man. Fredricka Helmstadter was also born in Baden, on October 16, 1870. She died at Beatrice, January 29, 1927.

With the intention of fitting himself for a teaching career, Carl W. Helmstadter, upon his graduation from Beatrice High School in May, 1919, entered the University of Nebraska, where in 1924 he received his A. B. In 1928 he received an A. M. from the same university. He received a letter in football and basketball from Beatrice High School two years, 1917 and 1918. In the university he was elected to Alpha Chi Sigma (secretary) and Phi Delta Kappa.

In 1919 he was secretary to agent of the Chicago, Burlington and Quincy R. R., and was promoted to private secretary of the superintendent of the Union Pacific Railroad in 1920. During 1924-25 he was principal of the Milford, Nebraska, High School; from 1925-27 he was coach and commercial instructor of the West Point, Nebraska High School, and headed the department of commerce of the Beatrice High School 1927-29. During 1929-30 he was assistant dean of the college of commerce of the University of Omaha, of which he is now registrar.

He is the author of *Some Trends in Commercial Education in Nebraska High Schools.*

He was married to Freda Vernita Coonley at Indianola, Iowa, February 21, 1925. Mrs. Helmstadter was born at Hoag, Nebraska, November 14, 1903, and was a teacher prior to her marriage. They have one son, Gerald, born November 28, 1925.

Mr. Helmstadter was a sergeant of Company C, Nebraska National Guard at Beatrice, 1927-30. He is a Republican, a member of the Beatrice Chamber of Commerce and the Omaha Junior Chamber. He attends Miller Park Presbyterian Church. A member of the Nebraska State Teachers' Association, he was vice-president of the commercial section in 1929, and president of that section 1931. His club is the Birchwood. He enjoys golf, while his hobbies are reading and vocational instruction. Residence: Omaha.

Foster Helvey

Foster Helvey, sheriff of Jefferson County, was born in Daykin, Nebraska, January 27, 1895. Mr. Helvey graduated from the Fairbury High School in 1914, attended Peru State Normal, Peru, Nebraska, and taught school two years.

Roscoe C. Helvey, father of Foster, was born at Helvey, Nebraska, June 27, 1869, and is now engaged in farming. Mamie E. (Church) Helvey, his wife, was born at Cascade, Iowa, December 12, 1876, of Irish parentage.

Mr. Helvey is married to Lucy E. Jones, who was born at Fairbury, Nebraska, July 15, 1899. They have three children, Benna, born August 19, 1921; Norbert, born February 16, 1923; and Loraine, born July 25, 1924.

He served in the United States Navy during the World War, and is now commander of the Jefferson County Post No. 24 of the American Legion. Mr. Helvey is a member of the State Sheriffs' Association, the Chamber of Commerce, and the Nebraskana Society. Golf is his favorite sport. Residence: Fairbury.

William Joseph Hemphill

For the past thirty years William Joseph Hemphill has been in active practice as a physician at North Loup. He was born in Potter County, Pennsylvania, July 11, 1873, son of Silas Paul and Mary (Clare) Hemphill. His father died in Pennsylvania in October, 1916, and his mother in 1896.

Dr. Hemphill attended country school at Hebron Centre, Pennsylvania, and received the Bachelor of Letters, and Master of Science at Milton College, Milton, Wisconsin. He received his medical degree from Hahneman Medical College, Chicago. There he was president of his class and a member of the Philomathean Literary Society.

He was married to Cora Ellen Hurley. Mrs. Hurley was born in Humboldt, Nebraska, April 17, 1872. There are three children, Paul Hurley, born April 17, 1899; George Kenneth, born August 13, 1905; and Gertrude, born August 30, 1912. Both sons are graduate phyisicans. Paul is practicing in Pawhuskee, Oklahoma, while George is practicing in Philadelphia.

Dr. Hemphill is a Republican. He is a member of the Seventh Day Baptist Church at North Loup, the Odd Fellows, the American Automobile Association and the Young Men's Christian Association. Residence: North Loup.

Ashton Fremont Henderson

Ashton Fremont Henderson, newspaper editor and publisher at Wood River, Nebraska, has been a resident of this state all his life. He was born at Callaway, Nebraska, September 21, 1888, the son of William Henry and Alice Laura (Pinnell) Henderson. His father, who was a farmer and fruit grower, homesteaded in Custer County, Nebraska, in 1876; he was born in Illinois, September 17, 1852, and died at Ashdown, Arkansas, January 18, 1919; his great-grandparents came to America from Scotland.

His mother, whose ancestry is English and German, was born at Terre Haute, Indiana, July 27, 1867, and is living at Twin Falls, Idaho, today.

Mr. Henderson attended the public schools of Callaway, and studied journalism and advertising by correspondence. He has owned and published newspapers at Oconto and Stapleton, Nebraska, was publisher of a paper at Blanchard, Oklahoma, and was editor of papers at Covington, and Mountain View, Oklahoma. He is editor of the Wood River Sunbeam at this time.

He holds membership in the Chamber of Commerce, the Nebraskana Society, and the Masonic Lodge. His hobby is collecting old coins. On July 26, 1912, he married Ada Elizabeth Bybee at Kearney, Nebraska. Mrs. Henderson, who is a reporter and news writer, was born at Memphis, Missouri, August 27, 1891. She is of English and German descent. To their marriage two children were born: Mildred, August 2, 1914; and Dale, October 24, 1921. Residence: Wood River.

Robert Gilbert Henderson

Robert G. Henderson was born December 12, 1871, at Verdon, Nebraska. His father, Charles G. Henderson was born of Scotch and German parents in New Jersey, September 23, 1833, and died at Verdon, August 21, 1921. He was a carpenter and farmer. Julia (Wilkinson) Henderson, his mother, of Welsh descent, was born in Kentucky, January 20, 1853, and died at Verdon, February 28, 1929.

Robert G. Henderson was graduated from the Verdon High School in May, 1893, was a student at the University of Nebraska for two years, 1894 and 1895, and in 1900 was graduated from the Kansas City Medical College. He was admitted to the practice of medicine at Rulo, Nebraska, December 20, 1900, and for the last thirty years has been a physician in Richardson County. In 1915 he spent some time in post graduate work in Chicago.

Dr. Henderson was married to Carrie Louise Staver at Salem, Nebraska, June 27, 1900. Mrs. Henderson was born at Salen, July 15, 1878, and is the daughter of Captain H. G. and Ellen (Tisdel) Staver.

He is a member of the county and state medical societies, and is an Elk and Odd Fellow. His hobby is playing checkers and cards. He is a Democrat. Residence: Falls City.

Bertin Ellsworth Hendricks

One of Nebraska's leading lawyers, Bertin Ellsworth Hendricks has been engaged in legal practice at Wahoo, for the past 32 years. He was born at Butler, Indiana, November 23, 1868, the son of Salathiel Pritchard Hendricks and Elizabeth Jane (Baker) Hendricks. Salathiel Hendricks, who was born in Columbiana County, Ohio, July 14, 1843, and died at Ashland, Nebraska, October 25, 1924, was a teacher and farmer. He served as a private in Company F, 182nd Ohio Volunteer Infantry during the Civil War. His German ancestors settled in Pennsylvania in the early history of that state.

Elizabeth (Baker) Hendricks, his mother, was born at Butler, Indiana, September 14, 1846, and died at Ashland, August 6, 1921; she was a teacher. Her ancestors were among the puritan settlers in Massachusetts.

Mr. Hendricks attended the public schools in Andrew County, Missouri, was graduated from Western Normal College, Shenandoah, Iowa, in 1891, receiving the B. S. degree, and was graduated from the University of Nebraska in 1896, receiving the degree of Bachelor of Law. He has been engaged in general practice of law at Wahoo, Nebraska, for 32 years, and has handled many important

cases, both in the lower court and Supreme Court. Since 1922, he has been senior member of the firm Hendricks & Kokjer. He is connected with a number of banks in Saunders County as director and stockholder, and is president of the Wahoo Mutual Loan and Building Association.

He is a member of the American Bar Association and the Nebraska State Bar Association, having served as one of the vice presidents of the state association, and holds membership in the Chamber of Commerce at Wahoo. He is affiliated with the First Congregational Church of Wahoo, is a member of the order of Knights of Pythias, and has served his district as member of the board of education for seven years.

A Republican, Mr. Hendricks served as county attorney of Saunders County, 1905-07, and was presidential elector from Nebraska, in 1924. He was a member of the Four Minute Men Speakers during the World War, acted as United States Fuel Administrator, and was chairman of the Victory Loan Drive Committee.

On March 29, 1893, he was married to Christine Fischer at Tekamah, Nebraska. Mrs. Hendricks, who was a teacher prior to her marriage, was born at Allentown, Pennsylvania, October 22, 1872, of German parents. Their children are Lorene A., born April 23, 1897, who is supervisor of the lower grades in the public schools at Boise, Idaho; Madalene D., born June 30, 1900, who is head of the Latin department at Albuquerque, New Mexico; and Lucile M., born October 22, 1911, who is a junior at the University of Nebraska. Residence: Wahoo. (Photograph on Page 537).

Pirlh Wagor Hendricks

Born at Belleville, Kansas, April 17, 1894, Pirlh Wagor is the daughter of Lester LaVern and Fannie (Simmons) Wagor. The father, born in North Branch, Sullivan County, New York, February 27, 1865, lived at Chester, Nebraska, several years, and now resides at Manhattan, Kansas. One of Republic County's model farmers, and a breeder of registered Herefords, he is now retired and travels extensively in the United States. The mother, Fannie Simmons, was born in Illinois, March 28, 1870, She was a teacher prior to her marriage.

Pirlh Wagor attended rural schools in Kansas, was graduated from Chester (Nebraska) High School in 1913, and was graduated from a two year course at Peru State Normal School with a life certificate (Bachelor of Arts equivalent) in 1919. The summers of 1917, 18, 19 and 20, she attended Boulder University. She is a life member of the Philomathean Society, and was captain of the championship Volley ball team at Peru, 1914-15.

Beginning to teach in 1915, she spent a year in a rural school in Box Butte County, after which she went to Giltner, as teacher of science and coach of girl's basketball and school plays. In the fall of 1917, she went to Western where she held a like position. Feeling equal to a little larger position in 1918, she became principal at Clear Water, and upon resignation of the superintendent there a few weeks after school began, was elected to fill his place. Re-elected the following year, she met with great success in her work, due to her own efforts. Among the most outstanding of her improvements were the introduction of chemistry and the beginning of a reference library.

The following year, feeling that she wanted a little less responsibility, she became principal at Upland, and at that time began working on a method of attracting every child to school work. Extremely successful in this, she was elected superintendent there the year following, and had in school every child of school age and a few post graduates who took such work as bookkeeping or shorthand.

Raymond Benson of her bookkeeping class went to Chillicothe, Missouri, to complete a business course and was the scholarship student of his class. Mildred Larson, who took chemistry under her, was one of the three best students in chemistry at the University of Nebraska,

Anderson—Wahoo

BERTIN ELLSWORTH HENDRICKS

and is now a member of the faculty at the University of Minnesota. Many others have proved themselves in their chosen fields.

On June 7, 1922, she was married to Jyles Clair Hendricks at Munden, Kansas. He was born at Riverton, Nebraska, August 4, 1895. He served in France, during the World War. He is a farmer and dairyman. They have one son, Dwaine Clair, born January 16, 1925. Mrs. Hendricks has resided in Upland twelve years, teaching some each year except one or two until 1925. Since that time she has filled vacancies only.

Aside from her home duties she assists in church work and community activities, and finds time to do reporting for the *Hastings Tribune*, the *Upland Eagle* and the *Franklin County Sentinel*. She is a member of the Nebraskana Society, the Methodist Church, the Friendship Quilting Club (secretary-treasurer 1931), and the American Legion Auxiliary of which she was secretary-treasurer in 1930, and is present chaplain. Mrs. Hendricks helped organize the Junior Red Cross in Upland, about 1920, and assisted with all Red Cross activities during the World War period. Residence: Upland.

John Martin Hengstler

John Martin Hengstler, prominent Knox County farmer, was born at Creighton, Nebraska, August 31, 1874, son of Andrew and Martha (Zept) Hengstler. Andrew Hengstler was born at Aldingen, Germany, July 27, 1838, and came to America September 24, 1867. He farmed in Knox County until his death at Creighton on February 23, 1918. His wife, Martha, who was born in Aldingen, January 23, 1843, is living.

Educated in the public school at Creighton, John Martin Hengstler has farmed in Nebraska most of his life. He was married to Florence May Rafferty at Creighton on February 14, 1900, and to them were born two children, Helen, July 12, 1909, and Lawrence February 13, 1907.

Lawrence was a graduate of the University of Nebraska in 1931 with the degree of Bachelor of Science in Mechanical Engineering. Helen will receive her Bachelor of Science degree in Home Economics in 1933. Mrs. Hengstler was born at Lindsay, Ohio, July 14, 1879, of German and Irish parentage.

Mr. Hengstler has resided in Nebraska fifty-seven years, is a member of Zion Evangelical Lutheran Church and The Nebraskana Society. Residence: Creighton.

Guy Nelson Henninger

Guy Nelson Henninger, clerk of the district court of Buffalo County, was born at Shelton, Nebraska, July 16, 1895, son of Stephen A. D. and Elizabeth Jeannette (Quest) Henninger.

Stephen A. D. Henninger was born in Warren, Ohio, July 18, 1861, and until his retirement in 1921, was the owner of the Shelton Milling Company. His wife, Elizabeth, was born in Lancaster, Pennsylvania, November 10, 1876.

Mr. Henninger was graduated from the Shelton High School in 1914, and in 1918, received the degree of Bachelor of Science in Electrical Engineering from the University of Nebraska. He is a member of Sigma Tau, honorary engineering society, and for a time, was a student at the University of California at Berkeley.

He was admitted to the practice of law by the Supreme Court of Nebraska in 1930. He is a Democrat, and from January 10, 1921, has served as clerk of the district court. He was re-elected in 1922, 1926, and 1930.

His marriage to Mae L. Marshall was solemnized at Lexington, August 30, 1922. Mrs. Henninger was born at Cozad, March 11, 1897, and before her marriage was a school teacher. She is a member of the Episcopal Church. They have two children: Vernelle Jeanette, born

January 13, 1925, at Kearney; and Barbara Mae, born May 2, 1931, at Kearney.

During the World War, Mr. Henninger held the rank of second-lieutenant in the air service. He is at present time captain in the Nebraska National Guard and commander of the 120th wagon company, 35th division, quartermaster train. He is a member of the American Legion, the Chamber of Commerce, the Elks, and the Presbyterian Church. His hobbies are radios and automobiles. Residence: Kearney.

Henry Yoachum Henningsen

Henry Yoachum Henningsen was born at Yutan, Nebraska, June 16, 1888. He is the son of Peter Claus Henningsen and Wolver (Eggers) Henningsen. His father was born in Germany, February 24, 1854, and died at Yutan, August 2, 1924. Peter Henningsen came to this country in 1880 with his wife. She was born in Germany, August 20, 1852, and died at Yutan, March 11, 1925.

Mr. Henningsen attended the public schools of Yutan. On March 11, 1914, at Wahoo, he was united in marriage with Agnes Sophia Rohde. She was born in Germany, September 1, 1894. To this union six children were born: Henry, March 3, 1915; Arthur, April 13, 1916; Alice, August 16, 1918; Pearl, September 23, 1920; Evelyn, December 29 1925, and Glenn, March 5, 1931.

Mr. Henningsen is proprietor of a meat market at Yutan, where he was police magistrate 1927-28. He was precinct assessor 1925-28.

His religious affiliation is with the St. John Evangelical Lutheran Church, at Yutan. He is a volunteer fireman in the Yutan Fire Department. Residence: Yutan.

George Henrichs

George Henrichs, farmer in Gage County, Nebraska, was born at Bremen, Kansas, November 1, 1890, the son of Hye Henrichs and Alitye (Melmen) Henrichs. His father, who was also a farmer, was born in Germany, and died at Wymore, Gage County, Nebraska. His mother was born in Germany.

Mr. Henrichs is a member of the local school board, is affiliated with St. John's Lutheran Church, and holds membership in the Nebraskana Society. His hobby is machines. His political affiliation is with the Republican Party.

He married Tina Nickers at Wymore. Mrs. Henrichs, whose parents were farmers, was born in Germany. Their children are: Alma, Dean, Doris, Edgar, and Luetta. Residence: Wymore.

Clarence Emanuel Henrickson

Clarence Emanuel Henrickson, who has lived in Nebraska nearly all his life, has been engaged in business since he was 16 years of age, and has taken a prominent part in civic affairs for many years. He was born at Swedeburg, September 26, 1890, the son of Andrew and Amanda Charlotta (Anderson) Henrickson. His father, who was born at Besinge Township, Sweden, March 26, 1856, is a painter and decorator; who came to this country in 1883. His mother was born at Harlof, Kristianstad, Sweden, August 3, 1860, and died at Swedeburg, August 6, 1896.

Mr. Henrickson attended school in Sweden, and for a time was a student at the Luther College in Wahoo, Nebraska. He began work with his father at the age of 12 years, and four years later entered business for himself. Since 1920 he has been a partner and associate manager of the Henrickson Paint and Wallpaper Company at Wahoo. He is secretary of the Wahoo Temple Craft Association.

During the World War he served in the United States

Army Suppy Company, 134th Infantry, 34th Division, as supply sergeant; he was in France for about 4 months. In 1923 he acted as commander of the Herbert Beaver Post Number 736 of the Veterans of the Foreign Wars. He is a director in the Wahoo Chamber of Commerce, is a member of the Nebraskana Society, and is affiliated with the Lutheran Bethlehem Church at Wahoo. He is a Mason. From June, 1924, to June, 1925, he served as master of the Wahoo Lodge Number 59, and in 1928 was high priest of Wahoo Chapter No. 43 Royal Arch Masons.

Mr. Henrickson is a Democrat. On August 25, 1930, he was united in marriage with Ellen Erickson at Sioux City, Iowa. Mrs. Henrickson, who was born at Wahoo, is the daughter of Martin Erickson, pioneer farmer and cattle feeder. Residence: Wahoo.

Levi Barton Henriksen

Levi Barton Henricksen was born at Hampton, Nebraska, December 19, 1886, the son of Peter Anders Henriksen and Anna (Peterson) Henriksen. His father, a farmer, was born in Denmark, February 21, 1841, and died at Hampton, Nebraska, in November, 1912. His mother was born at Sillestrup, Denmark, February 24, 1847, anddied at Hampton in 1894.

Mr. Henriksen attended rural school and in 1904 was a student at Dana College where he was active in basketball and baseball. He has been a successful farmer since 1905 near Hampton. He is a member of the Hamilton County Farm Bureau of which he is now president, the Farmers Union, the Red Cross, and the school district of which he was president. He holds membership in the Nebraskana Society, is affiliated with the Lutheran Church of which he is deacon, and is a member of the Republican party.

His marriage to Maren Celie Hansen occurred at Hampton, September 21, 1910; she was born at Hampton, November 28, 1887. They have two children: Clarence, born January 20, 1913; and Gail, born October 25, 1918. Both are active members of the 4-H Club and have shown livestock at various county and state fairs. Mr. Henriksen was county committeeman for two years and in 1920 was elected precinct assessor. Residence: Hampton.

Alden Edson Henry

On June 29, 1877, Alden E. Henry, son of William Chester and Azelia Henrietta Henry, was born at Wilber, Saline County, Nebraska. His father, who was born in Michigan in 1840, and died at Lincoln, Nebraska, January 23, 1903, was a banker. He was captain of Company C, 7th Kansas Volunteer Cavalry in the Civil War.

His mother, who was born in Wisconsin, February 12, 1848, and died at Chicago, February 9, 1918, was a lineal descendant of the *Mayflower* passengers John Alden and Priscilla Mullins. She was a member of Deborah Avery chapter of the Daughters of the American Revolution.

Mr. Henry received his elementary education in the Pawnee City schools, and was graduated from the Lincoln High School in 1895. He received his bachelor's and master's degrees from the University of Nebraska in 1898 and 1899. He was awarded an LL. B, from the law school of Harvard University, where he was a graduate with the honor of *cum laude* in 1903. From 1899 to 1900 he attended the University of Wisconsin where he was a Fellow in political economy. He was also a Fellow in political economy at the University of Nebraska, and was a member of Alpha Theta Chi.

He was admitted to the Massachusetts bar in 1903; in Missouri in 1904; and Nebraska in 1915. He has lived in Nebraska many years, from 1877 to 1900 and from 1915 to the present time. He has engaged in the practice of law in New York City from 1903-04; in Kansas City, Missouri from 1904-15; and in Pawnee City, Nebraska since

1915. He is affiliated with the Democrat party and votes the party ticket. He is a member of the law firm Henry & Hawkins, and spends some time in the supervision of his farms in Pawnee County.

His marriage to Hallie Lillian Bates was solemnized at Kansas City, Missouri, December 23, 1911. Mrs. Henry was born at Kansas City, April 4, 1893, and is descended from English ancestors who settled in New York, early in the settlement of America. They have one daughter, Naomi, born November 21, 1914, who graduated from the Pawnee City high school this year and is a student at the University of Nebraska.

Throughout the World War he was county food administrator. He is a member of the Pawnee City Public Service Club, the Nebraskana Society, and the local and state bar associations. He is a Mason, Royal Arch, Knights Templar, Ancient Arabic Order Nobles of the Mystic Shrine (Sesostris Temple); he is patron of the Order of Eastern Star. He is a Unitarian. Residence: Pawnee City.

Benjamin Frank Henry

On August 30, 1855, Benjamin F. Henry was born at Lindport, Berks County, Pennsylvania. He is the son of David and Sarah (Smith)Henry. His father, who was born at Jacksonville, Pennsylvania, July 2, 1827, died at Klumsville, Pennsylvania, March 30, 1894. He was a stone mason and plasterer, whose parents migrated to Pennsylvania early in the 19th century from Germany. Sarah (Smith) Henry was born at Lynn Township, Lehigh County, Pennsylvania, and died in Berks County, Pennsylvania, November, 1881. Her parents also migrated to Pennsylvania from Germany.

Mr. Henry had few educational opportunities in his youth, but is a well read and highly intelligent person. He takes an active interest in community affairs, and is an outstanding citizen of the state. He was first married to Frances Wilhelm at Nebraska City, Nebraska, in 1879. To them one daughter was born, Martha. Mrs. Henry died in 1881.

His marriage to Catharine Burkey was solemnized at Leonardsville, Pennsylvania, February 25, 1882. Mrs. Henry was born in Berks County, Pennsylvania, June 5, 1853, and died at Daykin, Nebraska, April 16, 1918. Six children were born to them: Mary, Pearl Vesta, born December 16, 1885, who married William W. Fox; Charles, born October 1, 1888, who married Emma Babers; William Joseph, born August 17, 1890, who married Lulu Brinkman; Anna Louisa, born March 26, 1893, who married Milton C. Wessner; and Katy Mae, born December 21, 1899, who died April, 1929, who was married to Arthur G. Kirchoff.

Mr. Henry was married to Ida Ruhnke at Jansen, Nebraska, in 1919. He was a farmer near Dakin until his retirement in 1914, and served for 29 years as a member of the local school board. He is affiliated with St. John's Evangelical Lutheran Church of Daykin, and holds membership in the Nebraskana Society. Residence: Daykin.

John Richard Henry

For the past 59 years John R. Henry has lived in Nebraska, and for many years has been in business at Schuyler, Nebraska. He was born at Sterling, Illinois, March 8, 1870, the son of Richard Henry and Colonne (Doud) Henry. His father, who was born in Ireland, in 1839, and died at Schuyler, May 15, 1915, was a farmer. His mother was born in Ireland, in 1839.

Mr. Henry is now connected with the Farmers Mutual Insurance Company at Schuyler. A Democrat, he served as a member of the Nebraska legislature, 1915-17, and at a special session in 1917. He acted as chairman of the council of defense at Schuyler during the World War. He is a member of St. Augustine's Catholic Church at Schuyler; and holds membership in the Nebraskana Society, and the Modern Woodmen of America. His favorite sport is baseball, while his hobby is reading.

His marriage to Mary Murphy, was solemnized at Rogers, Nebraska, September 2, 1895. Mrs. Henry was born of Irish parentage in Colfax County, April 5, 1874. Residence. Schuyler.

Claude Pierce Hensel

Claude P. Hensel, a resident of Nebraska for the past 45 years, was born at Columbus, Ohio, December 8, 1874, the son of Frederick Christian and Elizabeth (Patrick) Hensel. His father, who was an accountant and traveling salesman, was born at Columbus, December 15, 1847; his ancestry is German. His mother, who was of Scotch Irish descent, was born at Belfontaine, Ohio, June 9, 1848, and died at Palacios, Texas, in 1921. The father died January 28, 1932.

Mr. Hensel attended the grade and high schools of Nebraska. He has been prominent in political and civic affairs throughout the state for many years and has held the following public offices: sheriff of Thayer County, Nebraska; deputy United States marshal, at Lincoln, Nebraska; and sheriff of Lancaster County, Nebraska. 1848, and died at Palacios, Texas, in 1921.

During the Spanish American War Mr. Hensel was in active army service, 1898-9, and in the recent World War took part in loan drives. He is a member of the Veterans of the Spanish War, Veterans of Foreign Wars. and Sons of the Veterans. His memberships in civic organizations include the Chamber of Commerce, Hiram Club, Optimist International Club, the Young Men's Christian Association, the Red Cross and the Nebraskana Society.

Mr. Hensel is a member of the Elks, the Knights of Pythias, and the Masons, (32nd degree, Sesostris Temple, and Lincoln Consistory). He is affiliated with St. Paul Methodist Church of Lincoln. Politically, he is a Republican.

On January 2, 1903, he was united in marriage with Mildred Marbelette Pratt at Hebron, Thayer County, Nebraska. Mrs. Hensel, whose ancestry is Scotch, was born at Geneva, Fillmore County, Nebraska August 21, 1880. Residence: Lincoln.

Joseph Aloysius Henske

Joseph A. Henske, one of Omaha's leading pediatricians was born at St. Louis, Missouri, April 2, 1886. His father, Andrew Adolphus, Henske, born in Germany, January 1, 1851, was a physician and a doctor of philosophy. He died at St. Louis, July 12, 1927. Theresa (Klaren) Henske, his mother, was born at St. Louis, September 15, 1858.

Dr. Henske was educated in the private schools of St. Louis, and later was a student at St. Francis Solanis College, St. Louis University, and Barnes University where he was awarded his M. D. degree. He was elected to membership in Phi Chi, medical fraternity.

Junior and senior interne at the City Hospital of St. Louis, 1907-09 he was surgeon for the Missouri Pacific Railroad at Kansas City and St. Louis, 1909 to 1913; division surgeon of the Missouri Pacific Railroad, 1913-17; and was associated with Dr. H. M. McClanahan from 1919 to 1929. He served as associate pediatrician at the Methodist Episcopal Hospital in Omaha, 1919-30, and since 1930 has been visiting pediatrician at this institution. Since 1922 he has been pediatrician at the Clarkson Memorial Hospital. He is now instructor of pediatrics in the medical department of the University of Nebraska.

The author of many contributions to pediatric literature, with Dr. H. M. McClanahan he published: *Pediatrics for the General Practitioner*. During the World War Dr. Henske was captain in the Medical Corps, 1917-19, and served in the hospital corps in the United States and in France.

His marriage to Kathryn Gwen McClanahan was solemnized at Omaha, November 3, 1915. Mrs. Henske was born in Illinois, the daughter of Dr. H. M. McClanahan, a pioneer pediatrician. They have three children: Kathryn Elizabeth, born November 12, 1916; Joseph Aloysius, born June 26, 1919; and John McClanahan, born June 3, 1923.

Dr. Henske is a member of the American Medical Society; the Central States Pediatric Society; Nebraska State Medical Association; the Douglas Omaha Medical Society and Association of American Teachers of Diseases of Children. He is a fellow of the American College of Physicians, and the American Academy of Pediatrics; holds membership in the American Authors and Writers Society; the Red Cross; and the Nebraskana Society. He is a member of the Omaha Chamber of Commerce; and of the Masons, Rural Lodge Number 316, at Kansas City, Scottish Rite and Shrine. His social clubs are the Omaha Club; and the Happy Hollow Country Club. He likes to golf and ride, while his hobby is farming. He is a Democrat, and is affiliated with the Lowe Avenue Presbyterian Church of Omaha. Residence: Omaha.

Aaron Jack Hepner

Aaron Jack Hepner, merchant, was born at Silver Plume, Colorado, May 26, 1892, son of Dave and Sarah (Jacobs) Hepner.

The father, born in Russia Poland, was a business man at Denver, until his death there on September 20, 1930. Sarah Jacobs was born in New York, of German Jewish ancestry.

Mr. Hepner was graduated from high school in June, 1911, and attended Woods Business College in New York City, until June, 1915. He has been in the mercantile business at Sidney, for the past six years.

On July 31, 1922, he was married to Lillian Joseph at Coalgate, Oklahoma. Mrs. Hepner was born at Hartshorn, Oklahoma, February 5, 1897. They have one son, Harold, born May 12, 1923.

During the late war, Mr. Hepner served in the aviation department. He is a member of the American Legion, the Red Cross, the Chamber of Commerce, the Country Club, and the Elks.

His favorite sports are golf and baseball, while his hobby is the radio. Residence: Sidney.

Kenis P. Herald

Born in Prestonsburg, Floyd County, Kentucky, October 20, 1860, Kenis P. Herald is the son of James H. and Eliza (Akers) Herald. His father was born at Prestonsburg, December 25, 1838, and died at Chester, Nebraska, June 19, 1909. Eliza Herald was also born at Prestonsburg, on February 7, 1842. She died at Chester, April 7, 1915. They were farmers.

Kenis Herald attended the elementary schools. He was united in marriage with Frances A. Goble, at Prestonsburg, on January 27, 1881. She was born at Prestonsburg, January 29, 1861. To this union six children were born: Corie Deve, April 11, 1882, who married L. D. Crandall, died April 8, 1920; Charley F., December 1, 1883, died July 14, 1885; Mary E., May 10, 1888, died May 10, 1888, Frank R., November 28, 1889, died November 20, 1909, Eunice, born December 23, 1891, died the same date, and Roy W., born September 23, 1891, who died the same date.

Mr. Herald has lived in the state for fifty-two years. He is a Democrat and at the present time is serving as postmaster having been appointed September 14, 1914, and is a member of the Nebraskana Society.

He is affiliated with the Methodist Episcopal Church at Byron, is a member of the Red Cross and is clerk of the Modern Woodmen of America Lodge at Byron. Mr. and Mrs. Herald celebrated their 50th wedding anniversary January 27, 1931. Residence: Byron. (Photograph in Album).

Henry William Herbek

A life resident of Nuckolls County, Henry William Herbek was born near Deweese, February 24, 1876. His father, Jakob Herbek, was born in Moravia, Austria, in 1825. Coming to Nebraska in 1870, he lived one year in Crete, and homesteaded in Nuckolls County in 1871. His death occurred at Deweese, June 11, 1900. Marie Svoboda, wife of Jakob, was born in Moravia, August 8, 1835, and died at Deweese, April 4, 1908.

Henry William Herbek attended public school to the ninth grade, and has since been a farmer. He was married on May 15, 1900, to Antonie Karmazin at Lawrence, Nebraska. Of this marriage there are seven children living and four deceased: Mary, born August 23, 1902, died January 6, 1903; George, born December 19, 1903, married Mary Drudik; Florence, born May 1, 1906, died October 6, 1906; Helen, born August 23, 1907, died December 20, 1907; Joe, born December 15, 1908; Albert, born March 15, 1911; Godfrey, born March 2, 1913; Stanley, born May 3, 1914, died May 6, 1914; Henry, born July 3, 1915; Bessie, born July 19, 1919; and Frank, born April 22, 1921. All the unmarried children are on the home farm at the present time. Mrs. Herbek was born in Hungary, October 28, 1878, and came to America in 1881.

During the World War Mr. Herbek participated in all loan and relief drives. A member of Assumption Catholic Church, he has served on various committees. During his entire life he has been a leader in his community, and has taken an active part in community affairs. He is a director of the local school board and a member of the Knights of Columbus, and was recently made a member of the Nebraskana Society. He also belongs to the Country Club. Residence: Lawrence.

Walter John Herbes

Born at Osmond, Pierce County, Nebraska, on March 7, 1891, Walter J. Herbes is the son of Henry John and Gertrude (Billerbeck) Herbes. He completed public school at Humphrey, Nebraska, and later attended Creighton University.

On November 21, 1911, Mr. Herbes was married to Margaret Dunker at Dodge, Nebraska. Mrs. Herbes was born at Dodge, on April 17, 1892. They have three children, Howard, born March 8, 1913; Maxine, born July 4, 1914; and Zona, born December 2, 1915.

An independent Republican, and active in politics, Mr. Herbes has served as secretary of the Republican County Central Committee for four years. He is editor and publisher of *The Osceola Record*, Osceola, Nebraska, at the present time, and has been active in the newspaper field for many years.

Mr. Herbes is a member of the Masons, and the Nebraskana Society. Baseball and football are his favorite sports. Residence: Osceola.

Friedrich August Hermsmeyer

Friedrich August Hermsmeyer was born at Cherokee, Iowa, October 14, 1874, the son of Henry Simon and Louise Caroline (Steinmeyer) Hermsmeyer. His father, who was born in Westphalia, Germany, April 9, 1840, served as a soldier in the War of 1864, in Germany, where he was a farmer; he died at Johnstown, Nebraska, April 27, 1906. His mother was born at Westphalia, July 2, 1845, came to America in 1867, and died at Johnstown, February 5, 1909.

Mr. Hermsmeyer received his education in the rural schools of Iowa and Nebraska, later attended the parochial school of the Zion Lutheran Church. Since his early youth he has been engaged in farming and since 1909, has lived on his 160-acre homestead in Brown County. He is affiliated with the Evangelical Zion Lutheran Church of the Missouri Synod. His hobby is mathematics.

His marriage to Dorette Friederike Wilhelmine Schelm occurred at Denison, Iowa, September 14, 1904. Mrs. Hermsmeyer, whose parents came to this country in 1868, was born at Denison, December 11, 1875. They have two children: Wilhelm, born October 16, 1912; and Friedrich, born October 31, 1914. Residence: Johnstown.

John Frederick Herold

On March 4, 1877, at Bern, Kansas, John F. Herold was born. The son of Bernard Michael and Katherine (Brookner) Herold, his father was born in Germany, and in his early boyhood came to America where he engaged in farming and breeding of fine livestock. He died at Lincoln, Nebraska, February 8, 1928. His mother was born in Germany, July 20, 1855 came to America in early childhood.

Mr. Herold's education was received in the public and high schools at Bern, Kansas. For the last thirty years he has lived in Nebraska where he is a farmer and grower of purebred stock.

His marriage to Eva Florence Hilt was solemnized at Bern, April 5, 1899. Mrs. Herald, who was born of German parentage at Bern, November 30, 1878, was a school teacher before her marriage. There are three children: Virginia, born January 15, 1901, who married Orval Dolph, now living at Los Angeles, California; Frances, born November 25, 1903, now at Hollywood, California; and John, born April 12, 1905, who married Rose Kessler, living in Los Angeles, California.

Mr. Herold enlisted as a private in the Spanish-American War, May 16, 1898. In the World War he was commissioned captain by Governor Neville. He served as committeeman of liberty loan drives and was active in all war-time affairs. He is a life member of the Red Cross, and a member of the United Spanish War Veterans; is president of the Tenant Farmers of America; past president of the Lewiston High School board; past president of the National Polled Hereford Breeders' Association, and in 1921 was president of the state association of this organization. He is a member of the Farmer's Union and various livestock and grain growers associations. He is fond of hunting, fishing, hiking, and traveling. His hobbies are reading and mechanics. Politically, Mr. Herold is an independent. Residence: Lewiston.

Henry Herpolsheimer

Henry Herpolsheimer, president of H. Herpelsheimer Company, was born in Tauensenov, Russia, November 28, 1843, the son of Christian O. and Anna Elisabeth (Smith) Herpolsheimer. The family emigrated from Herpolsheimer on Rhine, to Tauvensnov, about a hundred and fifty years prior to the birth of Christian Herpolsheimer, on July 28, 1805. He was a shoe manufacturer, who immigrated to the United States with his family, and settled in Michigan. He died at Grand Rapids on February 18, 1903, His wife, Anna, who was also a native of Tauensenov, and the mother of eight children, died at New Carlisle, Indiana, March 25, 1885. She was descended of the Smith and Hildebrand families of Germany.

Henry Herpolsheimer attended the public schools of New Carlisle, graduating in 1860. He married Caroline Wilhelmine Krause, who was born at Ann Arbor, Michigan, February 7, 1852. To their union ten children were born, five of whom are deceased. They are as follows: Hattie, who married William Lampbrecht; Ida, who married Al Barber; Albert, Alfred, Ervin, all unmarried, and Oscar, Walther, Robert, Theodore and Henry, deceased.

From New Carlisle he moved to Buchanan where he clerked in a store six years. He then was in business with his brother William G. Herpolsheimer for ten years. In

1880 he came to Lincoln where he established the first department store, H. Herpolsheimer Company.

During the Civil War Mr. Herpolsheimer enlisted with the 43rd Indiana Cavalry in 1861 and serving about one year. Residence: Lincoln.

Max Raymond Herrington

Born at Waterloo, Nebraska, June 7, 1895, Max Raymond Herrington is the son of James G. and Belle (Noyes) Herrington. His father, a native of Greenwich, New York, was a farmer many years in Nebraska, and died at Waterloo, January 2, 1916. His wife, Belle, who was also born in Greenwich, died at Waterloo, July 10, 1918.

Mr. Herrington was graduated from Waterloo High School in 1914 and received his Ph. G. from the Creighton College of Pharmacy in 1920. He is a member of Kappa Psi. His marriage to Elsie Meredith was solemnized at Omaha, where she was born, on July 3, 1899.

A registered pharmacist, Mr. Herrington is also serving as pastmaster at Millard. He is a life resident of the state, and is affiliated with the Republican party, and participates in local politics. During the World War he served overseas with the 42nd Ambulance Company, and he is a member of the American Legion. He is a Presbyterian and has been elected to life membership in the Nebraskana Society. Residence: Millard.

Adam John Herrmann

On January 11, 1874, Adam John Herrmann was born at Sandusky, Ohio. He is the son of John Martin and Katherine (Gegler) Herrmann. His father, a shoemaker, was born at Wurtemberg, Germany, November 23, 1845, and came to this country April 6, 1868. His death occurred Herrmann was born at Wurtemberg, July 9, 1845, and died at Osceola, October 6, 1921.

Mr. Herrmann's father homesteaded in Nebraska about fifty-five years ago. Because of poor health, most of the labor of the farm fell upon Mr. Herrmann, who helped his brothers to receive an education. He has resided in Nebraska for fifty-five years and is a successful farmer in Polk County.

His marriage to Hannah C. Timm was solemnized at Osceola, April 5, 1900. She is the daughter of Joacheir and Mary (Jannings) Timm, and was born at Three Rivers, Michigan, September 17, 1876. They have four children: Ruth Mae, born October 30, 1902; who is married to Phil W. Jacoby; Wesley P., born March 14, 1904, who is married to Veryle E. Foster; Arthur R., born May 30, 1907, who is married to Leona Lenhart; and Victor A., born December 2, 1915. Wesley P. is the undertaker at Tecumseh, Nebraska; Phil W. Jacoby is in the furniture and undertaking business at Alton, Illinois; and Arthur R. is the undertaker at McCook, Nebraska.

He is a member of the First Methodist Episcopal Church of Osceola, the Farm Bureau Association, The Nebraskana Society, and has been treasurer of his local school board for thirteen years. His favorite sport is baseball and traveling is his hobby. Residence: Osceola.

Joyce Hertzler

Joyce O. Hertzler, educator at the University of Nebraska, was born at Jordan, Minnesota, January 20, 1895, the son of Charles William and Lillie May (Zorn) Hertzler. His father, who was born at Burlington, Iowa, February 22, 1867, is head of the sociology department at the Baldwin Wallace College at Berea, Ohio; his Swiss ancestors settled in Ohio, and later moved to Iowa. His mother, who was a devoted homemaker, was born at Burlington, Iowa, February 11, 1874; her family was of old southern Indiana stock.

Professor Hertzler attended the public and high school at Berea, and later was graduated from Baldwin Wallace College, 1916. He was awarded a scholarship at Harvard University where he attended in 1916 and 1917, held a fellowship at the University of Wisconsin, where he was assistant instructor, 1918-20. He was awarded second honors at Baldwin Wallace College, was president of the graduating class there, and was active in music, basketball and track. He is a member of Alpha Kappa Delta.

He is now professor of sociology and chairman of the department of sociology at the University of Nebraska, and was formerly a member of the faculty at the University of Wisconsin. He is the author of the following: *History of Utopian Thought,* published by Macmillan, 1923; *Social Progress,* published by the Century Company, 1928; *Social Institutions,* published by McGraw-Hill, 1929; and various articles published in the *American Journal of Sociology,* the *Scientific Monthly,* and *Sociology and Social Research.* He is a contributor to the *Encyclopaedia of the Social Sciences.*

Professor Hertzler served as infantry drill sergeant during the World War, and was in the artillery officers school at the time the armistice was signed. He is a member of the American Association of University Professors, the Nebraska Writers' Guild, the Nebraska Conference for Social Work, and the Nebraskana Society.

His professional organizations include: American Sociological Society; American Association for Labor Legislation; and the American Academy of Political and Social Sciences. He is a member of the Lincoln University Club.

His sports are golfing and mountain climbing, while other interests include reading, gardening, and woodworking. Politically, he is an independent Republican.

His marriage to Flora Maria Louise Filtzer was solemnized at Milwaukee, Wisconsin, September 1, 1921. Mrs. Hertzler was born at Milwaukee, Wisconsin, and is a graduate of the University of Wisconsin. They have two children: Betty May, born August 22, 1924; and Robert Lincoln, born June 28, 1927. Residence: Lincoln.

Abe Herzberg

Abe Herzberg, merchant, was born in Franklin, Pennsylvania, October 6, 1875, son of Aaron and Henrietta (Marks) Herzberg. He is married to Celestine Schaufarber, who was born in Columbus, Ohio, November 25, 1888. They have one daughter, Angela.

For the past 25 years Mr. Herzberg has been a resident of Omaha. At the present time he is president of Herzbergs Incorporated, the Herzberg Realty Company, and the Herzberg Brothers Clothing Company. His clubs are the Highland Club and the Athletic Club. Residence: Omaha.

Oliver P. Hess

Oliver P. Hess, prominent merchant at Holdrege, Nebraska, was born at Barnsville, Ohio, July 17, 1877, son of James Milton and Elizabeth A. (Beabout) Hess. His father, who was born in Ohio, September 24, 1856, and died at Deshler, Nebraska, December 6, 1889, was a farmer. His mother was born in Ohio, October 10, 1854, and died at Hebron, Nebraska, March 5, 1915.

Mr. Hess received his education in the public grade and high schools of Hebron. He is now manager of the Hested Store Company at Holdrege, and is a member of the Christian Church and the Masonic Lodge No. 43 at Hebron. His political affiliation is with the Republican party.

On October 27, 1904, he was married at Geneva, Nebraska, to Bess Helen Wilcox, who was born at Belleville, Kansas, August 21, 1885. Their three children are: Wilma, born February 2, 1907; Donald, July 9, 1912; and Dean, April 13, 1914. Residence: Holdrege.

Harry Edward Hester

Harry Edward Hester was born at Beaver City, Nebraska, December 27, 1890, the son of Henry and Jeannette Lodema (Shafer) Hester. His father, who is a retired farmer, was born at Huntsville, Indiana, October 3, 1853, of Dutch parentage. His mother was born at Bellville, Ohio, May 25, 1858.

Mr. Hester was graduated from the Beaver City High School in 1910, and later attended the University of Nebraska. He has been a farmer near Beaver City for a number of years and has served as vice president and treasurer of the Beaver City Co-operative Creamery. He is secretary of the Furnas County Farm Bureau, is serving his fifth year as director of the school board of District 74, is affiliated with the Methodist Episcopal Church, and holds membership in the Independent Order of Odd Fellows.

He is vice president of the Furnas County Agricultural Society, and holds membership in the Nebraskana Society. He married Annie May Young at Beaver City, June 16, 1915. Mrs. Hester, whose ancestry is English, was born at Nemaha, Nebraska, October 5, 1892. Their three children are: Hazel Marie, born March 23, 1916; Max Raymond, born July 20, 1917; and Marjorie Jeannette, born February 23, 1921. Residence: Beaver City. (Photograph in Album).

Arthur B. Hestwood

Arthur B. Hestwood, wholesale dry goods executive of Omaha, was born at Jefferson, Iowa, July 17, 1864, the son of John and Anna (Griffith) Hestwood. His father, who was a clergyman in the Methodist Episcopal Church, was born in Ohio, and died at Indianola, Iowa, October, 1897. He was of English descent. His mother was born in Indiana and died in Indianola, Iowa, April, 1895. Her ancestry was Scotch-Irish.

Mr. Hestwood attended the Atlantic (Iowa) High School. He entered the wholesale dry goods business with the M. E. Smith Company where he remained for 9 years. In 1897 he became associated with the Smith-McCord Dry Goods Company at Kansas City, and was connected with this firm for 20 years. In 1917 he formed a connection with the Tootle-Campbell Dry Goods Company at St. Joseph, Missouri; he is now vice-president of the Omaha branch of this company, and is serving as manager.

He was married to May Lank at Dexter, Iowa, October 19, 1887. Four children were born to this marriage: Hazel, born August 28, 1889, who married Arthur P. Miller; Helen, born May 29, 1893, who married Harlan Thompson, who died July, 1924; Arthur, born April 23, 1903; and Clifford, born March 1, 1907. Mrs. Hestwood was born at Dexter, July 29, 1864, and died at St. Joseph, December 18, 1926.

Mr. Hestwood is a member of the Omaha Chamber of Commerce; The National Wholesale Dry Goods Institute of New York, and the Omaha Field Club. His favorite sport is golfing. He is a member of the Methodist Episcopal Church at St. Joseph. He is an independent Republican. Residence: Omaha.

Bruce Hudson Hewett

Bruce Hudson Hewett was born at Avon, Illinois, April 14, 1862, son of Leander Hudson and Hannah Wright (Morey) Hewett. The father was born in Ohio, and died at Gordon, Nebraska, March 1, 1910. He was a stock dealer, shipper, and feeder. His wife, Hannah, was born in Illinois, February 3, 1839, and died at Gordon, December 14, 1917.

Mr. Hewett was a rancher for a number of years and also a banker. He is a Republican, and has held the offices of county treasurer and county commissioner. He is a member of the Methodist Church, the Red Cross, the Modern Woodmen of America, and the Masons. His hobby is reading.

On November 7, 1911, he was married to Dora Etta Oehlmann, at Chariton, Iowa. Mrs. Hewett, who is of German descent, was born at Derby, Iowa, June 23, 1867. Residence: Rushville.

Leo Charles Hewitt

Leo Charles Hewitt was born at Elgin, Illinois, February 7, 1881, the son of Charles Alfred and Kate Belle (Knotts) Hewitt. His father, who was a jeweler, farmer, and optometrist was graduated from the Chicago Opthalmic College in 1894, was graduated from LaGrange School in 1906, and served as president of the State Board of Optometrists and president of the Nebraska Society of Optometrists. His English ancestors, who played an important part in the early history of America, first settled in Rhode Island in 1624. The family history is an interesting and varied one, and members of the family were inventors, financiers, politicians, and distinguished soldiers.

Kate Belle (Knotts) Hewitt was born at Leesburg, Virginia, October 2, 1855. She was engaged in business until 1920, and is now active in the following organizations at Neligh: Eastern Star; P. E. O., and Logas Club. She is a descendant of the McCabe family of Virginia and is the daughter of a Virginia manufacturer who served as county judge and was killed in the Civil War in 1864.

Mr. Hewitt was graduated from the Neligh High School in 1898, was a student at Gates College in 1899 and the University of Nebraska in 1900. He was agent and assistant superintendent of the Metropolitan Life Insurance Company, 1902-06, was associated with his father in the jewelry and optometry business from 1906 until his death in 1921, and has been engaged in business alone at Neligh since 1921.

He has been unusually prominent in professional organizations in the following positions: president of the Nebraska Optometrical Association, 1925-27; member of the board of Optometry Examiners, since 1928; chairman of the board of Optometry Examiners, two terms; chairman and examiner of the First Aid & Life Saving Department of the American Red Cross; secretary and treasurer of the North Nebraska Optometric Educational Extension Association, 1931. Mr. Hewitt is president of the Neligh Rotary Club, is a member of the Neligh Country Club, and served as vice president of the Chamber of Commerce.

His fraternal organizations include the Masonic bodies and the Order of Eastern Star. He is Past Master of Trowell Lodge Number 71, Past High Priest of Temple Chapter Number 40, Past Thrice Illustrious Master of Temple Council Number 20. A Republican, Mr. Hewitt has been mayor of Neligh since 1926. His sports include walking, swimming, and tennis.

He was married at Neligh, March 23, 1912, to Fannie Elizabeth Freeman, who was born at Neligh, November 11, 1887. Residence: Neligh.

Louis William Heyde

Louis William Heyde, prominent lawyer at Grand Island, Nebraska, was born there August 27, 1901, the son of Albert and Emily (Lucas) Heyde. His father was born at Bad Pyrmont, Germany, and his mother was also a native of Germany.

Mr. Heyde attended the Grand Island High School where he was graduated in 1920, received the A. B. degree at Grand Island College in 1924, and in 1927 received the LL. B. degree at the University of Nebraska where he is a member of Kappa Sigma. He played football at Grand Island College for four years, serving as captain of the college team in 1923. Since 1927 he has been independently engaged in the practice of law at Grand Island.

A Democrat, Mr. Heyde is serving as justice of the peace of Hall County. He is an Elk and Mason, and is past president of the board of directors of the Salvation Army of Grand Island. On August 17, 1930, he was married at Hays, Kansas, to Vera Woods. Residence: Grand Island.

August F. Heye

August F. Heye, was born near Glenvil, Clay County, Nebraska, January 11, 1882, and has always lived in that vicinity. His father, J. D. Heye, a farmer, was born in Germany, and died near Glenvil, November 11, 1891. Anna M. (Boltjes) Heye, his mother, was born in Germany, and died at Hastings, Nebraska, February 11, 1923.

Until 1905, Mr. Heye was a farmer, for four years, was a clerk, and for the last 22 years has been engaged in the hardware business at Glenvil. He is treasurer of the Commercial Club, is a member of the Nebraskana Society, and holds membership in Emanuel Luther Church of Glenvil. He served as treasurer of the school board from 1914 to 1923, and during the World War was agent for United States Thrift Stamps. He is a Democrat.

His marriage to Tena A. Kahman, occurred at Glenvil, April 12, 1905. Mrs. Heye was born near Golden, Illinois, December 17, 1883. Two children were born to them: Anna, born January 26. 1906, who married Walter Nowka; and Arnold, born July 22, 1912. Anna is assistant postmistress at Glenvil, and Arnold is clerk in his father's hardware store. Residence: Glenvil.

Albert George Heyhoe

Albert G. Heyhoe, distinguished educator of Nebraska, was born at Swaffham, Norfolk, England, the son of George and Lucy (Whiskerd) Heyhoe. His father, who was a cattle dealer, was born in Norfolk and died at Swaffham. His mother was born at Castleacre, Norfolk, England, and died at Swaffham.

Dean Heyhoe attended a private school in England, and for a time was a student at the Swaffham Public School. He holds the following degrees: A. B., Dartmouth College, 1906; A. M., Dartmouth College, 1908; B. D., Bangor Theological Seminary, 1915. He was a graduate student at Yale University, 1916-17, 1917-18; University of Colorado, during the summer session; Chicago Theological Seminary 1927, and the University of Chicago, 19278. He has been awarded the following scholarship honors; Phi Beta Kappa; *magna cum laude;* and special honors in philosophy at Dartmouth College.

He has held the following educational positions: assistant instructor in philosophy, Dartmouth College, 1906-07, 1907-08; instructor in Biblical literature and Christian evidences, Doane College, 1908-09; and professor of Biblical literature and Christian evidences, 1909-. Since 1919 he has been dean of men at Doane College, where he is also professor of philosophy and psychology. He is the author of *Relation of Mind and Body,* published in 1906, besides various magazine articles.

Dean Heyhoe was united in marriage with Anna Almena Wilgus, at Philadelphia, Pennsylvania. They have three children: Gordon, who attends law school of the University of Michigan; Kenneth Wilgus, who was graduated from Doane College; and Winston Brainerd, a student in engineering, University of Minnesota.

During the World War Dean Heyhoe was active in Liberty loan drives. He is a member of the Blue Valley Association of Congregational Ministers; was formerly a member of the Nebraska Schoolmaster's Club and the Nebraska Academy of Sciences; and is a member of the Nebraskana Society. He was a member of the Crete Rotary Club; is counsellor of the college Young Men's Christian Association; and was formerly a member of the board of trustees of the Crete Public Library. He was at one time a member of the American Philosophical Association.

He is affiliated with the First Congregational Church at Crete, and was moderator of the Nebraska Congrega-at Crete, and is moderator of the Nebraska Congrega-

tional Conference; he is chairman of the course of study committee of the Nebraska Congregational Conference; is a member of the Modern Woodmen of America, and a Royal Arch Mason. Residence: Crete.

John Herman Heyne

John Herman Heyne was born in Thurston County, Nebraska, February 11, 1886, the son of Henry and Christina (Meyer) Heyne. His father, who was born at Oldenburg, Germany, May 25, 1853, and died at Pender, Thurston County, Nebraska, came to America in 1884. His mother was born in Germany, April 10, 1868, and died at Pender, July 6, 1901.

Mr. Heyne, who has been a merchant, farmer, and livestock dealer in Thursday County for many years, is now president of the Heyne Service Station, and is vice president of the Heyne Lumber Company at Pender. He is a member of the Chamber of Commerce, is affiliated with the Lutheran Church, and holds membership in the Nebraskana Society. He is a Republican.

On April 12, 1907, he was married to Martha Nutzhorn, at Caron, Sask., Canada. Mrs. Heyne was born in Thurston County, November 20, 1885, and died at Pender, January 22, 1919. They have three children: Ember, born November 20, 1909, who married Arthur Budwig; Lloyd, born February 12, 1908; and Myra, born February 23, 1917. Mr. Heyne has remarried. Residence: Pender.

Daze Tracy Heynen

Daze Tracy Heynen, county clerk of Kimball County, was born at Tracy Ranch in Kimball County, November 11, 1883, daughter of Asa and Mary Ann (Shields) Tracy. Her father, a native of New York, died at Cheyenne, Wyoming, on January 26, 1888. He was a stockman, whose ancestors came over in the *Mayflower.* Her father was of Irish descent. Her mother was born in Illinois, August 2, 1853, and died at Pine Bluffs, Wyoming, February 19, 1906. She was of English descent, being related to Sir Walter Peacock of London, England.

Daze Tracy attended the public school, and was graduated from the school of music of the University of Nebraska. She was also graduated from Lincoln Business College, and thereafter was stenographer for Curtis, Towle and Paine Company of Lincoln (1902-1910).

On May 7, 1910, she was married to Frank Augustus Heynen at Lincoln. Mr. Heynen was born in Iowa, March 10, 1881, and died at Indianapolis, Indiana, September 11, 1913. His parents were born in Germany. He was a salesman for the Malleable Steel Range Company of South Bend, Indiana. There is one daughter, Dorothy, born January 1, 1912, who is in her senior year at the University of Chicago.

After her husband's death in 1913, Mrs. Heynen entered the office of the county clerk of Kimball County. She was deputy clerk from January 1, 1915, until July, 1917, and since that time has been county clerk. She was vice president of the Nebraska Association of County Clerks and Registers of Deeds for the year 1930, and is affiliated with the Congregational Church of Miles, Iowa. In her younger days, Mrs. Heynen enjoyed horseback riding, and now her favorite sport is golf. Residence: Kimball.

Clarence Wright Hiatt

Born at Odell, Nebraska, July 1, 1891, Clarence Wright Hiatt is the son of Colonel Johnson and Adelaide (Upson) Hiatt. Colonel Johnson Hiatt was born in Sidney, Iowa, June 6, 1859, and died at Beatrice, May 1, 1930. His father helped to settle southwestern Iowa. His father was of Quaker origin and originated in North Carolina. An influential man in the history of

Gage County, Colonel Johnson was a farmer and live stock buyer in Odell for more than twenty-five years.

Adelaide Upson was born in Seward Township, Illinois, March 11, 1859. Her father helped to establish the Upson Church which was the first in Gage County, which is still standing. His great grandfather, Joel Estes, discovered Estes Park, which bears his name; was one of the first white men in Colorado and was named Big White Chief by the Indians.

Clarence Wright Hiatt attended public school and was graduated from Odell High School. For one year thereafter he was a student at Cotner Business College at Bethany, and soon took up farming. He is now engaged, in addition to his agricultural work, in stock buying and hog raising, and in the purchase and sale of farms and farm lands.

During 1921-22, Mr. Hiatt served as deputy sheriff of Gage County, and for the past six years has served as a member and treasurer of school district No. 75. During the World War he held the rank of sergeant in the 3rd Military Training Camp at Camp Dodge, Iowa, and was to enter Officers Training School in California when the Armistice was signed.

Mr. Hiatt is a member of Homer A. Armstrong Post of the American Legion at Odell, is a Mason and a member of the Nebraskana Society. He likes sports of all kinds, especially outdoor activities. He is a Republican. His hobbies are farming and improving farms. Mr. Hiatt and his family attend the Methodist Church.

He was married first to Donna L. Baumgardener, daughter of William H. and Laura Baumgardener, early settlers in Wymore, the former for many years a house carpenter for the Burlington Railroad. Donna L. Baumgardner was born at Wymore, June 9, 1890, and died at Odell, February 24, 1917. There is one child of this marriage, Donna Doris, born February 22, 1917. She was an honor student all the way through junior high school at Beatrice and enters senior high school this fall.

On May 10, 1921, he was married to Mae Deck, at Oskaloosa, Iowa. Mrs. Hiatt was born at Oskaloosa, March 10, 1893, and is the mother of one son, Robert Deck, born July 26, 1926. During the World War she operated a Young Men's Christian Association food canteen for three months in London, later managing a food canteen at Nice, France. She received her high school education at Oskaloosa and later was a student at Penn College. For eight years she was a teacher in Iowa high schools and the high school at Beatrice, Nebraska.

Mrs. Hiatt is a member of the Eastern Star, the Woman's Overseas Service League, and the American Legion. She has held various offices in the Eastern Star, was president of the American Legion Auxiliary in 1930, and is now a member of the executive board of that organization. She holds membership in the Helen Sargent unit of the Woman's Overseas League. Residence: Diller. (Photograph in Album).

Charles W. Hickey

A physician and surgeon since 1903, Charles W. Hickey was born in Elkhorn, Nebraska, October 27, 1882. He is the son of Thomas J. and Louise E. (Knight) Hickey, the former born at Toledo, Ohio, April 11, 1854. Thomas J. Hickey, who engaged in farming all his life, died at Elkhorn, March 23, 1925. His wife, Louise, was born in Forest City, Nebraska, December 19, 1860. She is moderator of School District No. 12, and oracle of the Royal Neighbors of America, Camp No. 3498, which position she has held for fifteen years. She is also a member of the Order of Eastern Star.

Dr. Hickey was graduated from the Elkhorn High School in 1898, and received his M. D. from Creighton Medical College in 1903. He has been in the practice of medicine since May 3, 1903, and from 1905 to 1929, was a member of the drug firm of C. W. Hickey and Company at Bennington.

On January 9, 1906, he was married to Eda B. Witte, at Elkhorn. Mrs. Hickey, who is the owner of the Guernsey Dale Farm Dairy, and a breeder of registered Guernsey cattle, was born in Henry, South Dakota, January 11, 1884. They have two children, Elyzabeth Bernice, born October 10, 1907, and Roma Alice, born March 29, 1909. Both attended Omaha University and are talented musicians.

Dr. Hickey is a Republican. His fraternal organizations include Elks Lodge No. 39 at Omaha, the Woodmen of the World, Modern Woodmen of America, Royal Neighbors of America and the Masons. He is a member of the Nebraska State and Omaha-Douglas County Medical Societies, the Presbyterian Church and the Commercial Club at Bennington. During the World War he was a member of the Medical Advisory Board of Douglas County, rendering faithful and efficient service, and by reason of the discontinuance of all such boards pursuant to the act of Congress of May 18, 1917, he was honorably relieved from the duties of that office on March 31, 1919. He is a member of the Medical Veterans of the World War.

Dr. Hickey is fond of reading and enjoys baseball. He is a member of the Elks Club at Omaha. Residence: Bennington. (Photograph on Page 546).

John Donald Hicks

John Donald Hicks was born at Pickering, Nodaway County, Missouri, January 25, 1890, the son of John Kossuth and Harriett Gertrude (Wing) Hicks. His father, who was born near Quincy, Illinois, October 30, 1852, died at Mound City, Holt County, Missouri, March 19, 1919; he was a clergyman in the Methodist Episcopal Church, and was a member of the Missouri Conference and the Wyoming State Conference. He was descended from an old family in Virginia and North Carolina, originally of English and Scotch-Irish extraction.

His mother, who was born at Albany, Gentry County, Missouri, March 6, 1858, was a teacher in the Missouri schools before her marriage. She is descended from English colonial stock, the Wing and Otis families of New York.

Professor Hicks received his A. B. degree, 1913, and A. M. degree, 1914, at Northwestern University, and in 1916 was awarded the Ph. D. degree at the University of Wisconsin, where he was a member of Delta Upsilon, and Phi Eta. His early education was received in the public schools of Missouri, and in 1906 he was graduated from the high school at Hopkins.

He has held these positions: educator at Hamline, Wisconsin; at the North Carolina College for Women, 1922-3; at the University of Nebraska, 1923 to this date. He was a teacher in summer schools at Northwestern, University of Nebraska, University of Wisconsin, Syracuse University, University of Minnesota, and George Washington University. He is now professor of American history and is dean of the college of arts and sciences at the University of Nebraska.

He is a member of the American Historical Association, the Mississippi Valley Historical Association, the Nebraskana Society, and various other state historical societies. He is also a member of the University Club of Lincoln and the Woodmen of the World. Politically, he is an independent Republican.

On June 15, 1921, he was married to Lucile Harriet Curtis at St. James, Watonwon County, Minnesota. Mrs. Hicks, whose ancestry is English colonial and Scotch, was born at Kewanee, Illinois, June 7, 1899. They have three children: Jane Harriet, born March 11, 1922; Carolyn, born November 22, 1926; and Marjorie Curtis, born January 29, 1931. Residence: Lincoln.

CHARLES W. HICKEY

Heyn—Omaha

John Edward Higgins

John Edward Higgins, farmer and stockman, was born at Schuyler, Nebraska, June 18, 1878, son of William and Elizabeth (Casey) Higgins. William Higgins was born in Ballahagderen, County Mayo, Ireland, March 17, 1845, and came to America in 1860, at the age of 15. He was a farmer for many years in Colfax County, and died at Schuyler, December 8, 1910. His wife, Elizabeth, was born in Ballahagderen, June 6, 1848, and died at Schuyler, March 20, 1908. She was a home maker and church leader.

Upon finishing his rural school education, John E. Higgins attended Fremont Normal College from 1897-1900, and Creighton University 1902-04. A leading farmer in his community, he has served as secretary and director of the Farmers Grain Company of Schuyler 12 years, secretary of the Farmers Union 15 years, is past president of the Colfax County Farm Bureau and a director of the County Fair. A Democrat, he is precinct committeeman at the present time and has been chosen delegate to three state conventions. During the Republican landslide for Harding, he was defeated for the office of state representative. For four years he has served as precinct assessor in his home precinct.

It was through his efforts that the Nebraska Power Company built a high line into the rural districts to furnish them with light and power. Five different times he was sent as a delegate by the farm bureau to organize agriculture, and he was also a delegate to the Farmers Union State Convention four times, where he furnished old time selections on the violin. A school teacher for two years before going to Creighton Medical College, he still holds his credit for those years of study.

He was a member of the committee from Colfax County to send a carload of food to the drouth stricken area in 1931. A member of St. Patrick's Catholic Church and the Dublin Community, he is a committeeman in the latter, and has been a member of the Knights of Columbus for 27 years. President of a branch chapter of the Red Cross since 1915, he has served at the head of all Red Cross drives in his community. An oldtime fiddler, Mr. Higgins enjoys playing the violin, and has played over the radio many times and won many first prizes in fiddling contests.

When his father came to America he started working for $12 a month, and when he retired was worth $100,000. Mr. Higgins still lives on and owns part of the same farm upon which he was born 53 years ago. He is a stockholder in the Nebraska Power Company and the Farmers Union State Exchange.

He was married to Cora Mary Corcoran, at Denver, June 20, 1917. Mrs. Higgins was born at Rock Falls, Illinois, July 12, 1884, and was a school teacher at Denver, prior to her marriage. They have two children, John Edward, born June 6, 1918, and Sheila Elizabeth, born August 2, 1920. Both are musicians and play frequently in society and over the radio. John is a violinist and Betty a pianist. Residence: Schuyler. (Photograph in Album).

Merle C. Higgins

A merchant until 1917, Merle C. Higgins has, since 1919, been in the banking business. Born at Bethany, Missouri, July 14, 1892, he is the son of Milton A. and Mettie I. (Cornelison) Higgins. The father, a native of Bethany, born January 13, 1863, was for many years engaged in the mercantile business. He is now a banker. His ancestry is Irish.

Mettie I. Cornelison was born in Madison County, Iowa, January 13, 1868, of Swedish ancestry. Both parents reside in Benkelman. Upon his graduation from the Haigler, Nebraska, High School, Merle C. Higgins attended Cotner University for a short time. Thereafter for several years he was engaged in business with his father, leaving to enter military service in 1917. He served two years in the World War, as a sergeant in Company B, 355th Infantry.

Upon his return to Benkelman, Mr. Higgins became vice president of the Farmers & Merchants State Bank, which position he still holds. For a short period in 1928, he was bank examiner. He has held all offices in the American Legion, has been treasurer of the Red Cross since 1920, and treasurer of the Chamber of Commerce since 1925.

Mr. Higgins is a member of the Christian Church, the Masons, the Parent-Teachers' Association and the Nebraskana Society. His favorite sports are golf and horseback riding, and his social clubs are the Rod and Gun and the Golf Clubs.

On July 26, 1919, he was married to Inez R. Herring at Benkelman. Mrs. Higgins, who was a teacher before her marriage, was born in Cheyenne County, Kansas, March 21, 1896, and is descended through the maternal line to Lord Baltimore. They have one son, Val M., born May 17, 1925. Residence: Benkelman.

Ole E. Higgins

Ole E. Higgins was born on a farm near Brownville, Nemaha County, Nebraska, October 10, 1874. His father, David Higgins, who was a farmer and livestock breeder, was born in Cattaraugus County, New York, March 4, 1850 and died on his farm in Nemaha County, August 1, 1898. His parents were Welsh settlers who came from New York to Wisconsin and from there to Nebraska where they made homes in Nemaha County in 1859. They helped to develop Prairie Union into one of the finest rural communities in the state. Stella, which became the nearest town, was founded in 1882.

Elizabeth (James) Higgins, mother of Ole Higgins, was born at Pomeroy, Meigs County, Ohio, September 23, 1850. Of Welsh ancestry, she was the daughter of Rev. John T. James, a wealthy pioneer farmer and the founder of Penuell Church in Prairie Union. She died at Stella, May 1, 1914.

Mr. Higgins, who has always lived in this state, received his education at the Higgins' district school at Stella. Together with his sons he is owner and proprietor of the Evergreen Stock Farm, which is operated under the firm name O. E. Higgins & Sons, and is situated just six miles northeast of Stella. He is a member of the Nemaha-Richardson Dairy Herd Improvement Association; the Standard Poland-China Association; and the Holstein-Fresian Association of America.

His marriage to Harriet Louisa Wilkinson was solemnized at Auburn, Nemaha County, Nebraska, December 19, 1895. She was born of English parents, who were farmers, near Farmington, Knox County, Illinois, February 24, 1878. She came to Nebraska with her parents when one year old, and has since lived here. To this union ten children were born, all of whom are living. They are: Opal, born April 30, 1897, who married Jesse E. Moritz; Lilah, born November 22, 1898, who married James A. Simmons; Marie, born March 4, 1900, who married T. W. Overman; Ferne, born September 20, 1901, who married Elmer A. Moritz; Faye, born October 2, 1902, who married Loyal Parsons; Abigail, born October 23, 1905, who married John B. Coupe; Charles David, born August 9, 1907; Nellie, born November 14, 1910, who married Lawrence H. Winfrey; Ole Edwin, born September 25, 1912; and Elmer Estel, born May 1, 1914.

During the World War Mr. Higgins assisted in all local drives. He has always been active in the various civic and religious affairs of his community. He was reared in the Baptist Church, his mother being one of the first members of the Prairie Union Baptist Church, and his grandfather Thomas Higgins was the founder of the Sunday School of this church. At the present time he is affiliated with the new community church in Stella. He is a member of the Stella Chamber of Commerce, the Red Cross, and the Nebraskana Society. He is a Royal High-

Peterson—Auburn

OLE E. HIGGINS

lander. In 1928 he was awarded a silver medal for second highest ranking herd in Nebraska. Perhaps Mr. Higgins' most noteworthy achievement was the award he received in the form of a gold medal, presented to the owner of the prize dairy herd in Nebraska for the year 1929. He was also awarded a wall plaque for the third highest herd in the United States by the Dairy Tribune, a national farm organization. Residence: Stella. (Photograph on Page 548).

George Grover Hilder

George Grover Hilder was born at Wymore, Gage County, Nebraska, December 6, 1888, the son of John George and Martha (Garrett) Hilder. His father, who is a retired lumberman, was born at Burwash, Sussex, Old England, December 17, 1853, and has served as township clerk and president of the Wymore school board; he came to this country in 1872. His mother, who was born at Linwood, Saunders County, Nebraska, January 20, 1863, and died at Diller, Jefferson County, Nebraska, November 16, 1926, was a prominent club woman. She has an interesting genealogy which dates back to General Proctor of Revolutionary fame; many of her ancestors had much to do with the settlement of Kentucky and subduing the Indians. Her paternal ancestry dates to Joel Estes; she was eligible to membership in the Daughters of the American Revolution, and was active in the Eastern Star.

Mr. Hilder, who is a Master Farmer in Gage County, is moderator of the school board, is a member of St. Luke's Episcopal Church, and holds membership in the Nebraskana Society. He is a member of the Kiwanis Club, the Masons, Eastern Star, and the Geographical Society. During the war he was solicitor for loans in Gage County.

On August 18, 1909, he was united in marriage with Winnie Bertha Roberts at Wymore. Mrs. Hilder, whose ancestors were residents of Wales, was born at Wymore, June 9, 1889. They have three children: Esther, born June 12, 1910, who is a teacher; Harold, born January 29, 1914, who is a junior in the Wymore High School; and Wayne, born October 11, 1921. Residence: Wymore. (Photograph in Album).

Mortimer L. Hildreth

A physician and surgeon since 1880, Mortimer L. Hildreth was born in Lee, Massachusetts, January 9, 1850, and has resided in Nebraska since 1874. His parents, James Edgar and Sarah Ann (Bullock) Hildreth, were both natives of New York. His father was of French and English descent, his ancestors having come to America in Colonial times. His mother was descended from Colonial settlers from England and Holland. James Edgar Hildreth died at Tekamah, in 1906, and his wife died in Burt County, in 1876.

Dr. Hildreth attended public and private schools in New England, and received his M. D. from Rush Medical College in 1880. He has contributed articles to medical journals throughout his professional career, and has held many professional offices. He is former president and former secretary of the Nebraska State Medical Society and held the chair of medicine at the Sioux City College of Medicine for some time. He was a member of the house of delegates of the American Medical Association, has served as president of the Nebraska Society of Railway Surgeons, and was delegate from Nebraska to the Pan-American Medical Congress in Washington.

On October 25, 1882, he was married to Carolyn Elizabeth White, at Lyons, Nebraska. Mrs. Hildreth who was born at Milburn, Illinois, February 23, 1857, is descended from Scotch-English settlers in America about 1850. There are three children: Beulah, born March 20, 1885, who married Shepherd M. Dunlap; Raymond C., born October 8, 1888, who married Blanche Forrester; and Helene, born December 21, 1895, who married Edward Gillette .

Dr. Hildreth is a member of Lyons Presbyterian Church, and has served on the Lyons School Board, for many years, and is a member of the Red Cross, and the Young Men's Christian Association. Residence: Lyons.

Bertha Steele Hill

Bertha Steele Hill, daughter of Arthur Seth and Mertie Elvina (Monti) Steele, was born at Oberlin, Kansas, July 22, 1894. Her father was born at Platville, Wisconsin, January 24, 1865. He is a banker at Oberlin, and is chairman of the board of directors of the Oberlin National Bank. His ancestry is traced to William the Conqueror, and among his Revolutionary ancestors is Lieutenant Colonel Solomon Wills of Tolland, Connecticut. His wife was born at Lincoln, August 28, 1873, and is of the Sherrill family of Kentucky. She is a prominent clubwoman.

Bertha Steele was graduated from Decatur County High School in 1913, and attended Kansas University one year. On December 23, 1916, she was married to Ralph Wright Hill at Oberlin (see Nebraskana). A resident of Nebraska for the past four years, Mrs. Hill has always been active in club and civic organizations. A member of the Daughters of the American Revolution, she also belongs to the P. E. O., and the Order of Eastern Star, of which she is past matron. She is a member of the Red Cross, the Nebraskana Society, and the First Methodist Church of Hebron. For some time she has been active in Woman's Club work, and is now president of the Hebron Woman's Club. Her hobby is reading. Residence: Hebron.

Daniel T. Hill

Daniel T. Hill, dental surgeon, was born at Carmel, New York, July 19, 1857. His father, Daniel T. Hill, Sr., was a Baptist minister, born at Milton, Ulster County, New York, November, 1803, and who died at Syracuse, Nebraska, March 9, 1887. Sarah Jayne (Merritt) Hill, his mother, was born at Carmel, November 3, 1820, and died at Cornwall, New York, May 10, 1884. Both were of English descent.

Dr. Hill was graduated from Amenia Seminary in 1874, and in 1877 was awarded the D. D. S. degree at the New York College of Dentistry. He was admitted to the practice of dentistry at Cornwall, June 1, 1877, and from that date until 1883 was engaged in the dental practice at Cornwall. Since 1883 he has been a dentist at Syracuse, Nebraska.

He was married to Tella H. Capron at Purdys, New York, July 11, 1877. Mrs. Hill, whose ancestry is English and French, was born at White Plains, New York, October 31, 1857. Five children were born to their marriage, one of whom is living. They are: Ruby, born June 18, 1878, who died June 19, 1878; Pearl, born October 17, 1883; Myrtle H., born May 26, 1885; Clair L., born December 13, 1886, who was graduated from the Lincoln Dental College in 1910, and practiced with his father up until his death January 11, 1926; and Claud A., born March 13, 1893, who died August, 1893.

Dr. Hill is a member of the Sons of the American Revolution. He is also a member of the National Dental Association, the Nebraska Dental Association, the Red Cross, the Nebraskana Society and the I. O. O. W. His hobby is the American trotting horse. He is a Republican, and is now serving as mayor of Syracuse. Residence: Syracuse.

George Clayton Hill

George Clayton Hill, life underwriter, was born at Tabor, Iowa, November 25, 1869, and for more than 59 years has been a resident of Nebraska. He is the son of Edgar Strong and Delia Sophia (Jones) Hill, the former of whom was born at Wakeman, Ohio, January 23, 1834. He was a farmer, grain merchant and undertaker, county judge and surveyor, a Civil War soldier and a Nebraska pioneer. He died at Indianola, Iowa, August 29, 1929. He was of Puritan ancestry, descended from early English settlers who came on the ship *Mary and John* in 1632.

Delia Sophia Jones was born in Dover, Vermont, April 9, 1845, and died at Indianola January 7, 1928. In her younger years she was a teacher. She descended of Welsh and English Puritan settlers.

George Clayton Hill attended elementary school. He has been in the retail and grain merchandising business for many years and is now special agent of the Union Central Life Insurance Company. He is a liberal Republican, a member of the First Congregational Church, the Red Cross, the Chamber of Commerce, and the Kiwanis Club. In the latter he has held many offices including, president, 1929-30, lieutenant governor of the Sixth Division, Nebraska-Iowa District, 1931. He was president also of the Southwest Nebraska Historical Society in 1929. For several years he has been a director of the Young Men's Christian Association. His hobby is reading.

He was married on June 12, 1894, to Ella Maud Beardslee at Indianola. Mrs. Hill was born at Jerseyville, Illinois, July 29, 1869, and died at Indianola, May 30, 1923. Her ancestry was English. They had one daughter, Dorothy, born March 14, 1898, who died May 11 of that year. Residence: McCook.

James R. Hill

James R. Hill, a pioneer farmer of Clay County, Nebraska, was born in Shelby County, Illinois, January 13, 1874, the son of William and Nancy K. (Haggard) Hill. His father, who was born in Shelby County in 1846, and died at Edgar, Nebraska, August 14, 1885, was also a farmer; his ancestry was English. During the Civil War he served in Company G, 53rd Illinois Infantry and marched with Sherman to the sea. When he was one year old Mr. Hill's parents came to Nebraska and settled in Clay County, homesteading near Edgar, and he has lived in Clay County ever since. His mother, whose ancestry was French, was born at Nashville, Tennessee, May 9, 1853, and died at Edgar, February 25, 1916.

Mr. Hill was united in marriage with Jane E. Mann at Sutton, Nebraska, February 6, 1901. Mrs. Hill, who is of German descent, was born at Sutton, Nebraska, October 31, 1879. Both Mr. and Mrs. Hill are active members of the Evangelical Church of Clay Center. His early recollections of the Indians is one of continual uneasiness. They have three children: Loren, born December 17, 1901, who married Pauline Addler of Hastings; Viola, born March 1, 1906, who married Raymond Burklund, of Verona; and Maurice, born January 23, 1908. Residence: Deweese.

Ralph Wright Hill

Born at Hebron, Nebraska, August 7, 1893, Ralph W. Hill is the son of William McCuin and Annabelle (Wright) Hill. His father, who was born at Hannibal, Missouri, December 1, 1861, has been in the furniture and undertaking business in Hebron, for many years. One of the thirty-five leading undertakers in the United States, he is past president of the National Funeral Directors Association. His ancestry is Irish.

Annabelle Wright, his wife, was born at Pontiac, Illinois, January 8, 1869. She is descended from Revolutionary stock, including Ephriam Fairbanks, who was a member of the Boston Tea Party. Active in church and club work for many years, Mrs. Hill is a charter member of Chapter A. E. of the P. E. O., and past matron of the Order of Eastern Star.

Ralph W. Hill was graduated from Hebron High School in 1912, and attended the University of Nebraska three years, where he was a member of Phi Gamma Delta.

In 1917, he organized a furniture and undertaking business at Oberlin, Kansas, operating it until 1927, when he disposed of the business and returned to Hebron. The following year he entered into business with his father.

On December 23, 1916, he was united in marriage to Bertha Irene Steele, at Oberlin. Mrs. Hill was born there on July 22, 1899, and is descended from Lieutenant Colonel Solomon Wells of Connecticut, a Revolutionary figure. Two children were born to them, a son who died at birth, November 7, 1923, and a daughter, Joy Belle, born February 17, 1926.

Mr. Hill is a member of the First Methodist Episcopal Church of Hebron. He is a Royal Arch Mason, Knight Templar, and member of the Shrine, affiliated with Isis Temple at Salina. He also belongs to the Chamber of Commerce, the Kiwanis Club, the Hebron Country Club and the Red Cross, and in 1929 was elected member of the school board (1929-32). His favorite sport is golf. Residence: Hebron.

William M. Hill

William M. Hill, pioneer merchant of Thayer County, Nebraska, has been prominent in civic affairs at Hebron, for many years. He was born at Hannibal, Missouri, December 1, 1860, the son of Benjamin and Alice (Mannix) Hill. His father, who was also a merchant, was born in Ireland, and died at Hebron, June 14, 1908. His mother was born in Ireland.

Mr. Hill received his education in the schools of Hannibal. The owner of the Hill Furniture & Undertaking Establishment of Hebron forty years, until recent years he managed this organization; he is now retired from more active business life and has turned the management of the furniture store over to his son, Ralph W. Hill.

He is a member of the Hebron Chamber of Commerce, is affiliated with the Methodist Church of Hebron, is a Mason, and holds membership in the Nebraskana Society. His political affiliation is with the Republican party.

His marriage to Anna Belle Wright was solemnized at Hebron, November 27, 1887. They have four children: Nettie May, who married David Simms of Hastings, and who is a prominent lecturer, clubwoman, and artist; Ralph Wright, who is in business at Hebron; Ben James, who operates a store in Superior, and William John, who is engaged in the clothing business at Hebron. William married Ruth Wilmore, a lifetime resident of Hebron. Residence: Hebron.

Ethel Jane Hilton

Ethel Jane Hilton, assistant principal of Hastings Senior High School, was born at Blue Hill, Nebraska, daughter of Edgar and Alice Mary (Tyler) Hilton. Her father, who was born at Albia, Iowa, October 6, 1861 is engaged in business. Her mother was born at Pontypool, Monmouthshire, England, December 16, 1867.

Miss Hilton was graduated from Blue Hill High School in 1907, received her Bachelor of Arts degree from the University of Nebraska in 1911, and took post graduate work at the University of Colorado in 1929.

She has served as assistant principal at Culbertson, principal and superintendent at Hardy, principal at Red Cloud and assistant principal at Hastings.

She is a Democrat, a member of the P. E. O., the Royal Neighbors of America, the A. A. U. W. and the Nebraskana Society. Residence: Hastings.

Orlando Himebaugh

Orlando Himebaugh, railroad station agent, was born at Hooper, Nebraska, December 27, 1866, and has lived there all his life. His father, Orlando Allen Himebaugh, a grain and lumber dealer, was born at Erie, Pennsylvania, October 5, 1825, and died at Hooper, October 2, 1902; he was of Pennsylvania Dutch descent. His mother,

Elsina (Canaga) Himebaugh, was born in Ohio, November 5, 1857, and died at Hooper, March 21, 1922.

Mr. Himebaugh attended the Fremont Normal College, at Fremont, Nebraska. He has been a member of the Hooper school board for 20 years and for the past 15 years has been president of the board. He holds membership in the Maccabees and the Knights of Pythias. He is a member of the Nebraskana Society.

He was married at St. Edwards, Boone County, Nebraska, May 27, 1891, to Julia Magdeline Warner. Mrs. Himebaugh was born at Winnebago Mission, Nebraska, April 27, 1869. Her grandfather, Rev. Hamilton, was a Presbyterian missionary. Her father, Rev. Joel Warner, was a Presbyterian minister in Nebraska for 50 years. Six children were born to their marriage: Duke Orlando, born March 13, 1892, who married Lorene Poole; Roland Warner, born September 20, 1893, who married Hazel Goldberry; Gail Hamilton, born August 31, 1896, who married Will E. Rice; Genevieve Lorene, born June 23, 1898, who married Walter Strain; Jeanette, born May 7, 1904, who married Theodore Lovelady; and Wilma Julia born April 16, 1907. Duke Orlando is a commercial teacher in the high school at Casper, Wyoming. Roland Warner is a bookkeeper. Wilma is a graduate nurse. Residence: Hooper.

Minnie Grinstead Himes

Minnie Grinstead Himes, educator and distinguished stateswoman, was born at Summer Shade, Metcalfe County, Kentucky, May 19, 1868, daughter of George Rollans and Nancy Thomas (Wells) Grinstead. Her father, who was born at Glasgow, Barren County, Kentucky, February 5, 1837, is a farmer and has taken an interested part in community affairs, serving on the county board for many years and acting as elder in his church. He attributes his long life to total abstinence from drink and other bad habits. Early in the 17th century his ancestors came to America from East Grinstead, England, settling in Virginia where Philip Wade Grinstead, father of George, was born.

Her mother, who was born at Temple Hill, Barren County, Kentucky, March 25, 1844, and died at Humboldt, Nebraska, March 19, 1895, was a woman of energy and power in her home and community. Her father, William Wells, was born in Lexington, Kentucky.

Mrs. Himes attended the Lynchburg, Nebraska, country schools, the Dawson and Humboldt High Schools and was later a student at the Holton Normal School in Kansas. In 1901 she was graduated from Fremont Normal at Fremont, Nebraska, and in 1913 studied sociology and English at the University of Washington at Seattle. She received her A. B. degree from Cotner College in 1917. In 1918 she was awarded a master's degree in sociology and English at the University of Nebraska. From 1923-25 she was a student at George Washington University at Washington, D. C., and in 1924 studied through the extension department of Johns Hopkins University at Baltimore. She has lived at different periods for 30 years in Nebraska, and has been a teacher in country schools, principal of high schools and grade schools. At the present time she is saleswoman for the Lincoln Liberty Life Thrift Company of Lincoln, Nebraska. She is the author of a thesis *Influence of Mormons on Foreign Immigration into the United States.*

As a Republican, Mrs. Himes was an unsuccessful candidate in the primaries of 1930 for nomination to United States Congress. She is the first woman in Nebraska, either Democrat or Republican, to file for that office. Although defeated, she received one-half of the votes given the four candidates in Richardson County, and adjoining counties gave her an encouraging vote. Always a leader in civic and political affairs, she holds high principles as her standard. She believes that disobedience to moral and civic laws is the source of much civic trouble; and lack of thrift and the tendency to live beyond one's means is the cause of much financial trouble.

She was married on January 11, 1892 to Jacob Harvey Himes, at Washington, D. C. Mr. Himes is in the government service, as pension inspector. Two children were born to their marriage, one of whom is living. Philip Grinstead, born July 2, 1905, died July 26, 1905; and Lois Floy, born August 19, 1906, married Henry Cameron Lucas of Omaha. She received her master's degree from the University of Nebraska in 1927, majoring in the same subjects and studying under the same instructors as her mother.

Mrs. Himes is a member of the Columbia chapter of the Daughters of the American Revolution, at Washington, D. C., the Lincoln and Humboldt Woman's Clubs, and is a former member of the Parent-Teachers' Association. She is state director of morality of the social morality department of the W. C. T. U.; and in 1903-04 was on the Y. W. C. A. board at Spokane, Washington. She is a member of the National Educational Association, and the Nebraskana Society. She is a member of Humboldt chapter of the Order of Eastern Star, the Royal Neighbors and the Woodmen Circle of Lincoln. She is affiliated with the Humboldt Christian Church.

Mrs. Himes is very fond of reading and walking. She believes that obedience to moral and civil laws will help to solve our social and economic problems, and that industry, common sense and systematic spending and saving will bring independence. Residence: Humboldt. (Photograph on Page 552).

Joseph B. Hines

Joseph B. Hines, postmaster of Wahoo, was born at Morse Bluff, Nebraska, March 6, 1883, son of Frank and Mary (Bures) Hines. Frank Hines, a farmer, was born at Korita, Czechoslovakia, August 15, 1850, and came to the United States in 1868. He died at Morse Bluff, on October 22, 1926. His wife, Mary, was born at Sedlice, Czechoslovakia, July 20, 1850, and resides at North Bend, Nebraska.

Educated in the public and high schools of Morse Bluff, Mr. Hines has engaged in various occupations. He was for some time a clerk in a drygoods store, and was a bookeeper for a hardware firm. He has also engaged in farming. A Republican, he was county assessor from 1912-16, county clerk 1917-February 16, 1922, at which time he was appointed postmaster at Wahoo, and is now serving his third term.

He married Lillian Ruzicka at Schuyler, Nebraska, October 3, 1905. Mrs. Hines was born at Linwood, Nebraska, June 26, 1887, of Czech descent. They have one daughter, Lillian. She was born January 3, 1907, and was graduated from Wahoo High School. Later she received her B. S. degree from the University of Nebraska. She is now married to Dr. H. Gayle McMaster.

Mr. Hines was secretary of the local draft board during the World War, serving without pay, and was captain of the Home Guards and supervisor of explosives for Saunders County. He is a member of the First Presbyterian Church, the Red Cross and Salvation Army, the Chamber of Commerce, Masons and Shrine and the Knights of Pythias. His club is the Wahoo Golf Club. Residence: Wahoo.

Laurence Irwin Hines

Laurence Irwin Hines was born at Holstein, Nebraska, December 15, 1894, the son of Thomas Jefferson and Clara May (Powers) Hines. His father, a retired farmer, was born at Science Hill, Kentucky, April 1, 1871. His mother was born in Illinois, October 4, 1870.

Mr. Hines was graduated from the Hastings High School in 1913, and in 1918 was graduated with honors from the George Washington University where he received the degree, Doctor of Veterinary Medicine. He

Knight—Falls City

MINNIE GRINSTEAD HIMES

was awarded a surgery prize in college and was elected to membership in Omega Tau Sigma.

He served as a stenographer in departmental service of the United States Government from 1914 to 1918, was federal veterinary inspector in 1919, acted as Nebraska state veterinary inspector in 1922, and has been engaged in general practice of his profession since 1922. Dr. Hines is a member of the Nebraska State Veterinary Examining Board, and is prominent in many professional organizations.

He is a member of the Nebraska Veterinary Medical Association, the Interstate Veterinary Medical Association, the American Veterinary Medical Association, and the Medical Reserve Corps. He is president of the Spencer Commercial Club, is chairman of the Board of Education at Spencer, Nebraska, of which he was formerly secretary, and holds membership in the Nebraskana Society. His favorite sports are hunting and fishing.

His marriage to Sadie Mildred Hargleroad occurred at Minden, Nebraska, June 11, 1922. Mrs. Hines was born at Holstein, Nebraska. Their children are: June Elaine, born July 27, 1923; and Ramona Sari, born September 26, 1925. Residence: Spencer.

Leon L. Hines

Leon L. Hines, lawyer, was born in Imperial, Nebraska, September 25, 1891, son of David G. and Cordelia G. (Smith) Hines.

His father, a lawyer, was born in Winston-Salem, North Carolina, November 1, 1860, and died at Benkelman, March 28, 1928. His mother was born at Tabor, Iowa, March 24, 1868, and is still living.

His preliminary education was received in the public schools of Haigler, Benkelman and McCook. Upon his graduation from McCook High School in 1908, Mr. Hines entered the University of Nebraska from which he received his Bachelor of Arts degree in 1915. He is a member of Kappa Sigma and Phi Delta Phi.

Since his admission to the bar in 1915 Mr. Hines has been in active practice, and from 1926 until 1930 served as county attorney of Dundy County, elected on the Democratic ticket.

His marriage to Keturah Ellen Sipe was solemnized at Bartley, Nebraska, on June 20, 1917. Mrs. Hines was born at Cambridge, Nebraska, February 17, 1894. They have one son, Leon Clifford, born June 10, 1922.

Mr. Hines is a member of the American and Southwestern Nebraska Bar Associations, the Lions Club, the Masons, and the Knights of Pythias. Residence: Benkelman.

Alice Hamlin Hinman

Alice Hamlin Hinman, educator and clubwoman, was born in Constantinople, Turkey, daughter of Cyrus and Mary Eliza (Tenney) Hamlin. Cyrus Hamlin, who was born at Waterford, Maine, January 5, 1811, was a missionary and educator, founder and president of Robert College at Constantinople, and later president of Middlebury College in Vermont. He was a writer and lecturer, of English ancestry. His father was a captain in the war of 1812 and his two grandfathers served in the Revolution.

Mary Eliza, wife of Cyrus Hamlin, was born at Portsmouth, New Hampshire, April 12, 1828, and died at Lexington, Massachusetts, March 5, 1905. She was a teacher and writer, and prior to her marriage was assistant editor of the *National Era* at Washington, D. C. She was of English ancestry.

Alice Hamlin received her education in the public schools of New Haven, Connecticut and Bangor, Maine. She attended high school in Middlebury, Vermont, and was graduated from Abbot Academy at Andover, Massachusetts in 1887. In 1893, she received her A. B. from

Wellesley College, and in 1896, a Ph. D., from Cornell University. She was valedictorian of her class at Abbot Academy, a member of the Shakespeare Society at Wellesley and is a member of Sigma Xi. On July 21, 1897, she was married to Edgar Lenderson Hinman at Lexington, Massachusetts. They have one daughter, Eleanor, born December 9, 1899.

Miss Hamlin was a teacher in Abbot Academy three years, and a professor at Mt. Holyoke College 1896-97. During 1906 and 1927 she was instructor at the University of Nebraska; and during 1902-07, was a lecturer at the University. From 1928-32 she was a lecturer at the University of Nebraska School for Nurses.

During the World War she was a member of the Women's League of National Service, and was active in the establishment of a community kitchen, and was a speaker for food regulation, was goals, etc. A Congregationalist, she is affiliated with the First Plymouth Church. She is a member of the Young Women's Christian Association and has served as a member of the city board 1923-29, and the university advisory board 1903-31. She is a Republican in politics and a member of the League of Women Voters. In the latter she has served as chairman of the International Co-operation Department and as member of the state board.

Mrs. Hinman has been active in the advancement of educational work, and during 1906-18 was a member of the board of education. She has been high school chairman and president of the board of that organization. Among her educational memberships are the American Psychological Association and the American Association of University Women. Her clubs include the Sorosis and the Fortnightly.

At the present time Mrs. Hinman is chairman of International Relations of the American Association of University Women, and has so served in the past. She is a charter member of the Missionary Federation, was its secretary four years, and at one time was its president for four years. From 1903-08 she was educational chairman for the Nebraska Federation of Women's Clubs, and from 1921-29 was secretary of the Near East Relief Association in Lincoln. Residence: Lincoln. (Photograph in Album).

Edgar Lenderson Hinman

On September 5, 1872, Edgar L. Hinman was born at Afton, Chenango County, New York. For the past thirty-five years he has lived in Nebraska and has been engaged in the educational life of his community since he moved to Lincoln. His father, William Henry Harrison Hinman, who was a farmer, was born at Coventry, Chenango County, New York, March 8, 1840, and died at Coventry, February 12, 1902. His ancestors were Connecticut Yankees, descended from English settlers who came to America in 1650.

Mary Jane (Lenderson) Hinman, his mother, was born at Greene, Chenango County, New York. June 25, 1842. Her Dutch colonial ancestors settled in Schoharie County, New York, more than 200 years ago. She died at Afton, Chenango County, New York, December 15, 1904.

Professor Hinman attended a country school in Coventry until 1882, and then completed his high school course at Afton, 1889. He was awarded these degrees: A. B., 1892; and Ph. D., 1895; at Cornell University. He was president of the Classical Association at Cornell University; was president of the Philosophical Club, 1894-5; and was president of the Ethical Society, 1893-4.

He was teaching fellow at the University of California, 1895-6; and has been a member of the faculty at the University of Nebraska since 1896. He is now professor of logic and metaphysics, and is chairman of the department of philosophy and psychology at the University of Nebraska. He is the author of *The Physics of*

Idealism, 1904; and many articles in philosophical periodicals and in co-operative volumes; besides various book reviews.

He was married to Alice Julia Hamlin at Lexington, Middlesex County, Massachusetts, July 21, 1897. Mrs. Hinman was born at Constantinople, Turkey, December 20, 1870. Her ancestors were old New England settlers. She is active in various civic and social affairs in Lincoln. They have one daughter: Eleanor Hamlin, born December 9, 1899.

During the World War Professor Hinman was assigned to overseas service with the Young Men's Christian Association, but was requisitioned for other work at home. He taught war aims at the University of Nebraska. He is a member of the American Philosophical Association, and was president of the western division of this organization, 1915-16. He has held membership in the Nebraska Academy of Science, American Association for the Advancement of the Science, the American Institute of Archaeology, and the Nebraskana Society. He is a member of First Plymouth Congregational Church at Lincoln. Residence: Lincoln.

Alonzo Otis Hinson

Active in ministerial work for many years, Alonzo Otis Hinson has resided in Nebraska continuously since 1884. He was born in Filmore County, December 4, 1872, son of Newton and Sarah Alice (McLaughlin) Hinson. Newton Hinson, who was born in Allamance County, North Carolina, March 15, 1847, was the son of Joseph G. Hinson. He was a school teacher, a local and itinerant preacher, and served three years in the Civil War with Company D., 70th Indiana Infantry. He died at Holdrege, Nebraska, September 11, 1927. Sarah, his wife, was born in Virginia, August 11, 1851, and now resides at Kearney, Nebraska. Her family came to America with a group of colonists and settled at St. Mary's, Maryland, in 1637, under a grant made to Lord Baltimore.

Mr. Hinson was graduated from the Beaver City, Nebraska, High School in 1892, and was awarded a Bachelor of Letters degree from Nebraska Wesleyan University in 1896, and a Doctor of Divinity degree in 1918. He was valedictorian of his high school and college classes and a member of Everett Fraternity at Wesleyan. His honors include Phi Beta Kappa. During the years 1893 to 1896 inclusive he was a member of the baseball team at Nebraska Wesleyan.

A country school teacher during 1890-91, he served as principal at Hendley, Nebraska, 1896-97, and superintendent 1897-1901. From 1901 to 1903 he was superintendent of the Beaver City High School. In June, 1903, he entered the Methodist Episcopal ministry, and held the following pastorates: Daykin 1903-05; Chester, 1905-08; Dewitt 1908-1909; Syracuse 1909-14; Holdrege 1914-19. From 1919-22 he was district superintendent of the Beatrice District of the Methodist Church, and was pastor at Norfolk from 1921-27. Since September 1927 he has been superintendent of the Beatrice district.

During the World War Mr. Hinson served as a war loan speaker, etc. He served as a member of the Welfare Board at Norfolk six years, and as chaplain of the Norfolk Lions Club the same length of time. His fraternal organizations include the Masons, Odd Fellows and Modern Woodmen of America. He is a member also of the Y. M. C. A. His sports are hunting, fishing and golf, and his indoor recreation is reading. Residence: Lincoln.

Anthony Hirschman

Anthony Hirschman, mayor of Hartington, was born in Maustin, Juno County, Wisconsin, May 12, 1864, and has been a resident of Nebraska for fifty-nine years. He is the son of Franz and Thekla (Tawit) Hirschman, both of whom were born in Austria. His father was a farmer and carpenter, who settled in Nebraska in early days.

He died at Hartington in December 1896. His wife survived him until January 6, 1900.

Mr. Hirschman attended public school until 1884, and on May 14, 1889, was united in marriage to Anna Catherine Dreeson at Hartington. Mrs. Hirschman was born at Madison, Wisconsin, December 28, 1867, and to them were born six children, five of whom are living. Clara Thekla, born June 28, 1890, died February 19, 1892; Irene, born May 20, 1893, is a housekeeper; Leo H., born September 14, 1896, married Ida Irvin and is a practicing lawyer; Roman E., born February 25, 1902, married Harriett Adamiski and is in the drug business; Ivo J., born March 15, 1904, is an auto mechanic and Lucilla, born May 5, 1907, is a hairdresser.

A Democrat, Mr. Hirschman is serving as mayor, as stated above, and has held many civic and public offices. He is secretary of the Cedar County Fair Association, and has held all offices in the Chamber of Commerce. A member of the Eagles and the Sons of Herman, he is a member also of Holy Trinity Catholic Church, the Knights of Columbus, of Hartington, the Catholic Knights of America, of which he is secretary, the F. of E. of which he is also secretary, and is treasurer of the Sons of Herman. He was county chairman of the Knights of Columbus War Drive and sold bonds in the Victory Loan drive. His club is the Hartington Golf Club. His hobby is cards and his favorite sport is golf. Residence: Hartington.

Charles Daniel Hitch

Charles D. Hitch, lawyer, was born at Peoria, Illinois, December 10, 1898, the son of Charles Wesley and Catherine (Sherry) Hitch. His father, who was a printer, was born at Evansville, Indiana, and died February 3, 1931 at Peoria, Illinois. His ancestry is English. His mother, whose ancestry was Irish, was born at Peoria, and died there June 16, 1909.

Mr. Hitch attended parochial school and later was graduated from the Manual Training School at Peoria. He later was a student at Bradley Polytechnic Institute at Peoria, and Creighton University at Omaha, Douglas County, Nebraska. During his high school days he was captain of the track team, and at Creighton was elected to Delta Theta Phi.

Now attorney for the Omaha National Company, he has been engaged in the law practice since 1923, and has lived in Nebraska for the past 16 years.

On July 19, 1921 he was married at Omaha, to Helen May Travis. Mrs. Hitch was born at Sidney, Iowa, April 28, 1903. They have two children: Charles Travis, born December 28, 1925; and Thomas Sherry born March 3, 1928.

Mr. Hitch was a private during the World War. He is a member of the American Legion; the Omaha Chamber of Commerce; the Parent-Teachers' Association; and the Knights of Columbus. He is affiliated with the Blessed Sacrament Church. His sport is golf, and his hobby is reading. He is a Democrat. Residence: Omaha.

Gilbert Monell Hitchcock

Gilbert M. Hitchcock, newspaper publisher, and public figure for the past thirty years, was born at Omaha, Nebraska, September 18, 1859. His father, Phineas W. Hitchcock, was prominent in the political life of Nebraska, and served as United States senator from 1871-77. His mother was Annie Monell.

After public school study both in the United States and in Germany, Mr. Hitchcock attended the law school of the University of Michigan, where he received his LL. B. in 1881. He was married to Jessie Crounse, of Fort Calhoun, Nebraska, who died in May, 1925. His second marriage was to Martha Harris, at Memphis, Tennessee, on June 1, 1927.

Upon his admission to the bar in 1881, Mr. Hitchcock returned to Omaha and entered the practice of law, continuing until 1885. At that time he established the *Omaha Evening World*, and in 1889 he purchased the *Morning Herald*, consolidating it with the *Evening World* as the *Omaha World Herald*.

From 1903-05 and 1907-11 he represented the second Nebraska district in the 58th, 60th and 61st congresses of the United State. During 1911-17 and 1917-23 he was United States senator, and was unsuccessful candidate for re-election in 1930. He is a Democrat. Residence: Omaha.

Nova Elizabeth Hite

Nova Elizabeth Hite, former educator in the schools of Nuckolls County, Nebraska, is active in civic affairs at Nelson today. She was born at Nelson, October 27, 1888, the daughter of Valorus Arbie Thomas and Helena Grace (Coup) Thomas. (*See Nebraskana*). Her father, who is a physician, was born at Cambridge Springs, Pennsylvania, September 24, 1856, of Scotch-Irish, Welsh and German ancestry. Her mother, who was born at Woodcock, Pennsylvania, July 22, 1864, and died at Nelson, September 25, 1929, was past organizer of the P. E. O., and served as Past Worthy Matron of the Order of Eastern Star. She was a member of the Nelson Woman's Club, and before her marriage was a teacher in the public schools of Crawford County, Pennsylvania, and after coming to Nebraska, taught in the public schools at Nelson.

Mrs. Hite was graduated from the Nelson High School in 1905, received the A. B. degree at Nebraska University in 1911, where she was a member of the Nebraska Union Literary Society. She also received an A. B. degree from Nebraska Wesleyan. She was valedictorian of the graduating class in high school. She has held the following positions in educational activity; high school teacher at Blue Hill, Nebraska, 1911-12; principal of the high school at Nelson, 1912-13; principal of the high school at Bladen, Nebraska, 1913-14; rural school teacher, 1915-16, at which time she was holding a claim in Grant County, which she still retains.

She is an active member of the P. E. O. and one of its local past presidents; Order of Eastern Star, of which she is past worthy matron; is affiliated with the Nelson Methodist Episcopal Church, and holds membership in the Nelson Woman's Club. Mrs. Hite's political affiliation is with the Democratic party.

On December 26, 1917, she was married to Henry Herbert Hite at Nelson. Mr. Hite, who is district agent of the Bankers Life Company, was born at Wilber, Nebraska, March 26, 1882. They have two children; Carmen Grace, born July 16, 1920; and Mariah Elizabeth, born October 2, 1921. Residence: Nelson.

Walter Van Fleet Hoagland

Walter Van Fleet Hoagland, prominent Lincoln County lawyer, was born in Bunker Hill, Illinios, November 30, 1870, and is the son of Joseph and Marie Louise (Waples) Hoagland. He is descended from Dirck Jansen Hoagland, who came from Holland to New Netherlands in 1657, and on August 8, 1662, married Annetje Hansen Bergen, the daughter of Saraha Repelji Bergen, the first white woman born in New York.

Mr. Hoagland came to Lincoln, Nebraska, from Bunker Hill, Illinois, in 1873, and moved to North Platte in 1884. He attended the Lincoln and North Platte public schools, and received the Bachelor of Arts degree from the University of Nebraska in 1895. His Bachelor of Laws degree was awarded by the same university in 1896. Thereafter until 1920 Mr. Hoagland was in partnership with his father in the practice of law with the firm name of Hoagland and Hoagland, which in 1920, when his father died, became Hoagland and Carr. During the year 1931 the firm name was changed to Hoagland, Carr, and Hoagland by admission of his son, Robert V. Hoagland which partnership still continues.

Among Mr. Hoagland's professional memberships are the American Bar Association, the Nebraska State Bar Association, and the Western Nebraska Bar Association of which he was president in 1922. He is a member of all branches of the Independent Order of Odd Fellows. In 1917 he was grand master of the Independent Order of Odd Fellows of Nebraska and since then to the present time has represented Nebraska in the Sovereign Grand Lodge of Odd Fellows, the supreme legislative organization of the fraternity. During 1921 he was department commander of Nebraska Patriarchs Militant of the Odd Fellows. He is a life member of the Elks, a member of the Sons of Veterans, and is affiliated with the Presbyterian Church. His chief recreation is golf.

A Republican, Mr. Hoagland served as state senator, 1911-1915, 1919-1922, and in 1898 upon the passage of the National Bankruptcy Act, Mr. Hoagland was appointed Referee in Bankruptcy for Nebraska by Judge William H. Munger at Omaha and is still serving.

On August 17, 1898, he was married to Hattie Scott Singleton at North Platte. She was born at Allegheny, Pennsylvania, February 10, 1872. She is a member of the Presbyterian Church, the P. E. O. Sisterhood, the Rebekahs, of which she was president of the state assembly of Nebraska in 1917. She is also president of the L. A. P. M. of Nebraska. They have two children living, Eva, born November 25, 1900; and Robert, born May 7, 1905. One daughter, Marie, born August 5, 1889, died June 30, 1916. The children are both graduates of the University of Nebraska. Eva is director of kindergarten work in the Tulsa, Oklahoma, school system. Robert graduated from the Harvard Law School in 1930. Residence: North Platte.

William Wyman Hoagland

In the early spring of 1861, when Nebraska was a territory crisscrossed by buffalo tracks, George T. Hoagland and his son, George Appleton Hoagland, founded the first lumber business in Omaha, the then capital city. George Appleton Hoagland was born at Boonville, Missouri, May 20, 1843. He and his father came to Nebraska, where they soon built up a reputation for honesty and integrity which continues to this day. Of historical note is the following excerpt from an article by William Wyman Hoagland, grandson of the original founder of the lumber business.

"Pioneers with prairie schooners came from seventy and eighty miles around to haul lumber for their first Nebraska homes . . . Nebraska with its present boundaries was admitted to statehood in 1867, and Lincoln was made the capital, but Omaha remained the chief commercial center. The construction of the Union Pacific Railroad across the continent boomed business. . . With the completion of the Union Pacific in 1869 homesteaders and settlers thronged to Nebraska. In 1871 we established the first wholesale lumber business with branch yards throughout the state. . . Our lumber has helped build a majority of Nebraska's public buildings, churches, schools and homes."

George Appleton Hoagland in these early days married Ianthe Clementina Wyman, a native of Madison, Wisconsin, born April 20, 1842. She died at Omaha, February 7, 1919. To their union was born on February 4, 1870, William Wyman Hoagland. Mrs. Hoagland was active in charitable and civic work, and founded the Emma Hoagland Flower Mission at Omaha. William W. Hoagland was educated in the public schools of Omaha, and at St. Paul's School, Concord, New Hampshire.

He was married to Florence Jessie Boothroyd at Loveland, Colorado, July 2, 1902. Mrs. Hoagland was born near Fort Collins, Colorado, June 2, 1873, and is of English descent. There are three children: Helen Edith, born May 11, 1903, who married Loring Elliott; Emma Ianthe,

Heyn—Omaha

WILLIAM WYMAN HOAGLAND

born December 11, 1904, who married John Reed; and William B., born August 22, 1906, who is unmarried.

At the close of his school days William W. Hoagland entered the lumber business of his father, who in addition operated an investment business and was the builder of the Hoagland Block at 16th and Howard Streets and a warehouse at 9th and Douglas Streets. Upon the death of his father he took over the business, which is still operated under the trade name of George A. Hoagland and Company.

Mr. Hoagland is a Congregationalist. He is a member of the Chamber of Commerce, the Omaha Real Estate Board, the Nebraska Historical Society and the Nebraskana Society. His clubs are the Happy Hollow Country Club and the Omaha Athletic Club. His favorite sport is baseball. (Deceased). (Photograph on Page 556).

John Hoaglund

In the Spring of 1868, John M. Hoaglund and Sara (Vastling) Hoaglund, his wife, with their two children emigrated from Sweden to America. John M. Hoaglund, was born at Noravi, Ostergotland, Sweden, April 1, 1831, while his wife was born at Tiderssum, Ostergotlund, April 12, 1824. John Hoaglund, the son, was born in Noravi, September 15, 1861.

Upon reaching Gottenborg, where he was to purchase tickets for the family's passage to America, John Hoaglund was informed that he had not sufficient passage money to get to Burlington, Iowa, his destination, but that he could reach Jamestown, New York, where there was a Swedish settlement. The sea voyage was sixteen days, and later the mother became so ill that she was unconscious when the emmigrant train reached Jamestown. The family had just two dollars and a half in American money, and the railroad agent, being desirous of getting them off his hands, halted a one-horse dray and had the driver go after the Swedish Methodist minister.

When the minister was informed that the family had no relatives in that part of the country, he resolved to do his best for them and securing a dray, put the mother and children and their home made trunk into it and drove them up to the edge of town where there was an old vacant house. The mother continued ill part of the summer, and the father went to work on the railroad for $2.00 a day. John Hoaglund, the subject of this sketch, then seven years old, was a water boy for the men, while his mother, when she recovered, cooked for twenty-eight of them. Due to the fact that the contractor ran away with the pay roll, Mr. Hoaglund received no wages for his last two month's work. When winter weather made railroad work impossible, the father secured a job of wood cutting, while the mother took in boarders.

The following summer all worked for the railroad again, and in the fall the father had $300.00 saved. Going eighteen miles out of Jamestown he found a cheap farm which he purchased, making a down payment of $300.00. There they farmed until the Spring of 1878, when they sold out and came to what is known as the Looking Glass, in Nebraska. There mail was received twice a week, and Columbus was the nearest railroad town, forty-five miles away.

John Hoaglund, Senior, purchased railroad land, a half section a year before the family moved to Nebraska, at $2.75 an acre. In spite of the low price, however, they were forced to sell the only cow they had to make the small payment on a quarter section and to allow the railroad company to take back one quarter. Mr. Hoaglund recalls selling eggs for four cents, butter for three cents, and doing without coffee entirely. Until he reached 20 Mr. Hoaglund wore split leather boots. At that time he purchased his first pair of overshoes.

At first, in Nebraska, the family lived in a sod house, and built a sod barn. Drinking water was carried from the home of a neighbor eighty rods away. There was bad luck with the horses, and one of the best was lost when helping a neighbor thresh. The first seven years in Nebraska $1400 was used for the purchase of horses.

The baby sister died on May 5, 1883, while they still lived in the sod house, but finally things improved and at the present time Mr. Hoaglund lives in one of the most comfortable homes in Newman Grove, and is the owner of 700 acres of Nebraska land. His father died at Newman Grove, on January 7, 1921, and his mother also died at Newman Grove, November 4, 1917.

On June 6, 1894, Mr. Hoaglund was married to Hilda Augusta Peterson at Looking Glass, Nebraska. She was a native of Kastlosa, Oland, Sweden, daughter of Jonas and Johanna Peterson. Her brother, Charley A., was a prominent farmer in Platte County until his death on December 18, 1924. To them were born five children, four of whom are living: Edith, born November 3, 1894, married Victor Larson; Alice, born February 25, 1896, married Dr. Lloyd C. Blockman; Ethel, born September 5, 1897; Ada, born March 21, 1900, who died April 29, 1913; and John C., born September 15, 1903. The two oldest girls received a high school education, while the other two living children were graduated from the University of Nebraska. Ethel is a successful commercial teacher. John served two years as assistant secretary of a Young Men's Christian Association, was four and a half years in the Newman Grove Postoffice, and is now deputy treasurer of Madison County.

During the World War period Mr. Hoaglund's quota for Liberty bonds was placed, perhaps unjustly, at $5,000.00, and although he had to borrow the money, he purchased that amount. Educating his children also depleted his working capital, and his taxes became larger than his income. However, through the sale of two farms one at $100 and the other at $93 per acre, he readjusted himself. He believes now that in a few more years he will have his land entirely free from indebtedness.

Recently Mr. Hoaglund was elected to life membership in the Nebraskana Society in recognition of his work for the advancement of his community and state. Residence: Newman Grove. (Photograph in Album).

Matt Charles Hobza

Born at Vroketnici, Moravia, February 9, 1873, Matt Charles Hobza is the son of Frank Hobza and Antonia (Rombosek) Hobza. His father was born at Vroketnici, July 20, 1833, and died at Wahoo, Nebraska, July 14, 1912. His mother was born at Vroketnici, May 20, 1839, and died at Wahoo, Saunders County, Nebraska, June 20, 1921.

Matt Hobza attended public schools in Czechecoslovakia. On October 24, 1899, at Cedar Hill, Nebraska, he was united in marriage with Anne Agnes Sloup. She was born at Prague, Nebraska, June 24, 1881. To this union were born six children: Sister M. Alexia, December 31, 1900; Frank, July 7, 1902; Mary, February 24, 1904; Christine, July 24, 1905; Anne, January 14, 1907; and Ambrose, November 24, 1909. Sister Alexia is a nun of the Notre Dame Order, Frank is a mechanic, Christine is a stenographer, Anne is a teacher, and Ambrose attends College.

Mr. Hobza is affiliated with the St. Wenceslous Catholic Church. He was a member of the Red Cross during the World War. He holds membership in the Knights of Columbus and the Catholic Workmen Lodge. Reading and the farm are his chief interests. Residence: Wahoo.

Clyde Hanford Hodges

Clyde Hanford Hodges, postmaster at Superior, was born at Weldon, Illinois, September 18, 1875. He is the son of William and Sarah Catherine (Bosserman) Hodges. His father was born at Sandusky, Ohio, September 6, 1836, of Scotch-Irish descent, and died at Los Angeles, August 26, 1917. He was a retired farmer at the time of his death. Sarah Catherine Bosserman was born in Licking County, Ohio, May 21, 1844, and died at Superior, in February 1910. She was of Welch extraction.

Educated first in the rural schools of Illinois, Clyde Hanford Hodges attended Illinois State Normal School, and was graduated from Brown's Business College in May, 1893. A teacher for three years, he was in the general mercantile business twenty years, and is now postmaster. He is a Republican, and served on the Superior City Council two years.

On May 22, 1901, Mr. Hodges was married to Clara Everts at Trenton, Iowa. Mrs. Hodges, who was born at Trenton, March 13, 1875, traces her ancestry to Reverend Daniel Everts, officer in the Revolution, and Colonel Aranthus Everts, of the War of 1812. There are three children: Christine, born October 2, 1905, who married Robert L. Jackson; Hanford, born March 31, 1907; and Lawrence, born August 26, 1909.

Mr. Hodges was secretary of the Young Men's Christian Association at Great Lakes Station for a period of six months during the World War. He is a member of the Methodist Church, the Chamber of Commerce, the Kiwanis Club, the Social Study Club and the Masons. He is worthy patron of the Eastern Star at present. His favorite sport is golf. Residence: Superior.

Carl Archibald Hoefer

Carl Archibald Hoefer, physician and surgeon, was born at Friend, Nebraska, September 29, 1895. He is the son of Carl August and Elizabeth (Mullally) Hoefer, the former a blacksmith. Carl August Hoefer was born in New York City, July 29, 1867.

Dr. Hoefer was graduated from Friend High School in 1913, received his A. B. in 1921 and his B. S. and M. D. in 1924 from the University of Nebraska. His fraternities are Sigma Alpha Epsilon and Phi Rho Sigma. He is married to Beulah Merriam Martin, who was born at Shenandoah, Iowa, January 13, 1895.

Admitted to practice at Omaha on July 18, 1924, Dr. Hoefer has since been in general practice. During 1916 he was in Mexican Border Service, and served in the United States Navy during the World War. He is a fellow of the American Medical Association, and a member of the American Legion. Dr. Hoefer is a Catholic. His favorite sport is hunting and his hobby is music. Residence: Wisner.

Ernest Howard Hoel

For nearly forty years Ernest Howard Hoel has been an outstanding figure in the commercial and civic life of Omaha. He was born in Omaha, November 11, 1873, son of Aaron Robison and Catherine Marie (Durham) Hoel, and has lived his entire life in the city.

Aaron Robison Hoel, born in Hamilton County, Ohio, April 11, 1832, came to Omaha by steamboat on the Missouri River on April 28, 1858, with his parents. From 1857 to 1859 he engaged in the hotel business in Omaha, and in 1867 he was elected first sheriff of Douglas County. In 1871 he was made first warden of the Nebraska Penitentiary at Lincoln. His father was Dutch and his mother was Irish. He died at Omaha on August 5, 1912. Catherine Marie Durham was born at Elizabethtown, New Jersey, January 30, 1831, and died at Omaha, December 17, 1899. She was of Scotch descent.

Ernest H. Hoel attended primary schools and Central High School in Omaha. On November 21, 1895, he was united in marriage to Mary Elizabeth McLean, at Omaha. Mrs. Hoel, who is of Scotch and English descent, was born at Bellevue, Nebraska, December 16, 1873. There are two daughters, Lois Marguerite, born September 19, 1896; and Lucille Mary, born February 10, 1899, who married Dewey Anthony Hoadley.

Since he entered business in early manhood, Mr. Hoel has progressed steadily. For seven years he was associated with the Morse-Coe Shoe Company, and for the past thirty years has been connected with the Carpenter Paper Company. He is now vice president and general manager of the foregoing organization, and director of the following: Sioux City Paper Company, Sioux City, Iowa; Messinger Paper Company of Chicago; Carter, Rice & Carpenter Paper Company of Denver; Carpenter Paper Company of Des Moines; the Carpenter Paper Company of Utah; Kansas City Paper House, Kansas City, Missouri; and Federal Envelope Manufacturing Company of Omaha.

Mr. Hoel is a Republican. He is a member and elder in the Dundee Presbyterian Church, and a member of the Young Men's Christian Association, of which he was board member 12 years and president two years. He is especially active in commercial and fraternal organizations, and is a member of the following: The Omaha Chamber of Commerce, which he joined in 1905. He served as director and member of the executive committee in 1923, was chairman of the trade extension committee 1923-24, chairman of the traffic bureau in 1928, chairman of the executive committee in 1929, and president in 1930-1931. He belongs to the Greater Omaha Association, the Nebraska Tuberculosis Association, the Red Cross, the National Paper Trade Association, the Rotary Club, the Omaha Auto Club, the Knights of Ak-Sar-Ben, the Izaak Walton League, the Nebraska State Historical Society, the Nebraskana Society, the Iowa State Traveling Men's Association, and the Travelers Protective Association, of which latter he served as president for the Nebraska division in 1907.

His fraternal organizations include Elks Lodge No. 39; Masonic Lodge No. 1, Nebraska Consistory of the Scottish Rite Masons, Tangier Temple and Shrine. His sports are fishing and golf. His clubs are the Omaha Athletic Club, the Omaha Club and Happy Hollow Country Club. Residence: Omaha.

Alfred Christoper Hoff

The Reverend Alfred Christopher Hoff was born at Council Bluffs, Iowa, March 15, 1897, son of Henry Ernest and Catherine (Schneller) Hoff. His father, who was born in Thuringia, Germany, March 13, 1864, was a clergyman whose death occurred at Omaha, November 25, 1930. His mother was born in Mendota, Illinois, September 25, 1872, of Swiss descent.

Mr. Hoff was graduated from Council Bluffs High School in 1913 and attended Wartburg Pro-Seminary at Waverly, Iowa, 1913-15. From 1915-18 he attended Wartburg Normal College and Wartburg Theological Seminary.

A resident of Nebraska since June 1918, he was ordained at Millard on July 7, and has been pastor of St. Paul's Lutheran Church since that time. During his pastorate he has constructed a new church and parsonage and his membership has quadrupled in ten years. He is a member of the Omaha Lutheran Ministerial Association and the Nebraskana Society. A lover of golf, his favorite indoor diversion is the reading of history.

On July 10, 1919, his marriage to Laura Anna Pankow was solemnized at Wyoming, Iowa. Mrs. Hoff was formerly a normal and music instructor and is of German and early American ancestry. They have two children, Leon, born April 19, 1920, and Gloria, born January 10, 1929. Residence: Millard.

Ewalt Albert Hoff

Born in Galesburg, Illinois, September 27, 1872, Ewalt Albert Hoff has been a resident of Nebraska since 1880. He is the son of Henry and Louisa (Kramer) Hoff, the former born in Europe, October 31, 1841. Henry Hoff came to America in 1870, and at the time of his death at Leigh, Nebraska, November 1, 1921, was a retired pioneer farmer. His wife, Louisa, was born in

Frankfort, Germany, August 21, 1843, and died at Omaha, June 12, 1910.

Ewalt A. Hoff attended the public schools of Galesburg, Illinois, and was graduated from the St. Joseph, Missouri High School. He received his A. B. from Midland College at Atchison, Kansas in 1893, and his M. D. from Central Medical College at St. Joseph in 1898. He is a member of the Winn Society.

On June 21, 1911, he was united in marriage to Elizabeth Williams at Alda, Nebraska, her birthplace. Mrs. Hoff was born May 11, 1886, and before her marriage was a nurse. She is descended from settlers in America prior to the Revolutionary War, and is eligible to the Daughters of the American Revolution. They have an adopted daughter, Mildred, born February 1, 1910, who is a teacher.

Dr. Hoff has been engaged in the practice of medicine since 1898, and is the author of the following medical articles: *The Dangers and the Duties of the Hour in Pregnancy* (Nebraska State Medical Journal, December 1926) and *Reporting Five Cases of Pernicious Anemia* (American Journal of Clinical Medicine). His hobby is research work.

During the World War he participated in the usual civilian activities. He is a member of the American, and Nebraska State Medical Societies, and is a fellow of the American College of Physicians. He is a 32nd degree Scottish Rite Mason and an Odd Fellow and is a member of the North Bend Chamber of Commerce and the Red Cross. His religious affiliation is with the Methodist Episcopal Church. Residence: North Bend.

Michael Hoffer

Michael Hoffer was born at Hagerstown, Maryland, February 24, 1840, the son of Michael and Mary Ann (Cordiman) Hoffer. Michael Hoffer, Sr., was born at Mercersburg, Pennsylvania, November 4, 1816, and died at Stromsburg, Nebraska, September 11, 1891. Mary Ann Hoffer was born at Mercersburg, December 29, 1816, and died at Stromsburg, Nebraska, May 15, 1877.

On March 23, 1865, he was married to Lucinda Emily Fox, at Polo, Illinois. She was born in Frederick County, Maryland, May 15, 1844, and died at Osceola, in 1911. They had ten children: Mary Kate, born December 7, 1866, who is married to Leonidas Hennings; Clara V., born October 9, 1868, who died July 4, 1875; Oliver M., born March 6, 1870, who died September 17, of the same year; Albertus H., born January 18, 1872, who died on March 19, 1880; Charles E., born December 17, 1873, who is married to Maude Blake; Cora May born June 11, 1876, who is married to L. W. Obrist; Harvey B., born November 9, 1878, who died January 16, 1901; Effa J., born June 18, 1881, who died December 24, 1883; Alfred Clyde, born April 15, 1884, who is married to Stella Dunagan; and Olive Horah, born July 2, 1887, who is married to Erle E. Howley.

Mr. Hoffer has been a resident of Nebraska sixty years. He helped the early pioneers get settled in Nebraska by building houses, digging wells, and making brooms. He also made a honing block, where his neighbors could come and pound their grain.

He entered the Civil War as a Union soldier in October 1861. He was first a private, was promoted to corporal, and later was duty sergeant. He was captured with 11,000 of the Union men under McClellan at Harpers Ferry, and was paroled to Camp Annapolis at Maryland. His patriotic organizations are the Red Cross and the Grand Army of the Republic.

His religious affiliation is with the Church of God, in Maryland and Nebraska. He is ninety one years of age, and while he is unable to read on account of poor eye sight, he is still active in mind and body, and spends a great deal of time in beautifying his home. Residence. Osceola.

William Hoffman

Born at Milwaukee, Wisconsin, September 9, 1858, William Hoffman is the son of Augustus and Louisa (Hentz) Hoffman. His father, was a coal miner and farmer, was born at Darmstadt, Germany, March 7, 1831, and died at Berlin, Pennsylvania, in June, 1897; he came to this country in 1857 and settled in Milwaukee, Wisconsin and purchased land which is now a part of the city of Milwaukee. His mother was born at Darmstadt, October 5, 1853, and died at Berlin, July 30, 1920.

Mr. Hoffman moved to eastern Iowa at the age of 18 practically penniless, and after his marriage came to Nebraska where he acquired a quarter section of land south of Meadow Grove; he is now retired in his comfortable town home at Meadow Grove, Nebraska, which is partly furnished with several beautiful pieces of black walnut furniture made by him. He is a member of the Red Cross, attends the Methodist Church, and holds membership in the Nebraskana Society.

His marriage to Alice Ann Eckman occurred at Elwood, Iowa, November 21, 1883. Mrs. Hoffman was born near Elwood, May 8, 1862. The following children were born to their marriage: Myron Russell, February 14, 1885, who married Emma Louise Feldman; Leander William, July 11, 1886, who married Emma Shotwell; Louva, April 16, 1896; and Denton Otho, December 12, 1901. Myron is a farmer at Sacred Heart, Minnesota, Leander a mechanic at Sioux Falls, South Dakota, Louva a physician's assistant, associated with Dr. H. L. Kindred at Meadow Grove, Nebraska, and is an accomplished seamstress, and Denton a bookkeeper. Residence: Meadow Grove.

William Robert Hoffman

A resident of Nebraska for the past 51 years, William Robert Hoffman was born in Hunterdon County, New Jersey, April 4, 1856, the son of William and Mary Ann (Henderson) Hoffman. His father, who was a millwright, was born in Hunterdon County, August 30, 1807, and died at Ludlow, New Jersey, March 2, 1892; he spent the early part of his life making wooden machinery for grist mills; his ancestors were Holland Dutch soldiers in the Revolution. His mother, whose ancestry was Scotch, was born in Hunterdon County, New Jersey, February 8, 1816, and died at Ludlow, July 4, 1887.

Mr. Hoffman, who has been a furniture dealer at Norfolk, Nebraska, for many years, is prominent in civic and social affairs there. He is a director of the Humane Society, serving as its president at this time, is a member of the Lions Club, and is affiliated with the Methodist Episcopal Church of Norfolk. His fraternal organizations include Eastern Star; Modern Woodmen of America; and Blue Lodge, Royal Arch, and Knights Templar bodies of the Masons. His hobby is the study of the American Indians of the southwest.

His marriage to Katharine Ege Henderson occurred at Asbury, New Jersey, November 12, 1881. Mrs. Hoffman was born at Landsdown, New Jersey, June 14, 1860. They have two children: Lawrence, born August 24, 1888, who served in the World War as first lieutenant and was a soldier during the Mexican trouble in 1912; and Kathleen, January 22, 1903. Residence: Norfolk.

Leo A. Hoffmann

On December 5, 1880, Leo A. Hoffmann was born at Dubuque, Iowa, the son of Matthew Martin and Mary (Voelker) Hoffmann. His father, a mortician, served as county coroner at Dubuque for 14 years, and until his death was extremely active in educational affairs, serving as regent and member of the board of education of Columbia College at Dubuque, and president of the board of education for ten years. His mother, who was known throughout her community as a diligent church worker, was born at Dubuque, and died there in 1916.

Mr. Hoffmann was graduated from St. Mary's parochial school and later from Columbia College, at Dubuque. Active in music and debating during his college days, has served as president of the college alumni association, since graduation.

A resident of Nebraska for over 27 years he is now president of Hoffmann Mortuary at Omaha. He was at one time appointed county commissioner of Douglas County.

His marriage to Veronica Winifred Dougherty was solemnized at Omaha, May 6, 1908. Mrs. Hoffmann was born at Omaha, the daughter of pioneer Nebraskans, Charles and Mary Dougherty. They have five children: Mary Jeannette; Bernadette; Veronica; Leo A., Jr.; and Virginia.

During the World War Mr. Hoffmann was active in loan drives and war relief work. He is a member of the Red Cross; Chamber of Commerce; Advertising Selling League; and the Commercial Club; the Elks; Moose; Knights of Columbus; Catholic Order of Foresters; Independent Order of Foresters; Ancient Order of United Workmen; and Woodmen of the world.

He holds membership in the Nebraska Funeral Directors Association, and is a member of the National Selected Morticians. He is affiliated with St. Cecilia Cathedral at Omaha, and has served as Grand Knight in the Knights of Columbus. He is a member of the Athletic Club and Field Club. Residence: Omaha.

George Hoffmeister

George Hoffmeister, physician and surgeon, was born at Imperial, Nebraska, January 13, 1894, son of Fred and Mary (Krotz) Hoffmeister.

The father was born in Holzen, Germany, November 6, 1855, and died at Imperial, Nebraska, February 23, 1931. He was an early pioneer physician and surgeon in Nebraska, and a member of the Nebraska Legislature four terms, serving in 1913, 1915, 1917 and 1919. His wife, Mary, was born in Bohemia, and died in Imperial in September, 1926.

Dr. George Hoffmeister attended public school at Imperial and Aurora, Nebraska until 1910; and was graduated from high school there at that time. He received his Bachelor of Science degree from the University of Nebraska in 1914 and his medical degree from the same institution in 1916. While there he was a member of Alpha Omega Alpha, Kappa Sigma, and Nu Sigma Nu.

Since his admission in 1916, Dr. Hoffmeister has been in active practice. He is a member of the Nebraska State and American Medical Associations; the Lion's Club, the Masons, and the American Legion. During the late war he was a captain in the Medical Corps. He is a Democrat. He served in the 86th division, being stationed at Camp Grant, Rockford, Illinois. He served from September, 1918, until February, 1919, in France.

On July 18, 1923, he was married to Genevieve Lydia Todd, daughter of Louie C. and Jennie (Marx) Todd, at Imperial. Mrs. Hoffmeister was born at Nehawka, Nebraska, August 16, 1903. They have three children, George, born June 25, 1924; Charles, born November 30, 1926; and Rex, born July 30, 1928. Residence: Imperial.

Arthur Hofgaard

Arthur Hofgaard was born at Chicago, Illinois, March 17, 1880, the son of Andrew and Helene (Hadeler) Hofgaard. His father, who was a carpenter and farmer, was born at Reingerike, Norway, November 30, 1843, and died at Sweetwater, Nebraska, September 4, 1922. His mother, who was born at Oslo, Norway, May 17, 1845, is still living.

Rev. Hofgaard attended Trinity Seminary at Blair,

Nebraska, where he was graduated May 29, 1908. He served as pastor of the Danish Lutheran Church at West Branch, Iowa, 1908-11, was pastor of Our Saviors Lutheran Church at Owatonna, Minnesota, 1911-18, and was pastor of Nazareth Lutheran Church at Kenmare, North Dakota, 1918-26. Since 1926 he has been pastor of Bethany Lutheran Church at Minden, Nebraska, where he is also superintendent of the Old People's Home.

His marriage to Anna E. Larsen was solemnized at Hampton, Nebraska, June 3, 1908. Mrs. Hofgaard, who was a seamstress prior to her marriage, was born in Illinois, March 20, 1878. They have three children: Elna, born April 4, 1909; Alvin Herbert, born December 2, 1911; and Ethan Herluf, born March 9, 1918.

Rev. Hofgaard is affiliated with the Republican Party. He holds membership in the United Danish Evangelical Lutheran Ministerial Association. Residence: Minden.

Denis Patrick Hogan

Denis Patrick Hogan, one of Nebraska's foremost bankers, was born in Dubuque County, Iowa, August 29, 1869. His father, Michael Hogan, was born in County Limerick, Ireland, December 24, 1830 and was brought to America when an infant. He was a farmer, and died at Corning, Iowa, July 24, 1913. His wife, Mary Collins, was born in County Cork, Ireland, December 8, 1842, and died at Corning, June 21, 1916.

Denis Hogan attended the country schools of Adams County, Iowa, and was graduated from Corning High School in 1888, and from St. Benedict's College at Atchison, Kansas, in 1889. He was the winner of numerous prizes including one in commercial law and a premium in political economy.

He came to Nebraska in 1889 and became a clerk in the Bank of Wallace, Nebraska, continuing until 1894. He organized the Farmers Savings Bank of Massena, Iowa in 1897 and was cashier of that bank until 1907, when he was made president and which position he still holds. In 1917 he became president of the Federal Land Bank of Omaha, and still continues. He also operates a 640 acre farm in Cass County, Iowa, and his hobby is farm welfare. He keeps 200 head of registered Hereford cattle on his farm, and won second prize in the Hereford class of the Boys' Baby Contest at the Iowa State Fair in 1927. He was a member of the American Commission for the Study of Agricultural Co-operation in Europe in 1913, and spent four months abroad. The report of the American Commission was the basis of the Federal Farm Loan Act.

A Republican, he was a member of the house of the Iowa General Assembly from 1910-11. He has written numerous articles and pamphlets regarding the federal farm loan system during a period of thirteen years.

On October 9, 1901 he was married to Dolly Mary Snelson at Massena, Iowa. Mrs. Hogan, who is also a banker, was born at Massena, October 3, 1876. She was graduated from the Iowa State College at Ames, in 1898. She is of Scotch, German and English descent.

Mr. Hogan is a Catholic, and attends St. Margaret Mary Church. He is a member of the Knights of Columbus, and a director of St. James Orphanage. He has been a member of the Rotary Club since 1915, and is a member of the Chamber of Commerce. His clubs are the Happy Hollow Country, and the Omaha Athletic Clubs, and his favorite sport is golf. Residence: Omaha.

James Henry Hogan

James Henry Hogan was born at Chicago, Illinois, August 11, 1872, the son of John Bradner and Catherine (Baldwin) Hogan. His father, who was born at Nanaugh, Tipperary, Ireland, 1835, came to this country in 1863, and engaged in farming; he died at South Sioux City, Nebraska, October 10, 1887. His mother, who came to America in 1865, was born at Nanaugh, November 4, 1845.

Mr. Hogan was graduated from the South Sioux City High School in 1892, and was active in baseball there. For 14 years he was a plumber at South Sioux City, was chief of police there for one year, and for the past 14 years has been water commissioner. He holds membership in the Izaak Walton League, the Rod and Reel Club, Red Cross, and Saint Michael's Catholic Church. His favorite recreations are hunting and reading.

On January 11, 1909, he was united in marriage with Catherine Gertrude Carney at Wichita, Kansas. Mrs. Hogan was born at Jackson, Dakota County, Nebraska, December 30, 1884; they have one son, Robert, born July 1, 1920. Mr. Hogan is a member of the Nebraskana Society, and is independent, politically. Residence: South Sioux City.

Henry Hoheisel

The Reverend Henry Hoheisel was born at Klein-Schnellendorf, Silesia, Germany, June 30, 1860, and came to America with his father, Henry Hoheisel, Senior, at an early age. His father died at Leavenworth, Kansas, April 18, 1900, and was a farmer by occupation. His mother was Catherine (Blasius) Hoheisel.

Father Hoheisel was graduated from parochial school in June, 1874, at Leavenworth, Kansas, and from St. Benedict's College at Atchison, Kansas in 1880. In 1885 he was graduated from St. Francis Seminary at Milwaukee. He was ordained to the priesthood on June 29, 1885.

He has served as assistant pastor at West Point, and has also served at Chadron. He has held pastorates at Schuyler, and Oleyen, and from the last mentioned went to his present pastorate at Papillion, where he has been since 1897. He was the first pastor there, with Elkhorn as a mission. A rectory was built and in two years an addition made to the church. In 1917 the Elkhorn Mission was separated from Papillion and formed into a parish. On the 15th of July, 1912, a new location for the future buildings of the church, school and rectory was purchased, and was paid for with money derived from a legacy left to St. Columbkilles Church by Robert McCormick. In 1916 the Sacred Heart Academy, a boarding and day school, was erected. In 1923 a fine brick church was built and the following year the rectory.

Father Hoheisel is well known and highly regarded throughout Sarpy County. Residence: Papillion. (Photograph on Page 562).

Karl Siegfried J. Hohlen

One of Nebraska's leading surgeons, Karl S. J. Hohlen has lived in the state for 23 years and has been prominent in various civic and professional organizations for many years. He was born at Wilhelmshaven, Germany, April 24, 1886, the son of John Henry and Gesina (Bunting) Hohlen. His father, who is a cabinet maker, was born in Germany, December 2, 1858. His mother was born in Germany, March 23, 1856.

Dr. Hohlen attended school at Peoria, and Minonk, Illinois. He was graduated from the Minonk High School and in 1908 received his M. D. degree from Loyola University. He was later a student at Northwestern University and the University of Vienna, and was a charter member of the Phi Sigma chapter of Phi Chi at Loyola University, Chicago.

He is past president of the Nebraska State Medical Association; attending surgeon at Bryan Memorial Hospital; and surgeon for the Missouri Pacific Railroad Company. He was formerly president of the Lancaster County Medical Society, and in 1929 was president of the Nebraska section of the American College of Surgeons. He is the author of several surgical articles published in medical journals at various times.

He was united in marriage with Mina Eloise Kauf at Hastings, Nebraska, July 15, 1910. They have one son, Karl, born October 20, 1919.

Dr. Hohlen served as a member of the draft board at Lincoln during the World War. He is a member of the Nebraska State Medical Society; the Lancaster County Medical Society; American College of Surgeons; and the American Medical Association. He is a member of the Lincoln University Club and the Nebraskana Society, and is a Blue Lodge and Scottish Rite Mason and Shriner. Residence: Lincoln.

Carl Peter Hojbjerg

The Reverend Carl Peter Hojbjerg, clergyman and educator, was born in Denmark, Europe, June 12, 1873, and has been a resident of Nebraska two different times. He lived here from 1907 until 1912, and has been a resident since 1931.

His father, Ivor Hansen Hojbjerg, was a teacher, and his mother was Hausin Elizabeth Siersted. Mr. Hojbjerg attended the University of Copenhagen from which he was graduated in 1898. At the present time he is president of the Nysted Peoples College at Dannebrog, Nebraska, and Danish Lutheran minister, a member of the Danish Evanglican Church of America.

He is married to Hilda Giede Boving, who was born in Denmark, April 11, 1875. Her father was of Italian and German ancestry, his pedigree being traced to the seventeenth century. They have three children, Hans, born October 26, 1904; Otto Giede, born January 22, 1909; and Eva Giede, born July 30, 1910. Hans received his Bachelor of Arts degree at the Drake University of Des Moines and his Master of Arts degree from Columbia University. Otto received his Bachelor of Arts degree from Drake and is a member of Phi Beta Kappa. Eva is an art student.

Mr. Hojbjerg is the author of numerous articles, religious and otherwise, published in the Danish language. Residence: Nysted.

Lumir John Hokuf

Born at Wilber, Nebraska, August 22, 1888, Lumir John Hokuf is the son of Michael and Alice (Hinze) Hokuf. His father, born in Prague, Czechoslovakia, was a composer and a teacher of all brass and stringed instruments. He was a leader of bands and orchestras at Golden Gate Park prior to his death at Watsonville, California, in April, 1921. His wife, also born in Prague, died at Wilber, January 21, 1921. She operated a mercantile store, a millinery and later a bakery.

Mr. Hokuf attended the public school at Wilber, and after the war was head baker for E. W. LaShelle at Holdrege. He enlisted at Lincoln, for the World War, was corporal in Bakers Company 343, Quarter Masters Corps, saw active service in France, was sent to the United States as a casual in February, 1919, to hospital at Plattsburg Barracks, N. Y.

Prior to the War Mr. Hokuf was in business for himself in Wilber, and since 1921 has been in the bakery business at Bertrand. He is a Republican, a Methodist, a member of the American Legion, the Commercial Club, the Royal Highlanders, a Mason and Shriner. His favorite sports are baseball and football. His hobby is music.

On September 2, 1908, he was married to Bertha Belie Clements at Wilber. Mrs. Hokuf was born at Victor, Iowa, of Scotch-Irish descent. Two children were born to them, Thomas R. on March 26, 1910, who died July 30, 1910; and Grace L., born February 10, 1913. Grace was graduated from Bertrand High School in 1930, and was enrolled in the Arts and Science College at the University of Nebraska, in 1931. Residence: Bertrand.

Rudolph A. Hokuf

Rudolph A. Hokuf, who is now retired, was born at Wilber, Nebraska, March 14, 1881, son of Michael B. and Alice (Hinze) Hokuf. His father, who was a native of Czechoslovakia, was a farmer and musical in

HENRY HOHEISEL

structor. He died at San Francisco, California. His mother was a native of Germany.

Mr. Hokuf attended the elementary schools of Wilber, and at the age of 16 started in the bakery business. At the age of twenty-five he established his own business, and carried it on successfully until his retirement in January, 1927.

On September 26, 1906 he was married to Mary Sasek at Wilber. Mrs. Hokuf was born at Wilber, May 29, 1886. They have one daughter, Helen Marie, born November 12, 1911, who attends Doane College.

Mr. Hokuf is a Republican and in April, 1931 was elected city councilman of Crete for a term of two years. He is a Lutheran and former member of the Rotary Club. A Mason, he is a member of Sesostris Temple of the Shrine and the York Rite body. He is a Knight of Pythias, and a member of the Sokol and The Nebraskana Society. He is fond of outdoor sports. Residence: Crete.

Charles H. Holcomb

Born in Gibson County, Indiana, January 21, 1856, Charles H. Holcomb is the son of John C. and Julia A. (Skelton) Holcomb. His father, who served as county auditor of Gibson County, was born there in 1821, and died there, in 1878. His mother was born in Gibson County in 1832 and died in 1856.

Judge Holcomb taught school in Indiana for six years, and for the past 49 years has been prominent in the practice of law at Broken Bow, Nebraska. A Democrat, he served as county judge of Custer County for over 13 years, and has taken part in all civic projects in his community. He holds membership in the Public Service Club, is affiliated with the Baptist Church, and holds membership in the Independent Order of Odd Fellows. His chief recreations are golfing and reading.

He was united in marriage with Malinda Alice Finch at Gibson, Indiana, March 16, 1879; she was born at Gibson, April 9, 1863. Their children are Arthur W., born August 27, 1880, who married Florence E. Armstrong; Vessa C., born March 27, 1883, who married Clarence O'Bannion; Mabel, born October 16, 1885, who married William T. Darnell; Edna H., born June 27, 1889, who married Sidney S. Parkison; and Roy C., born June 13, 1895, who married Hazel D. Chiles. Residence: Broken Bow.

Tom Lawrence Holding

Tom Lawrence Holding, lumberman and banker, was born at Cambria, Wyoming, December 28, 1892, son of Thomas and Mary Jane (Wareing) Holding. The father was born at Glason, England, March 21, 1865, and came to America at the age of 20. He is a farmer. His wife was born in Blackburn, England, September 12, 1867, and came to America in 1868.

Mr. Holding attended public schools, Chadron Academy until 1910, and the College of Agriculture at Lincoln until 1914.

At the present time he is vice-president of the Farmers and Drovers State Bank and the owner of the Whitney Land & Lumber Company and the Cash Drug Store.

On February 14, 1917, he was married to Vera Adeline Cartwright at Whitney. Mrs. Holding was born at Whitney, September 21, 1894, and is a member of the Daughters of the American Revolution (four bars). They have three children, Wayne, born March 15, 1918; Phyllis, born September 1, 1920; and Caroline, born January 15, 1926.

Since 1914, Mr. Holding has been a member of the Reserve Officers Association. He is a member of the Nebraska National Guard, the Whitney Methodist Episcopal Church, the Northwest Nebraska Chamber of Commerce, the Masons and the Nebraskana Society. He enjoys hiking, tennis, and football, while his hobby is traveling. Residence: Whitney.

Carl Luther Holland

Carl Luther Holland, county clerk, of Burt County, was born at Chapman, Nebraska, August 14, 1894, son of John Swan and Mathilda Wilhelmina (Carlson) Holland. His father, who is a lawyer, was born in Sweden, came to the United States about 1880. His mother, also a native of Sweden, died at Sioux City, Iowa, December 21, 1921.

Upon his graduation from the public schools of Missouri Valley, Iowa, in April, 1907, Carl L. Holland entered Oakland, Nebraska, High School, from which he was graduated in May, 1912. A Republican, he was deputy district court clerk 1914-15, deputy county treasurer 1920-23, and since 1923 has been county clerk. During 1916-17 he was bookkeeper for the First National Bank at Tekamah.

He was married to Gretchen Thompson at Missouri Valley, July 27, 1924. Mrs. Holland was born at Tekamah, November 22, 1899. They have one son, Robert C., born April 7, 1925. Mr. Holland served fourteen months in the United States and ten months with the American Expeditionary Forces, in the World War as a first lieutenant in the M. A. R. C. He is a member of the American Legion, the Commercial Club and the Masons, and the Association of County Clerks and Registers of Deeds of Nebraska. He enjoys golf and baseball, while his hobbies are reading and mechanics. Residence: Tecumseh.

Dorothy Mandell Holland

Dorothy M. Holland was born at Cozad, Nebraska, October 9, 1903, the daughter of Milton Hamilton Brown and Mary Anna (Beunison) Hamilton. Her father, who was born in Illinois, July 2, 1864, is a banker. Her mother was born in Wisconsin, April 13, 1864.

Mrs. Holland attended the public and high schools at Cozad; the high school at Janesville, Wisconsin; the Anna Head School for Girls, at Berkeley, California; and later was graduated from the University of Nebraska with the degree, A. B. She was secretary and treasurer of the Pan Hellenic Council at the university; was president of the local chapter of Delta Gamma; and was chairman of the scholarship committee. She has lived in Nebraska for 25 years.

On October 7, 1926, she was united in marriage with Lyle Clifton Holland at Gothenburg, Nebraska. Mr. Holland, who was born at Seward, Nebraska, August 9, 1902, is a lawyer at Lincoln. Their daughter, Mary Sue, was born January 28, 1929.

Mrs. Holland is a member of the Nebraska Art Association and the Nebraskana Society. She holds membership in the Daughters of the American Revolution, and her social clubs are the University Club and the Lincoln Country Club. She is a member of the Methodist Episcopal Church. Her hobby is reading. Residence: Lincoln.

Lyle Clifton Holland

Lyle C. Holland was born at Seward, Nebraska, August 9, 1902, son of Clifton Earl and Sarah Lavina (Chenoweth) Holland. His father, born at Farmington, Illinois, May 19, 1859, was a lawyer and judge, of Scotch descent, who died at Lincoln on May 13, 1913 His wife, Sarah, was born at Williamsport, Indiana, April 28, 1861. She is of English descent and is still living.

Upon his graduation from Lincoln High School in 1920, Mr. Holland attended the University of Nebraska, and was graduated with the degree of LL. B. in 1925. During 1923 and 1924 he was manager of the baseball team and received his letter in that sport. He is a member of Delta Tau Delta, Phi Delta Phi and Theta Nu Epsilon.

Mr. Holland married Dorothy Mandell Brown at Gothenburg, Nebraska, October 7, 1926. Mrs. Holland was born at Cozad, Nebraska, October 9, 1903. They have one daughter, Mary Sue, born January 28, 1929. Since his admission to the bar in 1925, Mr. Holland has been actively engaged in the practice of law; and is a member of the firm of Chambers and Holland.

He is a Mason, a member of the Presbyterian Church, the Nebraska State and Lancaster County Bar Associations and the Chamber of Commerce. His clubs are the University and Lincoln Country Clubs, and his favorite recreations are golf and reading. Residence: Lincoln.

Frank E. Hollingsworth

As an executive and business man, Frank E. Hollingsworth has been prominent at Kearney, Nebraska, since 1915. He was born at St. Charles, Iowa, October 12, 1888, the son of Lewis N. and Jane (Downs) Hollingsworth. His father, who is a retired farmer, was born at St. Charles, October 8, 1855. His mother was born at St. Charles, June 23, 1853. His father and mother are residing in Kearney.

Mr. Hollingsworth received his high school education at Kearney, and later attended the Kearney State Teachers College of Kearney and was graduated in the class of 1911. He was a member of the high school debating squad there and acted as president of his commercial class in college 1910-11. He served as secretary and treasurer of the Kearney Baseball Club and engaged in clerical work until 1915 when he became secretary-treasurer of the Kearney Land & Mortgage Company, holding the latter position until 1918.

For two years, 1918-20, he was real estate manager of the City National Bank of Kearney, and from 1920 to 1928 acted as vice president and manager of the Guaranty Trust Company of which he is now president. He has served as city treasurer and treasurer of the school board for the past nine years, is chairman of the Buffalo County American Red Cross, and holds membership in the Kearney Chamber of Commerce. Mr. Hollingsworth is a member of the Parent Teachers Association, is affiliated with the First Methodist Episcopal Church as treasurer and board member, and for the past seven years has been treasurer of the Kiwanis Club. His outside interests include music and reading.

On September 8, 1915, he married Serena Myrtle O'Brien at Kearney. Mrs. Hollingsworth is a graduate of the Wesleyan University graduating in 1911, is president of the Parent Teachers Association, 4th district. They have two children: Gerald, born September 27, 1917; and Marjorie, born June 19, 1920. Residence: Kearney.

Grace Pearl Holloway

Grace Pearl Holloway, writer and executive, was born at Tobias, Nebraska, April 3, 1888, daughter of Louis Fremont and Carrie Elizabeth (Lewis) Holloway. Her father, who was born at Lawrence, Kansas, December 22, 1862, is a retail hardware dealer, and in his early days was a school teacher. Her mother, was born at Frankfort, New York, December 23, 1862. She was a teacher in her girlhood.

Educated in the elementary schools of DeWitt, Nebraska, Miss Holloway was graduated from Fremont High School in 1906, and received her B. A. from Doane College in 1911. She has studied advertising with the International Correspondence Schools; short story writing (2 courses) and magazine journalism with the Home Correspondence School. In earlier life she taught school, in the rural schools of Dodge County in 1907, and at Glen Cove, Long Island, 1911-12; at Howells, Nebraska, 1912-13, and for a short time thereafter was a teacher in country schools in Arkansas. In 1916 she worked for the Korsmeyer Company in Lincoln, as a stenographer, in 1917 for C. E. Abbott at Fremont, and in 1918 for the Pathfinder Hotel at Fremont. At the present time she is

stenographer, director and advertising manager of the L. F. Holloway Hardware Company at Fremont.

During the past ten years she has sold thirty stories, eighty-four articles, sixty-six short plays, thirty-seven pageants; sixty dialogues and exercises, and thirty-two poems in addition to those sold for recitations in special day programs and a contract for one page of verse each month for one year in the Hardware World; thirty-eight greeting card verses and three hundred and thirty-three recitations varying from four line jingles to rather long monologs. She is the winner of nineteen prizes in various contests, all of which involved writing.

She writes with more or less regularity for the *Hardware Retailer* of Indianapolis, the *Youth's Comrade* of Kansas City, the *Sunday School World* of Philadelphia, etc. The Paramount Line of program material published by the Meyer and Brother Company of Chicago, contains a large amount of her numbers. Their Christmas book for 1931 is exclusively hers. She has also sold plays or pageants to the Lorenz Publishing Company of Dayton, Ohio, George F. Rosche of Chicago, the Fillmore Music House of Cincinnati, the Eldridge Entertainment House of Franklin, Ohio, and others. She also appears in the *Evangelical Crusader,* published in Cleveland.

Miss Holloway is a member of the Congregational Church, and Christian Endeavor, of which she has been district vice-president, departmental superintendent in district, and state junior superintendent three terms in Nebraska and two in Arkansas. She is a member of the Inner Circle of the Order of Bookfellows, Miss Holloway is at the present time engaged in preparing a pageant for the South Dakota Baptist Convention for use at its Golden Jubilee to be held at Madison, in October, 1931.

She is fond of reading, writing and kodaking, and enjoys walking and driving. She belongs to the Nebraska Writers Guild, and the National Travel Club, and is a member of Epsilon Sigma Alpha and the Nebraskana Society. Residence: Fremont. (Photograph in Album).

Louis Fremont Holloway

Born at Lawrence, Kansas, December 22, 1862, Louis Fremont Holloway has been a resident of Nebraska forty-seven years. He is the son of James Clark and Mary Elizabeth (Roy) Holloway, the former born at Marion, Ohio, January 26, 1839. James Clark Holloway served in the Union Army in the Civil War with the rank of Sergeant, Company E., Kansas Volunteer Cavalry, three years. He was descended from English immigrants who probably came with the Jamestown colonists. His death occurred at Neodosha, Kansas, January 9, 1911. Mary Elizabeth Roy was born in Illinois in 1846, and died at Atchison, Kansas, February 1895.

Louis Holloway is self-educated. He taught school in Tobias and near Dorchester, and later worked in a lumber yard in Tobias and Strang. After serving a clerkship in a hardware store in Tobias he went into business for himself and operated stores at Ohiowa, DeWitt and Fremont. Since its organization he has been a director of the Nebraska Hardware Mutual Insurance Company, and has also served as its president. He is president of the L. F. Holloway Hardware Company at the present time.

His marriage to Carrie Elizabeth Lewis was solemnized at Tobias on September 8, 1886. Mrs. Holloway was born at Frankfort Hill, New York, December 23, 1862, of English and Welsh descent. They have had two daughters, Pearl, born April 3, 1888, has been a teacher and is now connected with her father in business. She is a member of the Nebraska Writers' Guild. Ruth, who was born February 26, 1893, married John Henry Bader. She died December 17, 1918.

During the World War Mr. Holloway was a member of the Home Guards. He is a former member of the Kiwanis Club, and a present member of the Modern Woodmen of America, the Odd Fellows and the Ancient

Order of United Workmen. He is affiliated with the First Congregational Church of Fremont, a member of the Young Men's Christian Association, and the Sons of Veterans. Formerly devoted to boy's work in Sunday School, he confines his energy to his business. Residence: Fremont.

George William Holmes

George William Holmes, banker, was born at Lincoln, Nebraska, February 29, 1880, son of William Winterston and Emma Frances (Hoagland) Holmes. The father was a banker and real estate operator.

Mr. Holmes attended the University of Nebraska and Notre Dame University and is a member of Beta Theta Pi. On March 1, 1905, he was married to Sarah Burnham at Lincoln. They have one daughter, Joan Eliza.

Mr. Holmes has resided in Lincoln all of his life. He is president of the First Trust Company of Lincoln He is a member of the Catholic Church. Residence: and the First National Bank of Lincoln. He is a member of the Catholic Church. Residence: Lincoln.

August C. Holmquist

August C. Holmquist, prominent grain executive of Nebraska, was born on a farm in Cuming County, February 19, 1875, the son of Anna Katherine (Johnson) and Olof Holmquist. His father, who was president of the Holmquist Company for many years, was born in Sweden, and died at Oakland, May, 1915. His mother was born in Sweden and died at Omaha, in 1917.

Mr. Holmquist attended the public schools at Oakland. He has lived in the state all his life and has been active in educational and civic affairs at Oakland. He is secretary and manager of the Holmquist Grain Company, and is vice president of the Coleson-Holmquist Company. He served as a member of the city council for 7 years; was mayor three terms; and has been a member of the school board for the past 27 years. He is a member of the Chamber of Commerce and the Nebraskana Society. He is past master and past high priest of the Royal Arch Masons, and holds membership in the Modern Woodmen of America. His hobbies are baseball, basketball, and football.

He was united in marriage with Ora Minier at Oakland, October 29, 1899. Mrs. Holmquist was born at Oakland, April 27, 1880. They have five children: Harold, born September 8, 1900; Menoyn, born January 28, 1902; August C., born July 28, 1905; Claude, born October 4, 1907; and Mary Helen, born April 8, 1918. Residence: Oakland.

Carl Arthur Holmquist

Carl Arthur Holmquist, postmaster at Wausa, Nebraska, has been a resident of Nebraska for the past 37 years. He was born at Mendota, Illinois, July 3, 1875, the son of Otto Holmquist who was born in Sweden, March 18, 1849.

Mr. Holmquist attended country schools, Wausa High School, and Northwestern Normal School at Le Mars, Iowa. He is now postmaster at Wausa, where he has been active in various community projects for many years. He served as secretary of the State Association of the County Commissioners and County Clerks, 1918-26, acted as highway commissioner of Knox County, 1923-24, and was connected with the department of public works, 1926-28.

He is a member of the Wausa Commercial Club, is affiliated with the Swedish Lutheran Church, and holds membership in the Nebraskana Society. His sports are baseball and basketball. On February 21, 1898, he was married to Anna E. at Cedar, Nebraska. Mrs. Holmquist was born in Sweden, August 25, 1880, and died at Wausa, April 22, 1926.

Their children are: Roy, born January 19, 1899; Ernest, born April 6, 1900; Walter, August 15, 1901; Clifton, June 3, 1903; Elmer, August 25, 1905; Melvin, September 3, 1907; Irene, August 23, 1910; Gladys December 8, 1912; Floyd, February 20, 1915; Viola, January 26, 1917; Loren, February 23, 1919; and Elaine, January 3, 1926. Residence: Wausa.

Herman Henry Holsten

Herman H. Holsten, a resident of Nebraska for the past 57 years, was born at Stover, Missouri, February 24, 1867, the son of Diedrich and Margareth (Behrens) Holsten. His father, who was born at Hanover, Germany, April 16, 1842, and died at Redlands, California, June 8, 1918, was a farmer and stockfeeder; he served four years in the Missouri Cavalry in the Civil War; he held membership in the Grand Army of the Republic. His mother was born at St. Louis, Missouri, March 22, 1848, and died at Redlands, June 1924. She was an expert needlewoman. Her ancestry was German.

Mr. Holsten received his education in the public schools, and in 1887 was graduated from the Fremont Business College at Fremont, Nebraska. He has been a farmer, live stock feeder, and banker at Dodge, Dodge County, Nebraska, for many years, and is today president of the Farmers State Bank at Dodge. He is connected with the Howells State Bank at Howells, Nebraska. A Republican, he served several years as a member of the Town Board, Township Board, and local school board at Dodge.

His marriage to Ella Dierker was solemnized at Snyder, Dodge County, Nebraska, September 11, 1890. Mrs. Holsten was born at St. Charles, Missouri, September 20, 1870. They have four children: Richard; Marguerite; Leona, and Viola.

Mr Holsten is a member of the Red Cross; is affiliated with the German Lutheran Church; and holds membership in the Nebraskana Society. Residence: Dodge.

Richard Harry Holsten

Richard H. Holsten was born at Dodge, Dodge County, Nebraska, August 31, 1891, the son of Herman H. and Elenora (Dierker) Holsten. His father, a banker, farmer, and livestock feeder, was born at Stover, Morgan County, Missouri, February 24, 1867; his German great grandfather landed in New Orleans in the early days and fought in the Mexican War; his grandfather was a soldier in the Civil War. His mother was born, of German descent, at St. Charles, Missouri, September 20, 1870.

Mr. Holsten was graduated from the Dodge High School, May 1907, and attended Boyle's Business College at Omaha. From 1909 to 1910 he was connected with the operating department of the Union Pacific Railroad Company, and since 1911 has been cashier in the Farmers State Bank at Dodge. For eight years he served as chairman of the village board at Dodge; he is a Republican.

He is a member of the Red Cross; the Dodge Commercial Club; and the Nebraskana Society. He is affiliated with St. Johns Evangelical Lutheran Church at Dodge. His hobby is flowers. On December 9, 1914, he was united in marriage with Lillian Karlen at Beemer, Cuming County, Nebraska. Mrs. Holsten was born at Beemer, July 23, 1893; her father was born in Switzerland, while her mother was born of Swiss parentage in Wisconsin. Residence: Dodge.

Lew Daniel Holston

Lew Daniel Holston, prominent lodge executive, now state manager of the Macabees Life Insurance Association, was born at Trenton, Nebraska, October 31, 1894, son of Jay Grant and Hattie (Jones) Holston.

The father, born in Monticello, Iowa, December 17, 1864, died at Kansas City, Missouri, November 8, 1931.

He was a farmer. His wife, who was born at Dawn, Missouri, November 22, 1873, survives him.

Mr. Holston attended public and high school at Trenton, and thereafter taught school five years. He was postmaster, at Trenton, five years, and the following six years was district manager of the Modern Woodmen of America. For four years he has held his present position.

A member of the Modern Woodmen, the Elks, Eagles and the Macabees, he is affiliated with the Congregational Church. He enjoys reading, while his favorite outdoor recreations include hunting, fishing and playing baseball.

On August 12, 1915, he was married to Zila Alberta Hurst at McCook. Mrs. Holston, who was born at Trenton, February 11, 1894. There are three children, Clayton, born September 15, 1922; Arvene, born May 18, 1918, and Hariett Ann, born December 17, 1929. Residence: Trenton.

Albert G. Holt

Albert G. Holt, who has been a resident of Nebraska for the past 47 years, was born at Missouri City, Missouri, January 15, 1861, the son of John D. and Martha M. (Peery) Holt. His father, who was born in North Carolina, was a merchant and produce shipper who traveled overland to California during the Gold Rush of 1849; he served in the Mexican War and the Civil War, and died at Long Pine, Nebraska, in August, 1890. His mother was born at Mexico, Missouri, and died at Holt, Missouri, in July, 1885.

Mr. Holt was graduated from the Holt High School in 1880, and attended the University of Missouri where he was active in debate events, and took a prominent part in athletics. He served as a telegraph operator and station agent at Johnstown, Nebraska, 1886-92, conducted a general store at Johnstown, and later served as postmaster there. He conducted a cold storage plant from 1895 to 1901, and from 1901 to 1921 served as president of the Citizens Bank of Johnstown. He is now engaged in the real estate and insurance business at Johnstown where he is a member of the Red Cross and the First Christian Church. He was formerly a member of the School Board, served as mayor of Johnstown for a time, and is a member of the local lodge of the Modern Woodmen of America. His hobby is bridge. During the World War Mr. Holt acted as the leader in all Liberty loan drives in his community, and contributed liberally to the Red Cross.

A Democrat, he attended the National Democratic Convention at Chicago in 1896 as a delegate, and has since attended all national conventions of his party. He served as postmaster at Johnstown under Cleveland's administration.

On October 21, 1885, he was married to Emma May Towne at Ticeville, North Dakota. Mrs. Holt, whose Scotch-Irish ancestors came to Ameriica in 1620, was born at Cresco, Iowa, April 20, 1866. Seven children were born to this marriage; Nellie Christine, March 6, 1887, who married Lewis I. Schell; Hazel May, May 8, 1889; John Albert, March 7, 1893, who married Mina Keister; Lewis Clinton, December 15, 1895, who married Carrie Hayes; Cleora Ruth, August 15, 1900, who married Elmo Olson; Grace Irene, December 17, 1903, who married Dean C. Norden; and Clifford Towne, January 15, 1907. Residence: Johnstown.

Nellie Lee Holt

Nellie Lee Holt, noted Nebraska educator, was born in Falls City, Richardson County, Nebraska, the daughter of William Robertson and Eva Lee (Giannini) Holt. Her father, who is a banker, stockman, and merchant, was born at Salem, Richardson County, Nebraska of English and Scotch parentage. Members of the Holt

family came to America from England and settled in Virginia in 1632.

Her mother, who was born at Milton, Atchison County, Missouri, is of Italian and English ancestry. She is an active club and church worker, and during the late war was awarded the Red Cross service medal.

Miss Holt received all her early education in the Falls City public schools and was graduated from the high school there in 1917. In 1921 she was awarded the B. A. degree at St. Mary's College at Notre Dame, Indiana, where she also received a diploma in piano. She received her master's degree at the University of Nebraska, June, 1922. In the summers of 1929 and 1930 she was a student at Columbia University. During her stay at the University of Nebraska she was a member of Chi Delta Phi, literary fraternity; Theta Sigma Phi, journalistic fraternity; and Delta Omicron, music fraternity. Her sorority is Kappa Kappa Gamma.

She has always lived in Nebraska and takes especial interest in the political life of the state. For several years she was active in the League of Women Voters, and still retains membership in this organization. She is the author of several articles published at various times, and is the author of *With Mahatma Ghandi in His Retreat*, published in the *New York Magazine*, March 11, 1928.

From 1922 to 1924, Miss Holt was English and Latin instructor in the Falls City High School. In the summer of 1925 she was sent on a special mission to England for Stephens College; she made a world tour for Stephens College, 1926-27. Since 1927 she has been professor of religious education at this school, and has been a professional lecturer with the Famous Speakers Incorporated of New York City.

Miss Holt is a life member of the Red Cross and in 1930 was made a member of The Nebraskana Society. She is affiliated with the First Presbyterian Church of Falls City. Her hobbies are: the theatre, reading, and writing. She is fond of swimming. She is an Independent. Residence: Falls City.

William Robert Holt

William R. Holt was born at Salem, Nebraska, December 7, 1877, the son of John White and Amanda M. (Oliver) Holt. His father, born in Boone County, Missouri, November 17, 1834, died at Falls City, Nebraska, June 16, 1911. A distinguished citizen and leader in his community, he served as state senator and treasurer of Richardson County, and for many years was president of the First National Bank of Falls City. His wife, who was active in church work, was born in Miami County, Indiana, January 29, 1847, and died at Falls City, July 11, 1929.

Upon his graduation from high school at Falls City, Mr. Holt studied for a year at St. Benedict's College at Atchison, Kansas, in 1894. From 1894-1896 he was a student at the Lincoln Business College at Lincoln, Nebraska. A resident of Nebraska for 53 years he has engaged in various enterprises. Among them he was connected with the First National Bank, 1896-1898; a farmer and fine stock breeder for 13 years; and in 1912 entered the hardware, plumbing and heating business, in which he is still engaged. At the present time he is a stockholder in the First National Bank, and in the Falls City Wholesale & Supply Company, and is still interested in farming and stock raising.

On June 1, 1898, his marriage to Eva Giannini was solemnized at Falls City. Mrs. Holt was born at Fairfax, Atchison County, Missouri. There is one daughter, Nellie Lee.

Mr. Holt took an especially active part in loan drives and other war-time activities. He is a charter member of the Rotary Club; is a member of the Ancient Order of United Workmen, and the Elks; and is a Mason. For the last twenty years he has been an elder in the Presbyterian Church. He is a Republican. Residence: Falls City.

Fred J. Homeyer

On January 4, 1869, Fred J. Homeyer was born at St. Louis, Missouri. Henry Homeyer, his father, whose ancestry was Teutonic, was born at Luepka, Germany, February 7, 1837, and came to America in 1856, where he became a private in the Union Army during the Civil War. He was a grocer and grain dealer.

Louisa Anna (Myer) Homeyer, his mother, was born at Burnighausen, Germany, October 3, 1840. Her parents were farmers.

Mr. Homeyer attended the Nebraska City High School and later was a student at the Nebraska City Episcopal College where he was graduated in 1885. He has lived in Nebraska for 60 years, and has taken an interested part in civic and business affairs in his community, and in Republican politics. He is now engaged in the shoe retail business, and is an orchardist. He is a stockholder and a director in the Merchants' National Bank at Nebraska City.

He was united in marriage to Clara Katherine Van Ells, February 3, 1910, at Nebraska City. Mrs. Homeyer was born at Milwaukee, Wisconsin, March, 1885, and died at Nebraska City, January 7, 1926.

In the recent war Mr. Homeyer was a member of the Nebraska City Home Guard, and later was active in soliciting for Armenian relief. He is a member of the Odd Fellows, Eagles, and Sons of Herman. His social clubs are the Nebraska City Country Club and the Golf Club. Reading is his hobby, and his favorite sport is golf. Residence: Nebraska City.

Joseph Josiah Hompes

One of Nebraska's leading physicians, Joseph Josiah Hompes is a native son. He was born at Chester, Thayer County, Nebraska, April 23, 1883, so nof Louis and Elma (Chambers) Hompes. Louis Hompes was born at Velsen, Germany, October 25, 1858. Prior to his retirement several years ago he was engaged in the real estate and farm mortgage business. His wife, Elma, was born at Lincoln on January 19, 1864, daughter of Josiah J. Chambers.

Dr. Hompes attended the Chester public school, and was graduated from the 10th grade in 1902. Thereafter he attended the Lincoln High School and Lincoln Academy but did not graduate. In 1908 he received his M. D. from the University of Nebraska, and during 1912-13 took post graduate work at the University of Vienna.

Since 1910 Dr. Hompes has engaged in the practice of medicine specializing in the eye, ear nose and throat. He is attending eye, ear nose and throat specialist to Lincoln General, Bryan Memorial and St. Elizabeth's Hospitals; consulting specialist to the U. S. Veterans Hospital and eye, ear, nose and throat specialist for the Missouri-Pacific Railroad. His professional organizations include the Lancaster County, Nebraska State and American Medical Associations, the Missouri Valley Eye and Ear Association, the Nebraska Eye and Ear Association, the American College of Surgeons, and the American Academy of Ophthalmology, Oto-laryngology and Otology.

During the World War he served with the Medical Corps from July 1918 to October 1919 with the rank of captain, as chief section head of surgery, U. S. Base Hospital. He now holds rank of Major in the Medical Reserve Corps.

During 1917 and 1918 he was secretary of the board of health of the State of Nebraska. He is president of the Hompes Investment Company, Inc., of Lincoln, a member of the Chamber of Commerce, the Elks, Masons, Young Men's Christian Association and the Nebraska State Historical Association.

He has written during his years in practice numerous articles on diseases of the eye, ear, nose and throat: *Roentgen Ray Examination in Mastoid Disease* (pub-

lished in the Journal of the American Medical Association May 1919) and *Toxic Otitis* (1930) etc.

His club is the Lincoln University Club, and his sport is golf. Residence: Lincoln.

Ralph Clifford Hon

Ralph C. Hon, educator at Nebraska Wesleyan University, was born at Jonesboro, Craighead County, Arkansas, January 29, 1903, the son of Earl Augustus and Mary Oma (Little) Hon. His father, who is a locomotive engineer, was born at Burnt Prairie, White County, Illinois, January 13, 1879; his German ancestors came to this country in 1774. His mother, whose ancestry is Scotch-Irish, was born at Jonesboro, July 29, 1881.

Professor Hon was graduated from the high school at Thayer, Missouri, 1920. He was a student at the University of Southern California during the summer of 1922, and attended American University, 1928-29. He holds the following degrees: A. B., University of Illinois, 1924; A. M., Harvard, 1926; Ph. D., University of North Carolina, 1930. He was a fellow in economics at the University of North Carolina, 1927-28, and the American University, 1928-29.

During 1924 and 1925, Dr. Hon served as teacher in the high school at Thayer, and was principal there, 1926-27. He is now professor of economics and business administration at the Nebraska Wesleyan University. He is a member of the American Economic Association, the Royal Economic Society, and the Nebraskana Society. He is affiliated with the Methodist Church. Politically, he is an Independent.

On July 14, 1930, he was married to Hazel Sada McLain at Thayer. Mrs. Hon was born at Thayer. Residence: Lincoln.

John S. Hooks

Born at Blair, Nebraska, April 1, 1892, John S. Hooks is the son of Robert Allen and Evelyn (Sutherland) Hooks. His father who is a farmer, was born at Edgwood, Illinois, January 9, 1867, and came to Nebraska a number of years ago. Evelyn Sutherland Hooks was born at Seymour, Indiana, July 21, 1868.

Mr. Hooks was graduated from the Blair public school on May 31, 1907, and afterward attended Blair High School and Dana College. He was married to Bertha Johanna Jacobson at Blair, on October 28, 1914. Mrs. Hooks was a native of Blair, born July 23, 1894. There are two sons, Leo, born April 18, 1918, and Ray, born December 9, 1919.

A farmer continuously since leaving school, Mr. Hooks has prospered steadily, and has taken an active interest in the advancement of his community. He is affiliated with the Democratic party, but always votes for the man he believes most capable regardless of party. He is a member of the Methodist Episcopal Church of Blair, and has been a member of its official board ten years.

For twelve years Mr. Hooks has been a member of the board of the Federal Farm Bureau, and is secretary and treasurer of the Dairy Herd Improvement Association of which he has been a member for the past six years. He is a Mason, a member of the Red Cross and the Nebraskana Society. His favorite sports are hunting and fishing. Residence: Blair.

Marcus Hoops

A leading professional man of Springview, Nebraska, is Marcus Hoops, who has been engaged in the practice of medicine and surgery since 1908. He was born at Staplehurst, Nebraska, May 3, 1879, the son of William Walter and Lydia Jane (McFadden) Hoops. His father who was born near Salem, Ohio, November 9, 1843, and died at Staplehurst, December 18, 1902, was a farmer and civic leader in that community for many years.

William Walter Hoops, whose ancestry was English, served as a member of the school board at Staplehurst for a number of years, was affiliated with the Presbyterian Church, and took an active part in political affairs. He was a member of the Republican party, originally, became affiliated with the Populists, and finally supported the Democratic principles.

Lydia Jane (McFadden) Hoops, who was born of Scotch Irish parents at Calhoun, Iowa, August 29, 1853, and died at Denver, Colorado, April 25, 1927, was the mother of a large family and was prominent in the Presbyterian Church organizations. She was a talented musician.

Dr. Hoops attended the Staplehurst High School, received the M. D. degree at Lincoln Medical College in 1908, took a post graduate course at Tulane University in Louisiana studied at the Surgical Technique Institute, and has attended clinics in various Chicago hospitals. He was a member of Tau Alpha Epsilon at the Lincoln Medical College.

He has been engaged in the practice of medicine and surgery at Springview since 1911, and owns a cattle ranch near there. He is a Master Mason, and was formerly affiliated with the Elks, Woodmen of the World, Modern Woodmen of America, the Ancient Order of United Workmen, and various medical societies. He is interested in raising pure-bred polled Hereford cattle.

During the World War, Dr. Hoops served as a member of the local exemption board in Keya Paha County. His favorite sport is fishing. His marriage to Nelly Blanche Smelser occurred at Central City, Nebraska, in March, 1909. Mrs. Hoops, who was a nurse prior to her marriage, was born at Marshalltown, Iowa, September 17, 1883. She is the daughter of Benjamin F. and Elvira Jackson Smelser. Their two children are: Sibyl Genevieve, born May 26, 1910, who was graduated from the Springview High School; and Eugene Herschel, born November 1, 1919. Sibyl studied at Penn College in Iowa for a year, and has taught school for two years. Residence: Springview.

Henry Harrison Hoover

Henry Harrison Hoover was born near Garrett, Somerset County, Pennsylvania, April 17, 1857, the son of Andrew Hoover and Sallie (Young) Hoover. His father was born in 1810, of German parentage, and died at Garrett, July 4, 1890.

Mr. Hoover attended public schools, and engaged in farming shortly thereafter. On October 24, 1894, at Davenport, Thayer County, Nebraska, he was united in marriage with Nettie Walker. She was born at Lavansville, Somerset County, Pennsylvania, February 11, 1867. To this union three children were born: Clarence, born January 2, 1896, who died January 5, 1896; Harold, born November 26, 1898, who died November 27, 1898; and Richard, born December 16, 1899, who is married to Evelyn Lowery.

Henry Hoover was a Democrat. He has been a farmer in Nebraska for forty-nine years. He is a member of the Red Cross and president of the Davenport, Nebraska, precinct. He also holds membership in the Nebraskana Society and is affiliated with the Lutheran Church. Henry Hoover died April 14, 1928.

Henry William Hopkins

Born at Tilden, Nebraska, August 1, 1870, Henry William Hopkins is the son of Allen Gardner and Frances Lucebra (Riley) Hopkins. His father, who was born in Artabula County, Ohio, June 28, 1847, is a farmer; he was a pioneer in Nebraska in the early days and his wedding was the first in Antelope County. His mother, whose ancestry was English, was born in Kentucky, August 5, 1851, and died at San Diego, California, March 31, 1927.

Mr. Hopkins, who is a successful stockman and farmer near Neligh, Nebraska, was the first white boy born in Antelope County. He received his education in the early-day rural schools of Nebraska. He is a member of the Elkhorn Valley Lodge of the Modern Woodmen of America, and is affiliated with the Baptist Church.

His marriage to Barbar A. Young occurred at Tilden, Nebraska, January 1, 1896. Mrs. Hopkins was born at St. Joseph, Missouri, February 14, 1877, and died at Tilden, August 12, 1907. To their marriage the following children were born: Albert C., born August 21, 1899, who died January 1, 1919; Wilma T., February 8, 1903, who married Webster Olson; and George A., February 22, 1905, who married Thelma A. Hopkins. On October 8, 1908, Mr. Hopkins married Lena M. Krape at Lock Haven, Pennsylvania. They have the following children: Elna E., born November 24, 1909; Dorothy N., born December 9, 1911; and Kenneth E., born April 13, 1914. Residence: Neligh.

Earl Eugene Hopping

Earl Eugene Hopping, druggist and undertaker of Beaver City, Nebraska, was born in that community, January 5, 1887, the son of Charles Edward and Anna May (Heston) Hopping. His father, who was born at Havana, Illinois, March 18, 1857, and died at Beaver City, March 9, 1930, was a druggist and undertaker who served as president of the Nebraska Druggists' Association, and the Nebraska Undertakers' Association at one time.

Mr. Hopping was graduated from the Beaver City High School, and in 1907 received the Ph. G. degree at Creighton, University College of Pharmacy. Since 1911 he has been proprietor of the Hopping Drug Company at Beaver City, and since 1930, has been manager of the Hopping Undertaking Establishment there.

He is affiliated with the Beaver City Presbyterian Church, holds membership in the Nebraska Undertakers' Association and the Nebraska Pharmaceutical Association, and is president of the Beaver City Rotary Club. He is a member of the Modern Woodmen of America, the National Geographic Society, and the Nebraskana Society.

His marriage to Selina Sarah Smith occurred at Beaver City, July 15, 1908. Mrs. Hopping, who is the granddaughter of B. C. Smith, Episcopal Rector of Holcote, England, was born at Beaver City, October 11, 1887. They have three children: S. Jean, born February 16, 1909; Charles E., born November 2, 1913; and Florence, born August 16, 1917. Jean is a student at the University of Nebraska, where she holds membership in Delta Delta Delta. Charles is also a student at the University of Nebraska. Residence: Beaver City. (Photograph in Album).

Philip Edward Horan

Born at Ottumwa, Iowa, June 24, 1885, Philip E. Horan has been a resident of Nebraska since his admission to the bar in 1913. He is the son of Philip Horan, a native of Ireland, who died at Ottumwa, in January, 1897. He was a farmer. His wife, Margaret (Sullivan) Horan, was born in Wapello County, Iowa, and died at Ottumwa, in 1891.

Mr. Horan attended the preparatory department of St. Ambrose College at Davenport, Iowa, from 1900-04. He later entered Creighton University, from which he received the degree of A. B. in 1908; A. M., 1909; and LL. B. in 1913. He has been a member of the law firm of Kennedy, Holland, DeLacey, and Horan, and a member of the firm of Sears, Horan and Shaw; and is now attorney for the Mutual Benefit Health and Accident Association, and the United Benefit Life Insurance Company.

He married Blanche A. Coffman, formerly a teacher in Central High School, at Omaha, June 24, 1916. There are three children, Philip E., born July 15, 1918; William C., born July 8, 1920, and Kathleen, born June 8, 1922. Mr. Horan is a Catholic and a Democrat. Residence: Omaha.

George Pancost Horn

Born at Tipton, Iowa, June 18, 1859, Geeorge Pancost Horn came to Nebraska in 1880. He is the son of James Clark Horn and Mary (Filson) Horn. His father, who was a farmer, was born at Somerset, Pennsylvania, January 24, 1817, and died at Tipton, March 15, 1884; he served as an elder in the Methodist Church at Tipton for many years; his ancestry was Scotch. His mother, who was also born at Somerset, Pennsylvania, March 1, 1818, and died at Tipton, September 1, 1876, came to Iowa with her husband in the early history of the state.

Mr. Horn attended the Tipton public schools. He has been a farmer near St. Edward, Nebraska, for many years and is now retired. He is a member of the Nebraskana Society, was Republican Central Committeeman for 16 years, and served as constable for 28 years. He has always been interested in fine stock.

On September 26, 1883, he was married to Mary Ellen Shaffer at St. Edward. Mrs. Horn is the daughter of Daniel A. and Letticia Margaret (Kennedy) Shaffer. She came with her parents to Boone County in 1879. Mr. Shaffer was born near Canton, Ohio, in 1839, and died at St. Edward, April 9, 1918. Mrs. Shaffer was born in 1846 near South Bend, Indiana. Mrs. Horn, who was born at Lexington, Illinois, March 20, 1864, is descended from the royal family of Scotland and Revolutionary ancestors. She holds membership in the Federated Woman's Club and the Daughters of the American Revolution at St. Edward.

To this marriage the following children were born, Homer Noble, August 31, 1885, who married Lillian Johnson; Robert Walter, July 14, 1888, who married Gertrude Kane; James Daniel, December 3, 1893, who married Marie Louise Beza; Edith Marguerite, December 9, 1897, who married Rank Ernest Poole; Erma Dale, January 3, 1902, who married Glenn Jennings Ronk; and Arnold Louis, September 30, 1907, who married Heraldine Laurent. The three younger children were graduated from St. Edward High School. Residence: St. Edward.

Matthaus Henry Horn

Matthaus Henry Horn, physician and surgeon, was born at Westerbergen, Schleswig-Holstein, Germany, January 27, 1871. His father, Nickolaus Friedrich Horn was born in Westerbergen, August 14, 1841 and died there August 12, 1884. He was a farmer whose ancestors had lived on the Island of Fehmarn for several generations. His wife, Anna Christina Mueller, was born in Burg, Schleswig, October 26, 1841, and died at Westerbergen, in January, 1917.

Upon his graduation from German Folk School in 1886, Matthaus Henry Horn entered the Kansas State Agricultural College, but did not graduate. He attended the Medical College of the University of Kansas at Rosedale and Washburn College at Topeka (these schools were merged in 1900), and received his medical degree in 1900. From that time until 1918 he practiced at Morrowville, Kansas.

In August, 1917, Dr. Horn entered the Medical Reserve Corps as a first lieutenant. On April 2, 1918, he was taken into active service, and received his honorable discharge on October 31, 1919. He was promoted to the rank of captain in the Reserves in December 1919, which rank he still holds. He is a member of the American Legion.

His marriage to Mary Maude Smith was solemnized at Morrowville, her birthplace on November 29, 1905. Mrs. Horn, who was born May 4, 1876, is German on the maternal side and English and German on the paternal side. There is one daughter, Maude Hildreth, born February 19, 1907. She is a graduate of Bethany High School and Cotner College, and is a school teacher.

Dr. Horn is a Republican. He is a Scottish Rite Mason and member of the Shrine and Eastern Star, as well as the Odd Fellows. His religious affiliation is with the Bethany Church of Christ. He is a member of the Nebraskana Society, and his hobby is floriculture and gardening. Residence: Lincoln.

Lulu Horne

Lulu Horne, city librarian in Lincoln, Lancaster County, Nebraska, was born at Kankakee, Illinois, the daughter of William Henry and Ellen Alzora (Titus) Horne. Her father, who was born at Milwaukee, Wisconsin, and died at Lincoln, October 7, 1907, was a farmer, banker, and ice and coal dealer; he was of Scotch descent. Her mother was born in Michigan and died at Lincoln, March 20, 1892; her ancestors were early English settlers of New York.

Miss Horne attended the public schools of Lancaster County. She was awarded the A. B. degree at the Nebraska Wesleyan University, and later was a student at the University of Nebraska and the University of Chicago. She was elected to membership in Phi Kappa Psi. In 1900 she was employed as an assistant in the Lincoln City Library, was made acting librarian, April 1910, and was elected librarian in September 1910. She is still employed in that capacity.

She is a member of the American Library Association, the Nebraska Library Association, the Lincoln Chamber of Commerce, the Business and Professional Women's Club, the Lincoln Automobile Club, the Social Welfare Society, Red Cross, and the Altrusa Club. She has been prominent in educational and welfare activities in Lancaster County for the past 30 years. She is a member of the Young Women's Christian Association and the Order of the Eastern Star. Her social and educational organizations include the American Association of University Women, University Club, and the Thursday Evening Club. Her political affiliation is with the Republican party. Residence: Lincoln.

Ralph Lester Horst

One of Nebraska's most distinguished citizens is Ralph Lester Horst, educator and chemist. He was born at Osceola, Nebraska, August 1, 1896, the son of George and Amalia Margaret (Buchta) Horst. His father, who was born at Green Bay, Wisconsin, May 13, 1854, and died at Osceola, Nebraska, January 3, 1908, was a teacher, farmer, and county superintendent of schools. He served in the Nebraska legislature for three terms. His German parents came to this country in 1851.

Amalia (Buchta) Horst, his mother, was born at Carpenter, Illinois, August 26, 1869. She was president of the Farm Woman's Club in 1929, is a member of Rebekah Lodge Number 88, and holds membership in the Independent Order of Odd Fellows Auxiliary. Her German ancestors came to this country in 1839, and her father was in the gold rush of 1849, traveling in a covered wagon from St. Louis, Missouri, to California.

Mr. Horst attended rural schools in Polk County, was graduated from the high school at Osceola, Nebraska, in 1914, received the A. B. degree at Nebraska Wesleyan University in 1918, and was awarded the Master of Science degree at the University of Illinois, in 1922. He was a member of the Henderson Club and the Chemistry Club at Nebraska Wesleyan University.

His career in the field of chemistry is as follows: chemistry assistant at Nebraska Wesleyan University, 1918; chemist in the meat inspection department, United States Department of Agriculture, 1918-19-20, at Washigton, D. C.; chemistry teacher in the high school at Mendota, Illinois, 1919-20; chemistry teacher at the

University of Illinois, 1920-22; chemist, Bureau of Chemistry and Food & Drug Administration, United States Department of Agriculture, at Chicago, New Orleans, and New York, since 1922. His present position is associate chemist, assistant supervisor of imports of food and drug products, United States Department of Agriculture.

Mr. Horst is a member of the Young Men's Business Club at New Orleans, was a member of the American Chemical Society, 1918-22, and held membership in the National Georgraphic Society, 1919-22. He is a member of The Nebraskana Society, the Methodist Episcopal Church of Osceola, and the Ancient Free and Accepted Masons. From 1914 to 1918 he was a member of the Young Men's Christian Association.

During the late war he served as a private in the Chemical Warfare Service at Cleveland, Ohio, and from 1919 to 1920 was a member of the American Legion. His chief recreations are tennis, reading, and the study of chemistry. Politically, he is independent.

His marriage to Irma Delord was solemnized at New Orleans, December 4, 1922. Mrs. Horst was born of French parentage at New Orleans, July 5, 1900. They have a son, Ralph Lester, born July 14, 1925. Residence: New York City.

Richard Scott Horton

Richard S. Horton, lawyer, was born in Cincinnati, Ohio, February 22, 1866. He is the son of B. J. and Virginia (Yeatman) Horton, the former also a lawyer.

Upon the completion of his public and high school work at Lawrence, Kansas, he entered the University of Kansas, where he received his B. A. degree. He then attended the Cincinnati Law School, from which he received his LL. B. He is a member of Phi Gamma Delta and Phi Delta Phi.

Mr. Horton was married to Evelyn Harrison of Lawrence, Kansas, at Kansas City, Missouri, and they have two children, Evelyn and Jane. Mr. Horton has been a resident of Nebraska for thirty years, and has been actively engaged in the practice of law since his admission to the bar. He is a Democrat, and active in party politics. Residence: Omaha.

Allen Harrison Hostetter

Allen Harrison Hostetter was born at Ladoga, Indiana, September 16, 1858. His father, Sherman Hostetter, who was born in Stark County, Ohio, in 1810, and died at Jamestown, Indiana, in 1866, was a farmer and a lawyer, and was in the Indiana legislature during the Civil War. His ancestors came to America from the Palatine, Germany, about 1650, and settled in Virginia. Later members of the family moved to Pennsylvania, and eastern Ohio.

Mary Ann (Byrd) Hostetter, his mother, was born in Kentucky, in 1819, and died at Crawfordsville, Indiana, in 1896. She was a member of the distinguished Byrd family, noted for many years in the history of the south. One of her ancestors was the author of the first history of Virginia, and an uncle, who was an officer in the army, was killed in the Revolution.

Dr. Hostetter, who has been a practicing physician in Nebraska for forty-four years, received his elementary education in the public schools of Indiana. He was graduated from Valparaiso Normal School, 1878, and graduated from Rush Medical College in 1886. On June 20, 1886, he was admitted to the practice of medicine at Crawfordsville, Indiana. For twenty-five years he has been vice president of the bank of Douglas.

His marriage to Cora Slosson was solemnized at Palmyra, Otoe County, Nebraska, June 16, 1891. Mrs. Hostetter, who was born at Cicero, New York, August 20, 1866, is descended on the maternal side from the Peabodie family of New York.

Four children were born to this union. Helen P., born

August 1, 1896, was awarded the A. B. degree from the University of Nebraska, and the M. A. degree from Northwestern University. She is now an instructor in the Lingnan University, Canton, China. Nina P., born January 7, 1898, is married to Dr. L. E. Brown. Doris, born October 16, 1900, is married to G. B. Flagg. Marjorie, born August 21, 1903, received the A. B. degree from Doane College at Crete, Nebraska, and is an instructor in a girl's school at Merzifun, Turkey.

Dr. Hostetter was a member of the Medical Reserve Corps during the late war. He is a member of the state and county medical societies, is a Mason, and is affiliated with the Methodist Church and the Parent Teacher's Association. His sports are golf and tennis. Raising chickens is his hobby. Residence: Douglas.

William Joseph Hotz

William Joseph Hotz, lawyer, was born in Iowa City, Iowa, October 15, 1885, son of William Joseph and Matilda (Ward) Hotz. His father was born in Iowa City, June 7, 1859, and died there on April 12, 1901. His mother was born in Iowa City, April 1, 1860.

Upon the completion of his public school education, Mr. Hotz attended Iowa University, from which, in 1909, he received the Bachelor of Laws degree.

On April 17, 1912, he was married to Florence Josephine Lynch, at Sioux City. Mrs. Hotz was born at Sioux City, August 17, 1885. They have one son, William J., Jr., born June 7, 1917.

At the present time Mr. Hotz is engaged in practice with his brother, Robert H. Hotz, under the firm name of Hotz and Hotz. He is a member of the American, Nebraska State and Omaha Bar Associations, the Red Cross, Chamber of Commerce, Degree of Honor, Ak-Sar-Ben, the Parent-Teachers' Association, and the Aeronautical Chamber of Commerce (New York).

Mr. Hotz is a Catholic, a fourth degree Knight of Columbus, and a member of the Holy Name and St. Vincent de Paul Society. Residence: Omaha.

Homer Roscoe Houchen

Homer Roscoe Houchen, physician and surgeon in Nebraska since 1905, was born at Edinburg, Indiana, April 20, 1881, son of Henry Addison and Ida Mae Belle (McKane) Houchen.

Henry Addison Houchen, an educator for more than forty years, attended normal school in Louisville, Kentucky, and college at Hartsville, Indiana. From 1885-87 he was principal of public schools at Greenwood, Indiana, and afterward taught in Seward and Butler Counties. He traced his ancestry to Edward Houchins, an Englishman who came to New Kent County, Virginia, in 1680; Edward Houchins, a Revolutionary War Soldier; and to Abram Martin, settler in Virginia in 1687, and his son, John, a member of the Virginia House of Burgesses. Henry Addison Houchen died at Lincoln, January 15, 1925.

His wife, Ida Mae, was born in Franklin, Indiana, October 28, 1858, and is prominent in civic and cultural circles. For a period of four years she was president of the Women's Christian Temperance Union, and she also belongs to the American Legion auxiliary, the Woman's Club, etc. She is a descendent from James McKane, settler in Pennsylvania, in 1734, and from John Chenoweth and his wife, Mary Calvert, daughter of Lord Baltimore, 3rd. Her father, a soldier in the Civil War, lost his life with the Union Army in 1863.

Dr. Houchen attended public school at Beaver Crossing and Milford, was graduated from high school at Beaver Crossing in 1901, and received his M. D. and Ph. G. from Lincoln Medical College in 1905. He also attended the University of Nebraska and Cotner College.

For the past twenty-six years Dr. Houchens has practiced medicine at Utica, and since 1913, when he built a drug store he has also operated that business. He is a member of the Nebraska State Medical Society and the Nebraska Pharmaceutical Associations, the Utica Commercial Club, and the Methodist Church. An Odd Fellow, he is a member of the encampment, and was recently made a member of The Nebraskana Society. His hobby is reading.

On April 11, 1906, Dr. Houchen was united in marriage to Elizabeth Vanderhook at Lincoln. Mrs. Houchen was born in Lancaster County, near Lincoln, on January 11, 1885. There are three sons, Ervin L., born January 25, 1908, who married Kathryn Hill; Homer R., born May 15, 1912; and Wayne L., born March 16, 1918. Ervin has had four years in medical college, and Homer has finished one year in pre-law work.

Dr. Houchen is a Republican, with an active interest in all public questions. Residence: Utica.

Paul C. Houchen

Born at Beaver Crossing, May 24, 1899, Paul C. Houchen is the son of Henry Addison and Mae Belle (McKane) Houchen. His father, born at Shelbyville, Kentucky, October 24, 1849, was a teacher by profession, who devoted forty years of his life to that calling. He attended normal school in Louisville, Kentucky, and Hartsville College in Indiana. Prior to his removal to Nebraska he was principal of schools at Greenwood, Indiana, and later in Seward and Butler Counties in this state.

Henry Addison Houchen was descended from Edward Houchins, who settled in New Kent County, Virginia, in 1680, and from Edward Houchins, 3rd, who was a soldier in the Revolution and who was wounded in the Battle of Camden. Maternally he was descended from Abram Martin, a settler in Virginia, in 1687, and of his son John, a member of the Virginia Burgesses.

Ida Mae Belle McKane, who was born at Franklin, Indiana, October 28, 1858, is a member of the American Legion auxiliary, and for four years served as president of the Women's Christian Temperance Union. She is a descendant of James McKane, who came to Pennsylvania, in 1700, and a daughter of John McKane, who died in the service of his country in 1863. Henry Addison Houchen died at Lincoln, January 15, 1925. 1922.

Paul C. Houchen attended school at Beaver Crossing, and was graduated from high school there in 1917. During the World War he was a private in the United States Army. He is a member of the American Legion and the Sons of the American Revolution. Upon the close of the war he entered the University of Nebraska, from which he received the degree of Doctor of Dental Surgery in 1922.

Since 1922 he has been engaged in the practice of dentistry at Beaver Crossing, his professional associations including the American, Nebraska State and Lincoln District Dental Associations. He is a member of the Red Cross, the Chamber of Commerce, the Independent Order of Odd Fellows and Encampment. His hobbies are tennis and reading. His religious affiliation is with the Church of Christ, and his political faith is Republican.

He was united in marriage with Elizabeth Pearle Bye at Central City, in 1928. Mrs. Houchen, who was born at Seward, October 10, 1903, is descended from Edmund Bye, who came from England to New Jersey in 1833, and maternally from Stephen Bradley, who came to Connecticut in 1642 and Eber Bradley, a Revolutionary War soldier. Dr. Houchen is the author of *Houchins Family History* (1931). Residence: Beaver Crossing.

Edward Charles Houdek

Edward Charles Houdek, banker, was born at Agenda, Kansas, March 1, 1902, son of Milo B. and Emma (Havel) Houdek. The father was born at Agenda, January 18, 1877, and is of Behemian ancestry. He is a member of the Odd Fellows and the Modern Woodmen of America, and since 1916 has been a member and president of the Agenda High School Board. Emma Havel was born in Cuba, Kansas, February 12, 1877, of Bohemian ancestry. She is a member of the Royal Neighbors of America.

Upon his graduation from public school at Agenda in 1916, Mr. Houdek entered the Agenda High School, being graduated in 1921. He was a member of the basketball and track teams in high school. Later Mr. Houdek attended the Concordia School of Business and Commerce, receiving a diploma. There he was a member of the basketball team.

In 1923 Mr. Houdek became cashier of the State Bank of Cuba, Kansas, and from 1925 until 1928 was manager of the Narka, Kansas, Gas and Oil Company. Since the last date he has been assistant cashier of the Hubbell Bank. He is agent for the National Union Fire Insurance Company, the Southern Surety and Massachusetts Protective (Masonic) Insurance Company.

On July 30, 1930, Mr. Houdek was married to Viola Ann Kern at Stanton, Nebraska. She was born at Cedar Rapids June 15, 1907 (*See Nebraskana*).

Mr. Houdek is a Democrat, and received the nomination for county clerk in 1926. He served as city clerk of Narka, Kansas, during 1926-27. He is a member of the Methodist Church, the Modern Woodmen of America, the Ancient Free and Accepted Masons) the Eastern Star (worthy patron, 1931), and the Nebraskana Society. He was made an entered apprentice Mason in April, 1925, and was raised to the sublime degree of Master Mason in August, 1925. He enjoys tennis, while his hobby is baseball. Residence: Hubbell.

Viola Ann Houdek

Viola Ann Houdek, teacher, was born at Cedar Rapids, Nebraska, June 15, 1907, daughter of Clarence C. and Ida (Noh) Kern. Her father was born in Colfax County, Nebraska, July 24, 1882, and is a real estate and livestock auctioneer of German and English descent. His wife, Ida, was born in Colfax County, Nebraska, February 20, 1882, is a member of the Womans Club and active in Sunday School and church work.

Mrs. Houdek attended Stanton grade school, and was graduated from Stanton High School in 1925. In 1930 she received the Bachelor of Arts degree from Doane College. She was a student at Colorado State Teachers College the summer of 1926, and at the University of Nebraska the summer of 1929. She was graduated from Doane College magna cum laude, with the title of Doane Scholar, as a member of Beta Lamba Sigma for special work in biology, as a member of Doane A Capella Choir, as a member of the Modern Language Club, as assistant in psychology, and a member and cabinet officer of the Young Woman's Christian Association. She is a member of Phi Sigma Tau, and was a member of the woman's tennis team at Doane. At high school she received a letter in basketball.

During 1925 and 1926 she taught in the rural schools of Stanton County, and during 1928 and 1929 assisted in the psychology department of Doane College. She was also library assistant. At the present time she is teacher of English, Latin and music in the Hubbell High School. She is a member of the Nebraska State Teachers Association and a member of the Classical Teachers Association.

On July 30, 1930, she was married to Edward Charles Houdek. (*See Nebraskana*) at Stanton. Mr. Houdek was born in Republic County, Kansas, and is assistant cashier of the Hubbell Bank.

Mrs. Houdek is a member of the Congregational Church, the Red Cross, Eastern Star, the Nebraskana Society, and the Parent Teachers Association. She enjoys basketball, while her hobby is reading. Residence: Hubbell.

Frank Houfek

Frank Houfek was born at Prague, Saunders County, Nebraska, October 8, 1886, the son of John and Rose (Mach) Houfek. His father, who is a retired farmer, was born at Vilimov, Bohemia, May 19, 1860. His mother was born at Cimone, Bohemia, September 12, 1860.

Mr. Houfek attended rural schools in Dodge County, and later was a student at Fremont Normal College, Fremont, Nebraska. He owns and farms 140 acres of Saunders County land, and is active in civic affairs at Prague. A Republican, he is at the present time, county commissioner of Saunders County, serving his second term.

He is a member of The Nebraskana Society, Modern Woodmen of America, Knights of Pythias, and the Presbyterian Church at Prague. He is serving as moderator of school district number 85 at this time.

On September 24, 1908, he was united in marriage with Mary Houfek at Prague. Mrs. Houfek, who is of Bohemian descent, was born at Weston, August 1, 1887. Their children are: Emil J., born July 29, 1909; Adolph, born July 17, 1911; Alice E., born February 2, 1914; and Sylvia, born May 13, 1918. One son is connected with an Omaha firm and the other son is a farmer. The girls are in school. Residence: Prague.

Willis Lorenzo House

Born at Waucoma, Iowa, May 25, 1856, Willis L. House is the son of John Nelson and Dency (Hunt) House. The former was born in New York on May 28, 1810, and the latter on May 11, 1817. John Nelson House died at Belvidere, Nebraska, January 31, 1882, and his wife on March 21, 1879.

Willis L. House has been a resident of Nebraska since 1872, when he came here with his parents, who were pioneer settlers. He has farmed continuously since early manhood, and is the owner of extensive farm lands.

He was married to Jennie James at Beatrice, Nebraska, on September 1, 1880, and to their union were born thirteen children, eleven of whom are living: Charles, born May 13, 1882, married Bessie Weaver; Clarence, born March 13, 1883; May, born March 13, 1886, who married Will Kenney, and died December 20, 1918; Bertha, born October 3, 1887, who married Oscar Weaver; Alice, born December 22, 1888, who married Louis Northrup; Louis, born March 9, 1890, who married Delia Harpe; Edna, born December 13, 1891; Ernest, born July 3, 1893, who died September 24, 1893; Laura, born June 14, 1896, who married Edward Arndt; Nettie, born November 28, 1897; Lena, born June 20, 1899, who married Paul Little; Ruth, born March 6, 1903; and Roy, born April 29, 1906, who married Gladys Fritchie. Mrs. House was born at Ebensburg, Pennsylvania, December 19, 1860.

Mr. House is a member of the Christian Church and The Nebraskana Society. Residence: Belvidere.

William Alvin Housel

William Alvin Housel, a leading professional man at Broken Bow, Nebraska, has been a resident of this state for the past 56 years and since 1904, has been engaged in the practice of dentistry. He was born at Stockholm, Nebraska, July 15, 1875, the son of Gardner and Mary Jane (Cook) Housel. His father, who was a farmer and stockman, was born in New Jersey, September 18, 1848, and died at San Benito, Texas, November 10, 1929. His mother, whose ancestry is English, was born at New York, December 2, 1854.

Dr. Housel was graduated from the high school at Ansley, Nebraska, in 1896, and received the D. D. S. degree at the University of Nebraska. He is affiliated with the Christian Church at Broken Bow and holds membership in The Nebraskana Society. His hobby is hunting. During the late war he did volunteer dental work for soldiers in his community and purchased Liberty bonds. Dr. Housel came to Custer County in 1879.

On September 4, 1900, he was married at Lincoln, Nebraska, to Florence Loretta Ford. Mrs. Housel, whose ancestry is English and Irish, was born at Blue Hill, Nebraska, April 8, 1881. Six children were born to this marriage: Alice, July 30, 1902, who married Roswell Jennings Bohner; Robert, born December 23, 1905, who married Grace Irene Lutgen; Dorothy, November 24, 1908, who married David Marcellus Witter; Lucile, January 17, 1911; Walter, October 10, 1915, who died March 4, 1916; Raymond, April 16, 1917. Robert is a practicing dentist and Alice teaches in kindergarten. He is a progressive Democrat. Residence: Broken Bow. Bow.

Ensley Clinton Houston

For half a century, Ensley Clinton Houston, banker, scientific farmer, writer, public speaker and legislator, has been identified with the progress of Burt County and northeast Nebraska. He was born on a farm in Monroe County, Indiana, January 8, 1861, the son of Clinton N. and Elizabeth A. (Woods) Houston.

The Houston family lineage has been traced to 1450, the most remote ancestor being House Son of Dublin, Ireland. The careers of the members of this family have been turbulent and identified with a number of the epic movements of the Old World as well as the Virginia colonies.

As a result of bitter religious dissensions, Alfred Houston came to Jamestown, April 12, 1612. His brother, Abner, embarked for the New World in 1616. The family later moved to what is now Fairfax on the Potomac. Members went into Pennsylvania as pioneers, went into the Shenandoah valley and formed a substantial portion of the pioneers led by Daniel Boone in settling Kentucky. E. C. Houston's ancestors went to Bloomington, Indiana, in 1825.

E. C. Houston attended the public schools of Indiana, and spent two years at the University of Indiana. He taught one year in the Indiana public schools and came to Nebraska in 1881. His first job was in the lumber yard of Thomas & Darst. He received the sum of $35 a month and held this job four years.

He started in the lumber business in 1885. In the early nineties he purchased his first farm and has since acquired three others. These he has continuously operated, is a pioneer sheep feeder and is deeply interested in the co-operative creamery idea. In the fall of 1919, he disposed of all of his interests except banking and agricultural holdings.

With all the movements to promote the welfare of Burt county, Mr. Houston has been closely identified. He has been an advocate of good roads and improved methods of production. He was a charter member of the Tekamah Volunteer Fire Department, president of the Burt County Fair Association, during the World's Fair, when Burt county exhibited and received a gold medal for her agricultural exhibit in 1892. He served as mayor of Tekamah, and made a record for economy and efficiency.

A firm believer in co-operation, he has been interested in all the associations for the betterment of farmers. He is a charter member of the Farmers' Elevator company of Tekamah, a director in the Farmers' Mutual Fire Insurance company and director in the Farmers' Independent Telephone company, and helped organize the Farm Bureau.

As state senator, he championed public road improvement, economy and efficiency. He was chosen for this position without solicitation on his part. Likewise he was

ENSLEY CLINTON HOUSTON

Heyn—Omaha

selected for presidential elector in 1920, selected to make the race for congress in the Third district on the Republican ticket in 1926, and urged to be a candidate for governor in 1932 on a business efficiency platform.

He is a 33rd degree Mason, Knight Templar and Shriner, and is affiliated with the Presbyterian Church, belongs to the State Historical Society, the Nebraskana Society, and the Old Settlers and Pioneer Associations of Burt county. His college fraternity is Phi Gamma Delta.

On June 4, 1885, he married Jennie Templeton Houston, daughter of R. A. Templeton, pioneer stockman and land owner of Burt county. Mrs. Houston was born at Mt. Pleasant, Iowa, October 23, 1864. They have one son, Richard Templeton Houston, born May 8, 1887. He attended Indiana University, and is now engaged in the sheep business in Colorado. There are two grandchildren, Jack Houston 17 years of age, who was graduated from Tekamah high school, 1931, as valedictorian of his class, and entered the University of Nebraska in September. Mary Jane Houston is 20 years of age. She was graduated of Christian College, Columbia, Missouri, in 1931, and was valedictorian of her class. She will finish her college career with two years at Northwestern University.

Mrs. Houston has taken a prominent part in the club, social and charitable movements of Burt county. She has aided and assisted her husband in his public work in every way. The Burt county chapter of the Red Cross was organized May 15, 1917, at Tekamah, with branches at Craig, Oakland, Lyons, Decatur and Bertha. Mrs. Houston was made president and held the office throughout the war period. The Burt county chapter was awarded a Red Cross flag by State Chairman F. W. Judson for having obtained the largest per cent of membership in 1917. Amounts aggregating $150,000 were furnished and Mrs. Houston acknowledged the co-operation of practically every man, woman and child in Burt County. The Tekamah chapter went over the top on practically every call, and made enviable record in all departments of the relief work. Residence: Tekamah. (Photograph on Page 573).

Everett Allen Houston

One of the distinguished lawyers of Knox County, Nebraska, is Everett Allen Houston who was born at Marion, Iowa, August 26, 1857, and for the past 47 years has been engaged in the practice of law at Niobrara, Nebraska. His father, Alexander P. Houston, who was a farmer, was born at Indianapolis, Indiana, April 14, 1833, and died at Cedar Rapids, Iowa, January 12, 1912. His mother, Catherine (Beckner) Houston was born at Williamsburg, Pennsylvania, February 9, 1834, and died at Coggon, Iowa, March 25, 1905.

Mr. Houston attended Cornell College in Iowa where he was a member of the Miltonian Literary Society. He is city attorney of Niobrara, is chairman of the Red Cross there, and holds membership in the Nebraskana Society, the Nebraska State Historical Society, and the Masons.

On December 29, 1886, he was married to Sarah A. McCulla at Niobrara. Mrs. Houston, who was born at Buffalo, New York, July 28, 1850, was a teacher in high school, served as a member of the board of education, and was leader in her community for many years; she died at Niobrara, August 8, 1926. Two children were born to them; Ruth Alice, September 12, 1887, who died June 2, 1930; and Everett T., November 14, 1893, who is a graduate of the University of Nebraska and is now a lawyer in Nebraska. He served in the U. S. Army for 18 months during the World War. Residence: Niobrara.

Frank A. Houston

For over thirty years Frank A. Houston has taken an active part in political and civic affairs at Fairbury, Nebraska. He was born at Wamo, Kansas, March 31, 1874, the son of John and Mary (Carr) Houston. His father, who was a master mechanic for the Union Pacific,

was born in County Tyrone, Ireland, May 15, 1823, and died at Zeandale, Kansas, July 27, 1901. His mother was born in County Tyrone, May 15, 1829, and died at Fairbury, May 29, 1918.

Mr. Houston received his education in the public schools and the Manhattan Business College. He has been clerk of the Rock Island Railroad, director of the First National Bank of Fairbury, secretary and director of the Fairbury Building & Loan Association. He is now a bonded abstractor and engaged in farm and city loans. He is a member of the Baptist Church of Fairbury; Chamber of Commerce; Young Men's Christian Association and the Nebraskana Society. He is treasurer of the Red Cross, and is a 32nd degree Mason.

He was married to Jessie Viola Davis, June 19, 1899, at Fairbury. Mrs. Houston was born at Fairbury, October 27, 1880; they have one daughter, Lucile, born April 1, 1901.

Mr. Houston has served as councilman, mayor, county clerk, registrar of deeds, and clerk of the district court in Jefferson County. Residence: Fairbury.

Harry Joseph Houston

One of Nebraska's leading business men and executives is Harry Joseph Houston of Plainview who has taken a prominent place in community and state commercial affairs. He was born at Plainview, December 9, 1899, the son of Walter Joseph and Clara (Michaelson) Houston. His father, who was a merchant at Plainview for 10 years prior to his death, was born at Hopkinton, Iowa, November 11, 1866, and died at Plainview, August 22, 1922; he was manager of the Dymond Simmons Hardware Company for the state of Colorado for many years, was mayor of Plainview 10 years, and was a leader in civic improvements at Plainview where he took part in promoting a city park, library, and other city establishments; his father, J. N. Houston, who was an influential and well-to-do business man, was descended from English ancestors who settled at Dover, Maine.

His mother, who is an active member of the Plainview Woman's Club, was born at Farnhamville, Iowa, February 26, 1876, of Norwegian and English ancestry. Her mother came to America in 1865 and settled at Chicago, Illinois.

Mr. Houston attended the public schools of Denver, Colorado, and Plainview, graduating from the high school at Plainview in 1918. He was a student at the University of Nebraska for a year, was a student at the Gem City College of Business Administration for a time, and was in an officer's training school during the World War. He received letters in athletics in high school.

He served as cashier of the First National Bank of Plainview for six years, was a merchant there for seven years, and is now *secretary* and *manager* of the *Associated Stores Wholesale Grocery Company*. He is an active member of the Federation of Nebraska Retailers, the Plainview Lion's Club, and the Plainview Commercial Club. He is affiliated with the First Congregational Church, has been a member of the Nebraska Red Cross for a number of years, is an officer in the Plainview Masonic Lodge, and is chairman of the activities committee of the Lion's Club. He holds membership in the National Travel Club, the National Geographic Society and the Nebraskana Society.

Mr. Houston's social Clubs are the Norfolk Country Club and the Plainview Country Club of which he is a director. He was winner of the North Nebraska Golf Tournament at O'Neill, Nebraska in 1930, was runner-up in 1931, and was champion of the northeast Nebraska Golf Tournament at Tilden, Nebraska and the Plainview Invitation Tournament in 1931. His hobby is experimental work in retailing, working with the United States Department of Commerce.

On April 22, 1922, he was married to Winifred Seabury Holbert at Plainview. Mrs. Houston, who is a musician, was born at Plainview, July 28, 1899. Her father, who was a native of New York, was president of the First National Bank for 42 years, and is a 32nd degree Mason and Shrine member; his ancestry was Scotch. Their son, Donald, was born July 10, 1924. Residence: Plainview.

William Brighton Houston

William Brighton Houston, pioneer farmer of Nebraska, was born at Buckinghamshire, England, October 1, 1869, the son of James Drummond and Mary (Lidington) Houston. His father, who was a farmer, was born at Edinburgh, Scotland, June 20, 1841, and died at York, Nebraska, June 1, 1923; he came to America in 1870. His mother was born in England, and died at York, February 14, 1920.

Mr. Houston attended public school and a business college. He has lived in York County for sixty years, and is a member of the Parent-Teachers' Association, the First Methodist Church, and the Nebraskana Society. He is a Mason, was active in the Red Cross during the World War, and was formerly a member of the Modern Woodmen of America. A Republican, he has served as township treasurer and assessor.

On October 1, 1903, he was married to Mary Jayne Sovereign at York. Mrs. Houston, who was born in York County, February 22, 1877, was a teacher for several years prior to her marriage. She is a member of the Daughters of the American Revolution. Their five children are: Helen, born February 12, 1905, who married Lloyd B. Zarr; Brighton, born July 6, 1910, who married Olive Denney; Margaret, born April 14, 1912; Milton, born September 10, 1917; and David, born June 25, 1920. Brighton was awarded second place in the state music contest two consecutive years, and is now studying music in New York. Residence: York.

George Thomas Houtby

George Thomas Houtby was born at Winterset, Iowa, October 4, 1875, and for the past 40 years has engaged in farming in Valley County, Nebraska. Edward C. Houtby, his father, who is a farmer, was born in Staten, Wisconsin, June 23, 1851, the son of English parents who came to this country from England in 1849. His mother, Mary Ann (Young) Houtby, was born at Barnesville, Ohio, April 1, 1853, and died at North Loup, Nebraska, September 27, 1930.

Mr. Houtby completed his education in 1880 and immediately began farming near Ord, Nebraska where he is now a member of the local school board, the Modern Woodmen of America, and the Red Cross. During the World War he took part in loan drives and purchased bonds.

Of his marriage to Hattie Grout, who was born at Winterset, December 20, 1873, and died at North Loup, October 15, 1909, three children were born: Mabel, November 10, 1899, who married Clifford Chubbuck; Guile, March 4, 1902, who married Eileen Rasmussen; and Hattie, October 15, 1909.

Mr. Houtby was united in marriage to Louise C. Newman at Ord, November 30, 1910. Their children are: Helen, born April 27, 1912; Chester, born May 11, 1914; and Frances, born September 1, 1923. Residence: Ord.

Herman Franklyn Hovland

Herman F. Hovland, prominent merchant at Lincoln, for the past 30 years, was born at Blanchardsville, Wisconsin, September 19, 1871, the son of Peter Johan and Martha (Soley) Hovland. His father, who was a cobbler, was born in Norway, and died at Madison, South Dakota, February, 1912; he was a Lutheran layman in Wisconsin in the early days. His mother was born in Norway, and died at Blanchardsville, in 1900.

Mr. Hovland attended elementary schools in Wisconsin, and was a student at the state normal school at Madison for three years. He is now president and a stockholder in the Sardeson-Hovland Company, a Delaware Corporation operating stores in several states. He holds membership in: Lincoln Chamber of Commerce; Kiwanis Club of Lincoln; the University Club; Lincoln Country Club; and the Young Men's Christian Association.

His religious affiliation is with the First Presbyterian Church of Lincoln, of which he is an elder. His favorite recreation is golfing. During the World War, Mr. Hovland was active in Red Cross drives and was a leader in war relief work. He holds membership in the Nebraskana Society, and is a member of the Republican Party.

He was united in marriage to Abbie Josephine Brundin at Albert Lea, Minnesota, June 19, 1895.

They have two children: Ruth, and Helen. Ruth married C. E. Swanson, who is in partnership with her father. Residence: Lincoln.

Albert Tompkins Howard

Born at Weeping Water, Nebraska, April 6, 1923, Albert Tompkins Howard is the son of Thomas Mentor and Deborah (Tompkins) Howard. His father, who was a real estate and insurance dealer, was born at Perry, New York, December 26, 1849, and died at Scottsbluff, Nebraska, December 4, 1918. His mother was born in Ireland, July 2, 1859, and with her family settled at Batavia, New York in 1871.

Mr. Howard attended grade schools at Weeping Water, Nebraska, and in 1910 was graduated from the Scottsbluff High School, where he was president of his senior class. He was employed as a clerk in the post office at Scottsbluff, 1910-12, was assistant post master, 1915-17, was chemist for the Great Western Sugar Company, 1918-19, and engaged in the grain and livestock business in Wyoming, 1920-25. Since 1925 he has been the owner of the Howard Greenhouse & Flower Shop at Scottsbluff.

During the World War Mr. Howard served as second lieutenant in the Field Artillery, and was instructor in the Officers Training Camp of Camp Zacharay Taylor in Kentucky. He is a member of the American Legion, has been a member of the Lions Club at Scottsbluff since 1925, and is affiliated with the Community Congregational Church at Scottsbluff. He holds membership in the Central Parent Teachers Association, the Masonic Lodge, and the Red Cross.

His marriage to Nelle Antha Taylor occurred at Denver, Colorado, June 21, 1919. Mrs. Howard was born at Erickson, Nebraska, October 11, 1890. She is the daughter of Dr. Edwin L. and Nellie (Wanser) Taylor. Mrs. Howard is a member of the Parent Teachers Association, and worthy matron of the Eastern Star. They have one son, Billy Reed, born May 26, 1922. Mr. Howard is a Republican and served as mayor of Scottsbluff in 1931. He is a member of the Nebraskana Society. Residence: Scottsbluff.

Edgar Howard

Edgar Howard is now serving his tenth year as a member of the United States congress, representing the Third District of Nebraska. He is a practical newspaper man, knows the value of publicity, yet no one has ever been able to induce him to write a biographical sketch of his life. The following sketch was written by a Nebraska newspaper friend of years:

He was born at Osceola, Iowa, September 16, 1858. His father was James Dakin Howard, a native of Ohio. His mother was Martha (Daniel) Howard, of Virginia.

He attended the village public schools in Glenwood, Iowa, and when he was expelled once too often, for mis-

EDGAR HOWARD

chievous conduct, never vicious, he was placed in a private school, the Western Collegiate Institute at Glenwood. Later he attended the Iowa College of Law at Des Moines. He was too much of a dreamer to become much of a scholar. I once heard him tell the members of a graduating class that he might have become splendidly educated during his many years of schooling, if he had only looked in his text books as earnestly as he had looked out of the school house windows.

At the age of fourteen years he began work as a printer's devil on the *Weekly Opinion,* at Glenwood, Iowa. Next he became a cub on the night shift of the *Iowa State Register.* Soon he was able to win a "case" on that sheet. Quickly he mastered the handwriting of Rhet Clarkson, who had a national reputation as being able to write a more unreadable hand that Horace Greeley. Only two other printers could with certainty decipher the handwriting of Clarkson, and when those three happened to be indisposed at the same time—well, the *Register* would appear the next morning without any of Rhet Clarkson's brilliant editorials.

By nature nomadic, Edgar Howard was soon caught by the lure of travel which held him fast. As a tramp printer and writer he visited all the great cities, finally settling down in one spot for more than a year. This was at Dayton, Ohio, where during that time he held the post of city editor on the *Dayton Daily Herald.* His was the dream in common of practically all metropolitan printers and writers—the dream of some day owning and editing a country newspaper. His dream came true. In 1883, in association with Hon. George A. Magney, now a distinguished Omaha attorney, he purchased the *Papillion* (Nebraska) *Times.* Three years later he established the *Dundy Democrat* at Benkelman, Nebraska, returning three years later to his old newspaper love at Papillion. There he remained until 1900, when he purchased the *Weekly Telegram* at Columbus, which ten years ago became a daily, and of which he is still editor. His devotion to the country newspaper game may be best portrayed by recalling a sentence taken from the official Blue Book of Congress, wherein appear the biographies of all the members. Following his customary peculiarity, Mr. Howard had refused to write his own biography, but he did enject two or three sentences into a biography written by a friend. All the political offices, low and high, which he had ever held, were listed, to which sentence Mr. Howard added these words: "Holding contemporaneously with all these official places, the higher office of editor of a country newspaper, and still in that estate."

In 1884, he was united in marriage with Elizabeth Paisley Burtch, a Nebraska girl. Coming of Quaker stock, and of late years in the Episcopal fold, he entertains fixed and firm views regarding marriage and divorce. This is illustrated by a two-word sermon which he preached in his brief biography in the Blue Book of Congress. His two-word sermon appeared at the close of the statement regarding his marriage as follows: "Still married." His living children are Findley Burtch Howard, for eighteen years residing in Central and South America, and at present customs financial advisor to the Republic of Guatemala, having formerly held like posts with the Republics of San Salvador and Chile; Mary Howard Rex, wife of Harry Rex of Creston, Iowa; Helen Howard Coen, wife of Clarence Coen, also of Creston, Iowa.

His first plunge into the political pond was at Lincoln, at the Democratic convention in 1890. He was a delegate from Sarpy County, and was selected by his delegation to speak in favor of the nomination of William J. Bryan. When Mr. Bryan went to Washington, in December, 1891, he took Mr. Howard with him as his private secretary. In those days a congressman had to pay the salary of his secretary. Howard would not accept any salary from the poor young congressman, but remained on duty for some months, as long as his own slim purse would permit.

In 1894, he won the Democratic nomination in Sarpy County for representative and was elected, being in the legislature of 1895, the only man elected as a straight Democrat to either house. In 1895, he was elected probate judge of Sarpy County, and was re-elected in 1897. In 1900, he was the Democratic nominee for congress in the Omaha district, but did not receive the certificate of election. In 1916, he was elected as a Democrat to the office of lieutenant governor of Nebraska. In 1922 he was the Democratic nominee for congress in the Third Nebraska District, and was elected in a three-cornered contest with Hon. Robert Evans, Republican, and Hon. John Havekost, independent. He survived the Coolidge landslide in 1923 and in the Hoover snowstorm in 1930, was elected to a fifth term by a majority of more than 30,000, although the district gave an average majority of more than 10,00 to the Republican state nominees.

In the national congress Mr. Howard has particularly devoted himself to three lines of effort: (1) a square governmental deal for agriculture; (2) belated justice in behalf of American Indians; (3) hospitalization and ample compensation to veterans of all wars and generous treatment of their widows and orphans.

Regarding foreign affairs he often refers to himself as a "George Washington Democrat", opposed to anything which looks like mixing by the American government in the politics of Europe. One day I was with him in Paris, France. We attended a meeting called by one of the great international civic societies. Privately he had been asked to express his views regarding the League of Nations, but had declined to do so. At this meeting, attended by men from more than a score of the nations of the world, he was thrice asked to publicly express an opinion which he had declined to express even privately. The request was repeated again and again. At last this prairie congressman yielded reluctantly, saying: "In a large measure I am regarding myself at this moment as a guest in the house of a friend. It is true that I am paying the freight, and yet I have hesitated to speak words which might distress the people of this great and ancient nation. However, since you have practically commanded me to speak, my reply to your question will contain but few words. Frankly I shall tell you that in my eyes the League of Nations is not more nor less than a wet nurse to the military ambitions of France." I shall never forget the consternation of that assembly following that statement by the Nebraskan, but through it all there stood Howard, calm and serene, smiling so winsomely that when he had spoken his thanks to his hosts for their hospitality of the day he retired amid plaudits which only moments before I had thought might be shouts of censure.

How shall I describe the personal appearance of Edgar Howard? It is always the same, always in black or grey clothes, with frock coat of the Chesterfield period. Smooth face, grey hair, speaking eyes, often taken for black, but indeed intensely blue. Always he wears a large black hat. Untutored persons have frequently referred to this hat as a "Bryan Hat." Absurd reference! The largest hat Bryan ever wore was a Fedora, while Howard's hat has a six-inch crown and a five-inch brim. Men carelessly have said that Howard apes William J. Bryan in dress. Impossible! Edgar Howard could not ape another if he should try. One day I asked Edgar why he always wore that black hat and his long hair. He was silent for a moment, and then he gently replied: "Perhaps only as a bit of ritualistic worship at the memory shrine of my Quaker forefathers."

When Edgar Howard gave me permission to write his biography for this official history of Nebraska, he exacted my promise that it would contain nothing laudatory. I have tried to obey his request literally, and yet I feel that he will not be offended if I shall append here the closing paragraph in a fine article recently appearing in that splendid magazine, *Time,* which carried a full page devoted to the Nebraska congressman and his work in the house of representatives. The closing paragraph in that article I deem particularly appropriate to reproduce at the close of my own estimate of my friend. That closing paragraph in the Time article ran as follows:

Impartial house observers rate Edgar Howard thus:

"A fine example of what congressmen were in the last century, plus a pointed, ubiquitous sense of humor. An adept at floor strategy, able to transcend House rules of debate by his witty, original methods, thus an insidious protagonist of minority measures. Perhaps the greatest 'character' in the House, and the most universally loved congressman." Residence: Columbus. (Photograph on Page 576).

Glenn Howard

Glenn Howard, editor and publisher at Ashland, Nebraska, was born at Pine Island, Minnesota, February 8, 1870. His father, Harry Green Howard, who was born at Columbus, Pennsylvania, April 11, 1831, and died at Marshall, Minnesota, January 28, 1890, was a farmer; he held membership in the Grand Army of the Republic; Isaac Howard an ancestor, came to America in 1722, from England, and members of the family served in colonial wars, the Revolution, and the Civil War. His mother was born at La Valle, Sauk County, Wisconsin.

Mr. Howard received his education in Minnesota. For the past 17 years he has been editor and publisher of the *Ashland Gazette* and has established himself in the newspaper world as a progressive editor. From 1893 to 1909, he was editor of the *Advance* at Alden, Minnesota, was editor of the *Sentinel* at Hooper, Nebraska, 1909-13. He has always been prominent in political and civic affairs, and has held the following positions: chairman of the Republican State Central Committee for seven years, Minnesota; member of the city council 14 years; mayor at Alden; member of the school board; and president of the Chamber of Commerce at Ashland, Nebraska.

Mr. Howard holds membership in the Nebraska Press Association, the National Editorial Association, the Red Cross, Parent-Teachers' Association at Ashland, and the Nebraskana Society. He is a member of the Young Men's Christian Association, is past president of the Ashland Chamber of Commerce, and is affiliated with the First Congregational Church at Ashland. His social club is the Ashland Golf Club, and his recreations include reading, hunting, fishing, and camping. His fraternal organizations are: Modern Woodmen of America; Pomegranite Lodge Number 110 of the Masons. During the World War, Mr. Howard was active in Red Cross work and assisted in loan drives. He has lived in Nebraska for 20 years. For two years he was secretary of the Dodge County Stock Show Association.

His marriage to Sarah Minnette Hulbert was solemnized at Wells, Faribault County, Minnesota, October 5, 1892; Mrs. Howard was born at Wells, June 9, 1874. Their children are: Harold, born December 9, 1894, who married Zelma Heine; Genevieve, born February 3, 1896, who married Joy A. McCartney; Sylvia, born April 25, 1905, who attended Doane College; and Dorothy, born March 13, 1908, a student at the University of Nebraska where she is a member of Kappa Delta and Theta Sigma Phi. She is associate editor of the *Ashland Gazette*. Dr. H. A. Howard is a dentist at Ashland, is a graduate of the University of Nebraska where he was elected to membership in Xi Psi Phi, and is past master of Pomegranite Lodge Number 110 of the Ancient Free and Accepted Masons. He is secretary of the Ashland Commercial Club. Residence: Ashland.

John Otis Howard

John Otis Howard was born at Nemaha, Nebraska, December 24, 1892, son of Thomas Jefferson and Martha Frances (Martin) Howard. His father was born in Polk County, Iowa, September 24, 1872, and has been a resident of Nebraska for more than sixty years. His mother was born at Shubert, Nebraska, October 22, 1876, and died there, July 10, 1929.

From early boyhood Mr. Howard has been engaged as a farmer. On December 2, 1911, he was married to Mabel Anna Boatman at Falls City, Nebraska. Mrs. Howard

was born at Nemaha, September 22, 1893. There are no children.

Mr. Howard is a Republican, and while not an office seeker, is active in the work of his party. He is more interested in his farms than anything else, but does enjoy hunting and reading. Residence: Nemaha.

Warren Harold Howard

Warren H. Howard was born at Reynolds, Nebraska, October 17, 1891, the son of Frank Albert and Margaret Elizabeth (Wood) Howard. His father, who was a grain merchant, was born at Washburn, Illinois, February 20, 1864, and died at Kansas City, Missouri, December 23, 1926; his ancestry was English. His mother, who was for many years a school teacher, was born at Perry, Ohio, April 13, 1864. She is of English and Dutch descent.

Mr. Howard attended Omaha grade schools and was later graduated from Omaha High School. Awarded his LL. B. degree in 1914 at the University of Nebraska, he was a member of Beta Theta Phi, Phi Delta Phi, and the Innocents. He played football, 1912-13-14, basketball, 1913-14, and took part in track events, 1913-14, at the University of Nebraska.

Admitted to the bar at Omaha, in February, 1915, he has been engaged in law practice there since that date. He is secretary of the Nebraska Land Investment Company; treasurer of the Lodgepole Lumber & Grain Company; and director of the Gardner-Miller Coal Company. He has lived in Nebraska all his life.

His marriage to Ruth C. Gould was solemnized at Omaha, April 9, 1917. Mrs. Howard, whose ancestry is English, was born at Omaha, December 16, 1891. They have three children: Suzanne, born June 30, 1921; Warren F., born February 20, 1924; and David G., born November 2, 1925.

Mr. Howard was lieutenant-colonel in the high school cadets; he was a member of the Officers Training Corps, Field Artillery, of the United States Army in 1918. He is a member of the American Legion, the Nebraska State Bar Association, the Omaha Bar Association, and the Nebraskana Society. He is a Mason. He is a member of the University Club of Omaha, and is affiliated with All Saint's Episcopal Church at Omaha. Residence: Omaha.

Herbert Howarth

Herbert Howarth, successful farmer and stockman at Exeter, Nebraska, has lived in Fillmore County for many years, and has been prominent in the life of his community. He was born near Friend, Nebraska, August 29, 1880, the son of Walter and Rebecca Howarth.

His father, who was born at Bolton, England, September 3, 1849, was a mechanic and draftsman in an iron foundry in England for several years, and in 1872 moved to this country. A little later he took up a homestead in Saline County, Nebraska, where he was a farmer and carpenter during the summer months and taught in the rural schools during the winter. Always prominent in the advancement of the state, he served as a member of the Grasshopper Relief Committee, (1874), was justice of the peace (1896), and was county supervisor (1892).

In 1877, he became a naturalized citizen of the United States and the following year returned to his home in England, where he married Rebecca Howarth. In 1884 he sold his homestead in Saline County and purchased land in Fillmore County in 1882, where he remained until his death at Exeter, March 22, 1926. He was influential in Fillmore County, and served as a member of various school boards and committees on public welfare. During the World War he assisted in loan drives. He acted as state representative in 1915, was the first president of the Exeter Elevator Company in 1911, continuing in that capacity until 1922.

Of his marriage seven children were born: Edith Alice,

who married James Francis Horne; Herbert; Emily, who is active in community affairs at Exeter; Anne, a registered nurse at Lincoln, Nebraska; Walter Jr., a banker at Friend, Nebraska. Two sons died in infancy.

Herbert Howarth attended rural schools of Fillmore County and was a student at the Lincoln Business College. He was employed by the Nye Schneider Fowler Company in 1909, at Martland, Nebraska, was employed by the Farmers & Merchants Bank at Exeter, in 1915, and since then has been a farmer and stockman. He is now a director of the Exeter Elevator Company, and farms land consisting of 240 acres, his father's original farm.

Mr. Howarth was a director in the Farm Bureau for two years, and in 1926 served as president of that organization. He holds membership in the Modern Woodmen of America, the Knights of Pythias, and the Nebraskana Society. He assisted in loan drives during the World War. He is interested in all athletic activities while his hobby is reading.

His marriage to Nell Clare Pflug occurred at Council Bluffs, Iowa, November 6, 1923. Mrs. Howarth, who was born at Exeter, November 8, 1884, was a teacher for 17 years before her marriage. Her mother, Hannah (Bayles) Pflug was born at Lyons, New York, and died at Exeter, in 1908. Her father, Jacob Pflug, was born in Milwoukee, and was a soldier in the 9th New York Heavy Artillery. At the close of the Civil war he came to Nebraska in 1865, and was a pioneer leader in Otoe County; he was engaged in the implement business for many years, served on the Exeter School Board, and was generally prominent in the early history of the state.

Hannah (Bayles) Pflug was the daughter of Dr. Charles Bayles, a graduate of Yale University, and was the great granddaughter of John Van Derbilt, a soldier in the American Revolution.

Among Mr. Howarth's ancestors were Richard and Adam Howarth whose father served as a British soldier under Wellington, at Waterloo; their ancestry traces back to the English nobility, Lord Willoughby. Residence: Exeter. (Photograph in Album).

Barton Church Howe

Barton Church Howe, banker, was born at Howe, Nebraska, December 9, 1882. He is the son of Herbert Rhodes Howe, pioneer farmer and banker, who came to Nebraska from England and at the time of his death in April, 1930, had been a resident of Nemaha County for more than fifty years. He was married to Mamie Francis Guerelle, at Howe, January 28, 1880. There were three children, Barton, the subject of this sketch, Hoxie N. and John Sedgwick.

Barton C. Howe attended the public and high school of Auburn and was graduated from the latter. On October 26, 1910, he was married to Mary Janet Fraser, at Storm Lake, Iowa. Mrs. Howe was born at Elizabeth, Jo Daviess County, Illinois, June 13, 1881. She is of Scotch descent. A member of P. E. O., she has served as its president and as state delegate. She is also a member of the Delphian Society and of the Auburn Woman's Club.

Their son, Marshall Church, was born November 29, 1912. He attended Kemper Military School at Booneville, Missouri. Upon his graduation from high school he was salutatorian of his class, and during his entire time in school he was extremely active in debate and a member of the debate societies. He is a member of the Hi-Y organization and has been its delegate to various conventions.

At the age of 16 Barton C. Howe entered the First National Bank of which his father was one of the original stockholders. He has continued with the organization since that time.

Mr. Howe is a Republican. Active in all of the affairs of his community, he is a member of the Nebraska Y. M. C. A., the Presbyterian Church, of which he is a deacon, the library board and the Chamber of Commerce. He is a charter member of the Kiwanis Club and is serving the third year as its secretary. A Mason and an Elk, he also holds membership in the Nebraska State Historical Society and the Nebraskana Society. He is interested in swimming, but his real hobby is kodaking. His social club is the Auburn Country Club. Residence: Auburn.

Edgar Franklin Howe

Edgar F. Howe was born at Owatonna, Minnesota, February 3, 1862, the son of LaFayette and Mary Jane (Tisdale) Howe. His father was a farmer and a carpenter, who served in the First Minnesota Volunteers in the Civil War. He was a descendent of John Howe, an Englishman who was the first settler in Marlborough, Massachusetts in 1638, and who was a selectman there. Gardner Howe, also an ancestor, was a lieutenant in the Revolutionary Army. He was born at Elyria, Ohio, July 3, 1824, and died at Fredericksburg, Iowa, in 1908. His mother was born in New York State in 1829.

Mr. Howe attended the public schools of Fredericksburg and Nashua, Iowa. He has been connected with the Fairmont Creamery Company since 1886, first living at Fairmont, Nebraska. In 1894 he moved to Crete, and in 1899 he settled at Omaha, Douglas County, Nebraska. Since 1903 he has been in charge of manufacturing and sales of the Fairmont Creamery Company, and is now vice president of this organization. He is president of the Don Lee Furniture Company of Omaha.

He was married at Hastings, Nebraska, on October 18, 1886 to Emma Miller. Mrs. Howe, whose parents came to Nebraska from Maryland, was born at Polo, Illinois, June 5, 1865. To their marriage six children were born: Harry, born January 19, 1889, who died March 13, 1894; Mae, born December 30, 1890, who died March 4, 1894; Donald, born September 6, 1893, who married Philip Chase; Edith, born September 2, 1898, who married John Kaemmeratin; and Marion, born October 27, 1902, who married Armand Gobiet.

Mr. Howe is a member of the Omaha Chamber of Commerce; and is a director in the United States Egg Society. He is a member of the Poultry Research Society of America, with headquarters at Chicago, is a member of the Independent Order of the Odd Fellows and the Modern Woodmen of America. He is a 32nd degree Mason. His social clubs are: Omaha Athletic Club; and Happy Hollow Club. Residence: Omaha.

Herbert Rhodes Howe

Herbert Rhodes Howe, pioneer banker and farmer of Nemaha County, Nebraska, was born at Chatteras, England, April 26, 1859. Both the maternal and paternal sides of his ancestry were English. As a boy he attended the country schools of Illinois, and later the Nebraska schools, after which he was graduated from the Nebraska City Episcopalian School, an organization which is now defunct.

A resident of Nebraska for over 50 years, Mr. Howe has had an interesting and varied life, and has always been active in the political and civic affairs of his community. During a short stay in Oklahoma he was one of the organizers and promoters of the K. T. highway, which now runs through the entire country. He was a member of the Good Roads Association in Nebraska in the early days when good roads were unknown and few people were interested in them.

A Republican, he was at one time a member of the Nebraska legislature for one term, and served several years as a member of the city council of Auburn. One of the original stockholders in the First National Bank, he served as president of the bank many years, and was a stockholder in various buildings in Auburn, and owned several sections of land in that vicinity.

He was united in marriage with Mamie Frances Guerelle, at Howe, Nemaha County, Nebraska, January 28, 1880. Mrs. Howe, whose ancestry is French, was born in Nemaha County in 1861. There are three children: Barton C., born December 9, 1882, who married Mary Janet Fraser; Hoxie N., born February, 1884, who married Alma R. Kleckner; and John Sedgwick, born December 10, 1897, who attended York College a year and was in the Naval Corps during the World War. He is married to Florence Hetrick.

Mr. Howe was at one time president of the Auburn Chamber of Commerce. He was a 32nd degree Mason, and a member of the Odd Fellows for several years. He was a member of the Episcopal Church at Auburn, and the Auburn Country Club. His favorite sport was golfing. Perhaps his greatest interest was his 50 acre apple orchard, situated outside of Auburn, which he planted 37 years ago and in which he took great pride. On April 7, 1930, he died after a life of service to his state and community.

Francis Singleton Howell

In public life since 1910, Francis S. Howell is an outstanding figure in the legal and political life of Nebraska. Born in Milton County, Georgia, July 17, 1863, he is the son of Singleton Gideon and Agnes Julia (Owsley) Howell. His father, born in Gwinnett County, Georgia, in 1825, was a planter of English and Welsh descent, his father, Evan Howell, having settled in the south in colonial days. He died at Duluth, Georgia, in 1878. Agnes (Owsley) Howell was born at Danville, Kentucky, April 18, 1825. Of Scotch, Irish and English descent, of the Bayne, Finley and Owsley families who came to America in 1652, 1688 and 1694 respectively. Many of her ancestors served in the Revolutionary War. She died May 20, 1898.

Francis S. Howell was graduated from the Atlanta public and high school in 1879, and attended Emory College, Oxford, Georgia, from 1880 to 1882. He is a member of the Phi Gamma and Chi Phi.

On January 9, 1887, he was united in marriage to Clara Julia Jones, at Norcross, Georgia. Mrs. Howell was born at Norcross, November 15, 1865. She was of Welsh and English ancestry, descended from settlers in America in the 16th century, and died at Omaha, September 24, 1927. To their union four children were born, Eunice, born September 8, 1888, married H. S. Pollard; Guy Robert, born July 10, 1890, served in the American Expeditionary Forces, and died on April 27, 1919, at Hoboken, N. J., upon his return to the United States; George L., born November 24, 1893, married Catherine Davenport; he is assistant manager of the Pittsburgh Plate Glass Company in Omaha: Frances Louise, born February 2, 1900, married Miles P. McSweeney.

Admitted to the practice of law at Ord, Nebraska, in May 1884, Mr. Howell has been consecutively member of the law firms of Redland & Howell, North Loup; Howell and Pratt and Howell and Spear, Albion; Davis and Howell, Blair; Jefferis and Howell, Omaha; Smith, Schall, Howell, Sheeban and Howard, Omaha; and Howell, Tunison and Joyner.

In 1910 he was made U. S. district attorney, serving until 1915; from January 3, 1928, to January 3, 1929, he was justice of the Supreme Court of Nebraska, and since January, 1930, he has been special assistant attorney general of Nebraska.

During the World War he was a participant in civilian war activities. He is a member of the American, Nebraska State and Omaha-Douglas County Bar Associations. Reared a Methodist he is not now affiliated with any church. He is a Mason and an Elk, and is a member of the Omaha Athletic Club. His favorite sport is baseball. Residence: Omaha.

Robert Beecher Howell

R. Beecher Howell, United States senator, was born in Adrian, Michigan, son of Andrew and Mary Adelia Beecher (Tower) Howell. The father was born in New York State in 1828 and died in Michigan in 1904. He was a lawyer, author and judge of the first judicial district in 1842 and died at Omaha in 1914.

Senator Howell attended public school at Adrian, and was graduated from the United States Naval Academy in 1885. In 1905 he was married to Allice Cullingham Chase at Denver, Colorado. She was born at Omaha in 1874. There is one son, James Sidney Cullingham, born in 1896.

During the Spanish-American War Mr. Howell held the rank of lieutenant junior grade, and during the World War was a lieutenant in the Naval Reserves. He is a member of the American Legion, the United Spanish War Veterans, the Masons and the Elks. He is a Republican and Presbyterian. His clubs are the Omaha Club and the Army and Navy Club of Washington, D. C. Residence: Omaha.

Frederick Hamilton Howey

Frederick Hamilton Howey, prominent in the banking business since 1887, has been a resident of Nebraska for the past 47 years. He was born in Ohio, December 9, 1868. His father, John Dagg Howey, who was born in Pennsylvania, November 21, 1831, and died at Lincoln, Nebraska, December 29, 1894, was a minister in the Presbyterian Church; he studied at Jefferson College in Pittsburg for four years, and was graduated from the Allegheny Seminary in 1858; his ancestry was Scotch Irish. His mother was born in Pennsylvania, August 15, 1835, and died at Beatrice, Nebraska, July 19, 1917.

Mr. Howey attended the public schools of Fairmont, Nebraska. In 1887 he began his career in banking as clerk in the State National Bank at Lincoln, and in 1897 was made vice president of the National Bank of Beatrice. He is now president of the First National Bank, Beatrice, the First State Savings Bank, and the State Bank of Liberty, Nebraska.

He served as treasurer of the Kiwanis Club at Beatrice for a number of years, was a member of the city school board for a time, and during the World War took an active part in loan drives. He holds membership in the Masons, Elks, Modern Woodmen of America, the Nebraskana Society, and the Beatrice Country Club. He is affiliated with the First Presbyterian Church of Beatrice and is a member of the University Club of Lincoln. His favorite sport is golfing.

His marriage to Eva Tamblyn was solemnized at Altona, Illinois, October 23, 1894. Mrs. Howey was born at Mason City, Illinois, February 3, 1870; she is descended from Cornelius C. Schoemaker of Revolutionary times. Their children are: Earle, born June 22, 1896, who is vice president of the First National Bank of Beatrice; Katharine, born July 28, 1897, who married Melvin Bekins; and Walden, born March 10, 1900, who married Gladys Sidles. Walden is engaged in the insurance business at Lincoln. Residence: Beatrice.

John M. Howie

John M. Howie, professor of mathematics at Nebraska Wesleyan University since 1924, was born near Bloomfield, Iowa, April 10, 1871, son of John and Hannah Olivia (Evans) Howie. John Howie, Sr., was born at Charlottetown, Prince Edward's Island, April 2, 1822, and died at Bloomfield, August 3, 1898. He was a farmer for many years, a member of the 3rd Iowa Cavalry in the Civil War, and a prominent Sunday School worker in his day. His father was Scotch, and came to America in 1820; was shipwrecked near the place where the Titantic was sunk. The Howie family has resided continuously since 1178 on the Lochgoin farm near Glasgow. Hannah Olivia Evans was born in Michigan, December 7, 1835, and died at Bloomfield, June 21, 1922. A homemaker, she was interested in art and was a carpet weaver of considerable ability. She was of Pennsylvania Dutch ancestry.

John Howie, Jr., attended country school, was graduated from Bloomfield elementary school in 1884, and from Bloomfield High School in 1887. He received his B. A. from Cotner University in 1896 (now Cotner College), his A. M., from the University of Nebraska in 1922, his A. M. from Columbia University in 1924; and an Ed. D. from Cotner College in 1930. He attended Southern Iowa Normal School, 1887-89, and was graduated in 1889, and was a graduate student at the University of Wisconsin in 1897. His fraternities include Phi Kappa Phi, Phi Delta Kappa, Pi Mu Epsilon and Kappa Sigma Pi, of which he is adviser as well as member. He played on the Cotner football team 3 years, and was captain one year.

From 1887-89, he was teacher at Southern Iowa Normal, from 1889-91, taught in country schools. From 1891-94 he taught at Cotner University. He was half-time instructor of mathematics at the Universities of Nebraska and Wisconsin 1894-95, 1895-97, and during 1897-98 had charge of the mathematic department of O'Clair High School, O'Clair, Wisconsin. He was head of the department of mathematics at Peru State Teachers College 1898-1922. During 1922-23 he was acting head of the mathematics department of Alma College, and since 1924 has been head of the mathematics department of Nebraska Wesleyan University. During the summers of 1923-24, he was professor of mathematics at the State Teachers College of Michigan and Colorado.

Professor Howie was married to Ida May Phillips at Yutan, Nebraska, June 18, 1894. Mrs. Howie was born at Yutan, April 3, 1875, and is of Welsh and Pennsylvania Dutch descent. They have one son, Clarence Alvia, born in 1895. He received his B. A. from Peru in 1916, his LL. B. from the University of Nebraska in 1922. He served as second lieutenant in the World War, and is now in the life insurance business.

Professor Howie is the author of a textbook in geometry. He is a Republican. At the present time he is a member of the First Methodist Episcopal Church of Lincoln. During 1918-19, he was active in army Y. M. C. A. work, and is still a member of the organization. His fraternal memberships include the Fraternal Aid Union, the Modern Woodmen of America, Royal Neighbors of America, the Masons and the Eastern Star. He is a member of the Sons of Veterans, the Nebraskana Society, the Nebraska State Teachers' Association, the National Education Association, the American Association of University Professors, the American Association for the Advancement of Science, the Nebraska Academy of Science, the Mathematical ssociation of America, National Council of Teachers of Mathematics, Central Association of Science and Mathematics Teachers and the Symposium. His sports are handball and swimming. Residence: Lincoln.

Charles Edward Hoyt

Charles Edward Hoyt was born in a sod house 13 miles southwest of McCook, Nebraska, June 3, 1900, and is a merchant and farmer in that community today. His father, James Llewellyn Hoyt, who was a farmer and teacher, was born at Syracuse, New York, March 10, 1846, and died at Cambridge, Nebraska, June 11, 1920; he was a member of the 9th Regular Heavy Artillery of New York during the Civil War. His mother, who was a teacher prior to her marriage, was born in Putman County, Ohio, November 30, 1860, of Scotch ancestry.

Mr. Hoyt was graduated from the McCook High School in 1917, received the B. S. of Business administration at the University of Nebraska, 1921, where he won a letter in football in 1918, three letters in wrestling for the years 1919, 1920, 1921 and was captain his last year at Nebraska. Further he won Western Intercollegiate heavy weight wrestling championship at Bloomington, Indiana with 16 universities competing, and for two years was athletic coach in the McCook High School. Immediately following his schooling, he was engaged in the operation of his parent's wheat and cattle ranch at the place of his birth for a period of two years. He has been a successful hardware merchant at McCook for the past seven years, and since 1927 has served as a member of the local Board of Education. He is a member of the executive committee of the Nebraska Alumnae Board, was formerly president of the Chamber of Commerce, and was a member of the Rotary Club. He is affiliated with the Methodist Episcopal Church, holds membership in the Nebraskana Society, and is a member of the Elks (exalted ruler 1931) and the Masons.

On August 28, 1924, he was married to Helen Edgecombe at Estes Park, Colorado. Mrs. Hoyt, who was a commercial teacher at McCook High School before her marriage, was born at Geneva, Nebraska, September 27, 1895, of New England parentage. Their two children are: John Edgecombe, born March 28, 1928; and Joan Priscilla, born January 12, 1931. Residence: McCook.

Susan Upson Hoyt

Susan Upson was born at Rockford, Illinois, September 27, 1855, daughter of Lyman Davis and Lucina Jane (Miller) Upson. Her father was born at Camden, Oneida County, New York, October 29, 1825, and died at Reserve, Nebraska, August 7, 1881. He was a lumberman, furniture manufacturer and ranchman, descended from Thomas Upson who came to Connecticut from England in 1632, and helped found the town of Farmington. Lucina Jane Miller was born at Lee, Oneida County, New York, December 23, 1829, and died at Rockford, Illinois, January 13, 1866. She was Scotch and English, a descendant of Thomas Miller who settled in Connecticut in 1634.

Susan Upson attended the Rockford High School, and in 1879 came with her father to Nebraska. She was married to Richard Cleveland Hoyt, at Reserve, Nebraska, June 4, 1884. Mr. Hoyt, was born at Holland Patent, Oneida County, New York, August 9, 1855. He was engaged in the lumber and coal business for many years, and for the past 33 years has been clerk of the United States District Court. They have one son, Edward Lyman, who attended Iowa State College at Ames. He married Marjorie R. Smith on November 9, 1911. They have two daughters.

Mrs. Hoyt is a member of the Colonial Dames of America, and is ex-regent of Omaha chapter of the Daughters of the American Revolution. She is president for Nebraska of the Daughters of Founders and Patriots. She is a member of the First Central Congregational Church of Omaha. She has always been active in welfare work, especially the Red Cross, the Old People's Home, the Social Settlement, the Visiting Nurses Association and the Young Women's Christian Association. Residence: Omaha.

William L. Hoyt

William L. Hoyt, prominent retired ranchman, was born at Cleveland, Ohio, May 3, 1863. He is the son of Jacob N. and Mary (Latimer) Hoyt, the former of whom was born at East Concord, New Hampshire, December 14, 1831, and died at Elburn, Illinois, May 7, 1907. He was a farmer.

Mr. Hoyt attended public and high school, and in 1888, came to Nebraska, where he was a rancher, until his recent retirement. He is a Democrat.

On November 18, 1896, he was married to Rosa De-Bock at Harrison. Mrs. Hoyt was born at DePier, Wisconsin, November 22, 1870, and died at Harrison, December 20, 1929. There is one daughter, Edith, born January 17, 1900, who is married to John O. Hanson. Residence: Harrison.

Charles Hrabak

Born in Prague, Czechoslovakia, December 28, 1858, Charles Hrabak has been a resident of Nebraska forty-eight years. His father, Joseph Hrabak was born there in June, 1830, and died in Dodge, Nebraska, September 22, 1892. He was a farmer. His wife, was born in Prague, in 1832, and died in Chelsea, Iowa, March 14, 1868.

Charles Hrabak attended country school, and entered the mercantile business in Dodge, continuing until his recent retirement. He was married to Josephine Christina Krutka at Wahkeeny, Kansas, November 5, 1879. Mrs. Hrabak was born in Racine, Wisconsin, April 1, 1862. There are five children living and one deceased: Julia, born August 14, 1880; Charles, born June 28, 1882, died October 9, 1918; Will Rudolf, born March 26, 1884; Carrie, born November 18, 1892; Mabel, born March 27, 1894, and Howard, born October 6, 1896.

Mr. Hrabak is a Catholic, and a member of Saint Wenceslaus Church. He is also a member of The Nebraskana Society. Residence: Dodge.

Frank Hrdy

Frank Hrdy, merchant, was born in Bohemia, November 14, 1860, son of Anton and Barbara (Sulc) Hrdy, and has resided in Nebraska since March 19, 1894.

On August 23, 1884, he was married to Louisa Stepanek at New York City. There are three children living and one deceased: Mamie, born November 12, 1885, who married J. D. Kopp; Frank, born November 25, 1887, who married Marie Holpuch; Lula, born August 8, 1889; and Vlasta, born April 11, 1899, who died December 25, 1901.

At the present time Mr. Hrdy is senior partner of the firm of Hrdy & Son. He is a member of the Chamber of Commerce, the Knights of Pythias, the Sokol, the Z. C. B. J., the Bohemian Historical Society, and the Dramatic Club of Milligan. Residence: Milligan.

Ernest Alfred Hubka

Ernest Alfred Hubka, well-known lawyer at Beatrice, Gage County, Nebraska, has lived in this state all his life and in prominent in civic affairs in his community. He was born at Virginia, Gage County, Nebraska, August 13, 1897, the son of Joseph S. and Frances Hubka. His father, who is retired, was born at Humboldt, Nebraska, August 18, 1871. His mother was born at Hanover, Marshall County, Kansas, December 4, 1874, and died at Virginia, March 24, 1919.

Mr. Hubka, who is serving as county attorney of Gage County at the present time, attended the public schools of Virginia, and in 1916 was graduated from the Beatrice High School. He was awarded the A. B. and LL. B. degrees at the University of Nebraska, where he held membership in Delta Tau Delta. He was active in football, basketball, track, and baseball at the University of Nebraska.

From 1922-23 he taught in Yuma, Colorado, high school; and from 1923-27 in the York, Nebraska, high school. He is a member of the Junior Chamber of Commerce, the Kiwanis Club, Young Men's Christian Association, and the Nebraskana Society. He is affiliated with the Christian Church at Beatrice, is a member of the Republican party, and holds membership in the Masons, Elks, and Eagles.

He was united in marriage at Blair, Nebraska, July 17, 1929, with Thelma Marie Underwood, who was born at Archer, Nebraska, June 13, 1903. They have one daughter, Mary Frances, born September 10, 1930. Residence: Beatrice.

Joseph S. Hubka

Joseph S. Hubka, prominent banker at Virginia, Gage County, Nebraska, has lived in this state all his life, and has been active as a farmer, grain buyer, implement dealer, and banker. He was born at Humboldt, Pawnee County, Nebraska, August 18, 1872, the son of Albert and Mary (Kovanda) Hubka. His father, a farmer and cattle feeder, was born at Kocin, Plzen, Cechoslovakia, April 12, 1844, and died at Virginia, September 28, 1897; he was a staunch Democrat, and was always active in politics; his ancestors came to this country in the 1860's. Mary (Kovanda) Hubka, his mother, was born at Striman, Plzen, Cechoslovakia, May 10, 1844, and died at Virginia, September 28, 1926. She came to this country and settled on a farm in Pawnee County, with her parents, in 1867.

Mr. Hubka attended rural schools. He is now cashier of the Citizens State Bank of Virginia, and has served on the local school board for many years. He is a member of the Virginia Cornet Band, and is affiliated with the Nebraskana Society.

He was united in marriage with Francis Vavruska at Beatrice, Gage County, Nebraska, November 5, 1896. Mrs. Hubka was born at Blue Rapids, Marshall County, Kansas, November 16, 1876, and died at Virginia, March 28, 1920. Four children were born to them: Ernest, born August 13, 1897, who married Thelma Underwood; Ladimer, born September 26, 1899, who is a graduate of the University of Nebraska, and is a lawyer at Beatrice; Albert, born December 15, 1902, who died August 12, 1909; and Elmer, born September 29, 1909, who is a student at the University of Nebraska. Ernest is a graduate of the University of Nebraska, and is now serving as county attorney of Gage County. All three sons are Republicans. Residence: Virginia.

Thelma Marie Hubka

Thelma Marie Hubka was born in Archer, Nebraska, June 13, 1903, the daughter of William Hewitt Underwood and Hannah Marie (Johnson) Underwood. Her father, born in Hamilton, Illinois, June 30, 1860, was a Methodist minister whose ancestors came from England, in 1770.

Marie Johnson Underwood, born in Christiansand, Norway, April 24, 1869, was active in literary work and belonged to the Eastern Star. Her father was the leader of the King's band in Norway. She died in Lincoln, Nebraska, June 28, 1931.

Thelma M. Hubka attended the Saunders School at Omaha, in 1916, the Blair, Nebraska High School, 1920, and in 1925, received her Bachelor of Arts degree at the University of Nebraska, where she again attended 1923-25. She is a member of the Delta Delta Delta at Nebraska Wesleyan University which she attended 1920-22. On July 17, 1929, at Blair, Nebraska, she was married to Ernest Alfred Hubka.

Mr. Hubka was born in Virginia, Nebraska, August 13, 1879, and is a lawyer. Mary Frances Hubka, born September 10, 1930, is the only child.

Mrs. Hubka taught in Plattsmouth, Nebraska, 1922-23; taught English and European history in Friend, Nebraska, 1925-28, and was biology teacher at South High School in Omaha, 1928-29. She has resided in Nebraska for twenty-eight years and is a member of the Nebraskana Society.

She is a member of the Centenery Methodist Church in Beatrice, and is on the Young Women's Christian Association board. She also belongs to the Eastern Star. Residence: Beatrice.

Lottie Belle Hudson

A resident of this state all her life, Lottie Belle Hudson is one of Nebraska's few women executives in the business world. She was born at Crete, Nebraska, August 25, 1889, the daughter of Isaac and Myrtle (Miller) Hudson. Her father, who was engaged in the garage business, was born of German parents at Munsie, Pennsylvania, October 22, 1864, and died at Crete, January 25, 1927. Her mother was born at Valparaiso, Indiana, June 22, 1871, of Scotch-Irish ancestry. She is descended from a family prominent in the early history of America.

Miss Hudson received her education in the public schools of Crete. She was connected with the Bell Telephone Company for five years at Crete, was transferred to the Independent Telephone Company, successor of the Bell Telephone Company, and served as chief operator for nine years. She was associated with the Lincoln Telephone Company for four years, and in 1928 became local superintendent of the Crete and Dorchester offices of the Iowa Nebraska Light & Power Company.

She is a member of the Pythian Sisters and the Royal Highlanders, and is past chief of the Pythian Sisters. She is affiliated with the First Methodist Episcopal Church of Crete, is a member of the Nebraskana Society, and holds membership in the Mizpah Club. Miss Hudson is a charter member and one of the organizers of the Business Women's Club of Crete. Residence: Crete.

Roy William Hudson

Roy William Hudson, business executive at North Loup, Nebraska, was born at Hayes Center, Nebraska, October 3, 1890, the son of William F. and Jane Eliza (Towne) Hudson. His father, who was a pioneer merchant and public leader in his community, was born in Michigan, and died at Kirkville, Missouri, July 6, 1906; his grandfather moved from New York to Michigan shortly after the Revolution. His mother, who was born on a farm near Northwood, Iowa, November 27, 1870, was the daughter of a soldier in the Civil War and traced her ancestry back to the early settlers of Massachusetts.

Mr. Hudson attended the Nebraska Wesleyan Academy, and in 1916 received the A. B. degree at Nebraska Wesleyan University where he was president of Theta Phi Sigma and member of Phi Kappa Phi, and held membership in the Glee Club. He studied at the University of Nebraska from 1916 to 1918, and since 1919 has been secretary-treasurer and manager of the Johnson and Company at North Loup. He has served as secretary-treasurer of the Loup Valley Independent Telephone Company of North Loup since 1926, and is now secretary-treasurer of the North Loup Co-Operative Cheese Company.

He is a member of the Parent Teachers Association, the Young Men's Christian Association, and the Modern Woodmen of America, and the North Loup Methodist Episcopal Church. His hobby is electricity, and his sports include golfing, hunting, and fishing.

He was married at North Loup, June 11, 1918, to Anna Ruth Johnson who was born there, November 1, 1894. Their children are: Florence Evelyn, born September 2, 1919; and Edward, born January 25, 1923. Residence: North Loup.

Otto Leonhart Huenefeld

Otto Leonhart Huenefeld was born at Aurora, Nebraska, May 13, 1885, the son of Carl Frederich and Anna Elizabeth (Bald) Huenefeld. His father, who has been a farmer and stock feeder, was born at Veldrome, Germany, October 6, 1853. He came to America in 1854 and in 1878 moved to Hamilton County, Nebraska as a pioneer farmer, breaking the virgin soil with oxen. He was interested in political affairs but has always refused to hold public office, and has given most of his efforts to

building up his community. He was for many years secretary of the Hamilton County Farmers Mutual Insurance Company, assisted in building the Prairie Gem Church which was erected on a corner of his farm near Aurora, Nebraska, and helped to secure the first rural free delivery of mail in Hamilton County. In 1901 he served as secretary of the Hamilton County Farmers' Telephone Company during its organization, a company which now owns and operates more than 3000 telephones.

Anna Elizabeth (Bald) Huenefeld, his mother, was born at Liberty, Wisconsin, March 1, 1858, of German parents. She is the mother of eleven children all born and reared on the same farm in Hamilton County. Mr. and Mrs. Carl Frederich Huenefeld are now residing at Augusta, Arkansas.

Mr. Huenefeld attended rural school near Aurora, was a student at York United Brethren College, 1903-04, and attended the University of Nebraska College of Agriculture, 1904-05. He is a farmer and stockman and is the proprietor of the Golden Hoof Farm near Aurora. He is interested in all community activities is president of the Farmers Union Association of Aurora and Marquette, Nebraska, has been secretary of the Farmers Elevator Company of Giltner, Nebraska, since 1918, and since 1920 has been president of the Hamilton County Farmers Union.

A Democrat, he has been a member of the county central committee, served as delegate to the county conventions at various times, has been a member of the election board, and was a delegate to the state convention at Lincoln, Nebraska where the first organized effort toward national prohibition was made in Nebraska.

Mr. Huenefeld has held membership in the Red Cross, and has always been a supporter of that organization and also the Child Saving Institute, the Society for the Friendless, and has taken a prominent part in welfare work in Hamilton County for many years. He holds membership in the Farmers' Educational and Co-operative Union, the Prairie Gem Community Club, the Nebraskana Society, and the Prairie Gem United Brethren Church. He and his wife are very much interested in religious activities. He specializes in certified small grain seed productions on his farm and woolen goods manufactured from home-grown wool.

On February 3, 1909, he married Nelle May Holmes at Aurora. Mrs. Huenefeld was born at Baylis, Illinois, March 27, 1889. Their three children are: Maynard Everett, born May 25, 1913; Phyllis Irene, born April 13, 1916; and Arnola May, born September 24, 1918. Maynard was graduated from the Aurora High School and the Northwestern School of Taxidermy. All the children are interested in religious and musical affairs. Residence: Aurora.

Lee Huff

Lee Huff is the son of one of Nebraska's foremost public men, the late James Huff. James Huff was born at St. John, Newfoundland, March 20, 1845. At the age of seventeen he came to the United States, and two years later enlisted for service in the Civil War. A clergyman, he served as chaplain of the Nebraska penitentiary. He was justice of the peace, police judge, county judge and clerk of the district court in Dodge County, and later served as a member of the Nebraska State senate. He was of Scotch-Irish descent, his family having settled in Canada, in its early days. He died at Omaha, February 2, 1929.

Laura Ellen Driscoll, wife of James Huff, was born in Sarpy County, Nebraska, June 3, 1849, and died at Omaha, September 24, 1919. She was also of Scotch-Irish descent.

Lee Huff entered the service of the Northwestern Bell Telephone Company at Fremont, in 1889, and served as manager of the company at Fremont, Crete, Grand Island and Lincoln, until his resignation in September, 1909. At that time he formed a partnership under which the

Nebraska Buick Auto Company was organized, for the sale of automobiles and accessories, without change, except in the name which is now the H. E. Sidles Company. Mr. Huff is also vice president of the Union Holding Company of Omaha.

In 1895, he was married to Adelaide Amanda Keasy, who was born at St. Petersburg, Pennsylvania, December 22, 1877, at Council Bluffs. They have one son, Lee, born July 15, 1899. He is married to Rosavere Menagh, and is engaged in the automotive supply business. Mr. Huff is a Democrat. During the World War he was in the United States Secret Service. He is affiliated with the Reorganized Church of Jesus Christ of the Latter Day Saints, and is a member of the Rotary Club, the Elks and the Masons. He is a member of the Nebraskana Society. Mr. Huff finds his recreation in golf and swimming. His hobby, however, is upland river navigation. His clubs are the Omaha Athletic Club and Happy Hollow Country Club. Residence: Omaha.

Ellis Harnden Hughes

Ellis Harnden Hughes, farmer in Boyd County, Nebraska, was born in Ontario, Canada, January 19, 1868, the son of Charles Wesley and Emily Louise (Harger) Hughes. His father, who was born in Ontario, December 2, 1825, of English parents, came to the United States in 1837, and died at Edwardsburg, Michigan, April 4, 1884. His mother, whose ancestry was English, was born at Troy, New York, December 13, 1837.

Mr. Hughes homesteaded in Boyd County in 1891, and has been a farmer near Naper, Nebraska, since then. He is affiliated with the Republican party, and is a member of the Masons, the Odd Fellows, and the Nebraskana Society.

He was married to Lida May Briggs at Beemer, Nebraska, May 12, 1925. Mrs. Hughes, who was a teacher and bank cashier before her marriage, was born at Scribner, Nebraska, October 15, 1874. Her ancestors were New Englanders. Residence: Naper.

Enos Thomas Hughes

Born at Scranton, Pennsylvania, December 1, 1875, Enos T. Hughes, banker, has been a resident of Nebraska for more than fifty-two years. His parents, Dominic and Mary (McDonnell) Hughes, were Irish. Dominic Hughes was born at Bellina, County Mayo, Ireland, in 1832, he died at Gretna, October 24, 1915, having been a farmer in Sarpy County for many years. Mary McDonnell Hughes was born at Corvoderra, County Mayo, Ireland, in 1842, and died at Gretna, February 10, 1915.

Enos Hughes received his early education in the rural schools of Sarpy County, and later attended the State Normal School at Fremont. On July 6, 1908, he was united in marriage to Cora Ellen Raker, at Lincoln, Nebraska. Mrs. Hughes was born at Salladsburg, Pennsylvania, July 6, 1879. There are two children: Gretna, born December 8, 1910, and Clark, born January 31, 1916.

A farmer in early life, Mr. Hughes was engaged as a general merchant from 1898 to 1908. In 1911 he entered the banking business in Platte County. He was one of the organizers of the Bank of Gretna, which handled all war loans during the World War. He is cashier of the Bank of Gretna at the present time.

During the World War Mr. Hughes was very active. He was a member of the committee finding valuations on farmers and others with regard to various war loans, and in the Red Cross of which he has always been a member. He is a member of St. Patrick's Catholic Church. He is also a member of the Chamber of Commerce, and active in all civic matters. He is an Elk. His philanthropic work is outstanding. His recreation is walking, but comes second to working in his peony garden, which is his chief hobby. Residence: Gretna.

Forrest L. Hughes

Born at Red Oak, Iowa, March 1, 1889, Forrest L. Hughes is the son of Lot J. and Martha Victoria (Francis) Hughes. His father, born at Wales, Great Britain, August 26, 1866, came to Iowa with his parents as an infant, and has been a farmer most of his life. He is now a clothing salesman, residing at Huntsman, Nebraska. His wife, Martha, was born in LaCross County, of Welsh parents, and resided near Red Oak, most of her life. There she taught school and was married, removing later, in 1895, to the family farm at Carroll, Nebraska. Her death occurred at Carroll, September 14, 1905.

Forrest L. Hughes attended public school and the State Teachers College at Wayne, Nebraska. From 1907-10, he was deputy county treasurer of Wayne County, and from 1910-20, was clerk of the district court of that county. Removing to South Dakota, in 1920, he engaged in banking there until 1926, and during 1927, was connected with the public relations and sales departments of the Northwestern Public Service Company at North Platte. Since 1927, he has been deputy clerk of the district court of Adams County, and engaged in the insurance business at Hastings. He is a Republican.

On June 1, 1915, Mr. Hughes was married to Opal E. Douglass, at Tekamah. Mrs. Hughes who is of English, Scotch and Pennsylvania Dutch extraction, was born at Tekamah, December 29, 1889. To them were born four children, three of whom are living: Forrest Douglass, born April 13, 1916, died April 16, 1916; Robert Forrest, born February 4, 1918; Neil Douglass, born March 10, 1923, and Martha Ellen, born November 30, 1926.

A member of the Methodist Episcopal Church of Hastings, Mr. Hughes is a member of its official board, and a member of the Young Men's Christian Association and the Ancient Free and Accepted Masons. During the World War he assisted in the selective draft during the entire period of the war, and was chairman one year of the Red Cross at Wayne. Residence: Hastings.

Frank Elsworth Hughes

A native of Swedeberg, Nebraska, Frank Elsworth Hughes was born December 6, 1889, son of Clinton Dewitt and Georgia Ellenette (Batchelder) Hughes. Clinton Hughes was born at Belmont, Ohio, May 26, 1845, and died at Hastings, August 30, 1906. Of English descent, he was a teacher and farmer, and a veteran of the Civil War. His wife, Georgia, was born in Worcester, Vermont, May 8, 1850, and was a teacher prior to her marriage. She is also of English descent.

Mr. Hughes attended the Wahoo public and high schools, and was graduated from the latter in May, 1906. Since early manhood he has been engaged in farming. He was married to Lola Mae Beaman, at Lincoln, on February 19, 1913. Mrs. Hughes was born at Ceresco, October 1, 1890, of English extraction. Three of their four children are living. They are: Eloise, born March 26, 1914, who was graduated with honors from Ceresco High School in May, 1931; Pauline, February 23, 1916, and Warren, born October 5, 1919. Eloise was valedictorian of her class and received the first scholarship. Pearl, born February 23, 1916, died August 21, 1916.

Music is Mr. Hughes' hobby, and he is leader of the Ceresco Concert Band, and has been leader of the Sunday School orchestra of the Methodist Episcopal Church for some time. He served as director of the School Board of District No. 40 during 1919-21, and is a former member of the Modern Woodmen of America. During 1917-18, he was a member of the Red Cross. He is now a member of the Nebraska Farmers Union and The Nebraskana Society. Residence: Ceresco.

Thomas Bennison Hughes

Born at Sterling, Illinois, August 14, 1888, Thomas Bennison Hughes has been a druggist at Cozad since 1912. His father, John Bamford Hughes, a merchant of Welch and English descent, was born near Bradford, Pennsylvania, March 23, 1856, and came to Nebraska in 1888 and settled at Cozad making his home here since. His mother, Mary Bennison, died at Cozad, Nebraska, in 1895.

Mr. Hughes attended public school at Cozad and then took a course in pharmacy in Fremont College. He has been in business for himself since he was twenty-one, and is numbered among the most prominent in the business world of his community. He is a Mason, a member of the Methodist Episcopal Church and the Nebraskana Society. His favorite sport is golf, and his chief indoor recreation is reading.

On July 9, 1912, he was married to Darlene Beulah Miller at Kearney. Mrs. Hughes, who is an instructor in piano, was born at Lexington, May 11, 1891. There are three children, Rae Arlene, born July 30, 1913; Mary Elizabeth, born October 31, 1914; and Duane Elbert, born June 26, 1917. Residence: Cozad.

Gerhard Hulsebus

Gerhard Hulsebus was born at El Paso, Woodford County, Illinois, April 1, 1872, the son of Berend and Rixte (Tarman) Hulsebus. His father, who was a farmer, was born at Steinfeld, Germany, June 7, 1847, and died at Defiance, Shelby County, Iowa, March 16, 1921; his family has lived in Germany for many generations. Rixte Tarman was born in Germany and died at Defiance, in 1918.

Mr. Hulsebus was graduated from Highland Park College at Des Moines, Iowa, in 1895, with the degree of Bachelor of Didactics. He received the Ph. B. degree at Western Union College, Le Mars, Iowa, and now is superintendent of the Hastings District of the Nebraska Conference of the Evangelical Church. He is the author of *Seven Days With Jesus, The Pathos Portrait of Jesus Christ,* and articles appearing in the *Evangelical Messenger.*

Mr. Hulsebus is chairman of the Hastings District Ministerial Association, is secretary of the board of trustees of Western Union College, and holds membership in the Nebraskana Society. He is a member of the Knights of Pythias, and has been district superintendent of the Nebraska Conference of the Evangelical Church since 1925. His hobby is reading.

He was married to Estella Florence Koenig, at Le-Mars, November 26, 1902. Mrs. Hulsebus, who is of German and English descent, was born at Le Mars, December 17, 1876. They have three children: Lowell Bernard, born June 20, 1906, who married Betty Clare Hedglin, and who is a teacher; Lois Cleone, born November 18, 1911; and Alice Estella, born February 25, 1915.

Mr. Hulsebus was pastor of various churches in Iowa and Nebraska prior to 1925; from 1904 to 1915, he was pastor of the Evangelical Church in San Francisco. In his position as district superintendent, he has 25 churches under his direction. Residence: Hastings.

John Albert Hultine

John Albert Hultine was born at Saronville, Nebraska, January 2, 1877, the son of pioneer parents, John and Emma Justine (Nelson) Hultine. His father, who was born in Sweden, January 14, 1840, and died at Saronville, January 3, 1892, was a farmer and pioneer homesteader in Clay County, Nebraska. Locating at Galesburg, Illinois, where he was married in 1869, Mr. Hultine's father first came West in the employ of the Burlington Railroad Company, helping to construct railroads as far west as Harvard. He came to America in 1868. His mother, who is still living on the farm which she settled with her husband, was born in Sweden, June 1, 1844.

Mr. Hultine attended country school and in 1897 was a student at Lincoln State Normal School, Lincoln, Nebraska. He is a farmer and stockman, and together

with his sons shows and sells registered Shorthorn and Polled Shorthorn cattle. Mr. Hultine has shown with marked success his Polled Shorthorn cattle in all corn-belt state fairs since 1911 and has won nine international grand championship prizes at the International Stock Show at Chicago. He has exported his cattle to Australia and Argentina. He is president of the Nebraska Shorthorn Breeders Society, and is a director of the Polled Shorthorn Society of America. He is a deacon in the Lutheran Evangelical Church of Saronville. His politics are Democratic.

On March 27, 1901, he was united in marriage with Hulda Charlotte England at Eldorado, Nebraska. Mrs. Hultine was born at Eldorado, October 4, 1881, of Swedish parentage. Their children are: Lloyd, born December 31, 1901, who married Judith Forsell at Clay Center, Nebraska, March 14, 1923; and Cleo, born April 14, 1905, who is at home. Residence: Saronville.

Frank Hummel

Frank Hummel was born at Bloom Township, Fairfield County, Ohio, April 17, 1860, son of David and Leah (Zaayer) Hummel.

His father, a native of Pennsylvania, was a farmer of Pennsylvania Dutch descent, whose death occurred at Sullivan, Indiana, in April, 1880. His mother was also born in Pennsylvania, and died at Sullivan in 1870.

Mr. Hummel attended country school in Indiana and 48 years ago came to Nebraska, settling in Sheridan County where he homesteaded. He was married on December 27, 1897, to Grace McCoy at O'Neill. Her father, Patrick McCoy, came to Holt County in October, 1875, where he homesteaded. Her mother, Mary Ann (McCrory) McCoy, came to Nebraska in April, 1876, with her family.

Mr. Hummel has five children, Ted L., born November 3, 1897, married Edna Galton; Mary, born April 4, 1900, married Karl Ledtyke; Claire, born February 24, 1903; Jim, born October 4, 1905; and Robert, born July 26, 1910. Ted is the editor of the *Algonac Courier* at Algonac, Michigan and is a member of the American Legion. Robert is associated with his brother on the *Courier.* Mary is a registered nurse and a graduate of St. Joseph's Hospital at Omaha.

In his earlier years, Mr. Hummel was in the livery business at Gordon. At the present time he is working in the carpentry department of Sherwood and Walrath Lumber Company. He is a Mason. His political affiliation is with the Democratic party. Residence: Gordon.

Grace McCoy Hummel

Grace McCoy Hummel, wife of Frank Hummel, was born in Fond du Lac, Wisconsin, October 9, 1870, the daughter of patrick and Mary Ann (McCrory) McCoy.

Before her marriage on December 27, 1897, she was a teacher. She is the heroine of the blizzard of 1888, which occurred on January 12, of that year, and is well known throughout the state for her courage in saving the lives of her eight pupils in Holt County. Mrs. Hummel kept the children in the schoolhouse, using the seats and furniture for fuel, while the fierce storm raged outside.

Remaining in the school all night, the inadequate fuel became exhausted and Mrs. Hummel, who was then only 16 years of age, realized the necessity of keeping the children's blood circulating. She instructed them to keep moving. It was not until the next morning, when the frenzy of the storm had abated, that she started out with her little brood to seek shelter and warmth. Mrs. Hummel's heroism remains as one of the most courageous experiences in the annals of teaching in Nebraska.

There are five children, Ted., born November 3, 1897, who married Edna Golton; Mary, born April 4, 1900, who married Karl Ledtyke; Claire, born February 24,

1903; Jim, born October 4, 1905; and Robert, born July 26, 1910. Ted is the editor of the *Algonac Courier* at Algonac, Michigan. Robert is associated with his brother on the *Courier*. Mary is a registered nurse and a graduate of St. Joseph's Hospital at Omaha.

At the present time Mrs. Hummel is librarian of the Gordon Library, and is the author of *Early History of O'Neill*, and *History of Gordon*, besides various other historical articles. She is a member of the Woman's Relief Corps and she and her children are members of St. Leo's Catholic Church. Residence: Gordon. (Photograph in Album).

Ray Orvin Hummel

Ray Orvin Hummel, prominent physician and surgeon at Lincoln, Lancaster County, Nebraska, was born at Humboldt, Richardson County, Nebraska, March 12, 1880, the son of Christian L. and Josephine (Beringer) Hummel. His father, who has been a banker and farmer and is now retired, was born at Allentown, Pennsylvania, December 6, 1852; he is of German descent. His mother was born at Menominee Falls, Wisconsin, July 17, 1856.

Mr. Hummel was graduated from the high school at Humboldt, in 1896, received his B. S. degree at the University of Nebraska in 1902, and was awarded his M. D. degree at Northwestern University Medical School in 1905. He was elected to membership in Delta Upsilon and Alpha Kappa Kappa. He has been engaged in the practice of medicine and surgery at Lincoln since his admission to the profession in 1905.

He is a member of the following: Lancaster County Medical Association; Nebraska State Medical Society; American Medical Association; The Nebraskana Society; and the National Geographic Society. His social club is the Lincoln University Club. He is a Mason, 32nd degree, Blue Lodge, and Shriner.

He was married at Lincoln, August 6, 1908, to Charlotte Eugenia Hulhorst. Mrs. Hummel, who is a talented musician, was born at Columbus, Platte County, Nebraska, March 17, 1882; she is of German ancestry. Two children were born to them: Ray Orvin, Jr., born October 22, 1909; and Paul Adrian, born March 14, 1911. Ray is now doing graduate work at the University of Nebraska in history, while Paul is a senior in the fine arts college.

Dr. Hummel is a Republican. He is a member of St. Paul's Church. Residence: Lincoln.

Arthur G. Humphrey

Arthur G. Humphrey, lawyer and former county judge and county attorney of Hooker County, was born at Drakesville, Iowa, May 10, 1880, son of Alfred H. and Charlotte (Runkle) Humphrey. His ancestry is English.

Upon the completion of his public school education, Mr. Humphrey attended Southern Iowa Normal School, and Des Moines University. He has the degree of Bachelor of Didactics and Bachelor of Laws.

On October 30, 1910, he was married to Clara C. Jeffords at Broken Bow, Nebraska. She was born there on November 28, 1884. There are three children, Carl G., born May 24, 1912; Phyllis Jean, born April 22, 1916; and Jack Alfred, born January 22, 1920.

Mr. Humphrey is a Republican. He is in active practice as a lawyer, and is an extensive land owner. He is a member of the Masons at Mullen where he has resided since 1905. Residence: Mullen.

Augustin Reed Humphrey

Augustin Reed Humphrey, lawyer and prominent figure in public affairs for many years, was born near Madison, Indiana, February 18, 1858, son of Augustin Reed and Hannah (Hicks) Humphrey.

His father was born near Frankfort, Kentucky, August 12, 1816, and died near Drakesville, Iowa, August 31, 1904. He was a farmer, whose English forebears came to America about 1750. His wife, Hannah, was born in England, March 20, 1824, and died near Drakesville, September 6, 1904. She was always an active worker in Sunday School.

Mr. Humphrey attended the common schools of Iowa and Southern Iowa Normal College, from which he was graduated on June 22, 1881. On June 4, 1882, he received his degree of Bachelor of Laws from Iowa State University. Since the last mentioned date he has been active in the practice of law. Since July, 1884, he has had a law office at Broken Bow.

From 1891 until 1895, Mr. Humphrey was commissioner of lands and buildings of Nebraska, and from 1906 until 1910 served as county judge of Custer County. He was mayor of Broken Bow 1916-1917, and a member of 67th congress of the sixth congressional district of Nebraska. From 1898 until 1914, he was president of the Broken Bow board of education.

His marriage to Nellie Nightingale was solemnized at Bloomfield, Iowa, June 28, 1883. Mrs. Humphrey was born near Drakesville, Iowa, November 11, 1860, and died at Broken Bow, May 30, 1914. She was a teacher, and was descended from early New England settlers from around Rhode Island. There are three children, Paul N., born November 30, 1885, who is a lawyer at Pawhuska, Oklahoma; Donald R., born June 28, 1894, who is an insurance agent at Fort Collins, Colorado; and Fred A., born March 17, 1896, who is a physician at Fort Collins, Colorado. All are Republicans.

Mr. Humphrey is not a member of any church, but attends several. He is a member of the Custer County and Nebraska State Bar Associations, the Red Cross, the Broken Bow Public Service Club, the Nebraska State Historical Society, the Young Men's Christian Association, and the Masons. He is a member of a whist club, and although too old for active sports, enjoys walking from two to five miles a day. His real hobby, however, is working in his garden and raising flowers. Residence: Broken Bow.

Clara C. Humphrey

Clara C. Humphrey, daughter of Charles H. and Mary Elizabeth (Price) Jefferde, was born at Broken Bow, Nebraska, November 27, 1884.

Her father was born in Beverly, Ohio, February 27, 1858, and is now a retired farmer of English descent. His wife, Mary, was born in Harrisburg, Ohio, February 26, 1859, and is principally of Scotch ancestry.

Clara C. Jefferde was graduated from high school at Broken Bow, Nebraska, and from 1907 until 1910 was teacher and postmistress at Mullen. She is a Republican, and in 1925 represented her district in the Nebraska Legislature.

She was married to A. G. Humphrey at Broken Bow, on October 30, 1910, and to them were born three children: Carl G., on May 24, 1912; Phyllis Jean, on April 2, 1915; and Jack Alfred, on January 15, 1920.

Mrs. Humphrey has been active in civic, fraternal and cultural organizations in her community for a number of years. She was chairman of liberty loan committee for Hooker County during the World War, is a member of the American Legion Auxiliary, St. Joseph's Episcopal Church, the Red Cross, and the Woman's Welfare Club of Mullen, the Eastern Star, the Nebraska State Native Sons and Daughters. Residence: Mullen.

Frank Charles Humphrey

The Reverend Frank Charles Humphrey, pastor of the Presbyterian Church of Stapleton, was born at

Osceola, Nebraska, August 25, 1885, son of Louis Elliott and Comora Virginia (Kingsolver) Humphrey.

The father, born at Tipton, Iowa, September 27, 1860, came to Nebraska in 1868 with his parents. He is a clergyman and for the past thirty-five years has been a Presbyterian minister. His present pastorate is the First Presbyterin Church of Sutherland. On the father's side, Mr. Humphrey is English on the paternal side, related to the noble Holt family. On the maternal side he is Scotch. Four generations on the father's side of the family have been clergymen.

Comora Virginia Kingsolver was born in Sullivan County, Missouri, March 15, 1862. She is of Scotch and Irish descent. She has always been interested in women's club work and has always taught a class in Sunday School and been a choir singer.

Frank Charles Humphrey attended elementary school in Chicago until the sixth grade, and was graduated from grammer school at Farwell, Nebraska. He attended the Academy of Hastings College until 1904 and received the Bachelor of Arts degree from Hastings College in 1908. In 1911 he received his diploma from the McCormick Theological Seminary at Chicago. There during the years 1909 and 1910 he sang baritone in the male quartet.

Ordained at Kanopolis, Kansas, on May 29, 1912, Mr. Humphrey has served in the following pastorates, Kanopolis until April 1, 1913; Bern, Kansas, until October 1, 1916; Ong, Nebraska, until April 1, 1919; Mt. Nebo and Kill Creek, Kansas, until September 1, 1921; Belle Plaine, Kansas, until September 1, 1924; Cambridge, Kansas, until January 15, 1927; Sylvan Grove, Kansas, until April 1, 1930. Since April 1, the last mentioned date, Mr. Humphrey has been pastor of the Presbyterian Church of Stapleton.

A member of the Kearney Presbytery at the present time, Mr. Humphrey was a member of the Solomon Presbytery until April, 1913, and the Highland Presbytery until October 1, 1916. He held the stated clerk's position for one year in Highland Presbytery. He was moderator from April 1, 1921, until September, 1921, of the Osborne Presbytery. As a member of the Wichita Presbytery until September, 1927, he was commissioner to the General Assembly in May, 1926, at Baltimore, Maryland.

Mr. Humphrey was president of war work activities at Ong, Nebraska, at the beginning of the World War. He is a membeer of the Stapleton Commercial Club, and in October, 1931, was elected president of the Stapleton Parent-Teachers Association. He is Past Grand of the Odd Fellows at Stapleton. In 1912 he joined the Masonic order at Alton, Kansas, and is still an active member. Since 1925 he has been a member of the Scottish Rite Consistory No. 2 at Wichita.

Mr. Humphrey has played a great deal of golf and tennis and enjoys ice and roller skating. His real hobbies, however, are piano and vocal music. For a number of years in Kansas he was a Scout Master and at two different times had charge of a group of boys at Brown Memorial Camp at Abilene.

On November 27, 1912, Mr. Humphrey was married to Ruth Beatrice Donnelly at Kanopolis. Mrs. Humphrey was born at Woodbury, Pennsylvania, December 26, 1890. She is a teacher in the Sunday School class and the secretary of the Ladies Auxiliary, as well as a member of the Ladies Club. There are five children: Ella Virginia, born December 12, 1913, is a student at Hastings College; Ruth Inez, born January 23, 1915; Helen Marie, born December 13, 1917; James Rae, born July 20, 1923; and Jeanne Louise, born May 7, 1927. Inez is a flute player with five years experience. Inez and Helen play the piano and have studied since the age of seven years. Virginia was graduated from Baker High School of Stapleton, as valedictorian of her class, and was the winner of a music scholarship in piano at

the conservatory of Hastings College in the fall of 1931. Residence: Stapleton.

Henry Albert Humrich

Henry Albert Humrich, farmer, was born in Pawnee City, Nebraska, December 26, 1883, son of John Wesley and Elizabeth (Clark) Humrich. The father was born in Illinois, June 20, 1854, and died at Pawnee City, July 2, 1931. He was a farmer. His wife, Elizabeth, was born at Planalp, Indiana, April 13, 1857. Her grandfather Jennings emigrated to the United States from England, while quite young.

Mr. Humrich attended public school and high school at Pawnee City and was graduated from business college at Pawnee City in 1904. He also attended Lincoln Business College at Lincoln in 1906.

From 1906 until 1914 Mr. Humrich was a bookkeeper for the Collins Ice Cream Company at Lincoln, Nebraska. From 1914 to 1918 he owned and operated a farm near Pawnee City, and since 1918 has operated his farm one and one-half miles northwest of Beaver City. He is a Republican, a member of the Methodist Episcopal Church, the Red Cross, and the Nebraskana Society. He enjoys athletics, baseball and football. Mr. Humrich recalls that during the month of February, 1919, a blizzard of great intensity visited the country. The snow drifted and buried 500 sheep for nearly 48 hours, however the sheep were released with but minor loss.

On November 3, 1909, he was married to Gladys Georgia Warner at Beaver City. She was born at Hendley, Nebraska, February 21, 1890. Her parents were natives of New York State. Mrs. Humrich is a member of the Methodist Choir, the Ladies Aid, and is past president of Chapter BV, P. E. O. at Beaver City also W. W. W. Club. They have one son, Verne, born December 15, 1910. Residence: Beaver City.

Algie Clarence Hunkins

Algie Clarence Hunkins, who is a banker at Cushing, Nebraska, is a lifetime resident of this state. He was born in Seward County, Nebraska, October 3, 1884, the son of Clarence William and Susan (Haney) Hunkins. His father was a farmer until the age of 35 and then entered business at Cordova, Nebraska, where he served as postmaster for a number of years.

Mr. Hunkins attended Hastings Business College for a time, having previously been graduated from the Cordova High School. He is cashier of the Cushing Bank at this time, and holds membership in the Masonic Lodge and the Nebraskana Society. He likes to hunt.

He was married at Lincoln, Nebraska, December 16, 1917, to Rosa E. Deahn who was born at Lincoln, July 7, 1892. To them two children were born: Helen, October 31, 1918; and Audrey, April 8, 1921. Residence: Cushing.

Lloyd Emerson Hunkins

Lloyd Emerson Hunkins, superintendant of schools at Exeter, Nebraska, is a lifetime resident of this state. He was born at Stratton, Hitchcock County, Nebraska, October 17, 1898, the son of Frank Benjamin and Ida May Hunkins. His father, a farmer, was born at Waukeshaw, Wisconsin, October 3, 1857; his English ancestors came to this country in 1659. His mother was born at Bushnell, Illinois, September 10, 1868, of Pennsylvania Dutch ancestry.

Superintendent Hunkins attended a rural school in Hitchcock County until 1912, and in 1916, was graduated from the Stratton High School. He received the B. S. degree from the University of Nebraska, in 1923, and the A. M. degree in 1931. He was elected to membership in Phi Delta Kappa at the University of Nebraska. He has held the following positions in the professional world: rural school teacher in Hitchcock County for one year;

teacher in the Wolbach High School for one semester; mathematics teacher in the Exeter High School, 1923-6; and since 1926, superintendent of public schools at Exeter.

He is the author of *Planning of Office Space in Small School Systems*. Mr. Hunkins is a member of the Nebraska State Teachers Association, the Nebraska Schoolmasters' Club, and the Exeter Commercial Club. He was secretary-treasurer of the Superintendents and Principals Association, 1929-30, is affiliated with the Methodist Church, and holds membership in the American Legion. He is a Democrat.

His marriage to Jennie Pearl Cleveland was solemnized at Trenton, Nebraska, June 24, 1923. Mrs. Hunkins, whose ancestry is English and Irish, was born at Stratton, December 14, 1898. They have two children: Vaughn, born September 1, 1925; and Dwain, born May 18, 1930. Residence: Exeter.

Edward Leontine Hunt

Edward L. Hunt was born at Fairfield, Iowa, August 10, 1884, the son of Ebenezer Warren Hunt and Katie (Bessel) Hunt. His father, who was born in Erie County, New York, May 3, 1851, and died at Omaha, Nebraska, November 19, 1913, was a minister and a professor at the University of Nebraska. His ancestors were Saxon English settlers in America in early colonial days.

His mother, whose ancestry was English, was born in Oswego County, New York, June 1861, and died at Lincoln, Nebraska, June, 1888. As a young woman she was a school teacher.

Mr. Hunt was graduated from the public school in 1896. He has lived in Nebraska 43 years and has always been a farmer. He has been in the Republican county organization for the last ten years and in 1929-31 served as state representative from the fifth district of Nebraska. He has always been interested in promoting the welfare and progress of his community and state.

He is a member of the Farmers Educational and Co-operative Union of Nebraska, and is secretary of the County Fair Association. He serves on the district school board and is a member of the Nebraskana Society. He is affiliated with the Methodist Church. Residence: Syracuse.

Frank Bradford Hunt

Frank Bradford Hunt, leading executive of Hastings, was born at Lenox, Iowa, December 15, 1874, and came to Nebraska about forty-eight years ago. He is the son of Clark Asberry and Frances (Wilcox) Hunt, both pioneer Nebraskans. Clark Asberry Hunt was born in Chagrin Falls, Ohio, May 11, 1847, coming to Iowa as a young man, and to Nebraska about 1884. He was a farmer, whose death occurred at Lincoln, on March 10, 1930. His wife, who was a native of New York, was born May 9, 1850, and died at Burchard, Nebraska, November 10, 1923.

Educated in the public and high schools of Burchard, Mr. Hunt was secretary and manager of the Burchard Telephone Company from 1905-16. Prior thereto and from 1902 to 1905, he was a member of the hardware and implement firm of Hunt and Hutton at Burchard. He was engaged in the general merchandise business at Burchard, from 1905-16 as a member of the firm of Hunt and Milks. Removing to Wymore, in 1916, for the following three years he engaged in the automobile business there, leaving in 1919 to become partner and manager of the Hunt Motor Company at Hastings.

A Republican, Mr. Hunt served as a member of the board of county commissioners of Pawnee County from 1906-13. He is a member of the First Methodist Episcopal Church of Hastings, and is a life member of the Nebraskana Society. He was united in marriage to Flora

Ada Milks at Burchard, on July 3, 1899, and has two children, Marvel, born September 4, 1901, who married Alvin C. Edwards, and Dorothy, born May 31, 1905, who married Homer Hubbard. Mrs. Hunt was born at Picatonia, Illinois, December 2, 1877. Residence: Hastings.

Glenn Howard Hunt

Born at Wilsonville, Nebraska, September 29, 1893, Glenn Howard Hunt is the son of William Austin and Mary Iola (McDonald) Hunt. His father was born in Ohio, September 22, 1866, and died at Wilsonville, December 24, 1902. A blacksmith and mechanic, he was of German and Scotch descent. His mother, a native of Wisconsin, was born September 30, 1872, and died at Hastings, July 26, 1930. She was of Scotch-Irish and German extraction and during the latter part of her life was active in the work of the Woman's Club.

Glenn Howard Hunt attended the Wilsonville public and high school, and was graduated from the latter in May, 1910. On June 6, 1914, he received his D. D. S. from the University of Nebraska, and has since been engaged in practice, except for two years after graduation when he taught at the University of Nebraska. His fraternity is Xi Psi Phi.

On June 1, 1916, Dr. Hunt was united in marriage to Edith May Randall at Kansas City, Missouri. Mrs. Hunt, who is of Scotch-Irish descent, was born at Lincoln, May 3, 1893. Dr. and Mrs. Hunt attend the Methodist Church.

During the World War period Dr. Hunt held the rank of first lieutenant in the Dental Reserve Corps, and at the present time is a captain in the Reserve Officers. He is a member of the national, state and district dental associations, the Red Cross and Salvation Army, the Chamber of Commerce and the Young Men's Christian Association. An Elk and a Mason, he is also a life member of the Nebraskana Society. He is fond of golf, and is a member of the Hastings Country Club. At the present time he is serving his sixth year as city councilman. He is a Republican. Residence: Hastings.

Loren Thomas Hunt

Loren Hunt was born at Atwood, Kansas, December 17, 1893, the son of James Edgar and Minnie (Moody) Hunt. His father, who was born at Raritan, Illinois, May 22, 1862, died at Friend, Nebraska, March 6, 1909. His mother was born at Taylorsville, Illinois, April 6, 1870.

Dr. Hunt was graduated from the Friend High School in 1911, and in 1915, received his D. D. S. degree at the University of Nebraska, where he was a member of Xi Psi Phi. He served as secretary of the Lincoln chapter of the latter organization. Entering the practice of dentistry at Lincoln, July 1, 1915, he has been there since that date.

He is a member of the District Dental Association; the Nebraska State Dental Association; the American Dental Association; the Cornhusker Study Club, the Lincoln Community Chest; the Lincoln Chamber of Commerce; the Red Cross; and the American Interprofessional Institute. His social club is the Lincoln University Club. He is a Republican. Residence: Lincoln.

Elga Van Camp Hunter

Elga Van Camp Hunter, a lifelong resident of Loretto, Nebraska, was born there, February 27, 1885, the daughter of G. V. and Laura E. (Whipple) Van Camp. Her father, who was born in Wisconsin, September 14, 1844, and died at Tilden, Nebraska, October 7, 1928, was a pioneer homesteader in Nebraska in 1872 and lived on the same farm in Boone County until his death. Her mother, whose ancestors were natives of New York, was born in Wisconsin, May 4, 1862, and died at Loretto, February 28, 1899.

Mrs. Hunter received her advanced education at

Doane College, Crete, Nebraska, where she was a student for two years. She is president of the Woman's Club of Loretto, is assistant postmistress there, and has been active in civic and educational affairs for many years. She is affiliated with the South Methodist Episcopal Church, serving as Sunday School superintendent, and was formerly president of the local Parent Teachers Association. Her hobby is reading.

Of her marriage to Irwin Hunter, who is a farmer, mechanic, and musician, three children were born: Irwin, November 6, 1908; Margaret E., March 27, 1910; and Robert David, June 6, 1913. Irwin is a master mechanic and is a graduate of the Lincoln Flying School. All the children are musically talented. Residence: Loretto.

Frank Le Roy Hunter

Frank LeRoy Hunter, general merchant, was born at Page, Nebraska, November 8, 1888, son of George Elmer and Eva Adeline (Farr) Hunter. The father, born at Victory, Wisconsin, August 9, 1862, was a merchant, farmer, and during the years 1880 until 1890 was constable. His ancestry is English and Scotch. His wife, Eva Adeline, was born in Schenectady, New York, September 30, 1860, and was the first school teacher in Page. Her ancestry is French and German.

Mr. Hunter attended public school, and was graduated from the commercial course at Nebraska Wesleyan University in 1909. During most of the time since he was 21, he has been a merchant and farmer. From 1924 until 1930 he was manager of the Farmers Union at Coleridge, and is now the owner and manager of the general merchandising business at Stuart.

On November 23, 1911, he was married to Olive Etta Wagers at Eugene. She was born at Page, Nebraska, October 15, 1888, and died at Lodi, California, November 7, 1918. There are two children of this marriage, Gordon, born November 25, 1913; and Glenn, born April 20, 1918. On January 5, 1920, Mr. Hunter was married to Tressa F. Townsend, and they have one child, Nondyce, born May 19, 1921.

Mr. Hunter has been a resident of Nebraska for 39 years. He is a member of the Methodist Church, the Lions Club and the Odd Fellows. He enjoys baseball and fishing. Residence: Stuart.

James Anderson Hunter

James Anderson Hunter, prominent Box Butte County ranchman, was born at Walshville, Illinois, September 17, 1862, son of Robert and Elizabeth (Anderson) Hunter. The father was born in Scotland, and died at Walshville, Illinois, in February, 1891. He was a farmer. The mother, also born at Scotland, died at Broken Bow, Nebraska, in 1900.

Mr. Hunter attended the public schools of Walshville, and afterward was a student at business college at St. Louis. On August 1, 1888, Mr. Hunter was married to Annie Sarah Harris at Farm Home, Nebraska. Mrs. Hunter was born at Petersburg, Illinois, December 24, 1868, and died on a ranch home near Hemingford, Nebraska, October 21, 1894. She was a teacher before her marriage. There were two children of this marriage, Robert Leroy, born August 29, 1889, who married Zillah Grace Stewart; and Grace Elizabeth, born May 21, 1891, who died April 22, 1892.

On June 29, 1897, Mr. Hunter was married to Nellie Harris in Dawes County, Nebraska. She was a sister of the first wife and was also a teacher. Twin boys, born of this marriage September 19, 1904, died at birth. A son, James Harris, born February 16, 1910, married Pauline Grace Pickerell. Robert is a ranchman, and James is part owner and manager of the Drake Hotel in Alliance.

For many years Mr. Hunter has been prominent in every activity in his community. For 25 years he has been retired. He is the owner of a ranch of more than 7000 acres on the Niobrara River, and is a part owner of the Drake Hotel of 70 rooms in Alliance, in addition to other property.

He is a Republican, a Methodist, and an Elk. Residence: Alliance.

Richard Charles Hunter

Richard C. Hunter, lawyer, legislator and judge, is the son of Jabez Richard Hunter, born in Catteraugus County, New York, August 1841. J. R. Hunter was in his earlier life the publisher of a daily Democratic newspaper in Milwaukee. While still a young man he came to Nebraska where he organized the Union Life Insurance Company, the first Life Insurance company in the state. He was of Scotch, Irish, Dutch and English descent. His death occurred at Omaha in February of 1919.

Sarah Frances Olmstead, wife of J. R. Hunter, was a native of Potsdam, New York, born in 1848. She came west with her husband and was a pioneer Nebraskan. She was descended from English settlers in the vicinity of what is now New York, prior to the Revolution. She died in Omaha in March, 1921.

Richard C. Hunter attended the Omaha public schools and was graduated from Omaha High School in 1904. He received his A. B. from the University of Nebraska in 1909, and his LL. B. from Columbia University in 1911; and also attended Harvard University College of Law one year. A member of the Columbia debating team in 1911 he debated against Cornell University, and is a member of Delta Sigma Rho and Sigma Alpha Epsilon.

Mr. Hunter has been engaged in the practice of law in Omaha for the past nineteen years. He is a Democrat, and served as member of the state legislature in 1915 During 1915-16 he was judge of the municipal court of Omaha. He was his party's nominee for attorney general in 1920 and for state railway commissioner in 1928.

He was married to Viletta G. Taylor at Lincoln, April 22, 1908. Mrs. Hunter, who was born at Eagle, Nebraska, September 12, 1888, is extremely active in civic club work in Omaha.

Mr. Hunter is a Protestant. He belongs to the Elks and to the Masonic lodge, is a member of the Nebraska State and Omaha-Douglas County Bar Associations. His favorite sports are golf and horseback riding. Residence: Omaha.

William Nuzum Hunter

William N. Hunter, editor, has lived in Nebraska for over 50 years. He was born at Davenport, Scott County, Iowa, November 22, 1867, the son of Elizabeth Peterman (Nuzum) and Charles Franklin Hunter. His father was a farmer whose ancestors came to America from Scotland, early in the hostory of the country. Quaker ancestors came to America with William Penn, and landed at Chester, Pennsylvania. He was an Indian Scout and from 1861, to 1866, was a government mail carrier in the Rocky Mountains. He was born in Delaware County, Pennsylvania, January 3, 1928, and died at Syracuse, Otoe County, Nebraska, February 16, 1897.

His mother, who was born in Delaware County, Pennsylvania, October 27, 1828, and died at Syracuse, October 17, 1919, was a clerk in Philadelphia, during her girlhood. Her ancestry was English and Irish.

Mr. Hunter attended the public schools of Iowa and Nebraska, and was later graduated from business college. He is the editor of the Syracuse *Journal-Democrat*. He was made clerk and treasurer of Syracuse, in 1925, and still holds this position. He was secretary of the Democratic Central Committee for six years. From 1917, to 1922, he acted as postmaster at Syracuse.

He was married to Bertha May Hall, at Nebraska City, Otoe County, Nebraska, July 27, 1883. Mrs. Hunter was born at Palmyra, Otoe County, Nebraska, July 27, 1883, and traces her ancestry directly to the Winslow

WILLIAM N. HUNTER

family and Miles Standish of Mayflower fame. Six children were born to this union, five of whom are living. They are: Charles Asbury, born January 4, 1902, who is with the Nebraska Highway Commission; William Albert, born April 21, 1904, who is in the United States Navy; Ruth, born January 19, 1906, who died September 14, 1920; Eugene Avery, born March 25, 1910, who has enlisted in the navy, is now in service in Pacific waters; Hugh Edward, born December 1, 1911; and Wesley Elmer, born January 16, 1914.

During the World War Mr. Hunter was in charge of the war savings drive in his city; was a minute man; and was a member of the Council of Defense. From 1922 to 1925, he was secretary of the Syracuse Chamber of Commerce. He was a member of the public library board since 1924 to 1927, and since 1925 has been secretary of the board of education. He is a member of the Otoe County Historical Commission and the Nebraskana Society. He has been co-operative observer of the United States Weather Bureau since 1890, making a monthly report. He is a Mason, Scottish Rite, 32nd degree, and is secretary of the local lodge of this organization. He is affiliated with the First Methodist Episcopal Church at Syracuse. Residence: Syracuse.

Ellsworth LeRoy Hurlbert

Ellsworth LeRoy Hurlbert, who is manager of the Co-operative Oil Company at Oxford, Nebraska, has lived in this state all his life. He was born at Sutton, Nebraska, April 21, 1888, the son of William Henry and Olean W. Hurlbert. His father, who was born at Rome, New York, September 14, 1858, and died at Edison, Nebraska, March 10, 1918, was a farmer and the manager of the North Platte Creamery Company. He came to Nebraska with his father, William Hurlbert, who homesteaded in Clay County in 1871, and was united in marriage to Orleana W. Bush at Edgar, Nebraska, in 1883. Mrs. Hurlbert, an active church worker, was born at Alton, Illinois, March 9, 1863, and resides at Inglewood, California.

Mr. Hurlbert attended the high school at Ong, Nebraska. He is the manager of the Oxford Co-operative Oil Company and owns a tourist camp at Oxford. He holds membership in the Independent Order of Odd Fellows, the Modern Woodmen of America, and the Nebraskana Society. His hobby is baseball.

On February 23, 1910, he was married at Holdrege, Nebraska, to Grace Viola Bard, who was born at Grant, Nebraska, June 19, 1889. Their children are: Charles, born December 18, 1910; Cleora, born June 10, 1912; Logan, born November 2, 1915; Irene, born August 1, 1920; Neal, born December 10, 1923; and Evelyn, born June 1, 1925. Charles is employed in a furniture store, and Cleora is a mercantile clerk. Residence: Oxford.

Clifford Job Hurless

Clifford Job Hurless was born at West Lima, Wisconsin, January 19, 1896, the son of Henry McLean and Emily Jane (Matthews) Hurless. His father, a livestock dealer, was born at West Lima in 1859, and died at LaCrosse, Wisconsin, in 1926; his grandfather came to America from England and settled in New England. His mother, a milliner and an active worker in the Women's Christian Temperance Union, was born at Viola, Wisconsin, in 1862. Her grandfather, who came to America in a sailing vessel, fought in the War of 1812, and her great-uncle was governor of Saxony.

Mr. Hurless attended the public schools of West Lima, and in 1915 was graduated from the high school at Lynch, Nebraska. He has been a successful clothing merchant at Lynch for the past 17 years, and is field agent for the Brotherhood of American Yeoman. A Republican, he is committeeman of the party in Lynch.

He is affiliated with the Methodist Episcopal Church of Lynch, is a member of the city council, has served as secretary of the Lynch Chamber of Commerce, and from 1923 to 1931 acted as president of the Red Cross. He is secretary and past master of Oak Leaf Lodge Number 312 of the Ancient Free and Accepted Masons, is Past Grand of the Ponca Valley Lodge Number 255 of the Independent Order of Odd Fellows, is a member of the Modern Woodmen of America, and is serving as correspondent for the Brotherhood of American Yeomen.

Mr. Hurless served as secretary of the Lynch School Board, 1930-31, is a member of the Parent Teachers Association and holds membership in the Hole-in-One Club and the Lynch Country Club of which he is president.

He was married to Grace Allene Duffy at Pierce, Nebraska, May 23, 1917. Mrs. Hurless, who is a business woman, was born at Carthage, Illinois, November 29, 1892. They have three children: Ruth Eloise, born May 2, 1919; Emma Jane, August 18, 1923; and Helen Adelle, October 1, 1926. Residence: Lynch.

Louis Jacob Husa

Born at Crete, Nebraska, November 9, 1882, Louis Jacob Husa is the son of Joseph and Barbara (Panek) Husa. His father, a pioneer Nebraska farmer, was born at Dobrejice, near Hluboka, Bohemia, November 19, 1833, and died at Crete on January 1, 1918. His mother was born in Bohemia December 4, 1845. Her death occurred at Barneston on May 20, 1906.

Louis Jacob Husa, the subject of this sketch, attended rural school near Crete and the Barneston public school. On September 11, 1907, he was married to Barbara Kunc at Crab Orchard. Mrs. Husa was born at Sedlec near Horovice, Bohemia, December 4, 1880.

There are three children, Arnold, born December 19, 1908; Melvin, born January 22, 1910, and Olga, born June 20, 1913. All were graduated from Otoe Consolidated High School, while Melvin is a student at the University of Nebraska.

Mr. Husa is a leading farmer in his community, is a member of the Farmers Union and various agricultural organizations. He is a member of the Board of Education, the Parent Teachers Association, the Z. C. B. J. and The Nebraskana Society. His favorite sport is baseball and his hobby is hunting. Residence: Barneston.

Joseph Amos Husak

Joseph A. Husak, retired farmer, was born in Zalesi, Nove Mesto, Moravia, July 20, 1858, son of Pancratius and Anna (Smatlan) Husak. His father was born in Paseky, Moravia, March 26, 1826, and died on his farm in Colfax County, Nebraska, after many years as a pioneer farmer, on November 9, 1908. Anna Smatlan Husak was born in Teleci, Policka, Bohemia, February 13, 1835, and died in Stanton County, Nebraska, February 4, 1912.

For the past fifty-eight years Joseph A. Husak has been engaged in farming in Colfax County, and an outstanding citizen in his community. He is descended from one of those few families who escaped extermination in the religious wars in early European history, and who came to the United States to enjoy freedom. Although not active politically, he has always taken a keen interest in public affairs, and has a well grounded knowledge of public questions. He is a Democrat.

Mr. Husak's farm is located in Stanton County, Reinsen precinct, and his sons, Frank and Lumir, are on the home place. Mr. Husak was morried to Joseph Rousar, at Schuyler, Nebraska, on March 4, 1889. Mrs. Husak was born in Milovy, Policka, Bohemia, March 22, 1866, and to them eight children were born, seven of whom are living: Miles, born January 27, 1890, married Mary Kroupa; Adelaide born February 22, 1891, married Peter Petitt, and lives in California; Olga, born July 11, 1892, married J. C. Lewis, and lives in California; Lumir, born September 29, 1893, married Clara Wecker; Joseph, born

October 7, 1895, enlisted in Company G, 61st Infantry, 5th Division, and took part in the St. Mihiel Drive and Argonne engagements; Frank, born March 26, 1898, married Anna Hayek; Julia, born January 12, 1905, died July 19, 1923; and Elsie, born January 17, 1907.

During the World War Mr. Husak was active in loan drives and for several years he served as precinct assessor. He is a Presbyterian, and a member of Signet Lodge No. 193, Free and Accepted Masons at Leigh. He is also a member of The Nebraskana Society. Residence: Leigh.

Earl Kenneth Husbands

Earl Kenneth Husbands, hardware merchant, was born at Madison, Nebraska, February 15, 1893, son of Charles Frederick and Hattie Martha (Howard) Husbands. The father, who was born in Shepshed, England, December 21, 1855, came to the United States about 1864 and has since engaged as a merchant. His wife, Hattie Martha Howard, was born in Vermont, and died at Gresham, Nebraska, December 16, 1913. She was a member and officer of the local Woman's Club and a teacher for a number of years. She was descended from early New England stock.

Mr. Husbands was graduated from Gresham High School, and attended Lincoln High School one year. From 1914 until 1921 he was a member of the firm of Husbands & Hawley, and since that time has owned and operated a retail hardware business of his own. He is a Democrat.

On March 23, 1929, he was married to Margaret Leota Davidson at Omaha. She was assistant cashier at the First National Bank, and was born at Gresham, April 7, 1894. One daughter was born to· them, Marianne, born January 15, 1931, who died the same day.

Mr. Husbands is a member of Gresham Presbyterian Church, the Red Cross (1917), the Morning Star Lodge No. 197 of the Ancient Free and Accepted Masons (master one year, secretary two years), and the Nebraskana Society. His sports are tennis, baseball, hunting, and fishing. Residence: Gresham.

Eugene Webster Huse

Eugene Webster Huse, editor and publisher, was born in Janesville, Minnesota, December 14, 1870, son of William and Ruth Elmina (Berry) Huse. William Huse, lawyer and publisher, was a native of Binghamton, New York, born in 1828. He came to Nebraska about 1871, where he was a pioneer newspaper man. His death occurred at Wayne, in October, 1906. Ruth Elmina, wife of William Huse, was born at Jamestown, New York, March 17, 1840, and died at Wayne, on March 28, 1911.

Educated in the public schools of Ponca, Nebraska, Eugene Webster Huse entered the newspaper business with his father, and was co-editor with him of the *Ponca Journal* for several years. From 1899, to 1903, he was editor of the *Klamath Falls Republican*, and from 1903-06, was editor of the *Wayne Herald*. He was editor of the *Beatrice Daily Express* from 1906-10, and since 1910 has been owner and editor of the *Wayne Herald*. Mr. Huse is a stockholder in the Stratton Hotel Corporation at Wayne.

On August 19, 1896, he was united in marriage to May Della Fisher, at Wymore, Nebraska. Mrs. Huse, a prominent clubwoman and a member of the Daughters of the American Revolution, was born at Belings Grove, Pennsylvania, January 6, 1873. There are four children, Olive, born April 17, 1898; Dorothy, born November 12, 1899, who married Fred Nyberg; Edith, born March 28, 1903, who married D. S. Whightman, and Miriam, born February 1, 1912.

Mr. Huse is a Republican, and a Blue Lodge Mason. He is affiliated with the Christian Science Church, and is a member of the Kiwanis Club and The Nebraskana Society. He is fond of hiking and is a member of the Wayne Country Club. Residence: Wayne.

Gene Franklin Huse

Born at Ponca, Nebraska, August 15, 1885, Gene Franklin Huse is the son of William Nathaniel and Mary (Leggett) Huse. The father, born at Albany, New York, was for many years the publisher of the *Norfolk Daily News*. His death occurred at Norfolk, January 13, 1913. He was of Welsh descent. His wife, Mary Leggett, was born at Marion, Ohio. She is of German descent.

Gene Franklin Huse attended the public schools of Norfolk being graduated from high school in 1904. Thereafter he attended the University of Nebraska three years, where he was a member of Phi Kappa Psi.

On September 20, 1911, he was married to Lucy Newbolt Harris at Reno, Nevada. Mrs. Huse, who is of Canadian ancestry, was born in Missouri Valley, Iowa, January 18, 1885. There are three children, Jean, born February 27, 1913; Charlotte, born September 28, 1915; and Gene, born January 17, 1927.

For some years Mr. Huse was associated with his father in the newspaper business, and since his death has been publisher of the *Norfolk Daily News*. He is a Republican. In 1919 he was decorated by the Belgian government for his work in war relief. He is affiliated with Trinity Episcopal Church, is a Mason, and a member of the Nebraskana Society. Residence: Norfolk.

Frederick Raymond Hussong

Frederick Raymond Hussong, was born at Sunnyside Farm, near Marshalltown, Iowa, February 24, 1870, son of John Jackson and Clarissa Alice (Bullman) Hussong. Mr. Hussong received his education in the country schools of Mound Valley, Kansas, and the high schools of Cathage, Missouri, and Nelson, Nebraska.

On April 29, 1898, he was married to Alice Katie Wankmiller, of Omaha. They have one daughter, Alice Eugenia. Mr. Hussong's religious affiliation is with Westminster Presbyterian Church, in which he has held various offices. He is a Democrat, a Mason, a member of the Kiwanis Club, and the Chamber of Commerce, and a former member and director of the Young Men's Christian Association.

For a number of years Mr. Hussong was associated with the firm of Rudge & Guenzel, and in 1916 became president and manager of F. R. Hussong, Incorporated, automobile dealers. Since 1930 he has been a member of the firms F. R. Hussong and F. R. Hussong Finance Company. Residence: Lincoln.

Charles Luke Hustead

Charles L. Hustead, one of Falls City's leading physicians, was born at Linn, Kansas, July 12, 1884. Silas Davis Hustead, his father, who was born at Fort Madison, Iowa, September 18, 1850, was a farmer and merchant; his father was English born and later lived in Virginia. Caroline Hustead, his mother, was born at Pleasant Ridge, Iowa, of English parentage, and was a resident of Vermont for many years.

Dr. Hustead was graduated from the Linn Public School in 1904. In 1905 and 1906 he was a country school teacher, and then became an employee of the Western Bridge & Construction Company of Omaha, 1907-08. He was a student at Creighton University, 1908-12, where he was granted his M. D. degree.

He has taken the following post-graduate courses: *Clinical Pathology* at New York Post Graduate Medical School & Hospital, 1919; *Medicine*, Nebraska University, 1920; *X-Ray*, Omaha, 1922; *X-Ray and Physio-Therapy*, Kansas City, 1925-26; *Pathology*, at Johns Hopkins University, 1930; and *X-Ray* and *Pathology*, Johns Hopkins University, 1930. He has attended the post-graduate courses of the Inter-State Post Graduate Medical Assemblies at Milwaukee, 1924; St. Paul, 1925; Cleveland, 1926; Kansas City, 1927; Atlanta, 1928; Detroit, 1929; and Minneapolis, 1930.

Dr. Hustead is surgeon and director of the staff at Falls City Hospital, Falls City, Nebraska, and is roentgenologist in this institution. He has been division surgeon of the Chicago, Burlington & Quincy Railroad since 1922. He is the author of: *The Acute Pelvis*, 1928; *Treatment of Carbuncles*, 1927; *Diverticulum of the Bladder*, 1927; *Thrombo Angiitis of the Hand*, 1925; *Gangrene*, 1929; and *Infectious Arthritis of the Elbow*, 1925.

United in marriage to Rosa Louise Kretzschmar at Omaha, Douglas County, Nebraska, February 26, 1913, their children are Charles Luke, Jr., born November 29, 1913, who is a senior in the Kemper Military School at Booneville, Missouri; and Claire Louise, born September 16, 1917, who is a student in the Falls City grade school.

Dr. Hustead was medical examiner of the local draft board throughout the World War. He is a member of the Richardson County Medical Society, having served as secretary and treasurer since 1922; Nebraska State Medical Society; American Medical Association; and Railway Surgeons Association. Active in the Rotary Club he has served as chairman of the boys' work committee, international services, and chairman of vacation service. He holds membership in the Falls City Chamber of Commerce, the Elks, Odd Fellows, and the Nebraskana Society. He is a member of the Falls City Elks Country Club. Residence: Falls City.

George Robert Huston

Born June 27, 1900, at Riverdale, Nebraska, George Robert Huston is the son of George William and Clara Mary (Lake) Huston. His father, who was a farmer, and road contractor, was born at Burlington, Iowa, March 18, 1859, and died at Kearney, Nebraska, January 9, 1928; his Irish, English, and German ancestors were in America prior to the Revolution. His mother, who was born at Shelburne, Vermont, August 5, 1867, is eligible to membership in the Daughters of the American Revolution through her English ancestry. She received her education in normal school, was a teacher for many years, and is prominent in the Kearney Woman's Club at this time.

Mr. Huston was graduated from the Kearney High School in 1917, received the A. B. degree at Nebraska Wesleyan University in 1921, and in 1924 was awarded the LL. B. degree at Columbia University. He is a member of Phi Kappa Phi chapter, and the Pi Kappa Delta chapter of the Nebraska Wesleyan University where he was active in the glee club, took part in college dramatics, and was president of the local fraternity, Everett. He is also a member of Story Inn, the Columbia University Chapter of Phi Delta Phi, a legal fraternity.

Since 1924 Mr. Huston has been engaged in the practice of law at Kearney where he has served as justice of the peace and police judge. He was a candidate for the state legislature in 1930, and is a member of the local Republican club. He is a member of the Kearney Chamber of Commerce, the Cosmopolitan Club, and the Nebraska State Bar Association.

Mr. Huston holds membership in the American Legion, is affiliated with the First Methodist Episcopal Church of Kearney, and is a member of the Grand View Golf Club. His sports include golfing, tennis and hiking, while his other recreations are music, drama, reading and philately.

His marriage to Grace Wilma Terhune was solemnized at Kearney, November 27, 1930. Mrs. Huston, who was born at Oblong, Illinois, December 15, 1901, comes of a long musical ancestry. She is a musician and radio artist of note. She was a participant in the finals of the national voice contest conducted by the National Federation of Women's Clubs at Boston in 1928. She is of French, English, and German ancestry, and is a member of the Hoover family of Iowa. Her father is Rev. Willard Ira Terhune, a Methodist minister at Nashville, Illinois. She is a graduate of Illinois Women's College and Chicago Musical College. Residence: Kearney.

John Evan Hutchins

John Evan Hutchins, superintendent of schools at Overton, was born at Cowles, Nebraska, June 27, 1894, son of John Nicholas and Charollet Eliza (Brimmer) Hutchins. The father, born in Ohio, December 11, 1865, was a railroader twenty-two years, and upon resigning received a recommendation which allows him to return at any time. A successful farmer since 1906, he has served as county commissioner three consecutive terms. He is of English, Scotch and German descent. Charollet, the wife of John Nicholas Hutchins, was a native of Iowa, born April 11, 1871. A strict adherant to moral and Christian principles, she is active in community projects, and has served as chairman of the Republican county committee three terms. Her ancestry is principally Scotch on the maternal side, while on the paternal side she was Yankee and Dutch.

Educated first in the grade and high school at Cowles, John Evan Hutchins was graduated from the Red Cloud High School in 1913; and attended Peru State Teachers College and the University of Nebraska. In high school he was active in basketball and track, and while in the university was a member of Palladian Literary Society, the University Band, and Kappa Lambda, honorary musician's fraternity. At Peru he was a member of Philomathean Literary Society.

From 1913-16 Mr. Hutchins taught in District No. 24, Webster County, Nebraska. On June 24, 1917 he enlisted in the United States Navy as a musician, 2nd class, serving nine months as a member of the band on *the U. S. S. Louisiana*, about eight months on the *U. S. S. Frederick*, and two months on the *U. S. S. New Mexico*. He also performed convoy duty while in war service, as well as taking part as a musician in various loan drives. Since 1920 Mr. Hutchins has been teaching continuously. In 1920-22 he taught in the Cowles High School, from 1922-29 he was city superintendent at Wilcox, and since that time has been superintendent at Overton. He is a member of the American Legion, the National Geographic Society, the Masons, Order of Eastern Star, and the Methodist Episcopal Church. He is a life member of the National Educational Association, a member of the Nebraska State Teachers Association, chairman of the Lions Club educational committee, and a Republican. He enjoys basketball, often serving as referee; is interested in mechanics, and fond of the saxophone.

On October 9, 1920, Mr. Hutchins was married to Marguerite Annette Jones at Lincoln. Mrs. Hutchins, who was born at Craig, Colorado, August 26, 1895, is Welch on her father's side and Scotch and German on her mother's. They have four children, Jean Dorothy, born July 24, 1921; Robert Evan, born July 31, 1922; Wilma Lucille, born April 21, 1924; and Eleanor May, born June 30, 1927. Residence: Overton.

Samuel C. Hutchinson

Samuel C. Hutchinson, real estate and insurance man, was born at Allerton, Iowa, March 14, 1870, son of William A. and Rebecca J. Hutchinson. He attended public and high school, and on October 11, 1900 was married to Elizabeth Eick at Diller. Mrs. Hutchinson was born at Lenox, Iowa, January 11, 1876. There is one son, Harold R., born July 27, 1901.

Mr. Hutchinson has resided in Nebraska forty years, and from 1896 until 1905 was in the mercantile business. He was postmaster from 1906-14, and in the farm implements and automobile business from 1914-19. From 1919-27 he was in the banking business. He is a Republican.

He is a member of the Presbyterian Church, the Commercial Club (president 1927-31), the Modern Woodmen of America and the Masons. From 1919 until 1925 he was president of the board of education. Residence: Diller.

George W. Hutchison

A leading business man at Red Cloud, Nebraska, is George W. Hutchison who has been a resident of this state since 1878. He came to Nebraska from Port Louisa, Louisa County, Iowa, in a covered wagon with his mother, two brothers and two sisters, and lived in a dugout near Red Cloud for about four years. He was born at Port Louisa, Louisa County, Iowa, July 21, 1867, the son of George and Mary Elizabeth (Huber) Hutchison, the former a merchant and steamboat agent, who was born in Iowa, February 12, 1820, and died May 17, 1871, at Port Louisa. His mother was born in Switzerland, November 30, 1826, and came to America aboard a sailing vessel at the age of six weeks. She died December 2, 1898, at Wilcox, Nebraska.

Mr. Hutchison has been engaged in the abstract, insurance and real estate business at Red Cloud for many years and has taken a prominent part in civic and political affairs there. He served as clerk of the district court in Webster County from 1904 to 1911 and at this time is city clerk of Red Cloud and a past member of the city council. He is a Mason, and past master of the Blue Lodge, past high priest of the chapter, past commander of the Knight Templars, and a member of the Mystic Shrine at Hastings.

His marriage to Anna Fogle was solemnized at Red Cloud in 1888. Mrs. Hutchison, whose ancestry is German, was born at Hollidaysburg, Pennsylvania, October 10, 1872. One son was born to them, Roy, June 6, 1889, who died in November, 1918; he was married to Bernice Heldman. Mr. Hutchison's grandson, George W., 3rd, has made his home with his grandparents since he was three years of age. Residence: Red Cloud.

John Huwaldt

John Huwaldt, successful farmer of Cedar County, Nebraska, is a lifetime resident of Nebraska. He was born in Pierce County on November 26, 1884, the son of August and Christina (Peterson) Huwaldt. His father, a farmer, was born at Passade-Holstein, Germany, August 2, 1853, came to this country in 1870, and died at Norfolk, January 27, 1929.

Mr. Huwaldt is a member of The Nebraskana Society, and is affiliated with St. John's Lutheran Church. He was united in marriage with Anne Marie Druhe at Pierce, Pierce County, Nebraska, May 22, 1907. She was born in Washington County, Nebraska, February 27, 1884. Their children are: Minnie, born May 8, 1908, who married Ernest Stratheman; Edna, born September 25, 1913; and Marvin, born September 25, 1921. Residence: Randolph.

James Martin Hyde

James M. Hyde was born at Waco, York County, Nebraska, August 3, 1882, the son of James Martin and Mary McClure Hyde. His father, a farmer, was born in County Armagh, Ireland, and died at Waco, July 19, 1887. His mother was born in County Armaugh, April 1, 1848, and died at Waco, March 13, 1928.

Mr. Hyde attended the public schools in York County and for three years was a student at York Business College. He has lived in York County all his life and for many years has been a farmer near Waco. He is moderator of the District Five School Board, is a member of the Red Cross, and holds membership in the Odd Fellows Lodge. He is a member of The Nebraskana Society and is affiliated with the Presbyterian Church of Utica, Nebraska.

He married Maud Edith Watson at Waco, York County, Nebraska, December 22, 1909. Mrs. Hyde was born at Corridon, Indiana, February 7, 1889. They have three children: Virgil, born September 26, 1910; Vyrle, born May 20, 1912; and Lowell, born June 30, 1914. Mr. Hyde is a Republican. Residence: Waco.

Mason Egbert Hyde

Born at Wilcox, Nebraska, November 16, 1884, Mason Egbert Hyde is the son of Henry Egbert and Minnie Jane (Norsworthy) Hyde. The father, a farmer, was born in Monticello, New York, January 23, 1853, and in 1875, came to Nebraska with an ox team, homesteading in Franklin County. His parents' ancestors came from England, with the first colonists, fighting under General Washington in the Revolution. Henry E. Hyde died at Gothenburg, Nebraska, May 11, 1931. His marriage took place at Gothenburg, on December 25, 1883.

Minnie Jane Norsworthy was born in Toronto, Canada, September 21, 1864. Her father was English, and her mother Scotch; they came to the United States from Canada, when she was a small child, settling in Dawson County. Mrs. Hyde is still living.

Educated in country school, Mason Egbert Hyde afterward attended Wilcox High School, Franklin Academy and Colorado College. He was a member of the Apollonian Debating Club, the Glee Club, and Gamma Delta chapter of Beta Theta Pi (member of local petitioning and receiving charter). During 1902-05, he was a member of the football and track teams at Franklin Academy, and the years 1908-10, was a member of the track team at Colorado College.

On June 19, 1912, Mr. Hyde was married to Fanny Almena Blank at Macon, Nebraska. Mrs. Hyde, who was born at Franklin, August 15, 1890, is the daughter of pioneer settlers in Franklin County, in 1872, from Germany. She is president of the local and county Women's Christian Temperance Union. There are three children: Henry Glen, born August 6, 1913; Rachel Elizabeth, born February 23, 1916; and Mason Egbert, Jr., born October 6, 1918.

Mr. Hyde was a country school teacher for a time after leaving school, and thereafter was teacher and athletic director in the Franklin High School. In 1910, he became cashier of the Macon State Bank, and at the same time was postmaster at Macon. He was assistant cashier of the State Bank of Farnam, for a time, and has since been the owner of the Gothenburg Nurseries. He was elected to the state legislature, 1923-24, on the Democratic ticket, and was defeated for a second term by a Republican.

Mr. Hyde held the rank of sergeant, Company L, 5th Nebraska National Guard on Mexican Border Service. He is a Mason (30th degree), an Odd Fellow, and is affiliated with the Banner Methodist Episcopal Church. For fourteen years he served as a member of the state executive committee of the Nebraska State Grange. He was an honorary member of the Nebraska State Historical Society 1923-24, and was recently made a life member of The Nebraskana Society. Mr. Hyde has been a member of the Young Men's Christian Association in years past, and has served as treasurer and as a member of the redistricting committee for the Consolidated Schools of Dawson County. His favorite sport is hunting, while his hobby is horticulture. Residence: Gothenburg.

Lester Ansel Hyland

Lester Ansel Hyland was born at Lowell, Oregon, August 9, 1893, son of Grant Noble and Catherine (Crugan) Hyland. The father, born in Lowell August 29, 1862, is a stockman of Scotch-Irish descent. His wife, Catherine, was born at Creswell, Oregon, October 27, 1862, of French and Pennsylvania Dutch descent. She is a school teacher.

Dr. Hyland attended grade school until 1909 and was graduated from High School in 1913 at Eugene. He received the degree of Doctor of Dental Surgery in 1919 from Northwestern University. Prior thereto he was a pre-medic student at the University of Oregon one year. Dr. Hyland is a member of Psi Omega.

His marriage to Clare Emily Melms was solemnized at Chicago on March 29, 1919. Mrs. Hyland was born at Chicago October 9, 1896. They have two children, Ruth Emily, born February 19, 1920, and Lester Robert, born June 30, 1926.

Dr. Hyland is a Republican. He served in the World War, is a member of the Methodist Episcopal Church, the American Dental Association, the Stapleton Commercial Club, the Masons, and the Parent-Teachers Association. His favorite sports are golf and football, while he devotes much of his time to hunting and fishing. Residence: Stapleton.

William N. Hylton

William N. Hylton who has been a physician at Gresham, Nebraska, since 1887, was born at New Virginia, Iowa, May 22, 1862. His father George, W. Hylton, a farmer and merchant, was born at Crawfordsville, Indiana, September, 1837, and died at Elmwood, Nebraska, in 1924. His family originally lived in Virginia. Letitia (Erwin) Hylton, mother of William, was born in Managhan, Ireland, in 1841, and died in Nebraska in 1924; she was a teacher prior to her marriage. Her ancestry was Scotch-Irish.

Dr. Hylton was graduated from the Elmwood High School and in 1886 received his M. D. degree at the University of Nebraska. He was valedictorian of his graduating class in medical school, and was active in baseball. He is president of the First National Bank at Gresham, and has been engaged in medical practice there for over 40 years.

He was married to Lulu Lanphere at Gresham, June 19, 1892. Mrs. Hylton, who was a teacher before her marriage, was born in Whiteside County, Illinois, December 9, 1866, and died at Gresham, June 24, 1924. They have three children: Harry, born May 10, 1893; Helen, born August 4, 1895; and George, born June 20, 1902, who attended the University of Nebraska, class of 1924. He is a farmer.

Harry is vice president of the First National Bank of Gresham. Helen is a graduate of the University School of Music at Lincoln, and is assistant professor of piano at the University of Wyoming.

Dr. Hylton has been mayor of Gresham and township clerk, a member of the school board 42 years, retiring voluntarily last spring. He was never defeated for any office. He is a Modern Woodman of America, a Woodman of the World, and a Presbyterian. Dr. Hylton has done post graduate work in the Post Graduate Medical School in Chicago, 1898, and at Mayo Brothers Clinic at Rochester, 1920. Residence: Gresham.

Lloyd F. Illingworth

Lloyd F. Illingworth was born at Fairfield, Nebraska, August 15, 1891, the son of George and Caroline (Doody) Illingworth. His father, whose ancestry was English, was a farmer and school teacher. His mother was of English descent.

When Mr. Illingworth was seven years of age he accompanied his parents on a trip abroad, visiting Scotland and England. He was graduated from the Fairfield High School in 1911, where he was active in debating. He also took a leading part in the graduating class play. Immediately upon graduating he farmed close to Fairfield for a period of five years.

Mr. Illingworth has lived in Nebraska all his life and for many years has been engaged in the insurance business at Fairfield. He is a member of the Nebraskana Society and is affiliated with the Fairfield Christian Church.

He married Mary Ransom at Fairfield, July 28, 1912. Mrs. Illingworth, whose ancestry was English, was born at Fairfield, December 28, 1892, and died there September 25, 1924. They have three children, Elton, born January 19, 1914, who graduated from Fairfield High School in 1931 and won first place in the state music contest and the contest held at Tulsa,

Oklahoma; Denton, born April 26, 1915, who was valedictorian of his graduating class, 1932; and Marie, born March 18, 1924. Residence: Fairfield.

Charles Reade Imler

Charles Reade Imler was born at Pavia, Pennsylvania, November 4, 1873, the son of Eli Whysong and Elizabeth (Ickes) Imler. His father, who was a merchant, was born in Blair County, Pennsylvania, February 17, 1849, the son of Isaac M. and Catherine (Whysong) Imler. He died at Shubert, Nebraska, April 8, 1917. His ancestor, George Michael Imler, arriver in America from Germany in 1732. His mother was born at Pavia, July 20, 1852, the daughter of Philip and Barbara (Weyant) Ickes, of German ancestry. She died at Shubert, December 26, 1910.

Mr. Imler was graduated from Nelson High School in 1894, and from 1896 to 1898 was a student at the University of Nebraska, where he held membership in Alpha Theta Chi. He has been engaged in the real estate, loan, insurance, and abstract business at Nelson since 1900, and at this time is an abstracter of titles.

During the late war Mr. Imler was chairman of the Four Minute men in Nuckolls County, and took part in Red Cross drives. He holds membership in the Nelson Chamber of Commerce, is affiliated with the Presbyterian Church, and is a director in the County Red Cross organization. He is a member of the Masonic Lodge at Nelson, Tadmor Chapter and Palmyra Commandery at Superior, Nebraska. His sports are golfing, hunting, and fishing, and his hobby is mechanics.

His marriage to Helen Hill occurred at Beaver Crossing, Nebraska, October 28, 1903. She was born at Clarinda, Iowa, in 1878, and died at Lincoln, Nebraska, May 3, 1920. She was the daughter of Joseph and Rhoda (Wright) Hill.

Two children were born to them, John Gordon, January 29, 1913, who is a student at Hastings College; and Charles Robert, April 18, 1920. On June 10, 1922, Mr. Imler was united in marriage with Minnie E. Hellner at Westfield, New Jersey. She died January 22, 1927. She was the daughter of Carl and Margaret (Nielsen) Hellner.

A Republican, Mr. Imler served as county treasurer from 1908 to 1912, and has been chairman of the Republican central committee of Nuckolls County for the past ten years. Residence: Nelson. (Photograph in Album).

Royal Clark Inger

Royal Clark Inger, hotel proprietor, was born in Strawberry Point, Iowa, August 18, 1878, and has been a resident of Hastings, Nebraska, fourteen years. He is the son of John Dawson and Elizabeth Maria (Bullock) Inger, the former a native of England, born in 1847. John Dawson Inger came to America, in 1849, with his parents, and engaged as a veterinary surgeon until his death at Waverly, Iowa, in February, 1912. Elizabeth Maria Bullock was born at Strawberry Point, on January 9, 1855, and is still living.

Mr. Inger attended the public schools of Waverly, Iowa, and also attended Waverly High School. Prior to becoming the owner of the Hotel Alexander, at Hastings, he was employed in hotels, clubs and in dining car service. Mr. Inger is a Republican, a member of the Sons of Veterans, St. Mark's Pro-Cathedral, the Elks, and the Masonic Order. In the last mentioned he is a member of the Scottish Rite, 32nd degree, the Knights Templar, Shrine and Eastern Star. He is a member of the Red Cross, the Nebraska Hotel Association and the Nebraskana Society, and his social club is the Hillside Golf Club, where he enjoys an occasional game of golf.

On September 12, 1898, he was united in marriage to

Allie May Greene at Vinton, Iowa. Mrs. Inger, who assists her husband in the operation of his hotel, was born at Woodstock, Kansas, January 27, 1879. They have one son, Clifford, born August 11, 1899, who is married to Esther Myrle Bielefeldt. Residence: Hastings.

Henry Ingerle

Prominent in Howard County for many years, Henry Ingerle has been postmaster at Elba since 1929. His father, Vencil Ingerle, was born in Vienna, Austria, August 27, 1837, and came to America with his wife, Marie Grecar, in 1872. He was a sergeant in the Austrian Army before coming to America. He settled in Saunders County, and died at Elba, July 27, 1917. Marie Grecar, born in Austria, January 17, 1835, died at Elba, February 6, 1920. The family came to Howard County in 1883.

Henry Ingerle was born at Weston, Nebraska, November 30, 1876, and was educated in country school. On July 27, 1904, he was married to Hattie Elizabeth Naprstek, at Elba, where she was born July 4, 1887. They have five children, Louis, born July 1, 1906, who married Jean Killenbarger; Augusta, born September 21, 1908, who married Joseph Spilinek; Clara, born October 22, 1910; Herbert, born March 16, 1912; and Albert, born April 3, 1919. Louis is a garageman, Augusta is a farmers' wife, while Clara is chief operator for the Northwestern Bell Telephone Company.

From January 1, 1921, until January 1, 1929, Mr. Ingerle was a member of the Board of Commissioners of Howard County. Since that time he has been postmaster at Elba. He was first lieutenant of Company A, Howard County Home Guard 1918-20, is a member of the United Brethren Church, the Masons (chapter, commandery, Shrine,) and The Nebraskana Society. His hobby is fishing. Residence: Elba.

Samuel Espy Ingram

Samuel Espy Ingram, a resident of Nebraska for the past 48 years, was born at North English, Iowa, April 5, 1872, the son of Henry and Mahatia (Reed) Ingram. His father, who was a farmer, was born in Indiana in 1842, and died at Millersburg, Iowa. His mother was born in Indiana in 1846, and died there in 1881.

Mr. Ingram was graduated from the high school at Clay Center, Nebraska, and in 1892 was a student at the Lincoln Business College. He was a farmer for 10 years, engaged in the mercantile business for over 23 years, and managed a garage for five years. He holds membership in the Modern Woodmen of America, the Red Cross, and the Presbyterian Church.

His marriage to Anna Florence Alford was solemnized at Clay Center, September 2, 1894. Mrs. Ingram, whose ancestry is English, was born at Palmyra, Illinois, June 14, 1875. Their three children are: Erwin, born November 1, 1895, who married Neva Moore; Will, born November 7, 1898, who married Iva Palmer; and Irene, born April 24, 1901, who married Walter Grebe. Erwin is a farmer, Will is engaged in the mercantile business, and Irene is a homemaker. Residence: Lebanon.

William M. Iodence

William M. Iodence, lawyer, farmer and rancher, was born at Taylorville, Illinois, October 27, 1860, son of Henry H. and Jane (Miller) Iodence.

His father came to America from Frankfort-on-the-Main, Germany, about 1835. His mother's family came from Kentucky. They were prominent pioneer settlers of Sangamon and Christian Counties, Illinois.

Mr. Iodence attended public school, and taught from 1880 until 1882. He was deputy county clerk of Seward County, 1883-84, and studied law the two years following. He was admitted to practice in 1886 in the district court of Seward County, by Judge T. L. Norval.

Mr. Iodence came to Box Butte County, in October, 1887, and was admitted to practice in Supreme Court in 1888. He continued the practice of law exclusively until 1902 when he moved on a ranch. He is now operating a ranch and farm with his son, Charles G., as a partner, farming about 1000 acres and running a herd of 400 registered Hereford cattle. Mr. Iodence's ranch comprises about 6000 acres.

Mr. Iodence is a Democrat, aand was the county attorney of Box Butte County during 1897 and 1898. He was elected to the Nebraska Legislature in 1930 from district No. 100, and served through the 47th session and the special session of 1931. He still appears occasionally as an attorney in district and supreme court.

On March 25, 1885, he was married to Mary Culliford at Seward, Nebraska. She is the daughter of Thomas and Mary (Millet) Culliford and a direct descendant of Oliver Cromwell. She helped organize the first Woman's Club of the state and served as its president for several years. Her hobby is painting.

Mrs. Iodence was born in Bath, England, April 15, 1859. Mr. and Mrs. Iodence have two children, Charles G., born June 13, 1887, who married Mary Kriz; and Mary, born April 3, 1890, who married Andrew Iversen.

Since 1894 Mr. Iodence has been a member of the Modern Woodmen of America. He was recently elected to life membership in the Nebraskana Society. Residence: Hemingford.

Fred Marshall Ireland

Fred Marshall Ireland, real estate and insurance man, was born at Gordon, Nebraska, April 18, 1888, son of George Henry and Alice Carey (Wilkinson) Ireland.

The father was born in Ohio, June 28, 1850, and was a farmer at Gordon, until his death there on March 8, 1930. His ancestry was English and Irish. His wife, Alice, was born in Illinois, June 13, 1854, and died February 9, 1923.

Mr. Ireland attended country school and Gordon High School, and later was a student at the School of Agriculture at Lincoln, Nebraska. Until 1919 he was a clerk in a store, and in 1920 became a cashier. Since 1921 he has been in the insurance business for himself. He has served as police magistrate and local justice of the peace. His politics are independent.

On December 24, 1913, he was married to Gladys Jean Case in Cherry County, Nebraska. Mrs. Ireland was born at Whitesville, Missouri, May 22, 1893. There are four children, Esther Elaine, born October 11, 1915; Evelyn Ruth, born April 14, 1917; Wilfred Case, born December 14, 1919; and Mary Jean, born December 18, 1927.

Mr. Ireland was active in various drives during the World War. He is a member and secretary of the Volunteer Fire Department of Gordon, secretary of the local Odd Fellows Lodge, a member of the First Presbyterian Church, and the National Geographic Society. He enjoys baseball, hunting and fishing, while his hobby is playing cards. Residence: Gordon.

George Albert Ireland

George Albert Ireland, county treasurer of Burt County, was born at Urbana, Illinois, March 11, 1871, son of Wallace Leroy and Minerva Nancy Johnson. At the age of four he came to Nebraska, and was educated in the public schools. He has been a continuous resident of the state for the past fifty-six years.

Elected clerk of the district court on the Republican ticket, he served from January 7, 1904, to May 18, 1909, when he served as county judge until June 4, 1918, Since 1927 he has been Burt county treasurer.

He was married to Rose Isabell Thorndike at Admah, Nebraska, May 30, 1893. Mrs. Ireland was born at Admah, October 29, 1873. They have four sons and daughters, Raleigh Clark, born August 20, 1896, who married Inez McDowell; Ethel May, born September 12, 1904; Ruby Grace, born August 10, 1908; and Amy Rose born March 2, 1911.

Mr. Ireland was a member of the Nebraska Council of Defense and active in all civilian projects during the World War. He is affiliated with the Church of Christ, and since February, 1925, has been a member of the board of education at Tekamah. He is a member of the Tekamah Chamber of Commerce, the Masonic Order, the Nebraskana Society and the National Geographic Society. He was city councilman of Tekamah four years, and city clerk two years. Residence: Tekamah.

Isaiah Whitset Irvin

At Bigelow, Marshall County, Kansas, Isaiah W. Irvin was born, April 2, 1876, the son of William Barrere and Mary Elizabeth (Boyd) Irvin. His father, who was born at Sabina, Ohio, August 14, 1843, and died at Lincoln, Nebraska, January 7, 1915.

In 1900 Dr. Irvin attended Cotner College, and in 1905 was graduated from the Lincoln Medical College. He was admitted to the practice of medicine in June, 1905, and since that time has been active in the medical field. A resident of Nebraska since 1900, he is now vice president of the Brownville Orchards Company, Incorporated.

His marriage to Jennie McDill Fullerton was solemnized at Lincoln, Nebraska, November 20, 1907. Mrs. Irvin was born of Irish and German parents in Peery County, Illinois, October 19, 1880. Before her marriage she was a nurse. Three children were born to this union, two of whom are living. They are: Gerald W., born October 22, 1911; Raymond F., born October 2, 1912, who died January 10, 1915; and Roy W., born July 28, 1921.

Dr. Irvin is past president of the Auburn Kiwanis Club; a member of the Chamber of Commerce; and the city library board. He is ex-mayor of Auburn, also. He is a member of the county and state medical societies and is a fellow of the American Medical Association. He is a Mason, an dis affiliated with the Auburn Church of Christ. He is a Republican. Residence: Auburn.

William Leland Irvin

A leading Republican, William Leland Irvin is at the present time a lawyer and first assistant clerk of the senate judiciary committee at Washington, D. C.

He was born at Rankin, Illinois, April 12, 1892, son of Joseph Hewins and Harriet Damaras (Palmer) Irvin. The father, born at Sheldon, Illinois, December 26, 1861, is a farmer, member of the school board and road commissioner. He is the son of Captain Abram Irvin who served in the Union Army during the Civil War, of Irish, English and Welsh descent. He was the only child.

Harriet Damaras Palmer, who was born in Adams County, Ohio, April 13, 1857, died at Ranking, Illinois, on September 22, 1930. A teacher prior to marriage, she was the youngest child of Cornelius and Harriet Palmer.

William L. Irvin attended the Schwartz rural school near Rankin, Illinois until 1910; was graduated from Grand Prairie Seminary at Onarga, Illinois in 1916; received his A. B. degree from North Western University in 1920 and his LL. B. from Harvard in 1923.

During his high school days he was active in basketball, baseball and track, was a member of the debating team three years, took part in several school plays, was the winner of an oratorical contest and was president of his senior class. He received Phi Beta Kappa honors from Northwestern University, but as he worked his way thru college, had no time for extra-curricular activities.

On April 28, 1929 he was married to Bertha Frances Eells at Rankin. Mrs. Irvin, who was born at Rankin, May 14, 1902, taught music and other subjects before marriage. She is the only daughter of Milton C. and Louella (Droll) Eells. They have one child, Leona Frances, born March 31, 1930.

Admitted to the bar at Lincoln, November 27, 1923, Mr. Irvin was until October 1, 1925, employed as a lawyer in the office of Edwin F. Myers of Broken Bow. Since November, 1925 he has had his own law office there. He was secretary of the Custer County Republican central committee 1928-30; candidate for the Republican nomination for county attorney 1926; Republican candidate for county attorney 1930; and city attorney of Broken Bow from November 1926 to April 1929. He maintains a law office at Broken Bow, and practices there between sessions of congress.

Entering the United States Army as a private during the World War, he later obtained the commission of second lieutenant of infantry at Camp Gordon, Georgia. He is a member of Joseph E. Palmer Post of the American Legion, the Harvard Law School Association, the Nebraska State and Custer County Bar Associations. His religious affiliation is with the Broken Bow Methodist Episcopal Church. He is a member of the Red Cross, the Nebraskana Society and the Ancient Free and Accepted Masons. His hobby is reading. Residence: Broken Bow.

Arthur James Irvine

For the past 35 years Arthur James Irvine has been a successful stockman near Hamlet, Nebraska. He was born in Polk County, Iowa, January 2, 1859, the son of James William and Rebecca Catharine (Furst) Irvine.

His father, who was a blacksmith and farmer, was born in New Brunswick, in 1818, and died in Polk County, Iowa, October 26, 1874; he came to this country in 1828 and settled at Philadelphia. His mother, whose ancestry was German, was born at Millerstown, Pennsylvania, October 21, 1822, and died in Polk County, Iowa, November 7, 1889.

In 1879 he left Polk County, Iowa in a covered wagon in company with J. T. Parks working on several ranches. He arrived at Hamlet, Nebraska in the spring of 1883, where he homesteaded and since that time has made his home on his ranch three miles north of Hamlet, consisting of 6000 acres. He now resides in a nine room home built of natural stone, the lime being burned on the premises, procured from the surrounding country. Within a hundred yards of Mr. Irvine's house is located a school house built in 1886 and made of the same material. His daughter, Grace, received her elementary education in that school.

Mr. Irvine was married to Ida May Heater in Hayes County, Nebraska, December 26, 1889; she was born at Wood, Ohio, November 7, 1864. Of the three children born to their marriage, only one is living: Grace, June 17, 1905, who received the Bachelor of Arts and Master of Arts degrees at the University of Colorado in 1926 and 1927 respectively. Albert H., born February 16, 1891, died October 1, 1891; and Florence, who was born December 6, 1897, died January 11, 1904.

In 1897 he was elected to the office of county clerk of Hayes County for a term of two years, which included the ex-officio office of clerk of the district court.

He holds membership in the Denver Athletic Club of Colorado, is a member of the Democratic Party, and holds membership in the Nebraskana Society. Residence: Hamlet. (Photograph in Album).

Joshua Alvin Isaman

A resident of Nebraska for the past 59 years, Joshua Alvin Isaman was born near Hillsboro, Iowa, July 4, 1869, the son of Benjamin Franklin and Mary (Newbold) Isaman. His father, who was born in West Moreland County, Pennsylvania, August 4, 1841, came to Nebraska in April, 1873, and homesteaded in Hamilton County about four miles west of Aurora. He retired from the farm in 1896 and made his home in Aurora until his death on October 6, 1900. The homestead is still retained by Joshua A. Isaman and his sister, Rachel F. Cole of Lincoln. He served as county commissioner for two terms and was a successful farmer. He was color sergeant in Company F., 14th Iowa Infantry during the Civil War. His mother was born in Pennsylvania, March 30, 1851, and died at Aurora, October 14, 1914.

Mr. Isaman attended the public schools of Aurora, and the high school at Mount Pleasant, Iowa, and later attended York Business College. He was engaged in the abstract of title business at North Platte, Nebraska, 1894-95, was a farmer in Hamilton County, Nebraska, 1896-1902, was elected county clerk of Hamilton County on the Republican ticket and served 1902-03. Since 1903 he has been in the real estate, insurance and abstract business at Aurora. He is president of the Farmers State Bank, has been secretary of the Farmers Mutual Insurance Company of Hamilton County since 1900, is a director in the Aurora Building & Loan Association of which he is also vice president, and is a director in the Protective Fire Insurance Company of Seward, Nebraska.

He served as president of the Aurora Rotary Club, 1928-29, is affiliated with the First Methodist Church, and holds membership in the Aurora Business Men's Club and the state Young Men's Christian Association. His social club is the Aurora Country Club and his fraternal organizations include: Modern Woodmen of America; Royal Highlanders, Order of Eastern Star and the Masons. He is a past patron of the Order of Eastern Star and is a 32nd degree Mason, member of the Shrine, and is serving his 20th year as secretary of Shekinah Chapter Number 32, R. A. M.

On April 17, 1895, his marriage to May Elizabeth Salisbury occurred at North Platte. Mrs. Isaman was born at Dwight, Illinois, December 23, 1869. She is affiliated with the First Methodist Church, is a member of the Worth While Project Club, and her fraternal organization is the Order of the Eastern Star of which she is past matron.

Mr. and Mrs. Isaman have two children, Frances, born March 19, 1896; and Emma, born July 13, 1897, who married McKinley Cooper Brown, and is the mother of six children of which there are two pairs of twins, Edwin, May 1, 1918; Earl G. and Donald J., born February 13, 1920; Mae Jean, December 9, 1924; Harold Allen and Gerald Alvin, April 25, 1929. Residence: Aurora. (Photograph in Album).

May Elizabeth Isaman

May Elizabeth Isaman, homemaker, was born at Dwight, Illinois, December 23, 1869, daughter of William Nelson and Philena Louise (Mathews) Salisbury.

The father was born in Georgetown, Ohio, March 8, 1835, and came to Nebraska in December, 1889. He purchased a ranch in Lincoln County, and retired to spend the last days of his life in North Platte. He died there on August 24, 1902. He was a farmer of Irish descent. His wife, Philena, was born in Georgetown, Ohio, November 30, 1839, and died at North Platte, Nebraska, February 25, 1924. She was a devoted wife and mother. Her ancestry was Scotch.

May Elizabeth Salisbury attended elementary school

in Tonica, LaSalle County, Illinois, and on April 17, 1895, was married to Joshua Alvin Isaman at North Platte. He was born near Hillsboro, Iowa, July 4, 1869. (*See Nebraskana*). There are two children, Frances, born March 19, 1896; and Emma, born July 13, 1897, who married McKinley Cooper Brown. Mr. and Mrs. Brown have six children, Edwin, born May 1, 1918; Earl G. and Donald J., born February 13, 1920; Mae Jean, born December 9, 1924; Harold Allen and Gerald Alvin, born April 25, 1929.

Mrs. Isaman is affiliated with the First Methodist Church. She is past worthy matron of the Order of Eastern Star, and is a member of the Worth While Project Club of Nebraska. Her hobby is needle work. Residence: Aurora. (Photograph in Album).

Andrew Grant Israelsen

Andrew Grant Israelsen one of a family of twelve children, came to Nebraska with his parents in the spring of 1878 and has been a farmer in Clay County most of his life. He was born at Swedona, Illinois, January 22, 1872, the son of Andrew Peter and Charlotta (Larson) Israelsen. His father, also a farmer, was born in Sweden, January 8, 1824, and died at Saronville, Nebraska, February 5, 1909. His mother was born in Sweden, August 6, 1833, and died at Saronville, August 3, 1906.

Mr. Israelsen was engaged in farming near Saronville until 1906 when he became local manager of the telephone exchange. He is a member of the Saronville Methodist Church, has been a member of the school board for over nine years, and is a member of the Red Cross.

His marriage to Emily Christina Backdahl occurred at Saronville, March 10, 1897. Mrs. Israelsen, whose parents were born in Sweden, was born at LaFayette, Indiana, December 2, 1875. Their children are: Verdie, born September 19, 1899, who married Fred E. Hansen of Saronville; Grant W., born September 4, 1901, who married Ethel Peterson of Saronville; and Ralph A., born March 20, 1909, who married Marguerite Claus of Sutton. Fred Hansen is manager for the Farmers Milling and Elevator Company of Aurora. Grant W. operates a garage at Saronville, and Ralph A. is employed by the Chicago, Burlington & Quincy Railroad. Mr. Israelsen is a Republican. Residence: Saronville.

William Israelson

William Israelson, who has been a business man in Nebraska for the past 38 years, was born at Soderham, Sweden, January 24, 1875. His father, Peter Eric Israelson, who was the manger of a lumber and saw mill, was born at Nearka, Sweden, April 15, 1841, and is still living; his ancestors were land owners in Sweden for several generations. His mother, who is also descended from an old family of landholders in Sweden, was born at Westmorland, Sweden, and died at Hartington, Cedar County, Nebraska, March 12, 1927.

Mrs. Israelson, who is a general contractor at Hartington, has been active in the advancement of his community for many years. For a time he was a lumber checker in Sweden, and after his arrival in America he was a general contractor and real estate man. He owned and managed a blacksmith shop and grocery store for a time, and now spends most of his time managing his farms and city property.

A master mechanic in the National Guard for seven years, he is a member of the General Associated Contractors, the Chamber of Commerce, the Nebraskana Society, Independent Order of Odd Fellows, and the Republican party.

On February 11, 1900, he was united in marriage to Louisia Sahara Schager at Hartington. Mrs. Israelson,

WILLIAM ISRAELSON

who is of the Nordic race, was born at Mecklin, Clay County, South Dakota, September 25, 1878. Five children were born to them: Christina, born July 1, 1900, who died November 11, 1931; Albert I., born September 25, 1901; Claude, born August 25, 1903; Carl Arvid, born September 25, 1908, and Wilma O., born November 11, 1915. Wilma is a student is Wayne Normal, while the three boys are in the general contracting business with their father. Claude and Albert are members of Right Angle Lodge No. 303 of the A. F. and A. M. at Omaha. The Israelsons are owners of various post office buildings in Iowa, Nebraska, and North Dakota, which they lease to the government. Residence: Hartington. (Photograph on Page 599).

Ernest Eugene Jackman

Born at Lowpoint, Illinois, March 4, 1884, Ernest Eugene Jackman, banker and lawyer, has resided in Nebraska 45 years.

His father, Ameal Jackman, was born in New Orleans, Louisiana, October 2, 1851, and moved to Nebraska in 1885, settling in Perkins County in 1887, and farmed in this state for many years prior to his death. He died at Grant, Nebraska, October 2, 1929. His wife, Katherine Dunn, native of Illinois, was born February 9, 1858, of Irish ancestors, and is still living.

Mr. Jackman attended the public schools of Grant, and graduated from Franklin Academy in 1904. He attended Doane College the following four years. He was married to Ruth Alice Waggener, who was born in Chase County, Nebraska, May 13, 1892, the daughter of Henry H. and Mary (Humphrey) Waggener. They have four children living and one deceased: Margaret Ruth, born February 3, 1914, and is now a freshman at Doane College, Crete; Fred Willard, born April 3, 1916; Charles Eugene, born in July, 1917; Herbert Lee-born December 29, 1929; and Kathryn Louise, who is deceased.

Mr. Jackman is a Republican and was a delegate to the National Republican Convention in 1916, and for two terms served as representative from the 88th district 1927-1930. He is the author of considerable bank legislation, including the measure abolishing the Guaranty Fund Commission and substituting in lieu thereof the State Receivership plan of handling defunct banks also the Bank Insolvency Act, which defines insolvency which made for better bank examination, and classification of bank papers; and the Bank Re-organization plan whereby 85 per cent of the depositors of a failed bank have the power to re-organize the bank. He has been cashier of the Grant Commercial Bank, of the Venango State Bank of Venango, and was one of the organizers and is the present cashier of the Farmers National Bank of Grant. In 1928 he was admitted to the practice of law in Nebraska.

Mr. Jackman was a four minute speaker during the World War. He is a member of the First Methodist Church, the Odd Fellows, and the Masons, while his sports are football, baseball and track. Residence: Grant. Residence: Grant.

Leo Vincent Jacks

Leo V. Jacks, educator and author, was born at Grand Island, Nebraska, March 14, 1896. His father, Porter Wellville Jacks, who was for many years in the United States Postal Department, is descended from a Welsh family which came to America in 1776. His mother is Margaret Genevieve (McMullen) Jacks.

Professor Jacks attended a parochial school at York, Nebraska, and in 1917 was awarded his A. B. degree at St. Mary's College in Kansas. He received his Ph. D. degree at the American Catholic University at Washington, D. C., in 1922. He is now an instructor at Creighton University. He is the author of: *Service Record,* published

by Scribner's, 1928; and *Xenopon,* published by Scribner's, 1930. He married Maxine Frances White.

He is a member of the American Philological Association, and L' Association Guillainne Bude, of Paris. He is a member of St. John's Catholic Church of Omaha. His favorite sport is rifle and pistol markmanship. Residence: Omaha.

George Washington Jackson

George W. Jackson has lived in Nebraska for the past 45 years and for over 20 years was engaged in the implement business at Nelson, Nebraska. He was born near Galena, Joe Davis County, Illinois, April 11, 1858, the son of William and Elizabeth (Beall) Jackson. His father died at Galena, in 1859, and his mother died at Beatrice, Gage County, Nebraska, 1916.

Mr. Jackson has been active in the political and business life of the state for many years and is now secretary of the State Board of Agriculture at Lincoln, Lancaster County, Nebraska. A Democrat, he served as county clerk of Nuckolls County for four years; was speaker of the Nebraska house of representatives for two sessions, and a member of the legislature three sessions; and in 1920 was vice president of the constitutional convention.

During the World War he made patriotic speeches in the Fifth Congressional District of Nebraska. He is a member of the Chamber of Commerce, in which he holds membership in the agriculture committee; the Young Men's Christian Association; the Rotary Club; the Nebraskana Society; and the Independent Order of the Odd Fellows. He is affiliated with the Methodist Church at Nelson.

His marriage to Anna Cora Hoskings was solemnized at Elizabeth, Joe Davis County, Illinois, November 18, 1885. Mrs. Jackson was born at Elizabeth. They have two children: Earl, who is a salesman for the Pittsburgh Plate Glass Company, at Dallas, Texas; and Winnie, who is a farmers wife. Residence: Nora.

Harold Tracy Jackson

Harold Tracy Jackson was born at Waverly, Iowa, October 6, 1887, the son of Elmore W. and Elizabeth Eunice (Pierson) Jackson. His father, who was a dry goods merchant, was born in New York and died at Waverly, Iowa, November 8, 1899. His mother was born in New York, January 18, 1854.

Mr. Jackson attended the public and high schools at Waverly. He entered the business world as clerk in the Citizens National Bank at Tecumseh, Nebraska, and in 1905 entered the employ of the United States National Bank of Omaha, Nebraska, where he was statement clerk, collection teller, exchange teller, receiving teller, and auditor. In 1912 he bought an interest in the Bank of Belgrade, Belgrade, Nebraska, and acted as cashier of that organization until 1922 when he sold his interest and became vice president of the Citizens State Bank at Cedar Rapids, Nebraska. He is still connected with the latter bank in that capacity.

A Republican, Mr. Jackson served as a member of the village board of trustees of Cedar Rapids for six years, and was a member of the board of education for five years. He holds membership in the Nebraskana Society and in 1928 was chairman of the Cedar Rapids Community Club.

On June 28, 1921, he was married at Ansley, Nebraska to Floreine Sarah McGowan; she was born at Ansley, August 13, 1899. Their two children are: Robert E., born February 8, 1924; and Richard T., born August 11, 1926. Residence: Cedar Rapids.

Henry Clay Jackson

Henry Clay Jackson rancher and farmer, was born at Salem, Indiana, November 14, 1877, son of John

Andrew and Elisabeth Jane (Haley) Jackson. His father, born in Connecticut, July 20, 1847, was the son of Nathan L. Jackson, who was of Irish descent, and whose wife was French. He was a farmer and rancher in Keya Paha County for a number of years prior to his death at Springview on June 18, 1928. His wife, Elisabeth, was born at Salem, January 4, 1849 and died at Springview, January 12, 1905.

Mr. Jackson attended rural school, Fremont Normal College, and for some time taught in the rural schools of his locality. On June 29, 1910 he was married to Vera Lorena Kenaston at Springview. Mrs. Jackson was born there on January 8, 1892, daughter of S. H. Kenaston. He was of Scotch descent, while his wife was German.

There are four children, Fern, born May 24, 1911, who is teaching school at the present time; Margaret, born December 18, 1914; Jean, born September 5, 1916; and Rolan, born July 2, 1918. Margaret and Jean are in high school, while Rolan is in grade school.

Mr. Jackson is a Republican. He is a prominent rancher and landowner, a member of the Parent Teachers Association and The Nebraskana Society. Residence: Springview.

David Carl Jacobson

David C. Jacobson, farmer and livestock feeder of Polk County, Nebraska, was born at Saby, Suioland, Sweden, December 7, 1876, the son of John Olof and Hedda Louisa (Johanson) Jacobson. His father, who was born at Bjorkebo, Sweden, January 16, 1836, came to this country in 1878 and settled in Illinois; later he homesteaded in Saunders County, Nebraska. His mother was born at Saby, and died at Osceola, Nebraska, March 30, 1907.

Mr. Jacobson was united in marriage with Mabel Alice Johnson May 4, 1910, at Stromsburg. Mrs. Jacobson, whose parents were born in Sweden, was born at Stromsburg, April 21, 1888. They have four children: Marion, born June 16, 1914; Laura Jane, born July 16, 1919; Doris Ruth, born August 7, 1922; and Carl David, Jr., born June 8, 1925.

He has lived in Nebraska for the past 45 years and is a member of the Masons, Red Cross, and The Nebraskana Society. Residence: Osceola.

J. H. Jacobson

J. H. Jacobson, now retired, was born at Pontiac, Illinois, March 28, 1861, son of Hans Boland and Annie (Johnson) Jacobson. The father was born in Bergen, Norway, November 6, 1825, and died at Randall, Iowa, July 10, 1903. He was a carpenter and ship builder, who settled in Illinois in 1854. His wife, Annie, was born at Bergen, September 16, 1824, and died at Randall, April 7, 1903.

For a number of years Mr. Jackson was a rancher, a contractor, and builder. He is a Republican, a Presbyterian, a member of the Masons, the Modern Woodmen of America, and the Odd Fellows, and from 1888 until 1895 was director of his local school board. His favorite sport is fishing and his hobby is carpenter work. During the late war he was a strong supporter of all civilian activities.

On September 14, 1887, he was married to Addie Lein at Rushville. She was born at Nevada, Iowa, February 7, 1863. Three children were born to them, Isabelle, born June 14, 1889, who married Leslie A. Peck, and who died January 25, 1930; Helen, born May 3, 1894, who died November 1, 1918; and Lein, who was born December 22, 1898, who married Helen Lindall. Lein is a lawyer. Residence: Gordon.

Lein Boland Jacobson

Lein Boland Jacobson, lawyer and county attorney of Sheridan County, was born at Desmet, South Dakota, December 22, 1898, son of J. H. and Addie (Lein) Jacobson. His father, who is a farmer and rancher, was born at Pontiac, Illinois. His mother in Story County, Iowa. She is a member of the Womens Club.

Mr. Jacobson attended the public schools of Gordon, Nebraska, was graduated from high school there in 1918, and received the Bachelor of Arts and Bachelor of Laws degrees from the University of Nebraska. He was awarded a scholarship in law school, and is a member of Phi Alpha Delta. Since his admission to the bar he has been in active practice.

He is married to Helen Caroline Lindall, who was born at Stanton, Nebraska. They have two daughters, Isabelle, born January 24, 1932; and Gloria, born April 1, 1931.

Mr. Jacobson served in the student army training corps in the World War and is a member of the American Legion. He is affiliated with the Presbyterian Church and is a Mason. His favorite sport is golf, while his hobby is smoking cigarettes. Residence: Gordon.

William Herman Jacobson

William Herman Jacobson, building contractor, was born in Schlesweig, Holstein, Germany, October 6, 1866, and has been a resident of Nebraska for the past sixty years. For more than 56 years he has resided in Waterloo, where he operates a contracting business.

Mr. Jacobson is the foster son of Knud Jacobson and his wife, the former a native of Germany, born October 31, 1832. Knud Jacobson came to America in the 1870's, conducting a brick yard at Waterloo, and later becoming a blacksmith. He died at Lincoln on January 16, 1929, at the age of 96 years, two months and fifteen days. His wife died at the age of 89 years and three months.

Educated in the public and high schools at Waterloo, Mr. Jacobson almost immediately went into business. A Republican, he has been prominent in local politics, serving eight years as mayor, and as a member of the board of education. He has been a member of the board for seventeen years, 15 of which were as secretary.

On September 28, 1898, Mr. Jacobson was married to Mary Ellen Bryant at Waterloo. She was born at Falls City, May 15, 1876, a direct descendant of Stephen Bryant who came from England in 1632 and settled at Plymouth. Mrs. Jacobson is a member of Lewis-Clark chapter of the Daughters of the American Revolution, past matron of the Order of Eastern Star, past grand of the Rebekahs and active in the Woman's Club, the Public Library and the Presbyterian Church.

Mr. and Mrs. Jacobson have two sons, Harold Bryant, born December 5, 1899; and Eugene William, born January 23, 1905, who married Miriam Isabell Stewart. Harold was graduated from business college, attended the University of Nebraska, where he was a member of the Student Army Training Corps, and is a member of the American Legion. Eugene was graduated in engineering from the University of Nebraska and is employed at Pittsburgh, Pennsylvania.

A Lutheran since childhood, Mr. Jacobson is a true Christian. For the past thirty years he has been band and orchestra leader at Waterloo, and recently he was made a life member of the Nebraskana Society. Residence: Waterloo.

Eugene Henry Sharp James

One of the pioneer merchants of Nebraska is Eugene Henry Sharp James who was born at Sesfurd, Sussex County, Delaware, August 21, 1855, and has lived in this state for the past 45 years. His father, John Sharp James, who owned a large plantation in Sussex County, Delaware, was born at Laurel, Delaware, August 7,

1819, and died at Seaford, April 23, 1867. His mother, Harriet (Wallace) James, was born at Seaford, June 12, 1816, and died there, July 20, 1899. Captain Henry Wallace served in the War of 1812.

Harriet (Wallace) James is a descendant of Captain Jacob Wright who was commissioned as captain of a militia in upper Dorchester Cunty, Maryland, May 20, 1778. Jacob Wright, who was the son of Edward and Nancy Wright, married Milcah Cannon, the daughter of Levin Cannon.

Mr. James learned the drug business as an apprentice of Tom Cottingham at Seaford. He has engaged in the drug business at Greenwood, Nebraska, Osceola, Nebraska, and since 1889 has been successful at Grafton, Nebraska in the firm of James & Fulmer. At this time his establishment is the Corner Drug Company of which he is independent owner and manager. He has always taken a keen interest in the political issues of his community and state, and enjoys reading current events. He is a member of the Modern Woodmen of America.

His marriage to Susie Elena Fisher was solemnized at Fairmont, Nebraska, August 21, 1890. Mrs. James, who was a teacher before her marriage, was born at New Columbia, Pennsylvania, January 31, 1864. She is descended from the following Revolutionary soldiers: Adam Smith, who served under Captain Joseph Green in Pennsylvania as a ranger on the frontier; Captain Gerlach Flick, who arrived in Philadelphia in 1751 and whose name appeared first on the muster roll of Colonel Cook Long of Northampton County, Pennsylvania; and Godfrey and Jacob Dieffenderfer, father and son, who served in Company 7, First Batallion, of the Northampton Militia, in Pennsylvania.

The following children were born to this marriage: Glen Hooper, who has been a Nebraska teacher for a number of years, serving as principal of the Exeter High School for a period of five years; Ruth, who married Carson Tanquary Patterson, and who is the mother of two children, Ruth Patricia, born August 27, 1923; and Suzan, born June 9, 1929. Residence: Grafton.

Richard C. James

Richard C. James was born at Lexington, Kentucky, October 14, 1878, son of Lafayette and Harriett (Lewis) James. His father, who was a school teacher, was born in Kentucky, February 3, 1854, and died there, March, 1884. His ancestors, who were English, came from Virginia to Kentucky during the time of the American Revolution.

His mother is descended from an old southern family, originally English. She was born in 1858, in Kentucky and died there in 1880.

Mr. James, who is a lawyer, was graduated from high school at Dunbar, Nebraska, June 1896. He is a graduate of the University of Nebraska where he received his A. B. degree, 1902, and LL. B., 1904. He was a member of the University of Nebraska debating team, 1902-04.

A Democrat, he held the position of county attorney in Richardson County for 12 years. He was admitted to the bar at Lincoln, Nebraska, 1904, and has practiced law in Nebraska since that time.

On April 28, 1917, he was married to Leona Garrett, at Falls City, Nebraska. Mrs. James, who was born at Mullen, Nebraska, is descended from English ancestors who came from Georgia, where they had settled, to Nebraska.

He was a soldier in the First Nebraska Volunteers, Company D., Lincoln, Nebraska, May 2, 1898, in the Spanish American War; was mustered out in San Francisco, August 23, 1899. Mr. James is an Elk and a Mason. He is a member of the Methodist Episcopal Church. His favorite outdoor sport is golf. Residence: Falls City.

Samuel McKinley James

Samuel McKinley James, prominent manufacturer at Hastings, has been active for several years in civic affairs in this state. He was born at Bala, Kansas, April 26, 1897, the son of Stephan and Ruth James. His father, a farmer, was born in Wales, August 15, 1844, came to this country in 1864, and died at Bala, July 5, 1911. His mother was born at Johnstown, Pennsylvania, April 1, 1856

Mr. James attended elementary school at Prairie Grove, Kansas, and in 1911 was graduated from the Kansas State Preparatory School. Later he was a student for three years at Kansas State Agricultural College, where he was a member of the varsity debating team and Pi Kappa Delta.

For a time he was employed by the dairy department of Kansas State Agricultural College. For two years he was the owner of a bottling company at Emporia, Kansas, and since then has been owner and manager of a Coca Cola plant at Hastings. He is a member of the Chamber of Commerce, the Red Cross, Salvation Army, Young Men's Christian Association, and The Nebraskana Society.

His marriage to Ethel Maude Pool was solemnized at Kansas City, Missouri, August 18, 1921. Mrs. James, who was born at Holton, Kansas, November 11, 1895, is secretary-treasurer of the Coca Cola Bottling Company.

Mr. James is a member of the board of directors of the State Bottlers Association, is affiliated with the Presbyterian Church, and holds membership in the Hillside Country Club. During the late war he served for six months; he is now a member of the American Legion. He is a Republican. Residence: Hastings.

Thomas Albert James

Thomas A. James, banker at Stromsburg, Nebraska, was born there August 8, 1888, the son of John William and Julia (Kent) James. His father's death occurred at Benedict, Nebraska, August 21, 1905; his mother died at York, Nebraska, October 29, 1928.

Mr. James was graduated from York High School in 1908 and in 1912 was awarded the A. B. degree at the University of Nebraska where he was elected to membership in Delta Upsilon. He has lived in Nebraska his entire life, and is now president of the First National Bank at Stromsburg. He was principal of Polk High School 1913-15; and superintendent of Polk Schools 1915-16. He is affiliated with the Methodist Episcopal Church, is secretary of the board of education, and holds membership in The Nebraskana Society and the Masons. At present he is chairman of the Polk County Republican committee.

He was united in marriage with Ruth Munger at Lincoln, Nebraska, June 5, 1917. Mrs. James was born at Lincoln, April 7, 1890, and is the daughter of the Honorable and Mrs. T. C. Munger of Lincoln. They have one son, John, born January 29, 1926. Residence: Stromsburg.

Walter Dudley James

A leader in the professional life of Cambridge, Nebraska, Walter Dudley James has been engaged in the practice of law there for 13 years as a member of the firm Butler & James. He was born at Council Bluffs, Iowa, April 17, 1897, the son of Walter Dudley and Minnie Margaret (Mitchell) James. His father was born at High Hill, Missouri, August 4, 1872, and died at Council Bluffs, January 4, 1898. His mother, who is librarian in the Carnegie Library at Brush, Colorado, was born at Ottumwa, Iowa, December 29, 1877.

Mr. James was graduated from the Brush High School in 1914, was a student at the University of Colorado, 1914-15, and in 1919 received the Bachelor of Laws degree at the University of Nebraska where he was a member of the Order of Coif and Phi Alpha Delta. He was active in track and basketball during his high school days.

He is a member of the 14th District Bar Association, the American Bar Association, and the Nebraska State Bar Association of which he was vice president in 1929. Mr. James has been a member of the Cambridge Commercial Club since 1920 and the Rotary Club since 1927, is a member of the Elks, and is affiliated with the Presbyterian Church. His hobby is tennis.

On September 10, 1919, he married Louise Builtte Weicher at Denver, Colorado. Mrs. James, who was born in Chicago, August 18, 1897, is descended from James Thornton and is a member of the Daughters of the American Revolution. They have four children: Walter D., born June 4, 1921; Vincent R., born July 16, 1923; Phillip, born October 11, 1925; and Muriel L., born July 2, 1928. Residence: Cambridge. (Photograph in Album).

Walter Gilbert James

Gilbert James, Nebraska educator, was born at Raritan, Illinois, January 29, 1880, the son of Stephen Price and Martha Elizabeth (Lynch) James. His father, who was a Methodist minister, was born at Baltimore, Maryland, December 9, 1842, and died at Omaha, December 28, 1924; his mother was descended from Lord Thomas Price and Captain Hicks Price. His mother was born at Baltimore, Maryland, October 29, 1843, and died at Abingdon, Illinois, March 22, 1910.

Dean James was graduated from the high school at Sparland, Illinois, in 1898. He holds the following degrees: B. L., 1902, Heddings College; A. B., 1903, Illinois Wesleyan University. He pursued post graduate courses at Northwestern University and received diplomas from the same institution in 1904 and 1907. In the summer of 1911 further post graduate work was done at Columbia College. He later studied at Highland College where the degrees of A. M., and Ph. D. were granted in 1910 and 1913, respectively. He was awarded many medals and ribbons for footracing at Heddings College, 1898-1902; was active in debating, dramatics, aand oratory, and was made member of Tau Kappa Epsilon at Illinois Wesleyan.

A professor at the Iowa Wesleyan University and at Bellevue College, later he was president of Highland College; he is now dean of Omaha University and acting president of that institution. He is a member of the Omaha Chamber of Commerce, the Ad-Sell League, the National Educational Association, and the Nebraska State Teachers' Association. A popular lecturer he is often called upon for literary lectures, recitals, and commencement addresses. He is a Mason, and a member of the North Presbyterian Church of Omaha. His sports include golfing, baseball and tennis. His hobbies are flowers and gardening, and reading poetry.

Dr. James was married November 27, 1907, at Galesburg, Iowa, to Cora B. Smith. Mrs. Smith was born at Ellisville, Fulton County, Illinois, October 29, 1884; her mother was descended from Civil War and Revolutionary leaders; Governor Torry of Louisiana, is an ancestor. They have one son, Edwin, born July 21, 1910. Residence: Omaha.

William Nicholas Jamieson

William Nicholas Jamieson, lawyer, was born at Grand Island, Nebraska, October 12, 1885, son of David F. and Delia (Dunphy) Jamieson.

Mr. Jamieson attended Grand Island public and high schools, and received his Bachelor of Laws degree from Creighton University in 1910. In 1907 he was awarded the Bachelor of Arts degree from St. Mary's College in Kansas.

On June 19, 1911, Mr. Jamieson was married to Mary Ann Lovely at Omaha.

A Democrat, Mr. Jamieson was nominee for congress on the Democratic ticket in 1924. He has engaged in the practice of law for nearly 25 years. He is a member of St. Margaret Mary Catholic Church, the Omaha Bar Association, and the Knights of Columbus. Residence: Omaha.

Joseph Jankowski

Born in Poland, December 19, 1869, Joseph Jankowski has been a banker at Ashton, Nebraska, for the past 22 years, and for 48 years has been a resident of this state. His father, Francis Jankowski, was born in Poland, came to America, in 1883, and died at Ashton, May 22, 1913. His mother was born in Poland, and died at Ashton, March 17, 1907.

Mr. Jankowski has served as township clerk for the past 15 years, and during the World War was district food administrator in Sherman County. He has been a director of the Ashton Schools, is local chairman for the American Red Cross, and is a member of St. Francis Catholic Church and the Knights of Columbus. He has been cashier of the Ashton State Bank for the past 22 years. He is a Democrat.

He married Anna Maciejewski at Farwell, Nebraska, September 25, 1894. Mrs. Jankowski was born in Poland, July 16, 1875. These children were born to their marriage: Clara, born November 1, 1895, who married Hubert Topolski; Paulina, born June 10, 1897, who married A. E. Kalkowski; Anton, born January 1, 1889; Alexander, May 30, 1900; Thomas, born November 29, 1902; Regina, born July 3, 1904, who married R. A. Gdanitz; and Andrew, born February 2, 1906. The two older girls reside on farms; Regina is the wife of a merchant; Alex is a civil engineer; and the two other sons are bankers. Residence: Ashton.

John Janovec

A lifetime resident of this state, John Janovec was born at Morse Bluff, Nebraska, October 12, 1876, the son of John Joseph and Marie (Roubal) Janovec. His father, who was born in Czechoslovakia, in 1848, and died at Morse Bluff, January 28, 1902, was a farmer who came to America in 1868. His mother, who came to this country in 1870, was born in Czechoslovakia, 1850, and died at Morse Bluff, May 9, 1914.

Mr. Janovec attended the public schools of Nebraska and later attended business college. He has been engaged in business for the past fifteen years at Morse Bluff, and for three years has been a member of the Morse Bluff school board. He is a member of the Ancient Order of United Workmen and The Nebraskana Society. He is a Republican.

On January 16, 1902, he was married to Emilie Soukup at Morse Bluff. Mrs. Janovec was born at Morse Bluff, June 16, 1879; her parents having emigrated to America in 1869. They have a son, Raymond, born November 21, 1903, who married Clara Hoffman. Residence: Morse Bluff.

Clark Jeary

Clark Jeary, lawyer at Lincoln, Nebraska, was born there April 25, 1892, and has lived there all of his life. His father, Edwin, Jeary, who was a retired banker for several years before his death, served as state representative from Cass County (1887) and Lancaster County (1913-15); he was born at Stalham, Norfolk, England, March 6, 1850, and died at Lincoln, January 6, 1930. His mother, Kittie (Sampson) Jeary was born in Iowa, August, 1860, and is still living.

Mr. Jeary attended the grade and high schools of Lincoln; was a student at the University of Michigan Law College, 1912; and received the LL. B. degree at the University of Nebraska in 1914. He held membership in Kappa Sigma at the University of Nebraska. A Republican, he has held the following public offices: state representative, 1919-21, from Lancaster County, state senator, 1925-27-29; and chairman of the Zoning Board of Appeals for the city of Lincoln.

His marriage to Marie Minor was solemnized at Hyannis, Nebraska, July 16, 1914. Mrs. Jeary was born at Hyannis, January 3, 1893. They have two children: Barbara, born in 1918; and Edward in 1931.

Mr. Jeary is a member of the Nebraska State Bar Society; the Lancaster County Bar Society; The Nebraskana Society; Lincoln University Club; and the Shrine Country Club. He is now serving on the budget committee for the Lincoln Community Chest, and holds membership in the Masons, Scottish Rite, Shrine; and the Elks. Residence: Lincoln.

Albert Webb Jefferis

Albert Webb Jefferis, lawyer, was born at Embreville, Pennsylvania, December 7, 1868, and came to Nebraska nearly 40 years ago.

He received his education at Pennsylvania State Normal School and the University of Michigan, from which he received the Bachelor of Laws degree.

On October 27, 1897, he was married to Helen Josephine Malarkey at Oregon, Illinois. There are two children, Albert W., Jr., and Janet.

A Republican, Mr. Jefferis has served as assistant county attorney, a member of the House of Representatives, and has been a candidate for the United States Senate. He has been engaged in the practice of law since 1893. Residence: Omaha.

Andrew Jay Jenison

Andrew Jay Jenison, physician, was born at Sastalia, Iowa, August 5, 1862, son of Luther Alonzo and Charlotte (Stowell) Jenison. He received his medical degree from the State University of Iowa in 1895, and has been in active practice since that time, until his recent retirement.

A Republican, he has served as coroner two terms, member of the board of the Insanity Commission two years, city mayor of Harvard, president of the board of education, and its secretary, president of the library board, state representative two terms (1907, 1919), acting postmaster two and a half years, and as a member of various state and local committees.

On January 10, 1900, he was married to Erma Johns at Fairfield. He is a member of Harvard Congregational Church, the Modern Woodmen of America, the Ancient Free and Accepted Masons, and has served as president of the Clay County Medical Society and chairman of the house of delegates of the Nebraska State Medical Association. Residence: Fairfield.

Erma Johns Jenison

One of Nebraska's most prominent clubwomen, Erma Johns Jenison has lived in this state all her life and has been active in civic and educational affairs for many years. She was born at Fairfield, Nebraska, the daughter of Joseph and Ernestina (Grambau) Johns. Her father, who is a farmer, was born in Cornwall, England, October 18, 1852, and came to this country April 12, 1873. Her mother, whose ancestry was German for many generations, was born in Germany October 11, 1854, and died at Fairfield, June 17, 1881.

Mrs. Jenison attended Fairfield High School and in 1895 was graduated from Fairfield College where she was interested in dramatics and was valedictorian of her senior class. She taught in rural schools for a time and was instructor in the high school at Harvard, Nebraska From 1916 to 1926 she served as librarian of the Harvard Public Library.

A Republican, Mrs. Jenison was a member of the Republican state executive committee from 1926 to 1930, and served as a member of the Republican state platform committee, 1924-30. She was chairman of the Harvard branch of the Nebraska Children's Home Society for a number of years, is a member of the Fairfield City Council, and has been a leader in the Nebraska Federation of Woman's Clubs.

She holds membership in the Harvard Woman's Club, the Fairfield Woman's Club, and the Fairfield Clover Club; she was the first president of the Harvard Club which she helped organize, and has served the other clubs as president. From 1921 to 1923 Mrs. Jenison served as president of the fifth district of the Nebraska Federation of Woman's Clubs, and during that time added 25 new clubs to the fifth district; this was the largest increase in membership during any administration in the history of the district. She was state corresponding secretary from 1923-25. She is a member of the Nebraskana Society, the Red Cross, P. E. O., Degree of Honor Protective Association, Order of the Eastern Star, and the Harvard Congregational Church, and is active in all of them.

During the World War she collected books for World War libraries, took a prominent part in Red Cross activities, and was chairman of the Clay County Council of Defense. She was married to Andrew Jay Jenison at Fairfield, January 10, 1900. Dr. Jenison, who was born in Iowa, is a physician.

Mrs. Jenison is now serving as fifth district chairman of legislation in the Federation of Women's Clubs, a position she has held several times in the past. Residence: Fairfield.

Justin Benjamin Jenkins

For the past 52 years Justin Benjamin Jenkins has been a resident of Nebraska where he has engaged in farming. He was born at Fairbury, Illinois, January, 30, 1874, the son of Benjamin and Lucy (Sanford) Jenkins. His mother was born in New York in 1836, and died at York, Nebraska, July 10, 1919. His father was born in New York in 1836, and died at York, February 16, 1891.

Mr. Jenkins is a member of the First Methodist Church of Holdrege, Nebraska, the Modern Woodmen of America, and the Nebraskana Society. Prior to 1903 he was a member of the York Public Band, and in 1912 he was state checker champion. His hobby is music.

On May 17, 1905, he married Amye Alma Armstrong at Holdrege. Mrs. Jenkins, who is a teacher, was born at Lincoln, Illinois, October 13, 1883; her grandfather was a soldier in the Union Army during the Civil War. Their three children are: Rollin Lusine, December 17, 1906; Newell Deane, March 26, 1916; and Lois Barbara, October 5, 1919. Rollin is a student in the University of Nebraska where he is a member of Tau Kappa Epsilon. Residence: Holdrege.

William W. Jenne

William W. Jenne was born at Lower Jay, Essex County, New York, March 20, 1849. Nehemiah Jenne, his father, who was born at Salisbury, Vermont, March 1, 1822, and died at Keene, Essex County, New York, was a carpenter. He was a sargeant in the 118th regiment of the New York Volunteers in the Civil War, and later held several public offices in his county. He is descended from an old Vermont family, of Scotch ancestry on his grandfather's side of the family, and of English ancestry through his grandmother.

Rebecca (Nye) Jenne, mother of William, who was born at Lower Jay, March 3, 1824, and died there March 7, 1910, was the daughter of Ziba Nye, who was English, and Abigail (Baker) Nye, direct heir to the Philadelphia estate of millions. She was a woman who was devoted to the church and was active in its work.

Mr. Jenne received his education in public high schools

and academy, and later taught schools in New York and Missouri. For nearly 48 years he has lived in Nebraska where he has carried on varied business activities. Having learned three trades, that of carpented and joiner, millright, and making sash-doors and blinds, he practiced his trades for some time and then became a clerk in stores in New York, and later in Missouri. In Sabetha, Kansas, he owned his first interest in a store, and in Falls City, Nebraska, he was owner and manager of two general merchandise stores and one ready-to-wear establishment. For twenty-five years he was employed by Charles Wolff & Company, owner of the Palace Silk Mills of Allentown, Pennsylvania, covering a district of fourteen states west of the Mississippi River. Mr. Jenne is now retired, and for the last twelve years has traveled for pleasure, and has visited every state in the union except Maine. A Democrat, he was chairman of the Democratic central committee of Richardson County for five years, and served two terms as supervisor of Richardson County.

His marriage to Florence Murch was solemnized at Clintonville, Essex County, New York, October 12, 1873. Mrs. Jenne, who was born at Lower Jay, May 10, 1852, and died at Falls City, December 24, 1928, was the daughter of English parents, Horace and Safronia Murch. Three children were born to this union, two of whom are living. Harry M., who was born August 25, 1876, and who married Mary Slocum, was a shoe dealer in Falls City for 12 years, and is now the owner of a 2,000 acre ranch in southern Kansas. William Nye was born April 3, 1881, and died September 2, 1905. Ralph H., born July 23, 1883, married Amy Bauer and owns a lady's ready to wear store in Falls City; he is a Democrat.

Mr. Jenne was active during the World War in various drives, acting as chairman of nearly all the liberty loan drives in his county. For six years he was chairman of the Red Cross, and is now vice-president and publicity chairman of this organization. He is a member of the Knights of Honor, the American Order of United Workmen, the Modern Woodmen of America, Eagles, the Royal Highlanders; he is a member of Elks, and Knights of Pythias, being past president of the state organization of Elks of the State of Nebraska. In 1881 he was united with the Congregation Church at Sabetha, Kansas. His favorite sport is golf; he is a member of the Elks Golf Club. Residence: Falls City.

Anna Vivian Jennings

Born at Van Meter, Iowa, January 30, 1874, Anna Vivian Jennings is the daughter of William Henry and Ruth Ann (Clayton) Jennings. Her father was born in Guernsey County, Ohio, February 14, 1845, and died at Lincoln, Nebraska, December 30, 1930. He was a prominent banker at Davenport, Thayer County, Nebraska, for more than 40 years, and was organizer of the Jennings State Bank now one of the outstanding banks of that country. He was a member of the Nebraska Senate in 1903 and 1905, and was president of the Senate in 1905. He was of English descent, and was a veteran of the Civil War. Her mother, who was a teacher before her marriage, was born at Salem, Indiana, January 7, 1847, and died at Davenport, Nebraska, September 22, 1912; her ancestry was German.

Miss Jennings was graduated from the high school, the first graduating class, at Davenport, Nebraska, attended York College, Peru Normal, and received the B. L. S. degree at the University of Illinois Library School in 1903. She taught in the rural schools of Davenport from 1893 to 1894, was a grammar grade teacher at Davenport from 1894 to 1897, and 1899-1900, and was assistant librarian of the Normal School at Peru, 1903-05. She organized the library of the State Teachers College of Kearney, Nebraska, in 1905, when the school was founded and has been head librarian since that time.

Miss Jennings is a life member of the American Asso-

ciation and has been chairman of the teachers college section at three national conferences. She is a member of the Nebraska Library Association and was president in 1910. She holds a membership in the National Educational Association, the Nebraska State Teachers Association, the American Association of University Women, and the Foreign Policy Association. She is state chairman of the international relations committee of the Business and Professional Women's Club for 1931, is a life member of the Kearney Women's Club, also a charter member of Chapter A. S. of the P. E. O., of which she was president in 1909. She is affiliated with the Methodist Episcopal Church of Kearney, and is a member of the Young Women's Christian Association, and a life member of the Nebraskana Society.

Anna Vivian Jennings has traveled extensively in the United States, spent the summer of 1910 in Europe, and made a world tour during 1926-27. Her political preference is the Republican party. Residence: Kearney.

Glenn Edwards Jennings

Glenn E. Jennings has lived in Nebraska for over 40 years and since 1903 has been an active business man at Omaha. He was born at Waukon, Allamakee County, Iowa, May 16, 1884, the son of John James and Jessie Benton (Edwards) Jennings. His father, who is a hardware merchant and banker, was born at Waukon, August 13, 1862, of English descent. His mother was born at Lansing, Iowa, July 20, 1862. Her ancestors were Welsh.

Mr. Jennings was graduated from high school at Gothenburg, Nebraska, 1901, and was a student at the University of Nebraska in 1902 and 1903. Since 1903 he has been associated with the Wright & Wilhelmy Company at Omaha, serving as salesman, 1906-15; vice president, 1918; vice president and secretary, 1926; and since 1929 president and treasurer. He is also a director in the United States National Bank at Omaha.

He married Meta Catharine Schomerus at Johnson, Nemaha County, Nebraska, December 22, 1908. Mrs. Jennings, whose ancestry is German, was born on a farm in Otoe County, Nebraska, May 27, 1885.

During the World War Mr. Jennings was active in all loan drives and Red Cross affairs. He is a director in each of the following organizations: Omaha Chamber of Commerce, National Hardware Jobbers Association, Young Men's Christian Association, and the Omaha Rotary Club of which he is also vice president. He is a member of all York and Scottish Rite bodies of the Masons; and the Shrine. He holds membership in the Omaha Athletic Club, the Happy Hollow Country Club, and is a member of First Methodist Episcopal Church of Omaha. He is a Republican. His favorite sports are golfing and fishing. Residence: Omaha.

John James Jennings

Born at Waukon, Iowa, August 13, 1862, John James Jennings has been a resident of Gothenburg, Nebraska, since 1890 and during that time has been successfully engaged in the hardware business. John Jennings, his father, who was a blacksmith, was born at Milton, New Jersey, September 12, 1811, and died at Armour, South Dakota, May 15, 1892. Sarah (Haines) Jennings, his mother, whose ancestry was English, was born at Peeksville, New York, September 16, 1821, and died at Greely, Iowa, January 2, 1913.

Mr. Jennings attended the grade school at Waukon. He has been in the firm of Jennings & Spaulding since his arrival in Nebraska 41 years ago, and is one of the oldest business men in Gothenburg. He is a director in the First State Bank of Gothenburg.

He holds membership in the Nebraska Retail Hardware Association of which he was president for a year, the Chamber of Commerce of which he was also president for a time, and the Kiwanis Club, acting as president of the latter organization at this time. Mr. Jennings was secretary of the local school board, is affiliated with the First Methodist Church, and holds membership in the Gothenburg Country Club. He is a member of the Odd Fellows and the following Masonic bodies: Blue Lodge, Chapter, Knight Templar, Scottish Rite, and Shrine. He likes to hunt and golf.

On May 16, 1883, he married Jessie Benton Edwards at Lansing, Iowa. Mrs. Jennings, who is a photograph retoucher, was born at Lansing, July 20, 1862, of Welsh and English descent. To this marriage four children were born: Glenn, May 16, 1884, who married Meta Schumaries; Clarence, April 3, 1886, who married Luberta Davies; Celia, January 2, 1889, who married Harry A. Lainson; and Caddy, March 11, 1891, who married Roger Williams. Glenn is president of the Wright & Wilhelmy Hardware Company of Omaha. Clarence has been connected with the Northwestern Bell Telephone Company of Omaha for 18 years. Residence: Gothenburg.

Anthony Louis Jensen

Anthony Louis Jensen, merchant and farmer, was born at Dell Rapids, South Dakota, April 27, 1889, son of Louis Anthony and Mary (Nesby) Jensen.

The father, born in Jutland, Denmark, came to the United States in 1873 and was a merchant until his death at Williamsburg, Virginia, February 12, 1918. His wife, born also in Jutland, died at Richmond, Virginia, May 26, 1929.

Mr. Jensen attended elementary schools in Virginia and Maryland, and afterward was a student at Boyles Business College in Omaha. During 1909 and 1910 he was a telegraph operator for the Union Pacific Railroad. Since that time he has been in business for himself. He is proprietor of the Jensen Mercantile Company at the present time.

On August 10, 1912, he was married to Bertha Mable Zimmerman at Big Spring, Nebraska. She was born there on January 19, 1895, of German and Irish ancestry, daughter of Andrew H. and Mary Jane (Henry) Zimmerman. Her father was born in Ohio, November 30, 1860, and died August 6, 1906 at Big Spring. He was a farmer near Big Spring for a good many years. Her mother was born in New York, August 9, 1871 and died July 26, 1926 at Big Spring. Mrs. Jensen is a member of the Methodist Episcopal Church, the Eastern Star, the Rebekahs, and the Royal Neighbors. They have four children, Lavern A., born February 17, 1914; Lyle R., born September 24, 1915; Dale C., born March 2, 1921; and Jimmie A., born March 15, 1925. Lavern is a student at the New Mexico Military Institute at Roswell, New Mexico.

Mr. Jensen is a Republican. He has resided in Nebraska for 24 years, and has been active in civic and fraternal organizations for some time. He is affiliated with the Methodist Episcopal Church, is a member of the Red Cross, the Federation of Nebraska Retailers, the Masons, the Odd Fellows, the Modern Woodmen of America, and from 1929 to 1931 was a member of the Big Spring School Board. His hobby is reading. Residence: Big Springs. (Photograph in Album).

Frank Jensen

A physician at Newman Grove, Nebraska since 1903, Frank Jensen was born at Council Bluffs, Iowa, July 22, 1880, the son of Lars and Mary (Sandstrom) Jensen. His father, who was a farmer, was born in Denmark in 1851 and died at El Reno, Oklahoma, July 10, 1915; he served as justice of the peace for years. His mother was born in Denmark and died at El Reno, Oklahoma, October 1, 1902.

Dr. Jensen attened rural school and was a student at Western Iowa College, Council Bluffs, for two years. In 1903 he received the M. D. degree at the University of Nebraska. He is past president of the Madison County Medical Society, and the Elkhorn Valley Medical Society, and is a member of the medical firm Jensen & Morris at Newmann Grove, Nebraska. He served as first mayor of the city and has been active in civic affairs there for several years.

He is a member of the American Medical Association, and the Nebraska State Medical Society. His fraternal organizations include: Odd Fellows; Modern Woodmen of America; Royal Neighbors of America; and Rebekahs. He has been a member of the Red Cross for many years He is a Scottish Rite Mason and Shriner.

His marriage to Rose Emoline Batten was solemnized at Plattsmouth, Nebraska, October 6, 1906. Mrs. Jensen, who was a milliner, was born at Plattsmouth, June 1, 1884, and died at Newman Grove, December 10, 1912. One son was born to them, Russell J., born November 23, 1909, who is a musician and instructor of piano at Norfolk, Nebraska. On February 15, 1928, Dr. Jensen was married to Inger Engelsgjerd at Newman Grove. They have a daughter, Frances Joan, born August 26, 1930. Residence: Newman Grove.

Jens Christian Jensen

Jens Christian Jensen was born in Denmark, January 12, 1885, the son of Jens Jorgen Jensen and Josena (Jergenson) Jenson, and for the past 39 years has been a resident of Nebraska. His father, who was a farmer, was born in Denmark, September 12, 1855, and died at Stanton, Nebraska, December 30, 1928. His mother was born in Denmark, June 8, 1861.

Mr. Jensen has been a carpenter and contractor at Ainsworth for the past 25 years, and at this time is a member of the Ainsworth Commercial Club, is serving as mayor of the city, and holds membership in the Red Cross. His hobby is building radios.

He was married at Ainsworth, July 18, 1906, to Amy Carolina Bower who was born at Ainsworth, June 14, 1887. Four children were born to them: Sibylia Jensen, December 2, 1908, who died December 12, 1908; Kenneth W., July 15, 1910; Peter, April 2, 1914; and Ruben Rolland, December 22, 1921. Residence: Ainsworth.

John Christian Jensen

One of Nebraska's leading educators, John C. Jensen has lived in the state all his life and has taken a prominent part in the educational and civic affairs in his community. He was born at Utica, on October 19, 1880, the son of Frantz Peter and Ellen (Jensen) Jensen. His father, who was born at Nestved, Denmark, December 16, 1842, and died at University Place, Nebraska, April 17, 1909, was a farmer; his father was a forester in the employ of the Danish government. His mother was born at Holbek, Denmark, December 9, 1842, and died at Lincoln, April 12, 1925; her father was a weaver.

Professor Jensen attended the rural schools of Seward County, and in 1897 was graduated from the high school at Utica. He was awarded the B. S. degree from Nebraska Wesleyan University, 1909; and received his A. M. degree at the University of Nebraska, 1916. He was a student at the University of Iowa, 1916; the University of Chicago, 1922; and the University of Nebraska, 1929-31. He was high school valedictorian and is a member of Sigma Xi, Phi Kappa Phi, Pi Mu Epsilon.

He has held the following positions in the educational field: teacher in rural schools in Seward County, 1897-01; superintendent of schools at Beaver City, Nebraska, 1903-07; professor of physics at Nebraska Wesleyan University from 1909 to the present time. Since 1921 he has been director of broadcasting at station WCAJ, and has written various articles on radio, lightning discharges, and spark potentials. He is a member of the Institute of Radio Engineers, the American Association of University Professors, American Interprofessional Institute, the Nebraska State Teachers Association, The Nebraskana Society, and the Symposium. He is a former scout master and commissioner of the Boy Scouts of America; and served as deputy commissioner in the Lnicoln Council of this organization for three years. He is a fellow in the American Association for the Advancement of Science; is representative of I. R. E., on the council of the American Association for Advancement of Science; is a fellow of the American Physical Society, and a member of the American Optical Society, the American Meteorological Society, the American Geophysical Union, and the Nebraska Academy of Science of which he was president in 1914 and 1922.

Professor Jensen is a member of the East Lincoln Business Men's Association. During the World War he served as civilian instructor in radio at the University of Nebraska. He is affiliated with the Methodist Episcopal Church of Lincoln. Politically, he is an Independent Republican.

On August 25, 1909, he was united in marriage with Susan Elizabeth Allington at Alma, Nebraska. She was born at Blue Springs, Nebraska, April 23, 1885, and died at University Place, December 25, 1918; before her marriage she was a teacher. Two children were born to this marriage; Robert R., born January 9, 1912; and Margaret Ruth, born March 27, 1917. Robert is a radio operator. Mr. Jensen was married to Emma Wilhelmsen at Omaha, August 22, 1922. Residence: Lincoln.

M. P. Jensen

M. P. Jensen, banker, was born in Denmark, December 22, 1885, son of Jens Peter and Caroline (Madsen) Jensen. The father, a farmer, died in Denmark, and the mother in Denmark also in 1895. Mr. M. P. Jensen came to the United States in 1903 landing in New York City. He then moved to Centerville, South Dakota where he lived until he went to Blair to attend school and has been a resident of Nebraska since.

In 1906 he was graduated from Blair college, and prior thereto attended public and high schools. From 1908 until 1917 he was in the lumber and hardware business at Chappell, and since 1917 has been vice president of the Chappell State Bank.

Active in civic and fraternal organizations, Mr. Jensen is president of the library board, a member of the board of regents of the Deuel County High School, and a member of the Deuel County Fair Board. He is a member of the Rotary Club, the Masons, the Eastern Star, and the Methodist Episcopal Church. His hobbies are trees and flowers, while his sports are trout fishing and golf.

On June 17, 1914, he was married to Mary Waneta Frederick, daughter of J. F. and Elizabeth (Stuart) Frederick, at Chappell. She was born at St. Paul, Nebraska, November 26, 1891. She is a member of the Methodist Episcopal Church, the P. E. O., the Eastern Star and is now president of the city school board. They have two children, Marie E., born July 27, 1915; and Mervin Paul, born May 19, 1920. Residence: Chappell.

Peter Jensen

Born in Denmark, March 7, 1877, Peter Jensen is the son of Anders and Karen (Pederson) Jensen. His father, a farmer, was born in Denmark and died at Dannebrog, Nebraska, November 24, 1908. His mother was born in Denmark and is living today at Boelus.

Mr. Jensen is a merchant at Boelus, and is serving as president of the Boelus State Bank and as vice president of the Citizens National Bank at St. Paul, Nebraska. He has been in business since 1893, and for many years has been a director in the State Bank of Dannebrog, Nebraska. He was treasurer of the local school board from 1900 to 1925, is a life member of the Red Cross, and holds membership in the Nebras-

kana Society.

He is interested in baseball, and in 1928 was manager of the winning Tri County League Baseball team at Boelus. He was united in marriage with Henriette F. Hatt at Dannebrog, December 20, 1899. Mrs. Jensen was born in Denmark, June 8, 1877, and died at Boelus, November 21, 1918. They have three children: Anna V., born January 30, 1901; Karen K., born July 26, 1905; and Anders H., born December 8, 1908, who married Lucille Christiansen.

Mr. Jensen is now married to Anna Klausen. To the latter marriage one daughter was born, Janet H., December 11, 1924. Residence: Boelus.

John Jeppson

For the past 46 years John Jeppson has been engaged in the drug business at Mead, Nebraska. He was born at Halland, Sweden, December 24, 1851, the son of Sven and Nilla Jeppson. His father, a farmer, was born in Sweden, November 11, 1815, and died at Mead, May 15, 1894; he came to this country in 1867. His mother was born in Sweden, September 17, 1813, and died at Ottumwa, Iowa, February 18, 1885.

Mr. Jeppson attended public schools and later took a course in pharmacy. He is engaged in business under the firm name of John Jeppson & Son, at Mead. From 1924 to 1929 he served as county chairman of the Republican party in Saunders County, and for six years he was secretary of the board of education there. He is affiliated with the Alma Lutheran Church and The Nebraskana Society.

He was married at Muntersville, Iowa, May 3, 1876, to Emma Knudson. Mrs. Jeppson was born at Muntersville, November 3, 1856, and died at Mead May 3, 1925. Their four children are: Alvin, born November 25, 1881, who is a graduate of the University of Iowa; Esther, born November 5, 1883, who married George H. Nelson, a farmer; Edna E., born November 21, 1886, who is a teacher; and Ruth V., born May 27, 1892, who married August Kling, a farmer. Residence: Mead.

Paul Jessen

Paul Jessen was born at Nebraska City, Otoe County, Nebraska, September 16, 1865, the son of Andrew and Margaret Jane (Martin) Jessen. His father, who was a farmer, was born in Denmark, November 29, 1827, and came to America in 1847. He died at Nebraska City, March 5, 1867.

His mother, who was born in Madison County, Indiana, July 1, 1829, and died at Nebraska City, February 22, 1898, was a teacher in one of the first schools for white children in the territory of Nebraska, in 1855.

Mr. Jessen was graduated from the Nebraska City High School in 1883, and later attended Cornell College, at Mount Vernon, Iowa, and Washington University at St. Louis, Missouri. He was admitted to the bar at Nebraska City, June, 1893, and since that time has practiced law there. For four years he served as city attorney of Nebraska City; was county attorney of Otoe County for four years; and was judge of the second judicial district for eight years. He is a director of the Merchant's National Bank at Nebraska City; has lived in this community for 65 years and for 38 years has been a lawyer and judge in Otoe County.

In the Spanish-American War he served as a first sergeant of Company C, second regiment, Nebraska Volunteer Infantry. He is a member of the Spanish War Veterans; is a member of the county, state and American bar associations and in 1924 was president of the Nebraska State Bar Association. He is a member of the Red Cross and the Nebraska City Chamber of Commerce, and is a Republican.

He was united in marriage with Emma Rose Schneider at Nebraska City, October 4, 1905. Mrs. Jessen, who was born of German parentage at Avoca, Iowa, October 24, 1873, was a clerk before her marriage. Two children were born to this union: Mary Louise, born August 31, 1908; and Margaret Jane, born January 30, 1914. Residence: Nebraska City.

Clifford Martin Jewell

Clifford Martin Jewell was born at Firth, Nebraska, September 24, 1900, son of Charles W. and Emma Viola (Martin) Jewell. The father, born in Ohio, February 27, 1868, is a salesman and a former member of the Nebraska National Guard. The mother was born in Madison County, Ohio, December 10, 1871.

Upon his graduation from the public school at Elmwood, Nebraska, in 1916, Mr. Jewell entered Elmwood High School, from which he was graduated in 1920. While there he received four letters in football. During the terms, 1920-21, Mr. Jewell was a student at Cotner College, and in 1925 received his Bachelor of Science degree from the University of Nebraska.

From 1923 until 1924 he was a teacher in the Gordon High School, and during the years 1925-29 was superintendent of schools at Hay Springs. In 1929 he became a member of the firm of Jewell & Stark, retail grocers at Gordon.

His marriage to Lelah Sarah Hutt was solemnized at Gordon, June 4, 1925. Mrs. Jewell was born at Gordon, July 19, 1900. She was a student of Simpson College in Iowa, and was a member of Mu Phi Epsilon. She is also a member of the P. E. O. and past president of the County Federated Club. They have a daughter, Jane, born December 11, 1926.

While at the University of Nebraska, Mr. Jewell was a member of the Reserve Officers Training Corps two years, and P. D. K. He is a member of the East Lincoln Christian Church at Lincoln, the Kiwanis International, The Nebraskana Society, the Parent Teachers Association (president 1925-26), and the Ancient Free and Accepted Masons at Gordon. His hobby is science. Residence: Gordon.

Joseph Jicha

One of Nebraska's pioneer merchants is Joseph Jicha, who has been engaged in business at Milligan for the past 37 years. He was born at Slatina, Szechoslovakia, November 11, 1863, the son of Thomas and Anna (Rezac) Jicha. His father, who was born in Czechoslovakia and died there in 1871, was a farmer most of his life. His mother was born at Slatina, and died at Ohiowa, Nebraska, December 10, 1910.

Mr. Jicha attended school in Europe and later studied at night school in this country. He holds stock in various banks, in addition to his private business ownership, and is a director of the Chamber of Commerce at Milligan. He is a member of the Knights of Pythias, has been a member of the school board for 13 years, and holds membership in the Nebraskana Society. His hobby is reading.

He was united in marriage with Mary Kohout at Omaha, Nebraska, October 12, 1889. Mrs. Jicha was born at Poline, Szechoslovakia, May 11, 1871. They have the following children: Mayme, born August 12, 1892, who married Joseph Vajrecka; Anna, born April 23, 1895; Joseph, born June 23, 1897; Libbie, born October 10, 1904; and Helen, born October 10, 1904. The four daughters are all well educated, three of them having taught school and one being a nurse. Joseph is a merchant.

Mr. Jicha served as chairman of the Liberty bond drive in the World War. His political preference is the Republican Party. Residence: Milligan.

Walter Lyman Jillson

Born at Heath, Massachusetts, September 21, 1857, Walter Lyman Jillson first came to Nebraska in 1879. In 1895 he went to Arkansas to live, returning in 1896, since which date he has resided in Nebraska.

His father, Lewis O. Jillson, was born at Whitingham, Vermont, September 23, 1823, and died there on August 25, 1875. He was a talented man, a farmer, carpenter, wheelwright, shoemaker and sawmill operator. He served three years and three months in the Civil War, in General Grant's Army, and was descended from early English settlers in the New England states.

His mother, Sarah Elvira Chase, was born in Heath, Massachusetts, December 23, 1836, of English ancestry. She made four trips from her home in Whitingham to Stuart, to visit her sons. Her death occurred at Vernon, Vermont, in January, 1913

Walter Lyman Jillson attended district and town school in New England until the age of 18. He was a merchant for three years in Stuart, was later a hay dealer, and for many years has owned and operated a farm at Stuart. He is an elder in the First Presbyterian Church, and has been superintendent of the Sunday School for many years. Recently he was made a life member of the Nebraskana Society.

On March 20, 1881, he was married to Anna Corlis at Linwood. She was born at Linwood and died at Orchard, in April, 1882. He was married to Laura Viola Baysinger at Canton, South Dakota on November 21, 1886, and to them were born nine children, seven of whom are living.

Elvira, born October 22, 1887, married Wilbert Smith; William Franklin, born February 11, 1890, died March 29, 1890; Ruth, born December 26, 1892, married Curtis Mohney; Susan, born April 19, 1894, married George Elwell; Paul, born June 19, 1896, married Juaneta Bartlet; Naomi, born April 28, 1898, married Fred Shefflette, and died November 3, 1931; Hester, born May 15, 1901, married Charles Timmons; Charlotte, born July 8, 1904, married Arthur Runnels; while Lyman, born May 9, 1907, married Phyliis Gavin.

Mrs. Jillson was born at Lena, Illinois, January 14, 1861. Her father was born in Kentucky of Scotch and German ancestry; and her mother in Indiana of Scotch and Irish descent. Her father was a minister and her brother a soldier in the Civil War. Mr. and Mrs. Jillson's children all attended the same district school and were graduated from Stuart High School. Elvira is a teacher, Ruth and Susan are teachers, Paul is a graduate in veterinary surgery from Ames, Naomi was a graduate nurse. Hester is a teacher and a graduate of Nebraska Wesleyan, while Lyman is a graduate in engineering from the University of Nebraska. Residence: Stuart.

John Allen Jimerson

John A. Jimerson, educator, was born at Miltonvale, Cloud County, Kansas, March 24, 1890. His father, James Lewis Jimerson, who was a farmer, was born in Iowa, July 17, 1863, and died at Liberty, Nebraska, in May, 1926. He is descended from Scotch settlers in America in 1800. Lillian Estella (Bowman) Jimerson, mother of John A., was born in Ohio, June 28, 1873. Her father was a member of the Grand Army of the Republic, and a Civil War veteran.

Mr. Jimerson was educated first in the Liberty High School, being graduated in 1906. In 1922 he was awarded his A. B. degree from Peru State Teachers' College, and in 1928 received his A. M. from the University of Nebraska. While in school he was a member of the glee club, the college orchestra and band, the dramatic club, the Philomathean Literary Society and Phi Delta Kappa fraternity.

On August 3, 1920, he was married to Hazel Georgia

Haywood, at Osakis, Minnesota. Before her marriage Mrs. Jimerson was assistant cashier in a bank. She was born in Dakota, May 21, 1895. There are two children: Meredith Blanche, born May 4, 1921, and Mary Shirley, born January 23, 1924.

A resident of Nebraska for 38 years, Mr. Jimerson has held various executive and educational positions. First a rural school teacher and high school principal, he has served as superintendent of schools at Shelby, Edgar, Stromsburg and Auburn. He is instructor at summer sessions of the Peru State Teachers' College, and is the author of many educational articles, including *Permanent Cumulative High School Record*. A public speaker and lecturer of note, he is much in demand as a speaker before graduating classes. Among his lectures are *The Salt of the Earth; Follow the Leader; Peace and Preparedness, or Piffle; Sharpening the Tools in Arithmetic* and *Quality and Quantity in Reading.*

During the World War he served two years in the infantry, and now holds the rank of major in the Infantry Reserve Corps of the United States Army. He is a member of the department of superintendents of the National Education Association, vice president of the Nebraska State Teachers' Association, and a member of the School Masters' Club. He is former president of district number two of the Nebraska State Teachers' Association.

Mr. Jimerson is a Mason, a member of the Chamber of Commerce, the Kiwanis Club and of the American Legion. He is affiliated with the First Methodist Episcopal Church of Auburn. He is a member of the Auburn Country Club. His out-of-door sports include tennis, golf, hunting and fishing. Residence: Auburn.

John Robert Jirdon

John Robert Jirdon, prominent merchant and executive, was born at Elk Creek, Nebraska, July 8, 1895, son of John and Nannie Elizabeth (Neal) Jirdon. The father was born in Pekin, Illinois, July 12, 1864, and is a farmer, whose parents came from Ireland about 1840. His wife Nannie was born near Elk Creek, February 14, 1866. Her father was Irish, and her mother Scotch-Irish and Welsh.

Mr. Jirdon attended the public schools of Gering and Morrill, and was graduated from Morrill high school in 1912. From that time until August, 1915, was employed by the R. S. Proudfit Company, at Minatare and Angus, Nebraska. From August 1915 until January 1, 1924, Mr. Jirdon was a partner with W. R. Preston at Morrill, in the grain and lumber business. Since January 1, 1924, he has been in the wholesale and retail grain, feed and coal business at Morrill.

Mr. Jirdon is the director of the First National Bank of Morrill, and president of the North Platte Valley Grain and Feed Dealers Association. He is a member of the Morrill Commercial Club, and a member of the National Grain and Feed Dealers Association. He is at the present time serving as president of the Morrill school board, and is a Mason (Royal Arch, Knight Templar). On September 7, 1920, he was married to Gladys Marguerite Remender, of Morrill, at Scottsbluff. She was born at Creston, Nebraska, on December 2, 1897, of German and Scotch-Irish ancestry. They have two children, Joyce Remender, born May 10, 1921, and Bonnie Jean, born December 3, 1924.

In politics Mr. Jirdon is independent. During the late war he served as a private, first sergeant and retired as 2nd Lieutenant in the United States Army. He served from August 1918 until January 1919. He is a member of the American Legion. His sport is golf, and his hobby is business. Residence: Morrill.

Joseph Frank Jirovec

Joseph F. Jirovec, executive and prominent band leader of Nebraska, was born at Morse Bluffs, Nebraska, March 20, 1884. His father, John Jirovec, a farmer, was born in Czechoslovakia, and died at Clarkson, Nebraska, November 10, 1919. Mary Jirovec, his mother, was born in Czechoslovakia.

Mr. Jirovec attended rural schools and was a student at the Fremont Normal School one year. He has studied music at home since he was 15 years of age and at the age of 19 organized and directed a band. He studied trumpet under Professor Don G. Berry of Lincoln and under Dr. Phelps of Omaha; and was awarded a diploma in band direction at the Vandercook School of Music at Chicago.

He was a restaurant manager for a time; owned a meat market; was manager of the Omaha Elevator Company at Brainard, Nebraska; served as manager of the Nye-Schneider-Fowler Company, and the Lumber & Grain Company of Clarkson; and since 1919 has been manager of the Farmers Union Co-operative Supply Company at Clarkson. He has also managed a lumber grain and coal business there during the past 12 years.

Mr. Jirovec is known throughout the state as the director of popular bands and dance orchestras, and has won a great deal of commendation from various parts of the middle west. He is the director of the Leigh Band, the Clarkson Band, and the Jirovec Orchestra, all of which have ranked high in musical contests. The Clarkson Band was placed in Class A in the Omaha Band Contest for two consecutive years, and the third year was awarded third prize. Mr. Jirovec is now giving private music lessons in addition to his other business activities.

During the World War he was a bugler in the home guard, and served on loan drives committees. He holds membership in the Red Cross; the Chamber of Commerce; the Modern Woodmen of America; and The Nebraskana Society. He is affiliated with Saint Cyril Catholic Church of Clarkson. Among his out of door sports are baseball and hiking. He is a Democrat.

On July 30, 1907, he was united in marriage with Tony Koza at Omaha, Nebraska. Mrs. Jirovec, who was born at Clarkson, January 21, 1886, is interested in home talent dramatic work. They have two children: Lambert, born November 25, 1908, who is studying music at the University of Nebraska, and will graduate this year in violin study; and Donald, born August 3, 1916, who is studying piano along with his public school work. Residence: Clarkson.

Albert E. Johansen

Albert E. Johansen, former rancher, was born at Yankton, South Dakota, January 13, 1883, son of Christian Andrew and Anna Marie (Wortman) Johansen.

The father was born in Denmark, March 1, 1841, and came to America at the age of 19. His parents, Peter and Augusta (Rovbye) Johansen, were married in the old church at Roeskilde, Dumkirke, Denmark. Christian Johansen was a farmer, whose death occurred at Hay Springs in October, 1914. His wife, Anna Marie, was born in Cincinnati, Ohio, July 6, 1843, and died at Hay Springs, August 10, 1922. She was the mother of ten children, and the daughter of Theodore Wortman and Kathryn Kohler. They were pioneer settlers of Sheridan County, settling there in 1886.

Mr. Johansen attended country school in Sheridan County, and was graduated from Hay Springs High School. He engaged in farming and ranching until 1920, when he was forced to stop on account of ill health. He spent considerable time in a hospital at Rochester, Minnesota, and after returning worked a few years in the local post-office. In the fall of 1929, he purchased a half interest in a hardware business, which he still owns, the firm being Hagedorn and Johansen. He is a director of the First National Bank at Hay Springs. He is a Democrat.

His marriage to Ethel Marcy, a daughter of Sidney S. and Harriet Jane (Blood) Marcy, was solemnized at Hay Springs, July 19, 1905. They were prominent pioneer settlers of Sheridan County, settling there in 1888.

Mrs. Johansen was born at Rowley, Iowa, October 31, 1882. She attended country schools and graduated from Hay Springs High School. She taught school for a number of years prior to her marriage. Mrs. Johansen is a member of the Eastern Star and Utopia Woman's Club.

Mr. Johansen is a member of the Hay Springs and Rural Improvement Club, the Lions Club, the Masons, and Order of Eastern Star (past master of Masons and past patron of Eastern Star), and from 1926-31 was director of the local school board. Residence: Hay Springs.

Rasmus Johansen

Rasmus Johansen, an implement dealer at Blair, for the past twenty-six years, was born at Knudstrus, Denmark, August 1, 1871, and came to America, in 1891. He is the son of Johannes and Eugene Josephine (Ankersen) Johansen, both natives of Denmark, the former born at Knudstrups and the later at Klosterlund. Johannes Johansen died at Hesselhus, Denmark, as did his wife. Johannes was a farmer, and a veteran of the Danish-German War of 1864. His father's father, Johan Vendel, was born in Germany.

Mr. Johansen attended common school, and for several years worked as a farmer and railroad man. For the past twenty-six years he has been in the implement business at Blair. He is married to Anna Georgina Kjellen, their marriage having been solemnized at Blair. Mrs. Johansen was born at Copenhagen, Denmark, January 25, 1879.

A Lutheran, Mr. Johansen is a member of the First Church at Blair, and is a member also of the Danish Brotherhood and the Nebraskana Society. Residence: Blair.

Clinton Walter John

Clinton Walter John was born at Cambridge, Nebraska, December 7, 1885, the son of James Henry and Caroline (Aaboe) John. His father is a druggist. Mr. John was graduated from the Cambridge High School in 1902, attended Nebraska Wesleyan University for two years, and was graduated from Northwestern University with the Ph. G. degree in 1907. He has been in the drug business at Cambridge since 1907.

Mr. John is a member of the Rotary Club, the Commercial Club, the Independent Order of Odd Fellows, and the Red Cross at Cambridge. He has served as secretary of the Cambridge School Board for the past two years, having been a member of that body for the past eight years, and is affiliated with the First Congregational Church. He is interested in music, and at this time is leader of the local band.

Of his marriage to Eva Dunkin, which occurred at Gibbon, Nebraska, one child was born, Eva, on May 17, 1912, who died May 21, 1912. Of his marriage to Caroline Thuman there are two children, Paulie, born May 28, 1918, and Marjorie, January 26, 1928. Residence: Cambridge.

Hattie Irene Johns

One of Hamilton County's pioneer leaders is Hattie Irene Johns who came to Nebraska in 1886 and has been prominent in civic affairs at Aurora for many years. She was born at Rochelle, Illinois, August 19, 1879, the daughter of Charles M. and Mary I. (Sawens) Johns. Her father, a farmer, was born of Welsh parentage at Darien City, New York, June 3, 1848 and died at Aurora, June 2, 1927. Her mother was born at Batavia, New York, October 19, 1855, and is residing at Aurora.

Miss Johns received her elementary education in the public schools of Hamilton County, was a student at the Lincoln High School for two years, and in 1898 was graduated from Lincoln Normal University. She was a teacher in the grade schools of Hamilton County from 1899 to 1923, from 1923 until 1931 served as deputy county

treasurer, and since 1931 has been treasurer of that county, elected on the Republican ticket.

She served as state treasurer of the Business and Professional Women's Club during 1929 and 1930, was a member of the Aurora Public Library Board, 1918-1931 and has served as a member of the board of the Red Cross for many years. She is affiliated with the Methodist Church of Aurora and holds membership in the Nebraskana Society. Residence: Aurora.

Harvey Johnsen

Harvey Johnsen has been a resident of Nebraska all his life and a leading lawyer of Omaha. He was born at Hastings, Adams County, Nebraska, July 16, 1895, the son of Peter C. and Marie (Jensen) Johnsen.

His early education was received in the public schools of Fremont, Nebraska, where he was graduated from the high school in 1913. At the University of Nebraska he was awarded the A. B. degree and LL. B. degree, 1919, and was distinguished as an honor student. The Order of the Coif was bestowed upon him and he was made a member of Phi Beta Kappa. He served as consul of Phi Delta Phi in 1919, and was Ivy Day orator.

Mr. Johnsen was admitted to the bar in Nebraska, June, 1919, and in 1920 became associated with the firm Montgomery, Hall and Young, at Omaha. From 1922 to 1925 he was instructor in the College of Law at Creighton University. He is now engaged in general legal practice as a member of the firm of Montgomery, Hall, Young and Johnsen.

He is a member of the Omaha Bar Association of which he was made president in 1931; is a member of the American Bar Association; and is secretary of the Nebraska State Bar Association. He is a member of the American Interprofessional Institute and the Co-operative Club. His social club is the University Club of Omaha. His hobby is biography an philosophy. He is a Democrat. Residence: Omaha.

Aaron William Johnson

Aaron William Johnson, prominent merchant and farmer at Loomis for many years, was born in Kronoberg, Sweden, August 31, 1851. He came to America in the spring of 1871, locating at Lockport, Illinois, where he resided until 1876. At that time, he removed to Nebraska, homesteading in Phelps County, where he lived until his death, on January 14, 1929, after a long illness.

Mr. Johnson was one of the earliest pioneers of what is now Phelps County, coming with the second colony of settlers in 1876.

On June 15, 1878, he was married to Augusta Granlund at Loomis, Nebraska, and to them 11 children were born; Ida, born March 9, 1879, who married Gust F. Carlson; Joseph, born May 3, 1880; Frank, born September 26, 1881, who married Iva Hitt, and who died January 29, 1931; Walter, born April 1, 1883, who married Esther Larson; Victor, born May 30, 1885, who married Esther Erickson; Julia, born November 30, 1887, who married Malcolm Abramson; Justus, born February 9, 1890, who married Florence Nelson; Harry, born August 24, 1892, who married Blanche Dahlstrom, and who died February 11, 1919; Henry O., born June 30, 1895, who married Julia Abramson; Mabel born September 18, 1897; and Loyd, born September 23, 1905. Mrs. Johnson was born at Ostergotland, Sweden, May 15, 1857. She is living on the original homestead two miles north of Loomis with her children, Joseph, Mabel, and Loyd.

Mr. Johnson was the first man to invite the Burlington Railroad to build through this part of the country, on what is called the high line, and pointed out the advantages and need of it to George W. Holdrege, the general manager of the road, while entertaining him on a hunting trip. He was the first merchant in Loomis, built and stocked the first general store in 1886. It featured hardware, chiefly, as that article was most needed by early pioneers. Later he bought livestock, grain and broom corn, using a pony to travel from place to place, often covering 50 to 60 miles in one day. In 1889 he was one of the founders of the flour mill at Loomis which burned in 1914.

After the organization of Phelps County, Mr. Johnson was active on the board of supervisors and held other minor offices, was especially active in the arrangement of the various school districts and the location and establishment of the schools, until age forced him to retire. He was one of the founders of the Loomis Swedish Mission Church in 1886, and also one of the founders of the Moses Hill Swedish Mission in 1877, and throughout his life was a faithful member and staunch supporter of the former institution. Mr. and Mrs. Johnson celebrated their 50th wedding anniversary recently.

Mr. Johnson was a man, fearless and unafraid to stand for what he knew to be right, and in times of defeat he was undaunted and ready to try again. He was always an aid to the weak and to the needy, and ready to do his share or more in times of distress and trouble. Residence: Loomis.

Albert Lytle Johnson

Albert Lytle Johnson, a resident of Nebraska for the past 65 years, was born at Albany, Green County, Wisconsin, June 19, 1864, the son of Andrew and Mary Ann (Lytle) Johnson. His father, who was a contractor, builder, and farmer, was born in Massachusetts, September 8, 1816, and died at Valparaiso, Saunders County, Nebraska.

In 1635 Edmund Johnson, the great great great great great grandfather of Albert L. Johnson, sailed with his wife, Mary, from London and settled in Hampton, New Hampshire. His son, James, was born in Hampton, in 1643, and later moved to Maine, where he was a millwright. There is no particular record of the Johnson family from that time until 1763, when Benjamin Johnson, grandfather of Albert Johnson, was born; he enlisted in the Revolutionary War at the age of 13, and was a private in Captain Jeremiah Fogg's Company, the Colonel George Reed's Regiment of New Hampshire.

Mr. Johnson's parents were married in Maine, November 26, 1840, where four of their ten children were born. In 1851 they moved to Ohio, where one son was born, and the same year moved on to Wisconsin; the five younger children were born there. In 1865 his father and his brother, R. K. Johnson, started for Nebraska with one horse and a light wagon looking for a suitable homestead; the brother had just been discharged from the army after service in the Civil War. Their means were limited and they paid expenses on the trip by mending clocks and tinware for the settlers.

Part of the trip was made on foot and the journey was a long one. They finally reached the southwestern part of Saunders County and homesteaded on land near the present site of Valparaiso. There they built the first frame house in that part of the state, hauling the lumber with ox teams from the Iowa side of the river and hewing the timbers from trees growing on the homestead. Since funds were low his father set out to find carpenter work, and as Lincoln began to grow found work on the first state capitol building; a little later he made a contract for part of the work on the first University of Nebraska building.

Mary Ann (Lytle) Johnson, mother of Albert L. Johnson, was born in New York, December 15, 1819, and died at Valparaiso, August 15, 1902. She was one of the finest types of pioneer women, and with no luxuries and few of the necessities of life contrived to make a home for her family of ten children. Her grandfather was a soldier in the Revolution, and in the War of 1812; her father was in the regular United States Army for a time. Her older brother, Robert Lytle, sailed around the Horn in 1849, and was in the gold rush of '49; he died in 1876. In 1850 her other two brothers, Benjamin Stevens Lytle and Albert

Waldo Lytle joined Robert, sailing from Belfast and crossing the Isthmus, where they left for Eureka, California. Albert died in 1896 and Benjamin in 1899.

Mr. Johnson, who has been a leader in the civic and business world at Crete, Saline County, Nebraska for many years, attended the public schools of Valparaiso, and the Nebraska Conference Seminary at York, Nebraska. He was a student at the University of Nebraska, 1880-81, and attended the Orchard City Business College at Burlington, Iowa, in 1881. He was employed by the Crete Mills as bookkeeper in 1883; was bookkeeper and cashier for David May at Lincoln, Nebraska; was assistant bookkeeper for Leighton & Clarke and the H. T. Clarke Company, wholesale druggists in Lincoln and Omaha; was cashier of the R. K. Johnson Bank at Valparaiso; and in 1888 returned to the Crete Mills as bookkeeper and assistant manager. In 1895 he became manager in full charge of activities of this organization. In 1901, when the Crete Mills were incorporated, he became president of the company; he holds this position today. He was formerly a director of the First National Bank at University Place, Nebraska; was formerly vice president of the Union Loan & Savings Company at Lincoln; was one of the organizers of the First Building & Loan Association at University Place; and is a stockholder in the Crete State Bank and several other corporations at Crete.

His marriage to Harriott Elizabeth Patmore was solemnized at Valparaiso, August 25, 1885. Mrs. Johnson, who was born at Elora, Ontario, Canada, October 11, 1861, is the daughter of Levi Patmore and Elizabeth (Bastedo) Patmore; her father was an architect. They have four children: Rodney Knox, born May, 1886, who married Mary Louise Crowe; Port Albert, born November 28, 1887, who married Edith May Cleveland; Ruth, born October 4, 1893, who married Evert Lee Stancliff; and Benjamin Lytle, born June 21, 1899, who married Helen Westlake.

Rodney is a physician and surgeon at Friend, Nebraska, and is senior captain of the hospital company of the 110th Medical Regiment of the Nebraska National Guards with headquarters at Lincoln. Port served in France during the World War and was commander of the American Legion Post at Crete for several terms; he is now eastern sales manager for the Crete Mills with headquarters at Huntington, West Virginia. Benjamin enlisted in the navy during the World War at the age of 16 and is now adjutant of the American Legion post at Crete. He is secretary of the Crete Mills.

Mr. Johnson is a member of the Sons of the American Revolution at Lincoln, the Nebraska Territorial Pioneers, and the Nebraskana Society. He is a life member of the Red Cross. From 1912 to 1922 he was a member of the board of education of the Methodist Episcopal Church. He was formerly a member of the school board at Crete, and at University Place. Since 1895 he has been a trustee of the Nebraska Wesleyan University, and from 1912 to 1929 was president of the board of trustees. He served as a member of the state committee of the Young Men's Christian Association from 1897 to 1926; he holds membership in the Lincoln society of this organization. His social club is the University Club at Lincoln.

Politically, Mr. Johnson is a Republican, and is an ardent temperance worker. He is affiliated with the Grace Methodist Episcopal Church at Crete. Residence: Crete.

Alvin Emanuel Johnson

Alvin E. Johnson was born at Omaha, Douglas County, Nebraska, February 18, 1893. His father, John Peter Johnson, who was a coal and grain dealer, was born at Filipstad, Wermland, Sweden, July 6, 1858. In 1879 he came to America; he died at Omaha, February 1, 1929.

Anna (Young) Johnson, his mother, was born at Filipstad, June 23, 1869, and came to America in 1885.

Mr. Johnson was graduated from the Hawthorne

School at Omaha, in 1905, and for the next two years was a student at South High School. On December 9, 1907 he became a messenger at the Livestock National Bank at Omaha, when that organization was first begun. In 1915 he was made assistant cashier, and in 1918 he became cashier. Since 1922 he has been vice president and director of this institution. He is director of the Commercial Savings & Loan Association and is a director of the Union Rendering & Refining Company, at Omaha.

He was united in marriage to Nina Myrtle McWilliams at Omaha, June 25, 1919. Mrs. Johnson was born at Maquon, Knox County, Illinois, May 12, 1894. She was graduated from the South Omaha public schools in 1912 and from Nebraska Wesleyan University in 1916. There are three children: Alvin Warren, born December 5, 1920; Myrtle Louise, born September 30, 1922; and Howard Mac, born April 12, 1924.

Mr. Johnson is a director of the Omaha Chamber of Commerce and the South Omaha Merchants Association. He is regent of the Municipal University of Omaha. He is interested in Young Men's Christian Association affairs, and at the present time is acting president of this organization. He is an Elk, Mason, Viking and Woodman of the World. He is a trustee of the First Baptist Church of Omaha. His social clubs are the Omaha Athletic Club and Happy Hollow Club. He is a Republican. His favorite sport is glf. Residence: Omaha.

Alvin Frederick Johnson

Alvin Frederick Johnson, lawyer, was born at Omaha, Nebraska, January 6, 1877, son of Andrew Frederick and Anna (Mortenson) Johnson.

Mr. Johnson received his early education in the Omaha public school, and was graduated from high school there in 1894. He received his Bachelor of Laws degree from the University of Nebraska, and has since been in active practice.

He was married on November 28, 1906, to Marie Stanfield Bryant at Toledo, Ohio. Mr. Johnson has served as a member of the Insanity Board of Douglas County, and as chairman of the executive committee and president of the Omaha and United States Chambers of Commerce. He has been active in the work of the Missouri River Navigation Association and has served as a member of the executive committee from Nebraska. Residence: Omaha.

Amos Frank Johnson

A physician and surgeon since 1904, Amos Frank Johnson was born at Scribner, Nebraska, September 15, 1874. He is the son of George and Mary (Jacobson) Johnson, the former of whom came to America in 1866. George Johnson was born at Copenhagen, Denmark, March 26, 1838, and was a pioneer Nebraska farmer. His death occurred at Leigh, Nebraska, May 12, 1920. Mary Jacobson was born in Denmark, August 14, 1848, and died at Dodge, Nebraska, August 13, 1903.

Educated first in country and public schools, Dr. Johnson attended high school at Dodge, and received his Bachelor of Science degree from Fremont Normal College in 1900. Active in debate and dramatics, Dr. Johnson spent several years as a teacher before studying medicine. In 1904, he received his medical degree from Creighton University, where he was valedictorian of his class.

He was married to Florence Hall at Exeter, Nebraska, on November 25, 1905, and to them was born one son, Frank Edward, born December 17, 1923. Mrs. Johnson, was born at Elgin, Illinois, May 24, 1882, was engaged in school work prior to her marriage. She is of English extraction.

Since June 15, 1904, Dr. Johnson has been in active practice. His professional organizations include the American, Nebraska State and York County Medical Associations. He is a Democrat, and a member of The Nebraskana Society. Residence: Gresham.

Carl Oscar Johnson

Carl Oscar Johnson, manufacturer and public man, was born in Sweden, August 19, 1867, son of Adolph P. and Clara Sophia (Swanson) Johnson. His father was born in Sweden, in 1842, and his mother in 1839, the former a shoemaker and harnessmaker.

Mr. Johnson attended public school, and came to Nebraska on May 24, 1883. He has been engaged in various businesses for himself since 1896, and at the present time is president and general manager of the Highway Maintainer Company. A Republican, he has held various local offices, among them, city treasurer, 1897, member of council, 1898, mayor two terms, 1899-1900; and was elected county commissioner of Lancaster County three terms, beginning November 15, 1909. He resigned from the last mentioned on October 1, 1919.

His marriage to Amanda Henrietta Faust was solemnized at Lincoln, on September 10, 1892. Mrs. Johnson was born in Sweden, October 1, 1867. To them were born three children, Nanny, born July 12, 1893, died on July 28, 1894; Olive, born July 21, 1894; and Clara, born December 5, 1904. Clara is a high school teacher, and Olive, secretary and treasurer of the Highway Maintainer Company.

Mr. Johnson's fraternal organizations include the Masons, Odd Fellows, Modern Woodmen of America, Scottish Rite, Shrine and Eastern Star. He is a member of Elm Park Methodist Episcopal Church, the Lincoln Chamber of Commerce and the Nebraskana Society. During the World War, Mr. Johnson was chairman of the local Young Men's Christian Association committee. Residence: Havelock.

Caroline Christine Johnson

Caroline Christine Johnson was born at Moen, Denmark, the daughter of Niels and Kristine (Jensen) Johnson. Her father, a farmer, who was born at Moen, June 20, 1851, came to America in 1882 and died at Marquette, Nebraska, March 6, 1917. Her mother was born at Moen, March 18, 1850, and died at Blair, Nebraska, May 25, 1928.

Miss Johnson attended the public schools at Hampton and Red Cloud, Nebraska, was awarded the A. B. degree at the University of Nebraska in 1904, and received the A. M. degree there in 1914. During 1912-13 she was engaged in European travel and study at Copenhagen and Berlin. At this time she is head of the foreign language department at Dana College, Blair, Nebraska.

She is a member of the Nebraska State Teachers Association, the Faculty Ladies Club, and the Nordic Reading Circle. She is affiliated with the First Lutheran Church of Blair, and holds membership in the Republican party. Residence: Blair.

Charles Elmer Johnson

One of the prominent stockman and farmers of Valley County, Nebraska, is Charles Elmer Johnson who has been a resident of this state since October, 1878. He was born at Newton, Iowa, June 29, 1878, the son of Robert and Mary Elizabeth (Watson) Johnson. His father, who was born at Utica, New York, and died at North Loup, Nebraska, was a farmer. His mother, whose father was killed in action during the Civil War, was born at Tonawanda, New York, December 19, 1838, and died at North Loup, March 24, 1921.

Mr. Johnson served as director of the North Loup School Board from 1921 to 1930, has been county commissioner since 1924, and has held membership in the Modern Woodmen of America since 1896. He is affiliated with the Davis Creek Methodist Church, is a member of the Democratic party, and holds membership in the Nebraskana Society.

He is married to Florence Brace Cummins who was born at Akron, New York, May 27, 1880, the daughter of Frank and Alsa Cummins. Their three children are: Merna, born February 19, 1903, who married Reuben Marvin Athey; Irma, born February 28, 1905, who attended Nebraska Wesleyan University and is now a teacher; and Eva, born April 14, 1909, who received the Bachelor of Science degree at the Nebraska Wesleyan University and is now a teacher. Residence: North Loup.

Charley William Johnson

Charley William Johnson, farmer, banker, merchant, and senator, was born in Sweden, January 21, 1864, son of Swen Dedrick and Carolina Sofia (Swanson) Johnson. The family came to America in 1867.

Mr. Johnson attended public and high school, and on April 21, 1886 was married to Ellen Christine Nelson at Kackley, Kansas. Mrs. Johnson was born in Denmark, April 3 1866.

Mr. Johnson has been a resident of Cheyenne County since 1886. He is a Republican, a member of the Methodist Church, the Masons and Odd Fellows. Residence: Potter.

Clarence Bruce Johnson

Clarence Bruce Johnson, dental surgeon of Alma, Nebraska, is a life-long resident of this state. He was born at Wilsonville, Nebraska, September 21, 1896, the son of Frank Bruce and Cora Bell (Austin) Johnson. His father, who was a physician and surgeon, was born at Rennselaer, Indiana, December 5, 1864, of Scotch and Irish parentage, settling in Wilsonville homesteading there. His mother, of New England descent, was born at Dwight, Illinois, April 9, 1874.

Dr. Johnson was graduated from the Wilsonville High School in 1915, and received the degree, Doctor of Dental Surgery, at the College of Dentistry, University of Nebraska, 1919, where he was a member of Xi Psi Phi. He has been engaged in the practice of dentistry at Alma since 1924 where he is prominent in civic affairs.

He holds membership in the Lions Club, of which he is serving as president, the Nebraska State Dental Society, the Southwestern Dental Society in which he has been president, secretary-treasurer and vice president, and the Scottish Rite body of the Ancient Free and Accepted Masons at Hastings. He holds membership in the Nebraskana Society and the American Legion. Politically, Dr. Johnson is a Republican. During the World War he was in the service of the United States Army, serving in the Dental Corps.

On August 7, 1922, he married Lela Lucile Haag at Alma. Mrs. Johnson, whose ancestry is German and Pennsylvania Dutch, was born at Stamford, Nebraska, September 2, 1898, and was a music instructor prior to her marriage being a graduate of the School of Music, University of Nebraska. Mrs. Johnson is affiliated with the P. E. O. having been president; the Order of Eastern Star, a past matron; a member of the Congregational Church where she is permanently identified with with the music. Residence: Alma.

Czar Clinton Johnson

Czar Clinton Johnson, physician and surgeon, was born at Sidney, Iowa, March 4, 1881, son of Clinton Darius and Laura Oliva (Caldwell) Johnson. Clinton Johnson was born in Chautauqua County, New York, September 18, 1858, and died at Colomb, South Dakota, in December, 1914. He was a farmer of Scotch and English descent. Laura Caldwell was born in Ashtabula, Ohio, September 7, 1860, and is of Dutch and Southern ancestry.

Dr. John was educated in the schools of Iowa and Nebraska. He was public school teacher in Madison County, Nebraska, from 1900 to 1903, and received his medical degree from Creighton Medical College in 1907, and is a member of Phi Rho Sigma. On September 12, 1907, he was united in marriage to Lena Marii Campbell at Creighton, Nebraska. Mrs. Johnson was born at Madison, Nebraska, December 23, 1886, of Dutch and Scotch ancestry. She attended the University of Nebraska, class of 1908, and was a Delta Delta Delta. They have one son, Harlan Allen, born September 16, 1911, who attends the University of Nebraska, and is a member of Sigma Phi Epsilon.

Dr. Johnson served as mayor of Creighton, Nebraska, 1909-10. He has lived in Nebraska 33 years. Among his writings are the following: *The Application of Business Principles in the Practice of Medicine; Some Problems in Reconstructive Surgery; Modern Measures; Complemental Jejunostomy in the Treatment of Ileus; Reorganizing the Profession; Industrial Bone and Joint Disabilities; Relation of Physiology to Surgery; A Physiological Empyema Tube; In the Promotion of Public Health Shall the Government be a Policeman or a Doctor; The Value of Chemistry to the Physician; Medical Service for Tourists; The Physician in Industry; The Teaching of Infectious Diseases in Public Schools; Acute Head Injuries; Breast Tumors; Fracture Splints; Resume of Present Views of Kidney Infections; Back Ache and Pain—1800 cases; Disabilities; The Reserve Medical Officer; The Reserve Army Nurse; The Training of Reserve Officers; Surgery—Surgeons and Hospitals; The Doctor and the Workmen's Compensation Law; Medical Mal-practice; Compensation a Big Medical Problem; Conservation of Energy; Hyperthyroidism and Exopthalmic Goiter; Adynamic Ileus; Your Boys Adventure; Proposed Changes that Should be Made in Claims Division of U. S. Veterans Bureau; Know Your Schools; Public vs. Blackstone and Hippocrates; The Army Cripple; Holding Fast; The Legion Invictus; Forgotten; Is the Compensation Patient Mentally or Physically Sick; Compensation Injuries under the Workmen's Compensation Act; Wanted a Leader.*

From 1907-1917, Dr. Johnson was in general practice at Creighton, Nebraska. From 1917-19 he was a Medical Officer with the 89th Division, American Expeditionary Forces, as 1st lieutenant, July 10 to November 8, 1917; captain November 8 to January 28, 1918; major, January 28, 1918 to January 28, 1919; lieutenant colonel, January 29, 1919 to June 10, 1919. He participated in the St. Mihiel and Meuse-Argonne engagements and served with the Army of Occupation. At the present time he holds the rank of colonel in the Officers Reserve Corps, and is a member of the Veterans of Foreign Wars, American Legion and Military Surgeons Association.

Dr. Johnson's professional memberships include the American Medical Association, the American College of Surgeons, the American Association of Medical Authors, the American Association of Industrial Surgeons, and others. He is a member of the Lincoln Chamber of Commerce, the Laymen's Club, the Nebraskana Society, and is a 32nd degree Mason and member of the Shrine. He is a Republican. His hobby is economics. Dr. Johnson is lecturer in industrial surgery in the Medical Department, Creighton University. Residence: Lincoln.

David August Johnson

David August Johnson, clergyman and author, was born at Tustin, Michigan, October 30, 1877, son of Peter August and Mathilda (Melin) Johnson. The father, born in Sweden, in 1837, was a farmer and clergyman of much ability. He died at Tustin in January, 1903. His wife, born in Sweden in 1834, died at Tustin in June, 1930.

Educated in the public school at Tustin until 1894, Mr. Johnson then attended Alma College from 1900-1905, and received his A. B. from Alma College in 1905. From that time until 1908 he was a student at McCormick Theological Seminary in Chicago. A letterman in track, football and basketball 1904-05, he was also a member of Phi Phi Alpha at Alma.

Mr. Johnson was married on September 7, 1910, to Bessie Hill at Grand Rapids, Michigan. Mrs. Johnson, who was born at Grand Rapids on November 8, 1885, is descended from the norble house of Hill, in England. There are four children, David A., Jr., born October 16, 1911; Phillip A., born December 5, 1913; F. Eugene, born December 2, 1915; and Elizabeth, born September 26, 1917.

Ordained to the Presbyterian ministry, Mr. Johnson has filled the following pastorates: Marengo, Iowa, 1908-14; Rock Island, Illinois, 1914-19; Englewood, New Jersey, 1919-25; and Kearney, Nebraska, (First Presbyterian Church) 1925—, of which he is now pastor. The author of a pageant *The Dream that Came True* (1924), he has also written scores of other pageants, Bible dramas and popular plays not yet published.

Mr. Johnson is extremely active in the advancement of his city, and during the late war was a captain in the Secret Service, and a four minute speaker. He is a life member of The Nebraskana Society, and his hobbies are dramatics and play writing. Residence: Kearney.

Dean R. Johnson

Dean R. Johnson, instructor of agricultural engineering at the Nebraska School of Agriculture at Curtis, Nebraska, was born at Crete, Nebraska, January 26, 1889, son of Frank and Ellie Maria (Davis) Johnson. His father was born on a farm in Green County, Wisconsin, May 31, 1852, and died at Denver, Colorado, October 1, 1922. He was a miller. His ancestors date back to the early colonial days in Massachusetts. He operated the first roller mill located west of the Missouri River. His wife, Ellie, was born on a farm in Rock County, Wisconsin, January 1, 1864, and is still living at Aurora, Nebraska. She taught school in her younger days, and for forty years has been a member of the Order of Eastern Star. She is much interested in club work. Her ancestry dates back to Governor Bradford of colonial fame.

Mr. Johnson attended the Crete grade schools to the eighth grade, and was graduated from Aurora High School at Aurora, Nebraska in 1906. He is a graduate of the Lincoln Auto and Tractor School and the Operative Millers Laboratories of Chicago, Illinois. At the present time he is working for his Bachelor of Science degree at the Colorado Agricultural College, and expects to qualify in the near future.

While in high school he was a member of the football team four years, and captained his team his junior and senior years, and afterward played two years of semi-professional football at Aurora, Nebraska. On June 8, 1911, he was married to Wilda Elsie Marsden at Curtis, Nebraska. Mrs. Johnson was born at Curtis, November 15, 1893. Her ancestry is traced to her grandfather, Joseph Marsden, of Marsden Row, Leeds, England. Mr. and Mrs. Johnson have four childen, Norma, born August 26, 1912, who was graduated from the Nebraska School of Agriculture at Curtis in 1929 and is now attending Doane College, Crete, Nebraska; Helen, born November 3, 1917; Eleanor, born April 17, 1920; and Dean, born October 25, 1922.

From 1906 until 1908, Mr. Johnson was a surveyor for the Chicago, Burlington and Quincy Railroad in Nebraska, Montana, Wyoming and Missouri. The following eight years he was a miller for the Curtis Mills, Curtis, Nebraska, and during 1916 and 1917 was a mechanic for the Ford garage at Curtis. He has held his present position since 1917. A Democrat, he has held local offices only, was a member of the school board four years, a member of the city council five years and still holds that office. He has been a trustee of the First Congregational Church of Curtis for the past twenty years.

During the late war he was a lieutenant in the Home Guards and participated in other civilian projects. In 1906 he attended the National Guard Encampment with the 2nd National Nebraska Guard, Company H. at Fort Riley. Among Mr. Johnson's civic and professional organizations are the Red Cross, the Chamber of Commerce, the Rotary Club, the Nebraska State Teachers Association, the Southwest Nebraska Schoolman's Club. For a number of years he was a member of the Ancient Order of United Workmen. He is a member at the present time of the Nebraskana Society, the Young Men's Christian Association (sponsor of school organization at the Nebraska School of Agriculture at Curtis). His favorite sport is golf, and he is football coach at the agricultural school. He devotes much time to reading, mechanics and architecture. Residence: Curtis.

Earle George Johnson

One of Nebraska's distinguished surgeons, Dr. Earle George Johnson is a lifelong resident of Hall County. He was born at Bellwood, Nebraska, May 30, 1887, the son of Edmund and Hariett Opal (Arasmith) Johnson. His father, who was a hardware merchant, was born at Coldwater, Michigan, May 10, 1863, and died at Grand Island, Nebraska, September 29, 1928. His mother was born at Oreon, Illinois, February 10, 1872. Her ancestors came from England and settled in Kentucky, later moving to Illinois and subsequently settling in Nebraska.

Dr. Johnson attended the public school at Clarks, Nebraska, and in 1905 was graduated from the high school there. He was a student at Nebraska Wesleyan University from 1905 to 1908, attended the University of Nebraska from 1908 to 1911 when he received the A. B. and A. M. degrees. He received a fellowship in physiology, histology, and embryology at the latter institution, and was elected to membership in Sigma Xi because of his scientific research work.

He was graduated from Rush Medical College in 1913 with the M. D. degree. Dr. Johnson was made a member of Sigma Alpha Epsilon and Nu Sigma Nu at the University of Nebraska, and served as president of Sigma Alpha Epsilon. He was a member of Theta Nu Epsilon at Rush Medical School, and a member of the Everett Society at Wesleyan University.

He has served as district surgeon for the Union Pacific Railroad at Grand Island, Nebraska, and as assistant surgeon for the St. Joseph & Grand Island Railroad since 1915, acting as chief surgeon for the Central Power Company since 1925. Dr. Johnson is chairman of the executive committee of the staff of St. Francis Hospital at Grand Island where he has been engaged in practice since 1914. He is the author of resolution adopted by the Nebraska State Medical Association requesting Governor Bryan to replace in the state budget the $25,000 item for continuation of tuberculosis eradication in cattle. During the World War he served as first lieutenant in the Medical Corps, was captain of the Medical Reserve Corps, and acted as chairman of the Hall County Medical Draft Board. He has been a member of the Officers Reserve and the American Legion since 1920.

Dr. Johnson served as president of the Hall County Medical Society in 1929, was delegate to the Nebraska State Medical Association Convention in 1928, is president of the Nebraska Chapter of the American College of Surgeons, and holds membership in the American Medical Association and the American College of Surgeons. He is a member of the board of directors of the Grand Island Chamber of Commerce of which he is president, is a member and past president of the Rotary Club of Grand Island, and was formerly president of the council of the Boy Scouts of America, 1929-30.

From 1926 to 1928 he served as a member of the Grand Island School Board, and in 1929 was a member of the board of directors of the Young Men's Christian Association. His fraternal and social organizations include: University Club of Grand Island; Woodland Golf Club; Riverside Golf Club of which he is vice president; Elks;

Blue Lodge, York Rite, Scottish Rite and Shrine bodies of the Masons. His chief recreations are golfing and fishing.

His marriage to Laura Melvina Huyck occurred at Grand Island, June 15, 1915. Mrs. Johnson, whose ancestry is Scotch and Dutch, was born at Grand Island, March 9, 1892. They have two children: Earle George, born August 2, 1917; and Beatrice Elizabeth, born February 16, 1920.

Dr. Johnson is a Republican, and since his college days when he was president of the Republican Club at Wesleyan University has taken an active part in political affairs in his community. Residence: Grand Island.

Edith Keeler Johnson

One of Nebraska's pioneer citizens and leaders is Edith Keeler Johnson who was born at Medina, New York, July 22, 1870. Her father, John Keeler, who was a farmer and a Civil War soldier, was born in England, January 20, 1834, and died in Platte County, Nebraska, June 17, 1914. Her mother, Mary E. (Bacon) Keeler, who was a milliner, was born at Ridgeway, New York, July 8, 1844, of English parents, and died at Wattsville, Nebraska, February 17, 1815.

Mrs. Johnson attended rural schools in Platte County and from 1889 to 1894 was a teacher in country schools near Monroe. Since 1926 she has been precinct assessor of Lost Creek Township, and has taken an active part in various community affairs. She is a member of the Monroe Union Church and holds membership in the Women's Missionary Society and the Ladies Aid Society of that organization. She was prominent in Red Cross work and Liberty loan drives during the World War.

Her marriage to Erick M. Johnson occurred at Wattsville, Nebraska, March 7, 1894. They have the following children: Lewis H., born July 8, 1898, who married Elsie Pearson; Stella May, born July 14, 1900, who married Fred A. Hobbensiefken; Fred Raymond, born April 2, 1902, who married Anna Pearson; Benjamin Wright, born September 9, 1904; Roy William, born September 27, 1907; who married Lorena Hoare; and Frank Leonard, born August 17, 1910. Four of the children are farmers, one a salesman, and one a practical nurse. Residence: Monroe.

Elmer Johnson

A lifetime resident of Nebraska, Elmer Johnson was born in Sweden, June 3, 1872, the son of Andrew and Elna Johnson. His faher, who came to Saunders County in 1880, was born in Sweden, in February, 1847, and died at Omaha, in 1929.

Mr. Johnson is in the clothing business at Wahoo, Nebraska. He is a member of the Nebraskana Society, the Independent Order of the Odd Fellows, and the Knights of Pythias. He is a Republican.

He is married to Harriet Isobel Lattin, daughter of J. W. and Martha Rider Lattin. She was born at Omaha, August 23, 1873, and attended College at Yankton, South Dakota. She is a Presbyterian. Residence: Wahoo.

Elsie Daisy Johnson

Born at Syracuse, Nebraska, September 19, 1897, Elsie Daisy Johnson is the daughter of David Delmore and Myrtle Rhoda (Miller) Duncan. Her father, who was formerly junior captain of the Omaha Fire Department, was born in Olin County, Iowa, May 30, 1867, and is now retired; his paternal great-grandfather came to this country from Scotland. Her mother, whose

family was prominent in religious affairs in Nebraska during pioneer days, was born at Syracuse, Nebraska, July 13, 1878.

Mrs. Johnson attended Brown Park School at Omaha, Nebraska, was graduated from South High School in 1916, and was a student at the University of Omaha for two summer sessions. She received a first grade county certificate, with honors, in 1916. She has taught the following schools: Glen, Nebraska, 1916; Whitney, 1916-18, Chandler School at South Omaha, 1919-21. At this time she is a homemaker and a leader in social and civic affairs at Page, Nebraska.

She has served as vice president and president of the Parent Teachers Association, has been a member of the Women's Christian Temperance Union for five years acting as chairman of the Scientific Temperance Instruction Department at Page, and was a director of the latter organization for several years. She is vitally interested in the mental, moral, and social development of children, and devotes most of her time to the care of her family. She engaged in the sale of thrift stamps and was active in Red Cross work during the late war.

Mrs. Johnson was married June 23, 1920, at West Point, Nebraska, to Clay Harold Johnson. Mr. Johnson, who is a farmer, was born at Brunswick, Nebraska, December 13, 1893, the son of pioneer Nerbaska parents and the grandson of the first county superintendent of schools in Antelope County. Their children are: Clay Harold, Jr., born September 2, 1923; Roy Duncan, born September 11, 1925; and Phyllis Myrtle, born April 11, 1927. Residence: Page.

Frank Johnson

Frank Johnson, general merchant at North Loup since 1901, was born at Newton, Iowa, December 27, 1873, son of Robert and Mary Elizabeth (Watson) Johnson.

The father was born at Penn Yan, New York, June 24, 1837, and died at North Loup, in January, 1915. He was a farmer and livestock shipper and breeder, who served as county supervisor of Valley County. His parents died when he was a child; his ancestors came to America before the Revolutionary War. His wife, Mary Elizabeth Watson, was born in Greenwich, New York, December 19, 1836, and died at North Loup, in March, 1921. She was a pioneer, who came to Chicago by boat and lived in Illinois and Iowa for a time. She settled in Nebraska about 1880, and reared a large family. Her parents died when she was a small child. She was distantly related to Secretary Seward.

Frank Johnson attended country school and the Grand Island Business College. A farmer's son, he worked for George E. Johnson in a grain, coal and implement business from 1896 until 1901. He has since been in the merchandise business. He is the director of the Loup Valley Independent Telephone Company at the present time.

On October 12, 1898, he was married to Grace Purdum at Burwell, Nebraska. She was born at Rockport, Missouri, August 1, 1876, a descendant of the Calverts of Colonial times, and of Judge Purdum. She was a teacher before her marriage. They have one daughter, Thelma, born October 16, 1906, who was married to Howard W. Hamilton. She was graduated from North Loup High School, and was a student at Nebraska Wesleyan University for three years where she was a member of Alpha Kappa Delta. She taught in high school prior to her marriage. Her husband is principal at the high school at Geneva at the present time.

Mr. Johnson has been elected three times as a member of the county board of supervisors. For many years he has been a member of the board of education. During the late war he was chairman for the sale of war saving stamps of his local district. He is a member of the North Loup Methodist Episcopal Church, the Red Cross, the Masons, the Odd Fellows, the Parent Teachers Association and the board of education of which he is now treasurer. Residence: North Loup.

Frank Bruce Johnson

Frank B. Johnson was born at Rensselaer, Indiana, December 5, 1864. His father, George Madison Johnson, a farmer and educator, was a teacher for over 50 years and served as county superintendent of public schools for several years. He was born at Terre Haute, Indiana, December 28, 1830, and was descended from English ancestors who came to America early in the history of the country and settled in Tennessee. He died at Wilsonville, Nebraska, July 30, 1904.

Anna Eliza Johnson, his mother, was deescended from English ancestors who settled in Kentucky several generations ago. She was born at Lost River, Orange County, Indiana, December 28, 1837, and died at Wilsonville, February 8, 1908.

Dr. Johnson has lived in Nebraska for 47 years and for over 35 years has been a practicing physician in this state. He was graduated from the Rensselaer High School, June, 1884, and in 1894 he was graduated from Keokuk Medical College with the degree M. D. He took post-graduate work at Chicago Polyclinic in 1901. He was admitted to the practice of medicine at Wilsonville, April, 1894. He has been a farmer, teacher, and is now engaged in the general practice of medicine at Lincoln.

His marriage to Cora Bell Austin was solemnized at Wilsonville, December 18, 1895. Mrs. Johnson was born at Dwight, Livingston County, Illinois, April 8, 1875. Her ancestors were English settlers in Rhode Island in the early days. Two children were born to this union: Clarence B., born September 21, 1896; who is a dentist; and George S., born September 10, 1899, who is a physician.

Dr. Johnson is a member of the Lancaster County Medical Association; the Nebraska State Medical Association; and the American Medical Association. He is a member of the Lincoln Chamber of Commerce, the Knife and Fork Club, and the Lincoln Young Men's Christian Association. He is a member of the Modern Woodmen of America; and the Masons, Shrine. His sport is golfing. He is a member of the Westminster Presbyterian Church. He is a Republican. Residence: Lincoln.

Frank McKinley Johnson

Frank McKinley Johnson, lawyer and insurance executive, was born at Seward, Nebraska, June 11, 1896, son of Louis Norton and Sarah Ellen (Stine) Johnson. Louis N. Johnson, born at Liberty, Illinois, May 11, 1850, died at Cozad, Nebraska, April 19, 1923. A pioneer in both Seward and Dawson Counties, he was a prominent farmer for many years, active in Republican politics, and after retiring from the farm was a member of the Cozad city council. He was of Irish and Pennsylvania Dutch descent. Sarah Ellen Stine was born in Metamora, Illinois, March 22, 1854, of German and Pennsylvania Dutch descent. She is living.

Educated in country school and the public school at Cozad, Frank McKinley Johnson was graduated from Cozad High School in 1912, where he earned letters in football, basketball, baseball and track. He was a member of the freshman football team at the University of Nebraska, where he received his Bachelor of Laws degree in 1925. While still in college he was delegate to the Republican national convention at Cleveland in 1924, and from 1927 to 1929 was secretary to Governor McMullen.

Mr. Johnson was reared on a farm, and after graduation worked as an apprentice at the depot of the Union Pacific Railroad. For a time he worked on a farm, later

resuming his course at the university. In 1926 he opened a law office in Lexington, leaving a few months later to become the governor's secretary, after which he re-established himself in the practice of law, at Lexington where he maintains his law office. He is vice president and counsel of the American States Life Insurance Company of Lincoln.

On August 31, 1930, he was married to Arvilla Melissa Johnson at Lincoln. Mrs. Johnson, who is of Revolutionary ancestry of Irish and Pennsylvania Dutch extraction, was born at Surprise, Nebraska, December 1, 1901.

Mr. Johnson is a member of the Nebraska State, the Western Nebraska and the Dawson County Bar Associations. He is a Scottish Rite Mason and member of the Shrine, a member of the Red Cross, Chamber of Commerce, Kiwanis Club and the Lexington Country Club. A lover of football, baseball, track and hunting, his hobbies are really reading and looking after farm lands. He is a lover of nature. Recently Mr. Johnson was made a life member of The Nebraskana Society. Residence: Lexington.

Frank P. Johnson

Frank P. Johnson, lawyer, was born at Valley, Nebraska, November 22, 1879, son of Charles Truman and Hannah Jane (Maus) Johnson. His ancestry is German and English, his family having come to America about 1700, settling in Pennsylvania.

Mr. Johnson attended the public schools of Nebraska, Fremont Normal School, and the University of Nebraska from which he received his Bachelor of Laws degree in 1910.

On June 22, 1904, he was married to Lora Cordelia Peters at Minatare. She was born at Madison, Nebraska, October 4, 1885. Mr. and Mrs. Johnson have two children, Charles T., born October 3, 1908; and Mabel Mary, born May 7, 1905, who married John T. Boatwright.

An independent and progressive Republican, Mr. Johnson takes an active interest in politics and has served as county superintendent of schools of Scotts Bluff County. During the years 1917-18 he was a member of the Council of Defense, and at the present time is a member of the Red Cross and the Methodist Episcopal Church. He enjoys golf, billiards, and football. Residence: Scottsbluff.

Frank W. Johnson

Since 1894 Frank W. Johnson has been engaged in the practice of medicine at Fullerton. He was born at Blue Earth, Minnesota, December 18, 1867, the son of Cyrus F. and Triphena (Cutting) Johnson. His father, who was a circuit rider and millwright, was born in England in 1798 and died and was buried in Cloud County, Kansas in 1870.

At the age of three years Dr. Johnson removed from Blue Earth to Cloud County, Kansas, where he lived with his family until 18874, when they removed to Hamilton County, Nebraska, residing at Lone Tree. They remained there until 1880, then moving to Fullerton, where Dr. Johnson has since resided.

Dr. Johnson was graduated from the Fullerton High School in 1890 and received his medical degree from Omaha Medical College in 1894. He has served as a member of the insanity commission since 1896, has been county health officer, a member of the city council, the firemen's association, and has been local surgeon for the Union Pacific Railroad. He is a member of the Old Timers Club, of the U. P. B. A., is city physician, and during the World War was a member of the local draft board.

He is married to Maude C. Matheson who was born of Scotch parentage at Hopkinton, Iowa, January 6, 1876.

Mrs. Johnson is the organizer of the Fullerton Pulblic Library, which was erected in 1913 and served as librarian until 1918. Dr. Johnson is a staunch Republican and a member of the Nebraskana Society. Residence: Fullerton.

Fred G. Johnson

Fred G. Johnson was born in Saline county, Nebraska, October 16, 1876. His father, Charles Johnson, was born in Sweden and died at Dorchester, Saline county, Nebraska, November 24, 1916. Descended from Swedish ancestors who came to America in 1850, he was a farmer and stock raiser and took an active part in the Civil War.

Mr. Johnson's mother, Jane Aurelia (Butler) Johnson was born in Wisconsin, December 3, 1850, and died at Dorchester, Nebraska, November 8, 1906. She was of Dutch and Irish descent.

A Republican, Mr. Johnson was a member of the state legislature, 1907-08; 1917-18; the state senate, 1919-20; lieutenant governor, 1923-24. He was elected to congress 1928. He has engaged in general real estate and law business for twenty-five years and has owned and operated ranches for about the same time.

On November 15, 1906 he was married to L. Maude Bridgman. Mrs. Johnson, whose ancestors were New Englanders, was born at Fairmont, Nebraska, February 18, 1881.

He was graduated from the Nebraska State University College of Law, in 1903 and was admitted to practice at Lincoln, on June 11, 1903. At the present time he engaged in the practice of law at Hastings.

Mr. Johnson is a member of the First Methodist Episcopal Church, American Automobile Association and the Young Men's Christian Association at Hastings. While in Congress, Mr. Johnson served as ranking new member on the irrigation and reclamation committee and was also a member of committees on patents and claims. Residence: Hastings.

George Edward Johnson

George Edward Johnson, lawyer, was born at St. Joseph, Missouri, November 9, 1905, son of George Edward and Minnie Ruby (Adams) Johnson. The father, a civil and electrical engineer, was born at Wymore, Nebraska, March 16, 1885 of English Canadian ancestry. He is manager of the Empire Bridge Company at this time. His wife, Minnie, was born at Neosho Rapids, Kansas, December 28, 1881, of English and Holland Dutch descent, and died in Denver County, Colorado, April 1, 1930.

George Edward Johnson attended the grade schools of Sabetha, Kansas and Falls City, Nebraska, and in 1920 was graduated from Elliott Grade School at Lincoln, Nebraska. He was graduated from the high school at Superior, Nebraska, and in 1929 received the Bachelor of Laws degree at the University of Nebraska where he was graduated with the honor *magna cum laude*. While at the university Mr. Johnson was a member of the debating team, served as secretary of his graduating class, and held membership in Delta Sigma Rho, Order of the Coif, Phi Gamma Delta and Phi Delta Phi.

Since his admission to the bar in June, 1929, he has been associated with the law firm of Root, Clark & Buckner in New York City. He is secretary of the Lincoln School of Aviation.

On January 6, 1930, his marriage to Betty Durisek was solemnized at West New York, New Jersey. Mrs. Johnson was born at Richfield Springs, New York, August 26, 1912. They have one son, George Edward, born September 27, 1931.

Mr. Johnson is affiliated with Westminster Presbyterian Church of Lincoln. His hobbies are radio, physics, and public speaking. Residence: New York.

George Robert Johnson

Born at Funk, Nebraska, December 31, 1885, George Robert Johnson is the son of Alfred and Louise (Hogerson) Johnson. His father, who was a pioneer farmer in Nebraska, was born in the province of Smalund, Sweden, January 6, 1851, and died at Funk, December 21, 1890. Louise (Hogerson) Johnson, one of the outstanding homebuilders of Nebraska, was born in Smalund, June 1, 1851, and died at Funk, June 9, 1909.

Mr. Johnson was a student at Bethany College, 1906-08, and attended Fremont College of Pharmacy, 1912-13, where he served as president of the senior class and engaged in semi-professional baseball. He was a farmer near Funk for over 25 years, served as a drug clerk for a period of four years at Salida, Colorado, was assistant cashier of the First State Bank at Bertrand, Nebraska, for two years, and for the past 16 years has owned and managed his own drug store at Bertrand.

He holds membership in the Nebraska Pharmaceutical Association, the Bertrand Golf Club, and the Community Club, of which he is president at this time. He holds membership in the Scottish Rite and Shrine bodies of the Masons. Mr. Johnson's chief recreations are golfing, fishing, and hunting.

On October 6, 1920, he was united in marriage with Grace McKee at Rayan, Nebraska. Mrs. Johnson, who was formerly a superintendent of schools, at Bertrand, was born of Scotch and Irish parentage at Fairfax, Missouri, January 13, 1893, the daughter of Jacob and Jeannette Elizabeth (Sellers) McKee. They have one son, George R., born December 20, 1925. Residence: Bertrand. (Photograph in Album).

Gus Johnson

Gus Johnson, postmaster at Ceresco, since 1927, was born in Sweden, March 30, 1884, and came to Nebraska at the age of two years. He is the son of Carl A. and Matilda (Erickson) Johnson, the former of whom was born at Smaland, Sweden, April 2, 1855, and came to the United States in 1886. He was a farmer until his death at Shickley, July 29, 1922. His wife, Matilda, was born in Smaland, May 23, 1857, and is living.

Mr. Johnson completed his common school education in 1900, and attended the International Law and Business Institute at Minneapolis in 1911. From 1907-10, he was manager of a grain station for the Updike Grain Company, and was auditor for them during 1910-11. From 1911-20 he was bookkeeper and assistant cashier of the State Bank of Ceresco, and from 1911-26, was city clerk of Ceresco. During the years 1921-25, he was manager of the Latta Grain and Lumber Company, and in 1926, was engaged in the insurance and loan business. Since 1927 he has been postmaster. He is a Republican.

On February 24, 1909, he was united in marriage to Lottie E. Gibbs at Lincoln. Mrs. Johnson, who is of English descent, was born at Ceresco, August 29, 1886. They have three children, Eunice, born September 6, 1911; Sylvia, born January 30, 1915, and Zelpha, born November 27, 1924.

Mr. Johnson is an outstanding citizen of his community, and takes an active part in civic and educational work. He participated in all Liberty loan drives, and was awarded special recognition in the Victory loan drive. He was also registrar of the local board for Saunders County. He is affiliated with the Red Cross and was president of the local advisory board of the Nebraska Children's Home Society, 1927. He has been a director of the Board of Education of Ceresco Schools since 1919, and a member of the board of directors of Luther College at Wahoo, since 1930. He is a Mason, Modern Woodman and member of the Eastern Star, as well as Commercial Club and The Nebraskana Society. His church is the Evangelical Lutheran Church of Ceresco. Residence: Ceresco. (Photograph in Album).

Harry Hanson Johnson

Harry Hanson Johnson, bank executive, manufacturer, and a leader in the business world of Nebraska, has been a continuous resident of this state for over 37 years. He was born at Lenox, Iowa, May 15, 1875, the son of Manander Matt Johnson and Charlotte (Ellis) Johnson. His father, who was born in Ohio in 1853, and died at Idaho Springs, Colorado, January 15, 1912, was an engineer, inventor, and manufacturer; he was of Holland Dutch and French descent. His mother was born of Irish parents in Pennsylvania, 1831, and is still living.

Mr. Johnson has been a miner, farmer, and stockraiser, and is today successful as a manufacturer. He is known to Nebraskans as the owner and announcer for radio station KMMJ at Clay center where he is president of the M. M. Johnson Company and of the Harry Johnson Company. He is serving as vice president of the Commercial State Bank of Clay Center at the present time, and takes an active part in community affairs.

He holds membership in the Nebraska State Historical Society, the Nebraskana Society, Clay Center Chamber of Commerce of which he was president for 12 years, and the First Congregational Church of Clay Center. His fraternal organizations include: Masons; Independent Order of Odd Fellows; and Modern Woodmen of America. Mr. Johnson is the author of various poultry articles and lectures on poultry, including *The Radio Visitor*. His hobby is livestock farming.

On October 27, 1902, his marriage to Lula Inez Holcombe was solemnized at Harlan, Iowa. Mrs. Johnson, who was born at Panama, Iowa, October 24, 1883, is a musician and is prominent in welfare and social activities in Clay County where she served as county chairman of the Red Cross. She is of Irish and German descent. Two children were born to this marriage: Dent K., July 1, 1903, who died October 11, 1931; and Manander M., June 21, 1908.

Mr. Johnson served as chairman of the Council of Defense during the World War, was a member of the draft board, and was prominent in county drives for the sale of Liberty bonds. Residence: Clay Center.

Herman Frank Johnson

Herman F. Johnson, orthopedic surgeon of Omaha, was born at Hall, Montana, January 8, 1897, the son of Frank and Sarah (Faulk) Johnson.

Dr. Johnson received his M. D. degree at the University of Iowa in 1922 where he was a member of Nu Sigma Nu, Alpha Omega Alpha and Sigma Xi. He was admitted to the practice of his profession in Nebraska in 1924. He is the author of several articles on bone and joint surgery. He is a member of the teaching orthopedic staff at the University of Nebraska, College of Medicine. His hospital appointments include the Clarkson, Methodist, Covenant Immanuel, Lord Lister, and Douglas County Hospitals in Omaha. He is the junior member of the firm Doctors Lord Schrock & Johnson. He is a member of the American Legion, having served in the Medical Corps during the World War.

He holds membership in the American College of Surgeons, American Medical Association, The Nebraska State Medical Society. He is a member of the Red Cross and the Nebraskana Society. He is a Republican.

On September 14, 1921, he married Maude Petersen at Cedar Rapids, Iowa. Mrs. Johnson was born at Mount Auburn, Iowa, August 27th, 1897. Her ancestry is German and Scotch. They have two children: Marjorie, born September 2, 1922, and Richard, born May, 1928. Residence: Omaha.

Irving Norton Johnson

Irving Norton Johnston, dentist at Broken Bow, Nebraska, was born at Sweetwater, Nebraska, October 22, 1901, the son of Julius and Ellen (Olson) Johnson. His father, a farmer and stockman, was born in Norway, August 28, 1856, and died at Sweetwater, September 23, 1913. He came to America in 1875, settling first in Minnesota and later in Nebraska. His mother was born in Norway, May 14, 1863, and came to Nebraska in 1882.

Dr. Johnson was graduated from the high school at Ravenna, Nebraska in 1918, and in 1923 received the D. D. S. degree at the University of Nebraska where he was a member in Delta Upsilon and Delta Sigma Delta. He has been engaged in the practice of dentistry at Broken Bow for the past 8 years, is a member of the American Dental Association, and holds membership in the Nebraska State Dental Society and the Bosworth Study Club. He is a member of the Lutheran Church. He is affiliated with the Emmet Crawford Lodge of the Ancient Free and Accepted Masons at Broken Bow and Horeb Chapter of the Royal Arch Masons.

On June 16, 1927, he was married to Helen Darlene Robb at Lincoln, Nebraska. Mrs. Johnson, who was a teacher and nurse, was born at Ong, Nebraska, December 1, 1903. Her great-great-grandfathers served in the Revolution. Residence: Broken Bow.

James Richard Johnson

James Richard Johnson, dean of McCook Junior College at McCook, Nebraska, was born on a farm near Kirksville, Missouri, May 30, 1898, son of William Lewis and Jennie Etella (Henry) Johnson.

William Lewis Johnson was born at Montrose, Iowa, August 23, 1866, and died at Kirksville, Missouri, April 17, 1928. He was a farmer whose father, John P. Johnson, was born in Vermont in 1828 of English descent. His mother, Mary Baggs, was born at Navoo, Illinois, 1832, and was of French Canadian descent.

Jennie, wife of William Lewis Johnson, was born in Adair County, Missouri, January 18, 1870. She resides at Lincoln, Nebraska. In her earlier years she was a rural school teacher. Her father, William Emory Henry a Methodist minister, was born in Philadelphia in 1813. His father came from Ireland. Her mother, Miranda Watts, was born in Ohio in 1843. Her mother's parents were named Van Horn and came from Holland. John Watts came from England.

James Richard Johnson received his elementary education in the rural schools of Adair County, Missouri, and was graduated from the Kirksville High School in 1917. There he was honored with letters in football, basketball and track, and also graduated with highest grades. He received the Bachelor of Science degree in education at Kirksville Teachers College in 1922; his Bachelor of Law degree from the American Extension University of Los Angeles in 1926; and his Masters degree from the University of Missouri the same year. During the summer of 1929 he was a student at the University of Nebraska. While in college Mr. Johnson was a member of Kappa Delta Pi.

From 1921 until 1923 Mr. Johnson was principal of the Unionville, Missouri, High School. From 1923 until 1925 he was superintendent of schools at Granger, Missouri, and since 1926 has held the position of dean of McCook Junior College, the first public junior college in Nebraska. He assisted in the organization of this institution in the fall of 1926.

On May 15, 1921, he was married to Cecile Ethel Croson at Kirksville. Mrs. Johnson was born at Downing, Missouri, December 19, 1896, daughter of Don C. Croson who was born on a farm near Lancaster, Missouri, and Elizabeth Hall, a native of Lancaster, Missouri. They have two children, Barbara Ettella, born January 1, 1925; and James Richard, Jr., born May 16, 1927.

Mr. Johnson is a Democrat. From May 20, 1917 until June 26, 1919, he served in the United States Army in Company I, 34th Infantry, 7th Division, and was discharged with the rank of sergeant. He is a member of the American Legion and the United States Army Reserve Officers (2nd lieutenant Chemical Warfare Service). He is a member of the First Congregational Church of McCook, the Nebraska State Teachers Association (secretary district five, 1930); and the American Chemical Society. Since 1926 he has been a member of the McCook Chamber of Commerce. He served as president of the Kiwanis Club in 1931 and since 1930 has been a member of the McCook Public Library Board, serving as president during 1931-32. He is a Mason, a member of the Young Men's Christian Association, and the Red Cross, president of the Southwestern Nebraska School Men's Club, 1930-31, which was organized some time previous to 1913.

Mr. Johnson's favorite sports include hunting, fishing, handball, and volley-ball. Much of his leisure time is devoted to reading. He is a member of the Nebraskana Society and the Southwestern Nebraska Historical Society. Residence: McCook. (Photograph in Album).

James William Johnson

James William Johnson, son of Frank C. and Jane (Armstrong) Johnson, was born at Randolph, Iowa, December 26, 1878, and for 43 years has resided in Nebraska.

The father was born in Quebec, Canada, May 12, 1846, and was a banker in Omaha until his death in September, 1896. His wife, Jane, was born in County Fermanagh, Ireland, April 14, 1846, and died at Omaha, in April, 1915. In her youth she was a rural school teacher.

Mr. Johnson was graduated from Omaha High School in 1896. He was, successively, connected with, the Omaha National Bank, the First National Bank of Omaha, the State Journal Company of Lincoln, the Hammond Printing Company of Fremont, Nebraska, S. D. Childs & Company of Chicago. He was later vice president of the Bank of Spearfish, South Dakota, and vice president of the American Bank at Sidney. Since 1920 he has been in the insurance and loan business by himself.

On December 20, 1911, Mr. Johnson was married to Helen Geneva Fowler at Deadwood, South Dakota. Mrs. Johnson was born at Rapid City, South Dakota, November 4, 1884. Her father was Irish and her mother of Pennsylvania Dutch descent. There are two children, Virginia F., born October 13, 1912, who is a sophomore at the University of Colorado and a member of Chi Omega, and who was a vocalist and salutatorian of her senior class at Sidney High School. Helen Jane, the second child, was born December 25, 1915.

For a period of 4 years Mr. Johnson was city treasurer of Sidney. He is a Republican. For four years he served as secretary of the Sidney Chamber of Commerce, and since 1925 he has been a member of the Rotary Club. He has served as sergeant-at-arms, a director, song leader, program chairman and now president. He is a 32nd degree Mason and a member of the Sidney Country Club. His hobby is music. Residence: Sidney.

Jennie Eliza Johnson

Jennie E. Johnson, distinguished in educational circles as a teacher of the blind, was born at Oakland, Burt County, Nebraska, January 1, 1880. Her father, Andrew Peter Johnson, a Civil War veteran and a shoe maker by trade, was born at Stockholm, Sweden, and died at Fremont, Dodge County, Nebraska, May, 1902. He came to this country at the age of 14.

Hannah Laura (Fleck) Johnson, her mother, was born at Philadelphia, Pennsylvania, February 11, 1854, and died at Grand Island, Nebraska, November 19, 1930. She was a teacher before her marriage. Her father, who was a lieutenant in the army in the Civil War, was of French and German descent. Her mother's ancestry was Pennsylvania Dutch and French.

Miss Johnson was graduated from the Nebraska School for the Blind at Nebraska City in 1899. In 1900 she returned to the school for a postgraduate course. A lifetime resident of Nebraska, she has for many years engaged in educational activities at the Nebraska School for the Blind, and at the present is associated with that organization as primary teacher. She has taken an active interest in welfare and civic affairs in Nebraska City and is beloved in her community for her unusual service.

She is president of the Altrusa Club at Nebraska City, and is affiliated with the Methodist Church. She is a Republican. Residence: Nebraska City.

Jennie L. Johnson

Jennie L. Johnson, educator and clubwoman at Harvard, Nebraska, has lived in this state for the past 38 years. She was born at Vermont, Fulton County, Illinois, November 1, 1865, the daughter of Henry Lee and Mary Catherine (Kennedy) Coulter. Her father, who was a merchant and mayor of his city, was born at Wellsville, West Virginia, September 20, 1828, and died at Harvard, Nebraska, January 5, 1905. He was of Scotch-Irish descent. Her mother was born at Pittsburgh, Pennsylvania, October 11, 1830, and died at Table Grove, Illinois, March 25, 1870; her Irish ancestors were farmers.

Mrs. Johnson was graduated from the Bardolph High School and was a student at Macomb Normal School, Macomb, Illinois, where she was active in debating, dramatics, and music. She taught school for five years in Illinois and for eight years in Nebraska. During the late war Mrs. Johnson served as chairman of the local Red Cross chapter, was a four minute lecturer, and purchased Liberty bonds. She was president of the Woman's Relief Corps in 1915, 1926, and 1927.

On June 20, 1901, she was married to Will Forrest Johnson at Ong, Nebraska. Mr. Johnson, who was born at Tippecanoe, Ohio, February 3, 1863, is a retired farmer. Mrs. Johnson is a member of the Harvard Woman's Club, the Pleasant Hour Woman's Club, the Mite Society, the Degree of Honor Protective Association, Modern Brotherhood of America, and the W. R. C.. She is a member of and is exceptionally active in the Congregational Church of Harvard, and holds membership in the Nebraskana Society. Her hobbies are reading and club work. Residence: Harvard.

John F. Johnson

John F. Johnson, hardware merchant, was born at Brady, Nebraska, October 23, 1882, son of William A. and Catherine (Carroll) Johnson. William A. Johnson was born in Sweden, October 1, 1846, and came to America in 1865. He worked in Illinois and Iowa for about two years and in 1867 located in Lincoln County, Nebraska. There he was a cowboy and cook on ranches until 1885, when he began farming. He retired and moved to Brady about 1920, where he resided until his death on May 28, 1923. His wife, Catherine, was born in Maple Wood, Ohio, September 27, 1856, and died at Brady, February 2, 1926.

Mr. Johnson attended public school in Lincoln County, and on March 22, 1909, was married to Matilda Elizabeth Kratzenstein at Lexington. She was born at Brady, September 9, 1887, daughter of Gus and Carolyn (Schuck) Kratzenstein. Her father was born in Muhlhausen, Germany, October 3, 1861, and in his early life was a cabinet maker. Later he was a farmer and afterward a merchant. He resides with his wife at Brady. Carolyn Schuck was born in Rintlen, Hessen, Germany, April 17, 1859, and is a member of the Methodist Episcopal Church, the Rebekahs and the Federated Women's Clubs.

Mr. and Mrs. Johnson have two children, Edna Pearl, born December 5, 1911; and Dean Leslie, born June 10, 1919. Mr. Johnson is a member of the Odd Fellows and the Methodist Episcopal Church. Politically he is a Democrat. His favorite sports are golf and fishing. Residence: Brady.

John Gottfrid Johnson

John Gottfrid Johnson, who has been a farmer, stockman, and builder at Ainsworth, Nebraska, for the past 22 years, was born in Sweden, July 3, 1884. His father, Jean Johnson, who was engaged in the express business for many years, was a native of Sweden. His mother, Marie Charlotte (Johanson) Johnson, was born in Sweden, and is still living there.

Mr. Johnson received his education in Sweden, and for 22 years has taken an active part in the business and educational affairs of his community in Brown County, Nebraska. He served as a director in the local school board from 1914 to 1916, and since 1921 has been a member of that organization. His fraternal organizations are the Masons and Modern Woodmen of America.

His marriage to Matilda Petterson took place at Lead, South Dakota, August 9, 1908. Eleven children were born to their marriage, all of whom are living: Mary Matilda, June 20, 1909; Harold Merle, June 16, 1911; Elsie Lillian, April 22, 1913; LeRoy Willard, June 7, 1915; Ruth Alice, February 24, 1917; John Robert, January 29, 1919; Martha Ragnhild Arlean, September 28, 1921; Lloyd Raymond, December 19, 1922; Eugene Kenneth, August 27, 1927; Doris Evelyn, August 3, 1929; and Donald, December 24, 1931. Residence: Ainsworth.

John Harvey Johnson

A lifetime resident of Nebraska, John H. Johnson has been prominent for many years in the political and business affairs of his community and state. He was born at Murray, Cass County, Nebraska, June 22, 1874, the son of Richard Thomas and Mary S. (Dunn) Johnson. His father was a farmer and stockman who was born at Oregon, Holt County, Missouri, January 14, 1852, of Scotch-Irish descent. His mother was born at Mound City, Holt County, Missouri, April 19, 1853, and died at Blair, Washington County, Nebraska, April 15, 1919; her ancestry was Irish. She was the mother of seven children.

Mr. Johnson attended grade and high school, and in 1895, was graduated from Rohrbaugh's Commercial College at Omaha. He was active in baseball and boxing during his school days. At the age of 18 he was editor and publisher of the *Murray Banner*, at Murray. Since January 1, 1907, he has been telephone superintendent at Herman. He owns farm and city property in Nebraska. In 1923 and 1925 he was a member of the Nebraska Legislature, and in 1925 was president of the Democratic House Organization.

He was united in marriage with Charrie Almedia Butler at Weeping Water, Cass County, Nebraska, November 26, 1896. Mrs. Johnson, who is of Quaker descent, the eldest daughter of Dr. M. M. and Stella Paine Butler, was born at Weeping Water, July 24, 1875. They have two children, Harvey B., born September 10, 1900; and Ralph Clare, born December 25, 1905. Harvey B., a graduate of the University of Nebraska, class of 1925, is assistant engineer in the mechanical department of the Burlington Railroad with headquarters in Chicago. Ralph Clare graduated in music and arts from the University of Nebraska, 1932.

Mr. Johnson has always been interested in the advancement of his community, and contributes to the Red Cross and other charity organizations. He is a member of the Lions Club at Herman; the Ancient Order of United Workmen; and the local Masonic chapter. His sports include baseball, boxing, and hunting. He is affiliated with the Methodist Episcopal Church at Herman. Residence: Herman. (Photograph in Album).

Leonard Lee Johnson

Leonard Lee Johnson, a leading merchant at Republican City, Nebraska, has lived in this state for the past 43 years and has taken an active part in the civic events of his community. He was born at Richland, Iowa, September 18, 1870, the son of Lot Morris and Jane (Hadley) Johnson. His father, who was a farmer, was born at Agency, Iowa, April 4, 1849, of Irish descent, and died at Almena, Kansas, May 20, 1928. His mother was born at Pleasant Plain, Iowa, March 3, 1852, of English parentage.

Mr. Johnson was a druggist at Beaver City from 1898 to 1900 and since then has been successfully engaged in the hardware retail business in Republican City. He is a member of the Republican City Commercial Club, the Nebraska Hardware Dealers Association, and the District Hardware Association.

His marriage to Ida Augusta Hickey was solemnized at Geneva, Nebraska, January 12, 1893. Mrs. Johnson, who was a teacher prior to her marriage, was born of Irish and English parents at Paw Paw, Illinois, June 10, 1867, and died at Republican City, March 1, 1923. Their three children are Howard, born September 8, 1893, who married Amy Viola Camp; Guy R., born January 25, 1901, who married Lucile Elizabeth Baker; and Hazel Mae, born August 26, 1906, who attended the University of Nebraska and is now a teacher at Superior, Nebraska. Howard was graduated from the business college at Hastings and is a banker at Hendley, Nebraska, while Guy R. attended the University of Nebraska and is also in the banking business, Ventura, California.

Mr. Johnson is affiliated with the Methodist Episcopal Church at Republican City, is a member of The Nebraskana Society, and holds membership in the following fraternal organizations: Masons; Modern Woodmen of America; and the Independent Order of Odd Fellows. His hobby is hardware mechanics. Residence: Republican City.

Merwin Oliver Johnson

Merwin Oliver Johnson, lawyer and county attorney of Sheridan County, was born at Stromsburg, Nebraska, December 12, 1893, son of Olaf J. and Betsy Belle (Nelson) Johnson.

The father was born in Sweden, December 23, 1851, and died at Stromsburg, January 11, 1931. His wife, born in Sweden, November 14, 1849, died at Stromsburg, July 27, 1930. The father was active in the business world and the mother was devoted to church work.

Mr. Johnson attended the public schools at Stromsburg and the Stromsburg and Lincoln High Schools. He completed a five year law course at the University of Nebraska and was a student at the University School of Music at Lincoln. While in university he was a member of the band and orchestra, a member of Phi Delta Legal fraternity and Sigma Phi Epsilon social fraternity. Since his admission in 1925, he has been active in the practice of law. He was elected county attorney in August 1930 and for the past three years has been city attorney of Rushville.

On April 11, 1925, he was married to Zoetta Blanch Ritchey at Marysville, Kansas. Mrs. Johnson was born at Lincoln, February 27, 1901. She is the daughter of Bert and Ella (Swanfelt), Ritchey of Lincoln, Nebraska, Mrs. Johnson is a member of the Eastern Star and the

Ladies Columbia Reading Club. She is a graduate of Lincoln High School, and took a course in a school of commerce.

During the late war, Mr. Johnson held the rank of sergeant, headquarters company, 355th infantry, 89th division, he is a member of the American Legion, the Nebraska State Bar Association, the Red Cross (county chairman two years), the Chamber of Commerce, the Masons and the Eastern Star. His religious affiliation is with the Baptist Church of Stromsburg. He enjoys fishing and hunting, while his hobby is music. Residence: Rushville.

Olaf O. Johnson

Olaf O. Johnson, farmer and stockman, was born at Hadley, Minnesota, July 15, 1877, and has resided in Nebraska for 23 years. His father, Claus O. Johnson, was born in Norway, January 15, 1833, and died at Carval, Colorado, October 12, 1927. He was a farmer and merchant. His wife, Ellen Anna Christianson, was born in Norway, August 15, 1835, and died at Hadley, February 6, 1880.

Mr. Johnson attended public school, and soon after engaged in farming. At the present time he is president of the board of directors of the Farmers Co-operative Oil Company at Gordon, and a member of the board of drectors of the Farmers Co-operative Creamery at Gordon. He is a Republican, and from 1925 until 1931 was a member of the Nebraska legislature. He was president of the County Farm Bureau 1920-1923, and is president at the present time of the taxpayers league of Sheridan County. In 1931 he was made a master farmer of America.

On February 14, 1904, he was married to Christine Louise Davidson at Webster, South Dakota. Mrs. Johnson was born at Montivido, Minnesota, June 7, 1885. They have six children, Melvin, born January 4, 1905, who married Hazel Wilber; Ernest, born September 23, 1907; Louise, born April 15, 1908; Arthur, born January 17, 1910; Herman, born February 16, 1912; and Ruth, born July 16, 1917.

Since 1914, Mr. Johnson has been a member and director of the board of education. He is a member of the Church of God. Residence: Gordon.

Orval Allen Johnson

Orval Allen Johnson was the first boy born at College View, Nebraska, the date of his birth being January 26, 1891. He is the son of Lincoln Elsworth and Alice M. (Allen) Johnson. Lincoln Elsworth Johnson is a resident of McPherson County, Nebraska, and has been county judge there for the past six years. His father, William A. Johnson, homesteaded in Hamilton County, the homestead being a part of Aurora town site. The house was located where the depot now stands. His great grandfather Johnson came to the United States from the northern part of Ireland.

Mr. Johnson attended public school in Nebraska and the Union College at College View. He taught school in McPherson County and was superintendent of schools there for about eight years prior to 1924. He is justice of the peace and truant officer and also in the insurance business at North Platte. He is a member of the Odd Fellows, and is affiliated with the Republican party.

On May 10, 1909, he was married to Bertha Mae Downs at Ringgold, Nebraska. She was born at Palmyra, Nebraska, September 12, 1890, and is the daughter of William H. and Mae (Kongdon) Downs of Palmyra. William H. Downs died in Sacramento, California, in 1927 and Mrs. Downs died there in 1929. Mr. and Mrs. Johnson have two children, Lloyd, born December 29, 1911; and Alice, born July 28, 1912. Residence: North Platte.

Peter John Johnson

Peter J. Johnson, postmaster at Rosalie, Nebraska, was born at Rankin, Illinois, November 5, 1881, the son of John S. and Betsy Johnson. His father, who was born in Norway, March 12, 1847, and died at Ashkum, Illinois, April 6, 1898, was a sailor and farmer. His mother died at Elliott, Illinois, February, 1890.

Mr. Johnson worked on a farm until 1900, was proprietor of a bowling alley at Bloomfield, Nebraska, 1900-01, worked in a flour mill at Hartington, Nebraska, homesteaded in Brown County, Nebraska, in 1906, and moved to Rosalie the same year. He was a stock dealer from 1912 to 1914, managed a general store, 1912-14, and in 1915, became postmaster of Rosalie, holding this position since that date.

He is a Republican. He holds membership in the Methodist Church and the Nebraskana Society. His hobby is reading. Residence: Rosalie.

Pleasant Lee Johnson

Pleasant Lee Johnson, son of Walter Samuel and Sarah Brannock (Gibson) Johnson, was born at Cincinnati, Iowa, October 12, 1860. His father was born at Liberty, Indiana, May 24, 1835, and died at Lincoln, September 13, 1904. A merchant, he held the rank of lieutenant in the Civil War, and was wounded in the Vicksburg campaign. He moved to Appanoose County, Iowa, in 1851, and later served three terms as clerk of the district court and several terms as mayor at Centerville, Iowa. He was also admitted to the practice of law in that state. Walter Samuel Johnson was the son of Dr. Samuel Henslee and Mary (Butler) Johnson; his grandfather, Nicholas Johnson, was born in Lynchburg, Virginia, in 1756; while his grandfather Butler was born in Nantucket, in 1690, removing to Lynchburg, Virginia.

Sarah Brannick Gibson was born at Greencastle, Indiana, November 14, 1836, daughter of James Gibson, and granddaughter of James Gibson, Sr. Her great grandfather, Brannock Gibson, came from old Virginia to Kentucky. She died at Lincoln, on November 27, 1917.

Educated first in the country schools of Cincinnati, Iowa, Mr. Johnson was graduated from the Centerville, Iowa, High School in 1878. In 1883, he received his Bachelor of Arts degree from the State University of Iowa, and in 1886, received his Master of Arts degree. He was a member of the Irving Literary Society, and of a university male quartet, and in 1927 was awarded an "I" sweater for baseball played in 1882 and 1883.

Since 1885, Mr. Johnson has been a resident of Hastings, and during the entire time he has lived there has been prominent in civic and educational affairs. From 1883 to 1884, he was a high school instructor at Fairfield, and Council Bluffs, Iowa, and from 1885 to 1893, was manager of the South Platte branch at Hastings, of Burnham Tulleys and Company. From 1893 to 1897, he was a member of the investment firm of Johnson, McLaughlin and Brown.

Since 1901, Mr. Johnson has been a member of the board of trustees and has served in varied capacities, including treasurer, financial representative and secretary of Hastings College. He was instrumental in the construction of the original field and stands, the athletic field, the Johnson Gynasium, the central heating plant; and in addition secured funds for the Carnegie Library and Alexander Hall. He secured in all $200,000 for endowment, buildings and expenses.

A farmer, he is also an extensive landowner, with holdings in Nebraska and Colorado. At one time he was president of a small bank in Colorado. Mr. Johnson is a member of the Chamber of Commerce, the Nebraska Water Conservation Association, the Young Men's Christian Association of which he has been director at various times, and is an officer of Hastings division of International Religious Education Association. He is a member of the First Presbyterian Church, is eligible to the Sons of Veterans of the Civil War, and is a member of Hastings Country Club. He is fond of golf, and was a member of the championship doubles team in the state tennis tournament of 1896. He also enjoys baseball and football. His hobby is engineering and construction.

On December 21, 1887, Mr. Johnson was united in marriage to Mary Louise Brown at Hastings. Mrs. Johnson who was born at Jacksonville, Illinois, June 29, 1865, is the daughter of Robert Brown and the granddaughter of Bedford Brown, of Jacksonville. They have one son, Walter Bedford, born October 7, 1889, who is married to Esther Bennett, of Lincoln. He was superintendent of schools for some time, held the rank of lieutenant in the World War, detailed to Fort Sill, Oklahoma, School of Fire, and took special work at Columbia University.

Walter Bedford Johnson is now operating his own farm eight miles north of Hastings, in Hall County. He has three children: Richard Bedford, Marcia Louise, and Robert Lee. Residence: Hastings.

Raymond Samuel Johnson

Raymond Samuel Johnson, prominent in all civic organizations at Beatrice, Gage County, Nebraska, has lived in this state all his life. He was born at Firth, Lancaster County, Nebraska, October 22, 1893, the son of George C. and Sarah Jane (Hull) Johnson. His father, who was a farmer, was born in Jefferson County, Missouri, August 7, 1859, and died at Crab Orchard, Johnson County, Nebraska, February 17, 1917; his ancestry was English. His mother, who was born at Firth, September 21, 1875, was of Pennsylvania Dutch descent. Her father, Rolander Hull, served two years in the Union Army during the Civil War, and was a homesteader in Lancaster County. Six of her daughters are public school teachers.

Mr. Johnson attended a rural school near Lincoln, and in 1911, was graduated from the Crab Orchard High School. Later he was a student at Boyles Business College at Omaha, and in 1923 was licensed to practice embalming in Nebraska. He now holds a partnership and half interest in the Harman-Johnson Funeral Home at Beatrice.

His marriage to Opal Maude High was solemnized at Beatrice, June 14, 1922. Mrs. Johnson, who was descended from President Andrew Jackson, was born at Mertilla, Meade County, Kansas, June 8, 1890. She was a teacher before her marriage.

Mr. Johnson is a member of the board of directors of the Chamber of Commerce, is affiliated with Centenary Methodist Episcopal Church, and holds membership in the Red Cross, the Young Men's Christian Association, and the Beatrice Country Club. He is a Republican.

He holds membership in the Masons, Eastern Star, serving as chairman of the advisory council of Order of DeMolay. His sports are golf and baseball, and his hobby is boys' activities. Residence: Beatrice.

Richard Conard Johnson

Richard C. Johnson, prominent farmer and stockraiser at Mead, Saunders County, Nebraska, was born there April 6, 1890, the son of Charles Peter and Ellen (Anderson) Johnson. His father, who was a farmer, was born in Sweden, April 4, 1861, and died at Mead, August 10, 1929. His mother was born in Sweden, October 1, 1862, and died at Mead, October 16, 1916.

Mr. Johnson attended the Mead Public School and in 1907, was graduated from the Mead High School. He began farming on the original home after leaving school. He is president of the Nebraska State Dairyman's Association, is a member of the Nebraska State Board of Agriculture, and is president of the Saunders County Fair

Association, and the Saunders County Livestock Breeders' Association.

He is a member of the Farmers' Union Association in Saunders County, the Saunders County Farm Bureau, the board of directors of the Saunders County Red Cross, the Nebraskana Society, and the First Baptist Church of Mead. In 1930, he served as president of the Mead Consolidated Schools. Mr. Johnson is affiliated with Wahoo Lodge Number 59, of the Ancient Free and Accepted Masons, the Stella Chapter of the Eastern Star, Royal Arch Chapter of Masons, Lincoln Consistory, and Sesostris Temple at Lincoln. Politically, he is a Republican.

In the state pig crop contest sponsored by the Agricultural College he was one of the eight successful contestants, and the next year raised his own record. He was awarded a production certificate by the National Dairy Association in 1927, and given a diploma in 1928. The Nebraska Live Stock Breeders' Association awarded him a certificate of recognition the same year. Mr. Johnson is still the champion heavy weight cornhusker of the state. On November 30, 1923, he husked 172 bushels of corn in 9 hours and 20 minutes. He weighed in at 288 pounds. His specialty has been the study of pure bred livestock.

Mr. Johnson was married to Neola Parson at Valley, June 16, 1915. She was born at Valley, September 8, 1892, daughter of Andrew and Hilma Peterson Parson. Mrs. Johnson, a member of the class of 1912 of the Peru Normal, taught one year at Walthill, and two years at Valley, before her marriage. She is a member of the Women's Christian Temperance Union, the Order of Eastern Star, and the Royal Neighbors; active in the work of the First Baptist Church of Mead, a teacher in Sunday School and interested in mission work. She is a former president of the Saunders County Homemakers, is a member of the Saunders County Farm Board, and has been an active member in the Pohoco Club and the Marietta Mothers' Club. There are two children, Maurine, born June 9, 1918, and Maxine, born July 6, 1923. Residence: Mead. (Photograph in Album).

Reuben A. Johnson

Born in Moody County, South Dakota, June 26, 1896, Reuben A. Johnson is the son of Rudolph Andrew and Alice (Aaker) Johnson. His father, who is a retired farmer, was born at Drammen, Norway, December 28, 1863; he came to this country in 1880. His mother, whose grandparents came from Norway, was born at Ridgeway, Iowa, September 23, 1874.

Mr. Johnson received the LL. B. degree at the University of Nebraska, in 1923; he attended the high school at Flandreau, South Dakota, where he was graduated in 1917, and in 1918 he was a student at the University of Washington, in Officer's Training School. He received letters in football, basketball, and track at Flandreau High School, and in 1922, served as steward of Phi Alpha Delta. From June 1, 1917, to June 1, 1918, he was deputy county treasurer of Moody County South Dakota.

Since 1923, Mr. Johnson has been engaged in the practice of law at Newman Grove, Nebraska, where he is city attorney; a candidate for county attorney in 1930, he was defeated by a close vote. He has been a member of the school board of Newman Grove for three years, is town chairman of the Boy Scouts of America, and holds membership in the Tri Community Club. He is a member of the Red Cross, the District Bar Association, and the Nebraskana Society.

During the World War he served as ensign in the United States Naval Reserve Force, commissioned in 1919. He has served as adjutant of the American Legion for six years, and is a service officer in Post Number 73 in Madison County; he is also county commander of that organization. Mr. Johnson is affiliated with Norwegian Lutheran Church of America.

On December 28, 1922, he was married to Vera Dale

Selway at Chicago, Illinois. Mrs. Johnson, who was born at Belle Fourche, South Dakota, August 18, 1903, of Welch and English parentage, is descended from Admiral Foote. She is the only child of Richard A. and Josephine (Reynolds) Selway. Their children are: Leon, born February 27, 1925; and Hartrice, born November 3, 1928. Residence: Newman Grove. (Photograph in Album).

Rynol Ben Johnson

For the past 18 years Rynol Ben Johnson has been a merchant at Gothenburg, Nebraska. He was born in that community, January 21, 1895, the son of Anton Johnson, a farmer who was a native of Sweden. Mr. Johnson came to Nebraska and settled in Custer County in 1874. He was united in marriage to Betty Lindberg in Sweden. He came to Dawson County in 1898 and has made his home there since.

Mr. Johnson received his education in the grade and high schools of Gothenburg. He is now the owner and manager of a general merchandise establishment at Gothenburg, is a trustee and deacon in the First Presbyterian Church there, and holds membership in the Chamber of Commerce and the Country Club.

He was married at Hot Springs, Arkansas, to Mae Jenkins who was born at Gothenburg, December 19, 1897. Their children are: Max, born June 18, 1924; Jaqueline, born September 26, 1928; and Maryland Anne, born March 9, 1930. Residence: Gothenburg.

Thomas Martin Johnson

Thomas Martin Johnson, banker and farmer, was born at Bethany, Missouri, February 15, 1871, the son of Joseph C. and Laura Carolyne (Lewellen) Johnson. His father, who was a farmer, was born at Caldwell, Missouri, November 14, 1837, and died at Chappell, Nebraska. His mother was born in Harrison County, Missouri, November 9, 1847, and died at Chappell, October 31, 1896.

Mr. Johnson was graduated from the Deuel County High School in 1889, and later attended the University of Denver Business College. He has been identified with banking enterprise at Chappell, Nebraska, since 1893, and owns several Deuel County farms. He is director and cashier in the Chappell State Bank, is affiliated with the First Methodist Episcopal Church of Chappell, and holds membership in the Modern Woodmen of America. He is affiliated with the Golden Fleece Lodge and Tangier Temple of the Ancient Free and Accepted Masons.

During the World War Mr. Johnson served as chairman of all Liberty loan drives in Deuel County. He was married to May Blanche Loveland at Julesburg, Colorado, October 10, 1898. Mrs. Johnson was born at Neoala, Iowa, October 1, 1874. To them were born: Laura Belle, born February 26, 1900, who married Samuel Reed Ferris, a druggist at Chappell; Dorothy May, born April 25, 1905, who is a domestic science teacher at Stambaugh, Michigan; and Joseph Lewis, born September 8, 1910, who is a student at Nebraska Wesleyan University.

Mr. Johnson is a member of the Republican party and holds membership in The Nebraskana Society. Residence: Chappell.

William Johnson

William Johnson, prominent business man at Minden, Nebraska, was born at Fremont, March 22, 1877, and has spent his entire life in this state. His father, Christian K. Jorgensen, a farmer, was born at Thisted, Denmark, November 23, 1847, and died at Fremont, Nebraska, April 15, 1890. His mother was born at Thisted, April 15, 1852, and died at Fremont, March 10, 1896.

Mr. Johnson is secretary of the Minden Chamber of Commerce, and is in the loans, insurance, and bonds business there. He holds membership in the Knights of Pythias, the Minden Presbyterian Church and the Nebraskana Society.

His marriage to Stella Johnson occurred at Denver, Colorado, May 1, 1900. Mrs. Johnson was born at Minden, September 14, 1882. Their children are: Gladys, born April 1, 1902, who married Fred Rasmussen; Merle, born March 17, 1905; Elmer, born May 17, 1907; and Grace, born September 23, 1916. Residence: Minden.

Albert Samuel Johnston

Born near Holdrege, Nebraska, July 1, 1893, Albert S. Johnston is the son of James Bishop and Emma Elizabeth (Myers) Johnston. His father born in Illinois, January 4, 1854, is a farmer and fine stockman. His mother was born in Piqua, Ohio, April 28, 1862.

He attended Phelps County rural schools until 1906, and was graduated from Holdrege High School in 1911. In 1916, he graduated from Kearney State Teachers College, and received his LL. B. from the University of Nebraska in 1920. He is a member of Pi Kappa Alpha and Phi Delta Phi.

On June 22, 1921, he was married to Juanita Lucile Campbell at Brock, Nebraska, her birthplace. There are three children, Albert M., born December 28, 1923; James B., born March 25, 1926, and Beth L., born July 18, 1929. They attend the First Baptist Church of Lincoln.

Mr. Johnston is a Republican, a member of the Lincoln Chamber of Commerce, the Knife and Fork Club, and Lincoln Lodge No. 19, Ancient Free and Accepted Masons. He is also a member of the state and county bar associations. He has been engaged in the practice of law since 1920. Prior to that time he taught school one year at McGrew, Nebraska. While attending the university he was associated with Burkett, Wilson & Brown. From 1920-26, he was with Claude S. Wilson, and since that time has been in private practice. Residence: Lincoln.

George Washington Johnston

A native of Detroit, Michigan, George Washington Johnston is the son of John William and Sarah Jane (Wood) Johnston. His father, a Canadian of Scotch-Irish descent, was a real estate dealer. He died at Detroit, October 22, 1872. Sarah Jane Wood was a native of Dumfries, Scotland, born April 29, 1829. Her father was a prominent physician, and she was an active worker in the Methodist Church. She died at Detroit in 1898.

George W. Johnston received his education in the public and high schools of Detroit. About forty years ago he came to Nebraska, where he now ranks high in the world of business and finance. He is president of the Mid-West Electric Company, president of the Omaha-Wyoming Oil Company, president of the Unita Petroleum Company, and director of the Stock Yards National Bank.

He was a captain in the Quartermaster Corps during the World War and is lieutenant-colonel of the U. S. Reserves. He is a member of the American Legion and Reserve Officers Association. One of the foremost Rotarians in the state, he is president of the local club and district governor of the 19th district of Rotary International. He is a member of Trinity Episcopal Church, and a member of the Red Cross and the Chamber of Commerce. A Mason, he is a member of the Scottish Rite and Shrine, Mount Calvary Commandery, St. John's Lodge, and Bellevue Chapter. He also belongs to the Sojourners Club and the Elks.

His clubs include the Omaha Club, the Omaha Country Club and the Happy Hollow Country Club.

Mr. Johnston is married to Isabelle Mary French, who was born at Storm Lake, Iowa, October 3, 1885. They have three children, Mary Alice, born March 10, 1912; Georgette French, born February 3, 1914, and Sarah Jane, born March 29, 1916. Residence: Omaha.

Grace Pheasant Johnston

Grace P. Johnston, clerk of the district court at Osceola, Nebraska, was born there November 3, 1883, and has lived in that county all of her life. Her father, Samuel Garrett Pheasant, who was a pioneer of Polk County in the 1870's, was born in Jefferson County, Iowa, July 17, 1846, and died at Osceola, November 28, 1922. He was prominent in political and civic affairs for many years, holding office as sheriff for four terms and later as postmaster; he was successful in the grain and livestock business at Osceola.

Her mother, Sarah J. (Stewart) Pheasant, who was born in Highland County, Ohio, February 26, 1852, and died at Osceola, January, 1913, was interested in church work and held membership in the Rebekah Lodge and the Order of Eastern Star. She was descended from the Stewarts of York County, Pennsylvania, some of whom served as soldiers in the Civil War and the War of 1812.

Mrs. Johnston was graduated from the high school at Osceola, in 1902, attended Wesleyan University, 1904-05, and was a student at the University of Nebraska, 1905-06. A Republican, she served as clerk of the county court in Polk County from 1915-18, was appointed clerk of the district court in 1918 to serve an unexpired term, and was elected to this position in 1920, 1924, and 1930. She acted as assistant postmistress at Osceola, from 1909 to 1914.

Her marriage to Wilber M. Johnston was solemnized at Osceola, September 14, 1922. Mr. Johnston who is a lawyer, was born at Greene, Butler County, Iowa, May 14, 1875. Mrs. Johnston served as secretary of the local Red Cross during the World War in the first loan drive. She holds membership in the National Federation of Business and Professional Women's Clubs, the Order of Eastern Star, and the Nebraskana Society. She is affiliated with the Methodist Church. Residence: Osceola.

Harry Clyde Johnston

Harry Clyde Johnston, retired power executive, was born at Boonesboro, Iowa, July 26, 1874. The son of Jacob Stenger and Ophelia (Speer) Johnston, his father was a merchant of early American descent. Jacob Stenger was for many years a prominent figure in business and fraternal circles, and was at one time past grand master of the Independent Order of Odd Fellows of Nebraska. His death occurred at Superior on December 15, 1906. His wife, Ophelia Speer, born at Zanesville, Ohio, July 20, 1852, is still living.

Educated in the public and high schools of Nuckolls county, Harry C. Johnston was valedictorian of his class in 1891. Ten years later, and on July 25, 1901, he was united in marriage to Margaret Hall Guthrie, at Superior. Mrs. Johnston, who was born at Ayr, Ontario, Canada, July 28, 1873, is decended from Scotch settlers in Canada.

From early manhood until 1914 Mr. Johnston was engaged as a merchant. During the ensuing twelve years he was secretary-treasurer and general manager of the Southern Nebraska Power Company at Superior. He is a member of the Chamber of Commerce, and of all degrees of Masonry, and has always taken an active part in local Republican politics. His favorite sport is golf, and his hobby is reading. Recently Mr. Johnston was elected to life membership in the Nebraskana Society, in recognition of his efforts toward the advancement of his community and state. Residence: Superior.

Nelle Frances Johnston

Nelle Frances Johnston, clubwoman, was born at Nashua, Iowa, April 17, 1886, daughter of Clarence Arthur and Abbie (Tracy) Thomas. Her ancestry is English.

In 1902 she was graduated from Nashua High School, and afterward attended the Iowa teachers college.

On November 2, 1907, she was married to Dan D. Johnston, at Sioux City, Iowa. Mr. Johnston was born at Royal, Nebraska, December 26, 1886. They have two children, Elinor, who was born at Royal, November 5, 1909, and Eloise, who was born at Norfolk, September 6, 1914.

Mrs. Johnston is a Democrat. She is vice-president and secretary of the Johnston Lumber Company, at Hay Springs, member of the Utopia Womans Club, the Congregational Church, the Order of Eastern Star, eligible to the Daughters of the American Revolution. Aside from her club activities, her favorite diversions golf, bridge, gardening and flowers. Residence: Hay Springs.

Norman Thomas Johnston

One of the leading physicians and surgeons of Kearney, Nebraska, is Norman Thomas Johnston who was born at Brantford, Canada, April 27, 1878. His father, Thomas Johnston, who was a manufacturer of farm implements, was born at Alma, Canada, November 9, 1849, and died at Guelph, Canada, July 7, 1907; his ancestry was Scotch and Irish. His mother, whose ancestry was Irish, was born at Port Hope, Canada, June 6, 1856, and died at Guelph, September 8, 1926.

Dr. Johnston was graduated from Brantford Public School in 1890, was graduated from the Brantford Collegiate Institute, 1894, and attended the Guelph Business College in 1895. He received the M. D. degree at Western University in London, 1902, and in 1905, was a student at the Chicago Eye, Ear, Nose & Throat College. He has been prominent in the practice of his profession at Kearney for some time and is serving as secretary of the American Electronic Research Association.

He served as secretary of the Franklin County Medical Association, 1909-22, was president of the Republican Valley Medical Association in 1914, served as vice president of the Republican Valley Medical Association in 1913 and as secretary, 1918-22, was vice president of the Nebraska State Medical Association in 1916, and acted as councillor of the latter organization from 1918 to 1922. At this time he is a member of the American Association of Medico-Physical Research and the American Electronic Research Association. His religious affiliation is with the St. Lukes Episcopal Church of Kearney.

A Republican, Dr. Johnston served as a member of the Franklin County Committee from 1910 to 1917, was a member of the Nebraska State Republican Committee, 1915-16, and was candidate for presidential elector in 1912. He is the author of many articles on professional subjects published in medical magazines.

He was married at Burlington, Canada, August 30, 1904, to Edith Jane Graham, who was born at Burlington, December 30, 1877, of Irish and English parents. Two children were born to them: Horace K., June 14, 1906, who was graduated from the Kirksville School of Osteopathy in 1928 and is now an osteopathic physician at Chicago; and Edith Kathleen, born July 12, 1908, who died May 10, 1921. Residence: Kearney.

Roscoe C. Johnston

A farmer near Lexington, Nebraska for the past 41 years, Roscoe C. Johnston was born at Lexington, Illinois, April 16, 1875, the son of George S. and Isabelle (Birney) Johnston. His father, also a farmer, was born at Deersville, Ohio, July 12, 1833, and died at Beatrice, Nebraska, June 30, 1911. His mother, whose ancestry was Scotch and Irish, was born in Harrison County, Ohio, September 12, 1839, and died at Lexington, Nebraska, November 1, 1905.

Mr. Johnston was married to Mary Laura Wilder at

Lexington, February 28, 1901. Mrs. Johnston, whose ancestry is English, was born at Beaver Crossing, August 9, 1876. Six children were born to this marriage: Ora, born January 2, 1902, who died November 8, 1902; Milton, November 9, 1904, who married Mildred E. Decker; Ruth, January 27, 1907, who married William Bluel; Adah, August 7, 1909, who married Fred H. Teets; Isabelle, April 26, 1911, who married Lloyd R. Smith; and Elizabeth Jane, February 12, 1919.

Mr. Johnston holds membership in the Lexington Kiwanis Club and is a member of the Nebraskana Society. Mr. Johnston was made a master farmer in the class of 1931. He moved to Dawson County from Lexington, Illinois in 1891 and has resided here ever since on the same farm named Walnut Grove Farm. He is a Republican. Residence: Lexington.

Wilber M. Johnston

Wilber M. Johnston, a continuous resident of Nebraska since 1888, was born at Greene, Iowa, May 14, 1876. He is the son of Hugh and M. Josephine (Ledyard) Johnston, the former a native of Long River, Canada. Hugh Johnston was born in 1840. His father settled in Canada in the first part of the nineteenth century, coming from Glasgow, Scotland. Hugh Johnston was a carriage and wagon manufacturer, and a skilled mechanic. His death occurred at Minneapolis, March 25, 1907.

M. Josephine Ledyard was born in Wayne County, Ohio, December 29, 1850. Assistant principal of city schools at Greene, Iowa, in 1883, she held this position until 1885. In March, 1888, she was graduated from Iowa State University as a physician and surgeon, and practiced at Osceola, until 1912. She is of Scotch and English descent.

Educated first in the public schools of Greene, Atlantic, Red Oak, and the Cedar Valley Seminary at Osage, Iowa, Mr. Johnston also attended public school at Osceola. He was admitted to the bar of Nebraska, at Lincoln, on November 17, 1908, and during 1907-08, was county attorney of Polk County. A Republican, he was appointed city attorney of Osceola, which position he held twelve years, and from February 14, to March 31, 1926, was acting county judge of Polk County.

Mr. Johnston was editor and owner of the *Polk County Republican* from December, 1900, to August, 1902, and editor of the *Osceola Record* from December, 1902, to August, 1903. Since the fall of 1904, he has been actively engaged in the practice of law.

In April, 1908, he enlisted as a private in Company E, First Nebraska Infantry, serving with his company at Camp Alvin Saunders until rejected for service in May, 1908. He always favored the entry of the United States into the World War on the side of the Allies, and was active in all war time projects.

Mr. Johnston is a member of Osceola Lodge No. 65, Ancient Free and Accepted Masons at Osceola. He is also a life member of The Nebraskana Society. His hobby is reading.

On September 14, 1922, he was united in marriage to Grace Pheasant at Osceola. Mrs. Johnston, who was born at Osceola, November 3, 1883, is clerk of the district court of Polk County. She is of Scotch, English, French and German descent. Residence: Osceola.

Peter Johnstone

A native of Hardgate, Scotland, born March 13, 1883, Peter Johnstone is the son of Francis and Maggie (McPherson) Johnstone. His father was born at Hardgate, and died there in 1887. His mother was born at Largs Argyleshire, Scotland, and is still living. Mr. Johnstone received his education in the public schools of Scotland, and came to American as a young man. For the past twenty-six years he has been a resident of Lincoln.

He was married to Mary Ellen Malone on July 8, 1912, at Lincoln. Mrs. Johnstone, who is the daughter of the late James Malone, was born at Lincoln, December 5, 1886. There are four children, James F., born May 25, 1913; Mary M., born August 7, 1914; Francis P., born June 11, 1916, and Emily D., born October 25, 1919.

Mr. Johnstone is a Republican. For three years he was with a local transfer company, and then was special agent for the Chicago, Burlington and Quincy Railroad for the same length of time. Thereafter he served as captain of detectives to May, 1916. From that date until January 15, 1918, he was superintendent of construction of public works, Malone Contractors. This position was succeeded by that of captain of detectives until December 11, 1918. From December 11, 1918, until November 1, 1930, he filled the office of chief of police of Lincoln. He is now guard of the First National Bank of Lincoln.

At the present time Mr. Johnstone is a member of the Red Cross and Community Chest, the Chamber of Commerce, Young Men's Christian Association, Hiram Club and Kiwanis Club, and the First Presbyterian Church. He is an Elk and a Mason, Scottish Rite and Shrine. He enjoys a little golf. Residence: Lincoln.

George Fedilis Jonaitis

George Fedilis Jonaitis, an immigrant boy, priest, patriot, and hero of the World War, has resided in Nebraska for the past 23 years, and was born at Kursenai, Lithuania, April 23, 1880, the son of George and Frances (Gricius) Jonaitis. His father, who was a grain farmer, was born at Kurtevenai, Lithuania, 1836, and died at Kursenai, Lithuania, 1890. His mother was born at Raudenai, Lithuania, and died at Kursenai, in 1901.

Father Jonaitis attended grammar school in Lithuania, and was a student at St. Bonaventure's College in New York, Louvain College, at Louvain, Belgium, and St. Paul's Seminary, St. Paul, Minnesota. He received the B. A. degree in 1905 at St. Bonaventure's College where he was a member of the debating team. He was ordained a priest in the Catholic Church in 1908, by the Right Reverend R. Sconnell of Omaha, and served his first parish at St. Anthony's Church, South Omaha, Nebraska. He organized and built the latter, and organized and built St. Peter's Church at Detroit, Michigan in 1920. From 1927 to 1931, he was pastor of St. Peter's Church at Stanton, Nebraska. He is now pastor of St. Francis Borgia Church at Blair, Nebraska.

He is the author of *My Experience in the World War* (1920) *Four Angels* (1927) and various articles published in Ford's magazine. He enlisted in the United States Army as a first class private in April, 1918; was trained at a chaplain's training school in May, 1918; was commissioned chaplain and first lieutenant, May, 1918; and was assigned to Camp Zachary Taylor, Louisville, Kentucky. He was sent to France as a casual, and was assigned to the 26th Division, 102 Infantry, 3rd Battalion. He served at Chateau Thierry. Aisne-Marne and St. Mihiel; and was transferred to the 313th Infantry, 79th Division, First Battalion. On November 7, 1918, Father Jonaitis was wounded in action in the Argonne Battle, and has lost the use of one forearm. He has been commissioned Major Chaplain in the United States Reserves.

He acted as lecturer for the Roman Catholic Church Alliance of America for six months in 1919, in the east, on the subject of Bolshevism. He is a member of the Veterans of Foreign Wars; the Disabled Veterans of Foreign Wars, Department Chaplain, American Legion (1929-1930); Emergency Officers of the World War; the American Legion; and the Knights of Columbus. He is an Elk and a Moose. His sports include football, wrestling, and boxing. His hobby is geography.

Father Jonaitis is a Democrat and holds membership in the Nebraskana Society. Residence: Blair.

Adeline Nelle Jones

Adaline Nelle Jones, registrar and secretary to the dean of the University of Nebraska College of Medicine, was born at Dallas, Texas. She is the daughter of John Bartlett and Nellie (Rust) Jones, the former of whom was born at Cincinnati, Ohio, July 1, 1864. He is president of the Midwestern Paper Company, a former director of the Western Newspaper Union, and its general purchasing agent at the present time.

Nellie Rust Jones was born at Winfield, Michigan, April 17, 1867. For some years she was department editor of the *Southern Mercury* at Dallas, and is a member of the Daughters of the American Revolution and the Delphian Society. She is of English and Scotch descent, and is listed in the *Rust Genealogy*.

Adaline Jones attended the public schools of Houston, and Dallas, until 1904; she was a student at the Houston High School and the Pasadena (California) High School. She was a graduate in normal training from the Northwestern University School of Music in 1913. While attending the university she was a member of the glee club.

From 1914-16 she was head of the music department at Margaret College, Versailles, Kentucky, and in charge of vocal department, Columbia Institute, Columbia, Tennessee, from 1918-19. She was vocal instructor at St, Mary's College, at Dallas, during 1919 and '20, and in charge of the music department at Rowland Hall, Salt Lake City, from 1920-24.

In 1925 she returned to Omaha, and became executive secretary of the Women's Division of the Chamber of Commerce for the term 1925-27, she is now vice president of that organization; and has been registrar and secretary to the dean of the University of Nebraska College of Medicine since 1927.

She is a member of the Daughters of the American Revolution, and a member of the board of the Altrusa Club. An Episcopalian, she attends Trinity Cathedral. Her social club is the Omaha College Club. Residence: Omaha. (Photograph in Album).

Carl Conant Jones

A resident of Nebraska for the past 47 years Carl Conant Jones was born at Oneida, Illinois, October 6, 1882, son of Charles Leonard and Octavia Howard (Conant) Jones.

His father was born in New York State in 1842, and prior to his death at Hastings, on November 26, 1931, was a livestock dealer. His wife, Octavia, was born in Vermont in 1852, and died at Sidney, in September, 1914. She taught Bible at Hastings College, and at one time was the editor of the *Union Worker*, a Woman's Christian Temperance paper. Two of her ancestors came over on the *Mayflower*.

Mr. Jones attended public school and high school and was a student for two years at Hastings College Academy. At the present time he is city water commissioner and city clerk of Sidney. He is a progressive Republican. He has been in the lumber and farm implement businesses, and engaged in auto sales.

On October 4, 1914, he was married to Lucy Irene Howard at Sidney. Mrs. Jones was born in Kankakee, Illinois, February 25, 1886. During the World War she was chairman of the Red Cross for the Gurley District. They have four children, Catherine, born August 23, 1915; Helen, born March 23, 1917; Robert, born September 14, 1919; and Jeanette, born June 27, 1921.

During the late war, Mr. Jones was food administrator for Gurley District of Cheyenne County. He is a member of the Lemon Memorial Methodist Church at Sidney, and the Masons. Residence: Sidney.

Charles Leonard Jones

Charles L. Jones, a resident of Nebraska for the past 52 years, was born at Prairie Du Chien, Wisconsin, April 4, 1875, the son of George William and Emma (Bonney) Jones. His father, who was born at North Hampton, England, October 20, 1849, and died at O'Neill, Nebraska, April 25, 1893, homesteaded in Holt County in 1879; he served as county sheriff in Wisconsin, and at the time of his death was engaged in the livery business. His mother was born in Pennsylvania, April 13, 1850, of Irish descent. She was a school teacher before her marriage.

Mr. Jones was graduated from a 10th grade school in 1889. He served an apprenticeship as machinist for the Case Threshing Machine Company; was employed by the Alis Chalmers Company, erecting machinery for three years; was with the Union Pacific Railroad for four years; and for seven years was engineer for the Wells Abbott Nieman Milling Company at Schuyler. He has spent some time in the employ of the United States government as railroad builder in the west. He is now a farmer near Schuyler, Nebraska.

He is a Republican, and was elected to the legislature as state representative in 1924-26-28-30. For the past 17 years he has been moderator of the Schuyler school board. He is a member of The Nebraskana Society; has been a member of the Young Men's Christian Association for many years; and is affiliated with the First Presbyterian Church at Schuyler. He holds membership in the Masons and the Royal Highlanders. During the World War Mr. Jones served as chairman of the precinct and school district committee in bond and stamp drives. His hobby is good horses.

On December 4, 1897, he was united in marriage with Phebe May Storts at Fremont, Dodge County, Nebraska. Mrs. Jones, whose ancestry is German, was born at Cutler, Ohio, June 26, 1876. They have one son, George W., born January 8, 1899, who is a farmer. Residence: Schuyler.

Charles Monroe Jones

Charles Monroe Jones, leading merchant at Hartington, was born at Richland, Iowa, August 13, 1855. He is the son of John W. and Almarinda (Gibbons) Jones, the former born at Mooresville, Indiana, in 1831. John W. Jones, who was a farmer, was of Welsh descent, and his death occurred at Hartington on May 22, 1909. Almarinda, his wife, was born in Indiana, in 1834, and died at Hartington on January 3, 1922. She was of Irish descent.

Educated in the public schools of Jefferson County. Iowa, Charles M. Jones later attended Central University of Iowa, at Pella. He came to Nebraska in 1883, and entered the mercantile business, in which he has continued for many years. He owns a controlling interest in the Globe Clothing Company at the present time, and is former president of the Hartington National Bank.

On September 23, 1886, he was united in marriage to Bessie Hogenson at St. James, Nebraska. Mrs. Jones was born in Sweden in 1865. To them were born five children, three of whom, Arthur, Paul and Minnie, died in infancy. Mary, their fourth child, was born January 14, 1897, and Charles M., Jr., was born August 1, 1903. He is in the clothing business with his father at present.

Mr. Jones is a Republican, a member of the First Congregational Church, a life member of the Red Cross and is active in all civic organizations. He served as sheriff and deputy sheriff over a period of ten years, and was a member of the local school board ten years. Residence: Hartington.

Charles Sandusky Jones

Charles Sandusky Jones, educator, was born at Prentice, Illinois, February 24, 1862, son of Cyrus Graham and Nancy Sandusky (Ferguson) Jones. His father, who was born in LaFayette, Indiana, March 15, 1830, died at Nevada, Missouri, October 13, 1905. A farmer, he was also a poet, and was a member of the Nebraska legislature. He was a descendant of John

Jones and of William Morris of Virginia, who fought in the Revolution. Nancy Sandusky Ferguson, his wife, was born in Kentucky, November 19, 1827, and died at Nevada, Missouri, June 17, 1912. Active in church and community affairs, she was descended from the Ferguson family of Kentucky and Virginia.

Educated first in rural schools, Charles S. Jones attended Humboldt High School and received his A. B. from Oskaloosa College in 1910. He was graduated from Peru State Normal School in 1893, attended Cotner College 1901-02 and spent several summers at the University of Nebraska. He was a member of the chorus at Peru and a life member of the Philomathean Society.

During the World War he was a member of the Home Guard and secretary of the County Council of Defense. He is a member of the Christian Church at Ord, and has held various offices in the Young Men's Christian Association, among them vice president 1889-90; president 1891-92, 1892-93; delegate to Lake Geneva 1892. He is a member of the Chamber of Commerce and the Nebraskana, and the Knights of Pythias, and Masons.

Active in civic affairs, he is a member of the Red Cross, and scoutmaster in the Boy Scouts of America, and in 1921 was secretary of the School Board at Ord. He is a member of the Nebraska State Teachers Association, and was at one time president and secretary of the district organization. His favorite sport is golf.

He married May M. Wyne, of Peru, in 1894. There are three children. Dora, born in 1896, attended Wesleyan university. She married Dr. K. C. McGrew and lives at Ord. Margaret Lillian, born in 1897, graduated from the Ord High School, married Dr. Glen D. Auble and lives at Ord. Howard E. was born in 1904; graduated from Clarkson High School and is on the *Ord Quiz*.

Clarence C. Jones

Clarence C. Jones, newspaper publisher, was born at Oskaloosa, Iowa, July 2, 1871, son of John Wesley and Anna E. (Irwin) Jones. The father was born in Zanesville, Ohio, September 30, 1850, and died at Rigby, Idaho, January 28, 1918. He was a newspaper man in Iowa, Nebraska, South Dakota and Idaho. The mother was born in Ohio, September 13, 1851.

Mr. Jones attended the public schools of Iowa and with the exception of three years (1899-1902), has been in the newspaper business. He began type-setting in 1887, at Gray, Iowa, and was later associated with his father at Gordon. In 1888 he went to Oelrich, South Dakota, and established the *Advocate*.

Later Mr. Jones was at Hot Springs with his father, who established the *Herald*. In 1893 they went to Lead, South Dakota, and the next year launched the *Lead Daily Call*. In 1902, after several years in a gold mine, he again took up newspaper work, as city editor of the *Daily Call* and *Lead Register*. In 1909 he purchased the Brown County Democrat at Ainsworth, and with his wife still publishes it.

His marriage to Lillian L. Hedrick was solemnized at Hot Springs, May 10, 1902. She was born at Marengo, Iowa, September 13, 1869, and before her marriage was a teacher.

Mr. Jones is a Democrat. He is a member of the National and the Nebraska Editorial Associations, the Red Cross, and the Chamber of Commerce. He is a Woodman of the World. Residence: Ainsworth.

Daisy Viola Jones

Daisy Viola Jones was born at Bryan, Williams County, Ohio, daughter of Lachyman Oscar and Sarah Malinda (Swift) Shouf. Her father was a native of Polk, Ohio, born August 15, 1846. He was a manufacturer of tile and brick, and died at Bryan, February 17, 1881. His father, John Breckenridge Shouf, published the first Democratic newspaper in Bryan, in 1855. The Shouf family

traced descent through the Breckenridges of Virginia, and the Culbertsons of Pennsylvania. Nancy Ann Franks, mother of Lachyman Shouf, was descended from Colonel Peter Livingood and from Jacob Franks, who built the first fort at Frankston, Pennsylvania. She was born June 11, 1809. John Breckenridge Shouf was born March 13, 1811, and died April 5, 1874.

Sarah Malinda Swift was born at North Eaton, Ohio, August 24, 1851, and died July 17, 1923. She was a poet and newspaper correspondent. On the paternal side she was descended from Richard Warren of the *Mayflower*, and on her mother's side from John Howland and Edward Fuller of the *Mayflower*.

Mrs. Jones was graduated from Bryan High School, and was valedictorian of her class. She later attended Ohio State University and Oberlin College. Coming to Nebraska, on November 25, 1906, the date of her marriage to Roland M. Jones (see *Nebraskana*), she has since resided here. She has one daughter, Sarah Ruth, born April 23, 1920.

She is a charter member of the Nebraska Society of Mayflower Descendants, ex-regent of Major Isaac Sadler chapter of the Daughters of the American Revolution, ex-state treasurer of the Daughters of the American Revolution, ex-state president of the United States Daughters of 1812, state registrar of the Daughters of American Colonists, ex-councilor and color bearer of the Daughters of Founders and Patriots, ex-board member of the American Legion Auxiliary and a life member of National Flag Association. She is a member of the Colony of New England Women and member of the Huguenot Society of South Carolina. Residence: Omaha.

David Pierce Jones

David Pierce Jones, prominent banker at Hastings, Nebraska, has been a resident of this state for 56 years. He was born at Pauline, Nebraska, October 2, 1874, the son of Thomas T. and Margaret (Davies) Jones. His father was born at Talyaarn, Wales, January 29, 1846. His mother, who was interested in church and educational affairs, was born at Beddgelert, Wales, December 27, 1845, and died at Pauline, Nebraska, March 10, 1910.

Mr. Jones attended rural school and later was a student at Fremont Normal School. He served as clerk, cashier, and vice president, successively in the Exchange National Bank at Hastings from 1903 to 1926, was connected with the First National Bank of Hastings from 1926 to 1928, and since 1928 has been treasurer and business manager of Hastings College. He holds membership in the Red Cross, Salvation Army, Chamber of Commerce, and the Nebraskana Society.

For six years Mr. Jones served as a member of the Hastings School Board, and at this time is affiliated with the Methodist Church and the Young Men's Christian Association. He was prominent as a member of the committee on Liberty bonds sale during the World War.

His marriage to May Bourne was solemnized at Pauline, September 6, 1899. Mrs. Jones, who was born in Morgan County, Indiana, October 23, 1873, is descended from Major Frederich Goss of the Revolution. They have two children: Mary Ellen, born December 30, 1902; and Margaret Ann, born November 12, 1906. Both are public school teachers. Residence: Hastings.

Edith D. Jones

Edith D. Jones, better known in the professional world as Mrs. Will Owen Jones, is an accomplished pianist and instructor at the University of Nebraska. She was born at Brattleboro, Vermont, the daughter of Benjamin Rush and Precepta M. (Austin) Jenne. Her father, who was a major in the Civil War, was born in Vermont, and died in New York. His English ancestors came to America in 1623. Her mother, who was born in Massachusetts, died at Brattleboro when Edith Jones was an infant, and the child was adopted by her mother's sister and took the name of Doolittle. She was a descendant of John and Elizabeth (Tilley) Howland of *Mayflower* fame.

Mrs. Jones attended the public schools of Massachusetts and Pennsylvania, and was a student at the University of Nebraska Preparatory School for two years. She attended the University of Nebraska for two years; was graduated from the New England Conservatory of Music at Boston; and later studied under Rafael Joseffy in New York City. Since 1897 she has been an instructor in the University School of Music at Lincoln; and since 1925, has been professor of piano at the University of Nebraska.

Her marriage to Will Owen Jones, a distinguished newspaper man in Nebraska, was solemnized at Lincoln, in 1889. Mr. Jones, who was born at Berlin, Wisconsin, in 1862, was for many years editor of the *Nebraska State Journal*. He died at Lincoln, January 29, 1928. One daughter was born to them, Mariel, who is instructor in piano at the University School of Music.

Mrs. Jones is a member of Pi Kappa Lambda, honorary musical fraternity, and the Clef Club. She holds membership in the Matinee Musicale and the Sorosis Club. She is affiliated with the First Plymouth Congregational Church at Lincoln. She is a Republican. Residence: Lincoln.

J. Arvid Jones

J. Arvid Jones was born at Vannas, Sweden, May 6, 1890, the son of Jonas and Erika Kristine Jonson. His father died in Sweden in 1897. His mother was born at Nordmaling, Sweden, and died at Vannas, September 8, 1918.

Mr. Jones attended school in Sweden, and in 1916 was graduated from the Theological Seminary at Chicago. He received the A. B. degree at Nebraska Central College, Central City, Nebraska, 1919. For three years he served the Siloa Mission Church, for five years was clergyman at Marquette, Kansas, and since 1924 has been pastor of the Ceresco Mission Covenant Church at Ceresco, Nebraska. He is chairman of the Evangelical Mission Association of Nebraska, is a member of the board of foreign missions of the Southwest Evangelical Mission Convenant of America, and is a member of the Nebraskana Society. He is a Republican.

On June 28, 1916, he was married to Hilder Ethyl Udd at Mead, Nebraska. Mrs. Jones was born at Mead, May 26, 1894. Two children were born to this marriage: Eleanor Arvida, May 29, 1918; and Rosalie, born September 2, 1920. Residence: Ceresco.

James Arthur Jones

James Arthur Jones was born at Peoria, Illinois, September 25, 1878, the son of Emanuel and Hester Medora (Deal) Jones. His father, who is a farmer, was born at Jackson, Ohio, January 10, 1846, of Welsh ancestry. His mother was born of German parentage at Jackson, Ohio, September 7, 1854, and died at Holdrege, Nebraska, November 28, 1931.

Mr. Jones completed a business college course and taught in a rural school for two years. He was connected with the First National Bank at Hastings, Nebraska for a year, was a clerk and time-keeper for the Chicago, Burlington & Quincy Railroad until 1907, and since 1907 has been engaged in farming in Phelps County, Nebraska. He is president of the Funk Oil Company, is township treasurer, and is president of the Funk and Haydon Telephone Company.

He is affiliated with the Evangelical Free Mission and holds membership in the Nebraskana Society. On June 2, 1908, he married Ellen Marie Norberg at Funk. Mrs. Jones was born of Swedish parents at Holdrege, September 25, 1885. They have one daughter, Mildred, born August 3, 1909. She was graduated from the Hol-

drege High School in 1927, attended teachers college for two years, and is now teaching school. Residence: Funk.

Mariel Theresa Jones

Mariel T. Jones, pianist of note and musical educator, was born at Lincoln, Nebraska, the daughter of William Owen Jones and Edith Precepta (Doolittle) Jones. Her father, who was born at Berlin, Wisconsin, October 6, 1862, was editor of the *Nebraska State Journal*. A member of the staff of this paper for over 40 years, he was an outstanding figure in editorial circles. He died at Lincoln, January 29, 1928. Her mother, who was born at Brattleboro, Vermont, was a *Mayflower* descendant. She is a talented pianist and has been instructor at the University School of Music for many years.

Miss Jones was graduated from the Lincoln High School, after which she began an extensive musical education. She was graduated from the University of Nebraska in 1912 with the degree, A. B.; was awarded her Bachelor of Music degree at the University School of Music, 1913-15; and took post graduate work there in 1918. She has attended the following schools: Chicago Musical College, 1919; Chautauqua Summer School, 1924; Matthay School at London, one of the foremost pedagogues of the world, 1927-28; and Shakespeare Studios at Chicago.

She was distinguished in college by election to various honor societies through scholastic achievement. Among them are: Phi Beta Kappa, Pi Kappa Lambda, Alpha Rho Tau, Mortarboard, the German Club, and the Latin Club. She is a member of Delta Gamma, and Sigma Alpha Iota, of which she is patroness. She has been presented in several piano recitals.

During the summer of 1917 Miss Jones was instructor at York College. She acted as accompanist at the Le-Baron-Wheatley Studios, 1916; and since 1919 she has been an instructor at the University School of Music at Lincoln.

She is a member of the Clef Club and holds membership in the following social and professional societies: Mortarboard Alumnae, Musical Art Club, Matinee Musicale, Delta Gamma Alumnae, and Sigma Alpha Iota Alumnae. Her favorite sports are hiking and swimming. Her hobby is cooking. She is affiliated with the First Plymouth Congregational Church of Lincoln. Residence: Lincoln.

Myrtillo Lester Jones

Myrtillo Lester Jones, optometrist, was born at Greeley, Iowa, December 12, 1869, son of Rollin James and Alice Sophia (Vernal) Jones. The father was born at Norfolk, New York, May 17, 1837, and was a farmer of unusual ability and success. He owned the first McCormick reaper and the first Beloit self rake harvester in Deleware County, Iowa. He died at Greeley, May 31, 1905. His ancestors, who were thrifty Welshmen, came to America about 1818. Alice Sophia Vernal was born in Glastenburg, Vermont, March 9, 1841, and died at Bennett, May 12, 1918. She taught school in her early life and was a natural musician. Her ancestry was English.

Mr. Jones attended rural school near Greeley, Iowa, and graduated from Greeley High School in 1886, and received the Bachelor of Science degree in 1890 from Epworth Seminary. During 1887 and 1888 he studied at Upper Iowa University. In college he was active in both debating and dramatics.

On October 14, 1895, he was married to Clara Luella Palmer at Fairfield. Mrs. Jones was born at Monmoth, Illinois, May 8, 1872, of early American ancestry. They have two children, Alton V., born August 3, 1899; and Frieda Pauline, July 6, 1915. Alton is a graduate of Drake University and also of the Institute of Musical

Art in New York. He is one of the most outstanding of the younger artists on the American concert stage, and was mentioned by Winthrop Tyron, New York correspondent of the *Christian Science Monitor,* as one of the twelve most important pianists now before the public. At the present time he is head of the piano department of Columbia University summer school, and a member of the faculty at the Institute of Musical Art. Frieda Pauline is still in high school and is also unusually talented musically.

Mr. Jones served his apprenticeship under J. H. Boyce of Fayette, Iowa, in watch repairing, and was later graduated from the Chicago Watchmakers Institute. He is also a graduate of LeGrange Optical Institute, and the owner at the present time of an attractive jewelry store a Fairfield, which is operated by G. T. Patton. He was admitted to practice in Nebraska in April, 1909, and for three years served as an examiner in optometry under appointment from Governor Shallenberger, and again served for three years, appointed by Governor Bryan. He is a member of the Nebraska Association of Optometrists (charter member), and served one term as president of the Nebraska Association in 1911. He is a member of the Fairfield Community Club (president 1929), a member of the local school board (1928-), and a member of the Fairfield board (1929-). He is also a member of the Central Nebraska Optometric Study Club which meets each month in Grand Island.

Mr. Jones is a member of the Red Cross and assisted in Red Cross drives during the late war. His religious affiliation is with the Christian Church of Fairfield. He is a 32nd degree Mason and member of the Shrine, and a member of the National Georgraphic and the Nebraskana Society. In his younger days he enjoyed playing baseball and still is a baseball fan. His hobby is devotion to the science of the conservation of vision. Residence: Fairfield.

Orel Jones

Orel Jones, druggist at Oconto, was born at Malvern, Iowa, February 6, 1877, son of Norvel and Ellen (Nelson) Jones. The father, born at New Windsor, Illinois, August 31, 1845, died at Grand Island, May 6, 1927. He was a farmer, whose father came to the United States from Canada in 1837, crossing the Chicago river on a pontoon bridge. Ellen, wife of Norvel, was born in Sweden and died at Logan, Iowa, March 21, 1909.

Educated first in the Madison public schools, Orel Jones was graduated from high school on May 26, 1893, and from 1899-1900 attended Highland Park College at Des Moines, where he studied pharmacy. He was admitted to practice in Iowa in August, 1900; in Wyoming in 1903; in Nebraska in June, 1905, and now holds a national certificate.

From 1893-98 Mr. Jones taught school. Since leaving college he has been engaged in the drug business continuously in Nebraska, except four years spent in that business at Loveland, Iowa. Since February 6, 1910 he has been the owner of a pharmacy at Oconto.

On January 6, 1904, he was married to Eva Pearl Hope at Little Sioux, Iowa. She was born there on December 26, 1879. Mrs. Jones is a pharmacist, attended the same college that her husband did, and was registered at the same times.

Mr. Jones is a Republican. During the World War he was vice president of the Custer County Council of Defense, a four minute speaker, and active in Red Cross and other drives.

He was president of the Nebraska Pharmaceutical Association in 1920, is a member of the National Association of Retail Druggists, was a member of the Pharmaceutical Examining Board 1913-17, and is now treasurer of the board of managers of the proprietors division of the Nebraska Pharmaceutical Association.

For twenty-two years Mr. Jones has been clerk of the Modern Woodmen of America. He is a trustee and superintendent of the Sunday School of the Evangelical Church, has served on the local school board eight years and as village clerk six years. He devotes much time to reading. Recently he was made a life member of the Nebraskana Society. Residence: Oconto.

Ralph Edward Jones

Born at La Fayette, Illinois, August 28, 1867, Ralph Edward Jones is the son of Rufus Sheridan and Mercy Jane Taylor Jones. His father, who was born at La Fayette, August 20, 1841, and died near Ainsworth, Nebraska, September 26, 1917, was a farmer and carpenter who came to Nebraska in 1883 as a homesteader. His mother, who was born at Kentontown, Kentucky, October 5, 1845, and died at Norden, Nebraska, December 28, 1929, received her early education in the public schools of Stark County, Illinois; her parents were Kentuckians who moved to Illinois in 1847.

Mr. Jones received his education in the public school at La Fayette, Illinois. He served as a clerk in a mercantile establishment at Ainsworth and Spencer, and a little later entered business independently at Norden, Nebraska. Until 1920 he owned a store at Springview, Nebraska; he is now retired on his country home near that community.

During the World War he served as chairman of the county Red Cross organization, was a member of the Council of Defense, and sold war bonds and savings stamps. He is chairman of the disaster relief committee for Keya Paha County, American Red Cross, and is consul of Camp Number 6194 of the Modern Woodmen of America.

He was united in marriage with Clara Eliza Swett at Ainsworth, July 26, 1892. Mrs. Jones, the daughter of Alanson R. and Susan Jane (Tinsley) Swett, was born at Bowman's Grove, Iowa, March 5, 1864. Their two children are: Leah, born June 20, 1893; and Beatrice, born July 25, 1897. Both daughters received their educations at the Springview School, as well as at Brownell Hall in Omaha, and studied at the University of Nebraska. Beatrice is married to a Lincoln business man. Residence: Springview.

Roland M. Jones

Roland M. Jones was born in Ottawa, Illinois, December 17, 1877, and shortly after his birth his parents moved to Ashtabula, Ohio. His father, John Page Jones, was the son of John Paul Jones, who was one of the "Squirrel Hunters" during the Civil War. John Paul Jones was the son of William Jedediah Jones, who served as a hundred day man in the War of 1812. He was the son of James Jones, captain, who helped in gaining American independence during the Revolution as naval inspector.

John Page Jones married Lillian Artemesia Morrill, daughter of Moses Morrill, a drummer boy from Ohio in the War of 1812. Roland M. Jones was graduated from Adelbert College, Western Reserve University in June, 1901. That fall he came to Omaha, and in 1902 began work on the *Omaha World-Herald.* He went to Toledo in 1904 and was on the staff of the *Toledo Blade* one year, returning to the *World-Herald* in 1905, where he has served continuously to date. He has been police reporter, city hall, state and national political reporter, night editor, city editor, and from the last mentioned enlisted in the World War. He was commissioned first lieutenant at Fort Snelling, served at Camp Dodge, and was overseas with the 88th Division, 351st Infantry. Upon his return to Omaha he became news editor of the *World-Herald.* He is now an editorial writer for the *World-Herald.*

On November 25, 1906, he was united in marriage to

Daisy Shouf, daughter of Lachyman O. and Sarah Malinda (Swift) Shouf, at Omaha. They have one daughter, Sarah Ruth, born April 23, 1920. Mr. Jones is a Democrat. Residence: Omaha.

W. Clark Jones

W. Clark Jones, retired banker and lumberman of Farnam, Nebraska, was born in Fayette County, Ohio, January 14, 1860. His father, Jonathan R. Jones, who was a farmer, was born of Welsh and Pennsylvania Dutch parentage at Ripley, Virginia, February 15, 1825, and died at Farnam, August 19, 1904. Mary Anne (Craig) Jones, his mother, was born at Greenfield, Ohio, September 2, 1837, and died at Farnam, August 19, 1907; her ancestry was English and Scotch.

Mr. Jones attended country schools and was a student at the Knoxville Academy, Knoxville, Iowa, for a short time. He taught in the public schools for four years, was a successful lumber dealer for over 20 years, and was engaged in the banking business for 20 years. He has served in various capacities in village and school offices at Farnam and at this time is village clerk and justice of the peace. Mr. Jones is affiliated with the Methodist Episcopal Church and the National Geographic Society. His hobby is reading.

On April 30, 1896, he married Mary Almina Carpenter at Knoxville. Mrs. Jones, who was a seamstress prior to her marriage, was born of English and Irish parents in Marion County, Iowa, April 26, 1862. They have a son, Wells Carpenter, born April 26, 1898, who married Jesse Maye Jones. He is a lawyer at North Platte, Nebraska. Residence: Farnam.

Wells Carpenter Jones

Wells Carpenter Jones, lawyer and former county attorney of Lincoln County, was born at Waldo, Arkansas, June 26, 1898, son of Wells Clark and Mina (Carpenter) Jones. His father, who is a retired banker at Farnam, Nebraska, was a stockholder and president of the Farnam Bank for many years. His mother died at Farnam in February, 1902.

Since his graduation from the University of Nebraska in 1921 with the Bachelor of Laws degree, Mr. Jones has been in active practice. From 1923 until 1927 he was county attorney of Lincoln County, elected on the Republican ticket. He is a member of the Nebraska State Bar Association, the American Legion, the Elks, and the Methodist Church. He is a veteran of the World War.

On December 27, 1922, he was married to Jessie Maye Jones at Council Bluffs, Iowa. She was born in Monroe County, Iowa, August 30, 1898. Theey have one daughter living, Beatrice Glenn, born November 15, 1924; and one son, Clark Oliver, born April 13, 1929, who died January 2, 1931. Residence: North Platte.

William Lloyd Jones

A leading merchant in Wymore, Nebraska, William Lloyd Jones was born in Wymore, Nebraska, November 19, 1886, son of Morris Jones, born in Wales, England, July 4, 1846, and Annie (Jones) Jones. The latter was born in Belmont, Iowa County, Wisconsin, December 18, 1857. Morris Jones was of Welsh parentage and came to America in 1867 where he became a farmer. He died in Wymore, Nebraska, December 25, 1928. His wife was also of Welsh descent and was a nurse.

William L. Jones received his education in rural schools. On June 3, 1914, he married Maude Ella Mitchell, who was born in Wymore, Nebraska, August 19, 1894. Mrs. Jones taught school before her marriage. Their eldest child, Evelyn Rhea, was born May 6, 1915, and Betty Marie, was born January 15, 1927.

Mr. Jones who has lived in Wymore all of his life, has served as state representative elected on the Republican ticket, and has always been active in party politics.

He is vice president of the Wymore Building and Loan Association, belongs to the Methodist Church of Wymore, and to the Wymore Community Club. Since 1922 he has belonged to the Kiwanis and he is also a member of the Ancient Free and Accepted Masons. Interested in educational work for nine years Mr. Jones has been on the Wymore school board. He is also a member of the Nebraskana Society. Residence: Wymore. (Photograph in Album).

Z. Harold Jones

Z. Harold Jones, clerk of the district court at Bridgeport, Nebraska, has lived in this state all his life. He was born at Gretna, Nebraska, March 28, 1891, the son of Zibe and Mary Inez (Stansbury) Jones. His father, who was a farmer, was born at Marshalltown, Iowa, June 28, 1848, and died at Gretna, March 7, 1900; his ancestry was Welsh. His mother, whose parents came from Maryland and were of English and Scotch descent, was born at Mount Pleasant, Iowa, January 12, 1850, and died at Bridgeport, November 25, 1919.

Mr. Jones was graduated from the Gretna High School in 1907, studied at Nebraska State Normal College, and studied in commercial training at York College, York, Nebraska. He was a teacher in the public schools until 1914, and since then has been in public office in Morrill County continuously.

He served as deputy county clerk from 1914 to 1917, was county clerk from 1917 to 1920, and since 1920 has been clerk of the district court of Morrill County. Mr. Jones owns a 320 acre farm in Morrill County, and is prominent in public affairs at Bridgeport where he is a member of the Lions Club, has acted as a member and secretary of the Board of Education for the past 13 years. He holds membership in the City Library Board, acting as president in 1921, the Presbyterian Church, of which he is trustee, former elder, and treasurer; and the Masonic Lodge of which he is secretary.

Mr. Jones has held all offices in the Masonic Lodge and is Past Master of Camp Clarke Lodge Number 285 at this time. He is a member of the Red Cross, Salvation Army, the National Georgraphic Society, and the Democratic party.

He was united in marriage with Nell Jeffords at Bridgeport, January 1, 1919. She is the daughter of John F. and Rose (Cordell) Jeffards. She was formerly a teacher of piano and studied at Damrosch Conservatory of Music in New York City. Mrs. Jones, who is a member of the order of the Eastern Star, the P. E. O. sisterhood and is eligible to membership in the Daughters of the American Revolution, was born at St. Paul, Nebraska, July 17, 1893. To their marriage three children were born: Robert Harold, October 25, 1919; Richard Arthur, August 25, 1922; and Margaret Virginia, January 3, 1926. Residence: Bridgeport.

Galin Elmer Jordan

Galin Elmer Jordan, clergyman, was born at Elmira, Oregon, November 24, 1903, son of Elmer Willoughby and Rena Mae (Inman) Jordan. The father was born at Halsey, Oregon, November 2, 1875, and has taught schools for approximately 40 years in the rural schools of Lane County, Oregon. He is descended from settlers from England and Wales. His wife, Rena, was born in Walla Walla, Washington, February 17, 1879. Her ancestry is principally Scotch.

Mr. Jordan attended the public schools of Eugene, Oregon, and was graduated from high school there in 1922. In 1926 he received the Bachelor of Arts degree from Eugene Bible University. For a time he was also a student at the University of Oregon. In 1926 Mr. Jordan represented the Eugene Bible University at the State Old Line Oratorical contest. In 1925 and in

1927 he was manager of Forensic. He was president of his graduating class, and debated three years. While at the University of Oregon he received honor grades, which gave him the privilege of independent study.

On June 24, 1928, he was married to Epha Monzella Soward at Sayre, Oklahoma. Mrs. Jordan was born at Lebanon, Missouri, April 26, 1908, and is of English descent. She was graduated from Eugene, Oregon, high school and attended the Eugene Bible University. Mrs. Jordan is a member of the Gering Woman's Club and the American Legion Auxiliary. She is the daughter of Henry and Mary (Vermillion) Soward. They have one daughter, Patricia Mae, born August 30, 1930.

Mr. Jordan is an independent Democrat. At the present time he is pastor of the Central Church of Christ at Gering. His favorite sport is fishing and his hobby is horticulture. Residence: Gering.

George L. Jordan

For the past 52 years George L. Jordan has lived in Nebraska where he has been engaged in the newspaper business since 1913. He was born in Schuyler County, Illinois, August 22, 1867, the son of John and Caroline (Garrett) Jordan. His father, who was a farmer, was born in Cass County, Illinois, in 1828, and died at Minden, Nebraska, in 1896. His mother was born at Louisville, Kentucky in 1829, and died at Minden, Nebraska in 1901.

Mr. Jordan attended the public schools of Franklin County and also attended Franklin Academy. He was a student for two years at American Cor School of Law. He taught in the public schools for 11 years, served as county judge of Kearney County for two years, and since then has been prominent in the newspaper field. Since 1919 he has been editor and publisher of the *Clarks Enterprise*.

Of his marriage to Nora May Adams in 1906, two children were born: Frances, May 27, 1909; and Dale E., April 16, 1916. Frances is a talened musician and singer, and Dale E. is also specializing in music. Mr. Jordan is interested in the study of life insurance. Mrs. Jordan was born at Minden. Residence: Clarks.

Loran Yateman Jordan

Loran Yateman Jordan, born near Panora, Iowa, July 11, 1872, is the son of David Chalmers Jordan and Sophia Jane (Wolfe) Jordan. His father was born in Millerburg, Holmes County, Ohio, May 25, 1831, and died in Chicago, Illinois, August 10, 1910. He was of Scotch-Irish ancestry and fought in the war of rebellion with the title of captain in Company G of the 40th Iowa Volunteers. Mrs. David Jordan was born near Vincennes, Indiana, June 6, 1830, and died at Salem, Ohio, June 23, 1918.

Mr. Jordan received his education in the David City elementary and high schools and attended Gibbon College in 1886 and 1887. He became a registered druggist in 1894 when he was admitted to the profession at Elm Creek, Nebraska, and then started in business for himself at Gresham, Nebraska. In 1905 he moved to David City, where he is owner of a drug store at present.

Bessie Lulu Willis became Mr. Jordan's wife, September 6, 1899, at Gresham, Nebraska. She was born near Palo Postoffice in York County, Nebraska, September 22, 1877. She is a descendant of Sir Peter Bulkley who came to this country from England in 1632. Mr. and Mrs. Jordan have one child; Dorothy Mildred, born July 25, 1902, who is married to James N. Livermore. She was graduated from the University of Nebraska and is a member of Alphi Phi. Her home is in Detroit, Michigan.

Mr. Jordan is a Republican and has lived in Nebraska since 1881; he is a member of the Nebraskana Society. During the World War he was a minute man in the War loan drive. He has been a member of the Nebraska Pharmaceutical Association since 1897 and was president in 1923-24. He was president of the David City Commercial Club in 1920-21, is a member of the David City Country Club and holds membership in the order of the Ancient Free and Accepted Masons. He is also a member of the Knights of Pythias and is a Modern Woodmen of America. Mr. Jordan enjoys golf as a sport. Residence: David City.

Albert James Jorgenson

Albert James Jorgenson, president of the American National Bank at Sidney, was born at Council Bluffs, Iowa, January 18, 1886, son of Christian and Anna (Fredricksen) Jorgenson. The parents were Danish and came to the United States in 1880.

Mr. Jorgenson attended public school, at Council Bluffs, Iowa, and business college two years. On September 12, 1907, he was married to Mary Ann Draper at Council Bluffs, Iowa. She was born at Council Bluffs, September 19, 1889. There are two children, Gwendolyn, born September 12, 1909; and Donald, born December 6, 1910.

Mr. Jorgenson is a Republican, and has served eight years on the city council of Sidney. He was engaged in the insurance and real estate business until 1921, when he was appointed a receiver of state banks, and an employee of the Guarantee Fund Commission. He is a 32nd degree Mason. Residence: Sidney.

Arthur Lawrence Joseph

Arthur Lawrence Joseph was born at Polk, Nebraska, September 26, 1885, the son of Fred J. and Minnie (Schroeder) Joseph. His father, who is retired from active business, was born in Germany. His mother was born in Germany, and died at Grand Island, September 2, 1923.

Mr. Joseph attended the public schools of Polk County, Nebraska, and was graduated from Concordia College, Milwaukee, Wisconsin. He was a student at the University of Nebraska, from 1906 to 1909, and since 1909 has been engaged in the practice of law at Grand Island, Nebraska, where he served as city attorney from 1917 to 1921, and has been serving as county attorney since 1927. He is a Democrat.

He is a member of the Trinity Methodist Episcopal Church of Grand Island, and holds membership in the Elks, Masons, and Odd Fellows. On September 26, 1912, he married Matilda Gertrude Schilling at Scotia. Mrs. Joseph was born at Scotia, October 30, 1887, and died at Rochester, Minnesota, February 21, 1931. Residence: Grand Island. (Photograph in Album).

Caleb Ressegue Judkins

A pioneer in the lumber business in Nebraska, Caleb Ressegue Judkins has been a resident of the state for the past 51 years. He was born at Fort Wayne, Indiana, September 16, 1867, the son of James T. and Sally Jane (Ressegue) Judkins. His father, an expert machinist, was born at Franklin, New Hampshire, July 3, 1826, and died at Syracuse, Nebraska, March 2, 1893. His mother, who was born at Benson, Vermont, August 24, 1836, and died at Unadilla, Nebraska, in April 19, 1928, was a teacher in early life and later was prominent in church activities. Her mother, Betsey Sheldon was the daughter of Joseph Sheldon and Diadema Preston of Suffield, Connecticut.

Mr. Judkins has been engaged in the lumber business since 1890 and is now president and general manager of the C. R. Judkins Lumber Company at Upland, Nebraska, where he has served as mayor and city councilman at various times. He is a member of the Upland Commercial Club, holds membership in the Upland Country Club, and is a member of the Tehama Temple and Ancient Arabic Order of the Nobles of the Mystic Shrine at Hastings. During the World War he was connected with Liberty loan drives and acted as investigator in his county.

On January 29, 1895, he married Vinnie E. Moore at Pawnee City, Nebraska. Mrs. Judkins, who was born at Pawnee City, July 12, 1872, is the daughter of Jacob W. and Emma Walbridge Moore of Revolutionary War lineage; she is a member of the Daughters of the American Revolution. They have one daughter, Jennie Milrae, born August 12, 1897, who married Michael D. Nolan. Mr. Judkins is a member of the Republican Party and the Nebraskana Society. Residence: Upland.

Anton C. G. Kaempfer

Born at Milwaukee, Wisconsin, July 8, 1869, Anton C. G. Kaempfer is the son of Anton and Wilhelmina (Pieritz) Kaempfer. His father, who was a mining engineer and business man, was born at Berlinbach, Germany, August 10, 1832, and died at Castle Rock, Colorado, March 23, 1915. He held the rank of sergeant in Company A, 26th Wisconsin Volunteer Infantry during the Civil War. His wife, who was a nurse and seamstress, was born February 24, 1841, at sea, and died in Douglas County, Colorado, October 3, 1894. Her ancestry was German.

Mr. Kaempfer has been a teacher, surveyor, stenographer, accountant, blacksmith, welder and farmer. He has lived at Bridgeport since 1903, and for five years was a teacher in the public schools of Colorado, where he was later a surveyor. He is a member of the Rocky Mount Teachers Association, the Redmen, the Independent Order of Odd Fellows, and the Modern Woodmen of America. His hobbies are music, dramatics, history, mathematics and science.

He was united in marriage to Ethlyn Emma Ford at Bridgeport, Nebraska, on November 25, 1903. Mrs. Kaempfer, who was formerly much interested in dramatics, was born at Hazel Dell, Missouri, July 24, 1882, and died at Bridgeport, May 19, 1931. Three children were born to them, Nina Madge, born November 12, 1904, who died March 5, 1930; Myron Anton, January 30, 1906; and Karl Kenneth, July 9, 1908. Residence: Bridgeport.

Gustave Julius Kahl

Gustave Julius Kahl was born at Sheboygan, Michigan, on August 28, 1870, son of Julius E. and Catherine (Senn) Kahl. Julius Kahl was born in Germany, and came to America in 1850, settling in Wisconsin. He was a minister of the gospel, and died at Big Stone City, South Dakota, in April, 1914. His wife, Catherine, was a native of Switzerland, who reared a family of six children. She died at Big Stone City in March, 1912.

Mr. Kahl received his early education in the public schools of Whitewater and Waukesha, Wisconsin. He later attended Evansville Seminary in Evansville, Wisconsin, for two years. On November 11, 1895, he was married to Lois Ethel Bassett, at Burr, Nebraska. Mrs. Kahl was born at Burr, November 5, 1876. There are five children, Edith Violet, born May 22, 1905; Pauline, born May 22, 1905; Lois E., born November 21, 1909; Elva June, born June 22, 1912, and Velma, born March 29, 1914.

Mr. Kahl has been a resident of Nebraska for the past thirty-five years and during most of that time has been engaged in the banking business. For the past 28 years he has served as cashier of The American Bank of Burr. He is a Republican and a member of the Burr Methodist Episcopal Church.

During the World War he was a minute man and captain of the Burr home guards. He took active part in all of the Liberty Loan drives and other war work. He is a member of the Masons and the Modern Woodmen of America. He has always been active in civic,

educational and welfare work, and for twenty years was president of the Burr School Board. He is a member of the Burr Parent-Teachers Association, also. Residence: Burr.

William Theodore Kahse

For 14 years missionary superintendent of the Nebraska Synod of the United Lutheran Church, the Reverend Theodore Kahse has been, since 1921, pastor of the Trinity Lutheran Church at Sidney.

He was born in Germany, June 27, 1870, son of Frederick William and Wilhelmine Josephine (Kolchohorst) Kahse. He came to America in 1893. His education was obtained in the public schools of Germany and of Beatrice, Nebraska, and he afterwards attended the academy at Atchinson, Kansas. His degrees of Bachelor of Arts and Doctor of Divinity were awarded by Midland College at Fremont.

On January 2, 1906, he was married to Bertha Lucile Jaedicke at Hanover, Kansas. Mrs. Kahse was born at Hanover, July 26, 1876. Dr. Kahse has three children, Luther William, born in December, 1906; Ruth Amelia, born in May, 1912; and Paul, born in September, 1913.

An earnest religious worker, Dr. Kahse was successful in establishing English Lutheran churches in many of our cities, and cared for the younger generation of the Lutheran Church in Nebraska for many years. For some time he was field secretary for Midland College. He is a member of the Chamber of Commerce, the Rotary Club, and the Parent Teachers Association. Residence: Sidney.

Rudolph Ladwig Kaliff

Rudolph Ladwig Kaliff, who is the owner and operator of the largest feeding plant in York County, Nebraska, is a lifelong resident of that county. He was born May 16, 1889, the son of August and Ida Louise (Johnson) Kaliff, the former a prosperous farmer and pioneer of York County. His father, who was born at Gammal Kil Parrish, Sweden, April 12, 1856, came to this country in 1869, settling in Iowa. He came to Nebraska with his father, John Kaliff, who homesteaded in York County in 1872. He later returned to Iowa and was placed in charge of a cattle feeding company. Returning to Nebraska in 1873, he bought railroad land and settled on his father's homestead which is now retained by his son, Frank Kaliff. August Kaliff died at Fort Collins, Colorado, December 10, 1917, while visiting with his sister, Mrs. Christine Johnson.

Ida Louise Johnson, who was an unusual mother and homemaker, was born at Hogakull, Sweden, September 9, 1857, came to York County in 1880. She died there, June 29, 1926. She was interested in flower gardening and beautifying her home.

Mr. Kaliff attended rural school and in 1909 was graduated from the United Brethren College at York. He is engaged in preparing commercial feed for livestock, and ships an average supply of 40 cars of livestock each year from his feed yards near York. He is a member of the Nebraska Crop Growers and Improved Breeders Association, the Farmers' Union, Young Men's Christian Association, the Red Cross, and the First Presbyterian Church (trustee 1925-1931).

His fraternal organizations include the Independent Order of Odd Fellows, Rebekahs, and the Modern Woodmen of America. Mr. Kaliff is especially interested in travel and together with his family has made many trips in the western part of the United States. He is affiliated with the Republican party and holds membership in the Nebraskana Society.

His marriage to Myrtle Naomi Seng was solemnized at McCool Junction, Nebraska, August 31, 1911. Mrs. Kaliff, who was a clerk and bank assistant prior to her marriage, was born at McCool Junction, July 30, 1891, the daughter of W. W. and Katherine (Kneiss) Seng, whose ancestry was German. She is a member of the Rebekahs, the Royal Neighbors, and is treasurer of the York department of the Federated Women's Club. She is also treasurer of the school board of district No. 75.

Three children were born to Mr. and Mrs. Kaliff, Kathryn Mae, April 22, 1916; Mildred Louise, February 26, 1920; and William Joyce, August 21, 1925. Kathryn is a junior in the York High School. Both daughters are interested in 4-H Club work, and Kathryn was awarded the prize of having the champion Angus heifer, which was also grand champion of the 4-H Club in the 1930 Ak-Sar-Ben stock show at Omaha. She was also awarded prizes in the 1931 stock show in Omaha. She is news reporter for the 4-H Club. Residence: York. (Photograph in Album).

Paul Homer Kannow

Born at Bazile Mills, Nebraska, May 3, 1895, Paul Homer Kannow has been prominent in banking circles for a number of year. He is the son of Adolph A. and Caroline Brooks (Saunders) Kannow, the former a flour miller and farmer.

Paul H. Kannow was educated in public school and attended Doane College at Crete, Nebraska, two years. From 1914 he was associated with the Bank of Keystone, Nebraska, and since 1929 has been an officer of the Fort Kearney State Bank, the Bank of Paxton, the Bank of Keystone and the Arthur State Bank. He is also a director of The Ravenna Bank, at Ravenna.

On September 12, 1917, he was married to Gertrude Phillips at Friend, Nebraska. Mrs. Kannow, who confines her activity to her home and family, was born at Friend, Nebraska, September 30, 1894. There are two children, Robert, born July 24, 1922; and Kathryn, born July 28, 1923.

From September 4, 1918, until April 11, 1919, Mr. Kannow was a private in the United States Army, stationed at Camp Grant, Illinois. He is a member of the Chamber of Commerce, the Rotary Club, the Masons and the Elks. Recently he was made a life member of the Nebraskana Society. Residence: Kearney.

John C. Kaschube

John C. Kaschube, merchant, was born at Cleveland, Ohio, January 31, 1877, and has resided in Nebraska for 23 years. He is the son of August and Lena (Schmidt) Kaschube, both natives of Germany. The father died in 1877 at Cleveland, Ohio, and the mother in 1925 at West Side, Iowa.

Mr. Kaschube attended public school and high school and for the past 38 years has engaged in the mercantile business. He was married to Alvina Hagge, their marriage having been solemnized at Arcadia, Iowa, October 28, 1904. Mrs. Kaschube died October 16, 1931. They have one son and one daughter.

Mr. Kaschube is a Republican; a Mason, a member of the Consistory and Shrine; an Odd Fellow; a Woodman of the World; a Modern Woodman of America; and a member of the Lions Club. His religious affiliation is with the Congregational Church. Residence: Hyannis.

Thomas James Kastle

For the past 65 years Thomas J. Kastle has lived in Nebraska and for over 23 years has been a merchant and banker at North Bend. He was born at Cedar Rapids, Iowa, November 26, 1866, the son of Peter and Anna (Frohner) Kastle. His father, who was a farmer, came to America in 1865 and died at Prague, Nebraska; he was of German and Bohemian descent. His mother, whose ancestry was German and Bohemian, died at Prague.

Mr. Kastle attended country schools and was a student at Fremont Normal School, Fremont, Nebraska, and Creighton College, Omaha. He was active in baseball and footracing in college. During the World War he took part in loan drives of all kinds. He is a member of the Red Cross; the North Bend Commercial Club; and The Nebraskana Society. He holds membership in the Ancient Order of United Workmen; the Modern Woodmen of America; and the Young Men's Christian Association. He is affiliated with Saint Charles Catholic Church. He is now retired from active business. He is a Democrat.

His marriage to Anna Mary Cusack was solemnized at North Bend, April 19, 1893. Mrs. Kastle was born of Irish and Scotch parents at North Bend. Their children are: Marion, who married J. D. Milliken; Alice, who married W. F. Brown; and Thomas. Residence: North Bend.

Carl C. Katleman

Carl C. Katleman was born at Omaha, Ferbuary 5, 1891, son of Jacob and Belle Rita (Siegel) Katleman. His father was born in Zasslav, Russia, Ferbuary 1, 1864, and settled in Omaha in 1885. His wife was born at Latzkava, Russia, May 1, 1870, and died at Omaha June 1, 1914.

Carl C. Katleman attended the Omaha public schools and was graduated from Central High School in 1907. He received his LL. B. from the Creighton University in May, 1914, and entered the practice of law at Omaha. He is a member of the law firm of Monsky, Katleman and Grodinsky.

He was a member of the F. A. C. O. T. S. at Camp Taylor, Kentucky, at the time of the signing of the Armistice, and is a member of the American Legion and Forty and Eight. He is a member of the American Bar Association, the Nebraska State Bar Association and the Omaha, Douglas County Bar Association. For some years he was a member of the executive committee of the Jewish Welfare Federation. His clubs are the Omaha Athletic and the Highland Country Club. Residence: Omaha.

Louis Harrison Kaub

Louis Harrison Kaub, clergyman, was born at Centropolis, Kansas, April 11, 1891, son of Jacob and Eleanora (Ford) Kaub.

The father, who is a farmer, was born in Maryland, August 14, 1853, descended from Jacob Kaub, who was born in America. The first ancestor of the family came to this country about 1795. Eleanora Ford was born at Independence, Iowa, December 8, 1861, of French and Scotch ancestry.

Mr. Kaub was graduated from Baker Academy of Baldwin, Kansas, 1912, and received his Bachelor of Arts degree from Baker University in 1916. In 1921 he received the degree of Bachelor of Sacred Theology from Boston University. During 1928 and 1929 he attended the University of Edinburgh, Scotland. He received numerous honors while in school.

Ordained to the Methodist Episcopal ministry in 1915, Mr. Kaub has held the following pastorates, Big Spring's Methodist Episcopal Church 1921-24; Sidney Methodist Episcopal Church 1924-28; Bayard Federated Churches (Methodist, Presbyterian) 1929-31. At the present time he is associated with the department of field cultivation of the Nebraska Wesleyan University. He is the author of *The Gift of God* (out door passion play). He is a Republican.

On August 2, 1916, he was married to Minnie Marie Weide at Yates Center, Kansas. Mrs. Kaub was born at Yates Center, January 21, 1892, of German ancestry.

They have one daughter, Frances Marie, born February 18, 1921.

Mr. Kaub is a member of the Red Cross, the Lions Club, the Chamber of Commerce, the Nebraskana Society and the Ancient Free and Accepted Masons. His favorite sport is mountain hiking. Residence: Lincoln.

Alfred Kaufmann

Alfred Kaufmann, clergyman and educator of Omaha, Douglas County, Nebraska, has lived in Nebraska for the past 17 years. He was born at Aaron, Argan County, Switzerland, December 11, 1878, the son of Leo and Adele (Adler) Kaufmann. His father, who was a business man, was born in 1848 and died in 1882; his ancestry was Swiss. His mother, was born in 1848; her ancestry was also Swiss.

Mr. Kaufmann attended the elementary schools of Switzerland and later was a student at the St. Louis University, St. Louis, Missouri, where he was awarded the A. M. degree. He was a teacher in Campion College, at Prairie du Chien, Wisconsin for a time. He is now professor of *European* history at Creighton University at Omaha. He is the author of: *Modern World*, 1918; *Modern Europe*, 1929; *Catholic Historical Review*; and many articles in other historical publications.

He is a member of the Catholic American Historical Association, and is affiliated with the Roman Catholic Church at Omaha. Residence: Omaha.

James W. Kaura

James W. Kaura, farmer and stockman, was born at DeWitt, Nebraska, September 26, 1886, the son of Frank and Mary (Tramba) Kaura. His father, who was born in Czechoslovakia, July 28, 1852, and died at Marsland, Dawes County, Nebraska, November 18, 1899, was a farmer and rancher. His mother was born in Czechoslovakia, October 11, 1861, and died at DeWitt, December 16, 1916.

Mr. Kaura was graduated from the Marsland High School in 1900. He has served his community as county commissioner of Saline County since 1926; was a member of the Court House building committee during the construction of the Saline County Court House in 1928 and 1929; and has been a member of the school board, district 93, for the past 12 years. He is president of the Saline County Farmers Union, and is secretary of the Blue Valley Chapter of the Farmers Union.

During the World War he served as a member of loan drives committees and the food conservation committee, and for many years has been active in the various civic organizations of DeWitt. He holds membership in the Evangelical Lutheran Church of DeWitt; is a member of the Republican Party; and is affiliated with the Nebraskana Society.

His marriage to Emma Katherine Inderlied was solemnized at DeWitt, January 28, 1915. Mrs. Kaura, whose ancestry is German, was born at DeWitt, February 25, 1894, and died at Beatrice, Nebraska, September 28, 1928. Two children were born to them: Arnold, born January 5, 1916; and Stanley, born September 9, 1928. Arnold is a sophomore in high school at DeWitt, and is a member of the school orchestra and the town band. Residence: DeWitt.

Charles Manning Kearney

Charles Manning Kearney, stockman and rancher, was born at Stanton, Nebraska, August 10, 1885, son of Alfred Allen and Jennie (Manning) Kearney.

The father was born in Eureka, Illinois, December 1, 1855, and has been a prominent citizen of Nebraska for a number of years and is a lawyer and former county attorney of Stanton County. His father and grand-

father were Masons, and he is past master and organizer of the Morrill Masonic Lodge.

Jennie Manning was born in Dublin, Indiana, in October 1858, and in her younger days was a school teacher and musical instructor. At the present time she is president of the Women's Literary Society, and a member of the Eastern Star. Her father, Joseph Manning, was an Iowa circuit rider in 1858, and the presiding elder in the Methodist Episcopal Church. He homesteaded and laid out an addition to the city of Jefferson, Iowa.

In 1897 Mr. Kearney was graduated from public school at Stanton, and in 1901 was graduated from high school there. He received his Bachelor of Arts degree from the University of Nebraska in 1907, and was also a student at Washburn College at Topeka, Kansas. He is a member of the Innocents and Sigma Chi.

For 22 years Mr. Kearney operated the Charles M. Kearney Lumber Company, which he organized. For the past eight years he has served as chairman of the Scotts Bluff County Republican central committee.

His marriage to Jessie May Chase was solemnized at Stanton, November 15, 1909. Mrs. Kearney was born in Stanton County, February 7, 1889. There are two children, Charles C., Jr., born October 5, 1910; and Allen A., Jr., born December 23, 1916.

During the late war Mr. Kearney was chairman of the Scotts Bluff County four minute speakers. He is a Protestant, a member of the Chamber of Commerce, past master of the Masons, and a member of the Red Cross. His hobby is purebred Jersey cattle. Residence: Morrill.

Frances D. Keefe

Frances D. Keefe, prominent clubwoman at Walthill, Nebraska, has lived in this state since 1898. She was born at Bentham, England, December 10, 1870, the daughter of Septimus Robson and Anne (Hodgson) Davis. Her father, who was born at Sagg Hill, Northumberland, England, October 11, 1818, and died at Springdale, Cedar County, Iowa, April 10, 1891, was a lecturer and organizer of British workmen, and for 15 years was a temperance missionary in England. He came to America in 1872.

Her mother, who was active in the Woman's Christian Temperance Union, was born at Liverpool, England, September 3, 1831, and died at Springdale, April 11, 1893. Her family history has been traced to the Norman Conquest, and at the time of the George Fox withdrawal, members of the family entered the Society of Friends.

Mrs. Keefe attended the Springdale Seminary and High School, and in 1895 was graduated from the University of Iowa. During the World War she served as chairman of the Woman's Division of the American Red Cross in East-Side Thurston County Chapter, and was active in welfare work at Camp Wadsworth. She is now past president and secretary of the American Legion Auxiliary, is chairman of the Library committee, and holds membership in the Nebraskana Society.

She has held following positions in the Woman's Club: past president of the local organization; president of the third district, 1904-6; president of the state organization, 1906-08; director of the General Federation of Women's Club, 1908-12; and recording secretary, 1912-16. She is secretary of the American Red Cross at Walthill at this time.

Her marriage to Harry Leonard Keefe was solemnized at Springdale, November 22, 1898. Mr. Keefe, who was born at Osage, Iowa, January 4, 1871, and died at Walthill, September 10, 1926, was a distinguished lawyer and progressive leader in Nebraska. From 1896 to 1926 he was prominent in legal practice in Cuming and Thurston Counties, and served as director in the First National Bank. He was a member of the Nebraska State Bar Association, the American Bar Association, and the American Legion. During the World War he served as hospital director for the American Red Cross at Camp Wadsworth, South Carolina, was acting chairman of the council of defense in Thurston County, and was morale officer in reconstruction service.

Mr. Keefe was a member of the Republican Party, and in 1919-20 acted as a member of the Nebraska Constitutional Convention. He secured the right of way for the Burlington Railway across the Omaha reservation, was instrumental in securing concession for the town sites of Winnebago, Walthill, and Rosalie, from the Indian Department. Perhaps his greatest claim to state recognition lies in the fact that he organized the counties of Nebraska into a federation which later became known as the Nebraska Farm Bureau Federationn. At the time of his death he was president of the latter organization in which he was especially active, and was well-known in various Nebraska societies, including: Potato Growers Co-operative Association of Northwest Nebraska; and County Poultry Co-operatives.

He held membership in St. Joseph's Catholic Church, was a member of the Knights of Columbus, and was affiliated with the State Historical Society.

Mrs. Keefe served as a member of the Walthill School Board from 1907-20. Residence: Walthill.

Harry Leonard Keefe

Harry Leonard Keefe, lawyer, was born in Osage, Iowa, January 4, 1871. From 1896 until 1926 he was a prominent lawyer in Cuming and Thurston counties, and was also associated with the First National Bank of Walthill in the capacity of director. He was a member of the Nebraska State Bar Association and the American Bar Association, and the American Legion. During the World War Mr. Keefe served as hospital director for the American Red Cross at Camp Wadsworth, South Carolina, was acting chairman of the council of defense in Thurston County, and was morale officer in reconstruction service.

A leading Republican, in 1919-20 he acted as a member of the Nebraska Constitutional Convention. He secured the right-of-way for the Burlington Railway across the Omaha reservation, was instrumental in securing the consession for the townsites of Winnebago, Walthill, and Rosalie from the Indian Department. His greatest claim to recognition perhaps lies in the fact that he organized the counties of Nebraska into a federation which later became known as the Nebraska Farm Bureau Federation.

At the time of his death on September 10, 1926, he was president of the latter organization and was well known in various Nebraska societies, among them the Potato Growers Co-operative Association of Northwest Nebraska and the County Poultry Co-operative.

He was married to Frances D. Davis at Springdale on November 22, 1898. (See *Nebraskana*). Mr. Keefe was a Catholic and a member of St. Joseph's Church. He was also a member of the Knights of Columbus and the Nebraska State Historical Society. Residence: Walthill. (Photograph in Album).

J. Jay Keegan

J. Jay Keegan, a physican at Omaha for the past 11 years, was born at Axtell, Kansas, January 8, 1889, the son of John A. and Agnes T. (Graney) Keegan. His father, who was born at Axtell, April 26, 1863, has been a farmer, publisher, real estate man, and county assessor; his ancestry is Irish. His mother was born at Seneca, Kansas, January 1, 1866, and died at Alliance, Nebraska, November 16, 1927; her ancestry was Irish. She was active in Woman's Christian Temperance Union affairs and served as delegate to conventions for this organization.

Dr. Keegan attended the public schools of Kansas and in 1907 was graduated from the Axtell High School. He was awarded his M. A. degree at the University of Nebraska in 1914 and his M. D. in 1915. There he was

elected to membership in Sigma Xi, Alpha Omega Alpha, and Phi Rho Sigma.

Instructor of anatomy at the University of Nebraska, 1915-17; he was a lieutenant in the United States Navy Medical Corp, 1917-19, during the World War; and served his internship at the Peter Bent Brigham Hospital at Boston, Massachusetts, 1919-20. Dr. Keegan has taken an active part in educational affairs, and from 1920 to 1929 was professor of clinical pathology and dean of the college of medicine at the University of Nebraska. He is now professor of neuro-surgery at the University of Nebraska and is engaged in private practice of neurological surgery at Omaha.

Dr. Keegan is the author of articles dealing with neurology, pathology, neurological surgery, and medical education. He holds membership in the American Medical Association, Society of Neurological Surgeons, and the American Association of Anatomists. During the war he was in charge of laboratory work in the United States Naval Hospital at Boston, Massachusetts. Politically, he is an Independent.

His marriage to Grace Gillilland was solemnized at Boston, Massachusetts, January 8, 1918. Mrs. Keegan was born at Glenwood, Iowa; her ancestry is Scotch, Irish, and English. They have two children: Nancy Jane, born November 9, 1924; and Norman Jay, born March 1, 1928. Residence: Omaha.

Emma Kees

Emma Kees was born in Nebraska City, on October 1, 1868, the daughter of Anton and Mary (Stohlnacker) Zimmerer. Her father, born in Germany, September 15, 1830, died at Nebraska City on June 15, 1912. An early settler, he was prominent among Nebraska's pioneers, and was a member of the state's first legislature. Her mother, Mary Stahlnacker, was of Pennsylvania Dutch descent, and was born at Bethlehem, Pennsylvania.

Educated in the public and high schools at Nebraska City, Emma Zimmerer was married to Frederick Daniel Kees at Nebraska City on May 6, 1880. To this union were born three children, John A., on March 10, 1881, who married Sadie Green; Clara, born January 17, 1885, and Dan, born May 20, 1900, who is married to Miriam Fogg.

Frederick D. Kees was a pioneer Nebraska manufacturer and one of the first gunsmiths in Beatrice. He died on October 23, 1927. Mrs. Kees is a director of the K. D. Kees factory at Beatrice, one of her sons is a mechanical engineer there and and the other is president of the organization.

Mrs. Kees is independent in politics, is a member of the First Baptist Church, and a life member of the Nebranskana Society. She takes great pleasure in gardening, and enjoys her home in which she has lived continuously since she came to Beatrice. Residence: Beatrice.

Riley Lytton Keester

A pioneer contractor and building supply dealer in Nebraska, is Riley Lytton Keester, who was born at Peekesville, Missouri, September 3, 1863, the son of William and Julia (Dixon) Keester. His father, a farmer, was born at Columbus, Ohio, April 4, 1832, of Scotch and Dutch parentage, and died at Medill, Missouri, July 18, 1914. His mother was born at Lennox, Ohio, June 10, 1834, and died at Medill, Missouri, April 15, 1916. Her parents were natives of England.

Mr. Keester attended rural school near Peekesville, was a student at the State Normal School of Kirksville, Missouri, 1881-84, and attended Pierce's Commercial School at Keokuk, Iowa. Except for two years at Plattsmouth, Nebraska, he has been in Alma, Nebraska, continuously since.

He studied law in the office of Judge Sullivan, at Plattsmouth, for two years and was admitted to the practice of law in 1908. In 1910, he moved to Alma, and formed a partnership with William Morning, remaining in that connection until Mr. Morning moved to Lincoln. He was later associated with various law firms at Alma, until 1920. He served as president and general manager of the Farmers & Merchants Telephone Company at Alma, from the time of its organization until 1927. At that time he owned the Wilsonville and Bloomington Telephone Company and a majority of the stock in the Farmers & Merchants Telephone Company.

Mr. Keester owns a number of farms and business buildings, and at this time devotes most of his time to managing them. He is a member of the First Christian Church of Alma, holds membership in the Red Cross and Lions Club there. He is a member of the Woodmen of the World, the Modern Woodmen of America, the Order of Eastern Star, and the Masons. He served as chairman of the Red Cross in Harlan County during the World War. His favorite sport is fishing.

His marriage to Nora M. Deans occurred at Alma, December 24, 1890. Mrs. Keester was a member of the first high school graduating class in Harlan County. She is the daughter of Dr. George Deans, pioneer physician in that county. Dr. Deans came to Harlan County in the spring of 1874, locating in Republican City. He was born in Durham County, England, coming to this country as a small boy. He died in Alma, May 4, 1888. Mrs. Keester's mother, Barbara Anna Stoddard, was born in Montgomery County, Indiana, November 24, 1853, and died in Alma, December 20, 1902.

Mrs. Keester was a teacher before her marriage. They have three adopted children: Opal, born November 10, 1903; Mildred, born March 21, 1904, and Carl, born March 14, 1908. Residence: Alma.

Joseph Warren Keifer, Jr.

Born at Springfield, Ohio, May 13, 1861, Joseph Warren Keifer, Jr., is the son of Joseph Warren and Eliza (Stout) Keifer. His father, born at Bethel Township, Ohio, January 30, 1836, was a lawyer. A major general by brevet, in the Civil War, he held the same rank in the Spanish American War, served in Congress fourteen years, as speaker of the 47th Congress, and was the author of *Slavery and Four Years of War*. His wife, Eliza Stout, was born in Springfield, July 11, 1834 and died there on March 12, 1899.

Joseph W. Keifer, Jr., was educated first in the public schools of Springfield, and attended Wittenberg College, Antioch College and Ohio State University. Coming to Nebraska in April, 1883, he has since engaged in stock farming.

Of his marriage to Julia Stevens Lowry, which was solemnized on October 20, 1886, four children were born: Joseph William, October 2, 1887. He married Thelma Amack, and served overseas in the World War. Lucy Stout, August 8, 1889, married John Ernest Bell; Margaret Eliza, April 1, 1891, married Joel E. McLafferty; and Oswin, July 26, 1893, was first married to Helen Kendall and second to Margaret Lang. He also served overseas, and served in the state legislature in 1923.

Mr. Keifer is a Republican. Chairman of the Republican state central committee in 1908, he was a member of the legislature in 1907. During the World War he was active in all civilian projects, and was chairman of his home district for the Council of Defense. He is a member of the Military Order of the Loyal Legion, the First Presbyterian Church, the Elks and is a 32nd degree Mason, the Nebraska State Historical Society and The Nebraskana Society. Residence: Bostwick.

Oswin Keifer

Oswin Keifer, grain dealer and livestock raiser of Nuckolls County, Nebraska, has resided in this state all his life. He was born at Bostwick, Nebraska, July 26, 1893, the son of J. Warren Keifer and Julia Stevens

(Lowry) Keifer. His father, who is a farmer and stockraiser, was born at Springfield, Ohio, May 13, 1861, and has served as a member of the Nebraska House of Representatives and chairman of the Republican State Committee. He is the son of General J. Warren Keifer of Ohio, a major general in the Civil War and Spanish-American War; the latter was a member of congress for 14 years, was speaker of the United States House of Representatives in 1881 and 1883, and was a prominent leader in national and state affairs.

Julia Stevens (Lowry) Keifer, mother of Oswin Keifer, was born at Ripley, Ohio, October 15, 1856. Her grandfather, Samuel Doak, founded the first college west of the Alleghenies at Tusculum, Tennessee, in 1778.

Mr. Keifer attended public schools at Lincoln, Nebraska, where he was graduated from the high school in 1910. He received the B. S. degree at the University of Nebraska in 1915. He was awarded a letter in basketball at the university. Since 1926 he has served as treasurer of the school board at Bostwick.

In 1917 Mr. Keifer enlisted as a private in the 110th Engineer Regiment, 35th Division of the United States Army, and served with this regiment in France throughout the duration of the war; he was discharged as a first lieutenant, May 19, 1919. In 1922 he served as commander of the American Legion Post at Superior, Nebraska. He holds membership in the Officers Reserve Corps, is affiliated with the First Presbyterian Church of Superior, and is a member of the Nebraskana Society. He is a Mason.

He married Helen Jane Kendall at Superior, July 19, 1919. The daughter of Wallace and Lillian (Bradshaw) Kendall. She was born at Superior, April 29, 1899, and died there, Septembeer 22, 1920. One child was born to them, Oswin, Jr., born September 13, 1920. Mr. Keifer was united in marriage with Margaret A. Lang at Gorn, Nebraska, March 17, 1928. Mrs. Keifer was born at Gorn, April 27, 1901, the daughter of John and Eva Leonard Lang.

A Republican, Mr. Keifer served as a member of the Nebraska house of representatives in 1923. Residence: Bostwick.

Baird Vinton Keister

Born at Essex, Iowa, August 13, 1895, Baird Vinton Keister is the son of William Edgar and Mary Ida (Baird) Keister. William Keister, who is a retired lumberman, was born of German parentage at McKeesport, Pennsylvania, April 2, 1855. Mary Keister, whose ancestry is Scotch Irish, was born at Nebraska City, Nebraska, July 26, 1857, and died at Essex, February 3, 1919.

Mr. Keister was graduated from the Essex High School in 1913, received the A. B. degree at Iowa State College in 1918, and was awarded the A. M. degree at the University of Chicago in 1928. He was a student at Coe College, 1913-14, and took post graduate work during the summer of 1920 at the University of Nebraska. He was active in the Iowa State College Band and Orchestra, and was a member of the Chicago Choir. His fraternity is Alpha Sigma Phi.

Since 1919 Mr. Keister has been prominent in educational activities in an executive capacity, holding the following positions: principal of the hgh school at Wagner, South Dakota, 1919-21; assistant principal of the senior high school at Norfolk, Nebraska, 1921-26; and superintendent of schools at Neligh, Nebraska since 1926. He is a member of the Nebraska Schoolmasters Club, is secretary of the Neligh Rotary Club, and is serving as a member of the state executive committee of the Nebraska State Teachers Association. He is a member of the National Educational Association, in 1930 was president of the Third District of the State Teachers Association, and is affiliated with the First Congregational Church of Neligh.

In 1918 he entered the United States Infantry as a private, was promoted to the rank of sergeant the following month, and served throughout the World War. He now holds membership in the American Legion. His social club is the Neligh Country Club and his sports include tennis and golf.

His marriage to Emma Eleanor Lindberg was solemnized at Essex, August 25, 1919. Mrs. Keister was born at Essex, March 1, 1895. Two children were born to them: Jean, August 31, 1922; and Thomas, May 1, 1927. Mr. Keister is a member of the Republican Party and the Nebraskana Society, and is interested in music and reading. Residence: Neligh.

Estial Chapman Keister

Estial Chapman Keister was born at Blackburg, Montgomery County, Virginia, December 3, 1871, and for the past forty-five years has resided in Nebraska. His father, John Henry Keister, was born at Blacksburg, February 14, 1841. He was a farmer of German descent, who moved from Virginia to Kansas. He died at Sabetha, April 24, 1916. He married Nancy Heavener, who was also a native of Blacksburg. She was born July 8, 1843, and was descended from the early English settlers of Virginia. She died at Tonganoxie, Kansas, May 17, 1917.

Estial C. Keister graduated from Stella High School in 1898, and later attended Lincoln and Western Normal Schools. During his school life he took active part in debate, and was a member of the debating societies. He married Lola Virdie Gilliland, at Auburn, December 5, 1894. She was born at White City, Missouri, March 4, 1872 and was of German and Scotch descent. There are three children, Robert Overton, born June 16, 1900, a mechanic; Joseph Chapman, born February 18, 1903, a farmer and Don D., born September 18, 1910, a professor of manual training.

Mr. Keister is a Republican and is now state representative from district number four. With the exception of five years spent as a teacher in public schools he has been a farmer all his life, and at the present time is an extensive landowner. During the World War he was active in all loan drives. He is affiliated with the Cumberland Presbyterian Church, is a member of the Red Cross, the Kiwanis Club, and the Nebraskana Society. His home is at Auburn.

M. Allen Keith

The Reverend M. Allen Keith, pastor of the First Methodist Episcopal Church of Alliance, was born at St. Louis, Missouri, February 6, 1885, the son of Menzo Harrison and Mary (Allen) Keith. Menzo Harrison Keith was born in Denver, Colorado, in 1839, and died in St. Louis in 1895. He held the rank of lieutenant in the Colorado Volunteers and was an insurance agent for the New York Life Company. His family came to America from Scotland about 1800. Mary Allen was born at Mt. Morris, Illinois, in 1846, and died at St. Louis, December 22, 1892. Her family was Spanish, coming to America about 1790.

Mr. Keith attended public school in St. Louis, Chicago and Mt. Morris, Illinois, graduating in 1898; he was graduated from the Academy of Taylor University at Upland, Indiana, in 1909; received his Bachelor of Arts degree from Nebraska Wesleyan University in 1916 and in 1921 was awarded the degree of Bachelor of Sacred Theology from Boston University School of Theology. During the year 1920-21 he was a student at Harvard University. He is a member of Phi Kappa Phi at Nebraska-Wesleyan where he was the winner of a medal in public speaking.

His marriage to Maude Mae Miller was solemnized at LaGrange, Indiana, June 3, 1921. Mrs. Keith was born at LaGrange March 21, 1882, and is of Pennsylvania Dutch, English and Irish descent. Two children were born to them, Allen, on July 14, 1922, who died the same day; Eleanor Elaine, on November 21, 1924.

Ordained to the ministry in September, 1911, from that date until 1914 he was minister at Salem, Nebraska, as he was from 1914 until 1917, at Alvo, Nebraska. From 1917 until 1920 he was pastor at Lawrence, Massachusetts, and from 1920 until 1921 at Lancaster, Massachusetts. Coming to Nebraska in 1921, he was for five years pastor at Omaha, removing in 1926 to Scottsbluff where he served two years. He has held his present pastorate since 1928. Politically he is a Republican.

Mr. Keith is a member of the Nebraska Annual Conference of the Methodist Episcopal Church, the Alliance Chamber of Commerce, the Scottsbluff Lions Club, and the Alliance Rotary Club. He is a Mason. His favorite sport is golf. Residence: Alliance.

James B. Kelkenney

James B. Kelkenney has lived in Nebraska for 50 years and for nearly 40 years has been a leading Omaha lawyer. He was born at Toledo, Ohio, August 2, 1883, the son of Patrick and Mary (Moran) Kelkenney. His father, a captain in the United States Army, was born in Ireland and died at Chicago. His mother was born in Ireland and died at Omaha.

Mr. Kelkenney attended the public and high schools of Nebraska, and in 1893 was admitted to the practice of law. He has been active in the civic affairs of Omaha since that time. He is a member of the Nebraska State Bar Association and the Douglas County Bar Association, the Omaha Commercial Club, the Chamber of Commerce and the Omaha Athletic Club. He holds membership in the Elks, and is affiliated with the Catholic Church.

His marriage to Leah Marie Cox was solemnized at Kansas City, Kansas. Mrs. Kelkenney, who is an artist, was born at Grand Island, Nebraska. Residence: Omaha.

William Frank Keller

William Frank Keller, pioneer Nebraska farmer, has lived in this state for the past 50 years. He was born in Westphalia, Germany, March 15, 1867, the son of Henry J. and Johanna M. (Euwens) Keller. His father, who was a farmer, was born in Rhineland, Germany, November 28, 1835, and died at West Point, Cuming County, Nebraska, June 29, 1919. He served in the German Army before coming to America in 1881. His mother, whose ancestors were Holland Dutch, was born in Rhineland, Germany, June 8, 1845, and died at West Point, July 27, 1923. She was active in all religious affairs, and was an energetic farm woman.

Mr. Keller was graduated from the elementary school in Germany, May 15, 1881. He is now a retired farmer in Cuming County, and holds an interest in the Farmers & Merchants Bank at West Point. He is a member and supporter of the Red Cross; was a charter member of the West Point Community Club; and was formerly a member of the local school board. He has been an active member of the Fair Board for several years; is affiliated with St. Mary's Catholic Church; and holds membership in the Knights of Columbus. His hobbies are reading and farm problems. Mr. Keller has always endeavored to further and support public and community affairs, and during the World War was especially active as a member of the Minute Men, and in the sale of Liberty bonds.

His marriage to Dorothy von Ackeren was solemnized at Humphrey, Platte County, Nebraska, May 22, 1900. Mrs. Keller was born in Westphalia, Germany, November 8. 1877. They have ten children: Anna, born March 10, 1901, who married Richard Johnson; Veronica, born June 17, 1902, who married Dale Kisling; John H., born January 17, 1904, who married Neva Robbins; Margaret, born March 16, 1906; Clara, born October 17, 1907, who married Anton Welding; Helen, born December 18, 1908;

Elizabeth, born April 13, 1912; Mary Ann, born December 16, 1913; Josephine, born September 25, 1915; and Florence, born January 8, 1918.

Nearly all of the children attended college, some of them later teaching school. The two youngest children are now attending high school at West Point. Residence: West Point.

Ernest Kelley

Ernest Kelley, specialist in nervous and mental diseases, was born at Des Moines, Iowa, December 20, 1883, son of John and Alice Ann (Frazer) Kelley. Dr. Kelley received his medical degree from Creighton Medical College, and was a post graduate student at Columbia University. He was married to Laura Bernice Carson at Omaha on January 29, 1908.

Dr. Kelley served as a member of the staff of St. Joseph's Hospital, Nicholas Senn Hospital, Lord Lister Hospital (chief of staff), and St. Bernard's Hospital, and also has been assistant professor of nervous and mental diseases at Creighton Medical College.

His professional organizations include the American Medical Association, the Nebraska State Medical Association, the Douglas County Medical Society, the Missouri Valley Society, and the Interstate Medical Society. Residence: Omaha.

Lee Kelligar

One of the eight children of William Henry Kelligar, one of Nemaha County's foremost lawyers and Democratic leaders, Lee Kelligar was born at Auburn, July 27, 1898. His father was born at Millstone, New Jersey, March 2, 1854, son of Nicholas and Ellen (Griffin) Kelligar. For almost fifty years he has resided in Nemaha County, where he has been an active member of the bar, served as district judge and been a political leader.

Mary Agnes Finn, mother of Lee, was born at St. Louis, March 12, 1862, and died at Auburn, December 11, 1923.

Lee Kelligar received his education in the public school of Auburn, and at St. Joseph's Parochial School. He was graduated from Auburn High School in 1917. During 1924 and 1925 he studied law at Creighton University, and was admitted to the practice of law at Lincoln, July 15, 1925.

On June 13, 1926, he was married to Irene Polsby at Omaha. Mrs. Kelligar was born at Wahoo, January 15, 1896, and at the time of her marriage was a teacher in the Omaha public schools. They have two children, William Lee, born March 1, 1927, and Robert Polsby, born March 14th, 1928.

A life time resident of Auburn, Mr. Kelligar, the year following his admission to the bar was elected county attorney of Nemaha County on the Democratic ticket for a term of four years; in November, 1930, he was re-elected for a second term. He is a member of St. Joseph's Catholic Church and of the Knights of Columbus. He is also a member of the Nebraska State Bar Association. His chief recreation is reading. Residence: Auburn.

William Henry Kelligar

William H. Kelligar, distinguished lawyer and judge of Nemaha County, was born at Millstone, New Jersey, March 2, 1854. His father, Nicholas Kelligar, was a contractor who came from southern Ireland and settled in Illinois, in the early days. He was the builder of several of the old landmarks in Illinois, many of which are today in perfect condition because of the splendid workmanship put into them; the asylum for the insane at Anna, Illinois, was constructed by him. Some of his ancestors came to America from Ireland in the early 1800's. He died at Pana, Illinois, March 17, 1905.

Ellen (Griffin) Kelligar, mother of William, was born in Ireland in 1824, and died at Pana, Illinois, December 31, 1860. She was an active church worker and a devoted home-maker.

Judge Kelligar received his elementary education in Illinois. He was graduated from the Pana High School after which he entered the law office of John W. Kitchell, a noted Illinois lawyer, where he received his entire legal education. He was admitted to the bar in Illinois, June 18, 1878, and since that time has engaged in the practice of law in Nebraska, in the following partnerships: Kelligar & Stowell, 1882-88; Kelligar & Ferneau, 1901-28, except for his service on the bench; Kelligar & Kelligar, since 1928.

Judge Kelligar is a staunch Democrat and has been prominent in political circles in Nebraska for over 40 years. In a recent newspaper article written by Richard Metcalfe, he was named as one of the four remaining Democrats who were the original party men in this state. He was at one time chairman of the Democratic county committee of Nemaha County, and has attended scores of conferences and conventions held by his party over a period of years. In 1890 he was elected county attorney and served this county for two terms. From 1904 to 1908 he was district judge, covering an area of six counties, Nemaha, Pawnee, Johnson, Gage, Jefferson and Richardson. He was retained as lawyer for several large drainage companies who came into Nemaha County several years ago when the course of the river was changed.

At one time he was one of our members of a committee made up of lawyers and judges for the purpose of assisting ex-convicts in finding work upon their release from prison. Four times each year this committee, of which Judge Frost was chairman, met and studied the prison problem, and placed as many men as possible in positions. There was no remuneration, and this work involved a great deal of time, effort, and thought.

His marriage to Mary Agnes Finn was solemnized at St. Louis, Missouri, December 2, 1883. Mrs. Kelligar was born at St. Louis, March 12, 1862, and died at Auburn, December 11, 1923. To this union eight children were born, all of whom are living. They are: Nellie, Josephine, Susie, Ruth, Agnes, William Griffin, Lee, and Pat, all born in Auburn. Nellie and Susie are the home makers of the family. Josephine is the owner and manager of the Kelligar Goodyear Service Station at Auburn. Ruth has been a kindergarten instructor in Omaha for nine years. Agnes has been cashier of the Western Public Service Company in Auburn for the last eight years. William G., who is with the Hydraulic Press Brick Company of St. Louis, was in the 89th division in the World War and saw active service in France. Lee, who is now entering his second term as county attorney of Nemaha County, married Irene Polsby, a former Omaha school teacher. Pat is co-owner of Kelligar Goodyear Service Station, at Auburn.

During the late war Judge Kelligar devoted all his time and energy toward loan drives, Red Cross relief work, and was especially active in rural sections where he made speeches and appeals for funds.

He is a member of the Nebraska State Bar Association; the Chamber of Commerce; and the Red Cross. He is an Elk, a Royal Highlander, and a member of the Nebraskana Society. He is affiliated with St. Joseph's Catholic Church at Auburn. His sports are hunting and fishing. He has always been a profound thinker and student, and is especially fond of reading. Residence: Auburn.

George Henry Kellogg

George Henry Kellogg, county extension agent of Lincoln County, was born at Cato, New York, April 28, 1881, son of Oscar Silas and Mary Jane (Shannon) Kellogg. The mother was born in Ira, New York, September 13, 1856, of Irish ancestry, and the father at Cato, February 8, 1842, his ancestors coming to America on the *Mayflower*.

In 1905 Mr. Kellogg was graduated from the Kansas State Agricultural College and at the present time is Nebraska county extension agent at North Platte. He is a member of the Nebraska Extension Agents Association, of which he was president in 1930, and Sigma Epsilon Phi.

On September 9, 1916, he was married to Wilma L. Lundt at Blair. She was born at Blair, April 18, 1892. Their three children are: George E., born April 4, 1920; Dean L., born April 14, 1922; and Kenneth H., born February 9, 1931, all of North Platte. Residence: North Platte.

Frank Kelly

Born at Ashkum, Illinois, September 28, 1881, Frank Kelly has been a resident of Nebraska since March, 1885. He is the son of Robert J. and Elizabeth C. (Carey) Kelly, the former a real estate and insurance man. Robert J. Kelly was born at La Salle, Illinois, October 27, 1856, his parents having come from Ireland about 1836. Elizabeth Carey was born in Cambridge, Massachusetts, March 3, 1858, and died at Merna, Nebraska, January 21, 1920. Of Irish descent, she was a school teacher and a member of the Shakespeare Club.

Frank Kelly attended Merna High School, Lincoln Business College, and received his Bachelor of Laws degree from Creighton University in June, 1906. From that time until January 1, 1915 he was in practice at Merna, and from April 1919 until May 1928 was in partnership with Arthur P. Schnell at Broken Bow. The balance of the time he has been in individual practice. A Democrat, he has served as county attorney of Custer County (1915-19).

His marriage to Ella S. Snyder was solemnized at Chatsworth, Illinois, April 27, 1908. Mrs. Kelly, who is a music teacher, is of French and Irish descent. She was born at Chatsworth, January 11, 1883. There are five children: Mary Frances, born April 24, 1909; Helen Louise, December 15, 1911; Kathleen Yvonne, April 7, 1913; James R., March 10, 1915; and John P., November 7, 1917. Helen is completing her last year of nurse's training, while Kathleen is in her second year at Kearney State Teachers College. The boys are in high school.

Mr. Kelly was a member of the council of defense and a four minute speaker during the World War. He is president of the Public Service Club, a member of the Knights of Columbus and the Modern Woodmen of America. Residence: Broken Bow.

Lloyd William Kelly

Born at Grand Island, Nebraska, November 10, 1901, Lloyd William Kelly is the son of William and Emma Rosetta (Gillming) Kelly. His father, who is an inventor and contractor, is serving as president of the Kelly Well Company, was born at DeSmet, South Dakota, November 17, 1880. His mother, who is active in the Woman's Club and the Civic League, was born at Ithaca, New York, May 18, 1878.

Mr. Kelly was graduated from the Grand Island High School in 1922, received the LL. B. degree at the University of Nebraska in 1927 where he was prominent in dramatic affairs and held membership in Kappa Sigma; Phi Delta Phi; and Pi Epsilon Pi. He served as bookkeeper for the William Kelly Company, 1927-29, was employed by the Kelly Well Company during the years 1922 to 1927, and is now engaged in the practice of law at Grand Island.

He is police judge of Grand Island courts, is associated in the practice of law with Edward F. Hannon, and is a director in the Kelly Well Company. He holds membership in the Hall County Bar Association, the Nebraska State Bar Association, the Cosmopolitan Club of Grand Island, the Parent Teachers Association, Civic League, and the City Improvement Association.

Mr. Kelly is affiliated with the following fraternal organizations: Elks; Masons; Eagles; Maccabees; and the DeMolay Alumni Association. He is a member of the Grand Island University Club, the Little Theatre Club, and the Nebraskana Society. His chief outside interests are the theatre and boxing.

On May 15, 1925, he was united in marriage with Vera Margaret Roberts at Wahoo, Nebraska. Mrs. Kelly, who is of German descent, was born at David City, Nebraska, June 29, 1903. They have two children: William L., born November 29, 1926; and James A., born February 27, 1929. Mr. Kelly, who is a Democrat, was elected police judge of Grand Island in 1931. Residence: Grand Island.

William Anthony Kelly

Director of education of Creighton University for the past two years, William Anthony Kelly was born at Harrison, New Jersey, August 9, 1900. He is the son of John Aloysius and Ellen Agnes (Brannin) Kelly, the former born at Newark, New Jersey, June 29, 1876, and the latter at Morristown, New Jersey, October 24, 1875.

He attended Holy Cross School at Harrison until June 1914, and was graduated from Harrison High School in June, 1918, whereupon he entered Seton Hall College at South Orange, New Jersey. He received his A. B. and A. M. from that college in 1923 and 1925 respectively, and his LL. B. from Fordham University in 1926. He was awarded a Ph. D. from New York University in 1929, and also attended Fordham Graduate School, Rutgers University and the College of the City of New York. He is a member of Phi Delta Kappa.

On August 6, 1927, he was married to Margaret Gertrude Reuther at Kearny, New Jersey. Mrs. Kelly was born at Harrison, New Jersey, July 4, 1902, and was a teacher prior to her marriage.

Mr. Kelly is a Democrat. He is the author of numerous educational articles in *The High School Teacher, Catholic School Journal, Catholic School Interests, Omaha School Forum*, etc. He attends St. Cecilia's Cathedral, and is a member of the National Educational Association and the Department of Superintendents. Residence: Omaha.

William J. Kelly

A leading business man of Wymore, Nebraska, William J. Kelly, was born April 21, 1876, in Peoria, Illinois, the son of John Edward Kelly and Esther Ann (Taylor) Kelly. John Kelly was born on the Isle of Man, on March 17, 1845, and was a tailor. He came to America in 1869, resided in Illinois for ten years and then came to Nebraska. Mrs. Kelly was born in England, July 31, 1851, and died at Monte Vesta, Colorado, October 18, 1929. Her parents came to America from England in 1871 and were very successful farmers.

William J. Kelly attended rural school and the Wymore, Nebraska, High School. He married Ida Rolena Paisley, (born in Dysert, Iowa, December 29, 1877) at Wymore, Nebraska, on February 8, 1899. To this union four children were born: Clarice, January 18, 1902, who is married to E. Lloyd Jones; Edna, July 14, 1903, now Mrs. Clifford Clark; Maude, June 26, 1908, the wife of T. Milton Lipscomb; and Harold, February 5, 1910, who died September 9, 1915. They have one adopted child, Billie, born May 10, 1920.

Since 1906 Mr. Kelly has been an implement dealer; formerly he was a farmer. For fifty-one years he has lived in Nebraska. His religious affiliation is with the First Baptist Church of Wymore.

He belongs to the Community Club, Independent Order of Odd Fellows, Rebekah Lodge and the Knights and Ladies of Security. He is a member of the Nebraskana Society and has been a member of the school board for twelve years. Mechanics is his avocation. Residence: Wymore.

Edwin Clair Kelso

Edwin Clair Kelso, secretary of the North Platte Chamber of Commerce, was born near Doniphan, Nebraska, August 12, 1884, son of Joseph and Mary Jane (Miller) Kelso. He of Scotch, Irish, and Dutch descent. His father served in the infantry during the Civil War. Upon moving to Nebraska he homesteaded in Hamilton County and later engaged in the broom manufacturing business at Grand Island, where he died in April, 1902. His mother resides in Pasedena, California.

Upon leaving school at Grand Island, Mr. Kelso became manager of the Nebraska Telephone Company there. He was afterward Nebraska State Fire Inspector, and manager of the Nebraska Telephone Company at McCook. After leaving McCook he was transferred to Omaha as district commercial agent for the Nebraska Telephone Company. He was thereafter district manager of the Equitable Life Association Company at McCook and secretary of the McCook Chamber of Commerce. He is a Republican.

On November 27, 1912, he was married to Mary Agnes Murphy at Cheyenne, Wyoming. She was born at Lincoln, Nebraska, June 29, 1883.

Mr. Kelso is a member of the Elks and the United Commercial Travelers. His hobby is fishing. Residence: North Platte. (Photograph in Album).

Edward L. Kemper

Since 1883 Edward L. Kemper has been a farmer and livestock feeder in Hamilton County. He was born at Lancaster, Wisconsin, June 27, 1859, son of George J. and Anna E. (Womelsdorf) Kemper.

George J. Kemper was born at Berleburg, Germany, June 14, 1823, and was a dyer in his native country. He came to America in 1847, settling in Philadelphia, and later removed to Wisconsin. He came to Nebraska in September, 1883.

He left Germany to avoid military training, and in Wisconsin took a leading part with others in building a church which they named the Liberty Ridge Church. He played an important part in the history of that state, and was a pioneer farmer in Nebraska. He died at Aurora, February 5, 1898.

Anna E. Womelsdorf was born in Berleburg, Germany. She was a well educated woman, and a devoted wife and mother. Her death occurred at Aurora, May 26, 1920.

Edward L. Kemper attended public and private schools, and soon thereafter entered farming in which he continued until his retirement. He has served as president of the Farmers Elevator Company at Aurora, as a member of the school board of rural district No. 77, and is a member of the Red Cross and the Federated Church of Aurora. He is also a member of the Modern Woodmen of America.

On December 19, 1883, Edward L. Kemper was married to Mary W. Althaus at Liberty Ridge. They left for Nebraska the same day, arriving at Aurora two days later, purchasing an 80 acre farm one and one-half miles west of Aurora. They have resided there continuously for forty-three years.

Mrs. Kemper, who was a teacher in the public schools, was born at Annaton, Wisconsin, March 31, 1862, of German parentage. Their children are: Clara M., born February 4, 1886; Alberta A., born October 4, 1887; Bessie M., born January 17, 1889, who attended the University of Nebraska one year; Clarence A., born December 10, 1890, who was first married to Mary Rockwell. They had one son, George W. She died May 16, 1923, and in 1927 Clarence married Marie Scott Torgensen. Walter L., was born October 31, 1895; and Carleton G., on February 20, 1898. Carleton married Miriam Hagelin. Clara married George H. Coy and has a son, George Walter. Albert married Claude Lantzer and has two children, Maurice Leon and Eileen Luree.

Bessie married Clarence Recknor and has three children, Edward E., Mary Elizabeth and Doris H.

Mr. Kemper is a Democrat and from 1923-25 served as a member of the Nebraska legislature. His hobby is hiking to the farm. He is a lover of trees, and woods in general. Residence: Aurora. (Photograph in Album).

William Kemper

William Kemper, who is a lifelong resident of this state, was born at Dorchester, Nebraska, April 17, 1873, the son of Wilhelm and Sophia (Baird) Kemper. His father, who was born at Sost, Germany, March 20, 1841, came to America in 1867 and three years later settled in Saline County, Nebraska, where he was a farmer at Dorchester until his death, May 16, 1909. His mother was born of Scotch parents at Springfield, Illinois, April 30, 1855, and died at Dorchester, June 1, 1919.

Mr. Kemper attended public and parochial schools at West Blue, Nebraska, and has been a farmer near Dorchester most of his life. He has served as a director of the local school board for three years, has been a member of the Maccabees since 1898, and plans to join the Saline County Historical Society soon. He is a member of the Nebraska Sportsman's Association, holds membership in the Nebraskana Society, and is a member of the German Evangelical Church.

On March 3, 1899, he was married to Lydia M. Johnson at Crete. Mrs. Kemper, whose ancestry was German, was born at Crete, July 27, 1880, and died at Dorchester, February 28, 1915. Two children were born to this marriage: Alvene W., April 28, 1900, who married Edith L. Mantey; Arthur J., July 16, 1902.

Of his marriage to Lillie Grace Younkin, which occurred at Dorchester, the following children were born: Evelyn L., April 10, 1917; Willard E., March 21, 1920; Orville C., June 23, 1923; and Lawrence B., August 21, 1926, who died December 5, 1931. Alvene is secretary of the Building & Loan Association of Grand Junction, Colorado, and Arthur is a farmer at Julesburg, Colorado. Residence: Dorchester.

George Edward Kennedy

Born at Oakland, California, October 19, 1881, George Edward Kennedy has been a resident of Nebraska for the past 48 years. He has three brothers, four half brothers and two sisters, of which two brothers and both sisters are living. His father, Charles Johnston Kennedy, was born at South Bend, Indiana, November 29, 1834, and died at Saint Edward, Nebraska, December 29, 1896. He served as manager of the Plasa Gold Mine in California, and was later a funeral director and retail furniture merchant. His ancestry was Scotch-Irish. His mother, Martha Jane (Kyle) Kennedy, was born in New York, November 25, 1851, and died at Saint Edward, Nebraska, November 30, 1906. She was also of Scotch-Irish descent.

Mr. Kennedy attended high school at Saint Edward for two years and upon the death of his father left school and began caring for the family. He is now the owner and operator of two service stations and a silver fox farm at Newman Grove. He is also the owner of two quarter sections of fine farming land. Mr. Kennedy is a member of the Odd Fellows and the Masons, is chairman of the Newman Grove Relief Committee, and is secretary of the Free Fair Board. He is affiliated with the Methodist Episcopal Church, and is serving as steward at this time. He is a director of the Co-operative Creamery Association of Newman Grove also.

He was married to Lillian Victoria Cain in Platte County, Nebraska, September 14, 1904. Mrs. Kennedy was born at Lindsay, Nebraska, August 9, 1886, and died at Newman Grove, July 12, 1924. She was the daughter

GEORGE EDWARD KENNEDY

of pioneer Nebraskans. Five children were born to them, Helen M., born September 26, 1905; George Edward, Jr., born January 16, 1911; Vivian L., born November 29, 1912; Thomas Cain, born October 12, 1914; and Margaret Lillian, born March 7, 1920.

On May 27, 1927, Mr. Kennedy married Esther L. Baker, the daughter of Charles and Ella (Hart) Baker who came to Nebraska in 1860. Mrs. Kennedy is a graduate of the University of Nebraska and was a teacher of mathematics for a period of ten years. She also served as principal of the Newman Grove High School from 1924 until 1927. They have a daughter, Ruth Marilyn, born June 14, 1931. George and Vivian manage their father's fox farm. Residence: Newman Grove. (Photograph on Page 641).

George Lincoln Kennedy

On December 17, 1861, George L. Kennedy was born at Brownville, Nebraska. His father, Stephen Wilkinson Kennedy, an ardent prohibitionist from the ranks of the Republican party, was a farmer and clergyman. He was born at Dayton, Ohio, June 12, 1816, and died at Auburn, September 1, 1903. He was of Irish descent. Eliza (Ware) Kennedy, mother of George L. Kennedy, was born in New Jersey, December 16, 1828. She was of English and Scotch descent, and during her early life was a teacher. She died at Brownville, May 13, 1911.

George L. Kennedy received his education in the public and high schools of Brownville. From early life he engaged in agricultural pursuits, and has been a successful farmer since early manhood. He has lived in Nebraska all his life, and is an extensive landowner in and around Brownville.

His marriage to Annie Isabelle Marsh was solemnized at Brownville, March 28, 1883. Mrs. Kennedy was born there on September 9, 1861, and died there on January 26, 1915. She was of English descent, coming from the line of John Marsh of Borton, England, who settled in America in 1635; her great-great grandfather, Jasper Marsh, was a soldier in the Revolution.

Of this marriage there are four children: Ethel, born May 19, 1884, who married Roscoe Russel Blankenship; Ilma, born December 3, 1886, who married Carl W. Biskel; Burtis, born October 12, 1890, and Cassius, born June 30, 1894, who married Ruth Anna Courtright.

Mr. Kennedy is a Bryan Democrat. For many years he has been active in the Masonic order, and is a 32nd degree member of the Scottish Rite body, a Knight Templar and member of the Shrine.

He is an earnest church worker, and is a member of the Peru Methodist Episcopal Church. He is a Kiwanian, and a member of the Nebraska Territorial Association. Residence: Brownville. (Photograph on Page 643).

Howard Kennedy, Jr.

Howard Kennedy, distinguished judge and lawyer of Nebraska, was born at Nebraska City, Otoe County, Nebraska, October 11, 1868, and has lived in this state all his life. His father, Howard Kennedy, who was born at Lansingburg, Rensselaer County, New York, August 14, 1832, and died at Omaha, Douglas County, Nebraska, April 18, 1905, was a prominent pioneer in the state. He served as the first superintendent of public schools at Omaha; the Howard Kennedy School of that city was named in his honor. He took an active part in the early settlement of Nebraska as receiver for the United States land office in Nebraska City and Lincoln; was secretary of the land department of the Union Pacific Railway Company; and was a member of the Omaha board of education, 1871-81. He was active in Presbyterian Church work throughout the state. His ancestry was Scotch and English; he was a descendant of Robert Kennedy of Ayrshire, Scotland, who settled in Maryland in 1755, and who was commander of a transport ship at the time of the French and Indian War.

His mother was born at Mount Joy, Lancaster County, Pennsylvania, July 31, 1836, and died at Omaha, December 22, 1905. She was graduated from the Cedar Hill Seminary at Mount Joy, and later taught an art class there. She was active in art and literary circles and in mission and church affairs. She was of English and German descent; one of her ancestors, George Long, came to America about 1760 settling first in Virginia and later moving to Mannhein, Pennsylvania, where his house, built of brick that was brought from England, still stands.

Judge Kennedy attended school at Omaha, and in 1885 was graduated from high school there. He was awarded the A. B. degree at Williams College in 1889 and the LL. B. degree at Washington University in St. Louis, 1891. He was editor of the Williams *Literary Monthly*, was president of the college literary society; was president of the junior class; and was valedictorian, 1891. He received Phi Beta Kappa membership and was elected to membership in the law fraternity, Phi Delta Phi.

He was admitted to the practice of law at Omaha, June 22, 1891 and continued in general practice until 1904 when he was elected judge of the 4th Judicial District of Nebraska. He held this position until 1913. He served as a member of the board of control of state institutions, 1913-17, acting as chairman of this board for two years; was a member of the Omaha board of public welfare, 1918-21; was chairman of the Nebraska Children's Code Commission, 1919-21; and in 1930 was defeated for clerk of the district court.

He resumed the practice of law December 1, 1930. He was vice-president of the Peters Trust Company from 1917-30. He is director of the A. Hospe Company, and is a trustee of the Forest Lawn Cemetery Association. During his service on the board of control he drafted and aided in the passage of laws providing for the commitment of feeble-minded persons to an institution, admission previously having been voluntary; a law requiring the payment of actual maintenance costs by persons who are able to pay their expenses in the state hospitals for the insane; and other laws affecting public welfare. These laws have proved a distinct benefit to the state.

Judge Kennedy was president of the Nebraska Conference for Social Work, 1914; is a member of the executive committee and is counsel for the Nebraska Humane Society; is vice-president of the Society for the Friendless; is a member of the executive committee of the Nebraska Civil Service Association; is on the executive committee of the Omaha Council of Social Agencies; was formerly a member of the board of governors of the Omaha Community Chest; and was formerly president of the Nebraska Child Labor Committee. He is a member of the American Bar Association, the Nebraska State Bar Association, and the Omaha Bar Association.

He holds membership in the Omaha Chamber of Commerce and the Ad-Sell League. He is on the executive committee of the American League of Good Will; is a member of the Nebraskana Society and the State Historical Society; was president of the Central High School Parent-Teachers' Association, 1926; was one of the incorporators of the University of Omaha, and was trustee of that organization for 21 years, having served as the first president of the board of trustees; and is president of the Omaha Chapter of the Phi Beta Kappa alumni.

He is a member of the American Academy of Political and Social Sciences and the National Geographic Society. He is an elder of the First Presbyterian Church of Omaha, and is a member of the advisory board of the Young Men's Christian Association. His social club is the University Club. During the World War he was a three-minute man and served as instructor of home service classes for the Red Cross. He is a Republican.

His marriage to Mary Radcliffe Cunningham was solemnized at Lincoln, Lancaster County, Nebraska, March 23, 1897. Mrs. Kennedy, whose ancestry is Scotch-Irish, English, and German, was born in Mifflin County, Pennsylvania, October 1, 1874. She is a church organist and is extremely active in music circles. She has always taken an active part in the civic and social affairs of Omaha, and holds membership in the following organiza-

GEORGE LINCOLN KENNEDY

Peterson—Auburn

tions: Tuesday Musicale; Friends of Music Club; Fortnightly Club; Nebraska Music Teachers' Association; P. E. O.; and Sigma Alpha Iota.

Four children were born to their marriage; Elizabeth, born September 29, 1902, who married Christian F. Dondore; Howard, III, born August 4, 1907, who is a law student; Anne, born April 8, 1910, who died February 25, 1916; and William Cunningham, born July 20, 1918. Elizabeth was graduated from the University of Nebraska with the B. F. A. degree in 1922, and took post graduate work at the New England Conservatory of Music in 1923. She is a church organist. Residence: Omaha.

James A. C. Kennedy

A native of Omaha, James A. C. Kennedy was born October 31, 1875, son of Thomas and Anna M. (Kennedy) Kennedy. Thomas Kennedy was a native of County Tipperary, born in 1843. He came to America when a young man, and served in the Civil War with Company K., 181st Ohio Volunteer Infantry. He was superintendent of the Willow Springs Distilling Company for many years, and died at Omaha, September 2, 1881. Anna M. Kennedy was born in County Tipperary, November 10, 1843. Left a widow with four small children, she reared and educated them all. She died at Omaha, August 15, 1917.

After being graduated from the Omaha public schools, James Kennedy attended Creighton College until fifteen years of age, when he entered the First National Bank of Omaha as a clerk. He later attended the University of Nebraska, and received his LL. B. in 1900. He was a member of Phi Delta Theta and Phi Delta Phi.

From 1900-01 he was a clerk with Montgomery & Hall, and from 1901-06 with T. J. Mahoney. In 1906 he entered the firm of Mahoney and Kennedy, continuing until 1917. Since the last mentioned date he has been a member of the law firm of Kennedy, Holland and DeLacey.

During his professional career he has been a member of the Nebraska House of Representatives, deputy county attorney of Douglas County, and from 1908 to 1916, Referee in Bankruptcy.

His marriage to Caroline Purvis was solemnized at Omaha June 1, 1905. Mrs. Kennedy was born at Omaha, June 1, 1886, and is of Scotch descent. There are three children, all of whom are attending college: Ann Marie, born January 29, 1910; Jean. born March 29, 1911, and James A. C., born September 27, 1913.

Mr. Kennedy served as first lieutenant, with Company G., 2nd Nebraska Volunteer Infantry in the Spanish-American War, and was judge advocate and ordinance officer of his regiment. During the World War he was on the appeal board at Omaha, and member of various draft boards in Douglas County. A Catholic, he is a member of St. Cecilia's Cathedral. He is a member of the American, Nebraska State and Omaha-Douglas County Bar Associations. His clubs are the Omaha Club and the Omaha Country Club, his sport is golf and his recreation is reading. Residence: Omaha.

James Madigan Kennedy

James Madigan Kennedy, dentist, was born at Caledonia, Haldimand, Ontario, Canada, son of Donald and Ellen (Madigan) Kennedy. His father is of Scotch, and his mother of Irish ancestry.

James Madigan Kennedy attended the public and high schools at Caledonia, and was graduated from Northwestern University at Evanston, Illinois, with the degree of Doctor of Dental Surgery. He has since been in active practice. He is a member of the American Dental Association.

On July 3, 1907, he was married to Adelaide Mary Forde at Chicago, her birthplace. There are five children, Mary A.; Jean V.; James F.; Ellen K.; and Virginia C.

Dr. Kennedy is a Democrat. He is a member of

Delta Sigma Delta fraternity, the Chamber of Commerce, and civic and fraternal organizations. Residence: Alliance.

John Lauderdale Kennedy

John L. Kennedy, one of Nebraska's foremost lawyers, was born in Ayrshire, Scotland, on October 27, 1854. At the age of 19 years he came to America, settling in LaSalle County, Illinois, where he farmed for four years. He is the son of John and Mary Barbour Kennedy, both natives of Scotland, who remained in the country of their birth. John L. Kennedy attended Uplawmoor public school, in Renfrewshire, Scotland, and after four years in America entered Knox College, but did not graduate. He has since received the honorary degrees of A. B., A. M., and LL. D. from that college; and LL. B. from the State University of Iowa.

On November 29, 1905, he was united in marriage to Marguerite Pritchett, daughter of George Edward and Harriet Georgia (Hanscom) Pritchett, at Omaha. (See *Nebraskana*). They have three children, John Hanscom, born October 12, 1906, and Edward Lauderdale, born May 3, 1908, both of whom attended the Hill School, at Pottstown, Pennsylvania, and Stanford University. Katharine Virginia, born December 2, 1914, attends The Bishop's School at LaJolla, California.

John L. Kennedy was admitted to the bar in 1882, and began active practice at Omaha. From 1888-1907 he was a member of the firm of Kennedy & Learned; and is now a member of the firm of Kennedy, Loomis & Offutt. In addition to his legal practice he has been prominent in Republican politics for many years. In 1905 he was elected to the 59th congress from the second district of Nebraska; from 1907-08 he was fire and police commissioner of Omaha. He served as chairman of the Republican state committee during 1911-12, and campaigned the state for woman suffrage in 1914. He was Republican candidate for United States Senator from Nebraska in 1916, and federal fuel administrator for Nebraska from October 17, 1917 to March 27, 1919.

He was president of the United States National Bank of Omaha from 1920-25, and president of the Omaha Chamber of Commerce from June, 1924 to June, 1925. He is counsel and a member of the board of directors of J. L. Brandeis and Sons and The Brandeis Investment Company. Mr. Kennedy is a Presbyterian. He is a member of the Omaha Athletic Club. Residence: Omaha.

Marguerite Pritchett Kennedy

Marguerite Pritchett, now Mrs. John L. Kennedy, is a native Nebraskan, born at Omaha, May 19, 1883. Her father, George Edward Pritchett, was born at Utica, New York, May 18, 1841. After serving as a lieutenant with the 126th New York Infantry he came to Nebraska, where he served as a member of the state legislature in 1877. He was city attorney of Omaha, and United States district attorney for Nebraska, appointed by President Cleveland. His father was the Reverend Edward C. Pritchett, born in India, on October 19, 1812. He came to America in 1833, and was graduated from Amherst College. He was ordained in 1848 and served as a chaplain in the Civil War.

George Edward Pritchett married Harriet Georgia Hanscom, who was born at Council Bluffs, Iowa, January 11, 1854. She was the daughter of Andrew J. and Catherine Ann (Young) Hanscom, who were married in Detroit, in 1848. Andrew J. Hanscom was born in Pontiac, Michigan, February 3, 1828, and served as first lieutenant of Company C., First Michigan Infantry, in the Mexican War. He came to Omaha in 1854, and was speaker of the first house of representatives of the Territory of Nebraska in 1855. In 1854 he was appointed colonel of the First Nebraska Regiment by Governor

Cuming. He gave the north thirty-five acres of Hanscom Park, which is named for him to the city of Omaha in 1872.

George Edward Pritchett died at Omaha on March 3, 1912, and Harriet Hanscom Pritchett died at Omaha on February 11, 1908.

Marguerite Pritchett was educated at the Academy of the Sacred Heart in Omaha, and the Masters School at Dobbs Ferry on the Hudson, New York. In 1905 she was married to John Lauderdale Kennedy at Omaha. (See Nebraskana.)

Mrs. Kennedy has been active in Republican politics for many years, and contributed liberally to the Nebraska Woman Suffrage campaign in 1914. During the World War she participated in Red Cross work, served on canteen committees and was chairman of the committee on Hospital Supplies at the Red Cross warehouse. She is an Episcopalian. Her social club is the Beach Club, at Santa Monica, California. Residence: Omaha.

James Rupert Kenner

James Rupert Kenner, bank executive and a leader in civic affairs, was born at Utica, Nebraska, July 17, 1895, and has spent most of his life in this state. His father, Dr. W. C. Kenner, who is a physician and surgeon at Glenvil, Nebraska, was born at Columbia City, Indiana, of German and Irish parents. His mother, who was a teacher before her marriage, was born at Bushnell, Illinois, and died at Utica, July 1896; her ancestry was French and English.

Mr. Kenner attended school at Utica, was graduated from the preparatory department of Bellevue College, and in 1917 was awarded the A. B. degree at the University of Nebraska. He was a student at the United States Naval Academy for a time, and later took up the study of law. He was active in basketball and football at Bellevue College and received letters in basketball and tennis at the University of Nebraska where he was a member of Phi Kappa Psi. He was elected to a commercial fraternity at Bellevue College.

His marriage to Dorothy Wetherald occurred at Hebron, Nebraska, September 22, 1920. Mrs. Wetherald was born at Hebron the daughter of Frank and Ivy (Green) Wetherald; her ancestry is English. She holds membership in the P. E. O., the D. W. Club, and the Hebron Woman's Club. Their children are: Margaret, born May 16, 1922; James Rupert Jr., born March 3, 1925; Ann Linwood, born November 9, 1927; and Jane, born March 12, 1931.

Mr. Kenner has held the following positions in the professional world; employee of the Lincoln State National Bank, 1919-20; teacher at Alexandria, Nebraska; superintendent of schools at Ririe, Idaho; assistant treasurer of the Puget Sound Power & Light Company of Wenatchee district, for six years; and since 1927, vice president of the Thayer County Bank at Hebron. He served as lieutenant junior in the United States Navy, in active duty for three years, and for several years has taken an active part in the affairs of the American Legion, in which he has been commander (at Hebron) and a member of the state committee for the department of Washington.

His membership in professional and civic organizations include Nebraska State Bankers Association; Chamber of Commerce; Red Cross; Kiwanis, in which he has been especially active; the actual organization of the National Geographic Society; and The Nebraskana Society. Mr. Kenner is a Scottish Rite Mason, is independent politically, and is affiliated with the University Club of Lincoln. His favorite sport is football. Residence: Hebron.

Bernard Vincent Kenney

A leading physician and surgeon in Dodge, Nebraska, is Bernard Vincent Kenney, who was born in Pocatello, Idaho, on July 13, 1896. His father is John Joseph Kenney, born in Roundout, New York, April 24, 1867, was a railroad engineer. His ancestors were Irish. He died in Pocatello on November 22, 1929.

Mary Honora (Moore) Kenney, born in Wood River, Hall County, Nebraska, is his mother. She is a direct descendant of Sir Thomas Moore.

Bernard Kenney was educated in the St. Joseph's parochial school in 1910, and then attended the Creighton University where he received the degree of Bachelor of Science in 1918, and Doctor of Medicine in 1922. He belonger to Phi Beta Pi.

Irene Cecilia Chapman, born in North Bend, Dodge County, Nebraska, on January 12, 1897, became Mr. Kenney's wife on August 22, 1923, in North Bend. To this union five children were born: Bernard Eugene, August 23, 1924; Jean Irene, December 28, 1925, who died August 31, 1928; Richard John, September 9, 1927; Jeannene Catherine, July 13, 1929, and Emmet Michael, January 13, 1931.

During the war Mr. Kenney was in the Student's Army Training Corps, and he is a member of the American Legion and the Red Cross. He is affiliated with the St. Joseph's Church and the Knights of Columbus. He holds membership in the Nebraska State Medical Association and in the Dodge County Medical Association. He is a Democrat, and a member of the Nebraskana Society. Mr. Kenney is interested in fishing and hunting. Residence: Dodge.

Walter J. Kent

Walter J. Kent, professor of biology at Hastings College, was born in America of English extraction. He attended public school and was a student at the University of Michigan and Wisconsin, receiving his degree of Bachelor of Arts from the former.

A resident of Nebraska for the past twenty years, Professor Kent has been a member of the faculty of Hastings College for some time, and is a leader in the educational field. He is unmarried. He has no political affiliation.

Mr. Kent attends the Methodist Episcopal Church of Hastings, is a member of the National Geographic Society, and was recently elected to life membership in The Nebraskana Society. Residence: Hastings.

Dallas E. Kepler

Dallas E. Kepler, merchant, was born at Argile, Wisconsin, January 9, 1882, son of John Adam and Flora Maria (Squires) Kepler. His ancestry is Scotch-Irish and German.

Mr. Kepler received his early education in public schools, and later attended the Shenandoah Business College at Shenandoah, Iowa.

On February 17, 1904, he was married to Stella Mae Miller at Doniphan, Nebraska. Mrs. Kepler was born at Reamsville, Kansas, October 25, 1882. There are two children, Florence, born May 3, 1906, who married Marvin J. McKole; and Velma, born April 27, 1905, who married Oscar W. Gilman.

Mr. Kepler has been a resident of Morrill County since 1910, when he homesteaded there. He enjoys hunting and fishing ond is much interested in geology, spending much time hunting for relics and arrow heads, soil formations and rocks.

A Republican, he is county commissioner of district

two of Morrill County, his term running from January 1, 1931 until 1935. For the past five years he has been engaged in the general mercantile business. He is a member of the Lions Club. Residence: Bridgeport.

Richard P. Kepler

Richard P. Kepler, prominent lawyer of Sidney, was born at Davenport, Iowa, May 10, 1872, son of John and Ann (Douglass) Kepler. His paternal ancestors were Dutch and German, who came to the United States about 1820, while his maternal ancestors are Scotch. His mother's ancestors came to the United States about 1760.

Mr. Kepler first attended the public schools of Davenport, Iowa, and in 1892 received the Bachelor of Science degree at Western College at Toledo, Iowa. In 1896 he received his Bachelor of Laws degree from the State University of Iowa.

On March 15, 1898, he was married to Bertha Davis at Gladbrook, Iowa. She was born at Garwin, Iowa, October 4, 1876. Three children were born to them, two of whom are living, Kenneth D., born December 15, 1902; Richard Gene, born February 7, 1905, who died April 6, 1928; and James Hollis, born April 1, 1908.

Since his admission to the bar, Mr. Kepler has been in active practice. From 1900 until 1906 he was county attorney of Tama County, Iowa, elected on the Republican ticket. From 1924 until 1927 he was county attorney of Cheyenne County, Nebraska, and for 8 years he has served as city attorney of Sidney.

From 1897 until 1900 Mr. Kepler was a member of the firm of Hitchcock & Kepler, and from 1922 until 1928 of the firm of Kepler & Kratz. From 1893 until 1898 he was a member of the Iowa National Guard.

Mr. Kepler's religious affiliation is with the Presbyterian Church. He is a member of the Ancient Free and Accepted Masons, the Odd Fellows, the Elks, the Sidney Chamber of Commerce, and the Sidney Country Club. He enjoys hunting, golf, and in his younger days was fond of football and baseball. His hobby is juvenile work. Residence: Sidney.

Ralph Bayard Keplinger

Ralph Bayard Keplinger, son of Emanuel and Margaret Rebecca (Gaskill) Keplinger, was born at Tecumseh, Nebraska, February 12, 1886. His father, a native of Lima, Ohio, was born August 21, 1844, of Pennsylvania Dutch ancestry. His family settled in Ohio about 1830. He was a rancher whose death occurred at Hay Springs, September 4, 1898. Margaret Rebecca Gaskill was born at Bluffton, Ohio, November 27, and died at Valentine, October 17, 1917.

Mr. Keplinger attended public school in Hay Springs, Nebraska, and was afterward a student at the Bradley Polytechnic Institute. At the present time he is the owner and operator of a jewelry store at Valentine.

On November 15, 1916, his marriage to Mildred Rose Dunn was solemnized at Valentine, her birthplace. She was born October 12, 1890, of English ancestry. There are two children, William Robert, born July 18, 1922; and Gretchen Jane, born November 1, 1923.

Mr. Keplinger is a Democrat. He is a member of the Masons and of the Cherry County Rifle Club. He enjoys outdoor life, especially hunting, fishing and shooting. Residence: Valentine.

William Raymond Kepner

William R. Kepner was born at Osceola, Polk County, Nebraska, August 8, 1900, the son of William Franklin and Lydia (Grindell) Kepner. His father, who was born at Port Royal, Pennsylvania, February 1, 1861, and died at Osceola, April 3, 1931, was superintendent of schools in Polk County from 1891 to 1895, and was engaged in the furniture business there; he was of Dutch descent. His mother, who was born at Platteville, Wisconsin, November 16, 1859, was a teacher in the Osceola High School for many years and helped organize the Woman's Club of which she is now a member. She is a direct descendent of Peter Cartwright, Sr., of Virginia.

Mr. Kepner was graduated from the Osceola High School in 1917, and was a student at the University of Nebraska for two years where he is a member of Sigma Alpha Epsilon. In 1917, he started in the furniture and undertaking business with his father, and is now sole owner and manager of the firm, W. F. Kepner & Son.

On August 11, 1926, he was united in marriage with Zella Olive Gillmor, at Denison, Iowa, where she was born May 12, 1902. Mrs. Kepner is a member of Kappa Alpha Theta, and Theta Sigma Phi, honorary journalistic sorority of the University of Nebraska, where she was awarded her A. B. degree in 1924. She is a member of P. E. O., the Daughters of the American Revolution, and the Legion Auxiliary. She is past president of the Osceola Woman's Club. Their daughter, Janet Louise, was born November 19, 1929.

During the World War, Mr. Kepner served as a private in Company D in the Student Army Training Corps at the University of Nebraska. He was a member of the home guard, and is now commander of William Wolfe Post Number 91 of the American Legion. He holds membership in the Funeral Directors' Association, the Nebraskana Society, University of Nebraska Alumni Association, and the Osceola Country Club. He was county chairman of the Red Cross in 1927, and chairman of the Osceola Chapter in 1928, is a 32nd degree Mason, and in 1928, was Master of Osceola Lodge No. 65, Ancient Free and Accepted Masons and a member of the Modern Woodmen of America.

His religious affiliation is with the First Presbyterian Church of Osceola. His favorite sport is golfing, while his hobby is philately. Residence: Osceola.

Robert Henry Kerkow

Robert Henry Kerkow, jeweler and engraver, was born in West Point, Nebraska, February 20, 1870. He is the son of John and Henriette (Brandt) Kerkow, both natives of Germany. His father was born in 1820, and came to America about 1868, settling in Nebraska. Here he farmed and followed the blacksmith's trade until his death in December, 1895. His wife was born on April 20, 1823, and died at Fremont, in February, 1907.

Mr. Kerkow attended public school and the School of Horology at Chicago. He has lived in Nebraska all his life, and for twenty-two years engaged in the jewelry business. For about twenty years he has engaged in the automobile, gas and oil business under the name of Kerkow & Ickman Company.

He is a Republican, and was city and school treasurer about nine years, and also served for a number of years as county supervisor. A Modern Woodman of America, and an Odd Fellow, he is also a member of the Sons of Herman, the Nebraskana Society, the Red Cross and the Community Club. He is fond of golf, hunting and fishing and is a member of the West Point Golf Club. His hobby is mechanics.

Mr. Kerkow was a charter member of the famous West Point band, organized by Professor Dusenberry 44 years ago. This organization has been playing since organized with practically the same personnel. C. Y. Thompson, and Rudolph Brazda are members and H. S. Radler is band leader.

Mr. Kerkow's wife, Mathilde Anne Kloeden, was born at Mayville, Wisconsin, April 20, 1871, and their marriage was solemnized there on August 28, 1895. There are two children, Winfred, born December 3, 1901, graduated from the University of Nebraska in 1924, and is a member of the

Delta Upsilon, and is now an efficiency expert with the Western Electric Company; Elsa, born September 12, 1906, graduated from University in 1927, and Pi Beta Phi, received Phi Beta Kappa honors at the University. Residence: West Point. (Photograph in Album).

Fred Heinrich Kerl

On May 30, 1867, Fred H. Kerl was born at Bocstedt, Hanover, Germany. He is the son of Heinrich J. and Lucie Anna (Harton) Kerl. Heinrich J. Kerl was born at Bocstedt, and died at Bruning, Nebraska, February 14, 1923. His grandfather served for eighteen years in the English Hanovarian Legion, and fought under Wellington at Waterloo. Lucie Anna Kerl was born at Duerte, Province of Hanover, Germany, December 7, 1836, and died at Danhollen, Germany, October 7, 1883.

He was united in marriage with Minnie Anna Kohlman at Bruning, Nebraska, February 25, 1892. She was born at Bloombury, Hanover Province, Germany, May 27, 1867, and died at Bruning, July 2, 1925. They had four children: William H., born August 20, 1892, who is married to Anna Wolken; Herman, born March 24, 1894, who is married to Frieda Middendorf; Lucie, born March 8, 1896, who is married to George R. Norder; and Nora, born August 18, 1904. All children live on farms near Bruning.

A Republican, Mr. Kerl served as committeeman for a number of years, and as precinct assessor for fourteen years. He has been a resident of Nebraska for forty-five years, and worked on a farm from 1886 to 1888. In 1889 he started farming for himself. Retiring in 1926, he moved to Bruning and became an insurance agent for several companies. He is director of the board of the Thayer County Insurance Company.

During the World War he served on various committees. He is affiliated with the Evangelical Lutheran Trinity Church at Bruning, and is a member of the Mission Board of the Central District of the American Lutheran Church. He served on his local school board until retiring, and is now a member of the board of the Hebron College and Academy. Reading and fishing are his favorite hobbies. Residence: Bruning.

Martin Edward Kerl

On November 10, 1866, Martin Edward Kerl was born at Omaha, Nebraska, the son of John and Caroline (Pfieffer) Kerl. John Kerl was born in Germany, and came to Nebraska in 1860. In 1866 he moved to Burt County and in 1890 to Cuming County where he engaged in farming until his death at West Point in 1892. His wife, Caroline, was born at Braunswei, Germany, and died at West Point, in June 1897.

Educated in country schools, Martin Edward Kerl has engaged in farming and as a hardware merchant for many years. He is a Republican, and has served as mayor of West Point, and as county supervisor and member of the board of education.

On February 23, 1888, he was married to Francis L. Ehrhardt at West Point. Mrs. Kerl was born in Jefferson City, Missouri, January 22, 1866, and died at Lincoln, November 24, 1926. There are three children, Walter Albert, born December 15, 1888, who married Lillian Chambers; Karl Konrad, born August 4, 1891, who married Rose Givens; and Eva Caroline, born November 26, 1893, who married Loring E. Gunderson. The two sons are jewelers, and Loring E. Gunderson is finance secretary of the University of Nebraska.

Mr. Kerl is a Protestant, a member of the Chamber of Commerce, the Sons of Herman and The Nebraskana Society. He is also a Mason and Shriner, and an Odd Fellow. His sports are hunting and fishing. Residence: West Point.

James Washington Kerns

James W. Kerns, executive and lumber dealer, was born at Ophir, Illinois, January 15, 1854, of Irish ancestry. He is the son of Peter and Margaret (Conlin) Kerns, both of whom are deceased. His father, a farmer, who was born in County Sligo, Ireland, in 1800, came to America in 1846. He died in LaSalle County, Illinois, in 1869.

Margaret Kerns, his mother, was born in County Mayo, Ireland, in 1815. She died in LaSalle County, Illinois, in 1895.

On December 25, 1879, he was united in marriage with Alice Josephine Crowley, at Mendota, Illinois. To this marriage was born the following children: Edward Mark, born December 19, 1880, married to Pearl Shipply; Laura S., March 8, 1883, married Edward H. Ely; Henry Francis, September 11, 1885, died February 9, 1892; Thomas L., September 27, 1889; Albert B., June 15, 1891; James W., December 26, 1892; Lawrence, July 26, 1894; Harold P., May 3, 1898; Alice F., November 16, 1899; Kathryn, May 20, 1902; Emily, January 14, 1905; and Mercedes, May 6, 1907.

A Republican, Mr. Kerns was city clerk of Auburn, and was member of the Nebraska state legislature, 1903-05. He has been a resident of Nebraska since March, 1872, except for one year, and is at the present time president of the J. W. Kerns Lumber Company. He is a Catholic, and a member of St. Joseph's Church, at Auburn, and the Knights of Columbus. Residence: Auburn.

Theodore J. Kerr

Theodore J. Kerr, physician and surgeon, was born in Union County, South Dakota, September 8, 1879, son of John R. and Anna C. (Clark) Kerr. His father homesteaded in Union County, and was engaged in building and contracting.

Dr. Kerr attended country school in Union County and later the high school at Akron, Iowa, graduating in 1898. In 1900 he was graduated from Highland Park College, after completing an electrical engineering course. In 1908 he was graduated from the University of Nebraska, College of Medicine, and after graduation was appointed house physician and surgeon for the Methodist Hospital in Omaha, 1908-1909, receiving his diploma in 1909. Since June 13, 1909, he has been practicing in North Platte.

On August 30, 1911, he was married to Selma Anderson at Vermillion, South Dakota. She was born in Union County, August 24, 1882.

Mr. Kerr is a Republican. He is a member of Platte Valley Lodge No. 32, Ancient Free and Accepted Masons, a member of the Gothenburg Lodge of Perfection, and Hastings Consistory, and is a 32nd degree Scottish Rite Mason. He is also a member of the Euphrates Chapter No. 15 and past commander of the Palestine Commandery No. 13 Knights Templar, and a member of Tehama Temple of the Mystic Shrine at Hastings. He is a member of the Elks Lodge at North Platte, the Rotary Club of which he was president in 1924, and the American Legion.

During the late war he received his training in the infantry. He was offered a commission as first lieutenant at Fort Snelling, Minnesota, in 1917, was transferred and commissioned captain in the Medical Corps of the United States Army, and was stationed at Fort Riley, Kansas, and Camp Humphreys, Virginia. He received his honorable discharge March 20, 1919.

His hobby is big game hunting, and he is an expert rifle shot. He has participated in hunting trips in northern and western Montana, western Idaho, Wyoming, Colorado, southwestern Utah, and northern Arizona. Residence: North Platte.

Charles Vernon Kettering

Charles Vernon Kettering, chairman of the department of music of Doane College, was born at Oxford, Kansas, September 22, 1889. He is the son of George and Minnie (Matthews) Kettering, the former a native of Pennsylvania, born in 1847, who died at Lecompton, Kansas, in May, 1903. He was a clergyman with the degree of Doctor of Divinity, and was of Pennsylvania Dutch descent. His wife, Minnie, was born in Ohio, in 1857, of New England ancestry.

Educated in the public and high school of Lecompton, Mr. Kettering was graduated from the latter in 1907. He was an accountant for the Atchison, Topeka and Santa Fe General Offices at Topeka, 1909-15, he became director of music of Miltonvale, Kansas, College 1916-19. In 1920 he received his B. M. from the Kansas University School of Fine Arts, and served as director of music of Marion College, Marion, Indiana, 1920-22. Mr. Kettering was a member of the basketball team at the Topeka Y. M. C. A., 1909-12, and a letterman on the Kansas University Freshman basketball team in 1908.

Since 1922 he has been chairman of the department of music of Doane College, and a member and director of music of Crete First Congregational Church. He is a member of the Nebraska State Music Teachers' Association and past vice president; and is past president of the Nebraska Academy of Teachers of Singing. While at Kansas University he was a member of the Dramatic and Glee Clubs. He is a member of the Commercial Club at Crete, and of the Nebraskana Society.

On August 2, 1914, Mr. Kettering was united in marriage to Blanche Merle Meade, at Kansas City, Kansas. Mrs. Kettering was born at Holton, Kansas, July 18, 1889, the daughter of O. M. and Catherine (Clippinger) Meade. The former is a descendant of General Meade of the Revolution. Mrs. Kettering is a piano teacher, specializing in children's work. They have one daughter, Kathryn Ann, born May 7, 1915, who is a talented young musician. Mr. Kettering is a Republican. He is author of *Singing Analyzed for Student and Teacher,* (MS). Residence: Crete. (Photograph in Album).

Oliver Morton Keve

Pastor of the Methodist Episcopal Church at York, the Reverend Oliver Morton Keve has been a resident of Nebraska for the past twenty years. He was born at McLean, Illinois, December 25, 1877, son of Henry Alfonso and Amanda Adeline (Preshaw) Keve. His father, a native of Allen County, Ohio, born June 20, 1837, is of French extraction. His death occurred at Abilene, Kansas, August 9, 1913. His mother, born of Scotch-Irish parents, at Woodsfield, Ohio, is living. She was born July 12, 1843, died February 7, 1932, at her home in Abilene, Kansas.

Dr. Keve received his Bachelor of Philosophy degree from the University of Chicago, his Master of Arts degree from the University of Denver, and his Doctor of Divinity from Nebraska Wesleyan University. His fraternities are Phi Beta Kappa and Pi Gamma Mu.

On June 7, 1916, he was united in marriage to Vera A. Moore, at Omaha. To them were born three children, John Moore, July 16, 1917; Grace Preshaw, November 23, 1919, and Miriam Latourette, June 20, 1921. There is one son, Paul Willard, born October 5, 1913, of a former marriage.

During the World War Dr. Keve served overseas with the Young Men's Christian Association. He is a member of the Nebraska Conference of the Methodist Episcopal Church, and is a life member of The Nebraskana Society. Dr. Keve takes an active part in the civic and social affairs of his community and is particularly interested in the training of young people. Residence: York.

Albert Marshall Keyes

A pioneer lawyer and banker of Nebraska is Albert Marshall Keyes who was born at Nebraska City, Nebraska, December 7, 1868, the son of Stephen Kittridge Keyes and Esther Lacy (Edom) Keyes. His father, who was a farmer, was born at Gouverneur, New York, April 20, 1836, and died at Zion, Illinois, February 20, 1916; he served as county commissioner of Furnas County, Nebraska, and was a Civil War veteran, holding membership in the Grand Army of the Republic; his English ancestors came to Watertown, Massachusetts in 1634. His mother, who is of English descent also, was born at Griggsville, Illinois, October 23, 1845. She is active in church and Sunday School affairs and resides in Holbrook, Nebraska.

Mr. Keyes was graduated from the Cambridge High School in 1890 and in 1893 received the LL. B. degree at the University of Nebraska where he was president of the Maxwell Debating Club. He taught school for three years, was deputy county treasurer for four years, practiced law for four years and served as county attorney of Furnas County for two years. He has been engaged in the banking business for the past 30 years at Holbrook, Nebraska.

He is a member of the Nebraska State Bar Association, the Nebraska State Historical Society, the Southwest Nebraska Historical Society, and the Nebraskana Society. He is a 32nd degree Mason and holds membership in the Red Cross and the Parent Teachers Association. His recreations are golfing and reading. During the World War Mr. Keyes acted as county food administrator for Furnas County, was chairman of the Third and Fourth Liberty Loan Drives, and held membership in the Four Minute Men Society. He is a Democrat.

His marriage to Elizabeth Wade Sipe was solemnized at Cambridge, Nebraska, December 25, 1895. Mrs. Keyes, who is of English and German descent, was born at Connellsville, Pennsylvania, July 24, 1873, and was a teacher prior to her marriage. Their children are: Charles S., born February 24, 1897, who married Katherine Cass; Mary E., born June 3, 1899, who married Burgess H. Orr; Evelyn W., born July 20, 1901, who married Cal D. Schulz; Albert Marshall, born September 27, 1906; John Rolland, born April 14, 1909; and Elizabeth, born November 7, 1912. Residence: Holbrook.

Edwin Randall Keyes

Edwin Randall Keyes was born at Milford, Nebraska, January 9, 1871, son of Stephen Kittredge and Esther Lacy (Edom) Keyes. The father, who was a farmer and stockraiser, was born at Gouverneur, New York, April 20, 1836, and died at Zion City, Illinois, February 3, 1916. He served in Company L, First Iowa Cavalry during the Civil War and was commander of the Grand Army of the Republic Local Post of Cambridge Nebraska for several years. His parents were Joel and Susan (Kittredge) Keyes. He is descended from one of two brothers, Solomon and Robert Keyes, who came from England to Chelmsford, Massachusetts about 1650. Joel Keyes died 1875, and his marking in the Cambridge Cemetery at Cambridge is the oldest one there.

Stephen Kittredge Keyes was chief bugler of the Cavalry and was with his regiment in the following engagements: Prairie Grove, Lone Jack, Montevallo, Clear Creek, Van Buren, Chalk Bluffs, Brownville, Cape Girardeau, Bayou Metoe, Little Rock, St. Francis River, Jenkens Ferry and Prairie Danna. On May 4, 1865, he was detailed as a clerk in the mustering office in Memphis, Tennessee, and was mustered out on December 4, 1865.

Mr. Keyes received an academic education. His wife, who was born at Griggsville, Illinois, October 23, 1845, resides at Cambridge at the present time. Her family came from England to Canada in 1830, and to the United

States in 1834, settling at Scott Falls, in Morgan County, Illinois. Her father, John Edom, was born in Yorkshire, England, December 28, 1806. He married Emeline W. Draper and died on December 12, 1899.

Edwin Randall Keyes attended early pioneer schools and was a student at Cambridge (Nebraska) High School, for a time. He served as secretary of the Farmers Elevator of Cambridge for thirteen years, has been a member of the board and president of the Cambridge Sales Barn for the past twelve years, and is connected with the Cambridge Co-operative Oil Company. A Democrat, he served as county commissioner several years, was state hail adjuster, precinct assessor at Cambridge, and Democratic committeeman ten years.

As the oldest resident of Cambridge, Mr. Keyes has been a loyal and progressive promoter of civic projects during the past thirty years, and still thinks Furnas County is the best part of the state. He is a member of the Nebraska State Historical Society, the South Western Nebraska Historical Society and was the first president of the Furnas County Old Settlers Organization. For the past four years he has been a member of the Furnas County Farm Bureau, and at the present time is serving as director of the Furnas County Fair Board. He holds membership in the Cambridge Community Club (board member and former president), the Red Cross, the Modern Woodmen of America and the First Congregational Church.

Mr. Keyes is vitally interested in history, especially of the state and community, and spends much time reading. During the World War he was a three minute speaker and active in Red Cross and loan drives. His sports are swimming and baseball.

His marriage to Christine Josephine Thompson occurred at Cambridge on October 23, 1895. Mrs. Keyes, whose parents came to the United States from Norway in 1860, settling in Illinois, was born at Capron in that state on June 26, 1871. She came to Cambridge in May, 1880. Mr. and Mrs. Keyes have a daughter, Esther Emma, born October 13, 1897, who married Harold Glenn Fee, October 23, 1919. Esther was graduated from Cambridge High School in 1916, attended the University of Nebraska in 1917, and taught school for two years. She is a member of the Order of Eastern Star and the Congregational Church. She was the first president of the local unit of the American Auxiliary, and is now vice president of the 9th district of the latter organization.

Mr. and Mrs. Keyes reside on their farm of 360 acres, two miles northwest of Cambridge. They have in their home all modern conveniences.

Harold Glenn Fee, husband of Esther Emma Keyes, enlisted in the Medical Corps of the United States Navy on May 31, 1918, at Denver, Colorado. He took his training at Goat Island, California, and served at Mare Island, California, and Bay Ridge, New York. He made one trip to Brest, France on the *U. S. S. President Grant*. He served at Base Hospital at Norfork, Virginia, where he was discharged on October 4, 1919. He held the rating of hospital corpsman first class.

Mr. Fee is a farmer and stock raiser and in partnership with his father-in-law. He is a member of the Congregational Church, the Masonic Lodge, and has held all offices of the American Legion Post at Cambridge No. 199. In 1928 he was elected commander of the 9th district of the American Legion Department of Nebraska for a term of two years. He was again reelected for another term in 1931.

Mr. and Mrs. Fee have two children, a son, Harold Glenn, Jr., born October 25, 1921; and a daughter, Margaret Esther, born November 3, 1924. Both attend the Cambridge Public School. Residence: Cambridge. (Photograph in Album).

George A. Keyser

George A. Keyser was born at Omaha, July 3, 1889.

He is the son of John and Elizabeth (Murphy) Keyser and has been a life resident of the city. John Keyser was born at Philadalphia, Pennslyvania, April 2, 1858, and was in the railway mail service at the time of his death at Omaha, July 8, 1922. Elizabeth Keyser was born in Cook County, Illinois, October 29, 1860.

Mr. Keyser attended Creighton University, where he received the degrees of A. B., A. M. and LL. B. Upon his admission to the bar in June, 1913, he took up the active practice of law, in which he was engaged until 1917. He was first lieutenant, 18th U. S. Infantry, First Division, from 1917-19. During 1919-21 he was government attorney, Virgin Islands, which were purchased from Denmark in 1917, and since 1921 has been assistant United States attorney at Omaha.

His marriage to Anna Marie Bennewitz was solemnized at Omaha, July 30, 1920. Mrs. Keyser was born at Grand Island, July 4, 1890. There are six children: Mary Dorothy, born April 11, 1921; Rite Jean, born November 15, 1922; George A. Jr., born May 3, 1924; John J., born May 11, 1926; Mary Margaret, born December 22, 1927, and Richard F., born September 11, 1929.

He is a Republican, a member of the Knights of Columbus, the American Legion and of St. Cecilia's Cathedral. He also holds membership in the American, Nebraska State and Omaha-Douglas County Bar Associations. Residence: Omaha.

Albertus Homer Kidd

Albertus Homer Kidd, distinguished lawyer at Beatrice, Gage County, Nebraska, was born at Ada, Ohio, March 19, 1863, the son of Jeremiah Wesley Kidd and Elmira Vandora (Lillibridge) Kidd. His father, who was a clergyman, was born at Marietta, Ohio, December 24, 1822, and died at Ohio, Bureau County, Illinois, June, 1912; his grandfather, who was English, lived in southwestern Pennsylvania during the Revolution and later moved to Marietta.

His mother, who was born near Athens, Ohio, October 21, 1829, and died at Princeton, Illinois, December 22, 1896, was actively interested in religious education and during the latter years of her life was a minister. Her grandfather, Thomas Lillibridge, of the fourth generation before herself, came from England and settled at Newport, Rhode Island, in 1699, where he was one of the founders of Trinity Church, the oldest religious institution in the state. Her maternal grandfather, Thomas Mansfield, was a soldier in the Revolution.

Albertus Homer Kidd received his early education in the public schools of Indiana and Illinois, and in 1884 was graduated from Giddings Seminary. Prior to his college work he was a teacher in the public schools of Illinois; he studied law at Monmouth in Illinois until his admission to the bar in 1887. He began the practice of law at Alma, Nebraska, in 1887, and in 1891 moved to Beatrice where he practiced continuously until 1928 when he retired to devote his time, for the most part as general counsel for the State Savings and Loan Association. He was engaged in independent legal activities until 1909, when he became a member of the firm Rinaker & Kidd; a little later the firm became Rinaker, Kidd & Delehant. He is now attorney for and president of the State Savings & Loan Association at Beatrice, is a member of the Young Men's Christian Association, and holds membership in the national, state, and county bar associations.

In 1904 Mr. Kidd served as editor of the *Beatrice Daily Express*. A Republican, he served two terms as city attorney, was a member of the board of education for six years, and was a member of the library board, for twenty years. His hobby is farming; he served as the first president of the Gage County Crop Improvement Association, now called the Gage County Farm Bureau. He is a member of the Red Cross, and during the World War was food administrator for Gage County. His favorite sport is golfing.

He was united in marriage with Sarah Elizabeth Gilliland, October 10, 1888, at La Harpe, Hancock County, Illinois. Mrs. Kidd, whose ancestry is English, was born at Littleton, Illinois, December 10, 1862, and died at Beatrice, June 10, 1926. They have two daughters: Dora Aldona, born January 18, 1890, who married Harold E. Shelley; and Norma Josephine, born January 12, 1893, who married Roy M. Green. Both daughters are graduates of the University of Nebraska and now live in Lincoln. Residence: Beatrice.

Grace Geneva Kidder

Grace Geneva Kidder, clubwoman, educator, and music teacher, was born at Weeping Water, Nebraska, November 11, 1897, the daughter of Thomas Fremont and Mary Louise (Hobson) Jameson. Her father, who was born at Warren, Ohio, April 2, 1858, is an architect and contractor who resides at Lincoln, Nebraska; he built and planned over half of the buildings of Weeping Water. Her mother, who was a club librarian for a number of years, was born at Mount Pleasant, Nebraska, April 15, 1864, and died at Lincoln, January 29, 1925.

Mrs. Kidder was graduated from the Weeping Water High School in 1917, received the A. B. degree at the University of Nebraska in 1921, and attended Columbia University in New York, 1926. She was valedictorian of her high school graduating class and was a member of Kappa Phi at the University of Nebraska. She taught at University Place, Nebraska, during 1921 and 1922, and was a teacher in the high school at Sargent, Nebraska, from 1924 to 1928.

She is affiliated with the Methodist Episcopal Church of Sargent, holds membership in the Order of Eastern Star and the Nebraskana Society, and was formerly county president of the Woman's Club. She likes to hike, and her chief interest is music. Politically, Mrs. Kidder is a Democrat.

On December 28, 1927, she was married at Murray, Nebraska, to William Ralston Kidder, who was born at Elmo, Missouri, January 18, 1893, of Dutch ancestry Mr. Kidder is manager of the Dierks Lumber and Coal Company of Sargent. Residence: Sargent. (Photograph in Album).

Henry Grant Kiddoo

Henry G. Kiddoo was born on a farm in Mercer County, Illinois, November 17, 1865, the son of William and Mary Appaline (Edgar) Kiddoo. His father, who was a farmer, was born in Lawrence County, Pennsylvania, July 26, 1841, and died on a farm in Adair County, Missouri, December 20, 1914; his Scotch grandparents were born in Pennsylvania early in 1800. His mother was born in Lawrence County, Pennsylvania, October 20, 1848. She was a farm woman who reared 9 children to maturity; eight children are still living.

Mr. Kiddoo, who has lived in Nebraska for the past 32 years and is a prominent business man at Omaha, Douglas County, Nebraska, attended district school and took a short course in a business college. He is now treasurer and local manager of the Byers Brothers Company, Livestock Commission Corporation. A Republican, he served two terms as clerk of Logan County, Kansas, 1892-96. He was a former member of the Omaha board of education, and is a member of the Omaha Chamber of Commerce, the Red Cross, and the Nebraskana Society. A 32nd degree Mason, he is also a member of the First Christian Scientist Church of Omaha. His hobby is old fashioned fiddling.

On April 13, 1887, he married Nora Alma Dodson at Joy, Illinois. Mrs. Kiddoo was born on a farm in Henderson County, Illinois, November 25, 1869. They have two children: Guy C., born February 26, 1889, who married Helen Sorenson; and Edgar D., born July 5, 1895, who married Esther Todd. Guy C. is an assistant vice president of the First National Bank of Chicago. Edgar D. is connected with the American Union Life Insurance Company of Omaha. During the World War Mr. Kiddoo served as a member of the Home Guards of Nebraska. Residence: Omaha.

Doane Fred Kiechel

Doane Fred Kiechel, lawyer and publisher, was born at Johnson, Nebraska, June 16, 1900. The son of Fred and Emma Alvina (Donze) Kiechel, his father a native of Alsace, Germany, born January 10, 1856. A farmer and business man, he has banking and grain elevator interests, and has always been prominent in Republican state and local politics. Coming to America in 1860, he settled immediately in Nebraska, where he was identified with every worthwhile pioneer movement.

Emma Alvina Donze, born at Bascow, Illinois, May 14, 1861, traces her ancestry to the nobility of France. Her family was among the first settlers of the French colony at Rock Creek in southeast Nebraska. She underwent the rigors of early pioneer life in the state, and recalls many of the early hardships incident to life here in the first days of the state. At the present time she is active in club, church and social life, and is president of the Cemetery Association and others.

Educated in the Clifton School at Johnson from 1906-1913, Doane Fred Kiechel was graduated from the 11th grade at Johnson High School in 1916, and the 12th grade at Auburn High School in 1917. A student at the University of Nebraska from 1917-22, he was graduated from its law school with the Bachelor of Laws degree in 1922. A member of Phi Alpha Delta, he served as its marshal, and was chief justice of The Squires (senior law organization). He was on the staff of the junior play, on the staff of the Awgwan and was president of his senior law class.

On June 16, 1923, Mr. Kiechel was united in marriage to Mary Elizabeth Boyd at Trenton, Nebraska. Mrs. Kiechel, who was born at Yuma, Colorado, is a graduate of Peru State Teachers College and the University of Nebraska, and a successful high school teacher. She is of Scotch-Irish and German descent. Their three children are: Barbara Donze, born at Superior, February 1, 1925; and Doane Frederick and Donna Elizabeth, twins born at Superior December 20, 1927.

A Republican, Mr. Kiechel has never been a candidate for elective office, but served two terms as city attorney of Superior, by appointment.

A member of the firm of Reeker and Kiechel, lawyers, at Norfolk, from 1922-24, he has been a member of the firm of Agee, Kiechel and Boyd, from January, 1924, to date. From March 10, 1926, to September 1, 1930, he edited the Superior Express. Among his contributions to literature are Four Years in the Saddle (poetry and prose); A Bird's Eye View of the American Bankruptcy Law; The American Flag, besides various poems and short stories.

During the World War Mr. Kiechel was a private in Company C., Student's Army Training Corps of the University of Nebraska, and at the present time he holds the rank of second lieutenant in the Infantry Reserves, and is on the executive board of the American Legion. A former member of the district, state and national bar associations, he is present member of the National Editorial Association, the Nebraska Press Association, and is past president and present counsellor of the Southern Council of the Nebraska Press Association.

In March, 1931, Mr. Kiechel retired from three years service as secretary and treasurer of the Superior Chamber of Commerce. Since he joined the Kiwanis Club in 1924 and is now its secretary. A Mason, he is a member of the York Rite bodies, and is past master of his lodge.

Townsend—Lincoln

ITA ELIZABETH CASEY KIECHEL

He is also an Elk and a Yeoman. Since the organization of the Superior Historical Society he has been secretary of that body, and since 1928 has been a member of the Superior Library board. A member for some years of the Superior University Club, Mr. Kiechel is past president and present secretary of the club. His religious affiliation is with the Methodist Episcopal Church. He is interested in all sports as a fan, but not as a participant. Residence: Superior.

Ita Elisabeth Casey Kiechel

Ita Kiechel was born at Johnson, Nemaha County, Nebraska, October 19, 1886, the daughter of Daniel and Laura Clementine (Noland) Casey. Her father, who was born in Buchanan County, Missouri, October 13, 1853, and died at Johnson, Nebraska, September 18, 1925, was a merchant and farmer. He organized and was the first president of the First National Bank at Johnson; and was a member of the county board of commissioners for several terms. His parents came from County Cork, Ireland, and died in America leaving him an orphan when he was two years old, after which he made his home with the Patrick family, pioneers of Holt County. An uncle, Thomas Landers, was a bishop in the Roman Catholic Church.

Her mother, who was born in Holt County, Missouri, August 10, 1856, was descended from the Noland family who came to Missouri from Kentucky with Daniel Boone. Delilah Briggs, mother of Laura, traced her ancestry to a pre-Revolution family in Maryland.

Mrs. Kiechel received her elementary education in the Johnson public and high schools, and was graduated in 1905 from the Nebraska Wesleyan University and taught in Sedalia College of Music at Sedalia, Missouri; and taught in the Jefferson City High School, Jefferson City, Missouri. From 1905-07, 1907-09 she was head of the department of expression of Cotner College, Lincoln, Nebraska.

She married Walter Kiechel at Johnson, Nebraska, June 30, 1909. Mr. Kiechel, who is a farmer, was born at Johnson, September 1, 1886. (See *Nebraskana*). There are three children: Mary Elizabeth, born August 8, 1910, a graduate of Nebraska Wesleyan, who teaches at Brock, Nebraska; Frederic Casey, born April 23, 1916; and Walter, Junior, born August 3, 1920. The two boys are in public school.

She is chairman of the drama division of the Nebraska Federation of Woman's Clubs; and is now president of the first district of this organization. Her political preference is the Republican Party. She is a member of the Methodist Episcopal Church of Johnson, Nebraska, a number of social and fraternal societies, and a member of the Nebraskana Society. Residence: Johnson. (Photograph on Page 651).

Walter Kiechel

On September 1, 1886, Walter Kiechel was born at Johnson, Nemaha County, Nebraska. His father, Frederic Kiechel, was a pioneer farmer and business man of western Nemaha County, and was vice president of the First State Bank. He is descended from a German family who traces its history to the 11th century. Born at Alsace, Germany, January 10, 1856, he came to America with his widowed mother when he was but three years of age. Arriving in Cass County they came to Nemaha in 1862.

Emma Alvina (Donze) Kiechel, mother of Walter, was born at Hancock, Illinois, May 14, 1860. She was a member of a French family who came to America a few weeks before her birth. The Donze family came to Nebraska in 1867 and became a part of the French colony in northern Nemaha County.

Mr. Kiechel, who is a farmer in Nemaha County, was educated in the country school and the public school at Johnson, and later was graduated from the high school at Auburn, Nebraska in 1903. In 1908 he was graduated from the Nebraska Wesleyan University with his A. B. degree. From 1904 to 1906 he served as principal of the Johnson (Nebraska) schools; and from 1908 to 1911 was superintendent of schools at Tecumseh, Nebraska. A Republican, Mr. Kiechel was a member of the Nebraska senate from 1913-17; was candidate for lieutenant governor in 1916; and was candidate for Congress, from the first district, in 1928. A resident of Nebraska all his life he has been a farmer and stockman since 1911.

He was united in marriage with Ita Elisabeth Casey, at Johnson, June 30, 1909. Mrs. Kiechel was born at Johnson, October 19, 1886, and is a member of one of Nemaha County's prominent pioneer families. They have three children. Mary Elisabeth, who was born August 8, 1910, was graduated from Nebraska Wesleyan in 1930 and is teaching in the high school at Brock, Nebraska. Frederic Casey, was born April 23, 1916. Walter, Junior, was born August 3, 1920.

Mr. Kiechel is a Mason, Shriner, and an Elk, and a charter member of the Kiwanis Club, at Auburn, Nebraska. He is a member of the Methodist Episcopal Church of Johnson, Nebraska. Residence: Johnson. (Photograph on Page 653).

Samuel Max Kier

Samuel Max Kier, son of Samuel K. and Minerva E. Kier, was born in Lincoln, September 19, 1895, and attended Lincoln High School and the University of Nebraska.

On July 4, 1918, he was united in marriage with Frances J. Duffy at Lincoln. They have one daughter, Mary Frances, who was born August 3, 1919. Mr. Kier is a Republican, and has been prominent in Nebraska politics for several years. He was a member of the house of representatives during the sessions of 1927, 1929 and 1931; during the 1931 session he was elected speaker of the house.

During his various political campaigns Mr. Kier has not neglected his law practice, and he has a wide reputation as a capable and conscientious member of the bar. He is a member of the law firm of Perrin & Kier, with offices at 502 Little Building, in Lincoln, at present.

For the duration of the World War Mr. Kier served as a lieutenant in the Air Service. He is a member of the American Legion, the Presbyterian Church, Cosmopolitan Club, and the Elks. A Mason, he is a member of the Scottish Rite and Shrine.

Mr. Kier has been active in supporting the Lincoln Chamber of Commerce for a number of years. He holds membership in the Lancaster County Bar Association and the Nebraska State Bar Association. Aviation is his hobby. Residence: Lincoln.

Theodore Alexander Kiesselbach

Theodore Alexander Kiesselbach, educator at the University of Nebraska, was born in Polk County, Nebraska, March 14, 1884, the son of Alexander and Caroline (Bayrhoffer) Kiesselbach. His father, who was a farmer, was born in Germany and died at Shelby, Nebraska, in 1887. His mother was born in Germany and died at Lincoln, Nebraska, in 1901.

Dr. Kiesselbach attended the public schools of Michigan and Nebraska, and in 1903 was graduated from the Lincoln High School. He received his A. B. degree at the University of Nebraska, 1907; B. S., 1908; A. M., 1912; and Ph. D., 1919. He is a member of Sigma Xi, Gamma Sigma Delta, Alpha Zeta, and Phi Sigma.

He was an instructor at the University of Nebraska in 1909, and since 1912 he has been professor of agronomy at that institution. He is the author of several experiment station bulletins and articles published in technical journals pertaining to crop production and improvement. He holds membership in the American Association for the Advancement of Science, the American Society

WALTER KIECHEL

Townsend—Lincoln

of Agronomy, the Nebraska Academy of Science, and
the Nebraskana Society.

His marriage to Hazel Hortense Hyde was solemnized
at Lincoln, June 30, 1909. Mrs. Kiesselbach, whose
mother was born at Cornwall, Illinois, and whose father
was born at Sturbridge, Massachusetts, was born at
Park River, North Dakota, August 19, 1886. They have
four children: Theodore, born October 19, 1910; Max,
born November 18, 1912; Katherine, born February 25,
1922; and Helen, born November 22, 1923. The two boys
are students at the University of Nebraska. Residence:
Lincoln.

Hubert Leo Kildare

Hubert Leo Kildare, lumberman, was born at
Ogallala, Nebraska, March 5, 1892, son of John Joseph
and Mary Elizabeth (Kavanagh) Kildare.

His father, a native of County Mayo, Ireland, born
December 24, 1858, came to the United States in 1870.
He was a farmer until his death at Ogallala, Nebraska,
February 8, 1904. His wife, Mary was born in Arklow,
County, Wicklow, Ireland, May 24, 1870, and is still
living, and resides at Ogallala.

Upon the completion of his public school education,
Mr. Kildare attended business college. For the past
twenty-two and a half years he has been in the retail
lumber business, and at the present time is the owner
of the Kildare Lumber Company at Paxton.

On September 1, 1912, he was married to Christine
Meyer at Paxton, Nebraska. She was born there on
November 20, 1886, and is of German descent. She is
a member of St. Patrick's Church, and the American
Legion Auxiliary. Six children were born to them, five
of whom are living, Veronica, on January 30, 1915; Mary
Huberta, November 12, 1916; Hubert Bernard, November 17, 1919; Lawrence James, September 15, 1922, who
died August 8, 1925; Christine, April 28, 1926; and
Dorothy, born February 5, 1929.

Mr. Kildare is a Democrat. He was a private in
Company B, 355th Infantry during the World War,
and is a member of the American Legion. His religious
affiliation is with St. Patrick's Catholic Church. He is
a member of the Elks, the Knights of Columbus, the
Modern Woodmen of America, the Nebraskana Society,
the Hoo-Hoo Club, the Lumber Merchants Association,
and the Commercial Club. His favorite sports are fishing and hunting. Residence: Paxton.

Albert Henry Kilmer

Albert H. Kilmer was born at Bellvue, Nebraska,
August 25, 1869, the son of John H. and Emma (Hodgson) Kilmer. His father, a farmer, was born in Columbia County, New York, September 22, 1833, and died at
Winnebago, Nebraska, February, 1914; his ancestry was
German. His mother, who was of English descent, was
born at Winterset, Iowa, in 1847, and died at Persia,
Harrison County, Iowa, January 31, 1877.

Mr. Kilmer has lived in Nebraska for 30 years and
has always been vitally interested in the progress of his
community and state. He is a member of The Nebraskana Society, and is a Mason.

On April 16, 1895, he was married to Amelia Jane
Chapman at Yorkshire, Harrison County, Iowa. Mrs.
Kilmer, who was born at Florence, Nebraska, is of English descent. They have a son, James Cornelius, born
June 4, 1906, who married Helen Brassfield. Residence:
Winnebago.

George Monroe Kilmer

George Monroe Kilmer was born at Shunk, Sullivan
County, Pennsylvania, July 27, 1848, and died at Western, Saline County, Nebraska, on October 3, 1927. He
was the son of George and Hannah (Battin) Kilmer,
both pioneer settlers in the middle west. George Kilmer
a native of New York, was born March 9, 1813, and died

at Western, March 17, 1888. He was of German and
Irish descent. Hannah, his wife was born in Sullivan
County, Pennsylvania, November 12, 1816, and died at
Western, September 19, 1876. She was of Scotch and
Irish descent.

The earliest record of George Monroe Kilmer's public service was in 1862 and 1863 when at the age of fourteen, he carried mail from Canton in Bradford County,
Pennsylvania, to Eaglesmere on top of the Allegheny
Mountains. It is recorded that New Years Day of 1863
was the coldest on record at that time, and he made the
entire route which covered fifty miles, on that day.

It was on May 1 of that year that his parents, together with their two sons and two daughters left their
home and started by train for Pella, Iowa. It is a notable coincidence that the family reached Springfield,
Ohio, at the time Abraham Lincoln's body was lying in
state. However, George and his father were unsuccessful in an attempt to force their way to the bier before
their train started. The family crossed the Mississippi
on a steamboat, landing at Keokuk, where the father
purchased a farm near Galesburg. After five years
spent on this farm they moved to Nebraska, where the
father and his two boys homesteaded.

While living in Iowa Mr. Kilmer had met and wooed
Mary Jane Fisher, and they were married at Galesburg,
April 12, 1870. Mrs. Kilmer was born in Southport, Indiana, January 28, 1854. There are eight children of
this marriage, all of whom are living except one: Murry
Orran, born March 19, 1870, who married Jennie Olive;
Marion Adett Leslie, born November 27, 1872, who married Cora Alma; Clara May, born January 3, 1875, who
died June 25, 1877; Maurice Ithamer, born February 9,
1877, who married Elizabeth Cruckchank; Morton Trueman, born August 2o, 1879, who married Lydia Witt;
Milo Jethro, born January 20, 1883, who married Mabel
Francis Wilson; Myrtle Donzella, born February 5, 1886,
who married Earl Alexander Wintermute; and Mabel
Lillian, born January 29, 1890, who married Elra Wilson
Miner.

Shortly after their marriage, on the 13th day of May,
they arrived at Beatrice where they camped with hundreds of settlers. After securing maps at the government land office Pat Farrel, Charles Lee, Theodore
Kilmer and George Monroe Kilmer started for Nuckolls
County. While at Meridian they were warned to protect themselves against the Indians. On May 16 they
camped on Spring Creek, near Hebron, when they were
ordered back by soldiers, who told them they were in
danger of being scalped. While talking with the soldiers
there appeared to the north across the valley what appeared to be a string of covered wagons and horsemen,
which were ascertained to be men who had been searching for a horse which had strayed during a buffalo hunt.
After they had crossed Spring Creek our party found
themselves surrounded by thirty-five hostile Indians. At
the command of the sergeant the soldiers shot down their
horses for breast works. In the skirmish, which lasted
about an hour the sergeant wounded one Indian and
killed another, after which the Indians left.

Afterward Mr. Kilmer and his party drove down to
Spring Creek to prepare their dinner, and while so engaged Mr. Kilmer noticed something circling around the
vicinity of the direction the soldiers had taken. He asked
Mr. Correll, deputy surveyor of Nuckolls County, what
it was and he said it was elks playing. Later they learned
that the soldiers and Indians had had a fight. Mr. Correll directed the party to leave the creek and follow the
ridge back, for their own protection. As they were
making their way they perceived some objects but were
unable to tell whether they were the Indians or the
soldiers. They soon picked up the soldiers and took them
along, and shortly thereafter found out that they were
following the trail of the Indians. A little farther down
the ridge the soldiers left the wagons and went north to
Kiowa, while the wagons went on to the homestead of

Mr. Correll's father, where they remained for the night. Learning from the older Correll that there was danger from the Indians in the vicinity, all the settlers were called in and breastworks erected out of logs.

The next morning Mr. Kilmer's party drove back to Beatrice where maps of Saline County were obtained. They selected homesteads, and returned to Beatrice where they filed their homesteads in person, and on the night of the 25th of May they returned with their families and slept on their homestead which still remains a part of Mr. Kilmer's estate. The year of 1874 was known as grasshopper year, but the family survived all the hardships, and in 1877 purchased another farm and moved onto it in 1878. In 1880 Mr. Kilmer took the government census for North Fork Precinct, and was tax collector for the same territory in 1884. In 1884 he was elected to the Nebraska legislature, taking office in January 1885, under a Republican administration. From 1878 to 1920 he was a member of the school board, twenty years of which he served as treasurer, and the balance of the time as director. He was a member of the Friends Church, while in Pennsylvania, and holds membership in The Nebraskana Society, The Nebraska Territorial Pioneer Association and the Legislative League.

When Mr. Kilmer and his wife came to Nebraska in 1870 he owned a span of mules and their halters. Together they bought and paid for 680 acres of land, and at the time of his death he still owned 360 acres which still remains as his estate. (Deceased).

Mary Jane Kilmer

Mary Jane Kilmer, daughter of Elijah Redden and Mary Margaret (McFarland) Fisher, was born at Southport, Indiana, January 28, 1854. Her father was born at Indianapolis, May 20, 1826, and died at Beloit, Kansas, April 4, 1894. He was a farmer, and served with rank of corporal in the Union Army under General Sherman in the Civil War. His wife was also a native of Indianapolis, born April 24, 1834. She died there on March 16, 1866.

On April 12, 1870, Mary Jane Fisher was united in marriage to George Monroe Kilmer, at Galesburg, Iowa. Together they homesteaded in Nebraska, and to them eight children were born. Murry Orran, born March 19, 1870, who married Jennie Olive Thomas; Marion Adett Leslie, born November 27, 1872, who married Cora Alma Slifer; Clara May, born January 3, 1875, and who died June 25, 1877; Maurice Ithamer, born February 9, 1877, who married Elizabeth Gruikchank; Morton Trueman, born August 20, 1879, who married Lydia Witt; Milo Jethro, born January 20, 1883, who married Mabel Frances Wilson; Myrtle Donzella, born February 5, 1886, who married Earl Alexander Wintermute, and Mabel Lillian, born January 29, 1890, who married Elra Wilson Miner. A sketch of Mr. Kilmer's life appears elsewhere in this volume. He died at Western, October 3, 1927.

Mrs. Kilmer has been a resident and a leading citizen of her community for more than 60 years. She is a Methodist, and a member of The Nebraskana Society. Her hobby is reading. Residence: Western.

Maurice Ithamer Kilmer

A lifetime resident of Western, Nebraska, Maurice I. Kilmer was born there on February 9, 1877, the son of George Monroe and Mary Jane (Fisher) Kilmer. His father, a farmer, was born at Shunk, Pennsylvania, July 27, 1848, and died at Western, October 3, 1927; he served as state representative in 1884-85. His mother was born of German and Scotch parentage at Southpert, Marion County, Indiana, January 28, 1854.

Mr. Kilmer attended the rural schools of Saline County and was a student at Western High School. He received his B. S. D. degree at McPherson College,

Kansas, where he was a member of the Irving Memorial Literary Society and the debating team. For five years he taught school; was director of the Western State Bank, 1916-26; and has been president of the Western Elevator Association for about 13 years.

His marriage to Elizabeth Cruckshank was solemnized at Lincoln, November 30, 1910. Mrs. Kilmer, who is of Scotch and English descent, was born at Elgin, Morayshire, Scotland, September 29, 1881. Their children are: Mary Elizabeth, born May 29, 1912; Donald Monroe, born January 31, 1914; Kathryn Elain, born April 11, 1916; and Helen Dale, born February 9, 1919.

Mr. Kilmer is vice president of the Community Club at Western; is president of school district number 106; and is financial secretary of the Methodist Episcopal Church at Western. He is a Democrat and holds membership in The Nebraskana Society. Residence: Western.

Charlotte Anne Wands Kilpatrick

Charlotte Anne Wands Kilpatrick was born at Newark, New York, November 8, 1852, and came to Nebraska in 1869 during the sod-house period.

Her father, Joseph S. Wands, was born in New York State, July 18, 1822, and moved to Illinois in 1854, settling in Marshall County, near Peoria. He homesteaded in Nebraska near Hebron in 1859 and died at Alexandria, May 9, 1890. He was of English and Scotch descent and was deacon at the Baptist Church at Alexandria during his entire lifetime. His wife, Elizabeth, was a dressmaker and the owner of a millinery store. She was born May 28, 1827, in New York State, the daughter of Herman and Ann Henderson and died at Alexandria, February 9, 1903.

Mrs. Kilpatrick was educated in the public schools of Lincoln, Illinois, and on March 14, 1875, was married to Henry Clay Kilpatrick in their neighborhood church and school building. Mr. Kilpatrick was born in Missouri, August 23, 1851, and died on his farm May 11, 1902. He was of Irish descent, the son of Samuel and Rachel (Thompson) Kilpatrick.

The following children were born to Mr. and Mrs. Kilpatrick, David Samuel, April 22, 1876; William Judson, January 18, 1878; Mark Nobel, September 21, 1879, who died August 4, 1884; Rebecca Rachel, August 14, 1881; Abraham, March 17, 1883, who died in infancy; Zada L., born March 13, 1885, who married J. T. McCuiston; Herman Roscoe, September 14, 1887; Leah Mabel, July 29, 1888; Dora Belle, April 20, 1890; Vesta Rebecca, born September 4, 1892; Ruth Charlotte, born December 29, 1894; and Nellie May, born September 22, 1898, who died March 19, 1931.

David Samuel, who is a farmer and rancher married Laura Hoiser. William Judson married Daisy Hoiser, and he is a rancher. Rebecca Rachel married Vern Worthen who is a farmer. Herman is a hotel man and is married to Roxie Scholle. Leah is a stenographer in Beatrice in the firm of Kilpatrick Contracting Company. Dora Belle married Roy Scoville, a hotel man. Vesta Rebecca is a postal clerk at Hebron. Ruth was a teacher before her marriage, and is married to O. H. Doyle, an attorney at Fullerton. Nellie May married Raymond Smith, an undertaker at Omaha. Mrs. Kilpatrick has twenty-nine grandchildren and thirteen great-grandchildren. Residence: Hebron.

Clarence Frederick Kilpatrick

Clarence Frederick Kilpatrick, rancher, was born in Gage County, Nebraska, June 22, 1897, son of Joseph M. and Augusta W. (Meitz) Kilpatrick. His father was born in Gage County, September 7, 1867, and his mother on August 26, 1869.

Upon his graduation from public school at Blakely, Nebraska, in 1912, Mr. Kilpatrick, entered the Beatrice High School from which he was graduated in 1917. At that time he enlisted, and served as a first class seaman in the United States Navy, receiving his honorable discharge on August 1, 1919. He participated in active foreign service, is a member of the American Legion and the Veterans of Foreign Wars.

Mr. Kilpatrick is a member of St. Matthews Episcopal Church of Alliance, the school board of District No. 23 of Box Butte County, the Elks and the Alliance Country Club. His favorite sport is flying and his hobby is mechanics.

On July 15, 1920, he was married to Naomi Green at Clatonia, Nebraska. Mrs. Kilpatrick, who was born at Clatonia, August 17, 1897, is a member of the Daughters of the American Revolution, descended from John Adam Walroth. They have one daughter, Mary Ellen, born March 9, 1924. Residence: Alliance .

Peter Henry Kilzer

Peter Henry Kilzer, farmer, was born at Germantown, Seward County, Nebraska, July 18, 1882, son of John and Helena (Honeig) Kilzer.

The father was born in Calgar, Old Louisendorff, Germany, March 26, 1849, and died at Germantown, Nebraska, August 19, 1899. His wife, Helena, was born in Calgar, February 29, 1852, and died at Garland, Seward County, Nebraska, February 17, 1932.

Mr. Kilzer attended public school about three months each year for about 12 years. He removed to Red Willow County in 1906 and located at Lebanon with no money and slight education. He took a 10 months course in banking and bookkeeping at the Lincoln Business College, earning a diploma. He now holds a deed for 3200 acres of land, which is nearly paid for. He is known as a wheat farmer, but also raises large acreages of corn, and bought the first combine in Red Willow County. He has a modern farm home, which is one of the oldest in the country, having been built 46 years ago when other houses were being made of sod.

He is director and secretary of the Lebanon Equity Exchange, and has taken an active part in local politics for a number of years. He was precinct assessor in 1909, deputy county treasurer of Red Willow County, 1912, 1913 and 1914, and agricultural census enumerator in 1925. He is a Republican.

On March 3, 1915, he was married to Mamie Bell Leist at McCook, Nebraska. Mrs. Kilzer was born in Brock, Nebraska, January 30, 1887, daughter of Lewis and Emma (Williams) Leist. Her father was born in Circleville, Ohio, November 17, 1835, and her mother in Missouri, February 18, 1862. Both made their home in Decatur County, Kansas.

Mrs. Kilzer is a member of the Legion Auxiliary, and is active in the affairs of the Methodist Church. She was graduated form Oberlin High School in Decatur County, Kansas, in 1908. She taught school for one year, thereafter attending Central Business College at Denver, Colorado, from which she received two diplomas, one in bookkeeping and one in shorthand.

Mr. and Mrs. Kilzer have four children, Helena, born March 3, 1918; Rosalie, born October 29, 1919; Maurine, born March 12, 1924; and John Lewis, born September 4, 1926. All the children were born at Lebanan.

Mr. Kilzer is a Methodist, and is a member of the Odd Fellows. His hobby is hard work. Residence: Lebanon. (Photograph in Album).

Thomas Rogers Kimball

Thomas Rogers Kimball, architect, was born in Cincinnati, Ohio, April 19, 1862, son of Thomas Lord and Mary Porter (Rogers) Kimball.

He received his education at the University of Nebraska and the Massachusetts Institute of Technology. He also attended the Cowles Art School at Boston, and studied with Harpignies in Paris. His marriage to Annie Lydia McPhail was solemnized at Brookline, Massachusetts, September 25, 1889.

Mr. Kimball is a Republican. Since January, 1928, he has been a member of the firm of Kimball, Steele and Sandham. He is a member of the American Institute of Architects (past national president), the Association of Professional Men's Clubs (national past president), the Chamber of Commerce, and the Omaha Civic League (past president). His clubs are the University, the Omaha and the Palimpsest. Residence: Omaha.

Walter Kimball

Walter Kimball, pioneer Nebraskan, was born in Andover, Massachusetts, June 27, 1852, son of Walter Henry and Mary E. (Gage) Kimball. The father was born in Boxford, Massachusetts, June 29, about 1820, and died at Andover, Massachusetts, in 1880. He was graduated from Dartmouth College, New Hampshire, and was descended from English settlers in New England prior to the Revolution. The ancestry of the Kimball family can be traced through books of genealogy in the public library at Andover, Massachusetts. His wife, Mary E. Gage, was born in North Andover, Massachusetts, about April, 1820, and died at Big Spring, Nebraska, in November, 1905.

Mr. Kimball attended common school until 1870 at Andover, Massachusetts. After leaving school Mr. Kimball traveled about, working for James A. Roberts Company, Pearly D. More and Company, and William Claflin Company, all Boston firms in the tanning business. He then came west to Nebraska and in September, 1884, took a homestead in Deuel County one mile south of Big Spring. At the time he moved to Nebraska, North Platte was a railroad center, Ogallala was a cattle town and cattle were shipped from the ranches there to the markets east. The cattle coming here were driven onto the range from Texas, and distributed through the valley regions. Mr. Kimball recalls many of the interesting occurrences of the pioneer days. His favorite diversion at the present time is reading.

In October, 1895, Mr. Kimball was married to Julia A. Stuart at Venango, Nebraska. She was born in Pittsfield, Illinois, December 9, 1852. Her father was Benjamine F. Stuart who crossed the plains in 1849 to California and of Scotch descent. Residence: Big Spring.

Richard Petring Kimmel

Richard P. Kimmel was born at Nebraska City, Otoe County, Nebraska, October 17, 1897, the son of Oliver Albright Kimmel and Cornelia (Petring) Kimmel. His father, whose ancestry was Pennsylvania German, was a land owner in pioneer days in Nebraska City. He was president of the Otoe County National Bank, and was qualified to practice law. He was born at Orwigsburg, Schuylkill County, Pennsylvania, June 4, 1858, and died at Nebraska City, March 18, 1911.

His mother was born in Nebraska City, November 3, 1862, the daughter of early settlers who came from Germany before 1850, and settled in St. Louis, Missouri. Later they moved to Nebraska City where they were prominent in civic and religious affairs. Her father was very progressive, especially in improvements on his home, having the first water system in this section of the country installed in his home. She is an interested church worker in the Lutheran Church at Nebraska City, and is a member of the P. E. O. She was a school teacher for nine years before her marriage.

Mr. Kimmel attended the public schools of Nebraska City and was graduated from the high school there in 1915. He then attended Cornell College at Mount Vernon, Iowa, where he was a member of the debating club, the debating team, and was one of the organizers of the Student Council there. He acted as secretary and treasurer of the Miltonian Society; and earned his college letter in tennis, was on the class basketball team, and engaged in cross country running and in swimming contests. He was awarded his A. B. degree, June, 1919.

Upon his graduation from college, Mr. Kimmel spent a year as manager of a lumber camp in the Ozarks in southern Missouri. He returned to Nebraska to enter the Otoe County National Bank where he stayed for five years. In 1925 he entered the fruit growing business, and since that time he has spent all his time on this business and on the management of the business and property of his mother and sisters. He is treasurer and director of the First Trust Company at Nebraska City.

He was married to Laurine Oetgen at Nebraska City, June 30, 1927. Mrs. Kimmel, who was born at St. Louis, November 3, 1900, was a clerk in a gift shop and drug store, and taught in the Omaha public schools before her marriage. Her grandfather on the maternal side was prominent in civic, religious, and business affairs in Nebraska City in the early history of the state. Her paternal grandfather was a noted pioneer business man of St. Louis. Her ancestry is German.

Mr. Kimmel was a member of the school cadets while in college; was in the Officers' Training Camp (Camp Grant) at Rockford, Illinois; and for three years was a member of the National Guard at Nebraska City.

A member of the Men's Glee Club of Nebraska City, the Nebraskana Society, he was at one time a member of the Y. M. C. A. He is affiliated with the First Evangelical Lutheran Church where he is financial secretary and a member of the church council. He is a Mason, and a Republican. Residence: Nebraska City.

Alva Vest King

A leader in religious and educational work for many years, the Reverend Alva Vest King is a native of Missouri. He was born at Trimble on August 3, 1889, the son of George Washington and Jennie Hawkins (Ross) King. His father was a native of Tennessee, who later migrated to Missouri, and died at Nashua on June 23, 1919. He was a farmer of Scotch-Irish ancestry. His wife, Jennie, was born in Clay County, Missouri, September 6, 1859, and is also of Scotch-Irish descent.

Dr. King attended the public schools of Trimble, Missouri, and in 1908 was graduated from high school at Edgerton, Missouri. In 1912 he received his Bachelor of Arts degree from Park College, in 1915 his Bachelor of Divinity degree from Auburn Theological Seminary (Auburn, New York), and in 1930 was awarded his degree of Doctor of Divinity from Hastings College. During the summer sessions of 1921 and 1922, the winter quarter of 1924, and the summer of 1930 he took postgraduate work at the University of Chicago.

Ordained to the Presbyterian ministry in April 1915, Dr. King served as pastor of the First Presbyterian Church of Trumansburg, New York, the following five years. During 1920-23 he was assistant pastor of the First Presbyterian Church at Chicago, and from 1923-29 was pastor of Roseland Presbyterian Church at Chicago. In 1929 he was made pastor of the First Presbyterian Church at Hastings. Dr. King is a member of the Hastings Presbytery, and is a trustee of Hastings College.

During 1917-18 he was sergeant in the New York State Guard, and participated in loan drives, war work census and as a four minute speaker.

Dr. King is a member of the Hastings Ministerial Association, the Chamber of Commerce, the Rotary Club, the Young Men's Christian Association, the Young Women's Christian Association, and The Nebraskana Society. A Mason, he is a member of Trumansburg Lodge No. 157 Ancient Free and Accepted Masons,

Oriental Consistory of Scottish Rite Masons, and Tehama Temple of the Shrine. His club is the Hillside, and his hobby is woodworking. Residence: Hastings.

Dexter D. King

For the past 17 years Dexter D. King has engaged in the practice of medicine and surgery at York, Nebraska. He was born at Bradshaw, Nebraska, September 19, 1884, the son of Bernard and Lillie Frances (Clark) King. His father, who was born at Union City, Pennsylvania, May 13, 1851, and died at York, March 31, 1926, was the first licensed embalmer and undertaker in York County; he served as mayor of York, 1896-1898. His mother, who was born at Cortland, Illinois, February 5, 1855, was secretary of the Grace Chapter of the Eastern Star at York for 31 years; her grandparents moved to Illinois from Connecticut.

Dr. King attended the public schools of Fremont, Nebraska, and York, and in 1904, was graduated from the York High School. In 1914 he was awarded the M. D. degree at the University of Nebraska where he was a member of Phi Rho Sigma. During his high school years he was active in football, baseball, and basketball.

In 1925 he began practice at Waco, Nebraska, and in 1916 moved to York and became a member of the York Clinic. Except for two years when he was active in the World War, Dr. King has been connected with the York Clinic continuously, and is now a partner in the York Clinic and Hospital and is physician to the State Odd Fellows Home at York. He holds membership in the county and state medical societies, is councilor-elect of the sixth district of the State Medical Society, and is past president of the York County Medical Society. He is a member of the Red Cross, the American Social Hygiene Association, the York County Commercial Club, and the York Rotary Club of which he is past president.

Dr. King is a member of the Knights of Pythias, Independent Order of Odd Fellows, and Ancient Free and Accepted Masons (Scottish Rite and Shrine). During the World War he was commissioned first lieutenant in the medical corps, was stationed at Base Hospital 39, Camp Beauregard, Louisiana, and in France was stationed at Base Hospital 19, where he was commissioned captain. He was in the army from October 8, 1917, to March 3, 1919, and was later active in the organization of the state department of the American Legion, serving as the first commander of Bolton Post Number 19 at York, Nebraska.

He is affiliated with the Methodist Church at York, holds membership in the York and Shrine Country Clubs, and is a member of the Nebraskana Society. He is interested in all athletic events and likes to golf, fish, and hunt. He is a Republican.

His marriage to Mary Agnes Anderson occurred at St. Joseph, Missouri, June 22, 1906. Mrs. King was born at Villisca, Iowa, July 28, 1886. Her mother's family came from Ohio, while her father's ancestry was Swedish. Two children were born to them: Boyd G., born June 9, 1908, who is a student at the University of Nebraska Medical College at Omaha; and Thomas A., born February 19, 1915, who is in his senior year at York High School. Residence: York.

Herbert Eugene King

Dr. Herbert E. King was born at Sandy Lake, Pennsylvania, February 3, 1882. He is the son of Henry Thomas King, born at Union City, Pennsylvania, March 24, 1853, who was one of the organizers of the Omaha Dental College. A practicing dentist, he was president and for many years treasurer of the Nebraska State Dental Society, and prominent in early state dental affairs. His ancestry was English and Scotch, the family prominent for several generations in Vermont and Pennsylvania. He died at Fremont, Nebraska, June 9, 1911.

Minnie Louisa Watson, wife of Henry Thomas King, was born at Tryonville, Crawford County, Pennsylvania, October 15, 1858. She came to Nebraska with her husband, bringing her family, and died at Colorado Springs, Colorado, June 22, 1915. She was of English descent.

Dr. King was educated in the Fremont public and high schools and received the degree of D. D. S. from the Omaha Dental College in 1905. He took the two year pre-medical course at the University of Nebraska. A member of Omicron Kappa Upsilon and Delta Sigma Delta, he is a fellow of the American College of Dentists. For many years he has been active in the professional life of Omaha. A teacher at Creighton University since 1913, he is now professor of prosthetic dentistry. He has held various offices in the Omaha District Dental Society, of which he has been a member since 1906. He was secretary of the Nebraska State Dental Society for 15 years, and was its president in 1922. He is a director of the Physicians Casualty Company. His other civic and professional organizations include the Omaha Odontological Society, the American Dental Association, the Central Parent-Teachers' Association, the Chamber of Commerce, etc. During 1917-18, he was a member of the dental examining board. He is a Mason, and a member of St. John's Lodge, and is active in the Red Cross and the Y. M. C. A. and attends the First Methodist Episcopal Church of Omaha. He was elected to the Omaha Board of Education in 1929. His clubs are the Professional Men's Club, the Continental Club and the University Club.

He was married to Nellie Agnes Kunkel at Osceola, Nebraska, June 26, 1912. Mrs. King was born in Polk County, Nebraska, August 8, 1882, and is of Irish and Pennsylvania Dutch descent. They have one son, Charles Herbert, born June 14, 1914. Residence: Omaha.

Marcus Lindsey King

Marcus L. King was born at Omaha, July 27, 1878, son of Jacob and Caroline Christina (Christenson) King. His father, born at Urbana, Ohio, September 3, 1832, was of English and German descent. He died at Omaha, January 19, 1910. His wife, Caroline, was born at Skagn, Denmark, September 6, 1837, and died at Omaha, April 22, 1912.

Dr. King was graduated from the University of Omaha with a D. D. S. degree in 1902. He is a member of Omicron Kappa Epsilon and Xi Psi Phi. Upon his admission to practice on June 15, 1902, he entered the dental profession in Omaha, where he has since been engaged. He is teacher at Creighton University, where he has filled various offices since 1913.

He was married to Margaret Josephine Phelan at Omaha, June 15, 1911. Mrs. King was born at Greeley, Nebraska, November 3, 1884, and is of Irish descent. They have three children, John, born May 22, 1912; William, born December 4, 1914, and Norma, born September 11, 1917, who died March 2, 1919.

Dr. King is a Republican. He holds the rank of first lieutenant in the Reserve Officers Training Corps. His professional organizations are the American and Nebraska District Dental Associations. He is also a member of the South Omaha Merchants Association. Residence: Omaha.

Milo D. King

Born at Goshen, Indiana, July 26, 1860, Milo D. King has been a leading lawyer at Minden, Nebraska, since 1886. His father, John King, who was a contractor and farmer, was born in Center County, Pennsylvania, August 5, 1812, and died at Topeka, March 21, 1906. His mother was born in Mifflin County, Pennsylvania, March 5, 1816, and died at Topeka, February 2, 1892.

Mr. King attended Hillsdale College in Michigan. A

Democrat, he served as county judge of Kearney County from 1895 to 1899, and later was county attorney for two terms. He has been city attorney of Minden, for 15 years, is a member of the Red Cross, and is affiliated with the First Presbyterian Church of Minden. He holds membership in the Nebraska State Historical Society, the Modern Woodmen of America, and the Nebraskana Society.

On October 5, 1887, he married Emma M. Bronson at Minden. Mrs. King, whose ancestry is Scotch, was born in Susquehanna County, Pennsylvania, July 1, 1866. Their two children are Ruth, born March 1, 1892, who married Walter A. Canaday; and Helen A., born June 16, 1900, who married Fred C. Palmer. Residence: Minden. (Photograph in Album).

Otis John King

Otis John King, one of the younger bankers of Whitman, Nebraska, was born at Torrington, Wyoming, November 26, 1900, the son of William David and Laura Elisa (Thompson) King. His father, who is a banker, was born of German parentage at Ava, Illinois, August 3, 1871. His mother, also of German descent, was born at Ava, June 15, 1871.

Mr. King was graduated from the Whitman High School in 1917, was a rancher for three years in Wyoming, and engaged in the mercantile business at Whitman for four years. He has served as cashier of the First State Bank of Whitman for the past five years and is a director in that institution.

He is a member of the Methodist Church, is treasurer of the school board, and holds membership in the Masonic Lodge of Hyannis, Nebraska, and the Odd Fellows Lodge at Whitman. During the World War he served as a first class private in the United States Army, and is adjutant and finance officer of the A. D. Fetterman Post of the American Legion of Hyannis, Nebraska. He is interested in reading, and his favorite sports are: golfing, baseball, hunting, and fishing.

On June 28, 1923, his marriage to Berniece Elsie Eriksen was solemnized at Mullen, Nebraska. Mrs. King was born at Council Bluffs, Iowa, April 17, 1902. She is the daughter of Eric P. and Laura Eriksen. Her father is a prominent ranchman and past county judge of Hooker County. She is secretary and treasurer of the American Legion Auxiliary and a member of the Rebekahs. They have two children, Otis John, born August 12, 1926; and Barbara Kay, October 2, 1928. Residence: Whitman.

Ralph Edward King

Born at Edgar, Nebraska, January 21, 1904, Ralph Edward King is the son of Edward Peck and Edith Nina (Manon) King. His father, who was a grocer and life insurance agent, was born at Delphi, Indiana, April 6, 1874, and died at Edgar, Nebraska, August 23, 1925. His mother, who was born October 5, 1882 at Beatrice, Nebraska, is active in the P. E. O. at Hastings, Nebraska where she is a member of the quartette in the Congregational Church and is interested in club work.

Mr. King was graduated from the Edgar High School in 1921, and took a post-graduate course at the same school. While in high school, he took an active interest in football and baseball, three years, and in his senior year was identified as a member of the cast in the class play. He attended Hastings College for three years, and while there served as president of the freshman class, president of the Pep Club, and held membership in Delta Phi Sigma Literary Society. He was employed as assistant manager of the Montgomery Ward Store at Hastings, at Claremore and Bartlesville, Oklahoma, was connected with the Valley Lumber Company at Superior, Nebraska, and is now manager of the Valley Lumber Company of Red Willow County, Danbury, Nebraska.

He holds membership in the Nebraska Lumber Dealers Association, the Nebraskana Society, the Southwest Nebraska Historical Society, the Red Cross, the Elks and the Masons. His social organizations are the Danbury Golf Club and the Indoor Baseball Club. His hobby is reading, and he is interested in all sports.

He was united in marriage with Phyllis Ruth Mousel at Hastings, Nebraska, June 12, 1929. Mrs. King was born at Cambridge, Nebraska, April 14, 1906, of German and French ancestry. She is a member of the P. E. O. and active in the affairs of the Presbyterian Church and Eastern Star. She is a graduate of Hastings College, Hastings, Nebraska, and attended the University of Nebraska, two years, being identified with the Gamma Phi Beta Sorority. Residence: Danbury.

William David King

One of the leading bankers in Grant County, Nebraska, is William David King, who was born at Ava, Illinois, August 3, 1871, the son of John Edwin and Eliza Elizabeth (Killion) King. His father, a farmer, was born of German parentage at Murphysboro, Illinois, April 2, 1849, and died there, December 25, 1922. His mother, whose ancestry was Scotch, was born at Ava, January 30, 1851, and died at Murphysboro, April 30, 1930.

Mr. King was a student in rural school and later attended the state normal college of Illinois. For 25 years he was a railroad operator, having taught in a rural school for several terms previously, and for the past 14 years has been cashier of the State Bank of Whitman, Nebraska, and is now active vice president. He holds membership in the Methodist Episcopal Church, the Red Cross, the Nebraskana Society, the National Geographic Society, and the Independent Order of Odd Fellows. He is a Mason.

On August 21, 1895, he was married to Laura Ella Thompson at Murphysboro, Illinois. Mrs. King, whose ancestry is German and English, was born at Ava, June 15, 1871. She attended public schools at Ava, Illinois, and the Illinois State Normal at Carbondale, Illinois; and was a teacher prior to her marriage. She is the daughter of Henry and Lavinia (Thomas) Thompson. Mrs. King is a member of the Eastern Star, Woodmen Circle, Royal Neighbors, the Red Cross and the Methodist Episcopal Church. To them were born the following children: Grace, April 15, 1896, who married Claus G. Johnson; Ruth, November 20, 1897, who married Victor H. Rathsack; Hazel, March 5, 1899, who married Dayton Sullenberger; Otis John, born November 26, 1900, who married Berniece E. Eriksen; and Edyth, April 11, 1902, who married Vern McCubbin. Otis is cashier of the First State Bank, Ruth is a bookkeeper, and Hazel is engaged in the advertising business. Mr. and Mrs. King have been residents of Nebraska for 27 years. All their children are high school graduates, except Otis John who had to leave school to serve in the World War. Mr. King's hobby is reading. Residence: Whitman.

Donaldson Wright Kingsley

Donald Wright Kingsley, physician and surgeon at Hastings, Adams County, Nebraska, has been a resident of this state all his life. He was born at Minden, Kearney County, Nebraska, March 16, 1899, the son of George Pomeroy and Mabel (Wright) Kingsley. His father, who was a banker, lumberman, and public leader, was born at Freeport, Illinois, November 11, 1865, and died at Minden, October 30, 1929; he was president of the Association for the Conservation and Utilization of Water Resources of Nebraska; his English ancestors came to America in 1700.

His mother was born at Elgin, Illinois, October 22, 1865, of English parentage; an uncle was a professor at Rush Medical College. She is vitally interested in various garden clubs in which she holds membership.

Dr. Kingsley was graduated from Minden High School in 1917. He holds the following degrees: A. B., Cornell University, 1922; A. M., Cornell University, 1923; M. D., Harvard University, 1926. He is a member of Kappa Alpha. Since his admission to the practice of medicine in 1926 he has been engaged in his profession, practicing at Hastings since 1928.

He was united in marriage with Myra Elizabeth Bowman at Lincoln, Lancaster County, Nebraska, December 17, 1928. Mrs. Kingsley, whose ancestry is English, was born at Quentin, Lebanon County, Pennsylvania, July 12, 1907. They have two children: Carolyn, born December 13, 1929; and Donaldson, born May 5, 1931.

Dr. Kingsley is secretary of the Adams County Medical Association, and holds membership in the Nebraskana Society and the Hastings Country Club. During the World War he was a member of the Student Army Training Corps at Hobart College. He is independent, politically. Among his recreations are golfing and hunting. Residence: Hastings.

Alva Raymond Kinney

Alva R. Kinney was born at Belmont, Ohio, October 4, 1870, the son of Elisha and Narcissa (McKirihan) Kinney. His father, born at Belmont, February 24, 1840, died at Milford, Nebraska, March 30, 1912. He was a farmer and school teacher; his Scotch-Irish ancestors came to America in 1812. His mother was born at Belmont, November 4, 1841; her ancestry was Scotch-Irish.

Mr. Kinney attended country schools and in 1897, was graduated from Doane College with the B. S. degree. He is now president of the Nebraska Consolidated Mills Company, and is a director of the Miller's National Federation, at Chicago. He is past chairman of the board of directors of the Southwestern Miller's League of Kansas City, past president of the Nebraska Manufacturers Association.

He holds membership in: Omaha Chamber of Commerce; Ad-Sell League; and the Nebraskana Society. He is a Modern Woodman of America and a Mason, Scottish Rite, Shrine. His social clubs are Rotary, Omaha, and Happy Hollow. He is a trustee of Doane College, and a member of First Central Congregational Church.

His marriage to Grace Catherine Barragar was solemnized in Chicago, April 20, 1898. Mrs. Kinney was born in Chicago, April 19, 1874; her father was born in Canada; her mother was born in Vermont. Their children are: Louise, who married H. J. Platt; Ruth, who married F. M. Ross; and Raymond Elisha. Mr. Kinney is a Democrat. During the World War he served as field agent for the food administration. He was captain of the Doane College Cadets, 1896-97. He is a director of Happy Hollow Club and is a member of the National Geographic Society. Residence: Omaha. (Photograph in Album).

Charles B. Kinney

A former banker at Elgin, Charles B. Kinney has been a resident of this state for the past 51 years. He was born at Marshall, Iowa, July 4, 1865, the son of Hiram W. and Mary (Burke) Kinney. His father, who was a farmer, was born at Rochester, New York, December 1, 1826, and died at Elgin, December 27, 1888. His mother was born in New York in 1830 and died at Ill Grove, Iowa, in 1870.

Mr. Kinney attended the public schools of Marshall and of Oakdale, Nebraska. For many years he was engaged in farming, but in recent years has taken an active part in business at Elgin, where he served as president of the Farmers and Merchants Bank. He was secretary treasurer of the Antelope County Telephone

Company for 20 years prior to 1928, and was secretary and director of the Farmers Corpoation in which he still holds a majority of stock.

He was married to Belle Frances Edwards at Neligh, Nebraska, January 1, 1889. Mrs. Kinney was born at St. Louis, Missouri, November 1, 1863, of Welsh and Holland Dutch descent. Six children were born to them: Albert E., July 25, 1890, who married Grace M. Jenkins; Ray H., November 7, 1892, who married Ethel Linton; Walter L., March 16, 1895 ,who married Ella Earl; Harvey C., January 22, 1898, who married Martha Johnson; Laura B., January 5, 1901, who married Raymond Elliott; and Charles E., November 22, 1903.

Mr. Kinney is a member of the Park Congregational Church at Elgin and holds membership in the Nebraskana Society. Residence: Elgin.

Hazel Gertrude Kinscella

Hazel Gertrude Kinscella, composer, writer, and noted music educator, has lived in Nebraska, since 1908, and has been prominent in educational fields for many years. She was born at Nora Springs, Iowa, the daughter of Samuel and Ella Gertrude (Quinn) Kinscella. Her father, who was a business man, was born at Cumberland, Ontario, Canada, May 19, 1854, and died February 26, 1930; he was of Scotch descent. Her mother, who was at one time a teacher and writer, was born at Freeport, Illinois, of English and Irish ancestry.

Miss Kinscella was graduated from the Nora Springs High School and Seminary, and in 1916, received the Bachelor of Music degree at the University School of Music at Lincoln, Lancaster County, Nebraska. In 1928 she was awarded the Bachelor of Fine Arts degree at the University of Nebraska; received her A. B. degree there in 1931; and is a graduate student at Columbia University, New York. She holds membership in Alpha Rho Tau; Pi Kappa Lambda; Mu Phi Epsilon; and Phi Beta Kappa.

Her professional activities are as follows: guest teacher at the universities of North Carolina; South Carolina; Michigan; Eastman School of Music, Rochester, New York; Kansas State Teachers College at Emporia, Kansas; Kearney State Teacher's College, Kearney, Nebraska; and Furman University, Greenville, South Carolina. She is now major teacher of piano at the University of Nebraska School of Music in Lincoln. She was one of three American pianists chosen to serve as piano consultant at the Anglo-American Music Conference at Lausanne, Switzerland, in the summer of 1931. She is a member of the advisory council for the Damrosch Music Appreciation Hour on the air.

She is the author and composer of the following: *Young Pianist's Library*, published by G. Schirmer of New York; *First, Second, Third, Fourth, Fifth, and Sixth Steps for the Young Pianist; Essentials of Piano Technic; My Very First Music Lessons; My Own Little Music Book; Velocity Studies for the Young Pianist; Ten Little Pieces for the Young Pianist; Ten Tiny Tunes for the Young Pianist; Ten Little Duets for the Young Pianist; Ten Tiny Tune Duets for the Young Pianist;* and *Ten Musical Tales for the Young Pianist*.

While Miss Kinscella has devoted most of her writing to Musical compositions for children, she has also written: six *Readers in Appreciation*, published by the University Publishing Company; two songs, *Longing*, and *Daisies*, published by G. Schirmer; and a college song, *Dear Old Nebraska*. She is the composer of *Music and Romance*, published by the RCA-Victor Company; has been recording pianist for the RCA-Victor and the Duo Art companies; and is the author of more than a hundred articles for *The Etude, Musical America, Musical Courier,* and *Better Homes and Gardens.*

Miss Kinscella is a life member of the National Educational Association; a member of the Supervisors' Conference; Writers' Guild of America; Nebraska Writers' Guild; the American Guild of Organists; the Lincoln Clef Club; is state president for Nebraska of Pen Women of America, and a life member of the Nebraska Alumni Association. She holds membership in the Red Cross; the Nebraskana Society; the Young Women's Christian Association; and the Second Presbyterian Church of Lincoln. Residence: Lincoln.

William Thorton Kinsey

A leading farmer in Franklin County, Nebraska, is William Thornton Kinsey, who was born at Leon, Iowa, March 19, 1868, the son of David Jacob and Mary Eliza (Linton) Kinsey. His father, who was a pioneer farmer in Kansas in 1871, was born in Ohio, December 25, 1837, and died at McDonald, Kansas, February 19, 1920; he served as sergeant in the Fifth Kansas Cavalry during the Civil War. His mother was born in Montgomery County, Indiana, August 11, 1843, of Scotch and Irish descent, and died at Phillipsburg, Kansas, November 7, 1903.

Mr. Kingsey completed his high school education at Sutton, Nebraska, in 1882. He has been successful in farming near Naponee, Nebraska, for a number of years, and is especially interested in Aberdeen Angus cattle. He is a member of the Aberdeen Angus Breeders Association, holds membership in the Naponee Elevator Company, and is affiliated with the Congregational Church of Naponee. He is a Mason.

On January 25, 1898, his marriage to Ella Florence Fogleman was solemnized at Phillipsburg, Kansas. Mrs. Kinsey, whose father was a surgeon in the Confederate Army during the Civil War, was born at Butler, Illinois, September 4, 1873, and died at Naponee, April 15, 1930. She was a teacher prior to her marriage. The two children born to this marriage are: Wayne, May 28, 1906; and Helen, July 26, 1909, who was graduated from Naponee High School in 1928. Residence: Naponee.

Thomas Jefferson Kirby

For the past 47 years Thomas J. Kirby has lived in Nebraska where he has been consecutively, a farmer, hardware dealer, and automobile dealer. He was born at Carman, Illinois, November 2, 1856, the son of James and Sarah (Butler) Kirby. His father, who was born in Maryland, July 18, 1819, and died at Carman, March 22, 1895, was a farmer who had 160 acres of farm land in Illinois, in 1850; he traveled by ox-team to California in the gold rush of 1849. His mother was born June 21, 1832, and died at Carman, January 12, 1861.

Mr. Kirby attended the grade school and then became engaged in farming. In 1890, he became active in the hardware business at Gresham, Nebraska, where he sold some of the first bicycles manufactured. He moved to Tobias, in 1918, and entered the automobile business in connection with a hardware store. Mr. Kirby has the distinction of selling the first radio and first automobiles in Saline County.

His marriage to Sophia Ruth Worden was solemnized at Carthage, Hancock County, Illinois, March 5, 1884. They have three children: Minda, born April 8, 1889, who married Harmon G. Eyestone; Thomas G. Jr., born November 2, 1895; and Nellie Ruth, born May 27, 1897, who married Harold J. Horney.

Mr. Kirby holds membership in the Nebraskana Society, the Woodmen of the World, and the Odd Fellows. He is a Republican. Residence: Tobias.

Sarah Seybolt Kirk

A resident of Nebraska for the past forty-five years, and principal of the Junior High School at Broken Bow for the past five years, Sarah Seybolt Kirk was born at Westtown, New York, September 27, 1880. She is the daughter of George Arnold and Mary Josephine (Thorn) Seybolt.

George Arnold Seybolt, born in Orange County, New York, May 10, 1843, was a real estate broker at Lincoln until his death there on January 23, 1931. His ancestry in America dates to 1730, when his great grandfather, John Mickle Seybolt, came from Wurtemburg, Germany. He later fought in the Revolutionary War.

Mary Josephine Thorn was also born in Orange County, but on April 16, 1847. She traces her ancestry to 1700 when her family came from England. Many of them served in the Revolution. She was a devoted worker in the Presbyterian Church, who died at Lincoln on August 21, 1904.

Educated in the public schools of Lincoln, Sarah Seybolt was graduated from high school in June, 1900. She later attended the Peru State Teachers College, the Kearney State Teachers College, the University of Nebraska and the University of Wisconsin. She has a life teacher's certificate.

On March 7, 1907, she was married to James Albert Kirk at Lincoln. He was born in Orange County, Indiana, January 30, 1878. There is one son, Harold, born February 2, 1908. She was an honor student at the Iowa State College, Ames, Iowa, where he was a member of Tau Beta Phi, honorary engineering fraternity, Eta Kappa Nu, honorary electrical fraternity and Phi Kappa Phi, scholastic fraternity. He is a member of Acacia, the Masonic Lodge and the Presbyterian Church, and at present is an electrical engineer at Waukegan, Illinois, with the Northern Illinois Light and Power Company.

A leading figure in civic and club work, Mrs. Kirk is a member of the Woman's Club, the P. E. O., the Eastern Star and the Degree of Honor. She is a member of the Red Cross, General George A. Custer chapter of the Daughters of the American Revolution, the Nebraska State Teachers Association and the National Educational Association. Recently she was made a life member of The Nebraskana Society. Residence: Broken Bow.

Howard Kirkpatrick

Howard Kirkpatrick, director of the University School of Music at Lincoln, has lived in Nebraska for the past 25 years. He was born at Tiskilwa, Illinois, February 26, 1879, the son of John and Honor (Grubbs) Kirkpatrick. His father, who was born in Ohio and died in Illinois, was a business man and a farmer of Scotch-Irish descent. His mother, whose ancestry was German, was born in Indiana and died in Tiskilwa in 1891.

Mr. Kirkpatrick attended elementary schools in Elmwood and Tiskilwa, Illinois, and in 1899, received the Bachelor of Music degree at Oberlin, Ohio. He studied music at the Royal Conservatory at Leipzig, Germany, was a student at Florence, Italy, for two years under Vincenzo Vannini. During 1902-03 he studied with and was assistant to Edmund J. Myer at Chautauqua, New York. In college he was elected to membership in Phi Kappa Lambda and Phi Gamma Delta. He is now director of the University of Nebraska School of Music and a teacher of singing. The author of many songs, and of *Applied Vocalization*, he has composed operas *Olaf and La Minuette*, anthems, and the Nebraska pagent the *Fire Worshippers*.

He is a member of the Nebraska Writers Guild, the Lincoln Chamber of Commerce, the Crucible Club, The Club, the Nebraskana Society and the Shrine Club. He is past president of the Nebraska Academy of Singing Teachers, is affiliated with the Congregational Church of Lincoln and is a member of the Republican party. He is a Mason and a member of the Shrine and an Elk. His favorite sport is golfing.

Mr. Kirkpatrick was married at Neligh, Nebraska,

to Vera Wattles, on June 23, 1907. One child was born to them, Jean, born on October 25, 1913. Residence: Lincoln. (Photograph in Album).

George A. Kittle

George A. Kittle, county clerk at Hayes Center, Nebraska, was born in Hayes County, November 10, 1897, the son of George Y. and Tillie (Larson) Kittle. His father, who was born at Cantril, Iowa, July 30, 1869, is an auctioneer and rancher, served as county commissioner four years, and is leader in county improvements. His mother, whose Norwegian ancestors moved to Hitchcock County, Nebraska in 1875, was born in Wisconsin, May 5, 1872. Her mother died in a Nebraska prairie fire.

Mr. Kittle was graduated from the high school at Palisade, Nebraska, 1918, attended the College of Business Administration for three years at the University of Nebraska, and taught school in Hayes County for three years. He received honors in high school and took part in athletic events, especially cross country running. Mr. Kittle has been a farmer and salesman for a wholesale grocery house, and since 1926 has served as county clerk of Hayes County, having been elected on the Democratic ticket by an overwhelming majority.

A member of the American Legion, he served as adjutant of that organization for two years 1928-29, and is now service officer. He holds membership in the Hayes County Commercial Club, the Masons and Odd Fellows, and is a director in the local school district. He is affiliated with the Hayes Center Congregational Church of which he is treasurer.

His marriage to Elva C. Birchall was solemnized at McCook, Nebraska, February 23, 1922. Mrs. Kittle, whose ancestry is English, was born at Hayes Center, September 5, 1898. She is a member of the Rebekahs Royal Neighbors, is treasurer of the American Legion Auxiliary, and is active in the work of her children. Their two children are: Keith, born November 26, 1923; and Bernard, born March 24, 1931. Residence: Hayes Center.

Henry Kitzinger

One of Nebraska's pioneer farmers is Henry Kitzinger who was born at Darmstadt, Germany, January 12, 1858, the son of Saervatius and Mary Cathrine (Miller) Kitzinger. His father, who was a farmer, was born in Germany and died at Lincoln, Nebraska, November 9, 1900; he came to America in 1860. His mother was born at Darmstadt, and died at Harvard, March 25, 1894.

Mr. Kitzinger attended the elementary schools of Stephenson County, Illinois, and for the past 55 years has lived near Harvard, Nebraska, where he has been active in political, civic, and business affairs. He served as a member of the city council for eight years, was a member of the school board for a number of years, and acted as township board-officer for a time. A Democrat, he was constable of Harvard for two terms.

He is a member of the Red Cross, the Nebraskana Society, the Congregational Church, and various other community societies. He served as director in the Harvard State Bank for four years, and for 44 years was an active member of the Modern Woodmen of America. During the World War he was interested in the sale of Liberty bonds.

His marriage to Mary Ann Gotheridge was solemnized at Harvard, October 30, 1881. Mrs. Kitzinger was born at Derbyshire, England, August 13, 1864. To this marmiarge the following children were born: Lottie May, July 5, 1882; Melvin E., April 3, 1886, who married Flora Waldorf at Western, Nebraska, December 27, 1918, and Edith, October 27, 1888, who married Frank Kightlinger on November 3, 1929. Residence: Harvard.

Albert A. Kjar

Born at Lexington, Nebraska, May 9, 1890, Albert A. Kjar is a farmer and wholesale dealer in grain and hay. He is also interested in the breeding and management of registered Holstein-Friesians and has a very choice herd on his ranch near Lexington. His father, who was born in Denmark, March 4, 1848, came to this country in 1872 and homesteaded in Dawson County where he has been a farmer for many years. He was united in marriage to Mrs. Mary Volk in Dawson County. She was born in Germany, May 12, 1850, and died at Lexington, May 20, 1919.

Mr. Kjar received his early education in country schools, was a student in high school for two years, and in 1911 was graduated from the University of Nebraska School of Agriculture. He is a director and vice president of the Chamber of Commerce, is affiliated with St. Ann's Catholic Church, and is a member of the Knights of Columbus, having served as state deputy in Nebraska during 1929 and 1930. His social club is the Lexington Country Club.

He was united in marriage with Veronica Stuart at Lexington, April 17, 1917. Mrs. Kjar was born at Lexington, April 11, 1894, and died there, August 19, 1919. They have one son, Albert William, born January 23, 1918. Mr. Kjar is a member of the Democratic party and the Nebraskana Society. Residence: Lexington.

Oliver Cecil Kleckner

Born at Firth, Nebraska, October 4, 1881, Oliver Cecil Kleckner is the son of Samuel and Lavina (Auman) Kleckner. His father was born at Union Town, Pennsylvania, August 4, 1851, and later moved to Nebraska. He was a farmer, whose death occurred at Firth on June 4, 1922. His wife, Lavina Auman, was born in Kent, Illinois, June 16, 1858, and died at Firth, December 14, 1930.

Oliver Cecil Kleckner attended country school and for a number of years engaged in farming. For some time he has been in the general merchandise business at Firth. He was married to Minnie Louise Damrow at Lincoln, on November 24, 1908, and to their marriage were born four children: Ethel, September 27, 1909; Irene, November 11, 1913; Leona, November 11, 1917, and William, September 14, 1920. The two oldest have just completed business college, one is in high school and the other in grammar school.

Mr. Kleckner is a Democrat. He is a member of the First Presbyterian Church of Firth and is a member of the Nebraskana Society. For two years he was a member of the Parent Teachers Association, and for four years was on the local school board. Residence: Firth.

Alois J. Klein

Born at Frantoly, Prachatice, Bohemia, February 6, 1866, the Reverend Alois J. Klein is one of Nebraska's most outstanding members of the clergy. He is the son of John and Catherine (Stepan) Klein, the former a native of Vitejice, Bohemia, born August 3, 1822, a master miller and a prominent member of the Millers' Guild at Lhenice, Bohemia. John Klein came of an unbroken line of millers who operated emphyteutic mills on the brook Zlaty Potok, beginning with the famed Forka Mill near Kralovice (Prachatice) Bohemia, under the Counts of Bucquoy and Schwarzenberg. John Klein came to America with his family in November, 1881, and died at Rosedale, Kansas, on April 24, 1887.

Catherine Stepan, who was born at Zernovice, Prachatice, Bohemia, April 4, 1838, died at Brainard, February 11, 1920, having made her home there since December 5, 1895.

Father Klein attended the German grade school in Frantoly, and was graduated from the German grammar school in Prachatice on July 31, 1878. On July 20, 1886, he was graduated *cum laude* from The Bohemian Gymnasium at Budejovice, and thereafter completed theological studies equivalent to a master's degree in America, in the seminaries of Budejovice and Klagenfurt, in Carinthia, and the German University at Prague, finishing in 1889. He was valedictorian in the Classical Gymnasium in 1886, and was ordained to the priesthood at Klagenfurt, Carinthia, on June 15, 1889.

Coming to Nebraska in November, 1889, he was appointed rector of St. Wenceslaus' Church at Wahoo, where in two years he paid off the last farthing of indebtedness on the rectory and erected a beautiful new church building. He had charge of the missions of Brainard and Weston, visiting each once a month. On December 10, 1891, he was transferred to St. Ludmila's Church at Crete, but retained charge of the missions at Brainard and Weston. The mission of Brainard prospering greatly Father Klein was determined to make a parish of it, and in 1893 secured a handsome building for a rectory. On September 5, 1893, he came to Brainard as its first resident pastor.

Weston formed, until February, 1901, a part of his ecclesiastical precinct. Father Klein was instrumental in enlarging the church building by extensive additions (1891), adding five lots to the church site, and increasing the membership from 32 families to 140. He founded three sodalities and completed the organization of the congregation.

During the "Bohemian Ethnological Exhibition" in Prague, Czechoslovakia, (1895), Father Klein paid a visit to the land of his birth. Upon his return he organized branches of the "Catholic Workman" at Brainard, Weston, Dwight, Touhy (1897), Loma (1902), and Bee (1909). Dwight was then a promising tributary of his Brainard church, and there Father Klein held services in the public schoolhouse until, owing to his tireless work, a frame church was erected in 1899. Then while in charge of St. Anthony's Church at Bruno, a new priest's house was built in 1901.

Turning his attention to Dwight, he furnished and improved the church structure, founded a number of benevolent societies, added an acre of land to the cemetery, enlarged the church site, purchased a residence for the parish house and erected a hall for the use of the organizations connected with the church.

In 1909, he founded a mission in Bee, where he saw a church arise in 1910. In the fall of that year the Dwight and Bee missions became independent pastorates. From St. Luke's branch of the "Catholic Workman" organized by him in Loma, in 1902, the present congregation sprang, a church for its use was erected in 1911, under his direction.

Though Father Klein has rendered valuable pioneer services to so many mission movements, still his main work has been founded in the upbuilding of Holy Trinity Church at Brainard, where hard working and faithful, he has embodied his ideals, and has poured forth lavishly the ardor of his youth. Through his untiring and enthusiastic efforts a vigorous campaign for funds was instituted and after long and persevering work, facing much opposition, the construction of a stately brick and stone church was completed in 1906, at a cost of $47,000. Its size, magnificence and interior elegance easily rank it among the most notable buildings of Omaha.

Being an ardent advocate of religious education, Monsignor Klein conceived a parochial school for Holy Trinity. He had provided a site beside the church for this, and after tireless effort, and many hardships, witnessed the dedication by Bishop Tihen on August 23, 1916. This beautiful structure, erected at a cost of $52,000, accommodates 180 pupils, and is a most cherished monument of Monsignor Klein's career.

In the year 1927, this zealous pastor turned his attention to a new rectory, and in the spring of 1928, completed what is perhaps one of the finest in the Lincoln Diocese, costing more than $30,000. The brilliant achievements of Monsignor Klein form a lasting memorial of his devotion

ALOIS J. KLEIN

Anderson—Wahoo

to the cause, these brilliant achievements being gained only through the hardest of hard work. Founding four congregations; organizing a dozen branches of different benevolent organizations; four new rectories, one model school and five church structures certainly constitutes a record of unusual attainments in the annals of missionary work. Father Klein is a man of talent and learning, and an enthusiast in all he undertakes.

He has served as Vicar General under three bishops, Administrator Apostolic of the Lincoln Diocese during vacancies in 1911 and 1917, chairman of the diocesan school board, examiner of the junior clergy, diocesan consultor and pro-synodical examiner. In 1913 he was named domestic prelate to the Holy See with the title of Monsignor, by Pope Pius X; was made honorary canon of the collegiate chapter of St. Maurice in Kromeriz, Moravia, by Archbishop Anton C. Stojan of Olomouc, in 1922, and in 1929, was made Protonotary Apostolic by Pope Pius XI, with the right of the Pontificals, being the first priest in the Diocese of Lincoln to be so honored.

Monsignor Klein is the author of numerous poems appearing in Bohemian periodicals and magazines, articles in both Bohemian and English on agricultural subjects, besides various translations of German and English into Bohemian. His linguistic acquirements and edifying zeal make him an efficient worker in the missionary field. In his younger days he often preached in three languages, English, Bohemian and German on the same day.

Although a busy clergyman, he nevertheless finds time for the Muses. Through poetic and prose contributions he is well and favorably known in the literary circles of America and Czechoslovakia. A collection of Bohemian poems *From the Domain of the Prairie* (Zoblastiprerijnich) is now ready for publication. He has translated Washington Irving's *Alhambra* and Charles Lamb's *Five Tales from Shakespeare*, besides Dr. Carl May's *In The Pacific Ocean* (from the German) into Bohemian.

From time to time he contributes various articles to *Vcelarske Rozhledy*, which is published monthly at Prague, Czechoslovakia. He was a contributor to *Ottuv Slovnik Naucny* (Otto's Encyclopedia) which is a monumental Bohemian educational work of twenty-eight volumes.

Father Klein, however, has not limited his activities to his mother tongue. He has contributed several English treatises on agricultural subjects, having gained distinction as an authority among bee keeping fraternities. These have appeared in the *Rural Bee Keeper, Bee Keeper's Review, The American Bee Journal*, and in the annual reports of the Nebraska State Board of Agriculture for 1911-1913. To him bee culture is an ideal recreation, and since 1911, he has served three terms as president of the former Nebraska State Beekeepers' Association.

Monsignor has a notable record of patriotic, educational and civic services. He was active during the World War. It has been his constant aim to inspire his compatriots, and to urge them to become American citizens, and to master the English language. But he also advises them to study that which is best in the mother tongue— the traditions and memories of their forefathers—and the history of their forebears. It was with glowing ardor that he furthered the Czechoslovak cause during the war.

During the years 1918 and 1919, he was director of the Brainard chapter of the American Red Cross, and during 1919-20, was a member of the Nebraska State Directorate of the Junior Red Cross Peace Program. In former years he was a regular speaker on patriotic and civic celebrations. In addition to the diocesan offices mentioned he is, at the present time, Vicar General Emeritus of the Diocese of Lincoln, and a member of the administrative board of St. Thomas' Orphanage at Lincoln. He is a member of the Catholic Workmen, the Nebraska State Historical Association, the Nebraskana Society, and the Knights of Columbus. His hobbies are agriculture and botany. Residence: Brainard. (Photograph on Page 663).

W. C. Klein

Wilhelm Carl Klein, prominent hardware merchant in Seward County for many years, was born at Milford. He is the son of Wilhelm Ludwig and Mary Josephine (Byrnes) Klein, the former a farmer, born in Germany. He came to Pennsylvania in 1868 and to Milford, in 1869, where he farmed until his retirement about 1900. In 1914, he removed to Milford, where he died on November 7, 1922. Mary Josephine Byrnes was born in Ireland, February 12, 1834, and died at Milford April 14, 1914. An ideal homemaker, she served her family in many capacities, and was active in the work of her church.

Mr. Klein received his education in a rural school and later attended Milford High School. In 1898 he entered the hardware business and shortly after added an implement department. In 1905 he purchased the local drug store and in association with Mrs. Klein engaged in the drug business until 1909. However, he still managed his hardware and implement business independently from 1898-1924, at which time he retired and disposed of his interests. Since then he has devoted his time to his land and city properties.

A Democrat, Mr. Klein served as precinct treasurer during 1900, member of the town board 1900, member of the cemetery board 1927 to date, and its president and vice president in both 1930 and 1931. He has been secretary of the Farmers Mutual Telephone Company since 1930, and for ten years was treasurer of the Nebraska Retail Hardware Association, of which he is an honorary member.

Mr. Klein was delegate to the National Hardware Convention in Denver, in 1910; to the Detroit convention in 1912, and again received the honor of being delegate to the convention in Boston, in 1916.

He is a Scottish Rite Mason and member of Sesostris Temple of Lincoln. Mr. Klein is a member of the Eastern Star, and is also affiliated with the Lutheran Church. He enjoys reading, history, travel and camping. On February 12, 1899, he was united in marriage to Meta Semler at Dorchester. Mrs. Klein, who was born at Sheboygan, Wisconsin, has always been associated with her husband in his business. She is the daughter of Erich Semler, a native of Hanover, Germany. He and his four brothers were clergymen. Erich Semler was educated for the ministry, but became an accountant and business man.

Mr. and Mrs. Klein have the following children: Clarence, born August 1, 1900, who died January 30, 1901; Lawrence, born August 1, 1900, who died February 1, 1901; Norma Louise, born February 24, 1910, and Maurice Eugene, born April 1, 1919.

Norma Louise attended the public school at Milford, and graduated from the Milford High School in 1926. Thereafter she entered the University of Nebraska, from which she was graduated in June, 1931. While at the university she was extremely active in all student affairs. She served as president of Delta Zeta, was secretary and treasurer of the Art Club, was made a member of the senior commissioners and the League of Women Voters, and is now vice president of the alumnae association of her high school graduating class. Residence: Milford. (Photograph in Album).

Ignatius Klima, Jr.

Born in Valley County, Nebraska, November 28, 1892, Ignatius Klima, Jr., is the son of Ignatius and Mary (Vodehnal) Klima. The father was born near Zahratka, Czechoslovakia, July 21, 1869, and came to America at the age of four. He was a farmer and pure-bred stock raiser until his death at his home in Valley County, January 1, 1923. His wife, born near Litomist, Czechoslovakia, May 2, 1872, resides at Ord. His mother came to this country at the age of four.

Ignatius Klima, Jr., attended public school and in

GEORGE W. KLINE

1912 was graduated from a two year commercial course in the St. Paul Business College. From May, 1913, until April, 1917, he was with the Fenner Abstract Company of Burwell, and from that time until July, 1918, was in the real estate business, loan and insurance business for himself in Morrill, Nebraska. From August 5, 1918, until March 30, 1919, he was in military service as a corporal in the Quartermaster Corps.

On April 1, 1919, Mr. Klima became assistant cashier of the Farmers Bank of Burwell, continuing in that capacity until January 1, 1920, when he became secretary and director of the First Trust Company of Ord. A Democrat, he was elected county clerk and register of deeds for Valley County for a four year term beginning January 1, 1927, and was re-elected in 1930 for a second term.

On November 17, 1919, he was married to Rebecca Lovina Williams at Burwell. Mrs. Klima, who is of Welsh, French Canadian and Pennsylvania Dutch descent, was born in Wales, Iowa, September 5, 1896. They have two children, Robert L., born February 7, 1923; and Doris L., born August 15, 1925.

Mr. Klima is affiliated with the Methodist Episcopal Church of Ord. He is a member of the American Legion, the Chamber of Commerce, and the Nebraskana Society, and is a 32nd degree Mason. He enjoys reading, fishing, hiking, and camping, while his hobby is honey bees and their culture. Residence: Ord.

Joseph J. Klima

Joseph J. Klima was born at Milligan, Nebraska, December 27, 1895, the son of Joseph and Josephine (Soufl) Klima. His father was born at Trtice, Czechoslovakia in 1853, and died at Milligan, November 22, 1897. His mother was born at Vejvanov, Czechoslovakia, July 13, 1863.

Mr. Klima attended the public schools of Milligan where he was graduated in 1913, was graduated from Peru State Teachers College in 1915, and attended the University of Nebraska during the summer months of 1916 and 1917. He served as president of the senior class in high school, was president of the Philomathean Society at Peru, and was a member of Phi Delta Kappa.

He was superintendent of schools at Bristow, Shelby, and Hildreth, Nebraska until 1919 when he became cashier of the Farmers & Merchants Bank at Milligan. He is now director and treasurer of the Milligan Auditorium Corporation. During the World War Mr. Klima served as apprentice seaman in the United States Navy, later being advanced to second class yeoman. He is a member of the American Legion.

Mr. Klima has been secretary of the Chamber of Commerce since 1924 and secretary of the Fillmore County Bankers Association since 1926. He is a member of the Bankers Association, the Nebraskana Society, and the Western Bohemian Fraternal Association of Cedar Rapids, Iowa. Since 1924 he has been secretary of the Milligan School Board. He is a Mason.

On June 2, 1921, he married Ada Stech at Omaha, Nebraska. Mrs. Klima, whose parents were natives of Czechoslovakia, was born at Milligan, February 9, 1898. Mr. Klima's chief recreations are golfing and swimming. He is a Democrat. Residence: Milligan.

George Washington Kline

George W. Kline, editor and author, was born at Jamesport, Davis County, Missouri, March 17, 1875, the son of Harmon and Mary Anna (Hevers) Kline. His father, who was a farmer, was born at Bloomsburg, Columbia County, Pennsylvania, December 24, 1830; a pioneer in Henry County, Ohio, he came to Nuckolls County, Nebraska, in 1884. He was a soldier in the Civil War, serving in Company B, 110th Pennsylvania Volunteers. His ancestry was Pennsylvania Dutch.

His mother, a pioneer homemaker and the mother of eight children, was born at Briara, Sligo, Ireland, August 25, 1834, and died at Edgar, Clay County, Nebraska, January 15, 1915.

Mr. Kline attended the country schools of Nuckolls County, but had no opportunity to attend high school. He was later a student at the University of Nebraska where he was graduated with the degree A. B., in 1910. He was a member of the English Club, at the University of Nebraska; was editor of the senior class book; and was chairman of the loan committee of the class of 1900. He served as secretary of the alumni association, 1911-13. He was a member of Pershing Rifles while in school there.

He was editor of the *Lincoln Star*, 1902-11; was editor of the *Alumni Journal*, 1911-13; he was publicity director for the State Board of Agriculture, and established *Nebraska*, the state official organ 1913-16; was editor of the Nebraska Highway Bulletin; and held various positions as a reporter. From 1913 to 1919 he was connected with the Lincoln Typesetting Company, and since 1919 he has been president and manager of the Kline Publishing Company.

Mr. Kline is the author of many short stories, features and essays. He is the author of biographies of Manoah B. Reese, W. B. Rose, Norris Brown, and other notables. Perhaps his most notable contribution to the literary world is *Bryan the Man*, published in 1908.

He has never aspired to public office, but has supported many other candidates. He proposed G. L. Sheldon for governor, and Norris for United States senator. He advocated the railway commission and the constitutional convention. In 1916 he served as assistant to the Republican State Committee. He has lived in Nebraska for 47 years and has been active in Nebraska's business, civic, and political affairs.

He was married to Orma Lulu Hull at Lincoln, Nebraska, August 12, 1902. Mrs. Kline, who is an editor and writer, is active in club work and social affairs in Lincoln. She is state chairman of the publicity department of the Daughters of the American Revolution for Nebraska. She was born at Humboldt, Nebraska, August 26, 1878, and is a descendant of the Rev. Joseph Hull of colonial fame. Joseph Hull was born in 1594, and in 1635 brought a colony to America. He was a minister at Weymouth, Hingham, and Barnstable, Massachusetts; he was an Oxford graduate. He died in 1665.

The Klines have a daughter, Dorothy Power, born July 21, 1915, who was the winner of the Native Sons and Daughters essay prize, January 5, 1931; also state winner in the essay competition of the National High School Awards for 1931.

During the World War Mr. Kline was a member of the American Protective Association. He is a member of the Nebraska Writers Guild; the Layman's Club; the State Historical Society; and the Nebraskana Society. He is secretary of the Popular Government League. He is a Mason (Liberty Lodge Number 300). His sports are fishing and boating. His hobby is promotion of interest in national parks. He assisted Enos Mills in the creation of Rocky Mountain Natural Park, and he is now compiling Nebraska political history from 1900-1930, and advocating parks and recreation centres in Nebraska. Residence: Lincoln. (Photograph on Page 665).

John Blaine Kline

John Blaine Kline, son of Isaiah and Libbie (Smith) Kline, was born at Bolivar, Ohio, December 29, 1876. His paternal ancestors in America settled first in Pennsylvania, and his grandfather migrated to Ohio, in 1807. His father was born at Coshocton, April 4, 1845, and is engaged in farming there. His mother, born in 1844, died in 1885.

Upon the completion of his preparatory work at Scio College, Ohio, Mr. Kline attended Wooster College, from

HARRY M. KNABE

Townsend—Lincoln

which he received his Bachelor of Philosophy degree in 1898. He was a student at the University of Chicago, in 1901, and in 1910, and at the University of Colorado, in 1903. His fraternity is Alpha Tau Omega.

Mr. Kline was a member of the faculty of Hastings College from 1901-12, and since that time has been engaged in the electrical contracting business. He has served as president of the board of education two years of the six he has been a member. Mr. Kline enjoys reading history, science and philospohy. He is a Presbyterian, a member of the Chamber of Commerce and the Rotary Club, and is a life member of the Nebraskana Society.

In 1906 Mr. Kline was married to Bessie Louise Duer, who was born in Illinois and died at Hastings, May 24, 1911. On December 16, 1916, he married Grace E. Hoppe of Hastings His children are as follows: Elizabeth, born October 4, 1907, who holds a secretarial position in Cambridge, Massachusetts; John, born May 17, 1911, who is an aviator; Mary, born May 11, 1919; Mildred, born December 14, 1921, and Robert, born March 26, 1923. Residence: Hastings.

Arthur Klingenberg

Arthur Klingenberg was born at Chapman, Nebraska, June 24, 1884, the son of Hans and Helena (Untiedt) Klingenberg. His father, who was a farmer, was born at Schleswig, Germany, October 13, 1834, and died at Chapman, April 23, 1917. His mother was born at Schleswig, June 26, 1840, and died August 11, 1924.

Mr. Klingenberg attended rural schools near Chapman, and was a student at the Nebraska State Agricultural College at Lincoln, Nebraska, 1901-03. He has been engaged in farming in Merrick County since 1903, and has been prominent in various civic and educational organizations at Chapman.

He served as a member of the school board from 1918 to 1927, is a member of the Farmers Educational and Cooperative State Union of Nebraska, and holds membership in the Chapman Co-operative Grain and Livestock Association. Since 1918 he has been a member of the Board of directors of the Chapman Co-operative Mercantile Association of which he also secretary. He is a Mason.

Mr. Klingenberg has lived all his life on the farm which his father homesteaded in 1871. His hobby is good stock and poultry. Politically, he is independent. On May 20, 1908, he was married to Cozetta Belle Kellogg at Grand Island, Nebraska. Mrs. Klingenberg, who was born at Chapman, October 3, 1889, is the daughter of Cyrus Kellogg (1848-1921) and Clarissa M. Shoemaker (born in 1852). To them were born three children: Donald A., born September 17, 1909, who married Grace Gladys Leeder; Arnold A., born May 21, 1912; and Harold H., born July 20, 1916. Residence: Chapman.

Harry M. Knabe

Harry M. Knabe was born at Nehawka, Cass County, Nebraska, November 12, 1902, the son of John C. and Anna M. (Hansen) Knabe. His father, who was born at Nehawka, February 29, 1868, was a farmer. His mother was born at Nehawka, February 12, 1880. His father's father, John C. Knabe, homesteaded the farm on which Harry M. Knabe is living, in 1856, living there until his death, and his father, John C. Knabe was born and reared on it, remaining there until Harry Knabe's marriage. Harry has resided there all his life.

Mr. Knabe was graduated from Nehawka high school in 1920. While he was in school he was active in basketball and other athletics. He was united in marriage to Fern Margaret Gansemer on September 12, 1927. They have had two children, one born December 3, 1928, who died that same day; and Margaret Ann, born December 15, 1930.

A lifetime resident of Nebraska, Mr. Knabe is a

breeder of purebred Hampshire hogs. He was a charter member of the first pig club in Cass County, and through this work he won a state championship giving him a free trip to Chicago in 1921. He was club leader from 1924-25, and is vice president of the Nebraska Hampshire Association. In 1925 he was voted the most outstanding 4-H Club member in the United States, and a booth entitled "Ambition" was sent to a number of state fairs including Iowa and Nebraska and other western states.

Mr. Knabe is a booster for 4-H Clubs and feels that he owes his present success to that organization, for if it had not been for them he would not have started with a little sow pig, weighing 60 pounds. He now owns one of the largest and best herds of purebred Hampshires in the United States, and in 1930 held top sale of all bred sows of all breeds for that year. His first bred sow sale in 1923 traced directly back to the original little pig with which he started. The sale above referred to is the only one tracing directly back to one sow.

Mr. Knabe's herd has been among the top winners at the Nebraska State Fair for the past ten years, winning many championships in the breeding stock, and he has been winner with grand champion carloads of barrows at some of the largest stock shows in the United States. He devotes much of his time to assisting boys and girls in getting started in 4-H Club work with hogs for he realizes its value to them.

He is affiliated with the Nehawka Methodist Church. He is a Republican. His favorite sport is basketball and his hobby is attending fairs and visiting other Hampshire breeders. Residence: Nehawka. (Photograph on Page 667).

Ray Howard Knapp

Ray Howard Knapp, merchant, was born at Loup City, Nebraska, November 7, 1902, son of Edward Aquilla and Elizabeth Emma (Flynn) Knapp. His father, born in Vinton, Iowa, December 22, 1872, is now a hardware merchant. For a number of years he farmed in Nebraska. His father, Will Knapp, served three years in the Civil War. His mother, Elizabeth Flynn, was born at Fort Laramie, Wyoming, March 14, 1880. She was a teacher for three years before her marriage. Her mother, Marilla Flynn was the first white woman to settle in Valley, and her father served in the United States Army 10 years during the Indian Wars.

Educated in the public schools of districts Nos. 1 and 43, until 1919, Ray Howard Knapp was graduated from high school at North Loup and later attended York Business College. During 1919 and 1920 he played high school football. On June 1, 1929, he was married to Dorothy Marie Nelson at Central City. Mrs. Knapp, who was a teacher, was born at Albion, Nebraska, October 31, 1908.

Upon returning from college in 1923 Mr. Knapp went to work in his father's hardware store, which in 1925, was purchased by him in partnership with his brother, Cecil. The firm name is now Knapp Brothers Hardware and Furniture Store. He is a director in the North Loup Building and Loan Association, and is serving his first term on the village board of North Loup. He is a Republican.

Mr. Knapp is a member of the Odd Fellows Lodge and the Nebraskana Society. His hobby is floriculture. He is an ardent baseball fan, and has served as secretary and treasurer of the North Loup Town Baseball Club. He has been a member of the Pop Corn Day Celebration committee for two years. Residence: North Loup.

John Knickrehm, Jr.

On January 18, 1890, John Knickrehm, son of John and Christina (Dohrn) Knickrehm, was born at Grand Island, Nebraska. His father, born in Kremp, Germany, March 20, 1857, came to America as a young man. While a citizen of Germany he had military service, and upon taking

JOHN KNICKREHM, JR.

up his residence in Nebraska, became a retail grocer and banker. He served two terms as a member of the Grand Island city council prior to his death on August 5, 1931. His wife, Christina, was born in Marne, Germany, in 1852, and died in Grand Island, January 31, 1922.

John Knickrehm attended the Platte and Howard schools, and when only eight years old worked in his father's store. A grocer all of his life, he has attained much prominence in his chosen work, is the owner of a number of stores, and during 1927-28, was president of the Nebraska Grocers' Association.

He is a member of the Chamber of Commerce (president retail section 1926-27); the Grand Island Advertising Club; the Federation of Nebraska Retailers and the National Grocers Association. A Republican, he served three terms as a member of the city council, and was its president 1926-27.

Mr. Knickrehm is an Elk, and a member of all Masonic bodies including Tehama Temple of the Shrine, and the Order of Eastern Star. He contributes to the Red Cross and Salvation Army, and during the late war took part in Liberty loans, the sale of thrift stamps and in all other civilian projects. His religious affiliation is with the English Lutheran Church.

Recently he was elected to life membership in The Nebraskana Society. He is a member of Plattdutsche Verein, the Liederkranz, and the Woodland Country Club as well as the Rotary Club. His favorite sport is golf, and his hobbies are baseball and football.

On August 20, 1913, Mr. Knickrehm was married to Miss Emma Stoppkotte, and to this union were born three children, Hubert John, born April 30, 1915; Marie, born October 30, 1918; and Rosa, born November 29, 1921. Mrs. Knickrehm died December 20, 1921. On June 17, 1926, Mr. Knickrehm was married to Miss Raamah Swartz of Lincoln. Residence: Grand Island. (Photograph on Page 669).

Augusta Henriette Knight

Augusta Henriette Knight, teacher of art in Omaha for the past twenty-three years, was born at Augusta, Illinois. She is the daughter of William S. and Anna M. (Mack) Knight, the former a native of Coshocton, Ohio, born August 17, 1840. William S. Knight was a clergyman with the degree of Doctor of Divinity, who furthered the cause of education in many ways, and for years was pastor of the Presbyterian Church at Carthage, Missouri, where he died on November 5, 1905. His ancestry was English and Scotch.

Anna Mack Knight was born at Carthage, Illinois, January 27, 1854, and died at Omaha, July 24, 1924. She was prominent in club and welfare work, especially the social settlement, as well as in missionary and church work. Of German ancestry, her great-grandfather was president of Jena University, Germany, and her father was a prominent lawyer. On the paternal side the family was Dutch, descended from Alexander Mack, founder of the Mennonite Colony in America.

Miss Knight was educated in the public schools of Carthage, Missouri, and received her A. B. from Carthage Collegiate Institute. She received a normal art diploma from Pratt Institute at Brooklyn, in 1908. She has studied art at the Chicago Art Institute at various times, the St. Louis School of Fine Arts, the Artist's Colony at Provincetown, Massachusetts, etc. In 1922 she attended New York University during the summer session. She was the holder of a scholarship to Pratt Institute, and the winner of the Robert Morseman prize for the best collective paintings at the Nebraska Art Exhibition; she received honorable mention in water color at the Midwestern Artists Exhibit at Kansas City, also.

From 1908-15, she was teacher of art at Brownell Hall. Since 1912 she has been teacher of art at the University of Omaha. She is represented in private collections, and has received honors in exhibitions at various times. She works in oil, water color and etching, and in leather and metal. She is a painter of landscape and still life. At the present time Miss Knight is director of art at the University of Omaha, and has classes at the Young Women's Christian Association.

She is a member of the First Presbyterian Church. Her professional organizations include the Omaha Art Guild, the Omaha Artists Association, the Art section of the Nebraska State Teachers Association and the Western Arts Association. Her particular interest, however, is in her pupils who have gone out to teach, and who have received honors in their work. She is fond of gardening in a small way, and in reading and sketching. Residence: Omaha.

Reuben Edward Knight

Reuben Edward Knight, banker and civil engineer, was born at Decorah, Iowa, April 27, 1885, and has resided in Nebraska since 1908.

He is the son of Aaron E. and Cora (Strayer) Knight. He was educated first in the public schools of East Denver and was graduated from the East Denver High School in 1903. He received the degree of Metallurgical Engineer from the Colorado School of Mines in 1907.

On November 9, 1910, he was married to Florence McKeen at Denver. To them were born two children, Edward McKean, born December 4, 1911; and Edith Elaine, born January 26, 1920.

Since 1908, Mr. Knight has been cashier of the Alliance National Bank. Prominent also in Republican politics, he has served as county commissioner two terms, as county surveyor and as city engineer. He is affiliated with the First Presbyterian Church, and is in his third term as a member of the school board. Residence: Alliance.

Fred Knobel

Born at Odessa, Nebraska, December 4, 1886, Fred Knobel has been a farmer there most of his life. His father, Andrew Knobel, who was also a farmer, was born in Switzerland in 1842, moved to Odessa in 1880 where he engaged in farming, and died at that place in October, 1891. He was married in New York State to Kathern Herty. The mother was born in Switzerland, December 10, 1843, and died at Odessa, November 6, 1929.

Mr. Knobel attended rural high school. He has been a director of the local school board for the past 18 years, is a member of the Parent Teachers Association and the Red Cross, and is an honorary member of the Lincoln Chamber of Commerce. He is actively interested in 4-H Club work, is fond of baseball and basketball, and spends much time in landscape gardening. During the late war he was chairman of loan drives in his community. In 1929 Mr. Knobel was made a Master Farmer of Nebraska.

His marriage to Lottie Anna Sear was solemnized at Odessa, December 15, 1912. Mrs. Knobel was born of English parents at Marysville, Missouri, December 15, 1894. They have three children: Dale William, born August 22, 1916; Jane Evelyn, born June 30, 1919; and Jean Alicia, born June 5, 1921. Residence: Odessa.

Louis Jarrett Knoll

Louis Jarrett Knoll, educator and banker at Liberty, Gage County, Nebraska, was born at Crete, Saline County, Nebraska, November 21, 1883, the son of August Louis and Mima J. (Young) Knoll. His father, who was born at Pekin, Tazewell County, Illinois, June 9, 1853, was a pioneer farmer and stockraiser in Nebraska; his ancestry is German. His mother, who was a devoted mother and homemaker, was born at Taylorville, Christian County, Illinois, March 7, 1853, and died at Crete, May 8, 1923. Her parents were pioneers in Illinois.

Mr. Knoll was graduated from the Crete High School

in 1903, Peru State Normal College, Peru, Nebraska, 1907, and was awarded the A. B. degree at the University of Nebraska in 1910. He was a student at Doane College for two years. During his high school days Mr. Knoll was prominent in debating, represented Doane College in debating, and was awarded first place in the Dawes Oratorical Contest, also represented the Peru State Normal in debating. At the University of Nebraska he won second place in an oratorical contest. He was active in athletics in both high school and college, and was elected to membership in Acacia, at the University of Nebraska.

Mr. Knoll has held the following positions in the educational world: superintendent of the public schools at Blue Springs, Nebraska, 1907-08; superintendent of public schools at Randolph, Nebraska, 1911-12-13; and superintendent of the public school at West Point, Nebraska, 1914-16. He entered the banking business in 1916 as cashier of the Ralston State Bank, was cashier of the Lebanon State Bank in Kansas, 1917-18, and in 1918 became cashier of the State Bank of Liberty, Liberty, Gage County, Nebraska. In addition to his financial interest in the bank he is connected with a number of local business firms at Liberty.

During the World War Mr. Knoll was given special recognition by the governor of Kansas for services to his country; he was a four minute speaker, and took part in all war activities in his home state. He was instrumental in organizing the local commercial club, and served as its secretary for many years. Mr. Knoll has always been identified with progressive movements in his community. He is affiliated with the Congregational Church, in which he has been treasurer and trustee for many years, is a member of the Nebraskana Society, and is a Mason. His political affiliation is with the Republican party.

His marriage to Marie Louise von Goetz was solemnized at North Platte, Lincoln County, Nebraska, September 23, 1916. Mrs. Knoll, who was born at North Platte, April 16, 1889, was a teacher before her marriage. She was graduated from the University of Nebraska, where she held Phi Beta Kappa honors. Their three children are: Allan Louis, born May 26, 1918; Robert Edwin, born February 3, 1922; and Eleanor Louise, born December 14, 1924. Residence: Liberty. (Photograph in Album).

Claus Frederic Knutzen

Born in Schleswig, Holstein, Germany, Claus Frederic Knutzen is the son of Henry and Maria (Brandt) Knutzen. His father's people were German and came to America in 1856. His mother was also of German parentage.

Mr. Knutzen attended the public schools and a business college in Nebraska, and is now a retired farmer and business man. He married at Colon, Saunders County, Nebraska, February 27, 1880.

Mr. Knutzen served as state representative in the Nebraska legislature for one term, elected on the Democratic ticket. He has lived in Nebraska for sixty years, is a member of the Nebraskana Society, and is affiliated with the Trinity Lutheran Church at Bruning. Residence: Bruning.

Frank Joseph Kobes

One of the prominent business men at Crete, Nebraska, is Frank Joseph Kobes, a lifelong resident of this state. He was born at Wilber, Nebraska, January 28, 1890, the son of Frank Joseph and Josephine (Kubes) Kobes, the former a merchant who was born at Manitawoc, Wisconsin, July 12, 1863, and died at Crete, November 3, 1903. His mother, who is active in the Bohemian Lodge, was born in Czechoslovakia, September 15, 1867.

Mr. Kobes was graduated from the Crete High School and later attended the Lincoln Business College. He served as assistant cashier of the First State Bank of Crete, 1918-28, and since 1928 has engaged in the surety, investment bonds, and insurance business independently. As a member of the Republican party he has held various offices: city clerk of Crete, 1919-22; mayor of Crete, 1922-28, and 1930-32; and president of the League of Nebraska Municipalities.

He is a member of the Saline County Red Cross, is sponsor of the board of the Boys Scouts at Crete, and holds membership in the Crete Commercial Club, the Nebraska Motor Club, and the Nebraska Good Roads Association. He served as president of the Rotary Club in 1928, and is affiliated with the following fraternal organizations: Masons; Order High Priesthood of Nebraska; Knights of Pythias; Z. C. B. J.; and the Order of Eastern Star. His sports include golf, baseball, football, hunting, and fishing.

On June 18, 1912, he was married to Otilie Vavra at Crete. Mrs. Kobes, whose parents came to this country from Czechoslovakia in 1869, was born at Crete, August 30, 1889. Their two children are: Frank, born May 27, 1914; and Mary Josephine, born April 1, 1923. Mr. Kobes is president of the Crete Park Association. Residence: Crete.

Frank Kobl

Frank Kobl, farmer and stockraiser, of Mason City, was born in Moravia, Austria-Hungary, in 1837, and in October, 1867, was married to Maria Jelinek. She was born in Moravia in 1847, and in the spring of 1881, she and Mr. Kobl left their pleasant home in Europe to come to America.

Arriving in New York Harbor safely after the usual time of waiting, they came directly to Nebraska. They remained for a short time in eastern Nebraska, in the meantime having filed a homestead in Custer County, about 65 miles from Kearney. They made the crossing over the state by covered wagon in the late summer of 1881. There they erected a small sod cabin with a thatched roof, made from the tall native grass of the state. This was the beginning of their new home.

Their oldest son, John, was born in June, 1868, and his death in 1898 was a great loss to them. Their second child, Frances, was born in December, 1870, and died in 1923. She was married to Joseph Kopecky. Mary, born in 1876, is married to Frank Tommicek, while Frank, born in 1878, is unmarried. Anna, born in 1879, is married to Victor Kucera, and Joseph, born in 1881, died in the same year. The four younger children were all born in Nebraska, Rosa, who married Joseph Melichar; Julia, who married A. L. Martin; and Josephine and Edward. Rosa is wheat farming in Montana with her husband. Julia is a Red Cross county nurse in New Mexico. Joseph is in the farming and poultry business, in Nebraska, while Edward is a farmer and stockman. Francis is a wheat farmer in Oklahoma, Mary and Frank are farming in Nebraska, while Anna is engaged in the farming and poultry business in Oklahoma.

As a boy in his native land Mr. Kobl received a good education which he followed with much reading and enterprise. In Europe he took vocational training in carpentry and mechanics.

When the Kobl family first settled in western Nebraska there was a large amount of wild land. The prairies grouse and little quail came up into their front yard and the wild geese and ducks migrated past here. Rabbits were plentiful, and provided ample meat for food in the long winter. Meadow larks cheered the place with their song.

During the fall of 1881 in addition to improving the place the family gathered chips and what sticks of wood could be found and twisted hay into knots to make fuel for the winter. With the exception of the stove, furniture was home-made and rough, but served its purpose. Store boxes were used for chairs and bunks were made for beds.

With a few carpenter's tools, a spade, a breaking plow, a sled and a yoke of oxen, the family started out to build up and improve the homestead. This, as years passed, became a lovely ranch home where strangers as well as friends were always welcome.

A well was dug and water drawn with buckets. The prairie was turned into fields, planted to corn, the ground being turned with a spade. It needed no further cultivation until harvest.

Kearney being the nearest trading point, supplies were brought back from there. Mr. Kobl supplemented his income by carpentry work, and that together with the sale of crops provided money for a milk cow, a team of horses, and a wagon. But with the coming of the Burlington Railroad in 1886 was the beginning of prosperity. A school was established in a vacant homesteader's shanty for three months of the year which was later increased to six months.

By honest endeavor Mr. Kobl helped to build up the community in which he lived. At the present time the land owned by Mr. Kobl is being homesteaded by his children. Residence: Mason City.

Harlan Clifford Koch

Harlan Clifford Koch, educator, was born at Barrs Mills, Ohio, July 9, 1891, son of George and Anna Cora (Penrod) Koch. The father, a blacksmith, was born in Shanesville, Ohio, January 8, 1865. His father came to America from Germany in 1850. Anna Cora Penrod was born in Union Hill, Ohio, August 28, 1866, and died at Blissfield, Ohio, December 1, 1922.

Mr. Koch attended rural school in Coshocton County, Ohio, high school at Nellie, Ohio, and academy at West Lafayette, Ohio. In 1919 he received his B. A. from Ohio University, in 1923 his M. A., and in 1926 his Ph. D. He is a member of Phi Delta Kappa, Tau Kappa Alpha, and Lambda Chi Alpha (chapter president).

On September 1, 1912, he was married to Cora May Bechtol at Coshocton. Mrs. Koch was born in Keene, Ohio, March 18, 1888. She is descended from General Joseph Reed, aide de camp to George Washington's staff, a member of Congress 1777, and a signer of the articles of confederation in 1778.

A teacher in rural schools and principal of high school until 1924, Professor Koch was research assistant, Bureau of Educational Research, Ohio State University 1924-26; associate professor and professor of secondary education University of Nebraska 1926. He is the author of *The Transmutation of Mental and Educational Scores on the Kental Principle in a General Educational Survey; The High School Principal in Budget Making; Practicable Cooperative Supervision; Lighting as a Phase of School Hygiene; Non-Newspaper Possibilities in Continuous School Publicity; The Determination of Problems in High-School Teaching; Is the Teacher a Publicist; Is There a Difference between the Problems of Men and Women Teachers?; How a Teacher's Subjects influence his Problems; The Influence of Experience and Graduate Training upon Teachers; From the Mouths of Latin Teachers; Some Aspects of the Department Headship in Secondary Schools; Is the Department Headship in Secondary Schools a Professional Myth; Culture and the Vocations; A Study of Deficiency in the Mount Vernon, Ohio, High School, etc., etc.*

Professor Koch is a member of the Kiwanis Club (chairman of the vocational guidance committee 1931-32), the American Association for the Advancement of Science, the Nebraska Academy of Science, the University Club, and the First Presbyterian Church. His favorite sports are golf and bowling. Residence: Lincoln.

Rudolph Koch

Rudolph Koch was born at Crete, Nebraska, June 23, 1876, the son of Fred Koch and Dorothea (Warnecke) Koch. His father was born at Rothenburg, Province of Hanover, Germany, January 14, 1849. He came to the United States in 1863, and died May 2, 1930, at Dshler, Thayer County, Nebraska. Rudolph Koch's mother was born in the Province of Hannover, Germany, September 28, 1854, and died at Deshler, August 19, 1910.

Mr. Koch attended public and parochial schools and was graduated from the Hastings Business College. He was united in marriage with Matilda Margaret Werner, June 7, 1900, at Deshler. To this union seven children were born: Arthur, March 2, 1901; Ida, August 15, 1902; Robert, February 16, 1906; Gertrude, March 24, 1908; Nora, March 7, 1911; Erna, May 5, 1913; and Edgar, March 29, 1915. Matilda Werner was born at Deshler, May 24, 1880, and died December 9, 1918. Mr. Koch married Matilda Buttner, October 1, 1919, and to this union two children were born: Hubert, June 23, 1921, and Phyliss, February 10, 1923.

Since 1901, Mr. Koch has been in the general retail business at Deshler. He is the owner of real estate in Kansas and Nebraska, and property at Deshler. He is president of the Farmers and Merchants Bank, and is a member of the Deshler Commercial Club. Mr. Koch is affiliated with the St. Peter's Lutheran Church. Recently, in recognition of his efforts, he was awarded life membership in the Nebraskana Society. Mr. Koch is owner, raiser and breeder of silver foxes, and operates the Deshler Silver Fox Farm. Residence: Deshler.

S. Jacob Koch

Born at Schenectady, New York, February 4, 1869, S. Jacob Koch is the son of Jacob and Regina (Schwilk) Koch. His father, who was a carpenter, was born at Wittenberg, Germany, in 1853, and died at Omaha, Nebraska, in February, 1906. His mother was born at Wittenberg and died at Lincoln, Nebraska, in September, 1883.

Mr. Koch, who has been a farmer and purebred stock dealer in Lincoln County, Nebraska, for the past 46 years, has served as county commissioner and chairman of the board of directors of the Farmers Co-operative Association at Hershey. He has been a director of the local school board for the past 42 years, was formerly a director in the Lincoln County Bank, and was one of the first ten Master Farmers of Nebraska.

He came to Nebraska, December 25, 1886, where he worked on a ranch for five years, acting as foreman the last three years. He then started in the ranching business for himself and at present is the owner of 3500 acres of fine land. Mr. Koch was the first president of the Lincoln County Farm Bureau and served in that capacity for six years. He was alternate delegate to the National Republican Convention at Kansas City in 1928 and cast the vote for Vice-president Curtis.

He is a member of the Hershey Community Club, holds membership in the board of directors of the Methodist Church of which he was chairman for four years, and is affiliated with the following fraternal organizations: Modern Woodmen of America; Independent Order of Odd Fellows; Masons; Royal Neighbors; and the Yeoman's Club. He is interested in music and reading.

On October 30, 1892, he was married to Maggie Belle Mason at Hershey. She was born at Prairie City, Iowa, October 13, 1868, the daughter of John S. and Mary Amanda (Elliott) Mason. Her father was born December 28, 1840, and died August 7, 1922. Her mother was born November 25, 1846, and died December 30, 1928. Both were natives of Indiana and were pioneer settlers of Iowa.

They have five children, Florence, born August 21, 1893, who married John Kracht; Frank, December 31, 1894, who married Hazel Barnett; Mabelle, December 18, 1897; Grace, March 19, 1900; and George, October 15, 1905. Residence: Hershey. (Photograph on Page 673).

S. JACOB KOCH

Ezra Edwin Koebbe

Ezra Edwin Koebbe, eye, ear, nose and throat specialist, was born at Manchester, Michigan, October 27, 1890. He is the son of Edwin John and Christina (Finkbeiner) Koebbe, who were born in Manchester on July 9, 1863, and February 1, 1868, respectively. Edwin J. Koebbe, a farmer, lumberman and grain dealer, died at Chelsea, Michigan, April 9, 1929. His parents came to America in 1840, from Germany.

Dr. Koebbe was graduated from Manchester High School in 1907; received his Bachelor of Science degree from the University of Michigan in 1913 and his medical degree in 1915. He was president of his class in 1914-15, participated in intra mural athletics and was a member of Phi Beta Pi.

The author of numerous medical articles since his admission to practice, Dr. Koebbe has always specialized in eye, ear, nose and throat. He is a member of the Platte County, Nebraska State and American Medical Associations, and is a fellow of the American Academy of Ophthalmology and Otolaryngology.

He entered the Medical Corps of the United States Navy 1916, and resigned with the rank of lieutenant-commander in 1922. At the present time he is a member of the American Legion. He is a Mason, Knight Templar and Shriner, Elk, Knight of Pythias, Eagle, and a member of the Sons of Herman. In 1928 he served as president of the Lions Club and at present is president of the Young Men's Christian Association. He is a director in the Red Cross, a member of the Chamber of Commerce and the Parent Teachers Association, and a life member of the Nebraskana Society. His club is the Columbus Country Club.

On September 4, 1917, Dr. Koebbe was united in marriage to Ethyl Nora Burkhart. Mrs. Koebbe was born at Chelsea, Michigan, December 2, 1891. They have one daughter, Mary Catherine, born June 18, 1923. Residence: Columbus.

Otto Koehler

Otto Koehler, retired farmer of Stanton County, Nebraska, has lived in the state since 1885. He was born at Fort Madison, Iowa, August 20, 1856, the son of George Henry and Margaret (Knauff) Koehler. His father, a cabinet maker, was born in Germany, and died at Macedonia, Pottawattamie County, Iowa, October 9, 1883. His mother was born in Germany, and died at Fort Madison, Lee County, Iowa, in 1862.

Mr. Koehler is a member of the Nebraskana Society; is affiliated with the Methodist Episcopal Church at Pilger; and is a member of the Democratic party. His favorite sport is skating. He has always been active in the advancement of his community and state.

He was married at Carson, Iowa, February 20, 1884, to Mary Sevilla Doty. Mrs. Koehler was born at Oxford, Iowa, January 21, 1863. They have the following children: Algia, born July 13, 1886, who married Charles M. Roe; Grover, born July 1, 1888, who married Birdie Mae Bordner; Irvin, born May 2, 1890, who married Alice O. Sabin; Ruth, born February 21, 1892, who married H. Lee Gaskill; Otto, born April 27, 1898; Harold, born September 17, 1902, who married Gladys Marie La Grange; and Erma, born August 27, 1907. Residence: Pilger.

George William Koehn

George William Koehn, son of Albert Herman and Anna Elizabeth (Heilii) Koehn, was born at Elkton, Brookings County, South Dakota, June 16, 1901. His father, born at Greifenhagen, Germany, January 5, 1865, came to America in 1877. A German of Prussian stock, the original name was Kohn. At the present time Albert H. Koehn is engaged in business. His wife, Anna, was born in Strassburg, Alsace, France, April 10, 1875, descended from the family of Thiers, in France, one of the

Thiers being the first president of France. In infancy she was kidnapped by a family by the name of Beaver, of Chicago, who were sojourning in Switzerland, at that time and was not aware of this fact until the death of her foster mother, which was on her 18th birthday.

Educated first in St. Mary's Convent at Elkton, George William Koehn was graduated from Elkton High School in 1919. Thereafter he attended Creighton University, from which he received his Ph. B. in 1923, and his LL. B. in 1928, was also a graduate student from 1925 to 1928. He was received into Alpha Sigma Tau, the Phi Beta Kappa of Jesuit Colleges, and is a member of Delta Theta Phi, of which he served as national officer in 1928. A member of the basketball team in high school in 1919, with the position of guard, it is to be noted that this team held the championship of South Dakota the same year. He was also editor of *Shadows* the Creighton magazine.

For the past twelve years Mr. Koehn has been a resident of Nebraska, and from 1923-25, was superintendent of schools at Waterbury, Nebraska. During 1928-30, he was professor of political science at Trinity College, and since June 1, 1930, has been engaged in the practice of law. He is the author of *The Administrator and his School* (1926) *Recent Movements in the Administration of Justice* (1929) and *The Basis of Civil Society* (1923).

Mr. Koehn was secretary of the Nebraska Collegiate Oratorical Association in 1921, its president in 1923, also a delegate from Nebraska to the national convention of the same year, business manager of the *Blue Jay* in 1928, and delivers commencement addresses. He holds the rank of first lieutenant in the 255th Infantry, Officers Reserve Corps, and attended six reserve camps, received his lieutenancy in 1923. A Catholic, he attends St. Michael's Church. He is a member of the American Inter-Professional Institute; the Tri-State College Club (9 colleges), of which he was secretary 1929-31; the Iowa Political Science Association, and the Nebraskana Society. He is a member of the Dakota County Bar Association and the Nebraska State Bar Association. His favorite sport is handball, and his hobby is the study of the developments in the administration of justice. He is a Democrat.

On June 16, 1928, Mr. Koehn was united in marriage to Genevieve Mary Collins at Omaha. Mrs. Koehn was born at West Bend, Iowa, August 9, 1906, and is a registered nurse, and a graduate of Lord Lister Hospital in 1928. They have one son, Paul, born June 28, 1929. Residence: South Sioux City. (Photograph on Page 675).

John B. Koenig

John B. Koenig, who has lived in Nebraska for over 40 years, was born at Newvienna, Iowa, June 16, 1870, the son of John and Elisebeth (Hoeffer) Koenig. His father, who was born at Cologne, Germany, and died at Newvienna, June 10, 1900, a farmer; he came to America in 1844 and settled in Iowa where he farmed the rest of his life. His mother was born at Coblenze, Germany, February 4, 1849, and came to the United States in 1850.

Mr. Koenig was graduated from elementary school in 1883 and later attended seminary. He is a director of the Bank of Petersburg, is connected with an insurance company, and is active in civic affairs at Petersburg. He holds membership in the Knights of Columbus, St. John the Baptist Catholic Church, and is a member of the National Geographic Society.

He has served as a director in the local school board for two years, acting as treasurer of that organization, has been president of the local order of Knights of Columbus, and is affiliated with the Roman Catholic Mutual Protective Association. His hobby is auction brdge.

He was united in marriage with Anna M. Koester at Raeville, Nebraska, January 28, 1896. Mrs. Koenig was born at Versailles, Missouri, February 15, 1874. They have 12 children; Marcella, Elizabeth, Margaret, Michael, Regina, Bernice, John, Anna, Paul, Ignatius, Isobel, and Marie. Residence: Petersburg.

GEORGE WILLIAM KOEHN

Albert William Koepff

Albert William Koepff, printer and journalist, was born at Beatrice, Gage County, Nebraska, October 6, 1889, the son of Gottlieb and Wilhelmina (Weingart) Koepff. His father, who was born in Germany and died at Beatrice, November, 1889, was an interior wood worker and finisher; he came to America in 1883, lived in Indiana for a year, and then moved to Nebraska. His mother, who was born at Rattenharz, Wurtemburg, Germany, July 23, 1861, and died at Beatrice, October 10, 1909, came to America in 1883.

Mr. Koepff attended the public schools of Beatrice, and in 1916 and 1917 was a student at the University of Kansas. During 1919 and 1920 he was a student at New York University. He is the author of *Snap It Up* and has been editor and publisher of *The Daykin Herald* at Daykin, Jefferson County, Nebraska, since 1927. He was connected with the Beatrice Daily Sun, 1905-16, the *Hebron Register-Champion*, 1917-18, *Daily Record* at Long Branch, New Jersey, 1919-23, *The Daily Princetonian*, 1923-26, Princeton, New Jersey, and the *Tribune*, 1926, at Great Neck, Long Island, New York. He is associated with the Koepff Printing Company at Plymouth, Nebraska.

On June 24, 1918, he enlisted in the signal corps and was a member of the 15th Service Band at Fort Leavenworth. He was stationed at Camp Meade, Maryland, and Camp Alfred Vail, New Jersey. He was honorably discharged at Camp Funston, Kansas, July 1, 1919; he held membership in Post Number 44, Long Branch, of the American Legion, 1920-23, was a member of Post Number 76, at Princeton, 1923-27, and is now affiliated with Post Number 194 at Alexandria, Nebraska.

Mr. Koepff is an independent Republican, and was formerly a member of the Centenary Methodist Church at Beatrice. He is a member of the following: Nebraska Press Association; Daykin Community Club; Nebraska Motor Club; Ancient Free and Accepted Masons; Young Men's Christian Association; Knights of H. H. U.; Wiggens Street Chowder and Marching Club, of Princeton; and the Daykin Bachelor Club.

His favorite recreations are tennis, golf, baseball, reading, and music. He conducts Vic's Band, sings in a male quartette, and plays a harmonica. Mr. Koepff is a member of the Nebraska Society. Residence: Daykin.

Lewis John Koepff

Lewis John Koepff, editor and publisher, was born in Beatrice, Nebraska, January 23, 1887. His father, Gottlieb Koepff, was born in Germany, came to America in his early twenties and began his trade as a carpenter. He died at Beatrice, Nebraska, in September, 1889. Wilhelmina (Weingart) Koepff, mother of Lewis, was born in Rattenharz, Germany, July 23, 1861, and died at Beatrice, Nebraska, October 10, 1909.

Mildred Edna (Hermle) Koepff, wife of Lewis J. Koepff, was born at Byron, Nebraska, January 3, 1889. Of their marriage two children were born. The elder, Robert, born June 21, 1916, and Phyllis, born September 19, 1921.

For forty-four years, Mr. Koepff has been a resident of this state, and during that time he has been in the printing business for thirty years. He was circulation manager of the *Beatrice Sun* for fifteen years and is now editor and publisher of *The Plymouth News*. He was mayor of Plymouth in 1929 and city clerk in 1930-31-32.

He is a Protestant and was baptized in the Lutheran faith. He is a member of the Nebraska Motor Club, and The Nebraskana Society. His hobby is reading and he is interested in electricity. Residence: Plymouth.

Henry William Koepke

Henry William Koepke, son of Julius and Meta (Dannaman) Koepke, has been a resident of Nebraska thirty-nine years, and has always engaged in farming. His father was born at Wilsnack, Germany, May 28, 1844, and came to America in 1869. Until 1892 he resided in Chicago, then coming to Nebraska where he engaged as a farmer until his death at Blue Hill on January 2, 1916. His wife, born in Germany, January 22, 1851, is still living.

Mr. Koepke attended the public schools of Adams County. On May 10, 1905, he was married to Alma Caroline Dahms at Blue Hill. Mrs. Koepke, who was born at St. Louis, Missouri, February 4, 1884, is the daughter of August and Caroline (Siebrass) Dahms. There are three children, Oscar, born May 12, 1907; Letha, born December 16, 1908, and Gilbert, born January 29, 1911. All of the children are high school graduates, and Oscar attends Seward College.

A Republican, Mr. Koepke is much interested in politics. He is a member and elder in the Trinity Evangelical Lutheran Church, and was recently made a life member of The Nebraskana Society. Residence: Blue Hill.

Gerhard Freidrich Koester

A citizen of the United States since December 5, 1899, Gerhard Friedrich Koester was born at Elsfleth, Oldenburg, Germany, May 7, 1876, son of John Herman and Sophie Johanne (Michael) Koester. John Herman Koester was born in Elsfleth, Germany, April 1, 1846, and served in the German Navy 1870-71. He came to Hooper, Nebraska, from Germany in 1890, engaging in farming in Cuming County for many years, and afterward moving to West Point. His death occurred at Council Bluffs, July 27, 1925. He is buried in Mt. Hope Cemetery at West Point, Nebraska. Sophie Johanne Michael was born in Elsfleth, January 14, 1851. An earnest church worker, and Sunday School teacher, she was interested in music. She died at West Point, February 25, 1917, and is also buried in Mount Hope Cemetery.

Gerhard F. Koester attended public schools in Elfsleth, Germany, and a winter term in English in the district school No. 60, north of Hooper. He has engaged in farming since reaching maturity, and is a successful farmer and landowner. At the present time he is a member of the board of directors of the Farmers Co-operative Elevator, a member of the Dixon County Farmer's Institute of which he was secretary 1912-15; director of school district 28, 1909-18, and member of the board of education, district 70, 1918-20. He is a charter member of the First English Lutheran Church at Allen, and has held the following offices: president of the Lutheran Brotherhood 1924-26; secretary 1926-27; president of church council 1912-20 and superintendent of Sunday School 1928-30.

Mr. Koester is a member of the Red Cross, and during the World War held 100% membership and subscribed to all loans. He is a member of the Nebraskana Society, and the Farmers Union. He rented for three years in Cuming County, and in 1905 came to Dixon County, where he purchased the farm on which his family still resides.

On February 12, 1902, he was married to Anna Mathilda Wessel, at Hooper. Mrs. Koester was born at Hooper, April 13, 1878; they have eight children as follows: Paul, born December 5, 1902, married Esther Black; Sophie, born January 23, 1905, married Percy Ole Lockwood; Oscar, born March 21, 1907, married Erma Wheeler; Herbert, born October 14, 1909; George, born October 15, 1912, attended Wayne Normal School; Martha, born December 30, 1914; Patience, born April 12, 1919; and Helen, born April 10, 1921. All the children are on the farm. Mr. Koester's hobby is reading and his favorite sport is swimming. Residence: Allen. (Photograph on Page 677).

GERHARD F. KOESTER   Craven—Wayne

Vaclav J. Kohout

Vaclav J. Kohout was born at Omaha, August 27, 1879, the son of Vaclav and Anna M. (Techacek) Kohout. His father, who was born at Nova Kdyn, Pilzensky, Czechoslovakia, January 1, 1854, and died at Wilber, October 26, 1929, was a farmer and nurseryman; he came to America, October 12, 1872. His mother was born at Merklin, Pilsenke, Czechoslovakia, 1857. She came to this country May, 1871; her family was in the textile mill business in Czechoslovakia. She has been active in club work for many years at Wilber.

Mr. Kohout, who has lived in Nebraska for 51 years, has been in the garage business for 22 years, and in the implement business for the past five years. He owns and manages his own garage; and is president of the Saline County Building & Loan Association. He is a member of the Commercial Club; the National Travel Club; the Nebraskana Society, National Geographic Society, Z C B J, and the Sokol.

He married Rose M. Tachovsky at Wilber, February 25, 1903. Mrs. Kohout was born at Wilber, October 28, 1880. Two children were born to them: Sylvia R., born June 12, 1903, who married Rudolf Hubka; and Otto J., born November 9, 1905, who died July 9, 1926. Sylvia received high honors in school, and was a piano instructor for several years. Residence: Wilber.

Vincent Kokes

Vincent Kokes, insurance and real estate dealer, was born at Bela, Czecho Slovakia, March 16, 1866, and is the son of Joseph and Anna (Borka) Kokes. The father was born in Czecho Slovakia, and died at Lincoln, July 9, 1896. He was a farmer who came directly to Valley County, Nebraska, upon his arrival in America in 1880. His wife, Anna, was born in Bohemia, and died there in 1880.

Mr. Kokes attended Bohemian schools until the age of 14. Upon coming to America, he was engaged in the drug business at Ord for 12 years, served as county clerk of Valley County from 1894 until 1900, and for 20 years was engaged in the banking business at Ord. At the present time he is president of the Bank of Scotia.

His marriage to Lydia L. Ledvina was solemnized at Wahoo, September 20, 1892. Mrs. Kokes was born at Green Bay, Wisconsin, July 22, 1870. They have one son, Edward L., born October 4, 1899, who married Helen Hamsa. He is assistant cashier of the Bank of Scotia.

Mr. Kokes is a member of St. Mary's Catholic Church of Ord, the Knights of Columbus and the Ancient Order of United Workmen. Recently he was made a life member of the Nebraskana Society. Residence: Ord.

Carl Albert Kollmeyer

Born at Quincy, Illinois, April 2, 1891, Carl Albert Kollmeyer is the son of John Henry and Catherine (Moenning) Kollmeyer. His father was born in Quincy, January 18, 1857. A traveling salesman 10 years, he was the owner of a fruit farm twenty years, and now owns a peony farm. His parents came to America from Germany in their youth. His wife, Catherine, was born in Quincy, September 19, 1859, and is of German parentage.

Carl Albert Kollmeyer attended St. Francis Parochial School, and was graduated from the Gem City Business College in 1909. In 1910 he was bookkeeper for the Quincy Stove Company, and was a salesman on the road for them until 1920. During 1920-21 he was western representative for the Rudy Furnace Company of Dowagiac, Michigan, and on January 1, 1922, became a partner of H. Doering in the Doering Hardware Company. On January 1, 1929, he bought the Doering interests and became sole owner.

On October 17, 1917, he was united in marriage to Rosalia Zita Stroot, at Quincy, Illinois She was born there, July 10, 1894, and before her marriage was secretary to her father, August C. Stroot. Mr. Kollmeyer is a Republican. He served as a private with the 122nd Infantry, 31st Division from June, 1918, to December, 1918. At the present time he is first vice commander of Henry Teigeler Post of the American Legion. During 1929-30 he was president of the Fremont Retail Merchants' Association, and served as treasurer of the Fremont Advertising Club 1927-28. He is a Catholic, and a member of St. Patrick's Church, and is grand knight of Phil Sheridan Council 1497, Knights of Columbus, at the present time. He is also a member of the Nebraskana Society, the Red Cross and the Young Men's Christian Association. His business is his hobby, and his sport is golf. Residence: Fremont.

William Arista Kommers

William Arista Kommers, a pharmacist at Hyannis, Nebraska, has lived in this state all his life. He was born at Firth, Nebraska, June 24, 1891, the son of John and Lillian May (Phillips) Kommers. His father, who was born at Sheboygan, Wisconsin, April 4, 1851, and died at Orange, California, June 21, 1927, was a blacksmith, carriage maker, and farmer who served as mayor of Firth and was an active church worker; he was past master of the Masonic Lodge and lectured for that organization; his father and brother were killed in action during the Civil War.

His mother, who was born in Iowa, November 20, 1864, is a clubwoman and church worker at Orange, California. She served in secretarial work for several years prior to her marriage. Her maternal ancesters came to Nebraska from Indiana in the early days of this state, making the trip overland in a covered wagon, and her grandfather was killed by the Indians while they were homesteading near Nebraska City, Nebraska.

Mr. Kommers was graduated from the high school at Ansley, Nebraska, and attended college at Fremont where he passed the examinations given by the State Board of Pharmacy in 1912 and was awarded the degree, Registered Pharmacist. In 1913 he settled on a homestead near Hyannis, and the following year purchased a drug store there. He has been successfully engaged in the latter business for the past 18 years, and is active in community affairs at Hyannis.

He is president of the Hyannis Lions Club, is president of the Hyannis School Board, holds membership in the Red Cross and the Nebraskana Society, and is past master of the local Masonic Lodge. Mr. Kommers was formerly mayor of Hyannis, is affiliated with the Presbyterian Church, and is a member of the Woodmen of the World. His recreations include golfing, tennis, radio mechanics, reading, and music.

On August 12, 1913, his marriage to Maybelle May Westover occurred at Lincoln, Nebraska. Mrs. Kommers, whose parents were settlers of the sand hills of Nebraska in early days, was born at Hyannis, October 27, 1895. Her parents were Robert J. and Elizabeth (Chrisman) Westover. Mrs. Kommers was graduated from Hyannis High School and is a member of the Woman's Club and the Booklover's Club. She attends the Congregational Church. Their two sons are, William, born July 30, 1915; and Howard, born June 1, 1917. Both boys are active in athletics in the Hyannis High School. Residence: Hyannis.

Anton Kopac

Anton Kopac, automobile dealer, and one of Nebraska's leading farm owners, was born at West Point, Nebraska, September 21, 1871, and has always lived in the state. His father, Mike Kopac, a farmer, was born at Klatovi, Bohemia, February 25, 1836, and died at Schuyler, July 28, 1894. He came to this country March 25, 1871. His mother, Jose (Janca) Kopac, was born at Klatovi, November 20, 1846, and died at Schuyler, April 25, 1888.

Mr. Kopac received his education in the rural schools of Nebraska, and since that time has been a farmer in Colfax County, where he has been active in the advancement of his community. During the Spanish-American War he served as a soldier in the Second Nebraska Volunteer Infantry. He is a member of the Nebraskana Society; is affiliated with the Republican Party; and holds membership in the First Presbyterian Church at Schuyler.

His marriage to Agnes Schultz was solemnized at Schuyler, September 26, 1911. Mrs. Kopac was born at Schuyler, November 23, 1885. Residence: Schuyler.

Lewis Kopecky

Lewis Kopecky, who is a farmer and hay dealer at Inman, was born in Omaha, May 15, 1883, the son of Frank and Anna (Cemper) Kopecky. His father, who was a blacksmith and farmer, was born at Skuparovski, Czechoslovakia, and died at Newman Grove, Nebraska. His mother, a native of Caslav, Czechoslovakia, died at Newman Grove.

Mr. Kopecky was employed in the South Omaha Public Library for a time, worked for the Thomas Kilpatrick Company there, and is now a farmer and hay dealer near Inman, where he is serving as moderator of the local school board. He is affiliated with the Methodist Church of Inman, and holds membership in the Nebraskana Society. He is especially interested in gardening.

He was united in marriage with Josephine Holub at Omaha, August 11, 1909. Mrs. Kopecky was born at Omaha, March 23, 1888. Two children were born to them: Lewis Frank, September 25, 1911; and Jerry John, August 4, 1913, who died January 7, 1931. Lewis F., who is a farmer, was graduated from the Inman High School with valedictory honors. Residence: Inman.

Andrew Kopperud

Andrew Kopperud, prominent banker of Omaha, was born at De Smet, Kingsbury County, South Dakota, October 8, 1880. His father, Niels Anderson Kopperud, was born at Oslo, Norway, came to America when a young man, and was a farmer and banker; he held various positions in local political offices. He died in June, 1917.

His mother, Mary (Hansen) Kopperud, was born at Drammen, Norway, and died at Rochester, Minnesota, in April, 1920.

Mr. Kopperud was graduated from the public schools at Milwaukee, and later was graduated from the Hoffman Business Institute at Milwaukee. He was a student at the State College at Brookings, South Dakota, for a time, and also attended the State Teachers College at Madison, South Dakota.

He has been connected with various country banks as cashier and president; was president of the Security Bank Trust Company at Webster, South Dakota; and is president of the Oldham National Bank at Oldham, South Dakota. He is now vice president and treasurer of the Federal Land Bank and the Federal Intermediate Credit Bank, of Omaha.

He has held various executive positions in professional organizations, among them treasurer and president of the South Dakota Bankers Association; member of the executive committee of the American Bankers Association. He served as school treasurer at Lake Preston, and Webster, for many years. He was alderman at Webster for six years.

His marriage to Mabel Laura Matthews was solemnized at Madison, Lake County, South Dakota, December 28, 1916. Mrs. Kopperud, whose ancestry is Scotch and Irish, was born at Madison, May 8, 1891. They have three children: Mary Jane, born February 10, 1920; Della,

born November 27, 1921; and Andrew, Jr., born July 4, 1924.

He is a member of the Rotary Club at Omaha. He is a member of the South Dakota Horticultural Society; the Young Men's Christian Association; the Athletic Club of Omaha; and the Nebraskana Society. He is an Odd Fellow, a Mason, and Shriner. He is affiliated with the First Presbyterian Church of Omaha. His hobby is fishing. He is a Republican. Residence: Omaha.

Walter William Korff

Walter William Korff, lumberman, was born at Lanham, Gage County, Nebraska, May 8, 1893. He is the son of Henry Korff, born in Germany, who has been prominent in the affairs of Thayer County for a number of years, and who was the organizer of the Korff Lumber Company. Henry Korff married Caroline Brockmeyer, who was born in Kansas, of German and English parentage.

Educated first in the public school at Odell, Nebraska, Walter W. Korff was graduated from Midland College Academy in 1911, and later attended Midland College. In 1913 he entered the lumber business, continuously at Waterville, Kansas, until 1922, and since that time in Hebron. He is now part owner and manager of the Korff Lumber Company.

On August 29, 1915, Mr. Korff was married to Margaret Sharpless, at Atchison, Kansas. Mrs. Korff, who is of English descent, was born in Kansas, on September 8, 1895. There are three children: Naomi, born August 29, 1917; William, born March 16, 1920, and Donald, born December 10, 1925.

Mr. Korff is a Republican. His present memberships include the Masons, the Nebraskana Society, and lumber and implement trade associations. Mr. Korff is affiliated with the Hebron Presbyterian Church, has served on the Hebron school board three years, and for two years was mayor of Hebron. Residence: Hebron.

Otto Albin Kostal

Born at Germania, Pennsylvania, March 5, 1899, Otto Albin Kostal is the son of Albin and Marie (Bower) Kostal. His father, a farmer, was born in Germany, came to this country in 1889, and died at Omaha, Nebraska, October 20, 1927. His mother was born in Austria in 1877.

Dr. Kostal attended the public schools of Sarpy County, Nebraska, was graduated from South Omaha High School in 1918, and received the B. S. degree at the Municipal University of Omaha, 1921. In 1923 he was awarded the degree Doctor of Medicine at the University of Nebraska where he was a member of Phi Chi. He served his internship at the Omaha Methodist Hospital, 1923, and in 1924 was a member of the staff of Gorgas Memorial Hospital in the Canal Zone. Since 1924 he has been engaged in general medical practice at Giltner, Nebraska.

He is a member of the Giltner School Board, the Hamilton County Medical Society, Nebraska State Medical Society, and the American Medical Society. He holds membership in the Red Cross and the Nebraskana Society; he is a 32nd degree Mason, holding membership in the Scottish Rite and Shrine bodies. In 1920 Dr. Kostal was president of the Science Club at Omaha.

In 1931 he was tennis champion of Hamilton County, Nebraska; his other sports include big game hunting. A Republican, he has served as chairman of the village board at Giltner since 1927. He was united in marriage with Florea S. Strickland at Lincoln, January 22, 1926. Mrs. Kostal, who is a nurse, was born at Kansas City, Missouri, September 19, 1897. To their marriage two children were born: Betty Joan, April 22, 1927; and Mary Lou, October 9, 1928. Residence: Giltner.

Otto Kotouc

Otto Kotouc, banker and author, was born at Humboldt, Nebraska, April 22, 1885. He is of Czech ancestry, his parents being Frank and Marie (Hon) Kotouc, the former born at Ransko, Bohemia, October 25, 1839, and the latter born at Hermanuv Mestec, Bohemia, April 24, 1850. Frank Kotouc was a harness maker by trade, who came to America in 1882. He was a teacher in the Bohemian school at Humboldt for about twenty years prior to his death on December 25, 1916.

After his graduation from the Humboldt High School in 1903, Otto Kotouc attended the University of Nebraska, receiving his B. A. in 1908. He is a member of Phi Beta Kappa and of Acacia. At the university he was a member of the Latin Club.

His marriage to Camille Cernik took place at Ord, Nebraska, August 29, 1912. Mrs. Kotouc was born at Ord, July 22, 1892. They have two children, Otto, Jr., born June 15, 1913; and Marie Louise, born March 1, 1917, who attends Humboldt High School.

Always active in the Democratic party, Mr. Kotouc served as member of the state legislature of 1909 and 1911. He is now chairman of the Democratic county central committee. From 1909-15 he was assistant cashier of the State Bank of Humboldt, and cashier of the Home State Bank, from 1915-25; since that time he has been president of that bank.

Poet and author, he made contributions to *Poet Lore* (1916, 17, 18), is the author of *Bohemian Settlement at Humboldt* in *History of Richardson County* (1917; *Songs of the Slav* (1919); contributions to *An Anthology of Czechoslovak Poetry* (Columbia University Press, 1929). He was associate editor of *Komensky Magazine* (1909-11).

During the World War he was a member of the Nebraska Council of Defense, chairman of Four Minute Men, chairman of loan drives, secretary of the local Red Cross, fuel administrator and advisory member of the draft board. He is a member of the Methodist Episcopal Church of Humboldt, past chairman of the Richardson County Bankers Association, past president of the fourth Nebraska Regional Clearing House Association, and president of the State Bankers Association. He was member of the advisory board, Richardson County Court House, 1923-24, and was secretary of the board of education six years, and of the Bruun Memorial Library several years. He is also past president of the Humboldt Chamber of Commerce. His fraternal organizations include the Odd Fellow, the Knights of Pythias and the C. S. P. S. He is a 32nd degree Mason and member of the Shrine, the Knights Templar and Order of Eastern Star. He is also affiliated with the state and university Y. M. C. A. His sport is fishing, and his chief recreation is reading. Residence: Humboldt.

Frank Koudele

One of Saunders County's most outstanding citizens, Frank Koudele was born at Wahoo, May 4, 1883, son of Frank and Frances (Vanous) Koudele. Frank Koudele, Sr., was born in Bohemia, December 3, 1849, and came to America about 1870. A butcher, he later became a successful business man and banker. He died at Wahoo, April 22, 1920. His wife, Frances, was born in Bohemia, in November, 1852, and is living.

Mr. Koudele attended the public schools, and Wahoo High School to the tenth grade. Since 1899 he has been associated with the Weston Bank, of which he is president. He is a director of that bank, and of the Weston Grain and Stock Company. A Republican, he was for some time chairman and member of the village board, and takes and active interest in community affairs. He is a former member and secretary of the Weston School Board, and during the World War was active in Red Cross and Liberty Loan drives. He is a 32nd degree Scottish Rite

Mason, member of the Shrine and Eastern Star, and of the Knights of Pythias and the Odd Fellows.

On June 19, 1907, he was united in marriage to Helen Henrietta Jacobs at Wahoo. Mrs. Koudele who is a bank director, was born at Yutan, Nebraska, June 2, 1884. They have two sons, Gordon F., born June 9, 1912, who is a bank clerk; and Joseph W., born August 21, 1920, who is a student in school. Mr. Koudele enjoys all forms of athletics, especially football and baseball. His favorite game is bowling. Residence: Weston. (Photograph on Page 681).

Denman Kountze

On October 28, 1899, Denman Kountze was born at Omaha, Nebraska, the son of Charles and May (Burns) Kountze. His father, who was born at Omaha, September 26, 1871, was a pioneer banker in Nebraska, and is still engaged in the banking business. His mother was born at Omaha, and died there.

Mr. Kountze attended Columbia High School at Omaha, and was a student at St. Paul's School at Concord, New Hampshire, and the University School at Cleveland, Ohio. Later he attended the University of Nebraska and Yale University, where he was a member of Beta Theta Pi and the Bergeluis Society. He has lived in Omaha all his life, and is now vice president of the First National Bank of Omaha. He is a partner in the firm Kountze Brothers of New York City.

His marriage to May Malloy Harris was solemnized at Memphis, Tennessee; Mrs. Kountze was born at Memphis. They have two children: Malloy, born November 17, 1924; and Denman, born June 10, 1929. During the World War Mr. Kountze served as a corporal in the tank corps. He is a member of the American Legion.

He holds membership in the Chamber of Commerce at Omaha, and the Kiwanis Club. His social clubs are: Omaha Club, Omaha Athletic Club, Omaha Country Club, Yale Club of New York, and Wiamco Club, at Wiamco, Massachusetts. He is affiliated with Trinity Cathedral at Omaha. He is a Democrat, and is a member of the Nebraskana Society. Residence: Omaha.

Anna Kovanda

Anna Kovanda was born at Pawnee City, Nebraska, February 28, 1873, the daughter of John and Mary (Vrtiska) Clema. Her father, who was born in Czechoslovakia, July 12, 1840, came to America in 1849 where he engaged in farming and stock raising. He died at Steinauer, Nebraska, January 5, 1924.

Her mother was born in Czechoslovakia, March 25, 1844, and died at Table Rock, Nebraska, October 27, 1927. She was active in church affairs; and took part in community and religious musical activities.

Mrs. Kovanda's education was received in high school with two additional years of academic work, and special training in dramatics. She has lived in Nebraska all her life and has always been interested in church and club affairs. For four years she was state vice president of the National American Woman Suffrage Association, prior to the enactment of woman suffrage, and during that time kept headquarters at the Lincoln Epworth Assembly and also at Pawnee City, during their Chautauqua. On February 16, 1920, she was awarded, by Carrie Chapman Catt, a certificate of honor for her services. She was assistant postmistress at Table Rock for nine years.

She was married to Anthony R. Kovanda, at Pawnee City, on August 18, 1891. Mr. Kovanda, who is a banker, was born at Czechoslovakia, May 6, 1863. Their son, Rudolph, who was born March 22, 1893, is a graduate of the University of Nebraska, is president of the State Bank of Elk Creek at Elk Creek, Nebraska.

During the World War Mrs. Kovanda was president of the local Red Cross, and took part in every drive for funds. She is a member of the Order of Eastern Star.

FRANK KOUDELE

Anderson—Wahoo

S. B. A., and the Western Bohemian Fraternal Association. Mrs. Kovanda is affiliated with the Methodist Episcopal Church, and is an interested worker in the Parent-Teachers' Association. She is a Democrat. Residence: Table Rock.

Anthony R. Kovanda

On May 6, 1863, Anthony R. Kovanda was born at Trimani, Czechoslovakia, the son of Albert and Frances (Hurt) Kovanda. His father, who was born at Trimani, April 9, 1815, and died at Table Rock, Pawnee County, Nebraska, July 15, 1892, was a farmer who came to America in 1867. His mother was born at Kric, Czechoslovakia, May 7, 1822, and died at Humboldt, Richardson County, Nebraska, December 10, 1914.

Mr. Kovanda received his education in the country schools, and later was especially interested in the study of music. He has lived in Nebraska for 63 years. A farmer for nineteen years and a bookkeeper for some time, he was for nine years postmaster. At the present time he is vice president of the State Bank of Elk Creek, at Elk Creek, Nebraska.

He married Anna Clema at Pawnee City, Nebraska, August 18, 1891. Mrs. Kovanda was born in Pawnee City, February 28, 1873; her ancestors were farmers and teachers. There is one son, Rudolph, born March 22, 1893, who is a graduate of the University of Nebraska, and is president of the State Bank of Elk Creek.

In the late war Mr. Kovanda was active in loan drives. He is a member of the Red Cross, the Security Benefit Association, the Western Bohemian Fraternal Lodge, and the Nebraskana Society. He is a Mason, and a Democrat. Residence: Table Rock.

Vratislav Joseph Kovarik

Vratislav Joseph Kovarik, druggist and postmaster, was born at Crete, Nebraska, June 30, 1876. He is the son of Mike and Mary (Kazda) Kovarik, Sr., who were born in Bohemia, the former in 1845, and the latter in 1855. His father died at Crete, in 1915, and his mother in 1916.

Born on a farm in Saline County, he lived there until he was nineteen years old, walked 2½ miles to country school until he graduated from eighth grade. He then attended Crete High School and had to walk 3 miles. In 1899 he won the first state prize in Crete Schools. The following 2 years he remained on the farm and then took up the drug business for 4 years. Later he attended St. Louis College of Pharmacy 6 months. Returning to Crete he passed the pharmacy examination and became a registered pharmacist. Mr. Kovarik worked 4 years at the Ed. J. Steidl drug store and then moved to Hallam. In 1897 he won first prize at Crete in the Sokol held for Bohemians from all over the state, including horizontal bars, parallel bars, etc.

On October 25, 1899, he was married to Barbara Anna Kubat at Crete. Mrs. Kovarik was born at Crete, April 23, 1880, and is now assistant postmaster at Hallam. They have one son, Robert Carl, born April 8, 1918, who attends high school.

A Republican, Mr. Kovarik participates in local politics. He clerked in a drug store at Crete eight years, from 1893-1901, and for more than thirty years has operated his own drug store at Hallam, and for twenty-nine years has been, and still is postmaster at Hallam. He is a member of the Modern Woodmen of America, the Masons and the Shrine, and is a member of the Sesostris Shrine Band of Lincoln. Playing in bands is his hobby.

He has been treasurer of the Modern Woodmen of America since 1915, and is still holding office. He was instructor in athletic work at Crete for eight years, 1888-1897; and had a band at Hallam for 10 years, 1910-1919. 1897; and had a band at Hallam for 10 years. 1910-1919. Residence: Hallam. (Photograph on Page 683).

Gustav A. Koza

Gustav A. Koza, who for the past seventeen years has served as postmaster at Clarkson, was born in Clarkson, May 8, 1880. He is the son of John and Antonie (Travnicek) Koza, the former a contractor and builder, who was born at Spelkov, Moravia, May 25, 1847. He died at Clarkson, March 18, 1930. Antonie, his wife, was born at Telecy, Europe, June 16, 1849, and died at Clarkson, March 13, 1929.

Educated first in the public schools of Colfax County, Gustav A. Koza later attended Western Normal College at Shenandoah, Iowa. On July 10, 1910, he was united in marriage to Anna Hubacek at Clarkson. Mrs. Koza, who was born in Policka, Bohemia, July 17, 1891, is active in club work and secretary of several civic organizations. There are three children: Gilbert L., born July 1, 1911, who is a junior at the University of Nebraska; Chester A., born September 6, 1913, who graduated in 1931 from the Clarkson public school, and Robert J., born February 15, 1924.

During the World War Mr. Koza was active in civilian drives and is a member of the Home Guard. His religious affiliation is with the New Zion Bohemian Presbyterian Church. He is a member of the Red Cross, the Commercial club and the Modern Woodmen of America. His favorite recreations are traveling and motoring, and his hobby is reading. Residence: Clarkson.

John A. Krance

John A. Krance, clergyman and educator, was born at Berea, Ohio, February 1, 1880. He is the son of Lawrence Krance who was born in Poland, on July 25, 1839. Lawrence Krance came to America in 1870, settling first in Ohio and later in Nebraska. He died on a farm at Farwell, Howard County, Nebraska, October 10, 1908. His wife, Susanna Margaret (Siedoff) Krance, was born in Poland, August 8, 1844, and died in Howard County, January 27, 1913.

Upon the completion of his elementary education in district and parochial schools John A. Krance entered St. Mary's High School, St. Mary's Kansas, from which he was graduated in 1898. He received his A. B. from St. Louis University in 1908, and his A. M. in 1916. His post graduate work was taken at Marquette University 1910-11, Armour Institute 1912, and the University of Wisconsin, 1924.

Professor Krance has been a resident of Nebraska intermittently since 1887. At the present time he is professor of organic chemistry and director of the department of chemistry at Creighton University. He is a member of the American Chemical Society, the American Association for the Advancement of Science, and the Nebraska Academy of Science. He is a Roman Catholic. Residence: Omaha.

Golden Paul Kratz

Golden Paul Kratz, county judge of Cheyenne County, was born at Randolph, Nebraska, September 14, 1892, son of George and Olive Annetta (Coats) Kratz. The father, born in Iowa, is a carpenter of German descent. The mother was born in Illinois of English ancestry.

Upon his graduation from Lyons High School in 1910, Mr. Kratz attended the University of Nebraska, receiving his Bachelor of Laws degree in 1916. He was president of his senior class in law school, was a member of the cross country team in 1915, and is a member of Phi Alpha Delta.

From 1920 until 1922 Judge Kratz was a partner in the firm of Kratz Land & Title Company, and from 1922 until 1928, was a member of the law firm of Kepler & Kratz. Since 1929 he has practiced alone in con-

VRATISLAV JOSEPH KOVARIK

Townsend—Lincoln

junction with his office of county judge. He was deputy county attorney, from 1922 until 1926.

His marriage to Clara Henrietta Paper was solemnized at Lincoln, November 1, 1919. Mrs. Kratz was born in Dodge County, Nebraska, January 11, 1893, of German ancestry. She is the daughter of Nicklaus and Augusta (Clausen) Paper. Mrs. Kratz is a member of Delta Delta Delta at the University of Nebraska, and was a student at Midland College. She is a member of the Eastern Star and the Parent-Teachers Association. They have two children, Kent, born April 28, 1923; and Dean, born June 26, 1924.

Mr. Kratz is a Republican. He enlisted in the Louiisiana National Guards in the spring of 1917 as a private, and was discharged in 1920 with the rank of second lieutenant. He is a member of the American Legion and was post commander, 1927-28; department executive committeeman, 1927-28. He is a member of the Reserve Officers Association of which he was president in 1927.

Among his professional, civic, and fraternal organizations are the following, Cheyenne County Bar Association, Western Nebraska Bar Association (vice president, 1929); Nebraska State Bar Association (advisory council, 1930); and the American Bar Association; the Chamber of Commerce; the Lions Club; the Blue Lodge Masons, Consistory and Shrine; Knights of Pythias (chancellor commander, 1927, grand chancellor, 1931). He is a member of the Parent Teachers Association and the Sidney Country Club. Residence: Sidney.

Alexander Rose Krause

Alexander R. Krause was born at West Point, Cuming County, Nebraska, February 7, 1898, the son of Alonzo L. and Jessie (Rose) Krause. His father, who was born at London, Ontario, August 24, 1870, is now a resident of Batesland, South Dakota, where he moved in 1926, and he is engaged in the real estate business. He has been a member of the city council, postmaster, and a civic leader in West Point for many years. His mother was of English descent, and his father's family was German.

Jessie (Rose) Krause was born at Greenbush, New York, April 27, 1872. She is of Scotch and English descent; her great grandfather, Colonel Zebulon Scriven, served in the American Revolution. She was organist for 40 years in her home church, and was active in club work in the community.

Mr. Krause was graduated from the West Point High School in 1915, and in 1920 was awarded the A. B. degree at the University of Nebraska, where he was prominent in school affairs. He was a member of the Glee Club; the Cornhusker Quartette; the Kosmet Club; and the Innocents, 1918. He took part in the spring vacation university road show; was president of Delta Upsilon, 1918, and held membership in Sigma Gamma Epsilon.

From 1920 to 1925, Mr. Krause was treasurer of A. L. Krause & Company; was president of this organization, 1925-27; and since 1927 has been in business for himself. A Republican, he was at one time a member of the city council at West Point, where he has lived all his life.

On October, 18, 1921, he was united in marriage with Lora Jean Thacker at Crowell, Texas. Mrs. Krause, who was born at Crowell, July 8, 1899, is of Norwegian and English descent. They have one daughter, Mary Elizabeth, born March 27, 1931.

Mr. Krause was a cadet officer, 1917-18; was commissioned second lieutenant in the United States Army Infantry, 1918; and was stationed at Camp Mebry, Texas, until the Armistice was signed during the World War. He is a member of the American Legion. He is at the present time treasurer of the West Point Community Club; was secretary of the Lions Club, 1929-30, deputy district governor, 1929-30, district secretary, 1930-31; and is a member of the Nebraskana Society. He is a Mason, Scottish Rite and Shrine. He is affiliated with Grace Lutheran Church of West Point, and is a member of the West Point Country Club. He is fond of golfing. Residence: West Point. (Photograph in Album).

Clyde Lauren Krause

Clyde Lauren Krause was born at Albion, Nebraska, July 2, 1893, and has been a resident of this state all his life. His father, Paul Athenial Krause, who was born in Wisconsin, February 26, 1860, has been a tinner, and implement and hardware dealer at Albion, for the past 52 years; his German parents immigrated to this country in 1852, where they settled in Wisconsin, later homesteading in Nebraska. His mother, Carrie Faulkner, who was born in Wisconsin, October 14, 1866, and died at Wahoo, Nebraska, February 14, 1927, was actively interested in nature study and club work. Her parents, who were of Scotch-Irish descent, were settlers in Wisconsin in the early days, and later moved to Nebraska where they were pioneer homesteaders.

Mr. Krause was graduated from the Albion High School in 1911, and was a student at the University of Nebraska, 1911-15, where he was a member of Kappa Sigma. He received letters in basketball and baseball, in high school and was actively identified with athletics during his university career. He also engaged in semi-professional baseball for a time. From 1919 to 1930, he was a partner in the hardware firm P. A. Krause & Sons, at Fullerton, Nebraska. At this time he is secretary-treasurer and a partner in the firm of P. A. Krause & Sons at Albion, acting as director in this organization.

He is a member of the Red Cross, was a member of the Lions Club at Fullerton, from 1927 to 1929, and holds membership in the Masons. He is affiliated with the Congregational Church of Albion, is a member of the Newman Grove Golf Club, and holds membership in the Nebraskana Society. His sports include hunting; fishing; golfing; volleyball; and basketball. His hobby is reading. During the late war Mr. Krause was a sergeant in the medical department of the United States Army, and at this time is a past commander of the American Legion.

He was united in marriage with Eleanor Marie Keenan, at Junction City, Kansas, May 10, 1919. Mrs. Krause, who is a registered nurse, was born at Peoria, Illinois, August 22, 1895, of Irish parentage. During the World War she was an active member of the United States Army Nurses' Corps, and as a member of the American Legion and its auxiliary, she is very active. Two children were born to this marriage: Margaret Louise, born January 19, 1920; and Janet Marion, born September 7, 1923.

Mr. Krause is a Republican, and served as a member of the Fullerton city council from 1924 to 1930. Residence: Newman Grove.

Chester A. Krebs

Chester A. Krebs was born at Scotia, Nebraska, July 13, 1896, the son of Morgan L. and Annie Viola (Reavis) Krebs. His father, who was a public spirited and progressive farmer and stockman, was born at North Manchester, Indiana, March 20, 1863, and died at Scotia, March 16, 1921. His mother was born at Warrensburg, Missouri, December 17, 1865. She was named for her maternal grandmother who settled in Missouri a hundred and ten years ago, and is a descendant of the Warren family of Virginia.

Mr. Krebs was graduated from the high school at Grand Island, Nebraska, in 1916, where he was president of the senior class and received letters in athletics. At this time he is manager of the Scotia Grain and Supply Company, is a member of the Scotia Business Men's Club, and holds membership in the Scotia Parent Teachers Association. He is a Mason.

During the World War Mr. Krebs served as a private in the Army Engineering Corps, and is now past commander and past adjutant of the American Legion. His hobby is mechanics and his favorite sport is football. Politically, he is a Progressive Republican. Residence: Scotia.

Frank John Kreizinger

Frank H. Kreizinger was born at Olmitz, Austria, August 28, 1874. He received his elementary education in a country school in Butler County, and was graduated in 1890, he then attended Fremont Normal College for one semester.

Joseph F. Kreizinger, father of Frank, was born in Olmitz, Austria, January 19, 1837, and died at Bellwood, Nebraska, June 10, 1910. He was a corporal in the Austrian Army for twelve years, and after coming to this country he was a farmer. Adalhide Josephine (Smith), mother of Frank, was also born at Olmitz, April 26, 1848, and is now living at the age of eighty-three at Bellwood, Nebraska, February 6, 1887. Their marriage took place on June 7, 1905, at Bruning, Nebraska. There were four children: Gladys, born March 25, 1906, and died April 21, of the same year; Everett, born September 15, 1907; Lloyd, born November 27, 1911; and Harold, born August 25, 1926. Everett is attending the University of Nebraska, and Lloyd is assisting on his father's farm.

Mr. Kreizinger has been a resident of this state for fifty-five years. He was township assessor from 1912 to 1918, and is president of the Farmer's Elevator of Bellwood. During the World War he was in charge of loan drives in his township.

He is affiliated with the Methodist Church of Bellwood. He was a member of the Red Cross from 1914 to 1924, is an honorary member of the Chamber of Commerce, and holds membership with the Royal Highlanders, the Odd Fellows, Ben Hur, and The Nebraskana Society. He was director of his local school district from 1906 to 1924. Carpentery is his hobby and baseball is his favorite sport. Residence: Bellwood.

Edward Stanley Krikac

Edward Stanley Krikac, editor and publisher of the *Comstock News*, was born at Comstock, Nebraska, June 27, 1903, son of Vencel Anton and Josephine (Klima) Krikac.

The father, born in Luzany, Prestice, Bohemia, December 29, 1866, came to America in April 1883, and is engaged in the banking and insurance business. The mother, born in Sabedraz, Kostelle, Bohemia, February 24, 1872, came to America in 1874.

Mr. Krikac attended public school at Comstock and was graduated from high school there in 1922. He attended Kearney State Teachers College the following summer. In high school he earned two letters in basketball and four in track.

From 1923 until 1925 he was employed on the *Creighton News*, from 1925-1926 on the *Wayne Herald*, and in February, 1926, purchased the *Comstock News* of which he has since been editor and publisher. From May, 1931 to May 1932 he served as a member of the village board. He is a member of the Nebraska State Historical Society and a life member of the Nebraskana Society. His favorite sports are football and baseball, while his hobby is fishing.

On May 18, 1928, he was married to Lillian Leone Pierce at Taylor. Mrs. Krikac was born at Bartlett, Iowa, September 18, 1905, daughter of Mr. and Mrs. Charles Pierce. Mrs. Krikac has an A. B. degree from Peru State Teachers College, graduating in 1927. She was a high school teacher prior to marriage. There is one son, Dennis Clair, born October 21, 1931. Residence: Comstock.

Mary Eleanor Krisl

Mary Eleanor Krisl was born at Milligan, Nebraska, February 1, 1886, the daughter of James V. and Mary B. (Hamouz) Krisl. Her father, who was born in Czechoslovakia, August 6, 1861, came to America with his father in 1870, and settled in the mining town of Braidwood, Illinois. When he was seventeen years of age his parents moved to Saline County and engaged in farming. He was a farmer, served as deputy county treasurer, precinct assessor nine terms and school director many years. He was always active in community affairs, and at the time of his death, November 17, 1912, was postmaster. However, due to poor health his daughter, Mary, has carried on his work as postmaster.

Mary B. Hamouz was born in Trtice, Nove Straseri, Czechoslovakia, February 2, 1862, and came to America with her parents as a girl of sixteen. With the exception of the years her husband served as deputy county treasurer, she lived in the vicinity of Milligan, her entire life. Both parents died in Lincoln Hospitals.

Miss Krisl was graduated from the Milligan High School in 1902, and for three years was a student at the University of Nebraska. For the past twenty years she has been postmistress at Milligan, where she is now serving as president of the Local Woman's Club. She is a member of the League of District Postmasters, is affiliated with the Catholic Church, and holds membership in the Nebraskana Society.

During the World War, through the efforts of Miss Krisl, $54,000 in War Saving Stamps were sold, and she received from the Treasury Department an award for distinguished service.

The postoffice at Milligan was started as a fourth class one, and in 1921, was made third class. In 1923, she built the Krisl Block which is a very beautiful building, modern in every way, which is occupied by the Charles J. Kotas general store and the Milligan Post Office, the latter being one of the finest and best equipped for size in the state. Residence: Milligan.

Oliver M. Krogh

Oliver M. Krogh, son of Jens Peter and Phena (Larsen) Krogh, was born at Dannebrog, Nebraska, May 14, 1900. His father was born in Denmark, December 19, 1866, and came to America in 1878. He is an extensive land owner, and is owner also of the Krogh Alfalfa Mills and the Krogh Feed Mill. His wife, Phena, was born at Farwell, Nebraska, May 16, 1875. Her parents homesteaded in Howard County, coming to America in 1873.

Upon his graduation from the Lothrop School at Omaha, on June 11, 1915, Mr. Krogh entered Central High School, from which he was graduated on June 13, 1919. He received his degree of Doctor of Chiropractic from the Palmer School of Chiropractic at Davenport, Iowa, on March 28, 1924, and the degree of Philosopher of Chiropractic on March 28, 1924. He has completed various extension courses from the University of Nebraska and Creighton University. In 1922, he was president of the Nebraska Alumni Association of the Palmer School of Chiropractic. He is a former scout master.

Since his admission to practice in 1924, Dr. Krogh has practiced most of the time at Chadron. During the year 1926 and 1927, he practiced at Kimball, and at one time, for a period of a year, was associated with Dr. Mortensen of Omaha. During the years 1919 until 1921, he was associated with the Omaha Alfalfa Milling Company, as bookkeeper.

On July 8, 1927, Dr. Krogh was married to Ethel Ann Schram at Madison. She is a graduate of Wesleyan University and a member of Alpha Kappa Delta and before her marriage was a teacher in the public schools at Kimball, Nebraska. She is the daughter of Charles F. and Ann C. (Broadbrooks) Schram. Mrs. Krogh was born at Foster, Nebraska, November 11, 1905, and is an educator of German descent. They have one son, Don Milton, born January 12, 1931.

Dr. Krogh is a Protestant, a member of the Lions Club, and of the Masonic Order. His favorite sport is golf. Residence: Chadron.

John Simon Kroh

John Simon Kroh, editor and publisher of the *Keith County News*, was born at Clearspring, Maryland, January 25, 1874, son of Courtney Hewit and Emma Cora (Schnebley) Kroh. His father was born in Franklin County, Pennsylvania in 1847, and died at Belle Plaine, Iowa, in 1905. His mother was born in Washington County, Maryland, in 1846, and died at Oswego, Illinois in 1926. His father is a farmer and stock grower of German descent, while his mother is of English and German.

Mr. Kroh attended public school at Clearspring, Maryland, and afterward was a student in the high school at Belle Plaine, Iowa. Starting as a clerk, he became manager of the grocery department of a department store, and afterwards had three years road work for Marshall Field and Company at Chicago, later he traveled for an advertising firm. He has resided in Nebraska for the past 17 years, and was state senator on the Republican ticket from the 31st district of Nebraska, 1923-24. He was president of the Nebraska State Press Association in 1923. At the present time he is county chairman of the Republican county central committee.

His marriage to Nellie E. Snyder was solemnized at Brule, Nebraska, December 31, 1910. Mrs. Kroh, who was born at Peru, Illinois, November 4, 1878, is of German and Irish descent. She is the daughter of George W. and Josephine (Wasson) Snyder. Her father died in July, 1916, at Brule, Nebraska, and her mother is making her home with her daughter, Mrs. Kroh. Mrs. Kroh is a member of the Congregational Church of which she has been chorister for the past sixteen years. She is a member of the Order of the Eastern Star and has served as a member of the school board. She takes a great interest in the public and county school work. Mrs. Kroh is interested in politics and is the committeewoman of the Republican State Central Committee from the 31st district and has more than average ability as a public speaker. She is a teacher and an instructor in voice and instrumental music.

During the late war, Mr. Kroh was a four minute speaker. He is a member of the Congregational Church, the Ogallala Commercial Club, the Ogallala Rotary Club (charter member), the Masons, and the Odd Fellows. His hobbies include gardening, reading, and public speaking. Residence: Ogallala.

William Krotter

One of Holt County's leading executives, William Krotter was born at Knoxville, Illinois, January 23, 1865. He is the son of John Baptiste and Anna Maria (Webber) Krotter, both natives of Germany.

John Baptiste, the father, was born at Riedenberg, Bavaria, November 3, 1826, and after military service as a curassier, followed his father's family to America. Locating in Chicago in 1854, acquired and operated a brewery and ice business at Knoxville. His death occurred there on February 11, 1890.

Anna Maria Webber, born at Brend, Ober Welzheim, Germany, November 18, 1838, died at Stuart, Nebraska, November 22, 1919. She migrated to Philadelphia in 1861, was married at Galesburg, Illinois, on June 17, 1862, rearing a family of eight, five of whom are living.

Educated in the primary and grammar schools of Knoxville, Illinois, until 1876, William Krotter graduated from high school in 1879. Coming to Nebraska in 1887, he was a lumber yard employee at O'Neill for a time and was later manager of Barnett and Frees at Emmett and at Stuart. In 1891 he purchased the business at Stuart, incorporating in 1905 with several branches. In 1906 he organized the Krotter & Hall Lumber Company with branches; the Atkinson Interstate Telephone Company in 1894, the Citizens Telephone Company in 1900, and at the present time is president of the William Krotter Company at Stuart with branches in Spencer and Naper, Nebraska, and St. Charles and Herrick, South Dakota.

Mr. Krotter is secretary-treasurer of the Stuart Federal Farm Loan Association, secretary of the Tri-County Improvement Association, and the author of various articles for lumber and implement journals. He has held various offices in state and national lumber and implement associations, including that of president; organized and operated the first telephone toll lines and exchanges in northern Nebraska and southern South Dakota, and the first federal farm loan association in that territory. His marriage to Mabel Adela Hall of Long Pine was solemnized on June 8, 1898.

He is chairman of the road committee of the Stuart Commercial Club, a Blue Lodge Mason, and a member of chapter, council and commandery. During the World War he was active in Red Cross, Liberty Loan, War Savings Stamp and other drives. From 1913-16 he was head of the board of education at Stuart. Mr. Krotter's religious affiliation is with the First Presbyterian Church of Stuart. Recently he was made a life member of the Nebraskana Society in recognition of his work in commercial and community activities. He devotes much of his leisure time to historical and geographic reading. Residence: Stuart. (Photograph in Album).

Joseph F. Krupka

For the past 53 years Joseph F. Krupka has lived in Nebraska, where he has engaged in farming in Colfax County. He was born at Ickovice, Czechoslovakia, March 20, 1874, the son of Joseph and Mary (Manak) Krupka. His father, a pioneer Nebraskan and prosperous farmer, was born at Ickovice, April, 1849, and died at Howells, July, 1921; he came to America, October, 1878. His mother was born at Ickovice, July 22, 1853.

Mr. Krupka attended the rural schools of Colfax County. He is a public spirited farmer, and has been interested in the advancement of his community for many years. Politically, he is an independent. He was recently elected to membership in the Nebraskana Society.

His marriage to Emilie Bohaboj, was solemnized at Howells, Nebraska, February 12, 1908. Mrs. Krupka was born at Ulkove, Ulyrske-Janovice, Czechoslovakia, February 8, 1883. Her parents are still living in Czechoslovakia. Three children were born to them: Emily J., born February 7, 1909; Adolph R., born April 17, 1910; and Joseph L., born June 27, 1913. Residence: Howells.

Theodore Kubart

Born at Chicago, Illinois, March 30, 1879, Theodore Kubart is the son of Joseph and Anna Kubart. His father, who was a cabinet maker, was born in Czechoslovakia and died at Atkinson, Nebraska, February 2, 1917. His mother was born in Czechoslovakia.

Mr. Kubart, who is a farmer and hay dealer, has been a resident of this state for the past 46 years. He is affiliated with St. Joseph's Catholic Church, is treasurer of the Society of St. Vincent de Paul, and holds membership in the Knights of Columbus.

On October 15, 1907, he married Effie Ella Pacha at Atkinson. Mrs. Kubart was born at Diagonal, Iowa, March 16, 1886. Their four children are: Josephine, born June 3, 1909; Helen, born December 8, 1910; Eva, born March 16, 1914; and Frank, born December 8, 1922. Josephine is a nurse. Residence: Atkinson.

Edward James Kubat

Edward James Kubat, lawyer, was born at Crete, Nebraska, July 23, 1903, son of James and Mary Julia

(Dredla) Kubat. The father was born at Ziline, Czecho Slovakia, October 18, 1874. He is a retired business man and prominent Republican. His wife, Mary was born in Crete, on August 22, 1878 of Czech and German descent.

Upon his graduation from high school in 1921, Mr. Kubat attended the University of Nebraska and the University of Arizona from which he received the degree of Bachelor of Laws in 1926. He is a member of Pi Delta Epsilon and Delta Chi. From 1926-28 he was associated with the law firm of Thomas J. Dredla at Crete, and since 1928 has been in independent practice at Friend. A Republican, he was defeated for office of county attorney in 1930, has served as state and county committeeman and is now city councilman of Friend.

On April 16, 1929, he was married to Mary Martha McGinley at Lincoln. She was born at Douglas, Nebraska, August 29, 1907. There was a son, born June 10, 1930 who died June 12, 1930.

Mr. Kubat is a member of the Plymouth Congregational Church of Lincoln, the Nebraska State Bar Association, the Chamber of Commerce (secretary 1928-30), the Masons and the Officers Reserve Corps. He holds the rank of 2nd lieutenant, attached to the 89th Light Tank Company. He enjoys golf, tennis, hunting and fishing, while his hobby is flower gardening. Residence: Friend.

Adolph Jacob Kubitschek

Born at Perry, Iowa, March 3, 1895, Adolph Jacob Kubitschek, is the son of Frank Joseph and Margaret (Feller) Kubitschek. His father, who was born in Germany, December 6, 1863, is a furniture dealer and was formerly a cabinet maker, who came to this country in 1870. His mother, whose ancestry was French and German, was born in Howard County, South Dakota, October 29, 1865.

Dr. Kubitschek was graduated from the Sacred Heart High School at Eagle Grove, Iowa, in 1914, and received the D. D. S. degree at Creighton University Dental College in Omaha in 1917. He was a member of Kappa Omicron Epsilon in college, and served as president of the freshman class. He received valedictory honors in high school.

Since 1917 he has been engaged in the practice of dentistry at Atkinson, and has been active in civic affairs in his community. He is a member of the National, state, and district dental societies, is local treasurer of the Lions Club, is vice president of the Knights of Columbus, and holds membership in the Red Cross and the Nebraskana Society. He is affiliated with St. Josephs Catholic Church and is a member of the Atkinson Country Club where he enjoys golfing. Dr. Kubitschek is present president of the Northern Nebraska Dental Study Club.

On August 29, 1917, he married Leone Isabelle Bollinger at Des Moines, Iowa. Mrs. Kubitschek, whose parents were of Irish and German descent, was born at Boone, Iowa, September 3, 1894, and died at Atkinson, May 10, 1927. Five children were born to them: John Douglas, October 5, 1918; Mary Kathryn, November 24, 1920; Ruth Leone, June 30, 1922; Joan Ann, March 24, 1924; and Paul Lynn, May 5, 1927. Residence: Atkinson. (Photograph in Album).

Carl Berthal Kugler

Carl Berthal Kugler, who was born at Minburn, Iowa, January 11, 1884, is the son of John and Emeline (Crane) Kugler. His father, a farmer, was born at Cadiz, Ohio, October 22, 1830, and died at Culbertson, Nebraska, August 22, 1911; he moved to California in 1849 by way of the Isthmus of Panama. His mother

was born in Wisconsin, March 30, 1846, and died at Culbertson, April 13, 1926.

Mr. Kugler is the sole owner of the Kugler Oil Company at Culbertson and holds ranching interests in Hitchcock County. He is a member of the local lodge of the Independent Order of Odd Fellows.

On November 29, 1910, he married Pearl Mabel Bright at McCook, Nebraska; she was born at St. Francis, Kansas, October 19, 1889. Mrs. Kugler is identified with the local Woman's Club, the Christian Church and the South Western Historical Society. Their children are: Charles, born April 20, 1912; Keith, born April 9, 1913; Merle, December, 1914; Arvine, April 28, 1920; and Russel, May 21, 1927. Residence: Culbertson.

Henry Frederick Kuhl

Henry Frederick Kuhl was born near Omaha, Nebraska, June 6, 1880, the son of Peter Hans and Sophia (Pluckhorn) Kuhl. Peter Kuhl, who was a farmer, was born at Holstein, Germany, February 26, 1854, and died at Plainview, Nebraska, June 11, 1912; he came to America in 1874. Sophia (Pluckhorn) Kuhl was born at Mecklenburg, Germany, August 7, 1856.

Mr. Kuhl attended rural school, was a student at Plainview Normal College, 1896-1900, and was a student at Hastings Business College, 1901-02. He has been a farmer and stockman in Knox County, Nebraska, for many years, and since 1904 has owned and operated the Evergreen Stock Farm near Plainview. He has been secretary of the Farmers Union Local Organization since it was first formed in 1911, and since 1925 has been secretary of the Farmers Union Shipping Association.

He is a director of the Nebraska State Board of Agriculture, is a member of the Knox County Fair Association of which he was president ten years and secretary four years, and since 1929 has been secretary of the Farmers Union Co-operative Association. Mr. Kuhl has acted as the leader of 4 H clubs for the past four years, and has been director of the Eden Valley Light Company for 10 years.

A Republican, he was candidate by petition for state senator from Knox and Cedar counties in 1930 and held a majority vote in Knox County. He is a member of the Bloomfield Community Club, is affiliated with the First Congregational Church of Plainview of which he was formerly a trustee, and holds membership in the Nebraskana Society. He served as a member of the local board of education from 1920 to 1923.

Mr. Kuhl is a member of the Sioux City Consistory and the Ancient and Accepted Scottish Rite Masonary, Planview Lodge Number 204 and Mount Vernon Chapter. During the World War he served as local district solicitor for the Red Cross. He is especially interested in choice livestock and is a breeder of purebred Duroc swine and Holstein cattle.

On July 25, 1906, his marriage to Elcy Mae Fulton was solemnized at Creighton, Nebraska. Mrs. Kuhl, who was a kindergarten teacher before her marriage, was born at Scribner, Nebraska, May 3, 1881. They have six children; Leonard, born June 4, 1907, who married Helen Ross; Dorothy, born October 16, 1909; Maurice, born September 20, 1911; Everett, born September 21, 1913; Hubert, born August 25, 1917; and Mabel, born August 17, 1921. The four older children are interested in music. Residence: Plainview.

Anna Reed Kuhle

Anna Reed Kuhle, editor, feature writer, and clubwoman of Nebraska, was born at Lyons, Burt County, Nebraska, October 31, 1882, the daughter of William Morris and Margaret Frances (Kennedy) Reed. Her father, who was born at LaPorte, Indiana, October 18, 1851, and died at Lyons, July 11, 1914, was a life-long Republican. George Reed, father of William Morris Reed, was a merchant at Westville, Indiana, 1850-60, and the Reed family was of English origin.

Amy Walton Underwood, wife of George Reed and the mother of William, was the daughter of John Underwood, a miller, and Mary (Clark) Underwood. The Underwoods were Quakers who came from England and settled at Baltimore, Maryland before moving to Indiana. The Clarks were descendants of *Mayflower* ancestors.

Margaret Frances (Kennedy) Reed was born at Pekin, Illinois, August 4, 1858, and died at Lyons, March 29, 1908. Her father, Captain Jack Kennedy, who was a native of Tipperary, Ireland, came to the United States when he was a young man. He enlisted in Company F., 55th Regiment, Illinois Volunteer Infantry, was promoted to captain and was killed in action, July 19, 1864, at the battle of Peach Tree Creek, Georgia. She was a clubwoman of prominence and served as one of the first secretaries of the Lyons Woman's Club.

Mrs. Kuhle was graduated from Lyons High School in 1900, and was a student at Fairchild, Wisconsin, for a year, where she took a course in normal training; she completed her study at the Fremont Normal School from which she received a kindergarten diploma. She was a public school teacher for five years in Wisconsin and Nebraska; is editor of the Writer's Guild Bulletin; served as vice president of the Third District of the Nebraska Federation of Womens Clubs and has written scores of feature articles for newspapers and women's publications. Among them are feature articles in the following: *Northwestern Bell* (1903); *Pathfinder* (1929); *National Printer Journalist* (1929); *Bookfellow Anthology* (1931); *General Federation News* (1929-30); *Clubwoman* (1930) and in metropolitan dailies.

Mrs. Kuhle is a Bookfellow and a member of the League of American Penwomen. She is affiliated with the Lyons Presbyterian Church. On August 8, 1906, she was united in marriage with Charles R. Kuhle, who is one of Nebraska's foremost newspaper man. He was born in London, England, August 27, 1881, of German parentage; his father was a professional musician in London. They have a daughter, Margaret Frances, born November 20, 1917, who is studying violin and is just entering high school. Residence: Leigh. (Photograph in Album).

Charles R. Kuhle

Charles R. Kuhle, distinguished editor and publisher of Leigh, Nebraska, has been a continuous resident of this state for the past 48 years. He was born at London, England, August, 27, 1881, the son of Anna Adolphina (Haarhues) Kuhle and Ernest Louis Kuhle. His father, who was a professional musician in London, was born at Schuettorf, Germany, and died at West Point, Nebraska in March, 1892; his ancestors were German merchants. His mother, whose family had lived in Germany for many generations, was born at Schuettorf, August 4, 1858.

Mr. Kuhle received his education in the West Point High School, and began his career in German and English journalism in the office of Nebraska *Volksblatt* at West Point where he was employed for 11 years. In 1907 he purchased the *Leigh World* and since that time has been active in state and community newspaper affairs. He has held various executive offices in newspaper associations throughout Nebraska and has taken an active interest in civic affairs at Leigh.

At the age of 14 Mr. Kuhle was forced to leave school because of the death of his father and become the sole means of support of his widowed mother and younger brothers and sisters. He was elected president of the Northeast Nebraska Editorial Association in 1926, was made president of the Nebraska Press Association in 1928, and for the past three years has been vice president for Nebraska of the National Editorial Association.

Today he is business manager of the Nebraska Press

and owns a printing plant at Leigh, the output of which is two weekly newspapers and four monthly publications. A Republican, he has been connected with central committees in an executive capacity and has been a regular attendant of county and state conventions for many years. In 1928 he served as official host to the National Editorial Association when he posed in special pictures with President and Mrs. Calvin Coolidge and Herman Roe, national president of the editorial association.

He holds membership in the Leigh Commercial Club, the Nebraska Historical Society, and the Nebraskana Society, while his fraternal organizations include the Odd Fellows and the Modern Woodmen of America. During the World War Mr. Kuhle served as a Four Minute speaker and Victory loan promoter. On two occasions his printing plant was completely destroyed by fire; he immediately rebuilt it each time and has since doubled his business.

On August 8, 1906, his marriage to Amy Anna Reed was solemnized at Lyons, Nebraska. Mrs. Kuhle, who was born at Lyons, October 31, 1882, is a prominent writer and clubwoman. Their one daughter, Margaret Frances, who is a violin student, was born November 20, 1917. Residence: Leigh. (Photograph in Album).

Luther Melanchthon Kuhns

Luther L. Kuhns was born at Omaha, December 10, 1861. He is the son of Henry Welty and Charlotta Josepha (Hay) Kuhns. His father was born at Greensburg, Pennsylvania, August 23, 1829, and died at Omaha, September 19, 1899; he was the first Lutheran missionary west of the Missouri River, was the founder of Kountze Memorial Lutheran Church, and traced his ancestry in America to 1723.

Charlotta Josepha Hay was born at Armagh, Pennsylvania, August 8, 1830, and died at Omaha, April 24, 1898. She was of English and Scotch ancestry, her forefathers having come to America with William Penn; Lieutenant Colonel John Hay, who settled in Virginia, prior to 1748, was an ancestor.

Dr. Kuhns graduated from Newberry Academy, South Carolina, in 1878. He has received the following degrees: Bachelor of Arts, Pennsylvania College, 1883; Master of Arts, 1886; Doctor of Literature, 1918; Doctor of Divinity, Newberry College, 1920. He is a member of Phi Gamma Delta.

He is the author of *Luther League Handbook* and various pamphlets and articles on religious subjects. He has been editor of *Luther League Review,* and *Luther League Topics.* He was ordained a minister of the Lutheran Church in 1885.

Dr. Kuhns was active in war drives during the World War. He is a Mason and holds membership in the University Club. Residence: Omaha.

Frank Anthony Kuhre

Born at Chicago, Illinois, February 27, 1869, Frank Anthony Kuhre has been a farmer in Keya Paha County, Nebraska for the past 47 years. His father, Anthony Frank Kuhre, who was a carpenter and farmer, was born at Benfeldt, France, July 20, 1838, and died at Johnstown, Nebraska, July 6, 1907; he came to America at the age of 17 and learned the carpenter trade in Chicago. His mother was born at Benfeldt, June 8, 1840, and died at Johnstown, March 22, 1919.

Mr. Kuhre is a rancher and general farmer at Norden, Nebraska where he has served as a member of the school board for the past 30 years. A Democrat, he served as precinct assessor in Keya Paha County for five terms and still holds that office.

On February 24, 1897, he married Mary Janet Thompson at Springview. Mrs. Kuhre was born at Manchester, Iowa, January 13, 1875. They have five children: Louis J., born October 6, 1899, who married Marie Langer;

Bernice, born August 7, 1902; Leon, August 22, 1905; Frank, Jr., May 2, 1912; and Ida, December 23, 1914. Residence: Norden.

David Henry Kunkel

One of Nebraska's prominent pioneers, David Henry Kunkel came to Polk County in 1873, and has resided there continuously since. He was born at Newberg, Pennsylvania, May 4, 1854, son of Martin and Agnes (Heffelbower) Kunkel.

His father, who was born at Lancaster County, Pennsylvania, April 8, 1928, died at Garrison, North Dakota, January 13, 1918. He was a hotel man, and the organizer and builder of the Young Ladies Seminary at Newburg, Pennsylvania in 1853. His ancestors came to the United States from Holland. His mother, whose ancestry was German, was born at Newburg, February 22, 1834, and died at Aurora, Illinois, May 31, 1879.

Mr. Kunkel arrived in Lincoln, on March 13, 1873 with $30.00 in cash, and a gold watch. He then contracted with Mayor E. E. Brown to break 80 acres of prairie land about 10 blocks southeast of the state capitol building. He then went to Grant Ensign, a horse dealer, and told him he wanted to buy a $400.00 team for $200.00. He happened to have that kind of a team, but no one could drive them, as one was balky and the other was a run-a-way.

However, Mr. Kunkel, purchased the team of horses, turning over his $30.00 in cash and his gold watch. It took about a week to break the horses so they could be hitched up alone. In July, Mr. Kunkel filed on a timber claim and planted about 40 trees. He proved up in eight years.

After the corn was husked, he went to Lincoln to get a job with hundreds of others. Finally he landed one in a grocery store with a salary of 25 cents a day and board and room. He worked from four in the morning until nine o'clock in the evening and it was real work. He stayed there until farm work in the spring, when he went to Polk County and broke up 140 acres on the family homestead and free claim.

In 1874 and 1875, the grasshoppers made things look discouraging, but the country was all right and they stayed with it, and the winter before the railroad came, Mr. Kunkel hauled 3500 bushels of wheat to Columbus, 27 miles away and sold it for 45 cents a bushel. For 16 years he was the owner of a drug store. He sold life insurance until 1917 and for the past 15 years has served as secretary of the Polk-Butler County Farmers Insurance Company.

He was elected as a delegate to the National general assembly of the Presbyterian Church in Chicago in 1914, and for many years has been an active worker in the First Presbyterian Church at Osceola. He is a member of the Odd Fellows, the Red Cross, and the Nebraskana Society. He and his father, together, organized the school district No. 48 in Polk County, of which he was director for 15 years. Upon his removal to Osceola, he was treasurer of the school board for nine years. During the late war, he collected thousands of dollars for the Red Cross and was a member of the home guard.

Mr. Kunkel likes to read, and his favorite sports are hunting, fishing, trap shooting. A Republican, he has always been interested in politics, and was nominated for county clerk at one time, but was defeated in the election. He has been a resident of Polk County for 57 years.

On January 14, 1879, he was married to Anna Mary Detweiler at Newburg, Pennsylvania. Mrs. Kunkel was born at Chambersburg, Pennsylvania, November 9, 1855, and was a teacher prior to her marriage. For the past 52 years she has been a devoted home-maker and active club woman. Mr. and Mrs. Kunkel celebrated their golden wedding anniversary in Osceola, January 14, 1929. They have the following children: Daisy Emma born December 20, 1879, who married Frank Higgie Anderson; Nellie Agnes, born August 8, 1882, who married Dr. Herbert

Eugene King; Charles David, born June 16, 1885, who married Lora Viola Smith; Margaret Anneta, born September 23, 1888, who married James Wilford Hartzell; and John Atley, born June 29, 1894, who married Barbara Swoboda. All of their children have received a college education. and are members of the Presbyterian Church. Margaret is a member of Phi Beta Kappa. Residence: Osceola. (Photograph in Album).

Donald Alden Kunkel

Donald Alden Kunkel, executive, was born in North Platte, Nebraska, May 12, 1902, son of John Adam and Bertha May (Bibleheimmer) Kunkel.

John Adam Kunkel was born in Carroll, Iowa, September 9, 1874, and is president of the Kunkel Wholesale Auto Supply Company. His ancestry is German and Dutch. His wife, Bertha May, was born in Pottsville, Pennsylvania, January 20, 1882, of Pennsylvania Dutch ancestry.

Mr. Kunkel attended public school, and afterward was a rancher. He later became employed in a garage, and still later entered the automotive wholesale supply and equipment business. This business increased rapidly until it is now one of the largest of its kind in western Nebraska. He is secretary and treasurer of this company, which is operated under the name of the Kunkel Auto Supply Company. He is a Republican.

He is a member of the Methodist Church, the Red Cross, the Chamber of Commerce, the Rotary Club, the Masons, and the Odd Fellows. He enjoys hiking and hunting, while his hobbies are reading and the study of history. Residence: North Platte. (Photograph in Album).

Leslie Lyman Kunkel

Leslie Lyman Kunkel, pharmacist and executive, was born at Osceola, Nebraska, July 10, 1893, son of Thomas Clark and Susie Matilda (Lyman) Kunkel.

The father was born at Newburg, Pennsylvania, December 8, 1868, and is a pharmacist, jeweler, and optician, chiefly of Holland Dutch ancestry. His wife, Susie, was born at Oconomawoc, Wisconsin, October 19, 1871, and is a teacher of piano and interested in club work. Her ancestry is mostly English.

In 1908, Mr. Kunkel was graduated from Venango Grade School, and in 1911, from Weeping Water Academy. He received his Bachelor of Arts degree in the school of business administration of the University of Nebraska in 1918. He was a member of the University Players, the Commercial Club, the Palladian Society, and first lieutenant in the Pershing Rifles, as well as a member of Acacia and Alpha Kappa Psi. In high school he was a member of the football and track team.

On May 18, 1920, he was married to Grace Edna Cassels at Denver. She was born at Denver, August 27, 1896, and is prominent in club work. Her ancestry is Scotch-Irish. Mr. and Mrs. Kunkel have three children, Dorothy Mae, born May 27, 1922; Virginia Grace, born March 25, 1924; and Marjorie Ann, born March 15, 1931.

Mr. Kunkel was first a school teacher, and next a registered pharmacist. At the present time, he is president and manager of the Kunkel Drug Company of Madrid, of Kunkel and Allen of Elsie, Kunkel and Davis of Grant, and the Dix Pharmacy of Dix.

He is a Republican, a member of the Nebraska and Colorado Pharmaceutical Association, the Masons, the Elks, and the Young Men's Christian Association. His religious affiliation is with the Congregational Church. His hobby is reading.

During the World War, he saw actual service, and held ranks of private to captain. At the present time, he holds the commission of captain in Infantry Reserve Corps, is a member of the American Legion and the Reserve Officers Association. Residence: Madrid.

John Winfield Kurtz

Born at Joanna, Berks County, Pennsylvania, April 2, 1894, John W. Kurtz has been a resident of Omaha since 1920. He is the son of Benjamin Franklin and Laura (Good) Kurtz, both natives of Pennsylvania. His father was born at Joanna, February 4, 1851, and died there December 8, 1929. He was a miller, and reared a family of eight children. His father and mother were natives of Germany, who came to America about 1820 and erected a four story mill which is still in use by the family. Laura Good Kurtz, also born at Joanna on February 1, 1858, is of French and Scotch descent. She is still living.

Educated in Caernarvon Township and rural schools until 1907, Mr. Kurtz was graduated from Caernarvon High School in 1910. He received his B. A. at the University of Omaha, and had previously graduated from Westchester State Normal School in 1913. He attended 2 years at Lehigh University studying Electrical Engineering, 1913-15, and studied mechanical engineering at Cornell University in 1916-17-19. He was a member of the Glee Club at Westchester and at Cornell and of the Glee Club and Orchestra at Lehigh. On May 26, 1922, he was married to Clarisse Browne at Omaha. Mrs. Kurtz was born at Omaha, September 8, 1897, and is of Danish, French and Quaker English descent. They have two children, Winfield, born December 14, 1923, and Joanne Helene born February 3, 1925.

Mr. Kurtz was electrician with the Berks Engineering Company, in 1915, and assistant engineer with Stewarts Contractors in 1920. He served 18 months during 1917 and 1918 with the Aviation Section, rank of 2nd lieutenant, balloon observer, World War.

From 1920-21 he was foreman, Corn Derivatives Company, and became a draftsman with the Omaha Steel Company in 1921. He was instructor in the wood shop at South High School, Omaha, 1922, and still continues, and is also instructor in engineering, drawing and shop at the University of Omaha, which position he has held since 1923. He is the author of *Shop Short Cuts, Clamp Racks* (August 1930).

Mr. Kurtz is a Democrat. He is a member of the American Legion, the Omaha School Forum, the National Educational Association, and the Nebraska State Teachers Association. He has belonged to the N. G. A. since 1925. He is a member of All Saint's Episcopal Church and is a Mason. He was elected secretary and treasurer of the Men's Club of All Saint's Church for the term 1930-31-32. He likes hunting and fishing, and his hobby is technical research. Residence: Omaha.

Albert LaBounty

A resident of Nebraska, since 1876, Albert LaBounty was born at Gilman, Illinois, October 1, 1867. He is the son of Peter and Mary (Demass) LaBounty, both natives of Canada. His father died at Blue Hill, Nebraska, April 29, 1899, and his mother at Nelson, on April 8, 1899.

Albert LaBounty attended country school, and for many years has been a hardware merchant. He is a Democrat, and served as a member of the Nebraska legislature in 1915 and 1917.

On March 6, 1890, he was united in marriage to Rillie Moffett, at Lawrence, Nebraska. Mrs. LaBounty, who was born at Shelby, Missouri, March 5, 1871, died at Rochester, Minnesota, February 8, 1920. Of this union there are five children: Ethel, born June 1892, who married Harold C. Ealy; Virgie, born August 8, 1894, who married C. R. Logan; Ina, born November 20, 1896, who married Lloyd Stonecker; Allen, born October 12, 1898, who is unmarried; and Marion, born December 23, 1904, who married Olive Keir. Allen is a rancher in Wyoming, and Marion is an electrical engineer.

Mr. LaBounty was married to Nora C. Crossgrove on June 11, 1922, at Farnam, Nebraska. She was the first white child born there.

During the World War Mr. LaBounty was a four min-

ute speaker. He is a member of the Farnam Commercial Club, the Modern Woodmen of America and The Nebraskana Society. Residence: Farnam.

Arthur W. Ladd

For 40 years Arthur W. Ladd was the editor and publisher of the *Albion Weekly News*, at Albion, Nebraska. He was born at Oneida, Illinois, July 29, 1858, the son of James M. and Sarah (Graves) Ladd, the former a shoemaker and farmer who was born at Unity, New Hampshire, June 1, 1818 and died at Albion, Nebraska, March 11, 1889. His mother, whose ancestors settled in New England in the early history of America, was born at Unity, New Hampshire, October 14, 1822, and died at Albion, June 30, 1910.

Mr. Ladd attended the public schools of Oneida, and in 1879 came to Nebraska, bringing his first printing press from Columbus, Nebraska, the nearest railroad point overland in a wagon, a distance of fifty miles. In 1919 he retired from active business. He is vice president of the Albion National Bank, has been mayor of Albion for eight years, has held membership on the school board and city council, and is a member of the Albion Lions Club. He is past master of the Masons.

He married Amy I. Fox, who was born in Dubuque County, Iowa, April 17, 1865. Her parents came to this country from England. They have one daughter, Della, born February 9, 1891, who married Warren B. Romans, of Lincoln, Nebraska. To this union two children were born, Elizabeth, July 7, 1916; and Warren, born October 19, 1918. Residence: Albion.

Eugene B. Laflin

On December 22, 1867, Eugene B. Laflin was born at Crab Orchard, Johnson County, Nebraska. His father, Lewis Hall Laflin, was a farmer who served in the first Nebraska regiment volunteers from 1862 to 1865 in the Civil War, and was a member of the Nebraska legislature in 1873. He was born at Rock Island, Illinois, August 21, 1843, and died at Crab Orchard, March 10, 1920.

America K. (Scott) Laflin, his mother, was born at Louisville, Kentucky, August 10, 1846, and died at Crab Orchard, July 27, 1905.

Mr. Laflin attended the public schools of Johnson County, but received most of his education through experience and private study. He was admitted to the bar at Falls City, Richardson County, Nebraska, June 10, 1895, and has practiced law in Nebraska since that time. Today besides his general law practice he is vice president of the American Aberdeen Angus Breeder's Association, and is engaged in farming and general stock raising. He has lived in Nebraska all his life.

He married Fannie M. Flory at Gibbon, Buffalo County, Nebraska, August 22, 1892. Mrs. Laflin was born at Smithburg, Washington County, Maryland, November 26, 1870. There are two children: Lewis Eugene, born August 7, 1895; and Ruth Mary, born July 4, 1898.

He is a Republican, and a member of the Nebraska State Bar Association and the Red Cross. He is a Mason, and a member of the Ancient Order of United Workmen. Residence: Crab Orchard.

Thomas Johnson Lahners

Thomas Johnson Lahners, retired farmer, was born in Golden, Adams County, Illinois, December 17, 1860, son of Oltman Johnson and Luka Catherine (Hofeling) Lahners. His father, who was born at Oldenburg, Germany, June 15, 1838, died at Flanagan, Illinois, December 3, 1868. He was a farmer. His wife, Luka Catherine, born in Germany, July 18, 1824, died at Flanagan, January 29, 1878.

Educated in public, private and parochial schools, Thomas J. Lahners was on November 23, 1882, married te Anna Bowman at Flanagan. Mrs. Lahners was born at Flanagan, May 29, 1867. Three of their five children were born in Illinois, and two in Nebraska: Oltman, born November 23, 1883, is a farmer; Folkert, born July 26, 1885, married Ollie Hawks. He died April 23, 1923; Thomas, born August 7, 1887; Carrie, born January 1, 1891; and George, born October 2, 1896. Falkert is a farmer; Thomas is a physician and surgeon, and a first lieutenant of Medical Reserve. Carrie is a housekeeper and George served as mess sergeant in Officers Training Corps. Both volunteered.

A resident of Nebraska, since 1890, Mr. Lahners has always been an outstanding resident of Thayer County. He has engaged in farming until recent years, and has been active in Republican politics for many years. He is a progressive, and in 1905 and 1907, served in the state legislature. He was state senator 1915-17, and the special session of 1918. A member of the Constitutional Convention of 1919-20, he was chairman of the agricultural committee.

His record in public affairs is exceptional. Much of the development of Thayer County agriculture and good roads may be traced to him. He was elected superintendent of Thayer Couny Good Roads Association in 1912 and while serving in this capacity was the leader of the movement for the building of the Meridian Highway.

In 1907 as a member of the legislature he introduced the good roads dragging bill which was signed by Governor George L. Sheldon, and which was really the beginning of improved highways in Nebraska, and in 1912 was one of the organizers of a good roads association, with Charles C. Fletcher, of Hebron, as president, Fred Hensel as secretary, William Miller as treasurer, and Mr. Lahners as superintendent. Mr. Lahners was at that time state senator and in 1915, introduced senate file No. 45, which made it unlawful to discharge fire arms on the public highways; senate file No. 211, which gave free music to towns, and which was signed by Governor Morehead. During the 1917 session he introduced senate file No. 27, which provided for watering stock at private tanks; and senate file No. 166, which gave soldiers the right to vote away from home. This bill was signed by Governor Keith Neville.

It is interesting to study the problem which confronted the development of the Meridian Highway in Thayer County, and credit should be given to all the members of the Good Roads Association for their untiring efforts, and particularly to Mr. Lahners. During the winter of 1912, he circulated a petition which was signed by many residents; road overseers were appointed, and 156 men pledged, 96 from Bruning, and sixty from Belvidere. All work done on the Meridian Highway was donated, and the road was kept in repair by Thomas Lahners, C. D. Mc-Kilip, F. E. Bailey and Earl Wilhelms, free of charge. As stated in the *Hebron Champion* of June 21, 1912, "It is indeed a great stroke of enterprise on the part of the projectors, and those having the matter in charge, especially Mr. Lahners, who projected the same, Homer Town of Belvidere, who had charge of the work out of Belvidere, and the men whose names are mentioned above as overseers. We doubt if there has been anything like it in the state, and if all parts of the state would take the same interest, it would not be long before Nebraska would be known as the best 'good roads' state in the world, and the property along the various roads would be enhanced in value.

In addition to his work for the county and state, Mr. Lahners has been active in civic, community and religious affairs. He was active in Liberty Loan work during the World War, is a member of the German Lutheran Church at Bruning, and from 1890 to 1915, was a member of the school board. He is a member of the Modern Woodmen of America, the Nebraska State Historical Society, and in recognition for his outstanding achievements has been made a life member of the Nebraskana Society. Residence: Belvidere. (Photograph in Album).

Earl Edward Laidig

Earl Edward Laidig, dentist, was born in Decatur County, Kansas, April 13, 1894, and since October 1, 1919 has been active in the practice of his profession. He is the son of William Franklin and Katherine (Lawless) Laidig, the former born in Illinois, January 28, 1861; his father was a farmer. His mother was also born in Illinois, in 1861 and died in Decatur County, Kansas, November 18, 1918.

Dr. Laidig attended the public schools of Decatur County, Kansas until 1910 and was graduated from Decatur County High School at Oberlin, Kansas, in 1914. He received his degree of Doctor of Dental Surgery at the University of Nebraska in 1919, where he was a member of Delta Sigma Delta fraternity. During his high school days he was active in basketball and football.

On May 20, 1920, he was married to Allie Fay Redfern at Marion, Nebraska. Mrs. Laidig was born at Marion, October 19, 1898. Her activities include church work connected with her membership in the Dorcas Society of Congregational Church and Sunday school, the Eastern Star and Woman's Club. They have one son, Clair Eugene, born July 23, 1928.

During the World War, Dr. Laidig was a member of the Medical Reserve Corps. He is a member of the National, District and State Dental Societies and is past master of Boaz Lodge of the Ancient Free and Accepted Masons No. 185, and past president of the District Dental Society. His favorite sport is golf. Residence: Danbury.

Fred Chester Laird

Fred Chester Laird was born at Tabor, Fremont County, Iowa, May 22, 1880, and for the past 26 years has been a resident of Nebraska. His father, Francis Marion Laird, who was born in Fremont County, February 7, 1855, is a retired farmer and stockman; he served in the Iowa legislature two terms; his great great-grandfather was a soldier in the Revolution, while two uncles were Civil War soldiers. His mother was born in Fremont County, Iowa, May 9, 1854; her father served in the Civil War.

Mr. Laird attended the high school at Tabor, Iowa, and in 1899 was graduated from the Tabor Academy. He received the Ph. B. degree at Tabor College, 1903, and the LL. B. degree at the University of Nebraska in 1906. He was awarded a college letter at Tabor College for football and baseball activities, and was exchequer of Alpha Tau Omega at the University of Nebraska.

From 1906 to 1913 he practiced law at Fremont, alone, and from 1913 to 1919, and from 1922 to 1929 was associated with George L. Loomis and H. W. Loomis in a law firm. He is now county judge of Dodge County. He has held the following public offices in Dodge County: police judge at Fremont, 1898-17; county judge 1929, to the present time; and revenue agent of the estate tax division, 1919-22, qualifying under Civil Service.

His marriage to Leo Alice Loomis was solemnized at Fremont, June 15, 1911. Mrs. Laird was born at Fremont, September 20, 1883. During the World War Mr. Laird served as a member of the registration board, the advisory board, four minute speaker, officer in the home guards, and Liberty loan man. He is a member of the Sons of the American Revolution while Mrs. Laird holds membership in the Daughters of the American Revolution.

He is a member of the Nebraska State Bar Association, is secretary of the Dodge County Bar Association, and has been a member of the Fremont Kiwanis Club since 1921. He is a member of the Fremont Chamber of Commerce, the Red Cross, and the Nebraskana Society. He is affiliated with the First Congregational Church of Fremont, and is a member of the Young Men's Christian Association.

For the past three years he has been a member of the Children's Hospital committee of Tangier Temple. He is also a member and chairman of the Kiwanis committee for under privileged children, and a member of the Elks general committee for crippled children. Most of the juvenile court work in the county is also handled by Mr. Laird.

Mr. Laird's fraternal organizations include the Elks, of which he is past exalted ruler; Fremont Lodge of the Masons, of which he is Past Master, Signet Chapter of Masons, Mount Tabor Commandery, and Shrine, and the Order of the Eastern Star. His social clubs are the Fremont Country Club; Happy Hollow Club of Omaha; and the University Alumni Association of Nebraska. He likes the out of doors and is particularly interested in golfing. Residence: Omaha.

Charles Allison Lambeth

Charles A. Lambeth was born at Nebraska City, Nebraska, December 7, 1878, the son of William Carey and Amanda (Fitz Allen) Lambeth. His father was a pioneer merchant in Omaha and Nebraska City and a freighter from Nebraska City to Denver. He was born at Lexington, Missouri, August 9, 1845, and died at Long Beach, California, February 29, 1928. His ancestry was English.

His mother was born in Kentucky, August 26, 1851, and is a member of the Daughters of the American Revolution.

Mr. Lambeth attended the Nebraska City public schools and the high school at Syracuse, Nebraska. Later he was a student at the Nebraska City Episcopal College. For a time he was a clothing salesman at Kansas City, Missouri, at St. Louis, at Prescott, Arizona, and Phoenix, Arizona. He is now the owner of a clothing store at Syracuse.

He married Alice Venters at Syracuse, September 6, 1911. Mrs. Lambeth was born at Stonington, Christian County, Illinois, September 3, 1882. Two children were born to them. William Allison, who was born December 12, 1912, is a student at the University of Nebraska. Stuart, who was born September 18, 1915, died January 3, 1917.

Mr. Lambeth is a member of the Syracuse Business Men's Association. He is a Modern Woodman and an 18th degree Scottish Rite Mason. He is a member of the Syracuse Golf Club, and a Democrat. Residence: Syracuse.

Frank S. Lamm

Frank S. Lamm, son of William and Nancy (Stonehocker) Lamm, was born in Scotland County, Missouri, September 28, 1869. When he was three weeks old, he with his parents, moved to Iowa, and when he was thirteen years old they moved to Thayer County, and lived on the farm where he is now living.

William Lamm, was born at Somerville, Preble County, Ohio, April 27, 1843, and died at Belvidere, Nebraska, February 13, 1914. Nancy (Stonehocker) Lamm was born at Coshoeton, Ohio, March 6, 1844, and died at St. Joseph, Missouri, August 21, 1917. They are both of American parentage.

Mr. Lamm has been a resident of Nebraska since November, 1882. He has always farmed and raised stock with his brother, Harlan M. Lamm. In November of 1931, Mr. Lamm will have lived on the same farm for forty-nine years.

During the World War he was active in war work, especially Red Cross and bond purchases. Residence: Belvidere.

Anton Kasper Lammers

Anton Kasper Lammers, a lifetime resident of Cedar County, Nebraska, was born June 23, 1870, the son of John and Mary Stratton Lammers. His father, who was

born at Hanover, Germany, in 1830, and died in Cedar County, July 9, 1896, was a farmer. His mother was born in Germany, in 1850, and died in Cedar County, December, 1906.

Mr. Lammers attended Quincy College, 1886-87. For 34 years he owned and operated a lumber yard at Hartington; he is now retired. He is a member of Holy Trinity Catholic Church, holding membership in the Knights of Columbus, is an active member of the Chamber of Commerce, and the Nebraskana Society. He is a Democrat. His hobby is gardening.

On May 22, 1900, Mr. Lammers was married to Clara Wolz, at Hartington, Cedar County, Nebraska; she was born at Plymouth, Iowa, in 1877. Their four children are: Aurelia, born 1903, a registered nurse at Nashville, Tennessee; Gertrude, born 1906; Dolores, born 1908; and Katherine, born 1910. Residence: Hartington.

Paul Harold Lammers

Paul Harold Lammers, practicing dentist, was born at Hartington, Nebraska, March 3, 1899, son of John W. and Ann (Kramer) Lammers. His father, who was a native of Dubuque, Iowa, was a farmer of German descent. He died in Milwaukee, Wisconsin, in January, 1913. His mother was born in Germany, about 1871, and is still living.

Dr. Lammers attended high school at Conception, Missouri, graduating in 1919, and during 1920, attended the University of Minnesota. He received his D. D. S. from Creighton University in 1925, and is a member of Psi Omega and Psi Alpha. During the time he was at Minnesota he was a member of the basketball team.

On November 1, 1925, Dr. Lammers was united in marriage to Mary Ida Kerken, at Norfolk. Mrs. Lammers was born at West Point, Nebraska, in 1898. There are two children: Hyacinth, born January 24, 1926; and Edward Joseph, born July 24, 1928. After five years practice at Norfolk, Nebraska, Dr. Lammers removed to Hartington, where he operates his own office.

He is a Democrat, and a member of Holy Trinity Catholic Church, and the Knights of Columbus. He is president of the Lions Club, and a member of the Chamber of Commerce and the Officers Reserve Corps. His professional organizations include the state, district and national dental associations. He is fond of golf, and is a member of the Country Club. Residence: Hartington.

Lane Lancaster

Lane Lancaster was born at Bellaire, Belmont County, Ohio, December 9, 1892, the son of Charles Warren and Josephine (Crow) Lancaster. His father, who is a manufacturer of glass products, was born at Marietta, Washington County, Ohio, April 7, 1866. His mother was born on a farm in Belmont County, Ohio, November 13, 1869. She has been active in religious work for many years; her ancestors were English and German settlers in Virginia and Pennsylvania.

Dr. Lancaster attended elementary schools in Ohio. He received the A. B. degree at Ohio Wesleyan University, 1915, was awarded the A. M. degree at the University of Illinois, 1918, and was graduated with the Ph. D. degree at the University of Pennsylvania, 1923. He was elected to membership in Phi Beta Kappa, Delta Sigma Rho, and Delta Tau Delta.

He was a scholar in history at the University of Illinois, 1917-18, held a fellowship in history at the University of Pennsylvania, 1919-20, was instructor in political science at the University of Pennsylvania, 1920-3, and served as assistant professor and associate professor of government at Wesleyan University, Middletown, Connecticut, 1923-30. Since 1930 he has been professor of political science at the University of Nebraska. During summer sessions he has taught in the Pennsylvania State College, and Bates College, Lewiston, Maine.

An Independent Democrat, Dr. Lancaster was unsuccessful candidate for the state senate of Connecticut, 1926. He was a private in the United States Army during the World War. He is a member of the American Political Science Association, the National Municipal League, and the Nebraskana Society. His recreations include golfing and reading.

On September 11, 1917, he was united in marriage with Mary Alice Brown at Cardington, Morrow County, Ohio. Mrs. Lancaster was born at Fulton, Ohio, June 2, 1892. Their two children are: Mary, born May 7, 1925; and Susan, born December 4, 1926. Residence: Lincoln.

Clarence Louis Landen

Clarence Louis Landen was born at Omaha, Nebraska, September 19, 1898, and has lived in that community all his life. His father, Ludwig Andrew Landen, who was born in Sweden, January 23, 1874, is a retired clothing merchant. His mother, Christina Emma Johnson, was born at Omaha, and died there June 10, 1916.

Mr. Landen attended the Lothrop School at Omaha; was graduated from Central High School; and later was student at the Omaha Business College. From 1916-24 he was engaged in the automobile business at Omaha, and he is now vice president and secretary of the Securities Investment Company. In addition he is president of the Motor Exchange Company, a director of the Securities Managers Corporation and the National Thrift Assurance Company; and is president of the Securities Managers Corporation.

He was united in marriage to Mereta Lucille Mathews at Omaha, June 19, 1918. Mrs. Landen was born at Albion, Nebraska, December 24, 1897. To them were born two children: John Louis, born June 5, 1920; and Clarence Leonard, born September 1, 1924.

Mr. Landen is a member of the Reserve Officers Corps and the Red Cross. His political affiliation is with the Republican party, and he holds membership in the following: Omaha Chamber of Commerce, National Association of Finance Companies, Omaha Auto Trade Association, Lions Club, and Ak-Sar-Ben. He is a member of the Parent-Teachers' Association of Dundee school, the North Presbyterian Church and the Young Men's Christian Association of Omaha. His clubs are the Omaha Athletic and Happy Hollow Country Club. He enjoys golf and swimming. Residence: Omaha.

Elwood Landis

Elwood Landis, postmaster, was born in Hill County, Texas, September 9, 1873, son of William Matchet and Sarah (Winters) Landis. William M. Landis, a farmer, was born in the state of Indiana, March 18, 1830, and died in Washington County, Kansas, October 30, 1909. His father was a soldier in the American Army in the War of 1812.

Sarah Landis, was born in Indiana, July 4, 1834, and died in Jefferson County, Nebraska, September 19, 1922. She was of German-Irish descent and her father was an officer in the American Army in the War of 1812.

On June 18, 1914, Mr. Landis was united in marriage to Elizabeth Lockhart, at her birthplace, Rochester, New York. Their only child died in infancy.

Mr. Landis is an independent and has been elected precinct assessor two terms. In early life, he was a farmer, a clerk, and a barber, and now is postmaster at Powell, Nebraska. A Protestant, he is a member of the Methodist Church at Powell. He is a member of The Nebraskana Society, Modern Woodmen of America, and the Independent Order of the Odd Fellows, and is interested in astronomy. Residence: Powell.

Harry DeWitt Landis

Harry DeWitt Landis, judge of the district court, was born at Sterling, Illinois, July 17, 1878, son of Elam Hershey and Alice Narcissa (Eschelman) Landis. The father was born in Lancaster County, Pennsylvania, November 17, 1846, and the mother at Strasburg, Pennsylvania, January 2, 1855. She died at Seward on October 17, 1930.

Judge Landis received his Bachelor of Science degree in 1899, his Bachelor of Laws in 1901, and his degree of Doctor of Jurisprudence in 1919 from the University of Nebraska. He is a member of Pi Gamma Mu, Phi Delta Phi and Sigma Chi.

On June 27, 1927, he was married to Alice Mabel Cattle at Seward. She was born at Seward, August 15, 1885. There are six children, Harry, born July 7, 1908, who married Eva Michelmore; Walter, born October 13, 1910; John, born September 11, 1912; Frank, born December 27, 1913; Alice, born August 16, 1920 and George, born August 6, 1927.

A Republican, Judge Landis was deputy county judge and deputy clerk of the Supreme Court of Nebraska, 1902; served as a regent of the University of Nebraska 12 years, and since 1925 has been district judge of the 5th judicial district elected on a non-partisan ticket.

He is a member of the First Presbyterian Church, the American and Nebraska State Bar Associations, a major in the Judge Advocate General's Reserves, president of the Social Welfare Association, treasurer of the Red Cross, a director of the Young Men's Christian Association and a director of the Nebraska Tuberculosis Association. He is an Odd Fellow and a Mason and a member of the University Club and the Magazine Club. Residence: Seward.

William J. Lane

William J. Lane, farmer, real estate operator and insurance man, was born in Iowa, November 29, 1876, and for the past forty-five years has been a farmer. He is the son of William and Polly A. (Kirkham) Lane, the former also a farmer.

Mr. Lane was educated in public schools, and soon thereafter took up his chosen occupation, in which he has been successful. He was married to June M. Marshall, and to them two children were born, Vernon, on July 5, 1914, and Vivian I., on January 17, 1917. Mrs. Lane was born in Michigan, December 6, 1887.

A Democrat, Mr. Lane has always been interested and active in local party politics. Recently he was made a life member of the Nebraskana Society. Residence: Newport.

Winthrop Bent Lane

Winthrop B. Lane was born at Omaha, Nebraska, December 11, 1893, and has lived there all his life. His father, Edmund C. Lane, who was born at Underhill, Vermont, July 20, 1854, and died at Omaha, April 14, 1898, was a lawyer. His mother, Mary Catherine (Bent) Lane, was born at Cornwall, Vermont. Her English ancestors came to America before the Revolution; she is descended from the Adams family of Massachusetts; her paternal grandfather was a minister, professor and landman.

Mr. Lane attended the public schools of Omaha and was graduated from South Omaha High School. He was awarded the B. S. degree at Nebraska Wesleyan University, and later was granted his LL. B. at Harvard Law School. He was a member of the Nebraska Wesleyan Debating Team for three years and was Ivy Day orator. He was also elected to membership in Pi Kappa Delta and Delta Omega Phi.

Admitted to the bar at Omaha, June, 1918, he was associated with the firm of Stout, Rose, Wells, and Martin and later became a member of the Omaha Bar Associa-

ELLA M. LANGDON

tion; Nebraska Bar Association; Ak-Sar-Ben; and the Omaha Young Men's Christian Association. He is a member of the First Central Congregational Church of Omaha. Serving in Officers Training Camp, Field Artillery, during the World War, he is a member of the American Legion. He is a Republican.

Mr. Lane was united in marriage at Harvard, Massachusetts, on September 27, 1919, to Frances Marr O'Brien. Mrs. Lane, whose Scotch-Irish ancestors were early settlers in Maine, was born at Somerville, Massachusetts, June 26, 1889. They have a daughter, Marjorie Louise, born May 25, 1927. Residence: Omaha.

George Winders Lang

A resident of Nebraska for the past 57 years, George Winders Lang is the son of James Riley and Rovilla Jane (Foster) Lang. He was born at Corydon, Indiana, February 13, 1874, and came to Nebraska with his parents. His father, who was born at Corydon, February 27, 1852, was a pioneer homesteader in Custer County in June, 1874, where he was a farmer and merchant for many years; his father, Francis Lang, came to America from England, in 1780, and settled in Indiana, in 1826. Rovilla Jane (Foster) Lang was born at Corydon, January 1, 1854. She was the daughter of Samuel Foster who moved to Indiana from Pennsylvania, about 1810, and Esther McCullom, who moved to Indiana from Kentucky in 1826.

Mr. Lang received his education at Muddy Mills, Grand Island, Nebraska, and in the Litchfield High School. From 1892 to 1898 he was engaged in farming, and from 1898 to 1916, was in the general merchandise, implement and hardware business. Since 1910, he has been a Ford automobile dealer and oil and gasoline retailer at Litchfield. He has been elected eight times to membership on the Litchfield School Board, making a total of 15 years service. In 1926 he served as chairman of the Commercial Club at Litchfield, of which he is still a member; and for the past 23 years he has been superintendent of the Christian Sunday School there. He holds membership in the Nebraskana Society, the Red Cross, the Ancient Order of United Workmen and the Masonic Order. His hobby is baseball. Mr. Lang has served as a member of the village board a number of times since 1898, and still holds office.

On September 2, 1901, he married Mamie Josephine Murphy at Lincoln, Nebraska. Mrs. Lang, who was a school teacher for a number of years before her marriage, was born at Newhampton, Missouri, November 25, 1873, a direct descendant of James Pleasant, Colonial Governor of Virginia, and B. S. Ewell, the first president of William and Mary's College, in Virginia, and whose grandfathers, William Shelton and Pleasant Murphy, served in the Revolutionary War and the War of 1812. They have three children: Byril, born June 8, 1902, who married Thelma D'Allemand; Ewell J., born December 2, 1903, who married Margaret Monroe; and Erroll F., born July 18, 1912. Residence: Litchfield. (Photograph in Album).

Ella Morgan Langdon

Ella Morgan Langdon was born at Canisteo, New York, January 2, 1866. She is the daughter of Giles and Eliza-Nancy (Hallet) Morgan, and was married to John H. Langdon at Rochester, Minnesota, October 24, 1883. There are five children, two of whom are deceased: Annette C., born September 21, 1885, married Henry F. Stahl, and died September 3, 1918; William M., born February 28, 1887, who married Gertrude Conner; Frederick Joseph, born November 16, 1889, died February 24, 1896; John LeRoy, born April 24, 1892, married Mary Thornbrough; and Ella Frances, born September 22, 1905, who married Joseph W. Koke.

Since her marriage Mrs. Langdon has acted as her husband's secretary. She is active in the life of her community, and is a member of St. Patrick's Catholic Church.

She is a third cousin of Robert Fulton, inventor of the steamboat, and in this connection it is interesting to note that her grandmother, Nancy Fulton Hallett, who was his first cousin, accompanied him on the first voyage of his steamboat in 1807, she being seven years old at the time.

Mrs. Langdon's uncle, Samuel Hallett, built the first 40 miles of the Union Pacific Railroad west of the Missouri River, which was completed in April, 1864. His brother, John Hallett, later built a railroad in Oregon, tunnelling a long distance through the Rocky Mountains. Mrs. Langdon is in possession of a letter of invitation sent by Samuel Hallett to her mother and father to attend the celebration held at Weston, Mo., on June 1, 1864. Residence: Gretna. (Photograph on Page 694).

John H. Langdon

John H. Langdon was born at Forest City, Sarpy County, Nebraska, June 23, 1858, the son of William and Margaret (Thomas) Langdon. His father, who was born at Lacken, Mayo County, Ireland, in 1821, and died at Forest City, August 18, 1884, was a farmer, who held large tracts of land. He was a Democrat. He came to America about 1846.

His mother, who came with her parents from Ireland, was born at Lacken, March 24, 1824, and died at Gretna, Sarpy County, Nebraska, December 21, 1917.

Mr. Langdon attended the public school in the early days when educational facilities were few and the students were placed at roughly hewn benches made of cottonwood. He early entered the business world first engaging in the implement business. Later he moved to a farm and after a time became engaged in general merchandise business. He was one of the organizers of the Bank of Gretna, and at the present time is in the real estate and insurance business at Gretna, Nebraska.

At Rochester, Ramsey County, Minnesota, he was married to Ella Mary Morgan, October 24, 1883. Mrs. Langdon was born at Canisteo, Steuben County, New York, January 2, 1866, the daughter of Giles and Eliza Nancy (Hallett) Morgan; she is a third cousin of Robert Fulton, inventor of the steamboat. She is secretary to her husband. Five children were born to them, two of whom are deceased. They are: Annette C., born September 21, 1885, who married Henry F. Stahl, and who died September 3, 1918; William M., born February 28, 1887, who married Gertrude Connor; Frederick Joseph, born November 16, 1889, who died February 24, 1896; John LeRoy, born April 24, 1892, who married Mary Thornbrough; and Ella Frances, born September 22, 1905, who married Joseph W. Koke.

Mr. Langdon is a Democrat and a lifetime resident of Nebraska. He is a member of the Red Cross and is affiliated with Saint Patrick's Catholic Church at Gretna. Residence: Gretna. (Photograph on Page 696).

Carl Marcus Lange

Born at Wall Lake, Iowa, January 4, 1900, Carl M. Lange is one of Nebraska's most illustrious soldiers. He is the son of William and Elizabeth (Schwartz) Lange, the former born at Schleswig, Holstein, Germany, April 15, 1878. He came to America as a young man, and died at Hartington, September 14, 1915. His wife, Elizabeth, was born in Andover, Iowa, July 12, 1880.

Carl M. Lange was graduated from public school at Hartington, in 1914, and attended Hartington High School. He has had a varied and interesting career, his first position after leaving school being as cashier with the C. St. P. M. O. Railway. He was thereafter chief clerk to the general yardmaster at Omaha, and chief clerk to the general foreman of bridge and building at Emerson, returning to Hartington in June, 1922, to engage in his present occupation as sales manager of the Ford Agency.

On November 11, 1922, he was united in marriage to

JOHN H. LANGDON

Bertha June Christiansen, at Hartington. Mrs. Lange was born at Blair, June 6, 1902. There were two children born to them: Gerald, born April 17, 1924; died the same day; and Shirley, born January 5, 1927.

At the age of 17, Mr. Lange enlisted in the United States Army and trained at El Paso, Texas, one of the youngest Nebraskans to enter the World War. Assigned Company B, 2nd Machine Gun Battalion, he embarked on June 2, 1917, and landed at Saint Naizaire, France, on June 26, to enter training at Gonderecourt. Mr. Lange's first action was on October 15, 1917, at Sommerville Sector. Thereafter he was in nine major campaigns, Ansauville sub-sector (Toul); Sector west of Montdidier (Picardy); Cantigny Operation (Picardy); Montdidier-Noyon Offensive (Picardy); Aisne-Marne Offensive (Soissons); Saizeraise sub-sector: St. Mihiel Offensive; Meuse-Argonne Offensive (September 30 to October 12, 1918) and Meuse-Argonne Offensive (November 5-8, 1918). On October 4, 1918, together with another soldier, he brought in about twenty Germans, captured as they worked around behind a machine gun nest which had been causing heavy casualties in the American Forces.

Mr. Lange received the following decorations: the *Distinguished Service Cross, Medaille Militaire* (two), *Croix De Guerre with palm,* the *First Division Service Medal,* the *Victory Medal,* and the *French Shoulder Cord Medal.* It is interesting to note that Mr. Lange was with the first group of soldiers to parade in France, and assisted in bringing out Merle Hay, the first American killed in action in France. After the Armistice he served nine months in the Army of Occupation, landing in the United States September 3, 1919.

At the present time a first lieutenant in the 134th Infantry, Nebraska National Guard, he served 1921 and part of 1931 as commander of the Hartington Post of the American Legion, filling the vacancy caused by the resignation of the commander. He was Nebraska's only Legion representative to the burial of the unknown soldier in Washington, in 1921.

Mr. Lange is a member of Trinity Lutheran Church, the Chamber of Commerce and the Nebraskana Society. His social club is the Hartington Country Club, his sport is golf and his hobby is the promotion of citizenship activities. Residence: Hartington. (Photograph in Album).

George Henry Lange

Born at Baven, Germany, October 31, 1869, George Henry Lange is the son of Peter Henry Christopher Lange and Mary (Koch) Lange. His father, who was a farmer and landowner, was born at Baven, in 1812, and died there in April 1892. His mother was born at Schmarbeck, Germany, May 7, 1834, and died at Baven, in May, 1919.

Mr. Lange attended school in Germany. He has been successfully engaged in farming and banking in Valley County for 33 years, and is now director in the Ord State Bank and the State Bank of Ord. He has served on the school board at various times, is a member of the Non-Partisan League, and is a member of the Farmers Club of Mira Valley. He is affiliated with St. John's Evangelical Lutheran Church and holds membership in the Nebraskana Society. His hobbies are reading and stockfeeding, and his favorite sport is baseball.

He was married at Ord, March 2, 1899, to August Wilhelmina Bremer who was born at Davenport, Iowa, July 15, 1878; her father served in the Civil War under General Sherman. The following children were born to them: Ernest, born January 21, 1900, who married Esther Marie Bredthaner; Arthur, December 6, 1901, who married Clara Plejdrup; Bertha, November 24, 1903, who married Russell Acton; Edgar, January 27, 1906; Cora, April 16, 1908; Henry, August 10, 1911; Ella, July 2, 1913. Arnold, an infant son, died in early childhood. Residence: Ord.

Millard Langfeld

Millard Langfeld, superintendent of laboratories for the Cudahy Packing Company at Omaha, was born in Glasgow, Missouri, October 7, 1872. He is the son of Daniel and Yette (Pretzfelder) Langfeld, the former of whom was born in Bavaria, Germany. He was a merchant of the Jewish faith, whose death occurred at Baltimore, Maryland, on January 22, 1894. He came to the United States in 1858. His wife, Yette, was born in Bavaria, and is still living.

Upon the completion of his public school education, Millard Langfeld entered college, receiving his Bachelor of Arts degree. He was awarded his degree of Doctor of Medicine from John Hopkins University in 1898. Since that time he has been in active practice, for many years associated with the Cudahy Packing Company.

His marriage to Mathilda Ash was solemnized at Baltimore, on September 22, 1899. Mrs. Langfeld was born at Baltimore, December 22, 1899. There are two children, Daniel, born March 10, 1902; and Millard, born April 29, 1912.

Dr. Langfelt has served for a number of years as city bacteriologist for the city of Omaha. He is the author of *Introduction to Infectious and Contagious Diseases.* He is a member of various civic, chemical and engineering societies. Residence: Omaha.

James Warren Lanning

James Warren Lanning, manufacturer, was born in Hildreth, Nebraska, January 25, 1888, son of James Edward and Martha (Erasom) Lanning. His education was obtained in the public schools, and in Hildreth High School. Afterward he took advanced work through correspondence and in university short courses.

On December 28, 1906, he was united in marriage to Mary Rebecca Sisler at Denver, Colorado. Mrs. Lanning was born in Bakerfield, Maryland. They have three children, Doris, J. Clair and Richard E.

For five years Mr. Lanning served as superintendent of the Western Brick and Tile Company at Nebraska City, and for a number of years has been plant manager for the Lincoln Brick and Tile Company, of which he is secretary.

Mr. Lanning is a member of the Chamber of Commerce, the Masons and East Lincoln Christian Church, in the last of which he has served as president of the financing association, chairman of the building committee and member of the official board. Residence: Lincoln.

Daniel M. Langston

Daniel M. Langston, contractor, was born at Kokomo, Indiana, January 5, 1857, son of George W. and Nancy (Willson) Langston. The father was born August 7, 1830, and died from wounds received at the Battle of Shiloh, April 8, 1862. His wife, Nancy, was born May 14, 1831, and died at Casville, Indiana, December 6, 1876. She was an expert weaver and spinner. Daniel M. Langston is the proud possessor of a letter written by his father to his mother on March 9, 1862, while at Nashville, Tennessee.

Mr. Langston attended public school in the vicinity of Kokomo, Indiana, and has been a contractor and farmer, for many years. He is married to Anna Minerva Umphress. She was born at Montpelier, Iowa, April 3, 1868. Their children are as follows, Harra, born October 8, 1886, who married Katherine Riley, and who is an electrician at Taft, California; Clarence, born April 13, 1891, who died May 7, 1891; and Harold, born July 14, 1895. He is a car inspector and is now located at Inglewood, California.

A Republican, Mr. Langston has always been active and interested in party politics. He is a member of the Methodist Episcopal Church and of the Nebraskana Society. Residence: Oshkosh.

Ronald William Lape

Born at Wymore, Nebraska, November 27, 1890, Ronald William Lape has been a resident of this state all his life and is a leader in community affairs at Lexington, Nebraska, today. William Addison Lape, his father, who died at Wymore, December 28, 1890, was a railway brakeman; his family was of German origin. Phylinda (Stickel) Lape, his mother, who is an active church worker and is prominent in various fraternal and social affairs, was born at Springfield, Illinois, August 2, 1865. Her ancestry is Scotch and Irish.

Mr. Lape attended the public schools of Seward, Nebraska, and studied at night school and through correspondence for a time. In 1925 he was graduated from the American Institute of Baking Technology at Chicago, and for 12 years was a journeyman baker. He engaged in the bakery business for himself at Blue Rapids, Kansas from 1919 to 20, was in business at Garnett, Kansas, 1920-21 and since 1921 has been at Lexington where he is proprietor and owner of the Blue Ribbon Bakery. He is president of the Lexington Finance Company, is president of the Kiwanis Club having served as trustee and vice president previously, and is past president of the Lexington Chamber of Commerce.

He holds membership in the United Commercial Travelers Association, the Independent Order of Odd Fellows, and the Masons. His religious affiliation is with the Methodist Episcopal Church and he is a member of the Men's Brotherhood of which he was formerly president. He is interested in golf, tennis, football, baseball, wrestling, and boxing, and is a member of the Lexington Country Club.

He was united in marriage with Adella Evalyn Turner at Bee, Nebraska. Mrs. Lape, whose ancestry is English and Irish, was born at Seward, May 10, 1891. Their two children, who are students in high school, are: Lowell, born June 28, 1916; and Bernice, born February 20, 1918. Residence: Lexington.

Harry H. Lapidus

Harry H. Lapidus, a leading manufacturer and business executive of Omaha, Nebraska, was born at Shavel Kovno, Lithuania, October 10, 1882, the son of Israel Mandel Lapidus and Esther (Rothouse) Lapidus. He came to America with his parents when he was a small boy and for many years has been a leader in the civic, welfare, and religious life of Omaha.

He is president and manager of the Omaha Fixture & Supply Company at Omaha. In 1902 he was united in marriage with Minnie Kooler at Omaha. They have three children: Estelle Joyce, who married Irvin Stalmaster; Lester; and Earl.

Mr. Lapidus is first vice president of the National Jewish Hospital for Consumptives, Denver, Colorado; is vice president of the Nebraska Tuberculosis Association; is a director of the Wise Memorial Hospital; is a trustee of the Jewish Community Center. He was made a member of the Boundary Commission created for the settlement of boundary disputes between the states of Nebraska and Iowa; and was chairman of the board of trustees created by the power of congress for the erection of interstate bridges between Iowa and Nebraska.

He was chairman of a committee for raising a fund of $250,000.00 for the Jewish Community Center and served as chairman of District Number 6 in a joint campaign with District Number 2 to raise $400,000.00 for the B'nai Brith Infirmary Building of the National Jewish Hospital at Denver. During the World War he was chairman of the Jewish Welfare Board of Nebraska, and was a member of the executive committee of the United Seven War Campaign.

He is a member of the following organizations: executive committee of the Jewish Welfare Federation; Jewish Social Service Committee; Omaha Lodge of B'nai Brith, of which he was formerly general committeeman of District Number 6, and of which he is past Omaha president; Omaha Hebrew Club; Modern Woodmen of America; Zionist Organization of America; National Conference of Jewish Social Service Work; Jewish Welfare Board; National Jewish Farm School; Jewish Theological Seminary of New York; Hebrew Theological Seminary of Chicago.

Mr. Lapidus is a member of the executive committee of the United Palestine Appeal; the executive committee of Jewish War Relief Campaigns, and director of the Omaha Manufacturers Association. He has won distinction in his community and throughout the country for his services in Jewish welfare work. (Deceased 1931).

Mary Eugenia LaRocca

Born at Brainerd, Minnesota, September 14, 1877, Mary E. LaRocca has been a resident of Nebraska for the past 12 years. She is the daughter of Thomas Chandler Fernald, born at Boston, February 13, 1848. He was a railroad clerk, and operated a trading post at Brainerd. He enlisted as a drummer boy in the Civil War, and was the son of Elihu Fernald, of Irish and English parentage, whose ancestors came to the United States during the Revolution, settling at Boston. He died in Napa County, California, December 22, 1927.

Thomas Fernald married Mary Alice Mills, born at Burlington, Vermont, July 30, 1851. She was the daughter of Asa Smith Mills, who was born on the Isle of Man, Scotland, and of Mary Jane Lyons, of Irish parentage. She died at Omaha, February 1, 1926.

Mary E. LaRocca received her elementary education in the public schools of St. Paul, Minnesota, and attended Garfield High School two years. She attended All Saints College at Sioux Falls, South Dakota four years. She was married at St. Paul, October 14, 1896, and has three children living, Harry B., born October 8, 1897; Richard Eugene, born July 13, 1899, deceased; Thomas Fernald, born January 12, 1916; and Mary Catherine, born May 28, 1917.

Her business career has been almost entirely with the Woodmen Circle. She helped organize and was first state president of Minnesota for the state convention of the Woodmen Circle. In 1907 she was elected national auditor at Norfolk, Virginia, and in 1911 chairman of national auditors at Rochester, New York. In 1915 she was made vice-president at St. Paul, Minnesota, and since 1919 has served as national president, being elected at the national convention in Chicago, with office in Omaha.

She is chairman of the committee for the Home For the Aged, Members and Orphan Children, and is editor of *Monthly Tidings,* official organ of the Woodmen Circle. During the World War she was active in Red Cross Work. She is a member of the Women's Relief Corps, the Auxiliary of United Spanish War Veterans, and War Mothers of America. She is eligible to the Daughters of the American Revolution. In religion she is a Congregationalist. The civic organizations in which she holds membership include the Y. W. C. A., the Woman's Club, the women's division of the Chamber of Commerce and the Business and Professional Women's Club. She is a member of the Women of Moose Heart Legion, the Degree of Honor, the Brotherhood of American Yeomen and the Maccabees. Fond of golf and all games, her hobby is reading. Residence: Omaha.

Percie Henry Larrick

A farmer and breeder of registered cattle, Percie Henry Larrick has lived near Bladen, Nebraska all his life. He was born at Bladen, August 22, 1883, the son of David H. and Annie Elizabeth (Richard) Larrick. His father, who was a pioneer farmer and homesteader in Webster County, Nebraska, was born at Winchester, Virginia, August 2, 1843, and died at Red Cloud, Nebraska, August 13, 1927. His mother, also a pioneer in Webster County, was born at Winchester, October 30, 1847, and is still living.

Mr. Larrick is a member of the board of directors

of the Webster County Fair Association, is a former member of the school board, and holds membership in the Parent Teachers Association and the Red Cross. He is a member of the Webster County Farm Bureau, the Nebraska Hereford Breeders Association, and is past president of the local society of the Farmers Educational and Co-operative Union of Nebraska. He is a football, basketball, and baseball enthusiast, is fond of hunting and fishing, and is especially interested in breeding Hereford cattle.

His marriage to Hattie Mabel Householder was solemnized at Bladen, Nebraska, September 9, 1908. Mrs. Larrick, who was a teacher before her marriage, was born at Bladen, March 2, 1884; her father was born in Pennsylvania of German ancestry and her mother was born in Ireland. Their children are: Richard, born July 9, 1909; Virginia, December 14, 1912; Percie, July 26, 1917. Richard was graduated from the Bladen High School in 1928 and attended Kearney Normal School. Virginia was graduated from Bladen High School and is now a student at the University of Nebraska. Percie Jr., is a freshman at Bladen High School.

Mr. Larrick served as local food administrator during the World War, and was prominent in Red Cross drives and war stamp sales. He is a Democrat. Residence: Bladen.

Fred Herbert Larson

Fred Herbert Larson, secretary and treasurer and general manager of the Heath Telephone Company, was born at Heath, Nebraska, August 9, 1898, son of S. M. and Emma (Mattson) Larson. The father, who was born January 4, 1854, came to America in 1878. He was a farmer and merchant whose death occurred at Omaha, December 20, 1917. His wife, Emma, was born in Knoxville, Illinois, February 12, 1863. Her parents came to America from Sweden in a sail boat.

In May, 1912, Mr. Larson was graduated from grade school, and in May, 1916, was graduated from Kimball County High School. During 1917 and 1918 he attended the Rubicon Business College at St. Louis, Missouri. A resident of Nebraska for 32 years, he has been active as a farmer. He is a Republican, a member of the Methodist Church, and the Knights of Pythias. His favorite sport is hunting while his hobby is mechanics.

On December 27, 1927, he was married to Evelyn Wilger at Denver. Mrs. Larson was born at Exeter, Nebraska, April 15, 1908. They have two children, Leonard, born November 4, 1929; and Kenneth, born February 1, 1932. Residence: Harrisburg.

Henry Larson

Henry Larson was born at Monmouth, Illinois, May 15, 1881, the son of Peter E. and Louis (Benson) Larson, the former a farmer who was born at Halmstad, Sweden, January 14, 1848. His mother was born at Lahalm, Holland, April 27, 1852.

Mr. Larson has been a farmer in Phelps County, Nebraska, most of his life and is today engaged in stockraising near Loomis. He is secretary-treasurer of the Loomis Farmers Co-operative Company, is a director of the Loomis Oil Company, and is serving as township clerk there. He is a trustee in the Westmark Evangelical Church and is treasurer of the local school board.

He married Agnes B. Brodine at Loomis, February 27, 1907. Mrs. Larson, who is active in farm work, was born at Loomis, April 27, 1882. The following children were born to them, all of whom are living: Clifton, March 23, 1908; Ralph, October 30, 1909; Raymond, May 5, 1912; Roland, May 5, 1912; Elliott, September 13, 1914; Elton, January 12, 1917; and Warren, April 21, 1920. Residence: Loomis. (Photograph in Album).

John Herman Larson

John Herman Larson, a farmer in Burt County since youth, was born in Sandviken, Sweden, December 20, 1877, son of Andrew Magnus and Anna (Ax) Larson. His father was born in Dalsland, Sweden, October 27, 1850, and is a farmer in Burt County. His mother who was born near Gifle, Sweden, August 22, 1857, died at Oakland, May 2, 1925.

Mr. Larson attended the district schools of Cuming County, and completed the commercial course at Fremont Normal College in 1900. He studied music and voice at Nebraska Wesleyan, and was first tenor and a member of the male quartet while there.

On May 19, 1910, he was married to Maude Thomas, a student of music and teacher of piano, at University Place, Nebraska. Mrs. Larson was born at Milwaukee, Wisconsin, June 7, 1885. Her great-great-grandfather edited the first newspaper in Quebec, Canada. There are five children of this marriage, Virginia, born June 9, 1911; Barbara, born May 7, 1914; Thomas, born October 24, 1915; Rosemary, born March 7, 1919, and Margaret Ann, born April 23, 1923. Virginia attends the University of Nebraska, Barabara attends Jackson High School in Lincoln, and Thomas is in the 10th grade.

Mr. Larson is a Republican, a member of Divide Center Presbyterian Rural Church, the school board and the Masonic order. He is fond of singing. Residence: Lyons.

Lauritz Augustin Larson

Lauritz Augustin Larson, a farmer and ex-merchant at McCook, Nebraska, was born in Stavanger, Norway, August 18, 1868, son of Augustin and Margareta (Pierson) Larson.

His father, Augustin Larson, was born in Honvaag, Norway, May 3, 1839, and died at Stockville, Nebraska, January 20, 1912. He was a navigator and a ship captain and after coming to America was a farmer. He homesteaded in Nebraska in 1885 in Frontier County, and was a member of the Farmers' Alliance. For 12 years he served as superintendent of Sunday school of Union Denominations.

His paternal ancestry was English, and his maternal old Norse-Viking stock. His paternal ancestors settled on an island called Witso (White's Isle) near Stavanger.

Margareta Pierson was born in Stavanger, February 26, 1842 and is still living at the age of 90 in Curtis, Nebraska. She was a professional mid-wife for many years both in Norway and the United States. Her paternal ancestors had lived in southern Norway for many generations. Her mother came from Bergen, and was of German ancestry.

Lauritz A. Larson came to the United States with his parents, while still a little lad. The father promptly secured naturalization papers and identified himself and his family with all the interests and institutions of his adopted country.

Going into the grocery business in New Sharon, Iowa, there the son grew to young manhood and under the influence of the Quakers, to which his parents belong, he received his education. He attended public school at New Sharon, though he whimsically says that he later majored in experience in the school of hard knocks.

In 1886 the family moved to Frontier County, Nebraska, homesteading in Laws precinct about 30 miles north of McCook. With the exception of seven years spent in the employ of a leading mercantile firm in Minden, Mr. Larson has been a constant resident of his home community for more than 40 years.

He understands to the fullest extent the privations and vicissitudes of pioneer life and has born his part in the taming of the wilderness and the development of southwest Nebraska, a land of beautiful homes.

Mr. Larson is a linguist of considerable ability, speak-

LAURITZ AUGUSTIN LARSON

ing German and the Scandinavian languages with ease and fluency. He has always taken an active interest in the social and educational welfare of his community and has been prominently identified with the good roads movement throwing all his energy and influence toward the construction of highways that will benefit the farm and local market town, rather than the passing tourists.

His friends esteem him for his personal integrity and he is known as a man who fearlessly champions his convictions. Questioned as to his stand on certain vital matters now occupying the popular attention, Mr. Larson has said: "I believe in the drastic reduction of tariff. I favor rigid law enforcement, whether on land or sea, so long as it is under the American flag, the 12 mile limit not-with-standing. America's policy toward world problems must be guided by the plain sign posts of history rather than by the well intentioned, but ill considered plans of enthusiasts who unknowingly voice the desires of sinister and selfish interests. I believe the brain and brawn of those who toil is the best asset of a nation, and should in all things receive first consideration and be valued above treasure."

On December 1, 1895, Mr. Larson was married to Anna Jane Sanders at Stockville. That was her birthplace. She was born on June 9, 1875, the first white child born in Frontier County. Her father represented the third generation of Scotch settlers in America. Her mother is descended from the old southern families of Lockwood and Lyon. Mr. and Mrs. Larson have three children living and two deceased, Wauneta, born November 22, 1896, died December 18, 1915. She was teaching school when she caught cold and died after only a 36 hour illness; Augustin, born March 13, 1899, died September 8, 1922; John S., born April 22, 1901, who married Frances Clawson. They have one child, John Lewis; Lauritz A., Jr., born December 19, 1903, who married Opal Grinnell; they have two children, Betty and Frankie; and Leon L., born April 7, 1906. Leon L. married Iola Scheidt, who died March 27, 1932. They had one child, Anna Jane.

Mr. Larson has always been a Democrat. He has served as school director ten years, as secretary of the board of education four years, and as police judge six years. At the present time he is associated with the department of public works as inspector in the highway department.

He was chief registrar during the World War for the draft board. He was brought up in the Society of Friends, but not attends the First Congregational Church of Curtis. He is a member of Curtis Lodge No. 168 of the Ancient Free and Accepted Masons, in which he has held membership for 40 years. His hobbies are off-hand drawing and portrait painting. Residence: McCook. (Photograph on Page 700).

Lewis C. Larson

Lewis C. Larson, veteran farmer and hardware dealer at Minden, Nebraska, was born at Joliet, Illinois, January 2, 1876, and for the past 48 years has resided in Nebraska. His father, Christ J. Larson, a clergyman, was born in Denmark, January 14, 1851, and died at Chicago, Illinois, in March, 1928. His mother was born in Denmark, February 25, 1848, and died in Michigan, in December, 1912.

Mr. Larson was married at Minden, December 6, 1898, to Mary A. Nelson, who was born at Blair, Nebraska, March 16, 1880. To this marriage three children were born: Durfee, October 8, 1900, who is assistant instructor at the University of Nebraska; Neota, January 1, 1903, a social worker; and Garnet, November 1, 1904, who is an instructor in the University of Kansas.

Mr. Larson is a member of the Nebraskana Society, the United Presbyterian Church, a member of the Minden City council from the second ward and a member of the Republican party. Residence: Minden.

Louis Peter Larson

Louis Peter Larson, a real estate man in Nebraska for the past 48 years, has lived in this state for 59 years. He was born at Lidkoping, Sweden, February 5, 1851, the son of Nelson Lars. His father, who was a farmer, was born at Lidkoping, in 1814, and died there in 1890.

Mr. Larson attended the public schools in Sweden, and in 1873, received a diploma from the Great Western Business College at Omaha. He is now connected with the Fremont Beverage Company, the Fremont Stock Yards and Land Company, and the L. P. Larson Real Property Company. He has been a director in the Fremont National Bank, Fremont, Dodge County, Nebraska, for the past 48 years.

A Democrat, he has served as city treasurer of Fremont, and member of the house of representatives in 1889. He is a member of the Nebraskana Society, is affiliated with the Christian Science Church at Fremont, and holds membership in the Elks and Knights of Pythias.

His marriage to Althea Granath was solemnized at Omaha, March 13, 1873; she was born at Linkoping, Sweden, April 20, 1849, and died at Fremont, May 9, 1907. Five children were born to this marriage: Lida, born March 5, 1874; Laura, born January 1, 1877; Louis P., born January 20, 1880; Lily, born April 26, 1882; and Luther C., born September 25, 1885. All the children are married. Mr. Larson was married to Ruth Wirsen at New York, September 16, 1910. Residence: Fremont.

Chelsea Ira Lathrop

Born at Inland, Nebraska, October 14, 1887, Chelsea Ira Lathrop is the son of Albert Milton and Anna Rowena (Lawton) Lathrop. His father, who was born at Griswold, Connecticut, July 11, 1841, is a farmer and a veteran of the Civil War; he was a pioneer in Nebraska in the early days and served as president of the Clay County Farmers Mutual Insurance Company for nearly 30 years; of English ancestry, he is descended from Judge Dixwell, one of the regicides who came to America from England. His mother was born of English and Scotch parents at Noriville, Connecticut, October 13, 1847, and died at Orange, California, September 6, 1918.

Mr. Lathrop attended the public schools of Inland and was a student in the academy of Hastings College, Hastings, Nebraska, for two years. He has been a progressive farmer near Inland for a number of years, and is now serving as a member of the town board as clerk. He is affiliated with the Methodist Episcopal Church, is a member of the Sons of Union Veterans of the Civil War, and holds membership in the Nebraskana Society. His hobby is horses.

On June 2, 1920, he married Bertha Emma Hiersekorn at McCook, Nebraska. Mrs. Lathrop, whose ancestry is German, was born at Beaver Precinct, Nebraska, November 10, 1897. Three children were born to them: Dixwell Albert, June 5, 1922; Betty Jean, July 26, 1924; and Rachel Wilhelmina, August 26, 1927. Residence: Inland.

Edith Anna Lathrop

Born at Inland, Nebraska, December 4, 1874, Edith Anna Lathrop is the daughter of Milton Albert and Anna Rowena (Lawton) Lathrop. Her father, who is a farmer and pioneered in Nebraska in early days, was born at Griswold, Connecticut, July 11, 1841; he served in the Civil War, and directly after the war was a teacher in the public schools of Connecticut. He is descended from Judge Dixwell who was one of the regicides who fled from England to America after the restoration of Charles to the throne of England.

Anna (Lawton) Lathrop, who was a teacher before

her marriage, was born at Norwich, Connecticut, October 13, 1847, of English and Scotch descent, and died at Orange, California, September, 1918.

Miss Lathrop attended the preparatory school of the University of Nebraska, and later was a student at the University where she received the A. B. and A. M. degrees, 1903 and 1917 respectively. She studied at George Washington University, 1926 and 1929, and took up work in the School of Library Science at Columbia University, 1931. Today she is one of Nebraska's foremost representatives in educational affairs.

She has held the following positions: teacher in rural schools of Clay County, Nebraska; teacher in high schools at Harvard and Hastings, Nebraska; county superintendent of schools in Clay County; rural school supervisor in the state department of education; and instructor at Johns Hopkins University, during the summer sessions. She is associated specialist of school libraries in the United States office of education at Washington, D. C. and is the author of bulletins and pamphlets published by the government and articles published in educational journals.

Miss Lathrop is a member of the National Educational Association, the American Library Association, and the American Association of University Women. She was the recipient of a grant-in-aid from Carnegie Corporation of $3000 for study of rural school libraries in 1931. Her hobby is reading, and her favorite sport is hiking. Residence: Inland.

James Oscar Latta

James Oscar Latta, physician and surgeon, was born at Plattsmouth, Nebraska, August 9, 1877, son of William Edmundson and Sarah Lee (Current) Latta. William Latta, whose parents were Ohioans, was born at Cincinnati, July 22, 1854. Now a retired farmer, he was for fifteen years in the mercantile, grain and implement business. His wife was a native of Indiana, born June 4, 1856, and until recently assisted her husband in his business.

Dr. Latta was graduated from Kenesaw High School in 1896, and from the medical department of Cotner University on April 2, 1902. For two years, 1900 and 1901, he was captain of the Cotner football team. On January 20, 1904, he was married to Ada Mae Bavinger at Clay Center. Mrs. Latta, who was born at Bradford, Illinois, October 27, 1876, was a stenographer prior to marriage. There are two children, Inez Mae, born November 25, 1906; and William Mitchell, born November 11, 1920. Inez Mae was graduated from the University of Nebraska in 1928, taught three years, and attended summer school at Columbia University the summer of 1931. She is teaching at Grand Island High School.

A Republican, Dr. Latta has been physician to the board of insanity of Clay County since 1908, was a member of the city council 1908-17, mayor of Clay Center, 1917-20, and county physician 1902-16, and 1924. From 1903-12, he was treasurer of the Clay County Telephone Company. During the World War, Dr. Latta was chairman of the conservation board for Clay Center.

Among his professional, civic and fraternal organizations are the following: Clay County, Nebraska and American Medical Associations (president Clay County 1910, secretary since 1924), Seventh District Medical Society (president), Chamber of Commerce (board member six years), Lions Club (chairman of activities committee). He is a Scottish Rite Mason and Shriner, a Knight of Pythias, Woodman of the World, Modern Woodman of America, Yeoman, and the Royal Highlanders. His club is the Clay Center Country, of which he is president. Golf, hunting, baseball and football are his favorite sports, while his hobby is mechanics. Residence: Clay Center.

John Diedrich Lau

John Diedrich Lau was born at Lincoln, Nebraska, March 5, 1881, son of Hans Peter Lau, who founded the firm of H. P. Lau, wholesale grocers. Educated first in the public and high schools of Lincoln, he later attended the University of Nebraska, and is a member of Phi Delta Theta, Phi Delta Phi and Theta Nu Epsilon.

On April 30, 1908 he was united in marriage to Cora Calista Whitesides at Lincoln. Mrs. Lau was born at Aurora, Nebraska, June 30, 1881. Her son, Willard Leroy, by a prior marriage has been adopted by Mr. Lau.

Since leaving college, Mr. Lau has been associated with H. P. Lau Co., and is now secretary-treasurer of the company. He is also a director of the National Bank of Commerce at Lincoln, and a member of the Chamber of Commerce. He enjoys tennis, golf, swimming, ice skating and football games. His clubs are the Lincoln Tennis Club of which he is president, the University and Lincoln Country Clubs, and is an Elk. Residence: Lincoln.

Loren H. Laughlin

Loren H. Laughlin was born at Mt. Ayr, Iowa, August 13, 1896, son of Lawrence Weldon and Belle (Hass) Laughlin. He attended public school at Mt. Ayr and Des Moines, and was graduated from the Mt. Ayr High School. He attended Drake University, where he engaged in the study of law, and in 1918 received his Bachelor of Laws degree while in Military Service. Mr. Lauglin was discharged from the army on March 20, 1919.

On May 28, 1918, he was married to Marie Chance of Eagle Grove, Iowa. Mrs. Laughlin is a graduate of the Fine Arts Department of Drake University, and a member of the Eastern Star.

A Republican, in 1924 he was elected a member of the Nebraska state senate from the 16th senatorial district. And in 1925 he was chairman of the committee on constitutional amendments. He was re-elected in 1926 without opposition.

Senator Laughlin is a member of the Masons, Sesostris Temple of the Shrine at Lincoln, and is active in the Elks and Odd Fellows. He is a member of the Gage County and the Nebraska State Bar Associations, and was president of the latter in 1922. He is also a member of the American Bar Association. His patriotic organizations include the American Legion in which he has held various offices and the Forty and Eight. His fraternity is Sigma Alpha Epsilon. He is a member of the Congregational Church, and has served as a member of the board of trustees. He is a member of the Chamber of Commerce and the Kiwanis Club. Residence: Beatrice.

Loren Hass Laughlin

Loren H. Laughlin, lawyer at Lincoln, Nebraska, was born at Mount Ayr, Iowa, August 13, 1896, the son of Lawrence Weldon and Sarah Belle (Hass) Laughlin. His father, who was born at Mount Ayr, April 11, 1868, has been a lawyer for many years, and was the organizer of the National Life Insurance Association at Des Moines, Iowa, and other insurance corporations; his English, Scotch-Irish ancestors came to America in the early New England period, and were professional men and business executives. His mother, whose German ancestors came to this country in the 19th century, was born at Allendale, Worth County, Missouri, August 16, 1874; her ancestors were business men, and farmers.

Mr. Laughlin attended the public school of Des Moines and Mount Ayr, and was graduated from high school at Mount Ayr, in 1914. He received the LL. B. degree at Drake University in 1918, where he was graduated with class honors. He received the highest honors attained in the history of the school at Mount Ayr High School; and was elected to membership in Sigma Alpha Epsilon at Drake University.

He studied law and the abstract business in his father's office during his boyhood; was a member of the law firm of Hazlett, Jack & Laughlin, at Beatrice, Nebraska, 1919-28; was a member of the firm Jack, Laughlin & Vette, 1928-9; and since 1929 has been a practicing attorney at Lincoln. He served as attorney for various corporations.

An active member of the Republican party, Mr. Laughlin has held the following public offices: assistant counsel, Iowa Railroad Commission, 1917-18; assistant to the Iowa Code Commission, 1919; state senator, 16th Nebraska district 1925-9; elected delegate to the National Republican Convention at Kansas City, Missouri, 1928.

During the World War he served in Battery A., 67th Artillery, and graduated at the Artillery Officers' Training School, Saumur, France, 1918; he is captain in the Judge Advocate General Reserves, is a member of the American Legion, the National Reserve Officers' Association; and the 40 and 8. He holds membership in the American Bar Association; the Lancaster County Bar Association; the Nebraska State Bar Association; and the Nebraskana Society.

From 1919-28, he was a member of the Beatrice Chamber of Commerce, of which he was director from 1923-1928; and since 1929, has been a member of the Lincoln Chamber of Commerce. He was a member of the Beatrice Kiwanis Club, 1921-8. His fraternal organizations include: Ancient Free and Accepted Masons; A. & A. S. R.; Shrine; Elks; Odd Fellows; Modern Woodmen of America; and B. A. Y. His social club is the University Club.

His marriage to Mildred Marie Chance was solemnized at Des Moines, Iowa, May 28, 1918. Mrs. Laughlin was born at Eagle Grove, Wright County, Iowa, May 25, 1898; her ancestry was English and Irish. Two children were born to this marriage: Betty Lucille, born February 26, 1930; and George William, born October 16, 1924. Residence: Lincoln.

Laurits Lauritsen

Laurits Lauritsen, farmer and former state representative, was born in Denmark, February 1, 1860, son of John and Meta (Hansen) Lauritsen. His father was born in Denmark, July 6, 1821, and died there in May, 1900. His wife, Meta, born in Denmark, September 15, 1823, died there May 15, 1918.

Mr. Lauritsen was educated in the public schools, and has engaged in farming ever since he came to America 42 years ago. He is president of the Farmers Union State Exchange at Omaha, and was elected to the house of representatives on the Republican ticket 1919 and 1921.

He was married to Hansine Schott at Omaha, and to them two children were born, John, born April 22, 1889, who married Mae Hansen; and Ann, born July 21, 1890, who married Marcus Peterson. Mrs. Lauritsen, who was born in Denmark, May 20, 1867, died at Omaha, August 20, 1891. Mr. Lauritsen's second marriage was to Maria Andersen, born in Denmark, May 15, 1867. They have had four children, Ellen, born May 20, 1892, who married Hans Pedersen, and who died August 28, 1929; Andrew, born March 8, 1895, who married Martha Reemers; Olga, born December 31, 1900; and Clara, born October 20, 1902, who married Al Buckman.

Mr. Lauritsen is a Lutheran, and a member of the Odd Fellows and the Danish Brotherhood. He is also a member of The Nebraskana Society. Residence: West Point.

George Wesley Lautenschlager

George W. Lautenschlager was born at Swanton, Saline County, Nebraska, July 20, 1880, and has always been a farmer there. His father, John Leonard Lautenschlager, who was a pioneer farmer in Nebraska, was born at Darmstadt, Germany, January 26, 1852, and came to America in 1866. The latter has been an important factor in the development of Saline County, and has the distinction of spiking the switch on the Chicago, Burlington & Quincy Railroad when the track was extended from Crete to Wymore, Nebraska. He built the first Methodist Episcopal Church in this section of the country.

Augusta Fredericka (Gutzmer) Lautenschlager, mother of George, was born in Wisconsin, October 27, 1857, and died at Lincoln, Lancaster County, Nebraska, April 8, 1924. Her German ancestors were pioneer settlers in Nebraska.

Mr. Lautenschlager received his elementary education in rural schools and later was a student at Swanton High School. He attended York College, York, Nebraska, 1899-1900, where he took part in track meets in which he distinguished himself. He is a member of the Western Community Club; is past officer of the local school board; and is a member of the Nebraskana Society. He is vitally interested in all organizations which have for their purpose the betterment of the community.

In the late war Mr. Lautenschlager assisted in Liberty loan drives. A Democrat, he was candidate for county commissioner, first district, in 1930, and was defeated by one vote. He is affiliated with the Swanton Methodist Church. His sports include practically every form of athletics.

Mr. Lautenschlager enjoys as his two hobbies, mechanics and singing. He likes especially male quartette work since he has been a member of some group of singers for over 30 years.

He has six children: William LeRoy, born March 4, 1907; Clarence Wesley, born February 22, 1909; Cecil Leonard, born November 25, 1911; Evelyn, born March 31, 1913; John L., born February 9, 1915, and Paul Herbert, born June 16, 1918.

Mrs. Lautenschlager before her marriage was Faye Alnora Force, and was born at Liberty, Nebraska, January 4, 1886, her father being one of the oldest settlers at Swanton, Nebraska. Residence: Swanton. (Photograph in Album).

Guy Laverty

Guy Laverty, county attorney of Garfield County intermittently for the past forty years, was born at La Porte, Iowa, November 2, 1868, son of Anson A. and Mary (McClintic) Laverty.

Anson A. Laverty, a lawyer of Irish descent, was born at Jackson, Michigan, and died at Omaha, January 13, 1912. His wife, a native of Ohio, was of Scotch-Irish ancestry. She died at Lincoln a number of years ago.

Educated in public school, Guy Laverty was graduated from Ord High School, and later attended Fremont Normal School. Engaged in the practice of law at Burwell since 1893, he has been county attorney approximately half that time. At the present time he is also attorney for the Farmers Bank at Burwell. He is a Democrat.

On August 31, 1892, Mr. Laverty was united in marriage to Emma M. Glover at Ord. Mrs. Laverty, who was a stenographer prior to her marriage, was born at Owassa, Michigan, October 27, 1872. There were two children born to them, Cecil Fay, October 9, 1894, who died February 13, 1921, and Carmen P., April 15, 1897. Cecil graduated from the law school of the University of Nebraska and was assistant attorney general under C. A. Davis. Carmen, who is a graduate of Nebraska Wesleyan University, and a commercial teacher, is married to Harvey B. Hornby.

During the late war Mr. Laverty was a member of the food conservation committee and a four minute speaker. He is a member of the Nebraska State Bar Association, the Red Cross, the Wranglers Club, the Odd Fellows and the Young Men's Christian Association. For about twelve years he was a member of the local school board.

Recently Mr. Laverty was elected to life membership in the Nebraskana Society. His favorite sport is golf, and his hobby is helping youngsters to get a start in life. Residence: Burwell.

Gerald Edward La Violette

Gerald E. La Violette was born at O'Neill, Nebraska, March 16, 1893. He is the son of William La Violette, born in New Brunswick, Canada. He was of French and Irish descent, and in his youth was a mining superintendent in Michigan. For many years he was a druggist at North Bend, Nebraska, and was active in Democratic politics. He died at North Bend, August 18, 1926. He married Ellen Hackett, who was born in Wisconsin, August 10, 1852. She was a school teacher, with more than an ordinary education. She is of Irish descent.

Gerald E. La Violette was graduated from St. Mary's Academy, at O'Neill in 1908. He attended St. Thomas Military Academy at St. Paul Minnesota, and was graduated from Creighton University High School at Omaha in 1912. He received his A. B. from Creighton University in 1916, and his LL. B. in 1919. He was the winner of five elocution medals and one oratorical medal at Creighton.

He was married to Henrietta Rita West at Omaha, February 25, 1923. Mrs. La Violette was born in Omaha, May 2, 1896, and is of English descent. There are two children, Frances Anne, born January 19, 1925, and William George, born November 9, 1926.

Since his admission to the bar in 1919, Mr. La Violette has been actively engaged in the practice of law, and a member of the law firm of La Violette and Mehrens. He is a Republican and a member of the Nebraska State and Omaha-Douglas County Bar Associations. He was a private in Base Hospital No. 49, during the World War. A member of the American Legion, and of St. John's Catholic Church, he is a member also of the Elks, Moose and Knights of Columbus. He likes football, and his hobby is public oratory. Residence: Omaha.

Frances Walker Lawritson

Frances W. Lawritson was born at Lincoln, Nebraska, July 23, 1900, the daughter of William F. and Jane Elizabeth (Hindley) Walker. Her father, who was for many years a salesman, was born at Ellsworth, Maine, December 7, 1856. Her mother was born at Manchester, England, February 6, 1868.

Mrs. Lawritson was graduated from Whittier Grade School in Lincoln, and in 1918 was graduated from the Lincoln High School. She was connected with the extension service department of the College of Agriculture, 1918-19, and with the Swallow Land Company, 1920. Since 1921 she has been with the Nebraska Farm Bureau Federation at Lincoln, and is at the present time president of the Federation.

She is an associate member of the Chamber of Commerce, and holds membership in the Nebraskana Society and the Red Cross. She is a member of the First Plymouth Congregational Church of Lincoln. Her marriage to Martin Nelson Lawritson was solemnized at Fremont, Dodge County, Nebraska, October 24, 1928. Mr. Lawritson is assistant manager of the Nebraska Daily Development Society. Residence: Lincoln.

Albertus Lay

Albertus Lay, son of Dirk G. and Margaretha (Bowman) Lay, was born at Leer, East Friesland, Germany, April 21, 1860. His father, born at Ven Hausen, East Friesland, August 18, 1832, was an architect who came to America in 1868. His death occurred at Hastings on March 21, 1905. Margaretha Bowman, his wife, was born at Ven Hausen, on June 17, 1833. Until the time of her death at Hastings on November 9, 1887, she was an ardent worker in her church.

Educated in the public schools of Nebraska, Albertus Lay left school to become a farmer. He has resided in Nebraska fifty-seven years, and during all of that time has taken an active part in the development of his community.

On April 18, 1885, he was united in marriage to Sara Gruis, at Hastings. Mrs. Lay was a native of East Friesland, also, born at Bunde, March 1, 1861. They are extremely proud of their family of eight children, who are as follows:

Dirk, born January 21, 1886, is married to Elizabeth Hilkeman; Dena, born April 22, 1887, married the Reverend August Cramer; Roelf, born April 20, 1890, married Amena DeVoogd, Siemon, born March 1, 1892, married Helen V. Tuttle; Margaretha, born January 10, 1895, married the Reverend William J. Grossheim; Lydia, born November 28, 1898, married George Sinning; Albertus A., born October 26, 1901, is unmarried, as is Sara, born December 11, 1904.

Dirk and Siemon are missionaries, Dirk in Arizona and Siemon in New Mexico; Dena and Margaretha are married to clergymen; Roelf and Albert are farmers; Lydia married a farmer, and Sara is a teacher.

A Republican, Mr. Lay has an active interest in the public welfare, and has served as school treasurer thirty years. As a member of the Council of Defense during the World War period he participated in all war time projects. He is an elder in the Presbyterian Church at Glenvil, and a member of the Nebraskana Society. His hobby is reading. Residence: Glenvil.

Joseph Lazure

Born in Washington County, Nebraska, January 25, 1872, Joseph Lazure has been a resident of the county since birth. He is the son of Adolph and Marie (Poissant) Lazure, both of French Canadian extraction. His father, who was born at Montreal, Canada, December 19, 1841, is a farmer and stockman who came to the United States in the Spring of 1866. His wife, Marie, was born in Montreal, September 24, 1845, and died at DeSota, Nebraska, March 28, 1924.

Joseph Lazure attended district school in Washington County, and the Western Normal School at Shenandoah, Iowa. He was married to May Allen at Omaha, on September 22, 1914. Mrs. Lazure was born at Fort Calhoun, June 11, 1872. She was a teacher in the schools of Washington County thirteen years, and is of German, Swiss and French Huguenot descent, and a member of the Daughters of the American Revolution.

Mr. Lazure is a Republican and was chairman of the Washington County Republican central committee 1910-12. He is a member of the Nebraskana Society, the Washington County Historical Society, and the Pioneers and Old Settlers Association of Washington County. His main interests are farming, stockraising and cattle-feeding. Residence: Ft. Calhoun.

Clyde Conner Leach

Clyde Conner Leach was born at Glendon, Iowa, May 14, 1880, and for the past 39 years has been a resident of Furnas County, Nebraska, where he is a merchant. His father, Joshua Brinton Leach, was born at Clinton, Indiana, October 16, 1850, and died at Beaver City, Nebraska, December 8, 1929; he was a merchant and served as postmaster for a number of years. His mother, Alice Ida Connor, was born at Dale City, Iowa, May 8, 1858, and resides at Beaver City at the present time.

Mr. Leach was a farmer for seven years, and for the past 22 years has been in the feed and produce business at Beaver City where he raises livestock. He is a member of the Red Cross and Community Club, is affiliated with the Methodist Church, and holds membership in the Ancient Order of United Workmen and the Masons.

His chief sport is hunting, and his hobby is mechanics.

On December 31, 1902, he was married at Beaver City, to Ethel Fern Ayars who was born at Beaver City, November 7, 1882. They have three children: Bernice, born June 10, 1904, who married Emmett Ira Sheets; Dorothy Fern, born December 5, 1917, and Clyde Conner, Jr., born November 26, 1920. Residence: Beaver City.

Martin Henry Leamy

Martin Henry Leamy, pioneer lawyer of Nebraska, was born at Gardner, Massachusetts, November 10, 1860, the son of Michael and Honora Elizabeth (Harty) Leamy. His father, who was a farmer, was born in Lemrick, Ireland, and died at Gardner, in August, 1895. His mother was born in County Tipperary, Ireland, and died at Gardner, February 1, 1904.

Mr. Leamy attended the public and high schools of Petersam, Massachusetts, and was a student at Western Normal College, Shenandoah, Iowa, Campbell Normal College, Holtan, Kansas, and Eastman Business College, Poughkeepsie, New York. He taught in the public schools of Massachusetts for three years and in the Nebraska public schools for four years. He was a bank cashier for three years and in 1895 was admitted to the bar. A Republican, he served as county attorney of Pierce County, 1896-98, and 1914-26.

He is a charter member of the Pierce Independent Order of Odd Fellows, is a member of the Nebraska Bar Association, and holds membership in the American Bar Association. He served as a member of the school board during his stay in Petersam, Massachusetts. His hobbies are reading and poultry raising. During the late war he was a member of the local registration board.

He was married at Plainview, Nebraska, December 22, 1897. Mrs. Leamy, who was a teacher before her marriage, was born at Louisville, Nebraska, September 7, 1871, of German, English and Scotch descent. Four children were born to them: Mary J., October 12, 1899, who is a graduate of the University of South Dakota Law College; Harold M., August 2, 1900, who died December 12, 1920; Florence J., November 25, 1903, who is a stenographer; and Manota E., July 2, 1908, who is a graduate of the School of Arts and Sciences of the University of South Dakota. Residence: Pierce.

George Edwin Leavitt

George Edwin Leavitt, farmer and pioneer, was born in Grant County, Wisconsin, October 9, 1855, the son of James and Mary (Nelson) Leavitt. His father, who was born in Massachusetts, died in Grant County, Wisconsin, in 1859. A carpenter, he was descended from a Puritan settler of the Leavitt family who came to America in 1628.

Mary Nelson, his wife, was born in a village near Glasgow, Scotland, August 2, 1828, and died in Green Lake, Wisconsin, February 20, 1913. For sixteen years she served as matron of Doane College. Two of her brothers served in the Civil War, one of whom, Joseph, was killed in battle. The other brother, William, was cited for bravery in the *Thwaite's Story of the State*, for holding a bridge against the enemy. He later became state senator of Wisconsin and U. S. Marshall of Utah. Thereafter he was editor of the *Salt Lake Tribune*.

For more than forty-nine years George E. Leavitt has been engaged in farming on the same homestead in Saline County. Since its organization in 1909, he has been a director of the City National Bank of Crete, and has been active in civic and community projects. In politics he is Independent. Without any capital he brought his wife and infant son to a one-room log cabin on a 120 acre farm. His life work has been the development of a 240 acre farm with well-equipped farm buildings.

He was married to Elizabeth Caroline McCallum in Grant County, Wisconsin, October 15, 1879. Mrs. Leavitt was born in Dubuque, Iowa, December 4, 1852, and was a teacher in the Grant County rural schools before her marriage. Her parents, with three children, came to Dubuque, from Scotland. There are two children, George Arthur, born September 2, 1880, who graduated from Doane College, and who married Sarah Jane Taylor; and Mary Orpha, who was born February 22, 1883, graduated from Doane College and married Raymond LeRoy McMillan. The family belongs to the First Congregational Church of Crete, of which Mr. Leavitt is senior deacon. He is a member of the Security Benefit Association and the Nebraskana Society. Residence: Crete. (Photograph in Album).

Adolph Lebsack, Jr.

For the past 29 years Adolph Lebsack has been engaged in the drygoods and shoe business at Lincoln. He was born at Frank, Saratoff, Russia, November 1, 1875, the son of Barbara (Amen) and Adolph Henry Lebsek. His father, who is a retired farmer, was born at Frank, October 16, 1856; he reared a large family and acquired one of the most extensive farm lands in Colorado. His mother was born in Frank, Russia, July 16, 1856.

Mr. Lebsack is now the owner of the Adolph Lebsack Dry Goods & Men's Furnishing Store at Lincoln; is secretary of the American Volga Relief Society; and is vice president and director of the Midwest Savings & Loan Association. He served as city councilman from 1911 to 1913; he is a Republican.

He was united in marriage with Anna Marie Amen at Lincoln, October 17, 1897. Mrs. Lebsack, who was born at Frank, August 7, 1878, came to America, April, 1888. To this marriage 11 children were born of whom eight are living: Adolph, born April 8, 1899, who died August 26, 1923; John, born May 15, 1901; Robert, born September 6, 1902, who died May 2, 1904; George Henry, born January 2, 1904; William Edward, born September 30, 1908; Rueben D., born June 23, 1906; Maria Magdalene, born February 21, 1911; Jacob Richard, born March 31, 1912, who died July 6, 1912; Martha May, born October 24, 1913; Ruth Charlotte, born March 7, 1918; and Robert Frederich, born January 25, 1921.

Mr. Lebsack conducted loan drives, made patriotic speeches, and served on the draft board during the World War. He is a member of the board of trustees of Midland College at Fremont, Nebraska; holds membership in the Nebraskana Society; and is a member of the American Foreword Association. He is affiliated with the German Evangelical Church of Lincoln, and is a member of the Modern Woodmen of America. His hobby is reading. Residence: Lincoln.

John James Ledwith

John J. Ledwith, the son of a pioneer Lincoln family, was born at Lincoln, Lancaster County, Nebraska, March 20, 1877. His father, James Ledwith, who was born at Elizabethtown, New Jersey, September 3, 1841, drove from Illinois to Lincoln with a mule team in 1869 before the railroad had entered that part of Nebraska. He was one of Lincoln's first merchants, and during his life in the state became a figure of prominence in the business and political world. He was delegate to the Democratic National Convention, 1884, which nominated Cleveland for president, was a member of the Lincoln City Council for 6 terms; and in 1886 built the Savoy Hotel. He died at Lincoln, March 30, 1890.

Anastatia (Maher) Ledwith, his mother, whose ancestry was Irish, was born near Madison, Wisconsin, in 1855, and died at Lincoln, May 14, 1884.

Mr. Ledwith was graduated from the Bryant Public School at Lincoln, 1890, and the Lincoln High School, 1895. He was graduated from the University of Nebraska with the B. S. degree, 1900, and LL. B., 1903. He was granted a scholarship in economics at the University of Nebraska, 1900-1. He was made a member of Order of

Coif, and Innocents. He served on the Athletic Board; and was a member of Phi Kappa Psi and Phi Delta Phi. He was admitted to the bar at Lincoln, June 13, 1903.

He began the practice of law with the firm Morning & Ledwith in 1903. Since 1917, he has carried on a law business alone. He has been professor of law at the University of Nebraska for nearly 30 years and for the past 15 years has been a member of the examining board of the Nebraska Bar Commission.

On June 30, 1909, he was married to Alvina Hoppe at Lincoln. Her ancestors were German and Bohemian. She was born at Lincoln, August 15, 1885. They have two children: Lucile, born April 18, 1910; and Charles E., born August 7, 1914. Both of the children are in school.

During the World War Mr. Ledwith was a member of the executive board of all seven war agencies, and was a Four Minute Man. He is a civilian member of the American Legion. He is a member of the American Bar Association and the Nebraska State Bar Association. For a number of years he was a member of the board of directors of the Lincoln Social Welfare Society. He is a life member of the Lincoln Chamber of Commerce; is a member of Native Sons and Daughters, and the Nebraskana Society. He served on the Lincoln Library Board. He is an Elk; was Exalted Ruler, 1915-16. He is a member of St. Mary's Cathedral of the Roman Catholic Church; he is a member of the Knights of Columbus. His sport is walking. He is a Democrat. Residence: Lincoln.

Daniel Robert Lee

A pioneer resident of Nebraska, Daniel Robert Lee was born near Lexington, Pennsylvania, September 24, 1856, the son of Daniel and Elizabeth (Ritter) Lee. His father, who was a farmer and stone mason, was born near Lexington, December 1, 1818, and died at Waverly, Minnesota, September 28, 1869; his ancestry was English. His mother was born at Hanover, Germany, in 1824, and died at Lexington, April 2, 1862.

Mr. Lee attended the public schools of Pennsylvania and was a student at Meyersdale Academy. He received the M. D. degree at the University of Iowa in 1890; he was a student at Ashland College from 1880 to 1881. Since 1890 he has been known as one of the leading physicians in Valley County, Nebraska, and saved hundreds of lives during the epidemic of influenza in 1918.

He is a member of the Community Club at Arcadia, Nebraska, is a Mason, and is ninth councilor of the District Medical Association. He holds membership in the Nebraska State Medical Association and the American Medical Association, and is affiliated with the Lutheran Church.

His marriage to Jennie Frances Allen was solemnized at Westcott, Nebraska, December 25, 1894. Mrs. Lee, who is the daughter of B. D. Allen, a pioneer settler in Nebraska, was born at Loup City, Nebraska, October 9, 1873. They have three children, Robert M., born August 13, 1899, who is a physician and surgeon; Miles N., born July 9, 1901, who is a lawyer; and Alvin B., born June 21, 1906, who is a lawyer. Residence: Arcadia.

Edward A. Lee

Edward A. Lee, prominent rancher, was born in Fremont, Nebraska, December 19, 1875, son of William B. and Maggie (Cassidy) Lee. The father was born in Ireland, September 13, 1832, and died at Douglas, Wyoming, June 30, 1918. He was a farmer. His wife, also born in Ireland in 1833, died at Fremont, January 30, 1918.

Mr. Lee attended public school and in 1896 was a student at Midland College. At the present time he is the owner of a 3000 acre cattle ranch in Cherry County. He has been justice of the peace there for about 25 years. He is a Democrat.

On April 9, 1900, he was married to Alice Euretta Lanning at Fremont. Mrs. Lee, who was born at Waverly, Iowa, July 18, 1877, is secretary-treasurer of the Federal Land Bank Association of Brownlee. They have four children, Francis, born July 22, 1901, who married Ina May Roberts; Margaret, born August 23, 1904, who married Cyril R. Richardson; Harold, born June 20, 1907; and Mary, born November 18, 1910, who married Joseph Hookham.

Mr. Lee has been prominent in civic and community affairs for many years. It is interesting to note that the town of Brownlee, Nebraska, was named for one of his ancestors, John R. Lee. Mr. Lee is a member of Joan of Arc Catholic Church and the Modern Woodmen of America. His favorite sport is baseball, while his hobby is reading. Residence: Brownlee.

Emmett Joseph Lee

Emmett Joseph Lee was born at Spalding, Nebraska, March 2, 1896, the son of William James and Delia Mary (Hannigan) Lee. His father, who was born at Chicago, September 3, 1868, came to Nebraska in 1883 and was prominent in the organization of the Co-operative Elevator Company at Spalding; he received his education at Valparaiso, Indiana, and taught school prior to coming to Nebraska. His mother, who was descended from Sarah Cook of the *Mayflower,* was born at Dunlap, Iowa, May 2, 1871, and died at Spalding, July 7, 1907.

Mr. Lee was graduated from Spalding Academy in 1913, and for years owned and managed a garage there. He is an enterprising farmer in Greeley County where he organized one of the first 4-H Clubs. He is president of the Spalding Livestock and Agricultural Association, is a member of the Spalding Commercial Club, and is affiliated with St. Michael's Catholic Church and the Knights of Columbus. He is interested in mechanics, while his favorite sport is baseball.

On July 31, 1918, he married Mary Ellen Darcy at Creighton, Nebraska. Mrs. Lee, whose ancestry is Irish and Scotch, was born at Creighton, June 21, 1896. Their children are: Margaret M., born December 3, 1919; Jean D., born June 29, 1921; William T., born January 1, 1923; Robert E., born August 28, 1924; Ann J., born March 12, 1927; and Claire A., born February 5, 1931. Residence: Spalding.

Francis Robert Lee

Francis Robert Lee, Episcopal clergyman and dean of Saint Marks Pro-Cathedral at Hastings, was born at Lee Hall, Lunenburg County, Virginia, October 5, 1882. He is descended from Col. Richard Henry Lee, the English Cavalier, who settled in Virginia in 1640. Col. Richard Henry Lee and Francis Lightfoot Lee, signers of the Declaration of Independence, and Gen. "Light-Horse" Harry Lee of the Revolutionary War, were also members of this famous Lee family of Virginia which has given many illustrious men to the American nation. He is the son of Major Henderson Lewis and Lucy (Scott) Lee, the former of whom was also born at Lee Hall, where he died in 1894. Henderson Lewis Lee was a lawyer who held the rank of major in the Civil War, and was a participant in Pickett's Charge at Gettysburg. Lucy Scott, wife of Major H. L. Lee, was born in Lunenburg, Virginia, and died there in 1885. She was of the Scott family which settled in Virginia, and whose members served in the Revolutionary War.

Educated in the public schools of Virginia, Francis Robert Lee attended Virginia Polytechnic Institute, received his A. B. from Roanoke College, and graduated from Virginia Theological Seminary. He is a member of Sigma Chi fraternity. Since his ordination to the Episcopal ministry he has filled various pastorates, and for the past six years has been dean of Saint Marks Pro-Cathedral at Hastings. This handsome Cathedral which cost nearly $150,000.00 has just been completed under his leadership. He is president of the Hastings Library Board, a member of the Kiwanis Club, the Elks and the Masons, and during the World War served with the rank of chaplain. His favorite sport is golf. Residence: Hastings.

James Parker Lee

James P. Lee was born at Omaha, Douglas County, Nebraska, January 19, 1890, the son of Michael and Mary Ann (Murphy) Lee. His father, who was born in Limerick, Ireland, in 1850, and died at Omaha, April 15, 1917, was a pioneer Omahan, and served as a member of the city council there in 1888; he was a member of the state legislature, 1907-09-13. His ancestry was Irish; and came to America in 1870. Mary Ann Lee was born at Columbus, Ohio, in 1860; she is the daughter of John and Johanna (Sullivan) Murphy.

Mr. Lee attended St. Patrick's School at Omaha, and later was a student at Creighton University. He began his career as messenger boy for the Merchants National Bank in 1907; was made assistant cashier in 1919; and in 1931 was appointed cashier of the Omaha National Bank. He is vice president of the Hamilton Corporation at Omaha.

On June 17, 1918, he was married to Hazel Irene Everett at Omaha. Mrs. Lee was born at Fairfax, Atchison County, Missouri, February 2, 1889, the daughter of John W. and Basha (Williams) Everett.

During the World War Mr. Lee was sergeant of the headquarters company at Camp Dodge, Iowa. He is a member of the American Legion, a member of Ak-Sar-Ben, and the Omaha Chamber of Commerce. He is affiliated with the Blessed Sacrament Church and is a director of the Knights of Columbus. He is a member of the Omaha Field Club and is director and treasurer of the Omaha Athletic Club. His favorite sport is golfing; and his hobby is reading. He is a Republican. Residence: Omaha.

Mabel Lee

Mabel Lee, noted Nebraska educator, was born at Clearfield, Iowa, August 18, 1886. Her father, David Alexander Lee, who was a coal operator, was born in New London, Iowa, May 18, 1853, and died at Norman, Oklahoma, June 19, 1924; the Lee family was prominent in the early history of Virginia in what is now Kentucky, as was the Williams family, from which Rosanna Williams, grandmother of Mabel Lee, came. Both families were of English origin. Jennie Aikman Lee, mother of Mabel Lee, was born in Vermillion County, Illinois, August 11, 1862; her ancestry is Scotch and English.

Miss Lee was graduated from the high school at Centerville, Iowa, in 1904; received the B. S. degree at Coe College, 1908; received the graduation certificate in physical education at Wellesley College, department of hygiene, 1910. She holds the following honors: membership in Phi Kappa Phi, honorary scientific fraternity; and *magna cum laude* at Coe College. She was elected to membership in Delta Delta Delta and Mortar Board.

She was director of physical education for women at Coe College, 1910-18; held the same position at Oregon Agricultural College, 1918-19; and at Beloit College, 1920-24. Since 1924 she has been professor of physical education and chairman of the department for women at the University of Nebraska. She is the author of articles on physical education and women's athletics published in the following magazines: *Pentathlon; Mind and Body; American Physical Education Review; Wellesley College Bulletin; Nebraska Club Woman; Nebraska Parent Teacher; Michigan Journal; Playground and Recreation; Women's Division National Amateur Athletics Federation and Physical Education and Research Quarterly. Physical Education and Research Quarterly.*

Miss Lee is listed in the 1929-30 issues of *Who's Who*

of North American Authors; is a member of the physical education committee of Hoover's White House Conference on Child Health and Protection; and represented the profession of physical education for women at the Third Race Betterment Conference in 1928. She was president of the Society of Physical Directors for Women in the Colleges and Universities of the Middle West, 1925-6; acted as president of the National Society of Directors for Women in Colleges and Universities, 1926-7; was vice president of the Middle West Society of Physical Education, 1928-9; president, 1924-30; was vice president, 1930, and president, 1931, of the American Physical Education Association, being the first woman ever elected to the latter position.

She has been a member of the Altrusa Club since 1925; is an associate member of the Nebraska Writers' Guild; and holds membership in the Nebraskana Society. She is a member of the executive committee of Nebraska State League of High School Girls Athletic Associations; is past state chairmen of the Wisconsin and Nebraska division of the National Amateur Athletic Federation; and is a member of the American Association of University Women. She is affiliated with Westminster Presbyterian Church of Lincoln, and the University Young Women's Christian Association. Her favorite sport is hiking; she is a member of the Rocky Mountain Alpine Club, and is a past member of the Green Mountain Club. Her hobbies are reading and traveling. Residence: Lincoln. (Photograph in Album).

Robert Stetson Lee

Robert Stetson Lee, rancher and Nebraska Master Farmer, was born at Fremont, Nebraska, September 26, 1874, son of John Richard and Mary Dorothy (Olsen) Lee.

The father was born in Ireland and came to America as a young man, ranching in Nebraska for a time. He died at Seattle, Washington, July 15, 1914. His wife, Mary, was born in Copenhagen, Denmark, August 8, 1855.

Mr. Lee was educated in the public schools of Nebraska and attended business college at Omaha two years. On March 15, 1900, he was married to Christine S. Lee at Brownlee. Mrs. Lee was born at Dennison, Iowa, March 14, 1875. They have seven children: Everett, born January 7, 1901; Marion, born November 26, 1902, who married Esther Higgins; Ava, born November 20, 1904; Seymour, born May 26, 1907; Forrest, born November 24, 1910, who married Grace LaMasters; Merrill, born December 15, 1913; and Annabel, born June 12, 1918.

Mr. Lee is a Republican and has always been interested in party politics and public affairs. He is a member of the Union Church of Brownlee, the Chamber of Commerce, has served as a director of the school board for 20 years, and is active in his church as an elder and superintendent of the Sunday School. Residence: Brownlee.

Joe W. Leedom

Joe W. Leedom, editor of the *Gordon Journal*, was born at Bartlett, Nebraska, July 19, 1889, son of Boyd and Ella (Wigton) Leedom.

The father was born in Oil City, Pennsylvania, and died at Gordon, January 10, 1924. A newspaper man, he worked on a paper at Ponca, Nebraska, in 1876, where he met and married Ella Wigton in 1878. He organized the *Wakefield Republican* in 1880, the *Wheeler County Independent* in 1885, and the *Osmond Republican* in 1891. He was editor of the *Gordon Journal* from 1913 until 1917. He was the son of Joseph and Margaret Leedom.

Ella Wigton was born in Delaware County, Ohio, August 19, 1856, and died at Gordon, June 13, 1919. She was president of the Federated Woman's Club of Gordon for four years. The family came from Wigtonshire, Scotland to the United States in 1705, settling first in New York and later in Ohio.

Mr. Leedom attended the Osmond, Nebraska, public and high schools and later was a student at the University of Nebraska and at Morningside College, Sioux City, Iowa. While in high school he was active in football and track. Learning the printers trade at Osmond, he took over the management of the *Osmond Republican* in 1907, continuing until 1913. That year he moved to Nebraska and has since owned an interest in the *Gordon Journal*. He is a Republican, and has served on the city council for two terms and as county commissioner of Sheridan County one term.

Mr. Leedom has a fine military record. He served as an enlisted man in the Nebraska National Guard, was captain of Company I of the Fourth Nebraska Infantry, Mexican border service, in 1916; captain of field artillery, an instructor in gunnery at School of Fire for Field Artillery, Fort Sill, Oklahoma, during the World War. He now holds the commission of lieutenant colonel of field artillery, United States Army Reserve. He is a charter member of Fred F. Sturdevant Post No. 34 of the American Legion and was post commander in 1929.

On June 3, 1910, Mr. Leedom was married to Jessie A. Smith, daughter of Adolph and Anne Smith, at Gordon. Mrs. Leedom was born at Wheatland, Iowa, July 31, 1888, and at the time of her marriage was a teacher in the public schools. They have three children, Marion, born February 4, 1913, a student at Nebraska Wesleyan University; Joe, Jr., born January 18, 1918; and Elizabeth Anne, born November 29, 1926.

Mr. Leedom is affiliated with the First Methodist Episcopal Church of Gordon, is a member of the Nebraska Press Association, the National Editorial Association, the Kiwanis Club, the Masons, and the Modern Woodmen of America. His hobby is aviation. Residence: Gordon.

Frederick DeLand Leete

Right Reverend Frederick D. Leete, bishop of the Methodist Episcopal Church, Omaha area, was born at Avon, Livingston county, New York, October 1, 1866. He is the son of Menzo Smith and Hannah Amelia (DeLand) Leete, both of whom are deceased. His father, who was a distinguished editor and preacher in Michigan, New York and Florida, was born at North Chili, Monroe county, New York, in 1834 and died at Jamaica, New York, in 1911. He was a pioneer preacher and the first editor in DeLand, Florida. Of English descent he was seventh in line from William Leete who was a graduate of Temple Bar, London, and Clerk of Court, Cambridge, England, in 1837; was governor of the Connecticut Colony and second governor of Connecticut.

Hannah DeLand Leete, mother of Bishop Leete, was born in Macedonia, Wayne county, New York, in 1836 and died in Philadelphia in 1915. Of Huguenot ancestry, she is a direct descendant of Philip DeLand who immigrated to Newburyport, Massachusetts in 1694. Her maternal grandfather was N. E. Tracy, a Revolutionary soldier. She was an educator and church worker.

Upon completion of his elementary school work at Homer Academy in 1883, Bishop Leete attended Syracuse University, where he was graduated in 1889. From 1903 to 1906 he studied in Utica and Rochester, New York. He holds the following degrees: A. B., Syracuse University; D. D., Syracuse; LL. D., Albion College, 1912 and Ohio Northern University, 1923; L. H. D., Syracuse, 1921. At Syracuse he was commencement orator in 1889. Among his scholastic honors are Phi Beta Kappa, Phi Kappa Phi, Pi Gamma Mu. He is a mem-

ber of Delta Kappa Epsilon. He was a member of the Syracuse Varsity baseball team from 1885 to 1887.

Bishop Leete was married to Jeanette Gertrude Fuller at Lima, New York, May 20, 1868. Before her marriage Mrs. Leete was an instructor. She is descended from Edward Fuller of the *Mayflower* through the line of Chief Justice Fuller. There are three children: Helen DeLand, born April 5, 1893, a graduate of Syracuse University, is married to William Dean Keefer. Jeanette Fuller, born November 17, 1894, and married to Lieutenant Colonel M. M. Andrews, is also a Syracuse graduate. Frederick DeLand, born November 12, 1901, completed a course at Wesleyan University and Harvard School of Business Administration.

In 1888 Bishop Leete was ordained to the ministry and since that time he has held various pastorates, among them: Little Falls, New York; Monroe Avenue, Rochester, New York; University Avenue, Syracuse; and Detroit, Michigan. He was elected bishop of the Methodist Episcopal Church in 1912. He was stationed at Atlanta, 1912-20; Indianapolis, 1920-28; and Omaha 1928. At various times he has been trustee of Clarks University, Chattanooga University, DePauw University, Cornell College, Nebraska Wesleyan College, and president of trustees at Evansville College, Gammon Theological Seminary and Wesley Foundations of Iowa.

He is the author of *Every Day Evangelism*, (1909); *Christian Brotherhoods*, (1912); *The Church in the City*, (1915); *Francis Asbury Itinerant, Centennial Addresses*, (1916); *Christianity in Science;* and *Immortality*, (Syndicated in the American Christian Advocate, Easter, 1930).

Bishop Leete is a member of the American Association for the Advancement of Science; American Historical Society; Y. M. C. A.; Omaha Chamber of Commerce; national board, Council of Churches; boards of the home and foreign missions of the Methodist Episcopal Church. During the war he was in charge of fifty Methodist camp pastors in Alabama, Georgia, South Carolina and Florida, 1917-18.

His hobby is the study of science, the Greek language, and literature. His social club is the Omaha Club. Residence: Omaha. (Photograph on Page 709).

Charles Edwin Legg

A physician and surgeon in Nebraska for the past twenty-six years, Charles Edwin Legg was born at Plattsburg, Missouri, September 21, 1875. He is the son of George Edwin and Mellissa Laura (Hazen) Legg. His father, born at Oroma Park, Illinois, October 12, 1846, was a farmer, whose great grandfather came to America in 1740. His death occurred at Aroma Park, August 28, 1918. Mellissa, wife of George E. Legg, was born at Columbus, Ohio, October 3, 1845, and died at Clearwater, Nebraska, November 20, 1907. A teacher prior to marriage, she traced her ancestry to Dutch settlers in America, about 1800.

Dr. Legg was graduated from the Neosho, Missouri, High School in 1894, and received his M. D. from the Hahnemann Medical College at Kansas City, in 1904. Thereafter he came to Nebraska where he has since engaged in practice. He is a member of the Sioux Valley Medical Association and the American Association of Railway Surgeons. He entered the United States Army as a first lieutenant in June, 1917, and was promoted to the rank of captain on October 1, 1918, and to major on February 25, 1919. He is a member of the American Legion, the Commercial Club, the Masons and the Odd Fellows. His favorite sport is golf and his hobby is birds.

On March 3, 1904, he was married to Ethel Blanche Twiss at Kansas City, Missouri. Mrs. Legg, a native of Newyago, Michigan, born August 30, 1879, is a descendant of John Rolfe and Pocahontas. They have one daughter, Clara Mellissa, born February 13, 1906, who is a

FREDERICK DeLAND LEETE

graduate of the University of Nebraska, with an A. B. degree, and teaches in the South Sioux City public schools. Residence: South Sioux City.

Clara Elsa Le Hew

Clara Elsa Le Hew, deaconess of the Protestant Episcopal Church, was born at Sutton, Nebraska, December 29, 1876, daughter of Joseph Snyder and Ellen (Pier) Le Hew.

Her father, born in Grandville, Ohio, March 14, 1841, died at Denver, Colorado, June 13, 1923. Joseph Snyder Le Hew was a lawyer and a veteran of the Civil War, who moved to Nebraska in May, 1871, homesteading in Filmore County. He was the first county judge of that county, and a first lieutenant and organizer of the Nebraska Militia. He drafted the first Nebraska military code under Governor Nance in 1881, was presented with a sword by the First Nebraska Regiment, and served nine years, at different times, on the governor's staff. He ranked as a colonel under Governor Boyd. The family settled at Fort Royal, Virginia, in 1799, some of them being Revolutionary soldiers under Lafayette.

Ellen Pier was born in Bristol, Ohio, June 20, 1846, and died at Denver, October 23, 1924. She was a teacher, and during the Civil War assisted in publishing a paper at Van Wert, Ohio. In her later years she devoted herself to her home and children, of whom there were nine.

Miss Le Hew attended the public schools of Sutton and McCook, and was graduated from the McCook High School in May, 1894.

She taught about four years in Red Willow County, and was trained as a deaconess in the Protestant Episcopal Church at St. Paul, Minnesota. In 1901 she was admitted to the order at Laramie, Wyoming, under Bishop Groves, and thereafter served as superintendent of the home for children at Utica, New York, and Laramie, Wyoming. At the present time Miss Le Hew is deaconess in charge of St. Joseph's Protestant Episcopal Church at Mullen, Nebraska. She has held several positions in church work under Bishop G. A. Beecher of Hastings.

Miss Le Hew is a Democrat. She is a member of the Order of Eastern Star and the Red Cross, (chairman of nursing activities for Hooper County). She is also a member of the American Legion Auxiliary and president of the Inter-county Woman's Club. Residence: Mitchell.

Frank E. Lehmer

Frank E. Lehmer, druggist and postmaster, was born at North Bend, Nebraska, April 24, 1893, son of David G. and Martha M. (Anderson) Lehmer. His father was born at Dillsburg, Pennsylvania, October 3, 1860, and was chief of police and water commissioner of North Bend for twenty-five years prior to his death on March 30, 1928. His wife, Martha, who was born at Dillsburg, August 27, 1863, is living.

Mr. Lehmer was educated in the public and high schools of North Bend, and was graduated from the latter in 1911. He was married to Hortense S. Inks, at Shelby, Nebraska, July 6, 1916. There are two children, Robert F., born April 20, 1918; and Carol P., born March 25, 1922.

A member of the school board, Mr. Lehmer takes an active part in educational and civic affairs, and is a member of the Nebraskana Society, and the Ancient Free and Accepted Masons. His favorite recreation is hiking. Residence: Morse Bluff.

Frank Lehmkuhl

Frank Lehmkuhl, county clerk of Saunders County, Nebraska, was born at Wahoo, April 26, 1877, the son of John D. Lehmkuhl and Minnie (Schoppe) Lehmkuhl. His father was born at Neimburg, Germany, October 27, 1833, and died at Wahoo, on February 16, 1906. Coming to America, in 1846, he settled in Nebraska, in 1868, where he engaged in stock raising and farming. His mother was born in Germany, on August 15, 1836, and died at Wahoo, January 22, 1908.

Mr. Lehmkuhl attended public school and business college. He was married to Georgia A. Isenberger, May 10, 1900, at Lodgepole, Nebraska. She was born at Kenesaw, Nebraska, November 23, 1879. They have five children: Frances M., born November 25, 1902; Alice L., born March 14, 1907; Doris V., born July 13, 1912; Howard P., born May 16, 1914; and Hillis F., born February 11, 1917. Frances is married to Lewis T. Oaks.

From 1900 to 1904, Mr. Lehmkuhl was cashier of the Peoples' Bank at Lodgepole, Nebraska. A Democrat, he was elected county clerk in 1926, and was re-elected in 1930. During the war he was active in the Red Cross and in Liberty Loan drives.

He is affiliated with the Presbyterian Church at Wahoo, and holds a membership in the Order of Ancient Free and Accepted Masons. A resident of Nebraska, since birth, Mr. Lehmkuhl was recently made a life member of the Nebraska Society in recognition of his work for the advancement of his community and state. Residence: Wahoo.

Henry John Lehnhoff

Henry John Lehnhoff was born at Louisville, Nebraska, December 10, 1871, son of Henry and Caroline (Ossenkop) Lehnhoff. The former, who was born at Hajen, Hanover, Germany, on February 12, 1836, came to the United States at the age of 12. He was descended from a line of Hanovarians, and homesteaded in Nebraska. He died at Lincoln, in May, 1908. Caroline, his wife, was also born in Hajen, in August, 1838, and died at Lincoln, in May, 1917.

Dr. Lehnhoff was educated first in district schools and later in the preparatory department of the University of Nebraska. He received his A. B. at Nebraska, and his M. D. at Northwestern University. He was ranking captain of the University Cadets under General Pershing in 1897, and is a member of Delta Tau Delta. Admitted to the practice of medicine in June, 1901, he is a member of the Lincoln Clinic, and has served as president and secretary of the Lancaster Medical Association, president of the Nebraska State Medical Association, and president of the Missouri Valley Medical Society. He is the author of numerous medical articles.

He attends All Soul's Unitarian Church, is a member of the Chamber of Commerce, the City Library Board, etc., and is a member of the Lincoln Tuberculosis Society and secretary of the State Board of Medical Examiners. He is a Mason. His club is the University.

Dr. Lehnhoff was married to Challis Ray, at Vienna, Austria, on May 22, 1910. Mrs. Lehnhoff was born at Onago, Kansas, January 10, 1884. They have two children, Henry John, born September 13, 1912, and Carolyn Elizabeth, born March 14, 1915. Residence: Lincoln.

Francis Marian Leibee

Francis M. Leibee, successful grain and coal operator, was born in Henry County, Illinois, June 23, 1857, and since 1878, has been a resident of Nebraska. His father, John Leibee, who was born in Butler County, Ohio, was a farmer and died as a soldier of the 9th Illinois Cavalry at Iuca, Mississippi, in 1865. His mother, Elizabeth (Israil) Leibee, was born in Decatur County, Indiana, and died at Shelby, Nebraska, in 1908.

Mr. Leibee was a grain dealer at David City, Nebraska, in 1878, and the following year moved to Shelby, where he worked for the Omaha Elevator Company until

1910. He is known as the oldest grain dealer in years of service in Nebraska, at this time. A Democrat, he was county clerk of Polk County from 1910 to 1915, and served as county assessor from 1917 to 1919.

He was married to Mary Ann Alberry at David City, Nebraska, September 4, 1883. She was born at Beverly, Ohio, August 5, 1868. Their children are: Margaret, born in August, 1884, who married William Yerty; John Ray, a physician at Beatrice; Venice Lillian, who married James Wilkes; Opal Lillian, who married B. W. Elgin; Deborah Ruth, who is a nurse in New York City; Francis M., who is in the oil business at Exeter; and Thelma, who married Herman O. Anderson, a farmer living near Stromsburg.

Mr. Leibee is a member of the Methodist Church at Shelby, and holds membership in the Nebraskana Society. He is a Mason. Residence: Shelby.

Enos R. Leigh

Enos R. Leigh was born at LaPrairie Center, Illinois, June 6, 1873, son of Alvin Lewis and Hannah Jane (Briggs) Leigh. His father was born at LaPrairie Center, October 27, 1851, and died at Bloomfield, Nebraska, November 30, 1927. He was a farmer of English and Scotch ancestry. His wife, Hannah Jane, was born in Duchess County, New York, March 4, 1853, and died at Bloomfield, in May 1919. Her ancestry was English and German.

Mr. Leigh received his elementary education in the country schools of Marshall County, Illinois, and attended the Sparland, Illinois, High School. His family moved to Nebraska in 1893, and he was graduated from the Omaha Commercial College in 1895. From 1897-98 he attended Peru State Normal School; he received his LL. B. from the University of Nebraska in 1900. He is a member of Phi Delta Phi.

On August 20, 1902, he was united in marriage to Etta Vitelle Fisher, at Brock, Nebraska. Mrs. Leigh was born at Glen Rock, Nebraska, December 22, 1877. She is of English descent, her father born in Missouri and her mother in Alabama. There are three children: Dorothy, born September 8, 1904, was graduated from the University of Nebraska with a B. A. degree, and is married to Dr. Edward M. Mark. Eleanor, the second daughter, was born February 7, 1906. She also received her A. B. from the University of Nebraska, and is a high school teacher at Louisville, Nebraska. Lewis, the only son, was born November 3, 1916.

Mr. Leigh was admitted to the Nebraska bar in June 1900, and took up the active practice of law at what was then the city of South Omaha. He is a Republican, and served as assistant city attorney of South Omaha four years; at one time he was deputy county attorney for Douglas County, which position he resigned to follow private practice exclusively.

He is a Methodist and attends Grace Methodist Church of Omaha; is a member of the Sons of the American Revolution, the Nebraska State Bar Association and the Omaha-Douglas County Bar Associations. Mr. Leigh is a Mason, Scottish Rite, 32 degree, and is serving as master of Bee Hive Lodge at South Omaha. He belongs to the Odd Fellows and to the South Omaha Business Men's Association. His favorite diversions are reading, raising flowers and attending lodge. Residence: Omaha.

Dean Richmond Leland

Dean R. Leland was born at Pendleton, New York, August 23, 1866. Herman Jay Leland, his father, who was a farmer and business man, was also born at Pendleton, on May 30, 1845, and died at Mayville, New York, April 16, 1907. He was descended from Henry Leland who came to America from England, and settled at Dorchester, Massachusetts in 1652.

Amelia (Van Slyke) Leland, his mother, who was born at Halls, New York, April 7, 1848, was of Dutch ancestry.

Dr. Leland was graduated from the Lockport Union School in 1885. He holds the following degrees: A. B., Hamilton College, 1889, at Clinton, New York; A. M., Princeton University, 1908; and D. D., Hamilton College, 1916. He was a student at Princeton Theological Seminary, 1891-1893, and attended Union Theological Seminary at New York City, 1905. In 1889 he was editor of the Hamilton Literary Magazine. He is a member of Alpha Delta Phi, and served as secretary of the Hamilton Chapter, 1888, and president of this chapter, 1889.

He was for a time pastor of the Second Presbyterian Church at Lockport, from 1898 to 1903 he was pastor of the Tyler Place Presbyterian Church at St. Louis, Missouri. He served as professor of history and Bible at Peekskill Academy, Peekskill, New York, 1903-1909. Since 1909 he has been university pastor of the Presbyterian Church at the University of Nebraska. He is the author of *The Faith of Our Fighting Men*, 1918, and *Lincoln's Gettysburg Speech*, 1919.

On June 3, 1903, he was married to Clara W. Walsh at Lincoln, Nebraska. Mrs. Leland, who was born at Lockport, June 2, 1868, is of English and Irish descent. They have two children: Dorothy E., born September 17, 1907, who was graduated from Wellesley College in 1928 with the degree A. B.; and Elizabeth S., born January 15, 1912, who is a student at the University of Nebraska, 1929-1933.

Dr. Leland served as chaplain of the National Service Commission at Camp Colt, Gettysburg, Pennsylvania, from April to November in 1918. He is a member of the Red Cross; is a director of the Social Welfare Committee; and a member of the Nebraska City Presbytery Synod of Nebraska. He is a member of the Chamber of Commerce at Lincoln, and the Lincoln University Club. Politically, Dr. Leland is independent. Residence: Lincoln.

Clair Leon LeMar

Clair L. LeMar, physician, was born at Aledo, Illinois, November 20, 1872. His father, Irvin Brush LeMar, was born in Indiana, September 9, 1851, and died at York, Nebraska, May 25, 1920. He was a farmer of French descent. Sarah Elizabeth (Dihel) LeMar, wife of Irvin LeMar, was born at Aledo, January 27, 1851, and died at Osceola, Nebraska, April 15, 1927. Her ancestors were early settlers in Virginia, and later in Illinois.

Upon his graduation from Mead High School in 1893, Dr. LeMar attended Wesleyan University and the University of Nebraska, and was graduated from the College of Medicine of the latter in 1903. He received honorable mention in surgery.

He is a member of the Pension board, is pension examiner for the Veterans' Bureau. He is also a member of the Polk County, Nebraska State, and American Medical Associations, the Osceola Community Club, Modern Woodmen of America, is a Mason, and a member of the board of education. His religious affiliation is with the First Methodist Church of Osceola. Gardening and collecting weapons are his hobbies.

On December 27, 1905, he was married to Helen Frances Dewey, at Des Moines, Iowa. She was born at West Union, Iowa, September 17, 1876, and died at Osceola, September 11, 1927. Three children were born to them: John D., who is a sophomore in the College of Medicine at the University of Nebraska; Carol E., who is in Methodist Hospital nurses training school at Omaha, Nebraska; and Richard B., who is at home. Residence: Osceola.

Anthony Adam Lembach

Anthony Adam Lembach was born at Wurzburg, Bavaria, February 27, 1870, the son of Ignaz Michael and Mathilda Louis (Nies) Lembach. His father, distinguished advisor to the Bavarian government, was born at Wurzburg, March 17, 1808, and died there November 26, 1885; the first record of his ancestors was in the 16th century when members of the family lived in Prague, Bohemia. His mother was born at Bischofsheim, Bavaria, July 7, 1841, and died at Wurzburg, August 14, 1891; she was descended from ancestors who were known as master woodcarvers for many generations.

Mr. Lembach attended private school and the King's Latin School in Germany, until 1885. He has held the following positions in the business world: decorator and floormanager for the F. W. Wurzburg Company at Grand Rapids, Michigan, until 1895; manager of Wolbach and Brach Department Store of Hastings, Adams County, Nebraska, until 1914; owner of accessory store at Hastings, until 1930; and at present, representative of the Continental Oil Company at Hastings. He is a stockholder and director in the Polenske Brothers Shellak & Company, brick manufacturers at Hastings.

His civic enterprises and offices include: president of the board of control of the Salvation Army; member of Red Cross; director of Chamber of Commerce for thirty years, and president in 1925; vice president of the Rotary Club at Hastings, 1931; and member of the Young Men's Christian Association since 1896. He is a member of the Nebraskana Society, is interested in theatricals, reading and singing, and holds membership in the Republican party. During the war he was a four minute speaker, and held membership in the Council of Defense.

Mr. Lembach was married on October 14, 1895, at Chicago, to Wilhelmina Knapp, who was born at Cincinnati, Ohio, November 16, 1862. Her parents came to this country from Prussia. Residence: Hastings. (Photograph in Album).

Edward John Lenger

A successful business man at Center, Nebraska, is Edward John Lenger, who has served as county clerk there since 1922. He was born at Niobrara, Nebraska, July 10, 1886, the son of Frank Henry and Caroline Blanche (Ferdinand) Lenger, and has been a lifelong resident of this state. His father, who was born in Bohemia, February 22, 1863, was a cattleman and farmer who served as superintendent of the Niobrara Packing House, was an implement dealer, acted as supervisor in District Two, and was an officer in the Knox County School Board; he is now retired. His mother died at Niobrara, April 11, 1910.

Mr. Lenger attended rural school in Knox County until 1902, was graduated from the Niobrara High School in 1905, and received the Ph. G. degree in 1913 at Creighton University where he took part in orchestra and band activities. He participated in debating during his high school days. After his graduation from high school Mr. Lenger studied business for a short time, was employed by the H. E. Bonestell Company as cashier and bookkeeper, and a little later served as clerk and timekeeper for the Chicago & Northwestern Railroad Company.

A Republican, he served as deputy county clerk of Knox County from 1913 to 1922, and since 1922 has been county clerk there. He is a member of the Independent Order of Odd Fellows, is affiliated with the Presbyterian Church of Creighton, and holds membership in the Nebraskana Society and the Muscovites. Mr. Lenger was a member of the Young Men's Christian Association from 1905 to 1909, was active in the Center Commercial Club from 1914 to 1919, and was formerly a member of the Creighton Golf Club. He is interested in scientific and mechanical affairs.

During the World War he served as county medical advisory board of Knox County, acted as clerk of the draft board throughout the war, and was a leader in Red Cross and loan drives. His favorite sport is golfing.

He is married to Anna Gertrude Vlasmik, who was born at Rapid City, South Dakota, July 1, 1887. Mrs. Lenger, who was a teacher before her marriage, is of Bohemian descent. They have one daughter, Marie, born

December 28, 1914, who was graduated from the Center High School with valedictory honors. She was awarded a county medal for scholastic honors, and is now studying music. Residence: Center.

Frederick William Lentz

Frederick William Lentz, automobile dealer, was born at Burlington, Iowa, October 10, 1897, son of Ludwig Carl and Elsie (Schick) Lentz. Ludwig Lentz, a native of Germany, came to America in 1893; he is a clergyman and is descended from a long line of ecclesiastics. His wife, Elsie, was born in Dixon County, Illinois, August 23, 1876, and her parents were teachers in Germany, prior to coming to America. At the present time she is active in the work of her church, and is president of the Women's Club at Deshler.

Educated in the rural schools of Gothenburg, until 1912, Mr. Lentz was graduated from the Gothenburg High School in 1916, and thereafter attended the University of Nebraska two years. He was a letter man in football and won class honors from high school in 1916.

On November 9, 1921, Mr. Lentz was united in marriage to Marcia Grace Renner, at Fairbury. Mrs. Lentz, who was born at Daykin, Nebraska, June 6, 1897, is the granddaughter of a pioneer physician, soldier and editor in Nebraska, who was a member of the constitutional convention of 1864, the editor of the first German newspaper in Nebraska, and a personal friend of J. Sterling Morton. Mr. and Mrs. Lentz have two children, Norma Arleen, born February 7, 1923, and Donald, born December 15, 1926.

On July 4, 1919, Mr. Lentz organized the Deshler Motor Company at Deshler, and continued in business there until January 10, 1928, at which time the Lentz Motor Company of Beatrice was organized. At the present time he is proprietor and manager of the Lentz Motor Company, and owns an interest in the Deshler Motor Company.

Mr. Lentz served in Section A, Company A, of the Student Army Training Corps at the University of Nebraska, in 1918, and is a member of the American Legion. He attends St. John's Lutheran Church at Beatrice, and is a member of the Young Men's Christian Association. During his residence in Deshler, he was a member of the school board the years 1927 and 1928, but resigned upon his removal to Beatrice. He is a member of the board of directors of the Beatrice Chamber of Commerce and the Beatrice Rotary Club, and holds membership also in the Parent-Teachers' Association and The Nebraskana Society. His hobby is airplanes, but he is interested in any speed machine. His favorite sports are golf and football. Residence: Beatrice.

Edward Joseph Leonard

Edward Joseph Leonard, registered pharmacist and merchant, was born at Tolono, Illinois, April 4, 1873, son of Andrew and Rosa A. (Kelly) Leonard.

Mr. Leonard attended public school, Riverton High School, and Franklin Academy. On December 31, 1901, he was married to Maud Lois Moore at Omaha. Mrs. Leonard was born at Columbia, New York, April 30, 1876. They have two children Edward, born July 2, 1904; and Byron, born November 22, 1911.

Mr. Leonard is a Republican. From 1896 until 1919, he was engaged in the drug and general merchandise business at Ruskin. He operated a grocery store at Sidney from 1923 until 1929, and since the last mentioned date has been in the retail furniture business. Residence: Sidney.

James Edward LeRossignol

James Edward LeRossignol was born at Quebec, Canada, October 24, 1866, the son of Peter and Mary (Gillespie) LeRossignol. His father, who was a merchant, was born at St. Mary's Parish, Isle of Jersey, May 7, 1824, and died at Quebec, October 13, 1874. His ancestry was Norman French. His mother, who was of Scotch-Irish descent, was born at Quebec, April 30, 1840.

Professor LeRossignol attended Huntingdon Academy, Prescott High School, and was graduatel from Montreal High School in 1884. In 1888 he received the A. B. degree at McGill College at Montreal, and holds the following others: Ph. D., University of Leipzig, 1892; LL. D., University of Denver, 1911; and LL. D., McGill University, 1921. He was given a fellowship in psychology at Clark University in 1892. He is a member of Phi Beta Kappa; and Alpha Kappa Psi.

Professor of psychology and ethics at the University of Ohio, 1892-94; he was professor of economics, University of Denver, 1894-1911; professor of economics at the University of Nebraska, 1911; was special lecturer in economics at McGill University, 1900; was lecturer in political science at the University of Wisconsin during the summer session of 1903; investigated economic conditions in New Zealand in 1906; was professor of political economy at the University of Nebraska in 1908 and 1909 during a leave of absence from the University of Denver; acted as professor of political economy at Stanford University in the summer session of 1923; was acting professor of political economy at the University of California, in the summer of 1926. At the present time he is dean of the College of Business Administration at the University of Nebraska.

Professor LeRossignol is a profound thinker and student. He is the author of numerous books on economic, social and literary subjects, among them: *The Ethical Philosophy of Samuel Clarke* (1892); *Monopolies, Past and Present* (1901); *Taxation in Colorado* (1902); *History of Higher Education in Colorado* (1903); *Orthodox Socialism* (1907) *Little Stories of Quebec* (1908); *State Socialism in New Zealand* (1910); *Jean Baptiste* (1915); *What Is Socialism?* (1921); *Economics for Everyman* (1923); *First Economics* (1926); *The Beauport Road* (1928); *The Flying Canoe* (1929); as well as articles on economic subjects and monographs.

He was united in marriage with Jessie Katharine Ross at Montreal, Canada, September 2, 1898. Mrs. LeRossignol was born at Montreal. Her ancestry is Scotch. Two children were born to this marriage: Edward Ross, born October 28, 1903, who married Blanche Marie Simmons; and Helen Marian Henderson, born April 14, 1909.

In the World War Professor LeRossignol was chairman of the Lancaster County Fuel Commission. He has lived in Nebraska for 21 years and has always been active in Lincoln's civic affairs. He is a member of the Lincoln Chamber of Commerce, and the Lincoln Association of Credit Men, the Rotary Club, the Nebraska Schoolmasters Club and the Nebraskana Society. He holds membership in the following scientific organizations: American Economic Association; American Political and Social Science; and the American Association of Collegiate Schools of Business. He served as president of the latter in 1925 and 1926. He is a member of The Club; the Round Table; the University Club, at Lincoln; the Authors' Club, London; the Canadian Authors' Association; and the Nebraska Writer's Guild, of which he is president. He is affiliated with the First Presbyterian Church. Politically, Professor LeRossignol is an independent. His favorite sport is angling, while his hobby is chess. Residence: Lincoln.

Glenn R. LeRoy

Glenn R. LeRoy, retail jeweler, was born at Fairbury, Nebraska, October 3, 1888, son of John H. and Jala F. (White) LeRoy. His father, who was of Holland Dutch descent, was born in Highland, New York, December 7, 1856. He was a jeweler in Fairbury from 1884 until his death on June 12, 1931. Jala F. LeRoy, was born

at Princeton, Missouri, March 12, 1862. Her ancestars were early Southern settlers.

Upon his graduation from the Fairbury High School, Glenn LeRoy attended the University of Nebraska where he received his Bachelor of Science degree. During part of the year of 1918 he attended Princeton War College. He was a member of the senior honorary society, the Innocents, and is a Sigma Chi.

While he is not active in political affairs, he is affiliated with the Republican Party, and has been a resident of Nebraska his entire life. He was an ensign in the United States Naval Reserve Force in the World War, and is a member of the Red Cross and the American Legion. He is also a member of the Chamber of Commerce, the Kiwanis Club, the Masons, and the Benevolent and Protective Order of the Elks. His social club is the University Club of Lincoln, Nebraska. He is a member of the Nebraskana Society. Residence: Fairbury.

Elmer Ellsworth Lesh

Elmer E. Lesh has lived in Nebraska for the past 47 years and has been engaged in business in Fairmont, York, and Lincoln, for many years. He was born at Newport, Perry County, Pennsylvania, July 9, 1861, the son of George Everette and Mary Margaret Lesh. His father, who was born in Berks County, Pennsylvania, was killed early in the Civil War where he was serving in the Union Army. He was a school teacher and printer. His German ancestors came to America in 1709. The name of the family was originally Loesch.

His mother was born at Newport, May 30, 1840, and died at Carrington, Foster County, North Dakota, November 13, 1910. She was a descendent of Balthazar Loesch who emigrated from Germany in 1709, and who was buried at sea before reaching America.

Mr. Lesh was a printer and publisher, 1876-96, in Pennsylvania, Illinois, and Nebraska. From 1897 to 1927 he was a traveling salesman for the Carpenter Paper Company of Omaha. In 1929 he was pensioned by this organization and is now retired. Since 1913 he has been a trustee of Nebraska Wesleyan University.

In 1880 he was editor of *The Home Guard* at Buda, Illinois. A Republican, he served as city clerk of Fairmont, Nebraska, 1887-90.

He was married to Emma Luella Banta at Oquawka, Henderson County, Illinois, October 4, 1880. Mrs. Lesh, who was born at Burlington, Iowa, February 15, 1859, is descended from Eqke Jacobe Banta who emigrated to America from Holland in February, 1659. They have the following children: William Walter, born June 6, 1882, who married Mary Edna Clymer; Luna Mary, born October 1, 1883, who died October 17, 1887; Clarence Banta, born October 7, 1885, who married Ola Frances Barr; Charles Wesley, born March 28, 1889, who married Ethyl Darling; Eva Lucille, born August 15, 1896, who married Henry Morris Jackson; Iva Luella, born July 4, 1899, who married Raymond Dewitt Lemon; and Edna Lucia, born December 3, 1901, who married Blaine Martin Allen.

Mr. Lesh is a member of the local Red Cross; the Nebraskana Society; and the Grace Methodist Episcopal Church of Lincoln, being a lay delegate of the Northwest Nebraska annual conference of the Church to the general conference held in Saratoga Springs, New York, in 1916. He served as a member of the school board at Fairmont, 1890-91; has been a member of the Young Men's Christian Association at various times; and is affiliated with the Odd Fellows and Modern Woodmen of America. He is a Mason. (Deceased).

Charles Blair Letton

Charles Blair Letton, clerk of the Supreme Court of Nebraska, was born in Edinburgh, Scotland, October 25, 1853, son of William Henry and Agnes (Michie)

Skoglund—Fremont

AUGUST J. LEUTHAUSER

Letton. A resident of Nebraska since July 1869, Mr. Letton's career has been interesting and varied. A Republican, he has served as city attorney of Fairbury, county attorney of Jefferson County, judge of the first judical district 8 years and was Supreme Court commissioner 1904 and 1905 and judge of the Supreme Court 19 years. He is the author of numerous legal addresses and articles and more than six hundred opinions of the Supreme Court of Nebraska. Prior to his election to the bench he practiced law in Fairbury 14 years, the last seven as a member of the firm of Letton and Hinshaw. Mr. Hinshaw later became a member of Congress, serving several terms.

On January 1, 1927 Mr. Letton was appointed clerk of the Supreme Court for a term of six years. A charter member of the American Institute of law, he served as president of the Nebraska State Bar Association in 1905, and as vice president for Nebraska of the American Bar Association 1925-26. He is a charter member of the Lincoln Kiwanis Club, a member of the Chamber of Commerce, the Nebraska Art Association, and since 1927 a member of the Nebraska Public Library Commission. In addition to the position of clerk of the Supreme Court, Mr. Letton is State Librarian. He is a member of the Nebraska State Historical Association, the Nebraskana Society, and belongs to the Lincoln University Club.

He was married to Althera Hosmer Pike of Carmel, Maine, at Fairbury, September 2, 1885. Mrs. Letton was born in Maine, and is descended from early settlers in Massachusetts. She was state regent of the Daughters of the American Revolution 1907-08; state president of the Daughters of Founders and Patriots 1928-30; and is a member of the Colonial Dames of America. There are two sons, Harry P., born in 1886, who was captain in the Engineers, American Expeditionary Forces in the World War; and William A., born in 1889, who is the auditor of a bank in Denver. Residence: Lincoln.

Harry Pike Letton

Harry P. Letton was born at Fairbury, Nebraska, May 28, 1886, the son of Charles B. and Althera H. (Pike) Letton. His father, who was born at Edinburgh, Scotland, October 25, 1853, is a former judge of the district court of Nebraska, and served as judge of the supreme court, 1906-24. He is now clerk of the supreme court and state librarian of Nebraska. He came to Nebraska with his parents and settled near Fairbury, in 1869.

His mother, who was born at Carmel, Penobscot County, Maine, July 5, 1863, is of New England ancestry. She served as state regent of the Daughters of the American Revolution, 1907-08, and was national vice president of that organization in 1914.

Mr. Letton was graduated from the Fairbury High School in 1904. He received his B. S. degree in civil engineering at the University of Nebraska in 1909. From 1910 to 1911 he was a student at Massachusetts Institute of Technology at Boston. He was elected to membership in Sigma Tau, honorary engineering fraternity, and to Kappa Sigma and is now alumnus advisor to the Nebraska University chapter of this society.

He was sanitary engineer of the New Jersey State Board of Health, 1911-13; held this position in the United States Public Health Service, 1913-1919; was a member of the engineering firm, Grant, Fulton & Letton, at Lincoln, 1919-28. Since 1928 he has been connected with the firm Burns Potter & Company, dealing in stocks and bonds at Omaha and Lincoln. He is the author of several articles on sanitary engineering subjects, published in technical publications. He has lived in Nebraska for 34 years.

On November 18, 1911, his marriage to Ethel M. Kirby was solemnized at Springfield, Illinois. Mrs. Letton was born at Liberty, Gage County, Nebraska, December 8, 1886. They have one son, Harry, born April 12, 1915.

Mr. Letton served as captain of the engineering corps

with the American Expeditionary Forces during the World War; he was engaged in water supply activities from 1917 to 1919. He is a member of the American Legion, serving as first commander of Lincoln Post Number 3. He holds membership in the Lincoln Chamber of Commerce; Lincoln Executives Club; Hiram Club; and Lincoln Collectors Club. He is a member of Masonic Lodge Number 54, Scottish Rite bodies of Lincoln. His favorite sport is golf, and ih sohbby is philately. Residence: Lincoln.

August John Leuthauser

August J. Leuthauser, a prominent banker at Beemer, Cuming County, Nebraska, has lived in this state all his life, and has been a farmer, teacher, and banker since 1908. He was born at Stanton, Stanton County, Nebraska, February 4, 1878, the son of Meta (Dammann) Leuthauser and August Leuthauser. His father, who was a clergyman, was born at Grumpen, Saxony, Germany, January 23, 1849, and died at Concord, Dixon County, Nebraska, December 17, 1909; he left Germany May 6, 1866, boarded the ship Bremen May 9, and arrived in New York, May 22, at the age of 17 years. His mother was born at Hanover, Germany, November 23, 1853, and died at Grand Island, Hall County, Nebraska, December 6, 1924.

Mr. Leuthauser attended the parochial and public schools at Cedar Bluffs, Nebraska, until 1891, and was a student at Lutheran Seminary at Milwaukee, Wisconsin. Since 1908 he has been cashier of the First National Bank of Beemer. He is also a director of this institution. He is a member of the Beemer Community Club; is secretary of the Beemer Lions Club; has been a member of the school board for many years and is now secretary of the board; and holds membership in the Nebraskana Society. He is a member of St. John's Evangelical Lutheran Church at Beemer, and for the past 21 years has been secretary of the congregation. He is an Independent Democrat.

He was married to Martha E. Piper at Wisner, Cuming County, Nebraska, December 4, 1902. Mrs. Leuthauser was born at Wisner, December 12, 1881, the daughter of August and Theresia (Breetzke) Piper; her parents were born in Germany. Four children were born to them: Agatha M., born August 27, 1905; Edna H., born October 30, 1906; Olive M., born September 8, 1910; and Norman A., born June 21, 1916. Agatha was graduated from Kansas Agricultural College, at Manhattan, Kansas, and is now a home economics teacher. Edna was a student at Ames and Kansas Agricultural College at Manhattan; she is now married to Carl Wendorf. Olive attended the University of Nebraska. Norman is in high school.

During the World War Mr. Leuthauser assisted in loan drives and war savings stamp campaigns. He is a member of the Beemer Red Cross and takes an active interest in community progress and welfare work. His hobby is reading. Golf is his favorite recreation. Residence: Beemer. (Photograph on Page 714).

Victor Emanuel Levine

Victor Emanuel Levine, prominent physician, scientist, and educator of Nebraska, was born at Minsk, Russia, August 4, 1891. His father, Israel Levine, was born at Minsk in 1864. His mother, Eva L. (Meisels) Levine, was born at Minsk in 1862.

Dr. Levine attended the public schools of New York City and in 1905 was graduated from Townsend Harris Hall at New York. He holds the following degrees: A. B., 1909, College of the City of New York; A. M., 1911, Columbia University; Ph. D., 1914, Columbia University; and M. D., 1928, School of Medicine, Creighton University. He was a student at Johns Hopkins University, 1919-21 and attended Toronto University, 1923. He is a member of Pi Gamma Mu, of Phi Delta Epsilon, and has

VICTOR EMANUEL LEVINE

Heyn—Omaha

been marshall and counsul of the Alpha Chi Chapter.

He has held the following positions through which he has distinguished himself in educational and professional circles: instructor in biological chemistry, College of Physicians and Surgeons, Columbia University, 1913-16, assistant professor of organic chemistry, Fordham University, 1916-17; director of the pathological laboratories, Beth Israel Hospital, New York, 1917-18; assistant professor of biological chemistry, School of Medicine, Creighton University, 1918-20; and since 1920 has been head of department and professor of biological chemistry and nutrition, School of Medicine, at Creighton. He is also advisory director of the Graduate School of chemistry at Creighton University.

Dr. Levine is the author of over 200 articles relating to original research and to general and special topics in the field of biological chemistry, nutrition, and public health. His researches in the field of nutrition has led him into the Arctic where he studied the health habits and dietary habits of the Eskimo. He is part author of *International Clinics*, Volume III, published in 1929 by J. B. Lippincott Company of Philadelphia, and also volumes I and II published in 1930. He is the editor of: *Dietary Administration and Therapy*, published in Cleveland, Ohio; and associate editor of *Archives of Physical Therapy*, published in Chicago. He is director of the Health Education department of the Dwarfies Corporation, at Council Bluffs, Iowa.

He is captain in the medical department of the Chemical Warfare Service of the United States Reserve Army, and holds a certificate of capacity for major. He is a member of the Reserve Officers' Association, of which he is historian. He holds membership in the following professional organizations: Douglas County Medical Society, Nebraska State Medical Association, Missouri Valley Medical Association, and the American Medical Association in which he holds a fellowship.

Dr. Levine also holds fellowships in the following scientific societies: New York Academy of Science, of which he was secretary of the section of physics, chemistry, and astronomy, 1914-16; American Public Health Association; Royal Society of Arts and Science of Great Britain; Royal Institute of Philosophic Studies, of Great Britain; American Geographical Society; the American Institute of Chemistry; American Congress of Physical Therapy, and the American Association for the Advancement of Science. He is a member of: the American Bacteriological Society; American Botanical Society; Society for the Study of Internal Secretions; Annual Biochemical Conference; Society for Experimental Biology and Medicine. He is also a member of the American Chemical Society and has been president of the Omaha section in 1925.

He has recently been appointed one of the five members that constitute the Research Council of the American Congress of Physical Therapy. It is the aim of this Research Council to plan and organize research in the various universities of America in the field relating to such radiations as ultra violet, infra-red, diathermy and X-Rays. The Research Council also has control of the funds available for research.

He is also an advisory member of the Committee for the Introduction of Nutrition in the Curriculum of the American Medical Schools. This committee, appointed by the American Dietetic Association at its annual meeting held in Toronto, in 1930, consists of three members representing the American Dietetic Association, one member representing the American Hospital Association, and one member (Dr. Levine) representing the medical schools.

He is at present (1931-32) president of the Nebraska Academy of Sciences. He is also serving as director of the Professional Men's Club at Omaha, and as director of the Society for the Friendless, a state organization that deals with the rehabilitation of convicts. He is a member of the Medical Editors' and Authors' Association and

of the Nebraska Writers' Guild. He is at present writing a syndicated column entitled "Keeping Fit for Success," which appears weekly in over four hundred newspapers.

Dr. Levine is listed in *Who's Who Among North American Authors*, in *American Men of Science*, in *Who's Who Among Educators*, and *Who's Who in America*. His sports include: hiking; tennis; swimming; and equitation. His hobby is literature. Residence: Omaha. (Photograph on Page 716).

Mark Levy

Mark Levy, retired merchant and salesman, was born at Malsch Ettlingen, Baden, Germany, December 15, 1854, and came to the United States in March, 1871. His father, Nathan David Levy, was born at Malsch, in 1800, and died there on July 4, 1874. He was a farmer and merchant. His wife, also born at Malsch, died there on January 4, 1894.

Mr. Levy attended German public and Hebrew schools. After leaving school Mr. Levi engaged in the mercantile business in Vermont, and later was a salesman in New England and the West. From 1885 until 1909, he was in the clothing business in Hastings, and from 1913 to 1925 operated a ladies' ready-to-wear establishment there. In 1888, Mr. Levy began to acquire the first of his extensive land holdings. Retiring in 1925, he devotes his time to looking after his farms in Nebraska, Oklahoma and Texas.

Always active in Republican politics, Mr. Levy was member of the Hastings city council 1891-1901; president of that council four years; chairman of the light committee at the time the municipal light plant was organized; chairman of the Republican county central committee in 1901; district committeeman for Captain Adams and Senator Norris when they first ran for office. Later Mr. Levy served two more terms in the city council.

A pioneer beet grower in Nebraska, he raised the first sugar beets in Adams County, in 1901, having learned how to raise them on his father's farm in Germany. He was agent for Exnard Beet Sugar Company at that time, and educated the farmers in that section of Nebraska in the art of growing sugar beets.

On October 31, 1886, Mr. Levy was married to Anna Sichl, at Nebraska City. Mrs. Levy, who was born at Carlsbad, Bohemia, in 1858, died at Hastings, on February 6, 1899. To them were born two daughters, Mabel, on April 9, 1890, who married Phillip Pizer; and Ruth, born July 18, 1893, who married Leopold Loeb.

On October 9, 1900, Mr. Levy was married to Alyne Friend at Lincoln. They have three children, Miriam, born October 31, 1901; Yetta Judith, June 15, 1903, and Nathan Simon, born November 21, 1909. All are high school graduates, and have attended college and the state university.

During the World War, Mr. Levy was local chairman for Jewish Relief Drives. President of the Hastings Commercial Club during 1895, 1896, he has served as president of Mount Sinai Cemetery Association since 1890. Of the Jewish faith, he is a teacher and organizer of the Jewish Sunday School. He is a master Mason, and the possessor of a fifty-year jewel, is a member of Hastings Consistory, 32nd degree, K. C. C. H., Tehama Temple, and is a member of Lincoln City Lodge of B'nai Brith.

Mr. Levy has always taken an interest in, and supported all worth while activities, and all efforts toward the betterment of his community. Residence: Hastings.

Charles E. Lewis

Charles E. Lewis, realtor, was born in Gordon, Nebraska, October 18, 1888, son of Harry H. and Arvilla (Bachelor) Lewis. His father is retired and is of Yankee ancestry. Arvilla Bachelor was born at Correctionville, Iowa, and is also retired. Her ancestry is Irish.

In 1907 Mr. Lewis was graduated from high school

at Valentine, Nebraska, and in 1908 completed a business course at Boyles Business College in Omaha. At the present time he is secretary and treasurer of the Northwestern Realty Company of Valentine, and secretary and treasurer of the Northwestern Livestock Sales Company of Valentine. He is a Republican.

He is married to Minnie C. Hornback, who was born in Valentine, in June, 1888. There are two children, Helen, born January 10, 1909; and Pauline, born November 21, 1919.

Mr. Lewis is a member of the Methodist Church, the Rotary Club, and the Masons. Residence: Valentine.

Edward Rust Lewis

Edward Rust Lewis was born at Little Rock, Arkansas, February 23, 1886, the son of Edward Samuel and Anna Carrie (Sparks) Lewis. His father, who was born at Natick, Massachusetts, August 24, 1855, is a doctor of divinity, author, and consulting editor in the Methodist Book Concern at Cincinnati, Ohio; his English ancestors settled in New England in the early history of the country. His mother, whose ancestry is English, was born near Cincinnati, July 2, 1856, and died at Cincinnati, in 1921.

Dr. Lewis attended the elementary schools of Cleveland and Cincinnati, and was graduated from the East High School at Columbus, 1903. He holds the following degrees: A. B., 1907; A. M., 1908; both from the Ohio State University. He was awarded the Ph. D. degree at Boston University in 1929. He was a student at Harvard University during the sammer sessions of 1907, was a student at Union Theological Seminary, New York City, 1908-11 where he was awarded *magna cum laude* honors, and Columbia University, 1910-12. He is a member of Phi Beta Kappa, Phi Kappa Phi, Pi Kappa Delta, and Phi Kappa Tau.

He was engaged in missionary educational work in Canada, under the Presbyterian Board, for a time, was a minister in New York, and southern Ohio, Methodist Conferences, 1912-22, was professor of philosophy at Wesley College, 1922-23, and was a lecturer in philosophy at Boston University, 1923-24. He has been professor of philosophy at Nebraska Wesleyan University since 1924.

Dr. Lewis is a member of the American Association of University Professors, is president of the local chapter of N. W. U., 1930-32, and is a member of the Nebraska Writers Guild. He holds membership in the Philosophy Club, the Nebraskana Society, and the Symposium. He has been a frequent lecturer and speaker on religious and educational themes, and from 1925-1932 was lecturer in the Bible department of the Lincoln Woman's Club. He is a member of Pi Gamma Mu, and is a contributor to the official publication of this organization. His hobby is travel.

On November 25, 1912, he was united in marriage with Susan Choate Van Vliet at New York City. Mrs. Lewis who was a kindergarten teacher before her marriage, was born at Brookville, Pennsylvania, July 10, 1887. They have three children: Edward, born January 6, 1914; Ruth born September 4, 1916; and Mary, born May 4, 1918.

Dr. Lewis is the author of numerous articles in journals published by the Abingdon Press at Cincinnati, Ohio, and several articles published in *Social Science*, a quarterly of the *Methodist Review*. Residence: Lincoln.

Nelson Hiram Lewis

Nelson Hiram Lewis, a prominent physician at Benkelman, Nebraska, was born at Bellcenter, Wisconsin, August 9, 1868, the son of John Bird and Rhoda Amanda (Thompson) Lewis. His father, who was a farmer and served in the Civil War, was born near Indianapolis, Indiana, February 4, 1836, and died at Owatanna, Minnesota, July 22, 1916; his Welsh ancestors were early settlers in Virginia. His mother, who was born at Bowling Green, Ohio, June 24, 1842, and died at Detroit, Michigan,

February 25, 1928, was descended from English ancestors who settled in Hartford, Connecticut, prior to the Revolution. Her grandfather served in the Revolutionary War. His grandfather went to California in the early days via the old Oregon Trail with an ox team, and his recollection of early life includes shooting bear cubs from a tree within a few rods of his home.

Dr. Lewis received the degree of Doctor of Medicine at Marquette University in 1905, practiced medicine at McDonald, Kansas, from 1905 to 1915, and since 1915 has been a physician at Benkelman, Nebraska. He holds membership in the Lions Club, the Nebraska State Medical Society, the Independent Order of the Odd Fellows, and the Masons.

He was united in marriage with Jeannette Korbmacher at Milwaukee, Wisconsin, October 3, 1906. Mrs. Lewis, whose ancestry is French and Dutch, was born at Milwaukee, May 10, 1880. She is a member of the Eastern Star and the Methodist Church. Two children were born to this marriage, Jerome B., March 7, 1909, at McDonald, Kansas; and Ruth K., February 10, 1912, at McDonald, Kansas. Residence: Benkelman. (Photograph in Album).

Samuel Arion Lewis, Jr.

Samuel A. Lewis was born at Omaha, Nebraska, January 27, 1900, the son of Samuel and Jessie (Anderson) Lewis. His father, who was born at Fort Wayne, Indiana, August 25, 1866, is a lawyer, whose ancestors came to America in 1600. His mother, who was born at Hull, England, March 19, 1873, is still living.

Mr. Lewis attended the Dundee grade school at Omaha, and in 1919 was graduated from Central High School there. He received his LL. B. degree from the University of Nebraska where he was graduated *cum laude* June 4, 1923. He was made a member of the Order of the Coif; was a member of the freshman and sophomore honorary societies; and was elected to Theta Chi and Delta Theta Phi.

A resident of Nebraska all his life; since 1923 he has been engaged in general law practice at Omaha. He is a member of the firm Webb, Kelley & Lewis at the present time.

His marriage to Fae Talmadge Cobb was solemnized at Glenwood, Iowa, June 21, 1924. Mrs. Lewis was born at Waterloo, Nebraska, June 15, 1902.

Mr. Lewis is a member of the Omaha Bar Association, the Nebraska State Bar Association, and the Commercial Law League of America. He is affiliated with the Dundee Presbyterian Church at Omaha; and is a member of the Knights of Pythias. He is a Republican. His sports are hunting, fishing and golfing. Residence: Omaha.

Walter Edward Lewis

Walter Edward Lewis, president of the Lewis Oil Company, was born at Dawson, Iowa, May 31, 1885, son of Charles Wesley and Florence (Gant) Lewis. His father, who was born in Illinois, is descended from early settlers in New York state. Florence Gant was born in Iowa, and was descended from early settlers in the eastern colonies.

Mr. Lewis attended country school and was engaged in the contracting business for fifteen years. For the past ten years he has been engaged in the oil business, and is president of the Lewis Oil Company, Incorporated, of Nebraska.

On January 22, 1914, he was married to Emma Nise at Dawson. She was born in Iowa, in 1883, and died at Fremont, December 18, 1926. There are five children of this marriage, as follows: Veldon, born February 22, 1906, who married Vera Johnson; Vernon, born May 25, 1909, who married Corabelle Graham; Metta, born May 27, 1912; Donald, born January 21, 1917, and Stephen, born December 5, 1920. Veldon is in the wholesale oil business.

Mr. Lewis is a member of the United Brethren Church, the Chamber of Commerce, the Odd Fellows and the Knights of Pythias. His hobbies are fishing and hunting. Residence: Fremont.

Rollie Walter Ley

Rollie W. Ley, banker and prominent citizen of Wayne, Nebraska, for over 50 years, was born at Jordan, Minnesota, May 15, 1879. His father, who was likewise a banker and merchant, was born July 5, 1850, in Wisconsin, and died at Wayne, February 13, 1925; his ancestry was German.

Mr. Ley attended the Wayne High School and later was graduated for the State Teachers College at Wayne, and the University of Nebraska. He is at present president of the State National Bank of Wayne. During the World War he served as chairman of the Liberty loan drives and War Savings campaigns. He is a member of the Episcopalian Church, The Nebraskana Society, and the Democratic party.

On October 8, 1902, he was married to Pearl Effie Reynolds, at Fullerton, Nebraska. Mrs. Ley, whose ancestry is English, was born in Iowa, October 1, 1877, and died at Wayne, February 1, 1930. Their children are: Henry, born October 25, 1903; Joy Margaret, born April 18, 1906; Mary Alice, born November 5, 1909; Marjorie, born June 21, 1912; and Josephine, born December 15, 1918. Residence: Wayne. (Photograph in Album).

E. E. Lichty

E. E. Lichty was born at Somerset, Pennsylvania, May 21, 1860. His father, Samuel A. Lichty, was born at Somerset, April 8, 1833, and died at Waterloo, Black Hawk County, Iowa, June 28, 1902. Cevilla Weitzel, wife of Samuel Lichty, was born in Germany, and died at Waterloo, Iowa, April 10, 1908.

Mr. Lichty attended public school, and on September 5, 1889, he was united in marriage with Rebecca M. Musser, who was born at Berlin, Pennsylvania. They have one child, Ralph, born October 21, 1890.

Mr. Lichty has been a resident of Nebraska for forty-five years. He is a Democrat, is affiliated with the Brethren Church of Carleton, Nebraska. He holds membership in the Nebraskana Society. Residence: Carleton.

Fred August Liebers

Fred August Liebers, farmer and veteran of the World War, was born at Minden, Nebraska, February 26, 1894, son of Christian August and Anna W. (Kohler) Liebers.

The father was born in Garnsdorf, Germany, February 22, 1853, and served in the German army, as a noncommissioned officer. He came to the United States in 1884, settling in Kearney County, where he was very successful as a farmer and business man. He died at Minden, March 8, 1908. His wife, Anna, was born in Auerswalde, Germany, February 8, 1851. Her father, an engineer, helped to construct and operate the important railroads in their province.

In 1915 Mr. Liebers was graduated from the Nebraska School of Agriculture, and latter attended the University of Nebraska until 1917, when he entered military service, lacking one semester of graduation.

From October 5, 1917, until June 12, 1919, Mr. Liebers served with Company F, 314 Motor Supply Train, 89th Division. He was with the American Expeditionary Forces, and participated in the following engagements, Lucey, August 8, to September 11, 1918; St. Mihiel, September 12, to September 16, 1918; Euzizes, September 17, to October 7, 1918; and the Meuse-Argonne, October 9 to November 11, 1918.

While in the school of agriculture Mr. Liebers was president of his second year class, president of the Young Men's Christian Association four years, president of his literary society, major of the first battalion, lieutenant colonel his fourth year at the university, president of the United Agricultural Society, 1917, president of the Kearney County Club, 1917, and member of the Agricultural Club. He is a charter member of Kappa Chapter of Alpha Gamma Rho.

On June 29, 1919, Mr. Liebers was married to Winifred Martha Randall at Bennet. She was a school teacher, born at Seattle, Washington, October 9, 1891. They have one son, Wayne Randall, born December 14, 1928.

With the exception of the two years spent in the army, Mr. Liebers has lived in Nebraska all his life. He is a former member of the board of directors of the Kearney Co-operative Creamery Company, and former secretary. He is a member of the American Legion, and was commander of Bennet Post No. 280, 1929, 1930, 1931, and commander of Lancaster County 1931. He is a member of the Presbyterian Church, the Bennet Community Club (president 1930-31). He is a Mason. Residence: Bennet.

Otto Hugo Liebers

In 1884 August Liebers and his wife, Anna (Koehler) Liebers, came to America from Germany and settled at Minden, Nebraska. It was here that Otto Hugo Liebers was born on June 25, 1887. He attended country grade school, the Minden High School, and Grand Island Baptist College. From 1906-09 he was a student at the State University School of Agriculture, graduating at the head of his class in 1909. From 1909-13 he was a student at the University of Nebraska from which he received his Bachelor of Science degree in June, 1913. During his time at the university he was president of the Agricultural Club, editor of the *Cornhusker Countryman*, a member of the livestock judging team in 1909, both the fruit judging and the dairy teams in 1910. He is a member of Alpha Zeta.

He was married to Ethel Leta Kindig at Holmesville, Nebraska, September 3, 1913. Mrs. Liebers, who was born at Benson, Illinois, July 25, 1888, is of English and German descent. There are three children, Laurence, born June 14, 1914; Harry, born December 6, 1916, and Ruth, born July 9, 1918.

During the years 1913-16 Mr. Liebers was county agricultural agent for Gage County, and from 1916-19 was agricultural and industrial agent for the Burlington Railroad at Denver. Returning to Lincoln in 1919 he organized and became president of the Liebers Equipment Company of Lincoln, continuing three years. Since 1924 he has been manager of the Nebraska Dairy Development Society.

In 1909 he was captain of the University Cadets, and served in the Food Administration during the World War. He is a member of the Second Presbyterian Church, the Lincoln Chamber of Commerce, and is an 18th degree Mason, and member of the Blue Lodge, Knights Templar and Scottish Rite bodies. His hobbies are flowers and boys. Residence: Lincoln. (Photograph in Album).

Chester J. Lienhart

For nearly three decades Chester J. Lienhart has been an outstanding citizen of Nebraska. Born at Akron, Colorado, April 28, 1890, he is the son of C. F. and Mary J. (Jones) Lienhart. His father, a druggist, and in later years a realtor and banker, was born in Stratford, Ontario, Canada, April 29, 1858, and settled in Kearney County in 1874. He was a leading Democrat, and at one time served as national committeeman. His death occurred at Hastings, April 3, 1918. His wife, Mary, was born in Rockford, Illinois, June 8, 1868, of pioneer Nebraska parentage. She resides at Hastings.

Mr. Lienhart, upon his graduation from Minden High School attended the National Institute of Pharmacy. He was enrolled for a time at the University of Nebraska, for the study of medicine, but dropped his enrollment to take up the study of pharmacy. For a number of years Mr. Lienhart was the owner and operator of three drug stores. In the period between 1922 and 1931 he has been president of the Hastings Chevrolet Company, of which he was the organizer. In April, 1926, he shipped a full trainload of Chevrolet cars from the factory at Saint Louis, and before the end of the month had sold them all.

The employer of 125 persons, during 1922-30 he sold 6422 new cars and 10,126 used cars, the total valuation of which was more than $13,000,000. Mr. Lienhart is the organizer, secretary and treasurer of the Great Plains Aircraft Corporation, and secretary-treasurer of the Hastings Loan and Finance Company. He is also secretary-treasurer of the Central Nebraska Golf Association (1931-32 season).

On April 15, 1909, he was united in marriage to Ema J. Winter, their marriage having been solemnized at Omaha. Mrs. Lienhart was born at Roseland, August 9, 1889. There are two daughters, Lois Evelyn, born January 2, 1911, who is married to Clyde D. Paul; and Gwendolyn Juanita, born February 23, 1912.

Mr. Lienhart is a Democrat, and has served as a member of various committees. He is a member of the Hastings Chamber of Commerce, and is a member of the good roads and the new industries committees. He is also a member of the Nebraska Good Roads Association, the Nebraska State Pharmaceutical Association, and the Young Men's Christian Association. His fraternal organizations include the Modern Woodmen of America, the Knights of Pythias, the United Commercial Travelers, Hastings Lodge No. 159 of the Elks, the D. O. K. K., and the A. M. O. B.

Among his favorite sports are golf, hunting, trap shooting and baseball, and he enjoys aviation, reading and travel. His hobby is mechanics. Residence: Hastings.

Guy Liggett

Born at Conway, Iowa, December 11, 1875, Guy Liggett is the son of Henry Bell and Helen Elizabeth (Shadrach) Liggett. His father, a physician and surgeon, and a private with the 85th Ohio Volunteers in the Civil War, was born at Akron, Ohio, September 30, 1844. He died at Los Angeles, April 7, 1924. He was descended from English ancestors in America before the Revolution.

Helen Elizabeth Shadrach was born in Delaware, Ohio, June 12, 1852, and is of Pennsylvania-Dutch descent on the paternal side and Scotch descent on the maternal side. She is still living.

Guy Liggett was educated in the public school of Conway, Iowa, and attended Creston High School. During the year 1893 he attended Iowa State College. On April 16, 1903, he was united in marriage to Jessie Leona Nelson. Mrs. Liggett was born at Conway, on January 1, 1877. On the paternal side she is Norwegian, and on the maternal side of pre-revolutionary English stock.

Mr. Liggett taught school in Taylor County, Iowa, two years, and then entered the Pratt and Green general store where he remained a year and a half as a clerk. He came to Omaha in March, 1898, where he became associated with The Pantorium, cleaners and dyers, where he has since remained. He is now president of that organization, and also engages as a real estate operator. Since 1910, he has been treasurer of the Nebraska State Association of Cleaners and Dyers, which was organized at that time. Having been totally deaf since 1915, he is not particularly active in commercial and other organizations. He is however, a member of the Chamber of Commerce, the National Geographic Society, The Nebras-

kana Society, etc. He is a Mason and Shriner and a member of the Elks. His sport is golf, and he is interested in reading, touring, and trap-shooting. His clubs are the Omaha Athletic Club and Happy Hollow Country Club. Residence: Omaha.

Chauncey Clark Lillibridge

Chauncey C. Lillibridge, dentist at Crete, Saline County, Nebraska, has lived in Nebraska all his life and for the past decade has been prominent in the civic and professional life of his community. He was born at Weston, Saunders County, Nebraska, May 10, 1894, the son of Cristopher Elra and Clysta Jane (Harrison) Lillibridge. His father, who was born at Waterford, Erie County, Pennsylvania, May 18, 1845, and died at Weston, September 14, 1908, was a stockman and hardware merchant; he was sheriff of Saunders County in 1880; his ancestors came to Rhode Island from Germany several generations ago. His mother was born in Clinton County, Iowa, February 28, 1849.

Dr. Lillibridge was graduated from the Wahoo High School in 1912, and received, in 1916, his D. D. S. degree at the University of Nebraska. He was a member of the wrestling squad and was elected to membership in Xi Psi Phi. In 1913 he was a school teacher and for two years practiced dentistry at Weston. Since 1919 he has been engaged in his profession at Crete. He has been city treasurer of Crete for the past five years.

He was united in marriage with Ella Elizabeth Ziegenbein at Memphis, Saunders County, Nebraska, August 29, 1917. Mrs. Lillibridge was born at Memphis, September 20, 1893. They have a daughter, Betty Ann, born April 27, 1901.

Dr. Lillibridge was in the Wyoming National Guards in 1911. During the World War he was commissioned first lieutenant in the Dental Reserve Corps. He is now first lieutenant in the Reserve Officers Corps. He is a member of the American Dental Association; the Nebraska State Dental Society; the Cornhusker Dental Study Club; and the Nebraskana Society. He is past secretary of the Crete Community Club; was secretary of the Rotary Club, 1927-30, and president, July, 1930, to July, 1931; and is treasurer of the Crete School Board. He is a member of the Shrine Country Club of Lincoln. He is a Mason; York Rite; Scottish Rite; Shriner. His sport is golfing. He is affiliated with the Grace Methodist Episcopal Church at Crete. Residence: Crete.

Lee Bennett Lilliedoll

For over 26 years Lee Bennett Lilliedoll has been engaged in the drug business at Sutton, Nebraska. He was born at Shickley, Nebraska, October 30, 1885, the son of Frank John and Cecilia (Peterson) Lilliedoll. His father, who was a farmer, was born at Trolle-Jung-Be, Sweden, April 25, 1834, and came to this country in 1867; he died at Shickley, March 14, 1898. His mother was born at Trolle-Jung-Be, March 14, 1854, and died at Shickley, May 24, 1927.

Mr. Lilliedoll was graduated from the high school at Oak, Nebraska, in 1903, and in 1906 was graduated from the pharmacy department of Creighton University. Since that date he has been successful as a druggist at Sutton, where he is an active member of the Chamber of Commerce, now known as the Lions Club. He is a supporter of the Unitarian Church, the Nebraskana Society, and the Elks. His social club is the Sutton Golf Club, and his favorite sports are golfing and hunting; and is the owner of several trophies, for a period of 10 years he played professional baseball, appearing in the uniform of many Nebraska towns. His hobby is mechanics.

His marriage to Chloe Anna Whitmore occurred at Lincoln, Nebraska, December 25, 1911. Mrs. Lilliedoll, whose ancestry is French and English, was born at Alliance, Nebraska, December 25, 1888. Mrs. Lilliedoll is a P. E. O., and is principally interested in her home and family. They have two children: Jarrold Donath, born August 5, 1919; and Joan Delore, born September 19, 1924. Both children are pupils at the public school in Sutton, Nebraska. Residence: Sutton.

Clarence Linch

Clarence Linch, a resident of Nebraska for the past 50 years, has been prominent in the business world for the past 23 years. He was born at Greenwood, Nebraska, June 15, 1881, the son of William A. and Arvilla Jenett (Foreman) Linch. His father, who was a grain dealer and farmer, was born at Burlington, Iowa, November, 1836, and died at Lincoln, Nebraska, December 24, 1906; he served in the Civil War; his ancestry was German and Irish. His mother, who reared a family of twelve children, was born in Iowa, March 18, 1856.

Mr. Linch has been an automobile dealer at Valparaiso, since 1908. He is a member of the Nebraskana Society, and is affiliated with the Republican party.

He was married to Mertie Hurlbut, at Valparaiso, April 3, 1904. Mrs. Linch, who was born at Coldwater, Michigan, May 16, 1882, is a devoted mother and homemaker. Their children are: Charley, born March 29, 1905, who married Goldie Caple; Bernice, born February 17, 1907, who married Russell A. Peterson; Laurence, born July 29, 1909; and Zelma, born May 9, 1914. Residence: Valparaiso.

George Wallace Lincoln

A resident of Nebraska all his life, George Wallace Lincoln was born at Willow Island, Nebraska, November 9, 1890, son of Dana Eugene and Jessie May (Hunt) Lincoln. His father, who is of English and Dutch extraction, was born at Sun Prairie, Wisconsin, April 12, 1867. A stockman, he has also served as a law enforcement officer and as deputy United States marshal. Jessie May Hunt, who was born at Battle Creek, Michigan, August 11, 1871, is of Scotch and English descent. She is prominent in club and church work in her community.

George Wallace Lincoln was graduated from Lexington High School in 1909, where he was a letterman in football for four years. He has served as a store clerk, a rural mail carrier, manager of a co-operative association, and is now owner of a men's clothing store and a cleaning and tailoring establishment.

On June 8, 1910, he was married to Edna Gertrude Stiner at Lexington. Mrs. Lincoln, who was a stenographer before her marriage, was born at Lexington, September 5, 1889. She is of Welch descent. They have one son, Harold Wayne, born February 10, 1912. He is married to Evelyn M. Norton, and is a pre-law student at George Washington University.

Mr. Lincoln is a Methodist, a Democrat and a Mason. He is a member of the Chamber of Commerce, the Kiwanis Club and The Nebraskana Society; is interested in football and basketball. He devotes much time to reading, and is a proponent of clean athletics. Residence: Lexington. (Photograph in Album).

John Lincoln

John Lincoln, clerk of the district court of Lincoln County since 1925, was born in Gothenburg, Nebraska, October 25, 1893, son of John Dalbert Ward and Mary (Fulton) Lincoln.

The father, who was born in Madison, Wisconsin, December 23, 1858, is living. His wife, Mary, born in New Glasgo, Cape Britton, September 3, 1870, is living also.

Mr. Lincoln was graduated from high school at North Platte in 1916, and the following year attended Kearney State Normal School. On November 17, 1921,

he was married to Elsie Sieman at North Platte. Mrs. Lincoln, who was born at Musleringen, Germany, August 23, 1893, is a registered nurse. They have one son, Arthur Fulton, born September 13, 1922.

Mr. Lincoln is a member of the Lutheran Church, chairman of the Lincoln County Red Cross, a member of the Chamber of Commerce, the Odd Fellows, and the Elks. Residence: North Platte.

John August Lindahl

A successful farmer in Antelope County, John August Lindahl has lived in Nebraska for the past 46 years. He was born at Lemnhutt, Sweden, June 24, 1867, the son of John Peter and Johanna Helena (Israelson) Lindahl. His father, who was a carpenter, was born at Oseda, Sweden, October 20, 1838, and died at Newman Grove, Nebraska, in November, 1908. His mother was born at Almasocker Parish, Sweden, November 1, 1832, and died at Newman Grove, December 5, 1919.

Mr. Lindahl attended elementary schools in Sweden. He has been moderator of the school board of District 31 at Tilden, Nebraska, since 1902, is a member of the Nebraskana Society, and is affiliated with the Free Mission Church at Tilden. His chief recreations are hiking, motoring, and reading.

On August 24, 1898, he was married to Ellen Christine Youngquist at Albion, Nebraska. Mrs. Lindahl was born in Chicago, November 16, 1875. Eight children were born to their marriage, of whom seven are living: Fred, born May 21, 1899, who married Myrtle Edith Grubb; Clarence, October 14, 1900, who died February 15, 1919; Leonard, March 4, 1902, who married Maxine Lillian Kinsey; Elmer, August 21, 1903; Arthur, August 16, 1907; Alys, October 17, 1909; Vivian, August 11, 1913; and Virgil, March 14, 1919. Mr. Lindahl has been township treasurer of Grant Township since 1917. Residence: Tilden.

Edwin O. Lindberg

Edwin O. Lindberg, superintendent of schools at Ceresco, was born at Broadwater, Nebraska, February 12, 1897. He is the son of Nils and Hannah (Swanson) Lindberg, born in Sweden. Nils O. Lindberg was born on January 27, 1866, and came to Nebraska in 1878, where he is engaged as a rancher. His wife was born October 7, 1865.

Mr. Lindberg attended rural schools at Broadwater, and was graduated from Luther Academy in May, 1915. He taught in rural schools near Oakland, 1915-16, and was superintendent of the Riverside Consolidated High School, 1921-24. He attended and took graduate work at the University of Colorado, and the University of Nebraska, and received his A. B. from Midland College in June, 1925. He is a member of the Wynn Literary Society and the Midland College Glee Club. During 1925-26 he was superintendent of the Dorchester public schools, and since 1926 has been superintendent of schools at Ceresco.

On June 16, 1925, he was united in marriage to Bertha Oliva Olson at Denver, Colorado. Mrs. Lindberg, who was born at Lodgepole, Nebraska, November 13, 1898, is a teacher of Swedish descent. They have one son, Edgar Leland, born March 30, 1929.

Mr. Lindberg is independent, politically. He takes an active interest in religious and educational work, and is a member of the National Educaional Association, Immanual Lutheran Church, the Lutheran Brotherhood and the Nebraskana Society. Residence: Ceresco.

Frederic Reinhold Lindberg

Frederic Reinhold Lindberg, rancher and banker, was born in Varmland, Sweden, January 25, 1866, and has resided in Nebraska 44 years. He is the son of Abraham and Anna Charlotte (Boxtrum) Lindberg,

Nelson—Alliance

FREDERIC REINHOLD LINDBERG

both natives of Sweden. The father died in Sheridan County, Missouri, in 1870, and the mother in Republic County, Kansas, in 1900. The family came to America in 1868.

Mr. Lindberg attended the elementary schools of Republic County, Kansas, and in 1888 came to Nebraska when he began work on a horse ranch on Lawrence Forks known as Laing Brothers Ranch. He worked for the Laing brothers for five years and at that time Guy Laing bought the older brother out. For three years Mr. Lindberg operated the ranch. Then Guy Laing died, and shortly after his death Mr. Lindberg purchased the ranch from Mr. Laing's widow. About ten years later Mr. Lindberg sold the ranch which comprised 4000 acres for $32,000.00 and he sold the cattle for about $10,000.00, reserving all the horses which were about 200 head. He then bought an adjoining ranch of about 10,000 acres which he now operates. At the present time Mr. Lindberg has about 500 head of cattle and 100 head of horses. For some time he has been chairman of the board of directors of the Bridgeport State Bank. For six years he served as county commissioner of Cheyenne County, and for 20 years was county commissioner of Morrill County. He is a Democrat.

He was married on February 1, 1906, to Lillian Pearl Waitman at Sidney. Mrs. Lindberg was born at Urbana, Iowa, March 29, 1879, and traces her ancestry to the Revolution. She attended school at Urbana, Iowa and attended country school near Redington, Nebraska. Mrs. Lindberg taught school for about eight years prior to her marriage. She is the daughter of Price P. and Minnie S. (Kelty) Waitman, is a member of the school board, Woman's Club, the Ladies Aid and the First Presbyterian Church. They have one son, Garland, born January 30, 1909, who was graduated from the Bridgeport High School and is now attending the Colorado Agricultural College, where he is a senior.

During the late war Mr. Lindberg was particularly interested in all civilian projects. He is a member of the First Presbyterian Church of Bridgeport, the Red Cross, the Chamber of Commerce, the Lions Club, the Modern Woodmen of America, and the Nebraskana Society. Residence: Bridgeport. (Photograph on Page 722).

William Carl Linden

William Carl Linden, farmer and dairyman, was born at Blair, Nebraska, December 26, 1881, son of Henry Bertrand and Henrietta (Hovendick) Linden. His father, who was born at Luxemburg, Germany, May 9, 1833, served in the War of the Rebellion with Companies B and L of the 2nd Missouri Volunteers. He died at Blair on October 4, 1887. His wife, Henrietta Hovendick, was born in Westphalia, Germany, October 22, 1843, and died at Blair March 4, 1922.

Mr. Linden was married to Mattie Sophie Rathmann at Blair, on December 21, 1904. Mrs. Linden was born at Bennington, Nebraska, May 22, 1886. They have three children: Mildred May, born May 25, 1909, who married Paul Jefferson and resides at Omaha; Raymond, born July 11, 1914, and Maurine Mae, born May 17, 1921.

Mr. and Mrs. Linden are members of the Congregational Church, and he is a member of the Modern Woodmen of America and the Nebraskana Society. Residence: Blair.

John Albert Linderholm

Born at Chicago, Illinois, April 14, 1870, John A. Linderholm has been an outstanding figure in the business life of Omaha, since 1909. He is the son of Nels Frederick and Anna Swenson Linderholm, the former of whom was born in Sweden, February 2, 1837, who came to America in 1869, bringing with him his wife, and settling in Chicago, and later in Nebraska. He was a cabinet maker and farmer by occupation. Anna Swenson was born in Sweden, in August, 1833, and died at Newman Grove, Nebraska, September 21, 1887. Nels Linderholm lived until February 1, 1916, and died at Newman Grove.

John A. Linderholm was educated in the public schools of Sterling, Illinois, and Newman Grove, Nebraska. He later attended Fremont Normal College for two years. He spent his first five years in Nebraska on a farm in Madison County, and then was engaged in the general mercantile business for three years. For the past thirty-five years he has been associated with the Crowell Elevator Company, for twenty years as manager at Omaha, of the grain department. He is secretary and director of the Crowell Elevator Company at the present time and is serving his third term as director of the Omaha Grain Exchange. During the World War in 1918, he was president of the Exchange, and also had charge of all war activities covering grain interests during the war. He assisted in the organization of a company of home guards and was a member of the company.

Mr. Linderholm attends the First Central Congregational Church and is active in Red Cross and other welfare work. He is a member of the Chamber of Commerce, the Ad Sell League, and of the Parent-Teachers' Association. He is a member of the Modern Woodmen of America and the Odd Fellows. His clubs are the Happy Hollow Country Club and the Omaha Athletic Club.

On April 5, 1896, he was married to Maude L. Hull at Burlington, Iowa. Mrs. Linderholm was a native of Burlington. She is a member of Mayor Isaac Sadler Chapter of the Daughters of the American Revolution, and a direct descendant of Lieutenant Joseph Peckham. Mr. and Mrs. Linderholm have two children, Edna, born July 8, 1900, who married Dr. C. E. Bloomberg, now deceased. Dr. and Mrs. Bloomberg have one daughter, Francis Marjorie, born February 3, 1920. Francis Linderholm, second daughter of Mr. and Mrs. Linderholm, was born December 3, 1902. Residence: Omaha.

Carl Reuben Lindgren

Carl Reuben Lindgren, farmer, was born at Bladen, Nebraska, July 8, 1883, son of Charles W. and Charlotte (Lundberg) Lindgren.

His father was born in Sweden, November 17, 1849, and came to the United States in 1868. He was a farmer and stock raiser, until his death at Campbell, Nebraska, April 27, 1907. His wife, Charlotte, was born at Kankakee, Illinois, in 1857, and died at Campbell, on May 10, 1888.

Mr. Lindgren attended public school and business college. He has been a prominent farmer at Riverton, for a number of years, and has taken an active part in Republican politics. He has served as precinct committeeman, and has held various minor offices.

On June 2, 1909, he was married to Bertha Caroline Erickson at Campbell. Mrs. Lindgren was born at Campbell, July 26, 1887. They have two children, Ruby, born October 19, 1910, who married Fred Brunke; and Charles R., born October 19, 1920.

Mr. Lindgren has always resided in Nebraska. He assisted with Red Cross and loan drives during the World War, has been treasurer of the local school board since 1910, and is a member of the Royal Highlanders and the Masons. His hobby is reading. Residence: Riverton.

Arthur Jennings Lindley

Born at Freeport, Illinois, March 22, 1877, Arthur Jennings Lindley has been a resident of Nebraska most of his life. Jotham Scudder Lindley, his father, who was a druggist, was born at Athens, Ohio, October 17, 1848, and died at Long Beach, California, January 12, 1930. His mother, Rachel Jane (Askey) Lindley, was born at Orangeville, Illinois, December 28, 1850, and died at Central City, Nebraska, March 9, 1889.

Mr. Lindley attended the high school at Central City,

and for many years has been a banker at Duncan, Nebraska, where he is now cashier of the Duncan State Bank. He is affiliated with Christ Church of Columbus, Nebraska, has been a member of the Shrine at Omaha since 1908, and holds membership in the Nebraskana Society. He is a Republican.

His marriage to Eola Lenora Jones occurred at Columbus, October 12, 1912. Mrs. Lindley, who is a music instructor, was born at Newton, Iowa, August 4, 1875. They have a son, Ralph Lewis, born September 1, 1915, at Duncan. Residence: Duncan.

Sigmond Hurst Lindley

Born near Nishna Station, Missouri, January 20, 1867, Sigmond Hurst Lindley is the son of Charles Benton and Caroline Adelia (Rich) Lindley. His father, a farmer and stockman, was born at Columbus, Ohio, September 13, 1842, and died at Elmo, Missouri; he served as cavalryman in Missouri during the Civil War. His mother was born at Lone Tree, Illinois, February 8, 1848, and died at Blanchard, Iowa, November 10, 1890. Her father came to this country from Ireland and served in the Civil War.

Mr. Lindley attended rural school in Atchison County, Missouri, and was a student at Tarkio College, Missouri. He is manager of the municipal coal and gas departments for the city of Lincoln, Nebraska, and is serving as treasurer of the Nebraska Building & Investment Company and secretary of the Midwest Grain Marketing Association.

He was a teacher at Lincoln from 1896 to 1904, taught in Nemaha County, Nebraska, for a time, and served as cashier of the Bethany State Bank. He is now a member of the Bethany Parent Teacher's Association, is chairman of the Safety Council, and holds membership in the Bethany Christian Church and the Young Men's Christian Association. His recreations are hiking, reading and gardening.

On August 6, 1907, Mr. Lindley was united in marriage with Huldah Jane Davis at Bethany. Mrs. Lindley, who is a physician and osteopath, was born at Essex, Iowa, May 23, 1865, of Welsh parentage. They have two adopted children: Lawrence, born September 15, 1909, who is a student at the Fort Monmouth Electric School in New Jersey; and Mary Elizabeth, born October 27, 1913, who is a student at Cotner College. Residence: Lincoln.

Carl Albert Lindstrom

Carl Albert Lindstrom, merchant at Gresham, Nebraska, for the past 35 years, was born at Princeton, Illinois, October 21, 1879. His father, Swan Lindstrom, was born at Jonkoping, Bjersferd, Sweden, July 23, 1849, and was a farmer in this country from 1868 until his death on August 21, 1922. His mother was born at Jonkoping, December 17, 1839, and died at Gresham, March 21, 1930.

Mr. Lindstrom attended a rural school in York County. He was a clerk for the Diers Brothers Company in Gresham, for 19 years, and since then has owned his own establishment there. He is a member of the Federation of Nebraska Retailers, the Nebraskana Society, the Osceola Country Club, and the Methodist Episcopal Church at Gresham. He is a 32nd degree Mason and Shriner, and is a member of the Independent Order of Odd Fellows. His sports include golfing, hunting, and fishing. A Democrat, he has been mayor of Gresham for the past year.

He married Martha Barbee at Gresham, June 20, 1906. Mrs. Lindstrom was born at Gresham, February 12, 1885. Four children were born to this marriage: Lucile, born September 27, 1912, a student at the University of Nebraska; Eleanor, born September 11, 1918, who died February 1, 1920; Gertrude, born December 23, 1920; and Stanton, born September 21, 1928. Residence: Gresham.

Jennie Lindsey Line

Jennie Lindsey Line, a resident of Nebraska since 1880, was born at Plainfield, Cumberland County, Pennsylvania, March 25, 1867, the daughter of Henry G. and Mary Ellen (Lindsey) Weigel. Her father, who was a teacher and farmer, was born at Carlisle, Cumberland County, Pennsylvania, 1840, of German parentage, and died at Diller, Jefferson County, Nebraska, April, 1904. Her mother was born at Plainfield, November 23, 1847, and died at Diller, May 2, 1906.

Mrs. Line attended rural school. She is a member of the Nebraskana Society, is affiliated with the Congregational Church at Diller, and is a member of the Republican Party. She was united in marriage with William Carothers Line at Diller, April 6, 1892. Mr. Line, a farmer, was born at Carlisle, November 27, 1850, and died at Diller, July 26, 1928; he was twice a successful candidate for the Nebraska Legislature on the Republican ticket.

To this marriage six children were born: William Harrison, born January 12, 1893; Henry Reid, born February 14, 1894, who died, July, 1894; Florence Belle, born March 28, 1895; Mary Ellen, born July 9, 1896; Eva Jane, born May 26, 1900; and Alice Matilda, born September 1, 1903. William H. is county attorney of Sherman County, and is married to Lulu May Gunderson. Eva J. is a physician at Niles Center, Illinois, and is married to Ardell Lorman Frowufelter. Alice is a teacher in high school. Mary Ellen, who married Paul Seibert Beckwith, is a graduate of Peru Normal, and Florence Belle, who is married to Clarence Richard Steffen, is a graduate of the University of Nebraska. Residence: Diller.

Thomas Henry Line

Thomas Henry Line, physician and surgeon in Nebraska for more than fifty years, was born in Boonsboro, Maryland, April 21, 1858, son of Reuben Henry and Margueret Rebecca (Thomas) Line.

Reuben Henry Line was born in Boonsboro, October 30, 1830, and died at Marquette, Nebraska, January 16, 1913. The earliest record of the family in America is in Lancaster, Pennsylvania, or thereabout in 1700. The family moved to Boonsboro, Maryland in 1760, purchasing a tract of land which is still owned by a member of the family. Margueret Rebecca Thomas was born at Keedysville, Maryland, May 29, 1834, and died at Marquette, Nebraska, September 5, 1917. Her father, who was of German ancestry, was born about 1755 and died about 1860. Her mother was of Irish extraction, born in America about 1780.

Dr. Line attended the college classes at Rush Medical College, from which he was graduated in February, 1881. He also attended the University of Michigan at Ann Arbor, the years 1878, 1879, and 1880. He has many post graduate diplomas.

From 1884 until 1887 Dr. Line was the editor and owner of the *Marquette Independent*, and from 1884 until 1886 was county coroner of Hamilton County. He was secretary of the United States pension board of medical examiners from 1888 until 1893 at Aurora, Nebraska. He laid out and fixed the boundary lines for the corporation of Marquette. He was the first chairman of the board of trustees, and wrote the first ordinances of the town.

For many years he was the owner of a drug store at Ogallala, but of late years has confined his activities closely to the practice of medicine. In early 1877 he taught a term of school in Douglas County, one in Illinois the same year, and a term in Maryland in 1876. He came to Nebraska prior to 1882 and has been in the state since December of that year continuously.

Dr. Line has served as city physician 12 years and health officer in Central City, Nebraska. He was county physician for several years, and during the World War was a member of the exemption board of Merrick County. He was also a physician at the Genoa Indian School during the World War.

On February 24, 1886, he was married to Mary Rebecca Brantner at Boonsboro. She was born there on July 26, 1861, and died at Central City, September 1, 1929. She was of Dutch descent, a seamstress and designer of women's clothing. There were three children born to them, Thomas Brantner, born February 28, 1888, who married Clara B. Tyier; Emma Kate, born January 1, 1890, who died June 20, 1890; and Alpha Amanda, born June 15, 1891. Thomas Brantner lives in California, where he is an accountant and painter. He has two girls, the oldest of whom was graduated from Omaha Technical High School.

Dr. Line has been a member of the Nebraska State Medical Association since 1886. He was a former member of the Commercial Club of Marquette, also of the Commercial Club of Central City. He is a Mason, a member of the Royal Highlanders and a former member of the Ancient Order of United Workmen, the Modern Woodmen of America, and the Redmen. At one time he was also a member of the State Historical Society. Residence: Grafton.

William Harrison Line

William Harrison Line, county attorney of Sherman County, was born at Diller, Nebraska, January 12, 1893, son of William C. and Jennie L. (Weigle) Line. The father was born in Carlisle, Pennsylvania, September 27, 1850 and died at Diller, July 26, 1928. He was a farmer and legislator (1905-1907). His wife, Jennie, was born at Plainfield, Pennsylvania, March 25, 1867.

Mr. Line received his Bachelor of Arts degree from the University of Nebraska in 1915 and his Bachelor of Laws degree in 1920. He is a member of Phi Alpha Delta.

On June 18, 1921, he was married to Lulu May Gunderson at Omaha. There are two children, William G., born July 19, 1927; and Marjorie Lou, November 29, 1931.

During the World War Mr. Line served as a member of the Pay Corps, United States Naval Reserve Forces June 12, 1917- May 27, 1919. He is a member of the American Legion, the Presbyterian Church, the Nebraska State Bar Association and the Masons. He is a Republican. Residence: Loup City.

Eric P. Lingren

Eric P. Lingren, for many years one of Knox County's prominent farmers, now retired, was born in Calmar, Sweden, March 4, 1851, son of Peter and Marie (Johnson) Pearson. His father, born at Calmar, March 2, 1801, died there on May 25, 1866. His wife, born in Calmar May 4, 1803, died at Calmar on July 2, 1867.

After the death of his parents, Eric P. Lingren set sail for America, landing in Detroit on the 21st of June 1869. Prior to coming to America he taught three years in the country schools of Sweden. Since he took up his residence in Nebraska he has engaged extensively in farming. For nine years he was assessor of Lincoln township in Knox County, for nine years he was chairman of the local school board, and in 1887 was justice of the peace for Lincoln township. He is a Republican.

On December 24, 1885, Mr. Lingren was married to Clara Sophia Nelson at Sioux City, Iowa. Mrs. Lingren was born at Linkoping, Sweden, May 2, 1852. To them were born seven children, as follows: Edna, born October 29, 1886, married Everett Ellingson; Ethel, born January 31, 1888, married Albin G. Johnson; Clarence, born June 9, 1889, married Hildur Wangstrom; Elvera, born February 20, 1891, married Gust Anderson; Ernest, born January 29, 1893, married Eva C. Lindstrom; Harold, born January 31, 1895, married Elna Nelson; and Carl, born July 5, 1897, married Irma Servine. Harold enlisted in the United States Army on July 5, 1917, was wounded in action on August 11, 1918, and honorably discharged on May 10, 1919.

Mr. Anderson served as chairman of the local Red Cross organization two years, is a member of Tabor Swedish Lutheran Church and the Nebraskana Society. He is an ardent baseball fan and now devotes much time to historical readings. Residence: Wausa.

Anton Link

The Reverend Anton Link, Catholic priest, was born at Waldernbach, Germany, February 6, 1883, and came to America in the fall of 1910. His father, George Wilhelm Link, was born in Hausen, Germany, March 29, 1853, and died at Waldernbach, January 8, 1932. He was a merchant. His wife, Catherina Mueller, was born in Waldernbach, in 1856, and died March 7, 1932.

Father Link received his elementary education in the public schools of Waldernbach, and afterward attended the Gymnasium Hadamar and Montabaur in Germany. From 1904 until 1910, he was a student at the University of Freiburg, Switzerland. Father Link came to America in October, 1910, and proceeded immediately to Omaha, where he received, from the Bishop of Omaha, Richard Scannell, the appointment as pastor of Saint Mary's Church at Prairie Center, Nebraska. Father Link was pastor at Prairie Center, until June, 1913, and since that time has been pastor of St. Patrick's Church at Sidney, and superintendent of the St. Patrick Academy.

He is state chaplain of the Knights of Columbus of the Nebraska jurisdiction, a charter member of Sidney Council 1861 of the Knights of Columbus, and a member of the Chamber of Commerce, the Red Cross, and the Sidney Country Club. Residence: Sidney. (Photograph in Album).

Karl Linke

Karl Linke, a lifelong resident of Rock County, Nebraska, has been a stock farmer and rancher near Hammond for many years. He was born at Perch, Nebraska, March 11, 1893, the son of Karl and Mary Elizabeth (Ammon) Linke, the former a stockfarmer and prominent banker at Bassett, Nebraska. His father, who was president of the State Bank of Bassett for a number of years, was born at Ochsenfurt, Germany, January 9, 1858, and died at St. Augustine, Florida, January 14, 1919. His mother was born in Crawford County, Indiana, and died at Bassett.

Mr. Linke was graduated from the Bassett High School in 1910, attended the Fremont College, and was a student at a business college at York, Pennsylvania. He has served as director of the school board at Hammond, Nebraska, since 1919, and is a member of the American Legion post there.

He was united in marriage with Viola Gay Barker at Centerville, South Dakota, January 30, 1918; she was born at Red Oak, Iowa, July 8, 1898. Their children are: Rose Mary, born November 16, 1918; Karl, born October 27, 1923; Marjory Marie, born May 2, 1927; and Francis Juanita, born March 6, 1929. Residence: Hammond.

Joseph William Linkhart

For the past 49 years Joseph William Linkhart has been engaged in the real estate business at Coleridge, Nebraska. He was born at Charleston, Coles County, Illinois, January 13, 1857, the son of Joel and Eliza Frances (Black) Linkhart. His father, who was a farmer, was born near Cambridge, Ohio, August 26, 1832, and died at Oxford, Iowa, February 1, 1901; his German and Irish ancestors came to this country in 1820. His mother was born near Cambridge, July 28, 1827, and died at Burlington, Kansas, November 5, 1926. She was the daughter of English and Irish parents; her father was born in Maryland, and served in the War of 1812; her mother was born in England.

Mr. Linkhart attended the public schools of Johnson County, and in 1881, was graduated from the law department of the University of Iowa. He has been associated with the firm of Linkhart Brothers at Coleridge, since 1884; this firm was active in the settlement of northeastern Nebraska, and especially of Cedar County. At this time he is a director in the Coleridge National Bank, is a member of the Nebraska State Historical Society, and holds membership in the Nebraskana Society. He has been chairman of the Red Cross since 1917, has served several terms as a member of the local school board, and is a member of the Masons and the Eastern Star. He is affiliated with the Coleridge Congregational Church and the Republican party.

He was united in marriage with Salome Rebecca Schaffer at Oxford, October 12, 1881. Mrs. Linkhart was born, of Pennsylvania Dutch ancestors, at Bellfonte, Center County, Pennsylvania, November 4, 1856. To this union three children were born: Anna Mable, born April 21, 1884, who died February 10, 1905; Blanche C., born July 28, 1885, who married James R. Whittier; and Alfred Rae, born January 19, 1887, who married Isa Ford. Mr. Linkhart acted as food administrator for Cedar County during the World War. Residence: Coleridge.

Thomas Jefferson Linn, Sr.

Thomas Jefferson Linn, Sr., farmer and stock raiser, was born at Kimball, Minnesota, October 23, 1885, son of James Edgar and Sarah Catherine (Campbell) Linn. His father and mother were united in marriage near Kimball, Minnesota in 1873. In 1886 they came to Nebraska and homesteaded in Keith County, nine miles southwest of Paxton. His father who was a stock raiser and farmer all his life, was residing two miles west of Paxton at the time of his death, August 7, 1928, and his mother was residing in Paxton at the time of her death, June 13, 1930.

He is married to Helen Etola Terry, who was born at Mercer County, Illinois, the daughter of William and Edna E. (Frank) Terry. Their marriage was solemnized at Ogallala, Nebraska, August 4, 1926. She is a member of the Lutheran Church, the Rebekahs, and the Royal Neighbors of America. They have three children, Thomas Jefferson, Jr., born March 31, 1927; Dorothy Marie and Donna Bell, born September 24, 1929.

A Republican, Mr. Linn has been county commissioner since January 8, 1925. His term expires January 1, 1933. He is a member of the Independent Order of Odd Fellows of which he was secretary 1923-29, and scribe in 1923-28, the Rebekahs, the Patriarchs Militant, and the Modern Woodmen of America of which he was clerk in 1919 and 1920. His religious affiliation is with the Lutheran Church. His favorite sport is huntng. Residence: Paxton.

Louis J. Lintz

Louis J. Lintz, prominent Deuel County farmer, was born in Louisville, Kentucky, August 4, 1861, of French ancestry. He is the son of Michael M. and Magdelena (Schmitt) Lintz. Michael M. came to the United States at the age of 16, and died at Wamego, Kansas, at the age of 92 in 1920.

On March 3, 1891, he was married to Lucile Helen Berlet at Omaha. She was born at Brock, Nebraska, October 15, 1868. They have four children, Alice born December 3, 1891, who married Lawrence Dirks; Opal, born July 3, 1893; Roy Peter, born May 20, 1895; and Mark Michael, born January 23, 1899, who married Irene Johnson of Big Spring, Nebraska, in January, 1926.

Mr. Lintz is a Republican. He has in previous years been engaged as a merchant at Talmage, and banker at Johnson, and is now a farmer. He is a member of the Odd Fellows and the Knights of Pythias, and has been a resident of Nebraska for 44 years. Residence: Big Spring.

Earle Lester Lionberger

Earle Lester Lionberger, prominent merchant at Superior, was born at Humboldt, Nebraska, April 11, 1890. He is the son of Frederick and Wilhelmina (Speiser) Lionberger, the former a traveling salesman for many years. Frederick Lionberger was born at Humboldt, July 13, 1861, his parents having come to America from Switzerland, in 1840, and having settled in Nebraska in 1857. Wilhelmina Speiser was also a native of Humboldt, born March 24, 1864. Her parents came from Germany, in 1855, pioneering in Richardson County, Nebraska in 1857. Prior to her death at Superior, on December 29, 1925, she took an active part in musical and study clubs, women's clubs, and the Order of Eastern Star of which she was past worthy matron.

Educated in the grade and high schools of Superior, Earle L. Lionberger was graduated in 1908, and in 1912 received his Bachelor of Science degree from the University of Nebraska. He was a member of the University Glee Club and of Alpha Chi Sigma. In 1913, he entered into the retail shoe business, in which he has since continued.

On March 25, 1919, Mr. Lionberger was united in marriage to Ina Marie Roe, at Webber, Kansas. Mrs. Lionberger was born at Superior, May 14, 1897. There is one daughter, Ruth, born September 22, 1927.

During the World War he was a private in the Nebraska detachment of the Provost Marshall Generals Department. He is a member of the American Retailers Association, the National Shoe Retailers Association, and the Superior Chamber of Commerce.

A Mason, and Shriner, he is affiliated with the First Presbyterian Church of Superior, is a member of the Nebraska State Historical Society, the Nebraskana Society, the National Geographic Society and the University Club. His hobby is reading. He is independent politically. Residence: Superior.

Philip Dodridge Littrell

A pioneer Nebraska farmer, Philip Dodridge Littrell has been a resident of the state for more than fifty-eight years. He was born on his father's farm in Mahaska County, Iowa, December 23, 1857, son of James and Margaret (Oldham) Littrell.

James Littrell, who was born of American parents, was of Scotch descent. He engaged in farming all his life, settling in Nuckolls County in its early days. On May 15, 1894, his death occurred at his home farm. His wife, Margaret Oldham, was a native of Indiana, her family having come originally from Kentucky. She died at Oak, Nebraska.

Philip D. Littrell attended country school in Mahaska County, Iowa, and came with his parents to Nebraska in 1873. Two years later, on April 28, 1875, he was united in marriage to Sarah Josephine Wehrman at Nelson. To them were born five children, Edna, born December 19, 1887, who married William Jensen; Jessie May, born September 25, 1892, who married Lloyd Roberts; Irvin J., born January 12, 1894, who married Romaine McVey; Paul M., born September 7, 1898, who married Hazel Mullet; and Verna G., born July 25, 1901, who married W. L. Eckles.

Mr. Littrell, who is now retired, was for many years one of Nuckolls County's most prosperous and successful farmers. He has always taken an active interest in civic affairs, is a member of the Republican party, the Christian Church and the Nebraskana Society. Residence: Nelson.

Guy Ernest Livermore

Guy Ernest Livermore, editor and publisher, was born near Mount Ayr, Iowa, October 17, 1875, son of Millard Filmore and Sophia Estella (Hatch) Livermore. The father was born on a farm in Louisa County, Iowa, August 27, 1850 and died in Custer County, Nebraska, March 13, 1892. The mother was born at Canton, Ohio, April 3, 1854, and died at Sargent, November 4, 1921.

Mr. Livermore attended public and high school and the University of Nebraska the summers 1908-11. In 1910 he obtained a state teacher's certificate. He taught in rural and city schools until 1903, farmed the following year, taught from 1904 until 1916, when he purchased the *Sargent News* and *The Sargent Leader*. On April 1, 1916 he combined the two papers, which he has owned and operated since under the name of *The Sargent Leader*.

On September 1, 1908, he was married to Mary Elizabeth Miller at Broken Bow. Mrs. Livermore was born near Moulton, Iowa, November 12, 1885, They have six children, Leland Clele, June 14, 1909, who married Madge May Coen; Clarice Wauneta, July 7, 1912; Roscoe Luverne, August 14, 1914; Wanda Floy, December 10, 1915; Lucille Marie, June 4, 1922; and Merwyn Miller, August 17, 1925.

Mr. Livermore is a member of the First Methodist Church, the Lions Club, the Odd Fellows and the Nebraskana Society. His hobby is raising flowers and gardening. Residence: Sargent.

Daniel Webster Livingston

A native of Otoe County, Daniel Webster Livingston is an outstanding figure in its legal and political life. He is the son of James and Euphemia (McLeod) Livingston, and was born February 13, 1873. James Livingston was born in Scotland, August 16, 1826, and settled in Indiana. In 1863 he came to Nebraska and homesteaded in Otoe County. He studied for the ministry in Scotland, and later taught school there. He died in Otoe County in 1901. Euphemia McLeod, his wife, was born at Prince Edward Island, Canada, about 1850. She was of Scotch descent. After her children were grown she devoted much of her time to caring for the sick and poor, and was greatly loved in her community. She died at Nebraska City, December 17, 1917.

Daniel Livingston was educated in the public schools of Otoe County, and taught school one year. He attended the University of Nebraska, where he was a classmate of Governor Weaver and other notables, and received his LL.B. in 1896. He was interested in literary work, and made a study of it also, while in school. He was also active in baseball.

On November 7, 1906, Mr. Livingston was married to Emma Schafer at Nebraska City. Mrs. Livingston was born at Nebraska City, January 1, 1874, and is of German descent. There are two children, Lucile Lydia, born December 8, 1907; physical director for girls in the Nebraska City school system; and Dale Wesley, born April 24, 1910.

Since his admission to the bar on June 11, 1896, Mr. Livingston has been engaged in the general practice of law at Nebraska City. He has filled various public offices and was elected city attorney for the term 1904-06; county attorney 1907-11 (2 terms); and served as a member of the Nebraska legislature in 1927. As a member of the lower house of the Nebraska legislature in 1927, he was one of the leaders in support of the measure for free bridges across the Missouri river, and in the debate in the lower house was one of those who took a leading part. He is a Democrat.

During the World War Mr. Livingston was chairman of the Otoe County Council of Defense; served as Government Agent, and was food and fuel administrator. He attends the Presbyterian Church, and is a member of the Nebraska State Bar Association and the Otoe County Bar Association. His fraternal organizations include

the Elks, Eagles, Modern Woodmen of America, the Woodmen of the World and the Masons. He is a member of the Ancient Free and Accepted Masons, the York Rite and Shrine Bodies. He is a member of the Nebraskana Society and the Nebraska State Historical Society. Since 1914 he has been a member of the school board, and was chairman from 1916-30. His favorite sport is football. His hobby is reading the histories of important trials. His club is the Nebraska City Country Club. Residence: Nebraska City.

Henry W. Locke

Henry W. Locke, owner of the Locke Studio at Grand Island, has been a photographer in Nebraska for many years. He has always taken an active part in the affairs of his community and was recently elected to membership in The Nebraskana Society in recognition of his achievements. Residence: Grand Island. (Photograph in Album).

Roy Randolph Lockwood

Roy Randolph Lockwood, son of Wellington Angevine and Marion Euletta (Goodrich) Lockwood, was born at Rock Rapids, Iowa, January 27, 1881. his father, born at Rice, New York, August 27, 1852, was the owner of a general mercantile business at Hebron for twenty-five years. His death occurred at Lincoln on May 22, 1919. Marion, his wife, was a native of Rolling Prairie, Wisconsin, born March 5, 1856. A graduate of Wayland University, she was also the composer of many beautiful poems. She died at Hebron, January 22, 1907.

Educated in the public and high schools of Hebron, Roy R. Lockwood was associated with his father's business in Hebron for ten years, and for fifteen years owned and operated a Ford Automobile Agency at Nelson. He is a Republican, and has served on the city council for eight years

His marriage to Iva Maebell Garmire was solemnized at Hebron on November 22, 1905. Mrs. Lockwood, who was born at Hebron, July 23, 1884, attended Lincoln Business College, and the Nebraska Conservatory, specializing there in piano and voice. Prior to her marriage she was a stenographer. There are two sons, Wilbur, born October 7, 1906, was graduated from Nelson High School in 1925. For two years he was a student at the University of Nebraska, taking a course in business administration, and at present is manager of the Mid West Commercial office at Rapid City, South Dakota. John D., born December 29, 1910 was graduated from Nelson High School. He has attended the University one year, studying medicine.

Mr. Lockwood has always lived in Nebraska, and during the mature years of his life has taken an active interest in all community and civic undertakings. He is a Mason, a member of the Red Cross and the Chamber of Commerce, and is also a member of The Nebraskana Society. His favorite recreation is golf. Residence: Nelson.

Frances Goodhue Loder

Frances G. Loder was born at Whitecloud, Michigan, September 18, 1904. George Harris Goodhue, her father, was born in Wisconsin, and her mother, Nellie Ella (Rockwood) Goodhue, was also born there.

Mrs. Loder received her elementary education in the grade school at Whitewater, Wisconsin. She attended high school at Goodland, Kansas, and in Chicago, and in 1927 was graduated from the Northwestern University School of Speech at Evanston, Illinois, with the degree B. L. She was awarded a diploma in the expression department of Nebraska Wesleyan University, 1926; and is a member of Pi Kappa Delta, Theta Alpha Phi, and

Phi Mu Gamma. She served as class treasurer during her junior year at Nebraska Wesleyan University; was a member of the grand council of Phi Mu Gamma and served as grand editor of this society, publishing *The Tri-Shield*.

She is now acting head of the expression department of Nebraska Wesleyan University. Her marriage to James Edwin Loder was solemnized at Lincoln, Lancaster County, Nebraska, December 23, 1930. Mr. Loder, who is an educator, was born at Waverly, Lancaster County, Nebraska, March, 1904. Mrs. Loder's hobbies are music and reading. She is fond of tennis. She is a Republican. Residence: Lincoln.

Maud Elizabeth Logan

Maud Elizabeth Logan was born at Montello, Wisconsin, February 4, 1882, daughter of Clarence Harvey and Eliza Ruth (Higgs) Pierce. Her father was born in Oneida County, New York, September 22, 1844, and died at Wilsonville, Nebraska, August 22, 1904. He was a banker at Wilsonville, from 1886 until 1898. He is descended from the Pierce family, who settled in Watertown, Massachusetts, in 1638.

His wife, Eliza Ruth Higgs, was born at Milwaukee, Wisconsin, October 12, 1848, and died at Lincoln, March 21, 1922. John Higgs, her father, came to Milwaukee from England in 1848. His wife, Sarah Barnette, was of English birth.

Maud Elizabeth Pierce attended Wilsonville High School until 1898, and afterward was a student at the University of Nebraska. There she was a member of Alpha Omicron Pi.

On January 27, 1915, she was married to William Henry Logan at Lincoln. Mr. Logan was born at Queen City, Missouri, September 15, 1882, and is state manager of the Peoria Life Insurance Company. He is descended from William Logan of Jo Daviess County, Illinois and James Powell Logan of Queen City, Missouri. Mr. and Mrs. Logan have one son, William Pierce, born November 2, 1915.

Mrs. Logan is a Republican. She is a member of Westminster Presbyterian Church, the State Historical Society, the State Genealogical Society, the University Club, and the Lincoln Country Club. Residence: Lincoln.

William Henry Logan

William Henry Logan, executive, was born at Queen City, Missouri, September 15, 1882, son of James Powell and Drusilla Mary Logan.

James Powell Logan was born at Elizabeth, Illinois, February 17, 1852, and was a merchant prior to his death at Amazonia, Missouri. His ancestry was Scotch-Irish. Mary Drusilla Logan was born in Greentop, Missouri, February 9, 1859. She is of English descent.

Mr. Logan attended public and high schools, and was graduated from business college at Quincy, Illinois, in 1899. From 1902 until 1904, he was associated with Ludlow-Saylor Wire Company at St. Louis, and with the McCormick Harvesting Machine Company of Ottumwa, Iowa. From 1904 until 1909, he was a traveling salesman for the International Harvester Company, and from 1909 until 1917 held the same position with the Parlin and Orendorff Plow Company. Since 1917 he has been with the Peoria Life Insurance Company, as manager for Nebraska at the present time. He is a Republican.

On January 27, 1915, he was married to Maud Elizabeth Pierce at Lincoln. Mrs. Logan was born at Montello, Wisconsin, February 4, 1882, and is of English descent. They have one son, William Pierce, born November 2, 1915.

Mr. Logan is a Mason, a member of the Hiram Club, the Lincoln Chamber of Commerce, the Kiwanis, and the Young Men's Christian Association. His religious affiliation is with Westminster Presbyterian Church of Lincoln.

He is a member of the Life Underwriters Association (director 1931), the Nebraska Life Agency Managers Association, and in 1930 served as president of the Nebraska Life Underwriters. His clubs are the University Club, and the Lincoln Country Club. His favorite sport is golf. Residence: Lincoln.

Hugh Latimer Lomax

Hugh Latimer Lomax was born at Cawker, Kansas, October 12, 1877, the son of Commodore Perry and Sarah Elizabeth (Latimer) Lomax. His father, who was born at Abingdon, Illinois, January 28, 1842, has been a farmer for many years, and later was court bailiff at Lincoln. He served in the 7th Illinois Cavalry during the Civil War. His mother, who was very active in the work of the Christian Church, was born at Abingdon, March 19, 1844, and died at Lincoln, December 23, 1923; she was descended from Captain Robert Latimer, who came to Boston, on the *Hopewell*, in 1635, and from William Brewster, who came to America on the *Mayflower*.

Rev. Lomax attended the public schools of Shenandoah, Iowa, and Bethany, Nebraska, and in 1896, was graduated from the Bethany High School. He received his A. B. from Cotner College, Lincoln, 1905; and was a student at Transylvania College, Lexington, Kentucky, 1907-08, and the University of Chicago, 1912. He represented Cotner College in four state oratorical contests and the state of Nebraska, in two interstate contests.

He has held the following positions: minister, Highland, Kansas, 1905-07; minister, Auburn, Nebraska, 1907-08; minister, Highland, 1908-13; minister, Abilene, 1913-15; minister of the Budd Park Christian Church, Kansas City, Missouri, 1915-19; field man for Cotner College, 1919-28; evangelist, Kansas Christian Missionary Society, 1928-30; and since that date, minister, Bethany Church of Christ.

Rev. Lomax is a member of the Nebraskana Society; the Bethany Church of Christ; and the Republican Party. He holds membership in Cotner Lodge Number 297, of the Ancient Free and Accepted Masons at Lincoln.

His marriage to Elsie Marie Hammill was solemnized at Bethany, August 3, 1903. Mrs. Lomax was born at Miller, Hand County, South Dakota, September 29, 1881. Their two children are: Louise, born August 18, 1909; and Ruth, born June 17, 1916. Louise was graduated from Cotner College in 1931. Residence: Lincoln.

Francis A. Long, M. D.

Born at Kreidersville, Pennsylvania, February 16, 1859, Francis A. Long is the son of Robert and Sarah Louise (Seip) Long. His father, who was successively a carpenter, miller and farmer, was born in Germany, about 1829, and died at West Point, Nebraska, September 9, 1903. He was descended from a family of note, and was a grandson of the minister to the King of Saxony. His mother was born near Danielsville, Pennsylvania, September 27, 1840, and died at West Point, August 31, 1927. Her ancestors were Revolutionary soldiers.

Dr. Long attended the public schools of Pennsylvania, and in 1878 finished the second year of high school at Moulton, Iowa. He received the degree of doctor of medicine from the University of Iowa in 1882. In 1894 and again in 1901, Dr. Long took post graduate work at the Chicago Post Graduate School and Hospital, and in 1915 received a fellowship in the American College of Surgeons.

Since 1882, Dr. Long has been engaged in general practice, including pioneer surgery, at Madison. He served as a delegate to the American Medical Association meetings at Atlantic City, 1907, Chicago, 1908, and Los Angeles, 1911, and was a delegate also to the Council on Medical Legislation and Education in the years 1909 and 1910. In 1910 he represented the Nebraska State Medical Association at the Second Conservation congress at St. Paul, Minnesota.

He probably performed the first operation for the removal of the appendix ever performed in north Nebraska, outside of Omaha, in December, 1892, and probably administered the first antitoxin in 1895. Dr. Long holds membership in the following organizations: Madison County Medical Society; Nebraska State Medical Association, and in 1906-07 was president of this organization; American Medical Association; Elkhorn Valley Medical Society; Missouri Valley Medical Society, and American College of Surgeons. He is a member of the American Association for the Advancement of Science, is president and a charter member of the Madison County Historical Society, and is a member of the Nebraska State Historical Society and the Nebraska Writers Guild.

Dr. Long is vitally interested in the Good Road Movement, and from 1923 to 1931 was vice president of the International Meridian Highway Association. He is the author of a number of articles on medical subjects, and since 1920 has been editor of the *Nebraska State Medical Journal,* for the creation of which publication Dr. Long was greatly responsible.

He has been president twice of the Madison Community Club, and is a member of the Norfolk Rotary Club.

His marriage to Maggie E. Miller occurred at West Point, Nebraska, December 2, 1884. Mrs. Long was born at Allentown, Pennsylvania, November 12, 1862, of Pennsylvania German parentage. Her ancestors came to America prior to the Revolution. She is a member of the Daughters of the American Revolution, has been active in Women's Club work, and is chairman of the endowment fund for the Nebraska Federation of Women's Clubs. She always has been active in Sunday School and Church work, and for the past 45 years has been an active Sunday School teacher in the Presbyterian Church, has been a member of the Madison Library Board since its inception, and for ten years during and following the war she was secretary of the South Madison County Chapter of the Red Cross.

Dr. and Mrs. Long have three children, Frances Louise, born September 7, 1885; Harriet Catharine, October 3, 1887; and Margaret Elenore, July 27, 1893. Frances received the Bachelor of Arts degree from the University of Nebraska, and the degree of Doctor of Philosophy from the University of Minnesota. She is now engaged in ecological research for the Carnegie Institution of Washington, D. C., at Santa Barbara, California. She is joint author with Dr. Frederick E. Clements of *Rubber Content of North American Plants,* and *Experimental Pollination.*

Harriet received the Bachelor of Arts degree from the University of Nebraska, attended the New York State Library school at Albany, receiving the degree of Bachelor of Library Science. Following the publication in 1925 of a volume on *County Library Service* she was given the degree of Master of Library Science by the same school. For ten years she was head of the Traveling Library Service of Wisconsin, and in 1931 became state librarian of Oregon, at Salem. During 1918 and 1919 she was in War Library Service, being first stationed at San Antonio, Texas, where she organized a library service for soldiers on the Mexican Border and the gulf coast. Later she was sent overseas and was in charge of the library of the A. E. F. (Doughboy) University at Beaune, France. Following the Army of Occupation into Coblenz, she took over an exclusive German officers clubhouse, and transformed it into a library for the American Army of Occupation.

Margaret, who received the Bachelor of Arts degree from the University of Nebraska is married to J. Wilbur Whisenand. Mr. and Mrs. Whisenand reside in Peoria, Illinois. They are the parents of three children, one son and two daughters. Residence: Madison. (Photograph in Album).

George M. Long

George M. Long was born at Kriedersville, Pennsylvania, April 9, 1864, the son of Robert and Sarah Louisa (Seip) Long. His father, who was a farmer, was born at Saxon, Germany, in 1829, and died at West Point, Nebraska. His mother was born in Pennsylvania, September 27, 1840, and died at West Point, August 30, 1927.

Mr. Long received his education in the public schools of Pennsylvania, and since 1879, has been a farmer in Cuming County, Nebraska. He is a member of the Congregational Church at Beemer; the Nebraskana Society; and the Modern Woodmen of America. He is a Democrat.

His marriage to Agnes Louis Fetzer was solemnized at West Point, July 28, 1888. Mrs. Long was born at Allentown, Pennsylvania, October 22, 1870. Four children were born to this union, two of whom are living: Charles H., born November 11, 1889, who died October 26, 1904; Emma E., born October 18, 1891, who married Percy C. Mellor, and who died June 8, 1930, Harvey V., born April 11, 1893, who married Laura Mae Trahm; and Zora Mae, born May 2, 1906, who is mathematics teacher in high school and a graduate of Hastings College in 1928. Harvey V. is a farmer near Beemer. Residence: Beemer.

John P. Long

John P. Long was born in Bedford County, Pennsylvania, February 19, 1857, the son of Joseph and Catharine (Pote) Long. His father, who was a farmer, was born in Bedford County, January 21, 1821, of Swiss ancestry, and died there October 18, 1892.

His mother, who was of Dutch descent, was born in Bedford County, March 21, 1824, and died there May 1, 1885.

Mr. Long, who is a merchant, has lived in Nebraska for 42 years. He is a member of the Chamber of Commerce at Tecumseh, and is affiliated with the Baptist Church there. He is a Republican. Residence: Tecumseh.

Rachel Ann Watkins Long

Rachel Ann Watkins Long, one of the few women physicians and surgeons of Nebraska, has lived in this state for the past 40 years. She was born at Neumedia, Pennsylvania, the daughter of Edward and Martha Permelia (Myers) Watkins. Her father, who was a farmer and stockraiser, was born in Columbia County, Pennsylvania, April 20, 1844, and died at Cambridge, Nebraska, August 4, 1922; he was a member of the Pennsylvania National Guards at the age of sixteen and a year later entered the Civil War as a member of Company H, 17th Pennsylvania Calalry.

Her mother was born at Mill Grove, Pennsylvania, July 29, 1846, and died at Holdrege, April 22, 1927. Her parents, whose ancestors came to this country with William Penn from England, were born in Pennsylvania.

Dr. Long received her education in the Lincoln Normal University, and the University of Illinois Medical College where she was graduated in 1906. She was a member of Nu Sigma Phi, the University Club of Illinois, the Writers Club of Chicago, the Speakers Bureau of Chicago; and served as vice president of her class at the University of Illinois.

At the age of 15 years she taught a rural school, was assistant principal at Curtis, Nebraska, served as dean of medicine at Dewey Camp, Washington, D. C., was instructor for the Red Cross from 1917 to 1924, and is now doctor of medicine and surgery at Holdrege, Nebraska, serving two years.

She is an outstanding figure in women's affairs at Holdrege, holding membership in the following organizations: Women's Club of which she is treasurer; Women's Christian Temperance Union; League of Women Voters; Legion Auxiliary of which she is district president; Professional and Business Women's Club; Red Cross, of which she has been treasurer for many years; the executive board of the City Welfare Society of Holdrege; the Young Women's Christian Association; Home and Foreign Missionary Society of the Methodist Episcopal Church; and the Ladies' Aid Society of which she was formerly president. She is a member of the Methodist Episcopal Church.

Dr. Long holds membership in the Phelps County Medical Society, the Nebraska State Medical Society, the American Medical Association, the Medical Women's National Association, is associate professor in neurology Club. She is regional director of the Medical Women's National Association, is associate professor in neurology of the University of Illinois Medical School, and from 1906 to 1911, was assistant superintendent of the Peoria State Hospital. She is a member of the Eastern Star, Royal Neighbors, and the Professional and Business Women's Club of Holdrege.

Her hobby is writing movies and public speaking. Her favorite sport is golfing. A Republican, she served as vice chairman of Phelps County Republican Committee for a number of years. She is the author of *What's In a Name*, and many short stories and poems. Her marriage to Charles Andrew Long occurred at Omaha, August 8, 1918. Mr. Long, who is a banker, was born of German and Scotch parents at Jackson, Ohio, August 8, 1870. Residence: Holdrege.

Thomas B. Long

Thomas B. Long was born in County Kilkenny, Ireland, December 8, 1865, the son of Thomas and Bridget (Butler) Long. His father, a pioneer farmer in Nebraska, was born in County Kilkenny, and died in Dakota County, Nebraska, April 15, 1883; he came to America, in 1875. His mother was born in County Kilkenny, and died there in 1873.

Mr. Long received his education in rural schools and through private study. He was employed by the Chicago, St. Paul, and Ohio Railway Company for 20 years, was a farmer for the next seven years, was in the grain and livestock business for about 10 years, and is now engaged in farming. He is also president of the Long Oil Company at Hubbard. A Republican, he served as county commissioner for 8 years, was precinct chairman of the Republican party, and was defeated for state railway commissioner.

During the World War he was a leader in Liberty loan campaigns, was active in Red Cross activities, and served as a member of the council of defense. He was director of the school board at Hubbard from 1910 to 1919, is a member of The Nebraskana Society, and is affiliated with St. Mary's Catholic Church. He is a member of the Knights of Columbus. His hobby is reading.

He was united in marriage with Mary Duggan, at Hubbard, February 12, 1890; she was born at Hubbard, March 17, 1866. They have six children, all of whom are living: Edward, born January 13, 1891, who married Gertrude Hall; Helen, born July 13, 1892; Frank, born May 31, 1894; Catherine, born March 10, 1896; Jettie, born November 27, 1897; Benedict, born May 18, 1900, who married Rose Hartnett. Edward is a grocer at Hastings Nebraska. Catherine teaches Latin in the South Sioux City Schools. Jettie, who maried Frank Walsh, is a home maker and teacher. Benedict is manager of the Long Oil Company. Residence: Hubbard.

Will Long

Will Long, publisher and editor of the *Hebron Register* at Hebron, Nebraska, has lived in this state all his life. He was born at Nelson, Nebraska, May 20, 1894, the son of Frank Warren and Rhoda (Tower) Long. His father, who was born July 25, 1871, was a farmer for many years and has been engaged in various business enterprises in Nebraska; his ancestry is Pennsylvania

Dutch and Irish. His mother was born December 23, 1872.

Mr. Long was graduated from the Nelson High School in 1914 and was a student in business college for a time. From 1920-3 he was the operator of a hydroelectric plant at Hebron, from 1917 to 1920 he was employed by the Hebron Roller Mills, and previous to that had been connected with the *Nucholls County Herald* at Nelson for two years. For the past seven years he has been editor of the *Hebron Register* formerly known as the *Register Champion*.

He is a member of the Nebraska Press Association, the South Central Press Association, the Chamber of Commerce, and the Nebraskana Society. He is affiliated with the First Christian Church of Hebron, is a member of the Red Cross, and holds membership in Lodge Number 43 of the Ancient Free and Accepted Masons, Blue Lodge. He is interested in football and is a member of the Hebron Golf Club. His hobbies are radio and electricity. He is independent in politics.

On July 29, 1917, he was united in marriage with Edna Carter at Nelson. Mrs. Long, who was born at Hebron, February 20, 1895, was a teacher before her marriage and has learned the linotype. Her ancestry is English, Spanish, and Irish. She is eligible to membership in the Daughters of the American Revolution and holds membership in the Hebron Woman's Club. Their children are: Lois, born March 21, 1918; Betty Jane, born March 5, 1921; and Thomas Carter, born June 18, 1923. Residence: Hebron. (Photograph on Page 729).

Carl Adolph Lonnquist

Since 1893, Carl Adolph Lonnquist has been a clergyman in Nebraska. He was born at Froderyd, Sweden, September 27, 1869, the son of Johan Reinhold Lonn and Johanna (Carlson) Lonn, the former a miller who was born in Sweden, in 1845, and died there in 1894. His mother was born in Sweden, December 25, 1849, and died there December 25, 1887.

Dr. Lonnquist was graduated from Wexio College in Sweden, studied at Upsala University in that country for a year, and for two years was a student at the Rock Island Seminary where he was ordained to the ministry. He came to America in 1891. He was awarded the D. D. degree at Augustana College in 1919.

He has taken part in the business and religious affairs of Nebraska in the following capacities: pastor, Stromsburg, 1893-1896; pastor, Axtell, 1896-1921; director of Bethphage Mission at Axtell, since 1917; director of the Lutheran College, 1914-20; director of the Augustana Book Concern, 1921-23; and statistician of the Nebraska Conference, 1893-1900. He is the author of four volumes of poetry, published in 1906, 1911, 1913, and 1916, and of various articles for papers and magazines. Since 1917 he has been editor of the monthly magazine *Guldax*.

Dr. Lonnquist is a member of the Augustana Historical Society and the Nebraskana Society. His hobby is writing poetry and his political affiliation is with the independent branch of the Republican party.

His marriage to Esther Cedilia Magnuson was solemnized at Orion, September 27, 1893. Mrs. Lonnquist was born at Swedona, Illinois, December 24, 1871. She is the daughter of Carl and Johanna (Hultgren) Magnuson. Four children were born to this union: Martha Flavia, August 2, 1898, who married John Rost, Jr.; Hilding Raymond, February 9, 1900, who married Leona Ingmanson; Doris Miriam Ingeborg, March 1, 1903; and Conrad Ivan, July 12, 1906. Hilding is a farmer, Doris is secretary to her father, and Conrad is employed in Omaha. Residence: Axtell.

Edward Lambert Loock

A general merchant at Diller for many years, Edward Lambert Loock was born at Peoria, Illinois, the son of Lambert Edward and Jana (Ojemann) Loock

WILL LONG

His father was born at Arle, Anst Berum, Ostfreslund, Germany, June 12, 1831. A baker and merchant, he came to America as a young man, settling at Peoria, where he died on May 1, 1916. His wife was born at Nordan, Ostfreslund, July 20, 1833, and died at Peoria, December 10, 1930, at the age of ninety-eight.

Edward Lambert Loock, Jr., attended public school, and soon thereafter entered the business world. In addition to his mercantile business, he is president of the Diller Telephone Company. For many years he was president of the Diller school board.

On July 23, 1885, he was united in marriage to Helen O. Murfin at Mount Pleasant, Nebraska. Mrs. Loock, was born in South Burgen, New Jersey, June 26, 1864, and came to Nebraska in September 1869. There were two children born to their marriage, Gertrude, born September 7, 1887, married Edward R. Henrichs; and Charlotte, born August 8, 1889, who died March 22, 1931.

Mr. Loock held the rank of colonel under Governor Morehead. He is a member of the Lutheran Church, the Red Cross, the Chamber of Commerce and the Knights of Pythias. His hobby is reading. Residence: Diller.

Lewis Samuel Loomer

Lewis Samuel Loomer, pioneer resident of York County, Nebraska, is a retired farmer and bank director at York. He was born at Sugar Creek, Wisconsin, February 22, 1855, the son of Timothy and Almira (King) Loomer. His father, a farmer, was born in Nova Scotia, Canada, September 3, 1819, and died at York, October 14, 1916. His mother was born at North Pomfret, Vermont, April 10, 1821, and died at York, October 4, 1913.

Mr. Loomer has been prominent in public activities for many years, and is now a director in the First National Bank of York, the First National Bank of Bradshaw, and the Farmers State Bank of Bradshaw. He is a member of the Elks, is affiliated with the Congregational Church, and holds membership in the Nebraskana Society. He is a trustee of York College.

He married Mary Ellen Wild at Geneva, Wisconsin, January 3, 1877. Mrs. Loomer, who was a teacher before her marriage, was born at Union, McHenry County, Illinois, June 6, 1857. She is descended from John Vandervost. To this marriage six children were born, four of whom are living: Lewis Earl, born August 8, 1878, who married Elizabeth Clark; Lila May, born December 20, 1879, who died January 14, 1884; George Edward, who died May 31, 1883; Hazel, who died September 18, 1888; Ruth Alda, born December 31, 1890, who married R. N. Gilbert; and Ruby Elva, born December 31, 1890, who died September 12, 1928. Residence: York.

Florence Geddes Loomis

Florence Geddes, daughter of Frederick Lyman and Kate Adele (Rosebrugh) Geddes, was born at Toledo, Ohio, July 7, 1890. Frederick Lyman Geddes, who was born at Adrian, Michigan, November 10, 1850, received his B. A. and M. A. degrees at the University of Michigan and was a corporation lawyer at Toledo for more than 50 years. His ancestry is traced to Scotch-Irish settlers in America in 1752. He died at Baltimore, Maryland, October 9, 1930.

Kate Adele Rosebrugh Geddes was born at Tecumseh, Michigan, September 18, 1853. She was president and one of the foremost in founding the Toledo Woman's Club. She resides at Toledo, Ohio.

Upon her graduation from public school, Florence Geddes entered the MacDuffie School at Springfield, Massachusetts, and received her B. A. from Smith College in 1913. She was active in dramatics, and member of the cast of *Taming of the Shrew.*

On December 18, 1915, she was united in marriage to John U. Loomis, at Toledo. Mr. Loomis is a lawyer (see *Nebraskana*). They have two children, John, born September 12, 1916, and Frederick, born February 26, 1926.

After her marriage Mrs. Loomis established her home at Omaha, where she has been very active in the social and cultural life of the city. A member of the Junior League of Omaha, she served as its president during 1929-30 and 1930-31. She is secretary of the Omaha Symphony Board, and since 1928 has been a member of the budget committee of the Community Chest, and a member of its board of governors. Mrs. Loomis is a Unitarian and a Republican. She is active in educational work and is a member of the Parent-Teachers Association. Her clubs are the Toledo Woman's Club, the Smith College Club, and the Book Club. Residence: Omaha.

George Linden Loomis

Born at Harmony, Chautauqua County, New York, November 28, 1849, George Linden Loomis has been an outstanding resident of Fremont for many years. He is the son of Daniel and Hannah (Scofield) Loomis, the former born at Tompkinsville, New York, August 25, 1805. Daniel Loomis was a Methodist clergyman who preached in the same church at Ashville, New York, 40 years. He also engaged in farming and was a quarryman. His death occurred at Harmony, in 1866. Simon Loomis, father of Daniel, was a soldier in the Revolutionary War, while his father and grandfather served in Colonial Wars. There have been ten generations of the family in America, and its genealogy is traced to England, in 1400. Hannah Scofield Loomis was born at Saratoga, New York, in 1813, and died at Harmony, December 22, 1895. A fine wife and mother, she reared fourteen children. She was the daughter of Josiah and Ann Scofield.

George L. Loomis attended the public schools of Blockville and Harmony, New York, and received his LL.B. from the Union University at Albany, in 1875. The following year he moved to Iowa, remaining but a year, and in 1876, settled in Fremont, and for fifty-five years has been head of the law firms of Loomis & Abbott, Loomis, Laird and Loomis, and at the present time Loomis & Loomis, with his son, Howard. In 1930, Mr. Loomis resigned as director of the Equitable Building and Loan Association after thirty-three years of service, being succeeded by his son, Howard. For many years he was a director of the Commercial National Bank and president of the Home Savings Bank. For eight years he was a director of the Union National Bank, but resigned in 1930. He has been a notary public fifty years.

A Democrat, Mr. Loomis served two terms as state representative, and was Democratic candidate for Supreme Judge in 1907. City and county attorney each two terms, he was appointed by President Wilson collector of internal revenue, serving seven years. He is the author of *History of Oddfellowship* in *Morton's History of Nebraska.*

Active in fraternal and civic organizations, Mr. Loomis served as grand master of the Odd Fellows, 1889-90, was national instructor 30 years (still holding), grand representative eight years, and trustee of the Odd Fellows Home fifteen years. For thirty-three years he was a director of Doane College, and for eleven years he was a member of the Fremont School Board.

A Son of the American Revolution he has held both state and local presidencies. He has served as state moderator of Congregational Churches, and is a life deacon of the Community Church at Fremont. One of the founders of the Commercial Law League of America, he is also a member of the Nebraska State and Dodge County Bar Associations, and was president of the latter from 1911-31. He is a member of the Chamber of Commerce, the Young Men's Christian Association, the Nebraskana Society, the Loomis Genealogical Association, and the Nebraska State Historical Society.

He was married to Alice Marie Hadley, daughter of Zela and Sarah (Scofield) Hadley, on July 21, 1880. Mrs. Loomis was born in Hillsdale County, Michigan, November 1, 1856, and formerly taught music. She was a church organist for seven years. There are five sons and one daughter: Bayard, born August 25, 1881, who is married to Florence Roberts, is associated with the Publix Theatres in Omaha. Leo Alice, born September 20, 1884, married Judge Fred C. Laird. Floyd, born July 18, 1886, married Vera Fulkerson, and for fifteen years has been associated with the *Oregon Journal* at Portland, Oregon. Zela Hadley, born February 10, 1891, married Svea Lindecranz, is associated with Hon. Edgar Howard, and is vice president of The Telegram Company at Columbus, Nebraska. Howard Waldron, born September 19, 1893, was graduated from the University of Nebraska Law School in 1915; is a past president of the Nebraska State Elks Association and was at one time city attorney of Fremont. Wayne is associated with the law firm of Loomis & Loomis. Mr. Loomis died at Fremont, March 22, 1932.

John Usher Loomis

John Usher Loomis was born at Salina, Kansas, April 2, 1893, son of Nelson Henry and Christie Addison (Campbell) Loomis. Nelson Henry Loomis, who is a native of Vermont, is general solicitor for the Union Pacific Railroad, and is of English descent. Christie Addison Campbell was born in Kansas and is of Scotch descent.

Mr. Loomis received his elementary education in the public schools of Topeka, Kansas, and was graduated from Central High School at Omaha. He received his A. B. from Dartmouth in 1915, and his LL. B. from Columbia University in 1918. He is a member of Psi Upsilon and was a letterman and manager of the football team at Dartmouth. In 1918 he was attache at the American Embassy in London.

He was admitted to the bar at Omaha in February, 1919, and has since been engaged in active practice. He is now a member of the law firm of Kennedy, Loomis and Offutt. He is a Republican. Since 1926 he has been a member of the Omaha School Board. For two years he was chairman of the teachers' committee, and is now vice-president.

On December 18, 1915, he was married to Florence Dority Geddes of Toledo, Ohio. They have two children, John U., Jr., born September 12, 1916 and Frederick G., born February 26, 1926.

Mr. Loomis is a member of the American, Nebraska State and Omaha-Douglas County Bar Associations, the Chamber of Commerce and the Pro Tem Club. Since 1927 he has been a member of the Omaha Council of Girl Scouts. His club is the University Club. Residence: Omaha.

Nelson Henry Loomis

Nelson Henry Loomis, general solicitor for the Union Pacific System, was born at Highgate, Franklin County, Vermont, June 28, 1862, son of Merle W. and Ellen Bradberry (Hungerford) Loomis.

Mr. Loomis attended public and high school in Chicago, and Evanston, Illinois, and received his degree of Bachelor of Laws from the Missouri Valley College at Marshall, Missouri, finishing at Hastings College at Hastings, Nebraska.

He was married to Mary Campbell of Salina, Kansas, September 23, 1885. She died June 12, 1888. There is one son, Alexander Campbell. Mr. Loomis was next married to Christie Campbell of Salina, Kansas, on August 12, 1891. Their children are, John Usher and Robert Henry.

In 1883, Mr. Loomis was admitted to the bar, and in 1885 entered the law department of the Union Pacific Railway at Lawrence, Kansas, as a stenographer and law clerk. He became assistant attorney general of the Union Pacific railway for Kansas and Missouri at Topeka, 1891-1902, and was general attorney for Kansas and Missouri until 1908. He was general solicitor May 1, 1908, until July 16, 1918, and since March 1, 1920.

Mr. Loomis is a member of the American Bar Association and the Nebraska State Bar Association and the Sons of the American Revolution. His clubs are the Omaha Club, the University Club, and the Dome Whites Club. Residence: Omaha.

Walter Phelps Loomis

Walter Phelps Loomis, district claim agent for the Chicago, Burlington and Quincy railroads, was born at Omaha, Nebraska, November 6, 1888, son of George Walter and Mary Lucy (Waggoner) Loomis. His ancestry is English.

Upon the completion of his elementary education in the Omaha Grade Schools, he attended the Omaha High School from which he was graduated in 1906. In 1910 he received his Bachelor of Science degree from the University of Nebraska.

His marriage to Isabel Elizabeth Treweek was solemnized at Omaha, May 29, 1926. Mrs. Loomis was born at Lead, South Dakota, July 1, 1891. She attended high school at Lead, South Dakota, and was a student of music at Columbia University in New York City. She was a prominent teacher of music prior to her marriage. There are two children, Walter P. Jr., born September 17, 1927; and Jean Elizabeth, born August 1, 1930.

Since leaving school Mr. Loomis has been in the law and claims department of the Chicago, Burlington and Quincy. He is a member of Alliance Lodge No. 183 of the Ancient Free and Accepted Masons, and Scottish Rite Alliance Consistory. His fraternities are, Beta Theta Pi, and Phi Beta Kappa.

During the late war Mr. Loomis served with base hospital No. 49 in France. His favorite sport is hunting. He is a Republican, and a member of the Nebraskana Society. Residence: Alliance.

Benjamin Franklin Lorance

One of Nebraska's most noted educators and physicians is Dr. Benjamin F. Lorance. Born at Gentryville, Missouri, December 8, 1858, he has been a resident of Nebraska for more than sixty-five years. He is the son of William Huston and Mary Minerva (Hill) Lorance. His father was French, born at Sweetwater, Tennessee, July 20, 1825. He died at Auburn, June 18, 1913. Dr. Lorance's mother was also born at Sweetwater, on January 20, 1832. She died at Brownville, October 10, 1886. Her parents were of English descent.

Dr. Lorance was graduated from Brownville High School May 30, 1878, and attended the University of Nebraska from 1879 to 1881. On November 2, 1882, he was united in marriage to Farie Blankenship. Mrs. Lorance was born at Peru, November 2, 1864, and died at Auburn, December 24, 1919. She was of English descent. Their children are as follows: Bertha B., born September 12, 1883, married W. E. St. John; Bessie, born December 5, 1885, married J. S. Wilson, M. D.; Ottie G., born October 17, 1888, married V. L. Strickland; Martha M., born March 14, 1893, married Raymond Kiechel; Helen, born December 3, 1894, married Wiley Langford; Celia, born September 3, 1898, married L. H. Hochhquertel; Benjamin F., Jr., born October 4, 1904, died November 11, 1911. On February 17, 1921, Dr. Lorance was married to Pearl Stevenson.

Identified with the educational interests of Nebraska for more than forty years, Dr. Lorance has served as principal of East School at Beatrice, 1887-92; as superintendent of Hebron city schools 1892-94; member Auburn board of education 1907-27; president Nebraska Association School Boards and School Executives 1927-28, etc.

Admitted to practice as a physician at Beatrice, on February 4, 1892, he has been engaged in the practice of medicine and surgery in Nemaha County 36 years, Brock 11 years and Auburn for the past 25 years. In 1904 and also in 1907 he took a post graduate medical course at Polyclinic Hospital in Chicago.

He is the author of *Medi-Cult, The A-B-C of The*

BENJAMIN FRANKLIN LORANCE

Medical Profession (Gorham Press, Boston, 1924); *Religious Instruction and the American Public School* (Gorham Press, 1924); *Another Case of Acromegaly* (Western Medical Review, 1898); *Cesarian Section With Report of a Case* (Western Medical Review, April 1905); *The Lower Femoral Epiphysis* (Western Medical Review, 1908); *A Few Facts about the Circulation System* (Nebraska State Medical Journal, February 2, 1924); etc.

Dr. Lorance is a member of the American Medical Authors Association, the American Medical Association, and the Nebraska State Medical Society. From 1896 to 1928 he was secretary of the U. S. Pension Board of Nemaha County. From June 20, 1917 until the close of the war he was a member of the Nemaha County local draft board, and was a four minute speaker. He is a member of the Voluntary Medical Service Corps, 1918. He is affiliated with the First Presbyterian Church of Auburn, and is a member of the Chamber of Commerce and Kiwanis Club. His annual address given in February, 1928, before the meeting of the Nebraska School Boards and School Executives Association was published by the association and given statewide circulation. The title of the address was *The American Public School and its Critics*. Among his fraternal organizations are the Masons, Odd Fellows, Modern Woodmen of America, Woodmen of the World, Royal Highlanders, Ancient Order of United Workmen, Order of Eastern Star, etc. He is a member of the Nebraska Historical Society and the Nebraskana Society, together with the Nebraska Y. M. C. A. Residence: Auburn. (Photograph on Page 734).

Joshua Speed Lord

On November 11, 1865, Joshua S. Lord was born at Rushville, Illinois. His father, Joseph Lord, was a weaver who came to America from England, in 1844. Born at Rochdale, England, in 1826, he died February 10, 1874 at Salem, Nebraska, where for many years he was a prominent farmer.

His mother, Anna (Boyd) Lord, was born at Boonville, Missouri, November, 1828, of Irish parents, and died at Salem, August 21, 1904.

Until 1884, Mr. Lord was a farmer. He entered the drug business in 1889 and continued in that work until 1904. A Democrat, he was a member of the state legislature in 1905; and from 1906 to 1910 was county treasurer of Richardson County. He became cashier of the First National Bank of Falls City, Nebraska, January, 1910, and has held this position since that time. He is also interested in farming and stock raising.

He was united in marriage with Eliza Price Boyd at Falls City, July 2, 1882. Mrs. Lord was born at Oregon, Holt County, Missouri, February 10, 1863. Three children were born to this union, two of whom are living: Vera, born November 15, 1887, who died November 10, 1916, was married to Russell Amos Hiatt, who died in 1924 from wounds received in the World War; J. Harold, born November 11, 1892, who married Vera M. Watson; and Mildred M., born October 5, 1895, who married Lewis W. Davies.

In the late war Mr. Lord was county chairman of liberty loan drives; he is a life member of the Red Cross. While he is not affiliated with any orthodox religious organization, he believes in practicing the golden rule. He is a member of the Odd Fellows and the Modern Woodmen of America. Residence: Falls City.

Gus Lorentz

A resident of Sherman County, Nebraska, for the past 42 years, Gus Lorentz was born in Sweden, February 25, 1873, the son of Nickolauson and Magalena (Jonasdotter) Lorentz. His father was a carpenter. Mr. Lorentz received his education in Sweden and since his arrival in Nebraska in April, 1889, has been the proprietor of a men's clothing and furnishing establishment.

He is a member of the Commercial Club, the Nebraska Retail Clothiers, the Nebraska Retail Association, and the Masonic Lodge. He is affiliated with the Presbyterian Church, is a member of The Nebraskana Society, and for nine years has been a member of the school board at Loup City, Nebraska. Mr. Lorentz's hobby is carpentry and some of his sports are hunting, fishing, golfing and skating. He is independent, politically.

His marriage to Libbie Erzim was solemnized at Loup City, June 25, 1905. Mrs. Lorentz was born at Ravenna, Nebraska, February 28, 1887, and died at Loup City, July 24, 1931. Their two children are Arnold, born August 12, 1908, who is a clothier; and Lucile, born September 6, 1913. Residence: Loup City. (Photograph in Album).

Grant Lothrop

Grant Lothrop, lawyer, and former superintendent of schools at Pilger, was born in Blair, Nebraska, October 17, 1890. His parents, John and Hortense (Landon) Lothrop, were natives of Michigan, the former born at Grand Rapids, February 23, 1853, and the latter at Pontiac, October 15, 1851. They resided in South Dakota several years, and brought their family to Washington County in 1881. John Lothrop died at Blair, December 22, 1929. His wife is still living. Hortense Lothrop's grandfather served as a soldier in the Revolutionary War.

Educated in the public and high schools of Blair, Grant Lothrop was graduated in 1910, and received his B. A. from the University of Nebraska, in 1914. He was admitted to practice by the Supreme Court of Nebraska on August 20, 1916, and has since been engaged in the practice of law. A Democrat, he is now living at Pilger.

Mr. Lothrop is married to Elma Adell Doty, their marriage having been solemnized at Council Bluffs, Iowa, April 22, 1926. Mrs. Lothrop, who was born at Pilger, February 6, 1900, is of Mayflower ancestry, and a member of the Daughters of the American Revolution. Their one child died at birth.

During the World War Mr. Lothrop was a private in the United States Army, and participated in the St. Mihiel offensive and the Meuse-Argonne engagement. He is a Methodist, and a life member of The Nebraskana Society. Residence: Pilger.

John Arthur Lothrop

John Arthur Lothrop, master farmer of Saline County, was born at Dubuque, Iowa, June 15, 1885, the son of Franklin B. and Katherine (McCallum) Lothrop. His father, who is a contractor, was born in Grant County, Wisconsin, July 3, 1844; he is a Civil War veteran; his English ancestors came to America on the *Mayflower*, and members of the family were prominent in the Revolution. His mother was born in Dubuque County, Iowa, August 15, 1850, and died at Crete, Saline County, Nebraska, May, 1925; her parents came to America from Scotland shortly before her birth.

Mr. Lothrop was graduated from high school in Dubuque, in 1902, and in 1908 was graduated from Doane College at Crete, with the B. S. degree. He was a member of Alpha Omega and was valedictorian of his college graduating class. He has lived in Nebraska since 1904, and for many years has been one of the outstanding poultry farmers of the state. He owns a 175 acre farm where he cares for 3000 laying hens. In 1929 he was one of the ten men in the state to receive the Master Farmer Award, a solid gold medal given in recognition of progress in farm work.

He is a member of the Crete Rotary Club; the Masonic Lodge; and the Nebraskana Society. He is a member of the Master Farmers of America. He is a deacon in the First Congregational Church of Crete. His hobby is beautifying his house and its surroundings. He is a Republican.

Mr. Lothrop was united in marriage with Edna Elinor

Cobb at Minneapolis, Minnesota, October 26, 1910. Mrs. Lothrop, who was born at Geneva, Nebraska, June 20, 1887, was a teacher for two years before her marriage; her ancestors were English and Connecticut Yankees. She is eligible for membership in the Daughters of the American Revolution; her children are members of the Children of the American Revolution. They have four children: Dorothy Mae, born July 27, 1911, who is a student at Doane College; John Arthur, Jr., born February 21, 1914, who is a student in the Crete High School; Helen Jean, born December 19, 1915; and Franklin Cobb, born October 27, 1928. Residence: Crete.

Edwin Jacob Loutzenheiser

One of Nebraska's leading bankers is Edwin Jacob Loutzenheiser, who was born at Chelsea, Iowa, June 4, 1882, and for the past 25 years has been an outstanding figure in the political, civic and professional life of his community and state, and served as mayor of Gothenburg 1921-1922. His father, William Reed Loutzenheiser, who was a farmer, financier and banking official, was born at Massillon, Ohio, January 11, 1843, and died at Gothenburg, Nebraska, November 14, 1931; his ancestors came to this country from Germany in 1764.

His mother, Martha Belle (Clem) Loutzenheiser, was born at Helena, Iowa, January 28, 1860, and died at Gothenburg, January 8, 1931. Her Scotch and Irish ancestors settled in the United States prior to 1800. Mr. Loutzenheiser received his elementary education in the public school of Iowa, and attended the business college at Cedar Rapids, Iowa, in 1900 and 1901.

He served as assistant cashier of the Chelsea State Bank from 1902 to 1903, was in charge of the bank at Elberon, Iowa, in 1903, served as assistant cashier of the First National Bank of Chelsea, 1904-05, and was cashier of the Gothenburg National Bank from 1906 to 1915. He is vice president of the Gothenburg State Bank at this time, and holds the following positions in community organizations there: past president of Group Number Five of the Nebraska Bankers Association; past president of the Kiwanis Club; and chairman of the local society of the American Red Cross.

Mr. Loutzenheiser is affiliated with the First Methodist Episcopal Church of Gothenburg, holding membership in the Men's Brotherhood of the church. He served as the first president of the Gothenburg Library Board in 1913 and aided in securing contributions toward establishing the library at Gothenburg. He is a 32nd degree Mason, serving as Past Master of Lodge Number 249, Past Venerable Master of the Lodge of Perfection at Gothenburg, and a member of Tehama Shrine of Hastings. He is a member of the Gothenburg Country Club, and is fond of golf and baseball. His hobby is reading.

He served for 15 months as a member of the Nebraska National Guard just before the World War and in 1917 and 1918 was active in Liberty loan drives and War Savings Stamp campaigns. On November 25, 1910, he was married at Gothenburg to Anna Wicklund. Mrs. Loutzenheiser, who is of Swedish descent, was born at Ogallala, Nebraska, February 25, 1889. Six children were born to them: June Bernice, June 30, 1912; Edwin, Jr., July 17, 1917; Carolyn, September 3, 1919; William Reed, August 28, 1924, who died April 2, 1925; Marian Anne, February 21, 1926; and Thomas Beaton, October 8, 1924. Residence: Gothenburg. (Photograph in Album).

Homer Clyde Loutzenheiser

One of the leading business men at Gothenburg, Nebraska is Homer Clyde Loutzenheiser who was born at Chelsea, Iowa, December 1, 1883, came to Gothenburg in April, 1909 and has made his home here since that date. His father, William Reed Loutzenheiser, who was a farmer and bank director, was born at Massillon, Ohio, January 11, 1843, and died at Gothenburg, November 14,

1931; his ancestry was Pennsylvania Dutch. His mother, Martha Belle (Clem) Loutzenheiser, was born at Helena, Iowa, January 28, 1860, the daughter of Richard M. and Mary (Hiatt) Clem, and died at Gothenburg, January 8, 1931.

Mr. Loutzenheiser attended rural school in Iowa, was a student at the Toledo High School for a year, and took a commercial course at Cedar Rapids Business College. He has been engaged in real estate and insurance business since his arrival in Gothenburg in 1909, and is now the owner and operator of the Gothenburg Real Estate Agency.

On October 16, 1907, he married Besse Lorraine Wilson at Chelsea, Iowa. Mrs. Loutzenheiser, who is the daughter of David W. and Jennie (Vickery) Wilson, was born at Belle Plaine, Iowa, October 26, 1885. There are four children, three of whom are living: Rex, born February 9, 1909, who died April 6, 1914; Donald Wilson, May 16, 1910; Homer Clyde, born August 26, 1915; and Ruth Lorraine, born February 29, 1920.

Mr. Loutzenheiser is past president of the Gothenburg Chamber of Commerce, is president of the Kiwanis Club, a member of the Red Cross, and a member of the First Methodist Episcopal Church of Gothenburg. He is a Master Mason, Past Master of Masons, and Scottish Rite Mason, was city clerk for seven years, served as a member of the board of education for nine years acting as secretary most of that time, and is a member of the board of directors of the Gothenburg County Club. During the World War he served in draft registrations, Red Cross drives, and loan activities. His hobby is golf.

Donald, Mr. Loutzenheiser's oldest son was graduated from the University of Nebraska School of Civil Engineering in 1931, and is now employed by the United States Department of Public Works as junior engineer in the Bureau of Roads. Residence: Gothenburg.

Don Lothrop Love

Don Lothrop Love, lawyer and banker at Lincoln, Nebraska, was born at Jonesville, Wisconsin, March 7, 1863. His father, Horace Love, who was a farmer, was born in Chautauqua County, New York, January 26, 1820, and died in Calhoun County, Ohio, October 27, 1880; his ancestry was English and Scotch. His mother, whose ancestors were English and Scotch, was born in Cayuga County, New York, October 10, 1824, and died at Malvern, Iowa, March 3, 1910.

Mr. Love was graduated from Centennial Academy at Malvern, and received the A. B. degree at the State University of Iowa, where he held membership in Delta Tau Delta. He was engaged in the practice of law from 1888 to 1916, was vice president of the Lincoln Safe Deposit and Trust Company, was vice president of the Lincoln National Bank, was treasurer of the Lincoln Joint Stock Land Bank, and served as president of the Lincoln Liberty Life Insurance Company.

He has been distinguished in public affairs for many years and has held a prominent place in Republican political activities in state, community, and national duties. Among the offices he has filled are: acting county judge, 1896; mayor of Lincoln, 1909-10; delegate at large to the Republican National Convention, 1910, 1916, 1920; committee on resolutions, 1920; member Republican State Committee, 1912; and mayor of the city of Lincoln, since 1929.

Mr. Love is treasurer of the Lincoln Joint Stock Land Bank, is president of the Lincoln Liberty Life Insurance Company, and holds membership in various civic organizations at Lincoln. He served as president of the local school board, 1907-08, was president of the Nebraska Art Association, 1910-12, and is serving as a member of the board of directors of the latter at the present time. He was president of the Nebraska State Historical Society from 1919 to 1921 and since 1921 has been a director in that organization. He holds membership in the Lincoln

Chamber of Commerce, the Red Cross, Kiwanis Club, and the Nebraskana Society. He is a 32nd degree Mason.

Mr. Love's social clubs include: University Club, Lincoln Country Club; The Club; Candlelight Club; and Laymen's Club. His favorite recreation is golfing, while his hobby is reading. During the World War he served as chairman of the draft board at Lincoln, 1917-18.

His marriage to Julia Larrabee was solemnized at Clermont, Fayette County Iowa, August 20, 1890. Mrs. Love, who is the daughter of Governor William Larrabee of Iowa, was born at Clermont, January 3, 1867. Residence: Lincoln.

Joseph Richard Love

Joseph Richard Love, son of George and Elizabeth (Allen) Love, was born in Madison County, Indiana, February 13, 1864. His father was born in County Tyrone, Ireland, July 13, 1834, of Protestant Irish parentage. He engaged in farming in Washington County until his death at Blair, September 2, 1892. Elizabeth Allen, his wife, was born in Ireland, of Protestant parentage, June 9, 1834, and died at Blair, March 30, 1896.

Educated in the rural schools of Nebraska, Mr. Love has been engaged in farming since manhood. He was married to Mattie Loreen Stewart, who is of Pennsylvania Dutch, Irish and Scotch descent, at Blair, July 12, 1899. Mrs. Love was born at Minden, Missouri, December 11, 1874.

There are eight children of this marriage, as follows: George Aubrey, born May 17, 1900, a graduate of Cotner, 1928; Stewart, born September 18, 1901, who attended the University of Nebraska for two years, and married Pauline Peters; Joseph Ross, born August 3, 1903, who married Lela Mae Burger; Drusilla, born June 19, 1906, who married Charles Harold French; Gertrude, born April 7, 1908, attended Cotner for two years and Nebraska University for one year; Mary, born July 31, 1910, who is studying nursing at the Methodist Hospital at Omaha; Elizabeth, born May 11, 1913; and Charles, born August 17, 1915.

Mr. Love is a Democrat and has been a continuous resident of the state since October, 1869. He is a Protestant, a Mason and a member of the Nebraskana Society. Residence: Blair.

George Washington Lovercheck

George W. Lovercheck, retired farmer of Belvidere, Nebraska, was born at St. Louis, Missouri, March 9, 1853, the son of Charles and Jane (Walton) Lovercheck. His father, who was born in Bohemia, came to Nebraska with his wife in the early nineties, and died at Belvidere. His mother was born near St. Louis, and died at Belvidere.

Mr. Lovercheck has lived in this state for 51 years, and for the past 22 years has been retireed from active farm life. He has been a trustee in the Christian Church of Belvidere for several years, was formerly a member of the Ancient Order of United Workmen, and is now a member of the Royal Highlanders and the Nebraskana Society.

He was married to Anna Eliza Brinnegar at St. Louis, August 17, 1880. Mrs. Lovercheck is an active member of the Christian Church and takes a prominent part in various women's societies in that organization. Four children were born to this marriage: Edwin Eugene, who resides at Los Angeles, California; Stella, who married James Day, and is now living at Lindell, Wyoming; Grover, who is married and lives at Guernsey, Wyoming; and Theodore, who resides at Hastings, Nebraska. In 1930 Mr. and Mrs. Lovercheck ceelebrated their golden wedding anniversary; they have ten grandchildren. Residence: Belvidere.

Raymond Fletcher Low

Raymond F. Low was born at Chicago, Cook County, Illinois, July 19, 1891, the son of Wilson Henry Low and Marion Ware (Fletcher) Low. His father, who is retired, was born in Massachusetts. His mother was born in Massachusetts.

Mr. Low began his business career as solicitor of insurance with the Foster-Barker Company, and later became vice president of this firm. In October, 1924, he organized and became president of the American Reserve Life Insurance Company and is still in this position. He has lived in Nebraska since 1898.

His marriage to Edith Norton Cornish was solemnized at Little Rock, Arkansas, April 9, 1919. Mrs. Low was born in Arkansas. They have two children: Richard, born February 12, 1923; and Marion Phoebe, born May 12, 1927.

He served in the First Officers' Training Camp, 1917, as first lieutenant; was aid de camp to General W. D. Connor in France, during the World War. He is a member of the American Legion. He is president of the Covered Wagon Area Council of the Boy Scouts of America, this area covering 30 counties. He is a member of the Omaha Chamber of Commerce; Omaha Club; Omaha Athletic Club; and the Omaha Country Club. Residence: Omaha.

Charles Riley Lowe

Charles Riley Lowe, a clergyman, was born near Gardner, Kansas, September 19, 1879. He received his elementary education in several Kansas towns, Waterville, Hutchison, Wichita, and Chapman. In 1894, he went with his parents to Jerico, Missouri, where he graduated from the high school in 1896. During the next three years he taught two terms of school, one at McDonald, Carter County, Missouri, and one in Cedar County, Missouri. The rest of the time he was studying at home under the tutelage of his father. In February, 1900, he entered Midland College, located then at Atchison, Kansas, now at Fremont, Nebraska. He received his Bachelor of Science degree from that institution in 1904. That same fall he entered Western Theological Seminary, graduating in 1907, and received his Bachelor of Divinity degree in 1908. Mr. Lowe was ordained by the Nebraska Synod of the United Lutheran Church in America September 15, 1907, at Grand Island, Nebraska.

While attending school he held the broad jump record, he was catcher on the baseball team during his whole college career, on the football team he was at center and guard one year, halfback one year, and fullback three years. He was interested in all the school activities.

James Angus Lowe, his father, a clergyman, was born at Smicksburg, Pennsylvania, October 22, 1851, and was educated at Wittenburg College at Springfield, Ohio, where he received his Master of Arts degree in 1874, and following that, his theological training. About 1899 he received his Doctor of Philosophy degree from the University of Arkansas.

Anna Eugenie (Wertz) Lowe, mother of Charles, was born in Oregon, Illinois, May 20, 1851. Before her marriage, she was a high school teacher in Rockford, Illinois. As a pastor's wife she was much interested in missionary work. Her death occurred at Wilber, June 4, 1912.

On May 17, 1907, Mr. Charles Lowe was united in marriage to Ava Lauretta Blessing of Auburn, Nebraska. She was born at Middletown, Maryland, July 15, 1882. She was a milliner before her marriage.

They have two daughters: Frances Eugenie, born at Rising City, Nebraska, August 14, 1909, who is at Midland, class of 1932; and Grace Louise, born at Benedict, Nebraska, July 5, 1913, at Midland, class of 1936, who is preparing to be a librarian.

Mr. Lowe has been in Nebraska during the years 1902 to 1909, and from 1912 to the present time. He was pastor of the United Lutheran Church at Rising City, three and a half years, at Waterloo, Iowa, two and a half years, at

Benedict, Nebraska, three years, at Dakota City, Nebraska, six years, stated supply at Hebron, Nebraska, Presbyterian Church one year. He is now pastor of the United Lutheran Church at Beatrice, where he has been since 1923. This is his home church, his father having been pastor there from 1902 to 1908, and he having been a member of that church when he entered the ministry. This has been Mr. Lowe's longest pastorate and the longest in the history of Trinity Lutheran Church.

The religious, civic and educational organizations to which Mr. Lowe belongs are The Ministerial Association of which he is president 1925 to 1932; Kiwanis, of which he was local trustee, 1928 and 1929, district trustee 1931, member of the international committee of Kiwanis Education, appointed 1931; city free library board, chairman since 1927-31.

Mr. Lowe is fond of outdoor life and camping, is a carpenter by trade. His hobbies are photography and bookbinding, and he has written numerous articles for photographic journals. Residence: Beatrice.

Clarence George Lowe

One of Nebraska's noted educators and authors is Clarence G. Lowe, professor of classics at the University of Nebraska. He was born at Columbus, Bartholomew County, Indiana, May 30, 1897, the son of Edward F. and Matilda (Pfeifer) Lowe. His father, who is an insurance agent, was born in Knox County, Indiana, in 1867. His mother was born at Columbus.

Dr. Lowe attended St. Peters Evangelical Lutheran School, and was graduated from the Columbus High School in 1915. He was awarded the following degrees: A. B., Franklin College, 1919; A. M., University of Illinois, 1921; and Ph. D., University of Illinois, 1924. He was elected to membership in the Alpha Society, honorary scholastic organization at Franklin College, and was a fellow in classics at the University of Illinois, 1922-4.

From 1924-5, he served as instructor in classics at Yale University, was assistant professor of Latin at Washington University, 1925-7, and was associate professor of the classics at the University of Nebraska, from 1927 to 1928. He has been professor of classics and chairman of that department at the University of Nebraska, since 1928.

Dr. Lowe is the author of: *Manuscript Tradition of Ps. Plutarch's Vitae Decem Oratorum,* (1924); *A Byzantine Paraphrase of Onasander* (1927). He has also written many articles and reviews published in philological journals. He is a member of the American Association of University Professors, the Classical Association of Middle West and South, Classical League, American Philological Association, Mediaeval Academy of America, the Linguistic Society of America, and American Archeological Association.

He is a member of the Red Cross and the Nebraskana Society. He is an Independent, politically, and is affiliated with the Lutheran Church. His hobbies include reading and travel. He was united in marriage with Clotilde Rose Pelkus at St. Louis, Missouri, August 15. 1926. Mrs. Lowe was born at Bellville, Illinois, March 25, 1906. Residence: Lincoln.

John Gibbons Lowe, Sr.

John Gibbons Lowe, Sr., banker, was born in Liverpool, England, October 19, 1865, and came to the United States in 1882. He is the son of Stephen and Ellen (Gibbons) Lowe. The family was Irish for several generations, but John Gibbons Lowe was born in England. He received his education in the Church of England and Wesleyan schools.

On November 20, 1900, he was married to Grace Smith at Kearney. She was born at Tuscola, Illinois, November 12, 1869. There are four children, John G., Jr., born March 5, 1902, who married Ethyl Spencer; Dorothy El-

len, born August 22, 1903; Marion L., born January 6, 1906; and Stephen, born May 29, 1910.

For several years in his younger days Mr. Lowe was connected with the Union Pacific railroad and the Western Union Telegraph Company. For 40 years he has been president of the Farmers State Bank of Kearney, and in 1931 was president of the Nebraska Bankers Association. He was president of the Buffalo County Bankers Association, 1929-30, and is treasurer of several local organizations. He is a member of all Masonic bodies, and in 1895 was a member of the Nebraska National Guards.

A Republican, Mr. Lowe has held several minor offices, and has served as a member of the board of education, and the city council at Kearney. Residence: Kearney.

Theodore Lowe, Jr.

Theodore Lowe, Jr., county clerk of Lincoln County, was born at North Platte, Nebraska, March 30, 1886, son of Theodore and Mary (Schwerdt) Lowe.

His father, who was born in Hamburg, Germany, June 16, 1850, served with the 3rd United States Cavalry from 1873 until 1878. He was an early homesteader near McCook, Nebraska, an early railroad worker, and was later the proprietor of a cigar store. His wife, Mary, was born in Alleghany, Pennsylvania, November 18, 1860. Her ancestry is also German.

Mr. Lowe attended public and high schools of North Platte, and from 1901 until 1913 was clerk for the Union Pacific Railroad. He was the organizer, in 1913, of the Artificial Ice and Cold Storage Company at North Platte, in which business he continued until 1917. From 1917 until 1922 he was general yard master of the Union Pacific Railroad.

A Democrat, Mr. Lowe has served continuously as county clerk the following terms: 1923-27; 1927-31; 1931-35. He has resided in Nebraska all his life.

On June 21, 1914, he was married to Lena Wangen at Rawlins, Wyoming. Mrs. Lowe was born at Aurland, Norway, August 30, 1888. They have two children, Donold, born June 30, 1915; and Robert, born February 2, 1928.

Since 1930 Mr. Lowe has been chairman of the Citizens Military Training Camp. He is affiliated with the First Lutheran Church, is a member of the Masons, Odd Fellows, and Elks, and is secretary and treasurer of the Lincoln County Historical Society. His hobby is tree planting. Residence: North Platte. (Photograph in Album).

B. Frank Lowery

B. Frank Lowery, clergyman and newspaper editor at Davenport, Nebraska, was born at Gridley, Illinois, February 7, 1874. He is the son of Walter W. Lowery and Mary E. (Young) Lowery. His father was born at Stark, Ohio, September 19, 1853, of German parentage, and died at Hansen, Idaho, August, 1922. His mother, who was of English and German parentage, was born in McClean County, April 26, 1853, and died there in March, 1885.

Mr. Lowery attended public schools and later studied at home. He was a teacher in Illinois, and in 1896, commenced preaching, continuing his private studies in English and Greek. He came to Davenport, in 1895, and has been prominent there in educational and religious activities since that date. He is the author of numerous articles published in religious and educational publications, and since 1909, has been the editor of the *People's Journal.* From 1927 to 1929, he was business manager for Harding College at Morrilton, Arkansas, which he helped organize in 1924.

He is affiliated with the Church of Christ at Davenport, and has served 13 years on the local school board. During the World War he was a four minute speaker, sold savings stamps and Liberty bonds, and was prominent in Red Cross work. He was chief of the fire department for five years at Davenport. Hiking, reading, and gardening, are his favorite recreations.

His marriage to Clara I. Padgett was solemnized at Davenport, July 10, 1898. Mrs. Lowery, who was formerly a school teacher, was born at Glascow, Barren County, Kentucky, December 16, 1872. To this union six children were born: Nellie Ruth, born February 3, 1900, who married Reuben L. Sanner; Rose Marie, born January 29, 1902, who was awarded the A. B. degree at Harding College, where she later taught; Frances Ruby, born February 27, 1904; Inez Lillian, born July 13, 1906, who married Delbert H. Sanner; J. Frank, born April 25, 1911; and Clara Frances, born January 3, 1913. Frances Ruby received the A. B. degree at Harding College, taught at Harding, and at Rockport, Missouri, and in 1931 was awarded the A. M. degree at the University of Oklahoma. Residence: Davenport. (Photograph in Album).

John Frederick Lubker

John Frederick Lubker, who has been a farmer in Nebraska for the past 35 years, was born in Saunders County, August 8, 1877, the son of Claus Henry and Frauke Odefy Lubker. His father, who was born March 26, 1842, in Germany, and died at Cedar Bluffs, Nebraska, June 27, 1919, was a farmer and in business at Wahoo and Cedar Bluffs, for seven years, and served as county commissioner for six years. He came to America in 1869. His wife, who also came to this country in 1869, was born in Germany, March 5, 1843, and died at Cedar Bluffs, October 15, 1910.

Mr. Lubker is now president of the Farmers Union Co-operative Association at Cedar Bluffs, is president of the Farmers Assessment Fire Insurance Company of Saunders County, is a director in the County Farm Bureau, and is secretary of the local Farmers Union Society. He has been a member of the local school board for 30 years, is affiliated with Salem Lutheran Church at Fremont, Nebraska, and holds membership in the Nebraskana Society.

During the late war he was active in loan drives and took a prominent part in Red Cross relief work. He is a Republican. His favorite recreation is reading.

His marriage to Alvina Martha Daufeldt was solemnized at Cedar Bluffs, March 16, 1902. Mrs. Lubker was born in Germany. To this union the following children were born: Henry, born January 27, 1903, who married Ruby McCauley; John, born March 17, 1907, who married Emma Johnson; Filda, born May 28, 1909, who died November 24, 1917; Arthur, born February 23, 1915; Alvena, born May 26, 1916; Francis, born March 6, 1918; Kathryn, born September 18, 1922; and Vernon, born May 6, 1924. Mr. Lubker has always been interested in educational affairs and is active in the progress of his community and state. Residence: Cedar Bluffs.

Emil Fred Luckey

Born at Columbus, Nebraska, February 27, 1897, Emil Fred Luckey has been engaged in the practice of law there since his admission to the bar in 1922. He is the son of Fred and Mary Catherine (Engel) Luckey, the former born in Germany, October 25, 1859, and the latter in Cincinnati, Ohio, April 5, 1868. Fred Luckey came to America at the age of seven, and has engaged in farming all his life. His wife is of German descent.

Emil F. Luckey attended country grade school in Platte County, was graduated from Columbus High School in 1916, and received his Bachelor of Laws degree from the University of Nebraska in 1922. He is a member of Sigma Phi Epsilon and Phi Alpha Delta.

A Republican, Mr. Luckey was elected state senator from the 20th district, comprised of Platte, Merrick and Nance Counties 1925-26, and is now serving his second term as county attorney of Platte County. He served a three year enlistment with the Nebraska National Guard, Collecting Company (medical unit) which was stationed at Columbus.

He is a member of the Platte County Bar Association, the Red Cross, Salvation Army, the Chamber of Commerce, Elks, Eagles and Knights of Pythias. He is a member of the Lutheran Church, the Young Men's Christian Association and the Wayside Country Club. He enjoys golf and bridge. Residence: Columbus.

J. Guthrie Ludlam

A resident of Nebraska since January 16, 1894, J. Guthrie Ludlam has been secretary of the Board of Education since 1916. He was born near Springfield, Illinois, December 9, 1875, son of Jeremiah Johnson and Laurenna Jane (White) Ludlam. His father, born near Springfield, was a general insurance agent whose ancestors came from Yorkshire, England, in 1640, settling at Southhampton, Long Island, and moving in 1692 to Cape May County, New Jersey.

Laurenna White Ludlam was born at Evansville, Indiana, July 4, 1852, and died at Chicago, May 14, 1908. For many years she was a business women in Bloomington, Illinois. Her mother was a native of New Jersey, and her father of Scotch-Irish descent, his ancestors migrating from the South of Ireland to Kentucky. He was a Presbyterian minister.

Educated first in the public schools of McLean County, Illinois, Mr. Ludlam was graduated from Stanford High School in McLean County in June, 1893. In 1894, he came to Nebraska, where he taught in the public schools of Hallam and Cortland. On February 5, 1898, he was united in marriage to Lena Caroline Dietrich at Lincoln. Mrs. Ludlam was born at Ironton, Ohio, May 8, 1878. Her parents came from Germany and settled at Ironton, later homesteading near Hallam, Nebraska. They have four children: Julius G. Guthrie, who married Florence Shondra. He is assistant manager of Schmoeller and Mueller Music Company and is an orchestra leader. Mabel Louisa, who married William D. Lamb, is a graduate of the University of Nebraska with a B. F. A., and an orchestral leader and teacher of violin. Helen Dorothy and Earl are both unmarried.

A Republican, Mr. Ludlam served as first assistant postmaster of Lincoln, appointed under the provisions of the Civil Service Act, and advanced during sixteen years of service 1900-1916 from city distributor to chief distributor, acting superintendent of money order division, postoffice of Lincoln; also acting custodian of postoffice, 1911-16. During 1915, he served as acting postmaster. Since 1916, he has been secretary of the Board of Education.

Mr. Ludlam has always been active in civic and community projects, and was a worker in Loan drives in the World War, worker and team captain in the Bryan Memorial Hospital drive, etc. Formerly he was a member of the Lincoln Advertising Club, the Chamber of Commerce, Rotary Club and Modern Woodmen of America. At the present time he is a member of the Knights of Pythias, Ancient Free and Accepted Masons, Lincoln Lodge No. 19, and the National Association of Public School Business Officials. Affiliated with Saint Paul's Methodist Episcopal Church, he is secretary of its official board. He enjoys hiking, and his hobbies are landscaping and picture taking. Residence: Lincoln.

Robert Arthur Luehrs

Robert A. Luehrs, lumber and coal executive at Fremont, Dodge County, Nebraska, was born at Kankakee, Kankakee County, Illinois, September 5, 1882. His father, Henry Christoffer Luehrs, who was born at Hanover, Germany, March 24, 1857, and died at Kankakee, December 6, 1923, was foreman of a tile and brick company for many years, and later was engaged in the coal business; he came to America from Germany in 1861. Margaret Barbara (Hess) Luehrs, his mother, was born at Louisville, Kentucky, December 9, 1857; her ancestry is Swiss.

Mr. Luehrs attended school at Kankakee, until 1898, when he became a carpenter. He was a building contractor for 32 years, and today is president of the Luehrs-Christensen Lumber & Coal Company. He is vice president of the Park Side Apartments, and is the owner of the Nearcourt Apartments, a business building, three residences, and a 160 acre farm. He is also president of the People's Co-operative Store at Fremont.

His marriage to Bessie Fauquet was solemnized at Wahoo, Saunders County, Nebraska, September 25, 1908. Mrs. Luehrs, who was a teacher before her marriage, was born at Cedar Bluffs, Nebraska, and died at Fremont, December 27, 1919; her ancestry was French. Four children were born to this union, Glen Clair, born April 10, 1910; Wilbur Ralph, born November 11, 1909; Arthur Robert, born February 28, 1917; and Bessie Marie, born December 27, 1919. Glen is a high school teacher. Mr. Luehrs was married to Adolphine Feichtinger, a trained nurse, at Wahoo, January 24, 1921.

He is a director of the Chamber of Commerce, the Retail Association, and the Young Men's Christian Association. Since 1929 he has been president of the Fremont School Board, and for several years has been trustee of Midland College and Grand Island College. He is affiliated with the First Baptist Church at Fremont, is a member of the Odd Fellows, and holds membership in the Nebraskana Society. He is a Republican. His sports include hunting, fishing, and boating. Residence: Fremont. (Photograph in Album).

Eric Luhn

A lifelong resident of this state, Eric Luhn was born at Blue Hill, Nebraska, September 18, 1894, the son of Peter and Wilhelmina Catherine (Frahm) Luhn. His father, who was born at Oconto, Wisconsin, February 28, 1865, is a retired farmer. His mother was born of German parents at Fuersville, Missouri, November 10, 1867.

Mr. Luhn was graduated from the elementary schools of Webster County in 1905 and was graduated from the Christian Day School in 1909. He is a member of St. Pauls Lutheran Church, is past director of the Blue Hill School Board, and holds membership in the Nebraskana Society and the Masonic Lodge.

During the World War he served as a private in the United States Army and at this time he is a member and Past Commander of the American Legion at Blue Hill.

On March 7, 1925, he married Helen Barbara Schulz at Blue Hill. Mrs. Luhn, who was a teacher before her marriage, was born of German parentage at Blue Hill, February 24, 1901. They have two children: Rodney Gene, born May 12, 1926; and Marion Suzanne, born June 7, 1931. Residence: Blue Hill.

William Albert Luke

William Albert Luke, general secretary of the Lincoln Young Men's Christian Association, has lived in Nebraska for the past 44 years. He was born at Swan, Iowa, April 11, 1885, the son of John Wister and Anna Elizabeth (Emery) Luke. His father, who was born in Scott County, Kentucky, February 28, 1858, has been a rancher in northwest Nebraska for many years, and was a pioneer railroad man in Nebraska; he is of English and German descent. His mother was born near Dayton, Ohio, March 27, 1860, and died at Phoenix, Arizona, March, 1925; her ancestors were German.

Mr. Luke attended the public schools of Holdrege, Nebraska; was a student at Crawford High School; and was graduated from Chadron Academy, 1906. He received his A.B. degree at Doane College, Crete, Nebraska, 1911, and took some graduate work at the University of Nebraska, later. He won his honor letter in athletics at Doane College, 1910-11, and was all-Nebraska captain both years. He was a member of Alpha Omega at Doane

and Alpha Sigma Phi at Nebraska.

He has been interested and active in educational-religious work for the Young Men's Christian Association for many years, and has held the following executive positions; lay committeeman, Chadron Academy, 1902-05; assistant secretary of the railroad Young Men's Christian Association, Chadron, 1905-06; community secretary, Crete, Nebraska, 1906-07; college Young Men's Christian Association secretary, Doane College, Crete, 1907-09; Nebraska state Young Men's Christian Association college field secretary, 1909-10; assistant general secretary, Lincoln, 1910; and general secretary, 1911 to date. His administration in this office has continued to the present day, during which time the Central Building has been financed and completed, the Hi-Y Branch Building has been built and the permanent boys camp known as Camp Strader has been added. Throughout, his leadership has been marked by splendid service of constructive order and of loyal enthusiasm.

In the opening period of the World War, Mr. Luke was assigned to the Central Department Y. M. C. A. work, with executive headquarters in the city of Chicago. In this position he was instrumental in helping organize Y. M. C. A.'s at many army posts and cantonments in the middle states. Near the close of the World War he was detailed to Y. M. C. A. service overseas, and was about to sail for France when the sudden death of one of his children resulted in a delay in sailing for this patriotic service. The Armistice in the meantime was declared.

In addition to the above he has been a member of the board of directors of Estes Park 1913 to date; member of the constitutional convention of the Young Men's Christian Association of the United States and Canada, held at Cleveland, 1923; national councilman of the Young Men's Christian Association of the United States, Chicago, 1926-8, 1930; member of the Estes Park Summer School Faculty of the National Young Men's Christian Association, 1922-29; member of the United Summer Schools of the Western Region of the National Young Men's Christian Asciation, 1930; member of the National Physical Education Committee of the United States, 1929-30; and member of the National Young Men's Christian Association of the Church Councilling Commission of the United States, 1930-31.

Mr. Luke is the editor of the *Red Triangle;* was editor of the *Rotary Propellor,* 1926-27; and is the author of many articles. During the World War he was a member of the home guards and took part in Young Men's Christian Association war work, attached to the central division. He is a member of the Red Cross; the board of directors of the Welfare Society; the executive committe of the Council for Social Agencies; Lincoln Chamber of Commerce; Rotary Club; State Historical Society; the Nebraskana Society; and the Lincoln Young Men's Christian Association. He was one of the organizers and a former member of the executive committee of the Lincoln Community Chest. He holds membership in these fraternal and social clubs: Odd Fellows; Masonic Blue Lodge; Candlelight Club; and the Lincoln Musical Association. He is an honorary member of the Central Labor Union, and has served as a member of the Labor Temple Board. He is affiliated with the Lincoln Ministerial Association, of which he was secretary in 1924, and is a member of First Plymouth Congregational Church of Lincoln. Mr. Luke's political preference is the Republican party. His favorite sport is trout fishing.

He was married at Lincoln, January 12, 1912, to Hester Lura Thorpe. Mrs. Luke, who was dramatic art instructor at Doane College before her marriage, was born at Watertown, South Dakota, October 15, 1885. She is of English Canadian ancestry. They have four children: Katherine, born November 23, 1913; William, born March 9, 1915; Jean, born June 12, 1920; and John, born December 27, 1922. Residence: Lincoln. (Photograph in Album).

O. P. Lund

O. P. Lund, a resident of Dixon County, Nebraska, for the past 36 years, was born in Norway, June 6, 1862, the son of Peter O. and Jartrud (Johnson) Lund. His father, a carpenter, was born in Norway, and died there in 1918. His mother was born in Norway, and died there in 1892.

Mr. Lund, harness maker and shoe repairer at Maskell, Dixon County, Nebraska, has always been interested in the progress of his state and community. He is affiliated with Zion Lutheran Church, is a member of the Republican party, and holds membership in the Nebraskana Society.

He was married at Yankton, South Dakota, to Mary O. Rodney, who was born in Norway, and died at Yankton, October 12, 1886. In 1891, he was married to Rosey O. Birkley at Maskell. To this marriage the following children were born: Martin P.; Peter O., who died in 1921; Helma, who married Joel E. Johnson; Oscar O.; Olaf M.; Geneva, who married A. B. Dahl; Rudolph; and Violet, who married Arthur Rysta. Residence: Maskell.

Frank Otto Lundstrom

Born at Omaha, Nebraska, Frank Otto Lundstrom is the son of Charles E. and Anna Stina (Anderson) Lundstrom. His father, a native of Sweden, born August 2, 1848, came to America in 1879. He engaged in the contracting business until his death at Omaha, on May 9, 1924. His wife, Anna, was born in Sweden, November 25, 1847, came to America in 1881, and died at Omaha, October 23, 1929.

Frank Otto Lundstrom was graduated from the Omaha High School in 1905. A resident of Burt County many years, he was elected clerk of the district court in 1926, and still holds that position. Prior to that time he served as deputy county treasurer in 1914, and from 1915-22 was county clerk of Burt County.

Mr. Lundstrom was married to Bessie L. Green at Council Bluffs, Iowa, on April 19, 1911. Mrs. Lundstrom was born at Council Bluffs, November 29, 1888. To them were born three children: Frances Louise, born August 30, 1912; Louis Carl, born June 7, 1915, and Justin Frank, born August 20, 1918.

Always active in civic and fraternal organizations, as well as in educational projects, Mr. Lundstrom is chairman of the executive committee of the Burt County Chapter of the Red Cross, is a member of the Chamber of Commerce, is vice president of the Board of Education of which he has been a member since 1924. He is Past Master of Tekamah Lodge No. 31, Ancient Free and Accepted Masons, and Past High Priest of Mackey Chapter No. 24, Royal Arch Masons at Tekamah. His religious affiliation is with the First Presbyterian Church of Tekamah. His hobby is mechanics. Residence: Tekamah.

Claude Harold Lundy

Claude Harold Lundy, rancher and breeder of registered Hereford cattle, was born at New Providence, Iowa, April 12, 1882, son of Daniel and Sarah Ann (Jackson) Lundy.

The father, born in Lafayette, Illinois, January 13, 1841, died at Whitton, Iowa, November 30, 1914. He was a farmer, whose English ancestors came to the United States before the Revolution. He served three years in the Civil War. His wife, Sarah Ann, was born in Bucyrus, Ohio, December 26, 1844, and is still living. She was a teacher in her younger days, and is a great neice of Benjamin Lundy.

Claude Harold Lundy attended the Sheridan County schools, and was graduated from Chadron Academy in 1901. There he was valedictorian of his class and active in basketball and track, afterward he was a student at Doane College two years.

On June 4, 1907, he was married to Alice Rachel

Denton at Chadron. She was born at Corning, Iowa, October 10, 1882, of Dutch and Scotch ancestry. There are four children, Lora, born May 12, 1908; Lester, born August 13, 1909; Lena, born December 9, 1910; and Doris, born March 2, 1913. The two oldest daughters are in nurses training at the Denver General Hospital.

Mr. Lundy is a Republican. He is a member of the Friends Church, and was recently elected to life membership in the Nebraskana Society. Residence: Chadron.

James William Lundy

James W. "Bill" Lundy, Sargent, Custer County, Nebraska, real estate operator, rancher, engineer and legislator was born at Atalissa, Iowa, October 30, 1872.

He came with his parents to Custer County, September 12, 1882, and they homesteaded at West Union. His father, Ira J. Lundy, was born at Atalissa, Iowa, in 1850, and died at Taylor, Nebraska, June, 1903. His mother, Maria Gregg (Ady) Lundy was born at Atalissa, Iowa, and died at Taylor, June, 1903.

Mr. Lundy attended district school near West Union, taught in district No. 189 of Custer County, in 1903 and 1904. He is a member of the Presbyterian Church.

He was married to Laura Etta Anderson (See Nebraskana) of Loup County, Nebraska, October 31, 1894. To them were born four children, Sadie, Alpha, Leila, and Albro L.

A self educated engineer, Mr. Lundy was a pioneer in the water power development of the state of Nebraska, having built the Lundy Hydro-Electric Power Plant on the Middle Loup river, six miles west of Sargent, one of the first successful water power plants in central Nebraska. This bears his name, but is now owned by the Western Public Service Company.

A Republican, active in politics and public service, he was mayor of Sargent in 1920 and 1921. He was elected to the house of representatives from the 79th district of Nebraska in 1921, re-elected in 1923. He was an active member of the highway committee both sessions.

Mr. Lundy has served as Sergeant-at-Arms of the house of representatives of Nebraska in 1925-27-29 and 1931. This service has given him a wide acquaintance throughout the state, and he is known everywhere as "Bill Lundy." He is an optimist: a collector of smiles. An ardent football fan, he played football until 56 years of age. His chief hobby is good roads. He is the father of United States Highway No. 83, north and south through central Nebraska. He is an ex-director and a member of the Nebraska State Good Roads Association. He is a member and past grand of the Independent Order of Odd Fellows Lodge No. 162 of Nebraska. He is an active member of the Exalted Order of Yellow Dogs, and chief solicitor of the Legislative Kennel at Lincoln. He is a life member of the Nebraskana Society. Residence: Sargent. (Photograph on Page 742).

Laura Etta Lundy

Laura Etta Lundy of Sargent, Custer County, Nebraska, was born at Andover, Illinois, March 18, 1875. She came to Nebraska with her parents in 1882, they homesteaded near Taylor in Loup County.

Her father, Frans Johan August Anderson was born November 19, 1849, in Sweden, and came to Illinois when 16 years of age. Her mother, Rebecca (Garrett) Anderson, was born in 1845 in Ohio, and died at Sargent in May, 1914.

Mrs. Lundy was educated in the district schools of Loup County. She was married October 31, 1894, to James W. Lundy (See Nebraskana). To them were born four children, Sadie on September 24, 1898, who is now Mrs. Floyd Pulliam of Sargent, Nebraska, and who has two children, Reed and Merleen; Alpha, born January 17, 1899, who is now Mrs. Robert Taylor of Sargent; Leila, born August 23, 1900, who is now Mrs. William Faith of Scotia, and who has three children, Billie, Jr.,

Townsend—Lincoln

JAMES W. LUNDY

Elaine and Lyle; Albro L., the youngest child of Mr. and Mrs. Lundy, was born June 23, 1902. He is married to Terry Huseman of Lincoln. They now reside in Los Angeles, California.

Mrs. Lundy has always been associated with her husband in business. She is the owner of Doris Lake ranch, a well known summer resort near Sargent. She is a member, and past noble grand of the Valley Queen Rebekah Lodge No. 154; an active member of the American War Mothers (attended the National War Mothers Convention at Long Beach, September, 1931); is a member and past president of the Justamere Womens Club of Sargent, and a member of the Christian Church. She is an active member of the Ladies Legislative League of Lincoln. Recently she was elected to life membership in the Nebraskana Society. Residence: Sargent. (Photograph in Album).

Axel Victor Erland Lunner

Axel Victor Erland Lunner, merchant, was born in Sweden, March 22, 1868, son of Johannes and Maja Stina Anderson. The father, born in 1833, was a farmer and county judge, who died in 1897. The mother, born in 1834, died in 1902.

On June 24, 1896, Mr. Lunner was married to Lillie O. Hallquist who was born in Henry County, Illinois, January 30, 1872. To them the following children were born: Robert E., February 3, 1899, who married Aneita Lavely; Myra G., June 23, 1901, who married William Schapers and who died October 6, 1928; Edmund L., June 3, 1904, who married Deane Gleason; Evelyn V., December 13, 1907, who married Lloyd E. Corp; and Lola, July 15, 1909, who married William A. Schapers.

Mr. Lunner is a Democrat and has served as mayor, city clerk, and as a member of the city council. He is a former member of the board of education and has been president of the library board since its organization in 1916. He has been in the mercantile business for thirty years in Stromsburg, now as a senior member of the firm of Lunner & Johnson.

He is affiliated with the Salem Lutheran Church, the Red Cross the Commercial Club (former president and secretary), Stromsburg Lodge No. 126 Ancient Free and Accepted Masons, the Parent Teachers Association and the Modern Woodmen of America. Residence: Stromsburg.

Edward Francis Lusienski

Born at Columbus, Nebraska, December 24, 1884, Edward Francis Lusienski is the son of Konstance and Katherine (Juskewiec) Lusienski. His father, born in Galicia, Poland, followed the shoemaker's trade. Coming to the United States in 1881, he settled at Columbus, removing to Platte Center in 1889. There his death occurred on November 2, 1903. Katherine, his wife, was born in Galicia, and died at Platte Center on June 13, 1917.

Edward Francis Lusienski attended St. Joseph's Parochial School where he completed a course equivalent to the twelfth grade. Forced by circumstances to go to work, he was a retail merchandise clerk and afterward engaged in the plumbing and heating business. From 1914-19 he owned and operated the Clother Hotel, and from 1920-22 managed the Farmers Union Co-operative store at Monroe. In May, 1922, Mr. Lusienski opened the first cash produce store handling a full line, adding, in February, 1924, the editing of the *Radiogram*, a weekly newspaper.

At the present time Mr. Lusienski handles poultry, eggs and cream, operates the *Platte Center Radiogram*, and engages in the insurance business. In early life a Republican, he is now affiliated with the Democratic party. He was unsuccessful candidate for Platte county clerk in 1905; was township clerk of Lost Creek precinct about twenty-five years ago, and at present is a member of the village board of trustees, elected in 1928 by having his name written in on the ticket by 111 electors. In 1932 he was nominated for the legislature on the Democratic ticket, and has no Republican opponent.

On November 4, 1914, Mr. Lusienski was united in marriage to Nell Regan at Platte Center. Mrs. Lusienski, whose parents are Irish, was born at Dhoon, County Cork, Ireland, November 28, 1885. There are two children, Edward J., born June 8, 1916, and Dean R., born January 24, 1922, who are at home; Maurine, the only daughter, is married to C. J. Hittner and resides at Battle Creek, Nebraska.

During the World War Mr. Lusienski was a member of the county council of defense, chairman of the local four minute speakers, chairman of the local selective service registration board, captain of the American Protective League and a captain in the Home Guards.

For a number of years he was president of the local Volunteer Fire Department, which he personally organized in November, 1907. Affiliated always with St. Joseph's Catholic Church, he has for more than a quarter of a century taken part in home talent plays, at least once or twice a year for the benefit of his church, Thanksgiving Day being an occasion in connection with its yearly bazaar.

Mr. Lusienski is a life member of the Nebraskana Society, a member of the Red Cross and the Community Club. His hobbies are reading, philanthropy and home-talent plays, while his present sports are baseball and football as a spectator. Residence: Platte Center.

Harry Detlef Lute

Harry Detlef Lute, farmer and stockman, was born at Holstein, Germany, January 8, 1870, and has been a resident in the United States for 61 years.

His father, John Lute, was born in Holstein, Germany, October 9, 1840, and came to the United States in 1869, where he was first a railroad section foreman. He was a stockman for many years prior to his death at Paxton, on August 2, 1901. His wife, Anna Christina Wulf, was born in Holstein, Germany, September 7, 1846, and came to the United States in 1871. She is a devoted wife and mother, and now resides at Paxton.

Mr. Lute attended public school and business college, and in 1904 was graduated from the Nebraska School of Agriculture. He has been prominent in agricultural circles for a number of years, for three years was executive secretary of the Nebraska Farm Bureau Federation, and for five or six years was on the state executive board and the state exchange board of the Farmers Union. He was president of the local and county Farmers Union. Since 1906 he has been a staff writer for the *Nebraska Farmer*, and in addition, has written numerous articles for farm papers and school papers.

A Republican, Mr. Lute has never been a candidate for public office, except when he served as a member of the Nebraska Constitutional Convention of 1919 and 1920.

On September 20, 1904, he was married to Emma Lulu Woods at Ogallala. She was born at Scotland, Indiana, November 26, 1875, and before her marriage was a school teacher. She is eligible to the Daughters of the American Revolution. They have two daughters, Marjorie, born December 7, 1911; and Harriet, born January 30, 1914, who attends Nebraska Wesleyan University.

Mr. Lute has been delegate to several national conventions of the Nebraska Farm Bureau Federation, and the Farmers Educational and Co-operative Union of Nebraska. He was Nebraska delegate to the dry farming congress at Lethbridge, Alberta, Canada, in 1913, a delegate to the agricultural conference call by President Harding, 1912. He represented the Nebraska shippers before the inter-state commerce commission in 1922, in the western hay and grain case. He was a lecturer for the Farmers Institute from 1905 until 1907.

During the late war he was chairman of the Paxton

Four Minute Speakers. He is a member of the Paxton Methodist Episcopal Church, the Red Cross, and the Commercial Club. In the Odd Fellows he has been through all the chairs and has the state degree on both the subordinate and encampment branches. He is a member of the Nebraska State Historical Society, the Nebraska State Young Men's Christian Association, and is in his ninth year of service on the Paxton School Board. He was president of that organization in 1918, and was its secretary in 1925. His favorite sport is hunting, and his hobby is reading. Residence: Paxton.

Clifford Athenius Lutgen

Clifford A. Lutgen, physician and surgeon of Auburn, Nebraska, was born at Plantsville, Ohio, November 7, 1872. Dr. Lutgen is descended from a long line of illustrious ancestors on the paternal side; his great grandfather, who was a distinguished army officer under Napoleon, came to America from Germany shortly after the close of the Naponleonic Wars. Upon the death of his wife he returned to Germany where he re-entered Napoleon's army as a special guard, leaving his two children in America. His son, Dr. James H. Lutgen, settled at Stockport, Ohio, in the early history of this country, and in the Civil War organized and was captain of a company, the 77th Ohio Volunteers. His son, Athenius Lutgen, one of eight children, who was born at Stockport, October 9, 1840, and was a pioneer homesteader in Kansas, was a farmer and contractor. An energetic farmer and a great home lover, he built a home at what is now Reixord, Thomas County, Kansas, but was killed by lightning in 1886 before his farm lands were cleared and improved.

Clifford A. Lutgen, son of Athenius Lutgen, was a small boy at the time of his father's tragic death, but he took over the entire work of the new farm, helped in the care of his brothers and sisters, and walked to the country school where he received his education. His mother, who was born of Scotch ancestry in Stockport, April 24, 1843, maintained a home for her children and was a hard working pioneer mother.

Dr. Lutgen was graduated from the Colby High School, after which he studied at the Salina Normal School, at Salina, Kansas. For the next four years he taught school, and was then a student at Cotner Medical College for three years, graduated with the degree M. D. in 1901. From 1903 to 1905 he was a post graduate student at the Chicago Medical College; he has taken numerous short post graduate courses in Chicago, New York City, and San Francisco.

A resident of Nebraska for 29 years he has been a practicing physician since 1901, when he was admitted to the profession. He was admitted to the practice of medicine in California in 1923. In 1914 he established the Auburn Hospital, and since that time has been chief surgeon of that institution. Dr. Lutgen has written various medical articles for medical journals and newspapers.

He was united in marriage August 5, 1903, at Tecumseh, Nebraska, with Myrtle B. Combs who was born at Tecumseh, in 1885, and died at Auburn, in 1918; she was a talented artist. To this union two children were born: Grace Irene, born August 5, 1905, who married Dr. Robert W. Housel; Arnold, born May 17, 1909. In 1919 he was married to Ada Pearl Hanks. Mrs. Lutgen, who is a woman of high ideals and character, is descended collaterally from the mother of Abraham Lincoln. Her great grandfather was a half brother to Nancy Hanks. There is one son, Marshall Hanks, who was born January 14, 1925.

Dr. Lutgen is a member of the county, state, and national medical associations, and the Missouri Valley Medical Association. He is a member of the Kiwanis Club, the Chamber of Commerce, and numerous fraternal organizations. He was at one time a member of the American Medical Research Association. He is affiliated with the Christian Church, the Y. M. C. A., and the Red Cross.

He is fond of golfing and likes especially any kind of sport which will take him close to nature. In 1909 he took an extensive trip into Canada, where he engaged in a bear hunt. He killed two large bears, and captured a cub bear. The cub he brought back to the United States at great cost and effort, and presented to the City of Lincoln. Today it is the most valuable bear in Lincoln's animal park. An article written by him entitled *Bear Hunting in the Canadian Rockies* was published in the *Outdoor Life* magazine in 1920. Residence: Auburn.

Sidney Anson Lutgen

S. A. Lutgen, a physician at Wayne, Nebraska, for the past 20 years, was born at Plantsville, Ohio, July 2, 1882, the son of Athenis and Sarah Kathryn (Asa) Lutgen. His father, who was a farmer, died at Oberlin, Kansas, July 5, 1883; of Scotch and Irish descent; he served as captain of Company F in the Ohio Volunteers during the Civil War. His mother, who was born in Ohio, was a pioneer in Kansas, coming to the west in 1882 from Ohio.

Dr. Lutgen attended rural schools in Kansas; was a student at Rexford School, Rexford, Kansas, for three years; attended school at Colby, Kansas, for three years, and in 1904 was graduated from the medical department at Cotner University, where he was a charter member of Tau Alpha Epsilon.

He practiced medicine at Elkcreek, Nebraska, 1904-08, built a small hospital at Wayne, in 1914, and successfully operated it until 1919, when he built a large hospital which accommodates 25 beds. He operated a radio broadcasting station at Wayne, 1925-7; and is now chief surgeon of the Wayne Hospital and surgeon for the Northwestern Railroad Company. He is a member of the Kiwanis Club, the Nebraskana Society, the Elkhorn Valley Medical Society, and Sioux Valley Medical Society. His social club is the Wayne Country Club. His hobby is mechanics, and his sports are golfing, rifling, and big game hunting. Dr. Lutgen is affiliated with the Methodist Church.

He was married to Grace Carolyn Welsh at Lincoln, Lancaster County, Nebraska, January 24, 1907. Mrs. Lutgen, who was formerly a teacher and writer, was born at Sterling, Johnson County, Nebraska, October 10, 1885. They have one son, Joe G., born January 12, 1912. Residence: Wayne. (Photograph on Page 745).

Emil Henry Lutt

Emil Henry Lutt, a prominent merchant for many years, was born in Comanche, Iowa, March 8, 1862. He is the son of Frederick and Sophia Marguerite Henrietta (Reese) Lutt. His father, born in Denmark, December 24, 1826, came to America from Germany in 1855, and became a naturalized citizen in 1859. Until his death at East Moline, Illinois, January 23, 1903, he was a farmer. His wife, Sophia, born in Germany, died at Comanche, Iowa, September 30, 1868.

Educated in the public schools of Comanche until he reached the age of fourteen, Emil Henry Lutt came to Nebraska, where he engaged in the mercantile business until 1919. At that time he retired, his sons succeeding him in business. He now devotes most of his time to supervising the working of his farming interests. He is vice president of the Bank of Niobrara, and since 1918 has been secretary of the local Red Cross.

On June 19, 1889, Mr. Lutt was united in marriage to Sophie D. Schroeder at Goose Lake, Iowa. Mrs. Lutt, who was born in Schlesweig, Germany, April 2, 1865, assisted in the store. There are four children, Elmer, born May 15, 1892; Harry, born December 26, 1894; Marvin, born December 20, 1899; and Lewis, born December 28, 1905.

Mr. Lutt was a member of the local Red Cross committee in 1918, is a member of Odd Fellows Lodge No. 82, and from 1920 to 1924 was a member of the Niobrara

S. A. LUTGEN

High School board. He is a Presbyterian. His favorite recreations are golf, hunting and fishing, and he devotes some leisure time to reading. Residence: Niobrara.

Ormond Ray Lutz

Ormond Ray Lutz, manager of Grand View Farm at Arcadia, was born at Stromsburg, Nebraska, September 18, 1882, son of Isaiah and Kate E. ((De Graff) Lutz. The father, born in Pomeroy, Illinois, November 14, 1843, was a miller by trade in his younger days, and in later life a farmer. On August 7, 1862, at the age of 19, he enlisted at Lincoln's call, served three years and eight days and was discharged August 15, 1865. He was a member of Company G, 124th Illinois Infantry.

Coming to Nebraska in 1873 he established a homestead. His death occurred at Arcadia, on June 14, 1921. His wife, who was born at Buffalo Prairie, Illinois, June 17, 1852, died at Arcadia, October 26, 1913. She was primarily interested in her family, but was widely interested also in the religious, educational and musical life of her community. Hospitality was a major part of her life. She was of French descent, while her husband was descended from early Dutch settlers in Pennsylvania.

Educated first in public school, Ormond Ray Lutz completed a commercial course at Lincoln Business College and later studied four years in the University of Nebraska School of Art. He studied elocution and expression under Professor Eugene Knox at Nebraska Wesleyan University and thereafter spent six years in Lyceum and Chautauqua as a cartoonist entertainer.

On June 24, 1918, he was married to Rowena Josephine Fuller at Arcadia. Mrs. Lutz was born at Arcadia, May 20, 1894, her mother born in Pennsylvania and her father in Ohio. They have three children, Josephine Mable, born June 22, 1919; Rosemary DeGraff, born June 6, 1920; and Orma Rae, born November 17, 1927.

Mr. and Mrs. Lutz are intensely interested in the bird and other natural wild life of Nebraska, and sincerely believe that our state has a beauty which is not fully appreciated. Mr. Lutz' hobby is outdoor sketching and working with flowers. He is a member of the First Methodist Episcopal Church, has been treasurer of the school board several years in the past, and is a member of Arcadia Lodge No. 208 of the Ancient Free and Accepted Masons. Recently he was elected to life membership in The Nebraskana Society. Residence: Arcadia.

Elton Lux

On September 4, 1900, Elton Lux was born at Chapman, Nebraska, the son of Clarence B. and Mary H. (Hansen) Lux. His father, who is a farmer, was born in Iowa, September 28, 1866. His mother, who was of Danish and English ancestry, was born at Wood River, Nebraska, December 22, 1871, and died at Omaha, in May, 1919.

Mr. Lux attended the rural schools near Chapman, 1905-10, the town school at Fountain, Colorado, 1910-13, and a rural school near Wood River, 1914. He was graduated from the Wood River High School in 1918, and later was a student at the University of Nebraska where he was graduated with the B. S. degree. While at the university he was editor of the college paper; was manager of the Farmers Fair, 1923; was a member of five college stock judging teams; and was a member of Gamma Sigma Delta and Alpha Zeta fraternities. He was winner of senior class honors in high school.

He has lived in Nebraska nearly all his life, and for the past several years has been extension service editor at the Agricultural College at the University of Nebraska; he is the author of numerous articles and circulars concerning news writing.

His marriage to Augusta M. Thaden was solemnized at Lincoln, Lancaster County, Nebraska, June 24, 1925. Mrs. Lux was born at Randolph, Cedar County, Nebraska, January 26, 1903. To this union four children were born: Ronald Sidney, born May 23, 1926; James Stanley, born June 24, 1927; John Elton, Jr., born December 27, 1928; and Kenneth Merlin, born September 29, 1930.

Mr. Lux is a member of the American Association of Agricultural College Editors, the Lincoln Junior Chamber of Commerce, and the Nebraskana Society. He is affiliated with the Methodist Church, and is a Republican. Residence: Lincoln.

Gladys Marie Lux

Gladys M. Lux, an artist and educator of some note in Nebraska, was born at Chapman, Merrick County, Nebraska, and has lived in this state practically all her life. Her father, Clarence Burton Lux, who was born at Toledo, Tama County, Iowa, and who is a retired farmer, is descended from a family that has been in America for generations. His parents were born in Indiana, and his father was a member of the 10th regiment in the Civil War, and was a member of the Grand Army of the Republic. Other ancestors of Clarence Lux were settlers in Ohio, in pioneer days.

Mary Hannah (Hansen) Lux, mother of Gladys Lux, who was a teacher in the public schools of central Nebraska before her marriage in 1897. Her father was born in Denmark, married an English girl and came to America, where he homesteaded at Wood River, Nebraska, in 1870. He was a soldier in the Civil War.

Miss Lux attended the rural school at Chapman, Nebraska, the public school at Fountain, Colorado, and later a rural school in Hall County, Nebraska. She was graduated from the high school at Wood River, Nebraska, in 1918. She was awarded the Bachelor of Fine Arts degree at the University of Nebraska in 1925, and has been a student at the State Teachers' College, 1918; School of the Art Institute, Chicago, 1927-29. She is a member of Alpha Rho Tau; the Art Club; College Council; Theta Alpha Phi; and was art chairman of Kappa Phi. In high school she was president of the junior and senior classes.

She was teacher in a rural school in Hall County for one year; was teacher in the summer session at the University of Nebraska, 1923-24-25; was art teacher and director at Central High School at Sioux City, Iowa, 1925-27. She is now director of the School of Art and professor of art at the College of Fine Arts, Nebraska Wesleyan University.

Miss Lux has won approval and distinction for her talent as an artist and has been presented in various exhibits in Nebraska and Missouri. She has been an exhibitor at the Omaha Art Institute since 1928; has been an exhibitor at the Kansas City Art Institute in 1930 and 1931. Her productions are in oil, water color and block prints. Her recent Omaha exhibit was given special comment in a late issue of the Christian Science Monitor.

She is a member of the Lincoln Artist Guild; the Western Arts Association; the Red Cross; and the Axis Club. She is affiliated with the First Methodist Church of Lincoln. Her outdoor sport is horseback riding, and hobby is collecting old household utensils possessing merit from an artistic standpoint. Residence: Lincoln.

Curtis Owen Lyda

Curtis Owen Lyda, county judge of Scotts Bluff County, was born at Atlanta, Missouri, January 17, 1891, son of Thomas and Sarah (Williams) Lyda.

He was educated in public and high schools, and in 1915 received the Bachelor of Arts degree from the University of Nebraska. He received his Bachelor of Laws degree from the same university in 1917. From 1922 until 1926 Mr. Lyda served as mayor of Gering, and at the present time is serving as county judge.

Mr. Lyda is a member of Scotts Bluff Lodge No. 201 of the Ancient Free and Accepted Masons, Oregon Trail Chapter No. 65 of the Royal Arch Masons, and

Bunah Commandery No. 26 of the Knights Templar at Alliance. He is a member of the Scottsbluff Kiwanis Club.

During the late war Mr. Lyda served in the United States Army, and was stationed at Camp Dodge, Iowa. He is a member of Gering Post No. 36 of the American Legion.

Mr. Lyda married Iva Eastman at Sturgis, South Dakota in August, 1917. She was graduated from Spearfish State Normal at Spearfish, South Dakota, and attended the University of Nebraska two years. She is a member of the Eastern Star and the American Legion Auxiliary. They have one son, Robert E., born March 19, 1920. Residence: Gering.

Gus Edward Lyden

Gus E. Lyden, photographer, was born in Ystad, Sweden, September 4, 1873. At the age of fourteen he ran away from home to become a sailor. Thereafter he spent seven years on the different oceans, making three trips around the world, and crossing the equator twenty-eight times.

Finally settling in Iowa, he took up photography as his life work, and has engaged in it since 1895. Since November 1, 1910, he has been located in Schuyler, where he is a leading photographer.

On September 27, 1920, he was united in marriage to Cora Genet Stockton, at Blair. Mrs. Lyden, who is of English descent, is also a photographer, and was born at Blair, October 10, 1897.

Mr. Lyden is a Republican. He is a Mason, and was master of his local lodge during 1916-17, and is now its secretary. He is a Shriner and a member of Au-Bu-Bekr Temple at Sioux City. He is a member of the Missouri Valley Photographers' Association and the International Association of America, the Chamber of Commerce and St. Mary's Episcopal Church at Schuyler. He holds life membership in the Nebraskana Society. Residence: Schuyler.

William Cranswick Lyle

William C. Lyle, a resident of Nebraska for the last 26 years, was born at Guysboro, Nova Scotia, September 6, 1867. His father, John Lyle, who was born at Guysboro, July 31, 1832, and died at Fall River, Massachusetts, June 2, 1916, was a seaman and cooper. Of Scotch ancestry, his family came from north Ireland to America about 1770, and settled in Virginia.

His mother, Ann Isabelle (Whitman) Lyle, who was of English descent, was born at Guysboro, September 14, 1832. In the 1770's her ancestors came to America and made their home in Connecticutt. She died at Gloucester, Massachusetts, January 3, 1895.

Mr. Lyle attended the public school at Gloucester, and at the age of 14 he began to work in a general store at Gloucester. When he was 23 years of age he entered the insurance business at Denver, Colorado, and on June 15, 1896, he was made special agent for the St. Paul Fire and Marine Insurance Company. In 1905 he was made general agent for this firm and moved to Nebraska. He is now general agent for the St. Paul Fire and Marine Insurance Company, the St. Paul Mercury Indemnity Company, and The Mercury Insurance Company, and is vice president of the Omaha Wimisett System Bank.

He was united in marriage with Emma Lantz at Gloucester, July 24, 1894. Mrs. Lyle, whose ancestry is Holland Dutch, was born at Gloucester, February 14, 1869. There are three children: Dorothy, born June 13, 1895; Donald W., born January 27, 1899, who married Dorothy Hipple; and John F., born August 5, 1911. Dorothy is a kindergarten teacher in the Dundee School at Omaha. Donald is special agent for the St. Paul Fire and Marine Insurance Company. John is a student at Brown University, at Providence, Rhode Island.

During the World War Mr. Lyle was chairman of the Conservation Association of Nebraska, 1917-18. He is a member of the Red Cross, the Omaha Chamber of Commerce, the Masons, Knights Templar, and Shrine. He is affiliated with the First Baptist Church and is serving as chairman of the board of trustees in the church; is a member of the University Club, Happy Hollow Club, and served as director and president of the latter for some time. His sports are golfing, hunting and fishing. Residence: Omaha.

Charles Fremont Lyman

Charles Fremont Lyman, real estate dealer, was born in Kearney, Nebraska, October 17, 1880, son of William Henry and Maria Jane (Van Kleek) Lyman.

The father was born in Massachusetts, in April, 1847, and engaged in insurance business until his death at Weeping Water, Nebraska, in October, 1917. His wife, Maria Jane, was born at Van Kleek Hill, Canada, March 10, 1847. She is of Holland Dutch ancestry.

Mr. Lyman attended public and high schools, and has been engaged in the banking, real estate, and insurance business all of his life. He established the town of Lyman, Nebraska, in 1921. He is secretary and treasurer of the Security Land Company, owners of the Lyman township and farm land. He is a Republican.

His marriage to Hazel E. Alling was solemnized at Lincoln, January 12, 1910. Mrs. Lyman was born at Youngstown, Ohio, March 26, 1887. She was graduated from Sterling, Nebraska, High School and attended the University of Nebraska conservatory of music. She is a member of the Eastern Star and the Christian Church. They have four children, Jack E., born November 18, 1913; Jayne A., born July 22, 1915; Charles W., born May 4, 1919; and Richard C., born August 26, 1923.

During the late war Mr. Lyman was awarded the government prize for his work in Liberty loan drives. He is a member of the Red Cross, the Masons, and of the Nebraskana Society. Residence: Gering.

Rufus Ashley Lyman

Rufus Ashley Lyman, one of Nebraska's leading educators and a lifetime resident of the state, was born at Table Rock, Nebraska, April 17, 1875. His father, William Graves Lyman, born at Nora, Illinois, December 12, 1847, was a farmer and a Nebraska territorial pioneer. He settled in what is now Pawnee County, the same year Nebraska was admitted to the union (1867), and not being of age or head of a family it was impossible for him to homestead, and he therefore purchased 160 acres at $1.25 per acre. William Lyman pioneered in Kansas, after spending thirty-four years in Nebraska, coming back to Lincoln, died January 4, 1919.

Sophie Lee (Allen) Lyman, his mother, was born in Green County, Kentucky, March 29, 1849. She was a pioneer in Nebraska territory. Her ancestry was Scotch and Irish.

Professor Lyman received his early education in the rural schools of Pawnee County, and was graduated from the Table Rock High School in 1892. He holds the following degrees from the University of Nebraska: A. B., 1897; A. M., 1899; M. D., 1903. He was valedictorian of his high school graduating class, and was elected to membership in Sigma Xi, Delta Sigma Phi, Phi Delta Chi; Nu Sigma Nu; Omega Beta Pi; and Phi Sigma.

He has taken an especially active part in the educational life of Nebraska since his admission to the practice of medicine, May 16, 1903, and has held the following positions: professor of pharmacology, at the College of Medicine, University of Nebraska, 1904-08; organizer of the School of Pharmacy of the University of Nebraska, 1908; director of the School of Pharmacy, 1908-15; and dean of the College of Pharmacy since 1915. He has been chairman of the department of physiology and pharmacology of the College of Pharmacy since its organization.

He was the organizer of the department of student

health of the University of Nebraska, 1919, and has been director of this department since its beginning. He was a member of the committee appointed by the war department, 1918, to formulate the program for the Pharmacy Unit of the Student Army Training Corp. He served as a member of the committee which, under the direction of the Commonwealth Fund, made a nation-wide study of pharmaceutical education and practice in 1923 to 1925.

Professor Lyman acted as president of the American Association of Colleges of Pharmacy, 1916-17; was chairman of the executive committee of that association from 1920-1923; and at the present time is vice chairman of the American Council on Education. He is one of the vice presidents of the United States Pharmacopoeial Convention. He is dean of the College of Pharmacy; chairman of the department of physiology and pharmacology; and is director of the Student Health Department, at the University of Nebraska.

He is the author of numerous articles dealing with various phases of pharmaceutical education and practice, published at various times since 1904. He holds membership in the following professional organizations: American Medical Association; Nebraska State Medical Association; Lancaster County Medical Society; American Pharmaceutical Association; Nebraska Pharmaceutical Association; American Public Health Association; American Student Health Association; American Association School of Physicians; Nebraska Academy of Sciences; and the American Association for the Advancement of Science.

He is a member of the Red Cross; is secretary of the Nebraska Society for the Friendless; and is a member of the Parent-Teachers' Association. He is a member of the Lincoln Chamber of Commerce; the State Historical Society; the Nebraska Art Association; and the Nebraskana Society. He is treasurer of the Westminster Foundation at the University of Nebraska. He is affiliated with the Westminster Presbyterian Church of Lincoln. He is a Republican.

His marriage to Caroline Day was solemnized at Lincoln, July 1, 1899. Mrs. Lyman, who was born at Keokuk, Lee County, Iowa, May 11, 1877, was formerly a teacher. Her ancestry is Welsh. Six children were born to their marriage: Esther, born July 23, 1902, who married Wilbur W. Knight; Caroline, born May 1, 1904, who died August 25, 1927; Elizabeth, born July 21, 1906; Louise, born April 21, 1910; Rufus Ashley, Jr., born February 28, 1916; and Edwin Day, born November 27, 1918. Esther, Caroline, and Elizabeth, are pharmacists. Residence: Lincoln.

William Patrick Lynch

William P. Lynch, a lifetime resident of Nebraska, was born at Omaha, August 15, 1881, the son of Patrick William and Ellen (Fitzpatrick) Lynch. His father, who was born in County Kerry, Ireland, March 9, 1849, and died at Omaha, December 13, 1906, came to this country in 1849, and engaged in business as U. S. storekeeper; he was Democratic candidate for sheriff of Douglas County in 1881. His mother was born in County Kerry, May 13, 1851, and died at Omaha, November 19, 1919.

Mr. Lynch attended the Omaha public and parochial schools and was graduated from Creighton High School. He was awarded the following degrees at Creighton University: A. B., 1902; LL. B., 1906; and A. M., 1906. He won his college letters in football and baseball at Creighton University and was captain of the football team there in 1899. Since 1906 he has been engaged in the practice of law in Omaha, and has held a prominent position in Nebraska politics for over 20 years. A Democrat, he has been a member of the Democratic county central committee for the past 15 years; served as temporary and permanent chairman of the Democratic county convention in 1920; and in 1912 was Democratic candidate for county

judge. He was Democratic candidate for public defender in 1918.

On January 15, 1912, he was united in marriage with Mary Fredricka Rauber at Omaha. Mrs. Lynch was born at Omaha, October 6, 1883. They have the following children: Eleanor, born February 18, 1913; Patrick, born September 14, 1914; James, born March 30, 1916; George, born July 21, 1918; William, born January 8, 1920; and Benjamin, born December 29, 1923.

During the late war Mr. Lynch served as a member of the county council of defense; was a four minute speaker; and was a member of the legal advisory board. He is a member of the Douglas County Bar Association and the Nebraska State Bar Association. He is a member of the Society of St. Vincent De Paul; is a member of the Superior Council of the United States; was president of St. Patrick's Conference, 1908 to 1919; and since 1919 has been president of the Particular Council of Omaha. He holds membership in the Vinton Street Commercial Club.

Mr. Lynch is affiliated with St. Patrick's Church of Omaha, and is a member of the Knights of Columbus. In 1914 he was president of the Nonpareil Athletic and Social Club, and also in 1930. He is a member of the Ancient Order of United Workmen. He is interested in practically all sports. His hobbies are reading and the study of history. Residence: Omaha.

Don William Lyne

Don William Lyne was born at Superior, Nebraska. April 10, 1894, the son of Philip Thomas and Mary M. (Burcher) Lyne. His parents were married in Ohio in 1881 and the following year came to Superior where they have lived continuously since that time. His father, a farmer, was born at Barnesville, Ohio, February 21, 1848; his Welsh ancestors came to America in 1700. His mother was born at Sarahville, Ohio, February 28, 1857 of English and Irish parentage.

Mr. Lyne was graduated from elementary school in 1910, and in 1914 was graduated from the Superior High School. During the World War he served as a corporal and was engaged in active service at Verdun, St. Mihiel, and Argonne; he is now a member of the American Legion.

On November 26, 1923, he was united in marriage with Orpha Hazel Craig, daughter of John and Clara (Clark) Craig, at Mankato, Kansas. Mrs. Lyne was born at Superior, September 22, 1895, of Irish descent. They have a daughter, Marjorie Ann, born November 8, 1924. Mr. Lyne is fond of baseball; he is especially interested in good livestock. Residence: Superior.

Carl William Lynn

Born near Norman, Nebraska, April 24, 1896, Carl William Lynn is the son of Charles and Hansina Carolina (Espersen) Lynn. His father, who was a pioneer Nebraska farmer and stockman, was born in Sweden, May 2, 1848, and came to this country in 1872 where he was employed in machine factories for a time prior to homesteading in Kearney County, Nebraska. His mother was born in Denmark, October 27, 1855, and came to America in 1874.

Mr. Lynn received his elementary education in rural schools and in 1914 was graduated from the Minden High School. He studied at the University of Nebraska for two years in the college of Agriculture. He has been engaged in farming on his father's homestead in Kearney County, near Norman, since 1918 and now specializes in poultry raising.

He is a member of the Nebraskana Society, the Independent Order of Odd Fellows, the Rebekah Lodge, and the Presbyterian Church of Norman. He has served as superintendent of the Presbyterian Sunday School since 1917 and has been a teacher of the adult Bible class since 1918.

His marriage to Nellie Josephine Branch was solemnized at Minden, October 9, 1917. Mrs. Lynn, who was a teacher before her marriage, was born in Taney County, Missouri, August 29, 1895. Two children were born to this marriage: William Joseph, January 27, who died at birth; and Donald Paul, born April 2, 1922. Residence: Norman.

Ray Orin Lyon

Ray Orin Lyon, merchant and postmaster at Clinton, was born at Edgar, Nebraska, October 26, 1885, son of Horace Greeley and Neva (Semans) Lyon. Horace Greeley Lyon was born in Iowa in January, 1860, and was a newspaper man at Gordon for a number of years prior to his death on December 12, 1924. He was of Scotch-Irish descent. His wife, Neva, was born at Faribault, Minnesota, in 1862. Her ancestry is also Scotch-Irish.

Upon the completion of his elementary education in the public school of Gordon, Mr. Lyon entered Gordon High School from which he was graduated in 1903. The following three years he attended Fremont Normal School and in 1905 was a student at the Agricultural College. At the present time he is the owner and manager of the largest Sioux Indian curio business in the United States; he is also postmaster. He is a Republican.

On June 15, 1908, he was married to Mildred L. Currie at Whitney, Nebraska, her birthplace. Mrs. Lyon, whose ancestry was Scotch, was born June 13, 1889. Mrs. Lyon was the daughter of Frank and Minnie (Richards) Currie. Her father was a member of the Nebraska State legislature for two terms. Mrs. Lyon is a graduate of the Gordon High School. She is a member of the Eastern Star and Rebekahs. They have four children, Glenn, born July 5, 1911; Clare, born April 5, 1914; Frank, born March 29, 1918; and Helen, born April 12, 1922.

A member of the Presbyterian Church at Gordon, Nebraska, Mr. Lyon is also a member of the board of trustees of the Methodist Church at Clinton and is a member of its board of directors. He is treasurer of the school board, finance chairman of the Sioux district, Nebraska, Boy Scouts, an Elk, a Mason, and a member of the Odd Fellows. His hobby is collecting Indian curios, stamps and coins. Residence: Clinton.

James Edmund Mabie

Born at Montour, Iowa, July 13, 1899, James Edmund Mabie is the son of Franklin Jeremiah and Rosalie (Elliott) Mabie. His father, who was a merchant, was born at Delavan Lake, Wisconsin, March 11, 1858, and died at Dickens, Iowa, December 24, 1921. Mr. Mabie was graduated from the high school at Nemaha, Iowa, in 1917, and later attended the Hamilton School of Commerce at Mason City, Iowa, for a time. He is manager of the Beaver City Co-operative Creamery at this time and takes an active interest in community affairs.

Mr. Mabie is a member of the Beaver City Community Club and the Beaver City Rotary Club, is affiliated with the First Methodist Church, and is a Mason and Odd Fellow. His sports are golfing and tennis, while his hobby is reading. During the World War he served as a private in the United States Army overseas for 19 months, and is now a member of the American Legion.

His marriage to Hazel Gladys Hotchkiss was solemnized at Spirit Lake, December 25, 1924, she was born at Eagle Grove, Iowa, December 15, 1903. She is the daughter of Willis R. and Ada (Gray) Hotchkiss. Their two children are: Howard Ted, born April 28, 1926; and Eleanor Jean, born January 25, 1928. Residence: Beaver City.

John Lawrence Mace

John Lawrence Mace, physician and surgeon, was born at Eldorado, Illinois, March 2, 1879, son of Willis L. and Eliza Jane (Smith) Mace. The father was born at Raleigh, Illinois, June 6, 1853, and died at Nashville, Tennessee, February 7, 1907. His wife died at Eldorado, June 2, 1892.

Dr. Mace received his medical degree from the University of Tennessee, and has been engaged in the practice of medicine in Nebraska for twenty-one years. He is a member of the American, Adams County and Nebraska State Medical Association, the Chamber of Commerce, the Lions Club, and the Masons (Scottish Rite, Shrine).

On June 1, 1911, he was married to Sarah Ella Deppe at Glenvil. She was born at Bey, Missouri, November 7, 1887. They have one child living and one deceased. Mary, born March 12, 1913, died March 13, 1913; and Glenn, born January 15, 1915.

Dr. Mace is a member of the Methodist Episcopal Church of Hastings and the Young Men's Christian Association. Residence: Hastings.

John Patrick Madgett

John Patrick Madgett, insurance specialist, was born at Binghamton, New York, March 3, 1881, and has lived in Nebraska for the past forty-seven years. He is the son of James and Mary (Hayes) Madgett, the former born in Limerick, Ireland. James Madgett, who was an employee of the English government, came to America in 1865, and died at Hastings on April 2, 1913. His wife, born in County Cork, May 5, 1843, died at Hastings in September, 1926. She was an ardent reader and student of political history.

Educated in the public schools of Hastings, John Patrick Madgett studies law at Hastings College, and while a student there was a member of the football team. For a period of ten years he served as assistant cashier of the First National Bank of Hastings.

On July 12, 1909, he was united in marriage to May Belle Parks, at Hastings. Mrs. Madgett, who was former city librarian there was born at Blue Hill, December 2, 1888. There are two sons, John Patrick, born October 2, 1910; and Albert Parks, born August 22, 1916. John is studying to be an engineer.

Mr. Madgett is a Republican, and active in the politics of his party. During 1916-17 he was in service on the Mexican Border, and in the World War held the rank of first lieutenant of Infantry. He was assistant division inspector at Camp Cody, New Mexico, as captain of the 6th Nebraska Infantry, and in 1918-19 served in the Department of the Inspector General.

In 1925 Mr. Madgett was commander of the Hastings Post of the American Legion. He is also a member of the Forty-and-Eight. Always active in civic, fraternal and commercial circles, he is a member of all bodies of Masonry, the Shrine, Knights of Pythias, Odd Fellows and Eagles, as well as the Chamber of Commerce (chairman insurance committee), the Red Cross, Salvation Army and the Lions Club. Mr. Madgett's religious affiliation is with the Congregational Church. His sports are football and golf. Residence: Hastings.

William Madgett

William Madgett, distinguished in public affairs at Hastings, Nebraska, for many years, was born at Riverside, Broom County, New York, July 9, 1878. His father, James Madgett, who was born at Killarney, Ireland, and died at Hastings, April 2, 1913, was an officer in the British navy yards at London; he was descended from an English and Irish sea captain, Nicholas Madgett.

His mother, who was born at Belfast, Ireland, May 1, 1850, and died at Hastings, December 5, 1926, was a descendant of John Hayes, a British army captain. After the death of her parents she was reared by her English uncles who were barristers in London.

Mr. Madgett attended the public and high schools at Hastings, and in 1895 was graduated from Hastings Business College. He played baseball in high school and college, was tennis champion of Hastings in 1897, and was semi-finalist in the state tournament, in 1898. He was accountant in the First National Bank of Hastings for nine years, and for more than 25 years has been engaged in the real estate, loan, and insurance business there. For the past 15 years he has been interested in the development of Oklahoma oil lands.

A progressive Republican, Mr. Madget was elected mayor of Hastings in 1915, 1917, and 1931. He is past president and director of the Nebraska League of Municipalities, is vice president of the Public Ownership League of America. He is also a member of the Hastings Chamber of Commerce of which he was formerly director. He holds membership in the Red Cross, Salvation Army, the Young Men's Christian Association, the Elks, and the Knight of Pythias. He was a charter member of the Hastings Country Club, and is a 32nd degree Scottish Rite Mason, holding membership in the Tehama Temple of the Mystic Shrine. Reading and political science are his hobbies.

His marriage to Pauline Edith Nance occurred at Savannah, Missouri. She is the daughter of Frank Nance, a banker. They have a daughter, Pauline Helen, who was graduated from Hastings High School, attended Hastings College, and was graduated from Grinnell College.

Mr. Madgett was active in all local patriotic affairs during the World War. He is affiliated with the First Presbyterian Church at Hastings. Residence: Hastings.

Martin Madison

Martin Madison, son of Martin and Carrie (Peterson) Madison, Sr., was born on his father's homestead near Beaver Crossing, Nebraska, on January 9, 1880. His father was born at Frejlev, Holland, Denmark, on September 29, 1847, and came to this country in 1867. He was on the first passenger train that came to Lincoln, Nebraska, where he worked on the first university building that was constructed there. He also worked on the state penitentiary building. He homesteaded near Beaver Crossing, Nebraska, in 1869, and later became president of the State Bank of Goehner, Nebraska. His death occurred December 28, 1921, at Lincoln. His wife was born at Frejlev, Denmark, August 21, 1846, and died at Lincoln, April 8, 1921.

Martin Madison, Jr., attended public school near Beaver Crossing and Goehner, Nebraska. In 1898-99, he was a student at the Lincoln Business College. He was united in marriage with Bertha Wussler at Boise City, Idaho, January 20, 1903. She was born at Paxton, Illinois, January 30, 1881, of German parentage. To this union five children were born: Velma M., December 12, 1909, Bernidene L., November 13, 1911; F. Lee, September 12, 1913, Marguerite H., August 23, 1915, and Stanley, December 21, 1918, who died May 11, 1919. Velma and Bernidene are graduated from the Wesleyan University; the former is assistant cashier in the Goehner State Bank, and the latter teaches school. F. Lee was valedictorian of the 1930 Goehner High School class. He also received the distinction of attending the 12 years without being absent or tardy. At the present time he is attending the Lincoln School of Commerce.

Mr. Madison is the cashier at the Goehner State Bank, which position he has held for fifteen years. He is connected with the First Trust Company of Seward, Nebraska, and holds the position of director and secretary.

During the World War he was a food administrator, chairman of a liberty loan, and treasurer of the Red Cross.

He is now chairman of the Village Board, and the Board of Education.

Mr. Madison is a Scottish Rite, and Royal Arch Mason, and is a member of the Shrine at Lincoln. Golf is his favorite sport, and he is interested in landscaping and mechanics. Residence: Goehner. (Photograph in Album).

Peter R. Madison

Peter R. Madison, leading farmer in Dakota County, was born at Sioux City, Iowa, July 10, 1887. He is the son of Rasmus and Kirsten Madison, both of whom were born in Denmark, and who came to America when young. Rasmus Madison was born at Langeland, Denmark, April 15, 1847, and died at South Sioux City on September 27, 1927. His wife, who was also born in Langeland, April 15, 1847, died at South Sioux City on November 28, 1928.

Educated to the seventh grade in the rural schools of Woodbury County, Iowa, Peter R. Madison afterward completed a commercial course at Sioux City, Iowa. He has been a resident of Nebraska for the past 19 years, and has engaged in farming during all that time.

On December 15, 1913, he was united in marriage to Olga Christine Petersen at Omaha. Mrs. Madison was born in New York City on September 1, 1894. To them were born the following children: P. Raymond, born November 17, 1914; Virginia, born November 29, 1916; Roy, born January 29, 1919; Doris, born April 27, 1921; Fern, born September 16, 1923; Wilbur, born November 3, 1925; Howard, born May 5, 1927, and Carol, born February 21, 1929.

Mr. Madison is Republican in politics, and is an attendant of the Lutheran Church. His fraternal organizations include the Masons, Odd Fellows and Modern Woodmen of America, his sports are hunting and fishing, and his hobby is mechanics. Residence: South Sioux City.

Albert Frederick Magdanz

Albert Frederick Magdanz was born at Pierce, Nebraska, March 8, 1880, the son of Albert Friederich and Maria Dorothea (Strelow) Magdanz His father, who was a farmer, was born at Braunsberg, Germany, in 1843, and died at Pierce, in 1910. His mother was born at Braunsberg, in 1845, and died at Pierce, in 1912.

Mr. Magdanz attended rural schools until 1893 and in 1899 was graduated from the high school at Pierce. He was graduated from the University of Nebraska with the A. B. degree in 1904. He became instructor in animal husbandry at the University of Nebraska in 1904, was given a promotion in rank each succeeding year until 1908 when he resigned as associate professor of animal husbandry.

He served as cashier of the Pierce State Bank until 1914 and from 1914 until 1930 was cashier of the newly organized Citizens State Bank of Pierce. He is now president and manager of Alsidon Farms, Incorporated at Pierce. He is a member of the Pierce Community Club, has been chairman of the Pierce Public Library board since 1910, and is a member of the Nebraskana Society. He is affiliated with the Congregational Church of Pierce and holds membership in the Masonic Lodge. His favorite sports are hunting and fishing, and his hobby is reading.

His marriage to Anna May Fowler was solemnized at Omaha, Nebraska, January 22, 1908. Mrs. Magdanz was born at Carrolltown, Missouri, September 23, 1880, the daughter of the late Judge James M. Fowler of Omaha Their three children are: Donald F., born April 24, 1915; Albert Sidney, born March 8, 1919; and Elizabeth Ann, born April 7, 1920. Residence: Pierce.

Nellie Throop Magee

A leader in civic and club work in Lincoln, Nellie Throop Magee is also an outstanding figure in its business life. She was born near Valparaiso, Nebraska, December 21, 1874, daughter of Henry E. and Ellen M. (Johnson) Throop. Her father, who was a native of Warsaw, New York, born May 26, 1828, was a successful farmer and cattleman, a carpenter and cabinet maker. He followed diversified farming, kept bees and had a fine orchard. After coming to Nebraska to make his home he helped to build its first capitol. He was descended from English ancestors who came to Hartford, Connecticut, in 1640. His death occurred at Valparaiso, July 27, 1896.

Ellen Johnson Throop was born in Maine, October 12, 1843, and died at Lincoln September 12, 1927. Before her marriage she was a teacher; as president of the Women's Christian Temperance Union she led in the erection of a reading room and the establishment of a library in Valparaiso. She was a leader in church and educational work. Her ancestry was English, the first members of her family in America settling at Hampton, New Hampshire, in 1635.

Nellie Throop Magee was graduated from Valparaiso High School in 1890; prior to that her entire education had been in country schools. She was valedictorian of her class and editor of a school column in the weekly paper. Her marriage to Oliver Nathan Magee took place at Valparaiso on June 20, 1894. Mr. Magee, who was born at Bloomfield, September 4, 1863, died at Lincoln, March 14, 1918. At the time of his death he was president of Magee's Clothing Company, which he founded. He was the son of John L. and Ann Magee, Nebraska pioneers. There are five sons and daughters, Oliver Harold, born June 23, 1895, who married Hazel Clemmons. He is manager of the shoe department of Magee's. Ethel, born January 24, 1897, married Alwin G. Amos. Elmer E., born November 3, 1900, married Evelyn Hegert. He is advertising man and secretary of Magee's. Helen, born January 8, 1911, and Woodrow R., born March 4, 1913, are still in school.

Mrs. Magee has lived all her life in Nebraska with the exception of six years of early married life spent in Seneca, Kansas. Since her husband's death she has been president of Magee's Clothing Company and of Magee's Shoe Company. She is the author of *Profitable Play Bible Games* (1905-31), and editor of *Various Bible Helps*.

Her welfare and civic endeavors are varied. As a member of the Red Cross, Salvation Army, Community Chest, Tuberculosis Association, Foundation for the Blind and in probation work her activities have been wide-spread. She is treasurer of Bryan Memorial Hospital, and a member of the Anti-Saloon League, the League of Women Voters, the Chautauqua Circle, a life member of the Young Women's Christian Association and a member of the Lincoln Woman's Club of which last she is treasurer at the present time.

The cultural and educational organizations to which she belongs include the Art Association, the P. E. O. Sisterhood, the Needlework Guild, the American Bible Association, the Wesleyan Educational Council in which she holds the position of first vice president of the state organization, and various others. She is a member of Deborah Avery Chapter of the Daughters of the American Revolution. Her religious affiliation is with the Warren Methodist Episcopal Church of Lincoln, and she is a member of the home and foreign missionary societies of that church. She is a member of the Nebraska State Historical Society, the Native Sons and Daughters, Territorial Association and the Nebraskana Society. She enjoys reading, writing, historical work and gardening, and is a member of the Lincoln Garden Club. She is a leader in the Early Nebraska History class connected with the Wesleyan Educational Council.

Perhaps her most profound interest is in her camp for boys on her father's farm at Valparaiso, which is called Camp KinniKinnik. The farm was purchased in 1866 with college scrip, and is a prized possession. Mrs. Magee at the present time is establishing a memorial to her pioneer parents on this farm. It has picnic grounds, swimming pool, fish ponds, tennis courts, a museum, cabins, and an old settlers' organization. Residence: Lincoln.

Jay L. Magill

Born at Woodlawn, Kansas, January 26, 1880, Jay L. Magill has been engaged in the practice of medicine for the past 32 years in Nebraska. He is the son of Samuel and Jane (Hooper) Magill, the former a stock feeder and farmer. His ancestry is Scotch and Welsh.

Dr. Magill was graduated from the high school at Seneca, Kansas, in 1896, was a student at the Kansas City University in 1900, and studied medicine in New York City, 1913-14. He engaged in medical practice at Gilead, Nebraska, from 1900 to 1912, and since 1912 has been prominent in his profession at Holdrege, Nebraska.

He holds membership in the Phelps County Medical Society, the Nebraska State Medical Society, the American Medical Association, and the Republican Valley Medical Society. He is a member of the American Red Cross, the Holdrege Chamber of Commerce, the Holdrege Rotary Club, and the Holdrege Country Club. He is a Mason. Dr. Magill served as secretary of the Medical Advisory Board, 10th Nebraska District, during the World War. His favorite sport is golfing.

He was united in marriage with Ethel Latimer, who was born at Bern, Kansas, June 6, 1880, and died at Gilead, September 5, 1910. Two children were born to that marriage: Grace, July 29, 1901; and Bernice Beth, July 11, 1904. Of his marriage to Orra A. Craft, which took place October 26, 1912, one daughter was born: Jean Lillian, August 14, 1912. Lucille is a professional singer, Bernice is a teacher, and Jean is a student at the University of Nebraska. Residence: Holdrege.

Robert Francis Magirl

Robert Francis Magirl, physician and surgeon at Jackson, Nebraska, has lived in this state for the past 47 years. He was born at Ryan, Iowa, July 3, 1885, the son of Bridget (McKenna) and Robert Emmett Magirl. His father was of Irish descent. His mother, who was also Irish, was born at Boston, Massachusetts.

Dr. Magirl was graduated from the O'Neill High School in 1905. He received the A. B. degree, 1908, and the M. D. degree, 1913, at Creighton University, Omaha, Nebraska, where he was a member of Phi Rho Sigma. He was a member of the Creighton football team, 1907-08-09-10, and served as captain of the team in 1910.

He was admitted to the practice of medicine and surgery at Omaha, December 10, 1913, and has been engaged in that profession since that date. He is affiliated with St. Patrick's Catholic Church and holds membership in The Nebraskana Society and the Modern Woodmen of America. His favorite sport is football. During the World War Dr. Magirl served as a member of the Medical Advisory Board at Jackson. He is a Democrat.

On September 29, 1915, he was married to Mildred Mary Sutton at Omaha. Mrs. Magirl who is Irish, was born at LeMars, Plymouth County, Iowa, February 23, 1890. Seven children were born to this union: Robert, born October 3, 1917; Elizabeth, born March 9, 1920; Mary Helen, and Ann Marie, born November 27, 1921; Catherine, born February 7, 1926; John Jo, born October 13, 1924; and Therese, born January 21, 1931. Anna Marie died in 1925. Residence: Jackson.

George A. Magney

George A. Magney, lawyer, was born in Scioto County, Ohio, September 29, 1857, and has been a resident of

GEORGE A. MAGNEY

Skoglund—Omaha

Nebraska since 1865. His father, John Magney, was born in Scioto County in 1836 and died in Cass County, Nebraska, May 10, 1895. He was a farmer of French descent. His wife, Mary (Searl) Magney was born in Scioto County in 1837, and died at Omaha, December 14, 1895. Her ancestry was English.

Educated in the country schools of Cass County, Mr. Magney was admitted to the bar of Nebraska at Plattsmouth in June, 1881. A Democrat, he was municipal judge of Omaha 1894-95, chief deputy county attorney of Douglas County 1902-12, county attorney 1913-19, and member of the constitutional convention 1920-21. From 1883-85 he was editor of the *Papillion Times*.

His marriage to Dora L. Ayer took place at Papillion, April 9, 1885. Mrs. Magney was born in New York State January 25, 1863, and died at Omaha, August 13, 1928. There are three children, Lloyd A., born July 11, 1890; Vernon P., born April 22, 1892 and Ethel G., born January 12, 1895. Vernon held the rank of first sergeant in the truck department at Camp Dodge in the World War.

Mr. Magney is a member of the Second Church of Christ, Scientist, of Omaha, and of the Knights of Pythias, the Modern Woodmen of America and the Woodmen of the World. He is a former member of the Chamber of Commerce. His favorite sport is baseball. Residence: Omaha. (Photograph on Page 752).

Thomas Ross Magowan

Thomas Ross Magowan, prominent grain dealer, was born in Hot Springs, South Dakota, January 31, 1899, son of William J. and Jennie (Coleman) Magowan. His father and morther are both living, the former of Scotch-Irish descent, and the later of Irish descent.

Mr. Magowan attended public and high schools at Hot Springs, graduating in 1916, receiving the degree of Bachelor of Business Administration from the University of Washington, at Seattle. He was business administrator of Beta Gamma Sigma, and a member of the Oval Club and Sigma Chi. A resident of Nebraska for nine years he is now manager and a member of the firm of the Farmers Grain Company of Gordon, and is associated with the Merriman Grain Company of Merriman, Nebraska. He is a Republican.

On May 10, 1922, he was married to Catharyn Cochran at Seattle. Mrs. Magowan was born at Seattle, August 30, 1898, of English descent. She is a member of the Woman's Club and the P. E. O.; is a graduate of the University of Washington, and a member of Kappa Alpha Theta. They have one son, Donald, born February 26, 1926.

Mr. Magowan served as a private in the United States Army during the World War, and is a member of the American Legion. At the present time he is roll call chairman of the Red Cross, and since 1929, has been a director of the Nebraska Grain Dealers' Association. He is a Mason, and in 1930, served as president of the Kiwanis Club. His favorite sport is golf. Residence: Gordon.

John Arthur Maguire

John A. Maguire, lawyer and Demcratic leader, and a resident of Lincoln 34 years, was born near Elizabeth, Jo Davies County, Illinois, November 29, 1870. He is the son of Francis and Margaret (Bough) Maguire, the former of whom was born near Enniskillen, County Fermanagh, Ireland, October 30, 1845. Educated in the country schools of Illinois and the state normal school at Platteville, Wisconsin, Francis Maguire was a teacher and educator, holding school and other local offices. His wife, Margaret, was born in County Cavan, Ireland, April 15, 1847, and with her and their family settled on a government homestead near Mitchell, Dakota Territory (now South Dakota) in 1882. He was a pioneer in its early settlement, development and civic growth and helped to shape the early school system of the state. Of

Irish ancestry, he came from Ireland with his parents in 1850 and settled near Elizabeth, Illinois. He died at Mitchell, October 8, 1925. His wife was educated in the public schools of Illinois and the Galena, Illinois, High School. A teacher prior to marriage she was, aside from her duties as a wife and mother, interested in school, church and charitable work in her community. She died at Mitchell, July 6, 1911.

Educated first in the country schools of South Dakota, Mr. Maguire was graduated from the Plankinton, South Datkota, High School in 1889, and attended South Dakota State College three years. He was awarded a B. Sc. from Iowa State College in 1893, an A. M. at the University of Nebraska in 1898, and his LL. B. from the latter in 1899. From 1891 to 1892 he was assistant at South Dakota State College. He taught in country schools in South Dakota during college vacations from 1900 to 1904 to earn his way through college. He served as superintendent of schools at Salem, South Dakota, in 1895, and taught in teachers normal institutes in South Dakota 1904-07. He was president of the South Dakota State Oratorical Association in 1893, vice president of the Inter-state Oratorical Association in 1898; president of the Union Boys Debating Club at the University of Nebraska in 1897; president of the University of Nebraska Alumni Association in 1904. In 1914 he was president of the University of Nebraska Almuni Association in Washington, D. C.

On June 6, 1918, Mr. Maguire was married to Nellie Murphy at Omaha. Mrs. Maguire was born at Schuyler, Nebraska. Outside of her duties as a home-builder, she is interested and active in school, church and welfare work. She is diocesan director in Nebraska of the National Council of Catholic Women. Both she and Mr. Maguire are members of St. Theresa's Church and he is a member of the board of trustees. There are three children, John Francis, born February 12, 1921, died February 15, 1921; Mary and Margaret who are in school.

In addition to the practice of law Mr. Maguire has served in various public offices and positions of public trust. He was elected on the Democratic ticket to Congress on November 4, 1908, and was re-elected in 1910 and 1912; he was deputy county treasurer of Lancaster County during 1900 and 1901; delegate from Nebraska to the Democratic National Convention at St. Louis in 1904; secretary of the Nebraska Democratic state committee in 1905; delegate to city, county and state Democratic conventions 1908-1930; secretary or chairman of city, and county Democratic committees 1899-1905; member of the National Democratic Congressional Committee for Nebraska 1914, etc.

He has been a member of the American, Nebraska State and Lancaster County Bar Associations, the Nebraska State Historical Society at various times, and was a member of the board of directors of the Social Welfare Society of Lincoln from 1918 to 1928.

Since 1904 he has been a member of the Knights of Columbus, and during 1904 and 1905 was grand knight of Fitzgerald Council, and from 1905-09 was district deputy for Nebraska. In 1918 he was president of the Catholic Educational Association, and in 1922 was president of the Lincoln branch of the National Council of Catholic Men. During the World War he was active in Liberty loan drives, Red Cross work, and other wartime activities. Residence: Lincoln. (Photograph in Album).

Andrew DeWitt Mahaffy

Born at Orland, Cook County, Illinois, March 2, 1865, Andrew DeWitt Mahaffey is the son of John and Mary Ann (Grange) Mahaffay. His father who was born at Orland, in November 1836, was a farmer of Irish descent, who died at Kirksville, Missouri. His mother, born in England, March 19, 1838, died at Kirksville, April 15, 1899. Her death occurred from a cyclone. She

Gale—Beatrice

THOMAS JEFFERSON MAJORS

was descended from English pioneer settlers in Illinois.

Dr. Mahaffay was educated in country grade school, and Brashear Academy at Brashear, Missouri. He attended State Normal School, taking a two year course in elementary education, and afterward attended the American School of Osteopathy and Surgery at Kirksville, Missouri, from which he was graduated in 1897, and in 1902 received his M. D. from Hahneman Medical College at Kansas City, Missouri. He is a member of the Conslintine Herring Medical Society.

On June 15, 1896, he was married to Mallie Gertrude Cunningham at La Plata, Missouri. Mrs. Mahaffay was born at La Plata, April 15, 1875, and before her marriage was an instructor in music. She is of German descent. Their three children are as follows: Mary, born March 25, 1900, who is musical supervisor at San Juan, Texas; Mallie, born April 15, 1902, who is a registered nurse at Omaha, and Charles, born March 15, 1907, who is professor of physics and electrical engineering at Pullman, Washington.

Since 1902 Dr. Mahaffay has been actively engaged in practice at Valparaiso. He is surgeon for the Union Pacific Railroad Company, and a member of the Red Cross. He is a member of the First Methodist Church of Valparaiso, the Modern Woodmen of America and the Odd Fellows. Residence: Valparaiso.

James Patrick Mahoney

James P. Mahoney was born at Hamilton, Illinois, February 13, 1870, the son of James and Margaret (Flynn) Mahoney. His father, who was a farmer and cattle man, was descended from Irish ancestors who came to America in 1864 and drove by mule team and covered wagon to a farm in Illinois, in 1869. In 1871 they homesteaded in eastern Butler County, Nebraska. He was born at Mitchelstown, County Cork, Ireland, and died near Bruno, Butler County, Nebraska, August 2, 1889. His mother was born at Mitchelstown, and died at Ulysses, Nebraska, December 28, 1925.

Mr. Mahoney attended the country schools at Butler County, and attended the high school at David City, Nebraska. Later he studied for six months at the Lincoln Business College, Lincoln, Nebraska. He has lived in Nebraska for 58 years and has always been an active participant in state and community affairs. In the late nineties he served on the county board in Butler County for two years, and he was unsuccessful candidate for the legislature in 1918. For a short time he served as cashier of the Bruno State Bank, and since then has been a farmer and purebred stockman. He has been a director of the Farmers Elevator Company at Palmyra, Nebraska, for the past 15 years.

He was united in marriage with Nellie Murray at Lincoln, February 22, 1898. Mrs. Mahoney, who was born at Stoughton, Wisconsin, July 4, 1872, is of Irish descent. There are eight children: Walter, born November 29, 1898; Joseph L., born July 22, 1900; who married Hilda Brinkman; James P., born January 30, 1902; Lucille, born January 17, 1904; John B., born July 19, 1906; Sylvester, born July 17, 1908; Dorothy, born September 22, 1910; and Edward M., born April 5, 1912.

In the late war Mr. Mahoney took part in loan drives and other war time activities in his precinct. He has served on the school board for 16 years, and is a member of the Old Settlers Organization at Palmyra. He is a member of St. Leo's Catholic Church. His hobby is the producing of better livestock on Nebraska farms. He is a Democrat. Residence: Palmyra.

Calvin George Mahood

A lifetime resident of this state, Calvin George Mahood was born at Petersburg, Nebraska, July 7, 1882, the son of James Nelson and Ellen Elizabeth (Lundy) Mahood. His father, who was a cabinet maker and bookkeeper, was born in County Down, Ireland, in 1840, and died at Petersburg, in 1888; he homesteaded in Nebraska in 1880. His mother was born in Virginia in 1846, spent her childhood in Pennsylvania, and died at Orchard, Nebraska, February 8, 1930.

Mr. Mahood attended the public schools of Neligh and in 1896 was graduated from the Gates Academy there. He was active in basball, track, and football in the academy. He worked for the Daxton Implement Company at Neligh for a time and in 1909 bought an implement and hardware store at Orchard. He was in charge of the Reo Automobile Agency in 1910, managed the Ford Automobile Agency in 1912 and expanded the latter business until 1917 when he built his present modern garage. In 1926 he took over the Ford Agency of Lynch, Nebraska, and at this time he is manager of the Mahood Brothers Garage at Orchard and the Lynch Motor Company. He is a member of the board of directors of the Orchard Alfalfa Co-operative Creamery, and is a member of the board of advisors of the Citizens State Bank of Orchard.

He is serving as president of the Orchard Chamber of Commerce, is a member of the Masonic Lodge, and is affiliated with the Congregational Church of Orchard. He married Mary Elizabeth Fraim at Sioux City, Iowa, April 16, 1924. Mrs. Mahood, who was a teacher for nine years, was born at Red Oak, Iowa, December 23, 1894. They have a daughter, Ellen, born November 26, 1929. Residence: Orchard.

Benjamin Maiben

Benjamin Maiben was born in Grant County, Wisconsin, June 7, 1871, the son of Jane (Children) and John Sandaman Maiben. His father, who was a farmer and Civil War veteran, was born at Peithshire, Scotland, in 1826, and came to America in 1845. He died in Otoe County, Nebraska, November 4, 1894.

His mother was born in County Kent, England, and died in Otoe County, April 6, 1906. Her father was a printer and a lecturer in astronomy.

Mr. Maiben attended the rural public schools and was graduated at the University of Nebraska College of Agriculture. He has lived in Nebraska for 57 years and has always been a farmer. He was married to Rachael Con, at San Francisco, California, June 2, 1909. Mrs. Maiben was born in Seward County, Nebraska, November 3, 1871.

During the late war Mr. Maiben was a precinct worker in classification and took an active part in all loan drives. He is a member of the American Association for the Advancement of Science; is a life member of the Nebraska Horticultural Association; and a life member of the American Genetic Association. He is affiliated with the Presbyterian Church. He is a Republican. Residence: Palmyra.

Winifred Price Main

Winifred Price Main, who has resided in Nebraska for the past 43 years, has taken an active part in the educational and civic affairs of her community. She was born at Vinton, Iowa, March 30, 1866, the daughter of Hays Hamilton and Sarah Maria (Redfield) McElroy. Her father, who was born at Trough Creek, Pennsylvania, April 13, 1841, and died at Vinton, April 13, 1920, was a merchant and postmaster; he served as a member of the Crockers Brigade, 13th Iowa Infantry, during the Civil War. His parents were James A. McElroy, born 1804, and Rebecca (Keith) McElroy, born October 14, 1818, and the family is of Scotch and Irish descent.

Sarah McElroy, mother of Mrs. Main, was born at Cazemovia, New York, March 26, 1844, and died at Wayne, Nebraska, December 23, 1928; she was a prominent church worker and a talented musician; the

ROSE MALTMAN

genealogy of the Redfield family has been preserved in book form.

Mrs. Main was graduated from the Vinton High School, and in 1882-84, was a student at Cornell College, Mount Vernon, Iowa. She is a member of the P. E. O., the Order of Eastern Star, and The Nebraskana Society. At one time she served as a member of the city library board, and has always been interested in the advancement of her community. She is affiliated with the Wayne Methodist Church, and is prominent in church society activities and mission work. Her social clubs are the Monday Club, at Wayne, and the Country Club. She is a Republican.

She was married to David Charles Main at Vinton, Iowa. Mr. Main, who was a banker, was born in Harrison County, Iowa, September 23, 1858, and died at Wayne, April 5, 1910. His parents, George and Ellen (Cook) Main, were both born in England. Three children were born to this marriage: Hays, born October 29, 1896; Helen, born June 29, 1900, who married John T. Bressler, Jr.; and Winifred, born August 22, 1902, who married John C. Carhart. Hays, who was a member of Sigma Chi at the University of Nebraska, is bank cashier at Vinton, Iowa. Helen was a member of Kappa Kappa Gamma at the University of Nebraska, and was later graduated from Smith College, Northampton, Massachusetts, 1922. Winifred was graduated from the University of Nebraska in 1925. Residence: Wayne.

Thomas Jefferson Majors

Thomas J. Majors, affectionately known throughout the state as "Colonel Majors", was born in Jefferson County, Iowa, June 25, 1841. His father, Sterling Perry Majors, was a lawyer and merchant, born in Simpson County, Kentucky, April 27, 1819. He died at Ainsworth, Nebraska, August 26, 1886. He was married to Ann Brown, who was also born in Simpson County, on March 19, 1820. She died at Peru, July 31, 1917.

Colonel Majors received his early education at Libertyville, Iowa, and later attended Peru Teachers College. A Republican, he was elected to the last territorial council of Nebraska Territory; to the first state senate, and was re-elected to the second senate. Later he was elected to the house of representatives; and thereafter served two terms as lieutenant-governor of Nebraska. He was assessor of Internal Revenue three years; again member of the house of representatives for a term, and state senator five succeeding terms. He was unsuccessful candidate for governor.

On August 28, 1870, he was united in marriage to Isabel Amelia Bushong at Bureau County, Illinois. Mrs. Majors was born in Bureau County, March 21, 1846, and died at Peru, July 15, 1922. Her father was French and her mother German. Of their marriage five children have been born: Franklin Perry, March 13, 1874, married to Emma Mae David; James Howard, born July 10, 1876, married Myrtle Robinson; Thomas Arthur, born May 23, 1879, married Ina Meade; Charles Wilson, born February 15, 1883, married Byrda Andre; and Gladys Lotta, born February 3, 1889, married Clarence W. Gale.

Colonel Majors was appointed to the state normal board about thirty years ago, and has been president of the board most of that time. He is a member of the Nebraska State Historical Society and The Nebraskana Society. He is past department commander of the Grand Army of the Republic. He enlisted under the first call in 1861, was made first lieutenant and later promoted to captain, major and lieutenant-colonel. He received his honorable discharge on July 1, 1866, having served five years and fifteen days.

He is a member of the Methodist Episcopal Church at Peru. On December 17, 1926, he was presented the Kiwanis Medal for distinguished service as a pioneer, soldier, citizen and statesman. He is a Mason and member of the Shrine. Residence: Peru. (Photograph on Page 754).

Idael Makeever

One of Nebraska's claims to distinction in the literary world lies in the fact that Idael Makeever, noted poet, educator, and author, is a Nebraskan. She was born at Valparaiso, Indiana, the daughter of George and Tryphena (Ferguson) Childers. Her father, who was a salesman and stockman, was born at Valparaiso and died there February 14, 1920; his ancestry was English. Her mother, whose ancestry was Scotch, was born at Chatham, Canada, and died at Valparaiso, July 7, 1918.

Mrs. Makeever received her high school and college education in schools at Valparaiso, and for several years taught in the public schools. She has been a saleswoman and homemaker, during which time she has constantly engaged in writing in addition to her many civic duties. She has taken a prominent part in the Young Women's Christian Association and Community Chest events, served as secretary of the Woman's Club at Boulder, Colorado, where she now resides, and was a member of the Business and Professional Women's Association during 1928 and 1929.

She acted as board member of the Young Women's Christian Association from 1921 to 1923, was secretary of that organization in 1926, and holds membership in the Order of Eastern Star and the Presbyterian Church. During the World War she worked on daily newspapers at Omaha, Nebraska, writing and selling advertising.

Mrs. Makeever has composed a number of short stories and feature articles, but is known throughout the east and west for her poetry of the middlewest. Her three volumes of descriptive and individual poems are: *Golden Rod and Dialect Poems; Prairie Flowers and Meadow Grasses.* In various critiques of her work it has been noted that in style and feeling her verse is closely associated with that of James Whitcomb Riley while her own individuality of pattern marks it as distinctly a new kind of literary achievement. The *Omaha World-Herald*, in reviewing her last volume, commented: "Her poems contain the incense of the prairies, the love of home and the pathos of partings that appeal to every heart that loves poetry."

Mrs. Makeever has demonstrated peculiar talent and adaptability as an impersonator and monologist and has won a national reputation through her performance on the Chautauqua stage. Her hobby is reading. On February 26, 1888, she was married to Milton Makeever at Valparaiso, Indiana. Mr. Makeever, who is a lawyer, and mining manager for the Makeever Brothers Company, was born at Rensselaer, Indiana, February 7, 1862, of Scotch-Irish parents.

There are two children: Merle, born December 1, 1889, who married Horace Blaine Putman; and Iva Lee, born May 25, 1894, who married Clarence McCloughan. Both are graduates of the Stromsburg High School and Kearney Normal School, and are teachers. Residence: Boulder, Colorado.

Ada C. Malcolm

Ada C. Malcolm, noted educator, was born at Clay Center, Clay County, Kansas, the daughter of Charles and Odille (Paranteau) Wingrove. Her father, who is a lawyer and farmer, was born at Clarksburg, West Virginia, January 6, 1846; he served in the 3rd Virginia Cavalry during the Civil War. Her paternal great-grandfather, Lord James Wingrove was prominent in England; his son, John, came to America at the age of 16 and served as colonel in the American Army during the Revolution, and was given a large tract of land in Virginia for his service.

On June 23, 1904, her marriage to Charles Calvin Malcolm was solemnized at Clay Center. Mr. Malcolm, who is a pharmacist, was born in Colorado, September 13, 1880, the son of Herman and Sopha Malcolm. They have three children: Donald Claude, born May 27, 1905, who was graduated from the Lincoln High School in 1922, and is now a medical student at the University of Nebraska; Bernard Leon, born November 19, 1908, who was second lieutenant in the Officers' Reserve Corps in the University of Nebraska, and is now studying mechanical engineering at the University of Nebraska; and Norman Adrian, born June 11, 1911. Donald holds membership in Theta Nu, Scabbard and Blade, Delta Sigma Lambda, and Phi Beta Pi. Bernard is a member of Delta Sigma Lambda, and is national vice president of Phi Tau Theta. Norman is studying pre-law work at the University of Nebraska, and is a member of Delta Sigma Lambda.

Mrs. Malcolm was a teacher in the public schools of Kansas for some time and from 1920 to 1925 was dramatic instructor at the University School of Music at Lincoln. In 1925 she was in charge of the Malcolm Studio. She has toured for Chautauqua companies for eleven seasons. During the late war she was especially active in Liberty loan drives and as junior and senior Red Cross organizer.

Mrs. Malcolm holds membership in the Lincoln Woman's Club, Drama League, the Nebraskana Society, and Trinity Methodist Episcopal Church. She is a member of the Electa Chapter of the Order of Eastern Star. Her hobbies are reading and gardening. Residence: Lincoln. (Photograph in Album).

William Robert Maloney

William Robert Maloney, merchant and funeral director, was born at Scranton, Iowa, September 18, 1883, son of William and Honora (Barrow) Maloney. The father was a native of Canada and the mother of Ireland.

On November 16, 1910, Mr. Maloney was married to Erma Vincent Dye at Salina, Kansas. She was born at Whiting, Kansas, October 10, 1880. There is one daughter, Maureen, born August 22, 1911.

At the present time Mr. Maloney is president of the W. R. Maloney Company, furniture dealers and funeral directors, vice president of the First National Bank of North Platte, the Federation of Nebraska Retailers of which he is a director, the Nebraska Funeral Directors Association (past president) the Chamber of Commerce (director 15 years), the Knights of Columbus, the Elks and the Brotherhood of American Yeoman.

He was made a master merchant in the class of 1931, being one of ten chosen for that honor. For the past nineteen years he has been a director of the North Platte Building and Loan Association. For fifteen years he has served as a member of the board of State Embalming Examiners. Residence: North Platte.

Rose Mizar Maltman

Rose Mizar Maltman was born at Craig, Missouri, July 20, 1888, daughter of Michael C. and Sarah Elizabeth (Chastain) Mizar.

She received her education in the public schools, and an November 24, 1905, was united in marriage to William Ward Maltman at Omaha. Mr. Maltman, who is president of the Democrat Printing Company, and publisher of *The Hastings Democrat*, was born at Sandy Creek, New York, June 17, 1878. (*See Nebraskana*).

Mrs. Maltman is a member of the Eastern Star and the Ladies' Shrine Auxiliary.

For a number of years she was actively engaged with her husband in the operation of newspapers in Nebraska.

She is an enthusiastic golfer, and during the year 1929-30, was city champion of Hastings. She is a member of the Hillside Golf Club. Residence: Hastings. (Photograph on Page 756).

William Ward Maltman

William Ward Maltman, a resident of Nebraska since 1878, was born at Sandy Creek, Oswego County, New York, June 17, 1878, the son of William and Ada Elizabeth (Weldon) Maltman. His father, who was born in Ontario, Canada, and died at Grand Island, Nebraska, 1925, was a farmer; his ancestry was Irish. His mother,

who was born at Sandy Creek, Oswego County, New York, and died at Wood River, Nebraska, December 24, 1918, is descended from English ancestors who settled in New York prior to the Revolution.

Mr. Maltman was graduated from the Wood River High School in 1896. He has been continuously engaged in newspaper work since 1907, and has owned and managed newspapers at Anoka, Shelton, Ansley, Broken Bow, Kenesaw, and Wood River. He is at the present time president and general manager of the Democrat Printing Company, printers and publishers of the *Hastings Democrat*.

A Republican, Mr. Maltman has served on Republican County Committee since 1912, was chairman of the Adams County Committee, 1928-30, and is now vice-president of the Nebraska Republican Club. He has been a member of the Rotary Club since 1923, served as director of the Nebraska Press Association, 1926-7, and is a member and director of the Hillside Golf Club at Hastings. He holds membership in the Nebraskana Society, and is a member of the Ancient Craft and Scottish Rite Masons and the Shrine. During the World War he served with the Adams County Registration Board and Council of Defense. He was a private in the Spanish American War; he now holds membership in the Sons of the American Revolution and the Hastings Camp of the United Spanish War Veterans.

His marriage to Rose Mizar was solemnized at Omaha, Douglas County, Nebraska, November 24, 1905. Mrs. Maltman was born at Craig, Holt County, Missouri, July 20, 1888. She is prominent in social and athletic affairs at Hastings, and is now city golf champion of Hastings. Mr. Maltman is fond of fishing, hunting, and golfing. Residence: Hastings. (Photograph on Page 759).

Stanley Maly

Stanley Maly was born at Schuyler, Nebraska, May 7, 1880, son of Vencl and Marie (Markovec) Maly. His father who was born in Bohemia (now Czechoslovakia) came to America about 1860. He engaged in the mercantile business at Schuyler for many years, but was retired at the time of his death at Lincoln, on September 1, 1926. His wife, Marie, was born in Dvory, Czechoslovakia, and died at Schuyler, May 12, 1924. She was a housewife and mother and active in the J. C. D. and Bohemian Woman's Club.

Mr. Maly attended the Schuyler public and high school, and entered the general merchandise business at Schuyler. He has been a banker since 1904, and is now vice president of the First National Bank of Lincoln, and a director of the Lincoln Trust Company. He is a Republican, member of the Chamber of Commerce, Lions Club and Hiram Club. In 1898 he served as a private with Company K, 2nd Nebraska Volunteer Infantry in the Spanish American War. He is a member of the Spanish American War Veterans. During the World War he was a member of the draft board, active in Red Cross, and a member of the Nebraska Council of Defense.

A thirty-second degree Mason, Mr. Maly is also a member of the Shrine. He enjoys golf and motoring and is a member of the Lincoln Country Club.

On October 24, 1917, he was married to Mary Frances Ketchmark at Glenwood, Iowa. Mrs. Maly was born at Omaha, June 16, 1889. There are three children, Mary Margaret, born September 5, 1918; Dorothy Frances, born February 6, 1921; and Stanley, Jr., born October 10, 1922. Residence: Lincoln.

Paul Ignatius Manhart

Paul I. Manhart, lawyer, was born at Mondamin, Iowa, October 23, 1894. He is the son of Lawrence and Catherine (Buckley) Manhart, and for the past sixteen years has been a resident of Nebraska. Lawrence Manhart, a

WILLIAM WARD MALTMAN

native of Alsace-Lorraine, was a harness and saddle maker, who came to America as a young man. He died at Panama, Iowa, November 23, 1911. His wife, Catherine Buckley, was born at Anamosa, Iowa, and died at Omaha, August 17, 1930. She was of Irish descent.

Mr. Manhart attended Georgetown University, at Washington, D. C., where he was awarded his LL. B. For three years he was in the Civil Service Department of the government at Washington, and prior thereto taught school and high school at Panama, Iowa. Since June 21, 1921, he has been engaged in the general practice of law. An independent Republican, he was candidate for nomination for congress from the first district of Nebraska in 1923.

He was married to Eleanor Catherine Steinauer at Omaha, on April 18, 1923. Mrs. Manhart was born at Steinauer, Nebraska, August 24, 1897, and is of German, Irish and Swiss descent. There are six children, Frances Ann., born March 1, 1924; Mary Eleanor, September 10, 1925; Paul Ignatius, Jr., January 2, 1927; David, June 10, 1928; Mary Jane, October 16, 1929, and John Nicholas, November 24, 1930.

During the World War Mr. Manhart served in the War Ordnance Department. He is a Catholic, and a member of Our Lady of Lourdes Church. Residence: Omaha.

George Brinton Mann

George B. Mann, editor and newspaperman of Plattsmouth, Nebraska, was born at St. Louis, Missouri, March 10, 1868. He is the son of Peter Mann, who was born at Bedford County, Pennsylvania, September 24, 1824, and died at Plattsmouth, December 21, 1891, and Elizabeth Caroline (Hooker) Mann, who was born at Desseldorf, Germany, March 22, 1835, and died at Plattsmouth, November 3, 1922. Peter Mann was the son of John Mann (1787-1845) and Sarah (McMullin) Mann (1800-1883). John Mann was the son of Peter Mann I (1759-1842) and Hanna (Haney) Mann (1764-1827). Elizabeth (Hooker) Mann was the daughter of Francis Hooker (died 1838) and Mary (Brightingham) Hooker (1814-1872). Francis Hooker was the son of Christopher Hooker. Mary (Brightingham) Hooker was the daughter of George and Elizabeth Brightingham.

Captain Peter Mann, father of George Brinton Mann, led a colorful and varied life. As a youth, he was apprenticed to the carpenter trade and after serving his apprenticeship built wooden tanks in which to store the coal oil then discovered near Bradford, Pennsylvania. A little later he moved to Pittsburgh, where he built his first boats, and from there he was engaged as a carpenter on a steamboat on the Ohio River. He was boat carpenter and pilot on the American Fur Company's boats shipping from St. Louis to Fort Benton, in 1848. In 1850 he traveled by steamboat to Fort Leavenworth, and from there journeyed overland to California, walking most of the way. In California he found little gold, but a great deal of steamboating on the Sacramento River. In 1855 he returned by way of the Isthmus of Panama to New Orleans, and St. Louis, and from that time until 1861 was a pilot on the Mississippi River. During the Civil War he was occupied in the navy yard at Carondlet, building Grant's fleet of gunboats. He was on the Union Pacific steamboats *Denver, Colorado, Kate Sweeney,* between St. Joseph and Omaha, from 1864 to 1865. In 1867 he raised the sunken steamboat *Benton,* near Florence, Nebraska, for an insurance company. In 1869 he brought the steamboat *Gallatin* from Memphis to Plattsmouth, to cross the C. B. & Q. railroad then being built from Plattsmouth to Kearney. He superintended the building of, and operated the transfer boat *Vice President* for the Burlington railroad at Plattsmouth.

George B. Mann has lived in Nebraska for 61 years, where he received his education, attending the Plattsmouth High School until 1881, and engaging in the newspaper business for the last fifty years. He has held the following positions: editor of the *Saturday Mirror,* 1891; editor *Evening News,* 1899; the *Elkhorn Exchange,* 1892; and the *Plattsmouth Journal,* 1896-1901. Together with Edgar Howard, of Columbus, Nebraska, he printed the first copy of the *Plattsmouth Journal,* November 5, 1881, on a Washington hand press. Today he is in the mechanical department of the *Plattsmouth Journal.*

At Kearney, Nebraska, he was married to Pearl Alice Nichols, September 4, 1913. Mrs. Mann, who was born in Buffalo County, Nebraska, February 10, 1879, the daughter of David and Ann Nichols, and now is principal of the high school at Clearwater, Nebraska.

They have one son, Robert M., born June 22, 1914, who has just been made an Eagle Scout.

Politically, Mr. Mann is an independent. Since 1886 he has been a member of the International Typographical Union. His favorite sport is boating on the Missouri River; having owned a houseboat for 20 years. His hobby is the collection of antiques. His home contains many pieces of old-fashioned furniture, many historical books and papers on early Nebraska history, and this collection is considered the finest of its kind in his county. Residence: Plattsmouth.

Martin Strange Mansfield

Martin S. Mansfield, merchant at Winnebago, Nebraska, for the past 30 years, was born at Homer, Nebraska, January 10, 1879, the son of Martin and Sarah C. (DeBorde) Mansfield. His father, who was a carpenter, was born at Springfield, Illinois, April 4, 1843, and died at Homer, January 10, 1910; he served for three years in the 25th Illinois Infantry during the Civil War. His mother was born in Wisconsin, September 15, 1852, and died at Homer, July 5, 1917.

Mr. Mansfield was a merchant at Homer for five years and for over twenty-five years engaged in the general merchandise business at Winnebago where he is also connected with the state bank. He is a member of The Nebraskana Society, is affiliated with the Presbyterian Church, and holds membership in the Democratic Party. He is a Mason.

On November 13, 1901, his marriage to Ethelyn Charlotte King was solemnized at Bottineau, North Dakota. Mrs. Mansfield was born at Fairbury, Nebraska, September 25, 1882; they had one son, Harold, born August 12, 1902, who died August 2, 1905. During the World War Mr. Mansfield served as chairman of the council of defense in Thurston County. Residence: Winnebago.

Charles B. Mantel

Charles B. Mantel, a hardware merchant at Malmo, Nebraska, since 1914, has always lived in that community. He was born at Malmo, August 31, 1885, the son of John B. and Barbetta Marie (Folk) Mantel. His father, who was a farmer and one of the first settlers in Saunders County, was born at Baden, Germany, December 25, 1840, and died at Malmo, February 18, 1899. His mother was born at Wurttemberg, Creglingen, Germany, May 5, 1844, and died at Malmo, January 24, 1919.

Mr. Mantel farmed until 1914 when he entered the hardware business in which he is still engaged. He is a member of The Nebraskana Society, and has always been interested in civic welfare. His sports are hunting and fishing. Residence: Malmo.

Orlando Bidwell Manville

Orlando Bidwell Manville, real estate and investment executive, was born at Watertown, Wisconsin, September 29, 1867. He is the son of Hiram Sage and Helen Frances (Nute) Manville, the former an importer of dry goods and notions until 1876, and general manager of

The Converse Cattle Company until 1903. Hiram Sage Manville was born at Great Barrington, Massachusetts on June 13, 1829, of old New England ancestry. He died at Oakdale, Nebraska, December 6, 1911.

Helen Frances Nute, his wife, was born at Farmington, New Hampshire, June 20, 1836, and died at Boston, March 17, 1927. She was also of old New England stock.

Orlando B. Manville attended Markham's Academy at Milwaukee, Wisconsin, one year; the public schools of Washington, D. C. two years; the public schools of Manchester, New Hampshire, three years; Chauncy Hall at Boston seven months; and Dartmouth College one year. He is a member of Beta Theta Pi.

On May 29, 1888, he was married to Alice E. Bittenger at Tilden, Nebraska. Two children were born to them, Richard B., December 25, 1889, who is unmarried. Hiram Sage, born October 21, 1891, was married in June, 1916, to Vera Regina Hudson of Omaha. To them were born three children, Betty Larie, born August 18, 1920; Barbara Lorraine, born March 2, 1923; and Beatrice Lucille, born November 2, 1925. Their youngest child, Florence was born July 7, 1905, and has completed a secretarial course at Stephens College. She is a stenographer. Divorced in 1900, Mr. Manville was married to Nora E. Nelson on May 3, 1902, at Neligh, Nebraska. She was born December 1, 1872.

Mr. Manville resided in South Dakota from 1890 until 1892, in Nebraska the summers 1882 to 1885, and became a permanent resident of Nebraska in 1885. The years 1904-06 he spent in California. Until 1906 he was engaged in the cattle business, and since that date has engaged in the real estate and investment business at Oakdale and Norfolk, Nebraska.

He is affiliated with the Congregational Church, is a member of the Chamber of Commerce, the Ancient Order of United Workmen and is a life member of the Nebraskana Society. Residence: Norfolk. (Photograph in Album).

Milton Hall Marble

Milton H. Marble, a direct descendant of Edward Doty, who came to America on the *Mayflower* in 1620, was born near Wooster, Ohio, March 16, 1839, the son of Hiram Sepcott and Anne (Stewart) Marble. His father, a minister in the Universalist Church, was born at Hoosick Falls, New York, June 10, 1810, the son of Jacob and Lydia Marble. He died at Mount Pleasant, Washington, in February, 1891. His mother, the daughter of Sylvester and Almira (Doty) Stewart, was born in Wayne County, New York, December 27, 1814, and died in Ohio, April 18, 1849.

Mr. Marble who is a pioneer Nebraskan, was educated in the Iowa public schools and was graduated from the Iowa City High School. He has been justice of the peace since 1895, and is the only police judge Table Rock, Nebraska has ever had. From 1886 to 1890, he served as county commissioner of Pawnee County. He has been a notary public for 48 years and since 1884 has been secretary of the cemetery board at Table Rock. A Republican, he cast his first presidential vote for Abraham Lincoln. For over 60 years he has been a contributor to magazines and newspapers.

On February 4, 1863, he was married to Maria Sarah Bump at Albany, Green County, Wisconsin. Mrs. Marble was born at Potsdam, New York, April 21, 1844, the daughter of John Orville and Sophronia Bump, and died at Table Rock, April 29, 1872. Two children were born to this union: Alice, born April 4, 1867, who married Edgar Woods; and Harmon, born November 5, 1870, who married Myrtle Woolsey. Harmon has been in the Indian Service as superintendent and assistant superintendent for 17 years. He was proprietor of the *Humboldt Leader* for fifteen years. Mr. Marble was married to Amanda J. Fairbank at Tecumseh, Nebraska, October 31, 1872, who died April 6, 1910; and on April 15, 1911, married Amy E. Linn, of Abilene, Kansas.

Mr. Marble has been a member of the Odd Fellows for 63 years and bears distinction of being the oldest member of this organization in Nebraska; was a charter member of the lodge of Table Rock. For 19 years he was president of school district number 51, and for 24 years has been a member of the Table Rock board of education, serving most of this time as secretary. At one time in his early youth, he served as deputy postmaster at Brodhead, Wisconsin, under Abraham Lincoln. Residence: Table Rock.

Thomas T. Marcott

Thomas T. Marcott, municipal judge, was born in Canada, October 21, 1857, son of John B. and Matilda (Mountain) Marcott. The father was born in Canada, and died at Brady, Nebraska in 1898. He was a retired farmer of Canadian French descent. His wife was born in Canada, and died at Brady in 1904. She was of French and Scotch descent.

On August 5, 1885, Mr. Marcott was married to Ruby Fidela Atkinson at Brady. She was born at Albany, Wisconsin, November 3, 1865, of English descent. There are three children, born to their union, two of which are still living, Nona M., born November 19, 1891, married W. T. Beatty of Brady. Two children were born to their union, William, December 5, 1915; and Irene, born December 31, 1916. Mrs. Beatty died in October, 1917. T. Logan, born May 10, 1895, married Gene Wardon and is residing on a ranch just south of Brady. Nina F., born June 21, 1902, married Tom Palmer who is maintainer of the public highways of Lincoln County residing at Brady.

Judge Marcott is a Democrat, and has resided in Nebraska since 1879. He was elected justice of the peace of Gaslin precinct in 1885 serving about 12 years, resigning to move to Brady where he went into the lumber business which he ran until 1896 at which time he returned to the ranch. In 1908 he retired from the ranch and has resided in Brady since. He was elected municipal judge in about 1922 and has served that office since. His fraternal organizations include the Modern Woodmen of America, the Elks and the Independent Order of Odd Fellows. Residence: Brady.

Clarence Sidney Marcy

Clarence Sidney Marcy, farmer and rancher, was born at Rowley, Iowa, November 18, 1872, and for 43 years has been a resident of Nebraska. His father, Sidney Stephen Marcy, was born at Marengo, Illinois, April 2, 1848, and died at Hay Springs, May 5, 1921. The family has been in America more than 125 years. Harriet Jane Blood, wife of Sidney Stephen Marcy, was born at New Hartford, Connecticut, April 11, 1849, her family having been in America about 150 years.

Educated in country schools in Iowa and Nebraska, Mr. Marcy was graduated from high school at Hay Springs. He taught country schools for three years, clerked five years in a general store and in a bank for about six months, and served as county treasurer for eight years, from 1923 until 1931. He was defeated at the primaries for a third term. He is a Democrat.

Mr. Marcy was united in marriage with Dora J. Johansen at Hay Springs, February 14, 1897. She is the daughter of Christian and Anna M. (Wortman) Johansen. Mrs. Marcy attended country schools and graduated from the Hay Springs High School. She is a member of the Federated Womans Club, the P. E. O. sisterhood and is a member and past worthy matron of the Eastern Star. Mr. and Mrs. Marcy have had five children, four of whom are living, Dorothy Claire, born October 18, 1900; Clarence Leslie, November 18, 1902; Opal Joyce, October 11, 1908; Deane Sidney, December 26, 1910; Irene Ethel, born May 1, 1916, who died May 18, 1916; and Eleanor Jane, born July 1, 1922. Deane Sidney is

CLARENCE SIDNEY MARCY

taking his pre-medical course at Rutgers University in New Jersey.

For six years Mr. Marcy served as a member of the board of trustees of Rushville, and one year was chairman of the board. For eight years he was chairman of the Sheridan County Corn Show, and served four years as chairman of the road committee for the Rushville Chamber of Commerce. Mr. Marcy was a proxy delegate to the Democratic state convention in 1924, and is a past president of the Nebraska State County Treasurers Association. During 1920 and 1921 he was treasurer of School District No. 35 of Sheridan County and since 1928 has been a member of the Rushville Chamber of Commerce. A Master Mason of Hay Springs Lodge Ancient Free and Accepted Masons, he is also a Knight Templar and Royal and Select Master. He is a member and past worthy patron of the Eastern Star. During the late war Mr. Marcy was extremely active in all civilian projects oversubscribing his quota in liberty bonds, and registering men, subject to draft, without remuneration. Mr. and Mrs. Marcy are affiliated with the Hay Springs Congregational Church. Residence: Hay Springs. (Photograph on Page 762).

Frank Mares

One of Nebraska's pioneer farmers and business men, Frank Mares has lived in this state for 67 years and has been prominent in various civic organizations. He was born in Czecho-Slovakia, October 11, 1864, the son of Jacob and Mary (Franek) Mares. His father, who was also a farmer, was born at Korita, Czecho-Slovakia, March 9, 1832, and died at Dwight, Nebraska, August 28, 1901. His mother, whose parents were pioneer settlers in Butler County, was born at Klatova, Czecho-Slovakia, August 26, 1838, and died at Dwight, September 26, 1920.

Mr. Mares received his education in a rural school. In 1900 he was a hotel keeper at Dwight, and at this time is a farmer and real estate dealer. He has served as Democratic delegate to county conventions, has been a member of the school board for 35 years, and was appointed county agent inspector by Governor Neville. During the World War he served as chairman of the loan drive committee and chairman of the Red Cross drives.

His marriage to Anna Kastl occurred at Weston, Saunders County, Nebraska, October 9, 1886. Mrs. Mares, who was a pioneer in Saunders County, was born at Weston, August 25, 1869, and died at Dwight, January 5, 1925. They have nine children, all of whom are living on farms: Albert; Frank C.; Barbara; James; Lewis; Fred; Helen; Eleanor; and Edward.

Mr. Mares is affiliated with the Dwight Catholic Church, and holds membership in the following organizations: Wester Bohemian Fraternal Association; Woodmen of the World; Modern Woodmen; Catholic Workmen and The Nebraskana Society. His hobby is pigeons. Residence: Dwight.

William Charles Margrave

On June 27, 1877, William C. Margrave was born near Preston, Richardson County, Nebraska. His father, William Addison Margrave, a farmer and rancher, was born at Peoria, Illinois, May 1, 1845, and died at Preston, July 30, 1906.

Margaret (Rubeti) Margrave, his mother, was born at Highland, Doniphan County, Kansas, January 19, 1848, the daughter of a French Canadian father and a Sac and Fox Indian mother. She was adopted at the age of three by a Presbyterian missionary, Rev. S. M. Irvin, who reared and educated her. She became the first teacher in the Sac and Fox Indian school on the Indian reservation near Preston, where she taught Indian children who could speak no English while she knew none of their language. She died at Hiawatha, Kansas, December 28, 1918.

Mr. Margrave received his early education at the Indian school where his mother had taught, later was a student in the public schools at Reserve, Kansas, and attended Hiawatha Academy.

For 46 years he has lived in Nebraska where for twenty years he was president of the W. A. Margrave Company and president of the Farmers' State Bank, at Preston. For the last twelve years he has been a director of of the Morrill and Janes Bank of Hiawatha.

He was united in marriage with Mary Julia Waller at Padonia, Brown County, Kansas, March 17, 1897. Mrs. Margrave was born August 28, 1877, and died at Preston, April 27, 1908. Three children were born to them: Howard J., born September 15, 1900, who married Marie Wasmand; Julia R., born September 12, 1903, who married Harold Kottman; and Martha M., born January 29, 1906, who married Madison Idol. His marriage to Ida Ernestine Pribbeno was solemnized at Preston, June 1, 1910. She was born at Preston, September 14, 1885, the daughter of Charles and Mary (Zoeller) Pribbeno. Three children were born to them, two of whom are living: Helen M., born December 21, 1911; William Addison, born April 9, 1914; and Warren Robert, born March 15, 1919, who died August 13, 1924.

For the past eight years Mr. Margrave has been a director on the school board, district 99, at Preston. He is a member of the Red Cross, the Modern Woodmen, and is chairman of the Republican national committee for Jefferson precinct. He is a member of the Methodist Church at Reserve, Kansas. His hobby is reading. Residence: Preston.

John Henry Markel

John Henry Markel was born at Nebraska City, September 10, 1891. His father, Henry Gustavus Markel, was born in Springfield, Illinois, August 7, 1851, of German descent. Engaged in the hardware business at Nebraska City from 1905 until his death on November 11, 1925, he was married to Amelia Mary Mohr, a native of Germany, born June 21, 1858. She came from a family of high military rank in her native country, and died at Nebraska City, March 5, 1909.

John H. Markel attended the Nebraska City public schools until 1907, and started as a Ford dealer at Nebraska City, August 3, 1908. On April 14, 1913, he took over the Ford dealership at Lincoln, which he sold in April, 1914. In November of 1914 he became Ford and Dodge dealer at Nebraska City. In March of 1915, he opened an office in Chicago, for the distribution of oil in the central west, and in December of 1916, sold his Ford Agency. In August, 1917, he sold his Dodge agency in Nebraska City, and his office in Chicago and entered the World War.

He enlisted as a private in headquarters company of the 355th Infantry, 89th Division and was promoted to sergeant on October 19, 1917; transferred to the 34th Division, National Guard Unit; on November 7, 1917, he was promoted to first sergeant Headquarters Company, 134th Infantry; May 1, 1918, he was promoted to regimental sergeant-major, 134th Infantry; September 11, 1918, he was promoted to second lieutenant of Regular Army Supply Office, transferred to 10th Supply Train, 10th Division under General Wood, and on October 18, 1918, received promotion to supply captain, 10th Division, Regular Army. He was honorably discharged January 23, 1919.

In December, 1927, he sold the Dodge Agency, taking the Hudson-Essex dealership at Lincoln, January, 1929. Omaha was then added for Hudson-Essex dealership, September, 1929, and he had taken entire distribution for entire state and western part of Iowa for Hudson-Essex Cars, with offices in Omaha and Lincoln.

During 1926-28 he was chairman of the campaign fund of the Community Chest. He has been a member of the Lincoln Kiwanis Club since 1927, and is a life member of the Lincoln Commercial Club and the Lincoln Auto Club. He is a member of the Omaha Chamber of Commerce, the Ad-Sell League, the Knights of Ak-Sar-Ben, the Aero-

nautic Association of the United States, and a director of
the Motor Trades Association of Omaha and Lincoln. His
hobby is aviation, and his sports are golf and hunting. His
clubs are the Omaha Club, the Omaha Athletic Club, and
the Lincoln Country Club. Residence: Omaha.

Miles R. Markley

Miles R. Markley, dentist, was born at Juniata, Nebraska, November 5, 1903, son of Melvin and Mildred
(Veley) Markley. His father Dr. M. Markley, was born
in Cass County, Michigan, August 1, 1862. In 1779 he
came to the state of Nebraska with his parents, Urias
L. Markley and Caroline Lutz Markley, his brother Lemon and sister Lennie. They settled on a farm in Adams
County near the towns of Juniata and Hastings. The
brother Lemon Markley, M. D., took his degree from
Omaha Medical College in 1887, and was the first resident
practicing physician in Kimball, Nebraska, 1887-1890.
He moved from there to Bellingham, Washington where
he now lives. The sister, Lennie (Markley) Saddler
lives in the same city.

Malvin Markley attended the Philadelphia College
of Dental Surgery, graduating in the class of 1896. He
was two years an instructor in this institution He
practiced in Juniata, Nebraska from 1896-1909, when
he and his family moved to Kimball. Of the three children in this family, Luella M. Markley is a graduate
of the University of Oregon School of Journalism, having
had training in the University of Colorado and Doane
College in Crete, Nebraska. She is at present the editor
of the Oregon State Board of Public Health publication,
Child Health. The younger brother Dick, is a graduate
of the Kimball Public Schools and is preparing for a
medical course.

Dr. M. Markley's wife, Mildred, was born in Otsego,
Michigan, August 12, 1883. She is secretary of the Kim-
ball school board and past president of the Kimball
Womans Club.

Dr. Miles R. Markley attended Kimball public and
high schools, graduating from the later in 1921. He attended the University of Nebraska during the years
1922-23, and the University of Denver from 1923 until
1927, receiving the degree of Doctor of Dental Surgery
in 1927. He is a member of Lambda Chi Alpha and
Delta Sigma Delta fraternities. Since July 1927 he has
been active in the practice of dentistry at Kimball.

On June 28, 1929, he was married to Winnifred F. Lute
of Denver She was born at Camden, New Jersey, September 23, 1905. She has the degree of Bachelor of Arts
and the degree of Bachelor of Science in Commercial
science. She taught in the Sidney, Nebraska high school
in 1926-27.

Dr. Markley is a member of the Kimball Methodist
Episcopal Church, the National, State, and District Dental Society, the Lions Club (secretary 1931, director 1932,
state secretary 1932) and is scout master of Scout Troop
No. 31. His club is the Kimball Country Club. He enjoys all outdoor sports especially fishing and skating,
while his hobbies are his garden and his work shop. Residence: Kimball.

John Prince Markoe

John Prince Markoe is a native of Minnesota, born at
St. Paul, November 1, 1890. He is the son of James
Cox and Mary (Prince) Markoe, the former a physician.
James Cox Markoe was born at St. Paul, August 13, 1856,
and is descended from French immigrants to the Danish
West Indies, who came to America prior to the Revolution
and settled in Philadelphia. Mary (Prince) Markoe was
born at St. Paul, September 19, 1856.

Professor Markoe attended the public schools of St.
Paul, until 1905, and was graduated from the High School
department of St. Thomas College in 1909. He attended

the United States Military Academy from 1910-14, where
he was a letterman in football 1912-13.

From 1914-15 he held the rank of second lieutenant,
10th United States Cavalry, Fort Huachuca, Arizona;
and captain Company F., 2nd Minnesota Infantry on the
Mexican Border, 1916-17. During the years 1922 and
1923 he was professor of mathematics at the University of
Detroit, and at the present time he holds the position of
professor of astronomy at Creighton University. He is a
member of the Society of Jesus. His hobby is
mathematics. Residence: Omaha.

Robert Howard Marks

Robert Howard Marks, farmer and pioneer resident
of Nebraska, was born at Sun Prairie, Wisconsin, June
4, 1876, son of Robert Henry and Ella (Pyncheon) Marks.
His father, who was born at Sun Prairie, September 27,
1842, was a volunteer in the 40th Wisconsin Infantry in
the Civil War. He was a farmer in Nebraska who died
at Alexandria, August 10, 1906. His parents came from
England in the 1830's, settling near the present town of
Sun Prairie, the trading point being Milwaukee, seventy-
five miles away. Ella Pyncheon was born in Clyde, New
York, February 6, 1844, and before her marriage was a
school teacher. She has always been interested in educational and church work. Her mother's ancestors
came from Scotland in early colonial days, while her
father, William Pyncheon, was of English descent. The
family moved to Thayer County in 1883, and Mr. Marks
was educated first in the country schools here, completing
the 11th year of the Ohiowa High School in 1897. In
1898 he completed a course at the Omaha Commercial
College, and during the year 1911-12 was a student at
the University of Nebraska.

Beginning as a hardware merchant at Ohiowa in 1898,
Mr. Marks continued until 1900, when he became assistant cashier of the Bank of Ohiowa. He retired from
the bank in 1904 to establish the Ohiowa telephone exchange, of which he retained management until 1912.
He moved to his present home in 1910, which is on the
same farm purchased by his father in 1880, and occupied
in 1883.

A Republican, he was a member of the House of Representatives, 1904-05, from Fillmore County, and was active in civic affairs in Ohiowa until 1910. He volunteered
in June, 1917, and served as a private with the 134th
Infantry, 34th Division, at Camp Cody, New Mexico,,
until August, 1918. He was transferred to Camp Dix,
New Jersey, on that date and sailed for France in October, 1918. After three months service he returned to
the United States with the 83rd Division and was mustered out at Camp Funston, Kansas, February, 1919.
Since 1919 he has been a member of the American Legion,
at Ohiowa.

He is a member of the Modern Woodmen of America,
the Nebraskana Society, and for several years a director
of the school board. His special interests include better
highways, better schools, better homes and communities.

On June 18, 1898, he was married to Clara Belle Clemons at Council Bluffs, Iowa. Mrs. Marks was born at
Carleton, Nebraska, April 2, 1879, the daughter of Albert F. and Laura (Babcock) Clemons. Her ancestors
were mainly English, one fought in the French and Indian
War and others in the Revolution. Albert F. Clemons
was born November 21, 1840 at Hartland, Connecticut,
and died November 13, 1914. He homesteaded in the
Ohiowa Community in 1870, where he was the first postmaster and was the originator of the name Ohiowa given
to the community and the postoffice. Three years later
he moved to the new Carleton settlement where he engaged in the general merchandise and implement business. He was very prominent in civic affairs. Later
he was elected county clerk and moved to Hebron, and
in 1885 removed again to Ohiowa, where he was an officer
and one of the founders of the Bank of Ohiowa. Laura

Babcock was born at Chardon, Ohio, August 7, 1851, and died at Carleton, July 5, 1884. Mr. and Mrs. Marks have two children, Robert Harold, born March 14, 1908, who was graduated from the University of Nebraska in 1929 with the Bachelor of Arts certificate in journalism; and Howard Clemons, born March 24, 1913, who is a high school graduate. Residence: Alexandria.

John Martin Markussen

Born at Moorehead, Iowa, March 29, 1892, John Martin Markussen is the son of Johannes and Anna Frederika (Neilsen) Markussen. His father, who was a Lutheran minister, was born in Denmark, October 12, 1855, and died at Cordova, Nebraska, in July, 1919. His mother was born in Denmark, April 22, 1860, and died at Cordova, in 1924.

Mr. Markussen attended school in South Dakota, was a student at Staplehurst, Nebraska, and was graduated from Dana College, at Blair, Nebraska. He attended the Chicago School of Watchmaking, 1910-1911 and the Chicago School of Optometry, 1914.

From 1911 to 1914 he was a watchmaker at Fremont, Nebraska, and since 1915 has been a jeweler at Minden, Nebraska. Mr. Markussen organized the Minden Ad Club and in 1916 was elected president of that organization, also was elected city clerk in 1917 serving for a four year period with the exception of the time he served in the army. In 1920 the Commercial Club and the Ad Club were consolidated and organized under the name of Community Commerce Club and served as the first president of the new society. He served as a first class private in Company F, 355th Infantry, 89th Division of the United States Army and was active in the Meuse-Argonne engagements in France, and in the Army of Occupation. He was a charter member of the American Legion serving as commander for two terms and later adjutant.

His marriage to Elizabeth Dagna Aabel was solemnized at Minden, August 20, 1919. Mrs Markussen was born at Minden, October 9, 1896. They have two children: Keith, born August 10, 1920; and Marilyn, April 7, 1925. Residence: Minden.

Charles Henry Marley

Born at Omaha, on November 14, 1879, for the past twenty years Charles H. Marley has been engaged in the practice of law. He is the son of Charles and Mary Jane (Leech) Marley, his father, a native of Bristol, England, born May 5, 1842. He came to Omaha and started work for the Union Pacific Railroad in 1864, and later pioneered in Montana. He died at Omaha, May 1, 1929. His wife, Mary Jane, was born in Manchester, England, June 26, 1844, and died at Omaha, September 22, 1918.

Charles H. Marley was educated in the public and high schools of Omaha, and studied law with General Charles F. Manderson. He was admitted to the practice of law at Omaha, on June 4, 1907. Mr. Marley started work in the office of General Manderson, then general solicitor for the Chicago, Burlington and Quincy Railroad, lines west of the Missouri River, in June, 1895, as office boy. He subsequently became secretary to the general solicitor, chief clerk in the law department and finally attorney. He left the railroad service in 1912 to enter the general practice of law, and is now associated in practice with Frank H. Woodland.

Mr. Marley was married to Marian Valetta Garvey at Omaha, November 30, 1928. Mrs. Marley, who is a registered nurse, was born at Albion, Nebraska, August 15, 1895. During the World War Mr. Marley was a four minute speaker and otherwise active. He holds the rank of major in the Judge Advocate General's Department, commissioned November 1, 1923, and was president of the Omaha Reserve Officers Association, in 1926. He is affiliated with All Saint's Episcopal Church, is active in the Red Cross and other welfare organizations, and is a member of the Omaha-Douglas County and Nebraska State Bar Associations.

A Mason, he belongs to all bodies of Masonry. During 1918-19 he was master of Nebraska Lodge No. 1, Ancient Free and Accepted Masons, and was commander of Mt. Calvary Commandery No. 1, Knights Templar, in 1920. He was grand commander of the Knights Templar of Nebraska, 1930-31, and sovereign of the Red Cross of Constantine in 1925. His club is the Happy Hollow Country Club, and his sport is golf. Residence: Omaha.

Robert O. Marnell

Robert O. Marnell, banker and business executive of Nebraska City, was born at Hannibal, Marion County, Missouri. His father, James E. Marnell, who was born at Philadelphia, Pennsylvania, August 25, 1822, and died at Hannibal, June 17, 1870, was a tinsmith. He was a Mexican War volunteer.

Katharine Sophia Frances (Hawkins) Marnell, his mother, was born at Georgetown, Kentucky, June 28, 1832, and died at Nebraska City, January 26, 1928. Her ancestors came to this country on the *Mayflower*, and have been prominent since Revolutionary days. Members of the family were active in the Civil War and in the reconstruction period.

Mr. Marnell has lived in Nebraska for 48 years and has led an interesting and varied life. In 1885 he left Nebraska City public school; even before the termination of his school days had found employment of various kinds. From 1880 to 1883, he was consecutively a picket-piler, tinshop boy, employed by the Hannibal Saw Mills, helper in a feed store, clerk, and driver of a delivery wagon. From 1883 to 1886 he was: a carrier and type-sticker for the *Nebraska City News,* and postoffice clerk. In 1886 he became connected with the Merchants' National Bank at Nebraska City, and has since become cashier and director in this organization. Since 1917 he has been a director in the Omaha Branch Federal Reserve Bank. He was for a time a theatre manager, and has handled accident, fidelity, health compensation, and life insurance.

On June 2, 1896, he was united in marriage with Georgia Hawke at Nebraska City. Mrs. Marnell was born at Nebraska City, and is descended from early Nebraskans. There is one daughter, Sue, born March 8, 1899, who married Frank D. Lowrey.

Mr. Marnell was active during the World War in all the loan drives, Red Cross affairs, and other war work necessary to carry on war successfully. He is a member of and a contributor to, the Red Cross: is a member of the Nebraska City Chamber of Commerce, the National Economic League, and the Nebraskana Society. He is affiliated with the Eagles, Elks, Odd Fellows, Modern Woodmen, Workmen, Yeomen, Herman Sohne, and Woodmen of the World. His club is the Omaha Athletic Club. He is a *Gold Standard* Democrat. His hobby is the study of human nature. Residence: Nebraska City.

Harry Miller Marquis

Since 1885 Harry Miller Marquis has lived in Nebraska most of the time, and has been in the practice of law at Osceola and Bridgeport. He was born at Dunkirk, Ohio, January 12, 1857, the son of David Lowry and Mary Ayers (Miller) Marquis, the former a carpenter. His father, who served with General George H. Thomas during the Civil War, was born at Beaver, Pennsylvania, September 6, 1832, and died at Denver, Colorado. His mother, whose ancestors were Pennsylvanians and Virginians, was born at Magnolia, Ohio, in May, 1849, and died at Denver, September 1, 1917.

Mr. Marquis was graduated from the high school at Dunkirk in 1876 and in 1884 was graduated from the University of Kansas law school. He has had a varied colorful career as a teacher, miner and lawyer. He engaged in the practice of law with M. A. Mills at Osceola for a time, practiced law in Washington, and is now county judge of Morrill County, having previously served as county attorney in Polk County.

Judge Marquis is the author of several stories published a few years ago. He holds membership in the Knights of Pythias and the state and district bar associations. His hobby is history. He holds membership in the Nebraskana Society.

His marriage to Jessie Catherine Ford occurred at Blair, Nebraska, June 10, 1886. Mrs. Marquis, who was a teacher, was of English descent. One son was born to this union: Vance William, September 3, 1891.

On November 30, 1922, Judge Marquis married Sylvia Sybil Hunt, widow of Frank N. Hunt, of Bridgeport, and daughter of John Ball Ball of Putney Heath, London, England. Residence: Bridgeport. (Photograph in Album).

Donald C. Marr

Donald Marr was born at Tekamah, Nebraska, July 8, 1893, the son of Peter G. and Rose E. (Babbitt) Marr. His father, who is of French, Canadian and English ancestry, was born on November 21, 1849, and died at Tekamah, Nebraska, June 29, 1903. His mother was born January 10, 1861. She is of English and Pennsylvania Dutch ancestry.

Mr. Marr was graduated from the Tekamah High School in 1914. On March 6, 1918, he married Irene Mason at Tekamah. She is a direct descendant of Captain John Mason and was born at St. Louis, Missouri, October 4, 1895. Their children are Donald R., born January 9, 1926; and Carolyn I., born August 4, 1929. Both children were adopted at the age of three months.

He is affiliated with the Tekamah Methodist Episcopal Church. He is a member of The Nebraskana Society, and is treasurer of school district No. 24. Residence: Tekamah.

Emmet Elmer Marr

One of Hastings' leading dentists, Emmet Elmer Marr has been a resident of Nebraska since June, 1915. His family on the paternal side, was originally Scotch, members of it migrating to Ireland, and thence to North Carolina. His father, James Carson Marr, was born in Missouri City, Missouri, December 23, 1828. He was a forty-niner in California and returned to Missouri after about two years. Later he served in the Confederate Army, while residing in Texas. He returned to Missouri soon after the close of the war and married Alice Caroline Poe about 1882; this was his second marriage. His death occurred at Liberty, Missouri, December 10, 1908. Alice Caroline, his wife, was born in Calloway County, Missouri, and now resides at Liberty. She is of English ancestry, and her chief interest is in her church.

Emmet E. Marr was born near Liberty, Missouri, October 26, 1884, and attended rural schools in Clay County. He was graduated from Liberty High School in 1904. In 1908 he received his Bachelor of Arts degree from William Jewell College, and in 1915 received his degree of Doctor of Dental Surgery from the Kansas City Dental College. Active in debating and dramatics, he also was his class president, and a member of Psi Omega.

From 1908 to 1912 Dr. Marr was a teacher in the government schools in the Philippine Islands. On June 19, 1912, he was united in marriage to Avis Ritchey at Cowles, Nebraska. Mrs. Marr, who is of English and German extraction, was born at Casey, Iowa, July 29, 1884. They have two children, Emmet Elmer, Jr., born September 25, 1914; and Marlos, born October 11, 1917.

Dr. Marr has engaged in general dental practice since 1915, and is a member of the national, state, district and county dental societies. During the World War he was a member of the Home Guard, and a four minute speaker. His religious affiliation is with the First Baptist Church, and he is a member of the Men's Inter-Church Reserve of Hastings. Dr. Marr is a member of the Red Cross, the Nebraska Conference of Social Work, the Chamber of Commerce and the Lions Club. He is an Odd Fellow, and a life member of The Nebraskana Society. His hobby is scouting. Residence: Hastings.

Fred Alexander Marsh

Of pioneer parentage, Fred A. Marsh was born at Central City, Nebraska, November 21, 1871, and for 60 years has lived continuously in Merrick County. William E. Marsh, his father, was born in Kent County, Ontario, Canada, November 8, 1832, and until 1852 remained there where he aided in clearing land on the family homestead. As a young man he moved to Detroit, Michigan, where he entered the practice of dentistry, but a little later gave up that profession because of his health and entered the service of the Western Union Telegraph Company. In 1869 he moved to Merrick County and homesteaded in Midland township where he was prominent in the progress of the middlewest; he was successful as a farmer and stockman until 1917 when he died at Archer, Nebraska.

Mary Ladoska Parker, mother of Fred A. Marsh, was born near Olean, New York, April 17, 1838, moving to Nebraska in 1858. She was engaged in the mercantile business in Denver, Colorada, for several years and later was the owner and manager of a hotel in Virginia City, Montana. She returned to Nebraska in 1867. She knew all the privations and hardships of early settlers in Nebraska, and was a typical pioneer home builder. Her death occurred at Archer, October 31, 1920.

Mr. Marsh attended rural schools in Merrick County, was a student at Central College for two years, and in 1892 was graduated from Fremont Normal School. He served as county superintendent of schools for eight years, and has been engaged in farming and stockraising in Merrick County for many years. At this time he is a regent of the University of Nebraska. He has been the teacher of the Men's Bible Class in the Methodist Episcopal Church for 35 years and has written many articles for the *Central City Republican* during that time

He is a member of K. O. T. M., contributes regularly to various welfare organizations at Archer, and until recently was president of the Merrick County Historical Association. During the World War he helped to secure funds for the Red Cross, Young Men's Christian Association, and Salvation Army.

He was united in marriage at Central City, April 19, 1893, to Virginia Ivy Crites. Mrs. Marsh, who was born at Central City, November 23, 1871, is the daughter of William H. and Phoebe (Saxton) Crites. To this marriage the following children were born: Earl C., June 19, 1894, who married Mary E. Perisho; Erma L., January 23, 1896, who married Raymond D. Mesner; Marion F., September 17, 1897, who married Lillie Belle Mesner; Elizabeth M., September 14, 1900; W. Warren, July 4, 1903; Portia, September 26, 1905, who married Theodore C. Reeves; Dorothy, January 10, 1913, who died January 17, 1913. All the children received liberal educations. Residence: Archer.

George Wesley Marsh

George W. Marsh was born in Saline County, Missouri, January 14, 1852, the son of Elijah Simeon and Delilah (Horner) Marsh. His father, who was born in Ohio, February, 1821, and died at Lincoln, Lancaster County, Nebraska, June 2, 1902, was a mechanic. His mother was

GEORGE W. MARSH

Dole—Lincoln

born in Pennsylvania, January 1, 1825, and died in Richardson County, Nebraska, August 9, 1901.

Mr. Marsh attended the Nebraska State Normal School. He has lived in the state since 1859, and for a time was editor of the *Falls City Journal* at Falls City, Nebraska. He is now state auditor. A Republican, he was county clerk of Richardson County, was county treasurer, and secretary of state, 1901-1905.

He was united in marriage with Anna Rutledge Stephens in Richardson County, February 4, 1877. Mrs. Marsh was born in Maryland, January 5, 1856, and died at University Place, Lancaster County, Nebraska, June 26, 1916. Five children were born to them, four of whom are living: Stella E., born January 15, 1878, who died March 6, 1888; Nellie M., born February 6, 1887, who married Charles F. Greenburg; Benton, born December 2, 1892, who married Hazel Sutton; Arthur, born August 9, 1897; and Wayne, born April 1, 1890, who married Beatrice E. Speier.

Mr. Marsh is a member of the Sons of Veterans and the Methodist Church at Lincoln. He is fond of baseball, fishing and hunting. Residence: Lincoln. (Photograph on Page 767).

Chester Chancy Marshall

Born at Cannonsburg, Hancock County, Ohio, September 23, 1862, Chester Chancy Marshall has been a resident of Nebraska since 1881. He is the son of Benjamin Clark and Catherine (Nonnamaker) Marshall, the former of whom was a farmer of Scotch-Irish ancestry, born in Warren County, Ohio, February 4, 1835. He died at Arlington, Nebraska, February 16, 1919. His wife, Catherine, was born in Cannonsburg, Ohio, December 10, 1836, and died at Arlington, November 7, 1904. She was of German descent.

Mr. Marshall was educated in the public schools of Cannonsburg, Ohio, and since 1887, has been associated with the Marshall Nurseries, of which he is vice president. From 1908 to 1927, he was president of the Arlington State Bank. He is now a director of the Arlington State Bank and the Fremont Union National Bank and president of Washington County Agricultural Society. A Democrat, he served as state representative from District 11, 1897-98, and was defeated by a narrow margin for the same office in the fall of 1898. He was defeated for the state senate from Dodge and Washington Counties in Lorengo Crounse 1900, and served as county supervisor 1895-96.

On July 1, 1886, he was married to Mary Catherine Fellers, at Findlay, Ohio. Mrs. Marshall was born at Findlay, March 31, 1859, and died at Fremont, May 6, 1928. There are three children living and two deceased: Herma Gail, born May 13, 1887, married Glen Leonidas Johnson; Leta Jane, born October 12, 1891, is a former public school teacher; Floyd Millard, born December 12, 1888, died February 15, 1890; Earl Fellers, born February 7, 1895, died January 6, 1899; Eva Constance, born January 13, 1898, married Jasper Hobson Ludwig. Eva is a teacher of public school music, and Gail teaches in the Fremont Public school.

Mr. Marshall was assistant food and fuel commissioner of Washington County, and assisted in all War Drives. He is a member of the First Congregational Church, the Nebraskana Society, Odd Fellows and Modern Woodmen of America. He belongs to the Young Men's Christian Association and is chairman of the rural committee of the Rotary Club. His hobbies are hunting and fishing. Residence: Fremont.

Chester George Marshall

Chester G. Marshall, a lifetime resident of Nebraska, has been active as a horticulture executive for many years. He was born at Arlington, Washington County, Nebraska, April 27, 1883, the son of Benjamin Ami and Minnie Wilhelmina (Marquardt) Marshall. His father, who is a retired farmer and nurseryman, was born at Bluffton, Hancock County, Ohio, January 27, 1859; his father was Irish. His mother whose ancestry was German, was born at Bluffton, September 6, 1866.

Mr. Marshall was graduated from the Arlington High School in 1901, and in 1901 and 1902 studied botany and horticulture at the University of Nebraska. He was president and secretary of the Nebraska State Horticultural Society for five years. He was editor of the horticultural department of the *Nebraska Farmer* from 1909 to 1917. For a number of years he has been interested in the development of county fairs, and has served as secretary of the County Fair Circuit of northeast Nebraska. With Val Keyser he organized the Central Fruit Growers' Association and was manager for two years and served as institute lecturer for the Farmers Association. He was connected with the horticultural department at the University of Nebraska for three years. He is now secretary and sales manager for the Marshall's Nurseries, at Arlington.

He is the author of several articles on horticultural subjects published in the Nebraska State Horticultural Society Reports, 1909-1920. He is a member of: Arlington Community Club; Parent-Teachers' Association; the Nebraskana Society; and the Young Men's Christian Association. He is serving as president of the Retail Nurseryman's Association of the United States; and is past president of the Western Association of Nurserymen. Mr. Marshall is affiliated with the Congregational Church at Arlington; is a member of Masons, Scottish Rite, and Shrine; and is an Independent, politically.

His marriage to Margaret Anna Brenizer was solemnized at Bennet, Lancaster County, Nebraska, November 26, 1912. Mrs. Marshall was born of German parentage at Bennet, May 6, 1885. They have two children: Betty, born November 12, 1914; and Frances, born September 1, 1917. Residence: Arlington.

Clarence LeRoy Marshall

Clarence LeRoy Marshall, newspaper publisher and writer, was born at Carroll, Nebraska, October 23, 1899, the son of Charles William Marshall and Mary Catherine (Mason) Marshall. His father, who was born at Fontanelle, Nebraska, March 6, 1874, was a garage proprietor, a mail carrier for many years, and a harness maker; he served in the Nebraska National Guard during his younger days, and is now retired; his ancestry is Irish. His mother was born at Cuba, Kansas, October 20, 1879. She is descended from the Mason family of Colonial days, and can trace her ancestry to the early land grants of Philadelphia. Her father was a soldier in the Civil War and her paternal grandfather served in the Revolution and the War of 1812.

Mr. Marshall attended Carroll High School, Boles Business College of Omaha, and the Naval Conservatory of Music at San Francisco, California. He learned the publishing business at an early age, and worked in various newspaper offices as an apprentice for several years. At one time he was agent for the Chicago, St. Paul, Missouri & Ohio Railroad Company and later served as messenger for this organization. He is now editor and publisher of the *Verdel News* at Verdel, Nebraska.

He is a member of the board of trustees of Verdel, the Modern Woodmen of America, Nebraskana Society, and the First Baptist Church of Carroll. His sports include baseball, basketball, boating, and motoring, while his hobbies are reading and writing. He served in the United States Navy as bandmaster the Mine Force Naval Band of the Pacific Coast from 1918 to 1922.

His marriage to Martha Amanda Peterson was solemnized at Creighton, Nebraska, June 21, 1923. Mrs. Marshall, whose ancestry is Norwegien, was born at Perkins, South Dakota, December 31, 1900. They have one daughter, Charlotte Elaine, born July 16, 1924. Residence: Verdel.

George Allison Marshall

George A. Marshall, a well known nurseryman and executive in Nebraska, was born at Cannonsburg, Ohio, December 20, 1864. His father, Benjamin Clark Marshall, who was a farmer, was born in Trumble County, Ohio, February 4, 1835, and died at Arlington, February 16, 1919; his ancestry was Scotch-Irish; his early geneaology includes Chief Justice Marshall and President McKinley. Catherine Howdeshell (Nonnamaker) Marshall, his mother, was born in Hancock County, Ohio, December 10, 1836, and died at Arlington, November 7, 1904; she was of German descent.

Mr. Marshall attended grade school in Ohio, and the Whitford School at Arlington. He was a student at the Fremont Business College for a time, 1887, and the same year entered the nursery business with his brother. He was a grower and salesman of nursery stock, 1897-1901, serving as president of the State Horticultural Society during that time; he was a member of the board of the latter organization several times. He has lived in Nebraska 50 years and is now president of the Marshall's Nurseries and president of the Loes, Land & Orchard Company.

He holds membership in the following: National Nurserymen's Association; American Association of Nurserymen; National Pomological Society; Western Retail Nurserymen; Nebraska State Nurserymen's Society; and the State Horticultural Society. For a number of years he was chairman of the Synonym Committee of the State Horticultural Society. For five years he served on the National Board of the American Association of Nurserymen and was president for one term. He also served as a member and as president of the board of the Western Association. As vice president and later as president of the State Horticultural Society; he assisted in the establishment and development of the plant at Halsey. He is a member of the Community Club; the State Historical Society; the Nebraskana Society; and the Parent-Teachers' Association. He has served as a member of the state committee and the Camp Sheldon committee of the Young Men's Christian Association. He is a Mason, Scottish Rite, and an Odd Fellow. His sports are fishing and coon hunting. He is affiliated with the First Congregational Church of Arlington, of which he is a trustee. He is an Independent Democrat.

Mr. Marshall was married to Dora Bertha Goltry at Tabor, Fremont County, Iowa, June 27, 1893. Mrs. Marshall was born at Missouri Valley, Harrison County, Iowa, April 16, 1875. Her ancestry is Scotch-Irish and English; her maternal grandfather was a Congregational minister and the organizer of Tabor College. Their children are: Victor Vernon, born April 28, 1894, who married Louise Anna Boker; Flora Catherine, born October 3, 1895, who married Edward Boker; Greeta Ruth, born December 17, 1896, who married Edward John Renard; Benjamin Ralph, born June 26, 1902, who married Victoria Huey, and who is ranching in South Dakota; Maurice Nonnamaker, born November 13, 1904, who married Lida Larson; and Sterling Todd, born November 30, 1908, who died January 4, 1912. Victor Vernon, Maurice, and Catherine, are in the nursery business. Greeta Ruth lives on a farm near Arlington. Residence: Arlington. (Photograph on Page 770).

Ralph Waldo Marshall

Ralph Waldo Marshall, banker, was born at Avoca, Nebraska, March 13, 1889, son of John Thomas and Loretta Medella (Smith) Marshall.

The father was born in Hull, Yorkshire, England, December 8, 1849, and came to the United States in 1872. He was president of the bank of Panama, state senator from Lancaster County in 1913 and 1915. He died at Panama, September 6, 1925. His wife, Loretta, was born in Meridian, Mississippi, May 14, 1859, and died at Panama, April 14, 1915.

In 1907, Mr. Marshall was graduated from Doane College Academy at Crete.

He was married on May 27, 1928, to Esther LaRue McLaughlin at York. She was born at Panama, July 14, 1904, and was a school teacher. Her father, the Honorable M. O. McLaughlin, is congressman from the 4th district of Nebraska.

At the present time, Mr. Marshall is cashier of the bank of Panama. He is a member of the Presbyterian Church, the Masons, and the Odd Fellows. Residence: Panama.

Virgil Albertus Marshall

Virgil Albertus Marshall was born at Nelson, Nebraska, July 24, 1901, the son of Robert Marshall and Ida (Linch) Marshall. His father was born at Monoga, Hala County, Pennsylvania, October 15, 1859, and is a successful farmer. Mrs. Marshall was born in Iowa, on January 2, 1859 and died at Nelson, January 7, 1927, after an active life in club and church work.

Mr. Marshall was graduated from the Nelson High School in 1918, and soon after his graduation he secured a position in the Bostwick State Bank. In 1921 he was appointed its cashier.

Holding this position until September, 1923 when he became connected with the Bankers Life Insurance Company of Lincoln, Nebraska. In 1927 he was appointed district manager, which position he now holds.

His marriage to Marie Katherine Diehl occurred July 22, 1922, at Nelson, Nebraska. Mrs. Marshall was born February 7, 1901, at McCook, Nebraska. Their son, Darrell LeRoy, was born October 18, 1928.

Mr. Marshall was active in the loan drives during the War. He is affiliated with the First Christian Church at Fairbury, Nebraska, and is a member of the National Underwriters Association, the Fairbury Chamber of Commerce, of which he is a director, the Kiwanis Club, of which he is vice president, the Ancient Free and Accepted Masons, the Royal Arch and the Knight Templars. He is a member of the Nebraskana Society and the Fairbury Country Club.

Mr. Marshall is especially interested in his beautiful lawn. He enjoys golf and other sports, and is a lover of music. Residence: Fairbury.

Alice Marshell

Alice Marshell, executive secretary of the Nebraska Tuberculosis Association, has lived in this state for the past 33 years and since 1917, has taken an interest in social and welfare work in her community. She was born at Osborne, Kansas, the daughter of Jacob William and Ada Byron (Johnson) Marshell. Her father, who was western agent for the Otto Gas Engines Works, was born at Pittsburgh, Pennsylvania, February 5, 1852, and died at Omaha, November 26, 1921. His Scotch ancestors came to America in the early settlement of the country and members of the family fought in the Revolution.

Her mother was born at Pittsburgh, September 26, 1855. Her great-great grandfather came to America from Ireland, and her great grandfather Johnson, was a pioneer in Pittsburgh, and a member of the first council of that city.

Miss Marshell was graduated from the Farnam School in 1897, and was graduated from high school at Omaha, in the class of 1901. She took short courses in social service work at the University of Nebraska, and the University of Chicago, and in 1918 became associated with the Nebraska Tuberculosis Association, being made executive secretary of this organization in 1925.

She took part in Red Cross activities during the late war; and was engaged in canteen work and tuberculosis prevention throughout the war period. She is a member of the American Association of Social Work, the Omaha Social Workers Club, and the Conference of Tuberculosis

GEORGE ALLISON MARSHALL

Secretaries. This year she was appointed state chairman of child hygiene of the Nebraska Congress of Parents and Teachers. She is a member of the Omaha Chamber of Commerce and the Altrusa Club, and is a Republican. Residence: Omaha.

Eva Jewett Marti

Eva Jewett Marti, personnel director of the Lincoln school of Commerce, was born at Wilbraham, Massachusetts, January 14, 1880, daughter of Henry Porter and Angeline Lucy (Jewett) Simonds.

Upon the completion of her public school education, Eva Jewett attended the State Teachers College of Mankato, Minnesota, and took special work at Cornell College. She also attended the conservatory there. On April 16, 1900, she was married to Col. Henry Grant Rising, who is deceased. On September 1, 1915 she was married to the late Alfred F. Marti.

She is a Republican, a member of the Chamber of Commerce, the Jewett Family Association, the Delphian Society (various offices), and is eligible to the Daughters of the American Revolution. Residence: Lincoln.

Frank Thomas Becket Martin

Frank T. B. Martin was born at Galesburg, Illinois, December 21, 1876. He is the son of Thomas Becket and Eliza Jane (Smith) Martin, the former an outstanding figure of Galesburg for many years. Thomas Becket Martin was born in Freeport, Pennsylvania, on December 29, 1832, and as a young man went to Galesburg, where he engaged in the insurance business. He was married at Pittsburgh, Pennsylvania, to Eliza Jane Smith, born at Tullow, County Carlow, Ireland. She died at South San Francisco, in November, 1901. Thomas Becket Martin was a Republican. He served as senior warden of Grace Episcopal Church of Galesburg for more than fifty years. His death occurred there on November 19, 1924.

Frank T. B. Martin attended the public schools of Galesburg, and at the end of his junior year at Knox College, left school and came to Omaha. He was a member of the varsity football team at Knox College and earned his letter as left half. He is a member of Phi Delta Theta.

In 1899 Mr. Martin entered the office of Martin, Perfect and Newman as a clerk, continuing there until February, 1902, when he and his brother purchased the firm, which has been operated as Martin Brothers and Company since that date. Mr. Martin is president of the Forest Lawn Cemetery Association and director of the Conservative Savings and Loan Association.

On April 15, 1903 he was married to Mary Ethel Barker, at Omaha. Mrs. Martin was born at Omaha, April 10, 1878, and is the daughter of George E. Barker, pioneer settler in Omaha in 1856. Their four children are Francis T. B., Jr., born November 29, 1904, who is in business with his father; George Barker, born November 6, 1905, who is also connected with Martin Brothers and Company; Charles Wellington, born March 27, 1909, who is associated with Crum and Forster of Chicago; and Alfred Joseph, born September 6, 1914.

One of Nebraska's leading insurance men, Mr. Martin is past president of the Insurance Federation of America, past president of the Nebraska Association of Insurance Agents and president of the Nebraska Insurance Federation. A member of the Chamber of Commerce, he is a member of the board of directors and is now a director and member of the executive committee, and a former chairman of the insurance division.

He is past president of the Continental Club, a trustee of Clarkson Memorial Hospital and a member of the board of regents of the Municipal University of Omaha. He is a vestryman of Trinity Cathedral of Omaha, and is a member of the Young Men's Christian Association. His clubs are the Omaha, of which he is a director, and the Omaha Athletic. In politics he is a Republican. His hobby is reading. Residence: Omaha.

George Ellsworth Martin

George Ellsworth Martin, an outstanding Nebraska educator and school executive, has been a lifelong resident of this state and since 1892 has taken a prominent part in professional affairs. He was born at Falls City, Nebraska, March 19, 1872, the son of Elza and Eliza Anne (Holland) Martin. His father, who was born in Meigs County, Ohio, October 29, 1831, and died at Nebraska City, Nebraska, June 10, 1916, was a farmer; he was descended from an old Virginia family which had settled in the south upon arrival in the country from England. His mother, whose ancestry was Scotch, was born in Delaware, August 26, 1835, and died at Falls City, March 3, 1904.

Mr. Martin attended school at Falls City, was graduated from the high school at Fort Scott, Kansas, in 1892, received the A. B. degree at the University of Nebraska in 1914, and was awarded the A. M. degree at Columbia University in 1919. He was awarded a prize in oratory in 1892, and was a member of Pi Delta Kappa and Kappa Delta Pi.

He has held the following positions in Nebraska: rural school teacher; principal of Dawson Public Schools; principal of the Nebraska City High School; superintendent of city schools of Nebraska City; professor of English, State Normal College, Kearney; and president of the Nebraska State Teachers College, Kearney, at this time. He is the joint author of *Searson-Martin Studies in Reading.*

Mr. Martin is a member of the Nebraska State Teachers Association, the National Education Association, the Kearney Chamber of Commerce, Illiteracy Board of the National Education Association, and the Kearney Country Club. He served as chairman of the Red Cross, 1927-29, was president of the Rotary Club in 1927 and is now a member of the board of directors of that organization. His hobby is reading, and his favorite outdoor sport is hunting.

On June 12, 1895, he was married to Alice Kriger at Clinton, Kentucky. Mrs. Martin, whose ancestry is French and German, was born at Paducah, Kentucky, April 13, 1868. They have four children. Alike, born May 4, 1896; Ruth, born February 22, 1898, who died June 13, 1920; Frances, born October 19, 1900, who married William W. Little; and Kathryn, born February 4, 1903, who married Harold Rondthaler. Residence: Kearney.

Jerry Lewis Martin

A resident of Nebraska since March 6, 1887, Jerry Lewis Martin is prominent in the lumber business at Edison today. He was born at Quitman, Missouri, February 15, 1871, the son of Wesley Bottom and Lilly Ann (Busby) Martin. His father, who was a farmer and a veteran of the Civil War, was born at Danville, Kentucky, and died at Edison, September 15, 1907. His mother was born at Canton, Ohio, and died at Edison, April 8, 1917; her ancestry was Irish.

Mr. Martin was a carpenter and contractor for many years at Edison and is now manager of the Byers Lumber Company of Minden, Nebraska, and a lumber yard at Edison. A Democrat, he served as chairman of the town board for four years. He is a member of the Christian Church, the Edison Chamber of Commerce, and the Nebraskana Society, while his fraternal organizations include: Masons; and Odd Fellows.

His marriage to Amber Ewing was solemnized at Denver, Colorado, November 23, 1923. Mrs. Martin, whose ancestry is Scotch, was born at Waco, Texas,

March 6, 1888. She is active in the affairs of the Christian Church of which she is a member; she is also a Rebekah. Residence: Edison.

John Martin

John Martin, a resident of Nebraska for the past fifty years, has been a stockman in this state for many years. He was born at West Jefferson, Ohio, January 13, 1863, the son of Frederick and Elizabeth (Linder) Martin. His father was born in Germany December 5, 1826, came to Saunder County September 25, 1882, and died at Waverly, Nebraska, February 21, 1903. His mother was born at Baden, Germany, August 18, 1834, and died at Lincoln, May, 1907.

Mr. Martin received his education in Ohio. He is now president of the Farmers and Merchants Bank at Ceresco, and is a successful stockman there. He is a member of The Nebraskana Society, is affiliated with the Methodist Church and holds membership in the Eastern Star, and the Masons. He has served on the town board 18 years and has twice been chairman of the board. During the World War he served as a member of the fuel committee of Saunders County, Nebraska. He is a Democrat.

On April 13, 1887, he was united in marriage with Nellie Blanche Robinson at Wahoo, Saunders County, Nebraska; Mrs. Martin was born at Erie, Pennsylvania, April 20, 1869. They have two children: Thurman, born August 26, a farmer, who married Ethel Lowell; and Thelma, born February 12, 1901, who married Joe R. Brown. Residence: Ceresco.

John Cooke Martin

Born at Belfast, County Down, Ireland, June 22, 1859, John Cooke Martin has been a resident of Nebraska forty-eight years. He is the son of William and Elizabeth (Cooke) Martin, the former of whom was born at Belfast in 1836, and died November 27, 1884. He was a ships carpenter and blacksmith. His wife, Elizabeth, was born in Belfast, and died in 1913.

John Cooke Martin was educated in public school, and since youth has engaged in farming. He has gained prominence in his chosen occupation, and is an outstanding citizen of his community. His political affiliation is with the Republican party. A Presbyterian, he is a member of the United Presbyterian Church at Superior. Recently he was elected to life membership in The Nebraskana Society.

On November 17, 1885, Mr. Martin was united in marriage to Agnes Speer at Superior. Mrs. Martin, who was born at Belfast, September 29, 1861, is a dressmaker. There are three children: Anna Mary, born November 27, 1887, married Thomas Howard Harvey; William James, born October 7, 1889, married Ivah Haught; and Floyd French, born July 22, 1908. Residence: Bostwick.

Melville Eugene Martin

A pioneer resident of Nebraska is Melville Eugene Martin who has lived in Fillmore County for the past 62 years. He was born at Kekoskee, Wisconsin, August 24, 1853, the son of Elisha Littlefield and Delight Adelia (Nichols) Martin. His father, who was a descendant of Captain Robert Martin, Revolutionary War soldier in New York, was born at Hornellsville, New York, August 22, 1827, and died at Fairmont, Nebraska, December 16, 1915. His mother was born at Hornellsville, and died at Fairmont, April 12, 1909.

Mr. Martin attended grade school and a part of high school in Nebraska. He was connected with the International Harvester Company for a time, was salesman for the Tropical Oil Company, and was salesman for the St. Paul Harvester Company. He is now retired. A Republican, he served as township clerk at Fairmont for four years and police judge for two years.

He is a member of the Ancient Order of United Workmen, was formerly a member of the Knights of Pythias, and is a member of the Nebraskana Society. He is affiliated with the Federated Church. During the late war Mr. Martin served in various loan drives.

He was married to Emma Gertrude Sexton at Fairmont, April 3, 1882; she was born at Auroraville, Wisconsin in 1857. Their children are: Eva Faye, born June 10, 1883; Elisha L., born September 26, 1885, who married Laura Cleveland; Julia Delight, born February 29, 1888, who married Ernest Temple Parnell; Allison Laurel, born May 11, 1892; and Edith Sexton, born October 16, 1896.

Elisha Littlefield Martin, father of Melville E. Martin, came to Nebraska in 1868, and homesteaded near Fillmore Mills where he laid out the village of Fillmore. He took a prominent part in the organization of the county, village, and state, serving as postmaster, mayor, and city councilman. He was a leader in the forming of the Odd Fellows Lodge at Fairmont. Residence: Fairmont.

Oscar Ross Martin

For the past 17 years Oscar Ross Martin has made his home in Nebraska. He was born at Farmington, Iowa, October 4, 1884, the son of Peter and Amelia (Ross) Martin. His father was a native of Pittsburgh, Pennsylvania, and was born in April, 1851. He was a clergyman of German descent and his death occurred at Brighton, Illinois, February 1, 1921. Oscar Martin's mother was born at Warsaw, Illinois, in April, 1856, and died in the same state at Altamont, in February, 1908. Her ancestry was German and Scotch.

As a boy Mr. Martin attended the public schools at various points in Illinois and Missouri. He received his Bachelor of Arts degree at Central Wesleyan College in 1907 and his Master of Arts degree at the University of Illinois in 1913. Mr. Martin has also studied at the University of Wisconsin. His fraternity is Delta Sigma Lambda and he holds membership in Beta Gamma Sigma and Alpha Kappa Psi.

Mr. Martin affiliates with the Republican party. He is the author of numerous articles on business subjects. His career as an educator began when he became an instructor in the Granite City, Illinois, high school. Later he became an instructor in the University of Illinois. Then he came to Lincoln and has been successively assistant professor, associate professor, and professor in the University of Nebraska; he is now chairman of the department of business organization and management at the University. Mr. Martin is a partner in the firm of Martin and Cole, public accountants, at Lincoln, Nebraska, is a member of the American Institute of Accountants, and has been recognized as a certified public accountant by the state of Nebraska.

Mr. Martin is a member of St. Paul's Methodist Episcopal Church, the Young Men's Christian Association, and the Lincoln Chamber of Commerce, the Polemic Club and the Crucible Club. He is active in club affairs and is particularly interested in Masonic affairs, being a member of the Scottish Rite and Shrine. He is a Kiwanian, and a member of the Nebraskana Society.

Mr. Martin is a past president of the Nebraska Chapter of the American Association of University Professors, and is a member of the American Economic Association and the American Association of University Instructors in Accounting.

The social clubs to which Mr. Martin belongs are the Lincoln University Club, the Lincoln Country Club and the Shrine Golf Club. His sports are golf and fishing.

On August 12, 1913, Mr. Martin was united in marriage to Hazel Hardin at Knightstown, Indiana. Mrs. Martin was born February 21, 1886, at Knightstown

There are four children, Ross, born May 21, 1916; Robert, born May 2, 1918; John, born June 25, 1921; and Marjorie, born June 18, 1923. Residence: Lincoln.

Wade Randall Martin

Wade Randall Martin, president of the Commercial Banking Company at Stratton, Nebraska, was born at Fremont, June 25, 1891, the son of Grant G. and Laura (Dickson) Martin. His father and mother were both born in Iowa and are still living at Lincoln, Nebraska. His father, former attorney-general of Nebraska, is a practicing lawyer and was a member of the Supreme Court Commission.

Mr. Martin atended the Fremont High School, Lincoln High School and received his Bachelor of Science degree from the University of Nebraska in 1911, where he is a member of Sigma Xi. Upon leaving college, he became assistant cashier of the Nebraska State Bank at Lincoln, Nebraska, resigning to enter the World War.

He attended the 2nd Officers Training Camp at Fort Snelling, Minnesota and was commissioned a first lieutenant of infantry on completion of the course. He was sent to Fort Brady, Michigan, and stationed with the 41st Infantry Regular Army on guard duty at the Sault Ste. Marie Locks and shortly afterwards was transferred to the 314th Cavalry at San Antonio, Texas, one of the fifteen cavalry regiments just created. He served with this regiment about seven months when orders from General Pershing converted all fifteen cavalry regiments into Field Artillery. He was sent to the School of Fire for Field Artillery at Fort Sill, Oklahoma, and upon graduation from this course of instruction was retained in the school of fire as instructor in gunnery and during this time was promoted to captain, Field Artillery. He is a member of the American Legion, organizinz the local post No. 281 at Stratton, Nebraska in 1920, and was commander of the local post, two years 1920-21, a member of the executive committee, four years, vice-department commander, and department commander, 1928-1929, of Nebraska.

On Eeptember 20, 1921, he was married to Emma Louise Mote at Denver, Colorado. She was born at Plainview, Nebraska, March 12, 1893. In 1912 she was graduated with honors from the Conservatory of Music at the University School of Music at Lincoln, and was a member of the Delta Delta Delta sorority. She is active in the Stratton Woman's Club and a member of the American Woman's Club and a member of the American Legion Auxiliary. She is also a leader in musical circles, having given instructions in the piano branch continuously since moving to Stratton.

Mr. Martin is a Republican. He is a member of the Methodist Church, the Chamber of Commerce, the Ancient Free and Accepted Masons, Robert Burns Lodge No. 173 served as its master in 1925 and is a life member of the Nebraskana Society. In 1925 Mr. Martin was partly instrumental in the organizing and building of a community building and dedicated to the veterans of all wars at the cost of $30,000.00, and the active management of same is in his hands. He is fond of golf. His club is the University Club of Lincoln. Residence: Stratton.

Warren Binney Martin

A resident of Nebraska all his life, Warren Binney Martin has been engaged in the grocery business at Albion for the past 31 years. He was born at Maxwell, Nebraska, and is the son of Thompson Frederick and Lydia Eliza (Thorpe) Martin. His father, who was born at Philadelphia, Pennsylvania, July 23, 1847, and died at Albion, September 29, 1921, was a telephone exchange manager; he moved to Nebraska in 1875 and was agent for the Union Pacific Railroad at Maxwell for many years. His mother was born at Gainsville, New

York, January 9, 1848, and died at Albion, March 18, 1890.

Mr. Martin received his elementary and high school education at Albion and later was a student at Elliotts Business College, Burlington, Iowa. He is the owner of a grocery store at Albion, owns a half interest in the Albion Silver Fox Company, and was a director in the First National Bank of Albion.

He is vice president of the Albion Lions Club, is a member of the Albion Chamber of Commerce, president of the Albion Building and Loan Association, and is affiliated with the Congregational Church there. His fraternal organizations include, Knights of Pythias, Royal Highlanders, and Scottish Rite and Shrine bodies of the Masons. His favorite sport is golfing, and his hobbies are flower gardening and woodwork. He is a Master Merchant of Nebraska, one of the ten merchants with this honor.

His marriage to Olga Pearl Whiting occurred at Albion, April 17, 1901; she was born at Albion, April 7, 1880, the daughter of George W. Whiting and Isadora (Havens) Whiting, early settlers of Boone County. Mrs. Martin first saw the light of day in a sod house. She is a member of the Eastern Star, having at times held various offices in the Albion Chapter. She is also active in her church and in the P. E. O.

Mr. Martin served in the Nebraska National Guard for seven years. Residence: Albion.

Josephine Sutton Marty

Born in Nemaha County, Nebraska, August 11, 1882, Josephine Sutton Marty is one of the five daughters of George Henry and Maria Catherine (Hughes) Sutton. Her father was born at Mount Vernon, Ohio, October 19, 1851, and was a miller and farmer, prominent in political and civic affairs. His parents came from Cornwall, England, to America in 1842, locating in Knox County, Ohio. George Henry Sutton's father learned the milling trade in England.

Maria Catherine Hughes, who was born in Nemaha County, August 2, 1857, died there on October 11, 1909. Her grandparents were also English, her mother's father a physician and slave holder of West Virginia, and her father's father a painter.

Josephine Sutton Marty received her elementary education in Nemaha County schools until 1894, and was graduated from Howe High School in 1896, having attended Auburn High School two years. Following this she had four years' experience as a teacher in the public schools. She has had extension work in history and parliamentary law, and was graduated from St. Joseph Business College in 1902. Her business career has been varied, and covers eight years with the Armourdale Foundry Company and the Kansas City Rubber and Belting Company in addition to her present position as special representative of the Bankers Life Insurance Company of Nebraska.

She was married to Edward L. Marty, at Auburn, Nebraska, on November 29, 1910. Mr. Marty is the head of a department in the Bankers Life Insurance Company, and the youngest son of Matthias Marty, one of the pioneers largely instrumental in the development of Kansas City, and the owner of much real estate.

Since her marriage Mrs. Marty has been active in the Lincoln Woman's Club, in which she held the office of president 1924-26, and secretary, 1922-24. She served as secretary of the State League of Women Voters 1929-31, and president of the Native Sons and Daughters of Nebraska 1930-31.

She is a member of St. Matthews Episcopal Church, the Nebraskana Society, the Young Women's Christian Association, the Thursday Morning Lecture Circle, the Tuesday Review Club, and a charter member of the Woman's City Club of Kansas City. Residence: Lincoln. (Photograph on Page 774).

JOSEPHINE SUTTON MARTY

Dole—Lincoln

Edward George Martz

A pioneer merchant at Hyannis, Nebraska, Edward George Martz has lived in this state all his life, and has been a leader in business and civic activities in his community for many years. He was born at Duncan, Nebraska, August 8, 1869, the son of Peter Joseph and Elizabeth Rose (Eisenhour) Martz, the former a farmer who was born at Zurich, Switzerland, in 1831, and died at Columbus, Nebraska, December 24, 1887. His mother was born at Darmsted, Germany in 1841 and died at Duncan, January 10, 1910.

Mr. Martz attended high school at Duncan, and since 1893 has been a merchant at Hyannis. He holds membership in the Red Cross, the Nebraskana Society, Woodmen of the World, and the Congregational Church of Hyannis. His sports are fishing and hunting.

Of his marriage to Emma Margaret Meedel on February 5, 1895, one child was born, George Andrew, March 13, 1896, who served in the World War, and is now engaged in the mercantile business with his father. Residence: Hyannis.

Archie Douglas Marvel

Archie Douglas Marvel was born at Giltner, Nebraska, May 26, 1892, the son of John S. and Mary Etta (Bedell) Marvel. His father, who is a farmer, was born at Wanesville, Illinois, July 9, 1862; his ancestry was French and English, and John Marvel, an ancestor, came to this country on the *Mayflower*. His mother was born in New York, September 10, 1868.

Mr. Marvel attended the public schools of Giltner where he was graduated from high school in 1908. He received the A. B. degree from Hastings College in 1912 and from 1912 to 1914 was a student at Harvard Law School. He was prominent in oratory, music, and debating, during his college days, was valedictorian of high school graduating class in 1908. He received letters in football at Hastings College and in 1911 was all-state end selection.

Born in a sod house in Hamilton County, Nebraska, Mr. Marvel has seen the entire growth of his state from a rough pioneer frontier land to the present day Nebraska. He has held various positions in banks, including: assistant cashier and cashier of the Bank of Commerce at Hastings, 1914-25; vice president of the First National Bank of Hastings, 1926-31; and since January 1, 1931, president of the General Credit Corporation. He is a trustee of Hastings College, is a member of the Red Cross and Salvation Army, and holds membership in the Young Men's Christian Association of which he is a director.

He served as president of the Hastings Kiwanis Club in 1923, is affiliated with the First Presbyterian Church of Hastings, and is an Elk and Mason. His hobby is gardening. His political affiliation is with the Democratic Party.

On June 19, 1915, he was married to Ruth Capps at Hastings; she was born at Hastings, October 19, 1891, and died there, October 19, 1920. Two children were born to this marriage: Richard Douglas, December 8, 1917; Robert James, November 24, 1919. Mr. Marvel married Beth Ellen Newell at Alexandria, Nebraska, June 1, 1925. They have a daughter, Marilyn, born January 30, 1928. Residence: Hastings.

Engalena Josephine Marvel

An outstanding leader in women's affairs in Hamilton County, Nebraska, is Engalena J. Marvel, a resident of this state for the past 28 years. She was born at Langdon, Missouri. October 8, 1888, the daughter of John Benhart Bowers and Matilda (Cooper) Bowers. Her father, who was a farmer, was born at Langdon, May 17, 1864, and died at Lincoln, Nebraska, June 19, 1928, his parents came to this country from Germany,

and his father served during the Civil War. Her mother, who was born in Nemaha County, Nebraska, October 8, 1866, was also of German parentage. Mrs. Marvel attended a rural school until 1903, and in 1906 was graduated from the Adams High School. She was a student at Northwestern Business College at Beatrice, Nebraska, 1907-08; she served as treasurer of the senior class at Adams. She was a teacher in the shorthand and typing department of the Northwestern Business College, 1908-09, and was a stenographer in the law office of Hainer, Craft, and Alysworth, at Aurora, from 1909 to 1914. At this time she is piano, violin, and cello instructor at Giltner. For many years Mrs. Marvel has contributed various items and articles to Hamilton County newspapers.

She has held executive positions in almost every phase of women's activities and is known throughout the state as an active Woman's Club worker. Among the positions she has held in the past few years are: captain of the Girl Scout Troop, 1914-18; secretary of the Women's Christian Temperance Union, 1930; first vice president of the Women's Christian Temperance Union, 1931; member of the executive committee of the Nebraska Christian Women's Missionary Society, 1929-31; secretary of the Fourth District Nebraska Christian Women's Missionary Society; secretary of the Hamilton County Sunday School Association; organizer and president of the local Music Study Club, 1926-30; chairman of the music department of the Nebraska Federation of Women's Clubs for District Four, 1930-31; and chairman of the Giltner Red Cross Drive Committee.

She has been particularly prominent in the Order of Eastern Star, holding the following positions: Grand Representative of Quebec, 1930; Worthy Matron, 1926-27-30, secretary, 1919-24. She served as local oracle of the Royal Neighbors of America for two terms, and was county oracle of this organization in 1921 and 1924. During 1929 Mrs. Marvel served as district secretary of the Rebekah Lodge. She is an active member of the Nebraska Music Teachers' Association, is a member of the Giltner Christian Church, and holds membership in the Nebraskana Society.

During the World War she acted as chairman of the Giltner branch of the Red Cross and was awarded a certificate and service pin in recognition of services rendered. Mrs. Marvel plays the piano, cello, and violin, and has directed various orchestras, choirs, and choruses in Hamilton County; she is especially interested in young people. A Democrat, she was committeewoman for Union Precinct in 1922 and 1930.

Her marriage to Perry Otto Marvel was solemnized at Filley, Nebraska, September 4, 1912. Dr. Marvel, who was born at Pennfield, Illinois, July 31, 1881. He has traced his lineage back 34 generations to the ninth century; members of his family came to America in 1650. Three children were born to them: Merton Eugene, born May 29, 1916, who died May 29, 1916; Alden Leroy, born March 30, 1918; and Wylda Maurine, born November 24, 1924. Residence: Giltner. (Photograph on Page 776).

Thompson Marvel

Thompson Marvel retired farmer of Hamilton County. Nebraska, has lived in this state for 48 years. He was born at Waynesville, Illinois, October 1, 1848, the son of James and Maria (Gambrel) Marvel. His father, also a farmer, was born at Springfield, Illinois, October 29, 1825, and died at Waynesville, February 6, 1876. His mother, the daughter of a Kentucky colonel, was born at Santa Ana, Indiana, September 27, 1829, and died at Phillips, Nebraska, March 30, 1898.

Mr. Marvel received his education in the public school of Waynesville. He has always farmed on a large scale and has been successful as a cattle feeder and hog raiser. In 1915 he retired from active work but still owns and maintains a 720 acre tract of land in Hamilton County.

ENGALENA JOSEPHINE MARVEL

He has served on various school boards during the last 20 years, and is now a member of Giltner Christian Church and the Nebraskana Society. He is a Democrat. In his youth Mr. Marvel was interested in wrestling; his hobby is reading.

His marriage to Margaret Jane French occurred at Potamac, Illinois, March 15, 1871. Mrs. Marvel, whose ancestors were among the earliest settlers in America, was born at Danville, Illinois, October 13, 1851. To this marriage the following children were born, James Asbury, December 2, 1871, a merchant at Giltner, who married Lula Cantrell; George Henry, June 21, 1873, a physician of Lincoln, who married Bernice Weekly of Lincoln; Lilie, born September 17, 1875, who died May 21, 1877; Stella, born February 19, 1878, who died May 17, 1880; Perry Otto, born July 31, 1881, physician of Giltner, who married Engalena J. Bowers; Irene Maria, born March 10, 1883, who married Claude D. Chapman, residing in Giltner; Maggie Ellen, born September 7, 1885, who married Lemoyne J. Gallentine, living in Fort Pierce, Florida; Della, born January 27, 1887, a cosmetician, living at home; and Delmar, born January 27, 1887, who died March 23, 1887. Mr. and Mrs. Marvel celebrated their sixty-first wedding anniversary March 15, 1932.

Mr. Marvel's ancestry dates back to the DeMarvel family of France, who moved to England and there took the name of Marvel. They came to the United States in the early 1699s, and came to Nebraska from Hamilton County, Iowa, in 1882. Residence: Giltner.

Charles Jacob Mary

Charles Jacob Mary, merchant, was born at Mullen, Nebraska, October 12, 1887, and has lived all of his life in Nebraska. His father, George Mary, was born in Cleveland, Ohio, July 3, 1856, and died at Oconto on October 10, 1919. He was a merchant whose French father and German mother came to America in 1850 on a sailing vessel, their trip taking about fifty-five days. Caroline Helmuth, wife of George Mary, was born in Germany, March 30, 1865. She is still living.

Mr. Mary attended public school and completed a two year business course at Kearney State Normal. While there he played right field with the first baseball team.

From the time he left school until his father's death in 1919, Mr. Mary was associated with him in the business known as George Mary and Sons Department Store. When he died Mr. Mary took over the business and changed the name to the Charles Mary Department Store. He is a Bryan Democrat. He resided at Mullen five years, at Lodi three years, and for thirty-six years has lived at Oconto.

On November 24, 1908, he was married to Lulu Catherine Kellog at Oconto. She was born at Waverly, Nebraska, June 16, 1890, of Scotch-Irish ancestry. They have three children, Agnes, born June 25, 1911, who is a clerk and who was graduated from St. Marys High Schol at Grand Island; Claudia, born March 6, 1914, who will graduate from the Immaculate Conception Academy of Hastings; and Maxine, born October 12, 1918.

Mr. Mary is a member of St. Mary's Catholic Church at Oconto, and the Merchants Hardware Association. He has always played ball and still enjoys it very much, he is fond of fishing and hunting, loves the things of nature, and has taken several trips to the Rocky Mountains. He also enjoys taking pictures. Residence: Oconto.

Anton John Masek

Anton John Masek, who was born at Newton, Nebraska, September 3, 1883, and for many years has been a farmer in this county. His father, Anton Masek, who was a blacksmith in Europe, and later was a farmer in America, was born at Sedlec, Hartikovic, Moravia, June 3, 1853, and died at Valparaiso, Nebraska, January 29, 1929. His mother was born at Sedlec, and died at Valparaiso, May 21, 1912.

Mr. Masek, who has always taken an active interest in the affairs of his community, has been a director of the school board for 23 years, is affiliated with St. Mary's Catholic Church, and holds membership in the Nebraskana Society. During the World War he was prominent in loan drives, and with his school district was awarded a German helmet and victory flag in recognition of service.

His marriage to Victoria Tejral was solemnized at Brainard, Nebraska, September 5, 1905. Mrs. Masek was born at Wahoo. Five children were born to this union: Emil, born July 19, 1907; William, born May 10, 1911; Anton, born September 9, 1914; Henrietta, born April 27, 1923; and Lawrence, born July 15, 1927. Residence: Valparaiso.

Edward John Mashek

Edward John Mashek, implement and hardware dealer, was born at Abie, Nebraska, September 16, 1878, son of Maty A. and Rose (Jaros) Mashek. His father was born in Posek, Bohemia, in 1848, and came to America in 1855. He was a pioneer blacksmith in Iowa, a stage driver and later a successful farmer. He came to Nebraska in a covered wagon in 1875, and thereafter held many public offices, among them county commissioner and justice of the peace. His death occurred at Norfolk in 1925. The father of Maty A. Mashek was a lumberman in Bohemia, who floated logs down the Votava River.

Rose, wife of Maty A. Mashek, was born in Bohemia in 1850, and died at Norfolk in 1927. She was primarily a wife and mother, but took an active interest in church and other activities.

Educated in the country schools of Butler County, Edward J. Mashek followed in his father's footsteps as a farmer. In 1914 he was united in marriage to Emma Rose Vaurina at Abie, her birthplace. She is the daughter of pioneer settlers in Butler County. Their daughter, Rose, was born August 27, 1915.

In addition to his agricultural pursuits, Mr. Mashek is a stockholder and vice president of the Abie State Bank. For the past thirty years he has been a member of the Modern Woodmen of America, and is a member of the Red Cross and The Nebraskana Society. He enjoys hunting, fishing and camping, and during the World War was a member of the Nebraska Council of Defense. Residence: Abie. (Photograph in Album).

Fred G. Mason

Fred G. Mason was born at Moline, Illinois, July 30, 1869, the son of Rasmus and Johanna (Hansen) Mason. His father, who was a farmer, was born at Magelby, Denmark, March 18, 1828, and died at Upland, Nebraska, November 15, 1904; he served in the war between Germany and Denmark in 1848-49-50. His mother was born at Moen, Denmark, March 15, 1835, and died at Moline, August 16, 1902.

Rasmus Mason came to America in the summer of 1862. The voyage across the Atlantic lasted for 13 weeks since the trip was made in the usual sailing vessel of that time. Upon his arrival in this country he traveled up the Mississippi River by steam boat to Moline, Illinois, where he made his home until the time of his death.

Mr. Mason received his education at Moline. He is president of the Telephone Company at Upland, Nebraska, is president of the District Farmers Co-operative Association, is a director in the Farmers Union Mercantile Company at Upland, and is a stockholder in the Farmers Grain Company there. He has been a farmer most of his life and is now retired.

He is affiliated with the United Brethren in Christ Church, holds membership in the Modern Woodmen of

America, and is a member of the Odd Fellows Lodge at Upland. His sports include hunting and fishing. As a member of the Republican Party, Mr. Mason has taken an active part in political affairs in his county, serving as a member of the State Legislature in 1931.

His marriage to Amelia Work occurred at Moline, June 30, 1897; she was born at Davenport, Iowa, December 20, 1870, and died at Upland, September 7, 1909. The four children born to this marriage are LeRoy, November 12, 1898, who married Creola Hadley; Ralph, June 1, 1900, who married Lila Saul; Ruby, born June 22, 1906, who married Theodore E. Daniels; and Lester, January 25, 1908, who died June 2, 1910.

On December 25, 1912, Mr. Mason was united in marriage with Minnie Steinke at Minden, Nebraska. Mrs. Mason, who is of German parentage, was born in Ford County, Illinois, June 14, 1882. They have two children, Lucille, born September 10, 1914; and Norma, born December 23, 1916. Residence: Upland. (Photograph in Album).

Margaret Jane Mason

Margaret Jane Mason was born at Rock Falls, Iowa, July 21, 1872, the daughter of John and Elizabeth (Thompson) Dolphin. Her father, who was a farmer, was born in Durham, England, September 15, 1842, and died at Bloomfield, Nebraska; he served as county sheriff and postmaster at Dolphin, Nebraska, was a Civil War soldier, and acted as the first mayor of Bloomfield; his English ancestors came to this country in 1850. Her mother, who was a music teacher, was born at Lancaster, England, March 3, 1850, and died in Knox County, August 4, 1888.

Mrs. Mason attended rural school and the high school at Hartington. She has been a resident of Nebraska since 1879. She is a member of the Woman's Club, Utile Dulce Club, the American Legion Auxiliary, and the Woman's Relief Corps. She is affiliated with the First Congregational Church of Bloomfield, Nebraska.

Her marriage to Edgar Hollest Mason occurred at Clinton, Iowa, March 17, 1893. Mr. Mason, who is a banker, was born of English parentage at Franham, England, November 15. The following children were born to them: Evelyn Caroline, May 5, 1894, who married Thomas Benton Watters; Margaret Marion, August 8, 1895; Richard Edgar, July 21, 1903, who died May 8, 1925; Mary Elizabeth, December 5, 1909. Margaret is music instructor in the public schools of North Platte, Nebraska. Residence: Bloomfield.

Myrtle Mason

Myrtle Mason, a lifetime resident of Nebraska, was born at Lincoln, Nebraska, and for the past 11 years has been prominent in newspaper work at Omaha. She is the daughter of Nathaniel Charles and Harriet (Mather) Keegan. She received her education at the University of Nebraska where she was a member of Theta Sigma Phi and Kappa Delta.

She is the author of many articles and for the past 11 years has been editor of the woman's section of the *Omaha Bee-News*. She is married to Cyrus Pollock Mason.

Frank George Massman

A farmer and cattle raiser for a number of years, Frank George Massman was born at New Melle, Missouri, May 13, 1878, son of Henry Chris and Mary (Schroder) Massman.

Henry Chris Massman, a farmer, was born at Melle, Hannover, Germany, and died at Battle Creek, Nebraska, October 22, 1925. He was a veteran of the Civil War,

vice president of the Battle Valley Bank from its organization until his death, and was a member of the school board for twenty-five years. He came to America at the age of 14. His wife, born at New Melle, January 24, 1850, died at Battle Creek on April 11, 1924.

Educated in the parochial school at Battle Creek until he was confirmed March 30, 1890, Frank George Massman attended Concordia Seminary also. He is an extensive farmer, land owner and cattle raiser and is vice president of the Federal Land Bank of Norfolk.

On December 27, 1909, he was married to Camilla Marion Christensen at Warrensburg, Missouri, and to them were born five children: Alvin, August 15, 1911; Edwin, July 16, 1913; Mildred, August 30, 1915; Frank, August 2, 1918; and Lois, November 26, 1920. Alvin and Edwin graduated from high school and are assisting their father. The others are still in school. Mrs. Massman was born at Fremont, Nebraska, May 1, 1887.

Mr. Massman is affiliated with St. John's Lutheran Church. He is a member of the Commercial Club, the Masons and the Nebraskana Society, and for nine years was president of the local school board. Residence: Battle Creek.

Clarence Edgar Masters

Clarence Edgar Masters, jeweler and optometrist, was born at Hartleton, Pennsylvania, June 12, 1874, son of Sam and Sarah Clara (Walter) Masters. His ancestry was Pennsylvania Dutch.

Mr. Masters attended public and high school at Milton, Pennsylvania, and since 1897 has been a jeweler and optometrist at Crawford. He is a member of the American and Nebraska state optometrist association, and the Nebraska Jewelers Association. He is a Republican and a Mason (Shrine and Consistory).

On July 1, 1901, he was married to Georgiana Gertrude Meredith at Crawford. Mrs. Masters was born at Ames, Iowa, January 24, 1878. They have two children, Meredith D., born January 15, 1904, who married Betty Roedel; Justin D., born October 12, 1906; and Sam A., born January 13, 1909. One was graduated from West Point in 1927, one is the junior civil engineer of the School of Mines, Rapid City, South Dakota, and the third is junior optical doctor at Penn State College of Optometry, Philadelphia.

Mr. Masters is a Republican. He enjoys athletics, dancing and cards. Residence: Crawford.

Joseph G. Masters

Joseph G. Masters has been prominent in Omaha's educational world for the past 16 years, and is one of Nebraska's leading educators. He was born at Newton, Kansas, February 20, 1873, the son of Joseph Tilford and Ellen (Mitchell) Masters. His father, who was a farmer and a Civil War veteran, was of Scotch ancestry. He was born at Nicholasville, Kentucky, October 4, 1842, and died at Newton, Kansas, December 30, 1919.

His mother was of Scotch-Irish parentage, in Harrison County, Ohio, April 8, 1843, and before her marriage was a school teacher. She died August 25, 1909.

Mr. Masters was educated in the rural schools of Kansas, and in 1900 he was graduated from the academic course of the Kansas State Normal. In 1904 he received his Latin degree from this institution; he was granted his Ph. B., 1912, and A. M., in 1915 by the University of Chicago. In 1908 he was a student at the University of California. He was twice president of his class, was editor of the school paper, and was a member of the debating team at Kansas State Normal. He was elected to Phi Delta Kappa at Chicago University.

He has held the following positions: story teller of western trails and battles; lecturer at the University of Pennsylvania; lecturer for state teachers' associations and teachers' institutes; principal of Central High School at Omaha, which position he now holds. Mr. Masters is a writer of distinction, and has made historical episodes of the west into intriguing stories that are read all over the country by biography and history lovers. He is the author of many educational articles published in the year book of the National Society for the Study of Education, and of articles published on the *Oregon Trail*. The stirring accounts of the old trails and heroic struggles of the pioneers with the Indians include the following: *Epic-Story Episodes* of the Far West, with the following stories: *Powder River, Beecher's Island, The Grand Old Man of the Rockies, High Noon on the Little Horn, Kit Carson;* and a general introduction to *Neihardt-Epic Series*.

He is the author of *Trails of Yesterday*, which included the two stories: *Romance and Tragedy of the Old Santa Fe Trail;* and *The Story of the World's Mightiest Highway* (Old Oregon Trail). He has told his historical stories at every sort of civic, educational, noonday and improvement club.

Perhaps his greatest achievement and claim to recognition in the educational world has been the founding of the National Honor Society for high schools. About ten years ago he made the first steps toward organizing this honor society, and today it is the one organization of its kind which has met with National approval and success. It is the only honor society to be sponsored by the National Principals Association, and is directly and completely recognized throughout the country.

Mr. Masters was president of Omaha Council of Churches for three years; was dean of the Standard Leadership Training School for three years; and was president of the State Teachers' Association of Oklahoma, 1914. He is a member of the National Educational Association, the Nebraska State Teachers' Association, and the Parent-Teachers' Association. During the World War he served as director of adult and citizenship education.

He is regional director of the Oregon Trail Memorial Association; is a member of the Colorado and Nebraska State Historical Associations; and holds membership in the Young Men's Christian Association and the First Baptist Church of Omaha. He is affiliated with most of Omaha's civic clubs including: Omaha Chamber of Commerce, Ad-Sell, and Ak-Sar-Ben. He likes to make camping trips; his hobbies are exploring western trails and battlefields, and hunting. He is a Republican.

On November 11, 1911, he was married to Helen Geneva Smith at Crown Point, Indiana. Mrs. Masters, who is a well known short story writer, was born at Smethport, Pennsylvania, April 23, 1885. Her ancestry is Irish and English. There are four children: Jose, born August 28, 1912; Jane, born November 7, 1913; Conrad, born August 16, 1918; and Helen Mitchell, born April 23, 1923.

Mrs. Masters has had her stories published in Munsey's publications, Midland, also written plays which have been produced by Omaha Woman's Club and various State Teachers' Associations and High Schools. Residence: Omaha.

Albert N. Mathers

Albert N. Mathers, farmer and banker, was born in Douglas, Nebraska, February 9, 1882, son of John and Mary (Cowles) Mathers. His father was born in Germany, in 1840, and came to the United States at the age of six with his parents. He was a farmer and retired land owner at the time of his death in Rogers, Arkansas, in June, 1924. His wife, Mary, who was born in New York, is of New England Yankee descent. She died in Douglas, Nebraska in 1918.

Upon his graduation from high school Mr. Mathers attended Nebraska Wesleyan University, and the University of Nebraska, College of Law. He was a member of Professor Fogg's debating squad at the university, and later taught school prior to entering business.

On November 11, 1907, he was married to Fern Johnston near Douglas. She was born in that vicinity July 23, 1887, her father of Scotch-Irish and her mother of New England Yankee descent. Mrs. Mathers attended Wesleyan University, and is now active in the Scottsbluff Chapter of the Daughters of American Revolution, and a member of the Episcopalian Church. There are two children, Albert L., born December 9, 1910, who received his Bachelor of Arts degree and his Bachelor of Laws degree from the University of Michigan; and Alice Elizabeth, born August 22, 1915, who is a senior in Gering High School.

A Republican, Mr. Mathers was speaker of the Nebraska House of Representatives in 1923. He is president of the Gering National Bank, a sheep and cattle feeder, and the owner and operator of nine improved farms. He has interests and investments in various corporations. He has done much legal work for irrigation districts, and was the advocate for reclamation projects before the departments and the United States Congress in Washington.

During the late war he devoted much time to local activities, was chairman of the county board, and the Red Cross organization, and was a member of the Hoover Food Commission. He is past president of the Associated Chambers of Commerce, the Nebraska Irrigation Association, the Scottsbluff Rotary Club, the Red Cross, and the Nebraska Bankers' Association. Mr. Mathers was the first mayor of Gering.

A 32nd degree Mason, he is a member of the Knights of Templar, the Shrine (Tanger Temple at Omaha). For ten years he was president of the board of education of Gering, and at the present time is custodian of the Scottsbluff National Monument. For several years he was district representative of the Young Men's Christian Association. His religious affiliation is with the Episcopal Church. His club is the Scottsbluff Country Club. His hobbies are reading and the irrigation law. Residence: Gering. (Photograph in Album).

Charles Edward Matson

Charles E. Matson was born in Dodge County, Nebraska, May 17, 1874. He has lived in this state all his life and for nearly 30 years has been engaged in the practice of law at Lincoln. His father, William Matson, who was born in Illinois, July 5, 1845, was a farmer, rancher and stock raiser who served in the Civil War. His ancestors were Swedish and Welsh; some of them in the Revolution. He died at Lincoln, October, 1914. Martha Jane (Riley) Matson, his mother, was born in Iowa, and died in Nebraska in 1889. Her grandfather Riley came to America from Ireland, and fought with the American troops in the War of 1812.

Mr. Matson was graduated from the high school at Ohiowa, Nebraska, in 1890. A student at Fremont Normal, 1890; Western Normal, 1896; and the University of Nebraska he was awarded the LL. B. degree in 1902. He served as a member of the Nebraska debating team in 1898; was editor of the senior law annual, 1902; and was elected to membership in Phi Delta Phi and Delta Sigma Rho. He held all offices, consecutively, in the local chapter of Kappa Sigma. He was center on the Nebraska University basketball team in 1898.

He has engaged in legal practice since his admission to the bar at Lincoln, June 10, 1902; has served as chairman of the citizenship committee of the Nebraska State Bar Association since its creation in 1924; and has served as a member of a similar committee of the American Bar Association for the past six years. He is past president of the Lancaster County Bar Association, and for three years was a member of the executive committee of the Nebraska State Bar Association.

He is the author of various articles on criminal law and procedure and other phases of administration of law, published at various times. A Republican, he served as chairman of the Lancaster County Republican Central Committee in 1898; was deputy county attorney of Lancaster County, 1904-09; was county attorney, 1919-27. He has been prominent in political affairs in the state for many years and has been a delegate to various county and state conventions of the Republican Party during his residence in Nebraska.

His marriage to Ethelyn Josephine Bignell was solemnized at Lincoln, June 8, 1904. Mrs. Matson was born at Lincoln, July 8, 1883; her ancestry is English and French. Her father, Edward Bignell, was for more than 25 years division superintendent of the Chicago, Burlington and Quincy Railroad at Lincoln.

Mr. Matson served as chairman of the Liberty loan committee for Nebraska District 14; he was a four minute speaker during the World War.

He is a member of the American Bar Association; the Nebraska State Bar Association; and the Lancaster County Bar Association. He holds membership in the Lincoln Chamber of Commerce; the Hiram Club; University Club; and the Lincoln Country Club. He is a Mason; Scottish Rite; 32nd degree; Knight Commander of Court of Honor; and Shrine. He is a member of the Nebraskana Society and the Nebraska State Historical Society.

His favorite sport is golf. His hobby is the study of the history of federal government and the federal constitution. He is affiliated with St. Matthew's Mission Episcopal Church at Lincoln. He is a member of the Sons of Veterans. Residence: Lincoln.

Richard A. Matteson

Richard A. Matteson has been a farmer and executive in farm organizations in Fillmore County for over half a century and today is retired at Geneva, Nebraska. He was born at Campbellsport, Wisconson, November 10, 1853, the son of Caroline (Harrington) and Isaiah Matteson. His father, who was born at Shaftsbury, Vermont, March 19, 1823, and died at Fairmont, Nebraska, October 10, 1900, was a farmer whose Welsh ancestors came to America in the early settlement of Rhode Island.

His mother was born at Shaftsbury, Vermont, August 15, 1833, and died at Geneva, December 2, 1915. She was of English and Scotch descent; her grandfather and six uncles served in the Revolution.

Mr. Matteson served as secretary of the Farmers Mutual Insurance Company for 22 years and is now president of this organization. A Republican, he has taken an active and important part in the political history of Fillmore County, holding the following positions: deputy clerk, 1888-92; county clerk, 1892-96; chairman of the county board, 1910-20; member of the constitutional convention, 1919-20; substitute county judge, 1927-29; and chairman of the Republican County Committee, for fifteen years.

He is a Knight Templer and 32nd degree Mason, holds membership in the Nebraskana Society, and is affiliated with the First Congregational Church of Geneva. He served as chairman of loan drives and Red Cross committees at Geneva five times during the World War. His marriage to Anna Mary Straley, occurred at Fairmont, February 10, 1884; she was born at New Enterprise, Pennsylvania, October 12, 1860, of German parentage. They have one child, Rosell Collis, born October 11, 1884, who is an electrical engineer. He was graduated from the University of Nebraska in 1922; at present time is taking post graduate work at the University of Minnesota. Residence: Geneva.

Ivan H. Mattson

Ivan H. Mattson, photographer, was born at Goteborg, Sweden, January 7, 1895, son of Herman and Ida (Person) Mattson. The father, an interior decorator, was born in Anneberg, Sweden, January 1, 1872, and arrived in America in 1904. His wife, Ida, was born in Goteborg, April 1, 1874. Her father, Peter Person, who lives in Sweden, is an old shipbuilder who in years past worked on many of the ships of the Swedish Navy.

Educated in public school until 1914, Ivan H. Mattson attended Kearney State Teachers College 1914-15. He served his apprenticeship as a photographer with the Anderson Studio in Kearney, from 1909-1920, the last five years as head of the printing department. In June, 1920, he started in business for himself under the name of Mattson Studio.

On August 21, 1929, Mr. Mattson was united in marriage to Ebba June Olsson at Kearney. Mrs. Mattson, who was born at Ord, June 17, 1908, is of Swedish parentage, her mother a teacher in the schools of Sweden.

A Democrat, Mr. Mattson was elected to the city council of Kearney in 1928 and is still serving. He is staff sergeant, Medical Detachment, 35th Division Train, in the Nebraska National Guard. For the past five years he has been a member of the Nebraska National Guard.

Mr. Mattson is a member of the First Lutheran Church, the Red Cross, the Chamber of Commerce, the Nebraskana Society, and since 1930 has been treasurer of the Nebraska Photographers Society. His club is the Kearney Country Club, his favorite sport is golf and his hobby is dramatics. Residence: Kearney.

Christ Matzen

Chris Matzen was born at Creston, Nebraska, March 29, 1876, the son of Theodore Konrad Matzen and Bertha Marie (Sverson) Matzen. His father, who was a sailor, miner, and farmer, was born at Tyn, Denmark, May 28, 1835, and is now retired; he homesteaded in Platte County in 1873. His mother was born at Veile, Denmark, May 3, 1851.

Mr. Matzen, who is a successful farmer in Boone County, Nebraska, attended rural school and Fremont Normal School. He is a member of the Parent Teachers Association at St. Edward, Nebraska, has been moderator of the school board for 14 years, is director and secretary of the Farmers Union Co-operative Association, and is an active member of the local Red Cross. He is affiliated with the First Presbyterian Church of St. Edward and is clerk of Woodville Township.

His marriage to Laura Marie Cartensen occurred at Leigh, Nebraska, June 10, 1908. Five children were born to their marriage: Maurice, May 4, 1909; Gordon, June 9, 1911; Kenneth, March 7, 1913; Stanley, February 15, 1917; and Steward, February 15, 1917, who died February 26, 1917. Maurice and Gordon are farmers, Kenneth is a student at Hastings College, and Stanley is a student at St. Edward High School. Residence: St. Edward.

John M. Matzen

John M. Matzen, assistant professor, school administration, of the University of Nebraska, was born at Moline, Illinois, son of Hans Christian and Albertina Fredericka (Mathiason) Matzen. The father was born in Denmark, November 27, 1839 and died at Hooper February 7, 1896. His wife, Albertina, was born in Sweden, August 20, 1838 and died at Hooper April 4, 1912.

In 1913 Mr. Matzen received the Bachelor of Science degree from Fremont College, and in 1927 and 1928 respectively received the Bachelor of Arts and Master of Arts degrees from the University of Nebraska. In 1931 he received the degree of Doctor of Philosophy from Columbia University.

A Republican he was county superintendent of Dodge County schools 1906-20, and from 1920 until 1927 was state superintendent of public instruction. He is a Scottish Rite Mason and Shriner, a member of the Knights of Pythias, the Nebraska State Bar Association, the National Education Association and the Department of Superintendence of the the later. Residence: Lincoln.

August Ferdinand Matzke

August Ferdinand Matzke, retired farmer, was born at Juda, Green County, Wisconsin, November 30, 1859, son of William Frederick and Hanna Louisa (Henning) Matzke. His father was born at Doelitz, Germany, June 5, 1833, and died at Juda, September 25, 1904. He came to America in 1856. Hanna, wife of William, was born at Doelitz, August 16, 1835, and died at Juda, in May, 1907.

Mr. Matzke received his education in the rural schools of Wisconsin, and in 1891, came to Nebraska, where he engaged in farming and stock raising on an extensive scale until his retirement. He was married to Wilhelmina Augusta Ziettlow, at Juda, Wisconsin, January 24, 1884. Mrs. Matzke was born at Juda, September 13, 1863, and died at Western, March 17, 1918. To their union ten children were born, one of whom, Adella, born June 10, 1885, died July 31, 1887. Those living are: Jasper F., born December 12, 1886. He is a farmer and is married to Ada R. Schultz. Stella May, born December 3, 1888, is active in the work of the W. C. T. U. She married Samuel Lange. Nettie Marie, born October 3, 1890, was graduated from Western High School, and taught seven years in rural schools. Anna Sylvia, born October 3, 1890, was graduated from Western High School, and taught 8 years in rural schools. She married John W. Dallas. Lawrence L., born December 16, 1894, finished high school at Western, and is a farmer. He married Ruby A. Dallas. Flossie W., born December 8, 1897, completed the course at Western High School, attended teachers training school, and taught in city and rural schools five years. She married Dewey Hibbert. Letha C., born June 14, 1900, attended Peru and Kearney Normal School and taught in city and rural schools seven years. She married Harvey Johnston. Edna Clara, born March 22, 1903, completed the course in the Kearney State Teachers College and taught in the high schools of Nebraska five years. Mabel M., born October 26, 1906, was graduated from the University of Nebraska in 1928, taught in a mission school at Beverly, Kentucky, one year, in Nebraska high schools one year, and is now engaged in religious educational work in the Methodist Episcopal Church. She is married to Nathaniel B. Burke. Laurence, the second son, served two years with the American Expeditionary Forces during the World War. All the children are interested in community and religious activities.

Mr. Matzke is a Republican. He is a member of the Evangelical Church, the Nebraskana Society, and during the World War participated in Liberty bond drives and Red Cross and Salvation Army work. He was a member of rural school boards for the years 1896-1912, and city schools 1920-23. For thirty years he was superintendent of Sunday School and for a like period was a trustee of his church. He enjoys reading, music and carpentry. Residence: Western. (Photograph in Album).

Murl M. Maupin

Murl M. Maupin, lawyer, was born at Stanberry, Missouri, February 21, 1901, son of Charles and Minnie (Shattuck) Maupin.

He attended Washington Grade School at North Platte, Nebraska until May, 1915 and was graduated from North Platte High School in 1919. In 1923 he received a Bachelor of Laws degree in the University of Nebraska, where he was a member of Phi Gamma Delta. He was admitted to the bar at Lincoln on June 5, 1923 and from 1927-1931 was county attorney of Keith County, elected on the Republican ticket. He is now a member of the board of education of Ogallala. He is a member of the Nebraska State and American Bar Association, the Rotary Club, and the Masons.

He was married to Viola Blonde at Ewing, Nebraska, February 24, 1925. In 1924 she received her Bachelor of Arts degree from the University of Nebraska. Residence: Ogallala.

Will Major Maupin

A noted newspaper man and editor of Nebraska, Will Major Maupin is the son of William Taylor and Sarah Ann (Miller) Maupin. He was born at Taylorville, Illinois, August 31, 1863, and for the past forty-six years has been a resident of Nebraska. William Taylor Maupin, who was born in Callaway County, Missouri, August 30, 1832, was a minister of the Disciples of Christ Church, and a veteran of the Civil War. His forbears came from France to Virginia in 1707. He died at Hennessey, Oklahoma, in March, 1911. Sarah Ann, his wife, was also born in Callaway County, on March 16, 1832. She died at North Bend in October, 1894.

Mr. Maupin attended the common schools of Missouri, leaving at the age of fifteen to be apprenticed to the printing trade. This he has always followed, and during the past fifty years has been editor of various newspapers. At the present time he is staff correspondent for the *Omaha World-Herald*. In addition to his newspaper editorial work, Mr. Maupin is the author of several volumes of verse and sketches, the last one being *Sunny Side Up*.

A Democrat, Mr. Maupin has always been active in the politics of his party, and during 1909-10 served as commissioner of Labor for Nebraska, and during 1917-18 was state director of the Bureau of Publicity. He has made an intimate study of Nebraska history, its resources and possibilities, and during the World War period was cited by President Wilson for meritorious work in connection with the National Council of Defense.

Mr. Maupin was married to Lettie Clifford Armstead at North Bend, Nebraska, on October 13, 1894, and to this union eight children were born, Louis of Salt Lake City; Lorena Elizabeth Lewellyn of Omaha; Dorothy Katherine Beindorff; Richard Metcalfe; Margaret Blanche; Charlotte May; Jack Robins; and Dan Whitmer. There are seven grandchildren at the present time. Mrs. Maupin, who was born at Columbus, Ohio, August 16, 1875, is of Pennsylvania Dutch and early New England ancestry.

Affiliated with the Disciples of Christ Church, Mr. Maupin is also a member of the Masons, the Knights of Pythias, the Lions Club and the Nebraskana Society. He devotes much of his leisure time to fishing, while his hobby is rare books and manuscripts. Residence: Hastings.

Irving Clayton Maust

At Myersdale, Pennsylvania, Irving C. Maust was born May 15, 1868. His father, Elias Abraham Maust, who was born in Somerset County, March 23, 1839, and died at Falls City, Richardson County, Nebraska, July 21, 1925, was a pioneer grain dealer in Falls City, and served as a corporal in the Civil War. Savilla (Miller) Maust, his mother, who was born at Myersdale, July 27, 1849, and died at Falls City, April 8, 1921, was a diligent church worker.

Mr. Maust, who has lived in Nebraska for sixty years, was educated in the public schools of Falls City. Since 1890 he has been continuously in the grain, livestock and coal business; in 1920 he became interested in the oil business and has carried on all of these enterprises since that date. He is vice president of the Hotel Realty Company.

On May 18, 1892, his marriage to Sara Blanche Norris was solemnized at Falls City. Mrs. Maust, a prominent clubwoman, is of English ancestry, descended from Sir William Norreys, and was born at Falls City, January 27, 1872. There are two children: June, born June 4, 1910, who is a graduate of the Christian College at Columbia, Missouri, and is now attending the University of Nebraska where she is a member of Pi Phi sorority; and Irving C., born August 18, 1914.

Mr. Maust is a Republican, a member of the Red Cross, the Chamber of Commerce, the Parent-Teachers' Association, and the Nebraskana Society. He is an Elk, a Mason, an Odd Fellow, and a Knight of Pythias. His club is the Falls City Country Club. Hunting and fishing are his hobbies. Residence: Falls City.

David Edward Maxwell

A prominent dentist in Nebraska for twenty-four years, David Edward Maxwell was born at Cedar Rapids, September 26, 1883, son of John and Anna (Dobson) Maxwell.

John Maxwell, born in Belfast, Ireland, March 10, 1847, married there and about 1866 left his wife and two children to come to America. A hard working, thrifty farmer, he afterward brought his family in 1869 to the United States, living near and in Cedar Rapids until 1925, then settling in Albion where he resided until his death. He, together with his brothers-in-law William Dobson and Hubert Reed, were the first settlers in Cedar Valley where they homesteaded in 1872, and when he died on May 18, 1928, he had amassed a comfortable fortune.

Anna Dobson was born in Belfast, and died at Cedar Rapids, January 9, 1924. She came to Boone County in the spring of 1872, with a team of oxen and a covered wagon, in which the family lived all summer. She reared a family of eight children, five of whom were born in a sod house in Cedar Rapids, which house is still standing at the present time. She was a devoted wife, mother, and a true pioneer.

Educated in public school, David Edward Maxwell was graduated from Cedar Rapids High School in 1904, and in 1908 received his degree of Doctor of Dental Surgery from the University of Nebraska. There he played baseball, and as he says "as a class of dentists we had a pretty good team."

He was married on March 12, 1909 to Grace Morris at Belgrade, who died at Cedar Rapids, July 9, 1909. His second marriage was to Lucy Elizabeth Farley, and was solemnized June 26, 1912 at Cedar Rapids. Mrs. Maxwell was born July 16, 1889. They have one daughter, Helen Lucile, born January 24, 1916. She is in high school.

Dr. Maxwell practiced nine and half years at Cedar Rapids, eight and half years at Albion and for the past six years has been at Columbus. In all three places he has enjoyed a large and lucrative practice. He is an extensive land and property owner in addition.

His fraternal organizations include the Modern Woodmen of America, the Masons, Eastern Star and Knights of Pythias. His religious affiliation is with the First Methodist Church of Columbus. He is a contributor to welfare organizations, is a member of the national, state and district dental associations, the Chamber of Commerce, and the Wayside Country Club. His favorite sport is golf and his hobby is his profession. He is also extensively interested in building both residents and business buildings, and at the present time is part owner of the Maxwell-Bratt building, on which extensive improvements are contemplated in the near future. Residence: Columbus.

Allan Daniel May

An editor and writer for more than thirty years, Allan D. May, was born at Mound City, Missouri, January 26, 1876. He is the son of Leonidas McKelvie and Martha Ellen (Hanna) May. His father was born at Findlay, Ohio, May 24, 1848, and was a railway postal clerk and editor. He served in the Civil War and was of Irish descent. Martha Ellen Hanna, his wife, was born at Hagerstown, Maryland, September 8, 1842. She was of Scotch descent, an earnest worker in the Presbyterian Church, whose main interest in life was the rearing of her family. She died at Falls City, May 27, 1918.

Allan D. May was graduated from the Falls City High

School on May 18, 1893, and studied at the University of Nebraska two years. In the newspaper business since leaving school, his first connection was with the *Falls City Journal* in 1896, which continued about seven years.

In 1907 Mr. May came to Auburn where he was connected with the *Auburn Republican* for several years, later becoming editor of the *Nemaha County Herald* in 1911. He is the author of considerable verse published in magazines at various times, and of newspaper articles, etc.

His marriage to Maude Alice Wylie was solemnized at Falls City, October 22, 1902. Mrs. May was born at Rome, New York, June 12, 1878, and is of English descent. They have one son, Edgar Wylie, born April 25, 1904, who married Mary Yvonne Sellers. Their son, Thomas Wylie, is now three years of age.

A Republican, Mr. May served as deputy county clerk 10 years. During the war he was active in various war drives. Affiliated with the Protestant Episcopal Church, he attends the Church of the Ascension at Auburn.

He is a member of the Nebraska Writers' Guild, the Nebraska State Historical Society and The Nebraskana Society. He is also a member of the Red Cross, the Chamber of Commerce and the Royal Highlanders. He is interested in sports, especially football. His hobbies, however, are reading, growing flowers and gardening. Residence: Auburn.

Clara Edith May

For the past 38 years Clara Edith May has lived in Nebraska, and is active in women's affairs at York. She was born at Buda, Illinois, December 4, 1881, the daughter of Joel Hulbert and Rebecca (Barnet) Foster. Her father, who was a farmer, was born in Onandaga County, New York, September 18, 1834, of Holland Dutch parentage, and died at York, Nebraska, April 8, 1916. Her mother, whose ancestry was English, was born at Lysander, New York, March 27, 1835, and died at York, September 30, 1910.

Mrs. May attended rural school in Illinois, and later was graduated from the York High School. She was a student at York College for a time. She is a member of the Young Men's Christian Association Auxiliary, the Eastern Star, Does, Pythian Sisters, Highlanders, and the First Presbyterian Church of York. She served as chairman of the York Hi-Y committee in 1930, and is now a member of the York Country Club. Her only business affiliation is with the York Floral Company.

She was married to Lemuel Elmer Dean at York, June 5, 1907. Mr. Dean, who was an electrician and farmer, was born at Blue Vale, Nebraska, January 24, 1879, and died at York, August 8, 1909. His ancestry was Pennsylvania Dutch. One child was born to this marriage: Helen Clarissa Dean, born June 25, 1909. On January 9, 1913, she was united in marriage with Grover C. May at York. Their two children are: Howard Bernhardt, born December 23, 1913; and Robert Foster, born January 30, 1916. Helen was graduated from York High School in 1927, was a student at Stephens College in 1929, and was graduated from the University of Nebraska, in June, 1931. She is a member of Alpha Phi at Lincoln. Howard was graduated from York High School in 1931. Residence: York.

Grover Cleveland May

Grover Cleveland May, a resident of Nebraska for the past forty-six years, was born in Richmond, Indiana, March 12, 1885, the son of August Henry and Augusta Fredericka (Bernhardt) May. His father, who was an iron moulder, was born in Baltimore, Maryland, April 14, 1848, and died at York, Nebraska, November 18, 1913. He was of German descent. His mother was born in Steinke, Germany, March 1, 1856.

Mr. May received his early education at Staplehurst, Nebraska, afterward attending York High School from which he was graduated in 1903. From 1906 until 1917 he was in the Railway Mail Service, resigning in 1917 to purchase the York Floral Company of which he is sole owner. For three years Mr. May served as secretary-treasurer of the Nebraska State Florists' Association; since 1928 he has been a director of the York County Commercial Club, and from 1927-29 was a director of the Young Men's Christian Association.

Several years ago Mr. May was a member of the York Rotary Club; and at the present time he holds the following memberships: Red Cross, Parent Teachers Association, Nebraskana Society, Masons (commandery and chapter), Knights of Pythias and the First Presbyterian Church of York. He is independent politically and is a member of the York Country Club.

On January 9, 1913, he was married to Clara Edith Foster at York. Mrs. May, who was born at Buda, Illinois, December 4, 1881, is of English descent. She has one child by a former marriage, Helen C. Dean, born June 25, 1909. Of their marriage two children were born, Howard B., on December 23, 1913, and Robert Foster, born January 30, 1916. Howard was graduated from York High School in 1931 and is now a student at York College. Residence: York.

Carl Burton McAndrew

Carl Burton McAndrew was born at Ainsworth, Nebraska, February 3, 1895, the son of William Davie McAndrew and Emily Dowding. His father, who was a rancher and farmer, was born at Glasgow, Scotland, June 16, 1843, and died at Ainsworth, December 11, 1919, having served as one of General Sherman's body guards during the Civil War; he was wounded twice and was cited for unusual bravery during that engagement.

William McAndrew came to America in 1849 where he acquired large land interests, most of which he gave to charity before his death. His wife, who was a faithful worker in the Congregational Church and who was a woman of high character and attainments, was born in England, October 8, 1851, and died at Ainsworth, February 20, 1908.

Mr. McAndrew was graduated from the Ainsworth High School in 1914, attended the University of Iowa in 1916, was a student at the University of Nebraska in 1917, and in 1922 studied at the Adcox School of Electricity. He owned and operated a dairy farm from 1920 to 1929, serving at the same time as a clerk in the Ainsworth Post Office. Since 1929 he has been city letter carrier in that community where he holds membership in the Commercial Club, the Red Cross, and the First Congregational Church.

He is a member of the National Association of Letter Carriers, the Nebraska Association of Letter Carriers, the Nebraskana Society, and the Masons. During the World War he served as corporal and sergeant in the United States Army and at this time is a member of the American Legion. He is interested in mechanics and is fond of fishing and hunting.

His marriage to Alberta Gail White was solemnized at O'Neill, Nebraska, September 9, 1919. Mrs. McAndrew, who is a talented organist, was born at Bassett, Nebraska, February 16, 1898. She is the daughter of Dr. H. J. White whose great-great-grandfather was killed by the Indians in New York in the early history of America. They have two children: Jean Harriet, born June 14, 1920; and William Davie, born January 2, 1928. Residence: Ainsworth.

Elizabeth May McBeth

Elizabeth May McBeth, for the past 43 years a resident of Nebraska, was born at Pilot Mound, Iowa, October 13, 1858. She is the daughter of William Marion and Sarah Collins (Scott) Petty, early pioneers.

William M. Petty was born in Miami County, Indiana, August 1, 1838, and held the rank of sergeant in the Civil War. A farmer in earlier life, he later entered the real estate and loan business, continuing until his death at Hebron. He was a member of the Petty family which came to the United States not later than 1700, and was descended from Sir William Petty, historian. His maternal grandfather, Peter Runyan, was an officer in the Black Hawk War.

Sarah Collins Scott was born in Virginia, June 21, 1836, and died at Hebron, in 1917. Her family came from the British Isles, her father a doctor, and her grandfather a minister.

On February 5, 1880, Elizabeth May Petty was united in marriage to James McBeth at Pilot Mound. He was born in Pennsylvania, May 25, 1856, and died at Hebron, May 1, 1903. There are two children, Pearl, born November 26, 1880, who married Henry Henning; and William, born August 6, 1893, who married Elizabeth Bowen.

A teacher in the public schools of Iowa in earlier life, Mrs. McBeth has been active in welfare, civic and social work for many years. For a number of years she has been city librarian, and since its organization has been secretary and treasurer of civilian relief. She is chairman of welfare work for the Hebron Woman's Club, and during the World War was especially active. She devotes much of her time to the attention of the sick and needy.

She is a member of the Presbyterian Church, the P. E. O. Sisterhood, and the Rebekahs, and is a member of The Nebraskana Society. Residence: Hebron.

Benjamin Franklin McBride

Benjamin Franklin McBride was one of the outstanding pioneers of Nebraska, and was recognized as the leader of the little band of settlers who came to Boone County in the spring of 1873. He was born in Noble County, Ohio, June 15, 1845, and during his boyhood moved with his parents to Iowa. At the age of 18 years he enlisted in Company B of the Fourth Iowa Cavalry and served throughout the duration of the Civil War.

In May, 1873, Mr. McBride left his native state of Iowa and with his wife and small children began the hazardous and difficult trip which was to establish him in the middlewest. He was the leader of a small band of pioneers who made the slow journey in the covered wagons of that era, fording the various streams they encountered and killing game for food.

He arrived in Boone County June 15, 1873, established his property claims, and made his homestead entry. Almost immediately the settlers began to build their temporary sod homes and to break the soil for their first crop of corn. Through the following years of grasshopper-destruction, drouth, and discouraging circumstances Mr. McBride continued to be the outstanding man in his little community, and is largely responsible for the fact that most of the settlers remained in the new country.

His youngest son, now a man of nearly 50 years, resides on the original homestead in Boone County, and it is a matter of pride among the McBride family that there has never been a mortgage attached to the farm. Mr. McBride died at Albion, Nebraska, November 23, 1915. Residence: Albion.

Edgar McBride

A banker most of his life, Edgar McBride was born at Blue Hill, August 6, 1892, son of Edward Joseph and Margaret (Uerling) McBride. His father, born in Lake County, Illinois, May 8, 1854, is president of the Commercial Bank of Blue Hill, treasurer of the Farmers Grain and Stock Company, director of the Glenwood Telephone Company, and was the originator of the Blue Hill Butter and Cheese Company, operating five cream-cries. His mother was born in Thiensville, Wisconsin, June 9, 1862. She is of German descent.

Edgar McBride attended Blue Hill High School and graduated from St. Marys College, academic course, at St. Marys, Kansas, in 1911 and took a post-graduate course in 1911-12. From 1912-17 he was assistant cashier of the Commercial Bank of Blue Hill and since that time has been cashier. He is also a director of the bank.

On February 14, 1925, he was married to Eva Theresa Conniff at Louisville, Kentucky. Mrs. McBride was born at Hawesville, Kentucky, April 1, 1902, the daughter of Thomas Edward and Margaret (Jarboe) Coniff. The former was a railroad contractor. The mother died when her daughter was seven years of age, and the father died in 1915, after which Mrs. McBride attended Immaculate Conception Academy of Hastings, where she graduated. There are three children, Edgar, born December 8, 1925; James, born September 17, 1928; and Margaret, born April 7, 1930.

Mr. McBride is a Democrat. He held the ranks of first class private to acting officer sergeant in Replacement Group, Headquarters Company, Camp Greenleaf, Fort Oglethorpe, Georgia, during the World War, is past commander and present finance officer and member of the executive committee of the American Legion.

He is a member of Holy Trinity Catholic Church, the Red Cross, Salvation Army, Community Chest, Chamber of Commerce (treasurer), the Elks, Modern Woodmen of America and the Knights of Columbus.

He has been a member of the city council eleven years, mayor six years, and still holds that office, and is vice president of the Nebraska Progress Association. He is a life member of the Nebraskana Society. Residence: Blue Hill.

Lewis Cass McBride

Lewis Cass McBride, who has lived in this state for the past 55 years, was born at Urbana, Champaign County, Ohio, May 25, 1847. He is the son of Andrew and Mary Kelley McBride. His father, who was a brick mason and a contractor, was born in Champaign County, and died at Marengo, Iowa County, Iowa, in 1895; he was of Scotch-Irish descent. His mother, who was born in Pennsylvania in 1886, was of Pennsylvania Dutch descent.

Mr. McBride attended the high school at Marengo. During his life he has held the following positions: brick mason; farmer; and business man. He is now retired. He married Mary Elizabeth Stoner July 4, 1868, at Brooklyn, Iowa. Mrs. McBride was born at Tiffin, Ohio, and died at Lincoln, Nebraska, November, 1913. She was the daughter of George W. and Hannah M. Stoner. To this marriage the following children were born: Jason E., born 1870; O. W., born 1876; Effie M., born 1880; and Maud M., born 1889.

During the Civil war Mr. McBride was a private in Company H, 12th Indiana Volunteer. He is a member of the G. A. R. and is the bass drummer in the Drum Corps and a member of quartet in Farragut Post No. 25. For the past sixty years he has been affiliated with the Methodist Church. He is a staunch Republican. Residence: Lincoln.

William Arthur McCain

William A. McCain, executive, was born in Rush, Pennsylvania, April 22, 1882, son of William Wallace and Orpha A. (Granger) McCain. Both were of Scotch-Irish ancestry.

From 1908 until 1926 Mr. McCain was the owner and manager of the Scottsbluff Overland Company, and since 1926 has been manager of the Platte Valley Loan and Investment Company. He is a member of the Community Congregational Church, and is affiliated with the Republican party.

On June 7, 1910, he was married to Leda A. Ross at Scottsbluff, Nebraska. She was born at Palmyra, Illinois, May 9, 1883. They have three children, Ross, born March 5, 1911; Jack, born December 12, 1912; and James, born August 11, 1914.

Mr. McCain's hobbies are fishing and hunting. Residence: Scottsbluff.

Frank Monroe McCarter

Frank Monroe McCarter, contractor, was born at Lexington, Nebraska, June 22, 1882, son of Charles Monroe and Ida F. (Johnson) McCarter. His ancestry is Scotch and Irish for several generations in America.

Mr. McCarter started in country school at Chimney Rock, and at the age of 21 was in the 6th grade. He finished High School in 1906, and for a short period of 1907 attended the Nebraska Wesleyan University. He later took up a commercial law and completed a business course. For a number of years he has been in the contracting business building highways, irrigation and drainage ditches.

On May 1, 1912, he was married to Ada Adell Smith at Lincoln, Nebraska. She was born at Bennet, Nebraska, December 3, 1887. Mrs. McCarter is a graduate of Lincoln High School and is a registered nurse. Prior to her marriage she was head nurse at the Central Hospital at Lincoln. They have five children, Verna Ilene, born February 9, 1913; Alice May, born October 17, 1915, who married Jonathan Franklin Lane; June, born July 17, 1917; Jacqueline, born March 10, 1919; and Betty Lou, born February 24, 1921.

Mr. McCarter is a Democrat. He is a 32nd degree Mason, a member of the Odd Fellows, the Modern Woodmen of America, and the Methodist Church. During the late war he served in the home guard. Mr. McCarter is a candidate for state senator. His favorite sports are hunting and golf. Residence: Bayard.

Anna Weber McCartney

Anna Weber McCartney, superintendent of schools of Boyd County, was born at Wapello, Iowa, June 10, 1890, daughter of Chris and Ella J. (Peters) Weber. Her father, born in Germany, January 10, 1849, was a farmer who came to America in 1851. His wife, Ella, was born in Bard, Iowa, March 14, 1858. She is a milliner.

Mrs. McCartney was graduated from Wapello High School in May, 1905, and received her Bachelor of Science degree from the Arizona State Teachers College. She was a student at Iowa State Teachers College, 1905-06, Missouri Teachers College, 1910-11, and the University of Colorado 1913.

A public school teacher for several years, Mrs. McCartney taught in Butte, Nebraska; Gregory, South Dakota; Winner, South Dakota; Fairfax, South Dakota; and Wapello, Iowa. Since 1923 she has been county superintendent of schools. She is a member of the First Christian Church, Wapello, the Nebraska State Teachers Association, the National Teachers Association and the State County Superintendents Association. She is a member of the Red Cross, Eastern Star, Parent Teachers Association, Young Women's Christian Association and the Nebraskana Society. Her hobbies are china, water color and pastel painting. Residence: Butte.

Fred Warren McCaw

A physician and surgeon in Nebraska since 1907, Fred Warren McCaw was born at Winfield, Iowa, March 23, 1882. He is the son of William Henry and Margaret Matilda (Serviss) McCaw. His father, born in Canada, July 26, 1844, practiced medicine in eastern Iowa almost fifty years, prior to his death. He died at Colon, Nebraska, December 16, 1925. Margaret M. Serviss was born in Michigan, in October, 1845, and died at Colon on March 27, 1922. Her father's parents came from Holland, and her father was born in New York State.

Fred W. McCaw attended the public schools of Winfield, Iowa, and was graduated from high school at Hooper, Nebraska, in 1898. His medical degree was awarded him by Creighton Medical College.

On September 29, 1910, he was united in marriage to Myra Russel Patterson at Winfield, Iowa. Mrs. McCaw, who was born at Winfield on October 3, 1891, is descended maternally from Patrick Henry. There are two children living and one deceased, Warren William, born February 28, 1912, who is taking a course in mechanical engineering at the University of Nebraska; Donald Hugh, born March 10, 1914, who died October 27, 1927; and Kenneth Russel, born March 23, 1920.

Dr. McCaw is a Republican and has served as mayor and a member of the council of Colon during most of the past twenty years. He has lived in Nebraska most of the time during the past thirty-nine years, and has always been an outstanding figure in his community. During the World War he was a member of the medical advisory board of Saunders County, and at the present time is a member of the Presbyterian Church, the American, Nebraska State and Saunders County Medical Societies, the Red Cross, The Nebraskana Society and the Masons. He enjoys a game of golf on the Wahoo course occasionally. Residence: Colon.

Harry Crawford McClellan

Harry C. McClellan, postmaster at Arlington, Nebraska, has lived in this state for the past 26 years. He was born at Salem, Indiana, January 27, 1883. His father, Emra Franklin McClellan, who was born at Salem, April 19, 1854, and died there April 27, 1924, was a rural letter carrier. Elizabeth Ellen (Walker) McClellan, his mother, was born at Salem, April 13, 1861; she is of English and Irish descent.

Mr. McClellan attended the grade school of South Boston, Indiana, and the high school at New Philadelphia, Indiana. He was a rural letter carrier four years; a post office clerk at Omaha for 12 years; a farmer for five years; and since 1924 has been postmaster at Arlington.

He was married at Salem, Indiana, April 13, 1902, to Gertrude Ethel Charles. Mrs. McClellan was born at Tekamah, Burt County, Nebraska, August 16, 1883; her ancestry was English and Irish. She is assistant postmaster at Arlington. Three children were born to their union: Merritt C., born February 5, 1903, who married Mildred Unland; Harry C., born September 16, 1910; and Rachel, born May 27, 1915. Merritt C., who is a civil engineer, was graduated from the University of Nebraska, and holds a position with the government as geological surveyor. Harry C., is a clergyman in the Methodist Church, and is now attending college.

Mr. McClellan engaged in secret service work during the World War. He is a member of the Commercial Club of Arlington, and the Nebraskana Society; was president of the Parent-Teachers' Association 1927-28; holds membership in the Masons, Eastern Star and Knights of Pythias. He is affiliated with the First Methodist Episcopal Church of Arlington. His hobby is mechanics. Residence: Arlington.

Emma McClelland

Emma McClelland, a lifetime resident of Furnas County, Nebraska, has taken a prominent part in the public affairs of her community for many years. She was born at Cambridge, Nebraska, December 14, 1873, the daughter of Thomas and Catherine (Munn) Andrews. Her father, who was a farmer and breeder of pure-bred stock, was born at Bideford, England, July 26, 1840, and was a pioneer in the development of Furnas County; he died at Cambridge, June 2, 1914. Her mother, who was an intelligent student and reader, was born of Scotch

parents at Appin, Ontario, Canada, February 9, 1838, and died at Cambridge, May 31, 1927.

Mrs. McClelland attended school at Ontario, Canada, where she was active in debating, dramatics, and music. She taught school for three years, was deputy clerk of the district court of Furnas County, 1891-92, and is a leader in social and civic affairs at Beaver City, Nebraska, today. She is chairman of the library board, is a member of the Beaver City Woman's Club, and is affiliated with the First Presbyterian Church of Beaver City.

In 1922 and 1923 she served as grand matron of the Order of Eastern Star. She is a member of the P. E. O. Sisterhood, the Red Cross, and The Nebraskana Society. Her hobby is books. During the late war she was unusually active and was awarded a Victory Loan medal in recognition of services rendered her country, as chairman of the Victory Loan drive.

On December 14, 1898, she married David Edmund McClelland at Cambridge. Mr. McClelland, who was born at Mount Vernon, Iowa, August 27, 1866, is of Irish ancestry, and is descended from a soldier in the Revolution. They have three children: Marion, born January 26, 1900, who teaches in the high school at McCook, Nebraska; Agnes, born February 7, 1903; and Althea Elizabeth, born July 16, 1910. They are all college graduates, and Agnes is teaching in junior college in New Jersey at this time. Residence: Beaver City. (Photograph in Album).

Daniel H. McClenahan

Daniel H. McClenahan, lawyer and referee in bankruptcy, was born in Toulon, Illinois, August 30, 1876, son of Elijah J. and Margaret (Thomas) McClenahan. The father was born in Polk County, Indiana. Mr. McClenahan attended rural school, and was graduated from academy at Toulon, Illinois. In 1899 he entered the University of Nebraska, and received his Bachelor of Laws degree in 1902.

Admitted to the bar in the same year, he later formed a partnership with Frederick C. Foster and in 1912 was appointed referee in bankruptcy by Judge W. H. Munger. He has been re-appointed several times and still holds this office in addition to his general law practice.

He is a Mason, a member of the Elks, and a member also of the Lincoln Chamber of Commerce. Residence: Lincoln.

Charles Albion McCloud

A banker since 1886, Charles Albion McCloud was born at Moravia, Iowa, May 14, 1860, son of William Escridge and Ann Maria (Sears) McCloud. William E. McCloud was a native of West Virginia, born August 26, 1839, of Scottish extraction. A farmer and stockraiser for many years in Nebraska, he died at York, June 2, 1902. His wife, Ann Maria, was born in Zanesville, Ohio, and died at York, December 2, 1912. She was a teacher of English descent.

Charles Albion McCloud attended the public schools of Moravia, Iowa, and the Centerville (Iowa) Normal School, being graduated from the latter in 1877. Later he was a student at Wesleyan University at Mount Pleasant, Iowa, and still later was graduated from Bryant & Stratton's Business College at Saint Joseph, Missouri.

On November 28, 1883, Mr. McCloud was united in marriage to Flora Saunders Bowman at Mount Pleasant. Mrs. McCloud, who is of English, Dutch and French ancestry, was born at Mount Pleasant on November 25, 1862. They have one daughter, Elsie, born on May 25, 1866. She is married to William T. Conley.

A banker of much prominence, Mr. McCloud is president of the First National Bank of York, president of the First Trust Company of York, president of the First State Savings Bank of York, president of the Bank of Thayer, president of the Farmers and Traders Bank of

Waco, president of the Blue River Bank of McCool, president of the Bank of Lushton, president of the First National Bank of Bradshaw, and president of the Farmers State Bank of Bradshaw. He is a director of the First National Bank of Lincoln, vice president of the York Mutual Building and Loan Association, president of the York Hotel Company, director and secretary of the Mutual Life Insurance Company of Lincoln, chairman of the board of trustees of York College, and director of the Security Mutual Life Insurance Companies and the Lincoln Trust Company of Lincoln.

A Republican, he was county commissioner 1888-93, mayor of York, 1902-06, and Republican national committeeman 1924-32. From 1882-86 he served as county treasurer of York County. During the late war Mr. McCloud was chairman for the 4th Congressional District in Liberty Loan drives, and he has always contributed to the Red Cross, Salvation Army and other welfare organizations.

A 32nd degree, Scottish Rite Mason and member of the Shrine, he is also an Elk, Odd Fellow and Knight of Pythias. His religious affiliation is with the First Congregational Church of York. Among his civic and cultural memberships are the Chamber of Commerce, the Rotary Club, the Elks Crippled Children's Association, the Young Men's Christian Association, the University Club of Lincoln, the York Country Club and the York Aviation Club. He is also a member of the Nebraska State Historical Society and The Nebraskana Society. Mr. McCloud is fond of golf, and devotes much time to reading. Residence: York.

Estella Ann McCloud

Estella Ann McCloud, educator, homemaker, and clubwoman, has been a resident of York County, Nebraska for the past 56 years. She was born near Waco, Nebraska, March 23, 1875, the daughter of Ezekiel and Martha Jane Evans. Her father, who was a farmer and minister, was born in Sussex County, Delaware, February 27, 1829, came to Nebraska and homesteaded, February County in 1871 and died at York, Nebraska, January 2, 1918; he was descended from a family of sailors on the Atlantic coast. He enlisted in the Civil War in Company I, 118th Regiment of Illinois Mounted Infantry and was discharged October 1, 1865 at Baton Rouge, Louisana. Her mother was born at Liberty, Illinois, June 5, 1835, pioneered in York County in 1872, and died at York, October 22, 1921.

Mrs. McCloud attended the rural schools of York County, was graduated from the Waco High School in 1892, and was a student at York College. She was connected with the First National Bank and other banks in various positions from 1905 to 1921. Prior to this she had served as teacher in country schools in York County and village schools at Waco and Bradshaw, Nebraska.

Her marriage to William Escridge McCloud occurred at Lincoln, Nebraska, December 24, 1896. Mr. McCloud, who is a banker, was born at Moravia, Iowa, January 6, 1872. They had a son, William, born May 3, 1898, who died in infancy.

Mrs. McCloud is past vice president of the Nebraska State Sunday School Association, has been a member of the board of the Nebraska Council of Christian Education, successor to the Nebraska State Sunday School Association for the past 25 years, and was treasurer of the council of this organization in 1930. She served as president of the York Woman's Club, 1927-8, is president of the York County Woman's Club, and holds membership in the Native Sons and Daughters of Nebraska and the Nebraskana Society. She served during the World War as a speaker in loan drives and from 1918 to 1920 was treasurer of the York County Chapter of the American Red Cross. A Republican, Mrs. McCloud was deputy county treasurer of York County from 1910 to 1915. She is a member of the Eastern Star and the Does,

auxiliary to the Elks, and holds membership in the Church of Christ. Her chief interests are reading and study clubs, while her hobby is helping young people secure education. Residence: York.

Flora Saunders McCloud

A pioneer clubwoman and civic leader at York, Nebraska, Flora Saunders McCloud has lived in this state since 1883 and has been prominent in York County organizations for many years. She was born at Mount Pleasant, Henry County, Iowa, November 25, 1862, the daughter of John Clark and Eliza Ann (Saunders) Bowman. Her father, a hardware and real estate dealer, was born at Warren, Trumbull County, Ohio, July 13, 1835, and died at York, February 24, 1917. He was of English, Scotch, and German ancestry, and was directly descended from Captain John Hull, who served in the Revolution.

Her mother was born at Mount Pleasant, December 19, 1842, and died at York, November 18, 1917. She was descended from Peter Mauzy and John Bowen, whose ancestry was French and English.

Mrs. McCloud received her education at Petaluma, California; she served as president and secretary of the Nebraska Alpha Chapter of Pi Beta Phi, and was the organizer of this chapter. She has been president of the library board at York since 1890, an organization which she organized in 1885, and is now a member of the Young Women's Christian Association Auxiliary, the Benevolent Patriotic Order of Does, (past supreme president), the P. E. O. and Eastern Star.

She holds membership in the Red Cross, is affiliated with the First Congregational Church, is Camp Fire sponsor at York, and is regent of Davis Bryant chapter of the Daughters of the American Revolution. Her social clubs are the University Club of Lincoln, and the Woman's Country Club at York. During the World War she served as York County chairman of the council of defense. She is a republican. Mrs. McCloud cared for and educated Elsie Metcalf, who is now Mrs. W. T. Conley of Columbia, Missouri. Residence: York.

William Escridge McCloud

William Escridge McCloud, prominent banker at York, Nebraska, was born at Moravia, Iowa, January 6, 1872, and for the past 53 years has been a progressive resident of York County. William Escridge McCloud, Sr., who was a farmer, stockraiser, and stock feeder, was born in West Virginia, August 26, 1839, and died at York, June 11, 1902. His mother, Ann Maria (Sears) McCloud, was born in Muskogen, Ohio, September 13, 1838, and died in York County, December 11, 1912.

Mr. McCloud attended business college at Omaha, Nebraska, and then became engaged in farming. He was a grain buyer, 1900-05, was bookkeeper for the Bradshaw Bank for a time, served as cashier of the Bank of Lushton, was assistant cashier of the Farmers National Bank of York, 1905-09, and for the past 11 years has been cashier of the First State Savings Bank at York. A Republican, he served as county treasurer of York County from 1910 to 1915, and acted as chairman of the county central committee in 1916.

He has taken a prominent part in civic affairs at York where he is a member of the Chamber of Commerce, the Red Cross, and the Isaac Walton League. He holds membership in the Young Men's Christian Association of which he was a member of the board of directors for five years and treasurer for four years. Mr. McCloud is affiliated with the Church of Christ at York, is a member of the Nebraskana Society, and holds membership in the York Country Club and the Shrine Club of Lincoln, Nebraska. He is fond of hunting. During the World War he took part in Red Cross and loan drives.

He married Estella Ann Evans at Lincoln, December 24, 1896. Mrs. McCloud, who was born at Waco, Nebraska, March 23, 1875, is active in social and civic affairs at York. She holds membership in the Woman's Club and Native Daughters of Nebraska. Prior to her marriage she was deputy county treasurer of York County and was employed in a bank at York. On the maternal side she is directly descended from Roger Williams. One child was born to them: William, May 1, 1898, who died in June, 1898. Residence: York.

Hugh Montgomery McClure

Hugh Montgomery McClure, architect and builder at Kearney, Nebraska, is the son of Hugh Marshall and Nellie Maria (Haines) McClure. He was born at Bladen, Nebraska, August 27, 1889, and has spent most of his life in this state. His father was a pioneer farmer in Nebraska where he took a keen interest in political situations and government affairs. He was born at Agahale, Ireland, January 15, 1856, of Scotch-Irish parents, and died at Kearney after a lifetime of business success.

His mother, who was born in Mount Hope, Township, Illinois, January 5, 1861, was descended from early New England stock and is a descendant of Stephen Hopkins and Captain John Carter of Revolutionary fame. She was intensely interested in the education of her children and had a great appreciation for the artistic.

Mr. McClure was a student at Kearney High School and the State Normal School at Kearney, and is a graduate of the Stout Polytecnic Institute of Menomonie, Wisconsin, 1913, where he specialized in architecture. He served as supervisor of industrial education in the public schools of Keokuk and Ft. Madison, Iowa, 1912-18, and since 1919 has been proprietor of the McClure Company, Architects and Builders at Kearney, specializing in domestic architecture and winning national recognition. He is a contributor to professional and trade publications and is the author of a song poem *In The Fields Of Old Nebraska*.

He is a member of the Red Cross, is a director in the Kearney Chamber of Commerce, is a director in the Fort Kearney Memorial Association, and holds membership in the Parent Teachers Association and The Nebraskana Society. He is a Mason and is a member of the First Presbyterian Church of Kearney.

Mr. McClure is vitally interested in history and has a profound admiration for the pioneer settlers who lived through the hardships of the early days and made Nebraska what it is today. During the World War he served as sergeant in the reconnaissance service, Engineer Corps in Alsace and Toul sectors in France. He is a member of the American Legion and the Veterans of Foreign Wars.

On January 15, 1920, he married Margaret Irene Dickerson at Evanston, Illinois. Mrs. McClure, who was a kindergarten teacher before her marriage, was born at Atlantic, Iowa; she is a descendant of Josephus Dickerson of Virginia, who served in the Revolution. To this marriage two children were born: Hugh, Jr., born November 23, 1920; and Marshall, born March 13, 1926.

Mr. McClure is fond of fishing and hunting. His hobbies are sketching and mechanics. Residence: Kearney. (Photograph in Album).

James McClure

Born at Arrowsmith, Illinois, January 5, 1880, James McClure is the son of William Montgomery and Eliza Rose (Heagler) McClure. His father, who was born at Ballymena, Ireland, August 15, 1848, is a farmer, and has served as a member of local school boards in both Nebraska and Illinois. His mother was born at Arrowsmith, July 10, 1860, and died at Blue Hill, Nebraska, June 2, 1890. She was eligible to membership in the Daughters of the American Revolution since her ancestors were early settlers in Rhode Island and Virginia. She was also a descendant of Abraham Lincoln and Daniel Boone of Kentucky.

Mr. McClure was graduated from the Cloverton

High School in 1898 and for a year studied at the Grand Island Business College. He has been a farmer near Blue Hill for a number of years and is secretary of the Farmers Union Co-operative Association there.

Since 1917 he has served as a member of the Cloverton School Board, is affiliated with the Methodist Episcopal Church, and holds membership in the Independent Order of Odd Fellows. He is fond of baseball and reading.

On September 23, 1908, he was married to Laura Belle Burroughs at Hastings, Nebraska. Mrs. McClure was born at Juniata, Nebraska, September 12, 1887. They have four children: Maxine, born July 9, 1910; Victor, born May 3, 1912; Glen, born April 15, 1918; and Marjorie, born February 22, 1926. Maxine, a graduate of Blue Hill High School, is a teacher in the public schools of Webster County. Victor is also a graduate of the Blue Hill High School. Residence: Blue Hill.

Harry Garfield McClusky

Harry G. McClusky was born at Boonville, New York, July 4, 1880. He is the son of Eli Hunt and Helen (Wiggins) McClusky. His father, who was born at Boonville, November 22, 1847, and died there November 7, 1916, was a carpenter. He was a Republican, and was active in church work and community affairs. His father coming from Ireland in the early days, homesteaded in New York state. His mother, born at Boonville, January 8, 1848, died July 19, 1911; she was the granddaughter of John Tinsley who came directly to New York from Ireland, in 1825.

Mr. McClusky's elementary education was received in the Boonville grade and high schools after which he attended Park College, where he was awarded his A. B. degree in 1904. In 1907 he received his B. D. degree from Princeton Theological Seminary. He has been an active clergyman since that date.

Mr. McClusky has lived in Nebraska for 23 years. He is former editor of the *Wheel*, a local Rotary publication, and is a Republican.

On July 2, 1907, he was united in marriage with Margaret Hughes at Burrton, Kansas. Mrs. McClusky was born at Ebensberg, Pennsylvania, February 3, 1880, and is descended from Welsh ancestors who came to America in 1870. To this union one son was born, Lawrence, September 14, 1911, and died September 21, 1911.

In the late war, Rev. McClusky was a four minute man, and was prominent in the various war activities. He is a member of the Nebraska City Presbytery, the Chamber of Commerce, the Rotary Club, The Nebraskana Society, and the library board, at Plattsmouth. He is a Mason, Blue Lodge, Royal Arch, and Knight Templar, Mount Zion Commandery number 5. His club is the Plattsmouth Country Club. Golf and tennis are his favorite sports. His hobby is reading newspaper and magazine sport articles. Interested in music, he has sung in quartettes at programs and clubs, and over the radio. In twenty-three years of ministry, he has had two churches; six and a half years at Laurel, and seventeen at Plattsmouth. Residence: Plattsmouth.

Edward McComas

Edward McComas, for many years a druggist at Broken Bow, now retired, was born in Nemaha County, Nebraska, January 22, 1861. His father, Edward Mitchel McComas, a druggist and physician, was born in Maryland, December 26, 1826, and died at Brownville, Nebraska, March 17, 1914. He was of Scotch descent on the paternal side. His wife, Almira Waggner, was born in Troy, Ohio, July 18, 1833, and died at Brownville, November 24, 1917. She was the daughter of W. W. Waggner.

Educated in the public school at Brownville, Edward McComas was graduated from high school in the class of 1878. Shortly thereafter he entered the retail drug business, and was a charter member of the Nebraska Pharmaceutical Association. Commencing business at Brownville on June 1, 1880, he came to Broken Bow in 1886 where he owned and operated a drug store until he sold out and retired on June 1, 1931.

On November 26, 1889, he was married to Clara A. Reese at Broken Bow. Mrs. McComas, who is the daughter of John Reese, was born at Bellefontaine, Ohio, July 27, 1872, and died at Broken Bow on July 21, 1927. There are two children, Clara Bernice, born September 9, 1890, who married Dr. Theodore Koefoot; and Helen L., born January 21, 1893. Helen is a graduate of the University of Nebraska, and is now in her eighth year as a teacher at Casper, Wyoming.

Mr. McComas is a Democrat. He is a member of the Rotary Club, the Degree of Honor, and a life member of the Nebraskana Society. Residence: Broken Bow.

Charles Marshal McCorkle

For the past 45 years Charles M. McCorkle has lived in Nebraska and since 1906 has been a clergyman in the Methodist Episcopal Church. He was born at Cincinnati, Ohio, November 21, 1868, the son of James A. and Ellen Louise (Smith) McCorkle. His father, born at Troy, Ohio, January 13, 1830, and died at Cincinnati, October 5, 1872, was an accountant; he was employed by the Quartermaster Department during the Civil War; his ancestry was Scotch. His mother, who was descended from Puritan stock, was born in Connecticut, September 27, 1831, and died at Dayton, Ohio, May 27, 1877. She devoted all her time to home-making.

Mr. McCorkle attended the elementary schools of Troy, Ohio, Crawfordsville, Indiana, and Hastings, Nebraska. Beyond that he was self-educated. In 1906 he was licensed to the ministry and in 1909 was ordained. In 1911 he was graduated from the Methodist Episcopal Conference Course of Study. He has held the following pastorates in the Methodist Episcopal Church: Stockville, Wauneta, Bertrand, Curtis, Juniata, Sutton, Harvard, North Bend, all of them in Nebraska. He is now pastor of the Methodist Episcopal Church at North Bend, Nebraska.

His marriage to Susie Catherine Meyers was solemnized at Hendley, Nebraska, July 6, 1892. Mrs. McCorkle, who was formerly a school teacher, was born at Foreston, Illinois, January 12, 1871. She is of Pennsylvania German descent, and holds membership in the Daughters of the American Revolution. They have an adopted daughter, Mela, born August 25, 1893, who married Clarence Paul Anton.

Mr. McCorkle was a four minute speaker during the late war. He is a member of the Omaha District of the Methodist Episcopal Conference, a Mason, and a member of The Nebraskana Society. He believes in the principles of the Republican party although he does not always vote a straight party ticket. Residence: North Bend.

Ross Samuel McCown

Ross Samuel McCown, clergyman at Beatrice, was born near Fayetteville, Lincoln County, Tennessee, April 26, 1880. His father, Samuel Sawyers McCown, who was born at Due West, South Carolina, February 2, 1837, and died at Fayetteville, June 13, 1896. He was a teacher and farmer who lived in Tennessee most of his life; he was a firm believer in states rights but was opposed to slavery; his ancestry was Scotch-Irish.

Dr. McCown's mother, Margaret Jane (Wyatt) McCown, who was a teacher and community leader, was born at Fayetteville, September 16, 1842, and died there May 30, 1929. She was descended from the House of Kent, England, directly; her grandfather was one of the first settlers of middle Tennessee.

Dr. McCown attended rural school, Moline Academy

in Tennessee, was a student at Cedarville College in Ohio for three years, and in 1906 was graduated from Westminster College in Pensylvania with the A. B. degree. He was a student at Princeton University for one year, was graduated from McCormick Theological Seminary in 1912, and was awarded the D. D. degree at Hastings College. He was prominent in debating and athletics, was college orator, and served as president of the Seminary class. He worked his way through school entirely from his freshman days in academy.

He is now pastor of the First Presbyterian Church at Beatrice, is a member of the Nebraskana Society, and is affiliated with the Republican Party.

On December 31, 1912, his marriage to Pauline Mae Collins was solemnized at Chicago, Cook County, Illinois; she was born of Scotch-Irish parents at Kenia, Green County, Ohio, April 26, 1881. Mrs. McCown was a Latin teacher in high school before her marriage. To this union the following children were born: Harvey Hale, born January 19, 1914; Robert Edwin, born July 10, 1916; Margaret Eunice, born June 20, 1919; John Ross, born January 27, 1922; and Jean, born September 29, 1923. Residence: Beatrice.

Alfred Thomas McCoy

Alfred Thomas McCoy, county judge of Hitchcock County, was born at Sutton, Nebraska, July 24, 1877, son of Alfred Absolom and Mary Jane (Ovington) McCoy.

The father was born at Mount Vernon, Iowa, April 12, 1845, and died at Trenton, October 18, 1915. He was a lawyer and a member of the state militia. He was rejected for service in the Civil War on account of physical disaility. His grandfather served in the Revolution. The great grandfather of Alfred A. McCoy was a Presbyterian minister. Mary Jane Ovington was born at Louisville, Kentucky, June 14, 1846, and died at Trenton, July 17, 1915. Her father was a native of England.

Mr. McCoy was graduated from Trenton High School in 1894, and was registered in the law office of Butler and James of Cambridge, Nebraska. A printer by trade, he was employed first by the Enterprise Printing Company of Geneva, Nebraska, and was afterward foreman of the *Hastings Daily News*. In 1900-01-02 he edited the *Palisade Press* of Palisade, Nebraska. A Republican, he has been county judge of Hitchcock County since January 7, 1921. He is a director of the Citizens State Bank of Trenton, Nebraska and the Trenton Loan and Building Association, served on the village board at Trenton from 1908 until 1915. He was chairman of Game and Fish of the Twin Valley Commercial Clubs during its existence, on the official board of the Methodist Episcopal Church since 1910, a county delegate of the Golden Rod Highway Association since the day of origin in 1917, on the road committee of the local commercial club for a number of years, a member of the Massacre Canyon Memorial Association, and delivered an address to the State Historical Society in an effort to persuade the state to appropiate a sum equal to the governments of $7,500, but to no avail. He volunteered for service in the World War, the only person in Hitchcock County over draft age that was accepted and served for the duration of the war, was past commander of Stellges-Baker Post No. 337 local legion and is present county commander, was a telegraph operator with three years employment to his credit with the Burlington Railroad at Trenton, Nebraska in 1910-11-12.

His marriage to Grace Effie Lant was solemnized at Denver, Colorado, January 4, 1922. Mrs. McCoy was born in Henderson County, Illinois, June 17, 1884, and taught school in Montana, Illinois, Nebraska and South Dakota, and was a teacher in the public schools at Seattle, Washington. For ten years she has been a member of the Order of Eastern Star, Bethel Chapter No. 109. Mrs. McCoy has been a member of the Library Board since its organization, and is head librarian devoting two half days a week to the work at this time.

Mr. McCoy was also county chairman for war saving stamps drive, county chairman of the American Red Cross, and participated in every liberty loan drive, each quota being over subscribed. He is a member of the Methodist Episcopal Church, and is an annual contributor to the Salvation Army.

He is a member of the Chamber of Commerce, the Odd Fellows, the Ancient Free and Accepted Masons, the Royal Arch Masons, the Knight Templars, and the Ancient Arabic Order of the Nobles of the Mystic Shrine, Tehama Temple Hastings, Nebraska, and the Southwest Nebraska Historical Society. He enjoys baseball and fishing, while his hobby is historical reading. Residence: Trenton.

Richard McCracken

Richard McCracken, farmer, rancher, and the enterprising sheriff of Keya Paha County, Nebraska, was born at Shenandoah, Iowa, February 23, 1870. His father, Andrew McCracken, who served for three months in the Civil War, was born in Ireland, March 14, 1833, and died at Springview, Nebraska, December 17, 1892. His mother, Laura (Cover) McCracken, was born at Cleveland, Ohio, September 16, 1834, and died at Burton, Nebraska, November 2, 1909.

Mr. McCracken came to Nebraska with his parents more than 48 years ago, and is one of the leading ranchers in Keya Paha County today. In 1904 he acquired land under the Kinkaid Act, and at this time owns and supervises 680 acres of farming land near Springview. He served as district school treasurer for 15 years and was a director for four years.

A Democrat, he was twice elected county sheriff and has proved to be an able and energetic factor in law enforcement in his county. One of his recent achievements was the capture of three hold-up men at Springview, for which he has received commendation from both state and county officers.

Mr. McCracken is probation officer at Springview, is a member of the Nebraskana Society, the Lions Club, and the Commercial Club, and is a contributor to various religious organizations. His favorite sport is baseball.

On February 24, 1901, he was married to Priscilla Koenig at Carns, Nebraska. Mrs. McCracken, who was a teacher before her marriage, was born at Niobrara, Nebraska, January 18, 1877. To this marriage were born: Henry F., July 6, 1902, who married Helena Christina Johnson; Ida, born June 4, 1904, who married Leonard Alonzo Woeppel; Frank E., October 3, 1906, who married Frances Hortense DeCorey; Nettie, November 13, 1908; Emma, January 3, 1912. Henry is a mail carrier, Frank is a western league baseball pitcher, and the three daughters are teachers. Residence: Springview. (Photograph on Page 790).

John Thomas McCuistion

John Thomas McCuistion, for many years a prominent member of the Thayer County Bar, was born near Bloomfield, Iowa, December 25, 1870, and died at Lincoln, April 20, 1927.

Mr. McCuistion spent his early life on a farm and attending public school. He was graduated from the Southern Iowa Normal School at the age of 17 and later from the Iowa City University, law department. He taught school both in Iowa and Nebraska, and after being admitted to the bar located at Hebron. He was associated there in the practice of law with T. C. Marshall for some time, and in later years practiced independently.

On January 24, 1895, he was married to Laura Stone, of St. Joseph. She died on April 20, 1906, leaving three children surviving, Mildred Niemeyer of Western, Ne-

braska; Margaret LeRoy of Crete; and Ruth Steffenson of Hebron.

On May 12, 1909, he was married to Zada Kilpatrick of Hebron and to this union three children were born, Maxine, on April 22, 1913; John James, on November 17, 1912; and Charles Henry on May 20, 1917. Maxine is stenographer in Lincoln, Jack is in college, and Charles Henry is in high school. Mrs. McCuistion was born at Hebron, March 13, 1885, and taught school before her marriage. She is a member of the Presbyterian Church, the Order of Eastern Star, and a former member of the Woman's Club and the Pollyanna Club.

Mr. McCuistion was prominent in political and civic affairs in Hebron for many years. He was a member of the Presbyterian Church, and enjoyed flower gardening and reading.

Anna Snyder McCullough

Anna Snyder McCullough, daughter of Jeremiah and Frances Elizabeth (Miles) Snyder, was born at Peru, Nebraska, May 12, 1869.

The father was born in Maslin, Ohio, April 5, 1830, and was a farmer and stockraiser until his death at Brady, May 22, 1918. His ancestry was Pennsylvania Dutch. Frances Elizabeth Miles was born at Bath, New York, April 16, 1834, and died at Maxwell, Nebraska, January 9, 1918. Her ancestry was English and German.

Anna Snyder attended public school at Maxwell, and the North Platte High School. She afterward attended summer sessions of normal schools and taught eight years in Lincoln County.

On February 20, 1897, she was married to James McCullough at North Platte. There are seven children, six of whom are living. (See Nebraskana).

Mrs. McCullough is a member of Sacred Heart Catholic Church, the county board of the Red Cross, the Phi Kappa Mothers Club, the American Legion Auxiliary, and the American War Mothers (past state president). During the late war she was active in Red Cross and Liberty loan drives. For two years she served as president of the Brady Woman's Club, and for several years was president of both the Woman's Benefit Association and the Woman's Christian Temperance Union. Her hobby is literature. Residence: Brady. (Photograph in Album).

James McCullough

James McCullough, ranchman and the former mayor of Brady, was born at Maxwell, Nebraska, December 14, 1870, son of John and Mary Ann (Gallagher) McCullough.

The father was born at Plumbridge, Ireland, November 12, 1847, and while living there was a cattle buyer. He came to America about 1862, arriving at Philadelphia. He operated the first pumping station for the Union Pacific Railroad at Brady, and was later a ranchman. He died at Maxwell, November 20, 1907. His wife, Mary Ann, was born at New Castle, North Umberland, England, December 22, 1847, and died at Maxwell, August 18, 1914. She came to America about 1867 and lived in Iowa for a time. She came to Nebraska and was married January 9, 1869, at McPherson, which is now known as Maxwell. Her family moved from Ireland to Scotland and then to England.

Mr. McCullough attended the public schools of Maxwell, and for a number of years has been the owner of a large ranch near Brady. He is a Democrat, and for a number of years was a member of the board of education (past president).

He was united in marriage to Anna Hester Snyder, daughter of Jeremiah and Frances Elizabeth (Miles) Snyder of Maxwell, at North Platte, February 20, 1897. Her father died at Brady, Nebraska, May 22, 1918, and her mother at Maxwell, January 9, 1918. Fannie Miles Snyder was a cousin of General Nelson A. Miles. Mrs. McCullough is a member of Sacred Heart

Stanley—Ainsworth

RICHARD McCRACKEN

Catholic Church, the American War Mothers, of which she is past state president, the Womens Benefit Association, of which she was president several years, the Women's Relief Corps, the American Legion Auxiliary, the Women's Christian Temperance Union (past president), and the Brady Woman's Club.

Seven children were born to Mr. and Mrs. McCullough, Mary Francis, born March 14, 1898, who is a graduate of St. Joseph's Hospital of Omaha. She took post-graduate work at the Laurentian Sanitarium, Ste. Agathe des Monts, Province of Quebec, and at Creighton University of Omaha. At the present time she is superintendent of the Platte Valley Hospital of North Platte.

John Jeremiah, the second child, was born February 10, 1900, and died August 20, 1929. He was a graduate of the Brady High School and enlisted and took training in the Reserve Officers Training School. James Donald, third child, was born February 27, 1902, and attended Creighton University. At the present time he is assistant cashier in the bank of Brady. Miles William, born November 18, 1903, completed an agricultural course at the University of Nebraska, and at the present time is general manager of his father's ranch. Maurine Annie, born May 17, 1905, completed a four year course at Mary Mount College, Salina, Kansas and the University of Nebraska. Maurine taught two years after receiving her Bachelor of Science degree and is now married. Miriam Ellen took one year post-graduate work after her graduation, two years at the University of Nebraska and one term at Kearney Normal. She is now employed by the Platte Valley Hospital. Doris June, born June 29, 1909, took one year post-graduate work after her graduation and taught four terms in rural schools. She attended summer school at Kearney and later took nurses training at Michigan City, Indiana. She is now employed by the Platte Valley Hospital.

Mr. McCullough is affiliated with the Sacred Heart Catholic Church at Brady, and is a member of the Knights of Columbus. He is also a member of the Red Cross and the Nebraskana Society. Residence: Brady. (Photograph in Album).

Theodore Wilson McCullough

A resident of Nebraska since February, 1889, Theodore Wilson McCullough was born at Kirksville, Iowa, September 26, 1861. He is the son of Samuel Clinton and Abigail Anne (Wilson) McCullough, the former a physician and surgeon, born at Morgan's Station, Kentucky, June 9, 1816. His father's father was born in Virginia, and his mother's father in Pennsylvania, and both served under General Washington.

Abigail Wilson was born at Callansburg, Pennsylvania, October 30, 1833, and died at Seattle, Washington, December 18, 1908. She was a teacher, whose Scotch-Irish Great-Great grandfather came to America in 1735, and was murdered by the Hessians at Trenton, January 2, 1777.

Mr. McCullough attended public school at Ottumwa, Iowa, and received his higher education under private tutelage. In 1889, he was city editor of the *Omaha Herald*, and in 1890 became night editor of the *World Herald*. In 1891, he became night editor of the *Omaha Bee*, and in 1897, city editor. In 1900, he was promoted to assistant managing editor, in 1906, to managing editor, in 1917, to associate editor, and to chief editorial writer in 1920, which position he still holds.

His marriage to Alice May Shaw was solemnized at Galesburg, Illinois, September 26, 1888. Mrs. McCullough was born in Knox County, Illinois, March 11, 1866, of English descent on the paternal side, and French Huguenot descent on the maternal side. They have three children, Alice, born September 7, 1889, who married Hubert Keyes Owen, was a Phi Beta Kappa at the University of Nebraska; Roger Shaw, born October 19, 1891, married Rosemarie Dalton. He received his B. Sc. from the University

of Nebraska, and is a captain in the Air Service; Phillip Morgan, born October 31, 1893, married Mary Hustead. He is a graduate in electrical engineering of the University of Nebraska and a member of the American Institute.

Mr. McCullough is a Republican. For many years he was a member of the Nebraska National Guard, in which he held the rank of lieutenant colonel. For four years he served as a member of the Nebraska Park Board, and during the World War was a member of the Excess Profits Tax Board at Washington. He is a director of the Omaha Welfare Association and a member of the Community Chest. He holds membership in the Concord Club and the American Academy of Social and Political Science. He is a Mason and member of the Shrine, a Knight of Pythias, and a member of the Modern Woodmen of America and the Royal Arcanum. His club is the Omaha Athletic. His hobby is forestry. Residence: Omaha.

Walter William McCutchan

Walter William McCutchan, stockraiser and farmer of Nuckolls County, Nebraska, has lived in this state for 53 years. He was born at Evansville, Indiana, June 19, 1871, the son of Paul Reuben and Carline Amanda (Johnston) McCutchan.

Paul Reuben McCutchan is the son of George Bond and Amelia (Yerkes) McCutchan who was descended from the McCutchans who landed in New York in 1812 from England and later emigrated to Indiana settling at what is now known as McCutchanville, Indiana; he died at Evansville in 1884, and his wife, Amelia, died in 1893. Mr. Paul McCutchan, who was a lawyer, was born at Evansville, August 8, 1838, coming to Nebraska in 1878, taking a homestead near Grand Island; his ancestry was Scotch-Irish and Pennsylvania Dutch. He enlisted in the Civil War August 10, 1861, Company A, 42nd Regular Indiana Infantry under command of the army of the Cumberland and met the enemy under General Bragg, September 19, 1863, at which time he was in the 14th Corps of General George H. Thomas, commander. He was wounded the following Sunday by a bullet striking him in the left hip and was taken captive and held in the Military Prison at Atlanta Georgia until he was exchanged at Rossville, Georgia, February 20, 1864. He carried this bullet in his hip until his death which occurred at Grand Island, Nebraska, October 10, 1917. Carline Amanda (Johnston) McCutchan was born at Evansville, September 28, 1839, and died at Nelson, March 31, 1925; she was of English and Irish descent.

Mr. McCutchan attended elementary school in Nebraska and was a student at Grand Island Business College for two years. For 15 years he was a teacher in the public schools, and since then has been engaged in stockraising and farming near Nelson. He is president of the Farmer Union Elevator Company of Nelson, and is now serving as county commissioner of Nuckolls County. He is affiliated with the Methodist Church, is a member of the Nebraskana Society, and holds membership in the Masonic Lodge.

His marriage to Alice Mary England was solemnized at Grand Island, December 27, 1892. Mrs. McCutchan, whose ancestry is Irish, was born at Eldenburg, Indiana, January 20, 1872. They have the following children, Irvin, born January 22, 1894, who married Isa Harris; Gertrude, born February 7, 1895, who married Field McPherren; Mary, born March 15, 1899, who married James Murphy; Alice, born January 2, 1900, who married Marice Vinning; Walter, born June 20, 1902, who married Audrey Demilt; Blanche, born June 24, 1910. Residence: Nelson.

Oscar Wiley McDaniel

Oscar Wiley McDaniel, county judge of Cherry County, was born in Radford, Virginia, April 15, 1866, and settled in Sarpy County, Nebraska, October 4, 1874.

His father, Jacob McDaniel, was born in Christiansburg, Virginia, May 19, 1837, and died at LaPlatte, Nebraska, January 5, 1912. A farmer and harness maker, he served as a private in the rebel army and fought in the battles of Lookout Mountain, Missionary Ridge, Bull Run, Chickamauga, Manassas Courthouse, and in several other battles of the Civil War. His father was Anthony McDaniel and his grandfather Bryant McDaniel.

Nancy Bradbury, wife of Jacob McDaniel, was born in Christiansburg, August 22, 1838. She was the daughter of Mark and Minerva (Dawson) Bradbury. Her grandfather, Thomas Dawson, was a soldier in the war of the Revolution and the War of 1812, and died at the beginning of the Civil War. Nancy Bradbury died at LaPlatte, Nebraska, March 20, 1880.

Upon the completion of his early education in the district school of LaPlatte, Judge McDaniel entered Bellevue College but did not graduate. He was a farmer and rancher, later a school teacher, and still later a hardware and lumber dealer. A Democrat, he has twice been elected county judge of Cherry County on a nonpolitical ballot and is candidate for re-election in 1932. He is a member of the firm Lausen & McDaniel, hardware, lumber, and furniture dealers at Wood Lake, and has served in various village and city offices.

On February 13, 1889, he was married to Mary Emily Rockwell at Wood Lake. Mrs. McDaniel, who was born at Toulon, Illinois, April 28, 1867, is the daughter of Seth and Hanna (Woodard) Rockwell. There are three children, Ethel Mae, born June 26, 1890, who was graduated from East Denver High School; Dwight Rockwell, born September 6, 1893, who was graduated from Lincoln High School, Wood Lake High School and is a veteran of the late war; and Ida Jeanette, born July 13, 1900, who was graduated from Wood Lake High School and Barnes Commercial School of Denver, Colorado, is secretary to her father.

Among Mr. McDaniel's fraternal organizations are the Woodmen of the World, the Ancient Order of United Workmen, the Ancient Free and Accepted Masons, the Royal Arch Masons, and the Knights Templar. During his lifetime he has been a member of various school boards. He is a Protestant. Residence: Valentine. (Photograph in Album).

Robert McKee McDill

Robert M. McDill, head of the department of mathematics of Hastings College, was born at Richland, Indiana, March 25, 1872. He is the son of N. C. and Nancy (McKee) McDill, the former a clergyman with the degree of Doctor of Divinity.

Mr. McDill received his A. B. in 1894 and his A. M. in 1898 from Indiana University, and has taken postgraduate work at the University of Colorado. From 1895-1907 he taught mathematics at New Castle, Indiana, and from 1907-1919 at Fremont Normal College. Since that time he has been a member of the faculty at Hastings College. Professor McDill is the author of *Exercises Introductory to Geometry* and several papers on mathematical subjects.

On August 19, 1896, he was married to Korah Kester at Lebanon, Indiana, and to their union one son was born, Homer K., December 6, 1899. He is married to Louella Goble, and is principal of Benedict High School.

Professor McDill is a member and an elder of the First Presbyterian Church of Hastings, is a member of the Nebraska Academy of Science, the American Mathematical Association and the Schoolmasters' Club He is a life member of The Nebraskana Society, and a Republican. Residence: Hastings.

Alan McDonald

Alan McDonald, architect, was born at Omaha, Nebraska, August 26, 1891, son of John and Martha (Tibbetts) McDonald. The father is an architect.

Upon his graduation from Central High School, Mr.

McDonald entered Harvard University, from which he received his Bachelor of Arts degree in 1912. He received the degree of Master in Architecture from Harvard University School of Architecture in 1915.

On September 11, 1917, he was married to Helen Scobie at Omaha.

He is a member of the First Unitarian Church, the Chamber of Commerce, the American Institute of Architects and the Community Playhouse. Residence: Omaha.

Guy Clinton McDonald

Guy C. McDonald was born at Camden, Minnesota, October 12, 1888, son of Clinton and Etta (Ward) McDonald. Clinton McDonald, who was of Scotch ancestry, was a salesman and mechanic. Etta Ward, his wife, a native of Worcester, Massachusetts, died at Portland, Oregon, in 1898. She was descended from William Ward who settled in Massachusetts, in 1630.

Guy C. McDonald was educated in the public schools of Omaha, and attended Central High School. He entered the employ of Beebe and Runyan as office boy, and was promoted through various positions to credit manager in thirteen years. He then became associated with the Omaha Crockery Company, as credit manager and has advanced to the position of general manager, secretary-treasurer and director of that company.

He was married to Nellie May Perry at Chicago, September 10, 1910. Mrs. McDonald, who was born at Charter Oak, Iowa, May 10, 1891, is of English descent. They have two sons, William Ward, born November 11, 1918, and Guy, Jr., born July 22, 1922.

Mr. McDonald is active in civic affairs, and is a member of the Chamber of Commerce, the Rotary Club, Ak-Sar-Ben, and is chairman of the Merchants Market Week Committee. He belongs to the Washington Parent-Teachers' Association and The Nebraskana Society. He attends the First Methodist Church of Omaha. His clubs are the Omaha Field and Omaha Athletic Clubs. His favorite sport is golf, and he enjoys reading and motoring. Residence: Omaha.

James Beauregard McDonald

An outstanding figure in the professional world of Nebraska is James Beauregard McDonald who has lived in the state for nearly 50 years and has taken a prominent part in political and civic endeavor for many years. He was born at Chatham Hill, Virginia, September 22, 1861, the son of James Van Buren McDonald and Emiline Ann Ganaway.

His father, whose ancestry was Scotch, was born at Chatham Hill, November 30, 1833, and died at Pierce, Nebraska, September 30, 1915; he was a carpenter, and during the Civil War was a Confederate soldier. His mother was born of English parentage at Cripple Creek, Virginia, April 7, 1836, and died at Council Bluffs, Iowa, December 1, 1917.

Judge McDonald has been a leading citizen of Pierce for many years. A Democrat, he served as county clerk from 1908 to 1914, was postmaster from 1914 to 1923, and since 1926 has been county judge of Pierce County. He acted as deputy postmaster from 1893 to 1897 and from 1897 to 1908 was engaged in the lumber business at Pierce. He is a member of the Community Club, the Independent Order of Odd Fellows, and the Rebekah Lodge. During the World War he served as chairman of the county Council of Defense.

On July 9, 1902, he was united in marriage at Pierce with Jessie Kerr who was born at Glasgow, Scotland, February 10, 1877. Three children were born to them: Suza Katherine, March 7, 1904, who is a registered nurse; Robert, who died in infancy; and James Howard, September 1, 1915. Residence: Pierce.

Lewis Weitzel McDonald

Born at Centerville, Ohio, April 8, 1879, Lewis Weitzel McDonald is the son of William Wallace and Anna Mary (Parcell) McDonald. His father, who served as general foreman for the Chicago & Northwestern Railway Company for many years, was born at Kingston, Illinois, January 4, 1855, and died at Elgin, Illinois, November 22, 1925; his ancestry was Scotch. His mother, who was prominent in the Order of Eastern Star, Rebekah Lodge, and the Women's Relief Corps, was born of Scotch and Irish parents at Centerville, December 15, 1859, and died at Elgin, January 1, 1916.

Mr. McDonald attended the high school at Troy Grove, Illinois, until 1894, and since then has been supervisory agent for the Chicago & Northwestern Railway Company at Long Pine, Nebraska. He is a Mason, was formerly president of the Chamber of Commerce and the local school board, holds membership in the Lions Club, and is a member of the Order of Eastern Star.

A Republican, Mr. McDonald is now serving his third term as mayor of his community. He is affiliated with the Congregational Church, and holds membership in the Nebraskana Society. His chief recreations are fishing, reading, and baseball.

On February 8, 1901, he was married to Bessie Marilla Clarke at Glen Ellyn, Illinois. Mrs. McDonald, who is descended directly from the Winthrop and Churchill families of Pilgrim days, was born at Beln Ellyn, April 1, 1884. They have one son, Charles Clarke, born November 15, 1901, who married Loretta Miller. He was graduated from Annapolis in 1923, and is now an instructor in the aviation school at Pensacola, Florida. Residence: Long Pine.

Milton Berlin McDowell

Milton Berlin McDowell, prominent physician and surgeon at Chadron, was born at Oil City, Pennsylvania, July 20, 1875, and came to Nebraska, in April, 1885.

His father, Cyrus F. McDowell, was born in Mercer County, Pennsylvania, February 19, 1842, and died at Long Beach, California, August 3, 1929. He was a veteran of the Civil War, and at the time of his death, was a retired farmer. His wife, Ella Berlin, was born in Venango County, Pennsylvania, July 12, 1849, and is still living.

Dr. McDowell attended country school of Sheridan County, and was graduated from Gordon High School. In 1902, he received his medical degree from the University of Nebraska, where he was a charter member of Iota Chapter of Phi Rho Sigma.

In addition to his practice, Dr. McDonald is the owner of a large ranch. At the present time, he is serving as city physician of Chadron. He is a Republican.

On February 12, 1908, he was married to Pearl A. Peacock at Hay Springs. Mrs. McDowell was born in Sheridan County, September 26, 1886. Mrs. McDowell is a member of the Eastern Star, Parent Teachers Association and the Does. She is the daughter of Frank and Zella (Dubbs) Peacock. Dr. and Mrs. McDowell are both members of the Congregational Church. They have two children, Cyrus, born September 6, 1909; and Betty, born March 2, 1916.

Among Dr. McDowell's civic and professional memberships are, the Nebraska State and Dawes County Medical Society, the Northwestern Nebraska Medical Society, of which he is now president, the Civic Relief Committee, the Chamber of Commerce, the Chadron Rotary Club, of which he is a charter member, the Masons, the Odd Fellows, and the Elks, of which he is exalted ruler. He is a member of the Chadron Country Club, enjoys hunting, fishing, and golf. His hobby is breeding hogs. Residence: Chadron.

Martin Slylvester McDuffee

Martin Sylvester McDuffee, son of G. N. and Ann (Layden) McDuffee, was born at Corning, Iowa, May 29, 1878, and since 1886 has resided in Nebraska.

His father was born at Rushville, Indiana, was a farmer and died at York, Nebraska in 1902. His mother was also born at Rushville. Both were of early American ancestry. Martin S. McDuffee attended public school, was a student at Fremont Normal College 1899-1903, and received his Bachelor of Laws degree from the University of Nebraska in 1906. He is a member of Theta Kappa Nu.

Upon his admission to the bar in June, 1906, Mr. McDuffee entered upon the active practice of his profession. From 1906 to 1912 he practiced at Madison, and from 1912 to 1923 served as county judge of Madison County, elected on the Democratic ticket. From 1923 until October, 1931, he was a member of the firm of McDuffee and Mapes at Norfolk. At the present time Judge McDuffee is engaged in practice alone.

He has been a member of the Board of Education since 1929, and at the present time is serving as its president. One of the organizers of the Carnegie Library, at Madison, he was active in all civilian projects during the World War period including Red Cross, Liberty loan drives, four minute speaking, etc.

He is a member and past president of the Kiwanis Club, served as president of the Chamber of Commerce in 1928, a member of the Madison County Historical Society, the Red Cross, Young Men's Christian Association and Boy Scouts. His professional memberships include the District, Nebraska State and American Bar Associations.

Judge McDuffee is affiliated with the First Presbyterian Church, is a Scottish Rite Mason and Knight Templar, and a life member of the Nebraskana Society. His social club is the Norfolk Country Club.

Of his marriage to Ida Belle Knoll there is one daughter, Ruth, born July 28, 1915. Mrs. McDuffee was born at Crete, on January 19, 1881, the daughter of A. L. and Mina (Young) Knoll. She is a graduate of Doane College, and before her marriage was a high school teacher and principal of the Madison High School for five years. She is a member of the Library board, past president of the Young Women's Christian Association, Madison, Norfolk, and Madison County Women's Clubs, and at present is president of the Women's Club for the third district. Residence: Norfolk.

Adelaide May McEachen

Adelaide May McEachen, clubwoman, was born in Cuming County, Nebraska, May 28, 1871, daughter of David Williams and Isabella (Gilmore) Burke. Her father, David W. Burke, was born in Perth, Ontario, Canada, September 15, 1838, and homesteaded in Nebraska in 1869. He was a teacher and member of the school board, commissioner of Cuming County and member of the Nebraska legislature. He died at Bancroft, Nebraska, August 14, 1911. Isabella, wife of David, was born at Almonte, Ontario, October 18, 1839, and died in Cuming County, October 15, 1882. She was of Scotch and her husband was of Irish descent.

Mrs. McEachen attended district school No. 21, which was located on part of her family homestead, and completed her education in June 1885. On June first of the following year she was married to Robert Allen McEachen, at Sioux City, Iowa. Mr. McEachen was born in Lanark County, Ontario, June 20, 1855, and was an outstanding farmer, of Scotch descent. His death occurred at Wayne on July 7, 1915. To their marriage the following children were born: George Allen, born in Cuming County, July 10, 1888, married Leone Copple; Benjamin C., born February 28, 1890, at Omaha, married Hazel Andrews; Esther I., born at Omaha, September 30, 1892; James A., born in Cuming County, June 12,

1894, married Edna Pegler; William Robert, born in Cuming County, February 3, 1896; Gertrude E., born in Cuming County, September 17, 1897; Howard D., born in Wayne County September 3, 1903, married Ada Bauman and Grant A., born in Wayne County, July 9, 1905. Two daughters, Mabel, born March 16, 1900, and Alice, born March 4, 1902, died in infancy.

Mrs. McEachen is a member of the American Legion Auxiliary, the Red Cross, and the First Presbyterian Church of Wayne, as well as the Federated Women's Club and the Eastern Star. Residence: Wayne.

Clyde McElmoil

Clyde McElmoil was born in Elkhart, Indiana, July 4, 1880, the son of James Henry and Mary Ellen (Gemberling) McElmoil. His father, who was a farmer in Adams County, Nebraska, was born at New York City, April 28, 1851, and died at Long Beach, California, July 21, 1931; he was the son of Robert McElmoil, who was born in Glasgow, Scotland, and Jennie (Miller) McElmoil, who was a native of Londonderry, Ireland. His mother was born in Elkhart County, Indiana, December 6, 1858.

Mr. McElmoil was graduated from the Juniata High School in 1899, and was a student for a year at the University of Nebraska, where he was a member of the University Cadet Battalion. He began work in a drug store at Lincoln, Nebraska, in the spring of 1900 and in 1905 became a registered druggist. In 1908 he bought a drug store at Farnam and is still the owner and proprietor.

He is past president of the Farnam Commercial Club and was secretary of the local Red Cross. His hobby is touring by motor. On October 30, 1907, he was married at Callaway, Nebraska, to Mable Irene Decker who was born at Galva, Illinois, July 23, 1880, and died at Rochester, Minnesota, July 2, 1921. She was a member of the Daughters of the American Revolution. Their son, Gordon Decker, was born December 25, 1912. In 1923 Mr. McElmoil married Mrs. Edith Hall at Wray, Colorado. Residence: Farnam. (Photograph in Album).

William George McFall

William George McFall, a pioneer resident of Nebraska, has taken a prominent part in the progress of his community and county. He was born at Palmerston, Canada, October 23, 1870, the son of Archibald and Ellen Morrow McFall. His father, who was a farmer, was born at Montreal, Canada, June 29, 1839, and died at Elmwood, Nebraska, January 9, 1926; his Scotch-Irish ancestors were natives of Canada. His mother, whose ancestry is English, was born at Montreal, Canada, October 1, 1837 and died at Elmwood, August 8, 1914.

Mr. McFall attended rural school in Cass County until 1890, and was a student at Cotner College, 1891-3, and at Lincoln Normal College, 1893-5. He taught school for four years, 1895-9, and has been a farmer and stockman near Brunswick, Nebraska, since that time. He is a member of the National Geographic Society, the Red Cross, Woodmen of the World, and Independent Order of Odd Fellows. He is a member and director of the Farmers Union, and is active in the interests of temperance education in Nebraska.

During the World War he served as a member of the council of defense and assisted in loan drives and military organizations. He is affiliated with the Brunswick Community Church and holds membership in the Nebraskana Society. His favorite sport is horseback riding, and his hobby is reading current magazines.

On January 1, 1900, he was married to Hattie Ella Rivett at Elmwood, Nebraska. Mrs. McFall, whose parents were born in England, was born at Unadilla, Nebraska, October 1, 1878. They have two children: Beatrice, born November 22, 1900, who married Fred Wilhelms; and Maurice, born October 19, 1902, who mar-

ried Ruth Ann McFall. Beatrice, who is a teacher, received the A. B. degree from Cotner College. Maurice was graduated from the State Agricultural School and is now an agent for the Metropolitan Life Insurance Company. Residence: Brunswick.

Elmer Warner McFarland

Elmer Warner McFarland, son of Cyrus and Lucy Ann (Warner) McFarland, was born at McLean, Illinois, October 5, 1861. The father was born at Providence, Rhode Island, July 24, 1835, and died at Lincoln, February 8, 1923. The mother was born at Hartford, Connecticut, May 30, 1834, and died at Lincoln, April 1, 1927.

Mr. McFarland attended public and high school until 1879, and for a number of years has been senior member of the mercantile firm of McFarland & Sons. He served as state senator in 1929-30, elected on the Republican ticket. Mr. McFarland is a Mason.

On December 24, 1882, he was married to Olive Jane Place at Rantoul, Illinois. She was born near Madison, Indiana, December 30, 1860. Their children are as follows: May, born October 24, 1883, married Edd DeVore, and is now deceased; John Warner, born July 1, 1885; Lee Ray, born January 17, 1888, died August 8, 1898; Cyrus, born June 15, 1891; and Harry, born August 17, 1898. Residence: Ohiowa.

William Irvin McFarland

Born at Falls City, Nebraska, January 14, 1877, William Irvin McFarland has been engaged in the practice of medicine since 1905. He is the son of William and Elizabeth (Knox) McFarland, both natives of Ireland. William McFarland, Sr., was born at Lindenberry, Ireland, February 27, 1832, and came to America in 1848. A farmer and stockman for many years, he was retired at the time of his death at Beatrice on September 1, 1901. His wife, who was born in the North of Ireland, August 26, 1844, died at Beatrice in 1914.

Educated first in country school, Dr. McFarland later attended Nebraska Wesleyan University, where he was a member of the Thiophanian Society. He was admitted to the practice of medicine at Beatrice on June 2, 1905, and is a member of the Nebraska State and Thayer County Medical Societies.

He was married to Hattie Laura Miller at Lexington, Nebraska, December 12, 1905, and to them was born one son, Osmyn W., who is a pre-medic student at Creighton. Mrs. McFarland was born at Neoshaye, New York, and before her marriage was a music teacher. She received her musical education at Nebraska Wesleyan. She is at the present time superintendent of Blue Valley Hospital, which is operated by Dr. McFarland. The hospital, the only one in the county, specializes in surgery only.

Affiliated with the Presbyterian Church, Dr. McFarland is also a Mason and Kiwanian, and is a member of the Chamber of Commerce and The Nebraskana Society. Residence: Hebron.

Alexander McFarlane

For the past 40 years Alexander McFarlane has carried on a successful mercantile business at Friend, Nebraska. He was born at Gartmoore, Scotland, June 11, 1854, the son of John and Janet (Sands) McFarlane. His father, who was a landholder and chief of the clan of McFarlane, was born at Gartmoore, September, 1815, and died there October, 1873. His mother was born at Gartmoore, in 1813, reared a family of ten children, and died there in 1896; for the past 100 years her family has lived on the estate of the Duke of Montrose.

Mr. McFarlane attended elementary school at Gartmoore; in 1870, was graduated from the high school in Glasgow, Scotland; and was president of Coleraine Lyceum, 1874-75. A resident of Nebraska for 50 years. During the World War he was appointed patriotic speaker at Friend, Saline County, Nebraska. He served as president of the Friend Chamber of Commerce for six years; is a Mason; Odd Fellow; and Modern Woodman of America. His social clubs are the Friend Country Club and the Burns Club. He is a member of the Methodist Episcopal Church. Mr. McFarlane is a Republican, and served as mayor of Friend in 1908, and from 1924 to 1930.

On January 2, 1882, he was united in marriage with Mary E. Malcolm at Lexington, Nebraska. Mrs. McFarlane, whose ancestry is Scotch, was born at St. Thomas, Canada, April 9, 1861. They have one son, Malcolm L., born August 30, 1886, who served in the United States Navy for seven months during the World War. Residence: Friend.

Claud Gwinn McGaffin

Born in Lincoln, Nebraska, October 21, 1874, Claud Gwinn McGaffin is the daughter of Garrett George Gwinn and Jerusha Rebecca (Wickens) Gwinn. Her father was born in Brown County, Indiana, December 23, 1845, of Irish and Dutch parentage, and died in Lincoln, September 10, 1916. Her mother was born in Buffalo, New York, December 21, 1846, of English ancestry, and died April 12, 1931, at Bellwood, Nebraska.

Mrs. McGaffin was educated in the Lincoln elementary and high schools. She was married to George Samuel Hagenbuch at Lincoln, Nebraska, October 21, 1895. He was born in Pennsylvania, March 15, 1872. To this union two children were born: Wilma, April 21, 1899, who died July 30, 1899; and George Gwinn, December 27, 1902, who is married to Pearl (Young) Hagenbuch. George was graduated from the State University in 1924, and was admitted to the bar in the same year.

On April 8, 1906, she was married to William Henry McGaffin, at Omaha. Mr. McGaffin was born in County Down, Ireland, April 22, 1845. Wesley Claude McGaffin was the only child of this marriage. He was born March 29, 1909, and died November 6, 1923.

Mrs. McGaffin is editor of *The Bellwood Gazette*. She is a Republican, a member of the Nebraska Press Association, and is secretary of the school board. Her religious affiliation is with the Methodist Episcopal Church of Bellwood. She is a member of the Red Cross and Rebekah Lodge No. 367. She also belongs to the Ladies' Aid Society and to the Nebraskana Society. Residence: Bellwood. (Photograph in Album).

Hugh M. McGaffin

Hugh M. McGaffin, prominent editor and publisher at Polk, Nebraska, has been a resident of this state for the past 45 years. He was born at Poughkeepsie, New York, March 29, 1872, the son of William Henry and Margery Clendenin (Martin) McGaffin. His father, one of the state's oldest publishers at the time of his death, was the founder, editor, and publisher of the *Bellwood Gazette*. He was born in Crobane, County Down, Ireland, April 22, 1845, and died at Bellwood, January 30, 1927. His mother was born at Donahmore, County Down, Ireland, January 4, 1849, and died at Bellwood, March 25, 1901.

Mr. McGaffin is the editor and publisher of the *Polk Progress*, and during President Wilson's administration was postmaster at Polk. He was a member of the home guard during the World War and took an active part in Red Cross work. He is a member of the District Council of Defense, the Nebraska Press Association (serving as chairman of the executive committee in 1921) and The Nebraskana Society. He was a member of the Polk School Board from 1923 to 1924, was president of the Polk Commercial Club from 1913 to 1922, and served as chancellor of the Knights of Pythias in 1923.

He is a member of the Independent Order of Odd Fellows, Modern Woodmen of America, and the Royal Highlanders. His marriage to Nellie Mae Derby was solemnized at Bellwood, November 11, 1894. Mrs. McGaffin, who was born at Bellwood March 10, 1875, is a direct descendent of Governor William Bradford and Elias Bingham of England. They have three children: Ruth C., born November 18, 1895, who married Daniel B. Carter; Nelle M., born May 2, 1898, who married Wallace M. Scott; and C. William, born October 2, 1910.

Mr. McGaffin's favorite sport is football, while his hobby is reading. He is a Democrat. Residence: Polk.

Florence Irwin McGahey

Florence Irwin McGahey, registrar of the University of Nebraska, was born at Lincoln, June 4, 1880, daughter of Thomas Harrison and Emeline Van Lear (Irwin) McGahey. The former was born in Butler County, Pennsylvania and died at Lincoln on August 5, 1924; while the latter, born in Franklin County, Pennsylvania, May 23, 1853, is still living.

Miss McGahey attended Lincoln public and high schools, and in 1901 received the Bachelor of Arts degree from the University of Nebraska. She is a member of Pi Beta Phi. Her religious affiliation is with the First Presbyterian Church. She is a member of the Red Cross, the Altrusa Club, the Young Women's Christian Association and the Nebraska Women's Educational Club. Residence: Lincoln.

James Adams McGeachin

James Adams McGeachin, who is a merchant at Orleans, Nebraska, is a lifelong resident of that community. He was born at Orleans, January 17, 1883, the son of James and Janet (Lorimer) McGeachin, the former a merchant who was born at Old Cummock, Scotland, in February, 1843, and died at Orleans, July 27, 1913. His mother was born at Ackensue, Scotland, May 8, 1843, and died at Orleans.

Mr. McGeachin was graduated from the Orleans High School in 1900, received the A. B. degree at the University of Nebraska, and served as president of the fraternity, Phi Gamma Delta at the latter institution. He was captain of Company D of the University Cadets. For a number of years he has been the owner and manager of the McGeachin Store at Orleans.

He is a member of the Orleans Commercial Club, the Rotary Club, the Masons, and the Modern Woodmen of America. His chief recreations are golfing and reading. Of his marriage to Nevile Margaret Rogers two children were born: Margaret, February 26, 1929; and James, May 27, 1931. Residence: Orleans.

Charles Hill McGee

Charles Hill McGee, son of Jesse Steed and Mary Anderson McGee, was born in Abbeville County, South Carolina, May 19, 1867. Jesse Steed McGee, also a native of Abbeville County, was born April 8, 1834. He was a farmer, and later a member of the state legislature. During the Civil War he served as orderly sergeant with Company B., 7th South Carolina Infantry. His death occurred at Greenville, January 21, 1915. Mary Anderson, his wife, was born in Greenville County September 27, 1839, and is still living. Both are of Scotch Irish descent.

Educated in rural schools, Mr. McGee came to Beatrice in February, 1897. He was a telegraph operator and train dispatcher for the Rock Island from 1886-1915, an insurance agent from 1915-21, at which time he retired to look after his personal affairs. He was a director of the Harbine bank until it was sold.

Mr. McGee is a Republican, and a member of the city council of Fairbury. During the Spanish-American war he was corporal and company clerk of Company D., 2nd Nebraska Volunteers from May 10-December 6, 1898. He is a member of the Guy Dodge Camp No. 3, United Spanish War Veterans, the Red Cross, and the Commercial Club. From 1919-25 he served as secretary of the Fairbury School Board. He is a member of the First Baptist Church, the Kiwanis Club and the Masons, of which last he is secretary.

On April 3, 1900, he was united in marriage to Nellie Eldridge at Fairbury, her birthplace. Mrs. McGee, who is of English extraction descended from Nathaniel Gardner, is a member of the D. A. R. She was born July 4, 1878. There is one daughter, Aileen, born February 8, 1907, who is employed in the Omaha City Library. Residence: Fairbury.

Edmund George McGilton

Edmund G. McGilton, born at Eau Galle, Wisconsin, February 10, 1859, is the son of John H. McGilton, who was born at Moores, New York, December 1, 1825. He was descended of Scotch-Irish settlers in early days, and when a young man moved to Wisconsin. A farmer and lumber manufacturer, he owned about one thousand acres in a high state of cultivation, and in his manufacturing operations employed from one hundred and fifty to two hundred men. He served on the board of supervisors of Dunn County, as chairman, and was a member of the Wisconsin state legislature. He married Gratia Eleanor Burke, a native of Hemmingford, Canada, who was born January 31, 1837. She was for many years superintendent of the Sunday School of her church, and a teacher of a Bible class. She was highly educated and a profound student of the Bible. Her ancestry is traced to Edmund Burke, and an ancestor came to America on the *Mayflower*.

Edmund G. McGilton received his early education in the public schools of Dunn County, Wisconsin, and was graduated from Menominie High School in 1878. He was graduated from the University of Wisconsin in June, 1883 with an LL. B. and in June, 1885, was awarded a B. L. by the same university. He was a member of the musical society, and of the debating society, and delivered an oration at his commencement. He is a member of Alpha chapter of Beta Theta Pi. While at the university he filled the positions of catcher, pitcher and first baseman on the baseball team at various times.

Admitted to the practice of law in Wisconsin, June 20, 1885, he is also admitted to practice in all the courts of Nebraska both steate ad federal and in the Supreme Court of the United States, where he has argued many cases.

Since July 1887, he has practiced law continuously in Nebraska, in connection with the following law firms: McGilton and Stoddart, McGilton and Lindsay; Cavanagh, Thomas and McGilton; McCabe, McGilton and Elmer; McGilton and Herring, McGilton and Gaines; McGilton, Gaines and Smith; McGilton and Smith, and Gaines, McGilton, Van Orsdel and Gaines, of which last named firm he is now a member.

His firm is general counsel for McCord-Brady Company, Wright and Wilhelmy Co., Eggers-O'Flyng Company; Beebe and Runyan Furniture Company, A. Y. McDonald Manufacturing Company; United States Fidelity and Guaranty Company and other insurance companies. Mr. McGilton is a member of the board of directors of Wright and Wilhelmy Company.

He was married to Lina Augusta Williams at Menomine, Wisconsin, April 4, 1889. Mrs. McGilton was born at Oshkosh, Wisconsin, January 31, 1856, and is descended from Charlemagne, Alfred the Great, Hugh Capet, and down to Governor Jeremiah Clarke of Rhode Island. While her interests are primarily in her home she is active in church and club work. There are three children: Edna Gertrude, born September 4, 1891, who died May 9, 1892; Harriet, born December 1, 1893, who died January 19, 1899; and Eleanor, born March 22, 1897, who was graduated from Smith College in June 1918, and was married to Edward J. Connor on October 1, 1921.

A Republican, Mr. McGilton has served as lieutenant governor of Nebraska for two terms, 1903-07. He was unsuccessful candidate for member of the board of regents of the University of Nebraska, and defeated candidate for the state senate.

He is the author of an address before the Nebraska State Bar Association and an address as president of the Commercial Law League of America. During his university days he was editor of the college paper known as *The Badger*. He was also a member of the University of Wisconsin military battalion for two years, and during that time was promoted to the rank of captain. Captain Charles King of the United States Army was commander of the university battalion of which Mr. McGilton was first lieutenant, and in June, 1880, this battalion was taken to Milwaukee to meet General Grant, who was a guest of the G. A. R. During the World War he was appointed four minute speaker by President Wilson and as such took active part in loan drives.

He is a member of the First Central Congregational Church, and for many years was active in the Y. M. C. A. He has always been a worker along educational and civic lines. For four years he was a member of the Omaha Board of Education, and was superintendent of city schools at Menominie, Wisconsin, in 1884. He has served on many committees of the Omaha Chamber of Commerce, of which he is a member, and is a contributor to the Red Cross, Salvation Army and Volunteers of America. For many years he has been a member of the Nebraska State Historical Society, and is a member of the National Geographic Society and of the Nebraskana Society.

His fraternal organizations include the Elks, Woodmen of the World and the Masons. He is a member of St. John's Lodge of the Ancient Free and Accepted Masons, Omaha Chapter, Commandery, Tangier Temple, Nobles of the Mystic Shrine of which he was potentate in 1910.

Mr. McGilton was an ardent golfer for fifteen years. His clubs were formerly the Omaha Club, the Omaha Athletic Club, the Omaha Country Club, Happy Hollow Country Club and the Omaha Field Club. He was, however, forced to resign his memberships on account of ill health. His chief interests at present are reading biographies and general literature, and automobile driving. Residence: Omaha. (Photograph in Album).

Bert B. McGinnis

Born at Norfolk, Nebraska, November 3, 1871, Bert B. McGinnis is the son of Andrew N. and Mattie M. (Figley) McGinnis. His father, who was a farmer and livestock raiser, was born at Richwood, Ohio, June 8, 1842, and died at Hutchinson, Kansas, November 30. 1923; of Scotch parentage, he lived in Nebraska for many years and during the Civil War served in the Ohio Volunteer Infantry. His mother, whose parents were natives of Pennsylvania, was born at Richwood, October 4, 1845, and died at Norfolk, August 23, 1904.

Mr. McGinnis attended public school and was a student at Wayne College, Wayne, Nebraska for a year. Since 1893 he has been successful as a farmer and livestock breeder near Norfolk in Warnerville Precinct. He is a member of the Nebraskana Society, is affiliated with the First Congregational Church of Norfolk, and is a Mason.

On April 29, 1896, he was united in marriage with Florence M. Nielson at Norfolk. Mrs. McGinnis, whose parents came to this country from Denmark, was born at Norfolk, June 10, 1873. They have three children: Lyle, born June 18, 1898, who married Hazel Horner; Fay, born July 24, 1908; and Helen, born August 2, 1910. All the children completed the high school course, and Fay and Helen are students in college at this time. Mr. McGinnis is a Republican. Residence: Norfolk.

James Wayne McGinnis

James Wayne McGinnis, veterinary surgeon, was born at Blue Springs, Nebraska, November 20, 1885, son of Harrison Lincoln and Zeporah Ann (Yowell) McGinnis.

The father, born in Muscatine, Iowa, July 27, 1860, is a farmer and rancher at Maywood. His ancestry is Scotch-Irish. His wife, Zeporah, was born in Iowa, June 23, 1865, and is an active member of the Rebekah Lodge. Her ancestry is English and Dutch.

Upon leaving country school, Mr. McGinnis entered York Business College, from which he was graduated in 1904. In 1909, he received the degree of Doctor of Veterinary Surgery from the Kansas City Veterinary College. There he was active as a member of the football team in 1907. From 1909 until 1912, Mr. McGinnis was in general practice at Ord. He moved to Grand Island in 1912, living there until 1916, when he again returned to Ord. A Democrat, he was a member of the Ord City Council 1917-21 (two terms). He was unsuccessful candidate for the state legislature in 1928. He is a member of the Nebraska Veterinary Medical Association, of which he was president one year and of which he has been a member of the executive and legislative committees. He is a member of the executive committee of the Missouri Valley Veterinary Association. He is a member of the Chamber of Commerce, served as its president one year, and as chairman of the good roads committee several years. From 1923 until the present time, he has been a member of the school board (1924-1928-1929). He is affiliated with the First Methodist Church, and is a member of the Knights of Pythias.

On September 14, 1907, he was married to Margaret Mae Tidyman at Hayes Center. Mrs. McGinnis was born at Maywood, October 31, 1887. Mr. and Mrs. McGinnis have four children, Selma Mae, born April 18, 1909; Velmer Wayne, born September 7, 1911, who married Ruth Maxine Babbitt; Kenneth T., born January 9, 1915; and Beulah, born June 3, 1917. Selma and Velmer are students at Kansas State Agricultural College, while Kenneth and Beulah attend high school at Ord. Residence: Ord.

Benjamin Robert McGrath

Since 1904 Benjamin Robert McGrath has been a practicing physician at Grand Island, Nebraska, and has taken a prominent part in the civic and professional life of his community. He was born in Jo Daviess County, Illinois, May 17, 1873, the son of Robert and Esther (Wier) McGrath, the former a farmer who was born in Bucks County, Pennsylvania in 1832, and died at Savanna, Illinois, June 1, 1902. His mother, whose ancestry was Irish, was born in Mercer County, Pennsylvania in 1836 and died at Savanna, in January, 1905.

Dr. McGrath was graduated from the Savanna High School in 1890, and received the M. D. degree at the University of Illinois in 1902. He served as principal of the school at Grant, Nebraska, 1894-98, and since 1904 has been engaged in the practice of medicine at Grand Island. He is a member of the American Medical Association and its subsidiary organizations, is a fellow of the American College of Surgeons, and in 1928 served as president of the Nebraska State Medical Association.

During the World War he served as surgeon in the United States Army with the American Expedition forces in France about one year. He was wih Base Hospital Number 116 and in charge of Operating Team No. 35. He was discharged with the rank of captain. He was promoted to the rank of major in the Medical Reserve, and is now a member of the American Legion.

On June 20, 1907, he married Susan Ellen Williamson in Jo Daviess County, Illinois, June 30, 1907; she was born in Jo Daviess County, January 1, 1875, and died at Grand Island, May 1, 1925. To this marriage the following children were born: William M., August 20, 1908, graduated from the Rush Medical College, Chicago, Illinois, in 1931; Esther L., November 23, 1909, graduate of the University of Nebraska, who married Raymond Flanagan; Benjamin, Jr., April 11, 1911, who is a student at Bucknell University; and James R., June 18, 1921.

Dr. McGrath married Dessie P. Shaffer May 31, 1928. One son was born to this marriage: Harvey C., July 9, 1929. A Republican, Dr. McGrath has served as a member of the Board of Education at Grand Island, 1908-17, acting as president of the board for five years. Residence: Grand Island.

Harriet G. McGraw

Harriet Goodman McGraw, one of Nebraska's few women physicians, was born in Iceland, the daughter of Finbogi and Margaret (Benedict) Goodman. Her father, who was a jeweler, was born in Iceland, and died at Winnipeg, Canada. Her mother was also a native of Iceland.

Dr. McGraw attended Canadian and American public schools, was a student at Union College, and holds degrees from Chicago Superintendent of Instruction and the Nebraska Superintendent of Instruction. Later she studied at Bennet Medical College and Loyola University in Chicago. She has been a resident of this state for the past 30 years and at this time is health officer for McPherson County, Nebraska, where she has been in medical practice since 1907. In 1909 she was married to Joseph A. McGraw at Lincoln. Mr. McGraw is county attorney of McPherson County.

She is a member of the American Medical Association, the Red Cross, the Lincoln County Medical Society, and the Republican party. Her local society is the Helping Hand Club. Residence: Tryon.

John Sylvanus McGraw

John Sylvanus McGraw, son of James and Frances (Walker) McGraw, was born at Sommerset, Indiana, September 29, 1867, and since September 1, 1880, has resided in Nebraska.

The father, born at Dublin, Ireland, January 1, 1844, was a farmer, who came to America in 1845 and served in the Civil War 1863-65. He settled first in Indiana and later in Custer County, his death occurring at Broken Bow in November, 1928. His wife, born in the country in Henry County, Ohio, was of German and Irish descent. She died at Broken Bow in 1915.

Educated in common school until 1886, John Sylvanus McGraw was a traveling salesman, later a farmer, and for a number of years has been engaged in real estate and insurance at Broken Bow. An independent Republican he has held minor political offices, and in 1912 was delegate to the national convention at Chicago. From 1918-23 he was president of the First Trust Company of Broken Bow, which dissolved in 1923.

On March 8, 1894, he was united in marriage to Lydia Ellen Brown at Gates, Nebraska. Mrs. McGraw, who was a school teacher before marriage, was born at San Pierre, Indiana, January 23, 1870, of Yankee and German descent. They have one daughter, Mildred, born March 4, 1907, who was graduated from the University of Nebraska in 1929 and who is now a member of the Bureau of Public Welfare in Chicago.

Mr. McGraw was a participant in wartime projects during the World War period. He is a member of the Methodist Church at Broken Bow, and for the past seven years has served as superintendent of its Sunday School. He is a Mason (Blue Lodge No. 148; Chapter No. 29; Knight Templar No. 25; and Sesostris Temple of the Shrine at Lincoln). At various times he has served on school boards at Broken Bow and Gates. He is a member of the Rotary Club and the Public Service Club. His favorite sports are golf and hunting; while his hobby is mechanics. Residence: Broken Bow.

Lillian Mae McGregor

Lillian Mae McGregor, musician and farm-woman, was born at Loup City, Nebraska, May 20, 1886, the daughter of John Henry and Mary E. (Boyd) Conhiser. Her father, who was a dealer in general merchandise, was born at Fort Plain, New York, April 21, 1848, of German parents, and died at Sargent, Nebraska, March 14, 1896. Her mother was born at Dewitt, Iowa, in 1858, and died at Omaha, Nebraska in 1888; her father was a physician.

Mrs. McGregor lived in Fort Plain, New York from 1888 until 1901 returning to Loup City, Nebraska where she was graduated from the Loup City School in 1904, and for the next 12 years was a clerk in various mercantile establishments in Sargent. She was employed in the following stores: A. L. Conhiser, three years; Peter Lakeman Clothing Company, 1 year; and Plin Metcalfe General Merchandise Company, six years. In 1915 she went to Wyoming, homesteading 320 acres near Torrington. This land is still retained by her. She returned to Sargent in 1917. She is a member of the Sargent Band, Sargent, Nebraska, and for a number of months served as leader of that group.

She was married to James S. McGregor at Sargent, April 30, 1916. Mr. McGregor, who is a farmer, was born at Sargent, November 15, 1886, the son of Robert and Stella (Livermore) McGregor. His parents are former residents of Iowa, coming to Nebraska in 1883 and homesteaded at Sargent. Residence: Sargent.

Walter Scott McGrew

Walter S. McGrew was born at Louisville, Nebraska, September 12, 1886. John Thomas McGrew, his father was born of Scotch Irish parentage in Fulton County, Illinois, January 17, 1840, and died at Louisville, March 20, 1909. His mother, Anna Ellen (Beckelheymer) McGrew, of Irish and German descent, was born in McDonna County, Illinois, December 12, 1845, and died at Louisville, February 25, 1905.

Mr. McGrew has lived in this state for 44 years, and received his education in the public schools of Louisville. For eight years he was a member of the village board at Louisville, and at the present time he is district manager of the Nebraska Power Company.

On March 28, 1910, he was united in marriage with Grace Mirriam Kinnison. Mrs. McGrew was born of English parents at Brock, Nemaha County, Nebraska, October 30, 1892. Seven children were born to them, six of whom are living. They are Mirriam Marie, born July 24, 1912; John Donald, born February 16, 1914; Dorothy Louise, born February 16, 1914, who died February 22, 1923; Larry Allan, born April 28, 1916; Grace Katherine, born January 19, 1925; Scott, Junior, born January 19, 1928; and Joan, born May 28, 1929.

He is a member of the Blue Lodge Masons at Springfield, and Chapter and Commandery at Plattsmouth; the Modern Woodmen of America; and Ancient Order of United Workmen. His hobby is horse races. Residence: Louisville.

Geore Berry McGuire

George Berry McGuire, son of Elisha and Julia Viola (Scott) McGuire, was born at Tekamah, Nebraska, September 4, 1871. His father was born in Carrolton, Ohio, July 18, 1833. From 1857-58 he drove a stage between Decatur and Henry Fontenelle's reservation, and from 1859-60 drove between Tekamah and Cuming City, Iowa. In 1862 he enlisted in Company B, 2nd Nebraska Volunteer Cavalry. He was married to Julia Viola Scott on September 2, 1860.

She was born at Marysville, Ohio, June 24, 1838. When her husband enlisted in the Civil War, she suffered the usual privations of being left at home with her infant child. She is a member of the Scott family, which originated in New England, and which has formed a Scott Family Association with more than three hundred members. The association holds a reunion on the 4th of July each year, the 52nd being held in 1931. Elisha McGuire died at Tekamah, March 27, 1920, and his wife on May 1, 1914.

George B. McGuire acquired his father's homestead and lived on it until 1910 when he moved to Tekamah, engaging in the livestock buying business twelve years. The home farm was sold to L. D. Baker who still resides there. It is interesting to note that the original homestead was secured by patent from President Buchanan, for $1.25 an acre. The patent is still in the possession of Mr. McGuire, who prizes it highly.

Mr. McGuire later engaged in various businesses, and on February 1, 1931, moved to his farm a half mile west of Tekamah, where he has all city conveniences, including electric light and water.

On September 14, 1904, he was united in marriage to Mary Ann Remington, at Tekamah. Mrs. McGuire was born at Blair, December 7, 1880, the daughter of Mr. and Mrs. O. N. Remington. She was secretary of the local and continued for several years. Since that time she has been chairman, and was so acting when the tornado swept over Tekamah on May 1, 1930. At that time she had charge of all the relief work.

There were three children, Kenneth Gordon, born February 4, 1906, who died February 15, 1906; William, born December 29, 1908, who died January 12, 1909; and Velna Evelyn, born March 10, 1907. Velna received her A. B. from the University of Nebraska in June, 1928. She is a member of Alpha Chi Omega, Pi Lambda Theta, Valkyrie, Mystic Fish and the Panhellenic Council 1927-28. She was married to Louis M. Hancock on November 9, 1929, and has one son, George Warren, born January 9, 1931.

Mr. McGuire was a member of the State Militia 1891-96, and was active in Red Cross work during the World War. He is affiliated with the First Presbyterian Church, and is a member of the Ancient Free and Accepted Masons and the Veteran Freemasons. Residence: Tekamah.

Howard L. McHatton

Howard L. McHatton, livestock farmer, was born at Oshkosh, Nebraska, January 23, 1892, and for 40 years has been a prominent resident of Nebraska. His father, James W. McHatton, was born in Ohio, October 24, 1861, and was a rancher of Scotch-Irish descent. His wife, Lillie Belle Brooks, was born in Illinois, April 17, 1871. Her ancestry was German.

Mr. McHatton attended public school until May, 1909, and since then has been engaged in the breeding of livestock. On September 30, 1914, Mr. McHatton was married to Nettie Irene Wolf at Denver. She was born at Chappell, March 13, 1894. They have two children, Doris Elaine, born August 2, 1917; and Henry Wolford, born September 27, 1923.

He is a Republican. During the late war he was a member of the home guard and active in other civilian projects. He is a member of the Chappell Methodist Episcopal Church, the Masons and the public school board. His club is the Chappell Golf Club, while his favorite sport is baseball. Residence: Chappell.

Harry Hall McHenry

Harry Hall McHenry, merchant, was born at Woodbine, Iowa, April 8, 1879, son of Oliver Orton and Mary Jane (Hall) McHenry. His father was Scotch-Irish, and his mother came from England about 1849.

Mr. McHenry was graduated from district No. 1 of Scotts Bluff County and Gering High School, and for a number of years has been engaged in the general mercantile business. He is a Republican, and a Mason. His favorite sport is baseball.

His marriage to Ella Jula Fossey was solemnized at Alliance, June 12, 1900. Mrs. McHenry was born at North Loup, Nebraska, March 5, 1879. They have three children, Sheldon, born October 25, 1901, who married Anita Vetam; Robert, born April 5, 1905, who married Mildred Sawyer; and Lucy Alice, born December 23, 1906, who married Leonard Roudebush. Residence: Lyman.

William Allen McHenry

William Allen McHenry, leading Nebraska dentist, was born in Nelson, on September 5, 1886. He is the son of William Canfield and Ella (Rowe) McHenry, the former a dentist of Scotch-Irish descent. William Canfield McHenry was born in West Bend, Wisconsin, February 2, 1852, and is still living. His wife, Ella Rowe, was born in Illinois, January 10, 1862, and is a member of the Daughters of the American Revolution, being descended from Ethan Allen.

Educated first in the Nelson public and high schools, William Allen McHenry was graduated in 1903, and attended the University of Nebraska, Northwestern University and Omaha University. He is a member of Xi Psi Phi, at the University of Nebraska, where he received his degree of Doctor of Dental Surgery.

On January 1, 1908, he was married to Maude Adams at Minden, Nebraska. Mrs. McHenry, who comes of the illustrious Adams family, was born at Minden, August 5, 1887. There were two children born to them, Willa, born May 30, 1911, who attends the University of Nebraska; and Edna, born May 30, 1913, who died in 1920.

Dr. McHenry, during all of his mature life, has been an outstanding resident of the state. In 1907 he was one of the organizers of the Southwestern Dental Society; he is a former editor of the *Nebraska Dental Journal;* and at various times has held the offices of president, secretary and treasurer of the Nebraska State Dental Society.

At the present time Dr. McHenry is president of the board of education at Nelson, president of the Nelson Chamber of Commerce, and president of the Nuckolls County chapter of the Red Cross. He is a thirty-second degree Mason and member of the Shrine, a Presbyterian, and a member of the American and Southwestern Dental Societies. He is interested in every civic and cultural movement in his community, and was recently elected to life membership in The Nebraskana Society. Dr. McHenry is fond of fishing and, devotes much of his leisure time to reading. He is a Republican. Residence: Nelson.

Ray Bishop McIllece

Ray Bishop McIllece was born at Van Cleave, Iowa, July 23, 1883, the son of John Barton and Eva Alice (Bishop) McIllece. His father, who was a farmer, was born at Bucks, Pennsylvania, October 1, 1855, of Irish ancestry. His mother was born at Newton, Iowa, November 12, 1860.

Mr. McIllece attended rural schools near Bladen, Nebraska, and in 1905 became a clerk in the Lawrence State Bank, Lawrence, Nebraska. In February of 1906 he bought his present hardware business and in 1920 added implements and harness to his stock. He is owner and manager of the company at this time.

He is a life member of the Red Cross, is affiliated with Sacred Heart Church, and is serving as a member of the board of education at Lawrence. He also holds membership in the Knights of Columbus and the Nebraskana Society. His sports include baseball, football, and golf.

His marriage to Blanche Ellen Cronin occurred at Lawrence, November 25, 1909. Mrs. McIllece was born at

Pauline, Nebraska, December 12, 1888. They have four children: Kathleen, born March 30, 1912; Raymond, born March 18, 1915; Patricia, born October 5, 1923; and Robert, born November 28, 1925. Kathleen is a sophomore in St. Theresa College at Winona, Minnesota. Residence: Lawrence.

William McIlnay

Born at Polo, Ogle County, Illinois, September 17, 1868, William McIlnay has been a resident of Nebraska 51 years. He is the son of Edward and Elizabeth (Bruebaker) McIlnay, the former born in Pennsylvania, March 19, 1844. On August 9, 1862, at the age of 18 he enlisted as a private in Company E, 92nd Illinois Volunteers, and was discharged at Concord on June 21, 1865. A farmer he came to Nebraska some time thereafter, and died at Dorchester in September, 1911. His wife, Elizabeth, was a native of Pennsylvania, of English descent. He was of Irish and Dutch ancestry.

Mr. McIlnay was educated in country schools, and has engaged in farming near Dorchester for many years. He is a Republican and active in local politics, and for 12 years was a rural school director. He was married to Orilla May Nichols at Wilber, August 24, 1898. She was born at Avon, Illinois, April 21, 1877, and is of English and Welsh descent. There are three children, Carrie E. A., born July 8, 1899; Edward W., born March 1, 1901 and Floyd M., born July 12, 1903. The daughter is a bookkeeper, and the two boys are farmers. Residence: Dorchester.

John Thomas McIntosh

John Thomas McIntosh, executive, was born at Potter, Nebraska, April 9, 1871, son of James J. and Mary J. (Heelan) McIntosh. His ancestry is Scotch-Irish.

Mr. McIntosh attended public school and the University of Notre Dame. He was appointed postmaster in 1911 and served until 1920. Since 1928 has been clerk of the district court of Cheyenne County, elected on the Republican ticket. From 1889 to 1903 he was cashier of the American Bank. His favorite sports are golf and baseball.

His marriage to Mary J. McFadden was solemnized at Sidney, Nebraska, October 25, 1899. Mrs. McIntosh was born at Philadelphia, Pennsylvania, December 26, 1873. They have two children, Clifton, born April 14, 1901, who married Estelle Harrington McIntosh; and Jean, born April 23, 1909.

He is a member of St. Patrick's Catholic Church at Sidney. His hobby is golf. Residence: Sidney.

Lillie Muir McKay

For the past eight years Lillie Muir McKay has been teacher of the seventh and eighth grades in the Haigler public school. She was born at Swanton, Nebraska, June 13, 1898, daughter of John C. and Lillie Alice (Kethcart) Muir.

Her father was born in Glasgow, Scotland, December 10, 1861, and came to America in 1866, settling in Lawrence, Massachusetts. As a young man, he came to Nebraska as a pioneer farmer in Jefferson County. Later he became a merchant at Adams, Nebraska for three years and Nora, Nebraska for 12 years. At the present time he is again farming near Dederick, Missouri. His wife, Lillie, was born in Shelby County, Ohio, August 11, 1878.

Mrs. McKay attended public school at Adams and Nora, Nebraska and afterwards attended Hastings College for two years. During her high school term she clerked in a store. Becoming a teacher in 1916, she taught four years in the rural schools of Nuckols County, Nebraska, three years at Pauline, one year at Roseland in Adams County. And for the last eight years has held the position given above.

On January 17, 1926, she was married to Hugh James McKay at Haigler, Nebraska. Mr. McKay, who is the owner of a garage, was born at New London, Prince Edward Island, Canada, August 23, 1893. They have one son, Wallace Fulton, born March 13, 1917, in Prince Edward Island, Canada by a former marriage.

Mrs. McKay is a member of the Parent-Teachers Association (chairman of program committee 1929-31), a member of the Nebraska Education Association, of the Eastern Star, and the Haigler Woman's Club. Her hobbies are reading, music and domestic arts. Residence: Haigler. (Photograph in Album).

Henry Clark McKee

Henry C. McKee was born at Palmyra, Otoe County, Nebraska, January 25, 1870. His father, John Randall McKee, who was a farmer and stock buyer, was born in Ohio, June 5, 1839, of Scotch ancestry, and died at Palmyra, June 22, 1922.

Sallie Rebecca (Lowe) McKee, his mother, was born in Pickaway County, Ohio, October 1, 1840, and died at Palmyra, February 26, 1921. Before her marriage she was a teacher.

Mr. McKee has lived in Otoe County all his life and since finishing high school has been a farmer. A Republican, he served two terms, 1919-21, in the Nebraska Legislature.

He was united in marriage with Kate Loper at Palmyra, January 1, 1893. Mrs. McKee was born at Hinesdale, Morgan County, Indiana, March 12, 1871. Seven children were born to their marriage, five of whom are living. They are: Clarke, born February 14, 1894, who married Ruth Sines; Kenneth, born March 6, 1896, who married Ethel Fink; Aubrey, born April 14, 1898, who married Effie Mecham; Stanley, born June 24, 1900, who married Myrtle Wisecup, and who died September 2, 1930; Dwight, born June 19, 1899, who died August 2, 1899; Ralph, born September 15, 1901, who married Opal Cryle; and Kathryn, born August 26, 1905, who married Roy Vernon Dwinell.

Mr. McKee is an honorary member of the Veterans of the Foreign Wars in recognition of his having five sons in the World War. He is a member of the Eastern Star and the Masons. He is affiliated with the Palmyra Presbyterian Church. During the World War Mr. McKee was active in all war work in his county. Residence: Palmyra.

Neal Patrick McKee

One of the outstanding professional men at Atkinson, Nebraska, is Neal Patrick McKee who has engaged in the practice of medicine in that community since 1914. He was born at Willow Island, Nebraska, January 16, 1890, the son of Charles and Mary Anne (McMullan) McKee. His father, a farmer, was born in Ireland, came to this country in 1872, and died at Willow Island, April 30, 1905. His mother was born in Ireland and died at Willow Island, September 22, 1908.

Dr. McKee was graduated from the high school at Cozad, Nebraska, in 1907, and received the M. D. degree at Creighton Medical College in 1914 where he was a member of Phi Beta Phi and was active in baseball. He is president of the Atkinson Commercial Club, is a member of the Nebraska State Medical Society and the American Medical Society, and is affiliated with St. Joseph's Catholic Church of Atkinson. He served as first lieutenant in the Medical Corps of the United States Army from 1917 to 1919, and is now vice state commander of the American Legion, having served as post commander at one time.

On January 9, 1918, he was married at Atlanta, Georgia, to Oliva Zoe Sturdevant, who was born at Atkinson, March 9, 1891. Their children are: Mary Ellen,

born August 22, 1920; and Neal S., born April 5, 1924. Residence: Atkinson. (Photograph on Page 801).

James Albert McKeeman

James Albert McKeeman has served as minister of Congregational Churches in Nebraska for the past 13 years and in Ainsworth for the past five years. He was born at Allerton, Iowa, January 29, 1882, the son of Madison Evans and Mary (Beasley) McKeeman, the former a farmer who was born of Scotch-Irish parentage in Ohio, January 10, 1848. His mother was born in Iowa in 1857 and died at Medford, Oklahoma, in July, 1916.

Mr. McKeeman attended rural school in Grant County, Oklahoma, was graduated from the Medford High School in 1904, received the A. B. degree at Kingfisher College in Oklahoma in 1911, and was awarded the B. D. degree at Hartford Theological Seminary in Hartford, Connecticut in 1914. He served as president of his senior class in college, was a member of the college football team at Kingfisher College, and in 1910 received the winning medal in the intercollegiate oratorical contest held in Oklahoma City.

He was ordained to the ministry at Medford, Oklahoma, in 1914, and has been active in both religious and civic affairs in Connecticutt, Oklahoma, and Nebraska. Mr. McKeeman was pastor at Geneva, Nebraska, 1919-23; at Blair 1923-25; at Waverly, Iowa, 1925-27; and since that time at Ainsworth. He is affiliated with the Elkhorn Valley Association of Congregational Churches of which he was moderator in 1927 and 1928, is a member of the Ainsworth Chamber of Commerce, and holds membership in the Masons and Odd Fellows.

For eight months during the World War Mr. McKeeman served in the Young Men's Christian Association. He was married to Evelyn M. Atkins at Stillwater, Oklahoma, July 13, 1914. Mrs. McKeeman, who aids her husband in her religious activities, was born at Niles, Kansas, February 2, 1885. She is descended from Rufus Putnam of Revolutionary fame and is eligible to the Colonial Dames and the Daughters of the American Revolution. Their three children are Katherine Louise, born April 21, 1917; James Madison, August 13, 1921; and Robert Lewis, born January 28, 1924. Residence: Ainsworth.

William Thomas McKelvey

William Thomas McKelvey, prominent farmer and stockman, was born in Martinsville, Illinois, February 17, 1857, son of Patrick and Mary (Campbell) McKelvey.

His father was born in County Donegal, Ireland, July 19, 1819, and died at Martinsville, December 29, 1881. His wife, Mary was born in Ohio, June 22, 1827, and died at Bayard, Nebraska, June 27, 1918.

Mr. McKelvey attended public school in Clark County, Illinois and for many years was a farmer and stockman. He is now retired. He is a stockholder of the First National Bank of Bayard. In 1908 at the time of the organization of Morrill County, he served as county commissioner two terms, elected on a Republican ticket. He was county chairman of the Young Men's Christian Association drive during the World War, is affiliated with the Methodist Episcopal Church, and is an Odd Fellow.

On December 25, 1892, he was married to Elizabeth Jane Webb at Martinsville, Illinois, her birthplace. She was born July 6, 1862, and died at Bayard, May 31, 1931. Mrs. McKelvey was a teacher before her marriage. She is the daughter of Isaac and Persis (Waren) Webb, who lived in Ohio before moving to Illinois. Residence: Bayard.

Samuel McKelvie

Since 1879 Samuel McKelvie has been a resident of Nebraska where he has been prominent for many years as a successful farmer. He was born at Tuscarawas Coun-

NEAL PATRICK McKEE

ty, Ohio, August 6, 1849, the son of Samuel and Jane (Sharon) McKelvie. His father, a farmer, was born and grew to manhood at Locknaw-by-Stranraur, Scotland, and in 1840 came to America where he settled in Ohio. He was married in 1844 to Jane (Sharon) McKelvie who was born in Tuscarawas County; he died in Schuyler County, Illinois, August, 1872.

Jane (Sharon) McKelvie was a typical pioneer mother and homemaker who wove her children's clothes from unfinished flax and lived through the various hardships common to early settlers. Her ancestors, the Eatons, were Ohio people who moved to Illinois about 1850. She died in Schuyer County.

Mr. McKelvie attended a rural school, and later was a student in normal school for a time. He taught in country schools for 12 terms. It is interesting to note that in 1923 the University of Nebraska presented him with a diploma in recognition of the interest he has taken in livestock and agriculture in Nebraska. Only seven other persons have been so recognized.

He has been a farmer and purebred stock grower and for over 36 years has been a member of the board of directors of the Standard Poland-China Record Association. He has been a member of the local school board for 15 years, and for 60 years has held membership in the Odd Fellows; he is the only charter member of Lodge Number 128 who is living today.

His marriage to Jane Belinda Glandon was solemnized in Schuyer County, December 25, 1872. Mrs. McKelvie, who was a devoted wife and home maker, was born in Ohio and died in Clay County, February 1919. They have nine children: Homer L., born May 27, 1874, who married Mary Hayes; Otis A., born February 19. 1876; Othello, born May 27, 1877; Samuel Roy, born April 15, 1881; Jennie Maud, born October 7, 1883; Hiram Claud, born October 11, 1884; Pearl, born July 13, 1886; Florence, born September 22, 1888; and Floyd, born December 26, 1889.

Mr. McKelvie has written his memoirs in a book *Seventy Five Years a Farmer,* originally published in the *Nebraska Farmer.* It is interesting both as a personal record and as a history of pioneer Nebraska. He is a Methodist. For the past 50 years he has exhibited livestock at fairs and exhibitions throughout the country. Residence: Fairfield.

Samuel R. McKelvie

Samuel R. McKelvie was born at Fairfield, Nebraska, April 15, 1881, son of Samuel and Jennie (Glandon) McKelvie.

On June 19, 1904, he was married to Flossie DeArnold at Table Rock, Nebraska.

From 1902 until 1905 Mr. McKelvie was with the Bee Publishing Company, and in 1905 became owner of the *Nebraska Farmer* of which he is president.

Mr. McKelvie served as a member of the Nebraska House of Representatives, 1911-13, was lieutenant governor of Nebraska, 1913-15, and governor of Nebraska, 1919-23. President Hoover appointed him a member of the Federal Farm Board in July, 1929. He retired in June, 1931.

He is a Republican, a Methodist, a Mason, and an Odd Fellow. He is also a member of the Elks, the Chamber of Commerce, the Chicago Athletic Club, and the Hamilton Club (Chicago). Residence: Lincoln.

Ferdinand W. McKenzie

Born in Nebraska, October 27, 1897, Ferd W. McKenzie is the son of Loyd Thomas and Catherine Mary (Wiedel) McKenzie. His father, who was born in Somerset County, Pennsylvania, December 11, 1873, is a dairy and poultry farmer. His ancestry is Scotch-Irish. Catherine Mary Wiedel was born at Sauk City, Wisconsin, April 15, 1878, of German parentage.

Mr. McKenzie attended Sacred Heart Parochial School at Hebron, and for some time engaged in farming. Later he was a baker, and thereafter worked in a grocery store. For some years he has been the proprietor of the Standard Market, and has engaged in livestock buying.

On July 29, 1919, he was united in marriage to Agnes Ellen Lockhart at Orleans, Nebraska, her birthplace. Mrs. McKenzie was born June 6, 1897. There are three children, Duane, born November 6, 1920; Virginia, born October 30, 1924, and Paul, born August 12, 1928.

Mr. McKenzie is a Democrat. He attends Sacred Heart Church, is a member of the Knights of Columbus, and was grand knight 1923-24. At the present time he is president of the Kiwanis Club. He is a member of the Hebron Commercial Club and The Nebraskana Society. Residence: Hebron.

Jesse William McKerney

Jesse William McKerney, live stock broker, was born at Bayard, Iowa, July 31, 1889, son of Bernard F. and Jessie Hamilton (Newlin) McKerney. Bernard, the father, a native of New York City, was born August 15, 1855, of Scotch-Irish descent. At the time of his death at Seattle, Washington, October 24, 1931, he was retired. Jesse Hamilton Newlin, born at Mendota, Illinois, July 1, 1858, died at Clarinda, Iowa, January 19, 1927. Her ancestry was French and Irish.

Educated in the public schools of Clarinda, Iowa, Jesse William McKerney soon entered the banking business, in which he remained until 1922. At the present time he is a member of the firm of Henline & Son and the Kearney Live Stock Company, both of Kearney.

His marriage to Lulu Blanche Henline was solemnized at Grand Island, January 3, 1914. Mrs. McKerney was born at Kearney, June 7, 1890. There are three children Bernard Franklyn, born January 13, 1915; Betty Jayne, born April 21, 1916; and Jesse William, born March 2, 1918. All are high school students.

Mr. McKerney is a Republican. He is a member of all Masonic bodies including the Shrine, is affiliated with the Methodist Episcopal Church, is a member of the Chamber of Commerce, the Kearney Country Club and the Nebraskana Society. His favorite sport is golf and his hobby is mechanics. Residence: Kearney.

Alexander McKie, Jr.

Alexander McKie is a native of Glasgow, Scotland, born July 23, 1903. His father, Alexander McKie, was born at Barrhill, Ayrshire, Scotland, April 22, 1876, and came to America May 5, 1910, where he is engaged in the real estate business. He brought to America with him his wife, Grace McCracken Galt, who was born at Barrhill, October 21, 1875.

Alexander, Jr., was graduated from Central High School in 1920, and attended Creighton University 1920-22. He received his A. B. from the University of Nebraska in 1924, and his LL. B. in 1926. President of Pi Kappa Alpha, 1925-26, and Ivy Day orator, 1926, he was president of the University Y. M. C. A., and a member of the varsity debate team at the University of Nebraska. He is a member of Delta Sigma Rho and Phi Delta Phi and of Scabbard and Blade.

Mr. McKie is a member of the firm of Finlayson, Burke & McKie. He was coach of debate at Creighton Preparatory School 1927-29, and at Omaha University 1929-30. He is professor of business law at the University of Omaha, and professor, University of Omaha Night Law School. A Republican, he was unsuccessful candidate for the state legislature from the 19th district.

During the World War he was a member of the R. O. T. C.; attended Reserve Officers Camp in 1928 and was instructor in Citizens Military Training Camp in 1929. He holds rank of first lieutenant in the Field Artillery Reserves.

He is a member of the Omaha, Nebraska State and

American Bar Associations, and has been elected president of the Barristers Club of Omaha for the term 1930-31. He is a member of Clifton Hill Presbyterian Church, a Mason and member of the Royal Arcanum, and is also a member of the Chamber of Commerce and of the Nebraskana Society. His club is the University, his sport is riding, and his recreation is reading. Residence: Omaha.

Sherman William McKinley, Jr.

Sherman William McKinley, Jr., lawyer, was born at Homer, Nebraska, November 11, 1901, son of Sherman William and Josie (Smith) McKinley, Sr. His father, a native of Illinois, was born May 27, 1879, and is county judge of Dakota County. His mother was born in Marcus, Iowa, June 18, 1882.

Mr. McKinley was graduated from the Sioux City, Iowa, High School in 1918, and received his A. B. from Morningside College in 1922. In 1925 he was awarded his LL. B. from the University of Nebraska, and is a member of Phi Gamma Delta and Phi Delta Phi.

Upon his admission to the bar, Mr. McKinley entered upon the active practice of his profession, and practices at Sioux City, Iowa, and South Sioux City, Nebraska. He is a Republican and a member of the Boals Methodist Church at South Sioux City. He is also a Mason and a member of The Nebraskana Society.

On July 5, 1930, he was united in marriage to Grace Harlan, at Lincoln. Residence South Sioux City.

Robert Lee McKissick

Robert L. McKissick was born at McKittrick, Montgomery County, Missouri, February 2, 1899. James S. McKissick, his father, was born at Fayette, Missouri, of Irish parentage. He was a merchant and railroad man. Ida Julia (Gruber) McKissick, his mother, who was born at McKittrick, was the owner and manager of a general merchandise store. Her ancestry is German.

Mr. McKissick received his education in the public and high schools of McKittrick. He has lived in Nebraska since 1917 and has held the following positions: telegraph agent in various towns of the St. Louis division of the M-K-T Railway, 1916-17; telegrapher and dispatcher in various towns of the Wymore division of the C. B. & Q. Railway, and since 1922 has been a farmer and stockman at Dunbar, Nebraska. He is at the present time vice president of the Farmers' Elevator Company at Dunbar. He also is an auctioneer.

On December 27, 1920, he married Pearl W. Knabe at Nebraska City, Otoe County, Nebraska. Mrs. McKissick was born at Nebraska City, November 26, 1899. They have one daughter, Arlene, born February 9, 1925.

He is a Royal Arch Mason, a member of the Dunbar Community Club and the Nebraskana Society. Since 1926 he has been treasurer of school district Number 11. Politically, Mr. McKissick is an Independent. His favorite sports are baseball, golf and racing. His hobby is reading. Residence: Dunbar.

Archie L. McLaurin

Archie L. McLaurin was born on a farm in Bruce County, Ontario, Canada, May 29, 1859. After completing his elementary education he was graduated from Tiverton High School at Tiverton, Ontario, Canada.

His father, Alexander McLaurin was born on a farm in Glengary County, Ontario, Canada, in the year 1827. Archie McLaurin, father of Alexander, came from Perthshire, Scotland, to this country June 15, 1815, the day of the Battle of Waterloo, and died in 1874 at the age of one hundred and two years. He farmed until his death at Tiverton on June 29, 1902.

Mary (McLaren) McLaurin, wife of Alexander, was of Scotch descent. She was born in Glengary County, Ontario, May 26, 1828, and died at Tiverton, July 23, 1918.

Archie L. McLaurin married Jennie Mary Campbell,

born at Maxwell, Ontario, August 26, 1864, and who died in Fairbury, Nebraska, August 26, 1926. Before her marriage she was a school teacher. To them was born one son, Colin C., on September 26, 1893, who is married to Clard Siders. He, with his father, is in the harness, saddlery, and shoe business, the oldest firm in Fairbury, known as McLaurin and Son. Mr. McLaurin has been in this business since June 21, 1888.

He is a Republican. A resident of Nebraska for forty-three years, he is a member of the first Baptist Church of Fairbury. He is a Modern Woodman of America and an Elk. Hiking is his favorite sport, and welfare work in Fairbury is his hobby. Residence: Fairbury.

John McLellan

John McLellan was born at Glasgow, Scotland, September 11, 1864, the son of James and Helen (Kelly) McLellan. His father, who was a farmer, was born at Glasgow, and in 1869 came to America where he settled in Illinois; he died at McAllister, Oklahoma, in 1815. His mother, whose father was a merchant in Scotland, was born in that country and died in Logan County, Illinois, in 1810.

Mr. McLellan attended business college in 1889, and for over 26 years was engaged in the mercantile business. He is now a real estate and insurance man at Grand Island. A Republican, he served as representative in the Nebraska Legislature from 1919-29, with the exception of 1923, and has always been extremely active in political affairs. He is a member of the Chamber of Commerce, Red Cross, Ancient Order of United Workmen in which he is a director, the Masons and Elks. He is a member of the board of directors of the Young Men's Christian Association, is an elder in the First Presbyterian Church of Grand Island, and holds membership in the Nebraskana Society.

His hobbies are horse races and reading. On December 18, 1892, he was married to Belle Jhunkie at Brookfield, Missouri. Mrs. McLellan, whose family has been prominent in the south for generations, was born at Knoxville, Tennessee, February 9, 1872. Their four children are: Agnes, born October 25, 1893, who married D. Williams; Myrtle, born November 9, 1896, who married Russell Halderman; John, born November 4, 1899; and Paul, born August 4, 1910. John is a revenue collector and Paul is a drafter in the highway department for the state of Nebraska. Residence: Grand Island.

Edward McLernon

Edward McLernon, who was born at Belfast, Ireland, October 24, 1849, is the son of John and Margaret McLernon. His father, who was a livestock broker, was a native of Scotland, and his mother lived in northern Ireland.

Mr. McLernon taught school in Ireland until 1869, was a teacher in Jersey City, New Jersey, for a year taught in the schools of Baltimore, 1870-74, and of Sidney, Nebraska, 1876-79. From 1881 to 1903 he engaged in the general merchandise business at Sidney, and from 1903 to 1911 was postmaster there. He has engaged in farming since 1911.

He is president of the Cheyenne County Historical Society, is affiliated with the Church of Christ at Sidney, and holds membership in the Nebraskana Society. His hobby is reading. He has written several articles on irrigation, the first one being in 1885, the main publication being the *Lodge Pole Valley*, and is still interested in developing irrigation in this district.

Of his marriage to Emma Johnson, which occurred at Fort Dodge, Iowa, March 21, 1891, two children were born: Irene, March 14, 1892; and John, April 7, 1898. Irene married C. F. Consigny, an executive of the Great Western Sugar Company of Denver, Colorado. John was graduated from the University of Arizona and teaches at a co-agricultural school at Young, Arizona.

Mr. McLernon has been a member of the Republican party since 1872 when he cast his first vote for Grant, and has voted for every Republican candidate for president since that year. Residence: Sidney.

Charles Gilbert McMahon

One of Nebraska's prominent surgeons is Charles Gilbert McMahon, of Brodstone Memorial Hospital at Superior. He was born at Peabody, Massachusetts, in 1880, the son of Thomas and Anna Josephine (Kelly) McMahon. Dr. McMahon received his early education in the public school at Adrian, Minnesota. He was a student at the University of Minnesota for two years in the pre-medical department, and in 1906 was awarded the M. D. degree there. He was elected to Nu Sigma Nu.

He was assistant surgeon in the Adams Hospital at Hibbing, Minnesota, for a time, acted as assistant chief surgeon for Miami Inspiration Hospital, at Miami, Arizona, was chief surgeon for the Tennessee Copper Company, and for 10 years has been chief surgeon at Brodstone Memorial Hospital at Superior. Dr. McMahon is the author of various articles on surgical subjects published in *Annals of Surgery, Tennessee State Medical Journal*, and *Nebraska State Medical Journal*.

He holds a fellowship in the American College of Surgeons, is a member of the Superior Kiwanis Club, and is a member of the Nebraskana Society. His political affiliation is with the Republican party. In 1907, Dr. Mahon married Grace Martha Cooper at Adrian, Minnesota. They have a daughter, Herma Wilhelmine, who was born in 1912; she is a student at the University of Nebraska. Residence: Superior.

Patrick Joseph McManus

Patrick Joseph McManus, general merchant at Valentine for the past forty-one years, was born at Benton, Wisconsin, October 27, 1860, son of Patrick and Ellen (Cassady) McManus.

His father was born in Ireland, came to America in 1854, and died at O'Neill, Nebraska, June 27, 1890. His mother, also born in Ireland, died at O'Neill January 12, 1902.

Mr. McManus is a member of the Red Cross and St. Patrick's Catholic Church. He is a Democrat. Residence: O'Neill.

Charles McMartin

Charles McMartin, educator and physician of Omaha, was born in Crawford County, Iowa, May 11, 1880. His father, Archibald McIntyre McMartin, who was a farmer, was born at Johnstown, New York, August 16, 1847, and died at Long Beach, California, November 9, 1928; his Scotch ancestors came to America before the Revolution. His mother, Harriet Amelia (Smith) McMartin, was born at Chelsea, Massachusetts, September 6, 1849, and died at Dunlap, Iowa, May 22, 1902. Her English ancestors were in America prior to the Revolution.

Dr. McMartin was graduated from Grinnell Academy at Grinnell, Iowa, in 1898; was awarded the Bachelor of Philosophy at Grinnell College in 1902; received his M. D. at Rush Medical College in 1906; and was a student at the University of Vienna in 1910. He has been engaged in the practice of medicine and surgery at Omaha since 1907; specializing in skin and urinary diseases. Since 1910 he has been professor of skin and genito-urinary diseases at Creighton Medical College.

He is married to Mary Elizabeth O'Kelly; she was born at Dublin, Ireland. They have one daughter, Harriet Margaret, born September 26, 1912. Dr. McMartin is a member of the Omaha-Douglas County Medical Society; the State Medical Association; the American Medical Association; and the American Urological Association. He is a member of the Omaha University Club; the Omaha Athletic Club; and the Omaha Country Club. He is a member of Lininger Lodge of the Masons, Scottish Rite, and Shrine; is affiliated with the First Central Congregational Church of Omaha; and is a Republican. Residence: Omaha

James Lloyd McMaster

J. Lloyd McMaster, legislator, lawyer and executive, was born in Hall County, Nebraska, November 13, 1888, son of Anderson Fremont and Margaret Alice (Stewart) McMaster. The former was a native of Iowa, a farmer and carpenter.

Upon the completion of his work at Central City High School in 1909, Mr. McMaster entered the University of Nebraska, receiving the degree of LL. B. in 1916. He received a letter in track 1913-14, and was a member, captain and winner of a letter in the Nebraska cross country team 1914.

He was married to Dessie Ellen Collins, who was born in Marshalltown, Iowa, October 28, 1888, on September 21, 1916. To them three children were born, Margaret Ellen, born March 6, 1918; J. Lloyd, Jr., born August 2, 1919, and Collins S., born March 3, 1921.

Mr. McMaster is a Republican and served as a member of the House of Representatives 1925-27, during which he was chairman of the judiciary committee and speaker pro tem in 1927. He is engaged in the practice of law and is president and director of the following: Western Good Roads Service Company, Nebraska Neon Company, and Iowa Flexlume Neon Company.

During the World War he served as chairman of the Lancaster County War Savings Stamp committee. He served as first secretary of the Lincoln post of the Reserve Officers Association. He is past commander of the Lincoln Camp of the Sons of Union Veterans. As a member of the Optimist International he was first president of the local organization and district governor of the 10th district 1929, 30, 31.

Mr. McMaster is a member of Grace Methodist Episcopal Church, the Nebraska State Bar Association, the Red Cross and the Masonic Order. In the last mentioned he is a member of the Scottish Rite and Shrine bodies. His sports are hiking and camping, and his hobby is boys' work. Residence: Lincoln.

Kenneth McMeen

Kenneth McMeen, a merchant at Lynch, Nebraska, has lived in this state for the past 30 years. He was born at Mount Vernon, Illinois, May 24, 1896, the son of James F. and Mattie J. McMeen. His father, a merchant, died at Gregory, South Dakota, in 1923.

Mr. McMeen was graduated from the Gregory High School in 1913, and during 1914-15 studied at Yankton College, Yankton, South Dakota. He is affiliated with the Methodist Church of Lynch, is active in the American Legion, and holds membership in the Nebraskana Society. During the World War he served as corporal in Headquarters Company 337 Field Artillery of the American Expeditionary Forces.

On March 16, 1920, he married Phyllis Alford at Pierce, Nebraska. Mrs. McMeen was born at Monowi, Nebraska, July 14, 1896. Residence: Lynch.

Duncan McMillan

Duncan McMillan, city treasurer of Chadron, was born at Tarbert, Scotland, November 21, 1869, son of Alexander and Misey (McDougal) McMillan. The father was born and died in Scotland, while the mother was born in Scotland, and died at Crawford, December 12, 1898. Her father was a farmer.

Mr. McMillan attended public school, and for more

than 30 years has been a merchant. At the present time he is serving as city treasurer. He is a Republican.

On November 4, 1897, he was married to Vida Bee Brockway at Crawford. She was born in Wisconsin, December 27, 1878, and her family have been in America for four generations. Mrs. McMillan in a member of the Eastern Star and the Woman's Club. She is the daughter of Herman and Ellen (Blackburn) Brockway. There are four children, Ellen, born August 4, 1898, who is a graduate of the University of Nebraska, and at present is department supervisor in Macey's Department Store in New York City; Misey, born March 13, 1900; Roy, born November 1, 1903; and Vida, born May 31, 1906.

Mr. McMillan is affiliated with the Congregational Church, is a member and secretary of the Chamber of Commerce, and a member of the Red Cross and the Masons. He is serving as treasurer of the local school board at the present time, and is a member of the Young Men's Christian Association. Residence: Chadron.

Eleanor Tynan McMullen

Of pioneer parentage, Eleanor T. McMullen was born at Peru, Nemaha County, Nebraska, June 30, 1870. Her father, Andrew Tynan, who was born at Kilkenney, Ireland, March 8, 1833, and died at Stella, Richardson County, Nebraska, June 15, 1912, was a pioneer homesteader and freighter. He saw and engaged in many interesting events and liked to tell stories of early Nebraska history.

Her mother, Ellen Jane Richardson, was born at Washington, Washington County, Pennsylvania, April 9, 1846. She was a student at the Peru College, before it was a normal school, and has been a teacher, homemaker and clubwoman. She resides in Lincoln, Nebraska.

Mrs. McMullen was educated in country schools and in the convent at Nebraska City, Nebraska. She studied teacher's training at Peru State Teachers' College for two years, and later was a student at the preparatory school of the University of Nebraska for two years. She has taught a country school; taught city grade work and high school classes, staying in the teaching profession for nine years; and for 35 years has been engaged in club work of various kinds.

She was united in marriage with Alexander Rankin McMullen at Stella, June 14, 1893. Mr. McMullen, who was born at Penn Run, Indiana County, Pennsylvania, December 6, 1862, is a farmer. Four children were born to them, three of whom are living: Mildred, born May 3, 1896, who died June 9, 1904; Richard, born December 29, 1903, a graduate of Iowa State College, who married Jessamine Hinds; Joseph, born August 24, 1906, who attended the Kansas Agricultural College at Manhattan, for two years; and Philip, born August 24, 1906, who is a graduate of the Kansas Agricultural College. All the children live on farms today.

Mrs. McMullen is a member of the Woman's Club and the Nebraskana Society. She is a member of the Eastern Star, and is affiliated with the community church of Stella, where she has been president of the church society and a member of the church council. She is a Republican. Writing letters, motoring, and reading are her hobbies. Residence: Stella.

Frederick Walter McNally

Born at Schuyler, Nebraska, June 1, 1887, Frederick Walter McNally is the son of William M. and Susannah Jane (Harris) McNally. His father, a farmer and a veteran of the Civil War, was born in County Langford, Ireland, July 12, 1847, and died at Schuyler, December 13, 1904; he came to this country on the ship *Old Ironsides* as a small boy. His mother, who was born at LaFayette, Indiana, January 6, 1847, and died at O'Neill, Nebraska, February 6, 1931, was the daughter of Benjamin Harris, a soldier in the Civil War.

Mr. McNally was graduated from Fremont Normal School in 1908, and for several years was engaged in

farming in Holt County, Nebraska. He is owner and manager of the O'Neill Gas & Oil Company now. A Democrat, he served as precinct assessor of Colfax County and was township treasurer from 1919 to 1922. He is vice president of the Lions Club at O'Neill and is affiliated with the St. Patrick's Catholic Church, acting as warden of the Knights of Columbus. His favorite sport is baseball.

On January 24, 1911, he was married to Emma Belle Webster at Schuyler, Nebraska. Mrs. McNally was born at Platte Center, Nebraska, February 6, 1885, the daughter of James and Margaret Ellen Webster. Their children are: James, born August 24, 1912; Doris, born October 24, 1913; Bernard, born June 26, 1919; and Betty, born May 4, 1923. James was graduated from St. Mary's College in 1931 where he was prominent in athletic events, and is now bookkeeper for the O'Neill Gas & Oil Company. Residence: O'Neill. (Photograph on Page 806).

Charles John McNamara

Charles John McNamara, civil engineer, was born at North Platte, Nebraska, August 27, 1880. He is the son of Michael and Mary (Keliher) McNamara, both natives of Kerry County, Ireland. The father was born November 15, 1847, and died at Peoria, Illinois, October 27, 1902. The mother was born April 15, 1849, and is still living at Peoria, Illinois.

Upon his graduation from elementary school at North Platte, Mr. McNamara entered North Platte High School, from which he was graduated in 1897. In February, 1906, he received the degree of Bachelor of Science in Civil Engineering from the University of Nebraska. There he was a member of Sigma Tau, Kappa Sigma, and Acacia.

From 1900 until 1912 he was civil engineer with the Union Pacific Railroad. Since May, 1912, he has been engaged in construction work, and the practice of civil engineering at North Platte.

On October 14, 1908, he was married to Rita Sally Clark at Omaha. She was born at Dunlap, Iowa, May 9, 1885. They have one son, Charles, born July 11, 1909, in Omaha, Nebraska. He was graduated with honors from the University of Nebraska, in June, 1931, with a Bachelor of Science degree in Civil Engineering. He is a member of Sigma Xi, and also Delta Sigma Lambda.

Mr. McNamara is a member of the Methodist Episcopal Church, the Chamber of Commerce, the Masons and Odd Fellows, the American Society of Civil Engineers, and the Nebraskana Society. He is a Republican. Residence: North Platte.

John G. McNamara

John G. McNamara was born at Wisner, Nebraska, March 1, 1872, the son of James and Margaret (Carpenter) McNamara, and has lived in this state all his life. His father, who is a farmer and stockman, was born at Mayo, Ireland, October 30, 1843, and came to America in 1861. His mother was born at Carlow, Ireland, August 7, 1852, and died at Wisner, April 1, 1909. She came to this country in 1868.

Rev. McNamara was graduated from Quincy College in 1892 and in 1897 completed a philosophical and theological course at Mount St. Mary's Seminary at Cincinnati, Ohio, having been admitted to this institution after submitting testimonials that he had satisfactorily completed a classical course in college. Since the above mentioned schools did not award degrees he was given a certificate to show he had received the education necessary for an A. M. and Ph. D. degree.

He was ordained to the ministry by the Right Rev. Richard Scannell at Omaha, Nebraska, March 4, 1897. He has been pastor of the Bloomfield parish for the past 31 years and is dean of the Bloomfield St. Andrews Church, and rector of that institution. Residence: Bloomfield.

O'Neill Photo Company—O'Neill

FREDERICK WALTER McNALLY

James A. McPherrin

James A. McPherrin was born at Knoxville, Illinois, December 19, 1858. George McPherrin, his father, who was a farmer, was born in Champagne County, Ohio, December 12, 1826, and died at Clarinda, Iowa, February 1, 1905. His mother, Eliza (Cherry) McPherrin was born in Rock Island County, Illinois, April 27, 1835, and died at Clarinda, November 12, 1914.

A resident of Nebraska for 38 years, Mr. McPherrin attended the country schools after which he was in the poultry, butter and egg exchange business for five years. For twenty years he engaged in the implement and coal retail business. For several years his chief activity has been farm work and flock feeding. Mr. McPherrin is a Republican and a member of the Masons and Odd Fellows.

He was married at Clarinda, June 16, 1892, to Myrtle Ray, who was born at Clarinda, February 5, 1868, and died at Tecumseh, Johnson County, Nebraska, August 7, 1892. Residence: Tecumseh.

Ralph Vern McPherson

For the past 53 years Ralph V. McPherson has lived in Nebraska and has taken part in the civic and welfare work of his community. He was born at Clearfield, Clearfield County, Pennsylvania, October 28, 1873, the son of John Hoyt and Hannah Jane (Hancock) McPherson. His father, who was a lumberman and farmer, was born at Clearfield, June 26, 1847, and died at Craig, Burt County, Nebraska, July 18, 1930; he was of Scotch descent. His mother, who was a teacher for a time before her marriage, was born at Clearfield, October 13, 1847, and died at Craig, September 18, 1911; her ancestry was Scotch-Irish.

Mr. McPherson received his education in the public schools of Nebraska. He engaged in farming in Burt County for many years; was postmaster at Craig from 1913 to 1922; has been president of the Craig Telephone Company for six years; and is one of the seven directors of the Farmers Union Corporation at Craig.

During the late war Mr. McPherson was active in loan drives. He was at one time president of the Commercial Club; has been a member of the Masons since 1899; and holds membership in the Nebraskana Society. Politically, he is a Democrat. He is affiliated with the Methodist Church, and is a member of the Red Cross.

His marriage to Flora Luella Loomis was solemnized in Burt County, October 1, 1902. Mrs. McPherson was born in Burt County, October 16, 1875, and is a descendant of Joseph Loomis who came from England to America in 1639. Residence: Craig. (Photograph in Album).

John McPhillips

Born at Darlington, Wisconsin, April 20, 1864, John McPhillips is the son of Thomas and Catherine (Lynch) McPhillips. His father, who is a farmer, was born in Monahan County, Ireland, and died in Platte County, Nebraska, October 8, 1888. His mother was born in County Monahan and died in Platte County in 1890.

Mr. McPhillips has been a resident of Nebraska for the past 61 years, and is moderator of the school board at Lindsay. He is affiliated with St. John's Catholic Church and has been a member of the township for 20 years and the school board for 33 years. He has been successful as a farmer in Platte County.

His marriage to Dina Donahy occurred at Omaha, February 4, 1902. Mrs. McPhillips, whose parents were farmers, was born in County Cook, Ireland, January 29, 1873. Six children were born to them: Thomas, June 29, 1903, who died February 13, 1904; Margaret, January 16, 1904, who died March 31, 1907; Elizabeth, October 12, 1905; Charles, May 11, 1908; Cecelia, May 8, 1910; Theresa, February 2, 1912. Residence: Lindsay.

James McQuillen

James McQuillen, one of Dixon County's most progressive farmers, was born at Ponca, February 26, 1876. The son of an Irish immigrant to America, Peter McQuillen, is a true lover of the soil. Peter McQuillen, who was born in Cerreck Macrosse, Monahan County, Ireland April 12, 1838, came to the United States in 1860, settling in Nebraska. Peter McQuillen married Catherine Mairon, who was also born in Cerreck Macrosse, on June 12, 1840. He died at Ponca, on August 10, 1883, and she on May 24, 1910.

Educated in rural schools, James McQuillen entered farming as a boy, and during his fifty-five years' residence has met with much success in his chosen field. He has always taken an active part in Republican politics in his locality, and served as director of the Martinsburg School Board for twelve years. He is a member of St. Paul's Catholic Church, and the Nebraskana Society.

On July 23, 1912, he was married to Mary O'Connor, at Ponca. A native of that city, Mrs. McQuillen was born March 26, 1878, of Irish parentage. To them were born two children: Mary, born May 10, 1913, and James, born April 8, 1915. Residence: Ponca.

Duncan Armour McQuiston

Duncan A. McQuiston was born in Calhoun County, Iowa, October 3, 1883, the son of Donald and Ann (Armour) McQuiston. His father, a farmer, was born in Argyleshire, Scotland, and in his boyhood came to America, where he acquired a thousand acre tract of land; he died at Pender, Nebraska, in November, 1917. His mother was born at Argyleshire, March 29, 1879, and died at Bloomfield, Nebraska, January 22, 1930.

Mr. McQuiston has been a farmer in Thurston County for many years, and is now president of the Farmers Co-operative Grain Association at Walthill. He is serving as vice president of the Thurston County Co-operative Service Company, is secretary-treasurer of the Thurston County Farm Bureau, and is treasurer of the local school board. He is the author of Christening O' the Bairnie.

His marriage to Mary Ann Duncan was solemnized at Bloomfield, April 7, 1909. Mrs. McQuiston was born at Campbelltown, Argyleshire, Scotland, September 9, 1887. Their children are: Kathryn Ann, born August 14, 1921; and Donald Duncan, born February 15, 1925.

Mr. McQuiston is a member of the Red Cross, Masons, the Captain of Walthill Home Guard, and the Nebraskana Society. He is interested in baseball, while his hobbies are: impersonation; writing poetry; and patenting. He is independent, politically. Residence: Walthill.

William McQuiston

William McQuiston was born at Stillman, Illinois, June 8, 1875, the son of Donald and Ann (Armour) McQuiston. His father, a farmer, who was born at Campletown, Scotland, April 7, 1848, and died at Pender, was of Scotch descent. His mother, whose Scotch ancestors were successful farmers, was born at Campeltown, April 29, 1847, and died at Bloomfield, Nebraska, January 22, 1929. She was a talented musician.

Mr. McQuiston has been a farmer in Thurston County for over thirty years. He is a member of the Nebraskana Society, is affiliated with the Pender Presbyterian Church, and is an independent. His hobby is reading.

He was married to Margaret McCarkindale at Odelbolt, Iowa, February 16, 1904; she was born at Odebolt, June 7, 1882, of Scotch descent. To this marriage nine children were born: Mary Lucille, born February 2, 1905; Edward Wallace, born January 5, 1907; Margaret Ann, born October 1, 1908, who married Sigfried Jacob North; Kathryn Mae, born May 13, 1910; Lloyd Donald, born December 8, 1912; William Gladstone, born March 2, 1914; Helen Marr, born May 5, 1915; Jean Francis, born

November 5, 1915; and Betty Lavonne, born March 20, 1923. Residence: Pender.

Hugh Gamble McVicker

Hugh Gamble McVicker, night editor of the *State Journal* at Lincoln, has lived in Nebraska since 1887. He was born on a farm in Carroll County, Ohio, April 27, 1864, the son of Robert and Margaret (McKee) McVicker. His father, who was born in County Antrim, Ireland, in 1820 and died at Fremont, Dodge County, Nebraska, September, 1893, was a commission merchant, farmer, real estate man, and insurance agent; he was a Union soldier in the Civil War; his Scotch Irish ancestors were engaged in the linen trade.

His mother was born on a farm in County Down, Ireland, December, 1825, and died at Peru, Nemaha County, Nebraska, March 1875. Her ancestry was Scotch, Irish, and English; two of her brothers were United Presbyterian missionaries in India for many years.

Mr. McVicker received his elementary education in country district schools and was a student at the teachers college at Peru, Nebraska, for a time. He has lived in this state continuously since 1887 and is now night editor of the *State Journal*. During the recent war he was a member of the Lincoln Home Guards. He is a Mason, a Republican, Modern Woodmen, and a member of the Lincoln Chamber of Commerce.

He was united in marriage at Lincoln, Lancaster County, Nebraska, December 7, 1892, to Lauretta Annie Harris. Mrs. McVicker was born at Nebraska City, Otoe County, Nebraska; she is active in religious work and instruction; her parents were born near London, England. They have two children: Hugh Harris, born December 13, 1894, who married Mary E. Gentry, and who is assistant manager of the Lincoln Paint & Color Company; and William James, born April 10, 1896, who married Ada J. Bemis. William is telegraph editor of the *Lincoln Star*. Residence Lincoln.

Ford McWhorter

Ford McWhorter, distinguished banker of Adams County, Nebraska, has lived in this state all his life, and is now active in civic affairs at Hastings. His father, James McWhorter, who is a farmer, was born in County Antrim, Ireland, August 2, 1855, and came to this country in 1863. His mother was born at Salem, Washington County, New York, November 12, 1856; her parents were born in Ireland.

Mr. McWhorter, who was born in Gage County, Nebraska, November 5, 1879, was graduated from the Pierce, Nebraska, High School in 1895, and in 1903, received the Bachelor of Arts degree at Bellevue College, Bellevue, Nebraska. He was awarded college letters in baseball, football, and track.

Today Mr. McWhorter is secretary of the Mortgage-Investment Company at Hastings, and is prominent in community activities. He is a member of the Chamber of Commerce, is affiliated with the First Presbyterian Church of Hastings, and holds membership in the Kiwanis Club of which he was president in 1929. He is an Elk and Mason, and is a member of the Republican Party. During the World War he was chairman of the Phelps County United War Work Drive, gave a great deal of his time to questionnaire detail service, and took part in loan drives.

His marriage to Lulu Lucretia Johnson was solemnized in Holdrege, Phelps County, Nebraska, January 5, 1910, she was born at Holdrege, June 4, 1888, of Swedish descent. Their three children are: Dean F., born October 12, 1912; Stuart J., born June 9, 1914; and James E., born June 9, 1914. They are all in school. Residence: Hastings.

Charles Wilbur Mead

Charles Wilbur Mead, banker of Omaha, Nebraska, was born at Long Pine, Nebraska, September 25, 1887, the son of Joseph Marshall and Lois Isabelle (Hill) Mead. His father, who was born May 15, 1845, at Gibson, Indiana, and died November 10, 1914, at Maskell, Nebraska, was a furniture merchant for 27 years; he was a Civil War veteran; his ancestors were early settlers in Indiana; his grandfather was a soldier in the War of 1812.

His mother was born October 13, 1850, in Warwick County, Indiana; she is a piano teacher and has been active in the Methodist Church at Long Pine, Maskell, and Omaha. Her parents were born in the British Isles and came to America when young.

Mr. Mead received his education in the public schools, and was valedictorian of his high school graduating class. Since 1919, he has lived at Omaha. He was assistant cashier of the Brown County Bank, 1904-06; was in the collection department of the First National Bank, 1906-07; was assistant cashier of the New Castle State Bank, 1907; was organizer and cashier of the Maskell State Bank, 1908-19. Since 1919 he has been connected with the Omaha Trust Company of which he is now vice president and secretary.

He is a stockholder in several country banks, and is a director of the Omaha Safe Deposit Company. During the World War he was active in loan drives in Dixon County. He holds membership in the Omaha Chamber of Commerce; the Ad Sell League; and the Nebraskana Society. He is a member of the Triangle Club; Athletic Club; and Happy Hollow Club. His favorite sport is tennis. Mr. Mead served as chairman of the Republican central committee for Dixon County for a time.

He was united in marriage with Ada Ellen Hardy at Omaha, September 22, 1915. Mrs. Mead was born in Harrison County, Iowa, November 7, 1895; her ancestry is French, Irish, and Dutch. They have one son, Wilber Marlow. Residence: Omaha.

Mary Mead

Mary Mead, a clubwoman, rancher and nurse, was born near Dannebrog, Nebraska, November 1, 1882, the daughter of Niels and Mary (Jensen) Mead. Her father, who was a rancher, was born near Arthus, Denmark, in 1841, and died in Garfield County, Nebraska, in July, 1917; he served in the Danish-German War and was awarded a medal for his achievements at the siege of Duppel in Schleswig, Prussia. Her mother, whose parents were natives of Denmark, and was born near Arthus, December 8, 1859; her son was killed during the World War, serving with the Princess Pat Regiment of Canada, and the family received a distinguished-service medal for his bravery.

Mrs. Mead was graduated from the public school of Boelus, Nebraska, and attended high school at St. Paul, Nebraska. She taught in public schools of Howard County for two years, has been a nurse and ranch manager for over 30 years, and has taken an active part in welfare work at Blake, Nebraska, during that time. She was cook and part-owner of the Lone Tree Ranch in Garfield County, and holds membership in the W. R. C.

She took a prominent part in Red Cross drives and loan campaigns during the World War, and devoted much time and energy toward helping her county raise its quota of war-relief money. A Democrat, she is committeewoman of her party in Garfield County, but is independent in local politics. Her hobby is reading.

Of her marriage to H. C. Mead, which occurred at Loup City, Nebraska, January 9, 1901, two children were born: Paul, born September 19, 1902; and Myron, born October 31, 1906. Both received education at the University of Nebraska School of Agriculture. Residence: Ballagh.

John Peter Medinger

On February 29, 1864, in Germany, at the city of Luxemburg, John P. Medinger, son of Nicholas and Mary

(Fiedler) Medinger, was born. Nicholas and Mary Medinger were both born in Europe at the city of Luxemburg. Nicholas Medinger was a farmer.

John Peter Medinger received his education in the elementary schools. While still a youth he came to this country and began his vocation of farming. Mr. Medinger is a Democrat, and has lived in the state forty-seven years. A Roman Catholic, he is a member of St. Mary's Church of David City. His hobby is reading.

On February 2, 1891, he was united in marriage to Sarah Bougger, of Omaha, Nebraska. She was born February 7, 1867, and died at her home at David City, Nebraska, May 1, 1930. To them were born eight children: Carolina, born February 28, 1892, who is married to W. W. Timms; Julia, born June 12, 1893, who is married to J. B. Speicher; Mary, born August 18, 1896; Nicholas, born February 8, 1898; Frank, born February 8, 1900; John Jr., born September 8, 1901; Joseph, born March 7, 1903; Edward, born January 10, 1905. Residence: David City.

Peter Anthony Meehan

Peter Anthony Meehan, retail shoe merchant at York, York County, Nebraska, was born there September 23, 1891, the son of Dennis and Mary Elizabeth (Gallagher) Meehan. His father, who was born at Morris, Illinois, August 6, 1863, is a distinguished bank executive, merchant, and community leader at York. He is a director in the First National Bank of York, served as president of the York Commercial Club for several years, was a four minute speaker during the World War, and from 1888 to 1921, was a successful merchant. He is descended from Dennis Meehan and Mary O'Connor who came to America from Ireland, in 1861.

Mary Elizabeth (Gallagher) Meehan, who was born at Canton, Illinois, January 1, 1870, was a teacher in the city schools of Canton before her marriage. She holds various offices in church societies. She is the daughter of Anthony and Mary (Martin) Gallagher, who came to Maryland from Ireland.

Mr. Meehan was a student at St. Ursula's Academy in 1906, and in 1910 was graduated from the York High School. He acted as clerk for Dennis Meehan, Sr., 1910-13, was a partner in the firm, 1913-21, and since 1921 has been a partner of Dennis Meehan, Jr. He is a stockholder in the First National Bank at York, and the McCloud Hotel Company.

For the past three years he has been a member of the board of the York County Red Cross, home service secretary, and a member of the health committee. He has been a director of the York Rotary Club since 1926, and president of this organization from July 1, 1929 to July 1, 1930. He is a member of the Federation of Nebraska Retailers, has served as director of the York County Commercial Club, acting as president of the latter at this time, and is a member of the Nebraskana Society. Trustee of Merici Junior College at York, he is secretary of St. Joseph's Parochial School Society, and is a member of the committee to raise funds for the Young Men's Christian Association.

Mr. Meehan is a member of Leo XIII Council of the Knights of Columbus, acting as recorder for three years, Grand Knight for two years, and district deputy, 1928-29. During the World War he served as corporal of a motor truck company in the American Expeditionary Forces, and saw service at Champagne-Marne, Aisne-Marne, St. Mihiel, and the Meuse-Argonne defensive sector. He was in charge of the first Knights of Columbus drive in York County. He has been first adjutant, second commander, historian and board member of the American Legion, and is a member of the Veterans of Foreign Wars.

He was united in marriage with Gertrude Agnes Crowley at Hastings, Adams County, Nebraska, May 2, 1922. Before her marriage Mrs. Meehan was clerk for the county judge in Adams County. She was born at Hastings, the daughter of Jerome Crowley and Agnes (Carney) Crowley. Her ancestry is English and Irish. Residence: York.

Louis Francis Meier

Louis Francis Meier was born in Lancaster County, Nebraska, April 16, 1889, son of Francis William and Susan Elizabeth (Harris) Meier. Francis W. Meier was a native of Hanover, Germany, born March 11, 1831, who came to America in 1858, and homesteaded in Nebraska. His death occurred at Lincoln, February 10, 1911. His wife, Susan Elizabeth Harris was born in Montgomery County, Tennessee, December 1, 1842, and died at Lincoln, September 18, 1925. She was the mother of fourteen children, and was descended from Colonial settlers who served in the Revolution.

Dr. Meier attended the Lincoln public schools and was graduated from Lincoln High School in 1908. His honors there included activity in dramatics, membership in the Ciceronian Debating Society, the track team and basketball team. He was captain of the last mentioned and president of his freshman class. At the University of Nebraska, from which he received the degree of B. Sc. in 1917, he was president of his sophomore class, president of Acacia and conclave representative; he won a reserve letter in basketball, and a numeral for championship class football. He was a member of the Dramatic Club, and belongs to Delta Sigma Delta. He received his D. D. S. degree at the University of Illinois in 1916.

On May 31, 1917, he was married to Mary Hazel Dickson at Panama, Nebraska. She was born at Panama, on May 30, 1895, of Scotch descent. They have one son, Duane, born March 26, 1918.

Since 1916, Dr. Meier has been engaged in practice at Lincoln, and is the author of *The Relation of Malnutrition to Dental Defects* published in the *Dental Summary*, 1923. His professional memberships include the Lincoln District Dental Society, the Nebraska State Dental Association and the American Dental Association. He was formerly a first lieutenant in the Dental Reserve Corps, and is a Blue Lodge, York Rite Mason, and Shriner, and a member of the Cosmopolitan International. He attends Trinity Methodist Episcopal Church. He belongs to the Shrine Country Club. Residence: Lincoln.

Bernard Meister

Bernard Meister, son of Charles and Catherine (Peatrowsky) Meister, was born at West Point, Nebraska, April 24, 1900. His father who was a farmer, died at West Point, on April 10, 1916. He received his education in parochial school, and upon the death of his father became a farmer.

On June 21, 1922, he was married to Gertrude Wilhelmina Kaup, at West Point. Mrs. Meister was born at West Point, October 1, 1903. They have adopted two children, Charles Louis, born January 24, 1926, and Helen Phyllis, born November 22, 1925.

Mr. Meister is a Catholic, and a member of St. Boniface Catholic Church. He is a life member of the Nebraskana Society, and an out-standing citizen in his community. His favorite sport is baseball. Residence: West Point.

John Edward Mekota

John E. Mekota, county attorney of Saline County, Nebraska, was born at Solon, Iowa, April 23, 1893. His father, Frank Mekota, was born in Czechoslovakia, January 66, 1860, and died at Solon, September 30, 1924; he came to America with his parents in 1869. Anna (Vlach) Mekota, his mother, was born at Iowa City, Iowa, June 3, 1867, of Bohemian ancestry.

Mr. Mekota attended the public school at Solon, and

in 1908 was graduated from the Iowa City Academy. He was awarded the A. B. degree, 1916, and LL. B., 1920, at the University of Iowa. He has engaged in general law practice at Crete, Saline County, Nebraska, since his admission to the bar in 1920. A Democrat, Mr. Mekota served as county attorney of Saline County from 1923 to 1927; he was re-elected to this position in 1931.

His marriage to Edna Dreyer was solemnized at Iowa City, August 25, 1917. Mrs. Mekota, whose ancestry is German, was born at Glencoe, Minnesota, October 28, 1892; her father is a minister. Two children were born to them: John Edward, born October 20, 1921; and Beth Anna, born November 9, 1924.

During the World War Mr. Mekota held the rank of first lieutenant, 129th Infantry, 33rd Division, in France; Villers-Bretteneux, Albert sector in the Somme offensive, Meuse-Argonne offensive, and Woevre Plain. He has been a member of the American Legion since 1920; and is a member of the Saline County Bar Association, Nebraska State Bar Association, and the Nebraskana Society. He was president of the Crete Community Club in 1925 and 1930, and is a member of the Knights of Pythias. Residence: Crete.

Eugene Patrick Melady

Eugene Patrick Melady, livestock commission merchant, was born at Fairibault, Minnesota, February 26, 1872, son of James and Catherine (Kane) Melady. His father was born in County Meath, Ireland, in 1835, and died at St. Paul, Minnesota, December 8, 1909. He came to the United States in 1848. His wife, Catherine Kane, was born in County Leithem, Ireland, in 1835, and died at St. Paul, Minnesota, July 2, 1897.

Mr. Melady attended parochial and Christian Brothers School at St. Paul, Minnesota. He was afterward a student at the University of Notre Dame, where he was active in baseball, football, and boxing.

He was married to Hilma Grace Anderson at Chicago, on November 22, 1911. Mrs. Melady was born in Omaha, May 25, 1876. They have one son, Eugene Patrick.

Mr. Melady is a prominent Democrat. He is a Roman Catholic and a member of the Knights of Columbus. He has been a livestock commission merchant at Omaha for a number of years, and is a member of the Livestock Exchange. His club is the Omaha Athletic Club. Residence: Omaha.

William Robert Mellor

William R. Mellor, lawyer and business executive of Lincoln, Lancaster County, Nebraska, was born in Porter County, Indiana, June 16, 1860. His father, William Mellor, who was born at Oldham, Lancastershire, England, May 15, 1832, came to America in 1854. He was a farmer for many years, and after serving as a private in the Civil War was a dry goods merchant until his death. He died at Michigan City, La Porte County, Indiana, April 21, 1891. Sarah Grace (Battye) Mellor, mother of William Robert Mellor, was born at Home Firth Yorkshire, England, August 8, 1836, and died at Michigan City.

Mr. Mellor received his education in the grade and high schools at Michigan City. He has lived in Nebraska since April 10, 1885. In 1885 he settled in Sherman County, Nebraska, and homesteaded, living in a sod house for the first five years. He is now vice president of the Lincoln Trust Company at Lincoln, and is secretary of the Shubert Orchards Company. He was admitted to the practice of law at Loup City, Sherman County, Nebraska, February 24, 1894.

Mr. Mellor was elected a member of the Nebraska State Board of Agriculture in 1898. In 1900 he was appointed a member of the board of managers by President S. C. Bassett, where he served until elected president of the State Board of Agriculture in 1904 and 1905. in January, 1906, he became secretary of the Board

where he served until 1917. In 1915 he was president of the International Association of Fairs and Expositions. During his term of service the Nebraska State Fair emerged from the county fair stage to that of one of the greatest recognized state fairs of the country, in which he was ably assisted by the late C. H. Rudge of Lincoln, and the late Peter Youngers of Geneva.

As a Republican, he was a member of the 40th and 41st sessions of the Nebraska legislature, representing Lancaster County in the house of representatives. He served on the committee of roads and bridges and suggested the present system of county auto numbers.

Mr. Mellor took a keen interest in baseball, and played on a number of teams in the state. He was one of the first pitchers to throw the curved ball in 1878—the first year the rules permitted the overhand throw from the pitcher's box. His favorite sport at present is golf.

His marriage to Mariamne Pyke was solemnized at Michigan City, October 16, 1883. Mrs. Mellor, who was the daughter of Jacob and Susan Pyke, was born at Lafayette, Tippecanoe County, Indiana. She died at Lincoln, June 13, 1913. On September 29, 1914, Mr. Mellor was married to Marietta Parrish, a daughter of George and Susan Parrish, at Lincoln.

He served on the exemption board during the World War. He is a member of the following organizations; Lincoln Chamber of Commerce; Rotary Club; Laymen Club; Current Topics Club; and the Young Men's Christian Association. He is a Mason, Scottish Rite, Shriner; and a Knight of Pythias. His social club is the Lincoln Country Club. He attends the Methodist Church. Residence: Lincoln. (Photograph on Page 811).

Bert C. Mendell

Bert C. Mendell was born at Tecumseh, Nebraska, April 1, 1875, son of George Henry and Margaret (Miller) Mendell. His father, born at Legnier, Pennsylvania, May 12, 1838, died at Superior, October 12, 1899. He was a farmer of English ancestry, and served through the Civil War. His mother, who was of German descent, was born at Stratton, Pennsylvania, January 16, 1838, and died at Superior, January 22, 1906.

Mr. Mendell was graduated from high school in 1895, and later attended Lincoln Normal School and also attended a business college at Kansas City. He started his career in business as a salesman for the Memorial Art Works at Superior, from the year 1896 to 1899, and that year engaged in the memorial art business at Superior. Since that time his business has expanded until today he is one of the leading memorial art dealers in the state. He is a member of the Nebraska Memorial Art Retail Dealers Association and has served as secretary for a number of years. He also owns real estate in Nebraska, Kansas and Wyoming.

He is active in all civic affairs at Superior, and has served as city official for four years. He is a member of the Kiwanis Club, the Chamber of Commerce, the Current Topics Club, and the Odd Fellows. He was appointed by the Chamber of Commerce with two other members on the committee to raise the funds for the purchasing of the real estate which was bought and donated as a site for the beautiful Nebraskan Hotel, and it was largely through their efforts that this magnificent hotel was built.

He is affiliated with the Christian Science Society in which he served as first reader for three years, and is a member of the Nebraskana Society. He is a Republican.

On May 28, 1918, he was married to Josephine Greenleaf Day at Superior. Mrs. Mendell, who is a musician, was born at Superior, October 10, 1882, daughter of Senator George L. Day. Residence: Superior.

George Newton Mendenhall

Among Nebraska's leading educators, George N. Mendenhail ranks as one of the foremost. Descended on the

Townsend—Lincoln

WILLIAM ROBERT MELLOR

paternal side from English settlers in America in the 17th century, he is of Irish lineage on his mother's side, her family being among the early pioneers in Pike county, Illinois.

Born at Jerico Springs, Mo., September first, 1878, he is the son of Jasper Newton Mendenhall, who was born near Bucklin, Missouri, October 23, 1855, and who is still living. Jasper Mendenhall married Margaret Ellen Rickey of Pittsfield, Illinois, who died at Rogersville, Missouri, August 28, 1894.

At the age of nineteen, after he had completed his elementary education, George N. Mendenhall attended Warrensburg State Normal School and Midland Academy until 1901. An A. B. degree was awarded to him by Midland College in 1905; a B. D. degree by Western Theological Seminary in 1908. In 1921 he was the recipient of a master's degree from the University of Iowa, and in 1922 he received a Ph. D. from that university. He attended the summer quarter of 1910 at Chicago University, and the summer session of 1928 at Northwestern. While attending Midland College he received a letter in football.

Dr. Mendenhall was married to Mamie Christina Johnson of Ericson, Nebraska, June 15, 1910. They have six children: Newell N., born June 30, 1912; Alfred L., born February 8, 1914; George Emery, born August 13, 1916; O. Wendell, born April 8, 1919; Mildred C., born March 22, 1921; and Helen E., born May 17, 1922. Newell is a junior and Alfred is a sophomore in college.

Ordained to the Lutheran ministry in 1908, he became pastor the same year, of the church at McCool Junction, Nebraska. During 1909-11 he served as principal of Midland Academy. Again entering the active ministerial field he accepted a pastorate at Pueblo, Colorado, which he filled until 1914, when he accepted a call to Muscatine, Iowa, 1914-18. During 1919-22 he attended the University of Iowa.

Returning to the educational field, Dr. Mendenhall has been head of the department of psychology and religious education at Midland College since 1927. From 1922-27 he was head of the department of education and psychology.

He is the author of *Wells by the Wayside,* (1913); *The Logos Idea in Philosophy and Theology,* (1921); *Self-Measurement Scales,* (1922). In addition he assisted in the preparation of the Iowa plan for moral instruction in public schools.

While he is not active in political affairs, he is affiliated with the Republican party. During the World War he was a member of the Four Minute Men Club, and the Muscatine Campaign Club, which was in charge of all drives.

A member of the Salem Evangelical Lutheran Church of Fremont, he is also a member of the Nebraska Association of Church Colleges, the Lutheran Synod of Nebraska, and the Platte Valley Ministerial Association. For two years he served as member of the local Red Cross board. During the years 1915-18 he served as board member of the Y. M. C. A. Dr. Mendenhall's chief recreation is reading, and his hobby is collecting old books. Residence: Fremont. (Photograph on Page 813).

Joseph Parsons Meredith

For the past 44 years Joseph Parsons Meredith has lived in Nebraska, and for many years has been a retail merchant at South Sioux City. He was born at Milford, Delaware, April 29, 1857, the son of John H. and Amelia (Parsons) Meredith. His father, who was a farmer, was born at Milford, where he died June, 1861. His mother was born at Milford, and is still living.

Mr. Meredith is a member of the Ancient Order of United Workmen in Nebraska, is affiliated with the Methodist Episcopal Church at South Sioux City, and holds membership in the Nebraskana Society.

His marriage to Frances Ellen Watson was solemnized at Paton, Iowa, September 6, 1889; she was born at Niles, Michigan, June 11, 1858. Their children are: Joseph, born July 8, 1883; Blanche, born June 26, 1886; and Oryntha, born August 3, 1890. Joseph is an electrician, while the girls are married to farmers. Mr. Meredith is a staunch Republican. Residence: South Sioux City.

John Andrew Merideth

John Andrew Merideth, one of Lincoln's rising young physicians and surgeons, was born at Bloomfield, Iowa, May 18, 1901, son of Stephen O. and Stella (Botts) Merideth. Stephen Merideth who is a farmer, was born at Pulaski, Iowa, in 1868, the son of Andrew and Mary Merideth. Stella, his wife, was the daughter of J. W. and Mary Botts, and died in 1903.

Dr. Merideth attended the public schools of Missouri and Colorado, and was graduated from the Colorado State Preparatory School in 1919. He received his A. B. from the University of Colorado, and his M. D. from Washington University. His fraternity is Alpha Kappa Kappa. On August 17, 1927, he was admitted to practice and served his internship at the Jewish Hospital and the Missouri-Pacific Hospitals at St. Louis. At the present time he is examiner for the Metropolitan Life Insurance Company, assistant surgeon for the Missouri-Pacific Railroad, and is engaged in private practice with Dr. K. S. J. Hohlen.

He holds the rank of captain in the Reserve Officers Training Corps, and in the Medical Department of the Nebraska National Guard. His medical organizations are the American Medical Association, the Lancaster County Medical Society and the Nebraska State Medical Associations. He is a member of The Nebraskana Society. Residence: Lincoln.

Isaac Johnston Merrick

Born at Meaford, Ontario, Canada, on September 10, 1858, Isaac J. Merrick is the son of Dorchester and Mary Ann (Johnston) Merrick. His father was born in Ottawa, Canada on February 26, 1821, and came to the United States in September, 1879. Mary Ann Merrick, born in Ireland July 25, 1828, came to Canada at the age of seven. Both parents died at Osceola, Dorchester Merrick on April 6, 1884, and his wife on February 17, 1900.

Isaac J. Merrick attended school in Canada, and later, on coming to Polk County, continued his education in a dugout and sod schoolhouse. Mr. Merrick attended Wesleyan University at Osceola for one year, and on March 15, 1893, was married to Mary Scott. Mrs. Merrick was born at Altona, Knox County, Illinois, March 27, 1873, and is now active in church and club work.

For the past sixty years Mr. Merrick has lived in Polk County. He taught in a country school for two years, farmed a number of years, and for the past twenty-five years has been engaged in insurance work. At the present time he is president of Polk and Butler Counties Farmers Insurance Company.

Active in liberty bond sales in Polk County during the World War, Mr. Merrick has been a member of the Red Cross since that time. He is affiliated with the First Methodist Episcopal Church and is a member of The Nebraskana Society. His hobby is reading. Residence: Osceola. (Photograph in Album).

Maurice Hitchcock Merrill

On October 3, 1897, Maurice H. Merrill was born at Washington, District of Columbia, the son of George Waite and Mary Lavinia (Hitchcock) Merrill. His father, born at Freeport, Maine, January 23, 1855, was a business man and farmer in Oklahoma for many years. A leader

GEORGE N. MENDENHALL

in local and state Republican politics, he was for five years postmaster at Stratford, Oklahoma. He was active in Farmers Union organization, and was vitally interested in civic betterment. He was descended from Nathaniel Merrill who came to Newbury, Massachusetts, in 1637. The family name was originally de Merle, an old French Huguenot refugee family.

His mother was born at Yarmouth, Maine, June 14, 1858; her ancestry including Gad Hitchcock, a noted Massachusetts clergyman of Revolutionary times, and General Benjamin Lincoln of the Revolution.

Professor Merrill derived a great deal of his educational training at home with his father, and later was a student at Stratford High School and Eastern University Preparatory School at Claremore, Oklahoma. He was graduated from Castle Heights School at Lebanon, Tennessee, 1915; and holds the following degrees: A. B., University of Oklahoma, 1919; LL. B., University of Oklahoma, 1922; and S. J. D., Harvard, 1925. He was awarded the S. T. Bledsoe ranking prize during his senior year in school; and was made a member of Phi Beta Kappa, Alpha Kappa Psi, Order of Coif, and Phi Delta Phi.

He was teaching fellow in government at the University of Oklahoma, 1919-22; instructor there, 1922; was engaged in the practice of law at Tulsa, Oklahoma, 1922-24; was associate professor of law at the University of Idaho, 1925-26; was assistant professor of law at the University of Nebraska, 1926-28; and since 1928 has been professor of law at the University of Nebraska. He taught in the summer sessions at the law schools of the University of California, 1927, and Cornell University, 1928. He was admitted to the bar at Oklahoma City, Oklahoma, June 6, 1922.

Since 1927 Professor Merrill has been editor of the *Nebraska Law Bulletin*. He is the author of the following: Chapters on *State Legislature, Judiciary, Regulation of Business and Labor, Highway Administration, Care of Special Classes,* and *Local Government,* published in *The Government of Oklahoma,* a publication edited by F. F. Blachly and M. E. Oatman in 1924; *Town Government in Oklahoma* (with J. E. McAfee), 1922; *Law of Convenants Implied in Oil and Gas Leases,* 1916; articles dealing with legal problems in *Agency, Constitutional Law, Public Utilities, Suretyship, Oil and Gas Law,* published in the *Harvard Law Review, the University of Pennsylvania Law Review, Cornell Law Quarterly, Southern California Law Review, Indiana Law Journal, Kentucky Law Journal, Minnesota Law Review; Iowa Law Review;* and *Nebraska Law Bulletin.*

He was united in marriage with Orpha Anita Roberts at Norman, Cleveland County, Oklahoma, June 4, 1922. Mrs. Merrill, who was born at South Fork, Howell County, Missouri, March 12, 1898, was formerly an educator. They have one daughter, Mary Jean, born July 6, 1926.

During the World War Professor Merrill served as private, Company D, of the Students Army Training Corps at the University of Oklahoma. He is a member of the American Bar Association, the Oklahoma State Bar, and the Lincoln Chamber of Commerce, The Nebraskana Society and the Southwestern Political and Social Science Association. He is affiliated with Trinity Methodist Episcopal Church at Lincoln. His favorite sport is tennis and his hobby is writing. Politically, he is an extremely independent Republican. Residence: Lincoln.

Edythe Dickson Merritt

Edythe Dickson Merritt, superintendent of Mary Lanning Memorial Hospital, was born at Atlanta, Georgia, December 25, 1883. She is the daughter of Robert and Renee (LaRue) Dickson, both of whom are deceased. Her father, a teacher, was descended from early settlers in the south, while her mother was of French extraction.

Mrs. Merritt attended public and high school, and was graduated from Nurses Training School. For many years she was a registered nurse, and for a number of years has been superintendent of Mary Lanning Memorial Hospital. Residence: Hastings.

Emil Merscheid

Emil Merscheid, florist and nurseryman, was born at Winkel, Rheingau, Germany, November 29, 1886, son of Friedrick and Barbara (Lorenz) Merscheid.

He attended elementary school and professional horticulture school, and came to Nebraska from Cambridge, Ohio, locating at North Platte in November, 1915. At the present time he is the proprietor of the North Platte Floral Company and president of the North Platte Nurseries. Incorporated, perhaps the youngest but one of the largest nurseries west of Fremont, Nebraska Emil Merscheid is the originator of the Weeping Chinese Elm, patent applied for, the only one of its kind known in the world.

On June 22, 1921, he was married to Helen Carolyne Scharmann at North Platte. She was born at Kearney, March 2, 1894. They have one daughter, Eva June, born June 28, 1928.

Mr. Merscheid is a Mason, a member of the Order of Eastern Star, the Odd Fellows, the Rebekahs, the Modern Woodmen of America, the Brotherhood of American Yeoman, the Society of American Florists, and the Nebraska State Florists Association of which he is vice-president. He is one of five directors of Mountain and Plains States Florists Society which includes 17 mid-west states, headquarters in Colorado and is also a member of the American Association of Nurserymen which is the largest organization of its kind in the world and the Florist Telegraph Delivery Association. He is also a member of the Chamber of Commerce, and is affiliated with the First Evangelical Lutheran Church. He is a Republican. His favorite sport is hunting, while his hobby is horticulture. Residence: North Platte. (Photograph in Album).

Peter Joseph Merten

Born at Blue Hill, Nebraska, August 26, 1881, Peter Joseph Merten is the son of Peter and Gertrude (Kick) Merten. His father, who was born at Milwaukee, Wisconsin, October 17, 1854, died at Blue Hill, June 9, 1925, was a funeral director and furniture dealer; he served as member of the city council and school board several years ago. His father, Peter Merten, was born in Germany, and came to this country around 1850, settling in Milwaukee. His mother was born in Germany, March 18, 1863, and died at Blue Hill, May 31, 1892.

Mr. Merten was graduated from the Blue Hill grade school in 1898, and the high school there in 1901. He served as secretary of the Nebraska Funeral Directors Association for 11 years and was its president for one year in 1928. He is successfully engaged in the furniture business and as funeral director at Blue Hill, where he holds membership in the Commercial Club, is committeeman of the Boy Scouts, is a member of the city council and for one year was a member of the Board of Education, and is affiliated with Holy Trinity Catholic Church and the Knights of Columbus. His favorite sport is golf.

He was married at Hastings, Nebraska, October 5, 1920, to Jessie Permelia Robinson. Mrs. Merten, who was a bookkeeper before her marriage, was born at Milledgeville, Illinois, September 11, 1885, the daughter of James H. and Julia (Berkholder) Robinson. Their children are: Julia Iona, born February 21, 1912; Vincent Peter James, born April 29, 1916; and Vivian Permelia, born April 29, 1916. Residence: Blue Hill.

Ernest Miles Merwin

Born at Beaver City, Nebraska, July 20, 1902, Ernest Miles Merwin is the son of Fletcher Newton and Merta Isadora (Foland) Merwin. His father, who is editor of the *Times-Tribune* at Beaver City, has been publisher and editor of that paper for over 40 years, and was the first secretary of Senator George W. Norris; he was born at New Haven, Connecticut, in 1872. His mother was born in Nebraska in 1876.

Mr. Merwin was graduated from the Beaver City High School in 1920, and was a student at the University of Nebraska during 1922-23. He is associate editor of the *Beaver City Times-Tribune*, holds membership in the Beaver City Community Club, and is a member of the Independent Order of Odd Fellows. He holds membership in the Nebraska Press Association, the Southwest Nebraska Press Association, the Red Cross, and the Methodist Church of Beaver City. His hobby is reading.

On August 5, 1931, he was married to Mary Myrtle Mitzner at Beaver City. Mrs. Merwin, who was a teacher prior to her marriage, was born at Emerson, Iowa, March 25, 1909. Residence: Beaver City. (Photograph in Album).

Fletcher Newton Merwin

One of the outstanding figures in the newspaper world of Nebraska is Fletcher Newton Merwin who was born at Woodbridge, Connecticut, October 2, 1868. His father, Henry Fletcher Merwin, who was a farmer and publisher, was born at Woodbridge, January 18, 1838, and died at Beaver City, Nebraska, February 6, 1927; he served as a corporal in Company A, of the 10th Connecticut Volunteers during the Civil War. His mother, Lucy Belden (Blakeslee) Merwin, who was a member of the original woman's suffrage organization, was born at Milford, Connecticut, November 25, 1838, and died at Beaver City, April 7, 1930.

Mr. Merwin established the first newspaper at DuBois, Nebraska in 1885, and at this time is editor of the *Times-Tribune* at Beaver City. He is past master of the Beaver City Lodge of the Ancient Free and Accepted Masons, served as secretary of the Beaver City School Board for 12 years, and served as secretary of the Nebraska Press Association for the past eight years. His hobby is reading.

A Republican, Mr. Merwin served as the first private secretary to Congressman George W. Norris during the latter's first term in Congress. On December 1, 1892, he married Merta Isadora Foland at Beaver City.

They have five children: Henry Chester, born August 27, 1893, who married Evelyn Pointon; Laurence Newton, born March 17, 1898, who married Fawn Weir; Ernest Miles, born July 20, 1902, who married Mary Myrtle Mitzner; Esther Lucile, born February 2, 1909, and Edith Barbara, born September 10, 1914. Henry Chester was graduated from the United States Naval Academy at Annapolis, and has served as first lieutenant in the United States Navy for 14 years. Laurence is postmaster at Beaver City. Residence: Beaver City. (Photograph in Album).

Merta Isadora Merwin

Born at East Cobleskill, New York, January 27, 1874, Merta Isadora Merwin is the daughter of Chester Henry and Ida Elizabeth (Miers) Foland. Her father, who served as a minister in the Presbyterian Church for over 40 years, was born in Schoharie, New York, August 3, 1853, and died at Mount Dora, Florida, September 25, 1924. Her mother, who was an active church worker, was born in Schoharie County, April 3, 1854, and died at Mount Dora, March 2, 1922.

Mrs. Merwin was graduated from the high school at Beaver City, Nebraska, in 1892, and since then has been a prominent clubwoman and writer in that community. She has contributed column and feature material to the *Times-Tribune*, and is the author of a book, *Day Dreams*, published in 1931.

She is a member of the Nebraska Writers Guild, the Beaver City Library Board, of the City Public Library,

and the Beaver City Woman's Club. She is affiliated with the Presbyterian Church and is past worthy matron of the Beaver City Chapter of the Order of Eastern Star. Her hobby is writing verse.

Of her marriage to Fletcher Newton Merwin, which occurred at Beaver City, December 1, 1892, six children were born: Henry Chester, born August 27, 1893, who married Evelyn Pointon; Lillian Evangeline, November 19, 1894, who died August 17, 1914; Laurence Newton, March 19, 1898, who married Fawn Weir, and who is postmaster at Beaver City; Ernest Miles, July 20, 1902, who married Myrtle Mitzner, and is editor of the Beaver City local paper; Esther Lucile, February 2, 1909, who was graduated from Hastings College and from the Library School of Madison, Wisconsin; and Edith Barbara, September 10, 1914, who is associate editor of the *Times-Tribune*. Residence: Beaver City. (Photograph in Album).

M. Myrtle Merwin

Born at Emerson, Iowa, March 25, 1909, M. Myrtle Merwin is the daughter of Edward O. and Orpha L. (Hughes) Mitzner. Her father, who was a farmer, was born at Fort Scott, Kansas, June 16, 1878, came to Nebraska March 3, 1919, and died at Beaver City, Nebraska, February 9, 1930. Her mother was born at Randolph, Iowa, June 6, 1883, and resides on a farm near Beaver City.

Mrs. Merwin attended rural school in Iowa, was graduated from the Beaver City High School in 1926, and attended Kearney State Teachers College, 1928-29. She was prominent in athletics both in high school and college, taught in the public schools of Furnas County, Nebraska, for three years, and was a teacher in Red Willow County for one year. At this time she is a member of the Beaver City Woman's Club, is affiliated with the Methodist Episcopal Church at Beaver City, and holds membership in The Nebraskana Society.

Her marriage to Ernest M. Merwin occurred at Beaver City, August 5, 1931. Mr. Merwin, whose ancestry is English and French, was born at Beaver City, July 20, 1902. Residence: Beaver City. (Photograph in Album).

Fred W. Messmore

Fred W. Messmore, lawyer and district judge, was born in Boone, Iowa, July 11, 1889, son of Hiram A. and Clara Jane Messmore. He attended public, business and normal training college, and in 1912 received the Bachelor of Laws degree from Creighton University. He was a member of Delta Theta Phi. Admitted to the bar at Omaha in 1912, he has been engaged in the practice of law in Nebraska for many years. He has served as county attorney of Gage County, county judge, and now is judge of the first judicial district of Nebraska.

He is a member of the Gage County Bar Association, the Red Cross, Salvation Army Board, Beatrice Chamber of Commerce, and Kiwanis Club (past president of local chapter). He is affiliated with the Methodist Church, the Young Men's Christian Association, the Parent-Teachers' Association. His fraternal organizations include the Elks, Masons, Odd Fellows and Eagles.

Of his marriage to Jane Frances Saxe three children were born, Hiram, born January 31, 1920; Ted, born November 14, 1921; and John, born July 27, 1924.

Judge Messmore served as a private in the World War and was a major in the Judge Advocate General Officers Reserve Corps. He is a member of the American Legion and the Reserve Officers Association. Residence: Beatrice.

Anna V. Cornish Metcalf

One of Omaha's most outstanding personages is Anna Cornish Metcalf, who was born in New York State. She is the daughter of Colonel Joel N. Cornish and Virginia

ANNA V. CORNISH METCALF

Raymond, and belongs to one of Nebraska's most prominent families. Her father was born at Rome, New York, May 28, 1828. He was a lawyer at Iowa City, and a banker in Omaha; during the Civil War he received the rank of colonel. He was descended in the line of Samuel Cornish who settled in Plymouth Colony in 1696.

Virginia Raymond was born in New York, April 2, 1827, and died in Omaha, December 14, 1903. She was a charter member of the Omaha Women's Club. Virginia Raymond Cornish, mother of Mrs. Metcalf, was of Scotch descent. Her mother's grandfather was Colonel Kennedy, and when he left Scotland his regiment presented him with a gold handled sword, which descended to his son, Captain Kennedy. Both were in the War of 1812. Captain Kennedy was the father of Virginia Raymond Cornish's mother. A town in New York State was named Kennedyville after this family.

Anna Cornish Metcalf was educated at Tabor College, Iowa, Brownell Hall at Omaha and Notre Dame at South Bend, Indiana. She was married at Hamburg, Iowa, to Joseph Maul Metcalf. Mr. Metcalf was born in Lewes, Delaware, February 20, 1846, a descendant of the Metcalfs of renown in that state. He was president and manager of the Metcalf-Lininger Implement Company at the time of his death at Omaha on January 25, 1905.

Mrs. Metcalf has been a resident of Nebraska forty-nine years, and during that time has been one of the foremost Omaha women. She is a charter member and former president of the Tuesday Morning Musical Club, the first musical being given on October 29, 1884, at Max Meyer's Music Hall. The club met twice a month. She is a former president of the Omaha Equal Franchise Society. She was a member of the board of lady managers of the Omaha Exposition in 1898. During 1917 and 1918 she was president of a division of the local Red Cross.

A member of the Daughters of the American Revolution, she is honorary regent of that organization, and has willed her sixteen room house to the Omaha chapter to be used as a future chapter house and museum. Her membership in the organization dates from October 7, 1907; she is eligible through Josiah Cornish Cornish, born October 15, 1760 and Thomas Cornish, born January 23, 1706.

The Metcalf home, which will go to the D. A. R., was constructed at a cost of seventy-five thousand dollars. It is situated at 1234 South Tenth Street, on River Drive midway between Omaha and Child's Point. Mrs. Metcalf has entertained the annual musical of the D. A. R. for the past twenty-one years.

Perhaps her outstanding achievement has been in the promotion of the appreciation and understanding of music and of art. She is a member of the Art Institute of Omaha, and of the Friends of Music. Among the paintings which Mrs. Metcalfe has in her unusual collection are the following: *Sheep*, by F. L. Guyot; *Cattle in Meadows of Holland*, by J. H. L. DeHaas; *In the Orchard*, by F. A. DeLobbe, pupil of Bouguereau; *Landscape*, by Jules Dupre; *The Shepherdess*, by Ponson E. Dupat; and *An Old French Village*, by the late L. G. Palouse. Affiliated with Trinity Cathedral, she was a president of the Altar Guild of that church for two years. She is a sister of the late Albert J. Cornish, supreme judge of Nebraska, and of Edward J. Cornish, former city attorney of Omaha, and for seventeen years a member of the park board; since 1911 he has been president of the National Lead Company of New York.

Mrs. Metcalf is a member of the Volunteer League of National American Women's Suffrage Association, of which she was president two years and a member of the board six years. She accepted the presidency of the Equal Franchise League in memory of her mother, Virginia Raymond Cornish, who was a personal friend of Susan B. Anthony and Katie Stanton.

In politics she is a Republican. She is a member of The Nebraskana Society and the Omaha Country Club. Residence: Omaha. (Photograph in Page 816).

Richard Lee Metcalfe

Richard Lee Metcalfe, mayor of Omaha, was born near Upper Alton, Illinois, October 11, 1861, son of Richard Lee and Ellen T. (Edwards) Metcalfe.

He was educated in public school, and on April 30, 1885 was married to Bessie Buehler, of Seymour, Indiana. Their children are, Ellen, who is married to Harley Conant; Buehler; R. Lee; Theodore W.; and Kenneth.

Mr. Metcalfe began his career as printer's devil on a country newspaper. At the age of 19, he edited a Democratic weekly, and in 1888 became a reporter on the *Omaha World-Herald*. In 1894 he became assistant to the editor, William Jennings Bryan, and during the years 1896 until 1905, was editor of the *World-Herald*. During 1913-14 Mr. Metcalfe was civil governor of the Panama Canal Zone.

He is the author of *Of such is the Kingdom; Other Stories from Life* (1906); and *Bishop Sunbeams* (1909). In 1928 Mr. Metcalfe was nominated as Democratic candidate for the United States Senate. Residence: Omaha.

Theodore Walter Metcalfe

Theodore Walter Metcalfe, lieutenant-governor of Nebraska, was born at Omaha, August 16, 1895. He is the son of Richard Lee and Bessie (Buehler) Metcalfe. Richard Lee Metcalfe, who is now mayor of Omaha, has been prominent in Democratic politics for many years. He was born in Upper Alton, Illinois, October 11, 1861, and is of Scotch-Irish ancestry.

Bessie Buehler Metcalfe was born in Seymour, Indiana, a daughter of Theodore von Buehler and Elizabeth Murphy. Theodore W. Metcalfe attended the public schools of Lincoln and Omaha, and was graduated from Lincoln High School. He attended the University of Nebraska, where he received his Bachelor of Laws degree. He is a member of Sigma Delta Chi and Phi Delta Theta.

At the age of 16 he was city editor of the *Fairbury Daily Times*, and later of the *Panama Daily Journal*. At the university he was editor in chief of the *Awgwan* (1917). Upon his admission to the bar he entered the business world and is secretary-treasurer of the Metcalfe Company, and the Country Club District, Inc. He was elected on the Republican ticket to the position of lieutenant-governor of Nebraska for the term 1931-33.

He was married to Helen Houston at Tekamah, Nebraska, May 6, 1919. Mrs. Metcalfe who is a native of Indiana, is the daughter of Charles D. Houston of Tekamah. They have two daughters, Joan, born April 21, 1922 and Marilynn, born May 9, 1926.

During the World War he was first lieutenant of Company C, 6th Nebraska National Guard, at Camp Cody, New Mexico. He entered the First Officers Training School at Fort Snelling in 1917. He was promoted to captain of Infantry and served at Camp Green, North Carolina. He is a member of the American Legion and was vice commander and one of the organizers of the Omaha post. He is an Elk and a Mason, and attends the First Presbyterian Church. His favorite sport is horseback riding. Residence: Omaha. (Photograph on Page 818).

Walter Roy Metz

Walter Roy Metz, lawyer, was born at Wakeeney, Kansas, February 16, 1889, the son of Pierce and Josephine Lois (Runyon) Metz.

Pierce Metz was born at St. Clair, Pennsylvania, July 12, 1852, and was formerly a merchant. He was captain at one time of the 5th Regiment of the Iowa National Guard and later held the rank of colonel in the 20th Regiment of the Kansas National Guard. He has served as clerk of the district court of Trego County, Kansas, and county auditor of Adams County, Iowa. His father and mother were both born in Pennsylvania, his mother of German descent, and his father of Quaker

THEODORE W. METCALFE

descent. His wife, Josephine Lois, was born at Martinsburg, Iowa, August 14, 1854, and died at Omaha, December 2, 1929. She was active as a clubwoman. Her ancestors were of Scotch and Irish descent.

Mr. Metz was educated in the public and high school of Corning, Iowa, and received the degree of Doctor of Jurisprudence from the University of Michigan in 1912 and the Bachelor of Arts degree, Grinnell College, in 1909. At the University of Michigan he was a member of Woolsack, the Barristers, and on the staff of the Michigan Law Review. At Grinnell College he was editor of the *Scarlet & Black*. His fraternities are Sigma Nu and Phi Delta Phi.

He was admitted to the bar of Michigan and Nebraska in 1912 and has since been in active practice. In 1918 he became a member of the law firm of Boyd and Metz, which later became Boyd, Metz and Meyer and since 1926, following the appointment of Mr. Meyer to the district bench, has again been known as Boyd and Metz. A Republican, Mr. Metz was city attorney of Alliance 1913-1914 and 1918-1924; and city counselor of Alliance 1928-.

He was married to Doris Rosine Young at Denver, on July 15, 1919. Mrs. Metz was born at Pacific Junction, Iowa, May 3, 1896, and is active in Catholic church work and charities. Her father, Edward E. Young, was general superintendent of the Wyoming district of the Chicago, Burlington, and Quincy railroad from 1909 until 1917. Mr. and Mrs. Metz have one son, Walter Roy, born October 13, 1924.

During the late war, Mr. Metz was a four minute speaker and a member of the legal advisory board. He is affiliated with the Congregational Church of Grinnell, Iowa, is a member of the Nebraska State Bar Association, The Nebraskana Society, the Alliance Rotary Club, the Elks, the Alliance Country Club, and the Ancient Free and Accepted Masons, the Royal Arch Masons, the Knights Templar, and the Ancient Arabic Order of the Nobles of the Mystic Shrine. His favorite sports are golf and tennis. Residence: Alliance.

William Walter Metz

William W. Metz, educator and executive of Nebraska City, was born at Shamokin, Northumberland County, Pennsylvania, February 23, 1864. His father, William Walter Metz, who was a moulder in an iron foundry, was born at Shamokin, January 3, 1833, of Holland Dutch ancestry. He died of black smallpox at Shamokin, January 26, 1864.

Nancy Ann (Lytle) Metz, his mother, who was a farmer's daughter, was born at Sunbury, Pennsylvania, January 23, 1831, and died at Riverton, Iowa, March 26, 1914. She was of English and Scotch descent.

Mr. Metz received his education at the district school of Riverton, Iowa. For three years he taught a district school in Fremont County, Iowa, and was a teacher in the Otoe County, (Nebraska) schools for four years. He was appointed railway postal clerk, April 26, 1889, and served continuously in this position until February 23, 1926, when he was pensioned and retired from government service. At the present time he is one of the three proprietors of the Nebraska City Bottling Works, Green's Ice Cream Factory at Nebraska City, and the Falls City Ice Cream Company of Falls City, Nebraska. He is president of the Nebraska City Building and Loan Association, organized in 1887.

He is a Republican and in 1926 was unsuccessful candidate for the state senate. He was married to Clara Josephine Vennemann at Nebraska City, December 12, 1889. Mrs. Metz was born of German parentage at Nebraska City, April 13, 1866. There are two children. William Walter, Junior, born March 8, 1897, was graduated from the Nebraska City High School and is an ex-service man, having been in active service overseas in the World War. Edwin John, born November 16, 1907, was graduated from Midland College in 1928 and since

then has been coach in the high school at Sumner, Nebraska.

During the World War Mr. Metz was a four minute man. He is a member of the Red Cross and the Nebraska City Chamber of Commerce having served in the latter as member of the board of directors for three years, and as executive secretary for two years. A member of the school board for nine years, serving as president one year; he is also a member of the Nebraska City Rotary Club; and is vice president of the local Parent Teachers Association. He is an Elk; Eagle; Modern Woodman; and Mason, 32d degree and Shriner. He holds the position of *Dad* to the Job's Daughters Society, and is a member of the Eastern Star.

Mr. Metz is affiliated with the English Lutheran church and has been superintendent of the Sunday School for the past twenty years. His social club is the Nebraska City Country Club. His hobby is golf. Residence: Nebraska City.

Henry Louis Meuret

Born at Orchard, Nebraska, May 28, 1889, Henry Louis Meuret is the son of Joseph Richard Meuret and Catherine (Merlet) Meuret. Joseph Meuret, a farmer and stockman, was born at Beloit, Wisconsin, March 30, 1856, and died at Orchard, May 24, 1927; his parents came to this country from Alsace-Lorraine, France, in 1852. His mother was born at Beloit, June 19, 1859, and died at Orchard, November 8, 1893.

Mr. Meuret attended rural school in Antelope County, Nebraska, was a student at Central Business College at Colorado Springs, Colorado where he was graduated in 1911. He was bookkeeper, stenographer, and general office manager for the Overburf-Davis-Miller Lumber Company at Bend, Oregon, 1912-14, was chief clerk for the Northern Pacific Railway Company in Missoula, Montana, 1914-19, and since 1919 has been a farmer and stockman at Orchard, Nebraska.

He was elected recently to serve on the depositors committee of the defunct Citizens State Bank of Orchard; he is a director of the Alfalfa Company of Orchard, is director of the Co-operative Creamery Company of Orchard, and is secretary-treasurer of the latter organization. He is moderator and treasurer of the local school board, is a member of the Nebraskana Society, and holds membership in the Democratic Party.

His father was one of the earliest settlers in Antelope County, and knew all the hardships and privations of the pioneers; from 1878 until his death in 1927 he was one of the leaders in the progress of the middlewest.

Henry Meuret was married to Waunita Dee Lane at Colorado Springs, Colorado, April 3, 1912. Mrs. Meuret, who is the daughter of W. D. Lane and Anna (Ayres) Lane, was born at Beloit, Kansas, June 20, 1894. Their three children are: Forrest Lee, born April 24, 1913; Ellinor Fay, born January 3, 1915; and Henry Louis, Jr., born November 16, 1928. Residence: Orchard.

Ernst Meyer

A leading flour miller at Superior, Ernst Meyer was born at Oak, Nebraska, December 26, 1887. He is the son of Ernst and Augusta (Ahrens) Meyer, the former a native of Germany, who was also a flour miller. He died at Oak, Nebraska, April 20, 1923. His wife, who was born in Iowa, still survives him.

Ernst Meyer, Jr., attended public school, and afterward followed the business started by his father. At the present time he is associated with and is president of the Superior Milling Company.

On July 12, 1911, he was united in marriage to Arva May Kincannon at Nelson. Mrs. Meyer was born at Angus, Nebraska, December 30, 1891. There is one son, Denny, born June 16, 1926. The family attends the Methodist Episcopal Church at Superior.

Mr. Meyer is a Mason, and Shriner, a member of the

Nebraskana Society, and is an ardent golfer. He is a member of the Commercial Club, the Kiwanis Club, and is a Republican. Residence: Superior.

Fred Meyer

Fred Meyer, retired merchant of Crete, Nebraska, was born at Harz Mountains, Hanover, Germany, June 27, 1846. His father, George Meyer, who was born in Germany, in 1823, and died there in 1875, was an architect. His mother, Elizabeth (Trude) Meyer, was born at Harz Mountains, Hanover, Germany, in 1818, and died there in 1880.

Mr. Meyer attended school in Germany; and was confirmed at the age of 14 years. He came to America in 1869 and settled in Pittsburgh where he worked in the railroad shops during the panic of 1873. Moving to Plattsmouth, Nebraska, in 1873, in 1874 he moved to Crete and homesteaded. In 1875 he was employed in a general merchandise store at Crete, and in 1878, organized a merchandise business of his own. A successful merchant for 32 years, in 1906 he retired. He is a member of the Lutheran Church, and the Nebraskana Society, and is a Republican.

His marriage to Jane Kennedy was solemnized at Crete; she was born at Sunderland, England, March 17, 1845, and died at Crete in 1924. Two children were born to this marriage: Lizzie, born September 7, 1871; and Maria, born June 7, 1870, who died in 1880. Mr. Meyer is now married to Catherine Kierse. Residence: Crete.

Harry Ferdinand Meyer

Harry Ferdinand Meyer, president of the Chadron Creamery Company, was born at Fort Garland, Colorado, May 22, 1893, and for the past 12 years has resided in Nebraska.

His father, Ferdinand Meyer, was born in Germany, April 22, 1837, and died at Costilla, New Mexico, March 20, 1920. He was a business man. His wife was born on the Island of Java, of Holland Dutch descent, January 16, 1867. She was a teacher.

Upon his graduation from public school at Colorado Springs, Colorado, Harry Meyer attended Colorado Springs High School one year. Afterward he was a student at business college, Fort Collins, Colorado.

From November, 1912, until March, 1915, he was a bookkeeper for the Intermountain Railway Light and Power Company, and during the year 1915 and 1916, was superintendent of light and water for the same company. He was traveling auditor for one year, and general cashier for the same organization at Navasota, Texas. On returning from the army, he became manager of their creamery company, the Chadron Creamery Company.

During the World War, Mr. Meyer held ranks from private to second lieutenant. He is a member of the American Legion, Grace Episcopal Church, the Red Cross, Commercial Club, Kiwanis Club, American Bottlers Association, International Ice Cream Manufacturers Association, the Masons, and the United Commercial Travelers. He enjoys fishing and hunting.

On October 20, 1923, he was married to Gertrude Elizabeth Chizek at Chadron. Mrs. Meyer was born at Chadron, June 6, 1898, and before her marriage was a bookkeeper. Residence: Chadron.

Henry Ferdinand Meyer

A native of Halle, Germany, Henry Ferdinand Meyer has been a resident of Nebraska since 1887. He is the son of Herman and Tana Mathilda (Rodenbrock) Meyer, and was born May 66, 1868. His parents both of whom remained in Germany are deceased, his father having died in 1886 and his mother in 1925.

Henry F. Meyer was educated in the public schools, he has been engaged in the hardware business for the past thirty-nine years. He has been extremely active in the civic and business development of Nebraska City. For the past thirty years he has been treasurer of the Nebraska City Building and Loan Association, and for four years he was vice president of the Otoe County National Bank.

He was married to Mary Thiele at Nebraska City, August 24, 1905. Mrs. Meyer was born at Plattville, Wisconsin, August 21, 1869. They have one daughter, Dorothy, born June 20, 1908, who is a teacher. Mr. Meyer is a member of the German Evangelical Lutheran Church. He is active in the various welfare drives of the city and is a member of the Chamber of Commerce and in educational organizations. His fraternal organizations include the Eagles, the Woodmen of the World and the Sons of Herman. His hobby is machinery. Residence: Nebraska City.

John Meyer

John Meyer was born October 14, 1856, at Benton, Missouri, the son of Henry Meyer and Margaret (Oelrich) Meyer. His father was a farmer who came to America with his parents at the age of thirteen.

He attended the public schools, and on April 25, 1888, he married Anna M. Scheve, at Beatrice. She was born near Beatrice, on April 22, 1869.

Mr. Meyer has resided in Nebraska for fifty years. Ordained on August 28, 1881, he is now affiliated with the Bethlehem Evangelical Lutheran Church at Kiowa, Thayer County, Nebraska, and holds membership in the Southern Nebraska District of Missionary Synod. Mr. Meyer's home is near Davenport, Nebraska. He is a member of the Nebraskana Society. Residence: Davenport.

William Charles Meyer

William Charles Meyer, general farmer and stock raiser, was born in Perry, Iowa, August 26, 1884, and for the past 40 years has resided in Nebraska. His father, Charles J. Meyer, was born in Germany, November 3, 1844, and came to America about 1866, coming to Nebraska in 1884. He was a farmer, whose death occurred at Hastings, Nebraska, February 14, 1924. His mother, Caroline (Timm) Meyer, was born in Germany, October 1, 1849, and died at North Platte, Nebraska, March 28, 1911.

Mr. Meyer has been a farmer ever since leaving district school and has always been interested in local Republican politics. At the present time he is living on a combined ranch and farm 14 miles from Maywood, on Rural Route No. 1, and is serving his third term as county commissioner of Frontier County. The home ranch has 840 acres. Previous to buying his present ranch he raised cattle on his 1,000 acre ranch north of Maywood, running as many as 150 head. He was a member of the White Community Club from 1927 until 1928 and is treasurer at the present time of the Bluff View Community Club. He is a member of the Odd Fellows and the Nebraskana Society and is now serving his tenth year as moderator of the local school board. His favorite sports are hiking and talking, while his hobby is reading. Residence: Maywood.

Sylvester Lynden Meyers

Sylvester Lynden Meyers was the first white child born in Furnas County, June 20, 1873, and is the son of Isaac Stein and Henrietta (Diebler) Meyers. His father, who was a farmer and insurance dealer, was born at Gratz, Pennsylvania, December 13, 1845, and served as a member of the Pennsylvania Volunteer Cavalry during the Civil War, spending over seven months in the Andersonville Prison; he died at Hendley, Nebraska, January 2, 1918. His mother, who was of Dutch descent, was born at Gratz, March 19, 1847, and died at Hendley, November 2, 1918.

Mr. Myers attended the Beaver City High School and in 1894 completed a course in telegraphy. He was a farmer until 1920 and since then has raised livestock and operated a grain elevator and an insurance business at Hendley. A Democrat, he served as assessor of Lynden precinct for seven years.

He holds membership in the Ancient Order of United Workmen, the Independent Order of Odd Fellows, and the local scool board for over 20 years, and as treasurer for three years.

His marriage to Myrtle Cathrine McKown occurred at Hendley, February 28, 1900; she was born at Hendley, December 22, 1881, and died there, September 13, 1912. She was the daughter of Jefferson and Sarah (Woodhirn) McKown. Her parents came from Red Oak, Iowa, in 1879. Four children were born to this marriage, Doris Evelyn, July 1, 1901, who married Fay Adams, and is postmistress at Norbeck, South Dakota; Sarah Maude, November 5, 1902, who married D. Jewett; Ella Genevieve, October 20, 1904, who married Allen W. Lair, Jr., and Lloyd Ivan, October 9, 1906, who manages the elevator for his father.

On December 23, 1914, Mr. Meyers married Bessie Hazel Schooler. They have two children, Nadine Irene. born September 28, 1915; and Victor Lyle, born November 11, 1918. Residence: Hendley.

Frank C. Middlebrook

An outstanding figure in the business world Frank C. Middlebrook of York, Nebraska, has engaged in the mercantile business for the past 31 years. He was born at Dunnegan, Missouri, February 28, 1878, the son of Horace and Matilda Elizabeth (Holmes) Middlebrook. His father, who was a school teacher and a farmer was born at Decorah, Iowa, and died at Humansville, Missouri, August 12, 1881. He was descended from a long line of ancestors noted in American history, among them, Joseph Middlebrook, who came to the country from England in 1635.

His mother Matilda Elizabeth Holmes, also a teacher in the public schools, was born at Humansville, February 6, 1856, and died at Hiawatha, Kansas, September 7, 1931. Her family had been prominent in Tennessee in early days.

Mr. Middlebrook was graduated from the Dunnegan Springs Training School in 1900. In 1901 he with his brother opened a store at Robinson, Kansas, which was successfully conducted as a partnership for 15 years. In 1916 he moved to York, from Robinson, and established the Middlebrook Department Store. He is owner of the latter and of the Middlebrook Department Store at Grand Island, Nebraska.

He is president of the York County Commercial Club, is a member of the Nebraska Retailers Association, a member of the York Rite and Scottish Rite Masonic bodies, and of the York Methodist Church. He is a Republican, has served as a member of the board of education, and is one of the board of directors of the Young Men's Christian Association of York.

His marriage to Ruby Clark occurred at Reserve, Kansas, November 22, 1910. She is a graduate of the Nebraska State University. She is a member of the Eastern Star, the York chapter of P. E. O., and the Methodist Church of York. Mr. and Mrs. Middlebrook have three children, Robert Clark, born March 27, 1912; Alice Elizabeth, born January 29, 1915; and Margaret Jean, born June 3, 1921.

In 1901 a store without charge accounts was unheard of, but Mr. Middlebrook started his business at that time as a cash upon delivery store. That policy has been maintained ever since. His main purpose was to eliminate all extra costs and deliver to his customers the best merchandise for the lowest possible prices. It is said of Mr. Middlebrook, that he has developed a new phase of merchandis-

ing—responsibility to the customer. His store is called the "Make-It-Right" store, because of his policy of making good to his customers on all claims. The old slogan of *Caveat Emptor* (let the buyer beware) has never applied to the Middlebrook stores. Residence: York. (Photograph on Page 822).

Edward J. Miille

For the past 26 years Edward J. Miille has served as postmaster at Loretto, Nebraska, where he has taken a prominent part in business and civic affairs. He was born at Ponca, Nebraska, March 31, 1884, the son of Gotleib and Pauline (Hecht) Miille. Gotleib Miille, who was born at Berlin, Germany, in 1834, and died at Ponca, February 22, 1897, was a merchant in Berlin and later homesteaded in Dixon County, Nebraska. Pauline (Hecht) Miille was born in Berlin in 1838, and died at Ponca, in August, 1892.

One of a large family with an ambition for an education, Edward Miille worked and saved his earnings so that he might attend school. His activities as an officer of the Ak-sar-ben Stock Show, as well as the Nebraska State Fair, have given a wide acquaintance among the pure bred stockmen of the middle west. Mr. Miille attended a country school near Ponca, and later attended the Nebraska Normal College at Wayne, Nebraska, for three years. He served as manager of the Edwards & bradford Lumber Company for 12 years. He has been connected with the firms: Miille & Bruner, at Elgin, Nebraska, two years; Miille & Barnes, Loretto, four years; and the Loretto State Bank of which he was president for five years.

A Republican, Mr. Miille acted as representative to the Nebraska Legislature two years. He has always been an active member of the Red Cross, is secretary of the county Parent-Teachers' Association, is a member of the camp committee of Camp Sheldon, and of the Young Men's Christian Association. He served as president of the Kiwanis Club at Albion, Nebraska, for a year, having previously served as secretary of that organization for five years. Mr. Miille is a Mason, and a member of the Modern Woodmen of America and the Order of Eastern Star. In 1920 Mr. Miille organized a Boy Scout troop of which he was scout master.

On November 16, 1906, he married Jennie H. Waddell at Meadow Grove, Nebraska. Mrs. Miille is a homemaker and a club leader at Loretto, where she has been guardian of the local Camp Fire organization. To their marriage two children were born, Beulah M., December 15, 1909, who is a graduate of the Wesleyan University; and Norris E., February 15, 1911, who is a graduate of the Albion High School. Residence: Loretto.

Herman Henry Miille

Herman Henry Miille, retired deputy sheriff of Dixon County, was born in Berlin, Germany, October 3, 1866, son of Gottlieb and Paulena (Hecht) Miille. His father was born in Stutgard, Germany, April 16, 1841, and came with his family to Ponca, on March 20, 1867. He was a successful farmer, and died at Ponca, February 7, 1899. His wife, Paulena, was also born in Berlin, April 9, 1844, and died at Ponca, July 12, 1896.

Educated in country school, soon thereafter Mr. Miille entered the business world. He farmed until the age of 26, and was engaged in the hardware business in Ponca, for 20 years. He was also interested in the hardware and furniture business in Wynot, Nebraska, for 10 years, and was engaged in the hardware business in St. James, for one year.

Mr. Miille served as mayor of Ponca for five years, vice president of District No. 1 in Dixon County three years, as a member of the school board of district No. 1, of Ponca, and as deputy sheriff of Dixon County. He has resided in Dixon County for more than 64 years. At the present time he is a director of the Bank of Dixon County and the Farmers State Bank, both at Ponca.

That Man Gale—York

FRANK C. MIDDLEBROOK

On June 13, 1892, he was united in marriage to Louise M. Wendte, at Newcastle, Nebraska, who was born near Belle Plaine, Iowa, August 22, 1872. To them were born nine children, Charles, March 27, 1893; Harry, November 13, 1894; Cassie, October 23, 1897; Edna, July 10, 1901; Ralph, March 1, 1904; Laura, June 19, 1906; Evelyn, December 28, 1908; Leo, July 11, 1911, Dorothy, May 7, 1914.

At the present time Mr. Miille is a member of Salem Lutheran Church, the Odd Fellows and The Nebraskana Society. Residence: Ponca.

Roselia Viola Mikkelsen

Roselia Viola Mikkelsen was born at Turney, Missouri, October 23, 1888, the daughter of Edgar Everett Althouse and Ethalena Viola (Damitz) Althouse. Her father, who was a farmer, and furniture dealer at Nelson, was born in New York state December 15, 1863, and died at Nelson, Nebraska, February 9, 1909. Her mother was born at Peoria, Illinois, April 15, 1870, and is still living; her ancestry was German.

Mrs. Mikkelsen was a student at the Nelson High School. She has been prominent in women's affairs at Edgar for several years and is now president of the American Legion Auxiliary there. She is affiliated with the Methodist Episcopal Church, and holds membership in the Nebraskana Society.

Her marriage to Charles Michael Mikkelsen occurred at Nelson, May 30, 1911. Mr. Mikkelsen, who is caretaker of the Edgar High School, was born at Silkeborg, Denmark, June 26, 1878. Their children are: Christine, born September 17, 1912; John, October 25, 1917; and Robert, June 10, 1920. Christine is a teacher. Residence: Edgar.

Albert W. J. Miksch

Born at Oconee, Nebraska, July 21, 1897, Albert W. J. Miksch is the son of Alois and Theresa (Lammel) Miksch. His father, who is a farmer, was born at Karle, Austria, January 17, 1857, came to America in 1888, and for two years was employed by a railroad company; he now owns 400 acres of Platte County land. His mother, Theresa Miksch, was born at Karle, November 17, 1856.

Mr. Miksch attended rural school and in 1913 was graduated from St. Joseph's Parochial School at Platte Center. He is an amateur author and has written a number of short agricultural articles published in *Cappers Weekly* and the *Daily American Tribune*. He is affiliated with St. Joseph's Catholic Church. His hobbies are reading, gardening, and flowers. Residence: Platte Center.

Albert Tillison Milburn

Albert Tillison Milburn, prominent executive at Beatrice, Gage County, Nebraska, has been engaged in business in this state for the past 45 years. He was born at Chebanse, Iroquois County, Illinois, March 22, 1874, the son of Thomas Hutchinson and Sarah Eliva (Fanning) Milburn. His father was born at Peterborough, Canada, December 2, 1839, and died at Beatrice, Gage County, Nebraska, February, 1901. His mother was born at Orilla, Canada, February 27, 1840, and died at Beatrice, August 3, 1928.

Mr. Milburn engaged in the bookbinding business for 14 years and in 1901 organized the printing and bookbinding company, Milburn & Scott, at Beatrice. Today, after thirty years service in this firm, he is president and senior partner of the organization. He holds membership in the Chamber of Commerce, Masonic Lodge, the Nebraskana Society, Lodge Number 619 of the Elks, and the Methodist Episcopal Church. He is a Republican.

His marriage to Martha McClellan was solemnized at Beatrice, June 2, 1909. Mrs. Milburn was born at Homesville, Gage County, Nebraska. To this union three children were born: Robert T., born May 17, 1910, who died October 13, 1930; William H., born March 22, 1912; and Martha Virginia, born May 30, 1916.

Mr. Milburn's favorite recreations are baseball and horseshoe pitching. Residence: Beatrice.

Clarence Gillespie Miles

Clarence Gillespie Miles was born at Beattie, Kansas, June 12, 1887, and has been a resident of Nebraska for the past thirty years. His father, Samuel Albert Miles, was born in Delta, York County, Pennsylvania, October 27, 1851, of Scotch-Irish and English descent. He is the son of Stephen B. Miles, an early settler in Richardson County, Nebraska, who had what was probably the first mail route from Atchison, Kansas, to Salt Lake City, which was called the Overland Route. Clarence Miles' mother was Flora Belle Carter. She was born at Schoharie, New York, on March 27, 1867, and is still living.

Mr. Miles received his B. A. from Cotner College in 1911, and his LL. B. from Harvard, in 1914. Since that time he has engaged in the practice of law, except during 1917-18, when he was professor of law at the Idaho State University, and served in the M. O. T. C. at Ft. Riley, Kansas. He was a candidate for the state legislature in 1920. In 1925 he served as president of the Lancaster County Bar Association. He is a member also of the Social Welfare Society of which he is a trustee. Mr. Miles' religious affiliation is with the Deciples of Christ Church; he is a member of the Odd Fellows, the Knights of Pythias, the Parent-Teachers' Association, the Young Men's Christian Association, and the American Legion. His club is the Professional Men's. His sports are baseball and tennis.

On September 15, 1920, he was united in marriage to Elsie Clarissa Ziese, who before her marriage was a teacher in the art department at the University of Washington. Mrs. Miles was born at Bellingham, Washington, July 16, 1894. Their three children are: James Gillespie, born June 23, 1921; Mary Louise, born August 30, 1923, and Richard Samuel, born January 28, 1925. Residence: Lincoln.

Fred Allan Miles

Born on the farm of his father near Roseland, Nebraska, April 2, 1880, Fred Allan Miles has always resided in Nebraska. His father, Richard Louis Miles, was born in England, August 6, 1848, and came to America in 1869. A farmer and carpenter, he was an early settler in Adams County, and died near Roseland on March 4, 1900.

Florence Emma Dailey, wife of Richard L. Miles, was born in Illinois, January 13, 1852, a descendant of John Hart, one of the signers of the Declaration of Independence. She died at the home farm near Roseland on October 28, 1917.

Fred Allan Miles was educated in the public schools of Adams County, and as a young man began work on the farm. He has always resided in the county of his birth, and was recently elected to life membership in the Nebraskana Society in recognition of his effort toward the advancement of his community and state. Residence: Roseland.

Willard Barrows Millard, Jr.

Willard B. Millard, Jr., was born at Omaha, September 24, 1900, son of Willard Barrows and Frances Barton. His father, who was a banker and mining executive, was the son of Senator Joseph H. Millard. Frances Barton, who was born at St. Joseph, Missouri, was the daughter of Guy C. Barton. She died at Omaha several years ago. Willard Millard, Sr., died at Berkeley, California, September 25, 1930.

Upon his graduation from Princeton Preparatory Mr.

Millard entered Yale University, and received his Ph. B. in 1924. He was elected to Alpha Delta Phi and is a member of the Wolf's Head Society. In 1924 he entered the employ of the Omaha National Bank, of which he is now vice president.

Mr. Millard was married to Claire Daugherty of Omaha, at Omaha, on June 28, 1924. He is an Episcopalian, and a member of the Y. M. C. A.; he is active in civic and welfare work and is a trustee of the Nebraska Humane Society, and a member of the Chamber of Commerce, the Red Cross, the Omaha Library Board and the board of the Art Institute. He is a member of the Elks and the Woodmen of the World. His clubs are the Omaha Club, the Omaha Country Club, the Omaha Athletic Club and the University Club. He finds his recreation in golf and tennis. Residence: Omaha.

Albert Rudolph Miller

Albert Rudolph Miller, prominent investment banker at Columbus, was born at Calmar, Iowa, March 1, 1874, son of Henry and Eliza (Herklotz) Miller.

Henry Miller was born in Germany, March 1, 1839, and came to America in 1842, settling in Calmar, Iowa, where he founded and became president of the Miller Wagon Company. He died at Calmar, in April, 1920. His wife, Eliza Herklotz, died in 1879.

Educated in public and high school at Calmar, Mr. Miller was graduated and during 1889-90 attended Upper Iowa University at Fayette, Iowa. From 1900 until 1908 he was cashier of the Fullerton National Bank, Fullerton, Nebraska, and from 1908 until 1925 was vice president and cashier of the First National Bank of Columbus. At the present time he is president of the Miller Allied Securities Company, investment bankers, of Columbus.

His marriage to Mertie Miller was solemnized at Fullerton, May 25, 1905, and to them was born one son, Leonard, on September 5, 1907. He was graduated from the University of Nebraska in June, 1928. Mrs. Miller was born at Vestal, New York, May 8, 1878.

Mr. Miller is a Republican. He has taken an active part in all state good road programs, and since the inception of the Lincoln Highway Association has been consul for Platte County. For many years he has been a trustee of the local Young Men's Christian Association, and has served as president of the Columbus Chamber of Commerce and of the Wayside Country Club.

He is a member of the Federated Church, the Masons, and the Lions Club, and was recently made a life member of the Nebraskana Society. Mr. Miller enjoys a game of golf, but his hobby is mechanics, and he has a complete workshop in his home. Residence: Columbus.

Annie Louise Miller

Annie Louise Miller, newspaper writer, was born at Worthington, Iowa, daughter of William C. and Emma (Butterworth) Miller. Her father, a wholesale hardware and paint dealer, was born at Massillon, Ohio, March 12, 1826, and died at Lincoln, March 13, 1908. He was of Holland descent. Her mother was born at Pittsburgh, Pennsylvania, March 11, 1831, and died at Lincoln, May 19, 1907. She was of English parentage.

Miss Miller attended the public schools of Cleveland, Ohio, Cleveland High School, and was graduated from Hathaway-Brown private school at Cleveland. She also attended the University of Nebraska. A resident of the state since 1888, she has been associated with the *Nebraska State Journal* as reporter, music critic, and department editor since August, 1898; on leave of absence since July, 1930. She is the author of a book of travel *"Across Three Oceans"* (1922); articles on India, (1915); and many feature stories and magazine articles. She was a writer for the *Lincoln Courier*, now defunct, and in 1917, was editor of the *Suffrage Messenger*.

An extensive traveler, Miss Miller made a trip around the world and to Australia 1909-10, and spent the winter of 1914-15 in India, and Burma. During the World War she acted as state secretary of the women's committee of the Nebraska Council of Defense, and served as trustee of the Nebraska Federation of Women's Clubs scholarship fund for ten years. She is a member of the Young Women's Christian Association, a charter member and director of the Matinee Musicale, member of Sorosis, member of the Nebraska Writers' Guild, charter member of the Woman's Club, and member of Sigma Alpha Iota, national professional musical fraternity. She belongs to the Episcopal Church of the Holy Trinity. Residence: Lincoln.

Arthur Scott Miller

Arthur Scott Miller, jeweler, optometrist and genealogist, was born at Lexington, McLean County, Illinois, April 29, 1866. He is the son of Jacob and Eliza (Lyons) Miller, Jr., the former born at Clarksburg, Virginia, January 20, 1816. He was a printer and publisher in Portsmouth, Ohio, before coming west; his descent was from settlers in Pennsylvania from Germany, prior to 1800. He died at Hollenburg, Kansas, February 18, 1893. His wife, Eliza Lyons, was born in Columbia County, Pennsylvania, January 11, 1822, and died at Hollenburg, June 17, 1908. A milliner prior to marriage, her mother was of the Miller family, and her father, James B. Lyons, was a descendant of the Leonne's of Rome, who immigrated to England and Scotland.

Mr. Miller attended the common schools of Illinois and Kansas, and came to Nebraska in 1893. He practiced optometry several years before the state law requiring examinations was passed, and was a charter member and one time president of the Nebraska State Optical Society. He has written several genealogies, among them those of the Babcock, Ludwick, Lyons and Miller families.

He was married to Zemira Urmina Babcock at Hollenburg, December 24, 1890. Mrs. Miller, who was born at Pierceville, Indiana, September 29, 1861, died at Lincoln, March 9, 1930. She was of the German family of Ludwick on the maternal side, and of the English Babcock family on the paternal side. There is one son, Joy Preston, born March 4, 1892, who married Elsie Dover. He is engaged as a jeweler and optometrist.

Mr. Miller's hobby is family history. He is a member of the Nebraskana Society, and attends Trinity Methodist Episcopal Church. Residence: Lincoln.

Benjamin George Miller

Benjamin George Miller, pioneer telephone man, was born on the homestead of his father, at Martell, Nebraska, October 3, 1877. His parents were John Gotlieb and Wilhelmina (Herzer) Miller. John Miller, whose father was connected with the German government, came to America in 1855. He was born at Nellmersbach, Baden, April 25, 1838, and died at Lincoln, March 28, 1924, one of Nebraska's earliest settlers. He came to Nebraska in the year 1869. Wilhelmina Miller, his wife, was a native of Baden, born May 16, 1839, and died at Lincoln, May 11, 1918. Her father was a wealthy miller, whose property was seized by the government during the Forty Year War. She came to America with her sister, Sophia, in 1855.

Benjamin Miller attended country schools and had one year at Lincoln High School. He worked his own way through school, attending Iowa Wesleyan University two years and the University of Nebraska three years, taking a course in electrical engineering. He has lived his entire life in Nebraska with the exception of five years spent with the Automatic Electric Company whose headquarters are in Chicago. During this time one year was spent in the factory and four years on the road installing and operating automatic telephone equipment, covering territory from coast to coast. During the year

1906, he built and promoted the first telephone exchanges at Denton and Kramer, and in the spring of 1907, erected a telephone exchange at Pleasant Dale. In the fall of 1907, he founded the Crete Telephone Company, with the position of secretary-treasurer and manager. At the present time he is president and manager of that corporation. In addition to the last mentioned position, in 1926 he purchased the Reynolds Telephone Company at Reynolds, and in 1927 the Frontier Telephone Company at Hubbell. At the present time Mr. Miller is principal owner and manager of these three companies. An active participant in other businesses, he has been director of the Nebraska State Telephone Association for several years, a director of the Crete Building and Loan Association and of the Tuxedo Park Association; president of the Centerville Cemetery Association, which he has reorganized, member of the city council, the Pioneers Telephone Association of America, and a director of the Martell Telephone Company. Recently he was elected to vice presidency of the Crete Swimming Pool.

His marriage to Florence Lenora Hazen was solemnized at Lawrence, Kansas, on November 16, 1911 (see *Nebraskana*). Mr. Miller attends the Congregational Church at Crete, and is a member of various civic and other organizations. These include the Red Cross, the Rotary Club, in which he has served as a director and as secretary, the Community Club, and the Boy Scouts. In the latter he has been active in the promotion of the Boy Scout Camp at Crete, and is especially interested in boys' work. He is a member of the Nebraskana Society also. His outdoor sports include golf, football, baseball, fishing and hunting. Residence: Crete.

Chester Arthur Miller

Chester Arthur Miller, physician and surgeon, was born at Chicago, Illinois, June 17, 1874, son of Austin and Helen M. (Phillips) Miller.

The father was born at Boonville, New York, January 12, 1840, and died at Greenfield, Iowa, August 8, 1916. He was a farmer, who served three years with Company F, 54th and 157th New York Infantry in the Civil War. His ancestry was English and French. His wife, Helen, was born at Charleston, South Carolina, March 29, 1844, and is of German and Irish descent.

Dr. Miller attended public school in Iowa, until 1891, was graduated from Keokuk Medical College of Physicians and Surgeons in 1902, and for two years was a student at the Nebraska Wesleyan University. He has been in active practice for more than 30 years.

He was married on September 16, 1903 to Louie Deweese at Fontanelle, Iowa. Mrs. Miller was born at Riverside, Iowa, August 25, 1880. She is the daughter of David and Margaret (Lemley) Deweese, and is a member of the Eastern Star and the American Legion Auxiliary. They have one daughter, Margaret Helen, born May 16, 1907, who married Kenneth Ryan. At the present time they are residing at Massena, Iowa.

Dr. Miller held the rank of first lieutenant in the Medical Corps in the World War, and is a member of the Medical Reserve Corps, and the American Legion. He is a Republican, a member of the Red Cross, the Masons, the American Medical Society, and the Congregational Church. His hobby is mechanics. Recently he was made a life member of the Nebraskana Society. Residence: Thedford.

Dr. Clinton James Miller

Dr. Clinton James Miller, physician and surgeon, was born in Benton County, Iowa, December 7, 1881, son of James Madison and Nancy Emily (Brown) Miller. James Madison Miller, born in Jo Daviess County, Illinois, in 1843, was descended from the mountaineers of Kentucky. He was a farmer and businessman until his death in Calhoun County, Iowa, in August, 1916. His wife, who was born in Henry County, Illinois, in 1850, came from a family which settled early in Kentucky.

Dr. Miller was graduated from public and high school, attended normal school two years, and was awarded his degree of Doctor of Medicine from the University of Nebraska in 1905, graduating with honors.

He was married on July 26, 1911 to Zona Estella McNutt at Ord. Mrs. Miller, who was born at West Liberty, Iowa, November 29, 1887, is of Pennsylvania Dutch descent. They have two children, Mary Louise, born April 25, 1925; and Roger James, born March 4, 1928. The children are adopted.

Dr. Miller has spent his entire professional life at Ord, where he is owner and surgeon of the Ord Hospital. He is a member of the American Medical Association, the Nebraska State Medical Association and the Valley County Medical Society. He is a Mason and a Presbyterian. For the past twenty years he has been interested in all sports relating to guns, his hobby being shotgun and big game hunting. Residence: Ord.

Edith Merle Miller

Born at Tecumseh, Nebraska, May 18, 1898, Edith Merle Miller is the daughter of Walter Elliott and Gertie Ann (Fink) Snyder. Her father, who is a farmer, was born at Galva, Illinois, July 19, 1873; his father served in the Nebraska legislature for two years. Her mother, an active club worker, was born at Elk Creek, Nebraska, October 7, 1878.

Mrs. Miller was a restaurant owner for six years, and taught in the public schools of Holt County for six years. She is a member of the Parent Teachers Association, having served as vice president of that organization in 1929 and 1930 and as president since 1930. Her religious affiliation is with the Methodist Episcopal Church of Page, and her favorite recreations are reading and studying.

She was married to Lowell Maxwell Miller at Page, December 25, 1917. Mr. Miller, who is a mechanic, was born at Sandburn, Iowa, January 29, 1894. They have a son, Maxwell, born October 14, 1920. Residence: Page.

Edwin Stanton Miller

Edwin Stanton Miller was born at Waterloo, Iowa, July 31, 1864. He is the son of Samuel Horner and Eliza (Beachley) Miller, the former a clergyman and farmer. Mr. Miller attended the public schools, and the University of Nebraska and University of Michigan.

He was married to Ida Arnold at Parsons, Kansas, March 10, 1887. Mrs. Miller was born at Ashland, Ohio, February 13, 1865. They have three children: Edna, born July 1, 1888, who married Henry Johnson; Eugene, born February 10, 1890, who married Mary Brown; and Max, born February 1, 1896, who married Phebe Folsom.

Mr. Miller has been engaged in the grain and milling business in Omaha for many years and is president of the Miller Cereal Mills. He is a Republican, and a member of the First Unitarian Church, is active in civic and educational work, and the Chamber of Commerce. He is a Rotarian and a Mason.

His clubs are the University Club and the Omaha Country Club, and his sport is golf. Residence: Omaha.

Florence Hazen Miller

A native of Sylvia, Reno County, Kansas, Florence Hazen Miller is the daughter of Daniel Webster and Frances Eliza (Kinnamon) Hazen. Daniel Webster Hazen, who is descended from a Revolutionary soldier, and whose family has been in America since 1649, was born at Azalia, Michigan, August 6, 1849. He is now retired. 1921. Her ancestors came to America in 1774, and her grandfather served in the war of 1812.

Mrs. Miller's mother who was born in North Carolina, on

FLORENCE HAZEN MILLER

Wagner—Crete

November 29, 1856, died at Lawrence, Kansas, March 6.

On November 16, 1911, Florence Hazen was united in marriage to Benjamin George Miller. Mr. Miller, who was secretary, treasurer and manager of the Crete Telephone Company, and now its president, was born in Lancaster County, In October, 1877.

For the past twenty years Mrs. Miller has been a resident of Nebraska, and has done much toward its advancement in civic lines. She was the proponent of the idea of the Living Christmas Tree, the first of which was planted under her direction, on April 23, 1923, in Central Park at Crete. A special program was prepared and historic soil taken from various spots in Saline County, together with some from Continental Hall and the Nation's Capitol, was placed beneath the tree. During the past several years the message of the tree has been recognized by many foreign countries, and has become an international project. Mrs. Miller was the organizing president of the Crete Society of the Children of the American Revolution, and it is through this organization that the work of the Living Christmas Tree Memorial has spread. The subject of this sketch has been for many years a member of the Daughters of the American Revolution, and for the past nine years has served as president of the Crete Society of the Children of the American Revolution and is now its state director.

Another of her outstanding accomplishments is the designing of the Nebraska State Flag. This banner displays the Great Seal of the State, in gold and silver, on a field of National blue. The bill became a law July 2, 1925, made it the official state flag for Nebraska. One of the original flags made by Mrs. Miller is being preserved at Arbor Lodge Museum; Governor McMullen also is the possessor of one of the first ones created by her.

Since 1925 she has written a condensed history of the Living Christmas Tree and the Nebraska State Flag. She is also the author of the international code, which provides that Christmas trees shall be burned as soon as they become useless, much in the same manner as the national emblem.

Among her various civic activities are included the following: From 1925 to the end of 1927, she served as councillor of the D. F. P. A., and during 1926, she was state chairman of national defense for the Nebraska organization of the Daughters of the American Revolution. She was appointed local chairman for Better Homes in America by Secretary of Commerce Herbert Hoover in 1927. She has served as state chairman of finance of the Nebraska Genealogical Society, a Rotarian Ann, and holds membership in the Woman's Club, the Nebraskana Society and the Crete Congregational Church.

Mrs. Miller suggested that Francis Scott Key Memorial Bridge at Washington display the national emblem at all times, in memory of the author of the national anthem, and create the depths of feeling in those who pass over the bridge that inspired Francis Key to write the song.

She is the author of the *Stars and Stripes Forever*, the national march, made famous by John Philip Sousa. The bill to honor Mr. Sousa was introduced by Honorable J. N. Norton.

It is interesting to note, in connection with Mrs. Miller's life, that during her research work she has discovered that the World Court was of American origin. There now is on file in the Congressional Library at Washington, through the courtesy of Mrs. Miller, a volume published nearly a century ago by her great grandfather, which contains an article by David Millard, in which he describes it as an International Congress, together with a photograph of himself, which was presented to the library.

In December, 1929, Mrs. Miller presented the Nebraska State Flag to officers and crew of the *U. S. S. Omaha* which is displayed in the Recreation Room among the numerous trophies won by the ship. Mrs. Miller served on first United States Flag Contest in 1929. It is interesting that out of 71 names submitted Mrs. Miller received the honor of naming Tuxedo Park. Residence: Crete.

Frank Joseph Miller

Frank J. Miller has lived in this state all his life and since 1901, has been engaged in business as a furniture dealer and funeral director in Colfax County. He was born at Dodge, Nebraska, January 25, 1881, the son of Vaclav and Margaret (Pojar) Miller. His father, who was a farmer for 45 years, was born in Bohemia, May 16, 1848, and died at Dodge, August 19, 1919. His mother was born in Bohemia, October 20, 1848, and died at Dodge, April 7, 1918.

Mr. Miller attended grade school at Glencoe, Nebraska, and then engaged in farming with his father. In 1901, he was a student at the Fremont Normal School at Fremont, Nebraska, and the following summer bought his present business from Faymon & Son. He also owns a one-half interest in the company Miller & Hunlicek, at Dodge.

He has taken an active interest in civic affairs at Clarkson, for many years, and holds membership in various community organizations. He was a member of the village council for seven years; is now president of the local Red Cross; and holds membership in the Nebraskana Society. He is a member of Z. C. B. J., the Modern Woodmen of America, and the Knights of Columbus. His favorite sport is baseball. He is a Catholic.

Mr. Miller was united in marriage with Mary M. Chieboun, at Schuyler, Colfax County, Nebraska, August 16, 1905. Mrs. Miller, who assists her husband in his business, was born at Prague, Nebraska, August 18, 1885. Their two children, who were born in Clarkson, are Lauretta, born December 26, 1907; and Frank Joseph, born August 26, 1910. Lauretta attended the School of Music at Lake Forest, Illinois, for two years, and was a student at the University of Missouri, for three years. Frank attended military school at Lexington, Missouri, and later was a student at the University of Missouri for two years. Residence: Clarkson.

Frederick Emanuel Miller

Frederick E. Miller was born at Opheim, Illinois, December 2, 1880, the son of Hjalmer Richard and Lizzie (Hanson) Miller. His father, who is a physician, was born in Stockholm, Sweden, July 27, 1855; his paternal grandfather, was active in the Danish Prussian War in 1864, and later was vice consul to Sweden. His mother was born in Hievle, Sweden, April 24, 1848, and died at Chicago, September 22, 1922. Her parents were farmers.

Mr. Miller has lived in Nebraska for 45 years and has been connected with the T. G. Northwall Company for 32 years. He has been assistant secretary, vice president, and is now president of this organization.

He was married at Red Oak, Iowa, July 23, 1913 to Amy Elenora Austin. Mrs. Miller was born in Page County, Iowa, May 2, 1883. They have one daughter, Dorothy, born November 28, 1918. Mr. Miller was a member of the Nebraska National Guard, 1919-20. He holds membership in the Red Cross; Omaha Chamber of Commerce; Lions Club; and Noon-day Luncheon Club. He is a member of the Zion Evangelical Lutheran Church of Omaha, and is a Republican. Residence: Omaha.

George Adelbert Miller

George Adelbert Miller, who was a pioneer farmer in Furnas County, Nebraska, was born at Albany, Illinois, September 17, 1872, the son of George Michels and Nancy Jane (Wilson) Miller. His father, who was a farmer, died at Wilsonville, October 20, 1901. His mother, whose ancestry was Pennsylvania Dutch, died at Wilsonville, April 15, 1901.

Mr. Miller engaged in farming near Wilsonville until his retirement in 1917. He still owns his original farm, and is acting as vice president of the Wilsonville State Bank. He is affiliated with the Wilsonville Presbyterian Church, holds membership in the Commercial Club and the Red Cross, and is a member of the Nebraskana Society. He is a Mason and a member of the Eastern Star.

On March 14, 1894, he married Minnie May Hoylman at Wilsonville. Mrs. Miller, whose ancestry is German, was born at Roseland, Nebraska, April 1, 1886. Three children were born to this marriage: Helen, February 14, 1895, who married Everett H. Wilmot; Millie Marie, January 12, 1898, who married Glenn R. Best; and Ruby Wilma, September 20, 1911. Residence: Wilsonville.

George Henry Miller

George H. Miller, son of George Miller and Elizabeth P. (Erford) Miller, was born at Peoria, Illinois, March 18, 1858. His father was born at Harrisburg, Pennsylvania, February 3, 1828 of Scotch parentage. He was a miller by trade, and later a farmer. He died at Surprise, Nebraska, January 19, 1888.

His mother was born in Harrisburg, Pennsylvania, December 1, 1827, and died at Surprise, on June 17, 1915. Her ancestors were German.

Mr. Miller had a limited education under private tutors in Indiana. Coming to Lincoln, in 1872, he traveled to Seward, by stage coach. For a year he worked in a mill at Ulysses, and afterward operated a mill at Central City, five years. In 1881, he came to Surprise, where he built the mill which he has operated for forty-two years. On May 8, 1881, at Central City, Nebraska, he married Anna F. Cummings. She was born at Central City, November 23, 1862. To this union four children were born: Myra O., March 6, 1883, who died August 24, 1888; Nellie M., July 26, 1885, the wife of John H. Hertel, of Los Angeles; Roy Earl, October 25, 1889, who is married to Margaret Murphy now of Omaha; and Georgia Anna, January 22, 1899, who became the wife of Allen W. Gubser, and lives on a farm northeast of Surprise.

George Miller is affiliated with the Democratic party and the Lutheran Church at Surprise. He has resided in Nebraska, fifty-nine years and is a member of the Nebraskana Society.

Mr. Miller is director of The State Bank of Surprise. He organized the Tuscan Lodge No. 130 in Surprise, and has been a member of the order of Ancient Free and Accepted Masons for more than fifty years. Residence: Surprise.

Harry Daniel Miller

Harry Daniel Miller, banker and executive, was born at Marengo, Iowa, October 9, 1869, son of Levi and Lucretia (Tutweiler) Miller. Levi Miller, who was born at Columbus, Ohio, October 28, 1938, was admitted to the bar of Nebraska in 1881, and served as county attorney and mayor of Stanton. He was president of the First National Bank from 1883 to the time of his death on February 18, 1920. During the Civil War he served 1862-65 as a captain of the 2nd Missouri Cavalry. His grandfather, Michael Miller, was a fifer in Peter Grubbs Junior Company and saw active service in the Battle of Long Island, in the Revolution, and at Schaefferstown, Pennsylvania. Lucretia Miller, wife of Levi, was born in New Lexington, Ohio, August 15, 1845. She is active in church work and has served as president of the Sorosis Club. Her father and grandfather served in the War of 1812, and came from the Green and Tutweiler families of Rockingham County, Virginia.

Harry D. Miller attended Stanton High School, and Eastman's College at Poughkeepsie, New York. In 1901, he was one of the organizers of the Stanton Electric Light Company, and upon the death of his father he became president of the First National Bank. He is secretary-treasurer of the Stanton Telephone Company, and a director of the Mountain Timber Company of Oregon, and treasurer of that organization. He is treasurer and director of the Stanton County Fair Association and secretary and director of the Odd Fellows Cemetery Association of Stanton.

A Democrat, Mr. Miller is active in party politics and has several times been chairman of the county central committee and a member of the Democratic State Committee. During the World War he was chairman of the Stanton County War Savings Stamps committee, and a member of the Nebraska Council of Defense.

A member of the Red Cross, the Commercial Club and the Volunteer Fire Department, he was president of the Bankers Association of the Third District in 1917, and for fourteen years was a member of the board of the Stanton Public Library. His fraternal organizations include the Elks, Eagles, Knights of Pythias, Sons of Herman, Ben Hur, Modern Brotherhood of America, Ancient Order of United Workmen and the Royal Highlanders. His social club is the Stanton Country Club. Residence: Stanton. (Photograph in Album).

Harvey Dunlap Miller

Harvey Dunlap Miller, a banker at Clearwater, Nebraska, since 1908, has lived in this state all his life. He was born at Clearwater, November 19, 1884, the son of George Putnam and Ida May (Dunlap) Miller. His father, who is of German descent, was born in New York, May 18, 1856, and has been a teacher and farmer for many years. His mother, whose ancestry is Scotch, was born at Kingston, New York, February 18, 1860.

Mr. Miller was graduated from the Clearwater High School in 1904, and was graduated from the Nebraska Normal College at Wayne, Nebraska where he was a member of Philomathean. During 1908 he attended the Norfolk Business College. He taught in the public schools, 1905-06, was employed in a drug store, 1906-07, and in 1908 entered the Citizens State Bank of Clearwater as bookkeeper. He was made assistant cashier in 1910 and since 1925 has served as cashier of that institution.

He was employed in the banking department of the Nebraska government as special agent of closed banks from 1927 to 1929. Mr. Miller is a member of the Board of Education of Clearwater, is treasurer of the Commercial Club, and holds membership in the Modern Woodmen of America and the Independent Order of Odd Fellows. He served as secretary of the local Red Cross during the World War and was formerly a member of the Young Men's Christian Association. Among his sports are baseball, tennis, hunting, and fishing.

On June 15, 1910, he was married at Clearwater to Edna Grace Hildebrand who was born at Stratton, Nebraska, October 20, 1896. To this marriage two children were born: Audrey, May 21, 1912, who is a teacher; and Helen, June 30, 1915, who is a student in the Clearwater High School. Mr. Miller is a Democrat. Residence: Clearwater.

Harvey J. Miller

Born at Berlin, Pennsylvania, November 4, 1867, Harvey J. Miller has been a resident of Nebraska for forty-six years. He is the son of Ananias Peter and Mary (Meyers) Miller, the former of whom was born at Berlin, Pennsylvania, and died at Carleton, Nebraska, on July 2, 1889. He was a farmer of German descent. His wife, Mary, was also born at Berlin, and died at Carleton on October 9, 1913. She was of German descent also.

Upon completion of his elementary education, Mr. Miller attended Berlin Normal School and was graduated in 1884. He is married to Zua Ava Hiatt, who was born at Mt. Victory, Ohio, April 30, 1868. Their marriage took place at Carleton, May 6, 1890.

Mrs. Miller's parents, T. E. and Eliza Jane (Williams) Hiatt, were pioneers, who lived in the community of Carleton for many years. They homesteaded there in 1872, coming from Bellfontaine, Ohio. Mrs. Miller received part of her education in Ohio, and the balance in Carleton, studied music at Nebraska Wesleyan University and was for many years a music teacher at Carleton.

Mr. Miller has been in business for many years. Admitted to practice embalming in 1903, he has been a part owner and manager of Miller Brothers Furniture and Undertaking business since 1899. For twenty years he was justice of the peace and police judge, and for two terms was mayor of Carleton.

He is affiliated with the Brethren Church of Carleton, is a Mason and Modern Woodman of America and a member of the Nebraskana Society. Residence: Carleton

Harvey M. Miller

Harvey M. Miller, railroad agent, was born in Berks County, Pennsylvania, the 5th day of September, 1863, and has been associated with the Chicago and Northwestern Railroad Company since August 3, 1887.

His parents, Samuel M. and Esther (Christman) Miller, were born in Berks County, the former on May 3, 1834, and the latter about that time, the exact date being unknown. Samuel M. Miller was an early day farmer in Iowa, on land southwest of Perry. He died there about May 25, 1909. Esther Christman Miller died about sixty years ago, while Harvey M. Miller was still very young. She was of German descent.

Educated in the public schools, Mr. Miller also attended Drake University, and while there played football. There were no organized athletics at that time, and no letters were awarded. As stated above, Mr. Miller became associated with the Chicago and Northwestern Railroad on August 3, 1887, as agent, and since August 7, 1892, has been its agent at Seward.

He is a Republican, and has served as a member of the city school board for about twenty years. He is a staunch pacifist, and during the World War was a four minute speaker, and was active in civilian propects of that period. A Presbyterian, he is a member of the Federated Presbyterian and Congregational Church of Seward. He has served at various times on the board of the Young Men's Christian Association, and is a member of the Blue Lodge of the Masons. Mr. Miller is also a member of the Red Cross, the Chamber of Commerce, the Magazine Club and the Nebraskana Society. His favorite recreation is chess or checkers.

On August 23, 1893, he was united in marriage to Grace Lohring Porter at Seward. Mrs. Miller, who was born in Warren County, Illinois, December 23, 1865, was principal of Seward High School at the time of her marriage. There are five children, Chauncey M., born October 9, 1894, who is a railroad telegrapher and is married to Viola Petrick; Harold V., born March 14, 1896, who is a Union Pacific agent and married Gertrude Neely; Maurine M., born June 18, 1898, who married Edward H. Wehrs; Elmer, born October 3, 1900, a civil engineer, who married Melda Perry; and Helen E., born June 14, 1903, who is at home. Residence: Seward.

Jay Calvin Miller

Jay Calvin Miller, a physician at Gresham, York County, Nebraska, has lived in this state for 39 years. He was born at Firth, Gage County, Nebraska, August 20, 1892, the son of David Jacob and Kate (Ellis) Miller. His father, who is a retired farmer, was born in Illinois, December 6, 1868. His mother was born in Ohio, October 13, 1868, and is still living.

Dr. Miller attended grade school at Sunny Side, Nebraska, and was graduated from the high school at Cortland. In 1915 he was awarded the M. D. degree at Cotner University and since that time he has been engaged in the practice of medicine in Nebraska. He is a member of the York County Medical Society, Scottish

Rite Masons, the Modern Woodmen of America, Odd Fellows, and The Nebraskana Society. His political affiliation is with the Democratic party.

He married Edna Alice Macrow at Lincoln, Lancaster County, Nebraska, June 15, 1916. Mrs. Miller was born at Huntley, Nebraska, August 22, 1898. They have two children: David, born August 8, 1918; and Ann, born November 8, 1922. Residence: Gresham.

John Elwood Miller

For over 45 years John Elwood Miller has been in the service of the Chicago, Burlington & Quincy Railroad, in Nebraska. He was born in Bedford County, Pennsylvania, November 15, 1857, the son of Michael C. and Margaret (Arnold) Miller. His father, a merchant, was born in Bedford County in 1831, and died at Buffalo Mills, Pennsylvania in 1886; he was descended from Elias Miller who served in the Revolution. His mother was born in Bedford County, July 1, 1832, and died at Point Marion, Pennsylvania, in 1918. She was a descendant of John Cessna, a volunteer in the Revolutionary War who was a member of the constitutional convention of 1774 which drafted the first constitution of Pennsylvania.

Mr. Miller was graduated from Schellsburg Academy in 1879, was graduated from Pennsylvania State Normal School in 1881, and attended Indiana State Normal College in 1884. He was elected to the Clio Debating Society. He gave 45 years of continuous service as station agent in the employ of the railroad company, stationed at Harvard, Nebraska, one year, Tamora, Nebraska, two and a half years, and at Waco, Nebraska, nearly 42 years. The last 19 years of this service were given without a day's absence.

He is a member of the Chicago, Burlington & Quincy Veterans. He was united in marriage with Jennie Belle Stuckey at Bedford, March 23, 1886. Mrs. Miller was born at Bedford, December 12, 1860. Their daughter, Marjorie Mae, born September 16, 1891, married Earl Clifton Beck. Residence: Waco.

John Harrold Miller

John H. Miller, Nebraska State Railway Commissioner, was born in Henderson, Chester County, Tennessee, on February 5, 1888, son of John Alexandria and Matilda (Ash) Miller. His parents were descended from early Irish and Scotch-Irish settlers in Tennessee, John Miller, born May 14, 1856, died at Henderson, on November 16, 1928. He was a plantation owner and stock breeder. His wife, Matilda, was born in December, 1866, and died shortly after her son's birth.

Upon the completion of his public and high school work Mr. Miller attended Freed Hardeman College. In 1910 he came to Nebraska where he took extension work in the University, while engaged in railroad work, which continued until 1921. In 1914 he was married to Vesta Mae Austin at Papillion, Nebraska. Mrs. Miller, who is of English descent, was born at Lincoln, May 24, 1892. There is one son, James Franklin, born October 16, 1916.

In 1916 Mr. Miller entered sales work continuing for less than a year when he was promoted to sales manager, filling that position until 1925. He then was engaged in the mercantile business for about a year. In 1924 he was candidate for the office of State Railway Commissioner against the Hon. H. G. Taylor, and was defeated at the primaries by a small margin. Two years later he filed again and defeated the then incumbent Hon. Thorne A. Brown for the Republican nomination by a large majority. He defeated Floyd L. Bolen his Democratic opponent on November 2, 1926, by a large majority, and was appointed by His Excellency, Governor Adam McMullen on November 6, 1926, to fill the unexpired term of Mr. Brown who had resigned. His present term of office expires on January 3, 1933.

In his periods of recreation Mr. Miller enjoys hiking, boating, fishing, and hunting, and has for his hobby gardening and flower growing. He is affiliated with the First Church of Christ, Scientist, of Boston, and while not a member assists financially and otherwise, with the work of the Salvation Army. He is a York Rite Mason and Knight Templar, an Odd Fellow, Rebekah, and member of the Eastern Star. His historical and educational organizations include the Parent-Teachers' Association, the American Association for the Advancement of Science, the Nebraskana Society and the Greater Nebraska Club. Residence: Lincoln. (Photograph in Album).

John Wesley Miller

Born at Waterloo, Iowa, June 10, 1860, John Wesley Miller is the son of William and Lydia (Fike) Miller. His father, a native of Myersdale, Somerset County, Pennsylvania, born September 26, 1827, was a pioneer farmer in Iowa. His death occurred at Waterloo, January 10, 1908. Lydia (Fike) Miller, also born at Myersdale, on May 9, 1829, died at Waterloo, March 18, 1862.

John Wesley Miller received his education in country schools, and soon thereafter engaged in farming, for some time in Iowa. On September 28, 1882, he was united in marriage to Celia Emily Nedrow, at Waterloo. Mrs. Miller was born at Preston, Minnesota, April 8, 1863.

There are four children living, and two deceased: Franklin I., born May 16, 1884, who married Maud E. Snyder, died April 2, 1928; Cuthbert R., born May 16, 1886, married Cordie B. Snyder; Ephraim G., born January 21, 1889, married Olive J. Keim; Lulu M., born February 22, 1891, married William W. Keim; Ethel F., born September 28, 1895, died Stpember 8, 1899; Gladys Marie, born January 15, 1898, married Oscar L. Bower.

During most of his forty years' residence in Nebraska Mr. Miller was a farmer. At the present time he is retired. Residence: Davenport.

Max Arnold Miller

Max Arnold Miller was born at Beatrice, Nebraska, February 1, 1896, the son of Edwin Stanton and Ida (Arnold) Miller. His father was born at Myersdale, Pennsylvania, July 31, 1865, and his mother at Ashland, Ohio, February 13, 1866.

Mr. Miller was graduated from the Lincoln High School, and for three years was a student at the University of Nebraska, where he was elected to membership in Phi Kappa Psi. Since 1917, he has been connected with the Miller Cereal Mills, and is now vice president of this organization.

During the World War he served as a sergeant in the United States Army. He is a member of the American Legion, Omaha Club of Omaha, the Omaha Chamber of Commerce, Trinity Episcopal Cathedral.

His marriage to Phebe Folsom was solemnized at Lincoln, Lancaster County, Nebraska, October 6, 1917. Mrs. Miller was born at Lincoln, May 19, 1895. They have two children: Morris F., born March 17, 1919; and Edwin Stanton, born April 16, 1920. Residence: Omaha.

Oscar George Miller

Oscar George Miller, insurance executive, banker and real estate dealer, was born at Crete, Nebraska, April 27, 1888. He is the son of Theodore Henry and Mary (George) Miller, the former born at Lengede Ampt Peine, Germany, April 8, 1846. He came to America on January 21, 1867, and enlisted in the 36th United States Infantry on the way to For Kearney, serving later at Salt Lake City. He received his honorable discharge in 1870. He was president of the Crete State Bank, served as mayor two years, councilman four years, and was a member of the school board. He died at Palo Alto, California, July 7, 1928.

Mary, his wife, was born at Sheboygan, Wisconsin, March 30, 1847, and died at Palo Alto, November 16, 1920. She was a member of the German Lutheran Church at Crete, and of the Old Settlers Club. Her father, Ludwig George, was born in Bergen, Saxony, June 1, 1809, and died there in September, 1887; her mother, Hannah Eilhardt, was born in Gesper, Saxony, April 26, 1808, and died there February 1, 1891.

Oscar G. Miller attended the Crete elementary schools, Doane College and the Lincoln Business College. On June 24, 1914, he was married to Grace Florence Holbrook at Firth, Lancaster County, Nebraska. Mrs. Miller attended Firth High School and Peru State Normal, and afterward taught school in Firth and Lincoln. She also attended the Nebraska School of Business in Lincoln. She is past historian and former vice president of the Nebraska chapter of Daughters of Founders and Patriots, a member of the local chapter of the Daughters of the American Revolution and of the Mayflower Society of Massachusetts. Her father, Enos Holbrook, was born at Vesta, Johnson County, Nebraska, May 13, 1858, and died December 11, 1928; her mother was Harriett (Goldsby) Holbrook, born March 20, 1861, died December 5, 1924. Enos Holbrook was the first white child born on Yankee Creek, Johnson County, Nebraska. Both Mr. and Mrs. Miller are members of the Congregational Church at Crete. They have one son, Robert, born August 17, 1915. He was graduated from the 8th grade in Crete, in 1929, and was his class president. He is a member of Crete chapter, Children of the American Revolution, and was its organizing chaplain. He attended school in Hollywood, California, in 1923, Los Angeles, in 1926, and Beverly Hills, in 1931. He is an expert rifleman, and a member of the National Rifle Association and the Junior Rifle Corps.

Oscar George Miller has resided in Nebraska 43 years, and since manhood has engaged in business there. He is engaged in the general insurance business, is the owner and supervisor of stores, office buildings and lands at Crete, and a director of the Crete State Bank. During the World War he served in France with the Medical Corps, and is a member of the American Legion. He is a member of the Crete Chamber of Commerce, the Knights of Pythias and The Nebraskana Society. He enjoys golf, while his hobbies are travel and beautifying his home grounds. His clubs include the Eastridge Country Club, Fifty-Fifty Dancing Club, and the Art Club, all of Lincoln. Residence: Crete.

Stephen Daniel Gear Miller

Stephen Daniel Gear Miller, prominent farmer and director of the Shickley State Bank, was born at Marshalltown, Iowa, May 18, 1877, son of Albert Martin Townsend and Mary Catherine (Price) Miller.

Albert M. T. Miller was born in Clear Springs, Maryland, November 22, 1847, and was a farmer and clergyman until his death at Beatrice, December 17, 1901. His grandfather, Samuel S. Miller, was a soldier in the Revolutionary War. Mary Catherine Price was born at Oregon, Illinois, September 28, 1845, and died at Pickrell, Nebraska, September 1, 1894. She was a teacher, an active church worker and a writer. Her family were German farmers.

Mr. Miller attended public school in district 57, of Gage County, and from 1897 until 1899, was a student at McPherson College, Kansas, graduating from the commercial department in June, 1899. He was also a student at Nebraska State Agricultural College.

On October 5, 1904, he was married to Clara Edith Stouffer at Mount Morris, Illinois. Mrs. Miller was born at Polo, Illinois, August 13, 1879. Her father was a farmer and clergyman, and her grandfather a clergyman, both in the Church of the Brethren. Mr. and Mrs. Miller have three children, Ruth, born June 20, 1907, who was graduated from McPherson College and is teaching in Bruning High School; Albert, born September 18, 1910, who is a farmer, while Pauline is a freshman in college.

Mr. Miller is a Republican. He was elected a master farmer of Nebraska in 1930, and is a member of the Thayer County Farm Bureau. He is a member of the Bethel Church of the Brethren, the Red Cross, and the Nebraskana Society. From 1901 until 1920, he was a member of the school board of district 57 of Gage County, and from 1924 until 1930, was a trustee at McPherson College. Residence: Carleton.

William Peter Miller

On May 29, 1880, William Peter Miller was born at Polk Nebraska, the son of Henry Peter and Matilda (Jones) Miller. His father, a farmer, was born in Sweden, and died at Polk, Nebraska, in October, 1918. Matilda Miller was born in Sweden, and died at Polk, in June, 1899. William P. Miller received his education in a country school.

His marriage to Anna Louise Rydson took place February 11, 1903, at Stark, Nebraska. She was born at Stark, February 3, 1882, and to their union two children were born: Orlie, born March 19, 1903; and Floyd, born October 18, 1904. Both reside on the homestead.

Mr. Miller, a life resident of the state, has engaged in farming many years. He served as treasurer of his school district during all the time he resided on the farm, taking the office from his father. His son, Orlie, now holds the office. He is a Mason, a life member of The Nebraskana Society and is a Republican. Residence: Polk.

William Forsyth Milroy

For the past 48 years William F. Milroy has been engaged in the practice of medicine in Nebraska. He was born at York, Livingston County, New York, December 28, 1855, the son of James and Sarah Ann (Cullings) Milroy. His father, who was a farmer, was born at Cambret, Scotland, August 4, 1818, came to America in 1819, and died at York, New York. His mother, whose Scotch ancestors settled at Schenectady, New York, before the Revolution, was born at York, September 7, 1827, and died there September 18, 1908.

Dr. Milroy received his early education at York, and in 1879 was graduated from the state normal school at Geneseo, New York. He was a student at the University of Rochester, 1879, Johns Hopkins, 1880, and Columbia Medical School in New York, where he was graduated with M. D. degree in 1883. He is a member of Alpha Omega Alpha and Delta Kappa Epsilon.

He is ex-president of the Nebraska State Medical Association, past president and member of the Missouri Valley and Douglas County Medical Societies. He is a member of the American Therapeutic Society and the American College of Physicians. He is visiting physician at Immanuel Hospital, and has been on the staff of the Clarkson Memorial Hospital, and Douglas County Hospital. He is professor of clinical medicine at the college of medicine at the University of Nebraska. He is serving as president of the Nebraska Children's Home Society.

Dr. Milroy is the author of numerous articles published in medical periodical journals, the most important of which is: *An Undescribed Variety of Hereditary Edema*, 1892, which was later known in the medical world as *Milroy's Disease*. He was a member of the medical advisory committee in connection with selection by draft for army service during the World War. He is a member of the American Medical Association. He holds membership in the Happy Hollow Club and the University of Omaha. He is affiliated with the First Presbyterian Church of Omaha; is a member of the Young Men's Christian Association; and is a member of the Nebraskana Society. He is a Republican.

He was united in marriage with Lillian Barton at Baltimore, Maryland, April 27, 1886. Mrs. Milroy, whose ancestry is French and Dutch, was born at Baltimore, July 9, 1858. They have two children: Isabelle, who married LeRoy C. Dunn, residing in Des Moines, Iowa; and Katharine, who married Melvin Uhl residing at Longbeach, California. Residence: Omaha.

Edward Allen Miner

One of the leading business men at Broken Bow, Nebraska, is Edward Allen Miner, who has resided in this state continuously for the past 39 years. He was born at Pleasantville, Iowa, September 13, 1876, the son of James and Margaret (Kamp) Miner. His father, who was a furniture dealer until 1878 and later was a farmer, was born in Indiana, July 16, 1842, and died at Pleasantville, Iowa, April 30, 1916; he served in Company K, Third Iowa Volunteer Cavalry, during the Civil War. His mother was born in Holland, December 5, 1845, and died at Pleasantville, June 14, 1930.

Mr. Miner attended a rural school in Marion County, Iowa, and later was a student in the public schools of Greeley County, Nebraska. He taught school from 1896 to 1901, worked for a mercantile establishment from 1902 to 1904, and from 1905 to 1909 was employed in a real estate office at Wolbach, Nebraska. He was cashier of a bank in Wolbach, Nebraska, 1908-09, and since 1917 has been engaged in the real estate and insurance business independently. He is secretary of the Coffman Farms Company and the Corn Belt Realty Company.

Mr. Miner is a member of the Public Service Club at Broken Bow, is affiliated with the Independent Order of Odd Fellows and the Red Cross, and holds membership in the Nebraskana Society. He is a Republican, but votes independently on local issues.

His marriage to Sena Madsen occurred at Central City, June 16, 1909. Mrs. Miner was born in Denmark, March 4, 1887. They have a son, Verdon McClure, born May 21, 1913, who is a student at the University of Nebraska. Residence: Broken Bow.

Henry Rufus Miner

Early in the 17th century Thomas Miner came from England and settled in the Plymouth Colony. Since the early days in American history members of the family have been prominent in civic and business affairs in this country. Ephraim Miner, pioneer business man and public leader of South Dakota, was the son of Rufus Miner and the grandson of Thomas Miner. Born at Scriba, Oswego County, New York, April 5, 1833, he was a member of the Dakota territorial legislature and was one of the founders of Yankton College in South Dakota. He was one of the organizers of a company to put down the first artesian well in the Dakotas, and organized the first electric light company in that territory. He died at Yankton, March 26, 1912. His wife, Amanda P. (Stock) Miner is descended from German ancestors who came to America in 1700. One branch of her family is Scotch, and several members served in the Revolution. Born at Marticville, Lancaster County, Pennsylvania, November 16, 1837, she went to the Dakotas where she took an active part in church and educational affairs, and was one of the founders of the First Congregational Church there. She was a life long student and was especially interested in the study of geology. She brought the first piano into the Dakotas on a Missouri River steamboat. She died at Yankton, April 7, 1917.

Henry Rufus Miner, son of Ephraim and Amanda Miner, was born at Yankton, September 27, 1869. His elementary education was received in the Yankton public schools, and in 1891 he was graduated from Yankton College with the degree B. S.; he was awarded the master's degree in 1900. His M. D. was received at the Chicago Homeopathic Medical School, 1894, and Hannemann College, Chicago, 1902. While he was in the army he was sent to post graduate school at Harvard University studying the special army course in bone and joint surgery for overseas assignment; and he had a six months course in the Children's Orthopedic Hospital at Harvard, 1920. He continued his post-graduate work for three months at the

Townsend—Lincoln

HENRY RUFUS MINER

University of Lyons, France. While in college he won the championship in 50 and 100 yard dash and high jump, and was a tennis enthusiast.

He was admitted to the practice of medicine at Fairfield, Clay County, Nebraska, in June, 1894, since which time he has practiced medicine constantly except for a brief period during the war when he served in the army. He is the author of many articles on medical subjects for various state societies and for the *Nebraska State Medical Journal*, among them: *Rehabilitation After Infantile Paralysis*, which was copied by the *International Clinical Medicine* at Baltimore, 1928. At the present time he is a member of the staff of the Falls City Hospital, Falls City, Nebraska, in the department of surgery.

He was united in marriage at Lincoln, Nebraska, October 17, 1899, to Maude I. Rathburn, who was born at Cleveland, Ohio, July 24, 1871. Mrs. Miner was graduated from St. Luke's Hospital in Chicago in 1897. She answered the first call for nurses in the Spanish American War and was among the first seventeen trained nurses to take the field in America. She is a cousin of Thomas Edison, famous inventor, and is related to the Marsh family and Commodore Perry. Their three children are: Dorothy, born March 21, 1901, studied at Nebraska and Wisconsin Universities, and was graduated from the New York School of Fine and Applied Arts and the Paris School of Fine and Applied Arts. Jean, born April 15, 1903, received her B. A. degree from the University of Nebraska and attended Sorbonne University in Paris, one year, specializing in French. She is now instructor in French at the University of Nebraska. Henry Richard, born May 9, 1910, was graduated from Shattuck Military Academy of Faribault, Minnesota, in June, 1930.

In the World War Dr. Miner was chief surgeon in the orthopedic service, Base Hospital 123, Mars-Sur-Allier, Rhone, France, with the rank of captain. He is a member of the American Legion and in 1922 was post commander. He is a member of the local chapter of the Veterans of Foreign Wars, and is local president of the Reserve Officers Association. He is president of the Richardson County Medical Society, and is a member of the state, tri-state and national medical associations.

In 1916 he was elected a member of the Falls City school board, serving three years, and in 1929 was again elected for a three year term. He is a member of the American Medical Editors and Authors Association of New York. In 1903 he was president of the Nebraska State Homeopathic Medical Society. He is a member of the Rotary Club and of The Nebraskana Society. A Master Mason, he is a member of the Army Consistory No. 1, Forth Leavenworth, Nobles of the Mystic Shrine, Scottish Rite at Salina, Kansas. He is affiliated with the Woodmen of the World, Royal Highlanders, the Ancient Order of United Workmen and the Elks. He is a member of St. Thomas Episcopal Church.

Dr. Miner's social clubs are the University Club, and the Elk's Country Club, at Falls City. His favorite sports are golf, hunting, fishing, and tennis. Keeping fit in the out-of-doors is his hobby. Residence: Falls City. (Photograph on Page 832).

Evelyn Mills Minier

Born at Neosho, Missouri, December 24, 1884, Evelyn Mills Minier is the daughter of James Marshall and Lucy Alice (Portlock) Mills. Her father, who was born at Peoria, Illinois, July 17, 1852, was a farmer and later a hotel manager, whose family came from England. They included professional people, especially clergymen. Lucy Alice Portlock, who was born at Table Grove, Illinois, May 26, 1866, comes from a family of German farmers.

Educated first in the public schools of Galesburg, Illinois, Mrs. Minier was graduated from Galesburg High School in 1901. She also attended country school in Rawlins County, Kansas, and upper grades in Table Grove, Illinois. In June, 1906, she received her A. B. from Knox College. During the summer of 1908, she attended the Columbia School of Expression at Chicago. Since her

college days she has been interested in debate and dramatics. She received scholastic honors and was president of her junior class at Knox College.

During 1906-07, she taught in the country schools of Galva, and in 1908, the seventh grade city school; during 1909 she taught seventh and eighth grades at Wolsenburg, Colorado, and during 1909-10-11, taught English and expression at the Whitewater, Wisconsin High School. Returning to Missouri, in 1911, she was teacher of English and expression in Central High School, at St. Joseph.

On August 14, 1914, she was united in marriage to W. E. Minier, at Monmouth, Illinois, and has since resided in Nebraska. A Republican she was vice-chairman for Nebraska of the Hoover-Curtis Clubs in 1928.

Active in club work, she was president of the Oakland Woman's Club 1917-19, Third District Federation president 1919-21; president of the Nebraska Federation of Women's Clubs 1925-27; director 1927-29, and community service chairman of the General Federation of Women's Clubs 1928-32. She was secretary of the Oakland Chapter of the Red Cross 1917-30, is a member of the Oakland Methodist Episcopal Church and a member of the Oakland Library Board (1920). She has served five years as superintendent of the Sunday School, and three as president of the Ladies' Aid Society. Residence: Oakland.

Thomas Alexander Minier

Thomas Alexander Minier, son of George Washington and Sarah (Ireland) Minier, was born in Minier, Illinois, November 25, 1858. George Washington Minier, a farmer, clergyman and president of the American Forestry Association, was born at Milan, Pennsylvania, October 8, 1813, and died at Austin, Illinois, February 18, 1902. George W. Minier came to Illinois in 1837, and was employed by the government to survey the Illinois River from Ottawa to the junction with the Mississippi. He was an intimate friend of Abraham Lincoln. His wife, Sarah, was born in Clark County, Virginia, November 19, 1819, and died at Minier, November 22, 1897.

Educated in the public and high schools of Minier and Atlanta, Mr. Minier received his LL. B. from Wesleyan University at Bloomington, Illinois, where he practiced law for one year, and in November, 1880, came to Nebraska. There he farmed and became a breeder and importer of Hereford cattle. He engaged in the banking business in 1907, and was president of the First National Bank of Craig, for 24 years.

On June 26, 1884, he was united in marriage to Mary Elizabeth Pumpelly, at McLean, Illinois, her birthplace. Her father, Thomas Bennett Pumpelly was born at Turner, Maine, July 1, 1828, and died February 12, 1912. Her mother, Harriet Eliza Pumpelly, was born at Windham, New Hampshire, July 31, 1836, and died January 27, 1927. They were married at Maysville, Kentucky, in 1856, coming from there to McLean, Illinois, where they purchased a farm on which they resided until their deaths.

There are three children living: William, born June 28, 1885, who married Cora Clark; Nan, born December 5, 1886; Ella, born November 22, 1888, who married David Thurber; and Imogen, born June 28, 1885, twin of William, who died April 25, 1916, at San Antonio, Texas.

Mr. Minier is a Republican, a member of the Presbyterian Church, and a Mason. During the World War period he was extremely active in civilian war measures, participating in all Liberty loan drives, and serving as chairman of both war fund drives in 1917-18. He also served as treasurer of the Burt County Council of Defense, and as a member of the Food Conservation committee. His hobby is reading. Residence: Craig.

Clarence Minnick

One of the outstanding physicians and surgeons of Furnas County, Nebraska, is Clarence Minnick, who has engaged in the practice of his profession since 1905. He was born at Republican City, Nebraska, August 17, 1879, the son of John Thomas and Caroline (Callum) Minnick, the former a retired farmer who was born in Ohio, October 6, 1852. His mother, who was born in Ohio, January 3, 1859, is a devoted homemaker.

Dr. Minnick was graduated from the high school at Cambridge, Nebraska, in 1901, and received the M. D. degree at Northwestern University Medical School in 1905. He has been in active practice of medicine and surgery for over 26 years, at Indianola, Curtis, and Cambridge, Nebraska, respectively. At this time he owns and manages The Republican Valley hospital at Cambridge.

He is a member of the American Medical Association, the Nebraska State Medical Society, the Missouri Valley Medical Society, and the Furnas County Medical Society. Dr. Minnick is a 32nd degree, Scottish Rite Mason, and holds membership in the Cambridge Chamber of Commerce. His sports include fishing and hunting. During the World War he served as captain in the Medical Corps and at this time is a member of the American Legion.

On April 22, 1908, he married Flossie V. Andrews at Lebanon, Nebraska. Their children are: John C., born November 7, 1912; and Jim S., born December 18, 1919. John is a student at the University of Nebraska. Residence: Cambridge.

Roy Logan Minnick

Roy L. Minnick, dentist, was born June 9, 1884, in Frontier County, Nebraska. He is the son of John Thomas and Carrie Elizabeth Minnick, the former born in Kentucky, October 30, 1852, a retired farmer. Carrie E. Minnick was born in Springfield, Illinois, January 10, 1862.

Upon his graduation from Cambridge High School in 1905, Dr. Minnick attended the University of Nebraska where he received the degree of Doctor of Dental Surgery in 1910. He is a member of Xi Psi Phi fraternity.

A resident of Nebraska his entire life, he was admitted to practice his profession in 1910; located in Stromsburg and has been in the same office continuously. He has served as mayor of Stromsburg and has been chairman of the Republican county central committee two terms. He served in the legislature during the years of 1929 and 1930, elected on the Republican ticket. In the legislature he served on the medical, the agricultural and the finance and ways and means committees. Dr. Minnick holds membership in the following clubs and organizations: National Dental Association, associated with the state of Nebraska; the Masons, Independent Order of Odd Fellows, Modern Woodmen of America, Commercial Club, City Improvement Club, and The Nebraskana Society. Fishing and hunting are his hobbies. On September 4, 1909, he was united in marriage to Gertrude Light Rosenfelt at Beaver City, Nebraska. To this union three children were born: John, born July 1, 1910; Robert, born May 19, 1914; and Roy, Jr., born December 4, 1917. John is attending the University of Nebraska, studying to become a doctor. Residence: Stromsburg.

Harry Joseph Minor

Harry Joseph Minor, rancher, was born at Hyannis, Nebraska, July 14, 1899, son of Joseph Henry and Elissa (Allison) Minor. The father was born at Atwood, Kansas, March 5, 1869, and is an influential rancher and banker. His wife, Elissa, was born in Illinois, May 16, 1860, and died at Lincoln, March 24, 1924.

Upon the completion of his public school education, Mr. Minor attended the University of Nebraska, two years, where he was a member of Kappa Sigma. At the present time he is vice-president of J. H. Minor and Son,

vice-president of the Stock Growers Lumber and Supply Company, and a director of the Bank of Hyannis.

On April 27, 1921, he was married to Neva Dahlstrom at Lincoln. She was born at Stromsburg, Nebraska, May 16, 1900, of Swedish parentage. They have one son, Richard, born October 21, 1930.

Mr. Minor is a member of the First Methodist Episcopal Church of Lincoln, and of the Masons. His favorite sport is flying, and he has an airship which he uses for covering his ranch when he is in a hurry. Residence: Hyannis.

August Ferdinand Mischnick

August Ferdinand Mischnick, pioneer farmer, was born in Rummelsburg, Pomerania, Germany, February 23, 1866. His father, John Mischnick was a native of Falkenhagen, Pomerania, born January 24, 1839. He died at Nebraska City, February 18, 1921. He was married to Lottie (Zulske) Mischnick, who was born in Pomerania, November 17, 1841; she died at Nebraska City, on October 20.

Mr. Mischnick's first marriage was to Minnie Werner, and was solemnized at Avoca, Nebraska, March 21, 1889. Mrs. Mischnick was also a native of Pomerania. She was born July 18, 1867, and died at Cortland, March 25, 1905. The following children were born to this marriage: John Carl, born December 29, 1890, married Alta Kuhn; Ernest August, born May 2, 1892, who married Etta Mischnick; Lydia Ida, born November 14, 1893, is unmarried, and is a nurse in Chicago; Carl Herbert, born December 22, 1894, is unmarried; William Paul, born March 19, 1896, married Mildred Lund; August Ferdinand, born October 27, 1897, married Hulda Lund; Hugo Herman, born February 28, 1899, married Marie Menken; Kurt Carl, born April 23, 1900, was accidentally shot to death on August 18, 1908; Minnie Lottie, born March 27, 1902, married John Broers, Jr.

On August 20, 1908, Mr. Mischnick was married to Louise Knees who was born in Holstein, Germany, in 1878. They have the following children: Walter, born March 22, 1907; Louise Anna, born September 3, 1909; Anna Margaret, born November 11, 1910, a teacher; Esther Dorothy, born September 6, 1913; Arthur Henry, born March 27, 1916, and Alfred John, born January 30, 1921. In all, fifteen children have been born to Mr. Mischnick, of whom fourteen are living.

Mr. Mischnick is a firm believer in the golden rule. He is a member of St. John's Lutheran Church at Sterling. For about 9 years he was director of school district 141, and for six years of district No. 11. He is a member of the Parent-Teachers' Association also. His fraternal organizations are the Modern Woodmen of America and Royal Highlanders. He is a Republican, but votes for the candidate he thinks best. Residence: Sterling.

John Perry Misko

John Perry Misko was born at Ord, Nebraska, October 12, 1904, the son of James and Katie (Hellbig) Misko. His father, who was born in Bohemia, September 26, 1863, is vice president of the First National Bank of Ord; he arrived in this country in 1886 and served as president of the First Trust Company and mayor of Ord. His mother, who was born in Chicago, June 22, 1872, is president of the Ord Woman's Club.

Mr. Misko was graduated from the Ord High School in 1921, received the Bachelor of Arts degree at the University of Nebraska, 1929, and in 1930 was awarded the Bachelor of Laws degree at that institution. He was a student at Nebraska Wesleyan, 1921-22, the University of Colorado, 1925, and the University of Nebraska College of Medicine, 1924-26. His fraternities were Phi Alpha Delta and Phi Chi. At this time he is a member of the law firm Hardenbrook & Misko at Ord.

On August 23, 1931, he married Mae Lee Puderbaugh at Ord. Mrs. Misko, who was born at St. Francis, Kansas, December 21, 1904, was a teacher prior to her marriage, and a member of the Alpha Phi. Mr. Misko's hobby is writing, and his favorite sports are golf and tennis. Residence: Ord.

Charles Mitchell

Charles Mitchell, son of John D. R. and Catharine S. (Evans) Mitchell, was born in New York City, August 26, 1850. John D. R. Mitchell was born at Hartford, Connecticut, March 27, 1812, and when a young man was a manufacturer of quill pens in New York City. His ancestors had come from Scotland, in the earlier days of our country. John Mitchell later came to Sauk City, Wisconsin, and engaged in farming until his death on December 21, 1865, Catharine Evans Mitchell was born in Birmingham, England, June 10, 1823, and died at Highland, Minnesota, December 1, 1883. A fine vocalist, she was the daughter of William Evans, a manufacturer of steel cutlery in the city of Birmingham, England.

Educated in the common schools of Wisconsin, Charles Mitchell has been a resident of Nebraska since October 11, 1877, when he brought his family in a covered wagon. He had married Laura J. Bennett at Reedsburg, Wisconsin, on September 19, 1877, and at the time they removed here there were three children, one of them an infant. The family took up government land in 1880. Mrs. Mitchell, who was born at Buffalo, New York, November 12, 1853, was of German descent. There were ten children born to them, two of whom are deceased; seven of whom were born in Nebraska.

Lillie, born July 2, 1872, married Thomas Cox; James, born May 25, 1874, married Emma McKune; Lucretia, born May 5, 1876, married W. F. Willard; Callie, born September 18, 1878, married Elwood Good; Charles, born April 24, 1880, married Mary Schultz, and died March 29, 1916; John, born February 17, 1882, died February 14, 1899; George, born December 10, 1886; Benjamin, born June 8, 1888; Clarence, born June 13, 1890, and Edith, born January 10, 1893.

For ten years Mr. Mitchell taught in the schools of Dixon County, and in 1891 went into the mercantile business. He has filled many local political offices, among them the following: county supervisor (1888), member of the county board two years; assessor 3 years; justice of the peace, school director and treasurer and delegate to conventions. He was also nominated for county clerk on the Republican ticket, but was unsuccessful. Four years ago he was elected police judge at Allen, and is still holding office. In 1931 he received his diploma from the Radio School of the Air at Norfolk, Nebraska. He is the composer of many unpublished songs, and two which were recently published: *Sunny California* (copyrighted 1927); and *When the Birds Come Again in the Spring* (published 1928). He is a violinist, and enjoys playing old time music, and won second prize in a state contest.

From 1878 until 1890 he was a director on the school board, and in the fall of 1903 was appointed rural mail carrier on Route No. 1 from Dixon, Nebraska. He circulated the petition and had the route established, and was the first carrier on it and circulated a petition for public roads. During the World War Mr. Mitchell was the purchaser of $500 worth of government bonds, and otherwise assisted in war work. He is a member of the Springbank Society of Friends, and has taken an active part in church and Sunday School work for twenty years.

Mr. Mitchell has written an autobiography which he hopes to have published. Residence: Allen. (Photograph in Album).

Edward Joshua Mitchell

Edward Joshua Mitchell was born at Fulton, Illinois, May 28, 1865, the son of John Calvin Mitchell and Caroline (Van Eaton) Mitchell. His father was an early Nebraskan, who traveled through Nebraska territory in 1860, when on his way to Pikes Peak, Colorado. The two following winters he taught school in Nebraska. A Civil War veteran, he was an officer and fought in the battle of Chancelorsville. In 1889, he died at Indianola, Nebraska, after having lived for nine years in Gage County, and two years at Indianola.

His wife, Caroline, taught school in Nebraska before her marriage. They were married in Sidney, Iowa, in 1864.

Edward Mitchell attended the Fulton public schools and the Shenandoah College. Of his marriage to Tillie Barnes, two daughters were born, both of whom are deceased. Beulah, born in 1895, was graduated from the Hebron High School and the Deshler College. She was married to Amos Stauffer; she died in 1923, and is survived by two children. The other daughter, Mary, was born in 1900 and died in 1910.

In 1893, Mr. Mitchell became editor and publisher of the *Indianola Courier,* and later was associated with his brother-in-law, C. W. Barnes, in McCook, Nebraska, where they published the *McCook Republican.* In 1910, he became editor and publisher of the *Deshler Rustler,* and has since continued.

Mr. Mitchell was president of the Deshler Commercial Club from 1911-25. He has been secretary of the County Fair Association of Thayer County since its organization in 1912, and since 1921 he has been a member of the State Board of Agriculture. In 1925 he was president of the County Fair Managers in Nebraska.

He is affiliated with the Presbyterian Church, and the Order of the Ancient Free and Accepted Masons. He is a Knight Templar, and is a member of the Nebraskana Society. Residence: Deshler.

Fred B. Mitchell

Fred B. Mitchell, pioneer resident of Nebraska, was born at Jacksonville, Illinois, June 1, 1874, the son of Charles W. and Mary (Libby) Mitchell. His father, who was born in Maine in 1840 and died at Chester, Nebraska, in 1884, was a carpenter and served as a soldier in the Civil War; his ancestry was Scotch and English. His mother, who was born in Maine, September 4, 1835, and died at Hebron, Nebraska, in 1925, was descended from the Libby family which settled in America among the first New Englanders; members of the family were prominent in the early history of this country.

Mr. Mitchell attended school in Thayer County. He has lived in Nebraska for 48 years and has been a merchant, automobile dealer, and farmer. Throughout his other business activities, however, he has always been a successful stockraiser and farmer in Thayer County. In 1925 he was manager for the Chevrolet Company at Hebron, was dealer in Whippet automobiles from 1927 to 1930, and since 1930 has been the proprietor of the Mitchell Chevrolet Company.

He was at one time a member of the Kiwanis Club and the Commercial Club at Hebron, and is now affiliated with the First Presbyterian Church of Hebron and the Nebraskana Society. He was formerly a member of the Modern Woodmen of America. Mr. Mitchell is interested in all outdoor sports, but is particularly fond of travel.

His marriage to Amy Margaret Kitt occurred at Hebron, March 4, 1903. Mrs. Mitchell, who was born at Eddyville, Iowa, February 18, 1877, was a public school teacher for eight years prior to her marriage. Her ancestry is English and Pennsylvania Dutch.

Five children were born to this marriage: Charles S., born May 22, 1904, who married Armelina Brin; Marie K., born November 4, 1905; Dorothy J., born August 16, 1907; Edna May, born August 21, 1910; and Wiley Eugene, born February 14, 1916. Charles is associated with his father in the automobile business. Marie, who is bookkeeper for the Mitchell Chevrolet Company, was graduated from Hebron High School, completed a course at Pasadena Business College in California, 1927, and was graduated from Hebron College in 1928; she was a teacher in Thayer County schools for two years.

Dorothy was graduated from Hebron High School in 1924 and from Hebron College in 1929. She was a student at Hastings College for a year and is now entering her third year as teacher in the public school at Chester. Edna was graduated from high school at Hebron in 1928 and is now a teacher at Hubbell, Nebraska. Wiley is a junior in high school. Residence: Hebron.

Emmet Charles Mitchell

The Reverend Emmet Charles Mitchell, pastor of the Crawford Methodist Episcopal Church, was born at Fremont, Nebraska, December 6, 1887, son of Oliver Huston and Sadie (Headrick) Mitchell.

His father, born in Missouri, July 30, 1861, was a farmer, descended from early settlers in America. He died February 19, 1932, at North Loup, Nebraska. His father was a minister, a veteran of the Civil War, and a member of the Missouri legislature. Sadie Headrick was born in Iowa, July, 1865, and is also descended from early settlers in America.

Mr. Mitchell was graduated from Fremont High School, and in 1914 received his Bachelor of Arts degree from Nebraska Wesleyan University. He was a member of the debating team while there, took part in state oratorical contests, and was elected to Pi Kappa Delta, an honorary debating and oratorical society.

In 1910 he entered the Nebraska conference of the Methodist Episcopal Church, and until 1914 was a student pastor. Since that time he has served at Epworth Church in Lincoln, and the Methodist Episcopal churches at North Loup, Friend, Peru, Broken Bow, and Valentine.

On November 4, 1914, he was married to Pearl Angie Phinney at Lincoln. Mrs. Mitchell was born at Tamora, Nebraska, February 12, 1892, the daughter of a physician who was a graduate of Rush Medical College. Mrs. Mitchell attended Wesleyan University, and is a member of the Eastern Star. To them were born four children, Lawrence Emmet, December 22, 1916; Rosamond Pearl, June 1, 1919; Harold Verne, March 2, 1922; and Donald Marion, May 14, 1924.

Mr. Mitchell is a Republican. He is chairman of the Crawford Boy Scout council, a member of the local Chamber of Commerce, a Mason and member of the Eastern Star. Residence: Crawford.

Hayden William Mitchell

Hayden William Mitchell, farmer and editor, was born at Salisbury, New York, March 12, 1864, son of Henry and Lois (Shedd) Mitchell. The father was born in Newport, New York, December 1, 1829, and died there on January 2, 1900. He was a harness maker, who enlisted in the Civil War and served nearly two years. He went as a Democrat and returned as a Republican, full fledged, and dyed in the wool. His father was born in Scotland in 1803, and came to the United States as a young man. He was a hatter by trade. His name was McMitchell, the father later changing the name to Mitchell.

Lois Shedd was born at Salisbury, New York, November 18, 1828, and died at Clearwater, Nebraska, June 14, 1898. She was a weaver. She came to Columbus, Nebraska in 1877, locating on a homestead in Frenchtown township in 1880.

Mr. Mitchell attended public school in Salisbury Center, Newport, and Elm Creek, New York, and Columbus and Bellwood, Nebraska. He completed his education in a log school house in Frenchtown township near Clearwater.

On December 25, 1887, he was married to Mollie Mulvina Mummert at Neligh, Nebraska. She was born at Logan, Iowa, November 4, 1865, and died at Clearwater,

February 7, 1911. She was a school teacher of French and German descent. To them were born the following children, William, on October 4, 1887; Josephine, on September 6, 1891; Goldie, January 6, 1893; Fred December 15, 1895; Katherine, October 10, 1897; Cressie, September 26, 1899; Rachael, July 28, 1905; Maude, August 1, 1889, who died in November, 1901; Marcelous, September 22, 1901, who died in November, 1906.

William is married to Jessie Rogers; Goldie is married to Homer McClellan; Katherine is married to Raymond Bennett; Cressie to Miles Snider; and Rachael to Charles Nolze. Fred enlisted in the Marines in the World War, serving two years, and was promoted to the rank of corporal.

At the present time Mr. Mitchell is serving as editor of the *Clearwater Record*. He has lived in Nebraska 53 years, one at Columbus, two at Bellwood and 50 at Clearwater. In his early days he was a farmer and teacher, and as a side issue engaged in the mercantile business. He is an extensive land owner and has never missed raising a crop on any of his farms, and in addition to running his paper is much interested in his agricultural interests. He is a Republican, but independent. He was candidate for state representative in 1930, but was defeated.

During the late war he was a member of the home guard, a four minute speaker, and active in all other civilian projects. As a child, Mr. Mitchell followed the Universalist religion of his mother, but has lately attended the Methodist Episcopal Church. He is a member of the Red Cross, the Community Club, the Modern Woodmen of America, and the Odd Fellows (30 years), the Nebraskana Society, and the Nebraska State Historical Society. He is a member of the Clearwater Fire Department. He is an ardent baseball fan. Residence: Clearwater.

William Frank Mitchell

William Frank Mitchell was born at Knoxville, Iowa, December 12, 1877, the son of John William and Celestia (Kelley) Mitchell. His father, who was a physician, was born at Salem, Indiana, June 19, 1847, and died at Superior, Nebraska, August 26, 1921. His mother was born in Ohio, January 25, 1851, and died at Superior, April 31, 1926.

Dr. Mitchell was graduated from Superior High School in 1895 and in 1899 received the B. Sc. degree at Ottawa University, Ottawa, Kansas. He was awarded the M. D. degree at the University of Illinois in 1902. Dr. Mitchell has been engaged in the practice of medicine at Superior since 1902. He is a member of the Nebraska State Medical Society, the Nuckolls County Medical Society, and various civic organization at Superior. He is a Mason.

On July 12, 1905, his marriage to Alice G. Felt was solemnized at Superior. Mrs. Mitchell was born at Blairstown, Iowa, January 13, 1879. Their two children are: Louise, born April 25, 1907, who married Herman F. Ottex; and Francis, born June 7, 1911. Residence: Superior.

Edward Rudolph Mittelstadt

Edward R. Mittelstadt was born at Dunajemzy, Russia, July 13, 1872. He was graduated from a church school in Dunajmzy, in 1888. Julius Carl Mittelstadt, father of Edward, was born at Westphalin, Prussia, June 15, 1831, and died at Dunajemzy, January 15, 1880. He was a cloth manufacturer. Emelia Augusta Torinus, mother of Edward, was born at Dunajemzy, June 5, 1839, and died at Norfolk, Nebraska, June 20, 1913.

On August 11, 1898, he was united in marriage with Helene A. Pockrandt, at Laurel, Nebraska. She was born at Dunajemzy, Russia, November 8, 1881. They have six children: Hila A., born October 27, 1899; Alfred E., born

March 28, 1902; Oscar L., born July 6, 1905; Edwin R., born August 13, 1907; Alma H., born March 23, 1910; and Paul H., born September 20, 1914. Alfred is a lumber salesman; Oscar an electrician, and Edwin is studying art in Chicago.

Mr. Mittelstadt is a Republican. He started in the lumber and hardware business at Laurel, on July 12, 1893. He now is manager of Mittelstadt Brothers Lumber and Hardware.

He is affiliated with the St. John's Lutheran Church. He served for ten years on the town board, and ten years on the school board. He is director of the Laurel Building and Loan, a member of the LoVal Lake Club, and is a Mason. His favorite sport is football, and his hobby is gardening. Residence: Laurel.

Albert Riser Modisett

Albert Riser Modisett, cattle rancher and Nebraska Master Farmer, was born near Phillippi, Barbour County, in what is now West Virginia, December 13, 1861, son of Augustus Bartlett and Nancy Celia (Stout) Modisett.

The father, born near Phillippi, October 15, 1817, was a farmer and cattle raiser and dealer, the son of Hannah and Uriah Modisett of English and Dutch descent. Augustus Bartlett Modisett served eight years as sheriff and one term in the West Virginia State Legislature. He was president of the Farmers Bank of Phillippi, where his death occurred on February 26, 1881.

Nancy Celia Stout was born near Clarksburg, West Virginia, February 24, 1830, and died near Rushville, Nebraska, March 25, 1920. When a young woman she taught school. After her marriage she lived on a farm in West Virginia and later in Nebraska. She was the daughter of Abner Stout who was of English descent.

Raised on a farm until the age of 20, Mr. Modisett went to business college at Poughkeepsie, New York, and after graduation there worked in New York City as a bookkeeper and assistant cashier for Nash Whiton & Company for a year. Returning to farming, he spent a year at Taylor, Texas, and then drove cattle up the Texas trails. After a year on a ranch in Montana, at the age of 25, he located on his own ranch at Rushville, Nebraska, where he has since resided. This ranch consists of more than 31,000 acres of deeded land and approximately 4000 acres of leased land. In 1931 Mr. Modisett was made a Nebraska Master Farmer.

For a number of years he was a director in the Stockmen's National Bank of Rushville. He is a member of the Rushville Commercial Club, vice president of the Nebraska Stockgrowers Association, and a member of the executive committee, and second vice president of the American National Livestock Association. Recently Mr. Modisett made a trip to Texas to attend the annual meeting of the American National Livestock Association.

One of Sheridan County's most outstanding citizens, Mr. Modisett has been treasurer of School District 137 in his county for years. He was finance committeeman for his local precinct during the World War, is a Scottish Rite Mason and a member of the Shrine. He is affiliated with the Democratic party. He enjoys hunting, but his hobby is really the livestock business. Residence: Rushville.

Ernest W. Moehnert

Ernest W. Moehnert, county judge of Sherman County, Nebraska, was born at Imogene, Iowa, December 10, 1891. August C. Moehnert, his father, who was a farmer, was born at Oldesleben, Germany, April 4, 1840, and died at Madison, Nebraska, September 23, 1917; he came to this country in 1866. Thresa (Huelle) Moehnert, his mother, was born at Erfurt, Germany, September 23, 1849, and came to America in 1861.

Judge Moehnert attended school in Mills County,

Iowa, until 1906, and in 1911 was graduated from the high school at Madison, Nebraska. He received the LL. B. degree in 1916 at the University of Nebraska where he was a member of Phi Delta Phi, Phi Delta Theta, and the Iron Sphinx. From 1911 to 1912 he engaged in teaching in Saline County, Nebraska, and since 1916 he has practiced law continuously. He holds membership in the Nebraska Bar Association, the Nebraskana Society, and the American Legion.

During the World War Judge Moehnert served as field artillery lieutenant in the 7th Division of the American Expeditionary Forces. His sports include golf, hunting and fishing, while his hobby is book collecting. He was elected county judge of Sherman County on the Non-partisan Ticket and is serving in that capacity.

His marriage to Betty Parker occurred at Julesburg, Colorado, March 18, 1924. Mrs. Moehnert, who was born at Julesburg, February 19, 1901, was born of an old southern family and is the granddaughter of J. H. Parker who served as colonel in the Confederate Army. Their son, Ernest, was born July 28, 1925. Residence: Loup City.

John Henry Moeller

John H. Moeller has been a business man and banker at Leigh, Nebraska, since 1907. He was born at Omaha, June 17, 1886, the son of Otto Friedrich and Anna Margretha (Warn) Moeller. His father, a farmer, was born at Borstel, Germany, February 22, 1834, and died at Leigh, October 6, 1910. His mother was born at Seth, Germany, November 22, 1844, and died at Leigh, May 5, 1929.

Mr. Moeller attended grade school and was a student at the Fremont Business College in 1904. From 1907 to 1916, he conducted a general merchandise store at Leigh; and since 1917, has been active in the First National Bank at Leigh, of which he is still cashier, and director. He is affiliated with the Zion Lutheran Church; is a member of the Republican party; and holds membership in the Nebraskana Society.

On June 29, 1915, he was united in marriage with Alva Elvira Nelson at Leigh. Mrs. Moeller was born at Leigh, January 14, 1892. They have a daughter, Lois Ann, born December 14, 1924. Residence: Leigh.

Herman Moellering

The Reverend Herman Moellering, pastor of the First Lutheran Church of Papillion, was born at Bazile Mills, Nebraska, April 3, 1888. He is the son of Theodore Conrad and Anna (Schust) Moellering. The former was born at Fort Wayne, Indiana, October 15, 1860, and died there February 14, 1927. Theodore Moellering was a clergyman, whose parents came from Germany. Anna Schust was born at Fort Wayne, August 1, 1862, and died at Cincinnati, Ohio, September 12, 1917. She was of German parentage.

Herman Moellering was graduated from the Lutheran parochial school at Hampton, Nebraska, in 1902, studied at the Lutheran Normal School in 1902-03, at Seward, Nebraska, and studied at Fort Wayne College 1903-08, and was graduated from Concordia College in June, 1908; thereafter he attended Concordia Theological Seminary at St. Louis, until 1919.

Except for the time he spent in college, he has been a life resident of Nebraska. On June 2, 1915, he was united in marriage to Anna Albrecht, at Oxford, Nebraska. Mrs. Moellering was born at Oxford, on December 31, 1894, of German parents. There are three children: Theodore, born March 16, 1916; Armin, born April 20, 1919; and Ralph, born February 10, 1923.

Ordained to the ministry at Arapahoe, September 3, 1911, the Reverend Moellering served there until 1921; from 1921-28 he was pastor at Snyder, Nebraska, and since February 12, 1928, he has served at Papillion. While attending college at Ft. Wayne, he was first lieutenant of Company D, in the S. A. T. C. at Concordia College; he also assisted in various loan drives during the war. He is secretary of the mission board of the northern Nebraska district, elected at the last district convention in August, 1930. His hobby is music. Residence: Papillion.

Dean McKinley Mohr

Dean M. Mohr was born at Ponca, Nebraska, November 2, 1887. He is the son of John A. and Margaret Jane (McKinley) Mohr. His father was born January 12, 1854; he is a mortician and furniture dealer; his uncle, Silas Garber, was governor of Nebraska, and his ancestry dates back to the Revolutionary War. Margaret Jane Mohr, mother of Dean M. Mohr, was born at Ponca, April 21, 1864. She was a school teacher before her marriage. Her parents both came from Ireland.

Graduating from Ponca High School in 1905, Dean attended Bellevue College from which he was graduated in 1910, receiving his B. S. degree. During his school career he took part in both football and baseball activities.

His marriage to Mary Beth Elliott was solemnized April 16, 1912, at Hartington, Nebraska. She was born at Coleridge, July 27, 1889. They have two children: John Elliott, born November 30, 1913; who was graduated from Coleridge High School in 1931; and Dean M. Jr., born April 12, 1918.

Mr. Mohr has been a resident of Nebraska his entire life. He was employed by the Edwards and Bradford Lumber Company for one year, and since 1911, he has been in the undertaking and furniture business.

His religious affiliation is with the Congregational Church of Coleridge. He is past president of the Boosters Club, is a Mason, a member of The Nebraskana Society and a member of the school board from 1918 to 1929, and 1931. Golfing and swimming are his favorite sports and wood-working is his hobby. Residence. Coleridge.

John Astor Mohr

John Astor Mohr, furniture dealer and mortician, was born at Elkport, Iowa, January 27, 1855, son of Daniel and Mary (Garber) Mohr. His father, a native of Lancaster, Pennsylvania, was born September 3, 1823, son of Conrad Mohr, who came from Germany in 1818. He was a cabinet maker and farmer, and a keeper of bees. His death occurred at Moulton, Iowa, October 25, 1902. Mary Garber, wife of Daniel, was born in Augusta County, Virginia, December 21, 1826, and died at Ponca, January 13, 1902. She was the daughter of Martin Garber, born April 28, 1793, and Magdalene Mohler, born December 23, 1801.

Educated in the country and high schools of Manchester, Iowa, in September, 1881, Mr. Mohr came to Nebraska, and has since been a resident. During much of this time he has been engaged as a furniture dealer and mortician. He has been active in the affairs of his community and served as secretary of the school board 9 years, and served three terms as mayor of Ponca.

His wife, Margaret Jane McKinley, was born at Ponca, April 21, 1865, daughter of John and Margaret (Campbell) McKinley. There are three children, Dean, born November 2, 1887, who is a furniture dealer and mortician at Coleridge; Donald, born October 20, 1891, a salesman and mortician; and Nora M., born August 1, 1896, who is a teacher of Latin at Beatrice. Donald served at Camp Joseph E. Johnson in Florida, and Camp Green North Carolina, in the World War.

Mr. Mohr is a member of the Modern Woodmen of America, the Masons and the Nebraskana Society. Residence: Ponca.

William Jennings Mohr

Born at Culbertson, Nebraska, July 4, 1889, William Jennings Mohr is the son of Peter John and Antonia (Pelikan) Mohr. His father was born at Munich, Bavaria, Germany, in 1837, and came to the United States in early manhood. He was a clergyman, affiliated with the church of Latter Day Saints, whose death occurred at Lamoni, Iowa, January 20, 1920. His wife, born in Czechoslovakia in 1852, died at Orchard, Nebraska, May 22, 1931.

Upon his graduation from the East Denver Grade School, Mr. Mohr attended Culbertson High School, graduating in 1909. Thereafter he was a student at the Nebraska Wesleyan University for six months. From 1909 until 1917, Mr. Mohr was a rural mail carrier at Culbertson. Since 1920 he has been in the Ford garage business and at the present time is president of the Imperial Motor Company, Incorporated, at Imperial, with branches at Wauneta, Palisade, Culbertson and McCook, Nebraska. His marriage to Martha Ruth Cathcart was solemnized at Denver, Colorado, June 20, 1917. Mrs. Mohr was born at Liberty, Nebraska, June 3, 1893, daughter of Joseph C., Cathcart, who was born in Pennsylvania, February 9, 1847, and died April 24, 1909, and Elizabeth (McFarren) Cathcart, who was born in Wells County, Indiana, September 24, 1851, and died November 7, 1920. Mrs. Mohr is a member of the Methodist Episcopal Church, and takes an interested part in its activities. They have two children, William Robert, born November 6, 1918, at Culbertson, Nebraska; and Dorothy Verneal, born September 19, 1923, at Imperial, Nebraska. Residence: Imperial.

James H. Monahan

James H. Monahan, rancher, was born at Percival, Iowa, August 11, 1873, and for the past 44 years has resided in Nebraska.

He is the son of Thomas and Fannie (Abbott) Monahan, the former born in County Monaghan, Ireland. He died at Percival in September, 1886 after an active life as a farmer. His wife, Fannie, was born at Wabasha, Minnesota, May 6, 1856, and is still living.

Mr. Monahan attended public schools and has since engaged in ranching. He is president of the Bank of Hyannis, director of the Bank of Bingham, and the principal owner of the Monahan Cattle Company. A Republican, he served as county commissioner for nine years and county treasurer for two years of Grant County.

On November 3, 1897, he was married to Cora Anna McCawley at Hyannis. Mrs. Monahan was born at Dorchester, Nebraska, August 4, 1878. She is the daughter of Judge John and Edna (Hagin) McCawley. She attended public school at Hyannis, and is a member of the Eastern Star.

They have one son, Earl, born December 20, 1899, who is married to Marie Coppersmith, and who is manager of a ranch.

Mr. Monahan is a member of the Red Cross, the Community Club, the Lions Club, and the Scottish Rite and Shrine bodies of the Masons. Residence: Hyannis.

Daniel Joseph Monen

On February 17, 1898, Daniel J. Monen was born at Charles City, Iowa, the son of Daniel and Julia (Hoye) Monen. His father, who was a farmer, was born of Irish parents at Galena, Jo Davies County, Illinois, February 9, 1860, and died at Charles City, May 12, 1926. His mother was born at Milwaukee, Wisconsin, March 17, 1857, her family having come to America in 1848, from Ireland.

Mr. Monen attended Immaculate Conception Academy at Charles City, where he was graduated in June, 1916.

He was awarded his LL. B. at Creighton University, June 3, 1922; was a student at Columbia College at Dubuque, Iowa, 1917-18. During his stay at Creighton was speaker of the Creighton Model House, and a member of Gamma Eta Gamma.

He is now trust officer of the Omaha National Bank. Admitted to the bar at Omaha, June 3, 1922, he is a member of the Douglas County Bar Association and the State Bar Association. He holds membership in the Omaha Chamber of Commerce, the Nebraskana Society and the American Legion, is affiliated with St. Margaret Mary's Catholic Church, and is a member of the Knights of Columbus. He is a member of Happy Hollow Country Club. His sports are golf and hunting. During the war he was a private in the sixth company, 4th battalion, at Camp Pike, Arkansas.

He was married to Agnes Ethel Monaghan at Osage, Mitchell County, Iowa, June 3, 1924. Mrs. Monen, who was born at Elma, Iowa, January 14, 1901, is of Irish descent. They have three children: Patricia Ann, born April 30, 1925; Daniel Joseph, born September 18, 1927; and Mary Agnes, born October 7, 1930. Reseidence: Omaha.

Henry S. Monke

Henry S. Monke, pioneer resident of Fontanelle, was born in Herford, Westfalen, Germany, April 1, 1869. He is the son of John Henry and Anna Friedericka (Tappe) Monke, both of whom were Germans. John Henry Monke was born in Herford, March 21, 1830, and died at Fontanelle, Nebraska, on December 12, 1916. His wife, Anna, was also born in Herford, on December 8, 1827, and died in Fontanelle, January 29, 1905. They emigrated to America in the fall of 1869, and arrived in Fontanelle in November of that year.

Educated first in public schools, Henry S. Monke afterward attended Fremont Normal College several terms. He has been a resident of the state sixty-two years, and in addition to his farming activities, has found time to take an active interest in the advancement of his community. He is a Republican, and is at the present time serving as chairman of the township central committee. He is a member of the Masons and the Young Men's Christian Association, and since 1908 has served as superintendent of the Salem Lutheran Sunday School. His hobby is floriculture.

Mr. Monke was married to Pauline Louise Ruwe at Fremont, Nebraska, March 10, 1896. Mrs. Monke, who is of German descent, was born on a farm near Fontanelle, on September 29, 1877. They have two children: Anna May, born May 8, 1900, who married Jojakim William Blatter, a druggist, and Luther H. W., born December 1, 1902. He is married to Wilmeth Williams, and is a farmer. Anna May completed her high school education at Brownell Hall in Omaha, and attended her freshman year of college at the University of Nebraska. Her sophomore and junior years were spent at Midland College. Luther Graduated from Midland College with the class of 1927, when he received his B. A. degree. Residence: Fontanelle.

Henry Monsky

Henry Monsky, a resident of Omaha all his life, was born there February 4, 1890, the son of Abraham and Betsy (Periznef) Monsky. His father was born in Russia in 1868 and came to America 48 years ago. His mother was born in Russia in 1862.

Mr. Monsky attended the Omaha public schools and was graduated from the Central High School of Omaha. He received his LL. B. degree at Creighton where he was graduated with "cum laude" honors. He was elected to membership in Delta Theta Phi, law fraternity. Since his admission to the bar in 1912 he has been engaged in the practice of law at Omaha. A Republican,

he has held various positions in the county and state organizations and was at one time a member of the Republican State Executive Committee.

He is a member of the Omaha Bar Association, the Nebraska Bar Association, the American Bar Association, and the Omaha City Welfare Board. He served as president of the Omaha Community Chest for two years, is a board member of the Family Welfare Association, and is vice president of the Jewish Community Centre and the Welfare Federation. He was a member of the board of directors of the Chamber of Commerce at one time, is now a member of the Professional Men's Club, and has been prominent as a leader in all civic and welfare affairs. He holds membership in the following: Elks, Masons (Scottish Rite and Shrine), B'nai Brith in which he has served as a member of the Executive Committee, and the Nebraskana Society.

During the World War he engaged in the United War Work campaign and was chairman of the Four Minute Bureau. He is a member of the Conservative Synagogue. His social clubs are, the Omaha Athletic Club and the Highland Country Club.

Mr. Monsky was married at San Francisco, California, May 2, 1915, to Sadie Lesser. Mrs. Monsky was born at Omaha, June 6, 1891. They have three children, Joy, born February 3, 1916; Hubert, born February 26, 1918; and Barbara, born August 12, 1920. Residence: Omaha.

Olof Monson

Olof Monson, banker and executive, was born at Onnekop, Sweden, December 28, 1859, the son of Mons and Inga Eskelson Monson. His father, a farmer, was born at Horby, Sweden, June 24, 1825, and died there, August 1, 1895. His mother was born at Swenkop, Sweden, April 28, 1825, and died at Onnekop, June 2, 1885.

Mr. Monson was graduated from high school in 1875. He served as president of the Farmers & Merchants Telephone Company from 1914 to 1917, was supervisor in his county from 1916 to 1924, was secretary of the Farmers Union Co-operative Association from 1920 to 1926, and acted as assessor at Anoka, Nebraska, from 1910 to 1916. At this time he is secretary of the Boyd County Farmers & Merchants Insurance Company, and is vice president of the Boyd County State Bank.

He is affiliated with Evangelical Lutheran Trinity Church at Anoka, is a member of the school board, and holds membership in the Nebraskana Society and the Red Cross. Mr. Monson is a member of the Republican party, and has been a resident of this state for the past 42 years. His marriage to Anna Olson was solemnized at Onnekop, Sweden, February 2, 1881. Mrs. Monson was born at Sallerup, Sweden, November 20, 1856, and died at Omaha, Nebraska, July 10, 1930. Their children are: Hannah, born April 1, 1882, who married Alfred L. Nordin; Olof T., born September 22, 1884, who married Magna Gustafson; Andrew N., born December 2, 1886, who married Josie Hammerlun; John E., born April 7, 1889, who married Esther Bengston; George W., born May 30, 1896, who married Hazel Broady; and Lowry D., born August 12, 1899. All the children received college educations.

Hannah is a missionary, Olof, Andrew, and John are farmers, and George and Lowry are bank cashiers. George served in the United States Army in France during the World War for two years, while Lowry was in training camp at the time of the Armistice. Residence: Anoka.

Charles Ellsworth Montgomery

Charlie Ellsworth Montgomery, editor and publisher of the Belden Progress, was born at Carson, Iowa, May 13, 1880, son of James E. and Luella May (Holland) Montgomery. The father was born in Indiana, March

8, 1844, and died at Marshalltown, Iowa, June 6, 1924. The mother was born in Ohio, in September, 1846, and died at Pilger, in September, 1925.

Mr. Montgomery attended public school at St. Francis, Kansas, and on April 2, 1890, was married to Veda Alice Atkinson at Pilger. They have two children Elwin, born November 29, 1908 and Lola Ruth, on May 7, 1924.

He is a member of the Business Men's Club of Belden, the Odd Fellows, and Rebekahs, the Nebraska State Historical Society, and the Parent Teachers Association. He was three years a member of Company B, of the State Guard at Stanton, and four years held the rank of first lieutenant in the Home Guard. Residence: Belden.

Ivil James Montgomery

Ivil J. Montgomery, educator and school executive, was born at St. Francis, Kansas, September 10, 1894, the son of William Cyrus and Carrie Dell (Moody) Montgomery. His father, who was born in Pennsylvania, was formerly the editor of the *Herald* at Pilger, Nebraska; his Scotch-Irish ancestors came to America several generations ago. His mother, who is directly descended from Daniel Boone, was born in Iowa, and died at Sidney, Nebraska, September 10, 1919; her ancestry was English.

Mr. Montgomery was graduated from the Pilger High School in 1912; was a student at Wayne Normal School for two years, and in 1916 was granted his A. B. degree at the University of Nebraska. He was awarded the A. M. degree at the latter institution in 1929, and is a member of Phi Delta Kappa, and the Palladian.

Superintendent of schools at Johnson, Nebraska, 1916-19; at DeWitt, Nebraska, 1920-22; since 1922 he has been superintendent of schools at Wilber. He is the author of: *Maximums and Minimums in Education; Maximums and Minimums in Arithmetic*, published in 1930; and of various educational articles published in the *Nebraska Educational Magazine* and several university issues. He was superintendent and manager for the Standard Chautauqua for three years.

Mr. Montgomery was radio operator aboard the United States ship *Kemah* during the World War. He is district commander of the 11th district of the American Legion, is a member of the libary board; is secretary of the Wilber Rotary Club; and is a member of the Nebraska State Teachers Association. He is affiliated with the Methodist Church. Politically, he is an independent.

He married Ethel Marian Clayton at Homer, Dakota County, Nebraska, July 4, 1917. Mrs. Montgomery, who was born at Homer, March 12, 1896, is of Irish, English, and Welsh descent; her maternal grandfather fought at the battle of Gettysburg, in the Civil War. Four children were born to them: Jean Carol, born November 29, 1921; Chloe Marian, born July 3, 1923; Neil Clayton, born April 30, 1925; and Morris Dean, born October 20, 1920, who died at birth. Residence: Wilber.

Robert R. Moodie

Robert R. Moodie, son of P. M. and Catherine Y. (Readinger) Moodie, was born at West Point, Nebraska, May 3, 1898. His father, a lawyer, was born at Craftsbury, Vermont, May 29, 1859, and was graduated from the University of Michigan in 1885. For more than forty years, preceding his death at Omaha, August 13, 1929, he practiced law in Cuming County. He was descended from Scotch immigrants who early settled on a farm in Orleans County, Vermont.

Catherine Y. Readinger was born at Allentown, Pennsylvania, May 26, 1874. She is a member of various women's clubs, and the Elkhorn Valley chapter of the Daughters of the American Revolution, of which she is regent. Her ancestry is traced to pre-Revolutionary days in America.

Mr. Moodie was graduated from West Point High School in 1915, and attended the University of Nebraska College of Law. He was a member of the Dramatic Club, and is a member of Phi Delta Phi, Phi Alpha Tau, active in debate. He is also a member of Delta Upsilon,

Upon his admission to the bar in 1921, Mr. Moodie and was its president his junior and senior years. entered active practice, first as a member of the firm of Moodie, Burke & Moodie, now Moodie & Burke, in association with Allen G. Burke, former speaker of the house of representatives.

Before his admission to the bar in 1921 Mr. Moodie was a reporter on the *Lincoln Daily Star*. A Democrat, he was city attorney of West Point four terms 1921-25; county attorney of Cuming County 2 terms, 1922-30, and was defeated for third term in 1931.

He was married to Clara B. Dickerson at Lincoln, on November 10, 1923. Mrs. Moodie, who was born at Ruskin, January 11, 1899, was a teacher prior to marriage, whose paternal ancestors were among the earliest settlers of Dodge County. There are three children, Mary Louise, born November 12, 1924; Robert D., born April 5, 1927; and Catherine Elizabeth, born March 14, 1930.

Mr. Moodie enlisted in the Student Naval Training Corps at Lincoln, in September, 1918, and served until the Armistice. He is a member of the American Legion, the Red Cross and the West Point Community Club, of which he was president 1929, and director 1927-33. He served as president of the local Lions Club 1928-29, and is district governor of the Nebraska district, his term expiring in 1931. A Blue Lodge and York Rite Mason, he is also a member of the Congregational Church, the Nebraska State and Cuming County Bar Associations and the Bar Association of the 9th Judicial District. He is a member of West Point Country Club, enjoys hunting and is interested in reading and study. Residence: West Point.

Clark Willard Moon

Clark Willard Moon, a lifetime resident of Nebraska, has been successful as a merchant at Shelby for many years. He was born at Friend, Nebraska, October 16, 1876, the son of Clark Willard and Harriett C. (Myers) Moon. His father, who was a farmer and pioneer homesteader in Nebraska in 1869, was born of English parentage at Dixon, Illinois, 1843, and died at Friend, June 6, 1876. His mother, whose parentage was Pennsylvania Dutch, was born at Dixon in 1844, and died at Friend, April 9, 1918. She was a typical pioneer home builder and spent much of her time nursing the sick in her community in the early days.

Mr. Moon received his education in the grade and high school of Friend. In 1892 he started working in a clothing store at Friend and has engaged in the mercantile business since then. He organized his own establishment at Shelby in 1906 and has worked continuously there for over 25 years. An ardent community booster he has served on the local school board as president and has acted as secretary of the Commercial Club at Shelby.

He is a member and active worker in the Methodist Episcopal Church, has donated liberally to the Young Men's Christian Church, and has tried to make Polk County and his community a better place for young people. His hobby is the study of present day problems in merchandising. During the World War Mr. Moon was in charge of the Young Men's Christian Association drives, war chest funds, and Liberty loan campaigns.

On June 14, 1900, he was united in marriage with Madge Edna Graham at Friend. Mrs. Moon, who was a school teacher before her marriage, was born at Sycamore, Illinois, February 21, 1878. She is of Scotch-Irish and Mohawk Dutch descent. They have three children: C. Graham, born April 20, 1902; Glen H., born January 15, 1906; and Helen I., born July 6, 1908. All the children have high school educations and college degrees.

Graham is in business with his father, Glen is athletic coach and teacher, and Helen is a high school principal. Residence: Shelby.

Louis Edwin Moon

Louis Edwin Moon, physician and surgeon, was born at Audubon, Iowa, May 27, 1888. His father, also a physician and surgeon, was William Edwin Moon, born in Illinois, November 10, 1861, and who died at Traverse City, Michigan, November 10, 1912. He was married to Lucetta Gertrude Bates, born in Iowa, in 1869. She died at Audubon, June 2, 1888. She was of French-Canadian descent.

Educated first in the public and high schools of Audubon, Louis E. Moon was graduated from the Atlantic High School in May, 1907. In 1912 he received his M. D. from the University of Michigan. His fraternity is Phi Chi. Upon his admission to the practice of medicine Dr. Moon was resident physician at the Nebraska Methodist Hospital at Omaha, from 1912-13; was associated with Dr. A. F. Jonas when he engaged in general practice for the next four years. In 1919 he took post-graduate work in proctology, and since that time his practice has been devoted to that specialty. He is instructor in proctology at Creighton University, and is a member of the staffs of St. Joseph's Hospital, Nebraska Methodist Hospital and Immanuel Hospital.

Dr. Moon was first married to Verda V. Sanborn, who died at Omaha, October 23, 1918. She was born at Gretna, Nebraska, May 9, 1893. There is one child of that marriage, Margaret, born October 21, 1918. Dr. Moon was married to Honore Norris at Omaha, on June 8, 1929.

He is a member of the Masonic and Elk lodges, and the Lions Club. His professional organizations include the American Medical Association, the Nebraska State Medical Association, the Omaha-Douglas County Medical Society, the American Proctologic Society and the Omaha Clinical Club. He is a Fellow in the American College of Surgeons.

His social clubs are the University Club, the Omaha Athletic Club and the Happy Hollow Club. His sport is golf. Residence: Omaha.

Leon A. Moonmaw

Leon A. Moonmaw, prominent farmer of Morrill County, was born in Nebraska, December 27, 1887, son of Austin and Agnes (Spriggs) Moonmaw.

The father was born in Pike County, Illinois, July 29, 1860, and is a pioneer farmer of western Nebraska. His wife, Agnes, was born in Missouri, March 15, 1860. She was very prominent in early educational work in Nebraska, and is a member of the Daughters of the American Revolution.

Mr. Moonmaw attended sod house schools in the early days of the state, and was graduated from Bayard High School in May, 1905. He received his Bachelor of Arts degree from Cotner College in 1911, and his masters degree from the University of Nebraska in 1916. He was a member of four intercollegiate debating teams, and winner of the Nebraska state prohibition oratorical contest. From 1913 until 1916 Mr. Moonmaw was professor of history and social science at Cotner College.

He is now the owner and operator of excessive farming interests in western Nebraska. He is an independent Democrat, and was unsuccessful candidate for state representative from the Ninth district of Nebraska. He is the author of the *History of Cotner College* (1916), besides various newspaper articles in the *Omaha Journal Stockman*.

On April 2, 1914, he was married to Minnie E. Young at Lincoln. She was born at Highmore, South Dakota, July 25, 1886. There are four children, Evelyn, born

April 14, 1916; Robert, born July 9, 1918; Phillis, born September 21, 1926; and Russell, born July 7, 1928.

Mr. Moonmaw is a member of the Bayard Christian Church. He is secretary of the Morrill County Historical Society, and a member of the Nebraska State Historical Society. Recently he was made a life member of the Nebraskana Society. Residence: Bayard.

George Ezra Moor

Born at Hartsville, Indiana, January 15, 1872, George Ezra Moor is the son of George Madison and Frances K. (Matthews) Moor. His father, who was a carpenter and farmer, was born at Brookville, Indiana, December 23, 1831, and died at Inman, Nebraska, April 26, 1921; his ancestry was Irish. His mother, whose ancestry was Scotch, was born at Brookville, Indiana, January 9, 1836, and died at Inman, August 21, 1884.

Mr. Moor has always been a farmer near Inman, and holds membership in the Methodist Episcopal Church of that community. He has served as director of the local school board for the past 36 years, is a member of the Parent Teachers Association, and is a member of the Independent Order of Odd Fellows and the Masons. His hobby is reading.

On August 16, 1894, he was married to Margaret Alice Davis at Orchard. Mrs. Moor was born at Monticello, Indiana, January 13, 1868. Their three children are: William, born June 20, 1895, who married Alma Dorste; Frances Evadne, born August 25, 1898, who married Sidney Ershine; and Lois, born December 2, 1909. William is a banker, and was formerly a high school principal.

Mr. Moor is affiliated with the Republican party, and holds membership in the Nebraskana Society. He has been a resident of Holt County, Nebraska, for the past 53 years, and has always been interested in the progress of his community and state. Residence: Inman.

Cleland Granger Moore

Cleland G. Moore, physician at Fremont, Nebraska, since 1909, was born at Waverly, Iowa, November 25, 1882. His father, Nathaniel G. Moore, was born at Waynesburg, Pennsylvania, August 8, 1850, and died at Fremont, April 5, 1911. His mother was born at Elmira, New York, June 9, 1849.

Dr. Moore was graduated from the Fremont Normal School in 1900, with the B. S. degree, and in 1909, was graduated from the medical department of the University of Maryland, where he was elected to membership in Phi Beta Pi. He is now president of the Union Drug Company in addition to his medical practice. A Republican, Dr. Moore served as mayor of Fremont, 1928-29.

He was married at Baltimore, Maryland, October 5, 1909, to Emma G. Lewis. Mrs. Moore was born at Frederick, Maryland, July 22, 1888. They have one child: Lerlain, born October 5, 1915.

During the World War, Dr. Moore served as first lieutenant of the medical corps, 35th division, base hospital. He holds membership in the Dodge County Medical Association. He is a member of the Elks, Masons, and the Young Men's Christian Association. Residence: Fremont.

Frank Ralston Moore

Frank R. Moore, a resident of Nebraska since 1885 was born at Altoona, Pennsylvania, February 6, 1877, the son of John Humphrey and Elizabeth Miller (Ralston) Moore. His father, who was a merchant, was born at Akron, Ohio, December 24, 1828, and died at Schuyler, Nebraska, July 23, 1911; his great grandfather, William Ralston, was born in Ireland and died at Waterside, Blair County, Pennsylvania, at the age of 102 years; his grandparents operated an old fashioned woolen mill at Waterside, before and during the Civil War.

His mother, who was born at Waterside, December 18, 1840, and died at Schuyler, December 29, 1929, served as postmistress under Abraham Lincoln's administration in the early 1860's at Waterside. She was the daughter of Mr. and Mrs. Robert Ralston, whose three sons served in the Civil War; one son David Emigh Ralston, was killed at the battle of Chancellorsville, May 3, 1863; another son, W. H. H. Ralston, is still living at the age of 95 at the National Military Home in California.

Mr. Moore was graduated from the Schuyler High School in 1896. From 1897 to 1901, he taught in the rural schools of Colfax County, and from 1901 to 1918, was teacher in the Schuyler City Schools. He served as city clerk of Schuyler, is now secretary-treasurer of the Schuyler Chamber of Commerce, and since 1921, has been clerk of the district court at Schuyler. He is a Republican.

During his adult life Mr. Moore has taken an active part in the civic welfare of his community. He is chairman of the Boys Scout Court of Honor; is a member of the Schuyler Chamber of Commerce; is a former secretary of the local Red Cross; and holds membership in the Lions Club at Schuyler. He is a member of the Nebraskana Society, and is affiliated with the First Presbyterian Church of Schuyler. His hobbies are writing and automobiling. Mr. Moore is especially interested in athletic contests of all kinds. He has written various feature articles for the *Schuyler Sun*, and for about 15 years has been a reporter and news writer. Residence: Schuyler.

George Washington Moore

George Washington Moore, retail merchant, was born at Columbus, Wisconsin, July 14, 1880, and has resided in Nebraska for 32 years. His father, George Washington Moore, was born at Waterloo, Wisconsin, in 1848, and died at Sidney, Nebraska, February 22, 1880. A railroad man, he also operated a freighting outfit between Sidney and the Black Hills from 1876 until 1880, part of the freighting was done with ox teams. His parents were born in the United States of Scotch-Irish descent. His wife, Jane Sweet, was born in Columbus, Wisconsin, February 24, 1850, and is active in club work.

Mr. Moore attended public school until 1896, and from 1900 until 1915 was a barber. He was a painter from 1915 until 1930, and for the past two years has operated a retail paint store at Sidney. He is now serving on the city council.

On May 27, 1903, he was married to Julia Ann Sanders at Sidney. She was born near Whalen, Iowa, July 9, 1882, of German descent. Their children are Clifford, born July 19, 1905; Inez, born February 27, 1907; and Kermit, born August 24, 1910.

During the late war Mr. Moore participated in all civilian drives. He is a member of the Rotary Club, and is a 32nd degree Mason. His favorite sport is hiking, while his hobby is reading. Residence: Sidney.

Ira Herbert Moore

Ira Herbert Moore, farmer and rancher, was born at Dunlap, Iowa, May 27, 1880, son of Ira Mendenhall and Harriett Eva (Cessna) Moore. The father, who was born at Peru, Indiana, May 23, 1845, was a livestock man and farmer. In 1876-77 he owned and operated a two ten-mule freight teams from Sidney, Nebraska, to the Black Hills.

Later he came to Long Pine (1884), homesteading near the village. He was a member of the Methodist Church, and took an active interest in church, county and school affairs. He died at Long Pine, August 27, 1906. His father, was Hiram Moore, a minister, who was killed by lightning near Dunlap. His mother was Elvira Mendenhall, who was of English descent.

Harriett Eva Cessna was born at Kenton, Ohio,

January 3, 1839, and died at Long Pine on March 8, 1925. A devoted mother, she was active in the work of the Methodist Episcopal Church. She was of French Huguenot parentage, descended from one of the two Cessna brothers who fled from France in 1680 to escape religious persecution.

Ira H. Moore completed his elementary education in the district schools of Brown County in 1894, and was graduated from Long Pine High School in 1898. On July 30, 1914, he was graduated from the Beery School of Horsemanship at Pleasant Hill, Ohio.

Mr. Moore has been a farmer and rancher since youth. For eighteen years he has been a member of the school board in District No. 2, where he attended as a boy. His hobby is training horses. He is a member of the Methodist Episcopal Church, and a life member of The Nebraskana Society.

On June 27, 1902, he was married to Clara Isabelle Taylor at Long Pine. She was born at Webster City, Iowa, in 1878. They were divorced in 1910. There are two children of this marriage, Herbert Mayne, born August 31, 1903; and Shelley Theodore, born December 15, 1904, who is married to Minnie Marguerite West. Shelley is farming south of Long Pine, while Herbert is attending Hastings College, and graduated this year. He is a member of the Nebraska National Guard.

Mr. Moore's second marriage was to Augusta May Ashley at Long Pine, and was solemnized on March 15, 1915. She is the daughter of Henry E. Ashley, of Long Pine, Nebraska. They have two children, Harriett Eve, born May 13, 1918; and Ira, Jr., born April 27, 1921. Residence: Long Pine.

Jay Curran Moore

Jay Curran Moore was born on a farm near Beatrice, Gage County, Nebraska, May 25, 1873, the son of William Harry and Rena Printhia (Anderson) Moore. His father, who was born in Cumberland County, Pennsylvania, in 1840, and died in Lancaster County, Nebraska, September 11, 1886, was a Civil War veteran who served in an infantry and a heavy artillery regiment. He was a druggist.

His mother was born in Sandusky County, Ohio, August 8, 1850, and died at Tecumseh, Nebraska, April 16, 1926.

Mr. Moore, who is a lawyer in Tecumseh, was graduated from the high school at Sterling, Nebraska, in 1892, and was awarded the LL. B. degree, in June, 1899, at the University of Nebraska where he was a member of Phi Delta Phi. A lifetime resident of Nebraska, and a Republican, he served as county attorney of Johnson County for three terms, was city attorney and city clerk at Tecumseh, for four years, and is at the present time chairman of the park board there.

He was united in marriage with Mary Varner at Sterling, Nebraska, June 26, 1901. Mrs. Moore was born in Ohio, May 6, 1878. Their two daughters, who reside in Lincoln, Nebraska, are: Pauline, born May 31, 1902, who married Dr. Floyd W. Ryman; and Margaret, born April 8, 1907, who married Donald G. Gorton. Pauline was graduated from the University of Nebraska, and later taught in the kindergarten at Sterling. Margaret was supervisor of music at the Ashland High School for two years following her graduation from the University of Nebraska.

Mr. Moore was chairman of the county council of defense in the late war; was a member of the home guards, a four minute man, and took part in all war drive activities. He is a member of the Sons of Veterans.

For six years he served on the school board at Tecumseh. He is a member of the county, state, and national bar associations, and the Nebraska Title Association. He is president of the Kiwanis Club, is an active member of the Chamber of Commerce, and is a member of the Nebraskana Society. He is a Mason, Commandery, Consistory, Shrine. He is affiliated with the Grace Episcopal Church at Tecumseh. He is fond of amateur golf. Residence: Tecumseh.

Orin Wesley Moore

Orin Wesley Moore, leading dairy farmer of Nebraska, was born at Minatare, May 1, 1892, son of James Lowery and Ella (Todd) Moore. The father was born in Ireland, November 5, 1861, and came to the United States in 1870. He farmed until his death at Gering on January 4, 1924. His wife, Ella, was born in Chautauqua County, New York, February 19, 1861. She is still living.

Mr. Moore first attended the district schools of Scotts Bluff County, graduating in 1907. In 1912 he was graduated from Gering High School, and the following year attended the John Fletcher College at Oskaloosa, Iowa. During the years 1913 to 1917 inclusive he attended Nebraska Wesleyan University where he was a member of the W. Club, Delta Omega Phi, and a letter man in baseball.

Mr. Moore has met with notable success in the breeding of purebred Holstein cattle. He began in 1921 and proved one of the first proven dairy herd sires in the state of Nebraska, with the increase of his first ten daughters over their dams by 13.3% in milk production and an increase in butter fat production, over their dams of 15.6%. His purebred sire is Marathon Bess Burke VIII. Mr. Moore is a member of the National Dairy Association and was the winner of an honor roll certificate for high fat, 1927, 1928 and 1929. He is also a member of the Nebraska State Dairymen's Association which ordered him a silver medal in 1927 for the second high fat producing herd in the state, 22 cows averaging 453 pounds of butter fat. He also won the Nebraska State Dairymen's silver medal in 1929, for a herd of 21 cows making an average of 503.7 pounds of butter fat. He is a member of the local cow-testing association known as the D. H. I. A., or Dairy Herd Improvement Association, in which he has held membership since 1920. He was president of that organization in 1928, and has been a director most of the time since its organization. Mr. Moore is the leader of the Gering Valley 4-H Dairy Calf Club, which at the Scotts Bluff county fair in 1931, took three first, one second, and one third places out of six entries. He is also a member of the Co-operative Beet Growers Association and a stockholder in the North Platte Valley Cooperative Cheese Company of Gering. On June 3, 1929, Mr. Moore sold part of his high grade registered herd of cows at public auction; they brought an average price of $222.00 per head, since then he has gradually increased his herd to 35 cows, headed by Sir Bess Ormsby Fobes, 78th.

Mr. Moore is a member of the Gering Methodist Episcopal Church. He is a Republican. He is fond of athletics, and for a number of years played baseball. He now attends football, basketball, and baseball games as often as possible.

His marriage to Amy Leota Baker was solemnized at Gering, June 4, 1919. Mrs. Moore was born at Geneva, Nebraska, December 5, 1891, the daughter of Francis A. and Jennie (Glasson) Baker. She attended country school at Prairie Grove, and graduated from Geneva High School in 1911. She graduated from Peru Normal School in 1913 and from the University of Nebraska in 1917. She taught school four years prior to her marriage. Mr. and Mrs. Moore have three children, Evelyn and Donald, twins, born February 18, 1920; and Francis, born May 12, 1923. Residence: Gering. (Photograph in Album).

Orville Milton Moore

Dr. Orville Milton Moore, one of Nebraska's most distinguished physicians, has been a resident of this state since 1869 and for many years has been prominent in public affairs at York. He was born at Ripley, Brown County, Illinois, the son of Servetus V. and Laura A. (Morris) Moore. Members of the Moore family have been noted for several generations as pioneers in the building up of the middlewest.

John Moore, the great-grandfather of Dr. Orville Moore, who spent his early life in England and Scotland, was an officer in the British Army and in that capacity came to America to take part in the French and Indian War. He settled in this country and at the outbreak of the Revolution joined the American forces, serving as captain. His son, John Moore II, became identified with agricultural interests in Ohio in pioneer times and maintained a home there for his family.

S. V. Moore, father of Orville Moore and son of John Moore II, was born in Ohio in 1835. He married Laura A. (Morris) Moore in Illinois; she was born at Fredricksburg, Virginia, in 1837, and died at York, Nebraska, October 25, 1918. Following their marriage Mr. and Mrs. Moore lived in Illinois until 1869 when they moved to York County, took up a homestead there, and built a sod house overlooking the valley of Lincoln Creek. Mr. Moore, who had studied medicine in Illinois had not planned to practice in the new country. However, because of the extreme need of his neighbors he acted as physician to most of York County and part of Polk and Hamilton County. He served as a member of the first county board of supervisors in York County, was a member of the Nebraska Legislature, 1875-82, and engaged in the hardware business, 1884-98.

Dr. Orville M. Moore attended the rural schools of York County and was graduated from York Academy. In 1884 he was graduated from the Eclectic Medical Institute of Cincinnati, Ohio, and began the practice of medicine at Bradshaw, Nebraska. In 1896 he moved to York and established a general practice in connection with Dr. G. W. Shidler. Since Dr. Shidler's death he has been associated with the firm Moore, Shidler, & King. Members of this firm are recognized as leading physicians at York, and now engage in clinical work and conduct the Clinic Hospital, which was organized in 1920.

He is a fellow of the American Congress of Physical Therapy, the American Medical Association, the American Association of Physical Therapy. He holds membership in the Nebraska State Medical Society, has twice served as president of the Nebraska State Eclectic Medical Society. He was the first president of the York Rotary Club, and during the World War was chairman of the Medical Advisory Board and was a four minute speaker. He holds membership in the following: Red Cross, Commercial Club, Nebraskana Society, Young Men's Christian Association, the York Country Club, and the Knights Templar.

Dr. Moore devotes most of his time to professional duties and business interests and is one of the oldest physicians in York County. At various times he has taken post-graduate work in the New York Post Graduate Medical School, Chicago Post Graduate School, and Mayo Brothers Hospital at Rochester, Minnesota. He is a member of the Royal Highlanders, and is affiliated with the Democratic Party in which he has always been active. He is the author of many articles published in medical journals.

His marriage to Marion Davis Carpenter was solemnized at York June 24, 1903. Mrs. Moore, who was born at Worchester, Massachusetts, October 21, 1879, is a music composer and publisher, and for 15 years has been connected with the J. A. Parks Company at York. Her grandparents were born in England, while her parents were natives of Rhode Island. To this marriage three children were born: Robert Hilton, born December 16, 1904; Marion Ruth, born January 27, 1910; and Orville Morris, born October 21, 1912. Robert is a graduate of the University of Nebraska. Ruth attended Stephens College. Orville is a student at York College. (Deceased February 19, 1932).

Harley Green Moorhead

Since 1902, Harley G. Moorhead has been a lawyer at Omaha. He was born at Dunlap, Iowa, September 3, 1876, the son of George Park and Annis (Bowerman) Moorhead. His father, a cattle man and banker, was born at Nelsonville, Ohio, March 23, 1837, and died at San Diego, California, April 13, 1923; his ancestry was English and Scotch. His mother was of English and Dutch descent born near Picton, Ontario, Canada, January 19, 1844; she is active in club work.

Mr. Moorhead attended grade school at Dunlap, and was graduated from the Woodbine Normal School at Woodbine, Iowa. He was a student at Oberlin College and the law school of Columbia University, and holds the degrees of Bachelor of Philosophy, Bachelor of Laws and Doctor of Laws. He won his letter in football at Oberlin College, and was a member of Phi Gamma Delta and Phi Delta Phi at Columbia University. Since his admission to the bar at Omaha, in September, 1902, he has been engaged in active law practice in Omaha. He was appointed election commissioner for Douglas County, Nebraska, in 1913, when the Honest Election Law was passed by the legislation, and served for eight years. He was also appointed as the first jury commissioner serving for six years.

A Democrat, he was candidate for the legislature from Douglas County, 1904; was candidate for judge of the district court, 1911; was appointed to the Metropolitan Utilities District, March, 1930, for the remainder of the term of James C. Dahlman. He has lived in Nebraska for 31 years.

Mr. Moorhead was united in marriage with Bertha Wallin at Grand Rapids, Michigan, April 24, 1907. Mrs. Moorhead, who was born at Grand Rapids, December 5, 1886, is active in Omaha club work, and is president of the League of Women Voters in Omaha; her ancestry is English. They have two children: Harley, Jr., born September 3, 1908; and George Chadbourne, born December 31, 1912. Harley was graduated from Oberlin College in 1930; was a member of Phi Beta Kappa; and is now a student at Harvard Law School. Chadbourne is in his last year's work at Howe School, preparatory for college.

Mr. Moorhead was delegated by Governor Neville to appoint and supervise five draft boards in Douglas County during the World War. He is a member of the Douglas County Bar Association; the Nebraska State Bar Association; and the American Bar Association. He is a member of the advisory board of the Salvation Army and the Boy Scout Honor Court. He was president of the Rotary Club, 1915-16; was president of the Central High School Parent-Teachers' Association, 1926; and is a member of the Omaha Chamber of Commerce. He is vicepresident of the Young Men's Christian Association at Omaha; and is an Elk and a Mason. He holds membership in: University Club; Omaha Country Club; and Phi Gamma Delta Club of New York City.

He is affiliated with the First Central Congregational Church of Omaha. His favorite sport is golf. He is a member of the Nebraskana Society. Residence: Omaha.

Edwin Francis Moran

Edwin F. Moran was born at Nebraska City, Otoe County, Nebraska, December 17, 1897, the son of William Francis and Maude Loretta (Canada) Moran. His father was descended from Irish ancestors who arrived in America in 1858. He was born at Wheeling, West Virginia, January 19, 1864, and died at Nebraska City, January 9, 1929. He was a lawyer who took an active part in political civic affairs. He was a Democrat.

His mother was born of a pioneer Nebraska family at Nebraska City, May 23, 1875. Her ancestry is Irish, Eng-

lish, and Dutch, and her father was a captain in the Union Army during the Civil War.

Mr. Moran was graduated from the Nebraska City High School in 1916. He was admitted to the bar by examination, June, 1923, and in 1925 was awarded the LL. B. degree at the University of Nebraska. He has been engaged in the practice of law at Nebraska City since 1923. He is a member of the Otoe County Bar Association, the Nebraska State Bar Association, and the American Bar Association.

He was married to Louise Gaskill at Nebraska City, September 5, 1928. Mrs. Moran was born at Lincoln, Nebraska, June 25, 1904. Her father is descended from English and Irish ancestors who came to America about 1800. Her mother is of French and Irish ancestry.

Mr. Moran is a World War veteran. He is a member of the American Legion where from October, 1928 to 1929 he was a service officer. He is at the present a service officer in this organization. He is a member of the Nebraska City Country Club. He is a Democrat. Residence: Nebraska City.

Ellen Elizabeth Moran

Ellen Elizabeth Moran was born in Marion County, Iowa, September 23, 1869, daughter of James Calvin and Ann Elizabeth (Evans) McIntire. Her father was Irish, while her mother was of English and Scotch descent.

On January 1, 1891, she was married to Robert M. Moran at Mullen. Robert M. (Bud) Moran was born November 24, 1860, near Grafton, West Virginia. His parents were Otha and Ellen (Malotte) Moran, who were prominent pioneer settlers of Marion County, West Virginia. Mr. Moran homesteaded in Grant County in 1885. Mrs. Moran and her daughter still retain the original homestead. He was the appointed sheriff by Governor Thayer for the unorganized territory of which Grant County is now a part. He had a very interesting and exciting career and served as sheriff for 18 years. He was a 32nd degree Mason. A prominent rancher of French and Irish descent, he was a noted pioneer and prominent character in his community, whose death occurred April 29, 1929, at Hyannis.

There is one daughter, Winnifred D., who married Edson W. Shaw, both are graduates of the state university.

Mrs. Moran is a Democrat. She is a member of the Congregational Church at Hyannis, the Order of the Eastern Star, and the Woman's Club. Her hobbies are planting trees and flowers. Residence: Hyannis.

John Morbach

John Morbach was born at Bellwood, Butler County, Nebraska, May 19, 1888, the son of John Morbach and Elizabeth (Schmit) Morbach. His father was born in Luxemburg, Germany, March 10, 1853. He came to this country and engaged in farming; his death occurred at Bellwood, February 16, 1931. His mother was born in Luxemburg, Germany, March 10, 1856, and died at Bellwood, May 31, 1926.

Mr. Morbach attended public school at Bellwood. He was united in marriage to Augusta Mary Pentz, April 4, 1891, at Bellwood. Their son, John M., was born June 9, 1914.

A Catholic, Mr. Morbach is a member of St. Mary's Church, and the Knights of Columbus. He is also a member of the School Board of which he has been treasurer since 1922, he is Democrat, and a member of the Nebraskana Society.

During his forty-three years continuous residence in the state, Mr. Morbach has done much toward the development of his community along educational and cultural lines. Residence: Bellwood.

John Henry Morehead

In public life since 1895, John H. Morehead is an outstanding figure in politics, nationally, and more particularly in Nebraska. He was born at Columbia, Iowa, December 3, 1861, and has been a resident of Nebraska since 1884. He is the son of Andrew and Frances Amelia (Cooper) Morehead, his father, a farmer and justice of the peace, was born in Steubensville, Ohio, in 1819; he died at Columbia in December, 1887. On the paternal side, John H. Morehead is Scotch, the family having settled in America in 1633. Frances Amelia Morehead was born at Kean, Ohio, April 30, 1829, of a German father and an English mother. She died at Des Moines, Iowa, September, 1922.

Educated in the public schools of Iowa, he attended business college and then entered the merchantile field. His marriage to Minnie Weisenreder was solemnized at St. Deroin, Nebraska, February 17, 1886. Mrs. Morehead was born at Aspenwall, Nebraska, December 31, 1869, and is of German descent. Their children are: Dorothy Lee, who was born August 15, 1887, and who died March 1, 1920; and Edwin John, born November 4, 1895.

A Democrat, Mr. Morehead was elected treasurer of Richardson County in 1895, and was re-elected upon the expiration of his term. He served as mayor of Falls City in 1897. Elected to the Nebraska state senate in 1910, he was president pro-tem of that body. In 1912 he became governor, and his campaign for re-election was successful in 1914. He was unsuccessful candidate for the United States senate in 1918 and was defeated for governor in 1920. Elected to the United States house of representatives in 1922, he was re-elected 1924-26-28-30.

A farmer, stockraiser and banker, he is at the present time president of the Nebraska State Bank. His hobbies are farming, fishing and hunting.

During the war he served as a member of the Nebraska State Council of Defense, Red Cross chairman and chairman of one Liberty Loan drive. His son was a volunteer, enlisted as private and promoted to second lieutenant, serving two years, about 8 months of which was overseas.

Congressman Morehead's fraternal affiliations include the Masons, Odd Fellows and Elks. He is an honorary member of the Woodmen of the World. His social clubs are the University Club and the Falls City Country Club. He is a member of the First Presbyterian Church. His home is at Falls City.

Edwin Morgan

Edwin Morgan, son of Peter and Martha (Hunt) Morgan, was born in Dakota County, Nebraska, November 3, 1861, and has been a resident of the state for sixty-nine years. His father, who was born at Monmouthshire, England, January 10, 1835, came to America in June, 1854, and was a pioneer farmer in Nebraska. He died in Dakota County on December 24, 1912. Martha, his wife, who was born in Edwards County, Illinois, September 30, 1825, died in Dakota County, December 6, 1900. Her family had been in America for several generations.

Edwin Morgan attended the district school and thereafter engaged in farming. He is independent in politics, and has held various local offices, among them county commissioner 6 years, 1906-11, and director of school district No. 3 for twenty-four years.

On December 6, 1894, he was united in marriage to Mary Emily Morgan at Sioux City, Iowa. She was a native of Monmouth, England, born July 11, 1869. There are four children, Vern, born May 23, 1896; Belle, born June 16, 1900, who married Joseph O. Culbertson; William

P., born August 27, 1902; and Edwin T., born August 14, 1905, who married Florence Sweet of Clarks, Nebraska.

An outstanding citizen, Mr. Morgan has always been active in the affairs of his community, and has worked continuously for the advancement of civic and educational projects. Residence: South Sioux City.

Joseph W. Morgan

Born at Washington, Indiana, April 15, 1890, Joseph W. Morgan has been a resident of Lexington, Nebraska, for the past 36 years. He is the son of Valentine Edgar and Mary Ann (Miles) Morgan, the former a retired farmer who was born at Fredericksburg, Indiana, December 8, 1849, and who came to Lexington in 1896. Mary Ann Miles was born at Washington, Indiana, October 24, 1865, and died at Lexington on July 16, 1910.

Joseph W. Morgan attended rural schools and on June 24, 1915, was married to Stella Amanda Shaw at Kearney. Mrs. Morgan, who is of German and Scotch-Irish descent, was born at Lexington, May 23, 1892. They have three children, Roland, born January 27, 1917; Merle, born June 27, 1921; and Barbara, born March 3, 1927. Mrs. Morgan is an officer of the Lexington Woman's Club and a member of the Lexington board of education, now serving her second term. She is very active in church work.

Mr. Morgan lived on a farm until eighteen years of age, was in the automobile business 22 years, and since leaving the automobile business has been operating the Morgan Oil Company of which he is sole owner. For the past six years he has been manager of the Lexington Co-operative Oil Company, which is the largest co-operative oil company in Nebraska. He is also a director and appraiser of the Lexington Finance Company. He is a Democrat.

For five years Mr. Morgan was a director of the Chamber of Commerce, and in 1929 served as its president. He has been a director of the Kiwanis Club two years, 1929 and 1932, and a chairman of the Boy Scout committee two years, 1931, 1932. At the present time he is a member of the local relief committee of the Red Cross, and a director of the Dawson County Fair Association. A Catholic, he is a member of St. Ann's Church. His club is the Lexington Country Club. He is fond of fishing and hunting, golf and auto racing, while his hobby is mechanics. Recently he was made a life member of the Nebraskana Society. Residence: Lexington. (Photograph in Album).

Paul Clellan Morgan

Paul Clellan Morgan, real estate operator and insurance executive, was born at Plattsmouth, Nebraska, May 3, 1889, son of Frank John and Gertrude Ellen (Swift) Morgan.

The father, born at Osceola, Iowa, February 27, 1863, died at Plattsmouth on October 7, 1904. He was in the clothing business, prominent in Democratic politics and was for many years grand receiver of the Ancient Order of United Woodmen in Nebraska. His father was Miles W. Morgan.

Gertrude Ellen Swift, wife of Frank John Morgan, was born in Markesan, Wisconsin, May 21, 1863, daughter of George and Amelia Swift, who came to Plattsmouth from Wisconsin. She died at Plattsmouth, February 8, 1931.

In June, 1903, Mr. Morgan was graduated from Plattsmouth elementary schools, and in June, 1907, was graduated from high school there. He completed two years engineering work at the University of Nebraska and one year of architecture at the University of Illinois. He is a member of Sigma Chi at Nebraska, and in high school was a member of the football and baseball teams.

Since 1912 Mr. Morgan has been secretary-treasurer

of the Hay Springs Commercial Company, a corporation organized at that time, the name of which was changed to Horn and Morgan, Incorporated in 1930. The company is engaged in the real estate, insurance and loan business. Since 1920 Horn and Morgan, Incorporated has been the owner of the Star Theatre which it still operates, and has been associated with and is the owner of the one-half interest of the Hay Springs Telephone Exchange. A Democrat, he served as postmaster of Hay Springs from 1915 until 1919.

His marriage to Ethel Florence Ballance was solemnized at Plattsmouth on June 4, 1913. There are two children, Marion, born June 24, 1915; and Jean, born May 22, 1919; both of whom are in school. Mrs. Morgan was born at Pana, Illinois, April 11, 1891, and is the daughter of William Ballance of Plattsmouth.

Mr. Morgan is a Methodist, a member of the Red Cross, the State Young Men's Christian Association and the Hay Springs Golf Club. He is a Mason (Blue Lodge, chapter and council), is secretary of the Hay Springs Lions Club and a member of the Hay Springs and Rural Improvement Club. Recently he was made a member of the Nebraskana Society. He was chairman of Red Cross drives during the World War, and served on the local draft board. His favorite sport is golf. Residence: Hay Springs.

Sylvester E. Morgan

Sylvester E. Morgan, son of William Seth and Ann Eliza (Bryan) Morgan, was born at Sloan, Iowa, February 28, 1877, and has resided in Thurston County since 1896. His father was born at Bloomington, Indiana, October 27, 1837, and engaged in farming for some years prior to his death at West Point, Nebraska, in 1924. His mother was a native of Ohio, born June 7, 1846, who died at Miles City, Montana, July 18, 1928. The father was of English and Dutch and the mother of Irish and Pennsylvania Dutch descent.

Mr. Morgan attended the public schools of Sloan and Lake Port, and was graduated from the 8th grade at Sloan in 1894. He was married to Clara Margreta Schlueter at Fremont, on December 28, 1910. Mrs. Morgan was born at Linden, Schleswig, Holstein, Germany, August 3, 1876, and came with her father, a farmer, to America, in 1883. They have one daughter, Gladys Vesta, born April 28, 1912. She has graduated from Winnebago High School is now attending college.

Mr. Morgan is an extensive farmer and landowner, and an outstanding citizen of his community. Since 1917 he has been a member of the Red Cross. He is active in the betterment of agricultural conditions, and has been a member of the Farm Bureau since 1912. Since 1911 he has been treasurer of the local school board. He is also a member of The Nebraskana Society. Residence: Winnebago.

William Brooke Morison

Born at Salem, Nebraska, November 22, 1875, William Brooke Morison is the son of Joseph H. and Emma F. (Roads) Morison, the father is a banker.

Mr. Morison attended public and high school, and the Kansas University. He is married to Maude U. Hopkins, their marriage having taken place at Centralia, Kansas. They have one son, Joseph M., born June 11, 1907.

Mr. Morison has been a resident of Nebraska for 22 years. He has been in the lumber business for some time, and is now the president of the Morison Lumber Company, Incorporated, of Crawford. He is a Mason, and a member of Sigma Nu. Residence: Crawford.

Richard Daniel Moritz

A resident of Nebraska for fifty years, Richard Daniel Moritz was born at Emden, Germany, May 10, 1872, son of Karl Robert and Martha Marie (Stahlhut) Moritz. His father, a native of Naumburg, Germany, died at Prosser, Nebraska, in March, 1910. His mother, who was born at Erfurt, Germany, died at Prosser, in February, 1911.

Professor Moritz was educated in country school and Hastings public school, and was graduated from Nebraska State Normal School in 1893. He attended Hastings College in 1899, and received the degrees B. Sc. and B. Ed., 1899-1900. Thereafter he took post graduate work at Columbia University. He was active in tennis, football and track and is a member of Phi Delta Kappa.

From 1897-1901, he was county superintendent of the Adams County Schools, and from 1914-16, was state inspector of secondary education. At the present time he is director of the Bureau of Educational Service and Summer Session at the University. He is the author of numerous articles of an educational nature, and is a member of the Nebraska State Teachers Association, the National Educational Association, the American Association of Summer School Directors, the Parent-Teachers Association and the Library Board.

He was married to Genevieve Richards at Roseland, Nebraska, on December 22, 1897. Mrs. Moritz was born at Dodgeville, Wisconsin, October 3, 1874, of English descent. There are three children, Alan Richards, born December 25, 1899. He maried Velma Boardman, and is pathologist at Lakeside Hospital, Cleveland, Ohio. John Richards, born May 31, 1904, is assistant resident surgeon at Lakeside; and Amelia Genevieve, born September 12, 1909, is married to Lowell F. Beer.

Mr. Moritz is a Democrat. During the World War he was chairman of the United Charities, member of a committee on war loan drives and a four minute man. He is a director of the Young Men's Christian Association, a Mason and a member of the Open Forum, the Candlelight Club and the University Club. His hobby is chess. Residence: Lincoln. (Photograph in Album).

Grace Stewart Morning

Grace Stewart Morning, a resident of Nebraska practically all her life, has been prominent in social and welfare work in Lincoln, for many years. She was born at Seward, Nebraska, February 9, 1878, the daughter of John Elsworth and Amanda Elizabeth (Rhodes) Stewart. Her father, who was a farmer, was a pioneer in York County in 1872; he was born in Clark County, Ohio, April 26, 1828, and died at Seward, October 26, 1911. His great great grandfather came to this county from Glasgow, Scotland, in 1723, and his great grandfather served in the Revolution. Her mother was born at Chambersburg, Pennsylvania, March 22, 1836, and died at Lincoln, January 14, 1924; she was of German ancestry.

Mrs. Morning was graduated from the Seward High School in 1894, and later was a student at Fremont Normal schools, the Lincoln Schools, and the public schools of Seattle, Washington. She is now chief juvenile officer juvenile court, Lancaster County, Nebraska.

She is a member of the Altrusa Club at Lincoln; the League of Women Voters; and the University Club. She served as treasurer of the Lincoln Woman's Club, 1920-21; was business manager of the Federation Bulletin of the Woman's Club, 1921, 22, 23, 24; and served as secretary of Sorosis, 1923, and president, 1924. She is a Democrat.

She was married to William McClellan Morning, at Golden, Colorado, July 16, 1914. Judge Morning, whose ancestry was Irish, was born in Lycoming County, Pennsylvania, June 23, 1863, and died at Lincoln, February 18, 1924. At the time of his death he was serving as district judge. Residence: Lincoln.

George Squire Morrell

George Squire Morrell was born at Brierfield, England, March 14, 1889, the son of William Fawcett and

Emma (Sanders) Morrell. His father, who was a cabinet maker, was born at Ripley, England, November 23, 1848, and died at Nelson, England, October 20, 1906. His mother was born at Nidd, England, March 31, 1853, and died at Nelson, December 27, 1907.

Mr. Morrell attended the public schools of England, was a student at Wesleyan Methodist Day School, and in 1916 was graduated from Nebraska Wesleyan University Academy. He received his Bachelor's degree in 1922. He received the Bachelor of Sacred Theology degree at Boston University School of Theology in 1922. He was valedictorian of the graduating class in 1916 at Nebraska Wesleyan Academy and received various prizes for scholastic attainment.

He has held the following pastorates in Nebraska: Methodist Episcopal Church at Douglas, Nebraska, 1916-19; St. James Methodist Episcopal Church at Manchester, 1919-23; Methodist Episcopal Church at Stratton, 1923-26; and since 1926 First Methodist Episcopal Church of Holdrege.

Mr. Morrell holds membership in the Nebraska Annual Conference of the Methodist Episcopal Church, acting as a member of various important committees in that body, the Rotary International, and the Ancient Free and Accepted Masons. His sports include swimming and fishing, while his hobby is mechanics. During the World War he served as associated legal advisor, a member of the questionnaire board, speaker for the Red Cross, and Liberty loan worker.

His marriage to Sarah Jeanette Ditchfield was solemnized at Trenton, New Jersey, April 17, 1909. Mrs. Morrell, whose parents were natives of England, was born at Leigh, England, January 23, 1888. They have two children: Margaret Emma, born October 29, 1910; and Douglas Willard, born May 15, 1919. Margaret is a student at the Nebraska Wesleyan University. Residence: Holdrege.

Frank Nathan Morrison

A resident of Nebraska for the past 50 years, Frank Nathan Morrison was born at Algona, Iowa, January 26, 1881, the son of Nathan Montgomery and Abbie (Hinds) Morrison. His father, who was a farmer and stockman, was born of Scotch parents at Stillman, Illinois, February 1, 1842, and died at Neligh, Nebraska, April 22, 1930. His mother, who was a teacher prior to her marriage, was born in Maine, May 25, 1842, and died at Neligh, September 8, 1911.

Mr. Morrison was graduated from elementary school in 1895, and since then has been engaged in farming in Antelope County, Nebraska. He is a member of the local advisory board for the Nebraska Children's Home Society, is a director of the local county fair organization, and is affiliated with the Fairview Methodist Church. He served as treasurer of the school board, 1906-15, and was director of that organization from 1916 to 1922. His sports include hunting and racing.

On June 8, 1904, he married Amanda Christina Forsberg at Magnet, Nebraska. Mrs. Morrison, whose father came to this country from Sweden in 1873, was born at Royal, Nebraska, March 10, 1881. Their children are: Anita, born August 4, 1905, who married H. Coutts; Opal, born December 29, 1910, who was a student at the University of Nebraska for two years and is now a teacher; and Dwight, born February 7, 1915, who is a senior in high school. Residence: Clearwater.

Ira Gillispia Morrison

A railroad man since early manhood, Ira G. Morrison was born at Diagonal, Iowa, May 9, 1877, and has been with the Burlington for the past thirty-two years.

He is the son of George Warfield and Nancy Meriam (Williams) Morrison, his father a native of Pennsylvania,

born February 10, 1845. George W. Morrison, who was of Scotch ancestry, was a blacksmith and hotel proprietor, and saw three years and eight months service in the Civil War. He died at Diagonal, November 27, 1898. Nancy, his wife, who was born at Zannesville, Ohio, April 6, 1847, died at Diagonal on October 26, 1922. She was a practical nurse.

Mr. Morrison was educated in the public and high school at Diagonal, and was valedictorian of his class of 1896. Beginning as a laborer with the Chicago, Burlington and Quincy Railroad in November, 1899, he was promoted to storekeeper in February, 1905, holding that position at Creston, Iowa, St. Joseph, Missouri, West Burlington, Iowa, and for the past fourteen years at Havelock.

On February 27, 1898, he was married to Mary Arminta McFarland at Diagonal, her birth place. Mrs. Morrison, who was born September 12, 1880, is the daughter of a clergyman. There are four children, Coyle W., born November 22, 1898, who married Katherine Lutz, Ruth, born October 9, 1901, who married Edwin Hook; Paul J., born August 12, 1904, who married Virginia Price; and Donald, born May 7, 1908. Coyle is a clerk with the Burlington. The other children attended the state university where Paul was prominent as a football player.

A member of the Havelock Methodist Episcopal Church, he is also a member of the Lion's Club, the Modern Woodmen of America and is intensely interested in Boy Scout work, serving at the present time as chairman of a troop committee. Mr. Morrison's hobby is reading. Residence: Havelock.

Richard Grant Morrison

Born at Hennepin, Illinois, September 26, 1868, Richard Grant Morrison is the son of Richard Wilson and Elisabeth (Getty) Morrison. His father, who was a farmer, was born in County Antrim, Ireland, November 5, 1834. He came to the United States in 1859, and for the two years following lived in New York State. A little later he moved to Putman County, Illinois, and resided there until 1884, when he came to Nebraska. Railroad land, which he bought in 1882, is still retained by members of his family. He died at Loomis, Nebraska, October 18, 1887. His mother, whose ancestry is Scotch and Irish, was born in County Antrim, May 16, 1838, and died at Loomis, December 14, 1908.

Mr. Morrison has been engaged in farming in Phelps County, Nebraska, for many years. He is president of the Loomis Farmers Co-operative Company, is a member of the local school board, and is independent in politics.

His marriage to Jessie R. Marshall occurred at Holdrege, Nebraska, December 14, 1898. Mrs. Morrison, who was a country school teacher prior to her marriage, was born of Canadian parents at Arnprior, Canada, November 29, 1875. She is a member of the Industrious Club. Their two children are, R. Forrest, born April 17, 1902, who married Violet Schrock, and is a farmer and stockraiser; and Bonnie B., July 8, 1905, who married Edward F. Stepp. Bonne is a graduate of the University of Nebraska, receiving her Bachelor of Home Science degree in home economics in 1929. She is a Red Cross nutritionist, serving in Tylor, Texas, and Havre, Montana, 1930; Lansing, Michigan, and Greeley, Colorado, 1931; and at present is at Weeping Water. Residence: Loomis. (Photograph in Album).

Robert McKeown Morrison

One of the leading farmers near Loomis, Nebraska, is Robert McKeown Morrison, who has been a resident of the state for nearly 50 years. He was born at Lexington, Illinois, June 12, 1877, the son of Richard Wilson and Elizabeth (Getty) Morrison. His father whose occupation was farming, was born in County Antrim, Ireland, November 5, 1834, came to America in July, 1859, and died at Holdrege, Nebraska, October 16, 1887. His mother was born in County Antrim, May 16, 1838, and died at Holdrege, December 14, 1908. She was the daughter of Andrew and Margaret (Norris) Getty.

Mr. Morrison was graduated from the Loomis High School in 1896. He is secretary and treasurer of the Co-operative Oil Company of Loomis, a director of the school board, and for the past four years has been leader of the Baby Beef 4 H Club in Phelps County. He has served as secretary-treasurer of the Phelps County Junior Fair Association, since 1929, was superintendent of the Sunday School in the Congregational Church at Loomis from 1903 to 1920, and has served as deacon and trustee in the church.

During the World War Mr. Morrison was registrar for the Union Township, sold bonds and war savings stamps, and solicited for the Red Cross. A Republican, he acted as township treasurer for two terms, was township clerk for a period of ten years and served as township assessor for nine years. Since 1914 he has been a notary public.

He was united in marriage with Ethel Grace McClymont at Loomis, March 6, 1900. Mrs. Morrison, whose ancestry is Scotch, was born at Onedia, Illinois, March 15, 1879. She is the daughter of James and Isabel (McDowell) McClymont. They have six children, all of whom were members of the 4-H Club and all have graduated from high school. They are: Helen Marguerite, born May 23, 1901, who married Simon Spongberg; Robert DeWitt, born May 20, 1903, who married Sybil Carlson; Ethel Miriam, born October 20, 1907; Doris Elizabeth, born September 29, 1910; Frederick Neil, born August 2, 1913; and James Ellis, born June 11, 1916. Miriam is teaching school and Doris is completing a nurse's training at the Methodist Hospital at Omaha. Residence: Loomis.

Walter Fredrick Morrison

Walter Fredrick Morrison, farmer and merchant, was born at Bradshaw, Nebraska, July 26, 1887, the son of Edmund Walter Morrison and Ada Leona (Pope) Morrison. His father was born at Westmoreland County, Pennsylvania, September 26, 1869, of German and Scotch parentage. He was a merchant and died at Bayard, Nebraska, in October, 1922. His mother was born at Salem, Iowa, May 31, 1860, and died at Broken Bow, Nebraska, October, 1915.

Mr. Morrison was educated in the public schools and was graduated from the Bradshaw High School in May, 1905. He attended Cotner University at Bethany, Nebraska, and was active in football and baseball while in school.

He was united in marriage to Chloe Dill, who was born at Belvidere, Nebraska, February 6, 1887. To this union three children were born: Mildred Louise, December 10, 1911; Marion Jane, September 10, 1913; and Walter Fredrick, April 4, 1922. Mildred has taught school two years and will attend the Wesleyan University.

Manager of the Farmer's Elevator in 1914, Mr. Morrison was a farmer some years, and was assistant cashier in the bank in 1919-20. He now owns a grocery and meat store which he purchased in 1927.

Mr. Morrison is captain of the Belvidere Home Guards and is a member of the Red Cross. He is affiliated with the Christian Church, and holds membership in the Independent Order of Odd Fellows and in the Masons Lodge.

He is associated with the Equity Life Insurance Company. Mr. Morrison was secretary of the school board in 1921-22. A Republican, he is now the city clerk and is interested in football and baseball. Residence: Belvidere.

Andrew Marcus Morrissey

A native of Livonia, New York, Andrew M. Morrissey came to Nebraska thirty-seven years ago. He is the son of Andrew and Catharine (Dowling) Morrissey. Andrew Morrissey, Sr., was a native of Ireland, who came to America when a boy, and became a farmer in New York State. He died at Livonia, in December, 1902. Catharine Morrissey, also a native of Ireland, died at Livonia, in June, 1908.

Andrew M. Morrissey has been a resident of Nebraska, since he was twenty years of age. He was admitted to the bar of Nebraska, in 1896, and has since been active in the practice of law, and ranks among the foremost in the state in his profession. A Democrat, and active in the politics of his party, he was twice elected chief justice of the Supreme Court of Nebraska, and held that office from 1915 to 1927.

At the present time he is a member of the law firm of Mullen and Morrissey at Omaha. He is president of the Home Guardian Life Insurance Company.

During the Spanish-American War he was a private in the U. S. Army. He is a Roman Catholic. His professional organizations include the American Bar Association and the Nebraska State Bar Association. At one time he was a member of the faculty of Northwestern University Law College. His club is the Omaha Athletic. Residence: Omaha.

Bert E. Morrow

Bert E. Morrow, physician and surgeon, was born at Murray, Nebraska, April 26, 1881, son of William and Artie Mesa (Shaw) Morrow. The father, a veteran of the Civil War, was born in Jackson County, Ohio, September 27, 1839, and died at Plattsmouth, August 28, 1901. His wife was born near Craig, Missouri, August 18, 1850 and died at Seward, January 1, 1918.

Dr. Morrow attended high school at Plattsmouth, and received his medical degree from Cotner University. He took post graduate work at the Chicago Polyclinic Hospital. At the present time he is in active practice at Seward. He is a member of the American, Nebraska State and Seward County Medical Associations, the Chamber of Commerce, the Young Men's Christian Association and the Masons. For five years he held the rank of major in the Medical Officers Reserve Corps.

On January 7, 1909, he was married to Edith Naomi Franzen at Funk. She was born there on August 18, 1884. To them were born five children, two of whom are deceased: Jay, born April 18, 1914, died August 26, 1917; Lloyd, born April 18, 1914; Gene, born April 1, 1919, died April 16, 1919; Jannet, born August 24, 1921; and Warren, born July 18, 1923. Residence: Seward.

Charles Kennedy Morse

Charles Kennedy Morse, superintendent of the Nebraska School of Agriculture, of the University of Nebraska, at Curtis, was born at Nebraska City, April 2, 1888. He is the son of Samuel Frances Smith Morse and Mary Elizabeth (Kennedy) Morse. The father was born in Haverhill, Massachusetts, August 21, 1849, and was superintendent of the Union Stock Yards at Nebraska City. His parents came from England and Scotland to New England early in the 17th century. Mary Elizabeth Kennedy was born at Fort Madison, Iowa, October 22, 1852, and before her marriage was a teacher. Her ancestry is Scotch and Irish, her family having immigrated to Pennsylvania and from there to Tennessee and Kentucky.

Mr. Morse attended the public schools of Nebraska City and graduated from high school in 1907. In 1914 he received a Bachelor of Arts degree from the University of Nebraska and in 1930 was awarded his Masters degree from Columbia University. He is now a matriculant for his Ph. D. at that University. He was graduated from the Nebraska State Normal School at Peru in 1909. He is a member of Phi Delta Kappa and

Acacia, and while in university he was assistant editor of the Student Daily and Annual.

He was married to Jean Elizabeth McGahey, who was born at Lincoln, January 13, 1891. There are two children, Thomas Irwin (Tim), was born June 1, 1921; and Jean Frances, born July 23, 1926. Mr. Morse has always resided in Nebraska. From 1909 until 1920 he was connected with Chautauqua work, and helped to survey the school system of the Panama Canal Zone. He also participated in the survey of the schools of the states of Missouri and Holyoke, Massachusetts. He held the rank of first lieutenant and captain of the United States Infantry during the World War. He was attached to the H. D. Q. Company 352 Infantry 88 Division, and was in active service in France. He is a member of the American Legion, the Congregational Church, the Nebraska State Teachers' Association, the National Educational Association, and the National Department of Superintendents. He is a member also of the Chamber of Commerce, the Rotary Club, and the Sons of the American Revolution. Since 1922 he has been secretary-treasurer of the Nebraska High School debating league. He is a member of the National Teachers of English Association, the Masons, the Knights Templar and Shrine. Residence: Curtis.

Cyrus Allen Morse

Cyrus Allen Morse was born in Oswego County, New York, March 19, 1864, the son of Guilson Dikeman and Eunice Elizabeth (Frost) Morse. His father, who was a farmer and a minister, was born of English parents in Oswego County, October 24, 1825, and died at Panama, Nebraska, March 6, 1918. His mother, whose ancestry was Scotch and Irish, was born in Oswego County, April 17, 1840, and died at Lincoln, Nebraska, December 19, 1923.

Mr. Morse served the following firms as traveling salesman: Nicols & Shepard Thresher Company, four years, 1900-1904; Huber Thresher Company, four years, 1904-08; Advance Rumely & Avery Company, 1909-1920. For the past 10 years he has been in the retail implement business at Oxford, Nebraska, and prior to entering the business world was a farmer in Lancaster County.

Mr. Morse is a self made man, who started in early life without any help and has grown successful solely through his own efforts. On April 10, 1890, he was united in marriage with Sarah May Hendrichs in Otoe County, Nebraska. Mrs. Morse, whose ancestry was English, was born in Otoe County, August 9, 1873, and died at Lincoln, Nebraska, May 19, 1923. Four children were born to this marriage, Roy E., June 10, 1891, who served in the medical department of the 11th Ammunition Train during the World War and died in service on October 2, 1918; Lenna E., February 8, 1893, who married Roy E. Tutty; Myrtle A., December 30, 1894, who married Harry L. Goit; and William J., July 8, 1899, who married Ruby Bloom. Lenna was a stenographer and bookkeeper for the Gooch Milling Company for eight years.

Mr. Morse married Pauline Barbara Bauer, daughter of Phillip and Caroline (Fandry) Bauer, at Oxford, May 12, 1928. Her father, Phillip Bauer, was born in Eden, New York, December 28, 1855, and came to Nebraska in 1876, settling in Thayer County. He was one of the pioneers and successful farmers of Thayer County. Mr. Phillip Bauer was united in marriage to Caroline Fandry on May 20, 1880, in Thayer County. Eleven children were born to them, eight of whom are still living. Mr. Bauer lived in Thayer County until he was 39 years of age. He then removed to Furnas County where he has since resided. Mrs. Philip Bauer died at Oxford, March 23, 1914.

Mrs. Cyrus Allen Morse was a professional nurse from 1912 until 1928. She graduated in Omaha, in 1912, and was superintendent of the David City Hospital in 1914. She spent a great deal of her time in Omaha as a private duty nurse in the various hospitals, and was sent to many vicinities of the state. She organized and established the first hospital in Oxford in 1921. Residence: Oxford. (Photograph in Album).

Edgar Martin Morsman, 3rd

Edgar Martin Morsman, 3rd, son of Edgar Martin Morsman, 2nd, was born at Omaha, May 3, 1905. His father, who was born at Omaha, September 24, 1873, is the son of Edgar Martin Morsman and Frances Ann Sharp. He is a lawyer, and served as a member of the Nebraska state legislature in 1903. He married Mary Eager Buck, who was born at Omaha, December 21, 1874. The Morsman family has been in America since 1660, and the Buck family since 1636.

Upon his graduation from Saunders School in 1917, Edgar Morsman 3rd entered The Hill School at Pottstown, Pennsylvania, from which he was graduated in 1922. He received his A. B. from Princeton University in 1926, and a J. D. from the University of Michigan in 1929, where he was a member of the Phi Delta Phi.

Since his admission to the bar in 1929, he has been associated with the law firm of Morsman and Maxwell. He is independent in politics, and is a member of the First Presbyterian Church. His clubs are the Omaha Club, the Omaha Country Club and the University Club. Residence: Omaha.

Robert Porter Morsman

Robert Porter Morsman, banker, was born at Omaha, Nebraska, February 28, 1883, son of Edgar Martin and Frances A. (Sharp) Morseman.

He received his Bachelor of Arts degree from the University of Michigan in 1904, where he is a member of Phi Kappa Psi.

A Republican, Mr. Morseman has taken an active interest in politics. He is president of the United States National Bank and the United States Trust Company. His clubs are the University, the Omaha, the Athletic and the Country Club. Residence: Omaha.

Marion Richard Mortensen

Marion Richard Mortensen, prominent educator at Long Pine, Nebraska, is a lifelong resident of this state. He was born near Wolbach, Nebraska, July 18, 1898, the son of Jorgen and Anne (Ernsten) Mortensen, the former a pioneer farmer in Howard County, Nebraska, who was born in Denmark. His mother was born in Denmark and is still living at Fremont, Nebraska.

Mr. Mortensen attended rural school in Howard County, was graduated from Midland Academy at Atchison, Kansas, in 1917, and in 1921 received the A. B. degree from Midland College at Fremont. He was awarded the A. M. degree in 1931 at the University of Nebraska where he was elected to membership in Phi Delta Kappa. He has held the following professional positions in educational work: graduate assistant at the University of Nebraska, 1921; superintendent of schools at Rising City, Nebraska, 1922-26; superintendent at Dodge, Nebraska, 1926-28; and superintendent at Long Pine, since 1928. His Master's thesis in 1931 was on the subject: *Problems of the New School Superintendent in Nebraska*.

He is secretary of the Lion's Club at Long Pine, holds membership in the Nebraska State Teachers Association and the National Educational Association, and is affiliated with the First Congregational Church of Long Pine. He is a Royal Arch Mason, holds membership in the Parent Teachers Association, and is a member of the Nebraskana Society. He served in the United States Army during the World War and at this time is

Commander of the Long Pine Post of the American Legion. Politically, Mr. Mortensen is independent.

On August 16, 1922, he was married at Chicago, Illinois, to Ruth Evelyn Dornblaser, who was born at Atchinson, Kansas, February 3, 1900. One child was born to their marriage: Richard Edwin, March 8, 1925, who died March 9, 1925. They have an adopted son, Harry William, born May 17, 1929. Residence: Long Pine. (Photograph in Album).

Boatie Payne Morton

Boatie Payne Morton was born at Boonville, Missouri, October 31, 1869. Her father, Robert Payne, who was a wholesale grocer and later a lawyer, was descended from Revolutionary War ancestors. He was born at Fayette, Missouri, April 30, 1843, and died at Nebraska City, March 15, 1919. Her mother, Lucy Ellen (Baskette) Payne, who was born at Fayette, August 16, 1844, and died at Nebraska City, June 10, 1910, was descended from prominent early Virginians.

Mrs. Morton was graduated from high school at Nebraska City, June 4, 1886, and later attended Baird College at Clinton, Missouri. She is a member of the Otoe Chapter of the Daughters of the American Revolution, the Civic Club at Nebraska City, and the Nebraska City Country Club. She is affiliated with St. Mary's Episcopal Church at Nebraska City.

She was married December 19, 1888, at Nebraska City, to Carl Morton. Mr. Morton, who was born at Nebraska City, February 18, 1865, and died at Waugkegan, Illinois, January 7, 1901, was the son of J. Sterling Morton the originator of Arbor Day. He was a manufacturer. Their two children are: Wirt, born June 3, 1890, who married Ada Whiteside; and Martha, born February 18, 1898, who married Frederic Lattner. Mrs. Morton's grandchildren are: Carl Morton, born October 10, 1917; and Morton Lattner, born September 9, 1929. Residence: Nebraska City.

Irene Simpson Morton

For the past 40 years Irene S. Morton has been active in the civic and social affairs at Nebraska City. She was born there December 19, 1870, the daughter of William Taylor Barry Simpson and Mary Elizabeth (Payne) Simpson. Her father, who was born at Richmond, Kentucky, November 13, 1836, and died at Nebraska City, March 21, 1915, and descended from Duke Williams Simpson and Louisa (Lipscomb) Simpson, and from Revolutionary ancestors, John Williams and William Lipscomb. Her mother, who was born at Fayette, Missouri, December 8, 1845, and died at Nebraska City, December 4, 1871, was the daughter of William and Albena D. (Viley) Payne, and was descended from Revolutionary ancestors, Robert Johnson and Jemima S. Johnson.

Mrs. Morton was graduated from the Nebraska City High School May 31, 1889. She is a member of the Daughters of the American Revolution, of which she was chapter regent for a time; and was organizing agent of the Otoe Chapter of this organization. She holds membership in the Red Cross, the Civics Club, and the Nebraskana Society, and has always been interested in the progress of Nebraska City, where she has spent her entire lifetime.

On October 18, 1898, she was united in marriage with Otoe Clay Morton at Nebraska City. Mr. Morton, who was born at Nebraska City, October 14, 1867, and died there, December 11, 1912, was for many years publisher of the Nebraska City Daily News; this paper was founded and published by his father in 1854. He was the son of Thomas and Caroline (Woodruff) Morton. One child was born to this union: Thomas Simpson, born October 2, 1905; he was graduated from the Nebraska City High School; received his A. B. and LL. B. degrees at the University of Nebraska; was engaged in the practice of law

from 1929 to 1931; and is now county judge of Otoe County. Residence: Nebraska City.

Thomas Simpson Morton

Thomas S. Morton, lawyer and judge of Otoe County, was born at Nebraska City, October 2, 1905, and has lived in this state all his life. His father Otoe Clay Morton was born at Nebraska City, October 14, 1867, and died there December 11, 1912, was for many years publisher of the Nebraska City Daily News, and at one time served as mayor. He was the son of Caroline (Woodruff) and Thomas Morton, the latter a pioneer Nebraskan and the founder and publisher of the first newspaper in the state. Irene (Simpson) Morton, mother of Thomas S. Morton, was born at Nebraska City, December 19, 1870, the daughter of W. T. B. Simpson and Mary Elizabeth Payne Morton) Simpson. She was organizing regent of the Daughters of the American Revolution.

Judge Morton attended Second Avenue Public School at Nebraska City, and in June, 1923, was graduated from the Nebraska City High School. He was awarded his A. B. and LL. B. degrees at the University of Nebraska in 1929; he was business manager of the Daily Nebraskan; served as president of Phi Kappa Psi; and was made a member of the Innocents and Phi Alpha Delta..

He was engaged in private law practice from June 8, 1929, to February 1, 1931, and since that date has been county judge of Otoe County. He is a Democrat, a member of the Otoe County Bar Association; the Red Cross; Nebraska City Chamber of Commerce; and the Nebraskana Society. His social club is the Nebraska City Country Club of which he is now president.

He is affiliated with St. Mary's Episcopal Church of Nebraska City. His sports include golf, bowling, and hunting. His hobby is reading. Judge Morton served as lieutenant in Company A of the 134th Infantry in the Nebraska National Guards, and is a member of the Reserve Officers' Association. Residence: Nebraska City.

Ralph Stuart Moseley

Ralph S. Moseley was born at Lincoln, Lancaster County, Nebraska, December 19, 1886, and for nearly 20 years has been one of Lincoln's leading lawyers. His father, Daniel Wesley Moseley, was a pioneer Lincoln business man who engaged in real estate there, was a member of the city council and a member of the County Board of Commissioners of Lancaster County. He was born at Franklinville, New York, February 11, 1849, and died at Lincoln, November 18, 1929. His English ancestors came to America in the 17th century.

Virginia (Witter) Moseley, his mother, was born at Freeport, Illinois, November 25, 1856. She is a member of the Women's Relief Corps.

Mr. Moseley attended the public schools of Lincoln and in 1906 was graduated from the Lincoln High School. He was granted the LL. B. degree at the College of Law at the University of Nebraska in 1912. He was a member of Sigma Nu. He was admitted to the bar at Lincoln, June 14, 1912, and in 1913 was appointed special examiner of the Department of Interior, Indian Affairs. He is now a member of the law firm Frampton & Moseley at Lincoln.

He was junior editor of the university publication Cornhusker, 1909, and was editor in 1910. He was the joint compiler of the Nebraska Law Digest, 1929.

A Republican, Mr. Moseley was a member of the house of representatives, 1915, 1917, and 1921. In 1928 he was candidate for representative in congress in the Republican primaries. He was Republican nominee for representative in congress in the First Congressional District of Nebraska in 1930. He has lived in Nebraska all his life.

His marriage to Florence Roth was solemnized at Lincoln, June 19, 1919. Mrs. Moseley, who was born at Rochester, Minnesota, November 12, 1884, is descended from Revolutionary War ancestors. Before her marriage she was a teacher in the Lincoln High School. They have one daughter, Priscilla Jean, born December 31, 1921.

Mr. Moseley is a member of the Sons of the American Revolution. Since 1925 he has been secretary of Liberty Lodge Number 300 at the Ancient Free and Accepted Masons. He is a member of the Lancaster County Bar Association and the Nebraska State Bar Association; Hiram International Club. His hobbies are philately and reading. He is a member of the St. Paul Methodist Episcopal Church of Lincoln. Residence: Lincoln.

Adolph M. Mosler

Adolph M. Mosler was born at Bauerwitz, Germany, April 21, 1875, the son of Frank and Julie Mosler. His father, who was born at Bauerwitz, February 14, 1840, and died there, July 19, 1914, was a shoemaker. His mother was born at Bauerwitz, June 5, 1845, and died there April 25, 1916.

Mr. Mosler attended school at Bauerwitz, until 1889, when he became a student at the Gregorian University in Rome. Later he attended the Catholic University at Louvain, Belgium. He served as assistant pastor of St. Peter and Paul Church at Abie, from October 3, 1901, to January 30, 1902; from January 30, 1902, to August 10, 1907, pastor of St. Wenceslaus Church, Wilber; from August 10, 1907, to September 18, 1914, pastor of St. Mary's Church, at Odell; from September 18, 1914, till the present time, pastor of Sacred Heart Church, at Crete.

During the World War he took an active part in relief work, and was especially prominent in Knights of Columbus drives. He is a member of the Democratic party and has always been interested in the advancement of his state and community. Recently, he was elected to membership in the Nebraskana Society. Residence: Crete.

George Fay Moss

George Fay Moss, cashier of the McCook National Bank, was born at Fenton, Illinois, November 18, 1892, son of George Henry and Mary (Cronklite) Moss. His father was born at Morrison, Illinois, March 8, 1863, and is a farmer and merchant of early American ancestry. His mother was born at Saranac, Michigan, November 23, 1868.

Mr. Moss attended the public schools of Miltonvale, Kansas, until 1908. From June 12, 1912, until the present time he has been with the McCook National Bank of which he is now cashier. He is also a director of the Masonic Temple Craft of McCook. A Democrat, he served as city clerk of McCook from 1917 until 1930, and at the present time is serving as mayor, having been elected in 1930.

On November 10, 1915, Mr. Moss was married to Callie Kramer at McCook. She was born at Imperial, Nebraska, October 23, 1892, of German descent. There are two children, Jack, born October 20, 1923, at McCook; and Robert, born April 15, 1927, at McCook. Mr. Moss is a member of the McCook Chamber of Commerce and of the Masons. He is a Protestant. Residence: McCook.

Harland Lester Mossman

Harland L. Mossman was born at Walker, Iowa, January 21, 1884, the son of David Conklin and Mary Elizabeth (Cross) Mossman. His father, who was a farmer, was born at Morris, Illinois, November 11, 1849, and died at Sioux City, Iowa, February 17, 1917; he was descended from Sir James Mossman, financier of the realm and jeweler to Mary, Queen of Scots; he also descended from John Mossman of Baltimore, 1790, and James Mossman of Boston, 1667.

His mother, who was the daughter of Rev. Solomon and Anne (Urmey) Cross, was born at Houston, Indiana, June 25, 1851, and died at Sioux City, July 6, 1910.

Mr. Mossman attended school in Iowa, and in 1900 was graduated from the Larchwood High School there. He holds the following degrees: A. B., Morningside College, Sioux City, Iowa, 1908; Creighton University, Omaha, Nebraska, LL. B., 1909; A. M., Creighton University, 1910. He was a member of the Philomathean Society, and was active in intercollegiate debate. He was awarded a college letter in basketball and track at Morningside.

He served as superintendent of school at Edgemont, South Dakota, in 1909-10, and at Sisseton, 1910-12. In 1912, he began the practice of law at Omaha, and has continued since that date. A Democrat, he served as assistant city attorney, 1918-21, and was candidate for county attorney in 1926. He is well known in Omaha as a gifted political orator.

Mr. Mossman is a member of the Nebraska State Bar Society, the Douglas County Bar Association, the Concord Club, and the Nebraskana Society. He is a member of the Woodmen of the World, the Yeoman Club, the Ancient Order of United Workmen, and Moose. For several years he has been affiliated with the First Methodist Church of Omaha, and is an active member of the Minne Lusa Parent-Teachers' Association and the Central High Parent-Teachers' Association.

His marriage to Oliva Helen Wilson was solemnized at Kingsley, Iowa, June 14, 1910. Mrs. Mossman, who is an exceptionally fine musician and concert soprano, was a teacher before her marriage. Among her distinguished ancestors are: James Presnell, 1699, Hugenot Virginia; Glavill Maupin; Daniel Daniell, 1634, Virginia; John Willson, 1667, new Jersey; Peter Atwood, born in County Surrey, England, in 1203; Harmon Atwood, Boston, 1642; William Copp, County Warwick, England, who settled in Boston in 1635; John Bartholomew, Philadelphia, 1730; Abraham Conell, New Jersey, French Hugonot, 1701; Walter Sower, Massachusetts, 1654; Deacon Ralph Sheppard, Charleston, 1635; and Solomon Keyes, Newberry, 1653.

To their marriage six children were born: Harland Lester, born January 24, 1912; Clayton Wilson, born August 9, 1914; Frank David, born May 12, 1916; Mary Ella, born February 1, 1918; John William, born January 8, 1920; and Thomas Bennett, born January 8, 1920. Residence: Omaha.

Fred Mostrom

Fred Mostrom, banker, was born in Sweden, September 30, 1874, son of Peter Fredrick and Mathilda (Forsberg) Mostrom. Peter F. Mostrom was born in Sweden, March 7, 1848, and arrived in the United States in 1879. He was a clergyman, whose death occurred at Ceresco, April 7, 1912. His wife, Mathilda, was born in Sweden, April 8, 1845, and is still living.

Educated in the country schools of Saunders County, Mr. Mostrom later took a commercial course at Winnepeg, Canada. From 1898-1906 he was a grocery clerk, and from 1906-12, engaged in farming. In the banking business since 1912, he is now cashier of the Farmers and Merchants Bank of Ceresco.

His marriage to Ida Martinson, of Swedesberg, took place there on February 8, 1899. Mrs. Mostrom was born September 4, 1877, of a family of farmers. They have four children, Ruth, born October 19, 1900, who married Joseph J. Nelson; Carl, born November 6, 1902, who is assistant cashier of the Farmers and Merchants Bank; and who married Lorene Flodman; Philip, born December 12, 1905, who is bookkeeper in the Farmers and Merchants Bank, and John, born November 20, 1914, who is a student.

Mr. Mostrom is a Democrat. He is chairman of the Ceresco High School Board, and during the World War was active in all loan drives. He is a member of Evangelical Mission Church and of the Nebraskana Society. Residence: Ceresco.

Henry L. Mousel

Born near Cambridge, in Frontier County, Nebraska, April 14, 1878, Henry L. Mousel has become one of the foremost cattle breeders in the state. His father, Michael M. Mousel, was born in Luxemburg, Germany, April 16, 1848, and came to the United States as a young man. He came to Cambridge in 1874. A farmer and stockman, he was of the finest character, and a leader in every effort to assist the needy. His death occurred at Cambridge, March 19, 1902. Mary Ann Lawler, wife of Michael, was born in Bellevue, Iowa, May 27, 1853. She came to Cambridge in 1875, and died there June 14, 1907. She was of Irish descent, a devoted wife and mother.

Henry L. Mousel attended Cambridge High School to the tenth grade, and was graduated from Lincoln Business College in 1900. Since 1898 he has been a member of the firm of Mousel Brothers, breeders of Anxiety 4th Hereford Cattle. The firm breeds cattle which have won highest honors at national stock shows for the past twenty-five years, breaking the world's auction sale price record for beef cattle, fifty bulls and cows averaging $3840.00 each at Cambridge, in January, 1920.

He is the author of *Prince Domino Mischief, Mousel Brothers Best Bull* (See American Hereford Journal, Kansas City, Mo. From the Herd Bull number, July 1, 1931). Mr. Mousel is a member of the Community Club, the Nebraskana Society and St. John's Catholic Church. He is a Democrat. His favorite sports are hunting, boxing and football.

On July 27, 1903, he was married to Mabel Estella Welty at Denver. Mrs. Mousel was born at Otley, Iowa, of Swiss and English descent. There are seven children, as follows: Paul W., born May 19, 1904, is a graduate of the Cambridge High School and of the College of Engineering of the University of Nebraska. He has practiced at Grand Island and at Chicago, and is married to Bernice Giesler of Lincoln, who is also a graduate of the University of Nebraska.

Lucille J., born September 17, 1905, is a graduate of Cambridge High School, and graduated from the Denver University of Denver, Colorado, and also attended University of Nebraska. She is teaching school in Ogallala at present; prior to this term she taught in Colorado.

Charles H., born March 22, 1907, is a graduate of Cambridge High School, where he was track champion. He has attended the University of Nebraska and the Colorado School of Mines at Golden, Colorado, where he was a rifle champion.

Ruth L., born September 9, 1908, is a graduate of Cambridge High School and attended the University of Nebraska, also graduated from Teachers College, Greeley, Colorado. She is also a teacher.

Madeline, born March 23, 1910, was graduated from Cambridge High School and is married to Donald J. Coder.

George A., born February 22, 1912, is a graduate of Cambridge High School and was all-state quarterback in the 1930 high school football team. He is a student at the state university.

Ashur M., born August 14, 1914, is a junior in Cambridge High School. Residence: Cambridge.

Fred Carl Mowinkel

On October 3, 1881, Fred C. Mowinkel was born at Gretna, Nebraska, the son of Henry and Doris Mowinkel. His father, whose ancestors came to America from Germany in 1868, was the owner and operator of a large farm in the choice agricultural section of Nebraska. He was born at Holstein, Germany, June 4, 1848. He was active in Nebraska politics.

His mother was born at Bahma, Holstein County, Germany, January 12, 1857, and died at Gretna, Nebraska, January 8, 1920.

Mr. Mowinkel has lived in Nebraska for 49 years. He is a farmer. A Republican, he served as county commissioner 1928, 1930, and was re-elected in 1930 for four years.

He married Celia Margaret Lembcke at Gretna, Nebraska, February 18, 1903. Mrs. Mowinkel, whose parents were farmers, was born in Germany, November 16, 1884. They have three children: Nellie Helen, born August 29, 1907, whose husband is a farmer, and resides at Winside, Nebraska; Henry Hans, born September 6, 1910; and Mae Lorraine, born May 19, 1919.

Mr. Mowinkel was on the war activity board during the World War. He has been a member of the school board in Sarpy County for twenty years, and for twenty-eight years has been affiliated with the Modern Woodmen of America. He is a member of the Lutheran Church of Gretna, Nebraska. Residence: Gretna. (Photograph on Page 853).

Carl Clarence Moyer

Carl Clarence Moyer, prominent educator at Ainsworth, Nebraska, was born at Findlay, Ohio, November 26, 1886, the son of Aaron L. and Ida May (Bolton) Moyer. His father, a traveling salesman for many years, was born at Des Moines, Iowa, March 12, 1857, and is now a rancher and merchant; his parents came to this country about 1825, from Germany. His mother, who was born at Martinsville, Illinois, May 25, 1865, is of English and Pennsylvania Dutch descent.

Mr. Moyer was graduated from the high school at Findlay, Ohio, and was a student at the University of Nebraska and Chadron State Normal School. In his early years he was engaged in carpentry, and later he was a salesman for several years. He has taught school in North Dakota and Nebraska continuously since 1913, and for the past nine years has been principal of the high school at Ainsworth. He is a member of the American Classical Association, the Ainsworth Commercial Club, the Red Cross, and the Ainsworth Congregational Church. His recreations include hiking, fishing, and reading. Mr. Moyer holds membership in the Modern Woodmen of America and The Nebraskana Society.

On September 1, 1908, Mr. Moyer was married to Laurel Edith Everingham. Mrs. Moyer, who was formerly a teacher, was born of English and Irish parents at Hutsonville, Illinois, April 26, 1888. Their three children are: Glenda L., born November 25, 1910, who married Elmer Nissley Skillman; Arthur L., born January 28, 1915; and Doris M., born June 25, 1921. Glenda was graduated from Ainsworth High School and prior to her marriage was a teacher. Residence: Ainsworth. (Photograph in Album).

Earl John Moyer

Earl John Moyer, lawyer and prominent Republican, was born in Madison, Nebraska, October 5, 1893, son of Morris Joseph and Anna Luella (Spence) Moyer.

His father was born in Carroll County, Illinois, July 21, 1855, and was a lawyer and judge of Madison County two terms, 1890-1894. He died at Madison on June 17, 1909. His wife, Anna, was born in Ontario, Canada, December 16, 1867. She is a past president of the Madison Woman's Club, and member of the local chapter of the Eastern Star.

Mr. Moyer attended Madison Public and High School and was graduated from the latter in 1911. He was afterward a student at the University of Nebraska where he is a member of Kappa Sigma. He was admitted to the bar on June 13, 1913, and at the present time is the senior member of the firm of Moyer & Moyer. A Republican, he has served as chairman of the Republican county central committee five years, and a member of the state executive committee two years.

On Jonuary 22, 1918, he was married to Genevieve Weesner at Fremont. Mrs. Moyer was born at Hastings, March 26, 1894. They have three children, Margaret,

FRED CARL MOWINKEL

Heyn—Omaha

born November 8, 1920; Jane Ellen, born July 12, 1923; and Mary, born May 23, 1927.

During the World War Mr. Moyer served from January 26, 1918, until May 28, 1919. He held the rank of sargeant in the 311th Supply Company of the quartermaster corps, and was over seas from June, 1918, until May, 1919. He is a member of the American Legion and the Veterans of Foreign Wars.

From 1926 until 1931, Mr. Moyer served as a member of the board of education of Madison. He is a Mason, a member of the Red Cross, the Nebraskana Society, and the Methodist Episcopal Church. His professional organizations include the Nebraska State Bar Association and the Bar Association of the Ninth Judicial District of Nebraska. Residence: Madison.

George H. Moyer

George H. Moyer, lawyer, was born at Madison, Nebraska, October 14, 1895, son of Morris J. and Anna L. (Spence) Moyer. His father was a lawyer and county judge of Madison County.

Upon his graduation from Madison High School, Mr. Moyer entered the University of Nebraska, from which he received his Bachelor of Laws degree. He is a member of Kappa Sigma and Phi Delta Phi. Since January 1925, he has been engaged in the practice of law at Madison. A Republican, he was a member of the state legislature 1927 and 1929, and the special session of 1930.

On January 3, 1930, he was married to Eunice F. Geiger at Dakota City. She was born at Oberlin, Kansas.

During the World War, Mr. Moyer held the rank of first sergeant of infantry. He is a member of the American Legion, the Madison Community Club, the Nebraska State and Ninth Judicial Bar Association, and the Nebraskana Society. Residence: Madison.

Willis Edwin Mudge

Willis Edwin Mudge, pioneer Nebraska farmer, was born on the Atlantic Ocean, April 23, 1855, while his parents were on the way to America from England. His father, a native of Chatham, England, came to Nebraska as a pioneer in May, 1861, bringing his family with him. He died at Beatrice, August 16, 1916. His wife died at Beatrice on March 10, 1906. She was of English parentage.

Mr. Mudge educated in the early pioneer schools of the state, and from his youth has been a farmer. He was married on July 4, 1881, to Elizabeth Barbary Mathias at Fairbury. Mrs. Mudge, who was born at Germantown, Illinois, March 9, 1856, died at Diller on July 29, 1925. She was of German and English descent.

To this union four children were born, Ray, on December 1, 1882; Muriel J., on November 7, 1884; Ethel M., on February 6, 1892, and Cordelia on July 2, 1889, who died on July 23, 1889. All of the children are farmers. Residence: Diller.

Hanns Bernhardt Mueller

Hanns B. Mueller, one of Nebraska's foremost physicians and child specialists, was born at Goettingen, Germany, November 21, 1893. His father, Adolf Mueller, who was a dentist and physician, was born in Bovenden, Germany, January 18, 1862, and died there, February 23, 1915; since the 16th century his ancestors have been blacksmiths, farmers, and medical men. Francisca (Hans) Mueller, his mother, was born in Fuerstenfeld, Germany, February 25, 1868; her ancestors were merchants and farmers.

Dr. Mueller attended the public school at Goettingen, for three years, and Gymnasium for nine years. He was awarded the M. D. degree at Georgia, Augusta University 1919, and was a student at the university of Goettinger, where he received honors. He was active in tennis

during his high school days, winning championship honors at Goettingen, in 1911 and 1912.

He was connected with the children's clinic in Laudeshut, Germany, 1920-21; was first assistant and teacher in the baby clinic at Cecilienheim, 1921-23; was first assistant and teacher at the University Children's Clinic at Goettigen, 1923; and from 1923-25, was professor of medicine at Ann Arbor, Michigan. He is now a specialist in children's diseases at Lincoln. He is the author of many medical pamphlets and magazine articles.

His marriage to Henny-Rita Cramer was solemnized at Lincoln, March 31, 1926. Mrs. Mueller was born at Hanover, March 31, 1903. They have a daughter, Anna Lee, born December 23, 1928.

Dr. Mueller served as volunteer and first lieutenant of the Medical Corps in the German Army from 1914-19, and received German war decorations for distinguished service. He is a member of: Lincoln Chamber of Commerce; Cosmopolitan Club; the Nebraska Pediatic Society; the Lancaster County Medical Society; the Nebraska State Medical Society; and the American Medical Association. He is a member of the Young Men's Christian Association and the Nebraskana Society. Politically, he is an Independent.

His sports include swimming; horseback riding; volley ball; and tennis. His hobbies are photography, gardening, hunting, and traveling. Residence: Lincoln.

William Henry Mueller

William H. Mueller, a resident of Nebraska for the past 51 years, was born at Mankota, Minnesota, March 11, 1873. Frank Mueller, his father, who was a carpenter and farmer, was born in Saxony, Germany, August 23, 1838, and died at Clearwater, Nebraska, September 8, 1908. His mother, Friederike (Nolze) Mueller, was born in Saxony, January 20, 1839, and died at Clearwater, January 11, 1924.

Mr. Mueller was a farmer for a time, was employed in a packing house at Omaha, Nebraska, and for many years has been a successful merchant at Hampton, Nebraska. From 1904 to 1910 he served as treasurer of the School Board, and at this time he is chairman of the Hampton Community Club. He is a trustee in St. Peter's Lutheran Church.

He was united in marriage with Dora W. Fenster at Hampton, May 30, 1900. Mrs. Mueller was born at Bradshaw, Nebraska, September 21, 1879. Their two children are Frank, born February 4, 1912; and Wilma, February 9, 1927. Frank is a student at the University of Nebraska. Residence: Hampton.

William Max August Mueller

A native of the Province of Pomerania, Germany, William M. Mueller has been a resident of Nebraska for the past forty-five years. His father, Joachim Christopher Mueller was born at Wilhelmshaven, Germany, November 8, 1815. He married Louise Mueller, born in Germany, November 1, 1825, and came to America with her October 14, 1876, bringing their young son. Joachim Mueller was an alderman in Germany, and was a roofer by trade. He died at Martinsburg, Iowa, November 21, 1900, as did his wife.

William Mueller who was born January 21, 1862, received his education in the German public schools. He was married to Caroline Schaller of Hazelgreen, Wisconsin, at Tripoli, Iowa, January 14, 1885. Their children are as follows: Clarence J., born March 7, 1886; Frederick William, September 10, 1887; Cora Louise, July 11, 1891; Frederika Marguerite, June 16, 1895; Clara Julia, March 18, 1898; William R., January 17, 1900; Stanley A. J., October 6, 1901. The children are either in business or the teaching profession.

Mr. Mueller is a Republican, and for 16 years served as village trustee at Springfield. During his residence in the state he has been manager of the grain and coal business of Mueller & Son, and has been a farm manager. He is one of the oldest and best known residents of Springfield, and has always been active in the public life of his community. He is affiliated with the Evangelical Lutheran Church and is a Mason. His hobby is reading. Residence: Springfield.

Harold Benton Muffly

Harold Muffly, lawyer, was born in York County, Nebraska, August 3, 1890, the son of Samuel F. and Mary M. (Sands) Muffly. His father, who was the son of George H. and Sarah E. (McBride) Muffly, was born at Earlville, Illinois, November 20, 1861. His mother, the daughter of Thomas H. B. and Elizabeth C. (Primrose) Sands, was born at Darlington County, Indiana, November 19, 1866.

He attended the country school, Nebraska Wesleyan Academy, graduated from Nebraska Wesleyan University in 1914, and received his LL. B. degree at the University of Nebraska, in 1916.

Admitted to the bar in 1916, he engaged in the practice of law at Lincoln. Upon his return from France, he practiced at Pierce, Nebraska, moving to Lincoln in 1926, where he has continued practicing law.

He was united in marriage with Madge Boyce, at Lincoln. Mrs. Muffly was born at Plattsmouth, Nebraska, June 29, 1889, the daughter of Luke L. and Ada S. (Lillard) Boyce. They have two children: Helen Patricia, born November 11, 1923; and Robert Benton, born February 2, 1928.

Mr. Muffly is a member of American Bar Association; the Nebraska State Bar Association; Lancaster County Bar Association; Lincoln Chamber of Commerce; North Star Lodge No. 227 A. F. & A. M.; Lincoln Consistory, Shrine; Eastern Star; Warren Methodist Episcopal Church and Nebraskana Society. He is a Republican, and was a member of the American Expeditionary Forces. Residence: Lincoln.

Conrad William Muhle

Conrad W. Muhle, who has lived in this state all his life, was born at Schuyler, Nebraska, January 26, 1886, the son of Henry and Anna Muhle. His father, who is a farmer, was born in Germany, March 15, 1859, and came to this country in 1865. His mother, who was born at Schuyler, March 1, 1861, is the daughter of one of Nebraska's earliest settlers who came from Germany in the early 1850's. She is the mother of ten children.

Mr. Muhle attended public school, and later took a course in business training and commercial law bookkeeping at the National Business Training School at Sioux City, Iowa. He has been a farm worker, mechanic, manager and field man for various tractor companies, and is now the proprietor of a garage, at Walthill, Nebraska.

He enlisted in the United States Army, April 11, 1917, was promoted to corporal August 7, 1917, and sergeant, September 9, 1917, and May 18, 1918, was made first class sergeant. He saw active service at the battles of Meuse-Argonne, Champaigne, and Baccarat. He is a member of the American Legion, the Lions Club, the Nebraskana Society, and the Red Cross. He is a Mason and Modern Woodmen. His sports include football and baseball, and his hobby is mechanics.

Mr. Muhle was married to Helen Mortensen Frisk at Norfolk, December 28, 1927. Mrs. Muhle, who was a business woman before her marriage, was born at Little Sioux, Iowa, October 22, 1900. They have a son, Glenn Jeppe, born October 27, 1928. Residence: Walthill.

Sarah Theodosia Muir

Sarah T. Muir, noted educator, speaker, and civic leader at Lincoln, Nebraska, was born at Racine, Wisconsin, the daughter of Daniel H. and Emma Annette (Kenaston) Muir. Her father, who was a practicing physician for many years in Lincoln died in January, 1923. Her mother who was born in Columbia City, Indiana, and who died at Lincoln, March 7, 1927, was intensely interested in political, social, musical, and educational affairs at Lincoln, and held membership in the Woman's Club and the Matinee Musicale. She was interested in collecting the works of Nebraska authors. Her father, who was a native of Vermont, was a clergyman in Indiana and Kansas.

Miss Muir attended the Lincoln Public Schols, and received her A. B. and A. M. degrees at the University of Nebraska where she held membership in Chi Delta Phi, Silver Serpent, Theta Sigma Phi, and numerous other organizations. She was a student for one year at Hillsdale College, in Hillsdale, Michigan.

Since 1917 she has been head of the English department at the Lincoln High Schol. She is the author of numerous articles on English, ethics, and politics, published in the *English Journal, Educational Review, Minnesota Educational Journal, Nebraska Educational Journal, Intelligent Voter,* and the *Proceedings of the National Educational Association.* A Republican, Miss Muir served as a member of the Nebraska Legislature in 1925. She sat in the first legislative session in which a woman ever served.

She was president of the Lincoln Teachers Association, 1929, was president of the Nebraska State Teachers Association, District Number One, 1930, and chairman of the committee on ethics of teaching of the National Educational Association, 1924-29. She is a member of the National Council of Teachers of English, the Nebraska Writers Guild, the League of Women Voters, Nebraska Women's Educational Club, the Civic Music Association, Wooden Spoon, Matinee Musicale, Mortar Board, the Red Cross and the Nebraskana Society.

She was a member of the committee on college entrance requirements of the North Central Association, 1930-31; member of the English committee on the unit courses and curricula of the North Central Association, 1922; member of the National Education Association committee on English, 1924; member of the national committee of the Council of Teachers of English to revise reading lists, 1922; was president of the Nebraska Women's Educational Club, 1919; was president of the Lincoln Branch of the American Association of University Women, 1910, 1911, 1916; and was president of the Nebraska Chapter of National Council of Teachers of English, 1922-24, and director of this council in 1931. She is a member of the First Presbyterian Church at Lincoln.

Miss Muir's sports include swimming, walking, and gardening. Residence: Lincoln. (Photograph on Page 856).

Alex Muirhead

Alex Muirhead, lumberman, was born in Grey County, Ontario, Canada, January 11, 1872, son of Gavin and Catherine (McPhail) Muirhead. The father was Saxon and the mother Celtic, both coming from Scotland to Canada. Mr. Muirhead came from Canada to Nebraska in 1894.

He attended rural schools and Owen Sound Collegiate Institute and the Durham Model School at Ontario, Canada.

On June 10, 1903, he was married to Georgia Alice Miller at Hemingford. She was born at Martinton, Illinois, July 15, 1876, the daughter of Alvin M. and Addie (Pearson) Miller. Her father is one of the few surviving veterans of the Civil War. Mrs. Muirhead is a member of the Woman's Club and the Methodist Church. There are two children, Ruth Adeline, born April 5, 1904, who was graduated from Hemingford High School and the University of Nebraska, and later took a post graduate course in the University of California. Faye Catherine, born October 28, 1906, married Harold Thomson and is a graduate of the Oregon Agri-

SARAH T. MUIR

cultural College and was a teacher prior to her marriage.

At the present time Mr. Muirhead is the manager of a lumber company at Hemingford. He is a member of the Methodist Church, the Masons, and the Lions Club. A Republican, he served as county treasurer, 1902-03, and has held various other minor offices. Residence: Hemingford.

Arthur Francis Mullen

A native of Canada, of direct Irish descent, Arthur F. Mullen has been a resident of Nebraska since early childhood. He was born at Kingston, Ontario, May 31, 1873, son of James Mullen, farmer and business man, whose father came from Ireland about 1800. His mother, Emily (Clancy) Mullen, was born near Kingston in 1853. Her parents settled in Canada from Ireland about 1840. She is still living.

Receiving his early education in Canadian public schools, he attended the Fremont and Nebraska Normal Schools, graduating from the latter in 1891. He received his legal education at the University of Michigan, completing his course in June 1900, with the degree of LL. B.

In 1901 he was elected county attorney of Holt county, serving three terms, and until 1907. Always active in the Democratic party, he has been an outstanding member of that organization for many years. After serving as attorney general of Nebraska during 1910-11, he was a member and secretary of the Nebraska Tornado Commission in 1913. Since 1916 he has served as Democratic national committeeman, and he was a member of the executive committee 1918-20.

Mr. Mullen has attained a distinguished position in his profession through participation in many notable cases. Some of these cases can be found in the official reports, under the following titles: State v. Weber, statutory constrn, 102 Neb. 103; McShane v. Douglas County, constl law, 95 Neb. 699, 96 Neb. 695; State v. Supreme Forest fraternal ins., 100 Neb. 632; State v. Donohue, ouster of public official, 91, Neb. 311; Krause v. Long, 109 Neb. 846 enjoining judgment secured by fraud; Nebraska v. McKelvie, constl law, 104 Neb. 93; Fricke v. International Harvester, fraud case, 247 Fed. 869; Shallenberger v. First State Bank, bank guarantee, 219 U. S. 114, 55 L. Ed. 117; United States v. I. H. Co. Federal ouster suit under Serman Trust Act, C. C. A. of 8th Circuit; Nebraska v. McKelvie, foreign languages, 262 U. S. 404, 672 L. ed. 1047; Meyer v. Nebraska, 262 U. S. 390, 67 L. ed. 1042, constl law; Shukert v. Allen, 72 L. ed 764, estate taxes; Gamble v. Daniel, constrn of law as to whether or not Nebraska trust companies were banking corporations, 39 L. ed. (2) 447.

Mary Teresa (Dolan) Mullen, his wife, was born in Clinton, Iowa, May 24, 1874, of Irish parentage. Of their marriage, on June 18, 1903, two children were born. The youngest, Margaret, born in 1909, died in 1914. The elder, Arthur J., was born June 17, 1905. He is a lawyer.

Mr. Mullen was admitted to the bar of Michigan in June, 1900 and in Nebraska, January, 1901. He is associated in practice with Andrew M. Morrissey, under the firm name of Mullen & Morrissey. He is a member of the American Bar Association, The Association of Bar of New York, and the Nebraska State and Douglas County Bar Associations.

A Catholic, he is a member of St. John's Church, and a member of the Knights of Columbus (state deputy 1910-11). He is an Elk. His clubs are Omaha Athletic, Omaha Club, and Happy Hollow Country Club. Residence: Omaha. (Photograph on Page 858).

Joseph Samuel Mullen

Joseph Samuel Mullen, a leading Democrat at Ashland, Nebraska, was born at McPherson, Kansas, June 18, 1884, son of Joseph Lawrence and Mattie Elizabeth (McFarland) Mullen. His father, a farmer and political leader, was born at Milwaukee, Wisconsin, July 27, 1844, of Irish parentage. He died at Canton, Kansas, February 12, 1912. His mother, born in Iowa, of Scotch and Irish ancestry, resides at Ashland.

Mr. Mullen attended high school at Canton, Kansas, received the Ph. G. degree from Fremont College of Pharmacy, and has been a successful druggist at Ashland for the past twenty-one years. He is past president of the Board of Education, is a member and former secretary-treasurer of the Chamber of Commerce, and holds membership in the Nebraska Pharmaceutical Association. Mr. Mullen is a member of the Modern Woodmen of America, the Odd Fellows, the Masons and the Nebraskana Society. His hobby is mechanics.

On August 12, 1908, he was united in marriage to Lola Fern Parker of Ashland. They have three children: Dorothy Fern, born September 8, 1911; Joseph Robert, born June 6, 1916; Richard Keith, born June 6, 1918.

Dorothy married Allyn J. Naviaux and now resides in Kansas City. They have one son, Joseph Flynn Naviaux, born April 22, 1930. Richard and Joseph are students at the Ashland High School. Residence: Ashland.

Mary Tresa Mullen

Mary Tresa Mullen, who is the wife of Arthur F. Mullen, was born in Clinton County, Iowa, May 22, 1874. Her parents, James and Mary (Clark) Dolan, were natives of Ireland. Her father was born May 20, 1824, and came to America in early youth. He was a farmer by occupation, and died in Bryant County, Iowa, October 30, 1880. Her mother was born September 30, 1834, and died in Clinton County May 31, 1906.

Mrs. Mullen was educated first in the country schools and St. Mary's parochial school at Clinton, Iowa. She was graduated from Mt. St. Clair College in 1904. Her marriage to Arthur F. Mullen took place at Clinton, Iowa, June 17, 1903. Two children were born to them, Arthur, born June 18, 1905, who is a lawyer, and Margaret, born July 20, 1909, who died July 28, 1914.

Before her marriage Mrs. Mullen was a teacher in the public schools of Iowa and Colorado. During the World War she was active in Red Cross and other civilian work. She is a Catholic, and member of Holy Cross Church. She is active in welfare and social work, especially in the Red Cross Community Chest and Girl Scouts, she is a member of the Parent-Teachers' Association, the National Council of Catholic Women, and the Catholic Daughters of America, of which she is past president. Her sport is golf, and her clubs are the Omaha Club and Happy Hollow County Club. Residence: Omaha.

Joseph H. Mullin

One of Nebraska's pioneer lawyers, Joseph H. Mullin has been a resident of this state for the past 53 years.

He was born in Des Moines County, Iowa, February 24, 1851, and since 1876 has been actively engaged in the practice of law at Grand Island, Nebraska. His father, Bernard Mullin, a merchant, was born in Adams County, Ohio, in 1824, and died at Iowa City, Iowa, in July, 1892. His mother, Mary (Brenan) Mullin, was born at Mullingar, Ireland, in 1827, and died at Iowa City, Iowa, July 31, 1900.

Mr. Mullin received the LL. B. degree at the University of Iowa in 1876, where he was a member of the Zetagathian Literary Society. He is affiliated with the St. Mary's Catholic Church, has held the offices of chancellor and grand knight of the Knights of Columbus, and was formerly district deputy of the organization.

On October 15, 1884, he married Alice E. Hooper, daughter of Edward and Sarah (Parcell) Hooper, at Grand Island. Mrs. Mullin, whose ancestry is English, was born at Central City, Nebraska, January 28, 1866

ARTHUR FRANCIS MULLEN

Their children are: Bernard, born September 26, 1885, who married Helen Furniss; Cecil W., born September 1, 1887; Alice, born May 13, 1893; Margaret, born May 20, 1895; Dorothy, born February 7, 1897, who married Art Ernstmeyer; George, born April 1, 1899, who married Wilma Coats; and Isabel, born July 31, 1907.

Mr. Mullin, who is a Democrat, was county judge of Hall County from 1900 to 1929. His hobby is reading. Residence: Grand Island.

Richard Francis Mullin

Richard F. Mullin, prominent physician of Snyder, Nebraska, has lived in this state practically all his life and for many years has been active in community affairs at Snyder. He was born at Omaha, November 19, 1888, the son of Richard and Bridget (Cannon) Mullin. His father was born at Woodford, County Galway, Ireland, and was a clerk for the Union Pacific Railroad at Omaha, where he died November 30, 1912. His mother was born at Woodford.

Dr. Mullin attended the parochial and public schools of Omaha, and was graduated from the high school of Creighton University there. He holds the following degrees: A. B., Creighton University, 1911; A. M., 1912; M. D., 1918. He was especially active in college where he held the position of class treasurer, 1917-18; treasurer of the Mixers Club, 1916; and president of the Mixers club, 1917. He held membership in Phi Beta Pi, medical fraternity, and was treasurer of Archon for two terms.

His marriage to Margaret Anne Ortman was solemnized at Omaha, March 26, 1919. Mrs. Mullin, who is the daughter of C. W. Ortman of Omaha, was born at Omaha, March 6, 1895. They have three children: Charline, born April 24, 1921; Genevieve, born December 2, 1922; and Marilyn, born August 29, 1924.

Dr. Mullin served as lieutenant of the medical corps in the United States Naval Hospital during the World War, and was a medical officer at the United States Naval Air Station at Key West. He is a member of the American Legion. His professional and civic undertakings include membership in the Dodge County Medical Society; Snyder Chamber of Commerce; the Red Cross; the D. L. Club at Snyder; and the Nebraskana Society. He is affiliated with St. Leo's Catholic Church and is a member of the Knights of Columbus. He is a Democrat.

Dr. Mullin's chief interest is working for the advancement of his community and state. His sports include golf, fishing and hunting. Residence: Snyder.

Tom Peter Mullins

Tom Peter Mullins, dental surgeon, was born at Omaha, Nebraska, January 10, 1891, son of Charles Love and Kate Belle (Coon) Mullins.

Charles Love Mullins is a physician, who served as captain in the medical corps with the 1st Nebraska regiment of the Nebraska National Guard in the Philippines during the Spanish-American War. He is past president of the Nebraska State Medical Society.

Tom Peter Mullins attended public school at Broken Bow, and was graduated from Grand Island Academy in 1908. He took his pre-medical work at the Nebraska State University, and received his degree of Doctor of Dental Surgery from Creighton Dental College in 1917. He is a member of Acacia, and Xi Psi Phi, and at Grand Island College was a letterman in track and football each two years.

Upon his graduation from Creighton Dental College, in June, 1917, Dr. Mullins practiced at Valparaiso, Nebraska, until January, 1920. He then removed to Chappell, where he remained until July, 1921, and from that time until 1929, practiced at Merna. Since 1929, he has

been in practice at Chadron. Of his marriage on June 12, 1914, to Betty Ray, one son, Charles Love, IV, was born on October 2, 1916.

He was married to Hazel Marie Kimes at Broken Bow, on November 21, 1922. Mrs. Mullins was born at Duning, Nebraska, December 6, 1900. She is a member of the Business and Professional Woman's Club and the Epsilon Sigma Alpha.

Among Dr. Mullins professional organizations are, the American Dental Association, the Nebraska State Dental Society, the 8th Nebraska District Dental Society, and the Chadron Dental Study Club. He is a member of the Junior Chamber of Commerce, the Kiwanis Club, and is a Master Mason. Active in Boy Scout work, he is registered scouter in the covered wagon area of the Boy Scouts of America, chairman of the district committee of the Sioux district of the same, and a member of the town committee of Chadron in the same district. His club is the Chadron Country Club. He is affiliated with Grace Episcopal Church. He enjoys golf, while his hobby is boys' work. Residence: Chadron.

Wendell E. Mumby

Wendell E. Mumby, lawyer, was born at Swanton, Nebraska, March 16, 1906, son of George H. and Emma A. (Truka) Mumby. The father was born at Swanton, Nebraska, January 16, 1881, and is a merchant of English ancestry. His wife, Emma, was born at Wilber, February 23, 1882, and is an active member of the Eastern Star. Her ancestry is Bohemian.

Mr. Mumby first attended school at Crab Orchard, Nebraska, and was graduated from public school at Sterling. He attended Sterling High School, graduating in 1922, and in 1928, received the Bachelor of Laws degree from the University of Nebraska, where he is a member of Phi Alpha and Pi Kappa Phi.

Since 1928, he has been in the general practice of law at Harrison, and at the present time, is a member of the firm of Schnurr and Mumby. A Republican, he was appointed deputy county attorney of Sioux County, in 1928, and elected county attorney in 1930.

On June 3, 1928, he was married to Edna Ruth Dorsh at Sterling. She was born at Cook, Nebraska, September 15, 1905, of German ancestry. They have one son, Keith, born May 27, 1931.

Mr. Mumby is affiliated with the Methodist Episcopal Church at Harrison, is a member of the Nebraska State Bar Association, the Lions Club (secretary 1930-1931), Odd Fellows. He is a member of the Harrison Golf Club, Red Cross (county chairman, 1930-1931), and enjoys golf and fishing. His hobby is reading. Residence: Harrison.

Mary Munchhoff

Mary Munchhoff was born at Mount Vernon, Indiana, daughter of Herman Richard and Anna Margaret (Schenk) Munchhoff. Herman Munchhoff was born at Morganfield, Kentucky, August 3, 1843, and was a business man of early American ancestry. He died at Omaha, April 29, 1919. His wife, Anna Margaret, was both at St. Phillips, Indiana, January 5, 1847. She died at Omaha, in October, 1916.

Mary Munchhoff was graduated from a private school in Indiana, and studied at Berlin, under Frau Professor Selma Niklass-Kempner. She continued her studies with Mme. Mathilde Marchesi at Paris, for two years and also with the famous R. Von Zur Mehlen. Later she made numerous concert tours through Germany, Russia, Great Britain, Austria, Denmark, Belgium, and Holland. She sang many times under celebrated conductors, Nikisch, Safonoff, Mengelberg, Weingartner, Steinbach, Hausegger, Panger, Hertz, Victor Herbert and others.

Miss Munchhoff is an accomplished linguist, and has

learned German, French and Italian languages so well that
it is impossible to tell her nationality from her singing.
She made a special study of Bach, Shubert, Mozart, Hugo
Wolf, and French composers and while at the height of her
career in Europe, where she had gained renown as color-
atura soprano, she was forced to return to the United
States to care for her mother. She is engaged as a private
teacher of voice and is also voice teacher at Duschesne
College.

She is a member of St. Mary Magdalene's Catholic
Church, of the Clef Club, the Tuesday Music Club, Friends
of Music, of the Nebraska State and Omaha Musical
Teachers' Association and the Beethoven House, one of
honorary societies in music. Her home and studio are at
201 South 32nd Avenue, Omaha.

Claude C. Munday

A general merchant since 1910, at Edison, Claude
C. Munday has resided in Nebraska for the past forty-
seven years. He was born at Princeton, Illinois, October 29, 1879, son of John Marion and Mary Uretta
(Johnson) Munday. His father, a pioneer school teacher,
and later a successful merchant, was born in Casey
County, Kentucky, July 22, 1848. Now retired, he resides at Edison. His wife, born in Dearborn County,
Indiana, April 6, 1858, was a teacher and musical instructor in her younger days. Her family were farmers and professional people in Illinois.

Claude C. Munday attended the public school at
Edison, high school at Arapahoe, and afterward taught
in rural school near Edison. For a time he engaged in
business with his father, and in 1910 entered the merchantile business for himself. He has been a member
of the Edison school board, is a member of the Federation of Nebraska Retailers, the Commercial Club and
the Nebraskana Society. Affiliated with the Christian
Church, and is an officer. Each year Mr. Munday and
his family take a ten day outing in the mountains.

He was married to Blanche Paine at Edison on June
15, 1910, and to them was born a daughter, Bernice
Blanche, on October 26, 1911. She was graduated from
Edison High School and attended Hastings College
and Kearney State Normal School. Mrs. Munday
was born at Ellwell, Iowa, July 11, 1885, and was formerly a teacher. Her parents are farmers near Edison.
Mr. Munday's politics are independent. Residence:
Edison.

Joseph M. Mundil

Joseph M. Mundil, son of Joseph and Antonie (Bren)
Mundil, was born in Frantisky, Skutec, Czechoslovakia,
August 14, 1856. His father, who was born in Frantisky,
August 26, 1826, came to America in September, 1879,
and was a pioneer farmer in Colfax County. He was a
Republican, and died at Clarkson, May 19, 1905. Antonie
Bren Mundil was born in Frantisky, and died there in
October, 1876.

Mr. Mundil attended the village school in Frantisky,
and after coming to America, attended the country schools
of Colfax County. He has lived in Nebraska fifty-two
years, and at the present time is vice president of the
Clarkson State Bank and vice president of the Farmers
and Merchants Bank of Linwood. He is a notary public,
and is engaged in the farm loans and insurance business.

His marriage to Frances Mundil was solemnized at
Schuyler, Nebraska, November 12, 1882. Mrs. Mundil
was born in Frantisky, Czechoslovakia, September 10,
1863. They have two children living, and two are deceased: Joseph, born October 7, 1883, died December 11,
1883; Frederick F., born March 6, 1887, is cashier of the
Farmers and Merchants Bank of Linwood; William, born
May 16, 1888, died March 3, 1896; Joseph, born December

27, 1889, is assistant cashier of the Clarkson State Bank.

Mr. Mundil is a Republican, and active in local politics.
He is a member of the Presbyterian Church, and for
twelve years was a member of the town and school boards,
and four years assessor of Colfax County. He is active
in the support of the Red Cross and Salvation Army, and
is a member of the Woodmen of the World, the Modern
Woodmen of America, the Bohemian Fraternal Association, and the Nebraskana Society. His son, Joseph, served
in the World War as a volunteer, and is a member of the
American Legion. Residence: Clarkson.

Alfred Case Munger

Alfred C. Munger was born at Lincoln, Nebraska,
October 13, 1891, the son of Thomas C. and Carrie Case
Munger. His father, who was born at Van Wert, Ohio,
in 1861, was United States district judge of the Lincoln
division for many years. His mother was born at Cedar
Rapids, Iowa, in 1864.

Mr. Munger, attended the public school at Lincoln,
and in 1908 was graduated from the Lincoln High School.
He was awarded his A. B. degree at the University of
Nebraska in 1911, received his LL. B. at Harvard, in 1915,
and is a member of Phi Beta Kappa and Delta Upsilon.

From 1915 to 1920 he was associated with the firm
Stout, Rose & Wells; and since 1920 he has been a member of the firm Crossman, Munger, & Barton. A Republican, Mr. Munger, served as assistant attorney general in 1917 and 1919.

He married Florence V. Russell at Omaha, September
18, 1920. Mrs. Munger was born at Omaha, March 15,
1896. They have three children: Charles, born January
1, 1924; Mary, born September 8, 1925; and Carol, born
June 5, 1928.

Mr. Munger was stationed at Base Hospital Number
49, during the World War, and served with the American
Expitionary Forces at Allerey, France, in 1918 and 1919.
He is a member of the American Legion; of the Omaha
Bar Association; the State Bar Association; and the
Omaha Chamber of Commerce. His social clubs are the
University Club; Omaha Club; and Omaha Country
Club. He is fond of golf and hunting. Residence: Omaha.

Arbor Day Munger

Arbor Day Munger, son of Simeon Roode and Polly
Ann (Cain) Munger, was born at Elkader, Iowa, April
25, 1890. He has been an intermittent resident of Nebraska since 1909, and has lived here constantly since
1919. His father, Simeon Munger was born in Conneaut
Township, Pennsylvania, June 27, 1851, and is still living.
At the age of 19 he migrated with a wagon train to Kansas, where he became active in the development of the
state. Later he engaged in the contracting business in
Iowa, from which he is now retired. The first ancestor
of the family in America is recorded as Nicholas Munger,
an Englishman who arrived in 1630 from Guilford, England, and founded Guilford, Connecticut.

Polly Ann Munger, whose father was an imigrant
from Ireland, was descended on the maternal side from
the Scoville family who early settled in New York State.
She was born at Cox Creek, Iowa, November 15, 1873, and
died at West Union on December 15, 1928. Always active
in civic, fraternal and church work, she devoted much
time to the study of ceramics in which she gained no little distinction.

Arbor Day Munger received his elementary schooling
in the Elkader and Oelwein, Iowa, public schools, and
was graduated from the Oelwein High School in 1908.
He attended the University of Nebraska from which he
received his B. Sc. in 1913. At that college he was a
member of Phi Rho Sigma. After completing the medical course at Columbia University in 1915 he was awarded an M. D. He was one of the founders of Alpha Beta

chapter of Phi Rho Sigma at Columbia. Dr. Munger then served two years as house surgeon at the Kings County Hospital of New York, majoring in genito-urinary surgery, and graduating cum laude.

During his course at the University of Nebraska he was a member of the Cadet Corps, graduating with the rank of captain. In June, 1917, he was commissioned a second lieutenant in the United States Reserves. He was promoted to first lieutenant Medical Reserve, U. S. Army in November, 1917, and served at Fort Benjamin Harrison, Indiana, from which he was transferred to the 77th Division at Camp Upton. After 8 months service with the American Expeditionary Forces he was commissioned captain Medical Corps, U. S. Army. He was for 8 months with the British on detached service, in an advance sector for eight weeks, and later commanding officer of the American Military Hospital No. 21 at Paignton, England. He received his discharge at Camp Merritt in 1919, and was re-commissioned with the rank of major, Medical Corps United States Reserves. From 1920-24 he was a member of the Nebraska National Guard, with the rank of major, commanding Hospital Company No. 130. His military organizations include the following: American Legion, Veterans of Foreign Wars, Reserve Officers Association and Sons of the American Revolution.

Since 1919, Dr. Munger has been in active practice in Lincoln, and holds membership in the following: He is a member of the staff and of the executive committee of Lincoln General Hospital, chief of the division of genito-urinary surgery of Lincoln General Hospital, attending genito-urinary surgeon Bryan Memorial Hospital. He is a fellow of the American Medical Association, and a member of the Nebraska State and Lancaster County Medical Societies. In the latter he was secretary three years. He is also a fellow of the American College of Surgeons, member of the American Urological Association, and secretary of its southwestern branch.

He is affiliated with the Westminster Presbyterian Church, of Lincoln, and numbers among his civic organizations the Chamber of Commerce and the Rotary Club. A Mason, he is a member of Lincoln Lodge No. 19, and and Sesostris Temple, 32nd degree. His clubs are the University and the Lincoln Country Club.

When he is able to seek recreation Dr. Munger finds it in golf and fishing. He also enjoys reading, particularly European history.

Dr. Munger was first married to Olive Ruth Lucas, who was born at Pierce, Nebraska, May 7, 1891, and who died at Cincinnati, December 18, 1918. She was graduated from the University of Nebraska in 1915, where she had majored in European history and music. On the maternal side she was descended from early Dutch settlers in Manhattan. Her father descended from a long line of illustrious soldiers and statesman, and was directly related to Sam Houston and her grandfather, Robert Lucas, was governor of Ohio and first governor of Iowa. There is one child of this marriage, Margaret Olive, who was born at New York City, June 25, 1917. On December 20, 1930, Dr. Munger married Catherine Louise Colby. Mrs. Munger is the daughter of Mr. and Mrs. George Detter of Harbine, Nebraska, pioneer residents of Jefferson County. Residence: Lincoln. (Photograph in Album).

Irvia Clarence Munger, Jr.

Born at Chicago, Illinois, March 21, 1900, Irvia Clarence Munger, Jr., physician and surgeon, is the son of Irvia Clarence and Myrtie Ann (Hatch) Munger. The former is a leading physician and surgeon of Lincoln, who was born at Volga City, Iowa, March 18, 1875. He is a fellow in the American College of Surgeons, and held the rank of first lieutenant in the Medical Officers' Reserve Corps in the World War. He is a Mason, member of the Scottish Rite and Shrine bodies. The first member of the Munger family in America came from England, in 1621. Myrtie Ann Hatch was born in New York on February 28, 1873, and is still living.

Dr. Munger was graduated from the Cozad High

School in 1917, received his A. B. from the University of Wyoming, in 1923, his B. Sc. from the University of Nebraska, in 1924, and his M. D. in 1925. He is a member and the founder of Theta Nu, honorary medical fraternity and member of Alpha Theta Phi, honorary dramatic, Sigma Alpha Epsilon and Phi Rho Sigma. He received a reserve "W" in football at the University of Wyoming, the year 1919-20.

The two years following his graduation from medical school Dr. Munger served his internship in the Kings County Hospital at Brooklyn; since that time he has been in private practice at Lincoln. He is a member of the staff of Lincoln General and Bryan Memorial Hospitals, a member of the board of directors of the Social Welfare Society, and a member of the Lancaster County Medical Society.

During the World War he was a private with the A. E. F. at Base Hospital No. 37. He now holds the rank of first lieutenant in the Medical Reserve Corps. He is a junior member of the American College of Surgeons, a Mason, and member of the American Interprofessional Institute.

On April 21, 1924, he was united in marriage to Anne Elizabeth Leonard of Harvey, Illinois, at Logan, Iowa. Mrs. Munger was born January 27, 1898, and is an instructor in voice; her ancestry is traced to William the Conqueror. There are two daughters: Judith Anne, born February 27, 1928, and Constance Ruth, born June 30, 1929. The family is affiliated with the Holy Trinity Episcopal Church. Dr. Munger enjoys golf and fishing. His hobbies are reading, photography, hiking and pipes. Residence: Lincoln.

Cornelius S. Munhall

One of Nebraska's pioneers, Cornelius Munhall of Callaway, has taken an active part in building up the middlewest. His father, who was a minister, was born in Pennsylvania and died at Cleveland, Ohio, in 1863; he delivered the first sermon at Champaign, Illinois, in 1854, in an old depot building which was used for religious services at that time. His paternal grandfather came to this country from Ireland in 1763 and settled in Pennsylvania, the original family name being Mulhali.

Two uncles of Mr. Munhall built the first mill at Millbrook, Ohio, in 1832. His mother came to this country from England during her childhood, and died at Urbana, Illinois, in 1878.

Sixty-two years ago he resided at Fort Leavenworth. The country west of the Missouri River was a wild frontier where hostile Indians were preying upon the white settlers. In August, 1861, Mr. Munhall enlisted in Company I, 26th Illinois Volunteer Infantry. This brigade consisted of the 26th and 47th Illinois, the 8th Wisconsin "Old Abe" Eagle Regiment, the 11th Missouri, and the 5th Minnesota infantries, all of which remained together until the siege of Vicksburg, Mississippi.

He served with the Union Army on the famed march to the sea with General Sherman, and during 1867-68-69, engaged in warfare with the Indians. Residence: Callaway.

George Alvin Munn

Born at Ord, Nebraska, June 25, 1891, George Alvin Munn is the son of Charles Almon and Ada Arvilla (Heffelman) Munn. His father, who was born at Plainwell, Michigan, February 17, 1865, and died at Lincoln, Nebraska, June 8, 1901, was a lawyer, served as county attorney of Valley County, Nebraska, and was district judge; his ancestry was English and French-Canadian. His mother, who was born at Doylestown, Ohio, September 8, 1866, is past president of the Woman's Club of Ord and for many years has been a business woman.

Mr. Munn attended the grade schools at Ord and in

1909 was graduated from the Ord High School, where he was active in debating and dramatics and was a member of the basketball team. He received the A. B. and LL. B. degrees at the University of Nebraska where he was a member of the legal fraternity Phi Delta Phi, and was consul of P. D. P. Since 1915 he has been engaged in the practice of law at Ord and since 1920 has been a member of the firm of Munn & Norman.

A Democrat, he served as county attorney at two separate times in Valley County. He is a member of the Nebraskana Society, the Ord Chamber of Commerce, the Commercial Law League, the Nebraska Alumni Association. He holds membership in the following fraternal organizations: Masons, Scottish Rite and Shrine, Knights of Pythias, of which he is Past Chancellor and Past Member of the Grand Lodge Board of Trustees. His hobby is mechanics.

During the World War he was commissioned first lieutenant of the infantry at the 2nd Officers Training Camp at Fort Snelling, Minnesota. He was discharged as First lieutenant at Camp Custer, Michigan, April 14, 1919, after nearly a year's service overseas. He is a member of the American Legion.

He was married to Alfhild Rigmor Moller at Lincoln May 24, 1923. Mrs. Munn, whose ancestry is Danish and Norwegian, was born in Valley County, Nebraska, July 2, 1898. They have four children: Phyllis Joy, March 1, 1924; Charlene Claire, February 10, 1926; Verda Zoe, August 7, 1929; and Charles Alvin, December 12, 1931. Residence: Ord.

Irving Eugene Munroe

A farmer, lumber and elevator man for many years, Irving Eugene Munroe is now retired. He was born at Fairfield, Wisconsin, July 4, 1869, the son of William and Katherine (Case) Munroe, his parents having been pioneer settlers in the middle west.

William Munroe was born at Calimus, New Brunswick, December 5, 1839, of Scotch ancestry. A soldier in the Civil War, he was later a farmer, and died at Hastings on May 27, 1924. His wife, Katherine, was born in Hebron, New York, June 5, 1840, and died at Hansen, Nebraska, November 15, 1911.

Irving Munroe attended the early country school in his locality, and soon thereafter went to work on the farm. From 1891 until 1892 he was in charge of the A. F. Boston Lumber Company, and in 1893 was with the Orcott elevator and mill at Doniphan, Nebraska. A Republican, he served fourteen years as town treasurer, twelve years as school director and eight years as justice of the peace at West Blue Township, in Adams County.

On November 14, 1894, Mr. Munroe was united in marriage to Claudea Barbara Lakin at Hastings. Mrs. Munroe, whose parents were natives of Wisconsin, was born at Doniphan, January 13, 1874. There were three children born to them, two of whom are living: Delatus, born April 27, 1896, died May 23, 1911; DeWayne, born December 15, 1901, and Lawrence, born March 24, 1911.

Mr. Munroe has always taken an active part in civic and community affairs; was chairman for West Blue Town war loan drives in the late war, and is a contributor to Red Cross and Salvation Army. He is a member of the Evangelical Church, the Woodmen of the World, the sons of Union Veterans of the Civil War, and was recently elected to life membership in The Nebraskana Society. His hobby is baseball. Residence: Hastings.

John Alexander Munroe

John A. Munroe was born at Bradford, Massachusetts, August 18, 1853, the son of Rev. Nathan and Lucile M. Munroe. He began his career as a clerk for the Green Bay and Minnesota Railroad Company in 1873, and since 1881, when he became general agent for the Chicago, St. Paul, Missouri & Ohio Railway Company, he has been a prominent railway man at Omaha. He was made assistant traffic manager of this company in 1882; assistant general freight agent for the Union Pacific Railway Company, 1882-1901; and freight traffic manager, 1901-11. He was vice president of this company from 1911 to 1918.

Mr. Munroe was traffic manager of the Union Pacific Railroad, Oregon Short Line Railroad, Los Angeles and St. Louis Railroad, and St. Joseph & Grand Island Railroad, 1918-20; and was vice president of the Omaha & Council Bluffs Street Railway Company. Now retired from this position he serves in the capacity of director of this company.

Mr. Munroe was married to Hattie Baker at Kansas City, Missouri, January 18, 1888. Mrs. Munroe died in 1921. He is a Republican. Residence: Omaha.

Arthur H. Murdock

Arthur H. Murdock, lawyer, was born at Penn Yan, New York, August 13, 1863, son of Rensselaer and Eliza (Page) Murdock. The father was born in Glenn Falls, New York in 1809 and died at Scipioville, New York in February, 1872. His wife, Eliza, was born in New York State in 1823, and died at Raymond, Nebraska, in April, 1912.

A member of the Nebraska bar since February, 1891, Mr. Murdock has been in active practice since that time. A Republican, he was city attorney of South Omaha 1902; deputy county attorney of Douglas County 1904; member of the fire and police commission 1906; and municipal judge 1916.

On November 19, 1893, he was married to Anna Merrill at Omaha. There are three children, Maurine, born October 6, 1894, who married Charles W. Hamilton, Jr.; Harry M., born June 8, 1903, who married Margaret Shaw; and Arthur Clark, born December 27, 1909.

Mr. Murdock is a member of Westminster Presbyterian Church, the American, Nebraska State and Douglas County Bar Associations, the Elks and the Masons. His hobby is farming. Residence: Omaha.

Cora Ellen Stone Murphy

Born at Muscatine, Iowa, November 18, 1861, Cora Ellen Stone came to Nebraska in a covered wagon during the summer of 1864, her parents taking a homestead a mile and half north of Crab Orchard.

Her father, Benjamin Franklin Stone, was born in Ohio, May 1, 1815, and died at Crab Orchard, November 8, 1900. He was a farmer and carpenter, a so-called water witch, locating many wells. Himself deprived of schooling, he was an earnest advocate of education.

Maria Kilbourne, his wife, was born near Dayton, Ohio, November 21, 1824. She was an excellent housewife and an expert needlewoman, and was much in demand as a nurse among the pioneer settlers. She was of the Kilbourne family of Pennsylvania-Dutch descent, which had many honors to its credit. Her death occurred at Crab Orchard, January 24, 1912.

Benjamin Franklin Stone was considered one of the most courageous of the early settlers of Nebraska. He was ever ready to help newcomers or those in need, and was instrumental in the forming of the first school district in Johnson County.

Beginning her education in a log school house at Crab Orchard, Cora Ellen Stone afterward attended the Wayland School, and received her high school education at Tecumseh. She began teaching in country schools at the age of sixteen, and later attended the university two years. Her teaching career lasted for 12 years.

On March 12, 1890, she was married to James L. Murphy at Crab Orchard. Following their marriage they lived on a farm at Todd Creek, where they resided for seven years. They removed from there to Crab

Orchard, remaining until 1909, at which time they took up their residence in Holt County. Mr. Murphy, who is a farmer, was born near Danville, Indiana, on July 23, 1861, of English, French and Irish descent. There are four children, as follows: Mary, born July 26, 1893, who married John Nathan Stauffer and who lives at O'Neill; Evelyn, born December 12, 1894, who married Walter Russell French; Lowell, born November 21, 1896, who married Bessie Bryan; and Annie Laurie, born March 5, 1902, who married William F. Thompson. Mr. French is superintendent of the Mead Consolidated Schools, and his wife is prominent in social work and is a leader in 4-H Clubs.

Mrs. Murphy wrote numerous articles on school work during her teaching career and later wrote on home topics, which articles were published in *The Nebraska Farmer*. She has always assisted in every effort toward the advancement of her community, is president of the Woman's Christian Temperance Union, a teacher in the Sunday School of the Methodist Episcopal Church, and a member of the Woman's Foreign Missionary Society and the Ladies Aid Society. She served six years on the Page Board of Education, was its president two years, and is a member of the Parent Teachers Association. She is a life member of the Nebraskana Society, and is a member of the Page Woman's Club. Her leisure time is divided between reading and good citizenship work. Residence: Page. (Photograph in Album).

Daniel M. Murphy

Daniel M. Murphy was born at Oakdale, Nebraska, October 25, 1882. He is the son of Maurice W. and Maria (Regan) Murphy, the former born at Syracuse, New York, in 1853. Maurice W. Murphy came to Nebraska as a young man and settled in Antelope County where he engaged in farming and served as county supervisor for twelve years. He was of Irish descent. At the time of his death on March 17, 1908, he was retired.

Maria Regan was born in Ireland in 1853. She came to America when a girl, and died at Oakdale September 19, 1903. Daniel M. Murphy was graduated from Oakdale High School in 1906 and received his LL. B. from Creighton University. He was admitted to the Nebraska bar at Omaha in June 1915, and has since engaged in the practice of law. He is a Republican and was county superintendent of Antelope County from 1912-17. Before coming to Omaha in 1921 he was associated in practice with Hon. J. F. Boyd of Neligh, Nebraska.

He was married to Anna L. Klink at Elgin, October 27, 1915. Mrs. Murphy was born at Rising City, Nebraska, in 1893. She was a teacher prior to her marriage, and is of German descent. To them three children were born, Daniel, born October 17, 1916; Leonard, born September 12, 1928, died December 3, 1928, and Genevieve born October 8, 1930.

Mr. Murphy is a Catholic and attends St. Margaret Mary Church. He is a member of the Nebraska State Bar Association and the Chamber of Commerce; is also an Elk and a member of the Knights of Columbus. He is fond of golf. His club is the University. Residence: Omaha.

Francis Patrick Murphy

Francis Patrick Murphy, physician, was born in Rogers, Nebraska, September 12, 1890, son of Patrick Joseph and Margaret (Conboy) Murphy.

He attended public school at Rogers, and was graduated from Creighton High School in 1907. In 1911 he received his Bachelor of Arts degree from Creighton University, and in 1915 his medical degree.

On July 9, 1918, he was married to Agnes Edna Klockars at Junction City, Kansas. They have several children. Since 1920 Dr. Murphy has practiced in Omaha,

specializing in obstetrics. He is a Catholic, and a member of St. Cecelia's Church. His professional organizations include the Omaha, Douglas County Medical Associations, the Officers Reserve Corps in which he holds the rank of captain. Residence: Omaha.

George H. Murphy

Railway agent for the Chicago, Burlington and Quincy Railroad at Lincoln, since June, 1919, George H. Murphy has been a railroad man since leaving school. He was born at Biggsville, Illinois, December 3, 1877, son of Henry Alexandria and Hannah (Holah) Murphy. His father was a native of Pennsylvania, of German and Irish parentage, who served in the Civil War and later entered the mercantile business in Nebraska. He died at York, Nebraska, in October, 1922. Hannah Holah, his wife, was born in London, England, in 1847, and is still living.

Mr. Murphy was graduated from the Bradshaw, Nebraska, High School in 1896, and has since worked for the Burlington Railroad, both as telegrapher and agent at various places. He was married to Stella Cordelia Smith at David City, on June 30, 1909. Mrs. Murphy was born at Elk Creek, in 1884. They have three sons, Frank, born June 30, 1910, who is attending the University of Nebraska where he is a member of Phi Sigma Kappa; George. Jr., born September 15, 1914, and Marvin, born September 5, 1922.

A resident of Nebraska for forty-seven years, he has been active in civic and community work, and is a member of the Chamber of Commerce, Red Cross, etc. He is particularly active in Boy Scout work, and is a member of Elm Park M. E. Church, and the Masonic Order. Residence: Lincoln.

John Harry Murphy

John Harry Murphy, physician and surgeon, was born at Omaha, Nebraska, September 10, 1889, son of James and Anna Josephine (Westroppe) Murphy.

He received his public school education in Omaha, was graduated from Creighton High School, received his Bachelor of Arts degree from Creighton University in 1910, his Masters degree in 1913, and his medical degree in 1915.

He is married to Iene Angela Langdon, their marriage having been solemnized March 4, 1919.

Among Dr. Murphy's professional organizations are the American Medical Association, the Central State Pediatric Society, the American College of Physicians, the American Association of Teachers of Diseases of Children, the Nebraska State Medical Association, and the Omaha and Douglas County Medical Association. Residence: Omaha.

Joseph Francis Murphy

Joseph F. Murphy has lived in Nebraska for 40 years and has been engaged in the real estate and insurance business for the past 35 years at Omaha. He was born at New York City, March 31, 1870, the son of Matthew John and Elizabeth (Halpin) Murphy. His father, who for many years was engaged in railroad construction work, was born at Dublin, Ireland, and died at Neola. Pottawattamie County, Iowa, June 2, 1880. His mother was born at Dublin and died at Omaha, October, 1893.

Mr. Murphy completed a bookeeping and commercial and scientific course and later was a student at Valparaiso College in Indiana. He is now owner and manager of his own real estate and insurance company. and is secretary and treasurer of the Palace Theatre at Omaha.

His marriage to Catherine A. Cassidy was solemnized at Omaha, May 12, 1903. Mrs. Murphy, who was born at Omaha, May 12, 1879, was formerly a school teacher. They have two children: Joseph F., born March 11, 1904;

and James W., born June 6, 1908. Joseph is in the real estate business. James is a law student.

Mr. Murphy is a member of the Chamber of Commerce; the Red Cross; and other welfare societies, including the Salvation Army. He holds membership in the South Omaha Merchants and the South Omaha Chamber of Commerce. He is a member of the Nebraskana Society; the Lakewood Club at Omaha; St. Rose Catholic Church. His hobbies are reading and golf. He is a Democrat. Residence: Omaha.

Mark William Murray

Mark William Murray, an outstanding figure in the newspaper world for more than 50 years, was born at New Berlin, Wisconsin, January 6, 1867, the son of James and Catherine (Slain) Murray. His father, who was postmaster at Fremont, Nebraska, and served as county clerk of Dodge County for a number of years died at Fremont; he served as captain in the Civil War.

Mr. Murray was prominent in civic affairs at Pender, Nebraska, where he was editor and publisher of the *Pender Times*. A Democrat, he served as postmaster of Pender for three terms, was a member of the Nebraska Legislature two terms, acted as state central committeeman, chairman of the Democratic County Committee, and was a delegate to the Democratic National Convention in 1912. At the time of his death, February 24, 1931, Mr. Murray had been in business at Pender longer than any other man, and had contributed much to the advancement of his community and state.

He was president of the Chamber of Commerce two terms, was Past President of the Northeastern Nebraska Press Association, served as clerk of the Modern Woodmen of America, and was affiliated with St. Johns Catholic Church of Pender. He was a member of the Nebraska National Guards at Fremont, Nebraska, for five years, and served as first sergeant of the company for two years. His hobby was reading.

On June 27, 1893, he married Mary Ellen Corrigan at Milwaukee, Wisconsin. Three children were born to them: Byron; Eleanor, who married Dr. Lawrence D. Quigley of Green Bay, Wisconsin; and Catherine, who married William C. Eddy. Byron is now editor of the *Ponder Times*

Frank Edward Mussehl

Frank E. Mussehl, who has lived in Nebraska for the past 14 years, has taken an active part in the civic and educational advancement of the state. He was born at Jefferson, Wisconsin, December 3, 1891, the son of William and Freda (Muller) Mussehl. His father was born at Mecklenburg, Germany, January 27, 1841, and died at Jefferson, December 1, 1925. His mother was born in Germany, and died at Jefferson, February 12, 1918.

Professor Mussehl received his education in Wisconsin, and in 1907, was graduated from the Jefferson High School. He received his B. S. degree at the University of Wisconsin, 1915, and holds membership in Sigma Xi, Gamma Sigma Delta, and Alpha Gamma Rho. Since 1917, he has been professor of poultry husbandry at the University of Nebraska.

His marriage to Inez Lenora Clough was solemnized at Madison, Wisconsin, June 20, 1917. Mrs. Mussehl was born at Mazomanie, Wisconsin, July 6, 1894.

He has been a member of the Kiwanis Club at Lincoln, since 1924, and holds membership in the Shrine Country Club. He is a member of the American Association for the Advancement of Science. He is a member of the Scottish Rite and Shrine bodies of the Masons, is affiliated with the Congregational Church, and politically is independent. His sport is golf. Residence: Lincoln.

Myrtle Edna Musser

Myrtle Edna Musser, clubwoman, was born at Beatrice, Nebraska, May 25, 1877, daughter of Thomas Baker and Sara Elizabeth (Hackler) Jamison.

Her father was born at Tarkio, Missouri, January 19, 1833, and died at Chandler, Oklahoma, July 23, 1920. He was a farmer. His wife was born in Tarkio, October 21, 1835, and died at Chandler, March 8, 1906.

Mrs. Musser attended the public and high schools of Nebraska, and on March 21, 1893 was married to John Benjamin Musser. To them were born five children, two of whom are living, Opal, born September 24, 1894, is a graduate of the University of Nebraska; Michael, born September 24, 1900, died February 27, 1902; Mabie, born December 19, 1904, is married to Fred Cloud, she is also a graduate of the university; Thelma, born June 5, 1908, died April 20, 1911; and an infant boy, born August 24, 1911, died the same day.

A Democrat, Mrs. Musser was elected to state legislature from district 93 in 1930. She was nominated by petition for state senator, being the first woman in her district to run for that office.

Mrs. Musser has various ranching interests. During the World War she had more than 800 hours of service in the Red Cross work. She is a member of the Rushville Methodist Episcopal Church, the Business and Professional Women's Club, the League of Women Voters, of the P. E. O., the Delphian Society, and the Ladies Columbian Reading Club. She is past president of the county federation of Women's Clubs, and a member of the Rushville Library Board. She is past state president of the Rebekah Assembly. Her main interest apart from women's club work is music.

Mrs. Musser, during her term as state legislator, was instrumental in passing the dormitory bill which applies to the provision of dormitories for university and normal schools through state aid. Residence: Rushville. (Photograph on Page 865).

Sterling Faan Mutz

Sterling F. Mutz, a lifelong resident of Nebraska, has been engaged in the active practice of law in this state for the past 20 years, and has been prominent in state and local politics. He was born at Burton, Nebraska, March 31, 1888, the son of Otto and Ella Porter (Russell) Mutz. His father, a ranchman, publisher, and author, served both as county judge and chairman of the LaFollette independent party in Nebraska. He served as state senator at one time; was the author of two books. Born near Glenwood, Iowa, October 16, 1855, he died at Lincoln, October 18, 1926. He was of Swiss, German, and English ancestry; his father was born in Pennsylvania and lived in Ohio and Indiana; his mother was born in Virginia.

Ella (Russell) Mutz, who was born at Plattville, Grant County, Wisconsin, November 14, 1855, was a teacher. She was president of the county Woman's Christian Temperance Union for a period and is a member of the Daughters of the American Revolution; and the Ladies Legislative League. Her father was county judge of Cass County for many years. She is a direct descendant of Lieutenant John Kays who served in George Washington's army during the Revolution.

Mr. Mutz attended the rural schools near Burton, Nebraska; the grade schools at Ainsworth, Nebraska; and was graduated from the Ainsworth High School in 1905. He was a student at the Nebraska State Normal School at Peru, and the University of Nebraska where he was granted the LL. B. degree in 1911. He was a member of the debating squad at Peru, and Phi Delta Phi at the University of Nebraska. He was admitted to the bar at Lincoln, June 16, 1911.

He has been engaged in the general practice of law since 1911. He is a director in the Cosmopolitan Old Line Life Insurance, and was formerly president of this

MYRTLE EDNA MUSSER

organization. A Democrat, Mr. Mutz served as chairman of the Lancaster County Democratic Central Committee for 8 years; was defeated candidate for district judge, 1912; and served as city prosecuting attorney at Lincoln, 1917-18.

He was married to Jessie Gontley Clarke at Auburn, Nemaha County, Nebraska, August 8, 1917. Mrs. Mutz, who was born at Auburn, October 1, 1889, is a direct descendent of Matthew James Clarke a Revolutionary War soldier. They have two children: Jessica Faan, born October 19, 1918; and Sterling Faan, born July 19, 1920.

Mr. Mutz was special inspector in the conscription department during the World War, and took part in all Liberty Loan drives and Red Cross drives. He is a member of the Sons of the American Revolution, the Lancaster County Bar Association, the Nebraska State Bar Association; the American Bar Association, and the Lincoln Chamber of Commerce. He is a member of the Parent Teachers' Association, the Young Men's Christian Association, and the Nebraskana Society, and is director and lawyer for the Nebraska Children's Home Society.

He is affiliated with St. Matthews Episcopal Church; he has been licensed lay reader since 1930. He is a 32nd degree Mason, Scottish Rite, Shrine; a member of the Woodmen of of the World, Ben Hur Society, and the Woodmen Circle. His social clubs include: Lincoln University Club; and Lincoln Eastridge Club. He is fond of golfing and hunting, and his hobbies are philosophy, antiques, and travel. Residence: Lincoln.

Edwin F. Myers

Since 1908 Edwin F. Myers has been engaged in the practice of law at Broken Bow, and has attained much prominence in his chosen profession. He was born at Georgetown, Nebraska, November 22, 1879, son of John E. and Amanda M. (Shedd) Myers. His father, a ranchman, was born in Sussex County, New Jersey, August 22, 1841, and died in Ada County, Idaho, May 12, 1928. His mother, born in Chester, Vermont, February 16, 1849, is living.

Edwin F. Myers attended country school in Georgetown, was graduated from Broken Bow High School in May, 1900, received his Bachelor of Arts degree from the University of Nebraska in 1904, and his Bachelor of Laws degree from Harvard Law School in 1907. At the University of Nebraska he was a member of the debating squad, the University Players and the university chorus, and was captain of his class football team. He was a member of the Harvard swimming team and the second football team 1904-05-06. He is a member of Acacia.

After his graduation from law school he worked six months in the collection department of Marshall Field's retail store in Chicago. Admitted to practice in Nebraska in 1908, he formed a partnership with former Governor Silas A. Holcomb with whom he practiced law two years 1908 and 1909. Since that time he has practiced law alone.

His marriage to Chrissie J. Haumont was solemnized at Broken Bow October 29, 1910. Mrs. Myers was born at Broken Bow, May 18, 1890. There are four children, Edwin J., born October 10, 1911; Kenneth L., born November 23, 1912; Frank M., born November 12, 1916; and John R., born April 30, 1918. Edwin won first place in extemporaneous speaking in the state contest, while Kenneth won district contests in extemporaneous speaking, oratory and constitution contests. Both were four years on their high school debating teams.

Mr. Myers is a Republican. A Son of the American Revolution through three ancestors, he is descended from Daniel Shedd of Quincy, Massachusetts, 1640, whose descendent, Joseph Shedd, was a member of the Bos-

ton Tea Party. He, with several members of the party, disguised themselves as Mohawk Indians in the Shedd store building, which at that time occupied the present site of the Equitable Life Insurance Building in Boston. Mr. Myers is also the son of a Civil War veteran. He is a member of the Methodist Episcopal Church, the Public Service Club, the Eastern Star, and the Nebraska State and Custer County Bar Associations. Recently he was made a life member of The Nebraskana Society. His favorite sport is tennis, while his hobby is hunting. Residence: Broken Bow.

Henry Dey Myers

For the past 25 years Henry D. Myers has been engaged in the practice of medicine in Colfax County, Nebraska. He was born at Anamosa, Linn County, Iowa, November 2, 1878, and has lived in Nebraska practically all his life. His father, Samuel Henry Myers, who was born at Mansfield, Ohio, January 12, 1842, and died at Des Moines, Iowa, November, 1927, was a farmer; he was a member of Company C, 24th Infantry of Iowa, during the Civil War; his ancestors came from Holland; he was a Republican and took an active part in the civic and political affairs of his community. His mother, Mary (Porter) Myers, was born at Martelle, Linn County, Iowa, August 8, 1846, and died at Dodge, Dodge County, Nebraska, September 3, 1888; she was one of 13 children.

Dr. Myers was graduated from Dodge High School in 1894; was a student at Gates College for a time; was graduated from the University of Nebraska, 1898; and was graduated from Drake Medical School, 1906. He was admitted to medical practice at Howells, Colfax County, Nebraska, August 8, 1906, and has been prominent as a surgeon and physician there since that date.

He was united in marriage with Mayme Sophia Busch at Fremont, Dodge County, Nebraska, March 25, 1908. Mrs. Myers was born at Schuyler, Nebraska, May 3, 1882; her ancestry is German. She has been active as a housewife and assistant in her husband's office. They have two children: Susann, born January 22, 1910; and Henry Dey, born December 25, 1912. Susann was graduated from the University of Nebraska, in 1931. Henry Dey is a premedic in his second year at the University of Nebraska.

Dr. Myers is a member of the Dodge County Medical Society; the Nebraska State Medical Society; and the American Medical Association. He holds membership in Howells Chamber of Commerce; local and county welfare organizations; and the Nebraskana Society. He is a member of the Masonic Lodge at Leigh, Nebraska; was formerly active in the Young Men's Christian Association; and has been a member of the school board for the past 18 years. He is affiliated with the Congregational Church of Howells. He is a Republican. His sport is tennis. His hobby is music: Dr. Myers is a talented musician. Residence: Howells. (Photograph in Album).

Preston Brown Myers

On December 14, 1869, Preston B. Myers was born in Cedar County, Iowa, the son of Harman M. and Evelyn (Brown) Myers. His father, who was a farmer, was born at New York City, September 30, 1845, and died at West Liberty, Muscatine County, Iowa, March 19, 1922; he was a soldier in the Civil War. His mother was born in Ohio, April 17, 1849, and died at West Liberty, July 11, 1918.

Mr. Myers, who has been a prominent druggist in Omaha for the past 40 years, attended the rural schools of Iowa, and later was a student at the University of Iowa. He was employed by the firm Kuhn & Company as a pharmacist from June 5, 1889 to November 5, 1895; he then organized the Myers-Dillon Drug Company. He is now president of that organization.

He is a member of the Nebraska Pharmaceutical Association; the American Pharmaceutical Association;

and the National Association of Retail Druggists. He holds membership in the Chamber of Commerce at Omaha, the Red Cross, and the Nebraskana Society. He is an Elk. His sports are hunting and fishing. He is a Democrat. Residence: Omaha.

Clement Joseph Augustine Nacke

The Reverend Clement Joseph Augustine Nacke, Catholic priest, musician and author, was born at West Point, Iowa, October 12, 1896. He is the son of Conrad C. and Elizabeth Catherine (Pogge) Nacke, the former born at St. Louis, Missouri, March 22, 1856, and the latter at West Point, Iowa, October 17, 1860. Conrad C. Nacke is a hardware merchant at Hebron.

Clement Nacke first attended parochial school at West Point, Iowa, and was later graduated from parochial school at Hebron. During 1912-13 he attended Creighton High School at Omaha, and was graduated from St. Benedict's College at Atchison, Kansas, in June, 1917. Thereafter he attended St. Paul Seminary for Philosophy and Theology at Kenrick Theological Seminary at St. Louis, being graduated in 1922. He was ordained a Roman Catholic priest on July 1, 1922, by Archbishop J. J. Harty, D. D., at St. Cecilia's Cathedral in Omaha. Father Nacke celebrated his first Mass in Sacred Heart Church at Hebron, July 4, 1922.

After his ordination he was pastor *pro tem* at Atkinson, Nebraska, and was made assistant at the Church of St. Margaret Mary in Omaha on October 17, 1922. From June 1, 1923, until November 1, 1923, he was pastor at Constance, Nebraska, and since November 1, 1922, has been pastor at Hooper. He is also pastor of St. Lawrence Church at Scribner.

Father Nacke is a composer of music both sacred and secular. He is a choir and orchestral director of exceptional ability, and an accomplished pianist and pipe organist. Among his contributions to literature are *Value and Power of Music* (book); and *Psychology of Teaching Music* (MS).

At the present time Father Nacke is director of music of the Diocese of Omaha, and in September, 1930, was director of music at the Sixth National Eucharistic Congress at Omaha. His particular interest is the practical study of psychology through the affiliation of music and professional interests. He has been teaching music for several years.

On March 17, 1930, Father Nacke became the proud possessor of the first pipe organ in the world to be installed in a residence in the form of a concert grand piano. Residence: Hooper. (Photograph on Page 868).

Ralph Clayton Nash

Ralph Clayton Nash, merchant and postmaster, was born at Byromtown, Forest County, Pennsylvania, December 4, 1887. He is the son of Murray A. and Margaret (McGregor) Nash, the former a lumberman. Murray A. Nash was born at Corry, Pennsylvania, and died at Canton, New York. His wife was born at Scranton, and died at Flemington, New Jersey, May 28, 1929. She was an ardent church and temperance worker, and her father was a captain in the Civil War.

Mr. Nash was educated in public school, and during his 23 years' residence in Nebraska has been engaged in the general merchandise business. He is a Republican, and at the present time is postmaster at Richland.

On September 20, 1910, he was united in marriage to Marie Anna Bures at Omaha. Mrs. Nash, who was born in Czechoslovakia, September 20, 1886, is a printer. They have one daughter, Mildred, born November 10, 1917.

Mr. Nash is a Republican. He is a Mason and a director of School District No. 12, and a member of the Nebraskana Society. His favorite sports are golf and football. Residence: Richland.

Emil Herman Naumann

A resident of Nebraska for the past 40 years, Emil Herman Naumann was born at Mautitz, Germany, February 17, 1863, the son of Adolph and Henriette (Hering) Naumann. His father, who was a stock dealer, was born at Eula, Germany, October 15, 1827, and died at Mautitz, February 14, 1886. His mother was born at Mautitz, July 24, 1828, and died at Boertewitz, Germany in December, 1912.

Dr. Naumann attended an elementary school at Mautitz and studied for three years at Ostrau, Germany. He received the Doctor of Dental Surgery degree at the University of Iowa in 1890. As a young man he learned the milling trade in Germany and was employed in various flour mills there until 1884 when he came to America where he studied to enter the University of Iowa. He is engaged in the practice of dentistry at Columbus, Nebraska, where he is also a director and vice president of the Miller Allied Securities Company.

He was a member of the Board of Education for nine years, served as secretary four years and as president one year. He holds membership in the county, state, and national dental associations, is affiliated with the Federated Church of Columbus, and is a member of the Chamber of Commerce and the Red Cross. He was a director in the Young Men's Christian Association for a number of years and is a member of the History Club, the Country Club, and the Waldonians at Columbus.

His marriage to Clara Martin occurred at Columbus, June 5, 1894. Mrs. Naumann, whose ancestry is Scotch, was born in Venango, Pennsylvania, October 28, 1864, the daughter of Joseph and Clara (Kuhn) Martin. They have raised two children: Margaret Anna, born October 28, 1888; and Walter Richard, born June 1, 1901. In 1901 two children of Mr. Naumann's brother came to this country from Germany and became members of the Naumann home. Margaret married L. R. Taylor and Walter married Rene Burgess. Walter is associated with his father in the practice of dentistry. Residence: Columbus.

Perry Thomas Naylor

Perry Thomas Naylor, civil engineer, inventor and manufacturer, was born at Ware, Massachusetts, December 13, 1887, and has been a resident of Nebraska twelve years. His father, Thomas Naylor, was born at Ware, December 12, 1861, and is a general merchant and city almonor. Of English and Welch ancestry, his family came from England about 1855. Harriett Elizabeth Perry, wife of Thomas Nayor, was born at Hardwick, Massachusetts, December 26, 1868, of English and Scotch descent. She is a descendant of Robert Browning, and is interested in social science and literature.

Upon the completion of his high school education in 1907, Mr. Naylor attended Worcester Polytechnic Institute two years. Thereafter he completed a course in civil engineering with the American School of Correspondence, and a modern business course with the Alexander Hamilton Institute.

Since 1920 he has been city engineer at Hastings. From August, 1918, to February, 1919, he was sergeant with Headquarters Company, 211th Engineers on special assignments.

He was acting chief engineer September 1917-May 1918; assistant chief engineer May 1915-May 1917, and instrument man from January 1914 to May 1915 for the following: Worcester Consolidated Street Railway Companies, Springfield Street Railway Company, Inter-State Consolidated Street Railways, and the Milford, Attleboro and Woonsocket Street Railways. He was also instrument and office man for J. K. Barker, civil engineer, and draftsman for the United Electric Light Company of Springfield, between years at Tech, and was foreman for the F. T. Ley Construction Company, clerk and timekeeper for H. P. Cummings Construction Company and

Matsus—Omaha

CLEMENT NACKE

foreman for P. J. Nelligan Construction Company. He is the inventor and manufacturer of the Naylor Sprayer.

He was married to Mary Rebecca Bruner at Hastings on December 22, 1919, and to them were born the following children: William, born February 25, 1922; Elizabeth, born December 8, 1924; Mary, born November 7, 1926, and Margaret, born January 13, 1931. Mrs. Naylor who is of French and German pre-Revolutionary ancestry, was born at Pellville, Kentucky, September 15, 1899.

Mr. Naylor is a member of the First Baptist Church, the Chamber of Commerce, the Lions Club (first vice president 1931), the American Legion, and the Young Men's Christian Association. He is a Mason, and a member of the Nebraskana Society. Among his favorite recreations are water sports and hiking. He devotes much of his time to mechanics and invention. Residence: Hastings. (Photograph in Album).

Welcome Welton Naylor

Welcome Welton Naylor, treasurer and manager of the Chadron Flour Mills, was born at Modesto, Illinois, December 21, 1878, son of Jacob Butler and Martha Ellen (Nighbert) Naylor. The father was born in Shelbyville, Kentucky, January 25, 1848, and was a farmer and merchant who died at Chadron in June, 1905. Some of his family settled in Delaware about 1775, later moving to Maryland, Virginia, and Kentucky. They were probably Scotch-Irish. Martha Ellen Nighbert was born in Macoupin County, Illinois, September 19, 1851, and died at Adams, Nebraska, December 28, 1888.

Mr. Naylor attended public schools of Nebraska up to the eighth grade and was graduated from Chadron Academy in June, 1900. He was married May 25, 1904, to Florence A. Click at Filley, Nebraska, who died August 17, 1917 at Chadron. On June 18, 1927, he was married to Winifred Beatrice Chizek at Chadron. Mrs. Naylor was born at Chadron, March 19, 1896. She is a member of the Eastern Star and is past noble grand of the Rebekahs. She is the daughter of John R. and Minnie (Rucker) Chizek. They have two children, Florence Lorraine, born July 17, 1929; and Welcome W., Jr., born December 30, 1930.

Mr. Naylor is a Democrat. He is the director of the Chadron Chamber of Commerce, a director of the Kiwanis Club, a Mason and a member of the Young Men's Christian Association. He is affiliated with the Congregational Church. Residence: Chadron.

George Neale

George Neale was born at Fort Calhoun, Nebraska, August 7, 1882, son of David and Alice Mary (Brain) Neale. David Neale, a native of Bredon, Worcestershire, England, was born January 2, 1833, and came to America in 1854. Of yeoman stock, he drove the Pony Express to Salt Lake City, and was agent for the Ponca Indians. In the 1870's he established a farm at Fort Calhoun and later invented the Anchor Rip Rap System for the protection of land against erosion. He contracted widely on the Mississippi, Missouri, and Red Rivers, and died at Fort Calhoun, in April 17, 1916.

Alice Mary, his wife, was born in Yellow Springs, Ohio, August 11, 1855, and died at Fort Calhoun, on February 9, 1920. A teacher in early life, she was a woman of high capability, and in her husband's absence assumed the management of his farm. Her parents were of English yeoman stock also.

George Neale graduated from Fort Calhoun High School in 1899, and took over the management of the home farm. Later he purchased a farm of his own, and still later acquired an adjoining one, both of which he manages. He is a director of the Fort Calhoun State Bank. He was married to Pauline Kruse at Fort Calhoun, her birthplace, on December 30, 1909. Mrs. Neale

was born June 22, 1884, of German parentage. They have two daughter: Mabel, born September 30, 1910, who is a graduate of the University of Nebraska, 1931, and Eleanor, born May 8, 1915.

Mr. Neale is a Democrat. He is active in community and educational affairs, and is a member of the Parent-Teachers Association and the School Board in District 54, twenty-eight years. His hobby is horseback riding. Residence: Fort Calhoun.

Sophus F. Neble

Sophus F. Neble, editor and publisher, was born at Stubbekobing, Denmark, December 15, 1859, son of Martin and Karen (Poulsen) Neble. He died at Omaha in 1931.

Mr. Neble attended public school, and on April 24, 1883, was married to Christine Larsen at Omaha. He was married on December 5, 1901 to Olivia Hansen. Their children are Sophus Neble, Jr.; Eywind M.; and Frances, who married Dr. Glen Miller.

A Democrat, Mr. Neble was active in politics, and was presidential elector from the 2nd Nebraska district, 1908-1912-1916. He held the rank of colonel of the governor's staff, 1908, 1913, 1915 and 1919, and was Douglas County commissioner from 1917 until 1922. From the year 1886 until his death he was the editor of *The Danish Pioneer*. He was also president of the Sophus F. Neble Publishing Company. He was a Christian, an Elk, a Mason and Shriner. (Deceased).

William Nedrow

For the past 25 years William Nedrow has been prominent in community affairs at Fairmont, and has been a successful dairyman there. He was born at Myersdale, Pennsylvania, February 23, 1866, the son of Jacob and Susanna (Lape) Nedrow. His father, who was a lumberman, was born at Rockwood, Pennsylvania, October 24, 1829, and died at Myersdale, August 12, 1906; his ancestors came to this country from Holland. His mother, whose ancestry was Scotch-Irish, was born at Somerset, Pennsylvania, October 25, 1831, and died at Myersdale, November 10, 1915.

Mr. Nedrow attended rural school in Pennsylvania, and later was a student at Vinton College at Vinton, Iowa. He has served as mayor of Fairmont for three terms and has always taken an active part in city government there. During the World War he assisted in the sale of Liberty bonds and contributed liberally to all loan funds. He is affiliated with the Nebraskana Society.

His marriage to Hattie Florence Muir occurred at Oregon City, Oregon, March 5, 1893; Mrs. Nedrow was born at Bolkow, Missouri, April 29, 1873, of Scotch-Irish parentage. Their two children are: Ray, born July 23, 1895, who is a lawyer; and William, born January 17, 1909, who is studying law at George Washington University. Residence: Fairmont.

Millard F. Needham

Millard F. Needham has lived on the same section of land in Nuckolls County, Nebraska, near Bostwick, for the past 43 years, and has always been interested in the progress of his community. He was born in Iowa, September 8, 1858, the son of Gordon Byron and Irene (Eldredge) Needham. Gordon Needham was born in Cayuga County, New York, April 5, 1815, was a farmer in Iowa for many years, and died at Madrid, Iowa, April 27, 1912; his English ancestors came to Massachusetts before the Revolution, and his great-grandfather was a soldier in that war. His mother, whose ancestry was English, died in Boone County, Iowa., in 1870.

Mr. Needham attended the elementary schools of Iowa. He still owns and manages his farm on state highway number three, and has in the past served for many years as a member of the local school board. He is a member of the Farmers' Union of Nebraska, is affiliated with the Methodist Episcopal Church of Bostwick, and holds membership in the Nebraskana Society. His hobby is reading.

In 1880, he married Mary Elizabeth Kirkpatrick at Homer, Illinois. Mrs. Needham, who is an amateur flower gardener, is of English and Scotch descent; her mother's home was Berwick-on-Tweed, England, while her father was a native of Scotland. Their son, L. K. Needham is a civil engineer at Portland, Oregon, a daughter, Daisy J., is a teacher, and the other daughter, Emma, is married to J. M. Gilmore of Red Cloud, Nebraska. Residence: Bostwick.

John Marshall Neely

On January 28, 1870, John M. Neely was born at Owensville, Indiana, the son of John Marshall and Ellen (Smith) Neely. His father, born in Indiana, was a physician and surgeon, who served as first surgeon in the 120th Indiana Volunteer Infantry. His paternal great grandfather came to America from Scotland in 1754 and served in the Revolution. John Marshall Neely died at Elmwood, Nebraska.

Ellen Neely, who was a teacher, was born at Vincennes, Indiana, and died at Owensville, October 10, 1883. Her maternal great grandfather, Daniel McClure, was a soldier in the Revolution.

Dr. Neely attended the elementary schools of Indiana and later was a student at Wentfield College in Illinois and the National Normal University at Lebanon, Ohio. He was awarded the M. D. degree at the Kentucky School of Medicine in 1896. He has lived in Nebraska for the past 35 years.

His marriage to Edna Perry was solemnized at Ashland, Saunders County, Nebraska, December 30, 1902. Mrs. Neely, who was born in Iowa, November 10, 1882, is a choir leader and music teacher. The following children were born to this union: John, Jr., born September 23, 1904, who married Mary Barlow; Elsie Sanderson, born April 12, 1905, who married H. A. Sanderson; Alene, born December 14, 1910; Orvis, born January 30, 1912; Katherine, born April 19, 1913; Elizabeth, August 26, 1916; and Patricia, born January 1, 1927. John was graduated in medicine in 1930, making the fourth physician in the Neely family.

Dr. Neely is a member of the Sons of Veterans and the Sons of the Revolution, the Lancaster County Medical Association, the Nebraska State Medical Society, and the American Medical Association. He is a member of the Elm Park Methodist Church of Lincoln, and is a Republican. Residence: Lincoln.

William Albert Kneer Neely

W. A. K. Neely, pioneer farmer in Wayne County, Nebraska, has lived there since February 17, 1878. He was born near Honey Grove, Pennsylvania, October 20, 1853, the son of John and Margaret Jane (Ewing) Neely. His father, who was a farmer, was born at Waterloo, Pennsylvania, June 6, 1814, and died near Honey Grove, May 30, 1892; Mr. Neely's great grandparents were John and Margaret (McFeaters) Neely; and his grandparents were William and Sadie (Harvey) Neely. William Neely, the grandfather, purchased land and settled in Juniata County on territory formerly belonging to the Indians. The Neely family was prominent in the progress of Pennsylvania, and came from Scotland and Ireland early in the history of the colonies.

His mother was born at Blaine, Pennsylvania, November 20, 1831, and died at Mercersburg, Franklin County, Pennsylvania, October 25, 1925. She was the daughter of William and Sarah (Allison) Ewing, who were also settlers of Pennsylvania.

Mr. Neely attended the Farmers Grove School at Tus-

carora, and later attended Tuscarora Academy. He has been a successful farmer in Wayne County for the past 50 years. He has been a member and treasurer of the local school board for the past 43 years. He is affiliated with the First Presbyterian Church, is a member of the Nebraskana Society, and holds membership in the Democratic party. He was active in liberty loan drives during the World War.

He was married December 29, 1881, to Azile May Burchfield at Mifflentown, Juniata County, Pennsylvania. Mrs. Neely was born at Mifflentown, February 23, 1856. She was a teacher before her marriage, and taught the first school at Wakefield, Nebraska. She was the daughter of Lewis and Jane (McKennon) Burchfield, who were Scotch and Irish, and was a direct descendant of Lord Burcham Burchfield.

They have two children: John Burchfield, born July 31, 1883, who married Grace Hacker, and who is a civil engineer at St. Louis; and William Harvey, born May 17, 1892, who married Gladys Gertrude Orr, and who is an auctioneer and farmer at Wayne. Mr. Neely's grandchildren are: William Harvey Neely, Jr., born July 27 1921; and John Orr Neely, born August 31, 1929. His hobby is reading. Residence: Wayne.

William Franklin Negele

William Franklin Negele was born at Walnut, Iowa, on December 2, 1866, the son of Charles Frederick and Mary Ann (Zollinger) Negele. His father was born in Germany, and died at Altoona, Pennsylvania, May 26, 1899; he was a clergyman.

His mother, Mary Ann Zollinger, was born at Sandusky, Ohio, and died at Cleveland, in December, 1891. Mr. Negele was educated in the public schools. On August 24, 1896, he married Olive Corinne Rhodes, who was born at Freeport, Illinois, in 1866. The marriage was solemnized at Freeport. They have one son, John Herbert, who married Martha Hanna.

Mr. Negele is a member of the Republican party. For many years he was associated with the Thompson-Beldon Company. He is a member of the Calvary Baptist Church, and has been treasurer of the building fund since 1918. He is affiliated with the Omaha Chamber of Commerce, the Travelers Aid, and is a member of Ak-Sar-Ben. He is active in the work of the Kiwanis Club.

For 45 years Mr. Negele has taken a leading part in the civic, social and commercial affairs of his community. Residence: Omaha.

John G. Neihardt

John G. Neihardt, poet laureate of Nebraska, was born near Sharpsburg, Illinois, January 8, 1881, son of Nicholas N. and Alice May (Culler) Neihardt.

He attended the Nebraska Normal College where he completed the scientific course. He was much encouraged by the two presidents of the school while he was there, J. M. Pile and U. S. Coun, who provided him with all possible facilities for an education.

His first volume of poetry to the public was *A Bundle of Myrrh* in 1908. He has written also *The Song of Hugh Glass* (1915), *The Song of Three Friends* (1919), and *The Song of the Indian Wars,* (1925). Listed below are his more important contributions to literature: *The Divine Enchantment* (1900); *The Lonesome Trail* (1907); *Man-Song* (1909); *The River and I* (1910); *The Dawn-Builder* (1911); *The Stranger at the Gate* (1912); *Death of Agrippina* (1913); *Life's Lure* (1914); *The Quest* (1916); *The Splendid Wayfaring* (1920); *Two Mothers* (1921); and *Laureate Address* (1921). Mr. Neihardt was honored by Nebraska appointing him poet laureate of the state, and by making him in 1923 an honorary professor of poetry at the University of Nebraska. In 1917 he was awarded the honorary degree of Doctor of Letters.

On November 29, 1908, Mr. Neihardt was married to Mona Martinsen, a sculptress, of New York City. They have four children. Residence: New York City.

Monroe Winfred Neihart

For the last 58 years Monroe W. Neihart has been a leading citizen of Nebraska. He was born in Lehigh County, Pennsylvania, November 13, 1853, the son of Daniel Peter and Eliza (Peters) Neihart. His father, a surgeon who served in the Civil War, was born on the Pacific Ocean and died at Nebraska City, Otoe County, Nebraska, June 18, 1905. His mother was born at Allentown, Pennsylvania, November 24, 1824, and died at Nebraska City, June 10, 1917. Her ancestry was German.

Mr. Neihart attended the public schools of Pennsylvania, Illinois and Iowa. Later he was a student at the Iowa City College, Iowa. For the past seven years he has been justice of the peace at Nebraska City, and has taken an active part in the political life of his community for many years. Since the age of 16 he has been engaged in the photography business, and much of his time has been devoted to government photography, photographing convicts and similar work.

He is the editor of the *Poultry Review* and the *Wyandotte Herald*. For 25 years he has been connected with community band and orchestra work in Otoe County. He is president of the Isaac Walton League, Chapter 76; he has been secretary and financier of Ancient Order of United Workmen for the past 30 years, and is a Grand Lodge officer of the state and *Great Chief of Record* of the Fraternal Order of Redmen. He is a member of the Red Cross, and the Ancient Order of United Workmen, the American Order of Redmen, the Chamber of Commerce, and is a member of the committee on State Forestration.

He was united in marriage with Matilda Hauber at Nebraska City, January 5, 1881. Mrs. Neihart was born at Alsace Lorraine, December 16, 1861. Her grandfather was professor in a college in Germany. She died at Nebraska City, August 7, 1924. They have two children: Grace, born October 30, 1880, who married Marshall Ingraham; and John W., born September 21, 1890. Residence; Nebraska City.

Elmer F. Neil

Elmer F. Neil, one of the outstanding farmers of Dawson County, Nebraska, was born at Berlin, Missouri, December 27, 1873, the son of Lloyd N. and Sarah Elizabeth (Jolly) Neil. His father, who was a farmer, was born at Easton, Missouri, January 6, 1845, and died at Cozad, September 8, 1921; his ancestry was Scotch and Irish. His mother, whose ancestry was Holland Dutch, was born in Breckenridge County, Kentucky, August 27, 1852.

Mr. Neil is president of the Dawson County Farm Bureau, is president of the Lexington Co-operative Company, and is a member of the Lexington Kiwanis Club. He was selected as one of the 1929 Master Farmers of Nebraska, and has always been a progressive citizen of Cozad. He is affiliated with the Methodist Episcopal Church of Lexington.

On October 20, 1898, he was married at Lexington, to Ethel J. Grafton. Mrs. Neil, whose ancestors came to this country from Scotland and England in the early history of America, was born at Lexington, October 20, 1880. They have three children: Harley G., born January 31, 1902, who married Helen Christianson; Noel J., born October 4, 1909; and Wayne F., born May 11, 1916. Residence: Cozad.

Erland N. P. Nelson

Born at Ruskin, Nebraska, July 28, 1897, Erland N. P. Nelson is the son of Hans and Frederikke (Olsen) Nelson. His father, who was born at Odense, Denmark, died in 1912, and his mother, born at Borhholm, Denmark, is living.

Erland Nelson was graduated from Ruskin High School, attended Hastings College, and received his Bachelor of Arts degree from Peru State Teachers College. His Master of Arts degree was awarded by the University of Nebraska. His post graduate work was taken at the University of Nebraska where he will take his doctor's degree.

Mr. Nelson's fraternities include Phi Delta Kappa, Sigma Tau Delta and Alpha Sigma Phi. While at Peru he was a member of the debating team in 1921. He is a member of the Nebraska State Teachers' Association, and at the present time is chairman of the research committee of the National Lutheran Educational Conference.

A rural school teacher in Dundy County, and superintendent of schools at Comstock from 1922 to 1924, he was superintendent at Juniata, 1924-26. Since 1926 Mr. Nelson has been associated with Dana College, as head of the department of commerce until 1929, and is acting president 1929-31. For the past year he has been president of the college.

Among his contributions to literature are *Success of Students Who Transfer from College to College* (1930); and *How to Improve The College Teacher* (1931).

On August 6, 1924, Mr. Nelson was united in marriage to Naida Editha Randall at Juniata. Mrs. Nelson, who was born at Sitka, Kansas, October 27, 1896, is an educator of English descent. There are two children, Isabelle Frederikke, born July 23, 1925; and Erland Randall, born June 4, 1928.

Mr. Nelson is a Democrat. His religious affiliation is with the First Lutheran Church of Blair. Residence: Blair. (Photograph in Album).

Grover E. Nelson

Grover E. Nelson, banker, was born near Bennington, Nebraska, February 3, 1892, and with the exception of two years has always resided in Nebraska. He is the son of Hans C. and Christiana (Rasmussen) Nelson, natives of Denmark. Hans C. Nelson was born at Langeland, Denmark, October 4, 1855, coming to the United States as a young man. A farmer by occupation, he spent his later years in Nebraska and died at Elkhorn, May 12, 1911. His wife was born in Langeland, April 15, 1859, and died at Bennington, January 13, 1900.

Educated in country school district No. 44 until twelve years of age, Grover E. Nelson was a student in district 58, and then attended Lutheran Parochial School two years, and six months at Elkhorn town school. From November, 1909 until August, 1914 he attended Fremont Normal College a total of 122 weeks. During this time he completed a commercial course and a teacher's course and took some arts and science, but did not finish.

Mr. Nelson taught school in St. Helena, Nebraska the school year of 1913 and 1914. On May 20, 1915 he commenced as janitor, and assistant to the bookkeeper at the Citizen's State Bank of Parker, South Dakota. He was made assistant cashier of the State Bank of Elkhorn in January, 1917, and on April 18, 1917 came to Millard to become cashier and director of the Farmers State Bank of Millard.

On June 4th of the following year he was married to Mary (Mayme) Dorothy von Dohren at Omaha. Mrs. Nelson, who was a bank bookkeeper four years before her marriage, was born at Millard October 28, 1894. There are two children, Grove Edwin, born July 3, 1920 and Dorothy Ann, born April 29, 1925.

A Republican, Mr. Nelson has been elected justice of the peace about ten times, but refuses to qualify, taking the position that business and politics do not mix. He is a Mason and a member of Nebraska Consistory of Scottish Rite Masons. His religious affiliation is with the St. Paul Evangelical Lutheran Church at Millard. During the late War Mr. Nelson was active in Liberty loan drives, exceeding his quota for the bank in every drive, whether for bonds, war savings stamps or treasury certificates. He enjoys hunting, particularly the annual fall hunt for migratory birds. Residence: Millard.

Lemist George Nelson

Lemist George Nelson, lawyer, has been in active practice since 1929. He was born at Fremont, Nebraska, June 2, 1906, the son of Louis and Marie (Forbes) Nelson.

His father was born at Marshalltown, Iowa, in November, 1875. He is district sales manager of the Harris Coal Company of Omaha where he was a member of the Board of Education from 1920-1924. His parents were Danish and came to America about 1860 where they were pioneers in Pierce and Antelope counties. Marie, wife of Louis, was born at Hooper, Nebraska, September 6, 1880. She was descended from early Dutch settlers of Pennsylvania.

Mr. Nelson attended Omaha Central High School from which he was graduated in 1924, and in 1929 received the Bachelor of Laws degree from Creighton University. He is a member of Delta Theta Phi, of which he was secretary and treasurer, and of Alpha Rho Upsilon.

On August 2, 1927, Mr. Nelson was married to Flora Bernice Jones. Mrs. Nelson was born at Harvard, Nebraska, August 11, 1905. They have one daughter, Shirley Mae, born August 19, 1930.

Mr. Nelson is a Republican and is now county attorney of Rock County. He has been a resident of Nebraska all his life. He is a member of the State Bar Association, and in 1931 and 1932 was a member of its advisory council. He was president of the Bassett Lions Club in 1930-31, is an Odd Fellow and Mason, and is a member of the Nebraskana Society. His hobbies are traveling and reading. Residence: Bassett. (Photograph in Album).

Oliver Nicolas Nelson

Oliver N. Nelson, merchant and banker of Nebraska City, Otoe County, Nebraska, has been a resident of this state for 65 years, and has been a leader in the civic and business affairs of his community all his adult years. He was born at Visby, Gotland, Sweden, April 11, 1859, and came to America with his parents in 1865. His father, Nicholas Peter Nelson, was born at Stockholm, Sweden, October 2, 1832. He was a shoemaker both in Sweden and at Nebraska City, where he died October 10, 1907.

Mary (Clawson) Nelson, his mother, was born at Visby, January 7, 1834, and died at Nebraska City, October 22, 1913.

Mr. Nelson attended the elementary schools in Nebraska City and then entered the business world. From 1886 to 1920 he was in the shoe retail business. He has been vice president of the Nebraska City National Bank since 1915; has been president of the First Trust Company since its organization in 1924; and has been a director in the Commonwealth Building and Loan Association since 1927. A Republican, he served Nebraska City as mayor in 1897-98-99.

On July 12, 1898, he was united in marriage with Margaret Gabrielle Hershey at Nebraska City. Mrs. Nelson, who was born at Nebraska City, February 21, 1871, is descended on the maternal side from Roger Williams. Three children were born to this union, two of whom are living: Josephine, born September 22, 1899, who died in infancy; Pauline, born May 31, 1902; and Karl, born May 19, 1905.

During the World War Mr. Nelson was active in loan drives, and at the present time is a member of the

Red Cross and the Salvation Army. He served as a member of the school board at Nebraska City from 1914 to 1929. He is an Elk and a Mason, and is a member of the Nebraska City Country Club. Residence: Nebraska City.

Robert Albert Nelson

Robert Albert Nelson, lawyer, was born at Omaha, August 27, 1890. He is the son of Nels J. and Annie (Peterson) Nelson. His father, a native of Sweden, came to America in 1882, and was associated with the Chicago, Burlington and Qunicy Railroad at the time of his death on March 17, 1927. Annie Peterson Nelson was also a native of Sweden, and resides at Omaha.

Robert A. Nelson was graduated from Omaha High School in 1908 and received his LL. B. from the University of Omaha in 1914. Upon his admission to the bar in that year he entered upon the active practice of his profession. In 1925 he was U. S. Commissioner for Nebraska. He is a Republican.

During the World War he was a yeoman first class in the United States Navy. He is a member of Omaha Post No. 1 of the American Legion, and is a Mason. He belongs to the Nebraska State and Omaha-Douglas County Bar Associations, and is a member of the First Baptist Church. His clubs are the Omaha Athletic and the Happy Hollow Country Club, and his hobby is golf. Residence: Omaha.

John Andrew Nepper

The Reverend John Andrew Nepper, Catholic priest, was born at Fort Atkinson, Iowa, November 30, 1877, son of Christopher and Catherine (Smith) Nepper.

The father was born at Port Washington, Wisconsin, and died at Gregory, South Dakota, January 22, 1924. He was a teacher and farmer, whose parents came from Belgium and Luxemburg in 1850. His wife, Catherine, was born in Wiennishiek County, Iowa, in April, 1856. Her family having settled in America, coming from Alsace-Lorraine.

Educated first in the elementary schools of Iowa, Father Nepper attended Randolph, Nebraska, High School graduating in 1897. He received his Bachelor of Arts and Master of Arts degrees from St. John's University at Collegeville, Minnesota, where he was a member of the choir and active in dramatics. Afterwards, Father Nepper attended the University of Innsbruck, Austria.

Ordained in 1908, Father Nepper was assistant pastor at Cedar Rapids, Nebraska, for two years, and since 1910 has been rector of St. Mary's Church at Rushville. He is superintendent and teacher in St. Mary's High School, and has erected a rectory enlarged his church and built several school and other buildings, during his present pastorate. For years he has been a member of the Diocesan school board and a member of the board of examiners for junior clergy.

He is the author of various magazine articles, and *School Legislation in Nebraska* (1919). During the late war, Father Nepper was a leader in his community in the Knights of Columbus war drives. He is a member of the Nebraska State Teachers' Association, the Chamber of Commerce, the City Library Commission, and the National Geographic Society. His hobby is economic and social questions, and educational progress. Residence: Rushville.

John Wallace Neslund

John Wallace Neslund has been a practicing physician and surgeon at Cozad since June 1, 1915. He was born near Galva, in Henry County, Illinois, June 19, 1882, son of Andrew O. and Carrie (Wexell) Neslund. The father, born in Sweden, March 11, 1831, came to

America with his parents in 1854, settling at Bishop Hill, in Henry County.

Andrew O. Neslund was a member of the old Swedish Bishop Hill Colony in Henry County, Illinois. This colony consisted of about 3000 Swedish settlers who came to the United States between 1846 and 1856. Most of them left the country of their birth in order to obtain religious freedom in the new world. After the Colony was dissolved in 1860 and 1861, the land the Colony had acquired was divided amongst its members and Mr. Neslund also received a small tract upon which he then made his home. In later years he purchased considerable more land adjoining this and continued in the farming and stock raising business until 1909 when he retired and moved to Galva. He died at Galva July 2, 1916. Mr. Neslund was first married to Helena Matilda Newstrand, at Bishop Hill, in 1859. She was born in Sweden, January 7, 1832, and died October 20, 1876. She left five children, two girls and three boys. Mr. Neslund married Carrie Wexell, September 11, 1878. She was born in Sweden, September 16, 1859, and came to this country with her parents in 1865. Two children were born to this union, John Wallace being the eldest. She still resides at Galva.

Upon his graduation from high school, John Wallace Neslund attended Mendota College at Mendota, Illinois, receiving his Bachelor of Arts degree in 1907. Educated for the ministry, he was ordained to the Christian Church at Davenport, Iowa in 1909. He held pastorates at Alexis and Rock Falls in Illinois, and at Cozad, Brock, Nebraska City and Valparaiso in Nebraska. He received his medical degree from Cotner University in 1915. He was valedictorian of his class at Cotner.

Dr. Neslund was married first to Grace Isador Dickinson at Davenport, Iowa, on December 31, 1907. She was born in New York City, June 28, 1884, and died at Grand Island, April 1, 1924. She was of English descent, active in church work, a member of the Woman's Club and the Women's Christian Temperance Union. There is one child to this marriage, June M., born June 29, 1912. She was graduated from Cozad High School in 1930. Since that time she has specialized in elocution, piano and violin. She is also her father's office assistant and secretary.

On June 19, 1925, Dr. Neslund was united in marriage to Grace T. Walford at Burwell, Nebraska. Mrs. Neslund's parents live near Burwell. She was born near Gresham, February 13, 1899. She is prominent in church and civic affairs, is a member of the Woman's Club, and a member and former state director of the Women's Christian Temperance Union. They have one child, Doyle Jo, born August 13, 1929.

Dr. Neslund served as municipal judge in Cozad from 1919-24. He is affiliated with the Cozad Christian Church, is a member of the national, state and local medical associations, the Modern Woodmen of America and the Nebraskana Society. His hobby is music, especially the piano-accordian. Residence: Cozad. (Photograph in Album).

Henry M. Nestor

Henry M. Nestor, a lifetime resident of Omaha, was born there on December 8, 1876, the son of Henry Frederich and Bertha (Windheim) Nestor. His father, who was a business man, was born at Gustrov, Germany, March 2, 1850, and died at Denver, Colorado, July 19, 1909. His mother was born at Chicago, Illinois, February 15, 1854. Her parents were born in Germany; her mother was descended from the Saxon nobility.

Mr. Nestor is director of the Orchard Wilhelm Company of Omaha. He has always been active in promoting the progress of his community and state. He is a member of the Red Cross, the Community Chest, the Omaha Chamber of Commerce, and the Continental Club.

He is a Mason, and is affiliated with the First Christian Church of Omaha.

On April 28, 1904, he was united in marriage with Mae Shields at Omaha. Mrs. Nestor, who was born at Omaha, is of Scotch descent. They have two children: Florence, born September 1, 1905, who married Rudolph Helgren; and Henry, born October 25, 1907, who is a student at George Washington University at Washington, District of Columbia. Residence: Omaha.

George Emile Neuhaus

George Emile Neuhaus, physician and educator at Omaha, was born at Berlin, Germany, February 27, 1866. His father, Carl Neuhaus, who was a physician was born at Stargard, Germany, and died at Berlin, Germany, in 1895. He is descended from an old Westphalian family; his grandfather built the Berlin-Hamburg railroad and was president of the railroad company until his death.

His mother was born at Danzig, Germany, and died at Berlin. Her father was a civil engineer who built the Rhenish Railway and the railway bridge at Coblenz, Germany. He built many railways in Turkey for the Turkish government who had applied to the Prussian government for an engineer capable of doing this work.

Dr. Neuhaus attended the Gymnasium at Gorlitz, Germany; was graduated from the Gymnasium at Berlin, 1886; and received his M. D. degree in 1891 at Bellevue Hospital Medical College in New York City. He was a student at the University of Berlin, 1890-1896-1901; and attended Harvard Medical College in 1909 and 1919. He is a member of Phi Rho Sigma.

He served his internship at Bellevue Hospital, New York, 1891; practiced medicine in New York City, 1892-1902; practiced in Denver, Colorado, 1903-22; and since 1922 has been prominent in the medical world at Omaha. He served as head of the department of neurology and psychiatry at the University of Colorado School of Medicine from 1907 to 1922, and is now professor in medicine at Creighton University School of Medicine. He was director of the Mount Airy Sanitarium at Denver. He is the author of many medical articles in different professional journals.

Dr. Neuhaus is a member of the Omaha-Douglas Medical Society; the Nebraska State Medical Society; the American Medical Association; the American Psychiatric Association; the American Psychopathological Association; and the Central Neuropsychiatric Association. He is a member of the Nebraskana Society and the Red Cross, and is a Mason. His sport is hiking, while his hobbies are photography, reading, and writing. He is affiliated with the First Unitarian Church of Omaha.

He was united in marriage with Clara Ruth Mozzar in 1922. There are two children born of a previous marriage: Ralph, born September 26, 1896; Karla Elizabeth, born January 26, 1905; and Ruth, born May 26, 1923; and Gisa Marie, born June 17, 1925, the latter two being born by the second marriage. Ralph, who graduated from Boston Technical Institute, is an engineer, Karla Elizabeth is a teacher of history in the high school of Boulder, Colorado. Residence: Omaha.

Arthur Lorenzo Neumann

Arthur Lorenzo Neumann, prominent in the banking world for many years, was born at Andover, Illinois, February 3, 1870, son of Valentine and Annie (Wickstrom) Neumann. Valentine Neumann was a native of Lagenlonsheim, Prussia, born April 15, 1841, who came to America in 1857, and served as a private in Company B, 42nd Illinois Infantry in the Civil War. After the war he came to Nebraska and settled near Oakland, where he died on July 1, 1917. Annie Wickstrom was born in Sweden, October 14, 1849, and came to America with her parents as a child. Her father was captain of Company B, 57th Illinois Volunteer Infantry in the Civil War. She died at Lynn Center, Illinois, September 6, 1877.

Educated in the public schools, Arthur Lorenzo Neumann came to Nebraska in October, 1881, and in 1892 entered the Farmers and Merchants National Bank at Oakland, as a clerk. He is now president of this bank, and has a wide public record. A Democrat, he served as assistant postmaster at Oakland, 1887-90, and as state senator 1927, session of 1929, special session of 1930, and the session and special session of 1931. He was chairman of the Burt County liberty loan committee in the World War, and for more than forty years has been the leader of the local band. He is a member of the Sons of Veterans of the Civil War, the Chamber of Commerce, and the Nebraskana Society, and his fraternal organizations include the Masons, Odd Fellows and Elks. Residence: Oakland. (Photograph in Album).

Gus E. Neumann

Gus E. Neumann, county clerk of Hall County, Nebraska, was born in Germany, July 1, 1876, the son of Ernest F. Neumann and Johanne Grabs. His father was born in Bohemia, April 4, 1833, and died at Grand Island, April 4, 1895. Johanne (Grabs) Neumann, a native of Germany, was born September 28, 1839, and died in 1923.

Mr. Neumann was connected with the *Grand Island Daily Independent* for over 20 years, served as deputy assessor at Grand Island for a time, was county treasurer of Hall County, and is now serving as county clerk. He has been active in the Volunteer Fire Department for more than 20 years, acting as chief for over two years, is a member of the Chamber of Commerce, and is affiliated with St. Paul's Evangelical Lutheran Church.

He holds membership in the Salvation Army, the Young Men's Christian Association, the Elks, Eagles, Odd Fellows, and the Masons. He is a member of The Nebraskana Society, and is connected with the Republican party.

On April 19, 1891, he was married at Grand Island to Edith Wutzler, who was born in Germany, December 15, 1878. Three children were born to this marriage: Irma, July 29, 1897, who married William Reese; and Ernest F., February 27, 1899, who married Margaret Ernest who is manager of the branch office of the Indemnity Insurance Company at Los Angeles. Edith Elane was born October 28, 1920, and died November 10, 1920. Residence: Grand Island.

William Richard Carl Neumarker

William Richard Carl Neumarker, physician and surgeon, was born at Luxemburg, Germany, May 18, 1878, son of Richard William, and Elizabeth O. (Roth) Neumarker. The father, born in Germany, November 6, 1844, died at Columbus, April 1, 1928. He came to Richardson County in 1884, and held the degree of Doctor of Divinity, serving as a chaplain in the Franco-Prussian War. His wife, born in Sonnenburg, Prussia, May 26, 1840, died at Columbus, June 1, 1924. She was a musician.

Dr. Neumarker received his medical degree from Central Medical College at St. Joseph, Missouri, and has been in active practice in Nebraska since 1909. He is a member of the American College of Physicians, the Association of Military Surgeons, the American, Nebraska State and Platte County Medical Associations.

He is a member of the Masons (Shrine), the Modern Woodmen of America, the Chamber of Commerce, the Lions Club and the Nebraska State Historical Society. He served in the World War from June, 1917 until 1919, with the ranks of captain, major and lieutenant-colonel,

Medical Corps, one year with the American Expeditionary Forces. He is a Lutheran.

On February 26, 1908, he was married to Meta Hensley at Columbus. She was born there on April 3, 1880. There are two children, William, born April 3, 1909 and Richard, November 23, 1925. Residence: Columbus.

Harry George Neumayer

Harry George Neumayer, superintendent of schools at Paxton, was born at Grand Island, Nebraska, March 10, 1901, son of Lewis and Elizabeth (Danner) Neumayer. The father was born at Mendota, Illinois, January 15, 1868, and is in the grocery business at Grand Island. His grandfather was born at Haslach Baden, Germany, in 1818, and his grandmother at Kuhr, Switzerland.

Elizabeth Danner was born at Geradville, Pennsylvania, August 2, 1874, and is still living. She is of German ancestry.

Mr. Neumayer attended Platt School until February, 1910 and the Howard School until February, 1914. He completed his public school education at Grand Island and attended Grand Island High School two years 1917 and 1919. During 1920 and 1921 he attended Grand Island College Academy, and in 1926 received his Bachelor of Arts degree from the Grand Island College. During the summer of 1931 he was a graduate student at the University of Nebraska. In 1925 he was president of the Young Men's Christian Association at Grand Island College, and from 1920 until 1926 was a member of the Amphyction Literary Society there. He was a member of the football team 1917 and 1919 and 1920-22-23-24.

Until he finished college he worked for his father in a grocery store and for Charles Schirkofsky of Grand Island. He started teaching at Ord, in 1926, continuing until 1929. Since that time he has been superintendent of schools at Paxton.

On August 11, 1927, he was married to Gladys Eleanor Patton at Broken Bow. Mrs. Neumayer was born at Ellsworth, Nebraska, February 27, 1902, her parents, Robert and Della (Facemire) Patton, being ranchers south of Ellsworth. She is affiliated with the Methodist Church and a member of the Eastern Star.

Mr. Neumayer is a Republican. He is a member of the Methodist Church at Paxton, the Nebraska State Teachers Association, the Commercial Club, and the Grand Island Lodge No. 318 of the Ancient Free and Accepted Masons. His favorite sports are football and basketball. Residence: Paxton. (Photograph in Album).

John William Neville

For the past 11 years John William Neville has engaged in the practice of medicine, three years in Stromsburg, and eight years in Utica. He was born at Lincoln, Lancaster County, Nebraska, January 17, 1895, the son of John William and Jeanette L. (Swann) Neville. His father, whose ancestry was Irish, was born at Fairview, Fulton County, Illinois, October 17, 1862, and died at Hildreth, Franklin County, Nebraska, March 7, 1909. His mother was born at Portage, Bowling Green County, Ohio, October 3, 1867, of Scotch parentage.

Dr. Neville was graduated from the Hildreth High School, was awarded the B. S. degree, 1917, and the M. D. degree, 1920, at the University of Nebraska, and took a post graduate course at Harvard Medical College. His interneship was served in the city and county hospitals of San Francisco and in Leland Stanford Service. His fraternity is Phi Chi.

He is a member of the American Medical Association, the Nebraska State Medical Association, and the Seward County Medical Society. He is a Mason, holds membership in the American Legion and the Nebraskana Society, and is independent, politically. Dr. Neville has lived in Nebraska for over 36 years, and in January, 1932, moved to York, to engage in practice.

On July 3, 1920, he was married to Irene Frances

Swearingen at San Francisco, California. Mrs. Neville, whose ancestry is Dutch and English was born at Creston, Iowa, April 17, 1897. Two children were born to this marriage: Patricia Jane, born January 11, 1928; and John William, born October 15, 1930. Residence: York.

Keith Neville

Keith Neville is the son of William and Mary Ann (Keith) Neville. He was born at North Platte, Nebraska, February 25, 1884. His father, who was born in Chester, Illinois, December 29, 1843, and died at Douglas, Arizona, April 5, 1909, is descended from an American ancestor who landed at Clefts, Maryland in 1633.

His mother's ancestry dates to Revolutionary times. Mary S. Lockwood, one of the founders of the Daughters of the American Revolution, was her aunt. Mary Ann Neville was born at Topeka, Kansas, November 13, 1858 and died at North Platte, March 1, 1884.

Mr. Neville was graduated from St. John's Preparatory School in June, 1901, after which he attended St. John's College, Annapolis, Maryland, where he received his A. B. degree. He was active in debating, received letters in football and baseball, and was a member of the Phi Sigma Kappa fraternity.

A Democrat, Mr. Neville's political and civic experience has been wide. He served as governor of Nebraska, 1917-18; was defeated for re-election in 1918.

He was receiver for the Skinner Packing Company 1922-23. At the present time he is president and treasurer of the Neville Company; and vice-president and director of the First National Bank at North Platte, Nebraska. He was war governor of Nebraska and in 1917 was elected colonel of the 7th Nebraska Infantry. This organization, however, was never mustered into Federal service.

On October 21, 1908, he was married to Mary Virginia Neill, at Charlestown, Jefferson County, West Virginia. To this union four children were born; Mary Nelson, born November 30, 1910; Frances Elizabeth, December 20, 1911; Virginia Neill, November 30, 1913; and Irene Morell, July 1, 1918. Mrs. Neville traces her ancestry to Revolutionary days. She was born at Charlestown, August 5, 1883.

Mr. Neville has been president twice of the North Platte Chamber of Commerce, is a member of the council; school board; and the Rotary Club. In 1929 he received the Rotary Club award for leadership in civic improvement. He is an honorary member of the United Spanish War Veterans.

He is a Mason, Knight Templar, 32nd degree Scottish Rite, a Shriner, Elk, and Odd Fellow. An Episcopalian, he is a member of the Church of Our Savior in North Platte.

His social clubs are: North Platte Country Club, Omaha Athletic Club, Omaha; St. Petersburg Tarpon Club, Florida, and the Izaak Walton League. Residence: North Platte. (Photograph on Page 876).

Chenia Alburn Newberry

Chenia Alburn Newberry, merchant and manufacturer, was born at New Baltimore, Michigan, April 9, 1869, son of Norman and Fanny Jane (Morris) Newberry. The father was born in McComb County, Michigan, October 15, 1852, and was a farmer in Nebraska until his death at Kearney, August 9, 1901. His wife was born at New Baltimore, Michigan, September 5, 1854, and died at Kearney, Nebraska, April 23, 1931. Her family originally came from England, two members serving in the Revolutionary War.

On July 23, 1893, Mr. Newberry was married to Ellen Marie Brennan at Alliance. She was born at East Saginaw, Michigan, February 27, 1870, of Irish ancestry.

Their children are as follows: Mary A., born July 27, 1895, married Franklin Abegg; Norman M., born January 16, 1898, married Genevieve Dotson; Agnes R., born May 17, 1902, married Edward McNulty, who died April 6, 1924; Helen E., born May 6, 1904; Edward A., born July 31, 1907, died August 6, 1924; William Leonard, born January 3, 1912; Dorothy Clare, born November 22, 1901, died February 26, 1902; and Charles Alburn, born March 1, 1909, died July 4, 1909. William is a student at Notre Dame University.

At the age of 19 Mr. Newberry entered the hardware business at Alliance and has continued in that business since. He is at the present time the president of the Newberry Hardware Company. He is a Democrat. He is a member of Holy Rosary Catholic Church, the Chamber of Commerce, the Rotary Club, the Knights of Columbus, the school board, and the Alliance Country Club. His sport is golf, while his hobby is business.

Mr. Newberry's death occurred at Alliance, March 31, 1932. He has always been a prominent citizen of his community. His outstanding characteristics were humility and generosity. He is known over the state as the man "who put Alliance on the map." (Deceased).

Anne Christina Newbigging

Anne Christina Newbigging, author and clubwoman, was born at Ogden, Utah, May 12, 1869, daughter of Augustus and Christina (Neilson) Isaacson. Augustus Isaacson, who was born at Wesby, Sweden, May 25, 1827, was a farmer and landowner, who crossed the plains by ox-team, secured a home and raised a large family. He was a true pioneer. His death occurred at Ewing, Nebraska, in 1891. His wife, Christina, was born in Gothenburg, Sweden, October 9, 1835, one of the early pioneers of the west. Twins were born to her in a prairie schooner on the plains of the middlewest, and six children were reared to maturity. She died at Chambers, Nebraska, in October, 1921.

Educated in the public and high schools of Omaha, she was married on December 12, 1888, to James Newbigging, at Wisner, Nebraska. Mr. Newbigging was born in Strathburn, Canada, March 9, 1863. A farmer, he settled near Wisner, in 1889, where the family still resides. There are seven children, as follows:

John J., who maried Selma Buskirk; Barbara G., who married Frank Stubbs; Jean J., who married Louis Foy, James T., who married Thelma Waddell; Helen C., who married Robert Patterson; Giles D., who married Mary Alice Ulery and Marcella H., born December 1, 1913, who is a student in the Wisner High School.

At the age of three, Mrs. Newbigging re-crossed the plains from Utah to Nebraska, where she has since resided. She is the author of *A Cry of the Soul,* besides many short stories, poems, etc., covering a period of forty-two years. *A Cry of the Soul* was reviewed at the tenth annual convention of the Cuming County Federation of Women's Clubs, and has received much praise from other sources. Letters of appreciation received by the author, from many prominent persons have been placed in many public libraries in the state.

Mrs. Newbigging is a member of the Royal Highlanders, while her husband is an Odd Fellow, Highlander and Woodman. She is a member of the First Congregational Church, the Woman's Club, Nebraska Writers' Guild, and a life member of the Nebraskana Society. She is interested in music, literature, art, and gardening. Residence: Wisner. (Photograph in Album).

Evalena Newbranch

Evalena Newbranch, prominent clubwoman of Omaha, was born in Harrison County, Missouri, June 10, 1875, the daughter of Wilbur Thomas and Catharine

KEITH NEVILLE

Francis (Doubrousky) Rolofson. Her father was born in Illinois, September 12, 1852. Her mother was born in Czechoslovakia, December 25, 1852.

Mrs. Newbranch attended the Wilbur Public School, the Lincoln Grade School and the University Preparatory School at Lincoln, Nebraska. She was awarded the A. B. degree at the University of Nebraska in 1896. She is a member of the American Association of University Women and in 1916-17 was president of the Omaha chapter of this organization. She has lived in Nebraska for the past 51 years and has taken a vital part in the civic and social affairs of Omaha for many years.

A Democrat, Mrs. Newbranch is now serving as a member of the Democratic state central committee. During the World War she worked at the State Red Cross Warehouse as receiver and censor of all knitted goods made for the army under Red Cross supervision. She is a member of the Family Welfare Association, of which she was director for 10 years and has served as president of the board of directors of this organization for the past five years.

She is a member of the Omaha Public Library board and from 1924 to 1930 served as its secretary. She holds membership in the Quota Club and the Omaha Club, and is a member of the Nebraskana Society.

On March 12, 1896, she was united in marriage with Harvey Ellsworth Newbranch, at Lincoln, Nebraska. Mr. Newbranch, whose ancestry is Swedish, was born at Swedesburg, Henry County, Iowa, April 11, 1875. He is one of Nebraska's best known and most distinguished editors, and is recognized through his editorials throughout the United States. Four children were born to them: Katharine, born March 7, 1897, who married Howard N. Douglas; Isabel, born January 19, 1900, who died March 23, 1900; Evelyn, born June 16, 1902; and Eleanor, born March 7, 1904, who married Chester A. Gerbracht. Residence: Omaha.

Harvey Ellsworth Newbranch

Harvey E. Newbranch, editor and newspaper executive of Nebraska is known throughout the newspaper world for his striking editorials on the events of the day. He has lived in Nebraska since 1884 and has been the editor of the *Omaha World-Herald* for many years. He was born in Henry County, Iowa, April 11, 1875, the son of Oliver Peter and Louisa Albertina (Rapp) Newbranch. His father, who was born in Sweden, was a miner, farmer, grain dealer, banker, and real estate dealer; he died at Long Beach, California, in 1920. His mother was born in Sweden and is still living.

Mr. Newbranch attended the rural schools of Henry County, Iowa, and in 1892, was graduated from the high school at Wymore, Nebraska. He was awarded his A. B. degree at the University of Nebraska in 1896; he received his LL. D. at Creighton University, 1929. He is now editor of the *Omaha World-Herald*, and is a director and secretary of the World Publishing Company. He is director and vice president of the Herald Building Company.

He was united in marriage with Evalena Pearl Rolofson at Lincoln, Lancaster County, Nebraska, in 1896. Mrs. Newbranch is active in social and welfare work in Omaha. Four children were born to their marriage: Katherine, born March 7, 1897, who married Howard N. Douglas; Isabel, born January 19, 1900, who died March 23, 1900; Evelyn, born June 16, 1902; and Eleanor, born March 7, 1904, who married Chester A. Gerbracht.

Mr. Newbranch is a member of the Omaha Chamber of Commerce and the Omaha Athletic Club. He is a member of Omaha Club. He is a Democrat. Residence: Omaha.

James Compton Newcomb

For the past thirty-two years James Compton New-

comb has been a resident of Saline County. Born at Augusta, Illinois, May 31, 1870, he is the son of Proctor Peter and Mercy (Compton) Newcomb. Proctor Newcomb, who was a banker and lumberman, was born at Rushville, Illinois, June 15, 1834, and died at Augusta, Illinois, September 15, 1914. His father was born at Bernardston, Massachusetts, May 19, 1804, and traced his ancestry to Governor Bradford. Mercy Compton was a native of Brooklyn, Schuyler County, Illinois, and was born October 5, 1841. She died at Augusta, Illinois, on March 30, 1926.

Upon his graduation from high school, James Compton Newcomb entered the lumber business with his father in Augusta. He was married first to Florella Grace Whitten. She was born at Edgar, Nebraska, March 11, 1876, and their marriage took place at Edgar, June 15, 1898. She died at Friend, January 22, 1905. Of this marriage there are two children, Mary C., born October 30, 1901, who married Fred H. Preston of Lincoln, July 3, 1929; and Winifred W., born January 5, 1905, who married Ted Johnson of Lincoln, August 5, 1929. They reside at Elko, Nevada, where Mr. Johnson is manager of the Boeing Air Transport Co. Mr. Newcomb's second marriage was to Clara Mae Swarr of East Petersburg, Pennsylvania, and took place July 17, 1907. They have one adopted son, John Swarr, born August 5, 1915.

Soon after his marriage in 1898, Mr. Newcomb moved to Friend, where he associated himself with S. J. Whitten in the lumber business. For twenty years he was connected also with the Merchants and Farmer's Bank of Friend, until its merger with the First National Bank in 1930. A Republican in politics he has served on the city council and for nine years was a member of the board of education. Mr. Newcomb is affiliated with the First Congregational Church, has served as its treasurer 32 years, and for 25 years was superintendent of its Sunday School. He is a Mason and a member of the Chamber of Commerce. Residence: Friend.

Harry Julius Newell

Born at Kalamazoo, Michigan, April 12, 1872, Dr. Harry Julius Newell is the son of Francis Albert Newell and Caroline Hannah (Frost) Newell. Francis A. Newell, who was born at Bradford, Lancashire, England, in 1837 came to this country with his parents in 1839. He died at Alexandria, Nebraska, January 9, 1913. His wife was born at Frankfort, Maine, in 1840, of English parentage, and died at Alexandria, on September 3, 1925.

Harry Newell attended rural schools, and was graduated from normal school April 30, 1898. He was married to Charlotte Douglas, September 11, 1901, at Daykin, Nebraska. Of English parentage, she was born at Postville, Iowa, and died at Manatau, Colorado, August 10, 1918. Their daughter, Elizabeth, was born June 1, 1904, and is married to Archie D. Marvel. Dr. Newell is now married to Edna I. Wilson, a trained nurse.

Dr. Newell has practiced medicine in Alexandria since May, 1903, when he was admitted to the profession He is a Republican and has resided in Nebraska since November 25, 1877. A member of the American, Nebraska State and Thayer County Medical Associations, he also holds membership in the American College of Physical Therapy.

He is affiliated with the Presbyterian Church, the Independent Order of Odd Fellows and the Ancient Free and Accepted Masons. During the World War Dr. Newell was a member of the Council of National Defense and the Four Minute Men, and was a committee speaker on the Loan Drives. He holds membership in the Nebraska Historical Society and the Nebraskana Society. Residence: Alexandria.

Ralph Arlington Newell

Ralph Arlington Newell is a native Omahan, born May 10, 1886. He is the son of Charles Lorenzo and

Allie Elizabeth (Cuer) Newell, the former born at Eden Corners, New York, May 15, 1854. Charles L. Newell was for many years credit manager of the Omaha Ice and Cold Storage Company, and died at Omaha on November 12, 1929. He was descended from early English and Irish settlers in America. His wife, Allie Elizabeth, was born at Muscatine, Iowa, July 21, 1857. She resides at Omaha, where she is active in club work, especially in the Omaha Woman's Club. She is of English descent.

Upon his graduation from the Omaha High School in 1904, Ralph A. Newell entered the employ of the Union Pacific Railroad where he remained eight years. He was sales manager for the George H. Lee Company for six years, and has been associated with the Universal Motor Company since 1918. Sales manager of the organization from 1918-21, part owner in 1921, since 1926 he has been president and manager. He is also a director of the Yellow Cab and Baggage Company.

He was married to Allis Stone Hall, at Omaha on December 24, 1912. Mrs. Newell, who was born at Bay City, Michigan, October 2, 1888, is a member of the Daughters of the American Revolution, the Mayflower Descendants, etc. They have one son, Charles, born August 21, 1914.

Mr. Newell is independent in politics. He was active in Red Cross and Liberty Loan drives during the World War, and is an elder and superintendent of Sunday School in the Miller Park Presbyterian Church.

He is particularly active in the Masonic Lodge and is past master of Right Angle Lodge No. 303 of Omaha, is a director of the Masonic Home for Children, and belongs to the Royal Arch body, the Knights Templar, Mt. Calvary Commandery and Tangier Temple of the Shrine.

His civic organizations include the Red Cross, the Chamber of Commerce, the North High School Parent Teachers Association, etc. He is fond of music and is active in musical circles, is an ardent tennis enthusiast and has been the city tennis champion. His hobby is salesmanship. His clubs are the Concord Club, the Carter Lake Club and the Birchwood Club. Residence: Omaha.

Everett J. Newkirk

Born at North Platte, Nebraska, June 8, 1892, Everett J. Newkirk is the son of William Leonard and Mary Elizabeth (Sullivan) Newkirk. His father, born in Leesville, Indiana, April 4, 1858, is a retired farmer and former county treasurer of Logan County, Nebraska. He comes of a family of fine cabinet makers of Scotch and English extraction. Mary Elizabeth Sullivan was born in Petersburg, Indiana, March 17, 1867, of Irish and English descent.

Everett J. Newkirk was educated in the public schools of Hastings and Juniata, and was graduated from high school at Hastings in 1913. After attending Grand Island College two years, and Kearney State Normal School one year, Mr. Newkirk was a student at Hastings Business College, graduated in 1914.

Since leaving school Mr. Newkirk has taught in the Hastings Business College for a year, was credit man for J. H. McGrath Hardware Company 3 years and was for eight years the owner of a grocery in Hastings. At the present time he is the proprietor of the Guernseydale Dairy.

On August 11, 1915, he was united in marriage to Lillian Lametha Mason at Hastings. Mrs. Newkirk, who was a teacher prior to marriage, was born at Hastings, January 29, 1892. She is descended from Sir Edward Head of Virginia, who was with Washington at Valley Forge, and is also a descendent of Dr. Jesse Head, of Kentucky, who married Thomas Lincoln and Nancy Hanks.

Mr. and Mrs. Newkirk have three children, Alice,

born February 12, 1918; Lillian, born March 7, 1925; Mason, born December 15, 1928. Alice is in the 10th grade at Hastings Senior High School at the age of 13. She is the youngest in her class, excelling in history and English. Lillian is talented in art and dancing. The family attends the First Presbyterian Church of Hastings. Mr. Newkirk is a Republican.

Most of Mr. Newkirk's time is devoted to improvement of his dairy, which is located at 20th and Elm Avenue in Hastings. He has a herd of eighty grade and purebred Guernsey cattle, the original stock having come from Wisconsin. The Newkirks possess the largest and best improved dairy farm in their part of Nebraska, and are justly proud of it. Mr. Newkirk is secretary and treasurer of the Clay-Adams County Dairy Herd Improvement Association at the present time. Residence: Hastings. (Photograph on Page 879).

John Hamilton Newlin

John Hamilton Newlin, retired newspaper editor, was born in Ripley, Ohio, May 22, 1853, son of Nathaniel and Melissa Gates (Hamilton) Newlin.

Nathaniel Newlin was born in Brown County, Ohio, March 4, 1820, the son of John Newlin. He was a farmer, who died at Jamacia, Iowa, July 31, 1898. His wife, Melissa, was born at Cincinnati, Ohio, September 30, 1823, and died at Bayard, Iowa, May 16, 1896. She was of Irish descent.

Mr. Newlin attended common country school, and for 26 years was a teacher. He was editor of the *Harrison Sun* for 18 years, and is now retired. Since Christmas, 1931, he has been blind. He is a member of the Methodist Episcopal Church, the Odd Fellows, and the Rebekah Lodge. He is also a life member of the Nebraskana Society.

He was married to Ella Miriam Conner at Harrison, Nebraska, on May 29, 1890, and to them were born three children, two of whom are living: Jessie Eva, September 10, 1893, married Milo E. Wolff; Bessie M., born May 1, 1895, married Glenn H. Kreman; and Nellie B., born May 6, 1901, who died September 26, 1903. Residence: Harrison.

William Shadrach Newmyer

For the past 56 years William S. Newmyer has lived in Nebraska where he has been engaged in banking. He was born at Mount Pleasant, Pennsylvania, July 8, 1861, the son of George Washington and Elizabeth (Parker) Newmyer. His father was born at Pennsville, Pennsylvania, November 4, 1822, and died at Central City, Nebraska, August, 1891. He was a merchant and farmer who served as captain of Company B, 28th Pennsylvania Volunteers, in the Civil War. His maternal ancestors were Germans who came to America in 1727; his father was born in this country, December 15, 1798.

His mother was born in England, and died at Colfax, Whitman County, Washington, May 4, 1903. Her father was English; her mother was Welsh.

Mr. Newmyer was graduated from high school at Central City. He is now president of the Farmers Bank at Lyons. He has held many local offices in his community and served in the legislature two terms, 1925 and 1927. During the World War he was active in loan drives. He is a Republican, a Mason, and is affiliated with the First Presbyterian Church of Lyons.

His marriage to Clara Ethel Everett was solemnized at Lyons, September 2, 1890. Mrs Newmyer was born on a farm in Burt County, November 6, 1870. Her ancestry is Scotch-Irish. They have three children: Clara Ann, born February 13, 1891, who married Emil J. Christensen; Clay Everett, born August 21, 1893, who married Clara B. Canfield; and Helen Marie, born June 14, 1898, who married Loran L. Shumway. Clay owns a lumber yard

Nebraska Photo Company—Hastings

EVERETT J. NEWKIRK

in Lyons. Helen has spent some time on Chautauqua circuit as a musician. Clara was graduated from the University of Nebraska 1915, with Phi Beta Kappa honors. Residence: Lyons.

Howard Chamberlain Newton

Howard C. Newton, educator at Omaha, was born at Southboro, Massachusetts, September 16, 1892. His father, Albro Warren Newton, who was a manufacturer, was born at Southboro, and died there in 1911. His mother, Cora Isabel (Howard) Newton, was born at Winthrop, Massachusetts, and for many years was a teacher in the public schools.

Dean Newton attended the public schools of Massachusetts and later was graduated from the high school at Peters, Massachusetts. He holds the following degrees: B. S., Creighton University; Ph. G., Massachusetts College of Pharmacy. He was a student at Harvard during summer session, and later attended Omaha University. He holds membership in Phi Delta Chi. He is now dean of the College of Pharmacy at Creighton University.

On June 16, 1916, his marriage to Myrtle Adelaide Wallace was solemnized at Marlboro, Massachusetts. Mrs. Newton was born at Marlboro, July 7, 1893. They have two children: Myrtle Isabel, born March 13, 1918; and Lois Edith, born June 16, 1919.

Dean Newton is a member of the American Pharmaceutical Association and the Nebraska Academy of Science. He is president of the Lothrop Parent-Teachers' Association of Omaha, is a member of Carter Lake Club, and is a Republican. He has lived in Nebraska for the past 16 years. His sports are tennis and golf. Residence: Omaha.

William Erastus Nichol

Born in Warren County, Illinois, November 15, 1857, William Erastus Nichol is the son of John and Jane (Robb) Nichol. His father, who was a farmer, was born in Belmont County, Ohio, March 1, 1820, and died in Warren County, August 7, 1888. His mother, whose ancestry is Scotch, was born in Belmont County, Ohio, December 17, 1819, and died in Warren County, Illinois, February 3, 1908.

Mr. Nichol was graduated from Monmouth Academy in Monmouth, Illinois, in 1877, and in 1882 received a degree in science at Monmouth College. Coming to Nebraska in the spring of 1884, he engaged in the undertaking, hardware, and furniture business in 1886, but since 1910 has been handling the undertaking business exclusively. In the summer of 1931 the Nichol Hotel and Funeral Home was erected by the Nichol Brothers and has since been operated by them. A resident of this state for the past 48 years, he is affiliated with the Minden United Presbyterian Church and the Young Men's Christian Association.

He was united in marriage with Ida May Ure in Linn County, Iowa, November 11, 1886. Mrs. Nichol, who is also a graduate of Monmouth College, was born in Linn County, December 14, 1862. Their children are, William Ure, born November 12, 1887; and David Robb, born May 17, 1892. Both are licensed embalmers and are in business in Minden, having been graduated from Monmouth College. Residence: Minden.

Jay Edward Nichols

Born at Waterloo, Nebraska, April 26, 1890, Jay Edward Nichols is the son of Clate Bradford and Millie R. (Wilde) Nichols. His father was born at Prophetstown, Illinois, January 25, 1856, and came to Nebraska where he has resided many years. He is now retired. Millie, his wife, was born in Sterling, Iowa, April 29, 1863, of Irish descent.

Jay Edward Nichols attended grade and high school

in Valley, Nebraska, and since 1910 has been associated continuously with the Valley State Bank. He started as bookkeeper, and has been advanced over a period of twenty years to vice president.

On December 19, 1919, he was married to Orpha Ellen Gaines, at Omaha. Mrs. Nichols was born in Blair, Nebraska, January 28, 1891. They have one daughter, Betty Jane, born August 20, 1921.

Mr. Nichols is a Democrat. He entered military service in the U. S. Army in January, 1918, with the rank of private, and was promoted to quartermaster sergeant, finance department, and served overseas sixteen months with the American Expeditionary Forces with Headquarters, First Army.

He is a member of the American Legion, the Valley Chamber of Commerce, and the Board of Education of which he has been treasurer since 1927. He is a York Rite Mason and member of the Shrine, and attends the Methodist Church. Residence: Valley.

Elbert Jerome Nickerson

Elbert Jerome Nickerson, who has been a clergyman in Nebraska for the past 14 years, was born at Inman, Nebraska, August 12, 1885, the son of John Edward and Amanda Jane Nickerson. His father, who was a physician and surgeon, was born in Iowa, and died at Eddemont, South Dakota; his family had lived in America for many generations. His mother, whose ancestry is Irish, was born near Malvern, Iowa.

Mr. Nickerson was graduated from the high school at Malvern, in 1903. He received the A. B. degree at Coe College, 1908, and received a certificate of graduation from the Omaha Theological Seminary and Princeton Theological Seminary. He attended the University of Nebraska during one summer term. In 1913 he delivered the valedictory sermon at the University of Omaha; he was awarded letters in track and football at Coe College and was the holder of the two mile record in track.

Mr. Nickerson has held the following pastorates: First Presbyterian Church at St. Joseph, Missouri. 1913-15; First Presbyterian Church at Norfolk, Nebraska, 1916-18; and First Presbyterian Church at Wahoo, Nebraska, since 1919. He is a member of the Platte Valley Ministerial Association, and the Omaha Presbytery, is a member of the Lions Club, and holds membership in the Nebraskana Society.

During the World War he served overseas with the Young Men's Christian Association force. Politically, he is a Democrat, but is somewhat independent in his voting. Residence: Wahoo.

Elmer S. Nickerson

At Greenville, Pennsylvania, Elmer S. Nickerson was born September 11, 1866, the son of Joseph Arnold and Margaret Louise (McClimans) Nickerson. His father, a farmer and stock raiser, was born at Willits, New York, July 22, 1828, and died at Greenville, March 9, 1907. He was descended from William Nickerson, the first settler of Chatham, Massachusetts, and of Samuel Gorton, provincial governor of Rhode Island.

His mother was born at Salem Township, Pennsylvania, July 17, 1840, and died at Greenville, September 22, 1882. She was the daughter of Samuel McClimans of Scotch ancestry, and a grand daughter of Hugh McCiymonds, an early settler in Butler County, Pennsylvania.

Mr. Nickerson attended the common school of Pennsylvania, the Fredonia Institute, later attended the Edinboro State Normal School of Pennsylvania, and Allegheny College, where he was graduated in 1892 with a B. A. degree; M. A. degree, 1895; Ph. D., 1900. He was valedictorian of his class at Allegheny College in 1892. He has been instructor of Greek and Latin at Indiana State College of Pennsylvania; and superintendent of schools at Papillion, Gretna, and Fullerton, Nebraska. A Republican, Mr. Nickerson served Sarpy County as county attorney, 1915-22. He has lived in Nebraska for 38 years.

At Papillion on July 14, 1896 he was united in marriage with Lulu P. Patterson. Mrs. Nickerson, who was born at Papillion, October 14, 1879, is a lineal descendant of William Findley, Revolutionary soldier. There are three children: Ralph Joseph, born May 14, 1897, who married Mae Baxter, and who is engaged in the practice of law; Edward Covel, born June 26, 1901, who married Margaret A. Oliver; and James Findley, born December 16, 1910, who is a student at Nebraska Wesleyan University.

He was a member of the advisory council of Sarpy County in the late war. He is a member of the Business Men's Club; the Nebraskana Society; the State Historical Society; the American Bar Association; the Nebraska State Bar Association. He was president of the Second Judicial District Bar Association in 1928 and 1929; and is a member of the Parent-Teachers' Association. He is a Mason and Modern Woodman of America. He is affiliated with the St. Paul's Methodist Episcopal Church of Papillion. Residence: Papillion.

Frederick Nielsen

Frederick Nielsen was born at Lexington, Nebraska, August 4, 1892, the son of Hans Peter and Karen Johanna (Frandsen) Nielsen. His father, who was born at Hjorring, Denmark, October 9, 1865, is a lifelong Republican, was councilman, mayor and postmaster at Lexington, and was active in the Council of Defense and Red Cross during the World War; he came to America in 1881, worked as a grocery clerk in Chicago and later homesteaded in Custer County, Nebraska.

His mother, who was born at Varde, Denmark, May 14, 1875, is interested in horticulture. She came to America in 1889 with her parents who were fishermen on the sandy west coast of Denmark; her mother, Anne Frandsen, is still living at Minden, Nebraska, at the age of 92. They are both members of the Danish Lutheran Church and have always lived in Nebraska since arriving in America.

Mr. Nielsen was graduated from the Lexington High School in 1910, was a student at Lexington Business College for a year, studied in the Central Young Men's Christian Association Night School of Accountancy, and also took a course from the American Extension University of Law. He served as a railway clerk for the Chicago, Burlington & Quincy Railroad in 1911, was postoffice clerk at Lexington, 1911-12, was railway mail clerk from 1912-13 at Omaha, and was departmental clerk for the Post Office Department in the office of the First Assistant Postmaster General at Washington, D. C. From September, 1916, to August, 1917, he was engaged in the feed and seed business at Lexington, and from 1919 to 1921 was secretary and treasurer of the Mid-West Grain Company at Omaha. Since 1923 he has been postmaster at Lexington. A Republican, he served as city clerk of Lexington during 1922, and is active in Republican committee work there now.

He is a member of the Red Cross, Legion Welfare committee, the Lexington Chamber of Commerce, Federal Building Committee, and The Nebraskana Society. He has been treasurer of the Lexington High School Alumni Association for the past six years, and holds membership in the Methodist Episcopal Church, the Ancient Free and Accepted Masons, and the Lexington Country Club. Mr. Nielsen's favorite amusements are golf and bridge; he is a football enthusiast.

During the World War he was commissioned as first lieutenant at the Second Officers Training Camp at Fort Snelling, Minnesota; was later assigned to Company I, 41st Infantry, at Fort Crook, Nebraska, and thereafter was transferred to Camp Funston, Kansas, where the new 10th Division was formed under General Leonard A. Wood. After seventeen months domestic service he was mustered out of the army in 1919, and since held a number of offices in the Reserve Corp. He is now serving under the active commission as first lieutenant, 119th Wagon Company, 35th Division Train, Nebraska National Guard. For the past five years he has been Finance Officer of the local American Legion Post at Lexington, and in 1931 was chairman of the national defense committee of the Nebraska department.

On August 14, 1918, he was married to Zella Evelyn Wicklund at Gothenburg. Mrs. Nielsen was born at Gothenburg, Nebraska, January 13, 1896. They have two children: Frederick, born February 12, 1920; and Warren W., born May 20, 1923. Residence: Lexington. (Photograph in Album).

Frederick Peter Nielsen

Frederick Peter Nielsen, leading banker at Oxford, Nebraska, was born there December 29, 1890. His father, Peter Nielsen, a hardware merchant, was born in Germany, March 25, 1861, and died at Los Angeles, California, January 25, 1928. His mother, whose ancestry is German, was born at Quincy, Illinois, September 26, 1865, and now resides at Oxford with her son, C. C. Nielsen.

Mr. Nielsen was graduated from the Oxford High School and studied for six months at the Lincoln Business College. He started working in a bank as bookkeeper in 1909 and has been engaged in the banking business since then. He is now vice president of the Security State Bank of Oxford, is treasurer of the Oxford Lions Club, and is treasurer of the local Red Cross. He is affiliated with the Presbyterian Church of Oxford, is a member of The Nebraskana Society, and is a Mason.

During the World War Mr. Nielsen served as sergeant in the 601 Aero Supply Squadron, and at this time is a member of the American Legion. His sports are hunting and fishing. On August 12, 1925, he was married at Omaha, Nebraska, to Opal Dettman. Mrs. Nielsen, whose ancestry is German, was born at Wabash, Nebraska, January 6, 1900, and prior to her marriage was a public school teacher. Residence: Oxford.

Johannes Whittier Nielsen

Johannes Whittier Nielsen, educator, was born at Farwell, Nebraska, December 17, 1898, son of Niels Christian and Wilhelmina (Sorensen) Nielsen. His father was born at Dannebrog, Nebraska, April 28, 1874, of Danish parents who were among the first homesteaders on Turkey Creek in Howard County. He was born and raised in a sod house. His wife, Wilhelmina, was born in Racine, Wisconsin, February 4, 1875. Her parents emigrated at an early date from Denmark to Wisconsin, where they established their first home in this country. Later they moved to Nebraska, homesteading in the Danish settlement near Dannebrog. Mrs. Nielsen was raised in a sod house.

Mr. Nielsen attended grade and high school at Boelus, Nebraska, and was graduated from high school in 1918. He attended Kearney State Teachers College one year, and received the degree of Bachelor of Science in Agriculture from the University of Nebraska in 1922. He received his Masters degree from Iowa State College in 1923.

He is a member of Gamma Sigma Delta, honorary scholastic society in agriculture, Alpha Zeta, honorary agricultural fraternity, the Nebraska N Club, and Alpha Kappa Delta, now Phi Kappa Tau at Iowa State College. He received a college track letter for a cross country run, and in high school was active as a member of the basketball team.

Mr. Nielsen taught one year in a country school in

Howard County, and from 1923 until 1927 was instructor in agronomy and botany in Nebraska School of Agriculture at Curtis. Since 1927 he has been instructor of vocational agriculture at Sidney High School. He received his state teachers certificate for Nebraska in 1922.

His marriage to Edith Virginia Burr was solemnized at St. Louis, Missouri, December 25, 1923. She was born at Lynchburg, Virginia, December 6, 1902. She is state thrift chairman officer in the Parent Teachers Association, and a direct descendant of the Burr family of colonial history. They have two children, Helane Jo, born December 5, 1924; and Niels Cecil, born May 17, 1926.

Mr. Nielsen was a private in the infantry in the World War and is now a member of the American Legion. He is a member of the Nebraska Vocational Association, the Nebraska State Teachers Association, the Lions Club (chairman of program committee 1931-32), the Masons and the Parent Teachers Association. He is affiliated with the Lemon Memorial Methodist Episcopal Church. His favorite sport is hunting, while his hobby is taxidermy. Residence: Sidney. (Photograph in Album).

John Peter Nielsen

John Peter Nielsen, president of Trinity Theological Seminary, was born in Denmark, Europe, December 18, 1877, son of Peter and Caroline (Petersen) Nielsen. The father was born in Denmark, February 17, 1849, and died at Weston, Iowa, October 21, 1911. He was a farmer. His wife was born in Denmark, March 14, 1852, and died April 11, 1926.

In May 1901, Mr. Nielsen was graduated from Dana College, and later received his Bachelor of Arts degree from Webster University in Atlanta, Georgia. In 1923 he received the Bachelor of Divinity and the Master of Sacred Theology degrees from Lutheran Theological Seminary at Maywood, Illinois. Later he took post graduate work in theology at the Biblical Seminary in New York City.

On April 7, 1905, he was married to Anna Nielsen, at Philadelphia. She was born in Denmark, March 20, 1872, and died at Blair, September 30, 1928. She was a public and high school teacher. His second marriage was to Gertrude Jensen, who was born at Alden, Minnesota, January 15, 1893. Her father was a clergyman. She received her education at Dana College and Iowa State Teachers College, and was a public school teacher before her marriage.

Mr. Nielsen is a Republican. He is a member of the First English Lutheran Church at Blair, and second vice-president of the American Lutheran Conference. He is serving at the present time as American committeeman of the Dan-America Archives Society. Residence: Blair.

Isaac Johnson Nisley

Isaac Johnson Nisley, judge of the 13th judicial district, was born in Dawson County, Nebraska, December 11, 1882, son of John Fred and Sarah (Johnson) Nisley. The father, who was born at Pittsburgh, Pennsylvania, is now retired and resides at Livingston, Nebraska. His ancestry is German. His wife, Sarah, was born in Clearfield, Pennsylvania, of English and German descent.

Upon his graduation from Lexington High School in 1905, Judge Nisley entered the University of Nebraska from which he received the degree of Bachelor of Laws.

On May 10, 1918, he was married to Edna Anderson at Lexington. They have two children, Robert James, born December 22, 1920; and Jane Johnson, born February 15, 1927.

During the late war Judge Nisley was chairman of the draft board and food administrator of Dawson County. He is a member of the Methodist Church, the Nebraska State Bar Association, the Red Cross, the Kiwanis Club and the Masons. He is a Republican. Residence: North Platte.

William J. Nissen

Born at Oxford, Nebraska, April 6, 1895, William J. Nissen is the son of Jacob Henry and Clara Rose (Alloway) Nissen. His father, who has been engaged in the general merchandise business at Oxford, for the past 45 years, was born in Germany, June 20, 1856, and came to this country in 1887. His mother, whose parents homesteaded in Furnas County, Nebraska when she was a small girl, was born at Newton, Iowa, August 13, 1870.

Mr. Nissen was graduated from the high school at Oxford in 1913. He entered the general merchandise business there with his father and brother in 1913 and has been connected with the firm since then. He is a member of the city board of trustees, serving as chairman for eight years, and is the author of various short articles on the *Conservation of the Great Outdoors*.

He served as secretary of the Oxford Chamber of Commerce from 1922 until 1926, has been vice president of the Fifth Congressional District of the Izaak Walton League for the past three years, having organized and served as president of the Oxford Chapter of that organization. Mr. Nissen is a member of Rewalt Lodge, Knight Templars, and Shrine of the Ancient Free and Accepted Masons, and holds membership in the Nebraskana Society.

He organized the Oxford Gun Club, serving as secretary for 10 years; is a member of the Oxford Country Club, and is interested in the conservation of game. His hobby is growing conifer trees. During the World War Mr. Nissen served as a non-commissioned officer with Company A, 24th Machine Gun Battalion, 8th Regular Army Division, was Commander of the local American Legion for four years, service officer of the local post for four years, and is County Commander at this time.

On June 12, 1928, he married Bernice Rhynalds at Kearney, Nebraska. Mrs. Nissen, who was a teacher prior to her marriage, was born at Oxford, March 7, 1905. To this marriage one child was born: Nancy Lee, May 30, 1930. Residence: Oxford.

Leslie Hugh Noble, Sr.

One of Gage County's younger lawyers, Leslie Hugh Noble, Sr., was born in Homesville, Nebraska, October 29, 1901. His father, Lucian Leeds Noble, was born in Lincoln, Illinois, August 14, 1872. He is a doctor of medicine, a justice of peace, director of the school board and deputized sheriff to enforce health laws. His parents were of Irish-Welsh ancestry, born in Kentucky, who migrated to Illinois, about the same time that the Lincolns moved there.

Minnie Sarah Will, who became the wife of Lucian Leeds Noble, was born in Woodford, Illinois, July 24, 1879. Her parents were born in Virginia, and migrated to Illinois. An uncle of Mrs. Lucian Noble was in one of General Robert E. Lee's regiments of sharpshooters.

Leslie Hugh Noble, Sr., was educated in the Homesville High School until June of 1917. He continued high school and was graduated in June, 1919. He went to the Nebraska University and in June, 1924, received the degree of Bachelor of Arts. The following June he received his degree in Bachelor of Laws. While in the university he was honored with the vice presidency of his freshman class in 1922. He belonged to Delta Chi of which he was secretary in 1921, and president in 1925.

Mr. Noble married Helen Minnie Rhoads on March 31, 1926, at Lincoln. She was born in Emerson, Iowa, April 19, 1903, the granddaughter of Daniel Rhoads, a Civil War veteran, and great granddaughter of Lewis W. Tubbs, one of the founders of the town of Emerson, Iowa.

They have one child, Leslie Hugh, Jr., born November 24, 1930.

Leslie Hugh Noble has lived in the state since birth, and commenced practicing law in Beatrice, on October 1, 1925, and continued until he was elected county judge of Gage County, Nebraska for the term 1929-33.

While in college, Mr. Noble had two years' training in the Reserve Officers' Training Corps and was corporal the second year. He was chairman of the Gage County membership drive for the Red Cross in 1929. His affiliation is with the Centenary Methodist Episcopal Church.

Mr. Noble is vice president of the Gage County Bar Association, member of the board of directors of the Beatrice Junior division of the United States Chamber of Commerce, and is a member of the Young Men's Christian Association. He belongs to the Elks Club, the Eagles, the Odd Fellows Lodge and is a past master of the Beatrice Masonic Lodge. He is a member of the Nebraskana Society, and is interested in golf, baseball and tennis. Residence: Beatrice.

Robert Ernst Noll

Robert Ernst Noll, a seed merchant at Ord, Nebraska, was born in that community, March 7, 1891, the son of Clayton Willard and Carrie Louise (Marks) Noll. His father, a farmer, was born of Dutch parents in Lancaster County, Pennsylvania, May 8, 1857, and is living today. His mother was born at Westphalia, Germany, October 24, 1862.

Mr. Noll was graduated from the Ord High School in 1910, and for three years was employed in a store at Ord. He engaged in farming from 1913 to 1928 and since 1928 has owned and managed the Noll Seed Company at Ord. He is affiliated with the First Methodist Church and holds membership in the Nebraskana Society and the Republican party.

He was married at Ord, October 5, 1913, to Ava Ruth Clark who was born at Ord, September 27, 1892. Mr. Noll's hobbies are philately and flower gardening. Residence: Ord.

Ernest Frederick Nomer

One of Elsie's most outstanding residents, Ernest Frederick Nomer was born at Lawrence, Nebraska, May 2, 1886, son of Adin Cyrus and Sarah Ann (Davisson) Nomer.

The father was born at Norwich, Connecticut, October 25, 1855, and died at Grants Pass, Oregon, August 13, 1921. He was a farmer. His wife was born in Indiana, October 11, 1856.

Mr. Nomer attended public school at Lawrence, Nebraska, and was graduated from high school in 1910. He has served as county commissioner for the past ten years, as village clerk for 17 years, and as a member of the school board for eight years. He is a Democrat, and is engaged in the real estate and insurance business.

His marriage to Bessie Anna Kirk occurred at Madrid, Nebraska, April 2, 1913. They have three children, Florence, born July 3, 1914; Ruby, born April 12, 1917; and Louise, born June 25, 1919. Twin boys were also born to them, both of whom were deceased in infancy. Mrs. Nomer was born at Duggar, Indiana, May 23, 1893, the daughter of Paris J. and Carrie Belle (Farnham) Kirk.

Mr. Nomer is a member of the Odd Fellows, Elsie Lodge No. 206. His favorite sports are fishing and hunting, while his hobby is croquet. Residence: Elsie.

Arthur Francis Nordberg

A lifelong resident of Nebraska, Arthur Francis Nordberg has been engaged in farming at Stromsburg for over 30 years. He was born at Stromsburg, November 5, 1878, the son of Peter and Kate (Erickson) Nordberg. His father, who was a pioneer homesteader and farmer in Nebraska in 1871, was born in Sweden, December 26, 1841, and died at Stromsburg, January 30, 1917. His mother was born in Sweden, April 23, 1843, and died at Stromsburg, March 23, 1927.

Mr. Nordberg attended the Stromsburg grade school and attended high school two years. He was a student at Bryant Normal and Business College at Stromsburg, 1897-98. He is a director in the Farmers Grain Association of which he has been president for four years, and holds membership in the Nebraskana Society.

On September 25, 1902, he married Selma Naomi Rydberg at Stromsburg. Mrs. Nordberg, who is a descendant of the noted Swedish poet Victor Rydberg, was born at Jonkping, Sweden, June 30, 1882. They have three children: Donald E., born April 2, 1903, who married Olline Waye; Francis A., born March 10, 1905, who married Fern Williams; and Ralph E., born June 10, 1907. Residence: Stromsburg.

Elmer Conrad Nordlund

Elmer C. Nordlund, who has been a banker at Stromsburg, Polk County, Nebraska, since 1907, was born there June 10, 1888, the son of Peter Olof and Hannah Erika (Headman) Nordlund. His father who was a contractor and builder, was born at Amot, Okelbo, Sweden, and came to America in 1882. His mother, an active church worker, was born at Amot, February 13, 1862.

Mr. Nordlund attended the public schools of Stromsburg, was graduated from Luther College in 1905, and completed a business administration course from the same college in 1907. He was active in debating and college baseball. Upon his graduation from college he was elected assistant cashier of the Stromsburg Bank. Since 1913 he has been a stockholder and cashier in that organization.

He has taken a keen interest in politics but has never had personal political aspirations. He was mayor of Stromsburg 1915-16 and served several terms as president of the Commercial Club. During the World War he served as a member of the county committee having charge of all Liberty loan drives, and was president of the county War Chest fund from 1917 until its disbandment in 1918. He is affiliated with the Salem Lutheran Church of Stromsburg, and holds membership in various civic organizations at Stromsburg.

Mr. Nordlund is a member of: the Red Cross, of which he was president for two years, treasurer for 12 years, and secretary for three years; the Stromsburg Community Club, of which he was secretary for three years, president for two years, and executive board member for five years; Modern Woodmen of America; Ancient Free and Accepted Masons; and Rob Morris chapter of the Eastern Star. He served as a member of the Republican state central committee in 1928. He is a member of the Scottish Rite Masons at Lincoln and has served as master of Stromsburg Lodge No. 126, Ancient Free and Accepted Masons. He holds membership in the Public Library Board, Parent Teachers' Association, and the Young Men's Christian Association. Since 1920 he has served on the local board of education.

His marriage to Edith Olive Peterson occurred at Stromsburg, June 4, 1913. Mrs. Nordlund, who was born in Polk County, May 30, 1888, takes an active part in church work and is an officer in the Eastern Star. Her parents came to this country from Sweden. There are three children: Vivian Bernice, born May 19, 1916; Edith Maurine, born April 10, 1919; and Donald Elmer, born March 1, 1922. Vivian, who is a student in the Stromsburg High School, was selected by popular vote of the students as the representative girl of her school.

Mr. Nordlund's chief interests are: fishing, coin collecting, and reading. Residence: Stromsburg. (Photograph in Album).

Charles John Noreen

Born in Sweden, November 8, 1868, Charles John Noreen is the son of Charles and Anna (Malm) Noreen. His father was born in Sweden, in 1839; his mother in 1847, and they came to this country in 1869.

Charles Noreen attended the public schools during the winter until he was seventeen years of age. On March 16, 1892, he was united in marriage with Emma Nygren, at Malmo. She was born at Sweden, October 28, 1868; came to America, in 1870, and her death occurred December 27, 1918, at Newman Grove, Nebraska. To this union six children were born: Elmer F., December 27, 1892; Hildur E., April 19, 1894; Femie E., May 18, 1896; Pauline A., August 6, 1903; Paul A., August 6, 1903; and Arnold G., October 22, 1908. Elmer is married to Maude Haris; Hildur, who died December 25, 1918, was married to Louis Johnson; Femie is married to Magne B. Goranson and Paul is married to Alta Hammer.

In 1919, he was elected representative in the Nebraska legislature, on the Republican ticket. At present he is justice of the peace at Malmo, Nebraska.

He was chairman of the Council of Defense of Walker township in Platte County, and was active in all liberty loan drives during the war, and is a member of the Red Cross. For five years he was president of the Platte County Farmers Union. He is president of a co-operative store at Newman Grove. For three years he was president of the Farmers Bureau in Platte county, during the World War. Mr. Noreen is affiliated with the Evangelical Lutheran Edensburg Church at Malmo, and for the past six years was a member of the Luther College Board at Wahoo. He is a member of the Nebraskana Society, also. On September 8, 1920, he was united in marriage to Lottie B. Rosengren, whose maiden name was Carlson. Residence: Malmo.

James C. Norgaard

Born at Randers, Jylland, Denmark, October 16, 1893, James C. Norgaard is the son of Christian Gotfred and Maren (Nielsen) Norgaard. His father, who was a miller, was born at Randers, March 6, 1861, and still lives in Denmark. His mother, also born in Randers on September 3, 1863, died at Bronderslev, Denmark, January 21, 1927.

James C. Norgaard was graduated from public school on April 1, 1908, and from Technical High School in 1910. From November 1915 until March 1916 he was a student at the University of Wisconsin, and from November 1917 to March 1918 was an instructor there.

On May 10, 1916, his marriage to Violet A. M. Rasmussen was solemnized at Harbor Beach, Michigan. Mrs. Norgaard, who was born at Green Bay, Wisconsin, April 28, 1893, is of Danish descent. There are two sons, Ormond, born June 26, 1918; and Harold, born August 7, 1920.

A newsboy, buttermaker, and engineer in the Danish Navy, Mr. Norgaard was a buttermaker also in Wisconsin and Michigan. Following the period spent at the University of Wisconsin, he was butter inspector for the United States Navy, and manager of the Farmers Union Creamery Company of Superior.

At the present time Mr. Norgaard is general manager of the Farmers Union Co-operative Creameries at Superior, Aurora, Norfolk and Fremont, and is a director of the Citizens Building and Loan Company of Superior, and the Farmers Union Life Insurance Company of Des-Moines.

His religious affiliation is with the Danish Lutheran Church. His sport is baseball and his hobby is reading. He is a member of the Red Cross, the Farmers Union of Nebraska, and the Nebraskana Society. Independent in politics, he has served on the local school board. Residence: Superior.

Charles August Norlin

Charles A. Norlin has been a resident of Nebraska for the past 50 years and has been a clergyman in the Methodist Episcopal church in this state for over 30 years. He was born at Andover, Henry County, Illinois, February 24, 1870, the son of Olof and Kathryn (Jones) Norlin. His father, who was a carpenter and farmer and who served in the Civil War, was born in Sweden, January 4, 1832, and came to this country in 1850. He died at Minden, Nebraska, September 23, 1909.

His mother was born in Sweden in 1834, and died at Minden, June, 1913. Rev. Norlin attended Minden High School and later was a student at Orleans College for three years, 1894-97. He is now pastor of the Methodist Episcopal Church in Surprise. He was at one time state secretary and national committee man of the Prohibition Party. He is a Republican, a Mason and an Odd Fellow.

His marriage to Lydia Otilia Curtis was solemnized at Minden, November 24, 1897. Mrs. Norlin, who has always been active in community affairs as a minister's wife, was born at Galesburg, Knox County, Illinois, January 24, 1868. They have seven children: Carl Curtis, born August 2, 1899; August Claire, born August 2, 1899; Lillie Caroline, born April 12, 1901; Frank Merrill, born May 26, 1902, who married Viola Mae Tellier; Milford Elmer, born April 21, 1904; Ivan Wesley, born August 14, 1905; and Lorene Kathryn, born December 20, 1908. Residence: Lincoln. (Photograph in Album).

Day C. Norman

Day C. Norman, light and water superintendent at Chester for the past eight years, was born at Rensslaer, Indiana, December 20, 1885. His parents are John W. and Louise (Day) Norman, the former born at New Cumberstown, Ohio, March 6, 1856. Of American stock, his ancestors were early settlers in Pennsylvania. He is a retired carpenter, still residing in Rensslaer. Louisa Day was born in Rensslaer, Indiana, April 19, 1862, and died there on February 21, 1901. She was of Scotch-Irish extraction.

A resident of Nebraska since December 1, 1911, Mr. Norman was a farmer for six years, a merchant for six, and for eight years has been light and water superintendent and chief of police. He was married to Elizabeth Martha Duey at Cleveland, Kansas, December 6, 1910, and to them were born three children: J. D., born December 21, 1911; Martha E., born February 4, 1913; and Zora Mae, born June 19, 1915. J. D. was graduated from Chester High School in 1930, and is an electrician. Zora May is a senior in high school. Mrs. Norman was born at Carlisle Springs, Pennsylvania, October 18, 1889, of Pennsylvania Dutch ancestry.

Mr. Norman is a Democrat, active in local politics. He attends the First Church of Christ of Chester, and is a member of the Masons, Odd Fellows, Modern Woodmen of America and the Ancient Order of United Workmen. During the year 1921-22 he was chairman of the village board, and during the World War was a member of the Home Guard. His hobby is reading. Residence: Chester. (Photograph in Album).

Dan Clifford Norris

A distinguished legislator and business executive of Brewster, Nebraska, is Dan Clifford Norris, who was born at Dansbury, New Hampshire, May 10, 1864, and has lived in this state for the past 48 years. His father, Ichabod Johnson Norris, who was a farmer, was born of Scotch and Irish parents at Danbury, November 27, 1827, and died at Merrimack, Wisconsin, December 29, 1919. His mother, Harriett A. (Leeds) Norris, who was a teacher in her younger days, was born at Danbury, June 15, 1840, and died at Merrimack, March 19, 1915. She was descended from the English family, Leeds.

Mr. Norris was graduated from the high school at Baraboo, Wisconsin in 1884. He taught school in Nebraska for 12 years, was station agent at Abie, Nebraska, in the employ of the Chicago & Northwestern Company for six years, and served as agent at Dunning, Nebraska, for six years. A Republican, he was county clerk of Blaine County from 1908 to 1927, and since 1927 has been state representative from the 91st district. He is affiliated with the Congregational Church, the Masonic Lodge, and the Nebraskana Society. During the World War he served as a member of the selective board.

His marriage to Verna Mary Treaster was solemnized at Schuyler, Nebraska, October 11, 1890. Mrs. Norris, whose ancestry was German, was born at Exeter, Nebraska, June 21, 1872, and died at Brewster, December 12, 1912. Five children were born to this marriage; Ethel, March 12, 1891, who died December 9, 1915; Mabel, May 27, 1896, who married Ross N. Wilkinson; Bernice, March 13, 1899, who married Herbert Moore; Harold, May 18, 1902, who married Virginia Lyons; and Dan C., Jr., March 13, 1911.

Mr. Norris' marriage to Olive S. Ball was solemnized at Brewster, May 7, 1914. Mrs. Norris was born at McCook, Nebraska, May 25, 1883. She is the daughter of Peter and Elizabeth (Rowe) Muntz. Her father was a pioneer settler of Red Willow County, Nebraska. She is a member of the Congregational Church at Brewster. She has one daughter by a former marriage, Wilma L., born May 20, 1901, who married Harold W. Cochran of Bartley, Nebraska. They now reside at York, Nebraska. Residence: Brewster. (Photograph in Album).

George William Norris

George W. Norris, lawyer and United States senator from Nebraska, was born in Sandusky County, Ohio, July 11, 1861. He is the son of Chauncey and Mary (Mook) Norris, both of whom are deceased. Mr. Norris was first married to Pluma Lashley of Mount Pleasant, Iowa, who died at McCook in 1901. There are three children of this marriage: Gertrude, born March 21, 1900, married to George Brandon Rath; Marian, born February 11, 1897, married to Harvey Frans Nelson, and Hazel, born January 10, 1895, married to John Porteus Robertson. His second marriage was to Ellie Leonard, 1903.

In his youth Senator Norris worked on a farm summers and went to country schools in winter, thus obtaining his elementary education. He attended Baldwin University and Northern Indiana Normal School. Later, while teaching, he studied law, afterward attending Valparaiso University, and was admitted to the bar.

A Republican, he was prosecuting attorney three terms. Later he was judge of the fourteenth Nebraska district, 1895-1902. In 1903 he was elected to United States Congress as representative from the fifth Nebraska district, and served during the 58th, 59th, 60th and 62nd congresses. Elected to the United States Senate in 1913, his third term expired in 1931; he was re-elected.

Senator Norris is a Mason, Odd Fellow and Modern Woodman of America. He resides at McCook. His hobby is reading. Residence: McCook. (Photograph on Page 886).

Viola Hinds Norris

On January 18, 1890, Viola Hinds Norris was born at Harrisburg, Banner County, Nebraska, the daughter of H. P. and Susie E. (Phillips) Hinds. Her father, who was born at Shabbona's Grove, Illinois, September 29, 1851, was a pioneer in western Nebraska in the early 70's. A teacher for twelve years and a county judge for four, he is descended from Scotch ancestors who came to America 14 years after the landing of the Mayflower, the Andre Revolutionary stock.

Susie Hinds, mother of Mrs. Norris, was born near Alton, Illinois, October 2, 1858. Her maternal grandfather was killed in the battle of Shilo during the Civil War.

Mrs. Norris was educated in the Wabash (Nebraska) grade schools after which she attended the Weeping Water High School. In 1907 and 1908 she was a student at the Nebraska Wesleyan University.

She is a Republican and has served on election boards at various times. She is manager of the poultry division of the Norris White Rock Farm, which is one of the outstanding exhibition flocks in the state; she has written many articles on 4-H club work, the care of poultry, published in farm magazines; and has been active in 4-H club work for many years. She has trained several 4-H club demonstration teams that have won championships at state fairs. In 1927 her team was chosen to represent Nebraska internationally at the Poultry Congress at Ottawa, Canada. Her son was a member of this team, which was declared the best at the meet.

She married Ray Ellsworth Norris at Wabash, Cass County, Nebraska, December 29, 1909. Mr. Norris, who is a farmer, was born at Avoca, Cass County, Nebraska, January 7, 1887. They have one son, Clarence, born November 24, 1910. He is a sophomore at the University of Nebraska where he is a member of Alpha Theta Chi Fraternity; was one of the four outstanding 4-H club members to represent Nebraska at the National Camp, at Washington, D. C., in 1929; and has taken an active part in the various university activities.

Mrs. Norris is a leader in clubs of all kinds; is a member of the Woman's Club, and now secretary and treasurer of the Cass County Federation of Women's Clubs, and the Project Extension Club; is a leader of boys' and girls' 4-H clubs, having taken charge of from one to three organizations of this kind every year for the last eight years. She is a member of the Red Cross, the Helping Hand Aid Society, holding offices in the latter, and the Avoca Parent-Teachers' Association, serving as treasurer in 1928 and 1929. She has taught in Sunday School and sung in the church choir for over twenty years; at one time was a member of the Y. W. C. A. She has served as one of the superintendents of the county fair, and is an officer of the Eastern Star and has taken active part in the Weeping Water Congregational Church. Swimming is her favorite sport; she has been swimming instructor for boys and girls at 4-H camps. Her hobby is helping boys and girls in 4-H club work. She is also guardian of a Campfire group. Residence: Weeping Water.

Bernard Alexander Norsworthy

Bernard Alexander Norsworthy, retail merchant, was born at Gothenburg, Nebraska, December 29, 1894. He is the son of John Henry and Anna Wilhelmina (Ihde) Norsworthy. The former a native of Ontario, Canada.

John Henry Norsworthy was born January 16, 1861, and has lived in Nebraska for a number of years. He is a retired farmer and stock buyer, at the present time, and is mayor of Gothenburg. His ancestry is English, Canadian and Scotch. His wife, Anna, was born in Plainfield, Iowa, January 1, 1868, of German and Danish descent.

Mr. Norsworthy completed his public school education at Gothenburg, in 1909, and was graduated from Gothenburg High School in 1913. While in school he was a member of the football, track and basketball teams, and during his term (1915-1916) at the University of Colorado, received a freshman numeral in football.

Since 1920, he has been the owner and manager of his own retail seed, feed and grain business at Gothenburg. He is interested also in a farm in Colorado and a ranch in Wyoming.

He is married to Mima Morris, their marriage having been solemnized at Carrol, Nebraska. Mrs. Norsworthy is a former school teacher of Welsh ancestry.

GEORGE WILLIAM NORRIS

They have four children, Bernard A., born November 13, 1926; Joan E., born August 8, 1929; Wynne E. and Milton J., twins, born November 21, 1931.

From 1915 until 1917, Mr. Norsworthy held the rank of second lieutenant in the Nebraska National Guard. He spent eight months of his service on federal duty on the Mexican border, near Brownsville, Texas. During the World War from July, 1917 until June, 1919, he served with the 134th Infantry as first lieutenant and captain. He is a member of the American Legion, the Officers Reserve Corps, the Military Order of Foreign Wars (Pennsylvania commandery). He is county chairman for Dawson County of the Citizens Military Training Camp for Nebraska.

At the present time, he is serving as president of the Gothenburg Chamber of Commerce, a member of the board of education, of which he is secretary at the present time. He is a Mason and a Shriner, and a member of the Modern Woodmen of America. He is affiliated with the Methodist Episcopal Church. Among his favorite sports are football, fishing and hiking while his hobbies are military work and reading. He is a member of Gothenburg Country Club. Residence: Gothenburg. (Photograph in Album).

Jacob Henry North

Since 1872 Jacob Henry North has been a resident of Nebraska, and for many years has been politically active in the state. He was born at Norwich, England, May 11, 1865, the son of Jacob and Hannah (Abel) North. His father, who was born at Norwich, March 17, 1838, was a printer and established the firm of Jacob North & Company. He died at Lincoln, September 11, 1899. His mother was born at Norwich, February 14, 1839, and died at Lincoln, October 4, 1908. Her mother was Irish and her father was English.

Mr. North received his education in the public schools of Norwich and Lincoln. He has been associated with the Jacob North Company since its organization in 1892 and since the death of his father he has been president of this firm. He is a director in the Dwelling House Insurance Company of Lincoln.

A Democrat, Mr. North served for four years as chairman of the Lancaster County Democratic committee; later he was defeated as Democratic candidate for the Nebraska house of representatives. He is a Democrat mainly on the principle of free trade. In 1928 he resigned as presidential elector in view of his opposition for Alfred E. Smith as candidate for president. He was an ardent admirer of William Jennings Bryan and the ideals of the Commoner.

He was married to Laura Belle Hill at Lincoln, September 30, 1903. Mrs. North, who was born at Lincoln, November 17, 1882, is descended on the maternal side from the Pennsylvania Sigfrieds of Revolutionary days. She is entitled to membership in the Daughters of the American Revolution. There are two children: Emma Ruth, born July 1, 1904, who was graduated from the University of Nebraska where she was a member of Alpha Phi Sorority; and Jacob Sigfried, born October 17, 1906, who was a member of Phi Kappa Psi at the University of Nebraska, and who is now employed in the Jacob North Company.

In the Spanish American War Mr. North was a private in Company F, second Nebraska Volunteer Infantry. During the World War he was first Sergeant in the Lincoln Home Guard. He is a member of the United Spanish War Veterans, is past commander of William Lewis Camp Number 2, U. S. W. V., and for two terms was Department Adjutant and quartermaster in this organization.

He is a member of the Lincoln Chamber of Commerce, the Democratic Noon Luncheon Club, and the Anti-Saloon League. He is a member of the National Geographic Society, the Society for the Prevention of Blindness, and the Birth Control League. Past chancellor of the local lodge of the Knights of Pythias; he is past master of Masonic Lodge Number 19, and member of Scottish Rite, and Shrine. His hobbies are politics and history. He is a non-active member of the Episcopal Church. Residence: Lincoln.

Rose North

Rose North, county superintendent of schools of Lincoln County, was born at Decatur, Michigan, January 28, 1878, daughter of Charles William and Mary Ann (Webster) Dennis.

Her father was born in Erie County, Pennsylvania, in November, 1840, and died at Decatur, Michigan, in November, 1921. He was a farmer and a veteran of the Civil War. His wife, Mary, was born in Cold Water, Michigan, December 2, 1838, and died at Decatur, in June, 1917. She was a teacher before her marriage.

Upon the completion of her early education in the public schools of Decatur, in 1891, Rose Dennis entered the high school there, from which she was graduated in 1895. In 1912, she received the degree of Bachelor of Pedagogy from the Normal College at Ypsilanti, Michigan.

She began her teaching career as elementary teacher in the public schools of Decatur, Michigan and Jackson, Michigan, and afterwards was critic teacher at Fort Wayne, Indiana. For a time, she was first grade supervisor in Warrensburg State Normal College of Warrensburg, Missouri.

In November, 1922, she was elected county superintendent of schools of Lincoln County, and still holds that office. She is a Republican.

On February 2, 1917, she was married to Ralph L. North, at Grand Rapids. He was born at Convoy, Ohio, May 10, 1878.

Mrs. North is a member of the United Spanish War Veterans Auxiliary, the United Presbyterian Church, the Nebraska State Teachers Association, the Altrusa Club, and the Delphian Society. At the present time, she is chairman of the Junor Red Cross of Lincoln County; president of the State Association of County Superintendents of Nebraska, 1930; author of child story *Dell and Dot in Fairyland;* and vice-president of District No. 4 of the Nebraska State Teachers Association, 1931 and 1932. Residence: North Platte.

Mrs. Charles Oliver Norton

Lottie Elouise Gove Norton, business woman and former banker, is descended from a splendid American ancestry, and takes much interest in applying to present day problems the ideals of the Puritans and other early settlers of America.

Her father, the Honorable Elijah Atwood Gove, eminent jurist was born at Weare, New Hampshire, September 22, 1832. In 1856 he was graduated from Dartmouth College with his Bachelor of Arts degree and Phi Beta Kappa honors. A sutler in the Army during the Civil War, he was later a lawyer and judge, and at the time of his death at Minneapolis, September 5, 1922, was the oldest living graduate of Dartmouth. (See page 231, *Gove Book.*)

Marie Louise Haynes, wife of Elijah Gove, was born at Wilmington, Vermont, July 4, 1836, and died at Watertown, South Dakota, September 15, 1916. She was a writer of much ability, and held many offices in the Daughters of the American Revolution, the Eastern Star, etc. Of English and Scotch ancestry, she was descended from the Campbell family of Argyle, the Frazer, Gordon, Haynes, Robinson and Carpenter families, all early settlers in the Massachusetts colony in 1636.

Educated in the public and high schools of Minneapolis, and later a student at St. Joseph's Convent under Mother Seraphim, a sister of Archbishop John Ire-

MRS. CHARLES OLIVER NORTON

land, she thereafter took post graduate work and studied the French language in Church School at London, Ontario. Brought up an Episcopalian, she was a member of St. Mark's Church at Minneapolis, where her father was junior and senior warden for several years.

On November 29, 1879, she was united in marriage to Charles Oliver Norton at Marshall, Minnesota. Mr. Norton, born at Fort Edward, New York, September 25, 1848, died at Kearney, on April 8, 1896. A banker and financier, and a man of wide business interests, principally in Minnesota, South Dakota, and Nebraska. he came of the English and Scotch families of Campbell, Frazer and Gordon. The ancestors of the Norton family came to America in 1637 from England.

Three children were born to this union, Charles Oliver, Jr., born September 27, 1882, who died January 24, 1883; William Strait, born September 13, 1884, who died January 12, 1892; and Oliver Gove Norton, born December 30, 1893. Oliver Gove attended Phillips Exeter Academy, and in 1915 was a graduate of Massachusetts Institute of Technology, being at that time its youngest graduate. His fraternity is Sigma Chi. He is a mechanical, designing and efficiency engineer, who served as a member of the Bolling Government Commission to France in April, 1916, and who was subsequently a first lieutenant and later a captain in the United States Aviation Service, American Expeditionary Forces, attached to the Second General Staff in Paris. He married Charlene Barton, and resides in Paris.

Upon the death of her husband, Mrs. Norton took over the banking interests and operated his banks for several years. She is a member of the Society of Founders and Patriots of America, the Colonial Dames (Massachusetts) and a charter member of its associate society in Nebraska. A member of the First Families of Virginia, the Colonial Daughters of the Seventeenth Century, and the Daughters of the American Revolution with twenty-four ancestral bars of service in that war, she is ex-state vice regent and ex-state regent of the Nebraska Society of the last mentioned organization. She was an organizing member and first vice president of the Nebraska Society of the Daughters of 1812; is a member of the Nebraska State Historical Society, the New England Historic Genealogical Society and holds orders of The Daughters of Colonial Governors through her ancestor, Governor Thomas Mayhew of Massachusetts, is a member of Americans of Armorial Ancestry and is eligible for membership in the Mayflower Society.

Mrs. Norton was vice president of the Oregon Trail Memorial Commission at the inception of the marking of the trail across Nebraska, and was instrumental in placing the first monument and tablet to mark this trail in the state. She also served as a member from Nebraska on the International Peace Arbitration Commission. She had the honor also of being the only woman in Nebraska who was an active member of a Commercial Club in early years.

Interested in charities and philanthropic work, she is well known as a genealogist, and is a newspaper and magazine contributor. She has had published several pamphlets on genealogical subjects, and is a member of the League of American Pen Women. She is secretary of the Kearney Cemetery Commission, is a life member the Kearney Woman's Club, the Nebraska State Historical Society and the Nebraskana Society. Mrs. Norton gave the land upon which the Kearney City Library is built, and also the land upon which the Fort Kearney Hotel is erected. Her favorite sport is hiking and her hobby is genealogy. Residence: Kearney. (Photograph on Page 888).

John Nathaniel Norton

John N. Norton is a true Nebraskan—born on the homestead his parents settled early in Nebraska's history, on May 12, 1878. His father, Charles O. Nor-

ton, was born in Sweden, September 28, 1842. At the age of six he started to America with his parents, but, his mother dying on the voyage, he continued with his father, who settled in Illinois. There he grew to manhood and married Mary S. Hurtig. He was an outstanding personage, active in the public and political life of the community. He served in the Civil War, and during its last days was appointed an officer of the military prison at Little Rock, Arkansas. He died on September 26, 1929.

Mary S. Hurtig was of Swedish parentage. Born in Illinois on November 15, 1849, in 1873 she came to Nebraska with her husband, and here they made their permanent home. On the homestead in Polk County, three children were born. Of the six born to their marriage, three are now living. After an exemplary life she died on July 17, 1910.

John N. Norton received his early education in the country schools of Polk County, after which he attended the Bryant Normal and Business College, then located at Stromsburg. After attending Nebraska Wesleyan University for some time, he entered the University of Nebraska, where he received his A. B. in 1903.

At Nebraska Wesleyan he was active in dramatics, while at the state university he was active both in debate and dramatics, the former being under the tutelage of Professor M. M. Fogg.

He married Selma Josephine Floodman, daughter of Charles F. and Hilma J. (Widga) Floodman, the latter of whom is still living. Their children are: William Wendell and Evelyn Maurine. William graduated from the University of Nebraska with an A. B. and LL. B. in 1925. He is a member of Phi Alpha Delta, and while at the university was active in dramatics and athletics. He was Ivy Day orator his graduation year. Evelyn, who majored in dramatics, was graduated from the University of Nebraska in 1926. She has taken post graduate work at George Washington University.

John Norton, while attending the state university, studied economics under Dean Ross, now of the Wisconsin State University, and perhaps one of the best known authorities on that subject in America. He has since that time devoted much effort to the study of agricultural economics, and in addition to his other endeavors has been active in the agricultural field.

He held his first public office as mayor of Osceola, Nebraska, 1908-09. Elected to serve as member of the Nebraska house of representatives in 1911, he was Democratic leader of the house two sessions and during one session was speaker pro tem. During this term he was chairman of two of the most powerful committees, the judiciary and the ways and means committees. He was the author of the resolution for the reform of legislative procedure, which was made a law in 1915, and which resulted in reducing the personnel by one-third.

He was the author of the resolution in 1917, which resulted in the calling of a constitutional convention. The resolution was approved in 1918, and the convention was held 1919-20. He was a member of the convention and chairman of the legislative committee.

In 1924 he was Democratic nominee for governor, after Charles W. Bryan had withdrawn to accept the Democratic nomination for vice president. Although defeated in the Coolidge landslide of that year he received a vote which exceeded that received by the head of the ticket by 45,000 votes.

Elected to the United States Congress in 1926, to represent the Fourth Nebraska district, he rendered a service to his district that was highly pleasing to his constituents. Always attentive to his legislative and departmental duties, he initiated the idea of a weekly news letter, which would report congressional activities, as a means of keeping the people informed as to what is going on in Congress.

Defeated in 1928 by the narrow margin of 218 votes

JOHN NATHANIEL NORTON

in which election Hoover carried the district by 18,653 votes, he was re-elected in 1930.

He has always been active in farm organizations and is a former president of the Nebraska Farm Bureau Federation. He has attended many conferences and conventions on farming. He is also a Chautauqua and Lyceum lecturer.

Residence: Polk. (Photograph on Page 890).

William Wendell Norton

William W. Norton was born in Polk County, Nebraska, December 24, 1900, the son of John Nathaniel and Selma Josephine (Flodman) Norton.

John N. Norton was born in Polk County, Nebraska, in May, 1878. In earlier years he was a farmer, and at the present time he is congressman from the fourth Nebraska district. His father, Charles O. Norton, who came to America, from Sweden, while a lad, was an early Nebraska pioneer and settler, who lived on a homestead in Polk County, until his death in September, 1929. Selma Norton was born in Polk County, Nebraska, in June, 1877.

William W. Norton attended a country school, and was graduated from Polk High School in 1918. He then attended the University of Nebraska and received his A. B. and LL. B. degrees in 1925. While in the university he was a member of the University Players, the Dramatic Club, Awgwan staff, the Cornhusker staff, the Senate Club, was Ivy Day orator, vice president of the senior class in 1925, and participated in interclass debate. He is a member of Phi Alpha Delta fraternity and was chief justice his senior year. He was active in basketball and baseball in high school, and in 1920 and 1921 he was a member of the University squad.

His marriage to Catherine Eleanor Hayden was solemnized at Council Bluff, Iowa, June 3, 1925. She was born at Bloomington, Nebraska, August 14, 1904. Their two children are: William, born March 29, 1926; and James, born May 7, 1930.

Mr. Norton was athletic director and instructor in Pierce High School 1925 and 1926, was appointed county judge of Polk County, in August, 1926, to fill a vacancy, and was elected in November, 1928, for a four year term. He is a Democrat.

Mr. Norton is affiliated with the Methodist Episcopal Church of Osceola. He holds membership in the Polk County Bar Association; the County Judge's Association of Nebraska (president); is secretary of the Osceola chapter of the Red Cross, and is past president of the Osceola Chamber of Commerce. He is a member of Osceola Lodge No. 65, Ancient Free and Accepted Masons, The Nebraskana Society, the University of Nebraska Alumni (board of directors), and is president of the Osceola Country Club. Golf is his favorite sport. Residence: Osceola.

Richard Sampson Norval

Richard Sampson Norval, lawyer and statesman, was born near London Mills, Fulton County, Illinois, October 18, 1849. He is the son of Oliver Johnson Washington and Mary Jane (Sampson) Norval, and has resided in Seward, Nebraska, since March 26, 1872. His father was born near Goldsboro, North Carolina, February 26, 1807, and left his native state when he became of age because he did not believe in human slavery. He moved to Indiana in a two-horse cart. There he remained for two years, locating at the end of that period in Fulton County, Illinois, and engaged in farming until his death on April 19, 1891.

The Norval family originated in the Highlands of Scotland, and emigrated to America long before the Revolution. Mary Jane Sampson, wife of Oliver J. W. Norval, was born in Somerset, Maryland, November 14, 1824. Of English origin, her family settled in America long prior to the Revolutionary War, and two of her ancestors served in it. She died at London Mills, Illinois, June 22, 1912.

Richard Sampson Norval attended public school in Illinois, and was a student at Hedding College at Abingdon, Illinois. He was later graduated from the University of Michigan, with the degree of Bachelor of Laws, and was admitted to practice at Detroit, in March, 1871. On May 6, 1872, shortly after his arrival in Nebraska, he was admitted to the bar of the state, and for fifty-nine years has been a member of the law firm of Norval Brothers, Attorneys.

A Republican, he has an enviable public record. He was a member of the state senate in 1889, and in 1919; was president protem of the 1919 session and acted as governor of the state during the absence of the Governor and Lieutenant Governor for a short period in that year. A member of the constitutional convention of 1919-20; he was delegate at large from Nebraska to the National Republican convention at Chicago, in 1888, which nominated Harrison for president, and Morton for vice president, and was a member of the notification committee, which notified them of their nomination, and was present at the ceremony.

During the World War he was a member of the Seward County Advisory Board, and the Council of Defense, and participated in various other civilian work. He is a member of the American and Nebraska State Bar Associations, a charter member of the Chamber of Commerce, and a member of the Nebraska State Historical Society, The Nebraskana Society and the Young Men's Christian Association.

A Mason, he is a member of the Ancient Free and Accepted Masons at Seward, Sesostris Temple of the Shrine at Lincoln, and Lincoln Consistory. His religious affiliation is with the Methodist Church.

Mr. Norval was married to Martha Ann Gray at Galesburg, Illinois, July 17, 1873. She was born near London Mills, April 28, 1850, and died at Seward, June 13, 1931. There are six children, Eva N., born February 14, 1879, whose husband, Bertrand S. Langworthy is now deceased; Oliver Gray, born March 31, 1881, who married Mae Norval; Ethel L., born October 19, 1883, who married Gustavus Babson; Leona B., born May 22, 1887, who married Julius V. Harpham; Richard Sampson, Jr., born December 1, 1889; and Mary Margaret, born March 29, 1893, who married Carl F. Holtz. Residence: Seward.

William Fred Novak

William Fred Novak, physician and surgeon, was born at Howells, Nebraska, September 9, 1897, son of Joseph and Mary (Prucha) Novak. Joseph Novak, who is a retired business man, was born in Bohemia, September 18, 1867, and immigrated to America in 1877. Mary, his wife, was born in Bohemia, September 6, 1868, and came to America in 1876.

Upon his graduation from the Howells public school in 1911, Dr. Novak entered Howells High School attending 3 years, and was graduated from Schuyler High School in 1915. From then until 1917 he was a student at Peru State Normal School. In 1923, he received his B. Sc. from the University of Nebraska, and in 1926 his M. D. He is a member of Omega Beta Pi and Phi Chi.

On June 12, 1926, he was united in marriage to Dorothy Mildred Oaks at Woodbine, Iowa. Mrs. Novak was born in Fremont, June 26, 1907. During 1917 and 1918, Dr. Novak taught in the Howells public schools and since July 31, 1926, has been engaged in the practice of medicine. He was a private in the 9th Field Artillery in the World War and is a member of the American Legion. A Catholic, he is a member of St. John's Church, and is a Knight of Columbus. He is president of the Howells Business Men's Club at the present time, and has served as a member of the board of education since 1929. His professional memberships include the American, Nebraska State and Colfax County Medical Associations. He is fond of reading, travel and sports. Residence: Leigh. (Photograph in Album).

Charles Novotny

Charles Novotny, retired farmer of Colfax County, has lived for the past 60 years on his original homestead in Nebraska. He was born at Cedar Rapids, Linn County, Iowa, November 1, 1862, the son of John and Terezie (Zvacek) Novotny. His mother was born at Teleci, Bohemia, November, 19, 1825, and died at Clarkson, Colfax County, Nebraska, May 17, 1903; she was active in church affairs, and was a typical pioneer mother and homemaker. His father, who was born at Policka, Bohemia, April 9, 1805, and died at Clarkson, August 12, 1888, served for 13 years in the Austrian Army.

In 1869 John Novotny, father of Charles, sold his 30 acre farm in Linn County, Iowa, and moved with his family to the west. Preparatory to the trip two of his sons traveled in a covered wagon to Schuyler, Nebraska, where they located homesteads for their father and themselves. The following September the entire family set out for Nebraska with five other families, all of whom made the trip in covered wagons, crossing the Missouri River on ferry boats.

Some of their buildings on the new homestead were made of sod, and during the first year several families lived in their house. They knew all the privations of pioneers and had many terrifying experiences with the neighboring Indians who bagged and stole food from them frequently. In 1874 and 1875 the grasshoppers destroyed their crops leaving them nothing but wild game and black bread for food, and many of the settlers moved back to their eastern homes. At times prairie fires swept out their entire stores and growing crops and destroyed their only source of fuel. Money was scarce and the mail was available sometimes only once in four weeks.

The Novotny children attended school in a two-room house, half of which was used as a home by some of the settlers; the school term was three months. Church services were held in neighboring homes and were conducted by the villagers themselves.

Charles Novotny has been active in Colfax County for the past 60 years and is still living on his father's homestead. An old cottonwood tree which his father planted 59 years ago is the only landmark remaining to mark the early day history. He is a member of the Zion Presbyterian Church of Clarkson, and holds membership in the Nebraskana Society. He is a Democrat.

He was united in marriage with Emma Lorence at Ely, Linn County, Iowa, December 26, 1893. Mrs. Novotny was born at Ely, November 27, 1876. They have three children: Bozena, born October 31, 1895; Esther, born April 19, 1897, who married George Filinger; and George C., born February 22, 1901. Bozena is a voice teacher in the Sherwood Music School at Chicago; Esther lives at Wooster, Ohio; and George is a fur farmer at Clarkson. Residence: Clarkson. (Photograph in Album).

Berton Frank Noyes

Berton Frank Noyes, musician and musical educator, was born at Prophetstown, Illinois, August 18, 1901, son of Charles and Mary Taylor (Foote) Noyes. Charles Noyes, a florist, was born at Mystic, Connecticut, and was descended on the paternal side from John Alden and Priscilla Mullins. His wife, Mary Taylor Foote, a native of Oneida, New York, traces her ancestry to the first settlers of New York State.

Educated first in Groton Heights School, Mr. Noyes attended Norwich Free Academy of Norwich, Connecticut, and Mount Hermon School at Mt. Hermon, Massachusetts, and is now working on his Bachelor of Arts degree. He had served years of private instruction in music in New York City, with Max Bendix, Scipioni

Guidi and Hans Letz, and was a scholarship student for a time at Curtis Institute in Philadelphia. He also has won prizes in music at Mount Hermon and a scholarship at Mannes School of New York.

Mr. Noyes has been a resident of Nebraska for the past six years, and is head of the violin department and conductor of the symphony orchestra at Hastings College, which was organized through the efforts of Mr. Noyes. He is married to Claire Jackson, who was born at Palmyra, New Jersey, November 15, 1897, and has one daughter, Priscilla Anne, born March 19, 1924. (See *Nebraskana*).

A Mason, Mr. Noyes is also a member of the Nebraskana Society, and is affiliated with the First Presbyterian Church at Hastings. His hobby is flying, and his favorite sports are swimming, hiking and baseball. He is a Republican. Residence: Hastings. (Photograph in Album).

Charles Edward Noyes

At Beverly, Illinois, Charles E. Noyes, was born December 30, 1866, the son of Elijah and Priscilla (Ayers) Noyes. His father, the son of Isaac Noyes, who was born in New Hampshire, is a descendant of Nicholas Noyes who came to America from England in 1636. He was born at Cairo, Illinois, in October, 1838, and died at St. Louis, Missouri, in 1920.

His mother, of Scotch and English ancestry, was born in New Jersey, August 9, 1837, and died at Louisville, Cass County, Nebraska, February 12, 1916. During the Civil War she was a school teacher in Adams County, Illinois.

Mr. Noyes was educated in public and high school and later supplemented his education with a Chautauqua course of study. While in school he was active in athletics. For sixty-two years he has lived in Nebraska, and is now a retired farmer. A Republican, he served two terms in the Nebraska legislature, 1907-09, and in 1911 was defeated for the senate on the wet and dry issue. Mr. Noyes is affiliated with the Methodist Episcopal Church.

He was united in marriage with Florence Alma Glover at Gordon, Nebraska, January 21, 1905. Mrs. Noyes, who is of Scotch and English ancestry, was born at Lawrence, Kansas, August 17, 1866, and before her marriage was a teacher. (Deceased March 23, 1931).

Claire Jackson Noyes

Claire Jackson Noyes, educator, was born at Palmyra, New Jersey, November 15, 1897, daughter of George Ayres and Anne Eliza (Valentine) Jackson. Her father, born at Bethayres, Pennsylvania, August 2, 1867, died at Baltimore, April 14, 1931. Of Quaker ancestry on the maternal side, he traced to William Penn in America. His paternal ancestry was Welsh. Until his death he was for a number of years secretary of the Hanover Fire Insurance Company of New York.

Anne Eliza Valentine was born at Philadelphia, August 5, 1871. She also traces her ancestry to William Penn, but on the paternal side, while her maternal line is English. She is an active clubwoman and greatly interested in politics.

Educated in the public schools of Brooklyn, New York, until 1911, Mrs. Noyes was graduated from Girls' High School there in 1915. In 1919 she received her Bachelor of Arts Degree from Adelphi College, and in 1922 her Master's degree from Columbia University. From 1915-19 she held a Long Island scholarship to Adelphi as well as a New York State scholarship.

Mrs. Noyes is a member of Delta Tau Alpha, of Phi Beta Kappa rank, and while in college was president of the Adelphia Glee Club, and active in literary publications and language clubs. She attended the University of Pennsylvania 1927-28, Middlebury French School

(Vermont) 1929, and Columbia University in 1930. She is married to Berton Frank Noyes (*see Nebraskana*).

The author of various articles on language study and French literature, Mrs. Noyes has taught French for a number of years. Part of her work was at Adelphi College, and she later taught at Mount Hermon School, Northfield, Massachusetts, the New York City High Schools and at Abington Friends' School at Jenkintown, Pennsylvania. At the present time she is head of the department of French at Hastings College.

Mrs. Noyes is a member of the National Association of University Women, the Nebraska State Teachers Association, the Nebraska Association of Church Colleges, the Young Men's Christian Association, the Young Women's Christian Association, the Parent Teachers Association, and the First Presbyterian Church of Hastings. She is a Republican, a member of the Nebraskana Society and the Red Cross. Mrs. Noyes is fond of swimming, while her hobby is philology. Residence: Hastings.

William Wallace Noyes

William Wallace Noyes, physician for the past 23 years, was born at Blair, Nebraska, November 19, 1882, the son of William Webster and Joan (Carter) Noyes. His father, who is a railroad engineer, was born at Monroe, Michigan, June 3, 1853, of English descent. His mother, whose parents were West Virginians, was born in Ohio, and died at Lincoln, Nebraska, June 24, 1887.

Dr. Noyes, was graduated from the Lincoln High School in 1902, and in 1908 was graduated from the Lincoln Medical College. He was active in football during his college days. In 1908 he began the practice of medicine in Holt County, Nebraska, where he continued until 1923, when he moved to Ceresco.

He is a member of the National Geographic Society, the Nebraskana Society, the Saunders County Medical Society, Nebraska State Medical Society, and the American Medical Association. His fraternal organizations include the Modern Woodmen of America, Ancient Order of United Workmen, and the Independent Order of Odd Fellows. He is affiliated with the Methodist Church at Ceresco, and is a member of the Republican party. During the World War he served on the Medical Advisory Board in Holt County.

His marriage to Hattie May Lippencott was solemnized at Red Cloud, Nebraska, October 20, 1909. Mrs. Noyes, the granddaughter of early settlers in Nebraska, was born at Blair, Washington County, Nebraska, May 2, 1882. To this union five children were born: Hazel Eugenia, born August 4, 1910; Cecil Ruth, born March 24, 1912; Julia Marie, born November 10, 1915; Veva May, born November 30, 1917; and William Wallace, born March 9, 1920. Residence: Ceresco.

Andrew F. Nuquist

On January 27, 1872, at Moline, Illinois, Andrew F. Nuquist, was born. He is the son of Andrew and Gustava (Wenstrom) Nuquist, the former a merchant, who was born at Kalmar, Sweden, November 22, 1835. He came to this country in 1867, settling in Illinois, and coming to Stromburg, Nebraska, in 1882. He died at Stromsburg, March 16, 1898. Gustava Nuquist was also born at Kalmar, December 19, 1846, and died at Stromsburg, February 14, 1926.

Mr. Nuquist received his education in the public schools of Moline, Illinois, and was graduated from Stromsburg High School, June 9, 1887. He attended Omaha Commercial College in 1887 and 1888.

While a lad he clerked in his father's store. He was marshal of Stromsburg, from 1893 to 1897, sheriff from 1898 to 1901, assistant cashier and later vice president of the Osceola Bank from 1902 to 1912, and since 1912 he has been a cashier of the First National Bank. A Democrat, he was defeated for state senator in 1902. He was city treasurer of Osceola for several years, was treasurer and later president of Polk County Telephone Company, and was a member of the school board for six years, serving as president part of the time.

He was married to Maud Selby Edgerton at Lincoln, Nebraska, September 28, 1904. She was born at Stromsburg, and is an active clubwoman, and the mother of four children: Andrew E., who received his A. B. degree from Doane College of Crete, Nebraska, and has taught in China for three years; Irma, who received her A. B. degree from Doane College, and her M. A. degree from the University of Chicago. She is married to Leroy T. Laase, who is head of the Department of Speech at Hastings College. Joseph who is a student of the University of Nebraska; and Robert, a high school student, and winner in debate and extemporaneous speaking.

Mr. Nuquist holds membership in the Osceola Community Club of which he was president for several years, the Polk County Bankers Association, and The Nebraskana Society. He enjoys all sports, and is a member of the Osceola Country Club. Reading and collecting coins are his hobbies. Residence: Osceola.

Maud Edgerton Nuquist

Maud E. Nuquist, distinguished civic leader of Nebraska, has lived in this state all her life and is a nationally known clubwoman. She was born at Stromsburg, Nebraska, September 10, 1882, the daughter of Joseph W. and Sarah Jane (Shelby) Edgerton. Her father, who was a lawyer and pioneer statesman, was born at Chesterhill, Ohio, September 4, 1852. He was a Quaker and was identified with the Knights of Labor movement and the Populist Party, and was defeated for supreme judge in the campaign of 1890.

Her mother, who was born at Bartlett, Ohio, December 26, 1850, and died at Osceola, December 10, 1922, was an active club and church worker. Her English and Irish ancestors were farmers, business men, and physicians.

Mrs. Nuquist was graduated from the Grand Island High School in 1900 where she was a honor student and a member of the debating team. From 1901 to 1904 she was a public school teacher. She has devoted a great deal of time and effort to the Woman's Club and is today one of the leaders of this organization in Nebraska. She was president of the local Woman's Club for two years, was president of the Fourth District in 1926-27, was vice president of the Nebraska Federation of Women's Clubs from 1927 to 1929, and was president of the Nebraska Federation of Women's Clubs 1929-31.

Her marriage to Andrew F. Nuquist was solemnized at Lincoln, Nebraska, September 28, 1904. Mr. Nuquist, who is a banker, was born in Rock Island County, Illinois, January 27, 1872. They have four children Andrew Edgerton, who has taught in China for three years; Irma, who received her master's degree in religious education, and who is married to Leroy T. Laase; Joseph E., a student at the University of Nebraska; and Robert, who is a high school student. The latter has won various honors in debating and extemporaneous speaking.

Mrs. Nuquist took an active part in Red Cross work during the World War, and is a member of the Daughters of the American Revolution. She holds membership in the Nebraskana Society, the P. E. O., the Native Sons and Daughters, and the Osceola Country Club. Her favorite sport is hiking, while reading and welfare work are her hobbies. She is an active member of the Methodist Church at Osceola. Residence: Osceola.

Edmund Peter Nuss

A resident of Nebraska all his life, Edmund Peter Nuss has been engaged in the practice of law at Hastings since 1924, and is active in political affairs in Adams County. He was born at Sutton, Clay County, Nebraska, July 3, 1899, the son of John George and Margared (Griess) Nuss. His father, who was born at Odessa, Russia, November 15, 1852, and died at Sutton, October 26, 1930, was a farmer. His mother was born in Russia, June 27, 1863.

Mr. Nuss attended rural schools in Clay County, was graduated from the Sutton High School in 1918, and received the bachelor of law degree at the University of Nebraska in 1923. He was a member of the law firm Snell, Northup, & Nuss, at Grand Island, Nebraska, 1923-24, and is now a member of the firm Stiner & Boslaugh at Hastings. A Republican, he served as substitute county judge of Adams County in 1925, and has been police magistrate at Hastings since 1926.

He married Pearl Wanda Bauer at Lincoln, Nebraska, December 10, 1921. Mrs. Nuss, who was formerly a stenographer, was born at Sutton, December 4, 1900. Mr. Nuss is a member of the Nebraska State Bar Association, the Adams County Bar Association, The Nebraskana Society, Masons, Elks, and Knights of Pythias. He served as an apprentice seaman during the World War and is now a member of the American Legion. His favorite sport is swimming, and his hobby is mechanics. Residence: Hastings.

Joseph Carl Nuss

For the past twenty-five years Joseph C. Nuss has been engaged in the mercantile business in Nebraska. He was born in Mergentheim, Germany, April 2, 1873, the son of Carl and Marie (Hofman) Nuss; both his parents were born in Germany. His father died at Mergentheim, Germany, in 1916, while his mother died there June, 1915.

Mr. Nuss received his education at Wurzburg, Germany. He opened a small store at Wayne, Nebraska, in 1909, where he owned only a small stock of merchandise, and began business on a small scale. Today he owns and manages a modern and well-equipped establishment at Wayne. He is secretary of Wayne Country Club, was formerly president of the Kiwanis Club and the Commercial Club, and is now chairman of a committee to establish a Chamber of Commerce.

He holds membership in the Knights of Columbus, is affiliated with St. Mary's Catholic Church, and is a member of the Woodmen of the World. His sport is golfing. Politically, Mr. Nuss is a Democrat.

On April 28, 1906, he was married at Wilkesbarre, Pennsylvania, to Marie Herdt, who was born in Dartmund, Germany, December 24, 1873. They have two children: Carl, born September 8, 1908; and Helen, born November 28, 1910. Both are graduates of Creighton University. Residence: Wayne. (Photograph on Page 895).

Fred Louis Nutzman

A resident of Nebraska for the past sixty-four years, Fred L. Nutzman came directly to the state from Germany in April, 1866. His parents, Christian and Louis Mary (Brandt) Nutzman were of German birth. His father was born May 25, 1809, and died in Otoe County, December 25, 1890. His mother was born June 22, 1821, and died in Otoe County, June 23, 1900. They were early pioneers in Nebraska, settling in 1866, when Fred L. Nutzman was about three years old.

Mr. Nutzman married Mary Ann Gruberin, Otoe County, April 25, 1882. She is a native of Germany and was born February 23, 1865. To their union the following children have been born: Amelia, on May 14, 1883, who married Carl Balfour; Irene, October 5, 1885, who married Henry Ross; Clara, November 7, 1888, who married William Ost; and Eugene, February 23, 1891,

who married Emma St. John. All are engaged in farming; two are graduates from Doane College.

Always active in politics Mr. Nutzman served four terms in the Nebraska house of representatives. Aside from his farming interests he is a banker and now serves as director and president of the Nehawka Bank and vice president of the Murray State Bank. He is a Lutheran but attends the Methodist Church. For the past thirty-five years he has been affiliated with the Odd Fellows Lodge. His chief recreation is cards. His residence is in Otoe County. Residence: Nehawka.

Fred A. Nye

One of the leading lawyers at Kearney, Nebraska, is Fred A. Nye, who has taken a prominent part in the professional, political, and civic affairs of his community for the past 40 years. He was born in Muscatine County, Iowa, June 26, 1862, the son of Alfred and Sarah Ribble (Silverthorn) Nye. His father, who was a farmer, was born in Vermont in 1812, and died at Iowa City, Iowa, in January, 1886. He settled in Muscatine County in 1835, he and his uncle erecting the first grist and saw mill in the county. He was descended from Benjamin Nye who settled at Sandwich, Massachussetts in 1635. His mother was born in Pennsylvania, in 1822, and died at Kearney in 1901.

Mr. Nye attended the University of Iowa where he received the Ph. B. degree in 1887 and the LL. B. degree in 1888. He was a member of Phi Kappa Psi at the University of Iowa. He was a member of the law firm Nye, Worlock, & Nye, at Kearney for a number of years and is now a member of the firm Nye & Nye. A Democrat, he served as county attorney of Buffalo County from 1896 to 1900, was a member of the Constitutional Convention in 1919 and 1920, and has held membership in various civic organizations at Kearney.

He was for six years a member of the Kearney Board of Education, for four years a member of the Kearney Library Board. He served on the Nebraska State Normal Board during 1909 and 1910, and is a member of the Kearney Chamber of Commerce. He holds membership in the Nebraskana Society.

His marriage to Helen M. Barlow was solemnized at Kenton, Ohio, May 17, 1893. Mrs. Nye, who was born at Kenton, Ohio, March 4, 1873, is a member of the Daughters of the American Revolution and is a descendant of Hugh Scott who came to America in 1667. Their children are: Lucile Elizabeth, born March 27, 1894, who married Horace J. Cary; M. Barlow, born April 29, 1896, who married Jeannette Cooke; John H., born February 27, 1898, who married Esther Edson; Mary N., born July 11, 1900, who married George P. Bristow; Sarah Gertrude, January 28, 1903, who married Frank B. Kemp; and Ben I., born June 18, 1909. Residence: Kearney. (Photograph in Album).

Julian Christopher Nyrop

The Reverend Julian Christopher Nyrop, clergyman, was born at Grand Island, Nebraska, June 12, 1886, son of Holger Ahlmann and Karan Marie (Hansen) Nyrop.

The father, born in Kjoge, Denmark, August 24, 1844, was a farmer. The family has contained a clergyman for six generations. He died at Grand Island, Nebraska, August 11, 1909. His wife, Karan, was born in Kjong, Denmark, April 27, 1858. She was of a family of blacksmiths and painters.

Mr. Nyrop attended the Omaha Public Schools and the academy of Grand Island College. He received the B. A. degree from Doane College in 1922, his Bachelor of Divinity Degree in 1925 from the Chicago Theological Seminary, and during 1923-25 attended the University of Chicago.

He was a stationary engineer for nine and a half

JOSEPH C. NUSS

Craven—Wayne

years, and then took his theological training. He has held the following pastorates: Oildale, California, two months in 1926; and Brule, Nebraska, from 1926 until the present time. He is ordained to the Congregational Church. Mr. Nyrop is an Odd Fellow and a member of the Red Cross.

On June 17, 1931, he was married to Dorothy Charlotte Gorder at Weeping Water, her birthplace. Mrs. Nyrop was born March 25, 1902, and before her marriage was a high school teacher. Her family was originally German. Residence: Brule.

Thomas Charles Oates

Thomas C. Oates, successful farmer of Gage County has lived in this state for over 64 years, and has always been interested in the progress of his state and community. He was born at Peoria, Illinois, January 12, 1867, the son of Thomas and Hanah (McGrale) Oates. His father, who was a farmer, was born in Ireland in 1828, and died in Nemaha County, Nebraska, November 27, 1872. His mother was born in Ireland in 1833 and died in 1889.

Mr. Oates received his education in the public schools of Marysville, Kansas. He is affiliated with St. Joseph's Catholic Church, is a member of the Democratic Party, and holds membership in the Nebraskana Society.

He was married to Katherine Ann Gallogly at Barneston, Gage County, Nebraska, January 26, 1898. Mrs. Oates was born at Fort Sarney, Canada, October 10, 1879. To their marriage five children were born: Dureen, born March 23, 1900, who is married to Charles Mack; Beulah, born April 26, 1902, who married Roy Bradsby; Gervis, born July 2, 1907, who died July 27, 1920; Mabel, born June 6, 1913; and Donald, born September 20, 1915. Beulah is a stenographer at Lincoln, Nebraska. Residence: Liberty.

John Cooper Ober

A pioneer sheep trailer between Oregon and Nebraska in the early days of the country, John Cooper Ober is, at the present time an extensive landowner and stockman. He was born at Newburg, Pennsylvania, July 11, 1859, son of Jonathan John and Mary Ann (Cooper) Ober.

Jonathan Ober, born in Newburg, February 1, 1828, was a coachmaker, whose ancestors came from Holland prior to the Revolution. He died at Newburg on February 22, 1900. Mary Ann, his wife, was born in Chambersburg, Pennsylvania, February 13, 1826, and died at Newburg on March 27, 1892. Her ancestry was Irish and Dutch; a brother, John Cooper, poet, historian and journalist, was private secretary to President Buchanan. The family was descended from the noted Peter Cooper.

Educated first in the public school at Newburg, John Cooper Ober was graduated from Stuart's Academy in 1876. On January 31, 1892, he was united in marriage to Eliza Ann Johnson at Silver Creek, Nebraska. There are two children, Bessie Irene, born December 25, 1896, and Lucia M., born September 6, 1902. Bessie, who is a graduate of Nebraska Wesleyan University, and a former teacher, is married to John B. Skinner. Lucia, a graduate of the University of Nebraska, is a teacher. Mrs. Ober is descended from pre-Revolutionary settlers in America. Mr. Ober is affiliated with the Republican party and he is a member of the Nebraskana Society. Residence: Fullerton.

Robert S. Oberfelder

Robert S. Oberfelder, farmer, ranchman and broker, was born in New York City, December 8, 1855, and came to Sidney in 1876.

His father, Tobias Oberfelder, was born in New York, October 10, 1817, and died there on December 15, 1905.

He was a merchant, whose father was born in Germany. His wife, Betsy Silverman, was born in New York, September 10, 1830, and died there on April 15, 1900. She was of German descent.

Mr. Oberfelder attended public school, and coming to Sidney opened an outfitting store for people going to the Black Hills. He was in that business more than 50 years and then entered the bond business. At the present time he is president of the Oberfelder Investment Company. Mr. Oberfelder is the owner of considerable real estate, including two ranches and a number of farms.

Always active politically, he was mayor of Sidney for some time and was president of the Nebraska State Fish Commission.

He is a Democrat. Among the organizations of which Mr. Oberfelder holds membership are, the Red Cross (life member), the Masons, the Elks, the Modern Woodmen of America, Cheyenne County Historical Society, United Service Club (New York), the Omaha Athletic Club, and the Sidney Country Club. His favorite sport is golf and his hobby is working 16 hours a day. Residence: Sidney.

Louis Clark Oberlies

A resident of Nebraska for the last 57 years, L. C. Oberlies has been prominent in business throughout Nebraska for over 30 years. He was born at Galesburg, Iowa, April 23, 1872. John Oberlies, his father, who was born in New York City, July 10, 1839, was a lumberman and banker, and a Civil War veteran. He was a widely travelled and unusually versatile man, and was a diarist of note. His ancestors were Germans who came to America from Bavaria in 1838. John Oberlies died at Lincoln, Lancaster County, Nebraska, May 11, 1913.

Wilhelmina Augusta (Rohrdanz) Oberlies, his mother, who was born at Stettin, Germany, July 10, 1848, came with her parents to America in 1857. She was always unusually active in Red Cross work, charities, and church affairs. She died at Lincoln, March 15, 1932.

Mr. Oberlies attended the grade school at Dorchester, Nebraska, and the University of Nebraska Preparatory School. In 1895 he was awarded his A. B. degree at the University of Nebraska, and in 1899 received his A. M. degree there. He was president of his class; was active in musical circles; and was a charter member and founder of Alpha Chapter of Phi Kappa Psi.

From 1895 to 1908 he engaged actively in the lumber business, and from 1908 to 1917 he lectured, part of this work being devoted to Young Men's Christian Association affairs. He took part in war time activities during 1917 and 1918. He has been interested in the banking and investment business. Since 1929 he has been personnel director of the Lincoln Telephone and Telegraph Company. He is the manager of a line of lumber yards, and is a director in the following organizations: National Bank of Commerce; Homestead Bonding Company; Bendix Publishing Company, of which he is president; the Dwelling House Insurance Company; Cornbelt Life Insurance Company. He is president of the Tobias State Bank; president of the Waco Lumber Company; president of the Home Lumber Company; a director in the Chappell Hardware Cmpany; and is president of the Union Lumber and Mercantile Company. In addition to his extensive business interests he owns and operates farming land in western Nebraska.

A Democrat, Mr. Oberlies served as a member of the state senate for some time, and was a member of the State Board of Control of State Institutions for eight years, from 1919 to 1927. He is a lecturer of some distinction and often addresses civic clubs and community groups. He is the author of *Addresses to Boys,* and has been the editor of various church and college publications.

His marriage to Ella Aurilla Hall was at Lincoln,

June 30, 1896. Mrs. Oberlies was born at Columbus City, Kansas. They have the following children: Ruth, born July 17, 1899, who married Marvin R. Schafer and teaches with him at the University at Peiping, China; Colombe, born February 4, 1902, who married Paul Lessenhop; Helen, born June 14, 1904, who married Dr. Clarence I. Drummond a physician in Oregon; Lois, born September 17, 1906, who married William M. Dunkak; Viola, born October 1, 1908; Clark-Elinor, born August 6, 1915.

Mr. Oberlies spent six years in the military unit at the University of Nebraska where he was commissioned first lieutenant. He was secretary of the War Work Campaign for relief agencies during the World War. He has led the Oberlies Forum, a class for men for 25 years; is a member of the Lincoln Chamber of Commerce, the Lincoln Rotary Club and the Hiram Club. He has been a member of the State Young Men's Christian Association for the past 12 years; and is a member of the local Young Men's Christian Association. He is a member of the Open Forum, of the Masons, Commandery, Consistory and Shrine. He is fond of golf. His hobby is boys' work and lecturing at father-and-son affairs. Residence: Lincoln.

Byron Bay Oberst

Byron Bay Oberst was born at North Platte, Nebraska, January 20, 1891. His parents are Martin and Belle (Howe) Oberst, the former a native of Strasburg, Germany, born April 15, 1841. Martin Oberst came to America in 1868, and was a scout and Indian fighter in the early days of Nebraska. Before coming to America he was a lieutenant in the German army. He died at York, Nebraska, April 10, 1929.

Belle Howe was born at Dayton, Virginia, May 10, 1858, a descendant of Lord Howe, British general during the Revolution. She was a teacher in North Platte High School, and active in the Woman's Club and in foreign missionary work. She died at Omaha, September 12, 1918.

Upon his graduation from the North Platte High School in 1907, Mr. Oberst entered Northwestern University from which he received his LL. B. in 1915. He was dean of Delta Theta Phi, member of the Wigmore Senate, dean of the Omaha Alumni and chairman of the student council at Northwestern.

He was promoted from private, infantry to captain, infantry, during the World War, and from captain, infantry to lieutenant-colonel in the Officers Reserve Corps. He is a member of the American Legion, Omaha Officers Reserve Corps, of which he was president in 1924 and again in 1927, Military Order of the World War, and Omaha chapter of the Sojourners, of which he was president in 1924. He was formerly editor of the *Army News*.

Upon his admission to the bar at Chicago he was associated in practice with Herrick, Allen and Martin. Returning to North Platte, he entered practice under the firm name of Muldoon and Oberst. In 1920 he became associated with William Baird and Sons, Interstate Oil and Refining Company of Omaha; then with the New York Title and Mortgage Company of New York, and is now attorney for the Federal Land Bank of Omaha.

He was married to Claire Mathilda Healy at Lincoln, July 6, 1912. Mrs. Oberst was born at Omaha, November 30, 1891, and is of Welsh and Irish descent. She is active in civic work, particularly the Camp Fire Girls. There are three children: Annabelle, born July 2, 1914; Virginia, born September 14, 1917; and Byron, Jr., born March 15, 1923.

Mr. Oberst is a Republican. He holds membership in the Nebraska State and Omaha-Douglas County Bar Association, American Title Association and the Nebraska Title Association. He is an Elk, a Mason and a Knight of Pythias. His sport is golf, and his hobby is reading. Residence: Omaha.

Edward James O'Brien

Edward J. O'Brien, physician and surgeon at Exeter, Nebraska, was born at Ranchester, Wyoming, November 16, 1896, the son of James Henry and Margaret (Haley) O'Brien. His father, who was a miner, was born at Allentown, Pennsylvania, January 14, 1861, and died at Cripple Creek, Colorado, May 20, 1910; his ancestry was Irish. His mother was born, of Irish parentage, at Missouri Valley, Iowa, October 3, 1861.

Dr. O'Brien was graduated from the Cripple Creek High School in 1915, was awarded the A. B. degree at Colorado College, 1923, and received the M. D. degree at Creighton University in Omaha, 1928. He is a member of Alpha Sigma Tau, Theta Phi Alpha, and Sigma Chi. From 1911 to 1924 he was a pharmacist at Cripple Creek, Colorado, Casper, Wyoming, and Colorado Springs. Since 1928 he has been physician and surgeon at Exeter.

He is a member of the Exeter Commercial Club, the Nebraskana Society, Fillmore County Medical Society, Nebraska State Medical Society, and Knights of Columbus, and is affiliated with St. Stephens Catholic Church. During the World War he served from June, 1918, to December, of the same year, and since 1930 has been vice-commander of the American Legion. His social club is the Country Club of Friend, Nebraska, while his favorite sport is golfing.

He married Lucille Moran Egan at Omaha, November 8, 1930. Mrs. O'Brien was born at Highland, Wisconsin, February 23, 1904. Dr. O'Brien is a Democrat. Residence: Exeter.

Thomas Jefferson O'Brien

Thomas J. O'Brien was born at Mount Pleasant, Iowa, December 2, 1865, the son of Moses and Bridgett (Brennan) O'Brien. His father, who was born at Wixford, County Carlo, Ireland, August 15, 1826, was a farmer; he came to America in 1848, and lived in New York for two years after which he moved to Mount Pleasant; he died at Ottumwa, Wapello County, Iowa, January, 1910. His mother was born in County Kilkenny, Ireland, 1832, and died at Ottumwa, June 15, 1874.

Mr. O'Brien, who has led in Omaha civic and business affairs for the past 35 years, was graduated from high school at Ottumwa, Iowa. He was engaged in the hotel business at Omaha, from 1895 to 1919; and since 1914 has been in the automobile business there. He is now president of the T. J. O'Brien & Son automobile firm. He is a member of the Omaha Auto Trade Association; the Chamber of Commerce; and was one of the organizers and a charter member of the Rotary Club at Omaha. His social club is the Omaha Country Club. His sport is golf. He is an Elk and Eagle, and a member of St. Cecilia's Cathedral at Omaha.

He was married to Helen C. McGuire, at Omaha, January 12, 1896. Mrs. O'Brien, whose ancestry is Irish, was born at Plattsmouth, Cass County, Nebraska, January 10, 1871. They have five children: Coreta, born January 12, 1897, who married John H. Markel; Willow, who married Edward J. Shoemaker; Grace, who married Chester Winn; Thomas; and Mildred. Residence: Omaha.

Rinehardt Otto Ochsner

Rinehardt Otto Ochsner, born August 6, 1901, at Sutton, Clay County, Nebraska, is the son of John Peter Ochsner and Margaretha Lee (Griess) Ochsner. His father, who was born in Neustadt, Germany, June 22, 1861, was a farmer, and later became a real estate and insurance agent. He came to America in 1866 and died at Sutton, March 5, 1917. Most of his family are farmers, and one a successful surgeon. His mother was born in Neustadt, Germany, January 10, 1862; her parents came to America in 1867.

Rinehardt O. Ochsner attended rural school, the Sut-

RINEHARDT OTTO OCHSNER

Day—Hebron

ton grade school and was graduated from the Sutton High School, May 25, 1921. He attended the Peru State Normal College the summer term of 1919 and on June 15, 1926, he received the degree of Doctor of Dental Surgery from the University of Nebraska. He was a member of Xi Psi Phi and the Green Goblin. While attending high school Dr. Ochsner was active in basketball and track.

On June 29, 1926, he was united in marriage with Margaret Lee Uter, at Hastings. Mrs. Ochsner was born at Fairbury, Nebraska, January 21, 1904, and was cash auditor at Rudge and Guenzel's store at Lincoln prior to her marriage. They have two children: Jacquelyn Lou, born March 28, 1927; and Thomas Stanley, born September 12, 1929.

Dr. Ochsner is a Democrat and is affiliated with the Presbyterian Church. He is a member of the national, state, and district dental associations and is a member of the Ancient Free and Accepted Masons. He holds membership in the Red Cross, Salvation Army, and the Nebraskana Society.

He is a member of the Chamber of Commerce at Deshler, the Luncheon Club, the Young Men's Christian Association and the Country Club. Golf, football and swimming are his favorite sports and he enjoys reading and traveling. Residence: Deshler. (Photograph on Page 898).

Frank Boyd O'Connell

Frank Boyd O'Connell, secretary of the Nebraska Game Forestation and Parks Commission, was born at Malcolm, Nebraska, February 19, 1892. He is the son of John and Emma (Bates) O'Connell, the former a retired farmer who was born at Bloomington, Illinois, March 4, 1850. His mother was born in Michigan, in 1860, and is still living.

Mr. O'Connell attended public school, Raymond High School, the University of New York, and the University of Nebraska. He has been and is active in Republican politics, and served as chief Game Warden of Nebraska, March, 1925-29; and as secretary of the Nebraska Game Forestation and Parks Commission, 1929. He has done much as a newspaper writer and as a lecturer, and is the author of the following: *When Peace Comes* (1930); *History of Nebraska American Legion* (1922), besides many magazine articles and stories. From January, 1919, to July, 1919, he was editor of the *American Embarkation News* (LeMans, France), and is now editor of *Outdoor Nebraska*. He held the rank of major in the Nebraska National Guard, 1920-1931. He was one of the founders of the American Legion, and one of the founders and first secretary of the commission authorized to disburse the $2,000,000 trust fund for World War veterans, given by the State of Nebraska.

Of his many memberships in fraternal, civic and other organizations the following are perhaps the most important: The Lions Club, Izaak Walton Club, Masonic Order, and Nebraska Writer's Guild. Mr. O'Connell attends Westminster Presbyterian Church. Residence: Lincoln.

Timothy Joseph O'Conner

Timothy Joseph O'Conner, retired farmer, was born at Old St. Johns, Nebraska, October 31, 1856. He is the son of Cornelius Constantine and Catherine Mary (Duggan) O'Conner, the former a captain in the United States Army during the Indian campaigns in Dakota County, in 1863. He was a member of the Nebraska legislature two terms while it was a territory, and another after Nebraska became a state. He was born in County Cork, Ireland, August 14, 1815, and came to America in 1820. His death occurred at Homer, Nebraska, August 16, 1903. Catherine Mary Duggan was born in County Cork, September 8, 1830, and died at Homer, December 17, 1916.

Mr. O'Conner attended country school, and became engaged as a farmer shortly afterward. He was married

to Mary Celestine Dillon at Sioux City, Iowa, April 18, 1889, and to them were born six children: Charles, born December 12, 1900, married Anna Rocheford; Helen, born December 8, 1902; Harry, born October 29, 1904; married Hazel Beatty; Harold, born September 10, 1906; Catherine, born November 9, 1908, married Vincent F. Harrington; and Charlotte, born November 5, 1910.

An ardent baseball fan, Mr. O'Conner is fond of horseback riding also. He is a member of St. Cornelius Catholic Church at Homer, and the Nebraskana Society. Residence: Homer.

Viola Emily Rosseter Odendahl

A business woman at Loup City, Nebraska, and a resident of this state for the past 62 years, Viola Emily Rosseter Odendahl was born in Illinois, March 1, 1862. Her father, C. E. Rosseter, a hotel proprietor, was born in Portage County, Ohio, July 30, 1838. He moved to Nauvoo, Illinois, was in California, during the gold rush of 1861, and came back to Illinois, the early part of 1862, remaining there until 1870. After that he located at Grand Island, Nebraska. In the year 1872-73, the people decided to form a county organization, named Sherman County, and he was the first treasurer elected. He died at Los Angeles, California, October 1, 1906. His ancestry was Pennsylvania Dutch. Her mother, Lydia (Williams) Rosseter, was born at Washington, Ohio, May 4, 1838, and died at Chicago, May 19, 1897.

Mrs. Odendahl attended the public school at Loup City, and for a number of years has been the proprietor of a hotel there. She was vice president of the Loup City Community Club in 1931, is active in the Order of Eastern Star, and holds membership in the Nebraskana Society.

Her marriage to Charles Julius Odendahl was solemnized at Loup City, at the home of her parents. Mr. Odendahl who was a descendant of William Williams, one of the signers of the Declaration of Independence, was born September 16, 1853. They have three children: Frederick, born November 30, 1880, who married Ella Stepnowski; Ernestine, born December 12, 1882, who married Charles Carter; and William, born April 23, 1889, who married Lulu Winkleman. Residence: Loup City. (Photograph on Page 900).

August R. E. Oelschlaeger

For the past 38 years August R. E. Oelschlaeger has lived in Nebraska where he has taken a prominent part in the religious welfare work of the state. He was born near Farley, Missouri, June 6, 1871, the son of Henry Frederick and Johanna (Jungblut) Oelschlaeger. His father, a farmer, was born in Westphalia, Germany, 1824, and in the early 1850's moved to America; he died near Farley, Missouri, in the fall of 1876. His mother, an active farm woman and the mother of a large family, was born in Westphalia, 1836, and died near Farley, October, 1875. Her father was a blacksmith in Westphalia.

Mr. Oelschlaeger attended the parochial and public schools of Missouri, and parochial school at Leavenworth, Kansas. His advanced education was received entirely in church colleges, St. Paul's College at Concordia, Missouri, 1884-85; Concordia College, Fort Wayne, Indiana, 1885-89; and Concordia Seminary, St. Louis, Missouri, 1889-90, 1891-93. All of the former were Lutheran Missouri Synod institutions.

He served as traveling pastor in Sheridan County, Nebraska, 1893-5, covering the territory of Rushville, Hay Springs, Gordon, and Chadron. Since 1895, he has been pastor of St. Paul's Lutheran Church, at West Point, Nebraska. St. Paul's has a membership of over 500 hundred people, and includes an eighth grade all English Church school with two teachers; both German and English services are held. Mr. Oelschlaeger is a member of

Locke—Grand Island

VIOLA EMILY ROSSETER ODENDAHL

Northern Nebraska District of the Missouri Synod; he is vitally interested in the advancement of religious education in his community and congregation.

His marriage to Fredericka Louise Roebker was solemnized near Wallula, Leavenworth County, Kansas, April 22, 1896. Mrs. Oelschlaeger, who was born near Farley, Missouri, November 6, 1875, was a devoted mother and homemaker. She died at the Fremont Hospital, Dodge County, Nebraska, September 20, 1917.

The following children were born to this union: Anna, born August 28, 1899, a parochial school teacher, who married Herman Meyerhoff, also a parochial school teacher; Frieda, born April 22, 1899, who married Rev. Elmer Thode, a missionary at Ichang, Hupeh, China; Marie, born January 10, 1901, who is a nurse in the medical mission at Shihnan, China, and who will soon be married to Rev. Arnold Gebhardt, also a missionary; Ruth, born March 14, 1903, who is a bookkeeper; Quinta, born October 11, 1904, who is a parochial school teacher; Adeline, born December 10, 1906, who married Dr. Holly H. Heitzman, of Omaha; Talitha, born March 30, 1909, who keeps house for her father; Erich, born August 27, 1911, who is a student at St. John's College, Winfield, Kansas; Roland, born August 11, 1913, who is taking a high school post graduate course; Lenore, born January 3, 1915, who died April, 1915; and Edward, born March 26, 1916, a sophomore in high school. Residence: West Point.

Joseph Patrick O'Furey

Active among Nebraska newspaper publishers of the two two decades is Joseph Patrick O'Furey, editor and publisher of the *Cedar County News*, Nebraska's best known prize-winning weekly. Mr. O'Furey was president of the Nebraska Press Association in 1923, and was for nine years a member of the board of directors. He is now serving his thirteenth term as secretary-treasurer of the Northeast Nebraska Editorial Association. He was the founder and first president of the Tri-State Editorial Association, and also served as vice president for Nebraska of the National Editorial Association for three years.

Mr. O'Furey was born at Wheatland, Pennsylvania, June 1, 1876, son of Martin and Bridget (Davis) O'Furey. The father was born in Oranmore, Ireland, May 10, 1846, and died at Cleveland, Ohio, September 14, 1905. The mother was born in Maryborough, Ireland, September 8, 1852, and died at Youngstown, Ohio, February 10, 1923.

On July 6, 1904, Joseph Patrick O'Furey was married to Lulu Mae Price at Bloomington, Illinois. There were two children, Geraldine Elsa, born April 30, 1907, who married James Paul Cody; and Joseph Daniel, born February 21, 1909, and died January 16, 1932.

In 1924 Mr. O'Furey served as assistant sergeant at arms at the Republican national convention at Cleveland, while on his way to New York as delegate to the Democratic national convention, representing the 3rd Nebraska district.

He is the democratic candidate for the state senate in the Tenth District.

He has served as a member of the Hartington Board of Education and also as president of the Hartington Chamber of Commerce. He is a member of the Elks, Modern Woodmen, Knights of Columbus, and Holy Trinity Catholic Church. Residence: Hartington.

Joseph Patrick O'Gara

Born at Lincoln, Nebraska, June 18, 1907, Joseph P. O'Gara is the son of Patrick and Mary (Corcoran) O'Gara. His father was born in County Donegal, Ireland, March 4, 1861, and came to America with his parents in 1863. His mother was born at Westport, County Mayo Ireland, March 6, 1874.

Mr. O'Gara was graduated from Cathedral High School in 1924, entered the University of Nebraska, receiving his A. B. in 1928 and his LL. B. in 1930. He was awarded the Order of the Coif and received the highest grade in his law class. He is a member of Phi Alpha Delta. In high school he received a letter in football in 1923 and in baseball and basketball in 1924.

Since his admission to the bar in 1930 Mr. O'Gara has been associated with the law firm of Perry, Van Pelt and Marti. He is a member of the Nebraska State and Lancaster County Bar Associations, and The Nebraskana Society. He is a Catholic, and a member of St. Mary's Cathedral. His sports are football and baseball. Residence: Lincoln. (Photograph in Album).

Peter Francis O'Gara

Born in a sod house in Cedar County, Nebraska, September 23, 1874, P. F. O'Gara is a son of early pioneers. His parents Roger Thomas and Bridget Susan (Hayes) O'Gara, were born in County Sliga, Ireland, Roger in 1838, and Bridget in 1848. Roger O'Gara came to America in 1852, and was an early educator and for fourteen years served as county superintendent of public instruction in Cedar County. He died at Laural, July 19, 1906. His wife died at Laurel, on August 18, 1900. Principally Irish, she was perhaps one-eighth Danish, as she traced her ancestry to the Danish Vikings.

Peter Francis O'Gara attended the public schools of Nebraska, and received his Bachelor of Laws degree from the University of Nebraska on June 14, 1906. For several years prior to his admission to the bar he taught in the public schools of Cedar County, and has since been engaged in active practice.

A Jeffersonian-Democrat of the ultra-progressive type, he was for four consecutive terms county attorney of Cedar County, and for a period of ten years was a member of the Democratic state central committee. At the present time he is local attorney for the Chicago, Burlingon and Quincy Railroad Company.

On July 3, 1911, he was united in marriage to Catherine McGrinn, at Hartington. Mrs. O'Gara, a native of Dennison, Iowa, was born November 30, 1882. She is of Irish descent, and was an educator prior to her marriage. There are six children, Frances, born May 20, 1912, who attends Wayne State Normal College; Margaret, born August 2, 1913, who is her father's secretary; Roger, born July 19, 1916; Gerald, born March 30, 1918; Gertrude, born April 4, 1920, and Hugh, born January 8, 1923. The four younger children attend school.

He is a member of the Knights of Columbus, and was grand knight of the Hartington Council 1913-14, and state advocate 1914, '15 and '16. He is a member of the Nebraska State Bar Association, the Chamber of Commerce, and the Nebraska State Historical Society, a member and secretary of the Cedar County Pioneer and Old Settlers Association, and the Native Sons and Daughters of Nebraska. He holds life membership in The Nebraskana Society. Residence: Hartington.

Howard E. Ohman

Howard E. Ohman, lawyer and clergyman, was born at Omaha, July 17, 1899, and is perhaps as well known as a chess player as a member of the ministerial profession. He is the son of Albert F. and Emma (Larson) Ohman, both natives of Sweden. He was educated in the Omaha public schools; was graduated from Central High School in 1918, and later attended the University of Omaha, where he was the winner of an award for scholarship.

Despite his lack of years he has had an extremely varied and interesting career. For seven years he practiced law with Montgomery, Hall and Young, the law department of the Union Pacific Railroad, with Johnson, Moorhead and Rine, and privately. He was then associate Boy's Work secretary of the Omaha Y. M. C. A. two years. For six years he was editor of the chess department of the Omaha World-Herald. He is pastor's assistant at the First Central Congregational Church, and is associated with the Chelby Colorado Camps for Boys and Girls during the summer months. For the past fourteen years he has been Nebraska State chess champion. In addition he is interested in astronomy, and has given many lectures on the subject. He is a member of the Y. M. C. A., the Red Cross and the Chamber of Commerce. He is president of the Omaha Chess Club, and a member of the University Club. His sports are tennis and handball. Residence: Omaha.

David Dane O'Kane

David Dane O'Kane, a leader in business affairs at Wood River, Nebraska, was a pioneer settler in this state in 1874. He was born at Polo, Illinois, December 8, 1868, the son of Joseph and Mary Davey O'Kane. His father, who was born at Philadelphia, Pennsylvania, December 25, 1826, and died at Wood River, February 15, 1886, was a farmer who came to Dawson County as a homesteader in 1874 and served as county commissioner there for a number of years. His mother was born in County Sligo, Ireland, March 10, 1830, and died at Wood River, January 11, 1888.

Mr. O'Kane received most of his education at home and at the age of 14 began the study of telegraphy. He served as station agent for the Union Pacific Railroad Company from 1883 to 1902, and for the past 28 years has been connected with the Northwestern Bell Telephone Company in an executive capacity. During this time has also engaged in the real estate and insurance business at Wood River where he is still active in civic affairs.

Although he is retired from business Mr. O'Kane is serving as secretary of the Chamber of Commerce, is Grand Knight of the Knights of Columbus, and holds membership in the Modern Woodmen of America and the Red Cross. He is affiliated with St. Mary's Catholic Church at Wood River.

On November 29, 1905, his marriage to Agnes Mary Whalen was solemnized at Wood River. Mrs. O'Kane was born in Iowa, March 12, 1878. They have the following children: Mary, born October 7, 1906, who is a graduate of St. Louis School of Technology; Leo, born August 11, 1908, who is a junior at Creighton College of Medicine in Omaha; Robert Harold, born May 10, 1910, who is also a student at Creighton; Gretchen, born May 2, 1913; and Charlotte, born March 5, 1917. Mr. O'Kane was postmaster at Wood River form 1916 to 1924. Residence: Wood River.

Thomas Wesley O'Laughlin

Born at Dubois, Nebraska, October 10, 1865, Thomas Wesley O'Laughlin is the son of James and Mary (Addamson) O'Laughlin. His father, who was a farmer, died at Pawnee City, Nebraska. His mother, who was a teacher, died at Dubois in 1880.

Mr. O'Laughlin is part owner of the O'Laughlin & Livingston Furniture Company at Grand Island, and in 1892 started a hardware business in Dubois. In 1902 he moved to Friend, Nebraska, and engaged in the furniture and undertaking business. Since 1912 he has been engaged in the furniture and undertaking business in Grand Island. He attended business college at Grand Island in 1888.

He is a member of the Rotary Club, the Grand Island Credit Association, the Chamber of Commerce, and the First Methodist Episcopal Church of Grand Island. He is secretary and treasurer of the O'Laughlin Livingston Company, and has served as a member of the board of directors of the Young Men's Christian Association for 10 years, and holds membership in the Elks, Modern Woodmen of America, Masons, and the Security Benefit Association. His social club is the Woodlawn Golf Club.

On July 12, 1893, he was married to Mary Dunlap at Tecumseh, Nebraska. Mrs. O'Laughlin, who was formerly a teacher, was born at Tecumseh, January 19, 1868. Their children are, Edith Lyle, born October 31, 1895, who married Paul L. Guggemus; and Alyne Grace, born January 7, 1898, who married W. A. Henry who is in the finance business. Mr. Guggemus is an automobile salesman.

A Republican, Mr. O'Laughlin served as committeeman in Pawnee County from 1888 to 1900. Residence: Grand Island.

Charles Henry Oldfather

Charles Henry Oldfather was born at Tabriz, Persia, June 13, 1887, the son of Jeremiah M. and Felicia N. (Rice) Oldfather. His father, who was a missionary in Persia, 1872-90, was born at Farmersburg, Ohio, October 7, 1842, and died at Hanover, Indiana, May 10, 1910; he was a missionary in Persia, 1872-1890, and a clergyman in Indiana, 1890-1910; he served during the Civil War. His mother was born at Covington, Indiana, August 16, 1848. She is descended from Scotch, Irish, Welsh, and English ancestors.

Dr. Oldfather attended school in Indiana, and was graduated from Hanover College Academy, 1902. He holds the following degrees: A. B., Hanover College. 1906; B. D., McCormick Theological Seminary, 1911; Ph. D., University of Wisconsin, 1922. He was a student at the University of Munich, 1911-12, the University of Chicago, 1910, and the University of Illinois, 1919. He was a member of the college glee club and quartette, and Phi Delta Theta fraternity. In 1908 he was tennis champion of North Dakota, and took part in football and basketball.

He was a teacher in high school from 1906-07, was engaged in business, 1907-08, was teacher in the Syrian Protestant College, 1912-14, served as professor of classics at Hanover College, 1914-16, and was professor of Greek and ancient history at Wabash College, 1916-26. Since 1926, he has been professor of ancient history at the University of Nebraska.

Dr. Oldfather is a member of the American Association of University Professors, the American Historical Association, the Nebraskana Society, the American Philological Association, and the Classical Association of the Middle West. From 1920 to 1924, he acted as a member of the Library Commission of Indiana. He is affiliated with the First Presbyterian Church of Lincoln. His favorite sports are golfing and tennis.

During the World War he was prominent in loan drives and war work of all kinds. Politically, he is an Independent. On September 7, 1914, he was married to Margaret Kinsey McLelland at Indianapolis, Indiana. Mrs. Oldfather was born at Madison, Indiana, November 13, 1887. She is a niece of the famous author David Graham Phillips. Their children are: Ellanor Newton, born February 29, 1916; Margaret Rebekah, born November 26, 1918; and Charles Henry, born February 10, 1920.

Dr. Oldfather is the author of *The Greek Papyri from Greco-Roman Egypts*, 1912, and other articles. Residence: Lincoln.

Oliver Oscar Olinger

Oliver Oscar Olinger, farmer and stockman, was born near Tekamah, Nebraska, July 30, 1893. His parents are James Preston and Isabel (Hanson) Olinger, the former a native of Blacksburg, Virginia, born June 21, 1849. He was one of the earliest Nebraska pioneers, settling in Burt County, in 1855. He left Virginia with his parents at the age of seven, traveling by rail to the Ohio River, down which they went in a river boat, and thence by ox team and covered wagon from Kansas City to Nebraska. He was of German and English descent. His death occurred at Tekamah, on March 20, 1925. Isabel Hanson was born in Kongsberg, Norway, December 1, 1856, and was brought by her parents to America at the age of two in a sailing vessel. She is a typical pioneer mother.

Mr. Olinger attended district school in Burt County, and was graduated from Tekamah High School in May, 1911. He attended the University of Nebraska College of Agriculture 1912-14, and the liberal arts college of Nebraska Wesleyan University a year and a half during 1917-18. In high school he was a member of the baseball team, and at Nebraska Wesleyan was made a member of Kappa Sigma Pi.

During 1911-12, and 1914-15, Mr. Olinger taught in rural schools. In 1923 he was county agent for Thurston County, and was student pastor from Nebraska Wesleyan University to Wabash, Nebraska in 1927. During the latter part of 1927 and 1928, he was student pastor at Wesley Chapel near Lincoln.

From 1916 to 1926, he was a breeder of Duroc-Jersey swine, and is now engaged as a farmer and stock raiser. On January 31, 1917, he was united in marriage to Mabel Irene Cornish at Tekamah. Mrs. Olinger was born near Tekamah, November 1, 1894, of English descent. They have four children, Ida Elvira, born February 5, 1918; William Oliver, born October 17, 1919; James Merritt, born March 18, 1922, and Kenneth Cornish, born August 5, 1925.

In politics, Mr. Olinger is independent. From 1912-14, he was a member of the cadet corps at the university, and during the same time was a member of the Young Men's Christian Association at the university. During 1927-28 he was a member of the latter organization at Nebraska Wesleyan.

One of the organizers of the Burt County Farm Bureau in 1924, he served as its secretary 1924-26. He was the organizer of the Co-operative Egg and Poultry Association of Oakland, in 1926, and is a member of the Farmers Union of Nebraska. Since 1928, he has been a director of School District No. 70, and from 1918-23, he was treasurer of school district No. 16. He was one of the organizers of the Burt County Co-operative Oil Company in 1928, and the Tekamah Co-operative Creamery in 1930.

Mr. Olinger's hobby is the study of philosophy. He belongs to the First Methodist Episcopal Church of Tekamah. Residence: Tekamah.

Theodore Olk

A pioneer wagon maker and implement dealer, Theodore Olk was born at Puklies, Germany, January 7, 1870. He is the son of Nicholas and Angela (Center) Olk, the former born at Butsweiler, Germany, in 1830. Nicholas Olk died in Germany in 1923. His wife, Angela, was born in Puklies, Germany, in 1835, and died there in 1880.

Theodore Olk attended the public school, and for forty years has been engaged in the implement business at Pilger. He is a Democrat and a Catholic, and is a member of the Woodmen of the World, and the Knights of Pythias. He enjoys visiting with his friends and neighbors, and is fond of fishing. He is an authority on some phases of pioneer history.

On October 3, 1912, his marriage to Miana Eckhart was solemnized at Omaha. Mrs. Olk, was born in Olenbush, Germany, in July, 1896. They have had three children, Bernard, born July 31, 1913, died December 18, 1918; Evelyn, born October 6, 1915, died December 18, 1918; and Angelen, born in 1916, died the same year. Residence: Pilger.

Robert Henry Olmsted

A native of Chilo, Ohio, Robert Henry Olmsted has been a resident of Nebraska since September, 1887. He was born January 8, 1863, son of Thomas Bingham and Irvenia E. (Porter) Olmsted. His father, a farmer, was born at Cadiz, Ohio, November 16, 1833, and died at Chilo, Ohio, March 15, 1890. He was of Scotch-Irish descent. His wife, Irvenia, was born in Brown County, Ohio, June 15, 1840, and died in Clermont County, Ohio,

December 23, 1911, and was also of Scotch-Irish descent.

Mr. Olmsted was graduated from Hanover College (Indiana), June 15, 1885, with an A. B. degree, and received his M. A. from the same college in 1912. He is a member of Delta Tau Delta. In June, 1887, he was admitted to supreme court of Ohio, and in September, 1887, he came to Omaha, and was admitted to the bar, both in the courts of Nebraska and the United States. He was elected on the Republican ticket as member of the house of representatives in 1899, and has been active in politics for many years.

He was married to Demaris Beatrice Birkhauser, of Omaha, November 23, 1889. Mrs. Olmsted was born at Hiawatha, Kansas, August 29, 1869, and is active in church and civic circles. There are three children: Florence, born December 1, 1890, married to Bentley G. McCloud, who is senior vice president of the First National Bank of Chicago. Robert H., born January 8, 1900, married Edith Royal Tyler, and is manager of the investment department of the Uptown State Bank of Chicago. Wilbert, born November 19, 1905, died May 15, 1907.

Mr. Olmsted was a participant in all drives during the World War. He is a member of the First Presbyterian Church of Florence, Nebraska, and of the American, Nebraska State and Omaha-Douglas Bar Associations. His favorite recreations are reading, working in his garden and enjoying nature. Residence: Omaha.

Hans Olsen

Hans Olsen, director of teacher training at Kearney State Teachers College, was born at Farwell, Nebraska, April 27, 1892, son of Fred and Petra Caroline (Jensen) Olsen. His father, who is now retired, was born in Fyn, Denmark, November 20, 1858, and came to the United States in 1878. His wife, Petra, was born in Fyn, April 8, 1862.

Upon the completion of his education in the Farwell Public Schools, Mr. Olsen attended high school. He received his Bachelor of Arts degree from the Nebraska State Teachers College at Kearney in 1920; in 1922 he received the degree, Master of Arts from Columbia University and in 1926 the degree, Doctor of Philosophy from the same institution. During the year 1919-1920 he attended Kansas State Agricultural College at Manhattan. He is a member of Phi Delta Kappa, Kappa Delta Pi, and Xi Phi.

During the years 1911-1913, Mr. Olsen was a teacher in the public schools of District No. 78, of Howard County. He became principal of Hope Consolidated District in Scotts Bluff County in 1916 and held that position two years. The following year he was instructor at the Bayard, Nebraska, High School. From 1919 until 1925 he was instructor at the State Teachers College at Kearney. In 1925 he was made director of Teachers Training in that institution, which position he now holds. During the summers since 1927 he has been instructor in summer sessions in the University of Kansas.

Mr. Olsen is the author of *A Study of Educational Inequalities, Being a Survey of Certain Aspects of Public Education in Buffalo County, Nebraska* (1921); *The Work of Boards of Education and How It Should Be Done* (1926); *Obstacles to School Consolidation—How These Can Be Avoided or Overcome* (1921).

On August 15, 1926, he was married to Florence Katherine Miller at Nebraska City. Mrs. Olsen was born at Nebraska City, September 25, 1900. They have one son, Hans Christian, 3rd, born April 20, 1929.

Among Mr. Olsen's professional organizations are the National Education Association and the Nebraska State Teachers Association. He is a Lutheran, a member of the Chamber of Commerce at Kearney, and a member of the Cosmopolitan Club (president 1929), and the Masons. Residence: Kearney.

Otto Frederick Olsen

Born at Fremont, Nebraska, May 3, 1894, Otto Frederick Olsen has been an editor and publisher for a number of years. He is the son of Zacharias and Mariana (Christianson) Olsen, the former a shoemaker, who was born in Humlun, Denmark, May 22, 1861. He came to America in 1885, and is now located at Fremont. Mariana, his wife, was born in Kjarby, Denmark, January 20, 1862, and came to America in 1885.

Otto Frederick Olsen was educated in the Fremont and Kennard Schools, and attended Kennard High School. He was employed six and a half years on a Danish publication at Blair, and for one year on the *Superior Express,* and for fifteen and a half years has been in business for himself, eight and a half years at Kennard, and for the past seven years as editor and publisher of the *Ceresco News.*

He was married to Minnie Rohwer at Blair, on October 21, 1914. Mrs. Olsen, who was born at Blair, July 15, 1895, is the daughter of Mr. and Mrs. Carl Rohwer of Fort Calhoun, and assists her husband in his newspaper work. There are two daughters, Lucile Marian, born November 28, 1915, who is a junior in high school; and Vera Louise, born November 4, 1918, who is a freshman.

Mr. Olsen is independent in politics. He is a musician, and has been a member of local bands since the age of twelve, and for two years was leader and clarinetist in the Ceresco band. He has also played the clarinet and violin in orchestral work for twenty years. His religious affiliation is with the Ceresco Methodist Episcopal Church. For three years he served as secretary of the Ceresco Commercial Club. He is also a member of the Volunteer Fire Department and The Nebraskana Society. Mr. Olsen's hobbies are mechanics and radio experimentation. Residence: Ceresco.

Albert Olson

Albert Olson, who has lived in Nebraska since 1905, was born at Lulea, Sweden, August 25, 1878, the son of Olof Anders and Mary Katherine (Jakobson) Olson. His father, who was a carpenter and fisherman, was born at Neder, Sweden, April 16, 1845, and died at Neder, November 24, 1918. His mother was born at Angesbyn, Sweden, January 6, 1850, and died at Neder, January 14, 1901.

Mr. Olson has been a carpenter and contractor at Cozad, Nebraska, for many years. He served as captain of a sailing vessel, *The Swan,* for two years prior to 1903. He is affiliated with the Methodist Episcopal Church of Cozad, and holds membership in The Nebraskana Society. His hobby is reading.

He was united in marriage with Hulda Margaret Nordstrom at Lincoln, Nebraska, July 29, 1905. Mrs. Olson was born at Person, Sweden, January 2, 1877. To them the following children were born: Hazel, May 26, 1906; Richard, August 29, 1907, who married Elsie Fleharty; Helen Elizabeth, March 12, 1909, who died in infancy; Lillian, February 1, 1911, who married Rex R. Young; Helen Frances, August 15, 1914; and Berniece, October 28, 1918, who died April 13, 1920. Helen was graduated from the Cozad High School, and Richard is a farmer. Residence: Cozad.

Charles Emanuel Olson

Charles E. Olson was born in Fillmore County, Nebraska, May 3, 1879, and except for a few years spent in Iowa, has lived in the state all his life. He is the son of Charles and Anna Charlotte (Johnson) Olson. His father, whose ancestry was Swedish, was a farmer, and died when Charles Olson was an infant. His mother, who was of Swedish descent, was born in Webster County, Iowa, September 15, 1858, and died at Omaha, June 4, 1910.

Mr. Olson was graduated from the public school at Marshalltown, Iowa, in 1898. A business man for many years he is now president and treasurer of the Olson Coffee Company of Omaha.

He was united in marriage with Daisy Belle Rogers at Omaha, November 26, 1910. Mrs. Olson was born of English parentage in DeWitt County, Illinois, May 11, 1881.

Mr. Olson is a member of the Omaha Chamber of Commerce; the Noon-day Luncheon Club; and the Omaha Field Club. He is a Mason, and a Democrat and is affiliated with the First Central Congregational Church of Omaha. Residence: Omaha.

George Emil Olson

George E. Olson, who has been a farmer and broom manufacturer for many years in Polk County, Nebraska, was born at Providence, Rhode Island, April 3, 1880. His father, John Olson, was born in Sweden, February 2, 1846, and came to America, May 5, 1871. His mother, Mary (Johnson) Olson, was born in Sweden, June 21, 1847, and died at Stromsburg, April 29, 1911.

Mr. Olson was a student at the Stromsburg High School, attended Bryant Business College, and later the Moody Institute of Chicago. He is a member of the Eden Baptist Church, and is independent, politically. Football and hiking are his favorite sports.

His marriage to Mayme Erontyna Swanse was solemnized at Stromsburg, June 4, 1912. They have two children: Winona Marie, who was graduated from Stromsburg High School in 1931; and Melburne Ulrick. During the World War, Mr. Olson took an active part in loan drives. Residence: Stromsburg. (Photograph in Album).

Harry Theodore Olson

Harry Theodore Olson, a leading professional man of Sargent, Nebraska, was born at Pontiac, Illinois, February 17, 1883, the son of Christian James and Louise Recka (Ipson) Olson. His father, who was a farmer, was born at Ronne, Denmark, August 24, 1844, and died at Fordland, Missouri, in October, 1926. His mother was born in Denmark October 23, 1850, and came to America in 1868; her ancestors were chiefly clergymen.

Dr. Olson was graduated from the Fremont High School in 1905, received the D. D. S. degree at the Lincoln Dental College in 1913, and for a year taught in the public schools of Minnesota. He studied telegraphy and was station agent for the Missouri and St. Louis Railway from 1906 to 1910. Since 1913 he has been engaged in the practice of dentistry at Sargent.

He is a member of the Lion's Club and the Nebraskana Society, is a member of the National Dental Association, the Nebraska Dental Association, and the district organization. He has served as a member of the board of education at Sargent since 1923, acting as secretary of the board since 1929. His sports include football, hiking, and fishing.

On August 3, 1916, he was married to Gyneth Elizabeth Wittemyer at Boulder, Colorado. Mrs. Olson, whose ancestry is German and English, was born at Sargent, February 15, 1892. Their children are: Donald, December 26, 1917; Harold, February 2, 1920; Meredith, August 3, 1923; and Marjorie, June 27, 1931. Residence: Sargent.

Nels H. Olson

Nels H. Olson, a resident of Nebraska for the past 60 years, has been a farmer near St. Edward for over 32 years, and has been active in community affairs during that time. He was born at Kristianstad, Sweden, February 23, 1866, the son of Hakan G. and Bengta (Giselson) Olson, the former a farmer who was born in Sweden, April 20, 1829, and died at Mead, Nebraska, August 10, 1909. His mother was born in Sweden, April

28, 1828, and died at Mead, Nebraska, January 5, 1912.

Mr. Olson attended the public schools at Mead, in a school on property owned by his father. He is president of the St. Edward Community Club, is a member of the City Council of St. Edward, and is a member of the council of the Woodmen of the World. He was director of the school board for over 11 years. His religious affiliation is with the Salem Lutheran Church.

His marriage to Thekla M. Isaeson occurred at Omaha, Nebraska, March 31, 1892. Mr. Olson, whose ancestry was Swedish, was born at Brookyln, New York, March 25, 1870, and died at Mead, Nebraska, July 18, 1895. To this marriage were born; Norvin, February 20, 1893; Myrtle, April 3, 1895; of his marriage to Alice Johnson at Grant, April 17, 1898, one daughter was born, Ruby, May 30, 1907. Both his sons are farmers, living near St. Edward. Residence: St. Edward.

Peter Clyde Oman

A continuous resident of Nebraska since February 17, 1882, Peter Clyde Oman was born near Bloomsburg, Pennsylvania, August 8, 1870. He is the son of Peter W. Oman, who was born at Bloomsburg, January 27, 1846, whose ancestors served in the War of the Revolution. Peter W. Oman was a farmer, and at one time was county commissioner of Wayne County. He married Martha Elizabeth Evert, who was born at Bloomsburg, July 21, 1850, and who is still living. He died at Winside, Nebraska, October 27, 1928.

Peter Clyde Oman attended public school and two terms at normal school. Since early manhood he has been engaged in farming, and is an extensive landowner. He is a member of the Methodist Episcopal Church, the Masons and the Modern Woodmen of America, and is a Democrat. He enjoys golf, and is a member of the Wayne Country Club.

He was married to Mabel Olive Prescott at Wayne, Nebraska, January 3, 1894. Mrs. Oman, who was born at Avoca, Iowa, September 29, 1875, is a musician, and active in club work, and is a member of the Daughters of the American Revolution. Her ancestors were English and came to America in 1660. Her father was Captain John H. Prescott of the Civil War, who fought in the Battle of Red River of the South, with Company G of the First New Hampshire Cavalry. There are two children, Mabel Fern, born June 10, 1896, who is a graduate of the University of Nebraska, with a Bachelor of Fine Arts degree, and who married Jason L. Gorst; and Frances Olive, born May 30, 1898, who also received a Bachelor of Fine Arts degree from the University, and who married H. Lynn Tuttle. Both are fine musicians, and are members of Alpha Rho Tau. Residence: Wayne. (Photograph on Page 906).

John Raymond O'Neal

John Raymond O'Neal was born at North Platte, Nebraska, August 24, 1891, son of Thomas and Nellie Genevieve (Walsh) O'Neal. Thomas O'Neal was born at Galesburg, Illinois, April 4, 1857, and died at Lincoln, August 15, 1921. He was interested in mechanics, and was expert in the construction of railway locomotives and boilers. His wife, Nellie Genevieve, was born at Holyoke, Massachusetts, April 20, 1867.

Mr. O'Neal was educated in the public schools of North Platte, and was graduated from Rock Island (Illinois) High School in 1906, after attending Lincoln High School three years. He was engaged in various enterprises prior to entering the automobile business in 1916. He has held the positions of salesman, sales manager, general manager of the Nebraska Oldsmobile Company and Greenlease Lied Motors. In 1928 he entered business for himself as president of the Marmon Omaha Incorporated. Since that time the name of the corporation has been changed to the J. R. O'Neal Motor Company.

On November 16, 1913 he was united in marriage to Florence Agnes Tooey at Lincoln. Mrs. O'Neal was born at Brookfield, Mo., December 17, 1891, and is of English and Irish-American ancestry. They have eight children: Mary Elizabeth, born June 13, 1915; Dorothy Anne, born June 20, 1917; Florence Lucille, born May 30, 1920; Patricia Jane, born March 2, 1924; Jean and Joan, twins, born February 28, 1926; and John Raymond Jr., and Janet Agnes, twins, born December 17, 1930. Mary Elizabeth and Dorothy Anne attend Duchesne College.

Although not an aspirant to public office, Mr. O'Neal is interested in government and government control. He is independent in politics, but his present preference is Democratic. He is a member of St. Margaret Mary's Church, and is a past member of the Kiwanis Club, Chamber of Commerce, International Sales Managers Associations, etc. His social clubs are the Omaha Athletic Club and the Omaha Field Club. He is interested in baseball and football, but enjoys no active sports himself. His hobby is political study, and the lives of prominent men. At the present time he is enjoying the *Life and Accomplishments of Alfred E. Smith*. Residence: Omaha.

William Henry O'Neill

William Henry O'Neill was born in Jackson, Nebraska, May 15, 1857, and died at Jackson, in 1931. He was the son of Patrick and Bridget (McNamara) O'Neill. His father was born in Ireland, and came to Nebraska from Ireland, with Father Tracy's Colony. After an active life as a pioneer farmer, he died at Jackson, March 10, 1908. Briget, his wife, was born in Ireland, and died at Jackson, September 29, 1909.

Educated in the public and high schools of Jackson, William Henry O'Neill became a farmer in early life, and continued until his death. He was married on January 20, 1886, to Mary Jane Mora, and since his death she has carried on the work of the farm. There are thirteen children living and four deceased.

Mr. O'Neill was a staunch Democrat, and active in the work of his party. A life resident of the state, he did much toward its development, particularly in his own community. He was a member of St. Patrick's Catholic Church of Jackson.

John Edward Opp

John Edward Opp, who has been engaged in educational work in Nebraska for the past 30 years, was born at Union, Nebraska, October 15, 1879, the son of Jacob and Ravina (Ervin) Opp. His father, who was a business executive, was born at Niederhausen, Germany, August 24, 1851, and died at Omaha, Nebraska, February 11, 1929; he came to America with his parents in 1868. His mother was born near Plum-Hollow, Fremont County, Iowa, August 15, 1855, of English and Scotch-Irish parentage.

Mr. Opp attended high school at Avoca and Weeping Water, Nebraska, was graduated from Lincoln Business College in 1902, received the Bachelor of Science degree at Fremont Normal College in 1906, received the Bachelor of Science in Education degree from the University of Nebraska in 1924, and the Master of Arts degree in 1925. He has attended summer sessions at the University of Colorado and the University of California. His fraternal organizations in college included: Phi Delta Kappa; Mathematics Club; and Pi Gamma Mu.

He has held the following professional positions: rural school teacher, one year; city teacher, two years; high school instuctor, three years; superintendent of schools at Cordova, Nebraska, 1905-09; superintendent of schools at Beaver Crossing, Nebraska, 1909-14; superintendent of schools at Sutton, Nebraska, 1914-17; superintendent of schools at Nelson, Nebraska, 1917-18; assistant instructor at the University of Nebraska, de-

Craven—Wayne

CLYDE OMAN

partment of mathematics, 1923-25; and superintendent of schools at Burwell, Nebraska, since 1926.

Mr. Opp holds membership in the National Educational Association, Nebraska Educational Association, Superintendents & Principals of Nebraska Association, and the Mathematics Association of America. He has been chairman of the Garfield County Junior Red Cross since 1928, is affiliated with the First Methodist Episcopal Church of Burwell, and holds membership in the Burwell Wranglers Club and the Masonic Lodge. His hobby is reading. His marriage to Lulu May Petty occurred at Omaha, Nebraska, April 7, 1911. Mrs. Opp, who is eligible to membership in the Daughters of the American Revolution through her paternal ancestry, was born at Wharton, Ohio, September 8, 1883, of English and German ancestry. Residence: Burwell.

John M. Opper

John M. Opper, automobile dealer, was born at Peru, Illinois, November 11, 1872, son of Christopher J. and Mary E. (Giese) Opper.

He was educated in the public school of Hastings, and was married to Rose E. Rodriguez, who was born at Lafayette, Indiana, September 4, 1888. Their only daughter, Edna May, born February 11, 1899, married Emil F. Nygaard.

Mr. Opper is a Republican. He is the owner of the J. M. Opper Motor Company, a member of the Dundee Presbyterian Church, the Chamber of Commerce, Ak-Sar-Ben, and the Omaha Auto Traders Association. His club is the Athletic Club. Residence: Omaha.

Stella Hart Organ

Stella Hart Organ, prominent in club affairs at Edgar, Clay County, Nebraska, was born there January 29, 1883, the daughter of Harris Charleton and Alice Adelaide (Hart) Organ. Her father, who is a retired banker, was born in Illinois, April 7, 1856. He served as mayor for several terms in Edgar. Her mother was born in Illinois, October 6, 1857.

Mrs. Organ was graduated from the Edgar High School in 1901. She is president of the Edgar Woman's Club, is president of the county council of the Parent Teachers Association Association, is serving as president of the Parent Teachers Association of District Number 77 in Clay County, and holds membership in the Eastern Star. She is affiliated with the Methodist Episcopal Church of Edgar, and holds membership in the Nebraskana Society. She is a Democrat.

She was married to Edgar Dean Organ at Lincoln, Lancaster County, Nebraska, November 26, 1903. Mr. Organ, who is a farmer, was born in Illinois, December 18, 1882. They have three children: Charles, born August 24, 1904, who married Myreta Kirkoff, and who is a telephone construction foreman at Fullerton, California; Lela, born September 10, 1912, who is a teacher at Harvard, Nebraska; and Dorothy Organ, who is a student at Peru State Teachers College. Residence: Edgar.

William Ormesher

William Ormesher, farmer and rancher, was born at Valentine, Nebraska, May 9, 1885, son of Henry and Elizabeth (Winstley) Ormesher. His father was born in Wiggan, England, May 5, 1849, and was a cattle dealer and rancher until his death at Chadron, August 21, 1925. His wife, Elizabeth, was born in Wiggan, England, March 4, 1851, and is still living.

Mr. Ormesher attended public school and has been in the ranching and cattle business for a number of years with his brothers under the name of The Ormesher Brothers. At the present time he is serving in his sec-

ond term as county commissioner of Dawes County. He is a Republican.

On November 28, 1907, he was married to Jessie Elizabeth Harrison at Oelrichs, South Dakota. Mrs. Ormesher was born at Chadron, August 30, 1887, and died at Boulder, Colorado, December 22, 1928. There are two children, Mary, born December 24, 1908; and Margaret, born March 25, 1911.

Mr. Ormesher is a member of the Seventh Day Adventists Church, the Chamber of Commerce, the Odd Fellows, the Masons, and the Eastern Star. His favorite sport is football. Residence: Chadron.

Margaret Holcomb Orr

Margaret Holcomb Orr was born in Shelby County, Iowa, April 22, 1865, the daughter of Zoroaster Burgess Holcomb and Eunice Elizabeth (Hankins) Holcomb. Her father, who was born in Essex County, New York, February 11, 1834, and died at Clay Center, Nebraska, May 6, 1922, was a teacher; he served as county clerk and county treasurer and was an ardent Republican; for many years he was a farmer. Mrs. Orr is a descendant of Sir John Holcomb who was a descendant of William the Conqueror through inter-marriage.

Mrs. Orr's mother was born, of Irish and English parents, in Lewis County, Missouri, November 11, 1840, and died at Clay Center, July 15, 1919. Mrs. Orr attended public schools of Shelby County and later attended the high school at Dunlap, Iowa. Later she was a student at Stanbury Normal School, Stanbury, Missouri. From 1883 to 1894 she engaged in teaching school in Iowa and Missouri.

Mrs. Orr is a member of the Reorganized Church of Jesus Christ of Latter Day Saints, was county president of the Woman's Christian Temperance Union until 1919, and holds membership in the Parent Teachers Association. She has been a member of the local Red Cross since 1916, and is a member of the Clay Center Woman's Club, and was formerly a member of the Royal Neighbors.

In 1913 she became a member of the Daughters of the American Revolution and organizing regent in the chapter at Clay Center, Nebraska. She holds membership in the American Legion Auxiliary, and was formerly especially active in temperance and women's suffrage work. Most of Mrs. Orr's leisure time is spent in gardening and landscaping.

On February 11, 1891, she was united in marriage to Edward Wilson Orr at St. Joseph, Missouri. Mr. Orr, who was a flour miller, was born at Janesville, Wisconsin, November 4, 1864, and died at Clay Center, November 8, 1929; his ancestry was English and German. Two sons were born to this marriage: Lesley Kenneth, April 24, 1896, who married Harriet Mae Ward; and Burgess Henry, May 3, 1899, who married Mary Esther Keyes. Both of them attended the University of Nebraska and served in the World War. They are now engaged in the occupation of their forefathers, since their great-grandfather was a flour miller in England, their grandfather was a miller in Wisconsin, and their father took up this occupation in Missouri and Nebraska.

They are proprietors of the Orr Brothers Mill, and two of the leading business men in Clay Center. Both enlisted in the World War and are members of the American Legion, the K. of P., and Kappa Sigma. They are Republicans. Residence: Clay Center.

William McCullough Orr

William M. Orr, son of Alexander and Mary Jane (McCullough) Orr, was born at Blairs Mills, Pennsylvania, October 19, 1857, and has been a resident of Nebraska for twenty-seven years. His father, Alexander Orr, was born in Blairs Mills, in 1832, and died at Concord, Pennsylvania, in 1903. He was a carpenter of Scotch-Irish descent, who served in the Civil War. Mary Jane McCullough was born in Blairs Mills, in 1828, and died at Concord, in 1896.

Educated in the public schools of Franklin County, Pennsylvania, William M. Orr has devoted his entire life to the mercantile business. A Republican, he has served as mayor of Wayne, for eleven years, and is treasurer of the Wayne County chapter of the Red Cross.

Of his marriage to Emma D. Morris there are two children, Carroll A., born November 24, 1889, who married Helen McCullough; and Neva J., born August 24, 1894, who married A. T. Cavanaugh. The family attends the First Presbyterian Church of Wayne, and Mr. Orr is a member of the Kiwanis and the Masons. Residence: Wayne.

Louis Ortquist

A successful merchant at Hebron, Nebraska, for the past 16 years, Louis Ortquist is now the owner and manager of The Ortquist Store. He was born at Fremont, Nebraska, February 26, 1886, the son of Alex and Lena (Johnson) Ortquist. His father, who was a railroad man, was born in Sweden, came to America in 1880, and died at Elgin, Nebraska, in 1901. His mother was born in Sweden, and died at Fremont, in 1915.

Mr. Ortquist was graduated from the Elgin High School in 1901, and almost immediately entered the business world as a clerk at Fremont. He remained in that capacity until 1914, when he moved to Hebron, and opened his own establishment of which he is still owner and manager.

He is a member of the Hebron Commercial Club, holds membership in the American Federated Retailers' Association, and was recently elected to membership in the Nebraskana Society. Mr. Ortquist is affiliated with the Republican party. Residence: Hebron.

Charlie Joe Osborn

Charlie Joe Osborn, retired farmer, was born near Butler, Illinois, June 30, 1862, son of Samuel Cumbest and Lydia Ann (Kendirck) Osborn, the former was a farmer.

Mr. Osborn attended public school and has been a farmer in Nebraska until his recent retirement. For a period of years he was a member of the state board of directors of the Farmers Educational and Co-operative Union of Nebraska, and was elected president of that organization, serving from 1921 until 1925. During that period he served on the board of the Farmers Educational and Co-operative Union of America. At the present time Mr. Osborn is affiliated with the Republican party. From 1894 until 1895 he was county clerk of Cheyenne County, and at one time was a candidate for state senator.

He is married to Iva Luticia Bewley. Mrs. Osborn was born near Honey Bend, Illinois, December 24, 1864. Seven children were born to them, five of whom are living. Leo E., born June 2, 1884, married Anna Stuht; Maynard Waldo, born July 16, 1888, married Jessie Huff; Viola Blanch, born April 14, 1891, married N. S. Miller; Jesse Rozel, born November 2, 1894, married Olga Gebauer; Clifford June, born June 18, 1906, married Mildred Gurr; Sidney Roscoe, born May 23, 1886, died March 8, 1888; and Tiny Ruth, born December 14, 1892, died January 1, 1893.

Mr. Osborn has been outstanding in his community for many years and was recently made a life member of The Nebraskana Society. His religious affiliation is with Lemon Memorial Methodist Episcopal Church. Residence: Sidney.

George Carlisle Osborn

George Carlisle Osborn, prominent Box Butte County farmer, was born at New Wilmington, Pennsylvania, December 20, 1886, son of Jacob Cyrus and Sarah Margaret (Moore) Osborn.

His father was born at Mercer, Pennsylvania, May 10, 1855, and homesteaded northeast of Hemingford in the fall of 1892. He made that homestead his home until his death at Kearney, September 13, 1926. His Scotch-Irish ancestors came to America about 1740, settling in New Jersey and later moving to Venango County Pennsylvania.

Sarah Margaret Moore, his wife, was born at Washington, Pennsylvania, April 13, 1859, and died at Hemingford, September 3, 1904. She was very musical and an active worker in Sunday school and church. Her ancestry was Scotch-Irish, and she was a descendant of General Mercer of the Revolutionary War, after which Mercer County and the city of Mercer in Pennsylvania were named.

Upon the completion of his common school education, Mr. Osborn attended high school two years at Hemingford. He is since engaged in farming. He is a Republican, a member of the First Congregational Church, the Modern Woodmen of America, the Nebraskana Society, and the school board. He was moderator of district No. 125 from July 1, 1910, until July 1, 1913. For eight years he has been a member of the church choir and has been superintendent of the Congregational Sunday School for four years. He enjoys music and at the present time sings in quartets for church and civic entertainments.

On November 21, 1907, he was married to Anna Lilly McBurney at Alliance. Mrs. Osborn was born at Pittsburgh, Pennsylvania, July 25, 1889, of Scotch-Irish and German descent. To them were born seven children, four of whom are living, Jacob Gilson, born November 16, 1908, died January 4, 1909; Alberta Virginia, born December 11, 1909; Bernice Elva, born December 21, 1911, died January 9, 1932; Lorena, born April 20, 1914; George Carlisle, born July 22, 1916; Evalyne Margaret, born August 19, 1919; and Phyllis Ione, born October 21, 1921, died the same day. Residence: Hemingford.

Thomas C. Osborne

Thomas C. Osborne, farmer and clergyman, was born near Bloomington, Illinois, September 9, 1876, son of Samuel H. and Emily Willis (Benson) Osborne. His mother's ancestry is Scotch-Irish and English, the first member of her family having come to America about 1780. His father's ancestors settled in Maryland about 1635, and were of English descent.

Mr. Osborne attended Hastings College until 1901, and the Omaha Seminary until 1904. He was later awarded an honorary degree of Doctor of Divinity from Hastings College. A Democrat, he was a member of the Nebraska Constitutional Convention of 1919-20, and in 1923 served as state senator from the 33rd district of Nebraska.

On December 21, 1903, he was married to Julia Mary Jones at Hastings. Mrs. Osborne was born at Oneida, Illinois, November 13, 1880. They have five children: Emily, born September 17, 1904; Charles, born September 25, 1906; Clifford, born June 21, 1908; Howard, born July 31, 1910; and John, born June 20, 1919. Residence: Alliance.

Joseph Benjamin Osbourn

Joseph Benjamin Osbourn, real estate and insurance man, was born at Chicago, Illinois, August 30, 1864, son of Lewis Grant and Mary Deans (Skeet) Osbourn. The

EDWARD JOSEPH O'SHEA

Nelson—Holdrege

father, a native of Philadelphia, born October 10, 1810, was a homesteader in Custer County, who served as postmaster at Pilot, Nebraska. He died at Mason City, May 24, 1894. His wife, Mary, was born near London, England, May 4, 1839, and died at Hastings in August, 1922.

Educated first in the public schools of Illinois, Joseph B. Osbourn was graduated from high school at Waverly, Illinois, in the class of 1881. The following year he came to Nebraska, and on April 19, 1888, was married to Methelide Ager at Kearney. Mrs. Osbourn who was born at Menasha, Wisconsin, November 25, 1970, was of Norwegian descent.

There are five children, Helen Josephine, born October 25, 1889, who married John Herstead; Elsie May, born December 31, 1891, who married E. C. Carothers; Lewis Allen, born December 29, 1893, who is unmarried; Mary Deans, born February 10, 1896, who married D. D. King; and Carl Edley, born February 15, 1899, who married Catherine White.

In the real estate and insurance business most of his life, Mr. Osbourn served as county clerk of Custer County 1900 and 1901. He is a member of the United Brethren Church at Broken Bow, the Broken Bow Public Service Club, the Odd Fellows and The Nebraskana Society. Residence: Broken Bow.

Edward Joseph O'Shea

A printer for more than forty years, Edward Joseph O'Shea was born at Boston, Massachusetts, July 26, 1876, son of William John and Mary Ann (Hughes) O'Shea. The father, born in Manchester, England, April 21, 1834, was a bookbinder, who came to the United States in 1871, and died at Chicago, October 14, 1912. His wife, Mary Ann, also born in Manchester, but on September 29, 1848, died at Lincoln, April 17, 1916. Both were of Irish descent.

Edward Joseph O'Shea attended public and parochial schools at Lincoln, and was graduated from St. Teresa's Parochial High School. On August 27, 1910, he was married to Laura Caroline Cooper at Holdrege. Mrs. O'Shea was born at Bloomfield, Iowa, February 14, 1882. To them were born four children: Frances Ann, born August 13, 1911; William James, born March 4, 1913, died June 20, 1931; Mary Elizabeth, born February 14, 1915; and Edward Joseph, Jr., born August 24, 1918.

During his long career in the printing business, Mr. O'Shea was employed by J. D. Calhoun, Sam D. Cox, J. D. Bushnell and many others, and had considerable early newspaper experience in California, Oregon and Washington. At the present time he is secretary-treasurer and business manager of The Progress Printing Company, and editor of its publication, *The Holdrege Progress.*

A veteran of the Spanish-American War, Mr. O'Shea served as a musician, Company D, First Nebraska Volunteer Infantry, in the Philippines. He is a member of the Veterans of Foreign Wars, and is now serving as adjutant of George R. Mitchell, Post No. 1365, United Spanish War Veterans.

Mr. O'Shea is a member of All Soul's Catholic Church, the Chamber of Commerce, Lodge No. 159 of the Elks, the Nebraskana Society and the Holdrege Country Club. A charter member of the Rotary Club, he resigned in 1931. He is a Democrat. Mr. O'Shea enjoys golf, while his hobby is mechanics. Residence: Holdrege. (Photograph on Page 909).

Eugene Daniel O'Sullivan

For the past 25 years Eugene D. O'Sullivan has been prominent in civic and political affairs at Omaha, and since 1910, has been engaged in the practice of law there. He was born at Kent, Reno County, Kansas, May 31, 1883, the son of John Edward and Josephine (Kluh) O'Sullivan. His father, who was born at Newport, Rhode Island, September 27, 1853, and died at Kent, December 31, 1892, was a cattle raiser and farmer; he was graduated

from high school in Rhode Island, and in 1872, moved from Newport, to Kansas; his ancestors were Irish people who lived in County Cork, Ireland, for centuries, and were chiefly priests, teachers, or scholars.

His mother was born at Hauscourz, Kreis Fulda, Germany, January 20, 1853, and is now living at Omaha. She received her high school education in Germany, and in 1872 came to America with relatives for the purpose of buying land. Her German ancestors were builders and contractors.

Mr. O'Sullivan attended the public school at Kent, and in 1896, was graduated from the grade school there, one of the youngest students to graduate; he was class leader in scholastic honors. In 1903, he was graduated from Christian Brothers College at St. Joseph, Missouri, with class honors of valedictorian; was a student at St. Benedict's College at Atchison, Kansas, 1905-06; and received his LL. B. degree at Creighton University in 1910. He was active in dramatics at St. Benedict's College and contributed to the school magazine.

He received his degree, *cum laude* from Creighton University where he held the highest class average and was an honor man. He played football and baseball at Christian Brothers College, and at St. Benedict's College, and was a member of the track team at the former. He was admitted to the bar at Omaha, Douglas County, Nebraska, May, 1910.

Mr. O'Sullivan was connected with the law office of Crane and Boucher at Omaha, 1910-11; was a member of the firm Jamieson & O'Sullivan, 1912-22; was a member of the firm Jamieson, O'Sullivan, & Southard, 1922-27; and since 1927 is a member of the firm O'Sullivan & Southard. A Democrat, he has always been vitally interested in the political life of the state. He served as deputy county attorney of Douglas County, 1918-19, under George A. Magney, and served as delegate to the Democratic national conventions at New York, 1924, and Houston, Texas, 1928.

His marriage to Ellen Katherine Lovely, was solemnized at Omaha, June 12, 1918. Mrs. O'Sullivan was born at Omaha, January 26, 1893. Her father was born in Canada, of Irish parentage; her mother was born at Carroll, Iowa, of Irish parentage. They have two children: Eugene Daniel, born December 20, 1919; and Mary Ann, born October 30, 1924.

He is a member of the Omaha Bar Association; the State Bar Association; American Bar Association; the Omaha Chamber of Commerce; and the South Omaha Merchant's Association. He is an Elk and an Eagle. He is affiliated with St. Bridget's Catholic Church, and is a member of the Knights of Columbus. His social clubs are the Lakewood Club and the 20-20 Club. His sports include hunting, fishing, and golf. Residence: Omaha. (Photograph on Page 911).

Lumir Fred Otradovsky

Born in Schuyler, Nebraska, December 13, 1906, Lumir F. Otradovsky is the son of Joseph Henry and Anna (Dudek) Otradovsky. His father, who was born at Caslav, Czechoslovakia, July 22, 1873, has been a grocer in Schuyler, for more than forty years, having come to Nebraska, in May, 1890. His wife, Anna, was born in Brno, Czechoslovakia, November 6, 1873, and is still living.

Lumir F. Otradovsky attended Schuyler public and high school and was graduated from the latter in 1924. In June, 1929, he received his LL. B., *cum laude,* from the Univerity of Nebraska, and was the recipient of the following honors: Order of the Coif, Pershing Award (1928), N Club, and photograph editor of the *Cornhusker* (1928-29). He is a member of Theta Chi and was president 1927-28, and is a Phi Delta Phi. During 1925-26,26-27, and 27-28, he was a member of the University Rifle Team and was captain the last mentioned year.

From June, 1929, to January, 1931, he was associated in law practice at Schuyler, and was elected county attorney of Colfax County in 1930. He has also served as

EUGENE DANIEL O'SULLIVAN

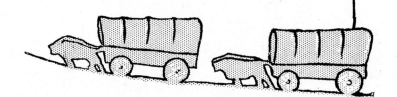

city attorney of Schuyler. He is a Republican. At the present time he holds the rank of second lieutenant in the 355th Infantry Reserves. He is a Mason, a member of the First Presbyterian Church, and the American and Nebraska State Bar Associations. He finds his recreation in golf, hunting and fishing, and his hobby is photography. Residence: Schuyler.

Daniel Lewis Ough

Daniel Lewis Ough, real estate, insurance and farm manager, was born at Green River, Illinois, May 4, 1875, son of John Clemins and Mary Ann (Moore) Ough.

The father was born near Princeton, Bureau County, Illinois, August 4, 1855, and died at Benkleman, May 31, 1919. He was a farmer, merchant, and hotel operator, who also served as county treasurer of Dundy County, Nebraska. His father came to America from Cornwall, England. The mother, born at Colona, Illinois, December 25, 1854, is of Irish descent.

Mr. Ough attended country district school, in Illinois and Nebraska, where he had the good fortune to study philosophy, Latin, algebra, surveying, music, and civics, with C. L. Brainard, a graduate of Nebraska University, after which he attended high school at Benkleman, Nebraska. He has a credit of one year in law, having studied in the law office of Judge J. W. James. During 1898 and 1899, and in 1905 he was associated with the John Roemmich General Merchandise store. He ranched during 1900, 1901, 1902, and 1903 and began a real estate and insurance business in 1910, which he has since conducted. During that time he has managed farms, organized the Farmers Exchange, and served three years as secretary of the County Fair Board. He is president of the local Federal Land Bank Association and has held other offices.

A Republican, he was county treasurer of Dundy County from 1906 until 1910, trustee of Benkleman, 1916-22, and state representative from the 87th district of Nebraska 1925-32, inclusive. He was a promoter of legislation, equalizing the tax burden and the opportunities of school children to obtain an education.

At the present time Mr. Ough is president of the Masonic Temple Association and a member of the depositors committee of the failed Farmers and Merchants Bank. He is a stockholder in the Farmers Grain Company.

For a number of years Mr. Ough has been prominent in every civic development in his community. He has written propaganda putting over the new court house, the Benkleman sewer, the high school, the modern city power plant, and the state highway through Dundy County. He is a member of the Ancient Free and Accepted Masons, the Royal Arch Masons and the Eastern Star. He is past master of Justice Lodge No. 180, Ancient Free and Accepted Masons, and also past patron of Holly Chapter No. 233, O. E. S. He was state clerk in 1912 of the Modern Woodmen and delegate to the Head Camp of the Woodmen at Toledo, Ohio, in 1914. He is a musician, his hobby is really music, and he plays the violin and sings in the choir of the Methodist Episcopal Church at Benkelman, where he holds membership. He is secretary of the Dundy County chapter of the Red Cross and a member of the Chamber of Commerce.

He was married on June 5, 1901, to Anna Elizabeth McDonald at Benkelman. Mrs. Ough was born at Marysville, Kansas, September 4, 1874; was a school teacher before her marriage also a teacher of music. She is of Scotch descent. There are five children, all living, Walter L., born March 16, 1902, an automobile mechanic; Marguerite E., born July 19, 1903; Helen R., born March 20, 1906; Melba I., born July 7, 1910; and Genevieve A., born February 24, 1913, all born in Benkelman, Nebraska. All of the girls have taught school, Helen and Melba have life certificates for teaching, Marguarite is

a student at the State University of Nebraska, and Genevieve is teaching in Dundy County. Residence: Benkelman. (Photograph in Album).

Albert Bernard Outhouse

Albert Bernard Outhouse was born at Huey, Illinois, May 22, 1862, the son of Oliver and Maria (Gerdes) Outhouse, and since 1887, has been a resident of Nebraska. His father, a farmer, was born in Clinton County, Illinois, June 26, 1826, and died there on November 18, 1882. He was the son of Joseph Outhouse (born July 20, 1802; died May 25, 1846), who was the son of Peter Outhouse, a Revolutionary soldier, born in 1757, and who died in 1836.

Marie Gerdes was a native of Hanover, Germany, born December 3, 1834, who came to America with her parents in 1850, settling at Vandalia, Illinois. There she married William Houseman who died in 1858. She married Oliver Outhouse in 1860, and died at Loup City, Nebraska, August 23, 1903.

Albert Bernard Outhouse attended country school in Clinton County, Illinois. In 1877 he entered into the retail merchandise store owned by his father at Huey, Illinois. He came to Loup City, Nebraska, in 1887. Here he organized and incorporated the Keystone Lumber Company, with headquarters at Loup City. From the date of the incorporation he was treasurer and manager. In 1907, he became owner of all the stock. He is now president of the Keystone Lumber Company, owning lumber yards at Loup City, Rockville, Arcadia, and Boelus, Nebraska. In addition he has served as director, vice president, and is now president of the First National Bank at Loup City.

A Republican, Mr. Outhouse has been prominent in local politics, and has held the following offices: member of the city council 1893-94, 1904-06; mayor, 1910-13. He is a member of the Nebraska Lumber Dealers Association (director 1906); the Patriarchs Militant, and the Independent Order of Odd Fellows, (treasurer 1893-1918).

Mr. Outhouse is interested in essays, likes to supervise the management of farms, and has devoted much time to tree planting. He has given more than a thousand trees to the local fair association, and to farmers in the vicinity of Loup City.

On November 28, 1887, he was married to Mary Rebecca Prather, at Huey, Illinois. Mrs. Outhouse, who is a descendant of James Prather, a Revolutionary soldier, was born in Clinton County, Illinois, December 19, 1862. She was a teacher before her marriage. To them the following children were born: Meroe, born August 25, 1889; Emma, born January 22, 1891, who died September 6, 1917; Winifred, born November 26, 1893, who married Frank J. Parr, on November 5, 1921; Orpha, born November 27, 1895, who married William H. Leininger, and who died November 25, 1922; Alberta, born June 1, 1898, who married Milo E. Daily; and A. Raymond, December 16, 1900, who married Louise Goodbrod, on February 11, 1922.

The elder daughters were formerly teachers, Meroe is principal of the high school at Stanton, while Alberta was formerly an active worker with the Red Cross Social Service. A. Raymond is treasurer of the Keystone Lumber Company, having been associated with the firm since 1922. He is serving as mayor of Loup City, and is a member of the local school board. Residence: Loup City. (Photograph on Page 913).

Ira Overstake

Ira Overstake, a merchant at Lebanon for a number of years, was born in Seward County, Nebraska, February 1, 1875, and is the son of Henry and Melissa Jane (Snyder) Overstake, who came to Nebraska in 1871.

The father was born at Hillsboro, Ohio, October 9, 1836, and died at Lexington, Nebraska, November 11, 1913. He was a pioneer Nebraska farmer, of Pennsylvania Dutch descent. His wife, Melissa, was born at

Locke—Grand Island

ALBERT BERNARD OUTHOUSE

Hillsboro, Ohio, August 29, 1834, and died at Lebanon, Nebraska, October 20, 1911.

Upon his graduation from high school, Mr. Overstake entered the mercantile business, in which he has since remained.

He was married on November 29, 1912, to Ruth Agnes Waugh at David City, Nebraska. Mrs. Overstake was born at Lebanon, Nebraska, January 17, 1895. They have one son, Henry Dean, born August 15, 1919, at Holdrege, Nebraska.

Mr. Overstake is a Methodist and a Democrat. He is interested in all sports, but his hobbies are fishing and hunting. Residence: Lebanon.

George T. Overton

George T. Overton was born at Laceyville, Pennsylvania, August 4, 1856, the son of Sanford B. and Matilda A. (Cox) Overton. His father, who was born in Bradford County, March 24, 1810, and died at Nebraska City, May 2, 1885, was a farmer. His mother was born in Bradford County, March 6, 1817, and died at Nebraska City, December 26, 1889.

Mr. Overton received his elementary education in the public schools of Bradford County, Pennsylvania. He came to Nebraska in 1880, and has lived in this state for 52 years. A farmer all his life. He is now retired.

He was married to Grace Pendleton at Nebraska City, January 5, 1885. Mrs. Overton was born in Nebraska City, August 14, 1865, and died there June 10, 1929. There are three children: Mabel, born November 9, 1887, who married C. H. Bickel; Carl Pendleton, born January 6, 1891, who married Arminta Nichols; and Ernest Truman, born July 3, 1894, who married Rachel Crow.

Mr. Overton is affiliated with the Methodist Episcopal Church at Nebraska City. He is a Republican. Residence: Nebraska City.

George Edwin Overturf

George Edwin Overturf, leading merchant and executive of Hastings, was born near Elk Creek, Nebraska, April 20, 1886, and has been a life resident of the state. He is the son of John Lake and Alzina M. (Sheldon) Overturf, the former a farmer, whose German ancestors came to the United States about 1790. John L. Overturf was born in Licking County, Ohio, September 25, 1850, and died at Bird City, Kansas, January 11, 1911. His wife, Alzina, also a native of Licking County, was born July 10, 1853, and died at Bird City, August 12, 1928. Of an early Kentucky family, she was the mother of fourteen children.

Educated in the country schools of Nemaha County until 1904, Mr. Overturf lived on a farm until the age of twenty-two, when he served a period of two years as bookkeeper in the German National Bank. From February, 1912, until January 1, 1919, he was employed in the County Treasurer's Office at Hastings as bookkeeper and deputy county treasurer. The following ten years were spent as secretary and treasurer of the Wolbach and Brach Department Store in Hastings, and for the past three years he has been secretary and treasurer of the City Fuel and Feed Company, Inc., of Hastings.

His marriage to Nellie McDonald was solemnized at Hastings on June 25, 1910, and of this marriage there are three sons, Lee Lake, born January 30, 1912; Donald Sheldon, born July 10, 1916, and George Edwin, Jr., born November 16, 1927. Mrs. Overturf, who is of Scotch-Irish descent, was born in Menard County, Illinois, February 2, 1888.

Mr. Overturf is a Republican, and was unsuccessful candidate for the city council. For five years he was a member of the Hastings school board, and during 1927 was president of the Hastings Lions Club. He participated in all civilian activities during the World War, and is still a member of the Red Cross. Among his civic and religious organizations are the Chamber of Commerce, the First Presbyterian Church and the Young Men's Christian Association, and he also holds membership in the Hastings Museum, of which he has been secretary and treasurer since 1926, the Knights of Pythias, and The Nebraskana Society. Mr. Overturf is fond of golf, and is a member of the Hillside Country Club. His hobby is reading. Residence: Hastings. (Photograph in Album).

Leonard Joseph Owen

Leonard J. Owen, surgeon, was born at Topeka, Kansas, November 21, 1892, the son of Ralph Orloff and Anna Elizabeth (Diettrich) Owen. His father, who was born in Shelby County, Indiana, September 21, 1864, has been a railroad man for many years. His Welsh ancestors came to America about 1800, and were pioneers in Indiana. Leonard Owen's mother was born at Topeka, February 23, 1867. Her ancestors were prominent in North Carolina during the Revolution, and were pioneers in Kansas in the pre-Civil War Period.

Dr. Owen was graduated from the high school at Colorado Springs, in 1910. He was a student at Colorado College from 1911 to 1915. In 1920 he was granted the M. D. degree at Washington University in St. Louis. He was active in footbal while he was in high school and college. He was admitted to the practice of medicine at St. Louis, May, 1920.

For a time he was resident surgeon at the Skin and Cancer Hospital at St. Louis; has been in private practice for about ten years; and for the last four years has been deputy superintendent of the Lincoln Health Department, and epidemiologist. He is the author of various articles on medical subjects. He has lived in Nebraska for 10 years.

On May 14, 1921, he was married to Ruth LaVerne Anderson at Minneapolis, Minnesota. Mrs. Owen, who was born at Girard, Kansas, June 15, 1894, is descended from an old Virginia family that has been in America for over 100 years. They have three children: Ruth Leota, born September 22, 1924; Leonard Jay, born February 24, 1926; and Lawrence M., born January 1, 1928.

Dr. Owen served in the medical corps during the World War. He is a member of the American Legion; the Lancaster County Medical Society; and the Nebraska State Medical Association; holds a fellowship in the American Medical Association; is a member of the Optimist Club, the Hiram Club, the Young Men's Christian Association, and the Nebraskana Society. He is a Mason, and a Modern Woodman of America, and a member of the training school staff of the St. Elizabeth Hospital. For many years he was a Seventh Day Adventist. He is fond of golf. His hobby is history. He is an independent Democrat. Residence: Lincoln.

Sidney Owen

Sidney Owen, who is supervisor of trade and industrial education for the State of Nebraska, was born at Walnut Grove, Missouri, son of Joseph Henry and Alice (Robinson) Owen. His father was born in Polk County, Missouri, in 1862, and died at Modesto, California, in 1917. He was a farmer and business man in Missouri until 1889 when he removed to California. Of Welsh descent, his ancestors came through Boonsboro, and Owensboro, Kentucky, and settled in Missouri. Alice Robinson Owen was also a native of Missouri, and is still living.

Mr. Owen received his education in the public and high schools of California, and received his B. S. from the Colorado Agricultural College; afterward he attended the University of Arizona. He was married to Clara Anita Peterson at Phoenix, Arizona, on May 28, 1928. Mrs. Owen was born at Badger, Iowa, May 7, 1901. She is a registered nurse and is of Norwegian descent. They have one son, Sidney, Jr., born February 12, 1930.

For the past year Mr. Owen has held the position of state supervisor of trade and industrial education. He has had extensive trade experience as an expert machinist, chief machinist in a copper mine in charge of the maintenance of mill, mine, filtration plant, and concentrator, and the short line railroad owned by the copper company by whom he was employed. For two years he was a machinery dealer, handling agriculural farm power machines, contractors supplies, mine and mill as well as road building machinery. In connection with this business he maintained a completely equipped service shop and had a small group of apprentices in training.

He was for two and a half years instructor in machine shop practice, forge shop, ox-acetylene welding, shop sketching, shop mathematics and blue print reading in day, evening and part time classes in the Phoenix Union High School. He came to Nebraska from Phoenix where he had been for four years director of vocational education. His responsibilities there were promotional, contacting industry, supervisory, administrative, selection and training of trade teachers and publicity of program. His field covered trades and industries, home economics, agriculture, retail selling and registered nurses training. The types of classes were all-day, general continuation, part-time and evening extension.

As part of his office as supervisor Mr. Owen has written numerous articles, bulletins, etc., on vocational education. For the past five years he has been a member of the Trade and Industrial Club, of which he was chairman during 1928-29. He is a Rotarian, and a member of the Knights of the Round Table International. His clubs are the University of Arizona Alumni Club, the Colorado Agricultural College Alumni Club, and the Lambda Sigma Fraternity. Residence: Lincoln.

Claire Estelle Owens

Dr. Claire Estelle Owens, one of Nebraska's most prominent women in professional and civic affairs, has resided in this state all her life. She was born in a sod house on her parents' homestead near Exeter, Nebraska, January 31, 1876, the daughter of Lewis Dudley and Harriet (Totton) Owens. Her father was born at Greensburg, Indiana, May 6, 1847, and was a pioneer farmer in Fillmore County, Nebraska; he died at Geneva, Nebraska, April 10, 1918. His parents, John and Joanna (Hummer) Owens, who were of Welsh descent, were Kentuckians.

Harriet (Totton) Owens, one of the early pioneer women in Nebraska, was born at Oxford, Butler County, Ohio, December 19, 1848, the daughter of Albert and Elibabeth (Bradford) Totton. She is still living.

Blind since the age of eight, Dr. Owens attended the public schools of Fillmore County for a time and in 1898 was graduated from the Nebraska School for the Blind at Nebraska City. She received the degree of Doctor of Osteopathy at Des Moines College in 1921.

A teacher in the public schools at Fairmont, Nebraska, from 1899 to 1902, she was supervisor of music in public schools at Exeter a period of seventeen years 1898 to June 1903; 1907-June 1909; and September 1913-June 1916. She taught from 1907 to 1917 at Geneva, and from 1905-07 was supervisor of music at Oakland and Macedonia, Iowa. In addition to her school work she taught piano, voice and dramatics in private classes. Since 1921 she has been an osteopathic physician at Exeter.

A Democrat, Dr. Owens has been unusually active in politics in Fillmore County, acting as legislative representative from District 54 in Fillmore County during the session held in 1930-31; regular and special; and candidate for that position in 1928. She was president of the Exeter Woman's Club for four years, was president of the Nebraska Association of Workers for the Blind for two years, served as a member of the board of di-

rectors of the Fillmore County Federation of Woman's Clubs for four years, and acted as director of the local Red Cross, two years. She is now president of the Nebraska Women's Osteopathic Association, is a member of the Exeter Commercial Club, and is affiliated with the First Presbyterian Church.

She is a member of the Fillmore County Red Cross, the American Association for the Workers for the Blind, the American Osteopathic Association, and the Nebraska Osteopathic Association. Dr. Owens was a member of the board of education at Geneva, 1922-23, and served in that capacity at Exeter, 1924-27. She was recently elected to membership in the Nebraskana Society. Her hobby is traveling. Residence: Exeter. (Photograph in Album).

Griffith John Owens

Griffith John Owens, prominent merchant and lumber executive at Benkelman, Nebraska, was born at Rewey, Wisconsin, December 7, 1877, the son of George Washington and Jane (Roberts) Owens. His father, who was a grain buyer for over 40 years, was born at Rewey, March 18, 1855; he has served as mayor and has held many offices in the Independent Order of Odd Fellows and the Knights of Pythias. His mother was born at Rewey, September 12, 1855, both are still living; she reared three sons, a soldier, an educator, and a successful business man.

Mr. Owens bought grain for the Hunting Elevator Company at Rosecreek, Minnesota, until 1905, when he came to Nebraska and managed a store and a ranch at Parks. He was engaged in the real estate and insurance business for two years, and for the past 18 years has been in the lumber business, acting as president of the Owens Lumber Company at this time. He has been a director in the Bank of Benkelman prior to its consolidation with the Farmers and Merchants Bank, and is connected with the Dundy County Telephone Company.

On June 3, 1903, he married Agnes Bagan at LeRoy, Minnesota, Mrs. Owens, who was born at LeRoy, May 10, 1877, is of Irish descent. She is actively indentified with the womans club as well as with the activities of her church. Her uncle, J. R. Phelan, built a railroad in the west and was general superintendent of the Chicago, Burlington & Quincy Railroad at Alliance, Nebraska. Four children were born to their marriage: Joseph, September 3, 1909, who is manager of a lumber yard at Parks; Daniel, May 26, 1911; Genevieve, June 25, 1904, who is a teacher, and Berneta, May 10, 1907, who died March 15, 1908. Daniel is a student at Creighton University, taking an Academic course.

Mr. Owens has never held public offices, but has always been active in securing able men to hold county and state positions. He has served as a member of the town board, the school board, and the county fair board, and has served as president of the Chamber of Commerce for a period of 10 years. He was secretary of the board of education for three years, and at this time is affiliated with St. Joseph's Catholic Church, was director in the Red Cross, and has been superintendent of the Salvation Army in Dundy County.

His chief outside interests are: geology; reading; poetry; nature studies; and agriculture. During the World War Mr. Owens sold Liberty bonds in every loan drive, and was prominent in the Red Cross. He was recently elected to membershiip in The Nebraskana Society. Residence: Benkelman.

Ferdinand Pacal

Ferdinand Pacal, banker and musician, was born in Moravia, Austria, July 20, 1878, son of John and Josephine (Horky) Pacal. His father, born at Preskov, Moravia, February 2, 1851, came to Wahoo, June 25, 1883, and located at Weston, on September 28, 1883. A weaver, railroad laborer, painter and paper hanger, he died at

Weston, on June 7, 1929. His wife, Josephine, was born at Mala Oslavicka, Velka Medric, Moravia, January 15, 1857, and died at Weston, June 8, 1927.

Educated in the public schools of Weston, Mr. Pacal was graduated in May, 1893, and attended Omaha Commercial College and a summer term at Fremont Normal College. He taught in the schools of District No. 76, Saunders County, from 1896-99, inclusive, and in District No. 103, at Weston, from 1900-10. From April 13, 1910, to April 15, 1930, he was cashier of the Farmers and Merchants Bank of Weston. At the present time he is in the insurance business, and teaches music. For more than thirty years he has been a correspondent of the *Wahoo Wasp*, and is the author of *Village Belles*, band march, copyrighted in 1906.

Mr. Pacal has always been active in politics and was secretary of the board of education 1914-15 (resigned), village clerk of Weston, 13 years, resigned about 1914. He was Republican candidate for county clerk, defeated by 38 votes in 1904; and was treasurer of the Saunders County Progressive (Bull Moose) party when Theodore Roosevelt and Hiram Johnson were candidates in 1912. He had been Republican committeeman from Chapman precinct for many years.

On October 27, 1912, he was united in marriage to Nellie Mae Madigan at Wahoo. Mrs. Pacal, who is of Irish and English descent, was born at Weston, September 9, 1879.

Mr. Pacal has been director and instructor in The 20th Century Band at Weston for about twenty years. He is a member of the Wahoo Lodge of the Masons, and St. George Lodge No. 95 of the Knights of Pythias, and a former member of the Royal Arch Masons and the Dramatic Order of the Knights of Khorasan. During the World War he was chairman of Chapman precinct Red Cross drive, and assisted in various loan drives. From 1892 to 1916, he played amateur baseball. His hobbies are music, bees and fishing. Residence: Weston.

John Stephen Pacal

John Stephen Pacal, a resident of Nebraska all his life, has been engaged in business at Weston, Nebraska, since February, 1910. He was born at Weston, December 26, 1883, the son of John and Josephine (Horky) Pacal. His father, who was a weaver, painter, paper hanger, and railroad laborer, was born at Preskov, Velka Medric, Moravia, February 2, 1851, and died at Weston, June 7, 1929. His mother was born at Mala Oslavicka, Moravia, January 15, 1857, and died at Weston, June 8, 1927.

Mr. Pacal was graduated from the Weston High School in 1899, and in 1909, was awarded the Ph. G. degree at Creighton University, where he received the award for the best sample case of products in manufacturing in pharmacy, 1909. He was a drug clerk in the Frank Johnson and Ben Smith drug stores at Valparaiso, Nebraska, was a teacher in Saunders County, 1902-04, was timekeeper on the Union Pacific Railroad, 1905-07, and since 1910 has been owner and manager of a drug store at Weston.

He is secretary of the board of education at Weston, is a member of the Nebraska State Pharmaceutical Association, and formerly held membership in the St. George Lodge Number 95 of the Knights of Pythias. For several years Mr. Pacal was a pitcher for the Weston Ball Club, one season was pitcher for the Wahoo Ball Club, and was manager of the Weston Ball Club in the Saunders County League, 1923-4. His hobbies and sports are: music, reading, mechanics, radio, tree culture, and hunting and fishing.

His marriage to Mildred Josephine Vlasak was solemnized at Weston, November 25, 1915. Mrs. Pacal, who was at one time a public school teacher, was born at Prague,

Saunders County, Nebraska, November 8, 1892, of Bohemian descent. They have three children: Louis, born September 24, 1916; Angela, born January 4, 1919; and Richard, born April 18, 1922. All the children are studying music; Louis plays the clarinet and assists in concerts given by the Wahoo Band. Angela is interested in 4-H Club work, and is secretary of the local society of this organization. Residence: Weston.

John McKinley Packer

J. McKinley Packer, physician and surgeon at Ashland, Nebraska, has lived in this state all his life, and is today active in various civic organizations at Ashland. He was born at Wakefield, Nebraska, June 9, 1883, the son of George Washington and Emily Elizabeth (Church) Packer. His father, who was a farmer, was born in Pennsylvania, February 6, 1830, of Irish ancestry, and died at Wakefield, April 7, 1929. His mother was born at Madison, Wisconsin, June 11, 1859, of English descent.

Dr. Packer was graduated from Cotner Academy in 1909, and in 1913 was awarded the A. B. degree at Cotner College where he was active in football and basketball. He received his M. D. from the Electic Medical College at Cincinnati. Since 1915, when he was admitted to the practice of medicine and surgery at Lincoln, he has been engaged in practice at Ashland.

He served as president of the Ashland School Board, 1924-25, and holds membership in the Parent-Teachers' Association, the Chamber of Commerce, the Young Men's Christian Association, and the Red Cross. He is affiliated with the Christian Church, is a Mason, an Odd Fellow, and is a member of the Nebraskana Society. Dr. Packer's favorite sports are golf and baseball.

During the World War he served as first lieutenant in the Officer's Training Corps at Fort Riley, Kansas, and acted as county examining physician for Saunders County. He was married to Mable Ellen Cutter at Lincoln, Lancaster County, Nebraska, September 21, 1915. Mrs. Packer, whose ancestry is English, was born at Avoca, March 25, 1890. They have one child, an adopted daughter, Virginia, who was born February 10, 1921. Residence: Ashland.

Bayard H. Paine

Bayard H. Paine, judge of the Supreme Court of Nebraska, was born on a farm near Painesville, Ohio, April 27, 1872, son of Ira T. and Ella M. (Huston) Paine.

His father, born near Painesville, January 31, 1847, of English ancestry, moved his family to Grand Island in 1873. His mother, born near Painesville, December 31, 1850, was of New England stock, and very active in the work of the Methodist Church. She died at Grand Island, October 21, 1911.

Judge Paine was graduated from Grand Island High School in 1889, attended Northwestern University (Bachelor of Science 1894), and was a student at Ann Arbor Law School part of one year. He is a member of Phi Delta Theta, and was editor in chief of the college annual and also of the *Northwestern*.

His marriage to Grace N. Bentley was solemnized at Grand Island, January 15, 1902. Mrs. Paine was born at Freeport, Illinois, and is of English descent. There are three children, Alice Ella, born April 15, 1903, who is librarian at Grand Island Senior High School; Charles Bentley, born May 1, 1905, who is practicing law at Lincoln; and Bayard H., Jr., born August 5, 1906, who is in business at Grand Island.

Judge Paine taught school four years, was official Court Reporter six years, then began the practice of law in June, 1904, served as police judge of Grand Island and was referee in bankruptcy for ten years. He was elected judge of the eleventh judicial district of Nebraska 1916,

1920, 1924 and 1928, and resigned in January, 1931, having been elected supreme judge of Nebraska in November, 1930 for the fifth supreme court district of eighteen counties.

He is president of the Grand Island Land Company and vice president of the National Bank of Doniphan. He was a private in the Home Guards at Grand Island, and a four minute speaker during the World War. Since 1911 he has been a member of the American Bar and for a number of years has been a member of the Nebraska State Bar Association and the American Judicature Society.

Judge Paine's civic organizations include the Chamber of Commerce, the Rotary Club (past president), and the Grand Island Public Library Board (trustee for more than 25 years). He is a Scottish Rite, and York Rite Mason and a member of the Shrine, and an Elk. For twenty-five years in the past he served as a member of the board of the Young Men's Christian Association, and was its president four years. He is a member of the First Methodist Church, being a delegate to the General Conferences of 1904 and 1908.

He was a member of the board of editors of the *History of Hall County*, and is a member of the Hall County, and of the Nebraska Historical Societies and of the Nebraskana Society. His clubs include the Lincoln University Club, the Riverside Golf Club, Grand Island, and the Executives Club of Chicago. During his summer vacations he has taken automobile trips over the greater part of the United States, and has driven his car through eleven European countries, in which trip he visited many European courts. Residence: Grand Island. (Photograph in Album).

Clara Audrea Paine

Clara Audrea Paine, librarian at Lincoln, was born near Normal, Illinois, April 5, 1875, the daughter of George Leonard and Elizabeth Ann (Vickery) Sibley.

She was graduated from the high school at Jacksonville, Illinois, in 1893, was a student at Brown's Business College, 1894, and attended the Illinois College at Jacksonville, 1893-94. Since 1916, she has been librarian of the State Historical Society, and has served as secretary of the Mississippi Valley Historical Association acting as business manager of its reviews.

She was united in marriage with Clarence Sumner Paine, December 16, 1905. Mr. Paine, who died in 1916, was superintendent of the Nebraska State Historical Society from 1907 to 1916. Three children were born to their marriage: Clarence Sibley; Ezra Kempton; and Elizabeth Audrea.

Mrs. Paine is deputy governor for the Society of Mayflower Descendants in Nebraska, and is state registrar of the National Society of Colonial Dames in Nebraska. She served as state regent of the Daughters of the American Revolution, 1925-27, was vice president general of the Nebraska society of this organization, 1927-30, and has been prominent in the society for many years.

She holds membership in the following: Kansas State Historical Society; Oklahoma State Historical Society; Illinois State Historical Society; Chicago Historical Society; Mayflower Descendants; Daughters of Founders and Patriots of America; Sons and Daughters of Pilgrims; Society of Daughters of Colonial Wars. She is a member of the Lincoln Woman's Club and the P. E. O. She is a member of the board of editors of the Nebraska Genealogical Society, and is the author of *The Vickery Family in America*. She has been a contributor to various magazines and newspapers. She is a Democrat. Residence: Lincoln.

William Henry Pallett

William H. Pallett, who has been a physician and surgeon at Crete, since 1898, was born at The Moat, Great Hadham, Hartfordshire, England, April 23, 1871. His father, William H. Pallett, who was a farmer, was born at Patchendon, Hartfordshire, England, August 11, 1844, and died at Dorchester, February 4, 1916; he came to America in 1873 with his parent. His mother, Lucy (Anthony) Pallett, the daughter of Juliana (Bigg) and E. H. Anthony, was born at The Moat, March 1, 1842, and died at Dorchester, July 3, 1899.

Dr. Pallett was graduated from the Dorchester High School; received the degree D. D. S. at the University of Iowa, in 1892; and in 1898 was graduated from the Kansas City Medical College. He has lived in Nebraska for 58 years. He served as surgeon in the Students Army training Corps at Doane College during the World War, and is a present captain of Medical Reserve Corps. Dr. Pallett is a former member of the Crete Board of Education. Politically, he is independent. He is affiliated with the First Congregational Church of Crete.

On June 26, 1895, Dr. Pallett was united in marriage with Carrie L. Cooper at Crete. Mrs. Pallett, who is the daughter of Rev. D. C. and Louisa J. (Tidall) Cooper, was born at Venango, Pennsylvania. Their children are: Donald H., born October 18, 1900, who married Maryna A. White; Merwin C., born January 19, 1902, who died January 22, 1920; Harold A., born August 29, 1903, who married Gladys Babcock; and James E., born November 19, 1906. Donald, Harold, and James, have received A. B. degrees. Residence: Crete.

Arthur Franklin Palmer

A resident of Nebraska all his life, Arthur Franklin Palmer was born at Raymond, March 12, 1876. His father, Joseph Thomas Palmer, who traced his ancestry to English immigrants prior to the Revolution, was born at Frankfort, Indiana, December 8, 1832. He was an early pioneer farmer in Nebraska, and died at Davey September 30, 1912. His wife, a native of Indiana, was Lydia Anna Brinson. She was born January 19, 1841, and died at Davey on December 8, 1918. Her family was German and Scotch and came to America prior to 1800.

Mr. Palmer attended public school in Nebraska, and has been a farmer at Davey for a number of years. At the present time he is the owner of considerable acreage in that vicinity. He was married to Georgia Alma Guthrie at Davey on October 16, 1901, and to them were born three children, two of whom are living: Arthur, March 28, 1907; Ethel, November 18, 1910, and Gerald, born November 22, 1913, who died April 8, 1929. Mrs. Palmer was born at Mendota, Iowa, December 22, 1879.

A Democrat, Mr. Palmer is active in local politics. He is a member of te First Christian Church of Lincoln, and the Nebraskana Society. Residence: Davey.

Claud Palmer

Claud Palmer, prominent physician and surgeon at Bridgeport, was born in Dallas County, Iowa, April 5, 1872, son of Daniel and Angeline (Stover) Palmer. The father was born in Noble County, Ohio, in 1847, and was a public school teacher and carpenter of Scotch descent. He died at Pacific Junction, Iowa, in 1915. His wife, Angeline, was born in Indiana in 1849, and died at Pacific Junction in 1907. Her ancestry was Pennsylvania Dutch.

Upon his graduation from Pacific Junction High School in 1890, Dr. Palmer entered the University of Nebraska where he received his medical degree in 1906. He passed the state board of medical examiners, making creditable grades in all branches of medicine and surgery, and was also awarded many scholarship prizes. He was tendered a position in the University of Nebraska as instructor by the chancellor at the time of his graduation, which was not accepted.

For 26 years Dr. Palmer has engaged in the practice of medicine and surgery at Bridgeport. Prior to that time he taught in the public schools for ten years. He is a Democrat and for 24 years has been County physician of Morrill County and from 1924 until 1926 served as mayor of Bridgeport.

He is married to Anroe Johnson, who was born at Weeping Water, Nebraska, March 28, 1871. She was a teacher before her marriage.

During the late war Dr. Palmer was examiner on the local draft board. He is a member of the Nebraska State and Scottsbluff Medical Society, and the Knights of Pythias. His favorite sports are hunting and fishing. Residence: Bridgeport.

Harry Oscar Palmer

Harry O. Palmer, distinguished lawyer, educator, and author, of Omaha, was born at Louisville, Cass County, Nebraska, June 10, 1886. His father, Emil Frederick Palmer, was a pioneer railroad man in Nebraska; was mayor of Louisville; and was a merchant there in the early days. He was descended from the nobility of Sweden of the families, Modernsvard, Liljehok, and Bage; he came to America in 1882. He was born at Kalmar, Smoland, Sweden, April 5, 1855, and died at Louisville, March 19, 1917.

Alma (Peterson) Palmer, his mother, was born at Omaha, Douglas County, Nebraska, December 15, 1863. She is an authority on the Franciscan Missions in California, and has widely traveled. Her Swedish and Norman French ancestors were seafarers and traders.

Mr. Palmer was graduated from the Louisville High School in 1904. In 1908 he was awarded the A. B. degree at Nebraska Wesleyan University, and in 1912 received his LL. B. at Harvard. He was made a member of Phi Beta Sigma, Oropilian, at Wesleyan; was a member of Lambda Phi at the Omaha University where he was a lecturer for a time; and was president of the Athletic Association at Wesleyan University. He was awarded the university scholarship at Harvard and was editor of the *Harvard Law Review* there. He was elected to Phi Kappa Phi at Wesleyan.

He was admitted to the bar at Omaha, in 1912, and since that date has been prominent in legal and educational circles in Omaha, practicing law with the firm Palmer, Taylor & Palmer, and later with the firm Palmer & Palmer. He was educational director of the American Institute of Banking, 1914-24; was for a time a lecturer in pleading and practice at Omaha University Law School; and is now attorney in Nebraska for the Federal Reserve Bank and the Prudential Insurance Company.

A Republican, Mr. Palmer has been outstanding in political activities in the state for several years. In 1910 he was secretary of the Cass County Republican Convention; was chairman of the Douglas County Republican Central Committee, 1928-30; and was candidate for governor of Nebraska in the 1930 primaries. He was president of the Republican Club at Wesleyan University. He was at one time city attorney of Louisville.

He began his career as a clerk in his father's store; was engaged by the Burlington Railroad; was cashier for the Redpath Chautauqua System; and has been a reporter and special writer for the *Nebraska State Journal, Omaha Bee News,* and other metropolitan newspapers. He is the author of: *The Law of the Air,* 1918; *Tenderest Lady,* 1919; *Chinese Chit,* 1920; and *Theodorus and Guacaro,* 1916. He has written scientific articles on *Nebraska Snakes,* including *Me and the Amoeba.* He was editor of *The Nebraska Wesleyan,* 1907-08.

Mr. Palmer held the ranks from private to major in the army during the World War; was assistant executive officer and commanding officer in the Judge Advocate General's Offices; and was judge advocate in the China and Siberian Expeditionary Forces. He saw service in the Philippine Department and in Japan. He was secretary of the Douglas County Food Administration, 1917; was secretary for the Nebraska Federal War Savings Organization and toured the southern and eastern states, 1917-18. He has been a member of the executive committee of the American Legion. He was director and national field organizer and speaker for the United States treasury department during the war.

He is a member of the Douglas County Bar Association; the Nebraska Bar Association; and the American Bar Association. He was chairman of the speakers bureau of the Omaha Chamber of Commerce; was educational director of the American Institute of Banking; and is a member of the Young Men's Christian Association. He is affiliated with the First Unitarian Church of Omaha. His favorite sport is tramping in the White Mountains. His hobby is the study of modern languages, especially German, French and Modern Greek. He is a member of the Masons and the Eastern Star. He is a member of the Noon-day Club and the Omaha University Club. Residence: Omaha.

Arthur Chester Pancoast

Arthur Pancoast, who has been a lawyer at Omaha, Douglas County, Nebraska, since June, 1901, was born in Saunders County, Nebraska, December 29, 1873. His father, Edward Clay Pancoast, who was a farmer and early settler in Nebraska, was born in Wayne County, Ohio, in 1842, and died at Ashland, Saunders County, Nebraska, March 25, 1902; he was a soldier in the Civil War; his English ancestors came to this country with William Penn. His mother, Sarah Elizabeth (Bryan) Pancoast, was born at Lebanon, St. Clair County, Illinois, and died at Ashland, Saunders County, Nebraska, December 28, 1912. Her ancestry was Irish and Welsh.

Mr. Pancoast was graduated from the Ashland High School in 1890. He holds the following degrees granted by the University of Nebraska: A. B., 1897; A. M., 1900; and LL. B., 1901. He was elected to Phi Gamma Delta at the university. He is now attorney for the Farmers Union of Nebraska and all of its subsidiaries, also of the Farmers and Merchants Bank of Ashland.

He holds membership in the Omaha Bar Society, the Douglas County Bar Society, and the Nebraska State Bar Association. He is a member of the Chamber of Commerce, is attorney for the South Omaha School Board. Mr. Pancoast's social club is the Happy Hollow Club of Omaha, while his fraternal organizations include the Odd Fellows and all Masonic bodies. He is affiliated with St. Barnabas Episcopal Church of Omaha, and is a member of the Republican party. His hobby is farming, while his favorite sport is golf.

His marriage to Selma Augusta Wiggenhorn was solemnized at Ashland, June 15, 1904. Mrs. Pancoast was born at Ashland. They have three children: Marjorie, born March 31, 1905; Helen Augusta, born December 5, 1906; and Elizabeth Dora, born January 26, 1912. The two older girls are graduates of Wellesley College and Elizabeth is a student there. Residence: Omaha.

Frederick Gerhard Panning

A lifelong resident of Nebraska, Frederick G. Panning was born at Hooper, Nebraska, February 14, 1874, the son of Henry and Meta (Meyer) Panning. His father was born at Hanover, Germany, April 15, 1844, and died at Hooper, September 15, 1929; he come to America from Germany, October, 1852, and settled at Watertown, Wisconsin; he moved to Nebraska in 1864, and bought 360 acres of land in Dodge County for $1,200. His mother was born at Oldenburg, Germany, and came to America in 1868.

Mr. Panning attended the public schools and Fremont Normal School. He managed a general merchandise store at Altona, Nebraska, for a time; was cashier of the Farmers State Bank at Altona for four years; and in 1914 returned to farming as his occupation. He is secretary of the Farmers Mutual Home Insurance Company of Hooper; is president of the Farmers Union Co-operative Company at Winslow, Nebraska; and is a director in the Winslow State Bank.

On June 29, 1909, he was married to Anna Emma Pflueger at Altona, Nebraska. Mrs. Panning was born of German parents in Cuming County, April 7, 1884. Seven children were born to their marriage, all of whom are living: Victor, born June 21, 1905; Leona, born December 30, 1906; Theodore, born August 28, 1908; Arthur, born May 20, 1910; Ester, born August 19, 1912; Ruth, born October 31, 1914; and Irvin, born May 21, 1919. Leona is employed as clerk at Lallman Brothers Merchandise Establishment at Winslow, Nebraska. The other children are employed at home.

Mr. Panning is a member of the Immanual Lutheran Church and is a director of the Church Extension Board; and a member of the Lutheran Layman League. He holds membership in the Nebraskana Society. He is a Republican. Residence: Hooper.

Ladimore Frank Papik

Ladimore F. Papik, a life time resident of Nebraska, was born at Crete, Saline County, Nebraska, December 7, 1894, the son of Frank Joseph and Barbara (Nedela) Papik. His father, who was born at Msene, Province of Prague, Czechoslovakia, December 19, 1854, and died at Crete, July 9, 1924, was a pioneer Nebraskan, and a prosperous farmer; he came with his parents, Frank and Katherine Papik, to America and in 1869 settled in Saline County where he became a prominent member of his community; he held membership in the Woodmen of the World and Z. C. B. J.

His mother, who was born at Msene, June 8, 1860, and died at Crete, December 16, 1927, came to America in 1866 with her parents, John and Barbara Nedela; they homesteaded near Crete in 1868. She was an active club worker, was a member of J. C. D., Z. C. B. J., and the Star Club. She was president of the latter and on the day before her death entertained the club at her home.

Mr. Papik was graduated from the Crete High School in 1915 with the largest class that school had known. He was a member of the high school baseball team for two years, and won many honors in track in which he took part for three years. He worked on his father's farm for a year, and from 1916-1918 farmed with his brother. In 1918 he moved on the farm he now owns; in the past decade, through thrift and energy he has built up his farm and made many improvements on it. He has specialized in hog raising and has made a most enviable record.

He was married to Bessie Lavina Pisar at Wilber, Saline County, Nebraska, November 28, 1916. Mrs. Papik, who is an energetic farm wife, was born at Dorchester, February 20, 1898, the daughter of Joseph and Rosie Pisar; she was graduated from school in 1912. She is active in her home and in community affairs. They have one son, Frankie Joseph, born February 27, 1923. He is in grade school and has won honor grades each year of his education.

Mr. Papik is a member of Z. C. B. J. and the Nebraskana Society. He has been district treasurer of school district Number 62 since 1926. His sports are baseball and basketball. His hobby is summer tours through the country. Residence: Dorchester.

Edmund McIntyre Parker

Edmund McIntyre Parker, veteran lumber dealer in Saline County, Nebraska, has lived in this state all his life and has taken an active part in civic affairs at Crete for many years. He was born at Dorchester, Nebraska, October 10, 1873, the son of Thomas Benton and Emma (Livingston) Parker. His father, who was a distinguished lawyer, was a member of the legislature of 1878 and served as deputy internal revenue collector for 11 counties in Nebraska; he was born in Pickaway County,

Ohio, October 8, 1843, and died at Steamboat Springs, Colorado, January 30, 1926; his ancestry was English.

His mother was born in Henry County, Illinois, November 19, 1849, came to Nebraska in 1858 with her parents and settled near Louisville. She died at Crete, February 22, 1922; her English ancestors were signers of the Declaration of Independence, and her father was a soldier in the War of 1812.

Mr. Parker attended the Dorchester Public Schools and was a student at Lincoln Normal School in 1893 and 1894. He has been engaged in the lumber business for over 30 years, acting as manager of the George A. Hoagland Lumber Company prior to 1908 and since then as treasurer and general manager of the Parker & Jacobsen Lumber Company. He is connected with the Paine Lumber & Coal Company at Beaver Crossing, Nebraska, as treasurer, and is vice president of the Crete Building and Loan Association.

He is a member of the Rotary Club, is past president and a member of the board of directors of the Community Club at Crete, and is affiliated with the Methodist Church there. He is interested in basketball and football and all outdoor sports, and holds membership in the Crete Country Club. During the World War he served as a member of various committees in loan and charity drives. Mr. Parker is a member of the Scottish Rite and Shrine bodies of the Masonic Order.

A Democrat, he served as mayor of Crete for two successive terms, 1914 and 1915. On August 12, 1903, he was united in marriage with Dora Mooberry at Dorchester. Mrs. Parker, whose ancestry is English and French, was born at Morton, Illinois, October 30, 1875, and died at Crete, February 5, 1915. Their elder son, Gerald, born November 27, 1905, was graduated from the University of Nebraska in 1929, and is now a high school teacher and coach at Osceola High School. Paul M., born April 13, 1910, is a student at Doane College, Crete, Nebraska. Residence: Crete.

Thomas William Parkin

Thomas William Parkin, clergyman at Ainsworth, Nebraska, was born at Rowlands Gill, England, April 16, 1890, the son of William and Josephine (Bell) Parkin. His father, who was a business man, was also born at Rowlands Gill. His mother was born at Winlaton, England, and died at Rowlands Gill, in 1918.

Mr. Parkin attended school in England, and in 1917 received the A. B. and A. M. degrees at the University of Toledo. He had formerly been a student at Ohio Northern University where he was prominent in debating and is a member of Phi Kappa Chi. He has been a minister in Nebraska for the past 15 years and has held a pastorate in Ainsworth for two years, and is active in community affairs there at this time.

He is a member of the Ainsworth Welfare Board, the Chamber of Commerce, the Young Men's Christian Association, and the Ministerial Association. He is a Mason, a member of the Eastern Star, and a recent member of the Nebraskana Society. Actively interested in Boy Scout work, he likes football, golf, and hiking. His hobby is reading.

He was united in marriage with Lillian Ruth Norgren at Des Moines, Iowa, July 21, 1918. Mrs. Parkin, whose ancestry is Swedish, was born at Ong Nebraska, November 21, 1897. Their two children are: Thomas, Jr., born April 16, 1920; and John Bell, born February 23, 1924. Residence: Ainsworth.

George Alanson Parkins

Since 1901 George Alanson Parkins has been established in business at Ord, Nebraska, as a jeweler and optometrist. He was born at Fontanelle, Iowa, March 24, 1881, but has lived in Nebraska most of his life. His father, John Parkins, who was born in Ontario, Canada, was a soldier in the Union Army throughout the duration of the Civil War; he is a wagon maker and carpenter. The Parkins family is of English descent.

Mr. Parkin was graduated from the high school at Elgin, Nebraska, in 1896, attended Hutchinson's Watchmaker School, and was a student in the Meyer School of Optometry. He holds membership in the scientific sections of Beta Sigma Kappa, the international honorary fraternity of optometrists, and is the author of various articles on the functioning and care of the human eye and its preservation.

He is a member of the Rotary Club, the Knights of Pythias, American Association of Optometrist, Nebraska Association of Optometrists, and the Red Cross at Ord. He is chairman of the Educational Committee of Central Nebraska Optometrists Club. During the World War he served as organizer and chairman of the Valley County Red Cross. His hobby is the study of the origin and the correction of various eye disturbances, and his favorite sport is golf.

His marriage to Mary Ann Purdum took place at Columbus, Nebraska, December 25, 1902; she was born at Rockport, Missouri, August 31, 1881. Their children are: John, born November 19, 1903, who married Sylvia Shoemaker; Mary, born April 23, 1908, who married Merle J. Olson; and George, born July 6, 1912. John is a watchmaker and jeweler at Los Angeles, California. Residence: Ord.

Harry Collins Parmenter

A leading farmer and stockman at Yutan, Nebraska, Harry C. Parmenter was born December 10, 1879, the son of George W. and Lillie Belle (Grisham) Parmenter. His father, a pioneer farmer and stockman, was born of English parentage, at Honesdale, Pennsylvania, February 16, 1843, and died at Fairfield, Nebraska, December 13, 1915; he served in the Civil War. His mother, an educator, was born at Fulton, Illinois, December 9, 1856.

Mr. Parmenter received his high school work at the preparatory department of Cotner University. He was awarded the A. B. degree at Cotner University, 1901, and the B. O. degree at the Nebraska College of Oratory, 1902. In 1902 he took post graduate work at the University of Nebraska.

He has served as a member of the school board, the Nebraska Farmers Union, is secretary of the Farmers Union Legislative committee, is secretary of the Corn Belt Federation, is president of the Farmers Union Elevator Association at Yutan, Nebraska, secretary of the Farmers Union Elevator at Wann, Nebraska, is a director of the Farmers Union Commission Company at Omaha, and the Farmers Union Credit Association, and is a director of the National Grain Commission at Omaha.

Mr. Parmenter was senatorial candidate in 1917, and in 1922 was progressive candidate for governor of Nebraska. He has always taken a prominent part in the economic and civic affairs of his state and community He holds membership in the Community Club, is affiliated with the Nebraskana Society, and is a member of the Christian Church.

His hobbies are reading and economics. His marriage to Martha Dora Hulfish was solemnized at Lincoln, Lancaster County, Nebraska, September 17, 1902. Mrs. Parmenter, who is a piano instructor, was born at Owensville, Indiana, November 10, 1876; her ancestry is English and German. They have one daughter, Annabelle, born January 14, 1914. Residence: Yutan.

James Milton Parrott

James Milton Parrott, prominent in Frontier County for the past quarter of a century, was born at Thurman, Iowa, June 7, 1860, son of Samuel and Anna (Tanner) Parrott. Samuel Parrott, born at Dayton, Ohio, February 16, 1835, was a music teacher, a farmer and a breeder of fine horses. His father was born in Maryland, and his paternal grand father in England. His father came to Nebraska in 1872, having traded a quarter section of land in Fremont County, Iowa, for a quarter section in Saline County, Nebraska, near Crete. When the family moved to Nebraska they made the trip in a covered wagon, camping along the way, stopping one night to camp along Salf Creek at Lincoln, which was a small village. Samuel Parrott died at Norton, Kansas, May 2, 1895.

Anna Tanner, wife of Samuel Parrott, was born in Lafayette, Indiana, August 16, 1841, daughter of Boyd Tanner, a farmer at Terre Haute, Indiana. She died at Norton, Kansas, June 5, 1908.

Dr. Parrott attended grade school at Nebraska City, and thereafter carried mail from Alma four years. Afterward he worked with Dr. M. L. Bancroft, of Alma, who taught him dentistry, and on December 2, 1895, he was registered in Nebraska. At that time Silas A. Holcomb was governor. Dr. Parrott has resided in Stockville forty years, and during sixteen years carried the rural mail out of Stockville. For the past seven years he has been a hotel operator and owner there.

Prominent in fraternal organizations, he was financier of the Ancient Order of United Workmen twenty years, and has occupied all chairs in the Odd Fellows Lodge. He was delegate to the Republican National Convention in 1928, helped to nominate Calvin Coolidge; served as justice of the peace ten years and as deputy sheriff four years. Dr. Parrott was mainly responsible for locating the body of Thomas Jensen of Stockville, in August 1898, and for the arrest of his murderer, Andrew Hawkins, who was sentenced to 99 years in prison by Judge George W. Norris, now U. S. Senator. In this connection he received a reward of $500.00 Recalling early experiences Dr. Parrott relates with pleasure his early associations when a boy with the Indians, many of whom became his friends.

During the World War Dr. Parrott was dental examiner for the government. He is a member of the Congregational Church, the American Dental Association, the Red Cross, Community Club, and The Nebraskana Society. For twelve years he was chairman of the local school board. His hobbies are reading, gardening and race horses.

On September 4, 1885, he was married to Cora May at Alma, Nebraska, from whom he is divorced. There are two children of this marriage, Carl, born at Alma, June 27, 1886; and Ethel, born at Alma, April 22, 1888, who married Wilbur Doughty of Colorado Springs, Colorado.

His marriage to Maggie Houghteling was solemnized at Stockville, January 23, 1898. Mrs. Parrott was born near Wilton, Wisconsin, October 26, 1875. They have four children: Anna, born October 26, 1898, who married Albert Covey; they reside at Farnam, Nebraska; Will, born July 17, 1900; James, born at Stockville, November 20, 1902; and Ella, born at Stockville, June 20, 1908, who married John Tinsman. They live at Reno, Nebraska. Residence: Stockville.

Antony Parsons

Born at Omaha, Nebraska, March 21, 1877, Anthony Parsons has been a physician since 1910. His father, Andrew Johan Parsons, was a native of Wenersborg, Elsborg, Sweden, born May 22, 1846, who came directly from Sweden to Omaha in 1869. Until his death at Valley on June 11, 1915, he was a farmer in Douglas County.

Martha Elizabeth Sword, wife of Andrew Parsons, immigrated to America in 1870, residing for a time in Southport, Connecticut before coming to Omaha. She was born at Wenersburg, July 24, 1842, and died at Valley on December 26, 1921. Essentially a homemaker, she was a true pioneer mother.

Antony Parsons attended public school in Douglas

County, was a student at Fremont and Grand Island Colleges during various periods between 1895 and 1902, and received his medical degree from Creighton University in 1910. After graduation he served a year's internship at the Omaha General Hospital, attended the London School of Tropical Medicine and spent 1912 and 1913 in England and Africa.

On December 16, 1911, he was married to Laura Schavland at Newman Grove. Mrs. Parsons, who was graduated as a nurse from Omaha General Hospital in 1910, was born at Stavanger, Norway, April 13, 1879. She came from Norway to America in 1894. During the World War she was chairman of the local Red Cross organization. There is one daughter, Helen Laurenze, born April 12, 1915.

Returning from abroad Dr. Parsons practiced one year in Uehling, and since that time has been in practice at Valley. In 1918 he was a member of the Nebraska Home Guard, and during 1917-18 was chairman of the rural department of the Douglas County Young Men's Christian Association drive, and assisted in the Red Cross.

A member of the First Baptist Church of Valley, he is chairman of the congregation and during 1912 was in medical mission service under the American Baptist Foreign Mission Society in Belgian Congo, West Africa. Dr. Parsons' professional and civic memberships include the American, Nebraska State and Omaha-Douglas County Medical Associations, the Welfare Board(chairman) the Commercial Club, the Valley School Board (member 17 years) and the Library board of which he is chairman. He is a member of the Nebraskana Society, and his hobby is amateur gardening. Residence: Valley.

Con Parsons

Con Parsons, prominent rancher, was born at Clearwater, Nebraska, October 6, 1880, son of Joseph Conrad and Martha Ann Parsons. His ancestors came to America from England in 1745.

Mr. Parsons attended grade and high schools at Harrison, Nebraska, graduating in 1897, and in 1899 was graduated from Chadron, Nebraska, Academy. He was graduated from Nebraska Wesleyan University in 1901.

His marriage to Susie Tupper was solemnized at Osmond, Nebraska, June 20, 1906 She was born at Grand Junction, Kansas, February 17, 1881. There are four children, Bruce Tupper, born September 28, 1908; Waldo Creg, born June 13, 1912; Charles Lowell, born October 1, 1916; and Susie Mae, born December 21, 1925.

A Republican, Mr. Parsons was county superintendent of public instruction, 1902, in Sioux County, Nebraska, and from 1903-1907 was deputy county clerk of Sioux County. He has always been a breeder of white face cattle. For 15 years until it closed in 1924, he was a director of the First National Bank at Harrison. He is a member of the Methodist Church. Residence: Harrison.

Fred C. Parsons

Fred C. Parsons, prominent executive, was born at Council Bluffs, Iowa, July 23, 1878, son of Asa A. and Ellen M. (Blaisdell) Parsons. The father was born in Parsonfield, Maine, October 13 1837 and died at Omaha December 25, 1912. He was an agricultural implement dealer of English ancestry. His wife, Ellen, was born in Wolfboro, New Hampshire, January 15, 1842, of Scotch and French ancestry.

On June 28, 1906, Mr. Parsons was married to Ruth Edwards. She was born at Kennard Nebraska and is a descendant of Jonathan Edwards. They have one daughter, Dorothy Ruth.

At the present time Mr. Parsons is president of the Kennedy Parsons Company. He is a Presbyterian, and a member of the Chamber of Commerce and the Masons. His clubs are the Concord Club and the Happy Hollow Country Club. Residence: Omaha.

Grant Parsons

Grant Parsons, building contractor, was born in Holly Meadows, Tucker County, West Virginia, December 7, 1865. He is the son of Cornelius and Laverna A. Parsons, both natives of Virginia. Cornelius Parsons, a school master, was born at Parsons Plantation, Randolph, Virginia, on June 21, 1839, and died at Petersburg, West Virginia, in March, 1914. English, he was descended from John Parr of London. Laverna A. Parsons was born in Randolph County, Virginia, October 16, 1848, and died at Petersburg, September 13, 1870.

Mr. Parsons attended the public and normal schools of West Virginia, and in a few years came to Nebraska. He returned to West Virginia, and on February 12, 1889, was united in marriage to Frances Lavina Dietz. Mrs. Parsons was born at St. George, Tucker County, West Virginia, February 19, 1867. She is of English, Dutch and German descent. The Parsons came to Nebraska where their five children were born. They are: Alice E., born August 2, 1890. She married Roy B. Tedrow, and died July 22, 1927. Marion L. was born April 28, 1892, married William J. DeWinter; Neal D., born March 16, 1894, died March 25, 1916. Marjorie I., born November 6, 1897, married W. Connor Gilbert; and Dorothy J. born February 8, 1900, married A. William Francis.

Since he first came to Nebraska, Mr. Parsons has been engaged in the construction business. He is president of the Parsons Construction Company at the present time, and is president of the Nebraska Master Builders and on the board of control of the National Association of Builders' Exchanges. He served as sergeant in the Nebraska National Guard for 9 years, and was chairman of the building committee in a loan drive during the World War.

In religion Mr. Parsons is a Unitarian and attends the Unitarian Church of Omaha. He is a director of the Chamber of Commerce, a member of the Hiram Club, a thirty-second degree Mason and member of the Modern Woodmen of America. His club is the Carter Lake Club, and his favorite diversions are gardening and automobile touring. Residence: Omaha.

William Curtis Parsons

William Curtis Parsons, veteran newspaper editor and publisher of Nebraska, was born in Wayne County, New York, May 16, 1873, the son of Henry Lewis and Mary A. (Beadle) Parsons. His father, who was a contractor and builder, was born in Wayne County, May 13, 1845, and died at Ord, Nebraska, August 5, 1911. His mother, whose ancestry was Scotch-Irish, was born in Wayne County, April 9, 1847, and died at Burwell, Nebraska, February 17, 1920.

Mr. Parsons was graduated from the high school at Papillion, Nebraska. He entered the newspaper field as an apprentice on the *Papillion Times,* under the direction of United States Congressman Edgar Howard, remaining there for five years. He was foreman of the *Ord Quiz* for 12 years, and since then has been editor and publisher of the *Burwell Tribune.*

He is a member of the Ancient Order of United Workmen, the Wranglers Club of Burwell, and the Red Cross, formerly serving on the local school board. He has been a member of the Masons for 24 years.

On June 23, 1904, he was married to Eleanor Mutter at Ord. Mrs. Parsons, who is his assistant and bookkeeper, was born of German and French extraction at Creston, Iowa, September 28, 1878. They have one son, Kenneth, born November 20, 1905, who married Marie

Katherine Spieth. Kenneth is an editor and publisher. Residence: Burwell.

Osborne Patterson

Osborne Patterson, retired farmer and politican, was born in Monaghan, County Monaghan, Ireland, December 26, 1851, son of George and Isabella (Kinnier) Patterson.

The father a native of Monaghan, came to the United States in 1872, and engaged in contracting and building. His death occurred at Philadelphia, March 2, 1880. His wife, Isabella, also born in Monaghan, Ireland, died at Dublin, Nebraska, in September, 1881.

John Patterson attended school in Monaghan, and was the first of that family to leave the old home in Clontibrat, Corner Brady, Monaghan, Ireland, and came to America. He arrived in the United States, five or six years before the Civil War, his object being to complete a medical course in Lynchburg, Virginia. His favorable reports of America were the magnet, which finally attracted his father and mother, George and Isabella Patterson and seven of their eight children remaining in Ireland, to America. Dr. John Patterson, who was then practicing medicine in Philadelphia, sent his family attractive circulars headed by the words given above.

On the 17th of March, 1872, the family of George and Isabella Patterson, together with their children, Robert, his wife and their two children, Richard G., Osborne, Mary, Hannah, Bella, and Rachel, set sail for America in the steamboat, *The City of Brussels,* which at that time was considered as risky traveling, as traveling in an aeroplane is generally considered today. The trip was made in record time, eight days and four hours. The trip was made from Liverpool, England, to New York City.

George Patterson gave up his work, as a contractor and builder, to come to America. His son, Robert, also sold his farm, which adjoined his fathers; Richard gave up his position in Manchester, as one of the Queen's life guards; Osborne, who was a youth of 17 or 18, and his sisters, Mary, Hannah, Bella and Rachel, were under the parental roof. The only member of the family, remaining in the British Isles at this time, was Adam Patterson, who together with his wife, Jane Livingston Patterson, niece of the explorer Livingston, were living in Manchester, where he was a minister. The family spent about two weeks in Philadelphia with Dr. John Patterson before they left for Fremont, Nebraska. Here George and his family lived for about two years on what was known as the Sioux City farm site, to which the present city of Fremont has been extended. From here they moved to township 19, which is a few miles north of the town of Primrose, and to their homestead, which is now owned by Osborne Patterson, Jr., a grandson of George and a namesake of Osborne, Sr.

On December 26, 1879, Mr. Patterson was married to Carrie Casper in Boone County. She was born on the Island of Rugan, Germany, September 29, 1865. To Mr. and Mrs. Paterson six children were born, four of whom are living: Minnie, on July 25, 1880, married Allen J. Randall; Jo Henry, on September 23, 1886, married Beulah Lull; Lizzie Belle, on December 28, 1889, who married Ralph Antisdel; Frank B., born September 30, 1892, who married Ina Lemon; George, born November 3, 1882, who died December 10, 1884; and Mary Jane, born July 12, 1885, who died July 14, 1885. Mr. Randall is a commission merchant, a member of the firm Cox, Jones and Randall, Henry is a farmer, Lizzie Belle a teacher, and Frank a ranchman.

One of the early experiences, which Mr. Patterson recalls, is that of the planting of trees on the homestead. One spring, early in the history of Cedar Valley, James McClain and Osborne Patterson went down into the Pawnee reservation, near Fullerton to dig up some cottonwood trees for replanting. On the way home they gave Hubert Reed an armful, which he planted around his buildings, on the Reed farm across the road from where now stands district schoolhouse No. 14. James McClain planted some on his homestead, and Osborne helped his father plant a grove of them on his father's homestead. The Patterson grove came up so thick the next spring, that one afternoon, after a good morning's rain, the grandfather said to Osborne, "Come, let's do a job, that will last long after we are gone." They then planted a row of trees on the west and south sides of the homestead, many of which are standing to this day. Later on Osborne extended the row on the south, so that the south line of his claim, which was directly east of his father's, was also lined with a border of these cottonwoods. And to quote Mr. Patterson, "Thus they stand, those sturdy trees planted by those early settlers, and long after they are gone will live the spirit of those early pioneers."

Mr. Patterson was one of the first members of the Presbyterian Church at St. Edward, Nebraska. It had happened that he had gone to a service there when the church was organized, and the Presbytery had a ruling that no church could be organized with a membership less than seven. There being only six persons there, Osborne Patterson let the organization go on with himself as a charter member. Until the church was built, in 1880, all meetings of the church as well as public meetings, of the settlement, were held in the sod house, belonging to Osborne Patterson. This was located about 80 rods from the homestead, in which the organization was completed. The Rev. Hood brought his song books with him from Columbus, and George Patterson, with his snow white hair, stood before them and led the singing, his clear, musical voice being the only accompaniment they had for the time being.

In the early days of the settlement, the government sent out herds of cattle from Texas to the Indian reservation in the Dakotas. They reached the part of the country, where the Pattersons lived, on Saturday evening. When the thirsty cattle smelled water, they made a rush for Cedar River, making it a seething mass of cattle. The drivers decided to rest over Sunday before going on. Mrs. Maxwell said she would be glad to sell them bread if she had any, but she had neither flour nor bread in the house. They said they would be glad to furnish the flour, if she would make the bread, so they brought a couple of 50 pound sacks of flour, and she spent all day Sunday making bread for the herders. The next day, when they were ready to start, they told Mr. Maxwell that there were seven or eight young calves that they might as well have, as they were too young to make the trip. Although Mr. Maxwell had only one cow, from which he got milk, he was glad to accept the calves, and this is how Maxwell got a start in cattle.

From his earliest days in Nebraska, Osborne Patterson took an active interest in politics. He was always Independent, and in 1897-1901, served as sheriff of Boone County. For many years until his recent retirement, he has been one of the leading farmers of his locality.

During his early days, he was a private in the Cedar Valley Rangers, and during the World War, was active in bond and stamp sales. He is a member of Clontibrat Presbyterian Church at Primrose, Nebraska, and a former member of the Woodmen of the World, the Modern Woodmen of America, and the Knights of Pythias. Residence: Omaha.

Frederick Joseph Patz

Frederick Joseph Patz was born at Crete, Nebraska, March 7, 1893, son of Thomas and Sophia (Stone) Patz. His father was born at Wilwerdingen, Luxemburg, Germany, April 12, 1847, and died at Crete on April 2, 1930. An educator, he served as an interpreter in the Franco-Prussian War; his paternal ancester, Michael

Patz, born in 1801 at Wilwerdingen, died in 1886; other ancestors are Magdalena Patz and Captain Lentz of Napoleon's Army, 1795.

Sophia Stone was a native of New York, born March 21, 1857. She also died at Crete. Coming from Switzerland in 1855, her parents lived for a time in New York State, and homesteaded near Denton, Nebraska in 1861.

A graduate of Crete High School in 1913, Mr. Patz attended Oberlin College 1913-15, and Ohio State University College of Law 1915-18, receiving his LL. B.; during the time he was at Ohio State he served as treasurer of Phi Kappa Psi, and as a member of the student council. He was married to Georgia Avery Sandusky at Sterling, Nebraska, August 30, 1922., Mrs. Patz was born at Sterling September 26, 1898.

During 1918-19 Mr. Patz served in the United States Navy on the *U. S. S. DeKalb*, a cruiser type of battleship, as seaman and radio operator, doing transport work between the United States and France. He was admitted to the bar in Columbus, Ohio on May 25, 1918, and at Lincoln, on October 6, 1919. Since his admission he has been in general practice beginning in 1924 with Sterling Mutz and Edward C. Fisher. He is now attorney for the following: Nebraska Radio Corporation, Conservative Mortgage Co., Zurich General Accident and Liability Insurance Co., U. S. Casualty Company, Constitution Indemnity Co., Yorkshire Insurance Association; State Auto Insurance Association; New York Indemnity Co.; Firemans Fund; Home Fire and Marine Insurance Co.; International Idemnity Co., Ocean Accident and Guarantee Association; Central Surety Insurance Co.; Continental Casualty Co.; Employer's Indemnity Corp.; Georgia Casualty Co.; Detroit Fidelity and Surety Company; Ohio Casualty Co.; National Casualty Co.; Hanover Fire Insurance Co.; Union Indemnity Company; Merchants Fire Assurance Corporation; and Merchants Indemnity Co. He is secretary and treasurer of the Arrow Aircraft Corporation of Havelock and treasurer of the Conservative Mortgage Co. of Lincoln.

He is a member of the American Legion, the Disabled American Veterans, the Nebraska State and Lancaster County Bar Associations, the Kiwanis Club, and the Masonic and Shrine bodies. He enjoys golf, and is a member of the Eastridge Country Club. Residence: Lincoln.

Mary Frances Paul

Born at St. Joseph, Missouri, April 20, 1849, Mary Frances Paul is the daughter of Samuel and Elmina (Mitchell) Paul. Her father, born at Harrisburg, Pennsylvania, of a family of Scotch Presbyterian farmers, died at St. Paul, Nebraska. At the time of his death he was a retired farmer and stockraiser. The mother, who was born July 4, about 1815, at Indianapolis, died at Leanvenworth, Kansas, in 1865. She was a devoted mother and homemaker.

Mary Frances Paul was educated in Loretto Convent at St. Louis, Missouri, finishing in 1866. She was married to J. N. Paul, December 22, 1866. He was born September 3, 1839, and died in St. Paul, Nebraska, March 9, 1922. He was a judge, and a prominent figure in his community. Four sons were born to them, Charles Howard, November 6, 1870, Herbert Jay, November 12, 1872; James Leonard, September 3, 1877, and Willard Samuel, January 24, 1880.

Howard was graduated from the University of Nebraska and from the law school at Ann Arbor, Michigan. He was in the immigration service thirty-eight or forty years when he retired. Herbert held the rank of colonel in the World War, after which he was appointed adjutant general by Governor McKelvie. Leonard was in the automobile business for a number of years. Willard is vice president of the St. Paul National Bank, is a Mason and Shriner, and has been eminent commander.

He is president of the Community Club and very active along all lines of public service.

Mrs. Paul has been prominent in the work of the Nebraska Federation of Women's Clubs for some time, and was state president 1916-18. In 1919 she was state chairman of the War Victory Commission. In addition she has held many minor offices. She served as vice president of the First Club of State Presidents of the Biennial of 1916 at New York City, and was delegate to the first National Republican Convention in Washington, D. C. She is a member of the P. E. O. Sisterhood, and was recently made a life member of the Nebraskana Society. Residence: St. Paul.

Willard Samuel Paul

Willard Samuel Paul, a banker for the past 32 years, has lived at St. Paul, Nebraska, all his life and is prominent in community affairs there at this time. He was born at St. Paul, January 24, 1880, the son of James Ney and Mary Frances Paul, the former a distinguished editor, lawyer, and judge. His father, who was born at Beaver, Pennsylvania, September 23, 1839, and died at St. Paul, March 9, 1922, served as United States Government Surveyor, and judge of the 11th Judicial District for 17 years. His mother, who is past president of the Nebraska Federation of Woman's Clubs, past secretary of this organization, and president of the P. E. O., was born at St. Joseph, Missouri, April 20, 1849.

Mr. Paul attended the St. Paul High School. He is vice president of the St. Paul National Bank of which he is also a director, is president of the Community Club, and is treasurer of the Howard County Historical Society. A Mason, he holds membership in the following bodies: Blue Lodge; Royal Arch; Knight Templars; Shrine. He is a former member of the St. Paul School Board, and holds membership in the St. Paul Golf Club.

During the Spanish-American War he served as a private in Company B., 2nd Nebraska Volunteer Infantry, and is now a member of the Spanish War Veterans. He was active in all loan drives during the World War.

He was united in marriage with Susan Thomas Paul at St. Paul, September 16, 1908; she was born at Niobrara, Nebraska, June 6, 1881. They have two children: Robert T., born November 8, 1909; and Willard S., Jr., born November 14, 1918. Residence: St. Paul.

Conrad Pauley

Conrad Pauley has been a resident of Nebraska for the past 52 years, and is today one of Lincoln's outstanding business men. He was born in Russia, November 27, 1862, the son of Henry and Lisbeth (Ross) Pauley. His father, who was born in Russia, was a farmer. He died at Harvard, Nebraska, December, 1915. His mother, who was born in Russia, died at Harvard, February, 1896.

Mr. Pauley received his education in the public schools of Harvard, Nebraska. For over 50 years he has been prominent in the lumber business; he was for a time engaged in farming. He is now owner and manager of the Pauley Lumber Company; is manager of the Belvedere Apartments at Lincoln; and is connected with the Home Owners Investment Company.

He was married at Harvard, February 27, 1886, to Alice Yost, who was born in Russia. Eight children were born to their marriage, all of whom are living. They are: L. H. Pauley, born February 13, 1886, who married Alberteena Ryder; Will, born December 8, 1887, who married Bessie Cattle; Pearl, born January 25, 1890, who married Adam Yost; Ray, born March 25, 1892, who married Lucile DeOgny; Ada, born July 16, 1901, who married Glen Crancer; Selma, born September 9, 1895, who married Joe Brehm; and Reon, born June 4, 1907, who married Helen Kulla.

EDWARD HENRY PAULEY

Mr. Pauley is a member of the Nebraskana Society; was a member of the school board at Harvard, and is affiliated with the Second Methodist Episcopal Church of Lincoln. He is a Republican. Residence: Lincoln.

Edward Henry Pauley

Edward Henry Pauley, farmer and lumberman at Henderson, York County, Nebraska, has been a resident of this state all his life. He was born at Harvard, Clay County, Nebraska, August 3, 1885, the son of Peter Pauley and Louise (Hamburger) Pauley. His father was born in Germany, October 20, 1859, and came to America in 1878 where he became a farmer. He died at Harvard, February 6, 1930. His mother was born in Germany, April 10, 1860.

Mr. Pauley was graduated from the public school at Harvard in 1898, was a farmer for several years, and later entered the lumber and grain business. He is now manager and owner of the Pauley Lumber & Grain Company at Henderson. From 1924 to 1928 he served as a member of the school board, and since 1918 he has been mayor of Henderson, retiring undefeated. He is a member of the Red Cross, (chairman of Henderson chapter) The Nebraskana Society, and the Congregational Church.

His marriage to Barbara Marie Hein occurred at Harvard, June 16, 1908. Mrs. Pauley was born at Harvard, July 9, 1886. They have a daughter, Berniece, born April 30, 1909, a student at the University of Nebraska where she is a member of Omega Pi. She is a member of G. F. S. at Doane College. Residence: Henderson. (Photograph on Page 924).

Ludwig Henry Pauley

A prominent lumberman in Nebraska for many years, Ludwig H. Pauley has lived in this state all his life. He was born at Harvard, Clay County, Nebraska, February 13, 1886, the son of Conrad and Alice (Yost) Pauley. His parents' ancestry is German.

Mr. Pauley was graduated from the Harvard High School in 1902. He is today president of the Pauley Lumber Company at Lincoln, Lancaster County, Nebraska; is president of the Home Owners Investment Company, and is vice president of the People's Savings & Loan Association. He holds membership in the Chamber of Commerce at Lincoln; the Hiram Club; Open Forum; and the Nebraskana Society.

His religious affiliation is with Trinity Methodist Episcopal Church at Lincoln. He is a Mason, Shriner. He is married to Albertina Righter and they have two children, Carroll, born December 22, 1908, and Gordon, born March 3, 1928. Mr. Pauley is a member of the Republican party. Residence: Lincoln.

William George Pauley

William George Pauley was born at Harvard, Clay County, Nebraska, December 8, 1887, the son of Conrad and Alice (Yost) Pauley. His father, a retired farmer and landowner, was born in Russia, and came to America in 1880. His mother was born in Russia. Their ancestry was German.

Mr. Pauley was graduated from the Harvard High School in 1905, and has been engaged in the lumber business continuously since that date. He is now manager and owner of the W. G. Pauley Lumber Company with headquarters at Hastings, Adams County, Nebraska, and is owner of the W. G. Pauley Lumber Company at Seward, in partnership with his father.

He is a charter member of the Kiwanis Club at Hastings, holds membership in the Hastings Chamber of Commerce, and is affiliated with the Methodist Episcopal Church. He is a Republican. Among his recreations are horseback riding and baseball.

Mr. Pauley was married to Bessie Willifer Cattle, at Seward, Seward County, Nebraska. Mrs. Pauley, whose ancestry is English, was born at Seward, August 23, 1893. Five children were born to them: Jacinth, born September 16, 1916; Harriet, born February 8, 1918; Mary Alice, born February 7, 1921; Margaret, born March 4, 1925; and William George, born April 28, 1927. Residence: Hastings.

Henry Pavlat

Henry Pavlat, county clerk of Cheyenne County, was born at Lodgepole, Nebraska, May 21, 1891, son of John and Mary (Tchel) Pavlat. His father was born in Europe of Bohemian ancestry, and before his death at Lodgepole was a farmer.

Mr. Pavlat attended the public schools of Lodgepole to the 11th grade, the Sidney High School until 1909, and had two years work in the Lincoln Business College. On May 10, 1914, he was married to Angeline G. Lawson at Cheyenne. She is the daughter of Alexander and Mary B. (Duncan) Lawson. Mrs. Pavlat is a member of the Eastern Star and Parent Teacher Association. Mrs. Pavlat was born at Cheyenne, Wyoming, May 28, 1894. There are two children: John H., born December 21, 1914, and Rose Marie, born May 20, 1926.

Mr. Pavlat is a Democrat. He is a member of Light Memorial Presbyterian Church, the Masons, Eastern Star, and Parent Teachers Association. For the past five years he has been secretary of the Chamber of Commerce. His favorite sport is fishing. Residence. Sidney.

Henry Allan Payzant

Henry Allan Payzant, retired farmer, was born at Black River, King's County, Nova Scotia, April 8, 1853, and has been a resident of Nebraska forty-seven years. He is the son of John and Mary Ann (Curry) Payzant, the former, a farmer, born at Antigonish, Nova Scotia, April 12, 1808. He died at Black River, March 13, 1885. His wife, Mary Anne, who was born at Falmouth, Nova Scotia, April 7, 1813, died at Black River, December 22, 1861. The father was of French descent, while the mother's people came from the north of Ireland.

Mr. Payzant was educated in the common schools, and until his retirement a short time ago engaged in farming. He was married to Mary Maud Ellis at Schuyler, Nebraska. She was born at Sheffield Mills, Nova Scotia, September 19, 1863, and died at Schuyler, September 20, 1912. He is a member of the Methodist Episcopal Church, and of the Nebraskana Society.

There are ten children of this marriage, nine of whom are living: Robie Arthur, born November 14, 1887, married Alma Nollman; George Allison, born July 5, 1889; Fred Henry, born December 20, 1891, married Eva Kunneman; Pearl Grace, born January 21, 1894, married George Bartz; Loyd Chester, born October 20, 1895, died August 5, 1896; John Austin, born February 27, 1898, married Louise Vetter; Thaddeus Freeman, born August 27, 1899, married Elizabeth Pederson; Perry Curry, born October 10, 1901, married Lenora Jungbluth; Burton Ells, born July 29, 1904, married Vera Stark; and Helen May, born August 7, 1906, who is unmarried. On September 7, 1915, Mr. Payzant was married to Mrs. Anna Wieland Williams. Residence: Schuyler.

Thomas James Peacock

A resident of Nebraska for the past 53 years, Thomas James Peacock was born at Jefferson, Iowa, December 4, 1875, the son of Thomas and Margaret Matilda (Bogardus) Peacock. His father, who was an orderly Sergeant under General McClellan in the army on the Potomac during the Civil War, was known as a gallant soldier and patriot; he was born in London, March 4, 1829, and in 1848, came to this country where he engaged in farming; he died at Mariaville, Nebraska, October 18, 1892. His mother, who was born at Albany, New York, October 27, 1837, was a pioneer farm woman in Nebraska and acted as mid-wife to pioneer women in her community. She is of Holland Dutch descent, and is the direct heir to the Bogardus estate in the heart of New York City near Trinity Church and Wall Street.

Mr. Peacock was a Methodist minister for several years, and is now a farmer at Newport, Nebraska. He is secretary of the Rock County Historical Society, is a member of the Red Cross, and is affiliated with the Methodist Episcopal Church at Long Pine, Nebraska. His hobbies are reading and writing.

His marriage to Grace Lucretia Vargason occurred at Bassett, Nebraska, July 2, 1898. Mrs. Peacock, whose ancestry is German, was born at Creighton, Nebraska, July 27, 1882. The following children were born to them: Ruth, May 19, 1899, who married Earl Cushing; Thomas, December 6, 1900, who died January 30, 1905; Agatha February 21, 1903, who married Walter Vargason; Oscar, July 10, 1906; C. Wesley, February 19, 1909, who died March 21, 1909; Leone, March 22, 1911; Velma, December 10, 1914; Grant, December 22, 1917; Grace, February 22, 1920; and Mildred, January 27, 1924.

Mr. Peacock took an active part in loan drives during the recent war. Politically, he is a Republican. Residence: Newport.

Jesse Leland Pearl

Born at Davenport, Nebraska, February 12, 1905, Jesse Leland Pearl is the son of Henry Arthur and Myrtella (MacDonald) Pearl. His father, who is a farmer near Burwell, Nebraska, was born at Buda, Illinois, May 26, 1873. William Henry Pearl, father of Henry Pearl, was of New England stock, was a volunteer in the Civil War, and was one of the early pioneers of Saline County, Nebraska. Myrtella (MacDonald) Pearl, who was born at Friend, Nebraska, September 18, 1874, is of Scotch and Irish descent; her father served in the Civil War for four years and participated in the famed march to the sea with Sherman.

Mr. Pearl served in the rural schools of Garfield and Thayer counties, was graduated from the Burwell High School in 1923, and lacks only a few credits towards an A. B. degree at the University of Nebraska, where he was secretary of Delta Theta Phi in 1928 and 1929. He also attended the Kearney State Teachers College.

For a number of years he taught in rural schools, and at this time is county treasurer of Garfield County. He is a member of the Wranglers Club of Burwell, is affiliated with the First Christian Church, and holds membership in the Nebraskana Society. His favorite sport is football, while his hobby is public speaking. Mr. Pearl's membership in Delta Phi, legal fraternity, is occasioned by his intention of entering the legal profession. He is a Republican. Residence: Burwell. (Photograph in Album).

Charles Elliott Pearse

Charles Elliott Pearse, one of Columbus's outstanding executives, was born at Negaunee, Michigan, April 10, 1883, son of Frank Ellery and Martha Cornell (Baker) Pearse. The father, born in Cleveland, Ohio, August 10, 1855, is a graduate of Columbia University and a leading lawyer. He traces his ancestry to English settlers in America about 1750. Martha Cornell Baker was born at Brooklyn, New York, April 22, 1859, and died at New York City, January 31, 1930. She was of Dutch and English descent.

Mr. Pearse attended high school at Chicago, and from 1897 until 1901 was employed by Marshall Field Company. From 1901 to 1918 he was secretary of the Hume, Robertson & Wycoff Company of Madison. He was made president of the organization in 1912. He

removed to Columbus in 1929, is director and auditor of the Nebraska Continental Telephone Company, and a director of several other corporations.

He was married to Myra Hume at Grand Heaven, Michigan, August 14, 1907, and to them were born three children, Margaret on November 24, 1909, Jean, on March 3, 1912; Emma H., on October 12, 1915. Margaret was graduated from the University of Nebraska in 1931, while Jean is a student at Grinnell, Iowa. Mrs. Pearse, who is the daughter of James Bailie Hume, was born at Madison, March 24, 1886.

Mr. Pearse is a Republican. During the World War he was a member of the Madison County Council of Defense, and for six year he was a member of the School Board. He is a Mason, a member of the Red Cross, Chamber of Commerce, Lions Club, and the Young Men's Christian Association. He is an Episcopalian.

Mr. Pearse's social clubs include the Athletic Club of Omaha and the Wayside Country Club at Columbus. His favorite sport is fishing. Residence: Columbus.

Robert Pease

Robert Pease was born at Somers, Tolland County, Connecticut, December 19, 1869, the son of Robert and Eliza Billings (Hall) Pease. His father, a farmer and a leader in his community, was born at Somers, March 28, 1808, and died at Niantic, New London County, Connecticut, January 21, 1888; he held local offices of trust and responsibility and, with the exception of his service in the legislature, refused to accept remuneration for public service; his ancestors came to this country from England, in 1633. Eliza Billings (Hall) Pease, mother of Robert Pease, Jr., was born at Somers, August 15, 1824, and died at Beatrice, December 30, 1910.

Mr. Pease attended the public schools of Connecticut, and later was a student at Morgan Academy, Clinton, Connecticut, where he was active in football. He received training in the mercantile business early in life, and after serving seven years in the railway mail service he engaged in the mercantile business. From 1903 to 1923 he was engaged in the grain business in Kansas and Nebraska. He is now postmaster at Beatrice, Gage County, Nebraska.

He is a member of the Young Men's Christian Association, the Red Cross, the Nebraskana Society, Beatrice Chamber of Commerce, and the Masons. He is interested in football and likes to hunt. His political affiliation is with the Republican party, but he has never been a candidate for an elective office.

On June 4, 1901, Mr. Pease was married to Bertha Ella Clark, at Cheyenne, Laramie County, Wyoming. Mrs. Pease, who was born at Olivet, Eaton County, Michigan, June 19, 1874, was a Latin teacher before her marriage. Her ancestry includes such notables as Abraham Clark, signer of the Declaration of Independence, and Lewis Clark, officer in the Civil War. Three children were born to this marriage: Robert, Jr., born July 10, 1906, who married Lorena Sherman; Florence C., born November 18, 1908, who was graduated from Doane College in 1930; and Geraldine, born March 28, 1911, who is a student at Doane College. All the children are graduates of the Beatrice High School. Robert, Jr., who was formerly a student at the University of Nebraska, is now manager of the Pease Grain and Seed Company at Beatrice. Residence: Beatrice.

Charles William Peasinger

Charles Peasinger, distinguished lawyer at Randolph, Cedar County, Nebraska, has lived in this state all his life and has been active in his community in civic and legal affairs. He was born at Omaha, on August 2, 1889, the son of Elizabeth (Reiter) and Jacob Peasinger. His father, a contractor, was born at Luxemburg, Germany, 1842, and died at Omaha, October 18, 1925. His mother

Genelli—Sioux City, Iowa

CHARLES W. PEASINGER

was born at Manistee, Michigan, 1856, and died at Omaha, July 8, 1910.

Judge Peasinger received his grade school and high school education at Omaha, and later was awarded the A. B., A. M., and LL. B., degrees at Creighton University. Prior to his receiving the LL. B. degree, Mr. Peasinger was principal of the high school at Treynor, Iowa, for one year, and during the time that he studied law he was engaged in newspaper work, as reporter for the Omaha World-Herald.

He practiced law at Omaha for five years following his admission to the State and Federal Bars, and was actively affiliated with the Omaha Commercial Club and Ak-Sar-Ben. He has been engaged in the practice of law since 1920 in Cedar County. In 1918 he was elected county judge, and since 1920 he has been city attorney of Randolph. He has revised, compiled, and published the ordinances, from the date of incorporation of Randolph. He is a Democrat.

Since 1930, he has been president of the Lions Club, and Deputy District Governor of Lions International. Since 1925 he has been secretary and treasurer of the Randolph Country Club, and since 1929 he has been president of Number 20 Federal Highway Association. He holds membership in the American Bar Association, the Nebraska State Bar Association, and the Nebraskana Society. He is affiliated with St. Frances de Chantel Catholic Church at Randolph.

His marriage to Elizabeth Marie Gentleman was solemnized at Omaha, May 8, 1917. The following children were born to them: Charles, born July 12, 1919; Helen, born July 10, 1921; Rosemary, born January 11, 1925; and George, born October 4, 1930. His favorite sport is golf. Residence: Randolph. (Photograph on Page 927).

Edward Porter Peck

One of Omaha's best known grain men, Edward Porter Peck was born at Akron, Ohio, October 22, 1855, the son of James Porter and Elizabeth Huntington (Ames) Peck. James Porter, Peck, a native of Summit County, Ohio, born October 11, 1821, was among the foremost of Omaha's early physicians and served as city physician from 1858 to 1861, and as president of the Omaha Medical Society in 1866, and trustee of that body in 1869. He was the son of Sherman and Anna Peck. He died at Omaha, February 20, 1887.

Elizabeth Huntington Ames was born December 15, 1824, and died at Omaha, September 1, 1908. She was the daughter of Elijah Ames of New London, Connecticut, and came to Nebraska with her husband in the early days of the state, bringing with her her year old son, Edward.

Edward Porter Peck was educated in the Omaha public and high schools. Entering the grain business soon after leaving school, he has been the vice president of the Omaha Elevator Company, president of the Terminal Elevator Grain Merchants Association, director of F. H. Peavey and Company, etc. Since 1927, he has been a director of the United States Chamber of Commerce. He is a director of the Union Stock Yards Co., Ltd., and the U. S. National Bank and National Security Fire Insurance Company, and is vice president and general manager of the Omaha Elevator Company.

He was married to Mary Ella Bishop, at Omaha, September 19, 1876. Mrs. Peck was born at Chicago, April 20, 1855, and died at Omaha, June 13, 1929. There are four children: Elizabeth Ames, born October 28, 1877, married Joseph Barker; Helen Bishop, born June 9, 1880, married the Rev. Robert B. H. Bell; Lyman, born October 15, 1885, married Aimee Kenny; and Louise Porter, born August 2, 1888, married Denise Barkalow.

Mr. Peck is a Republican. He attends Trinity Cathedral, and is a member of the Omaha Club, and the Chicago Club. Residence: Omaha.

Rich Stetson Peckham

Born at Brady, Nebraska, August 22, 1906, Rich Stetson Peckham is the son of one of Lincoln County's foremost citizens. His father, Herman Kossuth Peckham, was born in Soldiers Grove, Wisconsin, January 15, 1860. Now retired, he has been extremely successful as a rancher, and is looked upon as one of the most outstanding citizens of his community.

The ancestry of the Peckham family is traced to John Peckham, Archbishop of Canterbury (1279-1292), and to Sir John Peckham, his descendant, who came to America in 1638 and settled in Rhode Island. Stella Nevada Rich, wife of Herman Peckham, was born in Rockport, Missouri, February 5, 1874. An extensive traveler, Mrs. Peckham is a member of the Daughters of the American Revolution and the P. E. O. Sisterhood, and was formerly a teacher in rural schools. At the present time Mr. and Mrs. Herman Kossuth Peckham are residing in Omaha.

Rich Stetson Peckham attended the public schools of Brady, and was graduated from high school in 1924. He was a letterman on the basketball team there four years. Since leaving school he has been associated with his father, and upon his retirement assumed the management of the 79 Ranch. Politically he is independent. He is a member of the Methodist Episcopal Church, the Odd Fellows and the Nebraskana Society. His favorite sport is golf.

On December 20, 1925, he was married to Edith Carolyn Peterson at Washington, D. C. Mrs. Peckham was born at Brady, December 5, 1904. She is a member of the Methodist Episcopal Church, the Rebekahs, and the Nebraska Federation of Women's Clubs. They have two children, Rich, Jr., born May 28, 1927; and Marian, born October 1, 1929. Residence: Brady.

Hans Christian Pedersen

One of Fremont's leading physicians and surgeons, Hans Christian Pedersen was born at Saint Paul, Nebraska, December 3, 1883. He is the son of Soren Nort and Petrea Johanne (Zako) Pedersen. Soren Nort Pedersen was born at Tjaereborg, Jutland, Denmark, December 15, 1856, and died at Dannebrog, Nebraska, November 9, 1891. A section foreman on the Union Pacific, he came to America in the spring of 1876. His wife, Petrea, was a native of Farre, Jutland, Denmark, born January 29, 1856, who died at Dannebrog, July 16, 1888. She was the daughter of Peter and Barbara Zako.

Dr. Hans Christian Pedersen received his education in Dannebrog public schools, and attended high school two years. He received his A. B. and B. Sc. degree at the University of Nebraska in 1900, and attended the Nebraska University College of Medicine 1900-06. He was admitted to practice at Farwell, Nebraska, in 1906.

Engaged in practice since his admission, Dr. Pedersen is also surgeon to the Military Avenue and Richmond Hospitals, and is a member of the American, Nebraska State and Dodge County Medical Associations, the Mayo Physicians and Surgeons Club, and the Elkhorn Valley Medical Association.

He was married to Mayme Wilhelmina Werner at Chicago, June 1, 1914. Mrs. Pedersen was born at Boelus, Nebraska, March 6, 1894. They attend tthe First Lutheran Church of Dannebrog. A first lieutenant in the Medical Reserve Corps, Dr. Pedersen served oversees at Base Hospital No. 131, and was promoted to the rank of captain on September 21, 1918. He is a member of the American Legion, the Veterans of Foreign Wars and the Young Men's Christian Association.

His civic and fraternal organizations include the Chamber of Commerce, Rotary Club (former member), the Elks, Nebraska Consistory, Mount Tabor Commandery No. 9, Knights Templar, Tangier Temple of the Shrine, Royal Jesters, at Omaha, the Low Twelve Clubs of Omaha and Lincoln. He is a member of the American Association for the Advancement of Science, the Nebraskana Society and the Red Cross. He has served as president of the Dodge County Medical Association and also belongs to the Fremont Outboard Motor Club and the Izaak Walton League. He is fond of hunting, fishing, golf and football, and his hobby is reading. Residence: Fremont. (Photograph in Album).

Henry Pedersen

Henry Pedersen was born at Hardy, Nebraska, January 2, 1893, the son of Rasmus and Stina (Anderson) Pedersen. His father, who was a pioneer and successful farmer in Nuckolls County, Nebraska, was born at Laaland, Denmark, in 1847, and died at Ruskin, Nebraska, March 21, 1924. His mother was born at Falster, Denmark, in 1854, and died at Hardy, March 2, 1928.

Mr. Pedersen received his early education in the rural schools of Nuckolls County, Nebraska, and in 1913 was a student at the Nebraska College of Agriculture. He has been actively engaged in farming since 1915, at the same time owning and managing a meat market at Hardy. He has been manager of the Co-operative Shipping Association for two years, was a car dealer and salesman at Hardy, Nebraska, for a short time, and at this time is engaged in extensive farming in both Webster and Nuckolls County.

He is a director in the Guide Rock State Bank, and the Farmers Union Co-operative Creamery of Superior, Aurora, Norfolk, and Fremont, Nebraska. Mr. Pedersen is a member of the Nebraskana Society, the Methodist Church, Masons and Odd Fellows, and the University Club of Lincoln. He served as a member of the local school board from 1921 to 1924. A Democrat, he was elected state senator in 1931.

He was married to Minnie Swanson at Omaha, February 24, 1915. Mrs. Pedersen, who was a teacher before her marriage, was born at Oakland, Nebraska, September 10, 1892, and died at Hardy, October 15, 1925. Three children were born to them: Vernon, April 24, 1916, who died June 6, 1928; Walter R., July 1, 1920; and Norman C., July 13, 1923. On December 24, 1927, Mr. Pedersen was united in marriage with Doris May Sims, who was born at Edgar, Nebraska, July 15, 1902. They have one son, Charles E., born February 8, 1930. Residence: Guide Rock.

Lars Pedersen

Lars Pedersen was born in Nuckolls County, Nebraska, February 7, 1897, the son of Rasmuss and Stena (Anderson) Pedersen. His father, who was born at Olbier, Denmark, in 1846, and died at Ruskin, Nebraska, March 7, 1924, was a farmer and an early settler in Nebraska. His mother was born in Denmark in 1842 and died in Nuckolls County March 1, 1928.

Mr. Pedersen received his early education in rural schools near Ruskin and later attended Blair College for a year. He has been director of the local school board at Hardy, Nebraska, for the past three years, where he has engaged in farming. He holds membership in the Independent Order of Odd Fellows, the Rebekah Lodge, and the Danish Lutheran Church. He is actively interested in 4 H Club affairs, and is the breeder of Spotted Poland China Hogs.

During the World War Mr. Pedersen served as second class seaman, and since 1919 has been a member of the American Legion. His favorite sports are hunting, fishing, and horseshoe pitching, while his hobby is playing checkers.

He married Leta Bernice McKinney at Nora, Nebraska, June 1, 1921. Mrs. Pedersen, whose ancestry is Irish, was born at Nora, June 10, 1901. To this union the following children were born: Gene, born May 17, 1922; Elberta, August 31, 1923; Ruth, March 31, 1925;

Marie, November 24, 1926; Victor, March 8, 1928; Junior, November 23, 1929; Max, April 18, 1931. Residence: Hardy.

William Ross Pedley

Born at Thayer, Iowa, November 4, 1871, William Ross Pedley is the son of William Henry and Cynthia Hendrick (Butler) Pedley. His father, who was a farmer, was born of English parents at Hanley, England, February 8, 1842, and died at Bertrand, Nebraska, June 11, 1930. His mother was born at Fairfield, Vermont, March 4, 1844, and died at Bertrand, December 25, 1929.

Mr. Pedley was engaged in the drug business with the firm Axtell & Pedley, 1890-97, at Loomis, Nebraska, and the firm Pedley & Scranton, 1896-1910, at Bertrand. He is now postmaster there, and for four years was a member of the County Board of Supervisors. He holds membership in the Bertrand Commercial Club, the First Congregational Church, and the Masonic Lodge.

He was united in marriage with Carrie A. Axtell at Hastings, Nebraska, April 27, 1896. Mrs. Pedley, who is assistant post-master, was born at Rutland, Wisconsin, May 3, 1866. They have one son: Norris, born December 7, 1903. Residence: Bertrand.

Minnie Freeman Penney

Known to Nebraskans as the first woman to serve as a national committeewoman, Mrs. Penney is active in many other phases of public life. Born at Raymonds Corners, Pennsylvania, February 25, 1868, she has been interested in organization since girlhood. She is the daughter of William Elder and Sarah Lovica (Cushing) Freeman. Her father was a merchant and farmer, descended from English settlers. He made his first trip to Nebraska in 1868, and brought his family here in 1871. He died June 14, 1912.

Sarah Lovica Freeman, wife of William, was born in Potter County, Pennsylvania, April 8, 1833, and died at Cushing, Nebraska, in August, 1904. (See *Cushing Genealogy*). Upon the completion of her grade school education in the schools of St. Paul and Ord, Nebraska, Mrs. Penney attended York Methodist College, now the Wesleyan University at Lincoln. A member of Alpha chapter of Pi Beta Phi, she is active in the alumnae and is especially interested in its mountain school at Catlinburg, Tennessee.

On April 22, 1891, she married Edgar B. Penney, of Odell, Illinois, a merchant. They have two children: Freeman Seth, born October 17, 1895, who married Phyllis Gayle; and Fredric Doyle, born January 11, 1920, married to Janice Beck.

A Republican, Mrs. Penney was appointed by Senator Howell as national Republican committeewoman for a term of two years, 1922-24. In 1924 in the state primary she was elected for a four year term as Republican committeewoman and conducted the Woman's Department Campaign for the state in that year. During the war she was Nance County chairman of the Council of Defense and instructor in surgical dressing for the Red Cross.

She is a member of the Daughters of the American Revolution. She served as first president for the department of Nebraska of the American Legion Auxiliary. Her religious affiliation is with St. Alban's Episcopal Church of Fullerton.

A contributor to magazines and newspapers on club subjects, she is a member of the National League of American Pen Women. Honorary membership has been awarded her in the National Camp Fire Girls. She is a member of the Eastern Star. During 1921-23 she was state president of the Nebraska Federation of Women's Clubs. She was general federation director in 1923 and 1925. Her social club is the Omaha College Club. Her hobbies are reading and music. Residence: Chicago. (Photograph on Page 930).

MINNIE FREEMAN PENNEY

Gladstone Perkin

Gladstone Perkin, merchant, was born at Coldwater, Ohio, September 24, 1882, and has resided in Nebraska for the past 41 years. He is the son of Joseph Henry and Elizabeth Sproul Perkins, the former a native of Leeds, England, born December 3, 1849. He has been a merchant in western Nebraska for 40 years. He came to the United States from England in 1870. His wife, Elizabeth, died at Coldwater, about 1885.

Educated in the public schools at Grant, Mr. Perkin has worked in the store, owned by his father, since 1900, and before that was employed in a store at Grant. He is a member of the Maywood Commercial Club and the Odd Fellows.

His marriage to Ruby Elizabeth Fletcher was solemnized at Holdrege, March 2, 1914. Mrs. Perkin was born at Council Bluffs, Iowa, April 19, 1896. They have four children all in school, Richard, born December 4, 1914; Dorothy, born January 28, 1920; Marguerite, born April 14, 1923; and Willis, born February 9, 1927. Residence: Maywood.

Lyman Ormond Perley

For 40 years Lyman Ormond Perley was engaged in the practice of law at Omaha, Douglas County, Nebraska. He was born at Emporia, Lyon County, Kansas, February 28, 1866, the son of Isaiah Edward and Mary Jane (Allen) Perley. His father, who was born at Berlin, Vermont, March 12, 1834, and died at Emporia, July 11, 1894, was a banker and merchant; he was descended from Allan Perley who came to the United States with Governor Winthrop in 1630, having originally emigrated from Wales. His mother was born at New Hudson, New York County, New York, July 23, 1839, and died at Emporia. She was a teacher in Kansas before the Civil War; she was the daughter of Isabel (Frary) and Asaph K. Allen; the latter, together with his sons was an ardent anti-slavery advocate.

Mr. Perley attended the public schools of Emporia, and in 1881 was graduated from Emporia High School. He received the B. S. degree at Northwestern University, and the LL. B. degree at Yale University, 1886 and 1890, respectively. He held membership in Phi Kappa Psi and Phi Delta Phi.

He was interested in the live stock industry for several years, and since 1890 was engaged in the practice of law. He is a member of the Nebraskana Society, is affiliated with the First Central Congregational Church, and was politically a Progressive.

Mr. Perley was married at Omaha, December 10, 1895, to Nora Rachel Gibson. Mrs. Perley, who was the daughter of Edgar Milton and Julia Ann (Lawrence) Gibson of Maine, was born at Fairfield, Maine, July 24, 1869. Four children were born to this marriage: Edward Gibson, born October 11, 1896, who resides in Kansas City, Missouri; Constance, born March 12, 1902, who is living in New Haven, Connecticut. She is married to James A. Work; Anne Macgregor, born October 3, 1904, who is living in St. Louis, is a biochemist; and Nora, born November 17, 1908, who will complete her work at Grinnell College in 1933. Constance is a librarian. Residence: Omaha.

Benton Perry

Benton Perry was born at Alexandria, Madison County, Indiana, September 20, 1888, the son of William L. and Flora B. (Bennett) Perry. His father's ancestry was Irish, and his mother who was born in Adams County, Illinois, November 6, 1867, was of English and Dutch descent.

Mr. Perry attended the York grade school and in 1904 was graduated from the York High School. He was awarded the LL. B. degree at Cumberland Univer-

sity at Lebanon, Tennessee, in 1918. For 12 years he was connected with the City National Bank at York, and since that time has been a practicing lawyer there. He holds membership in the York County Bar Association, the Nebraska State Bar Association, the York County Commercial Club, and the American Bar Association.

He served as secretary of the York County Red Cross for two years and was York County food administrator during the World War. He is affiliated with the First Congregational Church at York, is a member of the Knights of Pythias, and holds membership in the Nebraskana Society. A Republican, Mr. Perry served as county attorney of York County for four years.

His marriage to Elizabeth L. Hart was solemnized at Enid, Oklahoma, September 22, 1915. Mrs. Perry, who was a teacher before her marriage, died at York, September 15, 1930. Three children were born to them: Thomas B., born July 14, 1916; Francis Hart, born June 18, 1918; and Betty Lee, born December 6, 1920. Residence: York.

Chester Arthur Perry

Chester A. Perry, one of Lincoln's most prominent executives, has lived in the state for the past 47 years, and today is recognized as a leader in civic and commercial affairs. He was born at Oakharbor, Ohio, January 31, 1884, the son of Arthur Villars and Nancy Jane (Goodsite) Perry. His father, born at Redfield, New York, September 13, 1854, is a successful lumberman, serving as secretary of the Perry Lumber Company, operating lumber yards throughout the state; his ancestors came to America from England, in the early days of this country.

His mother was born at Oakharbor, February 2, 1857, and died at Cambridge, Nebraska, March 12, 1911. She was of German and Scotch descent, and was one of the pioneers of Nebraska.

Mr. Perry was graduated from Cambridge High School and was a student at Lincoln Academy for a time; he was active in athletics and was engaged in semi-professional baseball at one time. Since 1906 he has been auditor of the Perry Lumber Company at Lincoln, Nebraska, and for the past 13 years has been secretary of the organization. He is president of the Nebraska Lumber Merchants' Association; secretary of the Perry-McIntire Lumber Company and the Perry-Sheets Lumber Company, and is president of the Moorish Tile and Supply Company.

A Republican, he served as mayor of Cambridge, from 1921-26. He is a member of the Lincoln Chamber of Commerce; the Lincoln Optimists Club; the Young Men's Christian Association; and the Nebraskana Society. His social clubs are: Eastridge Country Club; Shrine Country Club; and the Masons. His sports include golf, fishing and hunting, while his hobby is gardening. He is affiliated with the First Plymouth Congregational Church of Lincoln.

Mr. Perry was married at Lincoln, March 7, 1906, to Edna Amanda Clay. Mrs. Perry, who is a descendant of the distinguished statesman Henry Clay, was born at Farmington, New Hampshire, September 16, 1884. Their children are: Melvin, born June 24, 1908, who was graduated from the College of Agriculture at the University of Nebraska, in 1929; Leonard, born July 5, 1911; Evalyn, born March 11, 1914; Barbara, born June 22, 1918; and Paul, born January 30, 1923. Residence: Lincoln.

Claibourne G. Perry

Claibourne G. Perry, lawyer, was born at Wahoo, Nebraska, November 27, 1889, son of Thomas S. and Sarah A. (Watkins) Perry. The father was born in Angus, Canada, and is descended from Irish and English settlers in Ontario in 1790. He was in the agricul-

ERNEST BERT PERRY

tural implement business, and from 1898 until 1902 served as county surveyor of Saunders County. He died at Winner, South Dakota, August 31, 1922. His wife, Sarah, was born in Sketty, Swansea, South Wales, Great Britain, February 17, 1855, and is greatly interested in church work.

Mr. Perry attended the public schools at Wahoo, Nebraska, until June 1, 1903, and on June 7, 1907, was graduated from the Lincoln, Nebraska, High School. He received his Bachelor of Laws degree from the University of Nebraska on June 11, 1914, where he was a member of Phi Delta Phi and Phi Gamma Delta.

His marriage to Hazel M. Putman was solemnized at Golden, Colorado, March 10, 1923. Mrs. Perry was born in Morrill County, Nebraska, June 26, 1896. Her ancestry is American since pre-Revolutionary days on her father's side. Her mother's people came to the United States from England about 1830.

Mr. Perry began the practice of law at Bridgeport, Nebraska, in 1915, continuing until 1917. He was associated with William Ritchie, Jr., as a member of the firm of Ritchie and Perry. From 1919 until 1920 he was a member of the firm of Hunt and Perry in partnership with George J. Hunt, and since that time has practiced independently. He is serving as county attorney of Morrill County at the present time, and during 1920-21 served as mayor of Bridgeport. He is a Democrat.

During the World War Mr. Perry had 22 months service with the rank of first lieutenant in the 351st Infantry, 88th Division. He served in the American Expeditionary Forces under the army of occupation from January, 1919, until May, 1919. He is a member of the American Legion. His professional organizations include, the Nebraska state and western Nebraska bar associations. He is a member of the Episcopal Church of the Good Shepherd, the Lions Club, the Ancient Free and Accepted Masons, the Scottish Rite Masons, the Shrine, and the Knights of Pythias. His club is the Bridgeport Country Club. His sports are golf and hunting, while his hobby is reading. Residence: Bridgeport.

Ernest Bert Perry

One of Nebraska's most outstanding lawyers, Ernest Bert Perry was born at Haskins, Ohio, August 11, 1876. He is the son of Arthur Villars and Nancy Jane (Goodsite) Perry, the former of whom was born at Redfield, New York, September 13, 1854. The father locating in Gosper County in 1880, was one of the first county commissioners of that county, and a pioneer lumberman. He is president of the Perry Lumber Company; descended from settlers in Rhode Island in the 17th century. His family is of the same stock as Commodore Perry, and he is a direct descendant of George W. Perry of the War of 1812. Nancy Jane Goodsite was born at Oak Harbor, Ohio, February 2, 1857, daughter of Ernest Frederick and Marguerite (Welch) Goodsite. The former of German and the latter of Scotch descent. Nancy Goodsite died at Cambridge, Nebraska, March 24, 1911.

Upon his graduation from the public schools, Ernest B. Perry attended the University of Nebraska, from which he received his LL. B. degree. As *Who's Who in Jurisprudence* says of him, he "began practice of law at Cambridge, Nebraska, and after the first few years practice developed into trial business, extending over southern Nebraska and eastern Colorado. First he was in partnership with E. J. Lambe of Beaver City as Perry and Lambe, 1905-08; then B. F. Butler entered the firm and the name changed to Perry, Lambe and Butler, of which firm he remained senior member until he became district judge, 1912. He resigned as district judge in 1920 and resumed the practice of law in Lincoln, Nebraska, and was attorney in the Brown Will Case and the Starr-Gifford litigation and successfully defended, among others, George Critser, charged with the murder

of William Dillon; Ben Jussel charged with the murder of Peter Heagney, and Martin Morris, charged with the murder of Pearl Turner. He also successfully defended Dr. Abbott, Steve Carver and Kenneth Lanham. He is general attorney for the Nebraska League of Municipalities at the present time. He is senior member of the firm of Perry, Van Pelt & Marti, Lincoln, Nebraska.

A Republican, he was member of the Nebraska legislature from Furnas County 1903-07, chairman of the judiciary committee and majority leader, 1905; district judge of the 14th judicial district 1912-20, and declined appointment to the Supreme bench in 1920. During 1924-26 he was American member of the United States-Mexico Claims Commission, and for his work it is said of him, 'Honorable Ernest B. Perry has served the United States government exceptionally well in adjudicating property claims of United States citizens with the government and nationals of Mexico. His dissenting opinion in the celebrated Pringle case is one of the most lucid and searching revelations of the perfidy of Villa on the one hand, and the vacillating policy of the Carranza government on the other, to be found in the history of the western world. . . . . It is doubtful if the fallacy of a judicial decision was ever more clearly pointed out by the dissenting opinion than in this case.'"

Mr. Perry was president of the University of Nebraska Alumni Association in 1922, chairman of the Republican State Committee 1922-24 and chairman of the Nebraska delegation to the Republican National Convention in 1924. During the World War he was chairman of the legal advisory board of Furnas County. An author of note, among his works are *Local Ethics, The Little Fellow, The Interest Problem* and *The Santa Isabel Case*. He is a 32nd degree, Scottish Rite Mason, a member of the Kiwanis Club (president, 1931), the Chamber of Commerce, Red Cross and Community Chest. His professional memberships include the American, Nebraska State and Lancaster County Bar Associations, and his clubs are the University and Lincoln Country Clubs.

On June 23, 1904, he was married to Clara Wood Fowler, at Lincoln. Mrs. Perry, who was born at Illion, New York, December 9, 1877, was a teacher in the high school at Minden, and at Nebraska Wesleyan before her marriage. She is the daughter of Louis J. and Amelia E. (Wood) Fowler, both direct descendants of early New England colonists. There are five children: Lila Fowler, born September 1, 1905, married Wilson Watkins, and resides at Wichita, Kansas. Ernest Louis, born August 7, 1907, married Evelyn Anderson, and is engaged in the retail lumber business at Cambridge. Arthur Edwin, born March 12, 1910, A. B., 1931, and is now a law student at the University. Louise Bernice, born June 3, 1913, and Ralph Robert, born March 6, 1917, are students of the University and Lincoln High School. Mr. and Mrs. Perry are members of First Plymouth Congregational Church at Lincoln. Residence: Lincoln. (Photograph on Page 932).

John Joseph Pershing

General John Joseph Pershing, distinguished throughout the world for military service, was born in Linn County, Missouri, September 13, 1860, the son of John Fletcher and Anne Elizabeth Thompson Pershing. His father was born near St. Clair, Westmoreland County, Pennsylvania, March 1, 1834, and died at Chicago, Illinois, March 16, 1906. His mother was born at Maryville, Blount County, Tennessee, February 15, 1835, and died at Chicago, November 24, 1902.

General Pershing was graduated from the Kirksville, (Missouri) Normal School in 1880, and in 1886 was graduated from the United States Military Academy. He has been honored by recognition of his tremendous service to the world, by government leaders and execu-

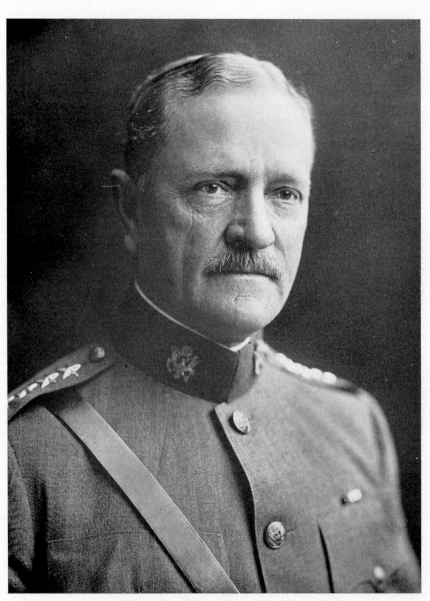

(GEN.) JOHN JOSEPH PERSHING

tives over the world, and has had an unusual brilliant career.

On September 30, 1886, he joined his regiment and served with it at Fort Bayard, New Mexico, in the campaign against the Apache Indians, 1886 to 1887. His next active service was in the field in South Dakota in the campaign against the Sioux Indians, 1891, and commanding Indian scouts at Pine Ridge Agency, South Dakota. He served as professor of military science and tactics at the University of Nebraska, 1891 to 1895. From 1897 to 1898 he was instructor of tactics at the Military Academy of West Point, and in 1898 served in Cuba in the Santiago Campaign. He was on duty at army headquarters at Washington, August 23, to December 20, 1898, was in the office of the assistant secretary of war, 1899, and removed to the Phillippine Islands by way of the Suez Canal, November 28, 1899.

He was adjutant general, district of Zamboanga, December 24, 1899, to April 24, 1900, was adjutant general of the Department of Mindanao, December 24, April 24, 1900, to August 3, 1901, was acting engineer of the same department, 1901, and was collector of customs at Zamboango, and ordinance officer and chief of the same department, to October 11, 1901. He served as commander of his squadron at Jolo, Philippine Islands, until 1902, was commanding provisional squadron at Camp Vicars, Philippine Islands commanding the expedition against the Moros, September 18, to October 3, 1902. He was on duty with the general staff at Washington, 1904, and was assistant to the chief of the staff, Southwestern Division, Oklahoma City, 1904.

In 1904 he was a student at the Army War College at Washington, sailed for Japan, February 14, 1905, and was military attache, Tokyo, from March 26, 1905 to October, 1906. He was commander of the department of California, until November 20, 1906, commander of the post, William McKinley Fort in the Philippines, January 3, 1907. In 1908 he sailed for Europe under special instructions pending the result of the situation in the Balkans and was designated as an observer in case open hostilities should ensue. After a leave of absence he was back on duty January 18, 1909, and the same year was on sick leave. On November 11, 1909, he was made commander of the Philippine Division, and from January 20, 1914 to March 15, 1916 he was commander of the expeditionary forces in Mexico, was commander of the district of El Paso, Texas, 1917, and commander of the southern department, February 21, to May, 1917. During the World War he was commander-in-chief of the American Expeditionary Forces in France, and on September 3, 1919, was appointed general of the armies of the United States. He was made chief of the staff, 1921.

Among the medals awarded him for distinguished service to his countrymen and the world are: Distinguished Service Medal, 1918; Indian Campaign Medal; Spanish Campaign Medal; Philippine Campaign Medal; Mexican Service Medal; Army of Cuban Occupation Medal. These foreign decorations have been bestowed upon him: Belgian Order de Leopold, (grand croix); Belgian Croix de Guerre; British Order of the Bath, the knight grand cross; Chinese Grand Cordon of the Order of the Precious Light of Chia Ho, first class; Czechoslovakia Croix de Guerre; French Legion d'Honneur, (grand croix); French Medaille Militaire; Greek Order of the Saint Savoir; Italian Order of St. Maurice and St. Lazarus, (grand cross); Italian Military Order of Savoy, (grand cross); Japanese Order of the Rising Sun (grand cordon of the Paulownia); Montenegrin Madaille Obilitch; Montenegrin Order du Prince Danila Ier, (grand cordon); Panamanian Order of La Solidaridad, (first class); Rumanian Order of Michael the Brave, (grand cross); Servian Order of Kara George, (first class); and the Polish Cross Virtuti Militari.

Special medals awarded him include a commemorative medal from Dr. Adolfo Mugica, president of the committee of the city of Buenos Aires, given in token of the profound admiration in which he was held by the people of that country. A resolution was passed at a public meeting of Wanganui, New Zealand, as an expression of their appreciation of the value of General Pershing's services in the World War. The Congress of the United States bestowed upon the general their thanks by a joint resolution.

General Pershing is now retired. He is chairman of the American Battle Monuments Commission, is affiliated with the Episcopal Church, and holds membership in numerous educational, welfare, social, and civic organizations.

His marriage to Helen Frances Warren was solemnized at Washington, D. C., January 26, 1905. Mrs. Pershing was born at Cheyenne, Wyoming, August 16, 1880, and died at San Francisco, California, August 27, 1915. Four children were born to this union: Helen, born September 8, 1906; Anna O., born March 25, 1908; Francis W., born June 24, 1909; and Mary M., born May 19, 1912. Mrs. Pershing and her three daughters were tragically killed in the burning of the Presidio. Francis W. is living.

General Pershing is the author of *My Experience in the World War*. He is a 32nd degree Mason, is a member of the Metropolitan Club at Washington, and holds membership in the Army and Navy Club, Washington and New York. He holds the following scholastic degrees: LL. B., University of Nebraska, 1923; LL. D., University of Nebraska, 1917; DCL., Oxford University, 1919; DL., Cambridge University, 1919; DL., University of St. Andrews, 1919; DL., University of Arizona, 1920; DL. University of Maine, 1920; D. L. George Washington University, 1920; DL., Harvard University, 1920; DL., Columbia University, 1920; DL., Williams College, 1920; DL,. Yale University, 1920; D. M. S., Pennsylvania Military College, 1921; LL. D., University of Pennsylvania, 1922; LL. D., McGill University, 1922; and LL. D., University of Maryland, 1922. Residence: Lincoln. (Photograph on Page 954).

Albert Benjamin Persinger

Born at North Port, Alabama, May 7, 1851, Albert Benjamin Persinger is the son of Elias and Louise (Curling) Persinger. His father was born in Virginia in 1807 and his mother in Tuscaloosa, Alabama.

Mr. Persinger came to Nebraska 56 years ago and at the present time is the owner of the Hardscrabble Ranch located two miles east of Lodge Pole in Duel County. He has always been active in every civic, educational, religious and political project in his community. He is a member of the Masons, the Knights Templar and the Shrine, and is vice president of the Historical Society of Cheyenne County.

In 1888 he was married to Mary Adams at Cornwall, Ontario, where she was born. Mrs. Persinger is a direct descendant of John Quincy Adams. She is a member of the Episcopal Church. There are two children, Charlotte, born in 1881, who died in 1896; and Mary, born in 1884, who was married to George Harris Searcy, who is a physician and surgeon residing in Tuscaloosa, Alabama.

Mr. Persinger is a Democrat and a member of the Red Cross. Recently he was made a life member of the Nebraskana Society. Residence: Lodge Pole.

Edwin B. Person

One of the prominent bankers of Phelps County, Nebraska, Edwin B. Person is cashier of the Funk State Bank. He was born at Chicago, Illinois, December 4, 1877, the son of Peter M. and Hanna (Erickson) Person. His father, who was a farmer, sailor, and carpenter, was born in Sweden, August 5, 1840, and died at Holdrege, Nebraska, in July, 1926. His mother was born in

Norway, August 23, 1850, and is a devoted homemaker.

Mr. Person was married at Funk, June 28, 1911, to Violet N. Johnson, who was born in Johnson County, Illinois, July 1, 1886. They have two children: John Paul, born June 19, 1912; who is a medical student at the College of Medicine of the University of Nebraska; and Richard Edwin, born August 14, 1916. The family is affiliated with the Friedhem Lutheran Church of Funk. Residence: Funk.

Jay Alvin Person

Jay Alvin Person, prominent Chase County farmer, was born in Wauneta, Nebraska, January 5, 1887, son of Hocan and Augusta (Carlson) Person.

The father was born in Sweden, March 22, 1861, and came to the United States in 1882. His death occurred at Wauneta, August 23, 1904. His wife, Augusta, born in Sweden, September 20, 1858, came to the United States on November 25, 1883. She is still living.

Upon the completion of his elementary education in the Chase County Rural schools, Mr. Person took high school work at the Nebraska State Normal School at Kearney, and attended business college at Grand Island. He was a member of the debating team at Kearney, and participated in the debate against Peru State Teachers Normal School, 1915-1916.

In his earlier years Mr. Person taught rural school two terms. He has been a farmer most of his life and is greatly interested in co-operative organizations. From 1910 until 1919 he was secretary and a director of the Farmers Produce and Supply Company at Enders, Nebraska, and at the present time is director of the Wauneta Equity Mercantile Exchange. He is also president and a director of the Wauneta Co-operative Oil Company. His politics is independently Republican.

On June 13, 1917, he was married to Orba Euceba Pflum at Wauneta, Nebraska. She was born at Plevna, Missouri, December 8, 1882, her family tracing directly to the Henry Clay famly. She is a member of the Womans Club, and is active in the affairs of the Methodist Church. There are two children, Phillys Evangeline, born June 27, 1918; and Bruce Alvin, born April 9, 1920.

During the years 1914-15 and 1915-16 Mr. Person was a member of the Young Men's Christian Association at Kearney, and was president of the local organization during the last mentioned year. He is a member of the local library board and of the board of trustees of Wauneta Rural High School. He attends the Methodist Episcopal Church, and is a member of the Wauneta Commercial Club. During the late war he was extremely active in raising funds for patriotic organizations and participated in loan and Red Cross drives. Residence: Wauneta.

Mary Belle Person

Mary Belle Person, educator, was born in Abingdon, Illinois, daughter of Michael and Mary Ellen (Shumaker) Dunigan. Her father, born in County Donegal, Ireland, May 1, 1836, came to America about 1853, settled in Nebraska and was county commissioner of Seward County for several years. He died at Nebraska City, May 23, 1926. His wife, Mary Ellen, was born in Abingdon, Illinois, October 1, 1843, and died at Bee, Nebraska, January 9, 1906. She was the daughter of Jacob and Charlotte Shumaker.

Educated first in the rural schools of Seward County, Mrs. Person attended hig school at Seward, and was graduated from the normal training department of the State Normal School of Peru in 1912. She received the A.B. degree. She also took teachers training at the University of Nebraska and the Wyoming State Teachers College. She is a member of Kappa Delta Pi, Alpha Mu Omega, and Sigma Tau Delta.

On April 5, 1900, she was married to Samuel J. Person at Lincoln, Nebraska. Mr. Person was born at Wilmington, North Carolina, and died at Bee, Nebraska, July 27, 1906. He was a traveling salesman and a lawyer, descended from Judge S. J. Person and General Thomas Person. There are three children, Samuel J., born October 10, 1901, who married Ola May Person; Clarence D., born April 9, 1904, who married Vernia Person; and Ellen Tyler, born June 15, 1905, who married George A. Fuerst.

Mrs. Person is a Democrat. She began her business career as a stenographer and bookkeeper for Duffie, Gaines and Kelby at Omaha, Nebraska. She has served as superintendent of schools at Oconto, Arnold, and Eddyville, Nebraska, and for a time was principal of the high school at Bayard, Nebraska. At the present time she is a teached of Mathematics and Latin in the Bayard High School. Mrs. Person is affiliated with St. Margaret's Episcopal Church, is a member of the General Federation of Women's Clubs, the Eastern Star and the Royal Neighbors of America. Recently she was made a life member of the Nebraskana Society. Residence: Bayard.

Owen H. Person

Owen H. Person was born at West Point, Nebraska, November 28, 1888, the son of Stephen and Catherine M. (Ehret) Person. His father, who was a teacher, farmer, and school superintendent in Cuming County, was born at Bethlehem, Pennsylvania, 1843, and died at West Point, March 21, 1922; he was a Civil War veteran. His mother was born at Bethlehem, December 18, 1848, and died at West Point, September 1, 1929.

Dr. Person was a student in Cuming County schools until 1901, and then attended the West Point High School. In 1913, he was graduated from the Kansas City Veterinary College with the degree of D. V. M. He has been engaged as a veterinary surgeon since that date at Wahoo, and is the author of several articles on veterinary subjects. A Republican, he is now serving his second term as mayor of Wahoo, is director of the Chamber of Commerce, vice-president of the Wahoo Lions Club, and is chairman of the executive committee of the League of Nebraska Municipalities.

He holds membership in the Nebraska Medical Veterinary Association, is affiliated with the Wahoo Presbyterian Church, and is a member of the Nebraskana Society. He holds membership in the Knights of Pythias, and all branches of the Masons. His recreations are hunting and baseball.

On September 17, 1918, he was united in marriage at Lincoln, Lancaster County, Nebraska, with Ruth Evelyn Williams. Mrs. Person, who was born at Des Moines, Iowa, November 22, 1889, is descended from Ethan Allen and General Putman. Residence: Wahoo.

Joseph Pestal

Born at Gerschdorf, Moravia, Czechoslovakia, January 16, 1874, Joseph Pestal is the son of Joseph and Eleanora (Trutna) Pestal. His father was born at Radosov, Moravia, March 1, 1839, and came to the United States in 1875. He located on a farm five miles southwest of Wahoo, where he resided 50 years prior to his death on November 18, 1927. His mother was born at Gerschdorf, in November, 1846, and died at Wahoo, November 10, 1917.

Dr. Pestal was graduated from Wahoo High School in 1889, and attended Nebraska Wesleyan University two years, 1896-98. In 1902 he received his M. D. from the medical school of Northwestern University, and entered the practice of medicine.

On October 3, 1905, he was united in marriage to Katheryn Elizabeth Radovick, at Chicago. Mrs. Pestal was born at Cleveland, Ohio, March 26, 1880, her father a Serb, and her mother a Czech. There are three children: Eleonora V., born September 3, 1906; Katheryn Vivian, born November 16, 1912, and Pauline E., born August 8, 1915.

Dr. Pestal is a Socialist. He is affiliated with Ali Soul's Unitarian Church at Lincoln, and is a member of the Masonic Order and the Nebraskana Society. During the spring of 1898, he was president of the Nebraska Wesleyan Young Men's Christian Association. Residence: Valparaiso.

Val J. Peter

Val J. Peter, editor and publisher, was born in Bavaria, Germany, April 24, 1875. He is the son of George and Katherine (Welzenbach) Peter. His father was born in Steinbach, Germany, and died at Rock Island, Illinois, November 21, 1891. He came to the United States in 1889. His wife, Katherine, was born in Hausen, Bavaria, and died at Rock Island, May 15, 1924.

Mr. Peter came to the United States on May 26, 1889, and became a naturalized citizen at Rock Island, Illinois, on July 22, 1896. He was married to Margaret Reese at Rock Island, on April 24, 1905. Mrs. Peter was born in New York City, January 18, 1884, daughter of Theodore Rudolph Reese, a conductor and composer. Their children are, Carl J., born March 13, 1906; Theodore Val, born December 5, 1907; Bernard George, born August 28, 1909; Arno Ernest, born August 3, 1911; Raymond Albert, born July 30, 1913; Theresa Katherine, born September 14, 1915; William A., born February 23, 1917; Anna Loretto, born June 20, 1919; Margaret Joan, born February 23, 1921; Paul Frederick, born November 11, 1922; Dorothea Josephine, born February 25, 1924; and Eugene Walter, born July 16, 1925.

A resident of Omaha for nearly 25 years, Mr. Peter is a prominent publisher. He is president of the Tribune Publishing Company, which publishes the following German language publication: the *Daily and Sunday Tribune, Nationales Farm Journal (Omaha), Die Welt-Post (Lincoln), Kansas City Presse (Kansas City)*, and *Volkesblatt (St. Joseph)*. He is also owner of the Val J. Peter Travel Bureau of Omaha and Kansas City. Residence: Omaha.

Alexander Peters

Alex Peters, farmer and stockman, was born at Bancroft, Nebraska, August 29, 1889, son of Claus and Mary (Rades) Peters. His father, who was a farmer, died at Bancroft, January 18, 1892. His mother, who was a native of Pomerania, Germany, March 27, 1857, is still living.

Mr. Peters was graduated from the Bancroft public schools in June, 1905, and has since engaged in farming and stock raising. He is a director of the First National Bank of Bancroft, and takes an active part in the affairs of his community.

He is a Republican and a Mason, and his hobbies are reading and mechanics. Residence: Bancroft. (Photograph in Album).

Claus F. Peters

Claus F. Peters, farmer and stockman, was born at Bancroft, Nebraska, March 16, 1890, son of Claus and Mary (Rades) Peters. Claus Peters, Sr., was a farmer, who died at Bancroft, January 18, 1892.

Mr. Peters attended the Bancroft public schools and was graduated in June, 1906. A Republican, he has lived in Nebraska all his life, and has been engaged in farming since maturity.

A veteran of the World War, Mr. Peters held the rank of sergeant, and is a member of the American Legion. He is also a member of the Masons, and the Order of Eastern Star. Residence: Bancroft. (Photograph in Album).

Emanuel Peters

A pioneer farmer in Webster County, Nebraska, Emanuel Peters has been a resident of this state for the past 62 years. He was born at Westpoint, Iowa, June 12, 1849, the son of Henry and Elizabeth Peters. As a leader in the community of Guide Rock, Nebraska he has served as county commissioner, sheriff, assessor, game warden, city marshall, and justice of the peace.

Mr. Peters is now retired from active farming and is a stockholder in the State Bank of Guide Rock. He is the author of *Early History of Webster County* contained in *Martin's History of Nebraska*, and holds membership in the Nebraska State Historical Society and the Nebraskana Society.

On May 6, 1844, he married Dora Dunbar at Guide Rock. Mrs. Peters was born at Lasell, Illinois, June 8, 1856. Three children were born to them: Alma, February 21, 1876, who married George Parker; Ralph C., July 22, 1881; and Roy C., October 11, 1884, who died December 30, 1918. Residence: Guide Rock.

George Steely Petersen

On August 16, 1895, George Steely Petersen, rancher and civil engineer, was born at Pocatello, Idaho. He is the son of William Christian and Caroline Helen (Catherine (Christensen) Petersen.

The father was born at Omaha, Nebraska, September 29, 1871, and was formerly superintendent of motive power of the Southern Pacific Railway Company at Tuscon, Arizona, and Los Angeles, California. Until his recent retirement, he was a round house foreman. He now resides at Santa Barbara, California. His ancestry is Danish, his parents having moved to Nebraska before the Civil War. Caroline Helen Catherine Christensen was born at Monmouth, Illinois, September 30, 1871. She is active in church work. Her family came from Denmark to Illinois in 1844.

Upon the completion of his grammar school work at Yuma, Arizona, in May 1909, Mr. Petersen entered Tucson High School, graduating in June, 1913. The following year he was a student at the University of Arizona, and the next year at the University of California. Mr. Petersen possesses a certificate from the University of California certifying that he left to enter the military forces in the World War, just before graduating. He never returned to finish his last few months.

In high school Mr. Petersen was manager of the school paper, *Tucsonia*, two years, and a member of the football, baseball, basketball and track teams each year from 1909 until 1913 inclusive. At the University of Arizona he was an officer in the Cadet Corps, president of his sophomore class, and a member of Tau Nu Epsilon and Sigma Phi Beta at the same university. At the University of California he was an officer in the Cadet Corps and a member of the varsity football team.

On May 13, 1917, Mr. Petersen entered First Officers Training Camp at Presidio, California, with a reserve commission of second lieutenant from the University of California. However, he was transferred to air service almost immediately and was in the first classes of the Aeronautic School at the University of California and remained in the air service until honorably discharged in 1919. Mr. Petersen was promoted to the rank of first lieutenant Air Service, December 17, 1917, was appointed commanding officer, 252nd Aero Service Squadron, January 18, 1918. He was discharged at Ellington Field, Texas, January 16, 1919. He is a member of the American Legion.

Coming to Nebraska in September, 1920, Mr. Petersen became superintendent of construction of the Arthur A. Dobson Company at Lincoln, continuing until 1926. Since that time he has been the owner and operator of a cattle ranch of his own in Grant and Sheridan counties. Mr. Petersen is a Republican. He is affiliated with the

Episcopal Church, is a member of Tucson Lodge No. 4 of the Free and Accepted Masons, and the Scottish Rite Bodies at Alliance. He is a member of the Nebraskana Society and a life member of the Alumni Association of the University of California at Berkeley.

On May 17, 1923, he was married to Dorothy Abbott at Wahoo, Nebraska. Mrs. Petersen was born at Hyannis, on June 16, 1901, and is of Irish and English descent, tracing her ancestry to the nobility of Ireland. There are two children, Georgia Shirley, born April 7, 1928; and Catherine Elizabeth, born November 29, 1930. Both were born at Alliance. Residence: Ashby.

John M. Petersen

John M. Petersen, farmer and stock breeder, was born near Carroll, Nebraska, October 22, 1890, the son of B. P. and Cecelia (Hargens) Petersen. His father, who was also a stock breeder, was born in Germany, November 4, 1866, and died at Sioux City Iowa, February, 1911; he came to Nebraska in 1888. His mother was born in Germany, September 30, 1869, and died at Colorado Springs, Colorado, October, 1906.

Mr. Petersen attended the public schools of Colorado, and later was a student at the Nebraska Normal College and the School of Agriculture in Nebraska. He has been prominent in civic affairs at Wayne for many years, and has lived in Nebraska all his life. In 1923 he served as secretary of the Carroll Community Club, and was the first active 4-H club worker in Wayne County. He has served as director and treasurer of the local school board for several terms, and is affiliated with Lodge Number 235 of the Ancient Free and Accepted Masons. He is vitally interested in the improvement of Poland China hogs.

His marriage to Jennie Annette Anderson was solemnized at Omaha, June 8, 1914. Mrs. Petersen, who was a teacher in Nebraska schools before her marriage, was born near Wakefield, Nebraska; her parents, who were Swedish, came to Dixon County in 1881. Three children were born to this marriage: Lorraine Cecelia, born December 4, 1915; Mabelle Jean, born September 17, 1917; Ruth Jeanette, born November 19, 1919. Residence: Wayne.

Alfred John Peterson

Alfred J. Peterson, a resident of this state all his life, was born in Cuming County, Nebraska, October 13, 1872, the son of Carl J. A. Peterson, and Emma (Nelson) Peterson. His father, who was born in Sweden, June 8, 1840, and died on his farm in Cuming County, February 19, 1920, came to America in 1864, and settled at De Kalb, Illinois; he served under Sherman in the Civil War, and in 1869 travelled overland to Nebraska, where he homesteaded. His mother was born in Sweden, October 10, 1849.

Mr. Peterson attended rural school, and in 1893 and 1894, was a student at Fremont Normal College, Fremont, Nebraska. Except for four years spent in Idaho, 1896-1900, he has lived in Cuming County all his life. During the late war he took a prominent part in Red Cross relief work, and has served many terms as school director. He is affiliated with West Side Methodist Episcopal Church at Oakland, Nebraska. He is a Democrat.

His marriage to Ida Swanson was solemnized at Lincoln, Lancaster County, Nebraska, September 2, 1903. Mrs. Peterson was born in Sweden, January 13, 1884. They have two children: Verrill, a graduate of West Point High School, born December 16, 1905, who married Muriel Birtwhistle; and Iona, born October 22, 1911. Verrill is a farmer on his father's original home; Iona attended the University of Nebraska for three years and will graduate in 1932. Residence: West Point.

Alfred Olaf Peterson

Alfred Olaf Peterson, physician, was born in Svanike, Island of Bornholm, Denmark, November 6, 1873, son of Jens and Ane K. (Lou) Peterson. Dr. Peterson received the Bachelor of Science, the Master of Arts, and the Doctor of Medicine degrees from the University of Nebraska. On June 11, 1901, he was married to Eva N. Bloshaw at Lincoln. They have two children, Ward Alfred and Richard L.

Dr. Peterson is in active practice. He is the author of various articles on medical subjects, and a lecturer in biology and embryology at the Omaha Medical College, 1898-1908, at the University of Nebraska, 1908-1916. His practice is now limited to internal medicine and physical therapy. He is a member of the American, Nebraska State Medical Association, the American Medical Association, the Omaha Roentgen Ray Society, and the American Association for Advancement of Science. His clubs are the Happy Hollow Club and the Athletic Club. Residence: Omaha.

Andrew R. Peterson

Andrew Rasmus Peterson was born at Cambridge, Dane County, Wisconsin, November 17, 1870, the son of Cornelius and Nicholena Sophia (Nelson) Peterson, and has lived in Nebraska practically all his life. His father, who was a farmer, was born in Finland, in 1838, and died in Cuming County, Nebraska, September 6, 1901. His mother was born in Norway, and died at Wisner, Nebraska, January, 1881.

Mr. Peterson attended the rural schools of Cuming County and the Wisner Grade Schools. He entered business as a candy merchant at Wisner, September 27, 1901, and is now proprietor and owner of a candy business there. He is a member of the Community Club of Wisner. He is an Elk. Politically, he is an Independent.

His marriage to Agnes Kathryn Neidermeyer, daughter of William B. and Catherine (Fleming) Neidermeyer, was solemnized at Wisner, December 30, 1903. She was born at Beemer, Cuming County, Nebraska, January, 1880, and died at Omaha, Douglas County, Nebraska, 1925. One son was born to them: Ross, born May 17, 1906, who is a graduate of Omaha Central High School and a florist in Omaha. On August 9, 1923, Mr. Peterson was united in marriage with La Vanda Palmer, daughter of Barton M. and Mary Goersch Palmer of Omaha, at Wisner. Residence: Wisner. (Photograph in Album).

C. Petrus Peterson

Born in Polk County, Nebraska, March 10, 1880, C. Petrus Peterson is the son of A. W. and Clara M. (Landstrom) Peterson. His father, who was born in Sweden, September 28, 1857, came to America in 1871, and is now retired. His wife, Clara, was also born in Sweden and died at Stromsburg, Nebraska, in 1922.

Educated first in the country schools of Polk County, Mr. Peterson was graduated from Luther Academy at Wahoo, Nebraska, in 1903, where he was valedictorian. In June, 1906, he received his A. B. from Augustana College, at Rock Island, Illinois, where he was also valedictorian. He attended then the University of Nebraska Law School. He is a member of Theta Kappa Nu and Delta Chi. Upon his admission to the bar in 1909 he entered practice at Wahoo, continuing there until 1911. At that time he came to Lincoln where he has since carried on his practice, during 1912-13 as a member of the firm of Whedon and Peterson, and since 1915 as a member of the firm of Peterson and Devoe.

Mr. Peterson is a Republican and served as a member of the house of representatives 1915 and 1917; and as state senator in 1919. He was a member of the Constitutional Convention of 1919-20 and city attorney of Lincoln 1915-29. He is general counsel for the Bankers

Life Insurance Company (1918) and a director of the corporation.

During the World War he was active in Food Administration in Lancaster County. He is affiliated with the First Plymouth Congregational Church, and is a member of the Chamber of Commerce, the Nebraska State Historical Society, Native Sons and Daughters (president 1930) and the Young Men's Christian Association.

His clubs are the Lincoln University and Lincoln Country Clubs, and his sport is fishing. He is a member of the American, Nebraska State Bar Associations, and the American Association of Life Insurance Counsels.

On January 29, 1910, he was united in marriage to Vera M. Melquist at Omaha. Mrs. Peterson was born at Omaha, May 22, 1887. There are three children, Breta, born in May, 1914; Vera May, born in January, 1916, and Patricia, born in December, 1922. Residence: Lincoln.

Clarence L. Peterson

Clarence L. Peterson, rancher, was born at Alliance, Nebraska, March 15, 1889, son of Frank Ferdinand and Christeen Maria (Johnson) Peterson. The father, born in Sweden, April 11, 1846, came to America as a young man and engaged in ranching. He died at Alliance, May 28, 1924. His wife, also born in Sweden, February 27, 1849, died at Alliance, October 22, 1926.

Upon the completion of his public school education Mr. Peterson attended Iowa Wesleyan University from 1910 until the end of 1911. He strted in the ranching business for himself in 1916 and has continued ever since, increasing the size of his ranch until it is now it is one of the largest and best in the state. He purchased 20,-000 acres in 1924 and 22,000 acres in 1925, together with several smaller tracts. His hobby is riding the range. Residence: Lakeside.

Earl J. Peterson

Earl J. Peterson, a lifelong resident of Nebraska, was born at Schuyler, February 25, 1897, the son of Oscar and Alice E. Bloomfield. His father, who was a rancher, farmer, and stockdealer, was born in Illinois, and died at Stuart, Nebraska, September 27, 1931. His mother, a teacher prior to her marriage, was born at Gailsburg, Illinois.

Mr. Peterson was a student in rural schools in Rock County, and studied at Wayne Normal College from 1913 to 1915. He has been a director and moderator of his community school board since 1926, and has engaged in ranching near Newport since 1915.

His marriage to Ethel Berta Ammon occurred at O'Neill, Nebraska, October 24, 1917. Mrs. Peterson was born in Rock County. To them were born the following children: Lorena, September 19, 1918, who died October 25, 1918; Lorence, December 19, 1920; and Betty, January 4, 1928. Residence: Newport.

Frank Leander Peterson

Born at Engathorp, Sweden, July 31, 1868, Frank Leander Peterson is the son of Andrew and Charlotte (Anderson) Peterson. His father was born in Sweden, in 1838, and was an extensive property holder and the owner of Engathorp Estate, where he had many tenant farmers. He homesteaded and farmed in Kansas, shortly after his arrival in this country in 1880, and then made his home at Wahoo, Nebraska, where he died, December, 1911. His wife, Charlotte, was born in Sharpe, Sweden, in 1841, and died at Waverly, Nebraska, in May, 1887.

Frank Peterson received instruction from tutors while living in Sweden, and after he came to the United States attended public school. He was united in marriage with Jennie Paul at Ceresco, Nebraska, October 31, 1901. She

was born at Odell, Illinois, January 10, 1870, of Scotch ancestry. They have two children: Russell Vernon, born September 22, 1902, who is married to Mrytle Bernice Linch, and Doris Genevieve, born October 13, 1903. Russell clerks in his father's store and Doris is a secretary.

Mr. Peterson has been in the mercantile business for the past thirty years and prior to, was a farmer. He served as vice president of the Farmers Elevator Company, and now owns and manages his general store and is vice president and member of the board of directors of the Valparaiso Grain and Lumber Company.

During the Spanish-American War he was in Company E of the First Nebraska Infantry, and served in the Philippine Islands. He is a member of the Veterans of Foreign Wars and the United Spanish War Veterans.

He is affiliated with the Mt. Zion Methodist Church at Ceresco; is a member in the Elks and Knights of Pythias, and was formerly a member of the Ancient Order of United Workmen. He is a life member of the Nebraskana Society. Horticulture and landscaping are Mr. Peterson's hobbies. Residence: Valparaiso. (Photograph in Album).

Fred Emanuel Peterson

On February 29, 1880, Fred Emanuel Peterson was born at Shickley, Nebraska, the son of Andrew William and Ida Maria (Johnson) Peterson. His father, who was a farmer and stockman, was born at Jonkoping, Sweden, November 7, 1849, and died at Shickley, August 1, 1929. His mother was born at Jonkoping, August 3, 1854, and died February 26, 1932 at Shickley.

Mr. Peterson attended Augustana College at Rock Island, Illinois, 1898-1901 where he was active in football. He was connected with the publishing department of Bettundorf Axel Company at Davenport, Iowa, in 1902, served as secretary of the American Company at Rock Island, 1902-07; was secretary of the Shickley Farmers Elevator Company, 1915-29, and served as vice president of the Farmers & Merchants Bank at Shickley from 1929 to 1930. He has been a farmer and stockman in Fillmore County for many years and is still connected with the bank there.

He is a member of the Red Cross, is affiliated with the Stockholm Lutheran Church, and holds membership in the Nebraskana Society. His fraternal organizations include Modern Woodmen of America and Independent Order of Odd Fellows. During the World War Mr. Peterson was in charge of local loan drives and acted as secretary of the Red Cross. His chief recreations are reading and football.

Mr. Peterson is a Republican, and has served as justice of the peace at Shickley and road overseer. Residence: Shickley.

Mrs. J. Fred Peterson

Mrs. J. Fred Peterson, formerly Agnes Marguerite Rasmussen, clubwoman and political leader, was born at Lincoln, Lancaster County, Nebraska, August 16, 1893, the daughter of Christian M. and Marie N. (Nielsen) Rasmussen. Her father was born at Aalborg, Denmark, March 17, 1860, and her mother was born at Aalborg, November 15, 1870.

In 1905 Mrs. Peterson was a student at Clinton School and in 1909 was graduated from the Lincoln High School. For the next three years she was a student at the University of Nebraska where she studied journalism under the tutelage of Professor Fogg. Upon completion of her college work she was connected with the *Lincoln State Journal* for seven years. A Republican, she has always taken an interest in state and county politics, serving in 1928 as a member of the state central committee; and in 1930 as executive member of the Republican state central committee of the first senatorial district. She is grand secretary and treasurer of the ladies' auxiliary of the

Brotherhood Railroad Signalmen of America, and international organization.

She married J. Fred Peterson of Wymore, at Lincoln, Nebraska, May 1, 1918. There is one son, Robert Legene, born August 12, 1921.

During the World War Mrs. Peterson was a member of the Veteran Relief Corps Number 129, of Falls City. Among her many club memberships are: Woman's Christian Temperance Union, of which she is president and county director of the Scientific Temperance Instruction; the Woman's Club of Falls City, in which she is chairman of the health department; the Nebraskana Society; and chapter Number 225 of the Order of the Eastern Star. She is a member of the Methodist Church at Falls City. She was very active in relief work during the World War.

Mrs. Peterson is a candidate for Republican National committee-woman from Nebraska. Her petitions have been sent out by her friends. Residence: Falls City.

Laurence Monnell Peterson

The son of John A. and Emma Josephine (Gustafson) Peterson, Laurence Monnell Peterson was born at Arlington, Nebraska, October 12, 1894. His father, born in Sweden, August 5, 1868, and was brought to America as an infant. He is a merchant. His mother was born in Dayton, Iowa, January 7, 1870.

Dr. Peterson attended the public and high schools of Arlington, and received his D. D. S. from the University of Nebraska, in 1917. There he was a member of Delta Sigma Delta and Beta Theta Pi.

On June 2, 1924, he was united in marriage to Violet Stella Warren, at Council Bluffs, Iowa. Mrs. Peterson, who is of English and German descent, was born at Craig, Missouri, August 14, 1902. They have one daughter, Jacqueline, born August 9, 1925.

Dr. Peterson has engaged in the active practice of dentistry since his admission on July 14, 1917. Among his professional memberships are the American and Omaha District Dental Associations. He held the rank of first lieutenant in the Dental Corps during the World War, is a member of the American Legion, and was first commander of Leslie W. Downs Post No. 71, at Arlington.

His religious affiliation is with the First Congregational Church, and he is also a member of Hiram Lodge No. 52 of the Masons, the Red Cross, Community Club, the Arlington School Board, and The Nebraskana Society. Dr. Peterson is fond of fishing and hunting. Residence: Arlington.

Nels W. Peterson

Nels W. Peterson, son of Hans Christian and Marin (Nielsen) Peterson, was born at Lake Forest, Illinois, December 2, 1879, coming to Nebraska forty-five years ago. His father, born in Als, Denmark, March 6, 1858, was a farmer and landowner, whose family came originally from Germany. He died at Mason City, August 14, 1928. His wife, born in Follerup, Jutland, Denmark, August 31, 1855, is living.

Mr. Peterson attended country school and grew up on a farm. He has been for some time engaged in the furniture and undertaking business in Mason City, has served as mayor several years, and is secretary of the school board there. He is a Democrat.

His marriage to Mary Theodocia Nicholas was solemnized at Mason City, November 24, 1904. Mrs. Peterson, whose parents were born in Wales, was born at Oldsburg, Kansas, October 15, 1883. Before her marriage she was a teacher. They have one son, Irwin Benjamin, born February 8, 1910, who attended college four years and is now athletic coach and teacher of history and mathematics.

Mr. Peterson is a member of the Commercial Club, the Odd Fellows and the Nebraskana Society, and enjoys football and hiking. Residence: Mason City.

Peter Homer Peterson

Peter Homer Peterson, lawyer, was born in Sweden, January 16, 1877, and has resided in Nebraska forty-five years. The son of Nels and Johanna (Pearson) Peterson, his mother was born in 1858 and his father on September 25, 1855. Nels Peterson came to America in 1887 with his wife, who died at Emerson in December, 1924.

Educated in the public schools of Emerson, Peter H. Peterson received his LL. B. from the University of Nebraska in 1906, where he was a member of Acacia and Phi Delta Phi. He was adimtted to the bar in June, 1906, and engaged in the practice of law immediately. He has practiced at Wausa continuously since 1906, and maintains an office at Center, Nebraska also. At the present time he is a member of the law firm of Peterson and Barta, in partnership with F. A. Barta of Center. A Democrat, he served as county attorney of Knox county for eighteen years.

He was married to Anna Mae Anderson at Lincoln, on April 20, 1908, and to them were born two children: Winston Keith, born January 24, 1909, is a lawyer practicing at Wausa. Duane, born July 16, 1912, is a student at the University. Mrs. Peterson was born at Elgin, Iowa.

Mr. Peterson was a member of the Council of Defense during the World War. He is a member of the American, the Ninth Judicial District and the Nebraska State Bar Associations, the Commercial Club, the Nebraskana Society, the Masons and Shrine. For ten years he was chairman of the Knox County Red Cross, and is its present vice chairman. Residence: Wausa.

John Petr, Jr.

John Petr, a farmer and stockraiser at Clarkson, was born there, January 12, 1876. His father, John Petr, who was born at Danhovice, Moravia, December 22, 1844, and died at Clarkson, December 11, 1926, was a farmer; he moved to America, May 25, 1874, and homesteaded in Colfax County. His mother, Josephine (Vlastovice) Petr, was born at Dankovice, September 27, 1846, and died at Clarkson, January 31, 1908.

Mr. Petr attended the public schools of Colfax County, and was a student at Fremont Normal School. He is president of the Farmers' Union at Clarkson, and was formerly president of the Farmers State Bank there. He has lived on the same farm, where he was born all his life. He is a member of the Red Cross, has been a director of the school board, 1905 to 1919, and 1921, is a member of Zion Bohemian Presbyterian Church, and the Nebraskana Society. He is especially interested in stockraising.

On February 22, 1905, he was united in marriage with Emma Schultz, at Clarkson. Mrs. Petr was born at Clarkson, October 23, 1883. Their children are: Elsie Emily, born October 21, 1905; Ethel Edith, born April 27, 1907; Eleanor Esther, born September 5, 1909; Leon John, born January 11, 1911; Agnes Olga, born July 11, 1919; and Betty Jeanne, born March 26, 1929. Elsie Ethel, Eleanor, and Leon, attended high school and the University of Nebraska. Residence: Clarkson.

John Christ Petrow

John Christ Petrow, retired merchant of Fremont, Nebraska, was born at Niata, Greece, March 3, 1882, and for the past 28 years has been a resident of Nebraska. His father, Christ Nick Petrow, who was a farmer, was born at Niata, Greece, and died there in the summer of 1919. His mother was born at Niata, March 1, 1853, and died there in 1919.

Mr. Petrow attended school until 1892. In 1903 he opened the Fremont Candy Kitchen which he successfully operated for 26 years. He served as president of the Arctic Ice Cream Company until that organization was bought by the National Dairy Company. At this time he is retired from active business, but still manages his various real estate holdings in Dodge County. In 1929 he visited his native country with his wife and children and made a six months tour of Europe.

He is a member of the Chamber of Commerce, the Nebraskana Society, Red Cross, and St. James Episcopal Church. He is a member of the board of directors of the Young Men's Christian Association, and holds membership in the Elks and Masons. His hobby is traveling, while his chief recreation is reading.

On September 14, 1914, he married Vasiliky Petroupulos at Tamaqua, Pennsylvania. Mrs. Petrow was born at Athens, Greece, July 26, 1893. To this marriage three children were born: Christ John, born October 7, 1915; Helen Jean, born October 7, 1916; and George John, March 11, 1920. All of the children read, write, and speak Greek freely.

Mr. Petrow is a Republican. Residence: Fremont. (Photograph in Album).

Willard Alonzo Petteys

One of the leaders in his community Willard Alonzo Petteys has lived in Harlan and Kearney Counties since 1885, when he homesteaded near Wilcox, Nebraska. He was born at Cambridge, Illinois, September 14, 1862, the son of John Teeple Petteys and Laurana E. (Field) Petteys. His father, who was born in Oneida County, New York, May 3, 1833, and died at Wilcox, October 10, 1910, was a farmer, who served as justice of the peace and county supervisor at Wilcox. His mother was born at Winchester, New Hampshire, August 15, 1839, and died at Wilcox, September 18, 1893.

Mr. Petteys has been a farmer for many years, and has served as secretary of the Wilcox Mutual Insurance Company which he helped organize for 25 years. He is president of the Mutual Oil and Gas Company, helped organize the Wilcox Telephone Company and was secretary for ten years. He is director and vice president of the First National Bank of Wilcox, and is prominent in civic affairs. He served on the school board in Harlan County from 1895 to 1915, and is now a member of the Red Cross, the Wilcox Community Church, Modern Woodmen of America and the Masons.

Elihu Field, grandfather of Mr. Petteys was a homesteader in Harlan County, Nebraska, in 1871. Cora Swain Petteys was admitted to the Midwest Chapter of Alden Kindred, and her son, John A. Petteys, served during the World War. Mr. Pettey's marriage to Cora Swain occurred at Geneseo, Illinois, April 3, 1884. Four children were born to them: Lloyd Milton, born April 23, 1886, who died March 25, 1887; Willard Alonzo, born November 25, 1887, who married Anna Federson, and who is cashier of the Farmers State Bank at Brush, Colorado, and was president of Colorado Bankers Association, 1929-30; he is a graduate of Grinnell College, Iowa. Lilah Althea, born September 24, 1889, died July 27, 1890; and John Alden, born August 7, 1899, who married Thelma Lewis; he is a graduate of the University of Nebraska.

Mr. Petteys has patented several devices, one the Elevator Dust and Chaf Collector, and he has placed a great many of them through Nebraska and Colorado. Residence: Wilcox. (Photograph in Album).

Charles Scott Pettit

Born at Red Oak, Iowa, June 16, 1872, Charles Scott Pettit is the son of Edmund Franklin and Harriet (Scott) Pettit. His father, who was a farmer, was born at Kaskaskia, Illinois, November 18, 1839, and died at Hot Springs, South Dakota, September 9, 1920; he served for four years in the Wisconsin Regiment during the Civil War and was wounded at the siege of Vicksburg; he was descended from John Pettit who came to

this country from France in 1730. His mother, who was a seamstress, was born at Dodgeville, Wisconsin, in 1842, and died at Fairbury, Nebraska, June 22, 1876.

Mr. Pettit was a blacksmith during his younger days and in 1901 purchased a half interest in a hardware store at Springview, Nebraska, where he remained until 1918 when he moved to Ainsworth, Nebraska, and established a hardware store there. He was owner and manager of this organization until 1930 when he sold the business. He has been a director in the Commercial National Bank of Ainsworth.

He has been a Mason for over 25 years, serving as Master of the local lodge for the past two years, and holds all Masonic degrees up to and including the Knights Templar. He held membership in the Ainsworth Commercial Club during his many years in business. Mr. Pettit's chief recreations are fishing and baseball.

On October 10, 1900, he was united in marriage with Stella Amelia Carr at Springview. Mrs. Pettit, who is the oldest child of John Frank and Amelia (Schutte) Carr, was born at Hiawatha, Kansas, November 30, 1878. She was president of the Ainsworth Board of Education and is district supervisor of the Order of Eastern Star. Six children were born to their marriage: Charles Carr, born July 22, 1901, who died July 19, 1902; Clarence Arthur, January 21, 1903; Frank Edmund, April 27, 1905; Carl Scott, February 15, 1908, who married Elizabeth Eileen Staal; Howard Thorley, December 2, 1915; and George Otto, November 21, 1917. Clarence and Carl are ranchers in South Dakota. Residence: Ainsworth.

Harrison McCurdy Pettygrove

Since 1895 Harrison McCurdy Pettygrove has been engaged in the retail lumber and coal business at Oxford, Nebraska. He was born in New Era Township, Nebraska, March 18, 1876, the son of Neal A. and Mary (Michel) Pettygrove. His father, was born at Calais, Maine, May 19, 1847, and died while visiting at Hansen, Idaho, September 12, 1924, was a Civil War veteran; he operated a general merchandise store at Oxford for 10 years, was in the hardware and implement business there for over 30 years, and was prominent in civic affairs in his community; his ancestry was Scotch and Irish. He was Oxford's first postmaster. His grandfather at one time held title to the land upon which the town of Calais was built. H. M. Pettygrove's great uncle Frank Pettygrove, founded the city of Portland, Oregon, and Pettygrove Street, in that city is named in his honor.

Mary (Michel) Pettygrove was born at Butler, Pennsylvania, April 5, 1851, and died at Oxford, January 10, 1920. She was of German parentage. Her father participated in the German rebellion in 1847, and soon after came to this country.

Mr. Pettygrove served as assistant cashier in the Commercial State Bank of Oxford from 1892 to 1894, and since 1895 has been successful as a retail lumber and coal merchant there. He is a member of the Modern Woodmen of America, the Ancient Free and Accepted Masons, and the Nebraskana Society, while his political affiliation is with the Republican party. Mr. Pettygrove served one term as mayor and member of the town board, and for years was a member of the school board.

On June 10, 1897, he married Georgia Francis Learn at Boulder, Colorado. Mrs. Pettygrove, whose parents were of German and English descent, was born at Laporte, Indiana, February 27, 1876; she was the daughter of Warren Edward and Lucy (Feese) Learn. They have the following children: Lucile, born May 18, 1898, who married Dr. Raymond M. Hergenrother; Laura, born November 1, 1899; Neal, born March 26, 1902, who married Fanchon Roepke; Irene, born March 1, 1904, who married Fred M. Janisch; George F., born August 12, 1906, who married Ruth Ahrendts; John W., born June 1, 1908; and Evelyn, born August 21, 1910. Neal L. and George F. are in the lumber and coal business with their father. Residence: Oxford. (Photograph in Album).

Elsie E. Pfeiffer

Editor and publisher of the *Nuckolls County Herald*, at Nelson, Elsie E. Pfeiffer is also a leader in club and child welfare work. Born at Beatrice, she is the daughter of Daniel B. and Selma R. (Arpke) Penrod. Her father who was born in Wooster County, Ohio, March 26, 1860, is a contractor, whose ancestors were among the first settlers of the country. Her mother was born at Sheboygan, Wisconsin, January 22, 1863, and died at Lincoln, April 18, 1929. Her ancestry was German.

Mrs. Pfeiffer was graduated from elementary and high school, and received teacher training. For a number of years prior to her marriage she taught in Gage County. She is a Republican, and participates in local politics. She is a member of the Nelson Woman's Club, Chapter No. 27 of the Order of Eastern Star at Nelson, and is a life member of the Nebraskana Society. She is a member of the Superior Country Club. Her favorite sport is golf, and her hobby is gardening.

Her marriage to John J. Pfeiffer was solemnized at Beatrice, on June 29, 1911. Mr. Pfeiffer was born at Cortland. (*See Nebraskana*). Residence: Nelson.

John J. Pfeiffer

John J. Pfeiffer, editor and publisher, was born at Roanoke, Illinois, June 11, 1883, son of Paul and Helena (Seibel) Pfeiffer. His father, who was of German descent, was born at Hesse Castle, Germany, October 12, 1852, and died at Cortland, Nebraska, in the Spring of 1930. His mother, also born in Hesse Castle, Germany, is still living.

Educated in the public and high schools of Gage County, John J. Pfeiffer was for a number of years a compositor in Lincoln and Beatrice. Since 1910, he has been publisher and editor of the *Nuckolls County Herald* at Nelson. He was married to Elsie E. Penrod, at Beatrice, June 29, 1911, (*See Nebraskana*).

Mr. Pfeiffer is a Republican. During his entire residence at Nelson he has been prominent in the civic development of his community. For five years he was a member of Company C, of the Nebraska National Guard, and during the World War was active in all wartime projects.

Affiliated with the First Congregational Church of Cortland, he is a member of Nelson Lodge of the Masons, and the Nelson Chamber of Commerce. Mr. Pfeiffer enjoyed baseball in earlier life, and is now an ardent golfer. He is secretary of the Nuckolls County Fair board, and a member of the Superior Country Club. Residence: Nelson.

Otto Pfeiffer

Born at Omaha, April 28, 1883, Otto Pfeiffer has always resided in Douglas County, where he is prominent dairy farmer. He is the son of Jacob Henry and Mary Pfeiffer. His father, born in Germany on September 1, 1850, came to America in March, 1883, and was a gardener until his death at Elkhorn on October 10, 1921. His mother, born in Germany, April 2, 1858, is living.

Mr. Pfeiffer attended public school in Douglas County, and on March 11, 1903, was united in marriage to Frances Blazek at Omaha. Mrs. Pfeiffer was born in Bohemia on May 25, 1880. There are five children, Grace, born February 18, 1904, who is a teacher; George, born March 20, 1909, a farmer; Gladys, born April 13, 1911, a

stenographer; Russell, born September 28, 1916 and Otto, Jr., born September 1, 1919.

Mr. Pfeiffer is president of the Nebraska-Iowa Non-Stock Co-operative Milk Association, a member of the Farmers Union, the Farm Bureau, a life member of the Nebraska Dairymen's Association and a life member of the Nebraska Dairymen's Association and a life member of the Nebraska Crop Growers Association.

For a period of four years he was president of the Douglas County Agricultural Association, and is now president of the Great Northeast Ten Circuit of County Fairs. During the World War he was chairman of Red Cross drives, and is a former member of the organization. He is a Mason and Knight Templar. For twenty years he was a member of the local school board, serving as president eight years, secretary two years and treasurer three years. Residence: Elkhorn.

Robert Frederick Pfeiffer

Robert Frederick Pfeiffer, district manager of the Central Power Company at Kearney, was born at Leavenworth, Kansas, July 18, 1882, the son of John and Barbara Pfeiffer. His father, who was a manufacturer, was born at Antweil, Switzerland, October 17, 1847, and died at Leavenworth, April 2, 1912; he came to America, in 1854. His mother was born at Lokenhaus, Austria, January 24, 1849.

Mr. Pfeiffer was graduated from the Leavenworth High School in 1900, and was a student at Leavenworth Business College for the next two years. He was engaged in the railroad clerical service from 1902 to 1908, was cashier of the Union Pacific Railroad from 1908 to 1910, and was auditor of the Electric Utility Company at Kearney for many years. He is now a director and district manager of the Central Power Company.

He is a member of the Kearney Retail Merchants Association of which he was president in 1926, was president of the Kiwanis Club in 1928, and served as president of the Kearney Chamber of Commerce in 1930. He holds membership in the Kearney Country Club, the Red Cross, and the Nebraskana Society. His hobby is reading.

He was married August 12, 1912, at Grand Island, Nebraska, to Hazel Burnadeen Fritts who was born at Omaha, Nebraska, April 6, 1892. Mr. Pfeiffer is a Republican. Residence: Kearney. (Photograph in Album).

Frank Emery Pfoutz

Frank Emery Pfoutz, clergyman, was born at New Sharon, Iowa, July 14, 1885, son of George William and Jestina Coquesa (Miller) Pfoutz.

George William Pfoutz, a farmer, was born in Frederick, Maryland, December 6, 1850, and died at New Sharon, Iowa, April 14, 1920. He was the son of Peter Pfoutz, who was born in Maryland. Jestina Coquesa Miller was born February 13, 1855, of Pennsylvania settlers, and died at New Sharon, Iowa, November 6, 1896.

Upon receiving his diploma in the common schools of Mahaska County in 1899, Mr. Pfoutz entered McPherson Academy in Kansas, remaining two years. In 1918, he received the Bachelor of Arts degree from Nebraska Wesleyan University, and afterward completed further studies in the Garrett Biblical Institute at Evanston, Illinois. At the present time, Mr. Pfoutz is the pastor of the First Methodist Church of North Platte, and a member of the North Platte Ministerial Association.

He was married to Saidee Emma Boone at Lyons, Kansas, on July 14, 1907, and to them were born two children, Helen, on June 14, 1908; and Irene, on September 13, 1912, who is married to Emery R. Pont. Helen is a registered nurse. Mrs. Pfoutz was born in Boone's Mill, Virginia, March 29, 1884. Her father and mother were born in Virginia, her father coming from the family of Daniel Boone.

Mr. Pfoutz has resided in Nebraska since 1913. He

is a member of the Chamber of Commerce, the Kiwanis Club, the Masons (Knight Templar), and the Red Cross. He enjoys golf and the radio. He is a Republican. Residence: North Platte. (Photograph in Album).

Harry Erastus Phelps

A newspaper editor and publisher since 1883, Harry Erastus Phelps is the son of Charles Julius and Sarah Elizabeth (Wells) Phelps. Charles Julius Phelps was born at West Hartford, Connecticut, September 13, 1839, and came to Omaha, in November, 1867. Shortly thereafter he settled in Colfax County, pioneering on a homestead in Maple Creek precinct. Taking up the study of law at Schuyler, the county seat, he left the homestead in the fall of 1874, and opened a law office at Schuyler, in partnership with the late Reuben Butler. While serving as grand master of the Masonic Lodge of Nebraska, he laid the cornerstone of the Trans-Mississippi Exposition at Omaha in 1895. His death occurred at Schuyler, on August 24, 1915.

Charles Julius Phelps was a direct descendant of William Phelps who sailed from Plymouth, England, on March 20, 1630, arriving at Nantucket, now Hull, Massachusetts, May 30, 1630. The colony of which he was a member settled at Dorchester, they being the founders of that town. Dorchester claims the honor of being the first town in a Massachusetts colony to organize a town government, and William Phelps took an active part in that work. He was the holder of various positions of trust in the administration of the town's business. In 1636, together with an unmarried brother, George, he removed to Windsor, Connecticut, settling on a grant of land, which Julius F. Phelps sold when he left Hartford, to come west in 1876. C. J. Phelps came to Nebraska in 1867, and Phelps County is named in his honor.

Sarah Elizabeth Wells was born in West Hartford, July 30, 1840. She attended college and taught school prior to her marriage. The organizer of Schuyler's first public library, she was active in Woman's Club, a member of the Order of Eastern Star, and active in the work of the Episcopal Church, prior to her death on December 6, 1921. Her ancestors came from England, in 1670, settling in Connecticut. Both sides of the family of Harry E. Phelps were represented by soldiers in the Revolutionary War.

Mr. Phelps attended school in a sod house in District No. 11, of Colfax County, and later was a student in the Schuyler public schools. In 1883 he entered the newspaper field as publisher of the *Schuyler Herald*. Later he formed a partnership and continued business under the firm name of Davis, Phelps and Davis, and in 1886, purchased the interests of his partners. In 1887, he formed another partnership, this time with his sister, the late Helen C. Reinecke, who purchased his interest in October, 1888, when Mr. Phelps removed to Howells, and founded the *Howells Journal*.

On August 16, 1904, Mr. Phelps founded the *Clarkson Herald*, operating it in conjunction with the *Journal* until September, 1916, when he disposed of it. A Democrat, he was United States storekeeper in the Internal Revenue Department at Omaha, from 1893-97. He has been active in Democratic politics many years, and has served as a member and chairman of the Colfax County central committee for thirty years, and as a member of the state central committee several years. In 1920, he was supervisor of census for the 3rd congressional district. Mayor of Howells for several years in its early days, he has also served as president of the board of education, and as president of the Old Settlers Association four terms.

His marriage to Bertha Minnie Luchow, was solemnized at Council Bluffs, Iowa, June 14, 1884. Mrs. Phelps, who was born at St. Louis, Missouri, December 1, 1865, assists her husband in his publishing business. Her parents came to the United States from Germany, while children. There is one daughter: Bertha Edna, born March 25, 1885, who is married to Rudolph Fred Busch. Prior to her marriage she taught five years in the Clarkson public schools. She is a member of the Congregational Church, and active in its work, and that of its auxiliary bodies.

Mr. Phelps is a member of the Commercial Club and Business Men's Club at Howells, is a member and former president of the local board of education and a member of Acacia Lodge No. 34, Ancient Free and Accepted Masons at Schuyler.

During the period 1890-91, he was a member of Company K, Nebraska National Guard, and was called for service in the Sioux Indian Uprising. He was a four minute speaker and a member of the state and county council of defense during the late war, and has been chairman of the annual county Red Cross drive the past four years. He also attends the First Congregational Church. His hobby is reading. Residence: Howells. (Photograph on Page 944).

Leland Albertus Phelps

Leland Albertus Phelps was born at Wahoo, Nebraska, November 10, 1899, son of Marion Albertus and Myrtle Louise (Nichols) Phelps. Marion Albertus Phelps, who was born at Cedar Bluffs, June 10, 1871, is president and general manager of the D. R. Phelps Lumber and Coal Company, and past president of the Nebraska State Lumber Dealers Association. He is the son of Douglas R. Phelps, born in Wyoming County, New York, April 25, 1844, who enlisted in Company C., 1st New York Regiment of Dragoons in 1862, and who moved to Nebraska in 1868.

Myrtle Louise Nichols was born in Jesup, Iowa, October 16, 1871, daughter of Wesley J. Nichols. He was born in Mexica Township, Oswego County, New York, August 16, 1835, and served in the Civil War with Company F, 1st Michigan Light Artillery in the Civil War. He came to Nebraska in 1871.

Educated first in the grade schools of Wahoo, Mr. Phelps was graduated from Wahoo High School in 1917, attended the University of Nebraska 1918-19, and Nebraska School of Business 1919-20. Upon the completion of his business course he went into the office of the D. R. Phelps Lumber and Coal Company of Wahoo, of which he was made secretary on April 2, 1923, and transferred to Fremont, to build a new yard, of which he is in charge.

He was married to Della Lucile Mapes at Council Bluffs, Iowa, on September 10, 1924. Mrs. Phelps was born at Inman, Nebraska, June 10, 1900, daughter of L. Sherman Mapes and Mary Christina (Coventry) Mapes, whose ancestry includes Ethan Allen and Isaiah Vail. During 1924 and 1925 she was Girl Scout troop captain, and in 1925-26 was secretary of a Girl Scout Council. She is a member of the Eastern Star, the Woman's Club, and the American Legion Auxiliary. Mr. and Mrs. Phelps have one daughter, Mary Louise, who was born at Omaha, March 24, 1927. They attend the First Methodist Episcopal Church.

Mr. Phelps has been active in the community life of Fremont, during his residence there. He is a member of the American Automobile Association, the Retail Merchants Association and the Chamber of Commerce. During 1921-22 he was secretary of tthe Wahoo Lions Club, and in 1920 was secretary of Hose Company No. 2, of the Wahoo Volunteer Fire Department, and its president 1921-22; during 1922 he also served as president of the department. Secretary of Fremont chapter of the Izaak Walton League in 1929, he was its president in 1930. A 32nd degree Scottish Rite Mason, he was vice president of William McKinley Class in May, 1922, and is senior deacon of Fremont Lodge No. 15, Ancient Free and Accepted Masons. He is a member of The Nebraskana Society. His hobby is community betterment and beautification. He is a Republican. Residence: Fremont. (Photograph in Album).

H. E. PHELPS

Chandler Noyes Philbrick

Chandler Noyes Philbrick, son of Chandler Noyes and Anna Christena (Veldboom) Philbrick, Sr., was born at Winona, Minnesota, March 20, 1866.

His father, born at Augusta, Maine, was a lumberman, who served with the Union forces in Tennessee, during the Civil War. Taken a prisoner, he was released and confined in Nashville Hospital. He received his honorable discharge on March 5, 1865. He came from a family of English shipbuilders who were early settlers in America.

Christena Veldboom was born in Holland, October 29, 1839. Prior to her death at Luverne, Minnesota, she was a nurse and a practicing physician. She died in May, 1904, while her husband died at Rochester, Minnesota, in May, 1866, little more than a year after being discharged from the army.

Educated in the public schools of Luverne, Chandler Noyes Philbrick, the subject of this sketch, continued his education into high school. On January 12, 1891, he was united in marriage to Anna Coles at Rock Springs, Wyoming. Mrs. Philbrick, who is of English descent, was born at Wheatland, Pennsylvania, July 1, 1867.

There are three children, Estelle, born January 13, 1892, who married Harold C. Koch, November 12, 1918; Fred C., born January 20, 1896, who was killed in action in an air combat at St. Miheil on September 18, 1918; and Shirley S., born April 10, 1900, who married Louis C. Barstow, a prominent dentist of Fullerton. Fred held the rank of first lieutenant in the 28th Aero Squadron, United States Army.

Coming to Fullerton twenty years ago, for a number of years Mr. Philbrick was the owner and operator of the electric power plant at Fullerton (1911-23). During that time he built a highline connecting a group of towns in his section of the state. At the present time he is district agent of the Bankers Life Insurance Company of Des Moines, Iowa.

A Republican, interested in national and local politics, Mr. Philbrick has had no special political aspirations. He is the author of an occasional poem, one on Nebraska having appeared in the *World-Herald* about 1929. During the World War he was a participant in Liberty Loan and Red Cross drives and was a member of the County Council of Defense. He is a member of the Sons of Veterans.

His fraternal organizations include the Odd Fellows, the Knights of Pythias, the Eagles and the Modern Woodmen of America. He is membership chairman of the local Red Cross organization, a member of the Lions Club and The Nebraskana Society, and a former member of the Fullerton Golf Club. Residence: Fullerton. (Photograph in Album).

Inez Celia Philbrick

Inez Celia Philbrick, educator and physician, was born at Tafton, now Bloomington, Wisconsin, May 14, 1866, daughter of Philetus Harvey and Malah Pamelia (Brackett) Philbrick. Her father, who was born at Machias, New York, March 8, 1839, was graduated from the University of Michigan in 1868, with the degrees of B. S. and C. E., and was professor of civil engineering at the University of Iowa, from 1873-87. He served four years in the Civil War, and was first post commander of the G. A. R. at Iowa City. Of English ancestry, he was descended from Thomas Philbrick, who came to America in 1630.

Malah Brackett, his wife, was born at Huntsberg, Ohio, February 16, 1840. A teacher for ten years before her marriage in 1862, she was a woman of literary ability and appreciation, and a member of various culture clubs. Philetus Philbrick died at Medford, Oregon, October 10, 1902, and his wife at Lincoln, on February 2, 1930. The latter was a descendant of Anthony Brackett, an Englishman who settled in Portsmouth, New Hampshire, several years prior to 1840, and was related to Thomas Brackett Reed, Secretary of the Navy, May Wright Sewell, Anna Brackett and John W. Weeks, at one time Secretary of War.

Dr. Philbrick received her education in the public schools of Iowa City, and was graduated from the Hiatt Academy in 1881. She received her B. S. from the University of Iowa, in 1886, and an A. M. in 1889. In 1891 she was graduated from the Woman's Medical College of Pennsylvania, with an M. D., receiving the highest grades in her class. She was salutitorian at the State University of Iowa. She was one of the first women to receive an appointment as interne in the Philadelphia General Hospital, receiving it by civil service examination.

An independent Democrat, she was chairman of the Woodrow Wilson Foundation for Lincoln. Her professional history is as follows: private practice, 1893; medical examiner of women, University of Nebraska, 1919; special lecturer, University of Nebraska, 1919. She was a member and former vice president of the Nebraska State Medical Society, and president of the Nebraska Association of Medical Women, and also the Lincoln Medical Women's Club. She has been a member of the Lancaster County, Nebraska State and American Medical Associations and was a member of the board of the Social Welfare Society for some time, and a member of the City Library Board for a time. Residence: Lincoln.

Bryce Alton Philips

Bryce Alton Philips was born near Bertrand, Nebraska, November 15, 1903, the son of Reed R. and Alice E. (Lenker) Philips. His father, who was born at Nebraska City, Nebraska, June 16, 1869, has been a farmer for many years and served as Phelps county supervisor in 1920. His mother, who is interested in woman's club work, was born at Dunbar, Nebraska, December 4, 1873.

Mr. Philips attended rural school in Phelps County, Nebraska, and in 1921 was graduated from the Holdrege High School. He was a student at Hastings Business College, and since completing his education has been engaged in farming near Bertrand, Nebraska. He is affiliated with the Methodist Episcopal Church being a member of the board of trustees, and holds membership in the Nebraskana Society. His hobby is mechanics.

On August 15, 1928, he was married to Louise May Canada at Bertrand, Nebraska, the daughter of Wesley W. and Anna C. (Schroder) Canada. She was born at Bertrand, June 23, 1909, and taught school before her marriage near Bertrand. Residence. Bertrand. (Photograph in Album).

Theodore Philippi, Sr.

Theodore Philippi, Sr., son of Martin Wilhelm and Dorothy (Orth) Philippi, was born in Oldenburg, Germany, August 15, 1860. His father, a native of Germany, came to America with his family in 1865, settling in Illinois. He was a politician, and died at El Paso, Illinois, in 1879. His wife, also born in Germany, was a talented musician, whose death occurred at El Paso in 1875.

Mr. Philippi attended public school. He has been a resident of Nebraska for the past forty-eight years, and has been an active participant of every effort toward the advancement of his community and state. He is a charter member of Trinity Lutheran Church, and a member of the Bruning Community Club and The Nebraskana Society.

His marriage to Mary J. Meyer was solemnized at Bruning, on August 14, 1888. Mrs. Philippi was born in Wisconsin, on June 19, 1870. There are three children, Martin H., born October 28, 1889; Stella, born September 7, 1894, and Hilda, born June 3, 1904. Residence: Bruning.

Albert Phillipson

For the past 27 years Albert Phillipson has been engaged in the real estate and insurance business at Holbrook, Nebraska, where he was born September 22, 1874. His father, Andrew Ellan Phillipson, who was a farmer, was born in Norway, February 1, 1844, and died at Holbrook, April 15, 1917; he came to this country in 1849 and settled on a farm with his parents in Wisconsin. His mother, Pauline (Olson) Phillipson, whose father achieved distinction during the Civil War, was born in Norway, December 10, 1849.

Mr. Phillipson attended the high school at Arapahoe, Nebraska, in 1896; he was prominent in debating and dramatics in high school. He has been a farmer, merchant, and real estate dealer at Holbrook for the past 27 years, and is now connected with a fire insurance company there. A Republican, he served as central committeeman for a number of years.

He is a member of the Royal Arch Masons, Consistory, and Shrine, and is affiliated with the Independent Order of Odd Fellows, the Woodmen of the World, and the Ancient Order of United Workmen. During the World War Mr. Phillipson served as a member of the fuel committee of Furnas County. He is interested in hiking and reading.

He was united in marriage with Grace Patterson at Holbrook, May 24, 1898. Mrs. Phillipson, whose parents were English, was born at Bloomfield, Iowa, January 15, 1880. Their one son, Adolph J., who was born April 31, 1899, was graduated from the Holbrook High School attended the Lincoln Business College, and was graduated from the School of Embalming at Des Moines, Iowa. He is now a licensed mortician in Nebraska. Residence: Holbrook.

Peter Phillipson

Peter Phillipson, veterinary surgeon and banker at Holbrook, Nebraska, was born in that community September 1, 1880, the son of Andrew Edward and Pauline (Olson) Phillipson. The father, who was a farmer, was born in Norway, September 30, 1846, and died at Holbrook, March 15, 1918. Dr. Phillipson's parents were pioneers in Nebraska in 1871. His mother was born in Norway, December 4, 1851.

Dr. Phillipson was graduated from Kansas City Veterinarian College in 1908. He was a farmer for nearly 20 years, was a clerk for a time, and was employed by the Beatrice Creamery Company from 1904 to 1905. At this time he is engaged in the practice of veterinary surgery, and is president of the Security State Bank. He holds membership in the Nebraska Veterinary Medical Association and the Missouri Valley Veterinary Association.

He is a member of the Board of Education, the Parent Teachers Association, the city council of Holbrook, the Red Cross and Deer Creek Lutheran Church. His fraternal organizations include the Independent Order of Odd Fellows, the Ancient Free and Accepted Masons (Scottish Rite, Consistory and a Shriner of Tehama Temple).

His marriage to Anna Sophia Olson occurred at Holbrook, December 28, 1902. Mrs. Phillipson, who came to this country in 1885 with her parents was born at Sunderland, Norway. One child born to this marriage died in infancy. Residence: Holbrook. (Photograph in Album).

Lawrence Grant Phipps

Lawrence Grant Phipps, sheriff of Burt County for many years, was born at Guthrie Center, Iowa, May 24, 1886. He is the son of Levi David and Hannah M. (Davis) Phipps, both natives of Illinois. Levi Phipps was born February 3, 1860, and came to Nebraska as a young man. A farmer by occupation, he served as sheriff of Burt County eleven years. He was of English and German descent. His death occurred at Tekamah, on December

31, 1916. Hannah, his wife, was born November 14, 1859, of Scotch and Irish parentage. She died at Tekamah, October 31, 1925.

Mr. Phipps attended school up to and including the first part of the 11th grade, when sickness made it necessary for him to be taken out. Afterward he attended business college a short time at Bellevue. From 1886, to 1917, and since 1923, Mr. Phipps has been a resident of Nebraska. He served as deputy sheriff under his father 9 years, was a farmer and owner of an ice plant five years, and ranched in Montana six years. He returned to Nebraska where he operated a restaurant at Tekamah was some time, and worked on the state highways.

He was elected on the Republican ticket as sheriff of Burt County, and is now serving his second term of four years. On January 25, 1911, he was married to Lola Dell Meador, daughter of W. T. and Bessie (Lamb) Meador, at Herman, Nebraska. Mrs. Phipps is a native of Blair, born July 31, 1890, of English descent. There are two children, Lorraine Frances, born June 15, 1915, and Willard Dale, born November 14, 1917. Mr. Phipps' favorite sports are baseball and football, and he enjoys reading. Residence: Tekamah.

James Snyder Pickett

James Snyder Pickett, son of Thomas Johnson and Kate Caroline (Snyder) Pickett, was born at Ashland, Nebraska, September 24, 1882. His father who was born at Peoria, Illinois, December 27, 1851, is a publisher and was a state senator from Sarpy and Saunders Counties in 1888. His mother was born at Fulton, Whiteside County, Illinois, November 12, 1852.

Mr. Pickett attended the Ashland and Wahoo, Nebraska public schools, from which he was graduated in 1900. He was married at Lincoln, on May 5, 1906, and has one daughter, Beatrice, born March 12, 1907. She was graduated from the Nebraska University in 1931, and is now teaching English in the Ainsworth High School.

James Pickett is a Republican and has resided in Nebraska since birth. He is editor of the *Cedar Bluffs Standard*, at the present time.

During the World War he was in charge of the loan drives and other war activities at Cedar Bluffs, where he was president of the Board of Education. He holds membership in the Ancient Free and Accepted Masons, the Modern Woodmen of America and in the Nebraskana Society. Fishing, football and baseball are his favorite sports. Residence: Cedar Bluffs.

William Thomas Pickett

William Thomas Pickett, distinguished editor and publisher at Wahoo, Nebraska, has lived in this state for over 50 years, and has been prominent in the political life of his county for many years. He was born at Fulton, Illinois, December 5, 1878, the son of Thomas Johnson, Jr., and Kate Caroline (Snyder) Pickett. His father, who was born at Peoria, Peoria County, Illinois, December 27, 1850, is a noted editor and publisher, and has been a political leader most of his life. He served as state senator, was printer expert for the state of Illinois, in 1872, held membership in the Illinois Press Association.

The mother of William Thomas Pickett was born in Whiteside County, Illinois, November 15, 1851, the daughter of Dr. William C. Snyder who was born of Quaker parentage in New Jersey. She served as county chairman of the Red Cross knitters during the World War and taught hundreds of women how to knit garments for overseas companies.

Mr. Pickett was graduated from the Wahoo High School in 1896 and Boyles Business College in 1898. He is the editor and publisher of the *Wahoo Wasp* which was organized at Wahoo, Nebraska, in 1875; he became the owner of the publishing business in 1923, and has been sole owner and manager since that date. He served as secretary of the Saunders County Republican committee for 20 years, was unsuccessful candidate for the Republican national convention, 1930, and served as city clerk of Wahoo, from 1904 to 1906. He was president of the city school board in 1920, is a member of the Lions Club and Chamber of Commerce, and holds membership in the board of directors for the Nebraska Press Association. He is a member of the Scottish Rite Masons, and Shrine, Knights of Pythias, Modern Woodmen of America, and the Nebraskana Society. His religious affiliation is with the First Presbyterian Church of Wahoo.

Mr. Pickett was married to Daisy E. Mielenz at Wahoo, April 24, 1906. Mrs. Pickett, whose ancestry is German, was born at Ithaca, Saunders County, Nebraska, July 1, 1878. They have one daughter, Katherine, born September 12, 1909, who was graduated from Wahoo High School and in 1931, was graduated from the University of Nebraska, where she was a member of Delta Gamma Sorority. She is now assisting her father in his newspaper work. Residence: Wahoo. (Photograph in Album).

Chester Arthur Pierce

Chester Arthur Pierce, son of Abraham Lincoln and Frances Kinsey (Stubbs) Pierce, was born in a sod house thirty miles north of North Platte, Nebraska, May 10, 1893. His father, who was born at Waukee, Iowa, October 8, 1860, was a carpenter. His death occurred at Des Moines, Iowa, September 15, 1911. His wife, who was born at Des Moines, August 11, 1866, is living.

Educated in the public schools of Des Moines, Chester Arthur Pierce was graduated from Des Moines Academy in June, 1916, and was graduated from the Palmer School of Chiropractic on March 24, 1922.

He was married to Edna Scott at Des Moines, on March 29, 1922, and to them the following children were born: Barbara Helene, born October 19, 1923; Sally Ann, May 4, 1925; Robert Lewis, May 4, 1925; Phillip Peter, Dec. 4, 1926; Richard Joseph, October 4, 1928; and William Thomas, April 4, 1931.

Dr. Pierce is a Democrat. He is president of the Nebraska Development Company and of the U. S. Drilling Company, and has practiced in Hastings since April 10, 1922. A sergeant in the United States Army, with Field Hospital No. 16, Second Division, Dr. Pierce participated in the Battle of Chateau Thierry, Soissons, St. Mihiel, Mont Blanc, and the Meuse Argonne, and served in the Army of Invasion and Army of Occupation.

He is a member of the American Legion, and served as vice commander of the Hastings Post in 1927; was president of the Nebraska Chiropractic Association in 1925, district governor 1927, 28, 29, 30 and 31, and is now first vice president of the National Radionic Association. He is a member of the Chamber of Commerce, the Lions Clubs, Knights of Pythias and the D. O. K. K., as well as the Young Men's Christian Association and The Nebraskana Society. His religious affiliation is with the First Methodist Church. His hobbies are his home and his family. Residence: Hastings. (Photograph in Album).

Walter Lawrence Pierpoint

Walter Lawrence Pierpoint, advertising executive, was born at Sistersville, West Virginia, December 13, 1880, the son of Jeremiah Stillwell and Mary Rose (Lazear) Pierpont. His father, who was born at Middlebourne, West Virginia, October 16, 1850, was a hotel proprietor, wholesale grocer and stock raiser. He died at Urbana, Ohio, July 9, 1925. Mary Rose Lazear was born at Sistersville, March 27, 1855, and died at Urbana, May 12, 1925.

Educated first in the rural schools of West Virginia, Mr. Pierpoint attended Marietta (Ohio) College and received his A. B. in 1900. He was a member of Phi Beta

Kappa, prize essayist and valedictorian, active in debate and member of Alpha Tau Omega.

On December 25, 1902, he was married to Lou Octavia Silvers at Butler, Missouri. They have one daughter, Evalyn Ruth, born August 29, 1911. In 1906 he established an advertising and sales service for merchants at Wichita, Kansas, removing to Omaha, in 1912. He is the owner of the Pierpoint Advertising Agency at the present time. He is the author of numerous pamphlets on selling and retailing.

Mr. Pierpoint is active in the civic and commercial life of Omaha. He is past chairman of the advisory board of the Salvation Army, member and past president of the Omaha Rotary Club, member of the executive committee of the Chamber of Commerce, and chairman of the bureau of publicity of that organization. He is president of the board of education and past president of Central High School Parent-Teacher Association, and director of the Young Men's Christian Association. He attends the First Central Congregational Church, and is a member of the Elks. His club is the University Club. Residence: Omaha.

Clarence Alexander Pierson

Clarence Alexander Pierson, physician and surgeon, was born at Minneapolis, Minnesota, May 14, 1897, son of Nels and Caroline (Bradley) Pierson. His father, who was born in Sweden, April 8, 1867, came to America at the age of 17, and is the owner and operator of a hotel. His mother was born in Fillmore County, Minnesota, April 22, 1869.

Dr. Pierson attended the public schools of Columbus, North Dakota, from which he was graduated in 1912. In 1915, he was graduated from the Minot, North Dakota High School, and attended Northwestern University from 1919-26. He received his M. D. from that university in 1924, and is a member of Sigma Nu and Phi Beta Pi, and was steward of the latter. During 1916-17, and 1917-18, he was a student at the University of North Dakota.

Since his admission to practice he has resided at Beemer, and has been active in his profession. He served a twelve month internship at the Illinois Central Hospital in Chicago, and six months at the Chicago Lying in Hospital. His professional memberships include the American, Nebraska State and Cuming County Medical Societies.

He married Frances Grinnell, October 28, 1924. There are two children: Mary Ann, born July 5, 1926, and Alice J., born January 8, 1929. Dr. Pierson is a Republican, and in religion is an English Lutheran. He is active in the Red Cross and the Nebraska Children's Home Society. A Mason, he is also a member of the Lions International, the Beemer Community Club, and the Nebraskana Society. He enjoys golf and reading. Residence: Beemer.

William Ernest Pierson

William E. Pierson has lived in Nebraska for the past 48 years and is now a successful grain dealer and feed manufacturer in Polk County. He was born at Melrose Park, Cook County, Illinois, March 23, 1882, the son of Peter Pierson and Nellie (Benson) Pierson. His father, who was of Scandinavian descent, was born in Sweden, May 22, 1847, and died at Holdrege, Nebraska, November 11, 1923. His mother, also of Scandinavian descent, was born in Sweden, July 14, 1847, and died at Holdrege July 11, 1927.

Mr. Pierson was graduated from high school at Minden, Nebraska, in 1899, and was a student at Nebraska Wesleyan University in 1900 and 1901. He was manager of the Farmers Grain Company of Osceola, Polk County, Nebraska, from 1918 to 1926, and since 1926 has been proprietor of the W. E. Pierson Flour and Feed Company.

He is a member of the Saint Paul Lutheran Church

JANE PINDER

of Osceola, the Osceola Community Club, Modern Woodmen of America, Independent Order of the Odd Fellows, and the Nebraskana Society: has served on the city council, and is affiliated with the Democratic party.

On March 2, 1910, he was united in marriage to Hilma Julia Nelson at Osceola. To this union five children were born: Wallace Everett, July 5, 1911, a graduate of Osceola High School and of the Lincoln School of Commerce; Byron Woodrow, born November 12, 1913, a graduate of the Lincoln School of Commerce; Leona Maurine, born August 20, 1916; Clinton Riley, born November 11, 1918; and Lois Birdell, born December 8, 1928. Residence: Osceola. (Photograph in Album).

Henry Home Pilgrim

Henry Home Pilgrim, a lifetime resident of Dakota County, Nebraska, was born at Homer, July 25, 1871, the son of Alfred and Ruth Corwin Pilgrim. Forty years ago, when Nebraska was still a comparatively new territory, he carried the United States mail from Homer to Winnebago Agency.

He was a farmer for ten years, was engaged in the livery business for 20 years, and at this time is an expressman and truck gardener. He is affiliated with Pentecostal Tabernacle at South Sioux City, Nebraska, and holds membership in The Nebraskana Society.

His marriage to Myrtle May McPherson was solemnized at Homer, December 9, 1897. Mrs. Pilgrim was born at Dakota City, March 1, 1877. They have two children: Harold, born November 3, 1898, who married Charlotte Olson; and Harry, born November 17, 1900, who married Cecil Lausom. Harry is a salesman at Rapid City, Iowa, and Harold is in business with his father.

Mr. Pilgrim's grandparents were the first white family to enter Dakota county, settling on Pilgrim Hill. He was born in North Carolina in 1820. Residence: South Sioux City.

Jane Pinder

A resident of Nebraska for nearly forty-four years, Jane Pinder is the daughter of Arthur and Henrietta Ida (Doughty) Pinder. She was born at Peabody, Massachusetts, August 8, 1878, and attended the grade schools of Newark, New Jersey, and Omaha, Nebraska . Thereafter she attended Omaha High School four years and completed a special course in languages there. She was for a time a student at Black Hills College in Hot Springs, South Dakota, and holds an honorary degree from Grand Island College.

Arthur Pinder, father of Jane, was born in Peabody, Massachusetts, December 16, 1856. His wife, Henrietta, was born in New York City, September 22, 1856, and died at Omaha on November 7, 1896. They both came from early settlers in America.

Jane Pinder has taught violin in Grand Island since 1899, with the exception of three years spent in the study of music in Chicago. For more than fifteen years she has owned and directed the Grand Island Conservatory of Music. During the period of time when the conservatory was part of Grand Island College she was its business manager. She is a teacher as well as a director, being a teacher of the ensemble playing of the conservatory. She is also a director of the Grand Island Symphony Orchestra.

She is an honorary member of the Grand Island Rotary Club, a member and former state president of the Nebraska State Music Teacher's Association, a member of the Grand Island Woman's Club, and former music chairman of the State Federation of Women's Clubs. At the present time she is a member of the advisory board of the Young Women's Christian Association; while during the World War period she was a four-minute speaker and active in canteen work. Recently Miss Pinder

was awarded life membership in The Nebraskana Society. Residence: Grand Island. (Photograph on Page 948).

Harry Robert Pinkerton

Harry R. Pinkerton has lived in Nebraska for the past 38 years, and has been engaged in business in Omaha, for many years. He was born in Peoria, Illinois, March 4, 1873, the son of John M. and Mary Jane (Stevenson) Pinkerton. His father, who was a farmer, was born in Prebble County, Ohio, February 3, 1836, and died in Peoria County, Illinois, in September, 1882; he was of Scotch-Irish descent. His mother was born in Prebble County, January 18, 1835, and died at Omaha, September, 1902. Her ancestry was German.

Mr. Pinkerton, who is a department manager and buyer at Omaha, was graduated from high school in Peoria, in 1891. On October 5, 1897, he was united in marriage with Laura Mary Schwartz at Omaha. Mrs. Pinkerton was born of German parentage at Atlantic, Iowa, January 15, 1873, and died at Omaha, December 20, 1930. Two children were born to their marriage: Robert, born September 29, 1898; and Harris, born June 6, 1905.

He is a member of the Omaha Chamber of Commerce, and is affiliated with the Church of Christ, Scientist. He is a Republican. Residence: Omaha.

Albert Francis Pinkley

A leader in civic and fraternal affairs for many years, Albert Francis Pinkley has been a resident of Nebraska since April 1, 1885. Born at Jelloway, Ohio, June 26, 1856, he is the son of Joseph and Sara (France) Pinkley.

Joseph Pinkley, who was born in Pennsylvania, October 30, 1814, was a school teacher who later took up farming. He held several minor public offices prior to his death at Fenton, Illinois, October 28, 1891. Of English descent, he was the son of David and Margaret (Brown) Pinkley.

Sara France, who was born in Pennsylvania, November 17, 1824, died at Fenton, Illinois, November 28, 1908. She was of German or Dutch descent, daughter of Fredrick and Margaret (Painter) France.

Educated in the elementary schools of Fenton until 1874, Albert Francis Pinkley attended the Janesville, Wisconsin, Telegraph and Commercial School 1875-76. From August 1, 1877, until August 1, 1930, he was railroad agent in various places for the Burlington. For the past forty years he has been located at Ansley, and on January 1, 1931, was retired on pension, and at this time wears a 53 years service emblem.

He was married on May 5, 1879, to Eliza Buena Vista Moss at Clinton, Iowa. Mrs. Pinkley, who was the daughter of Henry G. and Elizabeth (Eads) Moss, was born at Mt. Pleasant, Illinois, April 14, 1861, and died at Ansley, April 17, 1928.

To them were born five children Clyde, born March 2, 1880, who married Dessie Blowers; Elsie, born February 8, 1882, who married William S. Lawson; Ruby, born March 2, 1885, who married Jesse B. Hendrickson; Nellie, born August 24, 1890, who married Charles M. Garland; and Fern Olga, born February 1, 1895. Fern has followed the teaching profession and holds the degrees of Bachelor of Arts and Master of Arts from the University of Nebraska.

A Mason, Mr. Pinkley has held all offices in the Blue Lodge, and is a member of the Scottish Rite (32nd degree). He is at the present time secretary-treasurer and director of the Gladstone Temple Company, a Masonic organization. He has held all offices in the Modern Woodmen of America, is vice president of the Rotary Club, and a life member of The Nebraskana Society. From 1920-26 he served as a member of the library board, and from 1895 until the present time has been a member of the school board. He has been president or secretary continuously since 1927. Residence: Ansley. (Photograph on Page 950).

ALBERT FRANCIS PINKLEY

Locke—Grand Island

George LeRoy Pinney

George LeRoy Pinney, leading physician and diagnostician, was born at Michigan City, Indiana, August 5, 1894, son of Edward and Florence Bell (Metcalf) Pinney. His father was born at Wanatah, Indiana, February 3, 1861, and has been prominent in the political and commercial life of Bernalillo County and Albuquerque, New Mexico, for many years, and has among other things, served as treasurer of Bernalillo County. He is the son of Captain Horace Pinney of England. Florence Bell Metcalf, wife of Edward Pinney, was born at Wanatah, Indiana, October 21, 1861, of German extraction. She is active in club work and is a member of the Order of Eastern Star.

Educated in the public schools of Albuquerque, Dr. Pinney received his Bachelor of Science degree, and his Doctor of Medicine degree from Northwestern University. He was business manager of the Northwestern annual, a letterman in track at the University of New Mexico, and is a member of Pi Kappa Alpha, Phi Beta Pi and Theta Nu Epsilon.

On October 10, 1923, Dr. Pinney was united in marriage to Sarah Elizabeth Boone at Warren, Illinois. Mrs. Pinney, who is a graduate of the National Kindergarten College of Chicago, was born at Warren, January 9, 1896, of Scotch and Irish descent. They have three children: George LeRoy, Jr., born November 3, 1925; Gloria Ann, born March 22, 1928, and Sally Jane, born June 18, 1930.

Mrs. Pinney is a member of the Woman's Club, the Country Club, Eastern Star and Milk Fund Club. She is interested particularly in supplying proper food for the under-nourished child. After completing her education she taught two years in the public school of Gary, Indiana, as head of the kindergarten department.

Dr. Pinney is particularly interested in preventive medicine and was the 1930 chairman of the Adams County Fair Health Clinic, which examined about 200 babies and the same number of adults. Results in this field of research have been encouraging and Dr. Pinney has continued his study with the children of the public schools and students of Hastings College. He was chairman of the health clinic at the state fair for one day in 1931.

Dr. Pinney specializes in diagnosis, and at the present time is public school physician, physician to Hastings College, and consulting internist to Ingleside State Hospital, and chairman of medical staff of Mary Lanning Memorial Hospital, and is the author of *Blood Transfusion; Malnutrition* and *Cardiac Hypertrophy*. He is preparing an article for the Nebraska Dental Journal entitled *The Relationship Between the Interest and the Dentist*. During his ten years of active practice he has risen high in his profession and has filled various offices in medical organizations. He is a former president of the Adams County Medical Society, has served as delegate to the convention of the Nebraska State Medical Society, is a fellow of the American College of Physicians, is a fellow of American Public Health Association and is a member of the District Medical Society.

He is the representative of internal medicine in the Rotary Club and chairman of the social committee, chairman of the playground committee of the Chamber of Commerce, a 32nd degree Mason and member of the Divan of the Shrine. He holds membership in the Elks, the Young Men's Christian Association, the American Legion, and the Knights of Pythias. His religious affiliation is with the Presbyterian Church.

Dr. Pinney is interested in landscaping and enjoys golf and hunting. He is a Republican, and active in politics. His social clubs are the Northwestern University and the Hastings Country Clubs. Residence: Hastings.

Alva Sherman Pinto

Alva Sherman Pinto, physician, was born at Chilli-cothe, Ohio, May 29, 1872, son of Miles Augustus and Margaret A. (Reid) Pinto.

The father was born in Chillicothe, on March 4, 1826, where he spent his entire life. The mother was born in Chillicothe, August 12, 1835, and died there on December 7, 1879.

Dr. Pinto attended public school and received his medical degree from Creighton University. He was married to Mabel Belinda Spalding at Omaha, December 10, 1903. She was born at Elvaston, Illinois, August 28, 1877. There are two children, Sherman Spalding, and Harvey Elmore.

Dr. Pinto is a Republican, has been health commissioner of Omaha since 1921. He is a director of the Farmers and Merchants Bank, and the H. J. Hughes Company. During the late war he served on the exemption board. He is a member of the First Methodist Church, is a Spanish War Veteran, belongs to the American Legion, and the American, Douglas County, and Nebraska State Medical Association. His club is the Athletic Club. Residence: Omaha.

Emil Louis Pischel

Emil Louis Pischel, a resident of Nebraska for 61 years, was born in Bohemia, the son of Anton and Maria (Misliveacre) Pischel. His father, who was a merchant tailor, was born in Bohemia and died at Santa Rosa, California, March 2, 1900. His mother was born at Kutna Hora, Bohemia and died on a farm near Verdel, Nebraska, January 20, 1918.

Mr. Pischel was the owner and manager of a general merchandise store for several years, and was a successful farmer near Verdel for many years where he is now retired. He served as postmaster at Verdell from 1884 to 1927, was county supervisor, and chairman of the county board.

He married Theresa Dirz at Niobrara, Nebraska, October 15, 1884. Mrs. Pischel was born in Bohemia in 1865 and died near Verdel, May 6, 1929. They have six children: Anton, born February 1, 1886, who married Myrtle Addington; Otto, born July 7, 1888, who married Tillie Barta; Walter, born February 10, 1890, who married Grace Pischel; Arthur J., born June, 1902, who married Mary Pischel; Frank E., born September 1, 1904; and William, born January 2, 1900. Anton is bookkeeper for the Patterson Hardware Company at Fort Morgan Colorado. Otto, Walter, and Arthur are farmers. Residence: Verdel.

William Henry Pitzer

William H. Pitzer was born at Arizona, Nebraska, February 3, 1869, the son of Fletcher Bradley and Mary (Stringfield) Pitzer. His father, who was born in Kentucky, March 3, 1840, and died at Hillsdale, Mills County, Iowa, June 4, 1880, was a Methodist Episcopal territorial minister and circuit rider in Nebraska from 1864 to 1869. His family originally came from Virginia to Kentucky, and moved to Iowa in 1853.

His mother, who was born in Edmondson County, Kentucky, December 22, 1842, moved with her parents to Missouri, in 1843, and in 1852 moved to Iowa. She died at Nebraska City, November 27, 1920.

Mr. Pitzer attended the country and village schools of Iowa and Kansas, and was admitted to the practice of law in Iowa and Nebraska, in 1899. Since that time he has been engaged in the practice of his profession in Nebraska City. Since 1901 he has been secretary and chief executive officer of the Nebraska City Building and Loan Association. He is president of the Otoe County National Bank, and of the Farmers' Elevator Company at Nebraska City. He was formerly a member of the law firm Pitzer & Hayward, and thereafter was successively associated with Edwin Zimmerer, Earl Cline, V. E. Tyler, and L. E. Peterson.

A Republican, Mr. Pitzer has taken an active part in

the political and educational affairs of the state for many years. From 1919 to 1920, he was a member of the Nebraska Constitutional Convention, representing Cass and Otoe Counties; was a member of the Board of Education of the State Normal Schools, 1929-1930; and was elected state senator from the Second Senatorial District, composed of Cass, Otoe, and Sarpy Counties, for the term 1931-32.

His marriage to Ora Fern Miller was solemnized at Hillsdale, Mills County, Iowa, November 4, 1904. Mrs. Pitzer's father was a Tennesseean, and her mother was a Carolinian. She was born at Hillsdale, December 2, 1880. There are two children: Margaret Lawrence, born May 17, 1907; and John Marshall, born April 15, 1909, who received his A. B. degree at the University of Nebraska, and is now attending the law school there.

During the World War, Mr. Pitzer was in the Nebraska National Guard service, and was chairman of the omnibus war work in Otoe County. He is a member of the Nebraska State Bar Association and the American Bar Association. He is affiliated with the State Historical Society and the Nebraskana Society. His hobby is farming. Residence: Nebraska City.

Joseph Daniel Pivonka

For more than fifty-two years Joseph Daniel Pivonka has been a leading citizen of Swanton, Nebraska. He was born at Manitowoc, Wisconsin, June 29, 1869, son of Jacob and Helen Pivonka. His parents were natives of Czechoslovakia, the former born in 1840, and the latter in 1838. Jacob Pivonka died at Wilber, on November 10, 1921. His wife died there in 1888. At the age of ten years Joseph Pivonka came to Nebraska with his parents.

He was married to Mary Houser, at Wilber, January 10, 1893. Mrs. Pivonko was born in Czechoslovakia, June 19, 1870. There are two children: Adolph F., born January 11, 1894, who married Olga Fikar, and who is a banker. The daughter, Erma A., was born January 10, 1904, and is married to William Fitl.

Until 1919, Mr. Pivonka farmed in Saline County, and since that time he has been engaged in the banking business. He is at the present time president of the Bank of Swanton. In politics he is affiliated with the Democratic party. He is a member of the Swanton Commercial Club, thee Z. C. B. J. and The Nebraskana Society. Residence: Swanton.

Joseph Placek

Joseph Placek, retired farmer of Swanton, Nebraska, was born at Cleveland, Ohio, October 20, 1868, the son of John and Katherine (Sedivy) Placek. His father, who was a farmer, was born at Podebrady, Czechoslovakia, May 27, 1837, and died at Wilber, Nebraska, March 15, 1915; he came to America, May 27, 1867. His mother was born at Podebrady, November 23, 1839, and died at Wilber, April 20, 1913. She was active in her community and church affairs.

Mr. Placek, who has lived in Nebraska for the past 54 years, attended school at Cleveland, and in Saline County. He is a member of the Woodmen of the World and the Bohemian fraternal organization, Z. C. B. J. His religious affiliation is with the Catholic Church. Politically, he is a Democrat.

On February 3, 1891, he was united in marriage with Mary Emily Petrasek, at Wilber. Mrs. Placek was born at Wilber, February 1, 1871. Nine children were born to this union, all of whom are living: Edward, born March 23, 1892, who married Emma Bartos; Ladislav, born March 24, 1894, who maried Mary Slepicka; Bessie, born March 24, 1894, who married Frank Sasek; John, born February 4, 1896, who married Mary Hana; William, born June 22, 1898, who married Lydia Houser; Joe, born August 5, 1904; Jerry, born August 5, 1904, who married

Emma Vidlec; Rose, born September 7, 1906, who married Edward Jiskra; and Blanche, born January 25, 1911, who is a school teacher. Residence: Swanton.

Alden Charles Plantz

Alden Charles Plantz, prominent lawyer of Sheridan County, was born in Dodge County, Nebraska, February 4, 1882, son of Franklin Christian and Harriet Elizabeth (Pettegrew) Plantz. The father was born in Fulton County, New York, November 5, 1840, and served in Company C, 51st Infantry of New York, with the rank of corporal. He died at Hay Springs, Nebraska, February 5, 1909. His grandfather, who was born in Germany, came to America as an infant. Harriet Elizabeth Pettegrew was born near Marysville, Iowa, September 21, 1853, and in her younger days taught in the public school. Her ancestry was mixed; she was a descendant of John Alden and Priscilla Mullins.

In 1897 Mr. Plantz was graduated from Hay Springs High School at the age of 15, and three years later became assistant cashier of the Northwestern State Bank of Hay Springs. He continued in this capacity until 1903. From 1903 until 1910 Mr. Plantz was vice president, and later secretary and treasurer of the Maverick Loan and Trust Company of Rushville. Since 1910 he has been engaged in the practice of law there. At the present time he is attorney for the Stockmen's National Bank, the First National Bank of Hay Springs, and others. He is a Republican, and for six years was county attorney of Sheridan County. Among other offices which he has held are, justice of the peace, member of the school board, village trustee, and chairman of the Republican County Central Committee which he held for several years.

On January 1, 1908, he was married to Helen Watt at Rushville. Mrs. Plantz was born at Xenia, Ohio, May 16, 1885, and before her marriage was a teacher. Mr. and Mrs. Plantz are members of the Methodist Episcopal Church at Rushville.

During the late war Mr. Plantz was a member of the Legal Advisory Board and was government appeal agent, first president of the Sheridan County Red Cross, and secretary of the Sheridan County Council of Defense. A Mason, a member of the Eastern Star and the Royal Highlanders, he is also a member of the Woodmen of the World, the Nebraskana Society, and the Rushville Chamber of Commerce, and the American, Nebraska State and Sheridan County bar associations. At the present time he is a member of the Library Board also. His favorite sport is golf, and he holds membership in the Rushville Golf Club. Residence: Rushville. (Photograph on Page 953).

C. E. Plass

Born at Onedia, New York, September 15, 1857, C. E. Plass is the son of Edward and Margaret (Weeks) Plass. His father, who was a shoemaker, was born at Rome, New York, and died in Onedia County, New York, in 1862. His mother was born at Rome in 1860.

Mr. Plass was engaged in the bakery and grocery business for a number of years, and recently has bought and sold land in Madison County, Nebraska. He is a director of the First National Bank of Madison, has served as mayor of that city for two terms, and has been a member of the City Council for two terms. His sports include football and baseball.

On March 19, 1887, he was married to Mary Emma Reagan at Washington, Kansas. Mrs. Plass, whose ancestry is Pennsylvania Dutch, was born at Reading, Pennsylvania, November 23, 1863. They have seven children: C. E., Jr., born January 1, 1900; Hallie, born January 12, 1888; Mana L., born March 10, 1891, who married F. C. Jenkins; Clara I., born February 14, 1893, who married H. B. Brannian; Sadie, born July 13, 1896,

ALDEN CHARLES PLANTZ

who married T. F. Whiting; Madge, born June 12, 1899, who married E. G. Thiele. C. E., Jr., is a chemical engineer in the employ of the Western Electric Company. Residence: Madison.

George W. Platner

A veteran lumberman of Nebraska, George W. Platner, has been prominent in Omaha for the past 42 years. He was born at Glidden, Iowa, October 31, 1871, the son of William H. and Anna M. (Pierce) Platner. His father, who was born at Tipton, Iowa, March 4, 1838, and died at Omaha, was a lawyer. He was first lieutenant of the 13th Iowa Infantry until the Battle of Atlanta, when he was wounded. His ancestry was German and he claimed to be the third white child born in Iowa.

His mother who was born at Newton, Iowa, in 1853, and reared six children, all of whom are living, died at Omaha. Her ancestry was English.

Mr. Platner was graduated from high school at Glidden, Iowa, June, 1886, and was a student at Western Normal College at Shenandoah, Iowa, in 1887. He has been in business for himself for 37 years, and now owns and operates four lumber yards at Omaha.

He married Margaret Alice Bennett, who was born at Omaha, October 27, 1874; her ancestry is English on the maternal side and Irish through the paternal line. They have two children: Josephine, born July 3, 1903, who married J. Leslie Shear; and John, born January 12, 1906. Josephine was awarded a degree at Columbia University and is an archeologist. John is a member of Phi Beta Kappa, and holds a degree in mechanical engineering awarded at Princeton.

Mr. Platner was a private in the Home Guards during the World War, and entered almost every war activity during 1918. A member of the Chamber of Commerce, he was formerly a member of the Omaha Kiwanis Club. He is a member of the First Methodist Church of Omaha, and is a member of the board of trustees of the church. He holds membership in the Omaha Athletic Club and Happy Hollow Club. He is a 33rd degree Scottish Rite Mason. Politically, Mr. Platner is a Republican. Residence: Omaha.

Wilbur Harvey Plourd

Wilbur Harvey Plourd, educator and newspaper man, was born at Odell, Nebraska, September 18, 1893, the son of William Henry and Elizabeth (Hohman) Plourd. His father, who was born in Iowa, is the owner and manager of a theatre; his ancestry is French. Elizabeth (Hohman) Plourd was born in Germany.

Mr. Plourd attended the public schools of Indianola where he was graduated in 1911. He received the B. S. and B. P. degrees at Fremont College in 1916. He has held the following positions in the educational world: principal, Kimball, Nebraska, 1914-16; superintendent, Utica, Nebraska, 1916-17; superintendent, Loup City, Nebraska, 1919-20; superintendent, Fullerton, Nebraska, 1920-24. In 1924 he purchased the *News-Journal* at Fullerton, and in 1928 bought the *Fullerton Post*, consolidating the two newspapers to form the *Nance County Journal* of which he is now owner and publisher.

He is president of the board of education at Fullerton, was secretary of the Lions Club in 1927, and served as president of the latter organization in 1928. He was chairman of the Home Service Department of the Nance County Red Cross, 1931, assisted with the organization of the Nance County Homecoming Association, and is a member of the Nebraska Press Association. He is affiliated with the Methodist Church and holds membership in the Masons, Knights of Pythias, and Modern Woodmen of America. His social club is the Fullerton Golf Association.

Mr. Plourd served as first class sergeant, 310th Aero Squadron, overseas during the World War, and was commander of the Fred Philbrick Post of the Amer-

ican Legion in 1929. He is the author of *Paragon Plan System,* for use in the public schools.

His marriage to Hazelle Alta Mangan occurred at Kimball, Nebraska, August 16, 1916. Mrs. Plourd, who was a teacher until 1923, was born at Elkton, South Dakota, September 24, 1893. Her maternal grandfather was a descendant of Patrick Henry. They have a son, Marvin, born January 15, 1927. Residence: Fullerton.

Florando Ernst Poellot

Florando E. Poellot was born at West Point, Nebraska, May 24, 1884. After graduating from high school at West Point, he attended the Pharmacy College of Creighton, at Omaha, Nebraska, where he received his graduate pharmacist's degree.

Peter Poellot, father of Florando, was born at Aldorf, Germany, July 4, 1852, and came to this country in 1877. He is now a retired newspaper man. Ida (Krouse) Poellot, his wife, was born in Canada, August 16, 1862, and died at West Point, Nebraska.

On December 28, 1908, Florando E. Poellot was united in marriage to Blanche Scott, at West Point. She is interested in church and club work. They have a daughter, Doris Marie, born June 16, 1918.

Mr. Poellot has been a resident of Nebraska his entire life, and has been a druggist in Coleridge, for twenty-four years. He was mayor from 1922 to 1924. He is affiliated with the Congregational Church of Coleridge, and is a member and president of the Booster Club, and a member of The Nebraskana Society. His hobby is electrical work. Residence: Coleridge.

Ernest Mark Pollard

Born at Nehawka, Nebraska, April 15, 1869, Ernest M. Pollard has been active in the life of his community and state for many years. He is the son of Isaac and Viola (Welch) Pollard. Isaac Pollard was born at Plymouth, Vermont, June 30, 1830, a descendant of English settlers in America in 1690. An early settler in the middle west, he ran the original survey of Cass County for the government. He was a farmer, and served as clerk of Cass County and government surveyor. He died at Nehawka in November, 1916, after a useful and constructive life.

Viola Welch Pollard was born in New York State in August, 1838, of English parentage, and died at Nehawka, in July, 1914. Ernest M. Pollard attended country district school at Nehawka. Entering the first preparatory department of the University of Nebraska, he received his B. A. from that institution in 1893. While at the university he was president of his class, and president of the Palladian Society 1892-93, and senior captain of the University Cadet Battalion.

In 1896 he was united in marriage with Maude E. Rose of Millbrook, Pennsylvania. Mrs. Pollard died at Nehawka, on November 11, 1902. His second marriage was to Gertrude Waterman of Omaha, on July 27, 1905. To this marriage four children were born: Ernest Isaac, born November 11, 1906, married Helen Stahl, living at Irwin, Pennsylvania; Frank W., born October 11, 1909, married Helen Gansemer; Mary Caroline born November 30, 1911, and Halleck William, born January 8, 1914. Ernest is a graduate in electrical engineering from the University of Nebraska, and is now in the designing department of the Westinghouse Company.

A Republican, Mr. Pollard served in the state legislature from 1897-99, in 1905-1909 was a member of the United States Congress from 1st Congressional District of Nebraska, was a member of the Constitutional Convention of 1920, and was secretary of labor and welfare under Governor Weaver. From 1894, until 1927, he was manager of the Pollard Fruit Farm. From 1927-29, he was president of the Farmers Union State Exchange.

During the World War he was a member of the South Platte draft board. His religious affiliation is with the Christian Church.

Always active in the educational work of his community, he has been a member of the Nehawka School Board for twenty years, during eighteen of which he has served as president. He is a member of the Modern Woodmen of America, of the Odd Fellows and of the University Alumni Association. Residence: Nehawka.

Fay Hall Pollock

Fay Hall Pollock was born at Collison, Illinois, November 25, 1896, son of Henry William and Azubah (Hall) Pollock. His mother and father are living, and his mother is a descendant of Lyman Hall, a signer of the Declaration of Independence.

Mr. Pollock attended the public and high schools of Manning, Iowa, and was graduated from the latter in 1915. He attended the University of Nebraska, from which he received his LL. B. in 1921. He is a member of Sigma Nu of which he was commander 1920-21, and of Phi Alpha Delta.

Since June, 1921, Mr. Pollock has been engaged in the practice of law, and in 1925, was state representative from Douglas County (18th legislative district). Coming to Stanton, in 1925, since 1926 he has been county attorney of Stanton County. He is a Republican.

Mr. Pollock was married to Gladys Sharrar, at Sioux City, Iowa, March 18, 1927. Mrs. Pollock was born at Creston, Nebraska, March 31, 1903. There are two sons: James Hall, born February 1, 1928; and Jack Sharrar, born May 22, 1931.

From March 18, 1918, to December 10, 1918, he held the rank of second lieutenant in Air Service. He is a member of the American Legion, and was commander of Stanton Post No. 77, in 1930. His religious affiliation is with the Congregational Church of Stanton, and he is a member of the Masons and the Elks. His professional organizations include the County Attorneys' Association of Nebraska, of which he is president, the State Bar Association, and the Ninth Judicial District Bar Association. His favorite sport is fishing. Residence: Stanton.

Montgomery K. Pollock

Montgomery K. Pollock, who is a retired farmer at Hartington, Nebraska, has lived in this state for the past 65 years. He was born at Sterling, Illinois, April 25, 1863, the son of John and Elizabeth (Burnett) Pollock. His father, who was a farmer, was born at Myrshire, Scotland, December 23, 1824, and died at Fremont, Nebraska, July 16, 1880, his father who was a Scotch clergyman, came to this country at the age of 17 years. His mother was born at Glascow, Scotland, March 9, 1841, and died at Fremont, June 19, 1911.

Mr. Pollock was graduated from grade school in 1876. He has been a farmer until recently. He is a member of the Red Cross, the Nebraskana Society, and the Presbyterian Church. He has been a member of the Modern Woodmen of America for the past 35 years, and holds membership in the Odd Fellows. During the World War he served as a member of the draft board and was active in Liberty loan drives. He is especially interested in stock raising.

His marriage to Isabella Hindmarsh, was solemnized at Fremont, Dodge County, Nebraska, December 27, 1886. Mrs. Pollock, who is descended from the Rutherfords of New York, and the Grey family of England, was born at Sterling, Whiteside County, Illinois, July 6, 1866. Five children were born to them: Alice, born December 15, 1889, who married Ora Ray McColley; John, born November 16, 1892, who married Margaret Lynde; Edward, born March 24, 1896, who died December 24, 1918; Mary, born July 3, 1898, who married William Schwader-

er; and Ruth, born April 19, 1901, who married Nim Depue.

Alice is a licensed embalmer in Montana. John is a salesman, and Mary owns and operates a beauty parlor in Nebraska City. Ruth is a school teacher in South Dakota. Residence: Hartington.

Thomas Herbert Pollock

Thomas Herbert Pollock, banker, was born at Kankakee, Illinois, June 6, 1867, son of Thomas and Mary Rennick (Kerr) Pollock. The father was born in Ligonier, Pennsylvania, July 4, 1826, and died at Plattsmouth, October 22, 1913. He was descended from the Pollock family, whose ancestry is traced to Scotland in the 16th century. The mother was born in Florence, Pennsylvania, August 25, 1833, and died at Plattsmouth, January 20, 1914. She was a graduate of Washington and Jefferson College, and taught music in the seminary at Lexington, Kentucky. She was active in the First Presbyterian Church at Plattsmouth.

Mr. Pollock was graduated from high school at Plattsmouth in 1883. He owned and operated large independent telephone interests, built and owned a toll bridge at Plattsmouth, operated the Plattsmouth Water Company and at the present time owns large land interests in Nebraska and eastern Colorado. He is president of the Farmers State Bank of Plattsmouth.

On December 17, 1890, he was married to Lida Walker Patterson at Plattsmouth. She was born at Rock Bluff, Nebraska, February 20, 1870, and is of Scotch and Irish pre-Revolutionary ancestry. There are two children living, Ellen Campbell, born October 17, 1891, who married Lynn Overton Minor; and Alice Mary, born September 13, 1902, who married Virgil W. Perry. Edith Lillian, born March 7, 1909, died May 28, 1909.

For a number of years Mr. Pollock has been a member and director of the Chamber of Commerce. He is a Mason and an Elk, a member of the First Presbyterian Church, and the Omaha Athletic Club. Residence: Plattsmouth.

Daniel Edwin Pomeroy

Born at Avon, Wisconsin, February 2, 1861, Daniel Edwin Pomeroy is the son of Nelson Phineas and Jemima Minerva (Hutcheson) Pomeroy. Nelson Pomeroy was born in New York State in January, 1813. A riverman and lumberman, he was also a carpenter, and an early pioneer homesteader in Nebraska. Of Scotch-Irish and Dutch descent, his grandfather was a soldier in the Revolutionary War, and was in the battle of Bunker Hill. His wife was a sister of John Paulding. Jemima Minerva Hutcheson was born in New York State on March 5, 1822, and died at Allen, Nebraska, November 10, 1905. Active in her home and church, she was of Holland-Dutch descent.

Daniel Edwin Pomeroy was educated in country schools and has engaged in farming since reaching maturity. A Republican, he was a member of the quartette which sang campaign songs from 1888-92. On December 16, 1885, he was united in marriage to Ida May Hamlin in Dixon County. Mrs. Pomeroy, who is the daughter of a Civil War veteran, was born in Albertlea, Minnesota, February 6, 1866. There are four children, all of whom are farming. They are as follows: Glenn, born December 26, 1886, married Erma Joyce Green; Madge, born May 20, 1889, married Willard John Brandt; Ray, born December 8, 1890, married Neva Lorine Anderson; Florence, born March 20, 1893, married Paul A. Anderson. Residence: Allen.

Mary Lueta Pool

Mary L. Pool was born at Weeping Water, Nebraska, September 22, 1878, the daughter of James and Sarah Jane (Van Avery) Colbert. Her father was born in

Huntingtonshire, England, August 19, 1833, and in 1868 came from Michigan in a covered wagon to Cass County, where he homesteaded. He died at Weeping Water, September 5, 1912. Her mother was born at St. George, Canada, February 4, 1844, and died at Weeping Water, October 23, 1919.

On December 27, 1899, she married Clarence Edward Pool, at Wabash, Nebraska. Mr. Pool, who was born at Eight Mile Grove, Nebraska, July 18, 1878, is a farmer, and is president of the Farmers Grain & Supply Company at Weeping Water. He is of English descent. There are two daughters: Florence Eloise, born January 20, 1902; and Hazel Lueta, born February 13, 1904. Both of the girls are school teachers.

In 1928 and 1929 Mrs. Pool was president of the local Woman's Christian Temperance Union, and from 1922 to 1924, she was president of the Weeping Water Woman's Club. She is a member of the Nebraskana Society, the Eastern Star, and P. E. O., and is affiliated with the First Congregational Church of Weeping Water. Her political preference is the Republican party. Residence: Weeping Water.

Raymond John Pool

Born on a farm in Cass County, Nebraska, April 23, 1882, Raymond John Pool has spent his entire adult life as an educator. His father, William Henry Pool, was born on a farm in Ohio, and died at Weeping Water, Nebraska, October 12, 1912. He was a pioneer farmer and served as county recorder of Cass County. His ancestry was English and Scotch. Mary Louisa Burrows, wife of William Henry Pool, was born on a farm in Michigan. She died at Weeping Water, October 21, 1915, and was of English descent.

Professor Pool was educated in Cass County district school, and was graduated from Weeping Water High School in 1903. He received his A. B. in 1907, A. M. in 1908 and Ph. D. in 1913 from the University of Nebraska. He is a member and past president of the Nebraska chapter of Phi Beta Kappa, and Sigma Xi, and a member of Theta Nu, Phi Sigma and Alpha Theta Chi.

He was married to Martha Marie Stangland, who was born near Carroll, Iowa, at McCook, Nebraska, June 30, 1909. Since 1907, he has been a professor at the University of Nebraska, and since 1915 has been chairman of the department of botany. He was a member of the federal court commission in Salt Lake City in 1920, and since 1917 has been an investigator of the relation of metallurgical operations to vegetation. He is the author of *First Course in Botany, Handbook of Nebraska Trees, Vegetation of the Sandhills of Nebraska, Laboratory Guide in Plant Physiology, Flowers and Flowering Plants,* etc. and is the editor of the *Botanical Survey of Nebraska.*

From 1899-1903 he served in Company D, First Nebraska National Guard, with the ranks of private to first lieutenant. During the World War he participated in the usual civilian activities, loan drives, etc. He is a member of St. Paul's Methodist Episcopal Church, the American Interprofessional Institute, the Modern Woodmen of America, the Chamber of Commerce, and University Club of Lincoln. His professional memberships include the American Association of University Professors (president Nebraska chapter 1925), the Botanical Society of America, the American Pytopathological Society, the American Microscopical Society, the Ecological Society of America, the Torrey Botanical Club, the American Museum of Natural History, the Nebraska Academy of Science, the Society of American Foresters, and the American Association for the Advancement of Science, of which last he is a fellow. He is a member of the Colorado Mountain Club and the American Alpine Club, and is interested in Alpine vegetation and in mountain climbing. His hobby is the history of the Vikings. Residence: Lincoln. (Photograph in Album).

L. Thomas Poole

One of Sidney's most prominent residents, L. Thomas Poole was born at Riverton, Iowa, November 23, 1875, and is 1878 came to Guide Rock, Nebraska. His father, Thomas Jefferson Poole, was born at Platte City, Missouri, August 12, 1841, and came to Nebraska, locating at Auburn, Nemaha County, in 1855. He was a ranchman, a county politician, and a soldier in Company D, 5th Missouri Cavalry during the Civil War. He died at Sheridan, Wyoming, April 10, 1928. Thomas Jefferson Poole was the son of George Poole, born at Hazel, Yorkshire, England, in 1810. His mother was Catharine Hoover, a native of South Carolina. George and Catherine (Hoover) Poole, whose mother died on the Oregon Train in 1848, near the present site of Lexington, Nebraska, were united in marriage in Macoupin County, Illinois, in 1835.

Marian Maria Lytle, wife of Thomas Jefferson Poole, was born at Greentown, Indiana, August 12, 1845, and died at Sheridan, Wyoming, on March 10, 1922. She was an active club worker. Her father was Thomas Lytle and her grandfather, Francis Lytle, both natives of North Carolina. Thomas Lytle was married to Edith Louder.

Mr. Poole received his early education in country and village schools and afterward attended Chadron Academy. He was born on a farm and later was a cowboy, school teacher, railroad man, merchant, and traveling man. At the present time he is a sales manager and branch house manager for the John Deere Plow Company at Sidney.

His marriage to Minnie Ethelyn Smith occurred at Harrison, Nebraska, on April 4, 1895. Mrs. Poole was born at South Bend, Indiana, July 31, 1876. She is an educator, club woman and politician. Her father, David Rockefeller Smith, was born at Sunbury, Pennsylvania, February 2, 1830, the son of John and Eliza (Rockefeller) Smith. Her mother's maiden name was Clark, the daughter of Aaron Burr and Mary (Randolph) Clark.

Mr. and Mrs. Poole have seven children, Thomas Smith, born November 13, 1896, married Leila Hathaway; Mariam Jeannette, born August 23, 1898, married Lawrence Hensler; Clyde Harold, born April 3, 1900, married Violet Bayne; Ethelyne Elaine, born January 24, 1902, married Harold Colwell; George Basil, born November 24, 1903, married Virginia Hiett; Sydney Arthur, born August 18, 1905; and Jean Grant, born August 23, 1908.

In 1898 Mr. Poole was a private in Company H, 2nd Nebraska Volunteer Infantry. During the late war, 1917-18, he was vice president of the County Council of Defense. He is a member of the Veterans of Foreign Wars, the Red Cross, and the Chamber of Commerce, of which he was president, 1926-1930. He was first president of the Sidney Rotary Club and for 15 years was a member of the board of education. He is a member of the Parent Teachers Association, the Country Club, the Business Men's Club, the Elks, the Ancient Free and Accepted Masons, the Shrine and the Odd Fellows. Residence: Sidney.

Erwin Edward Popcke

Dr. Erwin Edward Popcke, eminent educator, lecturer, and editor of Nebraska, was born at Oxville, Scott County, Illinois, May 24, 1901, the son of William and Helen (Wilde) Popcke. His father, who was born at Berlin, Germany, June 26, 1871, is a clergyman, and is president of the New York Lutheran Synod. His mother was born at Posen, Germany.

Dr. Popcke attended the public schools of Detroit, and New York City, until 1915, and in 1919 was graduated from DeWitt Clinton High School at New York. He was awarded the Bachelor of Arts degree at Wagner College in 1923, where he was captain of the debating team and was valedictorian of his senior class; he earned a college letter in tennis. In 1925, he received the Doctor of Philosophy degree at the University of Berlin.

He has held the following professional positions, head of the classical language department of Luther Academy in New York, 1925-30; lecturer at Lutheran Teachers Conference, New York City, 1927-29, and since 1930, head of the social science department of Dana College at Blair, Nebraska. He is the author of *The Music Dramas of Richard Wagner*, 1930; and *The Germanic Sagas and Their Influence on Modern Literature*. He is assistant and advisory editor of *The Thinker*, a national periodical published and edited in New York.

Dr. Popcke is a member of the New York Scientific Society. His hobbies are book collecting, art, and archaelogy. He is a member of the Nebraskana Society, is affiliated with the Lutheran Church, and is independent, politically.

His marriage to Lillie Clara Weigelt was solemnized at New York City, August 31, 1924. Mrs. Popcke was born at Norwich, Connecticutt. They have one son, Richard, born September 17, 1927. Residence: Blair.

Carey Joseph Pope

Carey Joseph Pope, who has been a clergyman in Nebraska for the past 28 years, was born at Brownhelm, Ohio, January 23, 1858. His father, Josiah Pope, a farmer, was born at Clipston, Northamptonshire, England, August 11, 1833, and died at Grand Island, Hall County, Nebraska, November 27, 1903; he came to America in 1854. His mother, Phebe Ann Barnes, was born at Remsen, Oneida County, New York, April 29, 1824, and died at Osage, Mitchell County, Iowa. She was a teacher before her marriage. She was directly descended from Samuel Morse.

Dr. Pope attended rural schools, and in 1883, was graduated from Colgate University. He holds the following degrees: A. B., 1883, Colgate University; B. D., 1886, Divinity School, Chicago University; A. M., 1902, Shurtliff College; and D. D., 1920, Colgate University. He was class president at Colgate, in 1882, served as president of Beta Theta Pi, and was manager of the college paper, 1883. He was the holder of the three mile run record in college for ten years.

He was pastor of Valparaiso, Indiana, 1886-89, at Osage, Iowa, 1889-93, at Ottawa, Kansas, 1893-97, at Downers Grove, Illinois, 1900 to 1903, and at Grand Island, Nebraska, 1903-06. He was executive secretary of the Nebraska Baptist Convention, 1906-09, and from 1913 until 1930, when he retired, was Baptist University pastor at the University of Nebraska.

He is a member of the Nebraskana Society. From 1909 to 1930, he served as a member of the Nebraska Baptist Convention, from 1913-27, was trustee of the Grand Island College, and from 1920 to 1926, was a member of the Foreign Mission Board of the Northern Baptist Convention.

Dr. Pope was married to Margaret L. Lyndon at Eaton, Madison County, New York, September 2, 1884. Mrs. Pope was born at Belleville, Ontario, Canada, November 30, 1860. She was graduated from the Hamilton Ladies' Seminary in 1881; and was a teacher before her marriage. Five children were born to this marriage: Lawrence Clement, born April 9, 1887, who died October 27, 1887; Walter Lyndon, born January 26, 1889, who married Luella Platt; Mildred R., born January 8, 1892, who married Carrell Henry Whitnah; Ruth Margaret, born January 13, 1895, who married Roy William True; and Faith, born October 16, 1901, who died January 19, 1902. Walter is professor of law and a practicing attorney at Missoula, Montana. Dr. and Mrs. Whitnah were missionaries in Burma, for ten years, and he is now professor of chemistry at the Manhattan, Kansas, State College.

Dr. Pope is a Republican. His favorite recreations are hiking and reading. Residence: Lincoln.

John Edward Poquette

John Edward Poquette, district superintendent of the Western Public Service Company, was born at Longmont, Colorado, February 18, 1884, son of Mitchell E. and Ella A. (Work) Poquette.

His father was born in Grand Island, Lake Champlain, Vermont, May 8, 1860, and is residing at Las Animas, Colorado. He moved to Colorado in 1879 and homesteaded in Bent County. He was a miller until 1889 and since that time has been engaged in farming. His mother was born in Pennsylvania, April 10, 1862. His grandparents on his father's side came from Canada and on his mother's side they were Pennsylvania Dutch and Scotch-Irish.

On September 27, 1914, he was married to Nellie H. Holland at Alliance, Nebraska. She is a member of the Methodist Church, the Eastern Star and the Woman's Club. There are two children, Fern Lucile, born November 19, 1918; and Thomas Edward, born July 7, 1921.

Mr. Popuette attended elementary school in Bent County, Colorado, and took a short course in Highland Park College at Des Moines, Iowa, in 1908-09. Taking up electrical work in 1906 and first employed by the Las Animas Electrical Company, he was construction foreman for Marshall Brothers in 1910. In 1911 he was employed by the Laramie Electrical Light and Power Company, Laramie, Wyoming, and was transferred to Crawford, Nebraska, as superintendent in 1914. He was also manager of the Caney Electric Light and Power Company, 1915-17. In 1917 he came to Sidney as manager of the Sidney Municipal Service which was taken over by the Western Public Service Company in 1929 and he was made district superintendent. Politically he is Independent. He is a member of the Knights of Pythias, the Ancient Free and Accepted Masons, and the Rotary Club. Residence: Sidney.

Justin Edwin Porter

Justin Edwin Porter, lawyer, was born at St. Eleanors, Prince Edwards Island, Canada, December 25, 1866, and in 1894 came to Nebraska, where he has since resided.

His father, James Porter, was born at Newcastle, New Brunswick, Canada, January 20, 1835, and died at Victoria, British Columbia, September 19, 1922. He was a manufacturer of leathers, harness, and so forth, whose family came from Aberdeen, Scotland.

His wife, Caroline Alice Brown, was born at St. Eleanors, April 8, 1844, and is still living at Victoria. She is descended from the United Empire Loyalists, who went from Massachusetts to Nova Scotia upon the success of the American Revolution.

Mr. Porter attended common and parochial schools in Prince Edward Island, and was an articled student at law, Manitoba Law Society at Winnipeg. He was an attorney at law, on July 17, 1890, and a barrister on June 14, 1892.

From 1891 to 1892, he engaged in the practice of law at Emerson, Manitoba, and from 1892 until 1894, was a member of the firm of Monkman and Porter, Barristers, Winnipeg. Coming to Crawford, Nebraska, in 1894 he has since engaged in practice. At the present time, he is a director of the Crawford State Bank.

A Republican, active in local politics, Mr. Porter served as county attorney of Dawes County from 1907 until 1911, at which time he was elected mayor of Crawford. He is a member of the Nebraska State Bar Association, the Crawford Chamber of Commerce, the Masons, the Shrine, and the Modern Woodmen of America.

In 1885, Mr. Porter served as a private in the 90th Battalion, Canadian Rifles, in the Northwestern Rebellion, and participated in the battles of Fish Creek and Batoche. During the late war, he was a member of the draft board and a participant in various other war time activities. His religious affilation is with the First Congregational Church at Crawford.

On April 30, 1894, Mr. Porter was married to Edith Mabel Bickle at Winnipeg. She was born at Brooklin, Ontario, August 22, 1869, and died at Winnipeg, May 15, 1899. Of this marriage there was one son, Waldo J. B., born May 9, 1895, who was married to Jean G. Karnes and died at Lincoln, February 6, 1930.

On July 1, 1901, Mr. Porter was married to V. Genevieve Meredith, daughter of Dr. George A. Meredith at Crawford, Nebraska. They have two children, Caroline G., born October 25, 1903, who married Lieutenant Earl W. Barnes, United States Army; and George M., born January 6, 1915. Residence: Crawford.

Paul Banta Porter

The Reverend Paul Banta Porter, clergyman of the United Brethren in Christ Church at York, Nebraska, has been a resident of this state all his life. He was born at Culbertson, Nebraska, July 5, 1890, the son of William Lewis and Otie J. (Banta) Porter. His father, a farmer, was born in Illinois, March 17, 1854, of Pennsylvania Dutch and English ancestry, and died at York, February 4, 1924. His mother, who was a teacher before her marriage, was born at Stewartsville, Missouri, February 12, 1860, of English and Scotch-Irish parentage.

Mr. Porter attended country schools in Hayes County, was a student in the public schools of Culbertson, Nebraska, and Sabetha, Kansas, and was graduated from York Academy. In 1915 he was awarded the A. B. degree at York College, and in 1923 received the B. D. degree at Bonebrake Theological Seminary. He served as president of the senior class at York College, was president of the Literary Society there for two semesters, and received letters in football, basketball, and baseball.

He has held the following positions in the religious and educational world; pastor of Swanton, Nebraska, 1915-19; field secretary for York College, 1919-20; pastor, Merna, Nebraska, 1923-29; and college pastor of York College, since 1929. He was ordained to the ministry in 1919.

Mr. Porter is a member of the Young Men's Christian Association, is chairman of the board of Christian Education for the Nebraska Conference of the Church of United Brethren of Christ, and is president of the York Ministerial Alliance. He is a Mason.

His marriage to Nina Gwinn Francis was solemnized at Merna, June 26, 1918. Mrs. Porter, who was a teacher prior to her marriage, was born at Lillian, Nebraska, February 12, 1895, of Scotch and Welch parentage. Four children were born to them: Donald, July 5, 1921; Gordon, June 12, 1922, who died April 21, 1923; Warren, June 21, 1926; and Frances, March 1, 1929.

Mr. Porter is a Democrat. His sports are hunting, fishing, golf, and baseball, and his hobby is bees. Residence: York.

Robert James Porter

Robert James Porter, wholesale and retail oil dealer, was born in Lincoln, Nebraska, August 13, 1889, son of William and Anne (Seivers) Porter. His ancestry is Scotch and German. His father was born at Glasgow Scotland, March 4, 1855, and came to America in about 1873. He settled in Waterloo, Iowa, where he followed the trade of a brick mason. His mother was born at Peoria, Illinois, December 25, 1865. To this union were born four children, William D., born April 4, 1887 at Lincoln; Robert J., born August 13, 1889 at Lincoln; Myrtle Anne, born March 4, 1896 at Lincoln, and George P., born May 25, 1904 at Lincoln. All of whom are living.

Mr. Porter attended public school and business college at Lincoln, Nebraska, and until he entered business

for himself on March 15, 1920, was a traveling salesman for the Marshall Oil Company. During the late war he served in Company B, 415th Regiment. He is a member of the Scottish Rite and Shrine bodies of the Masons. His political affiliation is with the Republican party. Residence: Sidney.

John Edward Portwood

John Edward Portwood has been a resident of Nebraska for 48 years and since 1909 has been engaged in the retail business at Nelson. He was born at Macon, Illinois, January 20, 1880, the son of David and Nancy Jane (Culver) Portwood. His father, who was born at Macon, April 13, 1852, and died at Nelson, January 22, 1928, was a merchant and farmer; his German ancestors came to this country early in the history of America. His mother, who was an active church worker and home maker, was born at Zanesville, Ohio, September 15, 1853, and died at Nelson, March 15, 1918. She was of English, Scotch and Irish extraction; her family has been in this country for over a hundred years.

Mr. Portwood attended rural school near Edgar, Nebraska, and later was a student in the Nelson High School. In 1897 he taught school and from 1898 to 1909 was connected with the William A. Voight Mercantile Company at Nelson. Since 1909 he has been in business for himself at Nelson where he is now owner and manager of the Portwood Company. He is president of the Nelson Sewer Company and has insurance and land interests.

He was united in marriage with Alice Orner at Nelson June 25, 1905. Mrs. Portwood, who was a teacher and dry goods clerk before her marriage, was born at Martinville, Indiana, December 27, 1873, of French and German descent. They have four children: Helen Gail, born July 16, 1906; Donald Edward, born December 29, 1908; Joseph Laverne, born October 24, 1911; and Hannah Doris, born April 18, 1913.

Mr. Portwood is a member of the Red Cross, has been a member of the Nebraska Retailers Association for the past 25 years, and holds membership in the Nelson Chamber of Commerce. He served as president of the Nelson Commercial Club from 1924 to 1929, and for over 20 years has been an active member in the young Men's Christian Association. He is affiliated with the Methodist Episcopal Church of Nelson and since 1922 has been a member of Nelson Lodge Number 77 of the Ancient Free and Accepted Masons. His favorite sport is golf.

During the World War Mr. Portwood served as a member of the Four Minute Men, was county chairman of the war saving campaign, and took a prominent part in all relief work. He is a Democrat. His hobbies are reading and travel. Residence: Nelson.

John Frank Pospisil

John Frank Pospisil, superintendent of the University of Nebraska Experimental Station at Alliance, was born at Prague, Nebraska, February 1, 1902, son of Joseph Frans and Anna (Vavak) Pospisil. His father was born in Czechoslovakia, and was captain in the Hungarian Army. He died at Gregory, South Dakota, April 9, 1909. His wife, Anna, was born at Prague, Nebraska, July 25, 1879.

Mr. Pospisil attended the public schools of Wahoo and was graduated from Wahoo High School in 1922. He attended the College of Agriculture of the University of Nebraska three years. While in high school he was a member of the debating team, won three letters in football, four in basketball, two in baseball, and two in track. In college he received three letters in football and three in basketball.

On March 9, 1929, he was married to Bernice Faye Shelmadine at Hot Springs, South Dakota. Mrs. Pospisil was born at Shelby, Nebraska, November 7, 1908.

They have one son, Dennis Marx, born December 21, 1929.

Beginning as potato inspector for the Nebraska Central Potato Growers at Alliance, Mr. Pospisil was advanced to assistant manager and has since become superintendent of the Box Butte Experimental Farm. He was a member of the cadets at the University of Nebraska and has the necessary discharge papers to entitle him to enter the United States Army with the rank of corporal. He is a member of the Presbyterian Church, the Rotary Club (chairman of agricultural committee), and the Odd Fellows. His clubs include the Agricultural Club, the Agronomy Club, Kosinecokey Club. His favorite sports are football, basketball, baseball, and track, while his hobby is reading. Residence: Alliance.

Myron Jay Posson

Myron Jay Posson, county treasurer of Keith County, was born at Hinckley, Illinois, November 13, 1863, and has resided in Nebraska since December, 1885.

His father, Martin Luther Posson, was born in Knox, New York. He located in Joliet, Illinois and later moved to DeKalb County, residing there until his death in the spring of 1897. He was a farmer whose ancestry was Holland Dutch and English. Sophia Esther West, wife of Martin Luther Posson, was also a native of New York State, and died at Hinckley, Illinois, in June, 1868. She was a devoted homemaker of Irish and English descent.

Mr. Posson attended district school in Pierce Township, DeKalb County, Illinois, and high school at Hinckley, Illinois. He was active in football, boxing, and other athletics of the time.

Reared on a farm, he followed that occupation until the summer of 1912, when he accepted the position as cashier of the First National Bank of Hayes Center. He resigned this position in April, 1918 and opened a state bank at Paxton in May of that year. This was merged with the other bank on January 1, 1924. At that time Mr. Posson was elected county treasurer of Keith County on the Republican ticket and still holds that position.

He was married to Agnes Viola Snyder at Eureka, Nebraska, November 21, 1888. She was born at Slippery Rock, Pennsylvania, November 8, 1868, and is a member of the Methodist Episcopal Church. Mr. and Mrs. Posson have six children. Rutherford J., born February 27, 1890, married Ruth SinClair; they have one daughter, Joyce. Mr. and Mrs. Rutherford J. Posson are graduates of the University of Nebraska. He is now head of the dairy council residing in Washington, D. C. Zina B., born July 23, 1892, is a graduate of the Minneapolis High School. She is married to Frank L. Chase, who is farming near Montrose, Colorado. Mr. and Mrs. Chase have three children, Fannie, Robert and Margaret. Melancthon B., born August 28, 1894, married Roberta Rae Chipperfield; they have one daughter, Shirley Rae, and are both graduates of the University of Nebraska. He spent about seven years as extension agent in the department of agriculture of Lincoln after his graduation and they are now located in Dawes County, near Chadron on a ranch raising pure bred cattle. Esther W., born February 10, 1897, completed two and one-half years in the University of Nebraska and married William V. Lambert, who is professor of genetics residing at Ames, Iowa. They have two daughters, Marilyn Marie and Carol Anne. Dorothy L., born September 21, 1903 completed two years in the University of Nebraska and married William L. Lozier, who is manager of one of the Krueger Stores of Wichita, Kansas. Evelyn W., born September 1, 1908, completed two years in the University of Iowa and was a member of Sigma Alpha Iota and is married to George R. Friederick, mechanical engineer, employed by the Fisher Governor Company of Denison, Iowa. They now reside at Huntington Park, California.

Mr. Posson is affiliated with the Methodist Episcopal Church, the Ogallala Commercial Club, the Ancient Order of United Workmen, the Odd Fellows, and the Masons (32nd degree, chapter and consistory). Residence: Ogallala. (Photograph in Album).

Frank T. Post

Frank T. Post was born at Bloomington, South Dakota, January 19, 1891, the son of Mark T. Post and Emma M. (Sherman) Post. His father, who was born at Cincinnati, Ohio, March 8, 1847, and died at Monowi, Nebraska, March 2, 1931, was a lawyer and served as a member of the Nebraska house of representatives in 1905; he served with General Custer in the frontier warfare with the Indians and was in the Civil War for three years. His mother was born in Nebraska, January 16, 1859, and died at Monowi, December 5, 1926. Her father was of Dutch descent and her mother was of French and Indian descent.

Mr. Post attended elementary school until 1907 and studied law through the American Extension University and later was a student in his father's office. In 1912 he homesteaded in South Dakota, was assistant cashier of the Monowi State Bank from 1917 to 1919, worked in his father's law office in connection with a real estate and insurance business, and since 1927 has been postmaster at Monowi and caretaker for the Chicago & Northwestern Railway Company.

He has been a member of the Red Cross since 1919, serving as secretary of the local chapter and chairman of various committees at this time. During the World War he served as corporal in Battery C, 338th Field Artillery overseas for five months. He is a member of the American Legion and served as commander of the David R. Morgan Post Number 223 at Veriel, Nebraska in 1928. His hobby is reading. A Republican, he was unsuccessful candidate for county judge of Boyd County in 1924.

He was married at Creighton, Nebraska, June 24, 1919, to Edith E. Witwer. Mrs. Post, who was a teacher before her marriage, was born at Traer, Iowa, August 20, 1890; her Pennsylvania Dutch ancestors were early settlers in Knox County, Nebraska. Five children were born to them: LaVon, April 22, 1920; Mildred, April 8, 1922; Dolores, August 14, 1925; Mary Lou, August 30, 1927; and Kenneth T., March 10, 1929. Residence: Monowi.

Marcus L. Poteet

Marcus L. Poteet, son of Samuel William and Nora L. (Briles) Poteet, was born at Pawnee City, Nebraska, May 25, 1889. His father, who was a native of Ohio, was a farmer. Of French descent his family has resided in Maryland since 1790. He died at Pawnee City, in August of 1906. His wife, Nora, was born at Pawnee City, July 4, 1870, and since the death of her husband has carried on the work of the farm. She is of English and German ancestry.

Upon his graduation from the Pawnee City High School in 1910, Mr. Poteet entered the University of Nebraska, from which he received his B. A. in 1916, and his LL. B. in 1922. During his time in college he was business manager of the 1915 Cornhusker, and of the Daily Nebraskan and the Awgwan. He is a member of the Innocents, the Kosmet Club, the Helmet and Quill and of Phi Alpha Delta, Sigma Delta Chi and Phi Sigma Kappa. During 1915 and 1916 he was in the advertising department of the Lincoln Daily Star. From 1919-20 he was manager of the ship by truck department of the Firestone Tire and Rubber Company, and was organizing secretary of the stadium building campaign fund 1922-23. Since 1923 he has been engaged in the practice of law.

Mr. Poteet has a long and enviable war record.—On May 12, 1917, he enlisted as a private of infantry, and on August 15 of that year was commissioned a second lieutenant and assigned to the 166th Infantry with the 42nd (Rainbow) division. He landed in France on October 28, 1917, and participated in the following engagements.

Alsace-Lorraine, Aisne-Marne, St. Mihiel and Meuse-Argonne. He was promoted to rank of first lieutenant on August 22, 1917, and assigned as assistant in the first section of the General Staff, Rainbow division. On May 23, 1919, he was honorably discharged. In March, 1921, he enlisted in the Nebraska National Guard, and on April 26, was made first lieutenant of the 134th Infantry; he was promoted to captain 134th Infantry on July 8, 1921, and to major Quartermaster Corps, Nebraska National Guard, commanding the 35th division on May 11, 1923.

He was one of Nebraska's three representatives at the burial of the Unknown Soldier in Washington. He is a member of the Veterans of Foreign Wars and of the American Legion. In the latter organization he was vice-commander of Lincoln Post in 1921, past commander in 1928, and district commander of the 12th district 1929-30. He was elected department commander in 1931 and since 1919 has been chairman of the legislative committee.

On August 2, 1919, Mr. Poteet was married to Fay Stayner at Council Bluffs, Iowa. Mrs. Poteet was born at McCook, Nebraska, December 28, 1891, and was a teacher prior to her marriage. There are two sons, Marcus L., born August 6, 1922, and Samuel L., born October 22, 1924.

A Republican, he was manager of the campaign of Samuel R. McKelvie for governor in 1920, and field manager of Adam McMullen's campaigns in 1922-24-26. He is a member of the Nebraska State Bar Association and is on the executive committee of the Red Cross. He is a Mason and a member of the Scottish and York Rite bodies and the Shrine. In 1930 he served as master of Liberty Lodge No. 300, in 1928 was high priest of Lincoln chapter No. 6, and in 1927 master of Lincoln council. He is an Elk. His clubs are the Hiram Club and the Shrine Club. His hobby is gardening. Residence: Lincoln. (Photograph in Album).

Frederick Louis Pothast

Frederick Louis Pothast, the son of Philip and Mary (Wendt) Pothast, was born in Stephenson County, Illinois, June 4, 1878. His father, who was born in Germany, died in 1880, in Stephenson County, Illinois. He came to America from Germany, in 1866, and is still living. His mother was born in Germany, in 1850, and is still living.

In 1896, Frederick Pothast was graduated from the Cortland, Nebraska, High School, and in 1899, from the Omaha Business College. He was married to Delia Clark on December 12, 1900, in Cortland. She was born near Parkersburg, West Virginia, December 24, 1877. They have two children: Audrey, born September 16, 1903, and Mildred, born April 24, 1905, who is married to Donald D. Lock.

He taught school for two years, became a merchant in Cortland, for four years, then traveled for the International Harvester Company a year. In 1904, he organized the Farmer's State Bank in Pickrell, Nebraska, of which he is cashier, and at present he owns the controlling interest.

Mr. Pothast owns six Gage County, Nebraska farms and one farm in Pawnee County, and two farms in Colorado. He is connected with the National Bank of Commerce and the Commerce Trust Company in Lincoln. He holds a life membership in the Young Men's Christian Association, and the Nebraskana Society. He is a Republican in politics, and is affiliated with the United Brethren Church He is a member of the board of trustees of York College, and also of the Pickrell school board. Residence: Pickrell.

Bird Stephen Potter

A druggist since 1910, Bird Stephen Potter was born at Gothenburg, Nebraska, September 16, 1888. His father, Woodward Reynolds Potter, born at Smicksberg, Pennsylvania, June 18, 1851, was a farmer whose death occurred at Gothenburg, January 2, 1915. His mother, Christina Good, was born at Smicksberg, May 3, 1854, and resides at Gothenburg.

Bird S. Potter attended district school, was graduated from the Gothenburg High School in 1908, and received his Ph. G. from Creighton College of Pharmacy in 1909. For two years he worked in the Hinkley Pharmacy, then purchased his own business which he has since operated.

He was married to Hazel May Strahle at Gothenburg on June 10, 1914, and to them two children were born, Paul Edward on July 24, 1915; and William Charles on February 22, 1921. Mrs. Potter, who was a teacher prior to marriage, was born at Gothenburg, January 11, 1892.

Mr. Potter is a Republican, has been a member of the school board six years, and has served one term as a member of the Examining Board of Pharmacy. He is a member of the Nebraska Pharmaceutical Association (president 1932), and the National Association of Retail Druggists. During the World War he was active in loan drives and Red Cross work, and still holds membership in the latter organization. He is a 32nd degree Mason, and Shriner, a member of the Chamber of Commerce, the National Geographic Society, and The Nebraskana Society.

He is a member of the First Presbyterian Church and the Gothenburg Country Club, is fond of golf and enjoys fishing and gardening. He is a Master Farmer (1932). Residence: Gothenburg. (Photograph in Album).

Ernest Rollie Potter

In 1858 Charles R. Potter left his native state of New York and started on the long and dangerous trip which was to establish him in a new home in the middlewest. He lived at Streetor, Illinois, for a period of two years where he married, and knew many interesting experiences through the intense political excitement prevalent in Abraham Lincoln's home state at that time. After the Civil War he moved with his family to Iowa where he remained until 1874 when he homesteaded near Red Cloud, Nebraska. He built the first frame house in Harlan County, a building which is still in use today.

Ernest Rollie Potter, son of Charles R. Potter, was born at Grandview Iowa, February 21, 1867, and for the past 57 years has been a farmer in Kearney County, Nebraska. His mother, who was born in Quebec, Canada, April 8, 1843, and died at Alma, Nebraska, February 26, 1923, was an ardent member of the Women's Christian Temperance Union, and held membership in the Children's Home-finding Society; her ancestry was Scotch and English.

Mr. Potter served as a member of the school board at Pleasant View School in Franklin County, Nebraska, from 1889 to 1915, and is now a member of the Red Cross, the Nebraskana Society, the Community Church at Wilcox. His chief recreations are reading and touring. He is a member of the Sons of the American Revolution.

On February 26, 1888, he married Marv Ellen Griswold at Wilcox, Nebraska. Mrs. Potter, who is interested in painting, was born at Greensburg, Indiana, September 7, 1869. They have four children: Jennie E., born December 18, 1888, who married Fred B. Julanf; Ward Stanley, born November 9, 1890, who married Alice Gochnaur; Hazel May, born July 25, 1893, who married Alvin J. Cook; and Leah Evelyn, born December 10, 1903, who married Roland A. Drishaus. Residence: Wilcox.

Frank J. Potter

Frank J. Potter was born at Monroe, Nebraska, July 26, 1887, the son of John and Mary (Whitehouse) Potter. His father, who was a farmer, was born in Worchestershire, England, and died at Monroe. His mother, who was born in Worchestershire, England, was a nurse.

Mr. Potter attended rural schools and later was a student at the normal college at Fremont, Nebraska. He was manager of the Potter Hardware & Implement

Company for five years, and prior to that was prominent in Platte County as a farmer; he was named as one of the 1928 Master Farmers of Nebraska.

He is a member of the Lincoln Chamber of Commerce, is treasurer of the Monroe High School, and is affiliated with the Monroe Evangelical Church of Monroe, holding membership in the church brotherhood. He is an Odd Fellow and a member of the Republican party.

His marriage to Alice Pearl Hoare occurred at Columbus, Nebraska, March 1, 1910. Mrs. Potter, whose grandfather was a chaplain in the Civil War, was born at Platte Center, Nebraska, March 3, 1889. Their two children are: Elton Edwin, born August 29, 1916; and Ruby Lois, born March 20, 1922. Mr. Potter's favorite sport is hunting and his hobby is traveling. Residence: Monroe.

Verne J. Potter

Verne J. Potter, retail implement dealer, was born at Zumbro Falls, Minnesota, October 22, 1895, son of William and Clara (Stegner) Potter. His father, born in Scarborough, England, in 1866, came to America in 1883. A wagon maker by trade, he is at the present time engaged in the oil business. His wife, born in Rising Sun, Indiana, September 23, 1865, is descended from Dutch and German settlers in Pennsylvania.

Educated in the public schools of Lake City, Minnesota, Verne J. Potter afterward took a course in typing and shorthand in night school and has completed a course with the Alexander Hamilton Institute. In high school he received letters in basketball, baseball, and football.

Starting with a grain company in Minneapolis in 1913, Mr. Potter was transferred to Baudette, Minnesota, in 1915 as bookkeeper and accountant for a lumber firm. In 1917 he became associated with the John Deere Plow Company at Omaha in the credit and collection department. He was manager of the department during 1920 and 1921, and manager of the sales division until 1925.

Removing to Columbus in 1926, Mr. Potter started in the implement business for himself, adding branches at Genoa and Fullerton since that time. He is a member of the Chamber of Commerce, the Lions Club (director), the Elks and the Young Men's Christian Association (membership committee). He is a member of the Wayside Country Club and is fond of golf.

On June 6, 1917, he was married to Elsie B. Van Camp at St. Thomas, North Dakota. Mrs. Potter, a teacher prior to marriage, was born at St. Thomas, February 21, 1896. They have three children: William Van, born April 5, 1918; Vernice Jane, born August 8, 1919; and Kathryn Ann, born June 16, 1929. Residence: Columbus.

John Beekman Potts

John B. Potts, one of Omaha's most distinguished physicians and surgeons, was born at Morrisonville, Christian County, Illinois, July 4, 1876, the son of Thomas Franklin and Elizabeth (Stryker) Potts. He was graduated from the high school at Morrisonville, and in 1907 received his M. D. at the University of Nebraska College of Medicine, where he was a member of Alpha Omega Alpha, Beta Theta Pi, Phi Rho Sigma.

He acted as assistant to Dr. Harold Gifford from 1907 to 1910, and then began postgraduate work in New York, London, and Vienna. From 1907 to 1912 he practiced in ophthalmology and otolaryngology; since 1912 his practice has been limited to otology and oto-laryngology. He is now associate professor in oto-laryngology at the University of Nebraska, and is oto-laryngologist at the Bishop Clarkson Memorial Hospital of Omaha, the Nebraska Methodist Episcopal Hospital, and the University Hospital.

He is the author of a large number of papers on professional subjects, written for various medical societies, and most of them published later. They are: *Some Comparative Measurements of the Skull and Sella Turcica*, 1913; *Frontal Sinus, Ocular Relations*, Western Medical Review, December, 1915; *Report of Operated Pituitary Tumor*, Northwest Eye, Ear, Nose, and Throat Society, 1915; *Modern Methods of Tonsillectomy and Instruments*, read before the Missouri Valley Medical Society at St. Joseph, Missouri, March 24, 1916, and published in The Medical Herald; *The Use of Radium in Tuberculosis of the Larynx*, (a preliminary report) for The American Laryngological Rhinological and Otological Society, Denver, 1917; *Diagnosis of Pituitary Tumor*, Nebraska Medical Journal, 1916; *Mastoidectomy, Post-operative Treatment, By Use of Surgical Solution of Chlorinated Soda*, published in the Journal of the American Medical Association, 1919; *Nasal Infection, The Basis of Certain Ocular Lesions*, read before the Colorado Congress of Ophthalmology and Otolaryngology, 1919, and published in the American Journal of Ophthalmology 1920; *Maxillary Sinus, Conservative Treatments of Mastoids by Use of Carrell-Dakin's Solution, and Modification Necessary to Secure the Best Results*, published in the Journal of the American Journal of Ophthalmology 1920; *Post Operative Treatment of Simple Mastoidectomy*, read before the State Medical Society, Omaha, 1921; *Medicine of Yesterday*, read before the Nebraska State Medical Association at Lincoln, May 13, 1925, and published in the Nebraska Medical Journal, July, 1925; *Intracranial Complications Following Mastoiditis*, Transactions, American Laryngological Rhinological and Otological Society, 1925; *Globus Hystericus Frequently a Sexual Neurosis*, March 1926; *Report of Two Cases of Sinus Thrombosis with Operative Technique*, 1927; *Localization and Drainage of Brain Abscess of Otitic Origin*, read before the annual meeting of the American Laryngological Rhinological and Otological Society at Wichita, Kansas, 1928, and published in the Annals of Otology, Rhinology, and Laryngology, June, 1928; *Brain Abscess of the Temporo-Sphenoidal Lobe and Cerebellum with Comments on Operated Cases*, read before the annual meeting of the Nebraska State Medical Association at Hastings, Nebraska, May 15, 1928, and published in the Nebraska Medical Journal, October, 1928; *Angina Agranulocytosis*, published in the Transactions of the American Laryngological Rhinological and Otological Society, and read before the annual meeting of the American Laryngological Rhinological and Otological Society at Washington, D. C., May, 1928; *Angina Agranulocytosis*, published in Archives of Otolaryngology, March, 1929; *Brain Abscess and Meningitis Secondary to Acute Paranasal Sinusitis*, read before the Midwestern Section of the American Laryngological Rhinological and Otological Society at Denver, and published in the Annals of this society, June, 1929; *Results of Radical Sinus Operation on Asthmatics with Chronic Sinus Infection*, read before the Midwestern section of the American Laryngological, Rhinological, and Otological Society, January, 1930, and published in the Transactions of the society; and *Rational Operative Procedures for Chronic Hyperplastic Sinusitis in Asthma*, a preliminary report read before the annual meeting of the American Laryngological, Rhinological, and Otological Society at Atlantic City, New Jersey, May, 1930, published in the Annals of this society.

Dr. Potts was united in marriage with Goldie Claire Goddin, at Barhamsville, Virginia, June 28, 1913. Mrs. Potts, who was born at Barhamsville, is the daughter of Sylvanus and Susan Eliza Goddin.

During the World War Dr. Potts was captain in the United States Army, stationed at Base Hospital Number 49 at Allerey, France, and was in charge of otolaryngology and head wounds for a center comprising seven hospitals and concentration camp. He is a member of the Nebraska State Medical Society; the Douglas County Medical Society; the American College of Surgeons; the

Rinehart-Marsden—Omaha

DR. JOHN B. POTTS

American Medical Association; the Academy of Ophthalmology and Otolaryngology; the American Laryngoligical, Rhinological and Otological Society, is credited with the American Board of Otolaryngology, and a fellow of the American Laryngological Association and American Otological Society.

He is a member of the Omaha Chamber of Commerce; Omaha Club, and the Omaha Country Club. He is affiliated with the First Central Congregational Church of Omaha. Residence: Omaha. (Photograph on Page 962).

William Thompson Poucher

One of Burt County's most prominent men is William Thompson Poucher, who was born at Mooresville, Indiana, September 18, 1878. He is the son of John and Annie Martha (Cross) Poucher, the former a clergyman and educator. John Poucher was born in Boothby, Graffoe, Lincolnshire, England, March 4, 1843, and came to America about 1855. He received the degrees of A. M. and D. D. from Garret Biblical Institute, and was professor of theology at De Pauw University. His death occurred at Orleans, Indiana, June 29, 1918. Annie Martha Cross was born in Ohio, July 20, 1844, and was graduated from Cincinnati Wesleyan College. For several years she was a teacher. Her death occurred at Greencastle, Indiana, March 28, 1897. She was of French extraction.

Mr. Poucher attended Greencastle preparatory school from which he was graduated in 1894, and received his B. Sc. from DePauw University in 1898. In 1900 he took post graduate work at Cornell. His fraternity is Phi Kappa Psi. The year 1898-99, Mr. Poucher taught in Black Hills College, at Hot Springs, South Dakota, and from 1899-1902 was principal of the high school and superintendent of schools at Tekamah. From 1902-04 he was superintendent at Chadron, and 1904-06, at Weeping Water. A Republican, he was elected county superintendent of public instruction for Burt County, in 1911, and is still holding office. He has also served as mayor of Tekamah, 1917-1919; 1924-1930.

On July 27, 1904, he was married to Dorothy Lucy Mason at Decatur, Nebraska. Mrs. Poucher was born in Burt County, March 27, 1883. Her paternal grandfather was English. Her grandmother was American for several generations. There are two children: John, born July 26, 1915, and Lucy Anne, born August 31, 1919.

Mr. Poucher's professional memberships include the Nebraska State Teachers Association of which he has long been a member, the Northwest Nebraska Teachers' Association of which he became a member in 1903, and the Tekamah Library Board. He is a Mason, and served as deputy grand lecturer of the Royal Arch Masons 1928-29-30, and grand lecturer 1931. He is affiliated with the Methodist Episcopal Church, and during the World War was third district chairman of the W. C. C. S., county chairman of the United War Work Campaign and acting county chairman of the War Savings Stamps Campaign. His hobbies are reading and gardening. Residence: Tekamah.

Louise Pound

Louise Pound was born at Lincoln, Nebraska, June 30, 1872. Her father, Stephen Bosworth Pound, was a lawyer of note. He served as judge of the district court of Nebraska, as a member of its constitutional convention, and was a member of the state senate 1872-73. He came from a long line of colonial ancestors. Among the members of the family who settled in America in its early days are John Pound, founder, who came to New Jersey from England in 1686; Richard Hartshorne, who was appointed by William Penn as commissioner to lay out the province of West Jersey; and Joseph Moore, appointed by George Washington member of a commission to promote peace with the Indians.

Stephen Pound married Laura Biddlecome, who was also of colonial stock. Thomas Biddlecome came from England in 1630, and two of her ancestors, Lawrence and Cassandra Southwick, were Quaker martyrs.

Louise is a sister of Roscoe Pound, dean of Harvard Law School and of Olivia, who is assistant principal at the Lincoln High School. She received her early education under her mother's tutelage. She entered the University of Nebraska upon examination, and completed her preparatory course in 1888. In 1892 she was given her A. B., taking a diploma in music the same year, and she received her A. M. in 1895. Later she studied abroad for a year, and in 1900 received a Ph. D. from the University of Heidelberg. She was awarded an honorary Litt. D. from Smith College in 1928.

During her attendance at the University of Nebraska she was class orator, class poet, and associate editor of a college paper. A member of Phi Beta Kappa, she has served as corresponding secretary, and president of the local chapter. In addition she holds membership in Mortar Board, Theta Sigma Phi, Chi Delta Phi, Delta Omicron, Pi Gamma Mu and Kappa Kappa Gamma.

She entered the teaching profession as fellow in English at the state university in 1894. Appointed an instructor in 1897, she has received the following promotions: adjunct professor, 1900; assistant professor, 1906; professor, 1912. During the summer of 1923 she was instructor at the University of California, in 1928 at the Linguistic Institute of Yale, in 1929 at Chicago University, in 1930 at Columbia, and at Stanford University in 1931. She is now professor of English at the University of Nebraska.

She was vice president of the Modern Language Association of America in 1916 and in 1925, member of its executive council 1921-23 and 1925, and chairman of the comparative literature section 1923, 24, 27. She was director of the National Council of English Teachers 1916-19, and national treasurer in 1917. She acted as district secretary for Nebraska of the American Dialect Society from 1922-28. A charter member of the American Association of University Professors, she was a member of the national council in 1929-1932. She is also a charter member of the following: Humanistic Research Association (British), Linguistic Society of America, and is member of the International Phonetic Association, Medieval Academy of America, American Folk-Lore Society, serving as national president, 1928, member of national council 1925-27, and was vice president of the Spelling Reform Association in 1927-1931. She was head of the section of folklore and ethnology of the Nebraska Academy of Science in 1917, continuing until 1922.

She holds membership in the Nebraska Writers Guild. She was Nebraska director of the Association of Collegiate Alumnae 1906-08, and member of National Council 1913. She belongs to the American Association of University Women, Daughters of the American Revolution, and was acting state head and chairman of overseas relief committee, National League for Women's Service, 1918; member women's committee, State Council of Defense, 1918.

She is a member of the national council of the Guggenheim Memorial Foundation for Research, 1929-32, and of the National council of the Inter-American Institute for Intellectual Co-operation.

Among her cultural and social clubs are the National Arts (New York), Arts (Washington), Women's Press (Omaha), Lincoln Country, University, Copper Kettle and Wooden Spoon.

An ardent tennis enthusiast, she was women's city champion 1890, women's state champion 1891 '92, holder of university championship in men's singles 1891, 92; representative in intercollegiate men's singles and doubles, earning a man's N; men's doubles champion Wayne County, N. Y., 1894, with Charles Foster Kent, of Yale; city champion in women's singles, Chicago, 1897, 98; holder women's western tennis championship in singles, 1897, defeating the national and Canadian champion of that year, and defeating the national champions in doubles, which brought the western champion first rank in the

United States for that year; winner of several championships in Germany in women's singles and doubles and in mixed doubles, 1899, 1900; central western champion in women's doubles, Kansas City, and western champion in doubles with Carry Neeley, Chicago, 1915; champion in men's doubles with Guy Williams, Lincoln, 1913. She was director of the Nebraska State Tennis Association 1911-13, and president of the Lincoln Tennis Association 1919.

Among her honors in golf are the following: state golf championship 1916; ranking local woman golfer 1902-28, country club champion 1906-23, 1925-27 (did not enter 1923-24), city champion 1926. She is holder of a string of bars for riding 100 miles in 12 hours, from the Century Road Club of America, for cycling 1895-96, and of the Rambler gold medal for riding 5000 miles in 1896.

She is senior editor of *American Speech,* founded 1925, and acted as advisory editor of the *New England Quarterly* in 1928; *American Literature* 1929; *Folk-Say* 1930. She has been senior editor of *Nebraska Studies in Language, Literature and Criticism* since 1917, and is a member of the editorial staff of *University Studies.*

Author and editor of many publications on literary, linguistic, folk-lore and educational subjects, some of the publications to which she has contributed are: *Publications of the Modern Language Association of America; Modern Language Notes, Dialect Notes, English Journal, Anglistische Forschungen, Englische Studien, American Journal of Folk-lore, School and Society, Saturday Review of Literature, American Mercury.* She is the contributor of a chapter to the *Cambridge History of American Literature,* of articles to the *Encyclopedia Britannica, Dictionary of American Biography,* etc. Among her publications are *The Comparison of Adjectives in the XV and XVI Centuries* (Winter, Heidelberg); *Blends —Their Relation to English Word Formation* (Winter); *Poetic Origins and the Ballad* (Macmillan); *American Ballads and Songs* (Scribner); *Edition of Goldsmith's Deserted Village and Gray's Elegy* (Ginn); Coleridge's *Ancient Mariner* (Lippincott); Shakespeare's first part of *Henry the VI* (Macmillan); Homer's *Iliad* (Macmillan); Cooper's *The Last of the Mohicans* (Harlow), etc. Residence: Lincoln.

Olivia Pound

Olivia Pound, educator, has lived her entire life in the state, and has taken a prominent part in the progress of her community as an author and school executive. She was born at Lincoln, April 30, 1874, the daughter of Stephen Bosworth and Laura (Biddlecome) Pound. Her father, who was born at Farmington, New York, January 14, 1833, and died at Lincoln, May 14, 1911, was a lawyer; he served as judge of the district court, 1875-87; was a member of the constitutional convention in 1875; and served as a member of the state senate, 1872-73. His ancestors came to New Jersey from England, prior to 1686; one ancestor, Richard Hartshorne, was appointed by William Penn as commissioner to lay out west Jersey, while another ancestor, Joseph Moore was appointed by George Washington to make a treaty with the Indians in Ohio.

Miss Pound's mother, who was born at Phelps, Ontario County, New York, May 15, 1841, and died at Lincoln, Nebraska, was active in public affairs during her whole life; she served as state regent of the Daughters of the American Revolution, 1896-97 and 1901-02, was a member of the city public library board at Lincoln, 1880-90; and was a charter member of the Lincoln Woman's Club; she was descended from families that came to America from England in 1630, four members of which were signers of the compact for the government of Providence Rhode Island, in 1636; Laurence and Cassandra Southwick, other ancestors, were Quaker martyrs.

Miss Pound received her early education at home, and from 1889 to 1891, was a student at the preparatory school in the University of Nebraska. She holds the degrees:

A. B., 1895, University of Nebraska; A. M., 1897, University of Nebraska, where she was elected to Phi Beta Kappa, the Mortar Board, Chi Delta Phi, Pi Lambda Theta, and Kappa Kappa Gamma. She was a student at the University of Chicago, Harvard College, and Columbia University, during summer sessions.

From 1897 to 1914, Miss Pound was a teacher; was director of vocational guidance for girls, 1914-17; was advisor of girls, 1917-18; and since 1918 has been assistant principal of the Lincoln High School.

She is the author of the following: *Extra Curricular Activities of High School Girls,* A. S. Barnes & Company, 1931; *On the Application of the Principles of Greek Lyric Tragedy in the Classical Dramas of Swinbourne,* University Studies, Nebraska Volume 13, Number 14; *Hints for the Teaching of Beginning Latin,* Classical Journal, Volume 9, Number 8; *High School Latin and the Newly Formulated Aims of Education,* Classical Journal, Volume 14, Number 2; *The Need of a Constructive Social Program for the High School,* School Review, Volume 26, Number 3; *The Social Life of High School Girls,* School Review, Volume 28, Number 1; *Co-operation of Patrons in Solving the Problems of Social Life in the High School,* National Educational Association Report, 1919; *The Social Reconstruction in the High School,* School and Society; *Educational Lingo,* American Speech, Volume 1, Number 6, March, 1926; *Qualitative Standards for a Two Year Course in Elementary Latin,* North Central Association Quarterly, Volume 1, Number 4.

Miss Pound is a member of the National Education Association; the Nebraska State Teachers' Association; Lincoln Teachers Association; the Lincoln Public School Forum; Classical Association of the Middlewest and South; the National Association of Deans of Women; the Young Women's Christian Association; and the League of Women Voters. She was president of the National Association of University Women, 1913-14, and 1919-20. Her social clubs include: Wooden Spoon Club; Copper Kettle Club. She is an Independent politically; is a member of the Society of Friends; and holds membership in the Nebraskana Society. Her hobby is gardening. Residence: Lincoln.

James Louis Pounds

Since 1893, James L. Pounds has resided at Blair, Nebraska, where he has engaged in the clothing business. He was born in Harrison County, Iowa, December 22, 1878, the son of Samuel P. and Hester (Nichols) Pounds. His father was a railroad man for many years; he was born in Indiana, in 1846, and died at Arlington, Nebraska, December 10, 1887. His mother was born in Illinois, April 11, 1862, and died at Blair, October 27, 1927.

Mr. Pounds is treasurer of the local Red Cross, and from 1924-30, was president of the Blair School Board. He is a member of the Chamber of Commerce; Retail Clothiers Association; the Nebraskana Society; and the Blair Methodist Church. He is a Mason, and an Odd Fellow. His social club is the Blair Golf Club.

He married Margaret Marie Schmidt, at Blair, October 23, 1901. Mrs. Pounds was born at Blair, March 23, 1881. To this union four children were born, two of whom are deceased: Glen Ira, born February 2, 1905, died January 1, 1916; James W., born March 10, 1907, who married Thelma Joy Leonard; David Blair, born December 9, 1918, died January 12, 1919; and Margaret Marie, born March 28, 1919.

Elmer Joseph Power

Elmer Joseph Power, farmer and insurance agent, was born near Hordville, Nebraska, March 28, 1888, son of Eli and Lucinda (Ashby) Power. Eli Power was born in Wheeling, West Virginia, May 17, 1850, and died at Taylor, January 8, 1927. He had been a farmer there for a number of years prior to his death, and was of Dutch ancestry. Lucinda Ashby was born at Terre Haute, Indiana, February 12, 1850, and died at Taylor May 12, 1928. She was of Irish and Welsh descent.

Mr. Power attended public school, and on November 25, 1908, was married to Bessie Leola Karr at Grand Island. Mrs. Power was born at Marquette, March 20, 1890 and died there April 21, 1912.

On October 29, 1913, he was married to Alta Irene Fales at Taylor. She was born at Almeria, Nebraska, September 28, 1893. They have seven children, Leola, born March 3, 1915; Marcella, April 11, 1917; Leonard, September 19, 1918; Lester, March 1, 1920; Victor, August 17, 1921; Stanley, April 24, 1923; and Harold, June 25, 1929.

For the past twenty-five years Mr. Power has been a farmer and thresherman, and for eleven years has been engaged also in the insurance business. He is now president and member of the board of directors of the Farmers Co-operative Oil Company of Sargent, and is an ardent booster for the Farmers Union.

Mr. Power is independent in politics. He is affiliated with the Evangelical Church, is secretary of the local Farmer's Union, is a member of the Modern Woodmen of America, a member of the Nebraskana Society and moderator of his local school board. His hobby is mechanics. Residence: Taylor.

James Frederick Premer

James Frederick Premer, physician and surgeon, was born at Portland, Indiana, March 6, 1881, son of Solomon and Barbara Emeline (Halfhill) Premer. He came to Nebraska in 1886 with his parents settling in Bartley, Nebraska.

His father, a farmer, was born in Indiana, February 20, 1847, and died at Benkelman, Nebraska, December 28, 1921. His wife, Barbara, was also born in Indiana, on August 6, 1849, and died at Bartley, Nebraska, December 26, 1892.

In 1897 Dr. Premer completed his elementary education in the rural schools of district No. 68 of Red Willow County, Nebraska. He was graduated from the Bartley High School in 1902, and in 1908 received the degree of Doctor of Medicine from the University of Nebraska and served his internship at the Methodist Hospital at Omaha Nebraska. He located at Haigler, Nebraska, 1909, remaining there until 1919 when he located in Benkelman, Nebraska practicing his profession there continuously. He is a party owner of the Premer-Ough Drug Company store in Benkelman, Nebraska. During the year 1902-1903 he attended Nebraska Wesleyan University, and from 1915 until 1918 attended John Fletcher College, University Park, Oskaloosa, Iowa.

Among his professional organizations are, the Chase, Dundy, Hayes and Hitchcock Counties Medical Society serving as its president 1928-31, the Nebraska State Medical Society, and the American Medical Association. He is a member of the Benkelman Chamber of Commerce, the Lions Club and the Masons, Justice Lodge No. 180. From 1929 until 1931 he was secretary of the school board. He is a member of the Benkelman Methodist Episcopal Church and a member of the official board as its treasurer. During the late war, he was a medical examiner for the examining board for Dundy County.

On July 21, 1909, Dr. Premer was united in holy matrimony at Bartley, Nebraska to Lelah Fidler, daughter of Resin and Sadie (Phillips) Fidler, who was born November 3, 1884. To this union were born six children, Marlin J., born May 19, 1911; Veta P., born October 31, 1915; Leola R., born July 7, 1917, and died at Oskaloosa, Iowa, May 13, 1918; Eugene P., born June 29, 1920; Stanley D., born April 17, 1922; and Alta A., born September 4, 1924.

Dr. Premer is a Republican. Residence: Benkelman. (Photograph in Album).

Gustave Prestegaard

Gustave Prestegaard was born at Pratt, Steele County, Minnesota, January 12, 1880. His father, Peter Olsen Prestegaard, who was a farmer, was born in Norway, and came to America in 1867. He died at Owatonna, Steele County, Minnesota, October, 1922. His mother, Ingeleiv (Salthun) Prestegaard, was born in Norway.

Mr. Prestegaard was a student in the country district schools of Minnesota, and later attended The South Side High School at Minneapolis. He graduated from The Metropolitan Business College at Minneapolis, Minnesota, in 1898. He has lived in Lincoln for the past 22 years and has been engaged in the lumber business there during that time. He is president of the Prestegaard Lumber Company; is vice president of the Northern Machinery & Supply Company at Minneapolis, and was president of the Home Lumber Company at Potter, Nebraska, from 1917 to 1929. Also engaged in banking and farming.

On August 22, 1905, he was united in marriage with Carrie Nelsyne Nelson at Slater, Story County, Iowa. Mrs. Prestegaard was born at Slater, June 15, 1875, and is the daughter of Col. Oley Nelson, legislator and former commander Iowa G. A. R. They have four children: Pauline, born August 30, 1906, who was graduated from Midland College and received her A. M. degree at the University of Nebraska, now has charge of the English department of Waldorf College at Forest City, Iowa; Katherine, born November 30, 1907, who is a graduate of the University of Nebraska, and who married Edwin H. McGrew; Gerhard, born April 27, 1911; student University of Nebraska; and Helen, born August 27, 1913, attending Waldorf College, Forest City, Iowa.

During the World War Mr. Prestegaard was active in Liberty loan drives. He is a member of the Lincoln Chamber of Commerce; Lincoln Automobile Club; director in the Lincoln Rotary Club. He is vice gerent for the Nebraska district for the Concatenated Order of the Hoo Hoo, Lumbermen's Fraternal Order; is a member of the Twin Cities Hoo Hoo Club at Minneapolis. Was Treasurer Lincoln Council of Boy Scouts five years. He is affiliated with the Grace English Lutheran Church at Lincoln, and is a member of the executive committee of the Nebraska Synod of The United Lutheran Church in America. He is a member of the American Scandinavian Foundation, the Nebraska Art Association, and the Nebraskana Society.

He holds membership in the University Club at Lincoln, and the Shrine Country Club. He is a Mason, and Shriner. He is fond of golfing. Politically, Mr. Prestegaard is an independent Republican. Residence: Lincoln. (Photograph on Page 966).

Walter Grey Preston

One of Nebraska's leading insurance men, Walter Grey Preston was born at Omaha, October 10, 1871. His father, William Preston, was born at Worksop, Nottingham, England, November 17, 1838, and came to America in 1853. The remainder of his family remained in England. The tradition of the family relates that William de Preston came from Normandy to England with William the Conqueror in the tenth century. William Preston was a flour and grain dealer in the United States and died at New Orleans, April 26, 1914.

Emilie Victoria (Orchard) Preston, wife of William, was born at Livonia, Indiana, June 16, 1847, and died at Fresno, California, May 20, 1915. Her ancestors settled first in Pennsylvania, thence moving to Virginia, and on to Indian.a They were English.

Walter G. Preston was graduated from Omaha High School, and attended Bellevue College at Bellevue, Nebraska, and Phillips Academy at Andover Massachusetts. He received a Ph. B. from Yale University in 1891 and the same year was given a U. S. military certificate from that university. He was elected to membership in the Berzel-

Dole—Lincoln

GUSTAVE PRESTEGAARD

ius Society at Yale, the Colony Club and the Yale Glee and Banjo Club. He is a member of Pi Alpha Epsilon.

Entering the grain business with his father in 1891, under the firm name of William Preston and Company, Mr. Preston continued until 1898. From that time until 1903, he was a member of the firm of Preston and Company of Seattle and Dawson, Yukon Territory. Since 1903, he has been associated with the Bankers Reserve Life Insurance Company of Omaha, starting as vice president. He has served as first vice president and treasurer of the organization, and is now its president.

He was married to Myrtie Robison, at Omaha, on July 30, 1901. Mrs. Preston is a native of Tekamah, Nebraska, born December 10, 1875. They have one son, Walter Grey, Jr., born September 22, 1902. He was graduated from Phillips Academy, and from Yale University in 1925. He is assistant to the president of the University of Chicago, and is a licensed aviator.

Mr. Preston is a Republican. He attends the First Presbyterian Church of Omaha, is a member of the Chamber of Commerce, the Rotary Club, the Nebraska Pioneer Society and The Nebraskana Society. He is fond of golf and motor boating. His clubs include the Omaha Club, the Omaha Country Club, the Omaha Athletic Club, and the West Okoboji Golf and Country Club. Residence: Omaha. (Photograph in Album).

Comadore Edward Prevey

Comadore E. Prevey was born at Elroy, Juneau County, Wisconsin, December 30, 1871, the son of Frank and Mary (Bissett) Prevey. His father, a pioneer farmer in Wisconsin, was born at St. Johns, Quebec, Canada, October, 1822, and died at Elroy, May 7, 1903. He settled in Wisconsin in 1854. His mother was born at St. John, settled in Massachusetts, in 1840, and died at Elroy, May 27, 1900.

Mr. Prevey was graduated from the Elroy High School in 1888. He was awarded the B. L. degree at the University of Wisconsin, in 1895; received his A. M. degree at Columbia University in 1899, where he held a fellowship in sociology, 1898-1900; and was a student at the Yale Graduate School, 1897-98.

He served as general secretary of the Associated Charities of Fort Wayne, Indiana, 1895-97; was head lecturer and instructor in sociology at the University of Nebraska, 1900-06; was head resident of the College Settlements, Lincoln, 1902-08; was executive secretary of the Nebraska Children's Code Commission, 1920-21, and from 1900 to 1928 was general secretary of the Social Welfare Society at Lincoln. He is now agent for the Aetna Life Insurance Company, and the Folsom Brothers Company at Lincoln.

He was united in marriage with Medora Alice Whittington, at Lincoln, May 28, 1902. Mrs. Prevey was born at Princeton, Mercer County, Missouri, June 3, 1880. Her parents were West Virginians. Mr. Prevey has always been interested in the social welfare of his community and state and holds membership in the Social Service Club; Nebraska Conference of Social Work; the Open Forum, and the Lincoln Chamber of Commerce. Mr. Prevey spends has summer vacations with his family in the mountains of Colorado. He is a member of the Nebraskana Society, and is affiliated with the First Baptist Church of Lincoln. He is a Republican. Residence: Lincoln.

Frederick Homer Price

Frederick Homer Price, an educator and school executive for many years, and at this time an editor and publisher at Newman Grove, Nebraska, has lived in this state for nearly half a century. He was born at Avoca, Iowa, March 13, 1878, the son of Margaret Ann (Amerine) and Fletcher Price. His father, who was a farmer, was born in Franklin County, Indiana, October 27, 1837, and died

at York, Nebraska, July 14, 1923. His mother was born at Piqua, Ohio, March 23, 1845, and died at York, September 1, 1921.

Mr. Price received his early education in rural schools, was a student at Nebraska Wesleyan University, the University of Nebraska, and Peru State Teachers College, and in 1908 was graduated from Fremont College, Fremont, Nebraska. He was elected to membership in Phi Delta Kappa and the Schoolmasters Club.

He engaged in public school work for 18 years, and in 1918 resigned the superintendency of the Newman Grove schools to take charge of the *Newman Grove Reporter,* a weekly newspaper, of which he is editor and publisher. He served as president of the Nebraska State Press Association in 1930, was a member of the executive committee of the Nebraska State Historical Society, 1930, and acted as president of the Northeast Nebraska Teachers Association in 1914.

Mr. Price holds membership in the National Editorial Association, the Nebraskana Society, and the Methodist Episcopal Church of Newman Grove. He is a Mason, and during his years of teaching was active in all state educational societies. A Republican, he served as a member of the Board of Education for two terms and was city clerk of Newman Grove for 10 years.

Of his marriage to Matilda A. Miller, in 1905, the following children were born: Warren Miller, born December 15, 1906, who married Dolene Wills; Marvin Frederick, born May 26, 1908, who married Amy Louise Martin; Marian, born May 27, 1910; and Frances, born December 19, 1911. Mrs. Price died in 1913.

On August 18, 1915, he married Myrtle Faye Scott, at Pawnee City, Nebraska; she was born at Adrian, Missouri, daughter of Robert and Ida Scott, and was a public school teacher prior to her marriage. They have one daughter: Amy Annabel, born December 13. 1922. Residence: Newman Grove. (Photograph on Page 966).

Frank C. Prince

Frank C. Prince, superintendent of Bayard City Schools, was born in Valley County, Nebraska, January 11, 1894, son of Joseph and Antonia (Jankovec) Prince.

His father was born in Pacov, Tabor, Bohemia, November 17, 1868, and is a prominent farmer and member of his rural school board. His wife, Antonia, was born at Nova Ves, Pisek, Bohemia, May 11, 1872. She comes from a family of farmers.

Mr. Prince attended rural school in Valley County, until May, 1908, and was graduated from Ord High School, in May, 1912. In 1916, he received the Bachelor of Arts degree from Hastings College, and in 1932, received his M. A. from the University of Nebraska. He was president of his literary society in college, a member of the college student council, and active in athletics. He was a member of the football team four years, all state captain; in basketball four years, a member of the track team two years, and during the World War, was a member of the second all-American service football team.

On June 2, 1920, he was married to Fern Lymania Warner at Milford. Mrs. Prince was born at Milford, April 19, 1894, descended from the Warner family of colonial fame. She attended the University of Nebraska Academy, received her Bachelor of Arts degree from Hastings College in 1917, and took a post graduate course in home economics at the University of Nebraska. She was principal of the Burwell High School prior to her marriage. Mrs. Prince is past president of the Bayard Womans Club, and is an active member of the Eastern Star and the Bayard Federated Churches. They have three children, Doris, born April 9, 1921; Bernice, born January 3, 1923; and Donald, born November 11, 1924.

Active in educational work, Mr. Prince has served as secretary and president of the District Teachers Associations and as a member of the executive committee

FREDERICK HOMER PRICE

of the Nebraska State Teachers Association. He is a member of the National Education Association, the Red Cross, the Lions Club, and was a member of the Alliance Rotary Club. He is a Scottish Rite Mason.

During the World War, Mr. Prince was bayonet officer. He holds the rank of captain in the Infantry Reserve Corps, at the present time, is a member of the Reserve Officers Association, and the American Legion. His religious affiliation is with the Bayard Federated Churches. He is a Presbyterian. At the present time, he is serving as president of the Bayard Country Club. He enjoys all sports, particularly golf, tennis, hunting, fishing, and hiking. His hobby is gardening. Residence: Bayard.

Willard Ansel Prince

Willard Ansel Prince, an outstanding figure in the professional world of Grand Island, Nebraska, has been engaged in the practice of law there since 1888. He was born at Ashtabula, Ohio, September 3, 1864, the son of Ansel Willard and Maria (Aldrich) Prince, the former a farmer who died at Ashtabula, January 6, 1903. His father was of New England birth while his mother was a native of Canada.

Mr. Prince was graduated from Hillsdale College with the Bachelor of Science degree, June 15, 1886, and was a member of Phi Delta Theta there. A Republican, he served as prosecuting attorney for Hall County, city attorney of Grand Island, a member of the Nebraska house of representatives, and state senator. He is a director in the Commercial Bank of Grand Island.

He is a member of the Grand Island Bar Society and the Woodland Country Club. His recreations are fishing and golf. Mr. Prince is affiliated with the Presbyterian Church of Grand Island and holds membership in the Nebraskana Society.

His marriage to Carrie Belle Roberts was solemnized at Ulysses, Nebraska, December 26, 1888. Mrs. Prince, whose ancestry is Welsh, was born at Jefferson, Iowa, April 27, 1868. They have four children, Harold Aubrey, born April 6, 1891, who married Mary Carson; Hazel Mary, born June 6, 1895, who married Addison I. Bolton; Catherine Roberta, born February 11, 1901; and Elizabeth, born March 7, 1906. Residence: Grand Island.

Charles August Prinz

Charles A. Prinz was born at Chalco, Nebraska, June 22, 1883, the son of August Fred and Jetta (Stahl) Prinz. His father, who was a farmer, was born in Germany, and died at Millard, February 11, 1928. His mother was born in Germany, and died at Millard, December 31, 1929.

Mr. Prinz attended rural school in Sarpy County, and was a student at the University of Nebraska School of Agriculture. He has been a farmer near Chalco for the past 30 years. He is affiliated with St. Paul's Lutheran Church, and is a member of the Democrat party. Mr. Prinz is interested in mechanics. His favorite sport is baseball.

He married Louise C. Glasshoff, at Millard, August 16, 1905. Mrs. Prinz was born at Omaha, Nebraska, April 9, 1885. They have two children: Elmer, born March 16, 1907; and Florence, born April 26, 1908, who married Emory Megel. Residence: Chalco.

Leslie Richard Prior

Leslie Richard Prior, who is prominent in the business activities of Kearney, Nebraska, has resided in this state for the past 31 years. He was born at London, England, March 6, 1891, the son of William and Jennie (Napper) Prior, the former a business executive in London who died there in 1899. His mother was born at Mayfield, England, January 21, 1865, and died there in 1800.

Mr. Prior attended the city schools of Kearney, and has held the following positions in the business world of Nebraska: cashier of the Farmers Bank of Kearney, 1907 to 1918; cashier of the Maxwell State Bank, Maxwell, May 1, 1918 to May 1, 1928; special agent for the Northwestern Mutual Life Insurance Company of Milwaukee, at Hastings, Nebraska, 1928-29; and since 1929, secretary-treasurer of the Kearney Savings & Loan Association.

He is secretary of the Kearney Kiwanis Club, serving as editor of the *Kearney Kiwanian*, is a member of the Chamber of Commerce and the Red Cross, and is a member of the Kearney Country Club. Mr. Prior is a 32nd degree Mason and Shrine member, is affiliated with St. Lukes Protestant Episcopal Church of Kearney, and holds membership in the Nebraskana Society. During the World War he was active in the promotion of Liberty loan drives and in notarial work in connection with the draft. His political preference is the Republican party.

On June 21, 1916, he was united in marriage with Minnie Buerstetta at Red Cloud, Nebraska. Mrs. Prior, who was a professional reader and dramatist before her marriage, was born of German and Swiss parents at Tecumseh, Nebraska, January 18, 1889. Their two children are: Peggy Jane, born April 24, 1919; and Richard R., born October 3, 1922. Residence: Kearney.

Grace Wood Pritchard

For the past 15 years Grace Wood Pritchard has been prominent in public affairs at York, as a clubwoman and civic leader. She was born at Brownhelm, Ohio, February 29, 1872, the daughter of Edwin Austin Wood and Angeline (Cooley) Wood. Her father, who was born at Buffalo, New York, August 5, 1838, and died at Council Bluffs, Iowa, March 2, 1917, was a dry goods merchant at Brownhelm, for several years, and later was engaged in the dairy business at Avoca, Iowa. He served in the Civil War from 1861, to 1865. His Quaker ancestors came to this country in the *Mayflower*.

Her mother, who was of Puritan descent, was born at Brownhelm, September 28, 1841, and died at Avoca, July 19, 1911. She was a profound student and reader, and was actively interested in church work. Before her marriage she was a practical nurse.

Mrs. Pritchard received her education at Avoca, and Oakland, Iowa, and for 12 years before her marriage was assistant postmistress. Later she was engaged in the mercantile business for two years. She was married to Charles Daniel Pritchard at Avoca, December 19, 1906. Mr. Pritchard, who is a mechanic, was born at Avoca, August 9, 1875; he is of Welsh descent.

A Republican, she served as first ward committeewoman, and has always promoted civic organizations at York. During the World War she was chairman of various war committees at York, and was awarded a medal in recognition of her efficient efforts. She acted as president of the Women's Committee of the local Young Men's Christian Association for two years, was president of the York Woman's Club for two years, and served as superintendent of the Congregational Sunday School for over 12 years. She is now treasurer of the Order of Eastern Star, is acting committeewoman for the first ward at York, and is treasurer of Job's Daughters. In addition to her social and civic duties, Mrs. Pritchard is bookkeeper and assistant in the Pritchard garage. She is affiliated with the Congregational Church and the Nebraskana Society. Residence: York.

Ida Mae Pritchett

Ida Mae Pruitt was born at Bethalto, Illinois, April 30, 1856, and for the past sixty-four years has been a resident of Nebraska. Through both parents she traces her ancestry to pre-Revolutionary settlers in America.

The Preuitt family, whose first member in America was Martin Preuitt, Sr., has been prominent in the history of our country since the 16th century. Martin

Preuitt was a native of North Carolina, a soldier in the Revolutionary War, who participated in the Battle of Kings Mountain. After the war he moved to Virginia, remaining there several years, and later moving to Tennessee with his family. His sons were Abraham, William, Isaac and Martin, Jr.

The Preuitts took part in the Revolutionary War as soldiers under General Washington, and were with him when he crossed the Delaware and at Valley Forge. Martin Preuitt and his son Martin, Jr., also hunted with Daniel Boone in Kentucky, at which time Martin, Jr., was thirteen years old.

Martin, Jr., who was born July 15, 1752, married Mary Woods in 1771 and died at the age of 92 in Illinois. His son, Solomon, born January 7, 1790, was married to Rebecca Higgins in 1809 and thereafter to Elizabeth, her sister. He died in 1875. Wiley G., son of Solomon, was born February 12, 1827 at Bethalto, Illinois, and died at Bethalto on May 11, 1908.

Wiley Green Preuitt married Martha Helen Lyons on October 10, 1849. She was a native of Woodstock, Connecticut, born April 3, 1832, and who died at Fairbury on June 29, 1920. To this union were born six children, Mary, Edward and Emma, who died in infancy; Ida Mae, the subject of this sketch; and Elizabeth and Franklin.

The Lyon family originated in the British nobility. General Nathaniel Lyon descended, it is believed, in the direct male line from Sir Thomas Lyon of Auldbar, Forfarshire, North Britain, who was designated Master of Glamis, brother of John, eighth Lord Glamis. Sir Thomas was one of the principal agents in the seizure of James the Sixth at the Raid of Ruthren, on August 23, 1582, and was banished from England. Returning again to Scotland, with the Earls of Angus and Mar he seized Sterling Castle and again fled to England. In 1585 he was again received by the king and appointed captain of the guards, high treasurer of Scotland, and extraordinary lord of sessions, and in 1590 was knighted. He was married first to Agnes, daughter of Patrick the fifth Lord Grey and second to Euphemia, fourth daughter of William Douglas, Earl of Mreton.

Political and civil troubles forced members of the family to emigrate to New England in the seventeenth century, Thomas and Ephriam, brothers, coming together. General Nathaniel was descended from Ephriam, whose name was used in three successive generations. Nathaniel Lyon, a brave and loyal citizen died at the Battle of Wilson's Creek in Missouri on August 10, 1861.

Luther Wells Lyon and his brother, Isaiah, and their half brother, George, were, according to family tradition, third cousins of Nathaniel in the direct male line. The name of Lyon appears frequently in the records of Windham County, Connecticut, particularly with the part known as Ashford, Woodstrock and Ommfred townships.

Among the earliest recorded appearances of the name is one about the time Roxbury's colony was established. After the return to Roxbury of the men who had been sent to spy out Woodstock, and after the plans had been fully discussed and considered, articles of agreement were drawn up on July 21, 1686. Among those who fulfilled the agreement and took personal possession of land in the colony appear the names of William Lyon, Senior, Thomas Lyon and William Lyon, Junior.

The official register of Connecticut men in the War of the Revolution shows forty-five bearing the name of Lyon, thus demonstrating that the fighting qualities of the family had not degenerated since the days of its ancient progenitor, Sir Thomas.

William Lyon, Sr., married Sarah Ruggles and died about May 21, 1692; his wife, born in England, April 19, 1629, was the daughter of John and Mary (Curtis) Ruggles. John, his son, born in Roxbury, in April, 1647, married Abigail Polley on May 10, 1670. She

was born June 4, 1654, and died January 15, 1703. John died January 15, 1703, also. William, son of John, was born in Roxbury, September 15, 1675, and was first married to Deborah Colborn, diedApril 18, 1714, and he died in Woodstrock September 17, 1741. His son Aaron, born in Woodstock, January 11, in the year 1706 or 1707, married Elizabeth Allen. He died May 26, 1746.

Isaiah Lyon, born in Woodstrock, January 29, 1743, was undoubtedly identical with Isaiah Lyon, private in Captain Samuel McClellan's Company in the Lexington Alamer in April 1775. He married Sibyl Ranney, and died at South Woodstrock (Quasset), on August 25, 1813. Luther, son of Isaiah, born in South Woodstrock, married his cousin, Nancy, daughter of Henry (1753-1823) and Nancy (Shirtliff) Wells. He died about 1851. Nancy Wells was born April 17, 1781 and died January 3, 1815. His son, Luther, Jr., born May 5, 1802, at Quasset, married Martha Wardwell Fairfield, and died near Bethalo, Illinois, July 30, 1885. Martha, his wife, born about 1804 and died in 1870. She was the daughter of David and Hannah (Thurber) Fairfield.

Ida Mae Preuitt received her education in public and high school at Shurtleff College, Alton, Illinois. She was married to Gilbert Lafayette Pritchett, a physician and surgeon, at Bethalto, on January 20, 1876, and soon thereafter came with him to Nebraska. Dr. Pritchett, who was born at Fidelity, Illinois, August 25, 1848, died at Fairbury, July 28, 1916. There was one son, Albert Homer, born December 15, 1876, who died July 25, 1877.

Dr. Pritchett's first American ancestor was Johann Daniel Wendell who married a sister of John Jacob Astor. They had a daughter, Pamela, born April 8, 1794, who married Ebenezer Martin Pease. He was born December 2, 1786 in Ballston, New York. Pamela was married on March 31, 1811. Her daughter, Lydia Wendell Pease, born September 30, 1817, died at Jerseyville, Illinois, January 12, 1912. She was married to David Perry Pritchett, born March 1815 and who died September 7, 1890. They were the parents of Gilbert L. Pritchett.

Mrs. Pritchett is a member of the Fairbury Seventh Day Adventist Church and a life member of the Nebraskana Society. Her hobby is reading. Residence: Fairbury.

Rudolf Victor Prokop

Rudolph Victor Prokop, son of Joseph W. and Karolina (Kastanek) Prokop, was born in Wilber, Nebraska, September 5, 1892. His father, born at Podrezov, Kralu Kradec, Bohemia, October 30, 1859, was an early day farmer, and later operated a flour mill at Wilber, and a cattle ranch in southeastern Kansas. He came from Bohemia in 1866, and settled on a farm near Wilber. His death occurred at Lincoln on April 26, 1927. Karolina, his wife, was born at Hatline, Jindrichuv, Hradec, Bohemia, October 31, 1862, and died at Wilber, April 29, 1916.

Until 1908 Mr. Prokop attended country school nine and one-half miles northwest of Wilber, and during 1908-1909 attended Crete High School. From 1909 to 1912 he attended the Wilber High School from which he was graduated in May, 1912. In June, 1916, he received his A. B. from the University of Nebraska, and during 1915 attended the Lincoln Business College. He was president of the Komensky Klub at the University in 1915, and after graduation taught school in Dodge, Nebraska. Thereafter he taught in Clarkson, where he was superintendent of schools for several years. In 1921 he entered the banking business, and at the present time is vice president and cashier of the Hubbard State Bank.

On June 14, 1921, Mr. Prokop was married to Esther Marie Wolf at Schuyler, Nebraska. Mrs. Prokop was born at Clarkson, September 8, 1901, of Bohemian descent. To them were born three children, one of whom, Rudolf, born October 20, 1922, died on October 21, 1922.

Carolyn, born July 7, 1928, and Joseph Vincent, born August 7, 1930, are living.

Mr. Prokop is a Democrat. He served in the United States Navy in the World War, and was member of Y. M. C. A. and loan drives committees. He is a member of the American Legion, the Red Cross, National Geographic Society, Nebraskana Society, and Blue Valley Lodge of the Ancient Free and Accepted Masons at Wilber. He enjoys traveling. Residence: Wilber.

Louis Anton Proskovec

Louis A. Proskovec was born at Bruno, Butler County, Nebraska, January 18, 1889, the son of Vaclav Anton and Elizabeth Marie (Hlavac) Proskovec. Vaclav Proskovec, who is a business man, was born at Stryvkovice, Czechoslovakia, May 28, 1856; he and Mrs. Proskovec came to America, in 1870, the former dying at the age of 94 years and the latter at the age of 88. The mother of Louis A. Proskovec who was born at Maly, Porezany, February 14, 1863, came to this country in 1870.

Dr. Proskovec attended the Bruno public schools until his graduation in 1906; was granted the B. S. degree in 1910, by Fremont Normal College; and received the Ph. G. degree there in 1911. He was graduated from the University of Nebraska in 1919, with the degrees A. B. and D. D. S., and held membership in Xi Psi Phi. He served as principal of the Bruno schools for 9 years, and for the past 12 years has been engaged in the practice of dentistry at Schuyler, Colfax County, Nebraska.

During the World War he served in the E. M. R. C., and is now a member of the American Legion. He acted as chairman of the school board at Schuyler, 1928-29; is a member of the Nebraskana Society; and holds membership in the Chamber of Commerce and the Lions Club. His professional organizations include the Nebraska State Dental Association; and the American Dental Association. Politically, he is Republican.

On September 6, 1916, he was united in marriage with Ema Josephine Suchy, at Fremont, Nebraska. Mrs. Proskovec, who was born at Morse Bluff, Nebraska, May 20, 1893, was a school teacher and dental assistant before her marriage. Their children are: Marcella, born August 8, 1919; and Gloria, born July 4, 1926. Residence: Schuyler.

George C. Proud

George C. Proud, one of the leading lawyers of Furnas County, Nebraska, has been a resident of this state all his life and is today active in the professional life of Arapahoe. He was born in Frontier County, Nebraska, January 2, 1890, the son of John and Harriet Townsley Proud, the former a retired farmer who was born at Long Island, New York, November 18, 1851; his ancestry is Scotch, Irish, and English. His mother was born at Pittsburgh, Pennsylvania, October 19, 1856. Her parents came to Hamilton County and later came to Frontier County.

Mr. Proud was graduated from the high school at Holbrook, Nebraska, in 1906, and in 1910 was graduated from the Uiversity of Nebraska Law School where he received the LL. B. degree. He has been engaged in law practice at Arapahoe since his admission to the bar in 1912. He is a member of the Furnas County Soldiers Relief Commission, the Arapahoe Rotary Club, the Nebraska State Bar Association, and the Community Club.

He is secretary civilian relief of the Furnas County Chapter of the American Red Cross, is affiliated with St. Paul's Episcopal Church, and has served as a member of the School Board. He is a Mason. During the World War Mr. Proud was commissioned a first lieutenant of infantry at Fort Snelling and Camp Dodge; he organized the American Legion at Arapahoe and served as its commander for a number of years. His sports include tennis, basketball, golf, horseback riding.

On June 8, 1918, he was married to Florence Josephine French at Des Moines, Iowa, Mrs. Proud, whose ancestry is French and German, was born at Des Moines, February 3, 1892. Their son, Richard F., was born January 19, 1922. Residence: Arapahoe.

Robert Morton Proudfit

Robert M. Proudfit, distinguished lawyer and judge of Nebraska, has lived in this state for the past 49 years and has been engaged in the practice of law since 1892. He was born at Rockford, Winnebago County, Illinois, April 30, 1862, the son of Eliza Philena (Cilley) and Robert Proudfit. His father, who was a farmer and cooper, was born in York County, Pennsylvania, December 26, 1814, and died at St. Joseph, Buchanan County, Missouri, October 26, 1896; his Scotch grandfather came to America in 1754. His mother was born August 14, 1823, and died at Virden, Macoupin County, Illinois, March 13, 1870. She was a teacher and home maker; her ancestry was English.

Judge Proudfit attended the grade schools of Virden, Illinois, and in 1878 was graduated from the high school there. He obtained the rest of his education through private study. He was admitted to the practice of law in the Supreme Court of Nebraska, 1894; in the United States district and circuit courts, 1895; and in the Supreme Court of the United States and the Interior and Treasury Departments of the United States in 1901.

He began his business career as a salesman in a general mercantile establishment in 1881, and in 1884 entered the First National Bank of Friend, Nebraska, where he remained as bookkeeper and assistant cashier until January 1, 1904. From that date until 1924 he engaged in general law practice. He was elected district judge in 1924 and was re-elected to this position in 1928; has held various city and school district offices; and has always been keenly interested in the political life of the country and civic affairs in general.

During the World War Judge Proudfit acted as county chairman of the Saline County Chapter of the Red Cross and took part in the sale of war bonds. He is a member of the American Bar Association; Nebraska State Bar Association; and the American Judicature Society. He holds membership in the State Historical Society and the Nebraskana Society. He is a member of Friend Camp No. 439 of the Modern Woodmen of America and of Friend Lodge Number 73 of the Ancient Free and Accepted Masons. He is a member of the First Baptist Church of Friend. He was formerly active in baseball and tennis. His hobby is reading. He is a Republican.

His marriage to Ida Mae Dorwart was solemnized at Friend, August 28, 1889. Mrs. Proudfit, who is an efficient home builder, was at one time a teacher. She was born at North English, Iowa, September 17, 1865; her ancestry is German and English. They have three children: Helen Mae, born June 2, 1891, who married Windom A. Rosene; Robert Watson, born November 1, 1892, who married Margarita Carpenter; and Winifred Kent, born April 18, 1906, who married Robert Irving McWilliams.

Helen Mae, after completing her college course at Grand Island College taught in the Friend High School until her marriage in 1914, and is now living at Callaway, Nebraska, where her husband is superintendent of city schools. Robert Watson, after completing his college course at Grand Island College, was graduated from the College of Law at the University of Nebraska; in 1917 he enlisted in the United States Army and served as lieutenant in the Rainbow Division in France, in a machine gun battalion; he is now engaged in the practice of law at Los Angeles, California, where he is the junior member of the firm Swanwick, Donnelly, and Proudfit. Winifred Kent was graduated from Grand Island College in 1928, and is now living in Los Angeles, where her husband is studying law at the University of Southern California. Residence: Friend.

Vincent Joseph Prucha

Vincent Joseph Prucha, son of Joseph and Tina (Volenec) Prucha, was born in Bohemia, Chechoslovakia, August 14, 1871. His father who was born at Kutna Hora, Bohemia, November 11, 1844, is a cabinet maker. His mother, who was born in Chechozlovakia, died there in 1873.

From his earliest years Vincent Prucha spent most of his time in his father's cabinet factory, and was taught the trade. At the age of 17 he came to America, and upon arriving in New York learned the cigar business. In 1893 he opened a cigar factory with his uncle, Louis Prucha, at Perry, Oklahoma, and on July 1, 1894 opened a factory at Crete, which he still operates.

He was married to Francis Sedlacek at Wilber, Nebraska, May 21, 1896. Mrs. Prucha was born at Crete, December 15, 1872. They have two sons, Otto, born February 19, 1897, who is associated with the Addressograph Company at Denver; and Walter, born July 10, 1900, who married Nellia Morris. He is a machinist with the Union Pacific Railroad at Omaha.

Mr. Prucha is an outstanding citizen of Crete, where he is active in civic and community affairs. His main hobby is the training and trimming of trees, and rock garden work. He is an excellent landscape artist, and his home at Crete, Nebraska, is filled with beautiful examples of his art, particularly evergreen trees which he has trained and shaped in the forms of animals, birds, etc. His home is on one of Nebraska's main highways, and those traveling past it, throughout the Middle West, pause to admire it. Residence: Crete. (Photograph in Album).

Francis John Pryor, 3rd

Francis John Pryor 3rd, Episcopal clergyman, was born at Philadelphia, Pennsylvania, April 23, 1904, son of Francis John Pryor, Jr., and Florence Ella (Smith) Pryor.

Francis John Pryor, Jr., was born in Philadelphia, July 22, 1866, and died there, on April 11, 1926. He attended the University of Pennsylvania, from which he was graduated in 1887, and was treasurer, for a number of years, of the American Gas and Electric Power Company. English on the paternal side, his ancestors settled in Virginia during the 17th century. On the maternal side, he was Pennsylvania Dutch. His wife, Florence Ella, was born in Philadelphia, June 8, 1866, and is still living. She was educated in Quaker School in Philadelphia, and was a graduate of the School of Design for women, there. She descended from Welsh and Swedish settlers in Pennsylvania.

The Reverend Mr. Pryor attended the S. B. Huey School in Philadelphia, and was graduated from The Episcopal Academy at Overbrook, Pennsylvania, in 1922. In 1926, he received the Bachelor of Science degree from Trinity College, Hartford, Connecticut, and afterward, during 1926 to 1929, was a student at the Berkeley Divinity Schol at New Haven, Connecticut. He is a member of Delta Psi, and during the years 1923, 1924, 1925, and 1926, was a member of the football and baseball team.

Ordained in the diocese of Pennsylvania, on May 27, 1929, by the Rt. Rev. Thomas J. Garland, Doctor of Divinity, Mr. Pryor was priest-in-charge of St. Elizabeth's Mission at Holdrege and St. Mathew's Mission at Farnam, during 1929 and 1930. During 1930 and 1931, he was secretary of convocation, Diocese of Western Nebraska. At the present time he is rector of the Church of Our Savior at North Platte. He is a member of the Ministerial Association.

On June 17, 1929, he was married to Etta Marian Kart at Buffalo, New York. Mrs. Pryor was born at Buffalo, February 7, 1908, of German ancestry. Their one daughter, Susan Pryor, was born at Holdrege, May 3, 1930.

Mr. Pryor is a Republican. He is a member of the Platte Valley Lodge No. 32, Ancient Free and Acccepted Masons, the executive council of the DeMolay, the Red Cross, and the Nebraskana Society. He enjoys golf and tennis, while his hobbies are chess and reading. Residence: North Platte.

Jerome Martin Pucelik

Jerome Martin Pucelik, dentist at Spencer, Nebraska, is a lifelong resident of this state. He was born at Dodge, Nebraska, April 21, 1895, the son of Thomas and Kristina (Dostal) Pucelik. His father, a farmer, was born in Czechoslovakia, December 21, 1861, and came to America in 1881. His mother, whose parents were pioneers in Cuming County, Nebraska, was born at Racine, Wisconsin, December 6, 1868, and died at Spencer, May 14, 1931.

Dr. Puselik was graduated from the Spencer High School in 1913, received the D. D. S. degree at the University of Nebraska in 1918 where he was a member of Delta Sigma Delta, and was a rural school teacher for two years in Boyd County. He is director in the Spencer State Bank, is a landowner in Boyd County, and since 1918 has been engaged in the practice of dentistry at Spencer.

He has served as scoutmaster of the Boy Scouts of America for the past 10 years, acting as scout commissioner for a year, has served as chairman of the local School Board, and is a member of the Spencer Chamber of Commerce. Dr. Pucelik is secretary-treasurer of the North East Nebraska Dental Study Club, and holds membership in the Nebraska State Dental Society and the American Dental Association. His hobby is mechanics while his favorite sports are golf and baseball.

On June 30, 1926, he married Lola Meryl Brinkerhoff at Mitchell, South Dakota. Mrs. Pucelik, who was born at Exira, Iowa, March 14, 1897, is a member of the Daughters of the American Revolution. She served as vice president of the Woman's Club during 1929-30, and is now president of that organization. They have a daughter, Patricia, born June 10, 1928. Residence: Spencer.

John Louis Pucelik

John L. Pucelik was born at Dodge, Nebraska, June 21, 1898, the son of Thomas and Christina Pucelik. He was graduated from the Spencer High School, Spencer, Nebraska, in 1916, and in 1922 received his D. D. S. degree at the University of Nebraska. He was a member of the "N" Club, the Innocents, the student council, Alpha Sigma Phi, and Delta Sigma Delta, at the University of Nebraska, where he also took an active part in football during 1919-20-21.

He began the practice of dentistry at South Sioux City, in 1922, and has been active there in his profession since that date. In 1924, he served as president of the Chamber of Commerce, and he now holds membership in the Nebraskana Society, Masons, and the American Legion, of which he was commander in 1930.

He is married to Doris Carrol Knowlton, who was a dramatic instructor. Mrs. Pucelik was born at South Sioux City. Residence: South Sioux City.

Edwin Puls

Edwin Puls, educator, was born at Buffalo, New York, August 27, 1885. He is the son of Ferdinand Henry Puls, noted newspaper man and ornithologist, who was born at Buffalo, October 7, 1843, and died there January 25, 1926. Ferdinand Puls married Clara Boeckmann, also a native of Buffalo, born in 1853, who died there in August, 1913.

On completion of his preliminary education, Edwin Puls was graduated from Masten Park High School at Buffalo; he received a B. O. degree at the Buffalo School of Speech Arts, and an M. O. from Valpariso University, where he was president of his senior class and active in dramatics. He also received a letter in track from that university. Mr. Puls attended Cornell University and Keuka College.

His teaching career has covered positions as professor at Bellevue College, Central High School, the Young Men's Christian Association, the Young Men's Hebrew Association, the Knights of Columbus, the American Banking Institute, the Junior Chamber of Commerce, the Ad-Sell League, the Presbyterian Theological Seminary and Creighton University, of which last he is assistant professor of speech.

Mr. Puls was married to Lucile Tully at Charleston, West Virginia, on July 15, 1918. Mrs. Puls was born at Divide, West Virginia, February 28, 1891. Their son, Rodney, died January 11, 1922, at the age of fourteen months. They have a daughter, Virginia Maurine, born January 27, 1923.

Professor Puls is the author of a pocket manual of speech education, *Personal Power Through Expression*, and an article *Speech Training for Business Men*, which appeared in the *Quarterly Journal of Speech*.

He is a member of the Omaha Young Men's Christian Association, and during the World War was a Y worker at Camp Travis, San Antonio, Texas; a three minute speaker and physical director in the Students Army Training Corps. He is a member of the Bellevue Parent Teachers' Association, and the Bellevue Men's Club, of which he was president from 1926-28. He attends Bellevue Presbyterian Church, and is a member of the National Association of Teachers of Speech. His sports are hiking and handball, and his hobby is his men's Bible class. Residence: Bellevue.

Edward Thomas Purinton

Edward Thomas Purinton, farmer and stock raiser, was born at Hartford, Connecticut, July 30, 1872, son of Joseph Davenport and Jane Elizabeth (Coombs) Purinton.

The father was born in Hartford, January 12, 1846, and is a retired farmer now residing at Everett, Washington. His wife, Jane, was born at Colrain, Massachusetts, May 4, 1848. Her ancestors came over in the *Mayflower*; a great, great grandfather, Colonel Hugh McClellan, fought in the Revolution. In the early days he mustered a group of minute men and drilled them and they elected him captain, and when the Lexington alarm was given in 1775 they marched to Charleston, Massachusetts, and in April, 1777, marched to Saratoga and were in the battle fought there and were present at the surrender of Burgoyne (facts on record at the state house at Boston, Massachusetts). She is a distant relative of John Adams, president of the United States.

Mr. Purinton was graduated from Seward High School, and later attended Lincoln Normal College. He has been a farmer for many years. He is a Republican, and active in party politics, a member of the Congregational Church of Cambridge, of the Modern Woodmen, and the local school board. His favorite sport is hiking.

His marriage to Grace Ella Hutchison, daughter of V. T. and Cora B. Hutchison, occurred at Wilcox, Nebraska, April 16, 1911. Mrs. Purinton was born in Harlan County, Nebraska, August 17, 1885, a granddaughter of a Civil War veteran, Charles H. Potter, who died at Wilcox, August 1, 1931. They have two children living and one deceased, Elizabeth, born May 29, 1916; Helen, born April 17, 1918, and died September 23, 1930, of infantile paralysis; and Edward, born December 12, 1920. Residence: Cambridge.

Walter George Purtzer

Born at Lindsey, Nebraska, January 29, 1896, Walter George Purtzer has lived in this state all his life. John Purtzer, his father, who is a harness maker, was born at Evanston, Indiana, June 17, 1865, of German parentage. He is a Republican. Mary (Born) Purtzer, his mother, was born in Germany, October 20, and died at Madison, Nebraska, October 2, 1915.

Mr. Purtzer was graduated from high school at Lindsay, Nebraska in 1912. He owned a barber shop at Madison for several years, and in 1924 was elected clerk of the district court there on the Republican ticket. He still maintains the latter position. He is a member of Rotary International at Norfolk, the Community Club at Madison, and the Madison Firemen's Association. He is vice-chairman of the Welfare Board, is affiliated with Trinity Lutheran Evangelical Church, and holds membership in the Nebraskana Society. He is president of the Nebraska Clerks of District Court Association.

He served in the World War as a private for 17 months with the 34th Division, 134th Infantry at Camp Cody, New Mexico. He saw foreign service with the 103rd Infantry. At this time Mr. Purtzer is a member of two American Legion posts. His sports are baseball, golf-hunting, and football.

On August 17, 1920, he was married to Ruth Olive Davis at Lincoln. Mrs. Purtzer, who was formerly a school teacher, was born at Essex, Iowa, November 1, 1900, daughter of Benjamin F. and Maude (Pritchard) Davis. Her parents were farmers. Three children were born to them, Horace Chester, on July 19, 1921; Jean Walter, on August 17, 1924; and Dean Davis, on February 13, 1926. Residence: Madison. (Photograph in Album).

Frederick Arthur Putnam

Frederick Arthur Putnam, banker, came to this state in 1871, and has spent most of his life in Boyd County. He was born at Gratiot, Michigan, January 21, 1869, the son of Eri Carlton, and Eliza (Goodrich) Putnam. His father, whose ancestry was English, was born in Jefferson County, New York, January 12, 1812, and died at Ute, Iowa, August 26, 1896; he served as postmaster at Warren, Nebraska, from 1873 to 1877. His mother, of Pennsylvania Dutch descent, was born at Courtland, New York, in May, 1841, and died at Soldier, Iowa, May 11, 1904.

Mr. Putnam taught in the rural schools for a time, engaged in farming, was cashier of the Peoples Bank of Naper, Nebraska, served as cashier of the Citizens State Bank of Bute, Nebraska, and is now cashier of the First National Bank of Naper. He served as county clerk of Boyd County for four years, was county treasurer, by appointment, from January to December, 1904, and was elected county treasurer in 1914-1918.

He holds membership in the Modern Woodmen of America, the Royal Highlanders, the Independent Order of Odd Fellows, and the Madison County Historical Society. He is treasurer of the local school board at Naper, and holds membership in the Nebraskana Society. Mr. Putnam acted as representative to the Nebraska Legislature in the 47th Session. He is independent, politically.

He was united in marriage with Florence Gertrude Sanders at Scottville, Nebraska, November 2, 1892. Mrs. Putnam, whose ancestry is English, was born at Granite Falls, Minnesota, November 11, 1872. They have the following children: Ruth, born December 21, 1893, who married John Milton Johnson; Walter, born January 28, 1896, who died July 16, 1896; Eugene, born June 10, 1897, who married Gladys Andersen; Carlton, born October 21, 1900; Fred, born April 1, 1904, who married Alice Samuelson; Dorothy, born February 4, 1907; Wayne, born March 22, 1910, who was killed in an airplane crash at Wayne, Nebraska, May 24, 1931; Woodrow, born April 24, 1913, who died May 26, 1917; and Ward, born April 25, 1916. Residence: Naper.

Forest Bourne Putney

A lawyer at Tilden, Nebraska since 1894, Forest Bourne Putney has been a resident of this state for the past sixty-one years. He was born at Strawberry Point,

Iowa, October 12, 1857, the son of William Wallace and Rosina (Bates) Putney. His father, who was a farmer and civic leader, served as county clerk of Antelope County, Nebraska, from 1871 to 1875, and was a member of the legislature of Nebraska in 1880; he was born at Villenova Township, New York, March 6, 1834, and died at Neligh, Nebraska, December 19, 1912. His English ancestors came to America in 1737, and he is descended from Joseph Putney of New York, who was born in 1758. Judge Putney traces his ancestors direct to John Alden, of Puritan fame. Each Christmas time judge Putney writes to each of his grandchildren a story of his early boyhood in Nebraska, and the letters when completed will be a very interesting volume.

Rosina (Bates) Putney, mother of Forest L. Putney, was born at Stockton, New York, October 27, 1828, and died at Neligh, Nebraska, February 18, 1912. She was the daughter of Roswell Bates, a farmer, and a soldier in the War of 1812; her ancestry was English.

Judge Putney has been a farmer and editor of distinction and since 1894 has been one of the leading lawyers of Madison County, Nebraska. He is the author of *Four Chapters of Antelope County History*, and was formerly the editor of the *Oakdale Journal* and the *Willapa Republican*, published at Willapa, Washington. A Republican, he has been prominent in political affairs for many years and has held the following positions: member of the legislature of Washington; county judge of Madison County; member of the Board of Education of Tilden ten years; city attorney of Tilden for 25 years; and a member of the Madison County Council of Defense. He is a member of the Nebraskana Society.

He was united in marriage with Edith Hortense Wallington at Willapa, Washington, November 29, 1891. Mrs. Putney, who was born at Detroit, Michigan, January 18, 1872, and died at Tilden, February 15, 1902, is the daughter of Frederick and Sarah (Brown) Wallington; her ancestry is English.

Their children are: Fred W., born September 19, 1892, at Willapa, Washington, who married Cornelia Fraizer of Lincoln, Nebraska; William W., born December 2, at Oakdale, Nebraska, married Hazel Snell of Lincoln, Nebraska, daughter of the president of the Midwest Life Insurance Company of Lincoln; Leila G., born July 14, 1895, at Tilden, Nebraska, who married Lloyd E. Whitney; and Edward M., born July 12, 1898, at Tilden, Nebraska, who married Lois Shepherd of Lincoln, Nebraska. William W. is president of The Midwest Life Insurance Company of Lincoln, Nebraska. Residence: Tilden.

William Griffey Putney

William Griffey Putney, president of the Bank of Cedar Bluffs, was born at Ithaca, Nebraska, June 14, 1870, son of George Jewett and Elvira Maria (Griffey) Putney. George J. Putney was born at Conneaut, Ohio, November 5, 1844, and was a homesteader and farmer in Saunders County in 1867. He served four years in the 29th Ohio Regiment of Volunteer Infantry in the Civil War, and died at Wahoo, January 5, 1914. He was of English and Scotch descent, his ancestors having come to Massachusetts in 1635, and Vermont about 1700. His wife, Elvira, was born at Cherry Hill, Pennsylvania, February 13, 1845, and died at Wahoo, December 18, 1923. A teacher prior to marriage, she was of English, Welsh and German descent.

Mr. Putney received his elementary education in the rural schools of Saunders County, and was graduated from Wahoo High School on May 29, 1889. He later attended Elliott's Business College at Burlington, Iowa, and Fremont Normal College.

On March 8, 1893, Mr. Putney was married to Myrtella Eoline Bellows at Grant, Nebraska. Born at Arcade, New York, July 26, 1870, Mrs. Putney is descended from English settlers in Massachusetts, in 1635, and from one line of early French emigrants. She was a piano teacher

prior to her marriage. There is one daughter, Vera L., born December 27, 1895, unmarried.

A teacher in earlier years, Mr. Putney taught in Elliott's Business College in 1892, and in rural schools. He was superintendent of schools at Weston 10 years and at Cedar Bluffs eleven years. He has also engaged in farming, and is president of the Bank of Cedar Bluffs. A Democrat, he served two regular and two special sessions in the Nebraska House of Representatives, and was unsuccessful candidate for county superintendent in 1916.

During the World War he was a Four Minute Man and took part in all loan drives, and is a member of the Nebraska State Teachers Association, the State Historical Society, and the Sons of Veterans. He is a member and elder in the First Presbyterian Church, and a leader in religious activities. His fraternal memberships include the Ancient Free and Accepted Masons, Royal Arch Masons, Knights Templar and Shrine, and the Knights of Pythias. He enjoys golf and hunting. Residence: Cedar Bluffs.

William Wallace Putney

William W. Putney, insurance executive, was born at Oakdale, Nebraska, December 2, 1893, and has lived in this state all his life. Forest Lilbourne Putney, his father, who was born at Strawberry Point, Clayton County, Iowa, October 12, 1857, is a lawyer, editor, and educator. He served as state representative from Pacific County, Washington; was city attorney at Tilden, Nebraska, for 30 years; and served as county judge of Madison County, Nebraska. He is descended from Joseph Putney of Oneida County, New York; Salmon Putney of Chautauqua County, New York; and William Putney. His English ancestors came to this country in 1635.

Edith Hortense (Wallington) Putney, mother of William, was born at Detroit, Michigan, January 18, 1872, and died at Tilden, Nebraska, February 45, 1902. She taught in a private school in Pacific County, Michigan, before her marriage. Frederick Wallington and Sara (Brown) Wallington, her parents, were both born in London, England. Her father was assistant general baggage master for the Michigan Central Railroad several years.

Mr. Putney attended the public schools of Tilden, and was a student in the summer sessions of Colorado and Nebraska colleges. He was secretary and treasurer of the Star Van & Storage Company, 1919 to 1923; and from 1923 to 1927, was assistant secretary of The Midwest Life Insurance Company of Lincoln. Since 1927, he has been president of The Midwest Life Insurance Company.

On December 19, 1921, he was married to Hazel Frost Snell at Lincoln. Mrs. Putney was born at Lincoln, December 28, 1889. Prior to her marriage she was director of the public school extension department at Lincoln. Two children were born to their union: Hazel Patricia, born April 24, 1923; and Snell Wallace, born February 27, 1929.

Mr. Putney served as a member of the National Guard, 1913-14, and in 1917, enlisted in the 7th Nebraska Regiment, but was not called for service. In May, 1918, was called into active service and served until war ended. He took part in various loan drives during the war, and is at this time a member of the American Legion. His membership in civic organizations includes the Red Cross, Community Chest, Lincoln Chamber of Commerce, the Nebraskana Society, and the Kiwanis Club of which he was a director in 1929 and 1930. He holds membership in the Young in 1929 and 1930. He holds membership in the Young Men's Christian Association, is a Mason, Scottish Rite, Shrine. Among his social clubs are the University Club; and Eastridge Country Club, both of Lincoln.

He is affiliated with All Soul's Unitarian Church at Lincoln, and devotes a great deal of his time to the welfare of his community. He likes to hunt and fish. His favorite recreation is reading. Politically, Mr. Putney is a Republican. Residence: Lincoln.

E. Ruth Pyrtle

For over 50 years E. Ruth Pyrtle has lived in Nebraska, and for much of that time has taken an active part in the educational life of Lincoln. She was born at Charleston, West Virginia, the daughter of James Allan and Elizabeth Sarah (Davis) Pyrtle. Her father, who was born in Henry County, Virginia, May 14, 1837, was a Virginia planter who served in the Confederate Army in the Civil War and was a participant in the battles of Gettysburg and Petersburg. He was the great grandson of John Pyrtle who served in the 8th Virginia regiment in the Revolutionary War. He died at Plum Creek, Nebraska, December, 1875.

Her mother, who was born in Franklin County, Virginia, July 2, 1841, was an active church worker, was a member of the Women's Christian Temperance Union, and was a woman's suffrage advocate. She was the great granddaughter of Charles and Ann (Dent) Davis, of Charles County, Maryland; Charles Davis was a soldier in the Revolution. She was the daughter of Sampson J. and Basheba (Turner) Davis; the latter's grandfather served in the Revolution. She died at Lincoln, Lancaster County, Nebraska, January 10, 1898.

Miss Pyrtle attended the elementary schools at Lexington, Nebraska, and was graduated from the Lexington High School. Later she was a student at the University of Nebraska, where she was awarded the A. B. degree, 1904; A. M., 1909. She is a member of Pi Gamma Mu. She studied for three summers at Columbia University at New York.

From 1924 to 1929, she was chairman of the National Educational Association Retirement Committee. In 1927, she was made president of the department of the Elementary School Principals of the National Educational Association; she served as president of the latter organization in 1929-30. She is principal of the Bancroft School at Lincoln.

Miss Pyrtle is the author of *Early Virginia Families, Pyrtle-Davis-Turner-Martin*, 1930. She has written numerous magazine articles on educational topics. In 1922, she was a candidate for state superintendent of schools in Nebraska. She served as general secretary of the Young Women's Christian Association in Des Moines, Iowa, and at Camp Dodge, where she was in charge of women's welfare activities during the World War. She is a member of Deborah Avery Chapter of the Daughters of the American Revolution.

She is a member of the Red Cross, the Community Chest Organ of Lincoln, and the Social Welfare Society. She is a member of the Lincoln Woman's Club; the Lincoln Chamber of Commerce; and the Lincoln School Forum. She holds membership in the following organizations: Nebraska Woman's Educational Club; Nebraska State Teachers Association; National Council of Education of the National Education Association; and the Young Women's Christian Association. She has served on the board of the latter for the past four years.

She is affiliated with the League of Women Voters and the Nebraska Writers' Guild. She is a member of the Bruner Bird Club. She is a member of St. Paul's Methodist Episcopal Church at Lincoln, Nebraska. Her hobbies are hiking in the out of doors and the study of birds. Residence: Lincoln.

Loren Edwin Pyzer

Loren Edwin Pyzer was born at Elmwood, Nebraska, January 7, 1871, son of Alfred and Orilla (May) Pyzer. His father was born in England, came to America as a young man and served in the Civil War. He died at Elmwood in November, 1895. His wife, Orilla, was born in Cowell, Ohio, April 19, 1841, and died at Elmwood in 1873.

Mr. Pyzer attended country school, and until the last sixteen years of his life engaged in farming. He was then elected treasurer of McPherson County on the Republican ticket, serving eight years. He died at Tryon January 12, 1929. Mr. Pyzer was an outstanding citizen of his community. He was a member of the Odd Fellows and the Woodmen of the World, and in 1910 became a member of the Christian Church.

He was married on October 30, 1887, to Mary Esther Wood, daughter of Hiram N. and Martha (Foulks) Wood at Weeping Water. Hiram N. Wood was born in Malone, New York, and Mrs. Wood was born in Ohio. Mrs. Pyzer was born at Boscobel, Wisconsin, April 12, 1868. Her ancestors came from England before the Revolutionary War. There are five children, Walter, born August 30, 1888, who married Nellie Dobbins; Earl, born November 20, 1891, who married Merle Hall; Lisle Nelson, born January 13, 1896, who married Erma Childerson; Gladys, born February 27, 1897, who married Omer Dobbins; and Harry, born December 13, 1906, who married Dora Newberry. Residence: Tyron.

Daniel Thomas Quigley

Daniel Thomas Quigley, physician and surgeon, was born at Baraboo, Wisconsin, June 27, 1876, and has been a resident of Nebraska for the past twenty-seven years. He is the son of Thomas Bartlett Quigley, born at Boyle, County Roscommon, Ireland, March 10, 1840, who came to America in 1948. He was a farmer, and held the rank of colonel in the Civil War, in which he served in the Union Army. He died at Hot Springs, South Dakota, April 15, 1899. His wife, Elizabeth (Durnin) Quigley was born at Dundalk, Province of Ulster, Ireland, February 8, 1852, and is still living.

Dr. Quigley was graduated from the Lennox High School in 1896, and from Rush Medical College in 1902, with the degree of M. D. He took post graduate work at the University of Vienna, in 1913.

He was married to Helen Seyferth, at North Platte, on June 15, 1904. Mrs. Quigley was born at North Platte, December 8, 1883. She is of German descent, some of her paternal ancestors having been officers in the German army. They have one son, Thomas Bartlett, born May 24, 1908, who is a medical student at Harvard Medical College.

Since 1903, Dr. Quigley has been engaged in active practice in Omaha. He is the author of the first papers ever written on the following three subjects: *Focal Infection as a Cause for Rheumatism* (1907); *Treatment of Surgical Tuberculosis by Sunshine* (1908); and *Use of Sphygmomanometer by the General Practitioner and Surgeon* (blood pressure determination; 1908. In addition he is the author of *Conquest of Cancer*, a book (1929) and numerous articles in medical journals.

Since 1920 he has been medical director of the Radium Hospital. In 1908 he organized the Nebraska State Health Officers Association, and he served as its president four years. He is a member of the American Medical Association, the Nebraska State and Omaha-Douglas County Medical Associations, the American College of Surgeons, the American College of Radiology, the American Radium Society, Radiological Society of North America, and the American Medical Authors and Editors Association. His civic and commercial organizations include the Chamber of Commerce, the American Aeronautics Association, the Rotary Club, and the Interprofessional Institute. He is a member of the American Association for the Advancement of Science, and is instructor in surgery at the University of Nebraska Medical College. His clubs are the University Club, the Omaha Club, and the Omaha Country Club. His sport is golf. Residence: Omaha.

William Byran Quigley

William Bryan Quigley, lawyer, was born at Valentine, Nebraska, January 29, 1899. He received his Bachelor of Laws dgree from the University of Nebraska where he was a member of Delta Tau Delta.

Since his admission to the bar, Mr. Quigley has been engaged in active practice. He served in the United States Army during the World War. Residence: Valentine.

Friedrich A. Rabe

Friedrich A. Rabe, educator and clergyman of Lincoln, was born at Wenden, Hannover, Germany, July 1, 1863. His father, Heinrich F. Rabe, who was born at Wenden, in 1836, and died there in 1884, was a farmer, and was active in political affairs, serving as mayor of his community for years; his ancestors settled at Wenden, in 1600, and members of the Rabe family have lived there since that date. Marie S. (Hahne) Rabe, mother of Friedrich A. Rabe, was born at Wenden, February 1, 1837, and died there, December 5, 1876.

Dr. Rabe attended elementary schools in Germany, 1869-77; the gymnasium, 1877-84; and the University of Goettingen, 1884-1887. He received the D. D. degree from Midland College at Fremont, Nebraska, May 29, 1930. He was elected to membership in Akademische Sangerschaft, and Akademische Turnerschaft in Germany.

From 1906 to 1914, he was pastor at Bloomfield, Nebraska, and from 1914-30, was pastor of St. John's Evangelical Lutheran Church, at Lincoln. He is now professor of German, Hebrew, and the Old Testament, at the Martin Luther Seminary at Lincoln. He is the author of numerous short stories and several poems, published in the volume *Blumen der Praerie*. He is affiliated with St. John's Lutheran Church, and holds membership in the Nebraskana Society.

His marriage to Emma W. Feldmann was solemnized at Wartjenstedt, Hannover, Germany, January 5, 1893. Mrs. Rabe, whose father was a clergyman, was born at Bierbergen, Hannover, Germany, November 26, 1870. Her cousin, Wilhelm Feldmann, was an inventor and was the builder of the Schwebebahn, of Elberfeld-Barmen. Four children were born to their marriage: Friedrich, born June 14, 1896, who married Florence Weiss; Elizabeth, born October 3, 1897, who married Dr. W. H. Werkmeister of the department of philosophy at the University of Nebraska; Wilhelm, born October 24, 1900, who married Gertrude Wittstruck; and Heinrich, born in 1905 who died the same year. Friedrich was graduated from the University of Nebraska, mechanical engineering department, with the degree A. B.; was connected with the Westinghouse factory; was an instructor at Yale University, where he received his M. E. degrees; served as consulting engineer in New York; and is now chief engineer in St. Louis.

Wilhelm was graduated from the University of Nebraska with the A. B. degree, and is now an engineer in Minneapolis, Minnesota. Elizabeth received her A. B. degree at the University of Nebraska. Residence: Lincoln.

George A. Racely

George A. Racely, dental surgeon, was born at Center, Nebraska, April 7, 1889, son of Robert and Katie Eva (Jewell) Racely. His father, who was born in Pennsylvania, January 19, 1858, was descended from a family by the name of Root who came to America with William Penn. He is a retired merchant. His wife, Katie, was born in Michigan, July 14, 165, of English extraction.

Upon his graduation from the public schools of Pender, Mr. Racely attended Bellevue Academy until 1910. He received the Bachelor of Arts degree from the University of Nebraska in 1916, and the degree of Doctor of Dental Surgery from the University of Nebraska in 1927. While there he was chairman of the Junior Prom, assistant manager of the *Cornhusker,* a member of the

Spikes and the Viking and of Phi Gamma Delta and Xi Psi Phi. Active in athletics, he was a member of the track and football team, was head freshman coach in 1915, and assistant freshman coach 1923, 1924, and 1926.

He was a teacher and athletic coach for five years, and a salesman of hardware and furniture for three years. Since his admission in 1927 he has been in active dental practice.

On November 24, 1920, he was married to Lida Ione Couch at Fremont. Mrs. Racely is descended from Thomas Couch, a member of Washington's army of the Revolution. They have two children, Elizabeth Jean, born November 26, 1921, and George Jackson, born December 3, 1924. Mrs. Racely is past vice president of the Nebraska State Dental Auxiliary, is secretary of the American Legion Auxiliary, and secretary of the D. A. R. She attended the University of Nebraska, and is affiliated with the Westminster Presbyterian Church at Lincoln.

Dr. Racely is a Republican. He was a member of the University of Nebraska Cadet Corps, and at one time held the rank of first lieutenant in the Missouri National Guard. During the late war he was captain in the 59th Artillery Brigade, now retired. He is a member of the Disabled Emergency Officers of the World War, the American Legion, and the state committee of national defense. He is now mayor of Crawford (1932-34).

Dr. Racely's religious affiliation is with Westminster Presbyterian Church at Lincoln. He is a member of the American Dental Associaton and the Executive Council of the Nebraska State Dental Society. He is a member of the Chamber of Commerce, the Masons (Scottish Rite of Lincoln; Sesostris Temple of the Shrine). His favorite sports are fishing and huntng while his hobby is motoring. Residence: Crawford.

Wilbur A. Racely

Born in Blue Mounds, Wisconsin, July 10, 1885, Wilbur A. Racely is the son of Reuben Andrew Racely and Kate (Minnix) Racely. His father was born in Pennsylvania, May 10, 1855, and his ancestors were born in Bucks County, Pennsylvania. He was a farmer, and his father was a merchant. His mother was born in Wisconsin, and died in Pender, on January 3, 1931.

Wilbur Racely attended the Pender public schools and then the University of Nebraska from which he received his Bachelor of Science degree. He was an Acacia and a Phi Gamma Delta; he was also on the tennis team. He married Jennie Gervena McHerron in Yankton, South Dakota, and to this union four children were born: Jack, born March 22, 1916; Clay, born September 27, 1917; Jeanne, born February 3, 1920; and W. Erle, born August 13, 1926.

Mr. Racely belongs to the following fraternal organizations: the Elks, Ancient Free and Accepted Masons. Knight Templers, Modern Woodman of America, and is a Shriner. He is affiliated with the Presbyterian Church and the Republican party, belongs to the Pender school board, and is a member of the Nebraskana Society. Mr. Racely is interested in golf, football and tennis. Residence: Pender.

Gerard V. Rademacher

Gerard V. Rademacher was born at Crete, Nebraska, January 21, 1889, the son of Frank Joseph and Mary (Pavlik) Rademacher. His father, who was a furniture dealer and undertaker, was born at Olpe, Germany, April 22, 1845, and died at Crete, April 7, 1926; he was the son of Johann Rademacher and Catherine (Kramer) Rademacher. His mother was born at Volenic, Bohemia, February 3, 1852, and died at Crete, November 22, 1922.

Mr. Rademacher attended St. James Parochial School at Crete, was graduated from Crete High Schol in 1906, and in 1910 received the A. B. and B. S. degrees at Creighton University. He was awarded the A. M. degree in 1912 and the LL. B. degree in 1913 at the Omaha Law College where he was elected to membership in Gamma Eta Gamma. He was admitted to the bar in 1913. Since his graduation from school he has been engaged in the furniture and udertaking business at Crete.

He is a member of the Modern Woodmen of America, the Rotary Club, Crete Community Club, the Nebraskana Society, and the Red Cross. He holds membership in the Nebraska Funeral Directors Association, Federation of Nebraska Retailers, and the Crete Building & Loan Association of which he is a director. He is affiliated with St. James Parish of the Catholic Church and was formerly a member of the Knights of Columbus.

During the World War Mr. Rademacher served as corporal in the infantry, training troops and detached service, and in the officers' training school at Camp Pike, Arkansas. He is a member of American Legion Post Number 147 at this time. His chief recreations are golfing and reading.

Since the beginning of the state the Rademacher family has been prominent in Saline County, Nebraska. Frank Joseph Rademacher, father of Gerard Rademacher, learned the trade of cabinet making, draftsmanship, and architectural drawing, in Germany, and traveled through the entire country as an apprentice, studying at the various industrial centers. In 1868 he came to America and remained at Detroit, Michigan until 1870 when he moved to Nebraska and settled at Crete before the railroad was built.

His wife, Mary Pavlik, was the daughter of Adalbert Pavlik (1824-85) and Josephine (Bass) Pavlik (1824-1901) who came to this country in 1868 and settled in Maryland. In 1869 they moved to Nebraska City, Nebraska, and the following spring homesteaded in Lancaster County.

Both Frank and Mary Rademacher were prominent at Crete for many years; the former was in business there for 56 years, was a member of the school board, and was one of the organizers of St. James Parish. Residence: Crete.

Boyd Clyde Radford

Boyd Radford, a lifelong resident of this state, was born at Newark, Nebraska, February 2, 1884, the son of William H. and Lizzie M. Radford. His father, who is a farmer, was born in Heresfordshire, England, September 16, 1850, moved to Canada with his parents in his early childhood, and in 1873 homesteaded in Kearney County, Nebraska. His mother was born at Leesville, Ohio, September 19, 1861, of German parentage. She came to Nebraska in 1872, with two elder brothers, and took an active part in early western settlement.

Mr. Radford attended a rural school and studied in a private business college for two years. He has been a farmer in Kearney County all his life and since 1916, has served as secretary of the Nebraska Polled Hereford Breeders Association. He is a member of the Parent-Teachers' Association, is president of the school board at Newark, Nebraska, and holds membership in the Masonic bodies and the Modern Woodmen of America. During the World War he was active in the conservation of foodstuffs for the allied armies, and liberally contributed to loan funds. He is interested in music and holds membership in four community bands. His favorite sport is baseball.

On December 25, 1906, he married Edna M. Gormley, at Minden. Mrs. Radford, who is the daughter of a pioneer sheriff in Nebraska, was born at Lowell, Nebraska, November 24, 1886. They have ten children: Doris and Dallas, born October 29, 1907; Harold, born October 4, 1909; Ethel, born May 1, 1911; Alice, born January 11, 1915; Neal, born February 16, 1918; Marion, born December 5, 1919; Norman, born November 7, 1920; Robert,

born February 19, 1921; and Rex, born June 4, 1931. Residence: Newark.

Franz Christopher Radke

Franz C. Radke, lawyer, judge, and political leader of Tecumseh, Nebraska, was born at Wynot, June 23, 1889. His father, Carl Radke, who was born in Germany, and died near Wynot July 23, 1897, was a carpenter and farmer.

Mr. Radke attended the Cedar County district schools, and Hartington High School one year, after which he was a student at the Wayne Normal College. In 1914, he was graduated from the University of Nebraska with the A. B. degree, and in 1917 was awarded his LL. B. In 1909-10, he taught in a country school in Burt County, Nebraska. Upon his admission to the bar, June 11, 1917, he entered the practice of law at Hartington as a member of the firm of Burkett & Radke. In 1921 he moved to Tecumseh, where he is active in the legal field, and at present is city attorney of that city.

A Democrat, he was a member of the Nebraska legislature in 1917; was a member of the Nebraska constitutional convention, 1919-20; was county judge of Johnson County, 1925-29; and in 1930 was defeated for nomination as attorney general in the Democratic primary. He was private secretary to Governor Charles W. Bryan, 1923-24.

His marriage to Magdelene Craft was solemnized at Lincoln, June 26, 1921. Mrs. Radka, who was born at Tecumseh, August 8, 1893, is a lawyer. She is a member of the board of education and is president of the library board at Tecumseh. She was elected a member of the board of directors of Nebraska Writers Guild in November, 1930. She is also a member of the Quill Club of Lincoln. There are two children: Joanna Magdelene, born May 28, 1923; and Mark Francis, born December 24, 1928.

In August, 1917, Mr. Radke enlisted in the World War, was made second lieutenant in November, 1917; was stationed at Camp Dodge, Iowa, 1917-18; and in July, 1918, was promoted to rank of first lieutenant. He was trial judge advocate of general courts martial, and was active in victory loan and liberty loan drives.

He is a member of Kenneth A. Curtis Post No. 2 of the American Legion, the Tecumseh Chamber of Commerce, the Kiwanis Club, the Nebraska State Historical Society, and the Nebraskana Society. He is first vice president of the Native Sons and Daughters of Nebraska, and is on the board of directors of the Nebraska division of the Isaak Walton League. He is a member of the following organizations: Nebraska State Bar Association; American Judicature Society; Johnson County Bar Association; and Ancient Free and Accepted Masons, Lodge No. 17 at Tecumseh, and Scottish Rite Temple at Lincoln. Mr. Radke's hobby is the study of history and Nebraska aboriginal archeology. Residence: Tecumseh.

Frank L. Rain

A leading professional man in Fairbury, Nebraska, Frank L. Rain, was born at Marshall, Texas, August 5, 1877, the son of Frank M. Rain and Kate (Smith) Rain. His father, a railroad man, was born at Piqua, Ohio, in November, 1854, and died at Fairbury, Jefferson County, in October, 1856.

Frank Rain was graduated from the Fairbury High School in 1895 and then attended the University of Nebraska, where he received an A. B. degree. He also attended the University of Michigan, receiving the degree of Bachelor of Laws. There he was made a member of the Phi Delta Phi. At the University of Nebraska he was a member of Beta Theta Pi. On December 25, 1907, at Fairbury, Nebraska, he was united in marriage to Madge Merrell, who was born at Roca, Nebraska. They have two children: Francis M., born August 22, 1909; and

Maxine, born September 14, 1910.

Mr. Rain has been city attorney of Fairbury for twelve years, and county attorney of Jefferson County for thirteen years. He served as mayor two years and has lived in Nebraska since 1893. At the present time is a member of the law firm of Barnes and Rain.

Affiliated with the Presbyterian Church he is also a member of the Red Cross, and Benevolent and Protective Order of Elks, of which he was grand, exalted ruler, in 1919-20. He is an Ancient Free and Accepted Mason and is a member of the Chamber of Commerce. His clubs are the Lincoln University Club and the Fairbury Country Club. Residence: Fairbury.

Claude Raitt

Claude Raitt was born in Prague, Nebraska, March 7, 1887, the son of James Darward Raitt and Elizabeth, (Abbott) Raitt. His father was born in Arbroith, Scotland, October 3, 1840, and came to this country in July, 1871. He was captain on a ship. Elizabeth Abbott Raitt was born in Glamis, Scotland, August 30, 1843. Her husband died at David City, Nebraska, July 22, 1917.

Claude Raitt attended Wesleyan University one year. He married Tillie Belle Curry, March 3, 1909, at Garrison, Nebraska. Mrs. Raitt was born in Garrison, October 20, 1887. They have four children: Irene Curry, born October 12, 1912, Dean David, born October 27, 1915, Clarabelle, born May 20, 1919, and Richard Claude, born January 12, 1924, who are all at home.

Mr. Raitt is a democrat, and he and his family are affiliated with the Methodist Church. He belongs to the Red Cross, Odd Fellows, is treasurer of the Parent-Teachers' Association in Rising City, Nebraska, and has served on the school board for a number of years.

Baseball is Mr. Raitt's favorite sport. He has lived in Nebraska forty-four years, and is a member of the Nebraskana Society. Residence: Rising City.

Robert Rakow

Robert Rakow, son of William Fredrick and Johanna (Koeppe) Rakow, was born in Martinsburg, Nebraska, May 22, 1878. His father, William, was born in Schoenwalde, Pomerania, Germany, December 29, 1836, and died at Martinsburg, February 7, 1904. His wife, Johanna, was born in Schoenwalde, June 28, 1840, and died at Martinsburg, October 16, 1887.

Educated in public school, Robert Rakow has been a farmer since young manhood. On April 9, 1902, he was united in marriage to Mary Schultz, at Martinsburg. Mrs. Rakow was born there on September 6, 1881. They have one son, Kermit, born September 1, 1905, who married Anna Eva Reineccius.

Mr. Rakow is a Republican, and a member of Trinity Evangelical Lutheran Church of Martinsburg. Residence: Ponca.

William Fred Rakow

A retired farmer since 1919, William Fred Rakow was born in Pomerania, Germany, December 29, 1863, son of William and Annie (Cappey) Rakow. William Rakow, Sr., was born in Pomerania, December 29, 1834, and farmed in Nebraska until his death at Martinsburg, in February, 1901. His wife, was born in Germany, in 1850, died at Martinsburg, in March, 1890.

Mr. Rakow attended the public schools of Martinsburg, and engaged in farming until his retirement as above. He is a Republican, and a member of the Lutheran Church and the Nebraskana Society. His favorite sport is golf.

On April 17, 1888, he was united in marriage to Augusta Stark, at Martinsberg. Mrs. Rakow was born in Germany, August 12, 1869, and is a prominent church woman.

There are four children: Jessie, born January 16, 1889, who married Wilmer Harper; Edna, born November 5, 1890, who married Carl Anderson; Alice, born November 22, 1894, who married Walter Krause; and Gene, born February 22, 1891, who married Goldie Forman. Residence: Allen.

Sanford Eugene Ralsten

For the past 47 years Sanford Eugene Ralsten has lived in Nebraska, where he has been a farmer, merchant, postmaster and insurance man. He was born in Lewis County, New York, May 2, 1859, the son of George and Emily (McCarty) Ralsten. His father, who was born in New York, and died at Lincoln, in August, 1905, was a farmer and was descended from Scotch and Dutch ancestors. His mother was born of Irish-Canadian and New England Yankee parents in New York, and died at Holdrege, in 1922.

Mr. Ralsten has been postmaster at Geneva for the past eight years, and is still serving.

Active in various organizations for community progress, Mr. Ralsten is a member of the Red Cross, the Community Club, the Nebraskana Society, and the Young Men's Christian Association. He enjoys golf, while his hobby is reading. During the World War he took an energetic part in loan drives and other wartime projects.

He was married to Ida Ellen Dove at Monmouth, Iowa, on January 16, 1884. Mrs. Ralsten was born in Iowa, January 18, 1861, and died at Parkston, South Dakota, August 24, 1917. She was of English ancestry. One child was born to them, Maxwell, on March 21, 1898. For ten years he was superintendent of mail transfers at the Union Depot in Omaha, and for the past twenty years has been in mail service. Residence: Geneva.

Orville Alfred Ralston

Orville Alfred Ralston, who has been engaged in the practice of dentistry for the past 12 years, was born at Weeping Water, Nebraska, September 9, 1894. Charles A. Ralston, his father, who was a barber, was born in Pennsylvania, of English and Dutch parents, and died at Weeping Water, in 1908. Jeanette (Arnold) Ralston, his mother, was born in Iowa, of Scotch and Irish ancestry.

Dr. Ralston was graduated from the high school at Peru, Nebraska, in 1913, where he was a member of the Dramatic Club, and was active in athletic affairs, and in 1920 was graduated from the University of Nebraska with the D. D. S. degree. He served as grand master of Kappa Sigma in 1919, at the University of Nebraska. Dr. Ralston, who is the author of some articles on dentistry published in professional magazines, has been successfully engaged in the practice of dentistry at Ainsworth, Nebraska, for a number of years.

He is a member of the executive committee of the Ainsworth Chamber of Commerce of which he was vice president, is chairman of the aeronautics committee of the Nebraska American Legion, and holds membership in the Masons, Elks, and Modern Woodmen of America. Dr. Ralston is active in two dental study clubs and holds membership in the National Society of Denture Prosthetists, the American Full Denture Society, American Dental Association, and the Nebraska State Dental Association. He is now serving as mayor of Ainsworth.

During the World War he served as first lieutenant in many engagements overseas, was distinguished in the aviation service, and was awarded a Distinguished Service Cross; he was post commander of the American Legion at one time.

Dr. Ralston's chief outside interest is aviation, and his sports include game fishing and golfing. His marriage to Charlotte Belle Hanna, occurred at Wood Lake, Nebraska, November 20, 1920. Mrs. Ralston, who was born at Wood Lake, September 13, 1895, is descended from a

Scotch family connected with Alexander Hamilton. They have three children: Janet Muriel, born September 23, 1921; Robert, born September 13, 1924; and Patricia, born August 5, 1927. Residence: Ainsworth.

Albert Louis Ramacciotti

Born at Omaha, March 11, 1895, Albert L. Ramacciotti is the son of Hugo Louis and Nellie Ramacciotti. His father was born at Buffalo, New York, in 1855, and died at Omaha, September 7, 1907. Nellie Ramacciotti was born at Council Bluffs, Iowa, December 24, 1871, and is still living.

Upon his graduation from Omaha High School, Mr. Ramacciotti entered Notre Dame University. He attended Creighton University thereafter and received his LL. B. in 1922. He was a member of the debate team, etc., and a member of Gamma Eta Gamma. He has been engaged in active practice since his admission to the bar, and is now a member of the law firm of Reed, Ramacciotti and Robinson. He is a Republican.

On May 4, 1921, he was married to Hazel G. Bishop, at Papillion, Nebraska. Mrs. Ramacciotti was born at Beatrice, March 25, 1902. There are two children, Robert L., born March 29, 1922, and Patricia A., born May 3, 1924.

Mr. Ramacciotti served two years and two months during the World War and is a captain in the U. S. Reserve. He is a member of the Disabled Veterans of America, the American Legion, and the Reserve Officers Asociation. He is a Catholic and attends St. Margaret Mary Church, is a member of the Nebraska State and Omaha-Douglas County Bar Associations and the Knights of Columbus. His club is the Omaha Athletic, and his sport is golf. Residence: Omaha.

George Shelby Ramsay

George Shelby Ramsay, farmer and dairyman, was born at Newton, Iowa, September 28, 1869, and has been a resident of Nebraska fifty-three years. He is the son of George Lucas and Mary Jane (Sims) Ramsay, the former a native of Belvedere, Illinois, born in the early 1800's. He was a farmer, whose Scotch ancestors came to America shortly before his birth. He died at Seward, July 19, 1914. Mary Jane Sims, wife of George Lucas Ramsay, was born at Greencastle, Indiana, February 2, 1851, and died at Seward, November 1, 1921. Primarly a homemaker, she was interested in church work, and was the daughter of early settlers in Iowa.

Educated in the country grade schools, George Shelby Ramsay attended Seward High School, and thereafter engaged in farming. He is a purebred cattle breeder also and is a member of the board of the Seward County Farm Bureau. For twenty-five years he has served as a member of the school board, and was president of the Seward County Fair Board four years, and has been a member for ten years. Mr. Ramsay is interested in mechanics. He is affiliated with the Methodist Episcopal Church, and the Red Cross, and is a Modern Woodmen of America and a Mason. He is also a member of the Young Men's Christian Association and the Nebraskana Society.

On December 26, 1895, he was united in marriage to Jennie Frances Hickman at Seward. Mrs. Ramsay was born in Seward, May 16, 1870. Her father was a veteran of the Civil War, and her mother active in the suffrage and prohibition movements. They were of Scotch-Dutch extraction. There are three children: Thelbert H., born December 22, 1896, married Josephine Campbell; Elva Elizabeth, born February 23, 1899, married Raymond A. Hicks; and Robert S., born February 20, 1901, married Margaret E. Anderson. Thelbert runs the Ramsay Produce Company. Elizabeth, who is a graduate of the state university is a home economist, and Ro-

land, a purebred cattle breeder and dairyman, is vice president of the Nebraska State Holstein Association. All of the children graduated from Seward High School and have had musical training. They are all active in community affairs and in lodge work. Residence: Seward.

Ray Everett Ramsay

Ray E. Ramsay, one of Nebraska's better known university executives, has lived in this state for the past 12 years, and has taken a prominent part in the dramatic and executive affairs at the University of Nebraska. He was born at Rich Hill, Missouri, January 25, 1899, the son of Edward Everett and Ruth (Holdren) Ramsay. His father, who was born at Madison, Indiana, October 15, 1876, is in the wholesale grocery business. His mother was born at Spring Hill, Kansas, February 25, 1879.

Mr. Ramsay received his early education at the Longfellow School at Kansas City, and in 1917 was graduated from the Central High School there. He was awarded the A. B. degree at the University of Nebraska in 1928, where he was elected to membership in Alpha Sigma Phi.

During 1921, 22, and 23, Mr. Ramsay was an actor in New York City, and at various times between 1920 and 1924 was a chautauqua lecturer. From 1924 to 1929 he was in the dramatic department at the University of Nebraska, where he proved to be one of the university's most popular instructors. During 1929 he was a radio announcer, and for several years he has taken part in one act plays presented from the Lincoln radio broadcasting studio. Since 1929 he has served as secretary of the University of Nebraska Alumni Association.

His marriage to Florence Hapke was solemnized at Wahoo, Saunders County, Nebraska, October 4, 1922. Mrs. Ramsay, who was formerly a teacher, was born at Schuyler, Colfax County, Nebraska, June 12, 1899.

Mr. Ramsay is a member of the Lincoln Chamber of Commerce, the Lions Club, the Lincoln Young Men's Christian Association, and the Nebraskana Society. He is a Mason. During the World War he served as sergeant, 339 battalion, Tank Corps, and he is now a member of the American Legion. He is affiliated with the First Presbyterian Church of Lincoln. Politically, he is a Republican.

Among his favorite recreations are: golfing, tennis, baseball, and photography. Mr. Ramsay, who is a licensed air pilot, is intensely interested in aviation. Residence: Lincoln. (Photograph on Page 980).

Orva Chester Randall

Orva Chester Randall was born at Bowen, Illinois, September 6, 1873, and for the past 41 years has resided in Phelps County, Nebraska, where he was a farmer until his retirement in recent years. His father, Richard Sylvester Randall, was born at Gallopolis, Ohio, August 16, 1832, and died at Holdrege, Nebraska, August 9, 1903; he was a farmer. His wife, who was prominent in club work and Sunday School activities, was born in Adams County, Illinois, in March, 1840, and died at Holdrege, in July, 1912.

Mr. Randall served in two regular sessions and two special sessions of the Nebraska legislature, and has long been a leader in farm organization work in Phelps County. He is affiliated with the First Baptist Church of Holdrege, and holds membership in the Nebraskana Society.

He was married to Minnie Georgia Cain on December 22, 1896, who was born December 22, 1878, and died at Holdrege, June 13, 1920. Three children were born to them: Leslie, born July 19, 1899; Harry, born October 20, 1905; and Ralph, born October 26, 1908, who died August 9, 1926.

Mr. Randall married Nellie May Cain in 1921. Her

RAY EVERETT RAMSAY

Dole—Lincoln

Alberti—Cambridge

JOHN MURRAY RANKIN

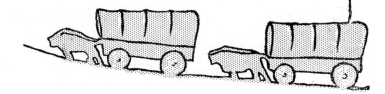

father, Isaac Leffer, was born near Canton, Ohio, August 12, 1851, and died in July, 1915. Her mother, Martha Alice Coffman, was born near Lincoln, Illinois, February 28, 1863. Mr. and Mrs. Leffer came to Nebraska in November, 1888, where they engaged in farming for many years.

Mrs. Randall is the mother of two children; Helen, born October 7, 1908, and who on November 25, 1930, was married to Otto H. Lank. They now reside in Omaha. Richard W. Cain, born August 16, 1910, was married December 21, 1931, to Dorothy Dreavor of York. They reside in York. Residence: Holdrege.

John Murray Rankin

John Murray Rankin, who has been a grain merchant at Cambridge, Nebraska, since 1888, was born at Haugh, Scotland, January 27, 1865, son of John and Jeanie Murray (Hillhouse) Rankin. His father, a farmer and merchant, was born at Kilmarnock, Scotland, April 4, 1834, and died at Cambridge, January 9, 1926. His mother was born at Catrine, Scotland, May 24, 1838, and died at Cambridge, September 28, 1904.

Mr. Rankin received his education in the public schools of Scotland. He arrived in America, in 1884, living in Albany, New York, for a year and a half, then moving to Cambridge, Nebraska, in March, 1886. He is manager of the Rankin Brothers Grain Company at Cambridge, is a member of the Cambridge Commercial Club, and was formerly president of the Rotary Club. He is a Scottish Rite and Shrine member of the Masons, and is affiliated with the First Congregational Church of Cambridge, of which he was choir leader for a number of years. He holds membership in the Red Cross and the Nebraskana Society.

For the past fifteen years Mr. Rankin has been a director of the Kansas Grain Dealers Association, representing that portion of Nebraska south of the Platte River which forms a part of the Kansas organization. In 1931, he was elected a director of the Nebraska Grain Dealers Association, and was also chairman of the committee of uniform grades of the Grain and Feed Dealers National Association for the years 1930-31.

During the World War, Mr. Rankin served as chairman of the four minute men of Cambridge, and was also chairman of the Cambridge branch chapter of the American Red Cross. He has acted in the later capacity ever since, his service extending over the past fifteen years. For the past seven years he has also been chairman of Furnas County chapter of the American Red Cross. He is affiliated with the Republican party. Residence: Cambridge: (Photograph on Page 981).

Robert Hillhouse Rankin

Robert Hillhouse Rankin, prominent grain and livestock dealer at Cambridge, was born at Catrine, Ayrshire, Scotland, May 28, 1858. His father, John Rankin, born in Kilmarnock, Ayrshire, April 4, 1834, was master foreman in a cotton spinning mill in his native land. He came to the United States as a homesteader, and later was a partner with his son Thomas M. Rankin in the Meat and Produce business at Cambridge. His death occurred there on January 9, 1926.

Jeanie Murray Hillhouse, wife of John Rankin, was born at Catrine, Scotland, May 24, 1838, and died at Cambridge on September 28, 1904. Her father was active in municipal affairs in his native town in Scotland. She was active in the work of the Free Church in Scotland, and later in the Congregational Church of Cambridge.

Robert H. Rankin was educated in the public schools of his native land, together with added study stimulated by active membership in literary societies there. A homesteader near Cambridge, he was later a member of the firm of Rankin Brothers, (consisting of R. H. Rankin and J. M. Rankin), grain and livestock dealers, which was established in 1884.

On September 25, 1890, he married Caroline Sidney Lenocker at Stuart, Iowa. Mrs. Rankin who was born at Mt. Hope, Ohio, November 4, 1864, is the daughter of Jacob and Barbara (Drushel) Lenocker. Her father, born in Switzerland, September 7, 1831, died November 1, 1907; while her mother, born in Mt. Hope, September 5, 1840, died March 10, 1878.

Mr. and Mrs. Rankin have eight children: Robert L., born September 6, 1892, an attorney and a veteran of the World War, married Verna Sparks; James H., born November 21, 1893, a merchant and a World War veteran, married Hazel Thorndike,; Walter M., born August 3, 1895, a grain dealer, married Angelette Barnes; Jeanie M., born May 16, 1897, is the wife of Monte C. Lockenour, a World War soldier; Annie L., born December 22, 1899, is an instructor at Centralia, Washington; Donald J., born April 9, 1902, is a pharmacist; Ruth M., born September 16, 1904, is the wife of Harry Fredricks, a World War veteran; and William A., born November 21, 1906, is a grain dealer.

Active in the development of Municipal Ownership industries in Cambrdge for forty years, Mr. Rankin has served on the board of the Congregational Church, the Board of Education, the village board, the Cambridge Telephone Company, and is chairman of the board of directors of the Enterprise Loan & Building Association on which board he has officiated for forty years. During the World War he participated in all loan and Red Cross drives. He is a member of the Red Cross, the Community Club, the Modern Woodmen of America, the Southwest Nebraska Historical Society, and the Nebraskana Society. His hobby is the study of literature, commercial and political reading. Residence: Cambridge. (Photograph on Page 983).

John Butler Raper

John B. Raper, lawyer and judge, was born in Pawnee County, October 5, 1861. William B. Raper, his father, who was born in Greene County, Indiana, October 29, 1832 and died at Pawnee City, December 30, 1914, was a merchant and government agent at the Ponca Agency. He enlisted in the 2nd Nebraska cavalry, October 16, 1862, in the Civil War, was commissioned 1st lieutenant and served until September 9, 1863. He was county clerk for some time, and was a member of the Nebraska house of representatives in 1907 and 1909. His ancestry was English and Irish; his paternal grandparents being members of an old North Carolina family.

His mother, Mary Jane (Butler) Raper, who was born in Greene County, Indiana, October 13, 1838, and died at Pawnee City, February 10, 1864, was descended from an old Kentucky family. Her father, John R. Butler, was a member of Nebraska's first legislature, in 1867.

Judge Raper received his elementary education in the public and normal schools. He was admitted to the bar in Pawnee County, in 1890. Since that time has engaged in the practice of law and has been active in the political life of Nebraska. He has been judge of the district court of the First Nebraska district, since 1905; has served as county clerk and county attorney of Pawnee County. He is a Republican.

He was married to Jennie Albright in Pawnee County, Nebraska, September 17, 1885. Mrs. Raper, who was born in Tazewell County, Illinois, March 27, 1864, is of English and German ancestry. They have one daughter, Pauline, born August 23, 1886. She is married to Edwin N. Van Horne; they have four children: Leonard Hugh; Betty; Pauline; and John Edwin Van Horne. Residence: Pawnee City.

Frank Washington Rapp

Frank W. Rapp was born at Springfield, Ohio, May 30, 1888, son of George Washington and Minne (Rains) Rapp. His father, a business man of German descent was born at Springfield, in 1866, and died there in 1917. Min-

ROBERT HILHOUSE RANKIN

Alberti—Cambridge

nie Rains Rapp was born at Villisca, Iowa, February 15, 1868, and is of English Quaker descent.

Frank W. Rapp attended parochial school eight years and high school two years at Springfield. Coming to Nebraska, he entered Fremont Normal College and was graduated in April, 1916. He received his D. D. S. from Creighton University in 1919. He is a member of Phi Kappa Omicron and Delta Sigma Delta.

Dr. Rapp has had an interesting and varied career. A Machinist, carpenter, stereotyper, piano plate finisher, salesman and chain restaurant operator, he also owned and operated an irrigated farm in central Utah, in 1911. Since 1919 he has conducted his own professional practice. He is president of Liberty Stands, Inc.

On July 22, 1920, he was married to Louise Babe Mackeben of Council Bluffs, Iowa. Mrs. Rapp was born May 22, 1888, and is of German descent. They attend Kountze Memorial Lutheran Church. During the World War Dr. Rapp was in the Medical Enlisted Reserve Corps. He is a member of the Interprofessional Institute, the Omaha District Dental Society, the Nebraska State Dental Society and the National Dental Association.

A Mason, Dr. Rapp is a member of Omaha Lodge No. 288, Ancient Free and Accepted Masons, Knights Templar, Nebraska Consistory, 32nd degree Scottish Rite, and Tangier Temple of the Shrine. He likes golf and hunting. His hobbies are reading and inventions. Residence: Omaha.

Melvin Earle Rasdal

One of the outstanding business executives of Nebraska in Melvin Earle Rasdal, who is a leader in civic and commercial afairs at Ogallala. He was born in Thurston County, Nebraska, July 7, 1891, the son of Harry Clarence and Ada Leila (Purdy) Rasdal, the former a farmer who was born in Minnesota, November 25, 1868. His father, whose French and English ancestors came to America prior to the French Revolution, has served as a member of the school board and as delegate to the Republican State Convention in pre-primary days. His mother, who has been active in educational and civic affairs in her community for a number of years, was born at Blue Earth, Minnesota, May 23, 1871. Her ancestors, who were descended from English, Welsh and Dutch settlers in America, were pioneers in Michigan, Indiana, Minnesota, and Nebraska.

Mr. Rasdal was graduated from the high school at Lyons, Nebraska in 1909, and received the Ph. G. degree at the University of Nebraska where he was chairman of the Pharmacy Week Committee, served as president of the Pharmacy Club, and held membership in Phi Delta Chi. He has been unusually prominent in Nebraska business affairs and has held the following positions: salesman for the Loose-Wiles Biscuit Company; manager of the Sioux City branch of the Loose-Wiles Biscuit Company; manager of the Farmers Union Store at Crofton; and owner of a retail drug store at Ogallala since 1924.

He has owned interests in drug stores at Lexington, Nebraska; Beloit, Kansas; and Sidney, Nebraska, and has written various articles on commercial subjects in trade journals. Mr. Rasdall is a member of the American Pharmaceutical Association, the National Association of Retail Druggists, also past president of Nebraska Pharmaceutical Association. He holds membership in the Ogallala Commercial Club, of which he was secretary, 1925-7, was secretary and a member of the board of directors of the Rotary Club for a year, and is a member of the Nebraskana Society. He is affiliated with the First Congregational Church of Ogallala, is a Master Mason, and was formerly a member of the Young Men's Christian Association. Until a few years ago he took a prominent part in semi-professional baseball and at this time officiates at various high school football games. Mr. Rasdal takes an active part in the Nebraska Rexall Club

and had a place on the program of the National Convention held at Boston, Massachusetts in 1928. He is interested in contract bridge and reading.

In 1930 Mr. Rasdal was awarded recognition as an astute and progressive business man by the Nebraska Merchant and Trade Review which presented him with a medal showing him to be one of the first class of ten Master Merchants of Nebraska. Since 1926 he has been a member of the board of managers, Unit Division, of the Nebraska Pharmaceutical Association; this division is for store owners only.

His marriage to Agnes Hofeldt occurred at Laurel, Nebraska, June 20, 1916. She is the daughter of Wm. F. and Anna (Bartels) Hofeldt. Henry Bartels, her mother's brother, served as state representative for several terms. Mrs. Rasdal, who is of German descent, was born in Wayne County, Nebraska, January 3, 1896. They have two children: Agnes Geraldine, April 4, 1918; and Earleen Jane, born September 1, 1923.

Mrs. Agnes Rasdal is a member of the P. E. O. Sisterhood and past matron of the Eastern Star. Residence: Ogallala.

Anton Nelson Rask

For over 44 years Anton Nelson Rask has been a resident of Howard County, Nebraska, and is now engaged in the implement business at Boelus. His father, Nels Nelsen Rask, who was a farmer, was born at Skjorping, Denmark, July 13, 1822, and died at Habro, Denmak, September 18, 1816; he served in the Danish and German War of 1848 in which he was wounded. His mother, Maren Kjerstine (Neldlatten) Rask, was born at Gunestruf, Denmark, April 16, 1832, and died at Habro, April 8, 1877.

Mr. Rask was married to Annie Schmaljohn at Alliance, Nebraska, February 25, 1899. Mrs. Rask was born at Rockville, Nebraska, January 21, 1875, of German and English parents who came to this country in 1872. To them were born: Leslie, July 18, 1900; Marguerite, September 24, 1902, who married Walter Nelson; Evelyn, November 6, 1904, who married Fred D. Lammers; Devona, April 5, 1911, who married Wilber Wickman; Anton, Jr., July 10, 1914; and Frances, November 22, 1906. Residence: Boelus. (Photograph in Album).

George Rasmussen

George Rasmussen, prominent lumber, coal, and grain executive was born at Idaho Falls, Idaho, the son of John and Caroline (Petersen) Rasmussen. His father, who was a general contractor, was born in Denmark and died in Omaha, January 29, 1902. His mother was born in Denmark.

Mr. Rasmussen was a student at the Lincoln grade school in Omaha, Nebraska, and later attended Omaha High School. He has lived in Nebraska since 1888 and is now president of the Atlas Lumber Company of Omaha and the National Cypress Pole & Piling Company of Cardwell, Missouri, and is connected with the Independent Lumber Company, the Western Securities Company, and several other Nebraska organizations.

He was united in marriage at Omaha, June 9, 1909, to Irma Springer. Mrs. Rasmussen was born at Beatrice, Nebraska, March 31, 1889. Their children are: Irma Georgene, born March 19, 1910; and George Paul, born July 24, 1914.

Mr. Rasmussen is a member of the Omaha Chamber of Commerce; the Nebraska Lumber Merchants Association; and is affiliated with most of Omaha's civic associations. He holds membership in the Nebraskana Society and the Young Men's Christian Association. His social clubs are the Happy Hollow Club and the Omaha Athletic Club. He is a member of the First Central Congregational Church. His sports are golf and tennis. He is a Mason and a Republican. Residence: Omaha.

Harry Rasmussen

Harry Rasmussen, manager of the Rasmussen Lumber & Coal Company, was born at Eagle Rock, Idaho, January 28, 1886, and for 46 years has resided in Nebraska. He is the son of John and Caroline Charlotte (Petersen) Rasmussen, the former a native of Denmark, born December 12, 1859, and the latter a native of Denmark, born March 17, 1860. John Rasmussen was a general contractor and the builder of the Pan American Building at Buffalo, New York. He died at Omaha, January 29, 1901.

Upon his graduation from Omaha High School, Harry Rasmussen attended Armour Technical Institute at Chicago. From 1905 until 1917, he was engaged in the contracting business. Entering the World War in 1917, he held the rank of second lieutenant in the air service. In April, 1919, he entered the lumber business at Nebraska City, and in 1925, came to Chadron to engage in the retail lumber and coal business. He is a member of the firm of Rasmussen Lumber & Coal Company and vice president of the Atlas Lumber Company of Omaha.

He was married to Henrietta Andrea Grandeek at Omaha, January 30, 1906. Mr. Rasmussen is a member of the American Legion, the Lutheran Church, the Red Cross, the Elks, the Brotherhood of American Yeoman, and the Masons. Always active in civic organizations, he served as president of the Kiwanis Club in 1929 and at the present time is a member of the school board (vice president) and a member of the municipal hospital board (vice president). His club is the Chadron Country Club. In 1931 Mr. Rasmussen was the winner of the golf championship for the year at the Country Club. Residence: Chadron.

Frederick John Rastede

Frederick John Rastede was born at Hampton, Illinois, October 22, 1877, the son of Frederick and Elisa (Wenke) Rastede. His father, who was a retail grocer, was born at Elsfleth, Germany, September 4, 1851, and died at Geneseo, Illinois, March 8, 1924; he was a member of the school board, city councilman, and a successful business man. His mother was born at Hampton Bluffs, Illinois, July 25, 1854, and died at Pierce, March 12, 1927. Her father was John Wenke who emigrated from Germany and established a farm home on the bluffs of the Mississippi River near Hampton, Illinois.

Mr. Rastede attended the Lutheran parochial school and in 1894 was graduated from the Geneseo High School. He was a grocery clerk, 1894, part owner of a grocery store at Geneseo, 1898-1901, partner in the firm of Fehlman and Rastede, at Glidden, Iowa, 1901-04, and partner in the firm Fehlman and Rastede, Pierce, 1904-07. Since 1907 he has been the sole owner of a general merchandise store at Pierce.

A Democrat by tradition and choice, Mr. Rastede served as councilman for nine years, mayor of Pierce, one term, and chairman of the Democratic central committee for one term. He is a member of the Lions Club of Pierce, the Federation of Nebraska Retailers, Pierce Community Club and the Geographic Society of Washington, D. C. He is president of the school board, has been chairman of the Pierce County Red Cross Chapter since 1920, and holds membership in the Nebraskana Society.

He is affiliated with the Zion Evangelical Lutheran Church of Pierce, and holds membership in Walther League and Lutheran Laymen's League. His social club is the Pierce Golf Club and his favorite sports are golfing, hiking, baseball, and football. His hobby is reading.

On June 27, 1906, he was united in marriage with Eva Lydia Mohrman at Pierce. Mrs. Rastede, who was a piano instructor until 1906, was born at Sterling, Nebraska, November 16, 1880, the daughter of Christian Mohrman a pioneer miller and merchant. Four children were

born to them: Luella Louise, February 13, 1909, who died April 30, 1909; Letha Marie, July 15, 1910, who was graduated from the fine arts department of the University in 1931; Winifred Alma, July 26, 1912, who is a student at the University of Nebraska; and Fredrick Leonard, September 3, 1914, who is a senior at Pierce High School. Residence: Pierce.

Kenneth Alberto Rawson

Kenneth Alberto Rawson, superintendent of Dix Rural High School, was born at Arlington, Iowa, December 10, 1905, son of Guy Lyman and Lilly (Walrath) Rawson.

The father, a school executive, banker and farmer, was born at Millgrove Hollow, 7 miles north of Arlington, Iowa, January 17, 1872. His ancestry is English, and the genealogy of the family is traced to John and Priscilla Alden.

Lilly Walrath was born at Arlington, in 1874, and died at Fayette, Iowa, January 22, 1927. She was a teacher in her early days, and was of Holland Dutch ancestry.

Mr. Rawson attended the public schools of Arlington, Iowa, and Fayette, Iowa, and was graduated from Fayette Consolidated High School in 1924. He received his Bachelor of Arts degree from Upper Iowa University, and in 1931 was a student at the State University of Colorado. During his high school days he received seven letters in athletics, and was captain of the basketball, two years. He was high school senior class president, president of the Young Men's Christian Association, at Upper Iowa Unversity, participated in eleven inter-collegiate debates and is a member of Pi Kappa Delta.

His first year after leaving college, Mr. Rawson taught in public school. He was promoted to the superintendency, which he has held for three years.

On June 11, 1930, he was married to Ruth Jessie Watson at Plainfield, Iowa. She was born at O'Neill. Nebraska, January 9, 1908, and is of English and Pennsylvania-Dutch descent.

Mr. Rawson is a Republican. He is affiliated with the Methodist Church, is a member of the National Education Association and the Nebraska State Teachers Association. He is an Odd Fellow. His hobbies are reading, hunting and fishing. He is an ardent golfer. Residence: Dix. (Photograph in Album).

Grant Thomas Ray

A resident of Nebraska, since 1887, Grant Thomas Ray was born at Darlington, Wisconsin, October 1, 1868, the son of Allen C. and Fannie (Dean) Ray. His father, a farmer, was born in Ohio, and died at Walnut, Iowa, January 1, 1890. His mother, who died in 1918, was a native of Liverpool, England.

Mr. Ray was graduated from Walnut High School in 1886, and the following year entered the drug business at Osceola. He is now a jeweler. He is a member of the Red Cross, the Osceola Community Club, Nebraskana Society, and the Ancient Free and Accepted Masons. He is affiliated with the Presbyterian Church of Osceola, is a member of the Republican party, and holds membership in the Modern Woodmen of America.

His marriage to Lizze B. Henderson was solemnized at Osceola, October 10, 1889. Mrs. Ray was born at Marshall, Michigan, July, 1868, and died at Osceola, February 20, 1920. To this marriage three children were born: Glenn S., who is employed by the government in the agricultural department at Columbus, Ohio; Donald H., who is manager of Kresge's Store in Ohio; and Allen G., who is a jeweler at Spokane, Washington. Residence: Osceola.

John Edward Ray

A leading lawyer and an outstanding citizen of Hastings, John Edward Ray has been a resident of Nebraska for more than thirty-eight years. Born in Fulton County, Illinois, May 19, 1882, he is the son of Archie and Rachel (McCormick) Ray. His father, a native of Belfast, Ireland, came to America at the age of five years with his parents, and was a successful farmer in Nebraska for many years. His death occurred in Webster County, on August 20, 1897. Rachel McCormick was born in County Donegal, Ireland, August 13, 1850, came to America when ten years of age, and is now living in Grand Island.

Mr. Ray attended public school, the Bladen High School and Peru State Normal School. Later he attended the law college of the University of Nebraska, and was admitted to practice on June 12, 1913. Among his honors at the university are Kappa Sigma, Phi Alpha Tau, Phi Delta Phi and the Vikings. At Peru, he was a member of the football, baseball and basketball teams.

For some time Mr. Ray was county superintendent of schools in Fillmore County. He has been engaged in practice for the past sixteen years, and has been elected and served as county judge of Clay County. During the World War he was attorney for the Council of Defense of Clay County, a member of the draft board, and was commissioned, but never called for active service.

Judge Ray's religious affiliation is with the Congregational Church. He is a Mason and Shriner, a member of the Nebraska State Bar Association, and was recently made a life member of The Nebraskana Society. Residence: Hastings.

Saunders Wilfley Ray

Saunders Wilfley Ray, cashier of the First National Bank of Fairbury and director of the Jefferson County Bank of Daykin, was born at Maryville, Missouri, November 21, 1888.

On November 2, 1909, he was married to Naomi Belle Armstrong at Maryville. She was born there on December 21, 1888 and is a member of the Daughters of the American Revolution. Mr. and Mrs. Ray have one daughter, Naomi, born December 28, 1913.

Mr. Ray is a Democrat, a member of the First Presbyterian Church, the Chamber of Commerce, the Kiwanis Club, the Masons and the Fairbury Country Club. Residence: Fairbury.

Clifford Downes Rayburn

Clifford Downes Rayburn was born at Roseville, Illinois, January 8, 1888, the son of James Alfred and Anna Elmira (Downes) Rayburn. His father, a farmer, was born at Spring Garden, Illinois, March 3, 1856, and died at Smithfield, Nebraska, April 6, 1927; his ancestry was Scotch and Irish. His mother was born of English and Irish parentage at South Prairie, Illinois, February 11, 1864.

Mr. Rayburn attended high school at Bertrand, Nebraska, and took a business course at Boyles College in Omaha. He has been a farmer near Elwood, Nebraska, for several years. He has been director in the local school board for the past four years, has been secretary-treasurer of the Farmers Union for three years, and is a member of the Modern Woodmen of America and the Ancient Free and Accepted Masons.

He is affiliated with the Methodist Episcopal Church of Elwood. His hobby is better schools. On June 3, 1917, he was united in marriage with Mattie Fern Johnson at Elwood. Mrs. Rayburn, who is of Scotch and English descent, was born at Macedonia, Iowa, May 20, 1888. Four children were born to this marriage: Shirley, January 15, 1922, who died January 16, 1922; Duane, January 25, 1924; Janet, May 1, 1926; and Allan, January 26, 1929. Residence: Elwood.

Thomas Middleton Raysor

Thomas M. Raysor, educator at the University of Nebraska, was born at Chapel Hill, Texas, March 9, 1895, the son of Paul Montgomery and Mary (Matthews) Raysor. His father, who was a physician, was born at Orangeburg, South Carolina, May, 1863, and died at Bryan, Texas, May, 1928. His mother was born at Chapel Hill, August 17, 1872.

Dr. Raysor was graduated from Allen Academy, Bryan, Texas, 1911. He holds these degrees: A. B., Harvard University, 1917; A. M., Harvard, 1920; Ph. D., Harvard, 1922. He is a member of Phi Beta Kappa.

He served as instructor at the Allen Academy, 1914-15, was instructor at A. and M. College of Texas, 1917-18; served as associate professor of the State College of Washington, 1924-29, and professor, 1929-30. Since 1930 he has been professor and chairman of the department of English at the University of Nebraska. He is the author of various articles published in professional journals, and is editor of *Coleridge's Shakespearean Criticism*.

During the World War he served as a private in the American Expeditionary Forces. He is a member of the Modern Language Association of America. His social club is the University Club. He is interested in literary history.

His marriage to Ellen Devereux Koopman, took place at Cohasset, Massachusetts, July 5, 1923. Mrs. Raysor was born at Katvijk, Holland, July 10, 1898. Their two children are as follows: Cecily, born September 18, 1826; and Joan, born October 11, 1928. Residence: Lincoln.

Micheal Edmund Rea

A pioneer farmer in York County, Micheal Edmund Rea has lived in this state for 51 years. He was born in DeWitt County, Illiois, February 14, 1871, the son of Thomas Edmund and Margaret Maria Rea. His father, who was also a farmer, was born in County Limerick, Ireland, December 21, 1825, came to America in 1843, and died at McCool Junction, York County, Nebraska, April 13, 1912; he was a Democrat and was interested in political and civic affairs; he served in the Civil War.

His mother was born in Tipperary, Ireland, June 22, 1836, and died at Chicago, Illinois, December 18, 1922. She was an ardent church worker and homemaker.

Mr. Rea attended elementary schools in Illinois and Nebraska. He has been a farmer for many years and is still active. A Democrat, he served as township road overseer in York County for several years. He is a member of the Farmers Union Association, Modern Woodmen of America, Ancient Order of United Workmen, the Red Cross, and the Nebraskana Society. He is affiliated with St. Patrick's Catholic Church and is an active member of the Knights of Columbus. During the World War Mr. Rea took a prominent part in Red Cross and Salvation Army activities. His sport is baseball, and his chief recreation is reading.

He was married to Mary Ellen McMahon at Aurora, Hamilton County, Nebraska, April 29, 1914. Mrs. Rea, whose Irish ancestors were farmers, was born at McCool Junction, April 22, 1892. To this marriage ten children were born: Thomas, born May 27, 1915; Cecilia, born October 13, 1916; Frank, born March 6, 1918; David, born December 10, 1919; Agnes, born July 26, 1921; Lawrence, born January 28, 1923; Eileen, born December 17, 1924; Margaret, born January 28, 1927; Gene, born April 17, 1929; and Roseanne, born April 7, 1931. Thomas, Cecilia, and Frank, are students in the McCool Junction High School. Residence: McCool Junction.

Elberti Ready

A leading professional man in Cedar County for forty years, Elberti Ready, born in Traer, Iowa, on March 12, 1868, is the son of William Lane and Rachel A. Ready.

His father was born December 1, 1842, and followed the occupation of a farmer. His ancestors came from Wales.

Mr. Ready attended the Cincinnati, Ohio, Law School after he had completed his elementary and high school work. There he received his degree of Doctor of Laws. He was united in marriage with Amanda Charlotte Hoese, on June, 11, 1895, in Hinton, Iowa. To this union three children were born: F. L., born May 25, 1896, who is married to Edith Shom; Dorothy, born in 1898, who died in 1909; and George, born December 1, 1901, who is married to Mildred McKnight. Dr. F. L. Ready is practicing medicine in Los Angeles, and George is with his father in his law office.

Elberti Ready is a Republican and has been county attorney of Cedar County. He is city attorney in Hartington, and several other towns in Cedar County, and is director of the First National Bank at Crofton. During the World War, Mr. Ready was active in drives and also in the Red Cross, giving addresses and speeches at various times. At one time Mr. Ready was mayor of Hartington, and a member of the library board, and is now a member of the Chamber of Commerce. He holds membership in the Independent Order of Odd Fellows Lodge, and was grand instructor in 1929-30. He is a member of the Nebraskana Society and the Hartington Country Club. Residence: Hartington.

Annie Dorrington Reavis

At Whitestown, Onedia County, New York, on October 24, 1845, Annie Dorrington Reavis was born, the daughter of David and Ann Barnard (Wood) Dorrington. Her father who was a carpenter and merchant and the first mayor of Falls City, Nebraska, under the statehood, was born at Chestnut, England, January 11, 1812, and died at Falls City, June 28, 1885.

Her mother was a colorful figure in pioneer history; she fed and assisted escaping slaves through the underground railway system. She was born at Ware, England, April 5, 1805, and died at Falls City, June 16, 1879.

Mrs. Reavis attended the Elmira Female Seminary in New York State, after which she taught school, in 1865, at Falls City. She has been a resident of Nebraska for 66 years. She is the author of a recent article on *Methodism*, published in the *Nebraska State Journal*.

Her marriage to Isham Reavis was solemnized at Falls City, May 19, 1864. Mr. Reavis, who was born in Cass County, Illinois, January 28, 1836, a lawyer and former judge of the United States Court of Arizona territory, whose family was originally from North Carolina. Five children were born to them, four of whom are living: Annie Minnie, born April 7, 1865, who married Thomas J. Gist; Isham, born October 19, 1866, who died December 14, 1866; David Dorrington, born December 19, 1867, who married Grace G. Yutzy; Charles Frank, born September 5, 1870, who married Myrtle Abbey, and who was congressman from the first district of Nebraska throughout the war period; and Burton Isham, born December 2, 1875, who married Lena Stites.

From 1883 to 1886 Mrs. Reavis was a member of the board of education of Falls City; has been on the board of stewards of the Methodist Episcopal Church for 35 years; has been superintendent of the primary department of the church for 20 years; and church organist for 10 years. She is a member of the Red Cross and the Eastern Star, the Sorosis Club, and the Nebraskana Society. Her hobbies are church work and reading. Residence: Falls City.

Charles Frank Reavis

Charles Frank Reavis, son of Isham and Annie Minnie Reavis, was born at Falls City, Nebraska, September 5, 1870. Isham Reavis was a native of Sangamon County, Illinois, born in 1836. who died at Falls City, on May 11, 1914; he was federal judge for Arizona Territory, appointed by President Grant. Annie M. Reavis was born in

New York State, October 17, 1846, and makes her home at Falls City.

Mr. Reavis was graduated from the Falls City High School in 1888, and attended Northwestern University. He was admitted to the bar of Nebraska, on March 7, 1892, and has since been engaged in the practice of law. A Republican, he was elected county attorney of Richardson County, member of congress four terms from the first Nebraska district, resigned June, 1922. He also served as assistant U. S. Attorney General at Washington, for two years, when resigned.

On June 25, 1895, he was married to Myrta Lee Abbey, at Falls City. Mrs. Reavis was born in Richardson County, April 13, 1871, of English descent. They have two sons, Charles Frank, born May 3, 1896, and John Wallace, born November 15, 1898.

In 1918, Mr. Reavis served as a member of the Commission to France. He is a member of Westminster Presbyterian Church. He enjoys golf and reading. Residence: Lincoln.

David Dorrington Reavis

David D. Reavis was born at Falls City, Nebraska, December 19, 1867, the son of Annie Dorrington Reavis and Isham Reavis. His father, who was a United States judge in the court of Arizona territory and a lawyer at Falls City, was born at Chandlersville, Illinois, January 26, 1836, and died at Falls City, May 8, 1914. His great grandfather was in the battle of King's Mountain in North Carolina in the Revolution; the family was originally Irish and English.

His mother was born October 24, 1845, at Elmira, New York. She was a teacher in the Falls City public schools, has been a Sunday School teacher for over 30 years, is worthy matron of the Eastern Star, and president of the Sorosis Club. Her father and mother, David Dorrington and Ann Wood of Cheshunt and Ware, England, came to Falls City in 1857, where her father was active in civic affairs and was the first mayor of the city.

Mr. Reavis was graduated from the Falls City High School in 1885. He then attended the Methodist Episcopal College in York, Nebraska, for two years, after which he was a student at the University of Nebraska. He has lived all his life in Nebraska where from 1887 to 1925 he engaged in the undertaking business. Since 1925, when he was admitted to the bar at Falls City, he has practiced law.

In the World War he assisted in all loan drives during which time he addressed farmers in three schools, arriving at the full quota at each meeting. He is a member of the Nebraska Bar Association, the Commercial Club of Falls City, the Rotary Club and the Red Cross. He is a Mason, an Elk, and Knight of Pythias. He was a member of the Falls City school board, the Nebraskana Society and the Nebraska Historical Society. Mr. Reavis takes a special interest in the latter since he is intimately acquainted with the history of Falls City and with the lives of many notable Nebraskans. He is also a student of Kansas and Arizona history in which he is well versed. He is a member of the Methodist Episcopal Church, and the Falls City Country Club. Reading, traveling, writing, painting and music are his hobbies. His sport is golf. Residence: Falls City.

August Louis Rebbe

August Louis Rebbe, farmer and banker, was born in Dodge County, Nebraska, February 28, 1880, son of Henry and Wilhelmine (Siever) Rebbe. His father, who was born in Hanover, Germany, May 12, 1841, was a pioneer farmer in Nebraska, and died at Hooper, March 22, 1908. His wife, Wilhelmine, was born in Germany, January 12, 1853, and is still living. Her father was a florist.

Mr. Rebbe attended the rural schools of Dodge County

and Fremont Normal School. He was married to Ida Carstens in Cuming County, Nebraska, January 29, 1907. Mrs. Rebbe, who comes of a family of farmers, was born at Scribner, November 2, 1884. There are three children: Emma, born December 9, 1907, married Raymond Voss; Lloyd, born September 6, 1909; and Carson, born August 20, 1910.

Active in the affairs of his community during his entire life, Mr. Rebbe served as a director of the First National Bank of Hooper, seven years, and for twelve years has been treasurer of School District No. 75. A Mason, he is a member of Hooper Lodge No. 72, Ancient Free and Accepted Masons at Hooper, and Tangier Temple of the Shrine at Omaha. He is a member of the Grace Lutheran Church and of the Nebraskana Society. Residence: Hooper. (Photograph in Album).

Edwin Barak Record

A resident of Nebraska for the past 46 years, Edwin Barak Record was born at New Portland, Maine, September 19, 1858, and since the 1880's has been engaged in farming and ranching near Osmond, Nebraska. His father, Barak Record, who was a farmer and school teacher, was born at Green, Maine, and died at Springfield, Massachusetts, in March, 1867. His mother, Esther Maria (Booker) Record was born at Hallowell, Maine, January 16, 1816, and died at Osmond, August 16, 1903. Her English ancestors came to this country prior to the Revolution and her paternal grandfather served as captain in that war.

Mr. Record has been a farmer, drayman, and rancher for many years, and has watched Nebraska grow from a pioneer frontier country to a well-organized group of cities and towns. He is a member of the Methodist Episcopal Church at Osmond, has been a member of the Ancient Order of United Workmen for 35 years, and holds membership in the Nebraskana Society. During the World War he bought Liberty bonds and was a three minute speaker for a time.

On April 12, 1880, he was united in marriage with Henrietta Morlan at Virginia, South Dakota. Mrs. Record, whose ancestry is English and Irish, was born at Fairmount, West Virginia, June 25, 1858. Their children are: Pearl Esther, born February 6, 1881; Elmer Marion, born August 22, 1883, who married Nicoline Nicolaison; Irwin McPherson, born July 30, 1886, who married Louise Thompson; Ralph Merton, born May 12, 1889, who married Florence Hendee; and Winifred Margaret, born June 19, 1899. Residence: Asmond.

Voyle Dixon Rector

Voyle Dixon Rector was born at Tobias, Nebraska, December 28, 1891. He is the son of Edgar Twilliger Rector, who was born at Oskaloosa, Iowa, June 5, 1870. Edgar Rector is president of the Fairmont Creamery Company of Omaha, and is descended from John Jacob Richter who came from Germany in 1714 and established Rectortown, Virginia. He married Tessie Belle Dixon, who was born at Hinkletown, Nebraska, December 8, 1872.

Mr. Rector attended the Omaha public schools and was graduated from Central High School in 1911. He received his B. S. degree from Dartmouth College in 1915, and attended Pomona College, Claremont, California, in 1916. He is a member of Alpha Delta Phi. Beginning his business career as salesman for the Fairmont Creamery at Syracuse, New York, he was promoted to superintendent at Buffalo, and manager at Detroit, and is now assistant general territory manager for the Fairmont Creamery Company, at Omaha.

He was married to Lillian Farnam Chapin at Philadelphia, September 15, 1917. Mrs. Rector was born at Lincoln, July 22, 1892, and is descended from Deacon Samuel Chapin of Springfield, Massachusetts. There are two children, Robert Chapin, born August 10, 1921, and Irving Chapin, born February 17, 1923.

During the World War Mr. Rector served as captain (battery commander) of the 350 Field Artillery. He is a member of the American Legion and is a Mason and Shriner. His clubs are the University Club and the Omaha Country Club. Residence: Omaha.

Arlie Clay Reddick

Born at Yutan, Nebraska, October 22, 1873, Arlie Clay Reddick has been engaged in the grocery business on North Cotner Boulevard, in Lincoln for the past thirty-six years. He is the son of Leander Marion and Mary Elizabeth (Saffer) Reddick, the former a retired grocer, born in Ohio, January 6, 1846. Mary, his wife, was born in Indiana, in 1849 and died at Lincoln, January 1, 1902.

Arlie Clay Reddick was educated in the rural schools of Saunders County, and at Cotner College Academy. On April 11, 1900, he was married to Grace May Olmsted at Holyoke, Colorado. Mrs. Reddick, who was of English descent, was born at David City, Nebraska, and died at Lincoln on August 29, 1930.

Six children survive her, Vera, born March 6, 1902; Edith, born October 29, 1903; Lawrence, born September 27, 1905, who married Frances Hansen; Mildred, born February 28, 1908; Lyle, born August 10, 1911; and Leah, born July 26, 1914.

Mr. Reddick is independent in politics. He is a member of the Lincoln Retail Grocers Association (director 1928, 1931), a member of Bethany Christian Church, and a life member of The Nebraskana Society. His favorite sports are hunting and fishing. Residence: Lincoln.

John Wood Redick

John W. Redick, a lifetime resident of Nebraska, was born at Omaha, Nebraska, June 26, 1884, the son of William A. and Mary (Otis) Redick. His father, who was born at Omaha, April 2, 1861, has been a judge of the district court at Omaha for many years; he is the son of John I. Redick, a pioneer Omahan. John W. Redick's mother, who is a member of the Colonial Dames and is connected with the Otis family, was born at Omaha, September 21, 1863.

Mr. Redick was graduated from the public schools of Omaha in 1899 and in 1903 was graduated from Culver Military Academy in Indiana; was awarded his A. B. degree at Williams College at Williamstown, Massachusetts in 1907, where he was a member of Theta Delta Chi. He was Nebraska state golf champion in 1919 and 1925.

For some time treasurer of the Merriam Commission Company, he is now president of the John W. Redick Company, is secretary of the O. K. T. Mines Incorporated, and is a member of the Omaha Chamber of Commerce and the Omaha Grain Exchange. He holds membership in University Club, the Omaha Country Club, and the Omaha Athletic Club. His sport is golfing. His hobby is horses. He is a Republican.

His marriage to Florence Mary Heap was solemnized at Williamstown, Massachusetts, June 21, 1910. Mrs. Redick, who was at one time president of the Oamha Junior League, was born in England, February 6, 1886, and died at Omaha, July 6, 1929. Two children were born to them, William, born February 14, 1911, who died in 1918; and John W., Jr., born March 9, 1917. Residence: Omaha.

William Armstrong Redick

William Armstrong Redick, lawyer and judge, was born in Omaha, April 2, 1859, and has been a prominent figure in the life of the state for the past fifty years. He is the son of John Irwin Redick, born at Wooster, Ohio, July 29, 1828. John Redick was a lawyer, and from 1875-

76 was judge of New Mexico. He was of Scotch-Irish descent. He died at Omaha, April 2, 1906. He was married to Mary Elizabeth Higby, a native of Alleghany, Pennsylvania. She died at Omaha in 1864.

William A. Redick attended Omaha public schools and studied at Omaha High School a year and a half. From 1870-71 he attended Cornell College, Iowa. He was admitted to the bar at Omaha, in June 1882, and has since been engaged in the practice of law, except at such times as he has been on the bench. A Republican he was district judge from 1904 to 1912, and was acting Supreme Court judge for three years or more. In 1915 he was again made district judge of the fourth judicial district, where he now serves. He is the author of more than one hundred opinions of the Supreme Court.

He was married to Mary Otis Wood at Omaha, September 12, 1883. Mrs. Redick is a native of Omaha, born September 20, 1864, and a daughter of Reuben and Philena Wood. They have one son, John, born June 26, 1884, who married Florence Heap. He is a grain commission merchant.

Affiliated with the Protestant Episcopal Church, he is a member of All Saints and is warden and vestryman of that church, and chancellor of the eastern diocese of Nebraska. He has been senior warden since 1920. He is a trustee of Brownell Hall, and a member of the Nebraskana Society and the Nebraska State Historical Society. He is a member of the Red Cross and of the Chamber of Commerce and of the Woodmen of the World. His professional organizations include the American Bar Association, the Nebraska State and Omaha Douglas County Bar Associations.

His sports are golf and billiards, and his clubs include the Omaha Club, the Omaha Athletic Club, the Omaha Country Club and the Elks Club. Residence: Omaha.

William David Redmond

William David Redmond, educator and banker, was born in Lee County, Illinois, February 14, 1870. He is the son of John and Katherine (Bassett) Redmond, the former a farmer. John Redmond was born in Ireland June 15, 1830, and died at Crab Orchard April 4, 1905. Katherine Redmond was born in Ireland August 30, 1830 and died at Crab Orchard, January 11, 1916.

Educated in the rural schools of Johnson County until 1888, Mr. Redmond completed a high school and collegiate course at Western Normal College, Shenandoah, Iowa, on August 18, 1890. He at that time received the degree of Bachelor of Didactics. Later, from 1892-93 he attended Western Normal College at Lincoln; during the summer of 1895 was a student at Fremont Normal, in 1896 spent a summer session at Lincoln Normal University, and in 1902 attended Peru State Teachers College.

A teacher in the rural schools of Nebraska 1890-91; he was superintendent at Crab Orchard 1891-92, Brock 1894-1900. He was deputy county clerk of Nemaha County 1900-02; registrar at Peru State Teachers College 1902-07; assistant state superintendent 1907-10 and registrar Wayne Teachers College 1910-18. From 1918 until the present he has been vice-president and manager of the Farmers State Bank of Mason City.

Mr. Redmond represented Nemaha County in the Nebraska legislature in 1907. He is a member of Lodge No. 170, Ancient Free and Accepted Masons, and served as grand orator of Grand Lodge of Nebraska, Independent Order of Odd Fellows, the Modern Woodmen of America, the Order of Eastern Star, and the Scottish Rite Masons.

He was director of the Thrift Association at Wayne during the World War, is secretary of the Mason City Community Service Club, a member of the Nebraska State Historical Sosiety and The Nebraskana Society. His relgious affiliation is with the Methodist Episcopal Church. Residence: Mason City.

Albert Alison Reed

Since 1883, A. A. Reed has lived in Nebraska, with the exception of two years, and has been prominent in the educational field for some years. He was born at West Lebanon, Pennsylvania, May 5, 1866, the son of Robert and Caroline (Fulton) Reed. His father, a farmer, was born in Indiana County, April 1, 1835, and died in Gage County, Nebraska, March 14, 1907. He served in the 206th Infantry of the Pennsylvania Volunteers during the Civil War, and held membership in the Grand Army of the Republic. His Scotch-Irish ancestors came to America during the Revolution. His mother, who was of English descent, was born in Indiana County, August 26, 1834, and died at Battle Creek, Michigan, October 4, 1915. Her ancestors were pioneers in Indiana County.

Professor Reed attended the rural schools of Knox County; the high school at Monmouth, Illinois; the preparatory department of Monmouth College; and the high school at Beatrice, Nebraska, where he was graduated in 1885. He received the A. B. degree, 1898, and the A. M. degree, 1912, at the University of Nebraska, where he was elected to membership in Phi Delta Kappa and of Acacia. From 1915 to 1916 he was a student at Columbia University.

He has held the following professional positions: rural school teacher, 1883-84; ward principal of the Beatrice schools, 1886-87; superintendent of schools at Crete, Nebraska, 1893-1900; county superintendent of schools in Gage County, 1892-93; principal of the Odell schools, 1888-91; principal of the Keokuk, Iowa, High School, 1900-02; and superintendent of city schools at Superior, Nebraska, 1902-07.

Since February 23, 1907, he has been connected with the University of Nebraska as director of the University Extension Division, professor of secondary education. university examiner, and member of the committee on advanced standing in all undergraduate colleges. He is co-author of *Essentials of Teaching Reading*, published by Sherman and Reed, 1905-17. A Republican, he was elected county superintendent of schools in Gage County, taking office in January, 1892.

Professor Reed is a member of the Nebraska Schoolmasters Club; served for five years as chairman of the commission on secondary education of the North Central Association of Colleges and Secondary Schools; and for the past 20 years has been chairman of the Nebraska commission of the North Central Association of Colleges and Secondary Schools. He holds membership in the Nebraskana Society; is a member of the Knife and Fork Club, of which he was president in 1928 and 1929; has served as a member of the board of directors, and is state manager of the Nebraska Reading Circle.

He is a life member of the National Educational Association and served as state director of that organization for a time. Professor Reed is a member of the First Presbyterian Church of Lincoln; was a member of the board of directors of the Young Men's Christian Association at the University of Nebraska; is a member of the religious welfare committee at the university; and is chairman of the committee on leadership training in the Boy Scouts of America. He is a member of the Lincoln Chamber of Commerce; is secretary-treasurer and trustee of the board of Presbytery of Nebraska City, in the Presbyterian Church; and is a member of the Lincoln University Club.

Since 1927, Professor Reed has been a member of the state board of examiners for life certificates. He is a Mason. From 1885, to 1892, he served as a member of Company C of the First Regiment, Nebraska National Guard, with rank from private to captain; from 1892, to 1897, was major and assistant adjutant general of the First Brigade, and served as colonel and aide-de-camp on the staff of Governor Sheldon. He commanded Company C in the Indian campaign in 1890-91. During the World

War he was appointed by the United States department of labor to organize the employment service.

His marriage to Mary Jane Bowles was solemnized at Clarence, Cedar County, Iowa, June 28, 1892. Mrs. Reed, whose ancestry is English, was born at Toledo, Tama County, Iowa, March 12, 1866. She is a member of the Daughters of the American Revolution. She is a graduate of Cornell College. They have three children; Merrill Vergil, born February 23, 1894, who married Jean Burroughs; Carolyn Elizabeth, born July 25, 1899, who married William McKinley Powell; and Donald Alison, born October 13, 1907, who married Mary Trude Bronson. Merril, who served in the 40th United States Infantry during the World War, attaining the rank of first lieutenant, served for a time as military instructor at Northwestern University, and is now eastern advertising manager for Sales Management in New York City. Carolyn was graduated from the arts and science college of the University of Nebraska, and from the music department at Nebraska Wesleyan. She is now teaching music at the Pasadena Junior College. Donald was graduated from the college of business administration at the University of Nebraska. He is in business at Los Angeles. Residence: Lincoln.

Alice Mae Reed

Alice Mae Reed, clubwoman, was born at Malvern, Iowa, May 7, 1868, daughter of Thomas Marlin and Jane (Whatt) Aistrope.

Her father was born in Wigift, England, December 11, 1928, and settled in White Cloud township, Iowa, in 1864. He was a farmer and stockman and a member of the Silver Creek Ranger Cavalry. His death occurred at Malvern on January 9, 1915. His mother, Marie Mason, and her father, George Aistrope, were born in England.

Jane Whatt was born in Wigift, England, December 3, 1830, and died at Malvern, Iowa, December 3, 1898. She was a mother of eleven children, a devoted house wife and a friend of everyone. She was descended from the Whatt, Wressle, and West families, of England.

Alice Mae Aistrope attended district school in Malvern, Iowa, and afterward attended Baptist Academy and Tabor College. She was graduated in music from Northwestern Normal College at Shenandoah, Iowa in 1888. While in college, she was a member of Delphian literary society.

On March 10, 1891, she was married to Willis Ellsworth Reed, lawyer and investor, at Malvern, Iowa. (See Nebraskana).

Mrs. Reed is a Democrat. During 1916 to 1918 she was treasurer of the Nebraska Legislative League of Lincoln. For four years she served as president of the Dalith Chapter of the Delphian Society in Madison, and was secretary to the first district Delphians of Nebraska for two years.

She is a member of the First Presbyterian Church of Madison, the Red Cross, the Madison County Historical Society, and for several years was a member of the Madison Library Board. She is a charter member of the Madison Woman's Club of which she was president 1905-1906; vice-president of third district of Women's Clubs 1906-07, which was organized under her administration. For one year Mrs. Reed was president of the Presbyterian Aid Society, and for two years superintendent of its Sunday school.

Mrs. Reed is a charter member of Piead Chapter No. 99 of the Order of Eastern Star, a member of the Madison County Golf Club, while her hobby is civic improvements. She has assisted greatly in farm organizations for the benefit of the farmer. During the late war she was an active member of the Red Cross, made heavy contributions to it not only in Madison, but did an immense amount of work as a member of the Red Cross in Lincoln, where Mr. Reed was attorney general. Both she and Mr. Reed were active workers in securing the Chautauqua at Madison when it was necessary to pay money to obtain outside talent, and Mrs. Reed has taken an active part in later work affording a free chautauqua each year for Madison. Residence: Madison.

Charles Seymour Reed

Charles Seymour Reed was born at Arnold, Nebraska, June 4, 1896. He is the son of Samuel H. Reed, who was born in Ohio, July 7, 1853, a farmer of Yankee descent. Samuel Reed married Alice Winwood, who was born in England, May 30, 1861, and who died at Arnold, December 10, 1923.

Charles Reed was graduated from Arnold High School in 1913, attended Kearney Normal School and the University of Nebraska, and was awarded his A. B. and LL. B. from the University. He was active in Athletics at Kearney in 1913, and is a member of Phi Delta Phi and Pi Kappa Phi.

Admitted to the Nebraska bar in 1921, the same year he was elected on the Republican ticket to the Nebraska legislature, and also served as assistant attorney general of Nebraska 1921-22 inclusive. He is now a member of the law firm of Reed, Ramaciotti and Robinson.

On August 18, 1928, he was married to Frances C. Wahl at Omaha. Mrs. Reed was born at Omaha, January 18, 1901. During the World War Mr. Reed was a second lieutenant of infantry, and is now a captian in the Infantry Officers Reserve Corps. He is a member of the American Legion, the Red Cross, the Chamber of Commerce and the Omaha Executives Association. He belongs to Calvary Baptist Church, is a member of the Scottish Rite and Shrine bodies of the Masons, and is a member of the American, Nebraska State and Omaha-Douglas County Bar Associations. His clubs are the Omaha Athletic and Happy Hollow Country, and his sports are golf and handball. Residence: Omaha.

E. Burkett Reed

Dr. E. Burkett Reed, member of the Lincoln Clinic, was born at Havelock, Nebraska, January 4, 1900, son of Anthony H. and Jane (Hornby) Reed. Anthony Reed was born at Madison, Wisconsin, November 9, 1858, and died at Lincoln, December 18, 1921. He was a farmer of Irish and English descent. His wife, Jane Hornby, was born in England, June 17, 1871, and is still living.

Upon his graduation from District School No. 62, in 1914, Dr. Reed attended Havelock High School, graduating in 1918. In 1923 he received his B. Sc. from the University of Nebraska, and in 1925, his M. D. He took post graduate work at Washington University in 1927; and at Tulane University in 1928. Dr. Burkett was valedictorian of his high school class. A member of Alpha Kappa Kappa, he has served as president, corresponding secretary and treasurer of its building fund.

On November 27, 1923, he was united in marriage to Iva Elaine Jenkins at Lincoln. Mrs. Reed was born at Louisville, Nebraska, January 11, 1900, and died at Lincoln, December 6, 1929. Dr. Burkett's second marriage was to Lora H. Coghill, a registered nurse, who was born at Rogers, Arkansas, January 5, 1904. They were married at Lincoln, May 9, 1930.

Since his admission to practice, Dr. Burkett has been actively engaged, and is associated with The Lincoln Clinic. He is a member of the American Medical Association, the Nebraska State Medical Association and the Iowa-Nebraska Pediatric Society. In connection with his practice he has written *Hypothyroidism in Children* (February, 1929). Dr. Burkett is a member of the Lincoln Chamber of Commerce, and a member of George Washington Lodge of the Ancient Free and Accepted Masons at Havelock, Rebekah Lodge No. 150, and Odd Fellows Lodge No. 244, at Havelock. Residence: Havelock.

Floyd B. Reed

Floyd B. Reed was born at Omaha, Douglas County, Nebraska, February 20, 1889, the son of Irving Lee and Mary Elizabeth (Holmes) Reed. His father, who is a carpenter, was born in Ohio, June 30, 1854; his ancestry is French and Scotch. His mother was born of Scotch and English parentage at McGrawville, New York, February 22, 1857.

Mr. Reed attended the Omaha High School, and for 14 years was connected with the firm of Wright & Wilhelmy Company at Omaha. For 11 years he has been affiliated with the W. M. Dutton & Sons Company at Hastings, Adams County, Nebraska, of which he is now vice president. He is a member of the Chamber of Commerce, the Kiwanis Club, (president 1932), Masons, York Rite and Council, and the Nebraskana Society. He is a member of the Republican Party while his religious affiliiation is with the Presbyterian Church.

On April 12, 1912, he was united in marriage with Alice Agatha Sawyer, at Omaha. Mrs. Reed was born at Fairmont, Nebraska, of English parentage. They have one daughter, Elizabeth Alice, born June 17, 1915. Mr. Reed is interested in kodaking and golfing. He is a member of the Hillside Golf Club. Residence: Hastings.

George Isaac Reed

George I. Reed was born at Montour, Iowa, March 14, 1880, the son of Hiram Isaac and Mary Catherine Rabb Reed. His father, a farmer, was born at Funkstown, Maryland, October 5, 1827, and died at Scotia, Nebraska, May 18, 1896; his ancestors came to this country from England, in 1776. His mother was born in Ohio, January 11, 1839, and died at Scotia, December 6, 1887.

Mr. Reed, who is a leading Nebraska executive, is now manage of the Reed Ice Cream Factory, and is connected with the Randolph Ice Company. He has lived in this state for 48 years, and is interested in community affairs, holding membership in the following organizations: Lion's Club; Red Cross; Nebraskana Society; Young Men's Christian Association; and the Randolph School Board, where he has served since 1924. He is affiliated with the Methodist Church, and holds membership in the Randolph Country Club. His sport is golfing.

His marriage to Elsa Louise Given was solemnized at Lincoln, Lancaster County, Nebraska, June 4, 1913. Mrs. Reed, who is a musician and teacher of piano, was born at Lincoln, August 2, 1890. Their children are: Bruce Vincent, born June 3, 1914; Francis Ann, born March 26, 1916; Willa Marjette, born January 1, 1918; Albert Tindale, born May 11, 1919; and George Dean, born March 21, 1927. Residence: Randolph.

Paul A. Reed

Paul A. Reed, physician, was born at Milo, Iowa, January 12, 1899, the son of Hugh Stephen and Elsie (Hammer) Reed. Hugh S. Reed, a successful physician, was born at Pleasantville, Iowa, September 22, 1879. His father, born in Ohio, in 1843 of Irish parentage, served as a soldier in the Civil War for three and one-half years. His mother was born in Iowa, in 1845. Elsie (Hammer) Reed was born at Swan, Iowa, November 17, 1873. Her father was of Irish descent, and was born in Illinois in 1845, and her mother was born in Iowa, in 1849, of German parentage.

Educated in the public schools of Guide Rock, Nebraska, Paul A. Reed was graduated from Guide Rock High School in 1916. He received his B. S. and M. D. degrees from the University of Nebraska in 1924, and is a member of Sigma Chi, national fraternity, and Nu Sigma Nu, national professional fraternity.

Dr. Reed is married to Beulah Adrienne Gunderson, a registered nurse, who was born at Vermillion, South Dakota, January 4, 1904, of Norwegian parentage. Their

marriage took place on January 6, 1926, at Plattsmouth, Nebraska. Their two children are, Stephen, born March 28, 1927; and Susan, born July 12, 1929.

During the World War he was a private in Company B, the Students' Army Training Corps, at Lincoln, Nebraska. Since 1925 he has held the rank of first lieutenant in the Medical Reserve Corps. He is a member of the Thayer County and Nebraska State Medical Societies, is an 18th degree Mason, and is a member of the Commercial Club and the Nebraskana Society. Dr. Reed is affiliated with the Presbyterian Church of Deshler. Residence: Deshler.

Perry A. C. Reed

Perry A. C. Reed, farmer, stockraiser, and political leader of York County, Nebraska, has been a resident of the state for over 55 years, and is well known in the middlewest for his activities in legislative affairs. He was born at Monroe, Wisconsin, January 22, 1871, the son of John Porter and Emma (Deveraux) Reed.

His father, who was also a farmer, was born at Monroe, July 28, 1847, and died at Henderson, Nebraska, April 16, 1910; his parents were natives of New York, and were of English descent. Emma (Deveraux) Reed, mother of Perry Reed, was born at Monroe, Wisconsin in 1851, and died there, April 22, 1872. She was a talented musician. Her father, who was of French descent, was a soldier in the Civil War; her mother's ancestry was English.

Mr. Reed has been a farmer, stockraiser, and breeder of thoroughbred horses for many years, has served as a member of the state board of agriculture since 1917, was a member of the board of managers of the Nebraska State Fair for seven years, and is today president of the Nebraska State Fair Board. As a Republican, he has held these positions: state representative from Hamilton County, 1917; state senator from Hamilton, York, and Polk counties, 1919-1931.

Due to his legislative activities he has accepted only honorary membership in most civic and community organizations. He is a member of the Nebraskana Society, and is affiliated with the Independent Order of Odd Fellows. His hobby is baseball. During the late war Mr. Reed served as district chairman of all war activities for men in Hamilton County.

His marriage to Abbie Lulu Westcott, occurred at Farmers Valley, Nebraska, March 11, 1896. Mrs. Reed, who was born at Farmers Valley, November 17, 1876, is vitally interested in gardening and poultry raising. Her mother was of New England descent, while her father was English and Dutch. They have four children: Emma J., born November 9, 1897, who married John Harrison; Mildred M., born September 27, 1900, who married Simon Terry Reed; Marjorie L., born October 28, 1903, who married Arthur A. C. Dobler; and Jeanette, born May 29 1906. Emma and Mildred were teachers in public schools for a time. Residence: Henderson.

William Elbridge Reed

For the past 40 years William E. Reed has lived in Nebraska and has been prominent in the banking and livestock commission service in Omaha. He was born at Fulton, Whiteside County, Illinois, May 10, 1872, the son of William and Anna Maria (Johnson) Reed. His father, who was a stone and brick mason, was born of English and Scotch parents at Amboy, Onandaga County, New York, May 13, 1828, and died at Fulton, April 17, 1872. His mother, who was born at Fulton, September 23, 1840, and died there, August 1, 1927, was a nurse, milliner and dressmaker. She endeared herself to her community and family by her kindness and consideration. Her ancestry was English.

Mr. Reed attended the grade and high schools in 1888. Since 1891 he has been connected with the John Clay Company. He became affiliated with this firm as a stenographer and is now manager of the organization. He is vice president of the Farmers National Bank at Central City, Nebraska, and of the Palmer State Bank at Palmer, Nebraska.

He served as a member of the board of education at Omaha for nine years, acting as president most of that time. During the World War he was captain of the home guard troop and was a member of the executive committee of the Omaha Chapter of the Red Cross. He is a member of the Red Cross, Volunteers of America, the Boy Scouts of America, the Young Men's Christian Association and the Omaha Chamber of Commerce. He is a Mason and a member of the Omaha Rotary Club. He holds membership in the Omaha Club. He is affiliated with the Church of Christ, Scientist at Omaha. His hobbies are sailing and all competitive games. He is a Republican.

On March 25, 1896, he was married to Anna Estelle Smith at Omaha. Mrs. Reed, who is of Holland Dutch descent, was born at Lincoln, July 13, 1872. They have two children: Helen, born April 28, 1900, a former librarian, who married Clifford T. McIntyre; and William Barton, born May 19, 1907, who is connected with the New York Life Insurance Company of New York City. Residence: Omaha.

William Iles Reed

William Iles Reed was born in Menard County, Illinois, August 26, 1863, the son of Andrew Jackson Reed and Sarah Jane (Sheneman) Reed. His father was born in Kentucky and died at Topeka, Kansas. His mother was born at Wooster, Ohio, and died at Paltonburg, Missouri.

Mr. Reed was a farmer in Gage County, Nebraska, near Beatrice until 1920. At this time he is mayor of Beatrice, is a member of the Chamber of Commerce and the First Baptist Church.

On October 15, 1885, shortly after his arrival in Nebraska, Mr. Reed was married near Wymore to Addie Clayton. Mrs. Reed, who is the daughter of Mr. and Mrs. Isaac Clayton of Beatrice, was born at Peoria, Illinois, July 30, 1867. They have six children: Ollie; Fred; Ada; Nora; Clarence; and Ethel. Residence: Beatrice.

Willis Ellsworth Reed

Willis Ellsworth Reed, lawyer, was born at Palmyra, Iowa, August 17, 1866, son of William Burton and Margaret Ann (Hamilton) Reed.

The father was born in Crown Point, Indiana, April 25, 1838, and died at Perry, Iowa, August 30, 1926. He was a carpenter and an early pioneer in Iowa. His family came to the United States, settling in Pennsylvania. The grandfather, Thomas Reed, was born in 1812, and his wife, Myria Myrick, was born in the state of Maine in 1814. His father fought in the American Revolution on behalf of the colonists (the father of Thomas Reed). Margaret Ann Hamilton, wife of William Burton Reed, was born near Crown Point, Indiana, July 2, 1843, and died at Des Moines, Iowa, February 4, 1930. She was the daughter of Sanford and Hannah (Linn) Hamilton, both of whose parents fought in the Revolution in America. The paternal grandfather of Hannah Linn served in the British army, deserting to join the American forces. He fought under General Washington.

Willis Ellsworth Reed attended public school at Palmyra, Iowa, and in high school was always active in debating. He was admitted to the bar at Madison, Nebraska, in October, 1888, and has since been in active practice.

On March 10, 1891, he was married to Alice Mae Aistrope at Malvern, Iowa. Mrs. Reed was born at Malvern, May 7, 1868, of English ancestry (See *Nebraskana*). An Independent Democrat, Mr. Reed has always been a figure in local political life. He was the first city attorney after Madison became a city, was attorney general of Nebraska two successive terms, January 7, 1915-January 9, 1919. He served as secretary and treasurer of the Attorneys General Association, which was comprised of one attorney general from each state, during his term of office.

He was campaign speaker for William Jennings Bryan for president in 1896, and for the Democratic party in each national campaign since that time, special attention being given to the campaigne of W. V. Allen for the United States senate and for Governors Powers, Holcomb and Poynter, and for Judge J. J. Sullivan for supreme judge, Judge Samuel Maxwell for congress, Gilbert M. Hitchcock, the United States senator. Mr. Reed was himself twice candidate for the nomination for the United States senate but failed to secure the nomination.

He is also the author of the uniform freight and passenger rate, the plan adopted by the United States government when it took over the railways during the war and which is in practice today. In 1912 Mr. Reed spoke in Omaha, Lincoln, and Alliance, his speech being published in the *Lumberman of St. Louis* and the *Omaha World-Herald*. In the 1880's Mr. Reed taught school in Guthrie and Audubon counties in Iowa. He taught in Madison County, Nebraska, during 1886, 1887, and 1888, and has since been engaged in the practice of law. He is admitted to all superior courts including the United States Supreme Court (1898).

During the late war he assisted in all local drives and was attorney for the State Council of Defense. He is a member of the American and Madison County District Bar Association, the Red Cross, and the Masons (past master, past worthy patron Order of Eastern Star, associate worthy patron 1932; Tangier Temple Ancient Arabic Order Nobles of the Mystic Shrine, Omaha (one of its life members). He is a life member of the Nebraskana Society. His hobby is economic reform. His favorite sport is golf. Residence: Madison.

Ernest Leonard Reeker

Ernest Leonard Reeker, county judge of Madison County, was born in Madison County, December 9, 1898, son of Frederick William and Rosa (Lucht) Reeker. The father, a farmer and stockman, was born in Germany, February 25, 1873, and came to America at the age of seven with his parents. He died in Madison County, December 16, 1921. Rosa Lucht was born in Madison County, December 10, 1878, her mother being one of the first white women to settle in Madison County, 1867.

Judge Reeker attended Deer Creek Public School. He entered Midland College in 1912, and thereafter took his pre-legal course in Valparaiso University. He received his Bachelor of Laws degree from the University of Indianapolis in May, 1921. He was active in debating and dramatic clubs, and became a member of Sigma Delta Kappa.

Admitted to the bar on June 21, 1921, he has since been in active practice. He is the author of *Big Business*, which relates to juvenile court, published in 1930 in the September issue of Kiwanis International Magazine. Mr. Reeker is a Republican and has been county judge of Madison County since January 1, 1925. He was re-elected without opposition in the year 1928, and was re-nominated in the primary of 1932.

On November 15, 1921, he was married to Cecilia Geraldine Huenergardt at Pierce. Mrs. Reeker was born at College View, Nebraska, March 8, 1897. They have one son, Ernest L., Jr., born October 12, 1924.

During the World War Mr. Reeker was in Officers Training Camp at Omaha, and did some dramatic work for the Red Cross. He is affiliated with Trinity Lutheran Church, is a member of the Community Club of Madison, the Lions Club, the Kiwanis Club (vice president 1931), the National Prohibition Association, and the Nebraska District and State Bar Association.

Judge Reeker enjoys hunting, fishing, and landscape gardening, the last mentioned being his real hobby. Residence: Madison.

David D. Rees

David D. Rees, a noted Nebraska educator and editor, was born at New London, Howard County, Indiana, May 4, 1871, the son of Melvina (Seward) and Joseph M. Rees. His father, who was born in Tennessee in 1844 and died at Washington, D. C., 1909, was a clergyman; he served in Company G, 89th Indiana Regiment, in the Civil War. His mother was born in Ohio in 1844 and died at Parkersburg, West Virginia, in 1909.

Mr. Rees was graduated from high school at Kokomo, Indiana; was awarded the A. B. degree at Battle Creek College in Michigan, 1895; and received the A. M. degree at Union College, Lincoln, 1903. He has held the following positions; professor of English, Union College, 1897-1905; professor of English at Mt. Vernon College, Mt. Vernon, Ohio, 1905-10; principal of the Forest Home Academy, Mt. Vernon. Washington, 1910-14; professor of English at Walla Walla College, Walla Walla, Washington, 1915-17; principal of the Campion Academy, Loveland, Colorado, 1917-18; educational secretary of the Central Union Conference at Lincoln, 1919-26; and since 1927 editor of the *Christian Record*, a national journal for the blind printed in Braille, at Lincoln.

He is the author of *How to Punctuate*, a textbook; *A Hint to the Wise*, a book dealing with the common errors in English; and numerous articles and poems printed in magazines and journals. He has been a resident of Nebraska for 21 years, and has been active in the educational and religious welfare of the state during that time. He is an ordained minister in the Seventh day Adventist Church. He is a member of the Nebraskana Society.

He was married to Anna Miller at Nashville, Tennessee. Mrs. Rees was born at Nashville, Tennessee, in 1873. Their children are: Virginia, who married Professor E. B. Ogden, a member of the Union College faculty; Dee Miller, who married Isabelle Wilson, and who is a practicing physician at Los Angeles, California; Edna, who is teaching in the high school in Bennet, Nebraska; and Conard, who is principal of the high school at Denton, Nebraska. Residence: Lincoln.

Harry A. Rees

Harry A. Rees, automobile dealer and executive, was born at Pilger, Nebraska, May 2, 1894, son of Howell and Alice (Holmes) Rees. Howell Rees, a native of Carmarthern, Wales, born March 16, 1854, came from Cardiff to Pilger in 1879. There he began as a farmer and stockman. He is Nebraska's leading pioneer Shorthorn cattle breeder, and has bred and shown more winners than any other Nebraskan. His wife, Alice was born at Malvern, Iowa, in January, 1865, of Yankee ancestry.

Educated in the public schools, Harry A. Rees was graduated from Pilger High School in 1912 and from that time until 1915 was a student at the University of Nebraska. While there he was active in track.

A rancher for three years at Long Pine, Mr. Rees entered the automobile business in 1919, when he purchased the Chevrolet Garage. He is a partner in the firm of Rees-Wegner Auto Company and president of the Blue Star Oil Products Company.

On October 16, 1916, Mr. Rees was married to Hanna M. Wegner at Lincoln. Mrs. Rees, who was born at Wisner, August 22, 1893, is of German descent. Her grandmother, who is 92 years of age, is still living. There is one son, Dale Willis, born May 16, 1918, who is a freshman in high school. An accomplished pianist, he is also athletic, and is a member of the football, basketball and track teams in school.

Mr. Rees is a Republican. He is a Mason, and an Elk, is a member of Creighton Federated Church, and is serving his third term as a member of the Creighton School Board. His club is the Field Club of Creighton and his favorite sport is golf. Residence: Creighton.

George Henry Reetz

George Henry Reetz, son of Theodore George and Bertha Jane (Long) Reetz, was born at Bloomfield, Nebraska, January 17, 1890. His father was born in Germany, August 4, 1861, and came to America in 1879. He is a farmer near Bloomfield, Nebraska. His wife, Bertha, was born at Marshalltown, Iowa, May 19, 1871. Her father fought in the Civil War, in which he lost his sight. Nevertheless he is accomplished in many ways.

On January 20, 1915, Mr. Reetz was married to Leora M. Aldrich at Potter. She was born in Nebraska, May 25, 1888, the daughter of Admiral Stuart and Ida M. (Noe) Aldrich. She is a member of the Methodist Episcopal Church, the Order of the Eastern Star, and has been director of the school board for the past 15 years. To them were born three children, two of whom are living. Alvin, born January 13, 1916, died May 19, 1919; Gayland, born March 8, 1920; and Bertha May, born October 24, 1923.

Mr. Reetz is a Democrat. He is a member of Grace Methodist Episcopal Church, the Woodmen of the World, and the Masons, and for the past 10 years has served and is still serving as moderator on the school board. Residence: Potter.

Frank Hill Reeve

Frank H. Reeve was born at Geneva, Nebraska, November 7, 1902, the son of Charles Bartley and May Rosa (Hill) Reeve. His father, who was born at Jacksonville, Illinois, December 5, 1872, was a dry goods merchant at Geneva, for 32 years, and is now retired; he was county chairman of the 3rd Liberty loan drive during the World War. His mother, who is active in musical circles and woman's club affairs at Geneva, was born at Central City, Nebraska, March 23, 1882.

Mr. Reeve attended the public schools at Geneva, and in 1919 was graduated from the Geneva High School. He was a student at the University of Nebraska, from 1919 to 1922. He was awarded the Junior Chamber of Commerce golf tournament, 1929 and 1930; and was golf champion of the Lincoln Country Club in 1928, 1930.

At this time Mr. Reeve is salesman for the Brown & Bigelow Advertising Company of St. Paul, Minnesota. He was employed by the Lincoln Trust Company for three years and the Nebraska Buick Auto Company for four years. He has lived in Nebraska all his life, and is prominent in civic affairs at Lincoln, holding membership in the following: Community Chest; Junior Chamber of Commerce; the University Club; and the Shrine Country Club. He holds membership in the Nebraskana Society and is a member of the Masons and Shrine. His favorite sport is golfing, and his hobby is reading. Mr. Reeve is a Republican.

On January 23, 1923, he was united in marriage with Carol Martha Cornell, at Lincoln. Mrs. Reeve was born at Lincoln, October 29, 1904, and is active in the social and and civic affairs of her community. Residence: Lincoln.

Alfred Edwin Reeves

Born at Spencer, Iowa, March 18, 1881, Alfred Edwin Reeves, physician and surgeon, is the son of Nelson Grant and Jessie Louise (Rose) Reeves. Nelson Reeves, a farmer, was born in Brown County, Kansas, October 9, 1853. His wife, Jessie, born at Ladoga, Indiana, November 21, 1856, died at Farnam, Nebraska, November 4, 1923.

Alfred Edwin Reeves attended rural schools in Missouri and Iowa; was graduated from high school at Ridgeway, Missouri, and received the degree of doctor of medicine from Ensworth Medical College on April 1, 1904. He played college football three years.

He was united in marriage to Maude Jennie Taylor at Curtis, Nebraska, June 7, 1905. She was born in Richardson County, March 14, 1881. There are two children, Richard E., born October 28, 1912; and Betty Lorraine, born December 12, 1918.

Dr. Reeves has been engaged in the practice of medicine in Nebraska for the past twenty-eight years. He is a member of the Nebraska State and Dawson County Medical Associations, the Farnam Commercial Club, the National Geographic Society (1922) the Nebraska State Historical Society and the Nebraskana Society.

He held the rank of captain in Company H, 5th Regiment of Infantry 1913-14; first lieutenant, Medical Corps, United States Army 1917-18, with service in France, and was promoted to the rank of captain, Medical Corps. He is a member of the American Legion, the Masons and Odd Fellows, and from 1925-28 was a member of the Farnam School Board. His favorite sport is hunting and his hobby is taxidermy. Residence: Farnam.

Peter Jensen Refshauge

Peter Jensen Refshauge, banker, was born at Cedar Falls, Iowa, June 14, 1886, son of Christian and Marie (Andreasen) Refshauge.

His father was born in Denmark, August 14, 1841, and was a professor of schools in Denmark, before coming to the United States. Later he was a farmer, whose death occurred at Cedar Falls, Iowa, in February, 1917. His wife, Marie Andreasen, was born in Denmark, May 4, 1850, and died in September, 1925.

Mr. Refshauge attended public schools, and spent two years in the Iowa State Teachers College, and one year at the Lincoln Business College.

From 1907 until 1908, he was assistant cashier of the First National Bank of Marquette, and cashier of the First State Bank of Hordville, Nebraska. Since 1918, he was vice-president of the First Trust Company of Aurora.

On May 10, 1911, he was married to Elfrieda Hansen at Davey. She was born at Dwight, Illinois, March 14, 1887, daughter of a pioneer Lutheran minister. They have one daughter, Adelaide, born July 16, 1912, who was graduated from Aurora High School in 1931, and is attending Iowa State College at Ames.

During the late war Mr. Refshauge was a patriotic speaker and active in other war-time drives. He is a member of the Lutheran Church, the Red Cross, Business Men's Club, the Rotary Club (president 1922), and is a 32nd degree Mason. He enjoys hiking in the woods, on the Platte River. He is a member of the Aurora Country Club. Residence: Aurora.

John Albert Reichenbach

John A. Reichenbach has lived in Nebraska for the past 54 years and has had an interesting and a varied career. He was born at Rowsburg, Ohio, February 18, 1854, the son of Benedict and Marie Emma (Rauvlaub) Reichenbach. His father, who was a tanner and served as lieutenant of artillery in Switzerland, was born at Sannen, Canton Berne, Switzerland, December 20, 1809, and came to America in 1852. He died at Rising City, Nebraska, December 30, 1900. His mother was born at Sannen, September 15, 1810, and died at Rowsburg, July 4, 1882.

Mr. Reichenbach attended the public school at Rowsburg. He has been a tanner, carpenter, farmer, lumber dealer, and banker. Formerly president of the Citizens State Bank at Ainsworth, Nebraska, vice president of the Bank of Petersburg, and cashier of the bank at Rising City, Nebraska, he is now vice president of the Lincoln Trust Company, the Lincoln Joint Stock Land Bank, and the Liberty Life Insurance Company.

He was united in marriage with Mabel Jennie Newcomer at Rising City, January 16, 1890. Mrs. Reichenbach, who was born at Lanark, Carroll County, Illinois, December 25, 1865, is the daughter of Maria (Hatfield) and George J. Follmer. Their daughter, Marie, who was born August 27, 1891, is active in civic and social affairs in Lincoln. She is a member of the Daughters of the American Revolution; Red Cross; Woman's Club; Young Women's Christian Association; Nebraska Sons and Daughters; League of Women Voters; Rocky Mountain Climbing Club; and Kappa Kappa Gamma.

Mr. Reichenbach is a member of the Lincoln Chamber of Commerce, the Red Cross, and Lincoln Kiwanis Club. He holds membership in the Lincoln Country Club. He is a Democrat. Residence: Lincoln.

William Frederick Reichenberg

William Frederick Reichenberg, contractor and builder, was born in Auhagen, Germany, November 10, 1860, and is the son of Heinrich and Wilhelmina (Stolze) Reichenberg.

His father was born in Auhagen, Germany, and died there in February, 1871. He was a weaver and beekeeper. His wife, Wilhelmina, was born in Cludebek, Germany, and died at Buchholtz, Germany in November, 1878.

Mr. Reichenberg attended public school seven years in Germany and came to Parkerburg, Iowa, October 1, 1893, and 24 years ago came to Nebraska. He is a contractor and builder, and the owner of a 1820 acre ranch. Independent in politics, he has served as county commissioner of Arthur County 1917-1918.

On November 14, 1885, he was married to Wilhelmina Augusta Shwerdtfeger at Hanover, Germany. Mrs. Reichenberg was born at Sifershausen, Germany, June 4, 1862. To Mr. and Mrs. Reichenberg were born nine children, William, on July 16, 1886, who married Hortense Rownd, August 24, 1910; Paul, on August 4, 1888, who married Elma Wemple, August 26, 1912; Carl, on May 16, 1890, who married Etta Kruger, December 25, 1917; Marie on October 25, 1891, who married Charley Engelbrecht, March 27, 1913; Frederick, on July 8, 1893, who married Lucille Dorris, October 10, 1919; August, on March 19, 1895, who married Fannie Hurlburt, June 1, 1920; Henry, on May 27, 1897, who married Esther Hurlburt, December 8, 1920; George, on September 21, 1900, who married Iva Bryant, May 10, 1923; and John, on November 21, 1902, who married Elizabeth Swett, November 4, 1929.

At the present time Mr. Reichenberg has 32 grandchildren living. Three of his sons served in the World War.

Before coming to the United States, Mr. Reichenberg served three years in the German army. He is a member and deacon in the Arthur Baptist Church, a member of the Red Cross, and the Nebraskana Society. His hobby is cabinet building. Residence: Arthur. (Photograph on Page 995).

John D. Reid

John D. Reid has been engaged in the practice of medicine at Pilger, Nebraska, for the last 29 years, and has taken an active part in the civic undertakings of his community. He was born at Cedar Rapids, Nebraska, September 23, 1874, the son of Hubert and Jane (West) Reid

Keith County Studio—Ogallala

WILLIAM FREDERICK REICHENBERG

His father, who was a farmer, was born in County Fermanagh, Ireland, January 21, 1846, and died at Primrose, Nebraska, February 18, 1928. He was a pioneer who homesteaded in Cedar Valley, in 1872, and who died on his original farm home. He was one of the leaders in educational and religious activiities in Nebraska, in the early days, and was instrumental in the progress of the state. His mother was born in Ireland, in 1850, and died at Primrose, August 18, 1893.

Dr. Reid attended school in a primitive sod house in Boone County. He was graduated from high school at Cedar Rapids, in 1894; was awarded the B. S. degree at the University of Nebraska, in 1899; received the M. D. degree there in 1902; and took post graduate work at Harvard Medical College in 1929. He was president of the Palladian Society, 1898, and was a charter member of the Pershing Rifles.

He was a cadet at the University of Nebraska, 1894-97; was local examiner during the World War; and was a Minute Man. He held membership in tne Red Cross, Young Men's Christian Association, and was a Liberty loan worker. He is a member of the American Medical Association; the Nebraska State Medical Association; Elkhorn Valley Medical Association; and the Five County Medical Society. His hobby is horticulture. He has served on the local school board for 20 years. He is a member of the Methodist Church at Pilger. Dr. Reid is not affailiated with any political party; he has voted for five Republican presidential candidates and three Democratic presidential candidates.

He was united in mariage with Elizabeth C. Jeter, at Omaha, October 21, 1903. Mrs. Reid was born in Orleans, Indiana, July 16, 1878. Her ancestry dates to the Revolution through both her parents; one of her ancestors, William Irving, was on the staff of General Washington. Their children are: Horace J., born November 23, 1905, who married Viola Isrealson; Margaret, born October 8, 1907, who married Loren Winship; Philip, born April 9, 1909; Kenneth, born April 27, 1912; Stuart J., born October 26, 1915; Marion F., born April 28, 1922. Horace is a lieutenant in the Air Corps of the United States Army, at Selfridge Field, Michigan. Margaret received the A. B. degree at Wesleyan University, 1928, while Philip and Kenneth attend Nebraska Wesleyan. Residence: Pilger.

John H. Reifenrath

John H. Reifenrath, prominent banker at Crofton, Nebraska, was born on a farm near Wynot, Nebraska, October 22, 1873, the son of Fredrick W. and Elizabeth M. (Becker) Reifenrath. His father, who was born near Cologne, Germany in 1835, and died in Cedar County, Nebraska, February 22, 1900, was a farmer who came to this country in 1853. His mother was born at Guttenberg, Iowa, October 7, 1851, and died at Wynot, January 4, 1930.

Mr. Reifenrath received the A. B. degree at Creighton University in 1904, and since then has held the following positions in public and business life in Nebraska: clerk in the office of the County Clerk of Hartington, 1905; bookkeeper in the First National Bank of Hartington, 1905-06; cashier in the First National Bank of Crofton, 1917-25; owner of a retail lumber yard at Crofton, 1913-17. He is now serving as president of the First National Bank of Crofton.

A Democrat, Mr. Reifenrath was a member of the Nebraska Legislature in 1915 and 1917, and in 1923 served as state senator. He is afiliated with St. Rose Church and holds membership in the Knights of Columbus.

On June 28, 1910, he married Nellie Casey at Crofton. She was born at Elkton, South Dakota, November 1, 1887, was a teacher before her marriage, and died at Crofton December 18, 1918. Four children were born to this marriage. Mr. Reifenrath married Bertha M. Gerlack at St. Louis, April 27, 1921; they have five children. Residence: Crofton.

George Joseph Reifert

George J. Reifert, undertaker, was born at Hartington, September 28, 1890. Upon the completion of his elementary and high school work, he attended the Chicago School of Embalming.

Fred W. Reifert, father of George, was a native of Germany. He was county coroner for eighteen years. The Reiferts have been in business in Cedar County over fifty years, Fred W. Reifert having been in the furniture and undertaking business until his death at Hartington, on February 9, 1921. Anna (Beste) Reifert came to this country from Germany, and died at Hartington.

Mr. Reifert is a Catholic, and is a member of the Holy Trinity Church. He is president of the Lions Club, is a member of the Country Club, and holds membership in The Nebraskana Society. Residence: Hartington.

Herman Ernst Reimers

Herman E. Reimers was born at Vail, Iowa, January 14, 1884, the son of Hans and Margaret (Schinkel) Reimers. His father was born at Lunden, Holstein, Germany, December 3, 1839, and came to America in 1875; he died at Manning, Iowa, March 1, 1927. His mother was born at Lunden, October 29, 1844, and died at Manning, February 6, 1927.

Mr. Reimers was graduated from the Manning High School in 1901, and was a student at Highland Park College, 1901-02. He entered business in 1902 as a stenographer for a New York wall paper company at Des Moines, Iowa. The firm moved to Omaha, in 1910, and was later called the Pan-American Wallpaper & Paint Company. He held the following positions with this firm: Stenographer; bookkeeper; credit manager; assistant manager; manager and treasurer. He holds the latter position at the present time.

He is a member of the Omaha Chamber of Commerce and the Concord Club. He is a Mason. His social club is Carter Lake Club of Omaha. He is affiliated with Westminster Presbyterian Church. He is a Republican.

On August 8, 1905, he was married to Lottie E. Ash, at Des Moines. Mrs. Reimers was born at Creston, Union County, Iowa, July 13, 1884. Their daughter, Lucille, was born May 25, 1906, and married Donald Hill. Residence: Omaha.

Lloyd Francis Reinecke

Lloyd Francis Reinecke, son of Francis C. and Helen C. (Phelps) Reinecke, was born in Schuyler, Nebraska, May 16, 1897. His father was born in New York City, about 1854, and his mother in Hartford, Connecticut, about 1855. They are both living.

Educated in the Cedar Rapids and Schuyler High Schools, Mr. Reinecke was graduated from the latter in 1913, and attended the University of Nebraska, where he was made a member of the Iron Sphinx and Sigma Nu. On October 19, 1917, he was married to Ferne Blanche Mattison at Fremont. Mrs. Reinecke was born at Linwood, April 30, 1899. They have three children, Jean Ellen, born July 22, 1912; John Morris, born April 26, 1925, and Robert Lloyd, born December 19, 1928.

Mr. Reinecke has always resided in Nebraska, and has engaged in business in Schuyler since leaving college. At the present time he is treasurer of the Eacker Motor Company, and president of the Progressive Finance Company. He is a Democrat. During the World War he held the rank of sergeant first class in the Medical Corps, and is now a second lieutenant in the Quartermaster Reserves and a member of the American Legion.

A leader in civic affairs, he served as president of the Chamber of Commerce 1928-29, secretary of the Lions Club in 1928, and president of the Schuyler school board 1929-30-31. He is a Mason, a Presbyterian, and a member of the Nebraskana Society. His social club is the Schuyler Golf Club, and his favorite sport is golf. Residence: Schuyler. (Photograph in Album).

George Oliver Remy

George Oliver Remy has been engaged in the practice of medicine for over half a century and has been a physician at Ainsworth, Nebraska, since 1884. He was born at Hope, Indiana, October 1, 1851, the son of John Taylor and Nancy (Jones) Remy, the former a successful farmer who was born at Brookville, Indiana, March 9, 1810, and died at Hope, August 10, 1893. His mother was born in Virginia, April 4, 1811, and died at Hope, March 10, 1879; her ancestry was Welsh.

Dr. Remy attended rural schools until 1870, and in 1877 received the Doctor of Medicine degree at Ohio Medical College. He was a student at Franklin College for two years where he was a member of the Periclesion Literary Society. He began the practice of medicine in Indiana in 1877, remaining in that state until 1884 when he came to Nebraska and settled in Brown County.

He has served as chairman of the Brown County Democratic central committee, and although interested in political affairs has never aspired to hold public office. Dr. Remy is the author of *Pioneer Doctors of Brown County, Nebraska*, and a poem *Lines to Life*, published in the *Nebraska State Medical Journal*. He is a member of the Holt County Medical Society, the Nebraska State Medical Society, and the following fraternal organizations: Modern Woodmen of America; and the Ancient Free and Accepted Masons. His hobby is reading and writing for his own amusement.

Dr. Remy served as a member of the Volunteer Medical Service Corps and was physician on the Selective Service Board of Brown County during the World War.

His marriage to Elizabeth Margaret Barrett was solemnized at Burrusville, Indiana, May 15, 1872. Mrs. Remy, whose ancestry is Scotch and Danish, was born at Hartsville, Indiana, February 12, 1852. Three children were born to this marriage: Nannie, January 30, 1873, the widow of John M. Cotton, who is successfully engaged in the insurance business at Ainsworth; Willie P., June 2, 1875, who died January 16, 1879; and Charles E., February 23, 1881, who married Florence House, and who is superintendent of the Minneapolis General Hospital. Residence: Ainsworth.

Carolyn Renfrew

Carolyn Renfrew, author, composer and musician, was born in Illinois, the daughter of Sylvester and Mercy (Clark) Renfrew, and came with her parents to Nebraska as a child. Her father, a native of Vermont, was of Scotch and English descent, a financier, singer and musician and a man of great intellectual attainments. Her mother, who was both musical and poetical, was born in New York State, and was descended from early English and Holland settlers.

Educated in public school and under private tutelage, Carolyn Renfrew studied music and literature especially, and was at one time a concert singer in New York and Illinois. She is a poet, composer, songwriter and author and has written one novel. Among her works are *Songs of Hope* (book of poems 1923); *The Last of the Strozzi* and *The Lure* (book of poetical plays 1923), and *Footprints Across the Prairie* (novel, 1930).

Miss Renfrew's present interests are in her home and her literary work. She is a member of the National League of American Penwomen, The Bookfellows, the London Poetry Review Society and the Hastings Woman's Club. She is also a member of the Nebraska State Historical Society and a life member of The Nebraskana Society, and is a Unitarian. Residence: Hastings. (Photograph in Album).

Edward Samuel Rennick

Edward S. Rennick was born at Pilger, Stanton County, Nebraska, February 2, 1892, and has lived there all his life. His father, James Rennick, who is a farmer, was born in County Fermanagh, Ireland, December 29, 1854, and came to America in 1868. Rebecca (Montgomery) Rennick, his mother, was born in New York, November 11, 1871, and died at Pilger, August 1, 1918.

Mr. Rennick, who is a successful farmer and stockman at Pilger, was a student at Wayne State Normal College for three years, and was a member of the basket ball team there in 1915. He is a member of the Young Men's Christian Association; is a director of the local school board; is affiliated with the First Baptist Church of Pilger; and holds membership in the Nebraskana Society. He is a Mason.

On September 8, 1915, he was married to Zora Elizabeth Patterson at Wayne, Wayne County, Nebraska. Mrs. Rennick was born at Hooper, Dodge County, Nebraska, October 22, 1892. Five children were born to them, four of whom are living: James, born June 7, 1917; Meredith, born June 8, 1918; Edward, born June 20, 1923, who died May 17, 1924; Marguerite, born April 16, 1925; and Roland, born August 31, 1930.

Mr. Rennick is a Democrat and is interested in the economic and civic progress of his state and community. Residence: Pilger.

Freddie Everett Replogle

Freddie Everett Replogle, a merchant for the past twenty years, was born at Papillion, Nebraska, January 11, 1889, son of Richmond Sylvester and Melvina E. (Beals) Replogle. The father, a farmer and stockraiser of German descent, was born at Charleston, Illinois, December 3 1855. His wife, Melvina, was born at Stewardson, Illinois, December 26, 1866. She is of English descent.

Mr. Replogle attended rural school, and had one year of high school in Illinois and one in Nebraska. He came to Nebraska forty-two years ago. On October 28, 1910, he was married to Edith May Poland at Taylor, her birthplace. She was born October 28, 1889, granddaughter of a soldier in the Civil War 1863-65. There are two children, Irene, born April 2, 1918; and Isla Mae, born March 18, 1922.

At the present time Mr. Replogle is chairman of the Loup County Chapter of the American Red Cross, and a member of the local school board. He is a Protestant, a Mason and a Democrat. He enjoys fishing and hunting, while his hobby is reading. Residence: Taylor.

Ray M. Rerucha

Born in Prague, Nebraska, August 7, 1886, Ray M. Rerucha is the son of Joseph and Mary (Coufal) Rerucha. His father was born in Valci, Terbic, Moravia, March 29, 1856, and his mother was born in Dalasie, Moravia. Joseph Rerucha came to America, on June 29, 1872, later settling in Nebraska where he was a pioneer farmer. His wife, Mary, came with him, and has always taken an active part in community affairs. At the present time she is president of the Busy Bee Club, and is a member of the Catholic Church.

Ray M. Rerucha was educated in the public schools, and on February 11, 1908, was united in marriage to Helen E. Yindrick, at Bruno, Nebraska. Mrs. Rerucha was born at Bruno, on September 18, 1887. To their union four children were born: Leonard, January 18, 1909; Edith, March 14, 1910; James, April 30, 1911, and Theodore, October 26, 1914. All of the children attended high school, and the three sons are engaged in farming with their father. The daughter married Joseph Havlovis, and her husband is also engaged in farming.

A Republican, Mr. Rerucha has held minor political

offices, among them three years as county supervisor (1929-31), and five years as clerk of the town board of Center Township, (1924-29).

Always prominent in the business life of his community, Mr. Rerucha has served as vice president of the Farmers Elevator Company sixteen years; was director of the Farmers State Bank two years, director of the Butler County board, the rural school board fourteen years, the Brainard High School board three years, and is a member of the Farmers Union.

Mr. Rerucha's religious affiliation is with the St. Mary's Catholic Church of David City. He is a member of the Knights of Columbus, and the organizer and a former president of the Centerville Parent-Teachers, Association. A member of the Red Cross and the Nebraskana Society, he was active in various civilian organizations during the World War. He is interested in mechanics and stockraising. Residence: Centerville.

Julius Reusch

For the past 41 years Julius Reusch has been prominent in business circles at Lincoln. He was born at Rodheim, Kreiss-Giessen, Germany, May 4, 1846, the son of William and Margaretha (Nicolai) Reusch. His father, who was born at Rodheim, December 25, 1812, and died there November 22, 1878, was a teacher in the same school for many years in Germany; members of his family were teachers in the same school for three generations. His mother, who was descended from farmers who had lived in one village for many generations, was born at Rodheim, June 9, 1815, and died there, February 18, 1879.

Mr. Reusch attended school in Germany, and was graduated from the gymnasium in Beudingen, August, 1865. After three years in the university at Giessen, he passed the examination for an office in the state service. He was a student at the University in Bonn, for a time, where he was president of the fraternity, Wingolfia.

He served for seven years in Germany as a public office holder; was a farmer in Iowa, for three years; was a druggist for a time; bought a flour mill in Iowa, and was the manager and operator of it; and in 1890, moved to Lincoln, Lancaster County, Nebraska. He became a partner in the Capitol City Coffee & Spice Mill; was president of the Lincoln Liquor & Cigar Company; and in 1904 organized the German-American State Bank, of which he was president. After a long trip abroad he organized the Midwest Savings and Loan Association of which he was president until March, 1931.

He is a member of the Lincoln Commercial Club; the Nebraskana Society; and the Elks. He is affiliated with St. Paul's Evangelical Church at Lincoln, and is a member of the Democratic party. Of his marriage to Margareth Appel, three children were born: Hermann, born January 26, 1884, who married Louise Hoppe; Emma, born March 23, 1886, who married H. C. Wittmann; and Juli, born June 27, 1889. Residence: Lincoln.

Ferdinand August Reuter

Ferdinand A. Reuter was born at Wetteborn, Province of Hanover, Germany, October 29, 1859, the son of William and Wilhelmina (Thurman) Reuter. His father, who was born at Wetteborn, May 10, 1827, came to America October 20, 1873, and settled at Platteville, Wisconsin, where he engaged in the retail shoe business. He died at Syracuse, Otoe County, Nebraska, June 8, 1903.

His mother, who was born at Eiershausen, Province of Hanover, Germany, May 12, 1830, came to America in 1873 and settled at Platteville. She was an efficient homemaker who reared a family of seven children. She died at Syracuse, April 25, 1906.

Mr. Reuter is a pioneer shoe merchant, financier and realtor at Syracuse. He was graduated from the elementary school at Wetteborn, in Germany, in 1873, and then came to America with his father. He entered the

shoe business with his father at Platteville, and there studied and completed a business course outside his working hours. With his father he was the founder and owner of his first store in Platteville, in 1881, and in 1884 removed to Syracuse, where he has since conducted the F. A. Reuter Shoe Store.

In later years he was obliged to find outdoor employment because of ill health. He entered the real estate business and was manager of both his shoe store and real estate office for some time. Later he sold the store to his son, F. H. Reuter. At the age of 71 he is still active in real estate and holds the record of selling 46 farms in one summer.

A Democrat, Mr. Reuter has taken an interest in state and community politics for many years. He served as a member of the state legislature two terms, 1912-14 and 1914-16, and was the author of the Electrocution Bill passed in 1913. His name was placed before the Democratic caucus for speaker of the house in 1915, but he declined the nomination. He was a member of the Syracuse City Council for four terms, and was Democratic central committeeman and treasurer for several years.

His marriage to Margareth E. Carl was solemnized at Platteville, Wisconsin, June 2, 1885. Mrs. Reuter was born of German parents at Platteville, December 11, 1859. Ten children were born to them: Nora, born August 22, 1887; Ferdinand H., born November 8, 1889, who married Clara Rose; Ruth, born November 4, 1892, who married Gus H. Bock; Rueben, born November 4, 1892, who died January 24, 1893; Eda, born September 6, 1894; Rosena, born October 5, 1898, who married Albert Albers; Carl, born March 8, 1900, who married Elizabeth Ott; Lester, born June 17, 1906; George who died in infancy and Marie, who died in infancy.

Mr. Reuter has been general superintendent of the Otoe County Fair Association, and in this position he carried on the work successfully over a period of years. He is affiliated with the First Lutheran Church of Syracuse, in which he was a deacon and active worker for fifteen years. He is very proud of his home, his church and his community and is vitally interested in their progress. His hobby is studying and reading history and the current events of the United States and other countries. Residence: Syracuse. (Photograph on Page 999).

John Walter Reutzel

John Walter Reutzel, son of Conrad and Sarah Anna (Schwab) Reutzel, was born at Clay Center, Nebraska, February 22, 1893. His father was born at Mendota, Illinois, April 17, 1864, and is a farmer and horseman. His wife was born at Mendota, February 19, 1871, and died at Clay Center, August 22, 1922. Both were of German descent.

Mr. Reutzel attended public school until June 4, 1910, and later attended the American Auction College at Kansas City, Missouri. At the present time he is completing a correspondence course in law from the University of California.

Mr. Reutzel has been a mail carrier for nine years, and a public auctioneer for twenty years. He is president of the Southwestern Nebraska Letter Carriers Association at the present time. He is a Republican and has served as county judge of Hitchcock County. He is an ex-member of the school board.

On October 18, 1916, he was married to Engeline Charlotte Rasmussen at Imperial, Nebraska. Mrs. Reutzel was born at Trenton, Nebraska, April 19, 1891, and taught in public schools for seven years. Her ancestry is Danish. They have two children, Maxine E., born September 18, 1918, at Clay Center, Nebraska; and Paul E., born February 1, 1923, at Trenton, Nebraska.

For a number of years Mr. Reutzel has been prominent in all civic and educational work in his community. He organized the Parent Teachers Association at Trenton, which is now extremely active and of which he is now president. He is a charter member of the Massacre

FERDINAND AUGUST REUTER

Pettinger—Syracuse

Canyon Memorial Association, was president five years and vice president four years of the Chamber of Commerce, and is a member of the Modern Woodmen of America.

On August 5, 1929, he was adopted into the tribe of Sioux Indians, christened "Chief Motaunka," "mo" meaning "big," "taunka" meaning "voice," an appropriate Indian name. He is a member of the Red Cross and is a Protestant. He enjoys baseball and for thirteen years served as manager of the local team. His hobby is fine stock.

In the early part of the World War, Mr. Reutzel took an active part in all wartime drives. He later enlisted as a farrier in the veterinary corps and served over seas. He is a member of the local post of the American Legion and served as its commander one term. In recent years Mr. Reutzel has been called upon to fulfill many engagements as a public speaker. Recently he was elected to life membership in the Nebraskana Society in recognition of his effort toward the advancement of his community. Residence: Trenton. (Photograph in Album).

Elmer Mortimer Reynolds

Elmer Mortimer Reynolds, druggist, was born in Spring Green, Nebraska, February 9, 1884, son of Milton Cyrus and Mary O. (Gamble) Reynolds.

The father, a registered pharmacist, was born at New Lisbon, Wisconsin, June 3, 1856, and d ied at Culbertson, November 27, 1921. His wife, Mary, died at Culbertson, April 19, 1907.

In May, 1901, Mr. Reynolds was graduated from the Culbertson High School, and August 7, 1908, received the degree of Ph. G. from Creighton University of Omaha, Nebraska. He passed the state board examination the same year.

A registered pharmacist since 1908, he owned and operated his own store from 1909 until 1917. From 1917 until 1921 he operated and managed the Reynolds Drug Store at Culbertson in the partnership with M. C. Reynolds, his father. He has owned the store alone since then. He is a Democrat.

On January 19, 1910, he was married to Esther M. Smith at Wray, Colorado. She was born at Amma, West Virginia, March 12, 1891, and assists her husband in the drug store. Mrs. Reynolds is the daughter of William A. and Mary A. (McCann) Smith. Her father, Mr. Smith was born July 15, 1853, in Dark County, Ohio. Mrs. Smith, born at Salem Center, Ohio, August 9, 1852, died at Boulder, Colorado, August 27, 1930. Mrs. Reynolds is Past Matron of the Order of Eastern Star of Bethel Chapter No. 109, Culbertson, Nebraska, serving in 1924 and 1931. They have one daughter, Mildred Mary, born March 15, 1911, who was married to W. S. Orton, on June 10, 1930. She graduated from Culbertson High School in 1928, and McCook Junior College, May 30, 1930. She is a member of the Eastern Star.

At the present time Mr. Reynolds is serving his third term as a member of the village board at Culbertson; he was chairman of the board in 1924. For the past five years he has been a member of the building committee of the local school board. He is a member of the National Association of Retail Druggists, the Nebraska Pharmaceutical Association, the Red Cross, the Culbertson Community Club, the Nebraskana Society, the Masons, including Royal Arch and Knights of Templar. His favorite sport is golf, while his hobby is hunting. Residence: Culbertson. (Photograph in Album).

Ralph K. Reynolds

Born at Barre, Vermont, August 28, 1902, Ralph K. Reynolds is the son of H. E. and Alma Martha (Silloway) Reynolds. His father, who was born at Strafford, Vermont, May 16, 1883, is a civil engineer and contractor at Barre. His great grandfather, William McReynolds, came from Ireland and settled at Strafford. The family were all natives of Vermont, four generations having lived on the same farm on which the great great grandmother settled.

Ralph K. Reynolds attended Spalding High School at Barre, and was graduated from the Kirksville College of Osteopathy and Surgery. Thereafter he had three post graduate courses at the same college, and there he also was made a member of Alpha Tau Sigma, and played three years' football. While still in high school he was active in athletics, and played football his entire four years.

Dr. Reynolds was united in marriage to Louise Howell at Kirksville, on August 21, 1925, and to their union one son, John Ralph, was born, January 27, 1927. Mrs. Reynolds, who was born at Kirksville, August 21, 1906, received her Bachelor of Science degree from Missouri State Teachers College. Her father, V. J. Howell, is a banker at Kirksville, and is listed in *Who's Who in America*.

Upon the completion of his internship, Dr. Reynolds came to Fairbury, where he has since engaged in practice. His professional organizations include the American and Nebraska State Osteopathic Associations; and he is also a member of the Junior Chamber of Commerce, a committeeman of the Boy Scouts of America, a member of the Fairbury Methodist Episcopal Church, and a life member of the Nebraskana Society. Dr. Reynolds enjoys golf and football, but his hobby is dogs. Residence: Fairbury. (Photograph in Album).

Wilson Benjamin Reynolds

Wilson Benjamin Reynolds was born at Fremont, Nebraska, January 19, 1888, son of Benjamin Willis and Mary (Davies) Reynolds. Benjamin Willis Reynolds was born at Fremont, son of Wilson and Morrilla S. Reynolds, the former born in Virgil Corners, Cortland County, New York, December 25, 1825, and who died May 9, 1909. Morrilla S. Reynolds was born in Warren, Ohio, July 3, 1834, and died July 4, 1877.

Many Ann Davies Reynolds, wife of Benjamin Willis Reynolds, was born in Wales, Great Britain, and is the daughter of James and Mary (Williams) Davies, the former a native of Cinderford, and the latter of Gilwern, Wales.

Wilson Benjamin Reynolds was graduated from grade school in May, 1901, and from Fremont High School in 1905. Thereafter he attended Fremont Normal College, and was graduated from the commercial course in 1906. He was pledged to Delta Tau Delta at Nebraska, but did not attend the university. During 1904-05, he was captain of the football and baseball teams at Fremont.

On October 14, 1920, Mr. Reynolds was married to Mary Livingston Carroll at Fremont. She was born there, August 16, 1887, daughter of William A. and Margaret (Livingston) Carroll. There are two daughters, Mary E., born October 16, 1921, an honor student thus far in her school work, and who plays the piano well. Susan J., born August 6, 1924, has always been an honor student in School.

A Republican, Mr. Reynolds has always been interested in politics, but has never aspired to public office. Since 1910 he has engaged in the insurance business, and is senior member of the general insurance agency of Reynolds Brothers; district agent for The Texas Company, president of the Red Arrow Cabin Camp Company, Inc., and vice president of Reynolds Brothers Martinson Company, Insurance and Real Estate.

He is past president of the Fremont Advertising Club and of the Chamber of Commerce, and a director of the latter 15 years. He is a former director of the Lincoln Memorial Bridge Company. He has served as member of committees and has aided all worthy welfare work in Fremont. A former member of the Kiwanis Club, he is also past president. He is a member of the Nebraska State Historical Society, in which his father is much interested, and is a member of the Elks. His sports are football, swimming, baseball and golf, while his hobbies are work, reading and children. Residence: Fremont.

Joseph Frank Reznicek

Joseph F. Reznicek, a resident of Nebraska for over 45 years, was born at Kirkov, Bohemia, October 12, 1874. His father, Vaclav Reznicek, was born at Jezov, Bohemia, 1844; he was active in fraternal insurance organizations, and takes a prominent part in church affairs; he came to America in September, 1886. His mother, Magdeline (Morstein) Reznicek, was born in Bohemia, 1845, and died at Dodge, Dodge County, Nebraska, July, 1924; she took an active part in social and religious affairs.

Mr. Reznicek attended school in Bohemia, until he was 12 years old, was a student at North Bend, Nebraska, for one year, attended rural school for two years, and in 1897 was graduated from the Joseph Medill High School, at Chicago. Later he was a student at Fremont Normal School where he received a first grade teachers state certificate. He was a rural school teacher from 1898 to 1902; was manager of a general store at Morse Bluff, Nebraska, 1902-14; and since 1914, has been the owner and proprietor of a general store at Dodge. He is now the owner of four stores, each of which is managed by one of his sons; they are located at Snyder, Wisner, Beemer, and Dodge.

He is a member of the Dodge Commercial Club; the Nebraskana Society; and the National Bohemian Catholic Organization. For 12 years he served as supreme president of K. D., an organization of Catholic Workmen, and for 16 years before that he was secretary. For 25 years he has been a member of Z. C. B. J., and for 4 years he has been an officer. He also holds membership in C. O. F., and is affiliated with the St. Wenceslaus Catholic Church at Dodge.

He was married at Abie, Butler County, Nebraska, February 6, 1899. Mrs. Reznicek was born at Abie, May 6, 1875; her parents were farmers. To this union ten children were born, of whom nine are living: Louis, born May 8, 1901, who married Julia Manarik, and who manages his father's store at Snyder; Joseph, born February 7, 1903, who married Cathrene Lodes, who manages his father's store at Wisner; William, born April 20, 1904, who married Elizabeth Svoboda, and who manages his father's store at Dodge; Helen, born November 22, 1905, who married James Melena; Ernest, born February 19, 1907, who died August 24, 1908; Rosie, born February 19, 1909, who married Marvin Jones; Albin, born April 8, 1911; Lucile, born February 7, 1913; Mary, born December 17, 1915; and Tillie, born September 4, 1918. Residence: Dodge.

John A. Rhoades

John A. Rhoades, son of Daniel Marion and Armilda (Bovee) Rhoades, was born in Harrison County, Iowa, November 20, 1874. His father, who was born in Atchison County, Missouri, August 28, 1841, died at Blair, Nebraska, in January, 1917. His mother is a native of Illinois.

Educated in high school and college, John A. Rhoades holds a professional life certificate and a city superintendent's life certificate. For twenty-two years he taught in the public schools, and for the past seventeen years he has been in the newspaper publishing business. He is editor of *The Enterprise* at Blair.

On January 6, 1905, he was united in marriage to Blanche Lozein Hilton, at Blair, her birth place. Mrs. Rhoades, who was born April 22, 1879, is assistant editor of her husband's newspaper. There are three children,

Lozein Marion, born July 16, 1906, who married Phillip O'Hanlon, a lawyer; J. Hilton, born August 30, 1908, who married Lucille Jensen, and who is a newspaper reporter; and Priscilla M., born March 11, 1913, who is in college.

Mr. Rhoades is a member of the Blair Congregational Church, the Nebraskana Society, the Masons and the Eastern Star. His hobby is gardening. Residence: Blair.

John Wallace Rhodes

John Wallace Rhodes, son of Lucian Millburn and Malvina (Acheson) Rhodes, was born at Winterset, Iowa, June 2, 1878. His father, born in Ohio, July 30, 1853, of German and Irish descent, is a farmer. His mother, born in Illinois, March 14, 1850, died at Stuart, Nebraska. She was of Pennsylvania Dutch ancestry.

Mr. Rhodes attended country schools. For the past twenty-nine years he has been in the employ of W. N. Coats, at Stuart, ten years in the furniture and undertaking business, and nineteen years as manager and bookkeeper of an implement and hardware business.

He was married to Rubina Jane Hutton at Lincoln on June 20, 1906, and to them one daughter was born, Phyllis Janet, on August 13, 1907. She is a pharmacy graduate at the University of Nebraska, and is taking post graduate work in chemistry there. She has a state license. Mrs. Rhodes, who is of Scotch descent, was born at York, New York, June 28, 1878.

Mr. Rhodes is a Republican. He is affiliated with the Stuart Presbyterian Church, is a member of the Commercial Club, and has served on the school board eight years and on the village board six years. He enjoys tennis and baseball, while his hobbies are reading and woodworking. Residence: Stuart.

Clarence Edward Rice

Clarence Edward Rice, physician and surgeon, was born at Orchard, Antelope County, Nebraska, December 8, 1892. After graduating from Orchard High School, he attended York College, York, Nebraska, for two years. He was superintendent of schools at Lushton, Nebraska, during the years of 1914 to 1916, and was a student at the University of Nebraska until he received his medical degree in 1921. Dr. Rice is a member of Alpha Psi chapter of Phi Beta Pi.

Dr. Rice's parents are George Washington and Mary Alice (Ludwick) Rice. George W. Rice was a farmer of English parentage. He was born at Grinnell, Iowa, March 9, 1869, and died at Orchard, Nebraska, March 8, 1931. Mary Alice Rice, mother of Clarence, was born in Marshalltown, Iowa, June 13, 1870. She was a school teacher before her marriage.

Irene Blanche (Dredla) Rice, the wife of Clarence, was born at Crete, Saline County, Nebraska, December 30, 1897. Mrs. Rice is a registered nurse and superintendent and anaesthestist of the Odell General Hospital. They were married at Omaha, Nebraska, May 6, 1922. They have one son, Edward Lee, born April 28, 1923.

Dr. Rice has taken an active part in the advancement of his community and state. He was president of the board of education at Odell, Nebraska, during the years of 1923 to 1928, and is now president of the Board of Health.

He is a member of the Methodist Church at Odell, Nebraska, an Odd Fellow, a member of the Nebraskana Society, and the Nebraska, Gage County, and American Medical Associations. He is now physician and surgeon to the Odell General Hospital. His political affiliation is with the Republican party. Residence: Odell. (Photograph in Album).

Ernest Joseph Axtell Rice

One of Nebraska's enterprising school executives,

Ernest Joseph Axtell Rice has been a resident of the state for fifty years. He was born at Grinnell, Iowa, January 7, 1866, son of John Newton and Amy Axtell Rice.

His father, a farmer, was born in Pennsylvania, October 10, 1833, and died at Harvard, November 16, 1920. His mother, whose family is closely connected with that of Abraham Lincoln, was born in Pennsylvania, in 1834, and died at Neligh, April 15, 1894.

Mr. Rice attended elementary school in Iowa, was graduated from Doane Academy at Crete, and received his Bachelor of Arts degree from Gates College and Doane College. He was a post-graduate student at the University of Wisconsin for two and a half years.

Upon leaving school Mr. Rice was in business for some time. Due to ill health he took up farming but always retained his interest in things educational. He has written some exquisite poems, and is the composer of a song *Fair Nebraska*.

He has served as manager of several commercial enterprises, has taught and been a school executive, and at the present time is superintendent of Brown County schools. He was president of the Nebraska County Superintendents Association for the year 1931-1932, a member of the Parent Teachers Association, and has served on various school boards.

Mr. Rice is a member of the Chamber of Commerce and the Young Men's Christian Association. He is a life member of the Horticultural Society of Nebraska, and a member of the Nebraskana Socety and the First Congregational Church of Ainsworth. His leisure time is largely devoted to writing poetry.

On December 26, 1900, he married Myrtice Mygatt at Long Pine. Mrs. Rice was born at Kenosha, Wisconsin, March 7, 1870. Three children were born to them, Meredith, on July 14, 1902, who died March 13, 1923; Albert Jesse, September 6, 1903, who was graduated from Hastings College in 1925, and is married to Olive Fullerton, a student of Hastings College; and Warren Lincoln, August 28, 1907, who completed a course in agriculture at the University of Nebraska, and is married to Burdetta Simmons, a student of Hastings College. Immediately following his college graduation, Albert spent several years in successful public school teaching.

Both boys are farming, Albert near Ainsworth and Warren near Hastings. While in school Warren was a member of Alpha Zeta, honorary agricultural society, a member of the stock judging team and prominent in athletics. Residence: Ainsworth. (Photograph in Album).

Frank Earnest Rice

Frank Ernest Rice, one of Blue Spring's leading merchants, was born at Monticello, Wisconsin, September 3, 1856. He is the son of Charles Rice, a farmer, born in New York, in 1818, and Eliza (Colton) Rice born in Pennsylvania, May 23, 1828. Charles Rice died in Exeter, Wisconsin, January 10, 1868, and his wife died July 7, 1915, in Santa Ana, California.

Frank E. Rice was educated in elementary schools. On November 27, 1881, at Blue Springs, Nebraska, he married Sarah Schock, born in Bellvue, Ohio, on June 10, 1858. To this union seven children were born· Laura, born April 2, 1883; Lydia, born July 16, 1886; Judson, born November 17, 1888, who married Ethel Pearl Gessell; Emma, born October 7, 1891, who married Leonard Colby Barnes, died on June 23, 1925; Lucq, born November 19, 1895, who married J. Elon Davis; Grace, born January 3, 1899; and Harry, born May 18, 1901, who married Charlotte Marguerite Funk.

Mr. Rice farmed and freighted until 1867, when he went into the hardware business with his brother. In 1889, he started in the mercantile business and continued until

1908, when he entered the F. E. Rice Company as president.

The Protestant faith is his preference. He is a Republican, and has resided in the state for fifty-nine years. He is a member of the Red Cross and is a member of the Nebraskana Society. Reading is his favorite recreation. Residence: Blue Springs.

Guy James Rice

For the past 45 years Guy J. Rice has lived in Nebraska, and in recent years has been a successful farmer in Merrick County. He was born at Decatur, Michigan, July 5, 1883, the son of Eugene Ernest and Mary Alice (Dorr) Rice. His father, who was born at Fort Wayne, Indiana, November 27, 1858, of Pennsylvania Dutch ancestry, is a farmer. His mother was born at Vandalia, Michigan, November 28, 1859, of German parentage.

After completing his elementary education Mr. Rice was a student at Grand Island Business College. He is a member of the Parent-Teachers' Association, and holds membership in the Chapman School Board, acting as treasurer in 1926-27-28. He is a Mason, holds membership in the Order of Eastern Star and is associate patron at the present time. He is affiliated with the Prairie Creek Baptist Church, where he has been superintendent of the Sunday School for 22 years. Mr. Rice has been a director of the Merrick County Fair Board, and is now serving as vice president of that organization. He is past president of the Merrick County Christian Association. A Democrat, he was elected as township clerk in 1909-10-11, and is now serving as president of Farmers Union, Local 900. He is a member of the board of directors of the Chapman Co-operative Grain Association and Chapman Co-operative Mercantile Association.

He was united in marriage with Edith Blanch Bettsworth at Archer, Nebraska, December 22, 1909. Mrs. Rice was born at LeMars, Iowa, November 3, 1884. She is a member of the Eastern Star, and Parent Teachers' Association, of which she is serving her second year as president. They have one son, Jasper, born August 15, 1911, who was graduated from Chapman High School in 1929, and attended Concordia Business College at Concordia, Kansas for one year. After leaving college he accepted a position with the Chicago Lumber Company, at Belgrade, Nebraska, and is now assisting his father in the management of the farm. Residence: Chapman.

Harold Oliver Rice

Harold Oliver Rice, wholesale grocer, was born at Burnside, Illinois, November 25, 1874. He is the son of Nathaniel Green and Evelyn (Ing) Rice, the former a farmer and merchant, and, prior to his death, for many years a traveling salesman. Nathaniel Green was born at Frederick, Illinois, October 17, 1851, and died at Chicago, December 20, 1913. He was of English descent. His wife, Evelyn, was born in Hancock County, Illinois, in 1851, and died at Nebraska City in 1923. Her father was a physician in practice in Hancock County. Mrs. Rice was a lover of home, and an active worker in the Methodist Church.

Harold O. Rice attended the public schools of Paton, Iowa, and Grand Island, Nebraska, and attended David City High School. From 1890 to 1892 he traveled for the Taylor Manufacturing Company of St. Louis, and from 1892 to 1893 for the Sloan-Johnson and Company of Omaha. From 1893 to 1895 he was associated with the Steele-Smith Grocery Company of Omaha and from 1895 to 1905 with Paxton and Gallagher Company.

On January 1, 1905, together with L. P. Utterback and William P. Sargeant, he organized the wholesale grocery business known as The Sargeant and Rice Company, of which he is now vice president.

He was married to Florence Alma Warren at Davenport, Nebraska, on May 26, 1897. Mrs. Rice was born at Lincoln, Illinois, March 13, 1878. They have two children, Phyllis born September 17, 1900, who is a graduate of Smith College and the University of Nebraska, and a teacher of geology and geography in Winthrop College, Rock Hill, South Carolina. For six years she was a teacher in the geography department of the University of Nebraska. Harold O., Jr., born July 28, 1908, is an artist in Chicago.

Mr. Rice has always been active in the civic and welfare work of his city. During the World War he was active in loan drives and in the Food Administration Bureau. He is a contributor to the Red Cross and Salvation Army and is a member of the Chamber of Commerce, the Rotary Club, (president in 1927). A Mason, he is a member of the Knights Templar and Shrine, and is a member of the Elks. His club is the Nebraska City Country Club. His favorite sport is baseball, and his hobby is music. Residence: Nebraska City.

Judson Leroy Rice

Judson L. Rice, one of Blue Springs leading merchants, was born at Blue Springs, November 17, 1888. He is the son of Frank Ernest and Sarah (Schock) Rice. Frank E. Rice was born in Monticello, Wisconsin, September 3, 1856. He was successful in the mercantile business. Sarah, mother of Judson, was born at Bellvue, Ohio, June 10, 1858.

Educated at Blue Springs High School until 1907, he thereafter took a commercial course at the Northwestern Business College. His athletic activities were confined to base ball and basket ball.

On June 15, 1915, his marriage to Ethel Pearl Gessell was solemnized at Blue Springs. Mrs. Rice was born at Beatrice, on July 18, 1892. They are the parents of a daughter, Loretta Sarah, born February 22, 1923.

Mr. Rice has been manager of the F. E. Rice store at Blue Springs for some years. He is a Republican, and has been a resident of the state of Nebraska for forty-two years. During the World War he was a member of the registration board, and took an active part in loan and Red Cross drives.

He is a member of the Blue Springs Methodist Episcopal Church, the Independent Order of the Odd Fellows, The Nebraskana Society, Red Cross, Commercial Club, (of which he is treasurer), and the school board (of which he was secretary in 1919 to 1925, and treasurer 1928 to 1931). His hobby is reading. Residence: Blue Springs.

Lawrence Raymond Rice

Lawrence R. Rice was born at Lexington, Missouri, January 27, 1890, the son of James Lee and Mary Elizabeth Rice. His father, who is a contractor, was born at Wellington, Missouri, June 3, 1873; his ancestry is Scotch and Irish. His mother was born near Houston, Texas, October 2, 1873.

Mr. Rice was graduated from the public school at Lexington in 1904. Since 1918 he has been connected with the Liggett Drug Company, and since 1925, has been senior manager of this firm at Omaha. He became a registered pharmacist in Iowa, Kansas, and Missouri in 1911.

His marriage to Helen Wagner Hainkel was solemnized at Kansas City, Missouri, April 27, 1915. Mrs. Rice, who is of German descent, was born at Qunicy, Illinois, February 1, 1890. They have one son: Lawrence Wagner, born October 27, 1923; he is in school in Omaha.

Mr. Rice is a member of the Omaha Druggists Association, the Nebraska Druggists Association, and is a director of the Omaha Retail Druggists Association. He holds membership in the Goodfellowship Club, the Omaha Chamber of Commerce, the Dundee Parent Teachers Association, and the National Geographic Society. He is a Mason, is fond of golfing and fishing, and is a Republican. Residence: Omaha.

Clarence W. Richard

Clarence W. Richard, who is *superintendent of public schools* at Anselmo, Nebraska, is a life resident of this state. He was born at Chambers, Nebraska, October 2, 1902, the son of Walter and Lillie (Wyant) Richard, the former a farmer in Holt County.

Mr. Richard was graduated from the Chambers High School in 1920, received the A. B. degree at Wayne State Teachers College, and was awarded the A. M. degree at the University of Nebraska where he held membership in Phi Delta Kappa. He taught in the public schools of Chambers for two years, served as superintendent of schools at Magnet, Nebraska, 1924-27, and since 1927 has been superintendent at Anselmo where he is a member of the Order of Eastern Star, the Service Club, and the Masonic Lodge.

He is the author of *Business Management of Student Activities*. On July 7, 1925, he married Eunice Marion Garwood at Carroll, Nebraska. Mrs. Richard, who is also an educator, was born at Carroll, October 17, 1905. Residence: Anselmo.

Charles Lawrence Richards

Charles Lawrence Richards, for many years a prominent lawyer, was born at Woodstock, Illinois, March 21, 1856, and died at Hebron, Nebraska, in January, 1927. His father, Thomas McDonald Richards, was born in New York State and died at Woodstock, Illinois. He was a farmer of English descent. Mr. Richards attended public school at Champagne, Illinois, and graduated from the Union Law School with the degree of Bachelor of Law in 1884. He came to Nebraska in 1886, and was a lawyer in Hebron from that time until his death. He was a Republican, and served as county attorney of Thayer County four terms, and was speaker of the house of representatives of the Nebraska legislature in 1895.

On July 2, 1890, he was married to Elizabeth Lowric at Chicago. Mrs. Richards was born in Chicago on July 26, 1854. She died at Hebron on February 21, 1932. There are three children, Carl, a farmer; Bess, who is court reporter in the district court at Lincoln; John L., who is a lawyer; and Webb, who is a bond salesman.

Mr. Richards was very active in the work of the Presbyterian Church at Hebron, and was elder for many years. He was active in all civic organizations and affairs, and was a member of the Nebraska State Bar Association.

Fred Hamilton Richards

Born at Fremont, Nebraska, April 8, 1901, Fred Hamilton Richards is the son of Fred Hills and Adaline E. (Brown) Richards. His father, who is a realtor, was born in Fremont, May 1, 1877, while his mother was born in Racine, Wisconsin, February 13, 1880.

Upon his graduation from Shattuck Military Academy in 1919, Fred Hamilton Richards attended the University of Nebraska, receiving his LL. B. in 1923. He is a member of Phi Delta Phi and Phi Delta Theta. Since his admission to the bar on June 4, 1923, Mr. Richards has engaged in active practice. He was elected Justice of the Peace two terms, 1927-29; 1929-31; and was elected on the Republican ticket as county attorney of Dodge County, taking office January 8, 1931.

He was married to Grace Mary Shephard, at Fremont, March 29, 1924. Mrs. Richards, who is a native of Fremont, was born July 17, 1898. They have one daughter, Mary Adaline, born February 13, 1926.

A member of the Reserve Officers Training Corps during the World War, Mr. Richards has held the rank of Second Lieutenant in the Officers Reserve Corps for the past ten years. He is a member of the Nebraska State Bar Association, and the Dodge County Bar Association (member of executive committee). At the present time he is a director of the Chamber of Commerce, a Mason and a member of the Nebraskana Society. His religious affiliation is with the First Presbyterian Church in which he is a member of the Pathfinder Bible Class. He is director and recording secretary of the local Young Men's Christian Association. His favorite sport is horseshoes. Residence: Fremont.

John L. Richards

John L. Richards, lawyer, was born at Hebron, Nebraska, March 22, 1893, son of Charles L. and Elizabeth (Lowrie) Richards. His father, for many years one of the most prominent members of Thayer County bar, was born at Woodstock, Illinois, March 21, 1856, and died at Hebron, January 7, 1927. His wife, Elizabeth, was born at Chicago, Illinois, July 26, 1858, and died at Hebron, February 21, 1932. She moved from Chicago to Hebron, Illinois, in her early youth, and in 1880 came to Hebron where she continued to make her home. She was married to Charles L. Richards of Hebron, on July 2, 1890, and to this union were born three sons, John L., James who died in infancy, and Webb of San Francisco. She was a member of the Presbyterian Church for forty-three years and deeply interested in all its activities. She was also a member of chapter A. E. of the P. E. O. Sisterhood and a member of the Hebron D. W. Club.

In 1911 John L. Richards was graduated from Hebron High School, and in 1916 received the Bachelor of Arts degree from the University of Nebraska. In 1917 he received the degree of Doctor of Jurisprudence from the University of Chicago. He has been in active practice in Hebron since that time.

On June 24, 1918, Mr. Richards was married to Edith Holcomb of Hebron. Mrs. Richards was born at Hebron, March 22, 1893, daughter of John J. and Mary J. Holcomb. They have three children, Jacquelin, born January 7, 1920; Mary Elizabeth, born August 22, 1925; and Charlotte, born November 18, 1929. Residence: Hebron.

Ira Frederick Richardson

Ira Frederick Richardson, was born in Saunders County, Nebraska, August 17, 1872, son of George and Lizzie (Husenetter) Richardson. His father was born in Rockford, Illinois, March 31, 1840, and died at Fremont, Nebraska. A merchant, he served as postmaster at Linwood, Nebraska, twenty-four years. His mother was of the Penhollow family, who were participants in the Boston Tea Party. His wife, Lizzie, was born at Burlington, Iowa, August 28, 1844, and prior to her marriage was a teacher. She is active in the work of the Congregational Church, and has taken part in community affairs all her life. Her parents were born in Germany.

Dr. Richardson attended the Linwood public school and Franklin and Weeping Water Academies. In 1903, he was graduated from the Hahnemann Medical College at Kansas City, and from the Still College of Osteopathy at Des Moines, in 1901. Since 1903 he has been engaged in general practice until 1927-28, when he took special work in proctology, specializing in it in addition to his regular practice.

He was married to Nina J. Phillips at Fremont, March 20, 1912. Mrs. Richardson was born in Dodge County, May 11, 1887, and is a member of the Order of Eastern Star. They are members of the Congregational Church. For several years Dr. Richardson was a member of the American Medical Association, and is now a member of the American Osteopathiic Association. A contributor to Salvation Army and the Young Men's Christian Association, he is past president of the Fremont Kiwanis Club, past exalted ruler of Elks Lodge No. 514, and past eminent commander of the Knights Templar. He is physician to the Midland Basketball Club, and the Fremont Ball Club, and is fond of both baseball and basketball. He

took the examination for service as a physician in the World War, but was rejected because of ear trouble. Dr. Richardson is a member and past president of the Fremont Trapshooting Club. Residence: Fremont.

Lloyd Clifford Richardson

Born at Wisner, Nebraska, June 3, 1888, Lloyd Clifford Richardson is the son of Charles Taylor and Lilly Rose (Sharp) Richardson. His father, who was a pioneer farmer and stockraiser in Nebraska, was born at Brier Hill, New York, December 7, 1850, and died at Cambridge, February 8, 1925; he served as postmaster at Wisner, and was president and manager of a lumber company in this community. His ancestry was English and Dutch, and he was descended from President Zachary Taylor on the maternal side.

His mother was born at Richland, Wisconsin, May 27, 1854, and died at Cambridge, August 7, 1914. Mrs. Richardson was a pioneer homemaker in Nebraska, and was interested in club work and beautifying her home with flowers. Her family was of English descent, and members of it settled in Virginia, in the early history of America.

Mr. Richardson was graduated from the Cambridge High School in 1904, where he was active in debating and dramatics. Later he attended the Central Business College at Denver, Colorado. He was helper and assistant manager of the Chicago Lumber Company, 1904-15, and since 1925, has been president and general manager of the Cambridge Lumber Company. He is vice president of the C. & B. Gravel Company of Bartley, Nebraska, is an extensive land-holder in Furnas County, and vice president and director in the Cambridge Telephone Company.

He has served as director and treasurer of the Cambridge Rotary Club, is a member of the Nebraska Lumber Merchants Association, was formerly president of the Cambridge Commercial Club, and served as a member of the Cambridge School Board from 1922 to 1928. He is affiliated with the Methodist Episcopal Church of Cambridge, holds membership in the Red Cross, and is chairman of the local Boy Scouts committee. His social clubs are the Cambridge Tennis Club, The Business Men's Gym Club, and the Cambridge Shrine Club, and his fraternal organizations include the Modern Woodmen of America, Odd Fellows, and the Masons.

During the World War he was a member of the Home Guard, was a member of the loan drive committees, and was active in Red Cross activities. Although he is not interested in office holding, he is a member of the Democratic party.

On March 24, 1909, he was united in marriage with Lola Edith Corell at Cambridge. Mrs. Richardson, who is descended from an English lord and French ancestors who settled in America in the early history of this country, was born at Springfield, Nebraska, December 7, 1889. Their two children are: Charles Paul, born June 29, 1915; and Betty Ann, born June 30, 1921. Both children are musically inclined. Residence: Cambridge. (Photograph in Album).

Presstman Gardner Richardson

For the past fourteen years Presstman Gardner Richardson has been cashier of the Security State Bank of Broken Bow. He was born at Broken Bow on November 8, 1895, son of Presstman Johnston and Kate (Deatherage) Richardson. His father, a farmer and stockman, was born in Culpepper County, Virginia, and died at Broken Bow, in 1910. His mother, also born in Clupepper County is living.

Presstman Gardner Richardson attended the Broken Bow public schools, was a student at the University of Nebraska two years, and at the Finlay Engineering College, Kansas City, Missouri, one year. On January 15, 1919, he was married to Margaret M. Murphy at Lincoln. Mrs. Richardson, who is of Irish descent, was born at

Anselmo, Nebraska, October 2, 1897. They have two children. Katherine Margaret, born October 25, 1919; and Harry Marcus, born May 30, 1921.

Mr. Richardson volunteered for selective service in June, 1918, and was discharged for physical unfitness at Vancouver Barracks, Washington in July, 1918. He is a member of the Masons, the Modern Woodmen of America and the Nebraskana Society, and is affiliated with St. John's Episcopal Church. His hobbes are mechanics and electricity. He is a Democrat. Residence: Broken Bow.

Jacob Rickard

Jacob Rickard, a general merchant at Max, Nebraska, during the past 30 years, was born at Letart, West Virginia, October 8, 1863, son of John and Louisa (Frye) Rickard.

The father, born at Letart, died there in 1913 at the age of 84 years. He was a farmer of Pennsylvania Dutch descent. His wife, Louisa, born in Letart also, died there in 1918 at the age of 86.

Mr. Rickard attended the elementary schools of Letart, was graduated from Point Pleasant, West Virginia High School in 1882, and taught the following year in Mason County, West Virginia. He came to Nebraska and taught in a rural school in Franklin County in 1884, after attending Bloomington Normal School at Bloomington, Nebraska.

In 1885 he homesteaded west of Benkelman, coming to that point overland in a spring wagon in company with a man named Franklin Koch. He taught rural school during 1885-86, and clerked for Robidoux Brothers and John Roemmich, while providing up his homestead, until elected county clerk in 1892. After the expiration of his term, he purchased the J. F. Lynch merchandise store at Max, Nebraska, which he has operated ever since. For several years he handled a lumber and coal business for the Barr Lumber Company, and for a short time, after this business was sold to the F. C. Krotter Company, he handled it until they secured a manager.

Mr. Rickard is a Republican. He was interested in local party activities from 1890-1900 and has served various times as county chairman and precinct chairman. He was clerk of Dundy County, 1892-93-94-95.

In February, 1892, he was married to Margaret Ann Hurlow at Letart, West Virginia. Mrs. Rickard was born at Letart, West Virginia, February 16, 1864, and died at Max, Nebraska, May 27, 1923. To this union were born two children, James Otis, December 10, 1893, who married Irma Jean Mills of Meadow Grove, Nebraska, on August 3, 1921. He is an extensive land owner, a clever and successful breeder and raiser of cattle, living with his family south of Max. To them were born two children, Derald, December 21, 1923, and Marjorie Ann, October 26, 1927. Anna Louisa, born May 10, 1895, who married Martin Brethouwer of Benkelman, Nebraska, in 1913. She was descended from early Welsh settlers in West Virginia.

Mr. Rickard is a Methodist, a member of the Red Cross, the Masons, the Modern Woodmen of America of which he has been secretary for several times, the Parent-Teachers' Association, and the Nebraskana Society. His hobby is reading, especially history. Residence: Max. (Photograph in Album).

Louis Franklin Rickard

Louis Franklin Rickard was born at Springfield, Illinois, October 13, 1856, the son of Henry Washington Rickard and Sarah Ann (Sims) Rickard. His father, who was a farmer, was born in Farquar County, Virginia, January 1, 1830, and died at Springfield, August 1, 1891. He was a pioneer in Nebraska, and his father was one of the early settlers of Illinois where he moved in 1831, by the covered wagon route. The grandfather of Louis

F. Rickard, John Sims, built the first house in Springfield, Illinois, in 1818, and was an intimate friend of Abraham Lincoln. Mr. Lincoln made his home with members of the Rickard family and at one time proposed marriage to Sarah Rickard, an aunt of Louis F. Rickard.

Louis F. Rickard has been engaged in the hardware business at Nelson, Nebraska, for many years, and has been active in civic affairs there. He is affiliated with the Republican party, holds membership in the Presbyterian Church, and is a member of The Nebraskana Society.

On January 13, 1881, he was married to Carrie B. Brown at Farmingdale, Illinois. Mrs. Rickard, whose ancestry was English, was born at Farmingdale, May 4, 1862, daughter of J. J. and Emily (Ralston) Brown, and died at Nelson, June 23, 1924. Their children are: Louis Peyton, born January 9, 1882, who married Adelaide Irvin; and Cyrus Dale, born June 24, 1884. Both sons are connected with the Rickard Hardware Company at Nelson. Residence: Nelson.

Ted Eugene Riddell

Ted Eugene Riddell, physician and surgeon, was born at Beatrice, Nebraska, June 17, 1896, son of Fred A. and Ella Mae (Hilton) Riddell. His mother was born in Ohio, in 1877, and died at Beatrice, April 7, 1907. Her ancestry was Irish and English.

Dr. Riddell attended the public and high schools of Beatrice, and in 1918 received his Bachelor of Arts degree from the University of Nebraska. In 1923, he received the Bachelor of Science degree, and in the same year received the degree of Doctor of Medicine. He is a member of Delta Tau Delta, Nu Sigma Nu, Innocent Society, and received four letters in four major sports 1916-17.

Since his admission to practice in 1923, Dr. Riddell has been very active. He is the organizer of the Scottsbluff clinic, of which he is a surgeon. He is the author of various medical articles, and is a member of the American College of Surgeons, the American Medical Association and the Nebraska State Medical Society. During 1927 Dr. Riddell took post graduate work in surgery in several European clinics.

His civic organizations include the Red Cross, the Scottsbluff Chamber of Commerce, and the American Legion. An aviator in the Naval Aviation during the World War, he is now a member of the Reserve Officers Association. He is a 32nd degree Mason. He is a director of Scottsbluff Country Club, and is interested in all sports.

On August 18, 1928, he was married to Miriam E. Gilligan at O'Neill. Mrs. Riddell was born at O'Neill, January 23, 1904, her parents having come to the United States from Ireland. She was graduated from O'Neill High School, and also from the University of Nebraska in 1925. She is a member of the Delta Gamma and P. E. O. Sisterhood. Mrs. Riddell is the daughter of the late Dr. John P. Gilligan who was past president of the Nebraska State Medical Association and a former state senator. They have two children, Sandra, born December 31, 1930; and Demaris, born August 9, 1931. Residence: Scottsbluff. (Photograph on Page 1006).

Charles E. Rider

Charles E. Rider, dentist, was born at McCook, Nebraska, June 10, 1894, the son of William L. and Francenia (Shepherd) Rider.

His father, who was born at Gatesburg, Pennsylvania, October 28, 1860, of German and Scotch descent, is now retired. His wife, Francenia, was born at Clarinda, Iowa, on November 20, 1872, of English and Irish ancestry.

Dr. Rider attended public school in Nebraska, and in 1913 was graduated from the Oxford High School at Oxford, Nebraska. He received the degree of Doctor of Dental Surgery from the University of Nebraska in 1919,

TED EUGENE RIDDELL

Steiner—Scottsbluff

where he was a member of Delta Sigma Delta Fraternity.

On August 25, 1919, he was admitted to practice in Nebraska. Prior thereto he was a drug store clerk, 1913-14; taught school one year; and was a drug clerk at the Orpheum Drug Company at Lincoln, while attending the University, 1915-19.

His marriage to Catherine Lofing was solemnized at Lincoln, December 24, 1919. Mrs. Rider was born at Seward, Nebraska, August 22, 1898, and died at Imperial, April 11, 1921. Their infant child, born April 11, 1921, died the same day. Dr. Rider's second marriage was to Lela Marie Downs of Fort Collins, Colorado, August 10, 1922. They have two children, Donald Charles, born May 23, 1924, at Imperial, Nebraska; and Stanley Dale, born November 4, 1928.

Dr. Rider is a Republican. He is a member of the Methodist Church of McCook, the Medical Reserve Corps, the American Legion, the National Dental Association, the Nebraska State Dental Association, the District Dental Association, and the Nebraska-Kansas Study Club. He is first vice president of the Lions Club of Imperial, Past Worthy Patron of the Eastern Star, a Mason, a member of the Nebraskana Society, and the Parent-Teachers' Association. His favorite sport is football, while his hobby is breeding silver foxes. Residence: Imperial. (Photograph in Album).

Arthur Louis Riedesel

Arthur Louis Riedesel, hardware and implement dealer, was born at Glidden, Iowa, April 24, 1896, son of Louis A. and Sophia (Wetter) Riedesel. His father died at Glidden, Iowa in 1921, and his mother is residing at Bertrand, Nebraska.

He attended country school and in 1914 was graduated from Glidden High School. On June 9, 1920, he received his Bachelor of Arts degree from Buena Vista College at Storm Lake, Iowa, magna cum laude. He was active in debating three years, and in dramatics and orchestra work.

At the present time Mr. Riedesel is a member of the firm of Hobbs & Riedesel at Brule and Ogallala. He is a Republican. During the World War he served 16 months with the 318th Engineers, 6th Division, 13 months of this was overseas. He is a member of the American Legion and the Congregational Church.

On June 10, 1920, Mr. Riedesel was married to Catherine Marie Lawrence at Carroll, Iowa. Mrs. Riedesel was born at Anita, Iowa, July 1, 1897. They have two children, Arthur, Junior, born October 6, 1921; and Lawrence Eugene, born April 30, 1925. Residence: Brule.

Franz Joseph Riesland

Franz Joseph Riesland was born at Wood River, Nebraska, March 17, 1877, the son of Henry and Caroline Marie (Bansbach) Riesland. His father, who was an evangelical minister and a farmer, was born at Berlin, Germany, January 17, 1817, and came to New York City in 1834. His marriage to Caroline Marie Bansbach was solemnized at New York City, April 4, 1841. They came to Nebraska in the spring of 1874 settling at Wood River, where he died January 23, 1893. His mother was born at Manheim, Germany, December 27, 1828, and died at Wood River, December 21, 1896.

Mr. Riesland is the youngest of the family of nineteen children. He was graduated from high school in 1894, served for three years as an apprentice plumber and fitter, and from 1896 to 1899 studied heating engineering by correspondence. He has always been active in the Republican party and served as assistant postmaster at Wood River, 1902-04, and postmaster since 1925.

He is a member of the Nebraska Association of Postmasters, the National League of District Postmasters, the Wood River Chamber of Commerce, the Nebraskana

Society, and the Red Cross. He is affiliated with the First Methodist Episcopal Church of Wood River, and holds membership in the following fraternal organizations: Masons, serving as financial secretary of the Woodmen of the World; the Hastings Consistory; Independent Order of Odd Fellows.

Mr. Riesland has set a record preforming a worthy cause, he has sung for 400 funerals, a great many of which have been those of personal friends. He was first called on at the age of sixteen.

His marriage to Leah Alice Miller was solemnized at Wood River, September 12, 1901. Mrs. Riesland, who was a teacher prior to her marriage, was born at Wood River, June 7, 1879. Their children are: Rex Reed, born July 14, 1902, who married Nell Lee Sadler; Lela Marie, born October 19, 1903, who married Dr. Walter Price Moore; Almerie June, born July 15, 1909, who is studying music at Hastings College; and Ruby Dot, who is assistant postmaster at Wood River. Rex was graduated from Creighton University and is now a registered pharmacist. Lela Marie majored in voice and public school music at Wesleyan University. Residence: Wood River.

Fred J. Riggert

Fred J. Riggert, who has been a farmer in Nebraska since 1910, was born in Marshall County, Kansas, March 5, 1881, and for several years engaged in farming in Kansas. His father, August Riggert, who homesteaded in Marshall County in 1875, was born in Germany, February 22, 1848, and came to America in 1868. His mother was born in Marshall County, December 31, 1858, and died at Bremen, Kansas, August, 1901.

Mr. Riggert attended parochial school until 1895 and later attended public schools in Kansas. He has served as a member of the school board in Gage County for 12 years, is president of the Odell Lumber Company, is vice president of the Farmers Elevator, and for ten years served as a member of the township board at Odell. He owns and farms 240 acres of land in Gage County, and owns registered Guernsey cattle.

He is a member of the Gage County Cow Improvement Association, for eight years has been a board member of the Lutheran Hospital of Beatrice, Nebraska, is a member of the Farmers Union Associaton, and is now serving as a member of the board of the Gage County 4-H Club. He has been an elder in the Bethlehem Church at Odell for the last six years. During the World War he was solicitor for Liberty bonds and war savings stamps.

His marriage to Mary Adam occurred at Hanover, Kansas, April 13, 1903. She was born at Odell, November 13, 1881, and died there, January 28, 1915. Seven children were born to them: Elsie, born February 14, 1904, who married Walter Oldehoeft; Edwin, born November 18, 1906, who married Lulu Duensing; Martha, born September 27, 1908, who is a stenographer at Beatrice; Alfred, born February 26, 1910, who married Florence Beckman; Clara, born February 9, 1912, who is a teacher in the public schools; and Paul, born January 10, 1915. He married Lena Adam at Beatrice, April 13, 1916. To their marriage were born the following children: Lilian, born July 15, 1917; Agnes, August 2, 1919; Alice, born November 1, 1921; and Ruby, born October 8, 1923. Residence: Odell.

Edwin Harvy Riggs

Born at Aroma, Illinois, November 7, 1859, Edwin Harvy Riggs has been engaged in the practice of law in Blaine County continuously since 1894. His father, Porter Riggs, a farmer and a veteran of the Civil War, died at Brewster, Nebraska. His mother died at Aroma, Illinois.

Edwin Harvy Riggs attended the common schools of Illinois, until 1878, and in 1883 came to Nebraska. Having studied law with local attorneys in Brewster, he took the bar examination at Thedford, and on April 13, 1894, was admitted to practice. Since 1895 he has been connected with the general mercantile business in connection with his legal practice.

A Republican, he has held various offices, including county clerk, county treasurer and county attorney, which last office he now holds. He was first elected county clerk in the fall of 1886, and has never been defeated for office.

On December 25, 1888, Mr. Riggs was married to Mary Dill, from whom he is now divorced. To them was born one daughter, Joy, in 1900. She is married to Jay Williams. On September 18, 1905, he was married to Mrs. Gertrude (Fitch) Yoste, at Omaha. They have one son, Harold, born in March 28, 1908, who married Adah Howard.

Mr. Riggs is a member of the Red Cross, and a life member of the Nebraskana Society. His hobby is baseball. Residence: Brewster.

Myron Michael Riley

Myron Michael Riley, physician, was born at Dawson, Nebraska, February 7, 1874, son of Michael and Bridget Maria Riley. He attended public and high school, received his Bachelor of Arts degree from St. Marys College (Kansas) in 1896, and his degree of Doctor of Medicine from Creighton University in 1900.

He has been instructor of medicine Catholic University 1901, professor of medicine Catholic Universty, 1908, instructor of materia medica, Catholic University College of Dentistry, 1910-11. He has served as professor of medicine and head of the department of the school of medicine at Catholic University, and as secretary of the university's administrative board, and as a director of the medical staff of St. Joseph's Hospital and the School of Nursing of St. Joseph's Hospital. In 1917 he was made secretary of the administrative board of St. Joseph's.

Dr. Riley is a member of St. Peters Catholic Church, the Knights of Columbus, the American College of Internal Medicine, the American College of Surgeons (fellow), the Omaha-Douglas County Medical Society (president), and the Nebraska State Medical Society. He is a member of Ak-Sar-Ben and the Elks. Residence: Omaha.

Lincoln Riley

For the past 43 years Lincoln Riley has been engaged in the practice of medicine at Wisner, Nebraska. He was born at Prophetstown, Whiteside County, Illinois, August 12, 1867, the son of John and Abigail (Burnet) Riley. His father, a physician, was born at New York City, September 30, 1818, and died at Erie, Illinois, June 10, 1903. His mother, was born at Saratoga, New York, December, 1825, and died at Eric, January 9, 1907.

Dr. Riley attended Northern Illinois College at Fulton, Illinois, and in 1888, received his M. D. from the University of Iowa. He served for 12 years on the board of education at Wisner, and was coroner for Cuming County for several years. He is president of the Cuming County Medical Society and holds membership in the Nebraska State Medical Society.

During the World War he was captain in the Medical Corps of the United States Army and served as a member of the medical advisory board and the selective draft board. He was captain of ordnance in the Nebraska National Guard, 1910-15. He is state director of marksmanship of the American Legion and from 1910 to 1930 was captain of the Nebraska Civilian Rifle Team. He is a member of Wisner Lodge Number 114 of the Ancient Free and Accepted Masons. His sports include fishing and rifle shooting. He is a populist Democrat.

His marriage to Martina Guthrie was solemnized at Clinton, Iowa, August 26, 1886. Mrs. Riley was born at Whiteside, Illinois, May 9, 1870, and died at Wisner, November 23, 1923. Their three children are: Charles Lewis, born May 21, 1888, who married Clara Helms; Ivy, born September 15, 1890, who married (John) Helms; and Wilbur Kirk, born September 23, 1892, who married Elizabeth Daly. Charles is a dentist at Fremont, Nebraska; and Wilbur is a physician and surgeon connected with the veterans' bureau. Residence: Wisner.

Samuel Rinaker

Samuel Rinaker was born at Carlinville, Illinois, September 14, 1860, son of John I. and Clarissa (Keplinger) Rinaker. John I. Rinaker was born in Baltimore, Maryland, in 1830, and died at Eustis, Florida, January 15, 1915. His wife died at Carlinville, September 5, 1920.

Samuel Rinaker attended public school at Carlinville, and entered the Blackburn College at the age of sixteen, graduating from the classical course in 1880. He then attended Brown Business College at Jacksonville, and later entered the law department of Yale University, where he was a student during 1882 and 1883.

In 1884, Mr. Rinaker was admitted to the bar of Illinois, and in 1885 came to Nebraska. There he formed a partnership with the late Nathan Kirk Griggs, under the firm name of Griggs and Rinaker. In 1893 the firm became Rinaker and Bibb, and following the death of Mr. Bibb in 1907, Mr. Rinaker practiced alone until 1909. At that time he became a member of the firm of Rinaker and Kidd. This partnership continued until 1916, when John W. Delehant became a member of the firm, which is now Rinaker, Kidd and Delehant.

Mr. Rinaker is a member of the Chamber of Commerce of Beatrice, the Elks, and the Country Club. He has been a member of the Board of Directors of the First National Bank of Beatrice, and the First Savings Bank, and is a member of the Nebraska and American Bar Associations. He is a Mason, a Knight Templar, a member of the Rotary Club and the Modern Woodmen of America.

He is married to Carrie Palmer Mayo, a native of Carlinville, and the daughter of Samuel T. and Elizabeth (Palmer) Mayo. They have two children, Samuel and Carrie. Residence: Beatrice.

William Jack Rinder

William Jack Rinder, manufacturer and executive, was born at Red Oak, Iowa, May 29, 1888. He is the son of George and Anna Ida (Eichler) Rinder, the former a native of Strassburg, Alsace Lorraine, who came to America in 1872. George Rinder was born October 18, 1861, and until his death at Manitou, Colorado, on February 10, 1929, was a retail merchant. His wife, Anna, was born in Saxony, Germany, December 24, 1864, and is living.

Mr. Rinder attended the public schools of Hastings, and was graduated from high school in 1906. Thereafter he attended college two years, and entered the commercial world, becoming connected with the manufacturing concern K and R Incorporated. He was elected to the presidency of that organization in 1925, and is also a director of the Nebraska National Bank.

On October 9, 1912, Mr. Rinder was married to Laura Hedwig Bixler, at Fort Wayne, Indiana. Mrs. Rinder, whose ancestry has been American for three generations, was born at Berne, Indiana, January 7, 1889. At the present time she is a director of the Young Women's Christian Association and an executive officer and director of the Red Cross. There is one son, William, born May 9, 1914.

Mr. Rinder is a member of the First Presbyterian Church, the National Economic League, the Red Cross, Salvation Army, the United States Chamber of Commerce and the American Institute of Meat Packers. He is also a Rotarian and a 33rd degree Mason and was instrumental in forming the Shrine in Hastings.

His social clubs include the Hastings Country Club and others. He enjoys golf and football, and his hobbies are reading and art. Residence: Hastings.

John A. Rine

For the past 30 years John A. Rine has been active in the legal and political world at Omaha, Nebraska. He was born in Dodge County, Nebraska, December 23, 1878, and has spent nearly all his life in this state. He was awarded his LL. B. degree at the University of Michigan, and in 1900 was admitted to the bar in Nebraska. He served as referee in bankruptcy from 1903 to 1906; was city attorney of Omaha, 1910 to 1918; was a member of the Nebraska legislature, 1918; was a member of the Charter Convention at Omaha, 1918; and since 1922 has been a member of the Omaha Planning Board. He is a Democrat.

He married Elizabeth Maybelle Christensen at Fremont, Dodge County, Nebraska, August 22, 1917; Mrs. Rine was born at Fremont, November 18, 1886.

He is a member of the Douglas County Bar Association; the Nebraska Bar Association; the American Bar Association; the Omaha Chamber of Commerce; the Red Cross; and the Nebraskana Society. He holds membership in: Omaha Automobile Club; Nebraska Good Roads Association; ;the Omaha Athletic Club; and the Isaac Walton League. He is a Mason and an Elk. Residence: Omaha.

Alexander Charles Ring

Alexander Charles Ring, pioneer Nebraskan and a leader in the early development of Hebron, was born at Belleville, Ohio, May 17, 1847, of French and Dutch descent. His father was killed in the Mexican War.

Coming to Nebraska in 1868, Alexander Charles Ring was one of the founders of the town of Hebron. One of two survivors of Old Fort Butler, he was a member of the state militia five months, and during his service was one of the builders of the stockade at Fort Butler.

On August 10, 1869, the town of Hebron was laid out in lots, and Mr. Ring was detailed to stand picket while they surveyed the town. Lumber was hauled from Marysville, Kansas, the nearest railroad station, and the first order of goods had to be hauled from Lincoln.

Together with W. P. Harding, Mr. Ring was appointed to canvass the county for a division of the two counties, which resulted in the division of Thayer and Jefferson, which at that time were one. On October 14, 1869, Mr. Ring and Mr. Harding went from Republican River to Elk Creek, and Mr. Ring recalled there being two inches of snow on the ground, which remained more than a week.

Mr. Ring was Hebron's first city librarian, appointed October 20, 1873, and about the same time served as town trustee. He was married to Averilla Hess, daughter of pioneer Nebraskans, at Hebron in 1876, and to them four children, three sons and one daughter, were born. The oldest, Dr. William Ring, was born December 2, 1877. The other three are deceased.

Elected city treasurer in April, 1893, Alexander C. Ring held that position many years. In partnership with F. J. Hendershot he operated the first drug business in Hebron, continuing for a number of years, until he was compelled to retire because of ill health.

Mr. Ring had the distinction of being the oldest Odd Fellow in point of membership in Thayer County, having been a charter member of the lodge at its organization in 1874. Prior to that time he had been a member of the order in Ohio. Altogether he had more than fifty years service in the lodge.

It was a consolation to his family that Mr. Ring lived to celebrate his golden wedding anniversary, which occurred in 1926. He died at Hebron, on March 10, 1927, and is buried in the old cemetery north of Hebron.

Averilla Ring

Born at Saint Joseph, Missouri, September 9, 1858, Averilla Hess came with her parents to Nebraska in 1863. Settling at Virginia Station, they for a two year period furnished meals for stage coach drivers and passengers going west. Her mother baked pies, cakes and doughnuts to supply the regiments of soldiers going through to fight the Indians, which at one time came within ten miles of the little station, but were turned back by the troops.

From Virginia Station the family moved to the Otoe Reservation, living for one year in the arsenal. Her father instructed the Indians in farming. A miller by trade he ground their wheat for them and helped run the saw mill. The following spring the family went to Beatrice where they operated a hotel. In 1874 the family removed to Hebron.

Averilla Hess was married to Alexander C. Ring in 1876, and their first child was born on December 2, 1877. There were four children born to their union, Dr. William A. Ring being the oldest. Her husband, one of the first settlers in what is now Thayer County, performed picket duty while the town of Hebron was being laid out. He, together with F. J. Hendershot, operated its first drug store. He assisted in building the Fort Butler stockade, southwest of Hebron and was the city's first librarian. Alexander C. Ring lived to celebrate his golden wedding anniversary, and died at Hebron on March 10, 1927.

Mrs. Ring recalls many of the early hardships connected with the settlement of this section. The grasshopper plague, the great snow storm of 1888, the Indian uprisings, and the privations incident to pioneer life. She still lives in the home built by her husband for her fifty years ago. Residence: Hebron. (Photograph on Page 1010).

William Alexander Ring

Born at Hebron, Nebraska, December 2, 1877, William Alexander Ring is the son of Alexander Charles and Averilla (Hess) Ring. Alexander Charles Ring was born at Belleville, Ohio, in 1847, and died at Hebron, March 10, 1927. Coming to Hebron in 1868 from Belleville, he assisted in laying out the present town, and was first city librarian on October 20, 1873. He was one of the two survivors of old Fort Butler, and a pioneer and Indian fighter in Thayer County's early days. He recalled hearing H. P. Harding cover the county with a petition when Thayer was divided from Jefferson County. One of his distinctions was that he was the oldest Odd Fellow in point of membership in Thayer County, having been a charter member of the lodge, which was organized in 1874. Of French and Dutch extraction, his father was killed in the Mexican War.

Averilla Hess was born in St. Joseph, Missouri, of pioneer parentage, and was herself a pioneer in this section. She is the daughter of William Hess, who came to Hebron in 1873. Prior to that time he served as commissioner of Gage County, when all this part of the state was included in it. Mrs. Ring relates many interesting occurrences in her girlhood, and recalls the meeting of twelve Indian tribes at her father's home near Hebron. She speaks the Indian language, which she learned as a girl. Her father was of an old Virginia family and her mother was of Welsh descent.

William A. Ring attended the Hebron public schools, completing his high school education in 1895. In 1901 he was awarded the degree of Doctor of Dental Surgery from the Kansas City Dental College.

On August 27, 1899, he was united in marriage to Emma Myrtle Willmore, daughter of Charles and Sarah Jane (Wright) Willmore, at Hebron. She was born at

AVERILLA RING

Lane, DeWitte County, Illinois. There are two children, Helen, is married to Dick McLean, who is in the insurance business at Fairbury. William K., attended Peru State Teachers College, and is principal of schools at Palmyra, Nebraska, serving his fourth year.

Since his admission to practice at Lincoln, in August, 1902, Dr. Ring has always been engaged in the practice of dentistry at Hebron. He is interested in athletics, and from 1908 to 1923 managed the Hebron baseball teams. He also managed the team which won the Nebraska state basketball championship in 1923. He is an expert skater and has acted as referee for football teams.

Interested in politics since boyhood, Dr. Ring has always taken an active part in the affairs of the Democratic party locally, and has held various positions in the Democratic central committee. He was also a member of the town board one year. During the World War he was one of three appointed by Governor Keith Neville, who selected the Council of Defense for Thayer County; in addition, he was medical advisor for selective service.

Dr. Ring is a member of the Nebraska State and Southeast District Dental Societies, and the National Dental Association. He is a life member and one of the founders of the Civil Legion, and a member of the Service Veterans. He belongs to the Hebron Commercial Club, the National Travelers Association and is a former member of the Knights of Pythias, Odd Fellows, Moose, Sons and Daughters of Protection and the Modern Woodmen of America.

The first president of the Avalon Golf Club, Dr. Ring is a former president of the Hebron Izaak Walton League, and a member of the Nebraskana Society. He is active in all out door sports, including hunting, fishing, golf, canoeing, etc., and enjoys bowling, trapshooting, billiards, horse racing, baseball, basketball and football. Residence: Hebron. (Photograph in Album).

John Dean Ringer

Dean Ringer, a pioneer lawyer of Nebraska, was born at Lincoln, Lancaster County, Nebraska, March 1, 1878, the son of Bradford and Susan Milward (Dean) Ringer. His father who was a real estate man, was born in Goshen County, Ohio, December 30, 1845, and died at Lincoln, April 5, 1908. He was a Civil War veteran, whose ancestry was English. His mother, who was of English and Dutch descent, was born at Alexandria, Huntingdon County, Pennsylvania, March 11, 1842, and died at Lincoln March 17, 1907.

Mr. Ringer attended public school at Lincoln and in 1899 was graduated from the Lincoln High School. He was awarded the A. B. degree at the University of Nebraska, 1903, and was graduated from the University of Nebraska Law School in 1905 with LL. B. degree. He was a member of the debating team, 1905, for which he was awarded the chancellor's prize; won letters in football and baseball; was elected to Phi Delta Phi and was a member of Phi Kappa Psi.

He has been engaged in the practice of law since his admission to the bar in 1905, was appointed postmaster and is now serving his second term as postmaster at Omaha. A Republican, he has been city commissioner of Omaha, serving commissioner of police of Omaha in February 23, 1925.

His marriage to Nelle Mae Trigg was solemnized at Lincoln, June 28, 1906; she was born at Charles City, Iowa, July 31, 1881. They have two children: John Dean, Jr., born August 26, 1908, who is specialinzing in chemistry at Rollins College, Winter Park, Florida; and Miriam S., born September 18, 1911, who is a student at Nebraska Wesleyan University.

Mr. Ringer is a member of the American, Nebraska State and Omaha Bar Associations. He holds membership in the Red Cross, the Young Men's Christian Association, is past master of Bee Hive Lodge No. 184 South Omaha, and Grand Senior Warden of Grand Lodge of Nebraska. He is a member of Grace Methodist Episcopal Church of Omaha. He is fond of golf. (Deceased 1931).

Martin Luther Ringer

Martin L. Ringer, real estate man of Wayne County, Nebraska, has lived in this state all his life. He was born on a farm in Richardson County, Nebraska, September 19, 1884, the son of Calvin Joseph and Susanna (Walters) Ringer. His father, who was a doctor of divinity in the Lutheran Church, was born in Somerset County, Pennsylvania, December 10, 1860, and died at Omaha, April 28, 1931; his ancestors came to this country from Germany, in 1750. His mother was born in Somerset County in 1861.

Mr. Ringer is the owner and manager of a real estate and insurance business at Wayne. He is affiliated with the Evangelical Lutheran Church. His marriage to Rose Marguerite Peipenstock was solemnized at Wayne, December 10, 1913. Mrs. Ringer, who is of German ancestry, was born at Wayne, February 16, 1890. They have one daughter, Mildred Rose, born April 9, 1920. Residence: Wayne.

Conrad Ringsted

Conrad Ringsted, veteran lumberman of Ainsworth, Nebraska, has been a resident of this state for nearly half a century, and has been prominent in his community in civic and business affairs. He was born at Middlefort, Denmark, September 13, 1868, the son of Sophus Peter Hannibal Ringsted and Christine (Poulsen) Ringsted. His father, who was a printer, was born at Copenhagen, Denmark, in 1847, and died at Middelfort, Denmark, in July, 1872. His mother was born at Hellevad, Denmark, in 1848, and died at Hadar, Nebraska, October 22, 1912.

Mr. Ringsted received most of his education in Denmark, and Germany, and came to America in 1884 at the age of 16. His early life was spent in farming and in 1900 he became manager of the Nye-Schneider-Fowler Company, and in 1925 the company was purchased by the Cornbelt Company in which organization Mr. Ringsted was manager. He is a member of the Methodist Episcopal Church and was elected city clerk in 1928.

On September 19, 1891, he was married at Neligh, Nebraska, to Florence Marcellus, who was born at Fulton, Illinois, September 2, 1872. Of the seven children born to them, five are living: Charles, July 27, 1892; Louis, March 20, 1894; Orville, February 12, 1896, who died February 14, 1896; Muriel August 13, 1897; Rachel, March 24, 1899, who died December 27, 1903; Loren, April 16, 1902; and Vera, October 8, 1908. Charles and Loren are lumbermen while Louis is a hardware merchant. Residence: Ainsworth.

George Hampton Risser

For the past 33 years George H. Risser has been engaged in the practice of law at Lincoln. He was born at Mount Pleasant, Iowa, March 20, 1877, the son of Daniel and Anna (Hampton) Risser. His father, whose ancestry is German, was born in Ohio, in 1844, and died at Lincoln, July 17, 1917. His mother was born of English parentage in Ohio, in April, 1847, and died at Lincoln, July, 1906.

Mr. Risser was graduated from the college of law at the University of Nebraska, in 1897, where he was a member of Sigma Chi and Phi Delta Phi. He was a student at Iowa Wesleyan University for a time.

A Republican, he served as justice of peace at Lincoln, 1904-07; was police magistrate, 1908-11; and served as county judge of Lancaster County, 1912-17. He has lived in Nebraska for the past 38 years. He holds membership in the Lancaster County Bar Association, and the Nebraska State Bar Association; is a member of the Knights of Pythias, and a former Elk; and holds membership in the Nebraskana Society. He is a Republican and a Methodist.

His marriage to Lulu Belle West was solemnized at Nebraska City, Otoe County, Nebraska, November 15, 1899. Mrs. Risser was born in Otoe County, June 25, 1880. They have one daughter, Marion, born December 28, 1900, who married Norman Curtice. Residence: Lincoln.

William Ritchie, Junior

Of distinguished parentage, William Ritchie, Junior, was born at Ravenswood, Cook County, Illinois, July 28, 1886. He is the son of William and Charlotte Ensign (Congdon) Ritchie. His father, born at Frederick, Illinois, August 26, 1854, is a figure of note, having practiced law in Chicago for 50 years. He is an uncle of Governor Albert C. Ritchie of Maryland, and is descended from Scotch ancestors who arrived in America in 1745.

Mr. Ritchie's mother, who was born at Amboy, Illinois, July 29, 1865, and died in Chicago, January 27, 1889, was a grand-niece of Colonel Prescott of Bunker Hill fame. Except for a great-grandmother who came from Spain to America, her ancestors were English people who arrived in this country in 1628.

His education was received in the Oak Park High School, where he was graduated in 1904. His LL. B. was granted him at the University of Nebraska, where he was secretary of Interfraternity Council, 1913-15, and was a member of Beta Theta Pi, and Phi Delta Phi.

Mr. Ritchie was county superintendent of schools in Cheyenne County, Nebraska, in 1908. In 1915 he was admitted to the bar and has been active in political and civic affairs since then. Since 1919 he has lived in Omaha where he is a member of the firm Ritchie, Chase, Canaday and Swenson.

On April 26, 1916, he was married to Eunice Arthur, at Grand Island, Nebraska. Mrs. Ritchie, who was born in Detroit, Michigan, August 4, 1888, is the daughter of Rev. L. A. Arthur of Grand Island.

During the World War Mr. Ritchie was a private in the Sixth Nebraska Infantry; 1st lieutenant in the 349th Infantry; captain of the 69th Infantry; serving from August 2, 1917 to February 4, 1919. He is a member of the American Legion, Disabled Veterans of America, and was department commander of the American Legion in 1922.

Mr. Ritchie is a member of the American Bar Association; Omaha Bar Association; the Nebraska State Bar Association; Omaha Chamber of Commerce; and Professional Men's Club.

His social clubs are The Omaha Club and The Omaha Country Club. Residence: Omaha. (Photograph on Page 1013).

William Henry Ritchie

William H. Ritchie, who has lived in Nebraska for the past 47 years, was born at Philadelphia, December 2, 1861, the son of Francis and Eliza (Wilson) Ritchie. His father, also a farmer, was born at Milford County, Donegal, Ireland, June 8, 1834, and died at Beaver Crossing, Nebraska, June 1, 1922. His Scotch-Irish ancestors came to America in 1852; he had been active in church for many years, and was superintendent of the Sunday School and delegate and trustee in the Evangelical Church over a long period of time. He was a Blue Lodge Mason, holding membership and offices in that organization most of his adult life.

His mother, Eliza (Wilson) Ritchie, was born in County Derry, Ireland, June 5, 1837, and died at Monmouth, Illinois, July 13, 1876. She came to America in 1852, on a sailing vessel where she met her husband for the first time. They were married in 1857.

Mr. Ritchie attended the rural school near Monmouth, and for the past 46 years he has been engaged in farming

on the land which his father purchased early in the history of the state. He is now especially active in livestock breeding. A Republican, he has served as tax assessor for many years, although he has not been active politically. He is a member of the board of directors of the Farmers Grain Company, and the Farmers Oil Company of Beaver Crossing, has been a member of the board of education there, and holds membership in the Nebraskana Society. He is affiliated with the Methodist Church, and is a 32nd degree Mason. His hobbies are reading and cattle raising.

On August 26, 1903, he was married to Sarah Margaret Smith, at Beaver Crossing. Mrs. Ritchie, who was born at Grinnell, Iowa, October 29, 1875, is the daughter of Anna Mary (Buck) Smith, a Pennsylvanian, and Charles Franklin Smith, a native of Vermont.

Three children were born to this marriage: Mary Josephine, born November 18, 1905; Lois Jean, born October 2, 1910; and Margaret Frances, born April 15, 1917, who died December 24, 1917. Mary Josephine was graduated from Beaver Crossing High School in 1923, and received her advanced education at Rockford College and Northwestern University, Chicago, 1927. She is now in the legal department of the Hartford Fire Insurance Company in Chicago. Lois Jean was graduated from the Beaver Crossing High School, was a teacher for one year, and is now a nurse in the Lincoln General Hospital. Residence: Beaver Crossing.

Josephine Cook Ritzmann

Josephine Cook Ritzmann, who was born at Wahoo, Nebraska, July 15, 1886, has lived in that community all her life, and is now a buyer and saleswoman for a Wahoo firm. Her father, Joel D. Cook, was born at Potterville, Pennsylvania, August 21, 1843, and died at Wahoo, March 1, 1925.

Joel D. Cook assisted in platting the city of Wahoo, and was a commanding figure in the development of Saunders county for many years. He was educated in district schools with six months at a private seminary. He enlisted in 1861, and served in the medical department of the army in the Civil War. In May, 1868, he came by steamboat to Omaha, and worked for the Union Pacific Railway. By economy he saved enough in 1869 to buy a team of oxen. He located on a homestead and pre-emption claim in Saunders County in the same year.

He took a leading part in organizing the First National Bank, the Masonic Lodge of Wahoo, and the Saunders County Fair Association. He was active in the contest that resulted in locating the court house at Wahoo. He moved to Wahoo, in 1895.

Rhoda (Upson) Cook, wife of Joel, was born at Burlington, Connecticut, December 3, 1841. On the homestead 3½ miles south of Wahoo, she encountered all the privations incident to homesteading. Neighbors were few. The men were compelled to freight supplies long distances. The women and children must stay alone. There were wild animals and prowling Indians to add to the terrors of loneliness. Later Mrs. Cook took a leading part in the club, social and religious life of the community.

There are four children besides Mrs. Ritzmann; Cora V. McKiem; Charles A.; Clate; and Caroline who was graduated from the University of Nebraska in 1903. All lived in or near Wahoo. Mrs. Cook died at Wahoo, November 6, 1927.

Mrs. Ritzmann received her education in the public and high schools of Wahoo. For a year she was a saleswoman for the Ernest Kerns Company at Detroit, Michigan, and for the past five years has been connected with the firm of Smith, Hultin, Anderson & Company. She is a member of the Wahoo Business and Professional Women's Club, serving as its president from 1929-31, is affiliated with the Presbyterian Church, and holds membership in the Republican party. Her social club is the Wahoo Golf Club, while her hobby is reading.

Her marriage to Adolph Carl Ritzmann was solemn-

WILLIAM RITCHIE, Jr.

ized at Wahoo, July 15, 1908. Mr. Ritzmann, who was born at Detroit, December 3, 1886, and died at Casper, Wyoming, April 19, 1925, was a Lutheran school teacher. Residence: Omaha.

James Rivett

James Rivett, who for many years was supervisor of building construction on the Chicago, Burlington and Quincy Railroad, and helped in naming many of the towns, was born at Podington, Bedfordshire, England, August 29, 1852. He is the son of James and Mary Ann (Terry) Rivett, both natives of England.

James Rivett, Sr., who was born on June 15, 1825, was a contracting builder, descended of a line of builders in England for many generations; they were of Norman descent. Mr. Rivett came to America in June, 1873, and died at Lincoln, on April 15, 1895. His wife, Mary Ann, was born in London, August 26, 1816, and died at Lincoln, January 10, 1890. She was graduated from Queen Katherine's School in Southwark, London, at the age of 15. Her family had been residents of London for many generations. Mr. Rivett had six brothers and three sisters, those living are: Charles of Bethany, Nebraska, William of Lincoln, Richard of the State of Washington, and Mary Ann of Scottsbluff.

James Rivett, Jr., took seven years Chautauqua studies and received a certificate of graduation. Almost immediately he entered the building business, and for forty-two years was supervisor of building construction for the C. B. and Q., during which time 3000 miles of new line were built west of the Missouri River in Nebraska, Kansas, Colorado and Wyoming. Mr. Rivett is now retired.

He was married to Carrie Louella Logan at Greenwood, Nebraska, January 14, 1882. A teacher prior to her marriage, she was of a pioneer Vermont family. There are two sons, Harry L., born March 19, 1883, who married Julia Bednar, and Paul S., born February 17, 1888, who married Frances Wyman. They are respectively president and secretary of the Rivett Lumber and Coal Company of Omaha.

Mr. Rivett is a Republican. Mr. Rivett was a member of First Congregational Church at 13th and L Streets until the organization of Plymouth Congregational Church, of which both Mr. and Mrs. Rivett are charter members, and Mr. Rivett a member of the board of Deacons. He is a former member of the Woodmen of the World and the Modern Woodmen of America. His trade as a builder has always been his hobby. Residence: Lincoln. (Photograph in Album).

Rudolph Rix

Rudolph Rix, physician and chief of staff of Evangelical Covenant Hospital, was born at Fort Calhoun, Nebraska, December 28, 1870. He is the son of Nicholas and Mary (Hagedorn) Rix, the former born at Schleswig-Holstein, Germany, September 19, 1830. Nicholas Rix was a farmer who came to America when a young man. He died at Fort Calhoun October 10, 1918. His wife, Mary, was born at Schleswig-Holstein, in 1830, and died at Fort Calhoun, June 7, 1907.

Dr. Rix attended country school and later entered Western Normal College at Shenandoah, Iowa, receiving his B. Sc. from Western Normal College at Lincoln. He then entered Creighton University where he was awarded his medical degree. In 1911 he took post graduate work at Johns Mopkins Medical College. Dr. Rix is a member of Phi Rho Sigma.

Entering the practice of medicine in 1900, he was engaged as a teacher in the anatomical, pediatric and gynecological departments of Creighton Medical College from 1900 to 1921. He has been on the surgical staff of Evangelical Covenant Hospital at Omaha for many years and is at present chief of staff.

On September 17, 1903, he was united in marriage to Olive Louise Arnold of Otoe, Iowa, at Logan, Iowa. Their two children are Margaret Olive, born November 23, 1905, who married Richard Barton Cole. They live at 45 Bishopgate Road, Newton Center, Massachusetts. Robert Rudolph, born January 6, 1908, is in his second year as a medical student in Dartmouth College.

Dr. Rix attends the First Central Congregational Church of Omaha. He is a member of the American Medical Association, the Nebraska State and Omaha-Douglas County Medical Societies. He belongs to the Chamber of Commerce, the Woodmen of the World and is a Mason. His club is the Omaha Field. Residence: Omaha.

Antonio R. Rizzuto

Antonio R. Rizzuto was born in the village of Rizzuti, Scigliano County, Calabria, Italy, October 21, 1877. His father, Salvatore Rizzuto, who was a rancher and a sergeant in the Italian Army, was born at Rizzuti. His mother, Letterina Caterina (Scarpino) Rizzuto, was born in the village of Coraci, Italy; she was the mother of a large family, and was active in civic affairs.

Mr. Rizzuto attended the elementary schools in Italy. Until 1900 he worked in a glass factory, and since that date has been a general constractor. He is president of Rizzuto Brothers & Company, Incorporated, and is president of the Denver Sand & Gravel Company of Colorado. He does contracting with the Union Pacific Railroad Company; the Chicago Burlington & Quincy Railroad Company; the Chicago Great Western Railway Company; the Cudahy Packing Company; Union Stock Yards; and Armour & Company.

He was the editor of *Corriere del Popolo,* an Italian newspaper, for some time and has lived in Nebraska for the past 24 years.

His marriage to Franceschina Scarpino was solemnized in 1900 at Colosimi, Calabria, Italy. Mrs. Rizzuto was born at Coraci. Four children were born to this union: Frank, born June 19, 1905, who is a lawyer; Angelo, born December 19, 1906; Samuel, born August 25, 1908, who is a member of the firm Rizzuto Brothers & Company; and Elena Maria, born December 25, 1909, who died July 5, 1910. Angelo is a college student.

During the World War Mr. Rizzuto worked with Judge Foster raising money for the Red Cross; he was active in loan drives and has assisted in Community Chest drives. He is a member and vice president of the Folk Art of the Omaha Social Settlement; is an honorary member of the Italian Benevolent Association, at Omaha; was president of the Italian Civic League, 1930; and is an honorary member of the Association Nazionale Combattenti. He holds membership in the Chamber of Commerce, the Omaha Athletic Club, and the Loyal Club.

He is a Mason, Shriner, and an Odd Fellow. He is very much interested in baseball, and is the backer of the Rizzuto Brothers Baseball Club. He is a Republican. Residence: Omaha.

Rosa Ann Lizenby Robb

Rosa Ann Lizenby Robb, clergyman, was born near Medaryville, Indiana, January 15, 1878, daughter of William Wesley and Stena (Weise) Lizenby. Her father, who was born near Medaryville, May 5, 1849, is a retired farmer of Scotch-Irish parentage. Her mother was born at Michigan City, Indiana, March 30, 1855, and died at Francesville, Indiana, May 11, 1926. She was the daughter of German farmers.

Mrs. Robb attended public schools in Indiana, until 1894, and from 1904-07 the Northfield, Massachusetts, Seminary. From October, 1901-03, she attended Moody Bible Institute at Chicago. At the same time she was class visitor of a Bible class of 200 in Chicago, and in 1905 a Presbyterian minister's assistant. From 1906-08, she was city missionary at Coffeyville, Kansas. As a result of the evangelistic work three churches, the United Brethren, the Methodist, and the Methodist Episcopal, were organized. She was ordained to the Congregational minis-try in 1909, and has held pastorates 1908-1931. She was pastor at the Butler Avenue Congregational Church in Lincoln, for 6 years, and at the present time is pastor of the Camp Creek Congregational Church near Nebraska City.

On February 20, 1920, she was married to Veston Robb, at Lincoln. Mr. Robb was born in Butler, Pennsylvania, December 12, 1872, and is Scotch-Irish. He is now in the lumber business in Julian. Mrs. Robb is a Republican, and especially active during political campaigns. She is a member of the League of Women Voters at Lincoln, and of the Parent-Teachers' Association (program com-mittee, 1929-30), the Young Women's Christian Associa-tion and the Woman's Christian Temperance Union. Her home is at Julian.

Thomas Bruce Robb

T. Bruce Robb was born in Saline County, Kansas, January 31, 1885, the son of Thomas and Charlotte (Seanor) Robb. His father, whose ancestry was Scotch-Irish, and his mother English-German, were farmers for many years.

Dr. Robb attended the public schools of Kansas until 1902, and in 1908 was graduated from Park College Academy. He holds the following degrees: A. B., Park College, 1912; A. M., Yale University, 1914; and Ph. D., Yale University, 1919. He is professor of statistics and business research at the University of Nebraska, and is chairman of the department of business research at that institution. He is editor of *Nebraska Studies in Business,* and is the author of *Guaranty of Bank Deposits* (1921).

On June 5, 1918, he was married to Sarah Lillian Spence at Oklahoma City, Oklahoma. Mrs. Robb was born in Peterborough County, Canada, June 1, 1887. Their children are Bruce, Jr., born July 28, 1919; and George Seanor, born February 5, 1922.

Dr. Robb is a member of the American Association of University Professors; the American Economic As-sociation; the Lincoln Chamber of Commerce, and The Nebraskana Society. He is a member of the Republican Party; and is affiliated with the Presbyterian Church. He has lived in Nebraska for the past six years and takes an active interest in state and community affairs. Resi-dence: Lincoln.

John Weimer Robbins

John W. Robbins was born at Kent, Indiana, Oc-tober 25, 1862, and for the past 45 years has lived in Ne-braska where he has been a prominent business man. He is the son of Harrison H. and Hester Ann (Clines) Robbins. His father, whose ancestry was English, was born in Scott County, Indiana, January 1, 1825, and died in Jefferson County, September 1, 1912; he was a stock-man and farmer. His mother was born of English par-entage in Jefferson County, January 22, 1832, and died there, August 15, 1902.

Mr. Robbins, who has taken an active part in the political life of Nebraska and Omaha for many years, was awarded his A. B. degree at Hanover College, Han-over, Indiana, in 1884, when he was valedictorian of his class. He received his A. M. degree at the former in-stitution in 1888. In 1884 and 1885 he served as district secretary of Beta Theta Pi.

He was a junior member of the real estate firm Hart-man & Robbins, 1889-1891; was secretary of the Omaha Board of Public Works, 1891; assistant inspector of the Nebraska Fire Insurance Inspection Bureau, 1892-95; and since 1895 he has been engaged in the real estate business. He served as president of the Omaha Fire In-surance Agents Exchange, 1904-05; was president Omaha Real Estate Board 1909-10; was president of the Omaha Federal Business Association, 1929-31. He is now United State Collector of Customs at Omaha, and is a member

of the board of directors of the Omaha & Council Bluffs Street Railway Company.

A Republican, Mr. Robbins served as state senator from Omaha from 1918 to 1927, and was president pro tempore during the 1925 session. He was, as state sena-tor, one of the introducers of the Omaha Charter Bill, now Omaha's Home Rule Charter, and guided its passage through the legislature. He introduced and promoted the passing of the Omaha City Zoning Bill, and the Ne-braska State Park Bill. The provisions of the latter bill have made it possible to preserve for all time Nebraska's places of scenic, historic and scientific interest; five state parks have thus far been acquired without cost for the sites.

During the World War Mr. Robbins was active in Liberty loan drives and other war activities; he has taken part in various Red Cross and Near East Relief drives in the past ten years. He is a member of the Red Cross; Community Chest; Omaha Chamber of Commerce; Om-aha Real Estate Board; Omaha Association of Insurance Agents; and the Omaha Federal Business Association. He is first vice president and member of the executive board of the Nebraska State Historical Society, and is a member of the Nebraskana Society.

He is a Mason, a member of the Scottish Rite Masonic Benefit Club, and the Scottish Rite Low Twelve Club. He is a member of the Happy Hollow Country Club, and is affiliated with the First Central Congregational Church.

On September 25, 1894, his marriage to Isabel Wy-man was solemnized at Omaha, Douglas County, Ne-braska. Mrs. Robbins was born at Cincinnati, Ohio, September 18, 1870. She is descended through the pa-ternal line from Francis Wyman who emigrated from County Hertford, England, to Woburn, Massachusetts, in 1640. They have four children: Lois, born May 23, 1896, who married Leo B. Bozell; Wyman, born August 15, 1897, who married Mildred Foote, and who is manager of the real estate loan department of the S. W. Straus & Company of Los Angeles, California; Polly, born July 7, 1903; and Dean, born December 8, 1907. Residence: Omaha.

Ralph Monroe Robbins

Ralph Monroe Robbins, banker, was born at Mar-quette, Nebraska, December 23, 1894, son of George and Martha Ann (Foree) Robbins. His father, who was a farmer, was born in Illinois, October 4, 1848, and died at Aurora, Nebraska, in April, 1913. His mother died near Aurora in March, 1905.

Mr. Robbnis attended the public schools of Aurora, Chappell High School and York Business College and Normal School from which he was graduated in June, 1916. For the past 16 years he has been in the banking business, and is now assistant cashier of the Cahppell State Bank. He is a Republican.

His marriage to Irene Louis Swanson occurred at Chappell, September 28, 1919. She was born there on September 28, 1896, of Swedish descent. Their only son, Donald Monroe, was born June 21, 1925.

During the late war Mr. Robbins served as regimental sergeant major in the United States Army for 18 months. He is a member of Clinton McAuliffe Post No. 217 of the American Legion, the Methodist Episcopal Church, the Red Cross, the Masons, and Eastern Star, and is on the state board of the Young Men's Christian Associa-tion. His favorite sport is golf, while he also enjoys gardening. Residence: Chappell.

William Albert Robbins

William A. Robbins, educator and school executive, was born at Pennville, Jay County, Indiana, January 11, 1874, the son of Charles Wesley and Martha Jane (Dug-dale) Robbins. His father, who was a farmer and county clerk in Thomas County, Kansas, was born near Camden, Jay County, Indiana, December 24, 1844, and died at Colby Kansas, March 15, 1904. He was of Welsh and English descent. His mother was born near Camden, January 10, 1848, and died at Colorado Springs, Colorado, October 12, 1908. Her ancestry was Irish.

Mr. Robbins attended high school at Colby until 1897; was graduated from the Thomas County High School in 1898, and was a student at the University of Kansas, 1899-1900. He was later granted the Nebraska professional life certificate in commercial sciences.

Instructor in accounting, salesmanship, and business law at the Lincoln Business College, for a time, he was secretary of this institution, 1909-14; president, 1924-25. In March, 1925, The Lincoln Business College and The Nebraska School of Business were consolidated to form The Lincoln School of Commerce. He was candidate for county superintendent in 1900 in Thomas County, Kansas. He has lived in Nebraska since 1903.

He was united in marriage with Jessie Myrl Bain at Elk Creek, Nebraska, August 21, 1901. Mrs. Robbins, who is of German descent, was born at Elk Creek, February 1, 1876.

Mr. Robbins was president of the Missouri Valley Commercial Teachers, 1923; was president of the Central Commercial Teachers Association, 1924; and was president of the Private Schools Division of the National Commercial Teachers Association, 1930. He was president of the Lincoln Rotary Club, 1930; and is chairman of the Young Men's Division of the Young Men's Christian Association. He holds membership in the Nebraska State Historical Society and the Nebraskana Society, is a member of the Shrine Country Club and the Eastridge Club of Lincoln. He is a Mason, Master of Lodge Number 210, 1917-18; and Master of Lodge Number 314, 1922-23-24. He is affiliated with the Disciples of Christ Church of Lincoln. His favorite sport is golf. His hobby is reading. He is a Republican. Residence: Lincoln.

Halbert Harris Roberts

Halbert H. Roberts, was born at Ashland, Nebraska, November, 7 1879, and has lived in the state all his life. He is the son of John Fitzhenry and Sarah Hazzeltin (Harris) Roberts. His father, who was born in Lewiston, Illinois, February 22, 1879, was a live stock merchant, a member of the Nebraska legislature, and president of the Omaha live stock exchange He was prominent in civic affairs throughout his life and served as a member of the State Board of Education and the Omaha School Board. He died at Omaha, May 17, 1925.

His mother, who was born in Quincy, Illinois, February 7, 1855, was a country school teacher before her marriage. She was of Pennsylvania Dutch extraction.

Mr. Roberts attended the public school of Ashland, and was graduated from the South Omaha High School. He was awarded the A. B. degree at the University of Nebraska, where he was a member of the Innocents, editor and business manager of the *Nebraskan,* and served on the junior prom, senior prom, and Pan-Hellenic council.

Starting in the live stock commission business June 17, 1901, immediately upon his graduation from the University of Nebraska, he has devoted all his time since then to this business, although he has farming and cattle interests in addition. He is manager of the firm Roberts Brothers & Rose, Livestock Commission Company.

On September 27, 1905, he was united in marriage with Janet Marriott at Omaha. Mrs. Roberts, who is of English and French Canadian ancestry, was born at Pierre, South Dakota, November 7, 1883. They have two children: Jane, born September 17, 1906, who married C. Don Prawit; and Ruth, born July 29, 1908, who married Carol Van Ness Casey.

Mr. Roberts was a university cadet for two years and served in the Nebraska State Militia for two years. During the World War he assisted in loan drives and community chest activities. He is a member of the Omaha Chamber of Commerce; has been a member of the board of directors of the Omaha Livestock Exchange for several years, and is now serving as vice president of this organization; is a member of the Omaha Field Club; and holds membership in the Omaha Athletic Club. Past master of Bee Hive Lodge Number 184 of the Free Masons at South Omaha, he is also an Elk. His favorite sport is horse back riding, and his hobby is bridge whist. Residence: Omaha.

James Russell Roberts

James Russel Roberts, who has lived in this state all his life, was born at Lincoln, Nebraska, May 29, 1876, the son of Artemus and Mary (Belangee) Roberts. His father was born at Richmond, Indiana, October 28, 1841, and has been a prominent architect at Lincoln for many years. His Welsh ancestors came to America about 1600; his parents, Solomon W. and Elizabeth (Bond) Roberts were Quakers.

His mother was born at Danse, Bereau County, Illinois, September 2, 1842, and died at Dade City, Parco County, Florida, March 3, 1927. Her French Huguenot ancestors came to America in 1688 and in 1690 settled in Pennsylvania; one of her ancestors, Evi Belangee, was a pioneer Quaker in this country.

Mr. Roberts attended the University of Nebraska. He organized and developed the Roberts Dairy Company of Lincoln, Omaha, and Sioux City, and is now president of that organization. He is the author of several books used in the dairy industry and publishes a paper called *The Milkman.* He is a member of the Omaha Chamber of Commerce, the Lincoln Chamber of Commerce and the Rotary Club. His social club is Eastridge Club. He is affiliated with the First Plymouth Congregational Church.

His marriage to Clara West was solemnized at Rubens, Jewell County, Kansas, October 26, 1904. Mrs. Roberts, whose ancestry is Scotch, Irish, and Dutch, was born at Oskaloosa, Iowa, June 13, 1871. Her grandfather on the maternal side was a McBride; she is the great granddaughter of Clement West, a Revolutionary War soldier. They have two children: Perry, born September 30, 1905; and Gordon, born July 20, 1909. Residence: Lincoln.

John Elmer Roberts

John Elmer Roberts, son of Samuel and Mary Jane (Williams) Roberts, was born at Allen, Nebraska, August 16, 1872. His father was born at Pleasant Plain, Iowa, July 25, 1844. He served in the Civil War, and participated in Sherman's march to the sea, and in 1867, took up a homestead in Dixon County. He died at Allen, June 28, 1919. Mary Jane, wife of Samuel, was born at Pleasant Plain, Iowa, February 7, 1849, and resides at Greenleaf, Idaho. She is the daughter of John Williams, early pioneer, who made and burned the brick to build his home. The brick of which is still in good condition.

Mr. Roberts attended country school to the age of 16 when he helped his father on his farm until he was 25. At that time he farmed for himself two years, and for two years operated a blacksmith shop in Waterbury. Upon the death of his wife's mother, the Roberts family moved to her farm in order to care for the small children she left, and later, Mr. Roberts purchased a forty acre farm. This he sold and purchased another farm of 144 acres which he now operates. He has been a resident of Nebraska fifty-nine years.

On December 1, 1897, he was united in marriage to Georgia Fegley, at Allen. Mrs. Roberts, who is the daughter of R. L. and the granddaughter of Jacob Fegley, was born in Jackson, Nebraska, August 30, 1877. There are eight children of this marriage: Sadie, born March 1, 1899, married Leslie L. Townsend; Richard, born April 22, 1901, married Ruth Johnston; Emma, born April 5, 1904, married Howard Kyes; BeAnna, born August 4, 1905, married Clarence Emery; Lawrence, born December 8, 1906; Russel, born May 23, 1907: Ruby, born December 19, 1910, and LeRoy, born March 27, 1915.

Mr. Roberts is a Republican. He is a member of the Spring Bank Church of the Society of Friends, overseer and clerk of the pastoral body; was treasurer of the Quarterly Meeting, 1903-27; and member of the permanent board of the Nebraska Yearly Meeting since 1921. He served nine years as director of the school board, and is secretary of the Parent-Teachers' Association, and a member of the Nebraskana Society. He enjoys baseball and swimming, and his hobby is mechanics. Residence: Allen.

Joseph Roberts

Joseph Roberts was born at Cornwall, England, August 4, 1854, and for the past fifty years has been a resident of Nebraska. He is the son of John and Catherine (Dungey) Roberts. John Roberts was born at Cornwall, in 1828, and died there in 1860. He was also a farmer. His wife, Catherine, was born in Cornwall, in 1833, and died in 1865.

Mr. Roberts was educated in the common schools and has been engaged in agricultural pursuits his whole lifetime, with the exception of time spent in public office. From 1899 he was a member of the Dodge County Board of Supervisors, and in the 1903 and 1905 sessions was state representative. He was county treasurer from 1918-26. From 1906 to 1926, he was a member of the Nebraska State Board of Agriculture and served as its president 1913 and 1914. He is a Republican.

On June 20, 1893, he was married to Emma Maria Hicks at Fremont. Mrs. Roberts was born at Warren, Jo Daviess County, Illinois, December 17, 1863. They have no children, but have adopted a boy.

Mr. Roberts was one of the original members of the board of directors of the Elkhorn River Drainage District of Dodge County, and served as vice president; on the death of R. B. Schneider he was elected to the presidency. He is an outstanding citizen, a member of the Presbyterian Church, the Rotary Club and the Odd Fellows. Residence: Fremont. (Photograph in Album).

Russell LaSalle Roberts

Russell LaSalle Roberts, farmer and stockfeeder, was born at Wahoo, Nebraska, July 18, 1899, son of Russell LaSalle and Martha Stokes (Dech) Roberts. His father was born at Conneaut, Ohio, August 21, 1842, and on August 28, 1861, enlisted for three years with the 2nd Ohio Battery of Light Artillery. He was mustered out on September 10, 1864, and re-enlisted for another year, with the rank of corporal. He died at Wahoo, in June, 1911. His wife, Martha, was born in Monroe County, Pennsylvania, December 17, 1853. She was the first school teacher in Ithaca, and she and her husband were the first ones to be married there. Her father, Elijah Dech, homesteaded in Nebraska where Ithaca now stands.

Mr. Roberts attended the public schools of Ithaca, and completed the 9th grade in 1913. He attended the Nebraska School of Agriculture at Lincoln, 1913-14, and interested in stock feeding, and has farmer for himself since he was 16 years of age.

On December 31, 1923, he was married to Mary Philena McAuley, at Wahoo. Mrs. Roberts was born at Wahoo, on January 29, 1902, of Mayflower ancestry on the paternal side. There are two children: Karyl, born August 12, 1926, and Lois, born March 14, 1931. A second son, born February 1, 1930, lived but a few hours.

Mr. Roberts is a Republican. He is active in Church and Sunday School work in the Methodist Episcopal Church, is interested in farm account work, and is a member of the Ithaca Community Club. He is a Mason, a member of the National Geographic and the Nebraskana Societies, and has been secretary of the school board since 1926. His hobby is orchestral and band music, and he plays the cornet. Residence: Ithaca.

Walter Freeman Roberts

Walter F. Roberts, real estate and insurance specialist, was born at O'Neill, Nebraska, November 25, 1894, the son of Erastus Freeman and Alice (Dartt) Roberts. His father, who was a farmer, was born in New York, September 18, 1856, and died at O'Neill, December 8, 1926; his ancestry was English and Welch. His mother was born in Wisconsin.

Mr. Roberts attended the College of Agriculture at the University of Nebraska where he received his B. S. degree in 1919. He was elected to membership in Alpha Zeta and Alpha Gamma Rho at the university. From 1921 to 1924, he served as county agent in Saunders County, Nebraska, was farm manager at Grand Island, Nebraska, 1924-26, and since 1926 has been in business for himself as real estate, insurance and loan agent. He is secretary and treasurer of the Saunders County National Farm Loan Association, and handles Federal Land Bank Loans.

A Republican, he is chairman of the Saunders County central committee at this time. He is a member of the Nebraskana Society, is a director of the Wahoo Chamber of Commerce, is acting as county chairman of the Red Cross for Saunders County, and is a past chancellor commander of the Wahoo Lodge of the Knights of Pythias During the World War he served in the Naval Aviation department, and was a four minute man prior to enlisting for active service. He also took part in council of defense work and was county agricultural agent of Washington County, Nebraska. He is past commander of Wahoo Post No. 82 of the American Legion. He is a member of Masonic Lincoln Lodge No. 19 and Scottish Rite, Lincoln Council No. 2.

On July 11, 1923, he was married to Mabel E. Bern, daughter of Axel and Emily (Nygren) Bern, at Wahoo. Mrs. Roberts, who was formerly a music teacher, was born at Wahoo, of Swedish parentage. They have two children: Howard Bern, born November 25, 1926; and Irene Eveline, born August 26, 1929. Residence: Wahoo.

Walton Barwick Roberts

Walton B. Roberts was born at Lincoln, Nebraska, August 27, 1898, the son of Walton Grant and Mary (Barwick) Roberts. His father who was born at Fulton, New York, August 27, 1867, is a mortician; a descendent of John Holland, *Mayflower* passenger. His mother was born at Saybrook, Illinois, December 21, 1867.

Mr. Roberts attended McKinley and Capitol Schools and was graduated from Lincoln High School, in June,, 1917. He attended the University of Nebraska, 1922-23, and is a member of Beta Theta Pi. Upon his admission to the bar in 1924, he entered upon the active practice of law in which he is now engaged. A Republican, he was candidate for election to the House of Representatives from the 35th district, but was defeated. He was president of the Young Men's Republican Club for the year 1931.

During the time October 12, 1918, to December 16, 1918, he was a member of the Student Army Training Corps at the University of Nebraska. He is a member of the American Legion and a first lieutenant in the Quartermaster Corps Reserves. He is serving as secretary of the local organization at the present time and during 1929-30 was state secretary and treasurer. He is past vice commander and member of executive committee of Lincoln Post No. 3, of the American Legion; grand chef de gare passe, Cheminot National Passe of the Forty and Eight; member of the Sons of the American Revolution and of the Society of Mayflower descendents.

His clubs are the University, the Lincoln Country and the Shrine Clubs, and his sports are golf and tennis. His religious affiliation is with the First Presbyterian Church. He is a member of the state and county bar associations, the Chamber of Commerce, the Young Men's Christian Association, and the Hiram Club. A Mason, he is a member of the Scottish Rite, Shrine and Jesters. He also belongs to the Nebraska Alumni Association, the Nebraskana Society and the Native Sons and Daughters of Nebraska. His hobby is politics. Residence: Lincoln.

Walton Grant Roberts

Walton Grant Roberts was born at Fulton, New York, August 27, 1867, son of Evan Theodore and Josie Rosetta (Barber) Roberts. Of Welsh descent, Even T. Roberts was born at Utica, New York, February 4, 1838, and died at Lincoln on January 24, 1915. He was first a cabinet maker, a mortician and later deputy state librarian. His wife, Josie Rosetta, was born in Cherry Valley, New York, March 10, 1841 a descendant of John Holland, *Mayflower* passenger. She died at St. Joe, Michigan, June 7, 1870.

Mr. Roberts received his education in the Lincoln public schools. He has resided in Lincoln since July 6, 1873, and for many years has been engaged in the undertaking business. At the present time he is owner of the Roberts Mortuary. From 1898-1900 he was president of the National Embalmers Association. He is at the present a member of the Nebraska State Funeral Directors Association.

His marriage to Mary Barwick occurred at Lincoln on April 2, 1890. Mrs. Roberts was born at Saybrook, Illinois, December 21, 1867. She is of English descent. There are two children, Genevieve, born December 12, 1894, who married Walter Ostegard Johnson; and Walton B., born August 27, 1898, who is a lawyer (see *Nebraskana*). The Roberts' are members of the Holy Trinity Episcopal Church, the University, Country and Shrine Clubs. Mr. Roberts is a 33rd degree Scottish Rite Mason and Shriner. His other fraternal organizations include the Elks, Modern Woodmen of America, Ancient Order of United Workmen, the Royal Highlanders and the Knights of Pythias. He is a member of the Kiwanis Club, the Hiram Club, the Chamber of Commerce (life member), Nebraskana Society and the Nebraska State Historical Society. He is past president of the Sons of the American Revolution, and a member of the Society of Colonial Wars. He is deputy governor of the state society of Mayflower. Residence: Lincoln.

Wilber Roberts

Born at Spring Bank, Dixon County, Nebraska, June 24, 1874, Wilber Roberts is the son of Elijah and Sitnah Jane (Paxon) Roberts. His father was born at Pleasant Plain, Jefferson County, Iowa, January 16, 1849, and died at Allen, Nebraska, in December 14, 1921. He was a pioneer farmer and stockman.

Wilber Roberts attended the district school of Dixon County, and since young manhood has been engaged as a farmer. He has spent his entire life in Nebraska, and on March 4, 1896, was married to Cora Bell Dutton, at Allen. Mrs. Roberts was born at Jackson, Nebraska, September 23, 1877. There are eight children of this marriage, as follows:

Ross, born September 22, 1903, married Hazel Margaret Ferguson; Francis, born May 1, 1905, married Irene Hulda Tedro; Iva, born June 1, 1907, married David Luther Emery; Gladys, born October 27, 1909; Errol, born October 13, 1911; Claude, born February 23, 1915; Donald, born September 20, 1918; and Marjorie, born September 17, 1923. One of the boys is a mail clerk, one a linotype operator, and one a service station employee.

Mr. Roberts is a member of the Spring Bank Society of Friends, and for the past twenty-five years has been treasurer of the Evangelistic Board of the Nebraska Yearly Meeting. He is also a member of the Nebraskana Society. Residence: Allen.

John A. Robertson

Born at Brownstown, Indiana, January 22, 1867, John A. Robertson came to Holt County in 1883, in a covered wagon, taking a pre-emption on eighty acres of land in 1886.

His father, George L. Robertson, was born in Virginia, May 23, 1823, and died at Brownstown, in 1869. He was a farmer, descended from early Scotch settlers in Virginia. His mother, Harriet Critchfield, was born in Ohio, May 5, 1838, and died at Joy, March 3, 1928. Her ancestry was Scotch and Dutch.

John A. Robertson attended common school. Two years after coming to Nebraska, on December 25, 1885, he was married to Rachel Rebecca Hindman at Niobrara. Mrs. Robertson was born at Colora, Maryland, February 5, 1870. To them twelve children were born, all of whom are living.

Lottie M., born in 1886, is married to F. J. Weidman of Plainview, Nebraska. Elsie Roberta, born June 10, 1888, married Harry Anderson; they live at Wakefield, Nebraska. George C., born July 28, 1890, married Esther C. Thomas; they live at O'Neill; Helen Ethel, born February 21, 1893, is married to Albert T. Sundell of Wakefield; Harriet Jane, born December 18, 1895, married E. C. McElhaney of Page, Nebraska; John Allen, born March 19, 1898, married Henrietta Wedel, they reside in Chicago; Samuel R., born September 9, 1900, married Louise Walters and resides at Joy; Raymond Ralph, born January 22, 1902, married Neva Armour, and they live at Dakota City; Rachel A., born July 19, 1904; Rebecca M., born August 8, 1906; James A., born September 6, 1908, and Richard W., born December 3, 1910, all live at home. Both boys are attending the University of Nebraska, and all of the children have attended college or university.

Mr. Robertson is a Democrat, and has been active in politics for a number of years. He served in the Nebraska house of representatives 1895-97, and in the senate 1913-15-17 and 25. He introduced and secured the passage of the first mother's pension law in Nebraska (senate file No. 116). He was a member of the Nebraska state board for District No. 1 in the World War (July 21, 1917-March 31, 1919).

He is a member of the Royal Highlanders, the Modern Woodmen of America and the Nebraskana Society. Residence: Joy.

Wallace Robertson

Wallace Robertson, banker at Beatrice, Nebraska, has been prominent in civic and business affairs in Gage County for over 40 years. He was born at Cambridge, Washington County, New York, June 30, 1869, the son of John and Minerva Susanna (Rice) Robertson. His father, a farmer, was born at Cambridge, May 12, 1923, and died at Beatrice, April 9, 1891; his Scotch ancestors came to America in 1775, and settled in Washington County, New York.

His mother was born at Greenrich, Washington County, New York, October 9, 1835, and died at Beatrice, September 4, 1914. Her English ancestors settled in Sudbury, Massachusetts, in 1639.

Mr. Robertson was graduated from the Beatrice High School in 1887. He has held every official position possible in the Beatrice National Bank of which he is now president. He is eligible for membership in the Sons of the American Revolution, is a member of the Nebraska Historical Association and the Nebraskana Society, and for the past six years has been a director in the Young Men's Christian Association.

He is affiliated with the First Presbyterian Church, of which he is a trustee, is a member of the Rotary Club and the Beatrice Chamber of Commerce, and is an Elk and Mason. His social club is the Lincoln University

Club, and his political affiliation is with the Republican party. He is interested in football.

Mr. Robertson was married to Elizabeth Cleland at Beaver, Pennsylvania, October 10, 1906. Mrs. Robertson was born at Beaver, March 6, 1870; her father came to this country from Scotland in 1820. They have one daughter, Jane Elizabeth, born July 30, 1910. Residence: Beatrice.

Edward John Robins

Born at Hecla, Brown County, South Dakota, November 7, 1891, Edward John Robins has been a resident of Nebraska since September, 1912. He is the son of Edward John and Mary Elmira (Thorp) Robins, the former a native of Chicago, born November 6, 1860. A building contractor until his death at Hecla, July 2, 1924, his father came from London, and served in the Civil War. Mary Elmira Thorp was born at Winona, Minnesota, May 2, 1866, and resides at Hecla. Of German and English descent, her father served in the Civil War.

Educated in the grade schools at Hecla, he was graduated from the Portage Township High School at Hecla, in 1910, and received his LL. B. from Creighton, in 1915. During 1910-11, he majored in liberal arts at the University of South Dakota, and in 1918, attended the military aeronautics department of the University of California. He represented the University of South Dakota in debate, was a member of the Creighton debate team two years, and was captain the second year. His fraternity is Gamma Eta Gamma.

After one year's law practice in Omaha, he came to Fremont, in 1916, and was associated with C. E. Abbott for seven months. He then opened his own office, which he closed during the war. A second lieutenant in the aviation section of the Aeronautics Reserves, as a military aviator, he also assisted as a speaker in loan drives at Berkeley and San Francisco. After the war he had a plane in Fremont, two years, and is a member of the Aero Club of America. He is a member of the American Legion, the Young Men's Christian Association, and for some time was a member of Kiwanis. Since 1919, he has been again engaged in practice, until 1924, as a member of the law firm of Abbott, Rohn and Robins, for a time in private practice, and now as senior member of the law firm of Robins and Yost, with William H. Lamme as associate.

He is attorney for the Globe Indemnity Company, the American Auto Company, the Southern Surety Company, Nebraska, attorney for the First National Bank of Scribner, the Farmers State Bank of Valley, the Winslow State Bank, Hooper State Bank, etc. He is the owner of a section of land in Brown County which he is planting to pine timber under supervision of the Federal Forestry Department. He is interested in farm operations, and owns a farm in Knox County.

Mr. Robins is a Democrat, and a member of the Eagles, and of the America, Nebraska State and Dodge County Bar Associations. He enjoys fishing and swimming, and spends all his free time in farming.

On July 22, 1924, he was married to Lois Florene Haas, at Omaha. Mrs. Robins was born at Alexandria, Nebraska, March 1, 1900, was graduated from Nebraska with a B. S. in Home Economics, in 1923, and taught that subject in the Junior High School at Fremont, one year. She is a member of Alpha Omicron Pi: They have one son, James Edward, born May 6, 1928. Residence: Fremont.

Charles Robinson

For nearly 60 years Charles Robinson has resided at Belgrade, Nebraska, where he has successfully engaged in farming and stockraising. He was born at Pittsburgh, Pennsylvania, December 15, 1850, the son of Thomas and Sahara (Hale) Robinson, the former a farmer who was born in England and died at Rockfall,

Illinois, in 1831. His mother was born of German parentage at Pittsburg, and died at Rockfall.

Mr. Robinson was married to Sarah Castle at Fremont, Nebraska; she was born in Pennsylvania and died at Cedar Rapids, Nebraska; her ancestry was Scotch. To this marriage were born: Fanny, November 22, 1877, who married Alex Burnside; Thomas, February 26, 1874; Mary, June 17, 1878, who married Earnest Dufoe; Ethley, April 9, 1880; and Will, September 15, 1883, who married Nell Wilkinson. Mr. Robinson is now married to Molly De Lancey. Residence: Belgrade.

Frank Oakum Robinson

Frank Oakum Robinson, dentist, was born at Plain City, Ohio, December 1, 1865, son of William Hunter and Elizabeth (McCampbell) Robinson.

He received the Bachelor of Science degree in 1888 and the degree of Doctor of Dental Surgery from the Louisville College of Dentistry in 1899. From 1898 until 1919 he engaged in practice, and since 1894 has been secretary of the local building and loan association and a member of the firm of Robinson and Robinson, Abstractors.

He was married on October 10, 1900, to Florence N. Smith at Villisca, Iowa. There are four children, Marian, born January 18, 1902; Philip, born December 10, 1903, who married Lucile A. Randall; Howard, born October 5, 1905; and Donald, born April 14, 1907.

Dr. Robinson has been active in the Republican party for many years, and has held various offices. He is a member of the Chamber of Commerce (president 1915-16). He is a Mason (Scottish Rite, 32nd degree). During the years 1929-30 he was president of the Hartington Country Club. Residence: Hartington.

Harold Wiley Robinson

A resident of Nebraska for the past 25 years, Harold Wiley Robinson is editor and publisher of the *Upland Eagle* at Upland, Nebraska. He was born at Franklin, Nebraska, October 13, 1906, the son of John Warnock and Emma Jane (Laws) Robinson. His father is also a published. His mother's ancestry is English.

Mr. Robinson attended Franklin High School, and in 1924, was graduated from the Upland High School. He attended the University of Nebraska from 1924 to 1927, and was a student at the University of Denver for a time.

He is a member of the Upland Community Club, is affiliated with the Methodist Church, and holds membership in the Nebraskana Society. His hobby is philately and his favorite sport is golf. On February 27, 1931, he was married at Topeka, Kansas to Alyce Leone Groshong. Residence: Upland.

Lawrence Roswell Robinson

Lawrence Roswell Robinson was born at Waterloo, Nebraska, October 3, 1891, the son of James Chauncey Robinson and Mary Cornelia (Temple) Robinson. His father was born at Belcher, New York, November 7, 1861, and his mother at Granville, New York, May 8, 1863. James C. Robinson died at Waterloo, Nebraska, May 2, 1928.

Lawrence R. Robinson attended Waterloo public school, the Bellevue College, and Kearney Military Academy, from which he was graduated in 1910. He also attended the University of Nebraska two years, where he was a member of Beta Theta Pi and the local inter-fraternities Iron Sphinx and Viking.

On August 16, 1916, he married Sarah Blanche Fenton at Rocky Ford, Colorado. Mrs. Robinson was born at Rocky Ford on April 9, 1895, of English parentage. They have two children, Lawrence Roswell, Jr., born March 12, 1921, and Ward Fenton, born February 15, 1927.

Mr. Robinson is secretary-treasurer of the J. C. Robinson Seed Company at Waterloo, Nebraska, which has branch offices in Colorado and California. He has lived in Nebraska forty years and has always been prominent in its civic and cultural growth.

A Presbyterian, he is affiliated with the Waterloo Community Church. He is a member of the Happy Hollow Club, the University Club, and the Athletic Club, all of Omaha. Mr. Robinson is a member of the Nebraskana Society, and is a 32nd degree Mason and member of the Shrine. Residence: Waterloo.

Paul Ray Robinson

Paul Ray Robinson, cashier of the North Loup State Bank, was born at Scotia, Nebraska, September 5, 1893, son of Joshua Martin and Gertrude Beatrice (Sturgeon) Robinson.

Joshua Robinson was born in Springfield, Illinois, October 17, 1871, son of E. G. Robinson, who served in the United States Navy under Farragut in the Civil War, and who later brought cattle from Texas to Nebraska. Joshua Robinson is a manufacturer of poultry and livestock feeders.

His wife, Gertrude, was born in Indiana, October 26, 1873, of Pennsylvania Dutch descent, and in her youth was a school teacher.

Paul Ray Robinson attended Arcadia High School two years, was graduated from Doane Academy in 1909, and attended Doane College two years. He is a member of Alpha Omega. He taught school two years in rural Valley County, and served four years as deputy county treasurer at Ord.

Thereafter he engaged in banking four years at Crete, and for the past eleven years has held his present position as cashier of the North Loup State Bank. He is a Republican, has held minor offices including a term on the town board and two terms as mayor.

Hs marriage to Inez Annette Tully was solemnized at Grand Island on October 30, 1917. Mrs. Robinson was born at Grand Island, November 11, 1891, of Irish, English and Scotch extraction. Her mother is of the Brown family, descended from John Brown of the Civil War.

Mr. Robinson paid his way through two years of school as a band leader, and has continued to direct the Ord, Grand Island, Dorchester and North Loup bands. He is a member of the Congregational Church, Ashlar Lodge of the Ancient Free and Accepted Masons, Chapter and Knights Templar. For the past five years he has been treasurer of the Valley County Red Cross. His favorite sports are golf and baseball, while his hobbies are reading, bridge and music. Residence; North Loup.

Russell Alexander Robinson

Russell A. Robinson, one of the leading lawyers of Dodge County, Nebraska, was born at Saratoga, Wyoming, January 23, 1896, the son of Alexander and Isabel Sutherland Robinson. His father was a clergyman in the Presbyterian Church and was an energetic home missionary in the early days of Wyoming, where his territory was large and activities difficult. He was born at Pictou, Nova Scotia, 1858, and died at Boulder, Colorado, 1904. His father came from Scotland, and the family name of Robertson was changed at that time.

His mother was born at Westville, Pictou, Nova Scotia, Canada, July, 1858. She has always been a devout church worker and has been especially interested in the work of the Woman's Christian Temperance Union. Her ancestors were Scotch, of the Sutherland family of Highland blood.

Mr. Robinson attended the public schools of Colorado, and was graduated from high school at North Bend, Nebraska, 1915. He was a student at Hastings College, 1915-17; was awarded the LL. B. degree at the University of Nebraska, 1921; received a certificate of study from Faculte Des Lettres, at the University of Toulouse, Tou-

louse, France, June 30, 1919; and received a law certificate at the latter institution. He was a member of the Hastings College debating team, 1915-16, and received his college letter; was a member of the University of Nebraska sophomore class debating team, 1917; and was secretary of the law class at the University of Nebraska, 1921.

Mr. Robinson was admitted to the bar, June 19, 1921, and immediately began the practice of law at Maybell, Colorado. A little later in the year he moved to North Bend, and in 1923, entered into a partnership with Vance A. Doty, continuing until 1926. He served as city attorney of North Bend, from 1922-31. A Republican, he has consistently refused to enter the political field and has devoted his entire time to the practice of law.

He was married to Mary Estella Baker at Carleton, Nebraska, September 19, 1920. Mrs. Robinson was born of Irish parentage at Carleton, October 26, 1899. Two children were born to them: Clark A., born February 18, 1923; and Gorden Kent, born February 22, 1926, who died June 26, 1930.

Mr. Robinson entered the United States Army service April 26, 1918, and was sent to Camp Funston, in charge of that quota; was a private in the headquarters platoon, Company 355th Infantry, 89th Division; and saw service in the Toul Sector, St. Mihiel, and Meuse-Argonne. He is town committeeman of the C. M. T. C., and a member of the Committee of Defense, of the American Legion. He is a charter member and organizer of the local American Legion Post.

He has served his community as a member of the Red Cross; the North Bend Community Club; Volunteer Firemen; Boy Scouts of America; and the Young Men's Christian Association. He is city committeeman, and holds membership in the Dodge County Bar Association, and the Nebraska State Bar Association. He is a Mason, and is affiliated with the United Presbyterian Church of North Bend. His sports include: hunting; fishing; hiking; baseball; and volley ball. His hobby is philosophy. He likes duck hunting. Residence: North Bend.

Lesle Ivan Roblyer

Born at Almeria, Nebraska, September 29, 1891, Lesle Ivan Roblyer is the son of Jacob Henry and Marian Mayfield (Copp) Roblyer. His father, who was a farmer, was born at Elmyria, Pennsylvania, January 19, 1854, and died at Taylor, April 12, 1914; he served in Company F, Pennsylvania Volunteer Infantry for three years during the Civil War; his ancestry was Pennsylvania Dutch and French. His mother, whose English ancestors came to this country with Cornwallis, was born at Mansfield, October 18, 1853, and is living at Taylor at the present time.

Mr. Roblyer was graduated from the Taylor High School in 1910 and later was graduated from Kearney State Normal School. He was a teacher for nine years after the completion of his education and for the past seven years has been manager of the Farmers Union Association at Taylor. He served as a member of the school board from 1927 to 1930, and in 1928 was unsuccessful candidate for county treasurer.

He was married to Fanny Lucinda Moon at Taylor, July 1, 1914. Mrs. Roblyer, whose ancestry is Pennsylvania Dutch, was born at Minco, Oklahoma, October 18, 1893. To them the following children were born: Harry, February 6, 1919; Margaret, June 17, 1921; Jean, October 2, 1922; and Curtis, March 25, 1925.

Mr. Roblyer is a Democrat, and a member of the Modern Woodmen of America. His hobby is mechanics. Residence: Taylor.

Palmer Oliver Robson

A resident of Nebraska since birth, Palmer Oliver Robson was born near Thayer, in York County, September 4, 1900. He is the son of Horace and Alice Annette (Paden) Robson, the former a native of England. Horace Robson was born in London, August 14, 1865, and died at York, November 13, 1928. His wife, born in Ottowa, Illinois, May 15, 1864, and died at Thayer, May 25, 1907.

Upon his graduation from Benedict High School, Mr. Robson attended Lincoln High School. On May 23, 1925, he was united in marriage to Pauline Lucille Lytle, at York. Mrs. Robson was born at York, July 2, 1905, and is a teacher. There are two sons, Howard, born April 26, 1926; and Donald, born July 21, 1927.

Mr. Robson is a member of the First Presbyterian Church at Thayer, and of the Masons and the Nebraskana Society. Residence: Thayer.

Carl Henry Rockey

Carl Henry Rockey, electrical engineer, and superintendent of municipal utilities of the city of Alliance, was born at Edgemont, South Dakota, January 30, 1894, son of Chris Henry and Lulu Anna (Hagerman) Rockey. His father was born in Des Moines, Iowa, March 5, 1861, and is a locomotive engineer. His mother was born in Mercer, Ohio, February 1, 1870.

Mr. Rockey is married to Mabel Virginia Grassman, who was born at Plattsmouth, Nebraska, January 13, 1900. They have one daughter, Susan, born August 29, 1924.

During the late war Mr. Rockey served with the 127th Heavy Field Artillery with the rank of Sergeant, from April 6, 1917, until January 24, 1919. He is a member of the American Legion, a member and commander of the Veterans of Foreign Wars, and a member of the Society of Military Engineers, and the American Institute of Electrical Engineers. He is a Methodist, a Rotarian, a Mason, and an Elk. His club is the Alliance Country Club. His favorite sports are golf, baseball, and football, while his hobby is reading. Residence: Alliance.

Thomas Harry Rockwell

Thomas H. Rockwell, county treasurer of Dakota County for the past five years, has lived in Nebraska all his life. He was born at Hubbard, Nebraska, October 19, 1888, the son of Susan (Myers) and Richard Douglas Rockwell. His father, who was born at Hudson, Indiana, January 13, 1851, and died at Hubbard, Nebraska, December 24, 1914, was a carpenter and farmer; his ancestry was Dutch, English, and Welsh. His mother was born at Hudson, October 20, 1856, and died at South Sioux City, Nebraska, July 1, 1930.

Mr. Rockwell attended the public schools and high school at Hubbard, Nebraska. A Republican, he has served as county treasurer for the past five years.

On March 24, 1920, he was united in marriage with Dorothea Esther Teager at South Sioux City. Mrs. Rockwell was born at LeMars, Iowa, July 8, 1896. She was a teacher before her marriage. Two children were born to this marriage: Richard, born September 26, 1922; and Donald, born August 6, 1925. Residence: South Sioux City.

Patrick Roddy

Patrick Roddy, pioneer farmer, riverman and legislator, was born at Mullingar, County Westmeath, Ireland, July 12, 1842. He is the son of Michael and Annie (Cormack) Roddy. Michael Roddy who was born at Mullingar, in 1800, came to America in 1864, and settled in Otoe County, where he engaged in farming and stock raising until his death at Nebraska City in April, 1878. Annie Cormack Roddy was born in Ireland, in 1812, and died there in 1853. Patrick Roddy received his education in the public schools of Ireland. He married Mary Elizabeth Henzie at Omaha, on January 9, 1870.

Mrs. Roddy was born in County Tipperary, Ireland, March 17, 1844. There were six children born to their marriage, four of whom are living. They are: Margaret,

born October 23, 1870; John H., born February 1, 1872, who died March 16, 1912; Thomas F., born December 5, 1874, who married Mary E. Leggett, and who was graduated from the University of Nebraska, who received his B. A. in 1898, and his LL. B., in 1900; Bary E., born August 21, 1881, who was graduated from the University of Nebraska, 1904; Katherine A., born September 26, 1883, who was a graduate of the Peru State Normal School; and James P., born November 15, 1885, who died March 4, 1890, was a Spanish-American War veteran; John H., who died in 1912, was also a Spanish-American War veteran.

In 1872, Patrick Roddy was captain of the *Kate C. Nutt,* transfer between Omaha and Council Bluffs, and holds a pilot's license for the Mississippi River and its tributaries. He was formerly a member of the Missouri River Transfer Company and the Hannibal and St. Joseph Packett Company. He was a Republican and served as a member of the Nebraska State legislature the sessions of 1895 and 1897.

He lived in Otoe County for sixty-eight years, and was closely identified with every worthy movement in the community, and state. He celebrated his 88th birthday on July 12, 1930. He was a member of St. Mary's Catholic Church, and the Nebraska Territorial Pioneer's Association. For more than 20 years he served as a member of the Walnut Creek School Board.

Patrick Roddy was a man extremely active in his state and community. He took pride in the possession of his neighbors and beautifying and improving his state. His death on February 17, 1931, was a distinct loss to his community and many friends. He came to Nebraska, on March 7, 1863, walking from Sidney, Iowa, to Nebraska City, as there were no railroads at that time.

James A. Rodman

James A. Rodman, lawyer and executive, was born at Salem, Indiana, May 6, 1887, son of Walter Benton and America (Robinson) Rodman.

He received his Bachelor of Laws degree from the University of Nebraska, and from 1913 until 1921, practiced law in Kimball County. He was county attorney of Kimball County from 1915 until 1919, and a member of the house of representatives, 1919-21-25-27, floor leader, 1925, and speaker of the house, 1927. In 1920 he was a member of the Nebraska Constitutional Convention.

His marriage to Helen Irene Lawrence was solemnized at Fremont, Nebraska, on August 15, 1914. Residence: Omaha.

Samuel Wesley Roe

Samuel Wesley Roe was born in Huron County, Canada, December 26, 1871, the son of Henry and Mary Ann McCracken Roe. His father, who was a farmer, was born in County Kilkarney, Ireland, June 28, 1834, and died at St. Paul, Nebraska, February 11, 1908. His mother was born at Peterborough, Canada, March 21, 1844, and is still living.

Mr. Roe attended rural school and later studied at the Central City College. He has been a member of the Ord School Board for the past 25 years, is president of the Farmers Grain and Supply Company of Ord, is vice president of the Valley County Fair Association, and is treasurer of the Enterprise Telephone Company.

He holds membership in the Ancient Order of United Workmen, is a Mason, and is affiliated with the First Methodist Church of Ord. His hobbies are reading and history. During the World War Mr. Roe was registrar and served in loan drives in Valley County.

His marriage to Jessie M. Ward occurred in Valley County, September 17, 1902; she was born in Valley County, August 29, 1880. They have the following children: Edgar Ward, born July 24, 1903, who married Edna Kill; Claude, born December 1, 1907; Howard, born June 9,

1909; Irma M., born November 1, 1913, who died November 9, 1916; and Dwight Harris, born January, 26, 1924, who died April 3, 1924. Residence: Ord.

Clyde Augustus Roeder

Dr. Clyde A. Roeder, born at Omaha, October 15, 1884, has won distinction in his profession both within and without the state. He is the son of George and Florence (Hurle) Roeder, the former a physician and surgeon of early American ancestry. Florence Hurle Roeder died at Grand Island, Nebraska, in November, 1903. She was of English descent.

Dr. Roeder received his elementary education in the public schools of Nebraska, and was awarded his M. D. from Yale University in 1908. He entered upon the practice of medicine, 1910, and was an associate surgical assistant at the Mayo Clinic in Rochester, Minnesota, 1914, 1915, and 1916, specializing in surgery in 1916, and for the past twenty years has been engaged in private practice. He is the author of more than thirty-eight articles on surgical subjects, and is associate professor of surgery at the University of Nebraska, and attending surgeon to University Hospital, Immanuel and Covenant Hospitals and the Clarkson Memorial Hospital.

An Episcopalian, Dr. Roeder is a member of Trinity Cathedral, a member of the Chamber of Commerce and of the Nebraskana Society and the State Historical Society. His professional associations include the Western Surgical Association, the American Medical Association, American College of Surgeons, Nebraska State Medical Association, and the Alumni Association of the Mayo Clinic. He is also a member of the Douglas County Medical Society.

He was married to Theresa Heinsimer, at Glenwood, Iowa, June 25, 1912. Mrs. Roeder was born at Glenwood, in 1894, and is of English and German descent. They have one daughter, Suzanne, born November 10, 1918. Residence: Omaha.

Elmer Frederick Roeder

A resident of Nebraska since 1892, Elmer Frederick Roeder was born at Schapville, Jo Daviess County, Illinoise, November 29, 1881. His father, Fred Roeder, born at Schapville, March 27, 1858 is a farmer whose parents came to America from Germany in 1852. His mother, Elizabeth Stiefel, was born in Hamburg, Germany in 1859, and died at Hickman, Nebraska, January 4, 1898.

Educated in the rural schools of Lancaster County until he reached the age of sixteen, Mr. Roeder has since engaged extensively in farming and for a number of years has been much interested in 4-H Club work. He is at the present time leader in that organization, is a member of the Bennet Parent Teachers Association, and for six years has served as a member of the local school board.

On October 2, 1912, he was united in marriage to Emma L. Baade at Bennett. Mrs. Roder, born at Bennet, March 5, 1893, is the daughter of German farmers in Lancaster County. There are four children, Lois, born August 3, 1913; Lewellyn, born May 29, 1917; Norma, born July 9, 1924; and Eldon, born August 8, 1926.

An independent politically, Mr. Roeder takes an interest in all public issues. He is a member of the Hickman Presbyterian Church, and was recently made a life member of the Nebraskana Society. Residence: Bennet.

Theresa Roeder

Theresa Roeder, a leader in Omaha social and civic circles, was born in Iowa, and for a number of years has lived at Omaha. She attended Lasell Seminary at Auburn Dale, Massachusetts, and later studied at the University of Iowa, where she was a member of Delta Gamma Sorority.

Mrs. Roeder is a member of the Omaha Junior League. She served as secretary of the Tuesday Musical Club at Omaha, 1928-29-30, was past president of the Woman's Faculty Club at the University of Nebraska in the department of medicine, 1929-30, is vice president of the Woman's Auxiliary to the Nebraska State Medical Association, and is a member of the board of the Omaha Art Institute.

She is married to Clyde Augustus Roeder, who is a prominent physician and surgeon in Omaha. They have one daughter, Suzanne. Residence: Omaha.

Erwin H. Roepe

Born at Corder, Lafayette County, Missouri, July 4, 1890, Erwin H. Roepe is the son of Louis and Mathilda Sophia (Lohoefener) Roepe. His father was born at Concordia, Missouri, February 4, 1873, and was a successful merchant in Beemer, and in Missouri, for many years. He is now retired and resides at Kansas City, Missouri. His wife, Mathilda, was born at St. Louis, Missouri, October 16, 1878, and is active in club and church work. Both are of German descent, for several generations in America.

Erwin H. Roepe attended St. John College at Winfield, Kansas, graduating in 1909, he attended Beemer High School, and also took a business course. In college he was especially active in dramatics and was a member of the basketball team.

On June 2, 1914, he was united in marriage to Margaret Anna Breetzke, at Beemer. Mrs. Roepe was born at Beemer October 16, 1889, of German parentage. They have one son, Robert, born March 9, 1916, who has studied piano especially, and plays many musical instruments. He intends to be a salesman.

For twenty-six years Mr. Roepe has engaged in general store work, and just recently has engaged in selling flour and feeds for the Norfolk Cereal and Flour Mills, still retaining his mercantile connection as junior member of the firm of L. Roepe and Son. He is a Democrat, and for seven years has been a member of the village council.

Mr. Roepe is a member of the Community Club, and is secretary and treasurer of the Cuming County Civic Club. He is president of the local Lions Club and a member of St. John's Evangelical Lutheran Church. He likes golf, and is a member of the Country Club, and is fond of reading, and music. Residence: Beemer.

William Henry Roether

William Henry Roether, county judge, was born in Clarkson, Nebraska, March 20, 1888, son of John and Christina Mary (Becker) Roether. John Roether was born at Mineral Point, Wisconsin, April 13, 1850. He was a farmer and business man and a Jeffersonian Democrat whose parents came from Germany. He died at Clarkson, on May 23, 1907. His wife, Christina, was born near Coblenz, Germany, April 15, 1849, and came with her parents to America. They died shortly thereafter. She was a real mother, who reared eleven children, and who devoted her entire time to their interests. Her death occurred at Clarkson, November 1, 1930.

Upon his graduation from Clarkson High School in June, 1904, William Henry Roether attended Fremont Normal School, and later taught three years in the rural districts. Thereafter he was an office man in a garage, wrote insurance and farmed. In 1916, he was elected Clerk of the District Court, serving until 1920; and served as deputy county treasurer, 1923-25. He was elected county judge of Colfax County in 1925, and is still serving. An independent in politics, he tends toward being a Jeffersonian Democrat.

Judge Roether was married to Emily Zelenda at Fremont, Nebraska, January 12, 1910. Mrs. Roether was born at Cedar Rapids, Iowa, August 27, 1887. Her parents came from Bohemia, and left her an orphan at the age of 12. There are two children, Geneva E., born October 30, 1910, who is a graduate of Schuyler High School as an honor student in the class of 1928, which numbered sixty-seven. She attended the American Business College at Omaha, and was graduated in 1930, and is now clerk of the Colfax County Court. The second child is Willette Elaine, born December 3, 1925.

Judge Roether was crippled at the age of four by having a heel crushed in a turntable, and as a boy worked with his parents, brothers and sisters in sugar beet fields of their own. Later as the children grew up they went into general farming.

At the present time Judge Roether is a member of the school board, and the First Presbyterian Church of Schuyler. During the World War he was chief clerk and secretary of the Colfax County Local Draft Board, and assisted in Red Cross, Y. M. C. A. and other drives. Aside from his profession his chief interest is farming and caring for stock, and at the present time he has several cows. Residence: Schuyler.

Elmer R. Rogers

Elmer R. Rogers, superintendent of schools at Bridgeport, was born at Jennings, Kansas, September 15, 1887, son of Isaac and Jennie Ellen (Goldsbury) Rogers. His father was born in Lawson, Missouri, and farmed there until his death. He was of Scotch-Irish ancestry. His wife, Jennie, was born in Lawson, Missouri, July 17, 1869.

Mr. Rogers attended the public and high schools at Inman, and received his Bachelor of Arts degree from the State Teachers' College at Wayne. He was later a student at the University of Iowa, and the University of Nebraska, and has completed his work on his thesis for his Masters degree. From 1912 until 1915, he was the only student member of the State Normal quartette, and during 1915 was guard on the football team.

From 1918 until 1920, Mr. Rogers was a salesman for the Standard Oil Company and the following two years was engaged in the insurance business. From 1908 until 1911, he taught in rural schools, and from 1915 until 1919 was superintendent of schools at Pilger. He also held this position from 1922 until 1924, and from 1925 until 1931, was superintendent at Madison.

On August 4, 1915, he was married to Ina Frances Clark at Winona, Minnesota. Mrs. Rogers was born at Inman, Nebraska, April 25, 1891. She is a graduate of Inman High School and attended Winona State Teachers College. She is the daughter of Edward A. and Anna M. (Green) Clark. Her mother is a resident of Inman, Nebraska. To them were born five children, four of whom are living, Helen, born May 28, 1916, died August 28, 1921; Maxine, July 25, 1919; Jeanette, July 17, 1922; Kenneth, April 8, 1925; and Shirley, July 3, 1928.

Mr. Rogers is affiliated with the First Baptist Church of Chambers. He is a member of the Chamber of Commerce and was secretary at Madison, 1925-1926. He is a member of the Lions Club, the Modern Woodmen of America, the Odd Fellows, the Ancient Free and Accepted Masons, and was president of the third educational district of the Nebraska State Teachers Association. He is director of the male quartette of the Lions Club, and is much interested in music. His favorite sport is golf. Residence: Bridgeport.

Richard Huntington Rogers

Richard H. Rogers, owner of the Rogers Motor Company, was born at Minden, Nebraska, November 18, 1896. He is the son of Noyes C. and Harriet C. (Sprague) Rogers, the former of whom, a banker and lumberman, was born at Walden, Vermont, in January, 1843, and died at Lincoln, in April, 1929. He was of English ancestry. Harriet Sprague Rogers was a native of Montpelier, Ver-

mont, who was born June 23, 1854, and died at Lincoln, in October, 1928.

Mr. Rogers was graduated from the Minden public and high schools and attended the University of Nebraska 3 years. At the university he was a letterman in baseball and a member of Sigma Chi. On August 9, 1917, he was married to Marie Meeker at Lincoln. Mrs. Rogers was born at Garland, January 16, 1898. They have two children, Richard H., born June 23, 1919, and Eloise, born December 16, 1924.

During 1920, Mr. Rogers was engaged as a banker at Puenta, California, and during 1919, was so engaged at Minden. Since 1921, he has been in the automobile business as owner of the Rogers Motor Company, Ford dealers. He is also a director of the Cornbelt Life Insurance Company. He is a Republican, a member of Westminster Presbyterian Church and the Young Men's Christian Association. He enjoys golf, and his hobby is horses. His clubs are the University and the Country Clubs. Residence: Lincoln.

Wallace Hector Rogers

Wallace Hector Rogers, past vice-president of the Rogers Lumber and Coal Company of Bayard, was born at Waco, Nebraska, January 29, 1882, son of Hector John and Agnes (Stevenson) Rogers. The father, born in Belfast, Ireland, January 1, 1844, came to America about 1869. He was a farmer and carpenter, whose death occurred at York, Nebraska, March 6, 1928. His wife, Agnes, was born at Mulinary, Ireland, December 25, 1854, and died at York, March 5, 1925.

Upon the completion of his public school education, Mr. Rogers attended the York Business College. He has been in the lumber business for the past 28 years, 16 years as yard manager, seven years as district manager for the Antrim Lumber Company of St. Louis, having supervision of 15 yards in Oklahoma. The balance of the time, he has been the owner of a lumber yard. He is a Republican.

His marriage to Rosa Jane Jones occurred at Shelby, Nebraska, October 4, 1905. Mrs. Rogers, who was a school teacher before marriage, was born at Rising City, Nebraska, February 29, 1884. To them were born four children, Elsie, born January 28, 1907, who is a registered nurse; Maurice, born May 8, 1909, who is married to Evelyne Reynolds and who is in the lumber business; LaVerne, born May 14, 1914, who is in school; and Wallace, born December 28, 1920, who is also in school.

For a number of years, Mr. Rogers has been prominent in fraternal and civic organizations in his city. He is a member of the Red Cross, the North Platte Valley Chamber of Commerce, the Lions Club, the Bayard school board, and the Masons (royal arch, knights templar). During the late war, Mr. Rogers passed all examinations for Young Men's Christian Association secretary, and served in that capacity. He is affiliated with the Methodist Episcopal Church. His favorite sports are hunting and fishng. Residence: Bayard.

Walter Scott Rogers

Walter Scott Rogers, who is a lifelong resident of this state, was born at Waco, Nebraska, March 17, 1880. His father, Hector John Rogers, who was born in County Armaugh, Ireland, January 1, 1843, and died at York, Nebraska March 6, 1928, was a pioneer farmer, carpenter and cabinet maker, who came to this country in 1869; he built the first store in Waco and Utica, and supervised the building of many stations for the Burlington Railroad. Agnes (Stevenson) Rogers, his mother, was born of Scotch parentage in County Armaugh, December 25, 1853, and died at York, March 5, 1926; she came to this country in 1871.

Mr. Rogers attended rural school in York County, was graduated from the York Academy, and studied commercial subjects at York Business College. He has been engaged in the retail lumber business for over 30 years, and has been a hardware dealer part of that time. He is now manager of the W. S. Rogers Lumber Company at Ainsworth, Nebraska, and is also a stock farmer in Brown County.

A Republican, he is serving as county committeeman of Brown County at this time. Mr. Rogers is a member of the Ainsworth Chamber of Commerce, was formerly a member of the Parent-Teachers' Association and the School Board, and has served twice as delegate to the General Conference of the Methodist Episcopal Church where he has been a regular attendant for the past 34 years.

On September 23, 1903, he married Nellie Irene Strickler at Waco. Mrs. Rogers was born at Waco, November 23, 1882, and is descended from Swiss ancestors, on the paternal side, who came to this country in 1700; her mother was of English descent. To this marriage were born: Vesper Agnes, September 20, 1904, who was graduated from the University of Nebraska in 1928; Helen, September 10, 1906, who attended Morningside College in Iowa, and is now married to Seth R. Thompson; Willard, September 19, 1913, who is a student at Ashbury College, Wilmore, Kentucky; and Doris, March 3, 1919. Residence: Ainsworth.

Julius William Ferdinand Roggenkamp

Julius William Roggenkamp, a farmer near Upland, Nebraska, for the past 36 years, was born at Davenport, Iowa, November 9, 1871, the son of George and Amelia (Untiedt) Roggenkamp. His father, who was born at Schleigwig, on the Island of Famam, Germany, August 12, 1833, and died at Davenport, February 14, 1920, was a farmer who came to this country in June, 1842. His mother, also of German descent, was born at Davenport, July 4, 1847, and died there in November, 1917.

Mr. Roggenkamp has been a farmer and stockman all his life, and for many years has been prominent in civic affairs at Upland, Nebraska. He served as county supervisor for 12 years in Franklin County, has held membership in the local lodge of the Odd Fellows for over 30 years, and is a member of the Upland Commercial Club, and was a member of the bridge committee nine years. He is a member of the German Lutheran Church, the Nebraskana Society, and the Upland Country Club.

On February 15, 1900, he was united in marriage with Elizabeth Sophia Hogeland at Upland. Mrs. Roggenkamp, whose relatives served in the Civil War, was born in Henry County, Iowa, January 19, 1880. They have six children: Blanche, born October 5, 1901, who married Sidney O. Hendricks; George, born January 19, 1903, who married Geneva Pinkham; Amy, born March 30, 1905, who married Ray L. Bunger; Estella, born September 23, 1906; Richard, born October 23, 1908; and Dorothy, born March 12, 1914. Mr. Roggenkamp's chief recreations are golf and reading. He is the owner of a golf course, located on his farm. Residence: Upland. (Photograph on Page 1025).

R. W. Rohrke

R. W. Rohrke, who is a lifelong resident of this state, was born at Norfolk, Nebraska, December 11, 1878, the son of Martin Gottlieb and Maria (Huebner) Rohrke. His father, who was born at Ixonia, Wisconsin, and died at Hadar, Nebraska, November 2, 1913, was the first blacksmith in northeastern Nebraska where he also engaged in farming; his parents were German born and settled in Wisconsin, later coming to Nebraska by covered wagon in pioneer days. His mother, who was also born at Ixonia, was a pioneer of the middlewest who knew all the hardships of those days, including the grasshopper invasion, Indians, and prairie fires common to the settlers. She worked on her parents homestead, breaking the new soil with an ox-team and crude plow. She

died at Hadar, January 21, 1911, after a useful and varied life.

Mr. Rohrke attended country school under the most difficult circumstances, often walking six miles to reach the pioneer school house of his neighborhood. He has always been a farmer, although at one time he sold stallions for an importing company, in connection with his farm work. He is a stockholder in the Farmers Grain & Livestock Company of Norfolk, Nebraska, was formerly constable for six years, and acted as road supervisor at Norfolk for two years.

He served as school director for 21 years, is a director in the Grain Elevator Company at this time, and for the past nine years has been a trustee in the Immanuel Evangelical Lutheran Church of Norfolk. He is a member of the Red Cross, and during the World War was prominent as a member of the Pierce Council of Defense and the Food Administration Committee. His hobby is good horses.

He married Anna Maria Kaiser, who was born at Norga, Russia, July 24, 1879, the daughter of Mr. and Mrs. Peter Kaiser. To them were born the following children: Wilhelm, March 15, 1898; Alma, August 24, 1899; Huber, September 27, 1911; Ewald, March 18, 1905; Fred, August 14, 1907; and Allen, January 15, 1910, who died October 10, 1911. Residence: Norfolk.

Hans Rohwer

A prominent banker at Ainsworth, Nebraska, is Hans Rohwer who was born at Jevenstedt, Germany, July 11, 1885, the son of Claus and Magdalene Maria (Kroeger) Rohwer. His father, who was a farmer, was born at Jevenstedt, January 6, 1829, and died at Gretna, Nebraska, July 6, 1911. His mother was born at Kiel, Germany, December 28, 1841, and died at Gretna, March 11, 1910.

Mr. Rohwer attended Grand Island Business College, Grand Island, Nebraska, from 1906 to 1908. He served as cashier of the National Bank of Ainsworth, for several years, was manager of the American Trust Company, Newman, California, and is again cashier of the Ainsworth bank at this time. He is secretary of the Ainsworth Commercial Club, holds membership in the Ainsworth Country Club, and is affiliated with the First Congregational Church of Christ. His fraternal societies are Knights Templar and the Modern Woodmen of America, and his favorite sport is golf.

He was united in marriage with Nora M. Wulf at Ainsworth, December 14, 1911. Mrs. Rohwer, who is a seamstress, was born at Ainsworth, December 30, 1884. Two children were born to them: Lillian M., October 12, 1912; and Rollin S., June 30, 1924. Lillian is a student at the Nebraska State Teachers College at Wayne, Nebraska. Residence: Ainsworth.

Henry Rohwer

For the past 50 years Henry Rohwer has lived on the same farm in Washington County, Nebraska, and has taken part in the civic and business affairs at Fort Calhoun. He was born at Holtdorf, Germany, November 18, 1856, and has lived in Nebraska for over 62 years. His father, Claus Rohwer, was born at Brammerau, Germany, September 18, 1823, and died at Fort Calhoun, September 5, 1911. A miller and millwright, he fought as a rebel against the Danish Government, in Germany. His mother, Kathrine (Sinn) Rohwer, was born at Nortorf, Germany, and died at Fort Calhoun, October 25, 1898.

Mr. Rohwer received his education in the public schools and under private tutors. He is now president of the Fort Calhoun State Bank. A Republican, he served as a member of the Washington County Board 6 years and was a member of the Nebraska legislature for 2 years, 1901-03. He is president of the Washington County Historical Society, a member of The Nebraska State Historical Society and the Nebraskana Society. He was secre-

JULIUS WILLIAM FERDINAND ROGGENKAMP

tary of the farm bureau of Washington County, took part in loan drives and was on the committee of military training camps, during the recent war. He is a member of the Woodmen of the World. His hobby is his home and garden.

He married Anna Olson at Central City, Merrick County, Nebraska. Mrs. Rohwer was born in Norway, and died at Fort Calhoun in 1926. Residence: Fort Calhoun. (Photograph in Album).

John Christen Romer

Descended from a large landholder of Bornholm, Denmark, John Christen Romer is the son of J. Christian Romer, who was born on the Island of Bornholm, Denmark, October 10, 1857. He came to the United States with his family in 1890, and has since engaged in farming. Hans Romer, the planter of the third largest grove in Denmark, is one of his ancestors. This grove is located on the Island of Bornholm, and is called Almindingen. Bornholm is the California of Denmark, and a resort for tourists. Petrea Christensen, wife of J. Christian Romer, was born in Jutland, April 26, 1854, daughter of a school teacher. She died at Minden, May 10, 1923.

John Christen Romer was born at Skjorping, Jutland, Denmark, February 9, 1886. He was educated first in the country grade schools of Freeborn County, Minnesota, and was graduated from the academy of Dana College at Blair, in 1913. Upon his graduation from the University of Nebraska, with the Bachelor of Arts degree in 1917, Mr. Romer entered Trinity Seminary at Blair, Nebraska, completing his course in 1920. He was president of his graduating class in 1920.

Since the spring of 1929, Mr. Romer has been and still is a member of the board of directors of Dana College and Trinity Seminary at Blair, and during the same period of time has been a member of the board of examiners of the seminary. For the past year and a half he has served on a debt retirement committee for the same institutions. He is pastor of the Fredericksburg Lutheran Church at Minden, at the present time.

Immediately after graduation in 1920, and continuously since, he has served as pastor in the United Danish Evangelical Lutheran Church of America, the first five and a half years at Duluth, Minnesota, and the remainder in his present pastorate. His church synod is a member of the American Lutheran Conference which numbers approximately one third of all Lutherans in America.

On May 29, 1920, Mr. Romer was married to Agnes Larsen at Sioux City, Iowa. Mrs. Romer who was a milliner and music student prior to marriage, was born at Mitchell, South Dakota, September 28, 1894. Her mother was born in Denmark, and her father in the part of Germany which has since the world war been restored to Denmark.

Mr. and Mrs. Romer have five children, Dorothy Ann, born March 28, 1922, who has shown more than usual interest in reading and in her general school work; John Carlton, born January 9, 1924; Robert Fred, born November 11, 1925; Harold Luther, born August 31, 1929, and Howard Philip, born August 31, 1929, twins.

The author of sermons, sermonettes and short articles published at various times in church papers, Mr. Romer is much interested in the development of the Nebraska District Pastors' Reading Circle of the United Danish Evangelical Lutheran Church of America. This Reading Circle has a circulating library which at the present time contains the following volumes, in addition to seven religious publications, most of which are quarterlies:

Hvorledes Blev Nye Testamente Til; Guds Riges Vaar; The Story of The Church; If I Had Only One Sermon to Preach; The Preachers His Life and Work; After Its Kind; Not Slothful in Business; The Proper Distinction Between Law and Gospel; All Quiet on the Western Front; The Successful Young People's Society; A Pre-

face to Morals; The Christian Way of Liberty; Why I Am a Christian; Beacon Lights of Prophecy; The Hidden Life; Outfitting the Teacher of Religion; The Theology of Crisis; Elmer Gantry and *The Word and The World.* Mr. Romer is librarian at the present time.

Normally a Republican, Mr. Romer cast his vote for Woodrow Wilson. He is a member of the Nebraskana Society, devotes much time to Bible study and Bible teaching, and enjoys reading books on general and religious psychology.

He was one of the promoters of the Lutheran Bible School, a summer Bible study conference which has been held annually for the past five years on the Young Men's Christian Association conference grounds at Estes Park, Colorado. Residence: Minden. (Photograph on Page 1027).

James Victor Romigh

James Victor Romigh, lawyer, was born at Rochester, Pennsylvania, June 28, 1881, the son of James Baker and Helen Sarah (Fezell) Romigh.

His father was born in Freedom, Pennsylvania, November 18, 1854, and died at Omaha, August 5, 1919. He was a construction foreman in the bridge department of the Union Pacific Railway Company. His father, Jacob Romigh, preceded by two other Jacob Romighs, settled in western Pennsylvania about 1770. The family was English and German.

Helen Sarah Fezell was born in Rochester, in March, 1854, and died in Omaha, Februaray 4, 1906. She was graduated from Mount Union College in Ohio, and taught school before her marriage. She was French through the paternal line, and German and Scotch through the maternal line, the Goehrings and Stewarts. Colonel George Stewart was an officer in the Revolutionary War, and was descended from Sir James Stewart of Ireland.

Mr. Romigh attended public schools of Omaha, and was graduated from high school there in 1898. In 1903, he received the Bachelor of Arts degree from the University of Nebraska, and while there was a member of Alpha Tau Omega fraternity. In 1906, he received the Bachelor of Laws degree from Harvard University.

On July 3, 1906, he was married to Viola May Luce at Vineyard Haven, Massachusetts. Mrs. Romigh was born at Vineyard Haven, September 15, 1881, a member of the Daughters of the American Revolution through 12 lines and belongs to the Mayflower Society. She is descended through the Dunhams from Governor Mayhew. To them were born three children, Victor Luce, June 5, 1907, who died November 22, 1922; Orin Lambert, born August 27, 1908, who is a student at the University of Nebraska; and Philip Stewart, born September 29, 1916, who is in school.

From 1906 until 1916, Mr. Romigh practiced law, at that time entering the automobile business, in which he continued until 1930. At the present time, he is engaged in the law and collection business. He is a very Independent Republican.

He is affiliated with the First Presbyterian Church of North Platte, is a member of various trade associations, and is president of the Great Plains (United States No. 83) Highway Association. He is an Elk, and a member of the Nebraskana Society. His hobbies are good roads, history and reading. Residence: North Platte.

Carey Addison Ronne

A resident of this state all his life, Carey Addison Ronne was born in York County, Nebraska, March 14, 1889, the son of Nelson Peter and Mary Jane (Kerr) Ronne. His father, a retired farmer, was born at Skive, Denmark, November 29, 1859, and came to this country in 1876. His mother was born in Scotland, December 18, 1856, and died at York, April 5, 1925.

Mr. Ronne attended the public school at York, and

JOHN C. ROMER

Smalley—Minden

later was a student at York College for a year. For many years he has been a farmer and has been actively interested in various civic organizations. At this time he is justice of the peace and chairman of the township board at Henderson, is affiliated with the United Brethren Church, and holds membership in the Odd Fellows Lodge. On December 14, 1910, his marriage to Mable Esther Gross was solemnized at York, Nebraska. Mrs. Honne was born at Waco, August 10, 1889.

There are three children: Wayne Addison, born April 26, 1913; Daniel Floyd, born December 8, 1916; and Wade LeRoy, born December 31, 1922. Residence: Lushton.

Lorenzen Peter Ronne

Lorenzen P. Ronne was born at Yorkville, Kendall County, Illinois, November 2, 1881, the son of Nelson Peter and Mary Jane (Kerr) Ronne. His father, a farmer, was born at Skieve, Denmark, September 29, 1857, and came to this country about 1875. His mother was born at Belfast, Ireland, December 18, 1853, and died at York, Nebraska, April 5, 1925.

Dr. Ronne attended the country schools in York County where he was graduated in 1894, and later was a student at the United Brethren College at York. For the next three years he taught school, and in 1905 he was awarded the D. D. S. degree at the University of Omaha. His fraternity is Xi Psi Phi. He was admitted to the practice of dentistry in Hamilton, York, and Otoe counties in 1905, and since May 3, 1909, has been in active practice at Lincoln, Nebraska.

On June 12, 1907, he was married to Mildred Olive Pratt, at Syracuse, Nebraska. Mrs. Ronne was born at Syracuse, May 22, 1888, and died at Lincoln, December 26, 1918. Five children were born to them, three of whom are living. They are: Kenneth, born February 25, 1910, who died July 10, 1911; David, born May 2, 1912; Mary Jane, born October 17, 1914, who died March 8, 1915; Robert, born December 17, 1916; and Mildred, born December 25, 1918. The children are all in school. On June 27, 1920, Dr. Ronne was united in marriage with Okolona Blanch Knerr, at Stromsburg, Nebraska; she was born at Stromsburg, September 21, 1897. She was a business woman and teacher before her marriage.

Dr. Ronne served in the national guard from 1910 to 1915 with the rank of dental surgeon for the state of Nebraska. He is a member of the district, state, and national dental association, and is a member of the Hiram Club. A Scottish Rite Mason and Shriner, he is a Modern Woodman of America. He is affiliated with the Trinity Methodist Episcopal Church of Lincoln. Residence: Lincoln.

Charles Henry Root

Charles Henry Root, physician, was born at Elgin, Illinois, December 25, 1875, son of Charles Marvin and Miranda E. (Burnidge) Root. His father, born in Connecticut April 27, 1837, died at Omaha, November 16, 1906. He was a gardener and farmer and descended from English settlers in New England, 1637.

His wife, Miranda, was born on Lake Huron, June 1, 1840, and died at Omaha, April 15, 1915. Her father was English and her mother New England Yankee.

Dr. Root attended the Beatrice grade school 1890, was graduated from the Beatrice High School in 1893; received his Bachelor of Science degree from the University of Nebraska in 1900, and his medical degree in 1903. He is a member of Phi Rho Sigma, and in 1899 received a letter in track.

On April 29, 1911, he was married to Lena Fike at Omaha. Mrs. Root was born at Newport, Nebraska, March 1, 1886, and died at Bassett, September 18, 1931. There are two children, Mildred, born November 29, 1912, and Charles, born October 16, 1920.

Dr. Root has been in the practice of medicine in Nebraska since May 13, 1903. He is a Republican. In the World War he was a member of the county exemption and examining board. He is a member of the Methodist Episcopal Church, the Holt County, Nebraska State, and American Medical Association and has served as president of the Holt County Association. He is a member of the Lions Club, Modern Woodmen of America, the Ancient, Free and Accepted Masons, the Royal Arch Masons and the Knights Templar. He is a member of the board of regents of the Rock County High School and past president of his local school board. Residence: Bassett.

Charles Henry Roper

Charles H. Roper was born at Exeter, Nebraska, August 16, 1874, the son of Scouler B. and Jennie S. (Abbott) Roper. His father, who was a farmer, was born at Lydd, St. Mary's Lincolnshire, England, December 15, 1849, and died at Exeter, October 28, 1885. His mother, who was a teacher before her marriage, was born at Jackson, Michigan, September 25, 1854; she is of English ancestry.

Mr. Roper was graduated from the Exeter High School, and is a member of Phi Kappa Tau. He is now president of the firm, Castle, Roper & Matthews, Morticians, at Lincoln. During the World War he served in all drives. He is a life member of the Lincoln Chamber of Commerce; is a charter member of the Rotary Club; and since 1929, has been president of the Nebraska State Funeral Directors Association.

He has been a member of the Detroit and Lincoln and Denver Highway Association for the past ten years, and is secretary of the Nebraska Good Roads Association. He served on the University School Board for 12 years; was a member of the official board of the Methodist Episcopal Church at Lincoln for over 20 years; and is a member of the Nebraskana Society. Mr. Roper is a member of the Eastridge Country Club; Shrine Country Club; and is a member of the Young Men's Christian Association; and the Republican party. He holds membership in: Scottish Rite, York Rite, of the Masons of which he is past master; is past patron of the Eastern Star, Lodge Number 94; and is a potentate of Sesostris Temple, and the Knights of Pythias. He is a member of the Woodmen of the orld and the Modern Woodmen of America. His sports include golf, hunting, and fishing.

He was married to Floy Elsie Clark at Lincoln, June 14, 1899. Mrs. Roper a teacher before her marriage was born at Woodburn, Iowa, December 18, 1873; she is the daughter of Daniel and Anna (Thomas) Clark. They have three children: Reginald C., born March 16, 1901, who married Esther McDowell; Marguerite H., born March 20, 1903, who married Earl G. Colton; and Max E., born October 20, 1906; who married Katherine Arnsberg. Residence: Lincoln.

Benjamin Ira Rose

Born at Norfolk, New York, August 17, 1856, Benjamin Ira Rose has lived in this state for over 67 years and is now a retired farmer at Brunswick. His father, who was a tanner, was born at Canton, St. Lawrence County, New York, November 10, 1827, and died in Cass County, Nebraska, May 14, 1877; he was a Civil War veteran. His mother, who was born at Pottsdam, New Work, March 8, 1832, and died in Cass County, March 11, 1909.

Mr. Rose attended school in a typical pioneer log school house in Antelope County, Nebraska. He is a member of the Nebraska Territorial Pioneers and the Nebraskana Society. He served as a member of the board of supervisors of Brunswick School District, 1893-94, and has always held a position of some kind on the various school boards in his county.

He was united in marriage with Irene Elizabeth Kuhn, March 16, 1882; she was born in Wayne County, Iowa, October 18, 1860, and died at Brunswick, Nebraska, March 10, 1922. Three children were born to them: William H., July 24, 1884, who married Ellen Nelson; Jesse A.,

November 14, 1885, who married Minnie Hansen; and David A., April 2, 1888, who married Esther Lundstrom. His marriage to Hulda Mohr occurred June 4, 1923. Mrs. Rose was born in Germany and spent most of her girlhood there. Residence: Brunswick.

Charles Danham Rose

Professor Charles Danham Rose, who has lived in Nebraska for the past 41 years, was born at Martinsville, Morgan County, Indiana, June 9, 1859. His father, Aaron Rose, who was a farmer, died at Martinsville. Elvira (Wetty) Rose, his mother, died at Martinsville.

Professor Rose completed his elementary education at Martinsville in 1878, and later was graduated from De Pauw University with the B. P. degree. He was professor of mathematics at the Nebraska Wesleyan University from 1890 to 1927, and is now professor emeritus of the department. He is affiliated with the First Methodist Episcopal Church at Lincoln, and is a member of the Nebraskana Society. He is a Republican.

His marriage to Cora Butler was solemnized at Noblesville, Hamilton County, Indiana, October 2, 1887. Mrs. Rose died at University Place, Nebraska, May 10, 1910. Three children were born to this union: Elizabeth, born September 5, 1893; Walter Butler, born October 2, 1895; and Julia, born May 31, 1897. Residence: Lincoln.

George Francis Rose

Born at Clarks, Nebraska, November 10, 1875, George Francis Rose is the son of Henry and Sarah Jane (Thomas) Rose. His father, a pioneer farmer in Merrick County, Nebraska, in 1870, was born in St. Lawrence County, New York, July 2, 1826, and died at Fullerton, Nebraska, April 6, 1912; his English ancestors settled in Massachussetts between 1620 and 1630. His mother, whose ancestors also settled in Massachussetts in 1620, was born in St. Lawrence County, New York, October 15, 1840, and died at Genoa, October 16, 1925.

Mr. Rose attended the rural schools of Merrick County, was graduated from Clarks High School in 1897, and received the LL. B. degree at the University of Nebraska in 1901. He was admitted to the bar in 1900, and since 1902 has been engaged in the practice of law at Genoa, Nebraska. In 1931 he moved to Fullerton and now maintains a law office in that city in connection with his practice at Genoa.

He is a member of the Nebraska State Bar Association, the Commercial Club, Nebraska State Historical Society, and the Knights of Pythias. He served as a member of the Council of Defense during the World War, was prominent in the Red Cross, participated in loan drives and was a lieutenant in the home guard.

On November 1, 1909, he married Daisy Blanche Lamb at Genoa. Mrs. Rose was a music instructor. She was born in Fremont County, Iowa, October 9, 1878, and died at Genoa, May 9, 1915. Her parents were pioneers of Iowa. To this marriage were born the following children: Forrest I., November 21, 1910, who was graduated from the Genoa High School in 1927, and is now a medical student at the University of Nebraska; Bowen F., August 5, 1913, was graduated from the Genoa High School in 1931, and is now a law student; and George D., April 24, 1915, a student in high school.

On June 30, 1928, Mr. Rose was united in marriage with Lillian E. Bake, an instructor in the city schools of Omaha. Her ancestors settled in Virginia, in 1637. Residence: Fullerton.

Halleck F. Rose

Halleck F. Rose, lawyer, was born at Grove City, Pennsylvania, November 15, 1863, the son of James McKinley and Maria Catherine (Brandon) Rose. The father was born in Grove City, on March 30, 1820, and died there on September 9, 1888. He was a farmer. His wife,

Maria, was born in Grove City, May 2, 1830, and died there in September, 1919.

On July 28, 1902, Mr. Rose was married to Catherine Cameron at Omaha. She was born at Scotch Center, Iowa, July 28, 1875. Their children are Halleck Lovejoy, Homer Cameron, and Hudson McKinley.

Mr. Rose is a Republican. He was admitted to the practice of law in Nebraska in 1887, and continued in practice at Lincoln, until April, 1908. He came to Omaha as assistant general solicitor for the Chicago, Burlington and Quincy Railroad, resigning in 1910 to enter general practice. He is a member of the American, Nebraska state and Douglas County bar associations, the Chamber of Commerce, the Professional Men's and the University Club. Residence: Omaha.

William Brandon Rose

William Brandon Rose, distinguished lawyer and judge of the Supreme Court of Nebraska, has been prominent in state affairs for over 40 years. He was born at Grove City, Mercer County, Pennsylvania, January 25, 1862, the son of James McKinley and Maria Catherine (Brandon) Rose. His father, who was born at Grove City, February 24, 1821, and died there, September 3, 1889, was a scholar and a teacher, was a farmer for many years and served in the Union Army in the Civil War. His paternal great grandfather came to America from England; his grandfather, Andrew Rose, was a soldier in the Revolution; and his father, who served in the War of 1812, was a double cousin of President McKinley's father.

His mother was born at Grove City, May 2, 1830, and for many years was active in civic affairs and in Presbyterian Church work. One of her paternal ancestors went from Prussia to England with William, Prince of Orange, upon his accession to the throne. She died at Millbrook, Mercer County, Pennsylvania, September 16, 1919.

Judge Rose attended the grade schools of Mercer County; was a student at Pine Grove Normal Academy; and was awarded an honorary degree, LL. D., by the Grove City College in Pennsylvania. He was admitted to the bar at Mercer, December 26, 1888. He has been judge of the supreme court since 1908, his present term expiring in 1937.

Judge Rose taught in the public schools in Pennsylvania, 1878-80; and 1884-85; served as chief clerk to Prothonotary in Mercer County, 1885-88; was deputy state librarian and deputy clerk of the Nebraska Supreme Court, 1888-99; and was assistant attorney general of Nebraska, 1900 to 1908. He was editor of *Supreme Court Reports,* volumes 35 to 59, and is the author of *Opinions Supreme Court Reports,* volumes 83 to 120; *Rules for Citation in Lawbooks;* and *James Rose, A Message to His Posterity,* a pamphlet.

His marriage to Genevieve Stevens, widow of Charles Eaton, was solemnized at Kansas City, Missouri, November 18, 1893. Mrs. Rose, who was a pianist of some note, was born at New London, Connecticut, September 23, 1866, and died at Lincoln, Nebraska, July 6, 1914. She was a member of the Society of Mayflower Descendants; was tenth in descent from Elder William Brewster, chief of the pilgrim band. They had one daughter: Genevieve, born June 20, 1896, who married Rev. David Earl Faust, Ph. D., of Mercersburg, Pennsylvania.

On June 21, 1919, Judge Rose was married to Lillian E. Trester at her home in Lincoln, Nebraska. Mrs. Rose was born April 1, 1872, near Lincoln, where her parents who came from Indiana entered upon a homestead in 1869. She was a teacher, accountant and merchant before her marriage and is a member of the Daughters of the American Revolution, the Order of Eastern Star, the Presbyterian Church and the Young Women's Christian Association. In the latter she was a member of the board of directors for seven years.

Judge Rose is a member of the American Bar Associations, Nebraska State Bar Association, Lancaster County Bar Association, and the Community Chest, of Lincoln. He is a member of the Lincoln Chamber of Commerce; is a director of the Nebraska State Library Board; and a Modern Woodman of America. He is an attendant and supporter of the First Presbyterian Church of Lincoln, a member of the University Club and the Eastridge Club. His sports are playing golf, horseshoes, and checkers. His hobby is law. He is a Republican. Residence: Lincoln.

William Henry Roselius

William Henry Roselius, head of the department of mathematics and the coach of Hebron College and Academy, was born at Pyrmont, Ohio, January 30, 1897, son of Henry and Anna (Purnhagen) Roselius.

His father was born in Bremen, Germany, December 10, 1845, and resides at Eaton, Ohio, where he is engaged in farming. His father's father was a Frenchman. Anna Purnhagen was born in Germany, May 13, 1862, and died at West Alexandria, Ohio, April 17, 1911. She was descended from German peasants.

Mr. Roselius attended the public schools of District No. 4 in Preble County, Ohio, until 1911, and was graduated from West Alexandria High School in 1915. He received his Bachelor of Arts degree from Capitola University at Columbus, and at the present time is working on his Master's degree at the University of Nebraska. During 1927, he studied at Ohio State University, and during 1923, 1926, 1930, and 1931, was a student at the University of Nebraska. He lettered in football three years, basketball two years, and baseball two years at Capitola University.

From 1920 until 1922, Mr. Roselius was an instructor at Hebron College and Academy, and since then has held his professorship. He has served as a member of the city council of Hebron, since 1929. He is a Democrat.

On June 18, 1921, he was married to Grace Koffer at West Alexandria, Ohio. Mrs. Roselius was born at Bachman, Ohio, June 26, 1897. Her father was German and her mother English, her grandfather served in the Civil War. They had two children, Marjorie Jane, born July 1, 1922, died January 14, 1931; and Roland Henry, born September 26, 1924.

Mr. Roselius is a member of the Nebraska State Teachers' Association, S. N. S. M. C., the Hebron Chamber of Commerce, the Kiwanis Club, and the Grace congregation of the Lutheran Church of Hebron. His sports include golf, tennis, baseball, football, and basketball. He is a member of the Hebron Country Club. Residence: Hebron.

William B. Rosenbaum

Born at Blair, Nebraska, December 15, 1878, William B. Rosenbaum has lived in the state all his life. He is the son of William and Helen (Weinbrandt) Rosenbaum, the former of whom was born in Germany, December 4, 1846, and came to America about 1870. He was a pioneer farmer and blacksmith in Washington County, and died at Blair, on April 13, 1886. Helen, his wife, was born in Slesvig, Holstein, Germany, October 5, 1859 and died in Blair, October 5, 1914.

William B. Rosenbaum was educated in Rose Hill School, and since youth has been engaged in farming. For some time he has been president of the Farmers Grain and Lumber Company. He is a Republican and active in party politics, and has been treasurer of his school district since 1915. His religious affiliation is with the Danish Lutheran Church.

On January 11, 1899, he was married to Anna Johanna Nelsen at Kennard. Mrs. Rosenbaum was born there March 15, 1878. There are ten children, as follows: Leslie, born February 19, 1900; Helena, born February 23, 1901, married H. F. McDonald; Chester, born April 17, 1903, married Dora Dierks, and is a farmer; Marie, born

July 17, 1905; Frieda, born September 10, 1906, married Herman Kruse; Clyde, born November 22, 1908, married Dorothy Widener; Walter, born April 30, 1910; Gladys, born January 17, 1912; Selma, born January 12, 1914; and Lola, born March 30, 1916. There was one child, Donald, born February 18, 1920, who died March 15, 1922. Merritt, born September 1, 1926, is an adopted grandchild. Residence: Kennard.

Charlotte Wilhelmina Rosencrans

Charlotte Wilhelmina Rosencrans was born at Nehawka, Nebraska, December 14, 1888, daughter of John George and Magdelena Caroline (Carsten) Wunderlich. Her father was born at Mechlenburg, Germany, July 2, 1867, and was brought to America by his widowed mother at the age of 12 to escape military duty. His wife, Magdelena, was born at Nehawka, December 26, 1867, and is of French descent.

Mrs. Rosencrans was graduated from Nebraska Wesleyan Elementary Normal School in June, 1906. While in school she played basketball three years. From 1906 to 1907, she taught school at Avoca, and from 1907-08, at Nehawka. She taught at Union, from 1908 to 1912, Eagle, 1912-13, and at Nehawka, 1913-14. On September 30, 1914, she was married to Clayton Arthur Rosencrans, at Plattsmouth. Mr. Rosencrans was born at Salladasburg, Pennsylvania, January 24, 1886, and descends in the line of General Rosencrans. They have one son, William Elsworth, born October 21, 1919.

Always active in the civic life of her community, Mrs. Rosencrans has capably filled many offices. She is School Attendance and Probation Officer of Cass County, having held this office three years and at present has six boys paroled to her from juvenile court. She is Department president of the American Legion Auxiliary, and secretary and treasurer of the Associated Charities. During the World War she was chairman of knitting in Cass County, and county inspector of surgical dressings, receiving her instruction and permit from the Omaha division. In the past she has served as secretary (1922-24), president, district secretary (1922-24), district president (1926-28), state chairman of rehabilitation (1929-30), of the American Legion Auxiliary. She is a member of the Women's Relief Corps, and secretary of the American Red Cross of Cass County, being the only woman on the executive board since 1918, and since 1926, has been a member of the Parent-Teachers' Association. She is a member of St. Luke's Episcopal Church. She was a member of the Degree of Honor 1906-17, Rebekahs, 1910-17, and since 1919, has been a member of the Order of Eastern Star.

She is a baseball and basketball enthusiast, and is interested in horse races. Her favorite recreations are reading and automobile driving. Mrs. Rosencrans is a Democrat. Residence: Plattsmouth. (Photograph on Page 1031).

George Walter Rosenlof

Since 1927, George Walter Rosenlof has been director of secondary education and teacher training in the State Department of Public Instruction. Mr. Rosenlof, who was born at York, Nebraska, January 16, 1891, is the son of Charles A. and Augusta Matilda (Magnusson) Rosenlof, both natives of Sweden.

Charles A. Rosenlof was born at Munka Ljungby, Sweden, May 31, 1863. A carpenter and builder, he came to America in the late 1800's, and settled in Nebraska. His death occurred at York, on June 3, 1905. Augusta, his wife was born at Smaland, Sweden, May 21, 1865, and died at York, on September 10, 1922.

Upon his graduation from York High School in 1910, George W. Rosenlof attended Hastings College, receiving the degree of B. Sc., in 1916. He attended York College during the summer of 1913. In 1922 he received his master's degree at the University of Nebraska, and in

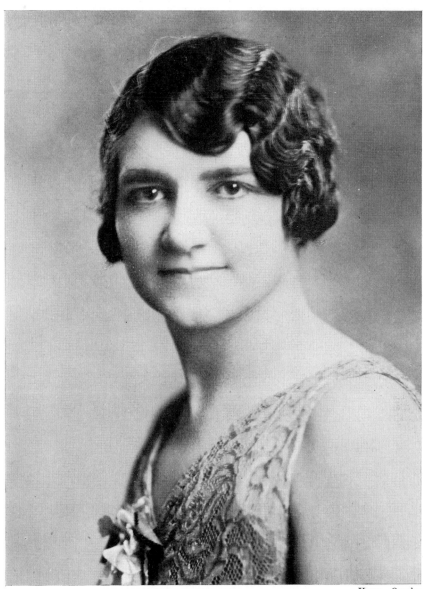

Heyn—Omaha

CHARLOTTE (LOTTIE) W. ROSENCRANS

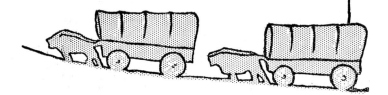

1929, his doctor's degree from Columbia University. At Hastings, he was a member of the Debating Society, and won many honors both in oratory and debate. He was also a member of the Glee Club and Chorus. His fraternities are Phi Delta Kappa, Kappa Delta Pi and is also a member of the Tawse Club of Columbia University Teachers College.

The educational experience of Dr. Rosenlof has been long and varied. He was a teacher in Nebraska rural schools from 1910-13; principal and superintendent of Chase County High School at Imperial, Nebraska, 1916-18; superintendent of schools at Nelson, 1918-21; instructor in the department of history and principles of education at the University of Nebraska, January, 1922, to September, 1927; instructor in summer sessions at the University of Nebraska, 1922-1927; associate in normal school education, Teachers' College, Columbia University, 1926-27; and director of secondary education and teacher training, 1927 to date.

He is the author of *Library Facilities of Teacher-Training Institutions.*

In addition to numerous educational articles he has written or co-operated in the writing of some twelve bulletins or courses of study published by the state department of public instruction. As secretary of the Nebraska High School Manual Revision Commission, he edited and assisted in preparing materials for the *High School Manual,* published under the joint authorization of the University of Nebraska and the State Department. He has written several articles appearing in current periodicals, among the most recent ones being *Why is a Library, Supplementary Study of Library Facilities of Teacher Training Institutions,* appearing in the tenth year book of the American Association of Teachers' College; *Rural Teacher Preparation in the Agricultural Midwest, Status of the Teacher in the Accredited High School of Nebraska,* both of which appear in the 31st biennial report of the State Superintendent of Public Instruction for January, 1931.

Dr. Rosenlof was married to Edna Mayo Lowry at Pawnee City, Nebraska, June 6, 1917. Mrs. Rosenlof was born at Wahoo, October 12, 1890. She is a musician and teacher, the daughter of Mr. and Mrs. O. P. Lowry. They are members of the First Presbyterian Church in which he is an elder. He is a member of the Scottish Rite Masons and Eastern Star lodges, and the American Inter-Professional Men's Institute. Mrs. Rosenlof is a member of the Eastern Star and of the P. E. O. Sisterhood. Due to physical disability, Mr. Rosenlof was discharged from draft at Camp Funston, Kansas, in August, 1918; he was a four minute man and director of War Savings activities in the public school of Nebraska, during the war period. He is a member of the Chamber of Commerce, the Nebraska Congress of Parents and Teachers, the Nebraska State Teachers Association, the National Educational Association, the National Society of College Teachers of Education, the North Central Association Commission of Colleges and Secondary Schools and the American Educational Research Association. He is also a member of the Order of Yellow Dogs, the Nebraska Writers' Guild and The Nebraskana Society.

Gardening is Mr. Rosenlof's hobby, and he enjoys golf and tennis, bowling, fishing and hunting. Residence: Lincoln.

Stanley M. Rosewater

Stanley M. Rosewater, lawyer, was born at Omaha, Nebraska, June 24, 1885, the only son of Andrew and Frances M. Rosewater.

He was graduated from the Central High School in 1903, and received his Bachelor of Laws degree from the University of Michigan in 1908. His marriage to Barbara Hamilton McAlvay was solemnized October 7, 1912 at Lansing, Michigan.

Mr. Rosewater is a Republican. He is a member of the American, Nebraska State and Omaha Bar Associations, the Chamber of Commerce (various offices), the Ad-Sell League, the Ak-Sar-Ben, the Elks, the Masons, and the Eastern Star. His clubs are: the University, the Professional Men's, the Carter Lake and the Omaha Tennis Club. Residence: Omaha.

James Abner Ross

Born at Waynesboro, Pennsylvania, February 13, 1875, James Abner Ross is the son of Daniel Newcomer Ross and Laura Katherine Ross. His father, who was a carpenter and potter, was born at Waynesboro, January 11, 1845, and died there, November 1, 1926; he served as a private in Company B., 21st Pennsylvania Cavalry, for a year; his ancestry dates to James Ross who came to this country from Scotland. His mother, the daughter of James Abner and Elizabeth Jain Hays, was born in Washington County, Maryland, August 17, 1841, and died at Waynesboro, May 25, 1925; her parents, who were of German and English descent, were inn keepers.

Mr. Ross, who has lived in Nebraska for the past 23 years, has been a telegraph operator for the Chicago & Northwestern Railway Company since 1901. He has served as a member of the school board at Long Pine, Nebraska, for the past 20 years, was mayor of the city, 1923-24, and has been a member of the Parent-Teachers' Association for over 2 years. He was a charter member and one of the organizers of the Chamber of Commerce and the Nebraska Good Roads Association in which he has been extremely active for a number of years.

He is assistant chairman of the Red Cross, has been a member of the Order of Railway Telegraphers since 1901, and holds membership in the following fraternal organizations: Elks; Woodmen of the World; Modern Woodmen of America; Masons; and the Civil Legion, of which he is a life member. Mr. Ross served in the Spanish-American War as a private, 1898-99. He acted as chairman of the Council Defense, was a Four Minute Man, and served as captain of the Home Guards, during the World War. He is now Commander of the United States War Veterans, Pine Camp Number 22, at Ainsworth, Nebraska.

He was united in marriage with Marietta Powell at Polo, Illinois, June 27, 1901. Mrs. Ross, who was a seamstress before her marriage, was born at Oregon, Illinois, June 20, 1874. Four children were born to this marriage: James K., June 10, 1903, who married Constance E. Eberly; Ardath, November 14, 1904; and Daniel U., April 11, 1906. James K. is an electrical engineer at Cincinnatti, Ohio. Ardath is a teacher in the public schools of Long Pine. Mr. Ross died January 20, 1932. (Photograph in Album).

George Scott Round

Born at Page County, Iowa, January 7, 1867, George Scott Round is the son of Solomon and Rebecca (Dean) Round. His father, who was a farmer, was born at Maryland, Ohio, in 1826, and died at Clarinda, Iowa, in 1906. His mother, who was born at Indianapolis, Indiana, February 4, 1828, and died at Alliance, Nebraska, in December, 1918, was the mother of 13 children, and was the daughter of Robert Dean of Kentucky, who fought with Jackson at New Orleans.

Mr. Round has served for four consecutive terms as sheriff of Valley County, Nebraska, and is active in the civic affairs of Ord. He is a member of the Ord Community Club, the Modern Woodmen of America, the Odd Fellows, and the welfare board of the Red Cross. He is affiliated with the Methodist Church of Ord, and holds membership in the Nebraskana Society and the Republican party. He likes football and baseball.

On December 24, 1893, he was married at Aurora, Nebraska, to Linda Jackson who was born of Scotch-Irish parents at Clarinda, Iowa, January 23, 1872. Five children were born to their marriage: Beulah Marie, May 3, 1896, who married W. D. Roberts; Tamar, April 11, 1900;

Alice Jane, January 9, 1905, who married F. S. Campbell; George, August 21, 1907, who is a senior in the University of Nebraska; and John, January 5, 1910, who is studying medicine at the University of Omaha. Residence: Ord.

Edwin Lincoln Rouse

Edwin Lincoln Rouse, educator, was born in Greenwood, Nebraska, May 27, 1868, son of John De Cullum and Fannie Sophia (Gilbreath) Rouse.

The father was born in Muskingum County, Ohio, November 6, 1842, and died at Peru, Nebraska, May 26, 1917. He served in the Civil War from 1861 until 1864, and later farmed in Nebraska. His wife, Fannie, was born in Heinzburg, Vermont, October 16, 1845, and died at Grand Island, on October 15, 1927. Her parents were both born in Ireland, while her husband's ancestry was pre-Revolutionary Dutch.

Upon the completion of his elementary education in the rural schools of Cass and Nuckolls Counties, Edwin Rouse attended Fairfield Academy. He received the Bachelor of Arts degree from Cotner College in 1910; his Masters degree from the University of Nebraska in 1919; and the degree of Doctor of Laws from Cotner College in 1923. During the summer of 1913 and 1915, he attended Columbia University. He is a member of Phi Delta Kappa.

After three years as a rural school teacher, Mr. Rouse was high school principal for the same period of time at Hebron, Nebraska. He was city superintendent of schools for 16 years at Weeping Water, Plattsmouth, and Scottsbluff, Nebraska, and for 15 years taught at Peru State Teachers' College. At the present time, he is director of college instruction of Chadron State Normal College.

On August 24, 1892, he was married to Rhoda Sarah Tunnicliffe at Shenandoah, Iowa. Mrs. Rouse was born at Kewanee, Illinois, August 14, 1869, of English and Scotch ancestry. Mr. and Mrs. Rouse have four children, Philip L., born July 13, 1893, who is an engineer and is married to Helen Houston, and is a veteran of the World War, with rank of first lieutenant; Laurance T., born March 27, 1901, who is a teacher. He is married to Elizabeth White. Marjorie, born February 15, 1909; and Kenneth E., born March 31, 1910.

During the late war, Mr. Rouse was conductor of the Student Army Training Corps at Peru. A member of the Council of Defense, and a four minute speaker; his professional organizations include the National Educational Association (life member), the Nebraska State Teachers' Association, and the Parent-Teachers Association. He is a member of the Disciples of Christ Church, the Red Cross, the Chamber of Commerce, the Rotary Club (Scottsbluff,-Chadron), and from 1907 until 1916, was a member of the Peru school board. His favorite sport is golf. He is a Republican.

Mrs. Rouse is a member of the Daughters of the American Revolution. She is a member of the P. E. O. Sisterhood, and has been active in Federated Women's Club. Residence: Chadron.

Dave D. Rowe

Born in Clay County, Nebraska, August 5, 1877, Dave D. Rowe is the son of Joseph and Mary (Whatton) Rowe, who were pioneers of Nebraska. Joseph Rowe was born in Leicester, England, May 20, 1835, a shoemaker and merchant. He died at Stockham, Nebraska, February 14, 1907. His wife, Mary Whatton, was born in Leicester, December 12, 1835, and died at Stockham, April 23, 1904.

Dave D. Rowe attended public school, Fremont Normal College and Lincoln Business College. A Republican, he served as a member of the Fremont school board 18 years. An organizer of the Fremont State Bank, now the Stephens National Bank, serving as cashier and now vice president. For thirty years an officer and director of the Nebraska State Building and Loan Association, of which he is now president and manager. He is also vice president of the Fremont Mortgage Company and president of the State Securities Company of Fremont.

On September 19, 1905, he was united in marriage to Mary E. Cameron at Stockham. Mrs. Rowe was born in Hamilton County, Nebraska, November 12, 1884, of Scotch pioneer parents. There are three children, Leicester, who is with the Fremont State Company; Grace, is attending Midland College; and Edythe is in the public school.

Always active in civic affairs, Mr. Rowe has been a director of the state and local Young Men's Christian Associations for twenty years, and at the present time is president of the Fremont Chamber of Commerce. A four minute speaker during the World War, he was active in loan and other drives, and is a member of the Red Cross. His religious affiliation is with the First Presbyterian Church, of which he has been an elder twenty-five years. A Rotarian, he is chairman of the student loan fund committee, and is an Elk and Mason. His favorite sports are golf and volley ball, and his club is the Fremont Country Club. Residence: Fremont. (Photograph in Album).

Edward Winfield Rowe

Edward Winfield Rowe, physician and surgeon, was born at Roberts, Ford County, Illinois, June 21, 1881, son of Clement Edward and Margaret Elizabeth (Alexander) Rowe. Clement Rowe, who was born at Carlow, County Carlow, Ireland, November 25, 1842, came from Ireland to America in 1865. He was a clergyman of English ancestry, and died at Lincoln, in April, 1916.

Margaret, wife of Clement, was born at Linneus, Missouri, in August, 1853, and died at Gresham, Nebraska, in January, 1905. Her grandparents were of Scotch-Irish descent, the original members of the family in America having settled in Virginia about the time of the Revolutionary War.

Dr. Rowe was graduated from the Palmyra, Nebraska, High School and received his B. Sc. from the University of Nebraska, in 1903. His M. D. was from Northwestern University in 1905. In 1918, he took post graduate work at Cornell Medical College. He is a member of Sigma Xi and Alpha Kappa Kappa.

On December 14, 1905, he was married to Sarah Belle Harper, at Randolph, Nebraska. Mrs. Rowe, who was born at Marengo, Iowa, January 18, 1878, is of Scotch, Irish, French and Dutch forebears who came to America in Revolutionary times. Their daughter, Gertrude, born November 7, 1906, received her B. A. and B. F. A. from the University of Nebraska. She is married to Charles F. Adams, and resides at Aurora, Nebraska.

Dr. Rowe has been in active practice since 1905, and is a member of the Lincoln Clinic, and chairman of the staff of Bryan Memorial Hospital. He is also medical director of the Midwest Life Insurance Company, and member of the following professional organizations: American, Nebraska State and Lancaster County Medical Associations, the American Roentgen Ray Society, the American College of Radiology, and the Radiological Society of North America.

He entered the World War as a captain in the Medical Corps in 1918, with nearly two years service. He is a major in the Medical Reserve Corps, saw overseas service, and was roentgenologist in Camp, evacuation and Base Hospitals on the western front and in Germany with the Army of Occupation. He is a member of the American Legion, the Chamber of Commerce, Kiwanis Club, American Society for the Advancement of Science, and a former president of the Lincoln Board of Education. He is a Republican and a Mason. His church is Trinity Methodist Episcopal at Lincoln, and his club is the University. He enjoys reading and orcharding. Residence: Lincoln.

Ruben Lee Roy

Ruben Lee Roy, county superintendent of schools of

Arthur County, was born in Frontier County, Nebraska, October 24, 1896.

His father, Joseph Roy, was born in Quebec, Canada, December 11, 1856, of Norman French descent. He was secretary and treasurer of the Nebraska Conference of Seventh Day Adventists. His wife, Eva, was born at St. Anne, Illinois, November 13, 1870, of French Canadian descent. At the present time his parents are residing at Lincoln.

Mr. Roy attended rural schools in McPherson County until 1911, and was graduated from Culbertson High School in 1916. In 1929 he received the Bachelor of Science degree from the University of Nebraska. While in high school he was valedictorian of his class, and a member of the basketball and baseball teams. Starting as a rural teacher, Mr. Roy was later a high school teacher and principal, and since 1928 has held his present position of county superintendent. He is Independent in politics.

He is a member of the Nebraska State Teachers Association, the Red Cross, the Masons and the Nebraskana Society. During the late war he was a member of the Students Army Training Corps.

On June 28, 1921, he was married to Irene Minnie Webb at Seward. Mrs. Roy was born at Tecumseh, February 23, 1900, of English descent. They have one daughter, Donna, born July 31, 1923. Residence: Arthur.

Abraham S. Rubnitz

Abraham S. Rubnitz, physician, was born in Russia, January 23, 1885, son of Meyer and Ann (Kushser) Rubnitz. He was graduated from the gymnasium of Slutzk, Russia, in 1908, and received his Bachelor of Arts degree from the University of Nebraska in 1915. In 1916 he received his medical degree from the same university.

He was married to Esther M. Yonich in Russia, on November 24, 1909.

Among Dr. Rubnitz's professional organizations are, the American, Nebraska State and Douglas County Medical Associations, the Missouri Valley Medical Association, and the American Society of Clinical Pathologists. Residence: Omaha.

Orla Oscar Rucker

Orla Oscar Rucker, purebred stock farmer, was born at Chadron, Nebraska, October 20, 1887, son of Warren and Amanda Jane (Crayton) Rucker.

The father, born in Summerfield, Ohio, February 27, 1841, died at Chadron, June 12, 1926. He was a farmer, who served in Company D, 42nd Ohio Infantry in the Civil War. He was a prominent citizen of Dawes County, served as county assessor, a member of the school board, and an active Sunday school worker. He was the son of Lemuel and Lucy Rucker, pioneers in Ohio. The family moved from Virginia where they had settled during the Revolutionary perod. The grandfather of Lemuel Rucker was a soldier in the Revolutionary War. Mrs. Rucker came with her parents from the Blakes, from Maine. She was a devout, industrious, pioneer mother.

Amanda Jane Crayton was born at Eureka, Illinois, January 14, 1851, and is still living. She was a Mehodist clergyman, and president of the Woman's Christian Temperance Union of Chadron and Crete. Her father was of Irish descent, an elder in the Christian Church. Her mother came from a well established family in Illinois.

Upon the completion of his early education in the city schools of Chadron, Mr. Rucker attended Chadron Academy and Doane Academy at Crete. During 1914-15 he was a student at Doane College, and during the year 1917 attended the University of Nebraska. He was a student at Iowa State College in 1919. Mr. Rucker was active in debating, a member of the Glee Club, and the Young Men's Christian Association Cabinet, and at Chad-

ron played football and basketball, while at Doane College he was active in football and track.

Mr. Rucker is a Republican. He is the director and treasurer of the Chadron Stock Pavilion Association, a member of the Chadron Hereford Breeders Association, the Northwest Nebraska Hereford Breeders Association, and is affiliated with Chadron Community Congregational Church.

Recently Mr. Rucker was elected to life membership in the Nebraskana Society. He is a Mason, and a member of the Sons of the American Revolution. He was first president of the County School District Officers Association, and from 1919 until the present time has served as treasurer of the rural school board. From 1910 until 1916 he was a member of the Young Men's Christian Association at Doane College, and from 1926 until 1929 was president of the Dawes County Sunday School Association. His hobbies are singing and reading. Residence: Chadron.

James Archie Ruddock

James Archie Ruddock, editor and publisher of the *Gazette* at Gresham, York County, Nebraska, has resided in this state for the past 40 years. He was born at Sergeant Bluffs, Iowa, September 20, 1880, the son of Thomas Henry and Albertina Elvira (Scovell) Ruddock. His father, who was a railroad man, was born in England, May 17, 1844, came to this country in 1861, and died at Boone, Iowa, August 1 1906; he was a soldier in the English Army and later served in the Civil War.

His mother was born in Iowa, July 19, 1853, and died at Sioux City, Iowa, January 7, 1925.

Mr. Ruddock attended the Gresham High School, and immediately entered the publishing business. He is a member of the Royal Highlanders, is affiliated with the Democratic party, and holds membership in the Nebraskana Society. For the past 17 years he has served as village clerk at Gresham and is now township clerk there. His sports include fishing and hunting.

He married Ruth Fontaine Pogue in Seward County, January 5, 1905. Mrs. Ruddock was born near Gresham, July 29, 1879. They have a son, Walter Donald, born December 10, 1905. He was graduated from the college of pharmacy at the University of Nebraska and is now a druggist at Grand Island, Hall County, Nebraska. Residence: Gresham.

Charles Ruden

Charles Ruden, son of Ole and Christena (Anderson) Ruden, was born in Knox County, Nebraska, March 16, 1871. His father, born in Sweden, October 29, 1831. Coming to America he engaged as a farmer and stockman, served as postmaster and operated a hotel. His death occurred at Bloomfield, Nebraska, August 31, 1903. The others of his family, with the exception of a sister who died at Seattle, remained in Europe. His mother, born in Sweden, August 10, 1845, died at Omaha, April 18, 1927.

Educated in country schools in Knox County, Charles Ruden attended Hartington High School. In 1889 he entered the employ of the Union Pacific at Omaha as a clerk. Removing to Bloomfield in July 1891, he worked in a lumber yard a year and a half, and was then associated with the Edwards and Bradford Lumber Company four years, as yard manager, two years of this period, and as collector two years.

In 1897 Mr. Ruden entered the implement business in Bloomfield and in 1900 was elected county clerk and register of deeds for six years, conducting a farm at the same time. From 1906 to 1908 he was cashier of the Farmers State Bank of Crofton, and then became postmaster of Crofton for six years. Since that time he has engaged in the real estate loans and insurance business, manages his own farm and others.

On May 5, 1897, Mr. Ruden was married to Anna

Buhrow in Knox County. Mrs. Ruden attended country school and Yankton College and was a student at the Conservatory of Music at Yankton. She is recorder of the Royal Neighbors of America, the Order of Eastern Star and has been an officer in various organizations. Her father was a corporal in Company K, Regiment of Missouri Artillery, and a member of the Grand Army of the Republic.

To Mr. and Mrs. Ruden were born five children: Edwin Dewey, born June 5, 1898, was stricken with spinal mengitis in May 1899 and was an invalid until his death on February 11, 1925. Donald, born August 25, 1899, died the same day. John Ralph, born November 22, 1900, was accidentally killed by a feed grinder on February 20, 1905. Walter Louis, born May 14, 1904, married Mildred Stanton. Daniel Charles, born September 24, 1907, is unmarried.

Walter was graduated from the Crofton High School, was valedictorian of his class and taught in the University of California for three years, and in the Salina, California High School two years. Daniel was graduated from the University of Nebraska as an electrical engineer, and is now working for the Iowa-Nebraska Light and Power Company at Lincoln. Walter was graduated from the University of Nebraska as an agricultural engineer.

Mr. Ruden is a Republican. For twenty years he has served as secretary of the local Masonic lodge. He is a member of Oriental Consistory at Yankton, and a life member of Tangier Temple of the Shrine at Omaha. He is now serving as secretary of the Crofton Community Club. Recently he was elected to life membership in The Nebraskana Society. Residence: Crofton.

Joseph Ruesing

The Right Reverend Joseph Ruesing, priest of the Catholic Church, has been a resident of Nebraska for the past 48 years. He was born at Faderbom, Westfalen, Germany, December 28, 1853, was graduated from the Faderbom Gymnasium in 1873, and was a student at the Catholic University of Muenster. For 30 years prior to 1914 he served as pastor of St. Mary's Church at West Point, and since that date has been director of the St. Joseph's Home and Hospital which he established in 1905. Residence: West Point.

Stephen James Rueve

Stephen J. Rueve, clergyman, philosopher, and educator, was born at St. Louis, Missouri, December 28, 1892. His father John Henry Rueve, who was born at St. Louis, July 11, 1867, for many years a government clerk in the post office. His ancestors were Germans who came from the Duchy of Oldenburg, in northwestern Germany, settling in America about 1850.

Sophia Josephine (Roos) Rueve, his mother, who was born at St. Louis, February 13, 1868, and died there, July 4 1928, was prominent in club and church work. She was a member of the National Catholic Women's Conference, and the Christian Mothers' Society. She was descended from Dutch and German ancestors who have been in this country for generations.

Father Rueve was graduated from St. Thomas Aquinas Parochial School at St. Louis, 1905, and in 1909 completed the high school course at the St. Louis University High School. He was awarded the A. B. degree at St. Louis University, 1915; A. M., 1917; and M. S., 1922. In 1922 and 1923 he attended the College de Saint-Jean Berchmans, at Louvain, Belgium, and from 1923 to 1926 was a student at Ignatiuskolleg, Valkenberg, Holland.

For a time he was an instructor at Rockhurst College, Kansas City, Missouri; from 1918-22, he taught at St. John's University, Toledo, Ohio; and from 1927-29, he was a teacher at St. Mary's College, Kansas. Since 1929

Father Rueve has held the position of assistant professor of Philosophy at Creighton University.

He is a member of the Mathematical and Philosophical sections of the Jesuit Educational Association; the Society of Jesus, and the Nebraskana Society. His favorite sports are golf, handball, and swimming. His hobby is music. Politically, he is an independent Republican. Residence: Omaha.

Walter Charles Rundin

Walter C. Rundin, who has been a clergyman in Nebraska for the past 20 years, was born at Norwich, Connecticut, July 12, 1885, the son of Aaron and Eliza Sophia (Johnson) Rundin. His father, who was born in Sweden, is retired and is living in Sweden at this time. His mother was born in Sweden, and died at Chicago, Illinois, June 3, 1911.

Mr. Rundin received his elementary education in Chicago, was a student at the Moody Bible Institute, was graduated from Bryant and Stratton College, 1902, and in 1909 was graduated from the Chicago Theological Seminary. He has held the following positions: pastor of Congregational Church at Crawford, Nebraska, 1912-17; pastor Federated Church at Mitchell, Nebraska, 1917-27; and pastor of the Congregational Church at Wahoo, 1927 to this date. He was connected with the Congregational Church at Port Byron, Illinois, 1909-12.

From 1914 to 1917, he served as secretary of the Crawford Chamber of Commerce, at one time was vice president of the Nebraska Chamber of Commerce, and for one year was president of the Associated Chambers of Commerce of the Platte Valley. He is a member of the Lincoln Association of Congregational Churches, is president of the Wahoo Lions Club, and holds membership in the Nebraskana Society. From 1913 to 1916, he was a member of the school board at Crawford; he is ex-president and present chaplain of the Nebraska State Volunteer Firemen's Association, and is an honorary member of the Iowa, Colorado, and Kansas firemen's associations. During the World War he was chairman of the Four Minute Men, and was active as secretary of the Red Cross at Mitchell. He is well known as an after dinner, commencement and community speaker.

He was married to Mae Bertha McMahon at Brunswick, Antelope County, Nebraska, June 22, 1910. Mrs. Rundin was born at Brunswick, May 1, 1888. They have two children: Bernice Fae, born February 27, 1913; and Walter Charles, born August 11, 1920. Residence: Wahoo.

Clifford Enfred Rundquist

Born at Royal, Nebraska, Clifford Enfred Rundquist is the son of Mathias John and Minnie Christina (Holm) Rundquist. His father, who is a retired farmer, was born at Dalerna, Sweden, April 23, 1852, came to America in 1877, and settled in Nebraska in 1885. His mother, whose parents were pioneer homesteaders in Nebraska, was born at Soderkoping, Sweden, May 3, 1865.

Mr. Rundquist attended the Nebraska Normal College during 1904 and 1905, was a student at Warriners Business College in 1906 and 1907, and taught a rural school for a time. He has been in the general merchandise business for 25 years at Royal, and is today manager of the firm Rundquist & Company. He is chairman of the Red Cross and a member of the State Drouth Relief Committee of Antelope County.

He is president of the Royal School Board, was formerly mayor of his community, and is Past Master of the Masons and Past Worthy Patron of the Eastern Star. For over 25 years he has been a member of the Royal Baseball Club, and still enjoys both baseball and football. His political connection is with the Republican party.

On June 14, 1911, he married Ollie Mae Boyd at Royal. Mrs. Rundquist, whose parents were pioneers of Antelope

County, Nebraska, was born at Royal, October 13, 1888. They have three children: Glenn, born April 4, 1912; Corinne, born November 22, 1914, who received honors in high school; and Gwendolyn, born October 22, 1916. Glenn is a clerk and farmer. Corinne is a student at Wayne State Teachers College, and Gwendolyn is still in high school. Residence: Royal.

Frank Oscar Rundquist

Frank Oscar Rundquist, a lifelong resident of Kearney County, Nebraska, was born in that vicinity, November 18, 1889, the son of Andrew Gustaf and Ulrika Carolina (Adolfson) Rundquist. His father, who was a farmer, was born in Sweden, July 6, 1856. He came to America in 1881, residing in Chicago for six years, then locating in Minden, where he died April 10, 1922.

His mother was born in Sweden, July 1, 1856. She came to America in 1882 and was united in marriage to Andrew Gustaf Rundquist at Chicago.

Mr. Rundquist is president of the Farmers Union Co-operative Association at Minden, is a director of district No. 27 school board, holds membership in the Parent Teachers Association, and is a member of the Farmers Educational & Co-operative Union of Nebraska. He is independent, politically.

His marriage to Emma Elizabeth Driscoll occurred at Minden, March 3, 1920. Mrs. Rundquist, who was born at Keene, Nebraska, September 17, 1888, is the daughter of pioneer settlers in Nebraska. Two children were born to this union: Ardyce, September 11, 1924; and Ardella, July 30, 1927. Residence: Minden.

Fred Bernhardt Runge

A resident of Nebraska for the past forty years, Fred Bernhardt Runge was born at Freetz, Germany, January 29, 1882. His father and mother were born at Freetz, the former on August 13, 1848, and the latter on September 1, 1854. The family came from Germany to America, arriving on May 31, 1891, and came direct to Nuckolls County. Albert Runge, the father, was a prominent farmer until his death at Oak, on February 4, 1927. His wife, Adeline Steve, preceded him in death, on March 24, 1917.

Fred Bernhardt Runge attended public school in Germany, and farmed with his father until he reached maturity. He was married on December 20, 1905, to Mary Jensen at West Point. She was born at West Point, January 6, 1884. To them were born five sons and daughters, Harold, born March 12, 1907; Martin, born October 28, 1908; Edna, born April 5, 1911, married William Paul Hineline; Melvin, born September 1, 1912; and Hilda, born November 4, 1916. Residence: Oak.

Robert P. Rusho

Robert P. Rusho, banker, was born at Fort Hartsup, Nebraska, September 1, 1876, son of Joseph and Josephine (Murray) Rusho.

The father, born May, 1859, is now retired and lives in Boulder, Colorado. He is of French descent and has been very successful as a farmer, rancher and business man. The mother, who was also of French descent, died at Boulder, Colorado.

Mr. Rusho attended common school, and afterward completed a commercial course at Western Normal College in Lincoln. He has been engaged in the mercantile business, in stock raising and banking, and is now president of the Bank of Taylor. He is a Republican.

On October 10, 1900, he was married to Elizabeth Anne Vinnedge at Taylor. Mrs. Rusho was born there September 28, 1881. They have two children, Robert Maxwell, born June 15, 1907, who married Mary Grier; and Jacquetta, born January 10, 1912. Robert operates a filling station at Houston, Texas, while Jacquetta is a student at Nebraska Wesleyan University. Residence: Taylor.

Fay Russell

Fay Russell, merchant, was born at Kearney, Nebraska, November 11, 1884, son of Robert and Ann (Flint) Russel. The father, a native of Clinton, Ohio, died at Kearney, April 4, 1919. He homesteaded eight miles east of Kearney, in 1873, and was the first judge of Sherman County. He was later a farmer and merchant, and was street commissioner of Kearney for 20 years.

His wife, Ann Flint, was born in Meppershal, Bedfordshire, England, July 5, 1852, and died at Ogallala, Nebraska, August 23, 1921. She was a charter member and active in the Royal Neighbors of America, and was a direct descendant of John Bunyan.

Mr. Russell was graduated from Kearney High School in 1903, and has since engaged in business in Kearney. At the present time he is a partner in the firm and the manager of the Princess Chocolate Shop. He is a Republican.

His marriage to Louise Ernestina Geisert was solemnized at Ogallala, February 20, 1918. Mrs. Russell was born in Ogallala, October 31, 1893, of German descent. Five children were born to them, three of whom are living, Boyd A., born December 9, 1918; Robert J., born February 7, 1920; Carol Annette, born December 21, 1930; Donald, born February 25, 1925, who died February 25, 1925; and Ronald, born February 6, 1932, who died February 7, 1932.

During the late war Mr. Russell was a first sergeant and first lieutenant of the Keith County Home Guard. He supported all war activities, and for a number of years has been a scout leader and active in boys' work.

His religious affiliation is with St. Paul's Evangelical Lutheran Church. He has contributed to the state Young Men's Christian Association, is a member of the Red Cross, the Rotary Club (president) and the Ogallala Commercial Club. His favorite sport is hiking while his hobby is gymnastics. Residence: Ogallala.

Harrison Frederick Russell

Harrison F. Russell, leading executive and lawyer of Hastings, has lived in Nebraska all his life. He was born at Kenesaw, Adams County, Nebraska, June 6, 1890, the son of Henry Maroni and Charlotte (Haller) Russell. His father, born at Steubenville, Steuben County, Indiana, on August 11, 1848, has been a banker and merchant at Kenesaw, Nebraska, for more than forty years. The Russells came to America from England, in 1810, Harrison F. Russell's grandmother being a member of the Chase family, and a descendent of men who were active in the Revolution. His own mother was born at Bridgmon, Berrien County, Michigan, on December 10, 1856, and was a public school teacher for sixteen years. Her father, who was a Civil War veteran, was born in Germany, while her mother was descended from Revolutionary War soldiers of the Stevens family.

Upon his graduation from Kenesaw High School in 1906, Mr. Russell attended Hastings College, from which, in 1910, he received the degree of Bachelor of Arts. He was valedictorian of his high school class, and was a letterman in college. From 1910-12 he was employed by the Exchange National Bank at Hastings, and thereafter purchased an interest in the Clarke-Buchanan Company, a loan and investment firm. After holding various offices in this organization, he was elected president and trust officer in 1930.

During the recent war Mr. Russell was a sergeant of Infantry, Machine Gun Officers Training School. Active in Red Cross work, he also served as a four minute speaker. He is a charter member of the Hastings American Legion, Post Number 11, the Sons of the American Revolution, and holds a commission in the United States Army Reserves.

Mr. Russell is a director and vice president of the Chamber of Commerce, is president and director of the Rotary Club, is a member of The Nebraskana Society, and of the First Presbyterian Church of Hastings. His hobby is boys' work and his favorite sport is golf.

His marriage to Mary Arthur Collins was solemnized at Hebron, Nebraska, June 4, 1913. Mrs. Russell, who was a talented musician, and an active participant in all musical affairs, was born at Hebron, January 3, 1889. She was descented from Revolutionary ancestors through both sides of her family. Her death occurred at Hastings, on March 31, 1924.

On June 30, 1926, Mr. Russell was married to Esther Rosalind Fuhr, at Pasadena, California. She was born at Macomb, Illinois, January 18, 1896, and is the mother of one son, Harrison Frederick, Jr., born September 27, 1930. Residence: Hastings.

Ralph Swisher Russell

Ralph Swisher Russell, physician and surgeon, was born at Metlaltoyuca, Old Mexico, March 22, 1900, son of Calvin Parker and Orissa Anna (Swisher) Russell.

The father, born at Glenns Falls, New York, April 18, 1857, is of English descent, a son of the American Revolution through Captain Parker of the battle of Bunker Hill. He is secretary and treasurer of the Lincoln Telephone and Telegraph Company; vice president of the Nebraska Anti-Saloon League; and treasurer of the building fund of the First Plymouth Church at Lincoln. His wife, Orissa, was born at Dayton, Ohio, August 31, 1864, and is very active in Woman's Club work. She is of Swiss German descent, representing the fourth generation in America.

Dr. Russell graduated from Cherry Street School in Lincoln in 1913 and from the Lincoln High School in 1917. He entered the University of Nebraska receiving his Bachelor of Arts degree in 1921, his Bachelor of Science degree in 1922, and his medical degree in 1925. He has been in active practice since that date. At the present time Dr. Russell is manager and owner of the Russell Hospital at Sutherland. He served his interneship at the University Hospital in 1925, and took a post-graduate course in surgery in 1926.

His marriage to Ruth Elizabeth Carpenter, daughter of A. W. Carpenter and Myrtle Tasker, was solemnized at Lincoln, July 20, 1926. Mrs. Russell was born at Denver, June 16, 1903, of Scotch-Irish descent, descended from General Bliss. They have one son, Ralph born July 23, 1928.

Dr. Russell is a Republican. He served at Camp Taylor, Kentucky, in the field artillery, during the World War and for the past ten years has been a leader of the Boy Scouts. He was commander of Post No. 208 of the American Legion in 1931, is a member of the Sons of the American Revolution, the First Methodist Church of Sutherland, the Lincoln County, Nebraska State, and American Medical Associations. He is also a member of the Red Cross, the Sutherland Commercial Club, the Masons, and the Odd Fellows. His favorite sports are hunting and fishing. Residence: Sutherland.

William Garfield Rutledge

William Garfield Rutledge, lawyer and former county judge of Nemaha County, was born near Rockford, Ohio, March 2, 1880. His father, William Mathew Rutledge, born near Rockford, October 1, 1836, was a soldier in the Civil War. He was descended from Edward Rutledge, signer of the Declaration of Independence. He died at Utica, Nebraska, May 9, 1900. His wife, Mary Ellen Eichar, was born near Rockford, September 11, 1845 and died at Brock, Nebraska, July 5, 1931.

Judge Rutledge was graduated from Utica High School in 1899 and from the commercial department of York College in 1901. He attended Lake Forest University, and received his LL. B. from Chicago-Kent College of Law at Chicago. He was admitted to the Illinois

Bar in October, 1904, and to the Nebraska Bar at Lincoln, in September, 1905.

Judge Rutledge has been a resident of Nebraska for the past fifty years, and during the course of his professional career has won a reputation in his community which is enviable. He is a member of the American and Nebraska State Bar Associations, and of the state Y. M. C. A. During the World War he was chairman of the Loyalty League of Nemaha County. He is a thirty-second degree Mason, and member of the Eastern Star. He is also affiliated with the Odd Fellows. His church is the Avenue Methodist Church of Auburn. He is a golf enthusiast and his hobby is reading. He is a Republican.

He was married to Frances Margaret Peuser-Geyer at Chicago, December 8, 1908. Mrs. Rutledge is a native of Chicago, born October 27, 1885. They have two children, Muriel Frances, born June 2, 1910, now attending the University of Nebraska; and Ruth Margaret, born February 18, 1915, attending Auburn High School. Residence: Auburn.

Calvin Taylor Ryan

One of the distinguished educators of Nebraska is Calvin Taylor Ryan, head of the English department of Kearney State Teachers College. He was born at Bishopville, Maryland, January 1, 1888, the son of David Davidson and Katherine (Timmons) Ryan. His father, whose ancestry was Irish, was a farmer who died at Bishopville, June 25, 1923. His mother, also of Irish descent, died at Bishopville, April 24, 1927.

Mr. Ryan was graduated from the Bishopville High School in 1905, received the Master of Arts degree at Washington College in Maryland in 1914, and was awarded the Master of Education degree at Harvard Graduate School of Education in 1922. He was a student at the University of Virginia during the summer session of 1908, and attended George Washington University from 1915 to 1918. His fraternities were Pi Kappa Delta, Sigma Delta Chi.

He was high school instructor at Cape Charles, Virginia, 1911-12, taught at Bridgeport, West Virginia, 1912-13, was instructor at Washington College at Chestertown, Maryland, 1913-15, and taught at Alexandria, Virginia, 1915-18. Mr. Ryan taught at Iowa Wesleyan College, 1922-28, and since 1928 has been head of the English department of the Kearney State Teachers College. He is the author of articles on education published in various professional and general magazines.

Mr. Ryan is a member of the Red Cross, the Knights Templar, and the First Methodist Episcopal Church. He served as a first class private in the Air Service of the United States Army, Photo-Unit, during the World War, and is a member of the American Legion. His favorite recreations are reading and hiking.

On June 23, 1920, he was married to Marie Bristowe at Cambridge, Massachusetts. They have a daughter, Zelda Jean, born June 6, 1929. Residence: Kearney.

Leo Edward Ryan

Leo Edward Ryan, who for the past thirteen years has been cashier of the Hazard State Bank, was born at Iowa City, Iowa, September 25, 1894. He is the son of James Edward and Cora Capitola (Hoover) Ryan, both born at Iowa City, the former on September 23, 1871, and the latter on November 5, 1876. James Edward Ryan was a barber, lawyer and police judge, whose death occurred at Douglas, Wyoming, October 10, 1924. His mother comes from the Horton and Hoover families, the history of the Horton's being traced back 600 years.

Mr. Ryan, who attended Holy Family School at Omaha, and the public school at Indianola, Nebraska, was graduated from Indianola High School on June 2, 1912. Thereafter he received two teacher's certificates and taught two years. In the banking business for many years, he was with the State Bank at Indianola, the State

Bank at Bartley and Cambridge State Bank at Cambridge, and for thirteen years has been cashier of the Hazard State Bank.

A Republican, Mr. Ryan has held minor town offices and has served as delegate to state conventions. During the World War he was a private in Company B, 23rd Machine Gun Batallion, 8th Regular Division. He has held local offices in the Red Cross, and has served on the Hazard School Board. Mr. Ryan is general agent of the American State Life Insurance Company of Lincoln, Nebraska. Residence: Hazard.

Mark Joseph Ryan

Mark J. Ryan was born at Coleman, South Dakota, May 7, 1889, the son of John and Agnes B. (Daley) Ryan. His father, who was born at Cincinatti, Ohio, May 25, 1854, and died at Madison, Lake County, South Dakota, July 4, 1929, was a school teacher in his early life and later was a farmer; his paternal great-grandfather came to this country from Ireland in 1830. His mother, whose ancestors came to this country from Ireland in 1840, was born at Madison, Wisconsin, May 24, 1852, and is now living at Madison, South Dakota.

Mr. Ryan attended the rural schools of Moody County, was a student at the State Normal School at Madison, and holds the following degrees: A. B., Creighton University, 1912; A. M. Creighton University, 1914; and LL. B., with *cum laude* honors, college of law, Creighton University, 1915. He was class valedictorian at the College of Arts and Sciences, Creighton, and held membership in the Theta Chapter of Gamma Eta Gamma.

He was engaged in the practice of law at Pender, Thurston County, Nebraska, from 1916 to 1924. A Democrat, he was United States Commissioner for Nebraska, 1920-24; was county attorney of Thurston County, 1922-25; and was elected judge of the 8th Judicial District 1924, re-elected, 1928. He is a member of the Pender Chamber of Commerce, the Lions Club, the Nebraska State Bar Association, The Nebraskana Society, and the Red Cross. He is an Elk and a member of the Woodmen of the World. He is affiliated with St. John's Catholic Church and is a member of the Knights of Columbus.

Judge Ryan enlisted in the air service, November 21, 1917, was discharged June 12, 1918, was inducted into service July 16, 1918, and discharged, March 29, 1919. He was regimental sergeant major at Camp Dodge, Iowa. Until he entered the service he was food administrator at Pender and acted as Four Minute Man. He is a charter member of Post Number 55 of the American Legion. His sports are tennis and golf.

His marriage to Anne Harrower was solemnized at Omaha, Dougles County, Nebraska, February 12, 1920. Mrs. Ryan, who was a stenographer before her marriage, was born at Omaha, October 15, 1894. Her ancestry is Scotch Irish, on the paternal side, and German through the maternal line. They have two children: John, born November 28, 1920; and Thomas Lee, born August 23, 1928. Residence: Pender. (Photograph on Page 1039).

William Hogan Ryan

On February 4, 1863, William H. Ryan was born in Dakota County, January 18, 1880; he was a prominent farmer and held the office of county commissioner at the time of his death. He came to America from Ireland, in 1846, at the age of 22. Margaret Hogan, the mother of William H. Ryan, was born in County Tipperary, in 1834, and died in Dakota County, Nebraska, October 11, 1871.

Mr. Ryan was married to Julia Ashford at Homer, on October 5, 1904. His wife is a native Nebraskan, having been born at Homer, on July 29, 1873. There are no children.

Since December, 1903, Mr. Ryan has been cashier of the Security State Bank of Homer. Prior to that time he served as county sheriff of Dakota County two terms covering four years as follows: 1890 to 1893; and from 1896, to 1900, was county judge. He is a member of the Republican party.

Mr. Ryan is a member of St. Cornelius Catholic Church of Homer. He has been prominent in the political, civic and religious affairs of his community for the past 40 years. Residence: Homer.

Charles Silcott Ryckman

Charles Silcott Ryckman, editor, was born at Fort Collins, Colorado, July 11, 1898, son of John Power and Ada (Silcott) Ryckman. John Power Ryckman, was a native of Johnstown, Pennsylvania, born December 28, 1858. He is a farmer, and former chief of Police of Fort Collins. Ada Silcott was born in 1870, and died at Fort Collins, in 1900. She was an accomplished pianist.

Mr. Ryckman attended Fort Collins public and high schools, where he was active in football and track. He is an associate member of Sigma Delta Chi, this honor having been bestowed by the Nebraska chapter He began his newspaper career on *Fort Collins Courier* in 1920, and since May, has been associated with the *Fremont Tribune* of which he is editor. He is a Republican, and a member of the city council, and has made his home in Nebraska for the past eleven years.

On August 12, 1922, he was married to Mary Elizabeth Redmond at Fremont. Mrs. Ryckman was born at Troy, Ohio, July 24, 1898. From April 16, 1917, to December 6, 1919, Mr. Ryckman served in the United States Navy, and at present holds the rank of captain in the United States Army Reserves. He is a member of the American Legion, the Veterans of Foreign Wars and the Reserve Officers Association. He is a Mason and an Elk, and is a member of the First Methodist Episcopal Church, the Y. M. C. A., and the Nebraskana Society.

He was the winner in 1931 of the Pulitzer award for having written the best editorial appearing in any American newspaper in 1930. It appeared in the *Fremont Tribune,* November 5, 1930 *The Gentleman from Nebraska,* dealing with the re-election of George W. Norris to the United States Senate. Residence: Fremont.

George Albert Rydlund

George Albert Rydlund, manager of the Funk Grain & Elevator Company at Funk, Nebraska, is a lifetime resident of Phelps County. He was born at Funk, October 26, 1883, the son of John Gust Rydlund and Matilda (Enquist) Rydlund. His father, who was a farmer, was born in Sweden, April 18, 1842, came to America, in 1856, and died at Funk, Nebraska, November 22, 1898. His mother was born in Sweden, April 9, 1855, and is now living at Boone, Iowa.

Mr. Rydlund attended Lutheran College at Wahoo, 1902-03. He has been a school director for the past eight years at Funk, is affiliated with Fredhem Lutheran Church, and holds membership in the Ancient Order of United Workmen, the Modern Woodmen of America, and the Masons. His sport is hunting.

On February 14, 1906, he was married at Ford Dodge, Iowa, to Evelyn Nafe. Mrs. Rydlund was born at Hampton, Iowa, January 18, 1885. Six children were born to them, Violet, born September 6, 1907, who married Rollo Bricker, of Lincoln; Garnet, born March 15, 1909, who married Vincent Hedstrom; Georgie, born September 19, 1910, who died October 2, 1910; Marjorie, born September 11, 1916; Linnea, born November 7, 1919; and George William, born June 30, 1929. Mr. Rydlund is a member of the Democratic party and holds membership in the Nebraskana Society. Residence: Funk. (Photograph in Album).

Clayton Arthur Rystrom

Clayton A. Rystrom was born at Stromsburg, Nebraska, November 4, 1901, the son of August Johannas and

MARK JOSEPH RYAN

Genelli—Sioux City, Iowa

Emma Josephine (Fusby) Rystrom. His father, who is a farmer, was born at Smalan, Sweden, January 2, 1857. His mother was born at Rome, Iowa, November 29, 1862.

Mr. Rystrom attended a rural school, was graduated from the Stromsburg High School in 1919, and in 1923 received the B. S. degree from the University of Nebraska where he was a member of Pi Kappa Alpha.

He is secretary and treasurer of the Rystrom Company, Incorporated, is a member of the Stromsburg Community Club of which he was secretary, 1926-28, and is affiliated with the Eden Baptist Church. He holds membership in the Nebraskana Society, and is a Mason. His hobby is reading.

Mr. Rystrom was married to Beulah Maud Tinker, August 18, 1926, at her home in Waco, Nebraska; she was born at Waco, July 17, 1905. They have two children: Clayton, Jr., born September 6, 1927; and Shirley Jean, born January 13, 1931. Residence: Stromsburg.

William Sack

One of the prominent business men at Ord, Nebraska, is William Sack, who was born at Sutton, Nebraska, May 4, 1889. His father, Phillip Sack, a carpenter, was born in Germany. Mary Elizabeth (Kaiser) Sack his mother, was born in Germany and died at Sutton, in September, 1908.

Mr. Sack received his education in the public schools of Sutton, and from 1908 to 1912 was an engineer in the electric light plant at Ord. From 1912 until 1916 he was bookkeeper of the Sack Lumber and Coal Company. Since 1912 he has been manager of the Sack Lumber and Coal Company at Ord, and is vice president of the Sack Lumber and Coal Company whose office is at Crete, Nebraska. He is affiliated with the Methodist Church, is city councilman of Ord, and holds membership in the Nebraskana Society. His sports include hunting and fishing.

He was united in marriage with Jessie Irene Moyer at Lincoln, Nebraska, June 15, 1916. Mrs. Sack, who was a teacher before her marriage, was born at Tecumseh, Nebraska, and died at Ord in December, 1923. Two sons were born to this marriage, Harold Lee, March 12, 1917, is a junior in the Ord High School; and Lloyd Lee, February 6, 1921, is in the 6th grade. Mr. Sack was married to Nora Cecelia Nygren Johnson, June 7, 1925, who has one daughter, Virginia Mary, born July 27, 1920, by a former marriage. Residence: Ord.

Harry Evans Sackett

Harry Evans Sackett, distinguished lawyer and political leader of Beatrice, Nebraska, has lived in this state since 1894, and has taken a prominent part in state and community affairs for many years. He was born at Warren, Trumbull County, Ohio, October 10, 1874, the son of Oliver P. and Mary (Evans) Sackett. His father, a farmer, was born at Canfield, Mahoning County, Ohio, January 19, 1828, and died at Beatrice, October 17, 1911; his English ancestors came to America in 1630, and both his grandfather and great-grandfather were soldiers in the Revolutionary War.

Mary (Evans) Sackett, mother of Harry Sackett, was born at Copley, Summitt County, Ohio, September 19, 1844. Her ancestry was Welsh and German.

Mr. Sackett was graduated from high school at Grant City, Missouri, in 1894, and in 1895 studied post graduate work at the Beatrice High School. He taught in the rural schools of Gage County during 1896, and a little later entered the College of Law, University of Nebraska. He was awarded the LL. B. degree at the University of Nebraska, where he represented the college in intercollegiate debate in 1898. Since his admission to the bar in 1898, Mr. Sackett has been active in legal practice at Beatrice.

A Republican, he served as county attorney of Gage County from 1901 to 1904, was state senator in 1907, and acted as chairman of the Republican state committee from 1924 to 1926. He has always been prominent in Republican state and national politics, and has held the following positions: delegate to the national convention, 1912; candidate for governor on the progressive ticket, 1914; delegate to the progressive convention, 1916; and delegate to the Republican national convention, 1920.

He is a member of the Beatrice Chamber of Commerce, the State Historical Society, the Nebraskana Society, and the Young Men's Christian Association. He holds membership in the American and Nebraska bar associations, and is one of the past presidents of the Beatrice Kiwanis Club, and is affiliated with the First Christian Church of Beatrice, and active in the Sunday School.

His marriage to Hermina Reynolds was solemnized at Beatrice, September 27, 1899. Mrs. Sackett, whose ancestry is English and Holland Dutch, was born at Beatrice, January 27, 1875. Their children are: Dean R., born November 6, 1902, who was a student at the University of Nebraska, Creighton University, and Georgetown University; Harry E., born September 24, 1906, who was graduated from the University of Nebraska with A. B. and LL. B. degrees; and Mary Louise, born October 3, 1914. Harry E. Jr., was awarded *Cum Laude* honors at the university, and was admitted to the Order of the Coif.

Mr. Sackett is a director in the Beatrice Building and Loan Association. An active member of the Nebraska Council of Defense, and a participant in other war relief work, Mr. Sackett was also a four minute man during the World War. His hobbies are gardening and flowers. Residence: Beatrice. (Photograph in Album).

Hermina Reynolds Sackett

Hermina Reynolds Sackett, a lifetime resident of Beatrice, Gage County, Nebraska, is prominent in civic and social affairs in her community. She was born at Beatrice, January 27, 1875, the daughter of Herman Meyer and Naomi (Barcus) Reynolds. Her father, who was a pioneer physician in Nebraska in 1857, was born in Sullivan County, New York, April 15, 1832, and died at Beatrice, April 27, 1875; he served as the first mayor of Beatrice, and was a member of the territorial legislature and the constitutional convention. His English and Holland Dutch ancestors came to America in 1671; he was the grandson of Revolutionary War soldiers.

Her mother, whose English ancestors were pioneers in America, was born at Covington, Indiana, October 20, 1841, and died at Beatrice, November 9, 1929. She was a typical pioneer home-maker.

Mrs. Sackett received her elementary education in the grade school at Beatrice, and in 1893 was graduated from the Beatrice High School where she was salutatorian. She is a member of the local board of the Young Women's Christian Association, holds membership in the Vesher Chapter of the Eastern Star, is affiliated with the First Christian Church at Beatrice. She is the teacher of a Sunday School class in her church.

During the World War, Mrs. Sackett took part in membership drives for the local Red Cross. She was regent of the Daughters of the American Revolution in 1928 and 1929, and compiled the directory of the Elizabeth Montague Chapter. She is a member of the Nebraskana Society and the Republican party.

She was married to Harry Evans Sackett at Beatrice, September 27, 1899. Mr. Sackett, who is a lawyer, was born at Warren, Ohio, October 10, 1874. His English ancestors came to America in 1630; members of the family fought in the Revolution. To this union three children were born: Dean R., born November 6, 1902, who is a lawyer; Harry E. Jr., born September 24, 1906, who was graduated from the University of Nebraska in 1931, with the honors *cum laude* and admitted to the Order of the Coif; and Mary Louise, born October 3, 1913. Residence: Beatrice. (Photograph in Album).

FRANK J. SADILEK

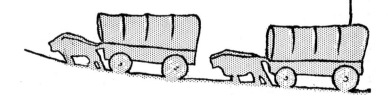

Frank J. Sadilek

Frank Sadilek was born at Ledec, Bohemia, December 1, 1851, and since 1874, has been a resident of Nebraska. His father, Jan Sadilek, who was a harness maker, was born at Ledec, and died at Wilber, Saline County, Nebraska, July 16, 1882. His mother, Barbara (Bradac) Sadilek, was born at Pavlov, Bohemia, December 4, 1813, and died at Chicago, Illinois, July 26, 1890.

Mr. Sadilek was graduated from high school in Bohemia, in 1866. He was engaged in the harness making business from 1864 to 1883. He was deputy county treasurer of Saline County from 1884 to 1887, and from 1887 to 1891 was county treasurer. He served as register of deeds, 1897-1919. A Republican, he was a member of the Nebraska legislature in 1882. He is now president of the Wilber State Bank.

He is the author of a little booklet, *From My Memories*, published in the Bohemian language, 1914. For several years he has been correspondent for the Bohemian newspaper *Hospodar*. He is a member of several Bohemian fraternal organizations, and holds membership in the State Historical Society and the Nebraskana Society. A Mason for the past 52 years, he is also a freethinker.

His marriage to Theresa Jurka was solemnized at Chicago, July 29, 1876. Mrs. Sadilek was born at Kralovice, Bohemia, July 19, 1857. Their children are: Antonie, born June 13, 1877, who married Edmil Folda, a banker; Olga, born September 13, 1887; Sylvia, born September 23, 1880; Frank J., Jr., born October 10, 1884, a salesman; Charles J., born November 22, 1882, who is a banker, and who married Millie Cihak; Walter B., born December 20, 1889, who is a lawyer; and Irma Deborah, born July 31, 1891, who married F. F. Mundil; Victor Hugo, born August 8, 1900, who married Elsie Armstrong.

Mr. Sadilek has delivered more funeral addresses than most clergymen. He is well known in every Bohemian settlement and enjoys the title of father of the Bohemian community. Residence: Crete. (Photograph on Page 1041).

Walter Byron Sadilek

Walter B. Sadilek, son of Frank J. and Theresa (Jurka) Sadilek, was born at Wilber, Nebraska, December 20, 1889. His father, who is now retired from active business, was born at Ledec, Bohemia, December 1, 1851; his mother was born in Bohemia, July 19, 1857.

Mr. Sadilek, who has been prominent in legal activities for the past sixteen years, was a student at Wilber High School 1906-07, and in 1910 was graduated from Highland Park College at Des Moines, Iowa. In 1913 he received his A. B. from the University of Nebraska, and in 1915, his LL. B.

Except for two years as an instructor in the Quaker Academy at Earlham, Iowa, Mr. Sadilek has lived in Nebraska all his life. Since June 15, 1915, he has been engaged in the practice of law at Schuyler, where he has served as county clerk and county attorney.

His first marriage was to Frances Barbara Schleis at Wilber. One child, Mary Theresa, was born to this union on January 2, 1918. On June 4, 1931, he was married to Exha D. Akins, of Western, Nebraska. She has an A. B. degree from Peru State Teachers College, and an M. A. from the University of Nebraska, 1930. Mrs. Sadilek is a native of Western, Nebraska.

During the World War Mr. Sadilek was a four minute speaker and later served as chairman of the Fuel Administration committee for Colfax County. He served as president of the local school board for some time, is a member of the Lions Club and the Nebraskana Society.

His professional associations include the American and Nebraska State Bar Associations and the State Abstractors Association. He is a Scottish Rite Mason.

Mr. Sadilek enjoys golfing, and is a member of the Schuyler Golf and Country Club. In politics his affiliation is with the Republican party. Residence: Schuyler.

Charles Jaroslav Safarik

Charles J. Safarik, son of Peter Safarik and Anna Barta, was born in Dayton, Ohio, May 15, 1866. His father was born in Czechoslovakia, March 20, 1829, and was an early settler in Nebraska. He was a painter, and deputy postmaster and land agent for the B. and M. Railroad at Crete. He died at Dewitt, after a long and useful life.

His wife Anna (Barta) Safarik was born in Czechoslovakia, January 29, 1836, and died at Dewitt, Nebraska. She was a clubwoman and active in civic affairs.

Charles Safarik received his education in public school and for a time served as clerk and later as telephone manager. For some years he has been engaged in the drug business, and is the owner and manager of a drug store at Schuyler.

He was married to Josephine Blanche Zerzan, at Schuyler, on October 8, 1888. Mrs. Safarik was born at Omaha, November 10, 1870. They have five children: Lumir, a graduate of the University of Nebraska, a member of Sigma Nu, was born September 29, 1892. He is a physician in Denver, and is married to Madge Dunnell; Ilda, born April 1, 1894, a graduate of St. Luke's at Denver, is a nurse in Schuyler; Vilma, born October 28, 1896, married Joseph Kadlicek, and lives at Englewood, Colorado; Joseph P., born July 30, 1900, is a druggist and is associated with his father. He was graduated from the Babcock School of Pharmacy in Denver. Charles J., born September 12, 1912, is studying pharmacy in Denver.

Mr. Safarik is a Democrat, and is active in party politics. He is a member of the Chamber of Commerce, the Royal League, the Z C B J, Modern Woodmen of America, and a charter member of the Knights of Pythias, and is a 32nd degree Mason. His hobby is reading. Residence: Schuyler.

Ira Ernest Sage

With the exception of about eight years spent in the Black Hills Ira Ernest Sage has been a continuous resident of Nebraska all his life. He was born at Ionia, Michigan, October 10, 1881, son of David and Helen Elizabeth (Worden) Sage.

The father, born in the province of Ontario, Canada, in December, 1840, was a farmer in Nuckolls County for many years prior to his death at Nelson in 1914. The mother was born in Michigan in 1847 and died at Nelson in 1916.

Mr. Sage attended the public schools of Nuckolls County, and received the Bachelor of Science and Bachelor of Arts degrees from Fremont College in 1907 and 1908 respectively. He was active in debating and dramatics in college.

From 1908 until 1910 Mr. Sage taught school at Maxwell, and from 1910 until 1912 he taught at Edgemont, South Dakota. From 1914 to 1918 he taught in the public schools of Terry, South Dakota, and from 1925 to 1926 taught in Wilsonville, Nebraska.

Entering the newspaper business at Edgemont, he edited the *Enterprize* and afterwards was the editor and publisher of the *Paxton Times*. From 1929 until 1931 he worked for the *Hooker County Tribune* at Mullen. At the present time Mr. Sage is the editor and publisher of the Arthur *Enterprise*. Mr. Sage is a Democrat.

From 1912 until 1914 Mr. Sage was secretary of the Fall River County Fair at Edgemont, South Dakota, and at the present time is secretary of the Shortway Highway Association. He is a former member of the Odd Fellows and the Modern Woodmen of America, and from 1919 until 1922 was a member of the Maxwell School Board. He is a member of the Mullen Golf Club and the Presbyterian Church. Residence: Arthur.

Lee Sage

Lee Sage, county treasurer of Nuckolls County since 1926, was born at Nelson, June 18, 1899. He is the son of

Madison and Roxana Lavina (Henderson) Sage, the former of whom was born at Ionia, Michigan, November 22, 1867. Madison Sage, who for a number of years was a public school teacher, is engaged at the present time in the grain, lumber and coal business. His wife, born at Pickneyville, Illinois, July 19, 1874, died at Nelson on March 9, 1916.

Educated in the public schools of Ruskin, Lee Sage was graduated from high school there in 1919. He has always resided in Nebraska, and since maturity has taken an active part in Democratic politics. He was elected treasurer of Nuckolls County in 1926, and still holds that office.

Mr. Sage is unmarried. He is a Mason, and past master of his lodge, a member of the Order of Eastern Star, the Modern Woodmen of America and The Nebraskana Society. Residence: Nelson.

Jerome Hamilton Sager

Jerome Hamilton Sager, one of the first settlers in Nebraska, has been a resident of the state for over 70 years. He was born in Mifflin County, Pennsylvania, August 15, 1850, the son of Samuel and Margaret (Wagner) Sager. His father, a farmer, was born in Mifflin County January 2, 1805, and died there January 9, 1866. His mother was born in Pennsylvania and died in Mifflin County in 1850.

Mr. Sager attended rural school and was a student at Kishacoquillas Seminary for four years where he was active in debating. He was a teacher for several years and later engaged in the insurance business. For the past 53 years he has been affiliated with the Independent Order of Odd Fellows, and for 12 years has been a member of the local school board. He is a member of the Methodist Church.

On April 4, 1878, he was united in marriage with Alice Emma Bales in Fillmore County, Nebraska. Mrs. Sager, whose Quaker ancestors came to America on the *Mayflower*, was born in Morgan County, Indiana, January 26, 1859, and died at Geneva, Nebraska, June 6, 1920. The following children were born to this marriage: Pearl, born September 25, 1882, who married Robert A. Case; Jerome, born April 21, 1884, who died February 25, 1887; Alfred, born June 23, 1888, who married Leona Morey; and Ethel, born March 5, 1891, who married Beverly N. Winston.

Mr. Sager holds membership in the Nebraskana Society and the Republican party. His hobby is mathematics. Residence: Geneva.

Frank Eli Sala

For the past 33 years, Frank E. Sala has been prominent in the religious and business world in Nebraska. He was born at Humboldt, Kansas, December 9, 1869, the son of John Adams Graves Sala and Priscilla (House) Sala. His father, who was a farmer, was born in Illinois, and died at Humboldt, Kansas, March 23, 1876; his family has been in this country for five generations. His mother, whose ancestry was Scotch-Irish and Pennsylvania Dutch, was born in Hamilton County, Ohio, in 1843, and died at Columbus City, Louisa County, Ohio, November 22, 1899.

Mr. Sala attended the public schools of Iowa, and there served as assistant secretary in the Y. M. C. A. at Muscatine, Iowa. In 1895, he was affiliated with the Children's Home Society, and was transferred to Nebraska, in April, 1897. In 1903 he was elected lay delegate by the lays conference of North Nebraska, to the General Conference of the Methodist Episcopal Church. Later he joined the Nebraska Annual Conference in September, 1913, and took the study in theology prescribed by the Methodist Episcopal Church. He has been a farmer and minister in Nebraska for many years and is now

financial secretary of the Bryan Memorial Hospital at Lincoln. A Republican, he has served as county committeeman, delegate to conventions, and in various other capacities. He holds membership in the Red Cross, the Nebraskana Society, the Parent-Teachers' Association, the National Geographic Society, and the Young Men's Christian Association. He is affiliated with the First Methodist Episcopal Church of Lincoln, and the Nebraska Annual Conference.

He was united in marriage with Anna Alice Bogardus, at Neligh, Antelope County, Nebraska, October 13, 1898. Mrs. Sala, whose ancestors were New Englanders, was born at Genoa, Nebraska, July 25, 1879. Their children are: Ruth Mary; Paul Franklin; Roy John; Ophie Esther; Ida May; Esther; Charles Watson; Grace Marie; Alice Lydia; Wendel Jonathan; Helen, and Beulah Evangeline. Paul Franklin, who holds a Master of Arts degree, is a teacher in the Hastings High School. Ophie Esther is a graduate of the Nebraska Teacher's College. Residence: Lincoln. (Photograph in Album).

James Henry Salsbury

One of the outstanding clergymen of Nebraska is James Henry Salsbury who has lived in the state for 33 years. He was born at Breckenridge, Missouri, August 8, 1871, the son of Anson and Rebecca (Guild) Salsbury, the former a farmer, stockraiser, and cattle shipper in Missouri. His mother, who was a leader in many religious activities in her church, was born at Woodstock, Canada, November 17, 1843, and died at Kansas City, Missouri, August 7, 1907; she was directly descended from the family of Lady Jane Grey of Scotland, and possessed many old family tokens which have been handed down for over 300 years.

Dr. Salsbury attended the rural schools of Caldwell County, Missouri, the academy at Kidder, Missouri, and Park College at Parkville, Missouri. He received his A. B. degree from Park College in 1896, and was awarded his D. D. degree by the Highland University at Highland, Kansas, in 1911 after having been graduated from Auburn Theological Seminary, Auburn, New York, 1899. He was manager of the college glee club for a year, was local editor of the college paper during his senior year, and served as president of the senior class.

He has held some of the best pastorates in Nebraska and is minister of the First Presbyterian Church at Wood River at this time. Dr. Salsbury as actively interested in agriculture and owns farming land in Missouri, Kansas, and Texas. Practically his whole life, however, has been devoted to the ministry since he has been engaged in uninterrupted service longer than any other clergyman of the Presbyterian denomination now in service in Nebraska. He was president of the Nebraska State Christian endeavor Union during 1908 and 1909, and at this time holds membership in the Hall County Ministerial Association and the Nebraskana Society.

He is a member of Skekinah Chapter Number 32 of the Royal Arch Masons of Aurora, Nebraska. He is affiliated with Esther Chapter Number 208 of the Order of Eastern Star. During the World War Dr. Salsbury engaged actively in all forms of war drives and relief affairs in his community.

On September 26, 1899, he married Cora George Downing at Breckenridge, Missouri. Mrs. Salsbury, whose parents were native Kentuckians, was born at Breckenridge, Missouri, December 3, 1870. They have one son: James Russel, born August 1, 1902, who married Grace Modlin of Ulysses, Nebraska. He was graduated from the University of Nebraska where he was first lieutenant of the University Band of the Reserve Officers Training Corps and is now a chemical engineer with the Proctor and Gamble Company in Kansas City, Missouri. Residence: Wood River.

Fannie Salsgiver

A resident of Nebraska for the past 48 years, Fannie Salsgiver was born at Linneus, Linn County, Missouri, September 18, 1858, the daughter of James J. and Elizabeth (Reid) Alexander. Her father, whose ancestry was Scotch Irish, was born in Boone County, Kentucky. Her mother was born in Boone County, March 28, 1834, and died at Lacled, Linn County, Missouri, March 20, 1872.

She is a member of S. B. A., and D. of H. Her religious affiliation is with the Methodist Episcopal Church of Wymore, Gage County, Nebraska. She holds membership in the Republican party and the Nebraskana Society.

Mrs. Salsgiver was married at Stanberry, Missouri, September 18, 1882, to Thomas Mabon Salsgiver, who was born March 7, 1858, and died at Wymore, December 16, 1929; his ancestry was Dutch. Three children were born to them: Thomas M., born January 13, 1885, who married Pearl Lavery; Maude M., born June 2, 1891, who married Frank R. Leighty; and Marie, born November 26, 1895, who married Robert S. Morse. Residence. Wymore.

Lester Miller Samples

Lester Miller Samples, superintendent of schools at Litchfield, was born at Edison, Nebraska, January 7, 1894, son of Eli J. and Virginia Adeline (Young) Samples. His father, born in Clay County, West Virginia, September 11, 1852, was a farmer of Scotch-Irish descent, who died at Edison, May 19, 1931. His mother, also born in Clay County, West Virginia, on December 22, 1859, died at Edison, May 5, 1928. She was of Scotch-Irish descent.

Educated in the public schools of Edison to 1913, when he was graduated from high school, Lester Miller Samples attended the University of Nebraska, Wyoming University and Kearney State Teachers College. In high school he was a member of the basketball and baseball teams.

Employed as a printer at Edison and at Pine Bluffs, Wyoming, Mr. Samples was at the age of seventeen editor of a newspaper at Edison. Constantly since 1913 he has been in school administrative work, three years as superintendent at Smithfield, one year at Holbrook, two years at Edison and twelve years at Litchfield. During the year 1924-25 he was editor of the *Litchfield Monitor*. He is the author of two short articles on special activities in school administration.

On December 20, 1919, Mr. Samples was married to Irma Sadie Smay at Hastings. Mrs. Samples, who was a teacher and a nurse before marriage, was born at Nevada, Iowa, December 26, 1900. There are three children, Althea, born September 11, 1921; Everett L., August 23, 1923; and Evan J., November 16, 1930.

Mr. Samples is a Republican. He served as a private in the World War with the 255th Field Hospital Company at Fort Riley, Kansas, and Camp Custer, Michigan. He is affiliated with the Christian Church at Litchfield, is a member of the Nebraska State Teachers Association, the Odd Fellows, the Nebraskana Society, and the Litchfield Commercial Club of which he was chairman in 1930. His hobby is printing. Residence: Litchfield.

Arvid Stanley Samuelson

For the past eight years Arvid Stanley Samuelson has served as postmaster at Axtell, where he was born, May 21, 1890. His father, Anders Samuelson, a native of Ostergotland, Sweden, was born April 23, 1841, came to Nebraska in 1885, and settled at Axtell. A farmer, he served several terms as district school director, prior to his death at Holdrege, on June 30, 1912.

Anna Gustava (Johnson) Samuelson, wife of Anders, was born in Ostergotland, Sweden, July 17, 1847, and died at Omaha, July 21, 1917. A devoted wife and mother, in later years she was much interested in church work.

Arvid S. Samuelson attended country school in Kearney County, and for two and a half years was a student at Franklin Academy, Franklin, Nebraska. He had one year at Holdrege High School, and thereafter attended Grinnell College for a year.

On June 3, 1925, he was married to Vivian Margurette Wilcox Carlson at Axtell. Mrs. Samuelson, who was born at Sayre, Pennsylvania, March 19, 1903, is a post office clerk. Her ancestry is English and Dutch. There are two children, Stanley Dorey, born April 22, 1926; and Ligne Lou-Aisne, born February 28, 1929.

A farmer for a time, Mr. Samuelson was in the general mercantile business for two years, and thereafter served in the World War. He served with the 355th Infantry, 89th Division at Camp Funston, and with the 4th United States Infantry, 3rd Division, with the rank of corporal, participating in the following: Champaigne-Marne, Aisne-Marne, St. Miheil, Meuse-Argonne and the Army of Occupation.

A member of the American Legion and the Veterans of Foreign Wars, Mr. Samuelson is also a 14th degree Mason, a member of the Presbyterian Church, the Nebraskana Society and the National Geographic Society. His favorite sport is golf, while his hobby is reading biographical, historical and scientific works. Residence: Axtell. (Photograph in Album).

Charles Edwin Samuelson

Charles Edwin Samuelson was born at Brobe, Sweden, September 1, 1864, and for the past 47 years has been a resident of Nebraska. Samuel J. Samuelson, his father, who for many years was engaged in secretarial work and farming, was born in Sweden, and died at Axtell, Nebraska. Johannah (Burman) Samuelson, his mother, who is descended from a princess of the royal family of France, was born in Sweden and died at Axtell in May, 1909.

Mr. Samuelson was a clerk in a general store at Holdrege, Nebraska, later becoming a partner in the company, and after several years purchased controlling interest in the organization. He is connected with the Hildreth Milling Company and the Trumbull Lumber Company, is vice president of the State Bank of Hildreth, and is engaged in the mercantile business there.

A Democrat, Mr. Samuelson served as colonel on the staff of Governor Morehead, and was elected to the Nebraska senate; he holds membership in the local Democratic Club. During his stay in this state he has always been active in projects for the betterment of his community and state, and has been a member of the Lutheran Church, the school board, Modern Woodmen of America, Knights of Pythias, and the Masons. He was county chairman of war loan drives during the World War.

His marriage to Gladys Harris occurred at Superior, Nebraska, December 7, 1890. Mrs. Samuelson, who was formerly a teacher, was born at Burr, Kansas, April 16, 1872, a descendant of the famous Cameron Clan of Scotland. To them were born three children: Leon, April 22, 1893, a lawyer, who married Velma Satchel; C. Ransom, July 19, 1900, and is county attorney of Franklin County, a lawyer and musician, who married Hazel Wilson; and Ruth, August 9, 1903, who is commercial instructor in the high school at Newman Grove, Nebraska. Residence: Hildreth.

Isaac Theodore Samuelson

Isaac Theodore Samuelson, a lifetime resident of Nebraska, was born at Stromsburg, Nebraska, January 21, 1877, the son of Matthew and Margaret (Hedman) Samuelson. His father, who was born at Ockelbo, Gestrikland, Sweden, September 22, 1831, and died at Stromsburg, June 30, 1903, was a pioneer homesteader in Polk County in 1872. His mother, who was a devoted

CHARLES FREDRICK SANDAHL

home maker, was born at Ockelbo, December 10, 1846, and died at Stromsburg, March 22, 1912.

Mr. Samuelson received his elementary education in rural schools, attended Bryant Normal and Business College at Stromsburg, and was a student at Fremont Normal College. He was engaged in a co-partnership business, hardware, furniture and undertaking, with the Victor Anderson Company, for seven years, was a farmer for two years, and entered the real estate and insurance business with the Polk Realty Company in 1916. He is now postmaster of Polk.

During the World War he was a member of the home guards, and served as chairman of the Red Cross Finance Committee. He is affiliated with the Baptist Church of Polk, and holds membership in the Polk Commercial Club, the Masons, the Odd Fellows, Royal Highlanders, and The Nebraskana Society. He was a member of the board of education, 1912-14. His favorite sport is baseball, while his hobby is promoting the progress of his community. Residence: Polk.

Charles Fredrick Sandahl

Upon his arrival in America, from Sweden, in 1881, the Reverend Charles Fredrick Sandahl took up his residence in Nebraska, where he has since lived. He was born November 17, 1871, the son of Claus William and Sophia (Anderson) Nelson. His father, born in Sweden, December 20, 1846, died there on May 26, 1875. His mother, born July 28, 1848, died at Cambria, Wyoming, April 27, 1893.

Dr. Sandahl received his Bachelor of Arts degree from Augustana College in 1898, his Bachelor of Divinity degree in 1901, and his degree of Doctor of Divinity from Bethany College, at Lindsborg, Kansas, in 1921.

Ordained to the ministry of the Lutheran Church, Augustana Synod in 1901, Dr. Sandahl has filled the following offices: pastor, Montclair, New Jersey, Oakland, Genoa and Kearney, Nebraska; member of the board of Upsala College, Orange, New Jersey, 1902-05; member Immigrant Home Board, New York, 1903-05; member Immanuel Deaconness Institute Board, Omaha, 1912-30; member Luther College Board, Wahoo, 1911; member Conference Mission Board 1919; member Bethphage Mission Board, Axtell, 1930; secretary Synodical Council 1914-21; vice president Nebraska Conference 1909-12; 1929; president Nebraska Conference 1913-22. He is the author of *Bible Study Quarterly* (1923); *Nebraska Conference History* (1931), and various newspaper articles in both the secular and religious press.

On July 10, 1901, he was united in marriage to Esther Mathilda Wallin at Stanton, Iowa. Mrs. Sandahl, who was formerly a teacher, was born in Page County, Iowa, July 10, 1901. There are three children: Marion Beatrice, born June 9, 1902, married Stuart Battles. She died October 1, 1927. Esther Dorothy was born October 5, 1904, and Clifford Fredrick, born on July 21, 1906. Dorothy is employed by Miller & Paine in Lincoln, Clifford was graduated from the University of Nebraska in 1929, was legislative reporter for the *Omaha Bee-News* in 1930, and is now one of its staff correspondents.

Dr. Sandahl is a member of the Nebraskana Society, and since 1930, has been a member of the Augustana Historical Society. Residence: Kearney. (Photograph on Page 1045).

Charles Edward Sandall

For the past 55 years Charles E. Sandall has lived in Nebraska, and since 1904, has been engaged in the practice of law here. He has been prominent in the political and civic world for many years at York and Omaha. He was born in York County, January 13, 1876, the son of Andrew Lawrence and Matilda (Kaliff) Sandall. His father, a farmer and stockraiser, was born at Smaland, Sweden, November 17, 1849, came to America with his parents in 1858. Settling in York County, in 1871, he married and reared a large family; he was a member of the town board for many years, and was a member of the Nebraska legislature from 1899 to 1901, elected on the Republican ticket; he acquired a section of York County land and was a prosperous farmer.

His mother was born in Sweden, in 1850. She was the mother of 12 children, one of whom, John Chester, died in service in France, in 1918. She died at York, June 15, 1915.

Mr. Sandall was a student at York College, 1897-1901, and was awarded his LL. B. at the University of Michigan, in 1904. He was the winner of a gold medal for oratory at York College, 1898; was active in debating; was a member of the Amphyction Society; was a member of the Law Presidents Club; and was president of the Good Government Club at the University of Michigan.

Since 1904, Mr. Sandall has been in the practice of law in York County, and has been a member of the following firms: White & Sandall; Sandall & Purinton; Sandall & Wray; Sandall & Webster; and in individual practice. A Republican, he served as county attorney for three terms; state senator two terms; supreme court commissioner one term. He is now United States District Attorney at Omaha.

He was united in marriage with Marie Elizabeth Romsdal at York, June 18, 1905. Mrs. Sandall, whose ancestry is Norwegian, was born in York County, February 6, 1882. They have eight children: Mildred Marie, born September 21, 1906, who married Homer Scott; Ruth Eileen, born January 22, 1908, who married Clyde Bolton; Esther Del, born June 23, 1910; Marion E., born July 29, 1916; Charles E., born January 12, 1918; John Chester, born March 5, 1920; Jerrol Genevieve, born November 1, 1921; and James Lawrence, born December 23, 1923.

Mr. Sandall was a member of the legal advisory board during the World War; and a member of various committees. He is a member of Nebraska State Bar Association; York County Bar Association; Douglas County Bar Association; American Bar Association; and the Omaha Chamber of Commerce.

He served as a member of the school board at York, 1926-30, is a member of the Knights of Pythias, and the Elks, and is affiliated with the First Presbyterian Church of Omaha. Residence: Omaha.

Carl August Sandberg

Carl August Sandberg, a resident of Nebraska for the past 50 years, was born in Sweden, January 3, 1866, the son of Carl John and Christine (Larson) Sandberg. His father, who was a farmer, was born in Sweden, December 4, 1837, and died at Ong, Clay County, Nebraska, March 23, 1907. His mother was born in Sweden, April 8, 1836, and died at Evanston, Cook County, Illinois, January 3, 1916.

Mr. Sandberg entered business as a clerk for Rudd & Woodhead Brothers in 1887, and in 1905 bought the store from the firm. From that time until 1930 he was a member of the firm F. O. & C. F. Rudd; at this time the firm name is C. A. Sandberg & Son. For 42 years Mr. Sandberg was a member of the Methodist Episcopal Church where he served as superintendent of the Sunday School. He is now affiliated with Gethsemane Lutheran Church at Ong, is a member of the Nebraskana Society, is president of Clay County Sunday School Association, and is president of the Red Cross. He is a Republican, has served as treasurer of the school board and a member of the town board.

He was united in marriage with Minnie Augusta Rudd at Ong, August 3, 1892. Mrs. Sandberg, whose father was a Methodist minister, was born in Sweden, October 8, 1868. They have one son: Wesley Orville Sandberg, born November 11, 1895, who married Nannie Harnett. He is a music teacher and studied violin under Steckelberg at Lincoln. During the World War Mr. Sandberg was a minute man, while his son served in the United States Army in France. Residence: Ong.

DANIEL P. SANDERS

Daniel Phillip Sanders

Daniel Phillip Sanders, who is sheriff of Hall County, Nebraska, and is prominent in civic projects at Grand Island, has lived in this state all his life. He was born at Grand Island, January 13, 1896, the son of Phillip Andrew and Emma Mary (Schimmer) Sanders, the former a farmer and stockman who came to America in 1883. Phillip Andrew Sanders was born at Hessen, Germany, November 20, 1867, and died at Grand Island, January 30, 1922. Emma (Schimmer) Sanders was born at Grand Island, September 12, 1872, the daughter of a stockman and farmer who built Schimmer's Lake at Grand Island.

Mr. Sanders was the proprietor of the Grand Island Hatchery for five years, and since 1930, has served as sheriff of Hall County. He holds membership in the Grand Island Chamber of Commerce, the Red Cross, Salvation Army, and St. Paul's Lutheran Church of Grand Island. During the World War he served as a private in Company 45, 161st Depot Brigade stationed at Camp Grant, Illinois, and at this time is a member of the American Legion.

He holds membership in the Nebraska State Sheriffs Association, the Elks Lodge Number 604, Masonic Order Number 33, of Grand Island, and the Cosmopolitan Club. His hobby is music.

On June 12, 1918, he was married at Central City, Nebraska, to Alma Louise Scherzberg, who was born at Grand Island, October 24, 1898. Their children are: Leo, born June 3, 1920; and Bernadeen, born August 21, 1924. Residence: Grand Island. (Photograph on Page 1047).

George Emory Newton Sanders

A resident of Nemaha County since his birth on February 13, 1860, George E. N. Sanders is known throughout his section of the state as an orchardist. He is the son of Thomas Newton and Julia Marie (Hickman) Sanders, the former born at Shelby, Indiana, February 16, 1832. He was a nurseryman and fruitgrower, and sold the first apple trees ever sold in the State of Nebraska in the spring of 1857. He died at Brownville, Nebraska, in 1885. Julia M. Sanders, his wife, was born in Ohio, on May 29, 1838, and died at Nemaha, in 1907.

George E. N. Sanders was educated in the schools of Brownville, and graduated in 1886. He was a resident of the town of Nemaha from 1881 to 1894, then removing to Brownville. On August 8, 1882 he was united in marriage to Anna Bertha Crother. She was born at Nemaha, June 26, 1863, and died at Brownville, December 15, 1895. Of this marriage the following children were born: George Edwin, born May 29, 1883, married Julia Hjelle; Bertha Grace, born October 7, 1881, married Everet Sperry and died July 1, 1928; Benjamin Harry, born October 19, 1891, married Viola Sanders; Albert Merle, born April 1, 1893, married Fern Pumel. On February 26, 1902, Mr. Saunders married Louisa Dora May Rains. To this union the following children were born: Francis Thomas, born April 15, 1904, who married Marjorie Vandevoort; and Dorothy Louise, born June 12, 1915.

Mr. Sanders is a Republican. He is a member and officer in the Central Fruit Association. During the World War he was a member of the Nebraska Council of Defense, and was active in the Red Cross. He is chairman at the present time of the Brownville County organization of the Red Cross. He is affiliated with the First Church of Christ at Brownville. Since 1899 he has been secretary-treasurer of the Royal Highlanders. He is a member of the Nebraska Historical Society and the Nebraskana Society, and of the Parent Teachers' Association. He is extremely interested in Sunday School work. His chief recreations are reading and music. Residence: Brownville.

Joseph S. Sanders

Joseph S. Sanders was born at Freeport, Illinois, September 6, 1860, the son of Fred and Frances Sanders. His father, who was born in Germany, came to America in 1830, and died at Freeport, in 1873. His mother was born in Germany, also, and died in Chicago, 1904.

Mr. Sanders attended parochial schools. He has lived in Nebraska for the past 23 years and is now manager of a summer resort, known as Sanders Beach. He is a member of The Nebraskana Society, the Elks, and the Eagles. His sports include hiking and swimming. Politically, he is a Democrat.

He was married to Delia Foley at Freeport, Illinois, in 1883. Three children were born to this marriage: Eva, born May 22, 1885; Katheryn, born November 16, 1891, who married Floyd Allen; and Fern, born August 26, 1899, who married Clare Cunningham. On October 8, 1930, Mr. Sanders was united in marriage with Beulah M. Lee. Residence: South Sioux City.

David Douglas Sanderson

David Douglas Sanderson, physician and surgeon, was born at Stillwell, Illinois, July 6, 1885, son of William Henry and Amelia (Wisch) Sanderson.

He received his medical degree from the Barnes University and has been in active practice since 1911. He is a member of the American, Nebraska State and Lancaster County Medical Associations, the Chamber of Commerce, the Rotary Club and the Masons. His club is the Eastridge Country Club.

On September 15, 1912, he was married to Bernice Potter at Red Cloud. She was born there on December 8, 1887. Residence: Lincoln.

Joseph Lacount Sanford

Joseph Lacount Sandford, rancher, was born at Newtown, Missouri, June 30, 1865, son of William and Barbara (Farley) Sandford.

The father was born in Kentucky, and died at Missouri in 1868. He was a farmer of Scotch descent. His wife, Barbara, was born in Ohio, and died at Newtown, Missouri, in 1881. She was Irish.

As a youth, Mr. Sandford helped to build the Chicago, Burlington and Quincy Railroad through the sand hills, and afterward worked on the section and in the round house. He was discharged for inefficiency and later started ranching in the Black Hills. He got starved out there, and started to return to Missouri, but going broke at Crawford, he stopped there where he engaged in the cattle business in a small way. He gradually increased his herd until now he has a large sized herd of excellent cattle.

Mr. Sandford has been highly successful in everything that he has undertaken. He is now president of the First National Bank at Mitchell, and a director of the First National Bank at Morrill. He is superintendent of Scotts Bluff County Fair Association also. He is a Mason, and a Baptist. Recently he was elected to life membership in the Nebraskana Society. His hobby is fast horses.

On January 19, 1887, he was married to Izilda Josephine Kinner at Unionville, Missouri. Mrs. Sandford was born in Pennsylvania, April 8, 1867, and died at Mitchell, July 13, 1928. She was the daughter of Silas E. and Phoebe (Morley) Kinner. She attended schools in Terre Haute, Missouri. She was of Dutch and Irish ancestry. To them were born six children, three of whom are living, Bessie, born December 17, 1888, is married to Walker M. Lee; Grace, born October 23, 1891, married Frank M. Elliott; Joseph, born February 25, 1896, is married to Marian Rohrig. Cora L., born October 16, 1901, died April 17, 1930; James S., born in 1889, and died in 1891; and Hugh B., born in 1888, died August 14, 1891. The three children are all ranchers. Residence: Mitchell.

Josiah Dow Sandham

J. Dow Sandham was born at Davenport, Iowa, November 11, 1880. He is the son of John and Josephine (Rockwood) Sandham. His father, a merchant, was born at Millbrook, Ontario, Canada, June 29, 1847, and is still living. The father of John Sandham was a soldier in the British Army who married an Irish girl in Killaloe, Ireland, and who came to Ontario, about 1840, where he was mustered out of service.

Josephine Rockwood Sandham, who was born in Janesville, Wisconsin, May 17, 1849, died at Omaha, June 29, 1926. At the time of her marriage she was a teacher of piano in a girl's school. She was of English, Irish and Welsh descent.

J. Dow Sandham was graduated from the Harlan, Iowa, High School in 1897. He studied architectural engineering at Rose Polytechnic Institute, Terre Haute, Indiana, during 1900, 1901 and 1902. He was orchestra leader, member of the glee club, etc., and is a member of Sigma Nu. He is a registered architect in South Dakota. He started as a draftsman with F. E. Wetherell of Oskaloosa, Iowa, and later was associated in that capacity with O. O. Smith and Smith and Gage of Des Moines. He was draftsman and architect with Thomas R. Kimball of Omaha, and is now a member of the firm of Kimball, Steele and Sandham.

He was married to Ella Suydam of Milwaukee, Wisconsin, at St. Paul, June 20, 1911. Mrs. Sandham is of Dutch descent on the paternal side and English on the maternal side. They have three children, James, born July 9, 1912, died July 31, 1912; John, born February 10, 1914; and Edwin, born March 13, 1917. The two living children are students at Central High School.

Mr. Sandham is a Republican. He has been a resident of Nebraska for the past twenty-five years. A member of the American Institute of Architects, he is past secretary and past president of the Nebraska chapter, and is a member of Omaha chapter of the American Interprofessional Institute. A member of the First Presbyterian Church, he also serves as trustee. He belongs to the Izaak Walton League of America, the National Geographic Society, and the Engineers Club of Omaha. His club is the Omaha Club. He enjoys mountain fishing and hiking, but his real interests outside of his professional work are archeology, paleontology and ethnology. Residence: Omaha.

Addie Ruth Sandman

Born at Harbine, Nebraska, December 18, 1892, Addie Ruth Sandman, teacher and clubwoman, is the daughter of Charles Henry and Agnes (Arpke) Sandman. Her father, who was born at Franklin, Wisconsin, July 28, 1860, died at Fairbury, June 10, 1931. Her mother, also born at Franklin, but on June 16, 1865, died at Harbine on October 15 1919. She was of German descent.

Upon her graduation from the public schools of Harbine in 1910, Addie Ruth Sandman attended Fremont Normal School, receiving her Bachelor of Science degree in 1911. She received a Bachelor of Science degree also from Kansas State Agricultural College in 1919. From 1919 to 1920 Miss Sandman taught in the high school at Clyde, Kansas, and from 1921 to 1924 at Clarinda, Iowa. At the present time she teaches in the Fairbury public schools.

Miss Sandman is affiliated with the First Baptist Church of Fairbury, is a member of the Axis Club, secretary of the Young Women's Christian Association Board, and is particularly active in the Woman's Club at Fairbury, and is its president. Her social club is the College Club, her favorite sport is hiking and her hobby is reading. Residence: Fairbury.

William G. Sandman

Born at Harbine, Nebraska, November 30, 1895, William G. Sandman is the son of Fred O. and Reka (Janssen) Sandman. His father was born at Harbine, December 2, 1873, and is engaged in farming at Harbine. He is of German descent. His wife, Reka Janssen, was born in Illinois, December 2, 1874.

Mr. Sandman attended the Harbine public school and was graduated from Diller High School in 1915. While in school he was a member of the football and basketball teams. From 1915-16 he was a teacher in the public schools of Nebraska, and since 1921 has actively engaged in farming and stockraising. During the World War he was a private in Headquarters Company, 127th Field Artillery, and served four months with the American Expeditionary Forces.

On December 25, 1921, he was united in marriage to Emma M. Koenig, at Plymouth. Mrs. Sandman, whose parents came from Canada in 1880, was born at Plymouth, December 17, 1900. There were two children born to their union, Leigh, born March 7, 1927, who died the same day; and Virginia, born January 26, 1928.

Mr. Sandman is a member of Zion Lutheran Church at Harbine, and of the Nebraskana Society. From 1923-29 he served as secretary of the Board of Education at Harbine. He is fond of baseball and football, and his hobby is reading. Residence: Harbine.

Mari Sandoz

A leading writer and educator of Nebraska, Mari Sandoz has lived in this state all of her life, and is prominent in various professional organizations in Lancaster County. She was born at Sandoz, Sheridan County, Nebraska, the daughter of Jules A. and Mary E. (Fehr) Sandoz. Her father, who was born in Switzerland, and died at Ellsworth, Sheridan County, Nebraska, was a well known horticulturist who came to America in 1881, and was nominated to the Nebraska Agricultural Hall of Achievement; he was known throughout the state as the "Burbank of the Sandhills." Her mother is the owner and manager of the Sandoz Fruit Farm in Sheridan County.

Miss Sandoz attended rural schools and was a student at the University of Nebraska for three and one-half years, where she was elected to membership in Chi Delta Phi, literary fraternity. A free lance writer, she is the author of a number of articles and novels, and is active in public school work. In 1927, 28, 29, she was associate editor of *School Executive Magazine;* and is the author of *Kinkaider Comes and Goes,* published in the *North American Review,* April and May, 1930.

She is a member of the Writers Guild, The Quill Club, Theta Sigma Phi, the Native Sons and Daughters of Nebraska, and the Nebraskana Society. Miss Sandoz is inclined toward socialistic political beliefs. Residence: Ellsworth.

Andrew J. Sandstrom

A veteran funeral director and furniture dealer at Bertrand, Nebraska, Andrew J. Sandstrom has been a resident of this state for the past 51 years. He was born in Sweden, February 24, 1863, the son of Carl G. and Ingry (Johnson) Sandstrom. Carl G. Sandstrom, who was a farmer, was born in Sweden, August 3, 1928, and died at Bertrand, April 22, 1884. Ingry (Johnson) Sandstrom was born in Sweden, June 23, 1836, and died at Bertrand, March 13, 1924.

Mr. Sandstrom is a member of the Bertrand Chamber of Commerce, is affiliated with the Swedish Lutheran Church, and holds membership in the Nebraskana Society. He was admitted to practice as a mortician January 1, 1903, at Bertrand.

He was united in marriage to Jennie J. Hoffstrand, at Bertrand, June 10, 1898. Mrs. Sandstrom was born in Sweden, January 17, 1874, and died at Bertrand, March

13, 1913. Three children were born to this marriage, Marguerite, born March 17, 1905; Carl, born November 24,
1906; and Dorothy, December 16, 1908. On November
11, 1915, he married Emily Carlson. Residence: Bertrand.

Frank R. Satterfield

Frank R. Satterfield, farmer and stockraiser, and
the founder of one of the first important herds of registered Hereford cattle in Loup County, was born at
Springfield, Nebraska, August 26, 1873.

His father, William Mead Satterfield, was born in
Maryland, December 15, 1826, and located in Sarpy
County in 1856. Prior thereto and in 1855, he was a
freighter with an ox team across the plains to Denver.
He was of Scotch descent. His death occurred at Spring-
field, January 28, 1908.

Rachel Augusta Jones, wife of William M. Satterfield, was born at Llennellen, Monmouthshire, England,
July 11, 1840, and came to the United States in 1856.
Prior to her death at Ord, July 7, 1931, she was active in
religious and temperance work.

Educated first in rural schools, Frank R. Satterfield
was graduated from Fremont Normal School and Business College on January 20, 1893, and for a time was a
rural teacher in Sarpy County. He is a member of the
Taylor School Board, the Masons, Woodmen of the
World, the Red Cross and the Nebraskana Society.

On January 2, 1895, he was married to Katherine E.
McLean at Brainard. Mrs. Satterfield, who is of Scotch
descent, was born at Pequanac, New Jersey, October 28,
1873. They have five children living, one deceased.
Everett, born October 3, 1895, married Florence Lewis;
George, August 31, 1899, married Olivia Moore; Harry,
December 4, 1901, married Marion Cole and died July
6 1930; Carrie, October 21, 1907; Stanley, October 22,
1912; and Doris, May 7, 1914.

Everett is county clerk of Loup County, George is
county treasurer of Valley County, Carrie is fifth and
sixth grade teacher in consolidated schools at Taylor;
while Doris is a rural school teacher. Mr. and Mrs.
Satterfield are justifiably proud of their fine family.
Residence: Taylor.

William Everett Satterfield

William Everett Satterfield, county clerk of Loup
County, was born in Springfield, Nebraska, October 3,
1895, son of Frank Richard and Katherine Ella (Mc-
Clean) Satterfield. His father, a farmer and breeder of
Hereford cattle, was born at Springfield, August 26,
1876, of pioneer English parentage. The mother, born
in New Jersey, October 28, 1876, of Scotch ancestry, was
a country school teacher in her youth.

Mr. Satterfield attended public school, was graduated
from Sargent High School in May, 1915 (football and
track 1914-15), and attended summer school at Kearney
State Teachers College. On November 2, 1926 he was
elected county clerk on the Republican ticket, and on
November 5, 1930 was re-elected to the same office.

He was married to Florence Esther Lewis at Burwell
on March 28, 1917, and to them two children were born.
Mildred on May 5, 1918; and Russell on November 6, 1920.
Mrs. Satterfield was born at Taylor, June 4, 1895.

During the World War period Mr. Satterfield was a
participant in loan drives, Red Cross and other civilian
projects. He is a Protestant, a member of the Modern
Woodmen of America and the Odd Fellows and was recently made a life member of the Nebraskana. His
favorite sports are baseball, hunting and football. Residence: Taylor.

John P. Sattler

Always active in the public life of Plattsmouth, John
P. Sattler has been mayor of the city for the past fourteen years. A native of Hiittenthal, Germany, he was
born November 18, 1864, a son of George Peter and Elizabeth (Lautenschlager) Sattler. His parents were born
and died in Germany.

Mr. Sattler received his education in the public schools
of Germany. His marriage to Anna Margeretha Prettig
took place at Plattsmouth, Nebraska, May 18, 1886. Mrs.
Sattler was born at Pekin, Illinois, September 8, 1865, of
German descent.

To their union ten children were born, all of whom
are living. They are Ella Marie, born May 2, 1887, who
married Jess F. Warga; Sophie, born October 11, 1888,
who married William Mason; Albert A., born March 28,
1890, who is unmarried; Olga, born May 13, 1893, who
married Harly Burdick; Karl C. born October 5, 1893, who
married Grace Sattler Fight; Amanda, born May 9, 1895,
who married Charles Lohman, Catherina, born July 12,
1897, who married Fred Herbester; Freda, born August
16, 1899, who married L. R. Sprecker; John P., Jr., born
March 3, 1902, who married Verle Sattler Becker; Dorothy, born September 7, 1904, married Bernard Meisinger.

Besides serving as mayor, as above, Mr. Sattler, who
has always been active in the Democratic party, served
as city councilman for twelve years. He has been a resident of Nebraska forty-five years.

In addition to his political duties, Mr. Sattler has been
engaged in the undertaking business at Plattsmouth, since
July, 1887.

During the World War Mr. Sattler was active in various drives and served as a four minute speaker. He is
a member of the German Lutheran Church. His civic organizations include the Chamber of Commerce and the
Rotary Club, and his fraternal affiliations include the
Elks, Eagles, Modern Woodmen, Odd Fellows, and Sons
of Herman. Residence: Plattsmouth.

John Dallas Saunders

John Dallas Saunders, a merchant at Kearney since
1908, is a native of Wilkesboro, North Carolina, born
June 14, 1873. His father, William Saunders, was born
near Statesville, North Carolina, January 22, 1847, his
father, Jacob Saunders, having come from England in
1812. A merchant, carpenter and miller, William Saunders died at Wilkesboro, July 19, 1931. Emily America
Hendren, wife of William Saunders, was born at Hunting Creek, North Carolina, June 17, 1846, and died at
Morgantown, North Carolina, April 1, 1928. She was a
country doctor, daughter of Oliver Hendren, who was
born at Meridian Falls, North Carolina.

Mr. Saunders has resided in Nebraska forty-two years,
and has been prominent in the development and growth
of his community and state. A farmer from 1889 to
1891, the following three years he was employed by the
George W. Franks Improvement Company, of Kearney,
a street railway company. From 1894 until 1908 he was
a stationary engineer, and since that time has been proprietor of the Club House Stores. He was director of
the old Kearney Canal Company 1896-97, and from 1923-
28 was a stockholder of the Brady State Bank.

A Republican, Mr. Saunders served as a member of
the city council at Kearney 1926-28, and was a member of
the Nebraska legislature, from the 75th district, its 45th
session. He is the author of the *Answer to Six Questions
Asked at the Twenty-eighth Convention of the National
Electric Light Association* (Volume 2, June, 1905).

On October 15, 1892, he was married to Mathilda
Sophia Lindbeck at Kearney. Mrs. Saunders, whose
parents came from Sweden, was born at Jonkoping,
Sweden, January 14, 1872. To them nine children were
born; Jennie, July 11, 1893, married John Harker Ball;
Nellie, July 4, 1894, married Walter Lee Miles; Margaret,
September 4, 1895, married Dean D. Gray; Eleanor, June
23, 1897, married Paul A. Dale; Louise, October 9, 1904,
married Donald A. Haase; Oliver George, September
21, 1911; Katherine, September 21, 1908; John William,

born November 19, 1909, died March 23, 1923; and Charles August, born February 6, 1913.

Mr. Saunders is interested in travel and exploration. From 1902-07 he was a member of the National Electric Light Association, and from 1898-1910 was a member of the National Association of Stationary Engineers. He is affiliated with the First Baptist Church of Kearney, is a member of the Nebraskana Society and is a Mason. Residence: Kearney.

Royal Ronald Savage

Royal Ronald Savage, manager of the Farmers Elevator Company at Elsie, was born at McComb, Illinois, September 27, 1876. He is the son of John Filmore and Ella (Scudder) Savage. His father, a carpenter and builder, was born in Virginia, Illinois, November 27, 1851, and died at York, January 20, 1932. His ancestry was Irish and English. His wife, Ella, was born in Cass County, Illinois, about 1856, and died at Jacksonville, Illinois, in 1880. She was a teacher in her early days.

Mr. Savage attended public and high school and for the past 35 years has been in the grain business. On April 6, 1906, he was married to Lina Williams, at Lincoln, Nebraska. Mrs. Savage was born near Springfield, Illinois, February 11, 1882, of English and Welsh descent. They have a daughter, Lucile, born March 30, 1908, who is married to W. C. Allen of Elsie.

Mr. Savage is a Republican. He is a member of the Odd Fellows and the Masons. His favorite sports are baseball and golf. Residence: Elsie.

Ashbel Shepherd Savin

Ashbel Shepherd Savin, now a retired farmer, was born at Alma Center, Wisconsin, April 7, 1855. The son of William and Clarinda Eunice (Hayden) Savin, his father was a native of Delaware, and his mother of New York. William Savin was a sailor in his youth, and a farmer during the remainder of his life. His death occurred at Liberty Center, Iowa, in 1886, and his wife in 1895.

Coming to Nebraska in October, 1878, Ashbel S. Savin has been a resident of the state fifty-three years. He was married to Alice May Henby at Nora, on September 17, 1884. They have two children, Ralph on April 26, 1905; and Ruth on October 27, 1897. Ralph died on December 10, 1924. Ruth, who is a graduate of the University of Nebraska with Phi Beta Kappa honors, is now a teacher.

A Democrat, Mr. Savin has always been active in the local politics of his party. He attends the Methodist Episcopal Church at Nora, and is a member of the Ancient Order of United Workmen and the Nebraskana Society. Residence: Nora.

Eli Marion Sawyers

Born at Knoxville, Tennessee, October 22, 1862, Eli Marion Sawyers has been a resident of Ainsworth, Nebraska for the past 50 years. His father, Nicholas Sawyers, who was a plantation and slave owner, was born at Knoxville, May 19, 1823, and died at Hillsdale, Iowa, January 14, 1905; he was descended from John Sawyers who moved to Virginia from England in 1745. His mother was born in Knox County, Tennessee, May 10, 1834, and died at Glenwood, Iowa, July 4, 1917.

Mr. Sawyers is affiliated with the Congregational Church of Ainsworth, is a member of the Modern Woodmen of America, and holds membership in the Nebraskana Society. His marriage to Mary Hagland occurred at Ainsworth, October 14, 1889. Mrs. Sawyers was born in Sweden and died at Ainsworth, April 1, 1900.

Three children were born to them: Nicholas, October 26, 1890, who married Phoebe Snell; Tilman, November 10, 1891, who married Bess Shaffer; Effie May, August 26, 1893, who died April 26, 1919. On July 1, 1902, Mr. Saw-

yer was married to Laura Dynell Curry. Three children were born to this marriage: Glenn, January 25, 1906; who died in infancy. Residence: Ainsworth.

Bessie Elizabeth Saxton

Bessie Elizabeth Robertson, daughter of Frank Leslie and Emma Kate (Guess) Robertson, was born at Kansas City, Missouri, August 12, 1885. Frank Leslie Robertson was born at Rising Sun, Indiana, September 8, 1860, and is a contractor and builder and the owner and operator of a planing mill. His father was born at Rising Sun, January 11, 1818, he was Scotch, and his wife was German. Frank Leslie Robertson married Emma Kate Guess, who was born near Bentonsport, Iowa, August 5, 1862. Her family moved to Red Oak, Iowa, when she was six years old. She is active in church and kindred work, and is an extensive reader. Her parents were born in Carrol County, Ohio, and her father was master of seven languages. Her mother was also a scholar.

Bessie Robertson was graduated from the Omaha public schools in May, 1901. She attended Brownell Hall and the American College, Drake University and the Lewis Hotel Training School, and specialized in dramatics, violin and voice. During her college days she was active in basketball, horseback riding and ice skating.

She was married to Howard Saxton, at Omaha, May 28, 1907. They have six children, Delmar, born May 26, 1908, who is bookkeeper for the Sinclair Oil Company; Dorothy May, born November 3, 1909, who is kindergarten director at Ashland Park School; Robert Howard, born October 11, 1911, who attends the University of Omaha; Charles Edward, born May 11, 1913, who is serving in the U. S. Navy; Margaret Phebe Emma, born November 17, 1916, who attends Central High School, and Ruth Elizabeth, born September 21, 1919, who attends Yates School.

Mrs. Saxton has always been active in the civic and educational work of the city, and has taken a particular interest in Parent-Teacher work. She was the organizer of the majority of the Parent-Teachers' Associations in Omaha, and is chairman of the teacher's committee of the Omaha Board of Education. She is sixth vice president of the Nebraska Congress of Parents and Teachers and a member of the Omaha school board. She was acting superintendent of the Saving Institute of Omaha. She is a member of the Young Women's Christian Association, and the First Christian Church.

A member of the board of the Omaha Council of Camp Fire Girls, she is a member also of the Red Cross and the Fontenelle chapter of the Order of Eastern Star, and also a member of the Girl Scout troup committee. At various times she has assisted in political campaigns and has always been active in the politics of the Democratic party. Her hobby is reading and gardening. The entire family is musical and Mrs. Saxton has organized an orchestra composed of members of her family. Residence: Omaha.

Howard Saxton

Howard Saxton was born at Granville Center, Pennsylvania, December 2, 1879, the son of Delmar and Phebe Ann (Bailey) Saxton. The former was born at Granville Center, March 28, 1854. Delmar Saxton was a merchant, descended from the earliest settlers in Massachusetts, who came to Nebraska in 1889, settling in Elmwood. He died at Elmwood, December 29, 1927. His widow, Phebe Ann Bailey Saxton, was born at Granville Center, August 5, 1856, and resides at Elmwood. She is descended from early Connecticut pioneer stock.

Mr. Saxton attended Elmwood High School, graduating in 1896. He received his LL. B. from the University of Nebraska, in 1901, and his LL. M. from Columbia University in 1904. In 1906 he received the degree of Doctor of Civil Law from George Washington University at Washington, D. C. He also took special courses in the

University of Chicago, in 1913. His fraternities are the Phi Delta Phi and Lambda Phi.

On May 28, 1907, he was married to Bessie Robertson, at Omaha. Mrs. Saxton was born in Kansas City, Missouri, August 12, 1885, and is of Scotch descent. She is very active in parent-teacher work, and is the organizer of approximately two-thirds of the Parent-Teacher Associations in Omaha. She was elected to the Omaha School Board in 1928, and has been chairman of the teachers committee of that organization. She has acted as superintendent of the Child Saving Institute of Omaha. Mr. and Mrs. Saxton have six children: Delmar, born May 26, 1908; Dorothy May, born November 3, 1909; Robert Howard, born October 11, 1911; Charles Edward, born May 11, 1913; Margaret Phebe, born November 17, 1916; and Ruth Elizabeth, born September 21, 1919.

Until 1916, Mr. Saxton practiced law in Thurston County, Nebraska, where he served as county attorney from 1909-15. He was assistant United States attorney, District of Nebraska, from 1916-19. After leaving that office he was a member of the firm of Baldrige and Saxton, until 1924, when the firm was dissolved. He has engaged in general law practice since that time. He is a Democrat.

Mr. Saxton's professional organizations are the Omaha, Nebraska State and American Bar Associations and the Commercial Law League of America. He is a member of the First Christian Church and was chairman of its official board for several years, he is a member of the Blue Lodge Masons, York and Scottish Rite bodies, and Nobles of the Mystic Shrine. His hobby is gardening. Residence: Omaha.

John Ralph Saxton

John Ralph Saxton, who has been engaged in the rea lestate business at Tilden, Nebraska, since 1901, was born at Wells, Minnesota, July 15, 1866, the son of Jay W. and Abby (Dorn) Saxton. His father, who was a pioneer in Minnesota in 1865, moved to Antelope County, Nebraska in 1870 and began farming; his ancestry was Irish, French, and German. His mother was born of German parentage near Gloversville, New York, October 7, 1837, and died at Tilden, Nebraska, April 23, 1915.

Mr. Saxton has been the owner, overseer, and dealer of a real estate business at Tilden for over thirty years. He is a Democrat. On February 15, 1888, he was married to Mary Wolff at Neligh, Nebraska. Mrs. Saxton, the daughter of Fredrich and Rosa (Whit) Wolff, was born at Champaign City, Illinois, February 8, 1868. Of their four children three are living: Tillie Rose, born November 15, 1890; Roy Rueben, born December 19, 1893, who died May 8, 1917; and Alvan Felix, March 10, 1898; and Darrell Lemly, September 20, 1907. Tillie is instructor in home economics at the Tilden High School. Residence: Tilden.

Ara Minta Louise Saylor

Ara Minta Louise Saylor was born at Grantsville, Garret County, Maryland June 1, 1874, the daughter of William and Katherine May (Daniels) Miller. Her father, who was born at Grantsville, June 3, 1838, and died at Sabetha, Kansas, November 11, 1924, a retired farmer; he was prominent in public affairs in Maryland, and served as county judge, sheriff in Maryland, and justice of the peace in Bruning, Nebraska. Her mother was born at Petersburg, Pennsylvania, May 2, 1843, and died at Sabetha, Kansas, January 11, 1914; her ancestry was Scotch Irish, while her husband's was German.

Mrs. Saylor was graduated from the elementary grade school in 1889 and later attended the Sabetha High School. She has been prominent in Woman's Club affairs, serving as fourth district president of the American Home, and is now affiliated with the Highlanders, the Eastern Star, and The Nebraskana Society. She is a member of the Methodist Church at Bruning, Thayer County, Nebraska, and since 1917 has been president of the Red Cross. She is especially interested in literature, and devotes a great deal of her time to writing.

Her marriage to Dr. Saylor was solemnized at Sabetha, October 8, 1893. Two children were born to this marriage: Alva Franklin, who was born April 5, 1895, and who died September 3, 1895; and Gladys Irene, born July 4, 1899. Gladys Irene, who is a junior high school teacher at Long Beach, California, was graduated from Hebron Academy and Nebraska Wesleyan University. She is a post graduate student at the University of Southern California, where she received her secondary certificate, and was graduated from the Univeristy of Nebraska public school music department, and has also received her California life certificate. Residence: Bruning. (Photograph in Album).

Harvey Wesley Saylor

Harvey W. Saylor, physician and surgeon, was born at Lanark, Illinois, February 25, 1872. He received his elementary education in the public schools of Brown County, Kansas, was graduated from the Kansas City Medical school in 1897, and was admitted to the practice of his profession in May 1897, at Fairview, Kansas.

Jonathan, father of Harvey W. Saylor, was born at Somerset, Pennsylvania, and died at Morrill, Kansas, a retired farmer. He was of Swiss ancestry. Mary (Whipkey) Saylor, mother of Dr. Saylor, was born at Somerset, Pennsylvania, of German ancestry, and died at Morrill, Kansas.

On October 8, 1893, Dr. Saylor was united in marriage to Araminta Louise Miller, at Sabetha, Kansas, born at Grantsville, Maryland, June 14, 1874. They had two children, Alva Franklin, born April 5, 1895, who died September 3, of the same year; and Gladys Irene, born July 4, 1899. Gladys graduated from Hebron Academy in 1916, and from Wesleyan University in 1922. She was valedictorian in high school, a post graduate of the University of Southern California, and is teaching junior high school in Long Beach, California. She is a graduate in public school music at the University of Nebraska.

During the World War Dr. Saylor was a medical examiner. He is a member of the Red Cross, Thayer County and Nebraska State Medical Societies, the Community Club, the Masons, Eastern Star, and holds membership with the Progressive Brethren. From 1905 to 1923 Dr. Saylor was chief of the Bruning Volunteer Fire Department. He is now county physician of Thayer County. His hobby is mechanics. Residence: Bruning. (Photograph in Album).

Arthur William Scattergood

An outstanding figure in the professional life of Ainsworth, Nebraska, Arthur William Scattergood has been a lawyer in that community for the past 35 years. He was born at Burton-on-Trent, England, December 13, 1865, the son of Arthur and Caroline (Blake) Scattergood. His father, who was a banker, real estate dealer and landowner, was born at Burton-on-Trent, March 18, 1841, and died at Johnstown, Nebraska, November 8, 1921. His mother was born at Yoxall, England, June 11, 1841, and died at Johnstown, March 27, 1926; her family had lived at Blakeswood on the ancestral estate for 250 years.

Mr. Scattergood was graduated from high school of Queen Mary in 1881, and was distinguished in scholastic honors in Latin, French, and Greek, at Cambridge University. He played cricket and football at Queen Mary's. He has served as deputy clerk of Brown County, four years, clerk of the United States Land Office, one year, and referee in bankruptcy, eight years. At this time he is United States Commissioner and is one of the leading lawyers of Brown County. He holds stock in the Citizens State Bank of Ainsworth, Nebraska, and is a member of the Ainsworth Commercial Club, and the Nebraska Bar Association. He is a member of the Modern Woodmen of America, is a Mason, and holds membership in the Olympic Club and the Ainsworth Country Club. His hobby is reading, and his sports include golfing, shooting and fishing.

During the World War Mr. Scattergood served as chairman of the legal advisory board of Brown County, was a four minute speaker, and took a prominent part in all war-time activities. He was elected an honorary member of the United Spanish War Veterans recently.

On November 12, 1900, he married Minnie Esther Emo at Ainsworth; she was born at Hornell, New York, and died at Ainsworth, February 20, 1908. Three children were born to this marriage: Mildred C., July 6, 1892, who married George W. Fiehn; Oswald A., April 1, 1895, who married Ruth Pauley; and Dorothy, November 12, 1899, who died November 20, 1899.

His marriage to Blanche Sara Davison occurred at Ainsworth, July 21, 1916. They have two children: Doris C., born April 17, 1917; and Roderick D., born January 28, 1921. Oswald Scattergood is traffic manager for the state of Minnesota for the Northwestern Bell Telephone Company. Residence: Ainsworth.

George Leonard Schaefer

Born at Oakland, Nebraska, May 10, 1891, George Leonard Schaefer is the son of Valentine and Elizabeth (Heilman) Schaefer. His father, who was born in Germany, February 4, 1848, was a veterinarian, who died at Tekamah, November 15, 1929. His wife, Elizabeth, was also a native of Germany.

Dr. Schaefer attended the Tekamah public school and was graduated in 1910, and received his D. V. M. from the Kansas City Veterinary College in 1913; in 1916, he received the same degree from Cornell University.

He is married to Lois Irene Snyder, daughter of Clarence and Leonora Josephine Snyder, and they have three children, Betty Jo, born January 16, 1923; Lois Norene, born December 4, 1926, and Lanora Jean, born May 23, 1928. During the World War, Dr. Schaefer held the rank of second lieutenant, veterinary, in the Medical Corps. He is a member of the American Legion, and the Ancient Free and Accepted Masons Lodge No. 31.

His religious affiliation is with the Presbyterian Church, and his professional memberships include the American Veterinary Medical Association and the Nebraska State Veterinary Association. Residence: Tekamah.

Benjamin Kurtz Schaeffer

Benjamin Kurtz Schaeffer, editor and publisher, was born at Tipton, Iowa, November 7, 1857, son of the Reverend J. G. and Nancy (Weimer) Schaeffer. The father was born at Senecaville, Ohio, April 9, 1832, and died at Rochester, New York, February 28, 1890. He was a minister, an educational promoter, a publisher, and a national platform lecturer and speaker. His wife, Nancy, was born at Janesville, Ohio, September 11, 1833, and died at Sharon, Wisconsin, November 3, 1870.

Mr. Schaeffer recalls his first sight of Curtis in March, 1886, a settlement of two rough buildings and many tents in anticipation of the building of the railroad, which was later completed. The first mixed train to arrive in Curtis rolled in that year in September, and was the occasion of a grand celebration.

He attended public school Hornellsville, New York, high school and academy, Barnesville, Ohio. For 40 years he has been engaged in newspaper work, 35 years as editor and publisher in the same town. His paper was the *Curtis Enterprize*. The first two issues of this paper were set up in a wagon box under a tent and run off on an old-fashioned Washington hand press.

Mr. Schaeffer has always been a leader in commercial, educational and religious work. For the past 30 years he has been a member of the Nebraska Press Association. As a member of the Chamber of Commerce he has held civic offices of trust and has been a member of various educational boards. He is a member of the State Historical Society, the town and school boards.

Mr. Schaeffer is a member of the First Congregational Church at Curtis, active in religious work. Two different times he was selected as national delegate to represent his church in Nebraska. He is a Republican, active in public affairs, and has served as district, state and county delegate to various political conventions.

On August 8, 1889, he was married to Effie M. Taylor at Grand Island, Nebraska. She was born at Altoona, Pennsylvania, March 20, 1867, and before her marriage was a teacher in the public schools. Two children were born to them, Howard, on August 9, 1890; and Nellie, on December 24, 1893, who died August 21, 1894. Howard resides at Everett, Washington, and is engaged as a commercial traveler. Residence: Curtis. (Photograph in Album).

Albert Frank Schaible

Albert F. Schaible was born at Falls City, Nebraska, October 4, 1876, the son of John and Catherine (Schaible) Schaible. His father, who was born in Germany, was a farmer, who died at Falls City, March 22, 1892. His mother was born in Germany, and died at Falls City, April 16, 1906.

Mr. Schaible was graduated from the Falls City High School in 1893; and he attended the Nebraska Wesleyan for two years, where he was a member of the Everett literary society.

A resident of Nebraska for 54 years, he has taken an active part in the civic and business life of his community. He has served two terms as city treasurer of Falls City, elected on the Republican ticket. He is employed as cashier of the Richardson County Bank, at Falls City.

Mr. Schaible's marriage to Magnolia Elizabeth Ewalt was solemnized at Falls City, October 4, 1905. Mrs. Schaible was born in Falls City, September 1, 1884. Their daughter, Jane, who was born May 24, 1910, is a student at the University of Nebraska.

Mr. Schaible was active during the late war in selling liberty bonds. He is a life member of the Red Cross, and a member of the Falls City Chamber of Commerce, a Mason, an Odd Fellow, and an Elk. He is affiliated with the First Methodist Episcopal Church. His club is the Falls City Country Club, and he is an ardent enthusiast of golf. Residence: Falls City.

Adolph Schainost

Adolph Schainost, farmer and stockman, was born at Wilber, Nebraska, November 16, 1876. He is the son of John and Anna Schainost, both natives of Bohemia. John Schainost was born May 1, 1840, and his wife in 1846. He served with Maxmilian's Army in Mexico, and was a prominent farmer in Thayer County prior to his death at Gilead, February 25, 1931. Anna Schainost died at Gilead in January, 1917.

Educated in the public schools of Thayer County, Adolph Schainost became a farmer as a young man. He has always resided in Thayer County, and in addition to his farming activities has gained much prominence as a stockraiser.

On March 24, 1904, he was united in marriage to Dora M. Hart at Hebron. Mrs. Schainost was born at London, England, January 22, 1882 (*see Nebraskana*). Mr. Schainost is a Democrat. His hobby is stockraising and his favorite sport is horse racing. Residence: Gilead.

Dora M. Schainost

Dora M. Schainost, educator and clubwoman, was born in London, England, January 22, 1882, daughter of Lewis A. (Law) Hart. Her father was born at Plumstead, England, March 8, 1851, and farmed in Thayer County many years prior to his death at Gilead on May 24, 1920. Her mother, who was born at Weston Favel, England, July 7, 1851, is living.

Educated in Fremont Normal College from 1899 to 1902, Mrs. Schainost taught for a time, and on March 24, 1904, was united in marriage to Adolph Schainost at Hebron. Of this marriage there are three sons, Roy L., who is married to Rose Hergott; John A., who was graduated from Hebron Academy; and Leland E., who is a Junior at Hebron Academy.

Mrs. Schainost, who has lived in Nebraska for the past forty years, is a Republican, and active in the politics of her party. Prominent as a clubwoman and as a civic leader throughout the state, she is president of the Fourth District of the Nebraska Federation of Women's Clubs, and in 1930 was appointed to the state illiteracy commission. She is president of the Gilead Red Cross, and Gilead Union Church.

For some time Mrs. Schainost has devoted much effort to Americanization work in Thayer County. Her hobbies are reading and adult education.

Mrs. Schainost has received a teacher's certificate from the state department of public instruction, and is highly qualified for this important specialized branch of educational work. Her services as state chairman of an organization for the Federated Women's Clubs of Nebraska has been outstanding, evidencing her aptitude for this technical teaching. Residence: Gilead.

Alfred Schalek

On April 12, 1865, Alfred Schalek was born at Prague, Czechoslovakia. His parents were Carl and Clara (Gerstel) Schalek, the former a business man, who died at Prague, in 1894. Clara Gerstel Schalek died at Vienna, in 1917.

Dr. Schalek received his early education in the schools of Prague, and was graduated from the University of Prague in 1890. He is a charter member of Nu Sigma Nu fraternity at Omaha.

His marriage to Claire Mary Bernhardi took place at Rock Island, Illinois, October 10, 1898. Mrs. Schalek was born in Rock Island, August 31, 1875. They have one daughter, Zoe Carola, born June 8, 1901, who is married to Warland W. Ingram.

Since his admission to practice at Chicago in 1893, Dr. Schalek has risen high in his profession. From 1898 to 1906, he was assistant professor of dermatology at Rush Medical College at Chicago, and since 1906 he has been professor of dermatology at the University of Nebraska. He is the author of *Diseases of the Skin* (1910; 2nd edition 1916) and *Fundamentals of Dermatology* (1926; 2nd edition 1931). He has been a resident of Nebraska for the past twenty-four years.

Dr. Schalek is a Mason. He belongs to the American Dermatological Association and the American Medical Association. His favorite sport is fishing, and his hobby is amateur photography. He is a charter member of Chicago Dermatological Society; the Mississippi Dermotological Association; Nebraska State Medical Association and Douglas County Medical Association. Residence: Omaha.

William C. Schaper

William C. Schaper, lawyer, was born near Mason City, Nebraska, October 4, 1890, and since June, 1914, has been active in the practice of law. He is the son of Henry E. and Louisa (Trobee) Schaper, the former of whom was born at Brunnenswick, Germany, February 16, 1865. He came to America at the age of 14 years, and was a merchant and farmer. His death occurred at Mason City, May 20, 1927. His wife, Louisa, is a native of Iowa.

Educated in the public schools of Mason City, William C. Schaper attended Grand Island College and received his Bachelor of Laws degree from the University of Nebraska in June, 1914. At the present time he is a member of the law firm of Schaper and Runyan, is a director of the Security State Bank of Ansley, the Seven Valleys State Bank of Callaway, the Broken Bow State Bank and the Broken Bow Building and Loan Association.

Altho independently inclined, Mr. Schaper affiliates with the Democratic party, and from 1919-27 held the office of county attorney of Custer County. His professional memberships include the American, Nebraska State and Custer County Bar Associations. He is a Mason and a member of the advisory board of DeMolay; a member of the Broken Bow Library Board and a former member of the board of trustees of Grand Island College.

Mr. Schaper is eligible to the Sons of the American Revolution, is a life member of the Nebraskana Society, and is a Baptist. He is a member of the Public Service Club of Broken Bow.

On June 17, 1914, he was married to Shirley M. Shires at Mead, Nebraska, her birthplace. To them three children were born: Carlos Elton on November 22, 1915; Lucile Arlene, April 12, 1917, and Leola Corrine, November 15, 1920. His hobby is horse back riding. Residence: Broken Bow.

Franklin Schaufelberger

Franklin Schaufelberger, physician at Hastings, Adams County, Nebraska, was born near Fostoria, Hancock County, Ohio, April 16, 1867, the son of Frederick Jacob and Margaretha (Fritcher) Schaufelberger. His father, who was a cabinet maker and farmer, was born at Vinegarten, Baden, Germany, May 31, 1815, and died at Fostoria, January, 1891. His ancestry dates back to 1544 when Ulrich Schaufelberger became a citizen of Zurich, Switzerland. The family coat of arms is on file in the city of Zurich.

The mother of Franklin Schaufelberger was born in Baden, Germany, September 5, 1822, and died near Fostoria, September 9, 1878. She was descended from a long line of artisans.

Both of Dr. Schaufelberger's parents are descended from men and women of prominence; his father's ancestors were lawyers, authors, and master tradesmen.

In 1884 Dr. Schaufelberger was graduated from the high school at Fostoria, and in 1888, he was awarded the Bachelor of Science degree at Heidelberg University. He received his Doctor of Medicine degree at Jefferson Medical College, Philadelphia, 1894. Until about 12 years ago he was engaged in general practice of medicine and surgery, and since that time he has limited his practice to the specialties of obstetrics and pediatrics. He is now obstetrician on the executive staff of the Mary Lanning Memorial Hospital at Hastings, Nebraska.

Dr. Schaufelberger has been engaged in the active practice of medicine in Hastings since 1894, which makes him the dean of physicians and surgeons in Adams County.

He holds a fellowship in the American Medical Association, is a member of the Adams County Medical Society. Since 1912 he has been a member of the American Red Cross, and during the late war was especially active in that organization.

His marriage to Wilhelmene Cameron was solemnized at Hastings, May 28, 1900. Mrs. Schaufelberger was born at Lincoln, Lancaster County, Nebraska, August 26, 1872, the daughter of Charles and Louise SeegMiller Cameron; her father was born in Scotland while her mother was a native of Canada.

Dr. Schaufelberger is a member of The Nebraskana Society. Politically, he is a Democrat. Residence: Hastings.

George Scheidel

George Scheidel, prominent merchant at Platte Center, Nebraska, was the first child born in that community, June 22, 1880, and has always lived there. His father, George Scheidel, who was a farmer and business man, was born at Crottweiler, Alsace Lorraine, December 25, 1846, and died at Columbus, Nebraska, May 3, 1929; he came to America in 1867. His mother, Magdalena (Siebler) Scheidel, was born at Nattingen, Alsace Lorraine, April 16, 1847, and died at Platte Center, November 28, 1899.

Mr. Scheidel attended the Platte Center High School and was a student at the Omaha Commercial College for a time. He was associated in business with the Bruckner Mercantile Company at Platte Center for 26 years, and in 1930 bought the Farmers Mercantile Company which he is operating under the firm name of Scheidel Mercantile Company.

He is treasurer of the First Baptist Church of Platte Center and holds membership in the Red Cross and the Nebraskana Society. For a number of years he has been city councilman at Platte Center, and was president of the Platte Center Volunteer Fire Department for a number of years.

He was united in marriage with Angelena Meyer at Humphrey, Nebraska, October 29, 1901. Mrs. Scheidel, whose ancestry is German, was born April 28, 1880. They have two children: Edna Lucille, born November 30, 1902; and Frederick George, born April 29, 1911, who married Claudine June Overturf, whose daughter, Mary Ellen is 15 months old. Residence: Platte Center.

Antone Fredrick Scheideler

Antone Fredrick Scheideler, county commissioner of Gage County, was born in Wymore, Nebraska, August 28, 1886, son of John and Anna Gracie (Lyble) Scheideler. The father was born in Berlin, Germany, July 8, 1850, and died in Wymore, January 21, 1908. He was a farmer. His wife, Anna, was born in Eagle, Wisconsin, October 31, 1860.

Mr. Schneider attended public school and at the present time is the owner of a recreation hall. He has been county commissioner of Gage County for the past sixteen years, elected on the Democratic ticket.

On February 11, 1914, he was married to Hazel Pernina Miller at Beatrice. She was born at Blue Springs, March 2, 1894. There are four children, Ruth, born July 18, 1916; Betty, born September 13, 1918; and Roy and Herbert, twins, born October 23, 1920.

Mr. Scheideler is a member of the Odd Fellows and the Community Club. Residence: Wymore.

Elizabeth Elma Schelkopf

Elizabeth Elma Schelkopf, noted Nebraska educator, has lived in this state all her life. She was born at Shickley, Nebraska, June 21, 1893, the daughter of Martin Louis and Elma Catherine (Beeson) Schelkopf. Her father, who was a Master Farmer and served as county supervisor of Fillmore County for 12 years, was born at Brimfield, Illinois, April 15, 1859, and died at Shickley, May 7, 1929. Her mother, who is a leader in civic affairs and is now serving as president of the local woman's club, was born in Ohio, November 2, 1862; her father was a Civil War soldier.

Miss Schelkopf was graduated from the Shickley High School in 1911 and in 1913 from the Peru State Teachers College. Later she was a student at the University of Nebraska. She taught in the public schools of Western, DeWitt and Craig, Nebraska, was principal of the Craig High School for three years, and is now serving her third term as county superintendent of schools in Fillmore County.

She is a member of the Young Women's Christian Association, is state director of the Inter-state Spelling Contest, and holds membership in the Martland United Brethren Church. She is a noble grand in the Geneva Rebekah Lodge. Her hobbies are reading and athletics. For eight years Miss Schelkopf was girls basketball coach. Her favorite sport is hiking. Residence: Geneva. (Photograph on Page 1056).

Charles Fredrich Schelm

Charles Fredrich Schelm, president of the Ainsworth Co-operative Creamery Company, was born at Dennison, Iowa, December 27, 1879, son of William and Elizabeth (Trumm) Schelm. The father, a retired farmer, was born in Hanover, Germany, October 16, 1856, and came to the United States in July, 1870. His wife, born at Cincinnati, Ohio, December 9, 1859, is of German descent.

Mr. Schelm attended rural school and soon thereafter engaged in farming and stockraising. He has resided in Nebraska forty-two years, and for twenty-two years as a member of his local school board. He is affiliated with the Zion Lutheran Church, and has been a deacon for the past sixteen years. His hobby is mechanics. He is a life member of the Nebraskana Society, and a Democrat.

On June 15, 1904, he was married to Lydia Sophia Uppmann at Ainsworth. Mrs. Schelm was born at Ainsworth, December 13, 1884, of German parentage. They have three children, Verna, born January 27, 1906; Alta, born May 25, 1907; and Adolph, born April 7, 1914. Residence: Ainsworth.

Robert Henry Schemel

Robert Henry Schemel was born at St. Benedict, Iowa, February 9, 1894, son of Philip Schemel and Pauline (Dietrick) Schemel. Philip Schemel was born in Baden, Germany, May 1, 1855, and is now retired. Pauline Dietrick was born December 8, 1858.

Robert H. Schemel was educated in the public schools of St. Benedict, Iowa, and attended Campion College, Prairie du Chien, Wisconsin. He received his D. D. S. at Creighton University in 1917, and is a member of Xi Psi Phi and Omicron Kappa Upsilon.

From 1920-28 Dr. Schemel served as instructor at Creighton Dental College and superintendent of the clinic at the college. Since that time he has been engaged in private practice.

He was married to Loretta Virginia Hirtes at Omaha, February 18, 1918. Mrs. Schemel was born at Council Bluffs, July 17, 1895. There are five children: Rita J., born September 5, 1919; Claire, born March 10, 1921; Loretta, born October 28, 1923; Robert, born July 14, 1926 and Margaret, born October 5, 1929.

Dr. Schemel holds the rank of captain in the Dental Officers Reserve Corps. He attends the Church of Our Lady of Lourdes and is a member of the Knights of Columbus. He belongs to the Omaha District Dental Society, the Nebraska State Dental Society and the American Dental Association. Residence: Omaha.

Henry Ernest Schemmel

Henry E. Schemmel, a lifetime resident of this state, was born September 7, 1892.

Mr. Schemmel attended the Hooper public schools, and completed a course at the Engineer Candidates School, at Langres, France, January 28, 1919. He is one of the organizers of the Elkhorn Valley League of Base Ball Clubs, and is the author of a baseball article *The Elkhorn Valley League* published in the August, 1925, issue of The Athletic Journal.

He enlisted in the United States Marine Corps at Denver, Colorado, August 18, 1911, and served in Hawaii and the Philippine Islands, and participated in skirmishes incident to the occupation of Santiago, Santo Domingo,

ELIZABETH ELMA SCHELKOPF

July 6, 1916; was in sea service on the United States Ships *San Diego*, and *Buffalo*, from November 25, 1915, to February 18, 1916; was awarded a good conduct medal August 17, 1915, and was honorably discharged at Norfolk, Virginia, August 17, 1916. He re-enlisted at Fort Logan, Colorado, October 2, 1917, and was assigned to D Company, 25th Engineers at Camp Devens, Massachusetts; served more than a year in France during the World War, and was with the First Army during the Meuse-Argonne engagement, September and October, 1918; was honorably discharged at Camp Dodge, Iowa, June 3, 1919, and now holds a commission as second lieutenant, Engineer Section, of the Officers Reserve Corps. During August, 1918, Mr. Schemmel was in charge of the construction of a 2500-bed unit at Base Hospital Number 8, Savenay, France.

He is a member of Hooper Lodge Number 72, Ancient Free and Accepted Masons; Friendship Chapter Number 122, Order of the Eastern Star; Emeth Lodge of Perfection Number 5, Scottish Rite; Longfellow Lodge Number 89, Knights of Pythias; the American Legion, and the National Association of the 25th Engineers. His sports include baseball and hunting.

On June 7, 1922, Mr. Schemmel was united in marriage with Lucile Estelle Cooper at Omaha, Douglas County, Nebraska. Mrs. Schemmel was a public school teacher from 1912 to 1922, and is now a member of the Board of Education, Hooper Public Schools. Members of her family have fought in every war for the United States except the Spanish-American War. Her ancestry includes: her parents, Grace (Mack) and Edgar Cooper; her maternal grandparents, Mary (Crist) Mack and Warren Mack who came to Nebraska from New York (Warren Mack's forefather came from Scotland before the Revolution); her paternal grandparents, Rebecca (Ford) Cooper and Andrew Cooper lived in Wisconsin. Andrew Cooper emigrated from Scotland, and was a descendant of the Douglas Clan. Mrs. Schemmel is a member of Friendship Chapter Number 122, Order of the Eastern Star; Pythian Sisters; R. N. A., and the American Legion Auxiliary. They have three children: Robert Edgar, born March 25, 1923; Mary Leah, born August 3, 1925; and Douglas Henry, born February 8, 1927.

Mr. Schemmel was acting postmaster at Hooper, from September 1, 1921, to February 5, 1922; was appointed postmaster February 6, 1922, by President Harding; was reappointed April 13, 1926, by President Coolidge; and reappointed April 15, 1930, by President Hoover. Residence: Hooper. (Photograph in Album).

Edward August Schenbeck

Edward August Schenbeck, farmer, was born in Rochester, New York, October 31, 1876, son of Frederick August and Johanna Henrietta (Kaufman) Schenbeck.

His father was born in Spect, Pomerania, Germany, March 10, 1844, and died at Aline, Oklahoma, on November 27, 1920. His parents, John and Louisa (Kamin) Schenbeck, were born in Germany, on April 7, 1816, and were pioneer settlers in the United States. Johanna Henrietta Kaufman was born in Stettin, Pomerania, Germany, November 24, 1844, and died at Aline, Oklahoma, June 15, 1929.

Mr. Schenbeck attended public schools in Gage County, and the Shenandoah, Iowa, Business College. He has resided in Nebraska for the past 41 years.

On January 14, 1903, he was married to Mary Katharine Spencer at Belleville, Kansas. Mrs. Schenbeck was born at Wymore, Nebraska, January 21, 1884. Her ancestors came from England, between 1620 and 1650, one of them being Judge Elizah Hatch of New York. Mrs. Schenbeck is the daughter of William Isaac and Belle (Henry) Spencer. They were prominent pioneer settlers of Gage County, Nebraska; they homesteaded there shortly after the close of the Civil War. Mrs.

Schenbeck's grandfather Marquis Spencer served in the Civil War.

She was graduated from the Wymore High School, is past secretary of the district Parent Teachers Association and past treasurer of the district school board. She is eligible to the Daughters of the American Revolution. Mrs. Schenbeck is affiliated with the Methodist Episcopal Church of Gering. They have three children, Frances, born October 21, 1905, who is married to James Earl Smith; Frederick August, born October 11, 1908, and Alice Marie, born October 6, 1923. Both of the older children attended the University of Nebraska.

Mr. Schenbeck is a Republican. He is affiliated with the Gering Methodist Episcopal Church, and is a member of the church board. He is a member of the Red Cross, and at the present time is serving as treasurer of the school board. His favorite sport is baseball. Residence: Gering.

Willis Wesley Schenck

Willis Wesley Schenck, son of Darwin Merriman and Elizabeth Moore (Crabb) Schenck, was born at Mount Pleasant, Illinois, September 12, 1867.

The father was born in Elbridge, New York, August 13, 1843, and died at Adair, Iowa, May 18, 1905. He was a shoemaker, a nursery tree salesman, and a soldier in the Civil War. His father, Garrett Schenck, was a Hollander and his mother, Emeline Raymond, was born in Vermont. The father lived in Illinois from Boyhood until April, 1869, when he moved to Iowa. He served in the Civil War three and one-half years and was married October 11, to Elizabeth Moore Crabb at Quincy. They made their home near Mount Pleasant when they moved to Adair County near Fontanelle, Iowa, and later to Adair, where his home was until his death. He served as justice of the peace about 12 years and was active in church and municipal affairs. He was the father of five girls and four boys.

Elizabeth Moore Crabb was born near Holland, Ohio, November 22, 1843, and died at Marshalltown, Iowa, May 17, 1928. She was a carpet weaver and later a church and missionary work. Her father was Edward Crabb of Irish descent, and her mother Eleanor Crabb of English and Welsh descent. Her parents were married October 11, 1864, at Quincy, Illinois, and lived at Mount Pleasant until April, 1869, when they moved to Adair County, Iowa, and pioneered in the new country. They lived in Adair County most of the time except a few years in Los Angeles. Elizabeth Schenck was the mother of nine children.

Willis Wesley Schenck attended public school in Iowa, Dexter Normal College, and completed a business course at Fontanelle, Iowa, in May, 1889. He came to Nebraska on June 1, 1890. In 1907 he became passenger conductor for the Chicago and Northwestern Railway, which position he has since held. Since 1921 he has been a director of the Chadron Building and Loan Association, and from 1904 until 1907 served as councilman of Chadron. He is a trustee of Elk Lodge No. 1399 and from 1915 until 1920 was a member of the Red Cross. At the present time Mr. Schenck is the third oldest passenger conductor on the Black Hills division of the Chicago and Northwestern Railway. He is a member of the Masons, the Order of Railway Conductors, Chamber of Commerce, the Kiwanis Club (song director), the Nebraskana Society, the Young Men's Christian Association (membership committee), and the Chadron Country Club (dancing and music committee). He is the possessor of a fine tenor voice, is much interested in music, mechanics, radio, and automobiles.

On June 29, 1893, he was married to Lein Lawrence at Rushville. They have one daughter, Pearl Beatrice, born September 19, 1895, who is married to E. J. Pennington. Residence: Chadron.

Henry F. Schepman

Henry F. Schepman, lawyer and civic leader of Falls City, Nebraska, was born at Lockwood, Dade County, Missouri, September 26, 1898. His father William Schepman, who was a farmer, was born of German parents at St. Louis, Missouri, October 30, 1872. His mother was born at Westphalia, Germany, September 10, 1873.

In 1918 Mr. Schepman was graduated from Tecumseh High School, and from 1918 to 1924 was a student at the University of Nebraska where he received his A. B. degree, 1923, and L. L. B., 1924. He was a member of the Dramatic Club and of the Pershing Rifles while at the University. Later he was a student at Chicago University.

On June 7, 1924, he was admitted to the bar at Lincoln, and has been engaged in the practice of law since that time. From 1925 to 1927 he served as state representative from Johnson County, having been elected in 1924 on the Democratic ticket. During the 69th congress he was appointed secretary to congressman John H. Morehead. In 1928 he was elected to the Nebraska State senate, and in 1930 was re-elected without opposition.

He married Sherlie Whitaker at Falls City, December 6, 1928. Mrs. Schepman, who was born at Falls City, May 30, 1901, is a descendant of Robert E. Lee.

Mr. Schepman was a soldier in the late war, and is a member of the American Legion, serving as adjutant of the local post in 1927. He is secretary of the Chember of Commerce, a member of the Rotary Club, the Nebraskana Society, the Nebraska Bar Association, and the Christ Lutheran Church of Falls City. He has lived in Nebraska for 23 years. Residence: Falls City.

Ralph Lipe Scherer

Born at Sidney, Nebraska, June 23, 1893, Ralph Lipe Scherer is the son of John Nelson and Henrietta A. (Lipe) Scherer. His father was born at Hillsboro, Illinois, March 15, 1860, and died at Dalton, January 25, 1928. He was a prominent farmer of North Carolina Dutch descent, and one of the first settlers in Cheyenne County. His wife, Henrietta, was born at Hillsboro, December 11, 1863, of English descent.

Until 1908, Mr. Scherer attended country school in Cheyenne County, and in 1912 was graduated from the South Denver, Colorado, High School. He later attended agricultural college at Curtis. While in high school he was active in track.

Until 1927, Mr. Scherer lived on a ranch, and at that time entered the automobile and farm equipment business at Dalton. He is a member of the firm of Scherer and Blome at the present time and is interested in the North Divide Farms Company.

His marriage to Genevieve Claire Armuth was solemnized at Dalton, June 23, 1914. Mrs. Scherer was born at Bancroft, March 10, 1895, of German descent. She is the daughter of Herman and Mary (Carr) Armuth. Her father is manager of the Dalton Co-operative Society. They have four children, Marguerite and Mary, born May 1, 1915; John, born February 24, 1922; and Frances, born January 25, 1928.

Mr. Scherer is a Democrat. He is a member of St. Mary's Catholic Church at Dalton. Residence: Dalton.

Harry Erwin Scherich

Harry Erwin Scherich lives on the farm his father homesteaded near Inland, Nebraska, in 1872. He was born near Harrisburg, Pennsylvania, June 19, 1869, the son of Jonathan Henry Clay Scherich and Margaret Rebecca (Kerr) Scherich. His father, who was born in York County, Pennsylvania, August 25, 1843, and died near Inland, April 8, 1914, was a farmer who served in the Union Army during the Civil War from 1864 until the close of the war. His father's people came from Germany before the Revolution. Through the maternal

line he was descended from Samuel Millard who came to America from England about 1750.

Margaret (Kerr) Scherich, mother of Harry E. Scherich, was born in Fulton County, Pennsylvania, December 2, 1842, and died near Inland, February 16, 1915. On her father's side of the family she was descended from George Kerr, who came to America from Scotland in the early part of the eighteenth century. On the maternal side she was descended from Alexander Blair, who came to America from Ireland in 1760 and who in turn was descended from Brice Blair, born in Scotland in 1600.

Mr. Scherich, who has been a prominent farmer in Clay County for many years, has served on the local school board and is a member of the Inland Community Club. He is a life member of the Red ross, is affiliated with the Inland Methodist Episcopal Church, and is a member of the Farmers' Union, the Modern Woodmen of America, the Nebraskana Society, and the Sons of Union Veterans.

His marriage to Ella March (Peterson) McCormick was solemnized at Inland, November 23, 1892. Mrs. Scherich, who is a leader in all civic, religious, and educational affairs at Inland, was born there, March 18, 1875, the daughter of John and Martha Peterson. Upon the death of her mother she was adopted, at the age of two years, by Thomas and Elizabeth McCormick. Mrs. Scherich is of Danish, Welsh, and German extraction.

To their union the following children were born: Rilla, who has been a foreign missionary; Clarence, who married Clara Baptiste and is a farmer; Esther, who has been a college instructor; Everett, who married Marian Metzger and is a debating coach and teacher; Bernard, who died in infancy; Millard, who is a theological seminary student; and Erwin Thomas, who is still in grade school. Residence: Inland.

Frank Aaron Scherzinger

Frank A. Scherzinger, editor and publisher, was born at Clarington, Monroe County, Ohio, April 7, 1865, the son of John B. and Rosa Ann (Yost) Scherzinger. John B. Scherzinger was born at Baden, Germany, August 24, 1841. He came to America with his widowed mother when he was a boy, settled in southeastern Ohio and worked as a skilled mechanic until in the Spring of 1888. He died in Nuckolls County, Nebraska, April 20, 1897. Rosa Ann Yost was born at Clarington, Ohio, July 26, 1842, and died at Nelson, Nebraska, August 18, 1917.

Frank A. Scherzinger received an elementary school education. At Nelson, Nebraska, on November 14, 1894, he married Bess Heath Bradley, who was born March 15, 1873, at Toulon, Stark County, Illinois. Two children were born to this marriage: Ruth Ione, June 28, 1897, now the wife of Lawson J. Wehrman; and Vic Bradley, May 28, 1908, who is now portraitist for Illustrina, Inc., publishers.

On February 1, 1886, Mr. Scherzinger took charge of the *Nelson Gazette* at Nelson, Nebraska, and has been editor and publisher of this newspaper since that time. During the World War he was a Four Minute man, was chairman of the War Savings Stamp drives for Nuckolls County, was local chairman of bond sales, and chairman of the United War Work Campaign.

A Republican, he has served as a party worker for that political organization but has never sought political office. He is affiliated with the First Presbyterian Church of Nelson, and holds a membership in the following organizations: Red Cross, National Editorial Association, Chamber of Commerce, the Nebraskana Society, and the Young Men's Christian Association, and has been affiliated with the Independent Order of Odd Fellows and the Knights of Pythias. Music is his hobby. Residence: Nelson.

Harry Schilling

Harry Schilling, cashier of the Hebron State Bank, was born at Strang, Nebraska, August 9, 1892, son of

James H. and Ida (Whistler) Schilling. The father, born in Cumberland, Maryland, is a retired business man. The mother born at Myersdale, Pennsylvania.

Mr. Schilling was graduated from Strang High School in 1910, and from that time until 1917 was connected with the Strang State Bank. He served in France with the 314th Supply Train, and was in the Central Record Office in France. He is a member of the American Legion, the Red Cross, the Chamber of Commerce and the Masons, and is a Presbyterian. He enjoys golf and hunting and is a member of the Hebron Golf Club. Residence: Hebron.

Albert Jensen Schjodt

Albert Jensen Schjodt, farmer and cattle feeder, was born in Bogeballe, Denmark, April 21, 1892, son of Jens Jensen and Kathrena (Knudsen) Schjodt. His father, a farmer, was born at Orum, Denmark, July 22, 1842, and served in the Danish-German War in 1864. He died at Bogeballe in July, 1907. Kathrena Knudsen was born in Uldum, Denmark, January 31, 1860, the daughter of a miller, and died at Bogeballe, in May, 1908.

Educated in the common and high schools of Denmark, Mr. Schjodt was graduated from the latter on May 1, 1911, at Hastev, Denmark, and had three years practice on an agricultural student farm in Denmark. He came to America in 1915, and took up his residence in Washington County, where he has since engaged as a farmer and cattle feeder.

On March 27, 1918, he was married to Andrea Marie Hansen at Blair. Mrs. Schjodt was born at Herman, Nebraska, March 3, 1900, and before her marriage was bookkeeper in a bank. She is the daughter of the treasurer of the Danish Evangelical Lutheran Church of the United States. There are four children living and one deceased: Veola, born May 13, 1919; Eulella, born April 7, 1922; Harold, born March 31, 1924; Margaret, born November 1, 1926, died November 23, 1926; and Rose-Marie, born July 5, 1929. The two older children are exceptional students, Veola having completed the 2nd and 3rd grades in one year, and Eulella the 4th and 5th the past year.

Mr. Schjodt is a member of the First Lutheran Church of Blair, and also a member of its finance committee. In June, 1930, he was elected director of school district No. 20, but because his naturalization papers were not complete he could not serve. He is a member of The Nebraskana Society. His hobby is reading. Residence: Blair.

William T. Schlife

William T. Schlife was born at Hubbell, Thayer County, Nebraska, September 20, 1870, the son of Nicholas C. and Catherine (Kelly) Schlife. He received a common school education.

Nicholas C. Schlife was born in Ohio, in 1839, and died at Hubbell, Nebraska, December 16, 1916. He was a merchant and a farmer. Catherine Schlife was born in Ireland, January 21, 1852, and died at Hubbell, January 21, 1928.

Mr. Schlife was united in marriage to Cecelia Martha Klaes, on May 1, 1906, at Hebron, Nebraska. Mrs. Schlife, who was born at West Point, Wisconsin, April 7, 1870, was a tailoress prior to her marriage, and was graduated from Hebron High School in 1887. They have two children Martin, born April 14, 1908, and Casper, born September 12, 1910. Both are graduates of the Chester High School and are now farming. A Catholic, he is affiliated with the Sacred Heart Church, and is a trustee and chancellor of the Knights of Columbus. He is treasurer of the local school board at the present time. Reading and mechanics are his hobbies. Residence: Chester.

John Daniel Schluntz

John Daniel Schluntz, a farmer near Huntley, Nebraska, is a lifelong resident of this state. He was born at Republican City, Nebraska, March 21, 1901, the son of Christian Henry and Katerine (Hoesch) Schluntz. His father, who was a cattleman and farmer, was born at Naponee, Nebraska, November 15, 1874, and died at Huntley, Nebraska, October 27, 1922. His mother, a nurse, was born April 19, 1877.

Mr. Schluntz was graduated from the public school at Huntley and since then has engaged in farming. At this time he is secretary of the local Telephone Company, is affiliated with the Zion Evangelical Church, and holds membership in the Nebraskana Society. His recreations are chess and baseball.

His marriage to Roma Boschult was solemnized at West Point, Nebraska, June 7, 1928. Mrs. Schluntz, who was a school teacher before her marriage, was born of German parents at Hooper, Nebraska, May 13, 1907. They have one daughter, Esther, born March 14, 1929. Residence: Huntley.

John O. Schmidt

John O. Schmidt, son of Marcus P. and Lena C. (Lush) Schmidt, was born at Wahoo, Nebraska, December 12, 1881. His father was born in Germany, December 23, 1845, and came to America in 1866, settling in Nebraska, where he engaged in the brickmaking trade. He died at Wahoo, November 11, 1908. His wife, Lena, was born in Sweden, October 10, 1856, and came to America in 1870. She is still living.

Mr. Schmidt attended public school, and afterward learned the brickmaking trade under his father. He started to farm in 1903, and at the present time is farming five hundred acres. He was the founder of the first Farmers Electric District, which has been recently declared unconstitutional by the Supreme Court.

He is president of the Farmers Union Co-operative Oil Association of Saunders County, and the Farmers Co-operative Company of Wahoo, the latter one of the largest and most successful co-operative companies in the state. A Republican, he served in the 37th session of the Nebraska legislature; assisted in the organization of the Progressive party, and was its treasurer and candidate for congress from the 4th district three times. He sought the Republican nomination for congress from the 4th district in 1928 and 1930, and is at present Republican county committeeman.

On April 28, 1909, he was united in marriage to Emma E. Keller. Mrs. Schmidt was born at Wahoo, December 21, 1889. There are four children living an one deceased: Kenneth E. born February 4, 1910, attends the University of Nebraska; Vernon A., born March 16, 1912, assists his father on the farm; Eileen V., born February 17, 1914, attends high school, as does Lucile E., born September 7, 1916; Melvin D., born December 24, 1919, died October 26, 1930. He was killed while playing in the sand, by being buried under a landslide.

Mr. Schmidt is a member of the Saunders County Farmers Union, and is county president of the organization at the present time. The Farmers Electric District, mentioned above, built thirty-five miles of electric line on bond issue, and operated seven years until declared unconstitutional. Mr. Schmidt is a member of the Wahoo Congregational Church, the Ancient Order of United Workmen, the Modern Woodmen of America, the Mystic Workers, and Lodge No. 58 of the Independent Order of Odd Fellows. He is a member of The Parent-Teachers Association and The Nebraskana Society, and is interested in economic problems for general improvement of conditions. Residence: Wahoo.

Charles Henry Schmitt

A leading merchant in Ulysses, Nebraska, Charles

Henry Schmitt was born at Ulysses, June 10, 1896. His father, Otto Schmitt, was born at Warsaw, Hancock County, Illinois, of German parentage, was a merchant, and died at Ulysses, November 10, 1914. His mother, Mary (Morrison) Schmitt, was born at Willimantic, Windom County, Connecticut, of Irish parentage, and died at Ulysses, February 6, 1928. She was an enthusiastic church worker.

Charles Schmitt attended the Ulysses public and high schools, and was valedictorian of his class in 1914. He attended the University of Nebraska, 1914-15. He was a member of the Ulysses football team in 1913.

A resident of Nebraska since birth, Mr. Schmitt is at present the owner and manager of a retail store at Ulysses. He has served on the council and was chairman one term. He is a Democrat. He is a member of St. Mary's Roman Catholic Church, the Ulysses Commercial Club, the Modern Woodmen of America, the Knights of Columbus, and the Red Cross, and is a life member of The Nebraskana Society. Residence: Ulysses.

Albert L. Schneider

Albert L. Schneider, physician and surgeon, was born at Langnau, Switzerland, April 4, 1887, and has been a resident of Nebraska for the past ten years. His father, Gottlieb Schneider, was born in Switzerland, where he died. He was a contractor. His wife, Liesette Schwander, was also born in Switzerland.

Dr. Schneider received his primary and secondary education in Langnau, and attended secondary school until 1903. He received his medical degree from Chicago College of Medicine in Chicago, Illinois, in the spring of 1918, and was admitted to the practice of medicine in Wyoming in June, 1919. He is a member of Alpha Phi Mu.

During the years of 1913 and 1914, Dr. Schneider was research chemist for the United Steel Company at Gary, Indiana. From 1916 until 1918, he was assistant professor of Histology at the Chicago Hospital College of Medicine. He held the rank of first lieutenant in the medical corps from 1918 until 1919 and engaged in the chemical warfare research work at the American University of Washington, D. C., during the later part of the World War.

From 1920 until the spring of 1922 Dr. Schneider was interne and house physician at St. Francis Hospital in Colorado Springs. In 1922 he was assistant superintendent of the Nebraska State Tubercular Hospital. Since 1923 he has been in private practice at Brady. Dr. Schneider is the author of *Eletro-Coagulation of Tonsils* (1932).

On May 15, 1929, he was married to Emma F. Lenke at Omaha. She was born in Germany in 1902. Dr. Schneider is a past member of the Chicago Anatomical Society and a member of the American Congress of Physical Therapy. He is a member of the Lincoln County and Nebraska State Medical Societies and in 1923 served as vice-president of the former. He is a Protestant and a member of the American Legion. He was first commander of Glendo, Wyoming Post in 1919. Since 1919 he has held the rank of captain in the United States Medical Reserve. He is a member of the Military Surgeons of the United States. Among Dr. Schneider's favorite sports are fishing, golfing, and shooting. He is a breeder of fancy game and fur and pure-bred St. Bernard dogs. Residence: Brady.

Fred David Schneider

Born at Minden, Nebraska, December 16, 1891, Fred David Schneider is the son of Rhynehart and Rebecca (Schafer) Schneider. His father, who was a farmer and stockraiser, was born at Peru, Illinois, March 30, 1866, and died at Hastings, Nebraska, May 7, 1930. His mother, whose father served in the Civil War, was born of German parentage at Iowa City, Iowa, July 22, 1874.

Mr. Schneider was graduated from the high school at Minden, in 1911, was a student at the University of Nebraska, and Kearney State Normal School, and later attended the University of Colorado. He taught in rural schools in Kearney County, Nebraska, for three years, and during the past 20 years has been prominent as an educator in the following schools: Riverton, Nebraska, three years; Cedar Rapids, three years; Loup City, the past 11 years. He is now superintendent of schools at Loup City, and is a member of the Rotary Club and Commercial Club of that city.

He is a member of the Nebraska State Teachers Association, the National Educational Association, North Central Music Supervisors Conference, and the Schoolmasters Club. He is a Mason, a member of the Knights of Pythias, and of the Loup City First Presbyterian Church. His chief interest is music.

On June 3, 1914, he was married at Miller, Nebraska, to Grace Darling Norcross. Mrs. Schneider, whose ancestry is English and Scotch, was born at Miller, November 3, 1894. She is descended from General George B. McClellan. They have two children: June Elizabeth, born July 23, 1916; and Fred David, Jr., born October 16, 1918. Residence: Loup City. (Photograph in Album).

Albert Louis Schnurr

Albert Louis Schnurr, lawyer, was born at Mount Pleasant, Iowa, August 21, 1879, son of William and Rosa (Rukgaber) Schnurr. The father was born at Portsmouth, Ohio, and the mother at Richmond, Virginia.

Mr. Schnurr attended the public school of Mount Pleasant, Iowa, and was graduated from high school there. Thereafter, he attended Iowa Wesleyan University, Mount Pleasant Academy, and the Omaha Law School. He was admitted to the bar, in 1906, and from 1908 until 1910, served as county judge of Sioux County. During 1926, 1927, 1928 and 1929, he was county attorney of Sioux County. He has been in the banking business for 14 years, and is now Sioux County deputy county attorney. He is secretary and treasurer of the Harrison National Farm Loan Association.

His marriage to Elsie Rohwer was solemnized, June 29, 1910. Mrs. Schnurr was born at Atlantic, Iowa. She is a member of the Eastern Star and Rebekahs. They have two children, William E. and Clarence A.

During the late war, Mr. Schnurr was chairman of all liberty loan and war savings drives in his county. He is a Protestant, a member of the Red Cross, the Masons, the Odd Fellows, the Foresters, and the Brotherhood of the American Yeoman. Residence: Harrison.

John Conrad Schoemaker

Born at Eagle Lake, Indiana, November 29, 1865, John Conrad Schoemaker has resided in Nebraska fifty years. His father, Martin Schoemaker, was born in New Orleans, Louisiana, in September, 1831, was reared in Chicago, Illinois, and worked in a barber shop there for five years. In 1870 moved to Benton County, Iowa, where he lived for 12 years. He then moved to Greeley County, Nebraska, in 1882, where he has since resided. When he first located he lived 50 miles from the railroad. He died at Scotia on October 23, 1924. Anna Meyer, wife of Martin Schoemaker, was born in Germany, August 3, 1844, and died at Scotia, October 20, 1919.

John Conrad Schoemaker attended rural school and until sixteen years ago was engaged in farming. At that time he became the owner of a mercantile business in Scotia. A Republican, he was mayor of Scotia two years. He is affiliated with the Evangelical Church, is a member of the Parent Teachers Association and the Nebraskana Society.

On August 28, 1889, he was married to Mary Louise Miller at Scotia. Mrs. Schoemaker, who is of German descent, was born in Racine, Wisconsin, April 3, 1871. To them were born three children, Alice, July 12, 1891; Walter, May 21, 1893, who married Elsie Hermsmeyer; and Roy, born June 30, 1896, who married Dorthea Piepho. Alice is a registered nurse; Walter ownes a meat market and Roy is in a general store at Scotia. Residence: Scotia.

Alfred B. Schoenauer

Alfred B. Schoenauer was born in Holmes County, Ohio, July 4, 1858, the son of Frederick and Sarah (Fabra) Schoenauer. His father, who was a shoemaker, mail carrier, and farmer in his native country, was born at Berne, Switzerland, April 3, 1831, and died at Whitley, Indiana, September 1, 1910; he was a Civil War veteran. His mother was born in Holmes County, January 14, 1838, and died at Whitley.

Mr. Schoenauer attended rural school in Whitley County and in 1884 moved to Nebraska where he became engaged in farming. He is a member of the Independent Order of Odd Fellows and is affiliated with the Friends Church at Plainview, Nebraska. He served as mayor of Plainview, elected on the Democratic ticket, 1909-13, 1925-26, and in 1926 was a candidate for the legislature.

On October 21, 1883, he was married to Evaline Brandenburg at Huntington, Indiana. Mrs. Schoenauer was born at Whitley, June 5, 1857, and died at Plainview, December 8, 1931. Their three children are: Arlen, born September 9, 1886, a farmer; Vilas, born September 12, 1888, a farmer; and Eber, born April 23, 1891, who is a disabled veteran of the World War. Residence: Plainview.

William Albert Schoeneck

William Albert Schoeneck, son of Carl Frederick and Emily (Radtke) Schoeneck, was born at Scribner, Nebraskana, March 27, 1871. His father was born in Germany, April 3, 1842, and came to America in 1860. A farmer, he homesteaded less than a mile south of Scribner in Dodge County, and died at Scribner in 1916. His wife, Emily, was born in Germany, December 2, 1850, and died at Scribner, January, 1931. She was a school teacher.

William A. Schoeneck was educated in the public schools of Dodge County, and has been engaged as a merchant and garage owner for several years. He was married to Sophie Henriette Siems at Fremont, November 25, 1893. Mrs. Schoeneck was born in the Province of Oldenburg, Germany, June 25, 1873. There are four children, Hilbert, born October 12, 1894, who married Gertrude Patiedl; Norma, born November 12, 1898, who married Fred Ebel; Arlan, born June 24, 1901, who married Inez Hall; and Eldon, born March 6, 1904, who is unmarried. All three sons are in business.

A progressive Democrat, Mr. Schoeneck has been interested in politics and active in the work of the party in a local way. He is a member of the Snyder Commercial Club, the Congregational Church, and has been elected to membership in The Nebraskana Society. He has served on the school board and has held various village offices. Residence: Snyder.

Louis Scholz

On July 25, 1870, at Braunseifen, Austria, Louis Scholz son of Joseph and Josephine (Stefan) Scholz, was born. His father, a farmer and freighter, was born at Altliebau, Austria, May 20, 1826, and died at Osceola, Nebraska, December 2, 1916. Josephine Scholz was born at Braunseifen, Austria, September 29, 1833, and died at Osceola,

Nebraska, July 2, 1895. Louis Scholz attended a pioneer school.

Mr. Scholz was united in marriage to Anna Solterberg on March 30, 1891, at Osceola. She was born at Omaha, December 20, 1874. They have five children: Martin, born July 14, 1892, who is married to Mary A. Scott; Lena, born October 2, 1899, who is married to Reuben C. Timm; Walter, born November 22, 1902; Evelyn, born July 2, 1906; and William, born August 4, 1908.

Mr. Scholz has been a resident of Nebraska for fifty-two years, and has been a farmer most of that time. He holds membership in the Modern Woodmen of America, the Red Cross, and The Nebraskana Society. He was a member of the Parent-Teacher Association from 1926 to 1928, and from 1892-1895 of his local school board. Reading history, and mechanics are his hobbies. Residence: Osceola. (Photograph in Album).

James Elvin Schoonover

Born in Pike County, Ohio, June 7, 1872, James Elvin Schoonover is the son of Isaac Wells and Mary Ann (Hyatt) Schoonover, the former a farmer in Ohio. His mother was born in Ohio, in 1848, of English parentage, and died at Aurora, Nebraska, in 1888.

James E. Schoonover was a student at Aurora High School, but was forced to leave school at the age of 16 to earn his living. He learned the printer's trade in the office of the *Aurora Republican* and continued with this paper until 1895. During 1895 and 1896, he edited and published the *Hampton Times* at Hampton, Nebraska, returning to Aurora, in 1897.

He was appointed assistant postmaster and served in that position under Alexander N. Thomas, 1898-99. In 1900 he returned to the printing business with the owner of the *Aurora Republican*, and in 1909 acquired Mr. Alden's interest in the newspaper. He served for two years as deputy state oil inspector, and in 1914 established a moving picture business at Aurora. Since 1922 he has been postmaster at Aurora.

Mr. Schoonover is secretary and director of the Aurora Building & Loan Association of which he was an organizer in 1902. He is a member of the Rotary Club, serving as president in 1927-28, the Nebraskana Society, Nebraska State Historical Society, and the Red Cross. He is past president and a board member of the Aurora Country Club. During the war he was active in all Liberty loan drives, food saving campaigns and all other civilian war activities.

A Republican, he has been active in politics since his boyhood when he organized a first voters club to support E. J. Hainer, candidate for congress. He has served as organizer, secretary, and chairman of county central committees, and in 1905 was the Republican candidate for county clerk.

Mr. Schoonover has had an interesting and varied career and has been an important factor in the progress of his state and community. In 1873, he was brought to Nebraska in a covered wagon, the family settling in Hamilton County. His childhood was spent in a sod house under the most trying and crude circumstances of pioneer life, and he remembers vividly the difficulties and dangers of Nebraska life in the early seventies.

On December 24, 1896, he was married to Maude Ann Matlock, at Aurora. She was born at South Bend, Indiana, October 14, 1875, of English and Scotch parentage. To their marriage the following children were born: Harold M., April 5, 1898, who married LaVerne Harris; Halga C., July 27, 1900, who married Walter C. Kenney; James M., July 30, 1905; and Evalyn M., September 30, 1909. Residence: Aurora.

Frank Theodore Schowengerdt

A physician at Cortland, Gage County, Nebraska, since 1912, Frank Theodore Schowengerdt has been active

Dole—Lincoln

FRED SCHREINER

in community affairs for many years. He was born at Hopewell, Warren County, Missouri, December 2, 1875, the son of John and Amalia (Schaake) Schowengerdt. His father, a farmer and merchant, was born in Warren County, Missouri, and died at Chamois, Osage County, Missouri, October 11, 1888; his ancestry was German. His mother was born in Germany and died at Hopewell, January 25, 1882.

Dr. Schowengerdt attended public schools and in 1898 was graduated from high school. He received his M. D. degree at Mariam Sime Beaumont College of Medicine, St. Louis, Missouri, May 1, 1902, and was admitted to the practice of medicine at St. Louis, Missouri. He has lived at Cortland for 20 years and has been engaged in general medical practice there during that time. He is a member of the Gage County Medical Society, and the Nebraskana Society. He is affiliated with Epworth Methodist Episcopal Church at Cortland, is a member of the Republican party, and holds membership in the Modern Woodmen of American and the Masons.

He was married to Mary Elisabeth Schmidt at Warrenton, Missouri, July 8, 1903. Mrs. Schowengerdt, who is of German descent, was born at Chamois, Missouri, February 20, 1875. Five children were born to this marriage: Irene, born November 27, 1904, who married John Wesley Lee; Waldo, born December 13, 1905, who died November 2, 1906; Gladys, born June 8, 1908, who died October 2, 1908; Grace, born April 21, 1910; and Frances, born August 2, 1916. Irene is a registered nurse, and Grace is a student and teacher. Residence: Cortland.

E. Frank Schramm

Born at DeWitt, Nebraska, September 7, 1883, E. Frank Schramm educator and geologist, has resided in Nebraska 35 years. He is the son of George W. and Mary Charlotte (Hawes) Schramm, the former a retired business man and farmer, who was born at Rushville, Illinois, April 19, 1856. He is of German descent. His wife, Mary Charlotte, was born at Council Bluffs, Iowa, in April, 1858, and died at Newkirk, Oklahoma, June 13, 1914. She was active in clubwork, and of early American ancestry.

E. Frank Schramm attended the grade schools of DeWitt and Newkirk, and was graduated from the Newkirk High School in 1902. He received his A. B. from the University of Oklahoma in 1906, and his M. A. from the University of Nebraska in 1908. Afterward he attended the law college of the university two and a half years. At Oklahoma he was president of the senior class, president of the Athletic Association, the Oratorical Association and the Forum Literary Society and associate editor and business manager of the college paper. He is a member of Sigma Xi, Alpha Chi Sigma, Sigma Gamma Epsilon, Phi Delta Phi, Phi Alpha Tau and Kappa Sigma. He has been grand vice president of Sigma Gamma Epsilon since 1920.

Since 1906 Mr. Schramm has been a member of the teaching staff of the University, and was field assistant, United States Geological Survery 1905, 07, 08, and 09, and member 1910-15. During the years 1906, 1912 and 1914 he was engaged in the Morrill Geological Expeditions, and in 1910 and 1911 was mineral expert in the United States Forest Service. During the year 1917-18 he was geologist for the Union Pacific Railroad Company.

He is now professor of geology at the University of Nebraska, consulting geologist and mining engineer for many oil and mining companies, and geologist for the Midwest Chemical Company and geologist and mining engineer for the Soil Tone Company of Utah.

During his professional career he has been the author of various articles, some of which are: *Building Stones of Oklahoma; Mining Claims; Oil Shales of Wyoming; Agate Anticline; Oil Possibilities of Nebraska and Well Logs of Nebraska* (co-author).

Professor Schramm's professional memberships in-

clude the American Institute of Mining and Metallurgical Engineers, the American Association of Petroleum Geologisits; American Association for the Advancement of Science (Fellow); American Forestry Association; Archeological Society of Washington; Nebraska Academy of Science; and the National Geographical Society. He is a member of the Unitarian Church, the Knights of Pythias, the Young Men's Christian Association and the Brotherhood of American Yeomen. His favorite recreations are fishing and hunting, and his hobby is the collection of minerals and gems. Residence: Lincoln.

Isaac Butler Schreckengast

Isaac B. Schreckengast was born at Danville, Des Moines County, Iowa, October 5, 1864, the son of Isaac and Sarah (Davis) Schreckengast. His father, who was a cobbler and merchant, was born at Lebanon, Pennsylvania, and died at Keota, Keokuk County, Iowa, in 1911; his ancestry was German. His mother was born at Annville, Pennsylvania, and died at Keota, in 1896. She was the daughter of Pennsylvania Dutch ancestors who lived in Pennsylvania.

Rev. Schreckengast attended school in Iowa, and received the B. S. degree at Iowa State College, 1885, and the S. T. B. degree at Boston University, 1895. He was awarded the honorary degree Ph. M. at Iowa State College, and the D. D. degree at Simpson College. He was elected to membership in Phi Kappa Phi. He has lived in Nebraska for the past 21 years, and is now chancellor at Nebraska Wesleyan University.

He is a member of the Lincoln Chamber of Commerce, and the Professional Men's Institute. He is affiliated with the First Methodist Episcopal Church of Lincoln, and is a member of the board of education of the M. E. Church with headquarters in Chicago.

His marriage to Genevieve Clarke was solemnized at Keota, May 1, 1889. Mrs. Schreckengast was born on a farm in Iowa County, Iowa, August 4, 1861; before her marriage she was a teacher. Her parents were born and reared in Vermont and New Hampshire. Three children were born to this marriage: Joy, born August 11, 1890, who married Lorne E. Jones; Carita, born August 13, 1892, who married Dr. J. D. Taylor; and Dorothy, born October 27, 1898, who married Dr. F. O. Hansen. Residence: Lincoln.

Fred Schreiner

Fred Schreiner has been a resident of Nebraska for over 46 years and has been engaged in the mercantile business in this state for 26 years. He was born at Peru, Illinois, July 14, 1874, the son of Wilhelmena (New) and Lorenz Schreiner. His father was born in Bavaria, Germany, February 24, 1842, and came to America with his parents in 1860. The trip was made in a sailing boat and lasted 63 days. He died at Syracuse, Otoe County, Nebraska, June 11, 1918. He was a farmer by occupation.

Fred Schreiner's mother, the sister of several Civil War veterans, was born in Paxton County, Pennsylvania, April 18, 1847, and died near Syracuse, April 16, 1928. She was a homemaker for her family of twelve children.

Mr. Schreiner came to Nebraska in February, 1884, and received his education in the country schools, completing school in 1894. He was graduated from the commercial department of the United Brethren College at York, Nebraska, 1903. Since that time he has been in the mercantile business.

His marriage to Grace Vivian Shaw was solemnized at York, Nebraska, September 1, 1904. Mrs. Schreiner was born at York, March 14, 1883. Her mother was of Quaker descent. Four children were born to this union, two of whom are living: Harold M., born October 8, 1905, who is a clerk in his father's hardware store; Evangeline, born June 7, 1909, who died September 1, 1910; Dwight E., born November 20, 1912, who died April 6, 1928; and Norman E., born August 10, 1915.

Mr. Schreiner served three years in the Nebraska National Guard, Company A, First Regiment, 1901-02-03, and was discharged as first sergeant. He served in the Nebraska Home Guards at Unadilla, Nebraska, 1916-1918, and was discharged in 1918 as second lieutenant by Governor Keith Neville. He is a member of the Ancient Free and Accepted Masons, Mount Moriah Lodge Number 57 at Syracuse, Ancient and Accepted Scottish Rite of Freemasonry, Valley of Lincoln.

He is a director of the Unadilla school board. He is affiliated with the Methodist Church. He is a Republican. Residence: Unadilla. (Photograph on Page 1062).

Robert D. Schrock

Robert D. Schrock, orthopedic surgeon, was born in Delaware, Ohio, August 22, 1884, son of William H. and Nettie M. (Patterson) Schrock.

He received his Bachelor of Arts degree from Wabash College in 1905, and his medical degree from Cornell University in 1912. He is a member of the American Orthopedic Association and the Chamber of Commerce. His clubs are: the University, the Country, and the Athletic Club. Residence: Omaha.

Herman Schroeder

Herman Schroeder was born in Noerenberg, Germany, January 24, 1867, the son of Herman Schroeder and Henrietta (Samme) Schroeder.

The father was a merchant in Noerenberg. He was born in Germany, February 24, 1845 and died at Elvershagen, Germany, in August, 1911. His mother was born in Noerenberg, December 26, 1844, and died at Elvershagen in 1926.

Mr. Schroeder came from Germany and settled in Omaha in 1888. He worked as a blacksmith for Andrew Murphy until September 1, 1889, when he began working for the Union Pacific Railroad Company at Omaha as a car repairer. In March, 1890, he was transferred to Sidney in the same capacity and was made car foreman in September, 1902. He was retired on a pension May 1, 1928.

He was united in marriage November 14, 1891, to Elizabeth Fix at Norfolk, Nebraska. Mrs. Schroeder was born near Norfolk, March 25, 1872, of German parentage. Six children were born to their union, Frank G., born March 3, 1893, who married Mable Closman, and is residing at Sidney; Sidney A., born October 20, 1894, who married Edna Bird, and is residing at Cheyenne, Wyoming; Elizabeth H., born October 15, 1896, who married N. K. Williamson, and is residing at Cheyenne, Wyoming; Florence B., born October 21, 1899, who married W. Turnbull, and is residing at London, England; Herman J., born December 18, 1902, who resides at Los Angeles, California; and Herald K., born July 17, 1921. Residence: Sidney.

Herman Gordon Schroeder

Born at Elwood, Nebraska, June 24, 1898, Herman Gordon Schroeder is the son of Frank David and Martha (Burt) Schroeder. His father was born near Springfield, Illinois, March 8, 1868, the son of a German settler in the early nineteenth century. His mother was born in Illinois, January 23, 1871.

Herman Gordon Schroeder attended the public and high schools of Lincoln, and received his Bachelor of Laws degree from the University of Nebraska in 1921. He is a member of Phi Delta Phi and Delta Tau Delta. Since his admission to the bar Mr. Schroeder has been in active practice in Hastings. From 1925 to 1929 he served as police judge of Hastings, having been elevated on the Non-Partisan ticket in 1925 and 1927. On January 8,

1931, took office as county attorney of Adams County, elected on the Democratic ticket.

Mr. Schroeder was married on March 28, 1922, to Hallie Virginia Minor at Hastings. Mrs. Schroeder was born at Nelson, Nebraska, December 8, 1901. There are three children, Jeanne, born May 30, 1923; Gretchen, born February 21, 1926; and Frank Minor, born November 29, 1928. The family attends the Episcopal Church.

During the World War Mr. Schroeder was a private in the radio service. He is a member of the American Legion, the Kiwanis Club, the Elks, and The Nebraskana Society, and his social club is the Hastings Country Club. Residence: Hastings. (Photograph on Page 1065).

Frank Schukar

On March 30, 1880, Frank Schukar was born at Shobonier, Fayette County, Illinois, the son of August Schukar and Bertha (Petermann) Schukar. His father, a farmer, was born at Koenigsberg, Germany, in 1848, and came to America in 1865, with his parents who died at the ages of ninety and ninety-one. He died at Evansville, Indiana, in 1914.

His mother was born in Germany, February 22, 1858. She came to the United States with her parents, at the age of seven, the family settling in Wisconsin. She died at Evansville, Indiana, in May 1928.

In 1905 Mr. Schukar was graduated from the Tobin College at Fort Dodge, Iowa. On March 21, 1906, his marriage to Johanna Bergstraesser was solemnized at Clarksville, Iowa. Mrs. Schukar was born at Ebersdorf, Germany, October 1, 1875. Her ancestors were keepers of the old Roman Highway known as the Bergstrasse. To this union six children were born: Dorothea, born March 1, 1907, who is married to Gus Rohrs; Magdalene, born September 24, 1908, who is a registered nurse at Wesleyan Hospital at Wichita, Kansas; Marie, born November 20, 1910; Gertrude, born April 23, 1912; Herbert, born December 9, 1914; and George, born October 26, 1916.

Mr. Schukar is affiliated with the St. Paul's Lutheran Church at Byron, Nebraska. He is a Republican, a member of the Nebraskana Society and is president of the Byron Commercial Club. Horticulture and foreign languages are his hobbies. Residence: Byron.

Henry F. Schulte

Henry F. Schulte, coach of athletics at the University of Nebraska, has lived in the state for 13 years. He was born in St. Louis County, Missouri, February 4, 1879, the son of Henry John and Elizabeth Schulte. His father, who was born in St. Louis County, in 1839, and died there in 1879, was a farmer, teacher, and judge, of German descent. His mother, who was born in St. Louis County in 1840, and died there in 1900, was manager of the home farm after her husband's death; her ancestry was German.

Mr. Schulte was graduated from Smith Academy at St. Louis, in 1897; was a student at Washington University for a time; and in 1907 received his A. B. degree from the University of Michigan. He was active in football during his college days. He is the author of various pamphlets on athletics; and is now coach of athletics at the University of Nebraska.

He was united in marriage at Marcellus, Michigan, June 9, 1909. Mrs. Schulte, who was born at Marcellus, March 13, 1899, is descended from English, Scotch, Dutch, French, and Welsh ancestors. Their son, Henry Frank, was born September 24, 1924.

Mr. Schulte is a member of the Football Association, the Track Association, and various other athletic societies. He holds membership in the Chamber of Commerce; the Lions Club; University Club; Red Cross; Nebraskana Society; and the School Masters Club. He is a Mason. His sports include fishing and hunting, while his hobbies are antique furniture and handicraft. Residence: Lincoln.

Nebraska Photo Company—Hastings

HERMAN GORDON SCHROEDER

Hermann von Wechlinger Schulte

Hermann von W. Schulte, distinguished educator of Omaha, was born at Utica, Oneida County, New York, August 9, 1876, the son of Bernard Schulte. His father, who was born at Hanover, Germany, June 24, 1848, and died at Omaha, April 6, 1927, was a clergyman of the Episcopal Church. He was awarded the following degrees: A. B., Hobart College, 1870; A. M., 1873; S. T. D., 1894; B. D., Berkely Divinity School, 1873. He was the son of Hermann von Schulte and Adelaide von Wechlinger.

His mother, the daughter of Edward Delevan Nelson, a landscape painter, and Susan Blanchard McDonald, was born in New York City, November 15, 1853, and died at Omaha, July 13, 1928. She held many offices in the Girl's Friendly Society and was a life member of the national board of this society. She was at one time president of the society for the home study of the Holy Scriptures and was co-author of the handbook of the Church's Mission to the Indians in 1898.

She was a descendant of: John Nelson, a resident of Flatbrush, Long Island, 1670; of Major Nathaniel Delevan, born in 1746, who with nine brothers served in the same regiment during the Revolution—they were called the ten sons of the Revolution. One of the brothers, Captain Samuel Delevan, commanded the West Chester White Horse escorting General Washington in the evacuation day parade after which General Washington took leave of his officers in Fraunces Tavern. She was a descendant also of Colonel Lewis McDonald who was born at Strathspy, Scotland, and came to America in 1732; of Peter Cornelius Low, who came to America in 1659; and of Jan Jansen Bleeker who came to America in 1658 and was mayor of Albany, New York, in 1700. Fourth in descent from Jan Bleeker was Anthony Lispenard Bleeker, 1742-1816, from whom Bleeker Street of New York City was named.

Dr. Schulte attended St. Paul's School at Concord, New Hampshire, 1888-1893. In 1897 he was awarded the A. B. degree at Trinity College, Hartford, Connecticutt; M. D., Columbia University, 1902. He was a student at the University of Berlin during the summer of 1904. He was elected to membership in Sigma Xi, Alpha Omega Alpha, Delta Psi, and Phi Beta Kappa. He was valedictorian of the senior class at Trinity College, and served as literary editor of the Trinity *Tablet*, 1896-97.

He has held the following professional and civic positions as one of Nebraska's foremost physicians and educators: successively demonstrator, adjunct professor, assistant professor, associate professor of Anatomy, member of the faculty of the pure science and of medicine Columbia University, 1904-17; was junior dean, 1917, professor of anatomy, 1917 to date, and dean, 1918 to date of the School of Medicine of Creighton University. Since 1918 he has been chief of the staff at St. Joseph's Hospital. He is now dean and professor of anatomy at Creighton University School of Medicine.

Dr. Schulte is a member of: Omaha-Douglas County Medical Society; having served as advisor to the council since 1927, chairman of municipal affairs committee, 1927-8, and chairman of the publicity committee, 1928-9; the American Medical Association; Association for the Study of Internal Secretions; Catholic Hospital Association, Harvey Society, Nebraska State Medical Society, in which he served as a member of the public affairs committee, 1928; the United States Public Health Association; National Tuberculosis Association; American Academy of Political and Social Science; Society for the Study of Internal Secretions.

He holds membership in: Nebraska Conference for Social Work, of which he was president, 1929-30; Society for the Relief of The Disabled of which he is trustee; and the Nebraska Writer's Guild, of which he was president in 1930. He is a member of the board of the Public School Lunch and Milk Fund; is a member of the board of governors of the Omaha Chamber of Commerce; also Councillor to Women's Division of Omaha Chamber; was

president of the Council of Social Work, 1929-30; and was president of the Omaha Chapter of the American Interprofessional Institute, 1924-26.

Dr. Schulte acted as board member of the Omaha Public Library, 1927 to 1930, and was president of the Omaha Art Institute, 1929-30. He is a fellow of the American Association for the Advancement of Science; was vice president of the New York Academy of Sciences, 1915-17; was vice president of the Nebraska Academy of Science, 1923-24, president 1924-5; is a fellow of the New York Zoological Society; and is a member of the American Museum of Natural History of New York City. He is a member of the Association of American Anatomists; and American Society of Mammologists. He was president of the University Club 1927-8, and is a member of the Omaha Athletic Club, and the Century Club of New York.

From 1918 to 1920 Dr. Schulte was a member of the Mayor's Committee on Communicable Diseases, and is a member of the Omaha World's Court Committee, and since 1930 secretary. Since 1922 he has been lieutenant colonel in the Medical Reserve, commanding General Hospital Number 55.. He is a member of the Omaha Chapter of the Reserve Officers' Association of the United States. He is a Democrat. His hobby is reading. He was arbitor in the wage scale dispute in the Typographical Union Number 190 versus the Omaha Daily Papers, 1927; was lecturer for the Omaha School Forum, 1928; and was lecturer on social work for the Episcopal Diocesan Conference of Nebraska, 1927 and 1928, and for the Episcopal Diocesan Conference of Iowa, 1930. Dr. Schulte was president of Council of Social Agencies from 1924-28.

Dr. Schulte is the author of scores of articles on medical subjects, most of them published in professional journals. Among them are: *The Range of Variations in Montromes and Australian Marsupials*, published in the Journal of Anatomy, Volume 6, 1906; *Further Communications on the Venous System of Marsupials Anatomical Record*, 1907; *The Development of the Human Salivary Glands, Studies in Cancer and Allied Subjects;* Columbia University Press, Volume 6, 1913; *The Development of the Salivary Glands in the Cat; The Mammalian Aveolingual Salivary Area; Early Stages of Vasculogenesis in the Cat* (Felis domestica with special reference to the Mesenchymal Origin of Endothelium), 1914; *Anatomy of a Foetus of Balaenoptera borealis* (Lesson), 1914, 1914; *The Fusion of the Cardiac Anlages and the Formation of the Cariac Loop in the Cat,* (felis domestica), American Journal of Anatomy, Volume 20, 1916; *The Development of the Neuraxis in the domestic cat to the state of twenty-one somites,* in collaboration with Frederick Tilney, 1915 published in the New York Academy of Science, Volume 29; *The Early Stages of the Development of the Great Veins and of the Hepatic Circulation in the Cat,* 1917; *The Skull of Kogia breviceps,* 1917; *A Note on the Lumbar Vertebrae of Scutisorex; The External Character, Skeletal Muscles and Nerves of Kogia breviceps* (Blainville), in collaboration with M. de Forest Smith; *Memoranda upon the Anatomy of the Respiratory Tract, Foregut and Thoracic Viscera of a foetal Kogia Breviceps,* 1918; *John Hunter,* The Creighton Chronicle, Volume 9, 1918; *The Spirit of Professionalism,* Junior American Institute of Architects, 1924, and Association of Professional Men's Quarterly, 1925; *Hospital Social Service,* 1925; *The Physician and His Community,* published in the Nebraska State Medical Journal, 1926; *Some Thoughts on Education,* 1926; *Social Aspects of Medicine,* published in the Nebraska State Medical Journal, 1927; *Building of a New County Hospital,* Omaha Bee News, November 20, 1927; *Fear and the Physician,* published in Shadows, 1928; *Medical Education as it strikes the Anatomist,* 1928; *Medicine and the Middle Class,* published in the Nebraska State Journal of Medicine, 1928; *The Future of Medicine,* published in the Association of Professional Men's Quarterly, 1928; *Professional Ethics,* address given at the annual meeting of the Iowa State Nurses' Association, 1928; *Obligation of the Hospital to the Doctor in Relation to his Patient,* published in Hospital Progress, 1929; *The Patient,* published in the American Journal of Nursing,

H. von W. SCHULTE

Heyn—Omaha

1930; and *Approval of Hospital for Residencies*, published in Hospital Progress, 1931.

Dr. Schulte was united in marriage with Susan Augusta Embury at New York City, September 10, 1907. Mrs. Schulte, who was born at Bridgeport, Connecticut, April 10, 1867, has been a leader in Omaha's social and civic affairs for the past 14 years. Residence: Omaha. (Photograph on Page 1067).

Susan Embury Schulte

Susan E. Schulte was born at Bridgeport, Connecticut, April 10, 1867, the daughter of James William and Phila Delaplane (Brett) Embury. Her father, who was born at Brooklyn, New York, April 24, 1830, and died at Salem, New York, October 9, 1889, was a distinguished landscape painter. His English and Dutch ancestors came to America about 1640; among his noted ancestors were Dr. Robert Manley, 1732, Catharine Popplesdorf, 1742, and Colonel Anthony Post, 1752.

Her mother was born at New York City, June 21, 1830, and died at Orange, New Jersey, March 11, 1922. She was of Dutch, English, and French descent; among her ancestors who were prominent in the very early history of the country were: Francis Rombonts, who served as mayor of New York City in 1678; Philip Milledoler, her grandfather, who was president of Rutger's College at New Brunswick from 1825 to 1840.

Mrs. Schulte received her education in private schools. On September 11, 1907, she was united in marriage with Hermann von W. Schulte. Dr. Schulte, who is dean of the Creighton University School of Medicine at Omaha, has been a leader in the civic and educational affairs of his state for some time. Mrs. Schulte has lived at Omaha for the past 14 years and has led in social and welfare work during that time. Residence: Omaha.

Frank B. Schultz

Frank B. Schultz has lived at Clarkson, Nebraska, all his life and for the past 30 years has been engaged in the practice of dentistry there. He was born April 8, 1878, the son of Anton and Teresa (Novotny) Schultz. His father was born in Czechoslovakia, and died at Clarkson, April 12, 1904. His mother was born in Czechoslovakia, and died at Clarkson, May 3, 1916.

Dr. Schultz attended country school in Colfax County, and on May 1, 1901, received the D. D. S. degree at the University of Omaha. He is a member of the American Dental Association, the Nebraska State Dental Society, the Red Cross, and the Clarkson Commercial Club. He is a Mason. During the World War he was a member of the draft registration board and took an active part in loan drives in Colfax County. He is first sergeant in the National Guards, a member of the Zion Presbyterian Church at Clarkson, and a Democrat.

His marriage to Josephine Bohac was solemnized at Clarkson, on November 28, 1901. Mrs. Schultz was born at Clarkson, July 27, 1878. Their children are: Alice J., born May 6, 1903, who married L. D. Stastny; and Frank A., born May 22, 1907. Residence: Clarkson.

William Will Schultz

William W. Schultz, sheriff of Cheyenne County, was born at Orient, Iowa, July 25, 1894, son of Otto A. and Christina (Leuers) Schulz.

The father, born in Germany, November 7, 1854, died at Orient, Iowa, April 20, 1923. He was a farmer. His wife, Christina, was born at Orient, Iowa, September 18, 1861 and died there on November 11, 1928.

Mr. Schulz has resided in Nebraska for 11 years. He is a Republican, and has served two years on the city council of Sidney. He was appointed as deputy sheriff by the late J. M. Nelson, who was shot February 20, 1930. On February 25, 1930 he was appointed sheriff, and

on November 4, 1930 was elected for a term of four years.

On February 16, 1916, he was married to Laura Laurana (Low) near Macksburg, Iowa. Mrs. Schulz was born near Winterset, Iowa, November 14, 1896. Their children are as follows: Wilma, born February 18, 1918; Lucile, born December 3, 1919; and Ada, born August 28, 1921.

Mr. Schulz is a member of the Methodist Church and the Odd Fellows. His hobby is baseball. Residence: Sidney. (Photograph in Album).

Rudolf Lorenz Schumacher

Born at Alexandria, South Dakota, June 1, 1887, Rudolf Lorenz Schumacher is the son of John Pierre and Mary Theresa (Schrupp) Schumacher. His father, who was a tailor, was born at Luxemburg, Germany, and died at Alexandria, South Dakota. His mother was born at Dyersville, Iowa, and died at Alexandria, South Dakota.

Mr. Schumacher completed a course at the Alexandria High School, and for the past 20 years has been engaged in the jewelry business at St. Paul, Nebraska, where he is a member of the Royal Arch and Knights Templar bodies of the Masons.

On July 16, 1911, he married Florence E. Tinkham at Fremont, Nebraska. Mrs. Schumacher, who is a daughter of O. B. Frances Tinkham is descended from Peter Brown, who came to America in the *Mayflower*, and John Brown, the abolitionist. She was born at Oak, Nebraska, November 22, 1887, and is a graduate of the University of Nebraska. Their children are: Montague Tinkham, born October 6, 1914; and Jack Rudolf, born July 12, 1917. Residence: St. Paul.

Albert Bernard Schuster

Albert Bernard Schuster, merchant at Virginia, Gage County, Nebraska, was born at Tecumseh, Nebraska, February 11, 1898, the son of Lawrence and Pauline Mary (Lempka) Schuster. His father, who was a farmer and dairyman, was born at Tecumseh, August 12, 1872, and is now living in Minnesota. His mother, whose ancestors were prominent in Germany for several generations, was born in Germany, September 12, 1872, and is still living.

Mr. Schuster was graduated from the Chokio High School in 1918, and was prominent in debating there. He served as class treasurer during his senior year. Later he attended the Sioux Falls Business College at Sioux Falls, South Dakota. He served as assistant cashier in the Farmers State Bank at Chokio, Minnesota, was head bookkeeper for the G. F. Bucke Company, in South Dakota, and at this time is president and manager of the Schuster Store at Virginia, Nebraska. He is director of the Virginia Cheese Company there.

Mr. Schuster is a strong supporter and promoter of progressive civic activities, and is now serving as president of the Virginia Commercial Club. He is secretary of the Chautauqua Association, was clerk of order in the Modern Woodmen of America for seven years, and for two years was township treasurer. He and his family attend the Christian Church. His hobby is reading history.

During the late war Mr. Schuster was assistant solicitor of government bond sales. He is an independent, politically.

His marriage to Nina Claire Burrows was solemnized at Adams, Gage County, Nebraska, June 25, 1924. Mrs. Schuster, whose ancestry is Scotch, Irish, and German, was born at Adams, March 19, 1901. She is vice president of the local Parent-Teachers' Association, and is a member of the Methodist Church of Adams. Their children are: Alberta, born May 17, 1925; Dean, born February 6, 1927; and Virginia, born September 30, 1929. Mr. Schuster is especially interested in biography. Residence: Virginia.

Henry Schwab

For the past 70 years Henry Schwab has lived in

Nebraska and for over 50 years has been engaged in farming in this state. He was born at Dellfeld, Reinish Bavaria, Germany, May 27, 1852. His father, Henry Schwab, was born in Bavaria, June 14, 1809 and died at Hooper, Nebraska, December 14, 1902, where he had been a farmer for many years. His mother was born at Dellfield December 16, 1816, and died at Hooper, February 27, 1902.

Mr. Schwab received his education in the public schools, and for the last 20 years he has been director of the school board, district 15 in Dodge County. He is a member of the Red Cross and the Nebraskana Society, a Mason, and a member of the Lutheran Church at Hooper. He is a Democrat, and in 1887 served as a member of the lower house of the Nebraska Legislature.

His marriage to Louisa Christina Weigle was solemnized at Fremont, Nebraska, June 2, 1874. Mrs. Schwab was born at Long Grove, Lake County, Illinois, July 16, 1855. Seven children were born to this union all of whom are living. They are: Minnie Hooper, born December 1, 1875, who married Henry Wagner; Harry, born April 22, 1877, who married Kate Schwein; Frank, born December 4, 1882, who married Anna Sommers; Edward, born August 21, 1885, who married Martha Bauer; Louise, born September 11, 1887, who married Peter Ewald; Robert, born March 25, 1893, who married Margaret Panning; and Elmer, born August 9, 1895, who married Ida Bolte. Residence: Hooper.

George Schwake

George Schwake, general manager of Grainger Brothers Company, is a native of Hannover, Germany, born on February 21, 1862, who came to Nebraska on June 27, 1879. He became a naturalized citizen in 1884. His father, Henry Schwake, was a farmer. George Schwake received his education principally in the public schools of Germany, although he attended school two winters in Lancaster County.

He was married to Mary D. Newton at Lincoln October 8, 1890. Mrs. Schwake was born at Princeton, Illinois, October 8, 1867, the daughter of Ezra Newton and Jane Ferguson Newton. She is a member of the P. E. O. Sisterhood, the Young Women's Christian Association, the Woman's Club and the Daughters of the American Revolution. There is one daughter, Florence, born October 20, 1891.

Mr. Schwake clerked in a general merchandise store from 1881-84; traveled on the road from 1884 to 1885; engaged in the retail grocery business from 1885 to 1886; served as assistant cashier of the German National Bank 1886-95. For the past thirty-five years he has been engaged in the wholesale grocery business as general manager of Grainger Brothers Company, in which he is also a director.

He is a member of St. Paul Methodist Church, the Chamber of Commerce, University Club, and the Masonic Orders. He enjoys golf and is interested in horticulture and farming. Residence: Lincoln. (Photograph in Album).

Mary Dell Schwake

Mary Dell Schwake, homemaker and clubwoman, was born in Bureau County, Illinois, October 8, 1867. She is the daughter of Francis Ezra and Jane (Ferguson) Newton. Her father was born at Marathon, Cortland County, New York, October 8, 1839, the son of Mary Tuttle and Caleb Newton. The family is descended from early English settlers in Amercia. Francis Newton was a farmer and business man, and served four years and six months in the Civil War with the rank of captain. His wife, Jane, was a native of Scotland, born in Glasgow, August 26, 1844. She died at Lincoln on March 10, 1923. Francis Newton died at Paden, Indian Territory, July 18, 1903.

Mrs. Schwake attended the Lincoln public and high schools and the University of Nebraska. Of her marriage on October 8, 1890, there is a daughter, Florence, born October 20, 1891. Mrs. Schwake is a member of the Daughters of the American Revolution and from 1916-18 was regent of Deborah Avery Chapter. She has been active for many years in the civic and educational life of Lincoln, and is a member of the Red Cross, the Lincoln Woman's Club (president 1912-14), the P. E. O. Sisterhood, the American Association of University Women and the Young Woman's Christian Association. She attends St. Paul's Methodist Episcopal Church. Residence: Lincoln. (Photograph in Album).

Elmore Charles Schweser

A leading merchant at Surprise, Nebraska, Elmore Charles Schweser was born at David City, on August 9, 1895, the son of John Carl and Linnie Adaline Schweser. His father, born in Mokena, Illinois, May 3, 1869, was a merchant who came to Nebraska, in 1886. His ancestry is German. Linnie Adaline Schweser was born in Ada, Ohio, April 24, 1876, of French parentage.

Elmore Schweser was graduated from David City High School in 1914, and then entered the University of Nebraska, remaining two years. In high school he earned a letter in athletics, and at the university was made a member of Delta Tau Delta and Xi Psi Phi. He is a graduate of the School of Military Aeronautics, situated at the University of Texas, and was commissioned an air pilot. In the World War he had eighteen months service with the rank of second lieutenant in the United States Army, was a member of the County Training Service, and is a charter member of Kregger Post No. 125 of the American Legion.

On January 2, 1921, Mr. Schweser was united in marriage to Theresa Nadine Dolgner, at Rising City. Mrs. Schweser, who was born at Rising City, August 19, 1898, was of German descent in the paternal line and Welch descent in the maternal line. She is a registered nurse, and is president of the Butler County Parent-Teachers' Association. Their only child, Vergene Gail, was born August 11, 1922.

Since the World War, Mr. Schweser has been engaged in the mercantile business, and at the present time is manager of Schweser's store at Surprise.

He is a Republican, a member of the Bethesda Baptist Church, the Red Cross and the Ancient Free and Accepted Masons. He is a member also of the Parent-Teachers' Association, the school board (treasurer), the Mid-Continent Retail Association, the Elks, Knights of Pythias and the State University Club. He is interested in football and golf and enjoys reading. He is a life member of the Nebraskana Society. Residence: Surprise. (Photograph in Album).

Ernest Sumner Scofield

Born at Blairstown, Iowa, February 22, 1872, Ernest Sumner Scofield is the son of R. H. and Charlotte (McDearman) Scofield. His father, born in Saratoga, New York, was a school teacher whose death occurred at Elgin, November 25, 1911. His ancestry was traced to Daniel Scofield who came from England to America with early Massachusetts colonists. Charlotte McDearman, also a teacher, was born in Chicago, and died at Madison, Nebraska, April 5, 1885.

Educated in the public schools at Syracuse, Nebraska, Mr. Scofield was graduated from high school in 1889 and from Western Normal College at Shenandoah, Iowa, in the class of 1891. For more than forty years he has been in the newspaper business in Antelope County, and is the founder of the *Elgin Review*, the *Neligh Register* and the *Neligh News*. He is at the present time co-editor with his son, Kenneth Alan, of the last mentioned paper. (*See Nebraskana*).

Mr. Scofield married Addie Lois Hodges, who was born at Owosso, Michigan, January 31, 1873. He is a

Democrat. Recently he was elected to life membership in the Nebraskana Society. Residence: Neligh.

Kenneth Alan Scofield

Born at Elgin, Nebraska, April 5, 1896, Kenneth Alan Scofield is the son of Ernest Sumner and Addie Lois (Hodges) Scofield. The father, born at Blairstown, Iowa, February 22, 1872, has been a newspaper publisher in Antelope County for more than forty years. He is descended from Daniel Scofield, an early Massachusetts settler. Addie Lois Hodges was born in Owosso, Michigan, January 31, 1873.

Kenneth Alan Scofield was graduated from Neligh High School in 1916, received his Bachelor of Arts degree from the University of Nebraska with the class of 1925, and from September 1916 to January 1917, attended Mechanics Institute at Cincinnati, Ohio. While in the university he was a member of the University Press Club, and was elected to Sigma Delta Chi. He is a member of Xi chapter of Alpha Sigma Phi.

On May 19, 1926, he was married to Nell Kathleen Whalen at Lincoln. Mrs. Scofield, a teacher prior to marriage, was born at St. Joseph, Missouri, December 19, 1901. She graduated from the University of Nebraska in 1924, and holds the degree of Bachelor of Arts. She is a member of Mu chapter of the Theta Phi Alpha. There are four children, Eleanor, born March 28, 1927; Alan, born June 8, 1928; Martin, born April 2, 1930; and Joel, born April 29, 1931.

Mr. Scofield is co-editor with his father of the *Neligh News*, and is president of the News Publishing Company, Inc. He is a Democrat. From July 6, 1917, to January 29, 1919, he served in the United States Navy on board the *U. S. S. Huntington*. In 1928 Mr. Scofield held the office of commander of American Legion Post No. 172.

A Mason, he was master of Trowel Lodge No. 71, Ancient Free and Accepted Masons in 1931-32. He was a member of the board of directors of the Rotary Club in 1930, and served as president of the Chamber of Commerce in 1929. He is a member of the Nebraskana Society and the Neligh Country Club. He enjoys football, baseball, and volley ball. Residence: Neligh.

Hazel T. Scoggin

Hazel T. Scoggin, treasurer of Morrill County since 1923, was born at Albion, Nebraska, July 31, 1888, daughter of Harvey L. and Sarah Louisa (Romine) Scoggin.

Her father was born in Piatt County, Illinois, March 15, 1858, and is a retired dentist, of English and Scotch descent. During the late war, he was county chairman of the dental examining board. His wife, Sarah, was born at Urbana, Illinois, July 27, 1860, and is prominent in church and civic affairs. She was district chairman of the Council of Defense during the World War, and also district chairman of a Liberty loan drive. She is descended from English Puritans, who came over on the Mayflower.

Miss Scoggin first attended grade school at Norfolk, Nebraska, next at Rantoul, Illinois, and later at Bridgeport, Nebraska. She was a member of the first graduating class of Bridgeport High School.

Her career has been interesting and varied. Beginning as a saleswoman, buyer and bookkeeper in various businesses, she was later an associate editor on a country newspaper. Later she served as deputy county treasurer and has held her present position for nine years. She is a Republican.

A member of the State County Treasurer's Association, she has held various offices in that organization. She is chairman of the business and professional women's department and active in the music department of the Bridgeport Woman's Club, and is past noble grand of

the Rebekah Lodge. Miss Scoggin homesteaded in western Nebraska under the Kinkaid Act. She is active in the Presbyterian Church. Residence: Bridgeport.

Allen Cecil Scott

Allen C. Scott was born at Omaha, August 16, 1882, son of William Wilbur and Elizabeth Scott. His father, born at New Cumberland, Ohio, December 12, 1855, died at Omaha, November 24, 1909. His father was a native of Belfast, Ireland while his mother was born in Ohio. Elizabeth, wife of William Scott, was born at St. Joseph, Missouri, June 26, 1865. Known as Mother Scott, she has been cateress at the Masonic Temple at Omaha for the past twenty-four years.

Upon the completion of his studies in the Omaha public schools Allen C. Scott entered the business world. He early made his mark in the business life of Omaha, and now is president of the Scott Omaha Tent and Awning Company, and the Scott Manufacturing Company, president of the Seattle Tent and Awning Company, president of the Stroud Road Machinery Company and the Little Red Wagon Manufacturing Company.

He was first married to Myra E. Smith who died February 28, 1919, leaving one adopted child, Jane Elizabeth, born December 23, 1915. On May 21, 1920, he was married to Gladys Thornton at Kansas City Kansas. Mrs. Scott was born at Thurman, Iowa, July 26, 1899. They have two children, Flora Catherine, born July 10, 1922, and Nina, born November 3, 1924.

During the World War Mr. Scott manufactured several million dollars worth of equipment for the government and operated seven plants engaged in this work, and was active in most drives, and was chairman of one Red Cross Drive.

He is a member of the National Tent and Awning Manufacturers Association and served as its president in 1918-19; was treasurer of the Nebraska Manufacturers Association for nine years, and was president of the Omaha Manufacturers Association in 1920. Mr. Scott also served as president of the Omaha Chamber of Commerce from 1922-23. He is a Mason and member of the Shrine, and a member of the Woodmen of the World.

He is president of the Municipal Baseball Association, 1930-31, composed of boys and men of amateur standing representing business houses.

His clubs include the Happy Hollow Country Club of which he is a director, the Seattle Golf Club, and the Omaha Athletic Club. His sports are golf and fishing. Residence: Omaha.

Anna Marie Scott

Born in New York, New York, November 20, 1849, Anna Marie Scott is the daughter of Patrick and Margaret (Nevill) Donahue. Her father, who was born in Dublin, Ireland, in 1820, was descended from a line of merchants. He himself was a farmer, and a Progressive in politics. His death occurred at Symerton, Illinois, in October, 1896. His wife, also a native of Ireland, died in New York City November 20, 1849. She was a teacher.

Anna Marie Scott received her education in the public schools of New York and Illinois. In October, 1871 she removed her family to Kansas, and since 1893 has been a resident of Nebraska. Her marriage to Edward Scott was solemnized at Symerton, on May 17, 1866. Mr. Scott, born at Belfast, September 14, 1845, was a farmer and stockman until his death at Hardy on August 4, 1907.

Of their marriage there are five children living and one deceased. Imogene, born March 29, 1869, married Frank E. Browning; Henry, born February 1, 1874, married Minnie Adaline Cramer, and died in 1930; Evalyn, born March 15, 1876, married Theodore Boehm; Pearl, born November 29, 1878, married C. L. Cramer; and Guy, born April 23, 1883, is unmarried.

Mrs. Scott is a Democrat. Affiliated with the Methodist Episcopal Church, she is a member of its Kensington Society, and in addition is a member of the Red Cross, the Woman's Club, the Rebakahs and the Security Benefit Association. She was recently made a life member of the Nebraskana Society. Residence: Hardy.

Arthur Inness Scott

Arthur Inness Scott, was born at Shelby, Nebraska, April 5, 1896, and has lived there all his life. His father, William Hugh Scott, who is a farmer, was born at Galesburg, Illinois, January 12, 1869, of Scotch parentage. His mother, Margaret Isabella (Inness) Scott, was born in Indiana, October 2, 1872; her parents were natives of England.

Mr. Scott is a director of the Shelby Co-operative Oil Company. He is affiliated with the Methodist Church of Shelby, was president of the Shelby Commercial Club for three years, and is a member of the Independent Order of Odd Fellows and the Nebraskana Society.

During the World War, Mr. Scott was a private for thirteen months in 838th Aero Squadron, and served nine months overseas. He is now finance officer of Post No. 296 of the American Legion and is a member of the Red Cross. He is serving his eleventh year as a member of the board of trustees of Shelby, and is treasurer of the board of trustees of the Shelby public schools. He is interested in all out-of-door sports and likes to farm.

On March 3, 1922, he was married to Dorothy Jane Reece at David City, Nebraska. Mrs. Scott was born at Maywood, Nebraska, September 12, 1897. They have two children: Stanley, born August 8, 1923; and Arthur, born April 10, 1927. Residence: Shelby.

Carrie Edith Scott

Carrie Edith Scott, daughter of a pioneer family was born in Genoa, Illinois, February 17, 1868. Her father, Charles Henry Moore, was born in Genoa, April 12, 1838. His father was one of the first settlers of De Kalb County, Illinois, in 1835. Later her father came to Nebraska where he was a prominent pioneer farmer, and died at Meadow Grove on January 3, 1919. His wife, Charlotte Athelia Doud, was born in Braceville, Ohio, May 20, 1841, and died at Meadow Grove August 29, 1913. She was of English descent.

Educated in the early day schools of Nebraska, Carrie Edith Moore taught six years on a second grade certificate. On December 10, 1889, she was united in marriage to Ira Jay Scott, a farmer, at Neligh. Mr. Scott, who was born at New London, Ohio, June 30, 1863, died at Meadow Grove on January 21, 1929.

There are six children, Fay, born March 4, 1891, who married Murl William Dow, and who died June 24, 1929; Nora, born September 10, 1895, who married Irvin L. Cloud, and who died October 23, 1926; Bernice, born August 30, 1898, wife of Melvin W. Kinne; Lillian, born October 25, 1900, who married Albert Schulz; Laurence, born October 26, 1901, who married Ruth Braun; and Evelyn, born March 19, 1906, who married William Burleigh Sesler. All were graduated from high school, some were teachers before marriage, and Laurence is a farmer.

Mrs. Scott, a resident of Nebraska nearly fifty years, is known throughout her entire community as an interested participant in the development of Nebraska. Recently she was elected to life membership in the Nebraskana Society in recognition of her efforts in the development of her state. She is affiliated with the Meadow Grove Methodist Episcopal Church and is a member of the Jefferson Homemakers, a country Club. Residence: Meadow Grove.

Harry William Scott

On July 3, 1891, Harry W. Scott was born at Pawnee City, Nebraska, the son of William and Jennie (Loch) Scott. His father was born in Scotland, January 20,

1848, and came to America with his parents in 1858. He was for many years a farmer in Pawnee County, where he died April 8, 1924. His mother was born in Illinois, July 3, 1855, the daughter of Scotch parents. She is living in Pawnee County now.

Mr. Scott received his education in the Pawnee County rural schools; was graduated from the Pawnee City High School; and was a student at Peru State Teachers College, 1912-13. From 1913 to 1916 he was principal of the schools at Virginia, Nebraska. He served as county clerk of Pawnee County, 1917-21; was assistant tax commissioner of Nebraska, 1921-23-25-29; was state tax commissioner, 1929-31; and was secretary of the Republican state committee from 1926 to 1928.

Now tax commissioner for the Northern Natural Gas Company and their affiliated companies, he is also a director of the American Thrift Assurance Company of Omaha, Nebraska.

He was united in marriage with Maud Elizabeth Hallingworth at Beatrice, Nebraska, August 25, 1915. Mrs. Scott, who was born at Beatrice July 18, 1890, was a school teacher before her marriage. Their children are: Clifford, born June 16, 1916; and Harold, born December 20, 1918.

Mr. Scott is a member of the Masons, Knight Templars, Chapter, Scottish Rite and Shrine. Residence: Lincoln.

Perlee W. Scott

A leading lawyer at McCook, Perlee W. Scott was born near Kirksville, Iowa, July 24, 1860, son of William and Martha (Biglow) Scott. William Scott, born in Londonderry, Ireland, April 27, 1798, came to America in 1800, where he became a minister. He died at Oskaloosa, Iowa, April 18, 1899. His wife, born at Fremont, Ohio, died at Oskaloosa, in 1864, when Perlee W. Scott was a small child. She was of Pennsylvania-Dutch descent.

Perlee W. Scott attended school at Oskaloosa, and the Parsons College at Fairfield, Iowa. Coming to Nebraska in February, 1885, he was admitted to the bar the following year, and from 1887 to 1920 practiced at Imperial, Nebraska. A Progressive Republican, he has held various public offices, among them, city treasurer 1889-90, city councilman 1903-15; city attorney 1915-20, member of the board of education 1905-20; county attorney 1899-1921, member of the constitutional convention of 1919-20; and state senator 1925-33.

On November 6, 1892, Mr. Scott was married to Jessie Ware at Imperial, Nebraska. She was born at Malvern, Iowa, August 28, 1867, and died at Imperial on July 1, 1917. A devoted wife and mother, she left three children who trace through her to Colonial ancestors. They are Roland, born October 3, 1893, who is in partnership with his father at McCook; Coryl, born March 25, 1895; and Judson, born April 3, 1899.

Mr. Scott served as member or chairman of all wartime drive committees. He is a member of the Nebraska State and Fourteenth District Bar Associations, the Chamber of Commerce, and the Young Men's Christian Association. He attends the Methodist Episcopal Church, is a member of the Ancient Free and Accepted Masons, the Royal Arch and Royal and Select Masters and the Odd Fellows. He is a member also of the Nebraska State Historical Society, the Southwestern Nebraska Historical Society and a life member of The Nebraskana Society. His social club is the McCook Country Club. Mr. Scott plays a good game of golf, enjoys fishing and attends baseball, basketball and football games. Residence: McCook.

Thaddeus Marvin Scott

Thaddeus Marvin Scott, was born at Nevada, Illinois, September 25, 1869, son of George Henry and Elizabeth (Hardy) Scott, the youngest of nine children.

The father was born in Fulton County, New York,

October 26, 1828, and died at Loup City, Nebraska, April 13, 1903. In his early life he was a paper manufacturer, later pioneering in Illinois, locating on a farm near now the City of Dwight, Illinois, and in 1880 moving fifty miles beyond a railroad to Sherman County, Nebraska, where he engaged in the cattle business. He was of Scotch and Dutch ancestry. The mother, Elizabeth, was born at Little Falls, New York, May 3, 1827, and died at Loup City, October 18, 1909. She attended a girl's seminary at Little Falls. Her father was an inventor and mechanic of Yankee descent.

Mr. Scott attended the pioneer country school and the Loup City High School. Thereafter attended the Western Normal College at Shenandoah, Iowa, graduating from the Western Normal College at Lincoln, Nebraska, in 1893.

On August 1, 1894, he was married to Daisy E. Childre, at Aurora. She was born at Delphi, Carroll County, Indiana, August 2, 1875, and died at Aurora, February 22, 1919. She was of German and French descent. There were four children of this marriage, L'Maree born December 7, 1895, educated in the Aurora public schools, Hastings College and the State Normal School at Kearney, Nebraska, and is the wife of Clarence A. Kemper; Dr. Hardy W. born February 18, 1897, educated in the Aurora public schools and the University of Nebraska, whose wife was Ruth Logue; Robert Allan, born August 10, 1899, educated in the Aurora public schools and the University of Nebraska; whose wife was Ruth Adams; and Josephine, born July 1, 1908, educated in the Aurora public schools, a graduate of Hastings College in 1930.

Mr. Scott is a Democrat. While at normal school at Lincoln, he was president of the Republican club. Resigning that position, he affiliated himself with the Democratic party. He was a member of the Nebraska legislature in 1913, and in 1915, elected on the Democratic ticket, and from 1922 until 1924, served as mayor of Aurora. Since January, 1925, he has been county judge of Hamilton County.

Raised on a farm, Mr. Scott became a teacher and superintendent of schools and studied law. In 1897, Mr. Scott's health became impaired from inside work and he took up the occupation of farming and stock raising, locating in Hamilton County, where he became active in civic and political affairs, being one of the organizers of the Aurora Elevator Company, one of the largest co-operative grain and milling businesses in the state, he holding the positions of president, vice president, salesman and business manager at various times. He has also served a number of terms on the board of directors of the Hamilton County Telephone Association. Mr. Scott has been a pioneer in the development of Nebraska, always allying himself with the progress and welfare of his adopted state.

Mr. Scott is affiliated with the First Presbyterian Church of Aurora, is a member of the Rotary Club, and the Royal Highlanders. Residence: Aurora. (Photograph in Album).

Edward Lees Scow

Edward L. Scow was born at Prague, Saunders County, Nebraska, April 4, 1891. His father, Christian Scow, who is a retired farmer, was born in Norway, July 21, 1848, and came to this country in 1870. His mother, Annie (Lees) Scow, was born at Mount Vernon, Iowa, March 23, 1858, of English parentage.

Mr. Scow received his education in a pioneer country school in Saunders County. He has always lived in Nebraska, and is now a farmer in Polk County. He holds membership in the Methodist Church of Shelby, the Nebraskana Society, and the Masons, and is moderator of the local school board. During the World War he served as secretary of the War Savings Society and was a member of the home guard. His hobby is reading.

On December 16, 1913, he was married to Anna Louise Christensen, who was born at Wahoo, Nebraska, December 13, 1889, and died at Shelby, June 21, 1917. Two children were born to this marriage: Lloyd, born December 16, 1914; and Louis, June 21, 1917. His marriage to Minne Juanita Berger occurred at Shelby, August 24, 1921. To this union two children were born: Annie Laura, born November 13, 1922, who died October 30, 1924; and Kenneth Berger, born May 2, 1928. Residence: Shelby.

Frederick J. Scow

Frederick J. Scow was born at Prague, Saunders County, Nebraska, September 6, 1885, the son of Christian and Annie (Lees) Scow. His father, who is a farmer and stock raiser, was born in Norway, July 21, 1848, and came to America in 1870, settling near Prague. At one time he owned and managed five hundred acres of land in Saunders County and adjoining territory. He was an expert seal hunter in Norway.

His mother was born at West Branch, Iowa, March 23, 1858, of English parentage. Her father, who liked to travel, made 13 trips across the ocean to visit his old home.

Mr. Scow was a student at Fremont Business College for a time. He is a member of the Masons, Eastern Star, and the Nebraskana Society. For the past 11 years he has been a member of the local school board.

He was married to Nellie Gertrude Roberts, December 29, 1909, at Cedar Bluffs, Nebraska. Mrs. Scow, who was a teacher before her marriage, was born at Cedar Bluffs, May 25, 1886. Five children were born to this marriage: Frederick, born March 3, 1911; Roland, born May 29, 1916; Eleanor, born February 14, 1918; Richard, born December 13, 1921, who died December 22, 1921; and David, born May 13, 1925. Frederick was a student at the University of Nebraska School of Agriculture for a year. Residence: Shelby.

Oliver Christian Scow

Oliver C. Scow, farmer and stock feeder, was born near Prague, Saunders County, Nebraska, October 20, 1879. His father, Christian Scow, was born in Norway, July 21, 1848, and is now a retired farmer and feeder, living at Wahoo, Nebraska. Annie (Lees) Scow, mother of Oliver C., was born in Iowa, March 23, 1858, and is living at Wahoo, Nebraska.

After attending a country school, Mr. Scow was a student at the Lutheran College of Wahoo, during the winter terms of 1904 and 1905.

His marriage to Clara May Christiensen was solemnized at Wahoo, December 28, 1909. She was born at Wahoo, August 1, 1885, of English and Norwegian descent. They have three children, Dale, born October 16, 1912; and twins, Ellen and Bessie, born October 5, 1915.

Mr. Scow has been a resident of Nebraska his entire life. He is affiliated with the Methodist Episcopal Church of Shelby, Nebraska. He is a member of the Red Cross and The Nebraskana Society. Residence: Shelby.

Benjamin Franklin Scroggin

Born at Mount Pulaski, Illinois, December 25, 1862, son of Leonard Kerby and Lavina (Buckels) Scroggin. His father, who was born at Schawnytown, Illinois, January 25, 1819, was a banker. His Scotch ancestors came to America before the Revolutionary War, and his father served in the Army. Leonard Scroggin died at Mount Pulaski, August 19, 1916. His wife was born at Mount Pulaski in 1827, and died there January 20, 1863.

Benjamin Franklin Scroggin attended public school in Illinois, and came to Nebraska in 1887. On March 1 of that year he was united in marriage to Arthilda E. Gasaway at Illiopolis, Illinois. Mrs. Scroggin was born at Illiopolis on January 17, 1866, of German and Welsh ancestry.

To them were born three children, Grover G., born February 22, 1888, who married Edith Allen; John L., born November 16, 1890, who married Artha Jones; and Doris E., born December 28, 1894, who married W. A. Schumacher. One is a banker, one a grain and cattle dealer.

Mr. Scroggin has extensive farm, cattle and grain interests, and is president of the Scroggin Bank at Oak, which he founded in 1898. He and his children are Democrats. He is affiliated with the Masons and Modern Woodmen of America, and is a life member of the Nebraskana Society. He was a delegate to the Democratic National Convention in 1912. He holds an interest in station KFEQ radio station at St. Joseph, Missouri, which was the 3rd station on the air in Nebraska where it was originally located. Residence: Oak.

Fred S. Seacrest

Fred S. Seacrest, business manager and vice president of the *Nebraska State Journal*, has lived in this state all his life, and is today outstanding in civic achievement. He was born at Lincoln, Lancaster County, Nebraska, July 17, 1895, the son of J. C. and Jessie E. (Snively) Seacrest. His father, who was born in Pennsylvania, is the publisher of the *Nebraska State Journal* at Lincoln; his ancestry is Pennsylvania Dutch. His mother, who was born at Shady Grove, Pennsylvania, is a member of the Daughters of the American Revolution.

Mr. Seacrest was graduated from the Prescott High School and attended the University of Nebraska; and was a student at Columbia University, School of Journalism at New York City. He holds membership in Sigma Delta Chi and Delta Upsilon. During the late war he served in the United States Army, and is now a member of the American Legion. He is a member of the Nebraska Art Association; the Lincoln Chamber of Commerce; the Lincoln Kiwanis Club; the Young Men's Christian Association; and the Nebraskana Society. He holds membership in the Lincoln University Club; the Lincoln Country Club; the Lincoln Garden Club; Modern Woodmen of America; Ancient Free and Accepted Masons, Scottish Rite, Shrine; and the Red Cross. He is affiliated with the First Plymouth Congregational Church of Lincoln. He is a Republican.

Of his marriage to Dorris Tilton there are three children: Mark T.; Jessie Ann and June. Residence: Lincoln.

Thelma Whitney Sealock

Thelma Whitney Sealock, fiction and article writer of Lincoln, Lancaster County, Nebraska, was born at Lowell, Washington County, Ohio, May 8, 1903. Her father, William Elmer Sealock, who is a noted educator was born at Zanesville, Ohio, February 9, 1877; he served as dean of the University of Nebraska Teachers College, and is now president of Omaha University; he is a Rotarian, and holds membership in Phi Beta Kappa, and Chi Delta Kappa; his Scotch ancestors settled in Virginia in early colonial days.

Her mother, Nancy (Whitney) Sealock, was born at McConnelsville, Morgan County, Ohio, April 27, 1880. She is a prominent clubwoman and writer, was the organizer of the Teachers College Club of the University of Nebraska, and holds membership in the Quill Club, the American Association of University Women, and the Eastern Star. Her English and Irish ancestors came to America and settled in New England during the colonial days.

Miss Sealock attended the public schools of Ohio, and was graduated from the high school at Oxford, Ohio, in June, 1917. She was awarded the A. B. degree at the University of Nebraska, 1921, and the A. M. degree, 1922, and was a student at the Iowa State College at Ames, Iowa, 1918-19, 1919-20. She was active in journalistic work in college, was vice president of the freshman class, secretary of the sophomore class, and held membership in Alpha Delta Pi and Chi Delta Phi. She served as president, secretary, and reporter of the local alumnae association.

She is the author of stories published at various times since 1924, articles for school papers, western magazines, and trade journals. Recently, she has been writing plays; three of her plays have been staged, the others having been sold to publishing houses.

Miss Sealock holds membership in the Quill Club of which she is now president. She is a member of the Nebraska Writers Guild, is a member of the temple chapter of the Eastern Star, and holds membership in the American Association of University Women. Together with the rest of her family she is a member of the University Club of Lincoln, and the Eastridge Country Club. Her sports include golfing, hiking, and swimming. Her interests are reading and writing, while her hobby is painting furniture.

She is a Republican. Recently she was elected to membership in the Nebraskana Society. Residence: Lincoln.

Willis G. Sears

Willis G. Sears, prominent Nebraska lawyer and former United States congressman, was born at Willoughby, Ohio, August 16, 1860. He is the son of Stephen S. and Mary (Wilson) Sears.

His father was born in Columbus, Pennsylvania in 1827, and died at Willoughby, in November, 1861. His mother was born at Meadville in 1830, of Scotch descent, and died in 1922.

Mr. Sears attended public school, and was admitted to the practice of law in Nebraska at Tekamah in 1884. He engaged in the active practice of his profession at Tekamah until 1904, during six years of which time he was county attorney. From 1901 until 1904 he was a member of the Nebraska house of representatives and was speaker of the house in 1901. He also served three terms as mayor of Tekamah.

He was judge of the 3rd judicial district of Nebraska from January, 1904 until March, 1923, and in November, 1922 was elected representative of the second Nebraska congressional district. In 1924, 1926, 1928, he was again elected. Since 1915 Mr. Sears has made his residence at Omaha. He is a member of the Nebraska State Bar Association, the Masons, Knights Templars, Scottish Rite and Shrine, and is past exalted ruler of the Elks.

In May, 1887, he was married to Belle Virginia Hoadley. She was born at Onawa, Iowa, in 1865, and died at Tekamah in May, 1902. His children are, Edgar A., who married Margaret Atkins; Mable, who resides at Leavenworth, Kansas; Flora, who married Henry A. Nelson; Sigsby S., who is a physician; and Charles, who resides at Council Bluffs. Residence: Omaha.

August Theodore Seashore

A leading educator and clergyman in Nebraska is August Theodore Seashore, who has been prominent in religious and school activities for over 20 years. He was born at Dayton, Iowa, December 24, 1871, the son of Carl Gustaf and Emily Charlotte (Swenson) Seashore. Carl Gustaf Seashore, who was a carpenter and also a minister, was born in Sweden in 1839, and died at Dayton, Iowa, March 24, 1897. He came to this country in

1812. His mother was born in Sweden in 1844, and died at Dayton in 1912.

Dr. Seashore attended grade school in Boone County, Iowa, was graduated from Gust. Ad. Academy and School of Commerce in 1892, and has received the following degrees: A. B., 1900; B. D., 1903; and D. D., 1924. From 1903 to 1906 he was pastor at Swea City, Iowa, from 1906 to 1911 he was instructor in Minnesota College, and since 1915 he has been president of Luther College. For five years he published *Our Church,* a religious pamphlet, and for over 30 years has been a contributor to newspapers and weekly magazines.

He is a member of the Wahoo Chamber of Commerce, the Ministerium of Augustana Synod, and the Nebraskana Society. His hobby is lectures. Dr. Seashore's political affiliation is with the Republican party.

His marriage to Jennie Caroline Rose was solemnized at Marine Mills, Minnesota, September 2, 1903. Mrs. Seashore, whose ancestors were millwrights, was born at Marine on St. Croix, Minnesota, December 29, 1878. Six children were born to their union: Rosel, December 17, 1904; Harold, August 4, 1906; Mauritz, January 6, 1908; Selma, 1912; Stanley, April 4, 1915; and Sylvia, October 7, 1919. Rosel is a student at the University of Minnesota where he will receive the M. D. degree in 1932. Harold received his Masters degree at the University of Iowa and is now working for the Ph. D. degree at the University of Iowa. Mauritz is studying botany and biology at the University of Minnesota where he expects to receive the Ph. D. degree. Residence: Wahoo.

Laurence Froyd Seaton

Laurence Froyd Seaton was born at Seaton, Illinois, March 26, 1887, the son of John Henry and Ida Jane (Palmer) Seaton. His father, a farmer, was born at Seaton, August 25, 1854, and died at Bancroft, Nebraska, August 6, 1906; his ancestry was Scotch. His mother was born at Keithsburg, Illinois, October 24, 1860, and died at Fremont, on June 25, 1926. She was active in club work, especially in the Masonic Order.

Mr. Seaton was graduated from the Bancroft High School in 1906; was awarded the B. S. degree in Mechanical Engineering at the University of Nebraska, in 1911; and in 1919 received the M. E. degree at the latter institution. He was elected to membership in Sigma Tau, Sigma Xi, and Gamma Sigma Delta, at the University of Nebraska.

He served as assistant professor at the University of Nebraska, 1912; professor, 1915; head of the department of mechanical engineering, 1917-18; chief engineer for Patriot Motors Company, 1918-20; and since that date has served as operating superintendent at the University of Nebraska. He is the author of a thesis on mechanical engineering published in the *American Society of Mechanical Engineers,* 1920. He has lived in Nebraska for the past 30 years.

During the recent war Mr. Seaton was in charge of training for engineering students at the University of Nebraska. He was president of the National Educational Buyer's Association, 1925, and secretary, 1923-24; is a member of the Chamber of Commerce at Lincoln, has been a member of the Lincoln Rotary Club since 1920; and holds membership in the Nebraskana Society. He is a Mason, Scottish Rite, Shrine; and his social club is the University Club of Lincoln. His hobby is mechanics.

His marriage to Pearl F. Erwin was solemnized at Bancroft, July 24, 1911. Mrs. Seaton was born at Bancroft, July 16, 1892. They have two children: Marjorie Elizabeth, born January 5, 1915; and Wanda Juanita, born July 19, 1920. Mr. Seaton is a Republican. Residence: Lincoln.

Premysl Otto Sedivy

As an agricultural executive and farmer, Premysl Otto Sedivy has been prominent for 30 years at Verdi-gre, Nebraska. He was born at Verdigre, March 6, 1881, the son of Joseph Paul and Marie (Jecminek) Sedivy. His father was a blacksmith and farmer who was a gifted writer and theatrical manager in his early years, contributing to magazines at various times; he was the author of *Recollections of Pioneer Times;* he was born at Numburk, Bohemia, October 28, 1856, and died at Verdigre, December 13, 1918.

His mother, who held prominent offices in the W. B. F. A. Lodge, was born at Pisek, Bohemia, and died at Gregory, South Dakota, November 18, 1929. She was a talented actress and made several theatrical appearances prior to her marriage.

Mr. Sedivy attended public school at Omaha, Verdigre, and in Virginia. He was a student at the University of Nebraska Agricultural College in 1901 and 1902 where he was active in debating and held membership in the Literary Society. He was a farmer until 1916 when he became assistant manager and president of the board of directors of the Farmers Co-operative Association. In 1919 he was made general manager of the latter organization, and today holds that position in addition to acting as mayor of Verdigre.

He served as director of rural schools from 1913 to 1916, was a member of the Young Men's Christian Association during his college days, and is now a member of the Chamber of Commerce, Red Cross, the Odd Fellows, and W. B. F. A. His hobby is baseball.

His marriage to Bessie Elenora Liske occurred at Verdigre, January 18, 1905. Mrs. Sedivy, whose parents were pioneer Nebraskans, was born at Niobrara, Nebraska, January 28, 1884. They have two children: Edmund, born December 16, 1911, who is in school; and Irvin, born July 26, 1921, who is a student in grade school. Edmund is a teacher and musician, and is talented in dramatic work. Residence: Verdigre.

William Alson Selleck

A resident of Nebraska for more than forty-six years, William Alson Selleck has had an interesting and varied career. He was born at Owatonna, Minnesota, May 30, 1857, the son of Alson and Mary Antoinet (Kent) Selleck. Alson Selleck was born at Potsdam, New York, December 20, 1823. A farmer and Republican leader, he traced his ancestry to David Selleck, the apparent head of the Selleck family in America. David Selleck, who lived in Boston, was born in 1638, and died in 1663. The name, which is Cornish-British, is first mentioned in 1086. Alson Selleck died at Owatonna, January 26, 1902. His wife, Mary A. Kent, born at Parishville, New York, December 31, 1831, was of the English family of Kent, which settled early in America. She died at Owatonna, April 14, 1895.

William Alson Selleck attended country district school and was graduated from the Owatonna High School. He received his A. B. and B. L. degrees from Carleton College at Northfield, Minnesota, in 1882. He was elected to membership in Phi Beta Kappa, was valedictorian of his class in 1882, and is a member of Phi Kappa Psi.

Upon his admission to the bar in 1884 at Owatonna, he entered the practice of law and was a member of the law firms of Selleck and Lane, and Abbott, Selleck and Lane from 1885 to 1897. On November 26, 1888, he was united in marriage to Nellie Woolworth Horton of Calais, Maine, at Lincoln. There are three children, John K., born October 9, 1889, who married Ardene Hammond, and who is manager of student activities at the University of Nebraska; Marjorie C., born January 25, 1890, who married George E. Clark; and Anna H., born December 17, 1892, who died June 21, 1894.

Three years prior to his marriage Mr. Selleck removed to Lincoln, where he has since lived. From 1909 to 1917 he was a partner and manager of the Western Supply Company, and from 1917 to 1923 he was president of the Lincoln State Bank. Since 1923 he has served as president of the Lincoln National Bank and Trust Company. He is also assistant trust officer of the Continental National Bank, member of the board of directors of the Midwest Life Insurance Company, the Lincoln Joint Stock Land Bank, the Fremont Joint Stock Land Bank, the Bailey Sanitarium, and the State Securities Co., of which last he is chairman of the board. He is also president of the Homestead Bond and Mortgage Company and the American Savings and Loan Association.

During his residence in Nebraska Mr. Selleck has been active in politics and has held various offices. He was elected state senator in 1911 and was unsuccessful candidate for nomination for Congress in 1912 and again in 1924. In 1920 he was a member of the Constitutional Convention and served as state delegate to the Republican National Convention in 1920.

Mr. Selleck has been active in civic affairs for many years, and among other things served as first secretary of the charity organization now known as the Social Welfare Society. He was president of this society in 1900. One of the early members of the Chamber of Commerce, formerly the Commercial Club, he was president of that organization during 1910-11. From 1900 to 1909 he was a member of the Lincoln School board, serving as president of the board in 1906. He is also a member of the board of trustees of Doane College, and has served as president of the board. Since 1904 he has been a member of the Young Men's Christian Association, and during 1917-18 was president of its board. He was a four minute speaker during the World War.

Mr. Selleck's religious affiliation is with the First Plymouth Congregational Church of Lincoln. He is a Mason and a member of the Woodmen of the World, the Nebraska State Historical Society and the Nebraskana Society. His clubs are the University and the Candle Light Clubs. Residence: Lincoln.

John Peter Senning

John Peter Senning, leading educator of Lincoln, Lancaster County, Nebraska, was born at Rotenburg, Hesse, Germany, August 4, 1883. His father, Wilehlm Senning, was of German descent.

Dr. Senning was awarded the A. B. degree at Union College, Le Mars, Iowa, 1908, where he was president of the senior class and class orator, and the Ph. D. degrees at the University of Illinois, 1924. He was a student at the University of Minnesota, University of Chicago, and Yale University, at various times. He is a member of Phi Alpha Delta.

He has held the following positions: secretary of the Chamber of Commerce, Middletown, Connecticut, 1913-14; an instructor in history and political science at Wesleyan University, Middletown, Connecticut, 1912-14; instructor in history and political science at Illinois College, 1910-11; the same position at the University of Nebraska, where he acted as instructor in American history, 1916. Since 1917 he has been instuctor in political science. He served as a member of the Preliminary Survey Commission for the Constitutional Convention of Nebraska, 1919-20, and was a member of the executive council for the American Political Science Association. He is at present professor of political science and chairman of the department at the University of Nebraska.

Dr. Senning is the author of *Party Disintegration in Illinois, 1850-60* (published in the Illinois State Historical Journal, 1912); *Administrative Reorganization in Nebraska* (published in the American Political Science Review, 1919); *Nebraska Constitutional Convention* (published in the National Municipal Review, 1920), the *Evaluation of Administrative Reorganization in Nebraska* (published in the National Municipal Review, 1923; *and Status of Home Rule in Nebraska* (1932).

He is a member of the Lincoln Chamber of Commerce, the American Political Science Association, and the Nebraskana Society. He is a Mason, and is a member of the Republican party. Dr. Senning's social club is the Lincoln University Club.

On June 13, 1913, he was united in marriage with Elizabeth Anna Stone at Joliet, Will County, Illinois. Mrs. Senning was born at Joliet, December 2, 1884; her English ancestors were among the first settlers in Connecticut in 1639. She is connected with the research department of the Nebraska Legislative Reference Bureau, and active in the League of Women Voters. Residence: Lincoln.

Ansel R. Settell

For several years Ansel R. Settell has been engaged in the practice of dentistry at Bloomfield, Nebraska. He was born at Ellsworth, Kansas, January 26, 1885, the son of Robert Philip and Helen (Valeau) Settell, the former a farmer who was born at Toronto, Canada, December 16, 1837, and died at Thurman, Iowa, February 19, 1925. His mother was born in Michigan in 1848 and died at Thurman, August 1, 1927.

Dr. Settell was graduated from the high school at Thurman in 1903, and in 1906 received the degree D. D. S. at the University of Iowa. He practiced dentistry at Crofton, Nebraska for a year and since then has been successful at Bloomfield. He is a member of the Methodist Church and holds membership in the Nebraskana Society.

On January 23, 1908, he married Bertha Mae Leigh at Sioux City, Iowa. Mrs. Settell was born at Chillicothe, Illinois, January 16, 1889. Their children are: Philip L., born April 29, 1909; Reynolds G., born December 16, 1912; Robert Louis, born July 8, 1915; and Marjorie Mae, born November 7, 1925. Residence: Bloomfield.

George Newton Seymour

One of Nebraska's outstanding bankers and executives, George Newton Seymour, now retired, was born at Gloversville, New York, May 7, 1865. His father, James Harvey Seymour, was born in New York State, February 20, 1822, and died at Meriden, Connecticut, July 5, 1896. A practicing dentist at Gloversville for twenty-five years, he was later in life in the lumber business at Meriden. He was descended from Richard Seymour who settled in Hartford, Connecticut, coming from England in 1636. His mother, Mary Leonard North, was born in Berlin, Connecticut, January 2, 1832, and died at Los Angeles October 8, 1911. She was a teacher in her youth, and was a member of the Daughters of the American Revolution.

George Newton Seymour attended Hartford public schools and was graduated from high school in the class of 1884. He received his Bachelor of Arts degree from Amherst in 1888, where he was active in dramatics, debate and public speaking, was a member of Chi Phi and of the football team.

On May 18, 1892, Mr. Seymour was united in marriage to Jessie Louise Butler at Meriden. To them were born two children, Alma Brooks, born March 6, 1893, who married Frank Latenser of Omaha, and Leonard North, born February 4, 1900, who married Vesta Beavers. Alma was graduated from Brownell Hall at Omaha, Bradford Academy at Bradford, Massachusetts, and Vassar College. Thereafter she took post-graduate work at Boston.

Mr. Seymour, who recently retired, has served as president of the Elgin State Bank, the Atlas Bank of Neligh and others, as well as president of the Northwestern Nebraska Bankers Association, and Nebraska Bankers Association. He is president of the Cratty Lumber and Grain Company of Elgin and Huffman-Seymour, Incorporated.

Mr. Seymour's hobbies are landscaping, architecture and art, and he is the author of the landscape plan of the University of Nebraska. For six years he was a member of the board of regents of the university, and for twenty-four years he served on the Elgin School Board. During the World War he was chairman of the North Nebraska Liberty loan committee and a member of the Antelope County Council of Defense. He is a Republican. His social clubs include the University Club at Lincoln, the Athletic Club of Omaha and Ak-Sar-Ben. He is a Mason, and was recently elected to life membership in the Nebraskana Society. Residence: Elgin.

Victor Seymour

For the past 57 years Victor Seymour has lived in Nebraska, and since 1892, has been prominent in the practice of law. He was born at Macomb, Illinois, May 28, 1870, the son of Henry and Weltha Victoria (Bell) Seymour. His father, who was born at Newark, Illinois, March 18, 1837, and died at York, Nebraska, February 2, 1893, was a grain and agricultural implement dealer. He enlisted in Company A, 14th Illinois Cavalry, in 1862, and was mustered out in 1865, with the rank of lieutenant. His family came from England, in the 17th century.

His mother, Weltha (Bell) Seymour, was born at Westfield, New York, September 7, 1838, and died at York, February 2, 1898. Her great great grandmother came to New England from Scotland, before the French and Indian War; her grandmother's great uncles were officers in the War of 1812; other ancestors came from England and Wales.

Mr. Seymour was graduated from high school at York, in May, 1889, and in 1892, received the LL. B. degree from the University of Nebraska. He served as stenographer for Sawyer & Snell, attorneys, for five years; was court reporter for Judge Albert J. Cornish, for 9 years; was deputy clerk of the Supreme Court of Nebraska; campaign manager for John L. Kennedy of Omaha, in his campaign for United States senator; and was partner in the firm of Maylard & Company, farm mortgage bankers at Norfolk, Nebraska. A Republican, he has served for 24 years in public office.

He is a member of the Nebraska State Bar Association; the Red Cross; and the Nebraskana Society. He is a member of the Sons of Veterans; the Masonic Blue Lodge, York Rite, Scottish Rite, Shrine; Modern Woodmen of America; and the Royal Highlanders. He is affiliated with the First Congregational Church of Norfolk, Nebraska.

His marriage to Jane Bawden was solemnized near Apple River, Illinois, September 1, 1896. Mrs. Seymour, who was born near Galena, Illinois, November 1, 1869, received her A. B. degree from the University of Nebraska.

Her ancestors were Cornish miners. Her father mined in California, Australia, Montana, Minnesota, and owned a lead furnace in Illinois. Four children were born to this marriage, two of whom are living: Ellanor Victoria, born August 16, 1897, who married Philip Gordon Jones, and who now resides in Buffalo, New York; Jane Bawden, born February 20, 1899, who died March 28, 1899; Richard Henry, born February 9, 1900, who died March 14, 1900; and Victor Reynolds, born July 24, 1908. Ellanor and Victor are both graduates of the University of Nebraska. Residence: Lincoln. (Photograph in Album).

Anna Dorothea Shadbolt

Anna Dorothea Shadbolt, clubwoman, was born at Davenport, Iowa, August 23, 1881, daughter of Peter and Anna Christian Maria (Rubien) Thomsen. Her father was born at Schleswig, Germany, December 6, 1850, and died in Scott County, Iowa, March 1, 1882. He was a farmer. Her mother was born in Jafenstedt, Holstein, Germany, December 2, 1854, daughter of Johanass and Anna John Rubien.

Mrs. Shadbolt attended country school, and on December 14, 1904, was married to George Everitt Shadbolt at Rushville, Nebraska. Mr. Shadbolt was born at Cascade, Wisconsin, October 8, 1858, and died at Gordon, March

16, 1923. At the time of his death Mr. Shadbolt was part owner of the Churn Ranch in Cherry County. He was the son of Seaman and Martha Parrish Shadbolt. Mr. and Mrs. Shadbolt have three children, Viola, born September 25, 1905, a graduate of the University of Nebraska, a member of Delta Zeta Sorority, and now a teacher in the Chadron High School. She was awarded a scholarship at the Colonial School for Girls at Washington, D. C. During her senior year at the University of Nebraska she served as president of her sorority. In 1928 she was delegate to the Delta Zeta convention which convened in Canada. Ella, the second daughter, was born February 18, 1908, and is married to Charles Loewenthal of Chadron. She was a graduate of Gordon High School and had three years dramatic work in Chadron Normal. Mrs. Loewenthal received the Stephens award for debating in 1930. She was a member of the winning Chadron Normal School debating team which debated against the University of Wyoming in 1929.

George, the only son, was born February 20, 1911, and is attending the University of Nebraska. He is a stockholder in the Shadbolt-Arnot Cattle Company. Now in his sophomore year at the University, he is a member of Sigma Nu Fraternity. He was awarded a scholarship to the Hastings Business College in 1929. He was also awarded the Kiwanis scholarship the same year.

Mrs. Shadbolt is a director of the Anchor Bank at Merriman, Nebraska, and president and director of the Shadbolt-Arnot Cattle Company. She is a Republican, a member of the Presbyterian Church, was president of the Gordon's Women's Club, 1923-1924, and is a member and secretary of the cemetery board. At one time she was a member of the Parent-Teachers' Association, and was a member of the library board for nine years. Residence: Gordon. (Photograph in Album).

Charles E. Shafer

Charles E. Shafer, pioneer farmer in Burt County, Nebraska, has lived in this state for 64 years. He was born at Tekamah, July 6, 1867, the son of Michael and Julia Ann (Lydick) Shafer. His father, a farmer and a Civil War veteran, was born at Mount Vernon, Ohio, March 21, 1832, and died at Tekamah, July 22, 1907. His mother was a teacher in the public schools for several years and took an active interest in church work; she was born at Mount Vernon, October 2, 1830, and died at Tekamah, November 9, 1906.

Mr. Shafer, who has lived on his father's homestead practically all his life, is a member of the Pioneers and Old Settlers Association of Burt County. He was treasurer of school his local district No. 18, 1904 to 1914, acted as chairman of the loan drives in that district during the World War, and took part in Red Cross affairs. He holds membership in the Independent Order of Odd Fellows and the Modern Woodmen of America. He is a Democrat.

He was united in marriage March 4, 1896, at Tekamah, with Evalyn Sisson who was born at Tekamah, August 17, 1877. One son was born to this marriage: Roland Lee, born April 29, 1898, who married Ethel E. Coons. She was born June 4, 1900. Residence: Tekamah.

Dean E. Shaffer

Born at St. Edward, Nebraska, July 17, 1903, Dean E. Shaffer is the son of Charles Johnston and Angie Chamberlain (Finch) Shaffer. His father is of Pennsylvania Dutch extraction, and is engaged as a dairy farmer. He is an elder and trustee of the Presbyterian Church, and has been a township and school officer. His wife was born of English parents, and was formerly president of her local Parent-Teacher's Association.

Mr. Shaffer was graduated from high school at St. Edward, and after receiving his A. B. degree from Hastings College in 1925, took graduate work at the University of California. While in Hastings he became a member of Pi Kappa Delta and Pi Gamma Mu, and in high school received letters in basketball 1919, 1920 and 1921. He was editor of the *Maroon* (high school paper) in 1921, and acting editor of the *Daily Californian* the summer of 1925.

From 1925 until 1927 Mr. Shaffer was instructor at Hastings College. During 1927 he was manager of Radio Station KFKX for the National Broadcasting Company, and since that time he has been manager of the insurance department of the Mortgage Investment Company of Hastings. A Republican, he is a participant in the work of his party locally, and during the years 1928-30 was secretary of the Adams County Republican Central committee. He received the U. S. Junior Chamber of Commerce civic award for Hastings in 1931.

A member of the Young Men's Christian Association, he is one of its directors, and head sponsor of the Hastings High School Hi-Y Club. He served as secretary in 1929 and president in 1930 of the Hastings Junior Chamber of Commerce, and is now a member of the Senior Chamber. His favorite sport is golf, altho he is also interested in all college and high school sports, while his hobby is boys work. During the years 1930 and 1931 he served as secretary of the Rotary Club. He is a Scottish Rite Mason and Member of the Shrine, a member of the First Presbyterian Church of Hastings and a life member of the Nebraskana Society. Residence. Hastings.

Norman Edward Shaffer

Born at Hooper, Nebraska, March 21, 1884, Norman Edward Shaffer is the son of Jacob G. and Elizabeth Mary (Winey) Shaffer. His father was born in Juniata County, Pennsylvania, October 18, 1848, and is now retired after an active life as a farmer and stock feeder. His mother was born at Richfield, Pennsylvania, August 8, 1856, and is still living.

Mr. Shaffer attended the public schools and Fremont Normal College, and from 1907-09 was bookkeeper for the Farmers Elevator. From 1909 to 1918, he engaged in farming, and since the last date has been cashier of the First National Bank of Hooper. He is a director of the Hooper Telephone Company, the Hooper Building and Loan Association, and the Community Finance Corporation.

A Democrat, Mr. Shaffer served as state representative in 1917. He was a participant in loan drives and local war activities in 1917-1918, and is a member of the board of education at Hooper. His religious affiliation is with Grace Evangelical Lutheran Church, and he is a Scottish Rite Mason. Mr. Shaffer is a life member of the Nebraskana Society also.

On February 23, 1909, he was married to Nettie Mary Monnich. Mrs. Shaffer was born at Hooper, March 20, 1889, and to them were born three children: Donald, Charlotte and Cornelius. Donald attended the University of Nebraska, and Midland College; Charlotte is taking a nurse's training course at the Methodist Hospital in Omaha, and Cornelius is in high school. Residence: Hooper.

Michael Shaheen

Michael Shaheen, merchant, was born near Beyrouth, Syria, September 19, 1877, son of Joseph and Helen (Lamone) Shaheen. The father and mother were both born near Beyrouth, Syria where the father was a farmer. He died there in 1922. His mother died there in 1882.

Mr. Shaheen received his education in the elementary schools of Syria, came to the United States landing in New York in the late spring of 1895, and for the past 30 years has been a resident of Nebraska. He has been a merchant continuously since 1902.

On April 8, 1908, he was married to Mable David in Syria, where she was born August 25, 1887. They have

ten children, all of whom were born in the United States except Toy J. Shaheen who was born in Syria. Toy James, born May 27, 1909; Gladys Anne, born March 7, 1911; Madelia, August 6, 1912; Marguerite Mary, March 21, 1914; Julia, December 25, 1915; Martha, February 22, 1918; Eve, March 14, 1920; Helen, November 9, 1923; George, May 17, 1924; and Kenneth Duane, born August 28, 1930. Madelia Julia is married to Charles Stevens who is a mechanic and merchant residing at Hardesty, Oklahoma.

Mr. Shaheen is a member of the Greek Orthodox Church, the Red Cross and the Odd Fellows. He devotes much of his leisure time to reading. Residence: Arthur.

Ashton C. Shallenberger

Ashton C. Shallenberger, congressman and farmer, was born at Toulon, Illinois, December 23, 1862. His father, Martin Shallenberger, born in Fayette County, Pennsylvania, February 23, 1825, was a lawyer and member of the legislature of 1856, descended from a Swiss-German family which came to Pennsylvania in 1830. He died at Toulon, in 1904. His mother, Eliza Hall, was born in Derbyshire, England, in June, 1830, and died at Toulon in 1900. She came to Stark County, Illinois, in 1836, with her father, Dr. Thomas Hall. The mother of six sons and two daughters, she was the author of *Stark County and Its Pioneers*.

Educated in the common schools of Toulon, Ashton C. Shallenberger attended the University of Illinois, and left the latter to come to Nebraska in 1881. The organizer of the Bank of Alma, he was its manager twenty-three years, and when elected governor of Nebraska in 1908, disposed of his interests in the bank. Since that time his only interests except those of a political nature, have been stockraising and farming.

A Democrat, Mr. Shallenberger was elected to the 57th congress in 1900, was candidate for governor on that ticket in 1906, was elected governor in 1908, and was candidate for the United States senate against Norris in 1912. He was elected to congress in 1914, 1916, 1922, 1924, and 1926, and was re-elected to the 72nd congress in 1930 from the Fifth Congressional District of Nebraska.

On May 24, 1885, he was married to Eliza Zilg at Osceola, Nebraska. Mrs. Shallenberger was born in Sauk County, Wisconsin, of German descent. They have three children, Martin Conrad, a major, general staff of the United States Army; Grace Pauline and Dorothy Elizabeth. Residence: Alma.

John Dee Shank

John Dee Shank, farmer and breeder of purebred livestock, was born at Osceola, Nebraska, February 1, 1889, the son of John Wesley and Emma Sophia (Rose) Shank. His father, who is also a farmer and stockman, was born at Agency City, Iowa, September 9, 1861; his parents were natives of Pennsylvania. His mother, whose parents came to Illinois from Sweden, was born at Swedona, Illinois, December 29, 1865.

Mr. Shank was graduated from the high school at Superior, Nebraska, in 1908, and for the following two years was a student at the University of Nebraska. He is a member of the Nebraskana Society, is affiliated with the Methodist Episcopal Church of Superior, and holds membership in the University Club. A Mason, he is past master and past commander Knights Templar.

He was married at Superior, December 6, 1911, to Grace Gossard, who was born at Omaha, Nebraska, November 18, 1892. She is the daughter of Charles H. and Effie (Hart) Gossard, direct descendants of John Hart, one of the signers of the Declaration of Independence. They have a son, Boyd, born November 5, 1914, who is a student at the University of Nebraska College of Agriculture. Mr. Shank is a Republican. Residence: Superior.

Charles Augustus Shannon

On August 19, 1879, Charles A. Shannon was born at Nebraska City, the son of Richard Thomas and Samuella Shannon. His father was born in Indiana and died at Cripple Creek, Colorado, in 1896; his ancestry was Irish. His grandfather was a spy in the American Revolution. He received a land grant from the government of Indiana. His mother was born in Missouri and died at Nebraska City, August 13, 1920. She came to Nebraska City in 1855 and her ancestry was Pennsylvania Dutch and English.

Charles A. Shannon was graduated from high school in 1897; from 1904 to 1908 he attended the University of Nebraska, receiving the degree of Bachelor of Science in Civil Engineering.

Since 1908 he has held the office of county surveyor of Otoe County, and has been city engineer of Nebraska City during the same period. Mr. Shannon is a Democrat, an Elk and a member of the Masonic lodge. His hobby is farming. Residence: Nebraska City.

Clara Amanda Sharp

Clara A. Sharp, who has lived in Nebraska for the past 67 years, was born near Maquaketa, Iowa, October 5, 1850, the daughter of Leonard and Mary (Dupray) Webb. Her father, a farmer, was born in New York, February 13, 1823, and died at West Point, Nebraska, June 26, 1882. Her mother was born at Dayton, Ohio, December 4, 1829, and died at Fort Morgan, Colorado, May 17, 1910.

Mrs. Sharp is prominent in social and civic affairs at Pilger, and holds membership in the Women's Federated Club, and the Nebraskana Society. She is affiliated with the Methodist Episcopal Church, and for many years has been active in the Ladies' Aid Society of the church. She is a Democrat.

Her marriage to Henry Clay Sharp was solemnized at West Point, October 20, 1867. Mr. Sharp, who was a farmer, was born in Bedford, Virginia, June 29, 1839, and died at Mountain Grove, Missouri, December 20, 1893.

Nine children were born to this marriage, eight of whom are living: Bertha May, born October 25, 1868, who married Ezra Bennett; Thomas Allen, born July 21, 1872, who married Daisy Ellen Bolton; Eugene Clay, born August 28, 1874, who maried Lola Cunningham; Henry Edward, born September 16, 1876, who married Bessie Baker; Roy Leonard, born May 15, 1878, who married Martha Headman; Claude Delbert, born August 2, 1882, who married Nell Russell; Mae Lee, born May 17, 1887, who married O. H. Cunningham; and Clara Belle, born August 28, 1893, who married Alva Wilson. Residence: Pilger.

Orson Jacob Sharp

Born at Eagle, Nebraska, August 3, 1894, Orson Jacob Sharp is the son of William and Pollie Sofia (Bahr) Sharp. His father, who was born at New York, September 1, 1856, is a retired farmer and grain dealer who lives at Trenton. His mother, who taught school for several years before her marriage, was born at Evans Mills, New York, May 2, 1864; she attended the University of Nebraska in 1883 and was an active Methodist Episcopal Church worker. Her grandfather served in the battle of Waterloo under Napoleon, and her maternal grandfather was a soldier in the War of 1812. His father, Henry L. Timmerman, was a soldier in Washington's Army.

Mr. Sharp was graduated from the Elmwood High School, Elmwood, Nebraska, in 1912. He taught school in Nebraska for six years, was connected with the Continental National Life Insurance Company of Denver for a time, and was district manager for Southwest Nebraska for the same company. He is engaged in farming at this time near Trenton. At one time Mr. Sharp was a member of the Republican central committee of Hitchcock County, but he has never aspired to public office.

He is chairman of the County Soldiers Relief Commission, is a member of the Red Cross, holds membership in the Southwest Nebraska Historical Society, and was formerly secretary of the local board of education, 1923-26. He is interested in reading, music, and art. During the World War Mr. Sharp served as corporal in Company C, 342nd Machine Gun Battalion, 89th Division of the United States Army, participating in the St. Mihiel and Meuse-Argonne offensives. He is a member of the American Legion, acting as vice commander of the 9th Nebraska District, was the first county commander of Hitchcock County, 1927-28, and first commander of Post 337 of the American Legion at Trenton.

His marriage to Ruth Langley Bratt was solemnized at Trenton, Nebraska, June 1, 1921. Mrs. Sharp, whose ancestors were natives of England, was born at Natrona, Illinois, April 17, 1898. She has taken an active interest in the American Legion Auxiliary, having held the following positions: secretary of the local unit, one year; president of the unit, three years; ex-county president; and district president at this time. They have one son: Warren Edward, July 14, 1922. Residence: Trenton.

Francis Thomas Shaughnessy

Born at Hartsgrove, Ohio, October 6, 1870, Francis Thomas Shaughnessy, Sr., is the son of Thomas and Ellen (Murphy) Shaughnessy. His father, born in County Tipperary, Ireland, December 14, 1842, came to America in 1848. He assisted in the building of the Union Pacific from Omaha to Promontory Point with General Casement. He was a farmer for a number of years prior to his death at Hartsgrove on October 11, 1918. Ellen Murphy was born in New York City, June 11, 1848, and died at Hartsgrove on April 19, 1924. She was of Irish descent.

Francis Thomas Shaughnessy attended public school at Hartsgrove until 1884. From 1888-97 he engaged in the lumber business, and from 1900-06 was a salesman. He was appointed clerk of the district court of Howard County in February, 1906, serving until January 8, 1910. From that time until the present he has been associated with the Citizens National Bank at St. Paul, of which he is now cashier. He is a Democrat.

On September 24, 1900, Mr. Shaughnessy was married to Anna Carraher at Wahoo. Mrs. Shaughnessy, who is of Irish descent, was born at Hartsgrove, June 14, 1866. There are five children, as follows:

Paul, born September 29, 1901, received his A. B., A. M., and M. D. degrees from Creighton University and is practicing in Cleveland, Ohio. He is married to Mary Martha Clark. Winifred, born March 22, 1905, has a Bachelor of Arts degree and is supervisor of music at St. Paul. Francis Thomas, Jr., born April 2, 1907, has his B. A. degree and is studying for the priesthood; Edwin John, born December 20, 1909, is studying medicine; while Cyril Patrick, born February 9, 1913, is studying law.

Mr. Shaughnessy is a member of SS. Peter and Paul Church, and is a Knight of Columbus (financial secretary 1918-). From 1907-13 he was a member of the city council, and since 1923 he has been secretary of the board of education. He is a member of the Red Cross and The Nebraskana Society. He enjoys golf, is a member of the St. Paul Golf Club, and is fond of reading. Residence: St. Paul.

Claude E. Shaw

Claude E. Shaw, son of Eugene Terry and Catherine (Fryer) Shaw, was born at Blue Mound, Illinois, September 8, 1879. His father, a railroad telegrapher and agent, was born at Cincinnati, Ohio, in May 1850, of Scotch and Irish parentage. He died at Poteau, Oklahoma, in October, 1915. Catherine, his wife, was a native of Bowling Green, Missouri, born July 27, 1853, and is still living.

Educated in public school, Claude E. Shaw came to Nebraska in 1900, and has resided here since. On May 9th of that year he was united in marriage to Ella Guthrie, at Superior. Mrs. Shaw, who is of Scotch descent, was born at Superior, May 27, 1881.

Mr. Shaw is a Democrat. At the present time he represents the Travelers Insurance Company, at Superior. He is a Mason and Kiwanian, a member of the Chamber of Commerce, and a member of Superior Country Club. His favorite sport is golf. Residence: Superior.

Guy S. Shaw

Guy S. Shaw, prominent farmer of Cheyenne County, was born in York, Nebraska, March 28, 1880, son of John and Hester (Denney) Shaw. His father, born in Ohio, April 24, 1854, was a farmer until his death at York, August 15, 1927. Hhis wife, Hester, died at York, in June, 1884.

Mr. Shaw attended public school and since that time has engaged in farming. He is a member of the Sidney Methodist Episcopal Church and the Sidney school board.

On February 21, 1906, he was married to Maud L. Huffman at York. Mrs. Shaw was born at LaFayette, Indiana, February 13, 1883. There are two children, Ruth E., born January 5, 1907, who married Walter S. Cork; and Ester J., born October 25, 1909. Both children are teachers. Residence: Sidney.

Lawrence Madison Shaw

A resident of Nebraska for the past 52 years, Lawrence M. Shaw has been engaged in the practice of medicine at Osceola, Nebraska, since 1889. He was born at Powershiek, Iowa, February 4, 1868, the son of Lanson and Mary Elizabeth (Valentine) Shaw. His father, who was a contractor and builder, was born at Berlin, Illinois, September 22, 1840, and died at Osceola, Nebraska, November 2, 1920. His mother was born at Degraff, Ohio, October 25, 1848, and died at Osceola, February 20, 1930. She is a member of the English family of Crane, and is descended from Lionel Gardner who came to Hemstead, Long Island, in 1657.

Dr. Shaw attended the grade school at Osceola, and in 1884 was graduated from the high school there. He attended Nebraska Wesleyan University, later, and in 1888 received the M. D. degree at the University of Iowa. He has been prominent in the medical world since his admission to practice at Osceola, and has held the following positions: president of the Nebraska State Medical Society, 1908-09; chairman of the board of counsellors of that organization; vice president of the society, 1908. In 1906 he assisted in the re-organization of the state association.

His marriage to Etta Moffett was solemnized at Osceola, January 15, 1890. Mrs. Moffett, whose ancestry is English, was born at Falmouth, Indiana, August 24, 1866. Their four children are: Marion A., who is a regent of the state university; Lawrence, who is assistant United States district attorney at Omaha, Nebraska; Leale, who is a teacher and aviatrix at Long Beach, California; and Irma. Marion is married to Laura J. Pratt; Lawrence married Emma J. Ritchie; Leah married William R. Shirey; and Irma married Elzie E. Calvin.

Dr. Shaw is affiliated with the Methodist Episcopal Church of Osceola, and takes an active part in the Young Men's Christian Association. He holds membership in the Red Cross, the Nebraska Medical Society, the American Medical Society, and the Masons. During the World War he was a member of the local board of examiners.

His favorite sport is golfing, while floral culture and reading are his hobbies. Residence: Osceola. (Photograph in Album).

Marion Ansley Shaw

A leading lawyer in Butler County, Marion Ansley Shaw, was born at Osceola, Nebraska, April 2, 1893. He is the son of Lawrence Madison and Etta (Moffett) Shaw. His father was born at Poweshiek, Iowa, February 4, 1868, and is a physician and a former president of the State Medical Association. His ancestors came to the United States before the American Revolution, and some of them fought with the American forces.

His mother was born at Falmouth, Indiana, August 24, 1867. She is active in Woman's Club, P. E. O., Daughters of the American Revolution, and in all local school affairs. Her ancestors were English and came to America prior to the Revolutionary war and fought in Washington's army.

Marion Ansley Shaw attended Osceola, Nebraska, grade and high schools and was graduated in 1911. At the University of Nebraska in 1917, he received a Bachelor of Laws degree. He was a Theta Nu Epsilon, president of Sigma Alpha Epsilon in 1917, and received an "N" for baseball while attending school.

On April 3, 1918, at Evanston, Illinois, he was united in marriage with Laura Josephine Pratt. She taught in kindergarten before her marriage. She was born in Lincoln, Nebraska, February 14, 1893, of Irish descent; her parents were born and reared in Ireland. They have three children; Jane, born February 11, 1919; Susan, born March 19, 1922; and Patricia, born November 16, 1925.

Mr. Shaw was appointed city attorney at David City, Nebraska, for 1930-31, and acted as Polk County judge in 1915. He is a member of the board of regents of the University of Nebraska, and chairman of the finance committee, and from 1919-23, he was a member of the legal firm of Roper and Shaw. Since that time he has been a member of the firm of Coufal and Shaw.

During the World War he was in the First Officers Training Camp, at Fort Snelling, and four months after he was commissioned second lieutenant he was promoted to first lieutenant. He served in battery A, 339th Field Artillery and was in France, from August, 1918, until January, 1919. He is a former member of the state executive committee of the American Legion, is a past post commander, and now service officer of Kregger Post No. 125.

Mr. Shaw is affiliated with the St. Luke's Methodist Church, and holds membership in the David City Commercial Club, of which he was president in 1929, and a member of the executive committee in 1927-28. He is a member of the Nebraska State Bar Association, the Masonic Blue Lodge at David City, the Scottish Rite at Lincoln, and is a Knight of Pythias.

He is a member of the Nebraskana Society, the Lincoln University Club, and holds membership in the David City Country Club. Golf, fishing and hunting are his sports. Residence: David City.

Relvia Ulysses Shaw

Relvia Ulysses Shaw, merchant now retired, was born at Redding, Iowa, November 7, 1863, son of Samuel Reed and Sarah (Phelps) Shaw. He settled at Cambridge three years before the railroad entered that section of the country.

Samuel Reed Shaw, a farmer and mason, was born at Bridgetown, New Jersey, February 26, 1814, and died at Cambridge, Nebraska, July 13, 1891. He owned a flour mill and a woolen mill at Clarinda, Iowa, and the family did their own weaving. His father came from England and settled on a homestead in Bridgetown, New Jersey. Samuel Reed Shaw came to Nebraska in 1878 and took a homestead in Furnas County, near Cambridge in September of that year and resided there until two years prior to his death.

Sarah Phelps was born in Courtland Village, New York, July 19, 1825, and died at Cambridge, in April, 1901. Before her marriage she taught school. Her parents came from Wales and settled on a homestead near Courtland Village.

Mr. Shaw attended country school which was a soddie covered with willow and dirt, graduating from the 8th grade in 1884. When a small boy he lived on a homestead with his parents, and since that time has always been a merchant. For the past 54 years he has made his home in Nebraska.

On February 13, 1902, he was married to Della Fair Downing at Omaha. Mrs. Shaw was born at Xenia, Missouri, February 24, 1870. Her grandfather was Scotch-Irish, and her mother's grandfather was a Frenchman from Paris.

For many years, Mr. Shaw has been a member and an active worker in the Methodist Episcopal Church of Cambridge. He is a member of the Red Cross, and a life member of the Nebraskana Society. His hobby is mechanics. Residence: Cambridge. (Photograph in Album).

Ernest Vincent Shayler

Ernest V. Shayler, bishop of the Episcopal church in Nebraska, was born in England, October 11, 1867. His father, Charles Shayler, was born in England, May 24, 1839, and came to America in 1880. He died at Columbus, Franklin County, Ohio, in 1918. His mother, Charlotte (Sherman) Shayler, was born in England, November 1, 1837, and died at Columbus December 24, 1897.

Bishop Shayler received his early education in the grade and high schools of England. He was awarded the D.D. degree at Kenyon College. He has been rector of Calvary Church at Sandusky, Ohio; Grace Church, at Oak Park, Illinois; and St. Mark's Episcopal Church at Seattle, Washington. He is now bishop of the Diocese of Nebraska. He is the author of: *Making of a Churchman;* and *History of the World.* He has lived in this state for eleven years. His marriage to Mignon Louise Knight was solemnized at Columbus, Ohio. Mrs. Shayler, who was born at Columbus, December 31, 1869, is descended from Revolutionary War ancestors. They have one daughter, Ernestine, born April 20, 1900, who married Marion C. Heath.

Bishop Shayler was civilian chaplain at Puget Sound Camps and was chairman of the committee on loan drives during the World War. He is a member of the Omaha Chamber of Commerce and the Kiwanis Club, and is a Mason. He holds membership in the Omaha Athletic Club and the Omaha Club. His favorite sport is golfing, and his hobby is gardening. Residence: Omaha.

Thompson Maple Sheaff

Thompson Maple Sheaff has lived in Nebraska since 1884, and since 1890 has been a resident of Nance County. He was born at Fulton, Illinois, December 31, 1852, the son of William L. Sheaff and Caroline (Efnor) Sheaff. His father, who was a farmer, was born in Delaware County, Pennsylvania, November 16, 1824, and died at Hastings, Nebraska, January 28, 1905; his great-great-grandfather came to this country from Germany in 1752. His mother was born near Utica, New York, March 4, 1833, and died at Bushnell, Illinois, February 5, 1884.

Mr. Sheaff attended school in an academy for two years and was a student in college for a year. He has been engaged in the implement business at Fullerton, Nebraska for over 40 years. At one time he held membership in the Knights of Pythias, and for over 40 years was a member of the Independent Order of Odd Fellows. He is a member of the Nebraskana Society.

His marriage to Amelia Evalyn Quigle was solemn-

ized at Prairie City, Illinois, February 5, 1874. Mrs. Sheaff was born in McDonough County, Illinois, February 21, 1851. Five children were born to them: Rosa, June 7, 1875, who died October 14, 1875; Olive, January 21, 1879, who married William C. Mangels; George L., November 12, 1881, who married Pearl Fuller; Frank, April 1, 1884, who married Grace Chalfant; and Arthur O., January 20, 1890, who married Ruby Corriell. Residence: Fullerton.

Eva Lydia Shearer

One of Nebraska's pioneer leaders in civic and social affairs, Eva Lydia Shearer was born at Exira, Iowa, February 18, 1861, the daughter of Andrew Moore and Elizabeth Potter (Clayton) Hardy. Her father was the first commissioner of Webster County, Nebraska, organized the first Sunday school there, and was justice of the peace for a number of years. He was born at Johnstown, New York, December 30, 1820, and died in White Cloud, Kansas, June 3, 1896, after many years of service to his community and his state. Her mother, a physician and homemaker, was born at Elizabethtown, New Jersey, July 12, 1824, and died at Atoka, Oklahoma, June 24, 1906.

Ten children were born to Andrew and Elizabeth Hardy, as follows: George W., born November 4, 1843; John W., born April 13, 1847; Amy Hoover, born August 18, 1849; Mina A. Connelly, born August 14, 1852; Mary E. Kelsay, born December 26, 1854; Laura J., born June 16, 1857; Eva L., subject of this sketch, born February 18, 1861; Clara J. Van Doran, born March 29, 1863; Ada B. Casteel, born November 23, 1865; and A. W. Hardy, born February 19, 1869.

Mrs. Shearer studied under the tutelege of her parents, since there were few schools in Nebraska during her early years. She later attended a sod school house in Webster County, and was a regular attendant at the pioneer Sunday School which her father helped organize. At this time she is compiling a history of the early days of Webster County which she expects to hand down to her children and many grandchildren.

During the past half-century Mrs. Shearer has held membership in nearly all the civic and religious affairs of her community, and at this time is a member of the Foreign Missionary Society of the Methodist Episcopal Church and the Women's Christian Temperance Union. She was recently elected to membership in the Nebraskana Society.

She was married to John B. Watt, who was a farmer, January 1, 1878. One daughter was born to this marriage, Lillian, November 2, 1878, who married E. L. Shuck.

Her marriage to F. A. Dickerson occurred at Webster, Nebraska in 1880, and the following children were born: D. F. Dickerson who is an educator, now residing at Winona, Minnesota, and who has been successful in his profession. He is now superintendent of schools at Winona and is the author of two books used in school work; Olive E., born October 3, 1883, who married Bernard McHugh; Ionn R., born February 2, 1888, who married Donald Bayles; and Ethel A., born April 22, 1890, who married Harold R. Cozier.

Five years after the death of Mr. Dickerson she married Horace F. Shearer, who is now retired from active business. Mr. and Mrs. Shearer are ardent advocates of temperance. Residence: Lincoln. (Photograph on Page 1081).

William Lete Shearer

William Lete Shearer, oral and plastic surgeon, was born at Fennimore, Wisconsin, July 6, 1880, son of John Edward and Mary Elizabeth (Ward) Shearer. He holds the degree of Bachelor of Arts, Doctor of Medicine, Doctor of Dental Surgery, Fellow of the American College of Surgeons, and Fellow of the American College of Dentists.

His marriage to Anna Katharine Wiley was solemn-

EVA LYDIA SHEARER

ized in Wyoming, October 30, 1907. There are three children, William Lete, 2nd, born April 26, 1910; Elizabeth Ruth, born January 10, 1914; and Katherine Jane, born March 22, 1915.

Dr. Shearer is a member of the First Central Congregational Church, the Nebraska State Dental Society, the American Dental Association, the American Medical Association, the American College of Surgeons, the American College of Dentists, the Omaha Douglas County Medical Society, the Omaha District Dental Society, the American Association of Oral and Plastic Surgeons, and the American Association of Oral Surgeons and Exodontists. He is a Mason, and a member of the Omaha Club, the Country Club, and the Happy Hollow Club. He belongs to the Chamber of Commerce (national affairs committee), the Rotary Club, and is a regent of the Municipal University. Residence: Omaha.

Thomas James Sheehan, Jr.

Thomas James Sheehan, Jr., lawyer, was born at Mount Carmel, Ohio, April 21, 1893, son of Thomas James and Elizabeth Teresa (Hoey) Sheehan. Thomas J. Sheehan, Sr., was born in New York City on September 7, 1848. His father's parents came from Ireland in 1848, and Thomas J. Sheehan, Sr., was the first child of the family born in the United States. He engaged in the hotel and restaurant business, and is now city road inspector. His wife, Elizabeth Teresa Hoey, was born at Newtown, Ohio, and died at Mount Carmel, April 21, 1893. Her parents were born in Ireland.

Thomas J. Sheehan, Jr., was educated first in the public and parochial schools of Cincinnati. He received his LL. B. from the McDonald Law Institute, which is now affiliated with the Cincinnati Law School, and also attended the University of Cincinnati. Admitted to the bar at Columbus, Ohio, on June 25, 1914, he practiced at Cincinnati, Ohio, until 1917. At that time he entered the First Officers Training Camp at Fort Harrison, Indiana, and was commissioned second lieutenant. He was promoted to first lieutenant and served until 1919, and now holds the rank of first lieutenant in the Reserve Officers Corps. He is a member of the American Legion.

In 1919 Mr. Sheehan came to Omaha, where he was admitted to the bar, and served as deputy county attorney of Douglas County in 1921. Previously, while in Cincinnati he was chief clerk to the United States Attorney from 1909-15. He is a member of the law firm of Lower and Sheehan at the present time.

Mr. Sheehan was first married to Margaret Wahosky, the marriage taking place at Omaha, on October 18, 1918. She was born at Omaha, April 11, 1896, and died there September 18, 1922. His second marriage was to Elizabeth Cogan, who was born at Omaha, January 6, 1896. They were married at Omaha, November 8, 1924. There are two children, Thomas J., III. born August 18, 1922, of the first marriage, and Elizabeth Patricia, born February, 9 1928, of the second marriage.

Mr. Sheehan is a Republican. He is a member of St. Margaret Mary Catholic Church, the Knights of Columbus and the Elks. He belongs to the Omaha, Nebraska State and the American Bar Associations, the Red Cross, and the Washington School P. T. A. His club is the Omaha Athletic, and his hobby is reading. Residence: Omaha.

Addison Erwin Sheldon

Addison Erwin Sheldon, was born at Sheldon, Houston County, Minnesota, April 15, 1861, the son of Rolland Fuller Sheldon and Mary Adel (Hassett) Sheldon. His father, who was a Baptist minister and a physician, was graduated from Rochester University in 1856; he is descended from Isaac Sheldon (1640) one of the original settlers of Windsor, Connecticut, and Northampton, Massachusetts, from Elijah Sheldon who was active in French and Indian Wars, and Moses Sheldon, Revolutionary soldier.

Mary Adel (Hassett) Sheldon, mother of Addison Sheldon, who was a musician and teacher, was descended from early settlers in New England. Mr. Sheldon received his early education in frontier Nebraska schools, and from 1878 to 1883 was a student at Crete Academy, and Doane College, Crete, Nebraska. He was a student at the University of Nebraska, 1883-1902, where he received his A. B. degree, and in 1904 was awarded his A. M. degree at that institution. In 1918 he was awarded the Ph. D. degree at Columbia University.

He was a homesteader in Cherry County near Cody from 1886 to 1888. On October 18, 1884, he was married to Jennie Almira Denton, who died July 20, 1907. His second marriage, to Margaret E. Thompson, occurred at Beaver Crossing, Nebraska, September 19, 1907. Mrs. Sheldon is past president of the Nebraska State Federation of Women's Clubs, and has been active in social and civic affairs at Lincoln. Their children are: Philip Lisle, who lives at Scottsbluff, Nebraska; and Ruth, who resides at Washington, D. C.

Mr. Sheldon was a member of the Republican party for many years, later was affiliated with the Populist party, and is now a Republican. He has held the following positions: member of the Nebraska house of representatives, 1897; chairman and secretary of the Populist County Committee, 1891-1901; founder and director of the Nebraska Legislative Reference Bureau. Since 1917 he has been superintendent and secretary of the Nebraska State Historical Society.

Mr. Sheldon has always been interested in editorial work, holding the following positions: editor of the *Burnett Blade* 1884-86; editor *Chadron Signal,* 1888-98; editor of the *Nebraska History Magazine;* overseas correspondent 1918-19. He is the author of the following books; *Semicentennial History of Nebraska,* 1904; *Nebraska Constitutional Conventions,* 1905-07; *Poems and Sketches of Nebraska,* 1908; *Report on Nebraska Archives,* 1910; *History and Stories of Nebraska,* 1913; *Documents of Nebraska Life,* 1910-20; *Nebraska Blue Book,* 1915-20; *Land Systems and Land Policies of Nebraska,* 1919; *Nebraska Civil Government,* 1925; *The Nebraska National Forest,* 1927; *New Standard History of Nebraska,* 1928-29; Editor *Nebraska History Magazine,* 1917-32; and articles on Nebraska in Encyclopedia Brittanica.

Mr. Sheldon holds membership in the Chamber of Commerce at Lincoln, Laymen's Club, Modern Woodmen of America, Nebraska State Teachers Association, American Historical Association, National Geographic Society, National Association for the Advancement of Sciences, Folk Lore Association, the Young Men's Christian Association, Sons of the American Revolution, Nebraska Authors Guild, and the Nebraskana Society. He is a member of the Lincoln University Club, and a charter member of the Kiwanis Club at Lincoln. Residence: Lincoln.

Burton Wallace Sheldon

Burton Wallace Sheldon, farmer, was born at Forreston, Illinois, November 8, 1880, and has been a resident of Nebraska for 31 years.

His father, Martin Van Buren Sheldon, was born in Stephentown, New York, February 29, 1840, and died at Denver, March 3, 1921. He was a railroad engineer, and a minister of the gospel of the Advent Christian Church. His family settled near North Kingston, Rhode Island, in the early days of northern colonization.

Abbie Howard Tanner, wife of Martin Van Buren Sheldon, was born at Stephentown, May 31, 1850, and died at Ogallala, June 25, 1920. She was a Sunday School teacher and active in church work. Her family was of English origin and settled in America in 1732. Members of the family served in Washington's army in the Revolution.

Mr. Sheldon attended public and high schools, and was graduated in 1898. He was a member of the baseball team for years.

On April 6, 1904, Mr. Sheldon was married to Minta May Sly at McCook. Mrs. Sheldon was born at Fisher, Illinois, December 6, 1882, and is of English descent. She is the daughter of John and Ella (Waite) Sly. Her father died December 25, 1901, and her mother is living with her at the present time. They have seven children, Wallace, born July 17, 1905, who married Marvel May Atkinson; Rosalie, born September 16, 1906, who married Theodore Roosevelt Lee; Burton, born June 29, 1909; Beulah, born March 10, 1912, who married Walter William Klemme; Keith, born September 6, 1915; Stanley, born July 19, 1917; and Robert, born November 16, 1920.

Mr. Sheldon was a farmer and rancher, and a breeder of purebred Shorthorn cattle. His main interest in addition to this, is highway construction and maintenance work. From 1918 until 1925, he was secretary-treasurer of the Keith County Shorthorn Breeders Association, and from 1917 until 1921, was secretary-treasurer of the Keith County Farm Bureau. From 1929 until 1931 he was president of the Keith County Agricultural Society. A Democrat, he served as county commissioner of Keith County from 1911 until 1914, and was elected state representative from the 94th district 1931-1932. He is prominent in party politics and at the present time is a member of the county central committee.

During 1917 and 1918 he was a sergeant in the home guard of Nebraska, and took part in loan drives and registration work. He is affiliated with the First Congregational Church, is a member of the Red Cross, the Ogallala Commercial Club, the Modern Woodmen of America and the Odd Fellows. From 1929 until 1932 he served as president of the Ogallala School Board, and from 1907 to 1927 was a member of the District School Board. Residence: Ogallala.

Harry Brooks Shellenbarger

Born of a long line of distinguished ancestors, Harry Brooks Shellenbarger is the son of David Porter and Anna Catharine Shellenbarger. He was born at Monmouth, Illinois, December 27, 1874, and for the past 50 years has been a resident of Harlan County, Nebraska where he has engaged in farming for many years. His father, who was also a farmer, was born in Pennsylvania, March 11, 1841, and died at Stella, Nebraska, April 23, 1904. His mother, whose parents were natives of Germany, was born in Pennsylvania, October 11, 1847, and died at Stella, August 30, 1931.

John Smilie, an ancestor of Harry Brooks Shellenbarger, was born in Lancaster County, Pennsylvania, in 1742, was a soldier in the Revolutionary War, assisted in establishing American independence as an officer in the civil service. He was a statesman of note, held important offices in the newly constructed American Government after the Revolution, served as a member of the assembly and was one of the signers of the constitution of Pennsylvania. He died in Washington, D. C. while on duty, and was buried in the Congressional Cemetery December 31, 1813.

Mr. Shellenbarger was graduated from the Stella High School. He has served as president of the Parent Teachers Association at Stamford for three years, and has served as a member of the Nebraska senate three consecutive terms, 1923-25 and 27 from the 28th district.

His marriage to Emma Myra Shrauger occurred at Humboldt, Nebraska, April 9, 1905. Mrs. Shellenberger, whose ancestry is Swiss, Dutch, and German, was born at Humboldt, February 23, 1880. They have one daughter, Vesta Pauline, born August 23, 1906, who married Lester Schwass. His hobby is the production of good live stock and reading political history. Residence: Stamford.

Dorsey Lincoln Shenefelt

Dorsey Lincoln Shenefelt, banker, was born in Huntington, Pennsylvania, February 20, 1866, son of Abram Burns and Nancy Rose (Pollock) Shenefelt. His father was born in Huntington County, and died there. He was a farmer of Pennsylvania Dutch descent. The mother, born in Union, Pennsylvania, died at Ewing, Nebraska, in 1907. She was a school teacher of Scotch-Irish descent.

Mr. Shenefelt attended grammar school in Jersey City, New Jersey, and came to Nebraska in 1881, homesteading in Antelope County. He was a merchant at Petersburg, Orchard, Neligh and Oakdale; was with the Farmers Union State Exchange in Omaha, for seven years, from 1922 to 1929. That year he went into the banking business at Oakdale, and is now president of the First National Bank.

Mr. Shenefelt is a Democrat. He has served as chairman of the county central committee of Boone and Antelope counties and was defeated for state representative and county treasurer on the Democratic ticket.

He was married in October, 1888, to Louisa True in Wheeler County, Nebraska. Mrs. Shenefelt was born at Audubon County, February 5, 1871. There are four children: Leona, Helen, Dorsey L., Jr., and Victor H. Mr. Shenefelt was raised a Presbyterian and was later a member of the Congregational Church. He is not now affiliated with any local organization. He is a member of the Red Cross, and for 18 years served on the school board at Petersburg, Nebraska. At the present time he is a member of the board of trustees at Gates College. His hobby is reading. Residence: Oakdale.

Fred Shepherd

For the past fourteen years the Honorable Fred Shepherd has been judge of the district court for the Third Judicial District of Nebraska. Born near Galesburg, Illinois, January 4, 1864, he is the son of Frederick Everest and Elizabeth Dickinson (Bull) Shepherd. Frederick Shepherd was a native of North Haven, Cannecticut, who went with the Forty Niners to California, and later pioneered in Nebraska. He was of Scotch and English descent. His death occurred at Lincoln. Elizabeth, his wife, who was descended of early English settlers in New England, was born at Milford, Connecticut, and died at Lincoln. She was an ardent church worker and homemaker.

Judge Shepherd attended the Lincoln public and high schools, and graduated from the latter in 1881. He thereafter attended the University of Nebraska. He was a member of the Palladian and Philodicean Literary Societies. There were no organized athletics at that time, and therefore no letters were granted. However, Judge Shepherd was captain of the baseball team during his entire time in college.

In 1890, upon his admission to the bar he entered the active practice of law, in which he engaged until he was elected district judge in 1916. He has written various opinions appearing in the Nebraska State Reports during the past fourteen years.

His first marriage was to Harriet Maria Curtiss of Lincoln, Nebraska, who died at Lincoln, on May 10, 1893. There is one daughter of this marriage, Helen, born in 1892, who is married. On September 30, 1904, he was married to Edna M. Curtiss, sister of his deceased wife, at Denver, Colorado. They, too, have a daughter Elizabeth, born July 28, 1906. She is also married.

Judge Shepherd has always taken an active part in the cultural life of Lincoln, and is a member of the University Club, the Country Club, the Round Table, Laymen's, Candle Light and the Low Twelve Club. He is a Mason, a member of the Ancient Order of United Workmen, the Modern Woodmen of America, the Chamber of Commerce, etc. His professional organizations include the Lancaster County Bar Association of which he is a former president, and the Nebraska State Bar Association of which he is now president. He attends the Plymouth Congregational Church of Lincoln. Residence: Lincoln.

Viola B. Shepherd

Viola B. Shepherd, county superintendent of schools of Morrill County, was born at Adams, Nebraska, October 21 1880, daughter of Silas and Clarinda (Young) Bryson. Her ancestry is Scotch, her family having come to the United States in 1770.

Graduated from Adams High School, Mrs. Shepherd afterward attended Peru State Normal School, Chadron State Normal School, and Nebraska Wesleyan University. She has the Bachelor of Arts degree.

Mrs. Shepherd has always been engaged in school work, and has held her present position of county superintendent for nine years. She is a Republican, a member of the Eastern Star, of the Rebekah Lodge, the Woman's Club, the National Educational Association (life member), the Nebraska State Teachers Association (president 6th district), the Daughters of the American Revolution, and the Bible Study organization. Her hobby is beautifying school grounds, while her favorite recreations are library work and out-door sports. She is a member of the Presbyterian Church. Residence: Bridgeport.

Charles Sumner Sherman

Charles Sumner Sherman, newspaperman, has lived in this state for the past 50 years, and has been prominent in the newspaper life of his community. He was born at Villisca, Iowa, March 10, 1871, the son of Charles Wheelan and Orilla (Groom) Sherman. His father, a newspaper publisher and editor, was born in Richland County, Ohio, June 6, 1841, and died at Los Angeles, in January 1921. He served as a member of the Third Iowa Cavalry for over three years during the Civil War. His ancestors emigrated from England in the 17th century, and his paternal great-grandfather was a soldier in the New Jersey troops during the Revolution.

Orilla Sherman, mother of Charles S. Sherman, was born in Marion County, Iowa, August 26, 1842, and died at Plattsmouth, Nebraska, May 31, 1900. Her family, of Scotch, Irish, and English extraction, in America for many generations.

Mr. Sherman first attended the public schools of Glenwood, Iowa, and in 1887 was graduated from the Plattsmouth High School. He has always been in the newspaper business and for 16 years has been sports editor of the *Lincoln Star*. Mr. Sherman first named the Nebraska University's athletic teams the *Cornhuskers*, a title by which they are known throughout the inter-collegiate sports world today. He is a member of the Lincoln Chamber of Commerce, the Lincoln University Club and the Nebraskana Society. His favorite sport is billiards, and his hobby is landscape gardening and beautifying his home.

His marriage to Nancy Ada Moore was solemnized at Davenport, Scott County, Iowa, August 16, 1893. Mrs. Sherman was born at Davenport, October 31, 1870; her ancestry is Scotch-Irish.

Mr. Sherman is a member of the Benevolent and Protective Order of Elks, Lodge Number 80, of Lincoln. He is a Democrat. Residence: Lincoln.

Lucius Adelno Sherman

Lucius A. Sherman, educator at the University of Nebraska, was born at Douglas, Worcester County, Massachusetts, August 28, 1847, the son of Asahel and Eunice (Walker) Sherman. His father, who was born at Burrillville, Providence County, Rhode Island, May 2, 1804, and died at Douglas, May 6, 1887, was a builder; Philip Sherman, who settled at Plymouth Colony in the early

history of America, came from southern Norfolk, England. His mother, whose ancestors were prominent in colonial America, was born at Douglas, September 14, 1810, and died there March 5, 1891.

Dr. Sherman attended the district school at Douglas, the high school there, and the East Greenwich Seminary, later attending Andover Phillips Academy. He received the A. B. degree at Yale, 1871, and the Ph. D. degree in 1875. He was awarded membership in Phi Beta Kappa and Alpha Delta Phi. He was professor of English and dean of the Arts College and later the Graduate College, and is now professor emeritus at the University of Nebraska. He was the founder and editor of *University Studies*, 1888. He holds membership in the Modern Language Association, the Nebraskana Society, and the St. Paul Methodist Episcopal Church of Lincoln, and holds membership in the University Club.

He was married to Antoinette Whittlesey at New Haven, Connecticut, July 6, 1875; she was born at New Haven, May 10, 1854, and died there August 14, 1900; she was descended from the Whittlesey family of Connecticut. To this marriage one child was born: Lucius, born July 22, 1876. On September 28, 1878, he was married to Anna Barber Williston, at Athens, Pennsylvania. Two children were born to this marriage: Horace, born October 21, 1879, who married Rosannah Cannon Sherman; and Winifred, born April 26, 1884, who married Robert Updike of Omaha. Dr. Sherman's marriage to Mrs. Josephine Fisher was solemnized at Boston, June 26, 1902. Residence: Lincoln. (Photograph in Album).

Nancy Moore Sherman

Nancy Moore Sherman was born at Davenport, Iowa, October 31, 1870, daughter of William Francis and Mary Ann (Treftz) Moore. Her father was born near St. Louis, Missouri, May 10, 1845, and died at Davenport, Iowa, February 4, 1881. He was of Scotch-Irish descent. Mary Ann Treftz was born at Johnstown, Pennsylvania, March 11, 1849, and died near Spokane, Washington, October 7, 1920. Her ancestry was Scotch-Irish and German.

Upon the completion of her elementary and high school work in the schools of Davenport, Iowa, Nancy Moore entered the University of Nebraska. There she was a charter member of the Dramatic Club, and vice president of her freshman class. On August 11, 1893, she was married to Charles Sumner Sherman, at Davenport, Iowa. Mr. Sherman, who was born at Villisca, Iowa, March 10, 1871, is sports editor of the *Lincoln Star*.

Mrs. Sherman taught in the public schools of Iowa and Nebraska for several years; during the World War she was a member of the first class in bandage making and taught four classes. At the present time she is assistant secretary of the Lincoln Trust Company of Lincoln.

She is a member of the First Presbyterian Church, and of the Altrusa Club, its secretary at the present time and was its president during 1929-30. Residence: Lincoln.

S. Toledo Sherry

S. Toledo Sherry, retired educator of Dakota County, Nebraska, was born at Mechanicsville, Missouri, March 3, 1862, the son of Thomas and Lorena (Sherry). His father, who was born at Brookborough, Ireland, and died in 1874, was a stone mason; he invented the check row corn planter and cultivator. His mother's ancestors were originally natives of Kentucky and Virginia.

Mr. Sherry received the B. S. degree in 1896 at Valparaiso University, Indiana, and the A. B. degree in 1920. He was later a student in universities in Missouri, Texas, Chicago, and Geneva, Switzerland. After twenty years in public school work and thirty years in the United States Indian Service he is retired on a federal annuity. He is the author of *The Model Farm Plan of Education;* and

The Movement to Issue Ten Billion Dollars in Prosperity Bonds and Place 5,000,000 Unemployed and others on Five to Forty Acre Tracts of Land.

He is a member of the South Sioux City Commercial Club, the Odd Fellows, Nebraska Teachers Association, the World Federation of Education Association. He holds membership in the Nebraskana Society, is affiliated with the Methodist Church, and is a member of the National Educational Associations. His ambition is to help make the United States a nation of happy homes, and the nations a United States of the world.

Of his marriage to Marcia K. Camp at Chicago, two children were born, Alice and Estelle. Mrs. Sherry is descended from ancestors who came to America on the *Mayflower*. Residence: South Sioux City.

Joseph V. Shestak

Joseph V. Shestak, a resident of Nebraska, since 1866, was born at Cooper, Wisconsin, January 19, 1861, the son of Vaciav and Frantiska (Woeab) Shestak. His father, who was born in Bohemia, in 1835, and died at Wilber, in 1905, was a farmer who came to this country in 1854. His mother was born in Bohemia, and died at Wilber, in 1887. Mr. Shestak's parents were the first Bohemian settlers in Saline County in 1865.

Mr. Shestak attended the grade and high schools of Saline County. He was engaged in the dry goods business for four years, and is now retired. A Democrat, he was justice of the peace at Wilber, from 1900 to 1926. His family has been prominent in Saline County since Vaclav Shestak homesteaded there in the early history of the state. He is a member of the Knights of Pythias and the Nebraskana Society. His favorite sport is hiking.

On September 13, 1884, he was united in marriage with Barbara Herian. Mrs. Shestak, whose parents were farmers, was born in Bohemia, April 24, 1866. They have three children: William J., born June 13, 1890, who married Clara Schleis Frances B., born March 17, 1888, who married Dr. Fred Barta; and Rose, born March 19, 1892. William J. served in the World War. Residence: Crete.

James Taylor Shewell

James T. Shewell was born at Nebraska City, Nebraska, October 8, 1878. Henry Nathan Shewell, his father, who was a banker, was born at Rootstown, Portage County, Ohio, January 16, 1846, and died at Nebraska City, August 22, 1914.

Jennie Terry (Taylor) Shewell, his mother, was the daughter of James H. Taylor of Charleston, South Carolina. She was born at Charleston, May 28, 1856, and died at Greenville, South Carolina, March 8, 1915.

Mr. Shewell attended the Nebraska City public schools and later was a student at Professor Bartlett's preparatory school for Yale at Blackhall, Connecticut. He has lived in Nebraska all his life, and since 1897 has been connected with the Merchants' National Bank at Nebraska City, serving the present time as its president.

His marriage to Elizabeth MacCuaig was solemnized at Nebraska City, March 12, 1906. Mrs. Shewell, who was born at Nebraska City, March 21, 1879, is of Scotch-English descent. They have one daughter, Corinne, born February 1, 1909, who was graduated from the University of Nebraska in 1930. Residence: Nebraska City.

John Grant Shick

John G. Shick was born at Parkville, Missouri, August 9, 1869, the son of Johnston Buckner and Joanna (Eby) Shick. His father, who was born in Brown County, Ohio, July 2, 1834, and died at Parkville, May 6, 1870, was a raftsman on the Missouri River; he served in the 19th Kansas Cavalry under General Price in the Civil War. His mother was born at Circleville, Ohio, August 22, 1833, and died at Neligh, Nebraska, January 13, 1915. Her ancestry is traced through her father's line, Joseph Eby,

and through her mother's family, the Dormans, to service in the continental armies during the Revolution.

Dr. Shick was graduated from the Gates Teachers College at Neligh, in 1896; was graduated from the Garrett Biblical Institute, Evanston, Illinois, 1899. He was awarded the D. D. degree at Nebraska Wesleyan University, June 1, 1921. Garrett Biblical Institute is now affiliated with Northwestern University. He is now pastor of the First Methodist Church at Cambridge, Furnace County, Nebraska.

He was married to Lizzie Harmon at Inman, Holt County, Nebraska, September 6, 1899. Mrs. Shick, who was a public school teacher and home missionary before her marriage, was born at Blandinville, McDonough, Illinois, August 27, 1869. Her father served in the Illinois Regiment during the Civil War under General Sherman. They have one daughter, Imogene Lydia, born June 26, 1900, who was graduated from Nebraska Wesleyan University, and who married Glendall Val Bailey, who was graduated from the University of Nebraska; she is an unusually fine singer.

Dr. Shick is a member of the Chamber of Commerce at Cambridge; is a member of the Nebraska Conference of the Methodist Episcopal Church; and holds membership in The Nebraskana Society. He was formerly a member of the Kiwanis Club at Wayne, Nebraska. His hobby is gardening. Residence: Cambridge.

Maurice Fisher Schickley

One of the most successful of the younger educators of Nebraska, Maurice Fisher Shickley is now serving as superintendent of city schools at Ainsworth. He was born at Geneva, Nebraska, May 21, 1901, the son of Clinton Richard, and Sarah Irene (Fisher) Shickley. His father was born at Springfield, Ohio, and died at Geneva, April 3, 1927. His mother was born at Davis, Illinois, and is living in Geneva.

Mr. Shickley was graduated from the Geneva High School in 1919, and received the Bachelor of Science degree from the University of Nebraska in 1925. During his university career he was a member of Gamma Lambda, captain of the university military band, business manager of the university symphony orchestra, and a member of the commercial club. He served as superintendent of public schools at Yutan from 1925-30, and since 1930 has held his present position.

He is a member of the Ainsworth Commercial Club, the Nebraska State Teachers Association, and the Shrine Country Club of Lincoln. He is a member, also, of Geneva Masonic Lodge No. 79, the Scottish Rite of Lincoln, and the Tangier Shrine Band, of Omaha. He is a member of the Congregational Church. His favorite sport is fishing.

On June 29, 1930, he was married to Gail Phyllis McCandless at Lincoln. Mrs. Shickley was born at Nemaha, Nebraska, October 17, 1907. Residence: Ainsworth.

Fred Shimerda

Fred Shimerda, furniture dealer and funeral director, was born in Wilber Precinct, Nebraska, September 28, 1891, son of Anton H. and Frances (Kostecka) Shimerda

He attended public and high school at Wilber, and in 1913 received the Ph. G. degree from Creighton University. He was in the drug business 1913-14; was assistant cashier of the Saline State Bank 1914-15; assistant cashier of the Wilber State Bank 1915-27; and since 1927 has been in his present business.

On June 4, 1913, he was married to Rose Sasek at Omaha. There are two children, Grace Frances, born July 16, 1914; and Faye Marie, born November 29, 1925.

Mr. Shmerda is a Democrat. He was a sergeant in the U. S. Army, stationed at Evacuation Hospital No. 12. He participated in the St. Mehiel drive and after the armistice was stationed at Treves, Germany. He is a member and was first commander of Louis Post, No.

101 of the American Legion, and was state vice commander in 1928.

He is a member of the Red Cross, the Masons, Knights of Pythias, Eastern Star, the Sokol, and the Library Board of which he was a director 1929-30. Residence: Wilber.

Marion Eugene Shipley

Born near Howard, Knox County, Ohio, July 16, 1868, Marion Eugene Shipley is the son of Benedict Francis and Mary Catherine (Anderson) Shipley. His father was born near Gambier, Knox County, Ohio, January 29, 1836, and died at Portland, Oregon, August 22, 1920. He was a mill-wright, lumberman and farmer. His great grandfather, Richard Shipley, came to America long prior to the Revolution, and as a civil engineer laid out much of the city of Baltimore. Mary Catherine Anderson was born in Knox County, Ohio, July 22, 1845, and died at Green Forest, Arkansas, October 4, 1902. Her father was Scandinavian and her mother Pennsylvania Dutch.

Marion Eugene Shipley attended the country schools of Ohio, and Nebraska, and the public schools of North Bend. He followed the profession of a printer for twenty years, and from 1894-98, was editor and publisher of the *Stanwood Herald* (Iowa). Thereafter he became interested in telephone engineering, and in 1901 became general manager of the Hooper Telephone Company which position he still holds. Until recently he has been connected with light and power corporations, and was president of the Hooper Electric Light and Power Company, and the owner of the Sheridan Electric Service Company of Rushville, Nebraska.

A Democrat, he served in the 33rd session of the Nebraska legislature as a member of the house of representatives, and during the World War was captain of the Hooper Company of the Nebraska Home Guards, chairman of Four Minute Men, holding a commission from President Wilson. His captain's commission was given him by Governor Neville. He was also active in loan drives and a member of the Nebraska Council of Defense.

On September 15, 1895, he was married to Lessie Alice Thompson, at North Bend. Mrs. Shipley was born at Marco, Indiana, September 17, 1876. She is a musician. They have one son, Trajan C., born August 20, 1897, who attended the University of Nebraska, and is an electrical engineer with the Central West Public Service Company of Omaha.

Mr. Shipley is a member of the Hooper Methodist Episcopal Church, the Ancient Free and Accepted Masons, the Odd Fellows, Knights of Pythias, and Modern Woodmen of America, as well as the Sons of the American Revolution and The Nebraskana Society. Residence: Hooper. (Photograph in Album).

Sherman Shipman

In the fall of 1879 Sherman Shipman homesteaded with his parents in Graham County, Kansas, where they remained until 1884 when they settled in Burr Oak, Kansas. He is now one of the leading farmers and stockraisers in the vicinity of Guide Rock, Nebraska, and takes part in all civic affairs in that community.

He was born in Iowa, March 4, 1878, the son of James John and Anna M. (Parrish) Shipman, the former a carpenter and farmer. His father, who was a soldier in Company B, 99th Indiana Infantry, was born at Springfield, Ohio, October 31, 1839, and died at Red Cloud, Nebraska, March 13, 1928. His mother, whose ancestry was Welsh and German was born at Cleveland, Ohio, February 27, 1847, and died at Red Cloud, January 15, 1931.

Mr. Shipman attended an elementary school at Burr Oak, Kansas. He is president of the Farmers Union Gas & Oil Company at Red Cloud, is president of the Farmers Union Co-operative Association of Guide Rock,

and for the past 18 years served almost continuously on the local school board. He is a member of the Independent Order of Odd Fellows and Rebekah Lodge, and holds membership in the Nebraskana Society.

During the World War Mr. Shipman assisted in loan drives and was a member of the home guards. His favorite recreation is reading the newspapers.

On January 18, 1905, he married Nora May Redden at Guide Rock; she was born of German and Irish parents at Davenport, Iowa, November 20, 1882. They have seven children: Elwin Lloyd, born October 26, 1905, who married Ruth Drake; Marvel Lucile, born April 29, 1908, who married Harold Smith; Erma Lavinda, born April 26, 1910, who married Elton Winemiller; Floyd, born May 27, 1912; Opal Verle, born June 18, 1915, who married Ralph Harris; Hazel Violet, born March 9, 1919; and Mildred Bernice, born April 7, 1922. Residence: Guide Rock.

Claude Joseph Shirk

Claude J. Shirk was born at Morrison, Illinois, August 18, 1875. Joseph Shirk, his father, was successively a carpenter, oil man, and farmer. He was born at Middlesex, Pennsylvania, April 4, 1832, and died at McPherson, Kansas, February 13, 1909. His Swiss ancestors came to America in 1610 and settled in Virginia. Later they moved to Pennsylvania where Joseph Shirks' father served in the War of 1812, was one of the survivors of Perry's flagship and was awarded a medal for bravery at the battle of Lake Erie.

His mother, Clarinda Alvira (Clark) Shirk, who was a teacher before her marriage, was born at Clarks Mills, Pennsylvania, November 27, 1840, and died at Dallas, Oregon, March 1, 1920. She was anactive worker in the Women's Christian Temperance Union. Her maternal grandfather was a snare drummer in the War of 1812, and the town of Clarks Mills was named in his honor.

Professor Shirk was graduated from the McPherson College Academy in 1896. He was awarded the following degrees at McPherson College: A. B., 1901; A. M., 1902; M. S. D., 1903. In 1909 he received his M. S. at the University of Chicago. He was awarded the degree Ph. D. at the University of Nebraska, 1924, and was a graduate student at the University of Kansas in the summer of 1904. He was made a member of Phi Kappa Phi, Pi Gamma Mu, and the Sem. Bot., University of Nebraska.

A district school teacher at McPherson, Kansas, 1896-1900, he was high school principal at Canton, Kansas, 1901; was superintendent of public schools at Inman, Kansas, 1901-04; professor of mathematics and chemistry, at McPherson College, at McPherson, Kansas, 1905-18; professor of mathematics at Ottawa University, 1911-13; professor of botany at Nebraska Wesleyan University, 1913-19; and since 1919 has been professor of biology at the Nebraska Wesleyan University. He is collaborator on *Biological Abstracts*; and is the author of *An Ecological Study of the Vegetation of an Inland Saline Area*, which was completed in 1924, unpublished as yet.

Professor Shirk is director and auditor of the Alliance Co-operative Insurance Company of Topeka, Kansas. A Democrat, he was nominee for county superintendent of McPherson County in 1904.

He was married to Jennie Elizabeth Bush at Inman, McPherson County, Kansas, June 14, 1905. Mrs. Shirk, who was born at Inman, June 17, 1884, is of English and German descent. Her father served four years in the Civil War. There are three children: Eldred Claude, born May 4, 1913; Wilmer Ray, born February 4, 1916; and Kathryn Jean, born October 3, 1919.

Professor Shirk is a member of the American Association of University Professors, the American Interprofessional Institute, American Association for the Advancement of Science, Nebraska Academy of Sciences, National Geographic Society, Botanical Society of

America, American Society of Plant Physiology, Ecological Society of America, and the British Ecological Society. He is a member of the First Methodist Episcopal Church of Lincoln. Residence: Lincoln.

Percy Chalmette Shockley

Percy Chalmette Shockley, ranchman and banker, was born at Fort Scott, Kansas, January 8, 1881, son of William Bridges and Anna Gertrude (Alexander) Shockley.

William Bridges Shockley was born at Maysville, Kentucky, October 11, 1840, and served through the Civil War and Indian campaign as a colonel of cavalry. He was a soldier and government employee whose death occurred at Fort Leavenworth, Kansas, August 16, 1915.

His ancestors came to the United States prior to the settlement of the Plymouth Colony and were officers in the Revolution and Indian wars. One paternal ancestor was killed in the Seminole Indian War.

Anna Gertrude Alexander was born at Hollidaysburg, Pennsylvania, September 12, 1843, and died at Brownlee, November 30, 1914. She was active in civic and welfare work. Her family were pressed into the English service during the Revolutionary War by a British press gang, and afterward deserted to the American forces and were pensioners of that war.

Mr. Shockley attended public school at Leavenworth, Kansas, and was graduated from Kemper Military School at Boonville in 1899. From that time until 1902, and during 1907 and the spring term of 1908, he attended the Missouri School of Mines at Rolla where he finished courses in surveying and mining, including metallurgy. Both in military school and college he was active in track and football.

Mr. Shockley began his career as a mining engineer for the Central Coal and Coke Company of Kansas City, Missouri. He was a mining engineer for the American Smelters Securities Company of Old Mexico, and next was manager of mines for the El Poriner Mining Company of Mexico. He has been a forest ranger, merchant, banker, and ranchman, and at the present time is president of the Goose Creek Cattle Company, a director of the Limestone Cattle Company, and is associated with the Stock Yards National Bank of Omaha.

On March 23, 1915, he was married to Zaidee Ina Guilfoil at Creighton, Missouri. Mrs. Shockley was born at Elliott, Iowa, October 2, 1895, and is of Revolutionary ancestry. They have one daughter, Frances Leila, born March 18, 1916.

Mr. Shockley is a Republican. He was captain of Company D, 38th Machine Gun Battalion, 13th Division, United States Army, during the World War, and had active service from August 23, 1917, until March 1, 1919. He is a member of the American Legion, the Masons, and the Nebraskana Society. His hobbies are dogs and horses. Residence: Brownlee.

Charles Albert Shoff

A lifetime resident of Nebraska, Charles Albert Shoff was born at Grafton, October 14, 1877, the son of John and Martha (Taylor) Shoff. His father, who is a veteran of the Civil War, was born October 27, 1840, and was the first commissioned postmaster at Grafton, serving intermittently from 1875 until 1914 at which time Charles Albert Shoff was appointed. His mother, who was a grand-niece of Zachary Taylor, was born at Coshocton, Ohio, June 11, 1844, and died at Grafton, February 3, 1901.

Mr. Shoff was graduated from high school in 1898. He has served as postmaster at Grafton since 1914 under the Wilson, Harding, Coolidge, and Hoover administrations. Mrs. Shoff has been his assistant during this time. During the World War he sold war saving stamps and liberty bonds and solicited for the Council of Defense.

He was awarded a Victory loan medal by the United States Treasury.

He was united in marriage with Mary Belle Standard at Geneva, Nebraska, July 2, 1907. Mrs. Shoff, whose father served in the Civil War, was born at Grafton, November 3, 1881. They have one daughter, Florence Ina, who was born December 23, 1917. She is a freshman in high school and is a member of the Children of the American Revolution, and upon reaching 18 years of age will automatically become a member of the Daughters of the American Revolution. Residence: Grafton. (Photograph in Album).

Frank William Shonka

Frank William Shonka, son of Mathias and Mary (Hajny) Shonka, was born in the village of Smolec, Okres Bachijn, Kraj Tabor, Cecho-Slovakia, May 15, 1858. His father, who was also born in the village of Smolec, on February 27, 1827, came to America in 1867, and assisted in the organization of the first Catholic Church in Butler County, in 1873, and the first school district organized the same year. A pioneer farmer, he died at Schuyler, June 7, 1907. Mary Hajny, wife of Mathias, was born in Okres Bachijn, Kraj Tabor, Cecho-Slovakia, in 1830, and died at Schuyler, February 14, 1906.

Frank W. Shonka was educated in the public schools, and on December 26, 1888, was united in marriage to Frances Emma Shimanek, at Crete. Mrs. Shonka, who was born at Omaha, May 24, 1869, is of Bohemian descent. There are four sons and daughters: Mary Frances, born October 10, 1889, graduated from Rohrbaugh Business College, and is married to Anthony Clement Wittera; Frank William, Jr., born October 29, 1893, served in the World War, and is married to Hattie Pelter; Irene Alice, born September 25, 1896, is a graduate of the University of Wisconsin, and is married to John Harold Tacki; John Charles, born December 30, 1907, is a graduate of Schuyler High School.

A Democrat, Mr. Shonka served as county clerk six years, county treasurer 4 years, and as a member of the board of education and the Schuyler city council. He has been engaged in the banking business for the past thirty years, and recently retired as president of the Richland State Bank. He is president and director of the Schuyler Savings Bank and vice president and director of the Schuyler State Bank.

By appointment of President Woodrow Wilson, he served as a four minute man during the World War for the purpose of supervising public speaking and keeping the administration informed regarding local war activities. His son, Frank, Jr., is a member of the American Legion, and is present district commander, 7th district, department of Nebraska.

A Catholic, Mr. Shonka was a member of the building committees of St. Mary's Church of which he is a member, and of St. Augustine's Church. He is a member of the Odd Fellows, the C. S. P. S. Lodge and the Nebraskana Society. His hobby is reading. Residence: Schuyler.

Judson Shook

Judson Shook, son of Jacob and Mary Elizabeth (Hyatt) Shook, was born in Ripley County, Indiana, May 14, 1870. Jacob Shook was born in Ripley County, Indiana, November 27, 1843, and died at Tipton, Indiana, November 27, 1920. He was a veteran of the Civil War and a farmer until ill health made it impossible. His family were among the first settlers in southern Indiana, all were farmers.

Mary Elizabeth Hyatt was born in Ripley County, December 4, 1850, and died at Tipton, December 2, 1891. They also were farmers and among the early settlers of Indiana.

Graduated from school in the spring of 1888, on Aug-

ust 15, of the following year he was married to Edith
A. Sparks at Sharpsville, Indiana. She was born in
Bartholomew County, March 22, 1872. Her father, W.
T. Sparks, was an early day school teacher and at 83 is
well and strong. He resides in Washington, D. C.

Mr. and Mrs. Shook have six children, Andrew, born
January 6, 1901, married Amelia Steffins; Mable, born
January 8, 1903, married William Lucke; Beulah, born
June 21, 1896, married Gordon Baber; Emily, born June
4, 1902, married Theodore Deetheardt; Harold, born
April 19, 1906, married Ann Lupton; and Mildred, born
February 15, 1909, married Wesly Robson.

Mr. Shook has resided at Gordon, Nebraska, since
September, 1913, and prior to that was farm agent in
Kansas for one year. Since 1913 he has been farm agent
on the Pine Ridge reservation in South Dakota, his work
in the Indian service being to a great extent missionary
work. His hobby is reading. Residence: Gordon.

William Edward Shook

William E. Shook was born at Hillsdale, a town now
extinct, Nemaha County, Nebraska, November 28, 1872.
John Hamilton Shook, his father, who was born at Carlinville, Macoupin County, Illinois, July 31, 1838, and died
at Livingston, Merced County, California, August 18,
1914, was a farmer and stockman, and a lumberman, furnishing many of the early settlers of southeast Nebraska
with lumber for their first buildings. He served in the
15th Iowa volunteers in the Civil War for over three years,
and was with Sherman on his famous march to the sea.
He acted as county commissioner of Nemaha County for
12 years; served one term in the state legislature. His
great great grandfather came from Holland before the
Revolutionary War, and settled in Pennsylvania. His
mother, Eleanor Ingram (Pike) Shook, was born in Jones
County, Iowa, March 14, 1852, and came to Nebraska
about 1870.

Dr. Shook attended the Nemaha and Auburn public
schools after which he attended business college for a
short time. He was a student at Cotner University for
some time, studied at the Omaha Medical College for
two years, and was graduated from the medical department of the University of Illinois, May 28, 1901. He was
admitted to the practice of medicine in Nemaha County,
Nebraska, October, 1901. Since 1903 he has been engaged in the medical profession at Shubert, Nebraska,
for the last twelve years he has been in partnership with
Dr. George W. Egermayer, under the firm name of Shook
and Egermayer, Physicians and Surgeons.

His marriage to Lizzie Belle Shurtleff was solemnized
at Humboldt, Nebraska, June 25, 1902. Mrs. Shook, who
was born at Humboldt, March 16, 1877, was a teacher before her marriage. The first Shurtleffs were colonists
in Massachusetts, and Mrs. Shook's parents came from
Virginia shortly after the Civil War, settling in Beardstown, Illinois. To this marriage were born two daughters:
Mildred Dorothy, born June 20, 1903, who is a graduate
of the University of Nebraska, and is a teacher in the
Falls City High School; and Eleanor Elizabeth, born October 17, 1907, a graduate of the University of Nebraska,
who is a teacher in the high school at Phillips, Nebraska.

Mr. Shook is a Republican. He served as official
court stenographer of the first judicial district of Nebraska in 1896 and 1897; was a member of the school
board for fifteen years; and has served several years on
the town board at Shubert. He is a member of the county and state medical associations, and the American Medical Association, holding various offices in the county organization, and serving as vice president of the state society. During the World War he served on the medical
advisory board for Richardson County, Nebraska. He
is a Mason, Shriner, Knight Templar. He is affiliated
with the Christian Church of Shubert. Residence: Shubert.

Abel Vail Shotwell

Abel Vail Shotwell, lawyer, was born at Marengo,
Iowa, January 7, 1883. He is the son of Hudson Burr
and Emma Jane (Noe) Shotwell. Hudson Burr Shotwell
was the son of Edward R. and Margaret Shotwell, whose
ancestors came to America in the early part of the 18th
century, and served in the Revolutionary War. Hudson
Burr Shotwell was born at Philadelphia, July 3, 1842.
He was a merchant, and held the rank of first lieutenant
in the Union Army during the Civil War. He died at
Marengo, Ohio in October, 1907.

Emma Jane Noe was born at Marengo, September 8,
1850. She is a daughter of George K. and Sarah J. (Doty)
Noe. Sarah J. Doty was a lineal descendant of Edward
Doty, who came to America on the *Mayflower*.

Upon his graduation from Marengo High School in
1900, Mr. Shotwell entered Ohio Wesleyan University.
He studied there one year, and entered the State Uni-
vrsity of Ohio, where he remained until 1905. He was
valedictorian of his high school class, and was awarded
a scholarship to Ohio Wesleyan. He was chairman of the
senior social committee at Ohio State University in 1905
and manager of the college publication *The Lantern* in
1904.

He was married to Hilda Eva Condron at Omaha,
June 7, 1907. Mrs. Shotwell was born at Bluff Center,
Iowa, November 8, 1885, and is of Scotch Irish descent.
They have four children, Ruth Vail, born August 17,
1908, married Roland Fletcher; Hudson Burr, born October 24, 1912; Gordon Stewart, born October 11, 1914;
and Anabel, born June 23, 1920.

Mr. Shotwell has been engaged in the practice of law
since 1905. From 1905-11 he was a member of the firm
of Shotwell & Shotwell, and from 1911-25 of the firm of
Lambert, Shotwell and Shotwell. At the present time
he is senior member of the firm of Shotwell and Vance,
successors to the firm of Shotwell and Ready, of which
he was a member from 1925-31. A Republican, he served
as county attorney of Douglas County from 1919-23. He
has been a member of the Republican State executive
committee since 1924, and has served as chairman during
that time of the executive committee of the Douglas County central committee since 1924.

He participated in all civilian war activities during
the World War. He is a member of the Mayflower Society and Sons of the American Revolution, the American, Nebraska State and Omaha-Douglas County Bar
Associations, the Red Cross and the Chamber of Commerce. His clubs are the Omaha Field Club, the Omaha
Club, the Omaha Country Club and the Omaha Athletic
Club. He is fond of golf, but his real hobby is fishing.
Residence: Omaha. (Photograph on Page 1089).

Berton T. Shoup

Berton T. Shoup, general manager of the Farmers
Union Co-operative Association at Sutherland, was born
there on July 24, 1904, son of James Milton and Etta
Florence (Ridgway) Shoup.

The father was born at Appleton City, Missouri,
September 26, 1874 and died at Sutherland, May 29,
1926. He was a farmer and stockman, prominent in
local affairs, a member of the board of directors of Sutherland schools and of the Farmers Union. His wife,
Etta, was born in Appleton City, October 13, 1872. She
was a teacher for nine years and is now active in the
Women's Club at Sutherland.

Mr. Shoup was graduated from Sutherland High
School in 1921 and attended the University of Nebraska
1921-22-23-24-25. He is a member of Farm House fraternity and was active in baseball, basketball, and tennis
of Sutherland High School. For the past seven years he
has been engaged in farming and the breeding of Hereford
cattle and at the present time is general manager of the
Farmers Co-operative Association in addition. He is a
Republican, a member of the First Methodist Episcopal
Church, and president of the Sutherland Commercial

ABEL VAIL SHOTWELL

Heyn—Omaha

Club. He is a member of Blue Lodge Masons, Royal Arch Masons, Knights Templar, and Eastern Star; and is pastmaster of the Blue Lodge. He is standard bearer of the Knights Templar and a member of Palestine Commandery Number 13 at North Platte. His favorite sport is tennis. Residence: Sutherland.

Emmett G. Shoup

Emmett G. Shoup was born at Pawnee City, Nebraska, June 5, 1904, the son of Charles Albert Shoup and Mary Anna (Hunzeker) Shoup. His father was born in Illinois, and died at Fairbury, Jefferson County, Nebraska, August 27, 1929. He was a carpenter and cabinet maker.

He was educated for the typographical and newspaper business under the supervision of the International Typographical Union. He married Mabel Grace Saulsbury at York, Nebraska, June 5, 1929. She was born at Shreveport, Maryland County, Pennsylvania, July 7, 1904, and was a dental nurse. They have one child, Robert Darrell, born February 5, 1931.

Mr. Shoup is editor and publisher of *The Carleton Enterprize*. He is independent in politics and has lived in Nebraska twenty-six years. He affiliated with the Methodist Church, is a member of the Elks Club, at Fairbury, Nebraska, and holds membership in the National Printer's Associations.

Mr. Shoup is a member of the Commercial Club, the Nebraskana Society, the National Educational Association and the Community Club at Carleton. He is interested in all sports, and reading and mechanics are his hobbies. Residence: Carleton.

Joseph M. Shramek

Joseph M. Shramek, surgeon, was born in Bohemia, December 22, 1879, son of Michael and Mary (Bohacke) Shramek. He attended public schools and Creighton University and is a member of Phi Beta Pi.

His marriage to Irma Mary Fay was solemnized at Omaha, on August 14, 1915.

Dr. Shramek has been a member of the faculty of Creighton University Medical College, and in 1913 was a lieutenant in the Medical Reserve Corps. He is a member of the American Legion, the American, Nebraska State, and Omaha Douglas County Medical Associations. Residence: Omaha.

William Ambrose Shreck

An outstanding figure in the professional world of Phelps County, is William Ambrose Shreck, who has been engaged in the practice of medicine at Bertrand, Nebraska, since 1896. He was born at Corydon, Indiana, September 3,1864, the son of Philip and Sarah Ann (Reed) Shreck. His father, who was a farmer and blacksmith, was born of Swiss parents in Rockingham County, Virginia, September 5, 1832, the son of George Shreck, and died in Harrison County, Indiana, September 1, 1897. His mother was born in Harrison County, May 2, 1836, and died at Corydon, in 1898. She was the daughter of Jesse G. and Barbara (Miller) Reed.

Dr. Shreck was graduated from the New Albany Business College in 1885, having previously taught in a rural school, attended Rush Medical College, 1893-94, and received the M. D. degree at the University of Louisville in 1896, where he was president of the graduating class.

He served as bookkeeper in the United States National Bank of Holdrege, Nebraska, 1886-89, was postmaster at Holdrege, 1889-93, and since 1896 has been a prominent physician at Bertrand, Nebraska. He is the owner of the Bertrand Telephone Company, a director of the First State Bank of Bertrand, is a member of the Phelps County Medical Society, the 10th Counselor District

Medical Society, the Nebraska State Medical Society, and the American Medical Association. He is a member of the Bertrand Community Club, the Red Cross, and the Modern Woodmen of America.

Dr. Shreck was secretary and president of the local school board from 1896-1930, and is a member of the Bertrand Golf Club and the Masonic Lodge. He is affiliated with the First Congregational Church of Bertrand, and during the World War was active in Liberty loan drives, and was secretary and treasurer of the Red Cross.

On December 29, 1896, he married Harriet Ardell Chittenden at Holdrege. Mrs. Shreck, who is a member of the Daughters of the American Revolution, was born at Durham, New York, January 11, 1874. She is the daughter of Horace K. and Julia (Montross) Chittenden, and the second great granddaughter of Captain Jairus Chittenden, of Guilford, Connecticut, who participated in the Revolutionary War. Wilham Chittenden was born at Marden, County Kent, England in 1594, and came to America from London in 1639 in the ship *St. John*, settling in Guilford, thus starting the Chittenden family in America.

Mrs. Shreck is active in the P. E. O. Lodge. They have two children: Neil C., born March 20, 1901, who married Lucyle Mae McGrath, and who is manager of the Bertrand Telephone Company, and who attended the University of Nebraska one year; and Horace W., born July 5, 1907, who is a graduate of Doane College and is now a student at Creighton Medical College. Residence: Bertrand. (Photograph in Album).

Frank William Shrimpton

For the past 50 years Frank William Shrimpton has been a resident of Nebraska and for a number of years has taken an active part in the civic and business affairs at Ainsworth. He was born at DeKalb, Illinois, December 29, 1874, the son of George and Ann (Freeman) Shrimpton, the former a flour miller who was born at Thames, England, April 9, 1839, and died at Salem, Nebraska, July 16, 1916. His mother was born at Crabs Cross, England, March 31, 1841, and died at Salem, February 22, 1922.

Mr. Shrimpton was graduated from high school and for 13 years was manager of the Greenewood Milling Company. For the past 18 years he has served as manager of the Shrimpton Milling Company at Ainsworth. He is chairman of the Brown County Chapter of the American Red Cross, and has served as president of the Ainsworth Commercial Club for two terms.

He has been a member of the Ainsworth Board of Education for the past 10 years, is past master of the Masons and a Knight Templar, and holds membership in the Ainsworth Country Club where he enjoys golfing. He likes to hunt and fish.

He was married at Salem, Nebraska, to Maude White Spurlock November 21, 1900. Mrs. Shrimpton, who was born at Salem, June 30, 1876, is a granddaughter of J. C. Lincoln, a cousin of Abraham Lincoln. They have two children: Alice, born October 16, 1904, attended Ward-Belmont School for a year, was graduated from the University of Nebraska, and is married to Ivan McKinley Stone; and Virginia Ann, born July 30, 1909, who attended Lindenwood School, St. Charles, Missouri, for two years and later was graduated from the University of Nebraska. Residence: Ainsworth.

J. Frank Shubert

On November 4, 1870, J. Frank Shubert was born in Richardson County, Nebraska, the son of Henry W. and Mary (Griffin) Shubert. His father, who was born in Bath County, Kentucky, June 2, 1834, and died at Shubert, Nebraska, April 19, 1909, was a farmer, commercial apple grower, live stock man, and banker. The town of Shubert was originally on his farm and was named for him. He was the son of John Shubert who was born in

Knight—Falls City

J. FRANK SHUBERT

Germany in 1806, and Rebecca Shubert who was born in Germany, in 1810.

Mary Griffin, his mother, was born in Mason County, Illinois in 1836, and died in Nemaha County, Nebraska, December 25, 1880.

Mr. Shubert attended the public schools of Nemaha County and was graduated from the Auburn High School. He has taken an active part in the political and business affairs of the state since he was a young man. Mr. Shubert is a Republican and has held the following offices: state senator 1906, state representative from Richardson County 1907, treasurer Shubert school district for the past 20 years. In 1928 he was unsuccessful candidate for the state senate.

For the past 22 years Mr. Shubert has been cashier of the Citizens Bank of Shubert; he is vice president of the Nebraska State Bank of Falls City, with which he has been affiliated for 10 years; for the past 15 years he has been treasurer of the Loess Land and Orchard Company. Like his father he is a commercial apple grower, live stock producer, farmer and banker.

On March 12, 1896, his marriage to Leona M. Athey was solemnized at Shubert. Mrs. Shubert was born in Mason County, Illinois, May 16, 1875. There is one daughter, Nina M., born December 12, 1896, who married Dearle Baker, a World War veteran and a district commander of the American Legion. She attended Shubert High School and was graduated from Falls City High School in 1916; two years later she completed the course at Peru State Teachers' College, Peru, Nebraska. She is an accomplished musician and is the composer of the well-known song *Nebraska*, and also the state song of the American Legion Auxiliary.

During the World War Mr. Shubert was chairman of the loan drives in his community and chairman of the local Red Cross, was active in United War Work, and sold Liberty bonds and war savings stamps. In 1925 he was commissioned a captain in the Quartermaster Reserve Corps in recognition of his wartime activities.

Mr. Shubert is a deacon and a member of the church board of the Shubert Christian Church. He is a member of the Commercial Club and a state member of the Y. M. C. A. He was recently re-elected to the State Board of Agriculture, and holds a life membership in the State Horticultural Society; he is a member of The Nebraskana Society, Shubert Parent-Teachers Association and the Masons, being affiliated with Hope Lodge No. 29, Ancient Free and Accepted Masons at Nemaha, Mount Sinai Commandery at Falls City, and Sesostris Temple, Ancient Arabic Order Nobles of the Mystic Shrine at Lincoln.

A sketch of Mr. Shubert's life appears in the *History of Richardson County* by Lewis C. Edwards (1917). Residence: Shubert. (Photograph on Page 1091).

Arthur Harold Shultz

Arthur H. Shultz, prominent banker of Nebraska, was born at Scribner, Dodge County, Nebraska, April 13, 1885, the son of John Wallace, and Mary Ellen Shultz. His father is a retired farmer who was born at Newtown, Fountain County, Indiana, September 25, 1853. His mother was born at Indianapolis, Marion County, Indiana, June 22, 1858, and died at Scribner, March 14, 1924. Her ancestry was German.

Mr. Shultz received his early education in the public schools of Scribner; was graduated from Fremont Normal College in 1900; and in 1903 was graduated from Highland Park College. From 1903 to 1905 he was a clerk in the store of W. Gibbs at Bellingham, Washington; managed the lumber yard at Toledo, Iowa, for the Northern Grain Company, 1905-07; farmed near Scribner, 1907-15; was president and manager of the Farmers Co-operative Mercantile Company of Scribner, 1915-21; operating a mill, elevator, and lumber yard there. In 1917 he organized the Farmers State Bank at Scribner. He is now president of the latter and spends some of his time managing several hundred acres of his farm lands near Scribner.

He was chairman of the local Republican committee and from 1916 to 1922 was chairman of the Dodge County Republican Central Committee. He was a member of the Council of Defense during the World War. He holds membership in the Scribner Chamber of Commerce and the Nebraskana Society. He is a Mason. He devotes most of his spare time to reading.

Mr. Shultz was married at Scribner, December 26, 1907, to Mary Ann Mohr. Mrs. Shultz was born at Scribner, March 21, 1883. They have a son, Harold Mohr, born December 27, 1909, who was graduated from the University of Nebraska in 1931; he attended Harvard Law School, Midland College at Fremont, and the University of Colorado, at Boulder. Residence: Scribner. (Photograph on Page 1093).

Simon Peter Shultz

Born at Murphysboro, Jackson County, Illinois, September 1, 1848, Simon Peter Shultz has resided in Nebraswa fifty-nine years. His parents, Jacob and Rebecca (Will) Shultz, who were of Pennsylvania Dutch extraction, were pioneers in Nebraska in its early days. Jacob Shultz was born in Somerset County, Pennsylvania, January 10, 1814, and at the time of his death at Schuyler, on February 22, 1890, was a retired farmer. Rebecca Will Shultz was born in Somerset County, December 26, 1814, and died at Schuyler, July 26, 1897.

Simon Peter Shultz attended a round log school house in Jackson County, Illinois, and in 1872 came west with his family. He farmed in Colfax County many years, and is now retired. On February 19, 1874, he was married to Esther Elisabeth Perrin at North Bend, Nebraska. Mrs. Shultz, who is of English descent, was born in Hazel Green, Illinois, April 20, 1852. To them the following children were born:

Rosa, born December 8, 1874, married J. Stephen Samis; Eva, born January 6, 1876, married Ben L. Peters, and died October 15, 1925; Walter, born January 1, 1878, married Louise Vincent; Bert, born October 1, 1880, married Minnie McVicker; Florence, born February 12, 1882 married Matt Richards and died May 29, 1916; Logan, born November 5, 1883, married Pearl Vanhousen and died in November, 1923.

Mr. Shultz is a Republican, a Mason and a member of the Methodist Episcopal Church at Rogers. He is also a member of The Nebraskana Society. Residence: Rogers.

Martin Le Roy Shumway

Martin LeRoy Shumway, for many years an outstanding citizen of Lyons, Nebraska, was born in Houston County, Minnesota, December 25, 1874, and died at Lyons, March 19, 1931. He was the son of Jeremiah and Mary Maria (Paine) Shumway, the former a native of Oxford, Massachusetts, born October 15, 1827. A lumberman, he enlisted in Company A, 5th Minnesota Regiment and served till the close of the war. He died in Lyons in 1921. His descent was traced to Peter Shumway a French Huguenot, who came to America in 1695 with Peter Faneuil and Sigourney. Mary M. Paine was born at Pascoag, Rhode Island, July 28, 1832, and died at Lyons, August 19, 1898, a descendant of Roger Williams. In the year 1890 Martin Shumway entered the firm of J. Shumway and Son, and after the death of his father continued in business until his death. He had been a resident of Nebraska fifty years, and his death was mourned by all who knew him. He was a Republican, a member of the Woodmen of the World, the Modern Woodmen of America, the Odd Fellows and the Masons. (Deceased).

Seymour Stephen Sidner

For more than 30 years Seymour S. Sidner has been engaged in the practice of law at Fremont, Nebraska. He was born at Stillwater, New Jersey, January 12, 1875, the son of John and Martha Elizabeth (Van Horn) Sid-

ARTHUR HAROLD SHULTZ

Skoglund—Fremont

ner. His father, a farmer, was born in Warren County, New Jersey, April 9, 1846, and died at Fremont, August 15, 1923; his ancestors were Quakers who came to America from Engiand and Holland. His mother was born of Holland Dutch parentage in Sussex County, New Jersey, January 23, 1846, and died at Fremont, May 20, 1923.

Mr. Sidner attended rural school and in 1897 received the B. S. degree at Fremont College. He was a member of the firm Courtright & Sidner for many years, and is now a member of the firm Courtright, Sidner, Lee & Gunderson, at Fremont. He is director of the Union National Bank, the Union Trust Company, and the Nebraska State Building & Loan Association. A Democrat, he served as county attorney of Dodge County, 1915-16, was a member of the Constitutional Convention of Nebraska, 1919-20, and for 12 years was a member of the board of education of the Fremont School Board.

He was united in marriage with Myrtle Ione Cramer at Fremont, October 31, 1899; she was born at Harrisburg, Dauphin County, Pennsylvania, August 28, 1879. Four children were born to this union: Arthur C., born November 5, 1900; John E., born December 4, 1901; Seymour S., Jr., December 15, 1910; and Robert D., born January 13, 1918, who died May 20, 1920.

During the Spanish American War Mr. Sidner served as corporal of Troop K, 3rd United States Volunteer Cavalry, and in the World War he was active as chairman of the County Chapter of the American Red Cross. He holds membership in the United Spanish War Veterans. He is a member of the American Bar Association, the Nebraska State Bar Association, the Dodge County Bar Association, the Fremont Chamber of Commerce, and the Rotary Club. He is a member of the national council and the state committee of the Young Men's Christian Association. He is a Mason. His religious affiliation is with the First Presbyterian Church of Fremont. (Photograph in Album).

Lawrence T. Sidwell

Since 1908 Lawrence T. Sidwell has been engaged in the practice of medicine and at this time is a leading physician at Kearney, Nebraska. He was born at Chicago, Illinois, May 19, 1883, the son of Alfred Thomas and Margaret Robertson (Martin) Sidwell. His father was born at Metamora, Illinois, March 30, 1857, and died at Omaha, Nebraska, April 16, 1922. His mother, whose ancestry is Scotch, was born at Mount Pleasant, Iowa, April 21, 1861.

Dr. Sidwell was graduated from the Omaha High School in 1902, received the B. S. degree, 1906, and the M. D. degree, 1908, at the University of Nebraska where he was president of his class and was a member of Phi Rho Sigma. He was employed in the office of the *Omaha Daily News* from 1898 to 1902, worked in the office of the auditor for the Burlington Railroad during the summer of 1902, traveled for the Cudahy Packing Company during the summer months of 1903, 1904, 1905, 1906, and 1907, and practiced medicine at Glenwood, Iowa, 1908-17.

He served as assistant physician in the Nebraska State Hospital for the Insane at Hastings, Nebraska, 1917, was assistant superintendent in the Insane Hospital at Lincoln, Nebraska in 1918, was superintendent of the Tuberculosis Hospital at Kearney from 1918 to 1923 and served as superintendent of the Nebraska Home for the Feeble Minded at Beatrice from 1923 to 1927. He has been superintendent of the State Hospital for Tuberculars since 1927.

Dr. Sidwell is a member of the Chamber of Commerce at Kearney, is vice president of the Rotary Club there, and holds membership in the First Presbyterian Church. He was president of the Gage County Medical Society, 1924, was president of the Buffalo County Medical Society, 1928-29, and holds membership in the Nebraska State Medical Society. He is an Elk.

On December 7, 1911, Dr. Sidwell was married to Florence Mosher Miller at Omaha. Mrs. Sidwell, whose ancestors were members of the Hyde family in England, was born at Whitehall, Wisconsin, June 3, 1884. She received the A. B. degree at the University of Wisconsin in 1907 and was a teacher before her marriage. Their two children are: Margaret E., born January 4, 1913; and S. Miller, born January 26, 1915. Residence: Kearney.

Fred Christian Siek

Born at Pleasant Dale, Nebraska, October 14, 1875, Fred Christian Siek is the son of Fred Christian and Johanna (Jess) Siek. His father was born at Osdorf, Kriess-Ekermforde, Germany, March 25, 1835, and came to America on August 15, 1865. Prior to his death at Pleasant Dale on June 27, 1913, he was a prominent farmer. His wife was also born in Osdorf, January 14, 1855, and died at Pleasant Dale August 17, 1917.

Fred C. Siek, Jr., was educated in the public and parochial schools of Seward County, and on December 15, 1899, was united in marriage to Dorthia Minnie Piening, at Emerald. Mrs. Siek, who is of German descent, was born at Emerald, July 12, 1877. They have six children: Hanna, born May 14, 1900, who married Richard Meusborn; Fred, born November 3, 1901, who married Verge Pool; Minnie, born August 27, 1904, who married Frank Ficke; Albert, born February 23, 1907, who married Malinda Lostrah; Amanda, born March 9, 1908, who married William Lintdner; and Ervin, born December 11, 1911, who is unmarried.

Mr. Siek is a Democrat and active in local politics. During the World War he was a member of the Nebraska Council of Defense and the Red Cross, and at the present time he is president of Bethany Evangelical Lutheran Church, which office he has held since 1923. From 1911-20, he was a director of school district No. 64, and recently he was awarded membership in the Nebraskana Society. Residence: Pleasant Dale.

Karl Friedrich Siemsen

Karl Friedrich Siemsen was born at Schleswig, Germany, April 9, 1873, and for the past 44 years has been a resident of Nebraska. His father, Henning Siemsen, who was a tavern keeper in Germany was born at Stabel, October 27, 1837, and came to America in 1887 where he engaged in farming; he died at Cedar Bluffs, Nebraska, December 27, 1910. His mother, Sophia Maria (Gefke) Siemsen, was born at Schleswig, April 7, 1835, and died at Cedar Bluffs, May 7, 1909.

Mr. Siemsen is engaged in the soda fountain business at Atkinson and is connected with the Atkinson Hatchery. He is a life member of the Red Cross, is president of O. D. H. S. Lodge Number 42, and holds membership in the Commercial Club. His political preference is the Democratic party.

His marriage to Bertha Albertine C. Ahrndt was solemnized at Scribner, Nebraska, December 30, 1903. Mrs. Siemsen, who is in business at Atkinson, was born at Scribner, September 29, 1884. They have five children: Emma, born January 1, 1905, who is a registered nurse; Dora, May 12, 1906, who married Ted Wright, and who is a business woman; Sophia, born January 6, 1908, a teacher; Clara, born February 9, 1911; and Martin, born May 17, 1916 a student in high school. One son, Karl, who was born November 9, 1913, died August 7, 1931. Residence: Atkinson.

Herbert Dutton Silsby

Herbert Dutton Silsby, civic leader and banker at Bayard, Nebraska, was born near Mondamin, Iowa, July 4, 1873, the son of Russell Dutton and Marinda Brown (Mason) Silsby. His father, who was born at Middlesex, Vermont, April 8, 1829, and died at Little Sioux, Iowa, May 1, 1894, was a merchant and undertaker; of

English ancestry, he was descended from early settlers in America who landed at Plymouth in 1630; he served with the Green Mountain Boys during the Civil War. His mother was born at Ackworth, New Hampshire, March 24, 1833, and died at Castana, Iowa, January 14, 1889.

Mr. Silsby was engaged in the harness trade for four years and clerked in a store for a time after completing his education. He was cashier of the Pisgah Savings Bank at Pisgah, Iowa, until 1906 when he moved to Mondamin, Iowa, where he served as assistant cashier of the Mondamin Savings Bank until 1917. He has been assistant cashier of the First National Bank of Bayard since 1917.

He has acted as city clerk of Bayard since 1923, was secretary-treasurer of the Boy Scouts there for several years, and served as a member of the library board for three years. He is a member of the Methodist Episcopal Church of Bayard, of which he has been treasurer for five years, and for the last four years has been treasurer of the Morrill County Republican Committee. He is clerk of the Woodmen of the World.

He was married at Castana, Iowa, October 10, 1894, to Fannie May Lown, the daughter of Philip and Martha Lown, who was born in Henry County, Illinois, January 21, 1874. Ten children were born to them: Phillip M., September 22, 1895, who married Cecil Baker; Lucille M., May 5, 1897, who married Floyd Black; Ruth L., April 3, 1898, who married Burle Gamet; Frank L., May 12, 1899, who died in November, 1918; Lloyd B., September 6, 1901, who died May 5, 1902; Harold H., born September 14, 1903, who married Jeanette Harrington; Lenore D., October 11, 1909, who married H. C. Upton; Carroll L., October 16, 1910; Robert D., October 26, 1912; and Kathryn L., February 9, 1915. Phillip served during the World War for 21 months and is now district commander of the American Legion at San Francisco, California. Residence: Bayard.

John Madison Silver

John Madison Silver, manufacturer, was born at Galveston, Indiana, September 17, 1869. He is the son of George Washington and Nancy Hanna (Kepner) Silver, the former a farmer of English and German descent. George W. Silver was born at Burlington, Indiana, November 29, 1842, and died at Russiaville, Indiana, April 6, 1925. His wife, born at Galveston, October 8, 1850, died at Darwin, Indiana, August 26, 1884. She was of German ancestry.

Graduated from public school in 1887, John Madison Silver was associated with the Burlington Railroad from September 10, 1888, until October 8, 1908, in the traffic and station departments. At the present time he is the owner of the Coca Cola Bottling Works at Superior, and is president of the Superior Building, Loan and Savings Association.

On June 12, 1893, he was married to Daisy Ventnor Conlee at Beatrice. Mrs. Silver, who was born at Cortland, Nebraska, November 29, 1873, is of Scotch descent. They have two daughters, Helen, born September 12, 1894, who is married to Ancel E. Green; and Elsie, born October 8, 1897, who is married to Edwin A. Frerichs.

Mr. Silver is a Republican and has served on the city council two years. He has lived in Nebraska forty-three years, and has always taken an interested part in the development of his community. For fifteen years he has served as a member of the board of directors of the Chamber of Commerce, and during the World War held the rank of lieutenant in the Home Guards. From 1920-25 he was a member of the Kiwanis Club, and during 1916-17 was president of the American Bottlers of Carbonated Beverages. From 1926-30 he was president of the Nebraska State Bottlers' Association. For fourteen years Mr. Silver was on the board of directors of the American Bottlers of Carbonated Beverages, and since 1916 has been secretary of the Nebraska Manufacturers Association.

A Mason, he is a Knight Templar and member of the Shrine. His religious affiliation is with the Presbyterian Church at Superior. Residence: Superior.

Harry Elmer Siman

Harry E. Siman, lawyer and former state senator, was born in Wennebago City, Minnesota, September 20, 1869, and for the past thirty-three years has made his home in Nebraska. He is the son of John and Ann Smart Siman, the former a native of Luxemburg, Germany, born September 8, 1835. John Siman was a miller, and died at Winona, Minnesota, August 24, 1894. His wife, born at Waksha, Wisconsin, January 20, 1838, of English descent, is living.

Educated in the public schools of New Libson, Wisconsin, Harry Siman was graduated from New Libson High School in 1888, and received his LL. B. from the University of the Northwest at Sioux City, Iowa. He was admitted to practice in June 1895, and has since been actively engaged. A Republican, he served as state senator 1918-20, and at the present time is president of the 9th Judicial Bar Association (February 1931-). He is a Methodist, a member of the Knights of Pythias, the Masons and Shrine, Eastern Star and Modern Woodmen of America. His favorite sport is boxing.

During the World War Mr. Siman was a speaker on loan drives and a member of the legal advisory board. He is a member of the Wayne Country Club. On January 25, 1899, he was united in marriage to May Sullivan at New Lisbon. Mrs. Siman who is of Irish, French and Scandinavian extraction, was born at New Lisbon, August 23, 1871, and was a teacher of music prior to her marriage. Their two sons, Victor, born May 13, 1891, and Paul, born December 23, 1897, are physicians at Norfolk and Wayne, respectively. Residence: Wayne.

George Frank Simanek

George Frank Simanek, surgeon, was born in Saunders County, Nebraska, May 16, 1880, son of George Thomas and Barbara Mary (Blaha) Simanek. He attended the Prague, Nebraska, public school, Creighton University preparatory department, and received his medical degree from Creighton University.

His marriage to Rose Anna Kirchman was solemnized at Wahoo, on May 17, 1905. From 1923 until 1928 Dr. Simanek held the rank of major in the Medical Officers Reserve Corps. He is a member of the American College of Surgeons, the Omaha and Douglas County Medical Association, the American Medical Association, the Nebraska State Medical Association, the Catholic Hospital Association, and the American Hospital Association. Residence: Omaha.

Edward Franklin Sime

Edward Franklin Sime, educator, was born at Morrison, Colorado, September 10, 1899. He is the son of Fred and Mary Rosina (Bissell) Sime, both of German parentage. Fred Sime was born in Mount Carroll, Illinois, May 8, 1860, and Mary his wife, at Mount Carroll on March 26, 1861.

Educated in public and high school, at Pauline, Nebraska, Mr. Sime was graduated from the latter in 1916, attended Kearney State Teachers College in 1923 and the University of Nebraska the year 1926.

After teaching ten years in the rural schools of Loup and Garfield Counties, Mr. Sime was elected county superintendent of Garfield County schools in 1927 for a term of four years. He was re-elected to this office in 1931. Mr. Sime is a Republican, and a Mason. His hobby is reading. Residence: Burwell. (Photograph in Album).

Joseph Simecek

For more than thirty-seven years, Joseph Simecek has been engaged in the practice of medicine in Saline County. He was born at Kostelec, Milevskv, Bohemia, November 26, 1866, and same to Nebraska in 1881. His parents, John and Anna (Hula) Simecek were both natives of Kostelec, the former, a farmer, dying there in 1890. After his death his wife, Anna, came to America, and she died at Wilbur on June 11, 1913.

Dr. Simecek received his degree of Doctor of Medicine from Rush Medical College of Chicago, and was admitted to practice at Wilber on July 15, 1894. He has served both as a druggist and physician, and is now engaged in the practice of medicine and surgery. He is a Democrat and from 1912-19 was coroner for Saline County.

He was married to Katie Korkel at Wilbur, September 20, 1894. Mrs. Simecek was born at Wilber, January 1, 1870. There are two children, Angeline, born November 24, 1903, and Victor, born May 8, 1907, both of whom are studying medicine and will receive their M. D.'s in two years.

Dr. Simecek has studied extensively at Prague University, at Prague, Czechoslovakia, and has made seven trips to Europe since 1921, his children accompanying him in 1924. He is a member of the Nebraska State and Saline County Medical Societies, the Community Club of Swanton, and the National Sokol Society. His hobby is reading. Residence: Swanton.

Philip Sheridan Simmons

Born at Winchester, West Virginia, December 5, 1860, Philip Sheridan Simmons has resided in Nebraska for more than sixty-five years. He was brought here by his parents, who were early settlers in the state. His father, Jacob Simmons, a physician, was born in Winchester, March 26, 1832. He served in the Civil War with the 43rd Ohio Volunteers. His ancestors came to America from Switzerland about 1680. Jacob Simmons died at O'Neill, January 15, 1905.

His wife, Liddy Anna Head, was born in Dark County, Ohio, February 22, 1833, of Scotch and English descent. For many years prior to her death at North Bend on December 15, 1888, she was choir leader in the Presbyterian Church.

Philip Sheridan Simmons was graduated from high school, took two years preparatory work, and completed his junior year at Lloyd's Medical College, where he received a letter in baseball. For a number of years he was engaged in ranching, but is now retired. A Republican, he was a silver Republican in 1896, and has been candidate for county judge and county sheriff. He is the author of *God's Reserve*, and numerous short historical stories of the state.

On January 16, 1888, he was married to Julia Ellen Thomas at Pierce, Nebraska. Mrs. Simmons, who is of Welsh descent, was born in Pottawattomie County, Iowa, June 8, 1871. They have ten children, Amy Pearl, born November 1, 1888; Elnora, born July 5, 1891; Charles Justice, born September 25, 1893; Zella, born March 1, 1896; Bryan, born September 23, 1898, Melvine, born November 4, 1901; Sarah, born February 6, 1903; Clarissa, born July 3, 1905; Philip, born January 15, 1907; and Maxine, born September 20, 1910.

Mr. Simmons has served as chief of police, and deputy state sheriff. He is a member of the Presbyterian Church, the Red Cross, the Volunteer Firemen, the Woodmen of the World and the Nebraskana Society. He enjoys fishing, hunting, baseball and bowling, while his hobbies are history and political economy. Residence: O'Neill.

Robert Glenmore Simmons

Robert Glenmore Simmons, lawyer, was born at Scottsbluff, Nebraska, December 25, 1891, son of Charles

H. and Alice M. Simmons. The father was born in New York State and is a merchant. The mother, born in New York State, died in Nebraska, March 1, 1918.

Mr. Simmons attended the public school and high school at Scottsbluff, and received his Bachelor of Laws degree from the University of Nebraska. He was also a student at Hastings College. At the State University he was a member of the Order of the Coif.

A Republican, Mr. Simmons has served as county attorney of Scotts Bluff County, and in 1922 was elected a member of Congress still holding that position.

He is married to Gladyce Weil, who was born at Hebron, Nebraska, their marriage having been solemnized at Scottsbluff, on June 23, 1917. They have three children, Robert G., born August 14, 1918; Marion Jean, born July 30, 1920; and Ray Clifford, born August 17, 1925.

Mr. Simmons served in the World War from October, 1917 until January, 1919 as a free balloon pilot and observer. He is a member of the First Presbyterian Church at Scottsbluff and is a 32nd degree Mason and Shriner. Residence: Scottsbluff.

Paris Marion Simms

Paris Marion Simms, clergyman, lecturer and author, was born at Lawrenceburg, Tennessee, May 2, 1869, son of Andrew Francis and Martha Ann (Bryan) Simms. He received his education at Cumberland University, from which he received the following degrees: A. B., 1899; B. D., 1902; Ph. D., 1907. He is a member of Pi Kappa Alpha.

Ordained to the Presbyterian ministry in 1893, he accepted a pastorate at Cornersville, Tennessee, which continued until 1896. On June 8, 1893 he was united in marriage to Edna Earl Johnson. Mrs. Simms is the daughter of J. S. Johnson, a prominent Mason, and the grand daughter of Robert Johnson, an officer in the War of 1812, from Tennessee. Her maternal great grandfather, Laban Abernathy, served in the American Revolution as did also her great great-grandfather, Isaac Drake. She is a member of the Eastern Star, P. E. O., Daughters of the Confederacy, Daughter of the American Revolution, and National Society. United States Daughters of 1812. During the World War Mrs. Simms was quite active at Camp Dodge, being known as one of the Camp Mothers, with 12 assistants. She has always been active as a member of the Woman's Club and in other civic affairs. There are two children, Burney Gilmore, born April 1, 1894, married to Merle Brown. He attended Coe College and is a Delta Phi Epsilon. At the present time he is in the hardware and sporting goods business at Sacramento, California. The second son, P. Marion, Jr., was born May 2, 1908. He attended Hastings College, is a member of the Eta Phi Lambda fraternity, Sons of Confederate Veterans, and is field secretary of the Nebraska Christian Endeavor Union.

Dr. Simms is the author of *What Must the Church Do To Be Saved?* (1913) and *The Bible From the Beginning* (1929).

From 1902-06 he served as registrar of Cumberland University, and also as its acting president. Thereafter he held various pastorates until 1917, when he became associated with the Y. M. C. A. for work in the World War. He spent several years raising money for Near East Relief, and is now pastor of the Presbyterian Church at St. Edward, Nebraska.

For four years he served as commissioner to the General Assembly of the Cumberland Presbyterian Church. He has been a Chautauqua lecturer since 1900, and a member of the International Lyceum and Chautauqua Associations. For many years he has been director of finance for the Nebraska Christian Endeavor Union. He is a Mason and member of the Royal Arcanum.

Perhaps his most prized possession is a collection of

PARIS MARION SIMMS

G. ELI SIMON

Alberti—Cambridge

120 versions of the Bible in England, or parts of the Bible, to which he is constantly making additions. He resides at St. Edward, Nebraska. (Photograph on Page 1097).

G. E. Simon

Gjulson Eli Simon, prominent lawyer, was born in Gosper County, Nebraska, August 29, 1877, and since 1914 has been engaged in the practice of law continuously at Cambridge. He has the distinction of being a Nebraskan, born in a log cabin and reared on a farm. He resides at Cambridge where his residence has been since 1902.

His father, Ole Simon, was born near Lillehammer, in Gudbrandsdal, Norway, October 6, 1847, and came to the United States in 1857. He settled near Madison, Wisconsin, and in 1873 came to Nebraska, where as one of the first settlers he established a home on Deer Creek northwest of Holbrook, leading the first Norwegian delegation into that section of Nebraska then a savage wilderness. He still maintains the original homestead there.

His mother, Barbara Julson, was born in Dane County, Wisconsin, September 7, 1853, and died at Holbrook, June 30, 1916. Her parents were born in Norway and her father, a soldier in the Civil War serving in a Wisconsin Regiment, was killed in battle.

Mr. Simon received his education in rural school, Arapahoe High School and was graduated at Franklin Academy in 1899. After teaching in public school two years, he later entered law school and in 1914 received his Bachelor of Laws degree from Creighton University College of Law. While at Franklin Academy he was a member of the football and track teams and for two years was captain. On June 3, 1929 he was elected a member of the Athletic Honor "D" Club of Doane College.

His marriage to Miss Sarah Grace McFadden was solemnized at Holbrook, Nebraska, July 29, 1903. She was born at Tuscola, Illinois, February 1, 1882, and died at San Diego, California, September 13, 1918. Until her marriage she was a teacher in the public schools. She was a graduate of Arapahoe High School and the State Normal College at Peru and was the daughter of the Reverend and Mrs. H. W. McFadden late of Holbrook, Nebraska. Her father, a Methodist Clergyman, was during his ministry, one of the most popular and eloquent preachers of the Methodist Episcopal Church.

He has one child by this marriage, Eldon McFadden Simon, born October 11, 1905, who is married to Pansy Lee Rea. He was graduated from Cambridge High School in 1924, and from Doane College where he received his Bachelor of Arts degree in 1929. Thereafter for a year he studied at the University of Nebraska and the University of Illinois. In athletics at college he lettered in football and track, and is now coach and director of athletics in the Cambridge High School.

Mr. Simon's second marriage was to Miss Susanne Thompson, daughter of Mr. and Mrs. Ole Thompson of Austin, Minnesota, who formerly resided at Holbrook, Nebraska. Mrs. Simon was a graduate of Arapahoe High School and the State Teachers College at Winona, Minnesota. She died at Cambridge on June 30, 1926.

Mr. Simon has always been active in Republican politics, and in 1930 was candidate for lieutenant governor. He served as county attorney of Furnas County one term, 1917-1919, and as city attorney of Cambridge nine years, 1922-1931. During five years of his business career he was associated with Judge Ernest B. Perry, formerly of Cambridge. Mr. Simon is a trustee of Doane College, elected in 1929, and is the donor of the athletic field of that college which bears his name, Simon Athletic Field.

Besides his regular profession and serving in various capacities to his community and the state, Mr. Simon has taken special interest in education, both from the intellectual and physical standpoints. It is his opinion that one of the chief functions is to train students in the development of physical power, as well as the mental and moral training necessary for competent leadership.

Reared in the Norwegian Evangelical Lutheran Church from childhood he held membership there until 1903, and since that time he has been a member of the Methodist Episcopal Church. Throughout his career Mr. Simon has taken a special interest in the religious activities of his community and has been for many years, and is at present, a loyal member and an active trustee of the First Methodist Episcopal Church of Cambridge.

As a recognition of such services among the tributes to him one follows; "He has been in his professional career a tower of strength to every righteous cause, tireless, fearless; he carrys on the fight for clean politics and good government. G. Eli Simon is the embodiment of all that is finest and best in our public life."

While in Franklin Academy Mr. Simon had three years service as a cadet. During the World War he was government appeal agent in his district under the Selective Service Act, and was chairman of the Legal Advisory Board of Furnas County. He was also enlisted in a branch of the United States Secret Service in which he rendered important services to the War Department. His professional organizations include the Nebraska State Bar Association and the 14th Judicial District Bar Association (president 1929).

G. E. Simon is a member of the Masonic Fraternity having united with Cambridge Lodge in 1903, and a member of the Scottish Rite Masons, Sesostris Temple of the Shrine, the Order of Eastern Star, the Odd Fellows, and the Modern Woodmen of America. He is a member of the Methodist Brotherhood, the Southwest Historical Society, and life member of the Nebraskana Society. His recreations are athletics, markmanship and hunting game. Residence: Cambridge. (Photograph on Page 1098).

Osborne Perkins Simon

A resident of Nebraska nearly all his life, Osborne Perkins Simon was born at Holbrook, Nebraska, March 16, 1885, son of Ole and Barbara (Juleson) Simon.

His father, who is a retired farmer, was born in Norway, October 6, 1847, and came to America in 1854. Making the trip overland to Nebraska in a covered wagon in 1873, he located on a homestead in Gosper County. The farm is still in his possession. His wife, Barbara, was born in Hollandale, Wisconsin, September 6, 1853, and died at Holbrook, Nebraska, June 30, 1916.

Mr. Simon attended public schools of Gosper County until 1901. At the present time he is cashier of the Culbertson Bank. He is a Democrat and served as county treasurer of Hitchcock County during the years 1915, 1916, 1917, and 1918. He takes an active part in the activities of his party in local as well as state and national affairs. He is a member of the Lutheran Church and the Masons. His favorite sport is golf, while his favorite diversion is Masonic work. On April 7, 1930, he was made deputy grand custodian by the Grand Lodge Ancient Free and Accepted Masons of Nebraska. He has served as master of the Culbertson Lodge No. 174 Ancient Free and Accepted Masons, and also as patron of the Bethel Chapter Order of the Eastern Star No. 109.

On March 21, 1906, he was married to Ethel May Fellows at Culbertson, Nebraska. Mrs. Simon was born at Aurora, Nebraska, March 1, 1883, of English descent on the maternal side and early American on the paternal side. Mrs. Simon is a member of the Order of Eastern Star, and is past matron of the Bethel Chapter No. 109 of Culbertson. She is a member of the Degree of Honor, and is active in the affairs of the Presbyterian Church and Sunday School, the Legion Auxiliary, the Red Cross, and in all civic affairs.

Mr. and Mrs. Simon have one son, Frank O., born May 23, 1907, at Kanona, Kansas, who was married to Elizabeth Bauer of Culbertson, Nebraska, November 25, 1927.

OSBORNE PERKINS SIMON

To them were born two children, Betty Lou, born January 2, 1929; and Frank O., Jr., born August 30, 1930. Frank is a graduate of the Culbertson public schools, Boyles Business College at Omaha, Junior College at McCook, and at the present time is coach in the public school at Oxford, Nebraska. Residence: Culbertson. (Photograph on Page 1100).

John Simpson

John Simpson, one of Fairbury's foremost manufacturers, was born in Burlington, Iowa, August 13, 1862, son of John and Anna (Herriott) Simpson. John Simpson, Sr., was born in Scotland and came to America in the 1860's. He was an early day freighter across Nebraska to Denver. His death occurred at Denver on May 10, 1907. His wife, Anna, was also born in Scotland, and died at Denver, November 16, 1889.

Educated in public schools, John Simpson, Jr., soon thereafter entered business. A resident of Nebraska since 1894, he has attained prominence in the manufacturing world, and at the present time is president of the Fairbury Windmill Company.

Mr. Simpson was first married to Dora M. Heath, at Washington, Kansas. Mrs. Simpson is now deceased. There is one daughter, Charlotte, born May 5, 1885, who is a music teacher. On May 1, 1895, Mr. Simpson was married to Dora M. Heath.

During the World War Mr. Simpson was active in loan drives and other civilian projects. He is a Democrat, a Christian, a member of the Red Cross, the Rotary Club, the Chamber of Commerce and the Masonic order. His hobbies are fishing and hunting. Residence: Fairbury.

John Rankin Simpson

John Rankin Simpson, cashier of the Harvard State Bank, Harvard, Nebraska, has lived in this state all his life. He was born at Orleans, Harlan County, Nebraska, April 27, 1891, the son of Charles T. and Bellie I. Simpson. His father, who is lawyer at Orleans, is of English descent.

Mr. Simpson was graduated from Hastings High School, and later was a student at Hastings College. He is a Mason, a member of the Episcopal Church, and a Republican. He is married to Clara J. Simpson who was born at Bloomington, Nebraska. Residence: Harvard.

Fred W. Sims

Fred W. Sims was born at Chillicothe, Illinois, September 10, 1874, son of Francis L. and Lucinda (Booth) Sims. His father, who was born at Salem, New Jersey, is a farmer, who settled in Saline County, where his family was reared. He died at Friend. His wife, Lucinda, was born at Toledo, Ohio, and also died at Friend.

Fred W. Sims was educated in country school and took up farming as a young man. Starting in a modest way he has increased his acreage and at the present time is quite an extensive landowner.

On May 26, 1897, he was married to V. Mina Roush at Friend. Mrs. Sims was born at Andersonburg, Pennsylvania, March 10, 1874. To their union six children were born: George, born February 22, 1898, died March 22, 1898; Francis, born May 9, 1899, married Esther Zieman; Edith, born October 18, 1900, married Leonard J. Kellough; Fannie, born June 9, 1902, married Guy H. Tobey; Foster, born December 16, 1907; and Aileen, who is deceased.

Mr. Sims is a Republican, and has been a resident of Nebraska forty-eight years. He is a member of the Methodist Church and of the Nebraskana Society. Residence: Friend.

Frank K. Sindelar

Frank K. Sindelar, retired farmer and merchant of Colfax County, Nebraska, was born in Czechoslovakia, March 19, 1862. His father, Josef Sindelar, a farmer, was born in Czechoslovakia, November 20, 1808, and died at Lincoln Precinct, Colfax County, Nebraska, January 20, 1883; he came to America in 1865 and settled in Baltimore, later moving to Colfax County, 1870. His mother, Marie Sindelar was born in Czechoslovakia, August 3, 1823, and died at Lincoln Precinct, February 28, 1888.

Mr. Sindelar served as precinct assessor, 1904-05-06-07, and was county commissioner of Colfax County, 1915-18. He is a member of The Nebraskana Society; the Red Cross; and the Modern Woodmen of America. He is affiliated with the Catholic Church at Tabor. He has lived in the same precinct since he was eight years of age and his son now lives on the family homestead.

He was married to Barbara Hajek at Lincoln Precinct, July 10, 1883. Mrs. Sindelar was born in Czechoslovakia, June 28, 1866. Six children were born to this union, four of whom are living: Charley, born November 8, 1884, who died January 3, 1889; Frank C. S., born August 5, 1899, who died November 16, 1924, and who was married to Emma Kaspar; Rose Koza, born October 30, 1886, who married Ed Koza; Bohumil F. S., born May 5, 1892, who married Lena Poyar; Charley F. S., born November 18, 1894, who married Marie Cech; and Christina, born December 20, 1897, who married James Zoubek. Residence: Howells.

John J. Sindelar

John J. Sindelar has lived in Nebraska for 60 years and has been a farmer and merchant at Howells for many years. He was born in Czechoslovakia in 1860, the son of Joseph and Mary (Strudl) Sindelar. His father, who was a farmer, was born in Czechoslovakia and died at Howells, November 5, 1894. His mother was born in Czechoslovakia and died in Colfax County in 1888; she was a weaver before her marriage.

Mr. Sindelar attended the public schools of Chicago. He was engaged in farming for a time and later became a merchant at Howells, where he now deals in hardware, furniture, plumbing and heating stock, and electric wiring. He took part in city affairs as mayor for 12 years and president of the high school board for 18 years. During the war he assisted through donations to loan funds. His religious affiliation is with St. John's Catholic Church at Howells.

He was married at Olean Church at Howells to Kathrena Bartak. Mrs. Sindelar was born in Czechoslovakia. They have five daughters and five sons all of whom are in business. The youngest is a nurse at Columbus, Nebraska, and the other children are farmers and clerks. Mr. Sindelar likes to hunt, fish, and dance. He is a Democrat. Residence: Howells.

Joseph E. Sindelar

Joseph E. Sindelar, merchant and music teacher at Howells, Colfax County, Nebraska, was born there October 23, 1878, the son of Joseph B. and Barbara (Kasper) Sindelar. His father, who was a distinguished historian and a merchant in Colfax County, was born in Bohemia, November 11, 1853, and died at Howells, February 8, 1931; he served as a member of the legislature for eight years; he came to America in 1867. His mother was born in Bohemia in 1858 and died at Howells, July 8, 1901.

Mr. Sindelar has been in the general merchandise business at Howells for the past 25 years, and for the past 32 years has been director of the Howells Band. He is affiliated with St. John's Catholic Church; is a member of The Nebraskana Society; and a Democrat. He has always taken an active interest in state and community civic affairs.

In November, 1904, he was married to Agnes Bohata at Howells. Mrs. Sindelar was born in Bohemia, October 24, 1884. Residence: Howells.

Henry Sinn

Henry Sinn was born at Moline, Illinois, May 31, 1868. He is the son of Jurgen and Elisa (Rung) Sinn, who were both born at Holstein, Germany. Jurgen Sinn was born January 24, 1841, and after coming to this country was a blacksmith, and worked for John Deere from 1865 to 1868. He then farmed in Iowa for several years, and has farmed in Nebraska since 1879. He is now living at the age of ninety years. Elisa Sinn was born May 27, 1844, and died at Alexandria, Nebraska, March 22, 1922.

Henry Sinn attended country school, and has engaged in farming during his fifty-two years in Nebraska, retired since 1927. He came to this state at the age of eleven years with his parents, living in a side hill dugout for five years. Following an old wooden beam walking plow, barefooted, he broke many acres of Nebraska sod.

He is married to Carrie Yoachim, who was born at Smithfield, Illinois, April 24, 1875. They have three children: Ray, born February 15, 1897, who is married to Bertie Pletcher; Dewey, born April 26, 1898, who is married to Emma Midert; and Lola, born August 19, 1901, who is married to Oliver Rosenau, a medical doctor. Both Dewey and Ray are graduates of Alexandria High School, and are now farming. Lola had two years at the University of Nebraska, and has taught domestic science at Hay Springs, Red Willow and Eustis, Nebraska.

Mr. Sinn is a Democrat. He is secretary and treasurer of the Farmers Telephone Company of Alexandria, Nebraska, of which he has been director since it was organized on April 1, 1904. He is a member of the Independent Order of the Odd Fellows and The Nebraskana Society. Residence: Alexandria.

John Edward Sinning

John Edward Sinning, physician and surgeon, was born at Lennox, South Dakota, September 5, 1905, son of Henry H. and Fanny (Bultena) Sinning.

The father, born in Illinois, July 1856, was a farmer of German descent, whose death occurred at Lennox, November 27, 1916. The mother was born in Germany, June 17, 1864, and died at Rock Valley, Iowa, January 1, 1924.

Dr. Sinning first attended public schools of Lennox, South Dakota, and from 1920 until 1924 attended Rock Valley, Iowa, High School. He was captain of the football and baseball teams and was active in track during his senior year. He received his medical degree from the University of Iowa in 1930. He was there a member of the Omega Beta Pi and Phi Beta Pi. He received a freshman numeral in track. He specialized in running both at high school and college where he received several medals in competition.

Dr. Sinning was an interne at the Cleveland Maternity Hospital at Cleveland, Ohio, in 1929, and at Tacoma General Hospital, Tacoma, Washington, 1930-31. He was a charter member of the Tacoma Pathological and Automatical Society.

He was married on April 19, 1930, to Helen Madolyn Hart at Clarinda, Iowa. She is the daughter of Annabel Lee Hart, the daughter of the first white girl born in Saunders County, Nebraska. Mrs. Sinning was born at Springfield, Massachusetts, April 5, 1908. She is a member of the Presbyterian Church.

Dr. Sinning is a Republican. In 1930 he was commissioned first lieutenant on the Reserve Officers Corps, United States Army. He is a member of the Red Willow County Medical Association, the Red Cross, and the Ne-

braskana Society. His favorite sports are golf and baseball, while his hobby is reading. Residence: Danbury

Fletcher Marion Sisson

Fletcher Marion Sisson, clergyman, was born at Benington, Indiana, November 21, 1851. His father, Zenas Bassett Sisson, a farmer and mechanic, was born in Switzerland, Indiana, October 9, 1829, and died at Garnet, Kansas, in 1910. His ancestry was Welsh and French.

Catheryne (Shaddy) Sisson, his mother, was born in Switzerland County, September 21, 1833, and died at Fremont, Nebraska, July 16, 1914. Her grandfather, who was German fought throughout the entire Revolutionary War.

Mr. Sisson, who is a retired minister of the Nebraska Conference, was graduated from Moore's Hill College and immediately entered his first pastorate. He is the author of *The Shepherd's Staff*, also the *Wooden Shoes* or the *Worth of the Common Man*. He has lived in Nebraska for 37 years, and for 10 years he was chaplain in the National Guards with the rank of captain. He is a Mason and an Elk, a member of the Nebraska City Country Club, and is a Republican.

Mr. Sisson was married to Sarah Elizabeth Whitson, on February 8, 1874. Seven children were born to this union, four of whom are still living. Two daughters living in New York City, and two sons in Columbus, Ohio. He is now married to Rachel (Larsh) Watson of Nebraska City, Nebraska. Residence: Nebraska City.

Lewis Henry Sixta

Dr. Lewis H. Sixta has been engaged in the practice of medicine at Schuyler, Colfax County, Nebraska, since June 17, 1897. He was born in Bohemia, January 21, 1867, the son of Frank and Anna (Kolinsky) Sixta. His father, who was a wholesale wine dealer, was born in 1838, and died in 1905 at Manitowoc, Wisconsin; he came to America in 1867. His mother was born in 1840 and died in 1929.

Dr. Sixta was graduated from the Manitowoc High School and in 1889 was awarded the M. D. degree at Chicago Medical College. Following the completion of his medical course in Chicago Medical College, Dr. Sixta studied general medicine in the Vienna Hospital and took post-graduate work in Obstetrics in Prague. He has studied at Northwestern University and the University of Wisconsin pharmacy department. He is now surgeon for the Union Pacific Railroad Company at Schuyler. During the World War he took a prominent part in war time activities as examining physician for recruits in Colfax County. He holds membership in: Colfax County Medical Society; the Nebraska State Medical Society; the American Medical Association; and the Nebraskana Society. He is a Republican.

He was married at Manitowoc, December 2, 1890, to Lottie Bertha Bem. Mrs. Sixta was born at Chicago, November 10, 1866. Three children were born to this union: Editha B., born September 21, 1892, who married Isaac Lee Pindell; Lottie, born April 6, 1893, who married Edward E. Ruzicka; and Florence, born June 21, 1895, who is a school teacher. Residence: Schuyler.

Charles McClellan Skiles

Charles McClellan Skiles, lawyer, was born in Lee County, Iowa, July 7, 1867. He received the degrees of B. L. and LL. B. from the University of Nebraska, and was admitted to the bar in 1895.

On June 29, 1904, he was married to Anna Witmeyer Swarr at Manheim, Pennsylvania. There are two children, John, born April 4, 1907, who is a lawyer in practice with his father; and Ruth, born January 4, 1914.

Mr. Skiles is a Democrat, has served as county judge of Butler County three terms, and as state senator. He was defeated for congress in 1912, and was delegate to the Democratic national convention of 1916. He was general council for bank receivership for eight years, and assistant attorney general 1929-31.

He is a member of First Plymouth Congregational Church of Lincoln, the Knife and Fork Club, the American, Nebraska State and Lancaster County Bar Associations, the Masons and the Lincoln Country and the Shrine Clubs. Residence: Lincoln.

James Van Wyck Skinkle

James Van Wyck Skinkle, superintendent of schools at Chadron, Nebraska, was born at Dorchester, Nebraska, June 1, 1887, son of Van Wyck and Bertha May (Vosburgh) Skinkle.

The father was born in Avon, Illinois, April 24, 1858, and is now retired and resides in California. His Dutch ancestors came into the province of New Amsterdam in 1649.

Bertha May Vosburgh was born in Aurora, Illinois, October 16, 1867, and is of German descent. Her family settled in Pennsylvania in 1750 in Luzenne County and members of it still reside there.

Mr. Skinkle was graduated from high school at Dorchester in 1904, and received the following degrees, a Bachelor of Arts from Fremont College, a Bachelor of Science from the University of Chicago in 1917, and his Master of Arts degree from Columbia University in 1931. He is a member of Phi Delta Kappa and was a member of the debating team at Fremont.

Mr. Skinkle has been superintendent of schools in Octavia, Glenvil, Davenport, Ulysses, Neligh, Blair and now at Chadron.

He was a member of the Reserve Officers Training Corps at the University of Chicago, and participated in all drives during the World War. He is a member of the National Educational Association, the Nebraska State Teachers Association, and has taught at Fremont College and Chadron State Teachers College.

Among his other memberships are the Chamber of Commerce, the Rotary Club, the Odd Fellows, the Knights of Pythias, the University Club of Chicago and the University Club of Columbia University of New York City. His hobby is motoring. He is affiliated with the Church of Christ.

On June 10, 1914, Mr. Skinkle was married to Ethel May Miller at Hastings. She was born at Davenport, Nebraska, August 17, 1894, of English and German ancestry. She is a teacher. There are two children, Lorraine, born September 2, 1918 at Neligh; and Jean, born November 23, 1924 at Chadron. Residence: Chadron.

Fred Walter Skinner

Fred Walter Skinner was born at Marshalltown, Iowa, July 15, 1877, the son of Henry John and Emily Adelia (Eastman) Skinner. His father, who was a newspaper editor and a Civil War veteran, served as the first sheriff of Keya Paha County, Nebraska; he died there in 1896. His mother, who was born in Illinois, in 1856, is still living.

Mr. Skinner has been, consecutively, a printer, stock buyer, butcher, and hardware merchant at Ainsworth, Nebraska, where he has resided for the past 52 years. A volunteer for service in the World War, at the age of 40, he is a member of the American Legion. He is also a Knights of Pythias, and a Modern Woodman of America. His sports include hunting and fishing.

His marriage to Ezada Phelps occurred at Springview, Nebraska, December 18, 1901. They have two children, Morris F., born September 14, 1906; and Ruby E., born September 11, 1909. Morris is an archeologist of some note, who has contributed many species as a result of his independent work. He is now employed by the New York Museum of Natural History. Among his discoveries are two pre-historic elephants. Residence: Ainsworth.

Morris Frederick Skinner

Morris Frederick Skinner, geologist and collector of fossils, was born at Springview, Nebraska, September 14, 1906, the son of Fred Walter and Ezada Janet (Phelps) Skinner. His father, who was born at Marshalltown, Iowa, in 1877, was a soldier during the World War, and for many years has been successfully engaged as a hardware merchant; he is fond of hunting and fishing and likes the out of doors.

Mr. Skinner was graduated from the high school at Ainsworth, Nebraska, in 1925, and received the B. S. degree at the University of Nebraska where he was a member of Alpha Chi Sigma and the N Club. Upon his graduation from high school, Mr. Skinner began collecting fossils under the direction of Childs Frick of the American Museum of Natural History.

He specialized in geology and paleontology at the University of Nebraska where he worked in the college museum during the summer months. At this time he is serving as collector in chief of a field party of the American Museum of Natural History.

He is a member of the Nebraska Society, is an associate member of the American Museum of Natural History of New York, and is devoting his life to work in the fossil collecting and paleontological field.

His marriage to Shirley Maria White occurred at Maryville, Kansas, October, 1930. Mrs. Skinner, who plans to complete her science course in the University of Nebraska, was born at Ainsworth, March 22, 1909. They have one daughter, Barbara, born August 17, 1931. Residence: Ainsworth.

Martin Victor Sklenar

Martin Victor Sklenar was born at Tekamah, Nebraska, February 19, 1892, son of Joseph and Barbara (Ourodnik) Sklenar. His father, who was a native of Bohemia, was born September 8, 1842, and came to America in June, 1864. He was a farmer for many years and died at Tekamah May 23, 1923. His wife, Barbara, was born December 4, 1854, and died at Tekamah, October 5, 1908.

Mr. Sklenar attended public school and afterward engaged as a farmer. He entered service for the World War July 22, 1918, and was assigned to Company 30, 8th Battalion, 163rd Depot Brigade at Camp Dodge, Iowa. On March 14, 1928, he was married to Julia Marie Jensen, at Tekamah, which was her birth place. They have two sons, twins, Charles and James, born December 14, 1929. Mr. Sklenar is a member of the First Baptist Church of Tekamah. Residence: Tekamah.

Willard Washington Slabaugh

Willard W. Slabaugh has had an interesting and varied career. Born at Nappanee, Indiana, February 29, 1856, he is the son of Amos L. and Julia Anna (France) Slabaugh. His father, born in Lancaster County, Pennsylvania, in December 1823, was a farmer of Swiss, Dutch and German descent. He died at Portage County, Ohio, August 19, 1909. His wife, Julia was born in Stark County, Ohio, in February, 1834, and died in Portage County, July 25, 1909. She was of French, German and English ancestry.

Willard W. Slabaugh received his early education in the country schools of Ohio and Indiana. He entered Mount Union College, and later attended Hiram College and Valparaiso Normal School. He received the degrees of B. Ph., and B. A. from Hiram College. He was admitted to the practice of law on August 5, 1885. He has been an editor, teacher, real estate man, lawyer and judge. He was editor of the South Omaha Times, the first newspaper in that city. He taught in country schools, select school and at Mount Union and Hiram Colleges. A Republican, he was chief assistant county attorney from 1892 to 1896, and district judge from 1896 to 1905. He is still in active practice, and is instructor in law at the University of Omaha.

On October 15, 1890, he was married to Anna Clayton. Mrs. Slabaugh was born at Hannibal, Missouri, in 1868. She is of English and German descent. Their four children are: Willard, born August 6, 1891; Ruth, born May 9, 1893; Grace, born October 12, 1895, and Eleanor, born October 30, 1899.

During the many years of his residence in Omaha Mr. Slabaugh has been a member of and active in civic, charitable and welfare organizations. He is a trustee of the Omaha Child Saving Institute, and a member of the First Christian Church. During the World War he was chairman of committees on departure of soldiers from Omaha, and of committees caring for returned dead.

He is a member of the Ad Sell League, a Mason, Knight of Pythias, Woodman of the World and Modern Woodman of America. He holds membership in the Nebraska State Historical Society and The Nebraskana Society. His hobby is health. He is an associate member of the Sojourners League of Omaha. Residence: Omaha.

Charles Eyster Slagle

Charles Eyster Slagle, one of the most prominent physicians and surgeons in Box Butte County, was born at Oregon, Illinois, July 10, 1870, son of Charles and Malinda (Oyster) Slagle. Charles Slagle was born at Hanover, Pennsylvania, February 12, 1809, and died at Oregon, Illinois, November 28, 1891. He was a farmer. The name was originally von Schlegel when the family lived in Saxony, Germany. The name was later changed to Schlegle, and in 1700 the family settled in Pennsylvania where the name was changed to Slagel, and later to Slagle. The family settled in Illinois in 1849. Malinda Oyster was born in Pennsylvania, and she died at Oregon, Illinois, March 20, 1909.

Dr. Slagle attended district school in Illinoiis, the preparatory department of Carthage College in 1886; he was graduated from Oregon High School in 1889, and in 1896 was awarded the degree of Doctor of Dental Surgery at Michigan University. He received the degree of Doctor of Medicine at the Keokuk Medical College in 1903, and a second degree of Doctor of Medicine from the University of St. Louis in 1906. He took postgraduate work in New York City, London, and Glasglow, Scotland.

Coming to Nebraska from Illinois in 1906, Dr. Slagle has since resided at Alliance. During the year 1903-04 he was professor of oral pathology at the Keokuk Dental College, was for a time president of the staff of St. Joseph's Hospital at Alliance, and at the present time is a lecturer on bacteriology to a class of nurses in training. Active in business as well as professional life, Dr. Slagle is at the present time a vice president of the Alliance Building and Loan Association and of the Alliance Loan and Investment Company. He is division surgeon and examiner for the Chicago, Burlington and Quincy Railroad, and is a past president of the Guardian State Bank, past director of the First National Bank, and past president of the Rotary Club. He is a Republican.

He was married to Myrtle Anna Shoop at Abingdon, Illinois, June 28, 1904. Mrs. Slagle was born at Abingdon, August 15, 1876. Her mother's name was Gaton, the family coming from Johnstown, Pennsylvania, to Illinois.

Dr. Slagle is a member of the American Association of Railroad Surgeons, the Nebraska State Medical Society, the Box Butte Medical Society, and is a Fellow of the American College of Surgeons. He is a 32nd degree Mason and a member of all Masonic bodies. His clubs are the Alliance Country Club, and the Rotary Hole in One Club. His favorite sport is golfing. Residence: Alliance.

Ivan Ray Sleigh

Born at Frankfort, Kansas, April 4, 1894, Ivan Ray Sleigh is the son of John Thomas and Laura Jane (Fowler) Sleigh. His father was born at Circleville, Ohio, January 27, 1861. He is now residing at Washington, Kansas. Mr. Sleigh was graduated from the high school at Washington, Kansas, in 1913. He is now manager of the Golden Rule Store at Lexington, Nebraska, where he is prominent in civic affairs.

He is a member of the executive board and the good roads board of the Chamber of Commerce, is affiliated with the Methodist Church of Lexington where he takes an active interest in Sunday School work, and holds membership in the Red Cross, the Independent Order of Odd Fellows, and the Masons. During the World War he served in the United States Naval Reserve Force, and at this time he is commander of the local post of the American Legion. He is a Democrat.

His marriage to Hazel Marie Philbrook was solemnized at Washington, Kansas, November 16, 1924. Mrs. Sleigh was born in Washington County, Kansas. They have two adopted children, Donald Keith, born October 22, 1928; and Richard Dale, born December 1, 1931. Residence: Lexington.

Charles Henry Sloan

Charles Henry Sloan, distinguished lawyer, civic leader, and statesman of Nebraska, was born at Monticello, Iowa, May 2, 1863, the son of James W. and Elizabeth (Magee) Sloan. His father, who was a farmer, was born at Bellamunna, Ireland, December 1, 1834, and died at Geneva, Nebraska, December 31, 1916; his parents were Charles and Jane (Weir) Sloan. His mother, who was a tailoress in Philadelphia, was born at Annaherin, Ireland, March 25, 1830, and died at Geneva, October 28, 1920. She was the daughter of Phillip and Ann (Murray) Magee.

Mr. Sloan attended rural schools, was a student at Monticello High School, and received the B. Sc. degree at Iowa State College. During his college years he was winner of numerous debates and oratorical contests, and was First Orator in the class of 1884. He was his debating society's tariff champion. His graduating thesis was on *Protection,* a doctrine then regarded almost exclusively Republican in the north. It is comforting to him now to see both great political parties and sections of this country, and every important nation in the world of that politico-economic belief. He was a member of Delta Tau Delta, and was a prominent baseball player, member of the College Military Company, and editor of the *Aurora,* a college paper.

A rural school teacher for four winter terms, he served as superintendent of the Fairmont, Nebraska, Schools for three years. Since 1887 has practiced law continuously and is a member of the law firm Sloans, Keenan and Corbitt. He served as city attorney at Geneva and Fairmont, was a member of the Nebraska State Bar Commission for three years, and for the past thirty years has been director of the Geneva State Bank, of which he is now president.

A Republican, Mr. Sloan has taken an important part in both state and national political affairs for many years in the following positions: county attorney of Fillmore County, two terms; member Nebraska State senate, 1894 to 1896; member 62nd to 65th Congresses, 1911 to 1919; member of 71st Congress, 1929-30; member of ways and means committee. In 1930 he was defeated for re-election. He has attended numerous state conventions, and has presided over their deliberations. His three most important successful measures while in the Nebraska senate were, (1) naming Nebraska the "Tree Planter's" State; (2) was author of Nebraska Anti-Oleomargarine Law; (3) was chairman of the Constitutional Amendment committee, and introduced seven amendments to our constitution which were submitted to the people and

Edward Davis—Geneva

CHARLES HENRY SLOAN

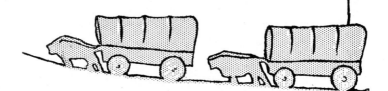

among which were verdict of civil jury by 5/6 of the panel; an elective Railway Commission; expansion of the Supreme Court; and provision for investment of the state school funds.

In congress he was the author of two great appropriating measures for the eradication of hog cholera, and eradication of tuberculosis in live stock. Among his important speeches delivered on the floor of the House were several tariff speeches: *Nebraska at Fifty; Washington, The Business Farmer; Corn Is King; John Ericsson*, and speech against the World War Resolution. Four of the eight public buildings in the Fourth District were provided during his ten year service, a comprehensive fish survey of the Fourth (Blue River) District was made at his instance by the Government Fisheries authorities.

He is a member of the American Bar Association, the Nebraska State Bar Society, Fillmore County Bar Society, Geneva Community Club, the Nebraska State Historical Society, and the Nebraskana Society. He is a 32nd Degree Mason, (Scottish Rite and Knight Templar) and is a member of the Knights of Pythias, Elks and Modern Woodman of America. He was in 1898 grand orator for the Nebraska Masonic Jurisdiction. Although a member of no church, his religious affiliation is with the Geneva Methodist Episcopal Church congregation. Mr. Sloan was opposed to the World War declaration but was an active supporter of our forces in and out of Congress, and aided and contributed liberally to various Red Cross and loan drives throughout Nebraska. His three sons were in the United States Service during the World War.

His marriage to Emma Margaret Porter was solemnized at Woodbine, Iowa, October 1, 1889. Mrs. Sloan, who was a teacher prior to her marriage, and a graduate of the Iowa State College with B. Sc. degree, was born in Harrison County, Iowa, December 25th, 1860, the daughter of Francis Joseph and Lucy (Frances) Porter. Four children were born to them: Ethel, born July 13, 1890, who married Grady Corbitt, now a member of Mr. Sloan's law firm; Frank Blaine, born May 14, 1892, who died overseas in the service of the United States in the World War, October 2nd, 1918; Charles Porter, born January 29, 1894, who married Lillian Steifer; and William McKinley, born August 28th, 1898, who married Esther Marshall. Charles P. is a successful farmer, and William M. is a member of his father's law firm. Residence: Geneva. (Photograph on Page 1105).

James Eldredge Sloss

James Eldredge Sloss, son of Robert Brown and Hattie May (Eldredge) Sloss, was born near North Bend, Nebraska, February 4, 1890. His father, Robert, was born in Cleveland, Ohio, September 19, 1856, of Irish parentage. He is a retired farmer, prominent in church and welfare work, who has resided in Dodge County for seventy-three years. His wife, Hattie, who was born at Salem, New York, December 3, 1860, has been prominent in church work all her life. She was a teacher prior to her marriage. Both her parents were of New England ancestry, descended from pre-Revolutionary settlers in America, and her father was a coal dealer in Fremont.

Upon his graduation from North Bend High School in 1908, James E. Sloss attended Tarkio College at Tarkio, Missouri, receiving his A. B. in 1912. On December 28, 1918, he was united in marriage to Fern Marion Elliott, at Lincoln. Mrs. Sloss was born at Mecklin, South Dakota, March 22, 1894. Her father's ancestry was Irish, and her mother traces her ancestry to pre-Revolutionary days in America. There are two daughters, Ruth Marion, born December 16, 1919, and Janet May, born July 9, 1925.

Mr. Sloss is a Republican. He is active in civic and educational projects and during 1929-30 was president of the Community Club, and served as a member of the executive committee from 1925-30. He is a member of

the United Presbyterian Church, the Parent-Teachers Association and the Nebraskana Society. He is a grain and livestock farmer with extensive interests. Residence: North Bend.

Robert Brown Sloss

Robert Brown Sloss, retired farmer, was born in Cleveland, Ohio, September 18, 1856, son of James and Nancy (Ritchie) Sloss. James Sloss was born in County Derry, Ireland, in 1820, and came to America about 1840, with his wife Nancy. She was also born in County Derry. They were early settlers in Dodge County and were pioneer farmers and quite extensive landowners. James Sloss died at North Bend July 21, 1902, and Nancy Sloss died there on April 11, 1907.

Robert B. Sloss who is now retired, has always been active in farming. He is an extensive landowner, and prominent in civic and religious affairs. He has lived in Nebraska seventy-three years, and at the present time is chairman of the local Boy Scout committee, and chairman of the North Bend branch of the Red Cross. He is a member of the United Presbyterian Church and of The Nebraskana Society. His favorite sport is swimming.

On May 13, 1886, he was married to Hattie May Eldredge at Fremont. Mrs. Sloss, who is of early New England ancestry, was born in Salem, New York, December 3, 1861. There are three children, Helen, born June 19, 1888, who died April 11, 1917; James, born February 4, 1890, who married Fern Marion Elliott (*see Nebraskana*); and Susie Valentine, born September 12, 1893, who married Harry Allan Luckhardt. Residence: North Bend.

Harry Theadore Sly

Harry Theadore Sly, newspaper man, was born at Iroquois, South Dakota, November 13, 1905, son of Lewis Bert and Laura Mae (Massey) Sly. The father is still living, while the mother died at Gordon, Nebraska, August 15, 1911.

Mr. Sly attended Chadron High School until his graduation in 1923, and was thereafter a student at Chadron Normal College for two years. While there he received two letters in track, 1921, and 1922. Since 1923 Mr. Sly has been associated with C. H. Pollard as editor of the *Chadron Chronicle*. He is news reporter and advertising manager for the *Chronicle*, Chadron correspondent for the Associated Press, the *World Herald*, the *Denver Post*, the *Sioux City Journal*, the *Rapid City Journal* and the *Norfolk Daily News*.

He was secretary of the Chadron Chamber of Commerce from June, 1929, until April, 1931, and at the present time is serving as secretary of the Northwest Nebraska Chamber of Commerce. During 1930-1931 and 1932 he has been secretary of the Dawes County Fair Association. He is also secretary of the Denver-Black Hills Highway Association. He is a Republican.

His marriage to Readith Mildred Babb was solemized at Hot Spring, South Dakota, June 22, 1929. Mrs. Sly was born at Macomb, Missouri, October 25, 1910. They have one daughter, Lorraine, born February 18, 1931.

Mr. Sly is a member of the Chamber of Commerce and Junior Chamber of Commerce of Chadron, the Odd Fellows, and The Nebraskana Society. He is a Methodist. His favorite sports include football, basketball, bowling, and baseball, while his hobby is mechanics. Residence: Chadron.

Clyde Chase Smalley

Clyde Chase Smalley, photographer, was born at Milligan, Nebraska, December 17, 1890, son of William Sherman and Nellie Grace (Chase) Smalley. His father, a native of Ohio, is a retired farmer living in Superior, Nebraska. His mother was a native of Illinois.

Mr. Smalley attended the high school at Milligan and during 1906-07 was a student at Hastings Business College. He is a graduate of the Southern School of Photography of McMinnville, Tennessee.

On September 25, 1911, he was married to Hazel Blanche Austin at Lawrence, Nebraska. Mrs. Smalley was born at Bertrand, Nebraska, November 21, 1891. Her father, Charles T. Austin, was a teacher, a depot agent, and later an attorney at law. Gertrude Purinton, her mother, was a graduate of York High School and a school teacher before her marriage. Her ancestry traces to Patrick Henry. Mrs. Smalley is a member of the P. E. O., and is active in the studio of her husband. Mr. and Mrs. Smalley have two children, Evelyn, born October 6, 1912; and Max, born July 8, 1914, who died August 5, 1918. Evelyn is teaching school in district number 81 of Webster County, Nebraska. She was graduated from Blue Hill High School in 1930 as valedictorian of her class.

Mrs. Smalley has two brothers who enlisted in the navy during the World War. They were wireless operators on destroyers and merchant ships. One brother, Spencer E. Austin of Chicago, convoyed President Wilson across the ocean and back again on the destroyer Lea. The other brother, Ralph, was sent to South America and also to France on a merchant ship. He is a graduate of the University of Nebraska, having received his Masters degree there. They both went to Harvard University, where Spencer received class honors. Ralph was at one time state food inspector for Nebraska while McKelvie was governor, and later held a position in the office of Dan Swanson, state land commissioner in the State Capitol Building. He is district superintendent for the Concordia Creamery Company and lives at Concordia, Kansas. Spencer is engineer of electrolosis for the Illinois Bell Telephone Company with offices in Chicago. Mrs. Smalley has a sister, Mrs. H. G. Stout, whose husband is an instructor in the Kearney State Teachers College.

Mr. Smalley started in the photography business with the Griffin and Day Studios at Hebron, Nebraska. He has owned and operated studios at Blue Hill, Red Cloud, Superior, and Alliance, and is now the owner of the Smalley Studio at Minden. After leaving Hebron, Mr. Smalley took charge of T. M. Mackey's Studio at Superior. With the exception of three years spent in Missouri, Mr. Smalley has been a continuous resident of Nebraska since his birth.

He is a member of the Methodist Episcopal Church, the Photographers International Association of America, and the Minden Chamber of Commerce. Residence: Minden. (Photograph in Album).

Joseph Smatlan

Joseph Smatlan, pioneer Nebraskan, and veteran lumber and coal dealer, has lived in this state since 1869 and has had a prominent part in the building up of his state and community. He was born at Telecim, Bohemia, on August 11, 1844, the son of Joseph and Anna (Zvacek) mother was born at Telecim, March 4, 1814, and died at Smatlan. His father, who was born at Telecim, August 7, 1793, and died there, June 9, 1864, was a farmer. His Schuyler, Nebraska, March 16, 1883.

Mr. Smatlan was engaged in the lumber and coal business at Schuyler from 1876 to 1900 when he retired from active business. He is the founder of the Colfax Bank at Howells, Nebraska, and has served as city treasurer and as a member of the board of education at Schuyler. He holds membership in the Nebraskana Society and the Red Cross, and is a member of the Woodmen of the World, the Modern Woodmen of America and the C. S. P. S.

He was married to Anna Telecky at Borove, Bohemia, October 28, 1866. Mrs. Smatlan was born at Sirokem,

Dole, Bohemia, August 6, 1849, and died at Schuyler, January 29, 1912. Six children were born to them, five of whom are still living: Anna, born born January 17, 1869, who married Thomas Molacek; Josephine, born September 12, 1870, who married Frank Woitishek, and who died May 5, 1918; Mary, born May, 3 1873, who married Adolph Kadletz; Joseph born December 19, 1876; Edward, born July 30, 1879; and Victor, born August 25, 1886. Joseph Edward, and Victor are all engaged in the lumber and coal business. Residence: Schuyler.

Joseph Edward Smatlan

Joseph E. Smatlan, prominent lumber and coal dealer at Schuyler, has lived in this state all his life. He was born in Colfax County, December 19, 1876, the son of Joseph and Anna (Telecky) Smatlan. His father, who is a farmer, lumber and coal dealer, was born at Telecim, Bohemia, August 11, 1844. His mother was born at Sirokem, Dole, Bohemia, August 6, 1849, and died at Schuyler, January 29, 1912.

Mr. Smatlan was graduated from the Schuyler High School, and later was a student at the University of Nebraska and the Lincoln Business College. He played baseball and tennis while in school. Since 1895 Mr. Smatlan has been engaged in farming and in the lumber and coal business at Schuyler, where he now is manager of his own lumber and coal organization. He is serving as a director of the Colfax County Bank of Howells, Nebraska.

He is an independent, politically, and has been a member of the Board of Education at Schuyler for many years. He holds membership in the Chamber of Commerce, the Nebraskana Society, and the Red Cross. His fraternal societies include the Eagles, Knights of Pythias, Odd Fellows, and Sokol. His hobby is mechanics, while his favorite sports are baseball and football. During the Spanish-American War Mr. Smatlan served as a private in Company K, Second Regiment, Nebraska Volunteer Infantry and was promoted to corporal and first lieutenant. In the World War he was active in loan drives.

His marriage to Emma Bartunek was solemnized at Schuyler, November 15, 1899. Mrs. Smatlan was born in Colfax County, November 11, 1878. To this marriage the following children were born: Emerson, born November 5, 1900, who married Edwina Lewis; Erma, born April 9, 1903, who is a graduate nurse; Alice, born November 30, 1906, who is a pharmacist; Joseph, born February 6, 1910, who is engaged in aviation; and Eleanor, born November 12, 1915, who is still in school. Emerson is in the lumber and coal business.

Mr. Smatlan is a member of the Veterans of the Foreign Wars. Residence: Schuyler.

Charles D. Smiley

Charles D. Smiley, veteran real estate and insurance dealer in Nebraska, has lived in this state for the past 40 years. He was born at Union, Erie County, Pennsylvania, October 27, 1852, the son of Robert and Eulzinia Smiley. His father, who was a veterinarian, served in the Civil War.

Mr. Smiley has been active in community affairs at South Sioux City for many years. He is a member of The Nebraskana Society, is affiliated with the Presbyterian Church, and holds membership in the Independent Order of Odd Fellows. His hobby is reading. He is a Democrat. He was married to Lillian E. Teter at Chattanooga, Tennessee. Residence: South Sioux City.

Erle Boyd Smiley

Erle Boyd Smiley, member of the Nebraska house of representatives in 1923, was born at Seward, Nebraska, December 5, 1890. His father, James Monroe Smiley, was born at Industry, Illinois, October 14, 1849, of Scotch-

Irish ancestry. He was married to Hattie C. Phillips, who was born at Vermont, Illinois, January 2, 1864.

Mr. Smiley attended the Seward and Beaver Crossing public schools. During 1917 and 1918 he was in the United States Air Service, with the rank of second lieutenant, and from 1920 to 1922 served as captain in the Nebraska National Guard.

A pioneer flyer, Mr. Smiley gave exhibitions for three years following the world war, and has the distinction of being the first politician to promote campaigns by air. In 1921, he was awarded a cup in an altitude test at York, Nebraska, and altho he is not flying at present, he is one of the state's most ardent air enthusiasts.

On August 5, 1923, he was united in marriage to Anna Marcella Peterson at York. To this union were born two children, JoAnn, born August 31, 1924; and Don Erle, born October 8, 1929.

Mr. Smiley is engaged extensively in the poultry business, and in 1915 was given a judge's general license, by the Poultry Association at the World's Fair. Since that time he has been engaged in judging some of the finest shows in America, including those held at Pomona, California, the Texas, Kansas, Oklahoma, Iowa and Nebraska State Shows, the Greater Omaha Auditorium Shows, snows at the Chicago Coliseum and the Sesqui-Centennial held at Philadelphia, and the show at Madison Square Garden which is the world's greatest. At the recent convention of the American Poultry Association Mr. Smiley was re-elected secretary and treasurer of the judge's section for the United States and Canada for the seventh time.

Mr. Smiley, in addition to his other business, breeds gold-fish and grows aquatic plants. He is much interested also in flower growing, but his hobby is Masonic work. He is a Republican, a member of the Chamber of Commerce, the American Poultry Association and the Nebraskana Society. Residence: Seward. (Photograph in Album).

Alvin Cordon Smith

Alvin Cordon Smith, civil engineer and contractor, was born at Lyons, Nebraska, January 20, 1891, son of Orange Cordon and Emily Serepta (Huckelberry) Smith.

His father was born in Dane County, Wisconsin, July 12, 1860, and was a miller until his death at Scottsbluff, December 13, 1930. His wife, Emily, was born in Valley County, October 18, 1864, and died at Lyons, September 16.

Upon his graduation from public school at Lyons in 1904, Mr. Smith attended Lyons High School, from which he was graduated in 1908. He received the degree of Bachelor of Science in civil engineering from the University of Nebraska in 1914, where he was a member of Sigma Xi, Sigma Tau, and Alpha Sigma Phi.

From 1913 until 1916, Mr. Smith was associated with the firm of Abel and Roberts, Contractors, and from 1916 until 1917 was associated with the Abel Construction Company. During 1918 he held the rank of second lieutenant with the coast artillery corps. He is a member of the American Legion.

His marriage to Edith Smith was solemnized at Lincoln, October 6, 1915. Mrs. Smith was born at Elwood, Nebraska, November 21, 1889. They have three children, Suzanne, born May 10, 1920; Robert, born July 1, 1922; and Margery, born November 23, 1925.

Mr. Smith is a member of the First Presbyterian Church of Scottsbluff, the Red Cross, the Chamber of Commerce, and the Scottsbluff Country Club. He is a member of Robert W. Furnas Lodge No. 265 of the Ancient Free and Accepted Masons, and from 1927 until 1930 was a member of the Scottsbluff School Board. Residence: Scottsbluff.

Archie Manley Smith

Archie M. Smith, lawyer and judge of Thurston County, has lived in Nebraska all his life, and has taken an active part in the political and civic life of the state. He was born at Hansen, Adams County, Nebraska, August 26, 1883, the son of Wilbur Heman and Sarah (Nichols) Smith. His father, who was born at Wyanet, Bureau County, Illinois, May 19, 1858, and died at Davenport, August 20, 1922, was a railroad station agent at Davenport, Hansen, and Verona, Nebraska; later he was a farmer. His wife, Sarah, was born at Markesan, Green Lake County, Wisconsin, January 26, 1861. Her father, who was born in New York, was a member of the legislature in Wisconsin and Kansas, and at various times between 1878 and 1903 resided in Clay and Thayer Counties, Nebraska.

Judge Smith was graduated from the Davenport High School in 1899, received the A. B. degree at Bellevue College, 1906, and was awarded the LL. B. degree at the University of Nebraska, 1910. He was a student at Fremont Normal School, Fremont, Nebraska, in 1901. He was employed in the station service of the C. B. & Q., and C. & N. W. Railroads from 1901 to 1913, except for time spent in college.

A Democrat, he served as county attorney of Thurston County, from 1917 to 1923, was appointed county judge of Thurston County in 1931, still holding the latter position. He was unsuccessful candidate for state senator on the Democratic ticket in 1924.

Judge Smith was chairman of the Four Minute Men at Pender, Nebraska, during the war; was a member of the legal advisory board, and took part in Red Cross drives. He is a member of the Nebraska State Bar Association, and the Thurston County Bar Association. He served as vice chairman of the Red Cross in 1917-18, and now is a member of the Pender Chamber of Commerce, and the Nebraskana Society. In addition to his legal activities, he is a bonded abstracter. He holds the office of grand marshal of the Ancient Free and Accepted Masons in Nebraska. He is affiliated with the First Presbyterian Church at Pender.

His marriage to Mittie Tucker was solemnized at Pender, March 27, 1923. Mrs. Smith was born at Pender, August 24, 1888. Residence: Pender.

Arthur Harris Smith

A pioneer farmer in Kearney County, Nebraska, Arthur Harris Smith was born in Ohio, May 31, 1866. He came to Nebraska in 1876 with his parents by train to Lowell and then to his present location where his father homesteaded. He is the son of Albert Franklin and Sarah (Holmwood) Smith. His father, a farmer, was born at North Adams, Massachusetts, and died at Las Vegas, New Mexico, January 15, 1881. He served as captain in the Civil War with the 116th New York Volunteers; his ancestry was Scotch. His mother, whose ancestry was English, was born in Sussex, England, June 30, 1839, came to America in 1850, and died at Minden, Nebraska, April 18, 1912.

Mr. Smith is a member of the National Geographic Society, the Farmers Elevator board, and the Nebraskana Society. He is treasurer of the local school board and takes an active interest in civic and community affairs at Campbell, Nebraska. His hobby is reading.

His marriage to Amanda Ellen Sallee was solemnized at Minden, January 6, 1892. Mrs. Smith, who was a teacher prior to her marriage, was born at Wayne, Wisconsin, September 23, 1870. They have six children: Ella Hazle, born October 26, 1892, who married Albert Hollander on October 9, 1914; Gertrude Lucile, born October 1, 1896, who is married to Herbert Ford; Sarah Sallee, born August 8, 1901, who married Chris Raun; Artie Holmwood, born March 10, 1907, who married John Faber, Jr., on February 3, 1926; Mary Jane, born October 2, 1908; and Marian Ellen, born August 27, 1911, who are teachers. Residence: Campbell.

Aubrey Adam Smith

A leading banker at St. Edward, Nebraska, Aubrey Adam Smith has lived in this state for over 52 years, and has taken a prominent part in the business and civic life of his community. He was born at St. Edward, January 7, 1879, the son of Pierson David Smith and Martha (Shaw) Smith. Pierson D. Smith, who was born in New York City, and died at St. Edward, October 15, 1927, was graduated from the Northwestern University, law department, and with his father, Adam Smith, bought 100,000 acres of Boone County land from the Burlington Railroad on which he settled in 1877; his grandfather, George Smith, came to this country from Scotland, about 1800.

Martha (Shaw) Smith, was born in Scotland, and died at St. Edward, July 19, 1930.

Mr. Smith was graduated from the preparatory school at Lawrenceville, New Jersey, in 1898, and received the Bachelor of Arts degree from Yale University in 1902. He was a member of Psi Mu. At this time he is the owner of 8000 acres of land in Boone County, and is president of the Smith National Bank at St. Edward. He is a member of the Omaha Club, holds membership in the Masons, Knights of Pythias, and Elks, and is a member of the Nebraskana Society. His hobby is reading. He served as a member of the most of the local committees at St. Edward during the World War.

A Republican, Mr. Smith was a member of the Nebraska house of representatives in 1907, and a member of the Nebraska senate in 1911. He was married to Lula Fisher at Norfolk, Nebraska, November 4, 1918. Mrs. Smith is the daughter of Paul F. and Sophie Fisher. Mrs. Smith was born of German parents at Grand Island, Nebraska, October 24, 1894. They have one daughter, Martha Margaret, who was born June 6, 1921. Residence: St. Edward. Residence: St. Edward.

Beaman Quincy Smith

Beaman Quincy Smith, educator and county extension agent of Frontier County, was born in Takoma Park, Prince George County, Maryland, February 7, 1906, son of Dr. Clarence Beaman and Lottie Lee (Smith) Smith.

The father, born in Howardsville, Michigan, September 21, 1872, is Chief of the United States Extension Service and assistant director. This includes 4-H work, women's work, county agents work, and all phases of extension. He is the author and editor of several books, poems, and agricultural encyclopedia. The family is related to Hamilton Wright Maybee on the paternal side and is almost purely English.

Lottie Lee Smith was born in Lawrence, Michigan, May 4, 1877; studied at Ann Arbor and Lansing and is a talented musician. She is a natural leader, having organized nearly ten clubs (both men's and women's) in Takoma Park, the family residence. She comes from an eminent family, which included four judges, two doctors, and an aunt who married a doctor on the father's side. The Quaker ancestry of the family traces back to the Black Finns of England. There is some Scotch as well as English blood.

Mr. Smith attended Takoma Park grade school in the District of Columbia, and in 1924 was graduated from Central High School at Washington, D. C. In 1929, after earning his way through college, he received a Bachelor of Science degree in Animal Husbandry at Michigan State College of East Lansing. His honors include Alpha Zeta, Seminarius Botanicus, the college orchestra, Alpha Gamma Rho, of which he was chaplain for two years and a service sweater for wrestling at Michigan State College in 1928. Mr. Smith has had eight years study on the violin, and was a candidate for the Rhodes scholarship, withdrawing because he felt that actual experience would be of greater assistance than further study. Prior to accepting his present position, Mr. Smith was assistant county agent at Fairbury, Nebraska, from April 10, 1930 until October 6, 1930. He then helped the State Exten-

sion Department with hog survey work and other tasks. On November 17, he was shifted to Stockville, Nebraska to fill the vacancy of county agent caused by the illness of Joe Kuska, and on April 6 he was given complete charge of the office.

Mr. Smith has had five years' military training in high school and college, with the ranks of private, corporal, sergeant, and first lieutenant in high school and corporal in college. From 1927 until 1929 he was chairman of hospital service and chairman of social service of the Young Men's Christian Association at East Lansing, Michigan. He is a member of Takoma Park Presbyterian Church, the People's Church of East Lansing, Michigan, the Fairbury Methodist Church, Fairbury, Nebraska, in addition to his membership in the Stockville, Nebraska Congregational Church. He enjoys all sports, especially tennis, wrestling, hiking, and canoeing. His hobbies are reading, the violin, friendship, and nature. Residence: Stockville.

Carson Rudolph Smith

Carson Rudolph Smith, vice-president of the Farmers State Bank of Ogallala, was born at Belgrade, Nebraska, August 20, 1902, son of Eugene A. and Mary L. (Kliese) Smith.

Eugene A. Smith was born in Illinois in April, 1875, and is a banker of German and English descent. His wife, Mary L., was born in Illinois in 1878. She is a devoted wife and mother and an active worker in her church. Both her parents were of Holland Dutch and German descent. Her mother was American born and her father was born in the Province of Prussia, Germany.

Mr. Smith attended the grade and high school at Columbus, Nebraska, finishing in 1918. Thereafter, he was a student at business college in Denver. For some time he engaged in ranching and later entered the banking business.

Mr. Smith is married to Mabel Gladys Antrim, who was born at Seward, Nebraska, March 27, 1900. Her parents are of Irish descent, the father a direct descendant of the landlords of County Antrim, Ireland. They have two children, Betty Lou, born March 16, 1927; and Roger Carson, born October 14, 1931.

At the present time, Mr. Smith is serving as president of the Ogallala Commercial Club, and treasurer of Ogallala Lodge No. 159 of the Masons. He is a member of the Methodist Church. His favorite sport is golf, while his hobbies are outdoor sports, hunting, fishing and reading. Residence: Ogallala.

Clara Lotspeich Smith

Clara Lotspeich Smith was born at Morning Sun, Iowa, daughter of Myron Chamberlin Smith and Amelia Judith (Lotspeich) Smith. Her father was born at Elmwood, Illinois, August 24, 1842. He was a farmer, a Republican, and served 3 years in the Civil War. His death occurred at Lincoln, on September 6, 1924. Of English descent, his ancestry is traced to Err Chamberlin, a Revolutionary soldier and to Sir John Wright of Kelvadon Hall, Essex, England, and from Joseph Wright who came to Massachusetts from London in 1630.

Amelia Lotspeich was born at New Salem, Illinois, March 22, 1844, and is descended from Ralph Lotspeich, a circuit rider in early Ohio Methodism, under whose guidance Peter Cortwright, well known Methodist minister, received his training.

Miss Smith received her early education in the county schools of Iowa, and was graduated from Woodbine, Iowa, Normal School in 1891. She has attended the University of Chicago and the University of Nebraska, and holds a life professional teacher's certificate.

Since 1895 she has been a resident of Nebraska, and during that time has been active in the political, civic and educational life of the state. From 1922-30 she was a member of the state Republican central committee and from 1922-24 was a member of the executive committee. She has taught in the city schools of Iowa and Nebraska, and has done clerical work in the University of Nebraska, and in the office of the state superintendent of schools. At the present time she is a realtor. During the World War she was vice president of the Red Cross organization at University Place. She belongs to the First Methodist Church at University Place, the Parent-Teachers' Association, Lincoln Woman's Club, and the Young Women's Christian Association. Her fraternal and patriotic organizations include the Order of Eastern Star, the Daughters of the American Revolution, the Daughters of Veterans, the Rebekahs, of which she is past noble grand, and the Patriarchs Militant Auxiliary of which she is secretary. She is also a member of the Women's Christian Temperance Union. Her hobby is gardening. Residence: Lincoln. (Photograph in Album).

Claude W. Smith

A prominent editor and publisher at Elwood, Nebraska, is Claude W. Smith, a lifetime resident of this state. He was born at Grant, Nebraska, December 1, 1889, the son of Charles F. and Jennie (DeVinny) Smith. His father, who was also an editor and publisher, was born at Charles City, Iowa, July 2, 1864, and died at Elwood, December 20, 1915; he served as president of the Madrid Exchange Bank and was postmaster at Elwood. His mother was born in Indiana County, Pennsylvania, March 18, 1868, and died at Elwood, in 1906.

Mr. Smith attended the Elwood grade and high school and entered the newspaper field with the Progress Printing Company at Holdrege, Nebraska. He remained there three years before locating permanently at Elwood in 1915. He has also been mechanical foreman of various newspapers, and is now editor and publisher of the *Elwood Bulletin*.

On September 8, 1921, he was married at Elwood to Ellen Umberger who was born at New Cumberland, Pennsylvania, March 16, 1891. Mr. Smith was awarded first place by the Nebraska Press Association for the best newspaper published in Nebraska towns of less than 1000 population, in 1926. He is president of the Elwood Community Club, past president of the Southwest Nebraska Press Association, and is a member of the Nebraska Press Association.

He holds membership in the following Masonic bodies: past master of Elwood Lodge, Number 167, Valley Scottish Rite Consistory of Hastings, Nebraska, and the Ancient Arabic Order of the Nobles of the Mystic Shrine. He is also a member of the Order of the Eastern Star, and the Nebraskana Society. Residence: Elwood.

Clayton Halsey Smith

Clayton Halsey Smith, son of Halsey Riley and Nancy Maria (Arnold) Smith, was born at Norwalk, Iowa, October 24, 1867. His father was born at Cleveland, Ohio, November 26, 1836, of English and Irish parentage. He was a farmer and taught school one term in Michigan and twenty-four terms in Butler County. His death occurred at Bellwood, Nebraska, February 11, 1911.

His mother was born at Cleveland, June 4, 1840, of Irish and Dutch parentage, and died at Bellwood, January 9, 1889. She was a wonderful mother and active in church work.

Mr. Smith attended rural schools in Butler County. On December 1, 1897, at David City, Nebraska, he was united in marriage with Fannie May Applegate. She was born at Schuyler, Nebraska, December 15, 1871, of Irish and Dutch parentage. To this union five children were born: Pearlie, October 8, 1898, who is married to Robert Runnion; Harlan, October 18, 1901; Auretha, March 4, 1905, who died April 5, 1910, who died May 11,

1911. Pearlie and Harlan are now residents of Douglas, Wyoming.

Clayton Smith is now a retired farmer, a resident of Nebraska sixty years. He has served two years as police judge and two years as township treasurer of Bellwood, Nebraska, and at present is mayor of Bellwood. He is a member of the Nebraskana Society, and the Independent Order of Oddfellows, and is a Protestant. Residence: Bellwood.

Daniel B. Smith

One of Nebraska's pioneer farmers is Daniel B. Smith who was born in Indiana, August 19, 1853, the son of Martin V. and Lucinda (Good) Smith. His father, who was a cooper by trade, was born March 19, 1818, and died December 1, 1862. His mother, whose ancestry was German, was born November 30, 1813, and died July 29, 1864.

Mr. Smith had been unusually successful in farming in Valley County, Nebraska, since 1868. He was affiliated with the Methodist Episcopal Church of Ord, Nebraska, and in the past had held various township and county offices. He died at Ord on June 4, 1932.

He was married to Martha I. Williams at Glenrock, Nebraska; she was born in Cedar County, Missouri, April 22, 1856. Their children are: Olive, born January 5, 1874, who died July 2, 1892; Frank W., born November 19, 1876, who died May 24, 1912; Ethel, born September 4, 1879, who married Germain Hoyt; Myrtle, born July 19, 1881, who married Eden F. Thompson; Charlie, born July 5, 1883, who married Ida Easterbrook; Lottie, born April 5, 1885, who married Harvey Friend; Evet A., born September 25, 1887, who married Mae Moyer; Nina S., born January 3, 1890, who married Harry Keasey; Dorah P., born September 10, 1891, who married Elmer Hallock; Minnie V., born June 13, 1893, who married Bert M. Hardenbrook; and Mamie L., born December 4, 1895. Residence: Ord.

David Jackson Smith

A pioneer physician in Nebraska, David Jackson Smith has been a resident in this state for the past 40 years. He was born at Washington, Pennsylvania, November 14, 1864, the son of David and Hannah (Snodgrass) Smith. His father, who participated in the Civil War, was born in Pennsylvania, April 17, 1827, and died at Claysville, Pennsylvania, January 21, 1884. His mother was born at Claysville, May 27, 1830, and died at Burnsville, January 19, 1887.

Dr. Smith attended the rural and normal schools of Pennsylvania, was a student at Iowa State University, and received the degree of Doctor of Medicine at the Omaha Medical College in 1898. He taught in a rural school in Polk County, Nebraska for eight terms, and since then has been actively engaged in the practice of his profession at Osceola, Nebraska.

He holds membership in the Osceola Chapter of the Red Cross, the Community Club, the Order of Eastern Star, Masonic Lodge, and the Nebraskana Society. He is a member of the American Medical Association, the Nebraska State Medical Association, and the Young Men's Christian Association of Osceola. His social club is the Osceola Country Club and his favorite sports are golfing and fishing. He is affiliated with the First Methodist Episcopal Church.

On June 29, 1897, he was married to Rose Elizabeth Allen at Osceola. Mrs. Smith, who was a teacher before her marriage, was born of Canadian parentage at Osceola, November 24, 1873. They have two children: Veda, born April 4, 1898, who married Charles R. Stanton; and Ruth, an adopted daughter, who married Kenneth A. Cornish. Residence: Osceola.

Earl William Smith

Earl William Smith, superintendent of schools at Red Cloud, Nebraska since 1927, was born at Trenton, Nebraska, June 28, 1891, son of William Jarvis and Mary Frances (Rutledge) Smith.

William Jarvis Smith's father, James Smith of Andrew, Iowa, was a Forty-niner. William J. Smith homesteaded along Bova Canyon, Hitchcock County in 1886, and was known to early settlers as "Bova Bill". The family came to the United States from England before the Revolution, settling in the Carolinas. The Smiths on the maternal side of the family come from the Palmers of New England and New York, whose ancestors were colonial soldiers in the Revolutionary War.

Mary Frances Rutledge, wife of William Jarvis Smith, was born in Somerset, Ohio, September 24, 1858. They observed their golden wedding anniversary at Sharpsburg, Iowa, in October, 1927. She is of American pre-revolutionary ancestry; a great grandfather having served in the Revolutionary War. Her father, William Rutledge, enlisted in the Civil War from Ohio. She was a pioneer in two states, Iowa and Nebraska.

Earl William Smith attended rural and village schools at Sharpsburg, Iowa, and was graduated from the eighth grade at Prairie Union Rural School in Hitchcock County, Nebraska in 1907. He attended the McCook and Trenton High Schools and was graduated from the latter in 1911. In 1914 he was graduated from the two year course at Peru Teachers College, and in 1925 received his Bachelor of Arts degree from Wayne State Teachers College. His Masters degree was awarded by the University of Nebraska in 1930. In 1931 Mr. Smith was awarded the service key of Phi Delta Kappa, honorary educational fraternity. He was president of the senior class at Trenton High School and a class officer of his senor class at Peru in 1914. He is a member of Phi Delta Kappa, and was a member of the college baseball team at Peru in 1914. He was for a time a student at Drake University, Des Moines, Iowa.

On March 20, 1915, Mr. Smith was married to Ulden Irene Tharp at Kearney, Nebraska. She was born at Surprise, Nebraska, June 15, 1894, and before her marriage was a teacher. Her ancestry is Welsh and Scotch-Irish. There are two children, Alice June, born June 14, 1916, at Thayer, Nebraska; and Robert Tharp, born February 23, 1918, at York.

An Independent Democrat, Mr. Smith is active in party politics, and has been a delegate to county and state conventions. He is the author of *Provisions and Characteristics of a Superintendent's Handbook* (1930), besides articles and comments on taxation reform. He has been superintendent of schools at Waterloo, Merna, Pierce, Wakefield, Hooper, and since 1927 at Red Cloud.

He is a member of the Congregational Church, the National Education Association, the Nebraska State Teachers Association, the Schoolmasters Club, the Red Cross, the Red Cloud Ad Club, the Lions Club, the Masons, the Nebraskana Society, the Nebraska Neihardt Club (president 1923), and was a member of the State Library Committee of the Nebraska State Teachers Association (1924-25). He enjoys golf and reading. Residence: Red Cloud.

Edward Alvin Smith

Edward Alvin Smith was born at Grand Island, Nebraska, April 30, 1876, the son of Walter and Sarah Jane (Garanger) Smith. His father, who was a pioneer farmer and carpenter in Nebraska, was born at Ontario, Canada, June 8, 1836, and died at Grand Island, February 2, 1913. His mother was born at Columbus, Ohio, March 2, 1838, and died at Omaha, Nebraska, February 14, 1913; her ancestry was German.

Mr. Smith attended the Grand Island public schools and later was a student at normal college. A clergyman of the Methodist Episcopal Church, he has held the following pastorates: Fullerton, Nebraska, 1904; Wolbach, 1905; Greeley Center, 1906-07; Woodriver, 1908; Purple Cane, 1909-12; Omaha, 1913; Purple Cane, 1914-24; Plainview, 1924 to date.

He is a member of the Red Cross, of which he was formerly a director, was a member of the Parent Teachers Association, 1928-30, and was at one time a member of the Dodge County Pioneer Association. He holds membership in the Nebraskana Society and is a 4-H Club leader. His hobbies are mechanics and radio. During the World War he served in Young Men's Christian Association work, was chairman of the township committee, and took part in Liberty loan drives.

Mr. Smith is the author of various articles on rural life. He was married to Addye Dell Copple at Fullerton, October 18, 1905; she was born at Centralia, Illinois, April 2, 1885. They have a daughter, Dorothy, born August 18, 1912. Residence: Plainview.

Eugene Allcott Smith

Eugene Allcott Smith, banker and mortgage loan and trust executive, was born in Hennepin, Illinois, April 10, 1874, son of James Anderson and Irene (Dickerson) Smith.

The father, born in Ohio, August 4, 1846, died at Cedar Rapids, Nebraska, July 18, 1918. He was a real estate and investment dealer, a veteran of the Civil War, having served with the 44th Iowa Infantry. His grandfather came from Germany about 1806. The mother, born in Ohio, September 13, 1856, died at Cedar Rapids, July 9, 1917. She was an ardent member of her church, of Scotch descent.

Mr. Smith attended public school to the tenth grade and was graduated from Cedar Rapids High School. He has been the owner and manager of the E. A. Smith Mercantile Company, the Clark Mercantile Company, the Haxton Mercantile Company, and at the present time is president of The Farmers State Bank and The Farmers Mortgage and Investment Company. He is a Republican and has served as central committeeman.

On June 18, 1901, he was married to Mary Louise (Kliese) at Belgrade, Nebraska. Mrs. Smith was born in Evanston, Illinois, October 30, 1876, of German descent. Four children were born to them, three of whom are living, Carson, born August 20, 1903; Millard, born November 4, 1906, who married Helen Beal and died February 16, 1929; Doris, born March 27, 1908; and Helene, born April 4, 1910. Carson is vice-president of The Farmers State Bank, Doris is a school teacher, and Helene is a music teacher.

Mr. Smith is a member of the advisory board of the Salvation Army, a member and past president of the Commercial Club, a member of the Rotary Club, the Elks Club, and is a director of the Omaha Stock Show. He is an Odd Fellow, a Modern Woodman of America, and a Woodman of the World. His favorite sport is golf, while his hobby is club houses, fishing and hunting. Residence: Ogallala.

Ezra Harold Smith

Ezra Harold Smith was born in Clay County, Nebraska, January 8, 1873, the son of Neri and Esther (Faires) Smith. His father, who was a farmer, was born in Bedford County, Pennsylvania, June 9, 1844, and died at York, Nebraska, November 28, 1927; he served in the 43rd Ohio Volunteer Infantry for over three years, during the Civil War. His mother, an active church worker and a member of the Women's Reserve Corps, was born in Morgan County, Ohio, June 11, 1852, and died at York, July 27, 1923.

Mr. Smith received his education in the rural schools of Clay County, and then engaged in farming for several years. For 15 years he was employed by the Chicago Burlington & Quincy Railroad Company. Since 1910, when he became secretary-treasurer of the Harrison Nursery Company, he has been engaged in the nursery businss at York, acting as vice president for six years. For the past three years he has been president of this organization.

He is secretary-treasurer of the York Investment Company, is past president of the Nebraska Horticultural Society, and is past president of the Western Association of Nurserymen. Mr. Smith is prominent in practically all civic and educational organizations at York and holds the following positions: president of the Young Men's Christian Association, since 1928; treasurer of the American Red Cross for York County, since January 1, 1931; and president of the board of education, since 1929.

Mr. Smith has been a member of the board of education for 10 years, serving as vice president of the board for eight years, has been a member of the board of directors of the Young Men's Christian Association for 15 years, serving on the state committee of the latter for 12 years, and has been a member of the Cotner College board for 10 years.

A charter member of the Rotary Club, he served as president in 1926, and is still a member of that society. He is affiliated with the Church of Christ at York, and for the past 15 years has been an elder in the church. His hobby is church work and civic enterprise.

Mr. Smith is a Mason, and Shriner, and past master of Lodge No. 56; past patron of Grace Chapter No. 87 of the Order of Eastern Star; past president of the Nebraska Horticultural Society; and past president of the Western Association of Nurserymen. During the World War he served on the county fuel committee, was enlistment chairman of the Young Men's Christian Association, and was chairman of the county Red Cross drive. He is a member of the Sons of Veterans. His sports are golfing and fishing.

His marriage to Myrtle Edna Zook was solemnized in Clay County, Nebraska, on October 27, 1897. Mrs. Smith was born in Clay County, December 26, 1876. They have two children: Vivian L., born March 21, 1899, who married Barton A. Johnson; and Leslie R., born July 16, 1904, who married Ruth Margaret Moss. Leslie is pastor of Tabernacle Christian Church at Lincoln, and is a graduate of Cotner College and Yale Divinity School.

Mr. Smith is a member of the Nebraska State Historical Society and the York Country Club. Residence: York.

Frank G. Smith

Frank G. Smith was born at Gilson, Knox County, Illinois, December 25, 1864. Oscar F. Smith, his father, was a clergyman born in Indiana and who died at Council Bluffs, Iowa, in 1907. Esther A. (Lynn) Smith, his mother, was born at Galena, Illinois, and died at Atkinson, Illinois, September, 1893.

Mr. Smith was graduated from the high school at Annawan, Illinois, and later received the B. S. degree from Northwestern Normal and Scientific College. He was awarded his Doctor of Divinity at Grinnell, Iowa, and was ordained at Neponset, Illinois, December 5, 1892. He has held the following pastorates, Neponset, Illinois, for three years; Abingdon, Illinois, three and one half years; Peoria, Illinois, two and one half years; Dubuque, Iowa, three years; Chicago, ten years; and Kansas City, Missouri, six years. For the past twelve years he has been pastor of the First Central Congregational Church of Omaha.

A Republican, Dr. Smith served as a member of the Illinois legislature, 1911-12. He has lived in Nebraska for the past 12 years and has taken an unusually active interest in civic and religious affairs in Omaha.

On August 19, 1886, he was united in marriage with Alma E. Palmer at Prairie Centre, LaSalle County, Illi-

nois. Mrs. Smith was born at Prairie Centre, May 3, 1863, and died at Omaha, June 23, 1930. There are two children: Leila B., born May 18, 1894, who married Robert F. Kirshner; and Xenophon P., born October 6, 1899, who married Irene Seery.

Dr. Smith is a member of the Omaha Fellowship Club, the Omaha Chamber of Commerce, and the Omaha Rotary Club. He is a member of the Masons; Blue Lodge, Chapter, Commandery, Consistory, Shrine, and is Knight Commander of Court of Honor. He is affiliated with the Omaha Young Men's Christian Association. His local clubs are the University Club, Omaha Club, and Happy Hollow Club. He is also a member of Crystal Downs Country Club of Frankfort, Michigan. His favorite sport is golf. Residence: Omaha.

Frank Henry Smith

Frank Henry Smith, retired merchant, was born at Manlius, Illinois, July 18, 1854, son of William Homer and Philinda (Stickell) Smith.

The father was born in New York State and died at Galesburg, Illinois, April 11, 1864. He was a farmer and carpenter, the inventor and manufacturer of the first two-horse corn cultivator. His father was English and fought in the Revolution at the Battle of Sacketts Harbor at the age of 17. His wife, Philinda, died at Chadron, August 5, 1909. She was of German descent.

Mr. Smith was educated in the common school. He was a merchant for 15 years and is now retired. A Republican, he was elected county clerk of Loup County two terms. He is a member of Union Congregational Church at Antioch, the Odd Fellows and the Nebraskana Society. Since 1918 he has been a member of the Antioch School Board.

On January 19, 1881, he was married to Rosetta Fidelia Aldrich at West Bureau, Illinois. Mrs. Smith was born at Wyanet, Illinois, October 9, 1858, and was formerly a teacher. They have seven children, all of whom are living, as follows: Ethel, born April 11, 1882; Gerald A., April 7, 1883; Fred V., November 21, 1886; Fenner, February 15, 1889; Homer, April 6, 1893; Zilma, August 20, 1894; and Frank, December 12, 1895. There are 14 grandchildren living. Residence: Antioch.

George Murray Smith

George Murray Smith, lumberman and banker in Nebraska for many years, was born at Racine, Wisconsin, the son of John Spence and Mary Ann (Higgie) Smith. His father, who was a lumberman, was born at Dundee, Scotland, April 25, 1831, and died at Shelby, Polk County, Nebraska, May 14, 1901; he came to this country in 1852. His mother was born at Newbourgh, Scotland, July 18, 1841, and died at Shelby, May 17, 1920.

Mr. Smith was a member of the Smith Brothers Lumber Company for 39 years, and is now president of the First National Bank at Shelby, and is a director in that organization. Mr. Smith and his brother, Frank E. Smith, are pioneer settlers of Shelby. F. M. Leibee was the first business man to locate and the Smith brothers were next to come to Shelby. He is a member of Sesostris Temple of the Shrine, at Lincoln, holds membership in the Republican party, and is a Mason and Elk. His sports are hunting and fishing, while his hobby is reading.

On December 12, 1901, he was married at Shelby to Florence Lockard, who was born in Polk County, April 28, 1878. She is a member of the Eastern Star. Residence: Shelby.

Hervey Foster Smith

Hervey F. Smith was born at Silver Lake, Kansas, March 14, 1886. His father, Benjamin O. Smith, who was born at Massillon, Ohio, February 29, 1856, was a school teacher and a farmer. His mother was born at Todd's Point Illinois, October 30, 1861.

Mr. Smith attended country school and was graduated from Baker University Academy in 1904. He received his A. B. degree at Baker University in 1908; was a student at the University of Chicago, 1909-10; and attended the University of Nebraska, 1929-30. Active in inter-collegiate debating and oratory, he was a member of Sigma Phi Epsilon.

He has been engaged in welfare and boys' work for several years; was associated with the Intercollegiate Prohibition Association, 1908-12; was engaged in newspaper work, 1912-14; and since 1914 has been in the Young Men's Christian Association activities, and is now boys' work secretary of the Lincoln association. He is the author of *Finding God in the Out of Doors* (1925).

His marriage to Emma May Garman was solemnized at Decatur, Macon County, Illinois, June 15, 1910. Mrs. Smith was born at Bethany, Shelby County, Illinois, June 12, 1886. Her ancestry dates to William Penn and Daniel Boone. They have two children: Harold Edwin, born May 16, 1914; and Eleanor Hervene, born April 6, 1919.

Mr. Smith is a member of the Association of Boys' Work Secretaries, and in 1926 served as president of the Nebraska Employed Officers Association of which he is still a member. He holds membership in the Hiram International Club. He is a Mason. Politically, he is an Independent Republican, is affiliated with Trinity Methodist Episcopal Church. Residence: Lincoln.

Hugh E. Smith

Hugh E. Smith, prominent rancher of Box Butte County, was born at Knoxville, Iowa, November 23, 1879, and has resided in Nebraska since March, 1910. He is the son of Bennett and Lily E. (Jones) Smith, both natives of Iowa. His father died there in 1881. He was a farmer. His mother was born April 9, 1861, and is Scotch on the maternal side.

Upon his graduation from the public schools of Knoxville, Iowa, Mr. Smith attended Knoxville High School where he was a member of the football team in 1901. Before coming to western Nebraska he was associated with the firm of Culver and Company, clothiers, for a period of seven years. He is now manager of his own cattle ranch.

While a resident of Knoxville, Iowa, Mr. Smith was a member of a fishing club situated in the beautiful Des Moines River, called the Mandalay Club. Upon his removal to Nebraska, his fellow clubmen promptly dubbed his ranch the Mandalay and it is so called by all their friends.

On February 28, 1908, Mr. Smith was united in marriage to Mary Ann Tucker at Knoxville, Iowa. Mrs. Smith was born at Marysville, Iowa, April 2, 1884, and is a member of the Daughters of the American Revolution through an ancestor, Thomas Fears. For three years Mrs. Smith served as leader for the Haekeri Pig Club, a girls 4-H Club. Both she and Mr. Smith served as chairmen of their precinct on various committees during the World War. They have one son, Adrian Bennett, born July 28, 1913. He was graduated from Alliance High School in 1931, was a member of the Glee Club for three years and played on the basketball team his second year.

Mr. Smith is a Republican. He is affiliated with the Methodist Episcopal Church of Alliance. Residence: Alliance.

James Joseph Smith

James Joseph Smith, who has been a practicing physician at Heartwell, Nebraska, since 1904, was born at New Lexington, Nebraska, February 14, 1875. His father, Michael Thomas Smith, a farmer, was born near New Lexington, September 20, 1848, and died at Sutton, Nebraska, December 29, 1906. His mother, Alice (Dean) Smith, whose ancestry was Irish, was born at New Lexington, June 19, 1847, and died at Heartwell, October 10, 1931.

Dr. Smith was graduated from the Sutton High School in 1896 and received the Doctor of Medicine degree at Creighton University in 1904. He is a member of the Holy Family Catholic Church, is serving on the local school board, and holds membership in the Nebraskana Society and the Modern Woodmen of America.

He was united in marriage with Catherine Joyce at Fairfield, Nebraska, May 31, 1905. Mrs. Smith, who is of Irish descent, was born at Streetar, Illinois, December 29, 1880. Their children are: Nellie, born August 19, 1906; Mary, born July 31, 1908; Catherine, born January 9, 1913; and James, born November 17, 1915. Dr. Smith is a member of the Democratic party. Residence: Heartwell.

James W. Barnum Smith

James W. Barnum Smith, physician and surgeon, was born at Kimball, New York, March 2, son of Joseph Henry and Mary Catherine (Barnum) Smith.

Joseph Henry Smith was born in Ontario, Canada, May 7, 1842, and died on his farm at Kimball, Nebraska, February 6, 1925. He was a pioneer physician and surgeon of Albion, coming there by stage coach in the fall of 1879, before railroad had been built. He practiced medicine at Albion continuously until failing health prevented. He was English; both father and mother were descended from the Tupper family.

Mary Catherine Barnum was born at Kendall, New York, August 25, 1845, and died at Albion, August 30, 1880. A teacher, she held a life certificate from the State of New York. She was a direct descendant of Thomas Barnum, the 15th son of Sir Francis Barnum, who was born in Kent, England in 1625. Thomas Barnum came to America in 1640 and is the original forebear of the Barnum family, in America.

Dr. Smith attended schools in Albion and was graduated from high school there in 1898. He received his medical degree from the University of Nebraska, where he was active in football.

Since May 14, 1903, Dr. Smith has been in active practice at Albion. He is a Republican, a member of the Albion Congregational Church, the Commercial Club and the Lions Club.

A Mason, he is a member of Albion Lodge No. 78, the Ancient Free and Accepted Masons, and is past master of that Lodge. He is a member of Scottish Rite at Omaha, the Elks, the Modern Woodmen of America, and the Y. M. C. A. and Parent-Teachers Association. During the late war, he was chairman of the Medical Advisory Board of his local country and assisted in Red Cross drive. He is a life member of the Red Cross.

Among his professional organizations are the Boone County Medical Association, which is a component part of the Nebraska State Medical Association, and the Missouri Valley Association. Dr. Smith's favorite sport is golf, while his hobby is fur farming.

On December 14, 1905, he was married to Julia L. Martin at Albion. Mrs. Smith was born at Maxwell, Nebraska, November 14, 1880, of Scotch-Irish and English descent. She was a stenographer and bookkeeper before her marriage. They have three children, Chauncey M., born October 4, 1906, who was graduated from Kemper Military School at Boonesville, Missouri, and is now attending the University of California; Lydia L., born November 3, 1908, who will graduate from the University of Nebraska in 1932; and LeRoy James, born February 3, 1919, who is in the eighth grade at the Albion Public School. Residence: Albion.

Leon Osmer Smith

Leon O. Smith was born at Miliedgeville, Carroll County, Illinois, January 17, 1889, the son of George James and Ida May (Wood) Smith. His father, who was a farmer, was born in Bradford County Pennsylvania, October 25, 1863, and died at Paullina, O'Brien County, Iowa, August 13, 1927. His ancestry was Irish.

His mother was born at Milledgeville, May 2, 1864. She is descended from the English family of Fitch, members of which came to Connecticut in 1638.

He was graduated from the high school in 1906 at Paullina; was awarded the A. B. degree at the University of Iowa in 1916; and the A. M. degree in 1918. He was a student at Iowa State College in 1913; was undergraduate assistant in English at the University of Iowa; and was elected to membership in Phi Delta Kappa.

Mr. Smith was superintendent of schools at Batavia, Iowa, 1910-12; at Keosauqua, Iowa, 1912-14; and at Onawa, Iowa, 1914-17; was a member of the faculty at Kearney State Teachers' College in the summer session of 1920; was on the faculty of the University of Montana, 1922; taught at the University of Wyoming, 1923; the University of Washington, 1924; San Diego State Teachers' College, summers of 1925-26; and Creighton University, summers of 1928-29-30. He has been assistant superintendent of city schools at Omaha since 1918. He is the author of *One Hundred Fifty Questions and Answers on the Constitution; The High School Library;* and *Score Card for High School Libraries.* He is editor of the book review department of the *Nebraska Educational Journal.*

He was married to Maude Alice Sumner at Fairfield, Iowa, June 12, 1912. Mrs. Smith, who was born at Cicero, Indiana, January 21, 1891, is a writer. Her ancestry is English and German. Two children were born to their marriage, Sumner, born December 29, 1915, who died August 5, 1928; and Carol, born May 9, 1930.

During 1909 and 1910 Mr. Smith was captain and commissary of the cadet regiment at the University of Iowa. He is a member of the National Educational Association and the Department of Superintendence; the Nebraska State Teachers' Association, of which he was president of Omaha District in 1928; and is a member of the legislative committee of the Nebraska State Teachers' Association.

He is a member of the Omaha Chamber of Commerce; Ak-Sar-Ben; and the Professional Men's Club of which he is president; is a life member of the Iowa State Historical Society; a member of the educational committee of the Omaha Young Men's Christian Association; the Nebraskana Society. He is affiliated with the First Unitarian Church of Omaha and is chairman of the board of trustees of this institution. He likes to hike, while his hobby is reading. Mr. Smith spent three summers as manager on the Chautauqua platform. He is a Republican. He holds membership in the Masonic Lodge, Royal Arch, Knights Templar, and Order of the Eastern Star. Residence: Omaha.

Thurman Amon Smith

For over 50 years Thurman Amon Smith has been prominent in civic and professional affairs in Nebraska, and has been a leader in various reform movements in the state. He was born at Warrenburg, New York, January 13, 1877, the son of Edwin B. and Anna L. (George) Smith. His father, who was a rancher and pioneer settler in Blaine County, Nebraska, was born in Vermont, August 14, 1858, and died at Taylor, March 27, 1929; he operated a hotel at Brewster, Nebraska, for a time, and served as county clerk of Blaine County for several years. His mother, an active church and Sunday School worker, was born at Lake George, New York of Scotch-Irish parentage.

Mr. Smith attended rural school and later was a student at Franklin Academy. He was a teacher in the public schools for 7 years, was prominent in religious movements for the Methodist Episcopal Church for a time, and for twelve years has been the editor and publisher of the *Taylor Clarion.* During the campaign to vote Nebraska dry he managed and edited a Woman's Christian Temperance Union newspaper, the *Search Light* in Cherry County, Nebraska. He is the owner and manager of the Pavilion Apartments at Taylor.

During the World War Mr. Smith was foreman of the *Antioch News* published at Antioch, Nebraska. During his resident there his son, Myrthe was drowned, and following a breakdown in his wife's health he moved to Taylor. He is a member of the Commercial Club, the Red Cross, the Nebraska Press Association, and the Fraternal Aid Union. He is affiliated with the Methodist Episcopal Church. Mr. Smith's hobby is good books, and he owns a private library of unusual quality.

On October 26, 1902, he was married to Laura Elnor Hoyt at Brewster, Nebraska. Mrs. Smith is a talented artist in oil painting. The six children born to their marriage are: Sidney C., January 23, 1904, who married Bessie Shelton; Myrthe C., August 7, 1905, who died November 13, 1918; Theodore H., November 11, 1909; Ivan L., July 28, 1907, who married Ellen Coleman; Ava L., November 26, 1911, who married Dr. J. I. McGregor; and Hazen E., March 15, 1915. Residence: Taylor.

Vance C. Smith

Born at Kearney, Nebraska, June 17, 1893, Vance C. Smith is the son of C. C. and Hannah M. (Carson) Smith. The father was born at Pella, Iowa, December 29, 1849, and died at Eddyville, Nebraska, April 8, 1923. He was a farmer of Scotch-Irish ancestry, for several generations in America. His wife, Hannah, was born in Richland, Iowa, January 21, 1858 the daughter of Albert Carson. She has been a Sunday School teacher since early womanhood.

Vance C. Smith attended public and high school at Kearney, and afterward was a student at Kearney Normal School for two years graduating in 1914. He was business manager of the annual, secretary-treasurer of his senior class and active in football and track in college.

For a year and a half Mr. Smith was principal of the Holbrook School, was superintendent there four years and has been superintendent of Elwood schools for the past nine years. In addition he has farming interests.

On December 27, 1921, he was married to Mabel Eunice Peterson at Gretna. Mrs. Smith, who is a teacher, was born at Gretna, May 24, 1897, the daughter of Chris A. and Jessie (Grell) Peterson. They have two children, Elinor Jean, born October 15, 1927; and Robert Elwood, born November 12, 1931.

Mr. Smith is a Democrat. From December 10, 1917 until January, 1919 he was a private of aviation, and served five months in England with Aircraft Acceptance Park No. 1. He is a member of the American Legion, the Community Club, the Parent Teachers Association, the Nebraska State Teachers Association and the Nebraskana Society. He is affiliated with the Elwood Methodist Episcopal Church and is a Mason. His hobbies are reading and mechanics. Residence: Elwood.

Villiers Deaver Smith

Villiers Deaver Smith, who is engaged in the insurance and real estate business at Beaver City, Nebraska, was born there, September 26, 1889. His father, Charles Edward Villiers Smith, who was a banker and stockman, was born at Aspley Guise, England, July 26, 1855, and died at Beaver City, Nebraska, October 1, 1930, having lived in America since 1875. His mother, was born at Stockport, Ohio, October 15, 1861, and died at Beaver City in October, 1927. She was Mary Lucretia Deaver, daughter of Charles E. and Sarah (Forsythe) Deaver.

Mr. Smith was graduated from the Beaver City High School in 1909, and in 1914 received the Bachelor of Arts degree at the University of Nebraska. He served as bookkeeper and assistant cashier of the First State Bank of Beaver City for 15 years, and since then has been engaged in the insurance and real estate business.

He is a member of the Community Club, the Beaver City Rotary Club, Scottish Rite and Shrine bodies of the Masons, and the First Presbyterian Church. He is a member of the school board, is chairman of the Boy Scouts committee, and holds membership in The Nebraskana Society. His political connection is with the Republican party.

On August 4, 1916, his marriage to Ruth Kimball was solemnized at Hastings, Nebraska, where she was born January 18, 1892. She is the daughter of George W. and Lilian (Yost) Kimball. Their children are: Mary Lilian, born May 30, 1918; and Paul Kimball, born August 1, 1920. Residence: Beaver City .

Walter DeLos Smith

For many years a lawyer and newspaper publisher, Walter DeLos Smith was born at Richland, Iowa, July 1, 1853, son of Alfred Hartwell and Mary Eliza (Woodward) Smith. Alfred Smith was born in Hendricks County, Indiana, July 6, 1828, and was an editor and publisher for many years. He died at Oakland, March 16, 1906. His wife, Mary Eliza, was a native of Indiana, born December 3, 1826, who died at Oakland, December 25, 1906. She was essentially a homemaker.

Walter DeLos Smith attended public and high school and was graduated from the Richland, Iowa, Academy. He was admitted to the bar at Tekamah, Nebraska, on October 3, 1887, and has been a school teacher, newspaper publisher and a lawyer. He is the editor of the *Craig News*, and for the past twenty years has been police judge and justice of the peace at Craig. He is a Republican.

On November 21, 1883, he was united in marriage to Etta Olevia Woodward at Union, Iowa. She was born in Hardin County, Iowa, April 4, 1862, and assists her husband in his newspaper work. There were six children born to this marriage, three of whom are deceased: Lena Vista Smith, born May 29, 1886; James L. Smith, born January 28, 1888; Loraine Harrison, born December 26, 1889, who died December 13, 1918; Shelley Wickersham, born March 9, 1892, who died March 26, 1908, Mary Etta, born January 6, 1894, who married Benjamin Harrison Eby, and who died December 15, 1918; and Walter M., born December 24, 1898. All his children assist him in his newspaper business.

Mr. Smith is a Republican, a member of the Burt County Bar Association, the Ancient Order of United Workmen and The Nebraskana Society. Residence: Craig,

Wilber S. Smith

Wilber S. Smith, banker, was born at Mattoon, Illinois, November 29, 1868. His father, James W. Smith, was born at Lancaster, Ohio, February 22, 1841, and died at Byron, Nebraska, December 17, 1917. For four and one-half years in the Civil War he was sergeant of Company F, 46th Ohio Volunteers. He is a direct descendant of the famous John Smith, who settled Virginia in 1620. Rebecca M. McCleery, wife of James W. Smith, was born at Lancaster, Ohio, April 17, 1849, and died at Byron, May 17, 1918. She was of Scotch descent.

Wilber Smith attended Normal school at Fort Scott, Kansas, and was graduated in 1892. On September 23, 1906, he was married to Grace M. Fisher, at Guide Rock, Nebraska. She is of English descent.

Mr. Smith has been cashier of the Farmers and Merchants Bank of Byron, Nebraska, since April 8, 1903. He is affiliated with the Methodist Church of Byron, Nebraska, and holds membership in the Modern Woodmen of America, and The Nebraskana Society. He is treasurer of the local Red Cross. Residence: Byron.

William Emerald Smith

William E. Smith, son of John M. and Caroline M. Smith, was born, May 28, 1887, in Moville, Iowa. His father was born in Germany, March 24, 1865, where he lived until 1883 when he came to America and followed the hardware business. He died in Sioux City, Iowa, on July 2, 1927. His mother was born in Battle Creek, Iowa, on October 20, 1875, and was of German parentage.

After graduating from the Moville High School in 1915, William Smith attended the University of Nebraska where he received a degree in dental surgery in June, 1918. He is a Delta Sigma Delta at the state university.

On August 14, 1919, his marriage to Eva S. Lorge was solemnized at Randolph, Nebraska. His wife was born in Randolph on January 6, 1888, of German and Belgian parentage. They have a son, Kenneth, born May 15, 1920.

Mr. Smith has resided in Nebraska fifteen years, practicing dentistry at Coleridge, for twelve years. During the World War he served in the United States Navy from July 10, 1918, until February 8, 1919. He holds membership in the American Legion, the American Dental Association, the Nebraska State Dental Society and the Ancient Free and Accepted Masons. He is a member of the Chamber of Commerce and School Board in Coleridge. Golf is Mr. Smith's favorite recreation. Residence: Coleridge.

William John Smith

W. J. Smith was born at Caledonia, Racine County, Wisconsin, June 14, 1869. His father, William Carl Smith, who was a farmer, was born in New York state, March 9, 1842, and died at Racine, November 8, 1918; his ancestry was German. Catherine (McClusky) Smith, his mother, was born at Tabor, Racine County, Wisconsin, in 1849, and died at Racine, December 14, 1893. Her ancestry was Austrian.

Mr. Smith was graduated from the public schools of Wisconsin, in 1883. He was telegraph operator for the Chicago and Northwestern Railway in 1887; was station agent for this railway at Green Lake, DePere, and Appleton, Wisconsin, until 1907. Since 1907 he has lived at Omaha, where he was local freight and general agent, 1907-23; and since 1923 has been manager of the American Railroad Association Car Service Division. He represents all railroads in car supply and freight service in Nebraska, Colorado, Utah, Wyoming, and Idaho.

He is a member of The Railway Guild; Red Cross; Community Chest; and the Omaha Chamber of Commerce. He is a member of the Young Men's Christian Association, the Omaha Athletic Club, and the Nebraskana Society. He is a York Rite Mason, and a member of the Modern Woodmen of America. He is a member of the First Congregational Church of Omaha. He likes to hike and his hobby is reading.

He was united in marriage with Elizabeth Remington at DePere, Brown County, Wisconsin, December 25, 1888. Mrs. Smith was born at DePere, January 8, 1871. She is of English and Welsh descent. They have the following children: Marjorie, born July 8, 1890, who married E. L. Hoyt; James, born April 12, 1899, who married Jean Groeger; and Thomas Robert, born September 9, 1907. James is joint owner of the Omaha Testing Laboratories. He was an honor student at the University of Illinois. Thomas Robert was graduated from the University of Illinois. Residence: Omaha.

Wilson Andrew Smith

Wilson Andrew Smith, merchant, was born in Holt County, Nebraska, October 9, 1885, son of Cord Melvin and Maggie (Dubert) Smith. The father was born at Wellsburg, Pennsylvania, in 1857, and died at Chambers, June 20, 1920. His wife, Maggie, was born at Wellsburg, June 20, 1860, and is still living.

Mr. Smith attended public school and has been a

merchant for a number of years. He is a Republican, a member of the Odd Fellows, the Red Cross, and the Chambers Baptist Church.

On May 1, 1909, Mr. Smith was married to Florence Anderson at Harold, Nebraska. She was born in Holt County, February 16, 1890. They have two children, Bernice, born August 31, 1913; and George, born October 18, 1907. Residence: Chambers.

Louis Benjamin Smoyer

Louis B. Smoyer, pioneer Nebraska farmer, has lived in this state for 64 years. He was born at Sancon, Leigh County, Pennsylvania, February 23, 1841. His father, Jacob Stephen Smoyer, a farmer, was descended from Dutch ancestors who came to America just before the Revolution. He was born at Macungie, Pennsylvania, October 17, 1800, and died at Parma, Michigan, January 5, 1875.

His mother, Anna Troxel (Beiry) Smoyer, was born at Galesburg, Pennsylvania, June 10, 1807, and died at Warren County, Ohio, April 3, 1854. Her ancestry was Dutch.

Mr. Smoyer was married to Addie Vatisha Sawtelle at Syracuse, Nebraska, October 17, 1866. Mrs. Smoyer, whose ancestry is French, was a teacher before her marriage. She was born at Battle Creek, Michigan, July 12, 1842. Seven children were born to this union six of whom are living. They are: George, born September 26, 1867, who married Eva Ingalls; Jesse, born March 24, 1869, who married Nettie Henry; Esther, born November 2, 1871, who married Claude D. Myers; Cora, born May 18, 1876, who married Albert Cross Armitage; Grace, born June 19, 1887, married Clarence Gilman Taylor; Gertrude, born June 19, 1882, who died March 16, 1903; and Nellie, born August 22, 1883, who married Sanford Batson (now deceased). All the children with the exceptions of George and Gertrude were students at the University of Nebraska.

Mr. Smoyer was active in loan drives and the buying of Liberty Bonds during the World War. He is a member of the Pioneers of Nebraska, and is affiliated with the Lutheran Church. He is a Democrat, and has been active in state politics for many years. Residence: Syracuse.

Charles Smrha

Charles Smrha, a resident of Nebraska since 1884, has been engaged in the banking business in Fillmore County since 1903. He was born at Styria, Czechoslovakia, September 14, 1876, the son of Charles and Katerina (Stulik) Smrha. His father, who was in the harness and saddlery business for many years, was born at Rabi, Czechoslovakia, November 9, 1894, and died at Milligan, Nebraska, June 18, 1908; he came to America in 1882. His mother was born at Maloveska, Czechoslovakia, August 2, 1874; she attended grade school and for two years was a student in a seminary. She speaks English and German in addition to her native tongue.

Mr. Smrha attended high school and normal school, was a teacher for two years, and served as county superintendent of schools for four years. He is now president of the Farmers & Merchants Bank at Milligan. He served for two years in the Philippines with the First Nebraska Volunteers during the Spanish American War, on special duty at the headquarters of Major General Arthur McArthur. During the World War he was a member of the South Platte exemption board, and later served as commander of the Nebraska department of the United Spanish War Veterans.

He has served continuously as a member of the school board, village board, or township board at Milligan since 1903, and is now a member of the Milligan Chamber of Commerce. His membership in fraternal organizations includes: Knights of Pythias; Masons; Independ-

ent Order of Odd Fellows; Ancient Order of United Workmen; Z. C. B. J., a Bohemian fraternal insurance society; and the Nebraskana Society. He has served as county chairman of the Red Cross of Fillmore County.

He was united in marriage with Agnes Barta at Lincoln, Nebraska, August 30, 1904. Mrs. Smrha, who was a teacher prior to her marriage, was born at Kamen, Czechoslovakia, March 3, 1876, and came to this country in 1881. Their children are: Robert V., born January 8, 1907; Albert C., born January 8, 1907; Mary A., born March 18, 1911; and Helen M., born March 6, 1913. Both daughters are students at the University of Nebraska. Albert was graduated from the University of Nebraska as an electrical engineer while Robert was graduated from the civil engineering department.

Mr. Smrha is a Democrat; he was a member of the state senate in 1923 and in 1927, and in 1930 was defeated candidate for state treasurer. Residence: Milligan.

Vaclav Vojtech Smrha

Vaclav Vojtech Smrha, physician and surgeon, was born in Kolinec, Czechoslovakia, November 7, 1878, and has resided in Nebraska since November, 1884.

He received his medical degree from Creighton University in 1905, and has been in private practice at Milligan since that time. He is the author of some medical papers, and insurance articles. He is supreme medical examiner for the Western Bohemian Fraternal Association (1911-).

On January 2, 1904, he was married to Anna Rose Hamouz at Exeter. She was born at Milligan, August 30, 1883. There are five children, Anna Rose, born May 28, 1904; Rose Marie, born July 2, 1906, who died December 8, 1918; Karel Frank, born December 2, 1907; James Albert, born February 17, 1911; and Marian Ruth, born March 6, 1918.

Dr. Smrha is a member of the American, Nebraska State and Fillmore County Medical Society, the Chamber of Commerce, the Council of the Czechoslovakia Society, the Knights of Pythias, the Sokol, the Modern Woodmen of America and the Nebraska Czechoslovakia Historical Society. He has received a decoration from the government of Czechoslovakia for assistance rendered in furthering its independence. He was secretary of the school board in 1913 and is a member of Z. C. B. J. Residence: Milligan.

Edgar Fudge Snavely

For the past 25 years Edgar F. Snavely, lawyer and executive, has been in the insurance and real estate business at Lincoln, Nebraska. He was born at Marion, Virginia, January 11, 1876, the son of Charles Winton and Mary Caroline (McGhee) Snavely. His father, who was a wagon maker, was born in Smyth County, July, 1849, and died at Chilhowie, Virginia, in 1921. His mother, who was of Scotch-Irish and Pennsylvania Dutch descent, was born in Smyth County, February 11, 1856, and died there.

Mr. Snavely attended the public schools of Virginia, an academy, and later the State Normal University. He received his LL.B. degree at the University of Nebraska where he was president of his graduating class and a member of the Palladium Society.

He has lived in Nebraska for 33 years and has engaged in the insurance business, handling bonds, and real estate loans. At the present time he is secretary of the Homestead Bond & Safe Deposit Company of Lincoln. A Democrat, Mr. Snavely, was precinct, county, and state committeeman for several years, and has been a member of several Democratic clubs.

Mr. Snavely married Cora Dell Coon at Manley, Nebraska, October 30, 1904. Mrs. Snavely was born in Iowa. During the World War Mr. Snavely was chairman of the county loan drive committee in Lancaster County. He is a member of the Lincoln Kiwanis Club, the Hiram Club, and holds membership in most of Lincoln's civic and welfare societies. He is a member of the Ancient Free and Accepted Masons, Shrine; and is a member of the Modern Woodfellows of America. He is serving on the board of the local Young Men's Christian Association, and is a member of the Nebraskana Society. His social club is the Lincoln Country Club. He is affiliated with the First Christian Church of Lincoln. Residence: Lincoln.

Arthur C. Snider

Born at Carthage, Illinois, January 1, 1868, Arthur C. Snider is the son of Hamilton and Mary (Aylshire) Snider. His father, who was a farmer, was born in North Carolina in 1841 and died at Springview, Nebraska, in August, 1892. His mother, whose ancestry was Scotch and English, was born in West Virginia, March 23, 1846, and died at Springview, April 21, 1905.

Mr. Snider has been a resident of Nebraska for the past 61 years and has been successfully engaged in farming near Mills for many years. He has served as a member of the local school board for the past 28 years, is a member of the Nebraskana Society, and is affiliated with the Republican party.

On April 24, 1894, he married Eliza B. Tweed at Springview. Mrs. Snider, who is an energetic farm woman, was born at Keithsburg, Illinois, November 21, 1876. Their children are: Lillie, born May 10, 1895, who married Frank Patton; Mildred, born August 29, 1897, who died June 2, 1917; William, born December 13, 1899, who married Delia Corneman; Mirriam, May 24, 1903, who married Elmer Blake; Irene, born December 8, 1909, who died April 2, 1919; Lucy, born March 22, 1911; and Thelma, born May 20, 1913. Residence: Mills.

Samuel Allen Snider

A prominent banker at Osceola, Nebraska, Samuel Allen Snider has been a resident of this state since March, 1871. He was born at Meaford, Ontario, Canada, January 30, 1864, the son of Mary Ann (Eagles) Snider and James Snider. His father, who was a carpenter, farmer, and county judge of Polk County, was born in Prince Edward County, Ontario, April 23, 1839, and died at Osceola, Nebraska, April 7, 1910. His mother was born in Grey County, Ontario, August 23, 1846, and died at Philomath, Oregon, May 18, 1924; her ancestry was German and English.

Mr. Snider has been engaged in the banking business since May 16, 1892, and until 1902 was connected with the Osceola Bank. He was one of the organizers of the First National Bank of Osceola in 1902 and acted as cashier of that institution of which he is now president. A Republican he was deputy county clerk and county clerk of Polk County for one year.

He is a member of the Community Club, is affiliated with the First Methodist Episcopal Church of Osceola, and holds membership in the following fraternal organizations: Odd Fellows; Osceola Lodge Number 65 of the Ancient Free and Accepted Masons, and Scottish Rite and Shrine bodies. His social club is the Osceola Country Club and his favorite sport is golfing. During the World War Mr. Snider served as chairman of the bond sale in his precinct and was first sergeant of the home guards. At this time he is completing his tenth consecutive year as mayor of Osceola.

On September 4, 1890, he was united in marriage with Marguerite Grass Tobias at Shelby, Nebraska. Mrs. Snider, parents were natives of Canada, was born at Green Garden, Illinois, October 1, 1866. Four children were born to them: Vera C., October 14, 1891, who married Walter D. Kirtley; Sidney L., May 26, 1896; Marjorie, March 17, 1898, who married Dr. Glenn C. Fonda; and Joyselan, September 12, 1901, who married Don R. Byers. Residence: Osceola.

Seymour Morgan Snider

For the past 32 years Seymour Morgan Snider has been engaged in active ministry in the United Brethren Church, and for over 22 years has been a clergyman in Nebraska. He was born at New Milton, West Virginia, August 15, 1869, the son of William Snider and Virginia (Morgan) Snider. His father, who was a farmer and carpenter, was born at Clarksburg, West Virginia, April 28, 1826, and died at West Union, January 7, 1912; his German ancestors came to America in 1760.

His mother, who was active in church work for many years, was born at Farmington, West Virginia, August 3, 1845, and died at Clarksburg, July 2, 1929; her ancestors were French and English.

Mr. Snider attended the grade and high schools and later studied through correspondence. From 1917 to 1921 he served as conference superintendent, and during 1921 and 1922 he built and organized the Calvary United Church at Lincoln. He is at present pastor of the United Brethren Church at Marquette, Nebraska, and for the past five years has been trustee of York College, and secretary of the conference board of trustees of the Nebraska Annual Conference of the United Brethren Church.

He is a member of the Lincoln Ministerial Association, is a member of The Nebraskana Society, and is affiliated with the Knights of Pythias and the Royal Arch Masons.

His marriage to Cora Belle Davisson was solemnized at West Union, West Virginia, March 23, 1893. Mrs. Snider, who was born at New Milton, West Virginia, December 18, 1868, is of Scotch and English descent. They have two children: Glenn, born January 2, 1894, who married Lois Wright; and Merle, born April 17, 1895, who married Arthur Gilbert. Glenn is clerk of the district court at Aurora, Nebraska, serving his second term. Merle is a graduate of the University of Nebraska while her husband is principal of the high school at Schuyler, Nebraska. Residence: Lincoln.

James Johnston Snipes

Born in Jackson, Madison County, Tennessee, February 24, 1880, James Johnston Snipes is the son of Farrington Burnett and Temperance (Johnston) Snipes. Farrington Snipes, who was born in Chatham County, North Carolina, September 7, 1828, was a lawyer, legislator, public speaker, essayist and planter who served in the Civil War. Of English descent, an ancestor was one of the first settlers of Charleston, South Carolina in 1670. He represented the seventh generation in America, all his male ancestors having served in the Revolutionary War. Farrington Snipes died at Denmark, Madison County, Tennessee, January 10, 1909.

Temperance Johnston was born at Denmark on June 15, 1846, and died there January 22, 1911. Active in her home and in church work, she was of Scotch descent, an ancestor having come to Pennsylvania in 1735 and to North Carolina in 1750. All her male ancestors served in the Revolution, and she represented the fifth generation of her family in America.

James J. Snipes attended the Denmark public and high school, and was graduated from the latter in June 1896. From then until 1899 he attended South West (now Union) University at Jackson, Tennessee, and from 1899-1900 Vanderbilt University at Nashville, Tennessee. He graduated in medicine at Tulane University, New Orleans, in 1903. His fraternity is Sigma Alpha Epsilon. Prior to the establishment of residence in Lincoln in 1909 Dr. Snipes practiced in Tennessee and Arkansas. Since 1909 he has specialized in diseases of the skin, and is a member and dermatologist on the staff of The Lincoln Clinic. He is the author of various medical and genealogical articles, and is a member of the American, Nebraska State and Lancaster County Medical Associations. During the World War he held the rank of captain in the Medcal Corps, and served as dermatologist on the staff of the Fort Riley, Kansas, Base Hospital. A major in the Medical Reserve Corps, he served as president of the Nebraska Society of the Sons of the American Revolution in 1929-30 and is a member of the American Legion.

A thirty-second degree Mason and Shriner, he also holds membership in the Chamber of Commerce, the Nebraska State Historical Society, the Nebraska Genealogical Society and The Nebraskana Society. He was married to Gertrude May Berry at Lincoln October 5, 1912. Mrs. Snipes was born at Topeka, Kansas, October 5, 1890, of English and French Huguenot descent; all her ancestors came on the Mayflower or ships following, prior to 1635. She is a member of the Society of Mayflower Descendants, Daughters of the American Revolution, and Daughters of Founders and Patriots of America; all her ancestors served in the Revolution. They have two sons, James Johnston, Jr., born September 21, 1915, in junior high school; and Allen Whitman, born December 6, 1917, in junior high school. The family attends the First Presbyterian Church.

Dr. Snipes is interested in history, genealogy, archeology, and allied subjects. He is a member of the University and Shrine Clubs. Residence: Lincoln.

Frederick Amos Snocker

Frederick Amos Snocker, superintendent of the Potter High School, was born at Cortland, Nebraska, March 25, 1886, son of Henry and Mattie G. (Balderson) Snocker. His father was born at Seneca, Illinois, February 19, 1861, and farmed until his death at Lincoln, July 15, 1927. His wife, Mattie, was born in Zanesville, Ohio, November 6, 1864, and died at Lincoln, March 29, 1918. She was a teacher and had studied at Doane College.

Mr. Snocker attended the public schools of Princeton, attended Warren Academy at Denver, and was graduated from Nebraska Weslyan Academy in 1912. In 1917 he received his Bachelor of Arts degree from the University of Nebraska. During the summer of 1927, Mr. Snocker attended the University of Colorado. He is a member of Phi Delta Kappa, and was a member of the football team at Nebraska Wesleyan Academy in 1911. Politically he is independent.

A teacher one year at Minatare High School, the following four years Mr. Snocker was superintendent of Chase County High School. The following four years he was superintendent at Lyman, and for the past four years has held his present position. He is a member of the Methodist Episcopal Church, the Nebraska State Teachers' Association, the Potter Commercial Club, the Nebraskana Society, and is a Mason and an Odd Fellow. He enlisted as a private in the 67th Coast Artillery Corps and served in the American Expeditionary Forces from September 1918 until February 1919. He is a member of the American Legion.

On August 13, 1919, he was married at Harrison, Nebraska, to Myrtle Rubie Phinney. She was born at Tamora, Nebraska, July 21, 1893, granddaughter of the Reverend Calvin Phinney. There are five children, Wendell, born February 2, 1921; Vernon, born December 7, 1922; Donald, born August 29, 1925; Charles, born April 16, 1928; and Frances, born September 23, 1931.

Mr. Snocker is interested in golf, hunting, and swimming, while his hobbies are reading, taking kodak pictures, and keeping crapbooks. Residence: Potter.

Charles Otis Snow

The Honorable Charles Otis Snow was born at Nemaha, Nebraska, March 1, 1858, and has been a resident of Nebraska continuously since 1881. He is the son of Charles V. and Margaret (Skeen) Snow, and his father, born at St. Johnsbury, Vermont, August 24, 1821, was

a physician and member of the Missouri legislature. He was the son of Levi and Lucina Snow. He died April 12, 1879.

Margaret (Skeen) Snow, mother of Charles Otis, was born in Buchanan County, Missouri, January 13, 1835, and died at Auburn, May 10, 1914. She was the daughter of Alexander and Mary (Blevins) Skeen, the latter a descendant of Pocahontas.

Charles O. Snow was educated in the public schools and attended Rockport High School, and from 1881 to 1888 was engaged in the mercantile business. On March 12, 1882 he was married to Anna Moore, at Sheridan (now Auburn) Nebraska. Mrs. Moore, who was born at Princeton, Illinois, June 4, 1861, died at Auburn, November 17, 1921. She was the daughter of John H. Moore. There were three children, one is still living. Edna Opal, born March 1, 1889, died October 25, 1918; Pearl U., cember 12, 1893, who married Walter Andrews. Mr. Andrews died in 1924.

A Democrat, Mr. Snow was elected county clerk of Nemaha County in 1900 for a term of two years; he was re-elected in 1915 and served four years, 1915-19. He was continuously engaged in the abstract business from 1907 to 1920, and since 1925 he has been county judge of Nemaha County.

During 1918 he was a member of the exemption board, and speaker in Red Cross drives. He is a member of the Nemaha County Red Cross organization and of the Auburn Commercial Club. His religious affiliation is with the Auburn Church of Christ.

He is a member of the Nebraska State Historical Society, The Nebraskana Society and the Native Sons and Daughters of Nebraska. He also holds membership in the Ancient Order of United Workmen. His social club is the Auburn Country Club, and his sport is golf. Residence: Auburn.

Marietta Snow

One of Nebraska Wesleyan's most beloved teachers, Marietta Snow was born at Clarion, Iowa, December 16, 1888. She is the daughter of Joseph Henry and Julia Alberta (French) Snow, the former born at Clinton, Maine, April 24, 1849. He was a clergyman of English descent, who died at Lincoln, on January 15, 1931. His wife, Julia, was born at Fairfield, Maine, April 19, 1858, and resides with her daughter in Lincoln. Her ancestry is English, three brothers of the French family having settled in America in the first third of the 17th century.

Marietta Snow attended the public schools of Malvern, Iowa, through the eighth grade, and received her secondary education in Nebraska Wesleyan Academy, graduating in 1907. In June, 1911, she received her A. B. from Nebraska Wesleyan University, and in January, 1927, her M. A. from the University of Nebraska. She attended Columbia University the summer of 1921, and the University of Wisconsin the summers of 1928 and 1929. For some time she has been a member of the Modern Language Association of the United States. She is a member of Alpha Gamma Delta, and was alumna advisor on scholarship and activities for three years. She has been secretary-treasurer of Nebraska Wesleyan Alumni Association since 1923.

Miss Snow has been a resident of Nebraska since September, 1903, and is assistant professor of German at Nebraska Wesleyan. He is a member of the First Methodist Episcopal Church of Lincoln. Residence: Lincoln. (Photograph in Album).

Charles Cook Snowden

A leading physician and surgeon in Davenport for many years, Charles Cook Snowden was born at Saltsburg, Pennsylvania, February 18, 1854. The son of Isaac Wayne and Harriett Elizabeth (Cook) Snowden. His father was born at Freeport, Pennsylvania, in 1832. Isaac Snowden comes of a family of soldiers of Scotch descent. His family was represented in the Revolution under General Washington, and his paternal grandfather held the rank of lieutenant in the War of 1812. Harriett Elizabeth Cook was born at New Alexandria, Pennsylvania, in 1832, and was a talented musician. She died at Nebraska City, June 15, 1865, her family having been pioneer settlers there. Isaac Snowden, who was a physician, died at Sacramento, California, in 1910.

Charles Cook Snowden attended public and high school in Nebraska, and attended the State University the two years 1871-72 and 1872-73. He was admitted to practice medicine in Nebraska at Davenport, on May 1, 1882. A resident of the state for sixty-eight years, Dr. Snowden recalls many of the rigors and hardships incident to pioneer life. He has always engaged in practice, and is a member of the American Medical Association and the Thayer County Medical Association.

On May 5, 1887, he was united in marriage to Mary Jesten Bean at Davenport. Mrs. Snowden was born at Plattsburg, Missouri, January 24, 1855. Both Mr. and Mrs. Snowden are members of the Davenport Methodist Church, and active in its work. Dr. Snowden is particularly active in the Masonic order, being a member of Lilly Lodge, Ancient Free and Accepted Masons at Davenport, and a member of the Knights Templar, Scottish Rite and Shrine Bodies at Hastings. He is a member of the Territorial Pioneers Association, and while at the University belonged to the Palladium Literary Society. Dr. Snowden is a Democrat, and an interested participant in the politics of his party. Recently he was elected to life membership in The Nebraskana Society.

During the late war he was active in all civilian wartime and relief projects, and members of his family were in the service. Residence: Davenport.

Francis Clark Snyder

The Reverend Francis Clark Snyder, clergyman, was born at Homestead, Michigan, August 23, 1895, son of Owen M. and Fannie A. (Seibert) Snyder.

The father was born in Berlin, Ontario, Canada, July 28, 1861. He was a graduate of Toronto Business College and attended the Oberlin Seminary, Oberlin, Ohio. He was a clergyman for more than 35 years prior to his death at Broken Bow, on September 21, 1927. The ancestry of the family was Swiss. Three brothers went to Canada from Pennsylvania in the early 1800s, E. W. B. Snyder having been a member of the legislative body of Canada. Fannie A. Seibert died at Fairfax, South Dakota, in the spring of 1921. She was of Pennsylvania Dutch ancestry, and was a teacher near Petoskey, Michigan, for several years.

In 1911 Mr. Snyder was graduated from public school at Pocahontas, Illinois, and in 1918 received the Bachelor of Arts degree from Carleton College at Northfield, Minnesota. He received the degree of Bachelor of Divinity from Chicago Theological Seminary in 1924. Active in debate, Mr. Snyder was a member of the Alethian Literary Society at Carleton College. He has served as vice president of Delta Theta Chi, and coached at Ward Academy, South Dakota, during 1919 and 1920.

His marriage to Lillie S. Larsen was solemnized at Chicago, June 17, 1925. Mrs. Snyder was born at Keene, Nebraska, October 21, 1895. There are three children, Myra Elaine, Anabel June, and Lois Jean.

For a time Mr. Snyder was director of young people's work in the Pilgrim Congregational Church of Oak Park, Illinois. He was ordained to the Congregational ministry at Chicago in May, 1924, and from that time until 1926 was pastor of the Green Street Congregational Church at Chicago. At the present time he is minister of the Loup Valley United Parish which includes three towns, Thedford, Halsey, and Seneca. He is the author of

The Reality of the Resurrection of Jesus (1924). He is a member of the Loup Valley Association of Congregational Churches, of which he has been scribe 1926-30 and 1931-32.

Mr. Snyder was a private in the 32nd service company in the Signal Corps in training at the Agricultural and Mechanical College at College Station, Texas, during the World War. He is a member of the Red Cross, the American Legion (commander 1927-29, chaplain 1930, 31, 32). In 1928 he was a member of the Parent Teachers Association and from 1914 until 1918 was a member of the Young Men's Christian Association. His favorite sports include basketball, football and tennis, while his hobbies are music and reading. Residence: Thedford.

Harry Amendus Snyder

For the past 20 years Harry Amendus Snyder has been a banker at Atkinson, Nebraska, where he is active in the civic affairs of his community. He was born at Scotia, Nebraska, November 24, 1885, the son of Edward H. and Blandia (Hilke) Snyder, the former a farmer who was born at Bethlehem, Pennsylvania, January 28, 1863. His mother, an active church and Sunday School worker, was born at Hustisford, Wisconsin, September 2, 1866.

Mr. Snyder attended the high school at Fremont, Nebraska, for two years, was railroad station agent at Atkinson for eight years, and for 20 years has served as assistant cashier in the Atkinson bank. He is president of the local Lions Club, has served as secretary of the Commercial Club for five years, and for 18 years has been secretary of the Atkinson Red Cross. He has been city clerk for the past 12 years.

He has been a member of the Modern Woodmen of America for 25 years, the Masons for 25 years, and the Independent Order of Odd Fellows for 18 years. Mr. Snyder has been secretary of the Atkinson Golf Club for 10 years having held membership in that society for 15 years, and is affiliated with the Presbyterian Church. He is a Republican.

On November 6, 1919, he married Helen Alice Ollerman at Atkinson. Mrs. Snyder was born at Carroll, Iowa, October 24, 1899. Their daughter, Jacqueline, was born March 19, 1925. Residence: Atkinson.

John P. Snyder

One of Nebraska's pioneer farmers is John P. Snyder who was born at Falls Village, Connecticut, April 7, 1854, the son of Joel and Mary Elizabeth (Shook) Snyder. His father, who served in Company B, Heavy Artillery, during the Civil War and was permanently injured at the battle of Cold Harbor, was born at Salisbury, Connecticut, April 7, 1822, and died at Ashley Falls, Massachusetts, August 5, 1899.

Mr. Snyder attended a rural grade school near Wilton Center, Illinois, came to Nebraska in August, 1875, homesteaded in Gosper County. He has been president of the Arapahoe Equity Exchange for 15 years, and for seven years has served as vice president of the Orleans Co-operative Creamery Company. For over 40 years he has been an active member of the district school board, and at this time is a member of the Independent Order of Odd Fellows there.

On January 12, 1879, he married Cynthia Jane Chambers at Arapahoe. Mrs. Snyder, who was born at Rensellaer, Indiana, April 21, 1854, is the daughter of J. B. and Mary Elizabeth Elston Chambers. Four children were born to them: Frank L., October 17, 1881, who died March 14, 1911; E. Ray, December 24, 1883, who married Dura Prime; John Percy, June 2, 1886, who died July 4, 1909, and Hervey W. born September 20, 1890, who married Kathryn Mayer.

Mr. Snyder served as the second treasurer of Gosper County, Nebraska, 1879-83, and was county commissioner from 1920 to 1924. He is independent, politically. Residence: Arapahoe.

Soren Nielsen Soelberg

Soren Nielsen Soelberg, a successful merchant and manufacturer at Elba, Nebraska, was born at Randers, Denmark, May 18, 1883, the son of Hans Nielsen and Inger Marie (Christensen) Soelberg. His father, who was a rope manufacturer, was born at Randers, March 23, 1852. His mother was born at Hjorring, Denmark, May 21, 1853.

Mr. Soelberg was graduated from the Randers High School in 1899, and later studied business at Randers. He learned the grocery trade in Denmark, and after his arrival in America clerked in a store at St. Paul, Nebraska, for a year. He served as clerk at Elba, from 1908 to 1909, bought an interest in the Nysted Store a year later, and in 1917 started a general merchandise store at Elba. He is also owner of the Elba Broom Factory.

He is a member of the Nebraska Retailers Association, the Danish Brotherhood, the Red Cross, and the Nebraskana Society. He is affiliated with the Danish Lutheran Church. From 1912 to 1917 Mr. Soelberg served as postmaster at Nysted. His hobby is reading.

On November 30, 1911, he married Mette Marie Henriksen at Elba. Mrs. Soelberg was born at Randers, April 9, 1884. Their children are: Margrethe, born November 28, 1912; and Lavern, January 3, 1925. Residence: Elba. (Photograph in Album).

Vallora Bundy Solts

Vallora B. Solts, clerk of the district court at Beatrice, Gage County, Nebraska, has lived in this state for the past 24 years and has been prominent during that time in civic service. He was born at Iodana, Clay County, Kansas, May 23, 1887, the son of James Henry and Mary Elizabeth (Bundy) Solts. His father, who is retired, was born in Jo Davies County, Illinois, Indiana, May 4, 1852, and lives at Morganville, Clay County, Kansas. His mother was born November 20, 1858, and lives at Morganville, Kansas.

Mr. Solts attended the public school at Beatrice and later studied at Northwestern Business College, Beatrice. From 1910 to 1924 he served as cashier for the Iowa-Nebraska Public Service Company, during 1924 was assistant to the city clerk of Beatrice. From 1924 to 1930 he was deputy clerk of the district court; he was elected to the office of clerk of the district court November 4, 1930.

He is a member of the Chamber of Commerce at Beatrice, the Parent Teachers Association, the Red Cross, and the Nebraskana Society. He is affiliated with the Methodist Church and holds membership in the Elks, Eagles, and Odd Fellows. His sports include fishing, baseball, and football. He is a Democrat.

His marriage to Zilpah Beatrice Skinner, was solemnized at Beatrice, March 11, 1914. They have one daughter, Jane Virginia, born October 4, 1920. Residence: Beatrice.

S. E. Sorensen

S. E. Sorensen, cashier of the Farmer's State Bank of Rockville, was born in Howard County, Nebraska, January 1, 1884, son of Hans and Johanna (Paulsen) Sorensen.

His father, who is a retired farmer and banker, was born in Denmark. His mother, born in Denmark also, died in Howard County, in September, 1888.

Mr. Sorensen was graduated from Broken Bow Business College in 1908, was a grain buyer for the Hord Grain Company from 1908-12, and from 1912-19 was in the hardware business for himself. Since 1919 he has been cashier of the Farmers State Bank.

He was married on September 12, 1911, to Marie Hehnke at Grand Island, and to them two children were born: Lillian, on September 4, 1912; and Dorothy on April 12, 1914. Lillian is a teacher, while Dorothy is in high school.

Mr. Sorensen is a Democrat. He has been city clerk for the past twenty years, is a member of the Comunity Church of Rockville, the Odd Fellows, Masons, and The Nebraskana Society. His favorite sport is golf. Residence: Rockville.

Thomas Sorensen

Thomas Sorenson, son of Nels and Anna (Goderum) Sorenson, was born at Gantrup, Jutland, Denmark, September 8, 1874. His father, born at Bjerreherred, Denmark, died at Sondervissing, Denmark, January 10, 1901. His mother, who was born at Voerlodegaard, Skov, Denmark, died at Sondervissing, July 25, 1923.

Educated in the public and high schools of Denmark, Thomas Sorenson came to Nebraska twenty-four years ago, and has gained much prominence in his community. Primarily a farmer, he has taken an active part in local Democratic politics, is moderator of the school board, a director of the Farmers Union store, and the Community Hall, and is active in his church, the Lutheran Church of Hardy. Mr. Sorenson is also a member of the Odd Fellows and the Rebekahs, and is a life member of The Nebraskana Society.

On January 25, 1902, he was united in marriage to Magdalena Elizabeth Simonsen, at Rankin, Illinois. Mrs. Sorenson, who was born at Synderjutland, Denmark, May 5, 1872, comes from a line of farmers. There were six children born to this union, Nels, born October 8, 1902, who married Marie Hansen; William, born April 18, 1905; Mabel, born December 30, 1907; Helen, born November 20, 1911; Harry, born March 27, 1913; and Gladys, born January 20, 1919. Nels and William are farming, Harry attends the university, and Mabel and Helen are teaching. Residence: Hardy.

J. Marenus Sorensen

J. Marenus Sorensen, banker of Dodge County, Nebraska, has lived in this state all his life and is prominent in civic and business affairs at Fremont. He was born at Ord, Valley County, Nebraska, June 20, 1890, the son of Lars and Anna (Olsen) Sorensen. His father, who was a farmer, was born in Denmark, January 16, 1850, and died at Long Beach, Los Angeles, California. His mother died at Oxnard, Ventura County, California, in March, 1929.

Mr. Sorensen attended country school and later was a student at Fremont Normal School. He is now vice president of the Stephens National Bank at Fremont, treasurer of the Fremont State Company, and secretary-treasurer of the Fremont Mortgage Company of Fremont.

He was married to Marie Peterson at Fremont, June 24, 1922. Mrs. Sorensen was born at Fremont, March 18, 1892. They have the following children: Robert M., born December 31, 1924; William Edward, born May 12, 1927; and Howard A., born June 1, 1930.

Mr. Sorensen was a member of the Nebraska National Guard, discharged as private; entered the World War and was discharged as sergeant, and was active in Liberty loan drives. He has been adjutant of the American Legion for two years and finance officer for the same time. He is a member of the Dodge County Bankers' Association, the Nebraska Bankers' Association, and is president of the First Nebraska Regional Clearing House Association. He was vice president of the American Bankers Association from Nebraska, in 1930; is a member of the executive council of the Nebraska Bankers Association, former chairman of the regional clearing house committee, and is chairman of the bank management committee.

He is former president of the Dodge County Chapter of the Red Cross, has been president of the Young Men's Christian Association for three years, and is a member of the board of directors of the latter. He served as president of the Kiwanis Club, 1929, and has served as treasurer and director. His fraternal organizations include the Knighs of Pythias and the Masons.

Mr. Sorensen is a Republican. He is affiliated with the First Baptist Church of Fremont, and is vice president of the Nebraska Baptist Convention. Residence: Fremont. (Photograph in Album).

Charles O. Soules

Charles O. Soules, farmer, was born at Wichita, Kansas, August 31, 1873, son of Oscar and Ellen Jane (Tosser) Soules. His father, born in Vigo County, Indiana, September 10, 1837, died in Lincoln County, Nebraska, April 20, 1906.

He was a farmer, a private in Lieutenant H. S. Millers Company (Company I), First Regiment of Indiana Cavalry, and served from July 4, 1861 until July 3, 1864. He was the son of William and Almira (Baker) Soules, who were married June 25, 1820. He was born February 28, 1796, and she on September 6, 1800.

Ellen Jane Tosser was a native of Kentucky, born December 8, 1851, and who died in Lincoln County, Nebraska, December 30, 1907. She was the daughter of David and Elmira Tosser.

Educated in country schools, Mr. Soules afterward engaged in the automobile business in Gothenburg for about sixteen years. He has since engaged in farming. He was married to Mary Bertha Middleton at Pleasant Valley, Lincoln County, Nebraska, on June 8, 1898.

Mrs. Soules was born at Troy, Iowa, November 22, 1877, daughter of Clarinda Lee Middleton. Her grandfather was Daniel Lee and her great grandfather Daniel Lee. They had one son, Willis, born November 27, 1901, who died April 19, 1924.

Mr. Soules was active in Red Cross and Liberty loan drives during the World War period. Politically, he is a Republican. He is a member of Banner Methodist Episcopal Church, the Banner Community Club and the Nebraskana Society. His hobby is purebred Hereford cattle. Residence: Gothenburg.

Miriam Southwell

Miriam Southwell, one of the leading educators of Scotts Bluff County, Nebraska, has lived in this state for the past 23 years. She was born at College Springs, Iowa, October 22, 1875, the daughter of Adam and Ann Corrett (Haskin) Grimes. Her father, who was a lawyer and probate judge in South Dakota, died at Des Moines, Iowa, in November, 1931; he served as county attorney of Charles Mix County, South Dakota, and was an outstanding figure in the professional affairs of his community.

Mrs. Southwell was graduated from high school in Iowa, and later studied at Chadron Normal College and the University of Nebraska where she held membership in Pi Gamma Mu. She is county superintendent of schools in Scotts Bluff County at this time, is active in the Order of Eastern Star, and holds membership in the National Educational Association, the Nebraska State Teachers Association, and is president of the Nebraska Women's Educational Club. She is affiliated with the St. Andrews Episcopal Church of Scottsbluff. Mrs. Southwell is a member of the American Legion Auxiliary. She was married to William Southwell at Wheeler, South Dakota, November 3, 1892. They have three children, Horace C., born October 6, 1893, who is a graduate of the University of Nebraska; Miriam Grace, born February 6, 1897, who married Millard J. Kittell; William Glenn, born April 5, 1900. Both boys saw active service in the navy during the World War. Residence: Gering.

Peter Spahn

Peter Spahn, general merchant at Culbertson, was born at Norka, Russia, and has been a resident of Ne-

braska since 1892. His father, George Spahn, was born in Norka, November 5, 1861, and came to the United States in 1892. He is a retired farmer. His wife was born in Norka, October 3, 1861, and died at McCook, Nebraska, April 4, 1930.

Mr. Spahn attended public school and since 1903 has been a general store manager for Conrad Walker at Culbertson, Nebraska. He is a Republican.

He was married to Lydia Wacker at Culbertson, Nebraska, on June 3, 1903. Mrs. Spahn was born at Culbertson, Nebraska, August 4, 1885. She is of German ancestry. Their children are as follows, Myrtle, Glen, Leona, Henrietta, Marcella, Gerald, Bernice and Richard.

He is a member of the Evangelical Church and the local school board. His hobby is work. Residence: Culbertson.

Edward Henry Spangler

Edward H. Spangler, master farmer of Cass County, was born at Plattsmouth, July 24, 1875. His father, Henry Spangler, who was born in Lancaster County, Pennsylvania, March 8, 1832, and died at Plattsmouth, August 5, 1907, was of German descent. Mary (Wadel) Spangler, his mother, was born at Hessen, Darmstadt, Germany, September, 4 1839, and died at Plattsmouth, April 4, 1925.

Mr. Spangler has been a resident of Nebraska for 55 years. During this time he has farmed, and was a master farmer of 1929. He is treasurer of the Co-operative Creamery Company, a director of the school board, and a member of the farm board.

He married Nellie Jean at Plattsmouth. Mrs. Spangler, who was born at Plattsmouth, August 5, 1884, is of French ancestry. There are two children: Jean Henry, born August 4, 1908, who is a recent graduate of the University of Nebraska; and Richard, born September 27, 1913, a graduate of the Plattsmouth High School.

Mr. Spangler is a Democrat. He is a member of the Red Cross, the Chamber of Commerce, The Nebraskana Society, and the United Brethren Church of Mynard. He is a Rotarian. His hobby is reading. Residence: Mynard.

Martin L. Sparks

A leading physician of Franklin County, Nebraska, is Dr. Martin L. Sparks, who was born at Martha, Kentucky, April 4, 1863, the son of Levi J. and Polley E. (Gambill) Sparks. His father, who was a physician, was born at Moelka, Kentucky, and died at Blaine, Kentucky.

Dr. Sparks attended school at Blaine, and received his professional education at Louisville Medical College in Kentucky, receiving his degree at Louisville in 1905. He has been a resident of Nebraska for the past 34 years and has practiced medicine at Bloomington since 1912. He is a member of the Franklin County Medical Society, the Nebraska State Medical Association, and the Nebraskana Society.

On February 18, 1886, he married Vessie L. Ferguson at Blaine; she was born at Blaine, October 29, 1869. To their marriage six children were born: Roy A., July 9, 1891, who married Grace McCabe; Herbert, March 30, 1894, who married Ida Kelly; Alonzo E., April 30, 1897, who married Ursel Morrhaus; Henry W., October 9, 1901, who married Pauline Holmes; Sarah E., December 13, 1904, who married Leonard Watkins; and Hillman, March 14, 1909, who married Ellanora Steck. Roy is a dentist and Alonzo is engaged in farming. Residence: Bloomington.

Edwin Josiah Spaulding

Edwin Josiah Spaulding, son of Gilman and Celia Johnson (Waterman) Spaulding, was born at Waukon, Iowa, July 28, 1862. His father, born at Dover, Maine, September 22, 1824, died at Gothenburg, December 8,

1892. He was a lumberman of English descent. His mother, born at Foxcroft, Maine, October 27, 1831, died at Waukon, February 25, 1912. She was also of English descent.

Educated in public and high school, Edwin Josiah Spaulding lived in Iowa until March 1, 1890, when he settled in Nebraska. He has been in the hardware business for a number of years. Active in civic and community affairs, he was local treasurer of the Red Cross during the World War period. He is a member of the Chamber of Commerce, the Kiwanis Club, the Masons (32nd degree, Knights Templar and Shrine), the Gothenburg Country Club and is affiliated with the Gothenburg Methodist Church.

On August 17, 1885, Mr. Spaulding was married to Martha Mary Rowe at Waukon. She is of German descent, born at Indiana, Pennsylvania on November 26, 1863. Before marriage she was a school teacher at Waukon. There are two children, Earle, born September 1, 1890; and Caryl, born May 3, 1893. Earle, who served in the World War and was discharged as first lieutenant, was united in marriage to Elsie Jerrison, November 8, 1919, and is living at Portland, Oregon. Mrs. Earle Spaulding served as a nurse during the World War at Camp Dodge and Camp Sheridan. Caryl married A. H. Williams, October 11, 1923, and resides at Kansas City, Missouri. Earle and Caryl are both graduates of the Nebraska State University.

Mr. Spaulding is a Republican. From 1880-87 he was a member of the Iowa National Guard. His Club is the Gothenburg Club. Recently he was elected to life membership in the Nebraskana Society. Residence: Gothenburg.

Allan Dale Speir

Allan D. Speir was born at Kilmornock, Scotland, January 8, 1878. His father, James D. Speir, who was born at Edinburg, Scotland, and died at Moberly, Randolph County, Missouri, August 7, 1823, was connected with the Wabash Railroad for 42 years.

Elizabeth Jane (Roy) Speir, his mother, was born at Beth, Scotland, June 9, 1859.

Mr. Speir received his elementary education at Moberly, and later was a student at Northwestern Normal at Stemberry, Missouri. He has lived in Nebraska for over 30 years and since June, 1900, has been in the cracker business. He is now sales manager for the Iten Biscuit Company.

He was united in marriage with Charlotte Gertrude Yocum at Hastings, Adams County, Nebraska, September 26, 1905. Mrs. Speir was born at Lloydsville, Ohio, July 26, 1879.

Mr. Speir is a member of the Red Cross, the Omaha Chamber of Commerce, and the Omaha Kiwanis Club. He is a member of the Methodist Church, Ak-Sar-Ben, and U. C. T., a Mason and Shriner. His social club is the Carter Lake Club. He is a Republican. His sport is bowling. Residence: Omaha.

Karl L. Spence

Karl L. Spence, newspaper editor and publisher of Nebraska, was born at Marion, Illinois, January 30, 1889, the son of Charles and Jennie (McBride) Spence. His father, who was engaged in the real estate, banking, and lumber business, was prominent in political affairs during his residence in Webster County, Nebraska; he was born in Johnson County, Illinois, November 4, 1862, and died at Hot Springs, Arkansas, February 26, 1931.

Charles Spence traces his ancestry to ancestors who fought in General Greene's army during the Revolutionary War. His ancestry is Scotch and English. Jennie (McBride) Spence, who was a teacher before her marriage, was born at Marion, June 8, 1866. Her grandfather, Samuel McBride was born at Dublin, Ireland, in 1795, and came to America in 1810 where he settled in Tennessee. Her father, James McBride, served in the Union Army

during the Civil War, and died October 17, 1929, leaving 92 direct descendants.

Mr. Spence was graduated from high school at Bladen, Nebraska, was a student at business college in Illinois, and for many years has been engaged in the newspaper business in Nebraska. He owned and published the *Eagle* at Upland, Nebraska, and at this time is the editor of the *Northwest Nebraska News* at Crawford, Nebraska. He is a member of the Nebraska State Historical Society, the Crawford Chamber of Commerce, the Nebraska Press Association and the National Editorial Association.

He has been an amateur archeologist for many years, is an inveterate collector of Indian artifacts and fossils which are on display in the museum at Hastings, Nebraska, and has written a number of articles describing them. He has made many important discoveries of Indian housesites in various parts of southern and northwestern Nebraska. Mr. Spence's sports include golfing, archery, and hiking. His social club is the Crawford Country Club.

During the World War he served as chairman of the Junior Red Cross in Franklin County, and assisted in loan drives. He is the author of *Passing of the Soddy*, an article published by the Western Newspaper Syndicate, and several feature articles published in the *Omaha World Herald* and the *Nebraska State Journal*. For nearly twenty years he was the editor and publisher of the *Franklin County News* which he established.

On February 25, 1908, he was united in marriage with Sadie Mae Doher at Franklin, Nebraska. Mrs. Spence, who traces her ancestry to soldiers in the Revolution, was born at Franklin, February 27, 1888. She is regent of the D. A. R. at Crawford and a member of the P. E. O. Sisterhood. They have four children: Loris, June 4, 1910; Katherine I., April 9, 1914; Charles Morton, May 24, 1922; and Stephen Thomas, June 17, 1925. Loris D. was a student at the University of Nebraska, and was a reporter for the Nebraska State Journal. Katherine is a student at the University of Nebraska. Residence: Crawford.

Leslie David Spence

On January 1, 1878, Leslie D. Spence was born at Radcliffe, Hamilton County, Iowa, the son of Alexander and Alice (Mace) Spence. His father, who was a merchant, farmer and live stock dealer, served for several years as county commissioner of Johnson County, Nebraska. He was born of Scotch parentage at Somers, Kenosha County, Wisconsin, February 1, 1846, and died at Crab Orchard, Johnson County, Nebraska, January 21, 1924. He was a Civil War Veteran, descended from ancestors who came to America from Scotland in 1845.

His mother was born in Greensboro, North Carolina, November 24, 1851, the daughter of Quaker parents. Her mother was a physician.

Mr. Spence, who is a farmer and livestock dealer, was educated in the public schools and business college. He has lived in Nebraska for 41 years and has been active in the political affairs of his state and community since his youth. He is a Republican; has served as precinct assessor, 1900; was county clerk of Johnson County, 1910-12 having previously served four years as deputy county clerk; in 1929 served in the regular session of the Nebraska legislature; and in 1930 served in a special session of the legislature.

In the recent war he was captain of the home guards and was active in Red Cross work. He is treasurer of the local branch of the Red Cross at the present time; is president of the board of education at Crab Orchard; and is a member of the Parent Teachers Association there. He is a member of the Methodist Church at Crab Orchard. Residence: Crab Orchard.

Charles Ralph Spicer

A leading physician and surgeon for many years, Charles Ralph Spicer was born at Springfield, Illinois.

May 18, 1870. He is the son of Thompson Clement and Melvina (Vigal) Spicer. Thompson C. Spicer was born in Indiana, of Pennsylvania Dutch ancestry, on December 1, 1825, and died in Sangamon County, Illinois, August 1, 1900. His wife, who was a native of Sangamon County, died there in 1872.

Educated first in the country schools of Illinois, Dr. Spicer was awarded his Bachelor of Science degree from Northern Indiana University in 1892, and his Doctor of Medicine degree from Rush Medical College in 1896. Thereafter he completed a clinical course at the Great Ormond Hospital for Sick Children at London, and at the Rotunda Lying-In Hospital at Dublin, Ireland. He also completed a similar course at Carolina Spittal, at Vienna, and had a year's post graduate work at Northwestern. He has since had two years work in the children's department of Rush Medical College.

A general practitioner at Taylorville, Illinois, for five years, Dr. Spicer spent a like period in the special practice of obstetrics and pediatrics at Springfield, Illinois, and five years at Aurora. For the past fifteen years he has been in special practice at Hastings. His professional organizations include the American, Nebraska State and Adams County Medical Societies. Dr. Spicer's hobby is the use of four devices employed by him in his practice, which he invented and has patented. He is a member of the First Presbyterian Church, a Mason and a member of The Nebraskana Society. His marriage to Florence Fletcher took place at Aurora, Illinois, August 10, 1910. Mrs. Spicer, who is of English and Scotch descent, was born at Saint Paul, Minnesota.

They have one son, Fletcher, born December 4, 1915, who is a student in high school. He is an Eagle Scout and has a hobby of making model airplanes and sailing yatches. He is interested in radio, television, photography and telegraphy. He also owns and operates a print shop. He has been awarded the merit badge for life saving and is an accredited master swimmer. Residence: Hastings.

Harry Oscar Spicknall

A resident of Nebraska for the past fifty-nine years, Harry Oscar Spicknall was born at Guilford, Indiana, December 11, 1867. His parents, Richard Surburn and Anna Rebecca (Proctor) Spicknall, were also born in Guilford, the former on March 6, 1832, and the latter on March 16, 1841. Richard Spicknall was a sergeant in the War of the Rebellion, of American ancestry for three generations, and a farmer by occupation. He died at Grand Island, July 8, 1910. His wife preceded him in death, on February 12, 1882, at Guilford. Anna Spicknall's father was English, and landed in the United States in 1820, at the age of 18. Her mother was of Pennsylvania Dutch extraction, born in Pennsylvania in 1808.

Harry Oscar Spicknall attended country school to the seventh grade, and thereafter took up his life work of farming. On March 4, 1896, he was united in marriage to Alice Elizabeth Mitchell at Hastings. Mrs. Spicknall who was of Scotch-Irish descent, was born at LeRoy, Nebraska, March 4, 1876 and died at Roseland April 8, 1919.

To them were born ten children, eight of whom are living: Mabel, born February 22, 1897, married A. Frank Grice and is living in Florida; Howard, born July 19, 1898, married Nattie Franzier, and resides in Colorado; Florence, born November 6, 1899, married Orville W. Joynt; Clifford, born September 20, 1901, married Frances Frazier; Amos, born October 9, 1904, died August 10, ???; Mildred, born August 24, 1906, married Cecil Evers and resides in Florida; Jeanette, born March 16, 1908; Robert, born February 8, 1910; Lila, born April 4, 1912, married Howard Franzier; and Laura, born December 28, 1913, died October 8, 1915.

Except for two years' residence in Florida during

1915 and 1916 Mr. Spicknall has always lived in Nebraska. He is much interested in farming and farm improvements, while his hobby is mechanics. He is a member of Holstein Evangelical Church, the Ancient Order of United Workmen, the Nebraskana Society, and was from 1888 to 1914 moderator of his local school board. Residence: Roseland.

Clarence Thompson Spier

Clarence T. Spier, was born at Trenton, Grundy County, Missouri, January 26, 1894. His father, William Clarence Spier, who was born at Battle Creek, Michigan, was in the operating department of the Chicago, Rock Island & Pacific Railroad for many years and was killed in a train wreck near Kansas City, Missouri, September 1, 1902. His Scotch ancestors have been in America for several generations. His mother was born in Taswell County, Virginia, March 6, 1871. Her father was a Confederate officer in the Civil War who was wounded at the battle of Shiloh; her English ancestors were early settlers in Virginia.

Mr. Spier attended the public schools of Trenton, Columbia, and St. Joseph, Missouri, and in 1910 was graduated from the high school at St. Joseph. He received his A. B. and LL. B. degrees from the University of Nebraska in 1916; was a student at Sarbonne University at Paris, France, 1919; and was made a Delta Upsilon and Phi Delta Phi.

Since 1916 Mr. Spier has been engaged in the private practice of law at Omaha, served as deputy county attorney of Douglas County, 1926-30. He is a member of the Omaha Bar Association and the Nebraska State Bar Association, is president of the Dundee Parent Teachers Association; and is a member of the Masons (past master of George W. Lininger Lodge No. 268 at Omaha). His social clubs are the University Club and Happy Hollow Club. His hobby is reading. He likes to golf. He is a member of the First Methodist Church of Omaha.

During the World War Mr. Spier was a first class sergeant in the American Expeditionary Forces in France, serving from January, 1918, to September, 1919, at Cantigny, Aisne-Marne, St. Mihiel, and the defensive sector of Meuse-Argonne. He is a member of the American Legion.

On November 29, 1919, he was married to Louise Coe at Nebraska City, Otoe County, Nebraska. Mrs. Spier was born at Nebraska City, September 10, 1894. Her English ancestors settled in Connecticut and later in Nebraska. They have two sons: William, born January 16, 1923; and Robert, born September 20, 1925. Residence: Omaha.

William Franklin Spikes

William Franklin Spikes, who has served as county attorney of Howard County since 1927, was born at Pocahontas, Arkansas, November 16, 1889. His father, born in Randolph County, November 18, 1854, was a public school teacher who later served as sheriff, county clerk and county terasurer. He died at Pocahontas on April 3, 1923. His ancestry was Scotch. His mother, Sarah Dalton, was born in Randolph County, March 18, 1869. She was a public school teacher.

Mr. Spikes attended the Pocahontas public high schools, and received his LL. B. from the University of Michigan in 1914. He was a member of Phi Alpha Delta, Order of the Coif, and was on the staff of the *Michigan Law Review* while at the Unversity of Michigan. During 1908-09 and 1909-10 he was a student at the University of Arkansas.

From 1909 to 1912 Mr. Spikes was superintendent of schools at Pocahontas, and from 1914-17 was a member of the law firm of Campbell, Pope and Spikes at Pocahontas. He was admitted to the bar of Arkansas in 1911, Michigan in 1914 and Nebraska in 1917.

Coming to Nebraska on March 3, 1917, he has since

been in active practice. He is a Democrat, and was elected to his present position on that ticket. His professional organizations include the Nebraska State and Howard County Bar Associations. He is affiliated with the First Presbyterian Church, is a member of the Red Cross, the Community Club, the Woodmen of the World, the Masons and the Nebraskana Society. For some time he has been an elder in his church. His favorite sport is golf, while his hobby is reading.

Mr. Spikes held the rank of second lieutenant, Field Artillery, United States Army, 1918, and was promoted to the rank of first lieutenant. On April 30, 1919, he was married to Genevieve Speice at Jonesboro, Arkansas. Mrs. Spikes was born at Paulding, Ohio, August 18, 1895. They have two children, Betty, born October 25, 1920, and Billy, born April 9, 1922. Residence: St. Paul.

Emanuel Joseph Spirk

For the past 33 years Emanuel J. Spirk has been a retail lumberman at Wilber, Saline County, Nebraska. He was born at Merklen, Czechoslovakia, January 1, 1865, the son of Joseph and Barbara (Brabec) Spirk. His father, who was a dealer in livestock, was born at Merklen, in 1826, and died at Crete, Saline County, Nebraska, in 1903; he came to this country June, 1874.

His mother was born at Merklen, in 1825, and died at Wilber, October, 1919. Mr. Spirk was graduated from business college in 1882. He has lived in Nebraska for the past 57 years and has always been interested in educational and civic affairs. A Republican, he served as state senator in the sessions of 1913-15-17, and was a delegate to the state constitutional convention. He was county treasurer of Saline County for two terms.

He married Mary Batta at Wilber, November 24, 1887; Mrs. Spirk was born at Cedar Rapids, Iowa, May 14, 1896. They have four children: Bertha, born April 30, 1889, who married Adolf S. Herman; Victor, born September 11, 1891, who married Flavel Ruth Bollman; Elsie, born August 14, 1893; and Hilda A., born April 12, 1895, who married Willard F. Cox.

Mr. Spirk took part in various loan drives and made speeches of a patriotic nature during the World War. He is now serving as president of one of the most successful Farmers Elevator Companies in Nebraska for twenty-six years; has served as treasurer of the local Red Cross for 10 years, as president of the school board, and as city councilman, and is now a member of the library board. He holds membership in the Rotary Club, the Community Club and the Nebraskana Society, is a member of the Modern Woodmen of America, the Knights of Pythias, the Royal Highlanders and Japadni Jednota.

While an ardent advocate of temperance, Mr. Spirk was never reconciled with the cause of prohibition and women suffrage. During the legislative session of 1917, he led a successful fight in the state senate against the ratification of the 18th Amendment, thus defeating the aims of William J. Bryan to force Nebraska to become the first state in the union to ratify that amendment, during legislative session of 1917. Residence: Wilber. (Photograph on Page 1125).

Victor E. Spittler

Victor E. Spittler, son of Ernest Joseph and Catherine M. (Kuhbacher) Spittler, was born at Ewing, Nebraska, May 13, 1898. His father was born near Belfort, France, October 25, 1855, of French and Swiss parentage, and came to America when a young man. He died at Ewing, January 23, 1926. His wife, Catherine, was born at Cologne, Germany, January 8, 1874.

Victor Spittler attended the public and high schools of Ewing and received his LL. B. from Creighton University. He was admitted to the practice of law in 1920, and is now a member of the law firm of Spittler and Nicholson.

He was married to Beryl M. Cooper, a native of Schuyler, Nebraska, born July 5, 1900. Mrs. Spittler is of English descent. They have two children living: Marilyn, born March 21, 1928, and Robert born April 2, 1930. Jean, born January 25, 1927, died June 28, 1930.

Mr. Spittler is a Republican and a member of the Catholic Church. He was a private in the Student Army Training Corps during the World War, is a member of the American Legion, and the Omaha and Nebraska and American Bar Associations. Residence: Omaha.

Myron Edgar Spooner

Born in Herkimer, Herkimer County, New York, October 28, 1857, Myron Edgar Spooner is the son of William Henry Spooner who was born in Herkimer, New York, September 5, 1819 and Amanda Malvina (Willard) Spooner who was born in Herkimer, New York, November 16, 1826. William H. Spooner was a successful farmer and died October 15, 1897 at Parkston, South Dakota. His wife who had formerly been a school teacher and was a capable house wife passed away the following year on June 12.

Myron Edgar Spooner received his education in elementary schools and on April 24, 1876, he married Alice Emely Robbins, who was born at Rockford, Illinois, February 6, 1858. They were married in Elk Point, South Dakota, April 24, 1876. Six children were born to this union: Addie, March 31, 1878, who became the wife of Will Oliver, Dealia, December 4, 1880, who is Richard William's wife; Ray, March 17, 1885, who is also married, Augusta, November 16, 1887, now Mrs. Lew Oliver; Raliegh, April 30, 1889 and Harry, September 30, 1897.

Mr. Spooner has resided for twenty-nine years in Nebraska working in the merchandising business and as a salesman. He belongs to the Barneston Commercial Club and has done much work in the Red Cross and in Democratic politics. He belongs to the order of the Ancient Free and Accepted Masons and is affiliated with the Presbyterian Church. His second marriage occurred in East Saint Louis, Illinois in 1904. Residence: Wymore.

Marion Wilson Spohn, M. D.

A leading professional man in Chester, Nebraska, Marion, Wilson Sophn was born in Keckuk, Iowa, April 17, 1855, the son of Adam Fisher Spohn and Angeline (Iler) Spohn. His father was born in Ohio, October 27, 1819, and died at Bloomfield, Iowa, March 29, 1890. He was of German parentage, and was a mechanic. His mother was born at Hartford, Ohio County, Kentucky, February 7, 1826, of English parentage, and died at Fairmont, Oklahoma, on September 10, 1915.

Marion Spohn attended the rural schools and Troy Academy in Iowa. In 1896-97 he attended the college of Physicians and Surgeons at Chicago, after he had attended the Keokuk Medical College in Iowa, a branch of the State University of Iowa. He also attended the Rush Medical School at Chicago and the West Side Medical School at Chicago. He is a member of the Des Moines Valley Medical Association and the Wapelo County Medical Association at Ottumua, Iowa.

Dr. Spohn was united in marriage to Joan B. McMains, July 4, 1878, at Bloomfield. She was born near Bloomfield, May 12, 1854, and died May 16, 1890. She was the mother of two children both of whom are deceased; Clara Ethel, born January 12, 1888, died March 11, 1930; and James Loyd, born April 17, 1890, who died in August, 1890. On April 1, 1894, Dr. Spohn was married to Eliza Etna McCuiston, who had taught school before her marriage. To this union three children were born: Beulah Marian, January 2, 1897; Berenice Mariesa, August 24, 1901, and Hubert Hiram, February 24, 1904. Berenice married Vern J. Wagor and is the mother of three daughters and one son who is deceased. Beulah is a musician, and Hubert attended the Babcock School of Pharmacy and is the father of two daughters and a son.

E. J. SPIRK

He is a graduate of Babcock School of Pharmacy and is registered in Montana and Nebraska.

Dr. Spohn taught school for a number of years and later engaged in farming. Since 1891, when he was awarded his degree he has practiced medicine, first at West Grove, Iowa, and since at Chester. He is a stockholder in the Chester State Bank and the Nebraska Light and Power Company.

Dr. Spohn was formerly affiliated with the Dunville Baptist Church in Davis County, Iowa, and now with the Methodist Episcopal Church at Chester. He is a member of the Independent Order of Odd Fellows, the Royal Highlanders, the Modern Woodmen of America, the Red Cross, and The Nebraskana Society. Raising bees is his hobby. Residence: Chester. (Photograph in Album).

Albert William Sprick

For over 50 years Albert W. Sprick has been a farmer in Washington County, Nebraska, and has been active in the political and educational life of the state. He was born at Fontanelle, Nebraska, March 18, 1871, the son of Henry A. and Sophie (Wilkening) Sprick. His father, who was born at Bielefeldt, Germany, March 1, 1826, and died at Fontanelle, July 27, 1906, was a farmer and landowner in Nebraska, who served three terms in the state legislature. He was engaged in military service in Germany until he came to America in 1852. His mother was born at Schaumburg, Lippe, Germany, and died at Fontanelle, September 12, 1916. She was the mother of ten children and a typical pioneer home maker.

Mr. Sprick received a public school education with additional religious instruction; was a student at Iowa College; and in 1894 was graduated from Midland College with the B. S. degree. Except for three years spent in the mercantile business he has always been a farmer. He served as a member of the Constitutional Convention 1919-20, and was a member of the house of representatives, 1921, 1927, 1929, and 1931. He has always been a member of the Republican Party.

He was united in marriage with Bertha Katherine Westhold at Quincy, Illinois, August 24, 1911. Mrs. Sprick, who is an able and energetic assistant to her husband, was born at Quincy, March 5, 1875; her ancestry is German.

Mr. Sprick took part in all civilian war activities in 1917-18 and served as chairman of the local Red Cross. He has been school treasurer for nine years and treasurer of the Salem Lutheran Church for 10 years. He is a Mason, 32nd degree, Scottish Rite. His hobby is reading. Residence: Fontanelle.

Edward Herbert Springer

Edward Herbert Springer, postmaster and ranchman, was born at Wilmington, Delaware, March 15, 1863, son of Joseph Whittaker and Rachel (Armstrong) Springer.

The father was born in Wilmington, Delaware, in 1826, and was a cabinet maker by trade. He died at Philadelphia, in February, 1899. His ancestry was Swedish, emigrating from Germany to Sweden some time in the 12th century and coming to the United States in the 17th century.

Rachel Armstrong was born in Wilmington, Delaware, February 12, 1826, and died at Philadelphia, October 17, 1918. Her English ancestors emigrated from Thuringia, in Germany during the 12th century. Mr. Springer's ancestry comes from the direct descendants of the Emperor of Germany, Louis I, who was imprisoned in a castle and made his escape by springing from a window of the castle and escaping by boat, through which the name Springer was derived. Mr. Springer has in his possession the Springer history. He also has in his possession the naturalization papers of Carl Christopher Springer with the original seal of William Penn, the first

governor of Pennsylvania, who was appointed by the King of England. The ancestry of the family is traced to 452.

In 1882 Edward Herbert Springer was graduated from the city schools of Philadelphia. In 1898 Florence Josephine Hempstill was united in marriage to James M. Pulliam at Jamestown, Colorado. Mrs. Springer was born at Jamestown, November 18, 1882, of English descent. Her second marriage was solemnized on May 1, 1919 at North Platte, Nebraska, to Edward Herbert Springer. She had three children by her first marriage, Harold H.; Dwight J.; and James D. Pulliam. The youngest son died November 19, 1919.

Mr. Springer has been active in Republican politics for a number of years. He has been road overseer and assessor for several years, and has served as county commissioner of Lincoln County for 17 years. He is a member of the Elks, the Odd Fellows, and the Modern Woodmen of America. Residence: Brady. (Photograph in Album).

Henry Monroe Springer

The Honorable Henry Monroe Springer was born at Green Castle, Missouri, March 3, 1860, son of Elihu Farrington Springer and Holly Ann (Jones) Springer. Elihu Farrington Springer was born in Macomb, Illinois, March 22, 1838, and was an early settler in Nebraska. He served as state representative one term. His death occurred at Mitchell, Nebraska, July 27, 1910. His forebears migrated from England to Germany, from there to Sweden, and from Sweden to America. Holly Ann Jones was born in Schuyler County, Illinois, August 12, 1838, and died at Wheatland, Wyoming, August 22, 1924.

Mr. Springer attended public schools in Sullivan County, Missouri, and about 42 years ago came to Nebraska. In 1902 he started construction on the Goshen Hole Irrigation ditch and reservoir in Goshen County, Wyoming, of which he is the owner and the builder. He is president of the First National Bank of Morrill, Nebraska, and chairman of the board of directors of the First National Bank of Mitchell, and a director of the Western Nebraska Livestock Feeders Corporation.

A Republican, he has served fifteen years as a member of the county board of commissioners of Scotts Bluff County, and at the present time is serving as state senator from the 33rd senatorial district. He is now mayor of Mitchell.

In 1879 Mr. Springer went to Idaho in a prairie schooner with his father and mother and brothers and sisters. They lived there five years, and spent three years buying, selling, and trailing horses from Oregon to the North Platte Valley. In 1885, while trailing horses, Mr. Springer filed on a tree claim in Mitchell Valley and made final proof on this tract of land. Mr. Springer lived in Wyoming from 1886 until 1889, twenty miles southeast of Douglas. He then located in Mitchell Valley where he has since resided.

He is a 32nd degree Mason, a member of the Order of Eastern Star and the Modern Woodmen of America.

On February 2, 1882, he was married to Alice Bottenberg at Green City, Missouri. She was born at Table Grove, Illinois, November 16, 1861. Mrs. Springer attended schools at Table Grove, Illinois, and in Sullivan County, Missouri. She is the daughter of Levi and Elizabeth (Cox) Bottenberg, and is a member of the Eastern Star and the Woman's Club. Mr. and Mrs. Springer celebrated their golden wedding anniversary February 2, 1932. They have three children living, Frank, born April 4, 1889, died September 8, 1889; Odessa Merl, born November 30, 1882, married Edward B. Dearing; Monroe, born April 10, 1884, died the same day; Ruby D., born April 18, 1885, married Lon D. Merchant; Vera Louise, born September 1, 1901, married Oliver Lewis Jones. Residence: Mitchell.

William George Springer

William George Springer, banker, was born at Pilot Township, Iowa, December 24, 1868, son of John Christopher and Margaret Elizabeth (Lortz) Springer. The father, born in Macon County, Illinois, January 19, 1845, died at Des Moines, Iowa, February 10, 1899. He was a farmer who served as corporal in Company I, 28th Iowa Infantry in the Civil War.

Margaret Elizabeth Lortz was born in Hessen Darmstadt, Germany, March 14, 1842, and died at Chicago, April 11, 1921. She was a teacher before her marriage. Coming to America with her parents in 1854, she came to Iowa in 1856.

William George Springer attended Pilot Center public school, the Marengo High School and the Capital City Commercial College at Des Moines. In 1890 he was a student at Drake University. On October 27 of that year he was married to Affie Belle Harrod at Des Moines. Mrs. Springer was born at Montezuma, Iowa, October 27, 1890. There were four children, Merlin L., born September 2, 1897, who married Lucile Cline; Willa Belle, October 28, 1907; and Maxwell John and Melville Daniel, born July 4, 1904, who died on October 23 and November 11, 1904, respectively. Merlin was graduated from the University of Nebraska in 1919 with his B. A., and received his LL. B. from Harvard University in 1922. Willa Belle was graduated from the University of Nebraska in 1930.

Mr. Springer came to Nebraska from Iowa on April 21, 1893, and has been a continuous resident since except for about three months residence in Idaho in 1920. He was cashier of the Commercial State Bank of Oxford, 1893-1903; owner and manager of the Springer Lumber Company at DeWitt, 1904-06; cashier of the First National Bank of Oxford, 1906-14. He organized and was made president of the Security State Bank of Oxford, continuing until 1920. Since 1920 he has been cashier of the First National Bank of McCook, of which he is also a director.

During the later war he was chairman of a liberty loan committee in Furnas County, a four minute speaker and a member of the Council of Defense. He is a Republican, a member of the Chamber of Commerce, the Rotary Club (past president), the American Red Cross (life member), the Ancient Free and Accepted Masons and the Young Men's Christian Association. His religious affiliation is with University Place Church of Christ at Des Moines. During the years 1925-31 he was a member of the McCook Board of Education, and for 15 years was a member of the board of education of Oxford. (Deceased, 1932). (Photograph in Album).

Edwin Eberhart Squires

Born at Hopkinton, Iowa, August 29, 1867, Edwin Eberhart Squires came to Nebraska in 1889 and has been engaged in active practice of law since 1893. He is the son of James Horace and Mary Ann (Eberhart) Squires.

Edwin E. Squires attended high school at Manchester, Iowa, during 1883 and 1884. He received his Bachelor of Science degree from Kansas University in 1889, and his LL. B. from the University of Nebraska in 1893.

Beginning the practice of law in Kearney in 1893, Mr. Squires moved to Broken Bow in 1907 where he has since resided. His biography appears in *The History of Custer County, Nebraska*. Formerly a member of the law firm of Sullivan and Squires (1907-13), he is now a member of the firm of Squires, Johnson & Johnson. A Republican, he became county attorney of Buffalo County in 1905, serving one term, and in 1913 was elected mayor of Broken Bow.

On April 24, 1926, he was married to Miriam Stanley Carleton, at Lynn, Massachusetts. Mrs. Squires, who was born at Lynn on August 23, 1886, is a violinist and lyric soprano. Her ancestry is traced to early colonists in Massachusetts. Residence: Broken Bow.

Frank Joseph Srb

Frank Joseph Srb, a resident of Nebraska since 1876, has lived at Dodge, since 1888, and for many years has been active in the civic and business affairs of his community. He was born at Opatovice, Caslav, Czechoslovakia, March 31, 1874, the son of Frank and Marie (Novotny) Srb. His father, who was born at Doubraveany, Caslav, Czechoslovakia, December 3, 1835, and died at Dodge, September 1, 1910, was a farmer and saloon proprietor for many years; he was a staunch Democrat, but never aspired to a political office. He moved to Cuming County in the fall of 1876, and was successful in both enterprises he undertook.

His mother was born at Opatovice, July 4, 1839, and died at Dodge, March 12, 1919. She was born of Czech parentage and came to America with her father. She had few interests outside her home, but was a good mother and home maker.

Mr. Srb attended rural and village school and then assisted his father in his business. He conducted a furniture and undertaking establishment for 29 years, part of the time in partnership with his brother. He was president of the First National Bank for about seven months before it closed. He is now connected with the Tichota Equalizer Company, a firm which makes and sells four and five horse equalizers.

For 20 consecutive years he was a member and treasurer of the board of education at Dodge; and a member of the board of trustees of Dodge for about ten years, part of that time acting as chairman. At this time he is serving his third year as justice of the peace for Webster Township, and is serving his second term as police magistrate for Dodge. He is a member of the Nebraska Funeral Directors Association. In 1925 he was treasurer of the Parents-Teachers' Association at Dodge. He is a member of Z. C. B. J., a Czech fraternal organization.

Mr. Srb's hobby is song and music. For a number of years he was manager and treasurer of the Bohemian Theatrical Society's Opera House now owned by Tel Jed Sokol. The latter is a Czech gymnastic association of which he is a member. He is a Catholic by baptism but is not a member of a local church.

His marriage to Louisa Talacko was solemnized at West Point, Cuming County, Nebraska, April 22, 1895. Mrs. Srb was born at Pabenice, Caslav, Czechoslovakia, December 6, 1874, and came to David City, Nebraska, in 1890. Six children were born to this marriage of whom five are living: Marie A., born April 22, 1896, who married Bohuslav Malec; Leon E., born August 18, 1897, who died September 28, 1909; Hugo F., born August 4, 1900, who married Frances G. Davey; Frank J., born November 22, 1908, who is studying law at the University of Nebraska; Luella, born November 4, 1910, who is a stenographer for the Aetna Life Insurance Company at Omaha; and Vivian, born December 16, 1917. Mr. Malec is part owner and manager of Peony Park. Hugo F. was graduated from the University of Nebraska, and is now state senator from Dodge and Washington counties. Residence: Dodge. (Photograph in Album).

Hugo Frank Srb

Born at Dodge, Dodge County, Nebraska, August 4, 1900, Hugo Frank Srb is the son of Frank Joe and Louisa (Talacka) Srb. His father, born at Opatovice, Bohemia, March 31, 1871, came to America in 1876, and was formerly a merchant and chairman of the village board, and member of the school board. At the present time he is justice of the peace and police magistrate (*see Nebraskana.*)

Mr. Srb attended Dodge public and high schools and was graduated from the latter in 1918. He attended Wayne Normal School, graduating in 1920, and received his LL. B. from the University of Nebraska in 1924. He was active in basketball in high school and at Wayne Normal, and a member of the University of Nebraska senior debating team. His fraternity is Phi Alpha Delta. Prior to his admission to the bar in 1924, he taught in the Elgin and Dodge High Schools. He is a Democrat, and was candidate for the state senate 1926, 1928, and was elected to that office in 1930.

On June 16, 1926, he was united in marriage to Frances Grace Davey, daughter of Mr. and Mrs. Frank S. Davey, at Lincoln. Mrs. Srb was born in Lancaster County, Nebraska, June 21, 1904. There are two sons, Richard, born August 3, 1927, and Arthur, born April 16, 1930.

Mr. Srb is a member of the Lewis Cerv Post No. 122, service officer, and past post commander. He is past president of the Dodge Commercial Club, and secretary of the board of education. He is a member of the Congregational Church, the Nebraska State and Dodge County Bar Associations, the Red Cross and The Nebraskana Society. Residence: Dodge. (Photograph in Album).

Joseph John Srb

Joseph John Srb, physician and surgeon, was born in Dodge, Nebraska, January 12, 1888, son of Joseph and Mary (Skala) Srb.

The father was born in Czecho Slovakia, March 19, 1859, and died at Dodge, August 1, 1922. He was a pioneer farmer in Cuming County, and established first furniture and undertaking business in Dodge, in 1894. He was a band leader for 30 years. He came from the family of Burgomasters of Czech descent. His wife, Mary, was born in Manitowoc, Wisconsin, January 29, 1863, and died at Dodge, March 11, 1921. Her family were pioneers in Cuming County, her father a veteran of the Civil War with the army of the Potomac.

Dr. Srb attended the public and high schools of Dodge, and was graduated from the latter in 1906. In 1907 he received the Bachelor of Science degree in Pedagogy at Fremont Normal School. In 1915 he received the degree of Bachelor of Medicine from Creighton Medical College, and was licensed to practice in Nebraska and Colorado by examination. He was valedictorian of his high school class, and music and band leader, while in college.

From 1907 until 1908 he was superintendent of schools at Nickerson, and from 1908 until 1909 was superintendent at Brainard, and from 1910 until 1911 was superintendent at Dwight. In 1909 he was vice-president of the Northwest Teachers Association.

Since 1915 Dr. Srb has been in active practice. He is also an extensive land owner. He is a Republican, and chairman of the township board.

On November 25, 1914, he was married to Agnes Martha Sabata at David City. She was born at Dwight, May 1, 1892, and was a public school teacher before her marriage. Her parents were pioneer settlers in Butler County. Dr. and Mrs. Srb have three children, Ellen, born in 1915; Hannah, in 1917; and Mary, in 1928.

On September 25, 1918, Dr. Srb was commissioned first lieutenant in the United States Army, Medical Corps and was discharged on December 27, 1918. He was chairman of the Red Cross drive of 1918. He is a member of Rejda Post of the American Legion at Brainard, and was offered a captaincy in the Medical Reserve Corps, which he refused.

His professional organizations include, the American Medical Association, and the Nebraska State and Butler County Medical Society. He is a member of the Mason and Shrine, and for ten years has been chairman of the board of education. He is a member of the David City Golf Club, and his hobby is wild flowers. Residence: Dwight.

Charles Elof Staberg

A pioneer farmer in Phelps County, Nebraska, Charles Elof Staberg was born at Motala, Sweden, September 11, 1862, the son of Herman and Maria Charlotte (Nordstrom) Staberg.

His father, who was also a farmer, was born at Motala, July 4, 1838, and died at Loomis, Nebraska, No-

vember 16, 1893. He homesteaded in Phelps County, Nebraska in 1879. His mother was born at Stockholm, Sweden, August 28, 1839, and died at Loomis, November 28, 1893.

Mr. Staberg has been farming the original Staberg homestead since 1893. The original sod house on the homestead stood until 1892, when it was replaced with the present home.

His marriage to Lydia Maria Edholm occurred at Loomis, November 28, 1901. Mrs. Staberg was born of Swedish parents at Hvetlanda, Sweden, August 16, 1868. Mrs. Staberg is very active in the affairs of her church, and is especially interested in her home.

Mr. Staberg is affiliated with the Westmark Evangelical Church. His hobby is reading. In 1896 he served as district supervisor in Phelps County. Residence: Loomis.

Ward Alan Stacy

Ward Alan Stacy was born June 18, 1883, on a farm near Edgar, Nebraska, and today operates the same farm. His father, Wright Milo Stacy, who homesteaded in Nebraska in the early days, was born at Painesville, Lake County, Ohio, January 15, 1850, and died at Edgar, Clay County, Nebraska, January 21, 1930; he was the son of Abyram and Puah (Stephens) Stacy, natives of New York. His mother was born at Baraboo, Sauk County, Wisconsin, October 2, 1856, the daughter of Asa and Jane (Tripp) Cole. She was a teacher before her marriage. Asa Cole, who was born in Michigan, was a mason by trade.

Mr. Stacy attended rural school in Clay County and in 1900 was graduated from the high school at Davenport, Nebraska. He worked on his father's farm for two years and in 1904 entered the University of Nebraska where he was a student for two years. He played with the cadet band at the university; he was president of the senior class in high school.

He is secretary of the Farmers Union Co-operative Association of Ong, Nebraska, and is secretary of the Davenport and Ong Co-operative Telephone Company. During 1930 Mr. Stacy served as president of the local Parent Teachers Association. He is a member of the Independent Order of Odd Fellows, is affiliated with the Methodist Episcopal Church, and holds membership in the Nebraskana Society. During the World War he was a member of the Home Guard and was active in the third loan drive.

Mr. Stacy's father homesteaded in Clay County in 1871 and was one of the few early settlers to hold his land until death.

Ward Allan Stacy was united in marriage with Lillie May Johnson at Davenport, December 12, 1906. Mrs. Stacy was born at Shickley, Filmore County, Nebraska, July 10, 1883, the daughter of Henry G. and Matilda (Hilgren) Johnson. Her parents were both born in Salina, Iowa. To this marriage the following children were born: Lorena Ruth, June 20, 1908, who married Owen Powell at Ong, Nebraska, January 3, 1929; Dorothy Lillian, on March 29, 1911, who married Clair Franson, at home on June 13, 1931; Opal Matilda, July 3, 1912; Alvera May, December 18, 1915; and Wright Henry, February 28, 1917. Residence: Edgar.

Ben Lynn Stahl

Born in Red Willow County, Nebraska, February 10, 1896, Ben Lynn Stahl has spent nearly all his life since leaving school in the lumber business. He is the son of Abraham Lincoln and Lillian (Loughridge) Stahl, both natives of Washington, Iowa. Abraham Lincoln Stahl was born on October 17, 1859, of German descent, and died at Cambridge, Nebraska, on July 21, 1924, after a long and successful life as a farmer.

Lillian Loughridge was born December 4, 1862, of Scotch-Irish extraction. Her entire life was devoted to her home, her family and to her church. Her death occurred at Cambridge, December 24, 1923.

Ben Lynn Stahl was graduated from rural school in Red Willow County in 1910, and from the Cambridge High School in 1914. With the exception of short periods as a teacher and clothing salesman, he was engaged in the lumber business. Starting with the Perry Lumber Company at Arapahoe, as helper and yard man, he became associated at a later period with the Holdrege Lumber Company as bookkeeper. In 1920, Mr. Stahl came to Nelson as resident manager for Day and Frees, retail lumber and coal dealers.

At the present time Mr. Stahl is secretary of the Nuckolls County Building and Loan Association, a member of the board of directors of the Chamber of Commerce, a member of the American Legion, the Red Cross, the Scottish Rite and Shrine bodies of the Masons, the First Presbyterian Church, and a life member of The Nebraskana Society. He is a Republican.

On August 10, 1921, he was united in marriage to Ida Grace Butler at Muscatine, Iowa. Mrs. Stahl was born at Muscatine, on June 24, 1897. To them were born three daughters, Barbara, September 25, 1923; Marilynn, December 25, 1924; and Eleanor, January 25, 1927.

During the World War period Mr. Stahl served in the United States Navy. Enlisting in the Hospital Corps on June 11, 1917, he was thereafter transferred to naval aviation, and was discharged on July 19, 1919, with the rank of Quartermaster First Class Aviation. Mr. Stahl's only hobby is reading and study. Residence: Nelson.

William Arnold Stahl

William A. Stahl, retired farmer and banker of Wymore, Gage County, Nebraska, has lived in this state for the past 43 years. He was born at Washington, Washington County, Iowa, November 19, 1857, the son of Zachariah and Nancy (Warfel) Stahl. His father, a farmer, was born at Lancaster, Pennsylvania, December 25, 1810, and died at Washington, July 25, 1876; his ancestors were German. His mother was born at Lancaster, November 21, 1815, and died at Washington, Iowa, April 18, 1894.

Mr. Stahl is a Mason, a member of the Modern Woodmen of America, and is affiliated with the Nebraskana Society. He is a Republican.

He was united in marriage with Martha Ann Custer at Washington, January 12, 1881. Mrs. Stahl, who was a teacher before her marriage, was born at Washington, October 23, 1859, of Scotch parentage. They have two children: Guy, born October 30, 1881; and Vena, born September 4, 1890. Residence: Wymore.

Alvah H. Staley

A prominent Nebraska educator, and at the present time superintendent of schools at Hastings, Alvah H. Staley was born in Branch County, Michigan, January 4, 1873. His father, Fredrick Staley was a native of Crawford County, Ohio, whose parents came from Germany. As a young man he migrated to Branch County, Michigan, where he engaged in farming. Sarah Jameson, wife of Fredrick Staley was a Scotch Covenantor.

Alvah H. Staley attended the rural schools of Branch County, and later was a student in the preparatory department of the Tri-State Normal College at Angola, Indiana. Upon his graduation from the Tri-State Normal College in 1895, he taught two years at Huntertown, Indiana, and then two years at Long Pine, Nebraska. He received a Bachelor of Arts degree in 1895 from Tri-State Normal. After four years of teaching Mr. Staley entered the University of Nebraska, where he remained two years, received a Bachelor of Arts degree from that institution in 1901.

For six years he was superintendent of schools at

Friend, and for eleven years at Superior. During 1918-19, he was assistant professor in charge of teacher training at the University of Nebraska, where he also took post graduate work. He has also had post graduate study at Columbia University, and is a member of Phi Kappa Delta. Since 1920, Mr. Staley has been superintendent of schools at Hastings. It is interesting to note that his teaching experience during the past thirty years has been confined to a radius of 100 miles.

A member of the Nebraska State Teachers Association, he has served as its president one year, as its treasurer three years, and as president of District Four one year.

Mr. Staley is also a member of the National Education Association, the Parent-Teachers' Association, the Young Men's Christian Association (board member), the Red Cross (board member and former chairman), and the First Presbyterian Church. He is a Scottish Rite Mason and Shriner, a member of the Chamber of Commerce and Rotary Club, and is the proud possessor of a letter signed by President Wilson commending him for active service in loan drives and other services during the World War.

Fond of golf and tennis, Mr. Staley is a member of the Hillside Golf Club. He is politically independent. On September 3, 1902, he was united in marriage to Helen Teresa Browne, at Lincoln. Mrs. Staley, who is of English and German descent, was born in Lincoln, October 1, 1881. They have a son and a daughter: Eugene, born July 3, 1906; and Helen, born June 7, 1914.

Eugene is assistant professor in the department of economics at the University of Chicago; he was graduated from Hastings High School in 1922; he received his Bachelor of Arts degree from Hastings College in 1925; after three and one-half years study at the University of Chicago, he was awarded his degree of Doctor of Philosophy in the field of economics. As a result of his research in this field he prepared a book entitled, *A History of the Illinois State Federation of Labor* which was published in 1929 by the University of Chicago Press. From 1929 to 1931 he did research work in Europe under a scholarship from the Social Science Research Council of the United States. In Europe his research was in the field of private international investments and their effect upon international relations. Residence: Hastings. (Photograph on Page 1130).

Irvin Abner Stalmaster

Irvin Abner Stalmaster, lawyer, and judge, was born at Odessa, Russia, June 5, 1897. He is the son of Louis and Esther (Forman) Stalmaster, the former born at Bardichev, Russia, February 17, 1869, and the latter born at Kishinev, Russia, August 5, 1875.

Educated in the public schools of Davenport, Iowa, he was graduated from Creighton University with an LL. M. from the University of Omaha in 1930. Since his admission to the bar, in the space of ten years, Mr. Stalmaster has gone far, both in legal practice and in the political world. A Republican, he served as judge of the district court from April 1928-January 1929; he was assistant county attorney of Douglas County from January 1924-December 1927, and assistant attorney general of Nebraska from January 1929 to date. In November, 1928, he was made a member of the Supreme Court of Nebraska, by invitation of the justices.

From 1924-30 he was associated with Sam Beber in the practice of law, under the firm name of Stalmaster and Beber; in 1931 the firm was re-organized under the firm name of Fradenburg, Stalmaster and Beber, in association with Joseph B. Fradenburg. Mr. Stalmaster is the author of two books, *The Jury System* and *What Price Jury Trials?* He is president and director of the Omaha Fixture and Supply Company, and instructor in Constitutional Law at Municipal University.

On December 28, 1925, he was married to Estelle Joyce Lapidus, daughter of Harry H. Lapidus, philan-

ALVAH H. STALEY

Nelson Studio—Hastings

thropist and civic leader. Mrs. Stalmaster was born at Omaha, September 7, 1904. They have one son, Lynn Arlen, born November 17, 1927.

Mr. Stalmaster is a Mason, and a member of the Scottish Rite and Shrine. He is an Elk, a member of the Omaha Hebrew Club, Temple Israel, the Zionist Organization of America, B'nai Israel Synagogue, the Independent Order of B'nai Brith, the National Conference of Jewish Social Service Workers, the Jewish Welfare Federation, the Jewish Community Center and the Conservative Synagogue of Omaha.

His civic and professional organizations include the Chamber of Commerce, the Ad-Sell League of America, the American League of Good Will, the Commercial Law League of America, the American, Nebraska State and Omaha-Douglas County Bar Associations, the American Interprofessional Institute, the National Probation Association, the American Judicature Society, the United States Federation of Justice, the American Academy of Political and Social Science, etc.

He is a trustee of the Jewish Community Center, and the National Jewish Hospital for Consumptives at Denver, as well as the Jewish Orphan Home at Cleveland, Ohio. He is a director of the Jewish Welfare Federation and former president of the Omaha Lodge of B'nai Brith. In 1925 he was chairman for Omaha of the Jewish Theological Seminary Campaign, and in the same year was chairman for the United Palestine Appeal. He was chairman for Omaha of the B'nai Brith Infirmary Building for the National Jewish Hospital for Consumptives at Denver in 1924, the National Jewish Orphan's Home Campaign in 1927 and the B'nai Brith Wider Scope Campaign of 1927. He was field representative for Nebraska in the Jewish War Relief Campaign for $14,000,000.00 in 1921. His clubs are the Highland Country Club and the Omaha Athletic Club. Residence: Omaha.

Ethzelda Rush Stanley

Ethzelda Rush Stanley, club women and welfare worker, was born on a farm in Wapello County, Iowa, December 27, 1868, and since 1885 has resided in Nebraska.

Her father, James Rush, was born on a farm in Perry County, Ohio, March 28, 1830, and died on his farm in Hamilton County, Nebraska, November 14, 1887. His father was Isaiah Rush, who was probably born in New Jersey from the same family as Dr. Benjamin Rush of the Declaration of Independence.

Malinda Gadd, wife of James Rush, was born on a farm in Perry County, Ohio, July 19, 1835, and died in Wapella County, Iowa, in 1865. She was descended from David Gadd, son of William Gadd, who was born in Maryland near Baltimore. They were a family of shipbuilders.

She attended the country school, and the Aurora High School, and the Peru State Normal. Later she was married to Marion Francis Stanley at Richmond. Mr. Stanley was born at Richmond, Virginia, December 5, 1862, and is a lawyer descended from Joseph Stanley. Mr. and Mrs. Stanley have three children, Lamar Rush, born May 2, 1892; Ethel Frances, born October 6, 1893; and Marion Edward, born January 31, 1903. Lamar is principal of the Newport News High School in Virginia, Ethel Frances is at home, while Marion Edward is associated press reporter in London, England.

For a few years before her marriage, Mrs. Stanley was a teacher in the public schools. During the late war she was a member of the council of defense, and helped organize the Red Cross in her county. She is a member of the Daughters of the American Revolution, and the Woman's Relief Corps. Her religious affiliation is with the United Brethren in Christ. She is a member of the local welfare committee, the Woodman Circle, and for a number of years was a member of the library board. She has been active for some time in the Woman's Christian Temperance Union. Residence: Aurora.

Fred James Stanley

A merchant at Nora, for many years, Fred J. Stanley was born there on December 27, 1875. His father, John Shields Stanley, was born in Pennsylvania, January 27, 1847, and served in the Civil War. In 1870 he pioneered in Iowa. A resident of Nebraska over a long period, he now resides at Selma, California. His wife, Susan Harris, was born in England, April 6, 1854, coming to America as a child. She died in Nuckolls County, March 27, 1887.

Fred J. Stanley attended public school in Nuckolls County, completed his high school course at Ruskin, in May, 1897. In 1904 he entered the grain business as an employee of a line company, and for ten years was manager of the Farmers Union Association at Nora. In 1925 he purchased his present grain plant, and operates another at Angus. In addition he is caretaker for the Chicago and Northwestern at Nora, and is a director of the Nora State Bank.

On December 25, 1898, he was married to Ida May Dickerson at Nora. Mrs. Stanley was born at North Bend, Nebraska, February 26, 1879. They have one daughter, Viola, born October 9, 1899, who is now teaching her ninth year in the city schools of Grand Island.

Mr. Stanley is a Republican, and was unsuccessful candidate for county treasurer in 1930. A member of the Nora Christian Church, he is president of the local school board, a member of the Masons, Modern Woodmen of America and The Nebraskana Society. Residence: Nora.

Marion Francis Stanley

Marion Francis Stanley, prominent lawyer of Aurora, was born in Richmond, Virginia, December 5, 1862, son of Joseph and Margaret (Morrison) Stanley. His father was born in Ross, Ohio, and died in 1880. He served one year under General Taylor and was in Company B third United States Dragoons in the Mexican War. He was of Irish descent. His wife, Margaret, was born in Virginia, and died at Portland, Oregon, in 1918. Her family came from Saxony.

Mr. Stanley was graduated from public school and attended Doane College and Peru State Normal. A Republican, he was county superintendent of schools six years, county attorney ten years, and has served on state Republican committee and county committees. He was admitted to the bar in Nebraska in 1895, and in the United States Supreme Court in 1907. He is a member of the Baptist Church, the American and Nebraska State Bar Association, the Commercial Club, the Ancient Order of United Workmen, the Knights of Pythias, the school board, and the Nebraskana Society. During the late war he received a medal for work on the Council of Defense, and is a member of the Legal Advisory Board of Hamilton County. Residence: Aurora.

Don Carlos Stansberry

Since 1918, Don C. Stansberry has been engaged in the practice of medicine and surgery at Geneva, Nebraska. He was born at Wells Mill, Iowa, April 9, 1861, the son of Grant Sperry and Rebecca (Cooksey) Stansberry. His father, who was also a physician, was born at Georgetown, Ohio, in 1828, and died at Dean, Iowa, May 19, 1917; his German grandfather came to America in 1778. His mother died at Dean, in 1926.

Dr. Stansberry was graduated from Iowa State University with the M. D. degree in 1890, and immediately entered into active practice. He practiced at Tobias, 1903-15, and at Dewitt, 1915-18. He is a member of the Fillmore County Medical Society, the Nebraska State Medical Association, and the Tri-County Medical Society. He holds membership in the Geneva Community

Club, Independent Order of Odd Fellows, and the Nebraskana Society.

His marriage to Rosina Corrick was solemnized at Dean, Iowa, September 11, 1884. Mrs. Stansberry, whose Scotch-Irish ancestry dates to the Revolution, was born at Coatsville, Missouri, September 10, 1867. They have seven children: Edal, born July 7, 1888; Glenn, born December 25, 1897; Georgia, born February 10, 1890, who married Charles Glaubets; Charles, born December 9, 1893, who married Gladys Britton; Verie, born August 24, 1895; Gladys, born May 24, 1899; and Vettna, born August 8, 1892. Residence: Geneva.

Elmer Ellsworth Stanton

An established lawyer at Stromsburg, Nebraska, is Elmer Ellsworth Stanton, who has been a resident of Polk County for the past 41 years. He was born at Hocking County, Ohio, July 16, 1861, the son of Thomas and Patience Campsedell (Hobbs) Stanton. His father, who was a farmer and a soldier in the Civil War, was born in Ohio, April 20, 1828, and died there October 2, 1903. His mother was born in Ohio, March 2, 1830, of German parentage, and died May 22, 1903.

Judge Stanton attended the public schools of Ohio and was a student at Bartlett Academy. He received his legal education through private study, and in 1886 was admitted to the practice of law at Stromsburg, Nebraska. He was a member of the firm Edgerton & Stanton for many years and is now senior partner of the firm Stanton and Stanton. He holds membership in the Nebraska State Bar Association, the Commercial Club, Young Men's Christian Association, and the Nebraskana Society. His fraternal organizations include: Masons, (Blue Lodge); Eastern Star; and Knights of Pythias.

During the late war Judge Stanton was captain of the Home Guard at Stromsburg. His favorite sports are hunting and fishing. A Democrat, he served as county judge in Hood River, Oregon, for one term, was county attorney of Polk County for ten years.

His marriage to Laura Etta Edgerton occurred at Stromsburg, December 24, 1885. Mrs. Stanton, whose ancestry was English and German, was born in Morgan County, Ohio, August 19, 1873, and died at Stromsburg, July 8, 1923. To them the following children were born: Gertrude E., November 4, 1886, who married Charles Floyd Moore; Charles E., February 10, 1888, who married Ella Newman; Hazel M., July 16, 1890; John Thomas, April 29, 1896, who married Mabel Anna Twarling; and Laura Ethel, April 12, 1901, who died January 11, 1902. Residence: Stromsburg.

John Thomas Stanton

John Thomas Stanton, lawyer at Stromsburg, Nebraska, has lived in this state all his life. He was born at Stromsburg, April 29, 1896, the son of Elmer Ellsworth and Laura Etta (Edgerton) Stanton. His father, who was born in Hocking County, Ohio, July 16, 1861, is a distinguished lawyer in Polk County, where he served four terms as county attorney. He also served one term as county judge of Hood River County, Oregon. He was a student at Bartlett Academy in Ohio, but received most of his legal education through private study.

John Stanton's mother was born in Morgan County, Ohio, August 19, 1873, of English parents, and died at Stromsburg, July 8, 1923. She attended college at Barnesville, Ohio, and later was active in the Woman's Club and Order of Eastern Star.

Mr. Stanton was graduated from the high school at Hood River, Oregon, in 1916, and in 1923 received the LL. B. degree at the University of Nebraska. He served as president of the legal fraternity of Phi Delta Phi, 1922-23, and was president of Lambda Nu Chapter of Phi Gamma Delta fraternity, 1922-23, at the University of Nebraska. He received letters in track and football at the Hood

River High School. Mr. Stanton enlisted in the United States Marine Corps, July 11, 1917, was promoted to quartermaster sergeant, attended the Marine Corps Officer's School at Quantico, Virginia, where he was commissioned first lieutenant, and was honorably discharged October 20, 1919. During his service he was stationed at various places in the United States and Nicaragua.

He is now junior member of the law firm of Stanton & Stanton at Stromsburg. A Democrat, he is serving his second consecutive term as county attorney of Polk County. He holds membership in the Nebraska State Bar Association, is affiliated with the Stromsburg Commercial Club, and is a member of the Nebraskana Society. Mr. Stanton is a Blue Lodge Mason, and is a member of the American Legion, Post No. 23, at Stromsburg. He likes swimming, tennis, hunting, and fishing, while his hobby is reading.

He was married to Mabel Anna Twarling at Stromsburg, July 27, 1923. Mrs. Stanton, whose ancestry is Swedish, was born in Polk County, July 11, 1897. They have a daughter, Elizabeth Ann, born October 16, 1924. Residence: Stromsburg.

Lucien Stark

Lucien Stark was born at Aurora, Nebraska, January 30, 1882, the son of William Ledyard and Gertrude (Ellsworth) Stark. They were married November 3, 1878, at Grand Island, Nebraska. His father, who was born at Mystic, Connecticut, July 29, 1853, and died at Tarpon Springs, Florida, November 11, 1922, was a distinguished lawyer; he served as county judge of Hamilton County, Nebraska, for 11 years, was congressman from the Fourth Nebraska District for six years, and served as colonel of the National Guard during the Spanish-American War. William Stark was of pure Scotch and English extraction and was descended from a family which has been prominent in America since 1722.

His mother, who was born at Malone, New York, November 4, 1857, was descended from English and Welsh ancestors who came to this country in 1724. She has been interested in political affairs and in music all her life.

Dr. Stark attended the Aurora High School, received the M. D. degree at Creighton Medical College in 1903, and took post-graduate course at various graduate medical universities. He has written many articles on medical subjects which have been published in the *Nebraska State Medical Journal* and the *Journal of the American Medical Association,* and has been engaged in the practice of medicine since 1903. He is a member of the Six-County Medical Society, the Nebraska State Medical Association, the American Medical Association, the Norfolk Chamber of Commerce, and the Norfolk Lions Club. Dr. Stark is the 63rd president of the Nebraska State Medical Association and is the first president ever elected by acclamation, unanimously.

He is a member of Hartington Lodge Number 155 and Consistory of Salina, Kansas, bodies of the Masonic Order, is affiliated with Holy Trinity Episcopal Church, and holds membership in the Nebraskana Society. Dr. Stark served as quartermaster, first class, in the United States Navy during the Spanish-American War, and was a captain in the Medical Corps during the World War.

A Democrat, he served as a member of the state board of Medical Examiners from 1915 to 1917. He was president of the Nebraska State Medical Association from 1931 to 1932, and is especially interested in medical research work. His sports are hunting and trap shooting.

His marriage to Marjorie Guilfoil was solemnized at Hyannis, Nebraska, December 16, 1903. Mrs. Stark, whose ancestry is Irish, English and Holland Dutch, was born at Elliott, Iowa, July 4, 1884. Mrs. Stark is the daughter of Frank and Ida (Dughman) Guilfoil. She is a graduate of the School of Music at the University of Nebraska, majoring as a violinist.

Two children were born to them: Ruth, January 19,

1905, who died at birth; and Howard, July 12, 1907, who is a student at the University of Nebraska. He earned letters in football and track at Hartington High School. Residence: Norfolk.

William Timothy Starkey

Since 1880 William Timothy Starkey has been a resident of Nebraska. He was born at Franklin, Ohio, November 1, 1878, the son of Wilson Cooper and Frances Virginia (Carter) Starkey, and has been engaged in railroad work since 1902. His father, who was an editor, merchant, and farmer, was born at Roscoe, Ohio, September 28, 1846, and died at Diller, Nebraska, April 3, 1916; he served in the 9th Ohio Cavalry during the Civil War. His mother was born at Franklin, April 14, 1848, and is still living today.

Mr. Starkey attended public school at Pawnee City, Nebraska. He has been employed by the Chicago, Burlington & Quincy Railroad since 1902 in the following Nebraska communities: South Bend, 1902-06; Utica, 1907-08; Louisville, 1908-20; and St. Paul, since 1920. He is a member of the Methodist Episcopal Church of St Paul, is vice president of the St. Paul Community Club, and holds membership in the Scottish Rite and Knight Templar bodies of the Masons.

His marriage to Mabel Florence Jackman occurred at Louisville, October 15, 1902. Mrs. Starkey was born at Louisville, July 14, 1884. Four children were born to this marriage: Glen, October 1, 1904, who married Amy Hakenson; Wilson, December 1, 1905, who died July 5, 1911; Lloyd, October 12, 1912, who married Verda Grimshaw. He is a musician. Neal was born May 17, 1917. Glen is manager for the Northwestern Bell Telephone Company at Randolph, Nebraska. Residence: St. Paul.

Olga Stastny

Dr. Olga Stastny was born at Wilber, Nebraska, September 13, 1878. She is the daughter of Frank John and Theresa (Jurka) Sadilek. Her father was born at Ledec, Czechoslovakia, December 1, 1851, and while he was but a child his family came to the United States. For the past thirty-three years he has held various public offices including county treasurer, county judge and clerk of the district court in Saline County. Dr. Stastny's mother is a native of Kralovice, Czechoslovakia, and was born July 19, 1858. She comes on the maternal side of a family of educators.

Dr. Stastny graduated from Wilber High School in 1895. On October 25, 1895, she married Charles Jan Stastny at Wilber, Nebraska. He was born at Slany, Czech-19, 1907, after his death. There are two children, Elsa Camilla who was born December 13, 1896, and who married to Ladislav Skocpol; a son, Robert Browning, born January 27, 1900, was killed in an aeroplane fire July 2, 1921, at Prague.

Dr. Stastny attended the University of Nebraska and University of Nebraska Medical College, receiving the degree of M. D., in 1913. Her internship was served at the New England Hospital for Women and Children at Boston. She later took postgraduate work at The Postgraduate College of Medicine at New York, and Mary Thompson Hospital of Chicago. She also studied abroad, principally at Prague and Berlin. At the University of Nebraska she was a member of the Dramatic Club, and was the organizer of Nu Sigma Phi, medical fraternity (Delta chapter) and has served as its president.

Dr. Stastny is a Democrat and was alternate delegate to the Democratic Convention at Houston in 1928. She has resided in Omaha since 1911. An author of some note, Dr. Stastny has written several pamphlets on health subjects which were prepared for the Czechoslovakia Army while she was serving there. She was for two years local editor of *Wilberske Listy* at Wilber, 1907-09. From 1913-18 she practiced medicine in Omaha. During 1918 and 1919, she was anesthetist in France,

with the American Women's Hospitals. During the years 1919 and 1920, she held the chair of hygiene at The School of Social Service at Prague. She was director of the Czechoslovakian Department of Health with the Y. M. C. A. from 1920 to 1922, and director of a quarantine station in Greece, from 1923 to 1924. Before going to France she was active in first aid instruction and organized the Department of Americanization, Council of Defense of Nebraska. She was awarded the Medaille de la Reconnaissace, (France) 1919; Cross of Saint George (Greece) 1923, and received special mention for service in Czechoslovakia.

She resumed her practice in Omaha in 1924. She is an instructor in the University of Nebraska College of Medicine. (See *History of Medicine in Nebraska*). In 1927 she was Nebraska's choice as the most prominent professional woman in the Business and Professional Woman's Club National Contest. A member of the Nebraska Association of Medical Women she served as first vice-president in 1917 and as president in 1927. She is a member of the Medical Reserve Corps; member and president of The Woman's Overseas League unit at Omaha; the Douglas County Medical Society; the American Medical Association. She was in 1930, president of The Medical Women's Association and was its delegate in 1924 to the International Medical Woman's Association Convention at London, and in 1931 to Vienna. She has been national health chairman of the Business and Professional Woman's Club for the past two years. She is a director of the Family Welfare Association of Omaha (formerly Associated Charities); a trustee of Doane College; and is serving as a member of the world service committee of the Y. M. C. A. In 1913 she was awarded the Noguchi medal for services in presentive medicine. She is a member of Eastern Star and of the Altrusa Club. Her hobby is the collection of foreign costumes, shawls, etc., and authentic copies of dolls, particularly.

A chapter of Esther Lovejoy's book, *Certain Samaritans*, entitled *Quality of Mercy* is devoted to Dr. Stastny's work abroad. Dr. Stastny resides in the Tadousac Apts., 418 S. 38th Avenue, and has her office at 1416-17 Medical Arts Bldg., Omaha. (Photograph on Page 1134).

Edwin Benjamin Stauber

Edwin Benjamin Stauber, son of Benjamin Christian Stauber, was born in Moravia, Iowa, December 21, 1862. His father was a native of Salem, North Carolina, born September 7, 1835. His ancestry was traced to Christian Stauber, born at Frankfurt, Germany, 1690. Christian Stauber was a saddler. His son, Paul Christian, was born in Frankfurt in 1726, and came to America, where his son, Christian Gottfried, was born May 28, 1761, at Fredrickstown, Hanover County, Pennsylvania. He had a son, Joseph, born at Salem, September 30, 1804, who was the grandfather of Edwin B. Stauber. Benjamin Stauber, a carpenter and farmer, came to Moravia, in 1849, to York, Nebraska in 1877, and to Hebron in 1880. He married Sylvia Ann Beatty, daughter of Michael Beatty. She was born at Magnolia, Illinois, November 5, 1840, and is living.

Educated in country school until 1884, Edwin B. Stauber has since been a farmer. He was married to Sophie M. Schorling at Deshler, Nebraska, May 5, 1889, and to them were born three children: Clarence, born May 13, 1890, who married Paula Wittenberger, and who died May 1, 1930; Irwin, born September 28, 1891, who married Leona Glasser, and Gertrude, born November 6, 1895, who married P. A. Chadwick. Mr. Stauber is a Republican and a member of The Nebraskana Society. Residence: Hebron.

Owen Chancy Stauber

Owen Chancy Stauber, a leading farmer at Chester,

OLGA STASTNY

was born at Moravia, Iowa, July 25, 1865, and came to Nebraska ten years later. He is the son of Benjamin C. and Sylvia Ann (Beatty) Stauber, his father born at Salem, North Carolina, September 7, 1835. He was an early settler in Nebraska, and died at Hebron on January 4, 1916. His wife, who was born at Magnolia, Illinois, November 5, 1840, is still living.

Mr. Stauber attended rural schools, and as a youth took up farming. For five years after coming to Nebraska he resided in York County, and for the past 51 years has been a resident of Thayer County. He is married to Mary Margaret Jones, who was born in Thayer County, November 26, 1872. Residence: Chester.

Carroll Orville Stauffer

Carroll O. Stauffer was born at Oakland, Nebraska, September 24, 1887, and has lived there most of his life. His father, Theodore Randolph Stauffer, was born at Iowa City, Iowa, December 25, 1856, of Swiss descent. His mother, Julia Mathilda (Steen) Stauffer, was born at Frankville, Iowa, September 27, 1856, and died at Oakland, September 17, 1917; her ancestry was Norwegian. She was a teacher and was active in church and club work.

Mr. Stauffer was graduated from the Oakland High School in 1905, and in 1912 was awarded the LL. B. degree at the University of Nebraska. He was admitted to the bar at Lincoln, June 13, 1912, and is now city attorney of Oakland. He served as judge of the Fourth Judicial District 1921-25, and was for some time chairman of the Republican central committee.

During the World War Judge Stauffer served as second lieutenant in the infantry. Prior to his enlistment he was active in loan drives for the Red Cross, and was a Four Minute Man. He is a member of the American Legion, and is a major in the Officer's Reserve Corps. He is a member of the Nebraska Bar Association and the American Bar Association. He is vice president of the Red Cross at Oakland, and from 1925-29, was a member of the board of education. He is a member of the Oakland Chamber of Commerce, the State Historical Society, and the Nebraskana Society. His hobby is reading.

His marriage to Nellie F. Hanson, daughter of Peter Hansen, and Breta Jaderberg Hansen was solemnized at Stromsburg, Nebraska, December 31, 1918. Mrs. Stauffer was born at Osceola, Nebraska, October 23, 1889; her ancestry is Swedish. Before her marriage she was a teacher. They have three children: Phyllis, born November 15, 1919; Russell, born May 29, 1921; and Mary Marie, born March 15, 1923. Residence: Oakland.

Albert Stauss

Albert Stauss, who is known throughout the newspaper world as an editor and executive, was born at Leutkirch, Wurttemburg, Germany, August 16, 1882. His father, George Johann Stauss, was born at Stuttgart, December 31, 1847, and died there on August 14, 1910. He was an educator who was descended from a long line of illustrious professional people, ministers, and teachers, all of them German. His mother, who was a middle class south German, was born at Bempflingen, Wurttemberg, Germany, and died at Stuttgart, May 5, 1887.

Mr. Stauss received his education at the Stuttgart Gymnasium and the Stuttgart Business College in Germany. He entered the newspaper business in 1912 as reporter; was correspondent for the *Baltimore Journal,* 1913-16; was editor of the *Buffalo Herald,* 1915-16; was editor of the *Green County Herald,* at Monroe, Wisconsin, 1916-19; editor *Lincoln Free Press* 1919-26; and was editor and manager of *Die Welt-Post* at Lincoln, Nebraska, for 11 years.

A member of the Lincoln Advertising Club, the Woodmen of the World, and various civic organizations, he was recently made a member of the Nebraskana Society. His hobby was reading. Mr. Stauss died September 21, 1930,

at Berlin, Germany. His death was a distinct loss to the newspaper world and to his community and state.

He was married to Dorothea Elizabeth Ober, at Flensburg, Germany, August 18, 1907. Mrs. Stauss was born at Grimma, Saxony, Germany, March 26, 1884. She is descended from a long line of ancestors who were artists and musicians. Their three children are: Hildegard, born June 30, 1908; George, born May 28, 1913; and Elfiela, born March 2, 1915. Hildegard was formerly instructor of German at the University of Nebraska. Residence: Lincoln.

Dorothea Elisabeth Stauss

Dorothea Elizabeth Stauss was born at Golzern by Grimma, Germany, March 26, 1884, the daughter of Freidrich Wilhelm Ober and Johanna Emilie Hoffman Ober. Her father was born at Neustadt, Germany, May 14, 1854, and is manager of a paper mill at the Free City of Danzig; he is an engineer and chemist. Her mother was born at Darmstadt, Germany, August 18, 1848, and was a teacher in London for eight years; her father was Lawyer Hoffman, cousin to Rudolph Hoffman the artist, and Clemens Brentano, the poet.

Mrs. Stauss attended the schools of Germany, and was a student at the Art College at Munich, Germany. She has lived in Nebraska 12 years, and is now editor and manager of *Die Welt-Post.* She is a member of the Advertising Club, is affiliated with St. Francis Catholic Church of Lincoln, and is a member of the Women's Catholic Order of Forester. She is a Democrat.

On August 18, 1907, she was united in marriage with Albert Stauss, at Flensburg, Schleswig, Holstein, Germany. They have three children: Hildegard, born June 30, 1908; George, born May 28, 1913; and Elfrieda, born March 2, 1915. Hildegard was German instructor at the University of Nebraska two years and is now the only instructor in German at the University of Omaha. Residence: Lincoln.

Lester Miles Stearns

Lester Miles Stearns, physician and surgeon since 1905, was born at Englewood, Illinois, November 16, 1883, son of Marcus Cicero and Nina Louise (Miles) Stearns.

The father, a lumber and coal dealer, was born at Chicago, October 10, 1858, and died at Philadelphia, June 14, 1905. He was descended from Isaac Stearns who emigrated from England in 1632 on the ship *Arabella,* and from Lieutenant Nathaniel Stearns of the Revolutionary Army.

Nina Louise Miles, who was born at Berea, Ohio, August 14, 1859, was of Revolutionary ancestry, and a member of the Daughters of the American Revolution. Her death occured at Altadena, California, May 14, 1925.

Lester Miles Stearns attended grade school in Chicago, Illinois, was a student at Lewis Institute in Chicago, and received his medical degree from the University of Illinois in 1905. He was class historian, a member of Alpha Kappa Kappa, and was elected to Alpha Omega Alpha in 1903. During the years 1905-07 he was house surgeon at the West Side Hospital in Chicago and in 1909 took post graduate work at the University of Vieinna.

A resident of Nebraska since September, 1908, Dr. Stearns has been active in professional, civic and fraternal organizations. He is a fellow of the American College of Surgeons, a member of the American, Nebraska State and Buffalo County Medical Associations, and is the author of numerous medical papers.

He was coroner of Buffalo County 1911-13, city physician 1915, member of the board of education 1925-31, and first physician, Kearney State Tuberculosis Hospital, 1912-14. At the present time he is attending surgeon, Good Samaritan Hospital, at Kearney.

Dr. Stearns is a 32nd degree York Rite and Scottish

Rite Mason and Knight Templar, and a member of the Elks, the Chamber of Commerce and the Red Cross. He was president of the Kearney School Board in 1930, was a contract surgeon 1917-18, and a four minute speaker. His club is the Kearney Country Club.

On June 20, 1906, he was married to Rosina Dickinson Alspaugh at Orland, Indiana. Mrs. Stearns, who is a member of the Daughters of the American Revolution, was born at Bronson, Michigan, March 10, 1884. There are two daughters, Francis J., born June 1, 1914, and Susanne M., born March 23, 1917. Residence: Kearney.

Albert Stebbins

Born in Story County, Iowa, March 10, 1864, Albert Stebbins is the son of Alanson and Mialmo Jane (Barkdull) Stebbins. His father, who was born at Geauga County, Ohio, February 3, 1830, was a preacher, blacksmith, and farmer, who moved from Story County to Antelope County, Nebraska, 46 years ago, and made a home for his family near Elgin; he died near Elgin, February 3, 1894; his ancestry was German. His mother was born of Scotch parentage in Ohio, August 28, 1823, and died in Antelope County, October 22, 1906.

Mr. Stebbins received his education in the rural schools of Story County. He has been a farmer practically all his life and is a member of the Farmers Union at Elgin. He is affiliated with the Park Congregational Church. Mr. Stebbins recalls vividly the pioneer religious services which were held in a sod school house in the early days and the various community activities which the early Nebraska settlers experienced. He was married to Charlotte Smiley Guthrie (Sapp) at Nevada, Iowa, August 28, 1902. Mrs. Stebbins, whose parents were Pennsylvania Dutch farmers, was born in Highland County, Ohio. She was married to Lewis Sapp November 16, 1887. Two children were born to their union: Flora May August 29, 1888, who married W. S. Armstrong and who died January 30, 1924; and William Aaron, April 10, 1892. Residence: Elgin.

Willis Irl Stebbins

Willis Irl Stebbins, postmaster at Gothenburg, was born there on March 29, 1895, son of Willis M. and Avis (Wilcox) Stebbins. The father, born in Oil City, Pennsylvania, January 21, 1863, is a merchant, and former state treasurer. He is descended from English settlers in America thirteen years after the landing of the Pilgrims. Avis Wilcox was born in Vermont, February 14, 1872.

Mr. Stebbins attended the Gothenburg public schools, was graduated from high school in 1914, and attended Nebraska Wesleyan University, the University of Nebraska and the University of Texas.

On April 11, 1925, he was married to Norma Thompson at Lincoln. Mrs. Stebbins was born at Central City, Nebraska, January 8, 1897. There are two daughters, Sally, born May 1, 1926; and Nancy, born March 10, 1930.

Mr. Stebbins is a Republican. He held the rank of 2nd lieutenant, Air Service, in the World War, serving at Kelley Field and Scott Field. He is a member of the American Legion, the Officers Reserve Corps, the Methodist Episcopal Church, the American Automobile Association, the Elks, Masons and Modern Woodmen of America. His club is the Gothenburg Country Club. He is a member of The Nebraskana Society. Residence: Gothenburg.

Willis Merrill Stebbins

Willis Merrill Stebbins, executive, was born at Wattsburg, Pennsylvania, January 20, 1863, and since April 12, 1884 has resided in Nebraska. He is the son of John C. and Dolly J. (Swetland) Stebbins.

Mr. Stebbins attended public school and Sherman Academy (N. Y.), and is an honorary member of Sigma

Phi Sigma at Lincoln. He homesteaded five years and for forty-two years has been in business in Gothenburg.

A Republican, he has been a member of the city council and school board, served in the Nebraska legislature 1911, 1913, and 1915; was a member of the constitutional convention of 1919-20, and served as state treasurer 1927-31.

On January 1, 1891, he was married to Avis Adelle Wilcox at Hastings. There are three children living, and two deceased: Verna, born October 20, 1891, married Arthur Greenslit, and died March 1, 1921; Guy L., born April 19, 1893, died September 15, 1914; W. Irl, born March 29, 1895, married Norma Thompson; Alice I., born May 14, 1904; Virge W., born May 28, 1906, married Florence Brooks.

Mr. Stebbins is a member of the Methodist Episcopal Church, the Kiwanis Club, the Hiram Club, the Knife and Fork Club, the Elks, Masons (32nd degree), and the Nebraska State Historical Society. Residence: Gothenburg.

Lester William Stecher

Lester William Stecher, farmer, was born in Dodge County, Nebraska, September 8, 1883, son of Joseph and Rosa (Wagner) Stecher. His father was born in Gutenberg, Bohemia, November 25, 1857, and came to the United States in 1869. His wife was born in Cleveland, Ohio, March 19, 1853. In her younger days she was a teacher. Her ancestry is German.

Mr. Stecher attended public school and for a number of years has been engaged in farming. He is married to Ethel Stephen, who was born at Valparaiso, Nebraska, August 13, 1883. They have one son, Joseph, born January 24, 1915.

Mr. Stecher is a Mason, a member of the Modern Woodmen of America. Residence: Potter.

Carl Frederic Steckelberg

Carl F. Steckelberg, musical educator and concert violinist of prominence, has lived in Nebraska for 47 years and has taken an active part in orchestra directing in Lincoln for many years. He was born in New York City, December 9, 1876, the son of John Henry and Mary (MacLean) Steckelberg. His father, who was born at Llsen, Hanover Province, Germany, August for Adolph Neundolph and Leopold Damrosch in New York. He was solo clarinetist with Gilmore, and was solo celloist with Theodore Thomas. He was descended from the German nobility.

His mother who was born at Scotsburn Station, Pictow County, Canada, February 2, 1847, and died on the home ranch Madison, Nebraska, and was buried at Lincoln, Lancaster County, Nebraska, November 13, 1923, was an active Eastern Star worker. She was a descendant of Gladstone through the maternal line, and Lord Hector MacLean on the paternal side.

Prof. Steckelberg attended the country schools and was a student at the Madison Normal and the Wayne Normal School. He studied in the University of Nebraska and Hochs conservatory at Frankfurt, Germany, where he obtained his A. M. degree, under Hugo Heerman; violin composition under Arrmand, ensemble under Carl Findley; then at Leipzig Conservatory was a special student with Amo Hilf (violin), Arthur Nickish conducting. He was a private pupil with Joachim in Berlin, with Ysaye at Brussels; with Sevcik in Prague; Pisek in Bohemia, and Leopold Auer in Chicago. He was a member of Sigma Chi and Acacia.

Since 1905 he has been at the head of the string department of the University School of Music at Lincoln. He is orchestral head at the University of Nebraska, and since 1927 has held the rank of professor. He is the author of: *Nemusier Method & Device; Why the Stiff Arm in Bowing;* and other musical articles.

On April 21, 1910, he was united in marriage with Onida Wiltse at Pender, Thurston County, Nebraska.

Mrs. Steckelberg, who was born at Walnut, Iowa, December 3, 1887, is accompanist to Mr. Steckelberg. There are two children: Carleen, born July 1, 1912; and Onida Janette, born March 10, 1920.

He is a member of the Lincoln Chamber of Commerce, and the Rotary Club. He is a 32nd degree Mason. He is a member of the East Ridge Country Club; the Nebraskana Society; and the First Presbyterian Church of Lincoln. Professor Steckelberg is vitally interested in building a huge loan fund for students by giving concerts and turning over the proceeds to this fund. His hobbies are: making violins; gardening; and doing research work in acoustics. His favorite sport is golf. Residence: Lincoln.

Lester Prescott Stedman

Lester Prescott Stedman was born at Oneida, Illinois, July 3, 1870, son of Volney Chapin and Julia Amanda (Prescott) Stedman.

For some time after leaving the Oneida High School, he engaged in farming and later was a hardware dealer in Woodhull, Illinois. He is now an employee of the firm of the Dempster O'Connell Hardware Company at Gordon, Nebraska. He has resided at Gordon, Nebraska, since 1916.

On January 12, 1898, Mr. Stedman was married to Lottie Belle Sterling at Utica, Iowa. She was born at Lima, New York, May 14, 1877, her father being one of the colony that founded the town of Gordon, Nebraska in 1884. There are two children, Win, born October 30, 1900, who married Jennie Pinkerton; and Stanford, born April 23, 1906, who married Grace Pohlman.

Mr. Stedman is a Republican and a Mason. His hobby is reading. Residence: Gordon.

Isaac Clinton Steele

Isaac C. Steele, pioneer business man in Nebraska, has lived in this state for the past 60 years. He was born at Shelbyville, Indiana, September 20, 1862, the son of Robert Robison and Mary Ellen (Croly) Steele. His father, who was a farmer, was born at Shelbyville, December 30, 1839, and died in Fillmore County, Nebraska, April 29, 1872. His mother, whose ancestry was Irish, was born in Lawrence County, Ohio, April 22, 1838, and died at Ohiowa, Nebraska, March 15, 1913.

Mr. Steele has been engaged in the furniture and undertaking business at Ohio for many years. He is a member of the Ohiowa Commercial Club, is affiliated with the Methodist Church at Ohiowa, and holds membership in the Nebraskana Society. He is connected with the Chester Telephone Company.

His marriage to Ora Belle Carter occurred at Friend, Nebraska, October 10, 1891. Mrs. Steele was born at Bushnell, Illinois, October 19, 1871, and died at Omaha, Nebraska, February 12, 1901. On August 31, 1902, Mr. Steele married Elda Dunn; three children were born to them: Edward Eloss, born June 23, 1903, who died November 15, 1903; Doretta Hope, born September 11, 1904, who died January 10, 1905; and Mary Vaunden, born March 30, 1906. Residence: Ohiowa.

William LaBarthe Steele

William LaBarthe Steele was born at Springfield, Illinois, May 2, 1875. He is the son of Robert Clingan Steele, born in Chester County Pennsylvania, March 13, 1836. He was an accountant, and merchant, and a member of the city council of Springfield. His father was a Pennsylvania farmer of Scotch descent, and his mother was of the Marsh family of Pennsylvania Dutch ancestry. Robert Steele married Mary Eleanor LaBarthe, born at Springfield, November 30, 1852. She is a musician and was for years organist of the Church of the Immaculate Conception at Springfield, and later soprano soloist. She

was also a teacher of piano and organ. Her father, Jules LaBarthe was born at Bordeaux, France, and her mother was Albina Mary Smith, born in Dublin.

Mr. Steele attended Rev. J. F. Brooks' Private School at Springfield, and was graduated from Springfield High School, of which William Helmle was principal, in 1892. He was valedictorian of his graduating class. In 1896 he received his B. S. in Architecture from the University of Illinois. He is a member of Sigma Chi, Kappa Kappa chapter. From 1893-96 he was a member of the university band, and was illustrator of *Illio* in 1896.

From 1896 to 1904 Mr. Steele was an architectural draftsman in the offices of Louis H. Sullivan and S. S. Beman of Chicago; Thomas Rodd, Alden and Harlow, S. F. Heckert of Pittsburg; W. W. Beach, Sioux City, and member of the firm of Beach and Steele at Sioux City from 1905-06. From 1906 to 1927 he practiced alone at Sioux City. Since 1928 he has been a member of the firm of Kimball, Steele and Sandham at Omaha. He is a registered architect in Iowa and South Dakota.

He married Mariana Green at St. Louis, April 30, 1901. Mrs. Steele was born at Champaign, Illinois, and is of English and Scotch descent. She was graduated from Champaign High School and the University of Illinois, and before her marriage was a teacher. They have six children, Mariana, born June 10, 1903; Melissa, born November 6, 1905, who joined the Dominican Order in 1929 and is known as Sister Mary Philip, and who is teaching at Faribault, Minnesota; William LaBarthe, Jr., born August 25, 1907; Jane Raymond, born March 26, 1910; Sallie Green, born February 7, 1914; and Philip Joseph, born April 23, 1916.

Mr. Steele is the author of various articles in the *American Institute of Architects' Journal, House Beautiful, Western Architect, Ecclesiastical Review*, etc. He is a member of the American Institute of Architects and is past president of the Iowa chapter; he served on the board of directors and as second vice president of the national organization. He is also a member of the Interprofessional Institute and of the Engineers Club. While living in Sioux City he was a member of the board of trustees of the City Library two terms, was president of the Rotary Club, and member of the board of directors of the Sioux City Chamber of Commerce. He is a member of the Knights of Columbus, and is Past Grand Knight of Epiphany Council of Sioux City.

In politics Mr. Steele is independent. He is a Catholic and member of St. Cecilia's Cathedral. He is a member of the Nebraskana Society. His present club is the University Club of Omaha. He is interested in archery and extremely fond of music. Residence: Omaha.

Ellis M. Steen

The Rev. Ellis M. Steen, clergyman, was born in Davis County, Indiana, May 26, 1879, son of John Franklin and Mary Catharine (Lock) Steen. His ancestry is Scotch-Irish and came to the United States about 1734.

In 1899 Mr. Steen was graduated from High School in Washington, Indiana, and the following two years attended Franklin College at Franklin, Indiana. The following year he was a student at James Millikin University.

On October 17, 1899, he was married to Dennie Bula Dale at Washington, Indiana, her birthplace. She was born October 1, 1878. Their children are: as follows, Lois, born March 18, 1901; Eunice, January 18, 1903; James Dale, January 27, 1904; Robert, October 18, 1906; Dorothy, March 17, 1909; and Ellis, Jr., April 15, 1914.

Mr. Steen has held eight pastorates, and during the years that he has been a clergyman he has added 1500 members to his various churches. He is a Republican, a member of the Kiwanis Club, the Commercial Club and the Knights of Pythias. His favorite sports are golf and fishing. Residence: North Platte.

Frank S. Stegge

Frank Stegge, prominent banker, was born in Pocahontas County, Iowa, December 31, 1878. Shortly after the Civil War his father homesteaded in Pocahontas County, Iowa. He died there on July 9, 1899, while his wife died there on September 9, 1896.

Mr. Stegge attended public school and on January 7, 1903, was married to Anna Meehan of Pocahontas, Iowa. Her parents were early settlers in that county. They have one daughter, Frances C., who was born November 3, 1915, at Randolph. She is a junior in St. Frances High School.

Mr. Stegge is an independent Democrat. He has been a resident of Nebraska since October 17, 1905, and at the present time is vice president and manager of the First National Bank of Randolph, of which he has been connected since October 17, 1905. This is one of the strongest banks in northeastern Nebraska. Mr. Stegge started as a bookkeeper, was made assistant cashier, and in July, 1909, was elected cashier and manager. This bank is affiliated with the Toy National Bank of Sioux City, Iowa, of which Mr. James F. Toy is the president.

Mr. Stegge is the owner of a farm and enjoys spending his spare time there. He is especially fond of good stock.

During the late war he assisted in all Liberty loan and other drives. He is a member of St. Frances Catholic Church, the Knights of Columbus, the Catholic Order of Foresters, and the Nebraskana Society. Residence: Randolph.

James Stehlik

James Stehlik, who was born at Olive Precinct, Lancaster County, Nebraska, October 8, 1870, is the son of Vaclav and Marie (Jarmon) Stehlik. His father, who was a pioneer farmer, was born in Kladno, Cecho Slovakia, and came to America in 1866. He died at Crete, May 10, 1908. His wife, Marie, was also born at Kladno, died at Crete, September 1, 1911.

Educated in the country grade schools of Nebraska, Mr. Stehlik has engaged in farming since a boy, and in Lancaster County thirty years. He was married to Mary Plouzek, at Crete, March 20, 1893. She was born at Crete, April 1, 1875, of Cech Slovak descent. There are four children: Marie, born July 15, 1897; Fred, born January 25, 1905; William, born August 1, 1907, and Emil, born February 26, 1910.

Mr. Stehlik is a Republican and a Catholic. He is a member of the Nebraskana Society, and is well known and highly respected in his community. Residence: Crete.

Fred Steinbach

Fred Steinbach, who has been a farmer in Saunders County, Nebraska, for over a half a century, was born at Delta, Ohio, March 10, 1864. His father, Werner Steinbach, was born at Hesse, Darmstadt, Germany, January 5, 1836, and died at Fremont, on March 23, 1927. His mother, Mary (Green) Steinbach, was born at Hesse, November 23, 1834, and died at Fremont, March 27, 1916.

Mr. Steinbach received his education in a rural school in Saunders County, Nebraska, and has always been interested in public affairs at Yutan. He was united in marriage to Mabel Bishop, at Wahoo, Nebraska, November 28, 1893. Mrs. Steinbach was born at Yutan, July 2, 1876. To this marriage three children were born: Orletha, who married Earl Goodwin; Everett, who married Mildred Ford; and Velma. Mr. Steinbach was recently elected to membership in the Nebraskana Society. Residence: Yutan.

John W. Steinhart

John W. Steinhart was born at Brunswick, Chariton County, Missouri, May 9, 1861, the son of John and Mary (Danne) Steinhart. His father, who was born at Westphalia, Germany, and came to the United States in his youth, was a merchant tailor. He died at Nebraska City.

His mother was born in Germany and at the age of four years came to Nebraska City with her parents. She was a devout church worker. She died at Nebraska City.

Mr. Steinhart, who has lived in Nebraska 66 years, received his education in the public schools of Nebraska City, and was a student at the Nebraska City Episcopal College, where he received a medal in rhetoric and elocution. In 1879 he became connected with the Nebraska City National Bank, and in 1881 he was made acting cashier. In 1890 he moved to New York City, and upon his return to Nebraska City a year later was made cashier of the Otoe County National Bank. In 1910 he was made postmaster at Nebraska City. In 1914 he organized and became president of the Otoe Food Products Company and today holds this position.

An earnest student of Nebraska history, Mr. Steinhart has devoted a great deal of time and thought to the beautifying and developing of Nebraska City and the adjoining country. He is the author of a book, *Nebraska City Beautiful,* in which he sets forth a tentative plan of his community developed with an eye to the future. In recognition of his book he was made a member of the American Civic Association in 1928.

A Republican, he was mayor of Nebraska City for one year. He was appointed by the governor of the state as a trustee for the school for the deaf at Omaha, and the school for the blind at Nebraska City, and served in this position for eight years.

He was united in marriage with Elizabeth Morton on May 23, 1888, at Nebraska City. Mrs. Steinhart, whose ancestry is English, was born at Nebraska City in 1861. She was at one time a teacher and organist, in the church and was active in Woman's Club affairs and the P. E. O. They have one son, Morton, born June 14, 1889, who married Ella Schwake. He was graduated from the University of Nebraska Law School in 1913, and is now associated with his father in business. Mrs. Steinhart died January 7, 1931. She was very active as a Red Cross worker in her community.

During the World War Mr. Steinhart was untiring in his efforts at raising loans and promoting Red Cross activities. He was president of the Nebraska State Association of Commercial Clubs, a war-time organization, from 1916 to 1918. He was formerly prominent in the Nebraska City Chamber of Commerce and was president and secretary for many years. For a number of years he was a member of the library board. He has been a member of the Nebraska Manufacturers Association for 18 years. He is a member of the Nebraska City Planning Committee, and the Nebraskana Society. He is an Elk. For 15 years he has been superintendent of the Sunday School in the Episcopal Church with which he is affiliated. His hobby is beautifying Nebraska City.

The Nebraska City Rotary Club made the following award: "In recognition of the life devoted largely to unselfish Public Service, the Rotary Club of Nebraska City on October 27, 1926, presents this formal award to John W. Steinhart. Residence: Nebraska City.

Hugo Robert Steinhaus

Hugo Robert Steinhaus, pharmacist, was born at Vanmeter, Iowa, September 28, 1879, son of Ed. H. and Carolena (Burgdorf) Steinhaus.

The father, born in Germany, November 24, 1848, came to the United States in 1874 and to Nebraska as a pioneer in 1883. He was a clergyman and an officer in the German army, and after coming to America was a livestock raiser. He is still living. Carolena Burgdorf was born in Germany, November 5, 1853, and is still living.

Educated first in country school, Mr. Steinhaus was a graduate in pharmacy of the old Fremont Normal Col-

FRANCIS J. STEJSKAL

Smith Studio—Crete

lege. Since 1904 he has been engaged in the drug business at Gordon.

Mr. Steinhaus has resided in Nebraska since 1884, and was in country school on 12th of January, 1888, the day of the big blizzard.

On August 26, 1909, he was married to Jennie E. Haynie at Pacific Junction, Iowa. Mrs. Steinhaus was born at Pacific Junction, December 14, 1881, and before her marriage was a teacher. Mr. and Mrs. Steinhaus have two children, Victor, born November 24, 1912; and Fay, born August 18, 1916. Victor was graduated from Gordon High School in 1929, while Fay will graduate with the class of 1933. Victor has had one year in business management at Nebraska Wesleyan University.

A Democrat, Mr. Steinhaus has always been interested in local party politics. He served three years in the Nebraska National Guard at Columbus, Nebraska, after the Spanish American War. He is a Baptist, a member of Odd Fellows Lodge No. 169, and of the Ancient Free and Accepted Masons Lodge No. 195. His favorite sports are hunting and fishing. Residence: Gordon.

John Jacob Steininger

John Jacob Steininger, clergyman, was born at Osage City, Missouri, October 22, 1861, son of John Nicholas and Catherine (Holzbierlein) Steininger. The father was a farmer.

Upon the completion of his public school education in 1877, John Jacob Steininger attended Central Wesleyan College at Warrenton, Missouri. He received his Bachelor of Arts and Master of Arts degrees in 1888 and 1891. On January 11, 1897 he was married to Louisa Steinmeyer at Lincoln. They have four children.

Mr. Steininger is a member of the Second Methodist Episcopal Church. For a number of years he has served as superintendent of the Lincoln district of the West German Conference, holding various charges. Residence: Lincoln.

Francis J. Stejskal

For the past 25 years Dr. Francis J. Stejskal has engaged in the practice of medicine at Crete, Nebraska. He was born at Borovany, Czechoslovakia, November 25, 1876, the son of Vaclav and Katharine (Bouska) Stejskal. His father, who was a farmer, was born at Borovany, March 6, 1842, and died there April 10, 1880. His mother was born at Borovany, November 10, 1856, the daughter of Anthony Bouska and Barbara (Hruska) Bouska; she died at Borovany, March 30, 1928.

Dr. Stejskal received his elementary and preparation education in Czechoslovakia, attended the Omaha Commercial College, and was a student at Creighton University Medical College at Omaha, for four years. He was admitted to the medical profession at Omaha, June 21, 1906, took internship at St. Joseph's Memorial Hospital at Omaha, 1906-07, and has practiced surgery and medicine at Crete, since then, serving as county physician for Saline County for several years.

He is a member of the Nebraska State Medical Society, the Saline County Medical Society, the American Medical Association. He is affiliated with Sacred Heart Catholic Church at Crete, the Knights of Columbus, and the Catholic Workmen.

During the World War Dr. Stejskal served as first lieutenant in the United States Army, and at this time is a member of the American Legion and the Disabled American Veterans. His sports are hiking, fishing, and hunting.

On January 24, 1924, he was united in marriage with Helen Agnes Krejci at Tabor, South Dakota. Mrs. Stejskal, who is a graduate nurse, was born at Crete. They have three children: Francis and Florence Katherine, twins, born November 7, 1924; and Robert Eugene, born September 6, 1931. Residence: Crete. (Photograph on Page 1139).

Charles Adam Stenglein

Charles Adam Stenglein, one of Waterloo's most prominent citizens, was born February 8, 1884, son of Adam and Johanna (Emmerick) Stenglein. Adam Stenglein was born in Bay Reuth, Germany, March 4, 1843, and held the rank of lieutenant in the German Army in 1866. He came to America in 1868 and became construction foreman on the Union Pacific Railroad which was nearing completion at Promontory Point. Afterward he engaged in farming until his death at Waterloo, on June 21, 1916. Johanna Emmerich was born in Hannover, Germany, December 7, 1851, and is still living.

Mr. Stenglein attended the Waterloo public schools to and including the 10th grade, and received his Ph. G. degree from Highland Park College of Pharmacy at Des Moines, in 1901. A resident of the state his entire life, he has followed the drug business continuously since 1899, although he has since become manager of the Postal Telegraph Company and handles estates and real estate loans.

He is a Democrat, and during the World War was a large purchaser of Liberty bonds and made liberal contributions to relief societies. He is a Lutheran, a 32nd degree Mason, and member of the Scottish Rite and Shrine, and is a member of the Elks. Mr. Stenglein enjoys fishing and big game hunting. He is a mineral rock collector and a lover of Indian lore. He also collects coins and stamps, is a dog fancier and trainer, a landscape artist and nurseryman, and enjoys mechanics of all types. Residence: Waterloo.

Dan Vorhees Stephens

Dan V. Stephens, banker, educational publisher, farmer and manufacturer, was born at Bloomington, Indiana, November 4, 1868. He comes of a line of pioneer settlers in Virginia, Tennessee, Kentucky and Indiana. He is the son of Richard Lewis Stephens, born in Indiana about 1830, a farmer, who died near Bloomington about 1912. His mother, Martha (Lambkins) Stephens, was born and died near Bloomington, Indiana.

He received his early education in the public schools of Indiana, and the city schools of Bloomington. He attended Valparaiso College from 1886-87. In North Bend, Nebraska on June 24, 1890, he was married to Hannah Boe. Mrs. Stephens was born in Bergen, Norway, May 10, 1866. She was formerly a teacher. Of the two children born to this marriage, one, Edith, is deceased; the other, Estella, is the wife of Benjamin Harrison of Omaha.

Always a Democrat, Mr. Stephens began his political career as delegate to the Democratic national convention in 1904. He was delegate at large and chairman of three following Democratic national conventions: Denver, in 1908; San Francisco, 1920; New York, 1924. Upon the death of James P. Latta, he was elected to the 62nd congress, 1911-13, to fill the unexpired term, and was re-elected to the 63rd and 65th congresses, 1913-19, from the third Nebraska district. During this time he was a member of the interstate and foreign commerce committee.

An author of considerable note, his published works include *Silas Cobb* (1902) and *Phelps and His Teachers* (1903), together with many articles on banking, appearing in the *American Bankers Magazine* and elsewhere.

He is the organizer of the Hammond & Stephens Company, educational publishers; the Fremont State Company and the Fremont Mortgage Company. He is president of the Fremont National Bank, etc.

Elected to United States Congress in 1926, to represent the fourth Nebraska district, he rendered a service to his district that was highly pleasing to his constituents. Always attentive to his legislative and departmental duties, he initiated the idea of the weekly news letter, which would report congressional activities,

DAN VORHEES STEPHENS

as a means of keeping the people informed as to what is going on in Congress.

Defeated in 1928, by the narrow margin of 218 votes, in which election Hoover carried the district by 18,653 votes, he was elected over Charles W. Sloan in 1930.

He has always been active in farm organizations and is a former president of the Nebraska Farm Bureau Federation. He has attended many conferences and conventions on farming. He is also a Chautauqua and Lyceum lecturer. Residence: Fremont. (Photograph on Page 1141).

Lamont L. Stephens

One of Nebraska's able lawyers is Lamont L. Stephens who has been engaged in legal practice at Loup City, Nebraska, since 1914. He was born at Rockville, Nebraska, December 8, 1887, and is the son of William Harrison and Anna Martha (Thompson) Stephens. His father, who was a farmer and stockraiser, was born at Durand, Illinois, January 17, 1851, and died at Hot Springs, South Dakota, December 24, 1908. His mother was born in Norway, November 12, 1852.

William Harrison Stephens was the son of William Harrison and Ruama (Randall) Stephens, who were natives of Onondaga County, New York. Theirs was the first marriage recorded in Wayne District and occurred October 26, 1836.

Mr. Stephens attended the Rockville Public School, was a student at Nebraska State Normal College at Kearney, Nebraska, and received the LL. B. degree in 1914 at the University of Nebraska where he received the Order of the Coif. He opened a law office in Loup City immediately after his admission to the bar and has been a leader in professional affairs since that date.

He was married at Ulysses, Nebraska, May 25, 1915, to Elizabeth Lucretia Warren, who was born at Rising City, Nebraska. Three children were born to them, of whom two are living: Ruth, born April 29, 1918; and Norman, July 21, 1920. Lowell Warren, who was born November 12, 1916, died January 20, 1917.

Mr. Stephens is a member of the Nebraska State Bar Association, the Masons, and the Independent Order of Odd Fellows. He served as county attorney of Sherman County, 1915-23, and was county judge there from 1925 to 1929. Residence: Loup City.

Samuel Zigmund Stern

Samuel Zigmund Stern, dentist, was born at Omaha, Nebraska, December 6, 1902, son of Morris and Toney (Feiler) Stern. He attended the high school at Billings, Montana, and received the degree of Doctor of Dental Surgery from the University of Minnesota.

Dr. Stern has been in active practice since 1925, and is a member of the national, state and local dental associations. He is also a member of B'nai Brith. Residence: Omaha.

William Sternberg

William Sternberg, lawyer and educator, was born at Underwood, Iowa, April 7, 1880. He is the son of Ludwig and Antonia (Hauber) Sternberg, both natives of Germany. His father, who was born at Mecklenburg, in 1824, came to America when a young man and settled in Iowa. He died at Earling, Iowa, January 21, 1905. His wife, Antonia, was born at Roehlingen, Stuttgart, Germany August 27, 1837, and died at Defiance, Iowa, January 19, 1919.

Upon his completion of the elementary courses in the parochial school at Earling, Iowa, Mr. Sternberg was graduated from Woodbine Normal High School. He attended St. Benedict's College at Atchison, Kansas, and

Drake University at Des Moines, receiving his A. B. and LL. B. from Creighton University.

Admitted to practice on April 30, 1910, he devoted ten years to the practice of law, as a member of firm of Crane, Boucher & Sternberg 1910-20, and since 1920 has given his entire time to educational work. He is professor of law at Creighton University at the present time.

He was married to Erica Louise von Lehenner, at Omaha, on November 15, 1924. Mrs. Sternberg was born at Hamburg, Germany, January 19, 1904. They have one daughter, Isabell, born June 18, 1926. Professor Sternberg is independent in politics. He is a Catholic, and a member of the Holy Name Parish. Residence: Omaha.

William Van Meter Steuteville

William V. Steuteville, lawyer at South Sioux City, Nebraska, has lived in the state since February, 1880. He was born in Grayson County, Kentucky, March 12, 1876, the son of Richard F. and Narcissa E. (Haynes) Steuteville. His father, who was a farmer, was born in Grayson County, November 5, 1844, and died at Brownville, Nebraska, April 16, 1930. His mother who was born in Hardin County, Kentucky, August 16, 1848, and died at Brownville, September 18, 1929, was a music teacher.

Mr. Steuteville attended the Brownville public school and was graduated from high school there in 1891; later he attended the University of Nebraska. For twelve years he was a teacher in rural and city schools, and since 1909 he has been engaged in the practice of law at South Sioux City. He is a member of the Nebraska Historical Society, is affiliated with the Boals Methodist Episcopal Church, and holds membership with the National Geographic Society, and the Nebraskana Society. He is a Democrat.

His marriage to Stella Vennum was solemnized at Stratton, Hitchcock County, Nebraska, July 21, 1915. Mrs. Steuteville was born at Exeter, Fillmore County, Nebraska, July 19, 1884. Their children are: Florence, born June 29, 1916; Fern, born November 10, 1927; Mary, born November 10, 1917; and William, born July 31, 1922. Residence: South Sioux City.

Harland Uriah Stevens

Harland Uriah Stevens, educator, was born at Knoxville, Iowa, August 8, 1884, son of Charles Freeman and Esther Meek (Kilgore) Stevens. His father, born at Paris, Maine, April 11, 1841, is a clergyman. His mother was born March 3, 1845. Both are living.

Professor Stevens attended the public schools at Knoxville, Iowa, and obtained his secondary education in the preparatory department of Union College. He holds the following degrees: Bachelor of Science, Union College, 1907; Master of Science, University of Chicago, 1912. A special student at the University of Nebraska for a time, he is now associate professor in the department of Bible and religion at Union College.

His marriage to Inez Leona Hoiland was solemnized at College View, Nebraska, on September 15, 1909. Mrs. Stevens was born at Anita, North Dakota, March 26, 1886, and died at Arequipa, Peru, South America, December 22, 1925. One child was born to this union, Helen, on January 15, 1918.

In August, 1912, Professor Stevens and his wife sailed for Argentina, to answer a call from the Seventh Adventist Day Mission Board to direct the River Plata Academy in Entre Rios, near Diamante, which is about 300 miles north of Buenos Aires. Here he was engaged for seven years, after which he was appointed educational secretary for the South American division of the Seventh Day Adventist General Conference, and in this capacity traveled over the greater part of South America.

Returning in 1922 to their World Conference in San

Francisco, he was there appointed superintendent of the Inca Union Mission of that church, which embraces the Republics of Peru, Ecuador and Bolivia. He moved with his family to Lima, Peru, and was engaged in this administrative work four years. After the death of his wife he returned with his daughter to the United States and was appointed associate professor of Bible and religion at Union College, which position he holds at the present time.

Professor Stevens was married to Grace A. Evans at Berrien Springs, Michigan, on May 30, 1928. Residence: Lincoln. (Photograph in Album).

Herbert Herman Stevens

Born at Cromwell, Iowa, February 4, 1895, Herbert Herman Stevens has resided in Nebraska for the past 22 years, and for a number of years has been a printer and publisher.

His father, William LeRoy Stevens, was born in Ohio and died at North Platte, Nebraska, in June 19, 1917. He served as superintendent of Potter public schools. His ancestry was Scotch-Irish. His wife, Margaret Mary Parry, was born in Ohio and died at Potter, Nebraska, September 9, 1927. She was also of Scotch-Irish descent.

Mr. Stevens attended the public high school of Potter. At the present time he is the editor of the *Potter Review*, and is village clerk and village treasurer. He is a Democrat.

His marriage to Elizabeth Johanna Meyers was solemnized at Kimball, June 19, 1923. She was born at Potter on June 25, 1902. There is one son, Wesley, born February 9, 1931.

During the World War Mr. Stevens held the rank of sergeant in the 341st Machine Gun Battalion. He is a member of the American Legion, Potter Post No. 291. He is also a member of the Methodist Church, the Nebraska Press Association, the Potter Community Booster's Club, the Potter Rifle Club, and the Masons. His hobby is mechanics. Residence: Potter.

Albert Ray Stevenson

Albert Ray Stevenson, merchant, and mayor of Thedford, was born at Westmoreland, Kansas, March 9, 1888, son of Francis Amsberry and Adelaide (Allen) Stevenson. The father was born in Pennsylvania in 1846, and is a veteran of the Civil War, of German and Scotch ancestry. The mother, born in 1848, died at Mullen on May 19, 1900. Her ancestry was French and Irish.

Upon the completion of his public school education, Mr. Stevenson became a farm laborer, continuing until 1908. The following two years he was a mail carrier, and for some time thereafter was connected with the firm of Moulton & Bass at Anselmo, four years as head clerk. Thereafter he was the manager of G. M. William's store for one year, resigning to start his own business. He first operated at Sweetwater and then at Thedford. At the present time he owns a store at Thedford, and another at Seneca which is being run by his brother.

Mr. Stevenson is a Republican, and has served as mayor of Thedford, 1925-26, 1931-32. He is a member of the Methodist Church, the Red Cross, the Nebraskana Society, and the Masons. His hobby is reading

On February 5, 1913, he was married to Zillah Fern Shankland at Callaway, Nebraska. Mrs. Stevenson was born at Callaway on October 1, 1893, of Scotch-Irish and Pennsylvania-Dutch parentage. There are five children, Frances Juanita, born August 14, 1913; Doris Evelyn, December 29, 1914; Alberta Valier, December 20, 1916; Alma Fern, October 10, 1922; and Gilbert Allen, June 21, 1926. Residence: Thedford.

Francis Chase Stevenson

Francis Chase Stevenson, general secretary of the Young Men's Christian Association at Hastings, was born at Lynn, Indiana, January 31, 1896. He is the son of James Elmer and Chloa Caroline (Kinsey) Stevenson, the former born at Modoc, Indiana, September 6, 1872, and the latter at Lynn, on September 19, 1872.

Mr. Stevenson was graduated from high school at Richmond, Indiana, in 1915, and received the degree of Bachelor of Science in Agriculture from Purdue University. He is a member of Alpha Zeta and Theta Chi.

From 1921 to 1926, Mr. Stevenson was secretary of the Young Men's Christian Association at Iowa State College, and from 1926-28, was state student secretary for Nebraska. He has held his present position since January, 1929.

His marriage to Ruth Mariam Simmons was solemnized at Russiaville, Indiana, September 3, 1921. To them were born three children: Charles William, born August 25, 1923, who died September 5, 1930; Betty Lou, born May 20, 1925; and Richard Lee, born January 3, 1929. Mrs. Stevenson was born at Kokoma, Indiano, March 20, 1897.

Mr. Stevenson entered Officers Training Camp at Fort Benjamin Harrison, on May 15, 1917, was made first lieutenant of infantry, assigned to Camp Shelby, Mississippi, until September 18, 1918, from which time until June, 1919, he served with the 5th Division, American Expeditionary Forces.

A member of the First Congregational Church at Hastings, Mr. Stevenson is also a member of the Young Men's Christian Association, General Secretaries Association, the Red Cross, Chamber of Commerce, Lion's Club, the Nebraskana Society, and the State Association of Employed Officers in which he is serving as president (1930-31). Among his sports are hand ball, fishing and hunting, and his hobby is reading. Residence: Hastings.

Oliver Stevenson

Oliver Stevenson was born of a pioneer Nebraska family, at Nebraska City, on February 14, 1883. Members of the Stevenson family have been in America since 1681. In the spring of 1860, Granville L. Stevenson, father of Oliver Stevenson, came with his parents to Nebraska, stopping first in Brownville, and a little later moving to Nebraska City, where they established the first steam powered flour and grist mill on the upper river. All machinery was shipped to them by boat from Mount Vernon, Ohio, and their business rapidly flourished. A large amount of flour and other mill products were shipped to the Mormans at Salt Lake City, and to Denver City. Granville L. Stevenson was born at Honesdale, Wayne County, Pennsylvania, and died at Nebraska City, in 1915.

Julia Catherine (Petring) Stevenson, his mother, came to Nebraska City with her parents in the spring of 1856. Her father, Herman H. Petring, established a store in Nebraska City, and until recently this business was managed by the family. In 1846, her father and mother came from Berlin, to St. Louis, Missouri. Her father was a son of a merchant in Germany, and owned an establishment which is still operated by his relatives in Berlin.

Mr. Stevenson was graduated from the Nebraska City public school, and he has been in business in this city all his adult years, has taken an active interest in community affairs and is connected with all civic movements of importance. A Democrat, he served for a time as County Clerk of Otoe County. At the present time he is vice president of the Otoe Food Products Company at Nebraska City.

His marriage to Maude Jane Metz was solemnized at Nebraska City, June 14, 1914. Mrs. Stevenson was born at Shamokin, Northumberland, Pennsylvania, October 26, 1886.

In the late war Mr. Stevenson served as secretary of the local draft board for Otoe County, working without compensation. He is a member of the executive committee of the Red Cross, the Chamber of Commerce, and is past president of the Nebraska County Clerks Association. He is a Mason, a member of the State Historical Society, and the Isaak Walton League.

Mr. Stevenson is vitally interested in the good roads movement, and is past president of the Nebraska Good Roads Association. His favorite sport is motorboating. Residence: Nebraska City.

Cloyd Laverne Stewart

A leading lawyer at Clay Center, Nebraska, is Cloyd Laverne Stewart, who has been a resident of Clay County most of his life. He was born at Hill City, Kansas, August 22, 1891, the son of Charles Bell and Millie (Stewart) Stewart. His father, who was born at Highland, Kansas, April 10, 1864, is a hardware merchant; his Scotch ancestors came to this country prior to the Revolution. His mother, whose ancestors were related to Benjamin Franklin, was born at Washington, Kansas, April 11, 1876. She has served as city librarian at Laramie, Wyoming, and in Albany County, Wyoming, for the past 10 years.

Mr. Stewart attended the Kearney Military Academy at Kearney, Nebraska, for four years from 1905 to 1909. He was awarded the LL. B. degree at the University of Nebraska in 1915, where he was prominent in dramatics and debating. He was president of the junior class in 1914, held membership in the Innocents Society, was a member of Phi Alpha Tau, and in 1914 acted as delegate to the national convention of Delta Upsilon.

Since his admission to the bar in 1915 Mr. Stewart has been engaged in the practice of law and at this time is city attorney at Clay Center. A Democrat, he served as county attorney of Clay County for three consecutive terms. He was formerly manager for the Redpath Horner Chautauquas. He holds membership in the Chamber of Commerce, the Lion's Club, Nebraska State Bar Association, and the Nebraskana Society. He is a Scottish Rite Mason and Shriner. His social club is the Clay Center Golf Club, and his favorite sport is golf.

He married Elma Charlotte Kinnison at St. Joseph, Missouri, April 14, 1914. To this union one son, James Bill Stewart, was born on February 20, 1915.

His marriage to Marie Wumenberg occurred June 20, 1926 at Swanton, Nebraska. One child was born to this marriage: Charles, born April 21, 1928. Residence: Clay Center.

Don Warner Stewart

Don W. Stewart was born at Lincoln, Nebraska, December 6, 1891, the son of John Minor and Alice Mary (Warner) Stewart. His father, born at Danville, Iowa, December 14, 1856, is a lawyer and former assistant Attorney General of Nebraska. He is of Scotch-English ancestry. Alice Mary, his wife, was born in Illinois, January 18, 1861, and died at Lincoln, October 27, 1907. She was of English and Dutch descent.

Mr. Stewart attended the Lincoln public schools and was graduated from Lincoln High School in 1909. He received his A. B. from Nebraska in 1913, attended the University of Michigan, in 1914, and returning to Nebraska, received his LL. B. in 1915. His fraternities are Beta Theta Pi and Phi Delta Phi.

He was married to Laura Kathleen McRoberts of Mound City, Missouri, October 22, 1919. They have three children, John W., born September 3, 1920; Donald W., born December 22, 1923, and Roger M., born July 9, 1927. He is a Republican and assistant United States Attorney for Nebraska, 1921-26. He is now a member of the law firm of Stewart, Stewart and Whitworth, and a

director of the Lincoln Trust Company, the Lancaster Hotel Company, the Union Real Estate Company, the Markel Hudsen-Essex Company, and the Stewart Investment Company.

His professional memberships include the American, Nebraska State and Lancaster County Bar Associations. He is a member of the Chamber of Commerce, Masons, Parent-Teachers' Association, and the Young Men's Christian Association. His sports are golf and tennis, and his clubs the University and Lincoln Country Clubs. Residence: Lincoln.

John Minor Stewart

John M. Stewart has been engaged in the practice of law in Nebraska for the past 52 years. He was born near Burlington, Des Moines County, Iowa, December 14, 1856. His father, James Andrew Stewart, who was born near Cincinnati, Hamilton County, Ohio, September 12, 1810, was a farmer. His ancestors came from Scotland about 1780. He died at Minden, Kearney County, Nebraska, September 23, 1893.

His mother, Lucinda (Cowles) Stewart, was born in Belmont County, Ohio, March 22, 1822 and died at Minden, October 14, 1899. The Cowles family came from England to Farmington, Connecticut in 1645.

Mr. Stewart attended the rural schools of Lee County, Iowa, until 1870. He was a student at Parsons College, at Fairfield, Iowa, 1877, and the Normal School at Kirksville, Missouri. He was admitted to the bar at Fairfield, Iowa, January, 1880, and began the practice of law at Minden, directly afterward.

A Republican, he served as county attorney at Minden, 1881-1885; was mayor of Minden, 1883-84; was deputy attorney general at Lincoln, four years 1887-1891; was city attorney of Lincoln, 1907 and 1908; and was chairman of the executive department of the Constitutional Convention, 1920. He is a director of the Lincoln Trust Company at Lincoln, and the Union Loan & Savings Association. He has been a trustee of the Nebraska Wesleyan University for the past 42 years.

He is a member of the American Bar Association; the Nebraska State Bar Association; and the Lincoln Chamber of Commerce. He holds membership in the Young Men's Christian Association, and the Nebraskana Society. He is a life member of the Nebraska State Historical Society. He is a member of the University Club and the Lincoln Country Club. He is affiliated with St. Paul's Methodist Episcopal Church of Lincoln. His sport is golf.

On October 22, 1881, he was united in marriage with Alice M. Warner, at Fairfield, Iowa. Mrs. Stewart was born at Campaign, Illinois, January 18, 1861, and died at Lincoln, October 27, 1907. She was of Dutch descent. Four children were born to them: Frances Edward, born September 22, 1882; Helen B., born August 16, 1885, who married Earl B. Day; Marcia L., born March 18, 1888, who married John Walter Mayo; and Donald W., born December 6, 1891.

Mr. Stewart was married to Harriet Gilyre Muir, June 3, 1915. Mrs. Stewart is a niece of John Muir, a great scientist and naturalist. Residence: Lincoln.

John Thomas Stewart

John Thomas Stewart, automobile dealer, was born at Council Bluffs, Iowa, July 23, 1876, son of Joel Littleton and Sara Isabella (Cory) Stewart. Joel L. Stewart was born at Mount Carmel, Illinois, February 19, 1837, of English parentage, his ancestors settling in Nova Scotia, about 1704. He was a wholesale grocer for many years and died at Council Bluffs, April 24, 1896. His wife, Sarah, was born in London, Canada, November 13, 1852, and is descended from English settlers in New Jersey, about 1700.

John T. Stewart was educated in the Council Bluffs public and high schools, and Yale University. He has been a resident of Omaha for twenty-five years, and during most of that time has been engaged in the automobile business. He is now president of the Stewart Motor Company.

Mr. Stewart was married to Gertrude Kountze, at Omaha, January 8, 1902. Mrs. Stewart, who is the daughter of Herman and Elizabeth (Davis) Kountze, was born at Omaha, May 21, 1877. There are three children: John, born November 4, 1902, who married Fredrica Nash; Gordon, born January 7, 1908; and Jane, born January 7, 1908, who married Ira L. Couch.

During 1917-18, Mr. Stewart was a member of the Nebraska Council of Defense. He is an Episcopalian, and a member of the Chamber of Commerce. His clubs are the Omaha Club and the Omaha Country Club, and his sports are golf and squash. His hobby is reading. Residence: Omaha.

William Clark Stewart

A leading business executive at Holdrege, Nebraska, is William Clark Stewart, who was born at Burlington, Iowa, April 19, 1875, the son of James and Ella (Clark) Stewart. His father, was a plumber and served in Company C, 65th Illinois Volunteers for three years during the Civil War. His mother, who is a descendant of the leader of the Lewis and Clark expedition, was born at Burlington, June 18, 1858, and is living today at Eugene, Oregon.

Mr. Stewart attended high school for two years at Junction City, Kansas. He was engineer-in-charge of the Kansas Deaf and Dumb School from 1899 to 1902, was a plumber and fitter during 1914, and for the next 14 years was a traveling salesman. He served six years with the Cornell Supply Company, three and a half years with the Western Supply Company, over four years with the Wolff Manufacturing Company, and three years as manager of the Hampton Hotel at Holdrege. He is manager of the Holdrege Credit Bureau at this time.

He is a member of the visiting committee of the local Welfare Association, is a member of the Chamber of Commerce, and holds membership in the State Association of Credit Bureaus. He is secretary of the Holdrege Rotary Club, is a member of the National Retail Credit Association, and is affiliated with the Presbyterian Church of Holdrege. Mr. Stewart is commander of Mount Elias Commandery Number 19, of the Knights Templar. He is grand conductor of the Grand Council of the United Commercial Travelers of Nebraska, and holds membership in the Spanish War Veterans Association of Grand Island, Nebraska. He served as sergeant in Company F of the Sixth Missouri Volunteers in the war with Spain.

His marriage to May McLinn occurred at Kansas City, Missouri, April 17, 1901. Mrs. Stewart was born at Flat Rock, Illinois, October 12, 1874. Residence: Holdrege.

Willis E. Stewart, M. D.

Willis E. Stewart, physician and surgeon, was born at Neoga, Cumberland County, Illinois, May 25, 1875, the son of Thomas Yates and Lucy M. (Fellows) Stewart. Dr. Stewart's father was a native of West Virginia, born January 23, 1842, and died at Neoga, Illinois, July 21, 1913. Mr. Stewart was a farmer and veteran of the Civil War. Lucy M. (Fellows) Stewart was born March 23, 1847, in Ohio, and died at Neoga, Illinois, October 10, 1930.

Dr. Stewart's elementary training was obtained in the Cumberland County, Illinois, public schools. He later attended The Friends Academy at Hiawatha, Nebraska, completing his college preparatory course there in 1893. In 1896 he was awarded his B. S. degree at Lamar College, at Lamar, Missouri, and his M. D. degree at Central Medical College at St. Joseph, Missouri, in 1900. While at Lamar he was elected president of his

graduating class, and was also president of his class in medicine in 1900.

During Dr. Stewart's student life up until the time of his graduation in medicine he was associated with the publication of country newspapers, working in all the various capacities in a country printing office, and remembers vividly the various duties of a printer's devil.

In February, 1902, he was married to Dolores Estella Sharp at Stratton, Nebraska. She was born at Parkersburg, Illinois, January 2, 1880, and before her marriage taught in the Stratton Public Schools.

To this union were born two children, Eugene Yates, born January 22, 1903, who married Mary M. Masters of Stratton on March 20, 1925; and John Noel, born February 17, 1909, who married Edna M. Burnstock of McCook, Nebraska, on January 9, 1928. Eugene is engaged in the lumber business at Wauneta, Nebraska. John is a member of the graduating class of 1932 in Medicine, of Nebraska University Medical School.

In 1900 Dr. Stewart began the practice of medicine in Stratton and in 1926 he erected a beautiful modern building to be used as a clinic in the heart of the town. Two blocks north of the clinic he erected a beautiful home and directly east, a modern private hospital with a 14 bed capacity. The grounds surrounding the premises are beautifully landscaped, being a spot of note. In addition to his professional practice he served for 20 years as president of the Board of Education at Stratton; he is president of the Veterans Memorial Hall (a community center) and for five years acted as president of the Citizens State Bank, and a member of the board of directors of the Stratton State Bank. He is also a breeder of livestock of note. His Poland China herd were judged world's champions at the National Swine Show in 1931, at Springfield, Illinois.

During the World War Dr. Stewart was medical examiner for the Government in Hitchcock County, Nebraska. He was chairman of the local Government Liberty Bond selling drives and chairman of the local Red Cross. His religious affiliation is with the Community Methodist Episcopal Church of Stratton and he is president of the Official Board. He holds membership in the county, state and national medical associations, is a life member of the Red Cross, member of the Chamber of Commerce of Stratton, a Mason, member of Tehama Temple at Hastings, Nebraska, and was elected in 1932 to membership in the Nebraskana Society. His politics are independent. Residence: Stratton. (Photograph in Album).

John Stibal, Jr.

John Stibal, Jr., son of John and Anna (Duda) Stibal, Sr., was born at Richland, Nebraska, in 1887. His father, born in Bohemia, in 1847, came to America in 1867, and homesteaded three miles north of what is now Richland in 1869. The homestead is still in the family. Mr. Stibal is now retired. His wife, Anna, was born in Bohemia in 1857 and came to the United States in 1873.

Educated in the Richland public school, John Stibal, Jr., was graduated in 1903, and from then until 1907 attended the University of Nebraska School of Agriculture, the Lincoln Academy, and the University of Nebraska School of Mechanic Arts. He is a member of Sigma Tau, and received his degree of Bachelor of Science in Civil Engineering from the University in 1912. From 1912-13 he was with structural steel firms in Omaha and Indianapolis, and from 1913-16 was associated with electrical power development in North Carolina. During the past years 1916-20 he engaged as a mining engineer in South America and the southern part of the United States. He is now engaged as an engineer and surveyor in Richland. His hobby is raising bees. Residence: Richland.

Daniel Brooks Stidworthy

A physician and surgeon since 1894, Daniel Brooks Stidworthy was born at Galena, Illinois, November 3, 1866. His father, William Stidworthy, was born in Devonshire, England, in 1830, and came to the United States as a young man, serving in the Civil War. He afterward engaged in business, and died at Sioux City, Iowa, in April, 1899. His mother, Sofia Elizabeth Brooks, was born in New Jersey, and was educated in Presbyterian Girls' School there. She died at Sioux City, in 1907.

Dr. Stidworthy attended the public and high schools of Sioux City, Iowa, and studied medicine at the Sioux City College of Medicine from which he was awarded his M. D. in April, 1894. He also attended Iowa State University 1890-91.

He has been a resident of Nebraska thirty-seven years, and actively engaged in the practice of his profession. During the World War, he held the rank of captain, and was promoted to major, 41st Railroad Artillery in command of Post Hospital at Fortress Monroe, Virginia. He is a member of the American Legion, and is a 32nd degree Mason and member of the Shrine.

On June 12, 1895, he was married to Alice Hallquist, a teacher in the Sioux City public schools. Mrs. Stidworthy was born in St. Paul, Minnesota, October 20, 1872. There are three daughters: Helen M., born April 18, 1896, who married Harry A. Fudge; Ada M., born June 7, 1899, who married Raymond N. Westover, and Margaret N., born September 22, 1901, who married Earl L. Coryell. All are graduates of the University of Nebraska.

Dr. Stidworthy is a Republican. His favorite sport is hunting. Residence: Homer.

Walter Savage Stillman

Walter Savage Stillman, lawyer, is the son of Walter Deming and Sarah Ann (Birch) Stillman. He attended the public schools of Council Bluffs, the preparatory department of Griswold College, the University of Michigan, from which he received his Bachelor of Arts degree, and the Harvard University College of Law.

His marriage to Anna Laura Martin was solemnized at Davenport, Iowa, September 20, 1893. There are four children, Walter Martin, Mary Birch, Hugh Deming, and Anna Johnston.

Mr. Stillman was admitted to the practice of law in Des Moines in 1891, and at Lincoln in 1899. He is a member of the American, the Council Bluffs, the Omaha, the Iowa, and the Nebraska State Bar Associations, the Elks, the Masons, and the Episcopal Church. His clubs are the Omaha, the University, and the Council Bluffs Country. Residence: Council Bluffs.

Carl Theobald Stimbert

Carl Theobald Stimbert was born at Inland, Nebraska, August 20, 1886, the son of David and Maria (Roser) Stimbert. His father, who is a farmer, was born at Chicago, Illinois, March 23, 1859, of German parentage. His mother was born at Colmar, Alsace Loraine, April 17, 1857.

Mr. Stimbert attended college at Wilton Junction, Iowa, for a year, 1903-04, was a rural mail carrier from 1906 to 1910 at Inland, engaged in the grain business from 1910 to 1912, and since 1912 has been postmaster at Inland. He is affiliated with the Methodist Church, is a Mason, and a Republican.

He was united in marriage with Clara Mathilda Schuck at Inland, March 15, 1907. Mrs. Stimbert was born at Inland, July 29, 1890, the daughter of Charles and Augusta (Fitzke) Schuck. To this marriage were born three children, Eldon Carl, September 25, 1908, who married Mildred Irene Crom and resides at Nehawka, Nebraska; Leola Maude, December 28, 1912; and Abbie Jean, May 19, 1919. Eldon was graduated from Nebraska

Wesleyan University in 1929, and Leola is a student there at this time. Eldon Carl has one daughter, Phyllis Ann, born January 25, 1932. Residence: Inland.

Lester B. Stiner

Lester B. Stiner, son of Henry and Mary (St. Clair) Stiner, was born at Cardington, Ohio, June 4, 1871. At the age of ten he came with his parents to Nebraska, and has since resided continuously in the state. His father, Henry Stiner, was a farmer, a native of Ohio, who died at Lexington, July 26, 1884. His wife, Mary St. Clair, was born in Ohio, also, and died at Lexington, March 14, 1901.

Educated in the public schools of Hastings, Judge Stiner attended Hastings College preparatory department, and was graduated from the college in 1884. Since his admission to the bar of Nebraska, in 1887, he has been engaged in the practice of law, for eighteen years as senior member of the law firm of Stiner and Boslaugh. A Republican, Judge Stiner served as county judge of Clay County two terms, as county attorney of Clay County two terms, and as mayor of Hastings two terms.

His marriage to Eva H. Robertson was solemnized at Harvard, Nebraska, December 22, 1910. There are three children: Lester R., 19; Roberta, 18; and Frederick K., 12. All three are students at the present time. Judge Stiner and his family attend the Hastings Congregational Church, while he is a member of the Chamber of Commerce, the Rotary Club, the Masons, Odd Fellows and Elks, as well as the Young Men's Christian Association. He was president of the Chamber of Commerce in 1928.

Judge Stiner is one of Hastings' outstanding citizens, and is known as the foremost lawyer of southern Nebraska. Residence: Hastings.

Allen Stark Stinson

Allen Stark Stinson has resided in Nebraska continuously for the past 52 years, and for 30 years has taken a leading part in both political and civic affairs in Knox County. He was born at Palo, Iowa, August 6, 1875, the son of Elizabeth Lovilla (Neihardt) and Truman C. Stinson, the latter a farmer. His father, whose ancestry was Scotch and Irish, was born at Sandusky, Ohio, October 12, 1835, and died at Crofton, Nebraska, May 12, 1892; he was a descendant of Ethan Allan and other distinguished New England ancestors. His mother, was born of Pennsylvania Dutch extraction; she was a member of the same family as John G. Neihardt, poet laureate of Nebraska.

Mr. Stinson finished his elementary education in 1892, and was graduated from the Creighton High School in 1896. As a teacher in Knox County, Nebraska, for 18 years, he held the highest grade certificate then issued in this state. He served as manager of the Farmers Union Store at Niobrara from 1924 to 1926, and since that time has been editor and publisher of the *Niobrara Tribune,* one of the leading weekly newspapers in Knox County.

A Democrat, Mr. Stinson served as deputy county clerk, 1912-14, county superintendent of schools, 1915-23, and a member of the state senate, 1927-31. He is a candidate for county judge at this time. During his service in the senate he was author of various school laws including the Character Education Law passed in 1927.

He is a member of the executive board of the Commercial Club of Niobrara, is a member of the publicity committee of the Nebraska Forestation Society, and holds membership on the Niobrara School Board. Mr. Stinson is affiliated with the Christian Church, is a Mason, and was recently elected to membership in the Nebraskana Society. His hobby is reading, and he is especially interested in politics and history.

On August 6, 1901, he married Regula Lena Ulrich at Bloomfield, Nebraska. Mrs. Stinson, whose parents came

Peterson Studio—Auburn

JAMES LEONARD STIVERS

to this country from Germany and settled in Knox County, was born at Herrick, Nebraska, Septembeer 12, 1880. Their children are: Crystal, born May 30, 1902, who married Oscar J. Rentzell; Winnifred, born November 13, 1903, who married George Sweigard, Jr.; born October 2, 1905; Kathryn, born January 1, 1907; and Ruth, born April 2, 1911. Residence: Niobrara.

James C. Stitt

In active architectural practice at Norfolk since 1889, James C. Stitt is a leading member of his profession. Hs was born at Mitchell Hollow, New York, September 28, 1866, son of Ransom and Elvira P. (Cooper) Stitt. His father, born at Medusa, New York, April 7, 1840, was a building contractor of Scotch and Irish descent, who died at Lincoln, Nebraska, May 4, 1911. His mother, who was of New England Yankee descent, was born at Berne, New York, February 6, 1840, and died at Norfolk, January 2, 1912. She was a zealous church worker. His grandfather, James J. Stitt, was an outstanding master builder, specializing in churches. His home was in Albany County, New York.

James C. Stitt attended elementary and high schooi at Canastota, New York, where he was active as a foot racer. On January 9, 1889, he took up his residence and the practice of his profession at Norfolk, and on October 20, 1890, was united in marriage to Cora May Holt. Mrs. Stitt, who was born at Hampton, Connecticut, March 8, 1870, daughter of Henry E. and Josephine (Carey) Holt, is descended from early English settlers in New England.

There are four children: Marian J., born November 28, 1892, married Frank T. Hughes; James C., August 11, 1897; Roger H., June 2, 1899; and Kathryn, January 30, 1911 is now completing her senior year in Rockford College, Illinois. James is an electrical engineer with the General Electric Company, while Roger is an acoustical engineer with the United States Gypsum Company.

Mr. Stitt is a Democrat, and from 1896-1900 was city clerk of Norfolk. He was vice president of the Norfolk Building and Loan Association 1914-29 and since that time has been president. From 1909-11 he was a colonel on the staff of Governor Shallenberger, and during the World War was secretary of the Norfolk Home Guards and a member of the United States Public Service Reserve.

A member of the Chamber of Commerce, he was its vice president in 1930 and has served three terms as a director. He is a charter member and former president of the Kiwanis Club, a Mason and Knight Templar, an Elk and a member of the Young Men's Christian Association. He belongs to the Red Cross, the Salvation Army, the First Congregational Church and the Norfolk County Club, and is a life member of the Nebraskana Society. He is an ardent baseball fan. Residence: Norfolk.

James Leonard Stivers

James Leonard Stivers, horticulturist, was born in Henry County, Kentucky, July 19, 1889, son of Charles Albert and Emma Jane (Moore) Stivers. His father, who was born in Henry County, Kentucky, April 12, 1845, and died in Mills County, Iowa, March 8, 1928, was a farmer and horse trainer in Kentucky. He was interested in fine-bred horses and in horse races, and was well versed in judging them. Strongly Democratic, he took an active part in Kentucky politics throughout his life. His ancestry was Scotch-Irish.

His mother, who was a devout Baptist Church worker, was born in Henry County, September 8, 1863, and died in Mills County, Iowa, August 1, 1926. She was of English ancestry.

Mr. Stivers was graduated from the high school at Glenwood, Iowa, in 1908, after which he attended the business college at Glenwood, for two years. He was active in football and baseball, and took part in the various phases of athletics in high school. He has been in the fruit business all his adult life. From 1910 to 1915 he was buyer and manager of a Minneapolis fruit company, and since 1915 he has been manager of the Central States Orchard Company, a corporation embracing Minnesota, Nebraska and Missouri, and also has been manager and secretary of the Brownville Orchard Company, since 1927, the latter a comparatively new but flourishing business. Mr. Stivers' coming to Nebraska renewed and revived the development of the fruit-growing industry in southeastern Nebraska. A resident of the state for 11 years, he has taken an active part in the civic and business affairs of his community. He is the author of various articles on horticulture published in magazines and newspapers. He is a member of the General Western Shipping Advisory Board.

His marriage to Pearl Olive Allen was solemnized at Plattsmouth, Nebraska, November 12, 1912. Mrs. Stivers was born at Bartlett, Iowa, November 19, 1892, daughter of Minor B. and Olive Nora Allen. Her ancestry is Dutch and English. She attended high school in Plattsmouth, Nebraska. She is a member of the Order of Eastern Star and the Woman's Club, and is active in church affairs. There are four children: Dick Allen, born August 13, 1913; Earl Maurice, born July 27, 1915; Charles Benjamin, born October 21, 1922; and Jane Lenora, born March 20, 1925. The three boys are in school.

Mr. Stivers is a member of the Missouri River Apple Growers Association, a member of the board of directors of the Auburn Chamber of Commerce and holds membership in the Red Cross. He is a Royal Arch Mason. For some time he has been treasurer of the Auburn Methodist Episcopal Church. With his wife he is a member of the Auburn Country Club. His favorite sport is baseball and his hobby horse racing and good horses. Residence: Auburn. (Photograph on Page 1147).

William Tolbert Stockdale

Born at Springfield, Illinois, William Tolbert Stockdale has lived in Nebraska since early childhood. His parents were natives of Illinois and were of Scotch and Irish descent. Mr. Stockdale attended rural schools in Saunders County, Nebraska, was graduated from the high school in connection with the Normal University at Lincoln, and holds the following degrees: A. B. Lincoln Normal University, 1898; B. S., Fremont Normal College, 1900; and A. M., University of Nebraska, 1921.

He served as superintendent of school at Wisner, Nebraska, 1901-09, was superintendent at Madison, Nebraska, 1909-11, and since 1911 has been director of the teachers training department of Nebraska State Normal College at Chadron, Nebraska. From 1911 until 1924 Mr. Stockdale was also head of the department of education, and from 1924-25 was on leave of absence and was on the regular faculty of the Nebraska State University, at the same time he was working toward obtaining his Ph. D. degree. Mr. Stockdale made five annual school surveys of the towns, 15 to 20 towns in each survey. These are called the Nebraska Panhandle School Surveys. He has been a member of the Chadron Chamber of Commerce for the past eight years, was formerly president of the Rotary Club, and for 14 years acted as local treasurer of the Junior Red Cross.

He is a member of the Nebraska State Teachers Association, the Odd Fellows, is affiliated with the Congregational Church, and holds membership in the Nebraska School Masters Club and Phi Delta Kappa. He was recently elected to membership in the Nebraskana Society.

On October 9, 1890, he was married to Ida May Vorse at Wahoo, Nebraska. Mrs. Stockdale, who was a teacehr prior to her marriage, was born at Erie, Pennsylvania. Two children were born to this marriage: Alva Percy, June 27, 1892, who died January 3, 1919; and Irma Lucile, December 8, 1903. Alva Percy was principal of the high school at Alliance, Nebraska, at the time of his death. Irma Lucile received her A. B. degree at Nebraska State Teachers College at the age of 17 years. She taught

WILLIAM TOLBERT STOCKDALE

three years in Scottsbluff High School, and received her
A. M. degree at the University of Nebraska at the age of
21 years, and is now a teacher in the Arthur Hill Senior
High School at Saginaw, Michigan. Residence: Chadron.
(Photograph on Page 1149).

Albert Edward Stocker

Albert E. Stocker was born at Marengo, Iowa County,
Iowa, September 6, 1870. His father, John Stocker, was
born at St. Neots, England, and died at Marengo, October 24, 1899.

His mother, Sarah Louise (Smith) Stocker, was born
in Ohio, August 3, 1840, and died at Marengo, October 10,
1929.

Mr. Stocker lived in Nebraska for over twenty years
and for several years was cashier of the Otoe County National Bank at Nebraska City. He was a Republican.
His death on July 15, 1930, was a distinct loss to his community and state.

John Denny Stocker

John Denny Stocker was born at Oskaloosa, Mahaska
County, Iowa, September 1, 1898, the son of Albert Edward and Helen J. (Gunn) Stocker. His father, whose
ancestry was English, was born at Marengo, Iowa County, Iowa, September 6, 1870, and died at Nebraska City,
Otoe County, Nebraska, July 15, 1930. He was a banker.

His mother who was born at Oskaloosa, September 2,
1870, was interested in civic and political affairs, and was
at one time committeewoman for the Republican party.

Mr. Stocker was graduated from the Nebraska City
High School in 1917, and later attended the University of
Nebraska, where he was a member of Phi Kappa Psi
Fraternity. He is now cashier of the Otoe County Na-
tional Bank.

He is married to Margery I. Menold. A resident of
Nebraska for twenty years Mr. Stocker has always been
interested in community affairs, and at the present time
is a director in the Nebraska City Chamber of Commerce.
During the World War he was a private in the United
States Artillery School Troops at Fortress Monroe, Virginia. He is a member of the American Legion, and is a
Mason and a Lion. His favorite sport is hunting. His
hobby is mechanics. He is a Republican. Residence: Nebraska City.

Joseph Orland Stockton

Joseph Orland Stockton, educator, was born at Wheaton, Illinois, December 2, 1900, the son of John Raymond
and Martha S. (Gauger) Stockton. His father, a building contractor, was born of English parents at Wheaton,
July 9, 1875. His mother, whose ancestry was German,
was born at Wheaton, February 17, 1882.

Mr. Stockton was graduated from the Wheaton High
School in 1918, was a student at Dakota Wesleyan University, and received the A. B. degree from Wheaton
College in 1923. He received four letters in football,
two letters in basketball, and four in baseball, at Wheaton
College, and was captain of the football team for two
years.

Upon his graduation from college Mr. Stockton became coach of athletics at Nogales, Arizona, where he
remained for a year. He served as coach at Alliance,
Nebraska for five years, and since 1930 has been superintendent of schools at Spencer, Nebraska.

He is affiliated with Gary Memorial Methodist Episcopal Church at Spencer, is a Mason, and holds membership in the Red Cross, Woodmen of the World, and the
Nebraska State Teachers Association. Hhis favorite
sports are football, hunting and fishing. During the
World War Mr. Stockton drove an ambulance in France
for 10 months, and is now a member of the American
Legion. He is a Republican.

On November 27, 1926, he married Helen Bertha

Hawes at Alliance, Nebraska. Mrs. Stockton, whose
ancestry is Irish and German, was born at Fremont,
February 4, 1906. Residence: Spencer.

Glenn Earl Stoddard

Glenn Earl Stoddard, who has been engaged in the
practice of dentistry at Alma, since 1919, if a life time
resident of Nebraska. He was born at Rising City, Nebraska, July 8, 1891, the son of Jay Ira and Edith Celesta
(Lemmon) Stoddard, the former a farmer who was born
at Orlando, Indiana, August 24, 1852. His forefathers
settled in Watertown, Connecticutt, in 1763, upon their
arrival from Scotland. His mother, whose parents were
natives of Pennsylvania, was born at Jamestown, Indiana,
March 22, 1862.

Dr. Stoddard was graduated from the Rising City
High School in 1907, was a student at Peru State Normal
College from which he was graduated in 1911, and in 1918
received the D. D. S. degree at Creighton University. He
received letters in football and baseball both in high school
and college.

He holds membership in the National Dental Society,
the Nebraska State Dental Society, and the District Dental Society. His fraternal organizations include: Independent Order of Odd Fellows, Masons, and the Modern
Woodmen of America. His favorite sport is golfing.

Dr. Stoddard taught in a rural school in 1909, was
superintendent of schools at Alexandria, Nebraska, 1911-
12, served as principal of the high school at Osceola, 1912-
14, and in 1918 was graduated from dental college. He
has been engaged in dental practice at Alma, since 1919.

His marriage to Lillie Martha Rasmussen was solemnized at Holdrege, Nebraska, August 9, 1925. Mrs. Stoddard was born at Bertrand, May 27, 1895. They have a
son, Glen Earl, born February 7, 1927. Residence: Alma.
(Photograph in Album).

Wayne Oliver Stoehr

Wayne O. Stoehr was born at Moline, Rock Island
County, Illinois, November 26, 1902, the son of Oliver and
Onieta (Poston) Stoehr. His father, who was a contractor, was born at Moline, March 21, 1876; his parents
came to America about 1860, from Germany. His mother,
whose ancestry is English, was born at Moline, November
19, 1882.

Mr. Stoehr attended the public schools of Moline,
where he was graduated from the high school in 1920. He
was a student at Augustana College, 1921-23, and the
University of Nebraska where he was awarded his LL. B.
degree in 1926. He was president of the senior class in
high school and took part in high school athletics; was
awarded his school letter in 1918. He was a member of
Phi Delta Phi, legal fraternity, and Phi Delta, social fraternity, at the University of Nebraska, and served as
president of the latter in 1926.

He has been engaged in active practice of law since
his admission to the bar at Lincoln, June 15, 1926. He
has been a resident of Nebraska for the last 6 years.

On June 27, 1927, he was married to Burdette Taylor at
St. Paul, Howard County, Nebraska. Mrs. Stoehr, who
was born at St. Paul, February 7, 1904, is of English descent. Mr. Stoehr is a member of the Omaha Bar Association; the Nebraska Bar Society; and the Barristers' Club.
He is a member of the Young Men's Christian Association, and the Presbyterian Church. He holds membership in the University Club of Omaha. His favorite sport
is golf. His hobby is reading. He is a Democrat. Residence: Omaha.

Arthur Charles Stokes

A leading member of the medical profession for many
years, Arthur Charles Stokes was born at Bury, Compton
County, Quebec, Canada, on December 24, 1869. He is the
son of Charles Henry and Mary Ann (Chapman) Stokes,

the former born at Bury, on March 8, 1840. He was a farmer and stockman whose father came to Canada, four years prior to his birth, and who died at Flaudreau, Moody County, South Dakota, October 10, 1924. His wife, Mary Ann Chapman was a native of Bath, England, born April 8, 1841, and who died February 14, 1930. Her father was a school teacher in Bath. She is particularly devoted to her home, and has reared seven children.

Dr. Stokes received his early education in the elementary schools of Canada, and was graduated from Rock Rapids High School in 1889. He received his B. Sc. from Ames, Iowa, in 1892, and his M. D. from the University of Nebraska, in 1899. He was a member of Phi Beta Phi, Alpha Omega Alpha, Phi Rho Sigma, and Delta Tau Delta. Upon the completion of his university studies in the United States, he took post graduate work in the Universities of Halle, Kiel, and Berlin, in Germany.

On December 17, 1910, Dr. Stokes was united in marriage with Bertha S. Shackleford, at Omaha Mrs. Stokes was born at Des Moines, Iowa, September 4, 1878, and her parents were natives of Kentucky. Since admission to practice in Nebraska June 1, 1899, Dr. Stokes has been actively engaged. He is the author of various medical articles. He is medical director of the Guarantee Mutual Life Insurance Company, and a member of the surgical staffs of various Omaha hospitals. In politics he is generally Republican. He is a member of the board of regents of the University of Nebraska. During the World War he organized Base Hospital No. 49, in Nebraska. Entering the active service in France as a major, he was promoted to the rank of colonel. He has been chairman of the Douglas County chapter of American Red Cross for ten years, and is a member of the Disabled Veterans of America, the American Legion, and the Reserve Officer Associations. His professional organizations include the Douglas County Medical Society, the American College of Surgeons; the American Medical Association and the Western Surgical Association.

In religion Dr. Stokes is an Episcopalian, and attends All Saint's Church. He is a member of the Chamber of Commerce, the Elks and the Masons, and the Nebraska State Historical Society. His favorite sport is hiking, and his hobby is trees and flowers. His clubs are the Omaha and Omaha Country Clubs. Residence: Omaha. (Photograph in Album).

Carl G. Stoll

A banker since 1912, Carl G. Stoll has been chief of the receivership division of the Department of Trade and Commerce since 1929. He was born at Brooklyn, New York, December 25, 1885, the son of Charles and Elizabeth Nancy (Markert) Stoll. Charles Stoll was also born at Brooklyn, in 1860, and died at Joliet, Illinois, in 1897. He was an architect whose parents came to America in 1840 from Germany. Elizabeth Markert Stoll was born at Mokena, Illinois, March 27, 1860.

In 1892, the family moved to Nebraska, and in 1904 Carl G. Stoll was graduated from the Beatrice High School. Afterward he attended the University of Nebraska for a year and a half. He is a member of Delta Tau Delta, and while at the university served as its chaplain.

From 1907 to 1912 he served as stenographer for the Chicago, Burlington and Quincy Railroad, and from 1912 to 1920 was engaged in the banking business at York and Bloomfield. Appointed receiver for the Citizen's State Bank of Kimball in 1923, he also served as assistant secretary of the Guarantee Fund Commission at Lincoln from 1923-29. Since 1929 he has been chief of the receivership division of the Department of Trade and Commerce.

His marriage to Myrtle Eleanor Hudson was solemnized at Lincoln, on December 31, 1913. Mrs. Stoll was born at Lincoln, May 22, 1886. There is one daughter, Susan Elizabeth, born July 8, 1915. They are members

of the Westminster Presbyterian Church in which Mr. Stoll is an elder and deacon.

Mr. Stoll is a Mason, and a member of Lodge No. 26, Ancient Free and Accepted Masons at Beatrice. He is a member of The Nebraskana Society. Residence: Lincoln.

Henry Stolting

Henry Stolting was born January 15, 1864, in Germany, the son of Dick Stolting and Altic (Freekine) Stolting, both of whom were born in Germany, and died at Golden City, Missouri. His father was born November 6, 1828, and died May 8, 1910, and his mother on June 10, 1833, and died December 4, 1913.

On July 11, 1892, he was united in marriage to Emma Emily Louis at Levant, Thomas County, Kansas. She was born at Germany, July 10, 1876. To this union thirteen children were born: Frances Emily, March 30, 1893, who is married to James L. Swartz; Anthon Frank, October 3, 1894; Cora Mary, July 11, 1896; Louise Ann, June 19, 1898, who is married to Ray L. Thomas; Bertha Amelia, March 23, 1900; George Washington, February 22, 1902; Anna Amanda, March 23, 1904; Alice Leora, October 17, 1909; Irene Mae, December 22, 1912; John Henry, February 22, 1915; Louis LeRoy, March 12, 1917; Marie Mable, March 6, 1919; and Emma Jean, January 8, 1922.

Mr. Stolting is a leading farmer. A Socialist in politics, he is the author of the articles *Twenty-five Cent Wheat* and *Cheap Corn*.

He is affiliated with the German Lutheran Church at Endicott, and is former treasurer of the school district No. 7, in Jefferson County. He is also a member of the Nebraskana Society. Residence: Endicott.

Charles Cain Stone

Charles Cain Stone was born in Welland County, Canada, May 12, 1861, the son of James Heber and Maria (Watts) Stone. James Heber Stone was born in Canada, of German and Irish descent on October 10, 1832, and died at Johnson, Nebraska October 1 1906, Maria Watts Stone was a native of Scotland, and died in Marshall County, Iowa, in 1865.

Educated in the country schools of Nebraska, Charles C. Stone attended Peirce's Business College at Keokuk, Iowa, from 1883 to 1884. He married Isadore Deal at Chicago, June 3, 1909. Mrs. Stone was born in Ohio, November 4, 1871. There are two children, Ada, born September 1, 1911, and Lenora, born June 16, 1915.

For the past fifty years Mr. Stone has been a resident of Nebraska and has been extensively engaged in the real estate, loans and investment business. He is a Mason, and a Spiritualist. Residence: Auburn.

Franklin Dudley Stone

Franklin D. Stone, newspaper editor at Hartington, Cedar County, Nebraska, has lived in this state for the past 24 years. He was born at Neguanee, Marquette County, Michigan, April 22, 1870, the son of Dudley Gray and Mary (Dewey) Stone. His father, who was a merchant and banker, was born at Richmond, Massachusetts, and died at Neguance, Michigan; his ancestry was traced to the *Mayflower*. His mother, also of *Mayflower* ancestry, was born at Pittsfield, Massachusetts, and died at Hartington, Nebraska.

Mr. Stone was graduated from the Negaunee High School in 1890, and two years later entered Wabash College. He holds the following degrees: A. B. and A. M., Princeton University, 1900; B. D., Princeton Theological Seminary, 1900. He was a student at Wabash College, Crawfordsville, Indiana, 1892-96; he held membership in Whig Hall at Princeton. At this time Mr. Stone is editor and publisher of the *Hartington Herald*.

A Republican, he is past chairman of the Republican county central committee. He is a member of the National Editorial Association, the Nebraska Press Association, the Hartington Chamber of Commerce, the Nebraskana Society, and is affiliated with the First Congregational Church at Hartington. During the World War Mr. Stone served as a member of the Home Guard, acted as chairman of the four minute speakers, and later was a member of Company F, 134th Infantry, Nebraska National Guard. He is now a member of the Civil Legion. His favorite recreation is reading.

His marriage to Catherine Eva Judge, was solemnized at Estelline, Hamlin County, South Dakota. Mrs. Stone, who was formerly a teacher, was born at Shieldsville, Rice County, Minnesota, January 25, 1878, of British, French and Canadian ancestry. They have two children: Dudley Judge, born April 9, 1904; and Elizabeth Mary, born September 11, 1906. Residence: Hartington.

David Daniel Stonecypher

David D. Stonecypher was born at Omaha, on April 21, 1895. His father, Abraham Lincoln Stonecypher, a printer, publisher, and editor, was of German descent and was the fifth generation of this family to be born in America. He was born in Nebraska, September 17, 1861.

Mary (Rodabaugh) Stonecypher, his mother, was born in Indiana, March 20, 1861, of a Pennsylvania-Dutch family who emigrated to Nebraska in 1870. She was awarded the A. B. degree at York College, York, Nebraska.

Dr. Stonecypher received his early education in the public schools of Omaha, and in 1913, was graduated from the high school at Lincoln. Later he was a student at the University of Nebraska, where he was awarded his B. S. degree in 1919, and his M. D. degree, 1921. He was a student at the Chicago Polyclinic in 1925, and in 1928-29 studied at the Colorado Eye, Ear, Nose and Throat Post Graduate School. His fraternity is Phi Rho Sigma.

A resident of Nebraska all his life, he has engaged in the practice of medicine since his admission to the profession at Peru, on June 13, 1921. From 1921 to 1924, he was in general practice at Peru; was an eye, ear, nose, and throat specialist at Auburn, for one year; and since 1925, has been in practice in Nebraska City, where he specializes in treatment of diseases of the eye, ear, nose, and throat. At the present time he is physician and surgeon at the Nebraska School for the Blind, at Nebraska City.

His marriage to Imogene Poynter was solemnized at Nebraska City, August 26, 1922. Mrs. Stonecypher, who was born at Mound City, Holt County, Missouri, January 9, 1904, is of Scotch, Irish, and German descent. She is the grand niece of a former governor of Nebraska. There were two children: Robert Lincoln who died in 1924; and David Daniel, Junior, born October 10, 1926.

In the late war Dr. Stonecypher was a first class private, Mobile Hospital 100, and was later commissioned first lieutenant. He is a member of the American Legion and the Officers' Reserve Corps. He is a member of the Otoe County Medical Society, acting as its president in 1927; the Nebraska State Medical Association; the National Academy of Eye, Ear, Nose and Throat, and the Sioux Valley, as well as Omaha, and Council Bluffs societies of this organization. He is local chairman of the Salvation Army; is a member of the board of directors of the Chamber of Commerce; and is active in Boy Scout work and Red Cross affairs. In 1925 he served as secretary of the Parent-Teachers' Association at Auburn; and in 1927, was president of the Methodist Men's Club of the First Methodist Church at Nebraska City, with which he is affiliated. He has been a member of the Ancient Free and Accepted Masons since 1922.

Dr. Stonecypher's favorite sport is golf. Short story writing is his hobby. He is a Democrat. Residence: Nebraska City.

Dale Perry Stough

Dale Stough, son of Charlie Bion and Mina (Bige-

low) Stough, was born at Bigelow, Holt County, Missouri, June 29, 1888. His father, who was a native of Bryan, Ohio, born October 30, 1861, was a conductor on the Chicago Burlington & Quincy Railroad until his death at Creston, Iowa, on November 12, 1913. The first Stoughs, two brothers, came from Germany, in the early seventeen hundreds; one married a refugee German princess. The first settler in Dixon County was a Stough. Charlie Bion Stough's great aunt was the wife of General Sterling Price of Missouri, who was the head of the Confederate Armies in the west.

Mina Bigelow was born at Strawberry Point, Iowa, July 4, 1865, and died at Creston, Iowa, May 29, 1904. A school teacher prior to marriage, she was descended from the Bigelow and Sargent families, and was a fourth cousin of John G. Sargent, Attorney General in President Coolidge's cabinet.

Mr. Stough attended the public and high schools of Creston, and was graduated from the latter in June, 1905. He afterward studied law and literature at the University of Nebraska (1908-09) and received his LL. B. from Creighton University in 1911. At Creighton he was registrar and librarian in the College of law, and therefore not eligible to scholastic honors.

A Democrat, Mr. Stough has been active in public life. During 1911-13, he was secretary of the Custer County Democratic committee, and in 1913, secretary of the 6th district Congressional Committee. From 1914-17, he was secretary to Chief Justice of the Supreme Court, and from 1917-22 was district court reporter at Grand Island. During 1922-25, he served as reporter for the State Railway Commission and Pardon Board.

Since that time he has been engaged in the practice of law, and manager of the Shorthand Reporter Service and the United Service Bureaus at Lincoln. During 1911 to 1914, he practiced law at Broken Bow, with Hon. J. R. Dean, now of the Supreme Court.

Mr. Stough is the author of the *Condensed History of Nebraska* (1921); *History of the Supreme Court of Nebraska* (1907); and has compiled histories of the following counties: Hall, Hamilton, Clay, York, Morrill, Kimball and Dawes, during the years 1919-22. He is a member and former secretary (1927-29) of the Nebraska Writers Guild, and is a member of the Nebraska State and Lancaster County Bar Associations.

During the World War period he was active as a four minute man, in Liberty loan drives, etc., and is active at the present time with various welfare organizations, particularly the Salvation Army. He is affiliated with the Lincoln Knife and Fork Club and is secretary of the international. His historical memberships include The Nebraskana Society and the Nebraska State Historical Society. He is a member of Westminster Presbyterian Church, the Elks and the Lincoln Advertising Club.

On June 29, 1913, he was married to Cassie Mary Beeler, at Davenport. Mrs. Stough was born at Perry, Iowa, February 16, 1889, and is a musician. They have one daughter, Ida Mildred, born February 24, 1914, Class of 1931, Lincoln High School. Residence: Lincoln.

Adolph Albert Stoural

Born at Verdigre, Nebraska, August 15, 1901, Adolph Albert Stoural is the son of John Karl and Antonie Frances (Beran) Stoural. His father, who was born at Verdigre, December 11, 1876, served as supervisor of the Third District of Knox County from 1916 to 1920 and was a farmer until his retirement in 1930; he was successfully engaged in raising Poland China hogs from 1920 to 1930. Antonie Frances (Beran) Stoural was also born at Verdigre, on May 11, 1881.

Mr. Stoural was graduated from the Verdel High School in 1918 and was a student at Grand Island Business College from 1923 to 1924. He served as manager of the John Lueshen Lumber Company in 1928, and since

1928 has been treasurer and manager of the Adolph Stoural Lumber Company at Verdel, Nebraska. He is a member of the Red Cross, the Catholic Workman Lodge, and the Assumption Catholic Church of Lynch, Nebraska. Mr. Stoural's favorite sports are baseball, hunting and fishing.

He was married to Rose Mary Vlcan at Lynch, November 13, 1928. Mrs. Stoural was born at Monowi, Nebraska, March 17, 1904. They have one child, Beta, born November 10, 1929. A Democrat, Mr. Stoural served as township assessor for two years, was a member of the board of trustees of Verdell for two years, and has been chairman of the latter board and director in the local school board since 1930. Residence: Verdel.

Richard Forbes Stout

Richard F. Stout was born at Lincoln, Nebraska, April 15, 1892, the son of Oscar Van Pelt and Edith (Forbes) Stout. His father was born in New Jersey in 1865, and for many years was dean of the College of Engineering at the University of Nebraska; he was major of engineers in the World War. He is of Irish and Pennsylvania Dutch descent; his grandfather was a direct descendant of Penelope Stout.

Edith (Forbes) Stout was born at Hillsdale, Michigan, in 1870. Her father, John A. Forbes, whose ancestry was Scotch, served as an officer in the Michigan Regiment of the Union Army during the Civil War.

Mr. Stout received his elementary education in the public schools of Lincoln; was graduated from the Lincoln High School; and in 1913 was graduated from the University of Nebraska, where he held membership in Phi Gamma Delta and Iron Sphinx. He was formerly a member of the law firms Reese, Reese & Stout, and Reese & Stout, and Stout & Baird. He was admitted to the bar at Lincoln, July, 1913.

A Republican, he was a member of the Nebraska house of representatives in 1919; was a member of the State central committee of the Republican party; served as secretary of the Lancaster County Republican central committee, 1920-22; and was chairman of the latter organization, 1922-30. He was assistant attorney general from 1923 to 1929.

His marriage to Ethel Edna Cornell was solemnized at Lincoln, June 17, 1915. Mrs. Stout was born in Chicago, May 29, 1891. During the World War Mr. Stout served as a private in the United States Army. Since 1927 he has been Major Judge Advocate General of the Nebraska National Guard, and is a member of the Officers Reserve Corp with the same rank. He holds membership in the Reserve Officers Association.

He is a member of the Lancaster County Bar Association, and was formerly vice president of the Nebraska State Bar Association, 1927-9. His social clubs are: Lincoln Country Club; and the Lincoln University Club of which he is a director. He was president of the latter organization in 1926. His sports include golfing and fishing. He is a member of the Scottish Rite and Shrine and of Lodge Number 19, Ancient Free and Accepted Masons. He is affiliated with the Plymouth Congregational Church of Lincoln. Residence: Lincoln.

Robert Irving Stout

Born at Hutchinson, Kansas, August 7, 1891, Robert Irving Stout has been a resident of Nebraska thirty-six years. He is the son of John Franklin and Lida Manary (Stitt) Stout, the former a native of Washington, Ohio, born July 12, 1861. John Franklin Stout was a lawyer whose ancestors, Dutch and English settlers, came to America in 1640. He died at Omaha, June 24, 1927. Lida, wife of John Franklin, was born in Cambridge, Ohio, September 12, 1863, and died at Omaha, September 15, 1917.

Robert Irving Stout attended Park School and Central High School, at Omaha, and the McKenzie School

at Dobbs Ferry, New York, from which he was graduated in 1909. He attended Amherst College, receiving his A. B. in 1913. While there he participated in junior and senior debating, was active in dramatics three years and was class secretary four years. He is a member of Chi Psi.

Since leaving school Mr. Stout has been engaged in banking, and for some time was associated with the Omaha National Bank, The National Bank of Commerce in New York. He is now president and director of the First National Bank of Tekamah, Nebraska. A Republican, he was alternate delegate to the Republican national convention of 1920, and delegate from the 3rd Nebraska district at the Republican National Convention of 1924.

On September 30, 1919, Mr. Stout was united in marriage to Anna Louise Knoedler at Chicago. Mrs. Stout, born at Augusta, Kentucky, October 27, 1892, is descended from the Buckners of Virginia. They have one daughter, Barbara, born September 11, 1920.

Mr. Stout has filled various civic and educational offices, and is president of the Tekamah Chamber of Commerce 1930-31, 1931-32; president of the Tekamah Library Board; member of the state executive committee of the Young Men's Christian Association, and president of the First Nebraska Regional Clearing House Association. He is a 32nd degree Mason and Knight Templar, member of the Red Cross and the Nebraskana Society. His favorite sport is golf, and his clubs are the Omaha Club, and the Omaha Country Club. His hobby is books. Residence: Tekamah.

Carl Strahle

Carl Strahle was born January 26, 1863, the son of Frederick and Christine (Wagner) Strahle. He has lived in Nebraska for the past 46 years, and until recently was a jeweler and watchmaker at Stanton, Nebraska. His father was born in Germany, in 1831, and died at Wurttemberg, Germany, 1884; he was a watchmaker. His mother was born in Germany, in 1842, and died there in 1901.

Mr. Strahle was graduated from high school in Germany, April, 1877. For 35 years he operated a jewelry store at Stanton. He has now retired to his 40 acre farm adjoining Stanton, where he is raising chickens. Politically, he is an independent; he was unsuccessful candidate for sheriff in 1895.

He was married at Fremont, Dodge County, Nebraska, August 16, 1885. Mrs. Strahle was born in Germany, 1857. They have four children: Carl, born January, 1886, who married Elinor Osler; Clara, born March, 1887, who married Richard Melcher; Elsie, born November, 1888, who married Harold Hansen; and Richard, born May, 1890, who married Muriel Rees.

Mr. Strahle was formerly a member of the Reform Lutheran Church. He is a member of Northern Light Lodge Number 41 of the Masons, and his hobbies are reading, mechanics, and electricity. He holds membership in the Nebraskana Society. Residence: Stanton.

Fred Jolly Strain

On July 25, 1868, at Chester, Indiana, Fred J. Strain, the son of David Fletcher and Mary Elma (Taylor) Strain, was born. His father was born in Highland County, Ohio, March 22, 1845, and died at Clifton, Colorado, November 20, 1925. In earlier life he was a contractor and builder and later was postmaster of Palisade, Colorado. He served with the 2nd Ohio Cavalry and the 9th Indiana Infantry in the Civil War, from 1863 to 1865. His ancestors came from Ireland, migrating to North Carolina in early days. Mary Elma Strain was born at Cedarville, Ohio, October 19, 1845, and died at Clifton, Colorado, September 25, 1924. She was an active club worker and teacher.

Educated in the public and high schools of Xenia, Illinois, he was graduated from the latter in 1884. His marriage to Bertha Marie Jarmin took place at Corpus, Christi, Texas, August 13, 1891. Her ancestors were Quakers, and came from England, in 1632. They had three children: Pearle, born June 18, 1892, who is married to O. D. Cator; Hazel, born July 10, 1897, who is married to D. W. McFadden; and Elma, born November 29, 1899, who died May 9, 1906.

Mr. Strain has lived in Shelby since August 19, 1899. During his boyhood he worked in a store between school terms. He entered the furniture and undertaking business May 20, 1906, and was granted his embalmer's license January 5, 1910, by the State of Nebraska. He was a farmer from 1887 to 1897, and from 1900 to 1905, and has been police magistrate since May, 1919.

Mr. Strain was a private in Company C, First Arkansas Volunteer Infantry in 1898, and in Schafter's Army in the Cuban Campaign in the Spanish-American War. He was on the local war board from 1917 and 1918, and was first lieutenant in the Shelby Home Guard Company from May 13, 1918, to May 13, 1919. he is a member of the United Spanish War Veterans, Nebraska department.

Affiliated with the Castle Memorial Church, he also holds membership in the Funeral Directors' Association, the Red Cross, Masonic Lodge No. 161 of Shelby, and The Nebraskana Society.

Mr. Strain erected the store and post office building at Shelby, in 1912, and the funeral home in 1929. Reading war history and traveling are his hobbies. Residence: Shelby.

Oscar Carl Strand

Born in Sweden, July 2, 1865, Oscar Carl Strand is the son of Swan Peter and Sophia Strand. He attended school in Sweden seven years, and three months in this country.

His father was born in Sweden, in 1828, and died at Saronville, Nebraska, in 1909. A farmer, he came to America in 1869, and remained for six years, went back to Sweden, and returned to America in 1884. Sophia Strand was born in Sweden, in 1824, and died at Saronville, February, 1911. She came to America with Mr. Strand in 1884.

Mr. Strand entered the lumber business in 1898, and is now president of the Aspregren & Strand Lumber Company, and is vice president of the Citizens State Bank of Polk, Nebraska.

On October 4, 1900, his marriage to Susanna Alfrieda Fried was solemnized at Lincoln, Nebraska. Mrs. Strand is a native of Sweden, born in March, 1871. Seven children were born to them: Paul, born August 31, 1901, who attended business college and is manager of the Strand Lumber Company at Polk; Harold, born July 7, 1903, who is a stock feeder; Melvin, born March 19, 1905, who died December 26, 1923; Warren, born October 19, 1907, who attended the State University, and is associated with the Citizens State Bank; Hilding, born May 7, 1909, who is connected with the Strand Lumber Company; Kenneth, born August 27, 1911, also connected with the lumber company; and Merrill, born July 27, 1916.

His religious affiliation is with the Methodist Church of Polk. A Democrat, he was a member of the city council fourteen years, was mayor for eight years, and has served on the local school board for ten years. He is a member of the Nebraskana Society. Residence: Polk. (Photograph in Album).

James Stuart Stringfellow

James Stuart Stringfellow was born at Jackson, Ohio, September 16, 1849, and for over 48 years has been a resi-

dent of Antelope County, Nebraska. His father, John Stringfellow, who was a farmer, was born at Lancashire, England, and died at Gallipoh, Ohio, September 8, 1884; he was the keeper in a glass factory in Pittsburg for several years. His mother, Hannah (Sperd) Stringfellow, whose family were natives of England, died at Jackson, Ohio, in August, 1876.

Mr. Stringfellow was brakeman on the railroad in Ohio, was a farmer for 30 years, and in 1901 moved to Oakdale and entered the hardware and implement business. He is now retired. He is chairman of the board of directors of the First National Bank of Oakdale, is a member of the Red Cross and Young Men's Christian Association, and is affiliated with the First Methodist Episcopal Church of Oakdale. He is a member of the Odd Fellows and Rebekah Lodge. His favorite sport is baseball.

On January 1, 1873, he was married to Eliza Ann Hughes at Centre Point, Ohio; she was born at Centre Point, October 7, 1851, and died at Oakdale, October 2, 1912. Their children are: Virginia Alice, born March 19, 1874, who married Everett O. Cunningham; Charles Everett, born August 19,1875, who married Ida Suell; William F., born August 7, who married Marie Theilen, and who died March 22, 1926; John Erving, born July 25, 1879, who married Ida Payne; Laura Ellen, born February 5, 1881, who married Charles Thomas; Nanette Viola, born January 12, 1883, who married Charles Wiest; Austin James, born April 20, 1885, who married Gladys Gano; LeRoy Walter, born June 21, 1887, who married Nellie Admire; Clarence DeWitt, born October 12, 1889, who married Nellie Kiman; Edna Blanch, born July 17, 1892, who married Walter H. Rose; and Lenora Murrel, born August 13, 1895 who died April 14, 1896.

Mr. Stringfellow married Esther R. Beers at Petersburg, Nebraska, July 7, 1926. She was postmistress and a teacher in the public schools before her marriage. Residence: Oakdale.

Leonard Stromberg

Leonard Stromberg, clergyman and author, was born in Arboga, Sweden, July 11, 1871, son of Per August and Sofia Adolfina (Mellander) Stromberg. His father was born in Sweden, March 9, 1839, and died there May 10, 1893. He was of an old and distinguished family. His wife, Sofia, was born in Sweden, November 23, 1833. She died May 16, 1887; her family was originally German, but had settled in Sweden several generations before her birth.

Educated in the elementary schools of Arboga, Sweden, Mr. Stromberg was graduated in 1884, and thereafter had private instruction. He was graduated from the Theological Seminary of Uppsala, Sweden, in 1894, and received the degree of Doctor of Divinity from Nebraska Wesleyan University in 1919. He has been a resident of Nebraska in all, twenty-nine years, and at the present time is pastor of the Swedish Methodist Church at Oakland. He is a member of the Central Northwest Conference of the Methodist Episcopal Church, president of the Oakland County Ministerial Association, and a member of the Burt County Ministerial Association.

Dr. Stromberg is the author of nearly fifty novels and hundreds of short stories and poems, most of which are written in Swedish; his first book was published in 1892. He is the editor of the local church paper the *West Side Herald,* and assistant editor of the *Sandebudet.*

His marriage to Mabel Evelyn Paulson was solemnized at Genoa, Nebraska, April 17, 1900. Mrs. Stromberg, who was born in Geneva, Illinois, April 22, 1879, is descended from an old family of farmers in Skane, Sweden. There are three sons: Edmund, born March 25, 1902; Eugene, born August 9, 1909; and Eleroy, born June 16, 1911, who are in Nebraska Wesleyan University, Eugene graduating in 1931, and one daughter, Bernice, born May 29, 1915, who attends high school.

Dr. Stromberg is a life member of the Red Cross, a

Mason and a member of the Swedish Historical Society, the Burt County and Nebraska State Historical Societies, the American Sons and Daughters of Sweden, and the Parent-Teachers' Association. His hobby is writing. Residence: Oakland. (Photograph in Album).

Allen Alfred Strong

Allen Alfred Strong, postmaster and prominent Republican, was born at Canadice Town, New York, May 9, 1884, the son of William Henry and Emma Cretta (McFarland) Strong.

The father, born at Victor, New York, April 30, 1845, was a farmer and ranchman whose grandparents came from Ireland about 1800. He died at Gordon, January 15, 1902. His wife, Emma, was born at Canandaigua, New York, May 27, 1850, and died at Gordon, June 4, 1930. Her grandparents also came from Ireland about 1800.

Mr. Strong was educated in school district number 90, of Sheridan County, graduating in 1899. He was graduated from high school at Gordon in 1902, and from that time until 1904 was a school teacher. From 1904 until 1909 he was a bookkeeper. He then entered the mercantile business continuing until 1922, when he was appointed postmaster.

Mr. Strong has held many political and public offices including, member of the city council at Gordon, 1916, 1917; member of the board of education at Gordon, February 1919-1922 (president one year); police judge, Gordon, 1918-1922; postmaster, Clinton, 1909-1910. Mr. Strong will retire as postmaster soon and has filed as Republican nominee for state representative from the 93rd district.

His marriage to Alyce Mary Leverenz was solemnized at Grand Island, Nebraska, September 5, 1916. She was born at Antigo, Wisconsin, June 7, 1890, and is a music teacher. Her father was born in Wisconsin of German descent, and her mother in Kansas of Bohemian descent. Mr. and Mrs. Strong had five children, four of whom are living, Ardath Marie, born January 16, 1918; Rex LeRoy, born June 19, 1920; Leland Dean, born December 8, 1921; and Allen Elwood, born September 24, 1926. An infant boy, born March 27, 1923, died the same day.

During 1917 and 1918, Mr. Strong was a member of the legal advisory board, and chairman of war saving societies in Sheridan County. Baptized into the Baptist Church at the age of 11, he now attends the Methodist Episcopal Church. For many years he has been a member of the Red Cross. He is a member of the Odd Fellows (Encampment branch), Kolo Sanctorum, and the Ancieint Free and Accepted Masons. Recently he was elected to life membership in The Nebraskana Society. His hobbies are Indian curios, gardening, and fishing.

Mrs. Strong is the daughter of John and Mary (Benish) Leverenz. Mrs. Strong is a prominent teacher of piano. She is a member of the Rebekah, (past noble grand and past district president). She is also a member of the home and educational department of the Woman's Club. Residence: Gordon.

Maurice Dickinson Strong

Maurice Dickinson Strong, who was born at Muncy Valley, Pennsylvania, November 9, 1881, is the son of Nehemiah Smith Strong and Charlotte Augusta (Mead) Strong. His father, a tanner, was born at Sullivan, New York, in 1838, and died at Wilcox, Nebraska, September 21, 1898. His mother, a teacher, was born at Liberty, New York, in 1844, and died at Williamsport, Pennsylvania, May 1, 1920.

Dr. Strong was graduated from the Wilcox High School, and later was a student at Franklin Academy, Franklin, Nebraska. He was a student at Kansas City Veterinary College, and since 1904 has been a farmer,

cattle feeder, and veterinarian. He has been a member of the local school board for three years serving as president for one year, and for six years has served as councilman at Stromsburg. He is a member of the Commercial Club at Stromsburg, and is affiliated with the Methodist Church.

He married Grace Fisher at Falls City, Nebraska, April 25, 1905. Mrs. Strong was born at Christenson, Illinois, in May, 1880, and died at Stromsburg, Nebraska in 1918. The following children were born to them: Helen, June 4, 1906, who married George Inness; Carol, March 24, 1908; Maurice, April 2, 1912; and Wallace, April 5, 1918.

Mr. Strong was married to Lois Browning Standing, April 20, 1919. She is the daughter of George Washington and Addie (French) Standing of York County. She was born in York County, April 2, 1892, and is eligible to the Daughters of the American Revolution. She served as Red Cross nurse at Camp Dodge, Iowa, and Camp Merritt, New Jersey, and is a former member of the American Legion. Their two children are Kenneth, born September 20, 1923; and Marilyn, born July 17, 1926. Residence: Stromsburg.

Roy Mead Strong

Born at Jeffersonville, New York, March 11, 1877, Roy Mead Strong is the son of Nehemiah Smith and Charlotte Adgate (Mead) Strong. His father, who was foreman for the Union Tanning Company, was a soldier with General Grant during the Civil War with the first New York Mounted Rifles. He died at Wilcox, Nebraska, September 21, 1898.

Mr. Strong attended the public school at Williamsport, Pennsylvania, finished a college preparatory course at Dickinson Preparatory School in 1897, and attended Dickinson College, Carlisle, Pennsylvania, the following year, where he held membership in Sigma Alpha Epsilon fraternity. Upon his arrival in Wilcox in 1898 he started farming south of Wilcox for a period of nine years, when he moved into town. He is a dealer in livestock, a farmer and stock feeder, and is the originator and proprietor of the Holdrege Sales Pavilion and Stock Yards, Incorporated at Holdrege. He is one of the largest shippers and feeders of livestock in the county.

He has served on the Wilcox city council for two terms, is a member of the Young Men's Christian Association, and holds membership in the Methodist Church. His hobby is reading. Of his marriage to Maude Jennie Sargent in May, 1903, two children were born, Charlotte, September 6, 1905, who married Clive Lantz; and Louise, November 9, 1906, who married Carl Hinrichs. Mrs. Strong died at Wilcox, Nebraska, in November, 1928.

On April 21, 1930, Mr. Strong married Esther Molly Olson at Wilcox, Nebraska. They have one son, Joseph Mead, born March 7, 1931. Esther Molly Olson, daughter of Olof and Bertha (Johnson) Olson, was born September 14, 1892, at Axtell, Nebraska. Before her marriage she was a graduate nurse. Residence: Wilcox.

Ralph William Strotheide

Ralph William Strotheide, hardware merchant and farmer, has lived in Nebraska all his life. He is the son of William Frederick and Louisa A. Strotheide.

His father was born in Germany, November 21, 1853, and came to the United States in 1860. He was a farmer until his death at Hay Springs, on February 5, 1931. His wife, Louisa, was born in Minden, Germany, in 1856. She is still living.

Mr. Strotheide attended rural school and the Agriculture College at Lincoln. He has been owner and manager of the Hay Springs Hardware Company for 16 years, is an extensive land owner and director of the Northwestern State Bank. He is a Republican.

On August 22, 1927, he was married to Nan Viola

Heaton at Peters, Nebraska. She was born at Moomaw, Nebraska, February 5, 1893, and at the time of her marriage was assistant cashier of the Northwestern State Bank. There are two children, Donald Gene, born August 9, 1928; and Ralph William, born August 5, 1929.

Mr. Strotheide is a member of the Red Cross, the Hay Springs Commercial Club, the Odd Fellows, the Masons, and Order of Eastern Star. Residence: Hay Springs.

Carl Kennedy Struble

Born at Reinbeck, Grundy County, Iowa, Carl Kennedy Struble has been a resident of Nebraska for more than 37 years. He is the son of Riley and Alice A. (Kennedy) Struble, the former born in Trumbull County, Ohio, August 26, 1844. Riley Struble, a farmer, enlisted in the Civil War at the age of 18 with Company B, 26th Iowa Volunteer Infantry, and was mustered out in 1865. He participated in the Siege of Vicksburg and Sherman's March to the sea. He was of Dutch descent, the first member of the family, Adrian Struble having settled in New Jersey. Riley Struble died at Maquoketa, Iowa, January 1, 1911.

Alice Kennedy Struble was born in Beaver, Pennsylvania, in 1847, and died January 11, 1911. Before her marriage she was a teacher. Her ancestry was Irish. Carl K. Struble attended the rural schools of Iowa and Nebraska, and York High School. He attended York College 1896-99, and received his D. O. from the S. S. Still College of Osteopathy in June, 1902. In June, 1919, he received his M. D. from the Kansas City University of Physicians and Surgeons, and in 1920 took post graduate work at Tulane University, and in 1921 at the Chicago Eye, Ear, Nose and Throat Hospital.

From 1902 to 1923, he practiced at Hastings, removing on the latter date to Fremont. He began the practice of eye, ear, nose and throat exclusively in 1920, and has confined his work to that branch since then. He is a member of the National Osteopathic and American Osteopathic Associations, the American Society of Opthalmology and Oto-laryngology, etc. On April 17, 1898, he enlisted in Company A, 1st Nebraska Volunteer Infantry, and served in the Philippines during the Spanish-American War and the Philippine Insurrection. During the World War he was on the Red Cross board and active in loan drives. He is a member of the United Spanish War Veterans and the Veterans of Foreign Wars. A member of the Hastings Board of Education for some time, he served as its president four years. He is a member of the board of the local Red Cross and Salvation Army, and is a member of the Retail Merchants Association, Kiwanis Club, Boy Scouts of America (board of directors), the Nebraskana Society, and the Young Men's Christian Association. He enjoys hunting, fishing, hiking and golf.

On June 24, 1903, he was married to Evelyn May Gilbert at Waco, Nebraska. Mrs. Struble was born at Waco, December 14, 1881, and is of English and Irish descent. Among her ancestors is Bishop Hugh Latimer, martyr (1490), who had an M. A. from Cambridge, and is buried in the public square at Oxford. There are five children: Dorothy, born April 26, 1905, who received her A. B. from the University of Nebraska, and is a member of Kappa Alpha Theta. Gilbert, born November 23, 1907, married Marion Margaret Coleman and received his B. S. and M. D. from the University of Nebraska. He is now a first lieutenant in the Medical Corps. Hazel, born July 28, 1909, is a member of Kappa Alpha Theta, and received her B. A. from Nebraska, in 1930. Helen, her twin sister, received her B. S. in 1930, and is a Phi Beta Kappa at Nebraska. Elizabeth, the youngest, was born June 10, 1913. She is a junior at the University of Nebraska, and is also a member of the Kappa Alpha Theta sorority. Residence: Fremont. (Photograph in Album).

Herman Strumpler

Born in Strohen, Germany, May 14, 1869, Herman Strumpler has been a resident of Nebraska for the past forty years. He is the son of Christ and Sophia (Summan) Strumpler, both natives of Strohen, the latter born November 15, 1845. Christ Strumpler died on May 18, 1909 and his wife on November 28, 1926.

During his entire residence in Thayer County Herman Strumpler has been a landowner and farmer, and is at the present time the owner of an extensive acreage. He was married to Clara Marie Thieme at Hebron, on May 18, 1893, and to them were born eight children, seven of whom are living.

Amelia, born November 15, 1895, married Walter Werner; Martin, born October 21, 1894, married Katherine Saberhorn; Matilda, born March 4, 1896, married Adolph Thurman; Johanna, born August 12, 1897, married Herman Hebbenhorst; Herman, born May 18, 1899, married Dorinda Bickoff; Emma, born September 15, 1900, married Rudolph Bartels, and died October 18, 1928; Hilda, born August 4, 1907, married Emil Malchow; and Edwin, born February 26, 1911, married Adalia Kellner.

Mrs. Strumpler was born at Decatur, Indiana, January 1, 1871, and came to Nebraska in her youth. They attend the American Lutheran Church, and Mr. Strumpler is a member of the Nebraskana Society. Residence: Hebron.

Herman John Struve

Herman John Struve, merchant and manufacturer, was born at Olean, Indiana, March 8, 1857, son of Wilhelm and Maria Marguretha (Fisse) Struve. The father and mother were natives of Hanover, Germany.

On November 28, 1880, Mr. Struve was married to Mathilda Nehrig at Friedensau, Nebraska. She was born at Lafayette, Indiana, and died at Deshler, Nebraska.

Mr. Struve came to Nebraska fifty-five years ago, and engaged in the general merchandising, manufacturing and banking business all of his life. At the time of his death he was president of the Deshler Broom Factory and vice president of the National Lutheran Educational Association of the United States.

He was a member of St. Peters Lutheran Church, and the Commercial Club.

William Struve

William Struve, prominent lumber dealer at Deshler, Thayer County, Nebraska, has lived in this state for the past 52 years. He was born at New Orleans, Louisiana, October 16, 1850, the son of William and Margaret (Fisse) Struve. His father, who was a farmer, was born at Hanover, Germany, came to America in 1850, and died in Ripley County. His mother was born at Hanover, came to this country with her husband, and died at Deshler, Thayer County, Nebraska.

Mr. Struve is affiliated with the Freidensay Lutheran Church at Deshler, and for many years has been a leader in community affairs at Deshler. He holds membership in the Red Cross, is a member of the Democratic party, and is a member of the Red Cross. His favorite recreations are croquet and cards.

His marriage to Emilie Hellmer was solemnized at Deshler. They have five children: William, Jr.; John; Anna; Albery; and Walter. Residence: Deshler.

Hird Stryker

Hird Stryker, son of the late Arthur Franklin Stryker, was born at Omaha, April 5, 1892. His father, who was born at Galena, Illinois, October 2, 1868, was of English and Dutch descent. He came to Nebraska when a young man, and was one of the organizers and prominent in the development of the Omaha livestock market. He was secretary of the Omaha Live Stock Exchange for twenty-one years, and during the World War served as a dollar a year man for the government. He married Barbara

HIRD STRYKER

Heyn Studio—Omaha

Hird, born at Hazel Green, Wisconsin, in 1869. Mrs. Stryker is of English descent, and is active in civic and church work.

Hird Stryker was graduated from South High School in 1910; he attended the University of Nebraska from 1911-13, and received a Ph. B. from the University of Chicago in 1914. He studied at Harvard Law School during the year of 1915, and returning to the University of Chicago, was awarded his J. D. in 1916. During 1911-12 and 1912-13 he was active in basketball at the University of Nebraska. He is a member of Phi Kappa Psi, Phi Delta Phi and Theta Nu Epsilon.

Since his admission to the bar of Nebraska in 1916 he has been associated with and a member of the law firm of Crofoot, Fraser, Connally & Stryker. On January 20, 1918 he was married to Ruth Estey Baume, at Galena, Illinois. Mrs. Stryker was born at Galena, April 15, 1894, and is of English descent. They have three children, Hird, Jr., born December 11, 1918; James Baume, born October 30, 1924, and Barbara Ruth, born February 19, 1928.

From May, 1917, until January, 1919, he served as captain of the 338th Field Artillery, and saw service in France. He was commander of the Omaha Post of the American Legion in 1923, that post being the largest in the world.

He is a member of the First Methodist Episcopal Church, Mason, and a Republican. His membership in professional organizations includes the Omaha-Douglas County Bar Association, the Nebraska State Bar Association and the American Bar Association. He is a member of the board of regents of the Municipal University of Omaha. He is fond of golf, and his clubs are the Omaha, and the Omaha Field Club. Residence: Omaha. (Photograph on Page 1157).

Dale K. Stuart

A leading professional man at Stuart, Nebraska, is Dale K. Stuart, who has been engaged in the practice of dentistry there since 1916. He was born at Springview, Nebraska, November 24, 1894, the son of David M. and Jennie (Boardman) Stuart, the former a business man and rancher who was born in Vermont, October 15, 1853. His mother, whose ancestry was Scotch and English, was born in Stark County, Illinois, March 3, 1856.

Dr. Stuart was graduated from the Stuart High School in 1913 and in 1916 received the degree Doctor of Dental Surgery at the University of Nebraska where he was a member of Xi Phi Psi. He is local committeeman for the Republican party at Stuart, is past master of the Masons, and is serving as vice president of the Parent Teachers Association there. He is treasurer of the school board, is chairman of the Village Board, is acting as vice president of the local Commercial Club. He holds membership in the American Dental Association, the Northern Nebraska Study Club, and the Red Cross. His social clubs are the Stuart Golf Club of which he is president, the Atkinson Golf Club, and the Rod and Gun Club. His hobby is entomology, and his sports are hunting and fishing.

He served as adjutant of the American Legion in 1920, was commander in 1921, and since 1922 has been finance officer of that organization. He served in the Dental Corps during the World War as first lieutenant.

On February 28, 1920, his marriage to Frances Emily Wefso was solemnized at Atkinson. Mrs. Stuart, whose ancestry is German, was born at Stuart, August 12, 1896. They have three children: Olline Mae, born December 12, 1921; Mary Ellen, born August 26, 1923; and Dale Brook, born January 31, 1931. Residence: Stuart.

Chresten Andersen Stub

Chresten A. Stub, educator and editor of Washington County, Nebraska, was born at Elk Horn, Iowa, February 26, 1891, the son of Jens and Maren Laurine (Kristensen) Anderson. His father, who was born at Stubberup, Denmark, and died at Elk Horn, October 4, 1897, was a farmer. His mother, who was born at Dolbey, Denmark, August 11, 1858, is still living. Her father served as a member of the first Danish district, signed the Danish constitution of 1848, and Dannebrogsmand, an order of merit.

Mr. Stub was graduated from the Elk Horn Academy in 1913, and in 1921 received the Bachelor of Arts degree at the University of Minnesota. He was publisher of the Nordic Press, serving as treasurer and manager, 1927-29, was editor of *Ungdom,* 1925-29, and was editor of *Ugebladet,* 1927-29. He has held the following educational positions: principal of the Elk Horn High School, 1921-23; teacher in Dana College, Blair, Nebraska, 1923-24; teacher in Dana College, (head of the department of Danish and the department of mathematics), since 1930. From 1915 to 1917, and from 1924 to 1927 he was a teacher in Grand View College, Des Moines, Iowa.

He is a member of the American Sociological Society, Sociology Discussion Club at the University of Minnesota, the Saturday Luncheon Club of Minneapolis, and the Nebraskana Society. He served as secretary of the D. S. U., 1915-21, and as district president of this organization, 1925-6. His hobby is reading.

During the World War Mr. Stub served in the air service, 1917-18. He was married to Anna Juhl at Minneapolis, April 3, 1921. Mrs. Stub was born at Hammerum, Denmark, November 16, 1888. To their marriage two children were born: Holger Richard, December 2, 1923; and Helen Elizabeth, May 26, 1925. Residence: Blair.

Roy Franklin Stuckey

A leading banker of Dawson County, Nebraska, is Roy Franklin Stuckey, who has lived at Lexington all his life. He was born August 18, 1873, the son of Henry Clay and Ida (Boblits) Stuckey, the former a stockman who was born at Bedford, Pennsylvania, August 2, 1844, of French and Dutch ancestry. His mother was born at Emmaville, Pennsylvania, February 7, 1853, of German parentage.

Mr. Stuckey attended rural schools in Dawson County and was a student at Hastings College during 1891-92. He is president of the Lexington State Bank, is president of the Dawson County Irrigation Ditch Association, and holds ranching interests in Dawson County.

He is a member of the Red Cross, the Chamber of Commerce, and the Kiwanis Club of Lexington, and served eight years on the school board at Lexington and on the First Library Commission which erected the Carnegie Library. He is affiliated with the First Presbyterian Church, holds membership in the Country Club and the Young Men's Christian Association, and is a member of The Nebraskana Society. His hobby is reading.

On June 18, 1901, he married Grace Winona Kennedy at Lexington. Mrs. Stuckey, who was a teacher before her marriage, was born of Scotch-Irish parentage at Osceola, Iowa, November 30, 1872. The following children were born to this marriage: Harold, December 9, 1904, who died June 21, 1918; Paul, October 11, 1906, who married Grace Pressley, who is manager of the Dawson County Irrigation Ditch Association, and Lyman, May 26, 1912, who is employed in the Lexington State Bank. Residence: Lexington.

Paul Frederick Stuefer

A resident of Nebraska sixty-eight years, Paul Frederick Stuefer was born at Watertown, Wisconsin, February 3, 1860, son of Martin and Johanna (Schweifel) Steufer. His father, who was born in Germany, in 1818, came to America and became a United States citizen in 1849. A merchant for some years in Wisconsin, he later came to Nebraska, where he was elected on the Republican ticket as state representative in 1865. His wife, Johanna, was born in Germany in 1819, and died at West Point, in 1878. Her husband survived her for twenty years, and died at West Point in 1898.

Paul Frederick Stuefer attended rural schools and has been a farmer since maturity. He was married to Julia Clara Wostoupal, at West Point, Nebraska. Mrs. Stuefer was born at Chicago, February 14, 1875. There were four children born to this union: Ruth, who died in 1910; Blanche, who married C. H. Kamrath, and Adah and Lulu.

Mr. Stuefer is a Republican and active in local politics. He is a member of St. Paul's Lutheran Church. His hobby is horses. Residence: West Point.

Frederick Ames Stuff

Frederick A. Stuff, noted educator and clergyman of Nebraska, has been a resident of this state for the past 45 years, and since 1894, has been prominent in religious and educational fields. He was born at Dixon, Illinois, June 18, 1865, the son of George Lynch Spencer and Elizabeth Naomi (Woodruff) Stuff. His father, who was born at Cincinnati, Ohio, April 21, 1822, was a clergyman. He served as chaplain of the 42nd regiment of the Illinois Volunteers with the rank of captain of cavalry, in the Civil War. His Dutch colonial and Revolutionary ancestors came to America in 1750; their names are on the muster rolls of Pennsylvania of the American Revolution. He died at Elgin, Illinois, May 7, 1893.

His mother, who was born at Burlington, Vermont, August 4, 1838, was a teacher in the public schools of Buffalo, New York, and Rockton, Illinois. Her ancestors came to Massachusetts in 1630, where the descendants served in the Indian wars and the Revolution. She died at Poplar Grove, Illinois, January 13, 1875.

Professor Stuff received his elementary education in the public schools of Illinois, and is 1893 was graduated from Nebraska Wesleyan University with the degree A. B. In 1900 he was awarded his A. M. degree at the University of Nebraska. The honorary degree, Litt. D O., was granted him in 1911 by Nebraska Wesleyan University. He was a student during the summer session at the University of Chicago, 1902, and Harvard University, 1903. He was elected to Phi Kappa Phi.

Principal of Nebraska Wesleyan Academy, 1894-96; he was pastor of Emmanuel Methodist Episcopal Church at Lincoln, 1896-98; professor of English, serving as chairman of the department of English at Nebraska Wesleyan University, 1898-1902; adjunct professor, assistant professor, and later associate professor of English at the University of Nebraska, 1902-1911; and in 1911 he was advanced to the rank of professor of English at the University of Nebraska. He was chaplain of the Hospital for the Insane at Lincoln, 1903-24. At the present time he is professor of English at the University of Nebraska. Since 1922, he has been a member of the board of trustees of Bryan Memorial Hospital at Lincoln.

Professor Stuff is the author of: *Pedagogy of College English; Proceedings of the Thirty-third Annual Meeting of the Nebraska State Teachers' Association,* (1899); *Induration of the Sensibility in Teaching Literature,* published in *The Monthly Review,* September, 1914, at Calcutta, India; *Sonnets to the Memory of James Thomas Lees,* published in the Nebraska *State Journal,* June, 1926; *Epic Quality in Neihardt's Songs of the Indian Wars; Present Day American Literature,* April, 1928; Editor of *Nebraska Studies in Instruction in English,* 1922-25.

His marriage to Minnie Julia Moore was solemnized at Lincoln, September 8, 1890. Mrs. Stuff was born at Rushville, Schuyler County, Illinois, August 23, 1866. Her Dutch ancestors came to America and settled in New York in 1624; her English colonial ancestors fought in the Revolution. Four children were born to this union: Freda Naomi, born January 30, 1893; Emily Marguerite, born March 27, 1897, who died March 28, 1897; Grace Hermione, born October 7, 1899; and **Marjorie Ann,** born

July 14, 1906. Freda Naomi married James Benedict Spaulding, and is a teacher of art in the public schools of Rochester, New York. Grace Hermione is a member of the national staff of the Young Women's Christian Association, serving in the Girl Reserve Division in New York City. Marjorie Ann is a graduate student at Bryn Mawr College.

During the World War, Professor Stuff was active in every loan drive and other patriotic affairs. He is a member of the Sons of the American Revolution, and is serving as director of correspondence and public safety of this organization. In 1931, he was made state president of this society. He is a member of the following professional and educational organizations: American Interprofessional Institute, serving as vice president of the Lincoln Chapter, 1929, and president, 1930; American Association of University Professors; Nebraska Writers Guild; American Oriental Society; and Modern Language Association of America, and American Folk-Lore Society. He is a member of the Red Cross, the Salvation Army, and the Nebraskana Society. He is a member of the Lincoln University Club, and is affiliated with Elm Park Methodist Episcopal Church. His favorite sport is fishing. He is a Republican. Residence: Lincoln.

Archibald Brantley Sturdevant

Archibald B. Sturdevant was born at Weston, Nebraska, December 22, 1895, the son of Edward Payson and Melissa Ellen (Smith) Sturdevant. His father, a railway station agent on the Union Pacific, was born near Wilkesbarre, Pennsylvania, in 1860, and died at Osceola, Nebraska, November 9, 1929. His ancestors were English and Dutch settlers who came to America in 1700. Melissa E. Sturdevant was born at Racine, Wisconsin, October 12, 1863. She is the mother of ten children, and the seven that are living are all Nebraska University graduates. Besides Dr. Sturdevant, the others are: Mary Louise, 1907; Charles Francis, 1909; Ralph Smith, 1912; Roger Edward, 1916; Florence Bertha, 1926; and Margery Ilene, 1929.

Mr. Sturdevant attended public school at Weston, and was graduated from Osceola High School in 1914. He attended the Dental College of the University of Nebraska, and received the degree of Dental Surgery in 1917. He is a member of Xi Psi Phi, professional fraternity.

Dr. Sturdevant has resided in Nebraska his entire life with the exception of seven months while he was in the Dental Department of the United States Army. He practiced dentistry at David City, from July, 1917, to July, 1918, at Lincoln, from January 22, 1919, to May 1, 1921, and since that time at David City, Nebraska. He holds membership in the American Legion, Modern Woodmen of America, Knights of Pythias, and The Nebraskana Society.

On May 22, 1918, he was united in marriage to Violet Frieda Ruckert, at Lincoln, Nebraska. She was born at Lincoln, September 9, 1895. To this union three children were born: Archibald, born December 15, 1919; Keith, born February 12, 1921; and Virginia, born October 15, 1922. Residence: David City.

Brantly Elijah Sturdevant

Born at Blackwalnut, Pennsylvania, December 11, 1852, Brantly Elijah Sturdevant is the son of James Benedict and Josephine Louisa (Mowry) Sturdevant.

James Benedict Sturdevant was born at Blackwalnut, May 24, 1824, and died at Atkinson on June 4, 1917. He was a teacher of voice and instrumental music as a young man, and later was an artist. His grandfather, the Reverend Samuel Sturdevant, was a soldier in the Revolution, who lived in Connecticut. His grandfather came from London, England, as a boy.

Josephine L. Sturdevant was born in Meshoppen,

McNally Studio—Long Pine

BRANTLY ELIJAH STURDEVANT

Pennsylvania, February 8, 1826, and died at Atkinson. May 17, 1914. She was primarily a devoted wife and mother, and reared seven sons and one daughter to maturity. Her father was Scotch and her mother was of Holland-Dutch descent.

In the year 1870, James B. Sturdevant with his son, Joseph, came to Nebraska, where the father purchased ten quarters of land in the Silver Creek Valley of Saunders County. They purchased a team for $400.00, broke the sod on one tract of land 12 miles south of Fremont, hired the rest broken, and in the spring of 1871 had 180 acres ready for a crop. That spring James Sturdevant brought his wife and eight children to Nebraska, crossing the Missouri on a ferry, there being no bridge at that time. The crops that year were excellent, wheat bringing a $1.00 a bushel at Fremont.

The following year they raised more than 8000 bushels of corn, and had a fine wheat and oats crop. Corn was low, bringing only ten cents so they used it for fuel in place of coal. The next two years came the grasshoppers which took all the corn, and the hogs had to be fattened on wheat.

A band, called the Sturdevant Band, was formed, and James Sturdevant and his seven sons with one or two others, constituted it. The boys did not seem to take to farming, and after securing an education drifted into different professions and lines of business. The father sold out in Saunders County, opening a photograph gallery, and in 1883 moved to Atkinson.

The family of James Sturdevant, on the paternal side, is traced through the Reverend Samuel to Blackwalnut, Pennsylvania, he having purchased a large tract on the Susquehanna River bottom, that was timbered with black walnut. These lands were handed down each generation, the father selling his after he got settled in Nebraska. James Sturdevant's grandmother on the paternal side was Fannie Jones, who was of Irish descent. His maternal grandfather was George L. Mowry, a Scotchman, and his wife was Hannah M. Hellenback, of Holland-Dutch descent. James and Josephine Sturdevant left twenty-four grandchildren and seventeen great grandchildren.

Brantly E. Sturdevant attended public and high school at Blackwalnut, but did not graduate, as he was needed to help on the new land in Nebraska. He did however take his brothers to the University in Lincoln, when there was only one little building. He was married to Ellen Ilivia Smith at Silvai, Pennsylvania, on August 24, 1876. She was born at Spring Hill, Pennsylvania, April 4, 1850, daughter of Charles and Jane Ann (Martin) Smith.

Their children are as follows: LaZelle Brantly, born June 4, 1879, who was the only one of 15,398 students who earned five degrees from the University of Nebraska. He is married and they have a daughter, Bobbette M., born September 18, 1912. She is in junior college in Los Angeles. Dr. Sturdevant, who is a practicing physician and surgeon, held the rank of major in the Medical Corps during the World War.

The second son, George Otis, was born December 25, 1882. He is married to Effie May Smoot, and is engaged in dental practice at Lincoln. The only daughter, Olivia Zoe, was born March 9, 1891. She married Dr. N. P. McKee, who is a physician at Atkinson. They have two children, Mary Ellen, aged 12, and Neal Sturdevant, aged 9.

Mr. Sturdevant has resided in Nebraska since March 10, 1871. He helped survey the Union Pacific Railway from Columbus to Norfolk, and opened up the Shelby Station for that railroad in July, 1879. Continuing as their agent for about three years and a half, he was then transferred to David City. There he remained until December 15, 1895, when he resigned to go into the mercantile business at Atkinson. He was in that business for twenty-five years, when he became active in politics, and represented Holt and Boyd Counties in the house of representatives 1919-23. He was state senator from

1923-25, for the 22nd Nebraska district. He has served on the Atkinson school board 12 years, was county supervisor one term and was register of the United States Land Office nine years. Since leaving the senate Mr. Sturdevant has been engaged in insurance, real estate and farm loans. He is connected with the following corporations in the capacity of director: Lloyd Oil Corporation of Fort Worth, Texas; the United Oils Company, Fort Worth, Texas; the North American Mining Company of Denver, and the Hermosillo Copper Company of Columbus, Ohio.

At the age of 79 he is extremely busy and in good health. He sings solos at the Methodist Episcopal Church, with which he has been affiliated for many years. He has been superintendent of its Sunday School, and is now a teacher of the Men's Bible Study class. He is a member of the Red Cross, holding two life memberships and for more than forty years has been a member of the Commercial Club. Always active in that organization, he has represented the Atkinson district at many state and district meetings. He was consul of the Modern Woodmen of America for about eighteen years, and has been a member of the Royal Highlanders and the Royal Neighbors.

Mr. Sturdevant is a Republican in politics, and a prohibitionist, believing that sobriety is a necessity to prosperity. He has served as a member of the city council and was mayor of Atkinson two terms.

He is a member of the State Historical Society and the Nebraskana Society, and is looked upon as one of the most outstanding figures in his community. Residence. Atkinson. (Photograph on Page 1160).

Andrew Frederick Sturm

On February 8, 1863, Andrew F. Sturm, son of Andrew and Minnie (Stoll) Sturm, was born at Nehawka, Nebraska. His father was born at Alsace, France, in 1832, came to America in 1855, and died at Nehawka, in 1905. He was a farmer. His mother was born in Germany, in 1834, and died at Nehawka, 1921.

Mr. Sturm received his elementary education in country schools, and for a time attended college at Nebraska City. Today he owns and operates a lumber concern at Nehawka. A Republican, he was a member of the state senate from 1919 to 1921.

He married Lola M. McCarthy at Wyoming, Otoe County, Nebraska, March 3, 1890. Mrs. Sturm, whose ancestry is Scotch-Irish and French, was born at Wyoming, October 17, 1869. Four children were born to this union: Victor A., born August 18, 1892, a lawyer and writer; Gertrude, born July 19, 1894, who married John O. Yeiser; Ralph M., born September 17, 1896, an oil geologist and engineer; and Justin C., born April 21, 1899, who married Katherine McCormick, and is a writer.

Mr. Sturm was a four minute speaker in the World War. He is a member of the Red Cross; is president of the Nehawka Commercial Club; is president of the Chautauqua organization; and for 18 years has been president of the local school board. He is a Mason, 32nd degree and Shrine; and a member of the Independent Order of the Odd Fellows. He is interested in mechanics, is fond of reading, and is a member of the Lutheran Church and the Nebraskana Society. Residence: Nehawka.

Chester Dwight Sturtevant

Chester D. Sturtevant was born at Chicago, August 5, 1877, son of Frank Hills and Lillian Chester (Keyes) Sturtevant. Frank Hills Sturtevant was a native of Chicago, born in 1849, who died there in March, 1893. He was a wholesale grocer, and a member of the firm of C. E. Robinson and Company. Of English descent, his first ancestor in America was Samuel Sturtevant who settled at Plymouth in 1640.

Lillian Chester Keyes was born at Chicago on May 1. 1858. She is still living. Chester D. Sturtevant was a student at Oak Park High School in Chicago from 1892-93 and received his LL. B. from the Chicago Law School in June, 1900. From 1893 to 1906 he was a clerk in the offices of Charles Counselman and Company of Chicago, and Des Moines, Iowa, and from 1906 to 1916 was secretary of the Cavers-Sturtevant Company of Omaha. Since 1916 he has been secretary of the Trans-Mississippi Grain Company, and since 1924 has been its president. He was admitted to the practice of law at Chicago, on December 31, 1900, and at Omaha, June 8, 1929. He is the author of numerous articles on the economics of grain distribution.

He was married to Augusta Marian Hall at Oak Park, Illinois, January 29, 1900. Mrs. Sturtevant was born at Kansas City, Mo., February 13, 1879, and is of English descent. They have three children, Austin D., born June 18, 1904, who married Catherine Bradley; Marian A., born August 16, 1908, who married W. H. Cox, and Elizabeth Jane, born February 26, 1917.

Mr. Sturtevant is a Republican. He has been especially active in his commercial organizations, and served as president of the Grain Dealers National Association two years, 1927 and 1928, president of the Omaha Grain Exchange in 1925 and president of the Omaha Chamber of Commerce one year, 1928-29, and has been elected to the board of governors of Ak-Sar-Ben, 1931. He attends Trinity Cathedral.

His clubs are the Omaha Club, the Omaha Athletic Club, the Omaha Country Club and the Union League Club of Chicago. He enjoys reading. Residence: Omaha.

Frank Lee Sturtevant

Frank L. Sturtevant, a resident of Nebraska for the past 28 years, was born at Dover, New Jersey, November 7, 1867, the son of Francis Davis and Jennie (Lee) Sturtevant. His father, who was a hotel man, was born at Rockaway, New Jersey, June 4, 1837, and died at Kansas City, Missouri, May 15, 1930; he was a Civil War veteran whose ancestry was Holland Dutch. His mother who died in 1902, was Irish.

Mr. Sturtevant attended school in Missouri, and served for five years in the Iowa national guards. He is now treasurer of the Lininger Implement Company of Omaha, Douglas County, Nebraska. He is a member of the Omaha Chamber of Commerce, a former member of the Rotary Club, an Elk, Modern Woodman, and a Mason. His favorite sport is golf, and his hobby is reading. He is a Republican.

On May 15, 1895, he was united in marriage with Elizabeth Bassett at Bedford, Iowa; she was born at Bedford, March 4, 1871, and died at Omaha, March 4, 1902. He was married at Kansas City, Missouri, November 28 1917, to Gertrude Snook. Two children were born by first marriage: Katherine, born July 28, 1919, who married Dr. E. W. Bantin; Elizabeth, born January 9, 1921, who married Clayton S. Nickols; and one child born by second marriage; Mary Virginia, born July 3, 1929. Residence: Omaha.

Blanche Alphaola Stutevoss

Blanche A. Stutevoss, clubwoman, was born in Cerro Gordo, Illinois, July 6, 1871. Her father, Robert Wilson Willett, was born at White Plains, Maryland, July 16, 1837, descended from Scotch and English settlers, some of whom came to America in 1666, and some at a later date. His mother was Elizabeth Adams, of the family of Samuel Adams; John Quincy and Samuel Adams were cousins. Until his death at La Place, Illinois, on April 10, 1890, Robert Wilson Willett was a farmer and mechanic.

Mary Elizabeth Cox, wife of Robert Wilson Willett, was born in Norfolk County, Virginia, July 16, 1847, and died at Fairbury, November 1, 1926. A teacher and homemaker, she was a writer of short stories and a student of

literature. Her family was originally English and settled in North Carolina and Virginia prior to the Revolution, where they were plantation owners.

Educated under private instruction in North Carolina, where she spent her girlhood, Blanche A. Stutevoss came to Nebraska in 1889, and on June 5, 1890, was united in marriage to Henry Stutevoss at Fairbury. Mr. Stutevoss was born at Muscatine, Iowa, February 15, 1859, of pioneer parentage. His father and mother came directly from Germany to Iowa, where Mr. Stutevoss grew to manhood and became a contractor and builder. He died at Fairbury, August 21, 1927. There are two children: Albert Henry, born September 19, 1891, who married Lois Estelle Mayhew, and who is a general contractor at Marysville, Kansas; and Florine, born October 7, 1896, who married Walter Cleveland Meyer. Both children served in the World War, the daughter at Washington, D. C., where she was employed in the War Department.

With the exception of the years 1911-17, Mrs. Stutevoss has been a continuous resident of the state since 1889. During the World War she participated in Red Cross work, and during 1922-27 served as supervisor of relief for her city and county, under appointment of the board of county commissioners. During her residence in Fairbury, she has always been a member of the Woman's Club, and was its president in 1909-10. She is a member of the Parent-Teacher Association, and from 1929-31, was a member of the Fairbury School Board. At the present time she is president of the Fairbury Board of Education.

For a number of years Mrs. Stutevoss has been active in local Republican politics, and has filled the offices of treasurer and vice chairman of the Republican County committee. She is a Rotary Ann, a member of the Christian Church, and the Young Women's Christian Association, and in the latter organization served as its first president, and held the same office from 1928-31. Mrs. Stutevoss enjoys working around her home, and is especially devoted to reading history. Residence: Fairbury.

Louis Suess

Louis Suess, owner of the C. L. Decroff Department Store and president of the McCook Milling Company, was born near Decorah, Iowa, April 1, 1870, son of William and Katherine (Barth) Suess.

The father was born in Baden, Germany, and was a clergyman of the German Congregational Church who came to the United States in 1867. He died at Crete, Nebraska, February 6, 1906. His wife, Katherine, also born in Baden, died at Crete, July 12, 1926.

Mr. Suess attended public country schools and the academy then located at Crete. He has been in the general merchandise business since 1888, 42 years in the same location. In 1930 he was elected a master merchant of a class of ten in Nebraska. He is a Republican.

On August 16, 1892, he was married to Catherine Schmidt at McCook, Nebraska. She was born in Germany, August 8, 1871, and died at McCook, February 5, 1899. There are two children of this union, Gertrude, born June 19, 1893, who is the librarian at the Oregon State College at Corvallis, Oregon; Martha, born December 4, 1895, who is a student in music at the Juilliard School of Music in New York.

On September 24, 1902, he married Ethel M. Oyster at McCook, Nebraska. To this union one child was born, Eleanor Louise, on April 4, 1912. She is living with her sister Martha, in New York.

During the late war Mr. Suess was active in liberty loan drives. He is a member of the Congregational Church, the Red Cross, the Chamber of Commerce (president, 1922, was former member of the board of directors), the Rotary Club (president, 1932, was former member of the board of directors), the Masons, the Knights of Pythias, the Southwestern Nebraska Historical Society, and the Young Men's Christian Association (which has been established six years and of which he has been president five years). Mr. Suess has served 11 years on the school board and for a number of years as a member of the library board. He is an extensive land owner in southwestern Nebraska. His hobby is Hereford cattle. Residence: McCook.

William Suhr

William Suhr was born at West Side, Iowa, January 31, 1886, the son of Hans and Dorothy (Bendixen) Suhr. His father, who was a lumberman and contractor, was born in Germany. Mr. Suhr attended high school at West Side, studied law at the University of Nebraska, and the University of Michigan, and is a member of Phi Delta Phi.

He has been engaged in the practice of law at Grand Island, Nebraska, since his admission to the bar in 1914, and was county attorney of Hall County for three terms. He is chairman of the Hall County Red Cross, is a member of the Chamber of Commerce and the Rotary Club, and holds membership in the following professional organizations: Hall County Bar Association; Nebraska State Bar Association; and American Bar Association.

Mr. Suhr is a member of Masonic Orders, Elks, and the University Club. Politically, he is a Democrat. Residence: Grand Island.

Thomas Earl Sullenger

One of Nebraska's leading educators is T. Earl Sullenger, head of the department of sociology at the University of Omaha. Mr. Sullenger was born at Irma, Crittenden County, Kentucky, November 19, 1893, son of James Ely and Clara (Perry) Sullenger. His father, also a native of Irma, was born February 9, 1867. He is a civil engineer. Clara Perry Sullenger was born at Tolu, Kentucky, February 15, 1874. She was a music teacher prior to her marriage. She died at Marion, Kentucky, March 4, 1914.

T. Earl Sullenger was graduated from Marion High School in 1915. He received a life state certificate in 1915, from Western Kentucky State Teachers' College; in 1920 he received his B. A. degree and M. A. degree from the University of Oklahoma, where he majored in sociology, psychology and education; a scholarship entitled him to attend the University of Chicago, where he took sociology and social work in the Graduate School of Social Service Administration the summer term of 1924. During the second semester of 1927-28, another scholarship enabled him to study sociology at the University of Wisconsin, and he received his Ph. D. from the University of Missouri, in 1929. During this time he held a teaching fellowship in the department of sociology.

On June 5, 1921, he was married to Flora Dorcas Fleming, at Norman, Oklahoma. Mrs. Sullenger was born in Monticello, Kentucky, February 20, 1892. During his teaching career, Mr. Sullenger has held the following positions: principal of public schools of Kentucky and Oklahoma, three years; instructor, Universty of Oklahoma, 1920-21; lecturer on methods of social research, Richmond, Virginia School of Social Work, 1921-23; and at the same time was executive secretary of Y. M. C. A. of Virginia State Medical College; professor and head of department of sociology, University of Omaha, 1923, and dean of men.

He is the author of *A Study of Divorce and its Causation in Douglas County, Nebraska* (1927); *Social Ministry in an American City—A Recreational Survey of the Churches of Omaha* (1924); *Social Determinants in Juvenile Delinquency* (1930); *A Syllabus and Notebook for the Study of Social Psychology* (1929); *Educational Survey of Crittenden County, Kentucky* (1915); *A Study of the Juvenile Delinquent in Omaha* (1925).

Mr. Sullenger is co-author of the following: *Cause and Extent of Crime Among Foreigners in Omaha* (1924); *A Survey of Illiteracy in Omaha* (1925); *Survey of Johnston County, Oklahoma* (1920); *Social Legislation in Nebraska, and Private and Public Welfare in Omaha* (1931). In addition he has written many published articles.

From May 4, 1918, until July 11, 1919, he served with the U. S. Navy, in recruiting work for six months, and psychiatric work which was pertaining to testing and observing shell shock cases, for nine months. He is a member of the First Christian Church of Omaha, and is a Republican. He is a golfer, and is interested in gardening. His professional organizations include: The Amerietn Association of Social Workers, the American Sociological Society, the American Association of University Professors, the Society for Social Research of the University of Chicago, the American Academy of Political and Social Science. He is a member of Alpha Pi Zeta, Alpha Kappa Delta, Kappa Delta Pi, and of the Omaha Council of Social Agencies; Omaha Social Worker, and is a director of Bureau of Social Research. Residence: Omaha.

James P. Sullivan

James P. Sullivan, a resident of Nebraska for the past 40 years, was born at Morrow, Kansas, January 10, 1889. His father, Patrick Sullivan who was born at Indianapolis, March 17, 1850, has lived in this state for the past 64 years; his ancestry is Irish. His mother, Nora (Rakes) Sullivan, was born at Rock Bluff, Nebraska, June 27, 1856; her father of German and English descent, and her mother was German and Irish. Mr. Sullivan is secretary of the South Omaha Merchants Association; is vice president of the Omaha Tanning Company; proprietor of Sullivans' Sanitary Towel Supply Company; and secretary of the Nebraska-Iowa Truckmen's Depot. He is editor of *The Spook*. A Democrat, Mr. Sullivan has been active for many years in the civic and political life of the state. He served as secretary of the South Omaha Board of Education from 1911 to 1914.

His marriage to Viola Morearty was solemnized at Omaha, on January 31, 1919. Mrs. Sullivan, who is of Irish descent, was born at Omaha. They have three children: James P., Jr., born September 27, 1923; Robert J., born September 10, 1924; and Ruth Eulalia, born November 8, 1926.

Mr. Sullivan was a corporal in the Field Artillery during the late war. He is a member of South Omaha Post 331, of the American Legion, the Omaha Chamber of Commerce, South Omaha Merchants Association, and the Nebraskana Society. He is an Elk, and an Eagle, and is affiliated with Our Lady of Lourdes Roman Catholic Church of Omaha, and the Knights of Columbus. He is a member of Carter Lake Club. Residence: Omaha.

John Edward Summers

John E. Summers, distinguished physician and surgeon of Omaha, was born at Fort Kearney, Nebraska, January 2, 1858, the son of John Edward and Caroline Jane (Stuart) Summers. His father, who was born January 24, 1822, and died October 1, 1908, was a member of an old Virginia family, and was a collateral descendant of Sir George Summers of Bermuda Islands fame; his ancestry was English; he was a surgeon in the United States Army, 1847-1886, and at the time of his death was a retired brigadier general in the United States Army.

His mother, who was born at Albany, New York, in 1827, was descended from the Stuart, Grant, and McKay families of Inverness-shire, Scotland. With her four sisters she was graduated from the Albany Female Academy. She died at Omaha, March 28, 1902.

Dr. Summers received most of his early education in private schools and was a student at the United States Military Academy at West Point, for over two years. He was awarded the M. D. degree at the Columbia University of Physicians and Surgeons, 1881, and the LL. D. degree at the University of Nebraska. For two years he took post-graduate work in Vienna, Austria, and later in other continental cities and those of the British Isles.

He is a fellow of the American Surgical Association, which is an honor for an American surgeon, since the membership is limited to one hundred and fifty surgeons of the United States and Canada, also a member of the Societe Internationale de Chirurgie. He is a member and past president of the Western Surgical Association, The Nebraska State Medical Society, The Douglas County Medical Society, and the Missouri Valley Medical Society. He has been in active practice at Omaha, since 1885, professor of Clinical Surgery, University of Nebraska College of Medicine; surgeon to the Clarkson and University Hospitals; surgeon and chief of staff of the Douglas County Hospital; consulting surgeon of St. Catherin's Hospital, and formerly, for a number of years, chief surgeon of the Immanuel and Wise Memorial Hospitals.

Dr. Summers served as Surgeon General for the Nebraska National Guard on the staff of Governor J. E. Boyd, and as colonel on the staff of Governor A. J. Shallenberger. From 1881 to 1883, he was acting assistant surgeon in the United States Army, and in 1890, held this position again. He is a member of the Military Surgeons of the United States. He holds membership in the Omaha Club, and the Country Club, and was formerly a member of the Omaha Library Board. He is a member of the Nebraskana Society.

The book, *Modern Treatment of Wounds* published in 1899, was written by Dr. Summers, in addition to numerous articles on surgical subjects appearing in Transactions of various Societies. He was a contributor to Binnie's Treatise on Regional Surgery. Dr. Summers' sport is hunting, and his hobby is bird dogs. He is an Episcopalian, and politically is an independent Democrat.

On April 24, 1895, his marriage to Laura Marion Hoagland was solemnized at Omaha. Mrs. Summers, who was born at Omaha, January 2, 1868, is of Dutch and English descent; her ancestors were early settlers in Massachusetts and Long Island. They have two children: John Hoagland, born July 11, 1896, and Stuart Wyman, born October 15, 1903. Residence: Omaha.

Pearle Ellis Summers

Pearle Ellis Summers, county superintendent of schools at Rushville, was born at Denison, Iowa, August 8, 1876, daughter of Camp Edward and Viola (Hawley) Ellis.

Her father was born in New York State, May 24, 1853, and was a merchant at Crawford, Nebraska, until his death there September 2, 1895. Her mother, Viola Hawley, was born in New York State, October 28, 1853, and is still living.

Mr. Summers attended Denison, Iowa, and Crawford, Nebraska, public schools and was graduated from high school at Crawford in 1895. Thereafter she attended Lincoln Normal University and Chadron State Teachers College. For nine years she was a grade teacher in rural schools at Crawford and Rushville. She has been county superintendent of schools fifteen years. Mrs. Summers is a Republican.

She was married to Harvey E. Summers at Crawford on January 1, 1900. They have one son, Paul, born January 19, 1902. Mrs. Summers is a member of the Methodist Episcopal Church, is president of the library board at Rushville, and superintendent of the Sunday School and a steward of the Methodist Episcopal Church. Residence: Rushville.

Gustav Sumnick

Gustav Sumnick, son of Michael and Rosella (Stude) Sumnick, was born in Hammer, Germany, May 5, 1865, and has resided in Nebraska for the past forty-six years. He came to Nebraska in 1884, at the age of twenty. His parents were natives of Germany, where his father died in 1869, and his mother in 1919.

Mr. Sumnick attended the public schools, and afterward became successively farm hand, renter and land owner. At the present time he is the owner of an extensive acreage in Douglas County, and is a stockholder in the local elevator company. He is a director of the Douglas County Farm Bureau, and has served as treasurer of the local school board for eighteen years.

On March 1, 1891, he was united in marriage to Mary Nettie Kenneway at Fremont. Mrs. Sumnick was born at Waterloo, Nebraska, September 12, 1872. Their children are as follows: Leo, William, Gustav, Jr., Hazel Ruth, Rose, John, Helen, Francis, Kathryn, Marie, and Alfred. The boys of the family are engaged in farming with their father on his 1200 acres.

As stated in a newspaper story of Mr. Sumnick's achievements, after his return from a trip to Germany, "It is no wonder that his friends in the old country consider him a very rich man. For he is even more, he is wealthy, wealthy not only in lands and property, but in having a fine large family, many friends and last, but not least, good health. His German friends were surprised to find not an old man, but a man truly in his prime."

During the World War period Mr. Sumnick was active in Liberty loan drives, and in donations to the Red Cross, and still maintains his membership in the latter. He is a member of the Four H Club, the Modern Woodmen of America, and a life member of the Nebraskana, the latter in recognition of his achievements. Mr. Sumnick is a Democrat, and active in local politics. His hobbies are ancient history, geography, archeology and astronomy.

Gustav Sumnick has made two trips to Germany, since first coming to America, one in 1901, and one on May 7, 1929, where he visited point of historical interest. His old home is near Schneidemuhl, in Germany. Residence: Waterloo. (Photograph in Album).

Peter Albert Sundbury

Peter Albert Sundbury, a distinguished physician of Phelps County, Nebraska, was born at Stockholm, Sweden, August 14, 1867, the son of Pehr and Johanna (Bjerstedt) Sundbury. His father, who was a farm estate manager in Sweden, was born February 8, 1844, and died May 22, 1910. His mother was born in Sweden March 16, 1839, and died there December 15, 1909.

Dr. Sundbury received his education in a Swedish gymnasium and through private tutors. He has been United States pension examiner, local surgeon for the Chicago Burlington & Quincy Railroad since 1898, and is successfully engaged in the practice of medicine at Holdrege, Nebraska. He is president of the local school board, is a member of the Rotary Club and the Chamber of Commerce, and at one time was a director in the Red Cross.

He holds membershipi in the Phelps County Medical Society, the American Medical Association, the First Methodist Episcopal Church of Holdrege, and The Nebraskana Society. His fraternal organizations include the Masons, Modern Woodmen of America, and the Royal Highlanders.

Dr. Sundbury was married at Keokuk, Iowa, May 19, 1893, to Iona Belle King. Mrs. Sundbury, whose ancestry is English, Irish, and German, was born at Powhattan, Ohio, March 10, 1872. To them were born two children: Anna Elizabeth, January 13, 1895, who married Louis John Brazda; and Paul William, April 13, 1900, who is a merchant at San Francisco, California. Residence: Holdrege.

James Albert Sunderland

For 48 wears James A. Sunderland has lived in Nebraska and taken part in the business and civic life of the state. He was born at Jamestown, Chautauqua County,

New York, September 3, 1860, the son of James and Mary Elizabeth (Partridge) Sunderland. His father, who was the son of Thomas and Sarah Sunderland, was a clergyman with the degree D. D. He was born near Kiethley, Yorkshire, England, December 16, 1834, and died at Oakland, California, April 23, 1924.

His mother, the daughter of Albert A. Partridge, was born at Worcester, Massachusetts, July 16, 1837, and died at Ottumwa, Wapello County, Iowa, January 31, 1879.

Mr. Sunderland attended the public schools of Vinton and Sioux City, Iowa; later he was a student at Fort Madison Academy, and in 1879 he was graduated from the high school at Ottumwa, where he was valelictorian of his graduating class.

From 1881 to 1883 he was connected with J. A. Sunderland and Company at Ottumwa, and from 1892 to 1929 he was president of Sunderland Brothers Company. He is now chairman of the board of directors of this company. He has been for many years vice president of Ash Grove Lime & Portland Cement Company. He is president of the Douglas Realty Company and of Home Realty Company, of Omaha.

He was united in marriage with Ada Elwood Youngs at Brooklyn, New York, September 24, 1885. Mrs. Sunderland was born at Brooklyn, April 5, 1862, and died at Omaha, December 30, 1891. Two children were born to this union, Edwin Milroy, born September 4, 1886, who was married to Florence Erford, and who died September 9, 1921. On February 10, 1897, Mr. Sunderland was married to Alice Edgerly, the daughter of John W. and Maria Edgerly. They have four children: John Edgerly, born January 16, 1898, who married Julie Bill; Helen, born January 20, 1901, who married Fred P. Curtis; Ruth, born March 15, 1903, who married Eugene C. Dinsmore; and Alice, born January 11, 1906, who married Lee Stevenson Davis. John is president of Sunderland Brothers Company; is treasurer of the First Baptist Church; and has been secretary of the Omaha Dartmouth Society.

Mr. Sunderland is a member of the Omaha Chamber of Commerce; is vice president of the Conservation Savings and Loan Association; and is a director in the Omaha Fine Arts Society. He is a member of the United States Chamber of Commerce, the Nebraska Historical Society. He is affiliated with the American Forestry Association and the National Geographic Society. He is a member of the First Baptist Church, where he is moderator and trustee. He is a member of Ak-Sar-Ben, the University Club, the Omaha Club, Happy Hollow Club, and Dewey Lake Club. He is fond of hunting and fishing. He is a Republican. Residence: Omaha.

Douglas Conger Sutherland

Born at Tekamah, Nebraska, July 14, 1888, Douglas Conger Sutherland is the son of James Robert and Mary Stuart (Conger) Sutherland. His father, who was born at Woodstock, Oxford County, Ontario, Canada, January 31, 1845, died at Tekamah, November 23, 1926. For more than thirty years he had served as editor of the *Burt County Herald*, was state senator, railway commissioner and author of the history *Burt County in the World War*. His parents, Donald and Margaret (Murray) Sutherland, migrated from Rogart, Sutherlandshire, Scotland, to Canada, in 1836. Mary Stuart Conger was born at Plymouth, Ohio, September 17, 1851. She is much interested in music and art.

Douglas C. Sutherland finished his work at Tekamah High School in June, 1908, and associated himself with his father in the newspaper business. Since his father's death he has continued as editor of the *Burt County Herald* and as a member of the firm of the Rogers Printing Company. The author of *The History of Burt County*, he is also interested in photography and in the study of sociology. His religious affiliation is with the First Presbyterian Church of Tekamah, and he is a member of the Red Cross, the Chamber of Commerce, and the Northeast

Nebraska Editorial Association of which he was president in 1930.

Mr. Sutherland is a Scottish Rite Mason, a member of the Native Sons and Daughters of Nebraska, the Nebraskana Society, the Nebraska State and Burt County Historical Societies. Residence: Tekamah. (Photograph in Album).

Earl Hale Sutherland

Earl Hale Sutherland, banker at Laurel, Nebraska, has lived in this state for the past 40 years. He was born at Battle Creek, Nebraska, April 5, 1890, the son of John Alfred and Alice (Hale) Sutherland. His father, who was born in Virginia, June, 1853, and died at Madison, Nebraska, February 16, 1924, was Scotch-Irish. His mother was born in Virginia, February 16, 1861, of English ancestry.

Mr. Sutherland was graduated from the Madison High School and later was a student at Wesleyan University. He served as deputy register of deeds in Madison County for three years, was cashier of the First National Bank at Tilden, Nebraska, for eight years, and cashier of the Citizens National Bank at Norfolk, for five years. He is now president of the Security National Bank at Laurel, and is a director in the Homes Security Company and the First National Bank at Madison.

He is a member of the Red Cross, Young Men's Christian Association, the Nebraskana Society, and the Presbyterian Church. He is a Mason, and an Elk, and is a member of the Laurel Country Club and the Norfolk Country Club. His favorite sport is golf.

Mr. Sutherland was married at Alliance, Nebraska, November 17, 1915, to Nell Estelle Grant, she was born at Madison, July 22, 1889, of English and German parentage. They have a daughter, Robinette, born March 25, 1917. Residence: Laurel.

Addison Edward Sutton

Addison E. Sutton, automobile dealer, was born at Elmcreek, Nebraska, May 6, 1902, son of Edward L. and Sadie A. (Beecroft) Sutton. His ancestry is English.

Mr. Sutton attended the public school, Elmcreek High School, Kearney Normal School one summer, and the University of Nebraska four years.

He was married on July 14, 1925, to Ruth Stuart at Council Bluffs, Iowa. She was born at Lexington, Nebraska, May 2, 1907. They have one son, Stuart, who was born at Lexington, September 13, 1929.

For some time after leaving school Mr. Sutton was a member of the firm of E. L. Sutton and Son Company, Ford Dealers at Elmcreek. He is now a member of the firm of the Sutton Chevrolet Company at Lexington and the Sutton Motor Company at Broken Bow. He is a Mason, a member of Lincoln Lodge Number 19, Ancient Free and Accepted Masons, the 14th degree Scottish Rite Mason of the Hastings Chapter. At the University of Nebraska he was a member of Phi Delta Theta, the Innocents, and the Scabbard and Blade. He is a Republican. Residence: Lexington.

Everette Samson Sutton, Jr.

Everette Samson Sutton, Jr., was born at Naponee, Nebraska, January 3, 1893, son of Everette Samson and Clara Pascal (Hughes) Sutton, Sr.

The father was born in Bloom, Wisconsin, February 3, 1859, and taught in Keokuk, Iowa, in 1878. He is an extensive land owner and agent for the Chicago, Burlington and Quincy Railroad. His wife, Clara, was born in Ellsworth, Ohio, March 29, 1872. She is active in politics, and is a member of the Republican county central committee, and is Adams County chairman. She is descended through her mother from President John

Adams and John Quincy Adams, and through her father from Daniel Boone.

Mr. Sutton attended public school, and when but two years old his family moved to Brush, Colorado. He returned to Nebraska in 1915, where he is a land owner at the present time, and agent for the Chicago, Burlington and Quincy Railroad. He is an Independent Democrat.

On July 16, 1916, he was married to Hazel Ava Gorthy at Benkelman, Nebraska. Mrs. Sutton was born at St. Francis, Kansas, August 20, 1892, of Scotch-Irish parentage. Three children were born to them, one of whom is living, Eldon James, born March 6, 1916, who died September 28, 1928; Ava Justine, born September 10, 1920; and Alyn Dent, born December 13, 1927, who died December 16, 1927. They are also caring for one boy, James Playford, born August 28, 1925.

Since 1926, Mr. Sutton has been director of Max Rural High School. He is a member of the Parent Teachers Association, the Red Cross, and the Methodist Church. In 1912 he was connected with the Signal Corps of the Colorado National Guard. Residence: Max.

Lonnie Orestes Swails

Lonnie Orestes Swails, well konwn merchant in Geneva, was born at Clarksdale, Missouri, August 3, 1882, son of John Charles and Ella Flora (Roles) Swails. John C. Swails, a farmer, was born in Indiana, September 12, 1859, his father of English and his mother of German descent. He died at Geneva, August 1, 1926. His mother, born in Nebraska, April 15, 1863, is of English descent.

Mr. Swails received his elementary education in the Geneva public schools and thereafter completed a two year course at York Business College. Until 1902 he lived on a farm, leaving to become a driver for Hitch's store at Geneva. He continued with that firm until 1909, working for a shoe store in Oklahoma about a year, and in 1910 purchased a half interest in the Hitch Store. In 1927 he bought the other half interest and since that time has been sole owner.

On April 3, 1910, Mr. Swails was married to Edna Elizabeth Leighton at Woodward, Oklahoma. Mrs. Swails, who was born at Osage City, Kansas, August 27, 1895, is of Irish descent. There are two children, Forrest, born June 19, 1911; and Marguerite, born August 20, 1914.

Mr. Swails has resided in Nebraska the past forty-seven years, and has always been active in every effort toward the advancement of his community. He is a Mason and Modern Woodman of America, a member of the Congregational Church, the Community Club and for ten years served as city treasurer. His favorite sport is golf. Residence: Geneva.

Harold W. Swan

Harold W. Swan, son of John Washington and Hattie (McKim) Swan, was born at Humboldt, Nebraska, October 4, 1893. The father, a native of Illinois, born October 22, 1851, settled in Nebraska, in 1857. He held various pastorates for the Methodist Church in Nebraska, and was for many years placing out agent for the New York Childrens' Aid Society. He is a member of the Nebraska Conference of the Methodist Church, and is of Scotch-Welch and German descent. His wife, born in Canada, November 15, 1865, was formerly agent for the New York Children's Aid Society. She is of Scotch-Irish descent. They live at Sedalia, Missouri.

Educated in public schools, Harold W. Swan was graduated from the Clinton, Missouri, High School in 1911, and received his Bachelor of Arts degree from Nebraska Wesleyan, in 1916. He was a member of the varsity football team, and a member of Everett fraternity there.

For four years after graduation he taught school, at

Phillips, Valparaiso and Kenesaw, Nebraska. The year following he was employed in the American State Bank at Kearney, and for two years thereafter was connected with a hardware and implement business at Upland. For a number of years he has been the owner of Swan's Furniture Store at Kearney.

On June 20, 1917, Mr. Swan was married to Lillian Pearl Volk, at David City. She was born at David City, September 13, 1892, of German parentage. To them were born three children: Harold Everett, born October 8, 1919; Norris Volk, born January 13, 1920; and Elaine Louise, born August 15, 1929.

Mr. Swan is a Republican, a member of the Methodist Episcopal Church, the Chamber of Commerce, the Cosmopolitan Club, the Parent-Teachers' Association, the Masons, and The Nebraskana Society. During the World War he was a four minute speaker. Residence: Kearney.

Paul Spencer Swan

Paul Spencer Swan, one of Nebraska's contributions to the world of art, was born near Ashland, Cass County, Illinois. At the age of nine he moved with his parents to Johnson County, Nebraska, where he received his elementary education, and was a student at the high school at Tecumseh.

After a year of teaching in Red Willow County, Nebraska Mr. Swan, became a student at the Art Institute in Chicago. By sheer pluck and perseverance he contrived to see the art centres of the world and has in the last few years won an enviable measure of fame.

Mr. Swan has various modes of artistic expression. Until late years he was conspicuous as a dancer, but recently his painting and drawing have demanded more than an equal share of his energies, as will be evidenced by the long list of portraits he has exhibited. Among them are such notabilities as Raquel Meller, Violet Heming, Anna Pavlowa, and Madame Cabanel. While he makes his home in New York City, where his work has been shown regularly at the National Academy of Design and the Architectural League, he makes frequent trips abroad and has held one-man exhibitions in London, Paris, Athens, ad Buenos Aires.

His marriage to Helen Gavit was solemnized in New York. They have two daughters, Flora and Paul. A portrait of the latter, painted by Mr. Swan, appeared on the cover of a recent issue of the *Literary Digest*. Residence: New York.

Carl H. Swanson

Carl H. Swanson, one of the leading lawyers in Hitchcock County, was born at Fulda, Minnesota, March 18, 1899, and has been a resident of Nebraska for the past 24 years. He is the son of Melker and Gustava Maria Sophia Vidolpha (Gyllenhammer) Swanson.

His father was born in Smaland, Sweden, June 2, 1865. He was a miller who came to America in 1884. His wife, Gustava, was born at Omberg, Sweden, May 14, 1869. A paternal ancestor was knighted by Charles the 12th of Sweden, and her father was cited and received an honorary title from Oscar II, the King of Sweden.

Mr. Swanson attended the public schools of Bode, Iowa, Central City, and York, Nebraska, until 1912, and was graduated from Ravenna High School in 1916. He received the Bachelor of Laws degree from the University of Nebraska in 1920 where he was treasurer of Phi Alpha Delta.

Mr. Swanson is a Democrat. He was candidate for county attorney in 1921, and a candidate in 1924 for state representative from the 87th District. He is precinct committeeman and has served as delegate to various state conventions. In 1930 he was a delegate to the Mississippi Valley Association, and in January, 1931, to the Chicago Flood Control Conference by commission from Governor Arthur J. Weaver.

Mr. Swanson is an authority on flood control which forms one of his hobbies. He is also devoted to history and to the full development of our water resources.

On June 7, 1920, Mr. Swanson was admitted to the bar, and since December of that year has been a member of the law firm of Lehman & Swanson. He is village attorney of Culbertson, attorney for the Frenchman Valley Irrigation district and the Twin Valley Co-operative Creamery Company among other corporations. He is a director and secretary of the Twin Valley Co-operative Creamery Company, also.

His professional organizations include the American Bar Association, the Nebraska State Bar Association (member Advisory Council, 1930-31) and the 14th Judicial District Bar Association of which he was president, 1930-31.

He is a member of the Red Cross, the Culbertson Community Club (was elected secretary and still holds that office, and is president of the Twin Valley Association of Commercial Clubs, and a member of the legislative committee of the Nebraska State Irrigation Association, 1930-31.

During the World War Mr. Swanson was a private of infantry. He is a member of the American Legion and served as post commander in 1925, county commander in 1931, and has been adjutant several terms. He is affiliated with the First Methodist Episcopal Church. His fraternal organizations include Culbertson Lodge 174 of the Ancient Free and Accepted Masons; King Cyrus Chapter Number 35 of the Royal Arch Masons, and Bethel Chapter 109, of the Order of Eastern Star. He is a member of the National Geographic Society, the Culbertson Golf Club, and the University of Nebraska Alumni Association. His favorite sports are tennis, golf, hiking, swimming, hunting and fishing. He also enjoys reading history. Residence: Culbertson.

Elmer Swan Swanson

Elmer Swan Swanson, graduate pharmacist, was born at Oxford, Nebraska, October 15, 1890, and has lived in Bushnell for the past 12 years. He is the son of Charles John and Clara Marie (Neuman) Swanson. The father having come from Sweden in 1880, and the mother in 1881. His father died at Oxford, October 30, 1921. His mother is now residing at Holdrege with her daughter, Mrs. F. J. Check.

In 1909 Mr. Swanson was graduated from the Oxford public schools, and in 1914 received the Ph. D. from Creighton College of Pharmacy.

He was married on August 17, 1917, to Marie Erickson at Holdrege, Nebraska. She was born at Farela, Sweden, November 19, 1890. They have two children, Mary Louise, born September 16, 1918; and Leonard Charles, born October 13, 1921.

Mr. Swanson has always been a Republican. He is a member of the Ancient Free and Accepted Masons at Kimball, and the Odd Fellows at Bushnell. He purchased the business of Dr. H. M. Bailey, now deceased, in Bushnell, in 1919, and has since operated the drug store. Residence: Bushnell.

Frank Theodore Swanson

Frank Theodore Swanson, prominent banker at Clay Center, Nebraska, is a lifetime resident of this state. He was born in Clay County, January 14, 1873, the son of Trued and Ellen (Lundahl) Swanson. His father, who was a retired farmer for several years before his death, was born in Sweden, October 25, 1843, and died at Creighton, Nebraska, March 1, 1919. His mother, who was vitally interested in educational affairs, was born in Sweden, May 24, 1843, and died at Verona, Nebraska, May 24, 1903.

Mr. Swanson attended rural school and Lincoln Business College but received most of his education through home study and reading good books. He has been engaged in the banking business since 1906 and until recently was active as president of the Clay Center State Bank. A Democrat, Mr. Swanson served as county treasurer of Clay County, 1901-05, was delegate from the Fifth Congressional District to the Democratic National Convention at Baltimore, 1912, and was delegate to the St. Louis Convention in 1916.

He is active in the Red Cross, of which he is a life member, is affiliated with the First Congregational Church of Clay Center, and holds membership in the Clay Center Chamber of Commerce. His fraternal organizations include: Ancient Free and Accepted Masons; Modern Woodmen of America; and Independent Order of Odd Fellows. His chief recreations are golf and reading.

On November 30, 1899, he was married at Sutton, Nebraska, to Martha M. Campbell, who was born at Peoria, Illinois, July 24, 1880, and died at Clay Center, July 28, 1909. To this marriage the following children were born: Franklin, October 28, 1900; Raymond, June 30, 1903, who died September 14, 1905; Howard L., February 8, 1905; Helen M., June 17, 1907; Martha M., July 16, 1909. Of his marriage to Mildred E. Deines, June 17, 1912, one child was born: Jean D., born November 30, 1915. Residence: Clay Center.

Leonard August Swanson

Leonard August Swanson, physician, was born at Clay Center, Nebraska, July 1, 1896, son of Samuel August and Amanda C. (Turner) Swanson. His father, born in Sweden, February 24, 1849, came to America at the age of twenty and has since engaged in farming. His mother, born in Sweden, July 24, 1858, has for some time served as president of the Clay County Women's Christian Temperance Union.

Upon his graduation from public school in district 34 of Clay County in 1910, Dr. Swanson entered Clay Center High School, being graduated from that institution in 1914. He received his Bachelor of Science degree and his degree of Doctor of Medicine in 1922 from the University of Nebraska, and is a member of Kappa Sigma and Phi Rho Sigma. He took post-graduate work at King's County Hospital and was house surgeon there in 1924.

On June 16, 1927, he was married to Betty Jane May at Glendale, California. Mrs. Swanson, who was born at Cripple Creek, Colorado, on June 22, 1906, is a dancer. They have one daughter, Betty May, born August 26, 1928.

Dr. Swanson is a member of the Nebraska National Guard and is commanding officer of the 130th Ambulance Company. He is also a member of the American Legion, the Junior Chamber of Commerce, the Elks, and Masons (Scottish Rite, Shrine). His social club is the Hastings Country Club. Residence: Hastings.

William Otto Swanson

William O. Swanson was born at Omaha, Douglas County, Nebraska, March 21, 1891, the son of Knute Victor Liljenstolpe and Anna Maria (Hadendahl) Liljenstolpe. His father, who was a railroad man, was born at Stockholm, Sweden, and died at Omaha, May, 1919; he came to America in 1882. His mother was born at Gothenburg, Sweden, and died at Omaha, August, 1928.

Mr. Swanson attended the public schools of Omaha, where he has lived all his life. He is secretary-treasurer of the Nebraska Clothing Company and is president of the United States Securities Company of Omaha.

On April 8, 1915, he was married to Christine Josephine Swanson at Omaha. Mrs. Swanson was born at Omaha, April 9, 1891. Their two children are: John William, born May 18, 1916; and Ellen Marie, born May 7, 1927.

Mr. Swanson is a member of the board of the Omaha

W. OTTO SWANSON

Heyn Studio—Omaha

Community Chest; the Rotary Club; Noon Day Club; Advertising Selling League; and the Nebraskana Society. He is a member of all the Masonic bodies and the Woodmen of the World. His social clubs are: Omaha Club; Athletic Club; Happy Hollow Club; Field Club; Del Mar Club of Santa Monica, California. He is a member of Zion Lutheran Church and is affiliated with the Omaha Young Men's Christian Association.

He is fond of golfing. His hobbies are reading, and boys. He is a Republican. Residence: Omaha. (Photograph on Page 1168).

Artie Olief Swartwood

Born near Columbus, Indiana, August 9, 1865, Artie Olief Swartwood, now county assessor of Dodge County, was for many years a clergyman. He is the son of Samuel and Ruth Eliva (Cooper) Swartwood. His father was born near Columus, Indiana, in 1844, and died there on March 26, 1918. Samuel Swartwood was a farmer of German descent, who served in the Civil War, 1861-65. His wife, Ruth, was born near Columbus, February 22, 1842, and died there May 26, 1898. She was of German and French extraction.

Educated in grade and normal schools Artie O. Swartwood attended Butler College in Indiana, and taught six years in the schools of Bartholomew County. He then entered the ministry and preached for about thirty years. He came to Nebraska in 1899 and is now a member and chairman of the board of elders of the First Church of Christ at Fremont.

A Republican, Mr. Swartwood is now serving his second term as county assessor of Dodge County. In addition to his other activities he has written extensively for newspapers. He was married to Mary Eva Johns at Pike's Peak, Indiana, October 3, 1888. Mrs. Swartwood was born near Columbus, December 5, 1866, of Scotch and Welch descent. There are three children: Pearl May, born August 17, 1889, a graduate of Cotner University, who married Henry W. Wehr; Francis Marion, born December 11, 1890, who married Clara DePue, and who served as a physician in the World War. He was stationed at Bordeaux, France, with the Heavy Artillery and is now practicing at Adams. Anna Blanche, the youngest child, was born August 16, 1894. She is a graduate of Cotner University, and is married to H. G. Wellensiek. All three children were graduated from high school and the daughters formerly taught in grade and high schools.

Mr. Swartwood is a Mason and Knight Templar, and a member of the Sons of Union Veterans, of which he is local commander. While in South Dakota he was president of the Society of the Disciples of Christ and built a new church house at Miller, South Dakota, and Mrs. Swartwood was state secretary of the missionary Society connected with the same church. Residence: Fremont. (Photograph in Album).

Francis Marion Swartwood

Francis Marion Swartwood was born at Columbus, Indiana, December 11, 1890, the son of Artie O. Swartwood and Mary Eva (Johns) Swartwood. His father, who was a clergyman and is serving as county assessor of Dodge County, Nebraska, was born in South Bethany, Indiana, August 9, 1865. His mother, whose ancestry is Scotch-Irish, was born in Brown County, Indiana, December 5, 1866.

Mr. Swartwood attended the public school of Miller, South Dakota, and was a student in the high schools at Miller, Rising City, and David City, Nebraska. He was graduated from the David City High School in 1910, and in 1915 was awarded the M. D. degree at the Lincoln Medical College.

He was united in marriage with Clara Lee DePue at Brock, Nebraska, June 12, 1917; she was born at Brock, Nebraska. Their children are: Beverly Ann, born March 30, 1926; and Frances Marian, born February 6, 1930.

During the World War, Mr. Swartwood served as first lieutenant of the Nebraska National Guard in border service at Llano Grande, Texas, and was first lieutenant in the medical corps of the United States Army. He is now major in the Medical Reserve, and is a member of the American Legion.

He is a director of the First National Bank at Adams, was formerly a member of the board of education, and is affiliated with the Church of Christ of Bethany, Nebraska. He is a member of the Chamber of Commerce, Nebraska State Medical Society, Nebraskana Society, and the Ancient Free and Accepted Masons. Residence: Adams. (Photograph in Album).

Edward Edmond Sweeney

Born at Sweet Home, Nodaway County, Missouri, June 23, 1873, Edward Edmond Sweeney has been a physician in Nebraska for the past twenty-three years. He is the son of Edward and Mary (Foley) Sweeney, the former a farmer. Edward Sweeney served ten years in the United States Army, from 1855-60, as a private in the United States Dragoons. From May 4, 1860, until May 4, 1865, he served with the 4th United States Cavalry under Generals Sherman, Buell and Thomas. His last period of service was under General Kilpatrick and General Wilson. He received his honorable discharge at Macon, Georgia, where he was body guard to the father-in-law of General Longstreet.

Edward Sweeney, Sr. was of Irish stock, some of his early ancestors having migrated to France in the 15th century, where the syllable "Mc" was dropped from the family name. Members of his family came to America in 1847 or 1848. He learned to read and write after his marriage at the age of thirty-five. His wife, Mary Foley, was born at sea, in May, 1849. Her parents were from County Kerry, Ireland. Her mother died when she was very young, and she received part of her education in convent school at Vincennes, Indiana. Her life was dedicated to the rearing and education of her children. It is believed that her step-mother was a distant relative of Captain John Paul Jones of the Revolution. Mary Foley died at Ravenwood, Missouri, March 7, 1891, and her husband on October 3, 1912.

Educated in the public schools of Missouri, Edward Sweeney, Jr., received his M. D. from the University of Medical College at Kansas City, Missouri, in 1908. Prior to that time he had attended Ensworth Medical College at St. Joseph, Missouri, two years. Dr. Sweeney was admitted to the practice of medicine in Nebraska, at Preston, on August 17, 1908, and for many years practiced in Thayer County, at Gilead. Recently he removed to Roseland, Nebraska. From 1919-12, he was coroner of Fillmore County, and from April 3, 1930, to July 29, 1931, was a notary public in Thayer County. Until the election of Herbert Hoover, he was a Republican.

On June 11, 1913, Dr. Sweeney was united in marriage to Johanna Mabel Lyhene at Sutton, Nebraska. Mrs. Sweeney, who was born at Sutton, on August 27, 1884, assisted her children in their education and musical training. Of Irish ancestry for generations, one of her family names is Hillard. There are four children: Margaret Mary, born July 12, 1914, who was graduated from the normal training course in Fairbury High School, third in her class; Edward Dennis, born July 23, 1916; Francis Joseph, born December 25, 1919; and Josephine, born February 5, 1923.

Dr. Sweeney served as a private in the Cadets of the University of Missouri, 1903-04, and held the rank of first lieutenant in the Medical Corps of the United States Army from March 19, 1918, to December 3, 1918. He is a member of the Catholic Church at Roseland. He enjoys reading, especially history, and raising bees. Residence: Roseland.

Charles Arthur Sweet

Charles A. Sweet, lawyer and banker, has lived at Palmyra, Otoe County, Nebraska, for 47 years and has taken an active part in the civic and business affairs of his community for many years. He was born at Milford, Otsego County, New York, November 7, 1855, the son of John and Maria (Eddy) Sweet. His father, a farmer, was born at Milford, March 22, 1820, and died there April 15, 1890.

His mother was born at Milford, in 1832, and died there in January, 1857.

Mr. Sweet attended Hartwick Seminary, Hartwick, New York, and the High School at Davenport, Iowa. He was appointed postmaster at Palmyra, January 1, 1899, and served in this capacity for 13 years during which time he also engaged in the practice of law. Since then he has been a banker and lawyer. At the present time he is cashier of the Bank of Palmyra.

His marriage to Minnie E. Hyde was solemnized at Cooperstown, Otsego County, New York, October 15, 1879. Mrs. Sweet was born at Jordansville, New York, November 3, 1860, and died at Palmyra, April 19, 1926. Four children were born to this union, three of whom are living. John Hyde, born September 1, 1880, who married Zelma Ringsby, is editor of the Nebraska City News Press. Evelyn, who was born March 15, 1882, died September 20, 1887. Grace was born October 28, 1884, and is a widow. Charles A., born June 23, 1888, married Floy A. Jones, and is assistant cashier of the Bank of Palmyra.

Mr. Sweet was active in loan drives during the late war. He is a member of the State Bar Association, and is president of the Otoe County Bar Association. He is a Mason. He is a Republican. Mr. Sweet is a profound thinker and student, whose hobby is reading. Residence: Palmyra.

John Hyde Sweet

John Hyde Sweet was born at Milford, Otsego County, New York, September 1, 1880. His father, Charles A. Sweet, has been a banker since 1883, and was recently honored in recognition of his 50 years practice as a lawyer. He was born at Milford, November 7, 1855, and is descended from Scotch ancestors who settled in Connecticut, in 1650. His paternal grandmother was one of the famous Eddy clan well known as ministers, educators and editors. He has lived in Otoe County over fifty years.

Minnie E. (Hyde) Sweet, who was born at Jordanville, Herkimer County, New York, November 3, 1860, and died at Palmyra, Otoe County, Nebraska, April 26, 1926, was a clubwoman of some prominence in her state and community. She was the organizer of a pioneer Woman's Christian Temperance Union, and a member of an early Baptist Church congregation. The Hyde family is of Irish extraction, and was founded by the famed Sir Edward Hyde, Earl of Clarendon who was beheaded by Bloody Mary. Members of the family settled in Massachusetts and Connecticut early in the seventeenth century.

Mr. Sweet attended high school both in Nebraska and California. He studied special work at the University of Nebraska, during a summer term. He has been editor of the Nebraska Daily News Press at Nebraska City, since 1909. He entered the office first as a stenographer and was later made an accountant. In the last twenty years he has built the business into a flourishing one, and is the author of a daily column that has increased the popularity of the paper. He is president of the Press Printing Company, and is part owner of a small town newspaper in an eastern mountain state. Mr. Sweet is a Republican, and is interested in political affairs, but has never aspired to public office. He has, however, helped scores of others attain political positions.

His marriage to Zelma Harriet Ringsby was solemnized at Auburn, Nemaha County, Nebraska, October 5, 1904. Mrs. Sweet was born at Sterling, Johnson County, Nebraska, November 4, 1880. They have one son, Arthur Rings-

by, born July 20, 1905, who was graduated from the University of Nebraska, in 1928. He is managing editor of the News Press.

At the age of seventeen Mr. Sweet attempted to enlist in the army in the Spanish-American War, but was rejected because of his youth. During the World War he was liberty loan driver for one district; was draft board adviser; and was head of the Otoe County department of justice in the secret service.

He is president of the Nebraska Press Association, and is vice president of the Inland Press Association at Chicago. He is past president of the Nebraska City Chamber of Commerce, and past president of the Nebraska City Rotary Club. From 1910 to 1925, he was secretary of the library board; he was at one time president of this organization. He was a charter member of the Nebraska State Historical Society and the Nebraskana Society. Golfing and mountain climbing are his favorite sports. Mr. Sweet likes contact with his fellow men. His hobbies are amateur photography, archeology, and literature. His club is the Kansas City Athletic Club. He is affiliated with the Unitarian Church. Residence: Nebraska City.

Myron Harmon Swenk

Myron Harmon Swenk, noted entomologist and educator of Nebraska, was born at Polo, Ogle County, Illinois, August 8, 1883. His father, Howard Swenk, was born at Norristown, Montgomery, Pennsylvania, August 27, 1858. He came to Nebraska, in 1885, and settled in Beatrice, where he engaged in the building contracting business. In 1901 he moved to Lincoln. He is descended from Pennsylvania German ancestors who came to America early in the 18th century, and helped in transporting supplies to Washington's army at Valley Forge.

Susanna (Harmon) Swenk, his mother, was the daughter of German immigrants who came to America in 1854, and settled in Illinois. Her ancestry is Hessian. She was born at Lancaster, Pennsylvania, May 8, 1860, and her interest was largely confined to her home, family, and church activities. She died at Lincoln, Nebraska, July 7, 1925.

Prof. Swenk received his education in the public schools of Beatrice, and in 1901 was graduated from the Beatrice High School. Later he attended the University of Nebraska, where he was awarded his A. B. degree, 1907, and his M. A. degree, 1908. He was made a member of Sigma Xi, Gamma Sigma Delta, Alpha Zeta, and Phi Sigma at the University of Nebraska. During his high school days he was a member of the debating team, 1900-01, and was class orator in 1901.

He was laboratory assistant in entomology at the University of Nebraska, 1904-07; was adjunct professor, 1907-10; was assistant professor, 1910-11; was associate professor, 1911-14; and from 1914-1932, was professor. He was made chairman of the department of entomology in 1919; was assistant station entomologist, 1913-19; was entomologist in the station, 1919; was made assistant state entomologist, 1908, serving until 1919; and was state entomologist from 1919 to 1927. At the present time he is professor of entomology, and is chairman of this department. He has lived in Nebraska 46 years.

On April 24, 1918, he was united in marriage with Jane Chandler Bishop. Mrs. Swenk, who was born at Clear Spring of La Grange, La Grange County, Indiana, October 13, 1885, is of Irish descent on the paternal side and English through the maternal line. Her great-great-grandfather, James Chandler, (1761-1835) was fife major in the Revolution.

Mr. Swenk served as entomologist in food crop conservation throughout the World War. He holds a fellowship in the American Association for the Advancement of Science; is a member of the American Ornithologists' Union, an organization which limits its membership by election; and is an active member of the American Association of Economic Entomologists. In 1918-19, he was president of the Wilson Ornithological Club; was president of the Nebraska Ornithologists' Union in 1907, and has been secretary since that date. He is a member of the Philadelphia Academy of Natural Sciences, Cooper Ornithological Club, the American Society of Mammalogists, and the Ecological Society of America.

His social club is the University Club of Lincoln. He is a Republican. His favorite sport is hiking. Residence: Lincoln.

Axel C. R. Swenson

Axel Swenson was born at Ramquila parish, Sweden, February 7, 1894, the son of Carl and Inga Swenson. His father, who was a farmer, was born in Sweden in 1848, and died there January, 1901. His mother was born at Backaby, Sweden, October 19, 1850.

Mr. Swenson immigrated from Sweden with his mother in 1901, and came to Oakland, Nebraska. He attended the Burt County rural schools and in 1910 was graduated from the high school at Oakland, Nebraska. He received his A. B. degree at the University of Nebraska, 1919, and his LL. B. degree at the University of Minnesota, 1921. He was made a member of Phi Beta Kappa and Innocents at Nebraska University, and was a member of the university debating team. He was admitted to the bar at Lincoln, Nebraska, June, 1922.

He is now a member of the law firm Ritchie, Swensen and Arey, at Omaha. He is attorney for the Swedish vice consulate for Nebraska, Iowa, Kansas, Colorado, and Wyoming. He has been a resident of Nebraska for 29 years.

His marriage to Geneva Seeger was solemnized at Glenwood, Mills County, Iowa, December 28, 1918. Mrs. Swenson, who is of German and English descent, was born at Glenwood, August 29, 1896. They have two children: John Richard, born May 23, 1920; and Edward William, born October 24, 1926.

Mr. Swenson served in the American Army from 1917 to December, 1918. He was commissioned 2nd lieutenant of infantry, and was twice promoted, having the commission of captain of infantry at close of war. He is a member of the American Legion, Omaha Bar Association, Nebraska State Bar Association, the Omaha Chamber of Commerce, and Ak-Sar-Ben.

He is affiliated with the First Central Congregational Church of Omaha, and is a member of the Omaha Club. In 1927 he was president of the Noon-day Club. He is a Mason and a Democrat. Residence: Omaha.

Samuel August Swenson

Samuel A. Swenson, distinguished physician of Nebraska, was born at Parish of Ramquilla, Province of Smaland, Sweden, May 22, 1879, the son of Carl John and Sophia (Peterson) Swenson. His father, who was chairman of the local school board, parish church warden, and song leader, was born at the Parish of Beckaby, Province of Smaland, September 17, 1850, and died at the Parish of Ramquilla, January 18, 1901; his ancestors were peasant farmers in Sweden. His mother was born at Beckaby, October 20, 1850, and was the mother of 12 children, two of whom died in childhood; her maternal grandfather was a merchant and a notary.

Dr. Swenson attended the common schools of Sweden; was a student in the Burt County schools; and in 1903 was graduated from Omaha Central High School. He was awarded the B. Sc. degree in 1908, and the M. D. degree in 1910, by the University of Nebraska, where he was elected to Sigma Xi, honorary society. Previously he attended the Omaha Commercial College. He was admitted to the practice of medicine at Wausa, Nebraska, June 10, 1910, and is now local surgeon for the Chicago, St. Paul, Minneapolis & Omaha Railroad Company.

He has held various civic and professional offices at Oakland, among them: president of the Oakland Chamber of Commerce, 1928; chairman of the Boy Scout commit-

tee, 1920-30; member of the local city council, 1923-4; and city physician for 10 years. He is the author of *On the Abortive Treatment of Pneumonia,* published in the *Western Medical Review,* (1914); and *The Bacterin Treatment of Pectussi,* published in the *Nebraska State Medical Journal,* October, 1925. He holds membership in the County Medical Society; Nebraska State Medical Society; American Medical Association; and the Sioux Valley Medical Society. In 1919 he helped organize the Burt County Young Men's Christian Association, and in 1920 was vice president of the organization.

Dr. Swenson served with the 10th Division of the Medical Corps as captain during the World War, stationed at Camp Funston, and at this time is captain of the Medical Reserves and is a member of the American Legion, having served as commander of the latter in 1922. His religious affiliation is with the First Methodist Episcopal Church of Oakland. He is a member of the Parent-Teachers Association; was recently elected to membership in The Nebraskana Society; and is a Mason. His favorite sport is golf.

On June 18, 1912, he was united in marriage with Anna Margaret Preston at Oakland. Mrs. Swenson was born at Oakland, November 11, 1884; her father is English and her mother is Scotch. They have four children: Anna Margaret, now a sophomore at the University, Anna Margaret, born July, 1913, now a sophomore at the University; Inga Rowena, born November 18, 1914; Samuel August, born January 14, 1917; and Jeanet Martina, born October 4, 1918. Residence: Oakland.

Erman Nathan Swett

Erman Nathan Swett, educator, was born at Ainsworth, Nebraska, August 19, 1890, son of Charles N. and Amanda Jane (Raper) Swett. His father, born near Yuba City, California, August 11, 1851, was a pioneer in Brown County, and took one of the first homesteads there. His grandfather went over the Oregon trail to California, in 1849. Of English descent, his ancestry is traced to pre-Revolutionary times, and some ancestors served in both the Revolutionary and the War of 1812. Amanda Jane Raper, was born in Bowling Green, Indiana, July 26, 1858, and died at Ainsworth, Nebraska, March 13, 1930. She was of Pennsylvania German descent.

Educated in the rural and village schools of Taylor County, Iowa, Erman N. Swett was graduated from the Grafton, Nebraska, High School in 1909, and received his A. B. from Nebraska Wesleyan University in 1917. His education was interspersed with teaching, and from 1915-18, he was superintendent of schools at Grafton. He was valedictorian of his class in 1909, and is a member and past president of Phi Beta Sigma, at Nebraska Wesleyan. Active in athletics, he earned three letters in baseball and was captain of his team one year.

From 1919-22, Mr. Swett was superintendent of schools at Homer, and from 1922, to the present time has been superintendent of schools at South Sioux City. During 1909-11, he taught in the rural schools of Fillmore County, and during 1911-12 in the grammar grades at Grafton. His professional memberships include the Nebraska State Teachers' Association, the Nebraska School Masters' Club, and the North East Nebraska School Men's Club of which he was president in 1930. He was a second lieutenant in Field Artillery during the World War, and is a member of the American Legion, and county chairman of the Citizens Military Training Camp. Mr. Swett is active in civic and fraternal work, and is a member and former director of the Commercial Club, and a member of Alpha Lodge No. 316 Ancient Free and Accepted Masons, and Laura Chapter of the Order of Eastern Star. He enjoys baseball and golf, and his hobbies are history, reading and new inventions.

On August 19, 1915, he was united in marriage to Bess Florence Gilbert at Grand Island, which is her birthplace. Mrs. Swett was born November 2, 1893, and was a teacher prior to her marriage. There is one son, Robert Earl, born August 22, 1928. Residence: South Sioux City. (Photograph in Album).

Goodwin Deloss Swezey

Goodwin D. Swezey has lived at Lincoln, Lancaster County, Nebraska, for the past 37 years, and has been prominent in educational circles there for many years. He was born at Rockford, Winnebago County, Illinois, January 10, 1851, the son of Lewis Samuel and Sarah (Cook) Swezey. His father was of the Massachusetts Colonial family, Swezey, originally spelled Suasey. His mother was descended from early New York residents.

Professor Swezey received his early education in the rural schools near Rockford, and later he attended the Rockford High School. In 1869 he was graduated from the Beloit College Academy, and in 1873, he was awarded his A. B. degree at Beloit College. He was a student at Yale Divinity School in 1873 and 1874, and he received his A. M. degree at Beloit, in 1876. His B. D. was awarded him at Andover Theological Seminary in 1880.

He is, and has been for many years, professor of astronomy at the University of Nebraska. During his years in educational work, Professor Swezey has written scores of articles and reports for various professional journals and other publications. He is the author of: *Catalog of the Plants of Wisconsin; Elementary Agriculture; Nebraska Board of Agriculture*, (1886-91); *Wisconsin Academy of Sciences; Nebraska Horticultural Society*, (1892-93-98); *Proceedings, Nebraska Academy of Sciences; Nebraska Irrigation Annual*, (1897); *Nebraska Agricultural Experiment Station*, (1902); and is the joint author with Bessey and Bruner of *Practical Exercises in Astronomy*. He is the author of scientific reports in *Geology of Wisconsin*. He has also written numerous scientific articles in *Popular Astronomy, Science, Nebraska Farmer*, and *Nebraska Blue Print*.

His marriage to Mary Frances Hill was solemnized at Beloit, Wisconsin, August 7, 1884. Mrs. Swezey was born at Janesville, Rock County, Wisconsin. There are the following children: Minnie Lucretia, who married George F. Elmendorf; Emma Josephine; and Marien Francis. Mrs. Swezey is deceased.

Professor Swezey is a member of the American Astronomical Society; the Nebraska Academy of Science; and the Nebraskana Society. He is a member of Beta Theta Pi, is a member of the Faculty Club, and is affiliated with the Y. M. C. A. He is a member of Vine Congregational Church where he is serving as trustee. Residence: Lincoln.

Elicha C. Swigert

Elicha C. Swigert, insurance man and cattle rancher, was born at Mineral Ridge, Iowa, April 1, 1886, son of Medill and Matilda (Johnson) Swigert.

The father, born in Mineral Ridge, December 25, 1854, was a cattle rancher, and owned and operated the first hotel and livery barn in Gordon for more than 20 years. He was of Pennsylvania Dutch ancestry. His death occurred at Gordon on November 24, 1931. His wife, Matilda, was born at Stratford, Iowa, March 31, 1856, of Swedish ancestry and died at Gordon, December 30, 1909.

From 1886 until 1891, Mr. Swigert attended grade school at Gordon, and from 1891 until 1893 attended high school there, graduating the last named year. Afterward he was a student at Black Hills College, Hot Springs, South Dakota. A trained athlete, he was a member of football and baseball teams while in school.

For the past 15 years Mr. Swigert has been in an insurance business at Gordon; prior thereto he was a general merchant for about 17 years. A Republican, he has served as justice of the peace of the city of Gordon for the past 12 years.

On August 13, 1893, he was married to Josephine Ada Sage at Clayton, Missouri. Mrs. Swigert was born at Bonaparte, Iowa, February 10, 1877, of English ancestry. She is past president of the P. E. O. and past grand matron, O. E. S., State of Nebraska. She is the daughter of Frank and Margaret E. Sage, pioneer settlers of Nebraska, who removed from eastern Nebraska to Hay Springs in 1886. Mr. Swigert is a member of Gordon Lodge No. 195 Ancient Free and Accepted Masons; Consistory No. 1 of Omaha, Shrine of Omaha, and Elks Lodge No. 961 of Alliance. He is a member of the Presbyterian Church, although baptized in the Swedish Lutheran Church. He is also a member of the Kiwanis Club. His hobby is travel. Residence: Gordon.

Raymond Clarence Swisher

Raymond C. Swisher, clergyman, was born at Woodstock, Ohio, May 25, 1880, the son of French and Sarah Viola (Unkefer) Swisher. His father, who was born in Ohio, January 6, 1855, had been in the mercantile business for several years until his death, November 4, 1882. He was a soldier in Company H, United State Infantry, stationed at Atlanta, Georgia, October 5, 1876, and was commissioned captain of Company D, 7th Regiment of the Ohio National Guard, August 12, 1882; his ancestry was Dutch; his great grandfather came to America from Switzerland.

Sarah Viola Unkefer, mother, was born at Urbana, Ohio, January 18, 1857, and died at Spencer, South Dakota, March 3, 1925. She possessed an unusual knowledge of house and garden plants and flowers. She was of German and Welsh descent.

Dr. Swisher attended the country school of Seneca County, Ohio, and in 1899, was graduated from the high school at Bloomville, Ohio. He holds the following degrees: Ph. B., Fenton College, 1902; A. M., Ohio Northern University, 1904; Ph. D., 1917, University of Southern Minnesota; D. D., Iowa Christian College, 1911. He was a student at Bonebrake Theological Seminary, 1900, and the Divinity School of the University of Chicago, 1910, 1911, 1913.

On October 4, 1908, he entered the Congregational ministry, and was consecutively missionary to the Lake Erie Islands; pastor at Vermillion and New London, Ohio; Dekalb, Illinois; Sedalia, Missouri; Austin, Minnesota; and York and Arlington, Nebraska. He is now pastor of the First Congregational Church of Arlington. He is the author of *The Boy and His Religion*, (1917); *The Influence of the Platonic Philosophy*, (1904); and *The Relation of Philosophy to Theism*, (1909).

He was united in marriage with Harriet Estelle Bates at Rising Sun, Ohio. Mrs. Swisher, whose ancestry is English, was born at Wayne, Ohio. She is instructor in dramatics and public speaking in addition to her homemaking activities. One child was born to them, Beatrice Elinor, who died in infancy.

Dr. Swisher was a four minute man during the World War and made addresses in various camps and cities. He is a member of the Platte Valley Ministerial Association; the Nebraska Congregational Conference; and the Omaha Association of Congregational Ministers. He is a member of the American Academy of Political and Social Science; the Arlington Community Club; the Nebraskana Society; the Knights of Pythias, and is an honorary member of the country clubs at Sedalia, Missouri, and Austin, Minnesota. Politically, he is independent. Residence: Arlington.

Robinson Merideth Switzler

Robinson Meridith Switzler, lawyer, was born at Omaha, Nebraska, November 19, 1885, son of Warren and Mary Duncan (Wilson) Switzler. The father, a practicing lawyer in Omaha for forty-five years, was born in Boone County, Missouri. The mother was born in Washington, D. C.

Mr. Switzler received his Bachelor of Arts degree from the University of Nebraska in 1910 and his Bachelor of Laws degree in 1912. On September 7, 1918, he was married to Kathleen Gilmore, daughter of Dr. Robert Gilmore, at Omaha.

Since his admission to the bar Mr. Switzler has been in active practice at Omaha. He is a member of the Red Cross, the Young Men's Christian Association, and the Omaha and Happy Hollow Clubs. Residence: Omaha.

William Bodine Tagg

W. B. Tagg was born at Waco, Nebraska, September 28, 1875, the son of Thomas Colter and Mary Elizabeth (Bodine) Tagg. His father, a stockman and merchant, was a farmer in York County for a time, and served in the Union Army in the Civil War. He was born in Chatham, England, September 15, 1838, and died at Omaha October 17, 1919. Mary Elizabeth Bodine, who was a music instructor, was born at Staten Island, New York, January 20, 1841, and died at New York City, February 14, 1926.

Mr. Tagg, who has been a prominent executive in Omaha, since 1894, attended high school at Waco. He is now president and manager of the firm Tagg Brothers & Rosenbaum, live stock commission agents at Omaha; is treasurer of Klink & Taylor Company and secretary of the Masonic Temple Craft of Omaha. He is also president of Walnut Grove Products Company at Atlantic, Iowa.

On November 23, 1907, he was married to Mary Alicia Leonard at Louisville, Kentucky. Mrs. Tagg, who was in the advertising business before her marriage, was born at Petersburg, Kentucky, February 23, 1879. There are three children: Richard, born September 4, 1908, who was graduated from the University of Nebraska in 1930; William, born January 4, 1911, who is a student at Annapolis; and Mary Elizabeth, born March 30, 1913, who attends Ferry Hall at Lake Forest, Illinois.

Mr. Tagg was active in all loan drives during the World War. He was chairman of the Omaha chapter of the Red Cross for one year; and is a member of the Omaha Chamber of Commerce. He was president for two years and director for nine years of the Omaha Live Stock Exchange. He was president two years and director for nine years of the Omaha Athletic Club. He was president of the National Live Stock Exchange for two years and a member of the executive committee six years; was a member of the National Live Stock and Meat Board for eight years. He is a member of the Masons, Elks, and Royal Arcanum, is affiliated with St. Martin's Episcopal Church at Omaha, and is a Republican. Residence: Omaha.

Paul F. Taggart

Paul F. Taggart, county extension agent at Red Cloud, Nebraska, has been a resident of this state all his life. He was born at Chambers, Nebraska, October 1, 1900, the son of Samuel and Edith May (Smith) Taggart. His father, who was a farmer, was born at Cordova, Illinois, September 28, 1861, and died at Chambers, September 26, 1914; his ancestry was Irish. His mother, who was born in Virginia, July 28, 1870, was an educator.

Mr. Taggart attended district school in Holt County, Nebraska, was graduated from the Chamber High School in 1917, and received the B. S. degree at the University of Nebraska in 1922. He held membership in Alpha Zeta at the university. He served as vocational agriculture instructor at Weeping ater, Nebraska, 1922-24, was superintendent of schools at Barneston, Nebraska, 1924-26, and was superintendent of schools at Dix, Nebraska, 1926-29. He is now county extension agent of Webster

County, is president of the Red Cloud Ad Club, and holds membership in the County Agents Association.

He has held membership in the Parent Teachers Association, of which he was formerly secretary, and now holds membership in the Nebraskana Society, School Board, Red Cross, and Masonic Lodge. His sports include golfing, baseball, basketball, and football, while his hobby is reading. Mr. Taggart is affiliated with the Congregational Christian Church of Red Cloud.

He married Louise Elizabeth Cook at Waverly, Nebraska, July 16, 1924. Mrs. Taggart, who was formerly an educator, was born at Waverly, November 30, 1900, of English parentage. Two children were born to them: J. Mark, October 12, 1926; and Donna Louise, August 31, 1928. Residence: Red Cloud.

Elias Fogle Talbert

Born at Shelbyville, Indiana, September 17, 1873, Elias Fogle Talbert has resided in Nebraska for more than fifty years. His father, Harrison B. Talbert, was born in Shelbyville, April 19, 1842, and died at Long Beach, California, February 22, 1922. He was a farmer of English descent who served in the Civil War 1861-65. His wife, Matilda Jane Rittenhouse, was born in Shelbyville, July 11, 1842, and died at Trumbull, Nebraska, May 1, 1917. She was of Dutch descent.

Elias F. Talbert attended district school in Adams County, attended Hastings College one year, and was graduated from Grand Island Business College in 1893. A traveling salesman from 1901 to 1927, he was with Martin Brothers and later with J. C. Slife both at Trumbull. He traveled for Doniphan and Company at St. Joseph and later the firm of Donald and Porter and The Donald Company at Grand Island for seventeen years.

During the latter part of 1919 he organized his own concern the Ulry-Talbert Company of Grand Island, and in January, 1926, opened a branch house at Columbus. Mr. Talbert is vice president and manager at Columbus.

He was married on December 14, 1899, to Erma Beatrice Ray at Marquette, Nebraska. Mrs. Talbert was born at Marquette, October 6, 1877, of Irish parentage. There are two children, William H. Ray, born December 10, 1912; and Elias Francis, Jr., born June 21, 1917.

Mr. Talbert is a member of the Grace Episcopal Church, the Red Cross, the Chamber of Commerce, the Modern Woodmen of America, the Masons, Knights Templar, and the Hastings Shrine. He is a member of the Wayside Country Club and a life member of the Nebraskana Society. His favorite recreations are golf and bridge. Residence: Columbus.

William Robert Talboy

William Robert Talboy, physician and surgeon, was born at Palmyra, Iowa, July 4, 1865, son of Benjamin and Martha (Garner) Talboy. His father, a native of Birmingham, England, came to America at the age of twenty-five and was employed in a woolen mill as a carder. He died at Silver City, Iowa, at the age of ninety-two years. Martha, his wife, was born in Lynn, England, and died at Silver City at the age of eighty. She was a homemaker and active in the work of her church.

Dr. Talboy attended Palmyra public school, and was graduated from high school in 1880. He received his medical degree from the Sioux City Medical College, and attended the Iowa City, Iowa, Medical College. Thereafter he taught in Iowa schools for four years. He is admitted to practice in both Texas and Nebraska, and has been a resident of this state 37 years. A Republican, he was state representative in 1925; has been chairman of the town board 20 years, and secretary of the school board twenty-five years.

On June 10, 1897, he was united in marriage to Lena

Schroer. Their marriage took place at Ponca, Nebraska. Mrs. Talboy was born at Victor, Iowa, September 18, 1873, of German parentage. There were five children born to this union, Marie, born April 5, 1896; Ruth, born in 1899; Esther, born January 2, 1902, married Paul Jacobsen, and died October 15, 1929; Willis, born September 18, 1905, and Margaret, born January 13, 1913. All are teachers or students.

Dr. Talboy is a member of the Nebraska State and Sioux Valley Medical Societies, the Masons, Modern Woodmen of America, and the Congregational Church. Residence: Newcastle.

Earl A. Talhelm

Earl A. Talhelm was born at Crete, Nebraska, October 30, 1885, son of Samuel B. and Mary M. (Casterline) Talhelm. Samuel Talhelm was born in Greencastle, Pennsylvania, August 11, 1856, and is a grain buyer for the Crete Mills. His family has been in America for several generations. Mary, his wife, was born at Hartford City, Indiana, April 5, 1864, of American ancestry for several generations.

Mr. Talhelm attended Crete High School from which he was graduated in 1904. He was a student at Doane College and Peru State Normal School, and was graduated from Doane in 1911. He represented that college in debate 2 years, was a member of its orchestra and glee club. At Peru, he was a member of the band. His fraternity is the I. D. C.

At Crete he won four first prizes in track, was center on the basketball team, and a member of the baseball team.

He was married to Lucretia May Smith at Crete, November 29, 1912. Mrs. Talhelm was born at Freeport, Illinois, October 12, 1886. They have one daughter, Ruth, born February 25, 1914. Mr. Talhelm is a Democrat. At the present time he is manager of the Crete Mills, at Crete, Nebraska. He is president (1929-31) of the American Corn Millers Federation; in 1929 was president of the Nebraska Millers Association; in 1930, was vice president of the Midwest Feed Manufacturers Association; and is now a member of the board of directors of the Crete Commercial Club, and the Nebraska Manufacturers Association. In 1930 he was president of the Crete Rotary Club. A member of the School Board for the past 10 years, he served as president one year and secretary eight years. He is a member of Grace Methodist Church, and for ten years was superintendent of its Sunday School. His fraternal memberships include the Modern Woodmen of America and the Security Benefit Association. He is a member of the Nebraskana Society, 1931-. His hobby is music. Residence: Crete.

Dora Alexander Talley

Dora Alexander Talley, national secretary of the Supreme Forest Woodmen Circle, was born in Franklin County, Alabama, November 14, 1879. She is the daughter of James D. and Nancy E. (Arnold) Alexander, the former of whom was state organizer of the Woodmen of the World for the state of Texas, and representative at six national conventions. He was born at Center Star, Alabama, June 15, 1851, and died at Garland, Texas, February 18, 1920. He is of Revolutionary descent, his uncle, Dr. Thomas Douglas being a member of the Sons of the American Revolution. His wife, Nannie, was born at Russellville, Alabama, April 5, 1858, and is a descendant of Matthew Smith, Revolutionary soldier.

Dora Alexander was educated in the public schools of Texas, where her parents settled when she was a girl, and attended summer normal courses. Until 1911 she was a teacher in the public schools of Texas. Her association with the Woodmen Circle began in 1904, when she joined the society. She was elected national secretary in 1911, and has been unanimously re-elected four times.

On August 19, 1919, she was married to John Robert

Talley, at Omaha. Mr. Talley, who was born near Gallatin, Tennessee, July 25, 1869, is in charge of the records of the Supreme Forest, Woodmen Circle.

Mrs. Talley is a Democrat. She is affiliated with the First Baptist Church of Omaha, and with the Young Women's Christian Association. She is a member of the Women's Division of the Chamber of Commerce, and the Business and Professional Women's Club, and the Omaha Woman's Club.

Her fraternal organizations include the Order of Eastern Star, the Rebekah Lodge, the Brotherhood of American Yeomen and the Women's Benefit Association. Her social club is the Happy Hollow Country Club. She is also active in the National Fraternal Congress of America, having served the Secretaries' section for several years. Residence: Omaha. (Photograph on Page 1175).

Edward Tanner

Dr. Edward Tanner, pioneer physician of Madison County, Nebraska, has been engaged in the practice of medicine at Battle Creek for the past 51 years. Born at Lacona, New York, February 6, 1855, he is the son of Charles and Mary (Hamer) Tanner. His father, a farmer, was born in England in 1817, and died at Lacona, September 1, 1896; he came to America in 1838. His mother was born in Wales in 1812 and died at Lacona, in 1898.

Dr. Tanner attended district school and in 1876 was a student at Union College, Schenectady, New York. He received the M. D. degree at the University of New York in 1879, and practiced medicine exclusively until 1919 when he assumed the duties of president of the Farmers Bank at Battle Creek. A Republican, he was county coroner for a number of years and served as a member of the school board for 12 years.

He holds membership in the Madison County Medical Association, Nebraska State Medical Association, American Medical Association, and the Nebraska State Historical Society. He is a member of the Battle Creek Commercial Club and the Red Cross. His favorite sport is golfing. During the World War Dr. Tanner served as a member of the Advisory Examining Board of Madison County and took part in all Liberty Loan and Red Cross drives.

He was married to Laura A. Hurford at Battle Creek, December 24, 1882; she was born at Canton, Ohio, April 6, 1858, of English and German parentage, and died at Battle Creek, July 11, 1920. Their daughter, Helen, born October 8, 1888, married John B. Dufphey. Dr. Tanner married Mary E. Berry, March 21, 1922. She is the daughter of George S. and Katherine (Hull) Hurford. She is a sister of Laura A. Hurford, Dr. Tanner's first wife. Residence: Battle Creek.

Harry H. Tappan

Harry H. Tappan was born at St. Clair, Michigan, on March 19, 1863, the son of Rochesly Tappan and Jane Catherine (Kunt) Tappan. His father was born in Onandaga County, New York, October 26, 1826, of English parentage. He was a rancher until his death in Grant County, Nebraska in October, 1908.

Mr. Tappan was educated in rural schools, and came to Nebraska in 1881, from Michigan. On July 4, 1885, at St. Clair, Michigan he was united in marriage to Anna A. Richmann, a native of Danzig, Germany.

Mr. Tappan is affiliated with the Republican party and is a member of the Nebraskana Society. He has been in the hardware business since he came to Nebraska, fifty years ago. Residence: Daykin.

Alfred Garfield Taylor

Since March 13, 1922, Alfred Garfield Taylor has been postmaster of Chappell. He was born at Nassagaweya,

DORA ALEXANDER TALLEY

Heyn Studio—Omaha

Ontario, Canada, July 28, 1883, and came to Nebraska 43 years ago.

His father, William Middleton Taylor, was born in Nassagaweya, Ontario, and is a veterinary surgeon. He is descended from Thomas Middleton Taylor, who was born in Yorkshire, England, February 21, 1820, and who died May 27, 1908, at Eden Mills, Ontario. His wife was Mary Knight Taylor who was born in Ireland, February 3, 1819, and died at Eden Mills, November 13, 1919.

Mary Ann Norrish, wife of William Middleton Taylor, was born at Nassagaweya, January 16, 1857, and now resides at Lincoln. She is past president of the Ladies Aid Society of her church and is prominent in church work. Her father was Nicholas Norrish, of Devonshire, England, who was born April 19, 1823, and died at Guelph, Ontario, June 13, 1901. His wife was Ann Youart Norrish who was born in Yorkshire, England, October 22, 1827, and who died at Nassagoweya, February 25, 1870.

Mr. Taylor attended the public schools of York, and the York High School and attended York College. He was graduated from York Business College in 1907. He played football during high school and at college was captain of the basketball and baseball teams.

On January, 1906, he entered the post office at York, Nebraska as a clerk. He resigned on October 1, 1918 to accept a position as bookkeeper with the First National Bank of Chappell. On February 3, 1922, he was appoited postmaster at Chappell, and is now serving in his third term. He is secretary of the Deuel County Poultry Association, and is a Republican.

He is married to Julia Avis Bryan who was born at Marion, Kansas, September 20, 1883. Four children were born to them, Laurence Bryan, on December 29, 1912, who died January 11, 1913; Phoebe Winifred, born September 22, 1915; Alfred Glenn, born July 22, 1918; and Charles Arthur, born October 21, 1921.

While living at York, Mr. Taylor was a member of the Young Men's Christian Association, and afterward held membership in the state organization for a number of years. He is president of the Chappell Golf Club, and president of the Logan-Sedgwick Golf League. In addition to golf, he enjoys skating, while his hobby is raising Rhode Island Red chickens.

For five years he was a member of the school board of Chappell. He is a Mason, a member of the Chamber of Commerce, the Red Cross, and the Methodist Church. Residence: Chappell.

Asahel Lysander Taylor

Asahel Lysander Taylor, editor of the *Republican Leader,* a weekly newspaper, was born at Franklinville, New York, August 2, 1861, son of Asahel Lysander and Polly Elizabeth (Rolph) Taylor. The elder Asahel Taylor was born in Franklinville, New York, October 16, 1832, and died there on October 11, 1862. He was a farmer of English descent. His wife, Polly, was born at Randolph, New York, March 16, 1838, and died at Trenton, Nebraska, December 24, 1917. She was of English and French descent.

Mr. Taylor attended the country schools of Michigan and Battle Creek College of Battle Creek, Michigan, for two years, 1877-79. On October 3 of that year he came to Nebraska where he has since resided. He taught country school from 1880 to 1881 and was in the mercantile business the two following years. He homesteaded in 1885 in Hitchock county, and from 1891 until 1902 was the manager of a general store. Since 1895 he has been a newspaper publisher.

His marriage to Amy Illione Livingston was solemnized at Shelton, Nebraska, May 14, 1882. She was born at Lowell, Massachusetts, July 27, 1865, and died at Trenton, July 30, 1895. She was of Mayflower ancestry.

To them were born five children, Nettie, June 19, 1883, who married Henry Owens, and lives in San Francisco; Lucy, October 14, 1884, who married Charles O.

Gammon, residing in Omaha; Percy, March 19, 1886, Uunion Pacific machinist at Salina, Kansas, who married Harriet Cook; Jessie, May 12, 1888, who married Paul F. Bischeld and lives in Denver; Merle, February 10, 1890, who married Henry Kirschke, and resides at Denver. She was widowed in July, 1924, and in August, 1929, married John W. Greenstreet. In April, 1896, Mr. Taylor was married to Belle E. Livingston, sister of his first wife, at Trenton. The following children were born to them, Elbert, June 21, 1897, who married Beulah Henderson, is a newspaper man at Cambridge, Nebraska; Charles, born March 22, 1899, who died November 19, 1906; Wayne, March 15, 1901, who married Pearl Brown, is deputy county clerk of Hitchcock County; Theodore, May 18, 1905, who died June 30, 1918; Amy, June 11, 1909, who is now teaching school; and Amelia Lucille, May 30, 1911, a student at Doane College.

Mr. Taylor is a Republican and active in party politics. Since 1920 he has been county chairman of the Republican party, and was unsuccessful candidate for state representative at two different times. From 1923 until 1925 Mr. Taylor served as secretary of the Trenton Commercial Club. He is a member of the Nebraska Press Association, the Odd Fellows, the Southwest Nebraska Historical Society, and for several years was a member of the School Board. He is the president of the Massacre Canyon Memorial Association, and the originiator of the idea of erecting a monument to commemorate the Battle of Massacre Canyon. His hobbies are baseball and reading. Mr. Taylor died April 6, 1932.

Charles E. Taylor

Born at Ashton, Illinois, December 9, 1872, Charles E. Taylor has been a leading banker at St. Paul for more than twenty-five years. His father, John P. Taylor, was born in Indiana, June 17, 1839, and served in the Civil War. His death occurred at St. Paul on August 17, 1923. His mother, born in Oregon, Illinois, in 1843, died at St. Paul in January, 1922.

Charles E. Taylor attended country schools in Sherman County, the St. Paul High School, and was graduated from Western Normal College at Lincoln in 1893. For five years thereafter he was cashier of the St. Paul State Bank, and the next five years was cashier of the Citizens State Bank at St. Paul. He has been active vice president of the Citizens National Bank for more than seventeen years.

Of his marriage to Vera I. Force, there are four children: Harriet and Cathryn, twins, born December 1903; and Charles, Jr., and Maydee, twins, born June 2, 1913. Cathryn, who married George J. Armstrong, resides at Grand Island, where her husband is associated with the Nebraska National Bank. Harriet teaches home economics in the Walnut Junior High School at Grand Island. Charles and Maydee are freshmen in Hastings College.

Mr. Taylor is an independent Democrat. He has always been active in local politics, and served two terms as county treasurer of Howard County and two terms St. Paul Chamber of Commerce two terms, and president of the local Lions Club two ters. During the World War he was chairman of Howard County Red Cross Drives.

He is a Presbyterian, but interested in Christian Science, is a member of the Young Men's Christian Association and the Nebraskana Society. An ardent golfer, he is a member of the St. Paul Golf Club. Residence: St. Paul.

Charles William Taylor

One of Nebraska's leading figures in the educational field, Charles William Taylor has been a resident of the state thirty-seven years. He was born at Red Oak, Iowa, June 3, 1874, son of James Henry and Tamar Ann (Ratliff) Taylor. James Henry Taylor was born at Mount Pleasant, Iowa, November 8, 1839, and was by occupation a farmer. During the Civil War he served three years and eleven month with the Union Army with Company M, Fourth Iowa Cavalry. He was descended from the Orange County, Virginia, Taylors, Hannahs, Morfitts and Waddels, all of whom were of Colonial stock. After the Civil War James Henry Taylor migrated west, settling in Iowa, where he met and married Tamar Ann Ratliff.

Tamar Ann Ratliff was born at Salem, Iowa, March 2, 1849. Aside from her duties in the home, a Quaker by birth, she was prominent in the Methodist Church, in the missionary society, Women's Relief Corps, and the Ladies of the Grand Army of the Republic. Before her marriage she was a student at Whittier College. Her ancestry was traced to the North Carolina Ratliffs, Fletchers, Nixons, Hobsons, and Provos, the first families of Virginia as early as 1609.

Charles W. Taylor was educated first in the rural schools of Montgomery County, Iowa, and was graduated from the Red Oak High School in 1893. He attended the University of Nebraska, from which he received his B. A. in 1898, and Columbia University where he took post graduate work. His scholastic honors include Phi Delta Kappa, membership on the Nebraska Intercollegiate Debating Team in 1898, and vice presidency of the State Oratorical Association in 1898. He is a member of Acacia, and of the Palladian Literary Society.

On July 3, 1899, he was united in marriage to Sarah Elizabeth Wert Smith at Lead, South Dakota. Mrs. Taylor was born at Humboldt, Kansas, March 18, 1874, and prior to her marriage was a teacher. She is descended from the Werts, Comptons, Hydes, Letz, Hankins and Runyons of colonial New Jersey, the McLeans of Scotland, and the Nordells of France. To their marriage six children were born: Seth Charles Henry, born April 24, 1900, married Ruth Lenore Hutton, and is the Cincinnati manager of the Sun Life Assurance Company of Montreal, Canada. Marie Provo, who was born May 16, 1902, died May 18, 1913. Hutch Nordell, born March 15, 1904, died October 13, 1918. John William, born December 21, 1906, married Mary Katherine Meier, and is an area traffic engineer for the Northwestern Bell Telephone Company at Omaha. James Ratliff, born February 28, 1909, died February 28, 1909. Beth Elaine, born January 23, 1915, is a student.

Mr. Taylor's military activities extend over a period of years. He enlisted in Company M, 3rd Iowa National Guard Infantry on October 18, 1893, and was honorably discharged on account of the expiration of his service on October 19, 1896. From September 1894, to June 9, 1898, he was a member of the University of Nebraska Cadet Regiment, and was a member of the Pershing Rifles two years. On October 3, 1902, he enlisted with Company G, First Nebraska National Guard Infantry, and was commissioned 2nd lieutenant on that date. He was honorably discharged on October 3, 1905.

On August 24, 1917, he enlisted in the Second Officers Reserve Training Camp at Fort Snelling, Minnesota, and was commissioned captain of Infantry on November 27, 1917. On December 15, 1917, he was assigned to the 88th Division at Camp Dodge and attached to Company F, Second Battalion, 163rd Depot Brigade. He was transferred to Machine Gun Training Center at Camp Hancock, Georgia, May 25, 1918, and commanded the 27th, 6th and 15th Companies at the Recruit Receiving Depot, Camp Hancock, and the 67th Company, Group 6, Main Training Depot, Machine Gun Training Center. On December 21, 1918, he was transferred to Officers Section, Machine Gun School and certified as a machine gun officer. He passed his overseas examination on September 13, 1918, and was honorably discharged from the rank of captain in the Army of the United States December 20,

1918. On August 19, 1919, he was commissioned captain of Infantry, Officers Reserve Corps of the Army of the United States, and still holds that commission.

Among his memberships in military and patriotic organizations are the Reserve Officers Association, the American Legion, the Sons of Veterans of the Civil War, Sons of the American Revolution, the Forty and Eight, of which last mentioned organization his membership is in Voiture No. 19.

Entering the teaching profession as a young man, Mr. Taylor taught in the rural schools of Iowa, 1893-94; was principal of the Ohiowa, Nebraska schools 1898-1901; was superintendent of city schools at Geneva 1901-07; superintendent of city schools at McCook 1908-11, and professor of school administration and director of teacher training at the University of Nebraska, 1911-26. In 1907, he was secretary-treasurer and manager of the S. R. Smith Furniture Company of Lead, South Dakota.

A Republican, he was defeated for nomination of State Superintendent of Public Instruction in the primaries of 1922; was nominated and elected to that office on the non-political ballot of 1926, and we re-elected in 1930. He is a member of the Nebraska State Teachers Association of which he was vice president one year; life member of the National Education Association.

He is also a member of the Nebraska Parent-Teacher Association, an executive officer of the State Board for Vocational Education, secretary of the State Illiteracy Commission, chairman of the Nebraska Committee on the Enrichment of Adult Life, and a member of the State Library Commission and the State Normal Board.

Since 1929 he has been chairman of the advisory board of the Lincoln Corps of the Salvation Army, and during 1924, was state commander of the American Legion, department of Nebraska. In fraternal organizations his memberships include the Ancient Free and Accepted Masons, the Scottish Rite Masons, the Grange, Royal Neighbors of America and the Eastern Star. He is a member of the Lincoln Chamber of Commerce and the Nebraskana Society. His hobbies are fishing and flowers. The Taylor family attends St. Matthew's Protestant Episcopal Church of Lincoln, of which Mr. Taylor is a member of the vestry. Residence: Lincoln.

Clyde Henry Taylor

Clyde Henry Taylor was born at Elm Creek, Nebraska, August 10, 1898, the son of John and Daisy (Losee) Taylor, the oldest son of a family of thirteen children, all living. His father, who was born at Rochester, New York, September 15, 1873, and died at Overton, Nebraska, November 13, 1931, was a farmer. His mother was born at Council Bluffs, Iowa, October 8, 1875.

Mr. Taylor, who has been the publisher of the *Overton Herald* at Overton, Nebraska, for the past 13 years, was graduated from the Overton High School in 1917. He has been active in various community affairs for several years and recently was made Republican precinct chairman at Overton. He was elected to membership on the Overton Board of Education in 1931, and is a member of the Overton Lions Club and the Nebraskana Society. His fraternal organizations are the Masons, Odd Fellows, and Modern Woodmen of America.

He holds membership in the Nebraska Press Association, and has received two important awards for achievement in the newspaper world: a loving cup presented to the best weekly newspaper in the Nebraska Press Contest for 1925; and first place in the "Best Front Page" contests of 1926 and 1927. He is interested in mechanics and gardening, and is fond of basketball and swimming. Mr. Taylor is the owner of the *Loomis Sentinel* at Loomis, Nebraska.

His marriage to Marguerite Gullion occurred at Lexington, Nebraska, May 19, 1917; she was born at Greenwood, December 31, 1898. To them two children were born: Dale, born April 19, 1918; and Clyde, born April 6, 1921. Residence: Overton.

Earl John Taylor

Earl John Taylor was born at Tobias, Nebraska, September 20, 1890, the son of William Henry and Lauretta Jane (Baker) Taylor. His father, who was born at Fort Edward, New York, May 19, 1855, was a grain dealer at Tobias and is now a resident of York, Nebraska. His ancestry is English and Irish. His mother was born at Odell, Livingston County, Illinois, June 6, 1859; her ancestry is English.

Mr. Taylor was graduated from the Tobias High School in 1907, and in 1913 was awarded the B. S. degree at the University of Nebraska, College of Agriculture. He was elected to membership in Sigma Phi Epsilon at the University. During 1914 and 1915 he was instructor in agriculture at the O'Neill High School, and from 1915 to 1918 was agriculture teacher at York High School, York, Nebraska. He was connected with the Keystone Creamery Company at York, 1918-29, and since 1929 has been manager of the Fairmont Creamery Company at York.

He is a member of the board of education at York, is president of the Nebraska Ice Cream Manufacturers Credit Association, and holds membership in the Masons and the Knights of Pythias. His social clubs are the Lincoln University Club and the York Country Club, while his favorite sport is golf.

On August 19, 1914, he was united in marriage with Bess Manon Stimson at Pawnee City, Nebraska. Mrs. Taylor, who is of English descent, was born at Pawnee City, October 6, 1891. They have three children: William, born May 20, 1915; Edwin, born January 1, 1917; and Barbara, born July 19, 1922. Residence: York.

Earl Sylvester Taylor

Earl Sylvester Taylor, leading merchant at Scottsbluff, was born at Holton, Kansas, July 14, 1883, son of George and Flora Ellen (Huff) Taylor. He is of English descent.

On June 12, 1910, he was married to Sarah Ellen Barrand at Horton, Kansas. Mrs. Taylor was born at Denton, Kansas, October 12, 1887. There are three children, Helen, born November 13, 1912; Billy, born December 26, 1919; and Bobby, born July 2, 1923.

Mr. Taylor is a Republican. He is a member of the Lions Club, the Elks and the Masons. He enjoys fishing, hunting and golf. Residence: Scottsbluff.

Elbert Lloyd Taylor

Elbert Lloyd Taylor, prominent in the educational world in Nebraska, was born in Gage County, Nebraska, November 13, 1882, the son of Lewis and Hannah Frances (Russell) Taylor. His father, who was a farmer, was born in Ohio, September 17, 1854, of English and Welsh parentage. His mother, whose ancestry is Irish and English, was born at Vandalia, Illinois, June 15, 1854, and died at Belvidere, Thayer County, Nebraska, February 6, 1903.

Mr. Taylor was graduated from the Belvidere High School in 1903, was a student at Cotner College, 1905-06, and attended Peru State Normal School, 1906-07. He was awarded the B. S. and A. M. degrees at the University of Nebraska, 1915, where he was affiliated with Alpha Zeta and Gamma Sigma Delta.

From 1918 to 1920 he was a member of the faculty of the University of Nebraska. He served as federal land appraiser for the Lincoln Joint Stock Land Bank, 1921-25, and from 1925 to 1928 was head of the schools at Alexandria, Bethany, and Belvidere, Nebraska. He is a member of the Christian Church at Belvidere, and holds membership in the Nebraskana Society. His favorite sport is football, while his hobby is the study of economics.

He was united in marriage with Mary Edna Hill at Lincoln, June 28, 1916. They have one daughter, Harriet Louise, born May 8, 1923. Residence: Belvidere.

Ellen Smoot Taylor

Ellen Smoot Taylor, daughter of William Harrison and Martha Sawyer (Bunnell) Smoot, was born in Lexington, Kentucky, April 5, 1852. For more than 62 years, she has been a resident of Nebraska.

Her father was born at Huntsville, Alabama, of English and Irish descent. He was a southern planter, a member of a distinguished family of landowners and slaveholders. He died at Lexington, in 1852. His wife, Martha, was born in Lexington, and died at Shubert, Nebraska, in 1909. Her grandfather came from France and helped to survey the state of Connecticut. Martha Bunnell was also descended from the May family, who came to Virginia 150 years ago from Ireland. She was extremely active in church work.

Ellen Smoot attended school in Louisville, Kentucky and Nebraska. She was a teacher for five years, one term in Indiana and four in Nebraska, and at the present time, manages her Nebraska and Colorado real estate holdings. She is a Democrat.

On July 8, 1875, she was married to John Wray Taylor at Brownville. Mr. Taylor, who was born at Bethany, Missouri, September 14, 1848, died at Auburn, Nebraska, February 13, 1907. He was a pharmacist, a descendant of early Virginia settlers from England. To Mr. and Mrs. Taylor, one son was born, Guy R., on December 16, 1877. He received his medical degree from Creighton Medical College in 1902, and is a leading physician at Hebron.

For more than 35 years, Mrs. Taylor has been a member of the Order of Eastern Star, and is still an active worker. She devotes much time to reading, is a profound student, and is keenly interested in the economic and political issues of the world. Her religious affiliation is with the First Presbyterian Church. Residence: Hebron.

Floyd Chesterfield Taylor

Floyd Chesterfield Taylor, county treasurer of Scotts Bluff County, was born at Merna, Nebraska, January 27, 1895, son of Frank Thomas and Mayme (Kitchen) Taylor. His ancestry is English and Dutch.

Mr. Taylor attended public and high school and was a student at business college for one year. Hhe has been a merchant, deputy county clerk, county assessor, abstractor, and is now serving as county treasurer elected on the Republican ticket. He is a Scottish Rite Mason. His favorite sport is fishing.

On April 27, 1917, he was married to Verle Opal Ray at Broken Bow. Mrs. Taylor was born at Anselmo, October 31, 1897. She is the daughter of George M. and Eva (Filley) Williams. She was graduated from Anselmo high school and is a member of the Eastern Star. He has a step-daughter, Eva Jean, born January 6, 1915. Residence: Scottsbluff.

Frank James Taylor

A distinguished lawyer at St. Paul, Nebraska, is Frank James Taylor, who has lived in this state for over half a century. He was born at Ashton, Illinois, February 12, 1866, the son of John P. and Susan K. (Bridge) Taylor. His father, who was a stock and grain dealer, was born at Terre Haute, Indiana, June 17, 1838, and died at St. Paul, August 17, 1923. His mother, who was born at Oregon, Illinois, May 27, 1843, was of Irish and Dutch descent, and died at St. Paul, January 22, 1922.

Mr. Taylor attended the St. Paul High School and in 1891, received the LL. B. degree at the University of Michigan. He was engaged in the practice of law for two years with the firm Kendall & Taylor at St. Paul, 1891-93; practiced alone from 1893 until 1917; and since that time has been a member of the firm of Taylor & Spikes. He is also president of the Citizens National Bank. He served as county attorney of Howard County for 12 years, was a candidate for congress in 1914, on the Democratic ticket, and is now serving his second term as regent of the University of Nebraska.

He holds membership in the Community Club, the Red Cross, the Royal Highlanders and the Modern Woodmen of America. He is affiliated with the Presbyterian Church of St. Paul, and holds membership in the Nebraskana Society.

He was married to Byrdie West, at St. Paul, June 27, 1895. Mrs. Taylor, who was formerly a teacher, was born at St. Paul, May 17, 1876. They have two children: Harold W., born July 23, 1899, who married Velma Hubbartt; and Burdette F., born February 7, 1903, who married Wayne O. Stoehr. Residence: Omaha. (Photograph in Album).

Harry Allen Taylor

Harry Allen Taylor, physician and surgeon, was born at Burr Oak, Kansas, January 9, 1883, son of William Allen and Martha Alice (Mitchell) Taylor. He received his Bachelor of Arts degree from Nebraska Wesleyan University in 1905; his Bachelor of Arts degree from the same institution in 1908. In 1905 he was a major in the Nebraska Wesleyan Cadet Battalion.

On May 1, 1913, he was married to Ruth Mary Maris at Newcastle, Wyoming. Admitted to the practice of medicine in 1908, he was pathologist to the Nebraska Hospital for the Insane, and has engaged in general practice since that date. He is a member of the American, Nebraska State and Lancaster County Medical Associations, the Hiram Club, and the First Methodist Church. He is a member of the board of trustees of Nebraska Wesleyan University, also. Residence: Lincoln.

James Taylor

Born at Lyons, County Kildare, Ireland, June 29, 1861, James Taylor, who died at Auburn, October 12, 1930, had been a leading citizen of his community for forty-three years. He was the son of Robert and Marcella (Doyle) Taylor. Robert Taylor, a miller by trade was born in Scotland. He died in 1892. Marcella, his wife was born in Ireland, and died in Newark, New York, 1904. James Taylor received his early education in Lyons, Ireland.

Coming to America while still a youth, he shortly afterward settled in Nemaha County. Here he married Lizzie E. Hughes, in 1895. Mrs. Taylor is the daughter of Peter and Mary Ann (Meath) Engles. Her father, a cabinet-maker, pre-empted a section of land in Nemaha County in 1860; prior to coming to America from Germany, he served three years in the German Army. Mrs. Taylor was born on the family homestead in 1865.

Mr. Taylor was active in the Democratic party, and in educational and civic organizations. He was a member of the Red Cross, and a trustee of the Knights of Columbus. From 1890 to 1896 he was a member of the local school board. He attended St. Joseph's Catholic Church.

At the time of his death he had owned and operated the Auburn Flour Mills for forty-two years, and had established an enviable reputation for integrity and honesty. His death was a distinct loss to his community and he is mourned by all who knew him.

Jay R. Taylor

Born at Wells, Minnesota, Jay R. Taylor is the son of Edward Henry and Elisa (O'Brien) Taylor. His father, who was a stockraiser and farmer, was born in New York, February 20, 1842, and died at Taylor, Nebraska, in 1907. His mother, whose ancestry was Irish, was born in New York, October 30, 1843, and died at Taylor in 1901.

Mr. Taylor has been a rancher and farmer for many years in Grant County, Nebraska, holds membership in the Independent Order of Odd Fellows at Whitman, and is a member of the Nebraskana Society. He is a member of the Republican party.

He is married to Lois Montas Bump who was born at Ackley, Iowa, August 5, 1883, of English parentage. By a former marriage the following children were born: Felix, April 10, 1889, who married Ruth Bolinger; Saide, April 22, 1890, who married Frank Dolin; Martha, February 22, 1893, who married Joe Francis; Bessie, 1892, who died December 1, 1911; William, 1894, who married Myrtle Castenson; Elias, 1901, who married Olive Lindburg; and Nelle, 1904, who married Herbert Cook. Residence: Whitman.

Mary L. Taylor

Mary L. Taylor, daughter of Benjamin Franklin and Sara Evelyn (Smith) Dill, was born in Cicero, Indiana, November 3, 1869. Her father was born in Cicero, March 24, 1844, a clergyman, and a descendant of Colonel George Matthew Dill, of the Revolutionary War, who came from Ireland about 1732. He died at Rector, Arkansas, December 23, 1929.

Sara Evelyn Smith was born in Cicero, May 7, 1851, and died at Thedford, Nebraska, March 31, 1910. She was of Irish descent, her maternal grandfather was killed at Lundy's Lane in 1812. They went to Indiana on their bridal trip about 1840.

Mrs. Taylor attended public and high school at Van Wert, Ohio, graduating in 1881. She thereafter attended business college and Fremont Normal School, and taught in the public schools of Nebraska fourteen years, in Blaine, Thomas, Hooker, Grant, Cherry, Rock and Brown Counties. For the past fifteen years she has been postmaster at Raymond. She is also the editor of the *Raymond Review*. She is eligible to the Daughters of the American Revolution, and is a member of the First Presbyterian Church, the Red Cross, and the Parent-Teachers' Association.

Mrs. Taylor has one daughter, Mrs. Jay Q. Williams, whose husband is supervisor of music at Appleton, Wisconsin, where they reside. They have four children: Robert F., born June 22, 1922; Stanley L., born October 19, 1924; Donald E., Born August 17, 1926; and Rawleigh J., born July 10, 1928.

A member of the publicity committee of the Raymond Woman's Club, Mrs. Taylor is also a member of the Nebraska Children's Home Society. Her hobbies are reading, history and psychology. Residence: Raymond.

Sherman Taylor, Jr.

Sherman J. Taylor was born at Wymore, Gage County, Nebraska, November 9, 1892, the son of Sherman and Helena Swick Taylor. His father, who was a farmer and banker, was born at Stark, Illinois, September 3, 1865, and died at Wymore, January 13, 1928. His mother was born at Lear, Germany, September 17, 1870.

Mr. Taylor was graduated from the Wymore High School in 1902, and later was a student at Nebraska Wesleyan University. From 1914 to 1928 he was engaged in the wholesale ice business, and since that date has been a farmer in Gage County. He is affiliated with the Methodist Church and holds membership in the Nebraskana Society. During the World War he was a member of Company C, Eighth Ammunition Train of the United States Army.

His marriage to Gladys Kara McMaken was solemnized at Plattsmouth, Nebraska, February 6, 1918. Mrs. Taylor was born at Plattsmouth, August 29, 1896, of Irish parentage. Three children were born to them: Margaret, born January 2, 1919; Edith, born January 4, 1920, who died September 9, 1920; and Joe, born September 5, 1922. Residence: Wymore.

William Taylor

William Taylor, retired farmer of Colfax County, Nebraska, was born at Haddenham, Cambridge, England, July 4, 1855. His father, John Taylor, was born at Haddenham where he died. Sarah (Pont) Taylor lived at Haddenham all her life.

Mr. Taylor received his education in the schools of England. He was a farmer in Nebraska for 48 years and upon his retirement moved to Howells where he is active in civic affairs. He is affiliated with the Howells Congregational Church; is a member of The Nebraskana Society; and is a member of the Modern Woodmen of America.

He was united in marriage with Leah Childrerey at Geneseo, Illinois, October 29, 1879. Mrs. Taylor, who is the daughter of Joseph and Eliza Childrerey, was born at Eltesly, Cambridgeshire, England, November 12, 1853. Their children are: Maggie, born October 17, 1880; Alfred, born July 15, 1883; and Frederick, born April 29, 1885. Residence: Howells.

William George Langworthy Taylor

William George Langworthy Taylor, professor emeritus of the University of Nebraska since 1911, was born in New York City, May 13, 1859. He is the son of George Henry and Sarah Elizabeth (Langworthy) Taylor, the former of whom was born at Williston, Vermont, January 4, 1821. A graduate of New York Medical College, he introduced Swedish massage in 1858, and was an author of considerable note. His family is traced to the Rev. Eldad Taylor (1642-1729), who settled in Westfield, Massachusetts, about 1669. He was a graduate of Harvard University in 1671 (See *Sibley's Harvard Graduates*).

Sarah Elizabeth Langworthy was born at Quanacontaug, near Westerly, Rhode Island, May 18, 1828, and died in Lincoln, August 21, 1906. A business woman, (she built the old Madison Avenue Hotel in New York City), she was graduated from Alfred Academy, later Alfred University, and served as principal of the Plainfield, New Jersey, Academy. She was descended from Robert Langworthy, born 1675-90, who was probably a son of Andrew Langworthy, born in England.

Professor Taylor attended the 22nd Street public school in New York City, the Institution Fezandie, New York, and D. S. Everson's College Preparatory School. In 1880 he received the degree of B. A. from Harvard University and in 1883 the degree of LL. B. In 1915 he was awarded an LL. D. from the University of Nebraska. At Harvard he was made a member of Phi Beta Kappa, 1879. He took second place in the mile run at Harvard 1879, was a member of his class crew at Harvard 1879, and took first place in the mile run at Columbia, 1881.

In 1886-87, he attended the Ecole des Sciences Politiques at Paris, the College de France, 1887, and the University of Leipsic, 1888-90. He spent eight years in Europe, most of which were devoted to travel and study.

Since August, 1893, he has been a resident of Nebraska, and has held positions from instructor to professor at the University of Nebraska. Since 1911 he has been professor emeritus, and has devoted his time to study and writing. He is the author of *The Credit System* (Macmillian, 1913), *The Saddle Horse* (Henry Holt, 1925); and numerous articles in economic and equestrian periodicals. He is the owner of Shibam (Arabian National Stud Book 125) and Martha Biggs (American Saddle Horse Association 1165), and is greatly interested in equitation. He is devoting much time to psychic research and has several books in preparation.

Mr. Taylor was married to Frances Chamberlain Brown at Winchester, Illinois, June 21, 1894. She was born at Saint Louis, Missouri, June 26, 1861, and died at Boulder, Colorado, July 28, 1925. She received her A. B. from Smith College in 1882, and was a teacher in the Saint Louis Latin High School before her marriage. She was the daughter of Major Charles Ferdinand Brown of the Missouri Volunteers, who was killed at Champion's Hill; she traced her ancestry to the Browns of the Mayflower. There is one child of this marriage, Edward Langworthy, born February 1, 1899, who received his A. B. at Nebraska in 1926. He attended Harvard three years, and studied four years in Europe. He is an actor.

On December 4, 1928, Mr. Taylor was united in marriage to Florence Dye Coles, widow of William Coles, Esquire. Mrs. Taylor attended the University of Nebraska, receiving her A. B. in 1910, and was also graduated from Peru State Teachers College. She had been a member of the school board at Newcastle, Wyoming.

Mr. Taylor is a Republican. He is a member of The Club of Lincoln, the National Institute of the Social Sciences, the University Club, and the Patriarchs Club of Lincoln. Residence: Lincoln.

William James Taylor

William James Taylor, farmer and former member of the Nebraska house of representatives, was born in Van Buren County, Iowa, December 3, 1862, son of Pleasant John and Nancy Elvira (Watson) Taylor.

The father, born in Missouri, March 22, 1839, was a farmer who died in Van Buren County, September 4, 1875. His wife, Nancy, born March 6, 1838, died in Van Buren County, October 29, 1872. He was of Scotch-Irish descent, while she was of English ancestry.

William James Taylor attended common school, and was a student at Whittier College, Salem, Iowa, two years. He was a country school teacher in his youth, later taking up farming. An independent Democrat, he was a member of the Nebraska house 1899, 1901, 1909, 1915, 1917, and two special sessions; was a member of the state senate in 1919; the constitutional convention of 1919-20; and received the Demo-Populist nomination for congress in 1912 and 1917, defeated in the election.

On October 26, 1882, he was married to Belle Collier Morris in Van Buren County, where she was born June 27, 1862. There were three children, Grace, born August 5, 1883, died September 6, 1912; Maud, born December 3, 1885, married William Kellenbarger and died August 31, 1912; and Wilma, born February 23, 1901, married Clarence Rama. There are six grandchildren and two great grandchildren.

Mr. Taylor is a life member of the Nebraskana Society. He is affiliated with the United Brethren Church. Residence: Merna.

Frederick F. Teal

Frederick F. Teal, senior member of the firm of Drs. Teal and Woodward, has been engaged in the practice of medicine, both in Omaha and Lincoln, since 1897. He was born at Council Bluffs, Iowa, January 21, 1875, son of Frank and Emma (Riley) Teal and has resided in Nebraska fifty-four years. His father was born in Duchess County, New York, June 14, 1854, and died at Oakland, California, in March, 1930.

Dr. Teal attended Omaha public schools, and the Omaha High School where he took post-graduate work also. In 1897 he received his M. D. from Hahnemann Medical College of Chicago. His post-graduate work in medicine was taken at Philadelphia Polyclinic. He is a member of Phi Alpha Gamma.

A specialist in eye and ear, he is the author of the following: *Pupillary Reflexes in Dementia Praecox; Teal's Test of Malingering in Unilateral Deafness; Retinal Signs of Tuberculosis, etc., etc.* His professional memberships include the Nebraska State and Lancaster County Medical Societies, the American Medical Association, the American College of Surgeons (fellow); and the American Academy of Ophthalmology. During the World War he was a member of the draft board and consulting oculist and aurist at the University of Nebraska and Agricultural College Training Schools. His sports are tennis and hiking. He is a Unitarian and a member of the Republican party. During 1901-02 he was superintendent of the Norfolk Hospital for the Insane, appointed by Governor Dietrich, and in 1898 was a member of the Omaha School Board.

His marriage to Maude Sedgewick Merriam was solemnized at Chicago, April 19, 1900. Mrs. Teal, whose family record is set out in the *Merriam Genealogy*, was born at Binghamton, New York, December 17, 1880. They have three children, Dorothy, Fritz and Philip. Residence: Lincoln.

Caroline Irene Tefft

Caroline Irene Tefft, educator and clubwoman, was born in Otoe County, Nebraska, January 3, 1876. She is the daughter of a pioneer farmer, Amsdel Sheldon, who was born in South Reading, Virginia, September 27, 1839. His English and Scotch ancestors came to America before 1640.

Celia Frances (Ellis) Sheldon, her mother, was born at Fon du Lac, Wisconsin, September 3, 1852, and before her marriage was a successful teacher in the public schools of Oshkosh, Wisconsin, and Nebraska City, Nebraska. She is a descendant of Andrew Ward, who came to America from England in 1630.

Mrs. Tefft attended the public schools of Avoca, Nebraska, was graduated from the Weeping Water Academy in 1895, and later was a student at the University of Nebraska. A resident of Nebraska all her life, she has taken an active interest in Community affairs, and has been especially interested in rearing her children to become useful citizens.

On June 29, 1898, she married Clarence Edwin Tefft at Avoca. Mr. Tefft, who was born at Avoca, May 24, 1871, is a lawyer. Their five children are: Sheldon, born May 7, 1900, who married Elizabeth Shephard; Carl Amos, born October 18, 1901, who married Anna Lois Norris; Ralph Francis, born September 28, 1903, who married Katherine Breen; Esther, born May 30, 1905; and Ward, born February 11, 1916.

Mrs. Tefft is a member of the Weeping Water Woman's Club, (president in 1925); was president of the Cass County Federation of Woman's Clubs, 1926, 1927, 1928; and is a member of the board of the Weeping Water public library. For several years she has been president of the Ladies' Aid Society of the Weeping Water Congregational Church, of which she is a member. She is a member of the Nebraskana Society; Johnathan Cass Chapter of the Daughters of the American Revolution; and B. T. Chapter of the P. E. O. She is a Republican. Residence: Weeping Water.

Clarence Edwin Tefft

On May 24, 1871, Clarence E. Tefft was born near Avoca, Nebraska, the son of Orlando and Elizzie H. (Kirkpatrick) Tefft. His father, a farmer and banker, was noted throughout the state for his political activities. He was state senator, 1879, 1881, 1893, and 1895, and was chairman of the Republican State Central Committee. Of English and Scotch ancestry, he was born at Elgin, Illinois, December 26, 1843, and died at Avoca, May 8, 1928. His family came to Rhode Island prior to 1771.

His mother who was of Scotch-Irish ancestry, was born at Wapello, Iowa, January 3, 1849, and died at Avoca, November 26, 1899.

Mr. Tefft, a distinguished lawyer attended the Avoca public schools and received the LL. B. degree at the University of Nebraska in 1896. He was a member of the First Pershing Rifles at the University, was a charter member of Sigma Alpha Epsilon, and was a member of Phi Delta Phi, legal fraternity. He was on the track team in 1892.

In June, 1896, he was admitted to the bar, and has been a practising attorney in Cass County since that date. He is a former member of the Weeping Water board of education, serving as president for two terms; is president of the Cass County Bar Association and a member of the Nebraska State Bar Association.

He married Caroline Irene Sheldon at Avoca, June 29, 1898. Mrs. Tefft was born in Otoe County, Nebraska, January 3, 1876. Five children were born to this marriage. Sheldon, born May 7, 1900, who married Elizabeth Shepherd, is a graduate of the University of Nebraska, College of Law; was a Rhodes scholar in 1924; received the Vinerian scholarship at Oxford University; and has been professor of law at the University of Nebraska, and the University of Chicago. Carl Amos, who was born October 18, 1901, married Anna Lois Norris. Ralph Francis, born September 28, 1903, married Katharine Breen, and was graduated from the University of Nebraska where he received his master's degree. He also attended the Massachusetts Institute of Technology, receiving his Ph. D. degree. There are two other children, Esther, born May 30, 1905, and Ward born February 11, 1916.

Mr. Tefft was local food administrator and a member of the legal advisory board for Cass County in the World War registration, 1917. A Republican, his hobby is good citizenship. He is a member of the Congregational Church at Weeping Water. Residence: Weeping Water.

Sheldon Tefft

On May 17, 1900, Sheldon Tefft was born at Weeping Water, Nebraska. His father, C. E. Tefft, who was a lawyer, and his mother, Caroline I. Tefft were born in Avoca, Nebraska.

Mr. Tefft received his elementary education in the public school of Weeping Water, after which he attended the University of Nebraska where he received the A. B. and LL. B. degrees. He was awarded the degrees of M. A. and B. C. L. at Oxford University where he spent three years as Rhodes Scholar from Nebraska. He received the distinction of election to Phi Beta Keppa and the Order of the Coif at the University of Nebraska. His fraternity was Sigma Alpha Epsilon; he is a member of Delta Sigma Rho debating fraternity and Phi Delta Phi law fraternity.

He was admitted to the bar in Nebraska in 1924. From 1927 to 1929 he was law instructor at the University of Nebraska. At the present time he is associate professor of law at the University of Chicago Law School. During the World War Mr. Tefft was a member of the S. A. T. C. at the University of Nebraska.

His marriage to Elizabeth Shepherd was solemnized at Lincoln, Nebraska, June 27, 1930. Mrs. Tefft was born in Lincoln, July 28, 1906. Residence: Weeping Water.

Frederic Lee Temple

Frederick Lee Temple, insurance executive, was born at Wadestown, West Virginia, August 28, 1864, son of Nathaniel and Henrietta (Rice) Temple. The name Rice was spelled Reis in Holland. The family came to America in 1690. Nathaniel Temple was born in Pennsylvania, and in early life was a contractor. He was a farmer until his death in West Virginia in 1867. Henrietta Rice was born in Pennsylvania, in 1832, and died at Lexington, September, 1899. She was the first president of a national bank in the United States, being head of the First National Bank of Lexington.

Mr. Temple attended public school and high school, and the Indiana State Normal at Valparaiso. He was married on February 18, 1891, to Josephine Krier at

Lexington. She was born at Trenton, New Jersey, November 2, 1872. There are four children, Harold Lee, born February 28, 1893, who married Maurine McAdam; Alice Clare, born July 27, 1900, who married John G. Nordgren; Mary Frances, born October 7, 1902, who married H. Schnell Harmon; and Philip, born January 2, 1905.

From 1885 until 1899 Mr. Temple was assistant cashier of the First National Bank of Lexington. He was cashier from 1899 until 1919, at which time he moved to North Platte. There he was president of the Fidelity Life Company until November, 1923. At the present time he is mayor of North Platte. He is a member and past grand master of the Masons, and is affiliated with the Republican party. Residence: North Platte.

Guy Allen Temple

Guy Allen Temple was born at Plum Creek, Nebraska, December 20, 1884, son of Harry V. and Jennie May (Reynolds) Temple. His ancestry is English, tracing on the mother's side to the *Mayflower*.

Mr. Temple attended the University of Nebraska two years, 1904-05, and the Cummings Art School at Des Moines, 1905. For 14 years he was associated with the First National Bank of Lexington, he was vice-president of the Farmers Security Bank of Maywood for 2 years, assistant cashier of the Chadron State Bank for 2 years, and in 1930 was the organizer and secretary-treasurer of the Lexington Finance Company which position he still holds. Since 1932 he has also been the owner and manager of his own insurance agency at Lexington. He is a member of the Chamber of Commerce, Tehama Temple of the Shrine at Hastings, and the Methodist Episcopal Church at Lexington.

On October 22, 1908, he was married to Julia G. Olsson at Lexington. They have two children, Dorothy, born November 21, 1911; and Harry V., born December 12, 1914.

Mr. Temple is a Republican. He was in the cadet corps at the University of Nebraska two years, and was a member of the Pershing Rifles. He enjoys golf, tennis, hunting and fishing. Residence: Lexington. (Photograph in Album).

Harry Joel Templin

Harry Joel Templin, banker, was born in Mahoning County, Ohio, October 25, 1867, and has resided in Nebraska since December 1889.

His father, James Wilson Templin, was born in Mahoning County, December 5, 1836, and died there on June 7, 1898. He was a shoe and harness maker and a farmer. His wife, Elizabeth Thompson Armstrong, was born in Mahoning County, February 18, 1840, and died there in December, 1925. Before her marriage she was a teacher in the public schools.

Mr. Templin attended district school, Northeastern Ohio Normal College at Canfield, and Mount Union College. He received his diploma from Mount Union about 1888.

On December 3, 1902, he was married to Letha Naomi Rouse at Wolbach, Nebraska. Mrs. Templin was born at Plainview, Nebraska, January 22, 1883. They have two children, Gwendolyn, born February 5, 1904, who married Dr. Earl N. Deppen, of Lincoln, Nebraska; and Evelyn, born April 2, 1908. Both daughters are graduated from the University of Nebraska, Evelyn is now teaching Latin and history at Shelton, Nebraska.

At the present time Mr. Templin is cashier at the Palmer State Bank. A Republican, he has held minor political offices such as treasurer of the village of Palmer, and a member of the school board there. He is a member of the Palmer Commercial Club, and enjoys golf. Residence: Palmer.

Samuel Oscar Templin

Born at Reynolds, Nebraska, June 18, 1888, Samuel Oscar Templin is the son of Elbert and Mary Malinda (May) Templin. His father, who is a prominent farmer in Holt County, Nebraska, was born at Jonesboro, Tennessee, February 26, 1846; his ancestry is Dutch. His mother, who was born at Jonesboro, September 17, 1849, and died at O'Neill, Nebraska, September 13, 1910, was a homemaker and the mother of 14 children all of whom are living; she was active in church affairs throughout her life.

Mr. Templin received his education in the rural schools of Jefferson County, Nebraska, and has been a farmer near Neligh, Nebraska, for many years. He is a member of the County Board of Farmers' Co-operative Union in Antelope County, is a director of the Farmers' Union Co-operative Oil Association, serving as secretary and treasurer of the latter organization at this time.

Since 1930 he has been treasurer of School District 44 in Antelope County. He is a member of the Red Cross, the Nebraskana Society, and the Lawn Ridge Club. His hobby is mechanics, and his favorite sports are football and baseball.

His marriage to Lola Glen Martin occurred at Pierce, Nebraska, May 10, 1905. Mrs. Templin, who was a teacher before her marriage, was born at Steele City, February 5, 1881, the daughter of Morris Martin, and the granddaughter of James Martin of Wisconsin. They have two children: Graydon Oscar, born August 16, 1906, who married Lois Marguerite Nicholson; and Elenor Cerese, born August 9, 1912, who married William J. Haynes. Both children are graduates of the Neligh High School. Graydon is a farmer. Residence: Neligh.

Hardin Sherman Tennant

Hardin Sherman Tennant, physician and surgeon, was born at Tuskeego, Iowa, April 23, 1895, son of Henry Stuart and Clara Naomi (Cash) Tennant. Henry Tennant, a native of Wisconsin, born November 9, 1864, is a merchant and former railroad dispatcher. His father was born in Toronto, Canada, of Scotch and English descent, and his mother was born in Sterling, Scotland, of the Stuart family. Clara Naomi Cash, who was born at Tuskeego, March 31, 1869, was a teacher in early life, and is active in civic, educational and club work. Her father was born in Kentucky, and was descended from early English settlers, and her mother, who belonged to the Edwards family of Wales and England, was born in Waverly, Illinois.

Educated in the public and high school at Pawnee City, Hardin Sherman Tennant was graduated from the latter in 1914, and attended the university. He received his B. Sc. degree in 1924, and his M. D. in 1926, and is a member of Omega Beta Pi (president 1921) and Phi Rho Sigma (house manager and steward, 1925).

On December 1, 1926, Dr. Tennant was united in marriage to Zira Van Pelt, at Omaha. Mrs. Tennant was born at Endicott, Nebraska, January 18, 1891, and prior to her marriage was a teacher. Her father is of Dutch and Irish extraction and her mother Welch and German.

A Republican, Dr. Tennant has been a member of the city council of Stanton, since 1929. He served as a radio operator in the United States Navy during the World War, and in 1930 was commander of Stanton Post No. 88 of the American Legion. During 1930-31, he was president of the Chamber of Commerce, and in 1931 was elected president of the Five County Medical Society. He is a member of the Nebraska State Medical Society, the Stanton Congregational Church, the Masons, Modern Woodmen of America, and The Nebraskana Society. Dr. Tennant enjoys baseball, golf and tennis. Residence: Stanton. (Photograph in Album).

James Leonard Tewell

The Honorable James Leonard Tewell, judge of the 13th Judicial District of Nebraska, was born at DeMossville, Kentucky, November 11, 1885, and has resided in Nebraska continuously since March 11, 1886.

His father, James Samuel Tewell, was born in Grant County, Kentucky, March 26, 1856, and resides at Holdrege, Nebraska. He is a retired farmer, the son of Elrod Tewell. The family name is said to have come from France, about the time of, or prior to, the American Revolution. Mary Alice Read, wife of James S. Tewell, was born in Fairfax County, Virginia, August 8, 1857, and died in Gosper County, Nebraska, April 26, 1901. Her family came from England, prior to the Revolution.

Upon the completion of his early education in country schools of Gosper County, Judge Tewell was graduated from the Elwood, Nebraska, school in May, 1905. Thereafter he attended three semesters at Holdrege. In June, 1912, he received his Bachelor of Arts degree from the University of Nebraska, and on June 12, 1913, received the degree of Bachelor of Laws at the same institution. There he was a member of the Order of the Coif, and of Phi Delta Phi and Sigma Alpha Epsilon.

Upon his admission to the bar, Judge Tewell entered active practice, and from December, 1914, until May, 1921, was a member of the law firm of Radcliffe & Tewell, at Sidney. A Republican, he was appointed city attorney of Sidney, holding office from 1916, until 1918. He was deputy county attorney of Cheyenne County, from 1915, until 1919, and since May 24, 1921, has been district judge.

His marriage to Pauline Lomitta Wesner was solemnized at Brighton, Colorado, October 14, 1920. Mrs. Tewell was born at North Manchester, Indiana, July 22, 1894. They have two children, William Hughes, born February 22, 1922; and Suzanne, born January 26, 1931.

From 1908 until 1910, Judge Tewell served in the Nebraska National Guard, and during the World War was a private of field artillery at Officers Training Camp, Louisville, Kentucky. He is now a major in the Judge Advocate General's Department, Officers Reserve Corps. He is a member also of the American Bar Association, the Nebraska Bar Association, the Rotary Club, the Elks and the Masons. His club is the Sidney Country Club. He enjoys golf and hunting. Residence: Sidney.

Victor Alcide Thibodeau

Victor A. Thibodeau was born at Campbell, Nebraska, May 1, 1894, the son of Gilbert and Delima (Choquette) Thibodeau, and has been a resident of this state all his life. His father, who was a farmer, was born in Canada, 1851, of French parentage, came to America 55 years ago, and died at Campbell, September 17, 1906. His mother was born in Canada of French ancestors in 1856, and died at Campbell, December 12, 1929.

Mr. Thibodeau attended high school at Campbell and business college in Lincoln and entered the business world as bookkeeper for the Bank of Campbell; after 13 years in that position he became cashier of the bank where he remained until recently. He is now a real estate and insurance man at Campbell, and is interested in all community projects and civic affairs.

He holds membership in the Nebraskana Society, the American Legion, and the St. Anns Catholic Church at Campbell. During the World War he was a corporal in the United States Marines for 19 months, serving overseas for 12 months. He enjoys hiking and golf.

On October 2, 1928, he was married to Emma Margaret Theis at Heartwell, Nebraska. Mrs. Thibodeau, whose ancestry is German, was born at Heartwell, September 15, 1904. She is very active in the affairs of her church, is director of the choir, and is a member of the American Legion Auxiliary. Residence: Campbell.

Andrew H. Thieme

Born in Adams County, Indiana, July 21, 1876, Andrew H. Thieme has lived nearly all his life in Nebraska. His father, Andrew Thieme, Sr., was born in Germany, coming to America as a young man. He settled first in Indiana, and later came west, where he engaged in farming until his death at Hebron on August 10, 1908. His wife, Sophia Klien, also born in Germany, died at Hebron on May 10, 1915.

Andrew H. Thieme, who attended the parochial schools of Thayer County, was married to Amelia Oltsen at Friedensau, on February 25, 1899. Mrs. Thieme was born in Iowa, on November 29, 1877, of German descent. To their marriage were born five children, Fred B., September 23, 1900, who married Minnie Peupans; Herbert, born October 12, 1905, who married Delsia Peupans; Walter, November 13, 1907, who married Florence Albrecht; Robert, born January 3, 1912; and Erma, born January 9, 1917. All of the sons are farmers.

In addition to his farming activities, Mr. Thieme has always taken an interest in Republican politics, serving as precinct assessor of Thayer County two terms. He is a member of the Red Cross, the Nebraskana Society and the Lutheran Church of Friedensau. Residence. Hebron.

James Alexander Thom

For the past 23 years James A. Thom has been a veterinary surgeon at North Bend, Nebraska. He was born at Paw Paw, Illinois, September 27, 1880, the son of William and Helen (Gardiner) Thom. His father, a farmer, stockman, and importer, was born at Dyce, Aberdeenshire, Scotland, April 7, 1838, and died at Omaha, December 13, 1919. His parents, William and Christine (Chalmers) Thom, came to America in 1870. His mother, the daughter of John and Jane (Wilson) Gardiner, was born in Banffshire, Scotland, February 20, 1848, and died at Libertyville, Illinois, December 6, 1913.

Dr. Thom attended school in Lake County and in 1898 was graduated from the high school at Antioch, Illinois. He received the D. V. M. degree at the Chicago Veterinary College in 1905; he took a short course in agriculture at the University of Wisconsin, 1899-1901. He was engaged in the practice of his profession at Antioch for three years and has been active at North Bend since that time.

A member of the Nebraska State Veterinary Association; the Missouri Valley Veterinary Association; the Belgian Horse Registery Association; and the North Bend Community Club, he was a member of the school board for six years, and from 1914 to 1917 was secretary of this organization. He is a member of the Parent-Teachers Association; The Nebraskana Society; the Modern Woodmen of America. His favorite sport is horseback riding. His hobbies are checkers and reading He is affiliated with the United Presbyterian Church.

Dr. Thom was married at Kenosha, Wisconsin, October 5, 1905, to Blanche Monteith Yule. Mrs. Thom, who is the daughter of Jessie (Strang) and B. F. Yule, was born at Somers, Wisconsin, June 27, 1884. Five children were born to them: Franklin, born November 2, 1906; Jeannie, born March 25, 1909; James G., born October 20, 1910; Katherine, born January 19, 1913; and Paul, born October 2, 1920. Katherine married Lyle Van Arsdol. Residence: North Bend.

Frank Charles Thomann

Frank C. Thomann, distinguished educator of Nebraska, was born at Summerfield, Kansas, May 16, 1893. His father, Frank Thomann, who was born in Alsace, France, March 27, 1847, and died at Summerfield, June 3, 1925, was a bank president for 26 years, and was at the same time engaged in the hardware business, owned a drug store and operated a grain elevator. He was a Democrat and was active in local politics, acting as mayor of his community for many years. He was a 32nd degree Mason, a Shriner, and past master. His father, who settled in Kansas in 1857, was a civil engineer and the first surveyor of Marshall County after Kansas became a state. The family came from France but some branches of it have been traced to Switzerland where his grandfather was a manufacturer.

Charlotte, wife of Frank Thomann, Sr., was born near Beattie, Marshall County, Kansas, December 16, 1865, of a German family which was made wealthy by the possession of a farm in Germany enclosing which four cities grew together increasing the value of the land tremenduously. Her father came to America to escape German Military service, but later purchased the privilege to return to his native country for a visit. An uncle of Mrs. Thomann's was a university professor in Germany.

Mr. Thomann was graduated from the Summerfield High School in 1913. Later he attended the University of Kansas, where he was awarded the A. B. degree in 1918; he also attended summer schools at the University of Nebraska, Chicago, and Colorado and was awarded a masters degree in 1928.

He was made a member of Phi Delta Kappa, Kappa Delta Phi, was awarded the Phi Delta Kappa Service Key, and was vice president and then president of the Acomas, a fraternity now called Sigma Phi Epsilon.

Instructor in the high school at Summerfield, 1915-16, he was superintendent of school at Maple Hill, Kansas, 1918-1919; at Wakefield, Kansas, 1919-1922; and in 1922 was made superintendent of city schools at Pawnee City, Nebraska, where he is now beginning his ninth year of educational service. He is the author of a thesis *Educational Survey of the Public Schools of Pawnee City.*

His marriage to Grace Rachel Smith was solemnized at Wray, Yuma County, Colorado, July 14, 1923. Mrs. Thomann, who is of Dutch and English ancestry, and is eligible for membership in the Daughters of the American Revolution, was born at Hartford, Michigan, July 19, 1898. Before her marriage she was a Pawnee County Red Cross nurse. Charles Edwin, their only son, was born September 4, 1926.

Mr. Thomann enlisted in the World War at Topeka, Kansas, December, 1917, but upon his arrival at Jefferson Barracks, St. Louis, Missouri, was rejected for military service. He is a member of the Nebraska State Teachers' Association, the Red Cross, the Pawnee City Service Club, and the Nebraskana Society. He is a Mason, 32nd degree, Scottish Rite. He was a member of the Y. M. C. A. cabinet at the University of Kansas in 1917 and 1918; was president of the Westminister Guild there, an organization with a membership of over 500 Presbyterian students. He is affiliated with the First Presbyterian Church, at Pawnee City. His social club is the Pawnee City Round Table. He is interested in all sports, especially hunting, fishing, football, and basketball. He is a Republican. Residence: Pawnee City.

Benjamin Franklin Thomas

One of Omaha's well known lawyers, Benjamin Franklin Thomas has been a resident of the state for more than forty-four years. He was born at Andrew, Iowa, November 10, 1861, son of Benjamin Franklin Thomas, Sr., and Mary Emma Gallow. A lawyer of Welsh descent, the elder Benjamin was born in Mercer County, Pennsylvania, October 9, 1833, and died at Maquoketa, Iowa, February 15, 1909. Mary Emma Gallow was born at Newberg, New York, July 1, 1838, and died at Maquoketa on March 10, 1910.

Mr. Thomas attended district school and Monmouth College and was graduated from Epworth Seminary in 1883. He was later made an honorary member of Phi

Delta Theta at Knox College, Illinois. A Republican in politics, Mr. Thomas has served his state and city in various offices. He was postmaster of Omaha from 1908 to 1913; state senator from Douglas County two terms, the 1905 and 1907 sessions; and was city prosecutor for Omaha three years 1906-09. He served also as a member of the Omaha School Board for seven years.

His career, although devoted principally to the practice of law, has been somewhat varied. During his forty-four years of residence he has held offices in many corporations, and at the present time is treasurer and director of the wholesale firm of Henry and Robinson Hardware Company.

On October 5, 1887, he was united in marriage to Ada Thomas, who was born at Truro, Cornwall, England, May 8, 1865. Six children were born to this marriage, five of whom are living: Howard F., born February 10, 1889, who married Lily May Turner; Rowland P., born April 26, 1890, married Geraldine Inmare; Bernice A., born February 13, 1893, married Martin Lloyd Minthorn; Lucille E., born February 18, 1895, married William Menken; Ruth Elizabeth, born April 20, 1898, died November 9, 1899; and Benjamin F., Jr., born April 5, 1901, who is unmarried.

Mr. Thomas is the author and compiler of a book entitled, *A Speech and Story for Every Occasion,* published in 1926. He is a thirty-third degree Mason and member of the Knights Templar and Scottish Rite bodies, and is also an Elk, Woodman of the World and Modern Woodman of America. He holds life membership in The Nebraskana Society. His religious affiliation is with the Hanscom Park Methodist Episcopal Church. His hobby is golf. Residence: Omaha.

Chalkley Bernard Thomas

The Reverend Chalkey Bernard Thomas, pastor of the Evangelical Church of Oconto, was born at Kent, Iowa, April 7, 1884, son of Chalkley and Margaret Asenith (Woolman) Thomas.

The father, who was born in Ohio, May 28, 1847, was a farmer, whose death occurred at Orleans, Nebraska, June 15, 1913. His wife, Margaret, was born in Mt. Pleasant, Iowa, in 1842, and died at Orleans, April 30, 1894. She was a teacher before her marriage.

Mr. Thomas attended public school, completed a ministerial course, receiving the orders of deacon and elder, and was ordained at Dawson, Nebraska, May 14, 1926. He is a Democrat.

On February 4, 1914, he was married to Vallie Pearl Miller at Phillips. Mrs. Thomas was born at Phillips, September 28, 1891. There are four children, Eustace, born November 19, 1914; Sterling, June 9, 1917, Rayme, September 10, 1922; and Floris, July 9, 1927.

Mr. Thomas enjoys golf, baseball and hunting. He was recently elected to life membership in The Nebraskana Society. Residence: Oconto.

Clay Henry Thomas

Clay H. Thomas was born at Council Bluffs, Iowa, July 21, 1890, the son of William Henry and Mary Ann (Peterson) Thomas. His father, who was a real estate man and mortgage broker, was born in Boxelder County, Utah, January 16, 1857, and died at Omaha, August 31, 1917; his ancestry was Welsh. His mother, whose ancestry is English and Danish, was born at Council Bluffs, Iowa, September 21, 1865.

Mr. Thomas, who has been a realtor and mortgage broker in Nebraska for the past 20 years, received his education in the public schools of Council Bluffs where he was graduated from high school in 1909. He attended the University of Nebraska class of 1914, and was elected to membership in Phi Gamma Delta.

His marriage to Margaret Helen Price was solemnized at Lincoln, October 2, 1915. Mrs. Thomas, whose ancestry is Welch and English, was born in Wisconsin, August 31, 1892. They have two children Margaret Helen, born October 18, 1919; and Janet Llewellyn, born July 19, 1921.

Mr. Thomas is affiliated with the First Presbyterian Church of Omaha. Residence: Omaha.

Dale L. Thomas

Dale L. Thomas, superintendent of Kilgore Public Schools, was born at Vaughnsville, Ohio, April 22, 1906, son of James G. and Cora L. (Sherrick) Thomas. His father, who is an agriculturist, was presidnet of the local school board, 1923-25, and is active in Republican politics. He was born at Kalida, Ohio, August 28, 1882, of Welsh ancestry. His wife, Cora, was born February 1, 1884.

In 1921 Mr. Thomas graduated from the consolidated schools of Sugar Creek Township, Ohio, and in 1925 was graduated from Vaughnsville High School. He received his Bachelor of Arts degree in education and science at Asbury College at Wilmore, Kentucky, in June, 1930. He was a member of Kappa Delta Kappa, Debating Club, the Club of Journalism, Synedria (charter member), all at Asbury, and received letters in basketball, 1928, 1929, 1930, and baseball, 1929 at college.

During 1930 and 1931 Mr. Thomas was coach of the Kilgore Public Schools, and since that time has been coach and superintendent. He is a Republican. During his college days he was circulation manager of the *Asbury Collegian*, a college weekly.

He is a member of the Nebraska State Teachers Association, the Red Cross, the Nebraskana Society, and the "A" Club of Asbury College. His favorite sports are basketball, tennis, and golf, while his hobbies are reading and the radio. Residence: Kilgore. (Photograph in Album).

Elmer Alonzo Thomas

Elmer Alonzo Thomas was born in Webster County, Nebraska, December 11, 1874, the son of Lorenzo Dow and Mary Anne (Chambers) Thomas. His father, who was a teacher, farmer and pioneer homesteader of Webster County, was born in Monroe County, Ohio, May 15, 1846, and died in Webster County, Nebraska, January 15, 1915; his Welsh ancestors settled in New Jersey before the Revolution. His mother was born in Illinois, February 2, 1855, and died in Webster County, March 15, 1917.

Dr. Thomas, who is a prominent dental surgeon at Hastings, received his education in the schools of Webster County, and in 1903 received his degree of Doctor of Dental Surgery at the University of Omaha. He took post graduate work at the University of Nebraska, 1916, and Northwestern University, 1918. In 1920, he attended Columbia University for a time. His fraternity is Delta Sigma Delta.

From 1902 to 1911, Dr. Thomas practiced dentistry at Red Cloud, Nebraska, and since 1911 he has been at Hastings. He has given numerous lectures on dental subjects, and is the editor of the *Journal of the Nebraska State Dental Society*. He served as superintendent of dental research at the Hastings State Hospital for ten years, doing scientific work for the American Dental Association, is retiring president of the Nebraska State Dental Society and research director and chairman of the history committee. At the present time Dr. Thomas is writing and publishing a history of dentistry in Nebraska. From 1909 to 1915, he served on the Nebraska State Dental Examining Board.

Dr. Thomas has held membership in the American Dental Association since 1905, is a member of the state and district dental organizations. He is a member of the Kiwanis Club, acting especially in the interests of underprivileged boys, and the First Presbyterian Church of Hastings. His hobby is science. During the late war

he served as Four Minute Man, and took part in loan drives of all kinds.

His marriage to Jessie Radley was solemnized at Nelson, Nuckolls County, Nebraska, June 9, 1902. Mrs. Thomas was born in Morgan County, Illinois, September 25, 1875. Their children are: Frances Muril, born May 15, 1905; and Charles Elmer, born May 29, 1907, who married Irene Sadler, and is established in the oil business at Hastings.

Dr. Thomas became interested in psychopathic research before he entered dental college. His first published article was accepted by the Western Dental Journal in 1908, after having been read by him before the Nebraska State Dental Society. He has written more than 25 articles which have been printed. Residence: Hastings.

Frederick Wagner Thomas

Frederic Wagner Thomas, banker, was born at Sargent, Nebraska, May 1, 1885, the son of Joseph William and Idella Edith (Wagner) Thomas. Joseph W. Thomas, also a banker, was born in London, England. November 17, 1852, and came to America when a young men. He died in Omaha, January 17, 1920. His wife, Idella, was born at Clinton, Iowa, December 12, 1863, and is a concert singer of some note. She is of German descent.

Frederic Thomas was educated in the public and high schools of Omaha, and received his B. A. from the University of Nebraska. He is a member of Phi Gamma Delta. Entering the banking business with the Union National Bank, he has been connected successively with Hayden Brothers, Bankers, the Corn Exchange National Bank, the Live Stock National Bank, and the First National Bank, of which he is vice president.

He is vice president of the Lininger Implement Company, the Douglas Investment Company and the Merchants Investment Company, a member of the board of directors of the First National Bank, and of the Security National Bank of Laurel, Nebraska. During the World War he was regional chairman of the War Finance Corporation.

On October 27, 1910, he was married to Marion Caroline Haller, at Omaha. Mrs. Thomas was born at Omaha, January 17, 1889. Mr. Thomas attends Trinity Cathedral. He is state treasurer of the Nebraska Children's Home Society and a charter member of the Triangle Club. He is a Mason and an Elk, and a member of the Nebraska State Historical Society and the Nebraskana Society. His clubs are the Omaha Club, the Omaha Athletic Club and the Omaha Field Club. Residence: Omaha.

Fredrick Ferdinand Thomas

On June 6, 1893, Frederick Ferdinand Thomas, postmaster and merchant, was born in Omaha, Nebraska, the son of Fred Conrad Thomas and Katherina Menshik. His mother was born in Moravia, Europe, and has made a profession of commercial cooking for which she is widely known.

Mr. Thomas has attended school in Omaha, Hastings and Linwood, Nebraska. August 24, 1916, he married Anna Wesely, in David City, Nebraska. She was born in Omaha, on August 16, 1893, of Bohemian parentage. To this union five children were born: Fredrick, March 5, 1917, Muriel, December 16, 1918, Conrad, March 30, 1922, Betty, June 1, 1924, and Elaine, April 23, 1926.

Fredrick Thomas was township assessor from 1915 to 1919 and would have been re-elected for a second term but declined because of his appointment as postmaster in 1920, which position he holds at present. Mr. Thomas began as a newsboy at the age of eight, and worked for four years. Later he became a professional musician and traveled for eight years doing Lyceum work.

He is connected with a grocery and confectionary

store in Linwood, where he has been prominent since 1910. He is a 32nd degree Mason, a member of the Shrine and a member of The Nebraskana Society.

During the late war Mr. Thomas contributed auctioneer services for the Red Cross in which he had phenomenal success. He is especially fond of baseball. Residence: Linwood.

Herman H. Thomas

Herman H. Thomas, insurance executive, was born in Hebron, Nebraska, August 12, 1898, son of Julius and Augusta Thomas. His father, who was a baker, was born in Germany of German and Welsh descent. His wife, Augusta, was born in Ohio and died at Hebron.

Mr. Thomas was graduated from Hebron High School in 1916, and received his Bachelor of Arts degree from the University of Nebraska in 1921. He attended the University of Illinois, and took graduate work in the University of Southern California, as well as at the University of Nebraska. He is a member of Sigma Delta Chi, Delta Tau Delta, and Phi Alpha Tau. He was a member of Kosmet Club and the Dramatic Club of the University of Nebraska, was stage manager of the university players two years, and prominent in dramatics, and was editor of *Awgwan*.

During the year 1921, Mr. Thomas was connected with the Potts-Turnbull Advertising Agency, and traveled with the Fritz Leiber Company (Shaksperian Repertoire Company). In 1922 he became associated with the Omaha Trust Company, and from 1922 until 1925 was principal of the Hebron High School. In 1925 he was appointed superintendent of schools, continuing until 1931. During five summers he traveled with various Chautauqua companies. At the present time Mr. Thomas is connected with the Travelers Insurance Company of Hartford, Connecticut, with offices at Omaha.

On August 18, 1925, he was married to Grace B. Duey at Chester. Mrs. Thomas was born at Chester, and before her marriage was a nurse. They have one son, John Duey, born September 8, 1929.

During the late war Mr. Thomas was a member of Officers Training Camp. He was a member and active in the American Legion, a member of the First Presbyterian Church (former trustee), the Schoolmasters Club, the Kiwanis Club (former president), and is a Mason (Knight Templar and Royal Arch). His hobby is cabinet making. Residence: Omaha. (Photograph on Page 1187).

James Right Thomas

James Right Thomas, farmer, merchant and miller, was born in Washington, Indiana, September 2, 1844. He is the son of Solomon and Eliza (Hawkins) Thomas, both of whom have been deceased for a number of years.

In the Civil War period he served with the Union Army, and has been successively a merchant, miller and farmer. He is a Republican, a member of the Methodist Church and a life member of the Nebraskana Society.

In January, 1869, he was united in marriage to Emma Wood Griswold at Anamosa, Iowa. Mrs. Thomas, who was born at Guilford, Connecticut, October 29, 1846; died at Osmond on January 8, 1917.

There were seven children born to them, five of whom are living: Edward, born in January, 1871, died in December, 1877; Abbie E., born February 2, 1873; Albert M., born October 12, 1874; Grace I., born December 18, 1875, married Lee Osborn; Arthur, born in April, 1879, died in October, 1879; Roy E., born July 28, 1881, married Ethel Leedom; and Frank W., born September 24, 1888, married Blanche Huey. Residence: Osmond.

Louis E. Thomas

Louis E. Thomas, jeweler and optometrist of Hebron, has been a resident of Nebraska all his life. He was born at Hebron, December 5, 1893, the son of Julius E.

and Augusta Thomas. His father, who died in 1900, was of English descent. His mother, whose ancestry was German, died at Hebron in 1911.

Mr. Thomas was graduated from Hebron High School in 1911, was a student at the University of Nebraska, 1911-12, and attended Bradley College at Peoria, Illinois, 1913-14. In 1915 he studied at Needles School of Optometry at Kansas City, Missouri. He was elected to membership in Delta Upsilon at the University of Nebraska, and was active in football and baseball at Hebron High School.

For two years Mr. Thomas was employed by a jewelry firm at York, and for four years worked in a jewelry store at Fairbury, Nebraska. Since 1921 he has been optometrist and owner of the Thomas Jewelry Store at Hebron. He is a member of the Nebraska Optometric Association, the National Jewelers Association, the Hebron Chamber of Commerce, and the Hebron Kiwanis Club. He holds membership in The Nebraskana Society, is affiliated with the First Presbyterian Church of Hebron, and is a member of the Boy Scout Advisory Board.

Mr. Thomas is a Mason (Blue Lodge, Chapter, Commandery). During 1924 and 1925 he served as a member of the local school board, and has always taken an active interest in educational affairs in his community. He is a member of the Hebron Golf Club and has won a number of cups and trophies in various golf matches.

His marriage to Ethel A. McKenzie was solemnized at Hebron in 1917. Mrs. Thomas, who was born at Hebron, April, 1893, is of Scotch descent. She is treasurer of the Hebron Woman's Club, holds membership in the Order of Eastern Star, and is a member of the Pollyanna Club. They have three children: Robert and Richard, twin boys, born April 28, 1918; and Ruth, born June 5, 1919. The three children are active in the school band at Hebron.

Mr. Thomas served in the Reserve Officer's Training Corp at the University of Nebraska. His political affiliation is with the Republican party. Residence: Hebron.

Minnie Florella Thomas

Minnie Florella Thomas was born at Newville, DeKalb County, Indiana, February 7, 1869. She is the daughter of Charles Leroy and Harriet Eliza (Fusselman) Thomas, both of Revolutionary ancestry. Her father was born at Newville, April 18, 1840. He was a realtor and councilman of Omaha from 1892 to 1896. He served with the 12th and 55th regiments of Indiana Volunteers in the Civil War. Of Welsh ancestry, he was descended from William Thomas, born in England, 1573, sailed from Yarmouth on the *Mary and Ann* in 1637, and settled in Marshfield, Massachusetts. He died in 1651. Charles L. Thomas died at Omaha, March 6, 1924. His wife, Harriet Fusselman Thomas was born at Newville, March 16, 1842. She was a descendant of Aaron Merrill who served with a Connecticut regiment in the American Revolution. Two of her brothers enlisted for service in the Civil War. She was a member of the Earnest Workers and of the First Christian Church of Omaha from 1881 until her death on June 4, 1908.

Minnie F. Thomas attended the Omaha public and high school, and was graduated in 1885. On April 27, 1886, she entered the service of the Union Pacific Railroad as stenographer, secretary and clerk and was retired after thirty-four years service, on May 1, 1920.

A member of the Omaha chapter of the Daughters of the American Revolution, she was local treasurer of that chapter 1924-25, and state chairman of the organization 1927-28. She belongs to Betsy Ross Tent No. 1, Daughters of Union Civil War Veterans. She is affiliated with Fontenelle Chapter No. 249, Order of Eastern Star.

A Republican, she is a member of the Douglas County Republican Woman's Club. During the World War she was a subscriber to Liberty Loan drives, and for several years was a member of Red Cross, and is a former mem-

HERMAN H. THOMAS

ber of the Carter Lake Club. She has served as secretary and treasurer of various departments, and as auditor of the Omaha Woman's Club (1927-28-31-32). She is a member of the First Christian Church of Omaha. Her hobby is genealogy. Residence: Omaha. (Photograph in Album).

Valorus Arbie Thomas

A leading physician at Nelson, Nebraska, now retired, is Valorus Arbie Thomas, who was born at Cambridge Springs, Pennsylvania, September 24, 1856, and for over 46 years has lived at Nelson. His father, Wilson Coulter Thomas, who was a farmer and stockman, was born at Cambridge Springs, October 31, 1832, and died at Woodcock, Pennsylvania, July 13, 1907; the ancestral home of the Thomas family was at Beckett, Massachusetts, where members of the family settled upon their arrival from Wales.

Helen Elizabeth (Doctor) Thomas, who was born at Cambridge Springs, February 7, 1834, and died there, September 19, 1919, was of Scotch-Irish and German descent. Her maternal great-grandmother came directly from Ireland to this country about 1812.

Dr. Thomas attended the rural and town schools of Crawford County, Pennsylvania, and was graduated from Cambridge Springs Academy. He was a student at Edinborough State Normal College for a time, and was awarded the Doctor of Medicine degree at Jefferson Medical College in 1897. Since 1897 he has been engaged in medical practice at Nelson with the exception of three years which time he took a claim in Grant County, Nebraska, which he now owns.

His marriage to Helena Grace Coup occurred at Woodcock, Pennsylvania, December 22, 1881. Mrs. Thomas, whose ancestry was French and Pennsylvania Dutch, was born at Woodcock, July 22, 1864, and died at Nelson, September 25, 1929. Their daughter, Nova, Elizabeth, (see Nebraskana), who was born October 27, 1888, married Henry Herbert Hite.

Dr. Thomas is a member of the Nelson Methodist Episcopal Church, and holds membership in the Nebraskana Society. He is a Mason (Scottish Rite and Shrine). Politically he is a Democrat. During the World War he was a member of the local examining board of Nuckolls County. Residence: Nelson.

Verne Nelson Thomas

Verne Nelson Thomas, lawyer and farm operator, was born at Adams, Nebraska, May 8, 1896, son of Nelson David and Laura Vivian (Dosie) Thomas.

His father was born in Indiana, February 22, 1851, and at the time of his death at Adams, March 20, 1928, was a retired farmer. His wife, Laura, was born in Nuckols County, Nebraska, and died at Lincoln, December 6, 1925. She was active in church work and in the Woman's Club and Women's Christian Temperance Union.

Mr. Thomas was graduated from Adams High School, attended Peru State Normal School, and the University of Nebraska, from which he received his degree of Bachelor of Laws. A member of Pi Kappa Phi, he was archeon in his senior year. Since his admission in August, 1924, Mr. Thomas has been active in the practice of law. He also has extensive farming operations.

On August 24, 1924, he was married to Margaret Anne Johnson at Sioux City, Iowa. Mrs. Thomas was born at Sterling, Nebraska, February 21, 1904. She is active in and holds office in the Eastern Star, and the P. E. O. Sisterhood. She is active in church work, the Woman's Club, and is also a devoted wife and mother. They have one child, David Edward, who was adopted March 23, 1930.

Mr. Thomas is a Republican. During the late war, he served in the United States Navy, and had oversea service. He holds a reserve officers commission in the United States Army, is a member of the Nebraska State Bar Association, the Chamber of Commerce and the Masons. He is a member of the committee of the local Salvation Army organization. He is a Methodist. Among his sports are fishing and hunting, while his hobby is pure bred stock. Residence: Crawford.

Albert Thompson

Born near Belleville, Illinois, October 9, 1860, Albert Thompson has been an outstanding lawyer at Fullerton, Nebraska, for the past 46 years. His father, Abel Thompson, a farmer, was at West Bowdoin, Maine, April 20, 1814, and died near Belleville, September 15, 1882. The Thompson family originated in America about 1643, settling in Maine, near West Bowdoin. His mother, Deliah Alexandra America (Charles) Thompson, whose parents were natives of North Carolina, was born at Alexandria, Illinois, October 6, 1820, and died at St. Clair County, Illinois, September 14, 1867. The Charles family were early settlers in North Carolina, near Gilford and members of this family fought in the Revolutionary War. The grandfather, Lavin Charles, lived in this community and bore a commission in the Colonial Army.

Mr. Thompson attended the public schools of St. Clair County, Illinois, was a student at Ewing College, 1878-79, and received the LL. B. degree at Washington University at St. Louis, Missouri in 1885. He is a member of the law firm Thompson and Thompson at Fullerton, Nebraska, where he served as county attorney for one term, 1906-07. He is a member of the State Historical Society, is affiliated with the Presbyterian Church, and was a member of the local school board for six years.

He served as chairman of the Nance County Council of Defense during the World War, was a local speaker, and took part in loan drives. Mr. Thompson maintains an unusual private library, containing over 1700 volumes of history, biography, economic treatises, and fiction. His hobby is reading.

On June 6, 1893, he was married at Burlington, Vermont, to Mary Kate Taggart who was born at Charlotte, Vermont, April 11, 1871, the daughter of Benjamin H. and Emma (Naramore) Taggart. They have two sons; Carroll N., born June 26, 1901, who was graduated from the University of Nebraska in 1924 and is serving his second term as county attorney of Nance County; and Dudley, born April 30, 1909, who is a student at the University of Nebraska Law College. Carroll married Pauline Gilmore, daughter of James T. and May Gilmore, of Fullerton, in 1925. They have a son, Don Gilmore, born April 16, 1926. Residence: Fullerton.

Charles Yoder Thompson

Charles Y. Thompson was born at Reading, Berks County, Pennsylvania, October 17, 1875, the son of Thomas Dick Thompson and Lizzie (Yoder) Thompson. He is descended from a long line of illustrious ancestors, most of whom were physicians. William Thompson, great-grandfather of Charles Y. Thompson, was an iron-master, and was the father of four sons, John, a farmer, Joel, a dentist, William, a dentist, and Levi, a physician. Levi Thompson, grandfather of Charles, was the father of six sons, four of whom were physicians, one a druggist, and one a farmer. Dr. T. D. Thompson, father of Charles, reared a family of eight children, four of whom were physicians; Warren was graduated from Rush Medical School, Richard, from Cornell University, Chester, from Harvard, and Kimball, from Creighton University.

Dr. Thompson moved to West Point, Cuming County, Nebraska, in 1876, and became a typical pioneer country doctor. Many of his calls were made in a lumber wagon and later in the first top buggy in Cuming County. For many years he travelled throughout a territory of 20 miles in the surrounding country near West Point caring for his patients both day and night. He was the confidante and advisor of many families in Cuming County, was highly respected for his integrity and progressive spirit, and has been given much credit for his part in the advancement of his community. He died at West Point, January 13, 1925. For many years he was a member of the school board at West Point; was president of the Nebraska State Bank; and took part in all civic affairs in that part of the state. His ancestry was Scotch-Irish and German.

Lizzie (Yoder) Thompson was born at Lyons Station, Berks County, Pennsylvania, December 18, 1853. In 1670 two Yoder brothers came to America, and during the Revolution members of the family were soldiers. Mrs. Thompson is a cousin to Nathan T. Schafer, superintendent of public instruction in Pennsylvania; the Schafers came to this country from Holland, in 1681.

Mr. Thompson attended the public schools of Cuming County, and later was graduated from the West Point High School, 1893, after a year in Central High School at Omaha. He was graduated from the University of Nebraska Law School, and admitted to the bar June 10, 1897. Later he took a short course in the College of Agriculture. He held membership in Phi Kappa Psi and Phi Delta Phi, at the University of Nebraska.

For many years he has been a farmer and feeder near West Point, and is active in 4-H Club work. He has been staff correspondent for the *Nebraska Farmer* since 1912. He holds membership in the Crop Growers Association (president), Improved Live Stock Breeders Association; West Point Community Club; the Business Men and Farmers Club, of which he was president for two years and director since its organization in 1921; and the County Fair Association of which he is president. He served as president of the Nebraska State Farm Bureau Federation in 1926, and is now a director of this organization. During the World War he acted as chairman of the Strong Arm committee. Mr. Thompson was elected to membership in the Nebraska Hall of Agricultural Achievement, January 17, 1928, and is known throughout the state as an efficient and progressive farmer. His hobbies are boys and girls clubs; and reading. He is a Republican.

He was married to Martha Helen Berthold at West Point, in 1899; she was born of German parentage at West Point, January 29, 1876, and died there June 2, 1924. Three children were born to their marriage: Margaret E., born May 9, 1900, who was graduated from Northwestern University and now teaches English and dramatics at Washington High School, Milwaukee, Wisconsin; Melvin, born May 7, 1901, who was graduated from the dental college of Northwestern University and is now practicing dentistry in Chicago; and Thomas D., born November 11, 1903, who was graduated from the University of Nebraska Medical College at Omaha, 1931.

Mr. Thompson was united in marriage with Maria E. Chamber, March 10, 1926. Mrs. Thompson is the daughter of A. H. and Margaret Chambers, who were among the earliest settlers of Cuming County, Nebraska. Residence: West Point. (Photograph in Album).

Edgar Thompson

Edgar Thompson, rancher and commission man, was born in Selma, Ohio, January 3, 1881, son of Elwood and Sarah (Wiemer) Thompson.

His father was born in Ohio, November 9, 1847, came to Nebraska and settled in York County in 1883, and died at York, March 20, 1917. He was a farmer, of Irish, English and Scotch ancestry. His wife, Sarah, was born in Germany, March 28, 1853, and died at York, September 14, 1903. Her ancestry was German and French.

Mr. Thompson was graduated from country school, and has since engaged in farming and ranching. At the present time, he is manager of the York Livestock Commission Company, and is a rancher in Cherry County. He is a Republican.

His marriage to Elsie Belle Weir was solemnized at

York, on October 5, 1904. Mrs. Thompson was born in Bradford, Illinois, December 2, 1881, daughter of William and Mary (Noies) Weir, of German and Irish ancestry. They have two sons, Howard, born June 19, 1906, who was graduated from the University of Nebraska in 1930; and Glen, born February 1, 1911, who is a student there.

During the World War, Mr. Thompson gathered in Cherry County the first car load of cattle to be given to the Red Cross in the United States. He is a member of the First Methodist Church, the York Chamber of Commerce, the Modern Woodmen of America, and the Ancient Order of United Workmen. Residence: York.

Frank Charles Thompson

Frank Charles Thompson, leading farmer in Washington County, was born at Omaha, December 7, 1879. His father, John Thompson, who was born at Kendall, England, June 4, 1829, came to America in 1849, settling in Nebraska where he engaged as a blacksmith and farmer. His death occurred at Blair, Nebraska, February 29, 1908. Susan Saunders, wife of John Thompson, was born in Torkey, England, December 30, 1838. Her life was devoted to the interests of her family, until her death at Blair on March 29, 1926.

Mr. Thompson attended the public schools to the 11th grade, and while in school played baseball. On February 17, 1904, he was united in marriage to Elnora Leona Bernhard, at Blair. Mrs. Thompson was born at Union, Illinois, October 18, 1883. They have two sons, Leslie, born May 17, 1908, who attends college; and Glenn, born February 12, 1913, who is also a student.

A farmer all his life, Mr. Thompson has been active always in the civic and educational life of his community. He is treasurer of the Sutherland School Board, and is a member of the Modern Woodmen of America, the Masons and the Eastern Star. During the World War he was active in loan drives and Red Cross Work. His political affiliation is with the Democratic party, and he is active in local politics. His hobbies are reading and history. Residence: Blair.

Harry Harold Thompson, M. D.

One of Nebraska's leading professional men, Harry Harold Thompson has been engaged in the practice of medicine at Oxford since 1908, and is at this time the owner and chief physician of the Republican Clinic in that community. He was born at Brock, Nebraska, March 21, 1883, the son of Daniel Caldwell ad Margaret Jane (Dysart) Thompson, the former a pioneer homesteader in Nebraska. His father, whose Scotch ancestors settled in New York in 1798 and homesteaded in Illinois in 1842, was born at Genoa, Illinois, March 22, 1855, and died at Talmage, Nebraska, March 31, 1924.

His mother, who was born at Delhi, New York, April 22, 1855, was a devoted mother and homemaker, and took an active interest in religious affairs until her death November 30, 1912. Her great-grandmother was the third daughter of Laird Thomas of Edinborough, Scotland.

Dr. Thompson attended Peru State Normal School and Nebraska Wesleyan Academy, and in 1904, was graduated from Creighton Academy at Omaha. He received the M. D. degree in 1908 at Creighton University where he was editor of the *Medical Bulletin*. He served as a general practitioner at Scribner, Nebraska, for three years, at David City, Nebraska, for five years, and since the recent war has been prominent as a specialist of the eye, ear, nose and throat at his clinic in Oxford.

He is a member of the Republican Valley Medical Society, was formerly coroner of Butler County, and holds membership in the Nebraskana Society. During the World War Dr. Thompson served as a lieutenant at Fort Riley, Kansas. He organized the American Red Cross in Butler County and served as a Four Minute Speaker in various loan drives. He holds membership in the American Legion.

On April 26, 1924, he married Elizabeth Shanks at Hiawatha, Kansas. Mrs. Thompson, who is of Scotch descent, was born at Auburn, Nebraska, March 21, 1893. He has one daughter by a former marriage: Margaret Katherine, born April 21, 1909, who was graduated from Grinnell College in Iowa and took a post graduate course at Chicago University. She is now engaged in secretarial work.

Dr. Thompson's chief sport is duck hunting along the Platte River. Residence: Oxford.

James E. M. Thompson

James E. M. Thompson, orthopedic surgeon, was born at Los Angeles, California, August 17, 1889, son of Edward and Ella Mary (Tarr) Thompson. Edward Thompson, who was born at Delaware, Ohio, in 1848, was a clergyman and educator, with the degrees of A. B., M. A., Ph. D., LL. D. and D. D. He was first president of York Seminary, and later associated with Nebraska Wesleyan University, and still later served as president of the University of Southern California. He died at San Antonio, Texas, January 16, 1916. His father, Edward Thompson, was a bishop in the Methodist Episcopal Church, and president of Ohio Wesleyan University. The family's ancestry is Scotch thruout.

Ella Mary (Tarr) Thompson, wife of Edward, was born at Albion, Michigan, in 1858, and died at Fort Worth, Texas, in 1912. Her mother was Dutch and her father Scotch. She held the degrees of A. B., M. D., and Ph. D., and served as dean of women at the University of Southern California, and dean of Arlington Heights College.

Dr. Thompson attended Northwestern Academy, Northwestern and Arlington Heights Colleges, receiving his A. B. at the latter, and his M. D. from Rush Medical College. He has taken post-graduate work at various European clinics. At Northwestern he played football, and is a member of Beta Theta Pi and Phi Chi.

On June 21, 1916, he was married to Helen Virginia Yoke at Adrian, Nebraska. Mrs. Thompson was born at Grafton, Virginia, March 19, 1896, and is descended from participants in the American Revolution. There are two children, Helen Jean, born March 29, 1924, and James E. M. born November 11, 1926.

Dr. Thompson is a member of the firm of Drs. Orr and Thompson, and has practiced orthopetic surgery exclusively since 1916. He is one of the leading orthopedic surgeons of the country, and is a member of the following professional associations: The American Orthopedic Association; Clinical Orthopedic Society; American College of Surgeons (fellow); American Medical Association (fellow); Nebraska State and Lancaster County Medical Societies. During 1930 he was president of the Nebraska section of the American College of Surgeons. He is the author of numerous medical essays appearing in the leading medical journals of the country; together with a chapter on foot disabilities in *Obts Pediatrics*.

At the present time Dr. Thompson is president of the Community Chest, a member of the Chamber of Commerce, the Lions Club, the Nebraska Arts Association of which he is a director, and the Masons in which he is a member of the Scottish Rite and Shrine Bodies. During the World War he held the rank of first lieutenant in the Medical Corps, attached to Base Hospital No. 49, American Expeditionary Forces at Allery, France. He is a member of the American Legion and the Veterans of Foreign Wars. For five years he was president of the Lincoln Boy Scout Council, and 8th region chairman Boy Scouts of America. He enjoys boating and fishing. His social clubs are the University and the Lincoln Country Clubs, and his hobby is art. Residence: Lincoln.

Lawrence Lewis Thompson

Lawrence Lewis Thompson, prominent Blaine County rancher, was born at Warwick, Kansas, June 6, 1886, son of Andy Charles and Linnet Adelaide (Glasgow) Thompson.

The father was born in Meadville, Pennsylvania, March 1, 1852, and is a farmer whose parents came to America from Ireland in 1848. Linnet Adelaide Glasgow was born in Oskaloosa, Iowa, January 24, 1859, and was a teacher in the early days of Kansas, 1878, 1879 and 1880. Her ancestry is Scotch, her family having come from Ohio to Iowa before that was a state, and then to Kansas in 1877. In a family of nine all were teachers except one.

Mr. Thompson received his elementary education in the schools of Republic County, Kansas, with a few months in grade school at Denver, Colorado. He settled in Blaine County, Nebraska on May 1, 1910, and since has been engaged in ranching there. He is Independent in politics.

On December 25, 1912, he was married to Fern Kennedy at Dunning. She was born at Merna, Nebraska, March 26, 1893, and is a teacher. There are two children, Edward Maxwell, born November 18, 1913; and Clifford Eugene, born September 21, 1918. Both are in high school at Dunning. Residence: Dunning.

Lynn Thompson

Lynn Thompson, druggist, was born at Java, New York, January 28, 1880, and has resided in Nebraska for the past 45 years. His father, Wellington Thompson, was born in New York, and died at Scottsbluff, March 26, 1926. His wife, Ellen Thompson, was born in New York State, and is still living.

Mr. Thompson attended public school and was graduated from Gordon High School, in June, 1898. On August 5, 1901, he was graduated from pharmacy from Highland Park College at Des Moines, Iowa. Since that time he has been in the retail drug business.

On October 26, 1926, he was married to Beulah I. Garman at Kansas City, Kansas. Mrs. Thompson was born in Iowa, May 26, 1883. She is a member of the Episcopal Church and the Eastern Star.

Mr. Thompson is a Republican. He was a private in the Iowa National Guard for some time, is affiliated with the Episcopal Church of Scottsbluff, and is an Elk and a Mason, and a member of the Eastern Star. His club is the Scottsbluff Country Club. His favorite sport is golf, and his hobby is hard work. Residence: Scottsbluff.

Theos Jefferson Thompson

For over fifteen years Theos Jefferson Thompson has been engaged in educational work. He was born at Northville, Spink County, South Dakota, November 1, 1886, the son of Charles Kare and Flora Belle (Torrence) Thompson. His father, who was a minister, farmer, and legislator, was born at Geneva, Illinois, February 2, 1860, and is still living; he came from West Virginia to Illinois, and later settled in South Dakota. His mother, who was an active missionary worker, was born at Senecaville, Ohio, May 21, 1869, and died at Northville, January 14, 1917; her parents moved from Pennsylvania to Ohio and from Ohio to South Dakota.

Dr. Thompson attended Northville elementary school in 1901 and completed his high school education at Regent Preparatory School at Houghton, New York. He was awarded the A. B., A. M., and Ph. D. degrees at the University of Nebraska. He was a student at Houghton College, New York, the University of Michigan, and the University of Chicago. He is a member of Sigma Xi, and the American Chemical Society, holding honorary membership in Alpha Chi Sigma and Phi Lambda Upsilon. He received letters in baseball and basketball at Houghton College.

He was a teacher at Miltonvale Wesleyan College, Miltonvale, Kansas, 1913-14, at Nebraska University, 1914-15, at Miltonvale Wesleyan College where he was a dean and professor of chemistry, 1915-18. He became graduate assistant in chemistry in 1918 and later instructor, professor, and at the present time is dean of student affairs and professor of chemistry at the University of Nebraska. He is also chairman of the Nebraska Basic Science Board in Medicine.

Dr. Thompson is the author of research articles in chemistry, published at various dates from 1920 to 1930, including these subjects: solubilities of fatty acid salts; hydrolosis of proteins; the relation of diet to the blood constituents synthesis of coumarins, hydantoins and substituted succinic acids; and benzyl esters. He has also written on philosophical subjects.

During the late war he served as four minute speaker and assisted in loan drives. From July 1918-December 1918, he was employed by the Hercules Powder company. He is now major in the Chemical Warfare Service Reserves. He is a member of the American Chemical Society, the American Association of University Professors, the Chamber of Commerce, the Rotary Club, and The Nebraskana Society. He holds membership in the Nebraska Educational Association, the State Teacher Retirement Committee, the American Association for the Advancement of Science, and the First Methodist Church at Lincoln. His social clubs are the University Club and the Eastridge Country Club, and his sports include golf, tennis, baseball and basketball. He is especially interested in flower gardening and reading.

A Republican, Dr. Thompson served for several terms as a member of the city council of University Place. He was married to Mabel Elizabeth Dow at Miltonvale, May 25, 1916. Mrs. Thompson, who is a teacher and educational executive, was born at Buffalo, New York, June 19, 1889. Her paternal grandfather settled in New York after living in Vermont for a time, and her maternal grandfather came to this country from Germany. They have three children; Theos Jardin, born August 30, 1918; John Rutherford, born April 16, 1921; and Richard Dow, born December 20, 1923. Residence: Lincoln.

William Henry Thompson

One of the distinguished professional leaders of Grand Island, Nebraska, is William Henry Thompson who has been engaged in the practice of law there for many years. His father, Eli Thompson, who was born in Carroll County, Ohio, in 1825, was a homesteader in Custer County, Nebraska, about 1889, and died in that county February 3, 1903; his ancestry was Scotch and Dutch.

Judge Thompson attended a private school in Iowa, supplemented his education with work in the Upper Iowa University, and enrolled in the law department of the University of Iowa in 1875, graduating with the LL. B. degree. In 1877 on his graduating, he opened up a law office at Brush Creek, now Arlington, in Fayette County and remained there until June, 1881, when he and his family moved to Grand Island, Nebraska, where they have resided ever since. He has served as a member of the Nebraska Capitol Commission since its organization, has served as a member of the Nebraska Supreme Court, and has always taken an unusually prominent part in state affairs.

A lifelong Democrat, Judge Thompson began his career in public office as county attorney for Hall County. In 1890 he was nominated for United States congress from the Big Third District, which then comprised all of the state north of the Platte River except Douglas and Sarpy counties. Since his arrival in Nebraska he has been a delegate to practically every state convention of his party and has been an outstanding figure in national conventions. He was delegate-at-large to the Democratic National Convention in 1892, serving as chairman of the Nebraska delegation, and was an ardent supporter of Grover Cleveland. In 1896 he was delegate-at-large to the party's national convention where he warmly supported William Jennings Bryan, and was chosen national committeeman. He held the same office in the national convention of 1900, and 1904, but was defeated for that position in the one of 1908.

In 1916 Judge Thompson was a member of the notification committee at the St. Louis Democratic National Convention where Woodrow Wilson was nominated for the presidency. He was nominated for the United States senate in 1900, and for governor in 1902, but in both cases was defeated by a small majority. From 1895 to 1899 he served Grand Island, and in 1924 was elected associate justice of the Supreme Court of Nebraska.

He is a member of the Nebraska State Bar Association, the American Bar Association, the Grand Island Chamber of Commerce, and the Nebraskana Society. He has served as a member of the Board of Trustees of the Grand Island Baptist College for 21 years, and is a member of the Kiwanis Club, the Red Cross, the Modern Woodmen of America, the Elks, and the Presbyterian Church of Grand Island. On September 7, 1879, Judge Thompson was united in marriage with Nettie I. Hutchison. Mrs. Thompson was born in Michigan, but was reared in Iowa. Her father, who was a lawyer, served as county recorder for a number of years and she acted as his deputy prior to her marriage. To this marriage were born: Edith L., who married Wallace E. Porter, and who died August 31, 1904; Mattie, who died in infancy; Grover, who married Lena Neifeldt has four sons; and Lloyd G., who married Aimee Ruth Schwyn, and now resides with his family in Los Angeles, California. In addition to their own children and their grandson, Judge and Mrs. Thompson also reared two of their nieces. Residence: Grand Island.

William Townsend Thompson

William T. Thompson was born at Fennimore, Wisconsin, the son of James and Charlotte (Hall) Thompson. His father, who was a farmer, was born in London, England, and died at Fennimore, in 1865. His mother died at Fennimore, September, 1871.

Mr. Thompson attended public school and later was a student at Simpson College where he was a member of Delta Tau Delta. He was admitted to the bar at Des Moines, Iowa, 1884, and since then has been active in the legal world. A Republican, he has held the following positions; member of lower house of the legislature, 1899-1903, deputy attorney general, 1904-06, attorney general, 1906-10, solicitor of the United States Treasury, 1910-14, supreme court commissioner from 1925 to 1929, and since 1931 has held this position.

He is a member of the Lancaster County Bar Association and the Nebraska State Bar Association. He is affiliated with the Westminster Presbyterian Church of Lincoln; holds membership in the Modern Woodmen of America; and is a member of the Lincoln Automobile Club.

His marriage to Florence Bell Bussell was solemnized at Indianola, Warren County, Iowa, April 21, 1885. Mrs. Thompson was born in Iowa. They have three children: Vivian, born April 6, 1887; Charlotte, born November, 1892; and Norma, born January, 1897. Residence: Lincoln.

Arthur Christian Thomsen

Arthur C. Thomsen, lawyer and judge, was born at Pierce, Nebraska, July 23, 1886. He is the son of Claus Christian and Catherine (Haman) Thomsen, both natives of Norderstapel, Schleswig, Germany. The father was born in 1850, came to America about 1880, and died here in 1889. His wife, Catherine, was born at Norderstapel, September 3, 1860. Her father was a general contractor in northern Germany and the inventor of a machine for road grading, patent for which was granted in the United States in 1887. The machine is substantially the same as those used today.

Judge Thomsen was graduated from Omaha High School in 1905, and attended the Omaha Law School until 1909. He received his A. B. and LL. B. at the University of Omaha in 1912. He is a member of Lambda Phi and Tau Delta Upsilon. He entered the active practice of law in 1909, associating with the firm of Montgomery, Hall and Young, which continued until 1912. He was a member of the firm of Searle and Thomsen 1912-13; Wakeley and Thomsen 1914-15; Thomsen, Horton and Standeven 1916-17 and 1919-20, and Thomsen, Mossman and Standeven 1920-27.

He was nominated for judge of the district court for the fourth judicial district in 1924. In 1928 he was elected to that office, which position he still holds. Judge Thomsen has been called by the Supreme Court to serve on the Supreme bench several times, and has written several Supreme Court opinions. He is also the author of *An Inquiry Directed to the Secretary of the Treasury* (1925), and is editor of the *Night Law Bulletin* of the University of Omaha. From 1920 to 1926 he was instructor in law at the Night Law School of the University of Omaha, and acting dean from 1914-28. Since 1928 he has been dean of the Night Law School of the University of Omaha. He was formerly its secretary.

At the beginning of the World War he was a four-minute speaker; later he was a second lieutenant, Air Service (balloon division), 1917-18. He is a licensed balloon pilot, member of the Society Aeronatique Internationale. He is a lieutenant in the Officers Reserve Corps of the Air Service of the Army of the United States. He is a member of the Nebraska State Bar Association, the American Bar Association and the Omaha-Douglas County Bar. He was formerly affiliated with the Commercial Law League of America. He is still a member of the International Association of Inventors, having had patents granted to him in the United States; also the American Title Association, the Nebraska Manufacturers Development Society, the International Transportation Association and the American Legion.

He is a member of the Ancient Arabic Order Nobles of the Mystic Shrine, 32nd degree, Scottish Rite, and of Covert Lodge No. 11 Ancient Free and Accepted Masons, Elks and Fontenelle Society of America. He is a trustee of the University of Omaha, and former president of the Alumni Association. He is a member of the Ad-Sell League and of Ak-Sar-Ben.

His marriage to Emily Susan Johnson was solemnized at Omaha, July 23, 1913. Mrs. Thomsen was born in England, January 26, 1880. She has taught in Omaha High Schools at various times. They have two children, Lystra Cecilia, 14 and Emily Margaret, 12.

Judge Thomsen's clubs are the Professional Mens, the A. B. C., the Concord and the Hiram Clubs. Residence: Omaha.

Ingebert Johansen Thomsen

Born at North Abild, Germany, August 4, 1873, Ingebert Johansen Thomsen is the son of Peter Hendick and Marie (Johansen) Thomsen. His father, who was born at Fahrenstedt, Germany, June 16, 1823, and died at Minden, Nebraska, July 17, 1905, was a stone mason and builder of bridges for 32 years, and then came to America, where he engaged in farming; he was descended from prosperous land owners and builders in Germany, and was active in political affairs there. His mother was born in Denmark, September 24, 1833, and died at Minden, September 4, 1907.

Mr. Thomsen was a farmer, specializing in full blooded stock, Percherson horses, and Shorthorn cattle until

1910, when he entered the land business. Four years later he became county clerk of Kearney County, Nebraska, and in 1923, was appointed postmaster at Minden. He is president of the Thomsen Pneumatic Collar Company, manufacturers of the pneumatic horse collar invented and patented by Mr. Thomsen.

During the World War, Mr. Thomsen served as secretary of the local board under very trying conditions. Shortly before war was declared it was discovered from the records that his father, who came to America as an old man, had been misinformed as to the requirements of the naturalization laws, and had failed to get what was called the "last papers." That made Mr. Thomsen technically a German citizen. The matter was reported to the governor, who was acting adjutant general of the state, but appreciating his loyalty to America and the faithful service he had rendered, the governor ordered Mr. Thomsen to continue. Although political opposition made an effort to have him removed, he was rewarded by being continued in the office of county clerk by a large majority at the next election.

He is president of the United Presbyterian Church Board at Minden, serving as a ruling elder, is a member of the Minden Commercial Club, holds membership in the Nebraska Historical Society and the Nebraskana Society, and in 1929, served as secretary of the Minden Parent-Teachers' Association. He is a member of the local Red Cross.

His marriage to Hedvig Ellen Holstein, occurred at Minden, November 18, 1903. Mrs. Thomsen was born at Rutland, Vermont, October 15, 1876. Five children were born to them: Vernon I., born May 24, 1905; Immanuel H., born December 16, 1907; Bernice M., born September 3, 1912; Eldoris S., born February 13, 1915; and Homer H., born December 31, 1918, who died in July, 1930. Residence: Minden. (Photograph in Album).

Soren Milton Thomsen

Sorne Milton Thomsen, head of the department of chemistry and physics at Dana College, Blair, Nebraska, was born at Milwaukee, Wisconsin, January 21, 1908. His father, Soren Christian Thomsen, who was born at Vinding, Denmark, March 23, 1872, is a building contractor; he came to this country in 1903. His mother, Johanna Marie Pedersen Thomsen was born at Vinding, August 3, 1881, and came to America in 1906.

Professor Thomsen attended Cass Street School at Milwaukee until 1921, and in 1925, was graduated from the Lincoln High School there. He received the Bachelor of Education degree at Milwaukee State Teacher's College in 1929, and in 1930, was awarded the Master of Science degree at the University of Wisconsin. Since 1930 he has been dean of men and head of the chemistry and physics department at Dana College.

In 1928 he was licensed by the Wisconsin State Board of Pharmacy as a registered assistant pharmacist. He is affiliated with the First Lutheran Church at Blair, and holds membership in the Nebraskana Society. He is independent, politically. Residence: Blair.

William Fred Thomsen

William F. Thomsen, who has lived in this state all his life and for many years has been a farmer in Saunders County, was born at Cedar Bluffs, December 17, 1875, the son of John Frederick and Anna M. (Wiegand) Thomsen. His father, who was a carpenter and farmer, was born at Flensburg, Schleswig, Denmark, November 30, 1842, and died at Cedar Bluffs, December 30, 1927; he came to this country in 1867. His mother was born at Holstein, Denmark, July 20, 1849, and died at Cedar Bluffs, December 6, 1930.

Mr. Thomsen has been interested in the general welfare of his community for many years, and has been active in improvement work at Cedar Bluffs. He has always been an industrious farmer, has been a school director for 15 years, and has made a hobby of better farming. He is affiliated with the Presbyterian Church at Cedar Bluffs, and is a member of The Nebraskana Society, and the Woodmen of the World. He is a Republican.

He was united in marriage with Mary Christena Lorenzen at Wahoo, Saunders County, Nebraska, June 2, 1909. Mrs. Thomsen, whose parents came to this country from Denmark in 1867, was born at Cedar Bluffs, September 2, 1880. Two children were born to this union: Adelbert F., born January 22, 1912; and Howard E., born January 22, 1914. Residence: Cedar Bluffs.

Bertha Evelyn Mangon Thomson

Bertha Evelyn Mangon, daughter of Charles Anthony and Margaret Anna (Habig) Mangon, was born at Brock, Nebraska, September 9, 1889. Her father, born near Bordeaux, France, July 20, 1849, came to the United States at about the age of two with his parents. A farmer and fruit grower, he served in the Union Army during the Civil War, and was active in politics and political reform. His death occurred at Lincoln, April 19, 1924. Anna Habig, whose parents were German, was born at Hollidaysburg, Pennsylvania, September 5, 1850, and died at Lincoln, on December 6, 1923. Primarily a homemaker, she was active in the life of her community, also. She came with her parents to Nemaha County in 1856, they being among the first settlers of the county, Nebraska City then being the nearest town.

Upon her graduation from Brock High School in 1906, as valedictorian of her class, Bertha Evelyn Mangon attended Peru State Normal School and then taught in country school two years before beginning the study of medicine. In 1913 she received her M. D. from Cotner University Medical College, since which time she has been actively engaged in practice. During 1914-15 she spent one year in post graduate work at the College of Missions and Butler University in Indianapolis, Indiana.

On July 26, 1914, she was united in marriage to Clinton Harris Thomson at North Platte, Nebraska. Mr. Thomson was born at West Side, Iowa, December 28, 1886, and was a minister and missionary to India. His death occurred at Hatta Damoh, District C. P. India, on December 24, 1927, from accidental drowning. Mr. Thomson was graduated from Cotner College in 1914. While a student there he was a participant in all activities, representing Cotner in state oratorical contests and being a member of her debating teams. He was an officer in the Young Men's Christian Association, the Student Volunteer Band and the literary societies. After his marriage he also took post graduate work at the College of Missions and Butler University.

There are five children, Paul Harris, born June 29, 1916; Margaret Evelyn, born March 14, 1918; Catherine Myrtle, born May 27, 1921; Alice Lucile, born December 8, 1923; and Ellen Mangon, born September 5, 1926. All of the children with the exception of Alice, were born in British India. The three older ones have crossed the Atlantic three times, once on the *S. S. Leviathan*.

During 1913-14, Dr. Thomson practiced medicine at North Platte, and in 1915 served an internship in the Methodist Episcopal Hospital at Indianapolis. In September, 1915, Mr. and Mrs. Thomson sailed from San Francisco, going by way of Japan and China to India, to take up missionary work. From 1916, until 1923, she had charge of a dispensary and thirty bed mission hospital at Mahoba U. P., India. She and her husband were under the United Christian Missionary Society of the Christian Church. At the present time Dr. Thomson is engaged in private practice at Bethany, Lincoln, Nebraska.

From June, 1923, until September 6, 1924, the Thomsons were on furlough in Lincoln. At the time of Mr. Thomson's accidental death in December, 1927, they had served since September, 1915, as missionaries. Dr. Thomson

has given many missionary addresses in and around Lincoln, since her return to the United States in 1928. She is a member of Bethany Christian Church, the Medical Woman's National Association, the National Electric Medical Association, the Nebraska State Electric Medical Association, of which she is secretary, and during 1928-29, was secretary-treasurer of the Nebraska Association of Medical Women.

Dr. Thomson is physical examiner for physical education department of the Lincoln Woman's Club, and of Cotner College girls. A member of the committee on health of the Bethany Parent-Teachers' Association, she is superintendent of the Loyal Temperance Legion, and a member of the Women's Christian Temperance Union. Dr. Thomson says her greatest object in life is to keep her five children busy and happy with their chickens, gardening and fruit, and to raise them to be valuable Christian citizens of their country. Residence: Lincoln. (Photograph in Album).

John Thomssen

Born at Alda, Nebraska, May 6, 1870, John Thomssen is the son of John and Anna (Stehr) Thomssen. His father, who was a farmer and a soldier in the Danish Army, was born in Germany, March 23, 1832, and died at Alda, in June 27, 1917. His mother was born in Germany, April 27, 1833, and died at Alda, August 19, 1925.

Mr. Thomssen was successfully engaged in farming in Hall County, Nebraska, for 33 years, served as cashier of the Alda State Bank for over ten years, and was vice president of the Farmers State Bank. He was a member of the Alda Board of Education for 11 years, acting as moderator part of that time, and is now a member of the Parent-Teachers' Association, the Masons, Royal Highlanders, and the Elks.

A Democrat, he has held the following positions: county treasurer of Hall County, 1898-1900; member of the House of Representatives, 1923-24, 1925-26, 1927-28; and unsuccessful candidate for Public Lands and Buildings commissioner, 1930. He is affiliated with the English Lutheran Church and holds membership in the Nebraskana Society.

His marriage to Christine Oltman was solemnized at Grand Island, Nebraska, March 8, 1894. Mrs. Thomssen, who is a homemaker, was born at Keil, Germany, August 2, 1876. To them were born: Eli, August 25, 1906, who was formerly employed in the First National Bank at Aurora, Nebraska; Emil, March 20, 1909, the owner of an oil station at Alda, and Arthur, July 2, 1913, a student. Residence Alda. (Photograph in Album).

Lindon Hackett Thornburgh

Lindon Hackett Thornburgh, who has been in public life as an educator and newspaper man for nearly 50 years, was born at Dalton, Wayne County, Indiana, November 11, 1856, the son of Lorenzo Rachel (McCrecken) Thornburgh. His father, who was born at Swann Creek, Tennessee, 1838, was an engineer for a saw mill in Indiana, and was killed August 30, 1862, while serving in the Civil War; he was descended from John Maulsby who came from England in 1869 in the *Bristol*, a merchant vessel. His mother, whose ancestry was Irish, was born in North Carolina in 1833 and died at Meckling, South Dakota, 1876.

Mr. Thornburgh was graduated from Fremont Teachers College, Fremont, Nebraska, with the B. S. degree. He has lived in Nebraska for 45 years and has been prominent in educational and newspaper work in this state for many years. He is now senior editor of the *Alexandria Argus*, Alexandria, Thayer County, Nebraska, and is retired from active service.

He is a member of the Independent Order of Odd Fellows, the Nebraskana Society, and the First Presbyterian Church at Alexandria. For thirty years he served as secretary of the local school board. Reading and editorial writing are his hobbies. Mr. Thornburgh married Mary Melrose, she was born at Eminence, Ohio, July 3, 1865, ad died at Alexandria, January 26, 1925. Twin sons were born to them January 8, 1898: Lewis, who died October 10, 1898; and Charles, who is publisher of the *Alexandria Argus*. Residence: Alexandria.

Wallace Gladstone Thornton

Wallace Gladstone Thornton, secretary of the Kearney Chamber of Commerce for nearly seven years, was born at Neligh, Nebraska, June 20, 1892. He is the son of Fred and Mary Serena (Wilcox) Thornton, the former born in Michigan, April 26, 1862. Fred Thorton moved to Illinois with his parents as a child, locating in Wennebago County. Now retired, he was for many years a building contractor and later engaged in the lumber and coal business.

Mary Serena Wilcox was born in Winnebago County, Illinois, September 12, 1860, and died at Neligh, October 1, 1926. A devoted wife and mother, she was the daughter of the Reverend John Wilcox, who was ordained a Congregational minister in London. He preached for nearly fifty years in a small country Congregational Church near his farm in Winnebago County, Illinois, with no remuneration for his services.

In June, 1906, Wallace Gladstone Thornton was graduated from the Neligh grade school, and in 1910 from the high school there. Shortly thereafter he became employed in the clerical department of the Northwestern railroad in Nebraska, and was next associated as clerk and bookkeeper with a Nebraska creamery. For seven years he was a commercial salesman in Nebraska territory. The ensuing five years Mr. Thornton was assistant secretary of the Lincoln Chamber of Commerce, leaving to become secretary of the Kearney organization.

His marriage to Carrie Delle Vesy was solemnized at Omaha, Nebraska, on April 8, 1916. Mrs. Thornton, who is the daughter of Mr. and Mrs. B. E. Vesy, was born at Gibbon, Nebraska, August 17, 1893. Her father died in 1899 and her mother now resides in Omaha. There are two children, Mary Elaine, born January 1, 1919, and Richard Wallace, born April 10, 1923.

Mr. Thornton is a Republican. He is secretary-treasurer of he Kearney Grain Exchange, secretary of the Nebraska division of the Central Western Shippers Advisory Board, and treasurer of the local Boy Scout organization. For the past four years he has been secretary of the Fort Kearney Memorial Association.

His religious affiliation is with the Kearney Methodist Church. He is a member of the National Association of Commercial Organization Secretaries, the Nebraska Association of Commercial Organization Secretaries, the Red Cross, the Travelers Protective Association, the Modern Woodmen of America and is a 32nd degree Mason. Recently Mr. Thornton was made a life member of The Nebraskana Society. Residence: Kearney.

Charles Duvawl Thorp

Charles D. Thorp, president of the Nebraska State Poultry Association for the past six years, is prominent in school activities and community affairs at McCool Junction, Nebraska. He was born in Hendricks County, Indiana, October 29, 1859, the son of Franklin and Martha Ann (Rawlings) Thorp. His father, who was a farmer, was born in Indiana of English and German parents, and died during service in the Civil War. His mother, who was of English descent, was born in Hendricks County, March 3, 1840.

Mr. Thorp came to Nebraska in 1880, having received his elementary and high school education in Indiana. As a successful farmer in York County he has always been interested in Nebraska public affairs. For the past 15 years he has served almost continuously as a member of the local school board. He is a Democrat, a Mason, and holds membership in The Nebraskana Society.

His marriage to Alice Missouri Heady was solemnized at Kokomo, Indiana, February 1, 1893. Mrs. Thorp, whose ancestry is English, was born in Hamilton County, Indiana, November 21, 1863. To this marriage ten children were born: Roy, born April 1, 1884; Ethel, born October 31, 1885; Leslie, born September 4, 1887; Earl, born January 8, 1889; Percy, born February 5, 1891; Martha, born September 11, 1894; Myrtle, born July 16, 1897; Esther, born October 26, 1899; Mildred, born December 30, 1904; and Ronald, born August 27, 1909. Residence: McCool Junction.

Milton Ralph Thorp

Milton R. Thorp has been active in the life of his community for many years. Born at Eastport, Iowa, February 15, 1867, he is the son of Edward Franklin and Martha Ann (Nicholson) Thorp. When he was a child his parents moved to Nebraska, where he has since been a resident. Edward Franklin Thorp was born at Cleveland, Ohio, August 31, 1834, and died at Nebraska City, December 14, 1913. He was a millwright and hotel proprietor. His wife, Martha Ann Nicholson, was born in Indiana, November 21, 1838, and died at Nebraska City, January 16, 1920.

Mr. Thorp was educated in the public and high schools of Nebraska City. From June 10, 1890, until December 1, 1909, he was a United States letter carrier. Since the last mentioned date he has served as assistant post master at Nebraska City.

He was married to LoRenna Perkins, at Nebraska City, October 4, 1896. She was born at Maquoketa, Iowa, October 20, 1868, and died at Nebraska City, May 18, 1921. There is one son, Ralph M., born December 11, 1897. Mr. Thorp's second marriage was to Carrie Browne on June 17, 1925. Mrs. Thorp had been a teacher in the public schools of Omaha for thirty-five years.

Mr. Thorp is a Republican, is active in the Red Cross, and the Boy Scouts of America, and is a director of the Chamber of Commerce. He is also former president of the Nebraska City board of education.

His fraternal organizations include the Elks Lodge No. 1049, of which he is past exalted ruler. He is past master of Western Star Lodge No. 2, Ancient Free and Accepted Masons; past commander of Mt. Olivet Commandry No. 2, Knights Templar, and a member of Sesostris Temple, Nobles of the Mystic Shrine, the Order of Eastern Star, and the Royal Arch Masons.

He is a baseball fan, and a member of the Country Club. Residence: Nebraska City.

Frank Dwight Throop

Frank D. Throop, publisher of the *Lincoln Star* at Lincoln, Lancaster County, Nebraska, was born at Mount Pleasant, Henry County, Iowa, September 23, 1878. His father, George E. Throop who was publisher of the Mount Pleasant *Daily News*, was born at Preston, Chenango County, New York, September 17, 1849, the son of D. W. C. Throop and Lydia Ann (Whipple) Throop; he died at Davenport, Scott County, Iowa, January 31, 1917.

His mother, Ida Carmeleta (Gimble) Throop, the daughter of O. J. and Clara Smith Gimble, was born at Peoria, Tazewell County, Illinois, August 21, 1856, and died at Davenport, March 5, 1929. Her father was born in Germany while her mother was a resident of Philadelphia.

Mr. Throop was graduated from the Mount Pleasant High School in 1895, received the B. S. degree in 1899 at Iowa Wesleyan College, Mount Pleasant, Iowa, where he was head of the debating club and advertising manager of the college paper. He is a member of Phi Delta Theta.

He entered the newspaper world as a reporter on the *Muscatine Journal*, Muscatine, Iowa, and in 1907, became publisher of this paper. He became publisher of the *Davenport Democrat*, 1915, and remained in that executive capacity until 1930 when he became publisher of the *Lincoln Star*. All the above papers together with seven others comprise the Lee Syndicate of which Mr. Throop is vice president.

Mr. Throop is a trustee of the Iowa Wesleyan College, a trustee of St. Katherine's School at Davenport, is vice president of the Journal Printing Company at Madi-Cross, Wisconsin, is secretary-treasurer of the Times Company at Davenport, is secretary-treasurer of the Democrat Publishing Company, at Davenport, is vice president of the Courier Printing Company, Ottumwa, son, Wisconsin, is vice president of the *Tribune*, at La-Iowa, is vice president of the Courier Post Printing Company at Hannibal, Missouri, is vice president of the Mason City, (Iowa) *Globe Gazette* and the Star Printing Company at Lincoln.

During the World War Mr. Throop was a captain of a Liberty Loan Team, was a four minute speaker, and was a member of the publicity committee of the Liberty Loan drives in Iowa. He is a member of the Sons of the Revolution, the Red Cross, the Lincoln Community Chest, and the Rotary Club. He holds membership in the Associated Press and American Newspaper Publishers Association, the Iowa State Historical Society, and the Nebraskana Society.

He is a member of the Young Men's Christian Association, is affiliated with the Universalist Church at Mount Pleasant, and holds membership in the University Club and the Country Club at Lincoln. He is a Democrat. Mr. Throop's favorite recreation is golfing.

He was married at Muscatine, June 21, 1905, to Mabel Zel Leverich. Mrs. Throop, who is the daughter of R. W. and Olive Garlock Leverich, was born at Muscatine, July 2, 1879. They have two children: Marjorie, born August 6, 1907, who married O. V. Calhoun; and Mary Katharine, born May 26, 1910. Residence: Lincoln.

Adolph John Thuman

Adolph John Thuman, president of the State Bank of Trenton, was born in Seward County, Nebraska, June 25, 1890. He is the son of John Herman, born at Northrup, Germany, September 30, 1850 and Anna (Flatemersch) Thuman, born in Germany, June 4, 1858. His parents came to America in 1870 settling in Illinois, and coming to Nebraska in 1884.

Mr. Thuman attended public school and high school at Cambridge, Nebraska. From 1910 until 1917 he was assistant cashier of the First National Bank of Cambridge, and in 1917 organized the State Bank of Trenton, serving as cashier until 1918. From 1919 until 1924 he was vice-president and since 1924 has been president of that bank.

On December 17, 1914, he was married to Elsie O. Exstrom at Axtell, Nebraska, who was born December 14, 1889. Mrs. Thuman is a member of the Eastern Star, and is active in the affairs of the Congregational Church of which she is a member. There are three children, Dale E., born April 7, 1916; Dean Roger, December 6, 1918; and Rachel Elsie, May 30, 1921.

Mr. Thuman is a Democrat. He is affiliated with the Congregational Church at Trenton, and is a member of Cambridge Lodge No. 150 of the Ancient Free and Accepted Masons. Residence: Trenton.

George Bartruff Thummel

A lifetime resident of Nebraska, George B. Thummel has been engaged in the practice of law at Omaha

since 1913. He was born at Grand Island, Nebraska, February 9, 1892, the son of George Hamilton and Stella Augusta (Bartruff) Thummel. His father, who was born in Lee County, Illinois, January 31, 1843, has been a lawyer, United States marshall, clerk of the United States Circuit Court, and chairman of the board of the First Trust Company of Omaha. His mother was born at Mount Pleasant, Iowa, July 14, 1854, and died at Omaha, November 5, 1924.

Mr. Thummel attended the Omaha public schools and the University Preparatory School at Ithaca, New York, 1909. He received his LL. B. degree at Cornell University in New York, 1913; and was a member of Sigma Phi. He was in partnership in law practice with John J. Sullivan, former chief justice of the supreme court of Nebraska, from 1916 until the death of Mr. Sullivan in 1926. He is director and general counsel, of the American Reserve Life Insurance Company.

He was married at Rochester, New York, February 9, 1916, to Gladys Eugenie Congdon. Mrs. Thummel, whose ancestry is English, was born at Syracuse, New York. Their children are: Marcia, born December 23, 1918; and Jean, born December 12, 1924.

Mr. Thummel was a first lieutenant in the air service during the World War. He is a member of the Omaha Bar Association; the Nebraska Bar Association; the American Bar Association; and the Omaha Chamber of Commerce. He is a member of Covert Lodge Number 11 of the Ancient Free and Accepted Masons. His social clubs are teh Omaha Club and the Omaha Country Club. An Episcopalian, he is affiliated with Trinity Cathedral at Omaha. He is a Republican. He holds membership in the Nebraskana Society. Residence: Omaha.

Clarence James Thurston

Clarence J. Thurston, lawyer, was born at Onawa, Iowa, November 1, 1896, son of Charles Augustus and Rose (Brody) Thurston. His father, Charles A. Thurston, was the son of James R. Thurston, who crossed Iowa in 1856 in a covered wagon and homesteaded in Monona County. Susan Williams, wife of James R. Thurston, was a direct descendant of Roger Williams. Charles A. Thurston was a hardware merchant twenty-five years, and is president of the Equitable Trust Company of Omaha, the Talmage-Thurston Company of Omaha and the Equitable Investment Company of Omaha.

Rose Brody Thurston was born at Cassopolis, Michigan, a direct descendant in the seventh generation of Anneke Jans. Mrs. Thurston is still living.

Upon his graduation from the Onawa High School in 1914, Clarence J. Thurston entered the State University of Iowa where he was awarded his B. A. in June 1918, and his LL. B. in June 1921. He was elected to Phi Delta Phi, held the offices of steward, secretary and president of Kappa Sigma, was a member of the University Players and cup winner of the All University Clay Bird Shoot 1914-15.

Upon his admission to the bar in 1921 he was employed as attorney with the Equitable Trust Company, continuing until 1926. Since that time he has been engaged in private practice. He was united in marriage with Edna Elizabeth Gingles, at Onawa, October 30, 1922. Mrs. Thurston was born at Seattle, Washington, February 3, 1901. Mr. Thurston enlisted through civilian application in the Infantry Central Officers Training School at Camp Pike, Arkansas, and had just completed his course when the armistice was signed. He is a member of the American Legion. He attends Trinity Cathedral and is a Mason. His professional organizations include the Nebraska State Bar Association and the Omaha-Douglas County Bar Association. His clubs are the University Club and the Dundee Dancing Club. He is fond of tennis, golf, horse-back riding and reading. Residence: Omaha.

Cynthia S. Thurston

A resident of Nebraska nearly sixty years, Cynthia S. Thurston was born near Meadville, Pennsylvania, December 1, 1851. She is the daughter of True Langdon and Amanda (Breed) Kelley, early pioneers in Nebraska. Her father was born in New Hampshire, in August, 1913, and came to Nebraska, dying in Saunders County. He was a teacher of Irish descent. Her mother was born in Vermont, October 31, 1813, and also died in Saunders County. She was a teacher of English ancestry.

Cynthia S. Kelley attended county school and the Academics of Saybrook and Conneaut, Ohio. Later she was a student at the University of Nebraska and Peru State Normal School. She was first married to Samuel Allen Bear at Fremont, on September 26, 1883. He was born in Missouri, May 21, 1849, and died in Hedgesville, West Virginia.

To them were born three children, Edith Alma, August 1, 1884, who married Ivar Shenefield; Edward Maxfield, August 2, 1886, who married Alice Barber; and Robert McCabe, May 27, 1893, who married Olga Schroder. Edward is a civil engineer and Robert is a farmer.

May 2, 1920, she was married to R. G. Thurston, a veteran of the Civil War, who is an invalid. Mrs. Thurston has been an outstanding personage in her community for many years. She is a member of the Community Church at Brunswick, and an ardent worker in the Women's Christian Temperance Union, in which she has held the office of president in times past. She is a member of the Nebraskana Society. Residence: Brunswick.

John Casper Thygeson

John Casper Thygeson, druggist, was born at Utica, Nebraska, September 7, 1876, son of Soren and Inge Thygeson. His father, born in Denmark, was in the hardware business for a number of years before his death at Utica, in 1880. His mother was born in Denmark, and died at Yakima, Washington, in 1918.

Mr. Thygeson attended public and high schools at Utica, and the Northwestern College of Pharmacy at Chicago. He commenced business in Nebraska City in 1900, and with one of his clerks purchased another store in 1922. He is a partner in the Thygeson and Glen Drug Store at Auburn, and the Stahlhut Drug Company of Crete.

He is a member of St. Mary's Episcopal Church, president of the Associated Charities, president of the Nebraska Pharmaceutical Association, and received the Master Merchant Award in 1931. He is a member of the Elks, the Chamber of Commerce, the Nebraska City Country Club, and is vice-president of the board of education. His favorite sport is golf.

On April 4, 1907, Mr. Thygeson was married to Minnie White at Plattsmouth. She was born at Plattsmouth, January 5, 1877. They have three children, Robert White, born June 20, 1908; Louise, born June 25, 1915; and Ruth, born November 30, 1916. Robert W. purchased an interest in his father's drug store, January 1, 1930, which is being continued as the Thygeson's Drug Store. Residence: Nebraska City.

Robert Tichy, Sr.

Robert Tichy, farmer and leading citizen in his community, was born at Wilber, Saline County, Nebraska, July 26, 1879. His father, Frank Tichy, who was born in Prague, September 27, 1850, was a pioneer Nebraskan who homesteaded in this state 75 miles from the nearest town in the early days; he came to this country in 1868, and for a time worked on the railroad at Nebraska City. His wife, Anna (Santin) Tichy, was born at Lobez, Germany, March 27, 1856; she worked in private homes and learned the English language by studying alone; she died at Wilber, January 13, 1931.

Mr. Tichy attended district school in Saline County,

and in 1900 was graduated from the Wilber High School where he won first place in his graduating oration. He has been interested in education and community improvement for many years and has promoted various meetings to encourage co-operation in civic affairs. For the past 27 years he has been a member of the school board, and has on several occasions acted as delegate to state conventions.

He is a member of the Farmers Union of which he was president for several years, and is now vice president of the Farmers Elevator Company. During the World War he was chairman of all the district committees in charge of Liberty loan drives. His hobby is reading. His political preference is the Democratic party.

On February 28, 1905, he was married to Rose Emma Schleis at Wilber. Mrs. Tichy, who was born at Wilber, September 27, 1883, is of Bohemian and German descent. Their children are: Robert, Jr., born February 10, 1906, who married Blanche Bartos; and Arline, born June 25, 1907, who married Stanley Chab. They have a daughter, Dolores, born October 21, 1929. Robert is an accomplished cornetist, orchestra leader, and music instructor. Arline was salutatorian of her high school class and was graduated from Doane College where she was awarded her A. B. with *Magna Cum Laude* honors. Both children are graduates of Wilber High School. Residence: Wilber. (Photograph on Page 1197).

James F. Tilden

James F. Tilden was born at White River, Vermont, April 23, 1849, the son of Orren E. Tilden and Orrel K. (Moore) Tilden. His father, whose ancestry was English, died at Woodhull, Illinois, April 25, 1879; he was a farmer.

Mr. Tilden has been active in the Farmers Co-operative Association for several years, and in the early 1890's was a member of the school board at Benedict several years. He holds membership in The Nebraskana Society, and is affiliated with the Presbyterian Church. He is independent, politically.

His marriage to Emma L. Frame occurred at Oneida, Illinois, October 23, 1878. Mrs. Tilden, who is a home maker, was born in Missouri, and died at Farm Home, York County, Nebraska, April 21, 1931. Seven children were born to this marriage: Orren E., born October 17, 1879, who married Rose J. Conway; George S., born September 19, 1881, who married Helen Church; Fred F., born August 1, 1883, who married Leona Legro; Roy E., born June 20, 1886, who married Blanche Schnarenger; Glen H., born August 23, 1888, who married Myrtle Harrington; Gladys L., born December 22, 1890, who married Ralph Stephenson; and Julius, born June 24, 1900. Residence: Benedict.

Bernice K. Tillett

Bernice K. Tillett, prominent club woman at Alliance, was born at Brooks, Iowa, July 18, 1879, daughter of John and Lyde (Spafford) Kridelbaugh. Her father was born in Indiana, December 23, 1852, and her mother at Harrisburg, Pennsylvania, August 5, 1852. Her mother was a teacher prior to marriage, is eligible to the Daughters of the American Revolution, and is active in club work.

Mrs. Tillett attended public and high school at Holdrege, Nebraska, and Black Hills College at Hot Springs, South Dakota, making a special study of music which she taught prior to her marriage.

On April 29, 1914, she was married to Samuel G. Tillett at Alliance. Mr. Tillett is chairman of the Nebraska State Legislative Board of the Brotherhood of Locomotive Engineers. Mrs. Tillett is independent in politics. She is a member of St. Mathews Episcopal Church and a local charity organization. Mrs. Tillett's mother organized Chapter A. H., Alliance, Nebraska, of the P. E. O. Sisterhood, and Mrs. Tillett was a charter

ROBERT TICHY, Sr.

Wagner Studio—Crete

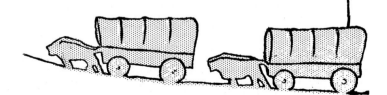

member. She has served as a member of the P. E. O. Sisterhood state board five years, and as past 2nd vice-president, past 1st vice-president and is now state president. She is an alternate candidate to the National Republican convention at Chicago, June 14, 1932. Mrs. Tillett is a member of the Nebraskana Society and the Alliance Country Club. Residence: Alliance.

William Isaac Tillinghast

William Isaac Tillinghast, lawyer and former county judge of Arthur County, was born in Hornick, Iowa, March 5, 1887, son of William Monk and Anna M. (Snyder) Tillinghast. The father, who was a mechanic, was born in Providence, Rhode Island, descended from Pardon Tillinghast, a Baptist minister who settled in Rhode Island with Roger Williams. The ancestry of the family is English, Irish, and Scotch. Anna M. Snyder was born at Foley, Minnesota, November 1, 1865, of German descent.

Judge Tillinghast attended common rural schools and business college, and supplemented his education by home study. A laborer until 1907 he then engaged in farming for seven years, and spent two years in the mercantile business. From 1917 until 1920, he was the editor and publisher of the *Arthur Enterprise* at Arthur. He was admitted to the bar of Nebraska in November, 1920, and has since been in active practice. He also handles real estate and abstract titles.

He is attorney for the Arthur State Bank, the Bills & Cline Investment Bankers of Nebraska, and the Bank of Keystone. A Republican, independently inclined, he was elected county judge of Arthur County in April, 1918, serving until December, 1920. He was elected county attorney of Arthur County in October, 1921, and is still serving. In 1920 he was candidate for state representative and was unsuccessful.

On June 27, 1906, he was married to Jessamine A. Rose at Rock Rapids, Iowa. Mrs. Tillinghast was born at Waterloo, Iowa, May 31, 1879, of French and Dutch ancestry. They have five children, Wayne, born August 11, 1908, who married Mildred Wade; Bess, born November 24, 1911, who married Garnet McCartney; Francis, born January 27, 1914; Arthur, born October 11, 1916; and William, born September 9, 1920.

During the late war Judge Tillinghast was a member of the legal advisory and local draft boards. He is affiliated with the Congregational Church, and is a member of the County Attorneys Association, the Western Nebraska Bar Association, and the Nebraska State Bar Association. He is an Odd Fellow and a member of the Board of Regents of the Arthur County High School. He homesteaded in what is now Arthur County, Nebraska, in 1910, reading law for several years while holding down his homestead, 30 miles from the nearest railroad station. He enjoys camping and hiking, while his hobbies are mechanics, reading and writing. Residence: Arthur.

August Mathew Tillman

August M. Tillman, the son of pioneer Nebraskans, has lived in this state all his life and for many years has been engaged in banking at Hooper, Dodge County, Nebraska. He was born in Ridgeley Township, Dodge County, August 1, 1870, the son of Frank M. and Anna (Enderly) Tillman. His father, who was born in Germany, May 10, 1824, and died at Hooper, October 1, 1915, was commissioner for Dodge County from 1873 to 1879; he came to America in 1851. His mother, who was born in Switzerland, November 25, 1826, and died at Hooper, October 8, 1908, came to this country in 1845.

Mr. Tillman attended the public school at Hooper. He has lived continuously in Nebraska except for four winters spent at San Antonio, Texas. He has been president of the First National Bank of Hooper since 1904; has

been vice president of the Logan Valley Bank at Uehling, Nebraska, since its organization in 1906; and is secretary and treasurer of the Hooper Land & Investment Company. He is one-third owner in a fine 35,000 acre ranch near Tampico, Tamps, Mexico, purchased in 1908.

During the World War he was unusually active in routine war service, assisting in loan drives, Red Cross drives, and filling out the various questionaires used by the government. He is a member of the Hooper Commercial Club and the Nebraskana Society. He is a member of Longfellow Lodge of the Knights of Pythias Number 89, at Hooper. He is affiliated with Grace Lutheran Church. He is a Democrat.

Mr. Tillman was married at Hooper, August 2, 1893, to Matilda Von Essen; she was born in Dodge County, June 3, 1874, the daughter of Henry and Mary Von Essen, and died at Hooper, August 8, 1896. Two children were born to this union: Luella, born June 19, 1894, who married Edward J. Monnich, who is in the automobile business at Oakland, California; and Cornelius H., born January 31, 1896. The latter was a senior at Oberlin College, Ohio, when he enlisted in the World War, 1917. He served in the Oberlin Ambulance Unit until his death, January 24, 1918.

On May 27, 1908, Mr. Tillman was united in marriage with Edna Hartung Uehling at Chicago. Mrs. Tillman was chairman of the Hooper Chapter of the Red Cross from 1917 to 1925, and served for two terms as a member of the board of education at Hooper. They have a daughter, Auralea, born November 25, 1909, who is a senior at the University of Nebraska. Residence: Hooper.

Mark Hillard Tilton

For the past 45 years Mark H. Tilton has been a leading merchant at Lincoln. He was born at Calais, Maine, April 30, 1856, the son of Edward Wilkins and Nancy Mana (Ellsworth) Tilton. His father, who was a sawmaker, was born at Charleston, Maine, June, 1826, and died at Oshkosh, Wisconsin, May, 1906. His ancestry was English. His mother was born at Calais, and died at Oshkosh; her ancestors came from the northern part of Ireland.

Mr. Tilton attended the public and high schools at Oshkosh. He was engaged in the wholesale furniture business for many years, and is now retired. He is a member of the Red Cross, The Nebraskana Society, the Lincoln Country Club and the Shrine Club of Lincoln. He is a Mason.

On December 17, 1890, he was married to Inez Dorris at Lincoln; she was born in Michigan and died at Lincoln, April 28, 1901. One child was born to their marriage: Dorris, born September 24, 1899. Mr. Tilton was married to Lucy Stickney, August 23, 1905, at Oshkosh, Wisconsin. Residence: Lincoln.

Markus Timm

Markus Timm, retired farmer of Polk County, Nebraska, was born at Three Rivers, Michigan, February 25, 1866, the son of Joachim Timm and Mary (Janing) Timm. His father, who was a farmer and clergyman, was born at Mecklen, Germany, November 7, 1831, and died at Osceola, July 26, 1913. His mother was born at Tatrow, Germany, and died at Osceola.

Mr. Timm, who has lived in Nebraska for 48 years, is retired from farming and is now engaged in the insurance business. He has been president of the Parent-Teachers Association for two years, and was formerly president of the Polk County Farm Bureau for four years.

During the World War he served as member of the home guards and as fuel commissioner. His religious affiliation is with the Methodist Episcopal Church of Osceola. He is independent, politically. His marriage

Genelli Studio—Sioux City, Iowa

EARLE A. TOLLES

to Margaret Schmoker was solemnized at Osceola, October 28, 1897. Mrs. Schmoker was born at Osceola, March 28, 1875. They have three children: Arvilla, born June 16, 1898, who is married to A. J. Manthey; Lloyd, born February 19, 1904, who married Zelda Fentress; and Robert, born October 4, 1914. Residence: Osceola.

Levi Goodsil Todd

Levi G. Todd, farmer, merchant and banker, was born at Three Groves, Cass County, Nebraska, on May 10, 1873. His father, Levi Goodsil Todd, Sr., was born at Stockton, New York, March 22, 1830, and came to Nebraska as a pioneer when a young man. He married Lydia Jones, who was born in Lee County, Iowa, December 4, 1833. She died at Union, August 17, 1908. Levi Todd, Sr., was prominent in the early life of Nebraska, and was candidate for governor on the "Greenback" ticket. He died at Union, February 24, 1906.

Levi G. Todd attended district school and the public school at Union. From 1893-94 he attended Lincoln Normal School. On January 7, 1903, he married Mary Anna Snyder, at Louisville. Mrs. Todd was born at Cedar Creek, Nebraska, March 1, 1880. They have two children, Alice, born January 13, 1904, who married Ernest M. Rathe, who lives at Gordon, Nebraska, and Melvin, born April 22, 1910, who married Ruth Irene Schanot, who live on the old Todd homestead.

Mr. Todd is a Democrat, active in politics, and served as a member of the Nebraska state legislature, the term beginning in 1917. He has been a farmer and merchant all his life, and is former president of the Bank of Union. During the orld War he was chairman of finance and was four-minute man of Liberty Precinct, Union, Nebraska. He is a member of the Red Cross and of the Union Methodist Episcopal Church. Residence: Union.

Irl Dentler Tolen

Irl Dentler Tolen was born at Moulton, Nebraska, March 25, 1887, the son of James Edward and Emma Cecelia (Dentler) Tolen. His father, who was a farmer, was born at Indianapolis, Indiana, February 16, 1850, of Pennsylvania Dutch descent. His mother, whose ancestry is German, was born at Rockford, Illinois, October 13, 1856, and died at Ord, January 13, 1911.

Mr. Tolen was graduated from the Ord High School in 1904. He served for seven years with the Koupal & Barstow Lumber Company, was manager of the Dierks Lumber & Coal Company for three years, was owner of an abstract of title company for six years, and was a publisher for five years. He was editor of the Ord Journal from 1924 to 1930.

A Democrat, he has held the following positions: city clerk of Ord, 1911-12-13; treasurer of Valley County, two terms; chairman of the Democratic county committee, and is a member of the Democratic state committee. He has been a member of the state board of agriculture since 1923, is now first vice president of the state board of agriculture, and is a member of the board of managers of the Nebraska State Fair Association. He is past president of the Rotary Club, is a member of the Ord Chamber of Commerce of which he was president in 1921, and holds membership in the Knights of Pythias and the Nebraskana Society. He is affiliated with the First Presbyterian Church of Ord.

Mr. Tolen's chief recreations are reading, golf, and baseball. During the World War he served as a member of the Council of Defense in Valley County. Of his marriage to Katherine Koupal the following children were born: Adrian, October 31, 1914; Robert, July 29, 1918, who died March 23, 1919; and Ruth, July 26, 1923. Mrs. Tolen, whose parents were Bohemian, was born at Ord, August 23, 1886. Residence: Ord.

Earle Ankeny Tolles

Earle A. Tolles, farmer, was born in Cedar County, Nebraska, February 6, 1881. He is the son of Louis Clark and Sarah Augusta (Ankeny) Tolles, pioneers in Nebraska. Louis Clark Tolles was born in Weatherfield, Vermont, November 17, 1847, and homesteaded in Nebraska in 1871. A leader in the development of his state, he died at Laurel on November 17, 1917. He was descended from English settlers in America, first in Connecticut, but prior to the Revolution in Vermont. Sarah Ankeny was born in Illinois, December 10, 1854, and died at Long Beach, California, February 17, 1925. Active in club work, she was a charter member and president of the Laurel Tuesday Club. The Ankeny family were French Huguenots and were among the early settlers of America. The ancestry of both the Ankeny and Tolles family is traceable to Revolutionary times.

Dewalt Ankeny, an ancestor of Sarah Ankeny, came to America from France with his brother in 1756. Millie Bowen, a Mayflower ancestor of Mr. Tolles, the wife of Matthew Walker, was the daughter of John and Mehitable Bowen and was the fifth in descent from Griffith Bowen who emigrated from Wales in 1628; she was fourth in descent from John and Sarah May who came from Mayfield, England, in 1640; and was sixth in descent from John and Margery Johnson who came from England with Winthrop in 1630. Other ancestors of Sarah Ankeny are Daniel and Joanna Brewer who came to this country in 1632. Captain Henry Tolles, from whom Louis Tolles is descended, was a private in Captain William Upham's Company of Vermont Militia. With his son, Clark Tolles, both natives of Weathersfield, Vermont, he served for several months during 1781.

Educated in the public schools of Nebraska, Mr. Tolles was graduated from the Agricultural College of the University of Nebraska in 1903. He has resided and operated on the same farm for the past fifty years. On December 18, 1923, he was married to Mary Ellen Rutherford, of Greeley, Colorado. Mrs. Tolles, who was born October 21, 1892, was of Scotch parentage on the paternal side, and on the maternal side was descended from early Pennsylvania Dutch settlers. There are three children, Mary Fae, born December 21, 1924; Louis Chester, born October 21, 1927, and James Rutherford, born August 16, 1929.

Mr. Tolles is a Republican. He has been a member of the First Presbyterian Church for many years, and an elder since 1918. His fraternal memberships include the Modern Woodmen of America and the Odd Fellows, and he is a life member of the Nebraskana Society. Residence: Laurel. (Photograph on Page 1199).

Edwin Frederick Tonsing

Edwin F. Tonsing was born at Okawville, Washington County, Illinois, February 15, 1886, the son of Frederick and Kathrine (Kerksieck) Tonsing. His father, who is a farmer, was born in Germany, February 27, 1840, and came to this country in 1854.

His mother was born in Germany, October 1, 1844, and died at Okawville, April 13, 1913.

Until he was grown Mr. Tonsing lived on a farm in Illinois, and received his early education in the grade and high schools. In 1906 and 1907 he was a student at the Southwestern Business College at Saint Louis, Missouri. He has lived in Nebraska for twenty-two years during which time he was a carpenter for seven years, and since 1915 has been a mortician and furniture dealer.

He was united in marriage with Clara Schreiner at Syracuse, Nebraska, January 19, 1916. Mrs. Tonsing was born of German parents at Unadilla, Otoe County, Nebraska, June 14, 1886. Five children were born to them, four of whom are living: Homer F., born March 14, 1917; Leota M., born April 11, 1918; Clara May, born January 6, 1920, who died January 10, 1920; Lucille M., born No-

EDWIN FREDERICK TONSING

vember 29, 1925; and Kathryn Ann, born September 2, 1927.

Mr. Tonsing is a member of the Syracuse Chamber of Commerce. He is a Mason and an Odd Fellow, and is affiliated with the St. John's Evangelical Church at Syracuse. He is fond of golf. His hobby is reading. His political preference is the Republican party. Residence: Syracuse. (Photograph on Page 1201).

Charles Brother Towle

Charles Brother Towle, son of Phineas Stewart and Mary (Brother) Towle, was born at Clinton, Iowa, September 10, 1875. His father was a native of New York State, born June 8, 1836, who died at Elmira, New York, in June, 1898. A merchant, he served as a major of Marines in the Civil War, and was of English descent. His wife, Mary, was born at Bath, New York, November 21, 1839, and died at Clinton, Iowa, in June, 1916. She was also of English ancestry.

Mr. Towle was graduated from Clinton High School in 1893, and received a B. S. from Rensslaer Polytechnic Institute in 1898. He is a member of Delta Kappa Epsilon. On January 4, 1902, he was married to Lucy Bonney Curtis at Clinton, Iowa. She was a native of Clinton, born February 5, 1878, of English descent. They have three children, Mary, born August 24, 1904, who married J. K. Cozier; Priscilla, born November 10, 1905, who married T. T. Varney, Jr.; and Curtis, born February 9, 1909.

Mr. Towle is a Republican. He has been engaged as a manufacturer for the past twenty-eight years in Nebraska, and is vice president of Curtis, Towle and Paine Company, a director of Curtis Companies, Inc., the Curtis and Yale Company, and the First National Bank. A member of various civic and commercial organizations he is a former president of the Chamber of Commerce, Community Chest, Nebraska Manufacturers Association and Lincoln Manufacturers Association. He is a 32nd degree Mason and past potentate of the Shrine. During the World War he was on the Exemption Board, a member of the Council of Defense, and active on the U. S. Employment Board. He was a corporal in the First Volunteer Engineers in the Spanish American War. His clubs are the University (president), Candle Light, Lincoln County Club and the Round Table. Residence: Lincoln.

John Webster Towle

John Webster Towle, civic engineer and executive, was born at Falls City, Nebraska, August 28, 1872. His father, Edwin Sargent Towle represents the eleventh generation from Phillip Towle who came to America from Ulster County, Ireland, about 1660 and settled at Hampton, New Hampshire. Edwin Sargent Towle was born at Mishawakee, Indiana, March 13, 1843, and has been prominent in Nebraska for many years. A lawyer, he was speaker of the Nebraska legislature in 1875, and served on the constitutional convention of 1873. He held the rank of sergeant with Company L, 2nd Nebraska Volunteer Infantry in the Civil War. He married Kittie Love Dorrington, a native of Whitestown, New York, born January 27, 1849. Her parents, David Dorrington and Ann Barnard Wood who came from England about 1841, moved to Falls City, Nebraska, in September 1857.

Upon the completion of his grade school education, John W. Towle entered the Falls City High School from which he was graduated in 1889. He later attended the Highland (Kansas) Academy, and received the degree of B. C. E. from Cornell University in 1894. He was a member of the baseball varsity team four years, a member of the Sphinx Head, honorary senior society and was elected to Alpha Tau Omega.

Returning to Nebraska in 1894 he engaged as a civil

engineer from that year until 1897 when he became general western agent for the Canton Bridge Company, continuing until 1904. In 1906 he organized the Omaha Steel Works, of which he since has been president. He is the organizer and is connected with various other corporations. He is the president of the Western Securities Company, vice president of the Western Bridge and Construction Company, president of the Towle Realty Company, vice president of the Independent Lumber Company, president of the Nebraska Bridge Supply and Lumber Company, treasurer of the Plattsmouth Bridge Company, etc.

A Republican, Mr. Towle is active in party politics. He was delegate to the Republican national convention of 1912 and delegate at large in 1920. He is the author of the *Erection of the Yuma, Arizona, Bridge Over the Colorado River*.

From 1917-19 he was a member of the Emergency Fleet Corporation, as plant engineer at Hog Island and Wilmington, N. C. He attends the First Methodist Church of Omaha, and is a member of the Young Men's Christian Association. From 1920-25 he was a Rotarian, and for the past twenty years he has been a member of the Elks. He is also a member of the Chamber of Commerce and the Nebraska State Historical Society. His outdoor recreations include golf, swimming, walking and baseball. He is also an ardent chess player. His clubs include the Omaha Club, the Omaha Athletic Club, the Omaha Field Club and the Omaha Country Club.

Mr. Towle was married to Naomi Frances Everts at Geneva, Illinois, on September 3, 1894. Mrs. Towle, who is a direct descendant of William Warner who settled at Ipswich, Connecticut in 1635, was born at Geneva, Illinois, March 19, 1873. To this union three children were born, two of whom are living. Marion R., born July 5, 1895, married D. J. Sibbernsen; Naomi N., born October 6, 1896, married F. H. Bucholz; Everts S., born April 24, 1903, died April 11, 1904. Residence: Omaha.

Max G. Towle

Max G. Towle, lawyer and county attorney of Lancaster County, Nebraska, was born at Annondale, Minnesota, September 9, 1889. Wilber W. Towle, his father, who is a lawyer, was born in Wisconsin, and is the son of W. H. Towle a Civil War veteran who was for many years postmaster at Annondale. His mother is Mae (Niles) Towle.

Mr. Towle attended the Clinton Grade School at Lincoln, and was graduated from the Lincoln High School. From 1909 to 1914 he was a student at the University of Nebraska where he received his LL. B. degree. He was a member of the Alpha Psi Chapter of Kappa Sigma. In 1913 he was captain of the university baseball team, and in 1912-13 he was quarterback on the football team. He was admitted to the bar at Lincoln, June 1914.

A Republican, Mr. Towle was justice of the peace at Lincoln, 1917-18; deputy county attorney, 1919-26; and since 1926 has been county attorney. He has lived in this state for 37 years.

His marriage to Ruth R. Scott was solemnized at Lincoln, November 26, 1917. Mrs. Towle was born at Brookfield, Missouri, January 25, 1895. Her father is a physician. Their daughter, Virginia, was born May 4, 1920.

Mr. Towle was in the Naval Aviation Training School at Seattle Washington, during the World War. He is a member of the American Legion. He is a member of the Lancaster County Bar Association, the Lincoln Chamber of Commerce, and the Parent-Teachers Association. He is an Elk, a Knight of Pythias, and an Odd Fellow. He holds membership in the local Young Men's Christian Association. He is fond of golfing, swimming and tennis. Residence: Lincoln.

Solon Rodney Towne

Solon Rodney Towne, physician and surgeon, was born at Stowe, Vermont, December 20, 1846, son of Jess and Salome Esther (Seabury) Towne. He was graduated from the Peoples Academy at Morrisville, Vermont, in 1868 and received the A. B., A. M., and M. D. degrees from Dartmouth College.

Since 1888 Dr. Towne has been in practice in Omaha. He was professor of public health, Creighton Medical College 1894-1900 and held the same position at the University of Nebraska 1900-13. He is now retired from active practice.

On July 23, 1873, he was married to Harriet Christiana Somers at Jericho, Vermont. She was born at Greensboro, Vermont, January 13, 1844, and died at Omaha, December 29, 1929. She was the organizer and served as president of the Omaha Woman's Club.

Their children are as follows: Jessie M., born July 5, 1874; Mary Agnes, born April 9, 1876; Robert Somers, born February 22, 1878, married Frances Dashiell and died April 27, 1925; Alice C., born April 3, 1884, married Fred Milo Deweese and died September 2, 1909.

Dr. Towne is a member of First Central Congregational Church, the Nebraska Tuberculosis Association (president 1908-28), the Nebraska Mayflower Society and the Audubon Society. Residence: Omaha.

Clinton Alonzo Townsend

Clinton Alonzo Townsend, president of Townsend Brothers, Incorporated, was born at Newton, Wisconsin, October 1, 1873. His father, Waldron Chaney Townsend, was a native of Zanesville, Ohio, born in 1846. He was a bridge builder, who served with Company C, 18th Wisconsin Infantry in the Civil War, as did his father. He was one of the first commissioners of Holt County. His death occurred at Page on June 14. Ida Alzina Farr, his wife, was born at Malone, New York, July 27, 1856. She is much interested in church work, the Women's Christian Temperance Union, etc.

Mr. Townsend was graduated from public school in 1891, and attended normal school in 1895 and 1896. From 1891 until 1898 he taught school, and since 1899 has been in the hardware and implement business continuously. He is a Democrat, a member of the Nebraska Hardware Dealers Association and the Midwest Implement Dealers Association.

Always active in civic and fraternal affairs, he has been treasurer of the Red Cross since 1920, is a member of the Woodmen of the World, the Modern Woodmen of America, the Odd Fellows, the Masons, the Rebekahs, the Royal Highlanders, Ben Hur, the Ancient Order of United Workmen and the Low Twelve Club. During the World War he was a member of the War Risk Insurance board, and a member of the advisory board of Holt County. He is a member of the Nebraska State Historical Society, the National Geographic Society and a life member of the Nebraskana Society. He enjoys reading.

On December 27, 1897, he was married to Carrie Helen Gallagher at Page. Mrs. Townsend was born at Lincoln, Illinois, September 16, 1878, and is of Scotch-Irish descent. They have two children, Clinton Alva, born April 10, 1900, who married June Elizabeth; and Helen Independence, born July 4, 1901, who married Franklin Joseph Chemler. Residence: Page.

June Elizabeth Townsend

Born at Sidney, Iowa, June 3, 188, June Elizabeth Townsend is the daughter of Amos N. and Mary Mercy (Moore) Travis. Her father was born of English ancestry at Sidney, and died there in December, 1908. Her mother, whose ancestry was Irish, was born at Sidney.

Mrs. Townsend attended the Sidney grade school and in 1917 was graduated from the high school there. She was a student at Nebraska Wesleyan University from 1917 to 1919, where she was a member of Omicron Rho Omicron and took an active part in athletics. She has held the following positions in Nebraska schools: teacher, Hordville, 1919; teacher, Fremont, 1919-20; teacher, Omaha, 1920-21; principal in the high school, Page, 1921-28.

She is affiliated with the Methodist Church of Page, is a member of the Eastern Star and Rebekah Lodge, and holds membership in the Nebraskana Society. Her marriage to Clinton Townsend was solemnized at Omaha, November 25, 1920. Mr. Townsend, who is a merchant, was born of English and Irish parents at Page, April 10, 1900. They have an adopted daughter, Patricia Ann. Residence: Page.

Frank Gordon Tracy

Born at Kearney, Nebraska, March 14, 1893, Frank Gordon Tracy is the son of Isaac Smith and Maria Elizabeth (Stowe) Tracy. His father, who was a farmer, was born in Licking County, Ohio, September 1, 1840, and died at Kearney, August 8, 1929; his ancestry was Scotch and Irish. His mother, whose ancestry was Scotch and Irish, was born in Hancock County, Illinois, September 3, 1859, and died in Polk County, Nebraska, October 9, 1912.

Mr. Tracy received his education in the public schools of Kearney. He is chief of police at Kearney, holds membership in the Chamber of Commerce, and is a member of the Nebraskana Society. He is a member of Tehama Shrine and Rob Morris Lodge Number 46, of the Ancient Free and Accepted Masons, and Buffalo Lodge Number 38 of the Independent Order of Odd Fellows.

During the World War, Mr. Tracy served as first lieutenant in the 127th Field Artillery and at this time is a member of the American Legion and the Veterans of Foreign Wars. A Republican, he served as deputy sheriff of Buffalo County, Nebraska, 1923-26, and in 1930 was candidate for sheriff of that county.

On August 24, 1922, he married Ethel Edna Madden at Hastings. Mrs. Tracy, whose ancestry is Irish, was born at Minneapolis, Kansas, June 24, 1894. They have one daughter, Gloria Lee, born January 27, 1930. Residence: Kearney.

Thomas Athur Tracy

A leading farmer in Lancaster County for many years, Thomas Arthur Tracy was born at Wilber, January 9, 1873. His father, George E. Tracy, was a prominent figure in the political and commercial life of Saline and Boone Counties. He was the general merchandise business, and for twelve years was postmaster at Wilber. Later he served five years as county assessor of Boone County. His death occurred at Albion, July 7, 1919. His wife, Julia Harriet Osborn, died at Wilber in March, 1884.

Raised on a farm, Mr. Tracy had but meager schooling. He was married to Ella May Leland at Valparaiso, Nebraska, on August 12, 1896. Mrs. Tracy, who is a true farmer's wife, was born at Wahoo, March 24, 1877. There are six children: Esther, born November 21, 1899, married Ray Rolfsmyer; Floyd, born December 23, 1901, married Rose Hermance; Dorothy, born May 11, 1904, married Ervin Broadwater; Thomas E., born November 20, 1909; Fred E., born June 21, 1911; and Helen M., born June 15, 1921.

Mr. Tracy is a Republican. He has always lived in Nebraska, and takes an interested part in every effort for the advancement of his community and state. Recently he was awarded life membership in the Nebraskana Society. Residence: Raymond.

Arthur Ray Transue

Arthur Ray Transue, dentist, was born at Summerfield, Kansas, August 10, 1898, son of George W. and Minnie M. (Manning) Transue. His ancestry is German and English.

Dr. Transue attended the University of Nebraska where he received the degree of Bachelor of Science in Dentistry and the degree of Doctor of Dental Surgery. He is a member of the Lions Club, the Nebraska State Dental Society, the United Presbyterian Church, the Masons, the Odd Fellows and Xi Psi Phi.

On September 15, 1923, he was married to Lela Fay Detweiler at Lincoln. She was born at Summerfield, Kansas, October 4, 1898. There are two children, Arthur Alan, born January 28, 1929; and Donna Jeanne, born March 15, 1926.

Dr. Transue served three months in the World War. He is a life member of the Nebraskana Society. His favorite sports are hunting and golf. Residence: Overton.

Nathan Evan Trego

Nathan Evan Trego, son of Evan and Elizabeth Rettew) Trego, was born in Cupola, Chester County, Pennsylvania, July 31, 1867. His father was born in Cupola in 1813, and died at Sadsburyville, Pennsylvania in 1873. He was a farmer of English ancestry. His wife, Elizabeth (Rettew) Trego, was born in Cupola, August 24, 1820, died at Sadsburyville, in March, 1908.

Mr. Trego came to North Platte, Nebraska 46 years ago, and worked for W. F. Cody (Buffalo Bill) until the fall of 1887.

He helped drive a herd of horses to western Iowa and returned to North Platte, where he went to work for W. C. Ritner who was then ranching northwest of North Platte. The following spring Mr. Trego entered the employ of John Bratt and Company, who were large ranchers for that period, and who owned ranches on the North Platte River and in the lake country in the sand hills. The home ranch was located on the South Platte River southwest of North Platte.

In 1895 another cowboy, John Schick, who worked for the Circle Ranch outfit, and Mr. Trego started ranching on a small scale in McPherson County on the old cotton wood ranch in the lake country about 1895. There Mr. Trego is still located with his two sons.

Mr. Trego has always taken an interest in public and community affairs and for 25 years served as a member of the board of county commissioners of McPherson County.

He was married to May Wilson at the Cody Ranch, June 30, 1896. Mrs. Trego was born at Dawson, Illinois, August 31, 1878. Her mother, Elizabeth Wilson, was born April 2, 1858, of Irish ancestry, and resides at Sutherland. Her father died at Sutherland, March 19, 1912. He is also of Irish descent.

To Mr. and Mrs. Trego were born five children, three of whom are living, Harriet, born July 31, 1897, died in August, 1918; Helen, born October 16, 1899; William, born September 23, 1901; and Morris, born January 1, 1904. The other child died in infancy.

A Mason, Mr. Trego is also a member of the Odd Fellows and the Modern Woodmen of America. He is a member of the Presbyterian Church at Sutherland. Residence: Sutherland.

Leonard Wallace Trester

Leonard Wallace Trester was born at Lincoln, Nebraska, March 9, 1895, son of Lewis Henry and Alice (Wallace) Trester. His father is manager of the Trester Mercantile Company and the president of the Trester Wrecking Company of Lincoln. Mrs. Trester is active in musical and club work in Lincoln.

Leonard Wallace Trester received his education in the public and high schools of Lincoln, and attended the University of Nebraska 1916, 1917 and 1918. He is a member of Alpha Theta Chi. He was married to Mary Milda Steele, of Hastings on May 7, 1919. They have two children, Patricia, born June 24, 1920, and Leonard born August 21, 1923.

Mr. Trester has been in the advertising business since leaving the university. Since 1920 he has been secretary-treasurer of the Omaha Outdoor Advertising Company; and since 1926 has been manager of the General Outdoor Advertising Company. He is president of the Outdoor Advertising Association of Nebraska, and a director of the Outdoor Advertising Association of America.

Always active in civic and welfare work, Mr. Trester has served as state chairman of the United States Boys Working Reserve, associate and later state director of the American Red Cross. He was also a director of the Junior Red Cross. He is a member of the Chamber of Commerce, the Ad-Sell League and the Rotary Club. He is a Mason. His clubs are the Omaha, the Omaha Country and the Omaha Athletic Clubs. His sport is golf, and his hobby is garden lilies. Residence: Omaha.

Volney Buchanan Trimble

Born at Clarksburg, West Virginia, October 9, 1856, Volney Buchanan Trimble is the son of Eldrege Clark and Mary Elizabeth (Radcliff) Trimble. His father, a farmer and banker, was born at Clarksburg, Virginia, December 12, 1832. His descent was traced to William Trimble, a Scotchman, who came to America as an officer in the army of Lord Cornwallis. Mary Elizabeth Radcliff was born at Fairfield, Virginia (now West Virginia), December 19, 1833, and died there on May 10, 1917. Eldrege Trimble died at Fairfield in June, 1906.

Volney B. Trimble attended private schools, Flemington (West Virginia) College, and was graduated from Fairmont State Normal School in West Virginia. Soon after his graduation he began teaching, continuing for three years; thereafter, for a period of six years owned and edited the *Randolph Enterprise*, a weekly newspaper, and *The Mystic Tie*, a Masonic Monthly. A Democrat, he served as mayor of Beverly, West Virginia, two terms, was delegate to the Democratic national convention in 1881, which nominated Hancock for president, and was admitted to the bar in 1880.

A resident of Nebraska since July 4, 1887, Mr. Trimble was a member of the wholesale grocery firm of Trimble, Blackman and Alexander in Hastings from 1887 to 1907, and since that time has engaged in the real estate and investment business. He has also served as a member of the city council and on the Hastings school board.

Of his marriage to Mary Burns Blackman there are two children living and one deceased. Wilfred B., born July 13, 1882, is married to Anna Blake, and is with Libby, McNeil and Libby, in Burbank, California. Estella M., born July 29, 1884, married Charles B. Duer, and died December 17, 1928. Helen M., born October 30, 1887, is married to J. Forrest Sims. They are in the life insurance business at Poughkeepsie, New York.

Mary Burns Blackman, who was born at Beverly, West Virginia, January 29, 1859, died at a hospital in Baltimore, Maryland, December 4, 1914. Of English and Scotch extraction, she was descended from the Reverend Adam Blackman, who came from England and settled in Connecticut in 1636.

Mr. Trimble has been a member of the Hastings library board since the establishment of the city library in 1903, and is at present secretary of the board, having served for a number of years as chairman. He is a charter member of the Lions Club, a member of the Chamber of Commerce and The Nebraskana Society, and is a Mason, Knight Templar and member of the Shrine.

His religious affiliation is with the First Presbyterian Church.

During the late war, Mr. Trimble was government appeal agent, and was chairman of the Adams County Council of Defense. He is a student of government and is interested in scientific literature. Residence: Hastings.

George Washington Trine

Born at Greenville, Pennsylvania, February 13, 1869, George Washington Trine is the son of Daniel and Elizabeth (Bash) Trine. His father, a farmer and stockraiser, was born in Lehigh County, Pennsylvania, September 28, 1837, and died at Blue Hill, Nebraska, May 23, 1909. He served with Company G, 145th Pennsylvania Volunteer Infantry in the Civil War, participating in the Battles of Antietam, Fredericksburg, Chancellorsville and Gettysburg.

Peter Trine, grandfather of George Washington Trine, was born in Lehigh County in 1815, and married Catherine Dunkel, born in 1805. Elizabeth (Bash) Trine was born in Pennsylvania, September 18, 1842, and died at Blue Hill, March 4, 1920. Her grandmother was a native Virginian. Elizabeth was the daughter of Rebecca (Jones) Bash, a first cousin of James G. Blaine, several times presidential candidate and a prominent statesman.

Mr. Trine attended the elementary schools of Illinois and Nebraska, coming here with his parents in 1884. He was a farmer for several years, was connected with the Beatrice Creamery Company for a time, and for the past nineteen years has been proprietor of a hardware store at Red Cloud.

He is a member of the National Retail Hardware Association, the Nebraska Retail Hardware Association, the Red Cross and the Knights of Pythias. Recently he was made a life member of the Nebraskana Society. He is a Democrat. Among his chief recreations are hunting and reading.

On October 20, 1901, his marriage to Lida Forst was solemnized at Nelson, Nebraska. Mrs. Trine was born in Clay County, Nebraska, May 3, 1883, daughter of John and Mary (Maruska) Forst. Her grandfather, Anton Forst, was born in Tyrol, Czecho-Slovakia, June 13, 1811, coming to America in 1858, settling at St. Louis, Missouri. He served in the Civil War being a member of Company C, First Missouri Volunteers. He came to Nebraska in 1874, homesteading in Clay County, near Fairfield. He died June 13, 1885.

Her father, John Forst, born at Pilsen, Czecho-Slovakia, March 3, 1848, came to America 1858, received his education in the elementary schools of St. Louis, where he married Mary Maruska, February 1, 1871. He also homesteaded in Clay County, Nebraska, in 1877.

Her maternal grandparents, John and Annie (Novak) Maruska came to America in 1853, settling at Waterford, Wisconsin. They brought a large fortune with them which was lost in the lumber business, after which the family removed to St. Louis, Missouri, in 1857. John Maruska died in 1877, and his wife in 1881. The family was prominent in the Catholic Church in Austria, there being twenty-two priests in the family.

Her mother, Mary (Maruska) Forst was born in Budweis, Czecho-Slovakia, February 12, 1853, and died in Nuckolls County, Nebraska, February 22, 1911.

Mr. and Mrs. Trine have one daughter, Verna, born August 29, 1902. She was graduated from the University of Nebraska with the degree of Bachelor of Arts, and Phi Beta Kappa honors. From the University School of Music, (Nebraska), Bachelor of Music degree, and Pi Kappa Lambda honors. She is a charter member of Chi Delta Phi literary sorority, and a member of Sigma Alpha Iota, musical sorority. She is a graduate of the Juilliard School of Music, New York City, and is now studying and teaching piano and harmony in the Christadora Music School in New York City. Residence: Red Cloud. (Photograph in Album).

James Allen Trowbridge

James Allen Trowbridge, physician and surgeon of Superior, Nebraska, has been a resident of the state for the past 21 years, and has taken a prominent part in professional and civic affairs in his community. He was born at Meredith, Kansas, August 7, 1875, the son of Leander Marion and Dorothy (Casseday) Trowbridge. His father, who was born in Preston County, West Virginia, February 1, 1837, and died at Clay Center, Kansas, April 18, 1909, was a teacher and farmer who served in the Civil War for four years; he was of English and Scotch descent. His mother was born at Preston County, December 12, 1832, and died at Clay Center, Kansas, September 22, 1904; her ancestors were Irish and German.

Dr. Trowbridge was graduated from the Clay Center High School in 1895, and in 1900 received the M. D. degree at the University Medical College in Kansas City, Missouri after which he did post-graduate work in London, England on eye, ear, nose and throat. He was a teacher from 1895 to 1897, and since his admission to the medical profession has been engaged in both Kansas and Nebraska professional life. He holds membership in the Nuckols County Medical Society, the Nebraska State Medical Society, at which he was president of the 7th councilor district, and the American Medical Association in which he holds a fellowship. For 16 years he has been secretary of the Nuckolls County society.

He is past president of the Kiwanis Club of Superior, is a member of the Superior Chamber of Commerce, and is affiliated with the Methodist Church of Superior. His fraternal organizations are: Masons, Blue Lodge, Scottish Rite, chapter and Shrine; Woodmen of the World; Security Benefit Association. For five years he served as an officer in the Kansas National Guard and during the World War he served as captain of the Medical Corps in the United States Army; having volunteered at the outbreak of the war; he is now a member of the American Legion of which he was vice commander in 1920. His hobbies are music and Masonic activities.

Dr. Trowbridge was united in marriage with Nancy Mabel Montgomery at Superior, October 4, 1917. Mrs. Trowbridge was born at Mankato, Kansas, November 9, 1888, of Scotch descent. They have a daughter, Allene Mabel, born November 11, 1920.

Dr. Trowbridge is a Republican. Residence: Superior.

David Hubert Troxel

Born at Ashland, Ohio, February 22, 1874, David Hubert Troxel has been a resident of Ainsworth, Nebraska since 1901. His father, Joseph Sherman Troxel, a carpenter, was born in Wayne County, Ohio, June 9, 1838, and died at Ainsworth, August 11, 1920; his parents were of Swiss and Irish descent. Mary Ann (Hunsicker) Troxel, his mother, was born at Harrisburg, Pennsylvania, February 26, 1845, and died at Melbourne, Iowa, June 22, 1915.

Mr. Troxel attended the high school at State Center, Iowa. Since August, 1901, he has been railroad station agent for the Chicago & Northwestern Company at Ainsworth, and is vice president of the Commercial National Bank in that community. He is affiliated with the First Methodist Church of Ainsworth, is a member of the Ainsworth Commercial Club, and holds membership in the Masons and the Modern Woodmen of America.

His marriage to Mae Eva Hayne was solemnized at Marshalltown, Iowa, February 22, 1899. Mrs. Troxel, whose ancestry is English, was born at Rhodes, Iowa, August 24, 1878. They have four children: Helen, born September 12, 1901; Jeanette, born October 14, 1902; Joseph, born December 5, 1905, who married Helen Stauffer; and Theodore, born March 16, 1913. Jeanette is married to John W. Lindsay, Helen is a teacher, Joseph is a telegraph operator, and Theo is a student in business college. Residence: Ainsworth.

Henry Truhlsen

Henry Truhlsen was born at Blair, Nebraska, April 20, 1891, son of Niels and Margaret (Hansen) Truhlsen. His father was a farmer who was born in Sweden, and died at Blair, in January, 1921. His mother, a native of Germany, died at Blair, August 9, 1910.

Mr. Truhlsen was educated in the public and high schools of Blair, and thereafter entered the Arlington State Bank at Arlington, where he remained for some time. For the past twenty years he has been engaged in the hardware, furniture and undertaking business, now in partnership with his brother Chris, in the firm of Truhlsen Brothers.

He was married to Lola Mollie Marshall of Lincoln, and they have three children, Stanley, born November 13, 1920; Marion, born December 21, 1922, and Joan, born August 13, 1928. Mrs. Truhlsen is a cousin of William McKinley, former president of the United States.

A Republican, Mr. Truhlsen served as county commissioner of Washington County from 1920-1924, and has served on the village board for many years. From February 13, 1918, to July 1, 1921, he served in the radio branch of the United States Navy, and is a member of the American Legion. He is a Mason, a member of the Lions Club, and of the Nebraska Funeral Directors' Association and the Nebraskana Society. His favorite sport is baseball. Residence: Herman. (Photograph in Album).

Lawrence Austin Trumbo

, Born at New Virginia, Iowa, July 13, 1882, Lawrence Austin Trumbo is the son of Washington Judson and Mary (Spencer) Trumbo. His father, who was a contractor, was born at Liberty, Iowa, December 25, 1856, of French parents and died at Liberty, March 28, 1897. His mother was born in Jefferson County, Illinois, May 13, 1863, and died at Liberty, June 16, 1926; her ancestry was Pennsylvania Dutch.

Mr. Trumbo was graduated from the high school at Osceola, Iowa. He is a member of the Holdrege Chamber of Commerce, the Holdrege Rotary Club, the Methodist Episcopal Church, and the Masonic Lodge. He has been successfully engaged in the contracting business at Holdrege for a number of years, has served as councilman for four years, was mayor of the city for two years, and holds membership in the local Red Cross. His political affiliation is with the Republican party.

On April 12, 1905, he married Nora Evalena Loving at Gunnison, Colorado. Mrs. Trumbo, whose ancestry is Irish, was born at Osceola, Iowa, March 6, 1884. Two children were born to them: Neva, January 20, 1906; and Milford, December 26, 1909, who died October 3, 1917. Residence: Holdrege.

Darrell Edward Trump

Darrell Edward Trump, mayor of Utica, was born at North Loup, Nebraska, January 18, 1895. He is the son of Charles Edward and Estella Maude (Smith) Trump, the former of whom, a grain buyer, was born in Greenville, Ohio, April 8, 1867. He is of Holland Dutch descent. Estella Maude Smith was born in Greenfield, Iowa, in June, 1870 and is of Scotch-Irish descent.

Educated in the public and high schools of Bradshaw, Nebraska, Dr. Trump was graduated from the latter in 1913 and received his D. V. M. from the Kansas City Veterinary College at Kansas City, Missouri, in 1917. He has since been engaged in practice, and is serving as mayor of Utica, elected on the Democratic ticket.

He was married to Alice Kathryn Vandeburg at York, Nebraska, on February 8, 1914, and to them three children were born: Murray, born January 2, 1915; Maxine, born December 29, 1917; and Dell, born December 6, 1919. Mrs. Trump was born at Elkhorn, Iowa, December 6, 1897.

A life resident of the state, Dr. Trump is a leader in civic and professional life. On August 8, 1917 he was commissioned 2nd lieutenant, was promoted to first lieutenant September 18, 1918, and is captain, Officers Reserve Corps, assigned to the 341st Field Artillery at the present time. He is a member of the American Legion, the Red Cross, the Ancient Free and Accepted Masons, the National Historical Society, the Nebraskana Society and School Board No. 60.

Dr. Trump's professional organizations include the American, Missouri Valley and Nebraska State Veterinary Medical Associations, and he is now serving as president of the last mentioned. Residence: Utica.

David Tuning

David Tuning, clergyman and farmer, was born at Springbank, Nebraska, February 9, 1877. A graduate of Springbank district school in 1892, he later attended Cleveland Institute from 1915 to 1918.

His father, William R. Tuning was born in Virginia, April 7, 1849, and died at Allen, Nebraska, June 10, 1917. He was of Scotch-Irish ancestry. Pheobe (Roberts) Tuning, mother of David, was born in Jefferson County, Iowa, August 25, 1852.

David Tuning was united in marriage with Nellie Kesian Ward on August 19, 1900 at Niobrara, Nebraska. She was born at Waukesha, Wisconsin, March 2, 1880, and was of English descent. Her parents were married in England. They have four children, Ruth, born August 27, 1901, who is married to Henry A. Engel; Joseph, born December 7, 1903, who is married to Martha A. Campbell; Arnold, born September 4, 1900, and Edna, born October 26, 1909. They are all college graduates, and have all been engaged in teaching.

Mr. Tuning was a farmer until 1915, clergyman at Deertail, Colorado, in 1918, and near Central City from 1919 to 1926. He is not active in pastoral work at the present time, but is living on his own farm near Allen, Nebraska.

He is a member of the Friends Church of Allen. He was president of the Nebraska Central College board of trustees from 1920 to 1922, and is chairman of the evangelistic and church extension board of Nebraska's yearly meeting of Friends. His favorite sport is football and reading is his hobby. Residence: Allen.

Minnie Eldridge Tunnicliff

Minnie Eldridge Tunnicliff, manager of the Omaha Symphony Orchestra and prominent clubwoman of Omaha, has lived in Nebraska for over thirty years. She was born at Stephentown, Rensselaer County, New York, December 24, 1884 the daughter of Eldorus Gorton Eldridge and Lelia (Potter) Eldridge. Her father who was born at Stephentown, July 3, 1856, is a descendant of Thomas Eldridge, born in 1734 at Exeter, Rhode Island. Thomas Eldridge was the son of John Eldridge who was born at North Kinston.

Lelia Potter, who was born at Stephenstown, January 26, 1861, is descended from Job Taylor who was born in 1756 at Kent, Connecticut.

Mrs. Tunnicliff was graduated from the Omaha High School in 1904. From 1905 to 1927 she was private secretary to the president of a wholesale and retail establishment in Omaha. For the past three years she has been manager of the Omaha Symphony Orchestra.

Her marriage to George Duffield Tunnicliff was solemnized at Omaha, September 15, 1927. Mr. Tunnicliff, who is engaged in the real estate business, was born at Galesburg, Illinois, January 22, 1874.

Mrs. Tunnicliff was active during the World War, serving as an instructor in Red Cross work, canteen worker, and as a member of the Women's Service League. She is a charter member of the Major Isaac Sadler Chapter of the Daughters of the American Revolution, and has held the offices of secretary and treasurer in this organization; but now a member of Omaha Chapter she has also held the office of treasurer of this chapter. She is eligible to the Colonial Dames, is a member of the Women's Division of the Omaha Chamber of Commerce, and is affiliated with the First Presbyterian Church of Omaha. All out of door activities interest her. Residence: Omaha.

George Thomas Tunnicliff

Born at Harvard, Nebraska, July 21, 1886, George Thomas Tunnicliff is the son of Ed Mear and Jessie Robinson (Oliver) Tunnicliff. His father, who was born of English parents at Kewanee, Illinois, May 22, 1858, was formerly county clerk and county judge of Garfield County. His mother, whose ancestry was Scotch, was born at Elmira, Illinois, January 28, 1857.

Mr. Tunnicliff was graduated from the Burwell High School, and at this time is postmaster in that community. He is a Scottish Rite Mason, is affiliated with the Nebraskana Society, and holds membership in the Red Cross. During the World War he served as first class chauffeur in the 318th Field Signal Battalion of the American Expeditionary Forces. He is a member of the American Legion.

On July 7, 1928, his marriage to Ada Ellen Ward occurred at Boston, Massachusetts. Mrs. Tunnicliff, whose ancestors were early New Englanders, was born at Boston, December 27, 1899. They have two children: Rowland Ward, born June 7, 1930; and David Ward, born September 18, 1931. Residence: Burwell.

Joseph Manson Turbyfill

Joseph Manson Turbyfill, former county judge of Adams County, was born at Waynesville, North Carolina, September 5, 1890, son of Pinkney Lafayette and Julia Catherine (Tate) Turbyfill. His father, a native of Catawba, North Carolina, is of English descent, and is now retired. His mother was born at Waynesville, North Carolina, of Scotch and English extraction.

Judge Turbyfill was educated in Waynesville public and high schools, and was graduated from the latter in 1909. During the years 1909-13 he was a student at Washington and Lee University, and from 1913-15 attended the University of North Carolina, where he was president of his senior law class. Judge Turbyfill received his Bachelor of Arts degree from Washington and Lee and his Bachelor of Laws from North Carolina. He was a member of the baseball team of Washington and Lee the years 1910, 1911, 1912 and 1913.

On May 8, 1918, he was united in marriage to Clara C. Chick at Columbia, South Carolina. Mrs. Turbyfill, who is an artist, was born at Hastings, July 11, 1893. Their two sons died in infancy.

From 1921-29 Mr. Turbyfill served as county judge of Adams County, and since November 1919 has been engaged in the practice of law at Hastings. He is a member of the Nebraska State and Adams County Bar Associations, a member of the Young Men's Christian Association (member of board of directors 1925-30), and a member and former president of the Lions Club. He is a trustee of the Hastings Post of the American Legion, and was post commander in 1930. During the World War Judge Turbyfill served from May 3, 1917, to June 19, 1919, with the rank of second lieutenant August, 1917, first lieutenant of field artillery January 1918. He was with the American Expeditionary Forces from August 8, 1918, to June 8, 1919, serving with 306th Ammunition Train of the 81st division and participating in the Meuse-Argonne Offensive.

Mr. Turbyfill is a member of St. Marks Pro-Cathedral at Hastings, the Red Cross, and the Knights of Pythias and D. O. K. K., and his club is the Hillside Golf Club. His favorite sports are golf and trout fishing. He is affiliated with the Democratic party. Residence: Hastings.

Elizabeth H. Turner

Elizabeth H. Turner, born at Richmond, Wayne County, Indiana, August 8, 1865, is the daughter of Rees J. and Lydia (White) Mendenhall. Her father was born at Richmond, December 13, 1823, and was a farmer and stock raiser. His ancestry was English, and is traced to an early date in America. His forebears came to America on the ship in which William Penn sailed. He died in Fairbury, Nebraska, July 4, 1894. Lydia White Mendenhall was also born at Richmond, Indiana, on November 7, 1827, of English parentage. She died at Fairbury, November 2, 1890.

Mrs. Turner attended the schools of Wayne County, Indiana, and later, in 1883-84, she attended several semesters at Earlham College, in Richmond. On December 28, 1896, she was married to James Plato Turner of Fairbury. He was born at LaPorte, Black Hawk County, Iowa, December 28, 1864, and died February 1, 1926, at Fairbury. To this union two children were born; Ruth, February 2, 1900, who is married to Francis L. Lyons and George H., January 29, 1902, now married to June (Sweney) Turner. Both children were graduated from the State University and George is deputy clerk of the Supreme Court of Nebraska.

Elizabeth Turner taught two years in rural schools in Jefferson County and two years in Fairbury. She is now hostess and has charge of the employment for the Young Women's Christian Association and also one of the board members of the Association at Fairbury.

She came to Nebraska in 1886, and is a member of the Nebraskana Society. She is an independent in politics, and is affiliated with the First Christian Church of Fairbury. Mrs. Turner holds membership in the Red Cross, Eastern Star, and is a member of the Welfare Board at Fairbury. Residence: Fairbury.

George Herrick Turner

On January 29, 1902, George H. Turner was born at Fairbury, Nebraska, the son of James P. and Elizabeth H. (Mendenhall) Turner. His father, who was a banker and creamery operator, was born at LaPort City, Iowa, December 28, 1864, and died at Fairbury, February 1, 1926. His mother, whose ancestry is English, was born at Richmond, Indiana, August 8, 1865.

Mr. Turner was graduated from the Fairbury High School, and in 1923 was awarded his LL. B. degree at the University of Nebraska where he was a member of Phi Delta Phi, the Kosmet Club, and Sigma Nu. He was admitted to the bar in Lincoln, June 4, 1923.

He served as private secretary of Chief Justice A. M. Morrissey, 1923-27, and since 1927 he has been deputy clerk of the Nebraska Supreme Court. He is a director of the Home Guardian Life Insurance Company of Lincoln, and a Democrat.

Mr. Turner was united in marriage with June Cornell Sweney at Fairbury, February 12, 1927. Mrs. Turner was born at Peru, Indiana, February 7, 1902, is of Irish descent. They have one son, George Herrick, 3rd, born June 23, 1930.

Mr. Turner is a member of the Nebraska State Bar Association, Lincoln Lodge Number 80 of the Benevolent and Protective Order of the Elks; and Fairbury Lodge Number 35 of the Ancient Free and Accepted Masons. He is a member of the First Christian Church of Fairbury. Residence: Lincoln.

John M. Turner

A leading business man at Thedford, Nebraska, is John M. Turner who was born at Bedford, Iowa, January 7, 1883, the son of William Jefferson and Nancy Jane (Little) Turner. His father, who was a farmer and carpenter, was born in Indiana, February 16, 1839, and died at Bedford, Iowa, April 13, 1911; he served in the 7th Indiana Infantry during the Civil War and was wounded in action in 1864; members of his family were in America prior to the Revolution.

His mother, whose father was a building contractor and completed the first lock in the Pittsburg River, was born at Frankfort, Kentucky, February 15, 1839, and died at Bedford, December 29, 1910. She was a milliner before her marriage. Interested in music, she assisted in perfecting the religious hymn *Night With Ebon Pinion,* written by Love H. Jamison.

Mr. Turner was graduated from the Bedford High School in 1903, where he played baseball and football. He served as auditor of the G. L. Turner Lumber Company of Broken Bow, Nebraska, 1904 to 1916, was president of the J. M. Turner Lumber Company at Thedford, Nebraska, 1917-22, and is now owner of the latter organization.

He is a member of the Thedford Community Club, Red Cross, the Congregational Church of Thedford, and the Modern Woodmen of America. He is interested in the development of his community, especially in the good roads movement, and in mechanical inventions. A Republican, Mr. Turner served as councilman at Broken Bow, 1911-12.

He was united in marriage with Sylvia D. Moore at Broken Bow, March 28, 1906. Mrs. Turner, who is a bonded abstracter at Thedford, was born at Sullivan, Illinois, June 4, 1883. She is the daughter of Joshua C. and Emily T. (Rowe) Moore. Mrs. Turner attended school at Broken Bow, and is a member of the Broken Bow Chapter of the P. E. O. Sisterhood and the Congregational Church of Thedford. Three daughters were born to them: Katharine, April 25, 1909, is a teacher at Broken Bow; Mary Jo, December 27, 1912, who teaches in the Thedford School; and Elizabeth Jean, February 11, 1920. The three girls are musicians. Katharine and Mary Jo attended school at Broken Bow and were graduated from Thedford High School and attended Cotner College at Lincoln. Residence: Thedford.

Paul Turner

Paul Turner, distinguished clergyman in the Presbyterian Church, is noted as a leader in civic and religious affairs at York, York County, Nebraska. He was born at Heyworth, McLean County, Illinois, November 21, 1894, the son of Frank and Harriet Emma (Cogswell) Turner. His father, who was born at Heyworth, March 3, 1868, and was killed there February 18, 1928, was a practising physician at Heyworth for 35 years; he volunteered for service in the World War directly before the Armistice was signed. His Scotch-Irish ancestors came to America early in the 17th century, and members of the Turner family fought in the Revolution.

Paul Turner's mother was born at Chatham, Illinois, May 12, 1870, and is still living. Her English ancestors came to America from England in the early part of the 18th century.

Mr. Turner was graduated from the Heyworth High School in 1911, was awarded the A. B. degree at Lake Forest College in 1915, and in 1925 received the B. D. degree at McCormick Theological Seminary. He was active in glee club work in college, was president of the college Young Men's Christian Association, took part in inter-class athletics, and was a member of Digamma Alpha Upsilon.

In 1917 he served as minister of the Presbyterian Church at Elfros, Saskatchewan, Canada, and from 1920 to 1927 held that position at Chippewa Falls, Wisconsin. Since 1927 he has been pastor of the First Presbyterian Church of York, Nebraska. Mr. Turner is the author of various magazine articles, has been active in Hi Y and Young Men's Christian Association work since 1910, and is serving his second year as president of the York Ministerial Alliance. He was a member of the Kiwanis Club for eight years, was formerly a member of the Chamber of Commerce, and at one time held membership in the

Odd Fellows Lodge. He is a member of the York Parent-Teachers Association, and in 1930 was grand orator of Grand Lodge of the Ancient Free and Accepted Masons in Nebraska.

During the World War Mr. Turner served in Company L, 123rd Infantry, 31st Division, in France. Prior to this he was secretary of the Young Men's Christian Association, and after the Armistice was engaged in work of this organization with the American Expeditionary Force in France. He has served as chaplain and service officer of the American Legion.

On February 18, 1918, his marriage to Elizabeth Catterlin was solemnized at Heyworth. Mrs. Turner, who was born at Clinton, Dewitt County, Illinois, December 11, 1895, is descended from Scotch ancestors who came to America in the 18th century and fought in the Revolution. Three children were born to this union: Donald Frank, born March 19, 1921; John Paul, born March 4, 1924; Elizabeth Anne, born June 7, 1925.

Mr. Turner's favorite sports are fishing and hunting, and his hobbies are guns, fishing tackle, radio, and carpentering. Politically, he is independent. Residence: York.

Ray Emmitt Turner

For a quarter of a century Ray Emmitt Turner has been a leading merchant at Kearney. Born at Erie, Kansas, August 22, 1888, he is the son of George Francis and Eliza Ann (Meloy) Turner. George F. Turner, a native of Indiana, was born October 5, 1853, and died at Canon City, Colorado, September 28, 1924. He was a farmer. His wife, born in Marshall County, Illinois, November 21, 1858, died at Canon City on June 28, 1930.

Ray Emmitt Turner was graduated from high school at Juniata, in 1903, and from business college in Colorado in 1906. For three years folowing he was associated with the Greenhill Orchards Commission firm of Colorado, and for the past twenty-five years has been general manager and part owner of the Twidale Shoe Company, which now owns and operates eight stores.

On October 26, 1909, he was married to Maude Adeli Rohrer at Hastings. Mrs. Turner was born at Lancaster, Pennsylvania, July 23, 1886. They have one daughter, Genevieve Esther, born October 20, 1910, who is married to Jack Dyas.

Mr. Turner is a Republican. His religious affiliation is with the First Christian Church. He is a member of all Masonic bodies, including the Shrine, and is president of the Kearney cemetery commission and secretary of the park commissions of Kearney, and is past president of the Nebraska Good Roads Association. He is a member of the Kearney zoning commission, a director and former president of the Chamber of Commerce and a member of the Nebraska State Historical Society and the Nebraskana Society. Twice president of the Kiwanis Club, he is also past lieutenant governor for his local district of that organization. He is a member of the Kearney Country Club. His hobby is his library. Residence: Kearney.

William Jay Turner

William Jay Turner, who homesteaded in Clay County, Nebraska, in 1871, has been prominent in business affairs at Harvard for many years. He was born at Byron, Illinois, November 2, 1849, the son of Thomas Ezra and Martha Eline (Pier) Turner. His father, who was a teacher in private and public schools, was born at Montville, Connecticut, May 5, 1811, and died at Quasquote, Iowa, January 3, 1861; he served in the Iowa legislature in 1854; his English ancestors settled in Connecticut in 1649. His mother was born at Cooperstown, New York, March 7, 1816, and died at Quasquote, October 26, 1898.

Mr. Turner attended school at Quasquote. From 1876 to 1886 he engaged in the grain and lumber business, and from 1886 to 1892 was a farmer. After eight years in

JOHN S. TWINEM, M. D.

the hardware business he retired. A Republican, he
served as village trustee, and was the first mayor of
Harvard. He was a candidate for the legislature in 1892.
He is a member of the Red Cross and the Nebraskana
Society, and for over 58 years has been an active Mason.

He married Eva Marie Hjelm at Harvard, July 14,
1896. Mrs. Turner was born at Christiania, Sweden,
July 4, 1860, and died at Harvard, Nebraska, June 26,
1925. Two children were born to them, both of whom
died: Pier, born March 17, 1898, who died March 27, 1898;
and Eva June, born June 4, 1900, who died February 26,
1930. Residence: Harvard.

William Leonard Turner

William L. Turner, real estate executive of Lincoln,
was born at Kearney, Nebraska, January 30, 1874, the
son of Bartlett and Mary Elizabeth (Standard) Turner.
His father, who was a retired farmer for several years
before his death, was born at Memphis, Scotland County,
Missouri, October 6, 1851, and died at Kearney, March
17, 1925; his Scotch-Irish ancestors moved from Virginia
to Missouri in the early days. His mother, whose ancestry was Irish, was born at Arbele, Missouri, October 25,
1857, and died at Lincoln, November 18, 1928; her father
died in the service during the Civil War.

Mr. Turner attended the public schools at Kearney
and was graduated from the Kearney Military Academy.
Later he secured a county certificate and taught in the
Buffalo County Schools. He was engaged in the grain
business at Kearney for 15 years and since 1916, has been
a realtor at Kearney and Lincoln. He is manager of
the Lincoln office of the State Savings & Loan Association.

He was married at Kearney, June 8, 1898, to Estella
L. Rizer. Mrs. Turner, who was born at Carleton, Nebraska, October 6, 1875, was a teacher in the schools of
Buffalo County for seven years before her marriage. Her
ancestry is German. Six children were born to this
union: Leonard, born June 4, 1899, was graduated from
Kearney State Normal School and is now a musician
playing in theatres at Los Angeles, California; Melvin,
born October 30, 1905, is associated with his father in
business; Keith K., born October 18, 1907, is a student
at the University of Nebraska; Neva Beth, born November 18, 1909, is attending the University of Nebraska;
Dwight, born December 10, 1915; and DeLon, born January 4, 1918.

Mr. Turner is past president of the Lincoln Real Estate Board; is a member of the present national, state,
and local real estate associations, and is a director of
the state organization. He holds membership in the Lincoln Chamber of Commerce; the Optimist Club; and the
Nebraskana Society. He is a member of the Modern
Woodmen of America, Trinity Methodist Church of Lincoln. Although his family has been affiliated with the
Democratic party, Mr. Turner is a Republican. Residence: Lincoln.

Nels Anton Tuveson

Nels Anton Tuveson, pioneer Nebraska grain dealer,
was born at Malmo, Sweden, September 29, 1868, the son
of Andres and Anna (Krok) Tuveson. His father, who
was born in southern Sweden, August 24, 1834, and died
at Mead, Saunders County, Nebraska, September 23,
1919, was keeper and forester for an estate in Sweden,
and served a term of compulsory military education
there; he was of Russian descent, and came to Nebraska
in 1887. His mother, who was a seamstress, was born at
Ludwigsburg, Sweden, 1840, and died at Metropolis,
Illinois, July 24, 1926.

For the past 38 years Mr. Tuveson has been connected
with the Weston Grain and Stock Company at Weston,
Saunders County, Nebraska, acting first as grain buyer
and later as manager of this organization. He holds

membership in the Nebraska State Historical Society, the
Nebraskana Society, the National Geographic Society,
the Bison Society, Red Wood League, Museum of Natural History of New York City. He is intensely interested in reading and collecting books, Indian relics, and
coins; his favorite sports are hiking, fishing, and hunting.

During the Spanish American War he served as a private under Colonel Stotsenburg, in the First Nebraska
Volunteers, and is now a member of the Veterans of Foreign Wars and United Spanish War Veterans. He is
a member of the Red Cross, the Izaak Walton League,
and the Masons. He is a Republican.

On November 27, 1907, he was married at Wahoo,
Saunders County, Nebraska, to Caroline Francis Mach-
acek who was born at Valec, Czechoslovakia; the latter
was a seamstress. They have one son, Leo, born February 18, 1911. He attended Creighton two years and is
now attending the Creighton University. Residence:
Weston. (Photograph in Album).

John S. Twinem

John S. Twinem, physician and surgeon, was born
at Portadown, County Armagh, Ireland, April 12, 1870,
and came to the United States in 1892. He is the son
of William and Mary Jane (McNally) Twinem.

Dr. Twinem attended the Irish National Schools and
Wheaton College at Wheaton, Illinois, working his way
through school. He received his medical degree from
the Hahnemann Medical College in 1905 and prior thereto attended the Chicago Homeopathic Medical College
from which he was graduated in 1903. Afterward he
took post graduate work in Chicago, 1926, and the American College, Chicago, and the Rotunda Hospital at Dublin, Ireland, in 1929.

On September 7, 1905, he was married to Martha Jane
Armstrong at Glidden, Iowa. She was born in Will
County, Illinois, January 23, 1879. There are four children, Linn Kenneth, born June 4, 1908; Mary Jane, born
September 4, 1910; William Armstrong, born October 24,
1913; and John Robert, born December 18, 1921. One
son, Linn Kenneth, is studying law in Boston. He is a
graduate of the University of Nebraska, where he was
a second lieutenant in the Pershing Rifles. Another son,
William Armstrong, is taking his pre-medic studies at
the University of Nebraska, and a member of the Pershing Rifles. A daughter, Mary Jane, is a graduate of
the University of Nebraska in 1929.

For a number of years Dr. Twinem was the owner
of the Platte Valley Hospital, which is now owned by
Wesleyan University at Lincoln. He is a practicing physician and the owner of the Twinem Building which
houses the J. C. Penney Store. He is a member of the
Kiwanis Club, the Elks, the Odd Fellows, the American
Institute of Homeopathy, and is a Methodist. He is a
member of the North Platte Country Club. Politically,
he is a Republican. Residence: North Platte. (Photograph on Page 1209).

Albert Franklin Tyler

Dr. Albert Franklin Tyler is one of Nebraska's most
outstanding physicians. Born in Logan County, Illinois,
March 14, 1881, he has been a resident of Nebraska since
early childhood, and has done much toward the advancement of the medical profession.

His parents, George Washington and Sarah Jane
(Tracy) Tyler, were both of English ancestry. George
Washington Tyler was a native of Indiana, born February 17, 1843. He was a farmer, who died at Lincoln,
March 17, 1917. Sarah Jane Tyler was born at Baltimore, March 15, 1847, and died at Lincoln, January 1,
1928.

Dr. Tyler received a B. Sc. from Nebraska Wesleyan
University in 1904, and his M. D. from Creighton Uni-

Rinehart-Marsden—Omaha

DR. ALBERT FRANKLIN TYLER

versity in 1907. He was admitted to practice on June 12, 1907, and from 1908 to 1913 was associated in practice with Dr. J. P. Lord. Since 1917 he has been professor of clinical radiology at Creighton University, and is attending radiologist to St. Joseph's and Swedish Immanuel Hospital.

An eminent contributor to the annals of the medical profession, a partial list of his works include: *Roentgeno-therapy* (C. V. Mosby, 1918); *Periostitis Detected by X-ray* (1912); *Cysts of Bone* (1914); *Backaches—Some Unrecognized Causes* (1914); *Urinary Calculi; Value of the X-ray in Their Diagnosis* (1914); *The Fulguration Treatment of Certain New Growths* (1914); *The X-ray an Aid to Diagnosis in Diseases of the Right Upper Quadrant of the Abdomen* (1915); *Colloid Cyst of the Appendix* (1915); *A Comparison of Roentgenological and Surgical Findings in Certain Abdominal Conditions* (1915); *Colles' Fractures—Important Features* (1915); *Positive Diagnosis of Abdominal Disease by the Roentgen Ray* (1915); *Dislocation of the First Cervical Vertebra* (1915); *Bone Pathology as Revealed by the Roentgen Ray, with Suggestions as to Treatment* (1915); *Bone Pathology as Revealed by the Roentgen Ray* (1916); *Viscera Transposed* (1916); *Positive Diagnosis in Diseases of the Chest* (1916); *Unusual Kidney Stone* (1916); *Fracture of the Ischium* (1917); *Pathological Fractures Due to Syphilis of Bone* (1917); *The New Light* (1917); *Dextrocardia with Mitral Stenosis* (1917) *Roentgen Therapy in Epithelioma* (1918); *Deep Roentgen Therapy* (1918); *Essential Principles of Deep Roentgenotherapy* (1918); *Multiple Sarcomatosis Secondary to Small Round cell Sarcoma of the Buttock* (1919); *Safety Pin in the Lung Five Years* (1919); *Syphilis of the Great Vessels* (1920); *Murphy Button Retained Four Years Complicated by Ulcer at Site of Gastro-enterostomy* (1920); *Injection of Gas into the Peritoneal Cavity for Diagnostic and Therapeutic Purposes* (1920); *The Treatment of Uterine Hemorrhage by Radiotherapy* (1920); *Diverticula of the Duodenum* (1921); *Focal Infection and its Relationship to Systemic Disease* (1921); *Recent Developments in Deep Therapy Technique—Facts and Fancies* (1921); *Cancers of the Skin and Mucous Membrane* (1921); *Pneumoperitoneum as an Aid in the Differential Diagnosis of Diseases of the Left Half of the Abdomen* (1921); *Radiation Treatment of Uterine Cancer* (1922); *Effect of Radiation Therapy on Lungs and Pleura* (1922); *Fracture of the Carpal Scaphoid* (1923); *Carcinoma of the Lingual Thyroid with Metastases in the Lung* (1923); *Electrothermic Coagulation* (1923); *Misplaced, Unerupted and Impacted Teeth* (co-author, 1924); *Principles Underlying Removal of Disease at Apices of Teeth* (co-author, 1924); *Surgical Diathermy in the Treatment of New Growths of the Face and Mouth* (1924); *X-ray Therapy in Actinomycosis* (1924); *Non-malignant Diseases of the Jaw* (co-author, 1924); *Sequelae of Radiation Therapy* (1924); *Surgical Diathermy in the Treatment of Benign Skin Blemishes* (1924); *Fundamental Principles in X-ray Diagnosis of Diseases of the Gastro-intestinal Tract* (1924); *Fundamental principles of X-ray Diagnosis of Diseases of the Pleurae and Lungs* (1925); *Malignant Degeneration of a Parotid Cell Rest in the External Auditory Canal* (1925); *What is Diathermy and How does it Act on Tissues?* (1926); *Pyelography as an Aid to Genito-urinary Diagnosis* (1926); *Roentgen Ray* (1926); *Report of Two Unusual Cases of Ascites Relieved by Diathermia* (1927); *Carcinoma of the Thyroid* (1927); *Physical Therapy in Industry* (1928); *New Growths in the Chest Wall, Pleura and Lungs* (1928); *Physical Therapy in Fungus Disease* (1929); *History of Medicine in Nebraska* (1929, editor); *Duodenal Stasis* (1929); *Recent Advances in Physical Therapy Service* (1930); *Radiation Treatment of Cancer of the Uterine Cervix* (1930).

Dr. Tyler was associate editor of the *Nebraska State Medical Journal* from 1917-19, editor of the *Journal of Radiology* 1921-22, *Archives of Physical Therapy, X-ray, Radium* 1923-26; managing editor, *Archives of Physical Therapy, X-ray, Radium* 1926-30.

During the World War he was chairman of the personnel department of the Y. M. C. A. He is a member of the First Methodist Episcopal Church, treasurer of the Nebraska State Y. M. C. A., trustee of Nebraska Wesleyan University and of the First Methodist Church. He holds membership in the American Roentgen Ray Society, The London Roentgen Ray Society, the American Radium Society, the American Congress of Physical Therapy, American College of Physicians, the American Medical Association, the Nebraska State Medical Association and the Omaha-Douglas County Medical Society. He is a member of the Chamber of Commerce, and during 1916-18 was a member of the publicity committee. His civic and fraternal organizations include the Elks, and the Rotary Club. He is a member of the National Geographic Society, the American Association for the Advancement of Science and the Nebraskana Society.

On September 23, 1908 he was united in marriage to Charlotte Ellen Roe, at Omaha. Mrs. Tyler was born at Omaha, May 7, 1883 and is of English ancestry. There are two children, Ellen Jean, born May 13, 1911, and Albert Edward, born October 1, 1909.

Dr. Tyler is a Republican. His social clubs are the University Club and the Omaha Club. Residence: Omaha. (Photograph on Page 1211).

Eugene Monroe Tyler

Eugene Monroe Tyler, physician and surgeon, is a native of Tennessee. Born at Sneedville, Hancock County, February 19, 1863, he is the son of Henry and Elizabeth (Jessee) Tyler. His father was born in northern New York, August 28, 1821. In early life he was a merchant, and later clerk of the county and district courts, and was descended from English settlers in Massachusetts in the late 1600's. Removing to Tennessee, he was active there for many years prior to his death on July 8, 1898. He was married to Elizabeth Jessee, a native of Lee County, Virginia, born March 28, 1835. Mrs. Tyler was of English and French ancestry, descended from early Virginia settlers. Her grandfather was of the Clark family which was distinguished in the Revolutionary War. Prior to her marriage she was a teacher, and through all her life was an active worker in the church. She died at Sneedville, December 26, 1890.

Dr. Tyler received his A. B. from Carson College in 1881, and his M. A. in 1894; in 1885 he was graduated from the medical college of the University of Tennessee. At Carson College he was a member of the Philomathean Society and represented this society two years. He was also a member of the baseball team. Dr. Tyler took post graduate work in Chicago, in 1908, and at New York, in 1922.

His marriage to Louisa Florence Quillen was solemnized at her home in Lee County, Virginia, May 6, 1886. Mrs. Tyler was born in Lee County, March 13, 1871. She is descended from Scotch and English settlers in Virginia. She is a member of the Auburn Woman's Club, the Eastern Star, the P. E. O., and the various church societies. There are four children: Ida Gertrude, born February 26, 1887, attended the University of Nebraska three and a half years. She is married to Frank C. Grant, lawyer and abstractor of Lincoln. Irene N., born February 17, 1889, was graduated from Peru State Teachers College and studied art at Omaha. She married Neal M. Cecil, a civil engineer. Varro Eugene, born January 6, 1891, is a graduate of the University of Nebraska, and later of the law school of Chicago University. During the World War he was in Officer's Training School and served overseas ten months. He married Venus Leamer, and is engaged in the practice of law at Nebraska City. Alonzo Lewis, born August 23, 1898, was graduated from Peru, and later from the U. S. Naval Academy. He then studied law at New York, where he is now engaged in practice. He is married to Ruth Townsend.

Since 1885, Dr. Tyler has been engaged in practice in Auburn. During the war he was on the medical examining board, and active in loan and Red Cross drives. He is still a member of the Red Cross. He was first president of the Kiwanis Club, and is a member of the Chamber of Commerce. He belongs to the Nebraska State Medical Associations, the American Medical Association and the Nemaha County Association.

He has always been active in educational work in the city, having been a member of the school board for fifteen years, and a member of Auburn's first library board 10 years. He is chairman of the board of trustees of the Methodist Episcopal Church. He is a Mason, and member of the Blue Lodge, chapter, council and commandery. He is affiliated with the Modern Woodmen of America, the Royal Neighbors, and of the Nebraskana Society. For many years he was a member of the Auburn Country Club. Residence: Auburn.

Harold Bertram Tyler

Harold Bertram Tyler, editor and publisher of three weekly newspapers in northern Nebraska, was born at Niles, Ohio, October 2, 1870, and has lived in Nebraska born July 27, 1820, in Staffordshire, England, and died in Cleveland, Ohio, November 30, 1890.

Susannah Tyler, his mother, was born of Scotch and Irish parents in Franklin County, Ohio, October 9, 1840, and died at Cleveland, October 12, 1921.

Mr. Tyler received his education in Westminister College, New Wilmington, Pennsylvania, where he was graduated with the B. L. degree in 1895, and was graduated from Xena Theological Seminary in 1898. For over 16 years he was a minister in the United Presbyterian Church, for twelve years he engaged in ranching, and for the past 11 years he has been prominent in newspaper work.

He is now publishing the following newspapers: *Wood Lake Stockman*, Wood Lake, Nebraska; *Ainsworth Star Journal*, at Ainsworth; and the *Long Pine Journal*, Long Pine, Nebraska. He is a stockholder in the National Bank of Ainsworth, is a member of the Ainsworth Commercial Club, and holds membership in the Red Cross and the Lions Club.

On November 16, 1895, he married Garretta Vanderwerf, at Cleveland. Mrs. Tyler, whose ancestry is Dutch, was born at Cleveland, June 14, 1870. To them were born: Dorothea Margaret, October 9, 1899, who married George W. Siebold; Gerrit V., December 22, 1904, who married Muriel F. Stringfellow; Norman Paul, August 6, 1909; Robert Harold, April 6, 1913; and Lida Pearl, August 25, 1906, who died August 15, 1907. Gerrit V. Tyler is a successful editor and publisher at Spalding, Nebraska. Residence: Ainsworth.

Venus Una Tyler

Venus Una Leamer, now Mrs. Varro E. Tyler, was born at Concord, Nebraska, daughter of David Cecil and Jessie Christensen Sterling (Cowie) Leamer. Her father was born at Hollidaysburg, Pennsylvania, September 12, 1857, and is a retired banker. He is French and Scotch, a descendant of one of Napoleon's aides and personal friends, James Leemar, born 1777. Jessie Cowie Leamer was born in Dane County, Wisconsin, November 25, 1862. She is Scotch, a direct descendant of Sir Walter Scott, and of King Bruce of Scotland.

Mrs. Tyler was graduated from Wakefield High School and received her B. A. from the University of Nebraska, in 1910. She is a member of Phi Beta Kappa, honorary fraternity, and Delta Zeta sorority. She was married to Varro Eugene Tyler at Des Moines, Iowa, May 29, 1918. There are two children: Jessie Lou, born August 22, 1924; and Varro Eugene, Jr., born December 19, 1926.

From 1910-13, Mrs. Tyler was a teacher in Syracuse High School, and from 1914-18 was library assistant in the Lincoln Public Library. She is a member of the Nebraskana Society, and the Women's Club, and is former member and was president in 1923 of the Music Club. She is at the present time president of the American Legion Auxiliary.

She is a member of the First Presbyterian Church, the P. E. O. and the Eastern Star. She is also a member of the Nebraska City Country Club. Residence: Nebraska City.

William Augustus Tyler

William Augustus Tyler, clergyman and church executive, was born at New Holland, Logan County, Illinois, June 5, 1867, the son of Sarah Jane (Tracy) Tyler and George Washington Tyler. His father, who was born at Raysville, Henry County, Indiana, February 17, 1841, and died at University Place, Nebraska, March 15, 1917, was a farmer; he served in Company G, 106th Illinois Infantry, from 1862 to 1865; his ancestry was English.

His mother was born at Baltimore, Maryland, March 15, 1847, and died at University Place, January 11, 1928. Her ancestry was French and English; her brother was prominent in the banking world at Springfield, Illinois, and was a director of the Baltimore & Ohio Railroad.

Dr. Tyler attended the rural schools of Logan County, received the M. D. degree at George Washington Universty, Washington, D. C., 1895, and was awarded the Bachelor of Divinity degree at Garrett Biblical Institute at Evanston, Illinois, 1904. He served as president of his class at the latter institution, and was a member of the debating team.

He taught school in Fillmore and Thayer counties for three years, was clerk in the war department at Washington for five years, and engaged in medical practice in Hamilton and Dawson counties for three years. He has been pastor of various Nebraska churches for 19 years, and has held pastorates in Illinois. After serving for three years as associate superintendent of the Nebraska Congregational Conference he became superintendent and still holds this position.

Dr. Tyler is a trustee of Doane College at Crete, Nebraska. He was an honorary member of the Adams County Medical Society and the Saline County Medical Society, and holds membership in the Lincoln Ministerial Association. He is a member of the Nebraskana Society, and was formerly a member of the library board at Crete for several years. During the World War he acted as Liberty loan speaker and solicitor, was prominent in Young Men's Christian Association work and the Red Cross, and was a Four Minute Man. He has held membership in the Sons of Veterans.

He is a member of Crete Lodge Number 37. of the Ancient Free and Accepted Masons, Valley of Hastings Consistory, Scottish Rite, Sesostris Temple of the Shrine. Politically, he is an independent.

On July 5, 1892, he was united in marriage with Ella Clara Kimball at Washington, D. C. Mrs. Tyler, who was born at Fort Wayne, Indiana, was cashier in a mercantile establishement before her marriage. Their children are: Tracy F., born January 16, 1895, who married Ruth Sherrerd; Harry E., born December 20, 1898, who married Jennie Hosford; Ralph W., born April 22, 1902, who married Flora Volz; and Ivory K., born February 18, 1905, who married Margaret Carey. Tracy has been superintendent of school in Nebraska for the past ten years. Harry has been superintendent of schools and is now dean of men at the Sacramento Junior College in California. Ivory holds a fellowship in Columbia University. Ralph is professor in the Ohio State University. Residence: Lincoln.

Robert Andrew Tynan

Robert A. Tynan was born at Peru, Nebraska, September 5, 1876. His father, Andrew Tynan, was born at Kilenney, Ireland, March 8, 1833 and came to America in 1845 where he engaged in farming. He died at Stella, Richardson County, Nebraska, June 15, 1912.

Mr. Tynan attended the Richardson County grade schools and the Stella High School. He later attended the University of Nebraska, being graduated in 1899. He was awarded an A. B. degree in 1922. All his life has been spent in Nebraska except for two years, when he lived in Montana. Until 1918 he farmed near Stella, and since that time he has been president of the State Bank of Stella. He is also secretary of drainage district number three in Richardson County.

On May 29, 1902, he was united in marriage with Della Loraine Harden at Verdon, Nebraska. Mrs. Tynan was born at Verdon, January 15, 1878. They have three children: Robert A., Junior, born August 10, 1904, who is a graduate of the University of Nebraska; Katherine C., born December 10, 1908, who received her A. B. at the University of Nebraska; and Eugene Harden, born June 26, 1914.

Mr. Tynan was captain in the home guards of Stella, in 1918. From 1901 to 1918, he was a member of the school board, district number 15, in Richardson County, and from 1920 to 1928, he was treasurer of the school board of district number 76. He is a member of the Y. M. C. A., the Stella Chamber of Commerce, the Masons (Scottish Rite Consistory No. 2, Shrine, Sesostris Temple), the Modern Woodmen of America, and the Order of Eastern Star. He is a Democrat. His hobby is farming. Residence: Stella.

Ace Vern Tyrrell

Ace Vern Tyrrell, automobile executive at Osceola, Nebraska, has lived in this state all his life. He was born at Beaver Crossing, March 14, 1898, the son of Henry Albert and Blanche (Howerton) Tyrrell. His father was born in Indiana, February 20, 1867, and died at Beaver Crossing, February 18, 1913. His mother was born at Goehner, Nebraska, August 15, 1877, and is still living.

Mr. Tyrrell attended high school at Beaver Crossing. He is a partner and manager of the Nielsen Chevrolet Company of Osceola and holds membership in various civic organizations, among them: Community Club, of which he is president; Masons; Elks; Odd Fellows; The Nebraskana Society. He is a member of the Democratic party, and holds membership in the Osceola Country Club, and the Osceola Gun Club.

On March 19, 1929, he was married to Esther M. Smith at Omaha, Douglas County, Nebraska. Mrs. Tyrrel was born at Inman, Nebraska, January 3, 1904. Residence: Osceola. (Photograph in Album).

Edward Uehling

Edward Uehling, banker, was born in Dodge County, Nebraska, March 13, 1863, son of Theodore and Kathrina (Schwab) Uehling. His father, who was born in Sax Meiningen, Germany, January 11, 1836, came to America with an older brother in 1847, his father and mother having died. He was a farmer and stock raiser until his death at Uehling, February 13, 1912. Katherine Schwab was born in Bavaria, Germany, February 28, 1838, and died at Uehling, April 2, 1927.

Mr. Uehling attended country school in the pioneer days of Nebraska, and was thereafter associated with the Dodge County Bank of Hooper for seventeen years. Since 1905 he has been associated with the Farmers State Bank of Uehling, as cashier and vice president. He is a Republican, and has served as a member of the school board at Hooper and Uehling, as a member of the board of trustees and as village treasurer.

He was married to Charlotte Herre at Fremont, Nebraska, July 13, 1890. Mrs. Uehling was born in New

Jersey, February 27, 1868, of German parentage. There are four children: Vera L., born May 6, 1892; Harold T., born January 27, 1896; Elletha, born October 2, 1900, and Clifton F., born May 11, 1903.

Mr. Uehling was chairman of all Liberty and Victory loans for Uehling and Logan township during the World War, and was chairman and treasurer of the Red Cross during the war period. He is a member of the Ancient Free and Accepted Masons. Residence: Uehling.

Ernest Clarence Uhlig

Ernest Clarence Uhlig, gas and oil merchant, was born at Adair, Iowa, June 7, 1880, and has resided in Nebraska 47 years. His father, Charles Uhlig, was born in Leipzig, Germany, June 1, 1842, and came to Nebraska homesteading in Frontier County in 1885. He resided there until his death at Eustis, Nebraska, in April, 1915. He came to America in 1860. His wife, Mary Ellen Lewis, was born in Des Moines, Iowa, April 27, 1862, and died at Eustis, Nebraska, September 2, 1920.

Mr. Uhlig attended public school at Eustis, and on April 2, 1900, was married to Marietta Martin at Farnam, Nebraska. She is the daughter of Miles F. and Rhoda Anne (Martin) Martin, and was born at Shickley, Nebraska, October 9, 1878. She is a member of the Christian Church and the Order of Eastern Star. They have one daughter, Bernice, born May 10, 1911, who is at present a student in the Colorado Woman's College.

Mr. Uhlig is a Republican, a member of the Commercial Club, the Modern Woodmen, and the Knights Templar. He is affiliated with the Christian Church and is secretary of the Board of Education at Sutherland. Residence: Sutherland. (Photograph in Album).

John Leonard Umberger

Born at Elwood, Nebraska, October 29, 1893, John Leonard Umberger is the son of William Miller and Mary Ellen (Barber) Umberger. His father, who was a ranchman and farmer, was born at Lisburn, Pennsylvania, March 30, 1855, and has served as county commissioner of Gosper County, Nebraska, for several years; his Pennsylvania Dutch ancestors have been in this country since the Revolution.

His mother, who took an active interest in all school and civic enterprises in her community, was born at Lisburn, May 30, 1858, and died at Lincoln, Nebraska, February 11, 1913. Her ancestry was Scotch-Irish and Pennsylvania Dutch.

Mr. Umberger attended school at Elwood and in 1913 was graduated from the Lincoln High School. He is now a farmer and rancher near Elwood and is a director in the Elwood Coal and Lumber Company. He holds membership in the Elwood Commercial Club, the Nebraskana Society, and the Methodist Church of Elwood. His fraternal societies include the Masons and Woodmen of the World. During the late war he served as a first class private in the infantry trained at Camp Funston and took an active part in the St. Mihiel and Argonne Forest offensives with the 35th Division in France.

His hobby is reading, and he is interested in all outdoor sports. His political affiliation is with the Democratic party. Residence: Elwood.

William Miller Umberger

William Miller Umberger was born at Lisburn, Pennsylvania, March 31, 1855, and for the past 41 years has been a resident of Nebraska. His father, who was a farmer, was born in York County, Pennsylvania in 1820 and died at Mechanicsburg, Pennsylvania, in 1897. His mother was born in York County in 1823 and died at Mechanicsburg, 1896.

Mr. Umberger attended rural school near Lisburn, Pennsylvania, and entered business there after his graduation. He was department manager of woolen mills at New Cumberland, Pennsylvania, from 1884 to 1889. He has served as county commissioner of Gosper County, Nebraska, from 1902 to 1906 and is now president of the Elwood Coal & Lumber Company and is vice president of the Elwood Equity Exchange.

He is the owner of a 2240 acre ranch west of Elwood, Nebraska, a 520 acre farm in Gosper County, and a 160 acre farm in Duel County, Nebraska, and has been in past years, an extensive breeder and feeder of cattle. He holds membership in the Methodist Episcopal Church at Elwood, is past master of Elwood Lodge of the Masons, and is a member of the Order of Eastern Star.

His marriage to Mary Ellen Barber occurred at Lisburn, Pennsylvania, April 11, 1889. Mrs. Umberger was born at Lisburn, December 2, 1858, and died at University Place, Nebraska, February 11, 1913. There are five children, Martha, born January 25, 1890, who married E. H. Ledyard; Ellen, born March 15, 1891, who married Claud Smith; Jessie, born July 8, 1892, who married H. A. Ringenberg; John L., born in October, 1893; and Perry J., born April 7, 1895, who married Alice Kolb. Residence: Elwood.

George Ralph Unthank

George R. Unthank was born at Arlington, Washington County, Nebraska, March 4, 1875, and has lived in this state all his life. His father, Oliver Nixon Unthank, who was born at Newport, now known as Fountain City, Indiana, November 18, 1842, was a government operator at Fort Laramie, Wyoming, 1869-1871. He freighted from Omaha to Denver in the early 60's, and was a member of the wagon train expedition to the Idaho gold fields with Jim Bridger acting as guide. He was descended from John Allen Unthank and Mary Jane (Curtis) Unthank, both of whom had Revolutionary War ancestors. The family came originally from England and has been in America for seven generations. He died at Arlington, November 21, 1928.

Emmaline Hummer (Brandon) Unthank, his mother, was born at Dayton, Ohio, November 30, 1845, and died at Arlington, November 13, 1900. She was a singer and artist of prominence and was active in the Women's Christian Temperance Union for many years. She was the daughter of John and Emmaline (Hummer) Brandon. The latter was of Scotch-Irish descent.

Mr. Unthank was graduated from the Arlington High School in 1893 and later was a student at the Peru Normal School. For five years he was a teacher; was in business with the Updike Grain Company for three years; was a civil service employee for 10 years; and was a contractor and builder for 18 years. In 1925 he organized and incorporated the G. R. Unthank Company, of which he is now general manager, secretary, and treasurer. A Republican, Mr. Unthank has served as county delegate for Washington County; county delegate of Saunders County; and senatorial delegate at large for Washington and Dodge counties.

He was united in marriage with Fanny Churchill Kettlewell at University Place, Lancaster County, Nebraska, December 25, 1901. Mrs. Unthank, who was born at Exeter, Fillmore County, Nebraska, September 4, 1877, is descended from the Churchill family of England, noted in Revolutionary times in America. Her paternal grandfather was a member of parliament in England. They have three children: Phyllis Arabel, born November 2, 1902, who was a student at the University of Nebraska where she was a member of Pi Beta Phi Sorority, and who married George Thomas Underwood; John Oliver, born August 3, 1904, who was awarded the A. B. degree at the University of Nebraska in architectural engineer-

ing, 1928, and who was a member of Alpha Tau Omega; and George Ralph, Jr., born July 29, 1914.

Mr. Unthank is a member of the Lincoln Chamber of Commerce. He is a member of the Masons and the Eastern Star. Residence: Lincoln. (Photograph in Album).

Fred Wilbert Upson

Fred Upson, noted educator at the University of Nebraska, was born at Byron, Ogle County, Illinois, February 2, 1883, the son of Richard Empey and Mary Williams (Johnston) Upson. His father, who was a farmer, was born at Camden, New York, in 1854, and died at Odell, Nebraska, July 26, 1896; he was descended from Thomas Upson who came to America and settled in Connecticut, in 1649; his mother was a member of the Putnam family, of Revolutionary fame.

His mother was born at Byron, September 23, 1853; she was descended from four *Mayflower* ancestors and the Copeland, Williams and Ames families.

Dean Upson attended country school at Odell, and in 1902 was graduated from the Lincoln High School. He holds the following degrees: Ph. D., University of Chicago, 1910; A. M., University of Nebraska, 1908; and B. S., University of Nebraska, 1907. He holds membership in Gamma Alpha and Sigma Xi.

He served as instructor in chemistry at the University of Cincinnati, 1910-12, was instructor of chemistry at the University of Chicago, 1912-13, and was professor of agricultural chemistry at the University of Nebraska, 1913-18. He has been chairman of the department of chemistry since 1918 and dean of the graduate college at the University of Nebraska since 1929. He is the author of numerous articles published in chemical journals, chiefly in the field of chemistry of carbohydrates.

Dean Upson is a member of the board of directors of the Nebraska Art Association, and the board of directors of the Lincoln Symphony Orchestra Association. He holds fellowship in the American Association for the Advancement of Science, is a member of the American Chemical Society, and holds membership in the American Association of University Professors. He is a member of the Lincoln University Club, is affiliated with the Republican party, and holds membership in The Nebraskana Society. His favorite sport is fishing, while his hobbies are reading and gardening.

On June 16, 1915, he was united in marriage with Georgia Baldwin Field at Lincoln. Mrs. Upson, the daughter of Judge A. W. Field of Lincoln, was born at Lincoln, May 6, 1885. They have one son, John Ames, born November 9, 1916. Residence: Lincoln.

Claude Thomas Uren

Claude T. Uren, distinguished physician and medical educator of Nebraska, was born at Lead, Lawrence County, South Dakota, June 18, 1887. His father, Thomas Uren who was born at Lands End, Cornwall, England, November 1, 1862, and died at Lead, May 25, 1894, was a cattleman. His mother, Gertrude R. (Huffman) Uren, was born at Hartford, Indiana, October 24, 1869. She was married to B. R. Stone in 1897.

Dr. Uren received his elementary education in the public schools of Lead, and in 1905, was graduated from the Lead High School. He was awarded the M. D. degree in 1910, at the University of Michigan, where he was a member of Phi Beta Pi. From 1910 to 1913, he was instructor in oto-laryngology at the University of Michigan. Since 1920, he has been professor of oto-laryngology at Creighton Medical College. He is a member of the staff of St. Joseph's Hospital, and at the Douglas County Hospital.

On January 16, 1916, Dr. Uren was united in marriage with Irma Wiedeman at Omaha, Nebraska. Mrs. Uren, who was born at Omaha, April 25, 1893, was the granddaughter of Fred Krug, a prominent pioneer Omahan. She died at Omaha, May 3, 1924. Three children were born to this marriage: Jane, born February 16, 1918; Thomas, born December 18, 1919; and Marjorie, born November 10, 1921. On January 28, 1926, his marriage to Gertrude Riedy was solemnized at Omaha. One daughter was born to this union, Sally, born January 23, 1927.

Dr. Uren served as captain of the medical corps in the World War, September, 1917, to April, 1919. He is a member of the American Legion. He is a member of the American Medical Association, the American College of Surgeons, American Academy of Ophtholmology and Oto-laryngology, and American Laryngological, Otological and Phenological Society. He is a member of the Omaha Chamber of Commerce, the American Institute of Professional Men, and the Nebraskana Society.

He is affiliated with Trinity Cathedral at Omaha. His clubs are the Omaha Club; Omaha Country Club; and Omaha University Club. His favorite sport is golf. He is a Republican. Residence: Omaha.

William George Vahle

The Reverend William George Vahle, pastor of St. John's Lutheran Church at Atkinson, was born at St. Louis, Missouri, February 20, 1884. He is the son of John Henry and Charlotte Anna Marie (Walkenhorst) Vahle, the former a native of Hanover, Germany, born November 20, 1842. John H. Vahle was a teamster, probably of Dutch parentage, but born in Germany, who came to the United States, in 1866, and died at St. Louis, on February 16, 1911.

His wife, Charlotte, was born in Washington, Missouri, February 7, 1853, and died at St. Louis, April 4, 1924. Her parents were born in Westphalia, and her father served in the Union Army during the Civil War.

Mr. Vahle was graduated from Zion Lutheran parochial school at St. Louis, in 1897, and from 1897, to 1901, had four years in German, English, and Latin, under a private tutor, taking public night school work at the same time. From 1901-07, he attended Concordia College and Seminary, at Springfield, Illinois, and in 1912, was a student at Coffeyville Business College for several months. He received his Bachelor of Divinity degree from the American University of Los Angeles, in 1923.

On August 4, 1909, Mr. Vahle was married to Emma Jane Mueller, at Stuttgart, Kansas. She was a native of Stuttgart, born August 22, 1885. Her father was born in Saxony, her mother in Illinois, her maternal grandmother in London, and her grandfather in Germany. They have one daughter, Dorothy, born October 1, 1910. She was graduated from Atkinson High School in 1928, taught two years in rural schools, and is now a sophomore at Midland College.

Mr. Vahle is a Democrat. He was graduated from the Crabtree Chiropractic College at Coffeyville, Kansas, in 1911, and practiced chiropractic in St. Louis, for 8 months, and during the same year taught at the St. Louis College of Chiropractic.

He is a member of the Red Cross, the Chamber of Commerce, the Nebraskana Society, and the Lutheran Mutual Aid Society of Waverly, Iowa. Mr. Vahle has for his hobbies carving in ivory, philately, and languages. He understands Swedish, Norwegian, and Dutch and has a working knowledge of French. Residence: Atkinson.

Clarence A. Valder

Clarence A. Valder, prominent Burt County farmer, was born in that county on November 30, 1872. He is the son of Edwin E. and Sarah Ann (Johnson) Valder, the former of whom was born in Leland, Illinois, February 4, 1841. Edwin Valder served in the Civil War and was a member of the Grand Army of the Republic. His father, the Reverend Hans Valder, organized the first Norwegian Baptist Church in America, founded the town of Newberg, and was a member of the state legislature. Edwin E. Valder died at Tekamah on May 2, 1914. His wife, Sarah Ann, was a native of Stavanger, Norway, born July 19, 1846. She was an active church worker, a member of the Women's Relief Corps and a nurse. Her death occurred at Tekamah on September 14, 1928.

A farmer since early manhood, Clarence A. Valder has also been active in Republican politics, and was a member of the house of representatives of Nebraska the sessions of 1929 and 1931. He is president of the Farmers' Telephone Company. The family attends the First Presbyterian Church, and Mr. Valder is a member of the Chamber of Commerce and the Odd Fellows. He has served as an elder in his church for some time, is treasurer of the local school board, and is president of the Burt County Historical Society. His hobby is reading.

On March 6, 1895, Mr. Valder was married to Ethel Ione McMullin in Burt County. Mrs. Valder, who was born in Burt County May 24, 1876, is of Scotch-Irish descent. There are three children: Clayton S., born May 14, 1898, is married to Sara Bassett, and is a Presbyterian minister; Ethel Pearl, born August 26, 1899, is a teacher of English; and Gerald C., born December 20, 1904, is a farmer. Clayton is a graduate of the University of Chicago and McCormick Seminary; Ethel is a graduate of the University of Nebraska in 1924, and is now attending Columbia University. Gerald is a graduate of Tekamah High School. Residence: Tekamah. (Photograph in Album).

Harm Van Boening

Harm Van Boening, farmer and prominent in agricultural circles, was born near Glenvil, Nebraska, January 7, 1882, son of Simon and Ida (Schmidt) Van Boening.

Simon Van Boening was born in Germany, February 26, 1857, and came to America, in 1869. He settled first near Lincoln, Illinois, and in 1879 came to Nebraska, pioneering in Hanover township of Adams County. He moved to a farm one mile west of Rosemont in Webster County in 1893, and is now retired. The title of Von was held by ancestors in Germany, and was changed to Van in America. Ida Schmidt was born in Peoria County, Illinois, July 21, 1860, of German parentage.

Mr. Van Boening attended public school in Hanover township of Adams County, and has since engaged in farming. He has been a member of the Farmers Union and the Farm Bureau as long as its existence in his community. He is always a promoter of the welfare of farmers, and is known as one of the most progressive farmers in Webster County. He is a faithful worker, a member of St. Paul's Evangelical Lutheran Church at Blue Hill, and is interested in the betterment of schools and in all good work for the development of public welfare.

In 1912, he became a member of the Modern Woodmen of America, in which he has held various offices. He has been treasurer of school district No. 45 of Webster County since 1919, and has always been a contributor to Red Cross and Salvation Army. He is a life member of the Nebraskana Society. His favorite sports are hunting and fishing, while his hobby is mechanics.

In January, 1905, he was married to Augusta M. Toepfer at Blue Hill. Mrs. Van Boening was born at Blue Hill, December 4, 1883, daughter of Mr. and Mrs. William Toepfer, who were born in Germany. Nine children were born to them, one of whom died in infancy. They are as follows, Charlotte, born January 7, 1906; Oscar, born June 15, 1908; Eleanor, born September 16, 1914, died February 27, 1915; Addelene, born November 11, 1911; Mildred, born May 17, 1913; Harlan, born November 21, 1915; Delbert, born January 16, 1918;

Elna, born August 3, 1920; and Dean, born April 15, 1926.

Charlotte taught school in the rural schools of Webster County and in Hallam. She was graduated from Blue Hill High School, and attended the University of Nebraska. Oscar was graduated from Blue Hill High School, and was employed in a drug store at Grant. Since 1929, he has been in the employ of the Blue Hill Auto Company. He writes insurance as a side line. Residence: Blue Hill.

John Harris Vance

John Harris Vance, physician and surgeon, was born at New Castle, Pennsylvania, October 24, 1858, and has been a resident of Nebraska for the past forty-four years. He is the son of William and Martha (Leslie) Vance. His father, William Vance, was born at New Castle, November 30, 1824, and died at New Wilmington, Pennsylvania, September 20, 1909. He was a farmer, whose parents came from County Antrim, Ireland.

Martha Leslie Vance was born at New Castle, April 28, 1826, and died at New Wilmington, November 29, 1909. Her father was of English, and her mother of Scotch descent.

Dr. Vance was educated in country schools and studied at Wooster, Ohio, and Westminster College at New Wilmington. He received his M. D. from Jefferson Medical College. He was married to Flora Gardner at New Castle, on November 28, 1888. Mrs. Vance was born at Portersville, Pennsylvania, May 31, 1866, and is of Scotch-Irish descent, and died October 30, 1931. They have three children: Harris G., born July 17, 1890, died May 23, 1927; William Brooks, born October 22, 1898, is a physician who is practicing in New York; and Mary, born September 27, 1006, married Dr. C. E. Thompson, a physician, and resides at Detroit.

During the World War, Dr. Vance was a member of the committee which organized Base Hospital No. 49, and an ambulance company. He is a member of the U. S. Medical Reserve Corps. He attends Central United Presbyterian Church, and during 1905-11, was a member of the Board of Education. He is a member of the Volunteer Medical Service Corps, the Nebraska State and Douglas County Medical Societies. His club is the University Club. Residence: Omaha.

Robert Cotton Vance

Robert Cotton Vance, farmer and humorist, was born at Crete, Nebraska, December 24, 1886, son of Robert Colville and Nellie Amelia (Cotton) Vance. Robert Vance, Sr., was born at Florence, Pennsylvania, July 4, 1836, of Revolutionary stock, and pioneered in Nebraska in 1868. His grandfather was a captain in the Revolutionary Army, and his ancestry was Scotch-Irish. Nellie Amelia, wife of Robert, was born in Saco, Maine, November 3, 1846, and died at Crete January 14, 1908. She was of English stock, her ancestors serving in the Revolution. Robert Colville Vance died at Hot Springs, Arkansas, February 4, 1908.

Robert Cotton Vance attended country school, and since his school days has lead an interesting and varied life. He was a railroad man in Pennsylvania, and a miner and prospector in Mexico. For some time he was postal clerk in El Paso, and in 1913 returned to Nebraska where he has engaged in farming and stock raising.

A humorous writer, he has contributed to many humorous magazines and agricultural papers and is the creator of *Idle Ike*. His social club is the Yellow Dog Club of Lincoln. He is fond of hunting, and devotes his leisure time to reading.

Of his marriage to Emma Amelia Sempf, at Pittsburg, Pennsylvania, there are four children living: Robert, born July 27, 1909; Helen, born December 16, 1907; Julius, born January 22, 1911, and Nancy, born March 1, 1914. John, twin of Julius died January 4, 1923. Residence: Milford.

Frank Ellsworth Van Cleave

One of the leading lawyers in Furnas County, Nebraska, Frank Ellsworth Van Cleave has been engaged in farming and the practice of law for the past 20 years. He was born in Furnas County, January 29, 1887, the son of Rachel Chenoweth and Cornelius Johnson Van Cleave. His father, who was a farmer, was born in Montgomery County, Indiana, May 14, 1836, and died at Holbrook, Nebraska, June 3, 1915. His mother, whose ancestry was English and Scotch-Irish, was born in Vigo County, Indiana, August 15, 1845, and died at Holbrook, Nebraska, June 29, 1915.

Mr. Van Cleave was graduated from the Wilsonville High School in 1905, and from 1910 to 1913, was a student at the University of Nebraska. A Democrat, he served as deputy county clerk from 1914 to 1916, was county clerk from 1917 to 1918, and was county judge from 1925 to 1932.

He was united in marriage with Lora Clair Munger in Furnas County, March 7, 1923. Mrs. Van Cleave, whose ancestry is English, was born in Hamilton County, Kansas, December 3, 1887; she is interested in art. They have the following children: Mary Esther, born January 27, 1924; and Ada Louetta, born April 2, 1928.

Judge Van Cleave is a member of the Nebraska State Bar Association, The Nebraskana Society, and the Masons. Residence: Beaver City.

George Dewey Van Cleef

George D. Van Cleef, leading banker of Thayer County, was born at Hubbell, Nebraska, August 2, 1898. His father, George C. Van Cleef, a farmer, was born at Vinton County, Iowa, January 16, 1854, of Holland descent. His mother, Margaret E. Van Cleef, was born in Vinton County, May 1, 1856, and died at Hubbell, Nebraska, August 19, 1929. She was of French ancestry.

Educated first in Hubbell public schools, Mr. Van Cleef was graduated from Hubbell High School in 1914 and afterward attended Fairbury Business College. There he took an active part in debating.

His marriage to Willa Alerta Holly was solemnized August 6, 1924, at her home in Narka, Kansas. They have one daughter, Bonnie June, born July 29, 1928.

Mr. Van Cleef has been a resident of Nebraska his entire life. He was associated with the Harbine Bank of Fairbury, Nebraska, from 1917 to 1920, and from 1920 until 1932, was with the Farmers and Merchants State Bank of Hubbell. He is now assistant cashier of the Hubbell Bank.

His religious affiliation is with the Methodist Episcopal Church of Hubbell. He is a member of the Nebraskana Society, a former member of the board of education, and his hobby is insurance. Residence: Hubbell.

Dana Burgess Van Dusen

Dana Burgess Van Dusen, lawyer, was born at Omaha, December 12, 1891, son of James Hamilton and Eugenie (Yawger) Van Dusen. His father, who was a native of New York, practiced law in Omaha until his death. He was descended from Holland Dutch settlers of the Van Dusen family in New Amsterdam about 1620, and the Burgess and Arnold families. Eugenie Yawger, who was born at Union Springs, New York, is descended from German Yawger and French deMersereau families settlers who came to America about 1725.

Mr. Van Dusen was graduated from Omaha High School in 1908, and received his A. B. from the University of Nebraska in 1912. He was managing editor and editor in chief of the *Cornhusker* during the year 1911-12, was president of the Nebraska Chapter of Phi Gamma Delta in 1912, and was elected to membership in the Innocents and the Iron Sphinx. He was also captain of cadets and a member of the English Club. He entered Creighton Law School for the year 1913, and attended Harvard 1914 and 1915.

Upon his admission to the bar in 1915 he entered the law department of the Union Pacific Railroad. He was later a member of the firm of Brown, Baxter and Van Dusen, and was city attorney and later corporation counsel of Omaha, serving from 1921-29. Since 1929 he has been general counsel of the Metropolitan Utilities District of Omaha. He is now a member of the firm of Brogan, Ellick and Van Dusen, and general counsel for the Northwestern Life Insurance Company of Omaha.

On April 21, 1919, he was married to Elise Maund Smith at Wilmington, North Carolina. They have two children, Jean Rowe, born in January, 1920, and Betty Jane, born in June, 1922.

Mr. Van Dusen held the rank of captain, 36th U. S. Infantry, 12th Division, in the World War. He is a member of the American Legion. His professional organizations include the American Bar Association and the Nebraska State Bar Association. He is a Presbyterian, but attends Trinity Cathedral. His clubs are the University Club, the Omaha Club and the Omaha Country Club. Residence: Omaha.

Rolla Clayton Van Kirk

Rolla Clayton Van Kirk was born at Brunswick, Nebraska, February 13, 1894, son of Clay B. and Mabel L. (Staples) Van Kirk. His father, who was born in Paris, Kentucky, is bailiff of the Federal Court at Lincoln. His ancestry is Holland. Mabel L. Van Kirk, his mother, was born at Stewartsville, Minnesota, and is of Scotch descent.

Mr. Van Kirk attended public and high school, Yankton College and the University of Nebraska, where he received his LL.B. He is a member of Alpha Sigma Phi and Phi Alpha Delta. Upon his admission to the bar in 1923, he entered active practice, and is at present associated with the law firm of Burkett, Wilson, Brown, Wilson and Van Kirk. A Republican, he served as a member of the house of representatives 1927-30 and member of the state senate 1931-33.

During the World War he served as a private in the United States Marines, 2nd Division; he now holds the rank of first lieutenant in the 134th Infantry, Nebraska National Guard, and is a member of the American Legion, Forty and Eight, Reserve Officers Association, Veterans of Foreign Wars and Disabled Veterans of America.

He was married to Lenore Catherine Burkett, a teacher of music at Lincoln, December 27, 1924. Their son, Clayton Burkett, was born September 17, 1929. They attend Trinity Methodist Episcopal Church. Mr. Van Kirk is a member of the Nebraska State Bar Association, the Elks and the Masons. His club is the Lincoln Country and his hobby National Guard activities. Residence: Lincoln.

Vernon Samuel Van Norman

Vernon Samuel Van Norman, who was born at Moville, Iowa, August 4, 1890, is the son of Samuel Seward and Sadie Anna (McKee) Van Norman. His father, who was born at Moscow, Wisconsin, April 1, 1868, is a farmer and stockman. His mother, a practical nurse, whose ancestry is Scotch, English and Irish, was born at Sioux City, Iowa, March 23, 1870.

Mr. Van Norman studied pedagogy at the high school of Pierce, Nebraska, and later attended Wesleyan University and Wayne Normal College. He was active in all athletics at Wesleyan University. For a time he engaged in farming in Rock County, was a teacher there for six years, and for the past six years has been manager and

bookkeeper of the Bassett Lumber Yard, Bassett, Nebraska.

He is vice president of the Lions Club, is secretary of the County Fair Board, is chairman of the Rock County High School Association, and is serving as president of the Bassett School Board. Mr. Van Norman holds membership in the Red Cross, is a member of the Board of Regents of the Parent-Teachers' Association, and is affiliated with the Odd Fellows, Masons, and Modern Woodmen of America. He is a member of the Bassett Methodist Episcopal Church and is serving as superintendent of the Sunday School in that denomination. A Republican, he served as county assessor of Rock County one term.

His marriage to Josephine Margaret Linke occurred at Bassett, January 1, 1914. Mrs. Van Norman, whose ancestry is German, was born at Bassett, December 28, 1894. They have three children: Robert, born October 18, 1917; Warren, born June 26, 1923; and Raymond, born December 8, 1927. Residence: Bassett.

Ralph Alexander Van Orsdel

Ralph Alexander Van Orsdel, lawyer, was born at Newcastle, Pennsylvania, February 6, 1884, son of Joseph G. and Hannah Elizabeth (Pomeroy) Van Orsdel.

Mr. Van Orsdel attended public school at Independence and Dallas, Oregon, and in 1906 received his Bachelor of Arts degree from the University of Nebraska. In 1910 he received the Bachelor of Laws degree from Creighton University.

His marriage to Esther Amelia Hunter was solemnized at Fremont, July 1, 1913. Mr. Van Orsdel is a member of the Second Church of Christ, Scientist, the Omaha, Nebraska State and American Bar Associations, the Chamber of Commerce, the Masons, Knights Templar, and Shrine. Residence: Omaha.

Robert Van Pelt

Robert Van Pelt, lawyer, was born on a farm in Gosper County, Nebraska, September 9, 1897. His father, Francis M. Van Pelt, was born near Perry, Illinois, July 11, 1857, of Pennsylvania Dutch ancestry. Sarah (Simon) Van Pelt, his mother, who was born in Dane County, Wisconsin, September 13, 1858, is Norwegian.

Mr. Van Pelt attended the public school at Stockville, Nebraska, and was graduated in 1910. In 1914, he was graduated from the Franklin Academy at Franklin, Nebraska. He was awarded the A. B. degree at Doane College, at Crete, Nebraska, in 1920, and received the LL. B. degree at the University of Nebraska in 1922. A letterman in track at Doane, he is a member of Delta Sigma Rho, Phi Sigma Kappa, and Phi Delta Phi.

A rural school teacher in Frontier County, Nebraska, in 1914 he was deputy county treasurer in Frontier County; 1915-16, was associated with Stewart, Perry & Stewart, lawyers at Lincoln, 1921-24; and was with the firm Stewart, Perry, Stewart & Van Pelt, 1925-1926. From 1927 to 1929, he was with Perry & Van Pelt, and since 1929, he has been associated with Perry, Van Pelt and Marti.

Mr. Van Pelt is a Republican. Since 1930, he has been assistant United States attorney.

His marriage to Mildred Ruth Carter was solemnized at Fullerton, Nance County, Nebraska, June 17, 1925. Mrs. Van Pelt was born at Genoa, Nance County, Nebraska, March 3, 1899. They have one son, Robert Van Pelt, born March 22, 1928.

In the World War Mr. Van Pelt served in the O. T. C. at Camp McArthur, Texas. He is a member of the Lancaster County Bar Association, (secretary of this organization for two years), the Nebraska State Bar Association, the American Bar Association, the Junior Chamber of Commerce at Lincoln, and has served on the board of directors of the Young Men's Christian Association since 1924. He is a Scottish Rite Mason and Shriner, and is affiliated with the First Plymouth Congregational Church of Lincoln. Residence: Lincoln.

Sarah Van Pelt

Born at Perry, Wisconsin, September 13, 1858, Sarah Van Pelt is the daughter of Nels and Ele (Olson) Simon. Her father, who was a carpenter and served in the Norwegian Army for four years, was born at Gubrandsdal, Norway, August 26, 1819, and died at Perry, Wisconsin, December 28, 1872. Her mother was born in Gubrandsdal, Norway, October 1, 1815, and died in Gosper County, Nebraska, February 25, 1902.

Mrs. Van Pelt attended the public schools of Wisconsin. She has been actively interested in civic and community affairs at Stockville, Nebraska, for over a half century. She came to Nebraska with her brother, Nels, in a covered wagon in 1874, locating in Gosper County. In the spring of 1875 she went to Moscow, Wisconsin, being employed with a family by the name of Flint, with whom she stayed until 1880; they moving to Iowa. Mrs. Van Pelt, after a visit with her parents at Burton's Bend in Gosper County, went to Dennison, Iowa, where she worked for a family by the name of Laub, then returning to Nebraska procuring a place of employment as cook in the old Arapahoe House, at Arapahoe, Nebraska. Having homesteaded previous to this time in Frontier County, she proved upon the same in 1891, disposing of it in March, 1898. She holds membership in the Royal Neighbors, the Southwest Nebraska Historical Society, the Red Cross, and during the World War was active in local organizations, serving and doing all possible to do her share. She also holds membership in the Nebraskana Society. She is affiliated with the First Congregational Church of Stockville, is past noble grand of the Rebekah Lodge and received the Decoration of Chivalry in York, 1923. She is an ardent prohibition enthusiast.

She was married at Cambridge, Nebraska, March 15, 1885, to Francis M. Van Pelt, who was born in Pike County, Illinois, July 10, 1857. They have one son, Robert Van Pelt, born September 9, 1897; on June 17, 1925, he was married to Mildred Carter at Fullerton, Nebraska. To them were born two children, Robert, born March 22, 1928; and Marjorie, born June 18, 1931. He is United States attorney at Lincoln, Nebraska. Residence: Stockville. (Photograph in Album).

Edward A. Van Steenberg

Edward A. Van Steenberg, banker, born at Hildreth, Nebraska, October 3, 1878, son of Robert and Cornelia M. (Cook) Van Steenburg. The father, born in Nunday County, New York, July 2, 1840, died at Hildreth, Nebraska, November 13, 1913. He was a farmer and a veteran of the Civil War. His wife, Cornelia, was born in Portgage, Wisconsin, July 9, 1842, and died at Hildreth, February 28, 1892. She taught in the first public school in Franklin County in 1872-73.

Educated in public school and at Franklin Academy, Mr. Van Steenburg was a farmer until 1905, and has since been a banker. He is president of the Franklin County Bank of Hildreth, and takes an active part in Republican politics. He has been a member of the school board twelve years, county treasurer 1912, 13, 14, 15; and from 1929-32 has been a member of the board of county supervisors.

On November 13, 1908, he was married to Frances M. Dennis at Auburn. She was born in New York City May 30, 1888. There are three children, Earl, born August 11, 1909; Edna, born October 19, 1910; and Ada, born June 6, 1916.

Mr. Van Steenburg is a member of the Methodist Episcopal Church, the Red Cross, the Odd Fellows and the Parent Teachers Association. Residence: Hildreth.

Guy Van Steenberg

Born at Macon, Nebraska, September 24, 1880, Guy Van Steenberg is the son of Robert William and Cornelia Melissa (Cook) Van Steenberg. His father, who served in the Civil War and who was a farmer for many years, was born in New York, July 2, 1840. Coming to Nebraska July 2, 1872, he homesteaded on Macon Prairie, and died at College View, Nebraska, November 2, 1913. His mother, who was a teacher before her marriage, was born in New York, July 9, 1842. She came to Nebraska on the same wagon train with Robert Van Steenberg and they were married in Franklin County, in 1873. She was one of the first school teachers of Franklin County, and died at Macon, February 27, 1892.

Mr. Van Steenberg attended rural school and was a student at Franklin Academy for two years. He served as director of the rural school board, 1910-27, and is a charter member and past president of the Rotary Club. He is a member of the Beaver City Chamber of Commerce, the Nebraskana Society, and the Methodist Episcopal Church. He is a Mason. As a farmer near Beaver City, he takes an active interest in all community affairs. His hobby is reading.

He was united in marriage with Armanda Jane Keim at Bloomington, Nebraska, December 24, 1903. Four children were born to them: Mildred, March 1, 1905, who is a teacher; Ivan March 7, 1907, a student in law school; Irma, July 26, 1911, who is a teacher; and Richard, March 15, 1917, who is a student in high school. Residence: Beaver City.

Ward Henry VanTilborg

On April 18, 1903, Ward Henry VanTilborg was born at Alva, Oklahoma, son of Harry Bismark VanTilborg and Elizabeth N. (Gitthens) VanTilborg. His father was born in Sheboygan, Wisconsin, August 22, 1869, of Dutch parentage, and is a salesman. His mother is of Scotch-Irish parentage and was born in Platte City, Missouri, March 15, 1868.

Ward Van Tilborg received his education in Loveland, Colorado, and Lincoln, Nebraska, and in 1931 he received the degree of Bachelor of Arts from the University of Nebraska. On July 9, 1926, he was united in marriage with Agnes Mae Meyers at Omaha. She was born at Hemingford, Nebraska, June 6, 1902, of German parentage. They have a son, Ross, who was born September 22, 1927.

Mr. VanTilborg was an intertype operator while he attended the university. He was principal of the high school at Rulo, Nebraska, in 1925, and from 1926-30, was superintendent of the schools at Hordville, Nebraska. At present he is superintendent of the schools in Ulysses, Nebraska.

He is affiliated with the Christian Church and the Democratic party. He holds membership in the Ulysses Commercial Club and is a member of The Nebraskana Society. Tennis and reading are his favorite recreations. Residence: Ulysses.

Emily Lucinda Van Valin

Emily Lucinda Van Valin, pioneer Nebraskan, was born at Hudson, Michigan, February 11, 1842, a daughter of Simon and Nancy (Warner) Piper. Her father, a native of Ontario, New York, was born June 5, 1817, and died at Hudson, March 12, 1857, after a successful life as a farmer. He was of Scotch-Irish descent. His wife, Nancy Warner, was born in Ontario, March 13, 1813, and died at Hudson, January 10, 1856.

Educated first in rural schools, Emily Piper later was a college student at Albion, Michigan. Following her marriage to Joseph Van Valin, and in 1871, the family removed to Saunders County, Nebraska, and two years later settled in Nuckolls County, where Mr. Van Valin died in 1905.

Of their marriage there are five children: Frank, born September 20, 1864, who married Bertha Williamson; John Isaac, born December 17, 1886, who married Susan Youngs; Alexander, born October 20, 1869, who married Anna Earle; Emily Esther, born January 3, 1875, who married Leroy Warren Knapp; and M. J. Inez, born February 28, 1881, who married Fred David James.

Mr. and Mrs. Van Valin made their first trip together into Nuckolls County with two wagons, one of which was drawn by oxen, the trip taking eight days. The first year corn was planted on the homestead, and the next year wheat and corn. It was those crops which were entirely consumed by the great hordes of grasshoppers which invaded the entire country that year.

Joseph Van Valin's family lived in a dugout for some six years after settling in Nuckolls County, and Mrs. Van Valin recalls, among the other hardships and privations incident to the times, the many soakings her family received when rain poured through their dirt roof. Some time thereafter Mr. Van Valin went to Edgar where he procured lumber and shingles and built a good roof for his underground home.

A resident of Nebraska for sixty years Emily Van Valin is now ninety years of age. However, her mental faculties are unclouded and she recalls still the building of the first school house in District No. 14, two miles east of Nelson, and the first teacher, who was then Miss Ola Carlson, afterward Mrs. Ethan Parker. She also remembers the erection of the first church, and the first newspaper, *The Inter Ocean* established by Dr. Case, Nelson's first physician. Dr. Case was assisted in his newspaper work by a young man named Oakley Maury.

Mrs. Van Valin has from girlhood taken an active part in church work, and for many years has been affiliated with the Methodist Church at Nelson. She is a charter member of Chapter No. 27, of the Order of Eastern Star, and was first worthy matron of the chapter. Recently she was elected to life membership in The Nebraskana Society. Residence: Nelson.

Thomas Vasey

Thomas Vasey, who has been a farmer in Nebraska for the past 48 years, was born at Scarborough, Yorkshire, England, January 9, 1867, the son of Thomas and Hannah (Dowsland) Vasey. His father, who was a farmer, was born at Brompton, Yorkshire, England, December 23, 1822, and died at Blue Springs, Gage County, Nebraska, July 1, 1894. His mother was born at Eberston, Yorkshire, England, September 17, 1822, and died at Holmsville, Gage County, Nebraska, August 13, 1888. She was active in church work.

Mr. Vasey received his education in the elementary schools of England and the rural schools of Gage County. A Republican, he was precinct committeeman for 30 years, and attended the territorial convention in Kansas City. For 16 years he was road overseer, and for over 15 years he has been director on the local school board.

He was a charter member of the Presbyterian Church and has been elder in the church and treasurer and teacher in the Sunday School. During the World War Mr. Vasey took a prominent part in Liberty loan drives and Red Cross work. He is a member of the Nebraskana Society.

On May 10, 1885, he was married to Cordelia Jones at Chester, North Wales. Mrs. Vasey, who was born in North Wales, May 10, 1867, is the daughter of G. V. Jones who served in the state legislature from 1897 to 1901. Residence: Blue Springs.

Byron B. Vaughan

Byron B. Vaughan, newspaper editor and publisher at Blue Hill, Nebraska, is a leader in civic and educational affairs in his community. He was born at Una-

dilla, Nebraska, December 24, 1894, the son of Charles E. and Lily M. (Becker) Vaughan, the former a native of Washburn, Illinois. His mother was born in Pennsylvania, in 1855. His parents are now residing at Guide Rock.

Mr. Vaughan attended Grand Island College Academy spent five years as assistant cashier of the State Bank of Edgar, Nebraska, 1913-20, and was assistant cashier of the Marcus State Bank, Marcus, Iowa, from 1920-25. He served as bookkeeper for the F. E. Scott Commission Company at Sioux City, Iowa, for eighteen months, and for nearly five years has been editor and publisher of the *Blue Hill Leader,* Blue Hill.

He entered the United States Army September 5, 1917, was commissioned second lieutenant in 1918, assigned to the 10th Division, Company K, 69th Infantry; at this time he is commander of the local American Legion Post. He is a member of the board of education at Blue Hill, the Red Cross, the Blue Hill Commercial Club of which he is secretary, and the Blue Hill Masonic Lodge. He holds membership in the Nebraska Editorial Association, is affiliated with the Methodist Episcopal Church, and is a member of the Nebraskana Society. His hobby is baseball.

On November 18, 1920, he married Opal Retta Brookley at Edgar, Nebraska. Mrs. Vaughan, who was associated with her father in the drug business and is a registered pharmacist, was born at Juniata, Nebraska, January 2, 1895. Two children were born to this union; William, March 24, 1922; and Thomas, November 8, 1925. Mr. Vaughan is a member of the Republican party. Residence: Blue Hill.

Miles Matthew Vaughn

Miles M. Vaughn was born at Carman, Illinois, November 25, 1866. His father, Matthew Vaughn, who was a farmer, was descended from English ancestors who settled in Dayton, Ohio, in 1849. He was born at Pontypool, Monmouthshire, England, November 10, 1829, and died at Burlington, Iowa, February 12, 1905. Mary Ann (Mardsen) Vaughn, his wife, was born at Dayton, and died at Carman, February 28, 1879. Her ancestry was English.

Mr. Vaughn received his elementary education in the public schools. In 1883 and 1884 he taught school after which he attended college at Quincy, Illinois, where he was graduated in 1888. He has lived in Nebraska for 42 years, and has always taken an active part in civic and educational affairs. He is engaged in the real estate business at Nebraska City, and is at the present time mayor of Nebraska City, elected on the Republican ticket.

He was united in marriage with Leonora May McAllister, at Nebraska City, October 5, 1898. Mrs. Vaughn was born at Charlottsville, Albemarie County, Virginia, September 7, 1878, and when a small child came to Nebraska with her parents. They have four children: Mary Ardis, born September 9, 1899, who married King Yates; Mildred Ila, born May 23, 1913; Miles Matthew, born September 5, 1916; and Charles Edward, born October 16, 1918.

During the late war, Mrs. Vaughn assisted the Red Cross workers in sewing and knitting. She is a member of the Child Welfare Organization. She is a member of the National Congress of the Parent-Teachers' Association, having served as vice president, 1927-28, and president, 1928-29. In 1929 and 1930, she served as president of District Number Two of this organization, a district covering 16 counties with a main office at Omaha. She is affiliated with the First Methodist Episcopal Church at Nebraska City. Residence: Nebraska City.

Charles Henry Velte

Charles Henry Velte, educator, was born at Lexington, Nebraska, August 7, 1889, son of Adam F. and

Minnie F. (Bauerkamper) Velte. His father, who was born in Wehrheim, Germany, September 8, 1854, resided at Hebron, Nebraska, until his death on November 1, 1918. He was a prominent farmer and served as county commissioner. His wife, Minnie, was born in Germany, in 1858, and is still living.

Educated in the public and high schools of Hebron, Charles Henry Velte received his A. B. from Hastings College, and in 1929 was awarded his M. A. from the University of Nebraska. During 1914-16 he was principal of the high school at Shelton, Nebraska, and during 1916-18 was superintendent of city schools at Stuart.

During the World War, 1918-19, Mr. Velte held the rank of second lieutenant in the United States Army Air Service, and in the spring of 1919 was principal of the Shelton High School. Since 1919 he has been superintendent of city schools at Crete, Nebraska.

On August 16, 1916, he was united in marriage to Eglantine C. Skillman at Broken Bow, her birthplace. Mrs. Velte was born August 16, 1892, and is of early American ancestry. They have three children, Clare, born September 6, 1917; Phyllis, born October 26, 1918, and Charles, born June 18, 1920.

Mr. Velte is a member of the American Legion, and served as commander of Crete Post No. 147 during 1928-29. His professional organizations include the National Education Association, and the Nebraska State Teachers Association, and he is a former president and present member of the executive committee of district No. 1, of the latter organization. From 1928-30 he was director of the Crete Chamber of Commerce, and in 1924 was president of the Rotary Club. Since 1930 he has been secretary of the Crete library board. Mr. Velte is a Republican and takes an active interest in the politics of his party, locally. He is interested in boys' work, and the Boy Scout organization, and is a member of the First Presbyterian Church of Crete. Residence: Crete.

Irvin E. Venell

Irvin E. Venell was born near Shickley, Nebraska, September 25, 1894, and has lived in this state all his life. His father, Nels John Venell, was born at Bravek, Kalmar Lane, Sweden, October 1, 1842, and is still living at Ong, Nebraska, where he is a carpenter and farmer; his father, one brother, and two sisters came to America in 1868. Minnie Wolstrom Venell, mother of Irvin Venell, was born in Sweden, March 29, 1854, and is still living at Ong, Nebraska.

Mr. Venell is a director of the school board at Ong, is a member of the Nebraskana Society, and is affiliated with the Shickley Methodist Church. He took part in Victory, Liberty, and Red Cross loan drives during the World War. He is a Republican.

On October 18, 1915, he was united in marriage with Edith E. Aspegren at Saronville, Nebraska. Mrs. Venell was born near Saronville, March 21, 1896. To their marriage three children were born: Cozette, August 17, 1917; Irvin E., Jr., December 24, 1918; and Curtis, January 3, 1926. Residence: Ong.

Frederick William Vennemann

Frederick William Venneman, physician, has been engaged in active practice at Spencer, Nebraska, since 1924. He was born at Vrasselt, Germany, February 9, 1889, the son of Frederick and Mathilde (Schulte) Vennemann. His father, a teacher, was born at Bienen, Germany, in 1855, and died at Oberd, Germany, July 15, 1916. His mother died at Oberdollen, January 6, 1918.

Dr. Vennemann was graduated from the high school at Emmerich, Germany, in 1910, and studied medicine at Bonn. He received the M. D. degree at Cologne, Germany, in 1916. He has been a physician and surgeon at Lynch and is now engaged in general practice at Spencer where he is chief surgeon in the local hospital.

He is affiliated with St. Marys' Catholic Church, is a member of Nebraska State Medical Society, and holds membership in the Nebraskana Society. He was an officer in the German Army during the World War. Residence: Spencer.

Ralph W. Venrick

Ralph W. Venrick was born at Noractur, Decatur County, Kansas, June 1, 1893, the son of David Frank and Alice (Stackhouse) Venrick. His father, who was born in Coshocton County, Ohio, was a pioneer homesteader in Decatur County, and later a grain dealer; he was engaged in the furniture business from 1900 to his death at DeWitt, Nebraska, February 1, 1928. His ancestry was Pennsylvania Dutch. His mother was born at Rennsalaer, Indiana, August 4, 1857; she is of English descent.

Mr. Venrick was graduated from the DeWitt High School in 1911, and later was a student at Doane College, Crete, Nebraska, for a year. He was graduated from the Hoenschu-Carpenter School of Embalming at Des Moines, Iowa, 1913. At the age of 18 he entered business with his father, and today is secretary-treasurer and general manager of the D. F. Venrick Furniture Company. Incorporated.

He has served on the city council of DeWitt for thirteen years, eleven years of which he was city clerk, and was Democratic precinct chairman for three years. He has lived in Nebraska thirty-three years, and holds membership in the following civic organizations: DeWitt Civic Service Club; Parent-Teachers' Association; Red Cross; and the Nebraskana Society. Mr. Venrick filled the unexpired term of his father as a member of the board of education, after his father's death in 1918, but refused to become a candidate for election to a full term.

He is a member of the Funeral Director's Association. He is affiliated with St. Augustine Episcopal Church; is at present master of the DeWitt Lodge Number 111 of the Ancient Free and Accepted Masons; and holds membership in Modern Woodmen of America and the Ancient Order of United Workmen. During the World War, Mr. Venrick served as secretary of the local Council of Defense, and was a four minute speaker. His sports include golf and kitten ball. His hobbies are the theatre and good music.

On December 26, 1914, he was united in marriage with Edna Alice Rossiter, at Lincoln, Lancaster County, Nebraska. Mrs. Venrick, who was born at DeWitt, October 16, 1891, acts as her husband's assistant in his business. Her English grandparents were pioneers of Gage County; her father served as a member of the Nebraska legislature. Four children were born to them, two of whom are living; Jean Margaret, born October 31, 1915, who died at birth; Jean Marjorie, born August 14, 1917; Virginia Ruth, born October 26, 1919; and Beryl Marie, born October 24, 1921, who died February 5, 1924. Both of the girls are talented musically, and are honor students in school. Jean Marjorie played before the State Musical Association at Omaha, when she was five years of age. Residenceff DeWitt.

Adolph Joseph Vierling

Born at Cincinnati, Ohio, May 16, 1852, Adolph J. Vierling has been an outstanding figure in the business life of Omaha for many years. He is of Alsatian parentage, his father, Francis Charles Vierling having been a native of Saverne, Province of Alsace-Lorraine, February 27, 1817. His mother was born at Saar Union, Province of Alsace-Lorraine, March 3, 1823, her maiden name being Caroline Vollmer. Her death occurred at Chicago, January 27, 1890 Francis Charles Vierling died at Chicago, October 20, 1863.

Adolph J. Vierling attended the public schools of Chicago, and when still a young man came to Omaha. He has been engaged in business here forty-five years, and is president of the Paxton and Vierling Iron Works. He is a Republican, a member of the Chamber of Commerce, the Young Men's Christian Association and the Elks. He attends St. Andrews Episcopal Church. His club is the Field Club.

He was married to Katie Luella Organ at Chicago, October 19, 1876. Mrs. Vierling was born at Washington, Iowa, March 18, 1853, and died at Omaha, July 23, 1913. There are four children: Ray W., born August 9, 1877; Frank Robert, born August 8, 1881; Luella Clara, born January 15, 1889; and Mable Claire, born June 6, 1890. Mr. Vierling's hobby is work and his sports are golf and dancing. Residence: Omaha. (Photograph in Album).

Edwin Vieselmeyer

A farmer and purebred stock raiser, Edwin Vieselmeyer was born at Yuma, Colorado, August 26, 1889. After finishing public school he attended North Western Business College at Beatrice, Nebraska, during the winter of 1906 and 1907.

His father, Fred William Vieselmeyer, was born at Westphalen, Germany, July 25, 1864. He is in the real estate and farm loan business, is a land agent, and a farmer and stock raiser. Carolina (Tatge), wife of Fred W. Vieselmeyer, was born at Waterloo, Iowa, November 15, 1868.

On May 6, 1915, Edwin Vieselmeyer was married to Ida Anna Jagels at Kiowa, Nebraska. They have three children, Alvin, born April 29, 1916; Leona, born November 10, 1918; and Norman, born March 15, 1921.

Mr. Vieselmeyer has been a resident of Nebraska for thirty-nine years, practically all of his life time. All these years he has spent on the same farm, the Pleasant View Stock Farm, four miles west of Deshler. It is Mr. Vieselmeyer's opinion that a farmer in order to succeed should is possible remain on one farm and in this way better its condition, and improve his own financial status. Besides taking an active interest in farming Mr. Vieselmeyer specializes in raising purebred Polled-Shorthorn cattle. He showed the first two Shorthorn cows and calves when the Thayer County Fair started at Deshler. He has shown good useful cattle every year since its organization, and has been awarded scores of ribbons and has received over a hundred dollars at a single showing.

Mr. Vieselmeyer attributes his success to the staying on one farm, and applying the aforementioned principles. He believes that one of the causes of our so-called depression is the fact that many farmers have gone too much into debt, mortgaged their farms and stock and lost all or part of them. Mr. Vieselmeyer believes that we must return to a cash basis, buy if we have the cash, if not, not to go into debt if there is any other way possible. His philosophy is that the secret of the success is to move toward the top little by little; climb the ladder from the bottom up, but not start from the top, for that spells ruin as time shows. Many a man has tried to raise the best show cattle in the world and gone broke simply by starting at the wrong end.

In conclusion it may be stated that Mr. Vieselmeyer has had Christian training and that it is his opinion that therein lies the answer to the question of success. He is glad that Thayer County does not fail to give its children good moral training in order to make future generations more useful and loyal citizens of state and country. During the 39 years of Mr. Veiselmeyer's residence in his locality there have been no divorces, murders, or thefts, an indication of what a Christian training means.

Mr. Veiselmeyer is a Democrat and is active in local politics. He is director of his local school district and of St. Mark's School. He is affiliated with the St. Marks Lutheran Church of Ruskin, Nebraska, and is a member of the Lutheran Aid Association. Baseball is his favorite sport and purebred stock raising is his hobby. Recently, in recognition of his efforts, he was awarded life membership in the Nebraskana Society. Residence: Deshler. (Photograph in Album).

Klas Torsten Vinell

Klas Torsten Vinell, Swedish vice consul, was born at Stockholm, Sweden, January 4, 1898, and was graduated from the University of Stockholm School of Law and the University of Stockholm School of Business Administration.

On April 16, 1921, he was married to Margareta Dorotea Theresia, a native of Stockholm, at New York, New York. Mr. Torsten is vice consul for the Kingdom of Sweden at Omaha, for Nebraska, Iowa, Kansas, Colorado, and Wyoming.

He is a member of the Swedish Lutheran Church, and a lieutenant in the Royal Life Guards of Sweden. Residence: Omaha.

Stephen Philip Visek

Stephen Philip Visek, dental surgeon, was born at Vinkovoi, Austria-Hungary, August 9, 1898, and is the son of Michel Andrew and Pauline Theresa (Dahlberg) Visek.

The father was born in Austria, September 12, 1866, and came to Omaha in 1906. The mother was born in Hungary. Stephen Philip Visek was graduated from Central High School at Omaha, and received the degree of Doctor of Dental Surgery from Creighton University in 1905. In 1912 he attended the Croatian Gymnasium in Slavonia.

His marriage to Mildred Eleanor Johnson was solemnized at Glenwood, Iowa, February 9, 1924. Mrs. Visek was born at Creston, Iowa, September 1, 1904.

Dr. Visek has been in active practice since 1925. He is a member of the Sons of Herman. He is a Christian. Residence: Omaha.

George Olien Virtue

George Olien Virtue, distinguished educator at the University of Nebraska, has lived in Nebraska since 1909, and has taken an active part in civic affairs and educational work. He was born at Abingdon, Knox County, Illinois, November 4, 1861, the son of John Freeborn and Cynthia (Jackson) Virtue. His father, who was a miller and farmer, was born at Mansfield, Richland County, Ohio, and died at Bedford, Taylor County, Iowa, in 1883; his ancestry was Scotch Irish. His mother, whose ancestry was Scotch, was born at Marietta, Ohio, and died at Bedford, Iowa, in 1906.

Dr. Virtue attended the public schools of Illinois and Iowa, and later received the following degrees: A. B., Kansas State University, 1892; A. B., Harvard, 1892; A. M., 1893; and Ph. D., 1897. He was a student at the University of Wisconsin during the summer of 1907, and of 1909. During his college days he took a prominent part in debating and glee club affairs, serving as president of the debating team, and was manager of the glee club.

In 1897 Dr. Virtue received an appointment to teach history and economics at the Teachers College, Winona, Minnesota, where he remained for twelve years. In 1909 he was appointed professor of economics and public finance at the University of Nebraska. During his term of service there he has taught in the summer sessions at the University of Chicago, Minnesota, and California.

While at Winona he served on the Board of Municipal Works, 1906-1909, and has in more recent years done investigational work for the United States Department of Agriculture and the Bureau of the Census. During the war he was for a year on leave of absence in the employ of the United States Shipping Board and the Federal Trade Commission, stationed at Washington. He was a member of Governor Morehead's Commission on Taxation and Revenue, 1913-14, and took an active part in preparing the report of the commission.

He is a member of the Lincoln Lodge Number 19, of the Ancient Free and Accepted Masons, is affiliated with All Souls Unitarian Church at Lincoln and is a member of The Nebraskana Society.

He was married to Meta Wilhemina Vogel at Green Island, New York, September 14, 1897. Mrs. Virtue was born at Danzig, Germany. They have two children: John Bernard, born September 26, 1901, who is a teacher in the English department of Northwestern University; John Bernard, born September 25, 1901, who is a teacher before her marriage. She is married to Gerald M. Almy who is a physics instructor at the University of Illinois. Residence: Lincoln.

Karl Eugene Vogel

Karl E. Vogel, civil engineer, was born at Chelsea, Michigan, May 3, 1883. Israel Vogel, his father, who was a blacksmith, was born at Pleinigen, Wurtemberg, Germany, March 15, 1843. He came to America July 3, 1859, and died at Chelsea, June 20, 1909.

His mother, Fredereiche (Wagner) Vogel, was born of German parents in Washtenaw County, in 1845, and died at Chelsea, May 20, 1909.

Mr. Vogel was graduated from the Chelsea High School in 1901, and then became a student at the University of Michigan, where he studied civil engineering. He was graduated with the A. B. degree in civil engineering in 1905. He has lived in Nebraska for 19 years, and has engaged in business in Omaha, during that time. From 1905 to 1911, he was engineer and shop executive for the American Bridge Company; since 1911 he has been connected with the Omaha Steel Works, acting first as superintendent, later assistant manager, general manager, and vice president. Today he is vice president and general manager of this concern. He is a director and chief engineer of the Plattsmouth Bridge Company.

He was married to Mary Celina Wood at Omaha, December 31, 1912. Mrs. Vogel was born at St. Joseph, Missouri. They have three children: John Phillip, born October 19, 1913; Mary Fredricka, born November 10, 1917; and Ann Elizabeth, born February 1, 1921.

Mr. Vogel is a member of the American Society of Civil Engineers, the American Society for Testing Materials, and the Omaha Engineers' Club. He is past president of the Nebraska Manufacturing Association; past president of the Structural Steel Society; and president of the Central Steel Fabricators. He is a vice president and director in the Omaha Builders Exchange, and is a director in the American Institute of Steel Construction.

He is a Mason, Knight Templar, and Shriner, and a member of the Nebraska State Historical Society, the Nebraskana Society, and the Omaha Commercial Club. His social clubs are the Happy Hollow Club, Carter Lake Club, and the Omaha Athletic Club. He is affiliated with the Kountze Memorial Church, at Omaha. His hobby is philately. He is a Republican. Residence: Omaha.

Rudolph Frederick Vogeler

Rudolph Frederick Vogeler, athletic instructor, was born in New York City, September 28, 1902, son of Rudolph Theodore and Martha Emilie (Kaiser) Vogeler. He attended Cornell University and in 1926 was awarded a diploma from the Ithaca School of Physical Educa-

tion. He has been an instructor in physical education since leaving college.

Mr. Vogeler is a member of the Red Cross, the Young Men's Christian Association, Phi Epsilon Kappa and Delta Sigma Phi. Residence: Lincoln.

Edward Louis Vogeltanz

Edward Louis Vogeltanz was born at Wahoo, Nebraska, October 12, 1895, the son of Joseph and Mary Jisa Vogeltanz. His father, who was a farmer, came to America from Bohemia, in 1865. His mother arrived in this country in 1853.

Mr. Vogeltanz was graduated from the Grand Island Business College in 1912, was a student at Peru State Normal College from 1914 to 1916, and received the A. B. and LL. B. degrees at the University of Nebraska in 1919. In 1918 he was a student at the University of California. His fraternity is Phi Alpha Delta. He has been associated with the following law firms: Norbal Brothers; Landis, Coleman & Mastin, at Seward, Nebraska, 1919; in practice alone, 1920-28, at Ord, Nebraska; and since 1928 Davis & Vogeltanz at Ord.

He is a member of the Rotary Club at Ord, the Chamber of Commerce, the Nebraska State Bar Association, and the Nebraskana Society. As a member of the Catholic Church he is affiliated with the Lady of Our Perpetual Succour Church at Ord, and is a member of the Knights of Columbus of which he has been grand knight for eight years and district deputy for two years.

Mr. Vogeltanz was a flying cadet in the aviation department of the Reserve Officers Training Corps and is now commander of the local American Legion Post. His political affiliation is with the Republican party.

On January 4, 1921, he was united in marriage with Amelia Polak at Wahoo. Mrs. Vogeltanz was born at Prague, August 1, 1897. Their children are: Elizabeth Janet, born November 15, 1922; Raymond, born October 24, 1925; and Rosellen, born April 28, 1921. Residence: Ord.

William August Voigt

Born at Peoria, Illinois, March 24, 1864, William August Voight has resided in Nebraska since 1884. His parents, William Diedrich and Catherine Josephina (Garenfeld) Voigt, were natives of Germany. William D. Voigt was born in Hagen, October 8, 1819, of a family of book publishers. A manufacturer of woolen cassimers in Germany, he emigrated to the United States in 1848, and engaged in the manufacture of tobacco and cigars at Peoria. Later, in 1884, he brought his family to Nebraska, where he entered the mercantile business. His death occurred at Burlington, Iowa, July 23, 1889. His wife, Catherina, was born in Geilenkirchen, near Cologne, Germany, April 12, 1824, and died at Burlington, August 3, 1874.

William August Voigt attended the public schools of Burlington, and was graduated from high school there. Coming to Nebraska in 1884, he served as clerk for Winger and Miller, general merchants in Lincoln for one years. In 1884 he went into the mercantile business with his father in Nelson, continuing until 1911, when he disposed of his stock and entered the real estate business. He is now engaged in farming and real estate operations.

On June 19, 1888, Mr. Voigt was united in marriage to Jennie May Baumbach, at Nelson. Mrs. Voigt, who is of English and German ancestry, was born at Cambridge Springs, Pennsylvania, January 30, 1866. There were two children born to this marriage, Edna M., born June 25, 1889, who died March 25, 1896; and Emma K., born November 10, 1890, who married Vernon C. Wade.

Mr. Voigt is a Democrat. For a number of years

he served as a member of the board of trustees of Hastings College, and for more than twenty-five years was a member of the state executive committee of the Young Men's Christian Association. An ardent Sunday School worker, Mr. Voigt is affiliated with the First Presbyterian Church. He is a member of the Chamber of Commerce, and the Nebraskana Society. His hobbies are philately and numismatics. Residence: Nelson.

Lawrence Vold

Lawrence Vold, professor of law at the University of Nebraska, was born at Dunlap, Brule County, South Dakota, April 11, 1886. His father, Asbjorn Vold, who was born in Norway, April 30, 1855, and died at Platte, South Dakota, January, 1921, was a farmer and architect; he served as a member of the school board and town board in South Dakota. His mother, Bertha Vold, who was a high school teacher and musician, was born in Norway, February 20, 1857, and died at Platte, South Dakota, May 1918.

Dr. Vold was graduated from the St. Paul High School in 1906. He holds these degrees: A. B., 1910; LL. B., 1913; S. J. D., 1914; all from Harvard University. He was a member of the Agora Debating Club, and played second squad football at Harvard. He is a member of Phi Beta Kappa and Phi Alpha Delta.

He was assistant professor and professor of law at the University of South Dakota, 1914-24, and has been professor of law at the University of Nebraska since that date. He is the author of a book on the law of sales and various articles on law and on legal education. He was co-editor of Supplementary Volumes to Cooley's Briefs on Insurance, 1919. Politically, he is a Republican.

During the World War Dr. Vold taught military law to the Student Army Training Corps at the University of North Dakota, was a Four Minute Man, and speaker in Liberty loan drives. He is a member of the Lincoln Chamber of Commerce, the Lincoln Professional Men's Club, the Nebraskana Society and the Association of University Professors. He served as a member of the local executive committee of the last named organization for the past two years. He is affiliated with the Westminster Presbyterian Church of Lincoln. Among his recreations are golf, tennis and reading.

His marriage to Margaret Anna Bryan was solemnized at Cambridge, Massachusetts, December 25, 1909. Mrs. Vold, who was born at Boston, of Scotch-English parentage, is a writer of occasional poems, and was formerly a teacher. She was a member of the People's Choral Union at Boston. They have two children: Robert D., born December 11, 1910; and Gordon A., an adopted child, born June 24, 1912. Robert was awarded the A. B. degree at the University of Nebraska in 1931, where he was a member of Sigma Xi, Pi Mu Epsilon, Alpha Chi Sigma, and was president of Phi Lambda Upsilon. Gordon is now a student at the University of Nebraska College of Engineers. He was granted his high school letter in swimming at Lincoln. Residence: Lincoln.

John C. Voline

For more than thirty years John C. Voline has been a newspaper publisher in Auburn. He was born near Stockholm, Sweden, October 24, 1878, he came to the United States with his parents while still a boy. The family settled in Iowa, where he attended the public schools of Creston. His father, Andrew Voline, died at Creston, in 1908, and his mother, an active worker in the Lutheran Church, died there in 1911.

Mr. Voline married Celine La Forgue at Prescott, Iowa, July 30, 1905. She was born at Corning, Iowa, December 31, 1884, of French parentage. She is a member of the Mental Culture Club and is active in community affairs. They have no children.

A Democrat, Mr. Voline served as postmaster of South Auburn, from 1913-1919. He has been a resident of the city since 1900. He started to learn the newspaper business on the *Gazette* at Creston, Iowa, in 1893, and came to Beaver City in 1898 to work on the *Beaver City Times*. Since coming to Auburn he has been continuously engaged in the newspaper business, and purchased the *Herald* in 1911, which in 1929 was consolidated with the *Auburn Republican,* and of which he is still owner and publisher. A modern building has just been erected to house the consolidated papers.

Mr. Voline is a member of the Lutheran Church. He is affiliated with the Elks and the Odd Fellows, and belongs to the Auburn Chamber of Commerce and the Kiwanis Club. He is a member of the Nebraska Press Association and the National Editorial Association. His social club is the Auburn Country Club. He is a lover of all sports. Residence: Auburn.

Alice Marie von Bergen

Alice Marie von Bergen, daughter of John F. and Anna Louise (Schultz) von Bergen, was born at Gordon, Nebraska, March 25, 1894. Her father was a native of Meiringen, Switzerland, born August 31, 1854, who died at York, Nebraska, March 17, 1929. An early pioneer he came to Nebraska in the Spring of 1871; his mother was an instructor in the household arts in the schools of Switzerland. Anna Louise Schultz was born in Stettin, Germany, May 13, 1869, and is the daughter of William Schultz, a German army officer who was awarded several medals for bravery.

Miss von Bergen was graduated from York High School in 1911 and received her B. A. degree at the University of Nebraska in 1919. She is a member of Phi Beta Kappa. Since graduation she has been associated with the Roberts Dairy Company of which she is secretary and a director. She is a member of a committee engaged in writing a sales manual for the International Association of Milk Dealers at the present time.

Her chief hobby is raising flowers, although she enjoys traveling and has made trips extensively through the United States, Canada and Europe. Golf is her favorite sport. She is a member of Eastridge Country Club, the Advertising Club, the Altrusa, The Nebraskana Society and is affiliated with Plymouth Congregational Church. Her home is in Lincoln. (Photograph in Album).

Arthur Elmer von Bergen

Arthur E. von Bergen, successful farmer of York County, Nebraska, has lived in this state all his life. He was born at Humphrey, Platte County, Nebraska, March 9, 1902, the son of John F. and Anna Louise (Schultz) von Bergen. His father, who was a farmer and a pioneer Nebraskan, was born at Meiringen, Switzerland, August 31, 1854, and died at York, March 17, 1929. His mother was born at Stettin, Germany, May 13, 1869. Her father, William Schultz, who was a German army officer, was awarded several medals for bravery.

Mr. von Bergen was a student in the public school at York until 1919 when he was graduated from the York High School. He was a student at the University of Nebraska College of Agriculture, 1919-25, where he was a member of the Nebraska Dairy Cattle Judging Team at the the National Dairy Show in 1924. His fraternity is Alpha Gamma Rho.

He was employed at the University of Nebraska in the dairy department, 1923-24, was herdsman for the Upland Dairy Farm at Palmyra, Nebraska, 1925-26, and since 1926 has been owner of the Vonca herd of registered Holstein-Friesen cattle on the von Bergen farm. He has been secretary-treasurer of the Seward-York-

Polk Dairy Herd Improvement Association since 1929, and holds membership in various civic organizations at York. He is a member of the York Rotary Club, the Nebraskana Society, Modern Woodmen of America, Independent Order of Odd Fellows, and the First Presbyterian Church of York. In 1919 Mr. von Bergen was a member of the Nebraska Reserve Officers Training Corps. His chief recreations are hunting and reading.

On October 23, 1926, he was united in marriage with Clare Atkinson at Pawnee City, Pawnee County, Nebraska. Mrs. von Bergen, who is a home maker and noted clubwoman at York, was born at Pawnee City, October 17, 1899. She was graduated from the University of Nebraska where she held membership in Phi Mu. She taught Smith-Hughes Home Economics from 1924 to 1926, and has been a leader in the 4-H Girls Club for some time. She served as president of the York County Federated Woman's Club, 1930-1931, and prior to that was secretary-treasurer of that organization. Mr. von Bergen is a Republican.

Mrs. Von Bergen is the daughter of Charles A. Atkinson who is a descendant of Sir John Peckham who came to America in 1638. John C. Atkinson, father of Charles Atkinson, was born in Yorkshire, England, July 27, 1834, and was one of the first settlers of Nebraska. Mabel Clare Godard, mother of Mrs. von Bergen, was a descendant of Ethan Allan.

One child was born to their marriage: Sherill Lenore, September 15, 1927. Residence: York.

Emil J. von Gillern

Emil J. von Gillern was born in Chicago, on February 20, 1879. His father, Emil Julius von Gillern, was born in Breslau, Germany, in May, 1847, and died at Chicago, May 30, 1885. He was a free born German baron and count and a German counseller. Ella Lenora (Schmidt) von Gillern, his wife, was born at Hoboken, New Jersey, November 28, 1852, and is now living at Beatrice, Nebraska.

Mr. von Gillern attended the Beatrice High School until 1895, and later attended the Kearney Military Academy. He has lived in Nebraska for 47 years, and for the last 30 years has been connected with the Duff Grain Company at Nebraska City. He is now manager of this organization, a director of the Nebraska City Building and Loan Association; and vice president of the Lawless Grain Company of Kansas City, Missouri.

He was united in marriage with Nellie Cannon at Omaha, Nebraska, October 22, 1911. Mrs. von Gillern, who was born at Omaha, January 25, 1881, is a niece of County Attorney John Creighton. Four children were born to this union: Emil, born July 22, 1903; Marion, born January 19, 1909; Gwen, born August 3, 1910, who died August 6, 1910; and Jack, born August 19, 1911.

During the World War Mr. von Gillern served on the Liberty Loan Drive committee. He is an Elk, a member of the Parent-Teachers' Association. Affiliated with St. Mary's Catholic Church he is a member of the church committee, and the Knights of Columbus. His clubs are the Nebraska City Golf Club and the Nebraska City Country Club. His favorite sports are baseball and golf. He is a Republican. Residence: Nebraska City.

Emil M. Von Seggern

Emil M. Von Seggern, publisher, was born at Hooper, Nebraska, February 28, 1882, son of Henry Bernard and Sophia Kathrina (Brockshus) Von Seggern. Henry Von Seggern was born in Oldenburg, Germany, in November, 1845, and came to the United States in 1869. He was a farmer and stock feeder, one of Nebraska's pioneer farmers and earliest livestock shippers. He died at Hooper, in May, 1891. His wife, Sophia, was born in Oldenburg, in November, 1848, and died at Hooper, July 3, 1918.

Educated in the public schools, Mr. Von Seggern worked on his home farm until 21, when he became the publisher of the *Nebraska Volksblatt* (German newspaper). A printer and publisher since that time, he became editor of the *West Point Republican* on January 1, 1917, and still continues. He is independent in politics and has been in the city council for eight years.

On January 2, 1908, he was married at West Point to Margaret Anna Romberg, who was born there on July 11, 1885. There are three sons, Boyd, born October 23, 1908; Marvin, born June 15, 1910, and Robert, born September 22, 1922. Boyd Von Seggern, a member of the journalism class of 1932, University of Nebraska, was chosen editor of the *Daily Nebraskan* for the first semester. He is also a member of the Innocents and of many honorary fraternities. Marvin Von Seggern is a senior in the Engineering College, an Innocent, and a member of a number of honorary fraternities.

Active in Red Cross, Y. M. C. A. and liberty loan work in the World War. Mr. Von Seggern is now a member of the Community Club, the Lions Club and the Masons. His hobbies are reading, mechanics and building.

Emil Von Seggern has a state-wide reputation as a brilliant editor. He has conducted a fight against the bridge trust, led a crusade for the protection of the local power plant and has fought for all public enterprises. For the past twenty-eight years he has taken a stand on all public questions. Residence: West Point. (Photograph in Album).

Carl Friedrich Voss

For 50 years Charles A. Voorhees has lived at Edgar, Nebraska, where he is president of the Clay County State Bank. He was born at Pennington, Mercer County, New Jersey, January 17, 1854, the son of Isaac and Helen Elizabeth (Hunt) Voorhees. His father, who was born at Blawnburg, New Jersey, October 11, 1824, and died at Pennington, July 23, 1895, was a farmer. His mother was born at Stoutsburg, New Jersey, May 5, 1823, and died at Edgar, February 28, 1910.

Mr. Voorhees was a student at Eastman Business College, Poughkeepsie, New York, for a time. He was engaged in farming in New Jersey until 1882 when he moved to Edgar where he has since been a banker. He has been a member of the local school board for 20 years, has been treasurer of the local Red Cross since 1917, and is now a member of the Nebraskana Society. He is affiliated with the First Presbyterian Church of Edgar, is a Mason and Knight Templar, and is a member of the Republican party. His hobby is flowers.

He was united in marriage with Lucy Anna Titus at Pennington, September 15, 1877; she was born at Pennington. The following children were born to them: Frederick, born February 9, 1881, who married Carrie L. Taylor; Bertha, born September 12, 1885, who married Orvie C. Johnston; Blair S., born July 14, 1890, who married Alice Thompson; Olita, born June 22, 1888, who married Frank J. Johnston; Edward R., born June 22, 1900, who married Claire Graul; Clarence W., born June 21, 1880, who died April 27, 1882. Frederick, Clair and Edward are all engaged in the banking business with their father. Residence: Edgar.

Carl Friedrich Voss

Born in Schwerin Mecklenburg, Germany, May 26, 1865, Carl Friedrich Voss is the son of Edward J. Voss and Elsie M. (Ausborn) Voss. His father was born at Schwerin, Mecklenburg, Germany, April 25, 1822, and was a customs officer and first sergeant in the German Army. He died in Germany, June 16, 1875. His wife, Elsie, was born in Mecklenburg, Germany, May 6, 1838, and died there, May 16, 1889.

Carl Voss was graduated from the elementary schools in 1881. On May 25, 1900, Ida E. G. Levermann became his wife at Byron, Thayer County, Nebraska. She was born in Zoelkow, Mecklenburg, Germany, November 31,

1874, and her father was a teacher. To this union five children were born: Fritz, May 20, 1901; Elsie, July 10, 1902, who is married to David R. Steinle; Frieda, January 5, 1904, now the wife of George Gundel; Erica, April 5, 1907, died April 19, 1907; and Otto, November 3, 1913. Fritz is married to Leona Holtzen and is with the Nebraska Light and Power Company. Otto is attending college.

Mr. Voss has been engaged in hardware and undertaking business at Byron for twenty-five years. He is a Republican and is affiliated with St. Paul's Evangelical Lutheran Church at Byron.

Before he came to America, Mr. Voss was a private in a Hunting Troup in Germany. He is a member of the Red Cross, Salvation Army, and holds membership in the Nebraskana Society. Residence: Byron.

Frank Patterson Voter

Frank P. Voter, lawyer and former member of the Nebraska state legislature, was born in Franklin County, Maine, December 28, 1869. He is the son of John R. and Augusta (Patterson) Voter, the former born in Franklin County, in 1832, and the latter in 1835. John R. Voter was a school teacher and died in September, 1907, his wife surviving him until February, 1914.

Educated first in the public schools, Mr. Voter attended the University of Nebraska from which he received his LL.B. in 1894. He has been a resident of the state since the Spring of 1882, and has been actively engaged in practice since his admission to the bar. A staunch Republican, he is active in politics, and served as a member of the state legislature in 1905, and was delegate to the National Republican Convention in 1908.

On October 17, 1898, he was united in marriage to Eva B. Brockway, of Battle Creek, Iowa, at South McAlister, Oklahoma. There are three children, Alma, born December 5, 1899; Gladys, born September 20, 1901, and Harold F., born August 11, 1907.

Mr. Voter is fond of golf, and is president of the Laurel Country Golf Club. During 1917-18 he was president of the Chamber of Commerce and is a member at the present time of the Nebraska State Bar Association, the Red Cross and Young Men's Christian Association. He is a former member of the Parent Teachers Association and was active in civilian projects during the World War. Residence: Laurel.

Francis Ira Waddell

Francis Ira Waddell was born in Dakota County, Nebraska, April 18, 1872, and for the past 60 years has lived in that county. His father, Christie Waddell, who was a pioneer farmer in Nebraska, was born in Ohio, July 3, 1834, and came to the western country in a covered wagon train with the late Gideon Warner; his ancestry was Welsh. His mother was born in Indiana, April 25, 1844, of Pennsylvania Dutch extraction, and died at South Sioux City, Nebraska, October 12, 1907.

Mr. Waddell knew all the experiences of early days in Nebraska, and most of the hardships. He recalls the grasshopper invasion and the disastrous flood of 1881. It is interesting to nite that he crossed the Missouri first in a ferry boat, later on the pontoon bridge, and now has seen the construction of the combination bridge.

He has always been interested in the progress of both his community and the state. During the World War he assisted in Red Cross and war savings drives, and together with his family, did everything possible to co-operate with the government. He is a member of the Republican party and the Nebraskana Society. His favorite sport is hunting.

He was united in mariage with Eve Belle Tunnicliffe, at Sioux City, Iowa, March 16, 1896. Mrs. Waddell was born at Antwerp, Ohio, November 16, 1878, and is descended from the Tunnicliffes who came from England,

in 1875; General Curtis was a relative of her maternal grandmother. Their children are: Ethel, born May 11, 1907, who married Charles Fox; John, born July 25, 1900, who married Lillie Pearl Cain; Sue, born March 18, 1902; Raymond, born January 25, 1904; Phil, born April 18, 1906, who married Sylvia Gertrude Lake; and Lois, born June 13, 1913. Residence: South Sioux City.

Olin Bennett Waddill

Olin Bennett Waddill, executive, was born in Coryal County, Texas, March 28, 1897, and for thirty years has resided in Nebraska. He is the son of Elias Marion and Elizabeth Melvina (Irwin) Waddill.

The father was born in Austin County, Texas, April 12, 1854, and was a rancher until his death at Gordon, on January 18, 1931. The family, which was Scotch-Irish, moved from Tennessee to Texas and settled in Austin County about 1827. Mr. Waddill's great-grandfather and great-grandfather rode to Texas from Tennessee by horseback. His grandfather brought the rest of the family through in a covered wagon. Elisabeth Melvina Waddill was born in Fayette County, Texas, March 6, 1856, and died at Gordon, October 31, 1930. She was active in the work of the Women's Christian Temperance Union. Her mother and father were pillars of strength and honesty through trying times in early days in Texas.

Mr. Waddill attended the elementary and high school at Gordon, graduating from the later in 1917. He was president of his graduating class and a member of the committee of eight. During the years 1918 and 1919 he attended Boyles Business College at Omaha.

At the present time Mr. Waddill is the manager and owner of a retail hardware store at Gordon. He has served as postal clerk, office manager, city clerk and city treasurer, and at present is a candidate for mayor. He has been active in every civic and cultural project in his community. He is affiliated with the Presbyterian Church at Gordon, and at the present time is assistant superintendent of the Sunday School there.

He is past secretary of the Gordon Welfare Board, president of the Gordon Kiwanis Club, an officer in Arcana Lodge No. 195 of the Ancient Free and Accepted Masons, is a member of the board of education, a trustee of his church, and a member of the Nebraskana Society. He is past chairman of the court of honor of the Gordon troop of the Boy Scouts.

His marriage to Alida Mosher was solemnized at Gordon, April 9, 1919. Mrs. Waddill is the daughter of Ward and Mary Mosher. She graduated from Gordon High School and attended Chadron State Normal College, and Boyles Business College at Omaha. Mr. and Mrs. Waddill have two children, Betty Mae, born September 2, 1920; and Olin Joel, born August 15, 1931.

During the late war Mr. Waddill was a first class seaman at the Naval Training Station at San Francisco, California, and in 1921 was a commander of the local post of the American Legion. His favorite sport is baseball, while his hobby is mechanics. Residence: Gordon. (Photograph on Page 1227).

John A. Waggener

John A. Waggener, physician and surgeon, was born at Burksville, Cumberland County, Kentucky, October 6, 1852. Louis Allen Waggener, his father, who was born at Burksville, July 27, 1825, and died there December 6, 1894, was a farmer. He was active in political and civic affairs serving as sheriff for 16 years and clerk of the court for 12 years.

Sarah Elizabeth (Alexander) Waggener, mother of John, was born at Smith's Grove, Warren County, Kentucky, July 21, 1834, and died at Burksville, February 24, 1898.

Dr. Waggener was a student at Alexander College, at

OLIN BENNETT WADDILL

Purdy Studio—Gordon

Burksville, and from 1874 to 1876 studied at Louisville Medical College, where he was graduated as salutatorian of his class. Since leaving school he has practiced medicine continuously, and in 1882, he helped to organize the first medical society in southeastern Nebraska, acting as president of this organization. He has been president several times of the Richardson County Medical Society, and has acted as councillor for the third district of the Nebraska State Medical Association.

He married Annie L. Grinstead at Summer Shade, Barren County, Kentucky, March 12, 1878. Mrs. Waggener was born at Summer Shade, April 3, 1863. They have three sons and one daughter: Hewitt A., born November 1, 1879, who married Ethel Miller; William R., born September 3, 1881, who married Nettie Shier; John T., born September 27, 1883, who married Mabel Shier; and Lillith V., born August 16, 1886. The three boys are all physicians, while the daughter is a graduate of the University of Nebraska, and assistant principal in the Beatrice city schools.

From 1918 to 1919, Dr. Waggener was a member of the Medical Reserve Board. He is a Knight of Pythias, an Odd Fellow, and a member of the Ancient Order of United Workmen, the Security Benefit Association, and the Chamber of Commerce at Humboldt. He is a Democrat. His favorite sport is fishing. Residence: Humboldt.

Joseph Henry Wagner

Born in Cedar County, Iowa, April 22, 1868, Joseph Henry Wagner is the son of Martin and Sarah Ann (Doman) Wagner. His father, born in Pennsylvania, July 21, 1831, was a farmer who settled in Iowa in the middle 1800's. He married Sarah Ann Doman, also a native of Pennsylvania, born November 9, 1831. She died in Richardson County, June 17, 1908.

Joseph Wagner received his education in the country schools of Cedar County, Iowa, and Richardson County, Nebraska, to which he came with his father in 1875. He has been engaged in farming extensively for nearly fifty-five years. Mr. Wagner is a Republican, and a member of the Chamber of Commerce of Stella.

He was united in marriage with Clara Fisher in Nemaha County, October 27, 1892. There are four children: Bertha, born September 26, 1894, who married Lowell Lambert; Elva, born July 12, 1896, married to William Albin; Earl, born June 13, 1902, married Georgia Hoppe, and Ray, born February 29, 1904, who married Ione Kapps. Residence: Stella.

Mary Ann Wagoner

A pioneer in Nebraska is Mary Ann Wagoner who has lived in this state for the past 68 years. She was born at Beardstown, Illinois, December 13, 1862, the daughter of William and Susan Elizabeth (Jones) Durell. Her father, a farmer, was born at Terre Haute, Indiana, October 18, 1833, and died near Auburn, Nebraska, October 14, 1902. Her mother, whose ancestry was Welsh, was born near Fort Madison, Iowa, December 22, 1844, and died at Oklahoma City, Oklahoma, September 30, 1922.

Mrs. Wagoner was one of the organizers of St. Stevens Church at Broadwater, which has now been discontinued. She is affiliated with the Church of the Good Shepherd at Bridgeport and holds membership in the Nebraskana Society. In 1864 she came to Nebraska with her parents, and in 1885 homesteaded in Cheyenne County with her husband.

Her marriage to Carl A. Wagoner was solemnized near Auburn, Nebraska, March 27, 1881. Mr. Wagoner, who was a stockraiser in his younger days, was born at Coshocton, Ohio, December 14, 1857, and died at Alliance, Nebraska, May 23, 1928. Mr. Wagoner's ancestry was German. His parents came to Nebraska in 1864 and settled near Peru. In 1884 they migrated to western Nebraska.

Mr. Carl Wagoner was the first man to raise sugar beets in the western part of the state. He lead a very active life and was a leading figure in solving the irrigation problems of the western people. At the time of his death he was engaged in the oil business at Broadwater.

To Mr. and Mrs. Wagoner was born one child, Thomas Leroy, February 11, 1882, who died June 14, 1882. Residence: Broadwater. (Photograph in Album).

Evard Oliver Waite

Evard O. Waite was born at Laurel, Nebraska, October 12, 1896. Oscar M. Waite, father of Evard was a pioneer merchant until his death at Laurel in 1904. Luella, his wife, was a teacher before her marriage. Oscar Waite was instrumental in the incorporating of Laurel in 1892.

After graduating from Laurel High School in 1917, he worked at the Laurel National Bank, and later he enlisted in the World War. He was employed at the Federal Reserve Bank of Omaha, Nebraska, in 1919, the Laurel National Bank from 1920 to 1926, the Standard Oil Company of Nebraska in 1927, and attended the University of Nebraska from 1928 to 1929. He attended Wayne Normal during the summer of 1928 to 1929.

Mr. Waite is a Republican. He is now the owner of the E. O. Waite Insurance Agency. He has been a member of the American Legion since the World War. He is secretary and treasurer of the Laurel Cemetery Association and treasurer of the city of Laurel. His religious affiliation is with the First Presbyterian Church of Laurel. He is a member of the Masonic Lodge and The Nebraskana Society. Residence: Laurel.

Harold P. Waite

One of McCook's most prominent citizens, Harold P. Waite was born at Swanton, Vermont, on September 28, 1855, and came to Nebraska in April, 1879, with his brother, Edwin, in a covered wagon locating five miles west of Wilsonville on a homestead. There he experienced all the hardships and pleasures of the early settlers. He recalls his first buffalo hunt in December, 1879, and has in his home the hide of his first kill.

His father, Pomeroy Waite, was born at Swanton, Vermont, December 28, 1828, and died at Nashua, Iowa, June 13, 1912. He was a descendant of Thomas Waite, who came to Rhode Island in 1610. Avis Niles, wife of Pomeroy Waite, was born at Swanton, Vermont, October 15, 1830, and died at Nashua, Iowa, May 26, 1910.

Mr. Waite attended common school and Bradford Academy, what was known at that time as Bradford in Chickasaw County, Iowa. From 1896 until 1925 he was in the hardware business at McCook. He is a director of the First National Bank at the present time. From 1873 until 1878 he taught rural school in Iowa, coming to McCook in 1888. A Republican, Mr. Waite has held many minor political offices, including a member of the city council, and was elected mayor in 1905, for two terms.

He is treasurer of the Associated Charities of McCook, a member of the Chamber of Commerce, a member of the Elks Lodge No. 1434, and is a former member of the Nebraska State Historical Society, also of the National Geographic Society.

On December 9, 1885, he was married to Jessie B. Randolph at Cambridge, Nebraska. Mrs. Waite was born at Indianola, Iowa, March 1863, and died at McCook, July 5, 1922. Her family came from Virginia to Indiana. They have two children, Edna, born October 10, 1886; and Edith, born June 15, 1888, who married Dr. Al Kee at McCook, December 9, 1914. Residence: McCook.

Willis Roseberry Waite

Willis Roseberry Waite, son of John Daniel and Juliette (Roseberry) Waite, was born at Palmyra, Iowa, July 22, 1870. His father, a farmer and steam engineer, served from 1862 until 1863 with the New Jersey Volunteers during the Civil War. He was born at Pittstown, New York, May 12, 1830, and died at Arcadia, October 20, 1891. His wife, Juliette, was born in Bethlehem, New Jersey, October 1, 1834, and died at Loup City, December 9, 1912. Both were of English descent.

Educated in public school at Palmyra, Iowa and Arcadia, Nebraska, Mr. Waite was later graduated from the Columbian Business College at Chicago and the Capital City Commercial College at Des Moines.

Coming to Nebraska from Palmyra, Iowa, with a team and covered wagon, he started on September 30, 1880, and arrived at Loup City nearly a month later, Sunday, October 24, 1880. He taught school and music, engaged in bookkeeping and then began farming. Strongly inclined to horticulture, he now has an orchard of 142 trees of 28 varieties. These include all the late improved apples, among them four varieties of Delicious trees, sixty-six in number.

For the past fifteen years Mr. Waite has been secretary and treasurer of the Hayes-Creek Threshing Machine Company, composed of himself and seven neighbors. A progressive Republican, he was a member of the Nebraska house of representatives 1925-26 (43rd session), but was defeated for a second term.

He was married to Abbie Grow at Loup City, October 25, 1899, and to them were born three children: Charles Edmund, born January 9, 1901, who married Frances Mildred Kennedy; Lucy Grow, born April 17, 1902; and Alice Helen, born June 3, 1916. Mrs. Waite was born at Loup City, October 18, 1879.

Mr. Waite's parents, John D. and Juliette (Roseberry) Waite, had five children, as follows: Charles Edmund, born in New Jersey July 16, 1854, died in Nebraska, February 2, 1883; William Henry, born in New Jersey, June 6, 1856, died in Mexico, April 4, 1912; Elmer Ellsworth, born in Minnesota, August 31, 1866, lives at Vancouver, Washington; Willis Roseberry, born in Iowa, July 22, 1870, the subject of this sketch; and Wilber Stanton, born in Iowa, July 22, 1870, who lives in Loup City.

During the World War period Mr. Waite was part time president and part time secretary of the local registration board. He is affiliated with the Methodist Episcopal Church and is a life member of The Nebraskana Society. He enjoys baseball and horseshoe pitching, while his hobbies are music and orcharding. Residence: Arcadia.

John W. Waitman

John W. Waitman was born at Webster City, Iowa, June 13, 1879, son of Watson L. and Lavinia (Wilcox) Waitman.

The father was born in Pennsylvania, July 29, 1849, and was a pioneer farmer in Nebraska. He died at Chappell, November 26, 1887. His wife, Lavinia, was born at Vinton, Iowa, April 12, 1852, and died at Bayard, Nebraska, February 8, 1915. She was a teacher of English descent. Mr. Waitman was graduated from school at Center Valley, in 1895. He has been with the reclamation department of the Department of the Interior for 20 years, beginning as a laborer, and being promoted to superintendent of irrigation. At the present time, he is watermaster for the Gering and Fort Laramie Irrigation District at Lyman, Nebraska. He is a Republican.

His marriage to Maud Fletcher was solemnized at Mitchell, on April 25, 1911. Mrs. Waitman was born at Atwood, Kansas, September 12, 1887, and is of English descent. There were six children born to them, five of whom are living, Ruth, January 13, 1913; Mearl W., Jan-

uary 6, 1915; Mary E., November 17, 1915; John F., born March 11, 1918, who died September 29, 1920; Dean L., April 2, 1926; and Billie L., March 10, 1928.

During the late war, Mr. Waitman was active in Red Cross and loan drives. He is a member of the Chamber of Commerce, the Odd Fellows, the Parent Teachers Association, and is a school trustee. His favorite sport is baseball. Residence: Lyman.

Clifton Henry Walcott

On February 26, 1882, Clifton H. Walcott was born at Hudson, Middlesex County, Massachusetts, the son of David Knights and Persis Victoria (Cutting) Walcott. His father, who was a farmer, was born at Bolton, Massachusetts, December 15, 1837, and died at Leominster, Massachusetts, September 11, 1897. His English ancestors came to America shortly after the arrival of the *Mayflower;* one of his ancestors was lord mayor of London, and was distinguished by defeating the King of England at chess, and was awarded a coat of arms, with a chessman worked on it, by the king; the coat of arms is still used by the Walcott family.

His mother was born at Berlin, Worcester County, Massachusetts, July 12, 1840, and died at Leminster, August 5, 1911. Her ancestry was English.

Mr. Walcott, who has been a clergyman for the past 20 years, attended the public schools of Leominster, and was graduated from the Mount Herman Preparatory School in 1906. He was awarded the A. B. degree at Brown University, 1910; the B. D. at Newton Theological Institution, 1913; and was a student at the University of Nebraska, 1929-30. He was a member of the Brown University debating team for three years; was president of Phi Gamma Delta; and was active in football, hockey, track and basketball at Brown University. He was a member of the Sphinx Club and Delta Sigma Rho, national intercollegiate debating society and Phi Beta Kappa.

He has held the following pastorates: First Baptist Church, Ashland, Massachusetts, 1911-13; First Baptist Church, Sharon, Massachusetts, 1913-20; First Baptist Church, Winchester, Massachusetts, 1920-26; and since 1926, First Baptist Church of Lincoln, Nebraska. He is the author of sermons in religious periodicals, papers written for the Boston Literary Society, and other religious publications.

He was united in marriage with Adelaide Eleanor Payton at Leominster, March 22, 1911. Mrs. Walcott, who is of English descent, was born at Waterloo, Quebec, Canada, March 8, 1883. They have two children: Jane, born June 2, 1917, and David, born September 18, 1921.

Mr. Walcott was awarded a medal for his unceasing efforts in loan drives during the World War. He was president of the Lincoln Ministerial Association, 1929; was a director of the Social Welfare Society, 1927-29, and is now vice president; and was a director and member of the headquarters committee of the Anti-Saloon League, 1926-31. He was a member of the Professional Men's Club, 1926-28. He holds membership in the Hiram Club; the Young Men's Christian Associtaion; and the Nebraskana Society. He is a Mason, Blue Lodge and Chapter. Formerly he was active in tennis, football, hockey, basketball, and baseball; his sports now include golfing and bowling. His hobby is the study of philosophy. He is an independent Republican. Residence: Lincoln.

Peter Waldorf

Peter Waldorf, a resident of the Nebraska since 1878, was born near Mendota, LaSalle County, Illinois, March 14, 1857, the son of Phillip and Margaret (Gudtt) Waldorf. His father was a farmer who was born in Germany, November 28, 1813, and died at Mendota, October 26,

Nelson Studio—Hastings

PETER WALDORF

1863. His mother was born in Germany, October 17, 1817, and died at Mendota, October 12, 1891.

Mr. Waldorf attended the rural schools through the eighth grade and then farmed until the age of 16 years when he served as an apprentice to a carriage builder at Chicago, Illinois. In 1875 he became a carriage builder at Morrison, Illinois, where he stayed for two years. From 1878 to 1884, he was in partnership with his brother, William Waldorf, at Wilber, Nebraska; and was in a hardware and furniture business of his own at Western, from 1884 to 1912, when he retired. He is now president of the Western Lumber Company at Western, Nebraska.

His marriage to Olive Flora was solemnized at Wilber, November 25, 1880; she was born in Pennsylvania, January 28, 1859, and died at Western, October 13, 1897. Four children were born to them: Flora May, born May 22, 1883, who married Melvin Kitzenger; Margaret, born June 6, 1886, who married Robert C. Ashby; Louis W., born June 12, 1890, who married Roxanna Wohrelsdorf, and who is in the mercantile business at Eugene, Oregon; and LaRhea, born November 1, 1894, who married Wylan Drewrey.

Mr. Waldorf is a member of the Red Cross, the First Methodist Church, and the Nebraskana Society. He is past master of Western Lodge Number 140, Ancient Free and Accepted Masons, and holds membership in the Shrine and Commandery. His political affiliation is with the Republican party.

On August 18, 1898, Mr. Waldorf was married to Mrs. Hattie Davis of Western, Nebraska. She was born March 3, 1862, at Albion, New York, of English descent. Mr. and Mrs. Waldorf have always been interested in the welfare of their community and are very well known throughout Saline County. Residence: Western. (Photograph on Page 1230).

Clement LeVerne Waldron

Clement L. Waldron was born at Great Bend, Pennsylvania, February 10, 1884. His father, Arthur K. Waldron was born in New York State, February 29, 1852. He was a railroad man, who came to Nebraska as a young man, and who died at Schuyler, Nebraska, in May, 1908. His wife, Carrie Nash Boone, was a native of New York State, born in 1856. She died at Omaha, in August, 1908.

Mr. Waldron received his elementary education in the grade schools of Lincoln, Omaha and Schuyler, and was graduated from Schuyler High School in June, 1902. He received his A. B. from the University of Nebraska in 1906, studied law there, and then entered the University of Wisconsin, where he continued the study of law and received his M. A. in 1907. He was president of his class at the University of Nebraska, and was a member of the Iron Sphinx, and the Innocents. His fraternities are Phi Gamma Delta, Phi Delta Phi, and Delta Sigma Rho.

On June 14, 1911, Mr. Waldron was united in marriage to Ramona A. Taylor, at Omaha. Mrs. Waldron who was born at Bloomington, Illinois, July 29, 1889, is a direct descendent of Zachary Taylor. They have four children: Dorothy, 18; Taylor, 16; Clement L. Jr., 12, and Barbara Jean, 4.

Mr. Waldron is a Republican. He was state's attorney of Golden Valley County, North Dakota, and city attorney of Beach, North Dakota, 1914-19. He is vice president of the Bankers Savings & Loan Association and of the Puritan Manufacturing Company, and a director of Nye and Jenks Grain Company.

During his university days he was a member of the Pershing Rifles, and in the World War he was a member of the draft board in North Dakota.

He is a member of Dundee Presbyterian Church, and vice president of the Men's Club. He is also a member of the Y. M. C. A. and presdent of the Benson High Parent-Teachers' Association. His professional organizations include the American, Nebraska State and Omaha-Douglas County Bar Associations. He is a member of

the Chamber of Commerce, and of the agricultural committee of that organization, and is greatly interested in farming and stock raising. He is a Mason and an Elk. His social club is the Omaha Club, and his sports are golf and football. Residence: Omaha.

John Albert Walford

John Albert Walford, farmer and general merchant, was born at Peoria, Illinois, February 25, 1863. He is the son of Charles and Martha Ann (Gregg) Walford, the former a native of London, England, born September 8, 1826. He came to America in 1854, where he engaged in farming and was active in all church work. He died at Des Moines, Iowa, June 10, 1918. His wife, Martha, died at Peoria, March 12, 1870.

Mr. Walford attended public country schools and for the past 21 years has been the owner of a general merchandise store at Dalton. He has a manager to operate the store while he lives on his farm of 880 acres. Mr. Walford is a stock holder in the Dalton State Bank and the Dalton Co-operative Company. He is a Republican, a Protestant, and for 30 years served as a member of the school board. Residence: Dalton.

Allan Walker

Allan Walker was born at Dunbar, Nebraska, November 5, 1898, the son of James C. and Adelia (Munn) Walker. His father, who was a farmer, was the son of an Irish sea captain who with his family came to America in 1840. He was born at Rock Island, Illinois, June 6, 1854, and died at Dunbar, March 12, 1922.

His mother, who was born at Wooster, Ohio, January 18, 1864, was a school teacher before her marriage. Her father, who was of Scotch and Welsh descent, journeyed to California in 1849, by way of Cape Horn, but returned east with the first immigrant train.

Mr. Walker was graduated from the Dunbar grade school in 1913, and in 1917, was graduated from the Dunbar High School. During his school days he was a member of the basketball team, four years, was captain two years; was a member of the baseball team; and was president of senior class. After his graduation he took an active interest in town athletics at Dunbar, where he has played on the city basketball team. He was a member of the American Legion team at Nebraska City for some time; has refereed many match games; and is interested in wrestling and other athletic affairs. He trained and managed his brother, Keith Walker, the state amateur boxing champion.

A lifetime resident of Nebraska, Mr. Walker is a farmer and horse trainer of some note. He is the owner and trainer of the famous Ritzie McDonald, the only horse in the world that does five gaits and can perform high school work without the use of a bridle. This horse has been shown and demonstrated at horse shows at Lincoln and Omaha, Nebraska, and Kansas City, Missouri.

Mr. Walker, who is a Democrat, has served on his local election board for several years. On September 16, 1924, he was married to R. Glyde Allen at Nebraska City, Otoe County, Nebraska. Mrs. Walker, who is a teacher, was born at Stella, Richardson County, Nebraska, March 24, 1897. There are two children: Norma Dee, born June 16, 1927; and Ruth Arvilla, born February 11, 1929.

During the late war he was a member of the Student's Army Training Corps at the University of Nebraska. He is a member of the American Legion and the Dunbar Community Club. He is a Mason, and past master of Lee Gillette Lodge No. 272, at Dunbar, and is affiliated with the Presbyterian Church at Dunbar, where he is an elder, and has been a teacher in the Sunday School for the last ten years. His favorite sport is horseback riding, and his hobby is the care and training of dogs and horses. Residence: Dunbar. (Photograph in Album).

Byron Milton Walker

An outstanding educator of this state Byron Milton Walker of Kearney, Nebraska, has been superintendent of schools in Buffalo County for the past five years. He was born at Buda, Nebraska, September 15, 1891, the son of Milton Addison and Amanda Jane (Knott) Walker. His father, who was born in Green County, Indiana, May 16, 1850, and died at Kearney, January 14, 1931, was a successful farmer; his ancestry was Scotch-Irish. His mother was born in Green County, March 9, 1855, and died at Holyoke, Colorado, in July, 1924.

Mr. Walker was graduated from the high school at Gibbon, Nebraska, in June, 1911, and received the Bachelor of Science degree at Kearney State Teachers College in 1931. He taught in public schools for 11 years, served as a bank cashier at Pleasanton for three years, and since 1927 has been county superintendent of Buffalo County.

He is affiliated with the First Christian Church, is a member of the Kearney Chamber of Commerce, and holds membership in the Masons and the Nebraskana Society. A member of the Red Cross, he served as secretary of the junior organization of that body from 1926 to 1932, and was secretary of the American Red Cross from 1926 to 1930. He is affiliated with the Buffalo County Sportsmen's League.

On June 10, 1924, he was married to Ethel Burell at Smith Center, Kansas; she was born at Miller, Nebraska, in April, 1905. To them one daughter was born, Twila, October 27, 1925. Residence: Kearney.

Frank Walker

Frank Walker, master farmer and prominent livestock breeder of Nebraska, has lived in this state for the past 56 years and has taken a prominent part in civic affairs in his community. He was born at Waverly, Lancaster County, Nebraska, May 11, 1875, the son of Peter Hayes and Sarah Helen (McMurry) Walker. His father, who was born at Lancastershire, England, March 13, 1841, and came to this country in 1850, was a farmer; he served as postmaster and was a Civil War veteran; he died at Waverly, January 29, 1908. His mother, whose ancestry was Scotch-Irish, was born at Vincennes, Indiana, April 9, 1848. She is still living.

Mr. Walker attended the rural and high schools of Waverly. He served as president of the Polled Shorthorn Breeders of America, 1913-16, was president of the American Spotted Poland China Record Association, 1926-27, is still director of the latter, acted as president of the Lancaster County Fair, 1927 to date, and since 1925 has been president of Nebraska S. P. C. Breeders Association. He is a Republican.

Among his civic and educational organizations are: Chamber of Commerce, Lincoln; Kiwanis Club, Lincoln; Parent Teachers Association, Waverly; Greater Nebraska Club; and the Nebraskana Society. During his life he has served more than 20 years on the school board. He served as secretary of the board of education for the Waverly Consolidated Schools, 1919-24. He is affiliated with the Waverly Methodist Episcopal Church, and at various times has held all offices in the church being a member for more than 35 years.

On July 11, 1899, he was united in marriage with Mary Lavina Packard at Wilber, Saline County, Nebraska. Mrs. Walker, who was born at Wilber, December 13, 1875, is descended from English ancestors who came to America in 1637. They have four children: Clyde, born January 3, 1901, who married Blanch Sophia Golz; Amy Helen, born July 18, 1903, who married Paul Leroy Griffith; Ivy Esther, born February 4, 1909, who was awarded the B. S. degree at Nebraska Wesleyan University, 1931; and Irving, who is now a junior at the University of Nebraska. Clyde received his A. B. and A. M. degrees at the University of Nebraska and is now

professor in the Oregon Agriculture College. Amy received her A. B. degree at Nebraska Wesleyan University in 1925. Residence: Waverly.

Gayle Courtney Walker

Gayle Courtney Walker, director of the school of journalism at the University of Nebraska, was born at Bison, Garfield County, Oklahoma, December 19, 1903. His father, Isaac Simeon Walker, who died at Clinton, Custer County, Oklahoma, August 29, 1918, was a country newspaper editor and was interested in civic affairs for many years. He served as secretary of the Chamber of Commerce at Clinton, was city food administrator, 1918, and was a member of the Custer County Council of Defense, 1917-18. His paternal ancestors were English.

Margaret Orabel Smith Walker, mother of Clyde, is descended from Pennsylvania-Dutch and Scotch-Irish ancestry. She was a teacher in the Nebraska and Oklahoma public schools for many years.

Professor Walker was a student in the public schools of Oklahoma, and in 1919 was graduated from the Clinton High School. He was awarded the A. B. degree at the University of Nebraska, 1924, and the A. M. degree at that institution, 1930. During the summer session of 1924 he was a graduate of the University of Missouri. He was elected to membership in Delta Sigma Rho, debating fraternity, 1924, and Sigma Upsilon, literary fraternity, 1928. He was senior class president and salutatorian in high school; he holds membership in Alpha Tau Omega, Sigma Delta Chi, and Kappa Tau Alpha.

He served as under-graduate assistant at the University of Nebraska, 1923-24; was acting director of the School of Journalism, 1926-30; was assistant professor in that department, 1927-30; and since 1930 has been director of the School of Journalism at the University. During 1929 Professor Walker served as vice president of the American Association of Schools and Departments of Journalism. He is the author of *A Yardstick for the Measurement of Country Weekly Service* published in the Journalism Quarterly, December, 1930; *The Country Weeklies Are Not Doomed*, published in the National Printer Journalist 1931; and was editor of *The Pyramid* of Sigma Tau, 1926-29.

He was a member of the Oklahoma National Guard, 1919. He is a member of the Junior Chamber of Commerce, the Inter-professional Institute, the Nebraskana Society, and the Westminster Presbyterian Church. He is a Mason. His favorite sport is golfing while his hobby is reading.

He was united in marriage with Wilma Fae O'Connell at Lincoln, June 12, 1926. Mrs. Walker, who was born in Lancaster County, Nebraska, October 25, 1904, is descended from Irish and colonial ancestors. Politically, Professor Walker is a Democrat. Residence: Lincoln.

Irving Seth Walker

Irving Seth Walker, president of the Kimball Irrigation District, was born in Saratoga County, New York, January 25, 1861, son of Seth Russell and Ruth (Baker) Walker.

Seth Russell Walker was born in Saratoga County, August 2, 1825, and died at Julesburg, Colorado, January 19, 1898. In his early days he was a merchant and lumberman, and in the last days he spent in Nebraska, was a farmer. He owned the farm on which the second battle of Bemis Heights was fought, October 7, 1777, and during which General Frazer was mortally wounded. The family landed at Scituate, Rhode Island, the second landing of the *Mayflower* in 1621. From there they traveled by water to Troy and Stillwater, New York, in 1622. While the father was living at Scituate, Rhode Island, in a storm at sea three transports were separated from the convoy. Supposing the city of Boston to be still in the hands of the British, they sailed boldly into the harbor, and were quickly captured by two privateers and an 18 gun brig belonging to the colonies. Here Archibald Walker surrendered with the others, and remained a prisoner on parole about two years. At this time he was exchanged and fought in the battles of Long Island and Kings Bridge, where he was again taken prisoner. He requested of the officer in command that he might not be exchanged, as his sympathies were with the colonists. The officer sent him to General George Washington at White Plains, to whom he related his life history requesting that he might not be exchanged but sent into the country to work among the farmers. Washington gave him a pass and sent him to Poughkeepsie to Governor Clinton, who gave him a general pass to go where he pleased. Mr. Walker's great-grandfather also fought in the Revolutionary War.

Ruth Baker was born in Saratoga County, November 7, 1821, and died at Champaign, Illinois, November 14, 1871. Her body was taken to New York and buried near Saratoga Springs in a cemetery where only Bakers are buried. Her family were Quakers coming to Nebraska in March, 1886, where they homesteaded 10 miles northwest of Potter. They resided here until 1892, when they moved to Kimball where Mr. Walker was employed as a bookkeeper in the bank of Kimball until 1898. He bought a ranch on Lodge Pole Creek in 1896 which he still owns. They resided on this ranch from 1898 until 1901 at which time they bought the Kimball Hotel, which is the oldest building in Kimball, and has been continuously occupied by the Walkers for the past 31 years.

In 1909, he promoted the organization of the Kimball Irrigation District making the filing for the appropriation of 20,000 acre feet of storage water, building a reservoir and all asseccories, which cost about $3,000,-000.00 in the year 1911. He has held his present position as president of the board of directors of the irrigation district for the past 24 years. He is also in the real estate and insurance business.

He was married to Hattie Emmaline Ainsworth at Kimball County, on April 6, 1887. Mrs. Walker was born at Wheaton, Illinois, October 23, 1865. To them were born two children, Ethel E., born February 16, 1889; and Ruth E., on May 21, 1891. Ethel is married to George F. Nugent. They have two children Richard Walker, born July 20, 1911; and Robert Irving, born April 17, 1913. Ruth is married to Vernon E. Linn, and they are among the largest and most extensive wheat and potato farmers in Kimball and Banner Counties.

Mr. Walker is a Republican. He is a member of St. Hilda's Episcopal Church at Kimball, the Ancient Order of United Workmen, and the Masons (secretary of Kimball lodge 16 years). He is a life member of the Nebraskana Society, and a member of the Kimball Country Club. His favorite diversion has been breeding and educating standard pure bred horses. Residence: Kimball. (Photograph in Album).

John Campbell Walker

On October 8, 1852, John C. Walker was born at Milan, Illinois, the son of William and Elizabeth (Campbell) Walker. His father, who was born at Mill Isle, Ireland, May 9, 1818, and died at Milan, June 9th, 1867, went to sea at the age of 14, and for the next 18 years sailed around Cape Horn to the Gulf of California. In 1851 he settled on a farm in Illinois. He was descended from George Walker of Yorkshire, England; a son of this noted ancestor was governor of Londonderry, Ireland, at one time.

His mother, a descendant of the Duke of Argyle, was born at Mill Isle, Ireland, February 15, 1828, and died at Douglas, Nebraska, August 30, 1908. William Campbell, her brother is still living, and is the last of the Pony Express riders.

Mr. Walker received his education at a time when most of the grade school work was limited to the study of the

McGuffy Readers. For about a year he was a prospector and miner in the Black Hills, and in 1882, he took a homestead and tree claim in Wheeler County, Nebraska. Now retired, he has been a land owner and farmer in Otoe County for many years, and has resided in Nebraska for 54 years.

He was united in marriage at Nebraska City, Nebraska, November 15, 1882, to Anna C. Tetan. Mrs. Walker was born at Hanover, Germany, December 25, 1862, and came to America with her parents in 1866, directly to Nebraska. Five children were born to this union: Bessie, born August 24, 1883, who married Arthur Money; Carl, born July 22, 1885, who married Mary Lowray; Joy, born July 19, 1895; Marie, born July 25, 1899, who married Frank Paap; and Nell, born July 2, 1901. All the children live on farms except Joy, who is a jeweler at Tekumseh.

Mr. Walker is a member of the Y. M. C. A. and the Red Cross, and is a Republican. Residence: Dunbar.

Lee Raymond Walker

Lee Raymond Walker, son of Robert Franklin and Christina (Nybroe) Walker, was born in Menard County, Illinois, April 12, 1885. His father, who was born at Georgetown, Indiana, January 13, 1860, is descended from Michael Waltman who served seven years and six months in the Continental Army during the Revolutionary War period. He is a farmer who served as sheriff of Franklin County five terms, 1909-22. Christina Nybroe was born near Oslo, Norway, and in earlier life was especially active in church work.

Educated in the rural schools of Fraklin County until 1901, Lee Raymond Walker later attended Bloomington High School. When he was eighteen years of age he learned the harness trade, and is now engaged in the harness and shoe business.

On October 26, 1910, he was married to Mable Martha Hanson at Bloomington. Mrs. Walker, whose parents came from Norway, was born in Bloomington July 24, 1884, and died at Red Cloud on December 25, 1928. She is the daughter of William K. and Martha (Holverson) Hanson. One child was born to them, Edward L., on October 5, 1926. He died December 6, 1929. On July 17, 1931, Mr. Walker was married to Miss Florence Burden. She was born at Campbell, Nebraska, November 16, 1892, and is the daughter of William and Nettie (Crosby) Burden.

Mr. Walker is a Democrat. He has served as a member of the city council at Bloomington, is a member of the Knights of Pythias, Delhi Temple No. 109 D. O. K. K., and the Nebraskana Society. He is eligible to the Sons of the American Revolution. His favorite sport is horse racing, and at one time was the owner of Ess H. Kay the fastest stallion ever owned in Nebraska. Residence: Red Cloud.

Sherman A. Walker

Sherman A. Walker, farmer and banker of Douglas, Otoe County, Nebraska, was born at Rock Island, Illinois, August 9, 1865. His father, William Walker, who was a sailor and a farmer, was born in County Down, Ireland, in 1818, and died at Rock Island, June 6, 1867. His ancestry was Scotch-Irish.

His mother, Eliza (Campbell) Walker, who was descended from the Duke of Argyle, was born in County Down, Ireland, January, 1834, and died at Douglas, September 4, 1908.

Mr. Walker attended the country schools of Illinois and Nebraska. Since 1875, he has lived in Nebraska where he has taken an active part in the business and civic life of his community. For several years he was engaged in the railroad construction business, and at the present time is president of the Farmers' State Bank at Douglas.

He is a member of the Nebraska State Historical Society and the Nebraskana Society. He is a Republican. Residence: Douglas.

Phillip Walla

Phillip Walla, son of Phillip and Barbara (Kunes) Walla, was born at Morse Bluff, Nebraska, November 17, 1884. His father, Philip, Sr., was born in Czechoslovakia, August 13, 1859, and came to America June 6, 1872. A farmer for many years, he is now retired. His wife, Barbara, was born in Czechoslovakia, April 10, 1862. She is living, as is her mother, who has reached the age of ninety-two years.

Educated in country schools, Phillip Walla, Jr., was graduated from the commercial course in Fremont Normal School in March, 1904. Since leaving school he has been engaged in banking, farming and grain dealing, and for twenty-six years has been manager of Walla Brothers, of which he is half owner. He is a director of the Bank of Morse Bluff, and the Farmers Elevator Company.

On February 7, 1910, he was married to Mary Georgie Bors at Geneva. Mrs. Walla, who was born at Milligan, March 24, 1888, is of Czech descent. To them two children were born, Marietta, born December 7, 1910, who has attended Nebraska University three years and is a member of Phi Mu; and Phill M., born April 22, 1914, who died May 1, 1931.

During the late war he was chairman of the United War Work drive, thrift committee, Red Cross and Y. M. C. A. drives. He is a Methodist. His fraternal organizations include the Ancient Free and Accepted Masons, the Modern Woodmen of America in which he has served as chairman; the Woodmen of the World of which he has been clerk, and the Z. C. B. J. of which he is chairman. He is village clerk at the present time. Residence: Morse Bluff.

Alvin Buril Wallace

Alvin Buril Wallace, lawyer, has been in active practice at Butte, Nebraska, since his admission to the bar in 1920. He was born at Belcherville, Texas, January 25, 1893.

Mr. Wallace was graduated from the Chickasha High School in Oklahoma, in 1913. He received the A. B. degree, 1916, and the LL.B. degree, 1920, at the University of Nebraska where he was a member of Phi Alpha Delta. During 1913 and 1914 he attended the University of Oklahoma. A Republican, he served as county attorney of Boyd County, Nebraska, from 1923 to 1927.

He is a Mason, is a member of the Woodmen of the World and the Nebraskana Society, and holds membership in the American Legion. Residence: Butte.

Charles Glenn Wallace

Charles Glenn Wallace, son of Henry M. and Margaret Jane (Scott) Wallace was born at La Rose, Illinois, December 8, 1871, Henry M. Wallace, who is of Scotch descent, was born at Greensburg, Indiana, August 26, 1847. A successful farmer, he is the owner of a well irrigated 220 acre farm near Lexington, Nebraska; his mother was a member of the Thomsen family who migrated to America from Scotland, in 1795; her husband, D. A. Wallace, was a Presbyterian clergyman, whose ancestors came from Scotland, much earlier.

Margaret Jane Scott, wife of Henry Wallace, was born on the farm of her parents in Marshall County, Illinois, October 31, 1847. She remained on the farm and reared a family of seven children to maturity. Her father, Harvey Scott, was born in Vermont, of Scotch extraction. He was a fine penman. Her mother, whose maiden name was McCuen, was of Irish descent.

Educated in the public schools of Illinois and Nebraska, Charles G. Wallace attended Lexington High School,

and soon thereafter became clerk and part owner of a hardware business at Lexington. For three years he was president and manager of the Hastings Foundry and Iron Works, and for nearly thirty years was associated with the Fairbanks Morse & Company, of Lincoln, is associated with the Western Brick and Supply Company of Hastings, and has many other interests.

Mr. Wallace has always taken an active part in constructive legislation. He assisted in organizing and having passed the initiative power bill Number 324, submitted to the people of Nebraska, in the election of 1930. The only public office he has ever held was that of chief enrolling clerk of the legislature which he held by appointment during 1896-97. An independent politically, he has voted for William Jennings Bryan three times, Theodore Roosevelt once, Woodrow Wilson twice, Robert LaFollette once and Herbert Hoover once.

Mr. Wallace is a member of the First Presbyterian Church of Hastings, the Young Men's Christian Association, the Red Cross, Chamber of Commerce and the Modern Woodmen of America. His hobby is politics.

He was united in marriage to Leona Idilla Jeffery at Denver, Colorado, June 19, 1902. Mrs. Wallace, who was born at Ottumwa, Iowa, December 16, 1871, was before her marriage librarian at Peru State Normal School, high school principal at Tecumseh, Nebraska, Lexington, Nebraska and Pueblo, Colorado. She received the degrees of Bachelor of Pedogogy at Peru; Bachelor of Fine Arts at the University of Nebraska, and Bachelor of Education. She is the daughter of William Scott Jeffery, who was of Scotch descent, and Louisa Dickey who was of French and English descent. William Scott Jeffery was the grandson of Sarah Wycoff, whose ancestry has been traced to 750 A. D.; Mary Scott Jeffery, his mother, was a second cousin of Mrs. Benjamin Harrison. Mr. and Mrs. Wallace have two children, Lura Lou, born April 7, 1908, who received the degrees of Bachelor of Fine Arts and Bachelor of Arts from the University of Nebraska; and who is a member of Kappa Alpha Theta; and Charles Glenn, Jr., born July 19, 1910, who is a graduate of Hastings High School and was a student at Kemper Military School. Charles at present is attending the University of Nebraska where he is affiliated with the Phi Kappa Psi fraternity. Residence: Hastings. (Photograph on Page 1235).

Hugh Elliott Wallace

A lifetime resident of Nebraska, Hugh Elliott Wallace was born at Omaha, on August 17, 1884, and since 1907 has been active in the business and civic affairs of his community. He is the son of George Gavin and Sarah Essie (Elliott) Wallace. His father, who was born at Morning Sun, Ohio, May 13, 1855, and died at Omaha, February 17, 1918, was descended from a Scotch pioneer South Carolina family; he was a realtor, was past president of the Omaha Real Estate Board, and was president of the State Sunday School Association. His mother was born at Morning Sun, October 17, 1856.

Mr. Wallace was graduated from the Omaha Central High School in 1903, and was a student at the University of Nebraska for two years. He was a member of the Glee Club, the Dramatic Club, and Alpha Theta Chi, served on the track team at the University of Nebraska, 1905-06, and participated in the Olympic games at St. Louis, 1904.

He was sales manager for a coal and building supplies firm, 1907-14; was assistant secretary of the First Trust Company, 1914-15; was manager of the First National Bank at Omaha, 1917-18; and since 1918 he has been district manager for the Equitable Life Insurance Company of Iowa. He is also secretary of the Fact Finding Institute.

His marriage to Maude Emily Matteson was solemnized at Duluth, Minnesota, October 10, 1914. Mrs. Wallace was born at Rochester, New York, January 27, 1890; her ancestry is Scotch. They have three children: Mary-

Nelson Studio—Hastings

CHARLES GLENN WALLACE

beth, born August 21, 1915; Jeanne, born September 6, 1917; and Eleanor, born July 24, 1921.

During the World War, Mr. Wallace served on all Liberty loan and Savings Stamps drives. He is a member of the Omaha Life Underwriters Association, of which he was president in 1928; and the Chamber of Commerce, of which he was director in 1928 and 1929. He was secretary of the Concord Club in 1920, and president, 1922; was director of the Camp Fire Girls, 1922-31; and is a member of the Dundee and Benson High School Parent-Teachers' Association. He has served as state treasurer of the Young Men's Christian Association.

Mr. Wallace is affiliated with Dundee Presbyterian Church of Omaha, and has served as music director of the choir for many years. He is a 32nd degree Mason, and in 1931 was made assistant director of the Shrine. He is a Republican. Residence: Omaha.

Stanley Paul Wallin

Stanley P. Wallin, physician and surgeon of Snyder, Dodge County, Nebraska, was born at Chicago, Illinois, March 15, 1899. His father, Charley Fredric Wallin, who was born in Sweden, October, 1870, is a licensed airplane mechanic; his ancestry is Scandinavian; he came to this country in 1890. His mother, Matilda (Swanson) Wallin was born in Sweden, July 7, 1873.

Dr. Wallin received his early education in the Beals Public School at Omaha, and in 1917 was graduated from Omaha Central High School. He was a student at the University of Minnesota, 1922, and in 1926 was awarded the M. D. and B. Sc. degrees at the University of Nebraska. He was a member of Upsilon Nu Chapter of Phi Chi at the University of Nebraska and Omega Beta Pi.

He was an airplane mechanic, 1919-20, at Omaha; was chief mechanic for Bellanca on the construction of auxiliary kings for mail ships, 1925. He is now physician and surgeon at Snyder, Nebraska. He is the co-author of, *Gall Bladder—Stomach Anastomosis,* published in *Surgery and Gynecology,* December, 1927. During the World War he was a member of the 266th Aero Pursuit Squad, First Division of the American Expeditionary Forces.

He is a member of the American Medical Association; the Dodge County Medical Society; and the Chamber of Commerce. He is a director of the Dodge County Red Cross; and of the Community Pavillion. He is a member of the Omaha Happy Hollow Club, and is affiliated with the Kountz Memorial Lutheran Church of Omaha. He is a member of the American Legion and the Disabled Veterans, and Scribner Lodge Number 132 of the Ancient Free and Accepted Masons. He likes golf and mechanics. Politically, he is a Republican.

Dr. Wallin was married to Kathleen McCrann in 1922. One son was born to them, Jerry, born on October 30, 1923. Mrs. Wallin died in 1924. On September 14, 1926, he was united in marriage with Virginia LeVeren Franklin at Omaha. A registered nurse before her marriage, she was born at Blue Hill, Nebraska, December 7, 1903, the daughter of Dr. W. A. Franklin who came from Illinois. They have one daughter, Jean, born April 7, 1928. Residence: Snyder. (Photograph in Album).

Eugene Artemas Walrath

Eugene Artemas Walrath, pioneer newspaper man in Nebraska, was born at Rochelle, Illinois, November 26, 1867, the son Jeremiah and Jennie Elizabeth (Fell) Walrath. His father, who was an engineer, was born at Sandy Creek, New York, September 2, 1831, the son of Anthony and Catherine Davis Walrath, and died at Osceola, August 11, 1920. Anthony Walrath was born August 20, 1796, and died April 25, 1870, and his wife was born May 29, 1802, and died October 31, 1881.

Mr. Walrath attended the high school at Rochelle, and in 1883 came to Nebraska where he has been prom-

inent in political and civic affairs. He is now editor and publisher of the *Polk County Democrat* at Osceola, and holds membership in the Osceola Community Club. A Democrat, he served as secretary of the Nebraska state senate for three terms and was state printer for two years. His fraternal organizations include the Modern Woodmen of America and the Ancient Free and Accepted Masons. He is affiliated with the First Presbyterian Church of Osceola.

On August 14, 1890, he was united in marriage at Payson, Utah, with Birdie Lorena Pulver. Mrs. Walrath was born at Springville, Wisconsin, June 16, 1868, the daughter of O. H. and Hannah Ann (Bixby) Pulver. They have two children: Maurine, born November 11, 1895; and Geralyn, born December 9, 1898. Residence: Osceola.

William Frederick Waltemath

William Frederick Waltemath, executive, was born at North Platte, Nebraska, July 19, 1889, son of Henry and Marie (Brant) Waltemath.

The father, who was born in Hanover, Germany, December 7, 1865, was an early settler in Nebraska coming to North Platte in 1882. He is president of the Waltemath Lumber and Coal Company. His wife, Marie, was born in Hanover, Germany, March 4, 1866. Both are still living.

Mr. Waltemath attended the public schools and high school of North Platte, graduating from the latter in 1907. From that time until 1911 he was a student at the University of Pennsylvania where he was a member of Sigma Nu fraternity.

At the present time Mr. Waltemath is vice-president of the Waltemath Lumber and Coal Company of North Platte and the Home Lumber and Supply Company of Hershey, Nebraska. He has resided in Nebraska all his life.

His marriage to Margaret Dorothy Ware was solemnized at Blair, on November 28, 1916. Mrs. Waltemath was born at Ogallala, Nebraska, August 1, 1890, and is the daughter of James Ware and a niece of the late W. A. Paxton, capitalist of Omaha. There are four children, Betty Marie, born September 26, 1917; William Ware, born March 11, 1919; Helen Louise, born September 14, 1923; and Mary Margaret, born January 5, 1925. Residence: North Platte.

Joe Walter

Joe Walter has been a farmer in Fillmore County, near Shickley, Nebraska, for the past 41 years, and has taken an active part in the religious and civic affairs of his community. He was born at Ohio, Illinois, August 25, 1876, the son of John and Otilda (Mueller) Walter. His father, who was born in Germany, December 11, 1843, and died at Grafton, Nebraska, February 5, 1923, was a farmer. His mother was born in Germany and died at Grafton, September 19, 1910.

Mr. Walter attended rural school in Illinois. He was elected county commissioner at Fillmore County on the Democratic ticket and is still serving in that capacity. He is affiliated with St. Mary's Catholic Church, holds membership in the Knights of Columbus, and is a member of the Nebraskana Society. During the World War he was prominent in all drives, especially those of the Red Cross.

His marriage to Anna Bartol occurred at Turkey Creek, Nebraska, April 27, 1904. Mrs. Walter was born at Shickley, Nebraska, October 28, 1881. Their children: Norma, born May 7, 1905, who married Harry Becker; Louetta, born March 5, 1907; Eugene, born February 28, 1910; and Linas, born September 22, 1915. Residence: Shickley.

Victor Walter

Victor Walter, son of Joseph Martin and Klotilda Marie (Hampl) Walter, was born at Crofton, Nebraska, February 14, 1884. His father, born in Zbirov, Bohemia, October 9, 1851, was, as a boy, apprenticed to the painter's trade there. After coming to America he engaged in farming until shortly before his death at Blyville (now Crofton). Joseph Walter, father of Joseph Martin Walter, was born in Cerovice, Bohemia, and was game warden of fisheries in Bohemia. Klotilda Marie Hampl was born in Seslove, Orkes, Kralovice, Bohemia, June 3, 1852, and resides in Knix County. Her mother was Marie Triner, born in Cerveny Zamek, Bohemia. She married at the age of seventeen and had twelve children. Her husband was a miller in Bohemia.

Educated in the rural schools near Blyville, Victor Walter has been a breeder of Hereford cattle, as well as a farmer for many years. When a boy he herded cattle over the unfenced prairies, and still recalls the devastating prairie fires and the roaming Indians. He remembers also something of the terrible blizzard of 1888.

On February 26, 1918, Mr. Walter was married to Agatha Evadna Svetc at West Point. She was born at Snyder, Nebraska, February 5, 1898. The Svetcs have been farmers for more than one hundred years and her mother's family includes many doctors and nurses. The family name is Brazda.

To Mr. and Mrs. Walter were born five children, Beatrice, born August 12, 1920; Stanley, born December 12, 1921; Milada, born August 5, 1923; Carol, born July 31, 1926; and Sterling, born March 5, 1928.

Mr. Walter is an independent voter. For many years he was a member of the board of directors of the Farmers Union in Crofton. In 1910, he was elected a member of the West Blyville School Board, and has since held that office continuously. On December 2, 1931, he was made a life member of the Nebraskana Society. He is affiliated with the Salem Evangelical Lutheran Church. His hobbies are reading, and collecting scenic cards and old coins. Residence: Crofton.

George Lawrence Walters

Born at North Manchester, Indiana, March 18, 1861, George Lawrence Walters has engaged in farming in Nebraska for the past forty-six years.

He is the son of Henry and Maria (Helm) Walters, the former born at Shippings, Pennsylvania, October 8, 1827. Henry Walters was a farmer, and faithful worker in the United Brethren Church, whose great-grandmather came from Hesse-Cassel, Germany, in the 1790's. His wife, Maria, was born at Shippings on July 4, 1829, and died at North Manchester on December 26, 1873. Her husband survived her until August 11, 1907.

George Lawrence Walters was graduated from public school in Wabash County, Indiana, in 1878. An independent in politics, he has held various township offices. He is affiliated with the Grace Evangelical Church at Hastings and is a member of the Nebraskana Society.

Of his marriage to Emma Coblenz there are eight children, all of whom are living: Blanche, born May 15, 1885, married Leonard F. Furgeson; Grace, born October 27, 1887, married William P. Sulzer; Rilla, born May 19, 1889, married J. Wyman Markin; Ralph H., born January 15, 1891, married Allameda Terhune; Carl J., born August 9, 1892, married Bernice Schmidt; Francis F., born April 21, 1894, married Florence Smith; Hazel, born August 9, 1897, married Merl McCoy; and Lawrence H., born November 2, 1899, is unmarried. Mrs. Walters was born at Springfield, Ohio, September 27, 1861.

Mr. Walters is fond of hiking, while his hobbies are gardening and fruitgrowing. Residence: Hastings.

William Ballou Wanner

On September 23, 1892, William B. Wanner was born at Falls City, Richardson County, Nebraska. His father, Albert Gottlieb Wanner, who was born at Woodland, St. Joseph County, Indiana, December 2, 1865, and died at Falls City, June 24, 1917, was a pharmacist. His ancestry was German.

Sarah Elizabeth (Easley) Wanner, his mother, was born in Halifax County, Virginia, May 3, 1867. She has been president of the Falls City Woman's Club at nine different times; is a member of the Daughters of the American Revolution; Sorosis; the Rebekahs; and the Eastern Star.

His elementary education was received in the Falls City public schools, and later was a student for three years at the University of Nebraska, leaving school because of the illness of his father. At the present time he is owner and manager of Wanner's Drug Store at Falls City.

Mr. Wanner was first lieutenant in the home guards during the World War, and drilled, drafted and enlisted men over all of Richardson County. He is a member of the Nebraska State Pharmacists Association; the Red Cross; Chamber of Commerce; and the Rotary Club. He is a member of the Ancient Free and Accepted Masons, Lodge No. 9, of which he has twice been Master; he has three times been High Priest of Eureka Chapter No. 5, Royal Arch Masons. He was twice eminent commander of Mount Sinai Commandery No. 8, and is at the present time grand generalissimo of the Nebraska Grand Commandery. He was for five years local patron of Falls City Chapter No. 225 Order of Eastern Star, and is grand sentinel of the Grand Chapter of the order. He is affiliated with the First Presbyterian Church, and the state Y. M. C. A. His hobby is mechanics. Residence: Falls City.

Leroy Emmette Wantz

Leroy Emmette Wants, merchant and dairyman, was born at Elliot, Illinois, September 5, 1879, the son of Peter E. and Emma Elizabeth (Hall) Wantz. His father, a rancher, was born of German parentage at South Whitley, Indiana, November 20, 1854. His mother, whose American ancestry dates to the Revolution, was born at Anthens, Illinois, August 26, 1854.

Mr. Wantz attended the Johnstown High School and studied at business college for a year. He came to Nebraska more than 30 years ago and settled on a homestead claim where he built a sod house typical of that period in the middlewest. He owns a dairy and store at Johnstown, Nebraska, where he is active in all community affairs. He holds membership in the Modern Woodmen of America, the Odd Fellows, I. W. L. A., and the Rebekah Lodge. He is a member of the Nebraskana Society, is affiliated with the United Brethren Church of Johnstown, and for two terms has served as chairman of the village board.

Mr. Wantz held membership in the Indiana State Militia, Company F, Third Regiment, at one time, and later was a member of the Johnstown Home Guard. His favorite sport is baseball.

His marriage to Clara Elaine Martin occurred at Johnstown, October 12, 1907. Mrs. Wantz, who was a teacher before her marriage, was born at Delphos, Ohio, September 28, 1882. She is descended from the famed Green family of Revolutionary times. They have a daughter, Lois Elaine, born October 6, 1911, who has taught in the same school in Cherry County for the past three years. Residence: Johnstown.

Charles Ward

Charles Ward, a resident of Nebraska forty-seven years, was born in Woodford County, Illinois, January 29, 1856. He was the son of Charles and Catherine (Bainbridge) Ward, both natives of England, who came to

America in 1851. Charles Ward, Sr., was born on March 3, 1823, and farmed for many years prior to his death at Western, Nebraska, December 8, 1900. Catherine Ward was born June 2, 1828 and died at Helvey, February 19, 1908.

Educated in public schools, Charles Ward, Jr., farmed for many years, and is now retired. He was married to Caroline Heinrich on February 10, 1881, in Woodford County, Illinois. Mrs. Ward, who was born in Henry County, Illinois, September 17, 1858, is of German descent.

In March, 1884, Mr. Ward started farming 2 miles north of Helvey, and at the present time the farm of 16 acres is in charge of George Ward, a son. George Ward, born February 5, 1884, is married to Louisa Ridder, they live on the home farm, and Roy Ward, born November 9, 1886, who is married to Jessie Olson, who lives on one of his fathers farms near Helvey, in Jefferson County. Myrtle Olive, born January 13, 1882, is married to Charles Beetley and they live in Aberdeen, South Dakota.

Mr. Ward is independent in politics. He has been assessor in his ward for the past 6 years. He is not a member of any church, but is a firm believer in an hereafter. He enjoys smoking and visiting with his neighbors. Residence: Helvey.

Nellie Marguerite Ward

Born at Lincoln, Nebraska, April 28, 1890, Nellie Marguerite Ward is the daughter of Arthur William and Mary Jane (Kelly) Ward, the former of whom was born at Markesan, Wisconsin, January 30, 1855, and died at Omaha, May 11, 1926. Arthur William Ward was an architect and contractor of English descent. His wife, Mary Jane Kelly, was born at Goldburn, Canada, May 1, 1856, of Scotch, English and Irish ancestry. She is still living.

Nellie Marguerite Ward was educated in the public and high schools of Lincoln, received her B. Sc. in 1913, and her M. A. in 1915, from the University of Nebraska. Her scholastic honors include membership in Iota Sigma Pi, and she is the organizer of Gamma Pi Sigma.

During 1915-16 she was high school principal, and from 1916-18 was professor of science at Central College. From 1918-28 she was professor of science at Central College. From 1918-28 she was professor of chemistry at the University of Omaha, and since 1928, she has been head of the department of chemistry.

She is a member of Westminster Presbyterian Church of Lincoln, and a member of the Red Cross. Her professional organizations are the American Chemical Society and the American Association for the Advancement of Science. She is a member of the Nebraskana Society. Her favorite sports are golf and riding. Her hobbies are principally her home and mother. Residence: Lincoln.

Wylie Ray Ward

Wylie Ray Ward, educator and farmer of Nebraska, has been a lifelong resident of this state. He was born near Overton, Nebraska, December 28, 1892, the son of William Eddy and Martha Alice (Ray) Ward. His father, who was born at Eureka, Illinois, August 16, 1859, was a member of the county board for three years and served on the local school board for 13 years. His mother was born at Washington, Illinois, January 22, 1862. They are now residing at Overton, Nebraska.

Mr. Ward was graduated from the Overton High School in 1911, was graduated from the University of Nebraska School of Agriculture in 1916, and studied at Nebraska Wesleyan University for a year. His fraternity in college was Alpha Zeta. He served as instructor in agronomy at the University of Nebraska, 1916-17, was engaged in government agricultural work as general organizer over the state, 1917, was district agriculture agent at Grand Island, 1918, and served as county agricul-

tural agent, 1919-20 at Holdrege, Nebraska. He is now a farmer, hog raiser, and alfalfa grower near Overton.

He is a member of the Red Cross, is affiliated with the Methodist Episcopal Church of Overton of which he has been Sunday school superintendent for six years; and holds membership in the Independent Order of Odd Fellows and the Masonic Lodge.

On September 2, 1920, he was married at York, Nebraska, to Helen Mary Plumb. Mrs. Ward, who is a registered nurse, is a graduate of the Methodist Hospital at Omaha. She was born at Fairmont, Nebraska, February 11, 1894, and is affiliated with the Methodist Episcopal Church and holds membership in the Order of Eastern Star. Residence: Overton.

Ellen Kinney Ware

Ellen Kinney Ware was born at Mount Vernon, Ohio, on July 25, 1841. John Fitch Kinney, her father, who was born at New Haven, Oswego County, New York, April 2, 1816, and died at Salt Lake City, Utah, August 16, 1902, was a lawyer and distinguished statesman in Utah. He served as county attorney in Iowa; was associate justice of the Supreme Court of Iowa; was chief justice of the Utah Supreme Court; and served as congressman from Utah. He was the son of Dr. Stephen Fitch Kinney and Abbey (Brockway) Kinney. His mother was the daughter of Rev. Thomas Clark Brockway, noted author, minister and poet. Eunice Lathrop, grandmother of John Fitch Kinney, was descended from Colonel Simon Lathrop who came to America from England in 1660, and settled in Virginia, where he was an outstanding figure in the colonial wars.

Hannah Dorothy (Hall) Kinney, mother of Ellen Kinney Ware, was born at Batavia, Genesee County, New York, November 12, 1816, and died at San Diego, California, May 1, 1895. She was the daughter of Samuel and Hannah (Chapin) Hall whose ancestry was English. Samuel Hall was captain of the Militia during the War of 1812.

Mrs. Ware was educated in the private schools of the south, and was graduated with honors from Virginia Female Institute, now called Stewart's Hall, in 1858. Since that date she has lived in Nebraska with the exception of several winters spent in California. She has always been an enthusiastic admirer of Nebraska, and has written articles on the early history of the state and various biographical papers for numerous societies and newspapers.

Her marriage to Jasper Anderson Ware was solemnized at Nebraska City, on October 10, 1861. Mr. Ware, who was born at Trenton, Kentucky, March 5, 1831, was a merchant, broker, and banker. He was the son of Edmond and Louisa Virginia (Anderson) Ware, and was descended from Nicholas Merriwether. Major Anderson of Fort Sumter fame, was also an ancestor. He died at Nebraska City, November 20, 1900. Four children were born to this union, three of whom are living. They are: Florence, who married Richard Smith Hall, was a student at Brownell Hall where she was awarded the scholarship medal and made the valedictory address. She died October 26, 1924. Ellen became a prominent teacher, and married Martin Schmaus. Grace Louise, was a teacher and studied music abroad. Norton, who is a civil engineer, was graduated from the University of Nebraska where he was made a member of Sigma Xi, honorary fraternity. He married Lola Wilson.

Mrs. Ware is a charter member of the Daughters of the American Revolution, Otoe Chapter, and during the World War was active in the work of the Red Cross. She is vitally interested in child welfare; is a member of the Associated Charities; and has been active in Woman's Club work. She has been a life member of the St. Mary's Episcopal Church at Nebraska City, where she has always taken part in all church affairs.

She is a Democrat by inheritance, but has become a

Republican. Her hobbies are reading, and the study of astronomy and history. As a girl her favorite sport was horseback riding. Residence: Nebraska City.

Samuel Delno Wareham

A pioneer farmer in Nebraska, Samuel Delno Wareham was born at Lowden, Iowa, November 12, 1871, the son of James and Sarah Melinda (Clayton) Wareham. He moved to Plum Creek, Nebraska, at the age of three. His father, who was a farmer and a soldier in the Civil War, was born in Pennsylvania, December 18, 1843, and died at Cozad, Nebraska, February 11, 1923; his ancestry was Irish.

Mr. Wareham attended a country school near Cozad. He was a farmer in Dawson County, near Cozad for many years, is an inventor and owns a blacksmith shop at Cozad. He has been chief and assistant fire chief for the past 20 years, is a member of the Cozad Chamber of Commerce, is affiliated with the Methodist Episcopal Church at Cozad, and holds membership in the Woodmen of the World. His favorite sport is hunting.

Of his marriage to Nellie Lewis three children were born: Glenn, who married Mary Kinnan; Elton; and George. He is now married to Carrie Elizabeth Boyd, who was at Pomona, Missouri, and attended school at Kansas City, Missouri. The following children were born to the second marriage: Deino, January 7, 1922; Boyd, October 27, 1925; and David, April 12, 1930. Mr. Wareham is a Democrat. Residence: Cozad.

Fred C. Warnemunde

Born at Plau, Germany, March 13, 1891, Fred C. Warnemunde is the son of Fred C. and Ida M. (Sellman) Warnemunde. His father who was a farmer, was born at Stettin, Germany, October 12, 1861. His mother was born at Plau, February 17, 1863.

Mr. Warnemunde attended grade and parochial school, and from 1910 to 1912 was a student at Fremont Normal School. He was a manager for the Nye Schneider & Fowler Company of Fremont, Nebraska, from 1912-15 at Clinton & Washington, Nebraska, and was manager of the F. H. Gilchrist Lumber Company at Oconto, Nebraska, 1915-18. From 1918-20 he was assistant cashier of the Oconto State Bank and of the Lexington State Bank. Since May, 1920, he has been owner of an insurance, real estate and loan business at Lexington, Nebraska.

He is a member of the Lexington Chamber of Commerce, is a director of the Red Cross, and is president of the board of education. He served as mayor of Lexington, Nebraska, 1925-26, and is past president and past secretary of the Kiwanis Club of Lexington. He is affiliated with the First Presbyterian Church, serving as elder 10 years and holding membership in its various service branches; and holds membership in the Nebraska State Association of Insurance Agents and the National Association of Insurance Agents. His fraternal organizations are: Thistle Lodge Number 61 of the Ancient Free and Accepted Masons, (master in 1928); Tyrian Chapter No. 29 Royal Arch Masons; Mt. Hebron Commandery No. 12, Knights Templar; Tehama Temple of the Shrine of Hastings, Nebraska; and the Independent Order of Odd Fellows of which he is a past noble grand.

On December 2, 1914, he was married to Olga Marie Rohwer at Rushville, Nebraska. Mrs. Warnemunde was born at Rushville, August 19, 1890. They have three children: Fred, born November 30, 1916; Ruth, born August 1, 1919; and Helen, born March 11, 1927.

Mr. Warnemunde's social club is the Lexington Country Club and his sports include golfing, football, and baseball. His hobby is reading. Residence: Lexington. (Photograph in Album).

Charles Joseph Warner

Charles Joseph Warner, prominent Lancaster County farmer, was born at Waverly, Nebraska, March 29, 1875, son of John and Christine (Magnuson) Warner. His father, born at Kisa, Sweden, December 21, 1842, died at Waverly on July 17, 1930. His mother, born at Ingatorp, Sweden, on June 16, 1838, died at Waverly on January 21, 1913.

Mr. Warner attended school in district No. 92 of Lancaster County until June, 1891, was a student at Luther College, Wahoo, 1892 and 1893, and received his Bachelor of Science degree from the University of Nebraska in 1899. In 1900 he studied law at the University of Nebraska, and in 1902 at Columbia University, Washington, D. C.

A Republican, Mr. Warner served ten terms in the Nebraska legislature, an unequalled record in Nebraska. During 1901, 1903 and 1906 he was state representative from Lancaster County, and 1919, 1921, 1923, 1925, 1927, 1929, 1931 served as state senator.

An extensive landowner and farmer, he is president also of the Lancaster County Bank and of the Prairie Home Co-operative Elevator Company, president of the Board of Education of Waverly Consolidated Schools and a member of the Parent Teachers Association.

On December 9, 1914, Mr. Warner was united in marriage to Esther Anderson at Lincoln. Mrs. Warner, a student at Nebraska Wesleyan, was a teacher prior to marriage. She was born at Virginia, Illinois, January 12, 1891, and is a former president of the Havelock Woman's Club. There are two children, Charles Leland, born January 14, 1922; and Phillip Jerome, born November 23, 1927.

Mr. Warner participated in all civilian projects during the World War. He is a member of the Congregational Church, the Red Cross, the Lincoln Kiwanis and University Clubs. He is a Scottish Rite Mason and Knight Templar, a Modern Woodman of America, and Odd Fellow and a member of the Vikings, and The Nebraskana Society. Residence: Waverly. (Photograph in Album).

Edwin Carlos Warner

Edwin Carlos Warner was born at Tremont, Illinois, May 8, 1863, the son of pioneer settlers of Madison County, Nebraska. His father, Hiram Warner, who was prominent in the early history of his community, was born at Canton, New York, August 4, 1839, and died at Warnerville, Nebraska, October 8, 1912; he was a farmer and merchant, and served for three years in the Union Army during the Civil War; he was descended from ancestors who came to America in the *Mayflower* in 1620. Rosalthe Lydia (Amsbary) Warner, mother of Edwin Warner, was born at Longs Landing, Virginia, June 6, 1839, and died at Warnerville, March 14, 1931; her ancestors were among the original English settlers of Virginia.

Mr. Warner attended the public schools and was graduated from the Illinois State Normal School in 1886. He was a public school teacher for five years, was cashier of the Tremont Bank at Tremont, Illinois for two years, and in 1887 helped to found the town of Warnerville. He engaged in a general merchandise business at Warnerville until 1894, was in the Railway Mail Service from 1894 to 1918, and since 1918 has farmed near Warnerville. At this time he is a member of the local school board. His chief recreations are golf and reading.

He was united in marriage with Lillie Belle Ashby at Onarga, Illinois, October 19, 1887. Mrs. Warner, who was a descendant of John Rolf and Pocahontas of colonial fame, was born at Indianola, Illinois, August 30, 1865, and died at Norfolk, June 17, 1929. Five children were born to their marriage: Edward H., November 3, 1888, who married Hazel Head; Marilla, June 2, 1890, who mar-

Crawford—Norfolk

FRANK AUSTIN WARNER

ried Bruce Dale; Frank A., April 2, 1892, who married Frances Colton; Bruce C., July 5, 1895, who married Bernice Ballantyne, and who died April 12, 1927; and George, April 6, 1898, who died June 6, 1891.

Mr. Warner is a Democrat. Residence: Norfolk.

Frank Austin Warner

Born at Warnerville, Nebraska, April 2, 1892, Frank Austin Warner is the son of Edwin Carlos and Lillie (Ashby) Warner. His father, born at Tremont, Illinois, May 8, 1863, is justice of the peace at Warnerville, and a farmer. He has also served as a railway mail clerk and has been a banker. He came to Nebraska from Tazewell County, Illinois, with his father, founding the town of Warnerville. His grandfather was a soldier in Company A, 108th Illinois Volunteers, in the Civil War.

His mother was born at Indianola, Illinois, August 30, 1865, and died at Norfolk, Nebraska, June 17, 1929. She was department president of the American Legion Auxiliary for the State of Nebraska, and was the daughter of Captain John Ashby who served with an Illinois regiment in the Civil War.

Mr. Warner, who is a prominent lawyer at Norfolk, attended high school in Jerseyville, Illinois, and North Division High School in Chicago. In 1909 he was graduated from Grand Prairie Seminary at Onarga, Illinois. He began the study of law in Chicago, and completed it in the office of United States Senator William V. Allen at Madison, and was admitted to the bar at Lincoln in 1915. He has been a member of the firms of Allen, Dowling and Warner; Dowling and Warner; and Dowling, Warner, Moyer and Schmidt. Since 1921 he has practiced independently.

A Democrat, he has served as county and city chairman, as a member and vice chairman of the state central committee and chairman of the permanent organization committee. His religious affiliation is with the First Presbyterian Church of Norfolk, while his professional organizations include the Nebraska State and American Bar Associations.

Mr. Warner enlisted in the Nebraska National Guard on May 13, 1917; organized Company I, 6th Nebraska Infantry (N. G.); was promoted to captain of infantry on June 25, 1917; was inducted into federal service on August 5, 1917; was transfered to 109th Engineers Train October, 1917; to 126th Field Artillery November, 1917; attended and instructed at the Fort Sill School of Fire January-June, 1918; was transferred to F. A. C. O. T. S. Camp Taylor, Louisville, Kentucky, June, 1918; was instructor, personnel adjutant, and executive, was promoted to major of Field Artillery and was transferred as assistant executive chief of Field Artillery, General Staff, Washington, D. C., October, 1918. He received his honorable discharge on January 27, 1919; and was made lieutenant colonel September 1, 1923.

A member of the Military Order of the World War, and of the Reserve Officers Association, he is former vice president of the latter, and a member of the state executive committee. He is president of the Elkhorn Valley Reserve Officers Association, past chef de gare of Norfolk Voiture, Forty and Eight; past grand chef de gare of the Nebraska Forty and Eight; organizer and past department vice commander and national executive committeeman of the American Legion and is now alternate national executive committeeman.

Mr. Warner is an Elk, an Odd Fellow, a member of the Chamber of Commerce, the Bull Run Society, the Volunteer Fire Department, the Young Men's Christian Association and the Nebraskana Society. Residence: Norfolk. (Photograph on Page 1240).

Minnie Estelle Warner

Minnie E. Warner was born on a farm near what is now known as Syracuse, Otoe County, Nebraska, August 13, 1859. Her father, George Washington Warner, who was born near Clay Corners, Onandaga County, New York, February 22, 1831, was a pioneer homesteader and horticulturist who migrated by overland stage team to Nebraska, in 1857. He died at Weeping Water, Nebraska, July 11, 1901. He was for many years justice of the peace in his community. His ancestry was distinguished and included Seth Orin Warner, grandfather of Minnie E. Warner, who was born in the Catskill Mountains in New York, and who was descended through the line of William Warner who landed at Ipswich, Massachusetts in 1637. Sarah Warner, wife of Seth Orin Warner, was of an old New York family.

Elizabeth (Brownell) Warner, mother of Minnie E. Warner, was born near Sparta, Ohio, April 28, 1834, and moved with her parents, by boat via St. Louis, to Nebraska City, in 1857. She was a pioneer woman's club worker in Nebraska, and was the daughter of Solomon Denton Brownell and Susan (Brinkerhoff) Brownell, and the great great granddaughter of a distinguished Revolutionary War soldier. She died at Syracuse, February 17, 1929.

Miss Warner has lived in Nebraska all her life and has taken an active part in club and welfare affairs. For twenty-five years she was a dressmaker, seamstress, and milliner.

Owing to ill health she was unable to take an active part in the World War loan drives, etc., but she assisted to the best of her ability in the local Red Cross organization. She was formerly a member of the Red Cross, the Good Templars, and is a member of the Woman's Christian Temperance Union. She is affiliated with the Federated Baptist Congregational Church. She is a Republican. Residence: Syracuse.

William Philip Warner

William P. Warner, a lawyer at Dakota City, Dakota County, Nebraska, since 1891, was born at Richland, Keokuk County, Iowa, April 28, 1866. His father, Gideon Warner, who was born at Worcester, Wayne County, Ohio, July, 1823, died at Edmonton, Alberta, Canada, February 3, 1903. He was a millright, carpenter, miner, farmer, and scout in pioneer days; served as scout and wagon master with General Crook in subjugation of the Sioux Indians in 1876-77 after the Custer massacre. He crossed the prairie lands three times. He was superintendent of construction of Fort Keough, west of Miles City. Andrew Warner, an ancestor, settled at Cambridge, Massachusetts, upon his arrival from England in 1630; other ancestors served in the Revolution and the War of 1812.

His mother, who was born in Lancaster County, Pennsylvania, June, 1833, and died at Allen, Dixon County, Nebraska, December 30, 1910; was descended from German pioneer farmers, and was the mother of twelve children.

Mr. Warner was graduated from the Sioux City Academy. He was admitted to the practice of law in 1891, and has been there since that date. He helped to organize the Nebraska State Bank at South Sioux City, in which he is still a director; he was formerly chairman of the board of directors.

A Republican, Mr. Warner has been active in politics, and he has held the following public offices and positions: chairman of the county, judicial district, congressional and state committee of the Republican party, 1905-06; county judge of Dakota County, Nebraska, 1890 to 1894; county attorney, 1895-1900; state senator, 1893-4; chairman commission to Lewis and Clark Exposition, 1905; United States Marshall of Nebraska 1905 to 1915; and regent of the University of Nebraska. He has lived in Nebraska for the past 63 years.

Aside from his legal and civic activities Mr. Warner owns and operates, together with his son, three farms; among them is one in Dakota County where he was born

Genelli Studio—Sioux City, Iowa

WILLIAM P. WARNER

and reared, which is now operated by him and his son. During the World War he was chairman of the Fuel Conservation Committee and the Food Conservation Committee in Nebraska. He took part in Liberty loan drives.

Mr. Warner is a member of the Red Cross, for over 20 years has been a contributor to the Salvation Army, and for many years has been president of the local school board. He is a member of the library board, and served as president of the board of regents at the University of Nebraska in 1927. He is a Mason, holding membership in Omadi Lodge Number 5, at Dakota City, Knights Templar, at Norfolk, Shrine and Tangier Temple at Omaha, Nebraska.

His hobby is reading, and his sports are fishing and hunting. For over 20 years Mr. Warner has maintained a hunting lodge on Lake Minnewawa in northern Minnesota.

His marriage to Alice Maggie Graham was solemnized at Sioux City, February 16, 1893. Mrs. Warner, who is Scotch, was born at Fairbault, Minnesota, April 5, 1869. Six children were born to them, Margaret, born June 30, 1895, died December 20, 1918; W. Graham, born April 7, 1898, who married Gladys Biermann; Herbert B., born June 30, 1900, who married Blanche Mathwig; Katheryn, born July 6, 1902, who married Dr. James W. Graham; William Philip, born September 9, 1910; and David Ross, born August 19, 1912. Residence: Dakota City. (Photograph on Page 1242).

John Clarence Warren

John Clarence Warren, successful druggist at Beatrice, Gage County, Nebraska, has lived in this state all his life. He was born at Thompson, Jefferson County, Nebraska, November 15, 1896, the son of Clarence Sylvester and Gertrude Corrine (Tipton) Warren. His father, who is a land owner in Gage County, was born at Minonk, Illinois, August 21, 1871, of English parentage. John Clarence Warren's mother, who was born at Glenwood, Mills County, Iowa, September 14, 1874, and died at Beatrice, October 12, 1924, was president of the American Legion Auxiliary for a number of years, and during the war was active in Red Cross work; her father, John H. Tipton, was active in the Iowa National Guard.

Mr. Warren attended the Beatrice High School and was a student at Fremont College of Pharmacy until 1917, when he volunteered for service in the World War. Later he attended the Babcock Institute Pharmacy at Des Moines, Iowa, 1919-20. From 1913 to 1916 he was employed by H. L. Harper and in 1921 he entered the drug business independently. He is the author of an article on merchandising, delivered before the 15th convention of the Nebraska Rexall Club, and published in the Rexall Ad-Van-tages, the international organ of the association of Rexall Clubs.

During the World War, Mr. Warren served as sergeant, battalion sergeant major, in the 134th Infantry. He was appointed to the officers training school at Langres, France, and was commissioned second lieutenant of the United States Army, April 17, 1919. He served as battalion adjutant, central records office, Bourges, France, and in 1919 was honorably discharged. He holds a copy of a supplementary statement taken from his officer's record book, which commends him for excellent service as a company officer and battalion adjutant. He is a member of the American Legion and is second lieutenant in the Infantry Reserve.

Mr. Warren was nominated Master Merchant of Nebraska, in 1931, and is the owner of a drug store which ranks second in the state of Nebraska, and tenth on the international honor roll for cities of this classification, from the United Drug Company. He holds membership in the Nebraska Rexall Club, the Chamber of Commerce, Junior Chamber of Commerce, Red Cross, Young Men's Christian Association, and the Nebraskana Society. He is first vice president of the Nebraska State Rexall As-

sociation, is affiliated with the Presbyterian Church, and is a Mason and Elk. His hobbies are reading and mechanics. Politically, Mr. Warren is independent.

On June 7, 1922, his marriage to Leilabeth Cecilia Farrell was solemnized at Lincoln, Lancaster County, Nebraska. Mrs. Warren, who is of Irish and Dutch descent, was born at Stuart, Iowa, November 20, 1895. Their children are: Betty Lou, born March 4, 1923; Mary Louise, born October 1, 1924; and John Clarence, born March 4, 1927. Residence: Beatrice. (Photograph in Album).

Simon Walter Warren

Simon Walter Warren, automobile dealer, was born near Dalton City, Illinois, July 28, 1876, son of Jesse Alexander and Martha (French) Warren.

The father, a native of Tennessee, born January 29, 1827, died at Edgar, Nebraska, in June, 1899. He was a farmer. His wife, Martha, was born in Tennessee, in 1837, and died at Edgar, on February 25, 1885.

Mr. Warren attended the public schools and spent one year at Fairfield College. On September 2, 1899, he was married to Bessie McFarland, at Nelson. Mrs. Warren was born at Fairfield, February 17, 1875, the daughter of Robert and Margaret (Wagner) McFarland.

Five children were born to them, four of whom are living, Robert J. born August 12, 1900, died May 20, 1917; Aubry W., born November 16, 1902; Orloe J., born March 12, 1905; E. Waldo, born May 24, 1910; and Doris B., born January 10, 1919. Orloe is an automobile mechanic at Tryon; Aubry is a student at the University of Nebraska, and Waldo is a newspaper man.

Mr. Warren is a Republican. He was county federal food administrator during the World War, is a regent of the county high school of McPherson County, and an Odd Fellow. Residence: Tryon.

Willard Bentley Warren

Willard Bentley Warren was born at Rising City, Nebraska, July 12, 1892, son of Lucius Artemus and Jennie Miller (Carpenter) Warren. His father, a banker, was born at Killingly, Connecticut, April 15, 1850, and died at Ulysses, Nebraska, December 2, 1906. He was descended from Arthur Warren of Massachusetts Bay Colony. His mother, whose ancestry was English, was born at Aurora, Illinois, March 6, 1854, and died at Ulysses, Nebraska, April 19, 1913.

Mr. Warren was graduated from the Ulysses High School in 1913, and farmed extensively until 1922. He was a stock buyer from that time until 1926 and since that time has been in the lumber business, for the past two years residing at Atkinson. He is a member of the Lions Club and of the Masons. His chief recreations are reading, football, and baseball.

His marriage to Fern Ruth Spelts occurred at Seward, Nebraska, February 28, 1918. Mrs. Warren, who is a descendant of Daniel Boone, was born at Wood River, Nebraska, February 8, 1897. She was graduated from the Ulysses High School in 1913 and taught school in Butler County in 1916 and at Gregory, South Dakota in 1917. Their children are, Georgia Fern, born March 11, 1919; Merritt Cleveland, born September 28, 1923; and Gerald Henry, born July 15, 1928. Residence: Atkinson.

John Wesley Warrick

Since 1887 John Wesley Warrick has been prominent in business in Madison County, Nebraska, and has taken an active part in civic affairs at Meadow Grove. He was born at Elk Creek, Virginia, May 7, 1858, the son of George and Elizabeth (Stone) Warrick. His father, a farmer of English descent, was born at Elk Creek, June

20, 1827, and died there, May 2, 1909. He was a teacher prior to his marriage. His mother was born at Elk Creek, February 13, 1836, and died there November 18, 1908. She was of Pennsylvania-Dutch descent.

Mr. Warrick attended school at Elk Creek until 1878 and taught school for a year in his native town. Later he entered the mercantile business, and in addition to it served as postmaster for five years. Coming to Nebraska in 1887, he settled in Meadow Grove where he has since resided, occupying the same homesite ever since his marriage.

For the past 20 years Mr. Warrick has been a member of the Meadow Grove School Board. He is a member of the Red Cross and the Ancient Order of United Workmen, and is affiliated with the First Methodist Church of Meadow Grove. He holds membership in the Nebraskana Society and the Battle Creek Country Club. His chief recreations are golfing and reading.

He was married to Grace Hanna Shafer at Meadow Grove, April 27, 1890. Mrs. Warrick was born in Garrison, Benton County, Iowa, August 16, 1870. They have four children, Elizabeth, born February 9, 1891, who married Vernon A. Dunlavy; Ruth, born September 6, 1894, who married George H. Lemon; Dorothy, born April 9, 1899, who married Charles Deuser; and John Wesley, Jr., born January 6, 1903, who married Ruth Hoflund. Elizabeth was graduated from Nebraska Wesleyan University, and Ruth was graduated from that institution and from Simmons College at Boston, Massachussets. Dorothy received her education at Nebraska Wesleyan University, also. John Wesley, Jr., attended Culver Military Academy at Culver, Indiana, two years and was a student at Nebraska Wesleyan University for the same period of time. He received his degree from the state university of Nebraska. Mr. and Mrs. Warrick have seven grandchildren. Residence: Meadow Grove.

M. C. Warrington

Born in Guthrie Center, Iowa, October 29, 1864, M. C. Warrington, editor and newspaper publisher, came to Mason City, August 19, 1886, before the town had a post office, helped organize the village government, the school district, and has been outstanding in community service ever since.

His father, William Warrington, was a native of Leeds, Yorkshire, England, born April 15, 1820, who died at Guthrie Center, July 26, 1905. His mother, Julia Cooper, born in County Tipperary, Ireland, in 1831, and died at Guthrie Center, in May, 1902.

M. C. Warrington received his education in town schools, Cornell College at Mount Vernon, Iowa, and in a printing office. On October 4, 1893, married Mena Agnes Mengel at Broken Bow, Nebraska. Mrs. Warrington was born at Springfield, Illinois, in February, 1862.

For a number of years Mr. Warrington has been owner, editor and publisher of *The Mason City Transcript*, and at times has been interested in other business ventures. He was register of the United States Land Office at Broken Bow five years, chairman of the village board three times, postmaster five years, at Mason City, member of the Nebraska legislature 1930, and has served as justice of the peace and police judge. He is affiliated with the Democratic party and has been an active political worker in state and local affairs.

He was a participant in all relief and other drives in the World War period, and was a four minute speaker. He is a member of the Community Club, the Red Cross, the Nebraska Press Association, the Nebraska State Historical Society and the Nebraska Society. A member of the Modern Woodmen of America, he is a charter member of Mason City Lodge No. 170, of the Ancient Free and Accepted Masons. Residence: Mason City. (Photograph on Page 1245).

Charles William Warwick

Since 1925 Charles William Warwick has been superintendent of schools of Valentine. He was born at London, Ohio, November 26, 1883, son of Luther Shelton and Emma (Rhodes) Warwick.

The father was born in Ohio, July 11, 1851, descended from English settlers in Virginia in colonial times. He possesses the genealogy of the family tracing to the original settlers. The mother was born in Ohio, April 21, 1856, of English and Pennsylvania German descent.

Educated in the country schools of Iowa, Mr. Warwick next attended Madison County, Nebraska, schools, and in 1902 was graduated from high school at Tilden. He received his Bachelor of Arts degree from Nebraska Wesleyan University, in 1911, and his Master of Arts degree from the University of Nebraska in 1916. He was valedictorian of his high school class.

From 1902 until 1905 Mr. Warwick was a teacher in rural schools in Antelope County, and from 1911 until 1912 was principal of the high school at Palmyra, Nebraska. He was superintendent at Silver Creek, 1913-15; Dodge, 1915-17; Elgin, 1917-20; North Bend, 1920-25; and at Valentine since 1925.

On August 10, 1916, he was married to Bessie Pearl Wait at Lincoln. She was born at Palmyra, Nebraska, September 21, 1891, and is of English ancestry. They have five children, Ruth Eleanor, born July 4, 1917; Virginia Beth, born April 20, 1920; Norman Wait, born July 21, 1923; Marjorie Jean, born September 25, 1926; and Mary Ellen, born April 21, 1928.

Mr. Warwick is a Republican. He is a member of the Presbyterian Church of Valentine, of the Rotary Club (secretary 1929-32), the Schoolmasters Club, and Phi Gamma Mu. Residence: Valentine. (Photograph in Album).

Sylvester Ambrose Wassum

Sylvester A. Wassum was born at Marion, Smyth County, Virginia, February 13, 1883. His father, William Washington Wassum, who was born in Smyth County, October 1, 1860, was a farmer in Nebraska for many years; he died at Sidney, Cheyenne County, Nebraska, July 5, 1930. Malissa Josephine (Rosenbaum), his mother was born in Smith County, Virginia, July 11, 1860, and is still living; her ancestors came from Germany, early in the 17th century and settled in Pennsylvania. William Washington Wassum was descended from English ancestors who settled in America in 1760, and were farmers.

Mr. Wassum was graduated from the Arlington High School in 1899, and was a student at the Omaha Business College for two years, 1900-01. He was employed by the Chicago, St. Paul, Minneapolis, and Omaha Railroad from 1901 to 1917 as station agent; was a member of the firm Cornish Auto Company, at Tekamah, Nebraska, 1917-26; and since that date has been sole owner of the Tekamah Oil Company, and retailer and jobber of petroleum products. He served as president of the Nebraska Independent Oil Men's Association, 1928-29-30, and is a member of the board of directors of that organization now. In April, 1931, he was elected a member of the board of trustees of Midland College, at Fremont, Nebraska.

He is an independent Republican and has held the following public offices: mayor of Tekamah, 1915-16-17; member of the board of education, 1914-31; president of the board of education since 1920. He is chairman of the home service department of the Red Cross; has been a member of the Commercial Club since 1914; of the local Lion's Club since 1925, serving as president in 1928; and is a member of the Nebraskana Society.

Mr. Wassum took an active part in Red Cross relief work and Liberty loan drives during the World War; he was a member of the home guards 1916-18. He is a Mason, holding membership in Tekamah Lodge Number 24, Royal Arch Chapter, and Jordan Commandery Number 16, at

M C. WARRINGTON

Blair, Nebraska. From 1915 to 1920, he held membership in the Burt County Young Men's Christian Association; it has since been disbanded.

He married Friedericka Christine Wisslicen at Fremont, Dodge County, Nebraska, June 22, 1905. Mrs. Wassum was born at Steinenbronn, Wurtemburg, Germany, June 30, 1878. Their three children are: Dorothy, born July 17, 1908, who received her A. B. degree at the University of Nebraska in 1931; Erma, born July 27, 1913; and Sylvesta, born November 26, 1914. Mr. Wassum is affiliated with Emmanuel Lutheran Church at Tekamah. His hobby is reading. Residence: Tekamah. (Photograph in Album).

Guttorm Ellingsen Wasthun

Born at Odde, Norway, November 28, 1841, Guttorm Ellingsen Wasthun is the son of Elling Hansen and Torbjor (Jordal) Washtun. His father was born in Norway, and farmed until his death at Odde, on June 2, 1891. His mother, also born in Norway, died at Odde, in 1884.

Guttorm Wasthun was educated in common school, and came to the United States, in 1864. On September 28, 1878, he was united in marriage to Martha Ann Pope, at Pierce City, Missouri. Mrs. Wasthun, born at Pulasky, Tennessee, May 28, 1853, died at Bostwick on October 28, 1916. Her paternal ancestors were Irish and her maternal ancestors English. Two children were born to them, Everet Ernest, born July 27, 1879, died September 28, 1880; and Lizzie Jane, born December 2, 1880.

A prominent farmer in Nebraska for the past twenty-five years, Mr. Wasthun is loved and respected by all who know him. He is affiliated with the Republican party, and was recently elected to life membership in the Nebraskana Society. Residence: Bostwick.

George Clarence Waters

George Clarence Waters, ranchman, was born at Frederick, Maryland, October 31, 1872, son of Peter Shlossor and Sarah Etta Catherine (Main) Waters. The father, born in Middletown, Maryland, June 27, 1848, was a farmer and ranchman in Nebraska for many years prior to his death at Brewster on January 28, 1902. His mother, born at Frederick, June 10, 1842, died at Aurora, July 7, 1918.

Mr. Waters attended the public school at Convoy, Ohio, until his graduation in May, 1855. From 1897 until 1898 he was a student at a normal school at Chillicothe, Missouri, where he received the degree of Master of Accounts.

He has resided in Nebraska for the past thirty-eight years, where he has engaged in ranching, and where he has served as county treasurer of Blaine County the past six years, elected on the Republican ticket.

During the World War period he was county food administrator, and legal advisor on the Blaine County draft board. He is a Protestant, a Mason, a member of the Eastern Star, the Ancient Order of United Workmen and the Nebraskana Society. For a number of years a member of the school board of Brewster High School, he has been chairman since 1929. His hobby is mechanics. Residence: Brewster.

Robert Orville Watkins

Robert Orville Watkins, leading professional man at Curtis, Nebraska, was born March 20, 1902, the son of Robert Clark and Elva (Whitehead) Watkins. His father who was a farmer, was born in Pennsylvania in 1865 of English stock. Dr. Watkins attended the Stockville Public Schools, Stockville, Nebraska, until 1923 when he was graduated from the high school there.

He received the Doctor of Dental Surgery degree at Kansas City Western Dental College, and in the Dental Departments of the Lincoln and Lee University of Kansas City, Missouri. He was a member of the Trowel Fraternity and was class president at Kansas City Western Dental College in his sophomore year. He has been engaged in the practice of dentistry at Curtis, Nebraska, for the past four years and holds membership in the Chamber of Commerce, the Rotary Club, and the Red Cross.

Dr. Watkins is affiliated with the First Congregational Church of Curtis, is a Master Mason a member of Stockville Lodge No. 196, and holds membership in the Nebraskana Society. His sports are hunting, fishing, and trap shooting. He has won several trophies at the trap.

On June 16, 1930, he was united in marriage to Neva Lou Taylor at Curtis, Nebraska. Mrs. Watkins was born at Edison, Nebraska, August 30, 1902, her parents having established their home there in the pioneer days. Her social activities include church and local civic affairs, and she is a member of the P. E. O. and Red Cross. They have one child, Luanne, born September 30, 1931. Residence: Curtis.

Charles J. Watson

Charles J. Watson, who has been a farmer in Nebraska for the past 50 years, was born at Majon, Illinois, April 2, 1860, the son of Thomas and Catherine (Kear) Watson. His father, who was a Methodist minister, was born in Ireland, and died in Mercer County, Illinois. May 1, 1879. His mother was born in Ireland and died at Lincoln, Nebraska, September 18, 1906.

Mr. Watson attended the grade schools of Illinois and was a student at Hedding College, and Northwestern University. He is a member of the Fairmont Commercial Club, was a member of the local school board for 12 years, and served as a member of the Fairmont city council for one year. He served three terms in the Nebraska legislature, elected on the Republican ticket.

He was united in marriage with Laura Catherine Hofrichter at Bellwood, Nebraska, September 21, 1891. Mrs. Watson was born of German parentage at Chatsworth, Illinois, February 10, 1870. To this marriage four children were born: Ruth, born September 3, 1892, who married Samuel Taylor; Frank H., born March 9, 1894, who married Frances Schemel; Florence, born April 2, 1896, who died; and Lee, born August 26, 1898, who married Clara Anderson. Frank is a farmer, while Lee is a teacher in public schools. Residence: Fairmont.

Earl Raymond Watson

Earl Raymond Watson was born at Northfield, Iowa, August 9, 1887, the son of John William and Amantha Belle (Houston) Watson, and for the past 30 years has been a farmer near Oxford, Nebraska. His father, who is a farmer, was born in Yorkshire, England, September 3, 1861, and his mother, who is a member of the Daughters of the American Revolution, was born at Louisa, Iowa, July 13, 1865. The latter is a relative of the Harrison family of Revolutionary fame and of Sam Houston, the founder of Houston, Texas.

Mr. Watson was graduated from the high school at Arapahoe, Nebraska, and took a short course in agriculture at the University of Colorado. He is a member of the Parent Teachers Association, is affiliated with the Methodist Episcopal Church, and was formerly a director in the local school board.

He married Leila Claire Richardson at Arapahoe, January 4, 1910. Mrs. Watson, who is an energetic farm woman, was born at Elwell, Iowa, April 1, 1889. Their children are: Edwin, born October 3, 1910; Helene, born November 29, 1914; and Eldon Earl, born May 18, 1928. Residence: Oxford.

Elsie A. Watson

Elsie A. Watson, graduate nurse and a leader in civic affairs at Albion, Nebraska, is a lifetime resident of this state. She was born at St. Paul, Nebraska, June 9, 1892, the daughter of Andrew D. and Mary M. (Polansky) Anderson. Her father, who was born in Denmark, has been engaged in business in this country for many years. Her mother, who was born at Prague, Bohemia, is musically inclined.

Mrs. Watson was graduated from the Minden High School in 1910, was graduated from the Wise Memorial Hospital at Omaha, and studied nurses training in New York City where she was an honor student in 1915. As a specialist in anaesthesia she held positions in Omaha over a period of six years.

She is president of the P. E. O., is a member of the Eastern Star and Parent Teachers Association, and holds membership in the Red Cross and the Nebraskana Society. Her hobbies are reading and needlework. During the World War Mrs. Watson served as a Red Cross nurse. She was the first vice president of the auxiliary and served as its treasurer during the years 1928, 1929, 1930, and 1931.

Of her marriage to William Burton Watson two children were born, William, October 1, 1923; and Howard B., October 1, 1923. Residence: Albion.

William Reeve Watson

William Reeve Watson, editor, was born at Delavan, Wisconsin, November 1, 1870, son of Joseph Jerome and Lucy Olin (Kendrick) Watson.

He attended the Burlingame, Beloit, and Kansas City public schools, and was graduated from Beloit High School in 1888. He received his Bachelor of Philosophy degree from Shurtleffe College at Upper Alton, Illinois, in 1892. On July 11, 1900, Mr. Watson was married to Coryell Wood at Milwaukee, Wisconsin.

Mr. Watson's newspaper career began as a reporter at Fort Smith, Arkansas on *News Record*. He was later associated with the *Salina Journal*, and has been reporter, night editor, Sunday editor, and finally managing editor of the *World Herald*.

Mr. Watson is a member of All Saints Episcopal Church, the Chamber of Commerce, the Rotary Club, and the Masons. His clubs are the University and Happy Hollow. Residence: Omaha.

William Henry Wearin

William Henry Wearin, who has been a successful farmer in Thayer County, Nebraska, for many years, was born near Hastings, Iowa, March 6, 1868, the son of Otha and Martha Jane (Wortman) Wearin. His father, who was a farmer, was born at Harrison, Virginia, March 22, 1826, and died at Hastings, April 8, 1902. His mother was born in Brown County, Ohio, May 18, 1837, and died at Hastings, September 30, 1870.

Mr. Wearin received his education in rural school and business college. He has lived in Nebraska for the past 29 years and is now a retired farmer and landowner. He holds membership in the Nebraskana Society and the Carleton Community Club.

His marriage to Cora Ella Woodrow was solemnized at Council Bluffs, Pottawatomie County, Iowa, October 18, 1904. Mrs. Wearin, whose parents were American born, was born at Malvern, Mills County, Iowa, September 18, 1867. They have one daughter, Edna, born September 10, 1905, who is married to Vern Christopher Armstrong. Residence: Carleton.

Arthur Lon Weatherly

Arthur Lon Weatherly was born at Simcoe, Canada, March 30, 1868, the son of John and Mary (Jackson) Weatherly. His father, who was a tailor, was born at Werwick-onTweed, England, and died at Osage, Mitchell County, Iowa. His mother was born at London, England, and died at Osage, November, 1892.

Dr. Weatherly, who has been a clergyman and welfare worker in Nebraska for the past 15 years, attended the Osage Public School and in 1888 was graduated from Cedar Valley Seminary. He received his A. B. at Grinnell College, and later was a student at Harvard University and Clark University. He was honored with Phi Beta Kappa membership and the D. D. degree; he was orator of his senior class.

He is now past minister of the All Soul's Unitarian Church at Lincoln, Lancaster County, Nebraska. He is the author of *Unity of the Race*, published sermons; and was the editor of The Co-operative Magazine, and editorial writer for *Unity*. He was secretary of the state board for dependent children, 1910-15, and was a member of the commission on workman's compensation.

On June 28, 1893, he was united in marriage with Clara Allyn Jones at Lancaster, Grant County, Wisconsin. Mrs. Weatherly was born at Lancaster, March 25, 1865. They have one son, John, born November 4, 1908.

Dr. Weatherly was director of the community service work at Southport, North Carolina, Wilmington, North Carolina, and Norfolk, Virginia, during the World War. He is a member of the Chamber of Commerce; the Candle Light Club; Laymen's Club; Philosophers' Club; and the Young Men's Christian Association. He is president of the Social Service Club, and holds membership in the Nebraska State Historical Society, and the Nebraskana Society. He is an Odd Fellow. His favorite sport is tennis. Politically, he is an independent. Residence: Lincoln.

Arthur J. Weaver

On November 18, 1873, Arthur J. Weaver, former governor of the state of Nebraska, was born on the old Weaver farm at Falls City, Nebraska. He is the son of Archibald J. and Martha (Myers) Weaver. The family, on both sides, is of pioneer stock. Abram Weaver, father of Archibald, came from Germany with his parents while still young. Archibald, left an orphan, was self-educated, graduating from Wyoming Seminary in Pennsylvania, and later completing the law course at Harvard University. In the spring of 1869 he came to Falls City where he soon developed the qualities which made him an outstanding personage in the community. He served in the constitutional conventions of 1871 and 1875, was district attorney of the first judicial district from 1875-76. At the age of thirty-two, and in 1857 he was elected district judge, serving seven years. He resigned when elected as member of congress from the first Nebraska district. He was re-elected for a second term and died during his encumbency, at the age of forty-three years.

Martha A. Weaver, mother of Arthur, was born on a farm in the Wyoming Valley, Pennsylvania. Her first colonial ancestor, Michael Myers, came from Germany in 1760, settling in Maryland. Two sons, Lawrence and Phillip, served in the Revolution, participating in the battle of Germantown. Phillip, grandfather of Martha, settled in the Wyoming Valley in 1785, where he married Martha Bennett. Her ancestors were among the early English settlers in Rhode Island.

Thomas Bennett, her father, was one of the builders and defenders of the famous Forty Fort on the banks of the Susquehanna. The Myers and Bennett families figured prominently in the many phases of the history of the Wyoming Valley. In 1864, Martha Weaver was graduated from the Wyoming Seminary. After her marriage she came to Falls City with her husband and for many years was known as a woman of usefulness and influence in her community.

Arthur J. Weaver was educated in the public schools

of Falls City; entered the University of Nebraska, receiving his B. A. in 1895, and his LL. B. in 1896. He then entered the legal profession, remaining in practice until 1904 when he became, successively, member of the Nebraska House of Representatives, city attorney of Falls City, county attorney of Richardson County, mayor of Falls City and member of the constitutional convention of 1920. He was chosen president of the last mentioned body, the work of which, submitted in the form of forty-one amendments, was approved by the people by a vote of three to one.

In 1905 he retired from the practice of law to engage in the fruit growing, livestock and farming business. He was for two terms president of the State Horticultural Society, and eight years a member of the State Board of Agriculture. From 1924-27 he served as agricultural director of the Omaha branch of the Federal Reserve Bank.

As a member of the state legislature, he introduced the constructive measure of providing for the permanent location of the state fair at Lincoln. He was one of the pioneers in securing drainage laws and construction thereunder of improvements in drainage district No. 1 of Richardson County. This has resulted in the reclamation of 20,000 acres of land. He was one of those instrumental in securing for his community the location of the Missouri Pacific shops and division as well as other industries, modern buildings, etc.

Elected on the Republican ticket in 1928 as governor he was unsuccessful candidate for re-election in 1930. During his term Mr. Weaver, as governor, for the first time in the history of the state, submitted a budget in two parts, one for appropriations which would come from general taxation, and one for the expenditure of moneys derived from the gasoline tax and miscellaneous fees. He advocated the system of code revision resulting in the elimination of two department heads and the abolition of bureaus and divisions, and the consolidation of others, resulting in an annual saving of over $72,000.00.

Among other things a bank re-organization law was suggested by the governor to the Department of Trade and Commerce and passed by the legislature, which has resulted in the re-organization of thirty-seven banks and a great saving to communities and the depositors of the banks affected. The Bank Guarantee Fund Commission was abolished and liquidation of failed banks consolidated. Other strengthening bank provisions were adopted as the result of his recommendations and that of chief examiner, former governor Shallenberger, as a result of the bank investigation. Under his leadership there has been consistent and energetic enforcement of the laws as disclosed by his record. Residence: Falls City.

Francis Louis Weaver

Francis L. Weaver was born at Anamosa, Iowa, December 16, 1861, the son of DeVolson and Nancy Lavina (Smith) Weaver. His father, who was born at Pitcher, Chenango County, New York, February 9, 1832, and died at Cedar Rapids, Iowa, in September, 1905, was an automobile dealer. Active in politics and civic affairs he served for a time as deputy sheriff and later as mayor. He was descended from English ancestors, two of whom served in the Revolution.

His mother, of German descent, homemaker and the mother of four children, was born at Cortland, New York, July 9, 1833, and died at Cedar Rapids, October 21, 1912.

Mr. Weaver received his elementary education in the public school at Anamosa, Iowa, and in 1882 was graduated from the high school at Ann Arbor, Michigan. He was awarded the degree Ph. B. at the University of Michigan in 1886, and the LL. B. in the law department of this institution in 1887. He was admitted to the practice of law at Ann Arbor, June, 1887. Since that time he has

lived in Nebraska, and since 1890 has been a member of the law firm of Weaver & Giller.

A Democrat, Mr. Weaver has taken an especially active part in the political life of his state. In 1902 he was candidate for the state senate. He has served as deputy county attorney, 1903-04; chairman of the Democratic county central committee, 1907; and city attorney, 1918-21. He was for several years president of the Jacksonian Club.

On June 26, 1889, he was united in marriage with Jeannette Martha Burgner. Mrs. Weaver was born at Richwood, Union County, Iowa, March 4, 1860. Her ancestry is Swiss. Three children were born to their marriage, two of whom are living. They are: Leonidas DeVolson, born February 22, 1893, who died June 29, 1930; Margaret Celestine, born October 30, 1895; and Frank Burgner, born July 16, 1901.

During the World War, Mr. Weaver was a four minute man. He is a member of the Sons of the American Revolution, Omaha Bar Association, the Nebraska Bar Association, and the American Bar Association. He is an Elk, and a member of the Red Cross. He is affiliated with the First Central Congregational Church of Omaha, and is a member of the Omaha Athletic Club and the Carter Lake Club. His favorite sport is hiking. His hobby is Shakespeare. Residence: Omaha.

John Ernst Weaver

John E. Weaver, a leading educator and botanist at the University of Nebraska, was born at Villisca, Iowa, May 5, 1884. His father, John Weaver, a farmer and a Civil War veteran, was born in Germany. Amelia (Theroff) Weaver, his mother, was born in Lee County, Iowa.

Professor Weaver was graduated from the University of Nebraska in 1909, with the degree B. S., and received his A. M., 1911. He was a student at the University of Chicago, in 1911; studied at Washington State College, 1912-13; and was awarded the degree Ph. D. at the University of Minnesota, in 1916. He has been awarded the following scholastic honors: Phi Beta Kappa; Sigma Xi; Phi Sigma; Botany Seminar; Who's Who in America; fellowship in the American Association for the Advancement of Science; and membership in the American Men of Science, starred in botany.

He was instructor of botany at Washington State College, 1912-13; was assistant professor of botany at this institution, 1913-14; was instructor of botany at the University of Minnesota, 1914-15, and assistant professor, 1915-17 Nebraska University, was made professor of plant ecology, 1917, at the University of Nebraska; and was made research associate in ecology, Carnegie Institute of Washington. He is now professor of plant ecology at the University of Nebraska.

Professor Weaver was married to Martha Helen Hasse at Wahoo, Nebraska. Two children were born to this union: Cornelia Marcia, born February 6, 1909; and Robert John, born September 20, 1917.

He is a member of the editorial board of Ecology and Ecological Monographs. He is a member of the American Association of University Professors; the Ecological Society of America, serving as vice president in 1924-25, and president in 1930; the Society of American Physiologists; Nebraska Academy of Sciences; and the Botanical Society of America. He is a member of the Lincoln Knife and Fork Club, is affiliated with All Souls Unitarian Church at Lincoln, and is a Republican.

Professor Weaver is distinguished throughout the scientific world by reason of the scores of articles he has written on professional subjects and his extensive study of botany. He is the author of the following:

Evaporation and Plant Succession in Southeastern Washington and Adjacent Idaho (1914); A Study of the Root-systems of Prairie Plants of Southeastern Washington (1915); Natural Reforestation in the Mountains of Northern Idaho (with Harry B. Humphrey, 1915);

The Effect of Certain Rusts upon the Transpiration of Their Hosts (1916) ; *A Study of the Vegetation of Southeastern Washington and Adjacent Idaho* (1917) ; *Ecological Studies in the Tension zone Between Prairie and Woodland* (with Albert F. Thiel, 1917) ; *Materials for Plant Studies in Nebraska Schools* (1918) ; *The Quadrat Method in Teaching Ecology* (1918) ; *Further Studies in the Ecotone Between Prairie and Woodland* (with R. J. Pool and F. C. Jean 1918) ; *Relative Transpiration of Coniferous and Broad-leaved Trees in Autumn and Winter* (with A. Mogensen 1919) ; *The Ecological Relation of Roots* (1919) ; *Root Developments in the Grassland Formation* (1920) ; *Development and Activities of Roots of Crop Plants* (with F. C. Jean and John W. Crist, 1921) ; *Experimental Vegetation* (with F. E. Clements, 1924) ; *Development of Root and Shoot of Winter Wheat under Field Conditions* (with J. Kramer and Maude Reed, 1924) ; *Absorption of Nutrients from Subsoil in Relation to Crop Yield* (with John W. Crist, 1924) ; *Relation of Hardpan to Root Penetration in the Great Plains* (with John W. Crist, 1922) ; *Direct Measurement of Water Loss from Vegetation without Disturbing the Normal Structure of the Soil,* (1924) ; *Plant Production as a Measure of Environment,* (1924) ; *Root Development and Crop Yield Under Irrigation* (with F. C. Jean, 1924) ; *Root Habits of Field Crops* (1925) ; *Investigations on the Root Habits of Plants* (1925) ; *The Transect Method of Studying Woodland Vegetation along Streams* (with H. C. Hanson and John Aikman 1925) ; *Some Ecological Aspects of Agriculture in the Prairie* (1927) ; *Root Development of Vegetable Crops* (with William E. Bruner, 1927) ; *Plant Ecology* (with F. E. Clements, 1929) ; *Plant Competition* (with F. E. Clements and H. C. Hanson, 1929) ; *Relative Development of Root and Shoot under Long and Short Day Illumination* (with W. J. Himmel, 1929) ; *Relation of Aeration to Root Development in Hydrophytes* (with W. J. Himmel, 1930) ; *Underground Plant Development in its Relation to Grazing* (1930) ; *The Environment of the Prairie* (with W. J. Himmel, 1931). Residence: Lincoln.

Adin Hilton Webb

Born at Loveland, Colorado, September 7, 1887, Adin Hilton Webb, physician and surgeon, has been a resident of Nebraska for twenty years. He is the son of Edward and Elizabeth (Williams) Webb, the former a farmer who was born at Bellvue, Ohio, September 10, 1851. His ancestry has been American for several generations, the Webbs having landed in Plymouth in 1630. Elizabeth, wife of Edward, was born at Minersville, Pennsylvania, August 4, 1861, her father being of Welsh blood, and her mother of Welsh extraction.

Dr. Webb attended the country schools near Hamilton, Missouri, 1902. Thereafter he attended Abilene High School and Dickinson County High School at Chapman, Kansas, graduating in 1908. In 1916 he received both his B. Sc. and his M. D. at the University of Nebraska. During 1910 and 1911 he attended Kansas State University. In 1928 he took post-graduate work at the Washington University. He played football in high school, was editor of his college paper and is a member of Phi Rho Sigma.

On November 26, 1919, he was married to Eda Bernice Myers at Lincoln. Mrs. Webb was born at Wayne, Nebraska, September 12, 1884 and was a teacher. On the paternal side her ancestors have been in America several generations; her mother came from Sweden. There is one daughter, Martha Joan, born July 2, 1929.

Medical director of Lincoln public schools in 1917-18, he was commissioned a lieutenant in the Medical Officers Reserve Corps on September 24, 1917, and in February, 1918, was called to active duty, serving overseas in England and France with the British Army until May 28, 1919. In January, 1919, he was promoted to rank of captain in the Medical Corps. From 1919 to 1924 he was

engaged in practice in Lincoln and served as medical director of the Midwest Life Insurance Company, and resident physician at the University of Nebraska. From 1924-27 he was director of a hospital at Yachow, West China. At the present time he is engaged in private practice and is attendant physician for University of Nebraska students.

Dr. Webb is a member of the First Baptist Church of Lincoln. His professional memberships include the American Medical Association, the Nebraska State and Lancaster County Medical Societies and the China Medical Society. He is district commissioner of Boy Scouts, a member of the Nebraskana Society and a charter member of the Nebraska Society of Mayflower Descendants. His sports are tennis and handball. Residence: Lincoln.

Katherine L. Webb

Katherine L. Webb, educator and executive of prominence in Nebraska, has been a resident of this state all her life. She was born at Beatrice, Gage County, Nebraska, March 27, 1886, the daughter of Joseph Luther and Kate L. (Sheppard) Webb. Her father, a physician, was born August 1, 1837, and died at Beatrice, May 12, 1912. His English ancestors came to America in the *Mayflower.* Her mother was born at Stockton, England, May 18, 1854, and is still living.

Miss Webb was graduated from the Beatrice High School in 1903, and in 1907 received her A. B. degree at Nebraska Wesleyan University, where she was elected to membership in Theophanian, now Alpha Kappa Delta. She took post-graduate work at the University of Nebraska. From 1907 to 1910 she served as principal of the high school at Davenport, Nebraska, and from 1912 to 1914, and 1918-19, was instructor in the Beatrice High School. She is now acting as general secretary of the Young Women's Christian Association at Beatrice.

She is the author of *Four Minute Talks for Superintendents,* 1926, and *More Four Minute Talks for Superintendents,* 1928. Her membership in civic organizations include: State Teachers Association; Business and Professional Women's Association; Parent Teachers Association; and the Beatrice Board of Education, of which she was president from 1925 to 1929. She has served as a member of the board of the Young Women's Christian Association for 12 years, and is now president of this organization. From 1915 to 1930 Miss Webb was general superintendent of the Centenary Methodist Episcopal Sunday School at Beatrice.

She has served as patriotic chairman and student loan-fund chairman of the Daughters of the American Revolution. Her religious affiliation is with the Centenary Methodist Episcopal Church at Beatrice. Residence: Beatrice.

Louis Harward Webb

Louis H. Webb was born at Oaks, North Carolina, August 2, 1888, the son of Junius Davis and Miriam Elizabeth (Harward) Webb. His father, who was born at Oaks, June 2, 1861, received his education at Duke University, Durham, North Carolina, and is a prosperous merchant and bank president today. His English and Welsh ancestors settled at Jamestown, 1607; one ancestor was a general in the Revolution.

His mother was born at Chapel Hill, North Carolina, November 1, 1868. She attended Peace College, Raleigh, North Carolina, and is a talented pianist and singer. Her paternal ancestors were English; her father was a Confederate soldier in the Civil War. Through the maternal line she is descended from the Scotch; one ancestor was a general in the Revolution.

Dr. Webb received his early education under a private tutor, and was graduated from the Chapel Hill High School in 1903. In 1910 he was awarded the M. D. degree at Jefferson Medical College at Philadelphia. He was a student at the University of North Carolina, 1904-08, and later took post-graduate work there; Tulane University, 1927; and Stanford University, 1919, 1928, 1929. He was a member of Omega Upsilon Phi, dialectic society; and won the southern championship for the one mile event in track at the University of North Carolina.

He is now medical officer in charge of the United States Veteran Hospital at Lincoln, Lancaster County, Nebraska, having been engaged in medical practice previously in North Carolina. He is the author of numerous medical articles. During the World War he served as lieutenant colonel of the Medical Reserve Corps of the United States Army, and was formerly surgeon of the Reserve United States Public Health Service. He now holds membership in the American Legion and the Reserve Officers Association.

Dr. Webb is a member of the American Medical Association; the American Hospital Association; the Nebraska Art Association; the Fifty Fifty Club of Lincoln; and the Nebraskana Society. He is an honorary member of the Royal Institute of Public Health of Great Britain. His sports include golfing and horseback riding. His hobby is military defense.

Of his marriage to Elsie Veronica Kester, three children were born: Louis Harward, Jr., born November 1, 1910; Frederick Alexander, born December 15, 1912; and Kathrene Kling, born December 17, 1913. On May 29, 1930, he was married to Mary Hall Twibel. Mrs. Webb, who was born at Montpelier, Indiana, July 10, 1904, received her education at the University of Cincinnatti, and was a graduate nurse before her marriage. Her ancestry is English. Residence: Lincoln.

Orie Lee Webb

Born at Bedford, Iowa, December 4, 1888, Orie Lee Webb is the son of William E. and Emma L. (Ferris) Webb. His father, born in Knox County, Illinois, February 7, 1855, died at Bellevue, Nebraska, October 13, 1929. A farmer and business man, he was the son of Luke and Melvina (Allen) Webb, who traced their ancestry in America to settlers coming before the Revolution.

Emma L. Ferris, born in Knox County, Illinois, March 24, 1856, is the daughter of Lorenzo D. and Elizabeth (Carpenter) Ferris. Her ancestors came to America before the Revolution, also.

Orie Lee Webb attended the public schools of Bedford, Iowa, and was graduated from high school there in 1907. He received his Bachelor of Arts degree from Bellevue College in 1914, and his master's degree from the University of Nebraska in 1928. During 1908-10 he was a student at Coe College, at Cedar Rapids, and in 1919 at Columbia University. At Bellevue he was prominent in debate, and was elected to Phi Delta Kappa. He also won football letters during 1911-13 at Bellevue.

From 1914 to 1916 Mr. Webb taught at Weeping Water, and from 1916 until 1922 was principal of the high school at Columbus. Since 1922 he has been superintendent of schools at David City, and during the summer sessions of 1929, 30, 31, has been instructor at the University of Nebraska.

Mr. Webb is a life member of the National Education Association, a member and treasurer of the Nebraska State Teachers Association, president (1930-31) of the David City Commercial Club, and a Scottish Rite Mason. He is affiliated with the Congregational Church. His favorite sport is golf and his hobby is reading.

On December 30, 1916, he was united in marriage to Olga M. Gereke at Seward. Mrs. Webb, who was born at Seward, August 3, 1886, is the daughter of J. F. and Minnie (Thomas) Gereke. A former teacher, she is at present state child welfare chairman for the American

Legion Auxiliary, and active in civic affairs. There are two sons, Richard, born November 18, 1917; and Herschel, born October 31, 1924. Residence: David City.

T. E. Webber

T. E. Webber, farmer and rancher, was born at Brooklyn, New York, October 15, 1871, son of H. H. and Helen (Dean) Webber.

The father was born in Bristol, England, and was a stone cutter and builder by trade. He died in Lancaster County, Nebraska, in 1890. His wife, Helen, was also born in Bristol, and died in Brooklyn, New York, in 1875.

Mr. Webber attended public school in Lancaster County, and from 1897 until 1910 engaged in mail contracting and staging in Wyoming. Since 1910 he has been a farmer and rancher near Mullen. He is a Republican, a Protestant, a 32nd degree Mason, and moderator of the school board of District No. 2 of Hooker County.

On December 31, 1902, Mr. Webber was married to Leona Hendricks at Douglas, Nebraska. She was born in Otoe County, October 15, 1874, of pioneer Nebraska parentage. They have three children, Laura N., born March 20, 1904, who married Leonard Decker; Doris C., born September 17, 1906; and Erwin E., born May 7, 1913.

Mr. Webber is a Republican. From 1883 until 1897 prior to his residence in Wyoming, he farmed in Nebraska. Residence: Mullen.

Thomas Edward Webber

Thomas Edward Webber, rancher and farmer, was born in Brooklyn, New York, in October, 1871, son of Henry Hadford and Helen (Dean) Webber.

The father, who was born in Bristol, England, was a contractor and builder, who died at Johnson, Nebraska, in 1889. His wife, Helen, also born in Bistol, was a well-educated woman and a devoted wife and mother. She died at Brooklyn in 1875.

The year of his mother's death, Thomas Edward Webber returned to England with his father, coming back to the United States in 1883. He completed his common school education in 1890. From 1897 until 1906 Mr. Weber was engaged in staging. He drove the C. M. Scribners six horse concord coaches at Fort Steele and Walcott, Wyoming, and during this time engaged also in prospecting and mining. From 1906 he was a mail contractor, carrying mail over the Continental Divide to Rambler, Wyoming, in the winter months crossing from 25 to 30 feet of snow. Since 1910 Mr. Webber has engaged exclusively in ranching and farming.

On December 31, 1902, he was married to Leona Hendricks at Douglas, Nebraska. Mrs. Webber was born at Douglas, on October 15, 1874. To them were born four children, three of whom are living: Laura, born March 20, 1902, is a beauty operator and is married to Leonard Decker. Doris, born September 17, 1906, is a musician. Helen, born December 12, 1908, died January 6, 1911. Erwin, born May 17, 1913, is a high school graduate.

Mr. Webber is a protestant and a Republican. He is a 32nd degree Mason, and is moderator at the present time of Hooker County School District No. 2. His hobbies are reading and athletics. Residence: Seneca.

Henry Augustus Webbert

Henry Augustus Webbert, who has lived in Buffalo County, Nebraska since 1872, was born at Dayton, Ohio, February 15, 1871, the son of David and Mary Ann (Arnold) Webbert. His father, who was a contractor, was born of French parents at Carlisle, Pennsylvania, October 15, 1831, and died at Kearney, Nebraska, July 24, 1893; he was a soldier in the Civil War. His mother, whose ancestry was Dutch, was born at Dayton, August 23, 1841.

Mr. Webbert is the proprietor of a commercial printing plant at Kearney, is director of the Kearney Savings and Loan Association, and is president of the Masonic Temple Association of Kearney. He holds membership in the Rotary Club and Red Cross, is director of the Kearney Chamber of Commerce, and is affiliated with St. Lukes Episcopal Church. His social club is the Kearney Country Club, and his fraternal organizations include the Elks and the following Masonic bodies: Blue Lodge; Chapter; Commandery; Consistory; Council; and Shrine.

His hobby is game conservation and his favorite sports are fishing and hunting. On March 22, 1893, Mr. Webbert was married at Kearney to Hattie Gertrude Taylor who was born at Aledo, Illinois, September 5, 1874. To them were born: David Arnold, July 22, 1894, who married Ethel Beardsley; Henry James, June 26, 1899, who married Clarissa Cleveland; and Marylouise, December 11, 1910, who married Robert J. Walker. Residence: Kearney.

Helen Blackman Webendorfer

Helen Blackman Webendorfer, for a number of years a missionary, was born in Beaver City, Nebraska, March 22, 1891, daughter of James Samuel and Mary Hopkins (Kuykendall) Blackman. Her father, a farmer and stockman, was born in Beverly, West Virginia, March 14, 1863, descended from English settlers in the American colonies in 1631. Her mother, born at Rommey, West Virginia, July 11, 1861, died at Beaver City, May 29, 1904.

Educated in the public schools of Beaver City, Helen Blackman was graduated from high school in 1910, and from the Los Angeles Bible Institute two year course in 1917. During the year 1911 and 1912 she taught in rural schools, and next taught one term in the first grade at Hendley, Nebraska. During 1913 and 1914 she was a governess in Los Angeles.

On April 17, 1918, she was married to Henry C. Webendorfer at Beaver City. Mr. Webendorfer, who was a missionary, was born at Poughkeepsie, New York, October 21, 1892, his father a native of Dresden and his mother born in New York State of French Huguenot stock. Mr. and Mrs. Webendorfer were missionaries in South America until Mr. Webendorfer's death at sea, near Callao, Peru, November 17, 1923.

There are four children, all born in Bolivia, except Douglas, who was born in Nebraska. They are as follows: Ellen, born August 21, 1919; Henry, Jr., born April 15, 1921; Muriel, born August 16, 1922; and Douglas, born February 9, 1924.

Returning to the United States after her husband's death, Mrs. Webendorfer spent five years in New York. She is at the present time missionary superintendent of Nebraska for Christian Endeavor, and is a member of the Beaver City Presbyterian Church. She is a member of the American Legion Auxiliary, the P. E. O. Sisterhood and The Nebraskana Society. She enjoys hiking, horseback riding and swimming, but her hobbies are reading, gardening, making hooked rugs and photography. Residence: Beaver City. (Photograph in Album).

Byron Talbert Weber

Byron Talbert Weber was born at Elm Creek, Nebraska, November 28, 1895, the son of Otto Talbert and Isabele Cora (Slice) Weber. His father, who was a railroad agent for the Union Pacific Company for many years, was born at West Welland, Canada, May 29, 1865, and died at Oconee, Nebraska, April 9, 1906; his ancestry was German and Holland Dutch. His mother, a practical nurse, was born at Thompson, Illinois, November 4, 1867, of Irish and Holland Dutch parentage.

Mr. Weber attended the grade school at Monroe, Nebraska, and later at Platte Center, Nebraska. He

has been grain buyer for the T. B. Hord Company since 1920 at Oconee, Nebraska, is the manager of a ranch near there. A Democrat, he served as committeeman to the county convention, and is now committeeman in Oconee Township.

He is the oldest resident of his community and has served in almost every civic enterprise. He is a member of the Red Cross, is affiliated with the Methodist Church, and holds membership in the Nebraskana Society. He is interested in reading and likes to memorize important dates in the history of the world. His favorite sports are hunting, and rifle shooting.

During the World War he was sergeant for 20 months and saw service in France. He is a member of American Legion Post Number 84 at Columbus, Nebraska. On April 21, 1925, he was married at Columbus to Helen Maria Boesiger. Mrs. Weber, whose parents were natives of Switzerland, was born at Columbus July 14, 1904. To them were born three children: Harold, May 12, 1926; Kenneth, July 28, 1927; and Luella, July 26, 1930. Residence: Oconee.

Fred D. Weber

Fred D. Weber was born at Adamah, Washington County, Nebraska, April 15, 1871, the son of Louis C. and Magdaline (Blentzinger) Weber. His father, who was prominent in Nebraska politics and civic undertaking for many years, was born at Louisville, Kentucky, June 8, 1846, and died at Arlington, Washngton County, Nebraska, August 13, 1909. He was a merchant and druggist, who served as state representative and was chairman of the county commissioners and a Civil War veteran. His mother was born at Evansville, Indiana, May 5, 1845, and died at Arlington, October 17, 1891.

Mr. Weber attended the public schools of Nebraska, and at the age of 13 became a clerk in a store. Later his father gave him a half interest in his general store at Arlington. In 1906 he purchased the remaining interest and has since been manager and owner. He is president of the First National Bank of Arlington, and for the past 20 years has been director of the board of federation of the Nebraska Retailers Association.

He is a member of the Arlington Community Club; holds membership in the Young Men's Christian Association; and since 1917 has been vice president of the Red Cross. He is a member of Hiram Lodge Number 52 of the Ancient Free and Accepted Masons, Scottish Rite, 32nd degree, Valley of Omaha. He is a member of the Nebraskana Society, and a Republican.

On November 9, 1892, he was united in marriage with Lois Mary Lewis at Arlington. Mrs. Weber was born at Middletown, Iowa, June 2, 1874. They have two children: Harold, born May 15, 1895, who served two years in France during the World War, and who married Dottie Winona Lowe; and Mildred, born January 23, 1899, who married William H. Hillegass. Mildred has been a teacher and clerk in a store. Residence: Arlington.

Pearl Louise Weber

Pearl Louise Hunter, one of Omaha's best known educators, was born at Toledo, Ohio, January 29, 1878. She is the daughter of Edgar Judson and Mira Lavina (Littlefield) Hunter. Her father was born at Ashtabula, Ohio, March 4, 1847, and was a railroad man of English and Irish descent. He died at Chicago, June 15, 1914. His wife, Mira, was born at Elmira, New York, March 27, 1847, and died at Chicago, June 1, 1928. She was of English, Dutch and French descent.

After attending Hyde Park High School in Chicago two years, Pearl Hunter entered Armour Institute of Technology, from which she was graduated in 1895. She received her Ph. B. from the University of Chicago, in 1899, and her A. M., from that university in 1920. She attended Cornell University from 1901-02. She was elected to Phi Beta Kappa at the University of Chicago, in 1899, and received a scholarship and fellowship at that institution. She was the winner of the Sage scholarship at Cornell. In 1898 she was basket ball star at Chicago, and was a member of Spelman House. She was elected to Pi Gamma Mu in 1929.

Her marriage to William James Weber was solemnized at Peckham, Oklahoma, February 6, 1902. Mr. Weber is a clergyman, and was born at Berksville, Pennsylvania, June 16, 1877. They have four children, Clarence, born May 2, 1903, married Mary Beaty, and is superintendent of schools at Hume, Illinois. Ruth, born August 18, 1905; married Lt. William B. Blaufuss; Rose, born June 26, 1911; and Esther, born March 21, 1913, holds an honor freshman scholarship in the University of Chicago.

Mrs. Weber's professional career started as a teacher in Southwest Kansas College 1900-01; she taught at Muncie Normal Institute from 1915-17; Aurora College 1917-20; Illinois Woman's College 1920-23; and since 1923 has been teaching at the University; in 1929 she was elected head of the department of philosophy at the University of Omaha. During the summer of 1922 she taught at the University of Colorado. She is the author of *Behaviorism and Indirect Responses* (1920) and *General Examinations* (1921). She is a member of Trinity Methodist Episcopal Church and is a member of The Nebraskana Society. Her hobby is the Little Theatre, to which she has devoted much of her time. Residence: Omaha.

Harvey Lawren Webster

A farmer and stock feeder of extensive interests, Harvey Lawren Webster, was born at Troupsburg, New York, March 21, 1867. His father, Albert Webster, was born at Troupsburg, June 21, 1844, came to Burt County in 1879, and farmed in Burt County many years prior to his death on April 6, 1926. His mother, Rhoda Delana Horten, was born in Howard, New York, February 27, 1849, and died at Tekamah, June 29, 1919.

Mr. Webster attended rural schools, and afterwards completed a business course at Fremont Normal College. For twelve years thereafter he was commercial traveler for an implement firm out of Council Bluffs and Omaha. At the present time he is manager of five farms comprising 700 acres in Burt County, is president of the Burt County Legislative and Taxation Committee, director of the Tekamah Co-operative Creamery and a stockholder in the Farmers State Bank.

A Republican all his life, he was township clerk and assessor for many years, and served in the 40th and 41st sessions of the Nebraska legislature. During the World War he was a member of the Home Guard and the Burt County Council of Defense, and chairman of all war loan activities in his district. A member of the Master Farmers organzation, he is also a member of the Burt County Old Settlers Club and Historical Society and is on the executive committee. He is an Odd Fellow, a Master Mason, and a member of Jordan Commandery at Blair, and is a member of the executive board of the Tekamah Chamber of Commerce.

Mr. Webster holds a life membership in the Red Cross, and is a member of the First Baptist Church. He was married to Mary Anna Gilbert at Tekamah on July 15, 1893, to them were born the following children: Everett W., born October 14, 1895; died October 19, 1895; Nora M., born November 2, 1897, who was graduated from Tekamah High School and attended Wayne Teacher's College; Alice R., born May 7, 1900, a graduate of Tekamah High School, who married Carl O. Carlson, a farmer living near Tekamah; Neva Mae, born March 12, 1913, and Kenneth L., born January 23, 1915. Mr. Webster is justly proud of his fine family. Residence: Tekamah. (Photograph in Album).

John Fabian Webster

Born at Sterling, Illinois, January 20, 1871, John F. Webster came to Nebraska in January, 1879. His father, James Webster, was born in Tipperary, Ireland, in 1851,

and came with his parents to America in 1866. His ancestors moved from Scotland to Ireland many generations ago. James Webster was a carpenter, railroad construction contractor and farmer, whose death occurred at Platte Center, Nebraska, December 17, 1885.

Margaret Pollard, wife of James Webster, was born in Tipperary, in 1848, and died at Platte Center, July 9, 1892. When her husband died she was left with seven small children to care for, and all her time was devoted to her family.

John Fabian Webster completed the eighth grade in country schools in the late eighties. As a boy he was a good baseball player, wrestler and foot racer. He still likes all sports but confines his activities to golf.

On July 1, 1902, he was united in marriage to Golda Ethel Barnes at Elba. Mrs. Webster was born at Scotia, January 12, 1885, of early American ancestry. There are four children, Marguerite, born December 17, 1903 who married Arthur H. O'Neill; Velma Alice, born May 31, 1905, who married Edward Gnaster, James Lavern, born February 11, 1907; and Cathryn, born November 6, 1915.

Until after the declaration of war with Spain in 1898 Mr. Webster farmed and worked with his father in railroad construction. On April 22, 1898, he enlisted with the Nebraska National Guard, and on May 10, was sworn into the service of the United States, for service in the Philippines. Upon his return he was employed with the Omaha Elevator Company, and bought grain for them until February 1, 1909, when he left to take charge of the *St. Paul Phonograph*.

An extremely independent Democrat, he was appointed state printer by Governor Keith Neville, and served two years, 1917 and 1918. During the years 1928 and 1929 he was a member of the Democrat state committee. He is a member in good standing of the United Spanish War Veterans, and in 1928 served as commander of Charles E. Norris Camp No. 6. A Catholic, he is affiliated with Sts. Peter and Paul's Church, and is a member (grand knight 1918-19) of the Knights of Columbus.

Always active in every effort toward the advancement of his community, Mr. Webster is a charter member of the St. Paul Community Club, and has been its president two terms. He is at the present time president of the local Lions Club, is a member of the Nebraska Press Association (president 1929), was first secretary of the Loup Valley Press Association 1913, and served as its president in 1919. He is a life member of the Red Cross and of The Nebraskana Society, and a member of the Ancient Order of United Workmen, the American Yeomen and the Parent Teachers Association. His social club is the St. Paul Golf Club, of which he has served as president two terms.

Mr. Webster enjoys all kinds of sport, including baseball, boxing, wrestling and of late years golf, and has parred ten different courses. His hobby is getting out a newspaper which tells his readers what is going on in public offices. Residence: St. Paul. (Photograph on Page 1253).

William Byron Weekes

William Byron Weekes, who has been a grain dealer and livestock raiser in Valley County, Nebraska, for 55 years, was born at Metropolis, Illinois, November 5, 1859. His father, Thomas Weekes, who was a cabinet maker, was born at Kent England, in 1826, and died in Libby Military prison in 1862; he was mortally wounded at Hartsville, Tennessee, in the Civil War. His mother was born at Kent, July 26, 1830, and died at Scotia, Nebraska, October 15, 1915.

Mr. Weekes attended rural school in Livingston County, Illinois, and latter took a night course after he had homesteaded in Nebraska at the age of 16. He is proprietor of the Weekes Seed Company at Ord at this time, is director of schools in his county, and since 1899

Kimber Studio—St. Paul

JOHN FABIAN WEBSTER

has been active in the Pioneers Association as secretary. He is a Royal Arch and Blue Lodge Mason, is active in the local Commercial Club, and holds membership in the Red Cross and the Methodist Episcopal Church.

He was united in marriage with Nora Almira Whitehead at Greeley, Nebraska, June 12, 1881. To them were born: Charles, born March 30, 1882, who married Ella Sears; Edward, June 12, 1883, who married Lillian Sautter; Edgar, June 12, 1885, who married Hattie Van Skike; Chester L., December 1, 1887, who married Jessie Pickett; Cecil C., September 14, 1889, who died May 1, 1907; Edith, July 29, 1893, who married John Aikman. Charles is a surgeon at Ord, Edgar is manager of the Bookwalter Estate at Beatrice, Nebraska; Edward is an insurance man, and Chester is the manager of the Farm Co-operative Board in Maryland. Residence: Ord.

Harry E. Weekly

Harry E. Weekly, county superintendent of schools at Broken Bow, Nebraska, has resided in this state all his life. He was born at Lincoln, Nebraska, August 16, 1892, the son of William L. Weekly and Margaret E. (Maxwell) Weekly.

Mr. Weekly received the A. B. degree at Cotner University at Lincoln in 1915, and has been an active leader in educational affairs in Custer County, Nebraska, since then. He served in the American Expeditionary Forces in France during the World War, and at this time is past commander of the American Legion Post at Broken Bow. He is a member of the Nebraskana Society, and holds membership in the Ancient Free and Accepted Masons.

Of his marriage to Jattie P. Hendricks, which occurred at Nelson, Nebraska, October 14, 1919, four children were born. Residence: Broken Bow.

Marie O'Donnell Weeks

Marie O'Donnell Weeks, newspaper publisher, writer and Clubwoman, was born in Cuming County, Nebraska, May 6, 1881. Her father, James O'Donnell, was born in Ireland of an old and distinguished family, and came to the United States in 1861. He served with the Union Army in the Civil War, and died in Cuming County, July 1, 1893.

Katherine Elizabeth McLaughlin, wife of James O'Donnell, was born in Hartford, Connecticut, March 25, 1862. She came of a family of many attainments in Ireland, and was a cultured woman and a fine mother. She died at Norfolk, May 29, 1930.

Educated in rural schools in Cuming County until 1896, Marie O'Donnell entered West Point High School from which she was graduated in June, 1900. On October 2, 1907, she was married to William Herbert Weeks, a newspaper publisher. Mr. Weeks was born in Brooklyn, New York, October 29, 1855, descended from Revolutionary War ancestors through both lines. Mr. Weeks died at Norfolk, September 25, 1927, leaving six children by a previous marriage. They are Charles, Anna, Gertrude, Ralph, Bryan and William H. Weeks.

Altho a Republican by inheritance, Mrs. Weeks is independent in politics. She has always taken an active part in public affairs, and was the first woman candidate for congress in Nebraska.

From the time of her marriage she was associated with her husband in newspaper work, and was editor and publisher of the *Norfolk Press* almost twenty-three years. In 1924 she was president of the Nebraska State Press Association, and was the founder of the Northeast Nebraska Editorial Association and the Nebraska Writers' Guild.

A member of the Native Sons and Daughters of Nebraska, she is also a member of the Madison County Historical Association and the Nebraskana Society. She is the possessor of a letter and medal for services rendered in the World War, is a member of the National and Nebraska State Press Associations, the Chamber of Commerce, and has for her hobby government. Residence: Norfolk.

Edward P. Weeth

Edward P. Weeth was born at Gretna, Nebraska, August 5, 1893, son of C. Stephen and Carrie C. Weeth. His father, who was born at Werneck, Bavaria, Germany, December 21, 1856, came to America in 1871, and was a pioneer in Sarpy County, where he engaged as a farmer, miller and coal dealer. He died at Gretna, June 24, 1924. His wife, Carrie Weeth was born at Chesterton, Indiana, September 15, 1856, and is still living. She is descended from Rebecca Prince of Leeds, England.

Mr. Weeth attended Gretnna public schools until 1908, and was graduated from Gretna High School in 1912. In 1917 he received the degree of B. Sc. from Armour Institute of Technology at Chicago. In that year he enlisted as a mechanic with the 35th Engineers, A. E. F., and had two years service in France. Upon his discharge he returned to Gretna, in 1919, to become manager of the Latta Grain Company, continuing until 1924. He is now part owner of a flour mill and two grain elevators.

He was married to Verda Derr Westenbarger at Ashland, Nebraska, on June 30, 1926. Mrs. Weeth was born at Mound City, Missouri, February 16, 1893.

Mr. Weeth is independent in politics. He is a Mason, and member of the Scottish Rite body and Nebraska Consistory, Valley of Omaha. He belongs to the Red Cross, the Nebraska Millers Association and the Nebraska Grain Dealers Association, and the Nebraskana Society. His sport is baseball. Residence: Gretna.

George Carl Wegener

George Carl Wegener, banker, was born in Will County, Illinois, October 2, 1860, the son of Fred Dietrich Wegener and Dorathea Marie (Bode) Wegener. His father, a farmer, who was born in Germany, January 27, 1838, came to this country in 1851. He died in Thayer County, Nebraska, January 3, 1910. George Wegener's mother was born in Germany, February 17, 1840, and died in Thayer County, on February 9, 1914.

Mr. Wegener was graduated from the elementary schools, March 21, 1875. He married Mary Helen Fricke, in Thayer County, October 6, 1887. Mrs. Wegener was born in Cook County, Illinois, February 17, 1869. To this union seven children were born: Henry, August 19, 1888; William, September 17, 1890, who died March 18, 1893; Emma, May 17, 1892; Fred, March 13, 1894; Walter, May 11, 1896; Dorothea, March 7, 1898, She died March 6, 1899. They have an adopted daughter, Marie Anna, who was born February 21, 1910. Henry is married to Alma Brase and Fred is married to Lydia Brase.

A banker many years Mr. Wegener is president of the Ruskin State Bank, director of the Ruskin Grain and Coal Company, and a member of the Farmer's Union Creamery Company at Deshler, Nebraska.

He is affiliated with the St. Marks Lutheran Church, of which he has been an elder for twenty-five years, and is a member of the Nebraskana Society. Residence: Deshler.

Ernest Solomon Wegner

Ernest S. Wegner, leading physician of Lincoln, was born at Milford, on February 15, 1889, the son of Herman Gustav and Mary Regina (Frei) Wegner. His father, who is a clergyman, was born at Stoewen by Falkenburg, Province of Pommern, Germany, February 10, 1859, and came to America in 1877. His mother was born in Illinois, July 3, 1869, and died at Loveland, Colorado, December 11, 1921. She was president of the State Woman's

Missionary Society of the Evangelical Church; her ancestry was German.

Dr. Wegner attended grade school in Saunders County, Nebraska, at West Point, Nebraska, and in Washington County, Nebraska. He was graduated from the Academy of North Central College at Naperville, Illinois, 1911. He holds the following degrees: M. D., 1919, University of Nebraska Medical School; B. S., 1915, North Central College; Ph. G., 1908, Creighton University College of Pharmacy. He took post-graduate courses at Washington University, at St. Louis, and at Harvard Medical School, Boston. He was a member of Upsilon Nu Chapter of Phi Chi, medical fraternity, 1918.

He was associated with the York Clinic and Clinic Hospital at York, Nebraska, as pediatrist, 1921-26. Since 1926 he has been connected with the Lincoln Children's Clinic. He is a member of Lancaster County Medical Society, Nebraska State Medical Association, American Medical Association, American College of Physicians (associate member), and the Nebraska Pediatric Society. He is a member of the Red Cross; the Nebraska Conference of Social Work; the Lancaster County Tuberculosis Society; the Lincoln Chamber of Commerce; and the Lincoln Rotary Club. He is a member of the board of directors of the Young Men's Christian Association, and is a member of the Parent-Teachers' Association. During the World War he was a member of the Medical Reserves. He is a member of the American Legion. He is affiliated with Calvary Evangelical Church of Lincoln. He is a Republican.

His marriage to Myrtle Laura Geier was solemnized at Biastone City, Grant County, South Dakota, December 22, 1921. Mrs. Wegner was born at Ortonville, Big Stone County, Minnesota, June 20, 1893. They have a daughter, Mary Jean, born October 21, 1924. Residence: Lincoln.

Irvin Johnson Wehrman

Irvin Johnson Wehrman, banker, was born at Decatur, Illinois, January 22, 1875, son of Henry and Elizabeth (McFeely) Wehrman. Henry Wehrman was born in Germany in 1833, and died at Nelson on July 31, 1910. Coming to America in 1845, he was a prominent farmer and stockman in Nebraska for many years. His wife was born in Stark County, Ohio, in 1842, and died at Nelson in 1908. She was of Scotch-Irish descent.

Educated in the public schools of Nebraska, Mr. Wehrman attended commercial school two years. A resident of Nebraska for fifty-seven years, he has been connected with the Commercial Bank of Nelson for some time as cashier.

In July, 1896, Mr. Wehrman was married to Leola Thomas at Weeping Water, Nebraska. Mrs. Wehrman, who was born at Weeping Water, died several years ago at Nelson. Three children were born to them, two of whom are living: Lawson J., born June 15, 1897, married Ruth Ione Scherzinger; Leone Maude, born in February, 1905, married Deforest Swanson; and Frank Casler, born April 3, 1903, died in July, 1912.

Mr. Wehrman is independent politically. He is a member of the Masons (32nd degree and Shrine), and the Nebraskana Society. He has been a member of the school board for over 25 years. Residence: Nelson.

James B. Wehrman

A resident of Nebraska since March 5, 1875, James B. Wehrman was born in Macon County, Illinois, October 16, 1866, son of Henry F. W. and Elizabeth (McFeely) Wehrman. His father, born in Germany in 1833, came to the United States in his early youth, and was a pioneer farmer in Illinois. He died at Nelson on July 31, 1910, after a residence of more than thirty years. His wife,

born in Dark County, Ohio, died at Nelson, March 19, 1908.

James B. Wehrman was educated in common school, and has since engaged in farming, until his recent retirement. He was married to Maude Ballard in 1888. Mrs. Wehrman was born in Labette, Kansas, June 13, 1870, and died at Nelson, February 20, 1921.

There were eight children born to their union, seven of whom are living: Basil C., June 1, 1889, married Dorothy Mauck; Henry E., january 14, 1890, married Myrtle Philpott; Ethel, September 21, 1894, married Robert Moore; W. ray, August 28, 1898, married Gwen Bottenfield; Hazel M., February 15, 1902, married Eugene McDonald; Homer, born August 13, 1903; Clifton E., October 21, 1905; and James B., Jr., born March 19, 1914, who died February 15, 1921.

Mr. Wehrman is a Presbyterian. He is president of the Commercial Bank at Nelson. Mr. Wehrman's ancestors on his mothers side were active in the Revolution. He is a Democrat. Residence: Nelson.

Herman Frederick Weigel

Herman Frederick Weigel who is a leading educator of Stuart, Nebraska, has been a resident of this state all his life, and in recent years has taken a prominent part in educational affairs in this state. He was born at Douglas, Nebraska, October 13, 1900, the son of Andrew and Anna Katherine (Besser) Weigel, the former a farmer who was born at Hessen-Nassau, Germany, January 25, 1861. His father served in the German Army from 1881 to 1884, and came to the United States in 1888 His mother was born at Hessen-Nassau, October 13, 1865.

Mr. Weigel was graduated from the Sterling High School in 1919, and received the B. S. degree in 1926 at the University of Nebraska where he was a member of Pi Kappa Phi. He served as rural school teacher in Otoe County in 1920, was department principal at Fullerton, Nebraska, in 1923, was athletic coach at Beaver Crossing, Nebraska, in 1924, and returned to the University of Nebraska as a student in 1925. He was athletic coach at Cedar Rapids, Nebraska in 1926, and since 1927 has served as superintendent of the Stuart public schools.

He holds membership in the following: Nebraska State Teachers Association; National Association; Niobrara Valley School Men's Association, of which he is president; High School Administration Section of the Nebraska State Teachers Association, District No. 3, of which he is chairman; and the Commercial Club of Stuart. He is chairman of the board of directors of the Lions Club, is treasurer of the Holt County School Activities Association, and holds membership in the local lodge of the Independent Order of Odd Fellows. He is vitally interested in educational research.

On August 25, 1926, he married Frances Louise King at Belgrade, Nebraska. Mrs. Weigel, who was a kindergarten teacher, was born at Silver Creek, Nebraska, August 25, 1906. Her paternal grandfather served as an officer in the Union Army during the Civil War, and her maternal ancestors were of Swedish descent. Residence: Stuart. (Photograph in Album).

Adolph Weiler

Adolph Weiler lived in Nebraska for nearly fifty years and took an active interest in business and civic affairs in his community from boyhood. He was born at Goeppingen, Wurttemberg, Germany, April 9, 1860, the son of John George and Dora Weiler. His father, who was a butcher, was born at Wurttemberg, April 6, 1820, and died at Goeppingen, December 2, 1883.

His mother was born at Goeppingen, and died there May 1, 1879.

Mr. Weiler was graduated from public school in 1874,

and since then had been engaged as a butcher, and banker, in the lumber business; farming; and cattle raising. He was president of the Farmers Bank at Dunbar, Nebraska, and was associated with the First National Bank at Omaha; Nebraska City National Bank, at Nebraska City; the Brdford Kennedy Lumber Company, at Omaha; and the Proudfit Radio Company, at Lincoln, Nebraska.

He was married to Christine Roos at Seward, Nebraska. Mrs. Weiler was born at Goeppingen, July 31, 1862. There are five children: Amalie, born November 24, 1885, who is an insurance agent and merchant; Fred, born August 9, 1887, who married Dorothea Garlip, and is a farmer; Carl A., born February 20, 1892, who married Minna Schmidt; Oscar, born October 13, 1894, who married Anna Griepenstroh, and is a farmer; and Irwin W., born August 5, 1902, who married Mabel Christensen, and who is a radio dealer and lumber man.

Mr. Weiler served as a sergeant in the artillery in Germany, from 1880 to 1883. He was a member of the Red Cross, the Bankers' Association, and the Lumbermen's Association. He was a Mason and Shriner, served as an elder in the Presbyterian Church at Dunbar, and was a member of the Sons of Herman and the Nebraskana Society. He is a Republican. (Mr. Weiler died June 28, 1931).

Andy J. Welch

Born at Milford, Nebraska, December 28, 1875, Andy J. Welch has lived there continuously fifty-five years. He is the son of John T. and Mary Jane (Alexander) Welch, the former a native of Kentucky, born October 21, 1842. He was a farmer and merchant, who died at Lincoln, July 7, 1898. Mary Jane (Alexander) Welch was born in Missouri, April 17, 1849, and died at Lincoln, January 25, 1928.

Mr. Welch attended the Milford public and high school, the Jones National School of Auctioneering and Oratory in 1908, and Western Normal School at Lincoln. A farmer all his life, he has in addition carried on a hardware, auctioneering, meat and ice business at various times. A leader in Democratic politics he served as state senator 1928-30, and 1930-31.

During the World War he was a four minute speaker, and active in Red Cross work, and is still a member of the last mentioned. He was chief of the Milford Fire Department for 6 years and is still an active member, and is a member of the town board, and for eighteen years 1906-16 and 1923-31, has served on the school board.

Mr. Welch is a member of the First Methodist Church, and during 1925-27 was a member of the board of stewards. During that period a new church building was erected, and Mr. Welch devoted much time to the project. He is a member of the Modern Woodmen of America and a life member of the Nebraskana Society. Among his sports are big game hunting, fishing and hiking. He is a breeder of pedigreed horses, and takes much interest in his avocation.

Of his marriage to Mary Birky, there are two children, Alvera, born January 4, 1897, and Lyle, born January 27, 1909. Alvera was instructor in piano for eleven years, and Lyle is assistant supervisor of music in the Lincoln Junior High Schools. Mrs. Welch was born at Clayton, Illinois, July 10, 1876, and was married at Milford, January 1, 1896. Residence: Milford. (Photograph in Album).

Henry Casper Wellensiek

Henry C. Wellensiek was born at Syracuse, Nebraska, March 11, 1882, the son of Henry Frederick and Marie Elsie (Kamopeter) Wellensiek. His father, who was born at Bierin, Germany, June 7, 1849, and died at Syracuse, August 6, 1921, was a farmer who came to America from Germany, in 1866. His mother, who was born at Bierin, November 8, 1849, and died at Syracuse, September 23, 1906, came to America in 1874.

Mr. Wellensiek, who has lived in Nebraska all his life, attended the rural schools of Otoe County, for two years was a student at the Nebraska State Agriculture College, and has always been a farmer. He was married to Louise Charlotte Schacht at Syracuse, February 15, 1906. Mrs. Wellensiek was born at Cook, Nebraska, April 16, 1884. Seven children were born to this union, six of whom are living. They are: Esther, born February 13, 1907; Alma, born July 29, 1908; Virgil, born March 14, 1910; Irene, born January 12, 1913, who died September 17, 1927; Louise, born December 10, 1915; Elsie, born April 30, 1919; and Henry, Junior, born March 2, 1923. Esther is a school teacher; Alma is in a nurses' training school; and Virgil is a farmer.

Mr. Wellensiek is affiliated with the St. John's Evangelical Church at Syracuse. Residence: Syracuse.

Hermann G. Wellensiek

Hermann G. Wellensiek, distinguished statesman and lawyer at Grand Island, Nebraska, has been a resident of this state all his life. He was born at Syracuse, Nebraska, September 28, 1884, the son of Henry F. and Marie C. (Kampeter) Wellensiek. His father, who was born at Bunde, Germany, June 7, 1849, and died at Syracuse, August 6, 1921, was a farmer who came to this country in 1865. His mother was born at Bieren, Germany, October 12, 1849, and died at Syracuse, September 23, 1906; she came to this country in 1873.

Mr. Wellensiek attended the rural schools of Otoe County, Nebraska, and in 1902 was graduated from the Syracuse High School. He received the Bachelor of Laws degree at the University of Nebraska College of Law in 1904. He served as cashier of the Bank of Avoca, Avoca, Nebraska, 1907-10, was president of the Harvard State Bank, Harvard, Nebraska, 1912-29, and since 1923 has been engaged in the practice of law at Grand Island with offices in the Cowton Building.

A Republican, Mr. Wellensiek is state senator from Hall, Howard, and Greeley counties, being elected for 1929-31, and 1931-33; and acts as chairman of the Banking Committee in both regular and special sessions during each term. He holds membership in the Nebraska State Bar Association, the American Bar Association, the Grand Island Chamber of Commerce, the Red Cross, and the Salvation Army. He is a life member of the Elks, and is a 32nd degree Mason and Shrine member. His social club is the University Club of Lincoln, Grand Island Riverside Golf Club, and his sports are golf and football.

Mr. Wellensiek is affiliated with St. Paul's English Lutheran Church at Grand Island. He was married to Adah Lanham at Hastings, Nebraska, October 5, 1915; she was born at Harvard, Nebraska, October 29, 1884, the daughter of Thomas and Jane Lanham who were pioneers of Nebraska, and was a teacher before her marriage. She died at Waukesha, Wisconsin, July 23, 1916.

On September 12, 1925, he was united in marriage with Anna Blanche Swartwood at Fremont, Nebraska. Their two children are: Paul Swartwood, born July 29, 1926; and Karl Wendell, born November 13, 1929. Mrs. Wellensiek, who was born at Columbus, Indiana, July 16, 1894, was graduated from Fremont High School and Cotner University, and taught in the public schools prior to her marriage. Residence: Grand Island. (Photograph on Page 1257).

Charles Arthur Wellington

Charles Arthur Wellington, rancher, was born at Murry, Iowa, April 8, 1874, son of Horace and Frances Esther (Whitlock) Wellington, the former an engineer, Civil War soldier, farmer and merchant. Horace Wellington was born at Concord, Massachusetts, September 6, 1849, and died at Hot Springs, South Dakota, April 11, 1912. His father was born in Boston, descended

Locke Studio—Grand Island

HERMANN G. WELLENSIEK

from early English settlers. At the age of 84 years Horace Wellington built a chimney thirty-two feet high.

Frances Esther Whitlock was born at Quincy, Illinios, September 6, 1847, and died at Waco, Nebraska, on July 5, 1894. Primarily a devoted wife and mother, she was also an active worker in her church.

Educated in country and public schools until May, 1886, Charles Arthur Wellington was graduated from Waco High School in May, 1889. He taught school in York County two years, 1894-95, 1895-96, and in 1903 homesteaded in the sand hills of Loup County. He is an extensive landowner there, and it has always been his ambition to see his hills covered with trees and fine cattle. Mr. Wellington is a Republican and was county commissioner 1922-27, defeated for re-election by three votes.

During the Spanish-American War, Mr. Wellington served in the Philippines, participating in nineteen engagements. He was promoted from private to corporal during his enlistment. He is a member of the Spanish War Veterans, the Church of Christ, the Nebraskana Society, and the school board. He was school director from 1906-09 and treasurer of his school district 1912-29. His favorite sport is baseball, while his hobby is breeding registered Polled Herefords.

On December 24, 1900, he was married to Nellie May Geiger at Waco. She was born there on April 18, 1880, and died at Taylor, April 8, 1905. There are three children of this marriage, Charles A., born October 6, 1901, who married Kathryn Sammons; Genevieve A., born June 12, 1903, who married Harry E. Simonsen; and Ora B., born November 17, 1904, who married George Fagan.

His second marriage was to Lulu Etta Wam, at Burwell, on December 19, 1912. They have six children, Fay E., born December 25, 1913; Marjorie F., born October 26, 1915; Arthur W., born September 28, 1917; Robert M., born May 12, 1922; Nola J., born June 29, 1924; and Dorthy P., born January 7, 1928. Residence: Taylor.

Robert Rider Wellington

Robert Rider Wellington, lawyer, was born at Albion, Maine, February 18, 1899, son of LeClaire and Ethel (Clark) Wellington. The father, who was born at Albion, April 3, 1872, is descended through Charles, John, George, Thomas, Thomas, Joseph, to Roger Wellington who settled in Watertown, Massachusetts, in 1630. His wife, Ethel, was born in Thorndike, Maine, September 10, 1873, and is descended through Dudley, Perley, Cudworth, John, Elisha, Josiah, to Elisha Clark who was a resident of Kittery, Maine, in 1690. Both Mr. and Mrs. Wellington reside at Harlowton, Montana.

Upon the completion of his elementary education in the public schools of Montana, Mr. Wellington entered the Harlowton High School, and in 1923 received the Bachelor of Arts degree from the University of Nebraska. He received his Bachelor of Laws degree from the University of Nebraska in 1926. He was a student for a time at Harvard Law School. His fraternities are Pi Kappa Phi and Phi Delta Phi.

On February 2, 1926, Mr. Wellington was admitted to practice in Lincoln. At the present time he is a member of the firm of Thomas and Wellington at Crawford, Nebraska, and is county attorney of Dawes County, elected on the Republican ticket. He is a member of the Chamber of Commerce, the Masons, and the New England Historic Genealogical Society. During the World War he was a private in the United States Army, and at the present time is a member of the American Legion.

His marriage to Katherine Morice Johnson was solemnized at Fremont, September 20, 1930. Mrs. Wellington was born at Fremont on June 15, 1906, and is a member of the Daughters of the American Revolution. They have one daughter, Nancy Jean, born February 27, 1932. Residence: Crawford.

Charles Hull Wells

Charles Hull Wells, civil engineer, was born at Boone, Iowa, March 5, 1882, son of Charles H. and Elizabeth Helen (Hull) Wells.

The father was born in Huntley, Illinois, in 1859, and died at Boone, Iowa, in February, 1926. He was English, a railroad cashier and telegrapher. His wife, Elizabeth Helen, was born at East Aurora, New York in 1851, and is a member of the Daughters of the American Revolution, and active in club and church work. She is descended from New England Yankees.

Mr. Wells attended common and high school at Boone and Iowa State College. From 1899 until the present time he has been civil engineer with the Chicago and Northwestern Railway, on construction valuation and general railway maintenance. He is division engineer for the Black Hills and Wyoming divisions of the Chicago and Northwestern. He is a Republican.

He married to Clyte Z. Kneeland at Boone, May 16, 1906. Mrs. Wells was born at Boone, July 11, 1882, of Yankee descent. She is the daughter of Howland P. and Capitola (Warner) Kneeland. She was graduated from high school at Boone, Iowa, and attended Normal Normal School at Cedar Falls, Iowa. She was a teacher in primary schools for several years prior to her marriage. They have three children, Helen, born November 6, 1907, who is a teacher; Elizabeth, born October 8, 1911, who is attending Iowa State College; and Charles, Jr., born July 4, 1920.

While a member of the Presbyterian Church, Mr. Wells is affiliated with the Congregational Church of Chadron. He is a Mason and a member of the Chadron Country Club. His favorite sports include golf, fishing and shooting. Residence: Chadron.

Adolph Eilert Wenke

Adolph E. Wenke, prominent lawyer at Stanton, Nebraska, has lived in this state all his life, and for the past decade has been active in the civic and political life of his community. He was born at Pender, Nebraska, January 22, 1898, the son of Frederick William and Henrietta (Athens) Wenke. His father was born at Oldenburg, Germany. His mother was born at Oldenburg, and died at Pender, June 7, 1916.

Mr. Wenke was graduated from the Pender High School in 1917, and in 1923, was graduated from the University of Nebraska with the LL. B. degree. He was elected to membership in Sigma Phi Epsilon; was a member of the football team at the University of Nebraska; and was active in track events. Admitted to the bar in Nebraska in 1923, since that date he has been engaged in the practice of law at Stanton. He was editor of the *Cornhusker* at the University of Nebraska. He is now county attorney of Stanton County.

On June 7, 1925, he was married to Gertrude Harriett Bauer at Suttoon. They have two children: Robert Adolph, born September 6, 1926; and William Frederick, born October 1, 1928. During the late war Mr. Wenke served overseas in the army for 10 months. He is a member of the American Legion.

He is a member of the Stanton School Board and the Nebraskana Society, is a Mason, and holds membership in Phi Delta Phi; Sigma Delta Chi; and the Stanton Country Club. He is a Democrat. His sport is golf. Residence: Stanton.

William Fred Wenke

A banker at Pender since 1908, William Fred Wenke is the son of Fred W. and Henriette (Aten) Wenke. He was born in Dodge County, February 12, 1888, and educated first in grade school. Thereafter he attended Pender High School, completing the 9th grade, and was a student at Omaha and Fremont business colleges.

Fred Wenke was born in Oldenburg, Germany, De-

ELIZABETH WENTZ

Hauck-Skoglund—Lincoln

cember 9, 1852, and came to America at the age of thirty. Now retired, he was for many years prominent in local politics, and held many county offices. His wife, Henriette, was born in Germany, in October, 1855, and died at Pender, June 15, 1916.

William Fred Wenke associated himself with the Pender State Bank in 1908, and this has been his only business connection. At the present time he is serving as cashier. He is also president of the Pender Chamber of Commerce, and is president of Group Three, Nebraska Bankers Association. He is past master of Roman Eagle Lodge No. 203 of the Masons, and has served as secretary of the Board of Education. He is a Democrat.

On June 14, 1911, he was united in marriage to Anna M. Rosacker at Omaha. Mrs. Wenke was born at Fort Calhoun, Nebraska, March 23, 1890, and to them three children were born: W. Sterling, born May 6, 1912, is attending the college of law at the state university, Paul E., born August 10, 1917 and Clark A., born February 6, 1920, are attending public school.

Mr. Wenke is a Lutheran. His sports are tennis and golf. Residence: Pender.

Elizabeth Wentz

Elizabeth Wentz, artist and civic leader of Nebraska, was born at Du Quoin, Perry County, Illinois, August 24, 1871. Her father, Harvey Stanton Lemen, who was a farmer, was born at New Design, Illinois, in 1827, and died at Lincoln, Lancaster County, Nebraska. His grandfather, James Lemen, was a Revolutionary War soldier from Virginia, who served with Washington in the White Plains campaign and was present at the surrender of Yorktown. After the close of the war he, with his five sons migrated to what is now Illinois. There they helped to lay the foundation for the spread of religion and established the first Baptist Church in the state. Her mother, who was a writer, died at Lincoln, December 28, 1930.

Mrs. Wentz attended the public schools of Illinois, and Lincoln, Nebraska, and attended college in Illinois for two years. Prominent in Lincoln educational and welfare work for many years, she was the first state president of the Nebraska Congress of Parents and Teachers, 1922-26, and was a member of the board of the National Congress of Parents and teachers, during that period. She was president of the local Hawthorne Parent-Teacher Association for six years and the first president of the Lincoln Council Parent-Teacher Association. She was state chairman of the American Child Health Association, 1925-8, a member of the Lincoln Board of Education, 1927-31, serving as vice president, 1931. She is a member of the State Historical Society, the National Education Association, the Woman's Club, and Young Women's Christian Association, the Woman's Christian Temperance Union, and the League of Women Voters. She is a member of the Nebraskana Society and a member of the Nebraska Commission on the Enrichment of Adult Life. She is a member of the Lincoln Chamber of Commerce, serving on the Educational and Planning committees of that body. She is affiliated with the First Baptist Church of Lincoln, of which she was a trustee from 1925-8.

Perhaps her most outstanding achievement was the founding of State Day in Nebraska. Mrs. Wentz was the originator of the state day idea, and had the support of the Nebraska Congress of Parents and Teachers in securing legislative enactment designating March 1, the anniversary of Nebraska's admission as a state to the Union, as official State Day. In conceiving the plan she had in mind a means of stimulating interest in the schools and citizens of Nebraska, in the history, industries, and resources of the state. Each year March 1, is proclaimed State Day by the Governor of Nebraska, with the suggestion that suitable programs, in honor of the day be arranged. Mrs. Wentz, who is State Day Chairman, was present at the time Governor Bryan signed the bill and

was presented with the pen which the Governor used in signing it.

On October 14, 1891, she was united in marriage with George Harrison Wentz at Lincoln. Mr. Wentz who was born at Pana, Illinois, December 6, 1865, is a heating engineer. They have two children: Harry Morris, born November 28, 1892; and Lawrence Eugene, born December 1, 1894.

Mrs. Wentz has lived in Nebraska for the past 48 years. Politically, she is a Republican. Residence: Lincoln. (Photograph on Page 1259).

Arthur Deboben Werner

Arthur Deboben Werner, assistant postmaster, was born at Hebron, January 8, 1895, son of Jacob Joseph and Katherine Elizabeth (Deboben) Werner.

The father was born in Frankfort, Illinois, March 24, 1856, and died at Hebron, January 16, 1927. His parents were born in Germany, and came to the United States shortly before the birth of Jacob Joseph Werner. For a number of years, Mr. Werner was prominent in Democrat politics and in the Masonic Lodge. His wife, Catherine Elizabeth, was born in Dayton, Ohio, May 7, 1855, and died at Hebron, February 24, 1927. Her parents were natives of Alsace-Lorraine.

In 1914, Mr. Werner was graduated from Hebron High School, and since that time has been assistant postmaster. He is a Democrat. His hobby is tinting (commercial art, portraits, and miniatures). Residence: Hebron. (Photograph on Page 1261).

Bernhard P. Werner

Bernhard P. Werner was born at Friedensau, Thayer County, Nebraska, November 15, 1887, the son of Jacob Werner and Julia (Schmidt) Werner. His father, a farmer of German parentage, was born at Joliet, Will County, Illinois, June 21, 1861. He died at Friedensau, April 17, 1886.

Bernhard Werner attended the Friedensau parochial school from which he was graduated in 1901. He married Caroline H. Vortman at Friedensau, on October 5, 1910. Mrs. Werner was born at Carleton, Thayer County, Nebraska, June 21, 1891. To this union three children were born: Norma, May 18, 1913; Earl, September 1, 1917; and Elmer, August 30, 1919.

Mr. Werner is a Republican and has lived in Nebraska since birth. He is affiliated with the Trinity Evangelical Lutheran Church at Friedensau, and is a member of the Nebraskana Society. Residence: Carleton.

Frank Werner

A resident of Nebraska for the past 52 years, Frank Werner was born at Corning, Iowa, son of Adam and Sallie (Van Valkenburg) Werner. His father, who was an architect, was born at Frankfort-on-Main, Germany, June 25, 1844, and died at Hebron, Nebraska, November 12, 1923. His ancestors were German farmers and weavers. Sallie Van Valkenburg, whose ancestors were English, Dutch and French pioneers, was born at Pecatonica, Illinois, August 4, 1854, and died at Hebron, December 26, 1929.

Mr. Werner was graduated from the Hebron High School in 1892, and thereafter attended the University of Nebraska two years. He was engaged in the drug business more than thirty years, fifteen of which were at Alma. Afterward he farmed for a time, and is now serving as county clerk of Harlan County and mayor of Alma. He is a member of the Alma public library board, the Red Cross, the Lions Club and the Odd Fellows, and is a trustee of the Boy Scouts.

On April 19, 1909, he was married to Mrs. Grace Evans at Alma. Mrs. Werner, a horticulturist, was born at

ARTHUR DeBOBEN WERNER

Schenectady, New York, September 29, 1878. She is
of Scotch parentage.

During the seven years Mr. Werner has served as
mayor of Alma he has done much toward putting the
public utilities on a paying basis, especially the light
plant which was hopelessly in debt at the time he took
office. He was elected county clerk in 1930. Residence:
Alma. (Photograph in Album).

Oscar Helmuth Werner

Oscar H. Werner, who has been prominent in educational circles since 1908, was born at West Point, Cuming
County, Nebraska, January 1, 1888, the son of Charles
and Minnie (Joekel) Werner. His father, who was a
clergyman in the Methodist Episcopal Church, was born
at Pommerania, Germany, November 2, 1862, and died
at Adams, Nebraska, July 20, 1898. His mother was
born at Sterling, Johnson County, Nebraska, November 8,
1865.

He was graduated from the Enterprise Normal Academy, 1907. He holds these degrees: A. B., Central Wesleyan University, 1910; A. M., Northwestern University,
1912; Ph. D., Columbia University, 1917; and A. M., in
education, University of Nebraska, 1924. He is a member of Phi Delta Kappa.

Dr. Werner has been a contributor to *School and Society, Modern Language Journal,* etc. He is the author
of *The Unmarried Mother in German Litterature* and
Every College Student's Problems. He taught in the
rural schools of Adams County, was instructor in the
commercial department of the school at Warrenton, Missouri, 1908-11, held a fellowship in German at Northwestern University, 1911-12, and was instructor in modern
languages at Upper Iowa Union, 1912-14. He was instructor at the Columbia University, 1914-16, 1916-17.
Since 1924 he has been professor of principles of education at the University of Nebraska. He was superintendent of schools at Arlington, Kansas, 1918-20, and at
Anthony, Kansas, 1920-4.

He is a member of the Nebraskana Society, is affiliated
with the Methodist Episcopal Church, and holds membership in the University Club and the Hiram Club. He
is a Mason, (Knight Templar), and is a member of the
University Club. He likes to golf.

His marriage to Anna Laura Yust was solemnized at
Sylvia, Reno County, Kansas, July 27, 1910. Mrs. Werner,
whose father was born in Germany, was born at Sylvia,
October 28, 1887. They have two children: Charles F.,
born December 25, 1913; and Margaret E., born May 18,
1917. Residence: Lincoln.

Phillip Werner

Philip Werner was born at Richton, Illinois, July 28,
1850. Henry Werner, father of Philip, was born at
Hessen, Germany, June 25, 1819, and died at Deshler,
Nebraska, August 29, 1906. He came to America in 1846,
and became a farmer. Margaret, mother of Philip, was
born in Hessen, September 13, 1823, and died at Deshler,
March 21, 1912. She came to America in 1847.

Mr. Werner attended parochial day school in pioneer
days and later attended a Lutheran Seminary until 1870.
He taught in a church school for three years, then went
back to farming on account of poor health.

He was married to Augusta Rotermund, May 20,
1872. Mrs. Werner died August 20, 1876, leaving two
daughters, Clara and Lydia. On February 10, 1878, he
was married to Elizabeth Nehrig, at Friedensau, Nebraska. She was born at Lafayette, Indiana, November
28, 1858, and died at Deshler, Nebraska, February 18,
1919. To them were born eleven children; Matlude, born
May 24, 1879, who was married to Rudolf Kock, and died
December 9, 1918; William, born November 3, 1881, who
is married to Anna Windhorst; Albert R., born June 5,
1883, who is married to Alvine Goerke; Louise, born June
24, 1885, who was married to George Bender, and died

February 23, 1921; Oscar H., born June 3, 1887, who is
married to Louise Buck; Emma, born November 6, 1890,
who is married to R. W. Vieselmeyer; Edward V., born
May 17, 1893; Flora, born April 13, 1895; Arthur P., born
March 2, 1897; Beata, born December 15, 1899; and
Herbert, born November 15, 1901.

Mr. Werner is an Evangelical Lutheran and is affiliated with St. Peters Church of the Missouri Synod.
Residence: Deshler.

Richard Phillip Werner

Richard P. Werner, son of John and Mary (Duehren)
Werner, was born in Thayer County, Nebraska, July 6,
1882. His father, a native of Illinois, was born June 16,
1854. He is now retired after a successful life as a
farmer. His wife, Mary Duehren, was born in Minnesota, January 9, 1864.

A resident of Nebraska his entire lifetime, Mr. Werner
has been a farmer since early youth. He is a member
of the board of Hebron College and Academy, a director
of school district No. 86, and a trustee of the Friedens
American Lutheran Church. For twelve years he was
secretary of the Farmers Union Creamery at Deshler, and
for fifteen years has been secretary of the Farmers Union.
He has served as a director of the Farmers Elevator.

He was married to Minnie Pauline Schmidt at Deshler,
Nebraska on March 1, 1906, and to their union were born
four children, two of whom are living: Rosa, born June
28, 1907; Albert, born December 23, 1910; Arnold, born
June 25, 1912, who died August 24, 1914; and Lorna,
born October 5, 1915, who died July 26, 1921. Residence:
Deshler.

Harry Jacob Wertman

Harry Jacob Wertman, leading professional man at
Milford, was born at Franklin Grove, Illinois, April 24,
1877, the son of Charles Henry and Sarah (Courtright)
Wertman. His father, born at Franklin Grove, January 3, 1852, of Dutch and Welsh parentage, was county
supervisor in 1898, and for many years was a farmer.
His mother, an interested club worker, was born at
Dixon, Lee County, Illinois, of German and English
parents.

Dr. Wertman attended elementary school and in 1894
was graduated from the Milford High School. He received the B. S. degree from the University of Chicago,
and later was a student at Rush Medical College, Chicago,
where he received his M. D. degree. He was elected
to membership in Alpha Kappa at Rush Medical College.
Since 1903, he has been engaged in the practice of medicine and surgery at Milford, Nebraska, and he is a member of the county, state and American medical societies.

He was married to Izora Mary Hollingsworth at Milford, May 12, 1908. Mrs. Wertman, whose ancestry is
German and English, was born at Milford, November
11, 1887. They have two children: Charles J., born April
19, 1910, who is a student at the University of Nebraska;
and Maxine H., born February 11, 1918.

Dr. Wertman, who has lived in Nebraska for 47 years,
is a member of the following civic organizations at Milford: Commercial Association; University Club; Board
of Education, of which he has been president since 1917;
the Nebraskana Society, the Nebraska Good Roads Association (president), and the Masons. During the
World War he served as a member of the Council of
Defense and the Red Cross, and was a three minute man.
He is affiliated with the Methodist Church at Milford.
His favorite sports are trap shooting, and hunting. Residence: Milford. (Photograph in Album).

George William Wertz

For the past 34 years George W. Wertz has been engaged in the practice of law at Schuyler, Colfax County.

Nebraska, where he is prominent in civic affairs. He was born at Carrollton, Green County, Illinois, April 3, 1868, the son of Seymour Solomon and Martha Elizabeth (Jones) Wertz. His father, whose ancestry was Holland Dutch, was born at Miami, Ohio, November 1, 1842, and died at Milford, Seward County, Nebraska, June 13, 1924; he served in Company F., 14th Illinois Infantry, during the Civil War. His mother was born at Woodville, Illinois, November 4, 1850, and died at Schuyler, May 13, 1915; her ancestry was English.

Mr. Wertz was graduated from the Kearney High School in 1889, and was a student in the law department of the University of Iowa, 1892-93. He was a member of the McClain Chapter of Phi Delta Phi. In 1897 he was admitted to the bar at Schuyler, and since that date has been one of Colfax County's leading lawyers. From 1899 to 1902 he was a member of the law firm Everitt and Wertz, and since that date has been in practice alone. He is an officer and director of the Finance Corporation at Schuyler. A Republican, he served as county attorney of Colfax County, 1903-05, and 1923-27.

During the World War Mr. Wertz acted as a member of the advisory board at Schuyler. He holds membership in the Commercial Law League, the Nebraska State Bar Association, the Schuyler Chamber of Commerce, the Nebraska State Historical Society, the Nebraskana Society, and the Red Cross. He served as a member of the Schuyler school board, 1910-15, and takes an active interest in all civic organizations. He is a member of the Masons, the Independent Order of the Odd Fellows, and the Knights of Pythias. His sports include baseball, duck hunting, and fishing. His favorite recreation is reading. He is a Republican.

He was married to Lottie Violet Guernsey at Sumner, Dawson County, Nebraska, June 29, 1896. Mrs. Wertz, who is of Scotch and English descent, was born at Manistee, Michigan, December 8, 1872. Residence: Schuyler. (Photograph in Album).

John Ross Wertz

John Ross Wertz, executive, was born in Bedford County, Pennsylvania, January 1, 1872, and came to Nebraska in 1890. His father, John W. Wertz, was born in Bedford County, September 10, 1832, and died there October 8, 1872. He was a farmer of German descent. His wife, Jane E. Oliver, was born in Bedford County, February 8, 1834, and died there on March 5, 1905. She was English. Her father came from England to the United States and was a veterinary surgeon. He lived to be 104 years old.

Mr. Wertz attended country school in Pennsylvania, and has been in business in Nebraska for a number of years. At the present time he is manager of the Wertz Brothers Hardware & Lumber Company, and is associated with the Omaha Life Insurance Company. A Democrat, he has served as county treasurer of Deuel County two terms, 1901-05.

His marriage to Blanche E. Francoeur was solemnized at Omaha, November 15, 1909. She was born at Concordia, Kansas, June 8, 1894, of French ancestry. They have two children, John D., born January 29, 1914; and Paul Ross, born August 14, 1917.

Mr. Wertz was chairman of thrift stamp sales during the late war. He is a member of Tangier Temple of the Shrine, the Eastern Star and the Masons, the Odd Fellows, and the Chappell Rotary Club. Since 1914 he has been chairman of the Deuel County Chapter of the Red Cross. Residence: Chappell.

Charles Clifford Wescott

Charles C. Wescott has lived in Nebraska for 51 years and has been prominent in civic affairs at Plattsmouth for many years. He was born at Brush Creek, Fayette County, Iowa, October 3, 1873, the son of Clar-ence Edgar and Mary Louise (Coffin) Wescott. His father, who was a merchant, was born at Cheshire, Massachusetts, October 14, 1841. His ancestry was English. He died on January 5, 1924.

His mother was born at Oswego, New York, April 21, 1848, and died at Plattsmouth, Cass County, Nebraska, December 24, 1929. She was prominent in the Woman's Christian Temperance Union. Her ancestry was English.

Mr. Wescott attended the public schools at Plattsmouth. He was a student at the University of Nebraska for a time. He has been active in community and state affairs and has been engaged in the clothing business at Plattsmouth all his adult years. He was secretary of the Cass County Council of Defense; was secretary of the State Sunday School Association; was secretary of the Nebraska Retail Clothiers Association; was secretary of the Allied Clothier and Jobbers; and is vice president of the Methodist Crowell Home, at Blair, Nebraska.

He is now senior member of the firm C. E. Wescott Sons, Clothiers, at Plattsmouth. He was married at Plattsmouth, October 8, 1901, to Edna Evelyn Eaton. Mrs. Wescott, whose ancestry in English, was born at Crete, Nebraska, October 31, 1873. To this union two children were born: Mason, born September 9, 1903; and Alice Louise, born April 3, 1906. Mason is professor of mathematics at Northwestern University, and is a member of Phi Beta Kappa and Sigma Xi. Alice Louise, is a graduate of Northwestern University, and is a member of Kappa Delta Sorority.

During the World War Mr. Wescott served as area secretary of the Young Men's Christian Association overseas; and later he was in charge of the uniform department of the Paris warehouse.

He is a member and president of the Plattsmouth Ad Club, and was president for three terms of the Plattsmouth Chamber of Commerce. He is a Mason and a Republican. His favorite sport is hiking. He is a member of the First Methodist Church of Plattsmouth. Residence: Plattsmouth.

Clara Street Wescott

Clara Street Wescott, musician and clubwoman, was born at Red Oak, Iowa, July 26, 1876, the daughter of William Lewis and Mary Amelia (McCulloch) Street. Her father, a Civil War veteran, was born at Bristol, Pennsylvania, March 10, 1844, and died at Plattsmouth, Nebraska, December 19, 1910. He was a Republican, and a member of the Grand Army of the Republic and the Modern Woodmen of America. His ancestry is traced to Daniel Street who was born in 1658.

Her mother, who is descended from Miles Standish, Increase Blake, Joseph McCulloch and David Vincent, of Revolutionary times, was born at Charlamagne, Massachusetts, June 8, 1849, and died at Plattsmouth, February 6, 1930. She was a business woman and a teacher; she was a student at Dover Academy, in Illinois. She was a member of the Daughters of the American Revolution and the Women's Relief Corps.

Mrs. Wescott was graduated from the Weeping Water High School in June, 1893. She taught school for three years and for two years was a music supervisor. For thirty-five years she has been a choir director, a voice instructor, and a popular soloist. Among her musical activities is that of convention song leader in various community clubs.

A resident of Nebraska since 1888, she has always been interested in political affairs. As a Republican, she served as chairman of the first district of the Hoover-Curtis Club; was defeated candidate for the city council of Plattsmouth.

In the late war she assisted in promoting the sale of bonds, and was connected with Y. M. C. A. drives. She is a member of the Women's Reserve Relief Corps, the Delphian Society, and the Daughters of the American Revolution, of which she is state regent. A member of the Mayflower Society, she is also a member of the Patriotic council. An ardent Woman's Club worker, she has been president of the local club of that organization, has written many articles on club activities, for four years served as state chairman of music, and was state chairman of community service for two years.

At Plattsmouth, September 28, 1904, she was united in marriage with Edgar Hilt Wescott, who is descended from an English ancestor, Sir Tristram Coffin. He was born at LaPorte, Indiana, July 25, 1878. There are two children: Helen Rude, born October 6, 1907, who is a graduate of Nebraska Wesleyan, where she was a member of Willard sorority (past president), Pi Gamma Mu, Theta Alpha Phi, a member of P. E. O. and the Daughters of the American Revolution; and Edgar Street, born March 18, 1910, who is a student at the University of Nebraska, where he is a member of Beta Theta Pi, (past president).

Mrs. Wescott is a member of the State Music Teachers' Association, the Woman's Christian Temperance Union, the P. E. O. and the Nebraskana Society. She is a member of the city park board, and is affiliated with the First Methodist Church of Plattsmouth, where she is connected with the home and foreign missionary societies. Her hobbies are genealogy, flowers, and birds. Residence: Plattsmouth. (Photograph in Album).

Milton Ralph Wessel

Milton R. Wessel, son of one of Nebraska's pioneer merchants, was born in New York City, February 1, 1882. His parents were Lewis and Sarah (Rheinheimer) Wessel, the former of whom was born in Austria, in March, 1836. He was a Jewish merchant, who settled in Nebraska City, in 1855, and established the firm of L. Wessei's Sons and Company. He married Sarah Rheinheimer, also a native of Austria, who died at Kansas City, Missouri, July 22, 1926.

Mr. Wessel, with his brother, Walter, have been engaged in the business organized by their father since 1903. He is now manager of the store. He was educated in the public schools of New York, and was graduated from the Nebraska City High School in 1899. He is unmarried.

In politics, Mr. Wessel is a Republican. He has been a resident of Nebraska City for forty years, and has been active in the business, civic and fraternal life of the city for many years. He is a member of the Red Cross, and the Elks, and the Nebraska City Country Club. His hobby is reading. Residence: Nebraska City.

Walter A. Wessel

In 1850, Lewis Wessel, a native of Austria, came to America, and in 1855 settled in Otoe County. He is reputed to be the first Jew to make his home in Nebraska. He was born in 1836, and died at New York City, May 30, 1906. The mercantile firm of L. Wessels Sons was formed by him in 1875, and for several years after his death was operated by his two sons, Walter A. and Milton Ralph. Lewis Wessel married Sarah Rheinheimer, who was born in Austria, and died at Kansas City, Missouri, July 22, 1926.

Walter A. Wessel was educated in the public schools of New York City, where he was born August 30, 1880. When his family came to Nebraska City, he entered the schools there, and was graduated from Lincoln Business College in 1898. At that time he entered the business organized by his father, and he and his brother purchased it in 1903. In 1928 he obtained the interest of his brother, and has since been the sole owner.

Mr. Wessel was married to Constance Sarbach at Lincoln, in May, 1906. Mrs. Wessel was born at Humboldt, Nebraska, in 1883, and is of German and French descent. There are three children: Louise, born July, 1907, married R. M. Gladstone; Helen, born in March, 1911, and Walter, Jr., born August 28, 1913.

Always active in the civic and welfare work of the city, Mr. Wessel is a charter member of the Chamber of Commerce, and a member of the Red Cross. He is an Elk, and a member of the Nebraskana Society. He enjoys tennis, and his hobby is traveling. He is a member of the Nebraska City Country Club. Residence: Nebraska City.

Dennison P. West

Dennison P. West, lawyer and banker of Syracuse, Nebraska, was born at Baldwinsville, New York, January 21, 1878. His father, Channing M. West, who was a lawyer, was born at Clay, New York, in 1851, and died there, April 4, 1913. His mother, Sarah A. (Phelps) West, was born at Sleepy Hollow, New York, in 1855, and died at Syracuse, July 19, 1914.

Mr. West was graduated from the Syracuse High School in 1895; and received his LL. B. degree at the University of Nebraska, in 1901. He is now president of the Bank of Syracuse.

His marriage to Eliza Ver Planck was solemnized at Clay, June 28, 1904. Mrs. West was born there, February 12, 1880. There are three children: Margaret, born January 31, 1906; Deforest F., born December 24, 1907, who married Vera Coupe; and Harry, born May 12, 1913.

Mr. West was a four minute man in the late war. He is a member of the state and county bar associations, and for several years has been treasurer of the Syracuse school board. He is an Odd Fellow, a Mason, and Shriner, and is affiliated with the First Methodist Church of Syracuse. He is a Democrat. Residence: Syracuse.

Elizabeth H. West

Elizabeth H. West, a pioneer business woman of Dawson County, Nebraska, was born at Chicago, Illinois, the daughter of Eric G. and Ingar (Benson) West. Her father, who was in the lumber, coal and grain business for many years, was born at Kristianham, Sweden, and died at Gothenburg, Nebraska, January 21, 1929. Her mother was born at Christianstadt, Sweden, and died at Gothenburg, February 15, 1902.

Miss West was graduated from the Gothenburg High School and attended Boyles School of Business at Omaha. She is an active member of the firm E. G. West and Company at Gothenburg, today, and takes an active part in the social and civic affairs of her community.

She is a member of the Woman's Club, serving as chairman of the tuberculosis seal committee, is former secretary of the City Relief Club, and holds membership in the Chamber of Commerce, and Chapter of the P. E. O. She is a Republican. The family attends the First Baptist Church. Her social club is the Gothenburg Country Club, and her favorite sport is skating. During the World War she served as secretary of the local Red Cross. Residence: Gothenburg. (Photograph in Album).

Frank William West

Frank W. West, pioneer grain and coal merchant in Nebraska, was born at Chicago, Illinois, March 2, 1858, the son of Francis Randall and Elizabeth Hanna (Hedges) West. His father, who was born in London, England, December 4, 1833, and died there February 14, 1867, was the proprietor of a plumbing shop; a life size portrait of him was brought from England in 1898 together with a portrait of his father, the grandfather of Frank William West.

His mother was born in London, October 10, 1834, and died in Chicago, at the age of 80 years. She was a typical English gentlewoman who devoted her life to making a home for her family; her father was a harness maker and manufacturer in England.

Mr. West attended the public schools of London and Chicago, but left school after his father's death to assist his mother in the support of the younger children. He has been many years in the grain and coal business with his brother, A. J. West, and is also a member of the West Brothers' Firm of automobile dealers. He has taken a prominent part in the civic and business life of Wisner, Cuming County, Nebraska, and has held the following positions in public life; member of the county board; member of the school board at Wisner; city councilman; member of the board of trustees of the Congregational Church; and non-political member of the local committee for city caucuses.

He is at present chairman of the County Red Cross Chapter; is a member of the Commercial Club at Wisner; and holds membership in the Nebraskana Society. During the World War he assisted in Red Cross work. He is a member of the Modern Woodmen of America; the Ancient Order of United Workmen; and the Royal Highlanders. His hobbies are reading and flower gardening.

He was united in marriage with Jeanetta Ruth Humphrey at Sutherland, Iowa, May 2, 1888. Mrs. West, who was a school teacher in Kansas and Iowa before her marriage, was born near Bellevue, Iowa, October 1, 1862. Her ancestors were teachers, farmers, and blacksmiths, and paternal grandfather made locks for the Erie Canal.

Their children are: Fern Genevieve, born February 14, 1890, who married A. F. Aitchison; Leota Elizabeth, born April 21, 1896, who is hospital dietician in Chicago; Helen Victoria, born July 14, 1897, who is city accountant at Omaha; Florence Eleanor, born July 10, 1899, who is hospital dietician in Chicago; Frances Jeanetta, born December 1, 1902, who is hospital dietician in Chicago; Harold John, born January 18, 1905, who is a high school teacher and athletic coach; and Lloyd Ellis, born January 21, 1908, who is chemistry instructor in the Agriculture College at Fargo, North Dakota. All the children are high school graduates and have from two to six years college training and are members of the Congregational Church. Residence: Wisner.

Ralph Millard West

A native of Albia, Iowa, born July 25, 1886, Ralph M. West is the son of Joel Wilcox and Ida Sarah (Cowles) West. Joel West, a lawyer, was born in Racine County, Wisconsin, July 28, 1856, and died at San Diego, California, December 25, 1917. Ida Cowles West was born at Bentonsport, Iowa, January 3, 1859, and died at Omaha, November 30, 1910.

Ralph M. West received his education in the Omaha public schools, and was graduated from Omaha High School in 1903. He entered Grinnell College and received his A. B. in 1907. In 1910, he received an A. M. and LL. B. from Creighton University.

He is a Republican, and has been engaged in the practice of law since 1910. On June 1, 1911, he was married to Mildred Warburton, at Grinnell, Iowa. Mrs. West was born at Jewell, Iowa, May 13, 1885.

Mr. West is a member of the First Central Congregational Church of Omaha, and of the American and Nebraska State Bar Associations. His clubs are the University Club, the Omaha Club and the Omaha Country Club. Residence: Omaha.

Chattie Coleman Westenius

Chattie C. Westenius, newspaper editor in Nebraska since 1892, was born near Redfield, Dallas County, Iowa, July 5, 1871, the daughter of Jacob Hesser and Nicy Lavonia (Farmer) Coleman. Her father, who was mayor of Stromsburg 2 terms, and police judge there for 34 years, was born in Green County, Illinois, November 5, 1841, and died at Stromsburg, Polk County, Nebraska, July 26, 1922; he served with the 91st Illinois Volunteers and from 1888 to 1890 was captain of Company I, 2nd Regiment of the Nebraska National Guards. His ancestors came from Rotterdom, Holland; the family has been represented in every war for the United States.

Her mother, who is descended from the Gooch family

of Virginia, was born in Illinois, in 1851, and died at Butte, Montana, in 1896.

Mrs. Westenius completed the elementary grades and later attended Bryant Normal University. She has been a resident of Nebraska since 1881 and since 1892 has been editor of the *Headlight* at Stromsburg, being the first woman in the state to own and control a weekly newspaper; since 1900 she has been a member of the Nebraska State Press Association.

Mrs. Westenius is the author of *History of Stromsburg*, a concise review of the early days and later developments of the town. This volume contains pictures of the early residence, the landmarks and the business blocks. The complete history of the business, the professional and financial progress of Stromsburg is set forth along with a complete history of each newspaper since the founding of the town. The work is especially valuable for its collections of pictures of buildings and landmarks of the pioneer days. Much interesting detail of life in the early days is given. The books also gives the firms in business in Stromsburg at the present time. She is at this time compiling a genealogical history of her own family.

She was active in Red Cross work and loan drives during the World War, was organizing regent of the local chapter of the Daughters of the American Revolution, and is a member of the Elijah Gove Chapter of this organization; in 1916, she served as state auditor for the society.

She holds membership in the Order of the Eastern Star, the Nebraska State Historical Society, Nebraskana Society, and the Woman's Club. She has been Red Cross secretary of the local chapter since 1917 and county chairman since 1929. Her hobby is flowers.

Her marriage to John Albert Westenius was solemnized at Omaha, Nebraska, February 17, 1922. Mr. Westenius, who was born at Gothenburg, Sweden, October 22, 1859, is the son of a distinguished editor, traveler, journalist, and lecturer in his native land. Residence: Stromsburg. (Photograph on Page 1266).

John Albert Westenius

John Albert Westenius was born at Gothenburg, Sweden, October 22, 1859, and for the past 45 years has been a resident of Nebraska. John Bernt Westenius, his father, who was born in Sweden, July 18, 1827, and died there in 1913, was a teacher, editor, and lecturer. Albertena (Westerberg) Westenius, his mother, was born in Sweden, January 12, 1826, and died there October 26, 1888.

Mr. Westenius served as printer for the *SwedishTribune* in Chicago, was foreman and editor of the *Stromsburg Republican*, 1891-3, and was foreman of the *Stromsburg Headlight* for 25 years. He is now assistant editor and publisher of the *Headlight*. He is a member of the Chamber of Commerce at Stromsburg, Red Cross, the Nebraskana Society, and is a 32nd degree Mason. He served as second sergeant of Company I, 2nd Regiment, of the Nebraska National Guards.

His marriage to Anna Sophia Johnson took place at Osceola, July 26, 1889; she was born at New Sweden, Iowa, September 21, 1870, and died at Stromsburg, March 21, 1921. Two children were born to them: Alvin, April 19, 1891, who married Ethel Severine; and Emma, December 12, 1896, who married Lloyd W. Hollister. On February 17, 1922, he married Chattie Coleman, who had been editor of the *Stromsburg Headlight* since October, 1892, at Omaha, Nebraska. Residence: Stromsburg.

John Christian Westerhoff

John Christian Westerhoff, retired farmer, was born at Alexandria, Nebraska, July 28, 1873. He is the son of William and Johanna Christianna (Gruetze) Westerhoff, the former a pioneer Nebraskan. William Westerhoff was born in Duesseldorf, Prussia, April 15, 1824, and

CHATTIE COLEMAN WESTENIUS

came to America in 1854, locating at Quincy, Illinois. He remained there until 1873 when he removed to Alexandria, where he died March 5, 1906. A retired farmer at the time of his death, he was prominent in his community, and served as county commissioner of Thayer County.

Johanna Christianna Gruetze was born in Dresden, Saxony, December 26, 1828, and came to America in 1855. She married William Westerhoff at Warsaw, Illinois, in 1860. A successful wife and mother, her death occurred at Alexandria, October 24, 1901.

Educated in the rural schools of District No. 30 in Jefferson County, Nebraska, John C. Westerhoff attended Nebraska Wesleyan University 1894-95, Lincoln Normal University 1897-98, and received his Ph. G. from Highland Park College at Des Moines, Iowa, in February, 1901. At Lincoln Normal he was a member of the male quartet, and at Nebraska Wesleyan was a member of the college chorus. He was also a member of the football team at Weselyan.

On June 1, 1911, Mr. Westerhoff was united in marriage to Flora Marie Wittenberger at Alexandria. Mrs. Westerhoff was born at Plattsmouth, October 1, 1883, her parents having immigrated to the United States from Germany as children. They have one child, Marlowe, born March 30, 1912, who is a junior at the University of Nebraska.

Mrs. Wittenberger is a registered nurse, and a graduate of St. Joseph's Hospital at St. Joseph, Missouri. Marlowe is a member of the Young Men's Christian Association, and since 1929 has been a member of the Reserve Officers Corps at the University. The family attends the First Presbyterian Church of Alexandria. Residence: Alexandria.

Victor Westermark

Victor Westermark, county attorney of Dundy County, was born at Oakland, Nebraska, June 16, 1895, son of Nels and Emma Sofia (Johnson) Westermark. The father, who was born in Vasterboten Lan, Sweden, November 27, 1858, came to the United States in 1888, and has since been engaged in farming near Oakland. His wife, who was born the same place on March 3, 1866, was a teacher in Sweden.

Mr. Westermark was graduated from Oakland High School in 1915, and received the Bachelor of Laws degree from the University of Nebraska, College of Law in June, 1923. Prior to that time he attended Wayne Normal School. He is a member of Delta Theta Phi.

From 1915 until 1917 Mr. Westermark taught in public schools. He held the rank of corporal in the United States Army from 1917 until 1919 attached to the 353 acre Squadron, and in 1923 he was admitted to the bar in Nebraska. He is a Republican.

His marriage to Corrinne Marie Robidoux was solemnized at Fort Collins, Colorado, September 4, 1926. Mrs. Westermark was born at Benkelman, Nebraska, January 21, 1892. She is a member of the Roman Catholic Church and is active in church affairs. She is much interested in her home and family, a daughter of Joe and Eliza Robidoux, early pioneers of Dundy County. They have one daughter, Celestine, born December 1, 1927.

Mr. Westermark is a member of the First Baptist Church of Benkelman, the American Legion, the Nebraska State Bar Association, the Red Cross, the Community Club and the Masons. He enjoys golf and fishing. His hobby is reading. Residence: Benkelman. (Photograph in Album).

Edgar M. Westervelt

Edgar M. Westervelt, railroad executive, was born at Buda, Illinois, May 17, 1861, son of Peter J. and Martha (Maycox) Westervelt.

His paternal ancestors came from Holland, and his maternal ancestors from England.

Mr. Westervelt was educated in the public and high schools at Buda, Illinois, and on January 27, 1887, was married to Rosamond B. Castor at Lincoln. Mrs. Westervelt is a native of Saline County. Her father, Tobias Castor, was a leading Democrat and served as a member of the national committee during President Cleveland's last term. He was an official of the Burlington Railroad. Mr. and Mrs. Westervelt have the following children, Frances C., now Mrs. Leonard A. Flansburg; and Edgar, who married Ruth C. Kallemeyn.

From 1884 until 1902 Mr. Westervelt was assistant right of way agent for the Burlington Railroad, and from 1902 until 1909 was right of way agent. He was a real estate agent from 1909 until 1912, and assistant land and industrial commissioner from 1912 until 1915. Since 1915 he has been land and industrial commissioner.

Mr. Westervelt is a Mason, Knight Templar, and Shriner. He is a member of the Chamber of Commerce and has served on various committees. His club is the Lincoln Country Club. He was an incorporator of the Bank of Commerce, and was director of the City National Bank for many years. He was also colonel on the governor's staff for a number of years. Residence: Lincoln.

Eugene Theodore Westervelt

Eugene Theodore Westervelt, prominent Nebraskan, was born at Greenfield, Massachusetts, January 16, 1865, son of James Henry and Loureana Amelia (Day) Westervelt.

James Henry Westervelt was born at Patterson, New Jersey, January 6, 1840, and died at Scottsbluff, July 14, 1908. He was a blacksmith of Dutch descent. His wife, Loureana, was born at Stanford, Vermont, May 3, 1848, and died at Scottsbluff, November 10, 1912. Her ancestry was Scotch-Irish.

Mr. Westervelt attended public school and from 1900 until 1925 was editor of the Scottsbluff Republican. He has always been active in Republican politics, and served as sheriff from 1896 until 1900. He was postmaster from 1910 until 1915, and from 1925 until 1931 was a member of the State Board of Control.

He was married on June 30, 1886, to Laura Belle Amos at Broken Bow. She was born at Carlton, Ohio, February 20, 1863, of Scitch and English descent. To them were born nine children, six of whom are living, Dessie May, born September 2, 1889, died August 17, 1916; Ethel Viola, born July 14, 1887, died July 11, 1888; Muriel N., born November 20, 1894; James William, born August 16, 1892, who married Myrtle Shumway; John M., born April 10, 1896; Laurence Eugene, born July 24, 1898, who married Esther Lind; Florence, twin sister of Laurence Eugene, born July 24, 1898, died July 25, 1898; Mendle Ely, born October 26, 1900, who married Anna Matlock; and Loureana Katherine, born July 1, 1904, who married Dale Henderson.

Laura Belle (Amos) Westervelt attended school at Perrysville, Ohio. She is the daughter of John and Catherine (Thompson) Amos, and is a member of the Methodist Episcopal Church.

Mr. Westervelt has always ranked among the most prominent personages in his state. He is a member of the Baptist Church, a Mason, and from 1900 until 1908 was a member of the school board. His hobby is fishing. Residence: Scottsbluff.

Plumer Parker Weston

Plumer Parker Weston, who has lived in Nebraska since 1902, has been engaged in business at Lincoln for the past 28 years. He was born at Elkpoint, Union County, South Dakota, July 11, 1884, the son of Alexis Ransome and Cornelia Maydora (Parker) Weston. His father, who was born in New York in 1859, is a farmer and plantation owner in Georgia; his ancestry is English. His mother was born in Pennsylvania in 1860 of Pennsylvania Dutch descent, and died at Lincoln, Lancaster County, Nebraska, in 1918.

Mr. Weston was graduated from the Elkpoint High School, in 1902 and later attended the Lincoln Business College. He served as stenographer and bookkeeper, 1903-04, for the Dwelling House Mutual Insurance Company, was employed in the office of the chief dispatcher and general superintendent for the Chicago, Burlington and Quincy Railroad, 1905-06, and was employed in the city clerk's office at Lincoln, 1907-08. From 1909 to 1920 he was secretary and business manager of the McKelvie Publishing Company at Lincoln, and since 1921 he has been senior partner of the Weston and Griffith Company, wholesale retail firm, at Lincoln.

He is a member of the Lincoln Chamber of Commerce, is affiliated with the Methodist Episcopal Church at Lincoln, and holds membership in the Nebraskana Society. In 1920 he was president of the Lincoln Credit Men's Association, and was a member of the Young Men's Chrstian Association, 1905-21, and the Rotary Club, 1910-21. He is a member of the Shrine Country Club, the Shrine Golf Club, and the Masons, (32nd degree Scottish Rite, Blue Lodge, and Shrine). His hobby is the radio and his favorite sport is golf.

On March 12, 1908, he was united in marriage with Eva Winifred Mitchell at Lincoln, Lancaster County, Nebraska; she was born at Red Cloud, Nebraska. To this union two children were born: Eva Jane, born July 28, 1914; and William M., born July 22, 1919. Mr. Weston was married to Emily K. Mayhugh at Omaha, April 16, 1927. Mrs. Weston was employed by the Western Electric Company, held a secretarial position in Congressman Sloan's office, was employed by the National Bank of Commerce, and the governor of Nebraska, She also was employed in the purchasing agent's and the state treasurer's office, later. Residence: Lincoln.

Frank Elmer Weyer

Born at Ainsworth, Nebraska, January 14, 1890, Frank Elmer Weyer is the son of John and Elizabeth (Sweitzer) Weyer. His father, a native of Berne, Switzerland, was born August 19, 1839, and came to America at the age of 10 years with his parents. Prior to his death at Ainsworth, on April 19, 1917, he had been a farmer for many years. His wife, Elizabeth, was born in New Philadelphia, Ohio, March 25, 1849. Her parents came to America from Switzerland, about 1835.

Upon the completion of his elementary education in the rural schools of Brown County and the grade schools of Ainsworth, Mr. Weyer attended Long Pine High School from which he was graduated in 1906. He was graduated from Crete Academy in 1907. In 1911 he was awarded his Bachelor of Arts degree from Hastings College, and in 1916 his Master of Arts degree, from the University of Nebraska. During the school year 1916-17, and the summer of 1917, he attended Teachers College, Columbia University, and during the summer of 1924, he attended Stanford University. He is a member of Phi Delta Kappa and Acacia fraternities.

On June 3, 1916, Mr. Weyer was married to Mabelle Claire Carey, of Hebron, Nebraska. They have three children, Mary Elizabeth, born September 2, 1917; Dorothy, born December 4, 1921, and Phyllis, born December 25, 1923.

Mr. Weyer was principal of the Newport, Nebraska, schools in 1911-13, superintendent of schools at Atkinson, from 1913-16, professor of education and psychology 1917-18 at Kendall College, Tulsa, Oklahoma, and since 1918 has been dean and professor of education at Hastings College. He is the author of *Status of Rural Teachers in Nebraska* (U. S. Bulletin No. 20, 1919).

Among Professor Weyer's professional organizations are the National Education Association, the Nebraska State Teachers Association, and the American Association for the Advancement of Science, the Nebraska Association of Church Colleges (Secretary since 1925), and the Nebraska Schoolmasters Club. He is a member of the First Presbyterian Church of Hastings. He is a Mason, a member of the Kiwanis Club, and a member of the board of Mary Lanning Memorial Hospital School of Nursing. Mr. Weyer is also a life member of the Nebraskana Society. Residence: Hastings.

Stephen Morris Weyer

Stephen Morris Weyer, physician and surgeon, was born at Ainsworth, Nebraska, August 3, 1886, son of John and Elizabeth (Schweitzer) Weyer. The father and mother both came from Berne, Switzerland.

In 1910 Dr. Weyer was graduated from Hastings College Academy, and in 1914 received his Bachelor of Science degree from Hastings. He received his medical degree from the University of Nebraska in 1918. He is a member of the American Medical Association, the Nebraska State Medical Association, and the Lincoln County Medical Association, and during 1918 was acting assistant surgeon of the United States Public Health Service.

On December 26, 1918, he was married to Dorris Elizabeth Roelse at Hastings. She is the daughter of Jacob and Margaret Roelse. Her parents both reside at Hastings. She was a native of Baldwin, Wisconsin. Two children were born to them, Jean Dorris, on November 4, 1919 at Omaha; and Ruth Elizabeth, on October 14, 1920 at Long Pine, Nebraska.

Dr. Weyer is a member of the Masons and the Odd Fellows. He is a Republican. His favorite sport is rifle range practice. He also enjoys hunting. Residence: Ogallala.

Jennings M. Wheat

For the past 60 years Jennings M. Wheat has been a resident of Sarpy County, Nebraska. He was born at Baltimore, Maryland, May 2, 1865, son of Marvin Timothy Wheat, lawyer and author. Marvin Wheat was born in New York, June 14, 1817, of English ancestry. He married Caroline Dyson, a native of Baltimore. She was of English and Irish descent, and was born March 24, 1838. She died at Papillion, May 7, 1910.

Judge Wheat was educated in the public schools of Nebraska, after which he attended college two years. Subsequently he took a law course, and was admitted to the Nebraska bar in June, 1909. During his youth and young manhood he was active in amateur baseball, boxing and wrestling.

A Republican, he has always been active in public life, and since January 4, 1912, has been county judge of Sarpy County; his present term expires January 4, 1933. Prior to his admission to the bar he was for eight years in the civil engineering department of the Burlington Railroad and was in the railway mail service about 10 years.

During the World War he was chairman of the legal advisory board for Sarpy County. He is a member of the Red Cross and of The Nebraskana Society. He is also a Mason. His particular hobby is reading.

On February 13, 1915, he was united in marriage to Clara Elvina Gehringer. She was born at Grimsville, Berks County, Pennsylvania, November 29, 1878. She is a member of the Order of Eastern Star, the Kensington Club, etc. Their marriage took place at Onawa, Iowa. There are no children. Residence: Papillion.

Walter Herbert Wheatley

Walter Herbert Wheatley, educator and musician, was born at Webb City, Missouri, January 12, 1878, son of William Alfred and Mary Lida (Street) Wheatley. William Wheatley was a native of Dayton, Ohio, and died at Joplin, Missouri, in July, 1912. His great-grandfather came from Yorkshire, England. His wife, Mary Lida, was born in Glenwood, Iowa, and died at Los Angeles, California, April 1, 1924. A church worker and clubwoman, she was also a talented singer. Her grandfather was one of the founders of Salem, Oregon, and a member of that heroic band who blazed the Oregon Trail.

Mr. Wheatley attended the Carthage, Missouri, public and high schools and studied music both in America, Chicago and New York, and abroad, in Paris under Jean de Reszke and La Pierre of the Paris Opera, and in Milan, Italy, with Antonio Colli, famous tenor of La Scalla and Betenelli, illustrious conductor and repetuer of La Scalla Opera. Mr. Wheatley, after singing at Covent Garden, London, in the Italian season, went to Italy where he was engaged at La Scalla and the Teatro Del Corso at Bologna, well known as the most musical city in Italy. More years were spent in England, after which he returned to New York where he sang in a big season of operas in English under the sponsorship of the Metropolitan Opera House. He later toured Australia and New Zealand after singing two seasons at Ravinia, Chicago. Through the medium of his voice he has circumnavigated the globe. He was leading tenor in grand opera in England, France, and Italy. While in London, on October 21, 1918, he was married to Fanny Florence Douglas, who was born in Edinburgh, Scotland, May 20, 1888.

After an operatic career in Europe, New York, and Chicago, Mr. Wheatley came to Lincoln, Nebraska, where he is professor of voice. He is the author of *Common Sense in Singing*. Because of the success of this book, he was brought to Chicago, where he lectured and taught at the Gunn School of Music. His religious affiliation is with the First Presbyterian Church. He is a member of the Nebraskana Society and the Chamber of Commerce. He enjoys golf, and is a member of the Lincoln Country Club. Residence: Lincoln.

Grace Mason Wheeler

Grace Mason Wheeler, a resident of Nebraska all her life, has been prominent in city, state, and national affairs since 1881. She was born at Nebraska City, August 26, 1864, the daughter of Oliver Perry Mason and Mary Jennie (Turner) Mason. Her father, who was born at North Brookfield, Madison County, New York, May 15, 1827, and died at Lincoln, August 18, 1891, was a distinguished lawyer, judge, and legislator. He served as the first chief justice of Nebraska, and was a member of the Constitutional Convention; was provost marshal during the Civil War; and was descended from ancestors who settled in New England in 1640 and were esteemed citizens of Connecticut and Rhode Island.

Mary Jennie Turner was born at Brattleboro, Vermont, March 24, 1835, and died at Nebraska City, May 15, 1874. She was a cultured pioneer woman, interested in musical and literary work, who was a leader in church and social affairs in Nebraska in the early days. Her New England ancestors were prosperous manufacturers and business men.

Mrs. Wheeler was graduated from Brownell Hall at Omaha, in 1881; and in 1881-82 was a student at the University of Nebraska. She has taken special work at the latter institution at later intervals. During her course at Brownell Hall she was awarded scholarship medals in literature, and was valedictorian of her graduating class. She has devoted most of her time to home making, and was for many years her husband's assistant in legal editorship.

Mrs. Wheeler is especially interested in the study of government current affairs, and has been active in politics and civic matters during the last 30 years. A Republican, she served as presidential elector in 1920; and in 1912 was campaign manager for the Suffrage Association. She was active in Parent-Teacher school work from 1893

to 1900; was legislative chairman for the Federation of Woman's Clubs, 1910-20; and made many speeches at educational meetings of women throughout the state. She is the author of *Handbook for Nebraska Citizens,* articles on *Nebraska's Constitution* published in *The Nebraska Farmer,* and lectures on current events, published in various magazines.

She was united in marriage with Hiland Hill Wheeler at Lincoln, May 20, 1885. Mr. Wheeler, who was born at New York City, New York, June 26, 1845, and died at Lincoln, February 11, 1928, was a lawyer and the publisher of the Nebraska Compiled Statutes. He was descended from Peter Bulkely and Jehu Burr of Connecticut. Three children were born to their marriage: Mason, born April 16, 1886, who married Helen Matteson, and who served as judge of the district court in Lancaster County, 1924-28; Margaret, born March 9, 1888, who married Simon Casady, Jr., and Hiland Hill, born September 15, 1889, who is chief engineer for the Lincoln Telephone and Telegraph Company.

Mrs. Wheeler is an honorary member of the Axis Club, and was state board member of the League of Women Voters, 1914-20. She holds membership in the Nebraskana Society, the State Historical Society, the Native Sons and Daughters, and All Souls Unitarian Church of Lincoln. She was a member of the city library board of Lincoln, 1899-1901. Her social club is the Sorosis Club. Her hobbies include: general reading; current events; and contact with her grandchildren. Residence: Lincoln.

Hiland Hill Wheeler, 3rd

Hiland Hill Wheeler, chief engineer for the Lincoln Telephone & Telegraph Company at Lincoln, has lived in this state all his life. He was born at Lincoln, September 17, 1889, the son of Hiland Hill Wheeler, II, and Grace (Mason) Wheeler. His father, who was a distinguished lawyer, was born at New York City, June 26, 1845, and died at Lincoln, February 11, 1928; he was a soldier in the Civil War; his ancestors settled in America in Colonial times. His mother was born at Nebraska City, Nebraska, August 26, 1864, and is still living. She is descended from American colonists.

Mr. Wheeler was a student at the University of Nebraska, 1905-09, where he was elected to membership in Delta Tau Delta. He is interested in the civic and social affairs of his community and holds membership in the Lincoln Rotary Club; the Lincoln University Club; and the Nebraskana Society. He is a 33rd degree Mason; a member of the Republican party; and a Unitarian. Residence: Lincoln.

Mason Wheeler

Mason Wheeler, a lifetime resident of Lincoln, Lancaster County, Nebraska, was born there April 16, 1886, the son of Hiland Hill and Grace (Mason) Wheeler. His father, who was a lawyer and served as deputy clerk of the Supreme Court of Nebraska, was born at New York City, and died at Lincoln, February, 1928; he was the compiler of the Nebraska Statutes; he served in the Civil War. His mother, who is a clubwoman and ardent suffragist, was born at Nebraska City, Otoe County, Nebraska. Her father, O. P. Mason, was chief justice of Nebraska.

He was graduated from the Lincoln High School and now holds the following degrees: A. B., 1906, University of Nebraska; LL. B., 1908, Columbia University. He was active in debating at the University of Nebraska, was class president and editor of the school paper. He was elected to membership in Delta Tau Delta.

Mr. Wheeler practiced law in New York City, 1908-16, was assistant attorney general, 1919-22, and practiced law at Lincoln, 1923. A Republican, he was elected assistant attorney general in 1919-22, and district judge

of Lancaster County District, 1924 and 1928. During
1929 he was engaged in legal practice at Seattle, Washington.

During the World War Judge Wheeler served as
lieutenant of the field artillery of the United States Army,
1917-19, and saw active service in France. He is a member of the county and state bar associations in Nebraska,
and of the Mountaineers Club of Washington. He was
married to Helen Matteson at Lincoln, July 12, 1927.
Mrs. Wheeler was born at Sutton, Nebraska. Residence:
Lincoln.

Thomas Ellsworth Wheeler

Thomas E. Wheeler, register of deeds at Lincoln, Nebraska, has lived in this state since 1868. He was born at
Butler, Pennsylvania, September 16, 1863, the son of John
Lewis and Maggie (Purvis) Wheeler. His father who
was born at Steubenville, Ohio, March 11, 1840, was a merchant and farmer who came to Nebraska in a covered
wagon in the early 1860's and homesteaded just north of
Bennet. He died at Bennet, September 13, 1913.

His mother was born at Butler, Pennsylvania, February 23, 1841, and died at Bennet, August 19, 1913. She
was an interested church worker and took an active part
in pioneer temperance work.

Mr. Wheeler received his education in the district
schools of Lancaster County. He was deputy register of
deeds at Lincoln for eight years and since 1914, has been
register of deeds. In 1930 he was re-elected for a four
year term to this position. He is a member of the Modern Woodmen of America and the Masons. His religious
affiliation is with the Normal Methodist Church of Lincoln. He likes to hunt and fish, and spends most of his
leisure time caring for his flowers and chickens. Residence: Lincoln.

Arthur Hutchison Wherry

Arthur H. Wherry was born on August 27, 1866, at
Wyoming, Jones County, Iowa, the son of James Bratton
and Nancy Jane (Moore) Wherry. His father, who was
born at Fairvue, Ohio, February 4, 1832, and died at Pawnee City, Nebraska, September 24, 1917, was a farmer and
stockraiser. He was descended from Scotch-Irish ancestors who came from North Ireland, about 1718, and
purchased land from William Penn, at what is now Chester, Pennsylvania. He devoted his life to fighting the
liquor interests.

His mother, who was born at Fairvue, September 22,
1833, and died at Pawnee City, May 29, 1901, was the
mother of seven children to all of whom she gave a college education. She was descended from Irish ancestors
on the paternal side and Scotch ancestors through the
maternal line.

Mr. Wherry was graduated from the Wyoming High
School in 1888, and in 1892 was awarded the A. B. degree at Monmouth College, Illinois, where he was active
in debating. Mr. Wherry, who has been a successful merchant and banker for 38 years, was a member of the firm
of Wherry Brothers, which he later sold to enter the
banking business. At the present time he is vice president
of the Citizens State Bank at Pawnee City. He is one of
four men owning large tracts of land in Canada.

He was united in marriage with Eva May Comstock at
Pawnee City, June 21, 1899. Mrs. Wherry, who was born
at Cascade, Iowa, July 24, 1875, is of Scotch and English
ancestry. Two children were born to this union. Evelyn,
born February 3, 1903, was graduated from Monmouth
College in 1924. She was a high school history instructor
at Kirkwood, Illinois, for two years after her graduation
from college, and for the next four years was history
teacher in the Pawnee City High School. Roland Comstock, born February 25, 1906, was graduated from the
University of Nebraska, in June, 1927; in 1928 entered

Northwestern Medical College at Chicago, and in 1930,
was appointed as an instructor in this school.

Mr. Wherry was chairman of the Pawnee chapter of
the Red Cross for two years, and during the World War
engaged in four loan drives. He is president of the Service Club; has been a member of the school board for 15
years, acting as president for the last seven years. He is
affiliated with the United Presbyterian Church at Pawnee City, where he has taught a Sunday School class for
25 years. Residence: Pawnee City.

Eva May Wherry

Eva May Wherry was born in Cascade County, Iowa,
July 24, 1875, the daughter of Abel and Isabelle Margaret
(Eckelson) Comstock. Her father, who was born at Putnam, New York, May 17, 1822, and died at Orchard, Nebraska, May 14, 1897, was a millwright, teacher, and landholder. He was an accomplished musician, and was cellist and song leader in his church for over 20 years. English ancestors of Mr. Comstock settled a tract of land in
Charlotte County, on the west coast of Lake Champlain,
in 1795. Other ancestors, who were weavers, came from
Paisley, Scotland.

Her mother, who was a teacher, was born at Burgetts-
town, Washington County, Pennsylvania, September 1,
1835, the daughter of James and Isabelle (McKinney)
Eckelson. She died at Pawnee City, Nebraska, December
2, 1899.

Mrs. Wherry attended the Liberty High School, at
Liberty, Nebraska, 1890-91, and the Pawnee City High
School, 1892-93-94. In 1898 and 1899 she was a student
at the University of Nebraska, where she studied piano.
She taught the public school at Riverside, Nebraska, from
1894 to 1897.

A resident of Nebraska all her life, she has taken part
in all civic, religious and educational affairs in her community. Upon completion of a trip abroad in 1927, she
was the author of a newspaper article, published in 1928,
entitled *Our Trip Abroad*.

Her marriage to Arthur Hutchison Wherry, was solemnized at Pawnee City, June 21, 1899. Mr. Wherry,
whose ancestry is Scotch-Irish, was born at Wyoming,
Jones County, Iowa, August 26, 1866. He is a banker
and landholder, and was formerly a furniture merchant.
Three children were born to this marriage, two of whom
are living: Margaret Evelyn, born February 3, 1903, who
was graduated from Monmouth College, and Monmouth
Conservatory of Music, Monmouth, Illinois, 1924, is history instructor at the high school of Pawnee City, Nebraska; Roland Comstock, born February 25, 1906, who was
graduated from the University of Nebraska, in 1927, was
a student at the Northwestern Medical College, Chicago,
where he is now instructor in anatomy; and an infant,
born January 26, 1911, who died January 28, 1911.

She was treasurer of the Pawnee County Red Cross
following the late war, and is a member of this organization today. She is past president of the Tuesday Afternoon Study Club and the Conservation Club; is treasurer
of the local welfare board; and is a member of the local
advisory board of the Nebraska Children's Home Society.
She is eligible for membership in the Daughters of the
American Revolution; is at the present time preparing
her family history for this membership. She is past president of Chapter A V of the P. E. O. She is affiliated
with the United Presbyterian Church, is secretary of the
Women's Missionary Society and for the past ten years
has taught in the Sunday School. Mrs. Wherry is interested in gardening, having planted over 700 tulips in the
last year. She is an extensive traveler; has toured the
United States, Canada, part of Mexico, Cuba, England,
and Scotland. Residence: Pawnee City.

Kenneth Spicer Wherry

Kenneth Spicer Wherry, merchant and legislator, was
born at Liberty, Nebraska, February 28, 1892, son of

KENNETH S. WHERRY

Dole Studio—Lincoln

David E. and Jessie (Comstock) Wherry. David E.
Wherry was born in Iowa, in 1856, and is a merchant
of Scotch-Irish descent. His wife, Jessie, was born in
Iowa in 1859, and is of Scotch-Irish and early New England ancestry.

Upon his graduation from Pawnee City High School
Mr. Wherry entered the University of Nebraska, where
he received his Bachelor of Arts degree. He later took
post graduate work at Harvard University. His fraternity is Beta Theta Psi. At the university he was a
member of Professor Fogg's debating team 1911, 1912
and 1913, and was a member of the track team.

A resident of Nebraska all his life, Mr. Wherry has
been active as a merchant and farmer during the past
twenty years. At the present time he is a member of
the firm of Wherry Brothers, general merchants. In
Politics a Republican, he has been prominent in party
politics, and has served as city councilman, and as mayor
and state senator. He was candidate for the office of
governor on the Republican ticket in the 1932 primaries.

In the legislature Mr. Wherry championed the fish
and game bill creating the present state commission. He
is the author of the fair practice bill which passed the
senate in 1931, and failed in the house. He opposed
Missouri River Navigation and debated the question in
a series of joint debates with ex-Governor Arthur J.
Weaver and others.

On September 20, 1920, Mr. Wherry was married to
Marjorie Colwell at Pawnee City. Mrs. Wherry was
born at Pawnee City on September 7, 1896, and is of
English descent. There are two children, Marilyn, born
May 21, 1925, and David, born December 18, 1926.

During the World War Mr. Wherry served one year
with the Naval Flying Corps. He is a member of the
American Legion, the First Presbyterian Church, the
Kiwanis Club, the Pawnee City Public Service Club and
the Pawnee County Agricultural Society of which he has
been president for six consecutive years. On June 30, 1931,
he was admitted to the bar of Nebraska. Residence: Pawnee City. (Photograph on Page 1271).

Thomas Uridge Whiffen

For more than 62 years Thomas U. Whiffen has lived
in Nebraska, and has taken an active part in the economic
and civic life of the state. He was born at Utica, Oneida
County, New York, September 5, 1847, the son of John
and Sarah (Seaton) Whiffen. His father, who was a
butcher, packer, livestock dealer, and farmer, was born
at Kimbolton, Huntingdonshire, England, October 14,
1815, and came to America in 1832; he died at Kewanee,
Henry County, Illinois, June 27, 1897. His mother was
born at Hoden, Yorkshire, England, October 25, 1820;
she came to America with her parents on the ship with
John Whiffen and his parents; she died at Wyoming,
Stark County, Illinois, February 23, 1854.

Mr. Whiffen had just completed the eighth grade in
school when he enlisted for service in the Civil War. He
was a recruit in Company A of the 124th Illinois Infantry
as a private, and was mustered out in December, 1865.
From 1873 to 1884, he operated a blacksmith shop at De-
Witt, Nebraska, and in 1884 entered the lumber business
there. He retired from active business in 1914, but is at
present president of the DeWitt Lumber Company, and
is a director in the Home State Bank of DeWitt. Mr.
Whiffen has been prominent in the development of the
city.

He was united in marriage with Nettie Waldo at Beatrice, Gage County, Nebraska, December 1, 1868. She was
born at Northwestern, New York, June 4, 1852, and died
at DeWitt, September 25, 1886. The following children
were born to them: John I., born October 14, 1869, who
married Emma Miller; Nora M., born February 7, 1871,
who married E. W. Tatum; Mary G., born May 15, 1873,
who married Jacob E. Carey; Charles V., born March 27,
1875, who married Kittie Travers; Ralph W., born August
27, 1877, who died August 11, 1882; Edna E., born No-

vember 24, 1878, who married F. P. Steele; Nettie M.,
born June 13, 1881, who married Jules A. Sire; Esther,
born May 5, 1884, who died August 8, 1884; Ona G., born
July 14, 1885, married Joseph W. Lindley and resides at
Lodgepole, Nebraska.

Mr. Whiffen was married to Frances E. Van Dusen,
at Beatrice, Nebraska, December 4, 1895; she died at De-
Witt, January 4, 1921. One daughter was born to them,
Norma L., born August 12, 1898, who married Eugene F.
Wilsey. His marriage to Mrs. Luella A. Leeper was
solemnized at Wilber, Nebraska, September 6, 1923.

During the World War Mr. Whiffen was a four minute
man. He was one of the two remaining members of the
S. R. Curtis Post of the Grand Army of the Republic of
which he has been adjutant for the past twenty-five years.
He is a member of the Red Cross; the Commercial Club
of DeWitt Lodge No. 111 of the Ancient Free and Accepted Masons; and the Nebraskana Society. For more
than twenty years he has been interested in education and
has served at various times on the local school board.
Politically, he is an independent. Residence: DeWitt.

Emma Boge Whisenand

Emma Boge Whisenand, a resident of this state for
the past 46 years, was born at Harvard, Clay County,
Nebraska, May 15, 1885. Her father, Fred Boge, who
was born in Germany, March 10, 1851, came to this country
in 1867 and was a pioneer farmer in Nebraska. Her
mother, Matilda (Holmes) Boge, was born in Sweden,
December 19, 1858, and died at Harvard, March 31, 1907.

Mrs. Whisenand was graduated from high school at
Harvard in 1902, attended a junior normal school, and
taught in rural schools for a time. She is prominent in
women's affairs throughout the state and is the author
of various poems and short articles published in national
and state magazines. In 1931 she was awarded an essay
prize for her study of the Nebraska Indian, by the General Federation of Women's Clubs. She served the Nebraska Federation of Woman's Clubs as president of 5th
district 1931-33, and as state chairman of rural clubs and
rural life, 1927-31.

She is a member of the Harvard Woman's Club, the
Progressive Woman's Club, the Nebraskana Society, and
the First Methodist Church. Her hobbies are painting in oils; flower gardening; reading; and the study of
poetry.

Her marriage to Paul Russell Whisenand was solemnized at Hastings, Nebraska, October 5, 1910. Mr.
Whisenand, who is a farmer, was born in Hamilton County, Nebraska, August 20, 1883. Their children are:
Keith, born September 6, 1913, who died May 29, 1919;
Mavis, born October 24, 1915, who is president of the 4-H
Club; and Neal, born July 20, 1918, who died July 23,
1918. Mavis was president of a 4-H Club in 1930; was
Clay County 4-H health champion in 1929; prize newspaper reporter 1927. She was graduated from high school
in 1932. Mrs. Whisenand is independent, politically. Residence: Harvard.

Douglas D. Whitcomb

Douglas D. Whitcomb, lawyer at Winnebago, Thurston County, Nebraska, has lived in Nebraska all his life.
He was born at Pender, Thurston County, Nebraska,
February 4, 1892, the son of Waldo E. and Clara E. Whitcomb. His father, who is a lawyer, was born at Hustisford, Wisconsin. His mother, who was born at Topeka,
Illinois, is still living.

Mr. Whitcomb received his early education in the
Pender and Winnebago public schools, and was a student
at Peru Normal School and the University of Nebraska.
He held membership in Sigma Chi and Phi Alpha Delta.
He is director in the State Bank of Winnebago, and is
engaged in general legal practice. He holds membership
in the Nebraskana Society, is a Mason, and is affiliated
with the Democratic party. Residence: Winnebago.

Charles Ray White

Charles Ray White, retail hardware merchant, was born in Champaign, County, Illinois, June 4, 1884, and has resided in Nebraska, continuously, since 1906. He is the son of James R. and Oliva Jane (Koch) White, the former of whom was born in Champaign County, January 17, 1862, and is a farmer. Oliva Jane Koch was born March 10, 1865, and died in Lincoln County, Nebraska, September 6, 1897.

Mr. White attended public school in Urbana, Illinois, and from 1893 to 1897, resided in Nebraska. He farmed until 1909, and engaged in banking from 1910 until 1916. During the years 1917 and 1918, he was state bank examiner, and since that time, has been in the retail hardware business at Sutherland, Nebraska. He is a member of the firm of Cowles White Lumber Company of Wallace and Elsie, Nebraska. He is a Democrat.

On December 11, 1911, he was married to Eva Retta Cox at Sutherland. Mrs. White was born in Mills County, Iowa, January 27, 1892. To them were born three children, Charles Marvin, on November 2, 1915; Lavone Lucile, on May 20, 1918; and Kenneth Warren, on April 28, 1924.

Mr. White is a member of the Presbyterian Church of Sutherland, the Red Cross, the Commercial Club, the Odd Fellows, the Parent Teachers Association, and the school board. He enjoys big game hunting, while his hobbies are reading and mechanics. Residence: Sutherland.

Elbert M. White

Elbert M. White, lawyer, was born at Fairbanks, Iowa, January 4, 1874, son of Ezra Albert and Mary Louisa (Miller) White. His father, born in Toronto, Canada, died at Bartley, Nebraska, in November, 1905. He was descended from early English settlers in America. His wife, Mary, was born in Valparaiso, Indiana, and died at Creston, Nebraska in 1898.

Mr. White attended country school, Long Pine High School and was a student at Highland Park College one year. He was admitted to the bar on June 11, 1903, and has since continuously engaged in the practice of law. A Republican, he has twice been elected county attorney of Garfield County, and also served as a member of the Nebraska house of representatives the session of 1927. He did not seek re-election.

On June 1, 1904, he was married to Nina Kate Young at Stanton. Mrs. White, who is of Scotch descent on the paternal side, was born at Stanton on June 28, 1883. They have four children, Ruth M., born September 5, 1905, married Kyle K. McCleery; they reside at Hamilton, Montana. Harold N., born December 31, 1906, is married to Madge King, and teaches at Blair; William Vance, born March 1, 1909, married LaVerne Fitton, and is in the mercantile business at Morrill; Marian O., born April 26, 1912, is at home.

During the late war Mr. White was a four minute speaker and active in various Red Cross and bond drives. He is affiliated with the Congregational Church, is a member of the Nebraska State Bar Association, the Wranglers Club, the Masons, Modern Woodmen of America, the Royal Highlanders and Ben Hur. For a number of years he was a member of the board of education, and was active in obtaining the Carnegie Library for Burwell.

Mr. White is an ardent baseball and football fan. He enjoys fishing and hunting and has a private lake stocked with game fish. Recently he was made a life member of the Nebraskana Society. Residence: Burwell.

Fred Sam White

Fred S. White, was born at Omaha, January 27, 1903. His father, Samuel White, who was engaged in the jewelry business for many years, was born at Shimsk, Russia, December, 1880, and died at Omaha, August 13, 1914. He came to America in 1900, and until his death was active in the business world.

Minnie Kurtzman, his mother, was born of Jewish parents at Zuromin, Poland, January, 1882, and is living.

Mr. White was graduated from Central High School at Omaha, in 1920. In 1921 he was a student at the University of Nebraska, and in 1924 was graduated from Creighton University, at Omaha, where he received his LL. B. degree. At Creighton he was a member of the debating team, 1922-24. He was admitted to the bar in Nebraska, June 6, 1924, and since that time has engaged in general law practice in Omaha.

He is a member of the Nebraska State Bar Association, and the Red Cross, and is affiliated with B'nai Israel Synagogue. Mr. White's clubs are the Omaha Athletic Club; and the Highland Country Club. He is a Republican. Residence: Omaha.

Harry Smith White

Harry S. White has been engaged in the farm loans and investment business at Lyons, Nebraska, for the past 23 years, and has been vitally interested in educational and civic affairs there during that time. He was born at Milburn, Lake County, Illinois, April 7, 1883, the son of Andrew J. and Abbie C. (Smith) White. His father, who was born at Milburn in 1850, and died at Boulder, Colorado, July 11, 1921, was in the real estate business for several years; his ancestry was Scotch. His mother was born at Milburn, and died at Lyons, January, 1898. She was descended from New England Puritan ancestors.

Mr. White received his education in the public and high schools of Nebraska, and was a student at Highland Park College, 1902-03, where he participated in football and track. He is the owner and sole member of the firm White Investment Company of Lyons. He has lived in this state for 45 years.

He was united in marriage with Sarah E. Paine at Lyons, November 24, 1910. Mrs. White was born at Lyons, July 10, 1883. They have three children: Andrew P., born January 4, 1912; Sarah A., born November 28, 1915; and Mary, born August 23, 1917. Mr. White was chief of the northeastern Nebraska department of the American Protective Association during the World War, and served in the secret service without compensation.

He is a member of the Lyons Community Club; Young Men's Christian Association; and the Nebraska Society. He was a member of the city council, 1916, and the school board, 1920. He is a member of the Presbyterian Church, a Republican, and holds membership in the Red Cross. His favorite sport is football. Residence: Lyons.

Henry Adelbert White

One of its most beloved teachers, Henry Adelbert White, professor of English and coach of debate at the University of Nebraska, was born at Oran, Onondaga County, New York, April 8, 1880. His parents, Edward Albert and Gertrude (Candee) White, are both descended from early American colonists. Edward Albert is ninth in line from the Whites of the *Mayflower* and his wife is of the Candee family which settled near New Haven about 1637. From this family are descended all persons of that name in America.

Dr. White has the following degrees: A. B., Wesleyan University, (Middletown, Conn.), 1904; A. M., 1905; A. M., Harvard University, 1912; Ph. D., Yale University, 1924. He is a member of Delta Sigma Rho and Delta Tau Delta. He received honors in English and was class poet at Wesleyan, 1904.

His marriage to Henrietta Davidson of New York City, grand-niece of John Zundel, hymn writer, took place in New York on June 28, 1916. Their children are: Muriel Gertrude, born September 27, 1917, and Donald

Townsend—Lincoln

HENRY ADELBERT WHITE

Davidson, December 20, 1920. Frank Adelbert, born February 7, 1923, died September 16, 1925.

He was professor of English at Lombard College and at Washington and Jefferson until he became associated with the University of Nebraska in 1926. He is the author of *English Study and English Writing; Sir Walter Scott's Novels on the Stage*, besides many magazine articles on the various phases of English. He assisted the blind hymnist, Fanny J. Crosby, in writing her biography. He has edited *Stevenson's Master of Ballantrae* and the *New Century Book of Facts*. He has been editor of *Gavel*, organ of Delta Sigma Rho since 1926.

His religious affiliation is with the Trinity Methodist Episcopal Church of Lincoln. He is a member of the Modern Language Association, Modern Humanities Research Association, Shakespeare Association of America, and the Society of Midland Authors, of which latter he is vice president for Nebraska. He is now serving as president of the Nebraska High School Debate League. He has been active in the Knife & Fork Club of Lincoln during his residence, and is past president of the organization. He resides at Lincoln. (Photograph on Page 1274).

Herbert Thoma White

Herbert T. White, lawyer, was born at Lockwood, Nebraska, November 21, 1897. He is the son of Elmer Orin and Mary (Thoma) White. Elmer Orin White, who was born at Ann Arbor, Michigan, July 27, 1862, was a farmer and stockfeeder, and served as a director of the school board and as mmeber of the legislature of 1907. He was a descendant of William White who came to America with his parents on the *Mayflower*. He died at Cairo, Nebraska, January 2, 1912. Mary Thoma was born in Atchison, Kansas, October 26, 1864. Her father served with the Union forces in the Civil War, sustaining wounds from which he later died. Both he and his wife were natives of Germany.

Herbert T. White was educated first in district school No. 14, Hall County, Nebraska, being graduated at the age of 10 in 1908. He was graduated from Grand Island High School at the age of 14. In 1918 he received his B. L. at the University of Nebraska, which he attended four years. He was vice president of his law class in his junior year and president in his senior year. He was a letterman in football in 1917, and is a member of Phi Delta Phi.

A Republican, he was elected to the Nebraska state legislature in 1927 from the 11th district, and was nominated for re-election both in 1928 and 1930. He was associated in practice with the law office of Mahoney and Kennedy for one year, and since 1919 has been engaged in private practice.

On September 20, 1919, he was married to Mary Frances Stefan, at Omaha. Mrs. White was born at Omaha, July 11, 1897, and died there April 12, 1922. She was of German and Bohemian parentage, her father having been a captain in the Austrian Army.

Mr. White is a Protestant. He is a member of the Nebraskana Society and during the World War was a four-minute speaker. His clubs are the Happy Hollow Country Club, and the Lake Shore Tennis Club. His favorite sports are golf and football. Residence: Omaha.

William Vance White

William Vance White, merchant at Morrill, Nebraska, was born at Burwell, March 1, 1909, son of Elbert Miller and Nina Kate (Young) White.

Elbert Miller White was born at Fairbanks, Iowa, January 4, 1874, and is an attorney and former state representative from the 77th district. His wife, Nina, was born at Stanton, June 28, 1883. She is president of the Burwell Woman's Club, a member of the American Legion Auxiliary, and past president and member of the P. E. O. Sisterhood. She was educated at Brownell Hall in Omaha. Her ancestry is Scotch. Her father W. W. Young, is a former state senator and a former state president of the Knights of Pythias. He was one of the founders of the North American Life Insurance Company.

Upon his graduation from Burwell High School, Mr. White entered the University of Nebraska, where he was a student 1926-27. He earned two letters each in football and basketball in high school, and at the university was a member of Sigma Chi.

Four years, Mr. White was employed in Walkers Pharmacy at Burwell. At the president time, he is owner and manager of Whites store at Morrill. He is a Republican.

On January 13, 1929, he was married to LaVerne Opal Fitton at Brewster. She was born at Grafton, April 21, 1908, and was supervisor of music in public schools at Burwell. She is the daughter of Mr. and Mrs. A. O. Fitton. She was a student at Doane College and is a member of the Woman's Club and the Daughters of the American Revolution. Her ancestry is English, three ancestors having fought in Revolutionary War. They have one daughter, Jane Harriet, born February 9, 1932.

Mr. White is a member of the Congregational Church, a member of the Commercial Club, the Masons, and the Nebraskana Society. His favorite sport is golf, while his hobby is reading. Residence: Morrill.

Edwin Newton Whitescarver

Edwin Newton Whitescarver, merchant, was born at Central City, Nebraska, March 21, 1898, son of Edwin Newton and Mattie Elsie (Weger) Whitescarver. The father, born at Stansbury, Missouri, April 5, 1862, is an advertising and circulation manager. The mother was born in Illinois, February 13, 1867.

Mr. Whitescarver was graduated from Central City High School in May, 1917, where he earned letters in football, basketball and baseball. From 1920-24 he was a traveling salesman for Grainger Brothers Company of Lincoln, and since the last mentioned date has been the owner of a general mercantile business at Dunning.

A Republican, Mr. Whitescarver is local secretary of the Republican national committee. He has been secretary of the Blaine County Fair Association since 1925, and was a member of the town board 1929-30. From 1925-30 he served as chairman of the local school board.

On May 31, 1923, he was married to Lucy Belle Chrisman at Lincoln. Mrs. Whitescarver was born at Broken Bow, Nebraska, September 11, 1897 and is a graduate of Broken Bow High School. She is the daughter of Abe R. and Emma (Tooley) Chrisman. They are pioneer settlers of Custer County. Her father is a descendant of Abraham Lincoln and her mother is a sister of the late senator C. S. Tooley. Mrs. Whitescarver is a member of the Eastern Star. To them were born two children, Charles Edwin, on January 16, 1925; and Leola Dean, born July 19, 1927. Residence: Dunning.

Elizabeth Edna Whitfield

Elizabeth E. Whitfield, vice president of the Nebraska Federation of Woman's Clubs, has been prominent in the social and civic life of the state since 1912. She was born at Beaver Falls, Pennsylvania, February 25, 1874, the daughter of Daniel Charles and Mary Catherine (Walsh) Barnard. Her father, who was born at Philadelphia, in 1819, and died at Beaver Falls, September 6, 1885, was the operator of stone quarries and coal mines. Her mother, who was a descendant of Andrew and Nathaniel Patterson, soldiers in the Revolution, was born at Pittsburgh, Pennsylvania, June 19, 1828, and died at Beaver Falls, August 9, 1918.

Mrs. Whitfield attended grade school at Beaver Falls, and in 1891 was graduated from high school. Later she stldied music at Beaver College for one year. In addition to her Woman's Club activities she is a member of the Young Women's Christian Association, the American Red Cross, the Daughters of the American Revolution and the Order of the Eastern Star at Lincoln. From 1922 to 1924 she was president of the Lincoln Woman's Club. Her religious affiliation is with the First Presbyterian Church of Lincoln. She is a Democrat.

Her marriage to William Wilson Whitfield was solemnized at Beaver Falls, December 27, 1892. Mr. Whitfield, who is a traveling salesman, was born at Dublin, Ireland, May 19, 1868. Their children are: Marion, born October 29, 1893, who married Guy E. Mickle; and Harold, born April 16, 1895, who married Edith Jump, and who is patent attorney for the Teletype Corporation. Residence: Lincoln.

J. W. Whitham

In 1849, J. W. Whitham was born in Broome County, Kentucky, the son of John Whitham and Caroline (Rowe) Whitham. His father, who was a farmer, was born in England, in March, 1812.

Mr. Whitham, a resident of Nebraska for 58 years, was county commissioner of Johnson County for several years. From 1904 to 1907, he served as representative in the Nebraska legislature, elected on the Republican ticket.

He was married at Cook, Nebraska, to Zereda Mavity. Mrs. Whitham's ancestry is Irish and English.

The family is affiliated with the Mount Hope Methodist Episcopal Church. Residence: Cook.

Roy Herbert Whitham

Roy H. Whitham was born at Raymond, Nebraska, July 14, 1899, and has lived in this state all his life. His father, George P. Whitham, a railroad agent, merchant, and farmer, was born at Aledo, Illinois, October 30, 1860. His ancestors settled in Pennsylvania about 1760. His mother, Rosa Belle (Stirk) Whitham, was born at Seneca, Kansas, December 27, 1865; her ancestors had lived in Pennsylvania for more than two generations.

Dr. Whitham was graduated from the high school at Fairfield, Nebraska, 1916; received his A. B. degree at the University of Nebraska, in 1920; and was awarded the M. D. degree at Harvard University, 1924. He was elected to membership in Phi Beta Kappa; Sigma Xi; the Innocents Society; and Beta Theta Pi, and was admitted to the practice of medicine at Lincoln, on November 16, 1926. He served his internship at the Massachusetts General Hospital, 1924-26; practiced at North Haven, Maine, during the summer of 1926, and since then has been a surgeon at Lincoln.

He is the author of a few scientific articles published in medical journals, is a member of the American Medical Association; secretary of the Lancaster Medical Society; and is junior candidate for membership in the American College of Surgeons. He is a member of the Lincoln Chamber of Commerce and the Nebraskana Society. He was a member of the Student Army Training Corps at the University of Nebraska, 1918. He is a Republican.

On July 23, 1924, he was married to Eleanore Virginia Fogg at Lincoln. Mrs. Whitham, who is a teacher and director of dramatics, was born at Providence, Rhode Island, May 30, 1898; her direct ancestors came to America and settled in New Jersey before the Revolution. They have a daughter, Anne Elizabeth, born September 11, 1927. Residence: Lincoln.

Edward Thomas Whiting

Edward Thomas Whiting, school administrator, was born at Juniata, Nebraska, February 21, 1901, son of George Noel and Maude May (Lanphere) Whiting.

The father, a farmer of English parentage, was born in Madison, Wisconsin, March 16, 1873. His wife, Maude, was born in Centerville, Iowa, December 22, 1880.

Mr. Whiting attended public school at Giltner and Juniata, and was graduated from Juniata High School in 1919. He received his Bachelor of Arts degree from the University of Nebraska in 1927; and his Master of Arts degree from the University of Nebraska in 1931. He attended Hastings College 1922-23. He is a member of Phi Delta Kappa, and was valedictorian of his high school class.

For the period of one year, Mr. Whiting was a high school teacher, and following that was principal of the Cowles High School. For eight years, he was superintendent of schools at Upland and Doniphan, and at the present, he is superintendent of city schools at Gordon. He is the author of *Codification of Controversial Items of School Expenditure* (1931) in addition to miscellaneous articles.

His marriage to Ethel Lucille Waller was solemnized at Superior, December 25, 1922. Mrs. Whiting was born at Cowles, June 27, 1901, of English descent. She is the daughter of Harry M. and Ola (Bailey) Waller. She graduated from Cowles High School and attended the Peru State Normal. She is a secretary of the Federated Woman's Club. They have two children, Donald, born September 6, 1923; and Marilyn, born March 18, 1928.

Among Mr. Whiting's professional organizations are, the National Educational Association (life member), Nebraska State Teachers Association (life member, secretary 6th district). He is secretary at the present time of the Kiwanis Club, and served as vice-president in 1930. He is a member of the Methodist Church, the Red Cross, and the Odd Fellows. His hobby is reading.

Mr. Whiting is second lieutenant in the 866th Field Artillery Reserve. He served as county chairman of the Citizens Military Training Camp for a period of three years. Residence: Gordon. (Photograph on Page 1277).

Fredrick Harvey Whitmore

Born at Valley, Nebraska, November 21, 1887, Fredrick Harvey Whitmore is the son of Frank and Mary (Gardiner) Whitmore, pioneer Nebraskans. Frank Whitmore was born at Sunderland, Massachusetts, October 14, 1853. In 1878 he came to Valley with his brother, William G. Whitmore, where he engaged in farming and stockraising. He was one of the organizers and for many years vice president of the Valley State Bank, and in 1901, with his brother, W. G. Whitmore, established the Valley Stock Yards and Grain Company.

Mary Gardiner was a native of Kilwiming, Scotland. Born May 26, 1849, she came with her family to America at the age of four, residing for some time in New York State. Later she removed to Holyoke, Massachusetts, remaining there until her marriage to Frank Whitmore in 1879. She is a member of the Order of Eastern Star and a charter member of the Valley Presbyterian Church.

Fredrick H. Whitmore attended public and high school at Valley, and in 1906 was married to Lurah Harrier at Des Moines, Iowa. She was born at Valley, September 4, 1887, and is assistant editor of her husband's newspaper. There are three children, Helen, born November 16, 1907; Mary, born February 1, 1911, who married Walter Allen; and Florence, born August 29, 1917.

At the present time the editor and publisher of the *Valley Enterprise*, the oldest legal weekly in Douglas County, Mr. Whitmore has always been active in public affairs. From 1912 to 1916 he served as postmaster, for six years he has been secretary of the commercial club, and has held the office of mayor of Valley. At the present time he is a member of the town board.

During the World War Mr. Whitmore assisted with the draft and participated in other civilian work. His religious affiliation is with the Valley Presbyterian Church. He is a member of Ak-Sar-Ben, a Scottish Rite

Purdy—Gordon

EDWARD THOMAS WHITING

Mason and member of the Shrine and Eastern Star, and a member of the Izaak Walton League.

Mr. Whitmore's hobby is philately. He enjoys golf, fishing, and hunting and is a member of a gun club. Residence: Valley. (Photograph in Album).

Howard James Whitmore

Howard James Whitmore, son of Joseph Knisely and Elizabeth Catherine (Gilbert) Whitmore, was born at Mount Pleasant, Iowa, March 4, 1857. His father, Joseph Knisely Whitmore, was born near Carlisle, Pennsylvania, October 2, 1826 and died at Lincoln, April 6, 1914, at the age of eighty-seven years and six months. He was a teacher, merchant and farmer, whose father was born in Pennsylvania. Elizabeth Gilbert was born in Gettysburg, Pennsylvania, September 14, 1831, and died at Lincoln December 11, 1925, at the age of 94. Her father and grandfather were born in Pennsylvania; and her mother in Wales.

Mr. Whitmore was educated in public and private schools in Ohio, and received his law degree from the State University of Iowa. Always affiliated with the Democratic party, he was appointed police magistrate of Lincoln in 1887; elected police magistrate in Lincoln 1916 for the terms 1917-20; re-elected twice on the straight Democratic ticket he served six years in all. Appointed United States commissioner in 1913 he has been re-oppointed several times and is still holding that office. In 1894 he was appointed national bank examiner, resigning in February, 1899. He has worked as an expert accountant at various times, but has mainly engaged in the practice of law.

On January 24, 1894, he was united in marriage to Myrta M. Osborn at Lincoln. She was born in Allegheny County, New York, January 28, 1862, and died at Lincoln, December 5, 1911. She was of early stock from Vermont and New York.

Brought up in the English Lutheran religion, Mr. Whitmore, is now a member of First Plymouth Congregational Church. He is past master of Lincoln Lodge No. 19, Ancient Free and Accepted Masons, a member of the Scottish Rite, Shrine and Odd Fellows. He belongs to the state and county bar associations, the Chamber of Commerce and the Open Forum. In the past he was fond of hunting, and now enjoys fishing once in a while. Residence: Lincoln.

Mark Evans Whitnah

Mark Evans Whitnah, son of Charles and Mary Evalyn (Richmand) Whitnah, was born in Seward County, Nebraska, January 4, 1894. His father, born at Spring Valley, Green County, Ohio, July 7, 1862, died at Rochester, Minnesota, March 11, 1929. His ancestors came to this country from Holland about 1663.

His mother was born at Guilford, Windham County, Vermont, April 9, 1863, of English parentage. She is living and taught school before her marriage.

Mark Whitnah attended the beaver Crossing elementary school, and from 1907-11 he was a student of the Grand Island Academy, from which he received the degree of Bachelor of Agricultural Science, in 1915. Later he attended the Grand Island College one year. On June 3, 1916, he was united in marriage to Evalana Melba Adams, at Grand Island. Mrs. Whitnah was born at Grand Island, November 22, 1895, of English parentage. Their daughters: Maydene, born September 17, 1918, and Eloise, born March 21, 1924, attende the Beaver Crossing school.

Mr. Whitnah has specialized in farming, in which he has been very successful. He is affiliated with the Methodist Episcopal Church and holds membership in the Community Club at Beaver Crossing, as well as the Nebraskana Society. His hobby is music. Residence: Beaver Crossing.

David Day Whitney

On August 6, 1878, David Day Whitney was born at Brookfield, Vermont. His father, Cyrus Hall Whitney, was a native of Brookfield, having been born there August 12, 1852. He was active in the business affairs of the community and was of English, Scotch and Welsh ancestry. His death occurred at Brookfield, March 23, 1908. The mother of David Whitney was Luthera Samantha Sprague, who spent her lifetime in Brookfield, where she was born February 23, 1850, and died April 5, 1926. She was descended from English, French, Irish and Dutch pioneers.

After completing the courses offered by the Brookfield public schools in 1895, David D. Whitney entered Montpelier Seminary, from which he was graduated in 1900. Wesleyan University awarded him the degree of Bachelor of Arts in 1904. He received the degree of Master of Arts in 1906, and Doctor of Philosophy at Columbia University in 1909. Dr. Whitney is a member of Delta Tau Delta, and of Sigma Xi fraternity and is a starred member of American Men of Science.

His marriage to Kathryn Stillman Bunce occurred at New Brittain, Connecticut, on June 17, 1914. Mrs. Whitney was born at Grant, Plymouth County, Iowa, December 10, 1877. Her ancestry is English. They have one daughter Elizabeth, who was born March 25, 1915.

At the present time Dr. Whitney is professor of Zoology at the University of Nebraska. From 1908 to 1916 he was an instructor and associate professor at Wesleyan University. In 1916 he moved to this state and became connected with the University of Nebraska.

During his career Dr. Whitney has written more than 30 articles for scientific journals concerning heredity and sex in rotifers. He is a fellow of the American Association for the Advancement of Science, a member of St. Paul Methodist Episcopal Church, the American Association of University Professors, the American Society of Naturalists, the Nebraska Academy of Sciences, and the American Society of Zoologists. Residence: Lincoln.

George Quinton Whitney

One of the leading business men at Ainsworth, Nebraska, is George Quinton Whitney who has lived in this state all his life. He was born at Tilden, Nebraska, July 12, 1879, and for the past 13 years has been a retail druggist at Ainsworth. Prior thereto he was in business at Beatrice five years, Norfolk a year and a half and Neleigh, three years. His father, Daniel Wing Whitney, who was one of the first railroad engineers for the Union Pacific Company west of Omaha, was born at Avon, New York, April 25, 1834, and died at Tilden, October 26, 1900; his parents settled in New York, later moved to Burr Oak, Michigan, and were pioneers in Nebraska.

His mother, Mary Anne (Quinton) Whitney, was born at Buffalo, New York, November 1, 1840, and died at Tilden, October 17, 1919. Her father, George Quinton, was of Scotch descent, and her mother, Bridget O'Callahan, was Irish.

Mr. Whitney was graduated from the Tilden High School in 1895 and in 1904 was a student at the Omaha College of Pharmacy. He is a member of the Ainsworth Commercial Club, was formerly a member of the local school board, and is affiliated with the Ainsworth Congregational Church. He is a Mason, is a member of the Nebraskana Society, and holds membership in the Ainsworth Country Club. Mr. Whitney's favorite sport is golfing.

On January 19, 1905, he was married to Susan Maria Gillespie at O'Neill, Nebraska. Mrs. Whitney, who is the daughter of Bennet Scott and Eleanor A. (Van Fleet) Gillespie, was born at O'Neill, January 29, 1885. To them were born: Donald G., July 11, 1906, who is an engineer with the American Telephone & Telegraph

Company, and Gale Q., November 7, 1908, who is an architectural draftsman at Omaha. Residence: Ainsworth. (Photograph in Album).

Helen Whitney

Helen Whitney, who is clerk of the district court in Furnas County, Nebraska, is a lifelong resident of this state. She was born at Beaver City, Nebraska, March 20, 1891, the daughter of William Butler and Isabel (Prime) Whitney. Her father, who was a lawyer and bonded abstracter, was born at Calais, Maine, May 2, 1857, of English ancestry, and died at Beaver City, July 5, 1930.

Her mother, the daughter of George and Ann Eliza Anderson Prime and the granddaughter of Robert Anderson, was born at Storey City, Iowa, September 5, 1859. She was of English and Scotch extraction.

Miss Whitney was graduated from the Beaver City High School in 1909, and in 1913 received the A. B. degree at Simpson College, Indianola, Iowa, where she was a member of the college orchestra and Pi Beta Phi. She served as secretary of the senior class at Simpson College in 1913, and was a member of the cabinet of the Young Women's Christian Association.

She served as mathematics instructor from 1913 to 1917, was government clerk in the code section of the Military Intelligence Bureau, 1918-19 in Washington, D. C., and again taught high school mathematics during 1919-20. Since 1921 she has served as clerk of the district court of Furnas County and since 1927 has been a bonded abstracter at Beaver City.

Miss Whitney is chairman of the Furnas County Volunteer Service department of the Red Cross, is affiliated with the Methodist Church, and holds membership in the P. E. O. She is a Republican. Residence: Beaver City.

William Ira Whitney

William Ira Whitney was born at Folsomedale, New York, September 22, 1871, son of Alva Rice and Angeline (Thomas) Whitney.

Alva Rice Whitney was born at Folsomedale, February 17, 1841, and was a farmer, coming to Nebraska in February, 1884. He died at Craig, Nebraska, February 17, 1890. His wife, Angeline, was born at Varysburg, New York, March 26, 1833, and died at Bayard, Nebraska, November 17, 1920.

On December 22, 1897, Mr. Whitney was married to Minnie Maud Plummer at Craig. She was born at Marshalltown, Iowa, September 9, 1877. Mrs. Whitney was the daughter of Anthony A. and Ellen Ora Plummer. Mr. Plummer was born at Dixon, Illinois, March 25, 1849, and now lives at Bayard, Nebraska. Mrs. Plummer was born in Columbiana County, Ohio, August 28, 1854 and died at Randolph, Nebraska, December 18, 1909.

They have three children, Claude J., born October 10, 1900; James A., born May 24, 1908; and Ellen Ora, born August 27, 1912. Claude and James are farmers; James attended the state university the year of 1925-26.

Mr. Whitney is a farmer at Bayard, Nebraska. He has resided in Nebraska for the past 48 years, and has been prominent in agricultural projects. At the present time, he is serving as president of the Chimney Rock Irrigation District. He is a member of the Federated Church of Bayard, the Masons, the Eastern Star, and the Morrill County Farm Bureau. His hobby is reading. He is a Democrat. Residence: Bayard.

Bernard Whitwer

Bernard Whitwer, who was a resident of Nebraska for 62 years, was born at Bern, Switzerland, December 20, 1845. He received his education in the public schools of Pittsburgh, Pennsylvania, where he attended night school. Upon his arrival in this country he settled at Pittsburgh where he remained until 1869 when he homesteaded in Antelope County, Nebraska.

Mr. Whitwer was the first blacksmith in Antelope County where he served as a member of the county board for a number of years and was a civic-minded and progressive leader in his community all his life. He was affiliated with the Friedens Evangelical Church, held membership in the Independent Order of Odd Fellows, and just prior to his death, on December 12, 1931, was elected to membership in The Nebraskana Society.

On February 16, 1872, he was united in marriage with Wilhelmine Caroline Draube in Stanton County, Nebraska. Mrs. Whitwer, whose parents were pioneers in Nebraska, was born at Stateen, Germany, October 10, 1852.

The following children were born to this marriage: Alfred A., born March 14, 1875, who married Mary Yenglin; Laura Anna, born October 17, 1876, who married John Fankhauser; Amel Herman, October 12, 1878, who married Maude Pierce; Will, September 29, 1880, who married Beulah Pierce; Minnie Flora, September 14, 1884, who married John Lamly, Sr.; and Clara Bertha, July 6, 1886, who married Charles F. Haudenshield. (Photograph in Album).

Herbert L. Wichman

Herbert L. Wichman was born at Pierce, Nebraska, September 6, 1889, the son of William and Bertha (Pasewalk) Wichman. His father, who was a blacksmith and wagon maker, was born in Wisconsin, September 21, 1857, and died at Pierce, January 9, 1891. His mother was born in Wisconsin, July 18, 1861, and died at Norfolk, Nebraska, October 28, 1919; her ancestry was German.

Mr. Wichman was appointed postoffice clerk in 1910 at Norfolk, was made assistant postmaster in 1920, and since 1924 has been postmaster. He is a Republican. He holds membership in the Red Cross, Chamber of Commerce, the Nebraskana Society, and the Young Men's Christian Association. He is affiliated with Mount Olive English Lutheran Church and is a member of the Meridian Heights Golf Club. His favorite sport is golfing and his hobby is mechanics.

His marriage to Irene Philena Stoltenberg occurred at Norfolk, Nebraska, September 27, 1910, the daughter of Peter and Philena (Newal) Stoltenberg. Mrs. Wichman, whose ancestry is German and French, was born at Ewing, Nebraska, August 4, 1890. They have one son, James H., born September 5, 1927. Residence: Norfolk.

Wilbur Atley Wickersham

Wilbur Atley Wickersham, farmer, was born at Marietta, Iowa, June 6, 1878, son of Tryon and Elizabeth (Groner) Wickersham. The father was born in Chester County, Pennsylvania, August 11, 1828, and enlisted in Company K, 32nd Iowa Infantry August 22, 1862. He was discharged August 24, 1865. He later came to Iowa and died at Marshalltown, December 23, 1903. His wife, Elizabeth, was born in Columbiana County, Ohio, in 1835, and died at Albion, Iowa, November 22, 1889. Her ancestors are Pennsylvania Dutch.

Mr. Wickersham graduated from public school in 1896 and has since engaged in farming. At the present time he is president of the Farmers Co-operative Elevator Company of Filley. He is a Democrat.

On May 28, 1903, he was married to Katheryn S. Bremer at Dresden, Kansas. Mrs. Wickersham was born at York, Nebraska, July 13, 1883, of German-Scotch ancestry. They have four children, Wilbur, born May 22, 1904; Maurine, born March 17, 1910; Earl, born February 24, 1914; and Fred, born December 10, 1918. The oldest boy is farming, Maurine is teaching in public school, while the two younger boys are still in school. Both of the older children have attended college.

Mr. Wickersham is a member of the Methodist Episcopal Church and the Masons. From 1908 until 1931 he was a member of the school board, and from 1929 until 1931 was president of the Parent Teachers Association. His hobby is reading. Residence: Filley.

Oscar Albright Wickert

A leading merchant in Rising City, Oscar Albright Wickert, was born at Mertztown, Berks County, Pennsylvania, February 23, 1859. He is the son of Charles and Lucretia (Albright) Wickert, the former born in Lehigh County, Pennsylvania. He died at Geryville, Bucks County, Pennsylvania. He had engaged in farming in Pennsylvania for many years, and was of Pennsylvania Dutch ancesry. His mother was born at Trexlertown, Lehigh County, Pennsylvania, and died at Spinnerstown, Pennsylvania. Her ancestors were German.

Oscar Albright Wickert attended public school and the Perkiomen Seminary. On November 28, 1895, at Monroe, Wisconsin, he was united in marriage with Medea May Musser, who was born at Orangeville, Illinois, April 18, 1870, of Pennsylvania Dutch parentage. She is a member of the Rebekah Lodge and a member of the Helen Gould Club, and is active in church work.

He is in the general merchandising business as a member of the firm, Wickert and Uhe, at Rising City, Nebraska. A Democrat, he has lived in Nebraska since 1888, and has been in business since that time. Mr. Wickert is affiliated with the Evangelical Lutheran Church, and is a member of the Nebraskana Society. He has served on the town board and the school board for many years. Residence: Rising City.

Edward Wiedel

Edward Wiedel, farmer, was born at Sauk City, Wisconsin, October 13, 1867, son of Stephan and Cathrina (Stutz) Wiedel. The father was born in Germany, and came to Nebraska as an early pioneer farmer. He died at Hebron, Febraury 26, 1919. His wife, who was born in Germany also, died in Thayer County, June 15, 1927.

Mr. Wiedel attended country school, and has since engaged in farming. He is a Democrat, and at the present time, is a director of the Stoddard bank and of the country school board.

On June 15, 1899, he was married to Rose Geopfrich at Hebron. Mrs. Wiedel was born at Newark, New Jersey, February 25, 1877, and was a country school teacher in her youth. She has resided in Nebraska for 53 years. They have eight children: Bernard, born May 1, 1900; Alvin, born September 6, 1901; Carl, born May 1, 1904; Louis, born April 29, 1906; Frank, born May 23, 1908; William, born March 7, 1911; Gertrude, born March 28, 1914; and Corneilus, born October 8, 1916.

Mr. Wiedel is a member of Sacred Heart Catholic Church, and Mrs. Wiedel is a member of the Hebron Country Club. Residence: Hebron.

Joseph Wiedel, Sr.

Joseph Wiedel, son of Stephen and Katherine (Stutz) Wiedel, was born at Honey Creek, Wisconsin, May 23, 1874, and came to Nebraska with his parents, who were pioneer settlers. Stephen Wiedel was a native of Germany, who came to America as a young man, and returned to Germany where he died. His wife was born in Germany, and is still living.

Mr. Wiedel attended public school and soon afterward engaged in farming. His interests have always been confined to agricultural pursuits, and to his family of which he is justly proud. He was united in marriage to Katherine Mary Willy at Hebron, on November 19, 1896, and to them were born eleven children, ten of whom

are living.

John, born December 12, 1897, married Gertrude Schmidt; Leon, born January 23, 1899, married Grace Dewald, and died in September, 1927; Joseph, Jr., born March 4, 1900, married Agnes Sponsel; Paul, born October 2, 1902, married Florence Shipman; Walter, born November 15, 1904, married Nellie Cooperrider; Marie, born July 14, 1906, is a nun; Albert, born September 3, 1907; Herman, born June 4, 1910; Benjamin, born August 3, 1912; Leona, born March 23, 1914; and Anna, born December 6, 1915.

Mr. Wiedel is a Democrat. He is a member of Sacred Heart Catholic Church and the Knights of Columbus, and is a life member of the Nebraskana Society. Residence: Hebron.

Fred Conrad Wiegman

The Reverend Fred Conrad Wiegman has been a resident of Nebraska since 1913. He was born at Wellsburg, Iowa, February 15, 1899, son of Frederick Conrad and Bertha (Hammerschmidt) Wiegman.

The father was born in Westphalia, Germany, October 13, 1857, and died at Hastings, September 14, 1917. He was a clergyman who came to America in 1878, and was superintendent of Synodical Missions. His wife, Bertha, was born at Monticello, Illinois, February 3, 1869. She is living at Hastings.

Mr. Wiegman attended the public schools of Newkirk, Oklahoma, and Howells, Nebraska, until 1912; was graduated from Hastings High School in 1916; received his Bachelor of Arts degree from Midland College at Fremont, Nebraska, in 1924; and his Bachelor of Divinity degree from Western Seminary in 1927. He was active in debating and dramatics, was a member of the literary society, and was college president of his senior class in 1924. On June 8, 1927, Mr. Wiegman was ordained to the Lutheran ministry. He is the author of *John the Baptist* (February, 1928).

Mr. Wiegman was married to Mary Clarinda Rangeler at Fremont, Nebraska, June 8, 1927. Mrs. Wiegman was born at Leipsic, Ohio, April 14, 1902, of German and Scotch-Irish ancestry. They have one daughter, Herma Jean, born October 12, 1929.

In 1916 Mr. Wiegman became a clerk for Wolbach and Brach at Hastings, and in 1917 was a driver for the American Railway Express Company. He was shipping clerk for the Fisk Rubber Company at Hastings in 1917, and billing clerk for the same company at Memphis, Tennessee, 1918-1919. During the same year he was manager of the Kirkendall Shoe Company at Omaha. At the present time he is pastor of the First Lutheran Church of North Platte.

During the World War Mr. Wiegman was a member of the home guard. He is a member of the First Lutheran Church of North Platte, secretary of the English Nebraska Synod and since 1927 has been a member of the Red Cross. He has also been a member of the Boy Scouts during this time and of the Rotary Club. He is a member of the Nebraskana Society, the Parent Teachers Association, and the Young Men's Christian Association. His hobby is mechanics. He is a Democrat. Residence: North Platte. (Photograph in Album).

John Henry Wiese

John Henry Wiese, Sr., father of the subject of this sketch, was born at Kiel, Germany, May 6, 1843, and came to America in April, 1860, settling in Nebraska territory. During the early days of the state he was a freighter, and later a surveyor on the Union Pacific Railroad from Omaha to the west. He married Anna Catherine Timmerman, who was born in Hamburg, Germany, December 31, 1848. He died near Omaha, October 1, 1890. His wife lived until February 8, 1914, and died at Omaha.

John H. Wiese was educated in the public schools of Douglas County. He married Mary Ernst, born July 8,

1878, in Douglas County, March 6, 1900. There are three children, Henry, born March 5, 1901; Clarence, born March 9, 1902; and Louisa, born September 18, 1903.

Mr. Wiese is a Democrat, and served as county commissioner of Sarpy County 1926-30, and was re-elected in 1930 for a term of four years. He has extensive farming interests in the county, and is otherwise active. He is a director of the First Lutheran Hospital at Omaha, and a member of the First Lutheran Church of Papillion. He is a member of The Nebraskana Society, of the Springfield Parent-Teachers Association, and in 1928 was elected a member of the board of education of Springfield. Residence: Papillion.

Edwin Charles Wiggenhorn

Edwin Charles Wiggenhorn, distinguished financier and civic leader at Ashland, Saunders County, Nebraska, has lived there since 1870. He was born at Hustisford, Wisconsin, October 18, 1865, the son of Ernest Alexander and Augusta (Niemeyer) Wiggenhorn. His father, who was born in Westphalen, Germany, March 23, 1830, and died at Ashland, September 23, 1904, came to Nebraska in 1867, settling first at Plattsmouth and later moving to Ashland. His mother, who was born in Hanover, Germany, May 4, 1837, and died at Ashland, August 3, 1881, came to Nebraska with her husband in pioneer days.

Mr. Wiggenhorn was graduated from the Ashland High School in 1881, was graduated from Northwestern University at Watertown, Wisconsin, 1884, and in 1887 received the Bachelor of Literature degree at the University of Nebraska. He was awarded the LL. B. degree at Georgetown University Law School, Washington, D. C., 1889, and the A. M. degree in 1890. From 1890 to 1904 he was in government service as field representative and special examiner for the Bureau of Pensions. He returned to Ashland in 1904 and became cashier of the Farmers and Merchants Bank, an institution founded by his father. He subsequently became vice president of the bank and held that position until his retirement from active business in 1928.

He was president of the Fremont Joint Stock Land Bank at one time, was a director in the Lincoln Joint Stock Bank, and was a director in the Midwest Life Insurance Company of Lincoln. A Democrat, he served as mayor of Ashland for four terms and during his administration Ashland streets were paved. He was largely instrumental in securing a Carnegie Library for the city of Ashland. Residence: Ashland.

Theron Leslie Wiggins

Born at Cole, Iowa, June 18, 1883, Theron Leslie Wiggins is the son of Charles Fremont and Emma Jane (Stark) Wiggins. They were married at Sycamore, Illinois, May 1, 1879. The father, who was a farmer and stockraiser, was born at Tunkhannock, Pennsylvania, March 12, 1857, and came to Gothenburg about 1902. He died at Grand Island, February 8, 1928. His wife, Emma Jane, was born in Sycamore, Illinois, November 15, 1858.

Mr. Wiggins attended high school in Iowa until 1899, and coming to Gothenburg in 1900 has been connected with the livestock business there ever since. He is a member of the Gothenburg Country Club and has been a director of the school board since 1913. He is a Mason and member of the Scottish Rite and Shrine bodies His hobby is reading.

His marriage to Grace Maude Homer was solemnized at Gothenburg, February 24, 1910. She was born at Mason City, February 10, 1882. Their children are, Harlan, born July 13, 1911; Raymond, born December 7, 1912; Ivan, born October 18, 1914; Dorothy, born July 11, 1917; Frances, born May 3, 1922; and Ruth, born September 3, 1925. Residence: Gothenburg.

Harrison Alonzo Wigton

Harrison A. Wigton has lived in Nebraska all his life and has been engaged in the practice of medicine in Omaha for over 25 years. He was born at Hastings, Nebraska, December 20, 1878, the son of Alonzo L. and Mary (Hunt) Wigton. His father, who was born in Delaware County, Ohio, January 19, 1841, was a newspaper and insurance man. He was a Civil War veteran and a pioneer in Ohio. His Scotch and English ancestors came to America before the Revolution. Alonzo Wigton died December 20, 1919, at Omaha. His mother was born in Delaware County, October 29, 1846, of English, Welch and Holland Dutch descent, and is a direct descendant of Captain Miles Standish.

Dr. Wigton was graduated from the Omaha High School in 1897. In 1900 he was granted the B. E. degree at Hastings College; in 1915, he studied in the New York Post-Graduate Medical School; and in 1905 he was awarded his M. D. degree at the University of Nebraska Medical College. In 1929, Dr. Wigton was made a fellow of the American College of Physicians.

He served as assistant superintendent at the Nebraska Sstate Hospital for the Insane at Lincoln, 1906-09, is now a specialist in neuropsychiatry and is medical director of the Omaha Life Insurance Company. He is the author of articles on Parkinsonian Syndomes and Epilepsy.

His marriage to Jessie May Mosher was solemnized at Lincoln, Lancaster County, Nebraska, December 19, 1907. Mrs. Wigton was born at Wessington, South Dakota, August 6, 1885. They have three children: Margaret Ruth, born September 17, 1909; Robert Spencer, born November 1, 1911; and Mary Elizabeth, born June 5, 1917.

In 1918, Dr. Wigton was a member of the Volunteer Medical Service Corps. He holds membership in the following professional organizations: Omaha-Douglas County Medical Society, American Medical Association, American College of Physicians, Missouri Valley Neuro-psychiatric Society, of which he is secretary. He is assistant professor of neuro-psychiatry at the University of Nebraska Medical School; is neuro-psychiatrist at Immanuel Hospital, Evangelical Covenant Hospital and Methodist Hospital, and is consultant at Bethphage Mission at Axtell, Nebraska.

Dr. Wigton is a member of the State Historical Society and The Nebraskana Society. He is a member of the Omaha Kiwanis Club; and is a member of the Masons, Scottish Rite and Shrine. He is a Republican. Residence: Omaha.

Elmer Dee Wiley

Elmer Dee Wiley, railroad station agent, was born at Storm Lake, Iowa, March 18, 1896, son of Isaac and Mary Elizabeth (Arndfelt) Wiley. His father, who was born at Deerfield, Indiana, June 4, 1861, is a retired farmer, descended from one of four brothers, John, James, Andrew, and Alexander Wiley, who came from County Down, Ireland, and settled in Rockbridge County, Virginia, during the Revolutionary War. They were farmers, inventors and gunsmiths. James Wiley came west with Daniel Boone and settled at Boonesboro, Kentucky; Andrew was a gunsmith; Alexander invented a ditching machine; and John Wiley, great grandfather of Elmer, was a farmer. One of Elmer Wiley's great uncles served in the War of 1812, and an uncle served in the Civil War. Mary Elizabeth Arndfelt was born in Elizabethtown, Ohio, December 10, 1860, and died at Endicott, Nebraska, February 21, 1927. She was of Irish and Pennsylvania Dutch descent.

Educated in the public schools of Ida Grove, Iowa, and Endicott, Nebraska, Elmer Dee Wiley has been a resident of Nebraska since December 28, 1911. During 1916-17 he was clerk with the Great Northern Railway, and during 1919-20 was a hostler helper with the Union Pacific System. Since 1920 he has been successively station helper, clerk, operator and station agent with the Chicago, Burlington & Quincy Railroad.

On October 10, 1923, he was married to Elizabeth Elma Gunderman at Denver, Colorado. Mrs. Wiley was born in Gotha, Germany, December 28, 1899. Her uncle, Ernest Gunderman, is a professor at the University of Gotha. They have one daughter, Bonnie Lou, born November 28, 1924.

Mr. Wiley served in the United States Army from September 19, 1917, to July 8, 1919, and was overseas from February 16, 1918 to June 30, 1919. During this time he was in General Pershing's Headquarters, at Chaumont, France, seventeen months. He was successively private, corporal and sergeant, and was recommended for promotion to battalion sergeant major, with Company G, Headquarters Battalion, General Headquarters, American Expeditionary Forces. He is a member of the American Legion (adjutant 1930-31). He is councilman of the Boy Scouts, and during 1930-31 served as secretary of the Community Club.

Mr. Wiley is a member of the Masons and the Order of Eastern Star, and a life member of the Nebraskana Society. He enjoys golf and football, and his hobbies are reading and woodcraft. He is an independent Republican. Residence: Bennet.

Ray Saunders Wilfley

Ray S. Wilfley, banker, was born in Maryville, Missouri, November 21, 1888. Upon completing his public school work he attended high school at Maryville, Missouri. George Lewis Wilfley, father of Ray, was born at Sedalia, Missouri, August 1, 1858, and has now retired from business. His mother, Jennie R. (Saunders) Wilfley, was born at Maryville, Missouri, in 1861. She is interested in club and community work and is a member of the 20th Century Club.

On November 2, 1909, Ray Wilfley was united in marriage to Naomi Belle Armstrong. She was born in Maryville, Missouri, December 21, 1888; is active in club work and is a member of the Daughters of the American Revolution. Their one daughter, Naomi, born December 28, 1913, is a student at the Fairbury High School.

Mr. Wilfley has been a resident of the state of Nebraska for sixteen years, during which time he was a banker at Steele City, thirteen years, and for the past three years he has been cashier of the First National Bank of Fairbury. He is also director of the Jefferson County Bank of Daykin, Nebraska. He is a Protestant and a member of the First Presbyterian Church of Fairbury.

He is chairman of the local board of Newton precinct in Jefferson County, a member of the Jefferson County Council of Defense, the Chamber of Commerce, Kiwanis Club, Masons and the Fairbury Country Club. Residence: Fairbury.

Charles M. Wilhelm

Charles M. Wilhelm, prominent executive of Omaha, has lived in Nebraska for nearly 40 years, and has taken an active interest in the progress of Omaha. He was born at Springwater, New York, November 22, 1858, the son of Benjamin F. and Samantha A. (Towne) Wilhelm. His father, who was owner and operator of a lumber and flour mill, was born at Sparta, New York, April 5, 1823, and died at Springwater, September 14, 1869; his grandfather was killed at the storming of Fort Erie in the War of 1812. His mother was born at Batavia, New York, June 30, 1833, and died at Indianapolis, January 7, 1901. She received her education at Batavia, and later taught school in Livingston County. She was directly descended from William Towne who was born in England, in 1600, and was believed to be the son of Richard Towne of Braceby, who came from England to Salem, Essex County, Massachusetts, in 1620.

Mr. Wilhelm attended district school at Springwater, was a student at the Rockford High School in Illinois, and later studied at Genesee Wesleyan College at Lima, New York. In 1919, he was awarded the degree of LL. D. by Bellevue College, in recognition of his service of fifteen years as president of the board of trustees of that institution.

He is now vice president and treasurer of the Orchard & Wilhelm Company, of Omaha. He is a director in the Conservative Savings and Loan Association, and the Metropolitan Utilities District. He is a member of the Sons of the American Revolution, the Omaha Rotary Club, and the Nebraska State Historical Society. He served as president of the Omaha Community Chest, 1927-28; was president of the Omaha Chamber of Commerce, 1907; and was for many years president of the board of trustees of Bellevue College.

He was a member of the board of governors of Ak-Sar-Ben, and was 36th King of Ak-Sar-Ben in 1930. He holds membership in George D. Lininger Chapter of the Ancient and Accepted Scottish Rite of Freemasonry. He is a member of the Nebraskana Society, and is affiliated with the following social clubs: Omaha Athletic Club; Omaha Club; Omaha Country Club; and the University Club. He is a member of the First Presbyterian Church of Omaha. He is a Republican.

On December 7, 1882, Mr. Wilhelm was united in marrage with Mary Eugenie Stocking at Lawton, Van Buren County, Michigan. Mrs. Wilhelm was born at Roscoe, Winnebago County, Illinois, March 26, 1862. Three children were born to them: Frank E., born September 25, 1883, who married Eugenia Cudahy, and who is vice president of the Cudahy Packing Company; Esther Eugenie, born August 20, 1897, who married Samuel L. Cooper; and Charles Hyde, born July 15, 1899, who died in infancy. Residence: Omaha.

Charles Martel Wilhelmj

Charles Martel Wilhelmj, noted educator, was born at East St. Louis, Illinois, December 17, 1896. He is the son of Charles Fredrich and Emma Elizabeth (Martel) Wilhelmj. Charles Fredrich Wilhelmj was born at Mayestown, Illinois, January 1, 1858, and is a physician and chief of staff of St. Mary's Hospital. He is of the Wilhelmj family of noted lawyers and statesmen, and is a cousin of August Wilhelmj, the German violinist. Emma Martel was born at East St. Louis, in 1875.

Dr. Wilhelmj was graduated from the East St. Louis High School in 1915, and received a Bachelor of Science degree, a Master of Science in Medicine and a Doctor of Medicine degree from St. Louis University. He has been a fellow in medicine and physiology at the Mayo Foundation, and the University of Minnesota. His fraternities include Sigma Xi, Chi Zeta Chi, and Phi Rho Sigma.

On March 8, 1916, he was married to Irene Katherine Mulconnery at East St. Louis. Mrs. Wilhelmj was born at Belleville, Illinois, April 8, 1897. They have one son, Charles, born November 29, 1928.

Dr. Wilhelmj was resident in medicine at the Jewish Hospital at St. Louis, from 1923-24, and instructor in bacteriology at the St. Louis University School of Medicine, 1924-25. He was a member of the permanent faculty of the Mayo Clinic from 1927-30, and instructor in physiology at the University of Minnesota, from 1928-39. From 1927-39 he was also associate in the division of experimental surgery and pathology of the Mayo Foundation. Dr. Wilhelmj has to his credit approximately thirty articles on the various phases of medicine, physiology and metabolism, published in American and foreign journals since 1920.

His professional organizations include the American Medical Association in which he holds a fellowship, the Minnesota State Medical Society, the Association of Residents and Ex-residents of the Mayo Clinic, and the American Inter-professional institute. He is a former member and secretary of the Salerno Club of the Mayo Foundation, and a member of the Nebraskana Society.

Dr. Wilhelmj's club is the University Club of Rochester, Minnesota. He is an Episcopalian. His favorite sports are hiking, camping and fishing. His hobbies are medical and general history and biography. Residence: Omaha. (Photograph in Album).

Fred Wilkins

Fred Wilkins, farmer and landowner, was born in Hanover, Germany and has been a resident of Nebraska since 1872. He was educated in the public schools of Germany, and since coming to America has continuously engaged in farming. On January 1, 1883, he was united in marriage to Elizabeth Eisenberg at Dakota City. Mrs. Wilkins was a native of Germany, and died at Homer, Nebraska, April 26, 1912. There were six children born to this marriage, four of whom are living.

Louis married Alma Eriksen; Minnie married Charles McGraw; Hattie, who married Will Kuhl is deceased, as is Emma; Grace married E. N. Maurice and Clara married Peter Maurice.

Mr. Wilkins has always voted the Republican ticket and is active in local politics. During the World War he participated in loan drives and other civilian war activities. He is a member of St. Paul's Lutheran Church, the Red Cross and the Independent Order of Foresters. In 1872 he operated a steamboat between Fort Benton and Sioux City on the Missouri, and in 1875 on the Yellowstone. Residence: Homer.

Harry Robert Wilkinson

Harry Robert Wilkinson, banker, was born at Weeping Water, Nebraska, September 9, 1889, and for a number of years has been outstanding in his community.

Robert Scott Wilkinson, the father, was born in Newcastle-On-Tyne, England, in 1850, and came to America with his father, Edward Wilkinson, in 1859. He was a merchant until his death at Weeping Water, November 5, 1906. His wife, Nettie Harriet Pearl, was born in Shepardsville, Michigan, in 1861, daughter of O. M. Pearl.

Educated at Weeping Water, Harry Robert Wilkinson was graduated from high school in 1906, and received his Bachelor of Arts degree from Doane College in 1912. He was a member of the debating team 2 years, the track team three years, and the football team four years while in college.

From 1912-19 Mr. Wilkinson was high school athletic coach at Wisner, Norfolk, and Curtis, Nebraska, and since June 1, 1919, has been associated with the Curtis State Bank of which he is now vice president. He is also secretary-treasurer of the Curtis Co-operative Creamery.

On August 15, 1916, he was married to Bertha Evalyn Penner at Lincoln, Nebraska. Mrs. Wilkinson is the daughter of Frank and Clara (Hay) Penner. Her father was born in Germany and her mother in America. She is a member of the Eastern Star, and is past worthy matron of the Curtis Chapter, is a member of the P. E. O., and is active in the affairs of the Congregational Church, of which she is a member. There are two children, Robert Scott, born July 2, 1917; and Donald Penner, born October 30, 1923.

Mr. Wilkinson is chairman of the Frontier County Chapter of the American Red Cross, a director of the Chamber of Commerce, vice president of the Rotary Club, and past master of Curtis Lodge No. 168, Ancient Free and Accepted Masons. In 1918 he served as a member of the Frontier County Liberty loan committee. Recently Mr. Wilkinson was elected to life membership in the Nebraskana Society. He enjoys golf, trap shooting, hunting and fishing, the last two being his special hobbies. Residence: Curtis.

Rees Wilkinson

Rees Wilkinson, son of Richard and Sarah (Rees) Wilkinson, was born in Hopkins, Nebraska, October 10, 1884. Richard Wilkinson was born in Dunfanaghy, County Donegal, Ireland, August 5, 1856, and is a retired capitalist (see Nebraskana). His mother was born in Huntington, England, August 6, 1882.

Upon his graduation from Lincoln High School in 1905 he entered the University of Nebraska and studied at the college of law in 1911. On November 25, 1919, he was married to Margaret Freeman. They have two children, Margaret 10 and Rees, Jr., 7.

After his graduation Mr. Wilkinson was associated with the Southern Pacific Railroad in the capacity of private secretary until he entered law school. In 1913 he purchased control of the Automobile Mutual Insurance Company of Omaha which at that time had over ten thousand dollars worth of debts. Mr. Wilkinson took over the company and completely reorganized it, moved it to Lincoln where the name was changed to the Indemnity Company of America, and in less than eighteen months he had over 600 producing agents and was doing a business of a quarter of a million in premiums yearly. This company is still in operation.

In 1916 he organized the National Automobile Insurance Company which has been in active operation since its incorporation and which he is now transforming into a life insurance company to operate under the name of the National Old Line Life Insurance Company. In 1917 in association with Dr. Atkinson, he developed the Frontier Accident Insurance Company, which interests were later sold to Dr. Atkinson. Mr. Wilkinson has holdings in many other Nebraska insurance companies, as well as real estate holdings in the city. He has always taken an active interest in the civic affairs of Lincoln, and gave to the city the pivot ground necessary to make possible the opening of Memorial Drive from South Street to Sheridan Boulevard. Mr. Wilkinson is considered one of the most oustanding and interesting men in the insurance business in the central west, and it is predicted that he and his company will meet with a complete success.

Mr. Wilkinson is a member of the Lincoln University Club, the Lincoln Country Club, the Lincoln Automobile Club, the Omaha Athletic Club, the Lincoln Chamber of Commerce, the Greater Nebraska Club, the Lincoln Advertising Club, and the Alumni Association of the University of Nebraska. Residence: Lincoln. (Photograph on Page 1284).

Richard Wilkinson

Richard Wilkinson, retired capitalist, was born in Dunfanaghy, County Donegal, Ireland, August 5, 1856. The son of Robert and Elizabeth (McElhiney) Wilkinson, his ancestry is traced to Richard Wilkinson, his great grandfather, for whom he was named. Robert Wilkinson, the father of the subject of this sketch, was born in Dunfanaghy, November 8, 1826. A country gentleman, he owned and represented the fourth generation of the Wilkinson family to inherit Rinclivin and surrounding lands in Ireland. The grandfather of Richard Wilkinson was also named Robert and married Catherine Irvine.

Elizabeth McElhiney, mother of Richard, was born at Carrigart, in County Donegal, on October 24, 1928. She was of Scotch ancestry originally, her father, Charles McElhiney, having been a professor and later a successful business man and property owner. She had many philanthropic interests, gave much to charity, and endowed a church at Blencoe, Iowa. Mrs. Wilkinson died at Tryon, Nebraska, 1909. Her husband died at Blencoe, Iowa, the home of the family after its migration to America.

Educated in the public schools of Dunfanaghy and under private tutelage, Mr. Wilkinson did not attend college, but traveled extensively. He came to America

REES WILKINSON

during the centennial exposition, and while traveling, met Sarah Rees, who later became his wife. She was also on a trip from the old world at the time. Sarah Rees Wilkinson was born at Huntington, Herefordshire, England, August 6, 1862, and is the granddaughter of the Reverend Thomas Rees, who was pastor for 56 years at Huntington Chapel, Herefordshire. He was the first college man to go to that part of the country and was famous in his day as an author and as a graduate of Carmathen College in Wales. Many books have been written about him and one side of the church at Huntington bears a marble memorial to his name.

As was customary in her part of the country Sarah Rees attended finishing school instead of college, and when she came to Lincoln satisfied one of her ambitions by attending the University of Nebraska where she was made a member of Kappa Delta. She is a woman of many avocations and hobbies, who takes an active interest in social and community affairs. Of her marriage to Richard Wilkinson, and April 26, 1882, there were born four children, three of whom are living.

Florence Maude Wilkinson, born May 17, 1883, died at the age of four and one-half years. Richard Rees, born October 10, 1884, married Margaret Freeman (See *Nebraskana*). David Eugene, born January 19, 1901, married Laveta Fritzlen, daughter of Clifford Fritzlen. Rees and David are insurance officials in various companies controlled by the Wilkinson interests. Gladys Bernice is a graduate of the University of Nebraska and has post-graduate work at Smith College, where she specialized in English, and Indiana University, where she studied music. Afterward she attended Les Hirondelles, at Geneva, Switzerland. At the University of Nebraska she was a member of the University Players, the Dramatic Club, Gamma Phi Beta, and Delta Omicron. Of her marriage to Paul William Lawrence there is one son, Paul William II, born November 2, 1922, at Des Moines, Iowa. He is the first-born grandson of Richard Wilkinson.

Mr. Wilkinson has been a resident of Nebraska for forty-nine years. Altho now retired from active business he acts in an advisory capacity in his many enterprises. For 13 years he was president of the Wilkinson Lumber Company, at Eagle, Nebraska, where he served as mayor for many years. During 1901-02 he was a member of the house of representatives from Cass County, elected on the Republican ticket. Among the various corporations with which he has been connected are the following: Ewart-Wilkinson Grain and Elevator Company, Federal Insurance Company, Nebraska Material Company, Auto Mutual Insurance Company, Lincoln Building and Supply Company, Merritt-Wilkinson Cement Company and National Auto Insurance Company. Mr. Wilkinson was president of the above companies and at the present time is president of the Nebraska Old Line Life Insurance Company. In addition he is the owner of an apartment house at 15th and E Streets and the Wilkinson Building at 16th and O Streets in Lincoln, besides land and farms in Colorado, Kansas, Nebraska, Alberta, and elsewhere.

Upon the death of his mother Mr. Wilkinson inherited the Wilkinson estate in Ireland, including the ancestral home. This particular property was part of the dowry settlement at the time of the marriage of his grandparents Richard Irvine and Catherine Weir.

An extensive traveler, Mr. Wilkinson has devoted much time to writing his experiences abroad. He is interested in reading and genealogy, but perhaps his favorite avocation was the breeding of horses, many of which have been prize winners. Mr. Wilkinson has always been an outstanding resident of Lincoln and has taken an active and interested part in civic and community projects. During the World War he contributed to the Red Cross, of which he is still a member, and purchased heavily of Liberty Bonds. He was a member of the Second Presbyterian Church of Lincoln, the Chamber of Commerce,

the Lincoln Country Club, the Parent-Teachers Association and the Young Men's Christian Association. For many years he was chairman of the Eagle school board and in recognition of his achievements he has been awarded a life membership in the Nebraskana Society. Residence: 230 South 27th Street, Lincoln.

Leroy D. Willey

Leroy D. Willey, county extension agent, was born at Lancaster, Wisconsin, April 8, 1887, son of Thomas Henry and Sophia Butterworth(Pendleton) Willey.

The father was born at Lands End, Cornwall, England, and died at Glidden, Iowa, February 23, 1893. He was a Cornishman, a coal and livestock dealer and a farmer. His wife, Sophia, was born at Oldham, England, March 26, 1847, and died at Wisdom, Montana, October 3, 1915. She was a practical nurse.

Upon the completion of his elementary education at School District No. 13 in Beaverhead County, Montana, in 1903, Mr. Willey attended the Beaverhead County High School, graduating in 1909. In 1913 he received the Bachelor of Science degree from Montana State College at Bozeman. During his senior year, 1912-13, he was instructor in wrestling. He was also active in dramatics.

From 1913 until 1920 Mr. Willey was employed by the United States Department of Agriculture from 1913 to 1916 he was in charge of dry land experiment at Archer, Wyoming, on an experiment station, from 1916 to 1920 he was superintendent of the Sheridan Field Station at Sheridan, Wyoming, and from 1920 until 1922 was on a ranch in Montana. He became county extension agent the last mentioned year, continuing until the present time. During the winter of 1922 he was assistant chief clerk of the Wyoming State Senate.

His marriage to Annette May Welsh was solemnized at Cheyenne, Wyoming, on July 30, 1915. Mrs. Willey was born at Cheyenne, Wyoming, August 26, 1895. Her mother was the second white girl born in that city. They have five children, Leroy, Jr., born April 19, 1917; Duane, born June 25, 1919; Melvin, born May 22, 1921; Charles, born April 15, 1923, and Kenneth, born June 8, 1925.

Mr. Willey is a member of Light Memorial Presbyterian Church, the Nebraska County Agents Association, the Red Cross, the Masons, and the Parent Teachers Association. For some time he was a member of the American Society of Agronomy. His hobby is reading. Residence: Sidney.

Donald Landon Willhoite

Donald Landon Willhoite, manager of the Scoular-Bishop Grain Company at Superior, was born at Pierson, Iowa, July 24, 1893. His father, Safe Chuse Willhoite, was a native of Bloomington, Illinois, born August 7, 1863. He was depot agent until his death at Pierson, on February 25, 1926. His mother, Alice Ermina Landon, was born March 4, 1867.

Educated in the public schools of Pierson, Iowa, Donald Landon Willhoite was graduated from the latter in 1910, and thereafter attended Moringside College at Sioux City. He is a member of the Othonian Society.

Since reaching maturity Mr. Willhoite has been associated with a number of railroads and grain firms in various capacities, and at present is manager of the Scoular-Bishop Grain Company. He has resided in Nebraska for the past ten years.

On June 11, 1921, he was united in marriage to Hilda Sabata at Omaha. Mrs. Willhoite was born at Dwight on November 23, 1895. There is one daughter, Betty, born May 9, 1922. The family attends the Methodist Episcopal Church at Superior.

Mr. Willhoite is a Republican. He is a member of

the Masons, the Chamber of Commerce at Superior, the Nebraskana Society and the Superior Country Club. His favorite sport is golf. Residence: Superior.

Benjamin Franklin Williams

Benjamin F. Williams was born at Creston, Iowa, October 2, 1875, the son of Richard Simon and Laura Eta (Sea) Williams. His father, who was a farmer, was born at Burlington, Iowa, in 1842, and died at Lincoln, Nebraska, August, 1924. His Scotch ancestors came to America in 1838 His mother was born at Mt. Pleasant, Iowa, and died at Des Moines, Iowa, in 1926.

Dr. Williams, who has been a prominent physician in Nebraska for the last 30 years, received his early education in the country schools of Iowa, and the high school of Indianola, Iowa. Later he attended Iowa State College at Ames, and Nebraska Wesleyan University, where he was made a member of Phi Kappa Tau. He was superintendent of the Lincoln State Hospital for 10 years and served as chairman of the Board of Control of State Institutions.

On June 22, 1899, he was united in marriage with Mary Delinda Joseph, at York, Nebraska. Mrs. Williams was born at Creston, March 26, 1876. Dr. Williams was a captain in the Medical Corps during the late war. He is now a major in the Reserve Officers Medical Corps.

He is a member of the following professional organizations: American Medical Association; Nebraska State Medical Society; Central Neuro-physyciatric Association; and Psychiatric Vienna-Austria Medical Association. He is a member of the Lincoln Chamber of Commerce, and a Mason. His social clubs are the University Club, and the Shrine Club of Lincoln. He is a member of St. Paul's Methodist Church of Lincoln, and a Democrat.

Dr. Williams is director of the neuro-physyciatric section at St. Elizabeth's Hospital, consultant at Bryan Memorial Hospital and consultant in neurology at the United States Veterans Hospital. Residence: Lincoln.

Cora Alice Williams

Cora Alice Williams, educator and musician, was born at Elmwood, Cass County, Nebraska. February 2, 1902. Her father, Harry Albert Williams, who was born at Marion, Iowa, July 11, 1875, is a dealer in Buick cars and an auctioneer. He is descended from English ancestors who fought in the Revolution.

Mary Wilhelmina (Kuehn) Williams, mother of Cora, was born at Louisville, Nebraska, December 10, 1877. Of German descent, she is an enthusiastic church worker and takes an active interest in civic affairs.

Miss Williams was educated in the public schools of Elmwood, Nebraska, graduating from the high school in 1920. At the University of Nebraska she majored in theory of music and in voice, and was graduated from the fine arts department in 1930. She studied voice under Walter Wheatley of Lincoln.

From 1920-22 she attended Nebraska Wesleyan and from 1922-27 was supervisor of music at Wilber, Nebraska. From 1927-29 she was supervisor of music in the Elmwood schools, at which time the music department won the silver loving cup at the M. I. N. K. Music Contest at Peru. She was a member of a quartet in the First Baptist Church at Lincoln, in 1929, 1930. At the present time she is director of the Presbyterian choir at Plattsmouth and music supervisor in the public schools. She gives private instruction in voice and piano. She sings many solos, and among them the contralto solos in the *Messiah* at Red Oak, Iowa, were rendered by her.

She is a member of the Daughters of the American Revolution, St. Leger Cowley Chapter, at Lincoln; is worthy matron of the Eastern Star and a member of the Rebekah Lodge. She is a member of the National Music

Association and is affiliated with Van Fleet Memorial Methodist Episcopal Church at Elmwood, where she is active in the Women's Home Missionary Society and the Ladies' Aid. She is a Republican, and a member of The Nebraskana Society. Her favorite sports are tennis and skating. Residence: Elmwood.

Edward Glen Williams

Edward Glen Williams, president of the North Platte Monument Company, was born at St. Paul, Nebraska, July 5, 1878, son of Warren Tilford and Allie R. (Houston) Williams.

The father was born in Bedford, Indiana, March 28, 1844, and died at Cook, Nebraska, April 9, 1910. He was a farmer and a veteran of the Civil War. His wife, Allie, was born in Bedford, Indiana, August 5, 1851, and died at Alda, Nebraska, December 17, 1915. She was an ardent church worker, a descendant of the Houston family, who were relatives of General Sam Houston.

Upon his graduation from common grade school, Mr. Williams attended Grand Island High School, from which he was graduated in 1901, and thereafter attended the University of Nebraska, for three years. He was married on June 4, 1909, to Marian Alexander Brown, at Alda. Mrs. Williams was born at Dumberton, Scotland, February 27, 1879. They have three children, Helen Mary, born May 23, 1910; Marion Allie, born March 27, 1913; and Betty F., born April 29, 1916. Helen is a kindergarten teacher at North Platte, Marian is a student at Greeley College, and Betty F., a student of North Platte High School.

Mr. Williams is a Republican. Before entering business for himself, he was a teacher and salesman. Residence: North Platte.

Frank D. Williams

Born at Mt. Carroll, Illinois, January 8, 1868, Frank D. Williams is the son of David and Mary Ellen (Sage) Williams. His father, who was a farmer and a lieutenant in the Union Army from 1862 to 1864, was born in Pennsylvania of Welsh and English parents, and died at Wagner, South Dakota. His mother, whose ancestry was Welsh and Dutch, was born in Pennsylvania.

Mr. Williams attended rural school, and in 1892 was graduated from the Fremont Normal School, Fremont Nebraska. He is now a member of the law firm Williams and Williams at Albion, is attorney for the First National Bank, the Citizens State Bank of Cedar Rapids, Nebraska, and the Farmers State Bank of Cedar Rapids, and is interested in various investments.

A Republican, he served as superintendent of county schools from 1894 to 1898, was delegate to the Republican national convention in 1904, and is a member of the resolutions committee of that body. He holds membership in the Albion Commercial Club, the Nebraska State Bar Association, the Red Cross, and the Kiwanis Club. He is a member of the Albion Golf Club, is a Mason, and holds membership in the Nebraskana Society. During the World War he acted as chairman of the Fuel Committee of Boone County and was a member of the Draft Board.

He was married to Fannie P. Roberts at Albion, September 2, 1896. Mrs. Roberts was born in Iowa, in March, 1876, of Pennsylvania-Dutch parents. They have one son, Dana R., born November 6, 1897, who is a member of the law firm William & Williams at Albion. Residence: Albion.

Frank L. Williams

Since 1868 Frank L. Williams, longtime newspaper editor of Nebraska, has lived in this state and has been prominent in the business and civic world. He was born at Granville, Indiana, December 29, 1866, the son of Sampson H. and Sarah Catharine (Brackin) Williams.

His father, who was a farmer, was born at Granville, December 31, 1842, and died at Lincoln, Lancaster County, Nebraska, August 18, 1927; he served as a soldier in the Civil War for three years as a member of Company B, 84th Indiana Infantry; his parents, whose ancestry was Welsh and Irish, were pioneers in Ohio and Indiana, and filed homestead papers in Delaware County, Indiana, in 1827.

His mother was born of Scotch-Irish parentage at Granville, March 14, 1848, and died at Franklin, Nebraska, January 1, 1900. During her girlhood she sang at rallies for Civil War volunteers after Lincoln's call for troops. Her parents were pioneers in Delaware County, moving there from Ohio in the early history of Indiana.

Mr. Williams received his education in the public schools of Nebraska; was a student at Franklin Academy for a time; and studied under private tutors. He has had a varied and successful career in the newspaper business. In 1884 he began newspaper work on the *Echo* at Franklin, Nebraska; later was a printer on several different papers; was connected with the *Kearney Hub*, Kearney, Nebraska, for 12 years; and from 1893 to 1894 was the owner of the first daily newspaper at North Platte, Nebraska, the *Daily Record*. Since 1898 he has been connected with the *Nebraska State Journal* at Lincoln, holding the following positions: reporter; city editor; and managing editor. He has been editor of the paper since January 28, 1928.

His marriage to Mattie Cora Crane was solemnized at Kearney, in 1889. Mrs. Williams, who is of English and Irish descent, was born at Cincinnati, Indiana, May 30, 1871. They have three children: Edith Blanche, born December 19, 1889, who is pharmacist at the Bryan Memorial Hospital at Lincoln; Jessie Leonard, born January 8, 1891, who married Hazel Carson; and Jay Irving, born December 8, 1894, who married Joy Riggs. Jesse is a business man and musician at Lincoln, and Jay is director of orchestra and vocal music at Appleton, Wisconsin.

Mr. Williams is a member of the Lincoln Chamber of Commerce and the Laymen's Club. He is affiliated with St. Paul's Methodist Episcopal Brotherhood; is a member of the Nebraskana Society; and holds membership in the Masons, Scottish Rite, 32nd degree. Politically, he is a Republican. During his years in the newspaper business Mr. Williams has written various feature stories and special articles. Residence: Lincoln.

George Arthur Williams

The Honorable George Arthur Williams, now retired, was born at Lafayette, Illinois, August 17, 1864, the son of Charles and Mary (Viney) Williams. His father, born at Mortlake, Surrey, England, January 26, 1824, was a direct descendant of Oliver Cromwell. Coming to the United States in 1852, he was a veteran of the Civil War, city alderman and assessor. His death occurred at Galva, Illinois, February 9, 1895. His mother, who was born at Breamore, Hants, England, January 4, 1824, died at Galva, Illinois, on March 9, 1895.

Mr. Williams was educated in the public and high schools of Galva, Illinois, and completed a business course at Graysville, Tennessee. He has had a successful business and farming career, about half of his life devoted to agricultural pursuits, and half to the mercantile business.

A Republican, he has been active in the politics of his party for years; was a member of the Nebraska house of representatives two terms (1919-22); lieutenant governor three terms (1925-31); was the author of the Nebraska Headlight Law; one of the introducers of the State Capitol Bill, and a leader in educational and state highway legislation. In 1923 Mr. Williams ran second in a list of four candidates for nomination to the office of secretary of state.

On October 25, 1888, he was united in marriage to Mabel Lucretia Grubb, at Burchard, Nebraska. Mrs. Williams was born at Galva, Illinois, November 8, 1870. To them were born eight children, seven of whom are living: Arthur F., born July 27, 1889, married Marian Lind-

borg; Mary Ada, born March 8, 1891, married Leonard Ray McIntyre; Lewis Victor, born May 30, 1892, died January 9, 1893; Ross, born April 13, 1894, married Malena Dewie Higgins; Estelle, born July 26, 1896, married Royal Joseph Jackson; Mildred, born September 16, 1901, married Richard Tipton Allen; George Aubrey, born February 15, 1904, married Florence Jarvis; and Ada Lucine, born May 29, 1910, is unmarried.

He has always expressed great faith in the potential greatness of Nebraska. For many years a deep student of Nebraska affairs, he is highly regarded as an authority on the progress and development of the state. His lecture *Nebraska Bountiful* has attracted wide-spread attention. He is a member of the Sons of Veterans of the Civil War and of the Seventh Day Adventist Church. Residence: Fairmont. (Photograph on Page 1288).

George W. Williams

George W. Williams, successful farmer in York County, Nebraska, has lived in this state for the past 57 years, and has taken a prominent part in educational and welfare activities in his community. He was born in Berkley County, West Virginia, November 4, 1869, the son of William W. and Eve (King) Williams. His father, who was a farmer, was born in Berkley County, May 22, 1824, of Welsh parentage, and died in York County, May 20, 1890. His mother was born in Berkley County, of Irish descent, and died in York County.

Mr. Williams received his education in the rural schools in York County, and has been engaged in various phases of farm work most of his life. He is now the owner of an improved farm and modern home in York County. A Republican, he served as justice of the peace at York, January, 1929, to January, 1931.

He holds membership in the Shorthorn Breeders' Association, has served as a member of School District Number 17 in York County for several years, and is affiliated with the First Christian Church of York. An active member of the Red Cross, he served as chairman of the chapter in Baker Township for two terms, 1917-19, and 1929-31. He is a member of the Nebraskana Society, and the Independent Order of Odd Fellows. Reading is his hobby.

Mr. Williams was united in marriage with Mattie Florence Graham at York, March 16, 1898. Four children were born to this marriage: Eva Grace, born April 1, 1899, who was graduated from the University of Nebraska and is now a teacher; Esther, born August 13, 1903, who attended the University of Nebraska; Gladys, born February 19, 1909, who was a student at the university and is now engaged in business; and Alma, born December 20, 1914. Mrs. Williams was born February 25, 1877, of Welsh and Scottish ancestry. Residence: York.

Henry Laurens Williams

For the past 30 years Henry Laurens Williams has been a prominent banker and rancher at Gothenburg, Nebraska. He was born at Gilbertson, Pennsylvania, March 12, 1879, the son of Henry Laurens and Catharine Ann (Phillips) Williams. His father, who was born at Uniondale, Pennsylvania, October 26, 1842, and died at Boulder, Colorado, October 24, 1912, was a teacher, coal operator, and ranchman; he served in the Union Army during the Civil War. Henry Laurens Williams, Sr., was a direct descendant of Roger Williams and Richard Warren of early American fame. His mother, whose parents came to this country from England in 1840, was born at Middleport, Pennsylvania, May 5, 1851.

Mr. Williams was graduated from the Pottsville High School in 1896. He was connected with the Williams McAdams Company as a contractor from 1896 to 1899, was employed by the Sterling Steel Company at Pittsburg, 1899-1901, and since then has been engaged in ranching near Gothenburg where he is president of the

Townsend—Lincoln

GEORGE ARTHUR WILLIAMS

State Bank. He holds membership in the Gothenburg Chamber of Commerce, the Red Cross, Community Chest, Society for the Friendless, the Young Men's Christian Association, the Gothenburg Country Club, and the First Presbyterian Church.

His marriage to Marian Bertha Mortimer was solemnized at Pottsville, Pennsylvania, September 27, 1905. Mrs. Williams was born at Pottsville, December 21, 1879. The following children were born to this marriage: Laurens, born December 14, 1906, who is a lawyer at Omaha, Nebraska; Mortimer, June 14, 1909, who is studying at Boston; and Robert, June 3, 1917, who is a student in high school at Gothenburg. Mr. Williams is affiliated with the Republican party. Residence: Gothenburg.

James Benjamin Williams

Born at Mayview, Kansas, July 28, 1889, James Benjamin Williams is the son of John Webster and Cora Belle (Donaldson) Williams. His father, who is a farmer, was born in Indiana, July 27, 1859. His mother was born at Wood River, Nebraska, July 18, 1870.

Dr. Williams was graduated from the Wood River High School in 1909, and in 1918 received his medical degree at Creighton University in Omaha. Prior to his medical work he attended the University of Nebraska where he was a member of Phi Chi. From 1920 to 1927 he was engaged in medical practice at Beaver Crossing, Nebraska, and since 1928 has been prominent at Polk, Nebraska.

He is affiliated with the Methodist Episcopal Church at Polk, holds membership in the Nebraskana Society, and is an Odd Fellow and Modern Woodman of America. His hobby is the violin. During the World War he served as lieutenant in the United States Naval Reserve Forces, was promoted to lieutenant of the Medical Corps, and is now service officer in the American Legion.

On July 20, 1918, he was married to Dorothy Esther Rowland at Washington, D. C. Mrs. Williams, who was a nurse prior to her marriage was born at Omaha, Nebraska, May 20, 1894; her ancestry is Swedish. Residence: Polk.

Lewis O. Williams

Lewis O. Williams was born at Shipman, Illinois, January 7, 1858, the son of Loring A. and Eliza Pickett (Wadhams) Williams. His father, who was born in Mississippi, July 9, 1828, and died at Glenwood Mills, Iowa, February, 1914, was a horticulturist. His ancestry was Welsh.

His mother, who was of English descent, was born in Connecticut, December 9, 1832, and died at Glenwood Mills. With her husband she moved from Illinois to Iowa where they lived a typical pioneer life, knowing the various experiences of the early settlers of that part of the middle west.

Mr. Williams attended the country schools of Iowa, and a little later studied at the Glenwood High School. In 1879-80 he was a student at Tabor College, and in 1881 attended the Iowa Agriculture College. One of Nebraska's leading horticulturists, he founded Williams Nurseries in 1905, recently established an additional organization, the Lowell Gardens, at Lincoln.

He is, among other things, interested in editorial work and poetry. He is the author of *A Life Survey at Seventy*, a poem depicting pioneer life and his own boyhood, *A Reverie;* and various other leaflets and pamphlets. For over ten years he was editor of the horticultural department of the *Nebraska Farmer,* and of the *Nebraska State Journal.*

His marriage to Clara Sarah Stillman at Plainview, Wabasha County, Minnesota, December 29, 1885. Mrs. Williams was of English ancestry and was descended from a New England Yankee family. She was born at Plain-

view, August 21, 1861, and died at University Place, Lancaster County, Nebraska, March 7, 1915.

Seven children were born to this union: Robert, born August 26, 1888, who died September 5, 1918; Iva, born July 25, 1891, who died December 7, 1907; Dwight, born July 19, 1893; Harvey, born March 13, 1896; Carol, born November 19, 1898; Rollin, born November 7, 1899; and Miriam, born July 2, 1902. Dwight, Carol, and Miriam are prominent in educational activities. Rollin is a practicing physician in Nebraska. Harvey is taking charge of the nursery established by his father.

All of Mr. Williams' sons were volunteers in the World War, and his oldest son, Robert, was killed in action in France, in 1918. Mr. Williams is a life member of the Nebraska State Horticultural Society; is a member of the Lincoln Garden Club; and holds life membership in the Nebraska Hall of Agricultural Achievement. He is secretary of the Anti-cigarette Advertising Campaign. He is a Modern Woodman of America. He is affiliated with the First Methodist Episcopal Church of Lincoln. Residence: Lincoln.

Mabel Denter Williams

Mabel Denter Williams was born at Brule, Nebraska, November 8, 1890, daughter of Joseph George and Mary May (Stirsky) Denter.

Her father was born in St. John, Austria, August 24, 1861, and is now a retired ranchman and farmer. He served as county commissioner several terms. His wife, Mary May Stirsky was born in St. John, Austria, May 26, 1868. The father and the mother came to America, one in 1864 and the other in 1869, settling close to each other near Iowa City, Iowa. In 1886, they married and came to Nebraska in a covered wagon, making the trip in six weeks. They homesteaded in Keith County, and have lived there nearly 40 years. They are now retired and live in Brule. They have four children, all of whom are living, of whom the youngest is Mrs. Williams.

Mable Denter attended public school until 1906, high school one year, and Kearney State Normal School two years, where she obtained a second grade certificate. She taught in public schools five years, a year in Big Spring, one in Brule and the other three in rural schools. She also took nurses training in North Platte in the general hospital for about one year.

On June 19, 1917, she was married to Fred T. Williams at Julesburg, Colorado. Mr. Williams, who is a cattle man and engaged in real estate and investment, was born at Whiting, Kansas, September 17, 1890. The family lives in their own home. Mr. Williams has a real estate office and also manages a large acreage in grain, and a small ranch. There are four children living, and one deceased. Beverly Bonham, born March 29, 1918, is ready for her junior year in high school and is accomplished both in piano and violin: Peggy Bernice, born June 20, 1925, is in public school; while Mary Lou and Frederick Thomas, twins, were born December 27, 1927. An infant son born July 31, 1919, died August 7, 1919.

During the late war Mrs. Williams participated in Red Cross and liberty bond drives. She is a member of the Congregational Church, the Red Cross, the Brule Woman's Club, of which she is president, the Ladies Aid Society, the Order of Eastern Star, and the Amusement Club, a social club. She enjoys golf and tennis, while her hobbies are bridge, flowers, and music. Residence: Brule.

Richard Owen Williams

Born at Mount Vernon, New York, July 13, 1869, Richard Owen Williams has been a citizen of Nebraska for nearly fifty years. He is the son of Owen and Mary (Piper) Williams, the former born at Carnarvonshire, North Wales, March 25, 1837. Owen Williams came to

America in June, 1857, and received his A. B. and A. M. degrees at Colgate University. Ordained in the Baptist ministry he was an early Nebraska pioneer preacher. From 1875 to 1881 he served the First Baptist Church at Nebraska City; and from 1886 to 1894 the First Baptist Church at Lincoln. In 1894 he was made superintendent of missions for Minnesota, Wisconsin, North and South Dakota, continuing until 1907. His death occurred at Albert Lea, Minnesota, on February 9, 1915. Mary Piper Williams was born at Wolfboro, New Hampshire, April 22, 1835, of Holland Dutch ancestors who came to New England in 1660. Before her marriage she was a teacher in New York State. After taking up her residence in Nebraska she conducted a private school at Nebraska City from 1877 to 1880. Her death occurred at Lawrence, Kansas, October 30, 1910.

Mr. Williams attended Knox Academy at Galesburg, Illinois, and later the University of Nebraska. He received his A. B. from the latter in 1891, and his LL. B. in 1893. In 1891 he was president of his class, and in 1893 was president of the glee club. While at the university he was a member of the Delian Male Quartet, and during 1914-15 was president of the Alumni Association.

Entering the practice of law upon his admission to the bar, in 1898 he became a member of the law firm of Flansburg and Williams which continued until 1910, when the firm was reorganized as Flansburg, Williams and Flansburg. Since 1913 he has been engaged in private practice. For the past thirty years Mr. Williams has been attorney for the Union Central Life Insurance Company of Cincinnati, Ohio, in Nebraska.

A Republican, Mr. Williams has never aspired to political office, but has taken an active part in professional and educational circles. Since 1920 he has been attorney for the Board of Education, and in 1927 was president of the Lancaster County Bar Association. He has been for many years a member of the Chamber of Commerce, and the Social Welfare Society and is a member of the Nebraska State Bar Association. His religious affiliation is with the First Baptist Church of Lincoln, of which he has been a member for many years. From 1914 to 1919 he took an active part in Boy Scout work and served as Scout Master for Troop No. 9. He is vice president of the Lancaster County Humane Society, and a member of the Open Forum and the Young Men's Christian Association. His hobby is music.

On June 20, 1900, Mr. Williams was married to Lina F. Cutts. She graduated from the University of Nebraska in 1900, and received the honor of membership in Phi Beta Kappa. Mr. and Mrs. Williams have three children, Dorothy, born May 26, 1903; Margaret, born March 20, 1905; and Owen, born June 28, 1906. Both daughters are members of Phi Beta Kappa, and Owen is a member of Sigma Xi. Residence: Lincoln.

Albert Williamsen

Albert Williamsen was born at Palmer, Nebraska, February 3, 1893, the son of Swen and Mary (Petersen) Williamsen. His father, who was born at Sandner, Norway, December 7, 1862, was a farmer for many years and has served as county commissioner of Howard County, Nebraska, for two terms. His mother was born at Feskebed, Denmark, September 13, 1869, and died in 1903 at Palmer, Nebraska.

Mr. Williamsen completed his high school education at Dannebrog, Nebraska, was graduated from the business and normal college at York, and has been prominent in civic and business affairs there since then. He was engaged in farming until 1914 when he entered the employ of the York Foundry where he remained until 1917. In 1918 he entered the nursery business as salesman for Harrison Nursery Company. In 1920 he was made sales manager of the latter organization and since 1927 has been secretary and treasurer.

He is a member of the board of directors of the York County Commercial Club, and holds membership in the Rotary Club, the Young Men's Christian Association, the Parent Teacher's Association, and the Nebraska Horticultural Society. His fraternal organizations are the Masons, Knights of Pythias, and the Eastern Star. Mr. Williamsen is affiliated with the Church of Christ at York, is a member of the Red Cross, and holds membership in the York Country Club. During the World War he served in 70th Spruce Squadron, stationed at Vancouver, Washington, and at this time is a member of the American Legion. His sports include golfing, fishing, and hunting, and his hobby is landscape gardening.

On September 14, 1916, he was united in marriage with Luella Pearle Wells at York. Mrs. Williamsen, who taught in the public schools prior to her marriage, was born at Palmer, Nebraska, March 11, 1895. Their children are: Gerald, born March 17, 1920, who died March 24, 1920; Donald, born May 30, 1921; Kenneth, born February 19, 1924; Huburt, born July 25, 1926; Dola, born April 26, 1928. Residence: York.

James Medford Willis

A distinguished physician of Nebraska is James Medford Willis who resides at McCook. He was born at Orick, Missouri, January 19, 1881, the son of John Franklin and Nannie C. (Petty) Willis, the former a farmer who was born in Maryland, March 8, 1832, and died at Arapahoe, Nebraska in 1915; his English ancestors came to this country prior to the Revolution.

His mother was born in Ray County, Missouri, in 1847, and died in Calloway County, Missouri, November 12, 1883, having taught in the public schools of that state for two terms. She was of English and Irish descent.

Dr. Willis holds the M. D. degree from Central Medical College at St. Joseph, Missouri, and is a fellow of the American College of Surgeons. He has been engaged in the general practice of medicine and surgery at McCook since 1903 when he was admitted to the practice of his profession. He is vice president of the Nebraska State Medical Association and owns the Willis Clinic at McCook.

He is a director in the Chamber of Commerce, was the first president of the McCook Kiwanis Club, and holds membership in the Red Willow County Medical Society, the American Medical Association, and the American College of Surgeons. He is affiliated with the Methodist Church, the Young Men's Christian Association, and the Southwest Nebraska Historical Society. His hobby is aviation, he being one of the first physicians over 50 years of age to receive a government pilot's license.

On August 20, 1902, he was united in marriage with Ethelyn Maud Keaton at St. Joseph, Missouri. Mrs. Willis, whose parents were Irish, was born in Montana, December 31, 1881. Two children were born to them: Lucile Leona, March 20, 1907; and Alma F., born July 13, 1913, who is a student at Ward Belmont Girls School. Lucile is married to L. A. Walker.

Dr. Willis is the author of various articles on professional topics published in the *Nebraska State Medical Journal*. He was recently elected to membership in the Nebraskana Society. Residence: McCook.

Robert Henry Willis

A pioneer resident of Nebraska, Robert Henry Willis was born at Cheyenne, Wyoming, March 22, 1869, the son of John Gregory and Cecelia Jane (Beck) Willis. His father, who was a merchant, was born at Charlton, New York, October 14, 1840, came to Omaha in 1865, immediately after the war. He was a freighter from there to Cheyenne and Denver until 1868, and in May, 1868, married in Cheyenne. During this year he was a merchant in Cheyenne, when his store burned down. He then moved to Omaha, where he entered the wholesale business, and was active in this until he retired in 1884. He died at Omaha, March 26, 1925. He served as a member of the city council at Cheyenne in 1868, and during the Civil War was second lieutenant in the 17th Illinois Cavalry, Company K. His father, Robert Frazier Willis, was born in Cork, Ireland, of Scotch-English ancestry.

Cecelia Jane (Beck) Willis, whose ancestry was English, was born at Muscatine, Iowa, May 1, 1850, the daughter of St. Ledger and Emily Jane (Vermilion) Beck, and died at Omaha, July 25, 1920. Emily Jane Vermilion Beck's ancestors were of English stock and came to America in 1812. She was born in Fairfax County, Virginia. St. Ledger Beck was born in Tennessee, and was a descendant of a Dr. Collyer, who practiced medicine in Dublin, Ireland.

Mr. Willis attended the Omaha High School during 1882-1885, was a student at Creighton College in 1886, and studied at Rensselaer Institute at Troy, New York, during 1887-90. His fraternity was Zeta Psi. He has held the following professional positions: civil engineer for the Union Pacific Railroad, 1890; in the city engineer's office at Omaha, 1891; employed by the Douglas County Engineering Department, 1892-93; state water commissioner of Nebraska, 1894-1909; state water superintendent, 1909-18; assistant state engineer, 1919; chief of the Bureau of Irrigation, Water Power and Drainage of Nebraska, 1902-to date.

He is a member of the American Association of Engineers and the Association of Western State Engineers. He served as a school board member at Bridgeport from 1896 to 1908, and holds membership in the Lions Club, the Nebraska State Historical Society, and the Red Cross. Mr. Willis is a Mason and Knight of Pythias, is affiliated with the Good Shepherd Episcopal Church, and is a member of the Nebraskana Society.

On December 30, 1891, he was married to Carrie Lee Melius at Rensselaer, New York; she was born at Rensselaer, October 14, 1869, a descendant of Holland-Dutch ancestors who came to this country in 1600; and died at Bridgeport, September 14, 1911. She was the daughter of Charles and Anna (Huyler) Melius. Her father was George Washington Huyler. His father, Jeremiah Melius, was born in Hudson, New York, in 1808; and his father, Jacob, was born in New York State in 1777.

One daughter was born to this marriage, Cornelia, September 17, 1893, who married Frank William Gordon. They have five children, Margaret Jane, born July 2, 1923; Jean Myro, June 11, 1926; Willis Gould, August 25, 1928; Frank Ameluis, March 26, 1930; and Robert Warren, September 19, 1931.

On January 6, 1914, Mr. Willis was united in marriage with Anna E. Hascall at Cheyenne. She is the daughter of Henry and Dorothea (Foellmer) Hascall, and was born at Grand Island, June 2, 1881. Residence: Bridgeport.

Tilford A. Willmore

For the past 42 years Tilford A. Willmore has been a resident of Thayer County, Nebraska, where he has been prominent in the civic, business, and political world. He was born at Clinton, Illinois, November 18, 1869, the son of Charles and Sarah J. (Wright) Willmore. His father, who was born in Essex County, Virginia, July 16, 1830, and died at Hebron, Nebraska, August 11, 1898, was a farmer, and was active in the Democratic party; his ancestors had lived in England for many generations prior to the founding of the new world. His mother was born in Illinois, February 14, 1836, and died at Hebron, August 21, 1924; her ancestors, natives of North Carolina, were of Irish descent.

Mr. Willmore was graduated from the Hebron High School in 1892, and until 1905 was a farmer near Hebron. He taught school for 12 years, and since then has been engaged in the real estate business. A Democrat, he has been one of the leaders of his chosen party in Thayer County both in state and national affairs, and has

held the following positions: chairman of the Democratic county committee, eight years; member of the state committee at this time; and postmaster for eight years under Woodrow Wilson's administration. He has attended three national Democratic conventions and practically all state conventions.

He is a member of the Hebron Commercial Club, is affiliated with the Christian Church, and holds membership in the Ancient Order of United Workmen and the Nebraskana Society. He is a member of the Red Cross.

His marriage to Maude Woodward occurred at Clinton, Illinois, September 14, 1893. Mrs. Willmore, who is a homebuilder, was born at Clinton, February 21, 1872, of English parentage. She is eligible to membership in the Daughters of the American Revolution and Order of Eastern Star, and is a member of the Hebron Woman's Club.

Three children were born to this union: Zelma and Velma, twin daughters, born February 26, 1903. One child, born December 3, 1901, died in infancy. Velma and Zelma have both been successful school teachers in the public schools and are now married. Residence: Hebron.

Allan Brittain Wilson

Allan B. Wilson was born at Nebraska City, Otoe County, Nebraska, September 28, 1876, the son of William Lewis and Josephine Catharine (Doud) Wilson. His father, who was an old time resident of Nebraska City, was born at Berwick, Pennsylvania, March 4, 1840, ad died at Nebraska City in 1912. He was an adjutant in the 142nd Pennsylvania Volunteers in the Civil War, and during his residence in Nebraska was president of the Nebraska City National Bank. Of Scotch-Irish descent, he was the son of a physician and the grandson of a Revolutionary War officer.

His mother, a member of the distinguished Doud family in Connecticut, was born at Madison, Connecticut, July 10, 1842, and died at Nebraska City on September 28, 1905.

Mr. Wilson received his education in the Nebraska City High School and the Shattuck Military School at Faribault, Minnesota. He has lived in Nebraska City all his life and is a grain dealer there. At the present time he is also president of the Nebraska City National Bank.

On June 17, 1908, he was united in marriage with Lula Janet Reed at Nebraska City. Mrs. Wilson was born in Nebraska City, October 3, 1884. There are three children: Robert, born March 1, 1910; James, born November 28, 1913; and Josephine, born May 29, 1919.

During the Spanish-American War Mr. Wilson was sergeant-major in the 2nd Nebraska Volunteers, and from 1899 to 1904 was first lieutenant and adjutant of the 2nd Nebraska Volunteers. He is a member of the Rotary Club, and is an Elk and Mason. He is affiliated with the Episcopal Church at Nebraska City. His hobby is orchard work. He is a Republican. Residence: Nebraska City.

Andrew Gordon Wilson

Andrew Gordon Wilson was born at Scotch Grove, Iowa, April 5, 1861, the son of James L. Wilson and Ellen (Gordon) Wilson. His father, who was a pioneer Presbyterian minister in Iowa, was born at Hopewell, Pennsylvania, January 20, 1824, and died at Eustis, Florida, November 24, 1890. James Wilson was graduated from Jefferson College in Pennsylvania, 1851, completed his education at the Allegheny Theological Seminary in 1854, and for many years served as president of the board of trustees of Lennox College, Hopkinton, Iowa; he was of Scotch-Irish descent.

Ellen (Gordon) Wilson, who received her education

at the Washington Ladies Seminary in Pennsylvania, was born at Hopewell, January 24, 1829, and died at Eustis, March 24, 1888. Her ancestry was Scotch-Irish.

Mr. Wilson was a profound student, was intensely interested in literature and research, and was an authority on most religious subjects. He was graduated from Lenox College and in 1884 was graduated from Wooster University, Ohio, where he received scholastic honors. He was county surveyor of Delaware County, Iowa, for a time, and for 20 years was a member of the faculty of Lenox College as geology instructor, and later as president. From 1901 until his death he was engaged in the abstract business at Hebron, Nebraska, where he was an elder in the First Presbyterian Church.

He married Elizabeth McKean who was born at Anamosa, Iowa, December 23, 1869. To their marriage the following children were born: Ruth Eleanor, July 13, 1900, who married Ove Peter Nielsen; Elizabeth G., January 18, 1906; Gordon McKean, July 30, 1908; and Frances Claire, June 29, 1912.

Mr. Wilson was a member of the American Association for the Advancement of Science, held a fellowship in a national organization of geologists, and was a member of the Sons of the American Revolution. He was the author of *Frozen Streams of the Iowa Drift Border*, published in the *American Geologist* in June, 1896.

His death occurred at his home in Hebron, April 19, 1922. Residence: Hebron.

Charles Malven Wilson

Charles M. Wilson was born at Garnett, Kansas, November 28, 1884, the son of James Lincoln and Floretta Ann (Davis) Wilson. His father, who was born in Ohio, January 19, 1856, has been a farmer for many years, and has always been interested in local politics; his ancestors came to America from Ireland. His mother, who was of English descent, was born at Woodsfield, Monroe County, Ohio, August 16, 1859, and died at Garnett, May 21, 1926; she was active in church affairs.

Mr. Wilson attended the public schools of Garnett; was a student at the Garnett High School for one year; attended the State Agricultural College at Manhattan, Kansas, one year; attended Sterling College for six years, where he was awarded his A. B. degree; and later studied for three winters at Xenia Theological Seminary, Xenia, Ohio. During his college days he took part in a number of state track meets.

Mr. Wilson has held the following pastorates: United Presbyterian Church of Jordan's Grove, Illinois, May 18, 1918 to November 30, 1921; United Presbyterian Church, Hanover, Illinois, December 1, 1921 to October 31, 1926; North Bend United Presbyterian Church, since 1926; and is also supplying the Webster Presbyterian Church. He was ordained to the ministry at Baldwin, Illinois, June 4, 1918 in the Jordan's Grove United Presbyterian Church by the Illinois Southern Presbytery.

He is now clerk of the Nebraska Presbytery of the United Presbyterian Church; is a member of the local Parent Teachers Association; and holds membership in the Nebraskana Society. In 1928 and 1929 he served as president of the Platte Valley Ministerial Association.

On February 27, 1912, he was united in marriage with Elsie Clara Whaley at Garnett, Kansas. Mrs. Wilson, whose ancestry is Irish and German, was born at Westphalia, Kansas, December 30, 1881. Residence: North Bend.

Clarence Oren Wilson

Clarence Oren Wilson, railroad executive, was born near Norton, Kansas, December 31, 1888. He is the son of John Cleve and Esther Ellen (Ridgway) Wilson, the former of whom was a farmer of Holland Dutch descent. John Cleve Wilson was born near Sparta, Wisconsin, April 4, 1865, and died at Endicott, Nebraska, May 15,

1930. His wife, Esther, was born on a farm in Jasper County, Iowa, November 3, 1867, of Irish descent on her father's side, and Pennsylvania Dutch on her mother's.

Mr. Wilson attended public school and business college, completing his course at Skelton's College, Salina, Kansas, on February 1, 1906. For two years thereafter he was a telegrapher with the Atchison and Santa Fe Railway. He then became associated with the St. Joseph and Grand Island, later taken over by the Union Pacific. With these companies he held all positions from station helper to his present position as supervisory agent of the Union Pacific System at Hastings. During the World War he was division agent and later train dispatcher.

On September 21, 1908, Mr. Wilson was united in marriage to America Queen Sweetland, at Marysville, Kansas. Mrs. Wilson was a native of Wetmore, Kansas, born June 17, 1892. She is of French descent. They have one son, Vernon, born December 21, 1910, who served an enlistment in the United States Navy on the *U. S. S. West Virginia*.

Rejected for military service in the World War because of physical disability (twice at St. Joseph, and once at Topeka), Mr. Wilson later organized and was captain of the State Guard company at Axtell, Kansas. He was a member of the first liberty loan drive at Axtell, and handled accounts for the central division of the Union Pacific which made intensive drives among its employees.

At the present time Mr. Wilson is a member of the Hastings Chamber of Commerce, the Young Men's Christian Association, the Ancient Free and Accepted Masons, the Royal Arch Masons, Knights Templar, Ancient Arabic Order Nobles of the Mystic Shrine, the Knights of Pythias, Elks and the Security Benefit Association. During 1909-10, he was director of the school board at Hansen, Nebraska. Mr. Wilson's hobbies are landscaping and decorating. He has resided at Hastings, since May 12, 1921. (Photograph in Album).

Eliza Means Wilson

Eliza Means Wilson was born at Springfield, Sarpy County, Nebraska, November 16, 1882, the daughter of James Ritchie and Sarah Charlotte (Means) Wilson. Her father, a leader in his community, was a farmer and postmaster at Gretna, county clerk, county judge, and clerk of the district court of Sarpy County, Nebraska. Born in Carroll, Ohio, April 18, 1855, he moved to Nebraska in early days and has served his county in various capacities for over twenty-five years. He was the great grandson of William Wilson, who was born in Maryland, in 1755, and was of Scotch descent, and Hester (Fickle) Wilson, whose Welsh ancestors served in the Revolution. He died at Papillion, Sarpy County, Nebraska, September 14, 1920.

Sarah Wilson, mother of Eliza, was born at Clarksdale, DeKalb County, Missouri, August 10, 1859, and died at Gretna, July 9, 1888. Before her marriage she was a school teacher. She was descended from the Means, Atterberry, Butler, and Walker families, all of Scotch and English extraction, who came to America during the colonial days. Jesse Walker, an ancestor, was a scout under General Francis Marion during Revolutionary times.

Miss Wilson was educated in a country school near Gretna, and later attended the Papillion High School where she was graduated as valedictorian, in May, 1901. During 1903-04-05 she was a student at Peru State Teachers' College at Peru, Nebraska.

Vitally interested in school work, Miss Wilson has held various educational positions. From 1901 to 1903, she was teacher in a country school; was in the kindergarten department at Crawford, 1905-06; and taught in the elementary school at South Side, Omaha, 1906-10. A Republican, she has entered the political field both for herself and for national candidates. She served as deputy clerk of the district court of Sarpy County, from 1912 to 1920; was clerk of the district court from 1920 to 1930; and in 1930 was a candidate for the latter position with no opposition. She has been a resident of Nebraska for 48 years except for a short residence in Tripp County, South Dakota, where she homesteaded in 1910 and 1911.

Miss Wilson is a member of the Red Cross, of which she has been secretary in Sarpy County since 1921. She is a member of the Papillion Community Club, serving on the executive committee in 1926; the Papillion Woman's Club; and the Royal Neighbors of America. She has been secretary of the clerk of the District Court Association since 1921. A member of the First Presbyterian Church, she is the teacher of the young people's class. She is fond of hiking. Her hobby is reading. Residence: Papillion.

Elizabeth McKean Wilson

Elizabeth McKean Wilson, abstracter, was born at Anamosa, Iowa, December 23, 1869, daughter of Francis Crawford and Jane Eleanor (Dunlap) McKean. Her father, born at Carrol County, Ohio, February 12, 1842, was the grandson of Hugh McKean, whose father emigrated from Scotland to County Antrim, Ireland at the close of the war of 1688-90. Francis Crawford McKean was a lawyer, and held the rank of captain in Company D, 9th Iowa Infantry. He died May 5, 1874, at Evans, Colorado. His wife, Jane Eleanor, was born in Shannon, Ohio, July 22, 1849, and died at Hebron, October 25, 1923. She was descended from Jeremiah Joseph and Polly Smith, who were married at Morgantown, West Virginia, in 1873.

Educated in public school, Elizabeth McKean received her Bachelor of Arts degree from Lenox College, at Hopkinton, Iowa, in 1889, and was a graduate in voice from the music department of that college in 1898. On June 25, 1890, she was united in marriage to Andrew Gordon Wilson, at Hopkinton. Mr. Wilson, who was for many years a prominent figure in the business life of Hebron, was born at Scotch-Grove, Iowa, April 5, 1861. He was of Scotch-Irish ancestry, his family settling early in Pennsylvania. Mr. Wilson died at Hebron April 19, 1922.

Of this marriage were born four children, Ruth Eleanor, born July 13, 1900, married Ove Peter Nielsen; Elizabeth, born January 18, 1906; Gordon McKean, born July 30, 1908 and Frances Claire, born June 29, 1912. Ruth was graduated from Stanford University in 1923 and is a high school instructor in English and Spanish. Elizabeth was graduated from the University of Nebraska in 1929, with Phi Beta Kappa honors.

Mrs. Wilson has resided in Hebron twenty-nine years. She is a Republican, a member of the First Presbyterian Church, the Order of Eastern Star, the P. E. O. Sisterhood and the Nebraskana Society. Her hobby is philately. Residence: Hebron.

Fredric Louis Wilson

Fredric Louis Wilson, physician and surgeon, was born at Petersburg, Nebraska, May 29, 1890, son of William Alexander and Louisa (Fanning) Wilson. The father, a native of Bland County, Virginia, was born in 1852. He was a Methodist minister, descended from a soldier in the War of 1812. His death occurred at Stuart, March 4, 1930. Louisa Fanning was born in Bland County, in 1856, and died at Stuart, March 2, 1931.

Dr. Wilson was graduated from high school at Stuart in 1907, and received his medical degree from Creighton University in 1917. There he was a member of Phi Rho Sigma, and president of his class. He was a student also at Nebraska Wesleyan University in 1912 and at the University of Nebraska in 1913.

He is the most outstanding physician in his section of the state, and is local surgeon for the North Western Railroad. Starting with a two bed hospital, he now has

twenty beds, and one of the best and modernly equipped hospitals in the state. The unique thing about it, is the fact that Stuart has a population of only 800 people. During 1931, 425 patients registered in the hospital. He maintains a staff of five registered nurses, a cook and laundress, at all times.

On June 25, 1915, Dr. Wilson was married to Bessie Myrtle Coats at Fremont. She was born at Stuart, October 6, 1895. There are two children living, Fredrick, born November 14, 1916, and Terrance, born December 24, 1930. Robert, born November 1, 1924, died February 2, 1929.

Dr. Wilson is a Republican. He is president of the Stuart Silver Fox Ranch, Incorporated, was a member of the school board (1930), and from 1921-23 was secretary of the Northwest Nebraska Medical Association. During 1923 he served as mayor of Stuart.

He is a Mason, a member of the Stuart Methodist Church, is a life member of the Nebraskana Society, and lion tamer of the local Lions Club, at Stuart, Nebraska. He enjoys fishing and hunting, while his hobby is painting. Residence: Stuart. (Photograph on Page 1294).

Harry Doud Wilson

Harry Doud Wilson, for many years one of Nebraska's prominent bankers, was born at Plymouth, Pennsylvania, December 2, 1866, and died at Nebraska City, February 24, 1928. He was the son of William Lewis and Josephine Catherine (Doud) Wilson. William L. Wilson was born at Berwick, Pennsylvania, March 4, 1840, and died at Nebraska City, October 18, 1912. He was a colonel in the Civil War, having served with the 142nd Pennsylvnia Volunteers, and was wounded at Gettysburg, July 1, 1863. For many years he was president of the Nebraska City National Bank. He was descended from William Wilson, who emigrated from Stewardstown, County Tyrone, Ireland, and settled near Philadelphia, in 1732.

Josephine Catherine Doud was born at Madison, Connecticut, July 10, 1842, and died at Nebraska City, September 28, 1905. She was active in the Presbyterian Church, and in all charities. Her son, Harry Doud Wilson attended the Nebraska City public schools and was graduated in 1886. He was married to Mabel Stafford, at Nebraska City, June 5, 1894. (See *Nebraskana*).

At the time of his death he was president of the Nebraska City National Bank, with which he had been associated since leaving school. He was always active in the civic, religious and educational life of the city. For many years he was treasurer of the Red Cross, serving up until the time of his death, and he served as a member of the school board and as its vice president for some years. He was a member of St. Mary's Episcopal Church and was its treasurer and vestryman. He was also a member of the Elks and the Nebraska City Country Club. His death was mourned by all who knew him.

Henry H. Wilson

Henry H. Wilson, a resident of Nebraska since 1871, was born on a farm in Sandusky County, Ohio, January 1, 1854. His father, Nathaniel Wilson, who was a teacher and a farmer, was born on a farm in Luzerne County, Pennsylvania, September 13, 1813, and died at Valparaiso, Saunders County, Nebraska, October 25, 1890. His ancestry was Scotch and Irish.

His mother, Mary (Feasel) Wilson was born on a farm in Franklin County, Ohio, May 23, 1819, and died in Saunders County, Nebraska, September 8, 1874. She was of English and Dutch descent.

Mr. Wilson attended the public schools of Ohio, was a student at Bryan Academy, Ohio, attended the Peru Normal School, and from 1873 until 1878 was a student at the University of Nebraska. He was awarded the

FREDRIC LOUIS WILSON

following degrees at the University of Nebraska: Ph. B., 1878; A. M., 1885; LL. M., 1895; and LL. D., 1929. He was president of the Union Debating Society, was editor of *Hesperian*, student paper, and was made a member of Phi Beta Kappa, Acacia, and Phi Delta Phi.

He was admitted to the bar at Lincoln, February 2, 1881. He served as professor of law at the University of Nebraska from 1889 until 1920 and is now a member of the law firm of Burkett, Wilson, Brown, Wilson and Van Kirk. He is the author of *"Occasional Addresses"*, a volume of public speeches delivered by him on various occasions covering a period of 50 years, and published in 1929.

A Republican, Mr. Wilson served as presidential elector in 1904. He was married to Emma Parks at Lincoln, Nebraska, June 22, 1882. Mrs. Wilson, who was born at Agency City, Wappello County, Iowa, June 23, 1856, and died at Lincoln, October 25, 1927, was the first dean of women at the University of Nebraska. She was descended from the Dudleys of Massachusetts and the Stouts of New Jersey. The following children were born to them: Henry Parks, born October 20, 1883, who died December 9, 1883; Helen, born October 26, 1884, who is head of the art department at Lincoln High School; Edith, born May 28, 1888, who married Paul T. Bell of Oakland, California; Ralph Parks, born November 5, 1890, who is a lawyer at Lincoln; and Walter Feasel, born October 1, 1892, who is a Lincoln architect. Walter was an ensign in the Navy, and Ralph was a private in the 89th Division during the World War.

On September 21, 1929, Mr. Wilson was united in marriage with Jennie S. Rinker at Omaha, Nebraska. During the World War he was a member of the Nebraska Home Guards and served as treasurer of the Lincoln Chapter of the Red Cross. He was president of the Nebraska State Bar Association, 1913-14, was president of the Lancaster County Bar Association, and has been a member of the American Bar Association since 1893.

He was president of the American Interprofessional Institute, is a member of the Chamber of Commerce, and holds membership in the Nebraska State Historical Society, and the Nebraskana Society. He is a member of Hiram International Club, the Round Table and the Patriarchs. He is a 33rd degree Mason, grand master, Scottish Rite, and past potentate of Shrine. He is interested in football and golf. His hobby is the study of international relations. Residence: Lincoln.

Howard S. Wilson

Howard S. Wilson, who has lived in this state since birth, was born at Lincoln, Lancaster County, Nebraska, November 16, 1894. He is the son of William Cook and Adele Almira (Stebbins) Wilson. His father on leaving college entered the lumbering business at Michigan City, Indiana; later he moved to Lincoln, Nebraska, as manager of Bankers Life Insurance Company, of Nebraska; in 1900 he was elected president of this company. He was born at Quincey, Michigan, October 11, 1858, and died at Lincoln, Nebraska, December 20, 1918; his father was English, and his mother was German.

Adele Almira (Stebbins) Wilson, mother of Howard Stebbins Wilson, was born at Port Huron, Michigan, on March 18, 1861. She is descended from Rowland Stebbins, born in England, 1594.

Mr. Wilson graduated from the Lincoln High School in 1913; and received his A. B. degree from the University of Nebraska in 1917, where he was a member of the University Players, Phi Kappa Psi. He also holds membership in the following organizations: Red Cross; Lincoln Community Chest; Masons, 33rd degree; Knight Templar; Shrine; Rotary Club; Nebraska State Historical Society; Nebraska Art Association; Young Men's Christian Association; Lincoln University Club; Lincoln Country Club; and Patriarchs.

During the World War, Mr. Wilson entered the United States Navy, as a second class seaman; later he was promoted to chief boatswain's mate; he was released to inactive duty January, 1919; and was honorably discharged in 1921. He is a member of the American Legion. His religious affiliations is with the First Plymouth Congregational Church where he has served two terms on the board of trustees and was a member of the finance committee for the new church building.

A member of the Lincoln Community Chest, he has served as its secretary since 1929; was a member of the board of directors of the Chamber of Commerce (1927-1931), and served as treasurer in 1929. He was master of the Lodge of Perfection in 1926, and master of Kadosh in 1930 in the Ancient and Accepted Scottish Rite of Freemasonry. Residence: Lincoln.

Mabel Stafford Wilson

Mabel Stafford was born at Hamburg, Iowa, June 25, 1873, daughter of Amos P. and Kate (Cotton) Stafford. Amos Stafford was born in Chinqua Concy, Canada, January 27, 1846, and for many years was in the lumber business and head of the Great Western Cereal Company at Nebraska City. For the past twenty-two years he has been retired. Kate Cotton Stafford was born at Shelbyville, Indiana, July 28, 1850, and died at Nebraska City, August 4, 1924. She was active in the Episcopal Church, and held one office in it for thirty years. She was head of the Associated Charities at Nebraska City for thirty years. Her family came from Kentucky, where they had settled three generations ago.

Mrs. Wilson was graduated from the Nebraska City High School on May 20, 1892. On June 5, 1894, she was united in marriage to Harry Doud Wilson at Nebraska City. (See *Nebraskana*). There are two children: Mark Stafford, born January 18, 1898, died August 13, 1907; William Lewis, born June 11, 1909, attended Nebraska City High School two years, and then entered Lake Forest Academy where he was graduated. At the age of 17 he entered Dartmouth College. He was made a member of Delta Upsilon. However, at the close of his sophomore year, when his father died, he returned to Nebraska City and entered the Nebraska City National Bank, where he is assistant cashier.

Mrs. Wilson has been a resident of Nebraska City for forty-two years, and has been active in Red Cross and charity work for a good many years. She served as treasurer and chairman for the children's relief committee for six years, in the latter organization. An Episcopalian, she is a member of St. Mary's Church, and served as president of the guild for many years. Residence: Nebraska City.

Oscar Lee Wilson

Oscar Lee Wilson, physician and surgeon, was born at Ladoga, Indiana, February 10, 1857, and for the past 37 years has resided in Nebraska. His father, Oliver Badger Wilson, was born in Kentucky, descended from early Scotch-Irish settlers there, on November 19, 1820. He was a Christian minister and a general merchant, whose death occurred at Ladoga, on September 10, 1874. His wife, Elizabeth, was born in Kentucky, May 30, 1825, and died at North Salem, Indiana, March 18, 1907.

Upon his graduation from the Ladoga Academy, Dr. Wilson attended the Medical College of Indiana from which he received his degree. He was a post-graduate student at the New York Post Graduate Medical School. While in school he was president of the college medical society, and a member of Esculapian Society. Dr. Wilson has devoted his entire life to the practice of medicine, and is a member of the Nebraska State and Wabash Valley medical societies.

His marriage to Mary Alpha Balch was solemnized at Janesville, Illinois, April 3, 1884. Mrs. Wilson was born at Farmington, Illinois, April 11, 1958. Her family was

OSCAR LEE WILSON, M. D.

born in Ireland and came to the United States, settling at Annapolis. Dr. and Mrs. Wilson have four children, James Lee, born August 16, 1885, who married Bertha McCrary; Mary Miller, born March 1, 1887; Beatrice W., born November 3, 1888, who married Robert Stookey; George Balch, born May 17, 1891, who married Helen Hart.

James Lee was graduated from the University of Nebraska and from Rush Medical College, and served as an County Hospital at Chicago. He afterward studied one interne in Bellevue Hospital, New York, and in the Cook year at Vienna. He is a member of the National Surgical Organization, the Indiana State Medical Association, and is now located at South Bend, Indiana, where he has a large practice. He was a first lieutenant in the World War.

George, who is chief examiner of building, loan and trust companies of Nebraska, served in the World War with the rank of first lieutenant in the signal service. He is now located at Lincoln. Mary Miller, who is a graduate of Rushville High School, also attended the University of Nebraska and was graduated therefrom, took a post-graduate course in Columbia University, and studied German in Berlin. She is now teaching in the high school at Evanston, Illinois, where she has been for the past twelve years. She is a member of the Parent Teachers Association, and of the P. E. O.

Beatrice Wilson Stookey graduated from Rushville High School and from the University of Nebraska, made a tour of several European countries, and is now located in Lincoln. She devotes her time to educate her children and to teaching at the business college. She was a member of the Rushville Columbian Society and the P. E. O. and worked in the county treasurer's office before her marriage. She was also assistant assessor for several years.

Mrs. Wilson is of illustrious ancestry. Her great-grandfather, William Goodwin Balch was born in Cecil County, Maryland, in 1850, and later moved to Mechlenburg, North Carolina. He served in the Revolutionary War. His son, the Reverend Hezekiah Balch, was one of the signers of the Mechlenburg Declaration of Independence which was largely written by him. His name is carved with the other signers on a monument to independence in Charlotte, North Carolina. The Mechlenburg Declaration of Independence was written a year before the Jefferson version, and they are very similar.

Another of her ancestors, John Rodgers, was in the battle of Alamance. Clark's Records of North Carolina and the war department of Washington carry this record. He served in both the colonial and Revolutionary wars. Her great-grandfather, William Goodwin Balch, whose ancestors came from Sommersetville to Annapolis, married the daughter of John and Martha Rodgers, whose ancestors had come from Ulster, Ireland. Both her grandfathers were in the Revolutionary War, and one, at least, in the colonial wars. Another ancestor was George Beal Balch, an admiral, and another had the honor of preaching George Washington's funeral sermon.

In 1885, when Mrs. Wilson's family came to Rushville, she helped organize a woman's club for reading and study, which is the oldest continuous woman's club in the state. She served 12 years as its president, and was elected unanimously each year until she refused to accept the nomination for another term. She served eight consecutive years as critic and also as parliamentarian. She has always worked in the Presbyterian Church and in its Sunday School as superintendent or teacher.

During the late war Dr. Wilson was medical examiner for drafted men, and United States pension examiner for four years. He is a member of the Rushville Presbyterian Church, and a life member of the Red Cross. He has served on the town council and school board, is an elder in his church and is a member of the National Geographic Society. His hobby is reading. Dr. Wilson has always affiliated with the Republican party. Residence: Rushville. (Photograph on Page 1296).

Ralph P. Wilson

For the past 15 years Ralph P. Wilson has been active in public life. He was born at Lincoln, November 5, 1890, the son of Henry H. and Emma (Parks) Wilson. Upon his graduation from Lincoln High School in 1907, he entered the University of Nebraska, receiving his A. B. in 1911, and his LL. B. in 1913. His fraternities are Beta Theta Pi, and Phi Delta Phi.

Since his admission to the bar in 1913, Mr. Wilson has been active in the practice of law. In addition, he served as county judge of Lancaster County 1916-1917; assistant attorney general of Nebraska 1919; and member of the house of representatives 1923-1924. At the present time he is a member of the law firm of Burkett, Wilson, Brown, Wilson, and Van Kirk.

As a private in Company I, 355th Infantry, 89th Division, he participated in the St. Mihiel and Meuse-Argonne engagements. He now holds the rank of major in the Judge Advocate General Reserves. His professional and civic memberships include the Lancaster County and Nebraska State Bar Associations, the Chamber of Commerce, and the Lions Club. Mr. Wilson is a member of the Masons, the Lincoln University Club, and Eastridge Country Club.

On August 14, 1919, he was married to Calla W. Johnson at Holdrege, Nebraska, her birth place. They have one son, Richard, born March 20, 1921. Residence: Lincoln.

William Henry Wilson

William Henry Wilson, physician, was born in County Londonderry, Ireland, July 24, 1855, son of Samuel and Ann (Henry) Wilson. He received his medical education at Keokuk, Iowa, New York City and Chicago, and his degree of doctor of medicine from the College of Physicians and Surgeons of Chicago.

On May 28, 1885, he was married to Phoebe Campbell at Martinsburg, Iowa. They have one daughter, Anna, who married Stuart K. Clark on November 7, 1918, while he was a lieutenant in the Aviation Service. He is now geologist for the Continental Oil Company. Both are graduates of the University of Nebraska.

A Republican, Dr. Wilson represented Pawnee County in the legislative session of 1903 (speaker), 1905. He is the author of the Nebraska Vital Statistics Law and other public health laws. He served in the state senate in 1907, was state health inspector for eight years beginning in 1907; was appointed state epidemiologist in 1917, serving until 1921, was appointed chief of the state bureau of health in January, 1925, serving four years, and has been a licensed pharmacist since the pharmacy law was passed.

He is a Mason, a member of the American, Nebraska State and Lancaster County Medical Associations, and the Red Cross. Residence: Lincoln.

Lowry Charles Wimberly

Lowry Charles Wimberly was born at Plaquemine, Iberville Parish, Louisiana, December 25, 1890, the son of Charles Perry and Betty Beeman (Lowry) Wimberly, His father, who was a minister in the Methodist Episcopal and Presbyterian churches is now retired. He was born at Coushatta, Red River Parish, Louisiana, February 25, 1860, and his ancestors were pioneer Georgians who originally came from Ireland. Professor Wimberly's mother was a school teacher in Louisiana in the early days. She was born at Winsboro, Franklin Parish, Louisiana, January 31, 1859. Her ancestry is Scotch.

Mr. Wimberly attended the public schools of Nebraska at Wauneta, North Platte, Ogallala, St. Edward, and was a student at the Woodbine Normal and High School, at Woodbine, Iowa. He was graduated there in 1908. In 1916 he received his A. B. degree at the University of Nebraska; A. M., 1920; and Ph. D., 1925. He was also a student at Morningside College, Sioux City, Iowa in 1911, and Columbia University, New York, 1918. He is a member of Tau Kappa Epsilon; is vice president of the alumni board of control; is a member of Sigma Upsilon, national literary fraternity; and was awarded Phi Beta Kappa honors.

A resident of Nebraska 27 years, Mr. Wimberly has had varied experiences in the business and professional world. He has been a farm laborer, bookkeeper, hotel clerk, stenographer, teacher, and clergyman. He is now professor of English at the University of Nebraska. He is the author of *Folklore in English and Scottish Ballads,* published in 1928, and has been a contributor to academic journals, to the *American Mercury, Forum, Harper's, Folk Lore, Saturday Review of Literature,* and others. He is the editor of *Prairie Schooner,* a midwestern literary magazine.

He was united in marriage to Ida May Boynton at Osmond, Pierce County, Nebraska, February 14, 1910. Mrs. Wimberly, who was born at Missouri Valley, Harrison County, Iowa, August 14, 1890, is descended from John Boynton, of Wintringham, England, and from Edward Griswold, of Malvern, England. Four children were born to this union: Ruth, born October 7, 1913; Steve, born February 26, 1916; Martha, born December 14, 1920; Ben, born December 14, 1920.

Mr. Wimberly was an instructor in the S. A. T. C. at the University of Nebraska during the World War. He is a member of the American Association of University Professors, the Modern Language Association of America, and the American Folk-lore Society. He is a Mason, (Blue Lodge); is a member of the Cosmopolitan Club, and the Nebraskana Society. He is affiliated with the Second Presbyterian Church of Lincoln. He is a Democrat. His hobby is exploring Nebraska Indian sites. Residence: Lincoln.

Ben Orlo Winslow

Ben Orlo Winslow was born at Cook, Johnson County, Nebraska, October 22, 1893, the son of George and Flavia (Brook) Winslow. His father, who was born at Hiawatha, Kansas, of New England ancestors, is a telegraph operator. His mother was born at Helena, Nebraska, and died at Canadian, Texas in 1910; she was of Scotch, Irish, and Dutch descent.

Mr. Winslow was graduated from the Cook High School in 1909, and for a time was in the drug store business in Texas. Since 1916 has been associated with his brother in the Winslow Drug Store at Hebron, Nebraska. He is a member of the Christian Church. the Nebraskana Society, and the Democratic party.

His marriage to Helen Louise Gerlach occurred at Canadian, Texas, December 28, 1916. Mrs. Winslow, who was born at Canadian, was a teacher in the public schools prior to her marriage; her ancestry is German. They have a daughter, Eleanor Elizabeth, who was born at Hebron, November 29, 1918. Residence: Hebron.

Orien Bennette Winter

Orien Bennette Winter, editor and publisher, was born in Ellery, Illinois, on August 5, 1892, and for the past 18 years has resided in Nebraska.

His father, John Jay Winter, was born in Minerva, Kentucky, in 1843, and died at Maysville, Kentucky, in 1917. He served as a Civil War soldier for three years and six months with the Union Army, and was honorably discharged. He was a tobacco buyer and farmer of Holland Dutch ancestry. His wife, Isadora Scott, was born in Scottsville, Illinois, in 1856, and died at Fairfield, Illinois, July 3, 1903. She was well-educated, a music teacher, a school teacher and writer. Her father was a captain in the Union Army in the Civil War.

Upon the completion of his elementary education in the public schools of Wabash, Illinois, Mr. Winter attended the Fairfield, Illinois, High School.

He was a job printer and linotype operator in Iowa prior to enlisting in the Marines for service in the World War. After 14 months and ten days service, he was honorably discharged on August 20, 1919. At the present time Mr. Winter is the editor of the *Herald-Clipper* at Thedford, the *Blaine County Booster* at Duning, and the *Enterprise* at Anselmo.

On February 20, 1924, he was married to Estella Anna Bates at Thedford. Mrs. Winter, who was born in New Jersey, is a music teacher and is experienced in printing and proof-reading. They had two children, both of whom are deceased, John Jay, born April 3, 1925, died April 5, 1925; and Marilyn, born January 13, 1931, died January 25, 1931.

Mr. Winter is a Republican. He is a member of the American Legion Post No. 230 at Thedford. He is also a member of the Congregational Church, the National Editorial Association, the Nebraska Press Association, the Modern Woodmen and the Odd Fellows. He is secretary of the Thedford Community Club at the present time. He enjoys hiking, while his hobby is printing. Residence: Thedford.

John Waldo Wintersteen

John Waldo Wintersteen was born at Harrisonville, Ohio, February 1, 1864, and has resided in Nebraska for more than sixty years. He is the son of James Horace and Mahala (Dunlap) Wintersteen, the former a native of Geauga County, Ohio, born May 16, 1821. James Horace Wintersteen was a shoemaker, merchant and farmer of Holland Dutch descent, whose death occurred at Fremont, May 9, 1913.

Mahala Dunlap Wintersteen was born in Meigs County, Ohio, October 28, 1825, and died at Fremont, June 3, 1903. Mother of ten children, she was as active worker in the Methodist Church. Of Scotch ancestry, her father and brothers were preachers, gunsmiths and soldiers.

Educated in country school, Mr. Wintersteen later attended the high schools of Lincoln, and Wahoo, and was admitted to the bar at Fremont, in June, 1895. A Democrat, he was secretary of the first Bryan Club in Dodge County; was presidential elector in 1912, and was the elector chosen to take the vote for Woodrow Wilson to Washington. He served as judge of the county court of Dodge County for twenty years, and has engaged in no other business than the practice of law since 1895, except two years as editor of the *Fremont Herald.* He is the author of an address *Early Days In Saunders County.*

On June 3, 1893, he was married to Grace May Palmer at Arlington, Nebraska. Mrs. Wintersteen was born at Spirit Lake, Iowa, July 9, 1874, of Scotch, Irish and Dutch descent. They have one daughter, Ruth, born June 23, 1895. She has an M. A. degree from Columbia University, and is a college instructor.

Judge Wintersteen served two enlistments in the Nebraska National Guard with Company E, First Regiment, and participated in the Battle of Wounded Knee in 1890-91. During the late war he was a member of the draft board and active in loan drives. He is a member of the Dodge County Old Settlers' Association, and for nineteen years has served as secretary of the Dodge County Bar Association. He is an Elk, Mason, Eagle, Royal Highlander and Modern Woodman of America and a member of the Rotary Club. He is a Congregationalist. His favorite recreations are reading and working in his garden. Judge Wintersteen has resided in the same house for 49 years and has always voted in the second ward of the City of Fremont. Residence: Fremont. (Photograph in Album).

Otto Allen Wirsig

One of the leading educators in Nebraska is Otto Allen Wirsig, a lifetime resident of the state. He was born near Taylor, Nebraska, August 26, 1886, the son of Frank A. and Mary E. (Britton) Wirsig. His father, who was born in Germany, September 27, 1852, and died at Taylor, Nebraska, March 7, 1903, served as county clerk and country treasurer, and was a teacher, farmer and stockman for many years; he came to Nebraska from Germany in 1861 and was actively interested in civic and religious affairs in Loup County. His mother was born in Ohio, January 15, 1862, and died at Taylor, March 8, 1921. Her father, who was a native of Ohio, was a Civil War veteran.

Mr. Wirsig attended the village school at Taylor and in 1908 was graduated from the high school at Ord, Nebraska. He received the A. B. degree at the University of Nebraska in 1914, was awarded the A. M. degree at Columbia University in 1924, and has since studied at the University of Southern California and Stanford University. He was valedictorian of his high school class, received letters in athletics, and was prominent in debating at the University of Nebraska.

He taught at Taylor, 1908-10, was superintendent of schools at Gering, Nebraska, 1914-16, was superintendent of schools at Brock, Nebraska, 1916-18, held that position at West Point, 1918-21, and since 1921 has been superintendent of city schools at Kearney, Nebraska. He is a director of the Boy Scouts, is past vice president of the State Teachers Association of District No. 4 of which he was president in 1926, and holds membership in the National Education Association. He is a member of the Parent Teachers Association, the department of school superintendents of the National Educational Association, the Rotary Club, Masons, and Young Men's Christian Association. He holds membership in the Kearney Country Club and is interested in golfing, tennis, hiking and traveling. His hobby is reading.

Mr. Wirsig is a member of the First Presbyterian Church of Kearney. He is the author of articles published in the *American School Board Journal* and other educational publications. He was married to Beulah Juliet Marohn at Lead, South Dakota, August 16, 1915. Mrs. Wirsig, who was a teacher before her marriage, was born at Lead, May 12, 1891. She is descended from Captain Farnam, a soldier in the Revolution, and William McClure who gave his entire fortune to the Revoluntionary cause. At this time she is president of the Kearney Woman's Club.

To this marriage three children were born: Woodrow M., June 28, 1916; Lucille Edith, May 18, 1918; and Otto A., Jr., August 10, 1920. Residence: Kearney.

Glen Ward Wise

Glen Ward Wise, police judge in Lodgepole, and light and water commissioner, was born at Seward, Nebraska, July 14, 1902, son of Victor Ward and Georgie (Dunten) Wise.

His father was born May 20, 1875, at Seward, Nebraska, and is a retired farmer and auctioneer. His mother was born October 27, 1883, at Lincoln, Nebraska.

Mr. Wise attended public and high school and was graduated from the latter in 1920. While there he received three letters in basketball. He is married to Margaret Florence Emanuelson, their marriage having occurred at Sterling, Colorado. Mrs. Wise was born November 30, 1907, at Lodgepole, daughter of William and Margaret Emanuelson. She was a teacher in rural schools in Cheyenne County.

Mr. Wise is a Republican, a member of Lodgepole Methodist Episcopal Church, the Community Club, the Four-H Club, and the Parent Teachers Association. He enjoys almost all sports but is especially interested in golf and fishing. His hobby is electrical mechanics. At the present time he is manager of the Lodgepole municipal light plant. Residence: Lodgepole.

Emil Wolbach

Born at Grand Island, Nebraska, August 24, 1882, Emil Wolbach has been a resident of this state all his life and is today prominent as a leading banker in Hall County. His father, Samuel Nathaniel Wolbach, who was born at New York City, November 18, 1851, and died at Grand Island, September 9, 1931, was a pioneer business man and banker of Grand Island. He was the founder of the largest department store in Grand Island, which is now S. N. Wolbach Sons, also of the First National Bank established in 1880, and for many years was prominent in the political activities of the state.

Rose Stein Wolbach, mother of Emil Wolbach, was born at Chicago, Illinois, January 30, 1856, and died at Grand Island, June 20, 1917.

Mr. Wolbach received his education in the grade and high schools of Grand Island. He is at the present time president of the First National Bank of Grand Island, president of the National Bank at Doniphan, Nebraska, and a partner in the department store firm, S. N. Wolbach Sons of Grand Island. He is a member of the Chamber of Commerce, the Hall County Historical Society, the Nebraskana Society, and the Red Cross. His hobby is aviation and his favorite sport is hunting.

During the World War he served as second lieutenant and is now major in the Officers Reserve Corps, and holds membership in the American Legion. His fraternal organizations are the Elks, Eagles and Masons. Residence: Grand Island.

Clara Buckstaff Wolcott

Clara Buckstaff Wolcott lives at Lincoln, Nebraska, and for many years has been a leader in the social and civic life of that community. She was born at Lincoln, October 4, 1877, the daughter of John Allen and Sarah Emily (Montgomery) Buckstaff. Her father was born at St. Johns, New Brunswick, June 16, 1852, and was a prominent business man in the early days at Lincoln. He was, consecutively, in the brick, paper, harness, and stove manufacturing business there and developed Capitol Beach. His great grandfather was an English sea captain; his mother was a member of the Bartlett family and was descendant of Stephen Hopkins who was a signer of the Declaration of Independence.

Mrs. Wolcott's mother was born at Sparta, Wisconsin, July 14, 1857, and died at Lincoln, October 26, 1915; she was the daughter of General Milton Montgomery, who was descended from an old Virginia family, and Ellen (Turner) Montgomery. The latter's father was a physician and was one of the first graduates of the medical college of the University of Pennsylvania.

Mrs. Wolcott attended Lincoln High School; was a student at the University of Nebraska for three years. She is a member of the League of Women Voters; the American Association of University Women; the Thursday Morning Lecture Circle, and All Souls Unitarian Church. She is also a member of the Daughters of the American Revolution. For many years active in the Lincoln Woman's Club, during that time she organized the Woman's Exchange, and was chairman of the committee which secured the present building site of the Woman's Club at 14th and L streets in Lincoln. She is a Democrat.

She was united in marriage with Robert Henry Wolcott at Lincoln, June 2, 1897. Mr. Wolcott, who was born at Alton, Madison County, Illinois, October 11, 1868, is an educator. His English ancestors settled in New England in 1630. They have two children: Robert Allen, born June 23, 1900, who married Julia Minnie Morrill; and Agnes Emily, born January 24, 1905, who married Gerald Jackson Carpender. Mr. and Mrs. Allen Wolcott have two daughters, Jamie Morrill, aged five, and Joan Morrill aged four. Residence: Lincoln.

Robert Henry Wolcott

Robert Henry Wolcott, who has been connected with the University of Nebraska since 1894, was born at Alton, Madison County, Illinois, October 11, 1868. His father, Robert Nelson Wolcott, who was born at Attica, Wyoming County, New York, April 5, 1838, and died at Batavia, Kane County, Illinois, September 30, 1907, was a telegrapher and railroad man in early life, and later was an insurance man and furniture manufacturer. He was descended from Henry Wolcott who came to America from England in 1630; his mother was a member of the Wright family who were early New Englanders.

His mother, Agnes Almina (Swain) Wolcott, was born at Nunda, Livingston County, New York, December 10, 1836, and died at Mountain View, Santa Clara County, California, June 13, 1903. Before her marriage she was a music teacher and soloist in a Chicago church. Her father, James Swain, who was a contractor, helped to build the first railroad west of Chicago. Her grandfather, who was of Irish descent, was a ship owner at Boston, Massachusetts.

Dr. Wolcott was graduated from the Grand Rapids High School, Grand Rapids, Michigan, in 1885. He holds the following degrees: B. L., University of Michigan, 1890; B. S., 1892; A. M. University of Nebraska, 1896; and M. D., University of Michigan, 1893. He was a student at the Michigan Agricultural College, June, 1893, to February, 1894. He was president of his graduating class in medical college, and holds membership in the honorary scientific society of Sigma Xi, Phi Delta Theta, and the Phi Rho Sigma Medical fraternity.

As a member of the faculty of the University of Nebraska he has passed through the several ranks to professor and department head. He was dean of the college of medicine, 1910-14, and is now professor of zoology and chairman of the department. He is the author of numerous articles on zoology, and has contributed to several books; was co-author of *Birds of Nebraska*, 1905. He has been the editor of *Proceedings of The Nebraska Academy of Science*, and *Transactions of The American Microscopical Society;* also *Proceedings of Nebraska Ornithologists' Union*.

Dr. Wolcott is a member of the American Association of University Professors, the Lancaster County Medical Society, The Nebraskana Society, and the Laymen's Club. His scientific associations include: American Association for the Advancement of Science; American Society of Zoologists; American Microscopical Society; American Ornithologists' Union; American Ecological Society; Nebraska Academy of Science; and Nebraska Ornithologists' Union.

He is a member of the University Club at Lincoln, and is affiliated with the All Soul's Unitarian Church at Lincoln. He is a Blue Lodge and a 33rd degree Scottish Rite Mason, and a Noble of the Mystic Shrine.

On June 2, 1897, he was married to Clara Corrine Buckstaff, at Lincoln, Lancaster County, Nebraska. Mrs. Wolcott, whose parents are of English descent, was born at Lincoln, October 4, 1877. They have two children: Robert Allen, born June 23, 1900, who married Julia Minnie Morrill; and Agnes Emily, born January 24, 1905, who married Gerald Jackson Carpender. Residence: Lincoln.

Frank Henry Wolf

Frank Henry Wolf, prominent retired banker, was born at North Platte, Nebraska, May 28, 1878, son of Henry D. and Mary A. (Ericson) Wolf.

His father was born in Holstein, Germany, April 11, 1849, and came to America at the age of 19. He was a breeder of registered and grade Hereford cattle, and his death occurred at Chappell, Nebraska, in January, 1931. Mary, his wife, was born in Germany, June 18, 1857, and at the present resides at Chappell. She is much interested in social work.

Mr. Wolf attended the public schools of Chappell, and the Fremont Normal College. For 17 years thereafter, he was engaged in the mercantile business at Big Spring, Nebraska. For 18 years he was a banker, and was associated with the Farmers State Bank of Big

Spring; and was cashier of the Cheyenne County Bank and the First State Bank of Lodgepole. Later he was cashier of the Liberty State Bank of Sidney. He is a Republican.

On September 9, 1902, he was married to Winifred E. Gunn at Sidney. Mrs. Wolf was born at La Salle, Illinois, October 19, 1880, (see *Nebraskana*), and is an active religious worker of English descent. They have four children, Gladys F., born September 15, 1903, is a teacher of languages at Sidney, Nebraska, a graduate of the University of Nebraska. She took her post-graduate work at the University of Southern California. Bonita Margaret, born March 27, 1906, married Harold K. Bond; Clifford E., born July 14, 1909, attended the University of Nebraska two years; Eugene Milton Wolf, the youngest child, was born April 27, 1910.

Mr. Wolf is a collector of old coins and pre-historic remains. He is past master of Goldenrod Lodge No. 306 of the Masons at Lodgepole, holds membership in the Shrine at Omaha, Nebraska, and attends Lemon Memorial Methodist Church. Residence: Sidney.

Henry Elmer Wolf

Henry Elmer Wolf was born on a farm in Frontier County, Nebraska, September 23, 1989, the son of pioneer Nebraskans. His father, Nelson Hicks Wolf, who was born at Asheville, North Carolina, September 20, 1849, raised tobacco and cotton in his native state prior to coming to Nebraska, farmed successfully in Nebraska many years, retired to California, and died there in 1930. His mother, Mary Frances (Tripplett) Wolf, whose family originally lived in Kentucky, was born at Jacksonville, Illinois, April 15, 1854.

Mr. Wolf received his elementary education in country schools of Frontier and Red Willow Counties, Nebraska, attended business and vocational schools, and obtained his higher education through good reading. He has been engaged in the railroad business most of his life in the employ of the Burlington railroad, and at this time is station agent at Hyannis, Nebraska.

He is secretary of the Hyannis school board, is a member of the Hyannis Lions Club, and holds a membership in the Nebraskana Society. During the World War he was station agent at Antioch, Nebraska, while this war boom town suffered acutely from fast growing pains caused by discovery and development of potash, so vitally necessary in the manufacture of war munitions. He served there as secretary of the local Council of Defense and was secretary of Antioch school board in 1922-1923. He is interested in reading, music, writing, and education for the young, and his sports include tennis, baseball, basketball, football, boxing, swimming and hunting.

His marriage to Louise Catherine Brahler occurred at Alliance, Nebraska, April 15, 1912. Mrs. Wolf, who was born at Indianola, Nebraska, October 4, 1892, was a daughter of a captain of German cavalry in the Franco-Prussian War, 1870. Their children are: Bernard Nelson, born February 15, 1913; William Kenneth, November 25, 1914; and Josephine Mary, July 27, 1916.

Seven of his uncles served through the Civil War; four on his father's side in southern armies, and three on his mother's side in northern armies. His disclaims any especial assets or abilities, and hopes he is an average citizen duly appreciative of the kind tolerances of his many friends among representative Nebraskans. His residence is Hyannis. (Photograph in Album).

Winifred E. Wolf

Born at La Salle, Illinois, October 19, 1880, Winifred E. Wolf is the daughter of Aaron Elihu and Mary Ann (Williams) Gunn. Her father was born at La Salle on March 8, 1851, and died at Chappell, Nebraska, March 10, 1889. He was a pioneer farmer in both Illinois and Nebraska, and at the time of his death was a teacher in the public schools. His wife, Mary Ann, was born in London, England, February 18, 1854. Her father was a Baptist minister both in England and the United States.

She attended elementary school and had seven years religious education under the Methodist Episcopal Church. She later attended normal school and has 15 hours credit in logic, psychology, and philosophy from the University of Nebraska, where she completed an extension course. For eight years before her marriage she was a teacher in the public schools. She was ordained local preacher in the Methodist Episcopal Church and has taught modern teacher training and religious education in state meetings (1918-1926).

On September 16, 1902, she was married to Frank Wolf at Sidney. They have four children, Gladys, born September 15, 1903; Bonita, born March 27, 1906, who is married to Harold Bond; Clifford, born July 14, 1909; and Jack, born April 27, 1913. Gladys is a teacher of languages, a graduate of the University of Nebraska, and the University of Southern California. Clifford attended the University of Nebraska 1929-30. Bonita attended the University during 1927-28.

Mrs. Wolf is a Republican. She is the author of numerous poems printed in local newspapers in addition to articles on education. She has always been a student and is intensely interested in public speaking. She recently discussed at length Russia's Five Year Plan before the Sidney Woman's Club of which she is a member. From 1919 until 1923 she was a member of the Lodgepole School Board. She is a member of the Parent Teachers Association, the Red Cross, and the Delphian Society. Her hobbies are extension courses, writing, and verse. Residence: Sidney.

Lois Wolfe

Born at Frederick, Iowa, August 6, 1867, Lois Wolfe has been a resident of Antelope County, Nebraska, for the past 51 years, and has been actively interested in welfare and clubwork at Neligh for many years. Her father, Hugh Lowrie McGinitie, who was a professor of science, was born at Limestone, Pennsylvania, March 9, 1840, and died at Neligh, Nebraska, January 5, 1927; he was a direct descendant of the House of Stuarts and Mary, Queen of Scots. Her mother, Theresa (Moore) McGinitie, who was a distinguished clubwoman, was born at Ottumwa, Iowa, December 2, 1846. William Orr, an ancestor of Theresa McGinitie, came from Londonderry, Ireland, before the Revolution, and served throughout the war. Another ancestor was Jacob Hedrick who came to America from Holstein, Germany and also served in the Revolution.

Mrs. Wolfe received her elementary education in the public and normal schools of Minnesota, and later (1888-89) was a student at Oberlin College, Oberlin, Ohio. She was engaged in teaching school for ten years, and since her marriage has been identified with all of the civic and social affairs at Neligh. She is county chairman of the Red Cross, is chairman of the Nursing Service of Antelope County, and holds membership in the Neligh Woman's Club of which she was president in 1928 and 1929. She is affiliated with the Neligh Congregational Church, is past matron of the Eastern Star, and is a member of the P. E. O.

Since 1914 Mrs. Wolfe has been Camp Fire Guardian and has been active in Camp Fire affairs of every kind. The Neligh court is the oldest active court since the organization of the Camp Fire Girls in 1913. During the World War she assisted in war savings and loan drives and worked with Camp Fire girls in the preparation of hospital supplies. She is a member of the Republican party.

On March 9, 1898, she married Emanuel Wolfe at Omaha, Nebraska. Mr. Wolfe, who is a merchant, was born at New York City, July 26, 1858; his ancestors came to this country from Germany. Their children are,

Priscilla, born March 9, 1899, who teaches history in the high school at Neligh, Nebraska. She attended Oberlin College, Oberlin, Ohio, where she received her Bachelor of Arts degree in 1921. Wayne received his Bachelor of Arts degree from Oberlin College in 1926. He is part owner and manager of the Star Clothing Store at Norfolk, Nebraska. Residence: Neligh.

Herman H. Wolken

A leading Barneston merchant is Herman H. Wolken, born in Barneston, Nebraska, April 15, 1891, the son of Melcher E. Wolken, born in Eibenhausen, Ostfreisland, Germany, December 8, and Anna Sophia Schoenheim, born in Bremen, Germany, February 25, 1855.

Melcher E. Wolken came from Germany and located at Nebraska City, Nebraska, in 1871, worked in a mill there and moved to Gage County, Nebraska, in 1889, where he became a farmer. Mr. Wolken was affiliated with the Democratic party and died in Barneston, Nebraska, June 11, 1911. His wife came to this country in 1871 with her mother, brothers and sisters and located in Nebraska City, Nebraska. Her father was a carpenter and died in Germany shortly before the family came to America. She died in Barneston, Nebraska, March 31, 1928.

Herman Wolken received his education in the Luthern school in Barneston until 1905 and the next year went to the Barneston, Nebraska, public school. He married Ida Ruth Bridgmon, March 14, 1923 at St. Joseph, Missouri. She had been a clerk and school teacher. They adopted one child, Gwendolyn, February 8, 1930.

Mr. Wolken began work in a general store in 1914, was elected manager of the farmer's general store in Barneston, which he managed for ten years. He then started a general store for himself, April 12, 1930. He has been successful in business for many years.

A successful military career is also to Mr. Wolken's credit. On June 3, 1917 he enlisted in Company C of the Fifth Nebraska National Guards, was transferred to the Regular Army in July of 1917, where he joined Company C of the One Hundred Thirty-Fourth United States Infantry. He was promoted in May, 1918, to corporal of the machine gun squad and was a sharpshooter with a rifle and Colt automatic. His company was stationed at Deming, New Mexico, until September, 1918. On October 13, 1918 he sailed for France where he served for nine months, arriving home in July, 1919.

Mr. Wolken belongs to the Disabled American Veterans and the American Legion, and was elected commander of the Barneston Post, No. 356 when it was organized in 1929. He has always been a member of the Lutheran Church until 1931 when he and his wife and daughter joined the Presbyterian Church in Barneston. He is a member of the Barneston Commercial Club, the Nebraskana Society and was made a Master Mason in the Ancient Free and Accepted Mason's order in January, 1913.

Mr. Wolken played a cornet in the Barneston Orchestra in 1921, is an extensive reader, and enjoys hunting. Residence: Barneston.

George Fred Wolz

George F. Wolz, pioneer resident of Fremont, Nebraska, was born at Philadelphia, Pennsylvania, December 30, 1861, and for the past 36 years has taken a prominent part in the civic and welfare work in his community. His father, George Wolz, who was born in Germany and died at Philadelphia shortly after he was mustered out of the Union Army, was a meat and produce dealer; he enlisted in Company D, 29th New York Infantry, Volunteers, and served for two years during the Civil War; his ancestry was German. Christiana (Basler) Wolz, mother of George F. Wolz, was born in Germany, and died at Fremont, June 26, 1904.

Mr. Wolz attended the Fremont grade and high

schools. A resident of Nebraska for the past 63 years, he was in the wholesale and retail bakery business for many years, was an ice-cream and fruit dealer for a time, and managed his own restaurant for 36 consecutive years. For the past 21 years he has been connected with the Fremont Chamber of Commerce of which he is now secretary. He is treasurer of the Fremont Dyking District.

A Republican, he was mayor of Fremont, 1903-09-11-13 and in 1913 was elected state senator; he was a defeated candidate for the legislature the second term. He is past president of the Nebraska League of Municipalities. He is a member of the advisory board of the Salvation Army, is active in Boy Scout work, is second vice president of the Covered Wagon Area of the Boy Scouts, and is serving as chairman of the local committee of the latter organization.

Mr. Wolz was the first president of the Nebraska Good Roads Association, is a member of the Rotary Club, and is both national and state chairman of the good roads committee. He holds membership in the following: Travelers Protective Association; the Nebraskana Society; Nebraska State Historical Society; Young Men's Christian Association; and the First Congregational Church of Fremont. He is a 32nd degree Scottish Rite Mason, (Knight Templar and Shrine), and is a member of the Odd Fellows, Knights of Pythias, Elks, Modern Woodmen of America; Woodmen of the World; Eagles; Ancient Order of United Workmen; and the United Commercial Travelers. He is past staee commander of the Sons of Union Veterans.

Mr. Wolz is fond of hiking, camping, and all outdoor life; his hobbies are good roads, boys and girls scout work, and civic improvement. His marriage to Maggie L. Pfeiffer occurred at Fremont, February 15, 1883. Mrs. Wolz, whose parents were German born, was born in Philadelphia, June 9, 1861. Three children were born to this marriage: Laura, January 14, 1891, who married Ray V. Stocks; Ida, April 4, 1886, who married Glenn O. Pope; and Will, who died in infancy. Residence: Fremont.

Asa Butler Wood

Asa Butler Wood was born at Ashland, Iowa, August 26, 1865, the son of Clay and Jane Warren Wood. His father, who was born in Pike County, Ohio, in 1836, and died at Agency, Iowa, in 1879, was a seminary instructor, and served as county superintendent of schools in Wapello County, Iowa; he served in the Civil War. His mother, who was also a teacher, was born in Delaware County, Ohio, in 1840, and died at Gering, Nebraska, in 1897.

Mr. Wood was graduated from the high school at Agency in 1882. He has been editor and publisher of the *Gering Courier* since 1887, and is president of the Star-Herald Printing Company at Scottsbluff, Nebraska. A Republican, he has served as both state and national delegate to the party's conventions, acted as postmaster at Gering for 15 years, and was senator from the 33rd district for four terms.

He holds membership in the Nebraska Press Association, of which he was president at one time, is past president of the Nebraska Irrigation Association and the Gering Chamber of Commerce, and is affiliated with the Central Church of Christ. Mr. Wood is a director in the Nebraska Historical Society, is chairman of the Old Settlers Association, and is a director of the Oregon Trail Days Association. His fraternal organization include: York and Scottish rite bodies of the Masons; and Independent Order of the Odd Fellows. His social clubs are the Gering Golf Club and the Scotts Bluff Country Club.

During the late war he served as secretary of the Council of Defense, was chairman of the Liberty loan committee, and acted as chairman of the Four Minute Men. He holds membership in the Sons of Veterans.

On October 11, 1888, he was married to Maggie Clay-pol at Cozad, Nebraska. Mrs. Wood, who was a teacher before her marriage, was born at Malta Bend, Missouri, in 1867. She is a member of the Daughters of the American Revolution. Their children are: Marie, born in 1900, who married William B. Sands; Dorothy, born in 1905, who married James W. Ponder; Lynette, born in 1907, who married Horton R. Colbert; and Warren Claypool, born in 1908, who married Della Reeder. William Sands is a manufacturer at Casper, Wyoming; J. W. Ponder is bookkeeper for the Great Western Sugar Company at Gering; and H. R. Colbert is a clergyman in California. Warren C. is associate editor of the *Gering Courier*. Residence: Gering. (Photograph on Page 1303).

Ed S. Wood

Ed S. Wood, county treasurer of Garden County since 1919, was born at Sutton, Nebraska, July 15, 1880, son of Samuel and Gertrude Wood. His father was born in County Tyronne, Ireland, in May, 1840, and came to America in June, 1867. He was a Methodist minister, whose death occurred at Tecumseh, January 3, 1885. His wife, Gertrude, was born at Waynesburg, Ohio, March 2, 1845, and died at York, September 26, 1931. She attended Jennings Seminary at Aurora, Illinois.

Mr. Wood attended the public and high schools of York. On June 8, 1909, he was married to Nora May Beaver at Des Moines, Iowa. Mrs. Wood was born at Greenwood, Nebraska, September 3, 1881. They have one son, Orien, born March 17, 1910.

A Republican, Mr. Wood has always been active in party politics. He was a member of the Nebraska National Guard 1898 and 1899, is a member of the Red Cross, the Chamber of Commerce, the Parent Teachers Association, the Modern Woodmen of America, the Odd Fellows, the Masons and the Eastern Star. His club is the Oshkosh Country Club, his sports are trout fishing, golf and hunting, while his hobby is reading. Residence: Oshkosh.

Ross Wilfred Wood

A dentist at Burwell since his admission to practice in 1917, Ross Wilfred Wood was born at Coburg, Nebraska, November 6, 1894. He is the son of Eli Murtin and Gusta Louise (Kaohn) Wood, the former a baker, painter and decorator of English descent. Eli M. Wood was born at Arlington, Iowa, June 6, 1868. His wife, born in Michigan, October 10, 1874, is of German descent.

Dr. Wood attended West High School at Des Moines, and was graduated from Sargent High School in 1913. He received his degree of Doctor of Dental Surgery from Creighton Dental College in 1917, where he was treasurer of his class and was elected to Xi Psi Phi. In high school he was a letterman in football and baseball.

On June 17, 1920, he was united in marriage to Ethel Ann Hill at Macomb, Illinois. Mrs. Wood, who is of Irish descent, was born in Sangamon County, Illinois, September 2, 1895. There is one son, Robert Wayne, born November 6, 1921.

Dr. Wood has been a resident of Nebraska his entire lifetime, and is a member of the Masons, the Parent Teachers Association, the Red Cross, the Nebraskana Society and the Wranglers Club. His religious affiliation is with the First Christian Church at Burwell. During the World War he served at Fort Riley, Kansas with the M. O. T. C. and for some years has been a member of the American Legion. His favorite sports are golf and hunting. Residence: Burwell.

Wilbur Fisk Wood

Wilbur Fisk Wood was born at Danville, Illinois, March 22, 1857, the son of Harvey Colcord and Ann Jane (Ellis) Wood.

The father, born in Portsmouth, New Hampshire, March 25, 1817, died at Aurora, Nebraska, March 19, 1910.

ASA BUTLER WOOD

He was a teacher and minister of English descent. His wife, Ann, was born in South Woodstock, Vermont, December 1, 1818, and died in Aurora, March, 1895. Her ancestry was also English.

Mr. Wood attended public school in the preparatory department of Northwestern University, Chicago, Illinois, graduating from the latter in June, 1876.

On June 13, 1881, he was married to Anna Duddles at Fremont Township, Illinois. They celebrated their golden wedding anniversary at Haigler, Nebraska. Mrs. Wood was born at Libertyville, Illinois, January 31, 1860. She is an active member of the Methodist Church. There are two children, Olin O., born October 27, 1882, at Libertyville, Illinois; and Lyle L., born August 20, 1895, at Haigler, Nebraska. Olin attended the Lincoln Academy at Lincoln, Nebraska, and for two years studied at the Moody Institute at Chicago. He was ordained into the ministry of the Congregational Church in 1909. Lyle attended Wesleyan University of Nebraska, graduating in 1921. He also attended the Medical School of that institution where he received his degree of Doctor of Medicine in 1925.

Mr. Wood is a Republican. He served as clerk of Dundy County from 1898 until 1902 and represented Hitchcock and Dundy Counties in the House of Representatives from 1921 until 1925. He is a member of the Haigler Commercial Club, the Golden-rod Booster Club, and the Twin Valleys Commercial Club. He is a Mason, and a member of the Methodist Episcopal Church. His hobbies are mechanics and politics. Residence: Haigler. (Photograph in Album).

Ernest Franklin Woodard

Ernest Franklin Woodard, a farmer and county commissioner of Thayer County, was born at Edgar, Nebraska, May 21, 1887, son of Franklin David and Rebecca (Turner) Woodard. The father was born in Canandaigua, New York, August 5, 1849, and came to Nuckolls County in 1876, where he has been a continuous resident. At the present time he is a retired farmer. His family came from England in 1646 and founded the first flour mill in Boston. Rebecca Turner was born in Fremont, Ohio, November 13, 1849, and was a pioneer school teacher in Nebraska and in the west. She taught in Republic County, Kansas, in 1871. Her grandfather served in the war of 1812.

Mr. Woodard attended country school and Edgar High School, and for a time was a student at the University of Nebraska. He is interested in all athletics.

On December 4, 1917, he was married to Beulah Ethel Olmstead at Lincoln. Mrs. Woodard was born at Liberty, Nebraska, March 20, 1888. Her ancestors came to America from England in 1630, and assisted in the founding of Hartford, Connecticut. They were a family of doctors and lawyers. Mr. and Mrs. Woodard have one son, Francis Olmstead, born November 16, 1918, who attends Chester public schools.

Mr. Woodard is an independent Republican. He is a member of the First Methodist Episcopal Church, the Red Cross, the Masons and the Eastern Star, the Parent-teacher Association, and the Nebraskana Society. His favorite sport is football, while his hobbies are reading and farming. Mr. Woodard organized and was first president of the Farm Bureau in Thayer County. Residence: Chester.

James Madison Woodard, Sr.

James Madison Woodard was born at St. Joseph, Missouri, September 30, 1881, the son of Daniel Samuel Woodard and Sarah Ann Casteel Woodard. His father, who was born near Winchester, Virginia, November 26, 1848, and died at Aurora, Nebraska, November 27, 1923, was a physician and the owner of a drug store at Hamp-

ton, Nebraska. He served as representative in the state legislature for three terms, and was superintendent of the hospital for the insane at Hastings and Lincoln, Nebraska. His Scotch ancestors arrived in America in 1780.

His mother, who was a teacher, was born in Marion County, Ohio, January 16, 1850, and died at Salem, Massachusetts, in February, 1930. She was of Irish and Scotch descent.

Dr. Woodard was graduated from the Aurora High School, was a student at Fremont Normal College for a time, and in 1907 was awarded the Doctor of Medicine degree at the Unversity of Nebraska. Later he studied at Northwestern University and Harvard School of Medicine; he was a member of Delta Tau Delta and Phi Rho Sigma at the University of Nebraska.

He was a teacher for two years, served as clerk in the county treasurer's office, was manager of the Woodard Drug Company, and was manager of the Woodard-Thomas Drug Company. He has been engaged in the practice of medicine at Aurora since 1907, and was grand medical examiner of the Ancient Order of United Workmen for a number of years.

A Democrat, he served as mayor of Aurora three terms, was a member of the local school board for two terms, was county health officer, and acted as county physician. His fraternal organizations include: Elks, Masons and Shrine, and the Modern Woodmen of America. He is a member of the Hamilton County Medical Society, Nebraska State Medical Society, the American Medical Association, and American Association of Railway Surgeons.

During the World War he served as captain of the Medical Corps in the United States Army, was major in the Medical Corps of the Third United States Infantry. Residence: Aurora.

Sands Forman Woodbridge, Jr.

Born at Omaha, Nebraska, August 26, 1895, Sands Forman Woodbridge, Jr., is the son of Sands Forman and Frances Edgar (Wilson) Woodbridge, Sr. His father, who was born at Candor, Tioga County, New York, April 28, 1853, is now retired. A pioneer Nebraska newspaper man, he was first city editor of the Omaha World-Herald, and was its assistant managing editor until his retirement. He is of English descent, one of his forebears having been the Reverend John Woodbridge, a Puritan, who settled in Massachusetts in 1634. Another ancestor was Jahliel Woodbridge, who held the rank of colonel of militia in the American Revolutionary Army.

Frances Edgar (Wilson) Woodbridge was born at Pittsburgh, Pennsylvania, April 29, 1855. She is of Scotch-Irish ancestry, and was a member of the first class to be graduated from the Omaha High School. She was extremely active in the early cultural development of Omaha.

Educated in Central School at Omaha, Sands F. Woodbridge, Jr., was graduated in 1909, and in 1913, was graduated from Central High School. From 1916-23, he served as advertising manager of Wright and Wilhelmy Company, at Omaha, and in 1923 became manager of the Woodbridge Advertising Company of that city. Since 1924 he has been advertising manager of W. M. Dutton and Sons Company at Hastings.

On December 31, 1917, Mr. Woodbridge was united in marriage to Margaret Jane McFarlane, daughter of W. P. and Jane Ann (McRae) McFarlane, at Omaha. Her father, who is of Scotch descent was a pioneer in the Chicago and Northwestern Railroad. Mrs. Woodbridge was born at Omaha, April 10, 1896. There are two children, Martha Jane, born December 5, 1919, and Margaret Forman, born July 17, 1921.

An author of considerable note, Mr. Woodbridge has written numerous articles on advertising and other allied subjects published in *Hardware Age, Hardware Trade*

Nebraska Photo Company—Hastings

SANDS FORMAN WOODBRIDGE, Jr.

Journal, New York Ad-Club News and Western Advertising. During 1926-27 he served as secretary-treasurer of the Hastings Advertising Club, and while a corporal of infantry at Camp Dodge, Iowa (1918-19) was a feature writer on *The Camp Dodger.*

Mr. Woodbridge is a member of the Chamber of Commerce, the Red Cross, the Board of Education, the Parent-Teachers' Association and The Nebraskana Society. He is also a member of the American Legion and is affiliated with the First Presbyterian Church of Hastings. He is a 32nd degree Scottish Rite Mason, and was master of Mid-West Lodge No. 317, A. F. & A. M. in 1931. He enjoys tennis, and his hobby is writing. Residence: Hastings. (Photograph on Page 1305).

Rolland Cecil Woodruff

Rolland Cecil Woodruff, physician, was born at Gibbon, Nebraska, August 13, 1888, son of Charles E. and Mary (Smith) Woodruff.

Charles E. Woodruff was born in Chippewa County, Wisconsin, and died at White Salmon, Washington, in October, 1918. He was in the retail and lumber business at Gibbon and Grand Island, and when he moved to White Salmon, continued in the same business. He was descended from pre-Revolutionary settlers in Connecticut.

Mary Smith was born in New York State, August 15, 1862, descended from pre-Revolutionary settlers in New York and Pennsylvania.

Mr. Woodruff was graduated from public school at Grand Island and from Grand Island Academy in 1905. In 1909, he received the Bachelor of Science degree from Grand Island College, and during the years 1909 and 1911, attended Chicago University. In 1913, he was awarded his medical degree from Rush Medical College, where he was a member of Phi Chi.

He was admitted to practice in Chicago in 1913, and in Nebraska, at Grand Island in 1915. From that time until the present, he has been a member of the firm of Drs. McGrath and Woodruff. He is specializing in internal medicine and X-ray diagnosis. During the year 1914 and 1915, he was interne at Cook County Hospital, and in 1931, was made president of the staff of St. Francis Hospital at Grand Island.

He is a Republican, and a member of the board of education of Grand Island.

On February 23, 1914, he was married to Laura Pauline Sutherland at Pierre, South Dakota. Mrs. Woodruff was born at Pierre, March 17, 1886, of Scotch-Irish descent. They have four children, Mary C., born March 18, 1915; Ralph S., June 27, 1916; Bradley, January 22, 1919; and Martha, September 15, 1922.

For a number of years, Dr. Woodruff has been prominent in every activity, both civic and educational. He is a member of the Hall County Medical Association, of the Nebraska State Medical Association, the American Medical Association, and the Radiological Society of North America. He is a member with the First Baptist Church, is a member of the board of trustees of the local Young Men's Christian Association, and the board of trustees of Grand Island College and Sioux Falls College. He is a member of the Chamber of Commerce, the Rotary Club, and the Masons. His club is the University Club, while his hobby is agriculture. Residence: Grand Island.

Frank Henry Woods

Frank Henry Woods, president of the Lincoln Telephone and Telegraph Company, was born in Boone County, Illinois, February 1, 1868, son of Fred M. and Eliza (Eddy) Woods.

Fred M. Woods was born in Belvidere, Illinois, August 13, 1844, and died at La Pointe, Wisconsin, August 1, 1928. He was a livestock engineer and real estate operator. His wife, Eliza Eddy, was born in Elmira, New York, December 3, 1845, and is still living.

Mr. Woods is married to Nelle Cochrane (*see Nebraskana*). He is one of Lincoln's leading business men and executives, and is a Republican. His clubs are the Lincoln Country Club and the Eastridge Country Club. Residence: Lincoln.

Nelle Cochrane Woods

Nelle Cochrane Woods, who has been prominent in the civic and social life of Lincoln, for many years, was born at Bushnell, Illinois, December 1, 1870. Her father, Thomas Cochrane, who was a grain merchant, was born at Porterdown, County Armagh, Ireland, October 17, 1846, and died at Lincoln, December 23, 1914; his Scotch ancestors came to America in 1851. Her mother, Hannah (Hartman) Cochrane, was born at Blairstown, New Jersey, September 6, 1846, and died at Lincoln, in 1919.

Mrs. Woods was graduated from the University of Nebraska where she was a member of Delta Gamma. She is a member of the Red Cross; the University Young Women's Christian Association; the Fortnightly Club; the Lincoln Woman's Club; and the Association of University Women. She is a member of the Athletic Club of Chicago. She is affiliated with the First Plymouth Congregational Church of Lincoln, and holds membership in The Nebraskana Society.

She was married at Lincoln, October 1894, to Frank H. Woods. Three children were born to them: Henry Cochrane, born October 24, 1895, who married Elouise Bixby; Thomas Cochrane, born October 24, 1895, who married Sarah Ladd; and Frank H., born May 2, 1905. Thomas and Henry were graduated from Yale University in 1918; Thomas was graduated from Harvard Law School in 1921. Frank was graduated from Yale University in 1928. Residence: Lincoln.

Sarah Ladd Woods

Sarah Ladd Woods, daughter of Charles Frank and Minnie B. (Latta) Ladd, was born at Lincoln, Nebraska, May 8, 1895. Her father who was born at Whitehall, Illinois, is a dentist, descended from one of the original English settlers in Haverhill, Massachusetts, in 1637. He is also descended from James Avery, a soldier in the Colonial Wars who lived in Groton, Massachusetts. Minnie B. Latta was born at Rockbluff, Nebraska, and is active in art and cultural affairs, and in church work.

Upon the completion of her public school work, Mrs. Woods attended Lincoln High School, being graduated in 1913. In 1917 she received a B. A. degree from Wellesley College. While there she was made a membr of Phi Sigma, played on the golf and hockey teams, and was listed on the honor roll. During the spring of 1913, and during 1917-18 she attended the University of Nebraska, and was elected to membership in Kappa Alpha Theta.

Of her marriage to Thomas Woods there are four children: Thomas Cochrane, Jr., born May 4, 1920; Shirley Ladd, born March 25, 1923; Latta and Lamora, twin girls born October 2, 1928, both lost in infancy. Residence: Lincoln.

Thomas Cochrane Woods

Thomas Cochrane Woods, lawyer, was born at Lincoln, Nebraska, October 24, 1895, son of Frank Henry and Nelle (Cochrane) Woods. (*see Nebraskana*).

The father is president of the Lincoln Telephone and Telegraph Company, chairman of the Board of the Addressograph and Multigraph Corporation, president of the O'Gara Coal Company, director of the Harris Trust and Savings Bank of Chicago, and the president of the Lincoln Telephone Securities Company.

Mr. Woods attended elementary school of Lincoln, and the Lawrenceville Preparatory School of Lawrenceville, New Jersey, until 1914. He received his Bachelor of Arts degree with honor at Yale University in 1918, and received his Bachelor of Laws degree from Harvard Law School. He was a member of Beta Theta Pi at Yale.

At the present time Mr. Woods is a member of the firm of Woods, Woods and Aitken, vice-president of the Lincoln Telephone and Telegraph Company; vice president of the Lincoln Telephone Securities Company, director of the Associated Telephone and Telegraph Companies, the General Telephone and Electric Corporation, the National Telephone and Telegraph Corporation, the First National Bank and Trust Company of Lincoln, and the Securities Investment Corporation of Omaha.

On September 9, 1918, he was married to Sarah Avery Ladd at Lincoln. Mrs. Woods was born at Lincoln, May 8, 1895, descended from Captain James Avery of Massachusetts. They have two children, Thomas Junior, born May 4, 1920; and Shirley, born March 25, 1923.

In 1917 Mr. Woods was a cadet in the Reserve Officers Training Corps, held the rank of second lieutenant with the 101st Field Artillery, 51st Brigade, 26th Division in France, and was promoted to first lieutenant in September, 1918. He participated in the engagements of Bois Boule, Chateau Thierry, and St. Mihiel. He is a member of the American Legion.

Mr. Woods' religious affiliation is with the First Plymouth Congregational Church. He is a member of the American Bar Association, the Chamber of Commerce of Lincoln (life member), the University Club of Lincoln (director and former president), Lincoln Country Club (president and director), the Chicago Club (Chicago), the Harvard, Yale, Princeton Club (Chicago). From 1922 until 1923 he was treasurer of the Red Cross, and he is a member of the Nebraska Tubercular Association of which he was director and vice-president in 1929. Residence: Lincoln.

Isaac Lawrence Woodward

Isaac Lawrence Woodward, county clerk of Keith County, was born in Philadelphia, Pennsylvania, April 17, 1864, son of Jacob Heald and Katherine (Farnum) Woodward. His parents and grandparents were Quakers. His father died at Philadelphia in June, 1877. His mother died at Media, Pennsylvania, Delaware County, in 1870.

Mr. Woodward attended public school and completed an academic course at Swarthmore College, at Swarthmore, Pennsylvania. He came to Nebraska as a young man with a state wide reputation as a sign man. Finding little to do in this line of work in the west, he was employed by the circle outfit, Coe, Carter and Bratt, for a number of years and became their foreman of their home ranch, south of North Platte, and after his marriage came to Ogallala, Nebraska, where he has since resided. For 10 years he was foreman of the bridge and building department of the Union Pacific Railroad.

W. F. "Buffalo Bill" Cody was one of his best friends and assisted him greatly in his younger days. John Bratt and his family deserve credit for giving him his start in life as he was left an orphan at the age of 12 years.

A Democrat, Mr. Woodward has served as county clerk of Keith County, his first nomination was given him in 1922 by writing his name in on the ballot. He carried the election by the largest majority of any name on the ticket of the state, county and national election. The county is normally 75 per cent Republican.

On October 22, 1898, he was married to Ella Josephine Fisher at North Platte. She was born at Princeton, Illinois, and died at Los Angeles, California, in July, 1919. There are two children, Keith, who married Kate Zahm; and Keene, who married Dorothy Pease. Both of them are residents of Los Angeles, and employed by the city as master painters.

On October 21, 1921, Mr. Woodward was married to Carrie F. Mead, daughter of William Mead of Fremont who for 25 years was county supervisor of Dodge County.

Mr. Woodward has been a member of the Odd Fellows for the past 35 years, and is past grand of that organization. Residence: Ogallala.

James Eugene Woodward

One of Chester's leading merchants, James E. Woodward was born at Mason City, Iowa, December 2, 1879. His father, William Woodward, was born at Guelph, Ontario, Canada, in 1854, and died at Hubbell, Nebraska, March 30, 1891. His mother, Alice (Grimell) Woodward, was born in New York State in 1850, and died at Hubbell on September 15, 1930. Her home was for a time in Ohio, where she attended McKinley's funeral and President Harding's funeral.

On May 25, 1904, Mr. Woodward was married to Millie Luella Elwell at Chester. Mrs. Woodward was born in Washington County, Kansas, July 20, 1884, and before her marriage was a teacher. They have seven children, Gladys, born October 26, 1905, who is married to J. Barclay Gallion; Doris born December 28, 1906, who is married to Glenn Segrist; Hazel, born September 11, 1908, who is married to M. M. Palmer; Wilma, born April 9, 1910; Helen Mae, born February 3, 1915; Burns Eugene, born September 30, 1919; and Norma Lee, born September 8, 1927.

The very unusual triple wedding of Doris, Hazel and Gladys was solemnized on June 2, 1931. All three of the girls were graduated from Nebraska Wesleyan University, where they are members of Alpha Delta Omega. Wilma also graduated from Wesleyan and is an instructor in the commercial department of Oxford High School. She is also a member of Alpha Delta Omega.

A Republican, Mr. Woodward was appointed county commissioner of Thayer County in 1917, and was elected to the same position in 1919, serving six years in all. During the World War he took part in Red Cross Work and was a member of the Home Guards. He is a member of the Chester Community Club, the Modern Woodmen of America, the Odd Fellows, and the Masons. He is affiliated with the Methodist Episcopal Church at Chester, was a member of the school board from 1918 to 1930, serving as its president nine years. Residence: Chester.

Alfonso William Woodworth

Anfonso William Woodworth, automobile dealer, was born at Bolivar, Missouri, December 22, 1886, son of James H. and Sarah Alwilda (Baney) Woodworth. The father was born in West Moreland County, Ohio, December 13, 1856, and was a farmer until his death at La Crosse, Kansas, October 31, 1929. His ancestry was German and English. His wife, Sarah, was born in Champaign, Illinois, October 16, 1865, and died at Benkelman, October 10, 1926. She was a school teacher in her early years, and was of German and Scotch descent.

Mr. Woodworth attended public school at Benkelman, and in 1908 was graduated from Grand Island Business College, at Grand Island, Nebraska. From that time until 1910 he was employed as an abstracter for the Chase Abstract Company, and from 1910 until 1912 was a member of the firm of Hines and Woodworth, Law and Real Estate. Since that time he has been the owner of the Benkelman Motor Company, Ford Dealers.

On December 25, 1910, he was married to Minnie Mabel Bremer at Imperial. She was born there on February 2, 1890, of German ancestry. There are two children, Tyrus Henry, born July 31, 1912; and Carroll, born May 19, 1915.

Mr. Woodworth is a member of the Commercial Club, the Lions Club (chairman), the Elks, the Woodmen of the World, and the Knights of Pythias. He enjoys baseball and hunting, while his hobby is guns. Residence: Benkelman.

Harry H. Woolard

Harry H. Woolard, postmaster at McCook, was born at Stratton, Nebraska, November 14, 1887, son of James Newton and Elizabeth G. (Hegeman) Woolard. The father was born in Shelby County, Illinois, November 24, 1862, of Scotch-Irish ancestry. He is the owner of a newspaper and cigar store in McCook. The mother, born in Oconee, Illinois, October 31, 1869, is of early American descent.

Mr. Woolard attended grade school of Hastings, McCook, and Stratton, Nebraska. He entered the post-office as a clerk at McCook on February 7, 1908, and on December 1, 1914 was appointed assistant postmaster. He received his appointment as acting postmaster on April 1, 1921 and on October 7, 1921 was appointed postmaster. He is a Republican.

On June 18, 1912, he was married to Hazel May Cox at McCook. Mrs. Woolard was born at Benkelman, Nebraska, September 13, 1891, and is of American-Canadian descent.

For three years, Mr. Woolard was a member of the Nebraska National Guard. He is a Protestant, a member of the Red Cross, the Chamber of Commerce, the Elks, and the Knights of Pythias. His hobby is baseball. Residence: McCook.

John William Woollen

John William Woollen, who has been a farmer in Nebraska, for the past 43 years, 8 years in Kearney County, three in Clay County and 32 in Harlan and Phelps Counties, was born in Madison County, Indiana, November 25, 1874. His father, John Henry Woollen, a farmer, stockraiser, and grain dealer, was born at Fairmont, Indiana, in 1842, and died at Fairfield, Nebraska, in January, 1894. His mother, Mary (Thurston) Woollen, was born at Summitville, Indiana, in 1854, and died at Lamar, Colorado, in 1888.

Mr. Woollen has been a successful farmer near Wilcox for many years, is president of the consolidated school district in his community, and holds membership in the Wilcox Community Church. He is a member of the Modern Woodmen of America, holds membership in the Nebraskana Society, and is affiliated with the Democratic party. His hobby is reading.

His marriage to Lillie May Fifford was solemnized in the home in which she was born on the homestead obtained in 1875 by her father, in Harlan County, March 22, 1899. Mrs. Woollen was born at Wilcox, April 7, 1881. Their children are: Cloie, born June 18, 1900, who married William Jensen, February 6, 1924; Loren, born January 11, 1902, who married Adryce Lindstrom, April 28, 1929; Gifford, born August 13, 1903; William, born December 2, 1910; Melvin, born October 21, 1916; and Bernard, born April 8, 1919; Lamoyne, born March 4, 1921; twins, lois and Louisa, born July 16, 1923; Lamont, born May 30, 1925; and Nordon, born December 21, 1926. Residence: Wilcox.

Dean Amory Worcester

Dean Amory Worchester, professor of educational psychology at the University of Nebraska, has been active as school executive, author, and instructor for several years. He was born at Thedford, Vermont, March 21, 1889, the son of George Steele and Ida Eldora (Kinney) Worcester. His father, who was born at Thedford, September 24, 1849, has been a recognized leader in the agricultural and civic affairs of his community, and has been a farmer and preacher for many years. His English ancestors settled with the Salem Colony in 1628, and members of the family have been eminent men in various professions. His mother, whose English ancestry has been traced to Governor Bradford, 1620, was born at Plainfield, Vermont, September 15, 1849, and died at Thedford, November 18, 1927.

Professor Worcester was graduated from Thedford Academy in 1905, and received the A. B. degree, 1911, and the A. M. degree, 1921, at the University of Colorado. He was awarded the Ph. D. degree at Ohio State University, 1926. He was manager of the baseball team, played basketball, and also served as president of the Young Men's Christian Association in undergraduate years. He holds membership in Sigma Xi and Phi Delta Kappa. In 1913 and 1914 he was supervisor of schools in the Philippines, was principal of the high school at Cheyenne, Wyoming, 1918-20, was professor of psychology of the University of New Mexico, 1914-18, and was professor of psychology at the Kansas State Teachers College, 1920-24. He held the position of instructor in psychology at Ohio State University, 1924-26, the Ohio University, 1926-27, and since 1927 has been professor of educational psychology at the University of Nebraska.

Dr. Worcester is the author of *Research Adventures in University Teaching* (with Pressey and others); *An Introduction to Educational Measurements* (with Fenton); and about 20 articles published in scientific and educational journals. He is a member of the American Psychological Association, is a fellow in the American Association for the Advancement of Science, a member of the American Educational Research Association, and the National Society of College Teachers of Education. He is affiliated with the First Plymouth Congregational Church, and holds membership in the University Club at Lincoln. He is an independent Republican. During the World War he served as a four minute worker and was active in loan drives.

On May 29, 1917, he was married to Elsie Rohwer at Boulder, Colorado. Mrs. Worcester was born at Telluride, San Miguel County, Colorado, February 10, 1892. Before her marriage she was a teacher. Her father was born in Germany, while her mother is descended from English ancestors who settled in America before the Revolution. They have three children: Dean, born May 1, 1918; Evarts James, born July 8, 1927; and Catherine Elsie, born July 19, 1929. Residence: Lincoln.

Clarence C. Worden

Clarence Claude Worden, insurance executive, was born in Perkins County, Nebraska, May 8, 1887, son of Elbert C. and Amy (Weaverling) Worden. His father and mother reside at Kearney, Nebraska.

He attended the public schools of Auburn and Columbus, Nebraska, and was graduated from high school at Columbus in 1906. Since leaving school Mr. Worden has been continuously in the banking, farming and insurance business, owning land in Keith and Perkins Counties which is under his personal supervision. At the present time he is serving as the city clerk of Ogallala.

His marriage to Ethel Farrand was solemnized at Columbus, August 3, 1910. Mrs. Worden was born at Fremont, June 30, 1888. They have three children, Marguerite, born December 19, 1914; Irene, born March 19, 1917; and Dorothy Ann, born April 17, 1929.

For a number of years Mr. Worden has taken an active part in civic and religious activities. He is a member of the First Congregational Church of Ogallala and has been a member of its board of trustees and its treasurer for many years. He is a member of the Commercial Club, the Rotary Club (president May, 1929-1930), is a member of the Blue Lodge of the Masons No. 159 at Ogallala, Tangier Temple of Scottish Rite Masons, and the Shrine, both of Omaha, Nebraska. Residence: Ogallala.

Dorsey Horatio Worden

Dorsey Horatio Worden was born at Superior, Nebraska, April 1, 1887, the son of Amariah and Ella R.

(Nash) Worden. His father, who was born at Delhi, New York, March 17, 1847, and died at Joplin, Missouri, October 21, 1926, was a farmer and stockman who came to Nebraska in the covered era in 1870, and was one of the leaders in pioneer days; he served in the New York Infantry during the Civil War. His mother, who was born at Clinton, Wisconsin, in 1848, and died at Superior, January 16, 1903, was descended from Colonel James Barrett of Revolutionary fame. She was related to the Barrett family of Concord and was entitled to two coats of arms, one of which dates to King James of England. Through the maternal line her ancestry dated to Charlemagne.

Mr. Wooden was graduated from grade school at Superior in 1901 and attended the Superior High School. He has lived in Nebraska for the past 44 years, and is active in educational and civic affairs at Superior. He holds membership in the Parent Teachers Association, has been a director of the school board of the Valley Home School for nine years, and is a member of the Superior Music Association. He is a member of the Sons of Union Veterans, holds membership in the Christian Science Society of Superior, and is a member of the Nebraskana Society.

His marriage to Erma Josephine Goodhue occurred at Superior, March 27, 1914. Mrs. Worden, who is a music supervisor, was born at Superior, January 14, 1894. Her parents were Mae (Burdick) and Louis Peter Goodhue. Her mother was descended from Ichobod Horace Burdick of Michigan (1832), while her father was a member of the same family as Grace Goodhue Coolidge. They have two children: Genevieve, born September 12, 1917, who is a member of the Girls Glee Club and the Art Club in high school; and Louis, born April 15, 1923. Residence: Superior.

Frank Worden

Frank Worden was born in Nuckolls County, Nebraska, December 11, 1874, the son of Amariah and Ella (Nash) Worden. His father, who was a farmer, was born in Delaware County, New York, in 1847, and died at Joplin, Missouri, October 19, 1926; he served in the Civil War. His mother was born in Wisconsin in 1853, and died in Nuckolls County, January 19, 1907.

Mr. Worden was graduated from the Superior High School in 1894, and since that time has been engaged in farming in Nuckolls County. At this time he is serving as vice president of the Security State Bank of Superior.

On September 25, 1901, he was united in marriage with Edith Emily Griffin. Mrs. Worden was born in Superior, July 11, 1882. They have one daughter, Wilma Grace, born February 22, 1907, who is a teacher in the Junior College at Grand Island, Nebraska. She is a member of Phi Beta Kappa, and was awarded honors by Sigma Xi at the University of Nebraska where she majored in mathematics and was active in dramatics, debating, and music. Residence: Superior.

Herman William Wriedt

Born in Germany, December 16, 1876, Herman Wriedt has lived in Nebraska for thirty-two years. He is the son of William Wriedt and Augusta (Detlef) Wriedt.

Herman W. Wriedt was united in marriage with Meta Carolyn Utemark in Wakefield, Nebraska, on December 18, 1902. She was born in Mecklenberg, Schwerien, Germany. To this union six children were born. Frances, August 21, 1903, who is married to William A. Barrett; Lester, January 22, 1905, Hermee, November 28, 1907; Inez, December 25, 1908; Cecil, February 20, 1912; and Ursula, May 14, 1915. The children all have musical ability and have a home orchestra. They have gone to high school and three of them have college educations. Two of the girls teach school and two of the boys are successful farmers.

Mr. Wriedt is president of the local Farmers Union

and of the local telephone company. He is a Republican, a shareholder in the Farmers Union, and is a deacon of the St. Lukes Evangelical Lutheran Church at Emerson, Nebraska. Reading is his favorite recreation. Residence: Emerson.

Clay Wright

Clay Wright, county clerk of McPherson County since January 1, 1927, was born at Culbertson, Nebraska, October 19, 1892. He is the son of Alexander Marion and Myrtle Emily (Jacobs) Wright. His father, a farmer and ranchman, was born at Maryville, Missouri, November 24, 1860, of English and French descent. His wife, Myrtle, was born at Hamburg, Iowa, November 13, 1872. She was a school teacher.

Upon the completion of his elementary education in the public schools of Hayes County, Mr. Wright attended York Business College from which he was graduated in 1913. Thereafter for a number of years he was a store keeper and a farmer.

On August 1, 1919, he was married to Marie Stone at North Platte. Mrs. Wright was born at Superior, Nebraska, September 8, 1898. They have no children.

During the World War from November 23, 1917, until July 8, 1919, Mr. Wright served in the United States Army with the rank of sergeant. He is a member of the American Legion, and is a Protestant. For the past two years he has served as treasurer of the county Red Cross organization. His hobby is reading. Residence: Tryon.

William Elza Wright

Born at Esbon, Kansas, September 27, 1896, William Elza Wright is the son of Thomas Jackson and Myrtle Jeanette (Mayfield) Wright. Thomas Wright, who is a farmer, was born in Pontiac, Illinois, May 23, 1864; while his wife, Myrtle, was born in Nebraska, December 27, 1874.

Dr. Wright was graduated from Esbon High School in 1914, and received his B. Sc. from the University of Nebraska in 1923, and his M. D. in 1925. During the years 1919-20 and 1920-21 he attended the University of Kansas. Dr. Wright is a member of Phi Chi medical fraternity. He was admitted to practice in Nebraska July 22, 1925, and for two years practiced in Utah, returning here where he has since resided. He is a member of the Washington County, Nebraska State and American Medical Associations.

On May 29, 1925, he was united in marriage to Claire Leone Reich at Marysville, Kansas. Mrs. Wright was born in Beemer, Nebraska, October 27, 1905. There are two sons, twins, born August 12, 1927.

Dr. Wright is a Mason, a Republican and a member of the American Legion. During the World War he served as a private in the Medical Corps, assigned to laboratory service. Residence: Kennard.

Herman O. Wulff

Herman O. Wulff, merchant, was born in Washington County, Nebraska, January 22, 1874. He is the son of Claus Henry Wulff, and Kathrina Schneider. His father who was a farmer and a native of Holstein, Germany, died in Washington County on April 5, 1897.

His mother was born in Holstein, Germany, and died at Blair, Nebraska, February 3, 1897. Mr. Wulff was educated in the public schools of Washington County and has been a resident of Nebraska all his life. He is influential in his community and has been engaged in the grocery business at Benson for many years. Mr. Wulff is a Republican and a Mason and a life member of The Nebraskana Society.

On October 18, 1899, he was married to Myrtle Alice Blaco, at Blair. Mrs. Wulff was born in Washington County, November 19, 1876. They have one daughter, Dorothy, born October 28, 1909. She is a school teacher. Residence: Benson.

Nellie Frances Wullschleger

Nellie Frances Wullschleger, daughter of James Stephen and Emma (Nye) Armstrong, was born at Albion, Nebraska, January 20, 1893. James Stephen Armstrong was born at LaPorte, Indiana, November 27, 1851, and was admitted to the bar at LaPorte, in 1872. He was the son of John L. Armstrong, who married Susannah L. Beggs, at Springhill, Indiana, May 6, 1830.

James Stephen Armstrong married Emma Nye, who was born at Springville, Indiana, July 14, 1852. She was one of his pupils, while he taught at Springville, and when he came to Nebraska, she promised to join him. They were married at Omaha, and went directly to Boone County, making the trip by stage coach. James S. Armstrong was a brilliant lawyer, and served as county judge of Boone County several terms. From the time of his admission to the bar he practiced continuously, and was regarded highly by contemporary members of the legal profession. In the hours just prior to his death he transacted important business and dictated letters that had to be taken care of. He was honored some time before his death by a resolution of the Boone County bar, in which his enviable record as a lawyer was commended, and he was designated as the pioneer lawyer of the sixth judicial district. His death occurred at Leigh, Nebraska, March 17, 1931.

His wife, Emma Nye, was a true pioneer. She taught school ten years in the early days of Indiana, six of which were in one room in LaPorte. She was the daughter of Ira C. and Elizabeth Ann (Pardee) Nye. For many years she was a member of the Order of Eastern Star at Albion. Her death occurred there on March 21, 1916.

Nellie Frances Wullschleger attended Albion grade school, and after two years in the grade schools of Hubbard, Minnesota, was graduated from the 10th grade; returning to Albion, she was graduated from the 12th grade in 1913. During 1915-16 she attended Kearney State Normal School. She taught in the rural schools of Minnesota one year, in Boone County 2 years, and two years in Leigh.

On May 26, 1918, she was married to Otto Herman Wullschleger at Omaha. Mr. Wullschleger, who is a farmer, is the son of John and Anna (Gruetter) Wullschleger. His father was born at Wynau, Aarwangen, Bern, Switzerland, and came to New York, at the age of 10, remaining seven years. He came first to Columbus, and then to Colfax county, and located on the farm where Otto H. now resides. Anna Gruetter was born in Rugsau, Ambte, Drechselwald, Bern, Switzerland, May 31, 1866, and came to Columbus, at the age of 18. They were married at Columbus, May 8, 1888.

Mr. and Mrs. Wullschleger have two children, Ema Jane, born September 22, 1920, and John Robert, born April 8, 1927. *The Leigh World,* of July 25, 1930, states that Ema Jane is an unusually well developed child for her age. In 1930, Ema Jane drove a tractor on her father's farm a non-stop run of eight hours, in the excessive heat, an unusual undertaking even for a grown person.

Mrs. Wullschleger is a member of the Church of Christ at Albion, and of the Leigh Woman's Club. She is a member of Maple Leaf Camp of the Royal Neighbors and has served as oracle and county oracle. She was past noble grand of the Rebekah Lodge at Leigh. She is a member of the Daughters of the American Revolution and the Daughters of 1812. She is also a direct descendent of Robert De Vere, Earl of Oxford, who was one of the signers of the great Magna Charta in 1215.

Her real interest is aiding rural women to become leaders in their communities, and to make them better homemakers. She is county chairman of extension work in Colfax County, and has given much time to the organization of clubs and in visiting clubs. She has seventeen clubs at the present time and several new ones for next year. She is also vice president of the Federal Farm Bureau of Colfax County, and a member of the 4-H committee for the county. She is a member of the Congregational Missionary Society and Ladies Guild. Residence: Omaha. (Photograph in Album).

Benjamin Franklin Wyland

The Reverend Benjamin Franklin Wyland, celrgyman, was born at Harlan, Iowa, March 16, 1882, the son of John Frank and Molly Eliza (Griffith) Wyland. His father was born in Indiana on September 14, 1852 of Dutch descent. His mother was born of Welsh ancestry on October 17, 1856 and died on February 12, 1894. Her family came to America with William Penn.

Mr. Wyland was graduated from the Harlan High School in 1900, and received his Ph. B. from the University of Iowa in 1905. He was a member of the Iowa-Nebraska debate team, editor of the *Daily Iowan,* president of the Irving Society and adjutant of the University of Iowa Battalion during the time at the university. At Yale University, where he received his B. D. in 1908, he was a member of the track and cross country teams and of Alpha Chi Rho.

He was married to Ada D. Beach, January 14, 1909, whose ancestors were among the founders of the colony at New Haven, Connecticut. There are four children, Gordon, born 1909; Hugh, born 1911; Molly, born 1919 and Robert, born 1923.

From 1910 to 1918 Mr. Wyland was associate pastor of the Tompkins Avenue Church of New York City, the largest Congregational Church in the World, and during 1917 and 1918 was religious editor of the *New York Tribune.* During the years 1918 to 1925 he was pastor of the Union Congregational Church at Worcester, Massachusetts. During his residence there he received the following honors: appointed chairman of food commission, disbursing $300,000 worth of food, and chairman of employment committee for returning soldiers, handling 10,00 soldiers; member of motion picture censorship board; president of the Congregational Club; president of the Interdenominational Ministers; chairman of Law Enforcement Committee; manager city relief to influenza sufferers; in 1923 exchange preacher between Great Britain and America; made life member of Knights Templar; made grand chaplain of the Massachusetts Grand Council of Royal and Select Masters of the Masonic Order; member Kiwanis Club.

At the present time Mr. Wyland is pastor of the First Plymouth Congregational Church of Lincoln, and is a member of the Lancaster County and Lincoln Ministerial Associations, as well as the Red Cross, Chamber of Commerce, Nebraskana Society and Y. M. C. A. Residence: Lincoln.

Joy Whitney Wymore

Joy Whitney Wymore, superintendent of the Curtis Public Schools, was born at Freedom, Nebraska, April 16, 1909, son of Ira E. and Sophia Adeline (Whitney) Wymore.

The father, born at Liberty, Nebraska, December 4, 1873, was formerly a teacher and is now engaged in farming. The mother was born in Wisconsin, July 30, 1883, and in her youth was a teacher also.

Mr. Wymore attended rural school of District No. 33 in Frontier County and was graduated from high school in Curtis in April, 1927. From 1928-29 he attended the Hastings College and the summers of 1930 and 1931 and the fall of 1931 was a student at Kearney State Teachers College. He was a member of Pi Kappa Delta, debating fraternity of Hastings College. He is a member of the First Congregational Church, the Rotary Club and the Nebraska State Teachers Association. Residence: Curtis.

Guy Austin Wynegar

Guy A. Wynegar was born at Pecatonica, Illinois, March 5, 1883, the son of Joseph Allen Wynegar and Hester Ann (Hulse) Wynegar. His father was born at Pecatonica, February 2, 1853. He was a farmer and stock raiser; was of German parentage and came to Nebraska, after living in Virginia, Ohio and Illinois, early in the 1880's. He died in Ulysses, Nebraska, January 27, 1931. Hester Wynegar was born in Texas, December 12, 1857.

Mr. Wynegar received his education in the grade schools. He was united in marriage with Ruth Ellen Sloan, March 1, 1906, at Hendley, Furnace County, Nebraska. She was born in Jewell City, Jewell County, Kansas, January 5, 1887, and is successful in farm work and is a chicken breeder. Their only child was John Allen, born June 30, 1907, who died March 1, 1920.

Mr. Wynegar is a general farmer but is especially interested in stock raising. He is township director of the county fair board and is a member of The Nebraskana Society. Residence: Ulysses.

Arthur B. Yates

Arthur B. Yates, automobile dealer and banker, was born at Ashkum, Illinois, February 16, 1874, son of Wilson W. and Mary E. (Whitesides) Yates. His ancestry is Welsh and early American.

Mr. Yates attended public school, and engaged in the general mercantile business for a time. He is also engaged in the automobile business, is a banker, and has some farming interests. He attended school in his early days in a rural sod school house.

On August 19, 1900, he was married to Mary F. Connelly at North Platte, her birthplace. She was born March 3, 1881. There are two children, Donald, born February 22, 1902; and Thelma, born June 3, 1912.

Ordinarily a Republican, Mr. Yates is at the present time independent. He is interested in mechanics and baseball, and is a member of Brotherhood of Locomotive Engineers, the Brotherhood of American Yoemen and the Knights of Pythias. Residence: Sutherland.

Frank Charles Yates

Frank Charles Yates, lawyer and executive, was born at Omaha, April 9, 1887, the son of John Thomas and Mary Katherine (Schuey) Yates. John Thomas Yates was born at Mt. Savidge, Maryland, and is secretary of the Woodmen of the World and past potentate of Tangier Temple of the Shrine. He is descended from Welsh settlers in America in 1840, who served in the Civil War.

Mary Catherine Schuey was born at Kittanning, Pennsylvania, of German parentage. Until her death at Omaha, she was active in the Omaha Woman's Club.

Frank C. Yates attended the public schools of Omaha, and was graduated from the preparatory department of Creighton University in 1904. He received his A. B. from Creighton in 1908, and an LL. D. in 1911. A Republican, he was elected member of the Nebraska house of representatives in 1913. Beginning his professional career as member of the law firm of Mulfinger and Yates, he later formed a law partnership under the firm name of Yates and Lones. In addition to his law practice, he is president of the Business Collection and Adjustment Company and president of The Joseph Speigel Company.

During the World War he was officer in charge of flying cadets and commanding officer of the 115th, 116th, 117th and 327th Aero Squadron, at Kelley Field. In 1916 he was captain of Company D, 4th Nebraska Infantry, on the Mexican Border. He is a member of the American Legion and is secretary of the Omaha chapter of the Reserve Officers Association. He is a member of the Omaha and Nebraska State Bar Associations, the Elks and the Woodmen of the World. His sport is golf and his hobby is reading.

On December 31, 1922, he was married to Kathryn G. Sneed, at Omaha. Mrs. Yates was born in Omaha, August 24, 1888. They have one daughter, Margaret Mary, born December 22, 1923. Residence: Omaha.

Henry William Yates

Henry William Yates, banker, was born at Omaha, December 24, 1879, son of Henry Whitfield and Eliza Barr (Samuel) Yates. Henry Whitfield Yates was born at Leonardtown, Maryland, January 1, 1837, and was a banker in Omaha, many years. He died at Omaha, on January 9, 1915. His ancestry was traced to English settlers in Maryland, in 1637.

Eliza Samuel Yates was a native of Columbia, Maryland, born November 19, 1840. She died at Omaha, on June 13, 1929. She was a granddaughter of Hon. David Todd of Missouri, and a great granddaughter of General Levi Todd, of Kentucky.

Upon the completion of his elementary education, Henry William Yates was graduated from the Omaha High School in 1897. He received his A. B. from Harvard University in 1901, and returned to Omaha, to enter the banking business. Until 1923 he was cashier and director of the Nebraska National Bank of Omaha. He is now assistant trust officer of the United States National Bank, and secretary and director of the Nebraska National Company. He is a Republican.

Mr. Yates is active in civic and welfare work, and is treasurer and director of the Omaha Chapter of the Red Cross and a member of the Chamber of Commerce. He is a member also of the Sons of the American Revolution, the Nebraska State Historical Society and The Nebraskana Society. He attends Trinity Cathedral. His clubs are the University, the Omaha Club, the Omaha Country Club and the Harvard Club of New York.

He is fond of golf and enjoys trout fishing. His hobby is reading. Residence: Omaha.

John Thomas Yates

John Thomas Yates was born at Mount Savage, Maryland, June 2, 1856, the son of Thomas and Mary Yates. His father, who was a merchant, was born in England, in 1817, and died at Mount Savage, October, 1881; his ancestry was English and Welsh.

His mother was born at Doulas, Glennongshire, Wales, in 1817, and died at Mount Savage, April 15, 1887.

Mr. Yates attended high school at Mount Savage. He has lived at Omaha for 49 years. He is now secretary of the sovereign camp of the Woodmen of the World, and is editor of the *Woodmen News*. He is the author of *The Hunchback* and many other short stories. He is a member of the Modern Woodmen of America, the Young Men's Christian Association, and the Masons. He is affiliated with All Saint's Episcopal Church of Omaha. His social clubs are: Happy Hollow; County; and Omaha University Club.

His marriage to Katherine Mary Shuey was solemnized at Pittsburgh, Pennsylvania, October 3, 1880; she was born of German parentage in Pennsylvania, March 23, 1860, and died at Omaha, December 3, 1904. Five children were born to them: Mary Frances, born November, 1881, who married H. E. Weil; Ann, born October 16, 1884, who married George Guild; Effa, born May 12, 1885; Frank, born April 9, 1887; and John T., born January, 1899. On October 12, 1908, he married Mary Elizabeth Free at Omaha. Residence: Omaha.

John Walter Yeager

John W. Yeager was born at Richland, Indiana, March 1, 1891, the son of Wilhelm Carl and Laura Elizabeth (Barton) Yeager. His father, who is a farmer, was born at Stuttgart, Germany, November 26, 1863, and came to America in 1880. His mother, whose ancestry is Scotch-Irish and Pennsylvania Dutch, was born at Booneville, Indiana, February 2, 1870.

Mr. Yeager received his early education in the country school near Richland, and in 1910, was graduated from the Richland High School. He was awarded his LL. B. degree at the Chicago Kent College of Law, 1913, and is a member of Delta Theta Phi, an honorary member of Lambda Phi, and of Delta Tau Epsilon at Omaha University where he is now an instructor.

Engaged in the practice of law at Evansville, Indiana, from 1913 to 1914; he was a farmer for a year, 1915; and since 1915 has practiced law at Omaha. For the past ten years he has been chief deputy county attorney of Douglas County. In 1928 he was unsuccessful candidate for judge of the district court, on the Republican ticket. He is vice president of the H. C. Noll Company.

On June 28, 1922, he was married at Denver, Colorado, to Lena E. Deeg, who was born at Eureka, Spencer County, Indiana, April 16, 1891. Mrs. Yeager, whose ancestry is German, was formerly a school teacher. They have one son: John Walter, Jr., born October 15, 1926, and one daughter, born February 23, 1931.

Mr. Yeager served as a first class sergeant in the World War, and for 11 days fought in the battle of St. Mihiel. He is a member of the American Legion, serving as judge advocate of the Omaha Post Number 1; and the Veterans of the Foreign Wars. He holds membership in the Omaha Bar Association, the Nebraska State Bar Association, and the American Bar Association, and has been a member of the Red Cross for several years.

He is a Mason, Odd Fellow, Elk, and Knight of Pythias, a member of the Omaha Athletic Club and the Omaha Field Club. He is affiliated with the First Presbyterian Church of Omaha. He likes to golf; his hobby is reading. Residence: Omaha.

John Yoachim

John Yoachim, son of Peter Yoachim and Dorothy (Maul) Yoachim, was born at Alexandria, Thayer County, Nebraska, April 5, 1892. His father was born in Premacens, Germany, February 6, 1846 and died at Alexandria, January 12, 1922. His family came to America in the neighborhood of 1866 and engaged in farming. His mother was born at Talischwailer, Germany, March 16, 1849, of German parentage.

Mr. Yoachim attended the public schools, and on April 27, 1921, he was united in marriage with Josephine Domeier, at Fairbury. She was born at Ohiowa, Fillmore County, Nebraska, February 28, 1896, of German parentage. They have two children: LaVerle, born January 17, 1922 and Marla Jean, February 7, 1928.

In addition to his agricultural activities, John Yoachim is a director of the State Bank of Alexandria. He has lived in Nebraska all of his life and is an outstanding citizen.

During the War he was a private in the ambulance service for ten months. He is a member of the American Legion, the Ancient Free and Accepted Masons Lodge, and also the Nebraskana Society. Reading is his favorite recreation. Residence: Alexandria.

Byron Ellsworth Yoder

Byron E. Yoder was born at Topeka, La Grange County, Indiana, August 21, 1882. Jonathan D. Yoder, his father, was a farmer, born at Topeka, May 24, 1854, and who died there September 3, 1916. His ancestry was Pennsylvania German. His mother, Elizabeth (Wenger) Yoder, whose ancestors were Pennsylvania German, also was born at Topeka, May 11, 1859. She is still living.

Mr. Yoder was graduated from high school in 1901, and attended Valparaiso University in Indiana, 1902, and was graduated from the University of Nebraska with the A. B. degree in 1908. A member of the interstate debating team, 1907, he was president of his senior class in 1908. He was elected to Phi Beta Kappa and Delta Sigma Rho at the University of Nebraska, and is a member of Delta Upsilon.

A resident of Nebraska since 1904, Mr. Yoder has had a varied career in the business and educational world. He was cashier of the State Bank of Melbeta, at Melbeta, Ne-

braska, 1914-21; was superintendent of schools at Ravenna, Nebraska, 1909-11; and from 1922 to 1929 was vice president of the Rathbone Company. He is now a member of the firm of Kimball-Yoder, Realtors.

On January 29, 1913, he was married to Irene Holland, at Lincoln, Nebraska. Mrs. Yoder, whose ancestry is Irish, was born at Friend, on October 29, 1886, and died at Lincoln, July 4, 1929. Three children were born to them, two of whom are living: Mary, born April 21, 1916; Byron, born March 29, 1919; and Ruth, born November 21, 1914, who died March 1, 1915.

Mr. Yoder is captain in the Quartermaster Corps of the Nebraska National Guard. He is captain in the Officers Reserve and a member of the Reserve Association. He is a member of the Lincoln Chamber of Commerce, the Lions Club, the Lincoln Club, the Lincoln Board of Realtors, and the Young Men's Christian Association. He is a 32nd degree Mason, Scottish Rite, a member of the Westminster Presbyterian Church of Lincoln, and holds membership in the University Club. He is a Republican. Residence: Lincoln.

Florence E. Yoder

One of Nebraska's veteran teachers in the public schools of Dawson County is Florence E. Yoder, who was born at Normal, Illinois, the daughter of Soloman H. and Lydia (Esh) Yoder. Her father, who was a teacher and minister in the Mennonite Church in Missouri, for years, was born in Mifflin County, Pennsylvania, June 24, 1844, and died at Elm Creek, Nebraska, June 16, 1925. He moved to Custer County, Nebraska, in 1886, and was a member and chairman of the county board of supervisors there; in 1895 he settled in Dawson County, and in 1907, removed to Buffalo County. His ancestry was Swiss.

Her mother, who was born in Mifflin County, January 19, 1840, and died at Elm Creek, January 26, 1918, was a teacher, an active church worker, and a member of the Women's Christian Temperance Union. Her ancestors came to America, from Switzerland, in 1746.

Miss Yoder has two brothers: Dr. C. A. Yoder and H. A. Yoder, living at Elm Creek. Miss Yoder was graduated from the Lexington High School, Lexington, Nebraska, in 1891, and as a young woman began teaching in rural schools. To advance in her profession she felt that she must have a higher education, and this she attained in the interims between teaching. She is today one of the most experienced and widely known teachers in the state, having taught over 1650 pupils during her years of service in public school work.

She taught one year at Callaway, Nebraska, six years at Elm Creek, Nebraska, and 28 years at Lexington, where she is now principal and teacher in the East Ward School. She holds membership in the Nebraska State Teachers' Association, the National Educational Association, the Rebekah Lodge, P. E. O., and the Lexington Country Club. She has served as secretary, vice president, and president of the Lexington High School Alumni Association which she helped organize in 1891.

Miss Yoder was active in Red Cross affairs during the World War, and is now a member of the Legion Auxiliary at Lexington, through her brother's war service. Dr. Charles A. Yoder, her brother, served as captain in the United States Army, Ambulance Company Number 20, 6th Division, commanding officer of the American Expeditionary Forces in France.

She is a member of the Nebraskana Society and is affiliated with the Mennonite Church. Residence: Lexington. (Photograph in Album).

Edwin Clarence Yont

Born at Nebraska City, April 12, 1868, Edwin Clarence Yont has been active as a banker and public man for the past forty years. He is the son of John and Sophia

(Atkinson) Yont. His father, born at West Newton, Westmoreland County, Pennsylvania, April 25, 1838, was a farmer and landowner of German descent, who died at Lincoln, September 13, 1913. His mother was born in Pennsylvania, October 11, 1845, and died at Lincoln, August 13, 1923. She was of German and Scotch descent.

Edwin C. Yont attended the public schools and business college, and later took a correspondence course in law. Born a Republican, he has always retained his affiliation with that party, and has twice been an unsuccessful candidate for the state legislature.

His marriage to Sella Norton took place at Talmage, Nebraska, December 24, 1898. Mrs. Yont was born at Victoria, Illinois, February 22, 1875. Their two children are: Helen, born August 2, 1900, a graduate of the University of Nebraska, and now an instructor in the Omaha High School; Gladys, born August 24, 1902, married Wilber Maclay, and is the mother of two children.

Mr. Yont began his banking career as cashier of the Bank of Brock, of which he is president. He is also president of the Fremont Joint Stock Land Bank, a director in the Lincoln Trust Company, and member of the advisory committee of the Lincoln Joint Stock Land Bank.

Mr. Yont is a 33rd degree Mason. He is particularly active in the order, and is president of the Masonic-Eastern Star Home for Children, at Fremont, Nebraska, and a member of the board of relief of the Grand Lodge of Ancient Free and Accepted Masons of Nebraska.

During the World War he was quartermaster sergeant of the local home guard company; chairman of all local war activities, and county vice-chairman of the Nemaha County Red Cross. He was county chairman of another war activity also.

He is a member of the First Methodist Episcopal Church, and is active in church and educational affairs. He was for two years president and three years vice president of the school board section of the National Educational Association, is a member of the Brock Community Club, and chairman of the Nemaha County Association of Bankers.

His social clubs include the J. O. C. Club of Lincoln, and the Fifty-Fifty Club of Lincoln. Residence: Brock.

Lewis Ernest York

Lewis Ernest York, successful farmer in Gage County, Nebraska, was born at Pine Valley, Chautauqua County, New York, July 31, 1875, the son of Warren Yeomans and Florence Malvina (Aldrich) York. His father, who is the owner of a chain of cheese factories in New York and Nebraska, was born at Brookfield, Madison County, New York, April 5, 1849, of Quaker parentage; he was a teacher in the public schools of New York during his youth. Lewis York's grandfather moved from Stonningson, Connecticut, to Brookfield, New York, where he built the first frame house in the settlement.

Florence Malvina (Aldrich) York, mother of Lewis York, was born at Warsaw, Wyoming County, New York, September 18, 1851, of English parentage, and died at Lincoln, Lancaster County, Nebraska, June 13, 1930. She received a musical education and was always prominent in the world of music. Members of the Aldrich family fought in the Revolution, and Mason Aldrich, father of Florence (Aldrich) York, drove a stage coach from Buffalo to Hamburg in the days of the plank road.

Mr. York was graduated from the Liberty High School in 1895 and for the next eight years he was a professional baseball player. He has been engaged in farm work intermittently since 1883 when his parents settled on the Otoe Indian Reservation in Gage County. He is a director in the Barneston Telephone Company, has been president of the Parent Teachers Association for several years, and has been township assessor at Barneston for some time. He holds membership in the Nebraskana Society, is a Master Mason, and is an active worker in the

Presbyterian Church at Barneston. His hobby is mechanics while his favorite sports are hunting and fishing.

His marriage to Mary Eliza Prettyman was solemnized at Marysville, Kansas, December 31, 1902. Mrs. York, who was born at Chillicothe, Missouri, February 10, 1884, is the daughter of Scotch and English parents. Her father was born at Knox, Indiana, of English parentage, and her mother was born on a Scottish estate near Edenburgh.

To their marriage four children were born: Ernest Garold, born November 17, 1903, who is married to Alice Jane Wolfe; Frances Belle, born September 16, 1910; Cenith Fern, born February 18, 1916; and Ruth May, born March 9, 1918. They have taken Leighton Arthur Parker from a children's home to care for him, but have not as yet adopted him. Garold York operates one of his father's farms; he has three sons. Residence: Barneston.

Charles Edward Yost

Born at Geneva, Nebraska, September 9, 1883, Charles Edward Yost is the son of Charles Henry and Sarah Jane (Bruce) Yost. His father, born at Goshen, Ohio, August 11, 1848, traces his ancestry in America to 1755. He was a farmer, who came to Nebraska in its early days, and died at Pauline, Nebraska, June 9, 1925. His wife, who was born May 17, 1849, traced her ancestry to *Mayflower* passengers. She died at Hastings in 1922.

Charles Edward Yost attended Hastings public and high schools and was graduated from Hastings Business College in 1903. He is a dairy farmer at the present time, and is president of the Adams County Livestock Breeders Association. His hobby is Jersey cattle.

On February 6, 1907, he was united in marriage to Clara Mary Drollinger at Hastings. Mrs. Yost was born at Gardner, Illinois, July 10, 1887. There are three children, Jessie, born January 18, 1908, who married Harold Alton Lundeen; Edward M., born July 2, 1911; and Ida Elizabeth, born February 25, 1919. The family attends the First Methodist Church at Hastings. Residence: Hastings.

H. S. Yost

H. S. Yost, manager of the P. L. Yost Lumber Company, was born at Harvard, Nebraska, August 28, 1895, son of P. L. and Christena (Glantz) Yost. P. L. Yost was born of German parents, and for many years has operated extensively in the lumber business in Nebraska. His wife is also of German parentage.

Mr. Yost was graduated from Lincoln High School in 1915, and attended the University of Nebraska, where he was made a member of Phi Gamma Delta; and later attended the University of Grenoble at Grenoble, France. For several years he has been associated with his father in the lumber business, and is now the manager of the P. L. Yost Company.

On June 9, 1920, he was married to Lula Shade, at Hebron, Nebraska. Mrs. Yost, who was born at Hebron, April 29, 1894, is of English descent. Mr. and Mrs. Yost have two children, Theodor, born December 27, 1924, and Marcia, born April 14, 1927.

Mr. Yost is a Republican. He served with the American Expeditionary Forces in the World War, and is a member of the American Legion and Forty and Eight. He belongs to the Junior Chamber of Commerce at Lincoln, the Lions Club, the Masons and the Odd Fellows. His religious affiliation is with the Congregational Church. He is a Mason and is a member of the Havelock Library Commission. His sports are golf and outboard motoring. Residence: Havelock.

John G. Yost

A farmer in Clay County, Nebraska, for the past 54 years, John G. Yost was born at Norka, Russia, June 27, 1845, the son of Catherine (Bott) and Henry Yost.

His father, who was also a farmer, was born at Norka, Russia, of German parentage, March 10, 1800, and died there April 20, 1865. His mother was born at Norka, September 5, 1804, and died at Harvard, Nebraska, November 25, 1882.

Mr. Yost received his education in a parochial school in Norka from which he was graduated in 1860. He is affiliated with the Harvard Methodist Episcopal Church, holds membership in the Nebraskana Society, and is a member of the Republican party.

On February 16, 1869, he married Christina Schwindt at Norka. Mrs. Yost was born at Norka, August 15, 1848, and died at Harvard, May 1, 1928. Eight children were born to their marriage, seven of whom are living: Alice, February 21, 1870, who died November 28, 1889; Henry G. May 24, 1876, who married Christiana Hamburger; Lew S., January 6, 1879, who married Anna Amelia Yost; John J., February 24, 1881, who married Mary Loos; Maggie, July 20, 1883, who married Conrad D. Yost; Conrad J., September 6, 1885, who married Ida Scheidt; William J., October 7, 1887, who married Anna Brehm; and Adam, January 26, 1890, who married Pearl Pauley. Residence: Harvard.

Alfred William Young

The Revered Alfred William Young was born at Omaha, December 28, 1899, and has resided continuously in this state all his life. His father, Alfred Vincent Young, was born in Potawatamie County, Iowa, August 10, 1880, and died at Omaha, October 23, 1923. His mother, Louise (Eschele) Young, was born at Omaha, September 25, 1882.

Mr. Young was graduated from Park School at Omaha in 1914, was graduated from Central High School in 1918, and in 1922 received the A. B. degree at Midland College, Fremont, Nebraska. He was graduated from Western Theological Seminary at Fremont in 1924, served the Lutheran Church at Verdon, Nebraska for three years, and for the past five years has been pastor of Trinity Lutheran Church at Stamford, Nebraska.

His marriage to Mary Marguerite Hanson was solemnized at Omaha, June 17, 1924; she was born at Omaha, August 29, 1899. Of the four children born to this marriage, three are living: Florence, born February 6, 1927; Evelyn, born April 8, 1929; and Dorothy, born July 26, 1931. Alfred W., who was born April 24, 1925, died May 18, 1929.

Mr. Young has been a member of the English Synod of Nebraska since 1923, is president of the Stamford Commercial Club, and is serving as a member of the Stamford School Board. He holds membership in the Nebraskana Society and is chaplain of American Legion Post Number 233 at Stamford. His recreations are hiking and reading. Residence: Stamford.

Arthur Farley Young

Arthur Farley Young, lawyer and deputy county attorney of Lancaster County, was born at Lincoln, September 10, 1895, son of Arthur N. and Rosa (Farley) Young. His father who was born in Missouri, November 8, 1872, is a railroad engineer, descended from the Edwards of England. His wife, Rosa Farley, a native of Wisconsin, died at Lincoln, March 4, 1930. She was a member of the Women's Republican Club, and the Eastern Star, and a descendant of the Farley family of Scotland.

Farley Young attended the public and high schools of Lincoln, being graduated in 1916. He entered the University of Nebraska, and in 1922 was graduated with an LL. B. He is a member of the Iron Sphinx, Phi Delta Phi and Kappa Sigma, and during 1917 and 1920, won three letters in athletics.

Upon his admission to the bar he became engaged in active practice, and served the following terms as assistant deputy county attorney: 1924, 1925 and 1926. Dur-

ing 1927, 1928, 1929, 1930 and 1931, he has been deputy county attorney of Lancaster County. He is a Republican.

During the World War he served as radio electrician, third class in the wireless telephone branch of the United States Navy, stationed at Base 27, Plymouth, England. His military organizations include the American Legion, Forty and Eight and Veterans of Foreign Wars. He is a member of the Nebraska State and Lancaster County Bar Associations, the Chamber of Commerce, Lions Club and Hiram Club. He is a Scottish Rite Mason, and a member of the First Christian Church of Lincoln.

On December 25, 1920, he was united in marriage to Bertha Marie Appleman at Lincoln. Mrs. Young was born in Cass County, Nebraska, October 10, 1896, and was a teacher prior to her marriage.

Mr. Young enjoys football and golf, and is fond of hunting and fishing. Residence: Lincoln.

Benjamin Franklin Young

Benjamin Franklin Young was born at Craig, Nebraska, April 21, 1888, son of Andrew and Clementine Henrietta (Lillie) Young, Jr. Andrew Young was born at Columbus, Ohio, April 21, 1855, and in 1856 was brought by his parents to Nebraska. The Young family settled six miles northeast of Tekamah, where Andrew Young remained until July 21, 1881, when he removed to his own farm near Oakland. Andrew Young, Sr., was born May 7, 1828, at Undenheim, Hesse, Darmstadt, Germany and came to America in 1849. He married Edwinna Brand on June 25, 1854. Andrew Young, Jr., was a prominent and successful farmer, whose aggressive personality made him a figure in the life of his community. He was noted for his charitable contributions, but his devotion to his family was perhaps his greatest charm. He died at Craig, Nebraska, January 30, 1928.

Clementine Henrietta Lillie was born at Corning, Iowa, April 6, 1858, and is still living. She is the daughter of Julius Henry Lillie, born March 31, 1823, at Hanover, Germany. Her ancestor was Josephine Louise Henry, born at Nantes, France, May 21, 1837. Her parents were married in the year 1857 and settled in Tekamah, in June, 1862.

A true son of these pioneer parents, Benjamin Franklin Young has carried on the heritage bestowed upon him. He attended country school and the Wayne State Normal School, and afterward went to the Agricultural College at Lincoln. He has always engaged in farming, of which he has made a great success, and has been active in community and civic affairs.

He was married to Lydia Mabel Friis at Fremont, March 22, 1911. Mrs. Young, who was born at Allen, March 8, 1893, is Danish on her father's side; while her mothers was a native of Illinois. They have six children, Forrest, born September 24, 1912, who joined the United States Navy April 22, 1931, and is stationed at San Diego, California; Helen, born July 10, 1914; George, born February 4, 1916; Chris, born December 4, 1917; Florence, born August 18, 1919; and Betty Alice, born July 30, 1927.

Mr. Young is a Democrat, a member of the Masons, the Eastern Star and the Woodmen of America. He belongs to the Craig Methodist Episcopal Church, and is fond of fishing and traveling by auto. Residence: Craig.

David Andrew Young

One of Nebraska's oldest pioneers is David Andrew Young, who was born at Glenwood, Iowa, March 22, 1851. His parents, William and Rebecca (McBroom) Young were among the first pioneers to settle in this section of the country. Both were natives of Kentucky. William Young was born on August 25, 1808, and died at Plattsmouth, April 25, 1899. He was of Scotch descent. His wife was born September 11, 1817, and died at Plattsmouth, February 19, 1865. She was of Scotch-Irish descent.

David Andrew Young is a pioneer farmer, whose parents settled on a homestead in what is now Cass County, on March 5, 1855, and where he has lived continuously since. When the family first homesteaded they lived in a tent while their log house was being constructed. Part of this house is still in existence, and all of the seven children born to his marriage were born in it except the youngest. They were married May 12, 1850.

Mr. Young married Anna Mann, who was born in Decatur County, Iowa, September 3, 1857. She died at Plattsmouth January 24, 1932. Their marriage was solemnized at Plattsmouth, March 22, 1876. Their children are as follows: Ona Mae, born April 10, 1878, married Seeley L. Lawton, who was killed March 26, 1914; Lucelia, born March 29, 1880, was killed July 18, 1893; Albert A., born January 22, 1882, married Pauline Oldham; Lena Ethel, born February 23, 1885, married Edward O. Lyman; William Rex, born December 20, 1887, married Pearl Hinton; Clara Lee, born September 20, 1893, married Guy C. White.

William Rex is deputy sheriff of Cass County, and during the month of October, 1930, was shot three times in trying to arrest a man wanted for murder. He recovered, however.

Mr. Young is a Republican. For the past thirty-seven years he has held membership in the Modern Woodmen of America. For twenty-five years he served on the school board. He is also a member of the State Historical Society. His home is R. F. D. 1, Plattsmouth, Nebraska.

Harry Raymond Young

Harry Raymond Young, former county treasurer of Nemaha County, was born at Brock, Nebraska, April 2, 1894. He is the son of George Valandingham and Ella Lucille (Cain) Young. His father was a native of Ohio, born May 27, 1864. A farmer and stockman of German descent, he was active in the affairs of his community until his death at Brock on November 30, 1904. Ella L. Young, mother of Harry R. Young, was born in Illinois, April 21, 1872. She was a public school teacher of Scotch and English descent. Her father enlisted for service in the Civil War at the age of 16.

Harry R. Young received his education in the public schools at Brock and Peru, and was graduated from the Model High School at Peru in 1910. He attended Nebraska Wesleyan University in 1913.

In 1916 he served on the Mexican Border, with rank of corporal, sergeant and first sergeant. On August 15, 1917, he was commissioned Second Lieutenant at Fort Snelling, Minnesota, and the same year went overseas with the 167th Infantry, 42nd (Rainbow) Division. He participated in the Lorraine defensive, and the Champagne-Marne and Aisne-Marne offensives. He was wounded in action July 26, 1918, and was thereafter promoted to first lieutenant.

After his discharge from the army he entered the University of Nebraska for the years of 1921 and 1922. On June 2, 1920, he was united in marriage with Ruth Ethyl Reeve at Brock. Mrs. Young was born at Talmage, December 14, 1894, and is of Scotch and English descent. They have two children, Phyllis Jean, born July 10, 1921, and Harold Raymond, born June 6, 1927.

Mr. Young is a Democrat, and was elected treasurer of Nemaha County, serving from January 6, 1923, to December 1, 1928, when he resigned to go into the abstracting business. He is now president of the Nemaha County Abstract Company at Auburn.

He is a member of the Disabled Veterans of America, and the American Legion, of which he is post commander of Post No. 23 for 1930, and member of the Drum and Bugle Corps. Mr. Young is a member of the Auburn Chamber of Commerce and of The Nebraskana Society. He formerly held membership in the Kiwanis Club. He is a Mason. His chief recreation is reading. Residence: Auburn.

Homer C. Young

Homer Cleveland Young was born at Highmore, South Dakota, December 14, 1884, the son of Hiram Boucher and Sarah Jane (Adams) Young. His father, who was a farmer and grocer, was born at Somerset, Pennsylvania, December 14, 1854, and died at Mitchell, Nebraska, November 18, 1922; his ancestry was Pennsylvania Dutch. His mother was born at Dariton, Ohio, December 2, 1861, and died at Lincoln, June 17, 1920; she was of Scotch-Irish descent.

Mr. Young took a course in agriculture at Brookings, South Dakota, in 1905. He is now engaged in the grocery business in Lincoln. He is affiliated with the Bethany Church of Christ, is a member of the Modern Woodmen of America, and holds membership in The Nebraskana Society. He is interested in baseball.

He was married to Ina Grace Gingles at Lincoln, June 14, 1917. Mrs. Young was born at Douglas, Otoe County, Nebraska, January 21, 1888; before her marriage she was a teacher. They have two children: Marguerite M., born July 14, 1918; and Max E., born May 8, 1921. Politically, Mr. Young is an Independent. Residence: Lincoln.

James Tilton Young

James Tilton Young, osteopathic physician of Fremont, Nebraska, was born in Kansas City, Missouri, March 7, 1874. Since 1905 he has made his home in Nuckolls and Dodge Counties, Nebraska. His parents were John Young and Kisiah Caroline (Allen) Young. His father, being of Irish and English ancestry, came to America in 1869. He was a farmer most of his life, but moved to Kansas City, Missouri, and died there about two years later, February 14, 1902.

Kisiah Caroline Allen was born at Hightown, Virginia, April 25, 1847, and lived there during the Civil War and until 1871, when she came to Dallas County, Missouri. There she met John Young to whom she was married at Bolivar, Missouri, April 2, 1872. Originally of Pennsylvania Dutch ancestry, she is closely related to the prominent Rexrode families of Virginia, and later of Missouri and Texas. She now resides with her son, James Tilton Young.

Educated in the rural schools of Missouri, in the Northwestern Normal School at Stanberry, Missouri, and, for a short period, at the Warrensburg Teachers College. Dr. Young taught in the rural schools of Gentry and Jackson Counties for six years. He was principal of the Ruskin High School near Hickman Mills, Jackson County, Missouri, in 1902, this being the first consolidated rural high school in Missouri. He was for two years president of the Jackson County, Missouri, Teachers' Association. In 1905 he received the degree of Doctor of Osteopathy from the Still College of Osteopathy at Des Moines, Iowa. He is a member of Iota Tau Sigma, and was president of his graduating class of eighty-one members.

Dr. Young practiced at Superior, Nebraska, from 1905 to 1910, when he removed to Fremont, where he continues to practice. President of the Nebraska Osteopathic Association from 1906 to 1908, he has been a member of the Osteopathic Board of Examiners beginning in 1908, for approximately sixteen years. For more than twenty years he has had a prominent part in securing legislation in this state which has widened the scope and more fully established and defined the legal standing of osteopathy. He is one of approximately a half dozen pioneer osteopathic physicians in Nebraska who have been most influential in establishing the legal and professional phases of osteopathy in the state. He is a member of the American and the Nebraska Osteopathic Associations and has appeared on many professional programs.

He has been active in Red Cross work, having served as chairman or member of the local board for several years, and is now president of the Rotary Club. He is a member of the Fremont Congregational Church, the Modern Woodmen of America, the Knights of Pythias, of the Y. M. C. A., of the Parent-Teachers' Association and the Nebraskana Society. Fond of reading, especially economics, he is a disciple of Henry George's economic philosophy.

On June 22, 1911, he was married to Jeanette Ann Dysart, daughter of William and Margaret (Twinem) Dysart, at Superior. Mrs. Young, who was born in Ohio, March 28, 1877, was formerly music teacher and supervisor in the schools of Superior and Nelson. They have two children, Jean, born April 10, 1912, graduate of Fremont high school 1929; and John, born December 9, 1913, graduate of Fremont high school 1930.

A Democrat, Dr. Young has served as chairman of the Dodge County Democratic committee several years, and has been a delegate to state conventions at various times. Residence: Fremont. (Photograph in Album).

Shaw Ruskin Young

Shaw Ruskin Young, farmer and livestock feeder, was born at Grant, Virginia, November 10, 1896, and has resided in Nebraska for 16 years.

His father, Floyd Steven Young, was born in Grant, May 5, 1854, and is a farmer. The first Young ancestor came to the United States with General Braddock and was in the French and Indian wars. Laura Ann Warrick, wife of Floyd Steven Young, was born at Elk Creek, Virginia, January 21, 1860, and died at Trontdale, Virginia, May 13, 1931. She was a school teacher before her marriage and afterwards a religious leader. She was descended from the family of Lord Warwick of England.

Mr. Young attended public and high school, completing his education in 1914. Since then he has been a prominent livestock feeder and farmer, and at the present time is serving as president of the Scottsbluff County Farm Bureau, and is director of the Beet Growers Association.

On August 22, 1922, he was married to Mary Ellen Yensen at Denver. Mrs. Young was born at Lowel, Nebraska, November 16, 1900, and until her marriage was a teacher. Her father, W. H. Yensen has served two terms in the Nebraska legislature. Her mother is of pre-Revolutionary English ancestry. Mr. and Mrs. Young have three children, Harden, born February 13, 1926; Charlotte, born August 17, 1927; and Miriam, born August 21, 1928.

A Republican, Mr. Young was candidate for county commissioner in 1930, and was defeated by 60 votes. He received 1100, while his opponent received 1160.

During the late war, Mr. Young held the rank of sargeant in the Engineering Corps. He is a member of the American Legion, the Cedar Valley Union Church (superintendent of Sunday School), the Gering Chamber of Commerce, the Nebraskana Society, and the school board (treasurer). From 1919 until 1922 he was a member of the Melbata, Nebraska, Red Cross committee. Residence: Gering. (Photograph in Album).

Libbie Delia Youngren

Libbie Delia Youngren was born at Corfu, New York, May 13, 1862, the daughter of Henry M. and Millie (Brown) Rich. Her father, who was a teacher and music instructor in early life, was born at LeRoy, New York, October 6, 1835, and died at Fairbury, Nebraska, July 13, 1927; he was a farmer and served as legislator and state senator from the 4th District 1883-85; his ancestry was Scotch-Irish.

Her mother, who was a teacher, and was interested in botany and music, was born at Corfu, May 24, 1839, and died at Fairbury, July 4, 1921; her ancestors settled in America in 1694; members of the Brown family served in the Revolution and in the Civil Wars.

She was united in marriage to Granville Samuel Merritt at Fairbury, May 1, 1881. Mr. Merritt, a lawyer, was born at Marion, Ohio, January 6, 1853, and was directly descended from General Wesley Merritt. His death occurred at Denver, Colorado, January 4, 1920. To this marriage one son was born: Glenn, born December 15, 1883, who served two enlistments in the United States Navy as wireless operator and chief electrician during the World War. He is married ao Emma J. Soderquist.

Her marriage to Fred Youngren was solemnized at Des Moines, Iowa, May 31, 1905. Mr. Youngren came with his parents from Sweden. Mrs. Youngren came to Nebraska 52 years ago, and has been prominent in civic and religious affairs at Fairbury for many years. She is a member of the Methodist Episcopal Church at Fairbury, is affiliated with the Nebraskana Society, and holds membership in the Women's Christian Temperance Union. In the latter organization she served as president, 1921-22, and secretary, 1927, 1928, and 1929. Before her marriage Mrs. Youngren was a public school teacher for fifteen years. She is independent politically. Residence: Fairbury.

Elmer Ellsworth Youngs

A resident of Nebraska for the past 35 years, Elmer Ellsworth Youngs was born near Higginsville, Missouri, January 16, 1869, the son of Joseph Linsay, and Lavina (Stahl) Youngs. His father, who was a farmer, was born at Newark, New Jersey, December 4, 1835, and died at Higginsville, May 28, 1929; his English ancestors came to this country just before the Revolution. His mother, whose ancestry is Pennsylvania Dutch, was born near Youngston, Ohio, June 12, 1843, and died at Higginsville, November 26, 1919.

Mr. Youngs attended district school, was a student at La Fayette College during 1884 and 1885, and was graduated from the Spaulding Commercial College at Kansas City, Missouri, in January 29, 1889. He served as president of the local Grange Society for six years at Lexington, Nebraska, was president of the County Farm Bureau, 10 years, served as president of the State Bureau Federation for two years, and for over 21 years was president of the Lexington Shipping Association. He is a stockholder in the Overton National Bank, Overton, Nebraska, and was president of the Dawson County Fair Association from 1908 until 1916.

In 1907 Mr. Youngs began planting forest trees on his farm in Dawson County, Nebraska, and today has more than 40,000 on his home place. He is a member of the Lexington Kiwanis Club, the Lexington Chamber of Commerce, and the Nebraskana Society. He is especially interested in trees and breeding Hereford cattle. He took an active part in the "Increased Pork Production Campaign" in Custer, Dawson and Phelps counties during the late war.

On March 10, 1897, he married Nellie Tyree near Mayview, Missouri. Mrs. Youngs was born of Scotch and English parentage near Mayview, October 31, 1870. He is a Republican. Residence: Lexington.

David Yung

David Yung, pioneer banker of York County, Nebraska, was born at Kohlsville, Wisconsin, March 12, 1870, the son of John and Fredericka (Hofer) Yung. His father, who was a farmer, was born in Germany in 1934, and died at Cedar Bluffs, Nebraska, February 11, 1899. His mother was born in Germany in 1835, and died at Cedar Bluffs, July 18, 1912.

Mr. Yung attended a rural school near Kohlsville, and in 1888 was graduated from Fremont Business College. He served as cashier of the Gresham State Bank from 1915 to 1931, and at this time was elected president of that institution, and is secretary of the Gresham National Farm Loan Association.

He is a member of the Masons, Order of Eastern Star, Odd Fellows Lodge, and the Rebekahs. He is affiliated with the Gresham Presbyterian Church, and holds membership in the Nebraskana Society.

His marriage to Louise Lampert occurred at Cedar Bluffs, August 23, 1893. Mrs. Yung, who was a teacher in Nebraska public schools for ten years before her marriage, was born at Hortonville, Wisconsin, August 15, 1870. They have a daughter, Huldah, born July 31, 1899, who married Rev. William H. Hunter and resides at Omaha. Huldah is a graduate of Hastings College. Residence: Gresham.

Charles Fred Zabel

Charles F. Zabel, a Nebraska farmer for the past 65 years, was born at Doelitz, Germany, October 25, 1855, the son of Hanna Justina (Wahl) and Christian Frederick Zabel. His father, who was also a farmer, was born at Doelitz, February 10, 1826, and died at Western, Nebraska, December 25, 1897; having come to this country from Germany, in 1866. His wife, Hanna, was born at Doelitz, May 16, 1829, and died at Western, July, 1905.

Mr. Zabel attended the country schools of Saline County, and farmed in Saline County until 1920, when he retired and moved to Western, where he is a director in the Saline County Bank. He is a member of the First Methodist Church of Western, and has always taken an interest in the civic and religious affairs of his community. He is a life member of the Nebraskana Society.

On January 17, 1878, he was united in marriage to Pauline Augustine Witt at Swan Creek Church, Saline County, Nebraska. Mrs. Zabel, who is of German descent, was born in Green County, Wisconsin, December 20, 1857, and died at Western, November 8, 1930. Eight children were born to them, all of whom are living: Ferdinand, born December 18, 1879; Herman, born December 18, 1879; Julia, born November 11, 1881; Lena, born June 13, 1883; John, born March 29, 1885; Sophia, born September 17, 1889; Esther, born April 30, 1894; and Hildreth, born October 28, 1899. Residence: Western. (Photograph on Page 1318).

Louise Shadduck Zabriskie

Louise Shadduck Zabriske, organist, violinist and teacher, was born at Cattaraugus, New York, January 14, 1884, daughter of Joseph and Alice (Bronson) Zabriskie. Her father was born at Erie, Pennsylvania, December 10, 1854, and died at Omaha, December 8, 1930. He was a teacher of the violin. The mother, a teacher of piano, was born at Hamlet, New York, October 15, 1860.

Upon the completion of her public school education in 1904, she studied with Hans Albert, Ben Stanley, J. H. Simms and Robert Cuscaden, and in Berlin studied under Arthur Hartmann (violin) and Edward Boehm (piano). She had organ study in New York with Clifford Demorest, Warren Hedden and Clarence Dickinson.

When she returned from Europe in 1907, she became a teacher of violin, piano and organ in Omaha. At the present time she is organist and director of music of the First Presbyterian Church. She is past dean of the Nebraska chapter of the American Guild of Organists, past president of the Omaha Clef Club and the Fortnightly Musical Club.

On December 6, 1908, she was married to Edgar Rudolf Zabriski, at Omaha. There are two children living, one deceased: Bettie, born July 19, 1910, who is a successful cellist; Helen, born April 4, 1912; and George, born March 7, 1916, who died April 16, 1916. Residence: Omaha.

William T. Zahradnicek

Born at Bison, Oklahoma, November 17, 1903, William T. Zahradnicek is the son of Mike L. and Mary (Semrad) Zahradnicek. His father, who was a landowner and farmer in Nebraska in the early days, was born in Austria Hungary, February 5, 1872, and is living today at Atkinson, Nebraska; his fathers grandfather was an ammunition and supply dispenser in the German Army during the Franco-Prussion War. His mother, whose father was a soldier in the German Army, was born in Austria Hungary, September 15, 1886.

Mr. Zahradnicek was graduated from Atkinson High School in 1922 as valedictorian of the class, and was graduated from Wayne State Teachers College in 1929, having attended the University of Nebraska for a year. He taught a rural school, 1922-23, was grade school teacher at Crofton, Nebraska, for two years, served as English instructor in the high school at Coleridge, Nebraska, for five years, and is now superintendent of public schools at Johnstown, Nebraska.

He has been unusually successful as coach of various basketball teams, one of them winning a district championship. Mr. Zahradnicek is a member of the Nebraska State Teachers Association, the North Central Nebraska School Men's Association, Red Cross, and the Nebraskana Society. He is a Mason, is affiliated with the Methodist Episcopal Church of Atkinson, and is president of the Parent Teachers Association at Johnstown. He is interested in all school athletics and sports.

On May 15, 1926, he was married to Ita Jay Watkins at Lincoln, Nebraska. Mrs. Zahradnicek, who was born at Plainview, Nebraska, October 20, 1903, is the daughter of John Watkins who served as corporal of Company G in the United States Army during the Spanish-American War. They have one son, William Bruce, born November 17, 1931. Residence: Johnstown. (Photograph in Album).

Rudolf Zajicek

Rudolph Zajicek was born at Medovim, Ojezde, Proske, Czechoslovakia, December 30, 1859, the son of Anton and Josefa (Veverkova) Zajicek. His father who was born at Medovim in 1828, died at Wilber, Nebraska, February 1, 1914. His mother was born at Medovim, December 4, 1838, and died at Wilber, May 4, 1920.

Mr. Zajicek has lived in Nebraska for the past 62 years; he is a retired farmer. He is a member of Z C B J and the Modern Woodmen of America. He is a Roman Catholic. During the World War he was chairman of loan drives for Saline County. He is a Republican.

He married Josefa Svoboda at Tecumseh, Nebraska, January 5, 1889. Mrs. Zajicek was born at Kraj, Proske, Czechoslovakia, October 20, 1864. When he was married he built a sod house in which he lived for 12 years and their four children were born there. Their children are: Mary, born October 10, 1884, who married Phillip Wenzel; Matilde, born October 10, 1886, who married Stephen Freouf; and Anna, born August 7, 1891, who married Anton Kostecka. All of them are farmers. Residence: Wilber.

Nicholas Edward Zehr

Nicholas Edward Zehr, son of Christian and Katherine (Roth) Zehr, was born at Pontiac, Illinois, March 30, 1871. His father was born in Alsace-Lorraine, France, March 6, 1835, and came to America at the age of twenty. He was a farmer, whose death occurred at Seward, Nebraska, November 14, 1907. His wife, Katherine, was born at Hamilton, Ohio, October 6, 1841, and died at Meadows, Illinois, June 1, 1910.

Mr. Zehr attended public school and on November 9, 1893, was married to Nancy Edna Roth at Chappell.

CHARLES FRED ZABEL

Mrs. Zehr was born at Archibald, Ohio, October 30, 1874. Her father was a Canadian. Mr. and Mrs. Zehr have three children, William, born June 29, 1894 (see *Nebraskana*); Edna, born February 3, 1898; and Nicholas, born September 14, 1903. William is mayor of Chappell at the present time, while Nicholas is assistant postmaster.

Mr. Zehr is a Democrat. He has resided in Nebraska for the past 50 years, is affiliated with the Methodist Church, is a member of the Red Cross, the Chamber of Commerce, the Modern Woodmen of America, and the Nebraskana Society. His hobby is willow weaving. Residence: Chappell. (Photograph in Album).

William Emanuel Zehr

William Emanuel Zehr, tractor and implement dealer, was born at Chappell, Nebraska, June 29, 1894, son of Nicholas Edward (see *Nebraskana*) and Nancy Edna (Roth) Zehr.

The father was born at Pontiac, Illinois, March 30, 1871, and the mother at Archibald, Ohio, October 30, 1874. She is president of the American Legion Auxiliary Unit of Chappell.

Mr. Zehr attended public school and since that time has been engaged in business. He is a Democrat, and at the present time is serving a mayor of Chappell, just completing his second term. During the late war he was corporal of ordanance detachment, 338th Field Artillery, 88th Division. He is a member of the American Legion, the Methodist Church, the Red Cross, the Chamber of Commerce, the Rotary Club, the Modern Woodmen of America, the Odd Fellows, the Masons, and the Nebraskana Society.

On August 18, 1921, he was married to Meta Dorothy Sick at Sterling, Colorado. Mrs. Zehr was born at Omaha, December 30, 1897, and was a teacher in the public schools at Chappell before her marriage. Mrs. Zehr is post president of the American Legion Auxiliary Unit at Chappell. Residence: Chappell. (Photograph in Album).

Frank Connell Zehrung

Frank C. Zehrung has lived in Nebraska for 60 years, and has been prominent in business and civic affairs during much of that time. He was born at Cedar Rapids, Iowa, October 7, 1858, the son of John and Mary E. (Connell) Zehrung. His father, a druggist, was born in Marion County, Ohio, February 15, 1831, and died at Los Angeles, California, March 11, 1908. His mother, who was of Scotch descent, was born at Greenville, Connecticut, October 7, 1835, and died at Lincoln, on September 13, 1893.

Mr. Zehrung attended the Lincoln High School and for two years was a student at the University of Nebraska. He has been a druggist, and a theatrical manager, and was president of the Western League. He is now president of the Zehrung Company, an outdoor advertising company.

A Republican, Mr. Zehrung has been prominent in politics in Lincoln and throughout the state for many years. He was elected mayor of Lincoln five times, and was defeated for this office twice.

He married Jessie Laura Voris at Lincoln, March 15, 1911; she was born at Geneva, Nebraska, July 11, 1881. He served as manager of the Liberty Theatre at Camp Stuart, Virginia, is a member of the Outdoor Advertising Association of America, the Advertising Club, the Lincoln Chamber of Commerce, and the Lincoln Rotary Club. He holds membership in St. Paul's Methodist Church of Lincoln and the Young Men's Christian Association, is a member of the University Club, the Country Club; and Eastridge Country Club. He is a member of the Elks. Residence: Lincoln.

Isidor Ziegler

Isidor Ziegler, lawyer, was born at St. Louis, Missouri, April 30, 1876. His parents, Jacob and Sally (Friedman) Ziegler were natives of Germany, who came to America in 1844.

Mr. Ziegler attended the public schools of Huntington, West Virginia, and the University of Preparatory School at Petersburg, West Virginia; was graduated from Huntington High School and attended Harvard University and the University of Michigan Law School, from which latter he received his LL. B. in 1899. For the past thirty years he has been engaged in the practice of law in Omaha, and is one of the city's outstanding lawyers.

He was married to Pearl Kiper at Chicago, in 1914. There are two children, Louise J., born January 6, 1912, and Julian, born May 30, 1921.

Mr. Ziegler is a Republican, a member of the Chamber of Commerce, and of the Elks and Masons. He is a member of Temple Israel of Omaha, the American Bar Association, the Nebraska State Bar Association and the Omaha-Douglas County Bar Association. His clubs are the Omaha Athletic and Highland Country Clubs. Residence: Omaha.

Elmo Murry Zike

Elmo Murray Zike, who has been engaged in the real estate business at Edison, Nebraska, for the past 20 years, was born at Shueville, Iowa, August 13, 1870, and since 1885 has been a resident of this state, locating at Edison arriving from Iowa in a covered wagon. His father, Samuel Pinkerton Zike, who served in the Civil War, a member of the Iowa Volunteers, was born at Louisville, Kentucky, and died at Hudson, Colorado, January 4, 1921. His mother, Kate Sophia (Hill) Zike, whose ancestry was German, was born at Pittsburg, November 10, 1841, and is still living at Edison at the age of 91.

Mr. Zike was a liveryman and stock buyer for 10 years, and for the past 20 years has been engaged in the real estate and insurance business at Edison. He holds membership in the Commercial Club, is a life member of the Red Cross, and for over 20 years has served as secretary of the Independent Order of Odd Fellows. His sport is golf.

On December 25, 1895, Mr. Zike was married to Cora Virginia Watkins at Edison, Nebraska. Mrs. Zike, who was a clerk prior to her marriage, was born at Missouri City, Missouri, September 8, 1874, of early American stock. To them were born two children, Eugene Eldrege, July 27, 1897, who married Emma Jensen of Minden on October 8, 1924, the parents of Patricia Lou, born September 13, 1927 at Minden, Nebraska; and Arva, born May 8, 1902, who married Roy C. Bendler of Oxford, Nebraska, June 20, 1923. Their son, Jack Charles, was born June 3, 1926. Residence: Edison. (Photograph in Album).

Clarence Howard Zimmerman

Clarence Howard Zimmerman was born at North Platte, Nebraska, August 24, 1908, the son of Thomas Franklin and Esther Retta (Masters) Zimmerman. His father, who homesteaded in western Nebraska in the early 1890's was born at Rensselaer, Indiana, April 9, 1878; his grandparents came to this country from England. His mother, who was a pioneer homemaker on Nebraska prairie land, was born in Ohio, September 24, 1878; her ancestry is English.

Mr. Zimmerman, attended the rural schools of Osgood, Nebraska, and in 1926 was graduated from the North Platte High School. He attended Cotner College where he was prominent in dramatics and oratory. Upon his graduation from high school he ran his father's dairy for a time, and was employed by the Piggly Wiggly Company and the Rush Mercantile Company. For one year he was a clergyman at Brownville, Nebraska, in the oldest Protestant church in Nebraska, and for the past two years has been pastor of the Christian Church at Virginia, Gage County, Nebraska. He plans to continue his education.

He is a member of the Parent Teachers Association, the Young Men's Christian Association, and the Nebraskana Society. He has been active for some time as leader in Hi-Y work and as a commissioned scout master. His sports include swimming, tennis, hiking, baseball, and basketball, while his hobby is commercial and private art. He is a Republican. Residence: Virginia.

Frank Zimmerman

Henry Zimmerman, father of Frank Zimmerman, was a native of Schleswig, Holstein, Germany, and was born October 25, 1856. In 1868 he came to America, settling in Sarpy County. He married Anna Busche, who was born at Cedar Creek, Nebraska, March 23, 1860. He died at Burwell, December 5, 1905. His wife survived him almost twenty-years, and died at Omaha, March 17, 1924. Her parents came from Switzerland.

Frank Zimmerman received his education in the public schools of Gretna and Millard. On February 20, 1901, he married Bertha Elizabeth Gottsch. Mrs. Zimmerman was born at Springfield, November 24, 1879, and died at Omaha, April 28, 1930. She was of German descent. She leaves the following children: Henry J., born October 9, 1901; Mabel H., born February 6, 1903, married to Randall Biart; Hazel A., born June 29, 1907, and Margaret A., born June 18, 1910.

Mr. Zimmerman has been a resident of Sarpy County since birth; and since early youth has been a stock feeder. From 1914 to 1919 he was a partner in the firm of Weeth & Zimmerman and from 1920 to 1928 was a member of

the firm of Zimmerman & Gottsch. Since that time he has owned and operated the Zimmerman Feed Yards. Mr. Zimmerman is a Lutheran and a Republican. Residence: Springfield.

Andrew Zoz

At Lincoln, Logan County, Illinois, Andrew Zoz was born on February 13, 1869. He is the son of Alois and Martina (Weber) Zoz. His father, who was born in Germany, came to America in 1858, and died at Murdock, Cass County, Nebraska. He was a farmer.

His mother was born in Germany, came to America in 1860, and died at Murdock, March 18, 1923.

Mr. Zoz received his education in the country schools and later attended Creighton University at Omaha for one year. A resident of Nebraska since 1881, he has engaged in farming here since that date. He has been a director on the school board for 12 years.

He was united in marriage with Anna Mae Bartz, at Manley, Cass County, Nebraska, April 30, 1907. Mrs. Zoz, of German descent, was born at Murdock, July 11, 1883. There are eleven children: John L., born April 13, 1908; Edna M., born May 12, 1909; Martin A., born March 4, 1911; Joseph A., born August 25, 1912; Gerald F., born February 5, 1914; Robert H., born March 2, 1915; Helen M., born September 27, 1916; Rose A., born December 16, 1917; Clara F., born March 9, 1919; Walter E., born March 23, 1920, and Lawrence D., born August 4, 1922.

Mr. Zoz is affiliated with St. Mary's Catholic Church at Elmwood. His hobby is reading. He is a Democrat. Residence: Murdock.

THE NEBRASKANA ALBUM

PHOTOGRAPHS OF MEN AND WOMEN
OF DISTINCTION
1932

WILLIAM JAMES ABBOTT
Whitman

ELLEN MURPHY ACKERMAN
Ainsworth

Stanley—Ainsworth

JAMES GEORGE ACKERMAN
Ainsworth

Day—Hebron

JOHN ADEN
Carleton

O'Neill Photo Co.—O'Neill

GEORGE SIMON AGNES
O'Neill

BOHUMIL WILLIAM AKSAMIT
Deweese

Day—Hebron

JOHN H. ALBRECHT

Deshler

Nelson—McCook

ARTHUR EURASHO ALLEN

Danbury

Krekeler—Gothenburg

CHARLES EDGAR ALLEN

Cozad

Krekeler—Gothenburg

KATHERINE FAY ALLEN

Cozad

Taylor—Madison

HENRY ALTSCHULER

Madison

CARL G. AMICK

Loup City

EDNA COCHRAN ANDERSON

York

Anderson—Kearney

IRA C. ANDERSON

Kearney

Clark—Stromsburg

VICTOR ANDERSON

Stromsburg

Dole—Lincoln

ORVILLE ALEXANDER ANDREWS
Lincoln

Locke—Grand Island

LESLIE C. ANSTINE
Wood River

Richards—Hartington

JOSEPH FRANK ARENS
Hartington

DR. CHARLES HARRISON ARNOLD
Lincoln

LEONARD E. ARNOLD
Sutherland

Bethscheider—West Point

CARRIE ARTHUR
Scribner

Ebers—Holdrege

WILBER STREMMEL ATEN
Holdrege

Ebers—Holdrege

WILBER WILLIAM ATEN
Holdrege

Olson—Newman Grove

OTTO G. AUSTIN
Newman Grove

JAMES ANDREW AXTELL
Fairbury

Townsend—Lincoln

LEON EMMONS AYLSWORTH
Lincoln

Gale—Aurora

W. H. BAKER
Aurora

GRACE BALLARD
Blair

Dole—Lincoln

GROVE ETTINGER BARBER
Lincoln

Genelli—Sioux City, Iowa

GEORGE EARL BARKS
Belden

Milenz—Stanton

JOHN D. BARNETT
Stanton

Anderson—Kearney

ARTHUR BARNEY
Kearney

Day—Hebron

JOHN E. BARUTH
Alexandria

Dedmore—North Platte
CONRAD LESLIE BASKINS
North Platte

Day—Hebron
HARVEY THEODORE BATES
Carleton

Day—Hebron
ROSCOE C. BEACHLER
Reynolds

Wagner-Crete
CHARLES EDWIN BEALS
Crete

Dole—Lincoln
JAMES O. BEAMAN
Ceresco

Anderson—Lincoln
PETER FRANKLIN BEGHTOL
Bennet

Stanley—Ainsworth
JESSE FRANCIS BEJOT
Ainsworth

Utter—Superior
JOHN ERNEST BELL
Superior

Rinehart-Marsden—Omaha
GRACE M. B. BENSON
Oakland

Phelps—Sidney
JOHN BENTLEY
Sidney

Genelli—Sioux City, Iowa
WILLIAM H. BERGER
Dakota City

Dedmore—North Platte
ARTHUR HERBERT BIVANS
North Platte

Westland—Neligh
SAMUEL C. BLACKMAN
Tilden

ANTON CHARLES BLATNY
Linwood

ALBERT ORR BOGGS
Gilead

HOMER BOWEN
Grand Island

Nelson—Holdrege
CHARLES ARTHUR BOWERS
Holdrege

HARRY EUGENE BOWMAN
Hastings

CLARENCE C. BOYES
Hebron

Day—Hebron
HERMAN LEE BOYES
Hebron

Day—Hebron
WILLIAM EDWIN BOYES
Hebron

Locke—Grand Island
ARCHIE LEE BRADSTREET
Grand Island

Townsend—Lincoln
CARMEN BRADY
Denton

Heyn—Omaha
GEORGE H. BREWER
Omaha

Day—Hebron
JOHN T. BRINEGAR
Belvidere

Dole—Lincoln
OTTO HERMAN BRINKMAN
Lincoln

Skoglund—Fremont
HARRY H. BROWN
Blair

Townsend—Lincoln

JAMES A. BROWN
Lincoln

LULU CLYDE BROWN
Stockville

Skoglund—Fremont

EDWARD CHARLES BRT
Abie

A. F. BUECHLER
Grand Island

Townsend—Lincoln

JOSEPH BURNS
Lincoln

Lyden—Schuyler

FRITZ J. BUSCH
Howells

Alberti—Cambridge

BENJAMIN F. BUTLER
Cambridge

JAMES ARTHUR BUTLER
Ewing

CONGRAVE C. CALLAWAY
Fairbury

ELIZA JANE CALLAWAY
Fairbury

BURTIS OAKLEY CALLENDER
North Platte

Townsend-Lincoln
JOSEPH ROBERT CAMERON
Bennet

Danskin—Osceola
H. H. CAMPBELL
Osceola

Dunham—Alma
JOSEPH NEW CAMPBELL
Stamford

Danskin—Osceola
P. B. CAMPBELL
Osceola

REV. R. S. CAMPBELL
Lincoln

SWAN CARLSON
Funk

STEWART EDGAR CARSKADON
Wilcox

Dole—Lincoln

HARRY GLEN CARTER
Lincoln

GUY C. CHAMBERS
Lincoln

Johnston—Fairbury

JAMES CHAMBERS
Fairbury

Kuhn—Blair

SAMUEL W. CHAMBERS
Blair

Keith County Studio—Ogallala

ANNA GRAY CLARK
Ogallala

Graves—Chadron

LUCY MARIE CLARK
Chadron

MORSE POWL CLARY
Lewellen

Rinehart-Marsden—Omaha

JOHN LEO CLEARY
Grand Island

HARRY JOSEPH COFFIN
Burwell

DR. ELBERT E. CONE
Oxford

Craven—Wayne
ULYSSES SYLVESTER CONN
Wayne

Genelli—Sioux City, Iowa
WILLIAM COOLIDGE
Rosalie

GERALD M. G. COOPER
Rushville

Heyn—Omaha
JOHN WILLIAM COOPER
Omaha

Ebers—Holdrege
CHARLES FINNEY COPELAND
Holdrege

Babcock—Shelby
WALTER A. CORNISH
Shelby

MABEL L. CORRELL
Cambridge

Townsend—Lincoln
MAJOR ALLEN P. COWGILL
Lincoln

Heyn—Omaha

FRANK B. COX
Waterloo

Nelson—Hastings

MABEL CRAMER
Hastings

ROBERT PLATT CRAWFORD
Lincoln

Day—Hebron

JOHN L. CURRIER
Hebron

Smalley—Minden

CARL T. CURTIS
Minden

Nelson—McCook

WILLIAM C. DAHNKE
Stratton

STANLEY OWEN DAILY
Minden

Townsend—Lincoln

FRANK TENNEY DARROW
Lincoln

Gale—Beatrice

ALLEN MANVILLE DARWIN
Virginia

O'Neill Photo Co.—O'Neill
EDWARD LLEWELLYN DAVIES
Ewing

Dedmore—North Platte
EDWARD SAMUEL DAVIS
North Platte

Genelli—Sioux City, Iowa
GROVER C. DAVIS
Homer

JOSEPH HORN DAVISON
Ainsworth

Taylor—Madison
IRWELL MONTGOMERY DAWSON
Madison

REUBEN ALWIN DAWSON
Randolph

Steiner—Scottsbluff
QUENTIN WARREN DEAN
Gering

Locke—Grand Island
WILLIAM THOMAS DEARING
Phillips

Hebrew—Lexington
BERT DECKER
Elwood

Day—Hebron

RUDOLPH F. DECKER, M. D.
Byron

Dedmore—North Platte

C. O. DEDMORE
North Platte

Hanson—Wakefield

FOREST RAY DILTS
Wakefield

CHARLES DOCEKAL
Abie

JOHN J. DOHRN
Grand Island

Keith County Studio—Ogallala

DAYTON HENRY DORN
Big Spring

Barnett—Lincoln

CHARLES LLOYD DORT

Dole—Lincoln

JOHN CHARLES DORT
Pawnee City

Crawford—Norfolk

GEORGE MARTIN DUDLEY
Norfolk

Terrell—Pender

GLEASON A. DUDLEY
Walthill

PETER WILLIAM DUFFY
O'Neill

Nelson—Holdrege

EDWARD E. DURYEE
Oxford

Ensign—Exeter

ALBERT WILLIAM DYER
Exeter

Dedmore—North Platte

GUY WALLACE EATON
Maxwell

Ebers—Holdrege

WILLIAM EBERS
Holdrege

Townsend—Lincoln

GOTTLIEB F. EBERSPACHER
Seward

DR. CHARLES DANIEL EBY
Leigh

Richards—Hartington

MILLARD ELMER EBY
Hartington

Smith—Crete

EDWARD HERMAN ECKERT
Crete

A. J. EDSTROM
Grand Island

Day—Hebron

FRANK LUDWIG EHLERS
Deshler

Jacobs—Oakland

OSCAR J. EKSTRAND
Oakland

WILBERT LESTER ELSWICK
Gurley

Krekeler—Gothenburg

J. W. EMBREE
Lodge Pole

LOREN WILLIAM ENYEART
Hayes Center

Gale—Beatrice

GUSTAVUS A. ERICKSON
Virginia

Moler—Red Cloud

CLIFFORD F. ESHELMAN
Red Cloud

WILLIAM FREDERICK EVERS
Plattsmouth

Nelson—McCook

SAMUEL MITCHELL EWING
Benkelman

Bartlett—Central City

WILLIAM FRANCIS FEEHAN
Clarks

Gale-Beatrice

ELBERT WESLEY FELLERS
Beatrice

Alberti—Cambridge

RUBEN O. FINCH
Cambridge

Hebrew—Lexington

J. S. FITZSIMMONS
Elwood

ALBERT CLAUS FLOTO
Seward

ERIC FORSLUND
Stromsburg

Day—Hebron

MATTIE E. FRANKS FOSTER
Hebron

VIRGIL SPRANKLE FREAS
Beaver City

WILLIAM FREIDELL
Dorchester

W. RUSSELL FREIDELL
Dorchester

Nelson—Holdrege

JOHN ALEXIS FRENCH
Edison

Skoglund—Fremont

ERNEST LESLIE FRIED
Beemer

WILLIAM THOMAS FRY
Holmsville

Ebers—Holdrege

BYRON SYLVESTER FULK
Atlanta

Johnston—Fairbury

GEORGE E. GARBER
Helvey

Keith County Studio—Ogallala

ORLIE ROBERT GARWOOD
Ogallala

Stanley—Ainsworth

CECIL LEON GATTEN
Ainsworth

Phelps—Sidney

META PAULA GEMEINHARDT
Potter

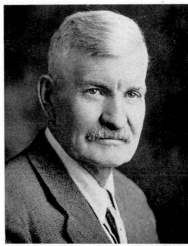

Steiner—Scottsbluff

BENJAMIN FRANKLIN GENTRY
Gering

Steiner—Scottsbluff

MRS. B. F. GENTRY
Gering

Seeman—Norfolk

JAMES WILLIS GILLETTE
Norfolk

Smalley—Minden

WILLIAM LARKIN GOODELL
Minden

Youngberg—Allen

JAMES R. GRAHAM
Allen

That Man Gale—York

ROBERT ARNOLD GRAHAM
York

Townsend—Lincoln

JOHN GRAN
Mead

Townsend—Lincoln
ALICE WINIFRED GRAHAM

Townsend—Lincoln
FRANCIS ANDREW GRAHAM

Genelli—Sioux City
EMMETT H. GRIBBLE
South Sioux City

Ebers—Holdrege
HENRY GROSENBACH
Mascot

MRS. HENRY GROSENBACH
Mascot

JOHN GUMB
Fremont

PLEASANT HUGH GUPTON
Oxford

Rinehart-Marsden—Omaha
CHARLES WILLIAM HADAN
Bennington

Skoglund—Fremont
H. P. HAESSLER
Leshara

Skoglund—Fremont
GUSTAVE HAHN
Neligh

Heyn—Omaha
JAMES M. HALL
Ithaca

Johnston—Fairbury
WILLIAM OTTO HALL
Reynolds

Nelson—McCook
J. O. HAM
Benkelman

Alberti—Cambridge
EDWARD JOSEPH HAMILTON
Wilsonville

JAMES WAVERLY HAMMOND
Geneva

JAMES WILLIAM HAMMOND
Holdrege

Kuhn—Blair
JAMES WALDO HANCOCK
Herman

ANTON HANSEN
Upland

Nelson—Hastings

ARTHUR TREVENNING HARRIS
Hastings

Skoglund—Fremont

GEORGE A. HASLAM
Fremont

Ebers—Holdrege

EMIL B. HASSEL
Holdrege

WILLIAM HAWLEY
North Platte

Hebrew—Lexington

MARSHALL EDDMON HEBREW
Lexington

Locke—Grand Island

CARL HEHNKE
Grand Island

BERTIN ELLSWORTH HENDRICKS

Day—Hebron

KENIS P. HERALD
Byron

HARRY EDWARD HESTER
Beaver City

Gale—Beatrice

CLARENCE WRIGHT HIATT
Diller

Lyden—Schuyler

JOHN E. HIGGINS
Rogers

Gale—Beatrice

GEORGE GROVER HILDER
Wymore

Hauck-Skoglund—Lincoln

ALICE HAMLIN HINMAN
Lincoln

Olson—Newman Grove

JOHN HOAGLUND
Newman Grove

Skoglund—Fremont

PEARL HOLLOWAY
Fremont

Nelson—Holdrege

EARL EUGENE HOPPING
Beaver City

Haberman—Friend

HERBERT HOWARTH
Friend

Gordon—Rushville

GRACE McCOY HUMMEL
Gordon

Pratt—Nelson

CHARLES READE IMLER
Nelson

ARTHUR JAMES IRVINE
Hamlet

JOSHUA ALVIN ISAMAN
Aurora

MAY ELIZABETH ISAMAN
Aurora

Alberti—Cambridge

WALTER DUDLEY JAMES
Cambridge

ANTHONY LOUIS JENSEN
Big Springs

Townsend—Lincoln

CARL OSCAR JOHNSON
Havelock

Ebers—Holdrege

GEORGE ROBERT JOHNSON
Bertrand

Dole—Lincoln

GUS JOHNSON
Ceresco

JAMES RICHARD JOHNSON
McCook

Townsend—Lincoln
JOHN H. JOHNSON
Herman

REUBEN A. JOHNSON
Newman Grove

R. C. JOHNSON
Mead

REV. GEORGE FEDILIS JONAITIS
In major's uniform of United States Army
Blair

WILLIAM LLOYD JONES
Wymore

ARTHUR LAWRENCE JOSEPH
Grand Island

That Man Gale—York
RUDOLPH LUDWIG KALIFF
York

Townsend—Lincoln
H. L. KEEFE
Walthill

EDWIN C. KELSO
North Platte

EDWARD LOUIS KEMPER
Aurora

Bethscheider—West Point
R. H. KERKOW
West Point

Hauck-Skoglund—Lincoln
CHARLES VERNON KETTERING
Crete

E. R. KEYES
Cambridge

Lumbard—Ord
GRACE GENEVA KIDDER
Sargent

Nelson—McCook
PETER HENRY KILZER
Lebanon

Smalley—Minden
MILO D. KING
Sargent

Heyn—Omaha
ALVA RAYMOND KINNEY
Omaha

Townsend—Lincoln

HOWARD KIRKPATRICK
Lincoln

Townsend—Lincoln

W. C. KLEIN
Milford

Gale—Beatrice

LOUIS JARRETT KNOLL
Liberty

Bethscheider—West Point

ALEX R. KRAUSE
West Point

CLYDE L. KRAUSE
Newman Grove

O'Neill Photo Co.—O'Neill

WILLIAM KROTTER
Stuart

ADOLPH JACOB KUBITSCHEK
Atkinson

ANNA REED KUHLE
Leigh

CHARLES R. KUHLE
Leigh

Danskin—Osceola

DAVID HENRY KUNKEL
Osceola

Dedmore—North Platte

DONALD ALDEN KUNKEL
North Platte

THOMAS JOHNSON LAHNERS
Belvidere

Anderson—Kearney

GEORGE WINDERS LANG
Litchfield

Richards—Hartington

CARL M. LANGE
Hartington

Nelson—Holdrege

HENRY LARSON
Loomis

Haberman—Crete

GEORGE W. LAUTENSCHLAGER
Swanton

Wagoner—Crete

GEORGE EDWIN LEAVITT
Crete

Townsend—Lincoln

MABEL LEE
Lincoln

Nelson—Hastings

ANTHONY ADAM LEMBACH
Hastings

Nelson—McCook

NELSON HIRAM LEWIS
Benkelman

Craven—Wayne

ROLLIE WALTER LEY
Wayne

Townsend—Lincoln

O. H. LIEBERS
Lincoln

Hebrew—Lexington

GEORGE WALLACE LINCOLN
Lexington

Phelps—Sidney

REVEREND ANTON LINK
Sidney

Locke—Grand Island

HENRY W. LOCKE
Grand Island

FRANCIS A. LONG, M. D.
Madison

Krekeler—Gothenburg

EDWIN J. LOUTZENHEISER
Gothenburg

Locke—Grand Island
GUS LORENTZ
Loup City

Dedmore—North Platte
THEODORE LOWE, JR.
North Platte

Day—Hebron
B. FRANK LOWERY
Davenport

Skoglund—Fremont
ROBERT A. LUEHRS
Fremont

WILLIAM ALBERT LUKE
Lincoln

LAURA ETTA LUNDY
Sargent

Gumbel—Seward
MARTIN MADISON
Goehner

Harris & Ewing—Washington, D. C.
JOHN ARTHUR MAGUIRE
Lincoln

Dole—Lincoln
ADA C. MALCOLM
Lincoln

O. B. MANVILLE
Madison

HARRY MILLER MARQUIS
Bridgeport

Skoglund—Fremont
EDWARD JOHN MASHEK
Abie

FRED G. MASON
Upland

ALBERT N. MATHERS
Gering

Johnston—Fairbury
AUGUST FERDINAND MATZKE
Western

Anderson—Kearney
EMMA McCLELLAND
Beaver City

Anderson—Kearney
HUGH MONTGOMERY McCLURE
Kearney

ANNA SNYDER McCULLOUGH
Brady

JAMES McCULLOUGH
Brady

Chaufty—Valentine
OSCAR WILEY McDANIEL
Valentine

CLYDE McELMOIL
Farnam

Daniels—Columbus
CLAUD GUINN McGAFFIN
Bellwood

EDMUND G. McGILTON
Omaha

LILLIE MUIR McKAY
Haigler

Jacobs—Oakland
R. V. McPHERSON
Craig

Danskin—Osceola
ISAAC JOHNSTON MERRICK
Osceola

EMIL MERSCHEID
North Platte

Nelson—Holdrege

ERNEST M. MERWIN
Beaver City

Nelson—Holdrege

FLETCHER N. MERWIN
Beaver City

Nelson—Holdrege

MERTA I. MERWIN
Beaver City

Nelson—Holdrege

M. MYRTLE MERWIN
Beaver City

HARRY D. MILLER
Stanton

Townsend—Lincoln

JOHN H. MILLER
Lincoln

CHARLES MITCHELL
Allen

Steiner—Scottsbluff

ORIN WESLEY MOORE
Gering

Hebrew—Lexington

JOSEPH W. MORGAN
Lexington

RICHARD GRANT MORRISON
Loomis

RICHARD DANIEL MORITZ
Lincoln

CYRUS ALLEN MORSE
Oxford

MARION RICHARD MORTENSEN
Long Pine

CARL CLARENCE MOYER
Ainsworth

ARBOR DAY MUNGER
Lincoln

CORA ELLEN STONE MURPHY
Page

H. DEY MYERS, M. D.
Howells

E. HERMAN NAUMANN
Columbus

Nelson—Hastings

PERRY THOMAS NAYLOR
Hastings

Skoglund—Fremont

ERLAND N. P. NELSON
Blair

McNally—Long Pine

LEMIST GEORGE NELSON
Bassett

JOHN WALLACE NESLUND
Cozad

Townsend—Lincoln

ARTHUR LORENZO NEUMANN
Oakland

Keith County Studio—Ogallala

HARRY GEORGE NEUMAYER
Paxton

ANNE C. NEWBIGGING
Wisner

Hebrew—Lexington

FREDERICK NIELSEN
Lexington

Phelps—Sidney

JOHANNES W. NIELSEN
Sidney

Dole—Lincoln

E. C. NORDLUND
Stromsburg

Dole—Lincoln

CHARLES AUGUST NORLIN
Lincoln

Day—Hebron

DAY C. NORMAN
Chester

DAN CLIFFORD NORRIS
Brewster

Krekeler—Gothenburg

BERNARD NORSWORTHY
Gothenburg

Skoglund—Fremont

WILLIAM FRED NOVAK
Howells

Lyden—Schuyler

CHARLES NOVOTNY
Clarkson

Nelson—Hastings

BERTON FRANK NOYES
Hastings

FRED A. NYE
Kearney

Townsend—Lincoln

JOSEFH PATRICK O'GARA
Lincoln

Danskin—Osceola

GEORGE E. OLSON
Stromsburg

JOHN EDWARD OPP
Burwell

Nelson—McCook

DANIEL LEWIS OUGH
Benkelman

Nelson—Hastings

GEORGE EDWIN OVERTURF
Hastings

CLAIRE ESTELLE OWENS
Exeter

BAYARD H. PAINE
Grand Island

Burwell—Burwell

JESSE LELAND PEARL
Burwell

Skoglund—Fremont

H. CHRISTIAN PEDERSEN
Fremont

Oakland—Oakland

ALEXANDER PETERS
Bancroft

Oakland—Oakland

CLAUS F. PETERS
Bancroft

Martin—Wisner

ANDREW R. PETERSON
Wisner

Gray—Lincoln

FRANK L. PETERSON
Valparaiso

JOHN PETRO
Fremont

WILLARD ALONZO PETTEYS
Wilcox

Ebers—Holdrege

HARRISON PETTYGROVE
Oxford

Anderson—Kearney

ROBERT FREDERICK PFEIFFER
Kearney

Dedmore—North Platte

FRANK EMERY PFOUTZ
North Platte

L. A. PHELPS
Fremont

Wilson—Fullerton
CHANDLER NOYES PHILBRICK
Fullerton

Nelson—Holdrege
BRYCE ANTON PHILLIPS
Bertrand

Alberti—Cambridge
PETER PHILLIPSON

Dole—Lincoln
WILLIAM THOMAS PICKETT
Wahoo

Nelson—Hastings
CHESTER ARTHUR PIERCE
Hastings

Dole—Lincoln
W. E. PIERSON
Osceola

Townsend—Lincoln
RAYMOND J. POOL
Lincoln

Keith County Studio—Ogallala
MYRON JAY POSSON
Ogallala

Townsend—Lincoln
MARCUS L. POTEET
Lincoln

Krekeler—Gothenburg
BIRD S. POTTER
Gothenburg

Nelson—McCook
JAMES FREDERICK PREMER
Benkelman

WALTER G. PRESTON
Omaha

Wagoner—Crete
VINCENT JOSEPH PRUCHA
Crete

WALTER GEORGE PURTZER
Madison

SANFORD EUGENE RALSTEN
Geneva

Locke—Grand Island
ANTON NELSON RASK
Boelus

KENNETH A. RAWSON
Dix

Skoglund—Fremont

AUGUST LOUIS REBBE
Hooper

Lyden—Schuyler

L. F. REINCKE
Schuyler

CAROLYN RENFREW
Hastings

JOHN WALTER REUTZEL
Trenton

Nelson—McCook

ELMER MORTIMER REYNOLDS
Culbertson

Johnston—Fairbury

RALPH K. REYNOLDS
Fairbury

Gale—Beatrice

CLARENCE EDWARD RICE
Odell

Stanley—Ainsworth

ERNEST JOSEPH AXTELL RICE
Ainsworth

Alberti—Cambridge

LLOYD CLIFFORD RICHARDSON
Cambridge

Nelson—McCook

JACOB RICKARD
Max

Nelson—McCook

CHARLES E. RIDER
Imperial

Day—Hebron

WILLIAM ALEXANDER RING
Hebron

Townsend—Lincoln

JAMES RIVETT
Lincoln

Skoglund—Fremont

JOSEPH ROBERTS
Fremont

Kuhn—Blair

HENRY ROHWER
Fort Calhoun

JAMES ABNER ROSS
Long Pine

Skoglund—Fremont

DAVE D. ROWE
Fremont

Ebers—Holdrege

GEORGE ALBERT RYDLUND
Funk

HARRY EVANS SACKETT
Beatrice

HERMINA REYNOLDS SACKETT
Beatrice

Townsend—Lincoln
FRANK ELI SALA
Lincoln

Smalley—Minden
ARVID STANLEY SAMUELSON
Kearney

Day—Hebron
ARA MINTA LOUISE SAYLOR
Bruning

Day—Hebron
HARVEY WESLEY SAYLOR
Bruning

BENJAMIN KURTZ SCHAEFFER
Curtis

Bethscheider—West Point
HENRY E. SCHEMMEL
Hooper

Nelson—Hastings
FRED DAVID SCHNEIDER
Loup City

Danskin—Osceola

LOUIS SCHOLZ

Phelps—Sidney

WILLIAM WILL SCHULZ
Sidney

Hauck-Skoglund—Lincoln

GEORGE SCHWAKE

Hauck-Skoglund—Lincoln

MARY DELL SCHWAKE
Lincoln

Townsend—Lincoln

ELMORE CHARLES SCHWESER
Surprise

T. M. SCOTT
Aurora

Townsend—Lincoln

WILLIAM ALSON SELLECK
Lincoln

Townsend—Lincoln

VICTOR SEYMOUR
Lincoln

Purdy—Gordon

ANNA DOROTHEA SHADBOLT
Gordon

Danskin—Osceola

LAWRENCE M. SHAW
Osceola

Alberti—Cambridge

RELVIA ULYSSES SHAW
Cambridge

LUCIUS A. SHERMAN
Lincoln

Skoglund—Fremont

MARION E. SHIPLEY
Hooper

CHARLES A. SHOFF
Grafton

Dedmore—North Platte

BERTON T. SHOUP
Sutherland

WILLIAM AMBROSE SCHRECK
Bertrand

SEYMOUR STEPHEN SIDNER
Fremont

Burwell Studio—Burwell

EDWARD FRANKLIN SIME
Burwell

Smalley—Minden

CLYDE C. SMALLEY
Minden

Dole—Lincoln

CLARA LOTSPIECH SMITH
Lincoln

ERLE BOYD SMILEY
Seward

Nelson—McCook

BEAMAN QUINCY SMITH
Stockville

Dole—Lincoln

MARIETTA SNOW
Lincoln

Kimber—St. Paul

SOREN NIELSEN SOELBERG
Elba

Skoglund—Fremont

J. M. SORENSEN
Fremont

Day—Hebron

MARION WILSON SPOHN
Chester

EDWARD HERBERT SPRINGER
Brady

Nelson—McCook

WILLIAM GEORGE SPRINGER
McCook

Brazda—Dodge

FRANK JOSEPH SRB
Dodge

Brazda—Dodge

HUGO FRANK SRB
Dodge

Dole—Lincoln

HARLAND U. STEVENS
Lincoln

Nelson—McCook

WILLIS EDIE STEWART
Stratton

Dunham—Alma

GLENN EARL STODDARD
Alma

ARTHUR CHARLES STOKES
Omaha

Danskin—Osceola

OSCAR STRAND
Polk

LEONARD STROMBERG
Oakland

Skoglund—Fremont

CARL KENNEDY STRUBLE
Fremont

Skoglund—Omaha

GUSTAV SUMNICK
Waterloo

Skoglund—Omaha

DOUGLAS C. SUTHERLAND
Tekamah

Skoglund—Fremont

ARTIE O. SWARTWOOD
Fremont

Townsend—Lincoln

FRANCIS MARION SWARTWOOD
Adams

Genelli—Sioux City, Iowa

ERMAN NATHAN SWETT
South Sioux City

Heyn—Omaha

FRANK JAMES TAYLOR
St. Paul

Hebrew—Lexington

GUY ALLEN TEMPLE
Lexington

Skoglund—Fremont

HARDIN S. TENNANT
Stanton

DALE L. THOMAS
Kilgore

Heyn—Omaha
MINNIE FLORELLA THOMAS
Omaha

Dole—Lincoln
CHARLES Y. THOMPSON
West Point

Smalley—Minden
INGEBERT JOHANSEN THOMSEN
Minden

BERTHA E. M. THOMSON
Lincoln

Locke—Grand Island
JOHN THOMSSEN
Alda

GEORGE WASHINGTON TRINE
Red Cloud

Heyn—Omaha
HENRY TRUHLSEN
Herman

Anderson—Wahoo
NELS A. TUVESON
Weston

Danskin—Osceola
ACE VERN TYRRELL
Osceola

Dedmore—North Platte
ERNEST CLARENCE UHLIG
Sutherland

G. R. UNTHANK
Lincoln

Skoglund—Fremont
CLARENCE A. VALDER
Tekamah

SARAH VAN PELT
Stockville

ADOLPH JOSEPH VIERLING
Omaha

Day—Hebron
EDWIN VIESELMEYER
Deshler

Townsend—Lincoln
ALICE MARIE VON BERGEN
Lincoln

Bethscheider—West Point
EMIL M. VON SEGGERN
West Point

McDermott—Broadwater

MARY ANN WAGONER
Broadwater

ALLAN WALKER
Dunbar

Lacy—Kimball

IRVING SETH WALKER
Kimball

Skoglund—Fremont

STANLEY P. WALLIN
Snyder

FRED C. WARNEMUNDE
Lexington

Hauck-Skoglund—Lincoln

CHARLES JOSEPH WARNER
Waverly

Gale—Beatrice

JOHN CLARENCE WARREN
Beatrice

Westland—Neligh

CHARLES WILLIAM WARWICK
Valentine

Skoglund—Fremont

S. A. WASSUM
Tekamah

Nelson—Holdrege

HELEN B. WEBENDORFER
Beaver City

Jacobs—Oakland

H. L. WEBSTER
Tekamah

HERMAN FREDERICK WEIGEL
Stuart

ANDY J. WELCH
Milford

Dunham—Alma

FRANK WERNER
Alma

Townsend—Lincoln

HARRY JACOB WERTMAN
Milford

Heyn—Omaha

GEORGE W. WERTZ
Schuyler

CLARA STREET WESCOTT
Plattsmouth

Krekeler—Gothenburg

ELIZABETH H. WEST
Gothenburg

Nelson—McCook

VICTOR WESTERMARK
Benkelman

Skoglund—Fremont

FREDERICK HARVEY WHITMORE
Valley

Stanley—Ainsworth

GEORGE QUINTON WHITNEY
Ainsworth

BERNARD WHITWER
Tilden

Dedmore—North Platte

FRED CONRAD WIEGMAN
North Platte

DR. CHARLES M. WILHELMJ
Omaha

Nebraska Photo Co.—Hastings

CLARENCE OREN WILSON
Hastings

Skoglund—Fremont

WALDO WINTERSTEEN
Fremont

HENRY ELMER WOLF
Hyannis

That Man Gale—York

WILBUR FISK WOOD
Haigler

Heyn—Omaha

NELLIE F. WULLSCHLEGER
Leigh

Hebrew—Lexington

FLORENCE E. YODER
Lexington

Skoglund—Fremont

JAMES TILTON YOUNG
Fremont

SHAW RUSKIN YOUNG
Gering

McNally—Long Pine

WILLIAM T. ZAHRADNICEK
Johnstown

Phelps—Sidney

NICHOLAS EDWARD ZEHR
Chappell

Phelps—Sidney

WILLIAM EMANUEL ZEHR
Chappell

Nelson—McCook

ELMO MURRAY ZIKE
Edison

Above is a photograph of the organ which was recently installed in the home of the
Reverend Clement J. Nacke at Hooper, Nebraska. Father Nacke is a musician of
note. This is perhaps the finest pipe organ located in a private home in the middlewest.

Engravings prepared by the
STATE JOURNAL COMPANY
Lincoln, Nebraska

≈

Printed by
THE DEMOCRAT PRINTING COMPANY
Hastings, Nebraska